W9-AZC-213

The grass withers, and the flowers fade,
but the word of our God
stands forever.

ISAIAH 40:8

Presented to

Jan Harper

BY Ruth Grimes (mom)

ON THE OCCASION OF

Allowing God back into my life!
Thank you Jesus.

DATE 1995

This explains why a man leaves
his father and mother
and is joined to his wife,
and the two are united into one.

GENESIS 2:24

Marriage

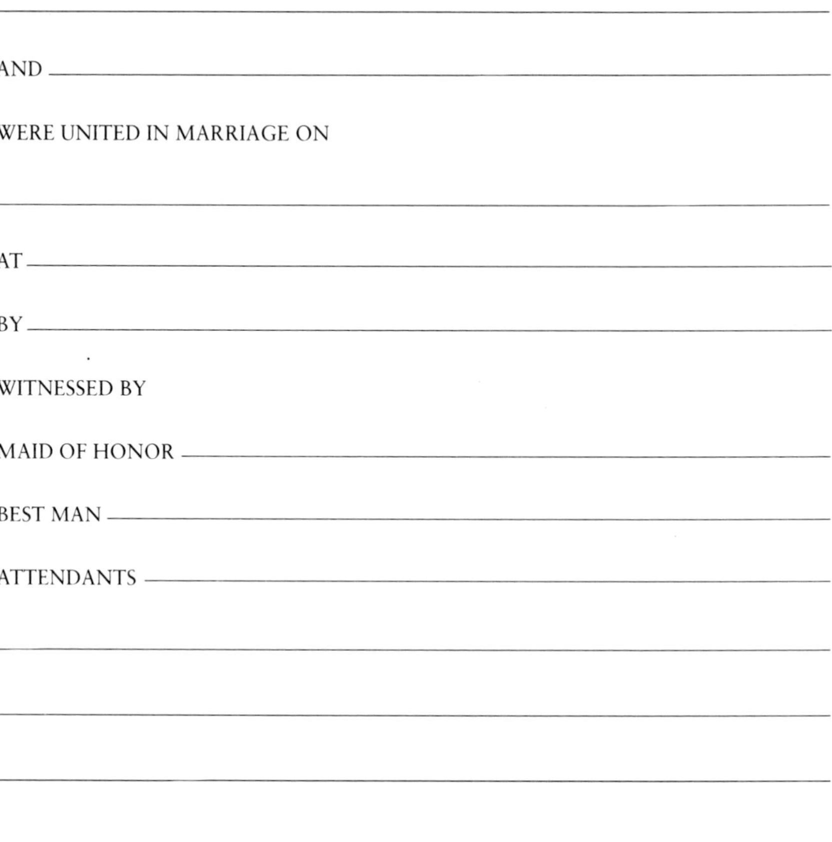

____

AND ______________________________

WERE UNITED IN MARRIAGE ON

____

AT ______________________________

BY ______________________________

WITNESSED BY

MAID OF HONOR ______________________________

BEST MAN ______________________________

ATTENDANTS ______________________________

Children are a gift from the Lord;

they are a reward from him.

PSALM 127:3

Nicole (niki-nik) 5-20-75
NAME DATE

mpls.
BIRTHPLACE

David (Dove) 2-8-78
NAME DATE

Eric (air-head) 12-80
BIRTHPLACE

NAME DATE

BIRTHPLACE

NAME DATE

BIRTHPLACE

NAME DATE

BIRTHPLACE

NAME DATE

BIRTHPLACE

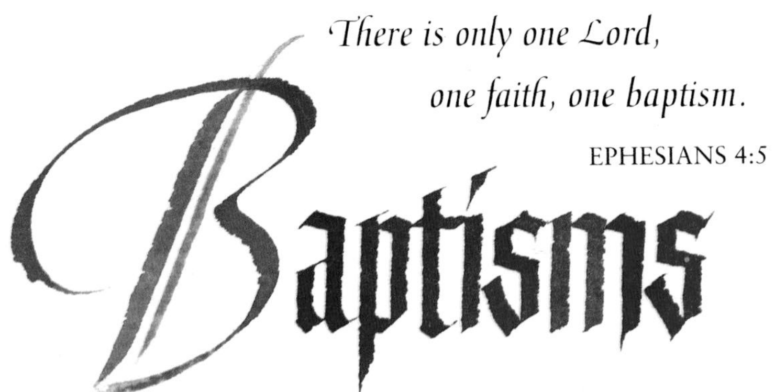
There is only one Lord,
one faith, one baptism.
EPHESIANS 4:5
Baptisms

____

WAS BAPTIZED ON ______________________________

AT______________________________

BY______________________________

____

WAS BAPTIZED ON ______________________________

AT______________________________

BY______________________________

____

WAS BAPTIZED ON ______________________________

AT______________________________

BY______________________________

____

WAS BAPTIZED ON ______________________________

AT______________________________

BY______________________________

And God will raise our bodies from the dead
by his marvelous power,
just as he raised our Lord
from the dead.

1 CORINTHIANS 6:14

NAME	DATE
Charles Grimes	January 1975

THE FAM

NAME BIRTHPLACE DATES

BROTHERS AND SISTERS

PARENTS

FATHER

NAME

BIRTHPLACE DATES

MOTHER

NAME

BIRTHPLACE DATES

GRANDPARENTS

PATERNAL

GRANDFATHER

BIRTHPLACE DATES

GRANDMOTHER

BIRTHPLACE DATES

MATERNAL

GRANDFATHER

BIRTHPLACE DATES

GRANDMOTHER

BIRTHPLACE DATES

GREAT-GRANDPARENTS

PATERNAL

GRANDFATHER'S FATHER

BIRTHPLACE DATES

GRANDFATHER'S MOTHER

BIRTHPLACE DATES

GRANDMOTHER'S FATHER

BIRTHPLACE DATES

GRANDMOTHER'S MOTHER

BIRTHPLACE DATES

MATERNAL

GRANDFATHER'S FATHER

BIRTHPLACE DATES

GRANDFATHER'S MOTHER

BIRTHPLACE DATES

GRANDMOTHER'S FATHER

BIRTHPLACE DATES

GRANDMOTHER'S MOTHER

BIRTHPLACE DATES

ILY TREE

NAME BIRTHPLACE DATES

BROTHERS AND SISTERS

PARENTS

FATHER

NAME

BIRTHPLACE DATES

MOTHER

NAME

BIRTHPLACE DATES

GRANDPARENTS

PATERNAL

GRANDFATHER

BIRTHPLACE DATES

GRANDMOTHER

BIRTHPLACE DATES

MATERNAL

GRANDFATHER

BIRTHPLACE DATES

GRANDMOTHER

BIRTHPLACE DATES

GREAT-GRANDPARENTS

PATERNAL

GRANDFATHER'S FATHER

BIRTHPLACE DATES

GRANDFATHER'S MOTHER

BIRTHPLACE DATES

GRANDMOTHER'S FATHER

BIRTHPLACE DATES

GRANDMOTHER'S MOTHER

BIRTHPLACE DATES

MATERNAL

GRANDFATHER'S FATHER

BIRTHPLACE DATES

GRANDFATHER'S MOTHER

BIRTHPLACE DATES

GRANDMOTHER'S FATHER

BIRTHPLACE DATES

GRANDMOTHER'S MOTHER

BIRTHPLACE DATES

Give thanks to the LORD,
for he is good!
His faithful love endures
forever.

PSALM 118:29

Special memories

EVENT

PLACE DATE

EVENT

PLACE DATE

EVENT

PLACE DATE

EVENT

PLACE DATE

EVENT

PLACE DATE

life APPLICATION® STUDY BIBLE

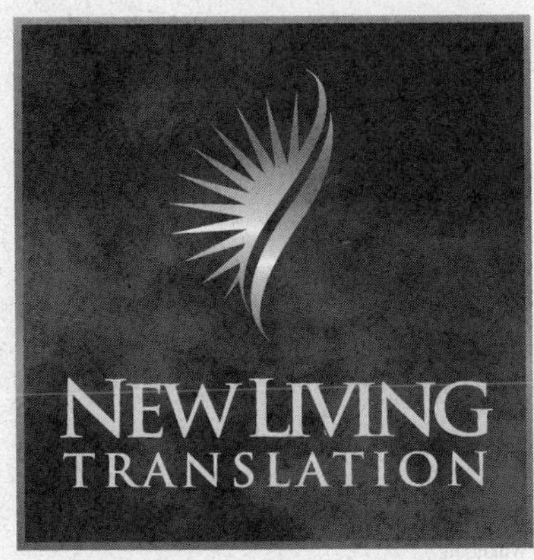

™

Tyndale House Publishers, Inc.
WHEATON, ILLINOIS

Tyndale House Publishers gratefully acknowledges the role of Youth for Christ/USA in preparing the Life Application Notes and Bible Helps.

The Bible text used in this edition of the *Life Application Bible* is the *Holy Bible,* New Living Translation.

Library of Congress Cataloging-in-Publication Data

Bible. English. New Living Translation. 1996.
  Life application study Bible : New Living Translation.
    p.   cm.
  Includes indexes.
  ISBN 0-8423-3267-7 (hardcover alk. paper).—ISBN 0-8423-3300-2 (hardcover indexed)
  I. Tyndale House Publishers. II. Title.
BS195.N394 1996b
220.5′208—dc20   96-20350

ISBN 0-8423-3263-4 Bonded Leather Burgundy
ISBN 0-8423-3301-0 Bonded Leather Burgundy Indexed
ISBN 0-8423-3264-2 Bonded Leather Black
ISBN 0-8423-3268-5 Genuine Leather Burgundy
ISBN 0-8423-3266-9 Genuine Leather Black

Printed in the United States of America

03 02 01 00 99 98 97 96
11 10 9 8 7 6 5 4 3 2 1

Each sale of the *Holy Bible,* New Living Translation, benefits Wycliffe Bible Translators, which completed its four hundredth New Testament in 1995 and is currently working in another one thousand languages. Tyndale House Publishers and Wycliffe Bible Translators share the vision for an understandable, accurate translation of the Bible for every person.

CONTENTS

LIST OF THE BOOKS OF THE BIBLE

A NOTE TO READERS

With 40 million copies in print, *The Living Bible* has been meeting a great need in people's hearts for more than thirty years. But even good things can be improved, so ninety evangelical scholars from various theological backgrounds and denominations were commissioned in 1989 to begin revising *The Living Bible.* The end result of this seven-year process is the *Holy Bible,* New Living Translation—a general-purpose translation that is accurate, easy to read, and excellent for study.

The goal of any Bible translation is to convey the meaning of the ancient Hebrew and Greek texts as accurately as possible to the modern reader. The New Living Translation is based on the most recent scholarship in the theory of translation. The challenge for the translators was to create a text that would make the same impact in the life of modern readers that the original text had for the original readers. In the New Living Translation, this is accomplished by translating entire thoughts (rather than just words) into natural, everyday English. The end result is a translation that is easy to read and understand and that accurately communicates the meaning of the original text.

We believe that this new translation, which combines the latest in scholarship with the best in translation style, will speak to your heart. We present the New Living Translation with the prayer that God will use it to speak his timeless truth to the church and to the world in a fresh, new way.

The Publishers
July 1996

INTRODUCTION TO THE **NEW LIVING TRANSLATION**

Translation Philosophy and Methodology

THERE are two general theories or methods of Bible translation. The first has been called "formal equivalence." According to this theory, the translator attempts to render each word of the original language into the receptor language and seeks to preserve the original word order and sentence structure as much as possible. The second has been called "dynamic equivalence" or "functional equivalence." The goal of this translation theory is to produce in the receptor language the closest natural equivalent of the message expressed by the original-language text—both in meaning and in style. Such a translation attempts to have the same impact on modern readers as the original had on its own audience.

A dynamic-equivalence translation can also be called a thought-for-thought translation, as contrasted with a formal-equivalence or word-for-word translation. Of course, to translate the thought of the original language requires that the text be interpreted accurately and then be rendered in understandable idiom. So the goal of any thought-for-thought translation is to be both reliable and eminently readable. Thus, as a thought-for-thought translation, the New Living Translation seeks to be both exegetically accurate and idiomatically powerful.

In making a thought-for-thought translation, the translators must do their best to enter into the thought patterns of the ancient authors and to present the same ideas, connotations, and effects in the receptor language. In order to guard against personal biases and to ensure the accuracy of the message, a thought-for-thought translation should be created by a group of scholars who employ the best exegetical tools and who also understand the receptor language very well. With these concerns in mind, the Bible Translation Committee assigned each book of the Bible to three different scholars. Each scholar made a thorough review of the assigned book and submitted suggested revisions to the appropriate general reviewer. The general reviewer reviewed and summarized these suggestions and then proposed a first-draft revision of the text. This draft served as the basis for several additional phases of exegetical and stylistic committee review. Then the Bible Translation Committee jointly reviewed and approved every verse in the final translation.

A thought-for-thought translation prepared by a group of capable scholars has the potential to represent the intended meaning of the original text even more accurately than a word-for-word translation. This is illustrated by the various renderings of the Hebrew word *hesed.* This term cannot be adequately translated by any single English word because it can connote love, mercy, grace, kindness, faithfulness, and loyalty. The context—not the lexicon—must determine which English term is selected for translation.

The value of a thought-for-thought translation can be illustrated by comparing 1 Kings 2:10 in the King James Version, the New International Version, and the New Living Translation. "So David slept with his fathers, and was buried in the city of David" (KJV). "Then David rested with his fathers and was buried in the City of David" (NIV). "Then David died and was buried in the City of David" (NLT). Only the New Living Translation clearly translates the real meaning of the Hebrew idiom "slept with his fathers" into contemporary English.

Written to Be Read Aloud

It is evident in Scripture that the biblical documents were written to be read aloud, often in public worship (see Nehemiah 8; Luke 4:16-20; 1 Timothy 4:13; Revelation 1:3). It is still the case today that more people will hear the Bible read aloud in church than are likely to read it for themselves. Therefore, a new translation must communicate with clarity and

power when it is read aloud. For this reason, the New Living Translation is recommended as a Bible to be used for public reading. Its living language is not only easy to understand, but it also has an emotive quality that will make an impact on the listener.

The Texts behind the New Living Translation

The translators of the Old Testament used the Masoretic Text of the Hebrew Bible as their stan dard text. They used the edition known as *Biblia Hebraica Stuttgartensia* (1977) with its up-to-date textual apparatus, a revision of Rudolf Kittel's *Biblia Hebraica* (Stuttgart, 1937). The translators also compared the Dead Sea Scrolls, the Septuagint and other Greek manuscripts, the Samaritan Pentateuch, the Syriac Peshitta, the Latin Vulgate, and any other versions or manuscripts that shed light on textual problems.

The translators of the New Testament used the two stan dard editions of the Greek New Testament: the *Greek New Testament,* published by the United Bible Societies (fourth revised edition, 1993), and *Novum Testamentum Graece,* edited by Nestle and Aland (twenty-seventh edition, 1993). These two editions, which have the same text but differ in punctuation and textual notes, represent the best in modern textual scholarship.

Clarity and Readability

The translators have made a conscious effort to provide a text that can be easily understood by the average reader of modern English. To this end, we have used the vocabulary and language structures commonly used by the average person. The result is a translation of the Scriptures written generally at the reading level of a junior high school student. We have avoided using language that is likely to become quickly dated or that reflects a narrow subdialect of English, with the goal of making the New Living Translation as broadly useful as possible.

But our concern for readability goes beyond the concerns of vocabulary and sentence structure. We are also concerned about historical and cultural barriers to understanding the Bible, and we have sought to translate terms shrouded in history or culture in ways that can be immediately understood by the contemporary reader. Thus, our goal of easy readability expresses itself in a number of other ways:

- Rather than translating ancient weights and measures literally, which communicates little to the modern reader, we have expressed them by means of recognizable contemporary equivalents. We have converted ancient weights and measures to modern English (American) equivalents, and we have rendered the literal Hebrew or Greek measures, along with metric equivalents, in textual footnotes.
- Instead of translating ancient currency values literally, we have generally expressed them in terms of weights in precious metals. In some cases we have used other common terms to communicate the message effectively. For example, "three shekels of silver" might become "three silver coins" or "three pieces of silver" to convey the intended message.
- Since the Hebrew lunar calendar fluctuates from year to year in relation to the solar calendar used today, we have translated Hebrew dates in a way that communicates with our modern readership. It was clear that we could not use the names of the Hebrew months, such as *Abib,* which are meaningless to the modern reader. Nor could we use a simple designation such as "first month," because the months of the Hebrew lunar calendar do not correspond with the months of our calendar. Thus, we have often used seasonal references to communicate the time of year when something happened. For example, "the first month" (which occurs in March and April) might be translated "early spring." Where it is possible to define a specific ancient date in terms of our modern calendar, we use modern dates in the text. Textual footnotes then give the literal Hebrew date and state the rationale for our rendering. For example, Ezra 7:9 pinpoints the date when Ezra arrived in Jerusalem: "the first day of the fifth month." This was during the seventh year of King Artaxerxes' reign (Ezra 7:7). We translate that lunar date as August 4, with a footnote giving the Hebrew and identifying the year as 458 B.C.

- Since ancient references to the time of day differ from our modern methods of denoting time, we used renderings that are instantly understandable to the modern reader. Accordingly, we have rendered specific times of day by using approximate equivalents in terms of our common "o'clock" system. On occasion, translations such as "at dawn the next morning" or "as the sun began to set" have been used when the biblical reference is general.
- Many words in the original texts made sense to the original audience but communicate something quite different to the modern reader. In such cases, some liberty must be allowed in translation to communicate what was intended. Places identified by the term normally translated "city," for example, are often better identified as "towns" or "villages." Similarly, the term normally translated "mountain" is often better rendered "hill."
- Many words and phrases carry a great deal of cultural meaning that was obvious to the original readers but needs explanation in our own culture. For example, the phrase "they beat their breasts" (Luke 23:48) in ancient times meant that people were very upset. In our translation we chose to translate this phrase dynamically: "They went home *in deep sorrow.*" In some cases, however, we have simply illuminated the existing expression to make it immediately understandable. For example, we might have expanded the literal phrase to read "they beat their breasts *in sorrow.*"
- Metaphorical language is often difficult for contemporary readers to understand, so at times we have chosen to translate or illuminate the metaphor. For example, the ancient poet writes, "Your eyes are doves" (Song of Songs 1:15). To help the modern reader, who might be confused or distracted by a literal visualization of this image, we converted the metaphor to a simile to make the meaning immediately clear: "Your eyes are soft *like* doves." Here we also added the modifier "soft" to help the modern reader catch the significance of the metaphoric expression. A few chapters later, the poet writes, "Your neck is like the tower of David" (Song of Songs 4:4). We rendered it "Your neck is *as stately as* the tower of David" to clarify the intended positive meaning of the metaphor.
- We did not feel obligated to display all Hebrew poetry in English poetic form. Only the book of Psalms is set entirely in poetic lines. Other books, though poetic in nature, are set in prose for the sake of easier reading. Nonetheless, these prose renderings reflect the poetic language of the original Hebrew. Where a portion of text is explicitly said to be a poem or song, however, it has usually been set as such.

Lexical Consistency in Terminology

For the sake of clarity, we have maintained lexical consistency in areas such as divine names, synoptic passages, rhetorical structures, and nontheological technical terms (i.e., liturgical, cultic, zoological, botanical, cultural, and legal terms). For theological terms, we have allowed a greater semantic range of acceptable English words or phrases for a single Hebrew or Greek word. We avoided weighty theological terms that do not readily communicate to many modern readers. For example, we avoided using words such as "justification," "sanctification," and "regeneration." In place of these words (which are carryovers from Latin), we provided renderings such as "we are made right with God," "we are made holy," and "we are born anew."

The Spelling of Proper Names

Many individuals in the Bible, especially the Old Testament, are known by more than one name or by a number of variant names (e.g., Uzziah/Azariah). For the sake of clarity, we have tried to use a single spelling for any one individual, footnoting the literal spelling whenever we differ from it. This is especially helpful in delineating the kings of Israel and Judah. King Joash/Jehoash of Israel has been consistently called Jehoash, while King Joash/Jehoash of Judah is called Joash. A similar distinction has been used to distinguish between Joram/Jehoram of Israel and Joram/Jehoram of Judah. All such decisions were made with the goal of clarifying the text for the reader. When the ancient biblical writers clearly had a theological purpose in their choice of a variant name (e.g., Eshbaal/Ishbosheth), the different names have been maintained with an explanatory footnote.

The Rendering of Divine Names

All appearances of *'el, 'elohim,* or *'eloah* have been translated "God," except where the context demands the translation "god(s)." We have rendered the tetragrammaton *(YHWH)* consistently as "the LORD," utilizing a form with small capitals that is common among English translations. This will distinguish it from the name *'adonai,* which we render "Lord." When *'adonai* and *YHWH* appear in conjunction, we have rendered it "Sovereign LORD." This also distinguishes *'adonai YHWH* from cases where *YHWH* appears with *'elohim,* which is rendered "LORD God." When *YH* (the short form of *YHWH*) and *YHWH* appear together we have rendered it "LORD GOD." The Hebrew word *'adon* is rendered "lord," or "master," or sometimes "sir."

In the New Testament, the Greek word *Christos* has been translated as "Messiah" when the context assumes a Jewish audience. When a Gentile audience can be assumed, *Christos* has been translated as "Christ." The Greek word *kurios* is consistently translated "Lord."

Gender-Inclusive Language

The English language changes constantly. An obvious recent change is in the area of gender-inclusive language. This creates problems for modern translators of the ancient biblical text, which was originally written in a male-oriented culture. The translator must respect the nature of the ancient context while also accounting for the concerns of the modern audience. Often the original language itself allows a rendering that is gender inclusive. For example, the Greek word *anthropos,* traditionally rendered "man," really means "human being" or "person." A different Greek word, *aner,* specifically means a male.

There are other occasions where the original language is male-oriented, but not intentionally so. For example, in the Pentateuch most of the laws are stated in language that is replete with masculine pronouns. But since it is clear in many cases that the recipients of these laws were both male and female, we have used gender-neutral language where appropriate. Another example is found in the New Testament epistles, where the believers are called "brothers" *(adelphoi).* Yet it is clear that these epistles were addressed to all the believers—male and female. Thus, we have usually translated this Greek word "brothers and sisters" or "Christian friends" in order to represent the historical situtation more accurately.

Finally, we have attempted to use a gender-neutral rendering where the text applies generally to human beings or to the human condition. For example, a traditional rendering of Luke 9:62 reads: "No man who puts his hand to the plow and looks back is fit for the Kingdom of God." We have translated it: "Anyone who puts a hand to the plow and then looks back is not fit for the Kingdom of God." In many instances we have used plural pronouns (they, them) in place of the gender-specific singular (he, him). For example, a traditional rendering of Proverbs 22:6 is: "Train up a child in the way he should go, and when he is old he will not turn from it." We have rendered it: "Teach your children to choose the right path, and when they are older, they will remain upon it."

Textual Footnotes

The New Living Translation provides several kinds of textual footnotes:

- All Old Testament passages that are clearly quoted in the New Testament are identified in a textual footnote in the New Testament.
- Some textual footnotes provide cultural and historical information on places, things, and people in the Bible that are probably obscure to modern readers. Such notes should aid the reader in understanding the message of the text. For example, in Acts 12:1, "King Herod" is named in this translation as "King Herod Agrippa" and is identified in a footnote as being "the nephew of Herod Antipas and a grandson of Herod the Great."
- When various ancient manuscripts contain different readings, these differences are often documented in footnotes. For instance, textual variants are footnoted when the variant reading is very familiar (usually through the King James Version). We have used footnotes when we have selected variant readings that differ from the Hebrew and Greek editions normally followed.

- When the meaning of a proper name (or a wordplay inherent in a proper name) is relevant to the meaning of the text, it is illuminated with a textual footnote. For example, the footnote at Genesis 3:20 reads: *"Eve* sounds like a Hebrew term that means 'to give life.'" This wordplay in the Hebrew illuminates the meaning of the text, which goes on to say that Eve "would be the mother of all people everywhere." If the meaning of the name is more certain, it is stated more simply. For example, the footnote at Genesis 16:11 reads: *"Ishmael* means 'God hears.'" In this case, Hagar named her son Ishmael after realizing that God had heard her cry for help.
- When we translate the meaning of a place name that is often simply transliterated from the Hebrew or Greek, we provide a textual footnote showing the transliteration that appears in many English translations. For example, the name usually transliterated "Havvoth-jair" in Judges 10:4 has been translated "the Towns of Jair," with a footnote that gives the traditional transliteration: "Hebrew *Havvoth-jair."*
- Textual footnotes are also used to show alternative renderings. These are prefaced with the word "Or." On occasion, we also provide notes on words or phrases that represent a translation that departs from longstanding tradition. These notes are prefaced with the words "traditionally rendered." For example, a footnote to the translation "contagious skin disease" at Leviticus 13:2 says, "Traditionally rendered *leprosy."*

AS WE SUBMIT this translation of the Bible for publication, we recognize that any translation of the Scriptures is subject to limitations and imperfections. Anyone who has attempted to communicate the richness of God's Word into another language will realize it is impossible to make a perfect translation. Recognizing these limitations, we sought God's guidance and wisdom throughout this project. Now we pray that he will accept our efforts and use this translation for the benefit of the Church and of all people.

We pray that the New Living Translation will overcome some of the barriers of history, culture, and language that have kept people from reading and understanding God's Word. We hope that readers unfamiliar with the Bible will find the words clear and easy to understand, and that readers well versed in the Scriptures will gain a fresh perspective. We pray that readers will gain insight and wisdom for living, but most of all that they will meet the God of the Bible and be forever changed by knowing him.

The Bible Translation Committee
July 1996

PENTATEUCH

Daniel I. Block, General Reviewer
The Southern Baptist Theological Seminary

GENESIS
Allan Ross, *Trinity Episcopal Seminary*
John Sailhamer, *Northwestern College*
Gordon Wenham, *The Cheltenham and Gloucester College of Higher Education*

EXODUS
Robert Bergen, *Hannibal-LaGrange College*
Daniel I. Block, *The Southern Baptist Theological Seminary*
Eugene Carpenter, *Bethel College, Mishawaka, Indiana*

LEVITICUS
David Baker, *Ashland Theological Seminary*
Victor Hamilton, *Asbury College*
Kenneth Mathews, *Beeson Divinity School, Samford University*

NUMBERS
Dale A. Brueggemann, *Assemblies of God, Division of Foreign Missions*
Roland K. Harrison (deceased), *Wycliffe College*
Gerald L. Mattingly, *Johnson Bible College*

DEUTERONOMY
J. Gordon McConville, *The Cheltenham and Gloucester College of Higher Education*
Eugene H. Merrill, *Dallas Theological Seminary*
John A. Thompson, *University of Melbourne*

HISTORICAL BOOKS

Barry J. Beitzel, General Reviewer
Trinity Evangelical Divinity School

JOSHUA/ JUDGES
Carl E. Armerding, *Schloss Mittersill Study Centre*
Barry J. Beitzel, *Trinity Evangelical Divinity School*
Lawson Stone, *Asbury Theological Seminary*

1 & 2 SAMUEL
Barry J. Beitzel, *Trinity Evangelical Divinity School*
V. Philips Long, *Covenant Theological Seminary*
J. Robert Vannoy, *Biblical Theological Seminary*

1 & 2 KINGS
Bill T. Arnold, *Asbury Theological Seminary*
William H. Barnes, *Southeastern College of the Assemblies of God*
Frederic W. Bush, *Fuller Theological Seminary*

1 & 2 CHRONICLES
Raymond B. Dillard (deceased), *Westminster Theological Seminary*
David A. Dorsey, *Evangelical School of Theology*
Terry Eves, *Calvin College*

EZRA/ NEHEMIAH/ ESTHER/ RUTH
William C. Williams, *Southern California College*
Hugh G. M. Williamson, *Oxford University*

POETRY

Tremper Longman III, General Reviewer
Westminster Theological Seminary

JOB
August Konkel, *Providence Theological Seminary*
Tremper Longman III, *Westminster Theological Seminary*
Al Wolters, *Redeemer College*

PSALMS 1–75
Mark D. Futato, *Westminster Theological Seminary in California*
Douglas Green, *Westminster Theological Seminary*
Richard Pratt, *Reformed Theological Seminary*

PSALMS 76–150
David M. Howard Jr., *Trinity Evangelical Divinity School*
Raymond C. Ortlund Jr., *Trinity Evangelical Divinity School*
Willem VanGemeren, *Trinity Evangelical Divinity School*

PROVERBS
Ted Hildebrandt, *Grace College*
Richard Schultz, *Wheaton College*
Raymond C. Van Leeuwen, *Eastern College*

ECCLESIASTES/ SONG OF SONGS
Daniel C. Fredericks, *Belhaven College*
David Hubbard, *Fuller Theological Seminary*
Tremper Longman III, *Westminster Theological Seminary*

PROPHETS

John N. Oswalt, General Reviewer
Asbury Theological Seminary

ISAIAH
John N. Oswalt, *Asbury Theological Seminary*
Gary Smith, *Bethel Theological Seminary*
John Walton, *Moody Bible Institute*

JEREMIAH/ LAMENTATIONS
G. Herbert Livingston, *Asbury Theological Seminary*
Elmer A. Martens, *Mennonite Brethren Biblical Seminary*

EZEKIEL
Daniel I. Block, *The Southern Baptist Theological Seminary*
David H. Engelhard, *Calvin Theological Seminary*
David Thompson, *Asbury Theological Seminary*

DANIEL/ HAGGAI/ ZECHARIAH/ MALACHI
Joyce Baldwin Caine (deceased), *Trinity College, Bristol*
Douglas Gropp, *Catholic University of America*
Roy Hayden, *Oral Roberts School of Theology*

HOSEA–ZEPHANIAH
Joseph Coleson, *Nazarene Theological Seminary*
Andrew Hill, *Wheaton College*
Richard Patterson, *Professor Emeritus, Liberty University*

GOSPELS AND ACTS

Grant R. Osborne, General Reviewer
Trinity Evangelical Divinity School

MATTHEW
Craig Blomberg, *Denver Conservative Baptist Seminary*
Donald A. Hagner, *Fuller Theological Seminary*
David Turner, *Grand Rapids Baptist Seminary*

MARK
Robert Guelich (deceased), *Fuller Theological Seminary*
Grant R. Osborne, *Trinity Evangelical Divinity School*

LUKE
Darrel Bock, *Dallas Theological Seminary*
Scot McKnight, *North Park College*
Robert Stein, *Bethel Theological Seminary*

JOHN
Gary M. Burge, *Wheaton College*
Philip W. Comfort, *Wheaton College*
Marianne Meye Thompson, *Fuller Theological Seminary*

ACTS
D. A. Carson, *Trinity Evangelical Divinity School*
William J. Larkin, *Columbia Biblical Seminary*
Roger Mohrlang, *Whitworth College*

LETTERS AND REVELATION

Norman R. Ericson, General Reviewer
Wheaton College

ROMANS/ GALATIANS
Gerald Borchert, *The Southern Baptist Theological Seminary*
Douglas J. Moo, *Trinity Evangelical Divinity School*
Thomas R. Schreiner, *Bethel Theological Seminary*

1 & 2 CORINTHIANS
Joseph Alexanian, *Trinity International University*
Linda Belleville, *North Park Theological Seminary*
Douglas A. Oss, *Central Bible College*
Robert Sloan, *Baylor University*

EPHESIANS–PHILEMON
Harold W. Hoehner, *Dallas Theological Seminary*
Moises Silva, *Gordon-Conwell Theological Seminary*
Klyne Snodgrass, *North Park Theological Seminary*

HEBREWS/ JAMES/ 1 & 2 PETER/ JUDE
Peter Davids, *Canadian Theological Seminary*
Norman R. Ericson, *Wheaton College*
William Lane, *Seattle Pacific University*
J. Ramsey Michaels, *S. W. Missouri State University*

1–3 JOHN/ REVELATION
Greg Beale, *Gordon-Conwell Theological Seminary*
Robert Mounce, *Whitworth College*
M. Robert Mulholland Jr., *Asbury Theological Seminary*

SPECIAL REVIEWERS

F. F. Bruce (deceased), *University of Manchester*
Kenneth N. Taylor, *Tyndale House Publishers*

COORDINATING TEAM

Mark R. Norton, Managing Editor and O.T. Coordinating Editor
Philip W. Comfort, N.T. Coordinating Editor
Ronald A. Beers, Executive Director and Stylist
Mark D. Taylor, Director and Chief Stylist

CONTRIBUTORS

Senior Editorial Team
Dr. Bruce B. Barton
Ronald A. Beers
Dr. James C. Galvin
LaVonne Neff
Linda Chaffee Taylor
David R. Veerman

General Editor
Ronald A. Beers

Tyndale House Bible Editors
Dr. Philip W. Comfort
Virginia Muir
Robert Brown
Del Lankford
Mark Norton
Steve Benson

Book Introductions
David R. Veerman

Book Outlines, Blueprints, Harmony
Dr. James C. Galvin

Megathemes
Dr. Bruce B. Barton

Map Development & Computer Operation
Linda Chaffee Taylor

Color Map Consultant
Dr. Barry Beitzel

Charts & Diagrams
Neil S. Wilson
Ronald A. Beers
David R. Veerman
Pamela York

Dictionary/Concordance
Dietrich Gruen

Personality Profiles
Neil S. Wilson

Design & Development Team
Dr. Bruce B. Barton
Ronald A. Beers
Dr. James C. Galvin
David R. Veerman

Tyndale House Production
Joan Major
Marlene Muller
Julee Schwarzburg
Jim Bolton
Linda Walz
Lois Rusch
Gwen Elliott

Tyndale House Graphic Design
Timothy R. Botts

A Chronology of Bible Events and World Events
Dr. David Maas

Theological Reviewers

Dr. Kenneth S. Kantzer
General Theological Reviewer
Dean Emeritus and
Distinguished Professor of Bible and Systematic Theology
Trinity Evangelical Divinity School

Dr. V. Gilbert Beers
President of
Scripture Press Ministries

Dr. Barry Beitzel
Associate Academic Dean
and Professor of Old Testament
and Semitic Languages
Trinity Evangelical Divinity School

Dr. Edwin A. Blum
Associate Professor of
Historical Theology
Dallas Theological Seminary

Dr. Geoffrey W. Bromiley
Professor
Fuller Theological Seminary

Dr. George K. Brushaber
President
Bethel College & Seminary

Dr. L. Russ Bush
Associate Professor
Philosophy & Religion
Southwestern Baptist
Theological Seminary

C. Donald Cole
Pastor, Moody Radio Network

Mrs. Naomi E. Cole
Speaker & Seminar Leader

Dr. Walter A. Elwell
Dean
Wheaton College Graduate School

Dr. Gerald F. Hawthorne
Professor of Greek
Wheaton College

Dr. Howard G. Hendricks
Professor-at-Large
Chairman
Center for Christian Leadership
Dallas Theological Seminary

Dr. Grant R. Osborne
Professor of New Testament
Trinity Evangelical Divinity School

A special thanks to the nationwide staff of Youth for Christ/USA for their suggestions and field testing, and to the following additional contributing writers: V. Gilbert Beers, Neil Wilson, John Crosby, Joan Young, Jack Crabtree, Philip Craven, Bob Black, Bur Shilling, Arthur Deyo, Annie Lafrentz, Danny Sartin, William Hanawalt, William Bonikowsky, Brian Rathbun, Pamela Barden, Thomas Stobie, Robert Arnold, Greg Monaco, Larry Dunn, Lynn Ziegenfuss, Mitzie Barton, Marijean Hamilton, Larry Kreider, Gary Dausey, William Roland, Kathy Howell, Philip Steffeck, James Coleman, Marty Grasley, O'Ann Steere, Julia Amstutz.

A special thanks also to the following people whose personal counsel, encouragement, and determination helped make this product a reality:

Dr. Kenneth N. Taylor
Translator of *The Living Bible*
Chairman of the Board
Tyndale House Publishers, Inc.

Mark D. Taylor
President
Tyndale House Publishers, Inc.

Dr. Wendell C. Hawley
Senior Vice President
Editorial
Tyndale House Publishers, Inc.

Virginia Muir
Retired Assistant Editor-in-Chief
Tyndale House Publishers, Inc.

Richard R. Wynn
Youth for Christ/Area Director
for Asia and Pacific

Dr. Jay L. Kesler
President, Taylor University

A CHRONOLOGY OF BIBLE EVENTS AND WORLD EVENTS

Creation
undated

Noah
builds
the ark
undated

Abraham
born
2166

Abraham
enters
Canaan
2091

2500 BC.
Egyptians
discover
papyrus
and ink
for writing
and build
the first
libraries;
iron objects
manufactured
in the ancient
Near East

2400
Egyptians
import gold
from Africa

2331
Semitic
chieftain,
Sargon,
conquers Sumer
to become
first "world
conqueror"

2300
Horses
domesticated
in Egypt;
chickens
domesticated
in Babylon;
bows & arrows
used in wars

2100
Glass made
by the
Mesopotamians;
ziggurats
(like the tower
of Babel)
built in
Mesopotamia;
earliest
discovered drug,
ethyl alcohol,
used to
alleviate pain

WHY THE *LIFE APPLICATION STUDY BIBLE* IS UNIQUE

Have you ever opened your Bible and asked the following:

- What does this passage really mean?
- How does it apply to my life?
- Why does some of the Bible seem irrelevant?
- What do these ancient cultures have to do with today?
- I love God; why can't I understand what he is saying to me through his Word?
- What's going on in the lives of these Bible people?

Many Christians do not read the Bible regularly. Why? Because in the pressures of daily living, they cannot find a connection between the timeless principles of Scripture and the ever-present problems of day-by-day living.

God urges us to apply his Word (Isaiah 42:23; 1 Corinthians 10:11; 2 Thessalonians 3:4), but too often we stop at accumulating Bible knowledge. This is why the *Life Application Study Bible* was developed—to show how to put into practice what we have learned.

Applying God's Word is a vital part of one's relationship with God; it is the evidence that we are obeying him. The difficulty in applying the Bible is not with

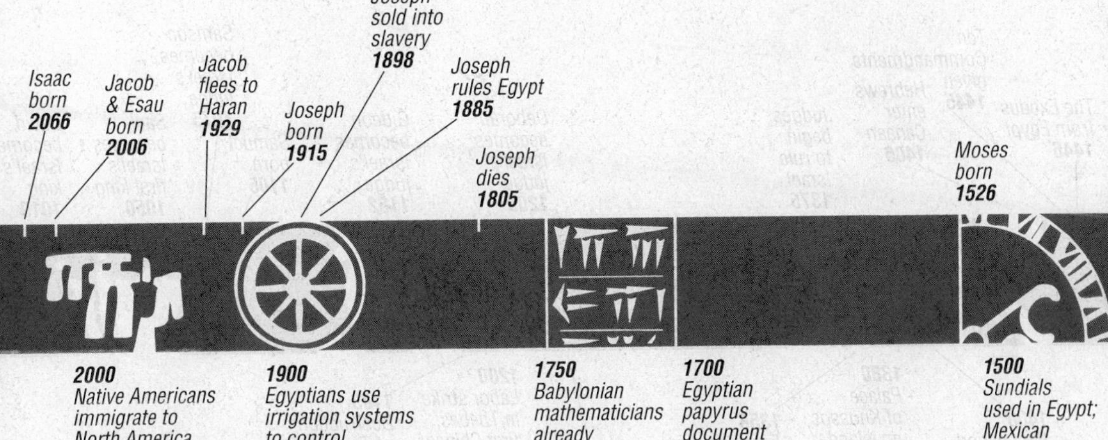

Isaac born 2066
Jacob & Esau born 2006
Jacob flees to Haran 1929
Joseph born 1915
Joseph sold into slavery 1898
Joseph rules Egypt 1885
Joseph dies 1805
Moses born 1526
2000 Native Americans immigrate to North America from northern Asia; stock breeding and irrigation used in China; Stonehenge, England, a center for religious worship is erected; bellows used in India, allowing for higher furnace temperatures
1900 Egyptians use irrigation systems to control Nile floods; spoked wheel invented in the ancient Near East; horses used to pull vehicles
1750 Babylonian mathematicians already understand cube and square root; Hammurapi of Babylon provides first of all legal codes
1700 Egyptian papyrus document describes medical and surgical procedures
1500 Sundials used in Egypt; Mexican Sun Pyramid built

the Bible itself, but with the reader's inability to bridge the gap between the past and present, the conceptual and practical. When we don't or can't do this, spiritual dryness, shallowness, and indifference are the results.

The words of Scripture itself cry out to us, "And remember, it is a message to obey, not just to listen to. If you don't obey, you are only fooling yourself" (James 1:22). The *Life Application Study Bible* does just that. Developed by an interdenominational team of pastors, scholars, family counselors, and a national organization dedicated to promoting God's Word and spreading the gospel, the *Life Application Study Bible* took many years to complete, and all the work was reviewed by several renowned theologians under the directorship of Dr. Kenneth Kantzer.

The *Life Application Study Bible* does what a good resource Bible should—it helps you understand the context of a passage, gives important background and historical information, explains difficult words and phrases, and helps you see the interrelationships within Scripture. But it does much more. The *Life Application Study Bible* goes deeper into God's Word, helping you discover the timeless truth being communicated, see the relevance for your life, and make a personal application. While some study Bibles attempt application, over 75% of this Bible is application-oriented. The notes answer the questions, "So what?" and "What does this passage mean to me, my family, my friends, my job, my neighborhood, my church, my country?"

Imagine reading a familiar passage of Scripture and gaining fresh insight, as if it were the first time you had ever read it. How much richer your life would be if you left each Bible reading with a new perspective and a small change for the better. A small change every day adds up to a changed life—and that is the very purpose of Scripture.

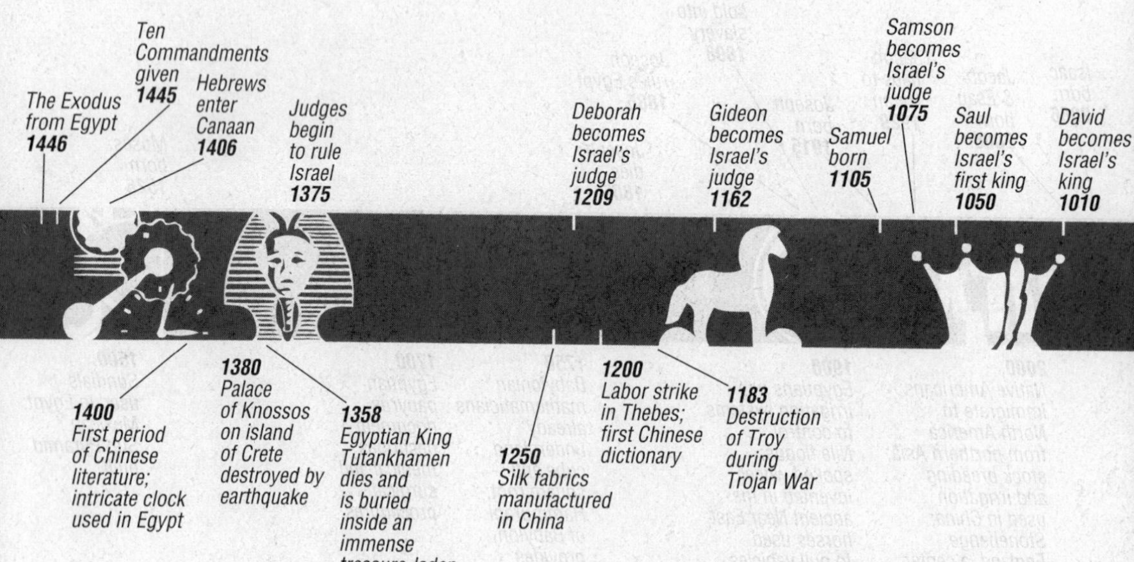

The best way to define application is to first determine what it is *not.* Application is *not* just accumulating knowledge. This helps us discover and understand facts and concepts, but it stops there. History is filled with philosophers who knew what the Bible said but failed to apply it to their lives, keeping them from believing and changing. Many think that understanding is the end goal of Bible study, but it is really only the beginning.

Application is *not* just illustration. Illustration only tells us how someone else handled a similar situation. While we may empathize with that person, we still have little direction for our personal situation.

Application is *not* just making a passage "relevant." Making the Bible relevant only helps us to see that the same lessons that were true in Bible times are true today; it does not show us how to apply them to the problems and pressures of our individual lives.

What, then, is application? Application begins by knowing and understanding God's Word and its timeless truths. *But you cannot stop there.* If you do, God's Word may not change your life, and it may become dull, difficult, tedious, and tiring. A good application focuses the truth of God's Word, shows the reader what to do about what is being read, and motivates the reader to respond to what God is teaching. All three are essential to application.

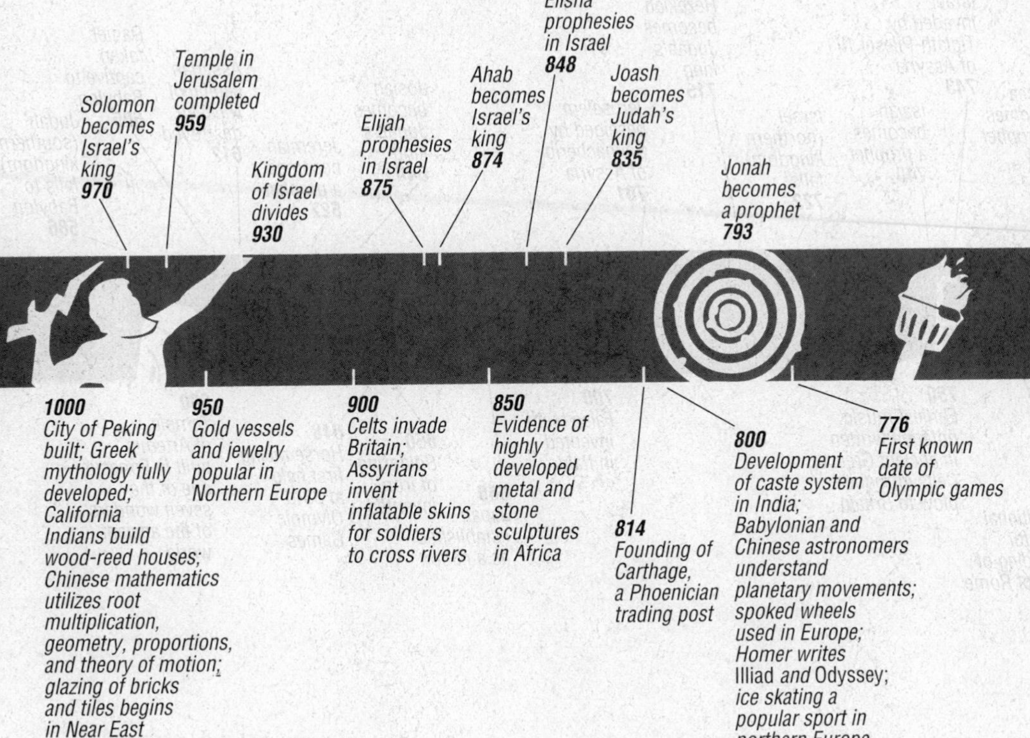
Solomon becomes Israel's king 970
Temple in Jerusalem completed 959
Kingdom of Israel divides 930
Elijah prophesies in Israel 875
Ahab becomes Israel's king 874
Elisha prophesies in Israel 848
Joash becomes Judah's king 835
Jonah becomes a prophet 793
1000 City of Peking built; Greek mythology fully developed; California Indians build wood-reed houses; Chinese mathematics utilizes root multiplication, geometry, proportions, and theory of motion; glazing of bricks and tiles begins in Near East
950 Gold vessels and jewelry popular in Northern Europe
900 Celts invade Britain; Assyrians invent inflatable skins for soldiers to cross rivers
850 Evidence of highly developed metal and stone sculptures in Africa
814 Founding of Carthage, a Phoenician trading post
800 Development of caste system in India; Babylonian and Chinese astronomers understand planetary movements; spoked wheels used in Europe; Homer writes Illiad and Odyssey; ice skating a popular sport in northern Europe
776 First known date of Olympic games

Application is putting into practice what we already know (see Mark 4:24 and Hebrews 5:14) and answering the question, "So what?" by confronting us with the right questions and motivating us to take action (see 1 John 2:5, 6 and James 2:17). Application is deeply personal—unique for each individual. It is making a relevant truth a personal truth, and involves developing a strategy and action plan to live your life in harmony with the Bible. It is the Biblical "how to" of life.

You may ask, "How can your application notes be relevant to my life?" Each application note has three parts: (1) an *explanation* that ties the note directly to the Scripture passage and sets up the truth that is being taught, (2) the *bridge* that explains the timeless truth and makes it relevant for today, (3) the *application* that shows you how to take the timeless truth and apply it to your personal situation. No note, by itself, can apply Scripture directly to your life. It can only teach, direct, lead, guide, inspire, recommend, and urge. It can give you the resources and direction you need to apply the Bible; but only *you* can take these resources and put them into practice.

A good note, therefore, should not only give you knowledge and understanding, but point you to application. Before you buy any kind of resource Bible, you should evaluate the notes and ask the following questions: (1) Does the note contain enough information to help me understand the point of the Scripture passage? (2) Does the note assume I know too much? (3) Does the note avoid denominational bias? (4) Do the notes touch most of life's experiences? (5) Does the note help me *apply* God's Word?

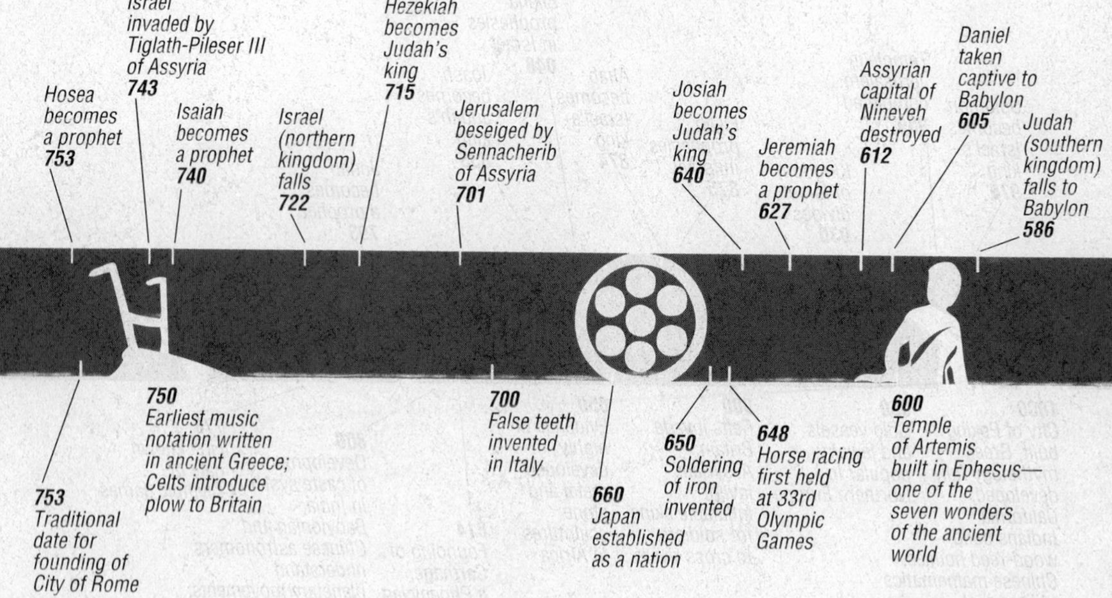
Hosea becomes a prophet 753
Israel invaded by Tiglath-Pileser III of Assyria 743
Isaiah becomes a prophet 740
Israel (northern kingdom) falls 722
Hezekiah becomes Judah's king 715
Jerusalem beseiged by Sennacherib of Assyria 701
Josiah becomes Judah's king 640
Jeremiah becomes a prophet 627
Assyrian capital of Nineveh destroyed 612
Daniel taken captive to Babylon 605
Judah (southern kingdom) falls to Babylon 586
753 Traditional date for founding of City of Rome
750 Earliest music notation written in ancient Greece; Celts introduce plow to Britain
700 False teeth invented in Italy
660 Japan established as a nation
650 Soldering of iron invented
648 Horse racing first held at 33rd Olympic Games
600 Temple of Artemis built in Ephesus—one of the seven wonders of the ancient world

NOTES

In addition to providing the reader with many application notes, the *Life Application Study Bible* offers several explanatory notes, which are notes that help the reader understand culture, history, context, difficult-to-understand passages, background, places, theological concepts, and the relationship of various passages in Scripture to other passages. Maps, charts, and diagrams are also found on the same page as the passages to which they relate. For an example of an application note, see Mark 15:47. For an example of an explanatory note, see Mark 11:1, 2.

BOOK INTRODUCTIONS

The Book Introductions are divided into several easy-to-find parts:

Timeline. This puts the Bible book into its historical setting. It lists the key events of each book and the date when they occurred. The alternative dates in parenthesis are based on a later dating of the Exodus.

Vital Statistics. This is a list of straight facts about the book—those pieces of information you need to know at a glance.

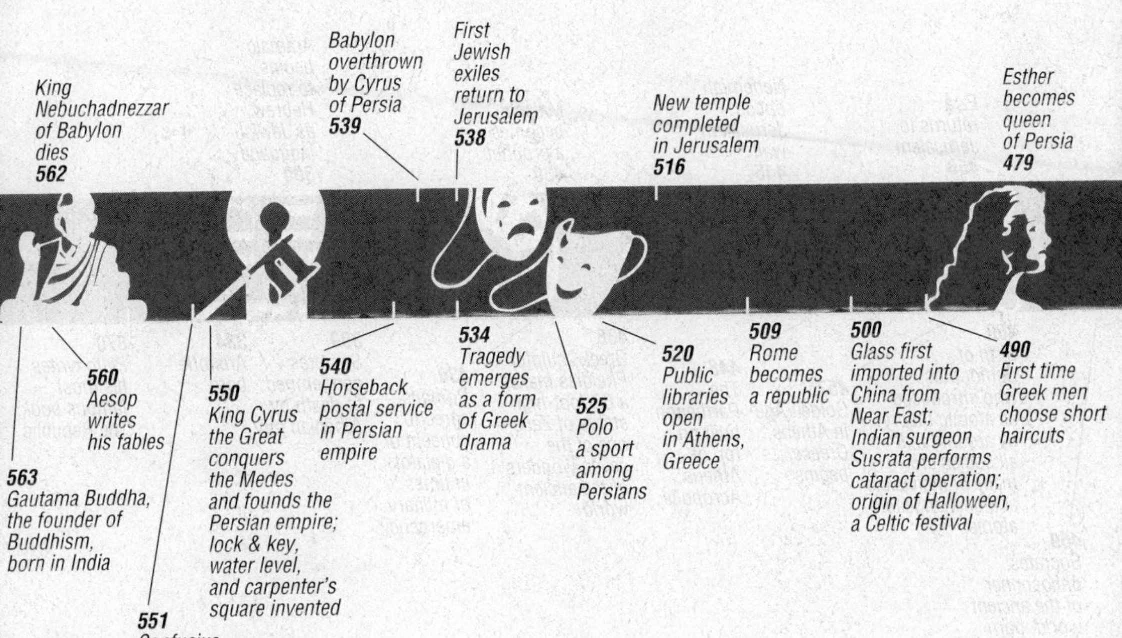
King Nebuchadnezzar of Babylon dies
562
Babylon overthrown by Cyrus of Persia
539
First Jewish exiles return to Jerusalem
538
New temple completed in Jerusalem
516
Esther becomes queen of Persia
479
563
Gautama Buddha, the founder of Buddhism, born in India
560
Aesop writes his fables
551
Confucius, famous Chinese scholar, born
550
King Cyrus the Great conquers the Medes and founds the Persian empire; lock & key, water level, and carpenter's square invented
540
Horseback postal service in Persian empire
534
Tragedy emerges as a form of Greek drama
525
Polo a sport among Persians
520
Public libraries open in Athens, Greece
509
Rome becomes a republic
500
Glass first imported into China from Near East; Indian surgeon Susrata performs cataract operation; origin of Halloween, a Celtic festival
490
First time Greek men choose short haircuts

Overview. This is a summary of the book with general lessons and application that can be learned from the book as a whole.

Blueprint. This is the outline of the book. It is printed in easy-to-understand language and is designed for easy memorization. To the right of each main heading is a key lesson that is taught in that particular section.

Megathemes. This section gives the main themes of the Bible book, explains their significance, and then tells why they are still important for us today.

Map. This shows the key places found in that book and retells the story of the book from a geographical point of view.

OUTLINE

The *Life Application Study Bible* has a new, custom-made outline that was designed specifically from an application point of view. Several unique features should be noted:

1. To avoid confusion and to aid memory work, each book outline has only three levels for headings. Main outline heads are marked with a capital letter. Subheads are marked by a number. Minor explanatory heads have no letter or number.
2. Each main outline head marked by a letter also has a brief paragraph below it summarizing the Bible text and offering a general application.
3. Parallel passages are listed where they apply in the Gospels.

Ezra returns to Jerusalem **458**

Nehemiah builds Jerusalem wall **445**

Malachi becomes a prophet **430**

Aramaic begins to replace Hebrew as Jewish language **390**

469 Socrates, philosopher of the ancient world, born

460 Birth of Democritus, who introduced an atomic theory by arguing that all bodies are made of indivisible and unchangeable atoms

457 Golden Age in Athens, Greece, begins

448 The Parthenon built on top of Athens' Acropolis

438 Greek sculptor Pheidias makes a 60-foot-high statue of Zeus—one of the seven wonders of the ancient world

430 Romans agree to concept of a dictator in times of military emergency

399 Socrates condemned to death by Athenian jury

384 Aristotle born

370 Plato writes his most famous book, The Republic

HARMONY OF THE GOSPELS
A harmony of the Gospels was developed specifically for this Bible. It is the first harmony that has ever been incorporated into the Bible text. Through a unique and simple numbering system, you can read any Gospel account and see just where you are in relation to the entire life of Christ. The harmony is located after the Gospel of John and explained in detail there.

PROFILE NOTES
Another unique feature of this Bible is the profiles of many Bible people, including their strengths and weaknesses, greatest accomplishments and mistakes, and key lessons from their lives. The profiles of these people are found in the Bible books where their stories occur.

MAPS
The *Life Application Study Bible* has more maps than any other Bible. A thorough and comprehensive Bible atlas is built right into each Bible book. There are two kinds of maps: (1) A book introduction map, telling the story of that Bible book. (2) Thumbnail maps in the notes, plotting most geographic movements in the Bible. In addition to these numerous black-and-white maps, there is an entirely new and comprehensive set of color maps and diagrams at the back of this Bible.

CHARTS AND DIAGRAMS
Hundreds of charts and diagrams are included to help the reader better visualize difficult concepts or relationships. Most charts not only present the needed information but show the significance of the information as well.

331 *Alexander the Great defeats the Persian empire*

312 *Romans build first paved road, the "Appian Way," from Rome to Capua*

255 *Hebrew Old Testament translated into Greek and called the "Septuagint"*

241 *Romans conquer Sicily and add their first non-Italian territory to the Roman empire*

215 *Great Wall of China built*

Temple of Jerusalem plundered by Antiochus IV ***169***

Judas Maccabeus begins a revolt against Antiochus IV ***165***

139 *Jews and astrologers banished from Rome*

102 *First Chinese ships reach east coast of India; ball bearings used in Danish cart wheels*

100 *Julius Caesar, first emperor of Rome, born*

55 *Romans conquer England and make it part of Roman empire until* A.D. *442*

51 *Cleopatra becomes last independent Egyptian ruler of the ancient world*

CROSS-REFERENCES
A carefully organized cross-reference system in the margins of the Bible text helps the reader find related passages quickly. A cross-reference marked by two slashes (//) indicates that the cross-reference is a parallel passage, largely identical to the identified text in content and wording. A cross-reference marked by a dagger (†) indicates that the identified text either quotes from the cross-reference or the cross-referenced text quotes the identified text.

TEXTUAL NOTES AND SECTIONAL HEADINGS
Directly related to the New Living Translation text, the textual notes examine such things as alternate translations, meaning of Hebrew and Greek terms, Old Testament quotations, and variant readings in ancient Biblical manuscripts. The NLT text also contains sectional headings in order to help you more easily understand the subject and content of each section.

INDEX
This book contains a complete index to all the notes, charts, maps, and personality profiles. With its emphasis on application, it is helpful for group Bible study, sermon preparation, teaching, or personal study.

DICTIONARY/CONCORDANCE
A concise concordance identifies terms of special interest and lists the important occurrences in context. Each word is followed by a brief definition.

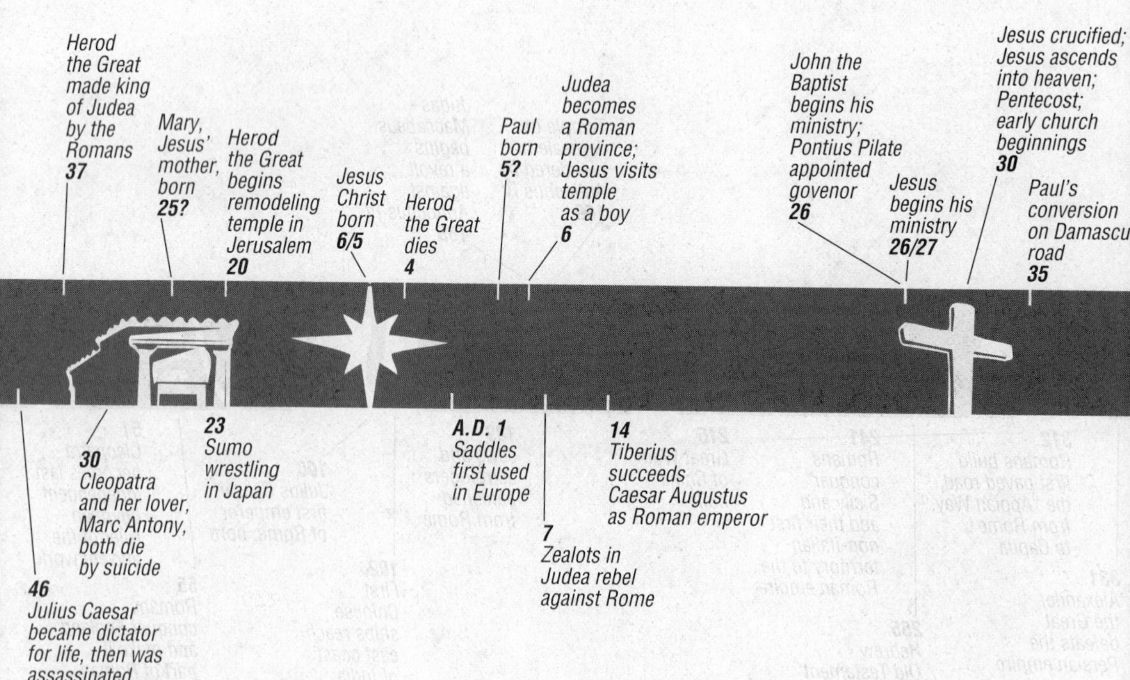

Herod the Great made king of Judea by the Romans 37
Mary, Jesus' mother, born 25?
Herod the Great begins remodeling temple in Jerusalem 20
Jesus Christ born 6/5
Herod the Great dies 4
Paul born 5?
Judea becomes a Roman province; Jesus visits temple as a boy 6
John the Baptist begins his ministry; Pontius Pilate appointed govenor 26
Jesus begins his ministry 26/27
Jesus crucified; Jesus ascends into heaven; Pentecost; early church beginnings 30
Paul's conversion on Damascus road 35
46 Julius Caesar became dictator for life, then was assassinated two years later
30 Cleopatra and her lover, Marc Antony, both die by suicide
23 Sumo wrestling in Japan
A.D. 1 Saddles first used in Europe
7 Zealots in Judea rebel against Rome
14 Tiberius succeeds Caesar Augustus as Roman emperor

Herod Agrippa appointed king of Judea
40

43
London founded; first definite reference to diamonds

Paul begins first missionary journey
46

50
Romans begin using soap

54
Emperor Claudius poisoned by order of his wife; Nero becomes emperor

Paul writes Romans; Paul imprisoned in Caesarea
57

Paul's voyage to Rome
59

Paul writes "prison letters"
60

Paul released from prison
62

64
Fire burns much of Rome. Nero blames Christians for setting it

66
Painting on canvas

Paul martyred
67?

68
Romans destroy a Jewish religious commune at Qumran. Before the Qumran community was captured, they hid their library of Bible manuscripts in a cave by the Dead Sea (discovered in 1948).

Romans destroy Jerusalem
70

960 Jews commit mass suicide at Masada while under Roman attack
73

74
China opens silk trade with the west

75
Rome begins construction of famous Colosseum

79
Mount Vesuvius in Italy erupts, killing 30,000 people and burying cities of Pompeii and Herculaneum

Apostle John writes Revelation
95

THE OLD TESTAMENT

GENESIS

Creation	Noah undated	Abram born 2166 B.C. (2000 B.C.)	Abram enters Canaan 2091 (1925)	Isaac born 2066 (1900)

VITAL STATISTICS

PURPOSE:
To record God's creation of the world and his desire to have a people set apart to worship him

AUTHOR:
Moses

TO WHOM WRITTEN:
The people of Israel

DATE WRITTEN:
1450–1410 B.C.

SETTING:
The region presently known as the Middle East

KEY VERSES:
"So God created people in his own image; God patterned them after himself; male and female he created them" (1:27). " 'I will cause you to become the father of a great nation. I will bless you and make you famous, and I will make you a blessing to others. I will bless those who bless you and curse those who curse you. All the families of the earth will be blessed through you' " (12:2, 3).

KEY PEOPLE:
Adam, Eve, Noah, Abraham, Sarah, Isaac, Rebekah, Jacob, Joseph

BEGIN . . . start . . . commence . . . open. . . . There's something refreshing and optimistic about these words, whether they refer to the dawn of a new day, the birth of a child, the prelude of a symphony, or the first miles of a family vacation. Free of problems and full of promise, beginnings stir hope and imaginative visions of the future. *Genesis* means "beginnings" or "origin," and it unfolds the record of the beginning of the world, of human history, of family, of civilization, of salvation. It is the story of God's purpose and plan for his creation. As the book of beginnings, Genesis sets the stage for the entire Bible. It reveals the person and nature of God (Creator, Sustainer, Judge, Redeemer); the value and dignity of human beings (made in God's image, saved by grace, used by God in the world); the tragedy and consequences of sin (the Fall, separation from God, judgment); and the promise and assurance of salvation (covenant, forgiveness, promised Messiah).

God. That's where Genesis begins. All at once we see him creating the world in a majestic display of power and purpose, culminating with a man and woman made like himself (1:26, 27). But before long, sin entered the world, and Satan was unmasked. Bathed in innocence, creation was shattered by the Fall (the willful disobedience of Adam and Eve). Fellowship with God was broken, and evil began weaving its destructive web. In rapid succession, we read how Adam and Eve were expelled from the beautiful garden, their first son turned murderer, and evil bred evil until God finally destroyed everyone on earth except a small family led by Noah, the only godly person left.

As we come to Abraham on the plains of Canaan, we discover the beginning of God's covenant people and the broad strokes of his salvation plan: Salvation comes by faith, Abraham's descendants will be God's people, and the Savior of the world will come through this chosen nation. The stories of Isaac, Jacob, and Joseph that follow are more than interesting biographies. They emphasize the promises of God and the proof that he is faithful. The people we meet in Genesis are simple, ordinary people, yet through them, God did great things. These are vivid pictures of how God can and does use all kinds of people to accomplish his good purposes—even people like you and me.

Read Genesis and be encouraged. There is hope! No matter how dark the world situation seems, God has a plan. No matter how insignificant or useless you feel, God loves you and wants to use you in his plan. No matter how sinful and separated from God you are, his salvation is available. Read Genesis . . . and hope!

Jacob & Esau born 2006 (1840)	Jacob flees to Haran 1929 (1764)	Joseph born 1915 (1750)	Joseph sold into slavery 1898 (1733)	Joseph rules Egypt 1885 (1720)	Joseph dies 1805 (1640)

THE BLUEPRINT

A. THE STORY OF CREATION (1:1—2:4)

God created the sky, seas, and land. He created the plants, animals, fish, and birds. But he created human beings in his own image. At times, others may treat us disrespectfully. But we can be certain of our dignity and worth because we have been created in the image of God.

B. THE STORY OF ADAM (2:4—5:32)
1. Adam and Eve
2. Cain and Abel
3. Adam's descendants

When Adam and Eve were created by God, they were without sin. But they became sinful when they disobeyed God and ate some fruit from the tree. Through Adam and Eve we learn about the destructive power of sin and its bitter consequences.

C. THE STORY OF NOAH (6:1—11:32)
1. The Flood
2. Repopulating the earth
3. The tower of Babel

Noah was spared from the destruction of the Flood because he obeyed God and built the boat. Just as God protected Noah and his family, he still protects those who are faithful to him today.

D. THE STORY OF ABRAHAM (12:1—25:18)
1. God promises a nation to Abram
2. Abram and Lot
3. God promises a son to Abram
4. Sodom and Gomorrah
5. Birth and near sacrifice of Isaac
6. Isaac and Rebekah
7. Abraham dies

Abraham was asked to leave his country, wander in Canaan, wait years for a son, and then sacrifice him as a burnt offering. Through these periods of sharp testing, Abraham remained faithful to God. His example teaches us what it means to live a life of faith.

E. THE STORY OF ISAAC (25:19—28:9)
1. Jacob and Esau
2. Isaac and Abimelech
3. Jacob gets Isaac's blessing

Isaac did not demand his own way. He did not resist when he was about to be sacrificed, and he gladly accepted a wife chosen for him by others. Like Isaac, we must learn to put God's will ahead of our own.

F. THE STORY OF JACOB (28:10—36:43)
1. Jacob starts a family
2. Jacob returns home

Jacob did not give up easily. He faithfully served Laban for over 14 years. Later, he wrestled with God. Although Jacob made many mistakes, his hard work teaches us about living a life of service for our Lord.

G. THE STORY OF JOSEPH (37:1—50:26)
1. Joseph is sold into slavery
2. Judah and Tamar
3. Joseph is thrown into prison
4. Joseph is placed in charge of Egypt
5. Joseph and his brothers meet in Egypt
6. Jacob's family moves to Egypt
7. Jacob and Joseph die in Egypt

Joseph was sold into slavery by his brothers and unjustly thrown into prison by his master. Through the life of Joseph, we learn that suffering, no matter how unfair, can develop strong character in us.

MEGATHEMES

THEME	EXPLANATION	IMPORTANCE
Beginnings	Genesis explains the beginning of many important realities: the universe, the earth, people, sin, and God's plan of salvation.	Genesis teaches us that the earth is well made and good. People are special to God and unique. God creates and sustains all life.
Disobedience	People are always facing great choices. Disobedience occurs when people choose not to follow God's plan of living.	Genesis explains why people are evil: They choose to do wrong. Even great Bible heroes failed God and disobeyed.
Sin	Sin ruins people's lives. It happens when we disobey God.	Living God's way makes life productive and fulfilling.

Promises	God makes promises to help and protect people. This kind of promise is called a "covenant."	God kept his promises then, and he keeps them now. He promises to love us, accept us, forgive us.
Obedience	The opposite of sin is obedience. Obeying God restores our relationship to him.	The only way to enjoy the benefits of God's promises is to obey him.
Prosperity	Prosperity is deeper than mere material wealth. True prosperity and fulfillment come as a result of obeying God.	When people obey God, they find peace with him, with others, and with themselves.
Israel	God started the nation of Israel in order to have a dedicated people who would (1) keep his ways alive in the world, (2) proclaim to the world what he is really like, and (3) prepare the world for the birth of Christ.	God is looking for people today to follow him. We are to proclaim God's truth and love to all nations, not just our own. We must be faithful to carry out the mission God has given us.

KEY PLACES IN GENESIS

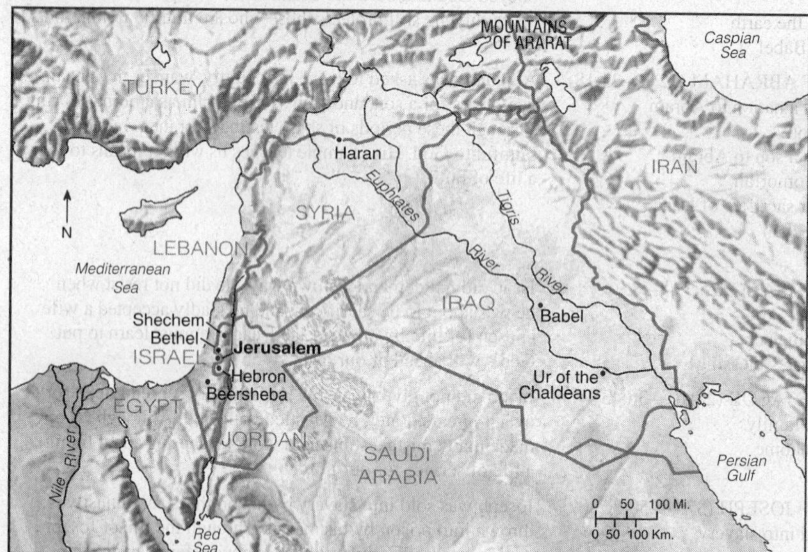

Modern names and boundaries are shown in gray.

God created the universe and the earth. Then he made man and woman, giving them a home in a beautiful garden. Unfortunately, Adam and Eve disobeyed God and were banished from the garden (3:23).

1 Mountains of Ararat Adam and Eve's sin brought sin into the human race. Years later, sin had run rampant and God decided to destroy the earth with a great flood. But Noah, his family, and two of each animal were safe in the boat. When the floods receded, the boat rested on the mountains of Ararat (8:4).

2 Babel People never learn. Again sin abounded, and the pride of the people led them to build a huge tower as a monument to their own greatness—obviously they had no thought of God. As punishment, God scattered the people by giving them different languages (11:8, 9).

3 Ur of the Chaldeans Abram, a descendant of Shem and father of the Hebrew nation, was born in this great city (11:27, 28).

4 Haran Terah, Abram, Lot, and Sarai left Ur and, following the fertile crescent of the Euphrates River, headed toward the land of Canaan. Along the way, they settled in the city of Haran for a while (11:31).

5 Shechem God urged Abram to leave Haran and go to a place where he would become the father of a great nation (12:1, 2). So Abram, Lot, and Sarai traveled to the land of Canaan and settled near a city called Shechem (12:6).

6 Hebron Abraham moved on to Hebron where he put down his deepest roots (13:18). Abraham, Isaac, and Jacob all lived and were buried here.

7 Beersheba The well at Beersheba was a source of conflict between Abraham and King Abimelech and later became a sign of the oarth that they swore there (21:31). Years later, as Isaac was moving from place to place, God appeared to him here and passed on to him the covenant he had made with his father, Abraham (26:23–25).

8 Bethel After deceiving his brother, Jacob left Beersheba and fled to Haran. Along the way, God revealed himself to Jacob in a dream and passed on the covenant he had made with Abraham and Isaac (28:10–22). Jacob lived in Haran, worked for Laban, and married Leah and Rachel (29:15–30). After a tense meeting with his brother, Esau, Jacob returned to Bethel (35:1).

9 Egypt Jacob had 12 sons, including Joseph, Jacob's favorite. Joseph's 10 older brothers grew jealous, until one day the brothers sold him to Ishmaelite traders going to Egypt. Eventually, Joseph rose from Egyptian slave to Pharaoh's "right-hand man," saving Egypt from famine. His entire family moved from Canaan to Egypt and settled there (46:3–7).

A. THE STORY OF CREATION (1:1—2:4)

We sometimes wonder how our world came to be. But here we find the answer. God created the earth and everything in it, and made humans like himself. Although we may not understand the complexity of just how he did it, it is clear that God did create all life. This shows not only God's authority over humanity, but his deep love for all people.

The Account of Creation

1:1 Pss 89:11; 102:25 John 1:1-2
1:2 Ps 104:30 Isa 45:18
1:3 Pss 33:9; 104:2 2 Cor 4:6

1 In the beginning God created* the heavens and the earth. 2The earth was empty, a
formless mass cloaked in darkness. And the Spirit of God was hovering over its
surface. 3Then God said, "Let there be light," and there was light. 4And God saw that it
was good. Then he separated the light from the darkness. 5God called the light "day" and
the darkness "night." Together these made up one day.

1:1 Or *In the beginning when God created,* or *When God began to create.*

BEGINNINGS

The Bible does not discuss the subject of evolution. Rather, its worldview assumes God created the world. The biblical view of creation is not in conflict with science; rather, it is in conflict with any worldview that starts without a creator.

Equally committed and sincere Christians have struggled with the subject of beginnings and come to differing conclusions. This, of course, is to be expected because the evidence is very old and, due to the ravages of the ages, quite fragmented. Students of the Bible and of science should avoid polarizations and black/white thinking. Students of the Bible must be careful not to make the Bible say what it doesn't say, and students of science must not make science say what it doesn't say.

The most important aspect of the continuing discussion is not the *process* of creation, but the *origin* of creation. The world is not a product of blind chance and probability; God created it.

The Bible not only tells us that the world was created by God; more important, it tells us who this God is. It reveals God's personality, his character, and his plan for his creation. It also reveals God's deepest desire: to relate to and fellowship with the people he created. God took the ultimate step toward fellowship with us through his historic visit to this planet in the person of his Son, Jesus Christ. We can know in a very personal way this God who created the universe.

The heavens and the earth are here. We are here. God created all that we see and experience. The book of Genesis begins, "God created the heavens and the earth."

Here we begin the most exciting and fulfilling journey imaginable.

1:1 The simple statement that God created the heavens and the earth is one of the most challenging concepts confronting the modern mind. The vast galaxy we live in is spinning at the incredible speed of 490,000 miles an hour. But even at this breakneck speed, our galaxy still needs 200 million years to make one rotation. And there are over one billion other galaxies just like ours in the universe.

Some scientists say that the number of stars in creation is equal to all the grains of all the sands on all the beaches of the world. Yet this complex sea of spinning stars functions with remarkable order and efficiency. To say that the universe "just happened" or "evolved" requires more faith than to believe that God is behind these amazing statistics. God truly did create a wonderful universe.

God did not *need* to create the universe; he *chose* to create it. Why? God is love, and love is best expressed toward something or someone else—so God created the world and people as an expression of his love. We should avoid reducing God's creation to merely scientific terms. Remember that God created the universe because he loves each of us.

1:1ff The creation story teaches us much about God and ourselves. First, we learn about God: (1) He is creative; (2) as the Creator, he is distinct from his creation; (3) he is eternal and in control of the world. We also learn about ourselves: (1) Since God chose to create us, we are valuable in his eyes; (2) we are more important than the animals. (See 1:28 for more on our role in the created order.)

1:1ff Just how did God create the earth? This is still a subject of great debate. Some say that there was a sudden explosion and the universe appeared. Others say God started the process and the universe evolved over billions of years. Almost every ancient religion has its own story to explain how the earth came to be. And almost every scientist has an opinion on the origin of the universe. But only the Bible shows one supreme God creating the earth out of his great love and giving all people a special place in it. We will never know all the answers to how God created the earth, but the Bible tells us that God did create it. That fact alone gives worth and dignity to all people.

1:2 The statement "the earth was empty, a formless mass" provides the setting for the creation narrative that follows. During the second and third days of creation, God gave *form* to the universe; during the next three days, God *filled* the earth with living beings. The "darkness" was dispelled on the first day, when God created light.

1:2 The image of the Spirit of God hovering over the earth's surface is similar to a mother bird caring for and protecting its young (see Deuteronomy 32:11, 12; Isaiah 31:5). God's Spirit was actively involved in the creation of the world (see Job 33:4; Psalm 104:30). God's care and protection are still active.

1:3—2:7 How long did it take God to create the world? There are two basic views about the days of creation: (1) Each day was a literal 24-hour period; (2) each day represents an indefinite period of time (even millions of years).

The Bible does not say how long these time periods were. The real question, however, is not how long God took, but how he did it. God created the earth in an orderly fashion (he did not make plants before light), and he created men and women as unique beings capable of communication with him. No other part of creation can claim that remarkable privilege. It is not important how long it took God to create the world, whether a few days or a few billion years, but that he created it just the way he wanted it.

6And God said, "Let there be space between the waters, to separate water from water."
7And so it was. God made this space to separate the waters above from the waters below.
8And God called the space "sky." This happened on the second day.
9And God said, "Let the waters beneath the sky be gathered into one place so dry ground
may appear." And so it was. 10God named the dry ground "land" and the water "seas."
And God saw that it was good. 11Then God said, "Let the land burst forth with every sort
of grass and seed-bearing plant. And let there be trees that grow seed-bearing fruit. The
seeds will then produce the kinds of plants and trees from which they came." And so it
was. 12The land was filled with seed-bearing plants and trees, and their seeds produced
plants and trees of like kind. And God saw that it was good. 13This all happened on the
third day.
14And God said, "Let bright lights appear in the sky to separate the day from the night.
They will be signs to mark off the seasons, the days, and the years. 15Let their light shine
down upon the earth." And so it was. 16For God made two great lights, the sun and the
moon, to shine down upon the earth. The greater one, the sun, presides during the day; the
lesser one, the moon, presides through the night. He also made the stars. 17God set these
lights in the heavens to light the earth, 18to govern the day and the night, and to separate
the light from the darkness. And God saw that it was good. 19This all happened on the
fourth day.
20And God said, "Let the waters swarm with fish and other life. Let the skies be filled
with birds of every kind." 21So God created great sea creatures and every sort of fish and
every kind of bird. And God saw that it was good. 22Then God blessed them, saying, "Let
the fish multiply and fill the oceans. Let the birds increase and fill the earth." 23This all
happened on the fifth day.
24And God said, "Let the earth bring forth every kind of animal—livestock, small
animals, and wildlife." And so it was. 25God made all sorts of wild animals, livestock,
and small animals, each able to reproduce more of its own kind. And God saw that it was
good.
26Then God said, "Let us make people* in our image, to be like ourselves. They will

1:6 Job 26:10; Ps 136:5-6; Isa 40:22; Jer 10:12
1:7 Job 38:8-11; Ps 148:4
1:9 Job 26:7; Ps 95:5; Jer 5:22; 2 Pet 3:5
1:10 Pss 33:7; 95:5
1:11 Gen 2:9; Ps 104:14; Matt 6:30
1:14 Pss 74:16; 104:19
1:16 Pss 8:3; 19:1-6; 136:8-9; 1 Cor 15:41
1:18 Jer 33:20, 25
1:20 Gen 2:19; Ps 146:6
1:21 Ps 104:25-28
1:24 Gen 2:19
1:26 Gen 5:1; 9:6; Ps 8:6-8; Acts 17:28-29

1:26a Hebrew *man;* also in 1:27.

DAYS OF CREATION

First Day	Light (so there was light and darkness)
Second Day	Sky and water (waters separated)
Third Day	Land and seas (waters gathered); vegetation
Fourth Day	Sun, moon, and stars (to govern the day and the night and to mark seasons, days, and years)
Fifth Day	Fish and birds (to fill the waters and the sky)
Sixth Day	Animals (to fill the earth) Man and woman (to care for the earth and to commune with God)
Seventh Day. . . .	God rested and declared all he had made to be very good

1:6 The "space between the waters" was a separation between the sea and the mists of the skies.

1:25 God saw that his work was good. People sometimes feel guilty for having a good time or for feeling good about an accomplishment. This need not be so. Just as God felt good about his work, we can be pleased with ours. However, we should not feel good about our work if God would not be pleased with it. What are you doing that pleases both you and God?

1:26 Why does God use the plural form, "Let *us* make people in *our* image"? One view says this is a reference to the Trinity—God the Father, Jesus Christ his Son, and the Holy Spirit—all of whom are God. Another view is that the plural wording is used to denote majesty. Kings traditionally use the plural form in speaking of themselves. From Job 33:4 and Psalm 104:30, we do know that God's Spirit was present in the Creation. From Colossians 1:16 we know that Christ, God's Son, was at work in the Creation.

1:26 In what ways are we made in God's image? God obviously did not create us exactly like himself because God has no physical body. Instead, we are reflections of God's glory. Some feel that our reason, creativity, speech, or self-determination is the image of God. More likely, it is our entire self that reflects the image of God. We will never be totally like God because he is our supreme Creator. But we do have the ability to reflect his character in our love, patience, forgiveness, kindness, and faithfulness.

Knowing that we are made in God's image and thus share many of his characteristics provides a solid basis for self-worth. Human worth is not based on possessions, achievements, physical attractiveness, or public acclaim. Instead, it is based on being made in God's image. Because we bear God's image, we can feel positive about ourselves. Criticizing or downgrading ourselves is criticizing what God has made and the abilities he has given us. Knowing that you are a person of worth helps you love God, know him personally, and make a valuable contribution to those around you.

be masters over all life—the fish in the sea, the birds in the sky, and all the livestock, wild
animals,* and small animals."

1:27 †Matt 19:4 †Mark 10:6

27 So God created people in his own image;
God patterned them after himself;
male and female he created them.

1:29 Gen 9:3 Pss 104:13; 136:25 · 1:30 Ps 104:14; 145:15 · 1:31 Ps 104:24

28 God blessed them and told them, "Multiply and fill the earth and subdue it. Be
masters over the fish and birds and all the animals." 29 And God said, "Look! I have
given you the seed-bearing plants throughout the earth and all the fruit trees for your
food. 30 And I have given all the grasses and other green plants to the animals and
birds for their food." And so it was. 31 Then God looked over all he had made, and
he saw that it was excellent in every way. This all happened on the sixth day.

2:2 Exod 20:11; 31:17 †Heb 4:4 · 2:4 Gen 1:3-31; 5:1; 6:9; 10:1 Job 38:4-11

2 So the creation of the heavens and the earth and everything in them was completed.
2 On the seventh day, having finished his task, God rested from all his work. 3 And
God blessed the seventh day and declared it holy, because it was the day when he rested
from his work of creation.
4 This is the account of the creation of the heavens and the earth.

B. THE STORY OF ADAM (2:4—5:32)

Learning about our ancestors often helps us understand ourselves. Adam and Eve, our first ancestors, were the highlight of God's creation—the very reason God made the world. But they didn't always live the way God intended. Through their mistakes, we can learn important lessons about the way God wants us to live. Adam and Eve teach us much about the nature of sin and its consequences.

2:5 Gen 1:11

1. Adam and Eve

When the LORD God made the heavens and the earth, 5 there were no plants or grain
growing on the earth, for the LORD God had not sent any rain. And no one was there

1:26b As in Syriac version; Hebrew reads *all the earth.*

WHAT THE BIBLE SAYS ABOUT MARRIAGE

Genesis 2:18–24	Marriage is God's idea
Genesis 24:58–60	Commitment is essential to a successful marriage
Genesis 29:10, 11	Romance is important
Jeremiah 7:34	Marriage holds times of great joy
Malachi 2:14, 15	Marriage creates the best environment for raising children
Matthew 5:32	Unfaithfulness breaks the bond of trust, the foundation of all relationships
Matthew 19:6	Marriage is permanent
Romans 7:2, 3	Ideally, only death should dissolve marriage
Ephesians 5:21–33	Marriage is based on the principled practice of love, not on feelings
Ephesians 5:23–32	Marriage is a living symbol of Christ and the church
Hebrews 13:4	Marriage is good and honorable

1:27 God made both man and woman in his image. Neither man nor woman is made more in the image of God than the other. From the beginning the Bible places both man and woman at the pinnacle of God's creation. Neither sex is exalted, and neither is depreciated.

1:28 To "be masters over" something is to have absolute authority and control over it. God has ultimate rule over the earth, and he exercises his authority with loving care. When God delegated some of his authority to the human race, he expected us to take responsibility for the environment and the other creatures that share our planet. We must not be careless and wasteful as we fulfill this charge. God was careful how he made this earth. We must not be careless about how we take care of it.

1:31 God saw that all he had created was excellent in every way. You are part of God's creation, and he is pleased with how he made you. If at times you feel worthless or of little value, remember that God made you for a good reason. You are valuable to him.

2:2, 3 We live in an action-oriented world! There always seems to be something to do and no time to rest. Yet God demonstrated that rest is appropriate and right. If God himself rested from his work, then it should not amaze us that we also need rest. Jesus demonstrated this principle when he and his disciples left in a boat to get away from the crowds (see Mark 6:31, 32). Our times of rest refresh us for times of service.

2:3 That God *blessed* the seventh day means that he set it apart for holy use. This act is picked up in the Ten Commandments (Exodus 20:1-17), in which God commanded the observance of the Sabbath.

to cultivate the soil. 6 But water came up out of the ground and watered all the land.
7 And the LORD God formed a man's body from the dust of the ground and breathed
into it the breath of life. And the man became a living person.
8 Then the LORD God planted a garden in Eden, in the east, and there he placed the
man he had created. 9 And the LORD God planted all sorts of trees in the garden—beautiful trees that produced delicious fruit. At the center of the garden he placed the tree of
life and the tree of the knowledge of good and evil.
10 A river flowed from the land of Eden, watering the garden and then dividing into
four branches. 11 One of these branches is the Pishon, which flows around the entire land
of Havilah, where gold is found. 12 The gold of that land is exceptionally pure; aromatic
resin and onyx stone are also found there. 13 The second branch is the Gihon, which flows
around the entire land of Cush. 14 The third branch is the Tigris, which flows to the east
of Asshur. The fourth branch is the Euphrates.
15 The LORD God placed the man in the Garden of Eden to tend and care for it. 16 But
the LORD God gave him this warning: "You may freely eat any fruit in the garden
17 except fruit from the tree of the knowledge of good and evil. If you eat of its fruit, you
will surely die."
18 And the LORD God said, "It is not good for the man to be alone. I will make a
companion who will help him." 19 So the LORD God formed from the soil every kind of
animal and bird. He brought them to Adam* to see what he would call them, and Adam
chose a name for each one. 20 He gave names to all the livestock, birds, and wild
animals. But still there was no companion suitable for him. 21 So the LORD God caused
Adam to fall into a deep sleep. He took one of Adam's ribs* and closed up the place
from which he had taken it. 22 Then the LORD God made a woman from the rib and
brought her to Adam.
23 "At last!" Adam exclaimed. "She is part of my own flesh and bone! She will be
called 'woman,' because she was taken out of a man." 24 This explains why a man

2:19 Hebrew *the man,* and so throughout this chapter. **2:21** Or *took a part of Adam's side.*

2:7
Gen 3:19
Job 33:4
Ps 103:14
John 20:22
†1 Cor 15:45

2:8
Gen 3:23; 13:10
Ezek 28:13

2:9
Gen 3:22
Ezek 47:12
Rev 2:7; 22:2, 14

2:10
Rev 22:1, 17

2:11
Gen 25:18

2:14
Gen 15:18
Deut 1:7

2:16
Gen 3:1-3

2:17
Deut 30:15, 19-20
Rom 6:23
Jas 1:15

2:18
Gen 3:12
Prov 18:22

2:22
1 Cor 11:8-9
1 Tim 2:13

2:23
Gen 29:14
Eph 5:28-30

2:24
†Matt 19:5
†1 Cor 6:16
Eph 5:31

2:7 "From the dust of the ground" implies that there is nothing fancy about the chemical elements making up our bodies. The body is a lifeless shell until God brings it alive with his "breath of life." When God removes his life-giving breath, our bodies once again return to dust. Therefore, our life and worth come from God's Spirit. Many boast of their achievements and abilities as though they were the originator of their own strengths. Others feel worthless because their abilities do not stand out. In reality, our worth comes not from our achievements but from the God of the universe, who chooses to give us the mysterious and miraculous gift of life. Value life, as he does.

2:9 The name of the tree of the knowledge of good and evil implies that evil had already occurred, if not in the garden, then at the time of Satan's fall.

2:9, 16, 17 Were the tree of life and the tree of the knowledge of good and evil real trees? Two views are often expressed:

(1) *The trees were real, but symbolic.* Eternal life with God was pictured as eating from the tree of life.

(2) *The trees were real, possessing special properties.* By eating the fruit from the tree of life, Adam and Eve could have had eternal life, enjoying a permanent relationship as God's children.

In either case, Adam and Eve's sin separated them from the tree of life and thus kept them from obtaining eternal life. Interestingly, the tree of life again appears in a description in Revelation 22 of people enjoying eternal life with God.

2:15-17 God gave Adam responsibility for the garden and told him not to eat from the tree of the knowledge of good and evil. Rather than physically preventing him from eating, God gave Adam a choice and, thus, the possibility of choosing wrongly. God still gives us choices, and we, too, often choose wrongly. These wrong choices may cause us pain, but they can help us learn and grow and make better choices in the future. Living with the consequences of our choices teaches us to think and choose more carefully.

2:16, 17 Why would God place a tree in the garden and then forbid Adam to eat from it? God wanted Adam to obey, but God gave Adam the freedom to choose. Without choice, Adam would have been like a prisoner, and his obedience would have been hollow. The two trees provided an exercise in choice, with rewards for choosing to obey and sad consequences for choosing to disobey. When you are faced with the choice, always choose to obey God.

2:18-24 God's creative work was not complete until he made woman. He could have made her from the dust of the ground, as he made man. God chose, however, to make her from the man's flesh and bone. In so doing, he illustrated for us that in marriage man and woman symbolically are united into one. This is a mystical union of the couple's hearts and lives. Throughout the Bible, God treats this special partnership seriously. If you are married or planning to be married, are you willing to keep the commitment that makes the two of you one? The goal in marriage should be more than friendship; it should be oneness.

2:21-23 God forms and equips men and women for various tasks, but all these tasks lead to the same goal—honoring God. Man gives life to woman; woman gives life to the world. Each role carries exclusive privileges; there is no room for thinking that one sex is superior to the other.

2:24 God gave marriage as a gift to Adam and Eve. They were created perfect for each other. Marriage was not just for convenience, nor was it brought about by any culture. It was instituted by God and has three basic aspects: (1) the man leaves his parents and, in a public act, promises himself to his wife; (2) the man and woman are joined together by taking responsibility for each other's welfare and by loving the mate above all others; (3) the two are united into one in the intimacy and commitment of sexual union that is reserved for marriage. Strong marriages include all three of these aspects.

leaves his father and mother and is joined to his wife, and the two are united into one.
2:25 Gen 3:7, 10-11 [25]Now, although Adam and his wife were both naked, neither of them felt any shame.

Adam and Eve Sin

3:1 2 Cor 11:3 Rev 12:9; 20:2 **3** Now the serpent was the shrewdest of all the creatures the LORD God had made.
"Really?" he asked the woman. "Did God really say you must not eat any of the fruit
in the garden?"

ADAM

We can hardly imagine what it must have been like to be the first and only person on earth. It's one thing for us to be lonely; it was another for Adam, who had never known another human being. He missed much that makes us who we are—he had no childhood, no parents, no family or friends. He had to learn to be human on his own. Fortunately, God didn't let him struggle too long before presenting him with an ideal companion and mate, Eve. Theirs was a complete, innocent, and open oneness, without a hint of shame.

One of Adam's first conversations with his delightful new companion must have been about the rules of the garden. Before God made Eve, he had already given Adam complete freedom in the garden, with the responsibility to tend and care for it. But one tree was off-limits, the tree of the knowledge of good and evil. Adam would have told Eve all about this. She knew, when Satan approached her, that the tree's fruit was not to be eaten. However, she decided to eat the forbidden fruit. Then she offered some to Adam. At that moment, the fate of creation was on the line. Sadly, Adam didn't pause to consider the consequences. He went ahead and ate.

In that moment of small rebellion something large, beautiful, and free was shattered . . . God's perfect creation. Adam was separated from God by his desire to act on his own. The effect on a plate glass window is the same whether a pebble or a boulder is hurled at it—the thousands of fragments can never be regathered.

In the case of Adam's sin, however, God already had a plan in motion to overcome the effects of the rebellion. The entire Bible is the story of how that plan unfolds, ultimately leading to God's own visit to earth through his Son, Jesus. His sinless life and death made it possible for God to offer forgiveness to all who want it. Our small and large acts of rebellion prove that we are descendants of Adam. Only by asking forgiveness of Jesus Christ can we become children of God.

Strengths and accomplishments
- The first zoologist—namer of animals
- The first landscape architect, placed in the garden to care for it
- Father of the human race
- The first person made in the image of God, and the first human to share an intimate personal relationship with God

Weaknesses and mistakes
- Avoided responsibility and blamed others; chose to hide rather than to confront; made excuses rather than admitting the truth
- Greatest mistake: teamed up with Eve to bring sin into the world

Lessons from his life
- As Adam's descendants, we all reflect to some degree the image of God
- God wants people who, though free to do wrong, choose instead to love him
- We should not blame others for our faults
- We cannot hide from God

Vital statistics
- Where: Garden of Eden
- Occupation: Caretaker, gardener, farmer
- Relatives: Wife: Eve. Sons: Cain, Abel, Seth. Numerous other children. The only man who never had an earthly mother or father

Key verses
"It was the woman you gave me who brought me the fruit, and I ate it" (Genesis 3:12). "Everyone dies because all of us are related to Adam, the first man. But all who are related to Christ, the other man, will be given new life" (1 Corinthians 15:22).

Adam's story is told in Genesis 1:26—5:5. He is also mentioned in 1 Chronicles 1:1; Luke 3:38; Romans 5:14; 1 Corinthians 15:22, 45; 1 Timothy 2:13, 14.

2:25 Have you ever noticed how a little child can run naked through a room full of strangers without embarrassment? He is not aware of his nakedness, just as Adam and Eve were not embarrassed in their innocence. But after Adam and Eve sinned, shame and awkwardness followed, creating barriers between themselves and God. We often experience these same barriers in marriage. Ideally a husband and wife have no barriers, feeling no embarrassment in exposing themselves to each other or to God. But, like Adam and Eve (3:7), we put on fig leaves (barriers) because we have areas we don't want our spouse, or God, to know about. Then we hide, just as Adam and Eve hid from God. In marriage, lack of spiritual, emotional, and intellectual intimacy usually precedes a breakdown of physical intimacy. In the same way, when we fail to expose our secret thoughts to God, we break our lines of communication with him.

2 “Of course we may eat it,” the woman told him. 3 “It’s only the fruit from the tree at
the center of the garden that we are not allowed to eat. God says we must not eat it or
even touch it, or we will die.”

4 “You won’t die!” the serpent hissed. 5 “God knows that your eyes will be opened
when you eat it. You will become just like God, knowing everything, both good and
evil.”

6 The woman was convinced. The fruit looked so fresh and delicious, and it would
make her so wise! So she ate some of the fruit. She also gave some to her husband, who
was with her. Then he ate it, too. 7 At that moment, their eyes were opened, and they
suddenly felt shame at their nakedness. So they strung fig leaves together around their
hips to cover themselves.

8 Toward evening they heard the LORD God walking about in the garden, so they hid
themselves among the trees. 9 The LORD God called to Adam,* “Where are you?”

3:3 Gen 2:17; Exod 19:12
3:4 John 8:44; 2 Cor 11:3
3:5 Isa 14:14; Ezek 28:2
3:6 2 Cor 11:3; 1 Tim 2:14; Jas 1:14-15; 1 John 2:16
3:8 Lev 26:12; Deut 23:14

3:9 Hebrew *the man,* and so throughout this chapter.

3:1 Disguised as a shrewd serpent, Satan came to tempt Eve. Satan at one time was an angel who rebelled against God and was thrown out of heaven. As a created being, Satan has definite limitations. Although he is trying to tempt everyone away from God, he will not be the final victor. In 3:14, 15, God promises that Satan will be crushed by one of the woman’s offspring, the Messiah.

3:1-6 Why does Satan tempt us? Temptation is Satan’s invitation to give in to his kind of life and give up on God’s kind of life. Satan tempted Eve and succeeded in getting her to sin. Ever since then, he’s been busy getting people to sin. He even tempted Jesus (Matthew 4:1-11). But Jesus did not sin!

How could Eve have resisted temptation? By following the same guidelines we can follow. First, we must realize that *being tempted* is not a sin. We have not sinned until we *give in* to the temptation. Then, to resist temptation, we must (1) pray for strength to resist, (2) run, sometimes literally, and (3) say no when confronted with what we know is wrong. James 1:12 tells of the blessings and rewards for those who don’t give in when tempted.

3:1-6 The serpent, Satan, tempted Eve by getting her to doubt God’s goodness. He implied that God was strict, stingy, and selfish for not wanting Eve to share his knowledge of good and evil. Satan made Eve forget all that God had given her and, instead, focus on the one thing she couldn’t have. We fall into trouble, too, when we dwell on the few things we don’t have rather than on the countless things God has given us. The next time you are feeling sorry for yourself and what you don’t have, consider all you *do* have and thank God. Then your doubts won’t lead you into sin.

3:5 Adam and Eve got what they wanted: an intimate knowledge of both good and evil. But they got it by doing evil, and the results were disastrous. Sometimes we have the illusion that freedom is doing anything we want. But God says that true freedom comes from obedience and knowing what *not* to do. The restrictions he gives us are for our good, helping us avoid evil. We have the freedom to walk in front of a speeding car, but we don’t need to be hit to realize it would be foolish to do so. Don’t listen to Satan’s temptations. You don’t have to do evil to gain more experience and learn more about life.

3:5 Satan used a sincere motive to tempt Eve: “You will become just like God.” It wasn’t wrong of Eve to want to be like God. To become more like God is humanity’s highest goal. It is what we are supposed to do. But Satan misled Eve concerning the right way to accomplish this goal. He told her that she could become more like God by defying God’s authority, by taking God’s place and deciding for herself what was best for her life. In effect, he told her to become her own god.

But to become like God is not the same as trying to become God. Rather, it is to reflect his characteristics and to recognize his authority over your life. Like Eve, we often have a worthy goal but try to achieve it in the wrong way. We act like a political candidate who pays off an election judge to be “voted” into office. When he does this, serving the people is no longer his highest goal.

Self-exaltation leads to rebellion against God. As soon as we begin to leave God out of our plans, we are placing ourselves above him. This is exactly what Satan wants us to do.

3:6 Satan tried to make Eve think that sin is good, pleasant, and desirable. A knowledge of both good and evil seemed harmless to her. People usually choose wrong things because they have become convinced that those things are good, at least for themselves. Our sins do not always appear ugly to us, and the pleasant sins are the hardest to avoid. So prepare yourself for the attractive temptations that may come your way. We cannot always prevent temptation, but there is always a way of escape (1 Corinthians 10:13). Use God’s Word and God’s people to help you stand against it.

3:6, 7 Notice what Eve did: She looked, she took, she ate, and she gave. The battle is often lost at the first look. Temptation often begins by simply seeing something you want. Are you struggling with temptation because you have not learned that looking is the first step toward sin? You would win over temptation more often if you followed Paul’s advice to run from those things that produce evil thoughts (2 Timothy 2:22).

3:6, 7 One of the realities of sin is that its effects spread. After Eve sinned, she involved Adam in her wrongdoing. When we do something wrong, often we try to relieve our guilt by involving someone else. Like toxic waste spilled in a river, sin swiftly spreads. Recognize and confess your sin to God before you are tempted to pollute those around you.

3:7, 8 After sinning, Adam and Eve felt guilt and embarrassment over their nakedness. Their guilty feelings made them try to hide from God. A guilty conscience is a warning signal God placed inside you that goes off when you’ve done wrong. The worst step you can take is to eliminate the guilty feelings without eliminating the cause. That would be like using a painkiller but not treating the disease. Be glad those guilty feelings are there. They make you aware of your sin so you can ask God’s forgiveness and then correct your wrongdoing.

3:8 The thought of two humans covered with fig leaves trying to hide from the all-seeing, all-knowing God is humorous. How could they be so silly as to think they could actually hide? Yet we do the same, acting as though God doesn’t know what we’re doing. Have the courage to share all you do and think with him. And don’t try to hide—it can’t be done. Honesty will strengthen your relationship with God.

3:8, 9 These verses show God’s desire to have fellowship with us. They also show why we are afraid to have fellowship with him. Adam and Eve hid from God when they heard him approaching. God wanted to be with them, but because of their sin, they were afraid to show themselves. Sin had broken their close relationship with God, just as it has broken ours.

3:12 Prov 28:13
3:13 2 Cor 11:3; 1 Tim 2:14
3:14 Deut 28:15; Isa 65:25
3:15 John 8:44; Rom 16:20; Heb 2:14
3:16 1 Cor 11:3; Eph 5:22; 1 Tim 2:15
3:17 Job 5:7; Eccl 1:3; Rom 8:20-22
3:18 Job 31:40; Heb 6:8
3:19 Gen 2:7; Pss 90:3; 104:29; Eccl 12:7; 1 Cor 15:47
3:20 2 Cor 11:3; 1 Tim 2:13
3:21 2 Cor 5:2-3

10 He replied, "I heard you, so I hid. I was afraid because I was naked."
11 "Who told you that you were naked?" the LORD God asked. "Have you eaten the
fruit I commanded you not to eat?"
12 "Yes," Adam admitted, "but it was the woman you gave me who brought me the
fruit, and I ate it."
13 Then the LORD God asked the woman, "How could you do such a thing?"
"The serpent tricked me," she replied. "That's why I ate it."
14 So the LORD God said to the serpent, "Because you have done this, you will be
punished. You are singled out from all the domestic and wild animals of the whole earth
to be cursed. You will grovel in the dust as long as you live, crawling along on your belly.
15 From now on, you and the woman will be enemies, and your offspring and her
offspring will be enemies. He will crush your head, and you will strike his heel."
16 Then he said to the woman, "You will bear children with intense pain and suffering.
And though your desire will be for your husband,* he will be your master."
17 And to Adam he said, "Because you listened to your wife and ate the fruit I told you
not to eat, I have placed a curse on the ground. All your life you will struggle to scratch
a living from it. 18 It will grow thorns and thistles for you, though you will eat of its
grains. 19 All your life you will sweat to produce food, until your dying day. Then you
will return to the ground from which you came. For you were made from dust, and to the
dust you will return."
20 Then Adam named his wife Eve,* because she would be the mother of all people
everywhere. 21 And the LORD God made clothing from animal skins for Adam and his wife.
22 Then the LORD God said, "The people have become as we are, knowing every-

3:16 Or *And though you may desire to control your husband.* **3:20** *Eve* sounds like a Hebrew term that means "to give life."

SATAN'S PLAN		
	Doubt	Makes you question God's Word and his goodness
	Discouragement	Makes you look at your problems rather than at God
	Diversion	Makes the wrong things seem attractive so that you will want them more than the right things
	Defeat	Makes you feel like a failure so that you don't even try
	Delay	Makes you put off doing something so that it never gets done

But Jesus Christ, God's Son, opens the way for us to renew our fellowship with him. God longs to be with us. He actively offers us his unconditional love. Our natural response is fear because we feel we can't live up to his standards. But understanding that he loves us, regardless of our faults, can help remove that dread.

3:11-13 Adam and Eve failed to heed God's warning recorded in 2:16, 17. They did not understand the reasons for his command, so they chose to act in another way that looked better to them. All of God's commands are for our own good, but we may not always understand the reasons behind them. People who trust God will obey because God asks them to, whether or not they understand why God commands it.

3:11-13 When God asked Adam about his sin, Adam blamed Eve. Then Eve blamed the serpent. How easy it is to excuse our sins by blaming someone else or circumstances. But God knows the truth, and he holds each of us responsible for what we do (see 3:14-19). Admit your wrong attitudes and actions and apologize to God. Don't try to get away with sin by blaming someone else.

3:14ff Adam and Eve chose their course of action (disobedience), and then God chose his. As a holy God, he could respond only in a way consistent with his perfect moral nature. He could not allow sin to go unchecked; he had to punish it. If the consequences of Adam and Eve's sin seem extreme, remember that their sin set in motion the world's tendency toward disobeying God. That is why we sin today: Every human being ever born, with the exception of Jesus, has inherited the sinful nature of Adam and Eve (Romans 5:12-21). Adam and Eve's punishment reflects how seriously God views sin of any kind.

3:14-19 Adam and Eve learned by painful experience that because God is holy and hates sin, he must punish sinners. The rest of the book of Genesis recounts painful stories of lives ruined as a result of the Fall. Disobedience is sin, and it breaks our fellowship with God. But, fortunately, when we disobey, God is willing to forgive us and to restore our relationship with him.

3:15 Satan is our enemy. He will do anything he can to get us to follow his evil, deadly path. The phrase "you will strike his heel" refers to Satan's repeated attempts to defeat Christ during his life on earth. "He will crush your head" foreshadows Satan's defeat when Christ rose from the dead. A strike on the heel is not deadly, but a crushing blow to the head is. Already God was revealing his plan to defeat Satan and offer salvation to the world through his Son, Jesus Christ.

3:17-19 Adam and Eve's disobedience and fall from God's gracious presence affected all creation, including the environment. Years ago people thought nothing of polluting streams with chemical wastes and garbage. This seemed so insignificant, so small. Now we know that just two or three parts per million of certain chemicals can damage human health. Sin in our lives is similar to pollution in streams. Even small amounts are deadly.

3:22-24 Life in the Garden of Eden was like living in heaven. Everything was perfect, and if Adam and Eve had obeyed God,

thing, both good and evil. What if they eat the fruit of the tree of life? Then they will
live forever!" 23So the LORD God banished Adam and his wife from the Garden of
Eden, and he sent Adam out to cultivate the ground from which he had been made.
24After banishing them from the garden, the LORD God stationed mighty angelic
beings* to the east of Eden. And a flaming sword flashed back and forth, guarding the
way to the tree of life.

2. Cain and Abel

4 Now Adam* slept with his wife, Eve, and she became pregnant. When the time
came, she gave birth to Cain,* and she said, "With the LORD's help, I have brought
forth* a man!" 2Later she gave birth to a second son and named him Abel.
When they grew up, Abel became a shepherd, while Cain was a farmer. 3At harvest
time Cain brought to the LORD a gift of his farm produce, 4while Abel brought several
choice lambs from the best of his flock. The LORD accepted Abel's offering, 5but he did
not accept Cain's. This made Cain very angry and dejected.
6"Why are you so angry?" the LORD asked him. "Why do you look so dejected?
7You will be accepted if you respond in the right way. But if you refuse to respond
correctly, then watch out! Sin is waiting to attack and destroy you, and you must
subdue it."
8Later Cain suggested to his brother, Abel, "Let's go out into the fields." And while
they were together there, Cain attacked and killed his brother.
9Afterward the LORD asked Cain, "Where is your brother? Where is Abel?"
"I don't know!" Cain retorted. "Am I supposed to keep track of him wherever he
goes?"
10But the LORD said, "What have you done? Listen—your brother's blood cries out

3:24 Ezek 10:1; Rev 2:7; 22:2, 14
4:2 Luke 11:50-51
4:3 Lev 2:1-2; Num 18:12
4:4 Exod 13:12; Heb 11:4
4:6 Jon 4:4
4:7 Rom 6:12, 16; Jas 1:15
4:8 Matt 23:35; 1 John 3:12
4:9 Gen 3:9
4:10 Num 35:33; Deut 21:1; Heb 12:24

3:24 Hebrew *cherubim.* **4:1a** Hebrew *the man.* **4:1b** *Cain* sounds like a Hebrew term that can mean "bring forth" or "acquire." **4:1c** Or *I have acquired.*

---

they could have lived there forever. But after disobeying, Adam and Eve no longer deserved paradise, and God told them to leave. If they had continued to live in the garden and eat from the tree of life, they would have lived forever. But eternal life in a state of sin would mean forever trying to hide from God. Like Adam and Eve, all of us have sinned and are separated from fellowship with God. We do not have to stay separated, however. God is preparing a new earth as an eternal paradise for his people (see Revelation 21–22).

3:24 This is how Adam and Eve broke their relationship with God: (1) They became convinced their way was better than God's; (2) they became self-conscious and hid; (3) they tried to excuse and defend themselves. To build a relationship with God we must reverse those steps: (1) We must drop our excuses and self-defenses; (2) we must stop trying to hide from God; (3) we must become convinced that God's way is better than our way.

4:1 Sexual union means oneness and total knowledge of the other person. Sexual intercourse is the most intimate of acts, sealing a social, physical, and spiritual relationship. That is why God has reserved it for marriage alone.

4:2 No longer was everything provided for Adam and Eve as it was in the Garden of Eden, where their daily tasks were refreshing and delightful. Now they had to struggle against the elements in order to provide food, clothing, and shelter for themselves and their family. Cain became a farmer, while Abel was a shepherd. In parts of the Middle East today, these ancient occupations are still practiced much as they were in Cain and Abel's time.

4:3-5 The Bible does not say why God did not accept Cain's sacrifice. Perhaps Cain's attitude was improper, or perhaps his offering was not up to God's standards. Proverbs 21:27 says, "God loathes the sacrifice of an evil person, especially when it is brought with ulterior motives." God evaluates both our motives and the quality of what we offer him. When we give to God and others, we should have a joyful heart because of what we are able to give. We should not worry about how much we are giving up, for all things are God's in the first place. Instead, we should joyfully give to God our best in time, money, possessions, and talents.

4:6, 7 How do you react when someone suggests you have done something wrong? Do you move to correct the mistake or deny that you need to correct it? After Cain's sacrifice was rejected, God gave him the chance to right his wrong and try again. God even encouraged him to do this! But Cain refused, and the rest of his life is a startling example of what happens to those who refuse to admit their mistakes. The next time someone suggests you are wrong, take an honest look at yourself and choose God's way instead of Cain's.

4:7 For Cain to subdue the sin that was waiting to attack and destroy him, he would have to give up his jealous anger so that sin would not find a foothold in his life. Sin is still waiting to attack and destroy us today. Like Cain, we will be victims of sin if we do not master it. But we cannot master sin in our own strength. Instead, we must turn to God to receive faith for ourselves and turn to other believers to receive encouragement and strength. The Holy Spirit will help us master sin. This will be a lifelong battle that will not be over until we are face to face with Christ.

4:8-10 This is the first murder—taking a life by shedding human blood. Blood represents life (Leviticus 17:10-14). If blood is removed from a living creature, it will die. Because God created life, only God should take life away.

4:8-10 Adam and Eve's disobedience brought sin into the human race. They may have thought their sin—eating a piece of fruit—wasn't very bad, but notice how quickly their sinful nature developed in their children. Simple disobedience quickly degenerated into outright murder. Adam and Eve acted only against God, but Cain acted against both God and other people. A small sin has a way of growing out of control. Let God help you with your "little" sins before they turn into tragedies.

4:11 Deut 27:15-26 to me from the ground! 11 You are hereby banished from the ground you have defiled
4:12 Deut 28:15-24 with your brother's blood. 12 No longer will it yield abundant crops for you, no matter
how hard you work! From now on you will be a homeless fugitive on the earth,
constantly wandering from place to place."
4:14 Gen 9:6 Job 15:22 13 Cain replied to the LORD, "My punishment* is too great for me to bear! 14 You have
banished me from my land and from your presence; you have made me a wandering
fugitive. All who see me will try to kill me!"
15 The LORD replied, "They will not kill you, for I will give seven times your
punishment to anyone who does." Then the LORD put a mark on Cain to warn anyone
who might try to kill him. 16 So Cain left the LORD's presence and settled in the land of
Nod,* east of Eden.
4:17 Ps 49:11 17 Then Cain's wife became pregnant and gave birth to a son, and they named him
Enoch. When Cain founded a city, he named it Enoch after his son.

4:13 Or *My sin.* **4:16** *Nod* means "wandering."

We know very little about Eve, the first woman in the world, yet she is the mother of us all. She was the final piece in the intricate and amazing puzzle of God's creation. Adam now had another human being with whom to fellowship—someone with an equal share in God's image. Here was someone alike enough for companionship, yet different enough for relationship. Together they were greater than either could have been alone.

Eve was approached by Satan in the Garden of Eden, where she and Adam lived. He questioned her contentment. How could she be happy when she was not allowed to eat from one of the fruit trees? Satan helped Eve shift her focus from all that God had done and given to the one thing he had withheld. And Eve was willing to accept Satan's viewpoint without checking with God.

Sound familiar? How often is our attention drawn from the much that is ours to the little that isn't? We get that "I've got to have it" feeling. Eve was typical of us all, and we consis- tently show we are her descendants by repeating her mistakes. Our desires, like Eve's, can be quite easily manipulated. They are not the best basis for actions. We need to keep God in our decision-making process always. His Word, the Bible, is our guidebook in decision making.

Strengths and accomplishments
- First wife and mother
- First female. As such she shared a special relationship with God, had co-responsibility with Adam over creation, and displayed certain characteristics of God

Weaknesses and mistakes
- Allowed her contentment to be undermined by Satan
- Acted impulsively without talking either to God or to her mate
- Not only sinned, but shared her sin with Adam
- When confronted, blamed others

Lessons from her life
- The female shares in the image of God
- The necessary ingredients for a strong marriage are commitment to each other, companionship with each other, complete oneness, absence of shame (2:24, 25)
- The basic human tendency to sin goes back to the beginning of the human race

Vital statistics
- Where: Garden of Eden
- Occupation: Wife, helper, companion, co-manager of Eden
- Relatives: Husband: Adam. Sons: Cain, Abel, Seth. Numerous other children

Key verse
"And the LORD God said, 'It is not good for the man to be alone. I will make a companion who will help him' " (Genesis 2:18).

Eve's story is told in Genesis 2:18—4:26. Her death is not mentioned in Scripture.

4:11-15 Cain was severely punished for this murder. God judges all sins and punishes appropriately, but not simply out of anger or vengeance. Rather, God's punishment is meant to correct us and restore our fellowship with him. When you're corrected, don't resent it. Instead, renew your fellowship with God.

4:14 We have heard about only four people so far—Adam, Eve, Cain, and Abel. Two questions arise: Why was Cain worried about being killed by others, and where did he get his wife (see 4:17)?

Adam and Eve had numerous children; they had been told to "fill the earth" (1:28). Cain's guilt fear over killing his brother was heavy, and he probably feared repercussions from his family. If he was capable of killing, so were they. The wife Cain chose may have been one of his sisters or a niece. The human race was still genetically pure, and there was no fear of side effects from marrying relatives.

4:15 The expression "seven times your punishment" means that the person's punishment would be complete, thorough, and much worse than that received by Cain for his sin.

18 Enoch was the father of* Irad.
Irad was the father of Mehujael.
Mehujael was the father of Methushael.
Methushael was the father of Lamech.

19 Lamech married two women—Adah and Zillah. 20 Adah gave birth to a baby named
Jabal. He became the first of the herdsmen who live in tents. 21 His brother's name was
Jubal, the first musician—the inventor of the harp and flute. 22 To Lamech's other wife,
Zillah, was born Tubal-cain. He was the first to work with metal, forging instruments of
bronze and iron. Tubal-cain had a sister named Naamah.
23 One day Lamech said to Adah and Zillah, "Listen to me, my wives. I have killed a
youth who attacked and wounded me. 24 If anyone who kills Cain is to be punished seven
times, anyone who takes revenge against me will be punished seventy-seven times!"
25 Adam slept with his wife again, and she gave birth to another son. She named him
Seth,* for she said, "God has granted me another son in place of Abel, the one Cain
killed." 26 When Seth grew up, he had a son and named him Enosh. It was during his
lifetime that people first began to worship the LORD.

3. Adam's descendants

From Adam to Noah

5 This is the history of the descendants of Adam. When God created people,* he made
them in the likeness of God. 2 He created them male and female, and he blessed them
and called them "human."*

3 When Adam was 130 years old, his son Seth was born,* and Seth was the very image
of his father.* 4 After the birth of Seth,* Adam lived another 800 years, and he had
other sons and daughters. 5 He died at the age of 930.

6 When Seth was 105 years old, his son Enosh was born. 7 After the birth of Enosh, Seth
lived another 807 years, and he had other sons and daughters. 8 He died at the age of 912.

9 When Enosh was 90 years old, his son Kenan was born. 10 After the birth of Kenan, Enosh
lived another 815 years, and he had other sons and daughters. 11 He died at the age of 905.

12 When Kenan was 70 years old, his son Mahalalel was born. 13 After the birth of
Mahalalel, Kenan lived another 840 years, and he had other sons and daughters.
14 He died at the age of 910.

15 When Mahalalel was 65 years old, his son Jared was born. 16 After the birth of Jared,
Mahalalel lived 830 years, and he had other sons and daughters. 17 He died at the
age of 895.

18 When Jared was 162 years old, his son Enoch was born. 19 After the birth of Enoch,
Jared lived another 800 years, and he had other sons and daughters. 20 He
died at the age of 962.

4:18 Or *the ancestor of,* and so throughout the verse. **4:25** *Seth* probably means "granted"; the name may also mean "appointed." **5:1** Hebrew *man.* **5:2** Hebrew *man.* **5:3a** Or *his son, the ancestor of Seth, was born;* similarly in 5:6, 9, 12, 15, 18, 21, 25. **5:3b** Hebrew *was in his own likeness, after his image.* **5:4** Or *After the birth of this ancestor of Seth;* similarly in 5:7, 10, 13, 16, 19, 22, 26.

4:23 Lev 19:18; Deut 32:35
4:25 Gen 4:8; 5:3; 1 Chr 1:1; Luke 3:38
4:26 Gen 12:8; 1 Kgs 18:24; Joel 2:32; Zeph 3:9; Acts 2:21
5:1 Gen 1:26; 6:9; 1 Chr 1:1
5:2 Gen 1:27; †Matt 19:4; †Mark 10:6
5:3 Gen 1:26; 4:25; 1 Cor 15:49
5:4 1 Chr 1:1
5:5 Gen 2:17; Heb 9:27
5:6 1 Chr 1:1; Luke 3:38
5:9 1 Chr 1:2; Luke 3:37
5:12 1 Chr 1:2; Luke 3:37
5:15 1 Chr 1:2; Luke 3:37
5:18 1 Chr 1:3; Luke 3:37; Jude 1:14

4:19-26 Unfortunately, when left to themselves, people tend to get worse instead of better. This short summary of Lamech's family shows us the variety of talent and ability God gives humans. It also presents the continuous development of sin as time passes. Another killing occurred, presumably in self-defense. Violence was on the rise. Two distinct groups were emerging: (1) those who showed indifference to sin and evil, and (2) those who worshiped the Lord (the descendants of Seth, 4:26). Seth would take Abel's place as leader of a line of God's faithful people.

5:1ff The Bible contains several lists of ancestors, called genealogies. There are two basic views concerning these lists: (1) They are complete, recording the entire history of a family, tribe, or nation; or (2) they are not intended to be exhaustive and may include only famous people or the heads of families. "His son" could also mean "his descendant."

Why are genealogies included in the Bible? The Hebrew people passed on their beliefs through oral tradition. For many years in many places, writing was primitive or nonexistent. Stories were told to children who passed them on to their children. Genealogies gave a skeletal outline that helped people remember the stories. For centuries these genealogies were added to and passed down from family to family. Even more important than preserving family tradition, genealogies were included to confirm the Bible's promise that the coming Messiah, Jesus Christ, would be born into the line of Abraham.

Genealogies point out an interesting characteristic of God. People are important to him as individuals, not just as races or nations. Therefore, God refers to people by name, mentioning their life span and descendants. The next time you feel overwhelmed in a vast crowd, remember that the focus of God's attention and love is on the individual—and on you!

5:3-5 All human beings are related, going back to Adam and Eve. All people form a family that shares one flesh and blood. Remember this when prejudice enters your mind or hatred invades your feelings. Each person is a valuable and unique creation of God.

5:21 1 Chr 1:3 Luke 3:37
5:24 2 Kgs 2:1, 11 Pss 49:5; 73:24 Heb 11:5
5:25 1 Chr 1:3 Luke 3:36
5:29 Gen 3:17 1 Chr 1:3 Luke 3:36 Rom 8:20
5:32 Gen 7:6; 9:18

21 When Enoch was 65 years old, his son Methuselah was born. 22 After the birth of Methuselah, Enoch lived another 300 years in close fellowship with God, and he had other
sons and daughters. 23 Enoch lived 365 years in all. 24 He enjoyed a close relationship
with God throughout his life. Then suddenly, he disappeared because God took him.
25 When Methuselah was 187 years old, his son Lamech was born. 26 After the birth of
Lamech, Methuselah lived another 782 years, and he had other sons and daughters.
27 He died at the age of 969.
28 When Lamech was 182 years old, his son Noah was born. 29 Lamech named his son
Noah,* for he said, "He will bring us relief from the painful labor of farming this
ground that the LORD has cursed." 30 After the birth of Noah, Lamech lived 595
years, and he had other sons and daughters. 31 He died at the age of 777.
32 By the time Noah was 500 years old, he had three sons: Shem, Ham, and Japheth.

C. THE STORY OF NOAH (6:1—11:32)

Earth was no longer the perfect paradise that God had intended. It is frightening to see how quickly all of humanity forgot about God. Incredibly, in all the world, only one man and his family still worshiped God. That man was Noah. Because of his faithfulness and obedience, God saved him and his family from a vast flood that destroyed every other human being on earth. This section shows us how God hates sin and judges those who enjoy it.

1. The Flood

6:1 Gen 1:28
6:3 Ps 78:39 1 Pet 3:20

6 When the human population began to grow rapidly on the earth, 2 the sons of God
saw the beautiful women of the human race and took any they wanted as their
wives. 3 Then the LORD said, "My Spirit will not put up with humans for such a long

5:29 *Noah* sounds like a Hebrew term that can mean "relief" or "comfort."

Abel was the second child born into the world, but the first one to obey God. All we know about this man is that his parents were Adam and Eve, he was a shepherd, he presented pleasing offerings to God, and his short life was ended at the hands of his jealous older brother, Cain.

The Bible doesn't tell us why God liked Abel's gift and disliked Cain's, but both Cain and Abel knew what God expected. Only Abel obeyed. Throughout history, Abel is remembered for his obedience and faith (Hebrews 11:4), and he is called "righteous" (Matthew 23:35).

The Bible is filled with God's general guidelines and expectations for our lives. It is also filled with more specific directions. Like Abel, we must obey regardless of the cost and trust God to make things right.

Strengths and accomplishments
- First member of the Hall of Faith in Hebrews 11
- First shepherd
- First martyr for truth (Matthew 23:35)

Lessons from his life
- God hears those who come to him
- God recognizes the innocent person and sooner or later punishes the guilty

Vital statistics
- Where: Just outside of Eden
- Occupation: Shepherd
- Relatives: Parents: Adam and Eve. Brother: Cain

Key verse
"It was by faith that Abel brought a more acceptable offering to God than Cain did. God accepted Abel's offering to show that he was a righteous man. And although Abel is long dead, he still speaks to us because of his faith" (Hebrews 11:4).

Abel's story is told in Genesis 4:1–8. He is also mentioned in Matthew 23:35; Luke 11:51; Hebrews 11:4 and 12:24.

5:25-27 How did these people live so long? Some believe that the ages listed here were lengths of family dynasties rather than ages of individual men. Those who think these were actual ages offer three explanations: (1) The human race was more genetically pure in this early time period, so there was less disease to shorten life spans; (2) no rain had yet fallen on the earth, and the expanse of water "above" (1:7) kept out harmful cosmic rays and shielded people from environmental factors that hasten aging; (3) God gave people longer lives so they would have time to "fill the earth" (1:28).

6:1-4 Some people have thought that the "sons of God" were fallen angels. But the "sons of God" were probably not angels, because angels do not marry or reproduce (Matthew 22:30; Mark 12:25). Some scholars believe this phrase refers to the descendants of Seth who intermarried with Cain's evil descendants. This would have weakened the good influence of the faithful and increased moral depravity in the world, resulting in an explosion of evil.

time, for they are only mortal flesh. In the future, they will live no more than 120
years."
4 In those days, and even afterward, giants* lived on the earth, for whenever the sons
of God had intercourse with human women, they gave birth to children who became the
heroes mentioned in legends of old.
5 Now the LORD observed the extent of the people's wickedness, and he saw that all
their thoughts were consistently and totally evil. 6 So the LORD was sorry he had ever
made them. It broke his heart. 7 And the LORD said, "I will completely wipe out this
human race that I have created. Yes, and I will destroy all the animals and birds, too. I
am sorry I ever made them." 8 But Noah found favor with the LORD.
9 This is the history of Noah and his family. Noah was a righteous man, the only
blameless man living on earth at the time. He consistently followed God's will and
enjoyed a close relationship with him. 10 Noah had three sons: Shem, Ham, and Japheth.
11 Now the earth had become corrupt in God's sight, and it was filled with violence. 12 God
observed all this corruption in the world, and he saw violence and depravity everywhere.
13 So God said to Noah, "I have decided to destroy all living creatures, for the earth is filled
with violence because of them. Yes, I will wipe them all from the face of the earth!
14 "Make a boat* from resinous wood and seal it with tar, inside and out. Then
construct decks and stalls throughout its interior. 15 Make it 450 feet long, 75 feet wide,
and 45 feet high.* 16 Construct an opening all the way around the boat, 18 inches* below
the roof. Then put three decks inside the boat—bottom, middle, and upper—and put a
door in the side.
17 "Look! I am about to cover the earth with a flood that will destroy every living
thing. Everything on earth will die! 18 But I solemnly swear to keep you safe in the boat,
with your wife and your sons and their wives. 19 Bring a pair of every kind of animal—a
male and a female—into the boat with you to keep them alive during the flood. 20 Pairs
of each kind of bird and each kind of animal, large and small alike, will come to you to
be kept alive. 21 And remember, take enough food for your family and for all the
animals."
22 So Noah did everything exactly as God had commanded him.

6:4 Num 13:33
6:5 Ps 14:1-3
6:6 Exod 32:14; Num 23:19; 1 Sam 15:11, 35; 2 Sam 24:16
6:7 Deut 29:20
6:8 Exod 33:17
6:9 Job 1:1; Ezek 14:14
6:11 Deut 31:29; Judg 2:19; Ezek 8:17
6:12 Ps 14:1-3
6:13 Isa 34:1-4; Ezek 7:2-3
6:14 Exod 2:3; 1 Pet 3:20
6:17 Ps 29:10; 2 Pet 2:5
6:18 Gen 9:9-16; 17:7; 19:12
6:20 Gen 7:3
6:21 Gen 1:29
6:22 Gen 7:5; Exod 40:16

6:4 Hebrew *Nephilim.* **6:14** Traditionally rendered *an ark.* **6:15** Hebrew *300 cubits* [135 meters] *long, 50 cubits* [22.5 meters] *wide, and 30 cubits* [13.5 meters] *high.* **6:16** Hebrew *1 cubit* [45 centimeters].

6:3 "They will live no more than 120 years" has been interpreted by some commentators to mean that God was allowing the people of Noah's day 120 years to change their sinful ways. God shows his great patience with us as well. He is giving us time to quit living our way and begin living his way, the way he shows us in his Word. While 120 years seems like a long time, eventually the time ran out, and the floodwaters swept across the earth. Your time also may be running out. Turn to God to forgive your sins. You can't see the stopwatch of God's patience, and there is no bargaining for additional time.

6:4 These "giants" were people probably nine or ten feet tall. This same Hebrew term was used to name a tall race of people in Numbers 13:33. Goliath, who was nine feet tall, appears in 1 Samuel 17. The giants used their physical advantage to oppress the people around them.

6:6, 7 Does this mean that God regretted creating humanity? Was he admitting he made a mistake? No, God does not change his mind (1 Samuel 15:29). Instead, he was expressing sorrow for what the people had done to themselves, as a parent might express sorrow over a rebellious child. God was sorry that the people chose sin and death instead of a relationship with him.

6:6-8 The people's sin grieved God. Our sins break God's heart as much as sin did in Noah's day. Noah, however, pleased God, although he was far from perfect. We can follow Noah's example and find "favor with the LORD" in spite of the sin that surrounds us.

6:9 To say that Noah was "righteous" and "blameless" does not mean that he never sinned (the Bible records one of his sins in 9:20ff). Rather, it means that he wholeheartedly loved and obeyed God. For a lifetime he walked step by step in faith as a living example to his generation. Like Noah, we live in a world filled with evil. Are we influencing others or being influenced by them?

6:15 The boat Noah built was no canoe! Picture yourself building a boat the length of one and a half football fields and as high as a four-story building. The boat was exactly six times longer than it was wide—the same ratio used by modern shipbuilders. This huge boat was probably built miles from any body of water by only a few faithful men who believed God's promises and obeyed his commands.

6:18 When God said, "I solemnly swear," he was making a promise or a *covenant.* This is a familiar theme in Scripture—God making covenants with his people. How reassuring it is to know God's covenant is established with us. He is still our salvation, and we are kept safe through our relationship with him. For more on covenants, see 9:8-17; 12:1-3; and 15:17-21.

6:22 Noah got right to work when God told him to build the huge boat. Other people must have been warned about the coming disaster (1 Peter 3:20), but apparently they did not expect it to happen. Today things haven't changed much. Each day thousands of people are warned of God's inevitable judgment, yet most of them don't really believe it will happen. Don't expect people to welcome or accept your message of God's coming judgment on sin. Those who don't believe in God will deny his judgment and try to get you to deny God as well. But remember God's promise to Noah to keep him safe. This can inspire you to trust God for deliverance in the judgment that is sure to come.

7:1 Gen 6:18; Matt 24:38; Luke 17:26-27; Heb 11:7; 1 Pet 3:20
7:2 Lev 11:1-47; Deut 14:3-20; Ezek 44:23
7:4 Gen 6:7, 13
7:6 Gen 5:32
7:7 Gen 6:18
7:9 Gen 6:22
7:11 Ps 78:23; Ezek 26:19; Mal 3:10
7:13 1 Pet 3:20; 2 Pet 2:5

The Flood Covers the Earth

7 Finally, the day came when the LORD said to Noah, "Go into the boat with all your
family, for among all the people of the earth, I consider you alone to be righteous.
2Take along seven pairs of each animal that I have approved for eating and for
sacrifice, and take one pair of each of the others. 3Then select seven pairs of every
kind of bird. There must be a male and a female in each pair to ensure that every kind
of living creature will survive the flood. 4One week from today I will begin forty days
and forty nights of rain. And I will wipe from the earth all the living things I have
created."
5So Noah did exactly as the LORD had commanded him. 6He was 600 years old
when the flood came, 7and he went aboard the boat to escape—he and his wife and
his sons and their wives. 8With them were all the various kinds of animals—those
approved for eating and sacrifice and those that were not—along with all the birds
and other small animals. 9They came into the boat in pairs, male and female, just
as God had commanded Noah. 10One week later, the flood came and covered the
earth.
11When Noah was 600 years old, on the seventeenth day of the second month, the
underground waters burst forth on the earth, and the rain fell in mighty torrents from
the sky. 12The rain continued to fall for forty days and forty nights. 13But Noah had
gone into the boat that very day with his wife and his sons—Shem, Ham, and
Japheth—and their wives. 14With them in the boat were pairs of every kind of
breathing animal—domestic and wild, large and small—along with birds and flying

In spite of parents' efforts and worries, conflicts between children in a family seem inevitable. Sibling relationships allow both competition and cooperation. In most cases, the mixture of loving and fighting eventually creates a strong bond between brothers and sisters. It isn't unusual, though, to hear parents say, "They fight so much I hope they don't kill each other before they grow up." In Cain's case, the troubling potential became a reality. And while we don't know many details of this first child's life, his story can still teach us.

Cain got angry. Furious. Both he and his brother Abel had given offerings to God, and his had been rejected. Cain's reaction gives us a clue that his attitude was probably wrong from the start. Cain had a choice to make. He could correct his attitude about his offering to God, or he could take out his anger on his brother. His decision is a clear reminder of how often we are aware of opposite choices, yet choose the wrong just as Cain did. We may not be choosing to murder, but we are still intentionally choosing what we shouldn't.

The feelings motivating our behavior can't always be changed by simple thought-power. But here we can begin to experience God's willingness to help. Asking for his help to do what is right can prevent us from setting into motion actions that we will later regret.

Strengths and accomplishments	• First human child • First to follow in father's profession, farming
Weaknesses and mistakes	• When disappointed, reacted in anger • Took the negative option even when a positive possibility was offered • Was the first murderer
Lessons from his life	• Anger is not necessarily a sin, but actions motivated by anger can be sinful. Anger should be the energy behind good action, not evil action • What we offer to God must be from the heart—the best we are and have • The consequences of sin may last a lifetime
Vital statistics	• Where: Near Eden, which was probably located in present-day Iraq or Iran • Occupation: Farmer, then wanderer • Relatives: Parents: Adam and Eve. Brothers: Abel, Seth, and others not mentioned by name
Key verse	"You will be accepted if you respond in the right way. But if you refuse to respond correctly, then watch out! Sin is waiting to attack and destroy you, and you must subdue it" (Genesis 4:7).

Cain's story is told in Genesis 4:1–17. He is also mentioned in Hebrews 11:4; 1 John 3:12; Jude 1:11.

7:1ff Pairs of every animal joined Noah in the boat; seven pairs were taken of those animals used for sacrifice. Scholars have estimated that almost 45,000 animals could have fit into the boat.

insects of every kind. 15Two by two they came into the boat, 16male and female, just
as God had commanded. Then the LORD shut them in.
17For forty days the floods prevailed, covering the ground and lifting the boat high
above the earth. 18As the waters rose higher and higher above the ground, the boat floated
safely on the surface. 19Finally, the water covered even the highest mountains on the
earth, 20standing more than twenty-two feet* above the highest peaks. 21All the living
things on earth died—birds, domestic animals, wild animals, all kinds of small animals,
and all the people. 22Everything died that breathed and lived on dry land. 23Every living
thing on the earth was wiped out—people, animals both large and small, and birds. They
were all destroyed, and only Noah was left alive, along with those who were with him
in the boat. 24And the water covered the earth for 150 days.

The Flood Recedes

8 But God remembered Noah and all the animals in the boat. He sent a wind to blow
across the waters, and the floods began to disappear. 2The underground water
sources ceased their gushing, and the torrential rains stopped. 3So the flood gradually
began to recede. After 150 days, 4exactly five months from the time the flood began,*
the boat came to rest on the mountains of Ararat. 5Two and a half months later,* as the
waters continued to go down, other mountain peaks began to appear.
6After another forty days, Noah opened the window he had made in the boat 7and
released a raven that flew back and forth until the earth was dry. 8Then he sent out a dove
to see if it could find dry ground. 9But the dove found no place to land because the water
was still too high. So it returned to the boat, and Noah held out his hand and drew the
dove back inside. 10Seven days later, Noah released the dove again. 11This time, toward
evening, the bird returned to him with a fresh olive leaf in its beak. Noah now knew that
the water was almost gone. 12A week later, he released the dove again, and this time it
did not come back.
13Finally, when Noah was 601 years old, ten and a half months after the flood began,*
Noah lifted back the cover to look. The water was drying up. 14Two more months went
by,* and at last the earth was dry! 15Then God said to Noah, 16"Leave the boat, all of
you. 17Release all the animals and birds so they can breed and reproduce in great
numbers." 18So Noah, his wife, and his sons and their wives left the boat. 19And all the
various kinds of animals and birds came out, pair by pair.
20Then Noah built an altar to the LORD and sacrificed on it the animals and birds that

7:15 Gen 6:19; 7:8
7:19 Ps 104:6
7:20 2 Pet 3:6
7:23 Matt 24:38-39; Luke 17:26-27; 1 Pet 3:20; 2 Pet 2:5
7:24 Gen 8:3
8:1 Gen 19:29; 30:22; Exod 2:24; 14:21; Job 12:15; Isa 44:27
8:2 Gen 7:4, 12
8:4 Gen 7:20
8:7 Lev 11:15; Deut 14:14; 1 Kgs 17:4; Luke 12:24
8:8 Isa 60:8; Hos 11:11; Matt 10:16
8:13 Gen 5:32
8:16 Gen 7:13
8:17 Gen 1:22
8:20 Gen 4:4; 12:7; 13:18; 22:2

7:20 Hebrew *15 cubits* [6.8 meters]. **8:4** Hebrew *on the seventeenth day of the seventh month;* see 7:11. **8:5** Hebrew *On the first day of the tenth month;* see 7:11 and note on 8:4. **8:13** Hebrew *on the first day of the first month;* see 7:11. **8:14** Hebrew *The twenty-seventh day of the second month arrived;* see note on 8:13.

7:16 Many have wondered how this animal kingdom roundup happened. Did Noah and his sons spend years collecting all the animals? In reality the creation, along with Noah, was doing just as God had commanded. There seemed to be no problem gathering the animals—God took care of the details of that job while Noah was doing his part by building the boat. Often we do just the opposite of Noah. We worry about details over which we have no control, while neglecting specific areas (such as attitudes, relationships, responsibilities) that *are* under our control. Like Noah, concentrate on what God has given you to do, and leave the rest to God.

7:17-24 Was the Flood a local event, or did it cover the entire earth? A universal flood was certainly possible. There is enough water on the earth to cover all dry land (the earth began that way; see 1:9, 10). Afterward God promised never again to destroy the earth with a flood. Thus, this Flood must have either covered the entire earth or destroyed all the inhabitants of the earth. Remember, God's reason for sending the Flood was to destroy all the earth's wickedness. It would have taken a major flood to accomplish this.

8:6-16 Occasionally Noah would send a bird out to test the earth and see if it was dry. But Noah didn't get out of the boat until God told him to. He was waiting for God's timing. God knew that even though the water was gone, the earth was not dry enough for Noah and his family to venture out. What patience Noah showed, especially after spending an entire year inside his boat! We, like Noah, must trust God to give us patience during those difficult times when we must wait.

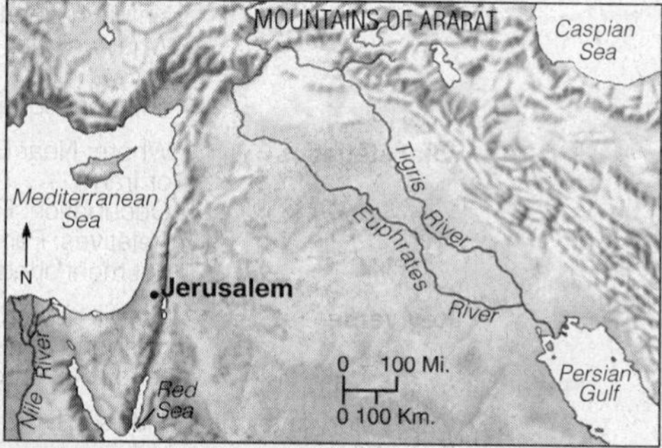

MOUNTAINS OF ARARAT The boat touched land in the mountains of Ararat, located in present-day Turkey. There it rested for almost eight months before Noah, his family, and the animals stepped onto dry land.

8:21 Gen 3:17 Exod 28:18, 25 Lev 1:9, 13 Isa 54:9
8:22 Ps 74:17

had been approved for that purpose. [21]And the LORD was pleased with the sacrifice and
said to himself, "I will never again curse the earth, destroying all living things, even
though people's thoughts and actions are bent toward evil from childhood. [22]As long as
the earth remains, there will be springtime and harvest, cold and heat, winter and
summer, day and night."

2. Repopulating the earth

God's Covenant with Noah

9:1 Gen 1:22
9:2 Gen 1:26-29
9:4 Lev 3:17; 7:26; 17:10 Deut 12:16
9:5 Exod 21:28-32
9:6 Exod 20:13; 21:12 Num 35:33

9 God blessed Noah and his sons and told them, "Multiply and fill the earth. [2]All
the wild animals, large and small, and all the birds and fish will be afraid of you.
I have placed them in your power. [3]I have given them to you for food, just as I have
given you grain and vegetables. [4]But you must never eat animals that still have their
lifeblood in them. [5]And murder is forbidden. Animals that kill people must die, and
any person who murders must be killed. [6]Yes, you must execute anyone who murders
another person, for to kill a person is to kill a living being made in God's image. [7]Now
you must have many children and repopulate the earth. Yes, multiply and fill the
earth!"

NOAH

The story of Noah's life involves not one, but two great and tragic floods. The world in Noah's day was flooded with evil. The number of those who remembered the God of creation, perfection, and love had dwindled to one. Of God's people, only Noah was left. God's response to the severe situation was a 120-year-long last chance, during which he had Noah build a graphic illustration of the message of his life. Nothing like a huge boat on dry land to make a point! For Noah, obedience meant a long-term commitment to a project.

Many of us have trouble sticking to any project, whether or not it is directed by God. It is interesting that the length of Noah's obedience was greater than the lifespan of people today. The only comparable long-term project is our very lives. But perhaps this is one great challenge Noah's life gives us—to live, in acceptance of God's grace, an entire lifetime of obedience and gratitude.

Strengths and accomplishments
- Only follower of God left in his generation
- Second father of the human race
- Man of patience, consistency, and obedience
- First major shipbuilder

Weakness and mistake
- Got drunk and embarrassed himself in front of his sons

Lessons from his life
- God is faithful to those who obey him
- God does not always protect us from trouble, but cares for us in spite of trouble
- Obedience is a long-term commitment
- A man may be faithful, but his sinful nature always travels with him

Vital statistics
- Where: We're not told how far from the Garden of Eden people had settled
- Occupation: Farmer, shipbuilder, preacher
- Relatives: Grandfather: Methuselah. Father: Lamech. Sons: Ham, Shem, and Japheth

Key verse "So Noah did everything exactly as God had commanded him" (Genesis 6:22).

Noah's story is told in Genesis 5:28—10:32. He is also mentioned in 1 Chronicles 1:3, 4; Isaiah 54:9; Ezekiel 14:14, 20; Matthew 24:37, 38; Luke 3:36; 17:26, 27; Hebrews 11:7; 1 Peter 3:20; 2 Peter 2:5.

8:21, 22 Countless times throughout the Bible we see God showing his love and patience toward men and women in order to save them. Although he realizes that their hearts are evil, he continues to try to reach them. When we sin or fall away from God, we surely deserve to be destroyed by his judgment. But God has promised never again to destroy everything on earth until the judgment day when Christ returns to destroy evil forever. Now every change of season is a reminder of his promise.

9:5 God will require each person to account for his or her actions. We cannot harm or kill another human being without answering to God. A penalty must be paid. Justice will be served.

9:5, 6 Here God explains why murder is so wrong: To kill a person is to kill one made in God's image. Because all human beings are made in God's image, all people possess the qualities that distinguish them from animals: morality, reason, creativity, and self-worth. When we interact with others, we are interacting with beings made by God, beings to whom God offers eternal life. God wants us to recognize his image in all people.

[8]Then God told Noah and his sons, [9]"I am making a covenant with you and your
descendants, [10]and with the animals you brought with you—all these birds and
livestock and wild animals. [11]I solemnly promise never to send another flood to kill 9:11 Isa 24:52
all living creatures and destroy the earth." [12]And God said, "I am giving you a sign
as evidence of my eternal covenant with you and all living creatures. [13]I have placed 9:12 Gen 17:11
my rainbow in the clouds. It is the sign of my permanent promise to you and to all the
earth. [14]When I send clouds over the earth, the rainbow will be seen in the clouds, 9:13 Ezek 1:28
[15]and I will remember my covenant with you and with everything that lives. Never
again will there be a flood that will destroy all life. [16]When I see the rainbow in the 9:15 Deut 7:9
clouds, I will remember the eternal covenant between God and every living creature
on earth." [17]Then God said to Noah, "Yes, this is the sign of my covenant with all the
creatures of the earth."

Noah's Sons

[18]Shem, Ham, and Japheth, the three sons of Noah, survived the Flood with their father.
(Ham is the ancestor of the Canaanites.) [19]From these three sons of Noah came all the
people now scattered across the earth.

[20]After the Flood, Noah became a farmer and planted a vineyard. [21]One day he 9:21 Gen 19:35
became drunk on some wine he had made and lay naked in his tent. [22]Ham, the father of 9:22 Hab 2:15
Canaan, saw that his father was naked and went outside and told his brothers. [23]Shem
and Japheth took a robe, held it over their shoulders, walked backward into the tent, and
covered their father's naked body. As they did this, they looked the other way so they
wouldn't see him naked. [24]When Noah woke up from his drunken stupor, he learned
what Ham, his youngest son, had done. [25]Then he cursed the descendants of Canaan, the 9:25 Deut 27:16
son of Ham:

"A curse on the Canaanites!
May they be the lowest of servants
to the descendants of Shem and Japheth."

[26]Then Noah said, 9:26 Gen 14:20

"May Shem be blessed by the LORD my God;
and may Canaan be his servant.
[27]May God enlarge the territory of Japheth, 9:27 Gen 10:2-5 Isa 66:19
and may he share the prosperity of Shem;*
and let Canaan be his servant."

[28]Noah lived another 350 years after the Flood. [29]He was 950 years old when he died. 9:29 Gen 2:17

10 This is the history of the families of Shem, Ham, and Japheth, the three sons of 10:1 Gen 9:18 1 Chr 1:4
Noah. Many children were born to them after the Flood.

Descendants of Japheth

[2]The descendants of Japheth were Gomer, Magog, Madai, Javan, Tubal, Meshech,
and Tiras. 10:2 1 Chr 1:5-7 Isa 66:19 Ezek 27:13; 38:2-3, 6
[3]The descendants of Gomer were Ashkenaz, Riphath, and Togarmah.
[4]The descendants of Javan were Elishah, Tarshish, Kittim, and Rodanim.* [5]Their 10:4 1 Chr 1:6-7

9:27 Hebrew *may he live in the tents of Shem.* **10:4** As in some Hebrew manuscripts and Greek version (see also 1 Chr 1:7); most Hebrew manuscripts read *Dodanim.*

9:8-17 Noah stepped out of the boat onto an earth devoid of human life. But God gave him a reassuring promise. This covenant had three parts: (1) Never again will a flood do such destruction; (2) as long as the earth remains, the seasons will always come as expected; (3) a rainbow will be visible when it rains as a sign to all that God will keep his promises. The earth's order and seasons are still preserved, and rainbows still remind us of God's faithfulness to his word.

9:20-27 Noah, the great hero of faith, got drunk—a poor example of godliness to his sons. Perhaps this story is included to show us that even godly people can sin and that their bad influence affects their families. Although the wicked people had all been killed, the possibility of evil still existed in the hearts of Noah and his family. Ham's mocking attitude revealed a severe lack of respect for his father and for God.

9:25 This verse has been wrongfully used to support racial prejudice and even slavery. Noah's curse, however, wasn't directed toward any particular race, but rather at the Canaanite nation—a nation God knew would become wicked. The curse was fulfilled when the Israelites entered the Promised Land and drove the Canaanites out (see the book of Joshua).

descendants became the seafaring peoples in various lands, each tribe with its own
language.

Descendants of Ham

10:6 1 Chr 1:8-10
6 The descendants of Ham were Cush, Mizraim,* Put, and Canaan.

10:7 Isa 43:3; Ezek 27:15, 20, 22
7 The descendants of Cush were Seba, Havilah, Sabtah, Raamah, and Sabteca. The
descendants of Raamah were Sheba and Dedan.

8 One of Cush's descendants was Nimrod, who became a heroic warrior. 9 He was
a mighty hunter in the LORD's sight.* His name became proverbial, and people
would speak of someone as being "like Nimrod, a mighty hunter in the LORD's

10:10 Gen 11:9
sight." 10 He built the foundation for his empire in the land of Babylonia,* with the

10:11 Mic 5:6
cities of Babel, Erech, Akkad, and Calneh. 11 From there he extended his reign to
Assyria, where he built Nineveh, Rehoboth-ir, Calah, 12 and Resen—the main city
of the empire, located between Nineveh and Calah.

10:13 Jer 46:9
13 Mizraim was the ancestor of the Ludites, Anamites, Lehabites, Naphtuhites,

10:14 1 Chr 1:12
14 Pathrusites, Casluhites, and the Caphtorites, from whom the Philistines
came.*

10:15 Gen 15:20; 23:3; 1 Chr 1:13; Jer 47:4
15 Canaan's oldest son was Sidon, the ancestor of the Sidonians. Canaan was also the
ancestor of the Hittites, 16 Jebusites, Amorites, Girgashites, 17 Hivites, Arkites,

10:16 Gen 15:18-21
Sinites, 18 Arvadites, Zemarites, and Hamathites. 19 Eventually the territory of
Canaan spread from Sidon to Gerar, near Gaza, and to Sodom, Gomorrah, Admah,

10:19 Gen 14:2
and Zeboiim, near Lasha.

20 These were the descendants of Ham, identified according to their tribes, languages,
territories, and nations.

Descendants of Shem

10:22 2 Kgs 15:29; Isa 66:19
21 Sons were also born to Shem, the older brother of Japheth.* Shem was the ancestor
of all the descendants of Eber. 22 The descendants of Shem were Elam, Asshur,

10:23 Job 1:1; Jer 25:30
Arphaxad, Lud, and Aram.
23 The descendants of Aram were Uz, Hul, Gether, and Mash.

10:24 Luke 3:35
24 Arphaxad was the father of Shelah,* and Shelah was the father of Eber. 25 Eber had
two sons. The first was named Peleg—"division"—for during his lifetime the
people of the world were divided into different language groups and dispersed. His
brother's name was Joktan.
26 Joktan was the ancestor of Almodad, Sheleph, Hazarmaveth, Jerah, 27 Hadoram,
Uzal, Diklah, 28 Obal, Abimael, Sheba, 29 Ophir, Havilah, and Jobab. 30 The
descendants of Joktan lived in the area extending from Mesha toward the eastern
hills of Sephar.

31 These were the descendants of Shem, identified according to their tribes, languages,
territories, and nations.

10:32 Gen 9:19; 10:1
32 These are the families that came from Noah's sons, listed nation by nation according to their lines of descent. The earth was populated with the people of these nations
after the Flood.

10:6 Or *Egypt;* also in 10:13. **10:9** Hebrew *a mighty hunter before the LORD;* also in 10:9b. **10:10** Hebrew *Shinar.* **10:14** Hebrew *Casluhites, from whom the Philistines came, Caphtorites.* Compare Jer 47:4; Amos 9:7. **10:21** Or *Shem, whose older brother was Japheth.* **10:24** Greek version reads *Arphaxad was the father of Cainan, Cainan was the father of Shelah.*

BIBLE NATIONS DESCENDED FROM NOAH'S SONS

Shem	*Ham*	*Japheth*
Hebrews	Canaanites	Greeks
Chaldeans	Egyptians	Thracians
Assyrians	Philistines	Scythians
Persians	Hittites	
Syrians	Amorites	

Shem's descendants were called Semites. Abraham, David, and Jesus descended from Shem. Ham's descendants settled in Canaan, Egypt, and the rest of Africa. Japheth's descendants settled for the most part in Europe and Asia Minor.

10:8, 9 Who was Nimrod? Not much is known about him except that he was a heroic warrior. But people with great gifts can become proud, and that is probably what happened to Nimrod. Some consider him the founder of the great, godless Babylonian Empire.

3. The tower of Babel

11 At one time the whole world spoke a single language and used the same words.
2As the people migrated eastward, they found a plain in the land of Babylonia*
and settled there. 3They began to talk about construction projects. “Come,” they said,
“let’s make great piles of burnt brick and collect natural asphalt to use as mortar. 4Let’s
build a great city with a tower that reaches to the skies—a monument to our greatness!
This will bring us together and keep us from scattering all over the world.”
5But the LORD came down to see the city and the tower the people were building.
6“Look!” he said. “If they can accomplish this when they have just begun to take
advantage of their common language and political unity, just think of what they will do
later. Nothing will be impossible for them! 7Come, let’s go down and give them different
languages. Then they won’t be able to understand each other.”
8In that way, the LORD scattered them all over the earth; and that ended the building of
the city. 9That is why the city was called Babel,* because it was there that the LORD
confused the people by giving them many languages, thus scattering them across the earth.

From Shem to Abram

10This is the history of Shem’s family.

When Shem was 100 years old, his son Arphaxad was born. This happened two years after the Flood. 11After the birth of Arphaxad, Shem lived another 500 years and had other sons and daughters.
12When Arphaxad was 35 years old, his son Shelah was born.* 13After the birth of Shelah, Arphaxad lived another 403 years and had other sons and daughters.*
14When Shelah was 30 years old, his son Eber was born. 15After the birth of Eber, Shelah lived another 403 years and had other sons and daughters.
16When Eber was 34 years old, his son Peleg was born. 17After the birth of Peleg, Eber lived another 430 years and had other sons and daughters.
18When Peleg was 30 years old, his son Reu was born. 19After the birth of Reu, Peleg lived another 209 years and had other sons and daughters.
20When Reu was 32 years old, his son Serug was born. 21After the birth of Serug, Reu lived another 207 years and had other sons and daughters.
22When Serug was 30 years old, his son Nahor was born. 23After the birth of Nahor, Serug lived another 200 years and had other sons and daughters.
24When Nahor was 29 years old, his son Terah was born. 25After the birth of Terah, Nahor lived another 119 years and had other sons and daughters.

11:2 Gen 10:10; 14:1; Isa 11:11
11:3 Gen 14:10
11:4 2 Sam 8:13
11:5 Gen 18:21; Exod 19:11
11:6 Gen 9:19; 11:1
11:7 Gen 1:26
11:8 Gen 9:19
11:9 Gen 10:10
11:10 Gen 10:22-25; Luke 3:36
11:12 Luke 3:36
11:13 1 Chr 1:17
11:14 Luke 3:35
11:16 Luke 3:35
11:18 Luke 3:35
11:20 Luke 3:35
11:22 Luke 3:34
11:24 Josh 24:2; Luke 3:34

11:2 Hebrew *Shinar.* **11:9** *Babel* sounds like a Hebrew term that means “confusion.” **11:12** Or *his son, the ancestor of Shelah, was born;* similarly in 11:14, 16, 18, 20, 22, 24. **11:12-13** Greek version reads *12When Arphaxad was 135 years old, his son Cainan was born. 13After the birth of Cainan, Arphaxad lived another 430 years and had other sons and daughters, and then he died. When Cainan was 130 years old, his son Shelah was born. After the birth of Shelah, Cainan lived another 330 years and had other sons and daughters, and then he died.*

11:3 The brick used to build this tower was man made and not as hard as stone.

11:3, 4 The tower of Babel was most likely a ziggurat, a common structure in Babylonia at this time. Most often built as temples, ziggurats looked like pyramids with steps or ramps leading up the sides. Ziggurats stood as high as 300 feet and were often just as wide; thus they were the focal point of the city. The people in this story built their tower as a monument to their own greatness, something for the whole world to see.

11:4 The tower of Babel was a great human achievement, a wonder of the world. But it was a monument to the people themselves rather than to God. We may build monuments to ourselves (expensive clothes, big house, fancy car, important job) to call attention to our achievements. These may not be wrong in themselves, but when we use them to give us identity and self-worth, they take God’s place in our lives. We are free to develop in many areas, but we are not free to think we have replaced God. What “towers” have you built in your life?

11:10-27 In 9:25 we read Noah’s curse on Canaan, Ham’s son, ancestor of the evil Canaanites. Here and in 10:22-31 we have a list of Shem’s descendants, who were blessed (9:26). From Shem’s line came Abram and the entire Jewish nation, which would eventually conquer the land of Canaan in the days of Joshua.

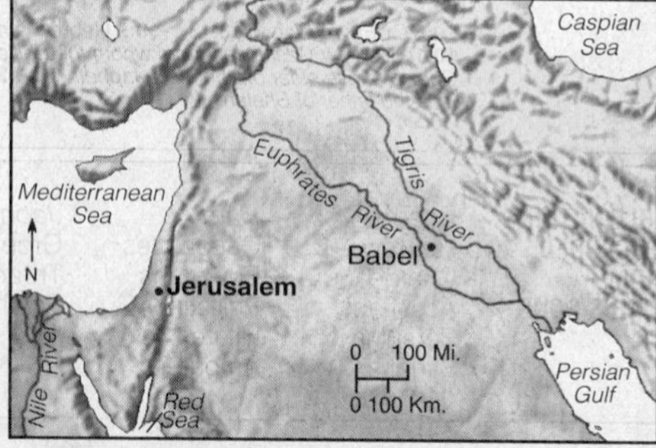

THE TOWER OF BABEL The plain between the Tigris and Euphrates Rivers offered a perfect location for the city and tower “that reaches to the skies.”

11:26 Gen 22:20; 1 Chr 1:26-27; Luke 3:34
11:29 Gen 17:15; 20:11-12; 22:20
11:30 Gen 16:1; 18:11; 25:21; 1 Sam 1:5; Luke 1:7
11:31 Gen 27:43; Josh 24:2; Acts 7:4

26 When Terah was 70 years old, he became the father of Abram, Nahor, and Haran.

The Family of Terah

27 This is the history of Terah's family. Terah was the father of Abram, Nahor, and Haran;
and Haran had a son named Lot. 28 But while Haran was still young, he died in Ur of the
Chaldeans, the place of his birth. He was survived by Terah, his father. 29 Meanwhile, Abram
married Sarai, and his brother Nahor married Milcah, the daughter of their brother Haran.
(Milcah had a sister named Iscah.) 30 Now Sarai was not able to have any children.
31 Terah took his son Abram, his daughter-in-law Sarai, and his grandson Lot (his son
Haran's child) and left Ur of the Chaldeans to go to the land of Canaan. But they stopped
instead at the village of Haran and settled there. 32 Terah lived for 205 years* and died
while still at Haran.

D. THE STORY OF ABRAHAM (12:1—25:18)

Despite God's swift judgment of sin, most people ignored him and continued to sin. But a handful of people really tried to follow him. One of these was Abraham. God appeared to Abraham one day and promised to make his descendants into a great nation. Abraham's part of the agreement was to obey God. Through sharp testing and an incident that almost destroyed his family, Abraham remained faithful to God. Throughout this section we discover how to live a life of faith.

1. God promises a nation to Abram

The Call of Abram

12:1 Gen 15:7; †Acts 7:3; Heb 11:8
12:2 Gen 13:16; 15:5; 17:4; 18:18; 22:17; Zech 8:13
12:3 Gen 22:18; 26:4; Exod 23:22; †Gal 3:8

12 Then the LORD told Abram, "Leave your country, your relatives, and your father's
house, and go to the land that I will show you. 2 I will cause you to become the
father of a great nation. I will bless you and make you famous, and I will make you a
blessing to others. 3 I will bless those who bless you and curse those who curse you. All
the families of the earth will be blessed through you."
4 So Abram departed as the LORD had instructed him, and Lot went with him. Abram
was seventy-five years old when he left Haran. 5 He took his wife, Sarai, his nephew
Lot, and all his wealth—his livestock and all the people who had joined his household

11:32 Some ancient versions read *145 years;* compare 11:26; 12:4.

11:27-28 Abram grew up in Ur of the Chaldeans, an important city in the ancient world. Archaeologists have discovered evidence of a flourishing civilization there in Abram's day. The city carried on an extensive trade with its neighbors and had a vast library. Growing up in Ur, Abram was probably well educated.

11:31 Terah left Ur to go to Canaan but settled in Haran instead. Why did he stop halfway? It may have been his health, the climate, or even fear. But this did not change Abram's calling ("the LORD told Abram," 12:1). He had respect for his father's leadership, but when Terah died, Abram moved on to Canaan. God's will may come in stages. Just as the time in Haran was a transition period for Abram, so God may give us transition periods and times of waiting to help us depend on him and trust his timing. If we patiently do his will during the transition times, we will be better prepared to serve him as we should when he calls us.

12:1-3 When God called him, Abram moved out in faith from Ur to Haran and finally to Canaan. God then established a covenant with Abram, telling him that he would found a great nation. Not only would this nation be blessed, God said, but the other nations of the earth would be blessed through Abram's descendants. Israel, the nation that would come from Abram, was to follow God and influence those with whom it came in contact. Through Abram's family tree, Jesus Christ was born to save humanity. Through Christ, people can have a personal relationship with God and be blessed beyond measure.

12:2 God promised to bless Abram and make him famous, but there was one condition. Abram had to do what God wanted him to do. This meant leaving his home and friends and traveling to a new land where God promised to build a great nation from Abram's family. Abram obeyed, walking away from his home for God's promise of even greater blessings in the future. God may be trying to lead you to a place of greater service and usefulness for him. Don't let the comfort and security of your present position make you miss God's plan for you.

12:5 God planned to develop a nation of people he would call his own. He called Abram from the godless, self-centered city of Ur to a fertile region called Canaan, where a God-centered, moral nation could be established. Though small in dimension, the land of Canaan was the focal point for most of the history of Israel as well as for the rise of Christianity. This small land given to one man, Abram, has had a tremendous impact on world history.

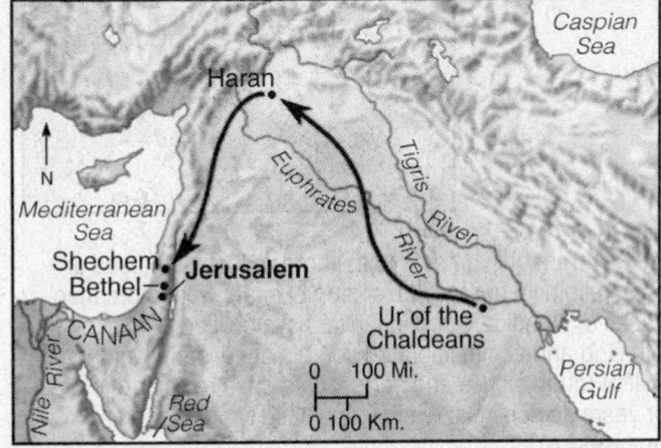

ABRAM'S JOURNEY TO CANAAN Abram, Sarai, and Lot traveled from Ur of the Chaldeans to Canaan by way of Haran. Though indirect, this route followed the rivers rather than attempting to cross the vast desert.

at Haran—and finally arrived in Canaan. 6 Traveling through Canaan, they came to a **12:6** Gen 33:18; 35:4
place near Shechem and set up camp beside the oak at Moreh. At that time, the area Deut 11:30
was inhabited by Canaanites.
7 Then the LORD appeared to Abram and said, "I am going to give this land to your **12:7** Gen 13:15
offspring.*" And Abram built an altar there to commemorate the LORD's visit. 8 After †Gal 3:16
that, Abram traveled southward and set up camp in the hill country between Bethel **12:8**
on the west and Ai on the east. There he built an altar and worshiped the LORD. 9 Then Gen 4:26; 8:20; 22:9
Abram traveled south by stages toward the Negev. **12:9** Gen 13:1; 20:1

Abram and Sarai in Egypt

10 At that time there was a severe famine in the land, so Abram went down to Egypt to **12:10** Gen 26:1; 42:5
wait it out. 11 As he was approaching the borders of Egypt, Abram said to Sarai, "You **12:11**
are a very beautiful woman. 12 When the Egyptians see you, they will say, 'This is his Gen 29:17
wife. Let's kill him; then we can have her!' 13 But if you say you are my sister, then **12:12** Gen 20:11
the Egyptians will treat me well because of their interest in you, and they will spare
my life."
14 And sure enough, when they arrived in Egypt, everyone spoke of her beauty.
15 When the palace officials saw her, they sang her praises to their king, the pharaoh, **12:16**
and she was taken into his harem. 16 Then Pharaoh gave Abram many gifts because of Gen 20:14; 24:35
her—sheep, cattle, donkeys, male and female servants, and camels.
17 But the LORD sent a terrible plague upon Pharaoh's household because of Sarai, **12:17** 1 Chr 16:21
Abram's wife. 18 So Pharaoh called for Abram and accused him sharply. "What is this Ps 105:14
you have done to me?" he demanded. "Why didn't you tell me she was your wife? **12:18** Gen 20:9-10
19 Why were you willing to let me marry her, saying she was your sister? Here is your **12:19**
wife! Take her and be gone!" 20 Pharaoh then sent them out of the country under armed Gen 20:5; 26:9
escort—Abram and his wife, with all their household and belongings.

12:7 Hebrew *seed.*

ABRAM'S JOURNEY TO EGYPT
A famine could cause the loss of a shepherd's wealth. So Abram traveled through the Negev to Egypt, where there was plenty of food and good land for his flocks.

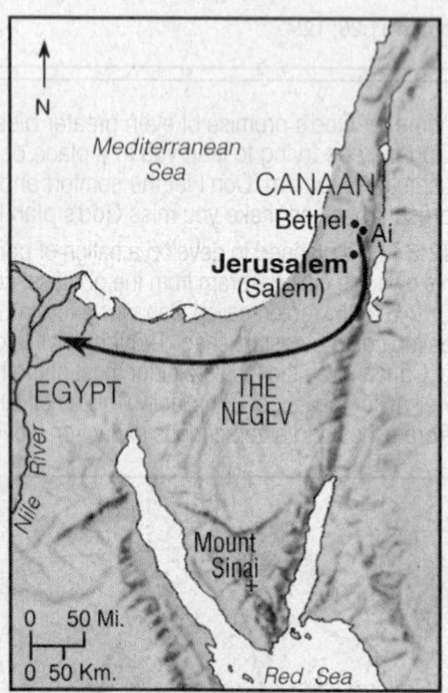

12:7 Abram built an altar to the Lord. Altars were used in many religions, but for God's people, altars were more than places of sacrifice. For them, altars symbolized communion with God and commemorated notable encounters with him. Built of rough stones and earth, altars often remained in place for years as continual reminders of God's protection and promises.

Abram regularly built altars to God for two reasons: (1) for prayer and worship, and (2) as reminders of God's promise to bless him. Abram couldn't survive spiritually without regularly renewing his love and loyalty to God. Building altars helped Abram remember that God was at the center of his life. Regular worship helps us remember what God desires and motivates us to obey him.

12:10 When famine struck, Abram went to Egypt where there was food. Why would there be a famine in the land where God had just called Abram? This was a test of Abram's faith, and Abram passed. He didn't question God's leading when facing this difficulty. Many believers find that when they determine to follow God, they immediately encounter great obstacles. The next time you face such a test, don't try to second-guess what God is doing. Use the intelligence God gave you, as Abram did when he temporarily moved to Egypt, and wait for new opportunities.

12:11-13 Abram, acting out of fear, asked Sarai to tell a half-truth by saying she was his sister. She *was* his half sister (see 20:12), but she was also his wife.

Abram's intent was to deceive the Egyptians. He feared that if they knew the truth, they would kill him to get Sarai. She would have been a desirable addition to Pharaoh's harem because of her wealth, beauty, and potential for political alliance. As Sarai's brother, Abram would have been given a place of honor. As her husband, however, his life would be in danger because Sarai could not enter Pharaoh's harem unless Abram was dead. So Abram lost faith in God's protection, even after all God had promised him, and told a half-truth. This shows how lying compounds the effects of sin. When he lied, Abram's problems multiplied.

2. Abram and Lot

Abram and Lot Separate

13:1 Gen 12:9
13:2 Gen 12:5
13:3 Gen 12:8-9
13:5 Gen 12:5
13:6 Gen 12:5; 36:7
13:7 Gen 12:6; 26:20
13:8 Prov 15:18; 20:3
13:9 Gen 20:15
13:10 Gen 2:8-10
13:13 Gen 18:20; Num 32:23; Isa 1:10; 3:9; 2 Pet 2:8
13:14 Gen 28:14; Deut 3:27; 34:1-4
13:15 †Gal 3:16; Gen 12:2, 7; 15:18; 17:7-8
13:16 Num 23:10
13:17 Num 13:17-25
13:18 Gen 14:13; 18:1

13 So they left Egypt and traveled north into the Negev—Abram with his wife and
Lot and all that they owned, 2 for Abram was very rich in livestock, silver, and
gold. 3 Then they continued traveling by stages toward Bethel, to the place between
Bethel and Ai where they had camped before. 4 This was the place where Abram had built
the altar, and there he again worshiped the LORD.

5 Now Lot, who was traveling with Abram, was also very wealthy with sheep, cattle,
and many tents. 6 But the land could not support both Abram and Lot with all their flocks
and herds living so close together. There were too many animals for the available
pastureland. 7 So an argument broke out between the herdsmen of Abram and Lot. At that
time Canaanites and Perizzites were also living in the land.

8 Then Abram talked it over with Lot. "This arguing between our herdsmen has got to
stop," he said. "After all, we are close relatives! 9 I'll tell you what we'll do. Take your
choice of any section of the land you want, and we will separate. If you want that area over
there, then I'll stay here. If you want to stay in this area, then I'll move on to another place."

10 Lot took a long look at the fertile plains of the Jordan Valley in the direction of Zoar.
The whole area was well watered everywhere, like the garden of the LORD or the
beautiful land of Egypt. (This was before the LORD had destroyed Sodom and Gomorrah.) 11 Lot chose that land for himself—the Jordan Valley to the east of them. He went
there with his flocks and servants and parted company with his uncle Abram. 12 So while
Abram stayed in the land of Canaan, Lot moved his tents to a place near Sodom, among
the cities of the plain. 13 The people of this area were unusually wicked and sinned greatly
against the LORD.

14 After Lot was gone, the LORD said to Abram, "Look as far as you can see in every
direction. 15 I am going to give all this land to you and your offspring* as a permanent
possession. 16 And I am going to give you so many descendants that, like dust, they
cannot be counted! 17 Take a walk in every direction and explore the new possessions I
am giving you." 18 Then Abram moved his camp to the oak grove owned by Mamre,
which is at Hebron. There he built an altar to the LORD.

Abram Rescues Lot

14:1 Gen 10:10; 11:2
14:2 Gen 10:19; 13:10; Deut 29:23

14 About this time war broke out in the region. King Amraphel of Babylonia,* King
Arioch of Ellasar, King Kedorlaomer of Elam, and King Tidal of Goiim 2 fought
against King Bera of Sodom, King Birsha of Gomorrah, King Shinab of Admah, King
Shemeber of Zeboiim, and the king of Bela (now called Zoar).

13:15 Hebrew *seed.* **14:1** Hebrew *Shinar;* also in 14:9.

13:1, 2 In Abram's day, sheep and cattle owners could acquire great wealth. Abram's wealth not only included silver and gold, but also livestock. These animals were a valuable commodity used for food, clothing, tent material, and sacrifices. They were often traded for other goods and services. Abram was able to watch his wealth grow and multiply daily.

13:5-9 Facing a potential conflict with his nephew Lot, Abram took the initiative in settling the dispute. He gave Lot first choice, even though Abram, being older, had the right to choose first. Abram also showed a willingness to risk being cheated. Abram's example shows us how to respond to difficult family situations: (1) Take the initiative in resolving conflicts; (2) let others have first choice, even if that means not getting what we want; (3) put family peace above personal desires.

13:7, 8 Surrounded by hostile neighbors, the herdsmen of Abram and Lot should have pulled together. Instead, they let petty jealousy tear them apart. Similar situations exist today. Christians often bicker while Satan is at work all around them.

Rivalries, arguments, and disagreements among believers can be destructive in three ways: (1) They damage goodwill, trust, and peace—the foundations of good human relations; (2) they hamper progress toward important goals; (3) they make us self-centered rather than love-centered. Jesus understood how destructive arguments among brothers could be. In his final prayer before being betrayed and arrested, Jesus asked God that his followers be "one" (John 17:21).

13:10, 11 Lot's character is revealed by his choices. He took the best share of the land even though it meant living near Sodom, a city known for its sin. He was greedy, wanting the best for himself, without thinking about his uncle Abram's needs or what was fair.

Life is a series of choices. We, too, can choose the best while ignoring the needs and feelings of others. But this kind of choice, as Lot's life shows, leads to problems. When we stop making choices in God's direction, all that is left is to make choices in the wrong direction.

13:12, 13 Good pasture and available water seemed like a wise choice to Lot at first. But he failed to recognize that wicked Sodom could provide temptations strong enough to destroy his family. Have you chosen to live or work in a "Sodom"? Even though you may be strong enough to resist the temptations, other members of your family may not. While God commands us to reach people in the "Sodom" near us, we must be careful not to become like the very people we are trying to reach.

3 The kings of Sodom, Gomorrah, Admah, Zeboiim, and Bela formed an alliance and
mobilized their armies in Siddim Valley (that is, the valley of the Dead Sea*). 4 For
twelve years they had all been subject to King Kedorlaomer, but now in the thirteenth
year they rebelled.
5 One year later, Kedorlaomer and his allies arrived. They conquered the Rephaites in
Ashteroth-karnaim, the Zuzites in Ham, the Emites in the plain of Kiriathaim, 6 and the
Horites in Mount Seir, as far as El-paran at the edge of the wilderness. 7 Then they swung
around to En-mishpat (now called Kadesh) and destroyed the Amalekites, and also the
Amorites living in Hazazon-tamar.
8 But now the army of the kings of Sodom, Gomorrah, Admah, Zeboiim, and Bela (now
called Zoar) prepared for battle in the valley of the Dead Sea* 9 against King Kedorlaomer
of Elam and the kings of Goiim, Babylonia, and Ellasar—four kings against five. 10 As it
happened, the valley was filled with tar pits. And as the army of the kings of Sodom and
Gomorrah fled, some slipped into the tar pits, while the rest escaped into the mountains.
11 The victorious invaders then plundered Sodom and Gomorrah and began their long
journey home, taking all the wealth and food with them. 12 They also captured Lot—
Abram's nephew who lived in Sodom—and took everything he owned. 13 One of the men
who escaped came and told Abram the Hebrew, who was camped at the oak grove belonging
to Mamre the Amorite. Mamre and his relatives, Eshcol and Aner, were Abram's allies.
14 When Abram learned that Lot had been captured, he called together the men born into
his household, 318 of them in all. He chased after Kedorlaomer's army until he caught up
with them in Dan. 15 There he divided his men and attacked during the night from several
directions. Kedorlaomer's army fled, but Abram chased them to Hobah, north of Damascus. 16 Abram and his allies recovered everything—the goods that had been taken, Abram's
nephew Lot with his possessions, and all the women and other captives.

Melchizedek Blesses Abram

17 As Abram returned from his victory over Kedorlaomer and his allies, the king of
Sodom came out to meet him in the valley of Shaveh (that is, the King's Valley). 18 Then
Melchizedek, the king of Salem and a priest of God Most High, brought him bread and
wine. 19 Melchizedek blessed Abram with this blessing:

14:3 Hebrew *Salt Sea*. **14:8** Hebrew *in Siddim Valley;* see 14:3.

14:3 Num 34:3, 12 Deut 3:17 Josh 3:16
14:5 Gen 15:20 Deut 1:4; 2:10, 20; 3:11 Josh 13:19
14:7 Gen 16:14; 20:1 Num 13:26 Deut 1:4 2 Chr 20:2
14:12 Gen 11:27
14:13 Gen 10:16; 13:18; 39:14
14:14 Gen 12:5 Deut 34:1
14:15 Gen 15:2
14:17 2 Sam 18:18
14:18 Heb 5:6, 10; 7:1
14:19 Gen 27:25; 48:9 Mark 10:16

14:4-16 Who was Kedorlaomer, and why was he important? In Abram's time, most cities had their own kings. Wars and rivalries among kings were common. A conquered city paid tribute to the victorious king. Nothing is known about Kedorlaomer except what we read in the Bible, but apparently he was quite powerful. Five cities including Sodom had paid tribute to him for 12 years. The five cities formed an alliance and rebelled by withholding tribute. Kedorlaomer reacted swiftly and reconquered them all. When he defeated Sodom, he captured Lot, his family, and his possessions. Abram, with only 318 men, chased Kedorlaomer's army and attacked him near Damascus. With God's help, he defeated them and recovered Lot, his family, and their possessions.

14:12 Lot's greedy desire for the best of everything led him into sinful surroundings. His burning desire for possessions and success cost him his freedom and enjoyment. As a captive to Kedorlaomer, he faced torture, slavery, or death. In much the same way, we can be enticed into doing things or going places we shouldn't. The prosperity we long for is captivating; it can both entice us and enslave us if our motives are not in line with God's desires.

14:14-16 These incidents portray two of Abram's characteristics: (1) He had courage that came from God; facing a powerful foe, he attacked. (2) He was prepared; he had taken time to train his men for a potential conflict. We never know when we will be called upon to complete difficult tasks. Like Abram, we should prepare for those times and take courage from God when they come.

14:14-16 When Abram learned that Lot was a captive, he immediately tried to rescue his nephew. It is easier and safer not to become involved. But with Lot in serious trouble, Abram acted at once. Sometimes we must get involved in a messy or painful situation in order to help others. We should be willing to act immediately when others need our help.

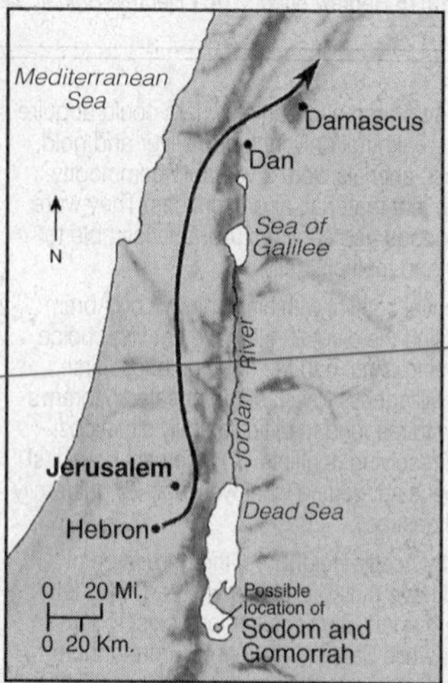

LOT'S RESCUE Having conquered Sodom, Kedorlaomer left for his home country, taking many captives with him. Abram learned what had happened and chased Kedorlaomer past Dan and beyond Damascus. There he defeated the king and rescued the captives, among them Lot.

14:18 Who was Melchizedek? He was obviously a God-fearing man, for his name means "king of righteousness," and king of Salem means "king of peace." He was a "priest of God Most

"Blessed be Abram by God Most High,
Creator of heaven and earth.
14:20 Gen 9:26; 24:27 †Heb 7:1-2
20 And blessed be God Most High,
who has helped you conquer your enemies."

Then Abram gave Melchizedek a tenth of all the goods he had recovered.
21 The king of Sodom told him, "Give back my people who were captured. But you
may keep for yourself all the goods you have recovered."
14:22 Gen 1:1
22 Abram replied, "I have solemnly promised the LORD, God Most High, Creator of
14:23 2 Kgs 5:16
heaven and earth, 23 that I will not take so much as a single thread or sandal thong from
14:24 Gen 14:13
you. Otherwise you might say, 'I am the one who made Abram rich!' 24 All I'll accept is
what these young men of mine have already eaten. But give a share of the goods to my
allies—Aner, Eshcol, and Mamre."

LOT

Some people simply drift through life. Their choices, when they can muster the will to choose, tend to follow the course of least resistance. Lot, Abram's nephew, was such a person.

While still young, Lot lost his father. Although this must have been hard on him, he was not left without strong role models in his grandfather Terah and his uncle Abram, who raised him. Still, Lot did not develop their sense of purpose. Throughout his life he was so caught up in the present moment that he seemed incapable of seeing the consequences of his actions. It is hard to imagine what his life would have been like without Abram's careful attention and God's intervention.

By the time Lot drifted out of the picture, his life had taken an ugly turn. He had so blended into the sinful culture of his day that he did not want to leave it. His drifting finally took him in a very specific direction—destruction. Then his daughters committed incest with him.

Lot, however, is called "righteous" in the New Testament (2 Peter 2:7, 8). Ruth, a descendant of Moab, was an ancestor of Jesus, even though Moab was born as a result of Lot's incestuous relationship with one of his daughters. Lot's story gives hope to us that God forgives and often brings about positive circumstances from evil.

What is the direction of your life? Are you headed toward God or away from him? If you're a drifter, the choice for God may seem difficult, but it is the one choice that puts all other choices in a different light.

Strengths and accomplishments
- He was a successful businessman
- Peter calls him a righteous man (2 Peter 2:7, 8)

Weaknesses and mistakes
- When faced with decisions, he tended to put off deciding, then chose the easiest course of action
- When given a choice, his first reaction was to think of himself

Lesson from his life
- God wants us to do more than drift through life; he wants us to be an influence for him

Vital statistics
- Where: Lived first in Ur of the Chaldeans, then moved to Canaan with Abram. Eventually he moved to the wicked city of Sodom
- Occupation: Wealthy sheep and cattle rancher; also a city official
- Relatives: Father: Haran. Adopted by Abram when his father died. The name of his wife, who turned into a pillar of salt, is not mentioned

Key verse
"When Lot still hesitated, the angels seized his hand and the hands of his wife and two daughters and rushed them to safety outside the city, for the LORD was merciful" (Genesis 19:16).

Lot's story is told in Genesis 11—14; 19. He is also mentioned in Deuteronomy 2:9; Luke 17:28–32; 2 Peter 2:7, 8.

High" (Hebrews 7:1, 2). He recognized God as Creator of heaven and earth. What else is known about him? Four main theories have been suggested: (1) Melchizedek was a respected king of that region. Abram was simply showing him the respect he deserved. (2) The name Melchizedek may have been a standing title for all the kings of Salem. (3) Melchizedek was a type of Christ (Hebrews 7:3). A type is an Old Testament event or teaching that is so closely related to what Christ did that it illustrates a lesson about Christ. (4) Melchizedek was the appearance on earth of the preincarnate Christ in a temporary bodily form.

14:20 Abram gave a tenth of the goods he recovered to Melchizedek. Even in some pagan religions, it was traditional to give a tenth of one's earnings to the gods. Abram followed accepted tradition; however, he refused to take any of the recovered goods from the king of Sodom. Even though this huge amount would significantly increase what he could have given to God, he chose to reject it for more important reasons—he didn't want the ungodly king of Sodom to say, "I have made Abram rich." Instead, Abram wanted him to say, "God has made Abram rich." In this case, accepting the gifts would have focused everyone's attention on Abram or the king of Sodom rather than on God, the giver of victory. When people look at us, they need to see what God has accomplished in our lives.

3. God promises a son to Abram

The LORD's Covenant with Abram

15 Afterward the LORD spoke to Abram in a vision and said to him, "Do not be afraid,
Abram, for I will protect you, and your reward will be great."
2 But Abram replied, "O Sovereign LORD, what good are all your blessings when I
don't even have a son? Since I don't have a son, Eliezer of Damascus, a servant in my
household, will inherit all my wealth. 3 You have given me no children, so one of my
servants will have to be my heir."
4 Then the LORD said to him, "No, your servant will not be your heir, for you will have
a son of your own to inherit everything I am giving you." 5 Then the LORD brought
Abram outside beneath the night sky and told him, "Look up into the heavens and count
the stars if you can. Your descendants will be like that—too many to count!" 6 And Abram
believed the LORD, and the LORD declared him righteous because of his faith. 7 Then the
LORD told him, "I am the LORD who brought you out of Ur of the Chaldeans to give you
this land."
8 But Abram replied, "O Sovereign LORD, how can I be sure that you will give it to
me?"
9 Then the LORD told him, "Bring me a three-year-old heifer, a three-year-old female
goat, a three-year-old ram, a turtledove, and a young pigeon." 10 Abram took all these and
killed them. He cut each one down the middle and laid the halves side by side. He did
not, however, divide the birds in half. 11 Some vultures came down to eat the carcasses,
but Abram chased them away. 12 That evening, as the sun was going down, Abram fell
into a deep sleep. He saw a terrifying vision of darkness and horror.
13 Then the LORD told Abram, "You can be sure that your descendants will be strangers
in a foreign land, and they will be oppressed as slaves for four hundred years. 14 But I
will punish the nation that enslaves them, and in the end they will come away with great
wealth. 15 (But you will die in peace, at a ripe old age.) 16 After four generations your
descendants will return here to this land, when the sin of the Amorites has run its course."
17 As the sun went down and it became dark, Abram saw a smoking firepot and a flaming
torch pass between the halves of the carcasses. 18 So the LORD made a covenant with Abram
that day and said, "I have given this land to your descendants, all the way from the border

15:1 Gen 21:17; 26:24 Deut 33:29 Ps 3:3
15:4 †Gal 4:28
15:5 Gen 12:2; 22:17; 32:13 †Rom 4:18
15:6 Ps 106:31 †Rom 4:3, 9, 22 †Gal 3:6
15:7 Gen 12:1; 13:17 Acts 7:2-4
15:8 Luke 1:18
15:9 Lev 1:14
15:12 Gen 2:21; 28:11
15:13 Exod 12:40 †Acts 7:6 Gal 3:17
15:14 Exod 6:5
15:15 Gen 25:8
15:16 Exod 12:40
15:17 Jer 34:18-19
15:18 Num 34:1-15 Deut 1:7-8

15:1 Why would Abram be afraid? Perhaps he feared revenge from the kings he had just defeated (14:15). God gave him two good reasons for courage: (1) He promised to protect Abram, and (2) he promised a great reward to Abram. When you fear what lies ahead, remember that God will stay with you through difficult times and that he has promised you great blessings.

15:2, 3 Eliezer was Abram's most trusted servant, acting as household administrator. According to custom, if Abram were to die without a son, his eldest servant would become his heir. Although Abram loved his servant, he wanted a son to carry on the family line.

15:5 Abram wasn't promised wealth or fame; he already had that. Instead, God promised descendants like the stars in the sky or the grains of sand on the seashore (22:17), too numerous to count. To appreciate the vast number of stars scattered through the sky, you need to be, like Abram, away from any distractions. Or pick up a handful of sand and try to count the grains—it can't be done! Just when Abram was despairing of ever having an heir, God promised descendants too numerous to imagine. God's blessings are beyond our imagination!

15:6 Although Abram had been demonstrating his faith through his actions, it was his belief in the Lord, not his actions, that made Abram right with God (Romans 4:1-5). We, too, can have a right relationship with God by trusting him. Our outward actions—church attendance, prayer, good deeds—will not by themselves make us right with God. A right relationship is based on faith—the heartfelt inner confidence that God is who he says he is and does what he says he will do. Right actions will follow naturally as by-products.

15:8 Abram was looking for confirmation and assurance that he was doing God's will. We also want assurance when we ask for guidance. But we can know for sure that what we are doing is right if we do what the Bible says. Abram didn't have the Bible—we do.

15:13, 14 The book of Exodus tells the story of the enslavement and miraculous deliverance of Abram's descendants.

15:16 The Amorites were one of the nations living in Canaan, the land God promised Abram. God knew the people would grow more wicked and would someday need to be punished. Part of that punishment would involve taking away their land and giving it to Abram's descendants. God in his mercy was giving the Amorites plenty of time to repent, but he already knew they would not. At the right time, they would have to be punished. Everything God does is true to his character. He is merciful, knows all, and acts justly—and his timing is perfect.

15:17 Why did God send this strange vision to Abram? God's covenant with Abram was serious business. It represented an incredible promise from God and a huge responsibility for Abram. To confirm his promise, God gave Abram a sign—the smoking firepot and a flaming torch. The fire and smoke suggest God's holiness, his zeal for righteousness, and his judgment on all the nations. God took the initiative, gave the confirmation, and followed through on his promises. God's passing through the pieces was a visible assurance to Abram that the covenant God had made was real.

15:19 Num 24:21

of Egypt* to the great Euphrates River—[19]the land of the Kenites, Kenizzites, Kadmonites,
[20]Hittites, Perizzites, Rephaites, [21]Amorites, Canaanites, Girgashites, and Jebusites."

The Birth of Ishmael

16:1 Gen 11:30 Gal 4:24-25

16:2 Gen 30:3

16:3 Gen 12:4-5

16 But Sarai, Abram's wife, had no children. So Sarai took her servant, an Egyptian
woman named Hagar, [2]and gave her to Abram so she could bear his children. "The
LORD has kept me from having any children," Sarai said to Abram. "Go and sleep with
my servant. Perhaps I can have children through her." And Abram agreed. [3]So Sarai,
Abram's wife, took Hagar the Egyptian servant and gave her to Abram as a wife. (This
happened ten years after Abram first arrived in the land of Canaan.)

15:18 Hebrew *the river of Egypt,* referring either to an eastern branch of the Nile River or to the brook of Egypt in the Sinai (see Num 34:5).

MELCHIZEDEK

Do you like a good mystery? History is full of them! They usually involve people. One of the most mysterious people in the Bible is the king of peace, Melchizedek. He appeared one day in the life of Abraham (then Abram) and was never heard from again. What happened that day, however, was to be remembered throughout history and eventually became a subject of a New Testament letter (Hebrews).

This meeting between Abram and Melchizedek was most unusual. Although the two men were strangers and foreigners to each other, they shared a most important characteristic: Both worshiped and served the one God who made heaven and earth. This was a great moment of triumph for Abram. He had just defeated an army and regained the freedom of a large group of captives. If there was any doubt in his mind about whose victory it was, Melchizedek set the record straight by reminding Abram, "And blessed be God Most High, who has helped you conquer your enemies" (Genesis 14:20). Abram recognized that this man worshiped the same God he did.

Melchizedek was one of a small group of God-honoring people throughout the Old Testament who came in contact with the Jews (Israelites) but were not Jews themselves. This indicates that the requirement to be a follower of God is not genetic but is based on faithfully obeying his teachings and recognizing his greatness.

Do you let God speak to you through other people? In evaluating others, do you consider God's impact on their lives? Are you aware of the similarities between yourself and others who worship God, even if their form of worship is quite different from yours? Do you know the God of the Bible well enough to know if you truly worship him? Allow Melchizedek, Abraham, David, and Jesus, along with many other persons in the Bible, to show you this great God, Creator of heaven and earth. He wants you to know how much he loves you; he wants you to know him personally.

Strengths and accomplishments
- The first priest/king of Scripture—a leader with a heart tuned to God
- Good at encouraging others to serve God wholeheartedly
- A man whose character reflected his love for God
- A person in the Old Testament who reminds us of Jesus and who some believe really was Jesus

Lesson from his life
- Live for God and you're likely to be at the right place at the right time.
- Examine your heart: To whom or what is your greatest loyalty? If you can honestly answer *God,* you are living for him

Vital statistics
- Where: Ruled in Salem, site of the future Jerusalem
- Occupation: King of Salem and priest of God Most High

Key verses
"This Melchizedek was king of the city of Salem and also a priest of God Most High. When Abraham was returning home after winning a great battle against many kings, Melchizedek met him and blessed him. . . . Consider then how great this Melchizedek was. Even Abraham, the great patriarch of Israel, recognized how great Melchizedek was by giving him a tenth of what he had taken in battle" (Hebrews 7:1, 4).

Melchizedek's story is told in Genesis 14:17–20. He is also mentioned in Psalm 110:4; Hebrews 5—7.

16:1-3 Sarai gave Hagar to Abram as a substitute wife, a common practice of that time. A married woman who could not have children was shamed by her peers and was often required to give a female servant to her husband in order to produce heirs. The children born to the servant woman were considered the children of the wife. Abram was acting in line with the custom of the day, but his action showed a lack of faith that God would fulfill his promise.

16:3 Sarai took matters into her own hands by giving Hagar to Abram. Like Abram she had trouble believing God's promise that was apparently directed specifically toward Abram and Sarai. Out of this lack of faith came a series of problems. This invariably happens when we take over for God, trying to make his promise come true through efforts that are not in line with his specific directions. In this case, time was the greatest test of Abram and Sarai's willingness to let God work in their lives. Sometimes we too must simply wait. When we ask God for something and have to wait, it is a temptation to take matters into our own hands and interfere with God's plans.

4 So Abram slept with Hagar, and she became pregnant. When Hagar knew she was pregnant, she began to treat her mistress Sarai with contempt. 5 Then Sarai said to Abram, "It's all your fault! Now this servant of mine is pregnant, and she despises me, though I myself gave her the privilege of sleeping with you. The LORD will make you pay for doing this to me!*"

6 Abram replied, "Since she is your servant, you may deal with her as you see fit." So Sarai treated her harshly, and Hagar ran away.

7 The angel of the LORD found Hagar beside a desert spring along the road to Shur. 8 The angel said to her, "Hagar, Sarai's servant, where have you come from, and where are you going?"

"I am running away from my mistress," she replied.

9 Then the angel of the LORD said, "Return to your mistress and submit to her authority." 10 The angel added, "I will give you more descendants than you can count." 11 And the angel also said, "You are now pregnant and will give birth to a son. You are to name him Ishmael,* for the LORD has heard about your misery. 12 This son of yours will be a wild one—free and untamed as a wild donkey! He will be against everyone, and everyone will be against him. Yes, he will live at odds with the rest of his brothers."

13 Thereafter, Hagar referred to the LORD, who had spoken to her, as "the God who sees me,"* for she said, "I have seen the One who sees me!" 14 Later that well was named Beer-lahairoi,* and it can still be found between Kadesh and Bered.

15 So Hagar gave Abram a son, and Abram named him Ishmael. 16 Abram was eighty-six years old at that time.

Abram Is Named Abraham

17 When Abram was ninety-nine years old, the LORD appeared to him and said, "I am God Almighty; serve me faithfully and live a blameless life. 2 I will make a covenant with you, by which I will guarantee to make you into a mighty nation." 3 At this, Abram fell face down in the dust. Then God said to him, 4 "This is my covenant with you: I will make you the father of not just one nation, but a multitude of nations! 5 What's more, I am changing your name. It will no longer be Abram; now you will be known as Abraham,* for you will be the father of many nations. 6 I will give you millions of descendants who will represent many nations. Kings will be among them!

16:4 Gen 16:15
16:5 Gen 31:53
16:7 Gen 21:17; 22:11, 15
16:8 Gen 3:9; 4:9
16:9 Gen 21:12; Eph 6:5; Titus 2:9
16:10 Gen 17:20
16:11 Gen 16:15; Exod 3:7-8
16:12 Job 39:5-8
16:13 Gen 32:30
16:14 Gen 14:7
16:15 Gen 21:9; 25:12
16:16 Gen 12:4; 16:3
17:1 Gen 12:7; 28:3; 35:11; 48:3; Deut 18:13; Matt 5:48
17:2 Gen 12:2; 15:18
17:3 Gen 17:17; 18:2
17:5 Neh 9:7; †Rom 4:17
17:6 Gen 35:11

16:5 Hebrew *Let the LORD judge between you and me.* **16:11** *Ishmael* means "God hears." **16:13** Hebrew *El-roi.* **16:14** *Beer-lahairoi* means "well of the Living One who sees me." **17:5** *Abram* means "exalted father"; *Abraham* means "father of many."

16:5 Although Sarai arranged for Hagar to have a child by Abram, she later blamed Abram for the results. It is often easier to strike out in frustration and accuse someone else than to admit an error and ask forgiveness. (Adam and Eve did the same thing in 3:12, 13.)

16:6 Sarai was angry with Abram, but she took it out on Hagar, and her treatment was harsh enough to cause Hagar to run away. Anger, especially when it arises from our own shortcomings, can be dangerous.

16:8 Hagar was running away from her mistress and her problem. The angel of the Lord gave her this advice: (1) to return and face Sarai, the cause of her problem, and (2) to submit to her. Hagar needed to work on her attitude toward Sarai, no matter how justified it may have been. Running away from our problems rarely solves them. It is wise to return to our problems, face them squarely, accept God's promise of help, correct our attitudes, and act as we should.

16:13 We have watched three people make serious mistakes: (1) Sarai, who took matters into her own hands and gave her servant to Abram; (2) Abram, who went along with the plan but, when circumstances began to go wrong, refused to help solve the problem; and (3) Hagar, who ran away from the problem. In spite of this messy situation, God demonstrated his ability to work in all things for good (Romans 8:28). Sarai and Abram still received the son they so desperately wanted, and God solved Hagar's problem despite Abram's refusal to get involved. No problem is too complicated for God if you are willing to let him help you.

17:1 The Lord told Abram, "I am God Almighty; serve me faithfully and live a blameless life." God has the same message for us today. We are to obey the Lord in every respect because he is God—that is reason enough. If you don't think the benefits of obedience are worth it, consider who God is—the only one with the power and ability to meet your every need.

17:2-8 Why did God repeat his covenant to Abram? Twice before, he had mentioned this agreement (Genesis 12 and 15). Here, however, God was bringing it into focus and preparing to carry it out. He revealed to Abram several specific parts of his covenant: (1) God would give Abram many descendants; (2) many nations would descend from him; (3) God would maintain his covenant with Abram's descendants; (4) God would give Abram's descendants the land of Canaan.

17:5 God changed Abram's name to Abraham ("father of many") shortly before the promised son was conceived. From this point on, the Bible calls him Abraham.

17:5-14 God was making a covenant, or contract, between himself and Abraham. The terms were simple: Abraham would obey God and circumcise all the males in his household; God's part was to give Abraham heirs, property, power, and wealth. Most contracts are even trades: We give something and in turn receive something of equal value. But when we become part of God's covenant family, the blessings we receive far outweigh what we must give up.

17:7 Gen 15:18 Lev 11:45; 26:12 Ps 105:8-11 †Gal 3:16

7“I will continue this everlasting covenant between us, generation after generation. It
will continue between me and your offspring* forever. And I will always be your God
and the God of your descendants after you. 8Yes, I will give all this land of Canaan to
you and to your offspring forever. And I will be their God.

The Sign of Circumcision

17:10 John 7:22 Acts 7:8

17:11 Exod 12:48 Deut 10:16

17:12 Gen 21:4 Lev 12:3 Luke 1:59; 2:21

9“Your part of the agreement,” God told Abraham, “is to obey the terms of the covenant.
You and all your descendants have this continual responsibility. 10This is the covenant
that you and your descendants must keep: Each male among you must be circumcised;
11the flesh of his foreskin must be cut off. This will be a sign that you and they have
accepted this covenant. 12Every male child must be circumcised on the eighth day after
his birth. This applies not only to members of your family, but also to the servants born

17:7 Hebrew *seed;* also in 17:8.

ISHMAEL

Have you ever wondered if you were born into the wrong family? We don't know much about how Ishmael viewed life, but that question must have haunted him at times. His life, his name, and his position were bound up in a conflict between two jealous women. Sarah (Sarai), impatient with God's timetable, had taken matters into her own hands, deciding to have a child through another woman. Hagar, servant that she was, submitted to being used this way. But her pregnancy gave birth to strong feelings of superiority toward Sarah. Into this tense atmosphere, Ishmael was born.

For 13 years Abraham thought Ishmael's birth had fulfilled God's promise. He was surprised to hear God say that the promised child would be Abraham and Sarah's very own. Sarah's pregnancy and Isaac's birth must have had a devastating impact on Ishmael. Until then he had been treated as a son and heir, but this late arrival made his future uncertain. During Isaac's weaning celebration, Sarah caught Ishmael teasing his half brother. As a result, Hagar and Ishmael were permanently expelled from Abraham's family.

Much of what happened throughout his life cannot be blamed on Ishmael. He was caught in a process much bigger than he was. However, his own actions showed that he had chosen to become part of the problem and not part of the solution. He chose to live under his circumstances rather than above them.

The choice he made is one we must all make. There are circumstances over which we have no control (heredity, for instance), but there are others that we can control (decisions we make). At the heart of the matter is the sin-oriented nature we have all inherited. It can be partly controlled, although not overcome, by human effort. In the context of history, Ishmael's life represents the mess we make when we don't try to change the things we could change. The God of the Bible has offered a solution. His answer is not control but a changed life. To have a changed life, turn to God, trust him to forgive your sinful past, and begin to change your attitude toward him and others.

Strengths and accomplishments
- One of the first to experience the physical sign of God's covenant, circumcision
- Known for his ability as an archer and hunter
- Fathered 12 sons who became leaders of warrior tribes

Weakness and mistake
- Failed to recognize the place of his half brother, Isaac, and mocked him

Lesson from his life
- God's plans incorporate people's mistakes

Vital statistics
- Where: Canaan and Egypt
- Occupation: Hunter, archer, warrior
- Relatives: Parents: Hagar and Abraham. Half brother: Isaac

Key verses
“Then God heard the boy's cries, and the angel of God called to Hagar from the sky, ‘Hagar, what's wrong? Do not be afraid! God has heard the boy's cries from the place where you laid him. Go to him and comfort him, for I will make a great nation from his descendants’ ” (Genesis 21:17, 18).

Ishmael's story is told in Genesis 16—17; 21:8–20; 25:12–18; 28:8, 9; 36:1–3. He is also mentioned in 1 Chronicles 1:28–31; Romans 9:7–9; Galatians 4:21–31.

17:9, 10 Why did God require circumcision? (1) As a sign of obedience to him in all matters. (2) As a sign of belonging to his covenant people. Once circumcised, there was no turning back. The man would be identified as a Jew forever. (3) As a symbol of “cutting off” the old life of sin, purifying one's heart, and dedicating oneself to God. (4) Possibly as a health measure. Circumcision more than any other practice separated God's people from their pagan neighbors. In Abraham's day, this was essential to develop the pure worship of the one true God.

in your household and the foreign-born servants whom you have purchased. 13All must
be circumcised. Your bodies will thus bear the mark of my everlasting covenant.
14Anyone who refuses to be circumcised will be cut off from the covenant family for
violating the covenant."

Sarai Is Named Sarah

15Then God added, "Regarding Sarai, your wife—her name will no longer be Sarai;
from now on you will call her Sarah.* 16And I will bless her and give you a son from
her! Yes, I will bless her richly, and she will become the mother of many nations. Kings
will be among her descendants!"

17Then Abraham bowed down to the ground, but he laughed to himself in disbelief.
"How could I become a father at the age of one hundred?" he wondered. "Besides, Sarah
is ninety; how could she have a baby?" 18And Abraham said to God, "Yes, may Ishmael
enjoy your special blessing!"

19But God replied, "Sarah, your wife, will bear you a son. You will name him Isaac,*
and I will confirm my everlasting covenant with him and his descendants. 20As for
Ishmael, I will bless him also, just as you have asked. I will cause him to multiply and
become a great nation. Twelve princes will be among his descendants. 21But my
covenant is with Isaac, who will be born to you and Sarah about this time next year."

22That ended the conversation, and God left Abraham. 23On that very day Abraham
took his son Ishmael and every other male in his household and circumcised them,
cutting off their foreskins, exactly as God had told him. 24Abraham was ninety-nine
years old at that time, 25and Ishmael his son was thirteen. 26Both were circumcised the
same day, 27along with all the other men and boys of the household, whether they were
born there or bought as servants.

4. Sodom and Gomorrah

A Son Promised to Sarah

18 The LORD appeared again to Abraham while he was camped near the oak grove
belonging to Mamre. One day about noon, as Abraham was sitting at the entrance
to his tent, 2he suddenly noticed three men standing nearby. He got up and ran to meet
them, welcoming them by bowing low to the ground. 3"My lord," he said, "if it pleases
you, stop here for a while. 4Rest in the shade of this tree while my servants get some
water to wash your feet. 5Let me prepare some food to refresh you. Please stay awhile
before continuing on your journey."

"All right," they said. "Do as you have said."

6So Abraham ran back to the tent and said to Sarah, "Quick! Get three measures* of
your best flour, and bake some bread." 7Then Abraham ran out to the herd and chose a
fat calf and told a servant to hurry and butcher it. 8When the food was ready, he took
some cheese curds and milk and the roasted meat, and he served it to the men. As they
ate, Abraham waited on them there beneath the trees.

9"Where is Sarah, your wife?" they asked him.

"In the tent," Abraham replied.

10Then one of them said, "About this time next year I will return, and your wife Sarah
will have a son."

Now Sarah was listening to this conversation from the tent nearby. 11And since

17:14 Exod 30:33 Lev 7:20
17:15 Gen 17:5
17:16 Gen 18:10
17:17 Gen 17:3; 18:11-13
17:19 Gen 21:2; 26:2-5
17:20 Gen 25:12-16
17:21 Gen 18:10, 14
17:22 Gen 18:33; 35:13
17:23 Gen 14:14
17:24 Rom 4:11
17:25 Gen 16:16
18:1 Gen 12:7; 13:18
18:2 Gen 32:24 Josh 5:13 Judg 13:6-11
18:4 Gen 19:2; 24:32
18:5 Judg 6:18-19; 13:15-16
18:10 †Rom 9:9
18:11 Gen 17:17

17:15 *Sarah* means "princess." **17:19** *Isaac* means "he laughs." **18:6** Hebrew *3 seahs,* about 15 quarts or 18 liters.

17:17-27 How could Abraham doubt God? It seemed incredible that he and Sarah in their advanced years could have a child. Abraham, the man God considered righteous because of his faith, had trouble believing God's promise to him. Despite his doubts, however, he followed God's commands (17:22-27). Even people of great faith may have doubts. When God seems to want the impossible and you begin to doubt his leading, be like Abraham. Focus on God's commitment to fulfill his promises to you, and then continue to obey.

17:20 God did not forget Ishmael. Although he was not to be Abraham's heir, he would also be the father of a great nation. Regardless of your circumstances, God has not forgotten you. Obey him and trust in his plan.

18:2-5 Abraham was eager to show hospitality to these three visitors, as was Lot (19:2). In Abraham's day, a person's reputation was largely connected to his hospitality—the sharing of home and food. Even strangers were to be treated as highly honored guests. Meeting another's need for food or shelter was and still is one of the most immediate and practical ways to obey God. It is also a time-honored relationship builder. Hebrews 13:2 suggests that we, like Abraham, might actually entertain angels. This thought should be on our minds the next time we have the opportunity to meet a stranger's needs.

18:12 1 Pet 3:6 Abraham and Sarah were both very old, and Sarah was long past the age of having
children, 12 she laughed silently to herself. "How could a worn-out woman like me have
a baby?" she thought. "And when my master—my husband—is also so old?"
13 Then the LORD said to Abraham, "Why did Sarah laugh? Why did she say, 'Can an
18:14 Gen 18:10; Jer 32:17, 27; †Rom 9:9 old woman like me have a baby?' 14 Is anything too hard for the LORD? About a year from
now, just as I told you, I will return, and Sarah will have a son." 15 Sarah was afraid, so
she denied that she had laughed. But he said, "That is not true. You did laugh."

Abraham Intercedes for Sodom

18:16 Gen 18:22; 19:1 16 Then the men got up from their meal and started on toward Sodom. Abraham went
with them part of the way.
18:18 Gen 12:2-3; †Gal 3:18 17 "Should I hide my plan from Abraham?" the LORD asked. 18 "For Abraham will
become a great and mighty nation, and all the nations of the earth will be blessed through

ABRAHAM

We all know that there are consequences to any action we take. What we do can set into motion a series of events that may continue long after we're gone. Unfortunately, when we are making a decision, most of us think only of the immediate consequences. These are often misleading because they are short-lived.

Abraham had a choice to make. His decision was between setting out with his family and belongings for parts unknown or staying right where he was. He had to decide between the security of what he already had and the uncertainty of traveling under God's direction. All he had to go on was God's promise to guide and bless him. Abraham could hardly have been expected to visualize how much of the future was resting on his decision of whether to go or stay, but his obedience affected the history of the world. His decision to follow God set into motion the development of the nation that God would eventually use as his own when he visited earth himself. When Jesus Christ came to earth, God's promise was fulfilled; through Abraham the entire world was blessed.

You probably don't know the long-term effects of most decisions you make. But shouldn't the fact that there will be long-term results cause you to think carefully and seek God's guidance as you make choices and take action today?

Strengths and accomplishments
- His faith pleased God
- Became the founder of the Jewish nation
- Was respected by others and was courageous in defending his family at any cost
- Was not only a caring father to his own family, but practiced hospitality to others
- Was a successful and wealthy rancher
- Usually avoided conflicts, but when they were unavoidable, he allowed his opponent to set the rules for settling the dispute

Weakness and mistake
- Under direct pressure, he distorted the truth

Lessons from his life
- God desires dependence, trust, and faith in him—not faith in our ability to please him
- God's plan from the beginning has been to make himself known to all people

Vital statistics
- Where: Born in Ur of the Chaldeans; spent most of his life in the land of Canaan
- Occupation: Wealthy livestock owner
- Relatives: Brothers: Nahor and Haran. Father: Terah. Wife: Sarah. Nephew: Lot. Sons: Ishmael and Isaac
- Contemporaries: Abimelech, Melchizedek

Key verse
"And Abram believed the LORD, and the LORD declared him righteous because of his faith" (Genesis 15:6).

Abraham's story is told in Genesis 11—25. He is also mentioned in Exodus 2:24; Matthew 1:1, 2; Luke 3:34; Acts 7:2–8; Romans 4; Galatians 3; Hebrews 2, 6, 7, 11.

18:14 "Is anything too hard for the LORD?" The obvious answer is, "Of course not!" This question reveals much about God. Make it a habit to insert your specific needs into the question. "Is this day in my life too hard for the Lord?" "Is this habit I'm trying to break too hard for him?" "Is the communication problem I'm having too hard for him?" Asking the question this way reminds you that God is personally involved in your life and nudges you to ask for his power to help you.

18:15 Sarah lied because she was afraid of being discovered. Fear is the most common motive for lying. We are afraid that our inner thoughts and emotions will be exposed or our wrongdoings discovered. But lying causes greater complications than telling the truth and brings even more problems. If God can't be trusted with our innermost thoughts and fears, we are in greater trouble than we first imagined.

him. 19 I have singled him out so that he will direct his sons and their families to keep the way of the LORD and do what is right and just. Then I will do for him all that I have promised." 20 So the LORD told Abraham, "I have heard that the people of Sodom and Gomorrah are extremely evil, and that everything they do is wicked. 21 I am going down to see whether or not these reports are true. Then I will know."

22 The two other men went on toward Sodom, but the LORD remained with Abraham for a while. 23 Abraham approached him and said, "Will you destroy both innocent and guilty alike? 24 Suppose you find fifty innocent people there within the city—will you still destroy it, and not spare it for their sakes? 25 Surely you wouldn't do such a thing, destroying the innocent with the guilty. Why, you would be treating the innocent and the guilty exactly the same! Surely you wouldn't do that! Should not the Judge of all the earth do what is right?"

26 And the LORD replied, "If I find fifty innocent people in Sodom, I will spare the entire city for their sake."

27 Then Abraham spoke again. "Since I have begun, let me go on and speak further to my Lord, even though I am but dust and ashes. 28 Suppose there are only forty-five? Will you destroy the city for lack of five?"

And the LORD said, "I will not destroy it if I find forty-five."

29 Then Abraham pressed his request further. "Suppose there are only forty?"

And the LORD replied, "I will not destroy it if there are forty."

30 "Please don't be angry, my Lord," Abraham pleaded. "Let me speak—suppose only thirty are found?"

And the LORD replied, "I will not destroy it if there are thirty."

31 Then Abraham said, "Since I have dared to speak to the Lord, let me continue—suppose there are only twenty?"

And the LORD said, "Then I will not destroy it for the sake of the twenty."

32 Finally, Abraham said, "Lord, please do not get angry; I will speak but once more! Suppose only ten are found there?"

And the LORD said, "Then, for the sake of the ten, I will not destroy it."

33 The LORD went on his way when he had finished his conversation with Abraham, and Abraham returned to his tent.

Sodom and Gomorrah Destroyed

19 That evening the two angels came to the entrance of the city of Sodom, and Lot was sitting there as they arrived. When he saw them, he stood up to meet them. Then he welcomed them and bowed low to the ground. 2 "My lords," he said, "come to

18:19 Neh 9:7
18:20 Gen 19:13
18:21 Gen 11:5; Exod 3:8
18:22 Gen 18:16; 19:1
18:23 Exod 23:7
18:25 Deut 1:16-17; 32:4; Ps 58:11
18:27 Gen 2:7; Job 30:19; 42:6
18:30 Exod 32:32
18:33 Gen 17:22; 35:13
19:1 Gen 18:2
19:2 Gen 18:4

18:20-33 Did Abraham change God's mind? Of course not. The more likely answer is that God changed Abraham's mind. Abraham knew that God is just and that he punishes sin, but he may have wondered about God's mercy. Abraham seemed to be probing God's mind to see how merciful he really was. He left his conversation with God convinced that God was both kind and fair. Our prayers won't change God's mind, but they may change ours just as Abraham's prayer changed his. Prayer helps us better understand the mind of God.

18:20-33 Why did God let Abraham question his justice and intercede for a wicked city? Abraham knew that God must punish sin, but he also knew from experience that God is merciful to sinners. God knew there were not 10 innocent people in the city, but he was merciful enough to allow Abraham to intercede. He was also merciful enough to help Lot, Abraham's nephew, get out of Sodom before it was destroyed. God does not take pleasure in destroying the wicked, but he must punish sin. He is both just and merciful. We should be thankful that God's mercy extends to us.

18:21 God gave the men of Sodom a fair test. He was not ignorant of the city's wicked practices, but in his fairness and patience he gave the people of Sodom one last chance to repent. God is still waiting, giving people the opportunity to turn to him (2 Peter 3:9). Those who are wise will turn to him before his patience wears out.

18:25 Was God being unfair to the people of Sodom? Did he really plan to destroy the innocent with the guilty? On the contrary, God's fairness stood out. (1) He agreed to spare the entire city if only 10 innocent people lived there. (2) He showed great mercy toward Lot, apparently the only man in the city who had any kind of relationship with him (and even that was questionable). (3) He showed great patience toward Lot, almost forcing him to leave Sodom before it was destroyed. Remember God's patience when you are tempted to think he is unfair. Even the most godly people deserve his justice. We should be glad God doesn't direct his justice toward us as he did toward Sodom.

18:33 God showed Abraham that asking for anything is allowed, with the understanding that God's answers come from God's perspective. They are not always in harmony with our expectations, for only he knows the whole story. Are you missing God's answer to a prayer because you haven't considered any possible answers other than the one you expect?

19:1 The entrance of the city was the meeting place for city officials and other men to discuss current events and transact business. It was a place of authority and status where a person could see and be seen. Evidently Lot held an important position in the government or associated with those who did because the angels found him at the city's entrance. Perhaps Lot's status in Sodom was one reason he was so reluctant to leave (19:16, 18-22).

my home to wash your feet, and be my guests for the night. You may then get up in the
morning as early as you like and be on your way again."
19:3 "Oh no," they said, "we'll just spend the night out here in the city square."
Gen 18:6-8 3But Lot insisted, so at last they went home with him. He set a great feast before them,
19:4 Gen 13:13; 18:20 complete with fresh bread made without yeast. After the meal, 4as they were preparing
19:5 to retire for the night, all the men of Sodom, young and old, came from all over the city
Lev 18:22 and surrounded the house. 5They shouted to Lot, "Where are the men who came to spend
Judg 19:22 the night with you? Bring them out so we can have sex with them."
6Lot stepped outside to talk to them, shutting the door behind him. 7"Please, my
19:8 Deut 23:17 brothers," he begged, "don't do such a wicked thing. 8Look—I have two virgin daughters. Do with them as you wish, but leave these men alone, for they are under my
protection."
19:9 Exod 2:14 9"Stand back!" they shouted. "Who do you think you are? We let you settle among
19:10 Gen 19:1 us, and now you are trying to tell us what to do! We'll treat you far worse than those other
men!" And they lunged at Lot and began breaking down the door. 10But the two angels

SARAH

There probably isn't anything harder to do than wait, whether we are expecting something good, something bad, or an unknown.

One way we often cope with a long wait (or even a short one) is to begin helping God get his plan into action. Sarah tried this approach. She was too old to expect to have a child of her own, so she thought God must have something else in mind. From Sarah's limited point of view, this could only be to give Abraham a son through another woman—a common practice in her day. The plan seemed harmless enough. Abraham would sleep with Sarah's servant, who would then give birth to a child. Sarah would take the child as her own. The plan worked beautifully—at first. But as you read about the events that followed, you will be struck by how often Sarah must have regretted the day she decided to push God's timetable ahead.

Another way we cope with a long wait is to gradually conclude that what we're waiting for is never going to happen. Sarah waited 90 years for a baby! When God told her she would finally have one of her own, she laughed, not so much from a lack of faith in what God could do, but from doubt about what he could do *through her*. When confronted about her laughter, she lied—as she had seen her husband do from time to time. She probably didn't want her true feelings to be known.

What parts of your life seem to be on hold right now? Do you understand that this may be part of God's plan for you? The Bible has more than enough clear direction to keep us busy while we're waiting for some particular part of life to move ahead.

Strengths and accomplishments
- Was intensely loyal to her own child
- Became the mother of a nation and an ancestor of Jesus
- Was a woman of faith, the first woman listed in the Hall of Faith in Hebrews 11

Weaknesses and mistakes
- Had trouble believing God's promises to her
- Attempted to work problems out on her own, without consulting God
- Tried to cover her faults by blaming others

Lessons from her life
- God responds to faith even in the midst of failure
- God is not bound by what usually happens; he can stretch the limits and cause unheard-of events to occur

Vital statistics
- Where: Married Abram in Ur of the Chaldeans, then moved with him to Canaan
- Occupation: Wife, mother, household manager
- Relatives: Father: Terah. Husband: Abraham. Half brothers: Nahor and Haran. Nephew: Lot. Son: Isaac

Key verse
"It was by faith that Sarah together with Abraham was able to have a child, even though they were too old and Sarah was barren. Abraham believed that God would keep his promise" (Hebrews 11:11).

Sarah's story is told in Genesis 11—25. She is also mentioned in Isaiah 51:2; Romans 4:19; 9:9; Hebrews 11:11; 1 Peter 3:6.

19:8 How could any father give his daughters to be ravished by a mob of perverts, just to protect two strangers? Possibly Lot was scheming to save both the girls and the visitors, hoping the girls' fiancés would rescue them or that the homosexual men would be disinterested in the girls and simply go away. Although it was the custom of the day to protect guests at any cost, this terrible suggestion reveals how deeply sin had been absorbed into Lot's life. He had become hardened to evil acts in an evil city. Whatever Lot's motives were, we see here an illustration of Sodom's terrible wickedness—a wickedness so great that God had to destroy the entire city.

reached out and pulled Lot in and bolted the door. 11Then they blinded the men of Sodom
so they couldn't find the doorway.
12"Do you have any other relatives here in the city?" the angels asked. "Get them out
of this place—sons-in-law, sons, daughters, or anyone else. 13For we will destroy the
city completely. The stench of the place has reached the LORD, and he has sent us to
destroy it."
14So Lot rushed out to tell his daughters' fiancés, "Quick, get out of the city! The LORD
is going to destroy it." But the young men thought he was only joking.
15At dawn the next morning the angels became insistent. "Hurry," they said to Lot.
"Take your wife and your two daughters who are here. Get out of here right now, or you
will be caught in the destruction of the city."
16When Lot still hesitated, the angels seized his hand and the hands of his wife and
two daughters and rushed them to safety outside the city, for the LORD was merciful.
17"Run for your lives!" the angels warned. "Do not stop anywhere in the valley. And
don't look back! Escape to the mountains, or you will die."
18"Oh no, my lords, please," Lot begged. 19"You have been so kind to me and saved
my life, and you have granted me such mercy. But I cannot go to the mountains.
Disaster would catch up to me there, and I would soon die. 20See, there is a small village
nearby. Please let me go there instead; don't you see how small it is? Then my life will
be saved."
21"All right," the angel said, "I will grant your request. I will not destroy that little
village. 22But hurry! For I can do nothing until you are there." From that time on, that
village was known as Zoar.*
23The sun was rising as Lot reached the village. 24Then the LORD rained down fire
and burning sulfur from the heavens on Sodom and Gomorrah. 25He utterly destroyed
them, along with the other cities and villages of the plain, eliminating all life—people,
plants, and animals alike. 26But Lot's wife looked back as she was following along
behind him, and she became a pillar of salt.
27The next morning Abraham was up early and hurried out to the place where he had
stood in the LORD's presence. 28He looked out across the plain to Sodom and Gomorrah
and saw columns of smoke and fumes, as from a furnace, rising from the cities there.
29But God had listened to Abraham's request and kept Lot safe, removing him from the
disaster that engulfed the cities on the plain.

19:22 *Zoar* means "little."

19:11 Deut 28:28-29; 2 Kgs 6:18; Acts 13:11
19:13 Gen 18:20; 1 Chr 21:15; Jude 1:7
19:14 Exod 9:21; Jer 5:12; 43:1-2
19:17 Gen 13:10; 19:26; Jer 48:6
19:22 Gen 13:10
19:24 Luke 17:29; Jude 1:7
19:25 Deut 29:23; Isa 13:19; Lam 4:6; 2 Pet 2:6
19:26 Gen 19:17; Luke 17:32
19:27 Gen 18:22
19:28 Rev 9:2
19:29 Deut 7:8; 9:5; 2 Pet 2:7-8

19:13 God promised to spare Sodom if only 10 innocent people lived there (18:32). Obviously not even 10 could be found, because the angels arrived to destroy the city. Archaeological evidence points to an advanced civilization in this area during Abraham's day. Most researchers also confirm some kind of sudden and devastating destruction. It is now widely thought that the buried city lies beneath the waters of the southern end of the Dead Sea. The story of Sodom reveals that the people of Lot's day had to deal with the same kinds of repulsive sins the world faces today. We should follow Abraham's example of trusting God. His selfless faith contrasts with the self-gratifying people of Sodom.

19:14 Lot had lived so long and was so contented among ungodly people that he was no longer a believable witness for God. He had allowed his environment to shape him, rather than he shaping his environment. Do those who know you see you as a witness for God, or are you just one of the crowd, blending in unnoticed? Lot had compromised to the point that he was almost useless to God. When he finally made a stand, nobody listened. Have you, too, become useless to God because you are too much like your environment? To make a difference, you must first decide to be different in your faith and your conduct.

19:16 Lot hesitated, so the angel seized his hand and rushed him to safety. Lot did not want to abandon the wealth, position, and comfort he enjoyed in Sodom. It is easy to criticize Lot for being hypnotized by Sodom when the choice seems so clear to us. To be wiser than Lot, we must see that our hesitation to obey stems from the false attractions of our culture's pleasures.

19:16-29 Notice how God's mercy toward Abraham extended to Lot and his family. Because Abraham pleaded for Lot, God was merciful and saved Lot from the fiery destruction of Sodom. A righteous person can often affect others for good. James says that the "earnest prayer of a righteous person has great power" (James 5:16). All Christians should follow Abraham's example and pray for others to be saved.

19:24 In the story of Sodom and Gomorrah, we see two facets of God's character: his great patience (agreeing to spare a wicked city for 10 good people) and his fierce anger (destroying both cities). As we grow spiritually, we should find ourselves developing not only a deeper respect for God because of his anger toward sin but also a deeper love for God because of his patience when we sin.

19:26 Lot's wife turned back to look at the smoldering city of Sodom. Clinging to the past, she was unwilling to turn completely away. Are you looking back longingly at sin while trying to move forward with God? You can't make progress with God as long as you are holding on to pieces of your old life. Jesus said it this way in Matthew 6:24: "No one can serve two masters."

Lot and His Daughters

19:30 Gen 13:10 30 Afterward Lot left Zoar because he was afraid of the people there, and he went to live
in a cave in the mountains with his two daughters. 31 One day the older daughter said to
her sister, "There isn't a man anywhere in this entire area for us to marry. And our father
will soon be too old to have children. 32 Come, let's get him drunk with wine, and then
we will sleep with him. That way we will preserve our family line through our father."
19:33 Gen 9:21 33 So that night they got him drunk, and the older daughter went in and slept with her
father. He was unaware of her lying down or getting up again.

34 The next morning the older daughter said to her younger sister, "I slept with our
father last night. Let's get him drunk with wine again tonight, and you go in and sleep

ISAAC

A name carries great authority. It sets you apart. It triggers memories. The sound of it calls you to attention anywhere.

Many Bible names accomplished even more. They were often descriptions of important facts about one's past and hopes for the future. The choice of the name *Isaac,* "he laughs," for Abraham and Sarah's son must have created a variety of feelings in them each time it was spoken. At times it must have recalled their shocked laughter at God's announcement that they would be parents in their old age. At other times, it must have brought back the joyful feelings of receiving their long-awaited answer to prayer for a child. Most important, it was a testimony to God's power in making his promise a reality.

In a family of forceful initiators, Isaac was the quiet, mind-my-own-business type unless he was specifically called on to take action. He was the protected only child from the time Sarah got rid of Ishmael until Abraham arranged his marriage to Rebekah.

In his own family, Isaac had the patriarchal position, but Rebekah had the power. Rather than stand his ground, Isaac found it easier to compromise or lie to avoid confrontations.

In spite of these shortcomings, Isaac was part of God's plan. The model his father gave him included a great gift of faith in the one true God. God's promise to create a great nation through which he would bless the world was passed on by Isaac to his twin sons.

It is usually not hard to identify with Isaac in his weaknesses. But consider for a moment that God works through people in spite of their shortcomings and often through them. As you pray, put into words your desire to be available to God. You will discover that his willingness to use you is even greater than your desire to be used.

Strengths and accomplishments
- He was the miracle child born to Sarah and Abraham when she was 90 years old and he was 100
- He was the first descendant in fulfillment of God's promise to Abraham
- He seems to have been a caring and consistent husband, at least until his sons were born
- He demonstrated great patience

Weaknesses and mistakes
- Under pressure he tended to lie
- In conflict he sought to avoid confrontation
- He played favorites between his sons and alienated his wife

Lessons from his life
- Patience often brings rewards
- Both God's plans and his promises are larger than people
- God keeps his promises! He remains faithful though we are often faithless
- Playing favorites is sure to bring family conflict

Vital statistics
- Where: Various places in the southern part of Palestine, including Beersheba (Genesis 26:23)
- Occupation: Wealthy livestock owner
- Relatives: Parents: Abraham and Sarah. Half brother: Ishmael. Wife: Rebekah. Sons: Jacob and Esau

Key verse
"But God replied, 'Sarah, your wife, will bear you a son. You will name him Isaac, and I will confirm my everlasting covenant with him and his descendants'" (Genesis 17:19).

Isaac's story is told in Genesis 17:15—35:29. He is also mentioned in Romans 9:7–10; Hebrews 11:17–20; James 2:21.

19:30-38 In this pitiful sequel to the story of the destruction of Sodom, we see two women compelled to preserve their family line. They were driven not by lust but by desperation—they feared they would never marry. Lot's tendency to compromise and refusal to act reached its peak. He should have found right partners for his daughters long before this; Abraham's family wasn't far away. Now the two daughters stooped to incest, showing their acceptance of the morals of Sodom. We are most likely to sin when we are desperate for what we feel we must have.

19:30-38 Why doesn't the Bible openly condemn these sisters for what they did? In many cases, the Bible does not judge people

with him. That way our family line will be preserved." 35So that night they got him drunk
again, and the younger daughter went in and slept with him. As before, he was unaware
of her lying down or getting up again. 36So both of Lot's daughters became pregnant by
their father.
37When the older daughter gave birth to a son, she named him Moab.* He became the
ancestor of the nation now known as the Moabites. 38When the younger daughter gave
birth to a son, she named him Ben-ammi.* He became the ancestor of the nation now
known as the Ammonites.

19:37 Gen 36:35; Exod 15:15; Num 21:29; Deut 2:9; Ruth 1:1
19:38 Num 21:24; Deut 2:19

Abraham Deceives Abimelech

20 Now Abraham moved south to the Negev and settled for a while between Kadesh
and Shur at a place called Gerar. 2Abraham told people there that his wife, Sarah,
was his sister. So King Abimelech sent for her and had her brought to him at his palace.
3But one night God came to Abimelech in a dream and told him, "You are a dead man,
for that woman you took is married."
4But Abimelech had not slept with her yet, so he said, "Lord, will you kill an innocent
man? 5Abraham told me, 'She is my sister,' and she herself said, 'Yes, he is my brother.'
I acted in complete innocence!"
6"Yes, I know you are innocent," God replied. "That is why I kept you from sinning
against me; I did not let you touch her. 7Now return her to her husband, and he will pray
for you, for he is a prophet. Then you will live. But if you don't return her to him, you
can be sure that you and your entire household will die."
8Abimelech got up early the next morning and hastily called a meeting of all his servants.
When he told them what had happened, great fear swept through the crowd. 9Then
Abimelech called for Abraham. "What is this you have done to us?" he demanded. "What
have I done to you that deserves treatment like this, making me and my kingdom guilty of
this great sin? This kind of thing should not be done! 10Why have you done this to us?"
11"Well," Abraham said, "I figured this to be a godless place. I thought, 'They will
want my wife and will kill me to get her.' 12Besides, she is my sister—we both have the
same father, though different mothers—and I married her. 13When God sent me to travel
far from my father's home, I told her, 'Wherever we go, have the kindness to say that
you are my sister.'"
14Then Abimelech took sheep and oxen and servants—both men and women—and
gave them to Abraham, and he returned his wife, Sarah, to him. 15"Look over my
kingdom, and choose a place where you would like to live," Abimelech told him. 16Then
he turned to Sarah. "Look," he said, "I am giving your 'brother' a thousand pieces of
silver* to compensate for any embarrassment I may have caused you. This will settle any
claim against me in this matter."

20:1 Gen 14:7; 18:1; 26:1
20:2 Gen 12:13
20:3 Gen 28:12; 31:24; 37:5
20:4 Gen 18:23-25
20:5 Gen 12:19; 1 Kgs 9:4; Pss 7:8; 26:6
20:7 1 Sam 7:5; Job 42:8
20:9 Gen 12:18
20:11 Gen 12:12; 42:18
20:13 Gen 12:1
20:14 Gen 12:16
20:16 Gen 23:15

19:37 *Moab* sounds like a Hebrew term that means "from father." **19:38** *Ben-ammi* means "son of my people."
20:16 Hebrew *1,000 shekels of silver,* about 25 pounds or 11.4 kilograms in weight.

---

for their actions. It simply reports the events. However, incest is clearly condemned in other parts of Scripture (Leviticus 18:6-18; 20:11, 12, 17, 19-21; Deuteronomy 22:30; 27:20-23; Ezekiel 22:11; 1 Corinthians 5:1). Perhaps the consequence of their action—Moab and Ammon became enemies of Israel—was God's way of judging their sin.

19:37, 38 Moab and Ben-ammi were the products of incest. They became the fathers of two of Israel's greatest enemies, the Moabites and the Ammonites. These nations settled east of the Jordan River, and Israel never conquered them. Because of the family connection, Moses was forbidden to attack them (Deuteronomy 2:9). Ruth, great-grandmother of David and an ancestor of Jesus, was from Moab.

20:2 Abraham had used this same trick before to protect himself (12:11-13). Although Abraham is one of our heroes of faith, he did not learn his lesson well enough the first time. In fact, by giving in to the temptation again, he risked turning a sinful act into a sinful pattern of lying whenever he suspected his life was in danger.

No matter how much we love God, certain temptations are especially difficult to resist. These are the vulnerable spots in our spiritual armor. As we struggle with these weaknesses, we can be encouraged to know that God is watching out for us just as he did for Abraham.

20:6 Abimelech had unknowingly taken a married woman to be his wife and was about to commit adultery. But God somehow prevented him from touching Sarah and held him back from sinning. What mercy on God's part! How many times has God done the same for us, holding us back from sin in ways we can't even detect? We have no way of knowing—we just know from this story that he can. God works just as often in ways we can't see as in ways we can.

20:11-13 Because Abraham mistakenly assumed that Abimelech was a wicked man, he made a quick decision to tell a half-truth. Abraham thought it would be more effective to deceive Abimelech than to trust God to work in the king's life. Don't assume that God will not work in a situation that has potential problems. You may not completely understand the situation, and God may intervene when you least expect it.

17 Then Abraham prayed to God, and God healed Abimelech, his wife, and the other
women of the household, so they could have children. 18 For the LORD had stricken all
the women with infertility as a warning to Abimelech for having taken Abraham's wife.

5. Birth and near sacrifice of Isaac

The Birth of Isaac

21 Then the LORD did exactly what he had promised. 2 Sarah became pregnant, and
she gave a son to Abraham in his old age. It all happened at the time God had said
it would. 3 And Abraham named his son Isaac.* 4 Eight days after Isaac was born,
Abraham circumcised him as God had commanded. 5 Abraham was one hundred years
old at the time.
6 And Sarah declared, "God has brought me laughter! All who hear about this will
laugh with me. 7 For who would have dreamed that I would ever have a baby? Yet I have
given Abraham a son in his old age!"

Hagar and Ishmael Sent Away

8 As time went by and Isaac grew and was weaned, Abraham gave a big party to celebrate
the happy occasion. 9 But Sarah saw Ishmael—the son of Abraham and her Egyptian
servant Hagar—making fun of Isaac. 10 So she turned to Abraham and demanded, "Get
rid of that servant and her son. He is not going to share the family inheritance with my
son, Isaac. I won't have it!"
11 This upset Abraham very much because Ishmael was his son. 12 But God told
Abraham, "Do not be upset over the boy and your servant wife. Do just as Sarah says,
for Isaac is the son through whom your descendants will be counted. 13 But I will make
a nation of the descendants of Hagar's son because he also is your son."
14 So Abraham got up early the next morning, prepared food for the journey, and
strapped a container of water to Hagar's shoulders. He sent her away with their son, and
she walked out into the wilderness of Beersheba, wandering aimlessly. 15 When the water
was gone, she left the boy in the shade of a bush. 16 Then she went and sat down by herself
about a hundred yards* away. "I don't want to watch the boy die," she said, as she burst
into tears.
17 Then God heard the boy's cries, and the angel of God called to Hagar from the sky,
"Hagar, what's wrong? Do not be afraid! God has heard the boy's cries from the place
where you laid him. 18 Go to him and comfort him, for I will make a great nation from
his descendants."
19 Then God opened Hagar's eyes, and she saw a well. She immediately filled her
water container and gave the boy a drink. 20 And God was with the boy as he grew up in
the wilderness of Paran. He became an expert archer, 21 and his mother arranged a
marriage for him with a young woman from Egypt.

A Treaty with Abimelech

22 About this time, Abimelech came with Phicol, his army commander, to visit Abraham. "It
is clear that God helps you in everything you do," Abimelech said. 23 "Swear to me in God's

20:17 Num 12:13; 21:7
20:18 Gen 12:17
21:2 Gen 18:10; Gal 4:22; Heb 11:11
21:4 Gen 17:10, 12
21:5 Heb 6:15
21:6 Isa 54:1
21:7 Gen 18:13
21:8 1 Sam 1:23
21:9 Gal 4:29
21:10 †Gal 4:30
21:12 †Rom 9:7; †Heb 11:18
21:13 Gen 16:10; 21:18; 25:12-18
21:14 Gen 16:1
21:16 Jer 6:26
21:17 Exod 3:7; Deut 26:7; Ps 6:8
21:18 Gen 26:24
21:20 Gen 28:15
21:21 Gen 25:18
21:22 Gen 26:26
21:23 Gen 24:2

21:3 *Isaac* means "he laughs." **21:16** Hebrew *a bowshot.*

20:17, 18 Why did God punish Abimelech when he had no idea Sarah was married? (1) Even though Abimelech's intentions were good, as long as Sarah was living in his harem he was in danger of sinning. A person who eats a poisonous toadstool, thinking it's a harmless mushroom, no doubt has perfectly good intentions—but will still suffer. Sin is a poison that damages us and those around us, whatever our intentions. (2) The punishment, striking all the women of Abimelech's household with infertility, lasted only as long as Abimelech was in danger of sleeping with Sarah. It was meant to change the situation, not to harm Abimelech. (3) The punishment clearly showed that Abraham was in league with almighty God. This incident may have made Abimelech respect and fear Abraham's God.

21:1-7 Who could believe that Abraham would have a son at 100 years of age—and live to raise him to adulthood? But doing the impossible is everyday business for God. Our big problems won't seem so impossible if we let God handle them.

21:7 After repeated promises, a visit by two angels, and the appearance of the Lord himself, Sarah finally cried out with surprise and joy at the birth of her son. Because of her doubt, worry, and fear, she had forfeited the peace she could have felt in God's wonderful promise to her. The way to bring peace to a troubled heart is to focus on God's promises. Trust him to do what he says.

21:18 What happened to Ishmael, and who are his descendants? Ishmael became ruler of a large tribe or nation. The Ishmaelites were nomads living in the wilderness of Sinai and Paran, south of Israel. One of Ishmael's daughters married Esau, Ishmael's nephew (28:9). The Bible pictures the Ishmaelites as hostile to Israel and to God (Psalm 83:5-6).

name that you won't deceive me, my children, or my grandchildren. I have been loyal to
you, so now swear that you will be loyal to me and to this country in which you are living."
24 Abraham replied, "All right, I swear to it!" 25 Then Abraham complained to Abimelech about a well that Abimelech's servants had taken violently from Abraham's servants.
26 "This is the first I've heard of it," Abimelech said. "And I have no idea who is
responsible. Why didn't you say something about this before?" 27 Then Abraham gave
sheep and oxen to Abimelech, and they made a treaty. 28 But when Abraham took seven
additional ewe lambs and set them off by themselves, 29 Abimelech asked, "Why are you
doing that?"
30 Abraham replied, "They are my gift to you as a public confirmation that I dug this
well." 31 So ever since, that place has been known as Beersheba—"well of the oath"—
because that was where they had sworn an oath. 32 After making their covenant, Abimelech left with Phicol, the commander of his army, and they returned home to the land of
the Philistines. 33 Then Abraham planted a tamarisk tree at Beersheba, and he worshiped
the LORD, the Eternal God, at that place. 34 And Abraham lived in Philistine country for
a long time.

Abraham's Obedience Tested

22 Later on God tested Abraham's faith and obedience. "Abraham!" God called.
"Yes," he replied. "Here I am."
2 "Take your son, your only son—yes, Isaac, whom you love so much—and go to the
land of Moriah. Sacrifice him there as a burnt offering on one of the mountains, which I
will point out to you."
3 The next morning Abraham got up early. He saddled his donkey and took two of his
servants with him, along with his son Isaac. Then he chopped wood to build a fire for a
burnt offering and set out for the place where God had told him to go. 4 On the third day
of the journey, Abraham saw the place in the distance. 5 "Stay here with the donkey,"
Abraham told the young men. "The boy and I will travel a little farther. We will worship
there, and then we will come right back."
6 Abraham placed the wood for the burnt offering on Isaac's shoulders, while he
himself carried the knife and the fire. As the two of them went on together, 7 Isaac said,
"Father?"

21:25 Gen 26:15
21:27 Gen 26:31
21:30 Gen 31:44
21:31 Gen 21:14; 26:33
21:33 1 Sam 22:6; 31:13; Ps 90:2; Isa 9:6; 40:28
22:1 Exod 15:25; 16:4; Deut 8:2, 16
22:2 2 Chr 3:1; John 3:16
22:6 John 19:17
22:7 Gen 8:20; Exod 29:38-42; John 1:29, 36; Rev 13:8

21:31 Beersheba, the southernmost city of Israel, lay on the edge of a vast desert that stretched as far as Egypt to the southwest and Mount Sinai to the south. The phrase "from Dan to Beersheba" was often used to describe the traditional boundaries of the Promised Land (2 Samuel 17:11). Beersheba's southern location and the presence of several wells in the area may explain why Abraham settled there. Beersheba was also the home of Isaac, Abraham's son.

22:1 God tested Abraham, not to trip him and watch him fall, but to deepen his capacity to obey God and thus to develop his character. Just as fire refines ore to extract precious metals, God refines us through difficult circumstances. When we are tested, we can complain, or we can try to see how God is stretching us to develop our character.

22:3 That morning Abraham began one of the greatest acts of obedience in recorded history. He traveled 50 miles to Mount Moriah near the site of Jerusalem. Over the years he had learned many tough lessons about the importance of obeying God. This time his obedience was prompt and complete. Obeying God is often a struggle because it may mean giving up something we truly want. We should not expect our obedience to God to be easy or to come naturally.

22:6 We don't know how Abraham carried the fire. Perhaps he carried a live coal or a flint to start a fire.

22:7, 8 Why did God ask Abraham to perform human sacrifice? Pagan nations practiced human sacrifice, but God condemned this as a terrible sin (Leviticus 20:1-5). God did not want Isaac to die, but he wanted Abraham to sacrifice Isaac in his heart so it would be clear that Abraham loved God more than he loved his promised and long-awaited son. God was testing Abraham. The purpose of testing is to strengthen our character and deepen our commitment to God and his perfect timing. Through this difficult experience, Abraham strengthened his commitment to obey God. He also learned about God's ability to provide.

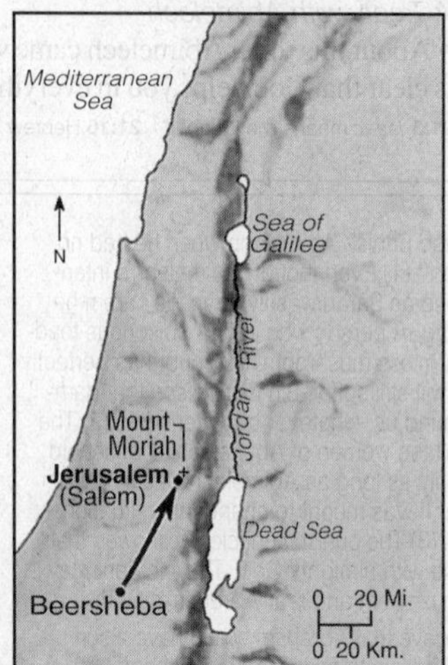

ABRAHAM'S TRIP TO MOUNT MORIAH
Abraham and Isaac traveled the 50 or 60 miles from Beersheba to Mount Moriah in about three days. This was a very difficult time for Abraham, who was on his way to sacrifice his beloved son, Isaac.

“Yes, my son,” Abraham replied.
“We have the wood and the fire,” said the boy, “but where is the lamb for the
sacrifice?”
8 “God will provide a lamb, my son,” Abraham answered. And they both went on
22:9 together.
Heb 11:17-19 9 When they arrived at the place where God had told Abraham to go, he built an altar
Jas 2:21 and placed the wood on it. Then he tied Isaac up and laid him on the altar over the wood.
10 And Abraham took the knife and lifted it up to kill his son as a sacrifice to the LORD.
22:11 Gen 16:7; 21:17 11 At that moment the angel of the LORD shouted to him from heaven, “Abraham!
Abraham!”
22:12 Heb 11:17 “Yes,” he answered. “I'm listening.”
12 “Lay down the knife,” the angel said. “Do not hurt the boy in any way, for now
I know that you truly fear God. You have not withheld even your beloved son from
22:13 Gen 8:20 me.”
22:14 13 Then Abraham looked up and saw a ram caught by its horns in a bush. So he took
Gen 22:7-8 the ram and sacrificed it as a burnt offering on the altar in place of his son. 14 Abraham

HAGAR

Escape of some kind is usually the most tempting solution to our problems. In fact, it can become a habit. Hagar was a person who used that approach. When the going got tough, she usually got going—in the other direction.

However, it is worthwhile to note that the biggest challenges Hagar faced were brought on by *other* people's choices. Sarah chose her to bear Abraham's child, and Hagar probably had little to say in the matter.

It isn't hard to understand how Hagar's pregnancy caused her to look down on Sarah. But that brought on hard feelings, and Sarah consequently punished Hagar. This motivated her first escape. When she returned to the family and gave birth to Ishmael, Sarah's continued barrenness must have contributed to bitterness on both sides.

When Isaac was finally born, Sarah looked for any excuse to have Hagar and Ishmael sent away. She found it when she caught Ishmael teasing Isaac. In the wilderness, out of water and facing the death of her son, Hagar once again tried to escape. She walked away so she wouldn't have to watch her son die. Once again, God graciously intervened.

Have you noticed how patiently God operates to make our escape attempts fail? Have you begun to learn that escape is only a temporary solution? God's continual desire is for us to face our problems with his help. We experience his help most clearly in and through conflicts and difficulties, not away from them. Are there problems in your life for which you've been using the “Hagar solution”? Choose one of those problems, ask for God's help, and begin to face it today.

Strength and accomplishment
- Mother of Abraham's first child, Ishmael, who became founder of the Arab nations

Weaknesses and mistakes
- When faced with problems, she tended to run away
- Her pregnancy brought out strong feelings of pride and arrogance

Lessons from her life
- God is faithful to his plan and promises, even when humans complicate the process
- God shows himself as one who knows us and wants to be known by us
- The New Testament uses Hagar as a symbol of those who would pursue favor with God by their own efforts, rather than by trusting in his mercy and forgiveness

Vital statistics
- Where: Canaan and Egypt
- Occupation: Servant, mother
- Relatives: Son: Ishmael

Key verse
“Then the angel of the LORD said, ‘Return to your mistress and submit to her authority’ ” (Genesis 16:9).

Hagar's story is told in Genesis 16, 21. She is also mentioned in Galatians 4:24.

22:12 It is difficult to let go of what we deeply love. What could be more proper than to love your only child? Yet when we do give to God what he asks, he returns to us far more than we could dream. The spiritual benefits of his blessings far outweigh our sacrifices. Have you withheld your love, your children, or your time from him? Trust him to provide (22:8).

22:13 Notice the parallel between the ram offered on the altar as a substitute for Isaac and Christ offered on the cross as a substitute for us. Whereas God stopped Abraham from sacrificing his son, God did not spare his own Son, Jesus, from dying on the cross. If Jesus had lived, the rest of humankind would have died. God sent his only Son to die for us so that we can be spared from the eternal death we deserve and instead receive eternal life (John 3:16).

named the place "The LORD Will Provide."* This name has now become a proverb: "On
the mountain of the LORD it will be provided."
15 Then the angel of the LORD called again to Abraham from heaven, 16 "This is what 22:16 †Heb 6:13-14
the LORD says: Because you have obeyed me and have not withheld even your beloved 22:17
son, I swear by my own self that 17 I will bless you richly. I will multiply your descendants Gen 12:2; 15:5; 26:4
into countless millions, like the stars of the sky and the sand on the seashore. They will †Heb 6:14
conquer their enemies, 18 and through your descendants,* all the nations of the earth will 22:18
be blessed—all because you have obeyed me." 19 Then they returned to Abraham's young †Acts 3:25 †Gal 3:8, 16
men and traveled home again to Beersheba, where Abraham lived for quite some time. 22:19
20 Soon after this, Abraham heard that Milcah, his brother Nahor's wife, had borne Nahor Gen 21:14
eight sons. 21 The oldest was named Uz, the next oldest was Buz, followed by Kemuel (the 22:20 Gen 11:29
father of Aram), 22 Kesed, Hazo, Pildash, Jidlaph, and Bethuel. 23 Bethuel became the father 22:23
of Rebekah. 24 In addition to his eight sons from Milcah, Nahor had four other children from Gen 24:15
his concubine Reumah. Their names were Tebah, Gaham, Tahash, and Maacah.

The Burial of Sarah

23 When Sarah was 127 years old, 2 she died at Kiriath-arba (now called Hebron) in 23:2 Josh 14:15
the land of Canaan. There Abraham mourned and wept for her. 3 Then, leaving her 23:3
body, he went to the Hittite elders and said, 4 "Here I am, a stranger in a foreign land, Gen 10:15
with no place to bury my wife. Please let me have a piece of land for a burial plot." 23:4 Lev 25:23
5 The Hittites replied to Abraham, 6 "Certainly, for you are an honored prince among us. 1 Chr 29:15
It will be a privilege to have you choose the finest of our tombs so you can bury her there." Ps 39:12 Heb 11:9
7 Then Abraham bowed low before them and said, 8 "Since this is how you feel, be so 23:6
kind as to ask Ephron son of Zohar 9 to let me have the cave of Machpelah, down at the Gen 14:14-16
end of his field. I want to pay the full price, of course, whatever is publicly agreed upon, 23:8-9 Gen 25:9
so I may have a permanent burial place for my family."
10 Ephron was sitting there among the others, and he answered Abraham as the others 23:10 Ruth 4:1, 11
listened, speaking publicly before all the elders of the town. 11 "No, sir," he said to
Abraham, "please listen to me. I will give you the cave and the field. Here in the presence
of my people, I give it to you. Go and bury your dead."
12 Abraham bowed again to the people of the land, 13 and he replied to Ephron as

22:14 Hebrew *Yahweh Yir'eh.* **22:18** Hebrew *seed.*

22:15-18 Abraham received abundant blessings because he did not hold back but obeyed God. First, God gave Abraham's descendants the ability to conquer their enemies. Second, God promised Abraham children and grandchildren who would in turn bless the whole earth. People's lives would be changed as a result of knowing of the faith of Abraham and his descendants. Most often we think of blessings as gifts to be enjoyed. But when God blesses us, his blessings are intended to overflow to others.

23:1-4 In Abraham's day, death and burial were steeped in ritual and traditions. Failing to honor a dead person demonstrated the greatest possible lack of respect. An improper burial was the equivalent of a curse. Mourning was an essential part of the death ritual. Friends and relatives let out loud cries for the whole neighborhood to hear. Because there were no funeral homes or undertakers, these same friends and relatives helped prepare the body for burial, which usually took place on the same day because of the warm climate.

23:4-6 Abraham was in a foreign land looking for a place to bury his wife. Strangers offered to help him because he was "an honored prince," and they respected him. Although Abraham had not established roots in the area, his reputation was above reproach. Those who invest their time and money in serving God often earn a pleasant return on their investment—a good reputation and the respect of others.

23:10-16 The polite interchange between Abraham and Ephron was typical of bargaining at that time. Ephron graciously offered to give his land to Abraham at no charge; Abraham insisted on paying for it; Ephron politely mentioned the price but said, in effect, that it wasn't important; Abraham paid the 400 shekels of silver. Both men knew what was going on as they went through the bargaining process. If Abraham had accepted the land as a gift when it was offered, he would have insulted Ephron, who then would have rescinded his offer. Many Middle Eastern shopkeepers still follow this ritual with their customers.

CAVE OF MACHPELAH
Sarah died in Hebron. Abraham bought the cave of Machpelah, near Hebron, as her burial place. Abraham was also buried there, as were his son and grandson, Isaac and Jacob.

23:15 Exod 30:13
23:16 Jer 32:9
23:17-18 Gen 25:9; 49:29-30; 50:13

everyone listened. “No, listen to me,” he insisted. “I will buy it from you. Let me pay
the full price for the field so I can bury my dead there.”
14“Well,” Ephron answered, 15“the land is worth four hundred pieces* of silver, but
what is that between friends? Go ahead and bury your dead.”
16So Abraham paid Ephron the amount he had suggested, four hundred pieces of
silver, as was publicly agreed. 17He bought the plot of land belonging to Ephron at
Machpelah, near Mamre. This included the field, the cave that was in it, and all the trees
nearby. 18They became Abraham’s permanent possession by the agreement made in the
presence of the Hittite elders at the city gate. 19So Abraham buried Sarah there in Canaan,
in the cave of Machpelah, near Mamre, which is at Hebron. 20The field and the cave were
sold to Abraham by the Hittites as a permanent burial place.

6. Isaac and Rebekah

24:1 Gen 12:2; 24:35
24:2 Gen 47:29
24:3 Gen 14:19

24 Abraham was now a very old man, and the LORD had blessed him in every way.
2One day Abraham said to the man in charge of his household, who was his oldest
servant, 3“Swear* by the LORD, the God of heaven and earth, that you will not let my

23:15 Hebrew *400 shekels,* about 10 pounds or 4.6 kilograms in weight; also in 23:16. **24:3** Hebrew *Put your hand under my thigh, and I will make you swear.*

REBEKAH

Some people are initiators. They help get the ball rolling. Rebekah would easily stand out in this group. Her life was characterized by initiative. When she saw a need, she took action, even though the action was not always right.

It was Rebekah’s initiative that first caught the attention of Eliezer, the servant Abraham sent to find a wife for Isaac. It was common courtesy to give a drink to a stranger, but it took added character to also fetch water for ten thirsty camels. Later, after hearing the details of Eliezer’s mission, Rebekah was immediately willing to be Isaac’s bride.

Several later events help us see how initiative can be misdirected. Rebekah was aware that God’s plan would be channeled through Jacob, not Esau (Genesis 25:23). So not only did Jacob become her favorite; she actually planned ways to ensure that he would overshadow his older twin. Meanwhile, Isaac preferred Esau. This created a conflict between the couple. She felt justified in deceiving her husband when the time came to bless the sons, and her ingenious plan was carried out to perfection.

Most of the time we try to justify the things we choose to do. Often we attempt to add God’s approval to our actions. While it is true that our actions will not spoil God’s plan, it is also true that we are responsible for what we do and must always be cautious about our motives. When thinking about a course of action, are you simply seeking God’s stamp of approval on something you’ve already decided to do? Or are you willing to set the plan aside if the principles and commands of God’s Word are against the action? Initiative and action are admirable and right when they are controlled by God’s wisdom.

Strengths and accomplishments
- When confronted with a need, she took immediate action
- She was accomplishment oriented

Weaknesses and mistakes
- Her initiative was not always balanced by wisdom
- She favored one of her sons
- She deceived her husband

Lessons from her life
- Our actions must be guided by God’s Word
- God makes use even of our mistakes in his plan
- Parental favoritism hurts a family

Vital statistics
- Where: Haran, Canaan
- Occupation: Wife, mother, household manager
- Relatives: Grandparents: Nahor and Milcah. Father: Bethuel. Husband: Isaac. Brother: Laban. Twin sons: Esau and Jacob

Key verses
“Isaac brought Rebekah into his mother’s tent, and she became his wife. He loved her very much, and she was a special comfort to him after the death of his mother” (Genesis 24:67). “Isaac loved Esau in particular because of the wild game he brought home, but Rebekah favored Jacob” (Genesis 25:28).

Rebekah’s story is told in Genesis 24—27. She is also mentioned in Romans 9:10.

23:16 Four hundred pieces of silver was a high price for the piece of property Abraham bought. The Hittites weren’t thrilled about foreigners buying their property, so Abraham had little bargaining leverage.

Ephron asked an outrageous price. The custom of the day was to ask double the fair market value of the land, fully expecting the buyer to offer half the stated price. Abraham, however, did not bargain. He simply paid the initial price. He was not trying to take anything he didn’t deserve. Even though God had promised the land to Abraham, he did not just take it away from Ephron.

son marry one of these local Canaanite women. [4]Go instead to my homeland, to my
relatives, and find a wife there for my son Isaac."
[5]The servant asked, "But suppose I can't find a young woman who will travel so far
from home? May I then take Isaac there to live among your relatives?"
[6]"No!" Abraham warned. "Be careful never to take my son there. [7]For the LORD, the
God of heaven, who took me from my father's house and my native land, solemnly
promised to give this land to my offspring.* He will send his angel ahead of you, and he
will see to it that you find a young woman there to be my son's wife. [8]If she is unwilling
to come back with you, then you are free from this oath. But under no circumstances are
you to take my son there."
[9]So the servant took a solemn oath* that he would follow Abraham's instructions.
[10]He loaded ten of Abraham's camels with gifts and set out, taking with him the best of
everything his master owned. He traveled to Aram-naharaim* and went to the village
where Abraham's brother Nahor had settled. [11]There the servant made the camels kneel
down beside a well just outside the village. It was evening, and the women were coming
out to draw water.
[12]"O LORD, God of my master," he prayed. "Give me success and show kindness
to my master, Abraham. Help me to accomplish the purpose of my journey. [13]See,
here I am, standing beside this spring, and the young women of the village are coming
out to draw water. [14]This is my request. I will ask one of them for a drink. If she says,
'Yes, certainly, and I will water your camels, too!'—let her be the one you have
appointed as Isaac's wife. By this I will know that you have shown kindness to my
master."
[15]As he was still praying, a young woman named Rebekah arrived with a water jug
on her shoulder. Her father was Bethuel, who was the son of Abraham's brother Nahor
and his wife, Milcah. [16]Now Rebekah was very beautiful, and she was a virgin; no man
had ever slept with her. She went down to the spring, filled her jug, and came up again.
[17]Running over to her, the servant asked, "Please give me a drink."
[18]"Certainly, sir," she said, and she quickly lowered the jug for him to drink. [19]When
he had finished, she said, "I'll draw water for your camels, too, until they have had
enough!" [20]So she quickly emptied the jug into the watering trough and ran down to the
well again. She kept carrying water to the camels until they had finished drinking. [21]The
servant watched her in silence, wondering whether or not she was the one the LORD

24:4 Gen 12:1
24:5 Gen 24:39
24:7 Gen 12:1, 7; 16:7; 22:11; Rom 4:13; †Gal 3:16
24:10 Gen 11:29; Deut 23:4
24:11 Gen 24:42
24:12 Gen 24:27, 48
24:14 Judg 6:17; 1 Sam 14:10
24:15 Gen 22:20-24
24:16 Gen 12:11; 29:17
24:17 1 Kgs 17:10; John 4:7
24:19 Gen 24:14

24:7 Hebrew *seed.* **24:9** Hebrew *put his hand under the thigh of Abraham his master and swore an oath.* **24:10** *Aram-naharaim* means "Aram of the two rivers," thought to have been located between the Euphrates and Balih Rivers in northwestern Mesopotamia.

24:4 Abraham wanted Isaac to marry within the family. This was a common and acceptable practice at this time that had the added advantage of avoiding intermarriage with pagan neighbors. A son's wife was usually chosen by the parents. It was common for a woman to be married in her early teens, although Rebekah was probably older.

24:6 Abraham wanted Isaac to stay in Canaan, but he didn't want him to marry one of the local girls. This contrasts to the way Hagar selected a wife for Ishmael in 21:21. To have Isaac stay and marry a woman from Canaan would have been easier. But Abraham wanted to obey God in the *who* as well as in the *where.* Make your obedience full and complete.

24:11 The well, the chief source of water for an entire village, was usually located outside town along the main road. Many people had to walk a mile or more for their water. They could use only what they could carry home. Farmers and shepherds would come from nearby fields to draw water for their animals. The well was a good place to meet new friends or to chat with old ones. Rebekah would have visited the well twice daily to draw water for her family.

24:12 Abraham's servant asked God for guidance in this very important task. Obviously Eliezer had learned much about faith and about God from his master. What are your family members, friends, and associates learning about God from watching you? Be like Abraham, setting an example of dependent faith. And be like Eliezer, asking God for guidance before any venture.

24:14 Was it right for Abraham's servant to ask God for such a specific sign? The sign he requested was only slightly out of the ordinary. The hospitality of the day required women at the well to offer water to weary travelers, but not to their animals. Eliezer was simply asking God to show him a woman with an attitude of service—someone who would go beyond the expected. An offer to water his camels would indicate that kind of attitude. Eliezer did not ask for a woman with good looks or wealth. He knew the importance of having the right heart, and he asked God to help him with his task.

24:15, 16 Rebekah had physical beauty, but the servant was looking for a sign of inner beauty. Appearance is important to us, and we spend time and money improving it. But how much effort do we put into developing our inner beauty? Patience, kindness, and joy are the beauty treatments that help us become truly lovely—on the inside.

24:18-21 Rebekah's servant spirit was clearly demonstrated as she willingly and quickly drew water for Eliezer and his camels. The pots used for carrying water were large and heavy. It took a lot of water to satisfy a thirsty camel—up to 25 gallons per camel after a week's travel. Seeing Rebekah go to work, Eliezer knew this was a woman with a heart for doing far more than the bare minimum. Do you have a servant spirit? When asked to help or when you see a need, go beyond the minimum.

24:22 Gen 24:47
intended him to meet. 22 Then at last, when the camels had finished drinking, he gave her
a gold ring for her nose and two large gold bracelets* for her wrists.
23 "Whose daughter are you?" he asked. "Would your father have any room to put us
up for the night?"
24:24 Gen 24:15
24 "My father is Bethuel," she replied. "My grandparents are Nahor and Milcah. 25 Yes,
24:26 Exod 4:31
we have plenty of straw and food for the camels, and we have a room for guests."
26 The man fell down to the ground and worshiped the LORD. 27 "Praise be to the LORD,
24:27 Gen 14:20; 24:12, 48
the God of my master, Abraham," he said. "The LORD has been so kind and faithful to
Abraham, for he has led me straight to my master's relatives."
24:28 Gen 29:12
28 The young woman ran home to tell her family about all that had happened. 29 Now
Rebekah had a brother named Laban. 30 When he saw the nose-ring and the bracelets on
24:29 Gen 25:20; 29:5
his sister's wrists, and when he heard her story, he rushed out to the spring, where the
24:30 Gen 24:10
man was still standing beside his camels. Laban said to him, 31 "Come and stay with us,
you who are blessed by the LORD. Why do you stand here outside the village when we
24:31 Gen 26:29
have a room all ready for you and a place prepared for the camels!"
32 So the man went home with Laban, and Laban unloaded the camels, gave him straw
to bed them down, fed them, and provided water for the camel drivers to wash their feet.
33 Then supper was served. But Abraham's servant said, "I don't want to eat until I have
told you why I have come."
"All right," Laban said, "tell us your mission."
24:34 Gen 24:1
34 "I am Abraham's servant," he explained. 35 "And the LORD has blessed my master
24:35 Gen 12:2
richly; he has become a great man. The LORD has given him flocks of sheep and herds
of cattle, a fortune in silver and gold, and many servants and camels and donkeys.
24:36 Gen 21:1-7; 25:5
36 When Sarah, my master's wife, was very old, she gave birth to my master's son, and
24:37 Gen 24:2-4
my master has given him everything he owns. 37 And my master made me swear that I
would not let Isaac marry one of the local Canaanite women. 38 Instead, I was to come
to his relatives here in this far-off land, to his father's home. I was told to bring back a
young woman from here to marry his son.
24:40 Gen 24:7
39 "'But suppose I can't find a young woman willing to come back with me?' I asked
him. 40 'You will,' he told me, 'for the LORD, in whose presence I have walked, will send
his angel with you and will make your mission successful. Yes, you must get a wife for
my son from among my relatives, from my father's family. 41 But if you go to my
relatives and they refuse to let her come, you will be free from your oath.'
42 "So this afternoon when I came to the spring I prayed this prayer: 'O LORD, the God
of my master, Abraham, if you are planning to make my mission a success, please guide
me in a special way. 43 Here I am, standing beside this spring. I will say to some young
woman who comes to draw water, "Please give me a drink of water!" 44 And she will

24:22 Hebrew *a gold nose-ring weighing a half shekel* [0.2 ounces or 6 grams] *and two gold bracelets weighing 10 shekels* [4 ounces or 114 grams].

ELIEZER: PROFILE OF A TRUE SERVANT
Have you ever approached a responsibility with this kind of single-mindedness and careful planning, while ultimately depending on God?

Accepted the challenge	24:3, 9
Examined alternatives	24:5
Promised to follow instructions	24:9
Made a plan	24:12–14
Submitted the plan to God	24:12–14
Prayed for guidance	24:12–14
Devised a strategy with room for God to operate	24:12–14
Waited	24:21
Watched closely	24:21
Accepted the answer thankfully	24:26
Explained the situation to concerned parties	24:34–49
Refused unnecessary delay	24:56
Followed through with entire plan	24:66

24:26, 27 As soon as Abraham's servant knew that God had answered his prayer, he prayed and thanked God for his goodness and guidance. God will also use and lead us if we are available like Eliezer. And our first response should be praise and thanksgiving that God would choose to work in and through us.

24:42, 48 When Eliezer told his story to Laban, he spoke openly of God and his goodness. Often we do the opposite, afraid that we will be misunderstood or rejected or seen as too religious. Instead, we should share openly what God is doing for us.

reply, "Certainly! And I'll water your camels, too!" LORD, let her be the one you have
selected to be the wife of my master's son.'

45"Before I had finished praying these words, I saw Rebekah coming along with her **24:45** 1 Sam 1:13
water jug on her shoulder. She went down to the spring and drew water and filled the
jug. So I said to her, 'Please give me a drink.' 46She quickly lowered the jug from her
shoulder so I could drink, and she said, 'Certainly, sir, and I will water your camels, too!'
And she did. 47When I asked her whose daughter she was, she told me, 'My father is **24:47** Gen 24:23-24
Bethuel, the son of Nahor and his wife, Milcah.' So I gave her the ring and the bracelets.

48"Then I bowed my head and worshiped the LORD. I praised the LORD, the God of
my master, Abraham, because he had led me along the right path to find a wife from the
family of my master's relatives. 49So tell me—will you or won't you show true kindness **24:49** Gen 47:29
to my master? When you tell me, then I'll know what my next step should be, whether
to move this way or that."

50Then Laban and Bethuel replied, "The LORD has obviously brought you here, so **24:50** Ps 118:23
what can we say? 51Here is Rebekah; take her and go. Yes, let her be the wife of your
master's son, as the LORD has directed."

52At this reply, Abraham's servant bowed to the ground and worshiped the LORD. **24:52** Gen 24:26
53Then he brought out silver and gold jewelry and lovely clothing for Rebekah. He also
gave valuable presents to her mother and brother. 54Then they had supper, and the **24:54** Gen 30:25
servant and the men with him stayed there overnight. But early the next morning, he said,
"Send me back to my master."

55"But we want Rebekah to stay at least ten days," her brother and mother said. "Then **24:55** Judg 19:4
she can go."

56But he said, "Don't hinder my return. The LORD has made my mission successful,
and I want to report back to my master."

57"Well," they said, "we'll call Rebekah and ask her what she thinks." 58So they called
Rebekah. "Are you willing to go with this man?" they asked her.

And she replied, "Yes, I will go."

59So they said good-bye to Rebekah and sent her away with Abraham's servant and **24:59** Gen 35:8
his men. The woman who had been Rebekah's childhood nurse went along with her.
60They blessed her with this blessing as she parted: **24:60** Gen 17:16; 22:17

"Our sister, may you become
the mother of many millions!
May your descendants overcome
all their enemies."

61Then Rebekah and her servants mounted the camels and left with Abraham's servant.

62Meanwhile, Isaac, whose home was in the Negev, had returned from Beer-lahairoi. **24:62** Gen 16:14
63One evening as he was taking a walk out in the fields, meditating, he looked up and saw **24:63** Ps 119:15, 27, 48
the camels coming. 64When Rebekah looked up and saw Isaac, she quickly dismounted.
65"Who is that man walking through the fields to meet us?" she asked the servant.

And he replied, "It is my master." So Rebekah covered her face with her veil. 66Then
the servant told Isaac the whole story.

67And Isaac brought Rebekah into his mother's tent, and she became his wife. He **24:67** Gen 23:1-2; 25:20; 29:18
loved her very much, and she was a special comfort to him after the death of his mother.

7. Abraham dies

The Death of Abraham

25 Now Abraham married again. Keturah was his new wife, 2and she bore him **25:1-4** //1 Chr 1:32-33
Zimran, Jokshan, Medan, Midian, Ishbak, and Shuah. 3Jokshan's two sons were
Sheba and Dedan. Dedan's descendants were the Asshurites, Letushites, and Leummites.
4Midian's sons were Ephah, Epher, Hanoch, Abida, and Eldaah. These were all descendants of Abraham through Keturah.

24:64, 65 When Rebekah learned that the man coming to greet them was Isaac, her husband-to-be, she followed two Oriental customs. She dismounted from her camel to show respect, and she placed a veil over her face as a bride.

25:1-6 Abraham took another wife, Keturah, after Sarah died. Although the sons and grandson of Abraham and Keturah received many gifts from Abraham, all his property and authority went to Isaac, his principal heir.

25:5 Gen 24:35-36 [5]Abraham left everything he owned to his son Isaac. [6]But before he died, he gave gifts
to the sons of his concubines and sent them off to the east, away from Isaac.
25:7 Gen 12:4 [7]Abraham lived for 175 years, [8]and he died at a ripe old age, joining his ancestors in
25:9-10 Gen 23:17-18; 49:29; 50:13 death. [9]His sons Isaac and Ishmael buried him in the cave of Machpelah, near Mamre, in
the field of Ephron son of Zohar the Hittite. [10]This was the field Abraham had purchased
25:11 Gen 12:2; 24:62 from the Hittites, where he had buried his wife Sarah. [11]After Abraham's death, God
poured out rich blessings on Isaac, who settled near Beer-lahairoi in the Negev.

Ishmael's Descendants

25:12-16 //1 Chr 1:29-31 [12]This is the history of the descendants of Ishmael, the son of Abraham through Hagar,
Sarah's Egyptian servant. [13]Here is a list, by their names and clans, of Ishmael's
descendants: The oldest was Nebaioth, followed by Kedar, Abdeel, Mibsam, [14]Mishma,
Dumah, Massa, [15]Hadad, Tema, Jetur, Naphish, and Kedemah. [16]These twelve sons of
25:17 Gen 25:8 Ishmael became the founders of twelve tribes that bore their names, listed according to
the places they settled and camped. [17]Ishmael finally died at the age of 137 and joined

ESAU

Common sense isn't all that common. In fact, the common thread in many decisions is that they don't make sense. Esau's life was filled with choices he must have regretted bitterly. He appears to have been a person who found it hard to consider consequences, reacting to the need of the moment without realizing what he was giving up to meet that need. Trading his birthright for a bowl of stew was the clearest example of this weakness. He also chose wives in direct opposition to his parents' wishes. He learned the hard way.

What are you willing to trade for the things you want? Do you find yourself, at times, willing to negotiate *anything* for what you feel you need *now?* Does your family, spouse, integrity, body, or soul get included in these deals? Do you sometimes feel that the important parts of life escaped while you were grabbing for something else?

If so, your initial response, like Esau's, may be deep anger. In itself that isn't wrong, as long as you direct the energy of that anger toward a solution and not toward yourself or others as the cause of the problem. Your greatest need is to find a focal point other than "what I need now." The only worthy focal point is God. A relationship with him will not only give an ultimate purpose to your life; it will also be a daily guideline for living. Meet him in the pages of the Bible.

Strengths and accomplishments
- Ancestor of the Edomites
- Known for his archery skill
- Able to forgive after explosive anger

Weaknesses and mistakes
- When faced with important decisions, tended to choose according to the immediate need rather than the long-range effect
- Angered his parents by poor marriage choices

Lessons from his life
- God allows certain events in our lives to accomplish his overall purposes, but we are still responsible for our actions
- Consequences are important to consider
- It is possible to have great anger and yet not sin

Vital statistics
- Where: Canaan
- Occupation: Skillful hunter
- Relatives: Parents: Isaac and Rebekah. Brother: Jacob. Wives: Judith, Basemath, and Mahalath

Key verses
"Try to live in peace with everyone, and seek to live a clean and holy life, for those who are not holy will not see the Lord. Look after each other so that none of you will miss out on the special favor of God. Watch out that no bitter root of unbelief rises up among you, for whenever it springs up, many are corrupted by its poison. Make sure that no one is immoral or godless like Esau. He traded his birthright as the oldest son for a single meal. And afterward, when he wanted his father's blessing, he was rejected. It was too late for repentance, even though he wept bitter tears" (Hebrews 12:14–17).

Esau's story is told in Genesis 25—36. He is also mentioned in Malachi 1:2, 3; Romans 9:13; Hebrews 12:16, 17.

25:21 As Isaac pleaded with God for children, so the Bible encourages us to ask and even plead for our most personal and important requests. God wants to grant our requests, but he wants us to ask him. Even then, as Isaac learned, God may decide to withhold his answer for a while in order to (1) deepen our insight into what we really need, (2) broaden our appreciation for his answers, or (3) allow us to mature so we can use his gifts more wisely.

his ancestors in death. 18Ishmael's descendants were scattered across the country from 25:18 Gen 16:12; 20:1
Havilah to Shur, which is east of Egypt in the direction of Asshur. The clans descended
from Ishmael camped close to one another.*

E. THE STORY OF ISAAC (25:19—28:9)

Isaac inherited everything from his father, including God's promise to make his descendants into a great nation. As a boy, Isaac did not resist as his father prepared to sacrifice him, and as a man, he gladly accepted the wife that others chose for him. Through Isaac, we learn how to let God guide our life and place his will ahead of our own.

1. Jacob and Esau

19This is the history of the family of Isaac, the son of Abraham. 20When Isaac was forty
years old, he married Rebekah, the daughter of Bethuel the Aramean from Paddan-aram
and the sister of Laban. 21Isaac pleaded with the LORD to give Rebekah a child because 25:21 Gen 21:2
she was childless. So the LORD answered Isaac's prayer, and his wife became pregnant
with twins. 22But the two children struggled with each other in her womb. So she went
to ask the LORD about it. "Why is this happening to me?" she asked.
23And the LORD told her, "The sons in your womb will become two rival nations. One 25:23 Gen 17:2-4; 27:29; 48:19 Num 20:14 Deut 2:4, 8 †Rom 9:11-12
nation will be stronger than the other; the descendants of your older son will serve the
descendants of your younger son."
24And when the time came, the twins were born. 25The first was very red at birth. He
was covered with so much hair that one would think he was wearing a piece of clothing. 25:25 Gen 27:11
So they called him Esau.* 26Then the other twin was born with his hand grasping Esau's 25:26 Hos 12:3
heel. So they called him Jacob.* Isaac was sixty years old when the twins were born.

Esau Sells His Birthright

27As the boys grew up, Esau became a skillful hunter, a man of the open fields, while
Jacob was the kind of person who liked to stay at home. 28Isaac loved Esau in particular
because of the wild game he brought home, but Rebekah favored Jacob.
29One day when Jacob was cooking some stew, Esau arrived home exhausted and
hungry from a hunt. 30Esau said to Jacob, "I'm starved! Give me some of that red stew 25:30 Gen 36:1, 8
you've made." (This was how Esau got his other name, Edom—"Red.")
31Jacob replied, "All right, but trade me your birthright for it." 25:31 Deut 21:16-17 1 Chr 5:1-2
32"Look, I'm dying of starvation!" said Esau. "What good is my birthright to me now?"
33So Jacob insisted, "Well then, swear to me right now that it is mine." So Esau swore 25:33 Gen 27:36 Heb 12:16
an oath, thereby selling all his rights as the firstborn to his younger brother. 34Then Jacob
gave Esau some bread and lentil stew. Esau ate and drank and went on about his business,
indifferent to the fact that he had given up his birthright.

2. Isaac and Abimelech

Isaac Deceives Abimelech

26 Now a severe famine struck the land, as had happened before in Abraham's time. 26:1 Gen 12:10; 20:1-2
So Isaac moved to Gerar, where Abimelech, king of the Philistines, lived.
2The LORD appeared to him there and said, "Do not go to Egypt. 3Do as I say, and stay 26:2 Gen 12:1, 7

25:18 The meaning of the Hebrew is uncertain. **25:25** *Esau* sounds like a Hebrew term that means "hair."
25:26 *Jacob* means "he grasps the heel"; this can also figuratively mean "he deceives."

25:31 A birthright was a special honor given to the firstborn son. It included a double portion of the family inheritance along with the honor of one day becoming the family's leader. The oldest son could sell his birthright or give it away if he chose, but in so doing, he would lose both material goods and his leadership position. By trading his birthright, Esau showed complete disregard for the spiritual blessings that would have come his way if he had kept it.

25:32, 33 Esau traded the lasting benefits of his birthright for the immediate pleasure of food. He acted on impulse, satisfying his immediate desires without pausing to consider the long-range consequences of what he was about to do. We can fall into the same trap. When we see something we want, our first impulse is to get it. At first we feel intensely satisfied and sometimes even powerful because we have obtained what we set out to get. But immediate pleasure often loses sight of the future. We can avoid making Esau's mistake by comparing the short-term satisfaction with its long-range consequences before we act.

Esau exaggerated his hunger. "I'm dying of starvation!" he said. This thought made his choice much easier because if he was starving, what good was an inheritance anyway? The pressure of the moment distorted his perspective and made his decision seem urgent. We often experience similar pressures. For example, when we feel sexual pressure, a marriage vow may seem unimportant. We might feel such great pressure in one area that nothing else seems to matter and we lose our perspective. Getting through that short, pressure-filled moment is often the most difficult part of overcoming a temptation.

26:1 The Philistine tribe would become one of Israel's fiercest enemies. The Philistines were one group of a number of

26:3 Gen 12:7; 15:15, 18
26:4 Gen 15:5; 22:17 Exod 32:13 †Acts 3:25 †Gal 3:8

here in this land. If you do, I will be with you and bless you. I will give all this land to you
and your descendants, just as I solemnly promised Abraham, your father. [4]I will cause
your descendants to become as numerous as the stars, and I will give them all these lands.
And through your descendants* all the nations of the earth will be blessed. [5]I will do this
because Abraham listened to me and obeyed all my requirements, commands, regulations,
and laws."

26:4 Hebrew *seed.*

JACOB

Abraham, Isaac, and Jacob are among the most significant people in the Old Testament. It is important to realize that this significance is not based upon their personal characters, but upon the character of God. They were all men who earned the grudging respect and even fear of their peers; they were wealthy and powerful, and yet each was capable of lying, deceit, and selfishness. They were not the perfect heroes we might have expected; instead, they were just like us, trying to please God, but often falling short.

Jacob was the third link in God's plan to start a nation from Abraham. The success of that plan was more often in spite of than because of Jacob's life. Before Jacob was born, God promised that his plan would be worked out through Jacob and not his twin brother, Esau. Although Jacob's methods were not always respectable, his skill, determination, and patience have to be admired. As we follow him from birth to death, we are able to see God's work.

Jacob's life had four stages, each marked by a personal encounter with God. In the first stage, Jacob lived up to his name, which means "he grasps the heel" (figuratively, "he deceives"). He grabbed Esau's heel at birth, and by the time he fled from home, he had also grabbed his brother's birthright and blessing. During his flight, God first appeared to him. Not only did God confirm to Jacob his blessing, but he awakened in Jacob a personal knowledge of himself. In the second stage, Jacob experienced life from the other side, being manipulated and deceived by Laban. But there is a curious change: The Jacob of stage one would simply have left Laban, whereas the Jacob of stage two, after deciding to leave, waited six years for God's permission. In the third stage, Jacob was in a new role as grabber. This time, by the Jordan River, he grabbed on to God and wouldn't let go. He realized his dependence on the God who had continued to bless him. His relationship to God became essential to his life, and his name was changed to Israel, "he struggles with God." Jacob's last stage of life was to *be* grabbed—God achieved a firm hold on him. In responding to Joseph's invitation to come to Egypt, Jacob was clearly unwilling to make a move without God's approval.

Can you think of times when God has made himself known to you? Do you allow yourself to meet him as you study his Word? What difference have these experiences made in your life? Are you more like the young Jacob, forcing God to track you down in the desert of your own plans and mistakes? Or are you more like the older Jacob who presented his desires and plans before God for his approval before taking any action?

Strengths and accomplishments
- Father of the 12 tribes of Israel
- Third in the Abrahamic line of God's plan
- Determined, willing to work long and hard for what he wanted
- Good businessman

Weaknesses and mistakes
- When faced with conflict, relied on his own resources rather than going to God for help
- Tended to accumulate wealth for its own sake

Lessons from his life
- Security does not lie in the accumulation of goods
- All human intentions and actions—for good or evil—are woven by God into his ongoing plan

Vital statistics
- Where: Canaan
- Occupation: Shepherd, livestock owner
- Relatives: Parents: Isaac and Rebekah. Brother: Esau. Father-in-law: Laban. Wives: Rachel and Leah. Twelve sons and one daughter are mentioned in the Bible

Key verse
"What's more, I will be with you, and I will protect you wherever you go. I will someday bring you safely back to this land. I will be with you constantly until I have finished giving you everything I have promised" (Genesis 28:15).

Jacob's story is told in Genesis 25—50. He is also mentioned in Hosea 12:2–5; Matthew 1:2; 22:32; Acts 7:8–16; Romans 9:11–13; Hebrews 11:9, 20, 21.

---

migrating sea peoples from the Aegean Sea who settled in Palestine. They arrived by way of Crete and Cyprus and were used as mercenaries by Canaanite rulers. These people, living along the southwest coast, were few but ferocious in battle. Although friendly to Isaac, this small group was the forerunner of the nation that would plague Israel during the time of Joshua, the judges, and David. This King Abimelech was not the same Abimelech that Abraham encountered (chapters 20–21). *Abimelech* may have been a dynastic name of the Philistine rulers.

6 So Isaac stayed in Gerar. 7 And when the men there asked him about Rebekah, he said, **26:7** Gen 12:11-13;
"She is my sister." He was afraid to admit that she was his wife. He thought they would 20:2, 12
kill him to get her, because she was very beautiful. 8 But some time later, Abimelech, king
of the Philistines, looked out a window and saw Isaac fondling Rebekah.
9 Abimelech called for Isaac and exclaimed, "She is obviously your wife! Why did you
say she was your sister?"
"Because I was afraid someone would kill me to get her from me," Isaac replied.
10 "How could you treat us this way!" Abimelech exclaimed. "Someone might have **26:10** Gen 20:7-10
taken your wife and slept with her, and you would have made us guilty of great sin."
11 Then Abimelech made a public proclamation: "Anyone who harms this man or his
wife will die!"

Conflict over Water Rights

12 That year Isaac's crops were tremendous! He harvested a hundred times more grain **26:12** Gen 26:3
than he planted, for the LORD blessed him. 13 He became a rich man, and his wealth only **26:13** Gen 24:35; 25:5
continued to grow. 14 He acquired large flocks of sheep and goats, great herds of cattle,
and many servants. Soon the Philistines became jealous of him, 15 and they filled up all **26:15** Gen 21:25
of Isaac's wells with earth. These were the wells that had been dug by the servants of his
father, Abraham.
16 And Abimelech asked Isaac to leave the country. "Go somewhere else," he said, "for **26:16** Exod 1:9
you have become too rich and powerful for us."
17 So Isaac moved to the Gerar Valley and lived there instead. 18 He reopened the wells
his father had dug, which the Philistines had filled in after Abraham's death. Isaac
renamed them, using the names Abraham had given them. 19 His shepherds also dug in **26:19** John 4:10-11
the Gerar Valley and found a gushing spring.
20 But then the local shepherds came and claimed the spring. "This is our water," they
said, and they argued over it with Isaac's herdsmen. So Isaac named the well "Argument,"* because they had argued about it with him. 21 Isaac's men then dug another well,
but again there was a fight over it. So Isaac named it "Opposition."* 22 Abandoning that **26:22** Pss 4:1; 18:19 Isa 54:2
one, he dug another well, and the local people finally left him alone. So Isaac called it
"Room Enough,"* for he said, "At last the LORD has made room for us, and we will be
able to thrive."

26:20 Hebrew *Esek.* **26:21** Hebrew *Sitnah.* **26:22** Hebrew *Rehoboth.*

26:7-11 Isaac was afraid that the men in Gerar would kill him to get his beautiful wife, Rebekah. So he lied, claiming that Rebekah was his sister. Where did he learn that trick? He may have known about the actions of his father, Abraham (see 12:10-13 and 20:1-5). Parents help shape the world's future by the way they shape their children's values. The first step toward helping children live right is for the parents to live right. Your actions are often copied by those closest to you. What kind of example are you setting for your children?

26:12-16 God kept his promise to bless Isaac. The neighboring Philistines grew jealous because everything Isaac did seemed to go right. So they plugged his wells and tried to get rid of him. Jealousy is a dividing force strong enough to tear apart the mightiest of nations or the closest of friends. It forces you to separate yourself from what you were longing for in the first place. When you find yourself becoming jealous of others, try thanking God for their good fortune. Before striking out in anger, consider what you could lose—a friend, a job, a spouse?

26:17, 18 The desolate Gerar area was located on the edge of a desert. Water was as precious as gold. If someone dug a well, he was staking a claim to the land. Some wells had locks to keep thieves from stealing the water. To fill in someone's well with dirt was an act of war; it was one of the most serious crimes in the land. Isaac had every right to fight back when the Philistines ruined his wells, and yet he chose to keep the peace. In the end, the Philistines respected him for his patience.

26:17-22 Three times Isaac and his men dug new wells. When the first two disputes arose, Isaac moved on. Finally there was enough room for everyone. Rather than start a huge conflict, Isaac compromised for the sake of peace. Would you be willing to forsake an important position or valuable possession to keep peace? Ask God for the wisdom to know when to withdraw and when to stand and fight.

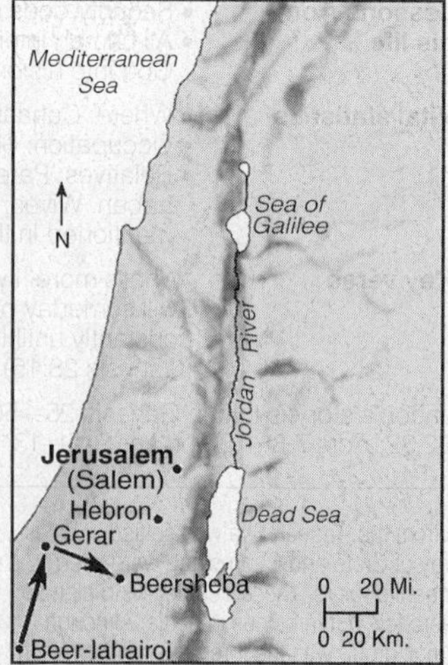

ISAAC'S MOVE TO GERAR
Isaac had settled near Beer-lahairoi ("the well of the Living One who sees me"), where his sons, Jacob and Esau, were born. A famine drove him to Gerar. But when he became wealthy, his jealous neighbors asked him to leave. From Gerar he moved to Beersheba.

26:23 Gen 22:19
23From there Isaac moved to Beersheba, 24where the LORD appeared to him on the
26:24 Gen 17:7; 22:17 Exod 3:6
night of his arrival. "I am the God of your father, Abraham," he said. "Do not be afraid,
for I am with you and will bless you. I will give you many descendants, and they will
become a great nation. I will do this because of my promise to Abraham, my servant."
26:25 Gen 12:7-8; 13:4
25Then Isaac built an altar there and worshiped the LORD. He set up his camp at that
place, and his servants dug a well.

A Treaty with Abimelech

26:26 Gen 21:22
26One day Isaac had visitors from Gerar. King Abimelech arrived with his adviser,
26:27 Gen 26:16
Ahuzzath, and also Phicol, his army commander. 27"Why have you come?" Isaac asked
them. "This is obviously no friendly visit, since you sent me from your land in a most
26:28 Gen 21:22-23
unfriendly way."
28They replied, "We can plainly see that the LORD is with you. So we decided we
should have a treaty, a covenant between us. 29Swear that you will not harm us, just as
we did not harm you. We have always treated you well, and we sent you away from us
26:30 Gen 31:54
in peace. And now look how the LORD has blessed you!"
30So Isaac prepared a great feast for them, and they ate and drank in preparation for
26:31 Gen 21:31
the treaty ceremony. 31Early the next morning, they each took a solemn oath of
nonaggression. Then Isaac sent them home again in peace. 32That very day Isaac's
26:33 Gen 21:31
servants came and told him about a well they had dug. "We've found water!" they said.
33So Isaac named the well "Oath,"* and from that time to this, the town that grew up
26:34 Gen 28:8
there has been called Beersheba—"well of the oath."
34At the age of forty, Esau married a young woman named Judith, the daughter of
26:35 Gen 27:46
Beeri the Hittite. He also married Basemath, the daughter of Elon the Hittite. 35But
Esau's wives made life miserable for Isaac and Rebekah.

3. Jacob gets Isaac's blessing

27:1 Gen 25:25; 48:10
27 When Isaac was old and almost blind, he called for Esau, his older son, and said,
"My son?"
"Yes, Father?" Esau replied.
27:2 Gen 47:29
2"I am an old man now," Isaac said, "and I expect every day to be my last. 3Take
27:3 Gen 25:27
your bow and a quiver full of arrows out into the open country, and hunt some wild
game for me. 4Prepare it just the way I like it so it's savory and good, and bring it here
27:4 Gen 24:60; 27:19; 48:9
for me to eat. Then I will pronounce the blessing that belongs to you, my firstborn son,
before I die."
27:5-6 Gen 25:27-28
5But Rebekah overheard the conversation. So when Esau left to hunt for the wild
game, 6she said to her son Jacob, "I overheard your father asking Esau 7to prepare him
a delicious meal of wild game. He wants to bless Esau in the LORD's presence before he
27:8 Gen 27:13, 43
dies. 8Now, my son, do exactly as I tell you. 9Go out to the flocks and bring me two fine
young goats. I'll prepare your father's favorite dish from them. 10Take the food to your
father; then he can eat it and bless you instead of Esau before he dies."
27:11 Gen 25:25
11"But Mother!" Jacob replied. "He won't be fooled that easily. Think how hairy Esau

26:33 Hebrew *Shibah,* which can mean "oath" or "seven."

26:26-31 With his enemies wanting to make a peace treaty, Isaac was quick to respond, turning the occasion into a celebration. We should be just as receptive to those who want to make peace with us. When God's influence in our lives attracts people—even enemies—we must take the opportunity to reach out to them with God's love.

26:34, 35 Esau married pagan women, and this upset his parents greatly. Most parents can be a storehouse of good advice, because they have a lifetime of insight into their children's character. You may not agree with everything your parents say, but at least talk with them and listen carefully. This will help avoid the hard feelings Esau experienced.

27:5-10 When Rebekah learned that Isaac was preparing to bless Esau, she quickly devised a plan to trick him into blessing Jacob instead. Although God had already told her that Jacob would become the family leader (25:23), Rebekah took matters into her own hands. She resorted to doing something wrong to try to bring about what God had already said would happen. For Rebekah, the end justified the means. No matter how good we think our goals are, we should not attempt to achieve them by doing what is wrong. Would God approve of the methods you are using to accomplish your goals?

27:11, 12 How we react to a moral dilemma often exposes our real motives. Frequently we are more worried about getting caught than about doing what is right. Jacob did not seem concerned about the deceitfulness of his mother's plan; instead he was afraid of getting in trouble while carrying it out. If you are worried about getting caught, you are probably in a position that is less than honest. Let your fear of getting caught be a warning to do right. Jacob paid a huge price for carrying out this dishonest plan.

is and how smooth my skin is! 12 What if my father touches me? He'll see that I'm trying
to trick him, and then he'll curse me instead of blessing me."
13 "Let the curse fall on me, dear son," said Rebekah. "Just do what I tell you. Go out
and get the goats."
14 So Jacob followed his mother's instructions, bringing her the two goats. She took
them and cooked a delicious meat dish, just the way Isaac liked it. 15 Then she took Esau's
best clothes, which were there in the house, and dressed Jacob with them. 16 She made
him a pair of gloves from the hairy skin of the young goats, and she fastened a strip of
the goat's skin around his neck. 17 Then she gave him the meat dish, with its rich aroma,
and some freshly baked bread. 18 Jacob carried the platter of food to his father and said,
"My father?"

"Yes, my son," he answered. "Who is it—Esau or Jacob?"

19 Jacob replied, "It's Esau, your older son. I've done as you told me. Here is the wild
game, cooked the way you like it. Sit up and eat it so you can give me your blessing."

20 Isaac asked, "How were you able to find it so quickly, my son?"

"Because the LORD your God put it in my path!" Jacob replied.

21 Then Isaac said to Jacob, "Come over here. I want to touch you to make sure you
really are Esau." 22 So Jacob went over to his father, and Isaac touched him. "The voice
is Jacob's, but the hands are Esau's," Isaac said to himself. 23 But he did not recognize
Jacob because Jacob's hands felt hairy just like Esau's. So Isaac pronounced his blessing
on Jacob. 24 "Are you really my son Esau?" he asked.

"Yes, of course," Jacob replied.

25 Then Isaac said, "Now, my son, bring me the meat. I will eat it, and then I will give
you my blessing." So Jacob took the food over to his father, and Isaac ate it. He also
drank the wine that Jacob served him. Then Isaac said, 26 "Come here and kiss me, my
son."

27 So Jacob went over and kissed him. And when Isaac caught the smell of his clothes,
he was finally convinced, and he blessed his son. He said, "The smell of my son is the
good smell of the open fields that the LORD has blessed. 28 May God always give you
plenty of dew for healthy crops and good harvests of grain and wine. 29 May many
nations become your servants. May you be the master of your brothers. May all your
mother's sons bow low before you. All who curse you are cursed, and all who bless you
are blessed."

30 As soon as Isaac had blessed Jacob, and almost before Jacob had left his father, Esau
returned from his hunting trip. 31 Esau prepared his father's favorite meat dish and
brought it to him. Then he said, "I'm back, Father, and I have the wild game. Sit up and
eat it so you can give me your blessing."

32 But Isaac asked him, "Who are you?"

"Why, it's me, of course!" he replied. "It's Esau, your older son."

33 Isaac began to tremble uncontrollably and said, "Then who was it that just served
me wild game? I have already eaten it, and I blessed him with an irrevocable blessing
before you came."

27:12 Gen 9:25; 27:21-22
27:13 Gen 27:8
27:15 Gen 27:27
27:19 Gen 27:31
27:21 Gen 27:12
27:23 Gen 27:16
27:25 Gen 27:4
27:27 Ps 65:10; Heb 11:20
27:28 Deut 7:13; 33:13, 28; Zech 8:12
27:29 Gen 9:25-27; 12:3; Isa 45:14
27:31 Gen 27:4
27:32 Gen 27:18
27:33 Gen 27:35

27:11-13 Jacob hesitated when he heard Rebekah's deceitful plan. Although he questioned it for the wrong reason (fear of getting caught), he protested and thus gave her one last chance to reconsider. But Rebekah had become so wrapped up in her plan that she no longer saw clearly what she was doing. Sin had trapped her and was degrading her character. Correcting yourself in the middle of doing wrong may bring hurt and disappointment, but it also will bring freedom from sin's control.

27:24 Although Jacob got the blessing he wanted, deceiving his father cost him dearly. These are some of the consequences of that deceit: (1) He never saw his mother again; (2) his brother wanted to kill him; (3) he was deceived by his uncle, Laban; (4) his family became torn by strife; (5) Esau became the founder of an enemy nation; (6) he was exiled from his family for years. Ironically, Jacob would have received the birthright and blessing anyway (25:23). Imagine how different his life would have been had he and his mother waited for God to work his way, in his time!

27:33 In ancient times, a person's word was binding (much like a written contract today), especially when it was a formal oath. This is why Isaac's blessing was irrevocable.

27:33-37 Before the father died, he performed a ceremony of blessing, in which he officially handed over the birthright to the rightful heir. Although the firstborn son was entitled to the birthright, it was not actually his until the blessing was pronounced. Before the blessing was given, the father could take the birthright away from the oldest son and give it to a more deserving son. But after the blessing was given, the birthright could no longer be taken away. This is why fathers usually waited until late in life to pronounce the blessing. Although Jacob had been given the birthright by his older brother years before, he still needed his father's blessing to make it binding.

27:34 Heb 12:17 34 When Esau understood, he let out a loud and bitter cry. "O my father, bless me, too!"
he begged.
27:35 Gen 27:19 35 But Isaac said, "Your brother was here, and he tricked me. He has carried away your
blessing."
27:36 Gen 25:26 36 Esau said bitterly, "No wonder his name is Jacob,* for he has deceived me twice,
first taking my birthright and now stealing my blessing. Oh, haven't you saved even one
blessing for me?"
27:37 Gen 27:28-29 37 Isaac said to Esau, "I have made Jacob your master and have declared that all his
brothers will be his servants. I have guaranteed him an abundance of grain and wine—
what is there left to give?"
38 Esau pleaded, "Not one blessing left for me? O my father, bless me, too!" Then Esau
27:38 Heb 12:17 broke down and wept.
27:39 Heb 11:20 39 His father, Isaac, said to him, "You will live off the land and what it yields, 40 and
you will live by your sword. You will serve your brother for a time, but then you will
27:40 2 Kgs 8:20-22 shake loose from him and be free."

Jacob Flees to Paddan-Aram

27:41 Gen 32:3-11; 37:4 41 Esau hated Jacob because he had stolen his blessing, and he said to himself, "My father
will soon be dead and gone. Then I will kill Jacob."
42 But someone got wind of what Esau was planning and reported it to Rebekah. She
27:43 Gen 27:8 sent for Jacob and told him, "Esau is threatening to kill you. 43 This is what you should
do. Flee to your uncle Laban in Haran. 44 Stay there with him until your brother's fury is
27:44 Gen 31:41 spent. 45 When he forgets what you have done, I will send for you. Why should I lose
both of you in one day?"
27:46 Gen 26:34-35 46 Then Rebekah said to Isaac, "I'm sick and tired of these local Hittite women. I'd
rather die than see Jacob marry one of them."

28:1 Gen 24:3 **28** So Isaac called for Jacob, blessed him, and said, "Do not marry any of these
Canaanite women. 2 Instead, go at once to Paddan-aram, to the house of your
28:2 Gen 25:20 grandfather Bethuel, and marry one of your uncle Laban's daughters. 3 May God Almighty
bless you and give you many children. And may your descendants become a great
28:3 Gen 17:1; 35:11 assembly of nations! 4 May God pass on to you and your descendants the blessings he
28:4 Gen 12:1-3; 15:7; 35:11 promised to Abraham. May you own this land where we now are foreigners, for God
gave it to Abraham."
5 So Isaac sent Jacob away, and he went to Paddan-aram to stay with his uncle Laban,
his mother's brother, the son of Bethuel the Aramean.
6 Esau heard that his father had blessed Jacob and sent him to Paddan-aram to find a
28:6 Gen 28:1 wife, and that he had warned Jacob not to marry a Canaanite woman. 7 He also knew
that Jacob had obeyed his parents and gone to Paddan-aram. 8 It was now very clear to
28:8 Gen 26:35 Esau that his father despised the local Canaanite women. 9 So he visited his uncle
28:9 Gen 36:2 Ishmael's family and married one of Ishmael's daughters, in addition to the wives he
already had. His new wife's name was Mahalath. She was the sister of Nebaioth and
the daughter of Ishmael, Abraham's son.

F. THE STORY OF JACOB (28:10—36:43)

Jacob did everything, both right and wrong, with great zeal. He deceived his own brother, Esau, and his father Isaac. He wrestled with an angel and worked fourteen years to marry the woman he loved. Through Jacob we learn how a strong leader can also be a servant. We also see how wrong actions will always come back to haunt us.

27:36 *Jacob* means "he grasps the heel"; this can also figuratively mean "he deceives."

27:41 Esau was so angry at Jacob that he failed to see his own wrong in giving away the birthright in the first place. Jealous anger blinds us from seeing the benefits we have and makes us dwell on what we don't have.

27:41 When Esau lost the valuable family blessing, his future suddenly changed. Reacting in anger, he decided to kill Jacob. When you lose something of great value, or if others conspire against you and succeed, anger is the first and most natural reaction. But you can control your feelings by (1) recognizing your reaction for what it is, (2) praying for strength, and (3) asking God for help to see the opportunities that even your bad situation may provide.

28:9 Ishmael was Isaac's half brother, the son of Abraham and Hagar, Sarah's maidservant (16:1-4, 15). After marrying two foreign girls (26:34), Esau hoped his marriage into Ishmael's family would please his parents, Isaac and Rebekah.

1. Jacob starts a family

Jacob's Dream at Bethel

10 Meanwhile, Jacob left Beersheba and traveled toward Haran. 11 At sundown he arrived **28:10** Gen 26:23
at a good place to set up camp and stopped there for the night. Jacob found a stone for a
pillow and lay down to sleep. 12 As he slept, he dreamed of a stairway that reached from **28:12** Gen 20:3
earth to heaven. And he saw the angels of God going up and down on it. Num 12:6
13 At the top of the stairway stood the LORD, and he said, "I am the LORD, the God of †John 1:51
your grandfather Abraham and the God of your father, Isaac. The ground you are lying
on belongs to you. I will give it to you and your descendants. 14 Your descendants will **28:14** Gen 12:2; 13:14;
be as numerous as the dust of the earth! They will cover the land from east to west and 22:17
from north to south. All the families of the earth will be blessed through you and your
descendants.* 15 What's more, I will be with you, and I will protect you wherever you **28:15** Gen 48:21
go. I will someday bring you safely back to this land. I will be with you constantly until Deut 7:9; 31:6, 8
I have finished giving you everything I have promised."
16 Then Jacob woke up and said, "Surely the LORD is in this place, and I wasn't even
aware of it." 17 He was afraid and said, "What an awesome place this is! It is none other **28:17** Exod 3:5
than the house of God—the gateway to heaven!" 18 The next morning he got up very Ps 68:35
early. He took the stone he had used as a pillow and set it upright as a memorial pillar. **28:18** Gen 35:14
Then he poured olive oil over it. 19 He named the place Bethel—"house of God"— **28:19**
though the name of the nearby village was Luz. Gen 12:8; 35:6; 48:3
20 Then Jacob made this vow: "If God will be with me and protect me on this journey
and give me food and clothing, 21 and if he will bring me back safely to my father, then **28:21** Exod 15:2
I will make the LORD my God. 22 This memorial pillar will become a place for worshiping **28:22**
God, and I will give God a tenth of everything he gives me." Gen 14:20; 35:7 Deut 14:22

Jacob Arrives at Paddan-Aram

29 Jacob hurried on, finally arriving in the land of the east. 2 He saw in the distance **29:1**
three flocks of sheep lying in an open field beside a well, waiting to be watered. Judg 6:3, 33 **29:2**
But a heavy stone covered the mouth of the well. 3 It was the custom there to wait for all Gen 24:10-11
the flocks to arrive before removing the stone. After watering them, the stone would be
rolled back over the mouth of the well. 4 Jacob went over to the shepherds and asked **29:4** Gen 28:10
them, "Where do you live?"
"At Haran," they said.
5 "Do you know a man there named Laban, the grandson of Nahor?" **29:5** Gen 11:29
"Yes, we do," they replied.
6 "How is he?" Jacob asked. **29:6** Exod 2:16
"He's well and prosperous. Look, here comes his daughter Rachel with the sheep."

28:14 Hebrew *seed*.

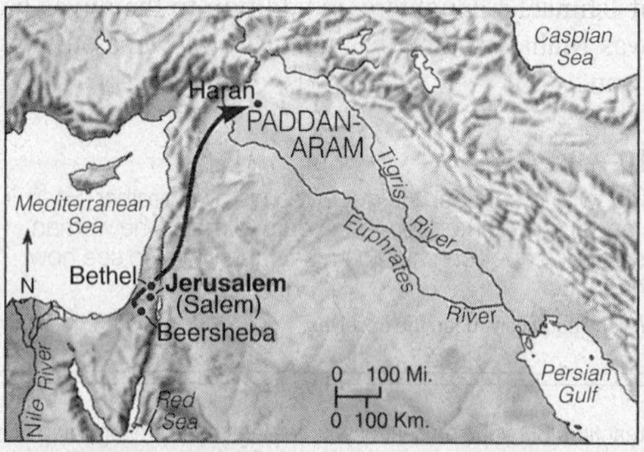

JACOB'S TRIP TO HARAN After deceiving Esau, Jacob ran for his life, traveling more than 400 miles to Haran, where an uncle, Laban, lived. In Haran, Jacob married and started a family.

28:10-15 God's covenant promise to Abraham and Isaac was offered to Jacob as well. But it was not enough to be Abraham's grandson; Jacob had to establish his own personal relationship with God. God has no grandchildren; each of us must have a personal relationship with him. It is not enough to hear wonderful stories about Christians in your family. You need to become part of the story yourself (see Galatians 3:6, 7).

28:19 Bethel was about ten miles north of Jerusalem and 60 miles north of Beersheba, where Jacob left his family. This was where Abraham made one of his first sacrifices to God when he entered the land. At first, Bethel became an important center for worship; later it was a center of idol worship. The prophet Hosea condemned its evil practices.

28:20-22 Was Jacob trying to bargain with God? It is possible that he, in his ignorance of how to worship and serve God, treated God like a servant who would perform a service for a tip. More likely, Jacob was not bargaining but pledging his future to God. He may have been saying, in effect, "Because you have blessed me, I will follow you." Whether Jacob was bargaining or pledging, God blessed him. But God also had some difficult lessons for Jacob to learn.

7 “Why don’t you water the flocks so they can get back to grazing?” Jacob asked.
“They’ll be hungry if you stop so early in the day.”
8 “We don’t roll away the stone and begin the watering until all the flocks and
shepherds are here,” they replied.
9 As this conversation was going on, Rachel arrived with her father’s sheep, for she
29:10 Exod 2:17 — was a shepherd. 10 And because she was his cousin, the daughter of his mother’s brother,
and because the sheep were his uncle’s, Jacob went over to the well and rolled away the
29:11 Gen 33:4 — stone and watered his uncle’s flock. 11 Then Jacob kissed Rachel, and tears came to his
29:12 Gen 28:5 — eyes. 12 He explained that he was her cousin on her father’s side, her aunt Rebekah’s son.
So Rachel quickly ran and told her father, Laban.
13 As soon as Laban heard about Jacob’s arrival, he rushed out to meet him and greeted
29:14 Judg 9:2; 2 Sam 5:1 — him warmly. Laban then brought him home, and Jacob told him his story. 14 “Just think,
my very own flesh and blood!” Laban exclaimed.

Jacob Marries Leah and Rachel

29:15 Gen 30:28; 31:7, 41 — After Jacob had been there about a month, 15 Laban said to him, “You shouldn’t work for
me without pay just because we are relatives. How much do you want?”
29:16 Gen 29:25-26 — 16 Now Laban had two daughters: Leah, who was the oldest, and her younger sister,
29:17 Gen 12:11 — Rachel. 17 Leah had pretty eyes,* but Rachel was beautiful in every way, with a lovely
face and shapely figure. 18 Since Jacob was in love with Rachel, he told her father, “I’ll
29:18 Gen 24:67; Hos 12:12 — work for you seven years if you’ll give me Rachel, your younger daughter, as my wife.”
19 “Agreed!” Laban replied. “I’d rather give her to you than to someone outside the
family.”
29:20 Song 8:7 — 20 So Jacob spent the next seven years working to pay for Rachel. But his love for her
was so strong that it seemed to him but a few days. 21 Finally, the time came for him to
marry her. “I have fulfilled my contract,” Jacob said to Laban. “Now give me my wife
so we can be married.”

29:17 Or *dull eyes.* The meaning of the Hebrew is uncertain.

JACOB’S CHILDREN
This chart shows from left to right Jacob’s children in the order in which they were born.

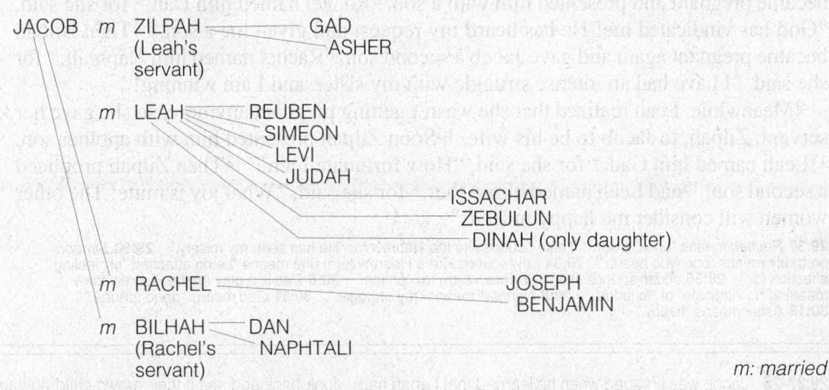

Jacob’s many wives (two wives and two “substitute” wives) led to sad and bitter consequences among the children. Anger, resentment, and jealousy were common among Jacob’s sons. It is interesting to note that the worst fighting and rivalry occurred between Leah’s children and Rachel’s children, and among the tribes that descended from them.

29:18-27 It was the custom of the day for a man to present a dowry, or substantial gift, to the family of his future wife. This was to compensate the family for the loss of the girl. Jacob’s dowry was not a material possession, for he had none to offer. Instead, he agreed to work seven years for Laban. But there was another custom of the land that Laban did not tell Jacob. The older daughter had to be married first. By giving Jacob Leah and not Rachel, Laban tricked him into promising another seven years of hard work.

29:20-28 People often wonder if working a long time for something they desire is worth it. Jacob worked seven years to marry Rachel. After being tricked, he agreed to work seven more years for her (although he did get to marry Rachel shortly after he married Leah)! The most important goals and desires are worth working and waiting for. Movies and television have created the illusion that people have to wait only about an hour to solve their problems or get what they want. Don’t be trapped into thinking the same is true in real life. Patience is hardest when we need it the most, but it is the key to achieving our goals.

22 So Laban invited everyone in the neighborhood to celebrate with Jacob at a wedding
feast. 23 That night, when it was dark, Laban took Leah to Jacob, and he slept with her.
24 And Laban gave Leah a servant, Zilpah, to be her maid.
25 But when Jacob woke up in the morning—it was Leah! "What sort of trick is this?"
Jacob raged at Laban. "I worked seven years for Rachel. What do you mean by this
trickery?"
26 "It's not our custom to marry off a younger daughter ahead of the firstborn," Laban
replied. 27 "Wait until the bridal week is over, and you can have Rachel, too—that is, if
you promise to work another seven years for me."
28 So Jacob agreed to work seven more years. A week after Jacob had married Leah,
Laban gave him Rachel, too. 29 And Laban gave Rachel a servant, Bilhah, to be her maid.
30 So Jacob slept with Rachel, too, and he loved her more than Leah. He then stayed and
worked the additional seven years.

Jacob's Many Children

31 But because Leah was unloved, the LORD let her have a child, while Rachel was
childless. 32 So Leah became pregnant and had a son. She named him Reuben,* for she
said, "The LORD has noticed my misery, and now my husband will love me." 33 She soon
became pregnant again and had another son. She named him Simeon,* for she said, "The
LORD heard that I was unloved and has given me another son." 34 Again she became
pregnant and had a son. She named him Levi,* for she said, "Surely now my husband
will feel affection for me, since I have given him three sons!" 35 Once again she became
pregnant and had a son. She named him Judah,* for she said, "Now I will praise the
LORD!" And then she stopped having children.

30 When Rachel saw that she wasn't having any children, she became jealous of her
sister. "Give me children, or I'll die!" she exclaimed to Jacob.
2 Jacob flew into a rage. "Am I God?" he asked. "He is the only one able to give you children!"
3 Then Rachel told him, "Sleep with my servant, Bilhah, and she will bear children for
me." 4 So Rachel gave him Bilhah to be his wife, and Jacob slept with her. 5 Bilhah
became pregnant and presented him with a son. 6 Rachel named him Dan,* for she said,
"God has vindicated me! He has heard my request and given me a son." 7 Then Bilhah
became pregnant again and gave Jacob a second son. 8 Rachel named him Naphtali,* for
she said, "I have had an intense struggle with my sister, and I am winning!"
9 Meanwhile, Leah realized that she wasn't getting pregnant anymore, so she gave her
servant, Zilpah, to Jacob to be his wife. 10 Soon Zilpah presented him with another son.
11 Leah named him Gad,* for she said, "How fortunate I am!" 12 Then Zilpah produced
a second son, 13 and Leah named him Asher,* for she said, "What joy is mine! The other
women will consider me happy indeed!"

29:22 Judg 14:10
29:23 Gen 24:65; 38:14
29:24 Gen 30:9
29:25 Gen 12:18
29:27 Judg 14:12
29:29 Gen 30:3
29:30 Gen 29:16
29:31 Deut 21:15-17
29:32 Gen 30:23; 37:21; 46:8
29:33 Deut 21:15
29:34 Gen 49:5
29:35 Gen 49:8 Matt 1:2-3
30:1 1 Sam 1:5-6
30:2 Gen 20:18; 29:31
30:3-4 Gen 16:2-4
30:6 Gen 30:23
30:8 Gen 32:28
30:11 Gen 35:26; 46:16; 49:19

29:32 *Reuben* means "Look, a son!" It also sounds like the Hebrew for "He has seen my misery." **29:33** *Simeon* probably means "one who hears." **29:34** *Levi* sounds like a Hebrew term that means "being attached" or "feeling affection for." **29:35** *Judah* sounds like the Hebrew term for "praise." **30:6** *Dan* is a play on the Hebrew term meaning "to vindicate" or "to judge." **30:8** *Naphtali* means "my struggle." **30:11** *Gad* means "good fortune." **30:13** *Asher* means "happy."

29:23-25 Jacob was enraged when he learned that Laban had tricked him. The deceiver of Esau was now deceived himself. How natural it is for us to become upset at an injustice done to us while closing our eyes to the injustices we do to others. Sin has a way of coming back to haunt us.

29:28-30 Although Jacob was tricked by Laban, he kept his part of the bargain. There was more at stake than just Jacob's hurt. There was Rachel to think about, as well as God's plan for his life. When we are tricked by others, keeping our part of the bargain may still be wise. Nursing our wounds or plotting revenge makes us unable to see from God's perspective.

29:32 Today parents usually give their children names that sound good or have sentimental appeal. But the Old Testament portrays a more dynamic use of names. Parents often chose names that reflected the situation at the time of the birth. They sometimes hoped their children would fulfill the meaning of the names given them. Later the parents could look back and see if their grown children had lived up to their names. Sometimes a person's name was changed because his or her character and name did not match. This happened to Jacob ("he grasps the heel," figuratively, "he deceives"), whose name was changed to Israel ("one who struggles with God"). Jacob's character had changed to the point that he was no longer seen as a deceiver, but as a God-honoring man.

30:3 Each of the three great patriarchs (Abraham, Isaac, and Jacob) had wives who had difficulty conceiving children. It is interesting to note how each man reacted to his wife's predicament. Abraham had relations with Sarah's servant in order to have his own child, thus introducing bitterness and jealousy into his family. Isaac, by contrast, prayed to God when his wife was barren. God eventually answered his prayers, and Rebekah had twin sons. Jacob, however, followed his grandfather's example and had children by his wives' servants, leading to sad and sometimes bitter consequences.

30:14 14 One day during the wheat harvest, Reuben found some mandrakes growing in a field
Song 7:13 and brought the roots to his mother, Leah. Rachel begged Leah to give some of them to
her. 15 But Leah angrily replied, "Wasn't it enough that you stole my husband? Now will
you steal my son's mandrake roots, too?"
Rachel said, "I will let him sleep with you tonight in exchange for the mandrake roots."
16 So that evening, as Jacob was coming home from the fields, Leah went out to meet
him. "You must sleep with me tonight!" she said. "I have paid for you with some mandrake
30:17 roots my son has found." So Jacob slept with her. 17 And God answered her prayers. She
Gen 25:21 became pregnant again and gave birth to her fifth son. 18 She named him Issachar,* for she
30:18 Gen 49:14 said, "God has rewarded me for giving my servant to my husband as a wife." 19 Then she
became pregnant again and had a sixth son. 20 She named him Zebulun,* for she said,
"God has given me good gifts for my husband. Now he will honor me, for I have given
30:22 him six sons." 21 Later she gave birth to a daughter and named her Dinah.
1 Sam 1:19-20 22 Then God remembered Rachel's plight and answered her prayers by giving her a

30:18 *Issachar* sounds like a Hebrew term that means "reward." **30:20** *Zebulun* probably means "honor."

RACHEL

History seems to repeat itself here. Twice a town well at Haran was the site of significant events in one family's story. It was here that Rebekah met Eliezer, Abraham's servant, who had come to find a wife for Isaac. Some 40 years later, Rebekah's son Jacob returned the favor by serving his cousin Rachel and her sheep from the same well. The relationship that developed between them not only reminds us that romance is not a modern invention but also teaches us a few lessons about patience and love.

Jacob's love for Rachel was both patient and practical. Jacob had the patience to wait seven years for her, but he kept busy in the meantime. His commitment to Rachel kindled a strong loyalty within her. In fact, her loyalty to Jacob got out of hand and became self-destructive. She was frustrated by her barrenness and desperate to compete with her sister for Jacob's affection. She was trying to gain from Jacob what he had already given: devoted love.

Rachel's attempts to earn the unearnable are a picture of a much greater error we can make. Like her, we find ourselves trying somehow to earn love—God's love. But apart from his Word, we end up with one of two false ideas. Either we think we've been good enough to deserve his love or we recognize we aren't able to earn his love and assume that it cannot be ours. If the Bible makes no other point, it shouts this one: God loves us! His love had no beginning and is incredibly patient. All we need to do is respond, not try to earn what is freely offered. God has said in many ways, "I love you. I have demonstrated that love to you by all I've done for you. I have even sacrificed my Son, Jesus, to pay the price for what is unacceptable about you—your sin. Now, live because of my love. Respond to me; love me with your whole being; give yourself to me in thanksgiving, not as payment." Live life fully, in the freedom of knowing you are loved.

Strengths and accomplishments
- She showed great loyalty to her family
- She gave birth to Joseph and Benjamin after being barren for many years

Weaknesses and mistakes
- Her envy and competitiveness marred her relationship with her sister, Leah
- She was capable of dishonesty when she took her loyalty too far
- She failed to recognize that Jacob's devotion was not dependent on her ability to have children

Lessons from her life
- Loyalty must be controlled by what is true and right
- Love is accepted, not earned

Vital statistics
- Where: Haran
- Occupation: Shepherdess, wife, mother, household manager
- Relatives: Father: Laban. Aunt: Rebekah. Sister: Leah. Husband: Jacob. Sons: Joseph and Benjamin

Key verse
"So Jacob spent the next seven years working to pay for Rachel. But his love for her was so strong that it seemed to him but a few days" (Genesis 29:20).

Rachel's story is told in Genesis 29—35:20. She is also mentioned in Ruth 4:11.

30:4-13 Rachel and Leah were locked in a cruel contest. In their race to have more children, they both gave their servants to Jacob as concubines. Jacob would have been wise to refuse, even though this was an accepted custom of the day. The fact that a custom is socially acceptable does not mean it is wise or right. You will be spared much heartbreak if you look at the potential consequences, to you or others, of your actions. Are you doing anything now that might cause future problems?

30:22-24 Eventually God answered Rachel's prayers and gave her a child of her own. In the meantime, however, she had given her servant to Jacob. Trusting God when nothing seems to happen is difficult. But it is harder still to live with the consequences of taking matters into our own hands. Resist the temptation to think God has forgotten you. Have patience and courage to wait for God to act.

child. 23 She became pregnant and gave birth to a son. "God has removed my shame," she said. 24 And she named him Joseph,* for she said, "May the LORD give me yet another son."

Jacob's Wealth Increases

25 Soon after Joseph was born to Rachel, Jacob said to Laban, "I want to go back home. 26 Let me take my wives and children, for I have earned them from you, and let me be on my way. You know I have fully paid for them with my service to you."

27 "Please don't leave me," Laban replied, "for I have learned by divination that the LORD has blessed me because you are here. 28 How much do I owe you? Whatever it is, I'll pay it."

29 Jacob replied, "You know how faithfully I've served you through these many years, and how your flocks and herds have grown. 30 You had little indeed before I came, and your wealth has increased enormously. The LORD has blessed you from everything I do! But now, what about me? When should I provide for my own family?"

31 "What wages do you want?" Laban asked again.

Jacob replied, "Don't give me anything at all. Just do one thing, and I'll go back to work for you. 32 Let me go out among your flocks today and remove all the sheep and goats that are speckled or spotted, along with all the dark-colored sheep. Give them to me as my wages. 33 This will make it easy for you to see whether or not I have been honest. If you find in my flock any white sheep or goats that are not speckled, you will know that I have stolen them from you."

34 "All right," Laban replied. "It will be as you have said." 35 But that very day Laban went out and removed all the male goats that were speckled and spotted, the females that were speckled and spotted with any white patches, and all the dark-colored sheep. He placed them in the care of his sons, 36 and they took them three days' distance from where Jacob was. Meanwhile, Jacob stayed and cared for Laban's flock.

37 Now Jacob took fresh shoots from poplar, almond, and plane trees and peeled off strips of the bark to make white streaks on them. 38 Then he set up these peeled branches beside the watering troughs so Laban's flocks would see them as they came to drink, for that was when they mated. 39 So when the flocks mated in front of the white-streaked branches, all of their offspring were streaked, speckled, and spotted. 40 Jacob added them to his own flock, thus separating the lambs from Laban's flock. Then at mating time, he turned the flocks toward the streaked and dark-colored rams in Laban's flock. This is how he built his flock from Laban's. 41 Whenever the stronger females were ready to mate, Jacob set up the peeled branches in front of them. 42 But he didn't do this with the weaker ones, so the weaker lambs belonged to Laban, and the stronger ones were Jacob's. 43 As a result, Jacob's flocks increased rapidly, and he became very wealthy, with many servants, camels, and donkeys.

2. Jacob returns home

Jacob Flees from Laban

31 But Jacob soon learned that Laban's sons were beginning to grumble. "Jacob has robbed our father!" they said. "All his wealth has been gained at our father's expense." 2 And Jacob began to notice a considerable cooling in Laban's attitude toward him.

3 Then the LORD said to Jacob, "Return to the land of your father and grandfather and to your relatives there, and I will be with you."

4 Jacob called Rachel and Leah out to the field where he was watching the flocks, 5 so

30:23 Luke 1:25
30:24 Gen 35:17
30:26 Gen 29:18; Hos 12:12
30:27 Gen 18:3; 39:2-5
30:28 Gen 29:15; 31:7
30:32 Gen 31:8, 12
30:37 Gen 38:41
30:43 Gen 13:2; 24:35; 26:13
31:3 Gen 28:15; 32:9

30:24 *Joseph* means "may he add."

30:27 Laban claimed to have learned by divination that God had blessed him because of Jacob. In other words, he thought his idols had given him this insight.

30:37-43 It is unclear what this method was or how it worked. Some say that there was a belief among herdsmen that vivid impressions at mating time influenced the offspring. Most likely, the selective breeding and God's promise of provision were the main reasons that Jacob's flocks increased.

31:1, 2 Jacob's wealth made Laban's sons jealous. It is sometimes difficult to be happy when others are doing better than we are. To compare our success with that of others is a dangerous way to judge the quality of our lives. By comparing ourselves to others, we may be giving jealousy a foothold. We can avoid jealousy by rejoicing in others' successes (see Romans 12:15).

31:4-13 Although Laban treated Jacob unfairly, God still increased Jacob's prosperity. God's power is not limited by lack of fair play. He has the ability to meet our needs and

31:6 Gen 30:29 he could talk things over with them. "Your father has turned against me and is not treating
me like he used to," he told them. "But the God of my father has been with me. 6 You
31:7 Gen 29:15; 31:41 know how hard I have worked for your father, 7 but he has tricked me, breaking his wage
31:8 Gen 30:32 agreement with me again and again. But God has not allowed him to do me any harm.
8 For if he said the speckled animals were mine, the whole flock began to produce
speckled lambs. And when he changed his mind and said I could have the streaked ones,
then all the lambs were born streaked. 9 In this way, God has made me wealthy at your
father's expense. 10 During the mating season, I had a dream and saw that the male goats
31:11 Gen 16:7-11; 22:11, 15 mating with the flock were streaked, speckled, and spotted. 11 Then in my dream, the
31:12 Gen 30:32 Exod 3:7 angel of God said to me, 'Jacob!' And I replied, 'Yes, I'm listening!' 12 The angel said,
'Look, and you will see that only the streaked, speckled, and spotted males are mating
with the females of your flock. For I have seen all that Laban has done to you. 13 I am
31:13 Gen 28:10-22 the God you met at Bethel, the place where you anointed the pillar of stone and made a
vow to serve me. Now leave this country and return to the land you came from.'"
14 Rachel and Leah said, "That's fine with us! There's nothing for us here—none of
31:15 Gen 29:20, 27 our father's wealth will come to us anyway. 15 He has reduced our rights to those of
foreign women. He sold us, and what he received for us has disappeared. 16 The riches
God has given you from our father are legally ours and our children's to begin with. So
31:18 Gen 25:20 go ahead and do whatever God has told you."
17 So Jacob put his wives and children on camels. 18 He drove the flocks in front of

---

LABAN

We're all selfish, but some of us have a real corner on the weakness. Laban's whole life was stamped by self-centeredness. His chief goal was to look out for himself. The way he treated others was controlled by that goal. He made profitable arrangements for his sister Rebekah's marriage to Isaac and used his daughters' lives as bargaining chips. Jacob eventually outmaneuvered Laban, but the older man was unwilling to admit defeat. His hold on Jacob was broken, but he still tried to maintain some kind of control by getting Jacob to promise to be gone for good. He realized that Jacob and Jacob's God were more than he could handle.

On the surface, we may find it difficult to identify with Laban. But his selfishness is one point we have in common. Like him, we often have a strong tendency to control people and events to our benefit. Our "good" reasons for treating others the way we do may simply be a thin cover on our self-centered motives. We may not even recognize our own selfishness. One way to discover it is to examine our willingness to admit we're wrong. Laban could not bring himself to do this. If you ever amaze yourself by what you say and do to avoid facing up to wrong actions, you are getting a glimpse of your selfishness in action. Recognizing selfishness is painful, but it is the first step on the road back to God.

Strengths and accomplishments
- Controlled two generations of marriages in the Abrahamic family (Rebekah, Leah, Rachel)
- Quick-witted

Weaknesses and mistakes
- Manipulated others for his own benefit
- Unwilling to admit wrongdoing
- Benefited financially by using Jacob, but never fully benefited spiritually by knowing and worshiping Jacob's God

Lessons from his life
- Those who set out to use people will eventually find themselves used
- God's plan cannot be blocked

Vital statistics
- Where: Haran
- Occupation: Wealthy sheep breeder
- Relatives: Father: Bethuel. Sister: Rebekah. Brother-in-law: Isaac. Daughters: Rachel and Leah. Son-in-law: Jacob

Key verse
"In fact, except for the grace of God—the God of my grandfather Abraham, the awe-inspiring God of my father, Isaac—you would have sent me off without a penny to my name. But God has seen your cruelty and my hard work. That is why he appeared to you last night and vindicated me" (Genesis 31:42).

Laban's story is told in Genesis 24:1—31:55.

---

make us thrive even though others mistreat us. To give in and respond unfairly is to be no different from your enemies.

31:14, 15 Leaving home was not difficult for Rachel and Leah because their father had treated them as poorly as he had Jacob. According to custom, they were supposed to receive the benefits of the dowry Jacob paid for them, which was 14 years of hard work. When Laban did not give them what was rightfully theirs, they knew they would never inherit anything from their father. Thus, they wholeheartedly approved of Jacob's plan to take the wealth he had gained and leave.

him—all the livestock he had acquired at Paddan-aram—and set out on his journey to
the land of Canaan, where his father, Isaac, lived. 19At the time they left, Laban was some **31:19** Judg 17:5
distance away, shearing his sheep. Rachel stole her father's household gods and took **31:20** Gen 31:27
them with her. 20They set out secretly and never told Laban they were leaving. 21Jacob
took all his possessions with him and crossed the Euphrates River, heading for the **31:21** Gen 37:25 Num 32:1
territory of Gilead.

Laban Pursues Jacob

22Laban didn't learn of their flight for three days. 23But when he did, he gathered a group **31:22** Gen 30:36
of his relatives and set out in hot pursuit. He caught up with them seven days later in the
hill country of Gilead. 24But the previous night God had appeared to Laban in a dream. **31:24** Gen 25:20
"Be careful about what you say to Jacob!" he was told.

25So when Laban caught up with Jacob as he was camped in the hill country of Gilead,
he set up his camp not far from Jacob's. 26"What do you mean by sneaking off like this?"
Laban demanded. "Are my daughters prisoners, the plunder of war, that you have stolen
them away like this? 27Why did you slip away secretly? I would have given you a farewell
party, with joyful singing accompanied by tambourines and harps. 28Why didn't you let me **31:28** Gen 31:55
kiss my daughters and grandchildren and tell them good-bye? You have acted very
foolishly! 29I could destroy you, but the God of your father appeared to me last night and
told me, 'Be careful about what you say to Jacob!' 30I know you feel you must go, and you
long intensely for your childhood home, but why have you stolen my household gods?"

31"I rushed away because I was afraid," Jacob answered. "I said to myself, 'He'll take **31:31** Gen 20:11
his daughters from me by force.' 32But as for your household gods, let the person who **31:32** Gen 44:9
has taken them die! If you find anything that belongs to you, I swear before all these
relatives of ours, I will give it back without question." But Jacob didn't know that Rachel
had taken them.

33Laban went first into Jacob's tent to search there, then into Leah's, and then he
searched the tents of the two concubines, but he didn't find the gods. Finally, he went
into Rachel's tent. 34Rachel had taken the household gods and had stuffed them into her
camel saddle, and now she was sitting on them. So although Laban searched all the tents,
he couldn't find them. 35"Forgive my not getting up, Father," Rachel explained. "I'm
having my monthly period." So despite his thorough search, Laban didn't find them.

36Then Jacob became very angry. "What did you find?" he demanded of Laban. "What
is my crime? You have chased me as though I were a criminal. 37You have searched through **31:37** Gen 31:33
everything I own. Now show me what you have found that belongs to you! Set it out here
in front of us, before our relatives, for all to see. Let them decide who is the real owner! **31:38** Gen 27:44

38"Twenty years I have been with you, and all that time I cared for your sheep and

---

31:19 Many people kept small wooden or metal idols ("household gods") in their homes. These idols were called *teraphim,* and they were thought to protect the home and offer advice in times of need. They had legal significance as well, for when they were passed on to an heir, the person who received them could rightfully claim the greatest part of the family inheritance. No wonder Laban was concerned when he realized his idols were missing (31:30). Most likely Rachel stole her father's idols because she was afraid Laban would consult them and learn where she and Jacob had gone, or perhaps she wanted to claim the family inheritance.

31:32 Do you remember feeling absolutely sure about something? Jacob was so sure that no one had stolen Laban's idols that he vowed to kill the offender. Because Rachel took them, this statement put her safety in serious jeopardy. Even when you are absolutely sure about a matter, it is safer to avoid rash statements. Someone may hold you to them.

31:38-42 Jacob made it a habit to do more than was expected of him. When his flocks were attacked, he took the losses rather than splitting them with Laban. He worked hard even after several pay cuts. His diligence eventually paid off; his flocks began to multiply. Making a habit of doing more than expected can pay off. It (1) pleases God, (2) earns recognition and advancement, (3) enhances your reputation, (4) builds others' confidence in you, (5) gives you more experience and knowledge, and (6) develops your spiritual maturity.

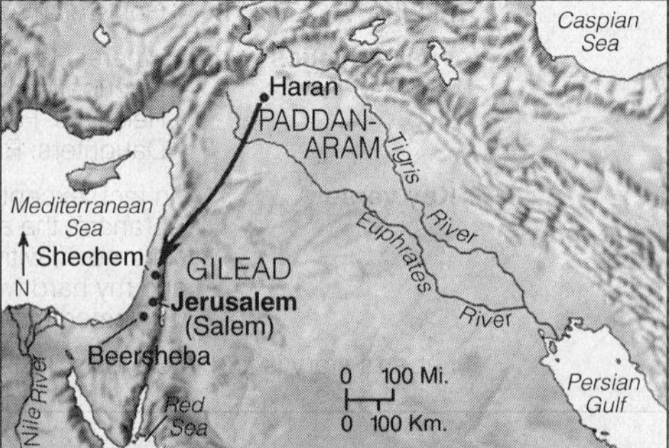

JACOB'S RETURN TO CANAAN God told Jacob to leave Haran and return to his homeland. Jacob took his family, crossed the Euphrates River, and headed first for the hill country of Gilead. Laban caught up with him there.

31:39 Exod 22:10-13 goats so they produced healthy offspring. In all those years I never touched a single
ram of yours for food. 39 If any were attacked and killed by wild animals, did I show
them to you and ask you to reduce the count of your flock? No, I took the loss! You
made me pay for every animal stolen from the flocks, whether the loss was my fault or
not. 40 I worked for you through the scorching heat of the day and through cold and
31:41 Gen 29:30 sleepless nights. 41 Yes, twenty years—fourteen of them earning your two daughters,
31:42 Gen 29:32 and six years to get the flock. And you have reduced my wages ten times! 42 In fact,
except for the grace of God—the God of my grandfather Abraham, the awe-inspiring
God of my father, Isaac—you would have sent me off without a penny to my name.
But God has seen your cruelty and my hard work. That is why he appeared to you last
night and vindicated me."

Jacob's Treaty with Laban

43 Then Laban replied to Jacob, "These women are my daughters, and these children are
my grandchildren, and these flocks and all that you have—all are mine. But what can I
31:44 Gen 21:27, 30 do now to my own daughters and grandchildren? 44 Come now, and we will make a peace
treaty, you and I, and we will live by its terms."
31:45 Gen 28:18; Josh 24:26-27 45 So Jacob took a stone and set it up as a monument. 46 He also told his men to gather
stones and pile them up in a heap. Jacob and Laban then sat down beside the pile of stones
to share a meal. 47 They named it "Witness Pile," which is Jegar-sahadutha in Laban's
language and Galeed* in Jacob's.
31:48 Gen 21:30 48 "This pile of stones will stand as a witness to remind us of our agreement," Laban
31:49 Judg 10:17; 11:29 said. 49 This place was also called Mizpah,* for Laban said, "May the LORD keep watch
between us to make sure that we keep this treaty when we are out of each other's sight.
31:50 Judg 11:10; 1 Sam 12:5; Jer 29:23; 42:5 50 I won't know about it if you are harsh to my daughters or if you take other wives, but
God will see it. 51 This heap of stones and this pillar 52 stand between us as a witness of
31:52 Gen 31:29, 42 our vows. I will not cross this line to harm you, and you will not cross it to harm me.
53 I call on the God of our ancestors—the God of your grandfather Abraham and the
31:53 Gen 24:12 God of my grandfather Nahor—to punish either one of us who harms the other."
So Jacob took an oath before the awesome God of his father, Isaac, to respect the
31:54 Exod 18:12 boundary line. 54 Then Jacob presented a sacrifice to God and invited everyone to a
31:55 Gen 31:28 feast. Afterward they spent the night there in the hills. 55 Laban got up early the next
morning, and he kissed his daughters and grandchildren and blessed them. Then he
returned home.

Jacob Sends Gifts to Esau

32:1 Gen 16:11; 2 Kgs 6:16-17 **32** As Jacob and his household started on their way again, angels of God came to
meet him. 2 When Jacob saw them, he exclaimed, "This is God's camp!" So he
32:2 Josh 13:26; 21:38; 2 Sam 2:8 named the place Mahanaim.*
3 Jacob now sent messengers to his brother, Esau, in Edom, the land of Seir. 4 He told
them, "Give this message to my master Esau: 'Humble greetings from your servant
32:3 Gen 27:41-42 Jacob! I have been living with Uncle Laban until recently, 5 and now I own oxen,
32:4 Gen 31:41 donkeys, sheep, goats, and many servants, both men and women. I have sent these
messengers to inform you of my coming, hoping that you will be friendly to us.'"
6 The messengers returned with the news that Esau was on his way to meet Jacob—
32:7 Gen 33:1 with an army of four hundred men! 7 Jacob was terrified at the news. He divided his
household, along with the flocks and herds and camels, into two camps. 8 He thought, "If
Esau attacks one group, perhaps the other can escape."

31:47 *Jegar-sahadutha* means "witness pile" in Aramaic; *Galeed* means "witness pile" in Hebrew. **31:49** *Mizpah* means "watchtower." **32:2** *Mahanaim* means "two camps."

31:49 To be binding, an agreement had to be witnessed by a third party. In this case, Jacob and Laban used God as their witness that they would keep their word.

32:1 Why did angels of God meet Jacob? In the Bible, angels often intervened in human situations. Although angels often came in human form, these angels must have looked different, for Jacob recognized them at once. The reason these angels met Jacob is unclear; but because of their visit, Jacob knew God was with him.

32:3 The last time Jacob had seen Esau, his brother was ready to kill him for stealing the family blessing (25:29—27:42). Esau was so angry he had vowed to kill Jacob as soon as their father, Isaac, died (27:41). Fearing their reunion, Jacob sent a messenger ahead with gifts. He hoped to buy Esau's favor.

9 Then Jacob prayed, "O God of my grandfather Abraham and my father, Isaac—
O LORD, you told me to return to my land and to my relatives, and you promised to treat
me kindly. 10 I am not worthy of all the faithfulness and unfailing love you have shown
to me, your servant. When I left home, I owned nothing except a walking stick, and now
my household fills two camps! 11 O LORD, please rescue me from my brother, Esau. I am
afraid that he is coming to kill me, along with my wives and children. 12 But you
promised to treat me kindly and to multiply my descendants until they become as
numerous as the sands along the seashore—too many to count."
13 Jacob stayed where he was for the night and prepared a present for Esau: 14 two
hundred female goats, twenty male goats, two hundred ewes, twenty rams, 15 thirty
female camels with their young, forty cows, ten bulls, twenty female donkeys, and ten
male donkeys. 16 He told his servants to lead them on ahead, each group of animals by
itself, separated by a distance in between.
17 He gave these instructions to the men leading the first group: "When you meet Esau,
he will ask, 'Where are you going? Whose servants are you? Whose animals are these?'
18 You should reply, 'These belong to your servant Jacob. They are a present for his master
Esau! He is coming right behind us.'" 19 Jacob gave the same instructions to each of the
herdsmen and told them, "You are all to say the same thing to Esau when you see him. 20 And
be sure to say, 'Your servant Jacob is right behind us.'" Jacob's plan was to appease Esau
with the presents before meeting him face to face. "Perhaps," Jacob hoped, "he will be
friendly to us." 21 So the presents were sent on ahead, and Jacob spent that night in the camp.

Jacob Wrestles with God

22 But during the night Jacob got up and sent his two wives, two concubines, and eleven
sons across the Jabbok River. 23 After they were on the other side, he sent over all his
possessions. 24 This left Jacob all alone in the camp, and a man came and wrestled with him
until dawn. 25 When the man saw that he couldn't win the match, he struck Jacob's hip and
knocked it out of joint at the socket. 26 Then the man said, "Let me go, for it is dawn."
But Jacob panted, "I will not let you go unless you bless me."
27 "What is your name?" the man asked.
He replied, "Jacob."
28 "Your name will no longer be Jacob," the man told him. "It is now Israel,* because
you have struggled with both God and men and have won."
29 "What is your name?" Jacob asked him.
"Why do you ask?" the man replied. Then he blessed Jacob there.
30 Jacob named the place Peniel—"face of God"—for he said, "I have seen God face
to face, yet my life has been spared." 31 The sun rose as he left Peniel,* and he was
limping because of his hip. 32 That is why even today the people of Israel don't eat meat
from near the hip, in memory of what happened that night.

Jacob and Esau Make Peace

33 Then, in the distance, Jacob saw Esau coming with his four hundred men. 2 Jacob
now arranged his family into a column, with his two concubines and their children
at the front, Leah and her children next, and Rachel and Joseph last. 3 Then Jacob went
on ahead. As he approached his brother, he bowed low seven times before him. 4 Then

32:28 *Israel* means "God struggles" or "one who struggles with God." **32:31** Hebrew *Penuel*, a variant name for Peniel.

32:9 Gen 28:13-15; 31:13
32:10 Gen 24:27
32:11 Gen 27:41
32:12 Gen 28:14
32:18 Gen 32:13
32:20 1 Sam 25:19
32:22 Deut 3:16 Josh 12:2
32:24 Gen 18:2
32:26 Hos 12:3-4
32:28 Gen 35:10 1 Kgs 18:31
32:29 Exod 3:13 Judg 13:17
32:30 Gen 16:13 Exod 24:10; 33:20 Num 12:8 Deut 5:24; 34:10 Judg 6:22 John 1:18
33:1 Gen 32:6-7
33:3 Gen 18:2; 42:6
33:4 Gen 45:14-15

32:9-12 How would you feel if you knew you were about to meet the person you had cheated out of his most precious possession? Jacob had taken Esau's birthright (25:33) and his blessing (27:27-40). Now he was about to meet this brother for the first time in 20 years, and he was frantic with fear. He collected his thoughts, however, and decided to pray. When we face a difficult conflict, we can run about frantically or we can pause to pray. Which approach will be more effective?

32:26 Jacob continued this wrestling match all night just to be blessed. He was persistent. God encourages persistence in all areas of our lives, including the spiritual. Where in your spiritual life do you need more persistence? Strong character develops as you struggle through tough conditions.

32:27-29 God gave many Bible people new names (Abraham, Sarah, Peter). Their new names were symbols of how God had changed their lives. Here we see how Jacob's character had changed. Jacob, the ambitious deceiver, had now become Israel, the one who struggles with God and overcomes.

33:1-11 It is refreshing to see Esau's change of heart when the two brothers meet again. The bitterness over losing his birthright and blessing (27:36-41) seems gone. Instead, Esau was content with what he had. Jacob even exclaimed how great it was to see his brother obviously pleased with him (33:10).

Esau ran to meet him and embraced him affectionately and kissed him. Both of them
were in tears.
5Then Esau looked at the women and children and asked, “Who are these people with
you?”
“These are the children God has graciously given to me,” Jacob replied. 6Then the
concubines came forward with their children and bowed low before him. 7Next Leah
came with her children, and they bowed down. Finally, Rachel and Joseph came and
made their bows.
8“And what were all the flocks and herds I met as I came?” Esau asked.
Jacob replied, “They are gifts, my lord, to ensure your goodwill.”
9“Brother, I have plenty,” Esau answered. “Keep what you have.”
10“No, please accept them,” Jacob said, “for what a relief it is to see your friendly
smile. It is like seeing the smile of God! 11Please take my gifts, for God has been very
generous to me. I have more than enough.” Jacob continued to insist, so Esau finally
accepted them.
12“Well, let’s be going,” Esau said. “I will stay with you and lead the way.”
13But Jacob replied, “You can see, my lord, that some of the children are very young,
and the flocks and herds have their young, too. If they are driven too hard, they may die.
14So go on ahead of us. We will follow at our own pace and meet you at Seir.”
15“Well,” Esau said, “at least let me leave some of my men to guide and protect you.”
“There is no reason for you to be so kind to me,” Jacob insisted.
16So Esau started back to Seir that same day. 17Meanwhile, Jacob and his household
traveled on to Succoth. There he built himself a house and made shelters for his flocks
and herds. That is why the place was named Succoth.* 18Then they arrived safely at
Shechem, in Canaan, and they set up camp just outside the town. 19Jacob bought the land
he camped on from the family of Hamor, Shechem’s father, for a hundred pieces of
silver.* 20And there he built an altar and called it El-Elohe-Israel.*

Revenge against Shechem

34 One day Dinah, Leah’s daughter, went to visit some of the young women who
lived in the area. 2But when the local prince, Shechem son of Hamor the Hivite,
saw her, he took her and raped her. 3But Shechem’s love for Dinah was strong, and he

33:5 Gen 48:9
33:8 Gen 32:14-16
33:9 Gen 27:39
33:14 Gen 32:3
33:17 Judg 8:5, 14; Ps 60:6
33:18 Gen 12:6; 25:20
33:19 Josh 24:32; John 4:5
34:1 Gen 30:21
34:2 Deut 21:14; 2 Sam 13:14

33:17 *Succoth* means “shelters.” **33:19** Hebrew *100 kesitahs;* the value or weight of the kesitah is no longer known. **33:20** *El-Elohe-Israel* means “God, the God of Israel.”

Life can bring us some bad situations. We can feel cheated, as Esau did, but we don’t have to remain bitter. We can remove bitterness from our lives by honestly expressing our feelings to God, forgiving those who have wronged us, and being content with what we have.

33:3 Bowing to the ground seven times was the sign of respect given to a king. Jacob was taking every precaution as he met Esau, hoping to dispel any thoughts of revenge.

33:4 Esau greeted his brother, Jacob, with a great hug. Imagine how difficult this must have been for a man who once had actually plotted his brother’s death (27:41). But time away from each other allowed the bitter wounds to heal. With the passing of time, each brother was able to see that their relationship was more important than their real estate.

33:11 Why did Jacob send gifts ahead for Esau? In Bible times, gifts were given for several reasons. (1) This may have been a bribe. Gifts are still given to win someone over or buy his or her support. Esau may first have refused Jacob’s gifts (33:9) because he didn’t want or need a bribe. He had already forgiven Jacob, and he had ample wealth of his own. (2) This may have been an expression of affection. (3) It may have been the customary way of greeting someone before an important meeting. Such gifts were often related to a person’s occupation. This explains why Jacob sent Esau, who was a herdsman, sheep, goats, and cattle.

33:14-17 Why did Jacob imply that he was going to Seir but then stop at Succoth? We don’t know the answer, but perhaps Jacob decided to stop there as they journeyed because Succoth is a beautiful site on the eastern side of the Jordan River. Whatever the reason, Jacob and Esau parted in peace. But they still lived fairly close to each other until after their father’s death (36:6-8).

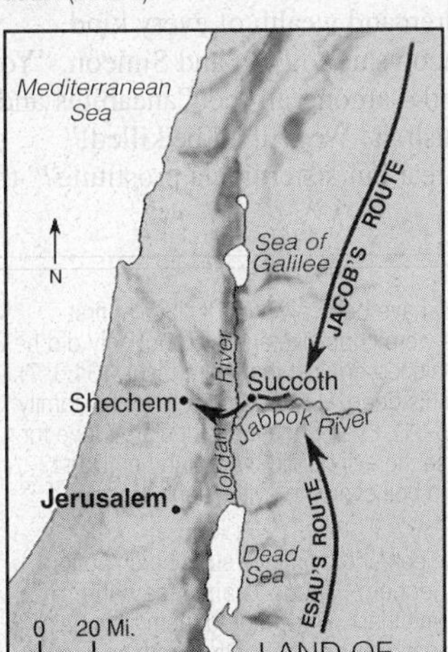

JACOB’S JOURNEY TO SHECHEM
After a joyful reunion with his brother, Esau (who journeyed from Edom), Jacob set up camp in Succoth. Later he moved on to Shechem where his daughter, Dinah, was raped and two of his sons took revenge on the city.

tried to win her affection. [4]He even spoke to his father about it. "Get this girl for me," 34:4
he demanded. "I want to marry her." Gen 21:21
[5]Word soon reached Jacob that his daughter had been defiled, but his sons were out
in the fields herding cattle so he did nothing until they returned. [6]Meanwhile, Hamor,
Shechem's father, came out to discuss the matter with Jacob. [7]He arrived just as Jacob's 34:7
sons were coming in from the fields. They were shocked and furious that their sister had 2 Sam 13:12
been raped. Shechem had done a disgraceful thing against Jacob's family,* a thing that
should never have been done.
[8]Hamor told Jacob and his sons, "My son Shechem is truly in love with your daughter,
and he longs for her to be his wife. Please let him marry her. [9]We invite you to let your
daughters marry our sons, and we will give our daughters as wives for your young men. 34:10
[10]And you may live among us; the land is open to you! Settle here and trade with us. You Gen 33:19
are free to acquire property among us."
[11]Then Shechem addressed Dinah's father and brothers. "Please be kind to me, and
let me have her as my wife," he begged. "I will give whatever you require. [12]No matter 34:12 Exod 22:16
what dowry or gift you demand, I will pay it—only give me the girl as my wife."
[13]But Dinah's brothers deceived Shechem and Hamor because of what Shechem had 34:13
done to their sister. [14]They said to them, "We couldn't possibly allow this, because you Gen 27:36 34:14
aren't circumcised. It would be a disgrace for her to marry a man like you! [15]But here is Gen 17:14
a solution. If every man among you will be circumcised like we are, [16]we will intermarry
with you and live here and unite with you to become one people. [17]Otherwise we will
take her and be on our way."
[18]Hamor and Shechem gladly agreed, [19]and Shechem lost no time in acting on this 34:19
request, for he wanted Dinah desperately. Shechem was a highly respected member of Gen 29:20
his family, [20]and he appeared with his father before the town leaders to present this 34:20
proposal. [21]"Those men are our friends," they said. "Let's invite them to live here Gen 18:1
among us and ply their trade. For the land is large enough to hold them, and we can
intermarry with them. [22]But they will consider staying here only on one condition. 34:22
Every one of us men must be circumcised, just as they are. [23]But if we do this, all their Gen 34:15
flocks and possessions will become ours. Come, let's agree to this so they will settle
here among us."
[24]So all the men agreed and were circumcised. [25]But three days later, when their 34:24
wounds were still sore, two of Dinah's brothers, Simeon and Levi, took their swords, Gen 28:15
entered the town without opposition, and slaughtered every man there, [26]including 34:25 Gen 49:5-7
Hamor and Shechem. They rescued Dinah from Shechem's house and returned to their Josh 5:8
camp. [27]Then all of Jacob's sons plundered the town because their sister had been defiled
there. [28]They seized all the flocks and herds and donkeys—everything they could lay 34:28
their hands on, both inside the town and outside in the fields. [29]They also took all the Gen 43:18
women and children and wealth of every kind.
[30]Afterward Jacob said to Levi and Simeon, "You have made me stink among all the 34:30 Gen 13:7; 49:5-7
people of this land—among all the Canaanites and Perizzites. We are so few that they Exod 5:23 2 Sam 10:6
will come and crush us. We will all be killed!" 1 Chr 16:19
[31]"Should he treat our sister like a prostitute?" they retorted angrily.

34:7 Hebrew *in Israel.*

34:1-4 Shechem may have been a victim of "love at first sight," but his actions were impulsive and evil. Not only did he sin against Dinah; he sinned against the entire family (34:6, 7). The consequences of his deed were severe both for his family and for Jacob's (34:25-31). Even Shechem's declared love for Dinah could not excuse the evil he did by raping her. Don't allow sexual passion to boil over into evil actions. Passion must be controlled.

34:25-31 Why did Simeon and Levi take such harsh action against the city of Shechem? Jacob's family saw themselves as set apart from others. God wanted them to remain separate from their pagan neighbors. But the brothers wrongly thought that being set apart also meant being better. This arrogant attitude led to the terrible slaughter of innocent people.

34:27-29 When Shechem raped Dinah, the consequences were far greater than he could have imagined. Dinah's brothers were outraged and took revenge. Pain, deceit, and murder followed. Sexual sin is devastating because its consequences are so far-reaching.

34:30, 31 In seeking revenge against Shechem, Simeon and Levi lied, stole, and murdered. Their desire for justice was right, but their ways of achieving it were wrong. Because of their sin, their father cursed them with his dying breath (49:5-7). Generations later, their descendants lost the part of the Promised Land allotted to them. When tempted to return evil for evil, leave revenge to God and spare yourself the dreadful consequences of sin.

Jacob's Return to Bethel

35 God said to Jacob, "Now move on to Bethel and settle there. Build an altar there
to worship me—the God who appeared to you when you fled from your brother,
Esau."
2 So Jacob told everyone in his household, "Destroy your idols, wash yourselves, and
put on clean clothing. 3 We are now going to Bethel, where I will build an altar to the God
who answered my prayers when I was in distress. He has stayed with me wherever I have
gone."
4 So they gave Jacob all their idols and their earrings, and he buried them beneath
the tree near Shechem. 5 When they set out again, terror from God came over the
people in all the towns of that area, and no one attacked them. 6 Finally, they arrived
at Luz (now called Bethel) in Canaan. 7 Jacob built an altar there and named it
El-bethel,* because God had appeared to him there at Bethel when he was fleeing
from Esau.
8 Soon after this, Rebekah's old nurse, Deborah, died. She was buried beneath the oak
tree in the valley below Bethel. Ever since, the tree has been called the "Oak of
Weeping."*
9 God appeared to Jacob once again when he arrived at Bethel after traveling from
Paddan-aram. God blessed him 10 and said, "Your name is no longer Jacob; you will now
be called Israel."* 11 Then God said, "I am God Almighty. Multiply and fill the earth!
Become a great nation, even many nations. Kings will be among your descendants!
12 And I will pass on to you the land I gave to Abraham and Isaac. Yes, I will give it to
you and your descendants." 13 Then God went up from the place where he had spoken to
Jacob.
14 Jacob set up a stone pillar to mark the place where God had spoken to him. He then
poured wine over it as an offering to God and anointed the pillar with olive oil. 15 Jacob
called the place Bethel—"house of God"—because God had spoken to him there.

The Deaths of Rachel and Isaac

16 Leaving Bethel, they traveled on toward Ephrath (that is, Bethlehem). But Rachel's
pains of childbirth began while they were still some distance away. 17 After a very hard
delivery, the midwife finally exclaimed, "Don't be afraid—you have another son!"
18 Rachel was about to die, but with her last breath she named him Ben-oni; the baby's

35:1 Gen 12:8; 28:19
35:2 Gen 31:19
35:3 Gen 28:15-22
35:4 Exod 32:3; Judg 8:24; Hos 2:13
35:5 Exod 15:16
35:6 Gen 28:19
35:7 Gen 28:19
35:8 Gen 24:59
35:9 Gen 28:13
35:10 Gen 32:28
35:11 Gen 12:2; 17:1, 6
35:12 Gen 13:15; 28:13
35:13 Judg 6:21; 13:20
35:14 Gen 28:18-19
35:16 Ruth 4:11
35:17 Gen 30:22-24
35:18 Gen 49:27

35:7 *El-bethel* means "the God of Bethel." **35:8** Hebrew *Allon-bacuth.* **35:10** *Jacob* means "he grasps the heel"; this can also figuratively mean "he deceives"; *Israel* means "God struggles" or "one who struggles with God."

35:2 Why did the people have these idols? Idols were sometimes seen more as good luck charms than as gods. Some Israelites, even though they worshiped God, had idols in their homes, just as some Christians today own good luck trinkets. Jacob believed that idols should have no place in his household. He wanted nothing to divert his family's spiritual focus.

Jacob ordered his household to get rid of their idols. Unless we remove idols from our lives, they can ruin our faith. What idols do we have? An idol is anything we put before God. Idols don't have to be physical objects; they can be thoughts or desires. Like Jacob, we should get rid of anything that could stand between us and God.

35:4 Why did the people give Jacob their earrings? Jewelry in itself was not evil, but in Jacob's day earrings were often worn as good luck charms to ward off evil. The people in his family had to cleanse themselves of all pagan influences, including reminders of foreign gods.

35:10 God reminded Jacob of his new name, Israel, which meant "one who struggles with God." Although Jacob's life was littered with difficulties and trials, his new name was a tribute to his desire to stay close to God despite life's disappointments.

Many people believe that Christianity should offer a problem-free life. Consequently, as life gets tough, they draw back disappointed. Instead, they should determine to prevail with God through life's storms. Problems and difficulties are painful but inevitable; you might as well see them as opportunities for growth. You can't prevail with God unless you have troubles to prevail over.

35:13, 14 This oil used to anoint the pillar was olive oil of the finest grade of purity. It was expensive, so using it showed the high value placed on the anointed object. Jacob was showing the greatest respect for the place where he met with God.

JACOB'S JOURNEY BACK TO HEBRON
After Jacob's sons Simeon and Levi destroyed Shechem, God told Jacob to move to Bethel, where God reminded him that his name had been changed to Israel. He then traveled to Hebron, but along the way, his dear wife Rachel died near Ephrath (Bethlehem).

father, however, called him Benjamin.* 19So Rachel died and was buried on the way to
Ephrath (that is, Bethlehem). 20Jacob set up a stone monument over her grave, and it can
be seen there to this day.

21Jacob* then traveled on and camped beyond the tower of Eder. 22While he was there,
Reuben slept with Bilhah, his father's concubine, and someone told Jacob about it.

These are the names of the twelve sons of Jacob:

23The sons of Leah were Reuben (Jacob's oldest son), Simeon, Levi, Judah, Issachar,
and Zebulun.
24The sons of Rachel were Joseph and Benjamin.
25The sons of Bilhah, Rachel's servant, were Dan and Naphtali.
26The sons of Zilpah, Leah's servant, were Gad and Asher.

These were the sons born to Jacob at Paddan-aram.

27So Jacob came home to his father Isaac in Mamre, which is near Kiriath-arba (now
called Hebron), where Abraham had also lived. 28Isaac lived for 180 years, 29and he died
at a ripe old age, joining his ancestors in death. Then his sons, Esau and Jacob, buried him.

Descendants of Esau

36 This is the history of the descendants of Esau (also known as Edom). 2Esau
married two young women from Canaan: Adah, the daughter of Elon the Hittite;
and Oholibamah, the daughter of Anah and granddaughter of Zibeon the Hivite. 3He also
married his cousin Basemath, who was the daughter of Ishmael and the sister of
Nebaioth. 4Esau and Adah had a son named Eliphaz. Esau and Basemath had a son
named Reuel. 5Esau and Oholibamah had sons named Jeush, Jalam, and Korah. All these
sons were born to Esau in the land of Canaan.

6Then Esau took his wives, children, household servants, cattle, and flocks—all the
wealth he had gained in the land of Canaan—and moved away from his brother, Jacob.
7There was not enough land to support them both because of all their cattle and livestock.
8So Esau (also known as Edom) settled in the hill country of Seir.

9This is a list of Esau's descendants, the Edomites, who live in the hill country of Seir.
10Among Esau's sons were Eliphaz, the son of Esau's wife Adah; and Reuel, the son
of Esau's wife Basemath.
11The sons of Eliphaz were Teman, Omar, Zepho, Gatam, and Kenaz. 12Eliphaz had
another son named Amalek, born to Timna, his concubine. These were all
grandchildren of Esau's wife Adah.
13The sons of Reuel were Nahath, Zerah, Shammah, and Mizzah. These were all
grandchildren of Esau's wife Basemath.
14Esau also had sons through Oholibamah, the daughter of Anah and granddaughter
of Zibeon. Their names were Jeush, Jalam, and Korah.

15Esau's children and grandchildren became the leaders of different clans.

The sons of Esau's oldest son, Eliphaz, became the leaders of the clans of Teman,
Omar, Zepho, Kenaz, 16Korah, Gatam, and Amalek. These clans in the land of
Edom were descended from Eliphaz, the son of Esau and Adah.

35:19 Gen 48:7
35:22 Gen 49:4; Lev 18:8; 1 Chr 5:1
35:23-26 //1 Chr 2:1-2
35:23 Gen 29:31-35; 30:18-20
35:24 Gen 30:24
35:25 Gen 30:5-8
35:26 Gen 30:10-13
35:27 Gen 13:18; 23:2
35:28 Gen 25:7-8, 20
36:1 Gen 25:30
36:2 Gen 26:34; 1 Chr 1:40
36:3 Gen 25:13
36:4 1 Chr 1:35
36:5 Gen 36:18
36:7 Gen 13:6
36:8 Gen 14:6; 25:30
36:9 Gen 36:43
36:10-14 //1 Chr 1:35-37

35:18 *Ben-oni* means "son of my sorrow"; *Benjamin* means "son of my right hand." **35:21** Hebrew *Israel;* also in 35:22a.

35:22 Reuben's sin was costly, although not right away. As the oldest son, he stood to receive a double portion of the family inheritance and a place of leadership among his people. Reuben may have thought he got away with his sin. No more is mentioned of it until Jacob, on his deathbed, assembled his family for the final blessing. Suddenly Jacob took away Reuben's double portion and gave it to someone else. The reason? "You slept with one of my wives; you dishonored me in my own bed" (49:4).

Sin's consequences can plague us long after the sin is committed. When we do something wrong, we may think we can escape unnoticed, only to discover later that the sin has been quietly breeding serious consequences.

36:9 The Edomites were descendants of Esau who lived south and east of the Dead Sea. The country featured rugged mountains and desolate wilderness. Several major roads led through Edom because it was rich in natural resources. During the Exodus, God told Israel to leave the Edomites alone (Deuteronomy 2:4, 5) because they were "relatives." But Edom refused to let them enter the land, and later they became bitter enemies of King David. The nations of Edom and Israel shared the same ancestor, Isaac, and the same border. Israel looked down on the Edomites because they intermarried with the Canaanites.

17 The sons of Esau's son Reuel became the leaders of the clans of Nahath, Zerah,
Shammah, and Mizzah. These clans in the land of Edom were descended from
Reuel, the son of Esau and Basemath.
18 The sons of Esau and his wife Oholibamah became the leaders of the clans of Jeush,
Jalam, and Korah. These are the clans descended from Esau's wife Oholibamah, the
daughter of Anah.

36:19 1 Chr 1:35

19 These are all the clans descended from Esau (also known as Edom).

Original Peoples of Edom

36:20-28 //1 Chr 1:38-42

36:20 Gen 14:6 Deut 2:12, 22

20 These are the names of the tribes that descended from Seir the Horite, one of the families
native to the land of Seir: Lotan, Shobal, Zibeon, Anah, 21 Dishon, Ezer, and Dishan. These
were the Horite clans, the descendants of Seir, who lived in the land of Edom.

22 The sons of Lotan were Hori and Heman. Lotan's sister was named Timna.
23 The sons of Shobal were Alvan, Manahath, Ebal, Shepho, and Onam.
24 The sons of Zibeon were Aiah and Anah. This is the Anah who discovered the hot
springs in the wilderness while he was grazing his father's donkeys.

36:25 Gen 36:2, 5, 14, 18 1 Chr 1:41

25 The son of Anah was Dishon, and Oholibamah was his daughter.
26 The sons of Dishon* were Hemdan, Eshban, Ithran, and Keran.

36:27 1 Chr 1:38, 42

27 The sons of Ezer were Bilhan, Zaavan, and Akan.
28 The sons of Dishan were Uz and Aran.

36:29-30 Gen 36:20

29 So the leaders of the Horite clans were Lotan, Shobal, Zibeon, Anah, 30 Dishon, Ezer,
and Dishan. The Horite clans are named after their clan leaders, who lived in the land
of Seir.

36:26 Hebrew *Dishan,* a variant name for Dishon; compare 36:21, 28.

JOSEPH

As a youngster, Joseph was overconfident. His natural self-assurance, increased by being Jacob's favorite son and by knowing of God's designs on his life, was unbearable to his ten older brothers, who eventually conspired against him. But this self-assurance, molded by pain and combined with a personal knowledge of God, allowed him to survive and prosper where most would have failed. He added quiet wisdom to his confidence and won the hearts of everyone he met—Potiphar, the chief jailer, other prisoners, the king, and after many years, even those ten brothers.

Perhaps you can identify with one or more of these hardships Joseph experienced: He was betrayed and deserted by his family, exposed to sexual temptation, and punished for doing the right thing; he endured a long imprisonment and was forgotten by those he helped. As you read his story, note what Joseph did in each case. His positive response transformed each setback into a step forward. He didn't spend much time asking why. His approach was "What shall I do now?" Those who met Joseph were aware that wherever he went and whatever he did, God was with him. When you're facing a setback, the beginning of a Joseph-like attitude is to acknowledge that God is with you. There is nothing like his presence to shed new light on a dark situation.

Strengths and accomplishments
- Rose in power from slave to ruler of Egypt
- Was known for his personal integrity
- Was a man of spiritual sensitivity
- Prepared a nation to survive a famine

Weakness and mistake
- His youthful pride caused friction with his brothers

Lessons from his life
- What matters is not so much the events or circumstances of life, but your response to them
- With God's help, any situation can be used for good, even when others intend it for evil

Vital statistics
- Where: Canaan, Egypt
- Occupation: Shepherd, slave, convict, ruler
- Relatives: Parents: Jacob and Rachel. Eleven brothers and one sister. Wife: Asenath. Sons: Manasseh and Ephraim

Key verse
"As they discussed who should be appointed for the job, Pharaoh said, 'Who could do it better than Joseph? For he is a man who is obviously filled with the spirit of God' " (Genesis 41:38).

Joseph's story is told in Genesis 30—50. He is also mentioned in Hebrews 11:22.

Rulers of Edom

31 These are the kings who ruled in Edom before there were kings in Israel*:

32 Bela son of Beor, who ruled from his city of Dinhabah.
33 When Bela died, Jobab son of Zerah from Bozrah became king.
34 When Jobab died, Husham from the land of the Temanites became king.
35 When Husham died, Hadad son of Bedad became king and ruled from the city of Avith. He was the one who destroyed the Midianite army in the land of Moab.
36 When Hadad died, Samlah from the city of Masrekah became king.
37 When Samlah died, Shaul from the city of Rehoboth on the Euphrates River* became king.
38 When Shaul died, Baal-hanan son of Acbor became king.
39 When Baal-hanan died, Hadad* became king and ruled from the city of Pau. Hadad's wife was Mehetabel, the daughter of Matred and granddaughter of Mezahab.

40 These are the leaders of the clans of Esau, who lived in the places named for them:
Timna, Alvah, Jetheth, 41 Oholibamah, Elah, Pinon, 42 Kenaz, Teman, Mibzar, 43 Magdiel,
and Iram. These are the names of the clans of Esau, the ancestor of the Edomites, each
clan giving its name to the area it occupied.

36:31-43 //1 Chr 1:43-54

G. THE STORY OF JOSEPH (37:1—50:26)

Joseph, one of Jacob's 12 sons, was obviously the favorite. Hated by his brothers for this, Joseph was sold to slave traders only to emerge as ruler of all Egypt. Through Joseph, we learn how suffering, no matter how unfair, develops strong character and deep wisdom.

1. Joseph is sold into slavery

Joseph's Dreams

37 So Jacob settled again in the land of Canaan, where his father had lived. 2 This is
the history of Jacob's family.
When Joseph was seventeen years old, he often tended his father's flocks with his half
brothers, the sons of his father's wives Bilhah and Zilpah. But Joseph reported to his
father some of the bad things his brothers were doing. 3 Now Jacob* loved Joseph more
than any of his other children because Joseph had been born to him in his old age. So
one day he gave Joseph a special gift—a beautiful robe.* 4 But his brothers hated Joseph
because of their father's partiality. They couldn't say a kind word to him.
5 One night Joseph had a dream and promptly reported the details to his brothers,
causing them to hate him even more. 6 "Listen to this dream," he announced. 7 "We were
out in the field tying up bundles of grain. My bundle stood up, and then your bundles all
gathered around and bowed low before it!"
8 "So you are going to be our king, are you?" his brothers taunted. And they hated him
all the more for his dream and what he had said.
9 Then Joseph had another dream and told his brothers about it. "Listen to this dream,"
he said. "The sun, moon, and eleven stars bowed low before me!"
10 This time he told his father as well as his brothers, and his father rebuked him.
"What do you mean?" his father asked. "Will your mother, your brothers, and I actually

37:1 Gen 17:8; 28:4
37:2 Gen 35:22-26; 41:46
37:3 Gen 37:23, 32; 44:20
37:4 Gen 27:41
37:5 Gen 28:12; Num 12:6; Dan 2:1
37:7 Gen 42:6, 9; 43:26
37:8 Deut 33:16
37:10 Gen 27:29

36:31 Or *before an Israelite king ruled over them.* **36:37** Hebrew *the river.* **36:39** As in some Hebrew manuscripts, Samaritan Pentateuch, and Syriac version (see also 1 Chr 1:50); most Hebrew manuscripts read *Hadar.* **37:3a** Hebrew *Israel;* also in 37:13. **37:3b** Traditionally rendered *a coat of many colors.* The exact meaning of the Hebrew is uncertain.

37:3 In Joseph's day, everyone had a robe or cloak. Robes were used to warm oneself, to bundle up belongings for a trip, to wrap babies, to sit on, or even to serve as security for a loan. Most robes were knee length, short sleeved, and plain. In contrast, Joseph's robe was probably of the kind worn by royalty—long sleeved, ankle length, and colorful. The robe became a symbol of Jacob's favoritism toward Joseph, and it aggravated the already strained relations between Joseph and his brothers. Favoritism in families may be unavoidable, but its divisive effects should be minimized. Parents may not be able to change their feelings toward a favorite child, but they can change their actions toward the others.

37:6-11 Joseph's brothers were already angry over the possibility of being ruled by their little brother. Joseph then fueled the fire with his immature attitude and boastful manner. No one enjoys a braggart. Joseph learned his lesson the hard way. His angry brothers sold him into slavery to get rid of him. After several years of hardship, Joseph learned an important lesson: Because our talents and knowledge come from God, it is more appropriate to thank him for them than to brag about them. Later Joseph gives God the credit (41:16).

37:11 Luke 2:19, 51 Acts 7:9
come and bow before you?" 11 But while his brothers were jealous of Joseph, his father
gave it some thought and wondered what it all meant.

12 Soon after this, Joseph's brothers went to pasture their father's flocks at Shechem.

37:13 Gen 33:19
13 When they had been gone for some time, Jacob said to Joseph, "Your brothers are over
at Shechem with the flocks. I'm going to send you to them."

"I'm ready to go," Joseph replied.

37:14 Gen 35:27
14 "Go and see how your brothers and the flocks are getting along," Jacob said. "Then
come back and bring me word." So Jacob sent him on his way, and Joseph traveled to
Shechem from his home in the valley of Hebron.

15 When he arrived there, a man noticed him wandering around the countryside. "What
are you looking for?" he asked.

16 "For my brothers and their flocks," Joseph replied. "Have you seen them?"

37:17 2 Kgs 6:13
17 "Yes," the man told him, "but they are no longer here. I heard your brothers say
they were going to Dothan." So Joseph followed his brothers to Dothan and found them
there.

Joseph Sold into Slavery

37:20 Gen 37:33
18 When Joseph's brothers saw him coming, they recognized him in the distance and

37:21 Gen 42:22
made plans to kill him. 19 "Here comes that dreamer!" they exclaimed. 20 "Come on, let's
kill him and throw him into a deep pit. We can tell our father that a wild animal has eaten

37:22 Gen 37:29
him. Then we'll see what becomes of all his dreams!"

21 But Reuben came to Joseph's rescue. "Let's not kill him," he said. 22 "Why should

REUBEN

Parents are usually the best judges of their children's character. Jacob summarized the personality of his son Reuben by comparing him to water. Except when frozen, water has no stable shape of its own. It always shapes itself to its container or environment. Reuben usually had good intentions, but he seemed unable to stand against a crowd. His instability made him hard to trust. He had both private and public values, but these contradicted each other. He went along with his brothers in their action against Joseph while hoping to counteract the evil in private. The plan failed. Compromise has a way of destroying convictions. Without convictions, lack of direction will destroy life. Reuben's sleeping with one of his father's wives showed how little he had left of the integrity he had displayed earlier in life.

How consistent are your public and private lives? We may want to think they are separate, but we can't deny that they affect each other. What convictions are present in your life at all times? How closely does Jacob's description of his son—"unruly as the waves of the sea"—describe your life?

Strengths and accomplishments
- Saved Joseph's life by talking the other brothers out of murder
- Showed intense love for his father by offering his own sons as a guarantee that Benjamin's life would be safe

Weaknesses and mistakes
- Gave in quickly to group pressure
- Did not directly protect Joseph from his brothers, although as oldest son he had the authority to do so
- Slept with one of his father's wives

Lessons from his life
- Public and private integrity must be the same, or one will destroy the other
- Punishment for sin may not be immediate, but it is certain

Vital statistics
- Where: Canaan, Egypt
- Occupation: Shepherd
- Relatives: Parents: Jacob and Leah. Eleven brothers, one sister

Key verses
"Reuben, you are my oldest son, the child of my vigorous youth. You are first on the list in rank and honor. But you are as unruly as the waves of the sea, and you will be first no longer. For you slept with one of my wives; you dishonored me in my own bed" (Genesis 49:3, 4).

Reuben's story is told in Genesis 29—50.

37:19, 20 Could jealousy ever make you feel like killing someone? Before saying, "Of course not," look at what happened in this story. Ten men were willing to kill their younger brother over a robe and a few reported dreams. Their deep jealousy had grown into ugly rage, completely blinding them to what was right. Jealousy can be difficult to recognize because our reasons for it seem to make sense. But left unchecked, jealousy grows quickly and leads to serious sins. The longer you cultivate jealous feelings, the harder it is to uproot them. The time to deal with jealousy is when you notice yourself keeping score of what others have.

we shed his blood? Let's just throw him alive into this pit here. That way he will die
without our having to touch him." Reuben was secretly planning to help Joseph escape,
and then he would bring him back to his father.
23 So when Joseph arrived, they pulled off his beautiful robe 24 and threw him into the
pit. This pit was normally used to store water, but it was empty at the time. 25 Then, just
as they were sitting down to eat, they noticed a caravan of camels in the distance coming
toward them. It was a group of Ishmaelite traders taking spices, balm, and myrrh from
Gilead to Egypt.
26 Judah said to the others, "What can we gain by killing our brother? That would
just give us a guilty conscience. 27 Let's sell Joseph to those Ishmaelite traders.
Let's not be responsible for his death; after all, he is our brother!" And his brothers
agreed. 28 So when the traders* came by, his brothers pulled Joseph out of the pit and
sold him for twenty pieces* of silver, and the Ishmaelite traders took him along to
Egypt.
29 Some time later, Reuben returned to get Joseph out of the pit. When he
discovered that Joseph was missing, he tore his clothes in anguish and frustration.
30 Then he went back to his brothers and lamented, "The boy is gone! What can I
do now?"
31 Then Joseph's brothers killed a goat and dipped the robe in its blood. 32 They took
the beautiful robe to their father and asked him to identify it. "We found this in the field,"
they told him. "It's Joseph's robe, isn't it?"
33 Their father recognized it at once. "Yes," he said, "it is my son's robe. A wild animal
has attacked and eaten him. Surely Joseph has been torn in pieces!" 34 Then Jacob tore
his clothes and put on sackcloth. He mourned deeply for his son for many days. 35 His
family all tried to comfort him, but it was no use. "I will die in mourning for my son,"
he would say, and then begin to weep.
36 Meanwhile, in Egypt, the traders sold Joseph to Potiphar, an officer of Pharaoh, the
king of Egypt. Potiphar was captain of the palace guard.

37:23 Gen 37:3
37:24 Jer 38:6; 41:7
37:25 Gen 31:21; 37:28; Jer 8:22; 46:11
37:28 Gen 39:1; 45:4-5; Lev 27:5; Judg 8:22-24; Acts 7:9
37:29 Gen 37:34; 44:13; Num 14:6
37:30 Gen 42:13, 36
37:32 Luke 15:30
37:33 Gen 37:20; 44:28
37:34 Gen 37:29
37:35 Gen 44:29; 2 Sam 12:17; Ps 77:2
37:36 Gen 39:1; 40:3

37:28a Hebrew *Midianites;* also in 37:36. **37:28b** Hebrew *20 shekels,* about 8 ounces or 228 grams in weight.

37:26, 27 The brothers were worried about bearing the guilt of Joseph's death. Judah suggested an option that was not right but would leave them guiltless of murder. Sometimes we jump at a solution because it is the lesser of two evils, but it still is not the right action to take. When someone proposes a seemingly workable solution, first ask, "Is it right?"

37:28 Although Joseph's brothers didn't kill him outright, they wouldn't expect him to survive for long as a slave. They were quite willing to let cruel slave traders do their dirty work for them. Joseph faced a 30-day journey through the desert, probably chained and on foot. He would be treated like baggage and, once in Egypt, would be sold as a piece of merchandise. His brothers thought they would never see him again. But God was in control of Joseph's life.

37:29, 30 Reuben returned to the pit to find Joseph, but his little brother was gone. His first response, in effect, was "What is going to happen to me?" rather than "What is going to happen to Joseph?" In a tough situation, are you usually concerned first about yourself? Consider the person most affected by the problem, and you will be more likely to find a solution for it.

37:31-35 To cover their evil action, Jacob's sons deceived their father into thinking Joseph was dead. Jacob himself had deceived others many times (including his own father; 27:35). Now, though blessed by God, he still had to face the consequences of his sins. God may not have punished Jacob immediately for his deceit, but the consequences came nevertheless and stayed with him for the rest of his life.

37:34 Tearing one's clothes and wearing sackcloth were signs of mourning, much like wearing black today.

37:36 Imagine the culture shock Joseph experienced upon arriving in Egypt. Joseph had lived as a nomad, traveling the countryside with his family, caring for sheep. Suddenly he was thrust into the world's most advanced civilization with great pyramids, beautiful homes, sophisticated people, and a new language. While Joseph saw Egypt's skill and intelligence at their best, he also saw the Egyptians' spiritual blindness. They worshiped countless gods related to every aspect of life.

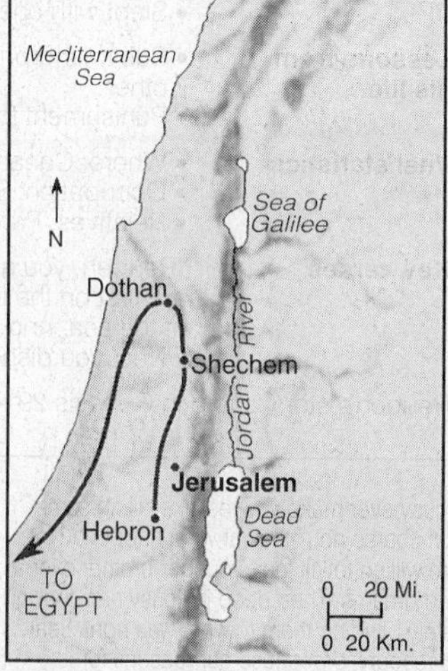

JOSEPH GOES TO MEET HIS BROTHERS
Jacob asked Joseph to go find his brothers, who were grazing their flocks near Shechem. When Joseph arrived, he learned that his brothers had gone on to Dothan, which lay along a major trade route to Egypt. There the jealous brothers sold Joseph as a slave to a group of Ishmaelite traders on their way to Egypt.

2. Judah and Tamar

38 About this time, Judah left home and moved to Adullam, where he visited a man named Hirah. 2 There he met a Canaanite woman, the daughter of Shua, and he married her. 3 She became pregnant and had a son, and Judah named the boy Er. 4 Then Judah's wife had another son, and she named him Onan. 5 And when she had a third son, she named him Shelah. At the time of Shelah's birth, they were living at Kezib.

6 When his oldest son, Er, grew up, Judah arranged his marriage to a young woman named Tamar. 7 But Er was a wicked man in the LORD's sight, so the LORD took his life. 8 Then Judah said to Er's brother Onan, "You must marry Tamar, as our law requires of the brother of a man who has died. Her first son from you will be your brother's heir." 9 But Onan was not willing to have a child who would not be his own heir. So whenever he had intercourse with Tamar, he spilled the semen on the ground to keep her from having a baby who would belong to his brother. 10 But the LORD considered it a wicked thing for Onan to deny a child to his dead brother. So the LORD took Onan's life, too.

11 Then Judah told Tamar, his daughter-in-law, not to marry again at that time but to return to her parents' home. She was to remain a widow until his youngest son, Shelah, was old enough to marry her. (But Judah didn't really intend to do this because he was afraid Shelah would also die, like his two brothers.) So Tamar went home to her parents.

12 In the course of time Judah's wife died. After the time of mourning was over, Judah and his friend Hirah the Adullamite went to Timnah to supervise the shearing of his sheep. 13 Someone told Tamar that her father-in-law had left for the sheep-shearing at Timnah. 14 Tamar was aware that Shelah had grown up, but they had not called her to come and marry him. So she changed out of her widow's clothing and covered herself with a veil to disguise herself. Then she sat beside the road at the entrance to the village of Enaim, which is on the way to Timnah. 15 Judah noticed her as he went by and thought she was a prostitute, since her face was veiled. 16 So he stopped and propositioned her to sleep with him, not realizing that she was his own daughter-in-law.

"How much will you pay me?" Tamar asked.

17 "I'll send you a young goat from my flock," Judah promised.

38:1 Josh 15:35; 1 Sam 22:1
38:2 Gen 24:3; 34:2; 38:12
38:3 Gen 46:12; Num 26:19
38:6 Matt 1:3
38:7 Gen 6:5; 13:13; 19:13; 38:10; 1 Chr 2:3
38:8 Lev 18:15; Num 36:8; Deut 25:5-10; †Mark 12:19; Matt 22:24
38:11 Ruth 1:13
38:12 Gen 31:19; Josh 15:10, 57
38:14 Josh 15:34
38:16 2 Sam 13:11
38:17 Gen 38:20

WOMEN IN JESUS' FAMILY TREE

Tamar	Canaanite	Genesis 38:1–30
Rahab	Canaanite	Joshua 6:22–25
Ruth	Moabite	Ruth 4:13–22
Bathsheba	Israelite	2 Samuel 12:24, 25

38:1ff This chapter vividly contrasts the immoral character of Judah with the moral character of Joseph. Judah's lack of integrity resulted in family strife and deception. In chapter 39, we see how Joseph's integrity and wise choices reflect his godly character. His faithfulness was rewarded with blessings greater than he could imagine, both for himself and for his family.

38:8-10 This law about marrying a widow in the family is explained in Deuteronomy 25:5-10. Its purpose was to ensure that a childless widow would have a son who would receive her late husband's inheritance and who, in turn, would care for her. Because Judah's son (Tamar's husband) had no children, there was no family line through which the inheritance and the blessing of the covenant could continue. God killed Onan because he refused to fulfill his obligation to his brother and to Tamar.

38:15-23 Why does this story seem to take a light view of prostitution? Prostitutes were common in pagan cultures such as Canaan. Public prostitutes served Canaanite goddesses and were common elements of the religious cults. Fornication was encouraged to improve fertility in crops and flocks. They were more highly respected than private prostitutes, who were sometimes punished when caught. Tamar was driven to seduce Judah because of her intense desire to have children and be the matriarch of Judah's line; Judah was driven by his lust. Neither case was justified.

38:15-24 Why was Judah so open about his relations with a prostitute, yet ready to execute his daughter-in-law for being one? To understand this apparent contradiction, we must understand the place of women in Canaan. A woman's most important function was bearing children, who would perpetuate the family line. To ensure that children belonged to the husband, the bride was expected to be a virgin, and the wife was expected to have relations only with him. If a wife committed adultery, she could be executed. Some women, however, did not belong to families. They might be shrine prostitutes supported by offerings or common prostitutes supported by the men who used their services. Their children were nobody's heirs, and men who hired them adulterated nobody's bloodlines.

Judah saw no harm in hiring a prostitute for a night; after all, he was more than willing to pay. He was ready to execute Tamar, however, because if she was pregnant as a result of prostitution, his grandchild would not be part of his family line. Apparently the question of sexual morality never entered Judah's mind; his concern was for keeping his inheritance in the family. Ironically, it was Tamar, not Judah, who acted to provide him with legal heirs. By seducing him, she acted more in the spirit of the law than he did when he refused to send his third son to her.

This story in no way implies that God winks at prostitution. Throughout Scripture, prostitution is condemned as a serious sin. If the story has a moral, it is that faithfulness to family obligations is important. Incidentally, Judah and Tamar are direct ancestors of Jesus Christ (see Matthew 1:1-6).

“What pledge will you give me so I can be sure you will send it?” she asked.
[18]“Well, what do you want?” he inquired. 38:18
She replied, “I want your identification seal, your cord, and the walking stick you are Gen 41:42 Hos 4:11
carrying.” So Judah gave these items to her. She then let him sleep with her, and she
became pregnant. [19]Afterward she went home, took off her veil, and put on her widow’s
clothing as usual.
[20]Judah asked his friend Hirah the Adullamite to take the young goat back to her and
to pick up the pledges he had given her, but Hirah couldn’t find her. [21]So he asked the
men who lived there, “Where can I find the prostitute* who was sitting beside the road
at the entrance to the village?”
“We’ve never had a prostitute here,” they replied. [22]So Hirah returned to Judah and
told him that he couldn’t find her anywhere and that the men of the village had claimed
they didn’t have a prostitute there.
[23]“Then let her keep the pledges!” Judah exclaimed. “We tried our best to send her
the goat. We’d be the laughingstock of the village if we went back again.”
[24]About three months later, word reached Judah that Tamar, his daughter-in-law, was 38:24
pregnant as a result of prostitution. “Bring her out and burn her!” Judah shouted. Lev 20:10; 21:9
[25]But as they were taking her out to kill her, she sent this message to her father-in-law:
“The man who owns this identification seal and walking stick is the father of my child.
Do you recognize them?”
[26]Judah admitted that they were his and said, “She is more in the right than I am, 38:26
because I didn’t keep my promise to let her marry my son Shelah.” But Judah never slept 1 Sam 24:17
with Tamar again.
[27]In due season the time of Tamar’s delivery arrived, and she had twin sons. [28]As they 38:27
were being born, one of them reached out his hand, and the midwife tied a scarlet thread Gen 25:24
around the wrist of the child who appeared first, saying, “This one came out first.” [29]But 38:29
then he drew back his hand, and the other baby was actually the first to be born. “What!” Gen 46:12 Num 26:20-21
the midwife exclaimed. “How did you break out first?” And ever after, he was called Ruth 4:12
Perez.* [30]Then the baby with the scarlet thread on his wrist was born, and he was named 1 Chr 2:4 Matt 1:3
Zerah.* Luke 3:33

3. Joseph is thrown into prison

Joseph in Potiphar’s House

39 Now when Joseph arrived in Egypt with the Ishmaelite traders, he was purchased 39:1
by Potiphar, a member of the personal staff of Pharaoh, the king of Egypt. Gen 37:25
Potiphar was the captain of the palace guard.
[2]The LORD was with Joseph and blessed him greatly as he served in the home of his 39:2
Egyptian master. [3]Potiphar noticed this and realized that the LORD was with Joseph, Acts 7:9
giving him success in everything he did. [4]So Joseph naturally became quite a favorite 39:4 Gen 40:4 Prov 22:29

38:21 Hebrew *shrine prostitute;* also in 38:21b, 22. **38:29** *Perez* means “breaking out.” **38:30** *Zerah* means “scarlet” or “brightness.”

38:18 A seal was a form of identification used to authenticate legal documents. Usually a unique design carved in stone and worn on a ring or necklace inseparable from its owner, the seal was used by the wealthy and powerful to mark clay or wax. Because Tamar had Judah’s seal, she could prove beyond a doubt that he had been with her.

38:24-26 When Tamar revealed she was pregnant, Judah, who unknowingly had gotten her pregnant, moved to have her killed. Judah had concealed his own sin, yet he came down harshly on Tamar. Often the sins we try to cover up are the ones that anger us most when we see them in others. If you become indignant at the sins of others, you may have a similar tendency to sin that you don’t wish to face. When we admit our sins and ask God to forgive us, forgiving others becomes easier.

39:1 The date of Joseph’s arrival in Egypt is debatable. Many believe he arrived during the period of the Hyksos rulers, foreigners who came from the region of Canaan. They invaded Egypt and controlled the land for almost 150 years. If Joseph arrived during their rule, it is easy to see why he was rapidly promoted up the royal ladder. Because the Hyksos were foreigners themselves, they would not hold this brilliant young foreigner’s ancestry against him.

39:1 *Pharaoh* was the general name for all the kings of Egypt. It was a title like “king” or “president” used to address the country’s leader. The pharaohs in Genesis and Exodus were different men.

39:1 Ancient Egypt was a land of great contrasts. People were either rich beyond measure or poverty stricken. There wasn’t much middle ground. Joseph found himself serving Potiphar, an extremely rich officer in Pharaoh’s service. Rich families like Potiphar’s had elaborate homes two or three stories tall with beautiful gardens and balconies. They enjoyed live entertainment at home as they chose delicious fruit from expensive bowls. They surrounded themselves with alabaster vases, paintings, beautiful rugs, and hand-carved chairs. Dinner was served on golden tableware, and the rooms were lighted with gold lampstands. Servants, like Joseph, worked on the first floor, while the family occupied the upper stories.

39:5 Deut 28:3-4, 11
39:6 Gen 29:17; 1 Sam 16:12, 18; Acts 7:20
39:7 Prov 7:15-20
39:8 Gen 39:5; Prov 6:23-24
39:9 2 Sam 12:13
39:10 1 Thes 5:22
39:12 Prov 7:13; 2 Tim 2:22
39:17 Exod 20:16; 23:1; Pss 37:14; 55:3
39:20 Gen 40:1-3, 15; 41:10; Ps 105:18
39:21 Ps 105:19; Acts 7:9
39:23 Gen 39:3
40:1 Neh 1:11
40:4 Gen 37:36; 39:1
40:5 Gen 20:3; 41:11

with him. Potiphar soon put Joseph in charge of his entire household and entrusted him
with all his business dealings. [5]From the day Joseph was put in charge, the LORD began
to bless Potiphar for Joseph's sake. All his household affairs began to run smoothly, and
his crops and livestock flourished. [6]So Potiphar gave Joseph complete administrative
responsibility over everything he owned. With Joseph there, he didn't have a worry in
the world, except to decide what he wanted to eat!

Now Joseph was a very handsome and well-built young man. [7]And about this time,
Potiphar's wife began to desire him and invited him to sleep with her. [8]But Joseph
refused. "Look," he told her, "my master trusts me with everything in his entire
household. [9]No one here has more authority than I do! He has held back nothing from
me except you, because you are his wife. How could I ever do such a wicked thing? It
would be a great sin against God."

[10]She kept putting pressure on him day after day, but he refused to sleep with her, and
he kept out of her way as much as possible. [11]One day, however, no one else was around
when he was doing his work inside the house. [12]She came and grabbed him by his shirt,
demanding, "Sleep with me!" Joseph tore himself away, but as he did, his shirt came off.
She was left holding it as he ran from the house.

[13]When she saw that she had his shirt and that he had fled, [14]she began screaming.
Soon all the men around the place came running. "My husband has brought this Hebrew
slave here to insult us!" she sobbed. "He tried to rape me, but I screamed. [15]When he
heard my loud cries, he ran and left his shirt behind with me."

[16]She kept the shirt with her, and when her husband came home that night, [17]she told
him her story. "That Hebrew slave you've had around here tried to make a fool of me,"
she said. [18]"I was saved only by my screams. He ran out, leaving his shirt behind!"

Joseph Put in Prison

[19]After hearing his wife's story, Potiphar was furious! [20]He took Joseph and threw him
into the prison where the king's prisoners were held. [21]But the LORD was with Joseph
there, too, and he granted Joseph favor with the chief jailer. [22]Before long, the jailer put
Joseph in charge of all the other prisoners and over everything that happened in the
prison. [23]The chief jailer had no more worries after that, because Joseph took care of
everything. The LORD was with him, making everything run smoothly and successfully.

Joseph Interprets Two Dreams

40 Some time later, Pharaoh's chief cup-bearer and chief baker offended him.
[2]Pharaoh became very angry with these officials, [3]and he put them in the prison
where Joseph was, in the palace of Potiphar, the captain of the guard. [4]They remained
in prison for quite some time, and Potiphar assigned Joseph to take care of them.

[5]One night the cup-bearer and the baker each had a dream, and each dream had its
own meaning. [6]The next morning Joseph noticed the dejected look on their faces.
[7]"Why do you look so worried today?" he asked.

39:9 Potiphar's wife failed to seduce Joseph, who resisted this temptation by saying it would be a sin against God. Joseph didn't say, "I'd be hurting you," or "I'd be sinning against Potiphar," or "I'd be sinning against myself." Under pressure, such excuses are easily rationalized away. Remember that sexual sin is not just between two consenting adults. It is an act of disobedience against God.

39:10-15 Joseph avoided Potiphar's wife as much as possible. He refused her advances and finally *ran* from her. Sometimes merely trying to avoid temptation is not enough. We must turn and run, especially when the temptations seem very strong, as is often the case in sexual temptations.

39:20 Prisons were grim places with vile conditions. They were used to house forced laborers or, like Joseph, the accused who were awaiting trial. Prisoners were guilty until proven innocent, and there was no right to a speedy trial. Many prisoners never made it to court, because trials were held at the whim of the ruler. Joseph was in prison two years until he appeared before Pharaoh, and then he was called out to interpret a dream, not to stand trial.

39:21-23 As a prisoner and slave, Joseph could have seen his situation as hopeless. Instead, he did his best with each small task given him. His diligence and positive attitude were soon noticed by the warden, who promoted him to prison administrator. Are you facing a seemingly hopeless predicament? At work, at home, or at school, follow Joseph's example by taking each small task and doing your best. Remember how God turned Joseph's situation around. He will see your efforts and can reverse even overwhelming odds.

40:1-3 The cup-bearer and the chief baker were two of the most trusted men in Pharaoh's kingdom. The baker was in charge of making the Pharaoh's food, and the cup-bearer tasted all of his food and drink before giving it to him, in case any of it was contaminated or poisoned. These trusted men must have been suspected of a serious wrong, perhaps of conspiring against Pharaoh. Later the cup-bearer was released and the baker executed.

8 And they replied, "We both had dreams last night, but there is no one here to tell us
what they mean."
"Interpreting dreams is God's business," Joseph replied. "Tell me what you saw."
9 The cup-bearer told his dream first. "In my dream," he said, "I saw a vine in front of
me. 10 It had three branches that began to bud and blossom, and soon there were clusters
of ripe grapes. 11 I was holding Pharaoh's wine cup in my hand, so I took the grapes and
squeezed the juice into it. Then I placed the cup in Pharaoh's hand."
12 "I know what the dream means," Joseph said. "The three branches mean three days.
13 Within three days Pharaoh will take you out of prison and return you to your position
as his chief cup-bearer. 14 And please have some pity on me when you are back in his
favor. Mention me to Pharaoh, and ask him to let me out of here. 15 For I was kidnapped
from my homeland, the land of the Hebrews, and now I'm here in jail, but I did nothing
to deserve it."
16 When the chief baker saw that the first dream had such a good meaning, he told his
dream to Joseph, too. "In my dream," he said, "there were three baskets of pastries on
my head. 17 In the top basket were all kinds of bakery goods for Pharaoh, but the birds
came and ate them."
18 "I'll tell you what it means," Joseph told him. "The three baskets mean three days.
19 Three days from now Pharaoh will cut off your head and impale your body on a pole.
Then birds will come and peck away at your flesh."
20 Pharaoh's birthday came three days later, and he gave a banquet for all his officials
and household staff. He sent for his chief cup-bearer and chief baker, and they were
brought to him from the prison. 21 He then restored the chief cup-bearer to his former
position, 22 but he sentenced the chief baker to be impaled on a pole, just as Joseph had
predicted. 23 Pharaoh's cup-bearer, however, promptly forgot all about Joseph, never
giving him another thought.

40:8 Gen 41:15-16; Dan 2:27-28
40:12 Gen 41:12
40:13 Gen 40:19-20
40:14 1 Sam 20:14
40:15 Gen 37:26-28; 39:20
40:18 Gen 40:12
40:19 Deut 21:22-23
40:20 2 Kgs 25:27; Jer 52:31
40:22 Gen 40:19
40:23 Gen 40:14

4. Joseph is placed in charge of Egypt

Pharaoh's Dreams

41 Two years later, Pharaoh dreamed that he was standing on the bank of the Nile
River. 2 In his dream, seven fat, healthy-looking cows suddenly came up out of the
river and began grazing along its bank. 3 Then seven other cows came up from the river,
but these were very ugly and gaunt. These cows went over and stood beside the fat cows.
4 Then the thin, ugly cows ate the fat ones! At this point in the dream, Pharaoh woke up.
5 Soon he fell asleep again and had a second dream. This time he saw seven heads of
grain on one stalk, with every kernel well formed and plump. 6 Then suddenly, seven
more heads appeared on the stalk, but these were shriveled and withered by the east wind.
7 And these thin heads swallowed up the seven plump, well-formed heads! Then Pharaoh
woke up again and realized it was a dream.
8 The next morning, as he thought about it, Pharaoh became very concerned as to what
the dreams might mean. So he called for all the magicians and wise men of Egypt and
told them about his dreams, but not one of them could suggest what they meant. 9 Then
the king's cup-bearer spoke up. "Today I have been reminded of my failure," he said.
10 "Some time ago, you were angry with the chief baker and me, and you imprisoned us
in the palace of the captain of the guard. 11 One night the chief baker and I each had a
dream, and each dream had a meaning. 12 We told the dreams to a young Hebrew man
who was a servant of the captain of the guard. He told us what each of our dreams meant,

41:2 Job 8:11; Isa 19:6-7
41:5 2 Kgs 4:42
41:6 Ezek 19:12
41:8 Exod 7:11-12; Dan 2:1-3; 4:5
41:9 Gen 40:14
41:10 Gen 40:2
41:11 Gen 40:5
41:12 Gen 40:12

40:8 When the subject of dreams came up, Joseph focused everyone's attention on God. Rather than using the situation to make himself look good, he turned it into a powerful witness for the Lord. One secret of effective witnessing is to recognize opportunities to relate God to the other person's experience. When the opportunity arises, we must have the courage to speak, as Joseph did.

40:23 When Pharaoh's cup-bearer was freed from prison, he forgot about Joseph, even though he had Joseph to thank for his freedom. It was two full years before Joseph had another opportunity to be freed (41:1). Yet Joseph's faith was deep, and he would be ready when the next chance came. When we feel passed by, overlooked, or forgotten, we shouldn't be surprised that people are often ungrateful. In similar situations, trust God as Joseph did. More opportunities may be waiting.

41:8 Magicians and wise men were common in the palaces of ancient rulers. Their job description included studying sacred arts and sciences, reading the stars, interpreting dreams, predicting the future, and performing magic. These men had power (see Exodus 7:11, 12), but their power was satanic. They were unable to interpret Pharaoh's dream, but God had revealed it to Joseph in prison.

41:13 Gen 40:22 13 and everything happened just as he said it would. I was restored to my position as
cup-bearer, and the chief baker was executed and impaled on a pole."
41:14 Ps 105:20 14 Pharaoh sent for Joseph at once, and he was brought hastily from the dungeon. After
41:15 Dan 2:25 a quick shave and change of clothes, he went in and stood in Pharaoh's presence. 15 "I had
a dream last night," Pharaoh told him, "and none of these men can tell me what it means.
But I have heard that you can interpret dreams, and that is why I have called for you."
41:16 Gen 40:8 16 "It is beyond my power to do this," Joseph replied. "But God will tell you what it
means and will set you at ease."
41:17 Gen 41:1 17 So Pharaoh told him the dream. "I was standing on the bank of the Nile River," he
said. 18 "Suddenly, seven fat, healthy-looking cows came up out of the river and began
grazing along its bank. 19 But then seven other cows came up from the river. They were
very thin and gaunt—in fact, I've never seen such ugly animals in all the land of Egypt.
20 These thin, ugly cows ate up the seven fat ones that had come out of the river first,
21 but afterward they were still as ugly and gaunt as before! Then I woke up.
22 "A little later I had another dream. This time there were seven heads of grain on one
stalk, and all seven heads were plump and full. 23 Then out of the same stalk came seven
withered heads, shriveled by the east wind. 24 And the withered heads swallowed up the
plump ones! I told these dreams to my magicians, but not one of them could tell me what
they mean."
25 "Both dreams mean the same thing," Joseph told Pharaoh. "God was telling you
what he is about to do. 26 The seven fat cows and the seven plump heads of grain both
41:27 2 Kgs 8:1 represent seven years of prosperity. 27 The seven thin, ugly cows and the seven withered
heads of grain represent seven years of famine. 28 This will happen just as I have
41:29 Gen 41:47 described it, for God has shown you what he is about to do. 29 The next seven years will
41:30 Gen 47:13 be a period of great prosperity throughout the land of Egypt. 30 But afterward there will
be seven years of famine so great that all the prosperity will be forgotten and wiped out.
Famine will destroy the land. 31 This famine will be so terrible that even the memory of
the good years will be erased. 32 As for having the dream twice, it means that the matter
has been decreed by God and that he will make these events happen soon.
41:33 Gen 41:39 33 "My suggestion is that you find the wisest man in Egypt and put him in charge of a
nationwide program. 34 Let Pharaoh appoint officials over the land, and let them collect
41:34 Exod 18:19 one-fifth of all the crops during the seven good years. 35 Have them gather all the food
41:36 Gen 47:14 and grain of these good years into the royal storehouses, and store it away so there will
be food in the cities. 36 That way there will be enough to eat when the seven years of
famine come. Otherwise disaster will surely strike the land, and all the people will die."

Joseph Made Ruler of Egypt

41:38 Dan 4:8, 18; 5:11, 14 37 Joseph's suggestions were well received by Pharaoh and his advisers. 38 As they
discussed who should be appointed for the job, Pharaoh said, "Who could do it better
41:39 Gen 41:33 than Joseph? For he is a man who is obviously filled with the spirit of God." 39 Turning
41:40 Gen 39:9 to Joseph, Pharaoh said, "Since God has revealed the meaning of the dreams to you,
Acts 7:10 you are the wisest man in the land! 40 I hereby appoint you to direct this project. You

---

41:14 Our most important opportunities may come when we least expect them. Joseph was brought hastily from the dungeon and pushed before Pharaoh. Did he have time to prepare? Yes and no. He had no warning that he would be suddenly pulled from prison and questioned by the king. Yet Joseph was ready for almost anything because of his right relationship with God. It was not Joseph's knowledge of dreams that helped him interpret their meaning. It was his knowledge of God. Be ready for opportunities by getting to know more about God. Then you will be ready to call on him when opportunities come your way.

41:16 Joseph made sure that he gave the credit to God. We should be careful to do the same. To take the honor for ourselves is a form of stealing God's honor. Don't be silent when you know you should be giving glory and credit to God.

41:28-36 After interpreting Pharaoh's dream, Joseph gave the king a survival plan for the next 14 years. The only way to prevent starvation was through careful planning; without a famine plan Egypt would have turned from prosperity to ruin. Many find detailed planning boring and unnecessary. But planning is a responsibility, not an option. Joseph was able to save a nation by translating God's plan for Egypt into practical actions (implementation). We must take time to translate God's plan for us into practical actions, too.

41:38 Pharaoh recognized that Joseph was a man "filled with the spirit of God." You probably won't get to interpret dreams for a king, but those who know you should be able to see God in you, through your kind words, merciful acts, and wise advice. Do your relatives, neighbors, and co-workers see you as a person in whom the Spirit of God lives?

41:39, 40 Joseph rose quickly to the top, from prison walls to Pharaoh's palace. His training for this important position involved being first a slave and then a prisoner. In each situation he learned the importance of serving God and others. Whatever your situation, no matter how undesirable, consider it part of your training program for serving God.

will manage my household and organize all my people. Only I will have a rank higher
than yours."
41And Pharaoh said to Joseph, "I hereby put you in charge of the entire land of **41:41** Esth 8:2
Egypt." 42Then Pharaoh placed his own signet ring on Joseph's finger as a symbol of Dan 6:3
his authority. He dressed him in beautiful clothing and placed the royal gold chain **41:42**
about his neck. 43Pharaoh also gave Joseph the chariot of his second-in-command, Esth 3:10; 6:8
and wherever he went the command was shouted, "Kneel down!" So Joseph was put
in charge of all Egypt. 44And Pharaoh said to Joseph, "I am the king, but no one will **41:44** Gen 45:8
move a hand or a foot in the entire land of Egypt without your approval." Ps 105:22
45Pharaoh renamed him Zaphenath-paneah* and gave him a wife—a young woman **41:45**
named Asenath, the daughter of Potiphera, priest of Heliopolis.* So Joseph took charge Ezek 30:17
of the entire land of Egypt. 46He was thirty years old when he entered the service of **41:46**
Pharaoh, the king of Egypt. And when Joseph left Pharaoh's presence, he made a tour of Gen 37:2
inspection throughout the land.
47And sure enough, for the next seven years there were bumper crops everywhere.
48During those years, Joseph took a portion of all the crops grown in Egypt and stored
them for the government in nearby cities. 49After seven years, the granaries were filled
to overflowing. There was so much grain, like sand on the seashore, that the people could
not keep track of the amount.
50During this time, before the arrival of the first of the famine years, two sons were
born to Joseph and his wife, Asenath, the daughter of Potiphera, priest of Heliopolis. **41:51**
51Joseph named his older son Manasseh,* for he said, "God has made me forget all my Gen 48:1
troubles and the family of my father." 52Joseph named his second son Ephraim,* for he Deut 33:17
said, "God has made me fruitful in this land of my suffering." **41:52** Gen 17:6
53At last the seven years of plenty came to an end. 54Then the seven years of famine **41:54**
began, just as Joseph had predicted. There were crop failures in all the surrounding Gen 41:30 Ps 105:16
countries, too, but in Egypt there was plenty of grain in the storehouses. 55Throughout Acts 7:11
the land of Egypt the people began to starve. They pleaded with Pharaoh for food, and **41:55**
he told them, "Go to Joseph and do whatever he tells you." 56So with severe famine Gen 41:41
everywhere in the land, Joseph opened up the storehouses and sold grain to the
Egyptians. 57And people from surrounding lands also came to Egypt to buy grain from **41:57** Gen 42:5; 47:15
Joseph because the famine was severe throughout the world. Ps 105:16

5. Joseph and his brothers meet in Egypt

Joseph's Brothers Go to Egypt

42 When Jacob heard that there was grain available in Egypt, he said to his sons, **42:1** Acts 7:12
"Why are you standing around looking at one another? 2I have heard there is **42:2**
grain in Egypt. Go down and buy some for us before we all starve to death." 3So Gen 43:2, 4
Joseph's ten older brothers went down to Egypt to buy grain. 4Jacob wouldn't let **42:3** Gen 43:20
Joseph's younger brother, Benjamin, go with them, however, for fear some harm **42:4** Gen 35:24

41:45a *Zaphenath-paneah* probably means "God speaks and lives." **41:45b** Hebrew *of On;* also in 41:50.
41:51 *Manasseh* sounds like a Hebrew term that means "causing to forget." **41:52** *Ephraim* sounds like a Hebrew term that means "fruitful."

41:45 Pharaoh may have been trying to make Joseph more acceptable by giving him an Egyptian name and wife. He probably wanted to (1) play down the fact that Joseph was a nomadic shepherd, an occupation disliked by the Egyptians, (2) make Joseph's name easier for Egyptians to pronounce and remember, and (3) show how highly he was honored by giving him the daughter of a prominent Egyptian official.

41:46 Joseph was 30 years old when he became second-in-command in Egypt. He was 17 when he was sold into slavery by his brothers. Thus he must have spent 11 years as an Egyptian slave and two years in prison.

41:54 Famine was a catastrophe in ancient times, just as it still is in many parts of the world today. Almost perfect conditions were needed to produce good crops because there were no chemical fertilizers or pesticides. Any variances in rainfall or insect activity could cause crop failure and great hunger because the people relied almost exclusively on their own crops for food. Lack of storage, refrigeration, or transportation turned a moderate famine into a desperate situation. The famine Joseph prepared for was severe. Without God's intervention, the Egyptian nation would have crumbled.

42:1, 2 Why was grain so valuable in those days? As a food source it was universal and used in nearly everything eaten. It could be dried and stored much longer than any vegetables, milk products, or meat. It was so important that it was even used as money.

42:4 Jacob was especially fond of Benjamin because he was Joseph's only full brother and—as far as Jacob knew—the only surviving son of his beloved wife, Rachel. Benjamin was Jacob's youngest son and a child of his old age.

42:5 Gen 41:57; Acts 7:11
42:6 Ps 105:16-21
42:7 Gen 42:30
42:8 Gen 37:2
42:9 Gen 42:16, 30-34
42:10 Gen 37:6-9
42:11 Gen 42:19, 31-34
42:13 Gen 37:30-33; 44:20; 46:31
42:14 Gen 42:9
42:17 Gen 40:4
42:18 Gen 20:11; Lev 25:43
42:20 Gen 42:34; 43:15
42:21 Gen 37:23-28; 45:3-5
42:22 Gen 9:6; 37:21-22
42:24 Gen 43:14, 23
42:25 Gen 44:1
42:28 Gen 43:23

might come to him. 5 So Jacob's* sons arrived in Egypt along with others to buy food,
for the famine had reached Canaan as well.
6 Since Joseph was governor of all Egypt and in charge of the sale of the grain, it was
to him that his brothers came. They bowed low before him, with their faces to the ground.
7 Joseph recognized them instantly, but he pretended to be a stranger. "Where are you
from?" he demanded roughly.
"From the land of Canaan," they replied. "We have come to buy grain."
8 Joseph's brothers didn't recognize him, but Joseph recognized them. 9 And he remembered the dreams he had had many years before. He said to them, "You are spies! You have
come to see how vulnerable our land has become."
10 "No, my lord!" they exclaimed. "We have come to buy food. 11 We are all brothers
and honest men, sir! We are not spies!"
12 "Yes, you are!" he insisted. "You have come to discover how vulnerable the famine
has made us."
13 "Sir," they said, "there are twelve of us brothers, and our father is in the land of
Canaan. Our youngest brother is there with our father, and one of our brothers is no
longer with us."
14 But Joseph insisted, "As I said, you are spies! 15 This is how I will test your story. I
swear by the life of Pharaoh that you will not leave Egypt unless your youngest brother
comes here. 16 One of you go and get your brother! I'll keep the rest of you here, bound
in prison. Then we'll find out whether or not your story is true. If it turns out that you
don't have a younger brother, then I'll know you are spies."
17 So he put them all in prison for three days. 18 On the third day Joseph said to them,
"I am a God-fearing man. If you do as I say, you will live. 19 We'll see how honorable
you really are. Only one of you will remain in the prison. The rest of you may go on
home with grain for your families. 20 But bring your youngest brother back to me. In this
way, I will know whether or not you are telling me the truth. If you are, I will spare you."
To this they agreed.
21 Speaking among themselves, they said, "This has all happened because of what we
did to Joseph long ago. We saw his terror and anguish and heard his pleadings, but we
wouldn't listen. That's why this trouble has come upon us."
22 "Didn't I tell you not to do it?" Reuben asked. "But you wouldn't listen. And now
we are going to die because we murdered him."
23 Of course, they didn't know that Joseph understood them as he was standing there,
for he had been speaking to them through an interpreter. 24 Now he left the room and
found a place where he could weep. Returning, he talked some more with them. He then
chose Simeon from among them and had him tied up right before their eyes.
25 Joseph then ordered his servants to fill the men's sacks with grain, but he also gave
secret instructions to return each brother's payment at the top of his sack. He also gave
them provisions for their journey. 26 So they loaded up their donkeys with the grain and
started for home.
27 But when they stopped for the night and one of them opened his sack to get some
grain to feed the donkeys, he found his money in the sack. 28 "Look!" he exclaimed to
his brothers. "My money is here in my sack!" They were filled with terror and said to
each other, "What has God done to us?" 29 So they came to their father, Jacob, in the land
of Canaan and told him all that had happened.

42:5 Hebrew *Israel's.*

42:7 Joseph could have revealed his identity to his brothers at once. But Joseph's last memory of them was of staring in horror at their faces as slave traders carried him away. Were his brothers still evil and treacherous, or had they changed over the years? Joseph decided to put them through a few tests to find out.

42:8, 9 Joseph remembered his dreams about his brothers bowing down to him (37:6-9). Those dreams were coming true! As a young boy, Joseph was boastful about his dreams. As a man, he no longer flaunted his superior status. He did not feel the need to say, "I told you so." It was not yet time to reveal his identity, so he kept quiet. Sometimes it is best for us to remain quiet, even when we would like to have the last word.

42:15 Joseph was testing his brothers to make sure they had not been as cruel to Benjamin as they had been to him. Benjamin was his only full brother, and he wanted to see him face to face.

42:22 Reuben couldn't resist saying, "I told you so." He thought they were being punished by God for what they had done to Joseph. Selling Joseph into slavery amounted to murder in their minds, for they did not expect him to have survived.

[30]"The man who is ruler over the land spoke very roughly to us," they told him. "He 42:30
took us for spies. [31]But we said, 'We are honest men, not spies. [32]We are twelve brothers, Gen 42:7
sons of one father; one brother has disappeared, and the youngest is with our father in 42:31 Gen 42:11
the land of Canaan.' [33]Then the man, the ruler of the land, told us, 'This is the way I will 42:32
find out if you are honest men. Leave one of your brothers here with me, and take grain Gen 42:13
for your families and go on home. [34]But bring your youngest brother back to me. Then 42:34 Gen 34:10
I will know that you are honest men and not spies. If you prove to be what you say, then
I will give you back your brother, and you may come as often as you like to buy grain.'"
[35]As they emptied out the sacks, there at the top of each one was the bag of money 42:35 Gen 43:12, 15, 18
paid for the grain. Terror gripped them, as it did their father. [36]Jacob exclaimed, "You 42:36
have deprived me of my children! Joseph has disappeared, Simeon is gone, and now you Gen 43:14; 44:20-22
want to take Benjamin, too. Everything is going against me!"
[37]Then Reuben said to his father, "You may kill my two sons if I don't bring Benjamin 42:37
back to you. I'll be responsible for him." Gen 43:9; 44:32
[38]But Jacob replied, "My son will not go down with you, for his brother Joseph is 42:38 Gen 37:35; 44:29, 34
dead, and he alone is left of his mother's children. If anything should happen to him, you
would bring my gray head down to the grave in deep sorrow."

The Brothers Return to Egypt

43 But there was no relief from the terrible famine throughout the land. [2]When the 43:1 Gen 41:56-57
grain they had brought from Egypt was almost gone, Jacob said to his sons, "Go 43:2
again and buy us a little food." Gen 42:25
[3]But Judah said, "The man wasn't joking when he warned that we couldn't see him 43:3 Gen 42:15; 44:23
again unless Benjamin came along. [4]If you let him come with us, we will go down and
buy some food. [5]But if you don't let Benjamin go, we may as well stay at home.
Remember that the man said, 'You won't be allowed to come and see me unless your
brother is with you.'"
[6]"Why did you ever tell him you had another brother?" Jacob* moaned. "Why did
you have to treat me with such cruelty?"
[7]"But the man specifically asked us about our family," they replied. "He wanted to 43:7 Gen 42:13; 43:27
know whether our father was still living, and he asked us if we had another brother so 43:8
we told him. How could we have known he would say, 'Bring me your brother'?" Gen 42:2
[8]Judah said to his father, "Send the boy with me, and we will be on our way. Otherwise 43:9 Gen 42:37
we will all die of starvation—and not only we, but you and our little ones. [9]I personally Phlm 1:18-19
guarantee his safety. If I don't bring him back to you, then let me bear the blame forever.
[10]For we could have gone and returned twice by this time if you had let him come
without delay."
[11]So their father, Jacob, finally said to them, "If it can't be avoided, then at least do 43:11 Gen 32:13; 37:25
this. Fill your bags with the best products of the land. Take them to the man as 43:12 Gen 42:25, 35
gifts—balm, honey, spices, myrrh, pistachio nuts, and almonds. [12]Take double the 43:13
money that you found in your sacks, as it was probably someone's mistake. [13]Then take Gen 43:3
your brother and go back to the man. [14]May God Almighty give you mercy as you go 43:14 Gen 42:24 Ps 106:46

43:6 Hebrew *Israel;* also in 43:11.

43:1 Jacob and his sons had no relief from the famine. They could not see God's overall plan of sending them to Egypt to be reunited with Joseph and fed from Egypt's storehouses. If you are praying for relief from suffering or pressure and God is not bringing it as quickly as you would like, remember that God may be leading you to special treasures.

43:9 Judah accepted full responsibility for Benjamin's safety. He did not know what that might mean for him, but he was determined to do his duty. In the end it was Judah's stirring words that caused Joseph to break down with emotion and reveal himself to his brothers (44:18-34). Accepting responsibilities is difficult, but it builds character and confidence, earns others' respect, and motivates us to complete our work. When you have been given an assignment to complete or a responsibility to fulfill, commit yourself to seeing it through.

43:11 These gifts of balm, honey, spices, myrrh, pistachio nuts, and almonds were highly valuable specialty items not common in Egypt. Because of the famine, they were even more rare.

43:12 Joseph's brothers arrived home from Egypt only to find in their grain sacks the money they had used to pay for the grain (42:35). Some months later, when it was time to return to Egypt for more food, Jacob instructed them to take extra money so they could pay for the previous purchase as well as for additional grain. Jacob did not try to get away with anything. He was a man of integrity who paid for what he bought, whether he had to or not. We should follow his example and guard our integrity. A reputation for honesty is worth far more than the money we might gain by compromising it.

before the man, that he might release Simeon and return Benjamin. And if I must bear
the anguish of their deaths, then so be it."
15 So they took Benjamin and the gifts and double the money and hurried to Egypt,
43:16 Gen 44:1 where they presented themselves to Joseph. 16 When Joseph saw that Benjamin was with
them, he said to the manager of his household, "These men will eat with me this noon.
Take them inside and prepare a big feast." 17 So the man did as he was told and took them
43:18 Gen 42:28, 35 to Joseph's palace.
18 They were badly frightened when they saw where they were being taken. "It's
because of the money returned to us in our sacks," they said. "He plans to pretend that
we stole it. Then he will seize us as slaves and take our donkeys."

A Feast at Joseph's Palace

19 As the brothers arrived at the entrance to the palace, they went over to the man in
charge of Joseph's household. 20 They said to him, "Sir, after our first trip to Egypt to
43:21 Gen 42:25, 35; 43:12 buy food, 21 as we were returning home, we stopped for the night and opened our sacks.
The money we had used to pay for the grain was there in our sacks. Here it is; we have
43:22 Gen 42:28 brought it back again. 22 We also have additional money to buy more grain. We have no
idea how the money got into our sacks."
43:23 Gen 42:24 23 "Relax. Don't worry about it," the household manager told them. "Your God, the
God of your ancestors, must have put it there. We collected your money all right." Then
he released Simeon and brought him out to them.
43:24 Gen 18:4; 24:32 24 The brothers were then led into the palace and given water to wash their feet and
food for their donkeys. 25 They were told they would be eating there, so they prepared
their gifts for Joseph's arrival at noon.
43:27 Gen 43:7; 45:3 26 When Joseph came, they gave him their gifts and bowed low before him. 27 He asked
them how they had been getting along, and then he said, "How is your father—the old
man you spoke about? Is he still alive?"
43:28 Exod 18:7 28 "Yes," they replied. "He is alive and well." Then they bowed again before him.
43:29 Num 6:25; Ps 67:1 29 Looking at his brother Benjamin, Joseph asked, "Is this your youngest brother, the
one you told me about? May God be gracious to you, my son." 30 Then Joseph made a
43:30 Gen 42:24; 45:2, 14-15; 46:29 hasty exit because he was overcome with emotion for his brother and wanted to cry.
Going into his private room, he wept there. 31 Then he washed his face and came out,
43:31 Gen 45:1 keeping himself under control. "Bring on the food!" he ordered.
32 Joseph ate by himself, and his brothers were served at a separate table. The
43:32 Gen 46:34; Exod 8:26 Egyptians sat at their own table because Egyptians despise Hebrews and refuse to eat
with them. 33 Joseph told each of his brothers where to sit, and to their amazement, he
43:33 Gen 44:12 seated them in the order of their ages, from oldest to youngest. 34 Their food was served
to them from Joseph's own table. He gave the largest serving to Benjamin—five times
as much as to any of the others. So they all feasted and drank freely with him.

Joseph's Silver Cup

44:1 Gen 42:25; 43:16 **44** When his brothers were ready to leave, Joseph gave these instructions to the man
in charge of his household: "Fill each of their sacks with as much grain as they
can carry, and put each man's money back into his sack. 2 Then put my personal silver
cup at the top of the youngest brother's sack, along with his grain money." So the
household manager did as he was told.
3 The brothers were up at dawn and set out on their journey with their loaded donkeys.
44:4 Prov 17:13 4 But when they were barely out of the city, Joseph said to his household manager, "Chase
after them and stop them. Ask them, 'Why have you repaid an act of kindness with such

43:23 How did the money get into the sacks? Most likely, Joseph instructed his household manager to replace the money and then explain it with this response. Note that the household manager credited their God, not some Egyptian deity.

43:32 Joseph ate by himself because he was following the laws of the Egyptians' caste system. Egyptians considered themselves highly intelligent and sophisticated. They looked upon shepherds and nomads as uncultured and even vulgar. As a Hebrew, Joseph could not eat with Egyptians even though he outranked them. As foreigners and shepherds, his brothers were lower in rank than any Egyptian citizens, so they had to eat separately, too.

44:2 Joseph's silver cup was a symbol of his authority. It was thought to have supernatural powers, and to steal it was a serious crime. Such goblets were used for predicting the future. A person poured water into the cup and interpreted the reflections, ripples, and bubbles. Joseph wouldn't have needed his cup, since God told him everything he needed to know about the future.

evil? 5 What do you mean by stealing my master's personal silver drinking cup, which **44:5** Gen 30:27
he uses to predict the future? What a wicked thing you have done!'" Lev 19:26
6 So the man caught up with them and spoke to them in the way he had been instructed. Deut 18:10-14
7 "What are you talking about?" the brothers responded. "What kind of people do you
think we are, that you accuse us of such a terrible thing? 8 Didn't we bring back the **44:8** Gen 43:21
money we found in our sacks? Why would we steal silver or gold from your master's **44:9**
house? 9 If you find his cup with any one of us, let that one die. And all the rest of us will Gen 31:32
be your master's slaves forever."
10 "Fair enough," the man replied, "except that only the one who stole it will be a slave.
The rest of you may go free."
11 They quickly took their sacks from the backs of their donkeys and opened them.
12 Joseph's servant began searching the oldest brother's sack, going on down the line to **44:12** Gen 44:2
the youngest. The cup was found in Benjamin's sack! 13 At this, they tore their clothing **44:13**
in despair, loaded the donkeys again, and returned to the city. 14 Joseph was still at home Gen 37:29, 34
when Judah and his brothers arrived, and they fell to the ground before him.
15 "What were you trying to do?" Joseph demanded. "Didn't you know that a man **44:15**
such as I would know who stole it?" Gen 44:5
16 And Judah said, "Oh, my lord, what can we say to you? How can we plead? How **44:16** Gen 42:11; 43:18
can we prove our innocence? God is punishing us for our sins. My lord, we have all
returned to be your slaves—we and our brother who had your cup in his sack."
17 "No," Joseph said. "Only the man who stole the cup will be my slave. The rest of
you may go home to your father."

Judah Speaks for His Brothers

18 Then Judah stepped forward and said, "My lord, let me say just this one word to you. **44:18** Gen 37:7-8
Be patient with me for a moment, for I know you could have me killed in an instant, as **44:19**
though you were Pharaoh himself. Gen 42:11; 43:7
19 "You asked us, my lord, if we had a father or a brother. 20 We said, 'Yes, we have a **44:21** Gen 42:11, 15
father, an old man, and a child of his old age, his youngest son. His brother is dead, and **44:23**
he alone is left of his mother's children, and his father loves him very much.' 21 And you Gen 43:3
said to us, 'Bring him here so I can see him.' 22 But we said to you, 'My lord, the boy **44:24**
cannot leave his father, for his father would die.' 23 But you told us, 'You may not see me Gen 42:29-34
again unless your youngest brother is with you.' 24 So we returned to our father and told **44:25** Gen 42:2
him what you had said. 25 And when he said, 'Go back again and buy us a little food,' **44:26**
26 we replied, 'We can't unless you let our youngest brother go with us. We won't be Gen 43:5
allowed to see the man in charge of the grain unless our youngest brother is with us.' **44:27** Gen 46:19
27 Then my father said to us, 'You know that my wife had two sons, 28 and that one of **44:28**
them went away and never returned—doubtless torn to pieces by some wild animal. I Gen 37:33
have never seen him since. 29 If you take away his brother from me, too, and any harm **44:29**
comes to him, you would bring my gray head down to the grave in deep sorrow.' Gen 42:38
30 "And now, my lord, I cannot go back to my father without the boy. Our father's life **44:30** 1 Sam 18:1
is bound up in the boy's life. 31 When he sees that the boy is not with us, our father will **44:32**
die. We will be responsible for bringing his gray head down to the grave in sorrow. 32 My Gen 43:9

44:13 Tearing clothes was an expression of deep sorrow, a customary manner of showing grief. The brothers were terrified that Benjamin might be harmed.

44:16-34 When Judah was younger, he showed no regard for his brother Joseph or his father, Jacob. First he convinced his brothers to sell Joseph as a slave (37:27); then he joined his brothers in lying to his father about Joseph's fate (37:32). But what a change had taken place in Judah! The man who sold one favored little brother into slavery now offered to become a slave himself to save another favored little brother. He was so concerned for his father and younger brother that he was willing to die for them. When you are ready to give up hope on yourself or others, remember that God can work a complete change in even the most selfish personality.

44:18-34 Judah finally could take no more and stepped forward to plead their case. This was risky because Joseph could have had him killed. But Judah courageously defended himself and his brothers and pled for mercy. And he offered to put himself in Benjamin's place. There are times when we should be silent, but there are also times when we should speak up, even if there could be serious repercussions. When faced with a situation that needs a strong voice and courageous action, remember Judah and speak up.

44:32, 33 Judah had promised Jacob that he would guarantee young Benjamin's safety (43:9). Now Judah had a chance to keep that promise. Becoming a slave was a terrible fate, but Judah was determined to keep his word to his father. He showed great courage in carrying out his promise. Accepting a responsibility means carrying it out with determination and courage, regardless of the personal sacrifice.

lord, I made a pledge to my father that I would take care of the boy. I told him, 'If I don't
bring him back to you, I will bear the blame forever.' 33Please, my lord, let me stay here
as a slave instead of the boy, and let the boy return with his brothers. 34For how can I return
to my father if the boy is not with me? I cannot bear to see what this would do to him."

Joseph Reveals His Identity

45:1 Gen 43:31 Acts 7:13 **45** Joseph could stand it no longer. "Out, all of you!" he cried out to his attendants.
He wanted to be alone with his brothers when he told them who he was. 2Then
he broke down and wept aloud. His sobs could be heard throughout the palace, and the
45:3 Gen 43:7 news was quickly carried to Pharaoh's palace.
3"I am Joseph!" he said to his brothers. "Is my father still alive?" But his brothers
45:4 Gen 37:28 were speechless! They were stunned to realize that Joseph was standing there in front
of them. 4"Come over here," he said. So they came closer. And he said again, "I am

---

JUDAH

People who are leaders stand out. They don't necessarily look or act a certain way until the need for their action is apparent. Among their skills are outspokenness, decisiveness, action, and control. These skills can be used for great good or great evil. Jacob's fourth son, Judah, was a natural leader. The events of his life provided many opportunities to exercise those skills. Unfortunately Judah's decisions were often shaped more by the pressures of the moment than by a conscious desire to cooperate with God's plan. But when he did recognize his mistakes, he was willing to admit them. His experience with Tamar and the final confrontation with Joseph are both examples of Judah's willingness to bear the blame when confronted. It was one of the qualities he passed on to his descendant David.

Whether or not we have Judah's natural leadership qualities, we share with him a tendency to be blind toward our own sin. Too often, however, we don't share his willingness to admit mistakes. From Judah we can learn that it is not wise to wait until our errors force us to admit to wrongdoing. It is far better to admit our mistakes openly, to shoulder the blame, and to seek forgiveness.

Strengths and accomplishments
- Was a natural leader—outspoken and decisive
- Thought clearly and took action in high-pressure situations
- Was willing to stand by his word and put himself on the line when necessary
- Was the fourth son of 12, through whom God would eventually bring David and Jesus, the Messiah

Weaknesses and mistakes
- Suggested to his brothers they sell Joseph into slavery
- Failed to keep his promise to his daughter-in-law, Tamar

Lessons from his life
- God is in control, far beyond the immediate situation
- Procrastination often makes matters worse
- Judah's offer to substitute his life for Benjamin's is a picture of what his descendant Jesus would do for all people

Vital statistics
- Where: Canaan and Egypt
- Occupation: Shepherd
- Relatives: Parents: Jacob and Leah. Wife: The daughter of Shua (1 Chronicles 2:3). Daughter-in-law: Tamar. Eleven brothers, at least one sister, and at least five sons

Key verses
"Judah, your brothers will praise you. You will defeat your enemies. All your relatives will bow before you. Judah is a young lion that has finished eating its prey. Like a lion he crouches and lies down; like a lioness—who will dare to rouse him? The scepter will not depart from Judah, nor the ruler's staff from his descendants, until the coming of the one to whom it belongs, the one whom all nations will obey" (Genesis 49:8–10).

Judah's story is told in Genesis 29:35—50:26. He is also mentioned in 1 Chronicles 2—4.

44:33 Joseph wanted to see if his brothers' attitudes had changed for the better, so he tested the way they treated each other. Judah, the brother who had stepped forward with the plan to sell Joseph (37:27), now stepped forward to take Benjamin's punishment so that Benjamin could return to their father. This courageous act convinced Joseph that his brothers had dramatically changed for the better.

45:4-8 Although Joseph's brothers had wanted to get rid of him, God used even their evil actions to fulfill his ultimate plan. He sent Joseph ahead to preserve their lives, save Egypt, and prepare the way for the beginning of the nation of Israel. God is sovereign. His plans are not dictated by human actions. When others intend evil toward you, remember that they are only God's tools. As Joseph said to his brothers, "God turned into good what you meant for evil. He brought me to the high position I have today so I could save the lives of many people" (50:20).

Joseph, your brother whom you sold into Egypt. 5 But don't be angry with yourselves
that you did this to me, for God did it. He sent me here ahead of you to preserve your
lives. 6 These two years of famine will grow to seven, during which there will be neither
plowing nor harvest. 7 God has sent me here to keep you and your families alive so that
you will become a great nation. 8 Yes, it was God who sent me here, not you! And he
has made me a counselor to Pharaoh—manager of his entire household and ruler over
all Egypt.
9 "Hurry, return to my father and tell him, 'This is what your son Joseph says: God has
made me master over all the land of Egypt. Come down to me right away! 10 You will
live in the land of Goshen so you can be near me with all your children and grandchildren, your flocks and herds, and all that you have. 11 I will take care of you there, for
there are still five years of famine ahead of us. Otherwise you and your household will
come to utter poverty.'"
12 Then Joseph said, "You can see for yourselves, and so can my brother Benjamin,
that I really am Joseph! 13 Tell my father how I am honored here in Egypt. Tell him about
everything you have seen, and bring him to me quickly." 14 Weeping with joy, he
embraced Benjamin, and Benjamin also began to weep. 15 Then Joseph kissed each of
his brothers and wept over them, and then they began talking freely with him.

Pharaoh Invites Jacob to Egypt

16 The news soon reached Pharaoh: "Joseph's brothers have come!" Pharaoh was very
happy to hear this and so were his officials.
17 Pharaoh said to Joseph, "Tell your brothers to load their pack animals and return
quickly to their homes in Canaan. 18 Tell them to bring your father and all of their
families, and to come here to Egypt to live. Tell them, 'Pharaoh will assign to you the
very best territory in the land of Egypt. You will live off the fat of the land!' 19 And
tell your brothers to take wagons from Egypt to carry their wives and little ones and
to bring your father here. 20 Don't worry about your belongings, for the best of all the
land of Egypt is yours."
21 So the sons of Jacob* did as they were told. Joseph gave them wagons, as Pharaoh
had commanded, and he supplied them with provisions for the journey. 22 And he gave
each of them new clothes—but to Benjamin he gave five changes of clothes and three
hundred pieces* of silver! 23 He sent his father ten donkeys loaded with the good things
of Egypt, and ten donkeys loaded with grain and all kinds of other food to be eaten on
his journey. 24 So he sent his brothers off, and as they left, he called after them, "Don't
quarrel along the way!" 25 And they left Egypt and returned to their father, Jacob, in the
land of Canaan.
26 "Joseph is still alive!" they told him. "And he is ruler over all the land of Egypt!"
Jacob was stunned at the news—he couldn't believe it. 27 But when they had given him
Joseph's messages, and when he saw the wagons loaded with the food sent by Joseph,
his spirit revived.
28 Then Jacob said, "It must be true! My son Joseph is alive! I will go and see him
before I die."

6. Jacob's family moves to Egypt

Jacob's Journey to Egypt

46 So Jacob* set out for Egypt with all his possessions. And when he came to
Beersheba, he offered sacrifices to the God of his father, Isaac. 2 During the night
God spoke to him in a vision. "Jacob! Jacob!" he called.

45:5 Gen 50:20
45:6 Gen 41:30
45:8 Gen 41:41; Judg 17:10
45:9 Acts 7:14
45:10 Gen 46:28, 34
45:11 Gen 45:8; 47:12
45:13 Acts 7:14
45:14 Gen 45:2
45:16 Acts 7:13
45:17 Gen 42:26
45:18 Gen 27:28
45:19 Gen 45:27; 46:5
45:20 Gen 46:6
45:22 Gen 24:53; 2 Kgs 5:5
45:23 Gen 43:11
45:24 Gen 42:21-22
45:26 Gen 37:31-35
45:27 Gen 45:19
45:28 Gen 44:28
46:1 Gen 21:14; 26:24; 28:13; 31:42
46:2 Gen 22:11; 31:11; Num 12:6

45:21 Hebrew *Israel;* also in 45:28. **45:22** Hebrew *300 shekels,* about 7.5 pounds or 3.4 kilograms in weight.
46:1 Hebrew *Israel;* also in 46:30.

45:17-20 Joseph was rejected, kidnapped, enslaved, and imprisoned. Although his brothers had been unfaithful to him, he graciously forgave them and shared his prosperity. Joseph demonstrated how God forgives us and showers us with goodness even though we have sinned against him. The same forgiveness and blessings are ours if we ask for them.

45:26, 27 Jacob needed some evidence before he could believe the incredible news that Joseph was alive. Similarly, Thomas refused to believe that Jesus had risen from the dead until he could see and touch him (John 20:25). It is hard to change what you believe without all the facts—or sometimes even with the facts. Good news can be hard to believe. Don't ever give up hope that God has a wonderful future in store for you.

"Here I am," Jacob replied.
46:3 Gen 17:1; 26:2 — 3"I am God," the voice said, "the God of your father. Do not be afraid to go down to
46:4 Gen 28:13; Exod 3:8 — Egypt, for I will see to it that you become a great nation there. 4I will go with you down
to Egypt, and I will bring your descendants back again. But you will die in Egypt with
Joseph at your side."
46:5 Gen 45:19 — 5So Jacob left Beersheba, and his sons brought him to Egypt. They carried their little
46:6 Num 20:15; Deut 26:5; Acts 7:15 — ones and wives in the wagons Pharaoh had provided for them. 6They brought their
livestock, too, and all the belongings they had acquired in the land of Canaan. Jacob
and his entire family arrived in Egypt—7sons and daughters, grandsons and grand-
daughters—all his descendants.

46:8 Gen 29:32; 35:26 — 8These are the names of the Israelites, the descendants of Jacob, who went with him
to Egypt:

46:9 1 Chr 5:3 — Reuben was Jacob's oldest son. 9The sons of Reuben were Hanoch, Pallu, Hezron, and Carmi.

46:10 1 Chr 4:24 — 10The sons of Simeon were Jemuel, Jamin, Ohad, Jakin, Zohar, and Shaul. (Shaul's mother was a Canaanite woman.)

46:11 1 Chr 6:19 — 11The sons of Levi were Gershon, Kohath, and Merari.

46:12 1 Chr 2:5 — 12The sons of Judah were Er, Onan, Shelah, Perez, and Zerah. (But Er and Onan had died in the land of Canaan.) The sons of Perez were Hezron and Hamul.

46:13 1 Chr 7:1 — 13The sons of Issachar were Tola, Puah,* Jashub,* and Shimron.

46:14 Gen 30:20 — 14The sons of Zebulun were Sered, Elon, and Jahleel.

46:15 Gen 30:21 — 15These are the sons of Jacob who were born to Leah in Paddan-aram, along with their
sister, Dinah. In all, Jacob's descendants through Leah numbered thirty-three.

46:16 Gen 30:11; Num 26:15 — 16The sons of Gad were Zephon,* Haggi, Shuni, Ezbon, Eri, Arodi, and Areli.

46:17 Gen 30:13 — 17The sons of Asher were Imnah, Ishvah, Ishvi, and Beriah. Their sister was named Serah. Beriah's sons were Heber and Malkiel.

18These sixteen were descendants of Jacob through Zilpah, the servant given to Leah by
her father, Laban.

46:19 Gen 44:27 — 19The sons of Jacob's wife Rachel were Joseph and Benjamin.

46:20 Gen 41:45, 50-52 — 20Joseph's sons, born in the land of Egypt, were Manasseh and Ephraim. Their mother was Asenath, daughter of Potiphera, priest of Heliopolis.*

46:13a As in Syriac version and Samaritan Pentateuch (see also 1 Chr 7:1); Hebrew reads *Puvah.* **46:13b** As in some Greek manuscripts and Samaritan Pentateuch (see also Num 26:24; 1 Chr 7:1); Hebrew reads *Iob.* **46:16** As in Greek version and Samaritan Pentateuch (see also Num 26:15); Hebrew reads *Ziphion.* **46:20** Hebrew *of On.*

JACOB MOVES TO EGYPT
After hearing the joyful news that Joseph was alive, Jacob packed up and moved his family to Egypt. Stopping first in Beersheba, Jacob offered sacrifices and received assurance from God that Egypt was where he should go. Jacob and his family settled in the region of Goshen, in the northeastern part of Egypt.

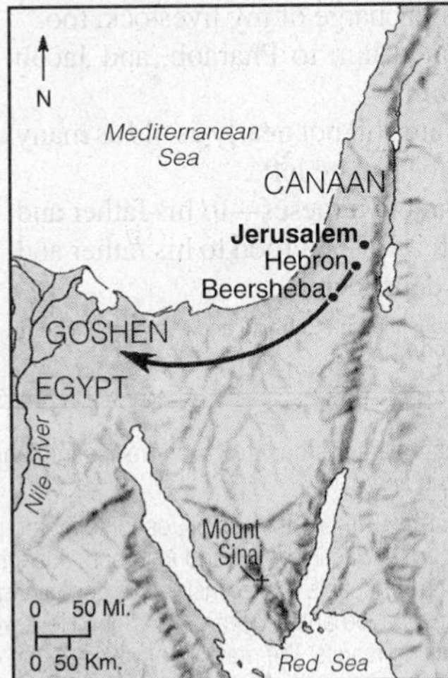

46:3, 4 The Israelites did become a great nation, and Jacob's descendants eventually returned to Canaan. The book of Exodus recounts the story of Israel's slavery in Egypt for 400 years (fulfilling God's words to Abraham in 15:13-16), and the book of Joshua gives an exciting account of the Israelites entering and conquering Canaan, the Promised Land.

46:3, 4 God told Jacob to leave his home and travel to a strange and faraway land. But God reassured him by promising to go with him and take care of him. When new situations or surroundings frighten you, recognize that experiencing fear is normal. To be paralyzed by fear, however, is an indication that you question God's ability to take care of you.

46:4 Jacob never returned to Canaan, but God promised that his descendants would return. That Jacob would die in Egypt with Joseph at his side was God's promise to Jacob that he would never know the bitterness of being lonely again.

[21]Benjamin's sons were Bela, Beker, Ashbel, Gera, Naaman, Ehi, Rosh, Muppim,
Huppim, and Ard.

[22]These fourteen were the descendants of Jacob and his wife Rachel.
[23]The son of Dan was Hushim.
[24]The sons of Naphtali were Jahzeel, Guni, Jezer, and Shillem.

[25]These seven were the descendants of Jacob through Bilhah, the servant given to Rachel
by her father, Laban.

[26]So the total number of Jacob's direct descendants who went with him to Egypt, not
counting his sons' wives, was sixty-six. [27]Joseph also had two sons* who had been born
in Egypt. So altogether, there were seventy* members of Jacob's family in the land of
Egypt.

46:21 Num 26:28-37; 1 Chr 7:6-12
46:22 Gen 35:24
46:23 Gen 30:6
46:24 Gen 30:8; Num 26:42
46:25 Gen 35:2
46:27 Exod 1:5; Deut 10:22; Acts 7:14

Jacob's Family Arrives in Goshen

[28]Jacob sent Judah on ahead to meet Joseph and get directions to the land of Goshen.
And when they all arrived there, [29]Joseph prepared his chariot and traveled to Goshen
to meet his father. As soon as Joseph arrived, he embraced his father and wept on his
shoulder for a long time. [30]Then Jacob said to Joseph, "Now let me die, for I have seen
you with my own eyes and know you are still alive."

[31]And Joseph said to his brothers and to all their households, "I'll go and tell
Pharaoh that you have all come from the land of Canaan to join me. [32]And I will tell
him, 'These men are shepherds and livestock breeders. They have brought with them
their flocks and herds and everything they own.' [33]So when Pharaoh calls for you and
asks you about your occupation, [34]tell him, 'We have been livestock breeders from
our youth, as our ancestors have been for many generations.' When you tell him this,
he will let you live here in the land of Goshen, for shepherds are despised in the land
of Egypt."

46:28 Gen 43:3; 45:10
46:29 Gen 45:14-15
46:30 Gen 44:28
46:31 Gen 47:1
46:32 Gen 37:2; 47:3
46:33 Gen 47:3
46:34 Gen 13:7; 26:20; 37:2

Jacob Blesses Pharaoh

47 So Joseph went to see Pharaoh and said, "My father and my brothers are here from
Canaan. They came with all their flocks and herds and possessions, and they are
now in the land of Goshen."

[2]Joseph took five of his brothers with him and presented them to Pharaoh. [3]Pharaoh
asked them, "What is your occupation?"

And they replied, "We are shepherds like our ancestors. [4]We have come to live here
in Egypt, for there is no pasture for our flocks in Canaan. The famine is very severe there.
We request permission to live in the land of Goshen."

[5]And Pharaoh said to Joseph, "Now that your family has joined you here, [6]choose any
place you like for them to live. Give them the best land of Egypt—the land of Goshen will
be fine. And if any of them have special skills, put them in charge of my livestock, too."

[7]Then Joseph brought his father, Jacob, and presented him to Pharaoh, and Jacob
blessed Pharaoh. [8]"How old are you?" Pharaoh asked him.

[9]Jacob replied, "I have lived for 130 hard years, but I am still not nearly as old as many
of my ancestors." [10]Then Jacob blessed Pharaoh again before he left.

[11]So Joseph assigned the best land of Egypt—the land of Rameses—to his father and
brothers, just as Pharaoh had commanded. [12]And Joseph furnished food to his father and
brothers in amounts appropriate to the number of their dependents.

47:1 Gen 46:31
47:2 Gen 43:15
47:3 Gen 46:32-33
47:4 Gen 46:34
47:6 Gen 45:18; Exod 18:21, 25
47:7 Gen 47:10; 2 Sam 14:22; 1 Kgs 8:66
47:10 Gen 14:19
47:11 Exod 1:11; 12:37
47:12 Gen 45:11; 47:24

46:27a Greek version reads *nine sons,* probably including Joseph's grandsons through Ephraim and Manasseh (see 1 Chr 7:14-20). **46:27b** Greek version reads *seventy-five;* see note on Exod 1:5.

46:31-34 Jacob moved his whole family to Egypt, but they wanted to live apart from the Egyptians. To ensure this, Joseph told them to let Pharaoh know they were shepherds. Although Pharaoh may have been sympathetic to shepherds (for he was probably descended from the nomadic Hyksos line), the Egyptian culture would not willingly accept shepherds among them. The strategy worked, and Jacob's family was able to benefit from Pharaoh's generosity as well as from the Egyptians' prejudice.

47:1-6 The faithfulness of Joseph affected his entire family. When he was in the pit and in prison, Joseph must have wondered about his future. Instead of despairing, he faithfully obeyed God and did what was right. Here we see one of the exciting results. We may not always see the effects of our faith, but we can be sure that God will honor faithfulness.

Joseph's Leadership in the Famine

13 Meanwhile, the famine became worse and worse, and the crops continued to fail throughout Egypt and Canaan. 14 Joseph collected all the money in Egypt and Canaan in exchange for grain, and he brought the money to Pharaoh's treasure-house. 15 When the people of Egypt and Canaan ran out of money, they came to Joseph crying again for food. "Our money is gone," they said, "but give us bread. Why should we die?"

16 "Well, then," Joseph replied, "since your money is gone, give me your livestock. I will give you food in exchange." 17 So they gave their livestock to Joseph in exchange for food. Soon all the horses, flocks, herds, and donkeys of Egypt were in Pharaoh's possession. But at least they were able to purchase food for that year.

18 The next year they came again and said, "Our money is gone, and our livestock are yours. We have nothing left but our bodies and land. 19 Why should we die before your very eyes? Buy us and our land in exchange for food; we will then become servants to Pharaoh. Just give us grain so that our lives may be saved and so the land will not become empty and desolate."

20 So Joseph bought all the land of Egypt for Pharaoh. All the Egyptians sold him their fields because the famine was so severe, and their land then belonged to Pharaoh. 21 Thus, all the people of Egypt became servants to Pharaoh.* 22 The only land he didn't buy was that belonging to the priests, for they were assigned food from Pharaoh and didn't need to sell their land.

23 Then Joseph said to the people, "See, I have bought you and your land for Pharaoh. I will provide you with seed, so you can plant the fields. 24 Then when you harvest it, a fifth of your crop will belong to Pharaoh. Keep four-fifths for yourselves, and use it to plant the next year's crop and to feed yourselves, your households, and your little ones."

25 "You have saved our lives!" they exclaimed. "May it please you, sir, to let us be Pharaoh's servants." 26 Joseph then made it a law throughout the land of Egypt—and it is still the law—that Pharaoh should receive one-fifth of all the crops grown on his land. But since Pharaoh had not taken over the priests' land, they were exempt from this payment.

7. Jacob and Joseph die in Egypt

27 So the people of Israel settled in the land of Goshen in Egypt. And before long, they began to prosper there, and their population grew rapidly. 28 Jacob lived for seventeen years after his arrival in Egypt, so he was 147 years old when he died. 29 As the time of his death drew near, he called for his son Joseph and said to him, "If you are pleased with me, swear most solemnly that you will honor this, my last request: Do not bury me in Egypt. 30 When I am dead, take me out of Egypt and bury me beside my ancestors." So Joseph promised that he would. 31 "Swear that you will do it," Jacob insisted. So Joseph gave his oath, and Jacob* bowed in worship as he leaned on his staff.*

Jacob Blesses Manasseh and Ephraim

48 One day not long after this, word came to Joseph that his father was failing rapidly. So Joseph went to visit him, and he took with him his two sons, Manasseh and Ephraim. 2 When Jacob heard that Joseph had arrived, he gathered his strength and sat up in bed to greet him.

3 Jacob said to Joseph, "God Almighty appeared to me at Luz in the land of Canaan and blessed me. 4 He said to me, 'I will make you a multitude of nations, and I will give this land of Canaan to you and your descendants as an everlasting possession.' 5 Now I am adopting as my own sons these two boys of yours, Ephraim and Manasseh, who were born here in the land of Egypt before I arrived. They will inherit from me just as Reuben and Simeon will. 6 But the children born to you in the future will be your own. The land they inherit will be within the territories of Ephraim and Manasseh. 7 As I was returning

47:13 Gen 41:30; Acts 7:11
47:14 Gen 41:36
47:15 Gen 47:18-19
47:17 Exod 14:9
47:19 Neh 5:2; Job 2:4; Lam 1:11
47:22 Gen 41:45; Deut 14:28-29
47:24 Gen 41:34
47:25 Gen 32:5
47:26 Gen 47:22
47:27 Exod 1:7
47:29 Gen 24:2, 49; 50:24-25
47:30 Gen 23:17-20; 25:9; 49:29; Acts 7:15-16
47:31 Heb 11:21
48:1 Gen 41:51-52; Heb 11:21
48:3 Gen 28:13-19; 35:9-12
48:5 Gen 29:32-33
48:7 Gen 35:19

47:21 As in Greek version and Samaritan Pentateuch; Hebrew reads *He moved the people into the towns throughout the land of Egypt.* **47:31a** Hebrew *Israel.* **47:31b** As in Greek version; Hebrew reads *bowed in worship at the head of his bed.*

47:29-31 Jacob had Joseph promise to bury him in his homeland. Few things were written in this culture, so a person's word then carried as much force as a written contract today. People today seem to find it easy to say, "I didn't mean that." God's people, however, are to speak the truth and live the truth. Let your words be as binding as a written contract.

from Paddan, Rachel died in the land of Canaan. We were still on the way, just a short
distance from Ephrath (that is, Bethlehem). So with great sorrow I buried her there beside
the road to Ephrath."
8 Then Jacob* looked over at the two boys. "Are these your sons?" he asked.
9 "Yes," Joseph told him, "these are the sons God has given me here in Egypt."
And Jacob said, "Bring them over to me, and I will bless them."
10 Now Jacob was half blind because of his age and could hardly see. So Joseph
brought the boys close to him, and Jacob kissed and embraced them. 11 Then Jacob said
to Joseph, "I never thought I would see you again, but now God has let me see your
children, too."
12 Joseph took the boys from their grandfather's knees, and he bowed low to him.
13 Then he positioned the boys so Ephraim was at Jacob's left hand and Manasseh was
at his right hand. 14 But Jacob crossed his arms as he reached out to lay his hands on the
boys' heads. So his right hand was on the head of Ephraim, the younger boy, and his left
hand was on the head of Manasseh, the older.
15 Then he blessed Joseph and said, "May God, the God before whom my grandfather
Abraham and my father, Isaac, walked, the God who has been my shepherd all my life,
16 and the angel who has kept me from all harm—may he bless these boys. May they
preserve my name and the names of my grandfather Abraham and my father, Isaac. And
may they become a mighty nation."
17 But Joseph was upset when he saw that his father had laid his right hand on
Ephraim's head. So he lifted it to place it on Manasseh's head instead. 18 "No, Father,"
he said, "this one over here is older. Put your right hand on his head."
19 But his father refused. "I know what I'm doing, my son," he said. "Manasseh, too,
will become a great people, but his younger brother will become even greater. His
descendants will become a multitude of nations!" 20 So Jacob blessed the boys that day
with this blessing: "The people of Israel will use your names to bless each other. They
will say, 'May God make you as prosperous as Ephraim and Manasseh.'" In this way,
Jacob put Ephraim ahead of Manasseh.
21 Then Jacob said to Joseph, "I am about to die, but God will be with you and will
bring you again to Canaan, the land of your ancestors. 22 And I give you an extra portion*
beyond what I have given your brothers—the portion that I took from the Amorites with
my sword and bow."

Jacob Blesses His Sons

49 Then Jacob called together all his sons and said, "Gather around me, and I will
tell you what is going to happen to you in the days to come.
2 "Come and listen, O sons of Jacob;
listen to Israel, your father.

48:9 Gen 33:5
48:10 Gen 27:1
48:11 Gen 44:28
48:12 Gen 33:3; 42:6
48:14 Gen 41:51-52
48:15 Gen 17:1; 49:24
48:16 Gen 22:11; 28:13-15; 31:11 †Heb 11:21
48:19 Gen 28:14; 46:3
48:20 Ruth 4:11
48:21 Gen 28:15; 46:4; 50:24
48:22 Josh 24:32 John 4:5
49:1 Num 24:14

48:8 Hebrew *Israel;* also in 48:10, 11, 13, 14, 21. **48:22** Or *give you the ridge of land.* The meaning of the Hebrew is uncertain.

48:8-20 Jacob gave Ephraim, instead of his older brother Manasseh, the greater blessing. When Joseph objected, Jacob refused to listen because God had told him that Ephraim would become greater. God often works in unexpected ways. When he chooses people to fulfill his plans, he always goes deeper than appearance, tradition, or position. He sometimes surprises us by choosing the less obvious person, at least by human reasoning. God can use you to carry out his plans, even if you don't think you have all the qualifications.

48:11 When Joseph became a slave, Jacob thought he was dead and wept in despair (37:34). But eventually God's plan allowed Jacob to regain not only his son but his grandchildren as well. Circumstances are never so bad that they are beyond God's help. Jacob regained his son. Job got a new family (Job 42:10-17). Mary regained her brother, Lazarus (John 11:1-44). We need never despair because we belong to a loving God. We never know what good he will bring out of a seemingly hopeless situation.

48:15 Jacob spoke of God as his shepherd throughout his life. In his old age, he could clearly see his dependence upon God. This marks a total attitude change from that of his scheming and dishonest youth. To develop an attitude like Jacob's, let God shepherd you as you trust in his provision and care. When you realize that all good thing come from God, you can quit trying to grab them for yourself.

48:20-22 Jacob was giving these young boys land occupied by the Philistines and Canaanites. His gift became reality when the tribes of Ephraim and Manasseh occupied the east and west sides of the Jordan River (Joshua 16).

49:3-28 Jacob blessed each of his sons and then made a prediction about each one's future. The way the men had lived played an important part in Jacob's blessing and prophecy. Our past also affects our present and future. By sunrise tomorrow, our actions of today will have become part of the past. Yet they will already have begun to shape the future. What actions can you choose or avoid that will positively shape your future?

49:3 Num 26:5; Deut 21:17; Pss 78:51; 105:36
49:4 Gen 35:22; Deut 27:20
49:5 Gen 29:33-34; 34:25-30
49:6 Gen 34:26
49:7 Josh 19:1, 9; 21:1-42
49:8 1 Chr 5:2; Heb 7:14
49:9 Num 24:9; Mic 5:8

3 "Reuben, you are my oldest son,
the child of my vigorous youth.
You are first on the list in rank and honor.
4 But you are as unruly as the waves of the sea,
and you will be first no longer.
For you slept with one of my wives;
you dishonored me in my own bed.

5 "Simeon and Levi are two of a kind—
men of violence.
6 O my soul, stay away from them.
May I never be a party to their wicked plans.
For in their anger they murdered men,
and they crippled oxen just for sport.
7 Cursed be their anger, for it is fierce;
cursed be their wrath, for it is cruel.
Therefore, I will scatter their descendants
throughout the nation of Israel.

8 "Judah, your brothers will praise you.
You will defeat your enemies.
All your relatives will bow before you.
9 Judah is a young lion
that has finished eating its prey.
Like a lion he crouches and lies down;
like a lioness—who will dare to rouse him?

PARALLELS BETWEEN JOSEPH AND JESUS
Genesis 37—50

Joseph	*Parallels*	*Jesus*
37:3	Their fathers loved them dearly	Matthew 3:17
37:2	Shepherds of their fathers' sheep	John 10:11, 27
37:13, 14	Sent by father to brothers	Hebrews 2:11
37:4	Hated by brothers	John 7:5
37:20	Others plotted to harm them	John 11:53
39:7	Tempted	Matthew 4:1
37:25	Taken to Egypt	Matthew 2:14, 15
37:23	Robes taken from them	John 19:23
37:28	Sold for the price of a slave	Matthew 26:15
39:20	Bound in chains	Matthew 27:2
39:16–18	Falsely accused	Matthew 26:59, 60
40:2, 3	Placed with two other prisoners, one who was saved and the other lost	Luke 23:32
41:46	Both 30 years old at the beginning of public recognition	Luke 3:23
41:41	Exalted after suffering	Philippians 2:9–11
45:1–15	Forgave those who wronged them	Luke 23:34
45:7	Saved their nation	Matthew 1:21
50:20	What people did to hurt them God turned to good	1 Corinthians 2:7, 8

49:4 The oldest son was supposed to receive a double inheritance, but Reuben lost his special honor. Unstable and untrustworthy, especially in his younger days, he had gone so far as to sleep with one of his father's concubines. Jacob could not give the birthright blessing to such a dishonorable son.

49:8-12 Why was Judah—known for selling Joseph into slavery and trying to defraud his daughter-in-law—so greatly blessed? God had chosen Judah to be the ancestor of Israel's line of kings (that is the meaning of "the scepter will not depart from Judah"). This may have been due to Judah's dramatic change of character (44:33, 34). Judah's line would produce the promised Messiah, Jesus.

[10] The scepter will not depart from Judah,
nor the ruler's staff from his descendants,
until the coming of the one to whom it belongs,*
the one whom all nations will obey.
[11] He ties his foal to a grapevine,
the colt of his donkey to a choice vine.
He washes his clothes in wine
because his harvest is so plentiful.
[12] His eyes are darker than wine,
and his teeth are whiter than milk.

[13] "Zebulun will settle on the shores of the sea
and will be a harbor for ships;
his borders will extend to Sidon.

[14] "Issachar is a strong beast of burden,
resting among the sheepfolds.*
[15] When he sees how good the countryside is,
how pleasant the land,
he will bend his shoulder to the task
and submit to forced labor.

[16] "Dan will govern his people
like any other tribe in Israel.
[17] He will be a snake beside the road,
a poisonous viper along the path,
that bites the horse's heels
so the rider is thrown off.
[18] I trust in you for salvation, O LORD!

[19] "Gad will be plundered by marauding bands,
but he will turn and plunder them.

[20] "Asher will produce rich foods,
food fit for kings.

[21] "Naphtali is a deer let loose,
producing magnificent fawns.

[22] "Joseph is a fruitful tree,
a fruitful tree beside a fountain.
His branches reach over the wall.
[23] He has been attacked by archers,
who shot at him and harassed him.
[24] But his bow remained strong,
and his arms were strengthened

49:10 Num 24:17; Pss 2:6-9; 60:7
49:11 Deut 8:7-8; 2 Kgs 18:32
49:13 Deut 33:18-19
49:14 Judg 5:16; Ps 68:13
49:15 Josh 19:17-23
49:16 Deut 33:22; Judg 18:26-27
49:19 Deut 33:20
49:20 Deut 33:24-25
49:21 Deut 33:23
49:22 Deut 33:13-17
49:23 Gen 37:24
49:24 Ps 132:2, 5; Isa 41:10; 49:26

49:10 Or *until tribute is brought to him and the peoples obey;* traditionally rendered *until Shiloh comes.* **49:14** Or *saddlebags,* or *hearths.*

49:10 "Until the coming of the one to whom it belongs" may also be translated, "until Shiloh comes." What is *Shiloh?* The meaning of this difficult passage is disputed. *Shiloh* may be another name for the Messiah, because its literal meaning is "sent." *Shiloh* might also refer to the Tabernacle set up at the city of Shiloh (Joshua 18:1).

49:18 In the middle of his prophecy to Dan, Jacob exclaimed, "I trust in you for salvation, O LORD!" He was emphasizing to Dan that he would be a strong leader only if his trust was in God, not in his natural strength or ability. Those who are strong, attractive, or talented often find it easier to trust in themselves than in God who gave them their gifts. Remember to thank God for what you are and have so your trust does not become misplaced.

49:22 Joseph was indeed fruitful, with some heroic descendants. Among them were Joshua, who would lead the Israelites into the Promised Land (Joshua 1:10, 11); and Deborah, Gideon, and Jephthah, judges of Israel (Judges 4:4; 6:11, 12; 11:11).

49:23, 24 These verses celebrate the times God rescued Joseph when his enemies attacked him. So often we struggle by ourselves, forgetting that God is able to help us fight our battles, whether they are against men with weapons or against spiritual forces. Joseph was able to draw closer to God as adversity mounted. To trust God to rescue you shows great faith. Can you trust him when injury or persecution is directed at you? Such spiritual battles require teamwork between courageous, faithful people and a mighty God.

by the Mighty One of Jacob,
the Shepherd, the Rock of Israel.
49:25 Gen 28:13 — 25 May the God of your ancestors help you;
may the Almighty bless you
with the blessings of the heavens above,
blessings of the earth beneath,
and blessings of the breasts and womb.
49:26 Deut 33:15-16 — 26 May the blessings of your ancestors
be greater than the blessings of the eternal mountains,
reaching to the utmost bounds of the everlasting hills.
These blessings will fall on the head of Joseph,
who is a prince among his brothers.

49:27 Deut 33:12 — 27 "Benjamin is a wolf that prowls.
He devours his enemies in the morning,
and in the evening he divides the plunder."

28 These are the twelve tribes of Israel, and these are the blessings with which Jacob*
blessed his twelve sons. Each received a blessing that was appropriate to him.

Jacob's Death and Burial

49:29 Gen 23:16-20; 25:8-9 — 29 Then Jacob told them, "Soon I will die. Bury me with my father and grandfather in
the cave in Ephron's field. 30 This is the cave in the field of Machpelah, near Mamre
in Canaan, which Abraham bought from Ephron the Hittite for a permanent burial
49:31 Gen 23:19; 25:9; 35:29 — place. 31 There Abraham and his wife Sarah are buried. There Isaac and his wife,
Rebekah, are buried. And there I buried Leah. 32 It is the cave that my grandfather
49:33 Gen 25:8 Acts 7:15 — Abraham bought from the Hittites." 33 Then when Jacob had finished this charge to
his sons, he lay back in the bed, breathed his last, and died.

50:1 Gen 46:4 — **50** Joseph threw himself on his father and wept over him and kissed him. 2 Then
50:2 Gen 50:26 — Joseph told his morticians to embalm the body. 3 The embalming process took
forty days, and there was a period of national mourning for seventy days. 4 When the
50:3 Num 20:29 Deut 34:8 — period of mourning was over, Joseph approached Pharaoh's advisers and asked them
to speak to Pharaoh on his behalf. 5 He told them, "Tell Pharaoh that my father made
50:5 Gen 47:29-31 — me swear an oath. He said to me, 'I am about to die; take my body back to the land of
Canaan, and bury me in our family's burial cave.' Now I need to go and bury my
father. After his burial is complete, I will return without delay."

49:28 Hebrew *Israel.*

JACOB'S SONS AND THEIR NOTABLE DESCENDANTS
Jacob's 12 sons were the ancestors of the 12 tribes of Israel. The entire nation of Israel came from these men.

Son	Notable descendants
REUBEN	none
SIMEON	none
LEVI	Aaron, Moses, Eli, John the Baptist
JUDAH	David, Jesus
DAN	Samson
NAPHTALI	Barak, Elijah (?)
GAD	Jephthah (?)
ASHER	none
ISSACHAR	none
ZEBULUN	none
JOSEPH	Joshua, Gideon, Samuel
BENJAMIN	Saul, Esther, Paul

50:1-11 When Jacob died at the age of 147, Joseph wept and mourned for months. When someone close to us dies, we need a long period of time to work through our grief. Crying and sharing our feelings with others helps us recover and go on with life. Allow yourself and others the freedom to grieve over the loss of a loved one, and give yourself time enough to complete your grieving process.

50:2, 3 Embalming was typical for Egyptians but unusual for nomadic shepherds. Believing that the dead went to the next world in their physical bodies, the Egyptians embalmed bodies to preserve them so they could function in the world to come. Jacob's family allowed him to be embalmed as a sign of courtesy and respect to the Egyptians.

50:5 Joseph had proven himself trustworthy as Pharaoh's adviser. Because of his good record, Pharaoh had little doubt that he would return to Egypt as promised after burying his father in Canaan. Privileges and freedom often result when we have demonstrated our trustworthiness. Since trust must be built gradually over time, take every opportunity to prove your reliability even in minor matters.

6 Pharaoh agreed to Joseph's request. "Go and bury your father, as you promised,"
he said. 7 So Joseph went, with a great number of Pharaoh's counselors and
advisers—all the senior officers of Egypt. 8 Joseph also took his brothers and the
entire household of Jacob. But they left their little children and flocks and herds in
the land of Goshen. 9 So a great number of chariots, cavalry, and people accompanied
Joseph.

10 When they arrived at the threshing floor of Atad, near the Jordan River, they
held a very great and solemn funeral, with a seven-day period of mourning for
Joseph's father. 11 The local residents, the Canaanites, renamed the place Abel-mizraim,* for they said, "This is a place of very deep mourning for these Egyptians."
12 So Jacob's sons did as he had commanded them. 13 They carried his body to the
land of Canaan and buried it there in the cave of Machpelah. This is the cave that
Abraham had bought for a permanent burial place in the field of Ephron the Hittite,
near Mamre.

Joseph Reassures His Brothers

14 Then Joseph returned to Egypt with his brothers and all who had accompanied him to
his father's funeral. 15 But now that their father was dead, Joseph's brothers became
afraid. "Now Joseph will pay us back for all the evil we did to him," they said. 16 So they
sent this message to Joseph: "Before your father died, he instructed us 17 to say to you:
'Forgive your brothers for the great evil they did to you.' So we, the servants of the God
of your father, beg you to forgive us." When Joseph received the message, he broke down
and wept. 18 Then his brothers came and bowed low before him. "We are your slaves,"
they said.

19 But Joseph told them, "Don't be afraid of me. Am I God, to judge and punish you?
20 As far as I am concerned, God turned into good what you meant for evil. He brought
me to the high position I have today so I could save the lives of many people. 21 No, don't
be afraid. Indeed, I myself will take care of you and your families." And he spoke very
kindly to them, reassuring them.

The Death of Joseph

22 So Joseph and his brothers and their families continued to live in Egypt. Joseph was
110 years old when he died. 23 He lived to see three generations of descendants of his son
Ephraim and the children of Manasseh's son Makir, who were treated as if they were his
own.

24 "Soon I will die," Joseph told his brothers, "but God will surely come for you, to
lead you out of this land of Egypt. He will bring you back to the land he vowed to give
to the descendants of Abraham, Isaac, and Jacob."

50:8 Gen 45:10
50:9 Gen 41:43
50:12 Gen 49:29; Acts 7:16
50:13 Gen 23:16-18
50:15 Gen 42:21-22
50:16 Gen 49:29
50:17 Gen 45:5, 7; Matt 6:14; Luke 6:27; Rom 12:19
50:18 Gen 37:7-10
50:19 Gen 30:2
50:20 Gen 37:26-27
50:21 Gen 45:11
50:23 Gen 30:3
50:24 Gen 13:15; 28:13

50:11 *Abel-mizraim* means "mourning of the Egyptians."

50:12, 13 Abraham had purchased the cave in the field of Machpelah as a burial place for his wife Sarah (23:1-9). It was to be a burial place for his entire family. Jacob was Abraham's grandson, and Jacob's sons returned to Canaan to bury him in this cave along with Abraham and Isaac. Their desire to be buried in this cave expressed their faith in God's promise to give their descendants the land of Canaan.

50:15-21 Now that Jacob (or Israel) was dead, the brothers feared revenge from Joseph. Could he really have forgiven them for selling him into slavery? But to their surprise, Joseph not only forgave them but reassured them, offering to care for them and their families. Joseph's forgiveness was complete. He demonstrated how God graciously accepts us even though we don't deserve it. Because God forgives us even when we have ignored or rejected him, we should graciously forgive others.

50:20 God brought good from the brothers' evil deed, Potiphar's wife's false accusation, the cup-bearer's neglect, and seven years of famine. The experiences in Joseph's life taught him that God brings good from evil for those who trust him. Do you trust God enough to wait patiently for him to bring good out of bad situations? You can trust him because, as Joseph learned, God can overrule people's evil intentions to bring about his intended results.

50:24 Joseph was ready to die. He had no doubts that God would keep his promise and one day bring the Israelites back to their homeland. What a tremendous example! The secret of that kind of faith is a lifetime of trusting God. Your faith is like a muscle—it grows with exercise, gaining strength over time. After a lifetime of exercising trust, your faith can be as strong as Joseph's. Then at your death, you can be confident that God will fulfill all his promises to you and to all those faithful to him who may live after you.

50:24 This verse sets the stage for what would begin to happen in Exodus and come to completion in Joshua. God was going to make Jacob's family into a great nation, lead them out of Egypt, and bring them into the land he had promised them. The nation would rely heavily on this promise, and Joseph emphasized his belief that God would do what he had promised.

50:25
Exod 13:19
Josh 24:32
Heb 11:22

50:26
Exod 1:6

25 Then Joseph made the sons of Israel swear an oath, and he said, "When God
comes to lead us back to Canaan, you must take my body back with you." 26 So Joseph
died at the age of 110. They embalmed him, and his body was placed in a coffin in
Egypt.

50:26 The book of Genesis gives us rich descriptions of the lives of many great men and women who walked with God. They sometimes succeeded and often failed. Yet we learn much by reading the biographies of these people. Where did they get their motivation and courage? They got it by realizing God was with them despite their inadequacies. Knowing this should encourage us to be faithful to God, to rely on him for guidance, and to utilize the potential he has given us.

EXODUS

Joseph dies 1805 B.C. (1640 B.C.)

S L A V E R Y I N E G Y P T

VITAL STATISTICS

PURPOSE:
To record the events of Israel's deliverance from Egypt and development as a nation

AUTHOR:
Moses

DATE WRITTEN:
1450–1410 B.C., approximately the same as Genesis

WHERE WRITTEN:
In the wilderness during Israel's wanderings, somewhere in the Sinai peninsula

SETTING:
Egypt. God's people, once highly favored in the land, are now slaves. God is about to set them free.

KEY VERSES:
"Then the LORD told him, 'You can be sure I have seen the misery of my people in Egypt. I have heard their cries for deliverance from their harsh slave drivers. Yes, I am aware of their suffering. . . . Now go, for I am sending you to Pharaoh. You will lead my people, the Israelites, out of Egypt'" (3:7, 10).

KEY PEOPLE:
Moses, Miriam, Pharaoh, Pharaoh's daughter, Jethro, Aaron, Joshua, Bezalel

KEY PLACES:
Egypt, Goshen, Nile River, Midian, Red Sea, Sinai peninsula, Mount Sinai

SPECIAL FEATURES:
Exodus relates more miracles than any other Old Testament book and is noted for containing the Ten Commandments

GET UP . . . leave . . . take off—these words are good ones for those trapped or enslaved. Some resist their marching orders, however, preferring present surroundings to a new, unknown environment. It's not easy to trade the comfortable security of the known for an uncertain future. But what if God gives the order to move? Will we follow his lead? Exodus describes a series of God's calls and the responses of his people.

Four hundred years had passed since Joseph moved his family to Egypt. These descendants of Abraham had now grown to over two million strong. To Egypt's new pharaoh, these Hebrews were foreigners, and their numbers were frightening. Pharaoh decided to make them slaves so they wouldn't upset his balance of power. As it turned out, that was his biggest mistake, for God then came to the rescue of his people.

Through a series of strange events, a Hebrew boy named Moses became a prince in Pharaoh's palace and then an outcast in a wilderness land. God visited Moses in the mysterious flames of a burning bush, and after some discussion, Moses agreed to return to Egypt to lead God's people out of slavery. Pharaoh was confronted, and through a cycle of plagues and promises made and broken, Israel was torn from his grasp.

It was no easy task to mobilize this mass of humanity, but they marched out of Egypt, through the Red Sea, and into the wilderness behind Moses and the pillars of cloud and fire. Despite continual evidence of God's love and power, the people complained and began to yearn for their days in Egypt. God provided for their physical and spiritual needs with food and a place to worship, but he also judged their disobedience and unbelief. Then in the dramatic Sinai meeting with Moses, God gave his laws for right living.

God led Moses and the nation of Israel, and he wants to lead us as well. Is he preparing you, like Moses, for a specific task? He will be with you; obey and follow. Is he delivering you from an enemy or a temptation? Trust him, and do what he says. Have you heard his clear moral directions? Read, study, and obey his Word. Is he calling you to true worship? Discover God's presence in your life, in your home, and in the body of assembled believers. Exodus is the exciting story of God's guidance. Read with the determination to follow God wherever he leads.

Moses born 1526 (1350)	*Exodus from Egypt 1446 (1280)*	*Ten Commandments given 1445 (1279)*	*Israel enters Canaan 1406 (1240)*	*Judges begin to rule 1375 (1220)*

THE BLUEPRINT

A. ISRAEL IN EGYPT (1:1—12:30)
1. Slavery in Egypt
2. God chooses Moses
3. God sends Moses to Pharaoh
4. Plagues strike Egypt
5. The Passover

When the Israelites were enslaved in Egypt, God heard their cries and rescued them. We can be confident that God still hears the cries of his people. Just as he delivered the Israelites from their captors, he delivers us from sin, death, and evil.

B. ISRAEL IN THE WILDERNESS (12:31—18:27)
1. The Exodus
2. Crossing the sea
3. Complaining in the wilderness

After crossing the Red Sea, the Israelites became quarrelsome and discontent. Like the Israelites, we find it easy to complain and be dissatisfied. Christians still have struggles, but we should never allow difficulties and unpleasant circumstances to turn us away from trusting God.

C. ISRAEL AT SINAI (19:1—40:38)
1. Giving the law
2. Tabernacle instructions
3. Breaking the law
4. Tabernacle construction

God revealed his law to the Israelites at Sinai. Through the law, they learned more about what God is like and how he expected his people to live. The law is still instructional for us, for it exposes our sin and shows us God's standard for living.

MEGATHEMES

THEME	EXPLANATION	IMPORTANCE
Slavery	During the Israelites 400-year stay in the land of Egypt, they became enslaved to the Egyptians. Pharaoh, the king of Egypt, oppressed them cruelly. They prayed to God for deliverance from this situation.	Like the Israelites, we need both human and divine leadership to escape from the slavery of sin. After their escape, the memory of slavery helped the Israelites learn to treat others generously. We need to stand against those who oppress others.
Rescue/ Redemption	God rescued Israel through the leader Moses and through mighty miracles. The Passover celebration was an annual reminder of their escape from slavery.	God delivers us from the slavery of sin. Jesus Christ celebrated the Passover with his disciples at the Last Supper and then went on to rescue us from sin by dying in our place.
Guidance	God guided Israel out of Egypt by using the plagues, Moses' heroic courage, the miracle of the Red Sea, and the Ten Commandments. God is a trustworthy guide.	Although God is all-powerful and can do miracles, he normally leads us by wise leadership and team effort. His Word gives us the wisdom to make daily decisions and govern our lives.
Ten Commandments	God's law system had three parts. The Ten Commandments were the first part, containing the absolutes of spiritual and moral life. The civil law was the second part, giving the people rules to manage their lives. The ceremonial law was the third part, showing them patterns for building the Tabernacle and for regular worship.	God was teaching Israel the importance of choice and responsibility. When they obeyed the conditions of the law, he blessed them; if they forgot or disobeyed, he punished them or allowed calamities to come. Many great countries of the world base their laws on the moral system set up in the book of Exodus. God's moral law is valid today.
The Nation	God founded the nation of Israel to be the source of truth and salvation to all the world. His relationship to his people was loving yet firm. The Israelites had no army, schools, governors, mayors, or police when they left Egypt. God had to instruct them in their constitutional laws and daily practices. He showed them how to worship and how to have national holidays.	Israel's newly formed nation had all the behavioral characteristics of Christians today. We are often disorganized, sometimes rebellious, and sometimes victorious. God's Person and Word are still our only guides. If our churches reflect his leadership, they will be effective in serving him.

KEY PLACES IN EXODUS

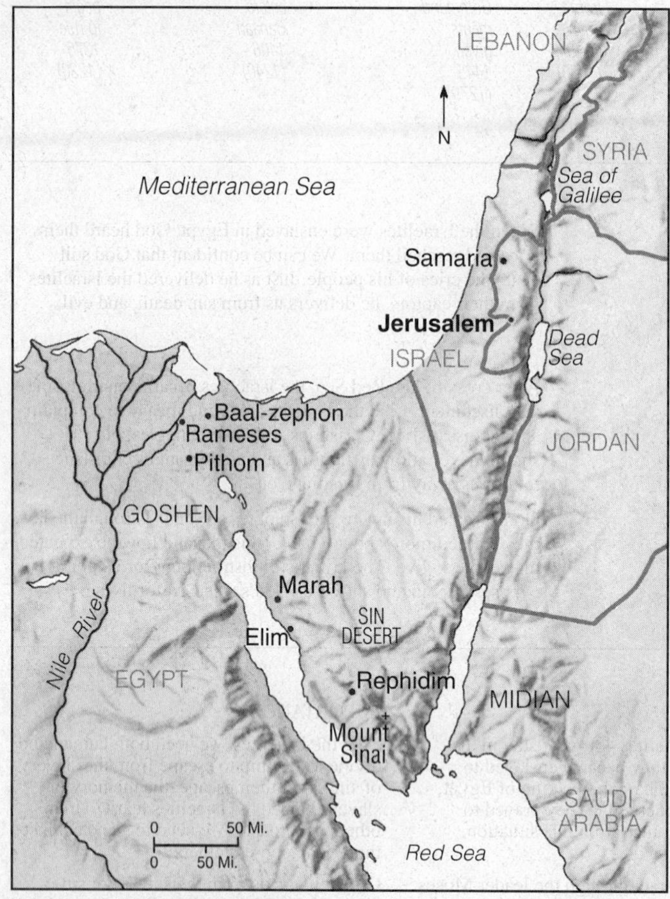

Modern names and boundaries are shown in gray.

1 Goshen This area was given to Jacob and his family when they moved to Egypt (Genesis 47:5, 6). It became the Hebrews' homeland for 400 years and remained separate from the main Egyptian centers, for Egyptian culture looked down upon shepherds and nomads. As the years passed, Jacob's family grew into a large nation (1:7).

2, 3 Pithom and Rameses During the Israelites' stay in the land of Egypt, a pharaoh came to the throne who had no respect for these descendants of Joseph and feared their large numbers. He forced them into slavery in order to oppress and subdue them. Out of their slave labor, the supply cities of Pithom and Rameses were built (1:11).

4 Midian Moses, an Egyptian prince who was born a Hebrew, killed an Egyptian and fled for his life to Midian. Here he became a shepherd and married a woman named Zipporah. It was while he was here that God commissioned him for the job of leading the Hebrew people out of Egypt (2:15—4:31).

5 Baal-zephon Slavery was not to last because God planned to deliver his people. After choosing Moses and Aaron to be his spokesmen to Pharaoh, God worked a series of dramatic miracles in the land of Egypt to convince Pharaoh to let the Hebrews go (5:1—12:33). When finally freed, the entire nation set out with the riches of Egypt (12:34–36). One of their first stops was at Baal-zephon (14:2), where Pharaoh, who had changed his mind, chased the Hebrews and trapped them against the sea. But God parted the waters and led the people through the sea on dry land. When Pharaoh's army tried to pursue, the waters collapsed around them, and they were drowned (14:5–31).

6 Marah Moses now led the people southward. The long trek across the desert brought hot tempers and parched throats for this mass of people. At Marah, the water they found was bitter, but God sweetened it (15:22–25).

7 Elim As they continued their journey, the Hebrews (now called Israelites) came to Elim, an oasis with 12 springs (15:27).

8 Sin Desert Leaving Elim, the people headed into the Sin Desert. Here the people became hungry, so God provided them with manna that came from heaven and covered the ground each morning (16:1, 13–15). The people ate this manna until they entered the Promised Land.

9 Rephidim Moses led the people to Rephidim where they found no water. But God miraculously provided water from a rock (17:1, 5, 6). Here the Israelites encountered their first test in battle: the Amalekites attacked and were defeated (17:9–13). Moses' father-in-law, Jethro, then arrived on the scene with some sound advice on delegating responsibilities (18).

10 Mount Sinai God had previously appeared to Moses on this mountain and commissioned him to lead Israel (3:1–10). Now Moses returned with the people God had asked him to lead. For almost a year the people camped at the foot of Mount Sinai. During this time God gave them his Ten Commandments as well as other laws for right living. He also provided the blueprint for building the Tabernacle (19—40).

God was forging a holy nation, prepared to live for and serve him alone.

A. ISRAEL IN EGYPT (1:1—12:30)

Joseph brought his family to Egypt and protected them there. But after Joseph's death, as they multiplied into a nation, they were forced into slavery. God then prepared Moses to free his people from slavery and lead them out of Egypt. To help Moses, God unleashed ten plagues upon the land. After the tenth plague, Pharaoh let the people go. On the night before the great Exodus, God's new nation celebrated the Passover. Just as God delivered Israel from Egypt, he delivers us from sin, death, and evil.

1. Slavery in Egypt

1:1 Gen 46:8-27 **1** These are the sons of Jacob* who went with their father to Egypt, each with his
family: 2 Reuben, Simeon, Levi, Judah, 3 Issachar, Zebulun, Benjamin, 4 Dan, Naph-
1:5 Gen 46:26 tali, Gad, and Asher. 5 Joseph was already down in Egypt. In all, Jacob had seventy*
direct descendants.
1:6 Gen 50:26 Acts 7:15-16 6 In time, Joseph and each of his brothers died, ending that generation. 7 But their
descendants had many children and grandchildren. In fact, they multiplied so quickly
1:7 Gen 12:2; 35:11; 46:3; 47:27; 48:4 †Acts 7:17 that they soon filled the land. 8 Then a new king came to the throne of Egypt who knew
nothing about Joseph or what he had done. 9 He told his people, "These Israelites are
becoming a threat to us because there are so many of them. 10 We must find a way to put
1:8 Acts 7:18-19 an end to this. If we don't and if war breaks out, they will join our enemies and fight
1:9 Ps 105:25 against us. Then they will escape from the country."
11 So the Egyptians made the Israelites their slaves and put brutal slave drivers over
1:10 Ps 105:24-25 Acts 7:17-19 them, hoping to wear them down under heavy burdens. They forced them to build the
cities of Pithom and Rameses as supply centers for the king. 12 But the more the
1:11 Exod 2:11; 3:7 Egyptians oppressed them, the more quickly the Israelites multiplied! The Egyptians
soon became alarmed 13 and decided to make their slavery more bitter still. 14 They were
1:14 Exod 2:23 ruthless with the Israelites, forcing them to make bricks and mortar and to work long
hours in the fields.
15 Then Pharaoh, the king of Egypt, gave this order to the Hebrew midwives, Shiphrah
1:16 Acts 7:19 and Puah: 16 "When you help the Hebrew women give birth, kill all the boys as soon as
they are born. Allow only the baby girls to live." 17 But because the midwives feared God,
they refused to obey the king and allowed the boys to live, too.

1:1 Hebrew *Israel.* **1:5** Dead Sea Scrolls and Greek version read *seventy-five;* see notes on Gen 46:27.

1:1 The children of Israel, or Israelites, were the descendants of Jacob, whose name was changed to Israel after he wrestled with the angel (see Genesis 32:24-30). Jacob's family had moved to Egypt at the invitation of Joseph, one of Jacob's sons who had become a great ruler under Pharaoh. Jacob's family grew into a large nation. But as foreigners and newcomers, their lives were quite different from the Egyptians'. The Hebrews worshiped one God; the Egyptians worshiped many gods. The Hebrews were wanderers; the Egyptians had a deeply rooted culture. The Hebrews were shepherds; the Egyptians were builders. The Hebrews were also physically separated from the Egyptians: They lived in Goshen, north of the great Egyptian cultural centers.

1:9, 10 Pharaoh was afraid the Israelites were becoming so numerous that they would organize and threaten his kingdom, so he made them slaves and oppressed them to kill their spirit and stop their growth. Slavery was an ancient practice used by almost all nations to employ conquered people and other captives. Most likely, the great pyramids of Egypt were built with slave labor. Although Israel was not a conquered nation, the people were foreigners and thus lacked the rights of native Egyptians.

1:11 There were levels of slavery in Egypt. Some slaves worked long hours in mud pits while others were skilled carpenters, jewelers, and craftsmen. Regardless of their skill or level, all slaves were watched closely by ruthless slave drivers, supervisors whose assignment was to keep the slaves working as fast as possible. They were specialists at making a slave's life miserable.

1:11 Ancient records indicate that these cities were built in 1290 B.C., which is why some scholars believe the Exodus occurred early in the 13th century. Looking at other evidence, however, other scholars believe the Hebrews left Egypt in 1446 B.C. How could they build two cities 150 years after they left? These scholars suggest that Rameses II, the pharaoh in 1290 B.C., did not build the cities of Pithom and Rameses. Instead, he renamed two cities that actually had been built 150 years previously. It was a common practice for an Egyptian ruler to make improvements on a city and then take credit for building it, thus wiping out all records of previous founders. Also see the second note on 13:17, 18.

1:12 The Egyptians tried to wear down the Hebrew people by forcing them into slavery and mistreating them. Instead, the Hebrews multiplied and grew stronger. When we are burdened or mistreated, we may feel defeated. But our burdens can make us stronger and develop qualities in us that will prepare us for the future. We cannot be overcomers without troubles to overcome. Be true to God in the hard times because even the worst situations can make us better people.

1:15-17 Shiphrah and Puah may have been supervisors over the midwives, or else these two were given special mention. Hebrew midwives helped women give birth and cared for the baby until the mother was stronger. When Pharaoh ordered the midwives to kill the Hebrew baby boys, he was asking the wrong group of people. Midwives were committed to helping babies be born, not to killing them. These women showed great courage and love for God by risking their lives to disobey Pharaoh's command.

1:17-21 Against Pharaoh's orders, the midwives spared the Hebrew babies. Their faith in God gave them the courage to take a stand for what they knew was right. In this situation, disobeying the authority was proper. God does not expect us to obey those in authority when they ask us to disobey him or his Word. The Bible is filled with examples of those who were willing to sacrifice their very lives in order to obey God or save others. Esther and Mordecai (Esther 3:2; 4:13-16) and Shadrach, Meshach, and Abednego (Daniel 3:16-18) are some of the people who took a

18 Then the king called for the midwives. "Why have you done this?" he demanded.
"Why have you allowed the boys to live?"
19 "Sir," they told him, "the Hebrew women are very strong. They have their babies 1:19 Josh 2:4-6
so quickly that we cannot get there in time! They are not slow in giving birth like 2 Sam 17:20
Egyptian women."
20 So God blessed the midwives, and the Israelites continued to multiply, growing 1:20 Exod 1:12
more and more powerful. 21 And because the midwives feared God, he gave them
families of their own.
22 Then Pharaoh gave this order to all his people: "Throw all the newborn Israelite 1:22 Acts 7:9
boys into the Nile River. But you may spare the baby girls."

2. God chooses Moses

The Birth of Moses

2 During this time, a man and woman from the tribe of Levi got married. 2 The woman 2:1 Exod 6:20
became pregnant and gave birth to a son. She saw what a beautiful baby he was and Num 26:59
kept him hidden for three months. 3 But when she could no longer hide him, she got a 2:2 Acts 7:20
little basket made of papyrus reeds and waterproofed it with tar and pitch. She put the Heb 11:23
baby in the basket and laid it among the reeds along the edge of the Nile River. 4 The 2:3 Gen 6:14
baby's sister then stood at a distance, watching to see what would happen to him. Isa 18:2; 19:6
5 Soon after this, one of Pharaoh's daughters came down to bathe in the river, and her 2:4 Exod 15:20
servant girls walked along the riverbank. When the princess saw the little basket among Num 26:59
the reeds, she told one of her servant girls to get it for her. 6 As the princess opened it, she 2:5 Exod 7:15; 8:20
found the baby boy. His helpless cries touched her heart. "He must be one of the Hebrew Acts 7:21
children," she said.
7 Then the baby's sister approached the princess. "Should I go and find one of the
Hebrew women to nurse the baby for you?" she asked.
8 "Yes, do!" the princess replied. So the girl rushed home and called the baby's mother.
9 "Take this child home and nurse him for me," the princess told her. "I will pay you
for your help." So the baby's mother took her baby home and nursed him.

---

bold stand for what was right. Whole nations can be caught up in immorality (racial hatred, slavery, prison cruelty); thus following the majority or the authority is not always right. Whenever we are ordered to disobey God's Word, we must "obey God rather than human authority" (Acts 5:29).

1:19-21 Did God bless the Hebrew midwives for lying to Pharaoh? God blessed them not because they lied, but because they saved the lives of innocent children. This doesn't mean that a lie was necessarily the best way to answer Pharaoh. The midwives were blessed, however, for not violating the higher law of God that forbids the senseless slaughter of innocent lives.

2:1, 2 Although a name is not mentioned yet, the baby in this story was Moses. Moses' mother and father were named Jochebed and Amram. His brother was Aaron and his sister, Miriam.

2:3 This tiny boat made of papyrus reeds was fashioned by a woman who knew what she was doing. Egyptian riverboats were made with these same reeds and waterproofed with tar. The reeds, which grew as tall as 16 feet, could be gathered in swampy areas along the Nile. Thus a small basket hidden among the reeds would be well insulated from the weather and difficult to see.

2:3ff Moses' mother knew how wrong it would be to destroy her child. But there was little she could do to change Pharaoh's new law. Her only alternative was to hide the child and later place him in a tiny papyrus basket on the river. God used her courageous act to place her son, the Hebrew of his choice, in the house of Pharaoh. Do you sometimes feel surrounded by evil and frustrated by how little you can do about it? When faced with evil, look for ways to act against it. Then trust God to use your effort, however small it seems, in his war against evil.

2:5 Who was Pharaoh's daughter? There are two popular explanations. (1) Some think that Hatshepsut was the woman who pulled Moses from the river. Her husband was Pharaoh Thutmose II. (This would match the earlier Exodus date.) Apparently Hatshepsut could not have children, so Thutmose had a son by another woman, and this son became heir to the throne. Hatshepsut would have considered Moses a gift from the gods because now she had her own son who would be the legal heir to the throne. (2) Some think the princess who rescued baby Moses was the daughter of Rameses II, an especially cruel Pharaoh who would have made life miserable for the Hebrew slaves. (This would match the later Exodus date.)

2:7, 8 Miriam, the baby's sister, saw that Pharaoh's daughter had discovered Moses. Quickly she took the initiative to suggest a nurse (her mother) who might care for the baby. The Bible doesn't say if Miriam was afraid to approach the Egyptian princess or if the princess was suspicious of the Hebrew girl. But Miriam did approach her, and the princess bought the services of Miriam and her mother. Their family was reunited. Special opportunities may come our way unexpectedly. Don't let the fear of what might happen cause you to miss an opportunity. Be alert for the opportunities God gives you, and take full advantage of them.

2:9 Moses' mother was reunited with her baby! God used her courageous act of saving and hiding her baby to begin his plan to rescue his people from Egypt. God doesn't need much from us to accomplish his plan for our lives. Focusing on our human predicament may paralyze us because the situation may appear humanly impossible. But concentrating on God and his power will help us see the way out. Right now you may feel unable to see through your troubles. Focus instead on God, and trust him for the way out. That is all he needs to begin his work in you.

2:10 1 Sam 1:20 2 Sam 22:17

10 Later, when he was older, the child's mother brought him back to the princess, who adopted him as her son. The princess named him Moses,* for she said, "I drew him out of the water."

Moses Escapes to Midian

2:11 Acts 7:23-24 Heb 11:24-26 · 2:12 Acts 7:24 · 2:13 Acts 7:26-28 · 2:14 †Acts 7:27, 35 · 2:15 Acts 7:29 · 2:16 Gen 24:11 Exod 3:1; 18:1 · 2:17 Gen 29:10 · 2:18 Num 10:29 · 2:20 Gen 18:5 · 2:21 Exod 4:25; 18:2 Acts 7:29 · 2:22 Gen 23:4 Heb 11:13

11 Many years later, when Moses had grown up, he went out to visit his people, the Israelites, and he saw how hard they were forced to work. During his visit, he saw an Egyptian beating one of the Hebrew slaves. 12 After looking around to make sure no one was watching, Moses killed the Egyptian and buried him in the sand.

13 The next day, as Moses was out visiting his people again, he saw two Hebrew men fighting. "What are you doing, hitting your neighbor like that?" Moses said to the one in the wrong.

14 "Who do you think you are?" the man replied. "Who appointed you to be our prince and judge? Do you plan to kill me as you killed that Egyptian yesterday?"

Moses was badly frightened because he realized that everyone knew what he had done. 15 And sure enough, when Pharaoh heard about it, he gave orders to have Moses arrested and killed. But Moses fled from Pharaoh and escaped to the land of Midian.

When Moses arrived in Midian, he sat down beside a well. 16 Now it happened that the priest of Midian had seven daughters who came regularly to this well to draw water and fill the water troughs for their father's flocks. 17 But other shepherds would often come and chase the girls and their flocks away. This time, however, Moses came to their aid, rescuing the girls from the shepherds. Then he helped them draw water for their flocks.

18 When the girls returned to Reuel, their father, he asked, "How did you get the flocks watered so quickly today?"

19 "An Egyptian rescued us from the shepherds," they told him. "And then he drew water for us and watered our flocks."

20 "Well, where is he then?" their father asked. "Did you just leave him there? Go and invite him home for a meal!"

21 Moses was happy to accept the invitation, and he settled down to live with them. In time, Reuel gave Moses one of his daughters, Zipporah, to be his wife. 22 Later they had a baby boy, and Moses named him Gershom,* for he said, "I have been a stranger in a foreign land."

2:10 *Moses* sounds like a Hebrew term that means "to draw out." **2:22** *Gershom* sounds like a Hebrew term that means "a stranger here."

2:12-14 Moses tried to make sure no one was watching before he killed the Egyptian. But as it turned out, someone did see, and Moses had to flee the country. Sometimes we mistakenly think we can get away with doing wrong if no one sees or catches us. Sooner or later, however, doing wrong will catch up with us as it did with Moses. Even if we are not caught in this life, we will still have to face God and his evaluation of our actions.

2:15 To escape punishment for killing the Egyptian, Moses ran away to Midian. He became a stranger in a strange land, separated from his home and family. It took many years after this incident for Moses to be ready to serve God. But he trusted God instead of fearing the king (Hebrews 11:27). We may feel abandoned or isolated because of something we have done. But though we feel afraid and separated, we should not give up. Moses didn't. He trusted God to deliver him, no matter how dark his past or bleak his future.

2:17 How did Moses handle these shepherds so easily? As an Egyptian prince, Moses would have been well trained in the Egyptian military, the most advanced army in the world. Even a large group of shepherds would have been no match for the sophisticated fighting techniques of this trained warrior.

2:18 Reuel is also called Jethro in 3:1.

2:23-25 God's rescue doesn't always come the moment we want it. God had promised to bring the Hebrew slaves out of Egypt (Genesis 15:16; 46:3, 4). The people had waited a long time for that promise to be kept, but God rescued them when he knew the right time had come. God knows the best time to act. When you feel that God has forgotten you in your troubles, remember that God has a time schedule we can't see.

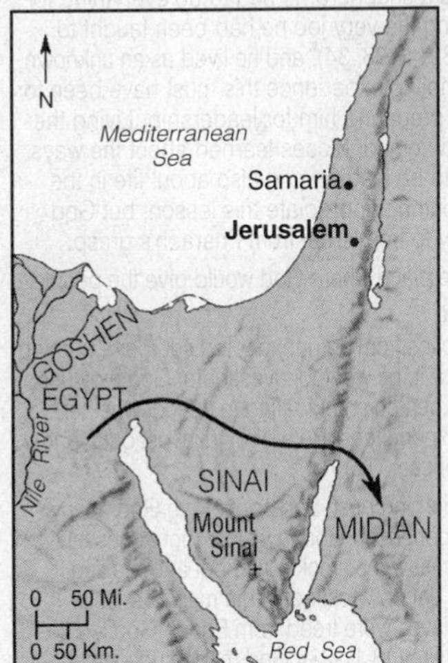

MOSES FLEES TO MIDIAN
After murdering an Egyptian, Moses escaped into Midian. There he married Zipporah and became a shepherd.

23 Years passed, and the king of Egypt died. But the Israelites still groaned beneath their
burden of slavery. They cried out for help, and their pleas for deliverance rose up to God.
24 God heard their cries and remembered his covenant promise to Abraham, Isaac, and
Jacob. 25 He looked down on the Israelites and felt deep concern for their welfare.

Moses and the Burning Bush

3 One day Moses was tending the flock of his father-in-law, Jethro,* the priest of
Midian, and he went deep into the wilderness near Sinai,* the mountain of God.
2 Suddenly, the angel of the LORD appeared to him as a blazing fire in a bush. Moses was
amazed because the bush was engulfed in flames, but it didn't burn up. 3 "Amazing!"
Moses said to himself. "Why isn't that bush burning up? I must go over to see this."
4 When the LORD saw that he had caught Moses' attention, God called to him from the
bush, "Moses! Moses!"

"Here I am!" Moses replied.

5 "Do not come any closer," God told him. "Take off your sandals, for you are standing
on holy ground." 6 Then he said, "I am the God of your ancestors—the God of Abraham,
the God of Isaac, and the God of Jacob." When Moses heard this, he hid his face in his
hands because he was afraid to look at God.
7 Then the LORD told him, "You can be sure I have seen the misery of my people in
Egypt. I have heard their cries for deliverance from their harsh slave drivers. Yes, I am
aware of their suffering. 8 So I have come to rescue them from the Egyptians and lead
them out of Egypt into their own good and spacious land. It is a land flowing with milk
and honey—the land where the Canaanites, Hittites, Amorites, Perizzites, Hivites, and
Jebusites live. 9 The cries of the people of Israel have reached me, and I have seen how
the Egyptians have oppressed them with heavy tasks. 10 Now go, for I am sending you
to Pharaoh. You will lead my people, the Israelites, out of Egypt."
11 "But who am I to appear before Pharaoh?" Moses asked God. "How can you expect
me to lead the Israelites out of Egypt?"
12 Then God told him, "I will be with you. And this will serve as proof that I have sent
you: When you have brought the Israelites out of Egypt, you will return here to worship
God at this very mountain."
13 But Moses protested, "If I go to the people of Israel and tell them, 'The God of your

2:23 Exod 6:5, 9; Acts 7:34
2:24 Gen 22:16-18; 26:2-3; 28:13; Ps 105:10, 42
3:2 †Acts 7:30
3:3 †Acts 7:31
3:5 Gen 28:17; Josh 5:15; †Acts 7:33
3:6 †Matt 22:32; †Mark 12:26; †Luke 20:37; †Acts 3:13; 7:32
3:7 †Acts 7:34
3:8 Gen 15:18-19; 46:4; 50:24; Exod 3:17; Deut 6:3; 8:7-9; 11:9; 26:9
3:10 †Acts 7:34
3:11 Exod 4:10; 6:12
3:12 Exod 4:12; 19:2; †Acts 7:7
3:13 Exod 15:3

3:1a Moses' father-in-law went by two names, Jethro and Reuel. **3:1b** Hebrew *Horeb,* another name for Sinai.

3:1 What a contrast between Moses' life as an Egyptian prince and his life as a Midianite shepherd! As a prince he had everything done for him; he was the famous son of an Egyptian princess. As a shepherd he had to do everything for himself; he was holding the very job he had been taught to despise (Genesis 43:32; 46:33, 34), and he lived as an unknown foreigner. What a humbling experience this must have been for Moses! But God was preparing him for leadership. Living the life of a shepherd and nomad, Moses learned about the ways of the people he would be leading and also about life in the wilderness. Moses couldn't appreciate this lesson, but God was getting him ready to free Israel from Pharaoh's grasp.

3:1 Mount Sinai is the place where God would give the people his revealed law (3:12).

3:2 God spoke to Moses from an unexpected source: a burning bush. When Moses saw it, he went to investigate. God may use unexpected sources when communicating to us too, whether people, thoughts, or experiences. Be willing to investigate, and be open to God's surprises.

3:2-4 Moses saw a burning bush and spoke with God. Many people in the Bible experienced God in visible (not necessarily human) form. Abraham saw the smoking firepot and blazing torch (Genesis 15:17); Jacob wrestled with a man (Genesis 32:24-29). When the slaves were freed from Egypt, God led them by pillars of cloud and fire (13:17-22). God made such appearances to encourage his new nation, to guide them, and to prove the reliability of his verbal message.

3:5, 6 At God's command, Moses removed his sandals and covered his face. Taking off his shoes was an act of reverence, conveying his own unworthiness before God. God is our friend, but he is also our sovereign Lord. To approach him frivolously shows a lack of respect and sincerity. When you come to God in worship, do you approach him casually, or do you come as though you were an invited guest before a king? If necessary, adjust your attitude so it is suitable for approaching a holy God.

3:8 This "land flowing with milk and honey" is the land of Israel and Jordan today. This was a poetic word picture expressing the beauty and productivity of the Promised Land.

3:10ff Moses made excuses because he felt inadequate for the job God asked him to do. It was natural for him to feel that way. He *was* inadequate all by himself. But God wasn't asking Moses to work alone. He offered other resources to help (God himself, Aaron, and the ability to do miracles). God often calls us to do tasks that seem too difficult, but he doesn't ask us to do them alone. God offers us his resources, just as he did to Moses. We should not hide behind our inadequacies, as Moses did, but look beyond ourselves to the great resources available. Then we can allow God to use our unique contributions.

3:13-15 The Egyptians had many gods by many different names. Moses wanted to know God's name so the Hebrew people would know exactly who had sent him to them. God called himself I AM, a name describing his eternal power and unchangeable character. In a world where values, morals, and laws change constantly, we can find stability and security in our

ancestors has sent me to you,' they won't believe me. They will ask, 'Which god are you
talking about? What is his name?' Then what should I tell them?"

3:14 Exod 6:3; John 8:58; Rev 1:8; 4:8

14God replied, "I AM THE ONE WHO ALWAYS IS.* Just tell them, 'I AM has sent me to
you.'" 15God also said, "Tell them, 'The LORD,* the God of your ancestors—the God
of Abraham, the God of Isaac, and the God of Jacob—has sent me to you.' This will be
my name forever; it has always been my name, and it will be used throughout all
generations.

3:15 Pss 72:17; 102:12; 135:13; †Acts 3:13

16"Now go and call together all the leaders of Israel. Tell them, 'The LORD, the God
of your ancestors—the God of Abraham, Isaac, and Jacob—appeared to me in a burning
bush. He said, "You can be sure that I am watching over you and have seen what is
happening to you in Egypt. 17I promise to rescue you from the oppression of the
Egyptians. I will lead you to the land now occupied by the Canaanites, Hittites, Amorites,
Perizzites, Hivites, and Jebusites—a land flowing with milk and honey."'

3:16 Exod 4:29

3:17 Exod 3:8; Josh 24:11

18"The leaders of the people of Israel will accept your message. Then all of you must
go straight to the king of Egypt and tell him, 'The LORD, the God of the Hebrews, has
met with us. Let us go on a three-day journey into the wilderness to offer sacrifices to
the LORD our God.'

3:18 Exod 4:23; 5:1, 3; Num 23:4, 16

19"But I know that the king of Egypt will not let you go except under heavy pressure.
20So I will reach out and strike at the heart of Egypt with all kinds of miracles. Then at
last he will let you go. 21And I will see to it that the Egyptians treat you well. They will
load you down with gifts so you will not leave empty-handed. 22The Israelite women
will ask for silver and gold jewelry and fine clothing from their Egyptian neighbors and
their neighbors' guests. With this clothing, you will dress your sons and daughters. In
this way, you will plunder the Egyptians!"

3:19 Exod 5:2; 6:1; 7:4

3:20 Exod 11:1; 12:31-33; Neh 9:10; Acts 7:36

3:21 Exod 11:3

3:22 Exod 11:2; 12:35

Signs of the LORD's Power

4:1 Exod 3:15-16, 18

4 But Moses protested again, "Look, they won't believe me! They won't do what I tell
them. They'll just say, 'The LORD never appeared to you.'"
2Then the LORD asked him, "What do you have there in your hand?"
"A shepherd's staff," Moses replied.
3"Throw it down on the ground," the LORD told him. So Moses threw it down, and it
became a snake! Moses was terrified, so he turned and ran away.
4Then the LORD told him, "Take hold of its tail." So Moses reached out and grabbed
it, and it became a shepherd's staff again.
5"Perform this sign, and they will believe you," the LORD told him. "Then they will

4:3 Exod 7:8-12, 15

4:5 Exod 4:31; 19:9

3:14 Or *I AM WHO I AM,* or *I WILL BE WHAT I WILL BE.* 3:15 Hebrew *Yahweh;* traditionally rendered *Jehovah.*

---

unchanging God. The God who appeared to Moses is the same God who can live in us today. Hebrews 13:8 says God is the same "yesterday, today, and forever." Because God's nature is stable and trustworthy, we are free to follow and enjoy him rather than spend our time trying to figure him out.

3:14, 15 God reminded Moses of his covenant promises to Abraham (Genesis 12:1-3; 15; 17), Isaac (Genesis 26:2-5), and Jacob (Genesis 28:13-15), and used the name I AM to show his unchanging nature. What God promised to the great patriarchs hundreds of years earlier he would fulfill through Moses.

3:16, 17 God told Moses to tell the people what he saw and heard at the burning bush. Our God is a God who acts and speaks. One of the most convincing ways to tell others about him is to describe what he has done and how he has spoken to his people. If you are trying to explain God to others, talk about what he has done for you, for people you know, or for people whose stories are told in the Bible.

3:18-20 The leaders of Israel would accept God's message, and the leaders of Egypt would reject it. God knew what both reactions would be before they happened. This is more than good psychology—God knows the future. Any believer can trust his or her future to God because God already knows what is going to happen.

3:22 The jewelry and clothing were not merely borrowed—they were asked for and easily received. The Egyptians were so glad to see the Israelites go that they sent them out with gifts. These items were used later in building the Tabernacle (35:5, 22). The promise of being able to plunder the Egyptians seemed impossible to Moses at this time.

4:1 Moses' reluctance and fear were caused by overanticipation. He was worried about how the people might respond to him. We often build up events in our minds and then panic over what might go wrong. God does not ask us to go where he has not provided the means to help. Go where he leads, trusting him to supply courage, confidence, and resources at the right moment.

4:2-4 A shepherd's staff was commonly a three- to six-foot wooden rod with a curved hook at the top. The shepherd used it for walking, guiding his sheep, killing snakes, and many other tasks. Still, it was just a stick. But God used the simple shepherd's staff Moses carried as a sign to teach him an important lesson. God sometimes takes joy in using ordinary things for extraordinary purposes. What are the ordinary things in your life—your voice, a pen, a hammer, a broom, a musical instrument? While it is easy to assume God can use only special skills, you must not hinder his use of the everyday contributions you can make. Little did Moses imagine the power his simple staff would wield when it became the staff of God.

realize that the LORD, the God of their ancestors—the God of Abraham, the God of Isaac,
and the God of Jacob—really has appeared to you."
6 Then the LORD said to Moses, "Put your hand inside your robe." Moses did so, and
when he took it out again, his hand was white as snow with leprosy.* 7 "Now put your
hand back into your robe again," the LORD said. Moses did, and when he took it out this
time, it was as healthy as the rest of his body.
8 "If they do not believe the first miraculous sign, they will believe the second," the
LORD said. 9 "And if they do not believe you even after these two signs, then take some
water from the Nile River and pour it out on the dry ground. When you do, it will turn
into blood."
10 But Moses pleaded with the LORD, "O Lord, I'm just not a good speaker. I never
have been, and I'm not now, even after you have spoken to me. I'm clumsy with words."
11 "Who makes mouths?" the LORD asked him. "Who makes people so they can speak
or not speak, hear or not hear, see or not see? Is it not I, the LORD? 12 Now go, and do as
I have told you. I will help you speak well, and I will tell you what to say."
13 But Moses again pleaded, "Lord, please! Send someone else."
14 Then the LORD became angry with Moses. "All right," he said. "What about your
brother, Aaron the Levite? He is a good speaker. And look! He is on his way to meet you
now. And when he sees you, he will be very glad. 15 You will talk to him, giving him the
words to say. I will help both of you to speak clearly, and I will tell you what to do.
16 Aaron will be your spokesman to the people, and you will be as God to him, telling
him what to say. 17 And be sure to take your shepherd's staff along so you can perform
the miraculous signs I have shown you."

Moses Returns to Egypt

18 Then Moses went back home and talked it over with Jethro, his father-in-law. "With
your permission," Moses said, "I would like to go back to Egypt to visit my family. I
don't even know whether they are still alive."
"Go with my blessing," Jethro replied.
19 Before Moses left Midian, the LORD said to him, "Do not be afraid to return to
Egypt, for all those who wanted to kill you are dead."
20 So Moses took his wife and sons, put them on a donkey, and headed back to the land
of Egypt. In his hand he carried the staff of God.

4:6 Num 12:10; 2 Kgs 5:27
4:7 2 Kgs 5:14; Matt 8:3; Luke 17:12-14
4:9 Exod 7:17-21
4:10 Exod 3:11; Jer 1:6
4:11 Ps 94:9; Matt 11:5
4:12 Deut 18:15, 18; Matt 10:19-20; Mark 13:11
4:14 Exod 4:27; 6:7
4:15 Isa 51:16; Jer 1:9
4:16 Exod 7:1; 18:19
4:17 Exod 14:16; 17:9
4:18 Exod 2:21
4:19 Exod 2:15, 23
4:20 Exod 18:3; Acts 7:29

4:6 Or *with a contagious skin disease.* The Hebrew word used here can describe various skin diseases.

4:6, 7 This contagious skin disease was leprosy, one of the most feared diseases of this time. There was no cure, and a great deal of suffering preceded eventual death. Through this experience, Moses learned that God could cause or cure any kind of problem. He saw that God indeed had all power and was commissioning him to exercise that power to lead the Hebrews out of Egypt.

4:10-13 Moses pleaded with God to let him out of his mission. After all, he was not a good speaker and would probably embarrass both himself and God. But God looked at Moses' problem quite differently. All Moses needed was some help, and who better than God could help him say and do the right things. God made his mouth and would give him the words to say. It is easy for us to focus on our weaknesses, but if God asks us to do something, then he will help us get the job done. If the job involves some of our weak areas, then we can trust that he will provide words, strength, courage, and ability where needed.

4:14 God finally agreed to let Aaron speak for Moses. Moses' feelings of inadequacy were so strong that he could not trust even God's ability to help him. Moses had to deal with his deep sense of inadequacy many times. When we face difficult or frightening situations, we must be willing to let God help us.

4:16 The phrase "you will be as God to him" means that Moses would tell Aaron what to say as God was telling him.

4:17-20 Moses clung tightly to the shepherd's staff as he left for Egypt to face the greatest challenge of his life. The staff was his assurance of God's presence and power. When feeling uncertain, some people need something to stabilize and reassure them. For assurance when facing great trials, God has given promises from his Word and examples from great heroes of faith. Any Christian may cling tightly to these.

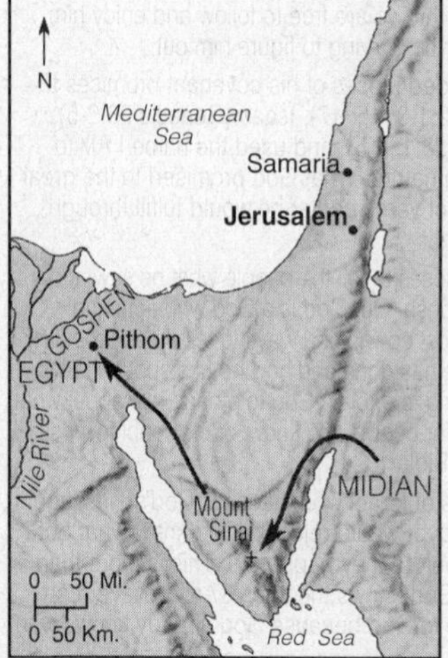

MOSES RETURNS TO EGYPT
God appeared to Moses in a mysterious burning bush on Mount Sinai. Later Aaron met Moses at the mountain, and together they returned to Egypt, a 200-mile trip.

4:21 Exod 7:3, 13; 9:12; Deut 2:30; John 12:40
4:22 Isa 63:16; 64:8; Jer 31:9; Hos 11:1; Rom 9:4
4:23 Exod 5:1; 6:11; 7:16
4:24 Num 22:22; 1 Chr 21:16
4:25-26 Josh 5:2-3
4:27 Exod 4:14
4:28 Exod 4:16
4:29 Exod 3:16
4:30 Exod 4:15
4:31 Exod 3:18; 12:27

21 Then the LORD reminded him, "When you arrive back in Egypt, go to Pharaoh and perform the miracles I have empowered you to do. But I will make him stubborn so he will not let the people go. 22 Then you will tell him, 'This is what the LORD says: Israel is my firstborn son. 23 I commanded you to let him go, so he could worship me. But since you have refused, be warned! I will kill your firstborn son!'"

24 On the journey, when Moses and his family had stopped for the night, the LORD confronted Moses* and was about to kill him. 25 But Zipporah, his wife, took a flint knife and circumcised her son. She threw the foreskin at Moses' feet and said, "What a blood-smeared bridegroom you are to me!" 26 (When she called Moses a "blood-smeared bridegroom," she was referring to the circumcision.) After that, the LORD left him alone.

27 Now the LORD had said to Aaron, "Go out into the wilderness to meet Moses." So Aaron traveled to the mountain of God, where he found Moses and greeted him warmly. 28 Moses then told Aaron everything the LORD had commanded them to do and say. And he told him about the miraculous signs they were to perform.

29 So Moses and Aaron returned to Egypt and called the leaders of Israel to a meeting. 30 Aaron told them everything the LORD had told Moses, and Moses performed the miraculous signs as they watched. 31 The leaders were soon convinced that the LORD had sent Moses and Aaron. And when they realized that the LORD had seen their misery and was deeply concerned for them, they all bowed their heads and worshiped.

3. God sends Moses to Pharaoh

Moses and Aaron Speak to Pharaoh

5:1 Exod 3:18; 4:23
5:2 Exod 3:19; Job 21:15
5:3 Exod 3:18; Deut 28:21
5:4-5 Exod 1:11; 2:11

5 After this presentation to Israel's leaders, Moses and Aaron went to see Pharaoh. They told him, "This is what the LORD, the God of Israel, says: 'Let my people go, for they must go out into the wilderness to hold a religious festival in my honor.'"

2 "Is that so?" retorted Pharaoh. "And who is the LORD that I should listen to him and let Israel go? I don't know the LORD, and I will not let Israel go."

3 But Aaron and Moses persisted. "The God of the Hebrews has met with us," they declared. "Let us take a three-day trip into the wilderness so we can offer sacrifices to the LORD our God. If we don't, we will surely die by disease or the sword."

4 "Who do you think you are," Pharaoh shouted, "distracting the people from their tasks? Get back to work! 5 Look, there are many people here in Egypt, and you are stopping them from doing their work."

4:24 Or *confronted Moses' son;* Hebrew reads *confronted him.*

4:24-26 God was about to kill Moses because Moses had not circumcised his son. Why hadn't Moses done this? Remember that Moses had spent half his life in Pharaoh's palace and half his life in the Midianite wilderness. He might not have been too familiar with God's laws, especially since all the requirements of God's covenant with Israel (Genesis 17) had not been actively carried out for over 400 years. In addition, Moses' wife, due to her Midianite background, may have opposed circumcision. But Moses could not effectively serve as deliverer of God's people until he had fulfilled the conditions of God's covenant, and one of those conditions was circumcision. Before they could go any farther, Moses and his family had to follow God's commands completely. Under Old Testament law, failing to circumcise your son was to remove yourself and your family from God's blessings. Moses learned that disobeying God was even more dangerous than tangling with an Egyptian pharaoh.

4:25, 26 Why did Zipporah perform the circumcision? It may have been Zipporah who, as a Midianite unfamiliar with the circumcision requirement, had persuaded Moses not to circumcise their son. If she prevented the action, now she would have to perform it. It is also possible that Moses became ill as a result of permitting disobedience, and so Zipporah had to perform the circumcision herself to save both her husband and son. This would not have made her happy—hence, her unflattering comment to Moses.

5:1, 2 Pharaoh was familiar with many gods (Egypt was filled with them), but he had never heard of the God of Israel. Pharaoh assumed that the God of the Hebrew slaves couldn't be very powerful. At first, Pharaoh was not at all worried about Moses' message, for he had not yet seen any evidence of the Lord's power.

5:3 Pharaoh would not listen to Moses and Aaron because he did not know or respect God. People who do not know God may not listen to his Word or his messengers. Like Moses and Aaron, we need to persist. When others reject you or your faith, don't be surprised or discouraged. Continue to tell them about God, trusting him to open minds and soften stubborn hearts.

5:4-9 Moses and Aaron took their message to Pharaoh just as God directed. The unhappy result was harder work and more oppression for the Hebrews. Sometimes hardship comes as a result of obeying God. Are you following God but still suffering—or suffering even worse than before? If your life is miserable, don't assume you have fallen out of God's favor. You may be suffering for doing good in an evil world.

Making Bricks without Straw

[6]That same day Pharaoh sent this order to the slave drivers and foremen he had set over the people of Israel: [7]"Do not supply the people with any more straw for making bricks. Let them get it themselves! [8]But don't reduce their production quotas by a single brick. They obviously don't have enough to do. If they did, they wouldn't be talking about going into the wilderness to offer sacrifices to their God. [9]Load them down with more work. Make them sweat! That will teach them to listen to these liars!"

[10]So the slave drivers and foremen informed the people: "Pharaoh has ordered us not to provide straw for you. [11]Go and get it yourselves. Find it wherever you can. But you must produce just as many bricks as before!" [12]So the people scattered throughout the land in search of straw.

[13]The slave drivers were brutal. "Meet your daily quota of bricks, just as you did before!" they demanded. [14]Then they whipped the Israelite foremen in charge of the work crews. "Why haven't you met your quotas either yesterday or today?" they demanded.

[15]So the Israelite foremen went to Pharaoh and pleaded with him. "Please don't treat us like this," they begged. [16]"We are given no straw, but we are still told to make as many bricks as before. We are beaten for something that isn't our fault! It is the fault of your slave drivers for making such unreasonable demands."

[17]But Pharaoh replied, "You're just lazy! You obviously don't have enough to do. If you did, you wouldn't be saying, 'Let us go, so we can offer sacrifices to the LORD.' [18]Now, get back to work! No straw will be given to you, but you must still deliver the regular quota of bricks."

[19]Since Pharaoh would not let up on his demands, the Israelite foremen could see that they were in serious trouble. [20]As they left Pharaoh's court, they met Moses and Aaron, who were waiting outside for them. [21]The foremen said to them, "May the LORD judge you for getting us into this terrible situation with Pharaoh* and his officials. You have given them an excuse to kill us!"

[22]So Moses went back to the LORD and protested, "Why have you mistreated your own people like this, Lord? Why did you send me? [23]Since I gave Pharaoh your message, he has been even more brutal to your people. You have not even begun to rescue them!"

Promises of Deliverance

6 "Now you will see what I will do to Pharaoh," the LORD told Moses. "When he feels my powerful hand upon him, he will let the people go. In fact, he will be so anxious to get rid of them that he will force them to leave his land!"

[2]And God continued, "I am the LORD. [3]I appeared to Abraham, to Isaac, and to Jacob as God Almighty,* though I did not reveal my name, the LORD,* to them. [4]And I entered into a solemn covenant with them. Under its terms, I swore to give them the land of Canaan, where they were living. [5]You can be sure that I have heard the groans of the people of Israel, who are now slaves to the Egyptians. I have remembered my covenant with them.

[6]"Therefore, say to the Israelites: 'I am the LORD, and I will free you from your

5:6 Exod 3:7; 5:10, 14
5:7 Gen 11:13
5:14 Isa 10:24
5:17 Exod 5:8
5:21 Gen 16:5; 34:30
5:22 Num 11:11; Jer 4:10
5:23 Exod 3:8
6:1 Exod 3:19-20; 11:1; 12:31
6:3 Gen 17:1; Ps 83:18; Isa 52:6
6:4 Gen 15:18
6:5 Exod 2:23-24
6:6 Exod 3:17; 13:3, 14; Deut 6:12; 26:8

5:21 Hebrew *for making us a stench in the nostrils of Pharaoh.* **6:3a** Hebrew *El Shaddai.* **6:3b** Hebrew *Yahweh;* traditionally rendered *Jehovah.*

5:7, 8 Mixing straw with mud made bricks stronger and more durable. Pharaoh had supplied the slaves with straw, but now he made them find their own straw and keep up their production quota as well.

5:15-21 The foremen were caught in the middle. First they tried to get the people to produce the same amount; then they complained to Pharaoh; finally they turned on Moses. Perhaps you have felt caught in the middle at work, or in relationships in your family or church. Complaining or turning on the leadership does not solve the problem. In the case of these supervisors, God had a larger purpose in mind, just as he might have in your situation. So rather than turning on the leadership when you feel pressured by both sides, turn to God to see what else he might be doing in this situation.

5:22, 23 Pharaoh had just increased the Hebrews' workload, and Moses protested that God had not rescued his people. Moses expected faster results and fewer problems. When God is at work, suffering, setbacks, and hardship may still occur. In James 1:2-4, we are encouraged to be happy when difficulties come our way. Problems develop our patience and character by teaching us to (1) trust God to do what is best for us, (2) look for ways to honor God in our present situation, (3) remember that God will not abandon us, and (4) watch for God's plan for us.

6:6 Small problems need only small answers. But when we face great problems, God has an opportunity to exercise his great power. As the Hebrews' troubles grew steadily worse, God planned to intervene with his mighty power and perform great miracles to deliver them. How big are your problems? Big problems put you in a perfect position to watch God give big answers.

6:7 Exod 16:12 Deut 4:20 Isa 60:16

slavery in Egypt. I will redeem you with mighty power and great acts of judgment. 7 I
will make you my own special people, and I will be your God. And you will know that
I am the LORD your God who has rescued you from your slavery in Egypt. 8 I will bring

6:8 Num 14:30 Josh 24:13

you into the land I swore to give to Abraham, Isaac, and Jacob. It will be your very own
property. I am the LORD!'"
9 So Moses told the people what the LORD had said, but they wouldn't listen anymore.

6:11 Exod 5:1; 7:2

They had become too discouraged by the increasing burden of their slavery.
10 Then the LORD said to Moses, 11 "Go back to Pharaoh, and tell him to let the people
of Israel leave Egypt."

6:12 Exod 4:10; 6:30

12 "But LORD!" Moses objected. "My own people won't listen to me anymore. How
can I expect Pharaoh to listen? I'm no orator!"
13 But the LORD ordered Moses and Aaron to return to Pharaoh, king of Egypt, and to
demand that he let the people of Israel leave Egypt.

The Ancestors of Moses and Aaron

6:14 Gen 46:9 Num 26:5-11

14 These are the ancestors of clans from some of Israel's tribes:

The descendants of Reuben, Israel's oldest son, included Hanoch, Pallu, Hezron, and
Carmi. Their descendants became the clans of Reuben.

6:15 Gen 46:11

15 The descendants of Simeon included Jemuel, Jamin, Ohad, Jakin, Zohar, and Shaul
(whose mother was a Canaanite). Their descendants became the clans of Simeon.

6:16 Gen 46:11 Num 3:17 1 Chr 6:1, 16-19

16 These are the descendants of Levi, listed according to their family groups. In the
first generation were Gershon, Kohath, and Merari. (Levi, their father, lived to be
137 years old.)

6:17 Num 3:18-20 1 Chr 6:17

17 The descendants of Gershon included Libni and Shimei, each of whom is the
ancestor of a clan.

6:18 Num 3:25-30 1 Chr 6:2, 18

18 The descendants of Kohath included Amram, Izhar, Hebron, and Uzziel. (Kohath
lived to be 133 years old.)

6:19 1 Chr 6:19

19 The descendants of Merari included Mahli and Mushi.
These are the clans of the Levites, listed according to their genealogies.

6:20 Exod 2:1-2 Num 26:59

20 Amram married his father's sister Jochebed, and she bore him Aaron and Moses.
(Amram lived to be 137 years old.)

6:21 Num 16:1

21 The descendants of Izhar included Korah, Nepheg, and Zicri.

6:22 Lev 10:4

22 The descendants of Uzziel included Mishael, Elzaphan, and Sithri.

6:23 Ruth 4:19-20

23 Aaron married Elisheba, the daughter of Amminadab and sister of Nahshon, and she
bore him Nadab, Abihu, Eleazar, and Ithamar.

6:24 1 Chr 6:22-23, 37

24 The descendants of Korah included Assir, Elkanah, and Abiasaph. Their
descendants became the clans of Korah.

6:25 Num 25:7, 11 Josh 24:33

25 Eleazar son of Aaron married one of the daughters of Putiel, and she bore him
Phinehas.

6:6-8 God's promises in these verses were fulfilled to the letter when the Hebrews left Egypt. He freed them from slavery, became their God, and accepted them as his people. Then he led them toward the land he had promised. When the Hebrews were rescued from slavery, they portrayed the drama of salvation for all of us. When God redeems us from sin, he delivers us, accepts us, and becomes our God. Then he leads us to a new life as we follow him.

6:9-12 When Moses gave God's message to the people, they were too discouraged to listen. The Hebrews didn't want to hear any more about God and his promises because the last time they listened to Moses, all they got was more work and greater suffering. Sometimes a clear message from God is followed by a period when no change in the situation is apparent. During that time, seeming setbacks may turn people away from wanting to hear more about God. If you are a leader, don't give up. Keep bringing people God's message as Moses did. By focusing on God, who must be obeyed, rather than on the results to be achieved, good leaders see beyond temporary setbacks and reversals.

6:10-12 Think how hard it must have been for Moses to bring God's message to Pharaoh when his own people had trouble believing it. Eventually the Hebrews believed that God had sent Moses, but for a time he must have felt very alone. Moses obeyed God, however, and what a difference it made! When the chances for success appear slim, remember that anyone can obey God when the task is easy and everyone is behind it. Only those with persistent faith can obey when the task seems impossible.

6:14-25 This genealogy or family tree was placed here to identify more firmly Moses and Aaron. Genealogies were used to establish credentials and authority as well as outlining the history of a family.

6:26 To bring the Israelites out of Egypt by their divisions means that they would be brought out in tribes, clans, or family groups.

These are the ancestors of the Levite clans, listed according to their family groups.
26 The Aaron and Moses named in this list are the same Aaron and Moses to whom the
LORD said, "Lead all the people of Israel out of the land of Egypt, division by division."
27 They are the ones who went to Pharaoh to ask permission to lead the people from the
land of Egypt.
28 At that time, the LORD had said to them, 29 "I am the LORD! Give Pharaoh the
message I have given you." 30 This is the same Moses who had argued with the LORD,
saying, "I can't do it! I'm no orator. Why should Pharaoh listen to me?"

Moses' Staff Becomes a Snake

7 Then the LORD said to Moses, "Pay close attention to this. I will make you seem like
God to Pharaoh. Your brother, Aaron, will be your prophet; he will speak for you.
2 Tell Aaron everything I say to you and have him announce it to Pharaoh. He will
demand that the people of Israel be allowed to leave Egypt. 3 But I will cause Pharaoh to
be stubborn so I can multiply my miraculous signs and wonders in the land of Egypt.
4 Even then Pharaoh will refuse to listen to you. So I will crush Egypt with a series of
disasters, after which I will lead the forces of Israel out with great acts of judgment.
5 When I show the Egyptians my power and force them to let the Israelites go, they will
realize that I am the LORD."
6 So Moses and Aaron did just as the LORD had commanded them. 7 Moses was eighty
years old, and Aaron was eighty-three at the time they made their demands to Pharaoh.
8 Then the LORD said to Moses and Aaron, 9 "Pharaoh will demand that you show him
a miracle to prove that God has sent you. When he makes this demand, say to Aaron,
'Throw down your shepherd's staff,' and it will become a snake."
10 So Moses and Aaron went to see Pharaoh, and they performed the miracle just as
the LORD had told them. Aaron threw down his staff before Pharaoh and his court, and
it became a snake. 11 Then Pharaoh called in his wise men and magicians, and they did
the same thing with their secret arts. 12 Their staffs became snakes, too! But then Aaron's
snake swallowed up their snakes. 13 Pharaoh's heart, however, remained hard and
stubborn. He still refused to listen, just as the LORD had predicted.

4. Plagues strike Egypt

A Plague of Blood

14 Then the LORD said to Moses, "Pharaoh is very stubborn, and he continues to refuse
to let the people go. 15 So go to Pharaoh in the morning as he goes down to the river.
Stand on the riverbank and meet him there. Be sure to take along the shepherd's staff that
turned into a snake. 16 Say to him, 'The LORD, the God of the Hebrews, has sent me to
say, "Let my people go, so they can worship me in the wilderness." Until now, you have
refused to listen to him. 17 Now the LORD says, "You are going to find out that I am the
LORD." Look! I will hit the water of the Nile with this staff, and the river will turn to
blood. 18 The fish in it will die, and the river will stink. The Egyptians will not be able to
drink any water from the Nile.'"
19 Then the LORD said to Moses: "Tell Aaron to point his staff toward the waters of
Egypt—all its rivers, canals, marshes, and reservoirs. Everywhere in Egypt the water

6:26 Exod 6:13
6:29 Exod 6:2, 6, 8; 7:2
6:30 Exod 4:10; 6:12
7:1 Exod 4:16
7:3 Exod 4:21
7:4 Exod 11:9
7:5 Exod 8:19
7:7 Deut 34:7; Acts 7:23, 30
7:9 Exod 4:3; Isa 7:11
7:11 Gen 41:8; Exod 8:7, 18; 2 Tim 3:8-9
7:13 Exod 4:21
7:14 Exod 8:15
7:15 Exod 2:5; 8:20
7:16 Exod 4:23
7:17 Rev 11:6; 16:4
7:19 Exod 14:21

7:1 God made Moses "like God to Pharaoh"—in other words, a powerful person who deserved to be listened to. Pharaoh himself was considered a god, so he recognized Moses as one of his peers. His refusal to give in to Moses shows, however, that he did not feel inferior to Moses.

7:11 How were these wise men and magicians able to duplicate Moses' miracles? Some of their feats involved trickery or illusion, and some may have used satanic power since worshiping gods of the underworld was part of their religion. Ironically, whenever they duplicated one of Moses' plagues, it only made matters worse. If the magicians had been as powerful as God, they would have reversed the plagues, not added to them.

7:12 God performed a miracle by turning Aaron's staff into a snake, and Pharaoh's magicians did the same through trickery or sorcery. Although miracles can help us believe, it is dangerous to rely on them alone. Satan can imitate some parts of God's work and lead people astray. Pharaoh focused on the miracle rather than the message. We can avoid this error by letting the Word of God be the basis of our faith. No miracle from God would endorse any message that is contrary to the teachings of his Word.

7:17 God dramatically turned the waters of the Nile into blood to show Pharaoh who he was. Do you sometimes wish for miraculous signs so you can be sure about God? God has given you the miracle of eternal life through your faith in him, something Pharaoh never obtained. This is a quiet miracle and, though less evident right now, just as extraordinary as water turned to blood. The desire for spectacular signs may cause us to ignore the more subtle miracles God is working every day.

will turn into blood, even the water stored in wooden bowls and stone pots in the
people's homes."

7:20 Pss 78:44; 105:29

20 So Moses and Aaron did just as the LORD had commanded them. As Pharaoh and
all of his officials watched, Moses raised his staff and hit the water of the Nile. Suddenly,
the whole river turned to blood! 21 The fish in the river died, and the water became so
foul that the Egyptians couldn't drink it. There was blood everywhere throughout the

7:22 Exod 8:7

land of Egypt. 22 But again the magicians of Egypt used their secret arts, and they, too,
turned water into blood. So Pharaoh's heart remained hard and stubborn. He refused to
listen to Moses and Aaron, just as the LORD had predicted. 23 Pharaoh returned to his
palace and put the whole thing out of his mind. 24 Then the Egyptians dug wells along
the riverbank to get drinking water, for they couldn't drink from the river. 25 An entire
week passed from the time the LORD turned the water of the Nile to blood.

A Plague of Frogs

8:1 Exod 5:1

8:2 Ps 105:30

8 Then the LORD said to Moses, "Go to Pharaoh once again and tell him, 'This is what
the LORD says: Let my people go, so they can worship me. 2 If you refuse, then listen
carefully to this: I will send vast hordes of frogs across your entire land from one border
to the other. 3 The Nile River will swarm with them. They will come up out of the river
and into your houses, even into your bedrooms and onto your beds! Every home in Egypt
will be filled with them. They will fill even your ovens and your kneading bowls. 4 You
and your people will be overwhelmed by frogs!'"

8:5 Exod 7:9-20

5 Then the LORD said to Moses, "Tell Aaron to point his shepherd's staff toward all the

8:6 Pss 78:45; 105:30

rivers, canals, and marshes of Egypt so there will be frogs in every corner of the land."
6 Aaron did so, and frogs covered the whole land of Egypt! 7 But the magicians were able

8:7 Exod 7:11

to do the same thing with their secret arts. They, too, caused frogs to come up on the land.

8:8 Exod 9:28; 10:10

8 Then Pharaoh summoned Moses and Aaron and begged, "Plead with the LORD to
take the frogs away from me and my people. I will let the people go, so they can offer
sacrifices to the LORD."
9 "You set the time!" Moses replied. "Tell me when you want me to pray for you, your
officials, and your people. I will pray that you and your houses will be rid of the frogs.
Then only the frogs in the Nile River will remain alive."

8:10 Exod 9:14; 15:11 Deut 4:35 Isa 46:9

10 "Do it tomorrow," Pharaoh said.
"All right," Moses replied, "it will be as you have said. Then you will know that no
one is as powerful as the LORD our God. 11 All the frogs will be destroyed, except those
in the river."

8:12 Exod 8:30; 9:33; 10:18

12 So Moses and Aaron left Pharaoh, and Moses pleaded with the LORD about the frogs
he had sent. 13 And the LORD did as Moses had promised. The frogs in the houses, the
courtyards, and the fields all died. 14 They were piled into great heaps, and a terrible

8:15 Exod 7:14 Eccl 8:11

stench filled the land. 15 But when Pharaoh saw that the frogs were gone, he hardened his
heart. He refused to listen to Moses and Aaron, just as the LORD had predicted.

A Plague of Gnats

8:16 Exod 4:2

16 So the LORD said to Moses, "Tell Aaron to strike the dust with his staff. The dust will

8:17 Ps 105:31

turn into swarms of gnats throughout the land of Egypt." 17 So Moses and Aaron did just
as the LORD had commanded them. Suddenly, gnats infested the entire land, covering the
Egyptians and their animals. All the dust in the land of Egypt turned into gnats.

7:20 Egypt was a large country, but most of the population lived along the banks of the Nile River. This 3,000-mile waterway was truly a river of life for the Egyptians. It made life possible in a land that was mostly desert by providing water for drinking, farming, bathing, and fishing. Egyptian society was a ribbon of civilization lining the banks of this life source, rarely reaching very far into the surrounding desert. Without the Nile's water, Egypt could not have existed. Imagine Pharaoh's dismay when Moses turned this sacred river to blood!

8:3ff Moses predicted that every house in Egypt would be infested with frogs. The poor of Egypt lived in small, mud-brick houses of one or two rooms with palm-trunk roofs. The homes of the rich, however, were often two or three stories high, surrounded by landscaped gardens and enclosed by a high wall. Servants lived and worked on the first floor while the family occupied the upper floors. Thus, if the frogs got into the royal bedrooms, they had infiltrated even the upper floors. No place in Egypt would be safe from them.

8:15 After repeated warnings, Pharaoh still refused to obey God. He hardened his heart every time there was a break in the plagues. His stubborn disobedience brought suffering upon himself and his entire country. While persistence is good, stubbornness is usually self-centered. Stubbornness toward God is always disobedience. Avoid disobedience because the consequences may spill onto others.

18 Pharaoh's magicians tried to do the same thing with their secret arts, but this time they — **8:18** Exod 7:11; 9:11
failed. And the gnats covered all the people and animals.
19 "This is the finger of God!" the magicians exclaimed to Pharaoh. But Pharaoh's — **8:19** Exod 7:5; 1 Sam 6:9
heart remained hard and stubborn. He wouldn't listen to them, just as the LORD had
predicted.

A Plague of Flies

20 Next the LORD told Moses, "Get up early in the morning and meet Pharaoh as he goes — **8:20** Exod 7:15
down to the river. Say to him, 'This is what the LORD says: Let my people go, so they
can worship me. 21 If you refuse, I will send swarms of flies throughout Egypt. Your
homes will be filled with them, and the ground will be covered with them. 22 But it will — **8:22** Exod 9:4; 10:23
be very different in the land of Goshen, where the Israelites live. No flies will be found
there. Then you will know that I am the LORD and that I have power even in the heart of
your land. 23 I will make a clear distinction between your people and my people. This
miraculous sign will happen tomorrow.'"
24 And the LORD did just as he had said. There were terrible swarms of flies in — **8:24** Pss 78:45; 105:31
Pharaoh's palace and in every home in Egypt. The whole country was thrown into chaos
by the flies.
25 Pharaoh hastily called for Moses and Aaron. "All right! Go ahead and offer — **8:25** Gen 46:34; Exod 8:8; 10:8
sacrifices to your God," he said. "But do it here in this land. Don't go out into the
wilderness."
26 But Moses replied, "That won't do! The Egyptians would detest the sacrifices that
we offer to the LORD our God. If we offer them here where they can see us, they will be
sure to stone us. 27 We must take a three-day trip into the wilderness to offer sacrifices to — **8:27** Exod 3:18
the LORD our God, just as he has commanded us."
28 "All right, go ahead," Pharaoh replied. "I will let you go to offer sacrifices to the LORD — **8:28** Exod 8:8
your God in the wilderness. But don't go too far away. Now hurry, and pray for me."
29 "As soon as I go," Moses said, "I will ask the LORD to cause the swarms of flies to
disappear from you and all your people. But I am warning you, don't change your mind
again and refuse to let the people go to sacrifice to the LORD."
30 So Moses left Pharaoh and asked the LORD to remove all the flies. 31 And the LORD — **8:30** Exod 8:12
did as Moses asked and caused the swarms to disappear. Not a single fly remained in the — **8:32** Exod 8:8, 15
land! 32 But Pharaoh hardened his heart again and refused to let the people go.

A Plague against Livestock

9 "Go back to Pharaoh," the LORD commanded Moses. "Tell him, 'This is what the — **9:1** Exod 8:1; 10:3
LORD, the God of the Hebrews, says: Let my people go, so they can worship me. 2 If
you continue to oppress them and refuse to let them go, 3 the LORD will send a deadly — **9:3** Exod 7:4
plague to destroy your horses, donkeys, camels, cattle, and sheep. 4 But the LORD will — **9:4** Exod 8:23; 9:26
again make a distinction between the property of the Israelites and that of the Egyptians.
Not a single one of Israel's livestock will die!'"
5 The LORD announced that he would send the plague the very next day, 6 and he did it,
just as he had said. The next morning all the livestock of the Egyptians began to die, but
the Israelites didn't lose a single animal from their flocks and herds. 7 Pharaoh sent officials — **9:7** Exod 7:14; 8:32
to see whether it was true that none of the Israelites' animals were dead. But even after he
found it to be true, his heart remained stubborn. He still refused to let the people go.

8:19 Some people think, "If only I could see a miracle, I could believe in God." God gave Pharaoh just such an opportunity. When gnats infested Egypt, even the magicians agreed that this was God's work ("the finger of God")—but still Pharaoh refused to believe. He was stubborn, and stubbornness can blind a person to the truth. When you rid yourself of stubbornness, you may be surprised by abundant evidence of God's work in your life.

8:25-29 Pharaoh wanted a compromise. He would allow the Hebrews to sacrifice, but only if they would do it nearby. God's requirement, however, was firm: The Hebrews had to leave Egypt. Sometimes people urge believers to compromise and give only partial obedience to God's commands. But commitment and obedience to God cannot be negotiated. When it comes to obeying God, half measures won't do.

8:26 The Israelites would be sacrificing animals that the Egyptians regarded as sacred, and this would be offensive to them. Moses was concerned about a violent reaction to sacrificing these animals near the Egyptians.

9:1 This was the fifth time God sent Moses back to Pharaoh with the demand "Let my people go!" By this time, Moses may have been tired and discouraged, but he continued to obey. Is there a difficult conflict you must face again and again? Don't give up when you know what is right to do. As Moses discovered, persistence is rewarded.

A Plague of Boils

8 Then the LORD said to Moses and Aaron, "Take soot from a furnace, and have Moses
9:9 Lev 13:18 Rev 16:2 toss it into the sky while Pharaoh watches. 9 It will spread like fine dust over the whole
land of Egypt, causing boils to break out on people and animals alike."
10 So they gathered soot from a furnace and went to see Pharaoh. As Pharaoh watched,
Moses tossed the soot into the air, and terrible boils broke out on the people and animals
9:11 Exod 8:18 throughout Egypt. 11 Even the magicians were unable to stand before Moses, because the
9:12 Exod 4:21 boils had broken out on them, too. 12 But the LORD made Pharaoh even more stubborn,
and he refused to listen, just as the LORD had predicted.

A Plague of Hail

9:13 Exod 8:20 13 Then the LORD said to Moses, "Get up early in the morning. Go to Pharaoh and tell
him, 'The LORD, the God of the Hebrews, says: Let my people go, so they can worship
9:14 Exod 8:10; 15:11 me. 14 If you don't, I will send a plague that will really speak to you and your officials
and all the Egyptian people. I will prove to you that there is no other God like me in
all the earth. 15 I could have killed you all by now. I could have attacked you with a
9:16 Exod 14:4, 17 †Rom 9:17 plague that would have wiped you from the face of the earth. 16 But I have let you live
for this reason—that you might see my power and that my fame might spread
throughout the earth. 17 But you are still lording it over my people, and you refuse to

THE PLAGUES

Reference	Plague	What Happened	Result
7:14–24	Blood	Fish die, the river smells, the people are without water	Pharaoh's magicians duplicate the miracle by "secret arts," and Pharaoh is unmoved
8:1–15	Frogs	Frogs come up from the water and completely cover the land	Again Pharaoh's magicians duplicate the miracle by sorcery, and Pharaoh is unmoved
8:16–19	Gnats	All the dust of Egypt becomes a massive swarm of gnats	Magicians are unable to duplicate this; they say it is the "finger of God," but Pharaoh's heart remains hard
8:20–32	Flies	Swarms of flies cover the land	Pharaoh promises to let the Hebrews go but then hardens his heart and refuses
9:1–7	Livestock	All the Egyptian livestock die—but none of Israel's is even sick	Pharaoh still refuses to let the people go
9:8–12	Boils	Horrible boils break out on everyone in Egypt	Magicians cannot respond because they are struck down with boils as well—Pharaoh refuses to listen
9:13–35	Hail	Hailstorms kill all the slaves and animals left out or unprotected and strip or destroy almost every plant	Pharaoh admits his sin but then changes his mind and refuses to let Israel go
10:1–20	Locusts	Locusts cover Egypt and eat everything left after the hail	Everyone advises Pharaoh to let the Hebrews go, but God hardens Pharaoh's heart and he refuses
10:21–29	Darkness	Total darkness covers Egypt for three days so no one can even move—except the Hebrews, who have light as usual	Pharaoh again promises to let Israel go but again changes his mind
11:1—12:33	Death of Firstborn	The firstborn of all the people and cattle of Egypt die–but Israel is spared	Pharaoh and the Egyptians urge Israel to leave quickly; after they are gone, Pharaoh again changes his mind and chases after them

9:12 God gave Pharaoh many opportunities to heed Moses' warnings. But finally God seemed to say, "All right, Pharaoh, have it your way," and Pharaoh's heart became permanently hardened. Did God intentionally harden Pharaoh's heart and overrule his free will? No, he simply confirmed that Pharaoh freely chose a life of resisting God. Similarly, after a lifetime of resisting God, you may find it impossible to turn to him. Don't wait until just the *right* time before turning to God. Do it now while you still have the chance. If you continually ignore God's voice, eventually you will be unable to hear it at all.

let them go. 18 So tomorrow at this time I will send a hailstorm worse than any in all
of Egypt's history. 19 Quick! Order your livestock and servants to come in from the
fields. Every person or animal left outside will die beneath the hail.'"
20 Some of Pharaoh's officials believed what the LORD said. They immediately brought
their livestock and servants in from the fields. 21 But those who had no respect for the word
of the LORD left them out in the open.
22 Then the LORD said to Moses, "Lift your hand toward the sky, and cause the hail to
fall throughout Egypt, on the people, the animals, and the crops."
23 So Moses lifted his staff toward the sky, and the LORD sent thunder and hail, and
lightning struck the earth. The LORD sent a tremendous hailstorm against all the land of
Egypt. 24 Never in all the history of Egypt had there been a storm like that, with such
severe hail and continuous lightning. 25 It left all of Egypt in ruins. Everything left in the
fields was destroyed—people, animals, and crops alike. Even all the trees were destroyed. 26 The only spot in all Egypt without hail that day was the land of Goshen, where
the people of Israel lived.
27 Then Pharaoh urgently sent for Moses and Aaron. "I finally admit my fault," he
confessed. "The LORD is right, and my people and I are wrong. 28 Please beg the LORD
to end this terrifying thunder and hail. I will let you go at once."
29 "All right," Moses replied. "As soon as I leave the city, I will lift my hands and pray
to the LORD. Then the thunder and hail will stop. This will prove to you that the earth
belongs to the LORD. 30 But as for you and your officials, I know that you still do not fear
the LORD God as you should."
31 All the flax and barley were destroyed because the barley was ripe and the flax was
in bloom. 32 But the wheat and the spelt were not destroyed because they had not yet
sprouted from the ground.
33 So Moses left Pharaoh and went out of the city. As he lifted his hands to the LORD,
all at once the thunder and hail stopped, and the downpour ceased. 34 When Pharaoh saw
this, he and his officials sinned yet again by stubbornly refusing to do as they had
promised. 35 Pharaoh refused to let the people leave, just as the LORD had predicted.

A Plague of Locusts

10 Then the LORD said to Moses, "Return to Pharaoh and again make your demands.
I have made him and his officials stubborn so I can continue to display my power
by performing miraculous signs among them. 2 You will be able to tell wonderful stories
to your children and grandchildren about the marvelous things I am doing among the
Egyptians to prove that I am the LORD."
3 So Moses and Aaron went to Pharaoh and said, "This is what the LORD, the God of
the Hebrews, says: How long will you refuse to submit to me? Let my people go, so they
can worship me. 4 If you refuse, watch out! For tomorrow I will cover the whole country
with locusts. 5 There will be so many that you won't be able to see the ground. They will
devour everything that escaped the hailstorm, including all the trees in the fields. 6 They
will overrun your palaces and the homes of your officials and all the houses of Egypt.
Never in the history of Egypt has there been a plague like this one!" And with that, Moses
turned and walked out.
7 The court officials now came to Pharaoh and appealed to him. "How long will you
let these disasters go on? Please let the Israelites go to serve the LORD their God! Don't
you realize that Egypt lies in ruins?"
8 So Moses and Aaron were brought back to Pharaoh. "All right, go and serve the LORD
your God," he said. "But tell me, just whom do you want to take along?"

9:18 Exod 9:23, 24
9:20 Prov 13:13
9:22 Rev 16:21
9:23 Gen 19:24; Josh 10:11; Ps 78:47; Rev 8:7; 16:21
9:25 Ps 105:32
9:26 Exod 8:22; 10:23
9:27 2 Chr 12:6; Ps 129:4
9:28 Exod 8:8; 10:16-17
9:29 Ps 24:1; 1 Cor 10:26
9:30 Exod 8:29
9:35 Exod 4:21
10:1 Exod 4:21; 7:14
10:2 Exod 13:8, 14; Deut 4:9; Ps 44:1
10:3 Exod 4:23
10:4 Rev 9:3
10:5 Exod 9:32; Joel 1:4; 2:25
10:7 Exod 7:5
10:8 Exod 8:8, 25

9:20, 21 If all the Egyptian livestock were killed in the earlier plague (9:6), how could the slaves of Pharaoh put their cattle inside? The answer is probably that the earlier plague killed all the animals in the fields (9:3) but not those in the shelters.

9:27-34 After promising to let the Hebrews go, Pharaoh immediately broke his promise and brought even more trouble upon the land. His actions reveal that his repentance was not real. We do damage to ourselves and to others if we pretend to change but don't mean it.

10:2 God told Moses that his miraculous experiences with Pharaoh should be retold to his descendants. What stories Moses had to tell! Living out one of the greatest dramas in biblical history, he witnessed events few people would ever see. It is important to tell our children about God's work in our past and to help them see what he is doing right now. What are the turning points in your life where God intervened? What is God doing for you now? Your stories will form the foundations of your children's belief in God.

9“Young and old, all of us will go,” Moses replied. “We will take our sons and
daughters and our flocks and herds. We must all join together in a festival to the LORD.”
10Pharaoh retorted, “The LORD will certainly need to be with you if you try to take
your little ones along! I can see through your wicked intentions. 11Never! Only the men
may go and serve the LORD, for that is what you requested.” And Pharaoh threw them
out of the palace.
12Then the LORD said to Moses, “Raise your hand over the land of Egypt to bring on
the locusts. Let them cover the land and eat all the crops still left after the hailstorm.”
13So Moses raised his staff, and the LORD caused an east wind to blow all that day and
through the night. When morning arrived, the east wind had brought the locusts. 14And
the locusts swarmed over the land of Egypt from border to border. It was the worst locust
plague in Egyptian history, and there has never again been one like it. 15For the locusts
covered the surface of the whole country, making the ground look black. They ate all the
plants and all the fruit on the trees that had survived the hailstorm. Not one green thing
remained, neither tree nor plant, throughout the land of Egypt.
16Pharaoh quickly sent for Moses and Aaron. “I confess my sin against the LORD your
God and against you,” he said to them. 17“Forgive my sin only this once, and plead with
the LORD your God to take away this terrible plague.”
18So Moses left Pharaoh and pleaded with the LORD. 19The LORD responded by
sending a strong west wind that blew the locusts out into the Red Sea.* Not a single
locust remained in all the land of Egypt. 20But the LORD made Pharaoh stubborn once
again, and he did not let the people go.

A Plague of Darkness

21Then the LORD said to Moses, “Lift your hand toward heaven, and a deep and
terrifying darkness will descend on the land of Egypt.” 22So Moses lifted his hand
toward heaven, and there was deep darkness over the entire land for three days. 23During
all that time the people scarcely moved, for they could not see. But there was light as
usual where the people of Israel lived.
24Then Pharaoh called for Moses. “Go and worship the LORD,” he said. “But let your
flocks and herds stay here. You can even take your children with you.”
25“No,” Moses said, “we must take our flocks and herds for sacrifices and burnt
offerings to the LORD our God. 26All our property must go with us; not a hoof can be left
behind. We will have to choose our sacrifices for the LORD our God from among these
animals. And we won’t know which sacrifices he will require until we get there.”
27So the LORD hardened Pharaoh’s heart once more, and he would not let them go.
28“Get out of here!” Pharaoh shouted at Moses. “Don’t ever let me see you again! The
day you do, you will die!”
29“Very well,” Moses replied. “I will never see you again.”

Death for Egypt’s Firstborn

11 Then the LORD said to Moses, “I will send just one more disaster on Pharaoh and
the land of Egypt. After that, Pharaoh will let you go. In fact, he will be so anxious
to get rid of you that he will practically force you to leave the country. 2Tell all the
Israelite men and women to ask their Egyptian neighbors for articles of silver and gold.”
3(Now the LORD had caused the Egyptians to look favorably on the people of Israel,

10:9 Exod 12:37
10:10 Gen 50:8; Exod 12:31
10:11 Exod 10:28
10:12 Exod 7:19
10:13 Pss 78:46; 105:34
10:14 Joel 1:4, 7; 2:1-11
10:15 Exod 10:5; Ps 105:35
10:16 Exod 8:8; 9:27
10:17 Exod 8:8, 29; 1 Sam 15:25
10:18 Exod 8:30
10:20 Exod 4:21; 11:10
10:21 Deut 28:29
10:22 Ps 105:28
10:23 Exod 8:22
10:24 Exod 8:8, 10
10:26 Exod 10:9
10:27 Exod 4:21; 14:4
10:28 Exod 10:11
10:29 Heb 11:27
11:1 Exod 12:31, 33, 39
11:2 Exod 3:22; 12:35-36
11:3 Exod 3:21; 12:36; Deut 34:10-12

10:19 Hebrew *sea of reeds.*

10:22 As each gloomy plague descended upon the land, the Egyptian people realized how powerless their own gods were to stop it. Hapi, the god of the Nile River, could not prevent the waters from turning to blood (7:20). Hathor, the crafty cow-goddess, was helpless as Egyptian livestock died in droves (9:6). Amon-Re, the sun-god and chief of the Egyptian gods, could not stop an eerie darkness from covering the land for three full days (10:21, 22). The Egyptian gods were (1) nonpersonal, centering around images like the sun or the river; (2) numerous; (3) nonexclusive. By contrast, the God of the Hebrews was (1) a living personal Being, (2) the only true God, and (3) the only God who should be worshiped. God was proving to both the Hebrews and the Egyptians that he alone is the living and all-powerful God.

10:27, 28 Why was Pharaoh so reluctant to let the people go? The Hebrews were Egypt’s free labor—the builders of their great cities. As Egypt’s leader, Pharaoh would not easily let such a great resource go.

and Moses was considered a very great man in the land of Egypt. He was respected by
Pharaoh's officials and the Egyptian people alike.)
4So Moses announced to Pharaoh, "This is what the LORD says: About midnight I will
pass through Egypt. 5All the firstborn sons will die in every family in Egypt, from the
oldest son of Pharaoh, who sits on the throne, to the oldest son of his lowliest slave. Even
the firstborn of the animals will die. 6Then a loud wail will be heard throughout the land
of Egypt; there has never been such wailing before, and there never will be again. 7But
among the Israelites it will be so peaceful that not even a dog will bark. Then you will
know that the LORD makes a distinction between the Egyptians and the Israelites. 8All
the officials of Egypt will come running to me, bowing low. 'Please leave!' they will beg.
'Hurry! And take all your followers with you.' Only then will I go!" Then, burning with
anger, Moses left Pharaoh's presence.
9Now the LORD had told Moses, "Pharaoh will not listen to you. But this will give me
the opportunity to do even more mighty miracles in the land of Egypt." 10Although
Moses and Aaron did these miracles in Pharaoh's presence, the LORD hardened his heart
so he wouldn't let the Israelites leave the country.

5. The Passover

12 Now the LORD gave the following instructions to Moses and Aaron while they
were still in the land of Egypt: 2"From now on, this month will be the first month
of the year for you. 3Announce to the whole community that on the tenth day of this
month each family must choose a lamb or a young goat for a sacrifice. 4If a family is too
small to eat an entire lamb, let them share the lamb with another family in the neighborhood. Whether or not they share in this way depends on the size of each family and how
much they can eat. 5This animal must be a one-year-old male, either a sheep or a goat,
with no physical defects.
6"Take special care of these lambs until the evening of the fourteenth day of this first
month. Then each family in the community must slaughter its lamb. 7They are to take
some of the lamb's blood and smear it on the top and sides of the doorframe of the house
where the lamb will be eaten. 8That evening everyone must eat roast lamb with bitter

11:4 Exod 12:29
11:5 Exod 12:12, 29; Pss 78:51; 105:36; 135:8; 136:10
11:6 Exod 12:30; Amos 5:17
11:7 Exod 8:22
11:8 Exod 12:31-33; Heb 11:27
11:9 Exod 7:3-4
11:10 Exod 4:21; Rom 2:5; 9:17
12:2 Exod 13:4; 23:15; 34:18; Deut 16:1
12:3 Mark 14:12; 1 Cor 5:7
12:6 Lev 23:5; Num 9:3; Deut 16:4, 6
12:7 Exod 12:22
12:8 Exod 34:25; Num 9:11-12; Deut 16:7

11:7 Moses told Pharaoh that God made a distinction between Egypt and Israel. At this time the distinction was very clear in God's mind: He knew the Hebrews would become his chosen people. The distinction was taking shape in Moses' mind also. But the Hebrews still saw the distinction only in terms of slave and free. Later, when they were in the wilderness, God would teach them the laws, principles, and values that would make them distinct as his people. Remember that God sees us in terms of what we will become and not just what we are right now.

11:9, 10 You may wonder how Pharaoh could be so foolish as to see God's miraculous power and still not listen to Moses. But Pharaoh had his mind made up long before the plagues began. He couldn't believe that someone was greater than he. This stubborn unbelief led to a heart so hard that even a major catastrophe couldn't soften it. Finally, it took the greatest of all calamities, the loss of his son, to force him to recognize God's authority. But even then he wanted God to leave, not to rule his country. We must not wait for great calamities to drive us to God but must open our hearts and minds to his direction now.

11:10 Did God really harden Pharaoh's heart and force him to do wrong? Before the 10 plagues began, Moses and Aaron announced what God would do if Pharaoh didn't let the people go. But their message only made Pharaoh stubborn—he was hardening his own heart. In so doing, he defied both God and his messengers. Through the first six plagues, Pharaoh's heart grew even more stubborn. After the sixth plague, God passed judgment. Sooner or later, evil people will be punished for their sins. When it became evident that Pharaoh wouldn't change, God confirmed Pharaoh's prideful decision and set the painful consequences of his actions in motion. God didn't force Pharaoh to reject him; rather, he gave him every opportunity to change his mind. In Ezekiel 33:11, God says, "I take no pleasure in the death of wicked people."

12:1-3 Certain holidays were instituted by God himself. Passover was a holiday designed to celebrate Israel's deliverance from Egypt and to remind the people of what God had done. Holidays can be important today, too, as annual reminders of what God has done for us. Develop traditions in your family to highlight the religious significance of certain holidays. These serve as reminders to the older people and learning experiences for the younger ones.

12:3ff For the Israelites to be spared from the plague of death, a lamb with no defects had to be killed and its blood placed on the doorframes of each home. What was the significance of the lamb? In killing the lamb, the Israelites shed innocent blood. The lamb was a sacrifice, a substitute for the person who would have died in the plague. From this point on, the Hebrew people would clearly understand that for them to be spared from death, an innocent life had to be sacrificed in their place.

12:6-11 The festival of Passover was to be an annual holiday in honor of the night when the Lord "passed over" the homes of the Israelites. The Hebrews followed God's instructions by smearing the blood of a lamb on the doorframes of their homes. That night the firstborn son of every family that did not have blood on the doorframes was killed. The lamb had to be killed in order to get the blood that would protect them. (This foreshadowed the blood of Christ, the Lamb of God, who gave his blood for the sins of all people.) Inside their homes, the Israelites ate a meal of roast lamb, bitter herbs, and bread made without yeast. Unleavened bread could be made quickly because the dough did not have to rise. Thus, they could leave at any time. Bitter herbs signified the bitterness of slavery.

12:10 Exod 23:18; 34:25
12:11 Num 28:16
12:12 Exod 11:4-5; Num 33:4
12:13 Heb 11:28
12:14-20 //Lev 23:4-8; //Num 28:16-25; //Deut 16:1-8
12:15 Exod 23:15; 34:18; Lev 23:5-6; Deut 16:3
12:16 Lev 23:7-8
12:17 Exod 13:3

herbs and bread made without yeast. [9]The meat must never be eaten raw or boiled; roast
it all, including the head, legs, and internal organs. [10]Do not leave any of it until the next
day. Whatever is not eaten that night must be burned before morning.
[11]"Wear your traveling clothes as you eat this meal, as though prepared for a long
journey. Wear your sandals, and carry your walking sticks in your hands. Eat the food
quickly, for this is the LORD's Passover. [12]On that night I will pass through the land of
Egypt and kill all the firstborn sons and firstborn male animals in the land of Egypt. I
will execute judgment against all the gods of Egypt, for I am the LORD! [13]The blood you
have smeared on your doorposts will serve as a sign. When I see the blood, I will pass
over you. This plague of death will not touch you when I strike the land of Egypt.
[14]"You must remember this day forever. Each year you will celebrate it as a special
festival to the LORD. [15]For seven days, you may eat only bread made without yeast. On
the very first day you must remove every trace of yeast from your homes. Anyone who
eats bread made with yeast at any time during the seven days of the festival will be cut
off from the community of Israel. [16]On the first day of the festival, and again on the
seventh day, all the people must gather for a time of special worship. No work of any
kind may be done on these days except in the preparation of food.
[17]"Celebrate this Festival of Unleavened Bread, for it will remind you that I brought

THE HEBREW CALENDAR

A Hebrew month began in the middle of a month on our calendar today. Crops are planted in November and December and harvested in March and April.

	Month	Today's Calendar	Bible Reference	Israel's Holidays
1	Nisan (Abib)	March–April	Exodus 13:4; 23:15; 34:18; Deuteronomy 16:1	Passover (Leviticus 23:5) Unleavened Bread (Leviticus 23:6) Firstfruits (Leviticus 23:10)
2	Iyyar (Ziv)	April–May	1 Kings 6:1, 37	Second Passover (Numbers 9:10, 11)
3	Sivan	May–June	Esther 8:9	Pentecost (Harvest) (Leviticus 23:16)
4	Tammuz	June–July		
5	Ab	July–August		
6	Elul	August–September	Nehemiah 6:15	
7	Tishri (Ethanim)	September–October	1 Kings 8:2	Trumpets (Numbers 29:1; Leviticus 23:24) Day of Atonement (Leviticus 23:27) Shelters (Leviticus 23:34)
8	Marcheshvan (Bul)	October–November	1 Kings 6:38	
9	Kislev	November–December	Nehemiah 1:1	Dedication (John 10:22)
10	Tebeth	December–January	Esther 2:16	
11	Shebat	January–February	Zechariah 1:7	Purim (Esther 9:24–32)
12	Adar	February–March	Esther 3:7	

12:11 Eating the Passover feast while dressed for travel was a sign of the Hebrews' faith. Although they were not yet free, they were to prepare themselves, for God had said he would lead them out of Egypt. Their preparation was an act of faith. Preparing ourselves for the fulfillment of God's promises, however unlikely they may seem, demonstrates our faith.

12:17, 23 Passover became an annual remembrance of how God delivered the Hebrews from Egypt. Each year the people would pause to remember the day when the Destroyer (God's angel of death) passed over their homes. They gave thanks to God for saving them from death and bringing them out of a land of slavery and sin. Believers today have experienced a day of deliverance as well—the day we were delivered from spiritual death and slavery to sin. The Lord's Supper is our Passover remembrance of our new life and freedom from sin. The next time struggles and trials come, remember how God has delivered you in the past and focus on his promise of new life with him.

your forces out of the land of Egypt on this very day. This festival will be a permanent regulation for you, to be kept from generation to generation. 18 Only bread without yeast may be eaten from the evening of the fourteenth day of the month until the evening of the twenty-first day of the month. 19 During those seven days, there must be no trace of yeast in your homes. Anyone who eats anything made with yeast during this week will be cut off from the community of Israel. These same regulations apply to the foreigners living with you, as if they had been born among you. 20 I repeat, during those days you must not eat anything made with yeast. Wherever you live, eat only bread that has no yeast in it."

21 Then Moses called for the leaders of Israel and said, "Tell each of your families to slaughter the lamb they have set apart for the Passover. 22 Drain each lamb's blood into a basin. Then take a cluster of hyssop branches and dip it into the lamb's blood. Strike the hyssop against the top and sides of the doorframe, staining it with the blood. And remember, no one is allowed to leave the house until morning. 23 For the LORD will pass through the land and strike down the Egyptians. But when he sees the blood on the top and sides of the doorframe, the LORD will pass over your home. He will not permit the Destroyer to enter and strike down your firstborn.

24 "Remember, these instructions are permanent and must be observed by you and your descendants forever. 25 When you arrive in the land the LORD has promised to give you, you will continue to celebrate this festival. 26 Then your children will ask, 'What does all this mean? What is this ceremony about?' 27 And you will reply, 'It is the celebration of the LORD's Passover, for he passed over the homes of the Israelites in Egypt. And though he killed the Egyptians, he spared our families and did not destroy us.'" Then all the people bowed their heads and worshiped.

28 So the people of Israel did just as the LORD had commanded through Moses and Aaron. 29 And at midnight the LORD killed all the firstborn sons in the land of Egypt, from the firstborn son of Pharaoh, who sat on the throne, to the firstborn son of the captive in the dungeon. Even the firstborn of their livestock were killed. 30 Pharaoh and his officials and all the people of Egypt woke up during the night, and loud wailing was heard throughout the land of Egypt. There was not a single house where someone had not died.

12:18 Lev 23:5-8 Num 28:16-25
12:19 Exod 12:15
12:21 Mark 14:12-16 Heb 11:28
12:22 Lev 14:4, 6 Num 19:18 Ps 51:7 Heb 11:28
12:23 Exod 12:12 Isa 37:36
12:24 Exod 13:5, 10
12:25 Exod 3:17
12:26 Exod 10:2; 13:14-15
12:27 Exod 4:31
12:29 Exod 4:23; 11:4 Pss 78:51; 105:36
12:30 Exod 11:6

B. ISRAEL IN THE WILDERNESS (12:31—18:27)

As Egypt buried its dead, the Hebrew slaves left the country, a free people at last. Pharaoh made one last attempt to bring them back, but the people escaped when God miraculously parted the waters of the Red Sea. But on the other side, the people soon became dissatisfied and complained bitterly to Moses and Aaron about their trek through the wilderness. Through these experiences of the Hebrews, we learn that the Christian life is not always trouble-free. We still have struggles and often complain bitterly to God about conditions in our lives.

1. The Exodus

31 Pharaoh sent for Moses and Aaron during the night. "Leave us!" he cried. "Go away, all of you! Go and serve the LORD as you have requested. 32 Take your flocks and herds, and be gone. Go, but give me a blessing as you leave." 33 All the Egyptians urged the people of Israel to get out of the land as quickly as possible, for they thought, "We will all die!"

12:31 Exod 8:8, 25
12:33 Exod 10:7; 11:1

12:29, 30 Every firstborn child of the Egyptians died, but the Israelite children were spared because the blood of the lamb had been smeared on their doorframes. So begins the story of redemption, the central theme of the Bible.

Redemption means "to buy back" or "to save from captivity by paying a ransom." One way to buy back a slave was to offer an equivalent or superior slave in exchange. That is the way God chose to buy us back—he offered his Son in exchange for us.

In Old Testament times, God accepted symbolic offerings. Jesus had not yet been sacrificed, so God accepted the life of an animal in place of the life of the sinner. When Jesus came, he substituted his perfect life for our sinful lives, taking the penalty for sin that we deserve. Thus he redeemed us from the power of sin and restored us to God. Jesus' sacrifice made animal sacrifice no longer necessary.

We must recognize that if we want to be freed from the deadly consequences of our sins, a tremendous price must be paid. But we don't have to pay it. Jesus Christ, our substitute, has already redeemed us by his death on the cross. Our part is to trust him and accept his gift of eternal life. Our sins have been paid for, and the way has been cleared for us to begin a relationship with God (Titus 2:14; Hebrews 9:13-15, 23-26).

12:34 A kneading bowl was a large bowl made of wood, bronze, or pottery and used for kneading dough. Bread was made by mixing water and flour in the bowl with a small piece of leavened dough saved from the previous day's batch. Bread was the primary food in the Hebrews' diet, and thus it was vital to bring the bowl along. It could be easily carried on the shoulder.

34The Israelites took with them their bread dough made without yeast. They wrapped their kneading bowls in their spare clothing and carried them on their shoulders. 35And the people of Israel did as Moses had instructed and asked the Egyptians for clothing and articles of silver and gold. 36The LORD caused the Egyptians to look favorably on the Israelites, and they gave the Israelites whatever they asked for. So, like a victorious army, they plundered the Egyptians!

37That night the people of Israel left Rameses and started for Succoth. There were about 600,000 men, plus all the women and children. And they were all traveling on foot. 38Many people who were not Israelites went with them, along with the many flocks and herds. 39Whenever they stopped to eat, they baked bread from the yeastless dough they had brought from Egypt. It was made without yeast because the people were rushed out of Egypt and had no time to wait for bread to rise.

40The people of Israel had lived in Egypt for 430 years. 41In fact, it was on the last day of the 430th year that all the LORD's forces left the land. 42This night had been reserved by the LORD to bring his people out from the land of Egypt, so this same night now belongs to him. It must be celebrated every year, from generation to generation, to remember the LORD's deliverance.

Instructions for the Passover

43Then the LORD said to Moses and Aaron, "These are the regulations for the festival of Passover. No foreigners are allowed to eat the Passover lamb. 44But any slave who has been purchased may eat it if he has been circumcised. 45Hired servants and visiting foreigners may not eat it. 46All who eat the lamb must eat it together in one house. You must not carry any of its meat outside, and you may not break any of its bones. 47The whole community of Israel must celebrate this festival at the same time.

48"If there are foreigners living among you who want to celebrate the LORD's Passover, let all the males be circumcised. Then they may come and celebrate the Passover with you. They will be treated just as if they had been born among you. But an uncircumcised male may never eat of the Passover lamb. 49This law applies to everyone, whether a native-born Israelite or a foreigner who has settled among you."

50So the people of Israel followed all the LORD's instructions to Moses and Aaron. 51And that very day the LORD began to lead the people of Israel out of Egypt, division by division.

12:35 Exod 3:22
12:36 Exod 3:22
12:37 Exod 38:26; Num 1:46
12:38 Num 11:4; Deut 3:19
12:39 Exod 11:1
12:40-41 Gen 15:13, 16; Acts 7:6; Gal 3:17
12:42 Exod 13:10; Deut 16:1
12:43 Num 9:14
12:44 Gen 17:12-13; Lev 22:11
12:46 Num 9:12; John 19:33, 36
12:48 Num 9:13-14; Gal 3:28
12:49 Lev 24:22; Num 15:15-16
12:50 Exod 12:28

Dedication of the Firstborn

13 Then the LORD said to Moses, 2"Dedicate to me all the firstborn sons of Israel and every firstborn male animal. They are mine."

3So Moses said to the people, "This is a day to remember forever—the day you left Egypt, the place of your slavery. For the LORD has brought you out by his mighty power. (Remember, you are not to use any yeast.) 4This day in early spring* will be the anniversary of your exodus. 5You must celebrate this day when the LORD brings you into the land of the Canaanites, Hittites, Amorites, Hivites, and Jebusites. This is the land he swore to give your ancestors—a land flowing with milk and honey. 6For seven days you will eat only bread without yeast. Then on the seventh day, you will celebrate a great feast to the LORD. 7Eat only bread without yeast during those seven days. In fact, there must be no yeast in your homes or anywhere within the borders of your land during this time.

8"During these festival days each year, you must explain to your children why you are celebrating. Say to them, 'This is a celebration of what the LORD did for us when we left Egypt.' 9This annual festival will be a visible reminder to you, like a mark branded on

13:2 Exod 13:12-13; 22:29; 34:20; Lev 27:26; Num 3:13; Deut 15:19; †Luke 2:23
13:3 Exod 3:20; 6:1
13:4 Exod 12:2
13:5 Exod 3:8, 17; 12:25-26
13:6 Exod 12:15-20
13:9 Exod 12:14; Deut 6:8

13:4 Hebrew *in the month of Abib.* This month of the Hebrew lunar calendar usually occurs in March and April.

12:37, 38 The total number of people leaving Egypt is estimated to have been about two million. The "many people who were not Israelites" may have been Egyptians and others who were drawn to the Hebrews by God's mighty works and who decided to leave Egypt with them.

13:2 *Dedicate* means to sacrifice or to consider something as belonging to God. This dedication practice described in 13:11-16 was to remind the people of their deliverance through God.

13:6-9 The Festival of Unleavened Bread marked the Hebrews as a unique people—as though they were branded on their hands and foreheads. What do you do that marks you as a follower of God? The way you raise your children, demonstrate love for others, show concern for the poor, and live in devotion to God—these actions will leave visible marks for all to see. While national groups are marked by customs and traditions, Christians are marked by loving one another (John 13:34, 35).

your hands or your forehead. Let it remind you always to keep the LORD’s instructions in
your minds and on your lips. After all, it was the LORD who rescued you from Egypt with
great power.
10“So celebrate this festival at the appointed time each year. 11And remember these
instructions when the LORD brings you into the land he swore to give your ancestors long
ago, the land where the Canaanites are now living. 12All firstborn sons and firstborn male
animals must be presented to the LORD. 13A firstborn male donkey may be redeemed
from the LORD by presenting a lamb in its place. But if you decide not to make the
exchange, the donkey must be killed by breaking its neck. However, you must redeem
every firstborn son.
14“And in the future, your children will ask you, ‘What does all this mean?’ Then
you will tell them, ‘With mighty power the LORD brought us out of Egypt from our
slavery. 15Pharaoh refused to let us go, so the LORD killed all the firstborn males
throughout the land of Egypt, both people and animals. That is why we now offer all
the firstborn males to the LORD—except that the firstborn sons are always redeemed.’
16Again I say, this ceremony will be like a mark branded on your hands or your
forehead. It is a visible reminder that it was the LORD who brought you out of Egypt
with great power.”

2. Crossing the sea

Israel’s Wilderness Detour

17When Pharaoh finally let the people go, God did not lead them on the road that runs
through Philistine territory, even though that was the shortest way from Egypt to the
Promised Land. God said, “If the people are faced with a battle, they might change their
minds and return to Egypt.” 18So God led them along a route through the wilderness
toward the Red Sea,* and the Israelites left Egypt like a marching army.
19Moses took the bones of Joseph with him, for Joseph had made the sons of Israel
swear that they would take his bones with them when God led them out of Egypt—as he
was sure God would.
20Leaving Succoth, they camped at Etham on the edge of the wilderness. 21The LORD
guided them by a pillar of cloud during the day and a pillar of fire at night. That way they

13:10 Exod 12:24-25
13:12 Exod 13:2; 22:29 Num 3:13 †Luke 2:23
13:13 Exod 34:20 Num 18:15-16
13:14 Exod 12:26-27 Deut 6:20
13:15 Exod 12:29
13:16 Exod 13:9 Deut 6:8
13:17 Exod 14:11 Num 14:1-4 Deut 17:16
13:19 Gen 50:24-25 Josh 24:32 Acts 7:16
13:20 Exod 12:37 Num 33:6-8
13:21 Exod 14:19, 24 Ps 105:39 1 Cor 10:1

13:18 Hebrew *sea of reeds.*

13:12-14 What did it mean to “redeem every firstborn son”? During the night the Israelites escaped from Egypt, God spared the oldest son of every house marked with blood on the door-frame. Because God saved the lives of the firstborn, he had a rightful claim to them. But God commanded the Israelites to buy their sons back from him. This ritual served three main purposes: (1) It was a reminder to the people of how God had spared their sons from death and freed them all from slavery; (2) it showed God’s high respect for human life in contrast to the pagan gods who, their worshipers believed, demanded human sacrifice; (3) it looked forward to the day when Jesus Christ would buy us back by paying the price for our sin once and for all.

13:17, 18 God doesn’t always work in the way that seems best to us. Instead of guiding the Israelites along the direct route from Egypt to the Promised Land, he took them by a longer route to avoid fighting with the Philistines. If God does not lead you along the shortest path to your goal, don’t complain or resist. Follow him willingly and trust him to lead you safely around unseen obstacles. He can see the end of your journey from the beginning, and he knows the safest and best route.

13:17, 18 When did the Hebrews leave Egypt? There are two theories. The *early* theory says the Exodus occurred around 1446–1445 B.C. The *late* theory suggests the Exodus happened between 1300 and 1200 B.C. Those who hold to the earlier date point to 1 Kings 6:1, where the Bible clearly states that Solomon began building the Temple 480 years after the Hebrews left Egypt. Since almost all scholars agree that Solomon began building the Temple in 966, this puts the Exodus in the year 1446. But those who hold to the later date suggest that the 480 years cannot be taken literally. They point to Exodus 1:11, which says that the Hebrews built the store cities of Pithom and Rameses, named after Pharaoh Rameses II, who reigned around 1290 B.C. Regardless of which date is correct, the fact is that God led the Hebrews out of Egypt, just as he had promised. This showed his great power and his great love for his people.

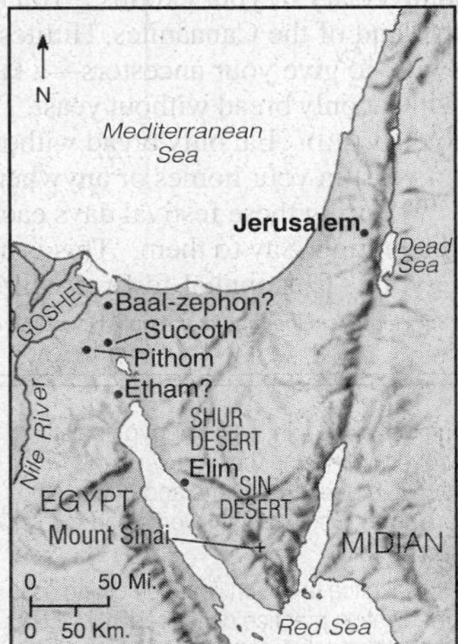

THE EXODUS The Israelites left Succoth and camped first at Etham before going toward Baal-zephon to camp by the sea (14:2). God miraculously brought them across the sea, into the Shur Desert (15:22). After stopping at the oasis of Elim, the people moved into the Sin Desert (16:1).

could travel whether it was day or night. 22And the LORD did not remove the pillar of
cloud or pillar of fire from their sight.

14:2
Num 33:7-8

14:4
Exod 4:21; 7:5
Rom 9:17, 22-23

14 Then the LORD gave these instructions to Moses: 2"Tell the people to march
toward Pi-hahiroth between Migdol and the sea. Camp there along the shore,
opposite Baal-zephon. 3Then Pharaoh will think, 'Those Israelites are confused. They
are trapped between the wilderness and the sea!' 4And once again I will harden Pharaoh's

MOSES

Some people can't stay out of trouble. When conflict breaks out, they always manage to be nearby. Reaction is their favorite action. This was Moses. He seemed drawn to what needed to be righted. Throughout his life, he was at his finest and his worst responding to the conflicts around him. Even the burning bush experience was an illustration of his character. Having spotted the fire and seen that the bush did not burn, he had to investigate. Whether jumping into a fight to defend a Hebrew slave or trying to referee a struggle between two kinsmen, when Moses saw conflict, he reacted.

Over the years, however, an amazing thing happened to Moses' character. He didn't stop reacting, but rather learned to react correctly. The kaleidoscopic action of each day of leading two million people in the wilderness was more than enough challenge for Moses' reacting ability. Much of the time he served as a buffer between God and the people. At one moment he had to respond to God's anger at the people's stubbornness and forgetfulness. At another moment he had to react to the people's bickering and complaining. At still another moment he had to react to their unjustified attacks on his character.

Leadership often involves reaction. If we want to react with instincts consistent with God's will, we must develop habits of obedience to God. Consistent obedience to God is best developed in times of less stress. Then when stress comes, our natural reaction will be to obey God.

In our age of lowering moral standards, we find it almost impossible to believe that God would punish Moses for the one time he disobeyed outright. What we fail to see, however, is that God did not reject Moses; Moses simply disqualified himself to enter the Promised Land. Personal greatness does not make a person immune to error or its consequences.

In Moses we see an outstanding personality shaped by God. But we must not misunderstand what God did. He did not change who or what Moses was; he did not give Moses new abilities and strengths. Instead, he took Moses' characteristics and molded them until they were suited to his purposes. Does knowing this make a difference in your understanding of God's purpose in your life? He is trying to take what he created in the first place and use it for its intended purposes. The next time you talk with God, don't ask, "What should I change into?" but "How should I use my own abilities and strengths to do your will?"

Strengths and accomplishments
- Egyptian education; wilderness training
- Greatest Jewish leader; set the Exodus in motion
- Prophet and lawgiver; recorder of the Ten Commandments
- Author of the Pentateuch

Weaknesses and mistakes
- Failed to enter the Promised Land because of disobedience to God
- Did not always recognize and use the talents of others

Lessons from his life
- God prepares, then uses. His timetable is life-sized
- God does his greatest work through frail people

Vital statistics
- Where: Egypt, Midian, wilderness of Sinai
- Occupations: Prince, shepherd, leader of the Israelites
- Relatives: Sister: Miriam. Brother: Aaron. Wife: Zipporah. Sons: Gershom and Eliezer

Key verses
"It was by faith that Moses, when he grew up, refused to be treated as the son of Pharaoh's daughter. He chose to share the oppression of God's people instead of enjoying the fleeting pleasures of sin" (Hebrews 11:24, 25).

Moses' story is told in the books of Exodus through Deuteronomy. He is also mentioned in Acts 7:20–44; Hebrews 11:23–29.

13:21, 22 God gave the Hebrews a pillar of cloud and a pillar of fire so they would know day and night that God was with them on their journey to the Promised Land. What has God given us so that we can have the same assurance? The Bible—something the Israelites did not have. Look to God's Word for reassurance of his presence. As the Hebrews looked to the pillars of cloud and fire, we can look to God's Word day and night to know he is with us, helping us on our journey.

13:21, 22 The pillars of fire and cloud were examples of *theophany*—God appearing in a physical form. In this form, God lighted Israel's path, protected them from their enemies, provided reassurance, controlled their movements, and inspired the burning zeal that Israel should have for their God.

heart, and he will chase after you. I have planned this so I will receive great glory at the
expense of Pharaoh and his armies. After this, the Egyptians will know that I am the
LORD!" So the Israelites camped there as they were told.

The Egyptians Pursue Israel

5 When word reached the king of Egypt that the Israelites were not planning to return
to Egypt after three days, Pharaoh and his officials changed their minds. "What have
we done, letting all these slaves get away?" they asked. 6 So Pharaoh called out his
troops and led the chase in his chariot. 7 He took with him six hundred of Egypt's best
chariots, along with the rest of the chariots of Egypt, each with a commander. 8 The
LORD continued to strengthen Pharaoh's resolve, and he chased after the people of
Israel who had escaped so defiantly. 9 All the forces in Pharaoh's army—all his horses,
chariots, and charioteers—were used in the chase. The Egyptians caught up with the
people of Israel as they were camped beside the shore near Pi-hahiroth, across from
Baal-zephon.

10 As Pharaoh and his army approached, the people of Israel could see them in the distance,
marching toward them. The people began to panic, and they cried out to the LORD for
help.

11 Then they turned against Moses and complained, "Why did you bring us out here
to die in the wilderness? Weren't there enough graves for us in Egypt? Why did you make
us leave? 12 Didn't we tell you to leave us alone while we were still in Egypt? Our
Egyptian slavery was far better than dying out here in the wilderness!"

13 But Moses told the people, "Don't be afraid. Just stand where you are and watch the
LORD rescue you. The Egyptians that you see today will never be seen again. 14 The LORD
himself will fight for you. You won't have to lift a finger in your defense!"

Escape through the Red Sea

15 Then the LORD said to Moses, "Why are you crying out to me? Tell the people to get
moving! 16 Use your shepherd's staff—hold it out over the water, and a path will open
up before you through the sea. Then all the people of Israel will walk through on dry
ground. 17 Yet I will harden the hearts of the Egyptians, and they will follow the Israelites
into the sea. Then I will receive great glory at the expense of Pharaoh and his armies,
chariots, and charioteers. 18 When I am finished with Pharaoh and his army, all Egypt
will know that I am the LORD!"

19 Then the angel of God, who had been leading the people of Israel, moved to a
position behind them, and the pillar of cloud also moved around behind them. 20 The
cloud settled between the Israelite and Egyptian camps. As night came, the pillar of cloud
turned into a pillar of fire, lighting the Israelite camp. But the cloud became darkness to
the Egyptians, and they couldn't find the Israelites.

21 Then Moses raised his hand over the sea, and the LORD opened up a path through

14:5 Ps 105:25
14:7 Exod 15:4
14:8 Num 33:3; Acts 13:17
14:9 Exod 14:2; 15:9; Josh 24:6
14:10 Josh 24:7; Neh 9:9
14:11 Exod 5:21; 15:24; Ps 106:7-8
14:13 Gen 15:1; Exod 14:30; 15:2
14:14 Exod 15:3; Deut 1:30; 3:22; Isa 30:15
14:15 Josh 7:10
14:16 Exod 4:17, 20; Num 20:8-9, 11
14:18 Exod 14:25
14:19 Exod 13:21-22
14:21 Exod 7:19; Pss 106:9; 114:3, 5; Isa 63:12-13

14:6-9 Six hundred Egyptian war chariots were bearing down on the helpless Israelites, who were trapped between the mountains and the sea. The war chariots each carried two people—one to drive and one to fight. These chariots were made of a wood or leather cab placed over two wheels, and they were pulled by horses. These were the armored tanks of Bible times. But even their power was no match for God, who destroyed both the chariots and their soldiers.

14:10, 11 Trapped against the sea, the Israelites faced the Egyptian army sweeping in for the kill. The Israelites thought they were doomed. After watching God's powerful hand deliver them from Egypt, their only response was fear, whining, and despair. Where was their trust in God? Israel had to learn from repeated experience that God was able to provide for them. God has preserved these examples in the Bible so that we can learn to trust him the first time. By focusing on God's faithfulness in the past, we can face crises with confidence rather than with fear and complaining.

14:11, 12 This is the first instance of grumbling and complaining by the Israelites. Their lack of faith in God is startling. Yet how often do we find ourselves doing the same thing—complaining over inconveniences or discomforts? The Israelites were about to learn some tough lessons. Had they trusted God, they would have been spared much grief.

14:13, 14 The people were hostile and despairing, but Moses encouraged them to watch the wonderful way God would rescue them. Moses had a positive attitude! When it looked as if they were trapped, Moses called upon God to intervene. We may not be chased by an army, but we may still feel trapped. Instead of giving in to despair, we should adopt Moses' attitude to "stand where you are and watch the LORD rescue you."

14:15 The Lord told Moses to stop praying and get moving! Prayer must have a vital place in our lives, but there is also a place for action. Sometimes we know what to do, but we pray for more guidance as an excuse to postpone doing it. If we know what we should do, then it is time to get moving.

14:21 There was no apparent way of escape, but the Lord opened up a dry path through the sea. Sometimes we find our-

14:22 Exod 15:19; Neh 9:11; Pss 66:6; 78:13; Heb 11:29
14:24 Exod 13:21
14:26 Exod 14:16
14:27 Exod 15:1, 7; Deut 11:4; Heb 11:29
14:28 Exod 15:19; Neh 9:11; Pss 78:53; 106:11
14:29 Ps 66:6; Isa 11:15
14:30 Pss 106:8; Isa 63:8, 11
14:31 Exod 4:31; 19:9; Ps 106:12

the water with a strong east wind. The wind blew all that night, turning the seabed into
dry land. 22 So the people of Israel walked through the sea on dry ground, with walls of
water on each side! 23 Then the Egyptians—all of Pharaoh's horses, chariots, and
charioteers—followed them across the bottom of the sea. 24 But early in the morning, the
LORD looked down on the Egyptian army from the pillar of fire and cloud, and he threw
them into confusion. 25 Their chariot wheels began to come off, making their chariots
impossible to drive. "Let's get out of here!" the Egyptians shouted. "The LORD is
fighting for Israel against us!"
26 When all the Israelites were on the other side, the LORD said to Moses, "Raise your
hand over the sea again. Then the waters will rush back over the Egyptian chariots and
charioteers." 27 So as the sun began to rise, Moses raised his hand over the sea. The
water roared back into its usual place, and the LORD swept the terrified Egyptians into
the surging currents. 28 The waters covered all the chariots and charioteers—the entire
army of Pharaoh. Of all the Egyptians who had chased the Israelites into the sea, not a
single one survived.
29 The people of Israel had walked through the middle of the sea on dry land, as the
water stood up like a wall on both sides. 30 This was how the LORD rescued Israel from
the Egyptians that day. And the Israelites could see the bodies of the Egyptians washed
up on the shore. 31 When the people of Israel saw the mighty power that the LORD had
displayed against the Egyptians, they feared the LORD and put their faith in him and his
servant Moses.

15:1 Ps 106:12; Isa 12:5; 42:10-12; Jer 51:21; Rev 15:3
15:2 Exod 3:15-16; Deut 10:21; 2 Sam 22:47; Pss 18:1; 48:14; Isa 12:2
15:3 Exod 14:14; Pss 24:8; 83:18
15:4 Exod 14:6-7, 17, 28
15:5 Exod 14:28; Neh 9:11
15:6 Exod 3:20; Ps 118:15-16

A Song of Deliverance

15 Then Moses and the people of Israel sang this song to the LORD:

"I will sing to the LORD, for he has triumphed gloriously;
he has thrown both horse and rider into the sea.
2 The LORD is my strength and my song;
he has become my victory.
He is my God, and I will praise him;
he is my father's God, and I will exalt him!
3 The LORD is a warrior;
yes, the LORD is his name!
4 Pharaoh's chariots and armies,
he has thrown into the sea.
The very best of Pharaoh's officers
have been drowned in the Red Sea.*
5 The deep waters have covered them;
they sank to the bottom like a stone.

6 "Your right hand, O LORD,
is glorious in power.

15:4 Hebrew *sea of reeds;* also in 15:22.

---

selves caught in a problem and see no way out. Don't panic; God can open up a way.

14:21, 22 Some scholars believe the Israelites did not cross the main body of the Red Sea but one of the shallow lakes or marshes north of it that dry up at certain times of the year, or perhaps it was a smaller branch of the Red Sea where the water would have been shallow enough to wade across. But the Bible clearly states that the Lord "opened up a path through the water with a strong east wind . . . turning the sea bed into dry land" (14:21; see also Joshua 3:15, 16; and 2 Kings 2:13, 14). Also, the water was deep enough to cover the chariots (14:28). The God who created the earth and water performed a mighty miracle at exactly the right time to demonstrate his great power and love for his people.

14:27, 28 No evidence of this great Exodus has been discovered in Egyptian historical records. This was because it was a common practice for Egyptian pharaohs not to record their defeats. They even went so far as to take existing records and delete the names of traitors and political adversaries. Pharaoh would have been especially anxious not to record that his great army was destroyed chasing a band of runaway slaves. Since either the Egyptians failed to record the Exodus or the record has not yet been found, it is impossible to place a precise date on the event.

15:1ff Music played an important part in Israel's worship and celebration. Singing was an expression of love and thanks, and it was a creative way to pass down oral traditions. Some say this song of Moses is the oldest recorded song in the world. It was a festive epic poem celebrating God's victory, lifting the hearts and voices of the people outward and upward. After having been delivered from great danger, they sang with joy! Psalms and hymns can be great ways to express relief, praise, and thanks when you have been through trouble.

Your right hand, O LORD,
dashes the enemy to pieces.
7 In the greatness of your majesty,
you overthrew those who rose against you.
Your anger flashed forth;
it consumed them as fire burns straw.
8 At the blast of your breath, the waters piled up!
The surging waters stood straight like a wall;
in the middle of the sea the waters became hard.

9 "The enemy said, 'I will chase them,
catch up with them, and destroy them.
I will divide the plunder,
avenging myself against them.
I will unsheath my sword;
my power will destroy them.'
10 But with a blast of your breath,
the sea covered them.
They sank like lead
in the mighty waters.

11 "Who else among the gods is like you, O LORD?
Who is glorious in holiness like you—
so awesome in splendor,
performing such wonders?
12 You raised up your hand,
and the earth swallowed our enemies.

13 "With unfailing love you will lead
this people whom you have ransomed.
You will guide them in your strength
to the place where your holiness dwells.
14 The nations will hear and tremble;
anguish will grip the people of Philistia.
15 The leaders of Edom will be terrified;
the nobles of Moab will tremble.
All the people of Canaan will melt with fear;
16 terror and dread will overcome them.
Because of your great power,
they will be silent like a stone,
until your people pass by, O LORD,
until the people whom you purchased pass by.
17 You will bring them in and plant them on your own mountain—
the place you have made as your home, O LORD,
the sanctuary, O Lord, that your hands have made.
18 The LORD will reign forever and ever!"

19 When Pharaoh's horses, chariots, and charioteers rushed into the sea, the LORD
brought the water crashing down on them. But the people of Israel had walked
through on dry land!
20 Then Miriam the prophet, Aaron's sister, took a tambourine and led all the women
in rhythm and dance. 21 And Miriam sang this song:

"I will sing to the LORD, for he has triumphed gloriously;
he has thrown both horse and rider into the sea."

15:7 Exod 9:16; 14:24; Ps 78:49-50
15:8 Exod 14:22, 29; Ps 78:13
15:9 Exod 14:5-9
15:10 Exod 14:27-28
15:11 Exod 8:10; Deut 3:24; 1 Sam 2:2; 2 Sam 7:22; Pss 22:23; 72:18; Isa 6:3; Rev 4:8
15:12 Exod 15:6
15:13 Neh 9:12; Ps 77:15, 20
15:14 Deut 2:25; Hab 3:7
15:15 Num 22:3; Deut 2:4; Josh 2:11; 5:1
15:17 Exod 23:20; 32:34; Pss 2:6; 78:54, 68; Isa 5:2; Jer 2:21
15:18 Pss 10:16; 29:10; Isa 57:15
15:19 Exod 14:22, 28
15:20 Exod 2:4; Num 26:59; 1 Sam 18:6; Pss 30:11; 150:4
15:21 Exod 15:1

15:20 Miriam was called a prophet not only because she received revelations from God (Numbers 12:1, 2; Micah 6:4) but also because of her musical skill. Prophecy and music were often closely related in the Bible (1 Samuel 10:5; 1 Chronicles 25:1).

3. Complaining in the wilderness

Bitter Water at Marah

15:22 Num 33:8; Pss 77:20; 78:52
15:23 Num 33:8; Ruth 1:20
15:24 Exod 14:11; Ps 106:13
15:25 Exod 14:10; 16:4
15:26 Exod 19:5-6; Deut 7:15; Ps 103:3
15:27 Num 33:9

22 Then Moses led the people of Israel away from the Red Sea, and they moved
out into the Shur Desert. They traveled in this desert for three days without water.
23 When they came to Marah, they finally found water. But the people couldn't
drink it because it was bitter. (That is why the place was called Marah, which means
"bitter.")
24 Then the people turned against Moses. "What are we going to drink?" they
demanded.
25 So Moses cried out to the LORD for help, and the LORD showed him a branch. Moses
took the branch and threw it into the water. This made the water good to drink.
It was there at Marah that the LORD laid before them the following conditions to
test their faithfulness to him: 26 "If you will listen carefully to the voice of the LORD
your God and do what is right in his sight, obeying his commands and laws, then I
will not make you suffer the diseases I sent on the Egyptians; for I am the LORD who
heals you."
27 After leaving Marah, they came to Elim, where there were twelve springs and
seventy palm trees. They camped there beside the springs.

FAMOUS SONGS IN THE BIBLE

Where	Purpose of Song
Exodus 15:1–21	Moses' song of deliverance and praise after God led Israel out of Egypt and saved them by parting the Red Sea; Miriam joined in the singing, too
Numbers 21:17	Israel's song of praise to God for giving them water in the wilderness
Deuteronomy 32:1–43	Moses' song of Israel's history with thanksgiving and praise as the Hebrews were about to enter the Promised Land
Judges 5:2–31	Deborah and Barak's song of praise thanking God for Israel's victory over King Jabin's army at Mount Tabor
2 Samuel 22:2–51	David's song of thanks and praise to God for rescuing him from Saul and his other enemies
Song of Songs	Solomon's song of love celebrating the union of husband and wife
Isaiah 26:1	Isaiah's prophetic song about how the redeemed will sing in the new Jerusalem
Ezra 3:11	Israel's song of praise at the completion of the Temple's foundation
Luke 1:46–55	Mary's song of praise to God for the conception of Jesus
Luke 1:68–79	Zechariah's song of praise for the birth of his son
Acts 16:25	Paul and Silas sang hymns in prison
Revelation 5:9, 10	The "new song" of the 24 elders acclaiming Christ as worthy to break the seven seals of God's scroll
Revelation 14:3	The song of the 144,000 redeemed from the earth
Revelation 15:3, 4	The song of all the redeemed in praise of the Lamb who redeemed them

15:23, 27 The waters of Marah are contrasted with the springs of Elim. Marah stood for the unbelieving, grumbling attitude of the people who would not trust God. Elim stands for God's bountiful provision. How easy it is to grumble and complain too quickly, only to be embarrassed by God's help!

15:26 God promised that if the people obeyed him, they would be free from the diseases that plagued the Egyptians. Little did they know that many of the moral laws he later gave them were designed to keep them free from sickness. For example, following God's law against prostitution would keep them free of venereal disease. God's laws for us are often designed to keep us from harm. Men and women are complex beings. Our physical, emotional, and spiritual lives are intertwined. Modern medicine is now acknowledging what these laws assumed. If we want God to care for us, we need to submit to his directions for living.

Manna and Quail from Heaven

16 Then they left Elim and journeyed into the Sin* Desert, between Elim and Mount
Sinai. They arrived there a month after leaving Egypt.* 2 There, too, the whole
community of Israel spoke bitterly against Moses and Aaron.
3 "Oh, that we were back in Egypt," they moaned. "It would have been better if the
LORD had killed us there! At least there we had plenty to eat. But now you have brought
us into this desert to starve us to death."
4 Then the LORD said to Moses, "Look, I'm going to rain down food from heaven for
you. The people can go out each day and pick up as much food as they need for that day.
I will test them in this to see whether they will follow my instructions. 5 Tell them to pick
up twice as much as usual on the sixth day of each week."
6 Then Moses and Aaron called a meeting of all the people of Israel and told them, "In
the evening you will realize that it was the LORD who brought you out of the land of
Egypt. 7 In the morning you will see the glorious presence of the LORD. He has heard
your complaints, which are against the LORD and not against us. 8 The LORD will give
you meat to eat in the evening and bread in the morning, for he has heard all your
complaints against him. Yes, your complaints are against the LORD, not against us."
9 Then Moses said to Aaron, "Say this to the entire community of Israel: 'Come into
the LORD's presence, and hear his reply to your complaints.'" 10 And as Aaron spoke to
the people, they looked out toward the desert. Within the guiding cloud, they could see
the awesome glory of the LORD.
11 And the LORD said to Moses, 12 "I have heard the people's complaints. Now tell
them, 'In the evening you will have meat to eat, and in the morning you will be filled
with bread. Then you will know that I am the LORD your God.'"
13 That evening vast numbers of quail arrived and covered the camp. The next morning
the desert all around the camp was wet with dew. 14 When the dew disappeared later in
the morning, thin flakes, white like frost, covered the ground. 15 The Israelites were
puzzled when they saw it. "What is it?" they asked.
And Moses told them, "It is the food the LORD has given you. 16 The LORD says that
each household should gather as much as it needs. Pick up two quarts* for each person."
17 So the people of Israel went out and gathered this food—some getting more, and
some getting less. 18 By gathering two quarts for each person, everyone had just enough.
Those who gathered a lot had nothing left over, and those who gathered only a little had
enough. Each family had just what it needed.
19 Then Moses told them, "Do not keep any of it overnight." 20 But, of course, some
of them didn't listen and kept some of it until morning. By then it was full of maggots
and had a terrible smell. And Moses was very angry with them.
21 The people gathered the food morning by morning, each family according to its
need. And as the sun became hot, the food they had not picked up melted and
disappeared. 22 On the sixth day, there was twice as much as usual on the ground—
four quarts* for each person instead of two. The leaders of the people came and asked

16:1 Exod 17:1; Num 33:11-12
16:2 Exod 14:11; 1 Cor 10:10
16:4 Deut 8:2, 16; Pss 78:24; 105:40; John 6:31; 1 Cor 10:3
16:5 Exod 16:22
16:6 Exod 6:6
16:7 Exod 16:12; Num 14:27; 16:11
16:10 Num 16:19
16:12 Exod 16:7
16:13 Num 11:31; Pss 78:27-28; 105:40
16:14 Num 11:7-9; Deut 8:3
16:15 Exod 16:31; Neh 9:5; John 6:31; 1 Cor 10:30
16:16 Exod 16:33, 36
16:18 †2 Cor 8:15
16:19 Exod 12:10; 23:18
16:20 Num 16:15
16:22 Exod 16:5; 34:31

16:1a Not to be confused with the English word *sin.* **16:1b** Hebrew *on the fifteenth day of the second month.* The Exodus had occurred on the fourteenth day of the first month (see 12:6). **16:16** Hebrew *1 omer* [2 liters]; also in 16:18, 32, 33. **16:22** Hebrew *2 omers* [4 liters].

16:1 The Sin Desert was a vast and hostile environment of sand and stone. Its barren surroundings provided the perfect place for God to test and shape the character of his people.

16:2, 3 It happened again. As the Israelites encountered danger, shortages, and inconvenience, they complained bitterly and longed to be back in Egypt. But as always, God provided for their needs. Difficult circumstances often lead to stress, and complaining is a natural response. The Israelites didn't really want to be back in Egypt; they just wanted life to get a little easier. In the pressure of the moment, they could not focus on the cause of their stress (in this case, lack of trust in God); they could only think about the quickest way of escape. When pressure comes your way, resist the temptation to make a quick escape. Instead, focus on God's power and wisdom to help you deal with the cause of your stress.

16:4, 5 God promised to meet the Hebrews' need for food in the desert, but he decided to test their obedience. God wanted to see if they would obey his detailed instructions. We can learn to trust him as our Lord only by following. We can learn to obey by taking small steps of obedience.

16:14-16 Manna (16:31) appeared on the ground each day as thin flakes like frost. The people gathered it, ground it like grain, and made it into honey-tasting pancakes. For the Israelites the manna was a gift—it came every day and was just what they needed. It satisfied their temporary physical need. In John 6:48-51 Jesus compares himself to manna. Christ is our daily bread who satisfies our eternal, spiritual need.

16:23 Gen 2:3; Exod 20:8; 23:12; Neh 9:14

Moses why this had happened. 23 He replied, "The LORD has appointed tomorrow as a day of rest, a holy Sabbath to the LORD. On this day we will rest from our normal daily tasks. So bake or boil as much as you want today, and set aside what is left for tomorrow."

16:24 Exod 16:20

24 The next morning the leftover food was wholesome and good, without maggots or odor. 25 Moses said, "This is your food for today, for today is a Sabbath to the LORD. There will be no food on the ground today. 26 Gather the food for six days, but the seventh day is a Sabbath. There will be no food on the ground for you on that day."

16:28 Ps 78:10

27 Some of the people went out anyway to gather food, even though it was the Sabbath day. But there was none to be found. 28 "How long will these people refuse to obey my commands and instructions?" the LORD asked Moses. 29 "Do they not realize that I have given them the seventh day, the Sabbath, as a day of rest? That is why I give you twice as much food on the sixth day, so there will be enough for two days. On the Sabbath day you must stay in your places. Do not pick up food from the ground on that day." 30 So the people rested on the seventh day.

16:31 Num 11:7-9; Deut 8:3, 16

31 In time, the food became known as manna.* It was white like coriander seed, and it tasted like honey cakes.

32 Then Moses gave them this command from the LORD: "Take two quarts of manna and keep it forever as a treasured memorial of the LORD's provision. By doing this, later generations will be able to see the bread that the LORD provided in the wilderness when he brought you out of Egypt."

16:33 Heb 9:4; Rev 2:17

16:34 Exod 25:16, 21; Num 1:50

16:35 Josh 5:12; Neh 9:20-21

33 Moses said to Aaron, "Get a container and put two quarts of manna into it. Then store it in a sacred place* as a reminder for all future generations." 34 Aaron did this, just as the LORD had commanded Moses. He eventually placed it for safekeeping in the Ark of the Covenant.* 35 So the people of Israel ate manna for forty years until they arrived in the land of Canaan, where there were crops to eat.

36 (The container used to measure the manna was an omer, which held about two quarts.)*

Water from the Rock

17:1 Exod 16:1; 19:2; Num 33:15

17:2 Exod 14:11-12; Num 20:3; Deut 6:16; 1 Cor 10:9

17 At the LORD's command, the people of Israel left the Sin* Desert and moved from place to place. Eventually they came to Rephidim, but there was no water to be found there. 2 So once more the people grumbled and complained to Moses. "Give us water to drink!" they demanded.

"Quiet!" Moses replied. "Why are you arguing with me? And why are you testing the LORD?"

16:31 *Manna* means "What is it?" See 16:15. **16:33** Hebrew *before the LORD*. **16:34** Hebrew *in front of the Testimony*. **16:36** Hebrew *An omer is one tenth of an ephah*. **17:1** Not to be confused with the English word *sin*.

JOURNEY TO MOUNT SINAI
God miraculously supplied food and water in the wilderness for the Israelites. In the Sin Desert, he provided manna (16). At Rephidim, he provided water from a rock (17:1–7). Finally God brought them to the foot of Mount Sinai, where he gave them his holy laws.

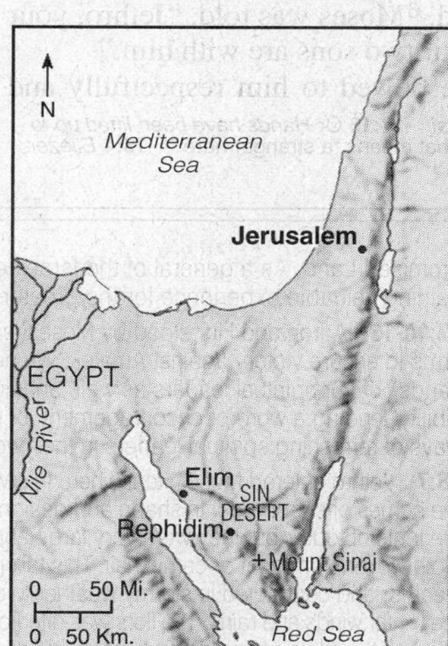

16:23 The Israelites were not to work on the Sabbath—not even to cook food. Why? God knew that the busy routine of daily living could distract people from worshiping him. It is so easy to let work, family responsibilities, and recreation crowd our schedules so tightly that we don't take time to worship. Carefully guard your time with God.

16:32 The Hebrews put some manna in a special jar as a reminder of the way God provided for them in the wilderness. Symbols have always been an important part of Christian worship also. We use special objects as symbols to remind us of God's work. Such symbols can be valuable aids to our worship as long as we are careful to keep them from becoming objects of worship.

17:2 Again the people complained about their problem instead of praying. Some problems can be solved by careful thought or by rearranging our priorities. Some can be solved by discussion and good counsel. But some problems can be solved only by prayer. We should make a determined effort to pray when we feel like complaining because complaining only raises our level of stress. Prayer quiets our thoughts and emotions and prepares us to listen.

3 But tormented by thirst, they continued to complain, "Why did you ever take us out
of Egypt? Why did you bring us here? We, our children, and our livestock will all die!"
4 Then Moses pleaded with the LORD, "What should I do with these people? They are
about to stone me!"
5 The LORD said to Moses, "Take your shepherd's staff, the one you used when you
struck the water of the Nile. Then call some of the leaders of Israel and walk on ahead
of the people. 6 I will meet you by the rock at Mount Sinai.* Strike the rock, and water
will come pouring out. Then the people will be able to drink." Moses did just as he was
told; and as the leaders looked on, water gushed out.
7 Moses named the place Massah—"the place of testing"—and Meribah—"the place
of arguing"—because the people of Israel argued with Moses and tested the LORD by
saying, "Is the LORD going to take care of us or not?"

Israel Defeats the Amalekites

8 While the people of Israel were still at Rephidim, the warriors of Amalek came to fight
against them. 9 Moses commanded Joshua, "Call the Israelites to arms, and fight the army
of Amalek. Tomorrow, I will stand at the top of the hill with the staff of God in my hand."
10 So Joshua did what Moses had commanded. He led his men out to fight the army of
Amalek. Meanwhile Moses, Aaron, and Hur went to the top of a nearby hill. 11 As long
as Moses held up the staff with his hands, the Israelites had the advantage. But whenever
he lowered his hands, the Amalekites gained the upper hand. 12 Moses' arms finally
became too tired to hold up the staff any longer. So Aaron and Hur found a stone for him
to sit on. Then they stood on each side, holding up his hands until sunset. 13 As a result,
Joshua and his troops were able to crush the army of Amalek.
14 Then the LORD instructed Moses, "Write this down as a permanent record, and
announce it to Joshua: I will blot out every trace of Amalek from under heaven." 15 Moses
built an altar there and called it "The LORD Is My Banner."* 16 He said, "They have dared
to raise their fist against the LORD's throne, so now* the LORD will be at war with Amalek
generation after generation."

Jethro's Visit to Moses

18 Word soon reached Jethro, the priest of Midian and Moses' father-in-law, about
all the wonderful things God had done for Moses and his people, the Israelites. He
had heard about how the LORD had brought them safely out of Egypt.
2 Some time before this, Moses had sent his wife, Zipporah, and his two sons to live
with Jethro, his father-in-law. 3 The name of Moses' first son was Gershom,* for Moses
had said when the boy was born, "I have been a stranger in a foreign land." 4 The name
of his second son was Eliezer,* for Moses had said at his birth, "The God of my fathers
was my helper; he delivered me from the sword of Pharaoh." 5 Jethro now came to visit
Moses, and he brought Moses' wife and two sons with him. They arrived while Moses
and the people were camped near the mountain of God. 6 Moses was told, "Jethro, your
father-in-law, has come to visit you. Your wife and your two sons are with him."
7 So Moses went out to meet his father-in-law. He bowed to him respectfully and

17:3 Exod 16:2-3
17:4 Exod 14:15; Num 14:10; 16:19
17:5 Exod 3:16, 18; 7:20
17:6 Num 20:8-10; Pss 78:15-16; 105:41; 1 Cor 10:4
17:7 Deut 6:16; 9:22; Pss 81:7; 95:8
17:8 Gen 36:12, 16; Num 24:20; Deut 25:17-19
17:9 Exod 24:13; Num 11:28
17:10 Exod 24:14; 31:2
17:12 Isa 35:3
17:14 Exod 24:4; 34:27; Num 33:2; Deut 29:19
17:15 Gen 22:14
17:16 Gen 22:16
18:1 Exod 2:16, 18; 3:1
18:2 Exod 2:21; 4:25
18:3 Exod 2:22; Acts 7:29
18:4 Gen 49:25
18:5 Exod 3:1
18:7 Gen 43:28; Exod 4:27

17:6 Hebrew *Horeb,* another name for Sinai. **17:15** Hebrew *Yahweh Nissi.* **17:16** Or *Hands have been lifted up to the LORD's throne, and now.* **18:3** *Gershom* sounds like a Hebrew term that means "a stranger here." **18:4** *Eliezer* means "God is my helper."

17:8 The Amalekites were descendants of Amalek, a grandson of Esau. They were a fierce nomadic tribe that lived in the desert region of the Dead Sea. They made part of their livelihood by conducting frequent raids on other settlements and carrying off booty. They killed for pleasure. One of the greatest insults in Israelite culture was to call someone "a friend of Amalek." When the Israelites entered the region, the Amalekites saw this as a perfect opportunity for both pleasure and profit. But this hostile tribe was moving in on the wrong group—a people led by God. For the Israelite slaves to defeat such a warlike nation was more than enough proof that God was with them as he had promised to be.

17:9 Here we meet Joshua for the first time. Later he would become the great leader who brought God's people into the Promised Land. As a general of the Israelite army, he was gaining valuable experience for the greater battles to come.

17:10-13 Aaron and Hur stood by Moses' side and held up his arms to ensure victory against Amalek. We need to "hold up the hands" of our spiritual leaders as well. Shouldering some responsibility, lending a word of encouragement, or offering a prayer are ways of refreshing spiritual leaders in their work.

18:7 Jethro entered Moses' tent where the two talked. Tents were the homes of shepherds. In shape and design, they resembled the tents of today, but they were very large and made of a thick cloth woven from goat or camel hair. This fabric breathed in warm weather and contracted in stormy weather to offer protection from the winter winds and rains. The floor was often covered with animal-skin rugs, while curtains divided the inside space into rooms.

18:8 Exod 15:6, 16; Num 20:14
18:9 Isa 63:7-14
18:10 1 Kgs 8:56; Ps 68:19-20
18:11 Exod 12:12; 15:11
18:12 Gen 31:54; Exod 24:5

greeted him warmly. They asked about each other's health and then went to Moses' tent
to talk further. 8 Moses told his father-in-law about everything the LORD had done to
rescue Israel from Pharaoh and the Egyptians. He also told him about the problems they
had faced along the way and how the LORD had delivered his people from all their
troubles. 9 Jethro was delighted when he heard about all that the LORD had done for Israel
as he brought them out of Egypt.
10 "Praise be to the LORD," Jethro said, "for he has saved you from the Egyptians and
from Pharaoh. He has rescued Israel from the power of Egypt! 11 I know now that the
LORD is greater than all other gods, because his people have escaped from the proud and
cruel Egyptians."
12 Then Jethro presented a burnt offering and gave sacrifices to God. As Jethro was
doing this, Aaron and the leaders of Israel came out to meet him. They all joined him in
a sacrificial meal in God's presence.

Jethro's Wise Advice

13 The next day, Moses sat as usual to hear the people's complaints against each other.
They were lined up in front of him from morning till evening.
14 When Moses' father-in-law saw all that Moses was doing for the people, he said,

JETHRO

People such as Jethro and Melchizedek—not Israelites, but nevertheless worshipers of the true God—play an important role in the Old Testament. They remind us of God's commitment to the world. God chose one nation through which to work, but his love and concern are for all nations!

Jethro's religious background prepared him for, rather than prevented him from, responding in faith to God. When he saw and heard what God had done for the Israelites, he worshiped God wholeheartedly. We can guess that for 40 years as Moses' father-in-law, Jethro had been watching God at work, molding a leader. Moses' and Jethro's relationship must have been close, for Moses readily accepted his father- in-law's advice. Each benefited from knowing the other. Jethro met God through Moses, and Moses received hospitality, his wife, and wisdom from Jethro.

The greatest gift one person can give another is an introduction to God. But that gift is hindered if the believer's attitude is, "I have the greatest gift to pass on to you, while you have nothing to give me in return." Real friends give to and receive from each other. The importance of introducing a friend to God does not make the friend's gifts to us insignificant. Rather, the believer is doubly blessed—first by receiving the gifts the friend wishes to give; then by growing in knowledge of the Lord. For we discover that in introducing another person to God, we increase our own awareness of God. As we give God away, he gives himself even more to us.

Is all you know about God a miscellaneous collection of trivia, or do you have a living relationship with him? Only with a vital relationship can you pass on to others the excitement of allowing God to guide your life. Have you reached the point of saying, with Jethro, "I know now that the LORD is greater than all other gods" (Exodus 18:11)?

Strengths and accomplishments
- As father-in-law to Moses, he came to recognize the one true God
- He was a practical troubleshooter and organizer

Lessons from his life
- Supervision and administration are team efforts
- God's plan includes all nations

Vital statistics
- Where: The land of Midian and the wilderness of Sinai
- Occupations: Shepherd, priest
- Relatives: Daughter: Zipporah. Son-in-law: Moses. Son: Hobab

Key verse
"Jethro was delighted when he heard about all that the LORD had done for Israel as he brought them out of Egypt" (Exodus 18:9).

Jethro's story is told in Exodus 2:15—3:1; 18:1–27. He is also mentioned in Judges 1:16.

18:8-11 Moses told his father-in-law all that God had done, convincing him that the Lord was greater than any other god. Our relatives are often the hardest people to tell about God. Yet we should look for opportunities to tell them what God is doing in our lives because we can have an important influence on them.

18:12 This reunion turned into a large celebration. The Israelites frequently shared a sacrificial meal among themselves. A burnt offering was sacrificed to God, and then the meal taken from the sacrifice was dedicated to God and eaten ceremonially as a fellowship dinner.

18:13-26 Moses was spending so much time and energy hearing the Hebrews' complaints that he could not get to other important work. Jethro suggested that Moses delegate most of this work to others and focus his efforts on jobs only he could do. People in positions of responsibility sometimes feel they are the only ones who can do necessary tasks; but others are capable of handling part of the load. Delegation relieved Moses' stress and improved the quality of the government. It helped prepare them for the system of government set up in Canaan. Proper delegation can multiply your effectiveness while giving others a chance to grow.

"Why are you trying to do all this alone? The people have been standing here all day to
get your help."
[15]Moses replied, "Well, the people come to me to seek God's guidance. [16]When an
argument arises, I am the one who settles the case. I inform the people of God's decisions
and teach them his laws and instructions."
[17]"This is not good!" his father-in-law exclaimed. [18]"You're going to wear yourself
out—and the people, too. This job is too heavy a burden for you to handle all by
yourself. [19]Now let me give you a word of advice, and may God be with you. You
should continue to be the people's representative before God, bringing him their
questions to be decided. [20]You should tell them God's decisions, teach them God's laws
and instructions, and show them how to conduct their lives. [21]But find some capable,
honest men who fear God and hate bribes. Appoint them as judges over groups of one
thousand, one hundred, fifty, and ten. [22]These men can serve the people, resolving all
the ordinary cases. Anything that is too important or too complicated can be brought to
you. But they can take care of the smaller matters themselves. They will help you carry
the load, making the task easier for you. [23]If you follow this advice, and if God directs
you to do so, then you will be able to endure the pressures, and all these people will go
home in peace."
[24]Moses listened to his father-in-law's advice and followed his suggestions. [25]He
chose capable men from all over Israel and made them judges over the people. They were
put in charge of groups of one thousand, one hundred, fifty, and ten. [26]These men were
constantly available to administer justice. They brought the hard cases to Moses, but they
judged the smaller matters themselves.
[27]Soon after this, Moses said good-bye to his father-in-law, who returned to his own
land.

18:15 Num 9:8; Deut 17:8-13
18:16 Exod 24:14
18:18 Num 11:14, 17; Deut 1:9
18:19-20 Deut 1:18
18:21 Deut 1:13, 15; Ps 15:1-5
18:22 Num 11:17; Deut 1:17-18
18:25 Deut 1:15; 16:18
18:26 Deut 16:18
18:27 Num 10:29-30

C. ISRAEL AT SINAI (19:1—40:38)

After escaping through the Red Sea, the Hebrews traveled through the wilderness and arrived at Sinai, God's holy mountain. There they received the Ten Commandments, as well as instructions for building a Tabernacle as a center of worship. Through Israel's experiences at Mount Sinai, we learn about the importance of obedience in our relationship with God. His laws help expose sin, and they give standards for righteous living.

1. Giving the law

19 The Israelites arrived in the wilderness of Sinai exactly two months after they left
Egypt.* [2]After breaking camp at Rephidim, they came to the base of Mount Sinai
and set up camp there.
[3]Then Moses climbed the mountain to appear before God. The LORD called out to him
from the mountain and said, "Give these instructions to the descendants of Jacob, the
people of Israel: [4]'You have seen what I did to the Egyptians. You know how I brought
you to myself and carried you on eagle's wings. [5]Now if you will obey me and keep my

19:1 Exod 12:51; 16:1
19:3 Exod 20:21; Acts 7:38
19:4 Deut 29:2; Isa 40:31; 63:9; Rev 12:14
19:5 Exod 15:26; Deut 10:14

19:1 Hebrew *in the third month . . . on the very day,* i.e., two lunar months to the day after leaving Egypt. This day of the Hebrew lunar calendar occurs in late May or early June; compare note on 13:4.

18:16 Moses not only decided these cases, he also taught the people God's laws. Whenever we help others settle disputes or resolve conflicts, we should also look for opportunities to teach about God.

19:2, 3 Mount Sinai is one of the most sacred locations in Israel's history. Located in the south-central Sinai peninsula, this mountain is where Moses met God in a burning bush, God made his covenant with Israel, and Elijah heard God in the gentle whisper. Here God gave his people the laws and guidelines for right living. They learned the potential blessings of obedience (34:4-28) and the tragic consequences of disobedience (34:7).

19:4-6 God had a reason for rescuing the Israelites from slavery. Now he was ready to tell them what it was: Israel was to become a kingdom of priests and a holy nation where anyone could approach God freely. It didn't take long, however, for the people to corrupt God's plan. God then established Aaron's descendants from the tribe of Levi as priests (Leviticus 8, 9), representing what the entire nation should have been. But with the coming of Jesus Christ, God has once again extended his plan to all believers. We are to become holy, a "kingdom of priests" (1 Peter 2:9). The death and resurrection of Christ has allowed each of us to approach God freely.

19:5 Why did God choose Israel as his nation? God knew that no nation on earth was good enough to deserve to be called his people, his "special treasure." He chose Israel, not because of anything they had done, but in his love and mercy he chose Israel in spite of the wrong the nation had done and would do. Why did he want to have a special nation on earth? To represent his way of life, to teach his Word, and to be an agent of salvation to the world. "All the nations of the earth" would be blessed through Abraham's descendants (Genesis

covenant, you will be my own special treasure from among all the nations of the earth;
for all the earth belongs to me. 6And you will be to me a kingdom of priests, my holy
nation.' Give this message to the Israelites."
7Moses returned from the mountain and called together the leaders of the people and
told them what the LORD had said. 8They all responded together, "We will certainly do
everything the LORD asks of us." So Moses brought the people's answer back to the
LORD.
9Then the LORD said to Moses, "I am going to come to you in a thick cloud so the
people themselves can hear me as I speak to you. Then they will always have confidence
in you."
Moses told the LORD what the people had said. 10Then the LORD told Moses, "Go
down and prepare the people for my visit. Purify them today and tomorrow, and have
them wash their clothing. 11Be sure they are ready on the third day, for I will come
down upon Mount Sinai as all the people watch. 12Set boundary lines that the people
may not pass. Warn them, 'Be careful! Do not go up on the mountain or even touch
its boundaries. Those who do will certainly die! 13Any people or animals that cross
the boundary must be stoned to death or shot with arrows. They must not be touched
by human hands.' The people must stay away from the mountain until they hear one
long blast from the ram's horn. Then they must gather at the foot of the mountain."
14So Moses went down to the people. He purified them for worship and had them
wash their clothing. 15He told them, "Get ready for an important event two days from
now. And until then, abstain from having sexual intercourse."
16On the morning of the third day, there was a powerful thunder and lightning
storm, and a dense cloud came down upon the mountain. There was a long, loud blast
from a ram's horn, and all the people trembled. 17Moses led them out from the camp
to meet with God, and they stood at the foot of the mountain. 18All Mount Sinai was
covered with smoke because the LORD had descended on it in the form of fire. The
smoke billowed into the sky like smoke from a furnace, and the whole mountain
shook with a violent earthquake. 19As the horn blast grew louder and louder, Moses
spoke, and God thundered his reply for all to hear. 20The LORD came down on the top
of Mount Sinai and called Moses to the top of the mountain. So Moses climbed the
mountain.
21Then the LORD told Moses, "Go back down and warn the people not to cross the
boundaries. They must not come up here to see the LORD, for those who do will die.
22Even the priests who regularly come near to the LORD must purify themselves, or I will
destroy them."
23"But LORD, the people cannot come up on the mountain!" Moses protested. "You
already told them not to. You told me to set boundaries around the mountain and to
declare it off limits."
24But the LORD said, "Go down anyway and bring Aaron back with you. In the
meantime, do not let the priests or the people cross the boundaries to come up here. If
they do, I will punish them."
25So Moses went down to the people and told them what the LORD had said.

19:6 Lev 11:44-45; Deut 33:3; †1 Pet 2:5, 9; Rev 1:6; 5:10
19:7 Exod 4:29-30; 24:9
19:8 Exod 24:3, 7; Deut 5:27; 26:17
19:9 Exod 19:16; 24:15; Deut 4:11; Ps 99:7
19:10 Gen 35:2; Lev 11:44-45; Num 8:7; 19:19; Heb 10:22; Rev 22:14
19:11 Exod 19:16
19:13 †Heb 12:20
19:15 1 Sam 21:4; 1 Cor 7:5
19:16 Exod 9:23; 20:18; Heb 12:18-19
19:17 Deut 4:11
19:18 Exod 24:17; Deut 5:4; Pss 68:7-8; 104:32
19:19 Ps 81:7
19:20 Exod 24:12; Neh 9:13
19:21 Exod 3:5
19:22 Lev 10:3; 21:6-8
19:24 Exod 24:1, 9

18:18). Gentiles and kings would come to the Lord through Israel, predicted Isaiah (Isaiah 60:3). Through the nation of Israel, the Messiah, God's chosen Son, would be born. God chose one nation and put it through a rigorous training program, so that one day it could be a channel for his blessings to the whole world.

19:5-8 In Genesis 15 and 17, God made a covenant with Abraham, promising to make his descendants into a great nation. Now that promise was being realized as God restated his agreement with the Israelite nation, the descendants of Abraham. God promised to bless and care for them. The people promised to obey him. The covenant was thus sealed. But the good intentions of the people quickly wore off. Have you made a commitment to God? How are you holding up your end of the bargain?

19:9-11 Moses was told to purify the people. This meant getting them physically and spiritually ready to meet God. The people were to set themselves apart from sin and even ordinary daily routine in order to dedicate themselves to God. The act of washing and preparing served to get their minds and hearts ready. When we meet God for worship, we should set aside the cares and preoccupations of everyday life. Use your time of physical preparation to get your mind ready to meet God.

The Ten Commandments

20 Then God instructed the people as follows:
2 "I am the LORD your God, who rescued you from slavery in Egypt.
3 "Do not worship any other gods besides me.
4 "Do not make idols of any kind, whether in the shape of birds or animals or fish.
5 You must never worship or bow down to them, for I, the LORD your God, am a
jealous God who will not share your affection with any other god! I do not
leave unpunished the sins of those who hate me, but I punish the children for
the sins of their parents to the third and fourth generations. 6 But I lavish my
love on those who love me and obey my commands, even for a thousand
generations.
7 "Do not misuse the name of the LORD your God. The LORD will not let you go
unpunished if you misuse his name.
8 "Remember to observe the Sabbath day by keeping it holy. 9 Six days a week are set
apart for your daily duties and regular work, 10 but the seventh day is a day of rest
dedicated to the LORD your God. On that day no one in your household may do any
kind of work. This includes you, your sons and daughters, your male and female
servants, your livestock, and any foreigners living among you. 11 For in six days the
LORD made the heavens, the earth, the sea, and everything in them; then he rested
on the seventh day. That is why the LORD blessed the Sabbath day and set it apart
as holy.
12 "Honor your father and mother. Then you will live a long, full life in the land the
LORD your God will give you.
13 "Do not murder.
14 "Do not commit adultery.
15 "Do not steal.
16 "Do not testify falsely against your neighbor.

20:1-17 //Deut 5:16-21
20:3 Exod 15:11; 20:23
20:4 Lev 26:1
20:5 Exod 23:13, 24; Num 14:18; Deut 4:24
20:6 Exod 34:6-7; Deut 7:9
20:7 Lev 19:12
20:8 Exod 16:23
20:11 Gen 2:2-3; †Acts 4:24
20:12 †Matt 15:4; †Mark 7:10; †Luke 18:20; †Eph 6:2
20:13 †Matt 5:21; 19:18; †Rom 13:9; †Jas 2:11
20:14 †Matt 5:27
20:15 †Matt 19:18; †Mark 10:19; †Luke 18:20
20:16 Matt 19:18

20:1ff Why were the Ten Commandments necessary for God's new nation? At the foot of Mount Sinai, God showed his people the true function and beauty of his laws. The commandments were designed to lead Israel to a life of practical holiness. In them, people could see the nature of God and his plan for how they should live. The commands and guidelines were intended to direct the community to meet the needs of each individual in a loving and responsible manner. By Jesus' time, however, most people looked at the law the wrong way. They saw it as a means to prosperity in both this world and the next. And they thought that to obey every law was the way to earn God's protection from foreign invasion and natural disaster. Law keeping became an end in itself, not the means to fulfill God's ultimate law of love.

20:1-6 The Israelites had just come from Egypt, a land of many idols and many gods. Because each god represented a different aspect of life, it was common to worship many gods in order to get the maximum number of blessings. When God told his people to worship and believe in him, that wasn't so hard for them—he was just one more god to add to the list. But when he said, "Worship only me," that was difficult for the people to accept. But if they didn't learn that the God who led them out of Egypt was the only true God, they could not be his people—no matter how faithfully they kept the other nine commandments. Thus, God made this his first commandment and emphasized it more than the others. Today we can allow many things to become gods to us. Money, fame, work, or pleasure can become gods when we concentrate too much on them for personal identity, meaning, and security. No one sets out with the intention of worshiping these things. But by the amount of time we devote to them, they can grow into gods that ultimately control our thoughts and energies. Letting God hold the central place in our lives keeps these things from turning into gods.

20:7 God's name is special because it carries his personal identity. Using it frivolously or in a curse is so common today that we may fail to realize how serious it is. The way we use God's name conveys how we really feel about him. We should respect his name and use it appropriately, speaking it in praise or worship rather than in curse or jest. We should not take lightly the abuse or dishonor of his name.

20:8-11 The Sabbath was a day set aside for rest and worship. God commanded a Sabbath because human beings need to spend unhurried time in worship and rest each week. A God who is concerned enough to provide a day each week for us to rest is indeed wonderful. To observe a regular time of rest and worship in our fast-paced world demonstrates how important God is to us, and it gives us the extra benefit of refreshing our spirits. Don't neglect God's provision.

20:12 This is the first commandment with a promise attached. To live in peace for generations in the Promised Land, the Israelites would need to respect authority and build strong families. But what does it mean to "honor" parents? Partly, it means speaking well of them and politely to them. It also means acting in a way that shows them courtesy and respect (but not to obey them if this means disobedience to God). It means following their teaching and example of putting God first. Parents have a special place in God's sight. Even those who find it difficult to get along with their parents are still commanded to honor them.

20:16 To testify falsely means lying in court. God knew that Israel could not survive unless its system of justice was incorruptible. We should be honest in our private dealings as well as in our public statements. In either situation, we "testify falsely" by leaving something out of a story, telling a half-truth, twisting the facts, or inventing a falsehood. God warns us against deception. Even though deception is a way of life for many people, God's people must not give in to it!

20:17 †Rom 7:7

17 “Do not covet your neighbor’s house. Do not covet your neighbor’s wife, male or
female servant, ox or donkey, or anything else your neighbor owns.”

20:18 Exod 19:18 Heb 12:18

18 When the people heard the thunder and the loud blast of the horn, and when they
saw the lightning and the smoke billowing from the mountain, they stood at a distance,
trembling with fear.

20:19 Deut 5:23-27

19 And they said to Moses, “You tell us what God says, and we will listen. But don’t
let God speak directly to us. If he does, we will die!”
20 “Don’t be afraid,” Moses said, “for God has come in this way to show you his
awesome power. From now on, let your fear of him keep you from sinning!”

20:21 Deut 5:22 Ps 97:2

21 As the people stood in the distance, Moses entered into the deep darkness where God
was.

Proper Use of Altars

20:23 Exod 32:4 Deut 29:17-18

22 And the LORD said to Moses, “Say this to the people of Israel: You are witnesses that
I have spoken to you from heaven. 23 Remember, you must not make or worship idols of
silver or gold.

JESUS AND THE TEN COMMANDMENTS

The Ten Commandments said . . .	*Jesus said . . .*
Exodus 20:3 “Do not worship any other gods besides me.”	Matthew 4:10 “You must worship the Lord your God; serve only him.”
Exodus 20:4 “Do not make idols of any kind.”	Luke 16:13 “No one can serve two masters.”
Exodus 20:7 “Do not misuse the name of the LORD your God.”	Matthew 5:34 “But I say, don’t make any vows! If you say, ‘By heaven!’ it is a sacred vow because heaven is God’s throne.”
Exodus 20:8 “Remember to observe the Sabbath day by keeping it holy.”	Mark 2:27, 28 “The Sabbath was made to benefit people and not people to benefit the Sabbath. And I, the Son of Man, am master even of the Sabbath!”
Exodus 20:12 “Honor your father and mother.”	Matthew 10:37 “If you love your father or mother more than you love me, you are not worthy of being mine.”
Exodus 20:13 “Do not murder.”	Matthew 5:22 “If you are angry with someone, you are subject to judgment!”
Exodus 20:14 “Do not commit adultery.”	Matthew 5:28 “Anyone who even looks at a woman with lust in his eye has already committed adultery with her in his heart.”
Exodus 20:15 “Do not steal.”	Matthew 5:40 “If you are ordered to court and your shirt is taken from you, give your coat, too.”
Exodus 20:16 “Do not testify falsely against your neighbor.”	Matthew 12:36 “You must give an account on judgment day of every idle word you speak.”
Exodus 20:17 “Do not covet.”	Luke 12:15 “Don’t be greedy for what you don’t have.”

20:17 To covet is to wish to have the possessions of others. It goes beyond simply admiring someone else’s possessions or thinking, “I’d like to have one of those.” Coveting includes envy—resenting the fact that others have what you don’t. God knows, however, that possessions never make anyone happy for long. Since only God can supply all our needs, true contentment is found only in him. When you begin to covet, try to determine if a more basic need is leading you to envy. For example, you may covet someone’s success, not because you want to take it away from him, but because you would like to feel as appreciated by others as he is. If this is the case, pray that God will help you deal with your resentment and meet your basic needs.

20:18 Sometimes God speaks to his people with a majestic display of power; at other times he speaks quietly. Why the difference? God speaks in the way that best accomplishes his purposes. At Sinai, the awesome display of light and sound was necessary to show Israel God’s great power and authority. Only then would they listen to Moses and Aaron.

20:20 Throughout the Bible we find this phrase: “Don’t be afraid.” God wasn’t trying to scare the people. He was showing his mighty power so the Israelites would know he was the true God and would therefore obey him. If they would do this, he would make his power available to them. God wants us to follow him out of love rather than fear. To overcome fear, we must think more about his love. First John 4:18 says, “Perfect love expels all fear.”

24 "The altars you make for me must be simple altars of earth. Offer on such altars your sacrifices to me—your burnt offerings and peace offerings, your sheep and goats and your cattle. Build altars in the places where I remind you who I am, and I will come and bless you there. 25 If you build altars from stone, use only uncut stones. Do not chip or shape the stones with a tool, for that would make them unfit for holy use. 26 And you may not approach my altar by steps. If you do, someone might look up under the skirts of your clothing and see your nakedness.

Fair Treatment of Slaves

21 "Here are some other instructions you must present to Israel:

2 "If you buy a Hebrew slave, he is to serve for only six years. Set him free in the seventh year, and he will owe you nothing for his freedom. 3 If he was single when he became your slave and then married afterward, only he will go free in the seventh year. But if he was married before he became a slave, then his wife will be freed with him.

4 "If his master gave him a wife while he was a slave, and they had sons or daughters, then the man will be free in the seventh year, but his wife and children will still belong to his master. 5 But the slave may plainly declare, 'I love my master, my wife, and my children. I would rather not go free.' 6 If he does this, his master must present him before God.* Then his master must take him to the door and publicly pierce his ear with an awl. After that, the slave will belong to his master forever.

7 "When a man sells his daughter as a slave, she will not be freed at the end of six years as the men are. 8 If she does not please the man who bought her, he may allow her to be bought back again. But he is not allowed to sell her to foreigners, since he is the one who broke the contract with her. 9 And if the slave girl's owner arranges for her to marry his son, he may no longer treat her as a slave girl, but he must treat her as his daughter. 10 If he himself marries her and then takes another wife, he may not reduce her food or clothing or fail to sleep with her as his wife. 11 If he fails in any of these three ways, she may leave as a free woman without making any payment.

Cases of Personal Injury

12 "Anyone who hits a person hard enough to cause death must be put to death. 13 But if it is an accident and God allows it to happen, I will appoint a place where the slayer can run for safety. 14 However, if someone deliberately attacks and kills another person, then the slayer must be dragged even from my altar and put to death.

15 "Anyone who strikes father or mother must be put to death.

16 "Kidnappers must be killed, whether they are caught in possession of their victims or have already sold them as slaves.

17 "Anyone who curses father or mother must be put to death.

18 "Now suppose two people quarrel, and one hits the other with a stone or fist, causing injury but not death. 19 If the injured person is later able to walk again, even with a crutch, the assailant will be innocent. Nonetheless, the assailant must pay for time lost because of the injury and must pay for the medical expenses.

20 "If a male or female slave is beaten and dies, the owner must be punished. 21 If the slave recovers after a couple of days, however, then the owner should not be punished, since the slave is the owner's property.

22 "Now suppose two people are fighting, and in the process, they hurt a pregnant

20:24 Exod 10:25; 18:12; 24:5; Lev 1:2; Deut 12:5
20:25 Deut 27:5-6; Josh 8:31
20:26 Exod 28:42
21:1 Deut 4:14
21:2-6 Lev 25:39-41; //Deut 15:12-18
21:2 Jer 34:14
21:5 Deut 15:16
21:6 Exod 22:8-9
21:7 Neh 5:5
21:10 1 Cor 7:3, 5
21:12 Gen 9:6; Lev 24:21
21:13 Num 35:22; Deut 19:4-5; Josh 20:9
21:14 Num 35:30-31; 1 Kgs 2:28-34
21:16 Deut 24:7
21:17 Lev 20:9; Deut 5:16; †Matt 15:4; †Mark 7:10
21:21 Lev 25:44-46

21:6 Or *before the judges.*

20:24-26 Why were specific directions given for building altars? God's people had no Bible and few religious traditions to learn from. God had to start from scratch and teach them how to worship him. God gave specific instructions about building altars because he wanted to control the way sacrifices were offered. To prevent idolatry from creeping into worship, God did not allow the altar stones to be cut or shaped into any form. Nor did God let the people build an altar just anywhere. This was designed to prevent them from starting their own religions or making changes in the way God wanted things done. God is not against creativity, but he is against us creating our own religion.

21:1ff These laws were given because everything we do has consequences. It is vital to think before acting, to consider the effects of our choices. Think of your plans for today and consider what their long-range results will be. As we deal with others, we should keep the principles of these laws in mind. We should act responsibly and justly with all people—friends and enemies alike.

21:2 The Hebrews, though freed from slavery, had slaves (or servants) themselves. A person could become a slave because of poverty, debt, or even crime. But Hebrew slaves were treated as humans, not property, and were allowed to work their way to freedom. The Bible acknowledges the existence of slavery but never encourages it.

woman so her child is born prematurely. If no further harm results, then the person
responsible must pay damages in the amount the woman's husband demands and the
21:23 Lev 24:19 judges approve. 23But if any harm results, then the offender must be punished according
21:24 Lev 24:20 †Matt 5:38 to the injury. If the result is death, the offender must be executed. 24If an eye is injured,
injure the eye of the person who did it. If a tooth gets knocked out, knock out the tooth
of the person who did it. Similarly, the payment must be hand for hand, foot for foot,
25burn for burn, wound for wound, bruise for bruise.
21:26 Job 31:13 26"If an owner hits a male or female slave in the eye and the eye is blinded, then the
slave may go free because of the eye. 27And if an owner knocks out the tooth of a male
or female slave, the slave should be released in payment for the tooth.
21:28 Gen 9:5 28"If a bull gores a man or woman to death, the bull must be stoned, and its flesh may
not be eaten. In such a case, however, the owner will not be held liable. 29Suppose, on
the other hand, that the owner knew the bull had gored people in the past, yet the bull
was not kept under control. If this is true and if the bull kills someone, it must be stoned,
and the owner must also be killed. 30However, the dead person's relatives may accept
payment from the owner of the bull to compensate for the loss of life. The owner will
21:32 Gen 37:28 Zech 11:12-13 Matt 26:15; 27:3, 9 have to pay whatever is demanded.
31"The same principle applies if the bull gores a boy or a girl. 32But if the bull gores
a slave, either male or female, the slave's owner is to be given thirty silver coins* in
payment, and the bull must be stoned.
21:33 Luke 14:5 33"Suppose someone digs or uncovers a well and fails to cover it, and then an ox or a
donkey falls into it. 34The owner of the well must pay in full for the dead animal but then
gets to keep it.
35"If someone's bull injures a neighbor's bull and the injured bull dies, then the two
owners must sell the live bull and divide the money between them. Each will also own
half of the dead bull. 36But if the bull was known from past experience to gore, yet its
owner failed to keep it under control, the money will not be divided. The owner of the
living bull must pay in full for the dead bull but then gets to keep it.

Protection of Property

22:1 Lev 6:1-7 2 Sam 12:6 Prov 6:31 Luke 19:8 **22** "A fine must be paid by anyone who steals an ox or sheep and then kills or sells
it. For oxen the fine is five oxen for each one stolen. For sheep the fine is four
sheep for each one stolen.
22:2 Num 35:26-27 2"If a thief is caught in the act of breaking into a house and is killed in the process,
the person who killed the thief is not guilty. 3But if it happens in daylight, the one who
22:3 Exod 21:2 killed the thief is guilty of murder.
22:4 Prov 6:30 Jer 2:26 John 12:6 "A thief who is caught must pay in full for everything that was stolen. If payment is
not made, the thief must be sold as a slave to pay the debt. 4If someone steals an ox or a
donkey or a sheep and it is recovered alive, then the thief must pay double the value.
22:5 Exod 21:34 5"If an animal is grazing in a field or vineyard and the owner lets it stray into someone
else's field to graze, then the animal's owner must pay damages in the form of high-quality grain or grapes.
6"If a fire gets out of control and goes into another person's field, destroying the sheaves
or the standing grain, then the one who started the fire must pay for the lost crops.

21:32 Hebrew *30 shekels of silver,* about 12 ounces or 342 grams in weight.

21:24, 25 The "eye for an eye" rule was instituted as a guide for judges, not as a rule for personal relationships or to justify revenge. This rule made the punishment fit the crime, thereby preventing the cruel and barbaric punishments that characterized many ancient countries. Jesus used this principle to teach us not to retaliate (Matthew 5:38-48). Judges, parents, teachers, and others who work with people must make wise decisions in order for discipline to be effective. A punishment too harsh is unfair, and one too lenient is powerless to teach. Ask God for wisdom before you judge.

22:1ff These are not a collection of picky laws but are case studies of God's principles in action. God was taking potential situations and showing how his laws would work in the Israelites' everyday lives. These case studies had several objectives: (1) to protect the nation, (2) to organize the nation, and (3) to focus the nation's attention on God. The laws listed here do not cover every possible situation but give practical examples that make it easier to decide what God wants.

22:3ff Throughout chapter 22 we find examples of the principle of restitution—making wrongs right. For example, if a man stole an animal, he had to repay double the beast's market value. If you have done someone wrong, perhaps you should go beyond what is expected to make things right. This will (1) help ease any pain you've caused, (2) help the other person be more forgiving, and (3) make you more likely to think before you do it again.

7 "Suppose someone entrusts money or goods to a neighbor, and they are stolen from
the neighbor's house. If the thief is found, the fine is double the value of what was stolen.
8 But if the thief is not found, God* will determine whether or not it was the neighbor
who stole the property.
9 "Suppose there is a dispute between two people as to who owns a particular ox,
donkey, sheep, article of clothing, or anything else. Both parties must come before God*
for a decision, and the person whom God declares* guilty must pay double to the other.
10 "Now suppose someone asks a neighbor to care for a donkey, ox, sheep, or any other
animal, but it dies or is injured or gets away, and there is no eyewitness to report just
what happened. 11 The neighbor must then take an oath of innocence in the presence of
the LORD. The owner must accept the neighbor's word, and no payment will be required.
12 But if the animal or property was stolen, payment must be made to the owner. 13 If it
was attacked by a wild animal, the carcass must be shown as evidence, and no payment
will be required.
14 "If someone borrows an animal from a neighbor and it is injured or killed, and if the
owner was not there at the time, the person who borrowed it must pay for it. 15 But if the
owner is there, no payment is required. And no payment is required if the animal was
rented because this loss was covered by the rental fee.

Social Responsibility

16 "If a man seduces a virgin who is not engaged to anyone and sleeps with her, he must
pay the customary dowry and accept her as his wife. 17 But if her father refuses to let her
marry him, the man must still pay the money for her dowry.
18 "A sorceress must not be allowed to live.
19 "Anyone who has sexual relations with an animal must be executed.
20 "Anyone who sacrifices to any god other than the LORD must be destroyed.
21 "Do not oppress foreigners in any way. Remember, you yourselves were once
foreigners in the land of Egypt.
22 "Do not exploit widows or orphans. 23 If you do and they cry out to me, then I will
surely help them. 24 My anger will blaze forth against you, and I will kill you with the
sword. Your wives will become widows, and your children will become fatherless.
25 "If you lend money to a fellow Hebrew in need, do not be like a money lender, charging
interest. 26 If you take your neighbor's cloak as a pledge of repayment, you must return it
by nightfall. 27 Your neighbor will need it to stay warm during the night. If you do not return
it and your neighbor cries out to me for help, then I will hear, for I am very merciful.
28 "Do not blaspheme God* or curse anyone who rules over you.
29 "Do not hold anything back when you give me the tithe of your crops and your wine.
"You must make the necessary payment for redemption of your firstborn sons.
30 "You must also give me the firstborn of your cattle and sheep. Leave the newborn
animal with its mother for seven days; then give it to me on the eighth day.
31 "You are my own holy people. Therefore, do not eat any animal that has been
attacked and killed by a wild animal. Throw its carcass out for the dogs to eat.

22:7 Lev 6:1-7
22:8 Exod 21:6; Deut 17:8-9; 19:17
22:9 Deut 25:1
22:13 Gen 31:39
22:16-17 Deut 22:28-29
22:18 Lev 20:27; Deut 18:10
22:19 Lev 18:23; 20:15
22:20 Exod 32:8; 34:15
22:21 Lev 19:33
22:22 Deut 24:17-18
22:25 Lev 25:35-37; Deut 23:19-20
22:26 Deut 24:6, 10-13
22:28 Lev 24:15-16; Acts 23:5
22:29 Exod 13:2; 23:16, 19; 34:20; Deut 26:2
22:30 Gen 17:12; Lev 12:3; 22:27
22:31 Exod 19:6; Lev 7:24; 17:15; 22:8

22:8 Or *the judges.* **22:9a** Or *before the judges.* **22:9b** Or *whom the judges declare.* **22:28** Or *Do not revile your judges.*

22:18 Why did God's laws speak so strongly against sorcery (Leviticus 19:31; 20:6, 27; Deuteronomy 18:10-12)? Sorcery was punishable by death because it was a crime against God himself. To invoke evil powers violated the first commandment to not worship any other god. Sorcery was rebellion against God and his authority. In essence, it was teaming up with Satan instead of with God.

22:21 God warned the Israelites not to treat foreigners unfairly because they themselves were once foreigners in Egypt. It is not easy coming into a new environment where you feel alone and out of place. Are there foreigners in your corner of the world? refugees? new arrivals at school? immigrants from another country? Be sensitive to their struggles, and express God's love by your kindness and generosity.

22:22-27 The Hebrew law code is noted for its fairness and social responsibility toward the poor. God insisted that the poor and powerless be well treated and given the chance to restore their fortunes. We should reflect God's concern for the poor by helping those less fortunate than ourselves.

22:26 Why did the law insist on returning a person's cloak by nightfall? The cloak was one of an Israelite's most valuable possessions. Making clothing was difficult and time-consuming. As a result, cloaks were expensive, and most people owned only one. The cloak was used as a blanket, a sack to carry things in, a place to sit, a pledge for a debt, and, of course, clothing.

22:29 The Israelites were to be prompt in giving God their offerings. The first of the harvest was to be dedicated to him. Since God doesn't send payment overdue notices, it is easy to take care of other financial responsibilities while letting our gifts to him slide. Giving to God first out of what he has allowed you to have demonstrates that he has first priority in your life.

A Call for Justice

23 “Do not pass along false reports. Do not cooperate with evil people by telling lies
on the witness stand.
2“Do not join a crowd that intends to do evil. When you are on the witness stand, do
not be swayed in your testimony by the opinion of the majority. 3And do not slant your
testimony in favor of a person just because that person is poor.
4“If you come upon your enemy’s ox or donkey that has strayed away, take it back to
its owner. 5If you see the donkey of someone who hates you struggling beneath a heavy
load, do not walk by. Instead, stop and offer to help.
6“Do not twist justice against people simply because they are poor.
7“Keep far away from falsely charging anyone with evil. Never put an innocent or
honest person to death. I will not allow anyone guilty of this to go free.
8“Take no bribes, for a bribe makes you ignore something that you clearly see. A bribe
always hurts the cause of the person who is in the right.
9“Do not oppress the foreigners living among you. You know what it is like to be a
foreigner. Remember your own experience in the land of Egypt.
10“Plant and harvest your crops for six years, 11but let the land rest and lie fallow
during the seventh year. Then let the poor among you harvest any volunteer crop that
may come up. Leave the rest for the animals to eat. The same applies to your vineyards
and olive groves.
12“Work for six days, and rest on the seventh. This will give your ox and your donkey
a chance to rest. It will also allow the people of your household, including your slaves
and visitors, to be refreshed.
13“Be sure to obey all my instructions. And remember, never pray to or swear by any
other gods. Do not even mention their names.

Three Annual Festivals

14“Each year you must celebrate three festivals in my honor. 15The first is the Festival
of Unleavened Bread. For seven days you are to eat bread made without yeast, just as I
commanded you before. This festival will be an annual event at the appointed time in
early spring,* for that is the anniversary of your exodus from Egypt. Everyone must
bring me a sacrifice at that time. 16You must also celebrate the Festival of Harvest,* when
you bring me the first crops of your harvest. Finally, you are to celebrate the Festival of
the Final Harvest* at the end of the harvest season. 17At these three times each year, every
man in Israel must appear before the Sovereign LORD.
18“Sacrificial blood must never be offered together with bread that has yeast in it. And
no sacrificial fat may be left unoffered until the next morning.
19“As you harvest each of your crops, bring me a choice sample of the first day’s
harvest. It must be offered to the LORD your God.
“You must not cook a young goat in its mother’s milk.

A Promise of the LORD’s Presence

20“See, I am sending my angel before you to lead you safely to the land I have prepared
for you. 21Pay attention to him, and obey all of his instructions. Do not rebel against him,

23:1 Exod 20:16; Ps 35:11
23:2 Deut 1:17; 16:19
23:4-5 Deut 22:1-4
23:6 Exod 23:2-3
23:7 Exod 20:13, 16; Deut 27:25
23:8 Deut 16:19
23:9 Exod 22:21; Lev 19:33-34
23:10 Lev 25:3
23:11 Lev 25:1-7
23:12 Exod 20:8-11
23:13 Deut 4:9, 23
23:14 Exod 34:23-24; Deut 16:16
23:15 Exod 12:15; 13:4; Lev 23:5
23:16 Exod 34:22; Lev 23:34; Deut 16:13
23:17 Deut 16:16
23:18 Exod 12:8; 34:25; Lev 2:11
23:19 Exod 22:29; Deut 14:21
23:20 Exod 32:34
23:21 Exod 3:14; 34:5; Num 14:10-11

23:15 Hebrew *in the month of Abib.* This month of the Hebrew lunar calendar usually occurs in March and April.
23:16a Or *Festival of Weeks.* **23:16b** This was later called the Festival of Shelters; see Lev 23:33-36.

23:1 Making up or spreading false reports was strictly forbidden by God. Gossip, slander, and false witnessing undermined families, strained neighborhood cooperation, and made chaos of the justice system. Destructive gossip still causes problems. Even if you do not initiate a lie, you become responsible if you pass it along. Don’t circulate rumors; squelch them.

23:2, 3 Justice is often perverted in favor of the rich. Here the people are warned against twisting justice in favor of the poor. Justice should be impartial, treating rich and poor alike. Giving special privileges to either rich or poor only makes justice for everyone more unlikely. Withstand the pressure of the crowd to sway your decision about a person. Let the fairness God shows to each of us guide your judgment.

23:4, 5 The thought of being kind to enemies was new and startling in a world where revenge was the common form of justice. God not only introduced this idea to the Israelites, he made it law! If a man found a lost animal owned by his enemy, he was to return it at once, even if his enemy might use it to harm him. Jesus clearly taught in Luke 10:30-37 to reach out to all people in need, even our enemies. Following the laws of right living is hard enough with friends. When we apply God’s laws of fairness and kindness to our enemies, we show how different we are from the world.

23:20, 21 Who was this angel that went with the Israelites? Most likely the angel was a manifestation of God. God was in the angel in the same way he was present in the pillars of cloud and fire (13:21, 22). “He bears my name” means the essential nature and power of God were made known in this angel.

for he will not forgive your sins. He is my representative—he bears my name. 22 But if
you are careful to obey him, following all my instructions, then I will be an enemy to your
enemies, and I will oppose those who oppose you. 23 For my angel will go before you
and bring you into the land of the Amorites, Hittites, Perizzites, Canaanites, Hivites, and
Jebusites, so you may live there. And I will destroy them. 24 Do not worship the gods of
these other nations or serve them in any way, and never follow their evil example.
Instead, you must utterly conquer them and break down their shameful idols.
25 "You must serve only the LORD your God. If you do, I will bless you with food and
water, and I will keep you healthy. 26 There will be no miscarriages or infertility among
your people, and I will give you long, full lives.
27 "I will send my terror upon all the people whose lands you invade, and they will
panic before you. 28 I will send hornets ahead of you to drive out the Hivites, Canaanites,
and Hittites. 29 But I will not do this all in one year because the land would become a
wilderness, and the wild animals would become too many to control. 30 I will drive them
out a little at a time until your population has increased enough to fill the land. 31 And I
will fix your boundaries from the Red Sea to the Mediterranean Sea,* and from the
southern deserts to the Euphrates River.* I will help you defeat the people now living in
the land, and you will drive them out ahead of you.
32 "Make no treaties with them and have nothing to do with their gods. 33 Do not even
let them live among you! If you do, they will infect you with their sin of idol worship,
and that would be disastrous for you."

Israel Accepts the LORD's Covenant

24 Then the LORD instructed Moses: "Come up here to me, and bring along Aaron,
Nadab, Abihu, and seventy of Israel's leaders. All of them must worship at a
distance. 2 You alone, Moses, are allowed to come near to the LORD. The others must not
come too close. And remember, none of the other people are allowed to climb on the
mountain at all."
3 When Moses had announced to the people all the teachings and regulations the
LORD had given him, they answered in unison, "We will do everything the LORD has
told us to do."
4 Then Moses carefully wrote down all the LORD's instructions. Early the next morning
he built an altar at the foot of the mountain. He also set up twelve pillars around the altar,
one for each of the twelve tribes of Israel. 5 Then he sent some of the young men to sacrifice
young bulls as burnt offerings and peace offerings to the LORD. 6 Moses took half the blood
from these animals and drew it off into basins. The other half he splashed against the altar.
7 Then he took the Book of the Covenant and read it to the people. They all responded
again, "We will do everything the LORD has commanded. We will obey."

23:22 Num 24:9; Deut 30:7
23:23 Josh 24:8, 11
23:24 Exod 20:5; 34:13
23:25 Exod 15:26; Lev 26:3-13; Deut 7:12-15; 28:1-14
23:27 Gen 35:5; Exod 15:14; Deut 7:23
23:28 Deut 7:20
23:29-30 Deut 7:22
23:31 Gen 15:18; Josh 21:44; 24:12, 18
23:32 Deut 7:2
23:33 Deut 7:1-5, 16
24:1 Exod 6:23; 19:24
24:2 Num 12:6-8
24:3 Exod 19:8; 24:7; Deut 5:27; 11:1
24:4 Deut 31:9
24:5 Exod 18:12
24:6 Heb 9:18
24:7 Exod 19:8; 24:3; Heb 9:19

23:31a Hebrew *from the sea of reeds to the sea of the Philistines.* **23:31b** Hebrew *the river.*

23:24, 25 If you're in the furnace, it's easy to catch on fire. God warned the Israelites about their neighbors whose beliefs and actions could turn them away from him. We also live with neighbors whose values may be completely different from ours. We are called to maintain a life-style that shows our faith. This can be a struggle, especially if our Christian life-style differs from the norm. Our lives should show that we put obeying God before doing what is praised and accepted by society.

23:29 Not all of God's solutions are instantaneous. Nor does delay justify inaction. In this case, God's cause would require constant cooperation, persistence, and effort by the Israelites. Success would come step by step.

23:32, 33 God continually warned the people to avoid false religions and false gods. In Egypt they had been surrounded by idols and sorcerers, but leaving that land did not mean they were free from pagan religious influences. The land of Canaan was just as infested with idol worship. God knew his people needed extra strength, so he continually emphasized guarding against the influence of pagan religions.

24:6-8 To understand this unusual covenant ratification ceremony, we need to understand the Bible's view of sin and forgiveness. God is the sovereign Judge of the universe. He is also absolutely holy. As the holy Judge of all, he condemns sin and judges it worthy of death. In the Old Testament God accepted the death of an animal as a substitute for the sinner. The animal's shed blood was proof that one life had been given for another. So on the one hand, blood symbolized the death of the animal, but it also symbolized the life that was spared as a result. Of course the death of the animal that brought forgiveness in the Old Testament was only a temporary provision, looking forward to the death of Jesus Christ (Hebrews 9:9–10:28).

In this ceremony described here, Moses sprinkled half the blood from the sacrificed animals on the altar to show that the sinner could once again approach God because something had died in his place. He sprinkled the other half of the blood on the people to show that the penalty for their sin had been paid and they could be reunited with God. Through this symbolic act God's promises to Israel were reaffirmed, and lessons are taught to us about the future sacrificial death (or atonement) of Jesus Christ.

24:8 Zech 9:11
Matt 26:28
1 Cor 11:25
†Heb 9:20
24:10 Exod 33:20
Num 12:8
Isa 6:5
Ezek 1:26
24:12 Jer 31:33
2 Cor 3:3
24:15 Exod 19:9
24:16 Exod 16:10
Num 14:10
24:17 Exod 3:2
Deut 4:24, 36
Heb 12:18, 29
24:18 Exod 34:28
Deut 9:9; 10:10
1 Kgs 19:8

[8]Then Moses sprinkled the blood from the basins over the people and said, "This
blood confirms the covenant the LORD has made with you in giving you these laws."
[9]Then Moses, Aaron, Nadab, Abihu, and seventy of the leaders of Israel went up the
mountain. [10]There they saw the God of Israel. Under his feet there seemed to be a
pavement of brilliant sapphire, as clear as the heavens. [11]And though Israel's leaders saw
God, he did not destroy them. In fact, they shared a meal together in God's presence!
[12]And the LORD said to Moses, "Come up to me on the mountain. Stay there while I
give you the tablets of stone that I have inscribed with my instructions and commands.
Then you will teach the people from them." [13]So Moses and his assistant Joshua climbed
up the mountain of God.
[14]Moses told the other leaders, "Stay here and wait for us until we come back. If there
are any problems while I am gone, consult with Aaron and Hur, who are here with you."
[15]Then Moses went up the mountain, and the cloud covered it. [16]And the glorious
presence of the LORD rested upon Mount Sinai, and the cloud covered it for six days. On
the seventh day the LORD called to Moses from the cloud. [17]The Israelites at the foot of
the mountain saw an awesome sight. The awesome glory of the LORD on the mountaintop
looked like a devouring fire. [18]Then Moses disappeared into the cloud as he climbed
higher up the mountain. He stayed on the mountain forty days and forty nights.

2. Tabernacle instructions

Offerings for the Tabernacle

25:1-7 //Exod 35:4-9
25:2 1 Chr 29:2-5
Ezra 2:68
Neh 7:70-72
2 Cor 8:11-12; 9:7
25:6 Exod 27:20; 30:23
25:8 Exod 29:45; 36:1-5
Deut 12:11

25 The LORD said to Moses, [2]"Tell the people of Israel that everyone who wants to
may bring me an offering. [3]Here is a list of items you may accept on my behalf:
gold, silver, and bronze; [4]blue, purple, and scarlet yarn; fine linen; goat hair for cloth;
[5]tanned ram skins and fine goatskin leather; acacia wood; [6]olive oil for the lamps; spices
for the anointing oil and the fragrant incense; [7]onyx stones, and other stones to be set in
the ephod and the chestpiece.
[8]"I want the people of Israel to build me a sacred residence where I can live among
them. [9]You must make this Tabernacle and its furnishings exactly according to the plans
I will show you.

Plans for the Ark

25:10-20 //Exod 37:1-9

[10]"Make an Ark of acacia wood—a sacred chest 3¾ feet long, 2¼ feet wide, and 2¼ feet
high.* [11]Overlay it inside and outside with pure gold, and put a molding of gold all

25:10 Hebrew *2½ cubits* [1.1 meters] *long, 1½ cubits* [0.7 meters] *wide, and 1½ cubits high.* In this chapter, the distance measures are calculated from the Hebrew cubit at a ratio of 18 inches or 45 centimeters per cubit.

THEOPHANIES IN THE SCRIPTURE

At the foot of Mount Sinai, God appeared to the people of Israel in a physical form. This is called a *theophany.* Here are some of the other times God appeared to Bible people.

Verse	*Theophany*
Genesis 16:7	The angel of the Lord appeared to Sarah's servant, Hagar, announcing the birth of Abraham's son Ishmael
Genesis 18:1–11	The Lord appeared to Abraham, foretelling Isaac's birth
Genesis 22:11, 12	The angel of the Lord stopped Abraham from sacrificing Isaac
Exodus 3:2	The angel of the Lord appeared to Moses in flames in a bush
Exodus 14:19	God appeared to Israel in pillars of cloud and fire to guide them through the wilderness
Exodus 33:11	The Lord spoke to Moses face to face
Daniel 3:25	One "like a divine being" appeared as the fourth man with Shadrach, Meshach, and Abednego in the fiery furnace

("Angel of the Lord" is a reverential way to refer to God in these passages.)

25:1ff Chapters 25 through 31 record God's directions for building the Tabernacle. Chapters 35 through 39 tell how these instructions were carried out. But what can all these ancient, complicated construction details show us today? First, the high quality of the precious materials making up the Tabernacle shows God's greatness and transcendence. Second, the curtain surrounding the Most Holy Place shows God's moral perfection as symbolized by his separation from the common and unclean. Third, the portable nature of the Tabernacle shows God's desire to be with his people as they traveled.

25:10 Much of the Tabernacle and its furniture was made of acacia wood. Acacia trees flourished in barren regions and were fairly common in Old Testament times. The wood was brownish-orange and very hard, making it an excellent material for furniture. Acacia wood is still used in furniture making today.

around it. 12 Cast four rings of gold for it, and attach them to its four feet, two rings on
each side. 13 Make poles from acacia wood, and overlay them with gold. 14 Fit the poles
into the rings at the sides of the Ark to carry it. 15 These carrying poles must never be
taken from the rings; they are to be left there permanently. 16 When the Ark is finished,
place inside it the stone tablets inscribed with the terms of the covenant,* which I will
give to you.

17 "Then make the Ark's cover—the place of atonement—out of pure gold. It must be
3¾ feet long and 2¼ feet wide. 18 Then use hammered gold to make two cherubim, and
place them at the two ends of the atonement cover. 19 Attach the cherubim to each end of
the atonement cover, making it all one piece. 20 The cherubim will face each other, looking
down on the atonement cover with their wings spread out above it. 21 Place inside the Ark
the stone tablets inscribed with the terms of the covenant, which I will give to you. Then
put the atonement cover on top of the Ark. 22 I will meet with you there and talk to you
from above the atonement cover between the gold cherubim that hover over the Ark of the
Covenant.* From there I will give you my commands for the people of Israel.

Plans for the Table

23 "Then make a table of acacia wood, 3 feet long, 1½ feet wide, and 2¼ feet high.
24 Overlay it with pure gold and run a molding of gold around it. 25 Put a rim about three
inches* wide around the top edge, and put a gold molding all around the rim. 26 Make
four gold rings, and put the rings at the four corners by the four legs, 27 close to the rim
around the top. These rings will support the poles used to carry the table. 28 Make these
poles from acacia wood and overlay them with gold. 29 And make gold plates and dishes,
as well as pitchers and bowls to be used in pouring out drink offerings. 30 You must
always keep the special Bread of the Presence on the table before me.

Plans for the Lampstand

31 "Make a lampstand of pure, hammered gold. The entire lampstand and its decorations
will be one piece—the base, center stem, lamp cups, buds, and blossoms. 32 It will have
six branches, three branches going out from each side of the center stem. 33 Each of the
six branches will hold a cup shaped like an almond blossom, complete with buds and
petals. 34 The center stem of the lampstand will be decorated with four almond blossoms,
complete with buds and petals. 35 One blossom will be set beneath each pair of branches
where they extend from the center stem. 36 The decorations and branches must all be one
piece with the stem, and they must be hammered from pure gold. 37 Then make the seven
lamps for the lampstand, and set them so they reflect their light forward. 38 The lamp
snuffers and trays must also be made of pure gold. 39 You will need seventy-five pounds*
of pure gold for the lampstand and its accessories.

40 "Be sure that you make everything according to the pattern I have shown you here
on the mountain.

Plans for the Tabernacle

26 "Make the Tabernacle from ten sheets of fine linen. These sheets are to be
decorated with blue, purple, and scarlet yarn, with figures of cherubim skillfully
embroidered into them. 2 Each sheet must be forty-two feet long and six feet wide.* All
ten sheets must be exactly the same size. 3 Join five of these sheets together into one set;
then join the other five sheets into a second set. 4 Put loops of blue yarn along the edge
of the last sheet in each set. 5 The fifty loops along the edge of one set are to match the
fifty loops along the edge of the other. 6 Then make fifty gold clasps to fasten the loops
of the two sets of sheets together, making the Tabernacle a single unit.

7 "Make heavy sheets of cloth from goat hair to cover the Tabernacle. There must be
eleven of these sheets, 8 each forty-five feet long and six feet wide. All eleven of these

25:12 Exod 26:29; 27:7; 37:5; 38:7
25:15 1 Kgs 8:8
25:16 Exod 16:34; Heb 9:4
25:17 Exod 37:6; Lev 16:13; Rom 3:25; Heb 9:5
25:20 1 Kgs 8:7; Heb 9:5
25:21 Exod 26:34
25:22 Exod 30:6, 36; Lev 1:1
25:23-29 //Exod 37:10-16
25:29 Exod 37:16; Num 4:7
25:30 Exod 39:36; 40:23; Lev 24:5-9; Num 4:7
25:31-39 //Exod 37:17-24
25:31 Exod 37:17; 1 Kgs 7:49; Heb 9:2; Rev 1:12
25:37 Exod 27:21; Zech 4:2; Rev 1:4, 12, 20; 4:5
25:40 Acts 7:44; †Heb 8:5
26:1-37 //Exod 36:8-38
26:3 Exod 36:10
26:5 Exod 36:12
26:7 Exod 36:14

25:16 Hebrew *place inside it the Testimony;* also in 25:21. **25:22** Or *Ark of the Testimony.* **25:25** Hebrew *a handbreadth* [8 centimeters]. **25:39** Hebrew *1 talent* [34 kilograms]. **26:2** Hebrew *28 cubits* [12.6 meters] *long and 4 cubits* [1.8 meters] *wide.* In this chapter, the distance measures are calculated from the Hebrew cubit at a ratio of 18 inches or 45 centimeters per cubit.

25:17 The cover of the Ark of the Covenant was called the atonement cover. This is where, between the two golden cherubim (mighty angels), the presence of God would dwell in a cloud above their outstretched wings. The atonement cover was where the highest and most perfect act of atonement would be made when the high priest would enter the Most Holy Place on the Day of Atonement to atone for the sins of all the people (30:10).

sheets must be exactly the same size. 9 Join five of these together into one set, and join
the other six into a second set. The sixth sheet of the second set is to be doubled over at
the entrance of the sacred tent. 10 Put fifty loops along the edge of the last sheet in each
26:11 Exod 36:18
set, 11 and fasten them together with fifty bronze clasps. In this way, the two sets will
become a single unit. 12 An extra half sheet of this roof covering will be left to hang over
the back of the Tabernacle, 13 and the covering will hang down an extra eighteen inches
26:14 Exod 36:19
on each side. 14 On top of these coverings place a layer of tanned ram skins, and over
26:15 Exod 36:20-34
them put a layer of fine goatskin leather. This will complete the roof covering.
15 "The framework of the Tabernacle will consist of frames made of acacia wood.
16 Each frame must be 15 feet high and 2¼ feet wide. 17 There will be two pegs on each
frame so they can be joined to the next frame. All the frames must be made this way.
18 Twenty of these frames will support the south side of the Tabernacle. 19 They will fit
26:20 Exod 36:23
into forty silver bases—two bases under each frame. 20 On the north side there will also
be twenty of these frames, 21 with their forty silver bases, two bases for each frame. 22 On
the west side there will be six frames, 23 along with an extra frame at each corner. 24 These
corner frames will be connected at the bottom and firmly attached at the top with a single
26:25 Exod 36:30
ring, forming a single unit. Both of these corner frames will be made the same way. 25 So
there will be eight frames on that end of the Tabernacle, supported by sixteen silver
bases—two bases under each frame.
26 "Make crossbars of acacia wood to run across the frames, five crossbars for the
north side of the Tabernacle 27 and five for the south side. Also make five crossbars for
the rear of the Tabernacle, which will face westward. 28 The middle crossbar, halfway up
the frames, will run all the way from one end of the Tabernacle to the other. 29 Overlay
the frames with gold and make gold rings to support the crossbars. Overlay the crossbars
with gold as well.
26:30 Exod 25:9, 40 Acts 7:44 †Heb 8:5
30 "Set up this Tabernacle according to the design you were shown on the mountain.
31 "Across the inside of the Tabernacle hang a special curtain made of fine linen, with
26:31 Exod 36:35 2 Chr 3:14 Matt 27:51 Heb 9:3
cherubim skillfully embroidered into the cloth using blue, purple, and scarlet yarn.
32 Hang this inner curtain on gold hooks set into four posts made from acacia wood and
overlaid with gold. The posts will fit into silver bases. 33 When the inner curtain is in
place, put the Ark of the Covenant* behind it. This curtain will separate the Holy Place
26:33 Exod 25:16; 40:21 Heb 9:5
from the Most Holy Place.
34 "Then put the Ark's cover—the place of atonement—on top of the Ark of the
26:34 Exod 25:21; 37:6 Heb 9:5
Covenant inside the Most Holy Place. 35 Place the table and lampstand across the room
from each other outside the inner curtain. The lampstand must be placed on the south
26:36 Exod 40:28
side, and the table must be set toward the north.
36 "Make another curtain from fine linen for the entrance of the sacred tent, and
26:37 Exod 36:38
embroider exquisite designs into it, using blue, purple, and scarlet yarn. 37 Hang this
curtain on gold hooks set into five posts made from acacia wood and overlaid with gold.
The posts will fit into five bronze bases.

Plans for the Altar of Burnt Offering

27:1-8 //Exod 38:1-7
27 "Using acacia wood, make a square altar 7½ feet wide, 7½ feet long, and 4½ feet
27:2 Exod 29:12 Lev 4:7
high.* 2 Make a horn at each of the four corners of the altar so the horns and altar
are all one piece. Overlay the altar and its horns with bronze. 3 The ash buckets, shovels,
27:3 Num 4:14

26:33 Or *Ark of the Testimony;* also in 26:34. **27:1** Hebrew *5 cubits* [2.3 meters] *wide, 5 cubits long, and 3 cubits* [1.4 meters] *high.* In this chapter, the distance measures are calculated from the Hebrew cubit at a ratio of 18 inches or 45 centimeters per cubit.

26:31-33 This curtain separated the two sacred rooms in the Tabernacle—the Holy Place and the Most Holy Place. The priest entered the Holy Place each day to commune with God and to tend to the altar of incense, the lampstand, and the table with the Bread of the Presence. The Most Holy Place was where God himself dwelt, his presence resting on the atonement cover, which covered the Ark of the Covenant. Only the high priest could enter the Most Holy Place. Even he could do so only once a year (on the Day of Atonement) to make atonement for the sins of the nation as a whole. When Jesus Christ died on the cross, the curtain in the Temple (which had replaced the Tabernacle) tore from top to bottom (Mark 15:38), symbolizing our free access to God because of Jesus' death. No longer did people have to approach God through priests and sacrifices.

27:1 The altar of burnt offering was the first thing the Israelites saw as they entered the Tabernacle courtyard. Here sacrifices were constantly made. Its vivid presence constantly reminded the people that they could only come to God by means of the sacrifice. It was the only way their sins could be forgiven and taken away. In Hebrews 10:1-18, Jesus Christ is portrayed as the ultimate sacrifice.

basins, meat hooks, and firepans will all be made of bronze. 4Make a bronze grating,
with a metal ring at each corner. 5Fit the grating halfway down into the firebox, resting
it on the ledge built there. 6For moving the altar, make poles from acacia wood, and
overlay them with bronze. 7To carry it, put the poles into the rings at two sides of the
altar. 8The altar must be hollow, made from planks. Be careful to build it just as you were
shown on the mountain.

Plans for the Courtyard

9"Then make a courtyard for the Tabernacle, enclosed with curtains made from fine
linen. On the south side the curtains will stretch for 150 feet. 10They will be held up by
twenty bronze posts that fit into twenty bronze bases. The curtains will be held up with
silver hooks attached to the silver rods that are attached to the posts. 11It will be the same
on the north side of the courtyard—150 feet of curtains held up by twenty posts fitted
into bronze bases, with silver hooks and rods. 12The curtains on the west end of the
courtyard will be 75 feet long, supported by ten posts set into ten bases. 13The east end
will also be 75 feet long. 14The courtyard entrance will be on the east end, flanked by
two curtains. The curtain on the right side will be 22½ feet long, supported by three posts
set into three bases. 15The curtain on the left side will also be 22½ feet long, supported
by three posts set into three bases.

16"For the entrance to the courtyard, make a curtain that is 30 feet long. Fashion it
from fine linen, and decorate it with beautiful embroidery in blue, purple, and scarlet
yarn. It will be attached to four posts that fit into four bases. 17All the posts around the
courtyard must be connected by silver rods, using silver hooks. The posts are to be set
in solid bronze bases. 18So the entire courtyard will be 150 feet long and 75 feet wide,
with curtain walls 7½ feet high, made from fine linen. The bases supporting its walls will
be made of bronze.

19"All the articles used in the work of the Tabernacle, including all the tent pegs used
to support the Tabernacle and the courtyard curtains, must be made of bronze.

20"Tell the people of Israel to bring you pure olive oil for the lampstand, so it can be
kept burning continually. 21The lampstand will be placed outside the inner curtain of the
Most Holy Place in the Tabernacle.* Aaron and his sons will keep the lamps burning in
the LORD's presence day and night. This is a permanent law for the people of Israel, and
it must be kept by all future generations.

Clothing for the Priests

28 "Your brother, Aaron, and his sons, Nadab, Abihu, Eleazar, and Ithamar, will be
set apart from the common people. They will be my priests and will minister to
me. 2Make special clothing for Aaron to show his separation to God—beautiful garments that will lend dignity to his work. 3Instruct all those who have special skills as
tailors to make the garments that will set Aaron apart from everyone else, so he may serve
me as a priest. 4They are to make a chestpiece, an ephod, a robe, an embroidered tunic,
a turban, and a sash. They will also make special garments for Aaron's sons to wear when
they serve as priests before me. 5These items must be made of fine linen cloth and
embroidered with gold thread and blue, purple, and scarlet yarn.

27:6 Exod 25:13
27:8 Exod 25:40; 26:30
27:9-19 //Exod 38:9-20
27:10 Exod 38:17
27:14 Exod 38:15
27:16 Exod 36:37
27:20-21 //Lev 24:1-3; Zech 4:11-12
27:21 Exod 25:22; Lev 3:17; 16:34
28:1 Exod 24:1, 9; Num 18:7; Ps 99:6; Heb 5:1, 4
28:2 Exod 29:5, 9; 31:10; Lev 8:7, 30; Num 20:26
28:5 Exod 25:3-4

27:21 Hebrew *in the Tent of Meeting, outside of the inner curtain, in front of the Testimony.*

28:1ff God was teaching his people how to worship him. To do so, he needed ministers to oversee the operations of the Tabernacle and to help the people maintain their relationship with God. These men were called priests and Levites, and they could only be members of the tribe of Levi. Chapters 28 and 29 give some details about priests. Not only was a priest from the tribe of Levi, but he also was a descendant of Aaron, Israel's first high priest. Priests had more responsibilities than Levites. As high priest, Aaron was in charge of all the priests and Levites. The priests performed the daily sacrifices, maintained the Tabernacle, and counseled the people on how to follow God. They were the people's representatives before God and thus were required to live worthy of their office. Jesus is now our High Priest (Hebrews 8). Daily sacrifices are no longer required because he sacrificed himself on the cross for our sins. Today ministers no longer sacrifice animals. Instead, ministers lead us in prayer and teach us about both the benefits and the commandments that characterize our new life as Christians.

28:3 The tailors who made Aaron's garments were given wisdom by God in order to do their task. All of us have special skills. God wants to fill us with his Spirit so we will use them for his glory. Think about your special talents and abilities and the ways you could use them for God's work in the world. A talent must be used, or it will diminish.

Design of the Ephod

28:6-14
//Exod 39:2-7

6 “The ephod must be made of fine linen cloth and skillfully embroidered with gold thread and blue, purple, and scarlet yarn. 7 It will consist of two pieces, front and back, joined at the shoulders with two shoulder-pieces. 8 And the sash will be made of the same materials: fine linen cloth embroidered with gold thread and blue, purple, and scarlet yarn. 9 Take two onyx stones and engrave on them the names of the tribes of Israel. 10 Six names will be on each stone, naming all the tribes in the order of their ancestors’ births. 11 Engrave these names in the same way a gemcutter engraves a seal.

28:12
Exod 39:7

Mount the stones in gold settings. 12 Fasten the two stones on the shoulder-pieces of the ephod as memorial stones for the people of Israel. Aaron will carry these names before the LORD as a constant reminder. 13 The settings are to be made of gold filigree, 14 and two cords made of pure gold will be attached to the settings on the shoulders of the ephod.

Design of the Chestpiece

28:15-28
//Exod 39:8-21

28:17
Exod 39:10

15 “Then, with the most careful workmanship, make a chestpiece that will be used to determine God’s will. Use the same materials as you did for the ephod: fine linen cloth embroidered with gold thread and blue, purple, and scarlet yarn. 16 This chestpiece will be made of two folds of cloth, forming a pouch nine inches* square. 17 Four rows of gemstones* will be attached to it. The first row will contain a red carnelian, a chrysolite, and an emerald. 18 The second row will contain a turquoise, a sapphire, and a white moonstone. 19 The third row will contain a jacinth, an agate, and an amethyst. 20 The fourth row will contain a beryl, an onyx, and a jasper. All these stones will be set in gold.

28:21
Exod 39:14

21 Each stone will represent one of the tribes of Israel, and the name of that tribe will be engraved on it as though it were a seal.

28:24
Exod 39:17

28:26
Exod 39:17

22 “To attach the chestpiece to the ephod, make braided cords of pure gold. 23 Then make two gold rings and attach them to the top corners of the chestpiece. 24 The two gold cords will go through the rings on the chestpiece, 25 and the ends of the cords will be tied to the gold settings on the shoulder-pieces of the ephod. 26 Then make two more gold rings, and attach them to the two lower inside corners of the chestpiece next to the ephod. 27 And make two more gold rings and attach them to the ephod near the sash. 28 Then attach the bottom rings of the chestpiece to the rings on the ephod with blue cords. This

28:29
Exod 28:12

28:30
Lev 8:8
Num 27:21

will hold the chestpiece securely to the ephod above the beautiful sash. 29 In this way, Aaron will carry the names of the tribes of Israel on the chestpiece over his heart when he goes into the presence of the LORD in the Holy Place. Thus, the LORD will be reminded of his people continually. 30 Insert into the pocket of the chestpiece the Urim and Thummim, to be carried over Aaron’s heart when he goes into the LORD’s presence. Thus, Aaron will always carry the objects used to determine the LORD’s will for his people whenever he goes in before the LORD.

Additional Clothing for the Priests

28:31-43
//Exod 39:22-31

31 “Make the robe of the ephod entirely of blue cloth, 32 with an opening for Aaron’s head in the middle of it. The opening will be reinforced by a woven collar* so it will not tear. 33 Make pomegranates out of blue, purple, and scarlet yarn, and attach them to the hem of the robe, with gold bells between them. 34 The gold bells and pomegranates are to alternate all the way around the hem. 35 Aaron will wear this robe whenever he enters the Holy Place to minister to the LORD, and the bells will tinkle as he goes in and out of the LORD’s presence. If he wears it, he will not die.

28:36
Exod 39:30-31
Lev 8:9

28:38
Lev 10:17; 22:16
Num 18:1
Heb 9:28
1 Pet 2:24

36 “Next make a medallion of pure gold. Using the techniques of an engraver, inscribe it with these words: SET APART AS HOLY TO THE LORD. 37 This medallion will be attached to the front of Aaron’s turban by means of a blue cord. 38 Aaron will wear it on his

28:16 Hebrew *1 span* [23 centimeters]. **28:17** The identification of some of these gemstones is uncertain.
28:32 The meaning of the Hebrew is uncertain.

28:6-13 The ephod was a kind of apron elaborately embroidered with two pieces, back and front, joined at the shoulder with a band at the waist. On each shoulder strap was a stone with 6 of the 12 tribes of Israel engraved on it. The priest symbolically carried the burden of the whole nation on his shoulders as he represented them before God.

28:30 The Urim and the Thummim were used by the priest to make decisions. These names mean “Curses” and “Perfections” and refer to the nature of God whose will they revealed. They were kept in a pocket and taken out or shaken out to get either a yes or no decision.

forehead, thus bearing the guilt connected with any errors regarding the sacred offerings
of the people of Israel. He must always wear it so the LORD will accept the people.
39"Weave Aaron's patterned tunic from fine linen cloth. Fashion the turban out of this
linen as well. Also make him an embroidered sash.
40"Then for Aaron's sons, make tunics, sashes, and headdresses to give them dignity
and respect. 41 Clothe Aaron and his sons with these garments, and then anoint and ordain
them. Set them apart as holy so they can serve as my priests. 42Also make linen
underclothes for them, to be worn next to their bodies, reaching from waist to thigh.
43These must be worn whenever Aaron and his sons enter the Tabernacle* or approach
the altar in the Holy Place to perform their duties. Thus they will not incur guilt and die.
This law is permanent for Aaron and his descendants.

Dedication of the Priests

29 "This is the ceremony for the dedication of Aaron and his sons as priests: Take a
young bull and two rams with no physical defects. 2Then using fine wheat flour
and no yeast, make loaves of bread, thin cakes mixed with olive oil, and wafers with oil
poured over them. 3Place these various kinds of bread in a single basket, and present
them at the entrance of the Tabernacle, along with the young bull and the two rams.
4"Present Aaron and his sons at the entrance of the Tabernacle,* and wash them with
water. 5Then put Aaron's tunic on him, along with the embroidered robe of the ephod,
the ephod itself, the chestpiece, and the sash. 6And place on his head the turban with the
gold medallion. 7Then take the anointing oil and pour it over his head. 8Next present his
sons, and dress them in their tunics 9with their woven sashes and their headdresses. They
will then be priests forever. In this way, you will ordain Aaron and his sons.
10"Then bring the young bull to the entrance of the Tabernacle, and Aaron and his sons
will lay their hands on its head. 11You will then slaughter it in the LORD's presence at the
entrance of the Tabernacle. 12Smear some of its blood on the horns of the altar with your
finger, and pour out the rest at the base of the altar. 13Take all the fat that covers the
internal organs, also the long lobe of the liver and the two kidneys with their fat, and burn
them on the altar. 14Then take the carcass (including the skin and the dung) outside the
camp, and burn it as a sin offering.
15"Next Aaron and his sons must lay their hands on the head of one of the rams 16as
it is slaughtered. Its blood will be collected and sprinkled on the sides of the altar. 17Cut
up the ram and wash off the internal organs and the legs. Set them alongside the head
and the other pieces of the body, 18and burn them all on the altar. This is a burnt offering
to the LORD, which is very pleasing to him.
19"Now take the other ram and have Aaron and his sons lay their hands on its head 20as
it is slaughtered. Collect the blood and place some of it on the tip of the right earlobes of
Aaron and his sons. Also put it on their right thumbs and the big toes of their right feet.
Sprinkle the rest of the blood on the sides of the altar. 21Then take some of the blood from
the altar and mix it with some of the anointing oil. Sprinkle it on Aaron and his sons and
on their clothes. In this way, they and their clothing will be set apart as holy to the LORD.
22"Since this is the ram for the ordination of Aaron and his sons, take the fat of the
ram, including the fat tail and the fat that covers the internal organs. Also, take the long

28:40 Exod 39:27-29 Lev 8:13
28:41 Exod 29:7-9 Lev 8:1-36 Heb 7:28
28:42 Lev 6:10; 16:4 Ezek 44:18
28:43 Exod 20:26; 27:21
29:1-37 //Lev 8:1-36
29:2 Lev 6:19-23
29:4 Exod 40:12 Heb 10:22
29:5 Exod 28:2, 5
29:6 Exod 28:36
29:7 Exod 28:41 Lev 8:12-13 Ps 133:2
29:9 Exod 40:15 Num 3:10; 18:7; 25:13 Deut 18:5
29:10 Lev 1:4; 8:14
29:12 Exod 27:2 Lev 8:15
29:13 Lev 3:3-5
29:14 Lev 4:11-12, 21 Heb 13:11
29:15 Exod 29:10
29:18 Gen 8:21
29:21 Exod 30:25, 31 Heb 9:22

28:43 Hebrew *Tent of Meeting.* **29:4** Hebrew *Tent of Meeting;* also in 29:10, 11, 30, 32, 42, 44.

29:1ff Why did God set up the priesthood? God had originally intended that his chosen people be a "kingdom of priests" with both the nation as a whole and each individual dealing directly with God. But the people's sin prevented this from happening because a sinful person is not worthy to approach a perfect God. God then appointed priests from the tribe of Levi and set up the system of sacrifices to help the people approach him. He promised to forgive the people's sins if they would offer certain sacrifices administered by the priests on behalf of the people. Through these priests and their work, God wished to prepare all people for the coming of Jesus Christ, who would once again offer a direct relationship with God for anyone who would come to him. But until Christ came, the priests were the people's representatives before God. Through this Old Testament system, we can better understand the significance of what Christ did for us (see Hebrews 10:1-14).

29:10-41 Why were there such detailed rituals in connection with these sacrifices? Partly it was for quality control. A centralized, standardized form of worship prevented problems of belief which could arise from individuals creating their own worship. Also, it differentiated the Hebrews from the pagan Canaanites they would meet in the Promised Land. By closely following God's instructions, the Hebrews could not possibly join the Canaanites in their immoral religious practices. Finally, it showed Israel that God was serious about his relationship with them.

29:23 Lev 8:26
29:24 Lev 7:30
29:26 Lev 7:31, 34; 8:29
29:27 Lev 7:31, 34 Num 18:11-12 Deut 18:3
29:29 Num 20:26, 28
29:30 Lev 8:35
29:33 Lev 22:10, 13
29:34-35 Lev 8:32-33
29:36 Exod 40:10 Heb 10:11
29:37 Exod 40:10 Matt 23:19
29:38 Num 28:3-31; 29:6-38 1 Chr 16:40 Dan 12:11
29:41 2 Kgs 16:15 Ezra 9:4-5 Ps 141:2
29:42 Exod 30:8
29:43 1 Kgs 8:11
29:45 Exod 25:8 Lev 26:12 Num 5:3 Deut 12:11 Ps 68:18 Zech 2:10 2 Cor 6:16 Rev 21:3
29:46 Exod 20:2

lobe of the liver, the two kidneys with their fat, and the right thigh. 23 Then take one loaf
of bread, one cake mixed with olive oil, and one wafer from the basket of yeastless bread
that was placed before the LORD. 24 Put all these in the hands of Aaron and his sons to be
lifted up as a special gift to the LORD. 25 Afterward take the bread from their hands, and
burn it on the altar as a burnt offering that will be pleasing to the LORD. 26 Then take the
breast of Aaron's ordination ram, and lift it up in the LORD's presence as a special gift to
him. Afterward keep it for yourself.

27 "Set aside as holy the parts of the ordination ram that belong to Aaron and his sons.
This includes the breast and the thigh that were lifted up before the LORD in the
ordination ceremony. 28 In the future, whenever the people of Israel offer up peace
offerings or thanksgiving offerings to the LORD, these parts will be the regular share of
Aaron and his descendants.

29 "Aaron's sacred garments must be preserved for his descendants who will succeed
him, so they can be anointed and ordained in them. 30 Whoever is the next high priest
after Aaron will wear these clothes for seven days before beginning to minister in the
Tabernacle and the Holy Place.

31 "Take the ram used in the ordination ceremony, and boil its meat in a sacred place.
32 Aaron and his sons are to eat this meat, along with the bread in the basket, at the
Tabernacle entrance. 33 They alone may eat the meat and bread used for their atonement
in the ordination ceremony. The ordinary people may not eat them, for these things are
set apart and holy. 34 If any of the ordination meat or bread remains until the morning, it
must be burned. It may not be eaten, for it is holy.

35 "This is how you will ordain Aaron and his sons to their offices. The ordination
ceremony will go on for seven days. 36 Each day you must sacrifice a young bull as an
offering for the atonement of sin. Afterward make an offering to cleanse the altar. Purify
the altar by making atonement for it; make it holy by anointing it with oil. 37 Make
atonement for the altar every day for seven days. After that, the altar will be exceedingly
holy, and whatever touches it will become holy.

38 "This is what you are to offer on the altar. Offer two one-year-old lambs each day,
39 one in the morning and the other in the evening. 40 With one of them, offer two quarts
of fine flour mixed with one quart of olive oil; also, offer one quart of wine* as a drink
offering. 41 Offer the other lamb in the evening, along with the same offerings of flour
and wine as in the morning. It will be a fragrant offering to the LORD, an offering made
by fire.

42 "This is to be a daily burnt offering given from generation to generation. Offer it in
the LORD's presence at the Tabernacle entrance, where I will meet you and speak with
you. 43 I will meet the people of Israel there, and the Tabernacle will be sanctified by my
glorious presence. 44 Yes, I will make the Tabernacle and the altar most holy, and I will
set apart Aaron and his sons as holy, that they may be my priests. 45 I will live among the
people of Israel and be their God, 46 and they will know that I am the LORD their God. I
am the one who brought them out of Egypt so that I could live among them. I am the
LORD their God.

Plans for the Incense Altar

30:1-5 //Exod 37:25-28 1 Kgs 6:20 Rev 8:3

30 "Then make a small altar out of acacia wood for burning incense. 2 It must be
eighteen inches square and three feet high,* with horns at the corners carved from
the same piece of wood as the altar. 3 Overlay the top, sides, and horns of the altar with
pure gold, and run a gold molding around the entire altar. 4 Beneath the molding, on

29:40 Hebrew *1/10 of an ephah* [2 liters] *of fine flour . . . 1/4 of a hin* [1 liter] *of olive oil . . . 1/4 of a hin of wine.*
30:2 Hebrew *1 cubit* [45 centimeters] *square and 2 cubits* [90 centimeters] *high.*

29:37 Notice the overwhelming emphasis on the holiness of God. The priests, the clothes, the Tabernacle, and the sacrifices had to be clean and consecrated, prepared to meet God. In contrast, today we tend to take God for granted, rushing into worship and treating him with almost casual disregard. But we worship the almighty Creator and Sustainer of the universe. Remember that profound truth when you pray or worship, and come before him with reverence and repentance.

29:45, 46 God's action in bringing the Israelites out of Egypt showed his great desire to be with them and protect them. Throughout the Bible, God shows that he is not an absentee landlord. He wants to live among us, even in our hearts. Don't exclude God from your life. Allow him to be your God as you obey his Word and communicate with him in prayer. Let him be your resident landlord.

opposite sides of the altar, attach two gold rings to support the carrying poles. [5]The poles are to be made of acacia wood and overlaid with gold. [6]Place the incense altar just outside the inner curtain, opposite the Ark's cover—the place of atonement—that rests on the Ark of the Covenant.* I will meet with you there.

[7]"Every morning when Aaron trims the lamps, he must burn fragrant incense on the altar. [8]And each evening when he tends to the lamps, he must again burn incense in the LORD's presence. This must be done from generation to generation. [9]Do not offer any unholy incense on this altar, or any burnt offerings, grain offerings, or drink offerings.

[10]"Once a year Aaron must purify the altar by placing on its horns the blood from the offering made for the atonement of sin. This will be a regular, annual event from generation to generation, for this is the LORD's supremely holy altar."

Money for the Tabernacle

[11]And the LORD said to Moses, [12]"Whenever you take a census of the people of Israel, each man who is counted must pay a ransom for himself to the LORD. Then there will be no plagues among the people as you count them. [13]His payment to the LORD will be one-fifth of an ounce* of silver. [14]All who have reached their twentieth birthday must give this offering to the LORD. [15]When this offering is given to the LORD to make atonement for yourselves, the rich must not give more, and the poor must not give less. [16]Use this money for the care of the Tabernacle.* It will bring you, the Israelites, to the LORD's attention, and it will make atonement for your lives."

Plans for the Washbasin

[17]And the LORD said to Moses, [18]"Make a large bronze washbasin with a bronze pedestal. Put it between the Tabernacle and the altar, and fill it with water. [19]Aaron and his sons will wash their hands and feet there [20]before they go into the Tabernacle to appear before the LORD and before they approach the altar to burn offerings to the LORD. They must always wash before ministering in these ways, or they will die. [21]This is a permanent law for Aaron and his descendants, to be kept from generation to generation."

The Anointing Oil

[22]Then the LORD said to Moses, [23]"Collect choice spices—12½ pounds of pure myrrh, 6¼ pounds* each of cinnamon and of sweet cane, [24]12½ pounds of cassia, and one gallon* of olive oil. [25]Blend these ingredients into a holy anointing oil. [26]Use this scented oil to anoint the Tabernacle, the Ark of the Covenant, [27]the table and all its utensils, the lampstand and all its accessories, the incense altar, [28]the altar of burnt offering with all its utensils, and the large washbasin with its pedestal. [29]Sanctify them to make them entirely holy. After this, whatever touches them will become holy. [30]Use this oil also to anoint Aaron and his sons, sanctifying them so they can minister before me as priests. [31]And say to the people of Israel, 'This will always be my holy anointing oil. [32]It must never be poured on the body of an ordinary person, and you must never make any of it for yourselves. It is holy, and you must treat it as holy. [33]Anyone who blends scented oil like it or puts any of it on someone who is not a priest will be cut off from the community.'"

30:6 Exod 25:21-22
30:7 Exod 27:21; 30:34-35; 1 Sam 2:28; Luke 1:9
30:10 Lev 16:8
30:12 Exod 38:25-26; Num 1:2; 26:2; 2 Sam 24:1; Matt 20:28
30:13 Matt 17:24
30:15 Prov 22:2
30:18 Exod 38:8; 40:7, 30
30:19 Exod 40:31-32
30:21 Exod 28:43
30:25 Exod 37:29; 40:9
30:26 Lev 8:10; Num 7:1
30:29 Exod 29:37
30:30 Lev 8:2, 12, 30
30:33 Gen 17:14; Exod 12:15; Lev 7:20-21

30:6 Or *Ark of the Testimony;* also in 30:26, 36. **30:13** Hebrew *half a shekel* [6 grams], *according to the sanctuary shekel, 20 gerahs to each shekel.* **30:16** Hebrew *Tent of Meeting;* also in 30:18, 20, 26, 36. **30:23** Hebrew *500 shekels* [5.7 kilograms] *of pure myrrh, 250 shekels* [2.9 kilograms]. **30:24** Hebrew *500 shekels* [5.7 kilograms] *of cassia, according to the sanctuary shekel, and 1 hin* [3.8 liters].

30:10 This once-a-year ceremony was called the Day of Atonement. On this day a sacrifice was made for the sins of the entire Israelite nation. This was the only day the high priest could enter the Most Holy Place, the innermost room of the Tabernacle. Here he asked God to forgive the people. The Day of Atonement served as a reminder that the daily, weekly, and monthly sacrifices could cover sins only temporarily. It pointed toward Jesus Christ, the perfect atonement, who could remove sins forever.

30:11-16 This money was like a census tax. It continued the principle that all the people belonged to God and therefore needed to be redeemed by a sacrifice. Whenever a census took place, everyone, both rich and poor, was required to pay a ransom. God does not discriminate between people (see Acts 10:34; Galatians 3:28). All of us need mercy and forgiveness because of our sinful thoughts and actions. There is no way the rich person can buy off God, and no way the poor can avoid paying. God's demand is that all of us come humbly before him to be forgiven and brought into his family.

The Incense

[34]These were the LORD's instructions to Moses concerning the incense: "Gather sweet
spices—resin droplets, mollusk scent, galbanum, and pure frankincense—weighing out
the same amounts of each. [35]Using the usual techniques of the incense maker, refine it
30:36 Exod 29:42; Lev 2:3
to produce a pure and holy incense. [36]Beat some of it very fine and put some of it in front
of the Ark of the Covenant, where I will meet with you in the Tabernacle. This incense
is most holy. [37]Never make this incense for yourselves. It is reserved for the LORD, and
you must treat it as holy. [38]Those who make it for their own enjoyment will be cut off
from the community."

Craftsmen: Bezalel and Oholiab

31:2-6 //Exod 35:30-36:1; 1 Chr 2:20
31 The LORD also said to Moses, [2]"Look, I have chosen Bezalel son of Uri, grandson
of Hur, of the tribe of Judah. [3]I have filled him with the Spirit of God, giving him
31:3 1 Kgs 7:14
great wisdom, intelligence, and skill in all kinds of crafts. [4]He is able to create beautiful
objects from gold, silver, and bronze. [5]He is skilled in cutting and setting gemstones and
in carving wood. Yes, he is a master at every craft!
31:6 Exod 35:34; 36:1
[6]"And I have appointed Oholiab son of Ahisamach, of the tribe of Dan, to be his
assistant. Moreover, I have given special skill to all the naturally talented craftsmen so
31:7 Exod 37:1-9
they can make all the things I have instructed you to make: [7]the Tabernacle itself; the
31:8 Exod 37:10-16; Lev 24:4
Ark of the Covenant;* the Ark's cover—the place of atonement; all the furnishings of
the Tabernacle; [8]the table and all its utensils; the gold lampstand with all its accessories;
the incense altar; [9]the altar of burnt offering with all its utensils; the washbasin and its
pedestal; [10]the beautifully stitched, holy garments for Aaron the priest, and the garments
31:11 Exod 30:23-32
for his sons to wear as they minister as priests; [11]the anointing oil; and the special incense
for the Holy Place. They must follow exactly all the instructions I have given you."

Instructions for the Sabbath

31:13 Lev 19:3, 30; Ezek 20:12-13
[12]The LORD then gave these further instructions to Moses: [13]"Tell the people of Israel
to keep my Sabbath day, for the Sabbath is a sign of the covenant between me and you
31:14 Exod 16:23; 35:2; John 7:23
forever. It helps you to remember that I am the LORD, who makes you holy. [14]Yes,
keep the Sabbath day, for it is holy. Anyone who desecrates it must die; anyone who
works on that day will be cut off from the community. [15]Work six days only, but the
seventh day must be a day of total rest. I repeat: Because the LORD considers it a holy
31:16 Exod 20:8
day, anyone who works on the Sabbath must be put to death. [16]The people of Israel
31:17 Gen 2:2-3; Exod 20:11
must keep the Sabbath day forever. [17]It is a permanent sign of my covenant with them.
For in six days the LORD made heaven and earth, but he rested on the seventh day and
was refreshed."
31:18 Exod 24:12; 32:15-16; 34:1, 28
[18]Then as the LORD finished speaking with Moses on Mount Sinai, he gave him the
two stone tablets inscribed with the terms of the covenant,* written by the finger of
God.

31:7 Hebrew *the Tent of Meeting; the Ark of the Testimony.* **31:18** Hebrew *the Testimony.*

30:34-38 The Israelites often burned incense, but this holy incense could be burned only in the Tabernacle. Here God gave the recipe for this special incense. The sweet-smelling incense was burned in shallow dishes called incense burners and was used to show honor and reverence to God. It was like prayer lifting up to God. It was also a vital part of the sacred ceremony on the Day of Atonement, when the high priest carried his smoking censer into the Most Holy Place. This incense, like the sacred anointing oil, was so holy that the people were strictly forbidden to copy it for personal use.

31:1-11 God regards all the skills of his people, not merely those with theological or ministerial abilities. Our tendency is to regard only those who are up front and in leadership roles. God gave Bezalel and Oholiab Spirit-filled abilities in artistic craftsmanship. Take notice of all the abilities God gives his people. Don't diminish your skills if they are not like Moses' and Aaron's.

31:12-17 The Sabbath had two purposes: It was a time *to rest* and a time *to remember* what God had done. We need rest. Without time out from the bustle, life loses its meaning. In our day, as in Moses' day, taking time out is not easy. But God reminds us that without Sabbaths we will forget the purpose for all of our activity and lose the balance crucial to a faithful life. Make sure your Sabbath provides a time of both refreshment and remembrance of God.

31:18 The two stone tablets contained the Ten Commandments. These were not the only code of laws in the ancient world. Other law codes had come into existence when cities or nations decided that there must be standards of judgment, ways to correct specific wrongs. But God's laws for Israel were unique: (1) They alleviated the harsh judgments typical of the day; (2) they were egalitarian—the poor and the powerful received the same punishment; (3) they did not separate religious and social law. All law rested on God's authority.

3. Breaking the law

The Calf of Gold

32 When Moses failed to come back down the mountain right away, the people went
to Aaron. "Look," they said, "make us some gods who can lead us. This man
Moses, who brought us here from Egypt, has disappeared. We don't know what has
happened to him."
2So Aaron said, "Tell your wives and sons and daughters to take off their gold
earrings, and then bring them to me."
3All the people obeyed Aaron and brought him their gold earrings. 4Then Aaron took
the gold, melted it down, and molded and tooled it into the shape of a calf. The people
exclaimed, "O Israel, these are the gods who brought you out of Egypt!"
5When Aaron saw how excited the people were about it, he built an altar in front of
the calf and announced, "Tomorrow there will be a festival to the LORD!"
6So the people got up early the next morning to sacrifice burnt offerings and peace
offerings. After this, they celebrated with feasting and drinking, and indulged themselves
in pagan revelry.
7Then the LORD told Moses, "Quick! Go down the mountain! The people you brought
from Egypt have defiled themselves. 8They have already turned from the way I commanded them to live. They have made an idol shaped like a calf, and they have worshiped
and sacrificed to it. They are saying, 'These are your gods, O Israel, who brought you
out of Egypt.'"
9Then the LORD said, "I have seen how stubborn and rebellious these people are.
10Now leave me alone so my anger can blaze against them and destroy them all. Then I
will make you, Moses, into a great nation instead of them."
11But Moses pleaded with the LORD his God not to do it. "O LORD!" he exclaimed.
"Why are you so angry with your own people whom you brought from the land of Egypt
with such great power and mighty acts? 12The Egyptians will say, 'God tricked them into
coming to the mountains so he could kill them and wipe them from the face of the earth.'
Turn away from your fierce anger. Change your mind about this terrible disaster you are
planning against your people! 13Remember your covenant with your servants—Abraham, Isaac, and Jacob.* You swore by your own self, 'I will make your descendants as
numerous as the stars of heaven. Yes, I will give them all of this land that I have promised
to your descendants, and they will possess it forever.'"
14So the LORD withdrew his threat and didn't bring against his people the disaster he
had threatened.

32:1 Exod 24:18; Deut 9:9-12; †Acts 7:40
32:2 Exod 35:22
32:4 Exod 20:23; Deut 9:16; Ps 106:19; Acts 7:41
32:6 Num 25:2; Acts 7:41; †1 Cor 10:7
32:7 Exod 19:24; 33:1; Deut 9:12
32:8 Exod 22:20; 34:15; Deut 32:17
32:9 Exod 33:5; Num 14:11; Acts 7:51
32:10 Num 14:12; Deut 9:14
32:11 Deut 9:18, 26; Ps 106:23
32:12 Num 14:13-16; Deut 9:28
32:13 Gen 15:5; 22:16-18; Heb 6:13
32:14 2 Sam 24:16; Ps 106:45

32:13 Hebrew *Israel.*

32:1-10 Idols again! Even though Israel had seen the invisible God in action, they still wanted the familiar gods they could see and shape into whatever image they desired. How much like them we are! Our great temptation is still to shape God to our liking, to make him convenient to obey or ignore. God responds in great anger when his mercy is trampled on. The gods we create blind us to the love that our loving God wants to shower on us. God cannot work in us when we elevate anyone or anything above him. What false gods in your life are preventing the true God from living in you?

32:4, 5 Two popular Egyptian gods, Hapi (Apis) and Hathor, were thought of as a bull and a heifer. The Canaanites around them worshiped Baal, thought of as a bull. Baal was their sacred symbol of power and fertility and was closely connected to immoral sexual practices. No doubt the Israelites, fresh from Egypt, found it quite natural to make a golden calf to represent the God that had just delivered them from their oppressors. They were weary of a god without a face. But in doing so, they were ignoring the command he had just given them: "Do not make idols of any kind" (20:4). They may even have thought they were worshiping God. Their apparent sincerity was no substitute for obedience or excuse for disobedience.

Even if we do not make idols, we are often guilty of trying to make God in our image, molding him to fit our expectations, desires, and circumstances. When we do this, we end up worshiping ourselves rather than the God who created us—and self-worship, today as in the Israelites' time, leads to all kinds of immorality. What is your favorite image of God? Is it biblical? Is it adequate? Do you need to destroy it in order to worship the immeasurably powerful God who delivered you from bondage to sin?

32:9-14 God was ready to destroy the whole nation because of their sin. But Moses pleaded for mercy, and God spared them. This is one of the countless examples in the Bible of God's mercy. Although we deserve his anger, he is willing to forgive and restore us to himself. We can receive God's forgiveness from sin by asking him. Like Moses, we can pray that he will forgive others and use us to bring them the message of his mercy.

32:14 How could God relent? God did not change his mind in the same way that a parent decides not to discipline a child. Instead, God changed his behavior to remain consistent with his nature. When God first wanted to destroy the people, he was acting consistently with his justice. When Moses interceded for the people, God relented in order to act consistently with his mercy. God had often told the people that if they changed their ways, he would not condemn them. They changed, and God did as he promised.

32:15 Exod 24:18 Deut 9:15
32:16 Exod 31:18

15 Then Moses turned and went down the mountain. He held in his hands the two stone
tablets inscribed with the terms of the covenant.* They were inscribed on both sides,
front and back. 16 These stone tablets were God's work; the words on them were written
by God himself.
17 When Joshua heard the noise of the people shouting below them, he exclaimed to
Moses, "It sounds as if there is a war in the camp!"
18 But Moses replied, "No, it's neither a cry of victory nor a cry of defeat. It is the
sound of a celebration."

32:19 Exod 32:6 Deut 9:16-17
32:20 Deut 9:21

19 When they came near the camp, Moses saw the calf and the dancing. In terrible anger,
he threw the stone tablets to the ground, smashing them at the foot of the mountain. 20 He
took the calf they had made and melted it in the fire. And when the metal had cooled, he
ground it into powder and mixed it with water. Then he made the people drink it.
21 After that, he turned to Aaron. "What did the people do to you?" he demanded.
"How did they ever make you bring such terrible sin upon them?"

32:22 Deut 9:24
32:23 Exod 32:1

22 "Don't get upset, sir," Aaron replied. "You yourself know these people and what a
wicked bunch they are. 23 They said to me, 'Make us some gods to lead us, for something
has happened to this man Moses, who led us out of Egypt.' 24 So I told them, 'Bring me

32:15 Hebrew *the Testimony.*

AARON

Effective teamwork happens when each team member uses his or her special skills. Ideally each member's strengths will contribute something important to the team effort. In this way, members make up for one another's weaknesses. Aaron made a good team with Moses. He provided Moses with one skill Moses lacked—effective public speaking. But while Aaron was necessary to Moses, he needed Moses as well. Without a guide, Aaron had little direction of his own. There was never any doubt as to who God's chosen and trained leader was. The pliability that made Aaron a good follower made him a weak leader. His major failures were caused by his inability to stand alone. His yielding to public pressure and making an idol was a good example of this weakness.

Most of us have more of the follower than the leader in us. We may even be good followers, following a good leader. But no leader is perfect, and no human deserves our complete allegiance. Only God deserves our complete loyalty and obedience. We need to be effective team members in using the skills and abilities God has given us. But if the team or the leader goes against God's Word, we must be willing to stand alone.

Strengths and accomplishments
- First high priest of God in Israel
- Effective communicator; Moses' mouthpiece

Weaknesses and mistakes
- Pliable personality; gave in to people's demands for a golden calf
- Joined with Moses in disobeying God's orders about the water-giving rock
- Joined sister Miriam in complaining against Moses

Lessons from his life
- God gives individuals special abilities, which he weaves together for his use
- The very skills that make a good team player sometimes also make a poor leader

Vital statistics
- Where: Egypt, wilderness of Sinai
- Occupations: Priest; Moses' second in command
- Relatives: Brother: Moses. Sister: Miriam. Sons: Nadab, Abihu, Eleazar, and Ithamar

Key verses
"Then the LORD became angry with Moses. 'All right,' he said. 'What about your brother, Aaron the Levite? He is a good speaker. And look! He is on his way to meet you now. And when he sees you, he will be very glad. . . . Aaron will be your spokesman to the people, and you will be as God to him, telling him what to say' " (Exodus 4:14, 16).

Aaron's story is told in Exodus—Deuteronomy 10:6. He is also mentioned in Hebrews 7:11.

32:19, 20 Overwhelmed by the actual sight of the blatant idolatry and revelry, Moses broke the tablets containing the commandments which had already been broken in the hearts and actions of the people. There is a place for righteous anger. However angry Moses might have been, God was angrier still—he wanted to kill all the people. Anger at sin is a sign of spiritual vitality. Don't squelch this kind of anger. But when you are justifiably angry at sin, be careful not to do anything that you will regret later.

32:21-24 Aaron's decision nearly cost him his life. His absurd excuse shows the spiritual decline in his leadership and in the people. Those who function as spokespersons and assistants need to be doubly sure their theology and morality are in tune with God so they will not be influenced by pressure from people. For more information on Aaron, see his Profile in chapter 32.

your gold earrings.' When they brought them to me, I threw them into the fire—and out
came this calf!"
25 When Moses saw that Aaron had let the people get completely out of control—and
much to the amusement of their enemies—26 he stood at the entrance to the camp and
shouted, "All of you who are on the LORD's side, come over here and join me." And all
the Levites came.
27 He told them, "This is what the LORD, the God of Israel, says: Strap on your swords!
Go back and forth from one end of the camp to the other, killing even your brothers,
friends, and neighbors." 28 The Levites obeyed Moses, and about three thousand people
died that day.
29 Then Moses told the Levites, "Today you have been ordained for the service of the
LORD, for you obeyed him even though it meant killing your own sons and brothers.
Because of this, he will now give you a great blessing."

Moses Intercedes for Israel

30 The next day Moses said to the people, "You have committed a terrible sin, but I will
return to the LORD on the mountain. Perhaps I will be able to obtain forgiveness for you."
31 So Moses returned to the LORD and said, "Alas, these people have committed a
terrible sin. They have made gods of gold for themselves. 32 But now, please forgive their
sin—and if not, then blot me out of the record you are keeping."
33 The LORD replied to Moses, "I will blot out whoever has sinned against me. 34 Now
go, lead the people to the place I told you about. Look! My angel will lead the way before
you! But when I call the people to account, I will certainly punish them for their sins."
35 And the LORD sent a great plague upon the people because they had worshiped the
calf Aaron had made.

33 The LORD said to Moses, "Now that you have brought these people out of
Egypt, lead them to the land I solemnly promised Abraham, Isaac, and Jacob.
I told them long ago that I would give this land to their descendants. 2 And I will send
an angel before you to drive out the Canaanites, Amorites, Hittites, Perizzites, Hivites,
and Jebusites. 3 Theirs is a land flowing with milk and honey. But I will not travel
along with you, for you are a stubborn, unruly people. If I did, I would be tempted to
destroy you along the way."
4 When the people heard these stern words, they went into mourning and refused to
wear their jewelry and ornaments. 5 For the LORD had told Moses to tell them, "You are
an unruly, stubborn people. If I were there among you for even a moment, I would
destroy you. Remove your jewelry and ornaments until I decide what to do with you."
6 So from the time they left Mount Sinai,* the Israelites wore no more jewelry.
7 It was Moses' custom to set up the tent known as the Tent of Meeting far outside the
camp. Everyone who wanted to consult with the LORD would go there.
8 Whenever Moses went out to the Tent of Meeting, all the people would get up and
stand in their tent entrances. They would all watch Moses until he disappeared inside.
9 As he went into the tent, the pillar of cloud would come down and hover at the
entrance while the LORD spoke with Moses. 10 Then all the people would stand and
bow low at their tent entrances. 11 Inside the Tent of Meeting, the LORD would speak
to Moses face to face, as a man speaks to his friend. Afterward Moses would return
to the camp, but the young man who assisted him, Joshua son of Nun, stayed behind
in the Tent of Meeting.

32:25 1 Kgs 12:28-30
32:26 2 Sam 20:11
32:27 Num 25:5; Deut 33:9
32:28 Num 16:32; 25:9
32:29 Deut 13:6; 33:9
32:31 Exod 20:23
32:32 Dan 12:1; Mal 3:16-17; Phil 4:3; Rev 3:5; 21:27
32:33 Deut 29:20; Ps 9:5; Rev 3:5
32:34 Exod 3:17; 23:20; Ps 99:8
33:1 Gen 12:7; Exod 32:7, 13
33:2 Exod 23:27-31
33:3 Exod 3:8, 17; 32:9-10
33:4 Num 14:1, 39
33:5 Exod 33:3
33:7 Exod 29:42-43
33:8 Num 16:27
33:9 Exod 13:21; 19:9; 25:22; Ps 99:7
33:11 Num 12:8; Deut 34:10

33:6 Hebrew *Horeb*, another name for Sinai.

33:5, 6 This ban on ornaments was not a permanent ban on all jewelry. It was a temporary sign of repentance and mourning. In 35:22 we read that the people had jewelry.

33:11 God and Moses talked face to face in the Tent of Meeting, just as friends do. Why did Moses find such favor with God? It certainly was not because he was perfect, gifted, or powerful. Rather, it was because God chose Moses, and Moses in turn relied wholeheartedly on God's wisdom and direction. Friendship with God was a true privilege for Moses, out of reach for the other Hebrews. But it is not out of reach for us today. Jesus called his disciples—and, by extension, all of his followers—his friends (John 15:15). He has called you to be his friend. Will you trust him as Moses did?

33:11 Joshua, Moses' aide, did not leave the Tent of Meeting, probably because he was guarding it. No doubt there were curious people who would have dared to go inside.

33:12 Exod 3:10; 32:34; John 10:14-15; 2 Tim 2:19
33:13 Exod 34:9; Pss 25:4; 27:11
33:14 Exod 13:21; Josh 22:4; Isa 63:9
33:16 Exod 34:10; Lev 20:24, 26; Num 14:14
33:17 Exod 33:12
33:18 Exod 33:20, 23
33:19 †Rom 9:15
33:20 Isa 6:5; John 1:18; 1 Tim 6:16
33:22 Ps 91:1, 4; Isa 49:2; 51:16
33:23 John 1:18

Moses Sees the LORD's Glory

12 Moses said to the LORD, "You have been telling me, 'Take these people up to the
Promised Land.' But you haven't told me whom you will send with me. You call me by
name and tell me I have found favor with you. 13 Please, if this is really so, show me your
intentions so I will understand you more fully and do exactly what you want me to do.
Besides, don't forget that this nation is your very own people."
14 And the LORD replied, "I will personally go with you, Moses. I will give you
rest—everything will be fine for you."
15 Then Moses said, "If you don't go with us personally, don't let us move a step from
this place. 16 If you don't go with us, how will anyone ever know that your people and I
have found favor with you? How else will they know we are special and distinct from
all other people on the earth?"
17 And the LORD replied to Moses, "I will indeed do what you have asked, for you have
found favor with me, and you are my friend."
18 Then Moses had one more request. "Please let me see your glorious presence," he
said.
19 The LORD replied, "I will make all my goodness pass before you, and I will call out
my name, 'the LORD,' to you. I will show kindness to anyone I choose, and I will show
mercy to anyone I choose. 20 But you may not look directly at my face, for no one may
see me and live." 21 The LORD continued, "Stand here on this rock beside me. 22 As my
glorious presence passes by, I will put you in the cleft of the rock and cover you with my
hand until I have passed. 23 Then I will remove my hand, and you will see me from
behind. But my face will not be seen."

34:1 Exod 24:12; 32:19; Deut 10:2, 4
34:3 Exod 19:12-13
34:5 Exod 33:19
34:6 Num 14:18; Neh 9:17; Pss 86:15; 103:8
34:7 Exod 20:6-7; Deut 5:10; Nah 1:3
34:9 Num 14:19; Deut 4:20; 32:9; Ps 25:11
34:10 Deut 5:2-3; Pss 72:18; 136:4

A New Copy of the Covenant

34 The LORD told Moses, "Prepare two stone tablets like the first ones. I will write
on them the same words that were on the tablets you smashed. 2 Be ready in the
morning to come up Mount Sinai and present yourself to me there on the top of the
mountain. 3 No one else may come with you. In fact, no one is allowed anywhere on
the mountain. Do not even let the flocks or herds graze near the mountain."
4 So Moses cut two tablets of stone like the first ones. Early in the morning he climbed
Mount Sinai as the LORD had told him, carrying the two stone tablets in his hands.
5 Then the LORD came down in a pillar of cloud and called out his own name, "the
LORD," as Moses stood there in his presence. 6 He passed in front of Moses and said, "I
am the LORD, I am the LORD, the merciful and gracious God. I am slow to anger and rich
in unfailing love and faithfulness. 7 I show this unfailing love to many thousands by
forgiving every kind of sin and rebellion. Even so I do not leave sin unpunished, but I
punish the children for the sins of their parents to the third and fourth generations."
8 Moses immediately fell to the ground and worshiped. 9 And he said, "If it is true that
I have found favor in your sight, O Lord, then please go with us. Yes, this is an unruly
and stubborn people, but please pardon our iniquity and our sins. Accept us as your own
special possession."
10 The LORD replied, "All right. This is the covenant I am going to make with you. I
will perform wonders that have never been done before anywhere in all the earth or in
any nation. And all the people around you will see the power of the LORD—the awesome

---

33:18-23 Moses' prayer was to see the manifest glory of God. He wanted assurance of God's presence with him, Aaron, and Joshua, and also he desired to know that presence experientially. Because we are finite and morally imperfect, we cannot exist and see God as he is. To see God's back means we can only see where God has passed by. We can only know him by what he does and how he acts. We cannot comprehend God as he really is apart from Jesus Christ (John 14:9). Jesus promised to show himself to those who believe (John 14:21).

34:6, 7 Moses had asked to see God's glorious presence (33:18), and this was God's response. What is God's glory? It is his character, his nature, his way of relating to his creatures. Notice that God did not give Moses a vision of his power and majesty, but rather of his love. God's glory is revealed in his mercy, grace, compassion, faithfulness, forgiveness, and justice. God's love and mercy are truly wonderful, and we benefit from them. We can respond and give glory to God when our characters resemble his.

34:7 Why would sins affect grandchildren and great-grandchildren? This is no arbitrary punishment. Children still suffer for the sins of their parents. Consider child abuse or alcoholism, for example. While these sins are obvious, sins like selfishness and greed can be passed along as well. The dire consequences of sin are not limited to the individual family member. Be careful not to treat sin casually, but repent and turn from it. The sin may cause you little pain now, but it could sting in a most tender area of your life later—your children and grandchildren.

power I will display through you. 11Your responsibility is to obey all the commands I
am giving you today. Then I will surely drive out all those who stand in your way—the
Amorites, Canaanites, Hittites, Perizzites, Hivites, and Jebusites.
12"Be very careful never to make treaties with the people in the land where you are
going. If you do, you soon will be following their evil ways. 13Instead, you must break
down their pagan altars, smash the sacred pillars they worship, and cut down their carved
images. 14You must worship no other gods, but only the LORD, for he is a God who is
passionate about his relationship with you.
15"Do not make treaties of any kind with the people living in the land. They are
spiritual prostitutes, committing adultery against me by sacrificing to their gods. If you
make peace with them, they will invite you to go with them to worship their gods, and
you are likely to do it. 16And you will accept their daughters, who worship other gods,
as wives for your sons. Then they will cause your sons to commit adultery against me
by worshiping other gods. 17You must make no gods for yourselves at all.
18"Be sure to celebrate the Festival of Unleavened Bread for seven days, just as I
instructed you, at the appointed time each year in early spring,* for that was when you
left Egypt.
19"Every firstborn male belongs to me—of both cattle and sheep. 20A firstborn male
donkey may be redeemed from the LORD by presenting a lamb in its place. But if you
decide not to make the exchange, you must kill the donkey by breaking its neck.
However, you must redeem every firstborn son. No one is allowed to appear before me
without a gift.
21"Six days are set aside for work, but on the Sabbath day you must rest, even during
the seasons of plowing and harvest. 22And you must remember to celebrate the Festival
of Harvest* with the first crop of the wheat harvest, and celebrate the Festival of the Final
Harvest* at the end of the harvest season. 23Three times each year all the men of Israel
must appear before the Sovereign LORD, the God of Israel. 24No one will attack and
conquer your land when you go to appear before the LORD your God those three times
each year. I will drive out the nations that stand in your way and will enlarge your
boundaries.
25"You must not offer bread made with yeast as a sacrifice to me. And none of the
meat of the Passover lamb may be kept over until the following morning. 26You must
bring the best of the first of each year's crop to the house of the LORD your God.
"You must not cook a young goat in its mother's milk."
27And the LORD said to Moses, "Write down all these instructions, for they represent
the terms of my covenant with you and with Israel."
28Moses was up on the mountain with the LORD forty days and forty nights. In all that
time he neither ate nor drank. At that time he wrote the terms of the covenant—the Ten
Commandments—on the stone tablets.
29When Moses came down the mountain carrying the stone tablets inscribed with the
terms of the covenant,* he wasn't aware that his face glowed because he had spoken to
the LORD face to face. 30And when Aaron and the people of Israel saw the radiance of
Moses' face, they were afraid to come near him.
31But Moses called to them and asked Aaron and the community leaders to come
over and talk with him. 32Then all the people came, and Moses gave them the

34:11 Exod 33:2; Deut 6:3
34:12 Exod 23:32-33
34:13 Exod 23:24; Deut 7:5; 12:3; 16:21; 2 Chr 34:3-4
34:14 Exod 20:3; Deut 4:24
34:15 Judg 2:17; Num 25:2; 1 Cor 7:10; 8:2
34:16 Deut 7:3; Josh 23:12
34:17 Exod 20:4, 23
34:18 Exod 12:2, 15-17
34:19 Exod 13:2; 22:29
34:20 Exod 13:13, 15; Num 3:45
34:21 Exod 31:15; 35:2
34:22 Exod 23:16
34:23 Exod 23:14-17; Deut 16:16
34:24 Exod 33:2; Josh 11:23
34:25 Exod 12:10; 23:18
34:26 Exod 23:19; Deut 26:2
34:27 Exod 17:14; 24:4
34:28 Exod 24:18; Deut 4:13; 10:4
34:29 Exod 32:15; Matt 17:2; 2 Cor 3:7, 13

34:18 Hebrew *in the month of Abib.* This month of the Hebrew lunar calendar usually occurs in March and April. **34:22a** Or *Festival of Weeks.* **34:22b** This was later called the Festival of Shelters; see Lev 23:33-36. **34:29** Hebrew *the Testimony.*

34:12-14 God told the Israelites not to join in religious rites with the sinful people around them, but to give their absolute loyalty and exclusive devotion to him. Pagan worship simply cannot be mixed with the worship of the holy God. As Jesus pointed out, "No one can serve two masters. . . . You cannot serve both God and money" (Luke 16:13). Love of money is the god of this age, and many Christians attempt to make a treaty with this enslaving god. Are you trying to worship two gods at once? Where is your first allegiance?

34:13 Sacred pillars were wooden poles that stood by Baal's altar (see Judges 6:25). Also called "Asherah poles," they were used to worship the goddess who was the consort (wife) of Baal. She represented fertility and good luck in agriculture.

34:28-35 Moses' face glowed after he spent time with God. The people could clearly see God's presence in him. How often do you spend time alone with God? Although your face may not light up a room, time spent in prayer, reading the Bible, and meditating should have such an effect on your life that people will know you have been with God.

34:33 2 Cor 3:13 instructions the LORD had given him on Mount Sinai. 33 When Moses had finished
34:34 2 Cor 3:16 speaking with them, he put a veil over his face. 34 But whenever he went into the Tent
of Meeting to speak with the LORD, he removed the veil until he came out again. Then
34:35 2 Cor 3:13 he would give the people whatever instructions the LORD had given him, 35 and the
people would see his face aglow. Afterward he would put the veil on again until he
returned to speak with the LORD.

4. Tabernacle construction

Instructions for the Sabbath

35:2 Exod 20:9-10; 23:12; 31:15; 34:21 Num 15:32-36 Deut 5:13-14 **35** Now Moses called a meeting of all the people and told them, "You must obey
these instructions from the LORD. 2 Each week, work for six days only. The
35:3 Exod 16:23 seventh day is a day of total rest, a holy day that belongs to the LORD. Anyone who works
on that day will die. 3 Do not even light fires in your homes on that day."

Gifts for the Tabernacle

35:4-9 //Exod 25:1-9 4 Then Moses said to all the people, "This is what the LORD has commanded.
5 Everyone is invited to bring these offerings to the LORD: gold, silver, and bronze;
6 blue, purple, and scarlet yarn; fine linen; goat hair for cloth; 7 tanned ram skins and
fine goatskin leather; acacia wood; 8 olive oil for the lamps; spices for the anointing
oil and the fragrant incense; 9 onyx stones, and other stones to be set in the ephod and
the chestpiece.

KEY TABERNACLE PIECES

Name	*Function and Significance*
Ark of the Covenant	• A golden rectangular box that contained the Ten Commandments • Symbolized God's covenant with Israel's people • Located in the Most Holy Place
Atonement Cover	• The lid to the Ark of the Covenant • Symbolized the presence of God among his people
Curtain	• The curtain that divided the two sacred rooms of the Tabernacle—the Holy Place and the Most Holy Place • Symbolized how the people were separated from God because of sin
Table	• A wooden table located in the Holy Place of the Tabernacle. The Bread of the Presence and various utensils were kept on this table
Bread of the Presence	• Twelve loaves of baked bread, one for each tribe of Israel • Symbolized the spiritual nourishment God offers his people
Lampstands and Lamps	• A golden lampstand located in the Holy Place, which held seven burning oil lamps • The lampstand lit the Holy Place for the priests
Altar of Incense	• An altar in the Holy Place in front of the curtain • Used for burning God's special incense and symbolic of acceptable prayer
Anointing Oil	• A special oil used to anoint the priests and all the pieces in the Tabernacle • A sign of being set apart for God
Altar of Burnt Offering	• The bronze altar outside the Tabernacle used for the sacrifices • Symbolized how sacrifice restored one's relationship with God
Basin	• A large washbasin outside the Tabernacle used by the priests to cleanse themselves before performing their duties • Symbolized the need for spiritual cleansing

35:5-21 God did not require these special offerings, but he appealed to people with generous hearts. Only those who were willing to give were invited to participate. God loves people who give cheerfully (2 Corinthians 9:7). Our giving should be from love and generosity, not from a guilty conscience.

10“Come, all of you who are gifted craftsmen. Construct everything that the LORD **35:10-19**
has commanded: 11the entire Tabernacle, including the sacred tent and its coverings, //Exod 39:32-41
the clasps, frames, crossbars, posts, and bases; 12the Ark and its poles; the Ark’s
cover—the place of atonement; the inner curtain to enclose the Ark in the Most Holy
Place; 13the table, its carrying poles, and all of its utensils; the Bread of the Presence;
14the lampstand and its accessories; the lamp cups and the oil for lighting; 15the
incense altar and its carrying poles; the anointing oil and fragrant incense; the curtain
for the entrance of the Tabernacle; 16the altar of burnt offering; the bronze grating of
the altar and its carrying poles and utensils; the large washbasin with its pedestal;
17the curtains for the walls of the courtyard; the posts and their bases; the curtain for
the entrance to the courtyard; 18the tent pegs of the Tabernacle and courtyard and their
cords; 19the beautifully stitched clothing for the priests to wear while ministering in
the Holy Place; the sacred garments for Aaron and his sons to wear while officiating
as priests.”

20So all the people left Moses and went to their tents to prepare their gifts. 21If their **35:21**
hearts were stirred and they desired to do so, they brought to the LORD their offerings of Exod 25:2; 35:5
materials for the Tabernacle* and its furnishings and for the holy garments. 22Both men
and women came, all whose hearts were willing. Some brought to the LORD their
offerings of gold—medallions, earrings, rings from their fingers, and necklaces. They
presented gold objects of every kind to the LORD. 23Others brought blue, purple, and **35:23** Exod 39:1
scarlet yarn, fine linen, or goat hair for cloth. Some gave tanned ram skins or fine
goatskin leather. 24Others brought silver and bronze objects as their offering to the LORD.
And those who had acacia wood brought it.

25All the women who were skilled in sewing and spinning prepared blue, purple, and **35:25**
scarlet yarn, and fine linen cloth, and they brought them in. 26All the women who were Exod 28:3
willing used their skills to spin and weave the goat hair into cloth. 27The leaders **35:27**
brought onyx stones and the other gemstones to be used for the ephod and the 1 Chr 29:6 Ezra 2:68
chestpiece. 28They also brought spices and olive oil for the light, the anointing oil, and
the fragrant incense. 29So the people of Israel—every man and woman who wanted to **35:29** 1 Chr 29:9
help in the work the LORD had given them through Moses—brought their offerings to
the LORD.

30And Moses told them, “The LORD has chosen Bezalel son of Uri, grandson of Hur, **35:30-35**
of the tribe of Judah. 31The LORD has filled Bezalel with the Spirit of God, giving him //Exod 31:2-6
great wisdom, intelligence, and skill in all kinds of crafts. 32He is able to create beautiful
objects from gold, silver, and bronze. 33He is skilled in cutting and setting gemstones
and in carving wood. In fact, he has every necessary skill. 34And the LORD has given **35:34**
both him and Oholiab son of Ahisamach, of the tribe of Dan, the ability to teach their Exod 31:6
skills to others. 35The LORD has given them special skills as jewelers, designers, **35:35** Exod 31:3, 6; 35:31
weavers, and embroiderers in blue, purple, and scarlet yarn on fine linen cloth. They 1 Kgs 7:14
excel in all the crafts needed for the work.

36 “Bezalel, Oholiab, and the other craftsmen whom the LORD has gifted with **36:1**
wisdom, skill, and intelligence will construct and furnish the Tabernacle, just as Exod 25:8
the LORD has commanded.”

35:21 Hebrew *Tent of Meeting.*

35:10-19 Moses asked people with various abilities to help with the Tabernacle. Every one of God’s people has been given special abilities. We are responsible to develop these abilities—even the ones not considered religious—and to use them for God’s glory. We can become skilled through study, by watching others, and through practice. Work on your skills or abilities that could help your church or community.

35:20-24 Where did the Israelites, who were once Egyptian slaves, get all this gold and jewelry? When the Hebrews left Egypt, they took with them the spoils from the land—all the booty they could carry (12:35, 36). This included gold, silver, jewels, linen, skins, and other valuables.

35:21, 22 Those whose hearts were stirred gave willingy to the Tent of Meeting (also called the Tabernacle). With great enthusiasm they gave because they knew how important their giving was to the completion of God’s house. Airline pilots and computer operators can push test buttons to see if their equipment is functioning properly. God has a quick test button he can push to see the level of our commitment—our pocketbooks. Generous people aren’t necessarily faithful to God. But faithful people are always generous.

35:26 Those who spun cloth made a beautiful contribution to the Tabernacle. Good workers take pride in the quality and beauty of their work. God is concerned with the quality and beauty of what you do. Whether you are a corporate executive or a drugstore cashier, your work should reflect the creative abilities God has given you.

36:2 Exod 35:21, 26; 1 Chr 29:5
36:5 2 Chr 24:14; 31:6-10; 2 Cor 8:2-3
36:7 1 Kgs 8:64

[2]So Moses told Bezalel and Oholiab to begin the work, along with all those who were specially gifted by the LORD. [3]Moses gave them the materials donated by the people for the completion of the sanctuary. Additional gifts were brought each morning. [4]But finally the craftsmen left their work to meet with Moses. [5]"We have more than enough materials on hand now to complete the job the LORD has given us to do!" they exclaimed.

[6]So Moses gave the command, and this message was sent throughout the camp: "Bring no more materials! You have already given more than enough." So the people stopped bringing their offerings. [7]Their contributions were more than enough to complete the whole project.

Building the Tabernacle

36:8-38 //Exod 26:1-37
36:14 Exod 26:7

[8]The skilled weavers first made ten sheets from fine linen. One of the craftsmen then embroidered blue, purple, and scarlet cherubim into them. [9]Each sheet was exactly the same size—forty-two feet long and six feet wide.* [10]Five of these sheets were joined together to make one set, and a second set was made of the other five. [11]Fifty blue loops were placed along the edge of the last sheet in each set. [12]The fifty loops along the edge of the first set of sheets matched the loops along the edge of the second set. [13]Then fifty gold clasps were made to connect the loops on the edge of each set. Thus the Tabernacle was joined together in one piece.

[14]Above the Tabernacle, a roof covering was made from eleven sheets of cloth made from goat hair. [15]Each sheet was exactly the same size—forty-five feet long and six feet wide. [16]The craftsmen joined five of these sheets together to make one set, and the six remaining sheets were joined to make a second set. [17]Then they made fifty loops along the edge of the last sheet in each set. [18]They also made fifty small bronze clasps to couple the loops, so the two sets of sheets were firmly attached to each other. In this way, the roof covering was joined together in one piece. [19]Then they made two more layers for the roof covering. The first was made of tanned ram skins, and the second was made of fine goatskin leather.

36:20-34 Exod 26:15-29; 40:18-19

[20]For the framework of the Tabernacle, they made frames of acacia wood standing on end. [21]Each frame was 15 feet high and 2¼ feet wide. [22]There were two pegs on each frame so they could be joined to the next frame. All the frames were made this way. [23]They made twenty frames to support the south side, [24]along with forty silver bases, two for each frame. [25]They also made twenty frames for the north side of the Tabernacle, [26]along with forty silver bases, two for each frame. [27]The west side of the Tabernacle, which was its rear, was made from six frames, [28]plus an extra frame at each corner. [29]These corner frames were connected at the bottom and firmly attached at the top with a single ring, forming a single unit from top to bottom. They made two of these, one for each rear corner. [30]So for the west side they made a total of eight frames, along with sixteen silver bases, two for each frame.

[31]Then they made five crossbars from acacia wood to tie the frames on the south side together. [32]They made another five for the north side and five for the west side. [33]The middle crossbar of the five was halfway up the frames, along each side, running from one end to the other. [34]The frames and crossbars were all overlaid with gold. The rings used to hold the crossbars were made of pure gold.

36:35-38 Exod 26:31-37

[35]The inner curtain was made of fine linen cloth, and cherubim were skillfully embroidered into it with blue, purple, and scarlet yarn. [36]This curtain was then attached to four gold hooks set into four posts of acacia wood. The posts were overlaid with gold and set into four silver bases.

[37]Then they made another curtain for the entrance to the sacred tent. It was made of fine linen cloth and embroidered with blue, purple, and scarlet yarn. [38]This curtain was

36:9 Hebrew *28 cubits* [12.6 meters] *long and 4 cubits* [1.8 meters] *wide*. In this chapter, the distance measures are calculated from the Hebrew cubit at a ratio of 18 inches or 45 centimeters per cubit.

36:8, 9 Making cloth (spinning and weaving) took a great deal of time in Moses' day. To own more than two or three changes of clothes was a sign of wealth. The effort involved in making enough cloth for the Tabernacle was staggering. The Tabernacle would never have been built without tremendous community involvement. Today, churches and neighborhoods often require this same kind of pulling together. Without it, many essential services wouldn't get done.

36:35 Cherubim are mighty angels.

connected by five hooks to five posts. The posts with their decorated tops and bands were overlaid with gold. The five bases were molded from bronze.

Building the Ark

37 Next Bezalel made the Ark out of acacia wood. It was 3¾ feet long, 2¼ feet wide, and 2¼ feet high.* 2It was overlaid with pure gold inside and out, and it had a molding of gold all the way around. 3Four gold rings were fastened to its four feet, two rings at each side. 4Then he made poles from acacia wood and overlaid them with gold. 5He put the poles into the rings at the sides of the Ark to carry it.

6Then, from pure gold, he made the Ark's cover—the place of atonement. It was 3¾ feet long and 2¼ feet wide. 7He made two figures of cherubim out of hammered gold and placed them at the two ends of the atonement cover. 8They were made so they were actually a part of the atonement cover—it was all one piece. 9The cherubim faced each other as they looked down on the atonement cover, and their wings were stretched out above the atonement cover to protect it.

Building the Table

10Then he made a table out of acacia wood, 3 feet long, 1½ feet wide, and 2¼ feet high. 11It was overlaid with pure gold, with a gold molding all around the edge. 12A rim about 3 inches* wide was attached along the edges of the table, and a gold molding ran around the rim. 13Then he cast four rings of gold and attached them to the four table legs 14next to the rim. These were made to hold the carrying poles in place. 15He made the carrying poles of acacia wood and overlaid them with gold. 16Next, using pure gold, he made the plates, dishes, bowls, and pitchers to be placed on the table. These utensils were to be used in pouring out drink offerings.

Building the Lampstand

17Then he made the lampstand, again using pure, hammered gold. Its base, center stem, lamp cups, blossoms, and buds were all of one piece. 18The lampstand had six branches, three going out from each side of the center stem. 19Each of the six branches held a cup shaped like an almond blossom, complete with buds and petals. 20The center stem of the lampstand was also decorated with four almond blossoms. 21One blossom was set beneath each pair of branches, where they extended from the center stem. 22The decorations and branches were all one piece with the stem, and they were hammered from pure gold. 23He also made the seven lamps, the lamp snuffers, and the trays, all of pure gold. 24The entire lampstand, along with its accessories, was made from seventy-five pounds* of pure gold.

Building the Incense Altar

25The incense altar was made of acacia wood. It was eighteen inches square and three feet high, with its corner horns made from the same piece of wood as the altar itself. 26He overlaid the top, sides, and horns of the altar with pure gold and ran a gold molding around the edge. 27Two gold rings were placed on opposite sides, beneath the molding, to hold the carrying poles. 28The carrying poles were made of acacia wood and were overlaid with gold.

29Then he made the sacred oil, for anointing the priests, and the fragrant incense, using the techniques of the most skilled incense maker.

Building the Altar of Burnt Offering

38 The altar for burning animal sacrifices also was constructed of acacia wood. It was 7½ feet square at the top and 4½ feet high.* 2There were four horns, one at each of the four corners, all of one piece with the rest. This altar was overlaid with

37:1-9 //Exod 25:10-20
37:1 Deut 10:3
37:10-16 //Exod 25:23-29; 40:22
37:17-24 //Exod 25:31-39; 40:24
37:17 Heb 9:2; Rev 1:12
37:25-28 //Exod 30:1-5
37:25 Heb 9:4; Rev 8:3
37:29 Exod 30:22-23; 40:9; Lev 8:10
38:1-7 //Exod 27:1-8; 40:10, 29

37:1 Hebrew *2½ cubits* [1.1 meters] *long, 1½ cubits* [0.7 meters] *wide, and 1½ cubits high.* In this chapter, the distance measures are calculated from the Hebrew cubit at a ratio of 18 inches or 45 centimeters per cubit. **37:12** Hebrew *a handbreadth* [8 centimeters]. **37:24** Hebrew *1 talent* [34 kilograms]. **38:1** Hebrew *5 cubits* [2.3 meters] *square at the top, and 3 cubits* [1.4 meters] *high.* In this chapter, the distance measures are calculated from the Hebrew cubit at a ratio of 18 inches or 45 centimeters per cubit.

37:1 The Ark (also called the Ark of the Covenant) was built to hold the Ten Commandments. It symbolized God's covenant with his people. Two gold angels called cherubim were placed on its top. The Ark was Israel's most sacred object and was kept in the Most Holy Place in the Tabernacle. Only once each year, the high priest entered the Most Holy Place to sprinkle blood on the top of the Ark (called the atonement cover) to atone for the sins of the entire nation.

bronze. 3 Then he made all the bronze utensils to be used with the altar—the ash buckets, shovels, basins, meat hooks, and firepans. 4 Next he made a bronze grating that rested on a ledge about halfway down into the firebox. 5 Four rings were cast for each side of the grating to support the carrying poles. 6 The carrying poles themselves were made of acacia wood and were overlaid with bronze. 7 These poles were inserted into the rings at the side of the altar. The altar was hollow and was made from planks.

Building the Washbasin

38:8
Exod 30:18

8 The bronze washbasin and its bronze pedestal were cast from bronze mirrors donated by the women who served at the entrance of the Tabernacle.*

Building the Courtyard

38:9-20
//Exod 27:9-19; 40:8

9 Then he constructed the courtyard. The south wall was 150 feet long. It consisted of curtains made of fine linen. 10 There were twenty posts, each with its own bronze base, and there were silver hooks and rods to hold up the curtains. 11 The north wall was also 150 feet long, with twenty bronze posts and bases and with silver hooks and rods. 12 The west end was 75 feet wide. The walls were made from curtains supported by ten posts and bases and with silver hooks and rods. 13 The east end was also 75 feet wide.

14 The courtyard entrance was on the east side, flanked by two curtains. The curtain on the right side was 22½ feet long and was supported by three posts set into three bases. 15 The curtain on the left side was also 22½ feet long and was supported by three posts set into three bases. 16 All the curtains used in the courtyard walls were made of fine linen. 17 Each post had a bronze base, and all the hooks and rods were silver. The tops of the posts were overlaid with silver, and the rods to hold up the curtains were solid silver.

18 The curtain that covered the entrance to the courtyard was made of fine linen cloth and embroidered with blue, purple, and scarlet yarn. It was 30 feet long and 7½ feet high, just like the curtains of the courtyard walls. 19 It was supported by four posts set into four bronze bases. The tops of the posts were overlaid with silver, and the hooks and rods were also made of silver.

20 All the tent pegs used in the Tabernacle and courtyard were made of bronze.

Inventory of Materials

21 Here is an inventory of the materials used in building the Tabernacle of the Covenant.* Moses directed the Levites to compile the figures, and Ithamar son of Aaron the priest served as recorder. 22 Bezalel son of Uri, grandson of Hur, of the tribe of Judah, was in charge of the whole project, just as the LORD had commanded Moses. 23 He was assisted by Oholiab son of Ahisamach, of the tribe of Dan, a craftsman expert at engraving, designing, and embroidering blue, purple, and scarlet yarn on fine linen cloth.

24 The people brought gifts of gold totaling about 2,200 pounds,* all of which was used throughout the Tabernacle.

38:25-26
Exod 12:37; 30:11-16
Num 1:46; 26:51

25 The amount of silver that was given was about 7,545 pounds.* 26 It came from the tax of one-fifth of an ounce of silver* collected from each of those registered in the census. This included all the men who were twenty years old or older, 603,550 in all. 27 The 100 bases for the frames of the sanctuary walls and for the posts supporting the inner curtain required 7,500 pounds of silver, about 75 pounds for each base.* 28 The rest of the silver, about 45 pounds,* was used to make the rods and hooks and to overlay the tops of the posts.

29 The people also brought 5,310 pounds* of bronze, 30 which was used for casting the

38:8 Hebrew *Tent of Meeting;* also in 38:30. **38:21** Hebrew *the Tabernacle, the Tabernacle of the Testimony.* **38:24** Hebrew *29 talents* [2,175 pounds or 986 kilograms] *and 730 shekels* [18.3 pounds or 8.3 kilograms], *according to the sanctuary shekel.* **38:25** Hebrew *100 talents* [7,500 pounds or 3,400 kilograms] *and 1,775 shekels* [44.4 pounds or 20.2 kilograms], *according to the sanctuary shekel.* **38:26** Hebrew *1 beka* [6 grams] *per person, that is, half a shekel, according to the sanctuary shekel.* **38:27** Hebrew *100 talents* [3,400 kilograms] *of silver, 1 talent* [34 kilograms] *for each base.* **38:28** Hebrew *1,775 shekels* [20.2 kilograms]. **38:29** Hebrew *70 talents* [5,250 pounds or 2,380 kilograms] *and 2,400 shekels* [60 pounds or 27.4 kilograms].

38:21 In the building of the Tabernacle, Moses laid out the steps, but Ithamar supervised the project. We all have different talents and abilities. God didn't ask Moses to build the Tabernacle but to motivate the experts to do it. Look for the areas where God has gifted you and then seek opportunities to allow God to use your gifts.

bases for the posts at the entrance to the Tabernacle, and for the bronze altar with its
bronze grating and altar utensils. 31 Bronze was also used to make the bases for the posts
that supported the curtains around the courtyard, the bases for the curtain at the entrance
of the courtyard, and all the tent pegs used to hold the curtains of the courtyard in place.

Clothing for the Priests

39 For the priests, the craftsmen made beautiful garments of blue, purple, and **39:1** Exod 35:23
scarlet cloth—clothing to be worn while ministering in the Holy Place. This
same cloth was used for Aaron's sacred garments, just as the LORD had commanded
Moses.

Making the Ephod

2 The ephod was made from fine linen cloth and embroidered with gold thread and blue, **39:2-7** //Exod 28:6-14
purple, and scarlet yarn. 3 A skilled craftsman made gold thread by beating gold into thin
sheets and cutting it into fine strips. He then embroidered it into the linen with the blue,
purple, and scarlet yarn.

4 They made two shoulder-pieces for the ephod, which were attached to its corners so
it could be tied down. 5 They also made an elaborate woven sash of the same materials:
fine linen cloth; blue, purple, and scarlet yarn; and gold thread, just as the LORD had
commanded Moses. 6 The two onyx stones, attached to the shoulder-pieces of the ephod,
were set in gold filigree. The stones were engraved with the names of the tribes of Israel,
just as initials are engraved on a seal. 7 These stones served as reminders to the LORD
concerning the people of Israel. All this was done just as the LORD had commanded
Moses.

Making the Chestpiece

8 The chestpiece was made in the same style as the ephod, crafted from fine linen cloth **39:8-21** //Exod 28:15-28
and embroidered with gold thread and blue, purple, and scarlet yarn. 9 It was doubled
over to form a pouch, nine inches* square. 10 Four rows of gemstones* were set across
it. In the first row were a red carnelian, a chrysolite, and an emerald. 11 In the second row
were a turquoise, a sapphire, and a white moonstone. 12 In the third row were a jacinth,
an agate, and an amethyst. 13 In the fourth row were a beryl, an onyx, and a jasper. Each
of these gemstones was set in gold. 14 The stones were engraved like a seal, each with **39:14** Rev 21:12
the name of one of the twelve tribes of Israel.

15 To attach the chestpiece to the ephod, they made braided cords of pure gold. 16 They
also made two gold rings and attached them to the top corners of the chestpiece. 17 The
two gold cords were put through the gold rings on the chestpiece, 18 and the ends of the
cords were tied to the gold settings on the shoulder-pieces of the ephod. 19 Two more gold
rings were attached to the lower inside corners of the chestpiece next to the ephod.
20 Then two gold rings were attached to the ephod near the sash. 21 Blue cords were used
to attach the bottom rings of the chestpiece to the rings on the ephod. In this way, the
chestpiece was held securely to the ephod above the beautiful sash. All this was done just
as the LORD had commanded Moses.

Additional Clothing for the Priests

22 The robe of the ephod was woven entirely of blue yarn, 23 with an opening for Aaron's **39:22-31** //Exod 28:31-43
head in the middle of it. The edge of this opening was reinforced with a woven collar,*
so it would not tear. 24 Pomegranates were attached to the bottom edge of the robe. These
were finely crafted of blue, purple, and scarlet yarn. 25 Bells of pure gold were placed
between the pomegranates along the hem of the robe, 26 with bells and pomegranates

39:9 Hebrew *1 span* [23 centimeters]. **39:10** The identification of some of these gemstones is uncertain. **39:23** The meaning of the Hebrew is uncertain.

39:1-21 The priests wore a uniform to the Tabernacle each day. Some of the pieces of their uniform were not only beautiful but also significant. Two parts of the high priest's uniform were the ephod and chestpiece. The ephod looked like a vest and was worn over the outer clothing. The chestpiece was fitted to the ephod (and sometimes was called the ephod). The chestpiece was made of colored linens about nine inches square. On its front were attached 12 gemstones, each inscribed with the name of a tribe of Israel. This symbolized how the high priest represented all the people before God. The chestpiece also contained pockets that held two stones or plates called the Urim and Thummim. The high priest could determine God's will for the nation by consulting the Urim and Thummim. (See the notes on 28:30 and Leviticus 8:8.)

alternating all around the hem. This robe was to be worn when Aaron ministered to the
LORD, just as the LORD had commanded Moses.
39:27 Exod 28:39-40, 42 27 Tunics were then made for Aaron and his sons from fine linen cloth. 28 The
turban, the headdresses, and the underclothes were all made of this fine linen. 29 The
39:30 Exod 28:36-37 sashes were made of fine linen cloth and embroidered with blue, purple, and scarlet
yarn, just as the LORD had commanded Moses. 30 Finally, they made the sacred
medallion of pure gold to be worn on the front of the turban. Using the techniques of
an engraver, they inscribed it with these words: SET APART AS HOLY TO THE LORD.
31 This medallion was tied to the turban with a blue cord, just as the LORD had
commanded Moses.

Moses Inspects the Work

39:32-41 //Exod 35:10-19 32 And so at last the Tabernacle* was finished. The Israelites had done everything just
as the LORD had commanded Moses. 33 And they brought the entire Tabernacle to
Moses: the sacred tent with all its furnishings, the clasps, frames, crossbars, posts, and
bases; 34 the layers of tanned ram skins and fine goatskin leather; the inner curtain that
enclosed the Most Holy Place; 35 the Ark of the Covenant* and its carrying poles; the
Ark's cover—the place of atonement; 36 the table and all its utensils; the Bread of
the Presence; 37 the gold lampstand and its accessories; the lamp cups and the oil for
lighting; 38 the gold altar; the anointing oil; the fragrant incense; the curtain for the
entrance of the sacred tent; 39 the bronze altar; the bronze grating; its poles and
utensils; the large washbasin and its pedestal; 40 the curtains for the walls of the
courtyard and the posts and bases holding them up; the curtain at the courtyard
entrance; the cords and tent pegs; all the articles used in the operation of the
Tabernacle; 41 the beautifully crafted garments to be worn while ministering in the
Holy Place—the holy garments for Aaron the priest and for his sons to wear while on
duty.
39:43 Lev 9:22-23 Num 6:23-26 1 Kgs 8:14 2 Chr 30:27 42 So the people of Israel followed all of the LORD's instructions to Moses. 43 Moses
inspected all their work and blessed them because it had been done as the LORD had
commanded him.

The Tabernacle Completed

40:2 Exod 12:2; 19:1; 40:17 Num 1:1 **40** The LORD now said to Moses, 2 "Set up the Tabernacle* on the first day of the
new year.* 3 Place the Ark of the Covenant* inside, and install the inner curtain
40:3 Exod 26:33; 40:21-30 Num 4:5 to enclose the Ark within the Most Holy Place. 4 Then bring in the table, and arrange
the utensils on it. And bring in the lampstand, and set up the lamps.
5 "Place the incense altar just outside the inner curtain, opposite the Ark of the
40:4 Exod 25:30 Covenant. Set up the curtain made for the entrance of the Tabernacle. 6 Place the altar
of burnt offering in front of the Tabernacle entrance. 7 Set the large washbasin between
40:7 Exod 30:18 the Tabernacle* and the altar and fill it with water. 8 Then set up the courtyard around
the outside of the tent, and hang the curtain for the courtyard entrance.
40:9 Exod 30:26 9 "Take the anointing oil and sprinkle it on the Tabernacle and on all its furnishings
to make them holy. 10 Sprinkle the anointing oil on the altar of burnt offering and its

39:32 Hebrew *the Tabernacle, the Tent of Meeting;* also in 39:40. **39:35** Or *Ark of the Testimony.* **40:2a** Hebrew *the Tabernacle, the Tent of Meeting;* also in 40:6, 29. **40:2b** Hebrew *the first day of the first month.* This day of the Hebrew lunar calendar occurs in March or early April. **40:3** Or *Ark of the Testimony;* also in 40:5, 21. **40:7** Hebrew *Tent of Meeting;* also in 40:12, 22, 24, 26, 30, 32, 34, 35.

39:32 The Tabernacle was finally complete to the last detail. God was keenly interested in every minute part. The Creator of the universe was concerned about even the little things. Matthew 10:30 says that God knows the number of hairs on our heads. This shows that God is greatly interested in you. Don't be afraid to talk with him about any of your concerns—no matter how small or unimportant they might seem.

39:42 Moses had learned his management lesson well. He gave important responsibilities to others and then trusted them to do the job. Great leaders, like Moses, give plans and direction while letting others participate on the team. If you are a leader, trust your assistants with key responsibilities.

39:43 Moses inspected the finished work, saw that it was done the way God wanted, and then blessed the people. A good leader follows up on assigned tasks and gives rewards for good work. In whatever responsible position you find yourself, follow up to make sure that tasks are completed as intended, and show your appreciation to the people who have helped.

40:1ff Moses was careful to obey God's instructions in the smallest detail. Notice that he didn't make a reasonable facsimile of God's description, but an exact copy. We should follow Moses' example and be fastidious about our obedience. If God has told you to do something, do it, do it right, and do it completely.

utensils, sanctifying them. Then the altar will become most holy. [11]Next anoint the
large washbasin and its pedestal to make them holy.
[12]"Bring Aaron and his sons to the entrance of the Tabernacle, and wash them with **40:12**
water. [13]Clothe Aaron with the holy garments and anoint him, setting him apart to Lev 8:1-13
serve me as a priest. [14]Then bring his sons and dress them in their tunics. [15]Anoint **40:15**
them as you did their father, so they may serve me as priests. With this anointing, Exod 29:9
Aaron's descendants are set apart for the priesthood forever, from generation to Num 25:13
generation."

[16]Moses proceeded to do everything as the LORD had commanded him. [17]So the **40:17**
Tabernacle was set up on the first day of the new year.* [18]Moses put it together by setting Exod 40:2
its frames into their bases and attaching the crossbars and raising the posts. [19]Then he Num 7:1
spread the coverings over the Tabernacle framework and put on the roof layers, just as
the LORD had commanded him.

[20]He placed inside the Ark the stone tablets inscribed with the terms of the cove- **40:20**
nant,* and then he attached the Ark's carrying poles. He also set the Ark's cover—the Exod 25:16
place of atonement—on top of it. [21]Then he brought the Ark of the Covenant into the Deut 10:5 1 Kgs 8:9 2 Chr 5:10
Tabernacle and set up the inner curtain to shield it from view, just as the LORD had Heb 9:4
commanded.

[22]Next he placed the table in the Tabernacle, along the north side of the Holy Place,
just outside the inner curtain. [23]And he arranged the Bread of the Presence on the table **40:23** Exod 25:30
that stands before the LORD, just as the LORD had commanded. Lev 24:5-8

[24]He set the lampstand in the Tabernacle across from the table on the south side of the
Holy Place. [25]Then he set up the lamps in the LORD's presence, just as the LORD had
commanded. [26]He also placed the incense altar in the Tabernacle, in the Holy Place in
front of the inner curtain. [27]On it he burned the fragrant incense made from sweet spices,
just as the LORD had commanded.

[28]He attached the curtain at the entrance of the Tabernacle, [29]and he placed the altar
of burnt offering near the Tabernacle entrance. On it he offered a burnt offering and a
grain offering, just as the LORD had commanded.

[30]Next he placed the large washbasin between the Tabernacle and the altar. He filled
it with water so the priests could use it to wash themselves. [31]Moses and Aaron and **40:31**
Aaron's sons washed their hands and feet in the basin. [32]Whenever they walked past Exod 30:19-21
the altar to enter the Tabernacle, they were to stop and wash, just as the LORD had
commanded Moses.

[33]Then he hung the curtains forming the courtyard around the Tabernacle and the altar.
And he set up the curtain at the entrance of the courtyard. So at last Moses finished the
work.

The LORD's Glory Fills the Tabernacle

[34]Then the cloud covered the Tabernacle, and the glorious presence of the LORD **40:34**
filled it. [35]Moses was no longer able to enter the Tabernacle because the cloud had Num 9:15-23 1 Kgs 8:11
settled down over it, and the Tabernacle was filled with the awesome glory of the **40:35**
LORD. 1 Kgs 8:1

40:17 Hebrew *the first day of the first month, in the second year.* See note on 40:2b. **40:20** Hebrew *the Testimony.*

40:16 God told Moses how to build the Tabernacle, and Moses delegated jobs in order to do it. God allows people to participate with him in carrying out his will. Your task is not just to sit and watch God work, but to give your best effort when work needs to be done.

40:17-33 The physical care of the Tabernacle required a long list of tasks, and each was important to the work of God's house. This principle is important to remember today when God's house is the church. There are many seemingly unimportant tasks that must be done to keep your church building maintained. Washing dishes, painting walls, or shoveling snow may not seem very spiritual. But they are vital to the ministry of the church and are an important part of our worship of God.

40:34 The Tabernacle was God's home on earth. He filled it with his glory—the overpowering sense of his presence. Almost 500 years later, Solomon built the Temple, which replaced the Tabernacle as the central place of worship. God also filled the Temple with his glory (2 Chronicles 5:13, 14). But when Israel turned from God, his glory and presence departed from the Temple, and it was destroyed by invading armies (2 Kings 25). The Temple was rebuilt in 515 B.C. God's glory returned in even greater splendor nearly five centuries later when Jesus Christ, God's Son, entered it and taught. When Jesus was crucified, God's glory again left the Temple. However, God no longer needed a physical building after Jesus rose from the dead. God's temple now is his church, the body of believers.

40:36 Num 9:17; 10:11
40:37 Num 9:19-22
40:38 1 Cor 10:1

36 Now whenever the cloud lifted from the Tabernacle and moved, the people of Israel
would set out on their journey, following it. 37 But if the cloud stayed, they would stay
until it moved again. 38 The cloud of the LORD rested on the Tabernacle during the day,
and at night there was fire in the cloud so all the people of Israel could see it. This
continued throughout all their journeys.

40:38 The Israelites were once Egyptian slaves making bricks without straw. Here they were following the pillar of cloud and the pillar of fire, carrying the Tabernacle they had built for God. Exodus begins in gloom and ends in glory. This parallels our progress through the Christian life. We begin as slaves to sin, are redeemed by God, and end our pilgrimage living with God forever. The lessons the Israelites learned along the way are ones we also need to learn.

LEVITICUS

Joseph dies 1805 B.C. (1640 B.C.)

S L A V E R Y   I N   E G Y P T

VITAL STATISTICS

PURPOSE:
A handbook for the priests and Levites outlining their duties in worship, and a guidebook of holy living for the Hebrews

AUTHOR:
Moses

DATE OF EVENTS:
1445–1444 B.C.

SETTING:
At the foot of Mount Sinai. God is teaching the Israelites how to live as holy people.

KEY VERSE:
"You must be holy because I, the LORD your God, am holy" (19:2).

KEY PEOPLE:
Moses, Aaron, Nadab, Abihu, Eleazar, Ithamar

KEY PLACE:
Mount Sinai

SPECIAL FEATURE:
Holiness is mentioned more times (152) than in any other book of the Bible.

"GOD seems so far away . . . if only I could see or hear him." Have you ever felt this way—struggling with loneliness, burdened by despair, riddled with sin, overwhelmed by problems? Made in God's image, we were created to have a close relationship with him; and when fellowship is broken, we are incomplete and need restoration. Communion with the living God is the essence of worship. It is vital, touching the very core of our lives. Perhaps this is why a whole book of the Bible is dedicated to worship. After Israel's dramatic exit from Egypt, the nation was camped at the foot of Mount Sinai for two years to listen to God (Exodus 19 to Numbers 10). It was a time of resting, teaching, building, and meeting with him face to face. Redemption in Exodus is the foundation for cleansing, worship, and service in Leviticus.

The overwhelming message of Leviticus is the holiness of God—"You must be holy because I, the LORD your God, am holy" (19:2). But how can unholy people approach a holy God? The answer—first sin must be dealt with. Thus the opening chapters of Leviticus give detailed instructions for offering sacrifices, which were the active symbols of repentance and obedience. Whether bulls, grain, goats, or sheep, the sacrificial offerings had to be perfect, with no defects or bruises—pictures of the ultimate sacrifice to come, Jesus, the Lamb of God. Jesus has come and opened the way to God by giving up his life as the final sacrifice in our place. True worship and oneness with God begin as we confess our sin and accept Christ as the only one who can redeem us from sin and help us approach God.

In Leviticus, sacrifices, priests, and the sacred Day of Atonement opened the way for the Israelites to come to God. God's people were also to worship him with their lives. Thus we read of purity laws (chapters 11—15) and rules for daily living concerning family responsibilities, sexual conduct, relationships, worldliness (chapters 18—20), and vows (chapter 27). These instructions involve one's holy walk with God, and the patterns of spiritual living still apply today. Worship, therefore, has a horizontal aspect—that is, God is honored by our lives as we relate to others.

The final emphasis in Leviticus is celebration. The book gives instructions for the feasts. These were special, regular, and corporate occasions for remembering what God had done, giving thanks to him, and rededicating lives to his service (chapter 23). Our Christian traditions and holidays are different, but they are necessary ingredients of worship. We, too, need special days of worship and celebration with our brothers and sisters to remember God's goodness in our lives.

As you read Leviticus, rededicate yourself to holiness, worshiping God in private confession, public service, and group celebration.

Exodus from Egypt 1446 (1280)	Ten Commandments given 1445 (1279)	Israel camps at Mount Sinai 1444 (1278)	Moses dies, Canaan entered 1406 (1240)	Judges begin to rule 1375 (1220)	United kingdom under Saul 1050 (1045)

THE BLUEPRINT

A. WORSHIPING A HOLY GOD (1:1—17:16) 1. Instructions for the offerings 2. Instructions for the priests 3. Instructions for the people 4. Instructions for the altar	God provided specific directions for the kind of worship that would be pleasing to him. These instructions teach us about the nature of God and can help us develop a right attitude toward worship. Through the offerings we learn of the seriousness of sin and the importance of bringing our sins to God for forgiveness.
B. LIVING A HOLY LIFE (18:1—27:34) 1. Standards for the people 2. Rules for priests 3. Seasons and festivals 4. Receiving God's blessing	God gave clear standards to the Israelites for living a holy life. They were to be separate and distinct from the pagan nations around them. In the same way, all believers should be separated from sin and dedicated to God. God still wants to remove sin from the lives of his people.

MEGATHEMES

THEME	EXPLANATION	IMPORTANCE
Sacrifice/Offering	There are five kinds of offerings that fulfill two main purposes: one to show praise, thankfulness, and devotion; the other for atonement, the covering and removal of guilt and sin. Animal offerings demonstrated that the person was giving his or her life to God by means of the life of the animal.	The sacrifices (offerings) were for worship and forgiveness of sin. Through them we learn about the cost of sin, for we see that we cannot forgive ourselves. God's system says that a life must be given for a life. In the Old Testament, an animal's life was given to save the life of a person. But this was only a temporary measure until Jesus' death paid the penalty of sin for all people forever.
Worship	Seven festivals were designated as religious and national holidays. They were often celebrated in family settings. These events teach us much about worshiping God in both celebration and quiet dedication.	God's rules about worship set up an orderly, regular pattern of fellowship with him. They allowed times for celebration and thanksgiving as well as for reverence and rededication. Our worship should demonstrate our deep devotion.
Health	Civil rules for handling food, disease, and sex were taught. In these physical principles, many spiritual principles were suggested. Israel was to be different from the surrounding nations. God was preserving Israel from disease and community health problems.	We are to be different morally and spiritually from the unbelievers around us. Principles for healthy living are as important today as in Moses' time. A healthy environment and a healthy body make our service to God more effective.
Holiness	*Holy* means "separated" or "devoted." God removed his people from Egypt; now he was removing Egypt from the people. He was showing them how to exchange Egyptian ways of living and thinking for his ways.	We must devote every area of life to God. God desires absolute obedience in motives as well as practices. Though we do not observe all the worship practices of Israel, we are to have the same spirit of preparation and devotion.
Levites	The Levites and priests instructed the people in their worship. They were the ministers of their day. They also regulated the moral, civil, and ceremonial laws and supervised the health, justice, and welfare of the nation.	The Levites were servants who showed Israel the way to God. They provide the historical backdrop for Christ, who is our High Priest and yet our Servant. God's true servants care for all the needs of their people.

A. WORSHIPING A HOLY GOD (1:1—17:16)

The Israelites have arrived safely at the foot of Mount Sinai, and the Tabernacle has been completed. The people will spend a great deal of time here as God shows them a new way of life with clear instructions on how sinful people can relate to a holy God. These instructions help us avoid taking our relationship with the same holy God too lightly. We learn about the holiness and majesty of the God with whom we are allowed to have a personal relationship.

1. Instructions for the offerings

Procedures for the Burnt Offering

1 The LORD called to Moses from the Tabernacle* and said to him, [2]"Give the following instructions to the Israelites: Whenever you present offerings to the LORD, you must bring animals from your flocks and herds.
[3]"If your sacrifice for a whole burnt offering is from the herd, bring a bull with no

1:1 Exod 25:22 Num 7:89
1:2 Lev 6:9-13; 17:1-8
1:3 Heb 9:14

1:1 Hebrew *Tent of Meeting;* also in 1:3, 5.

THE ISRAELITES AT MOUNT SINAI Throughout the book of Leviticus, the Israelites were camped at the foot of Mount Sinai. It was time to regroup as a nation and learn the importance of following God as they prepared to march toward the Promised Land.

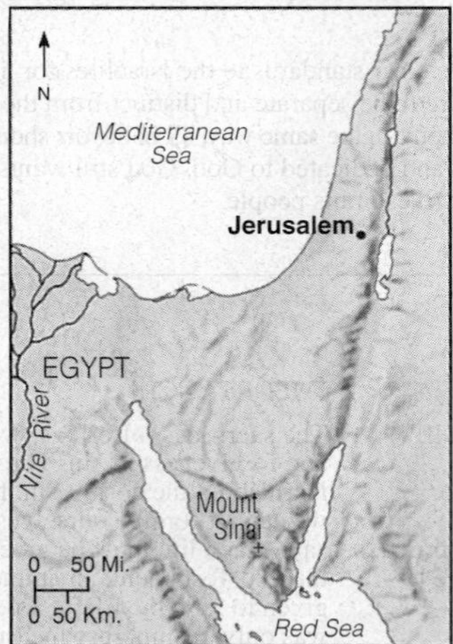

1:1 The book of Leviticus begins where the book of Exodus ends—at the foot of Mount Sinai. The Tabernacle was just completed (Exodus 35—40), and God was ready to teach the people how to worship there.

1:1 The "Tabernacle" where God met with Moses was actually the Tent of Meeting, a smaller structure inside the larger Tabernacle. The Tent of Meeting contained the sanctuary in one part and the Most Holy Place with the Ark in another part. These two sections were separated by a curtain. God revealed himself to Moses in the Most Holy Place. Exodus 33:7 mentions a "Tent of Meeting" where Moses met God before the Tabernacle was constructed. Many believe it served the same function as the one described here.

1:1ff We may be tempted to dismiss Leviticus as a record of bizarre rituals of a different age. But its practices made sense to the people of the day and offer important insights for us into God's nature and character. Animal sacrifice seems obsolete and repulsive to many people today, but animal sacrifices were practiced in many cultures in the Middle East. God used the form of sacrifice to teach his people about faith. Sin needed to be taken seriously. When people saw the sacrificial animals being killed, they were sensitized to the importance of their sin and guilt. Our culture's casual attitude toward sin ignores the cost of sin and need for repentance and restoration. Although many of the rituals of Leviticus were designed for the culture of the day, their purpose was to reveal a high and holy God who should be loved, obeyed, and worshiped. God's laws and sacrifices were intended to bring out true devotion of the heart. The ceremonies and rituals were the best way for the Israelites to focus their lives on God.

1:2 Was there any difference between a sacrifice and an offering? In Leviticus the words are interchanged. Usually a specific sacrifice is called an offering (burnt offering, grain offering, peace offering). Offerings in general are called sacrifices. The point is that each person *offered* a gift to God by *sacrificing* it on the altar. In the Old Testament, the sacrifice was the only way to approach God and restore a relationship with him. There was more than one kind of offering or sacrifice. The variety of sacrifices made them more meaningful because each one related to a specific life situation. Sacrifices were given in praise, worship, and thanksgiving, as well as for forgiveness and fellowship. The first seven chapters of Leviticus describe the variety of offerings and how they were to be used.

1:2 When God taught his people to worship him, he placed great emphasis on sacrifices. Why? Sacrifices were God's Old Testament way for people to ask for forgiveness for their sins. Since Creation, God has made it clear that sin separates people from him, and that those who sin deserve to die. Because "all have sinned" (Romans 3:23), God designed sacrifice as a way to seek forgiveness and restore a relationship with him. Because he is a God of love and mercy, God decided from the very first that he would come into our world and die to pay the penalty for all humans. This he did in his Son, who, while still God, became a human being. In the meantime, before God made this ultimate sacrifice of his Son, he instructed people to kill animals as sacrifices for sin.

Animal sacrifice accomplished two purposes: (1) The animal symbolically took the sinner's place and paid the penalty for sin, and (2) the animal's death represented one life given so that another life could be saved. This method of sacrifice continued throughout Old Testament times. It was effective in teaching and guiding the people and bringing them back to God. But in New Testament times, Christ's death became the last sacrifice needed. He took our punishment once and for all. Animal sacrifice is no longer required. Now all people can be freed from the penalty of sin by simply believing in Jesus and accepting the forgiveness he offers.

1:3, 4 The first offering God describes is the burnt offering. A person who had sinned brought an animal with no defects to a priest. The unblemished animal symbolized the moral perfection demanded by a holy God and the perfect nature of the real sacrifice to come—Jesus Christ. The person then laid his hand on the head of the animal to symbolize the person's complete identification with the animal as his substitute. Then he killed the animal, and the priest sprinkled the blood. He symbolically transferred his sins to the animal, and thus his sins were taken away (atonement). Finally the animal (except for the blood and skin) was burned on the altar, signifying the person's complete dedication to God. God required more than a sacrifice, of course. He also asked the sinner to have an attitude of repentance. The outward symbol (the sacrifice) and the inner change (repentance) were to work together. But it is important to remember that neither sacrifice nor repentance actually caused the sin to be taken away. God alone forgives sin. Fortunately for us, forgiveness is part of God's loving nature. Have you come to him to receive forgiveness?

1:4 Exod 29:10, 15, 19; Lev 4:13-35; Num 8:10-12; 15:25; 2 Chr 29:23-24
1:5 Lev 1:11; 3:8; Heb 12:24
1:6 Lev 7:8; Neh 13:31
1:8 Exod 29:13
1:9 Gen 8:21; Exod 29:17; Eph 5:2
1:14 Gen 15:9; Lev 12:8
1:15 Lev 5:9

physical defects to the entrance of the Tabernacle so it will be accepted by the LORD.
4 Lay your hand on its head so the LORD will accept it as your substitute, thus making
atonement for you. 5 Then slaughter the animal in the LORD's presence, and Aaron's sons,
the priests, will present the blood by sprinkling it against the sides of the altar that stands
in front of the Tabernacle. 6 When the animal has been skinned and cut into pieces, 7 the
sons of Aaron the priest will build a wood fire on the altar. 8 Aaron's sons will then put
the pieces of the animal, including its head and fat, on the wood fire. 9 But the internal
organs and legs must first be washed with water. Then the priests will burn the entire
sacrifice on the altar. It is a whole burnt offering made by fire, very pleasing to the LORD.
10 "If your sacrifice for a whole burnt offering is from the flock, bring a male sheep or
goat with no physical defects. 11 Slaughter the animal on the north side of the altar in the LORD's
presence. Aaron's sons, the priests, will sprinkle its blood against the sides of the altar.
12 Then you must cut the animal in pieces, and the priests will lay the pieces of the sacrifice,
including the head and fat, on top of the wood fire on the altar. 13 The internal organs and
legs must first be washed with water. Then the priests will burn the entire sacrifice on the
altar. It is a whole burnt offering made by fire, very pleasing to the LORD.
14 "If you bring a bird as a burnt offering to the LORD, choose either a turtledove or a
young pigeon. 15 The priest will take the bird to the altar, twist off its head, and burn the
head on the altar. He must then let its blood drain out against the sides of the altar. 16 The
priest must remove the crop and the feathers* and throw them to the east side of the altar
among the ashes. 17 Then, grasping the bird by its wings, the priest will tear the bird apart,
though not completely. Then he will burn it on top of the wood fire on the altar. It is a
whole burnt offering made by fire, very pleasing to the LORD.

1:16 Or *the crop and its contents.* The meaning of the Hebrew is uncertain.

THE OFFERINGS
Listed here are the five key offerings the Israelites made to God. They made these offerings in order to have their sins forgiven and to restore their fellowship with God. The death of Jesus Christ made these sacrifices unnecessary. Because of his death, our sins were completely forgiven, and fellowship with God has been restored.

Offering	*Purpose*	*Significance*	*Christ, the Perfect Offering*
Burnt Offering (Lev. 1—voluntary)	To make payment for sins in general	Showed a person's devotion to God	Christ's death was the perfect offering
Grain Offering (Lev. 2—voluntary)	To show honor and respect to God in worship	Acknowledged that all we have belongs to God	Christ was the perfect man, who gave all of himself to God and others
Peace Offering (Lev. 3—voluntary)	To express gratitude to God	Symbolized peace and fellowship with God	Christ is the only way to fellowship with God
Sin Offering (Lev. 4—required)	To make payment for unintentional sins of uncleanness, neglect, or thoughtlessness	Restored the sinner to fellowship with God; showed seriousness of sin	Christ's death restores our fellowship with God
Guilt Offering (Lev. 5—required)	To make payment for sins against God and others. A sacrifice was made to God, and the injured person was repaid or compensated	Provided compensation for injured parties	Christ's death takes away the deadly consequences of sin

1:3ff What did sacrifices teach the people? (1) By requiring perfect animals and holy priests, they taught reverence for a holy God. (2) By demanding exact obedience, they taught total submission to God's laws. (3) By requiring an animal of great value, they showed the high cost of sin and demonstrated the sincerity of their commitment to God.

1:3-13 Why are there such detailed regulations for each offering? God had a purpose in giving these commands. Starting from scratch, he was teaching his people a whole new way of life, cleansing them from the many pagan practices they had learned in Egypt and restoring true worship of himself. The strict details kept Israel from slipping back into their old lifestyle. In addition, each law paints a graphic picture of the seriousness of sin and of God's great mercy in forgiving sinners.

1:4ff Israel was not the only nation to sacrifice animals. Many other religions did it as well to try to please their gods. Some cultures even included human sacrifice, which was strictly forbidden by God. However, the meaning of Israel's animal sacrifices was clearly different from that of their pagan neighbors' sacrifices. Israelites sacrificed animals, not just to appease God's wrath, but as a substitute for the punishment they deserved for their sins. A sacrifice showed faith in God and commitment to his laws. Most important, this system foreshadowed the day when the Lamb of God (Jesus Christ) would die and conquer sin once and for all.

Procedures for the Grain Offering

2 "When you bring a grain offering to the LORD, the offering must consist of choice
flour. You are to pour olive oil on it and sprinkle it with incense. 2 Bring this offering
to one of Aaron's sons, and he will take a handful of the flour mixed with olive oil,
together with all the incense, and burn this token portion on the altar fire. It is an offering
made by fire, very pleasing to the LORD. 3 The rest of the flour will be given to Aaron
and his sons. It will be considered a most holy part of the offerings given to the LORD by
fire.
4 "When you present some kind of baked bread as a grain offering, it must be made of
choice flour mixed with olive oil but without any yeast. It may be presented in the form
of cakes mixed with olive oil or wafers spread with olive oil. 5 If your grain offering is
cooked on a griddle, it must be made of choice flour and olive oil, and it must contain
no yeast. 6 Break it into pieces and pour oil on it; it is a kind of grain offering. 7 If your
offering is prepared in a pan, it also must be made of choice flour and olive oil.
8 "No matter how a grain offering has been prepared before being offered to the LORD,
bring it to the priests who will present it at the altar. 9 The priests will take a token portion
of the grain offering and burn it on the altar as an offering made by fire, and it will be
very pleasing to the LORD. 10 The rest of the grain offering will be given to Aaron and his
sons as their food. It will be considered a most holy part of the offerings given to the
LORD by fire.
11 "Do not use yeast in any of the grain offerings you present to the LORD, because no
yeast or honey may be burned as an offering to the LORD by fire. 12 You may add yeast
and honey to the offerings presented at harvesttime, but these must never be burned on
the altar as an offering pleasing to the LORD. 13 Season all your grain offerings with salt,
to remind you of God's covenant. Never forget to add salt to your grain offerings.
14 "If you present a grain offering to the LORD from the first portion of your harvest,
bring kernels of new grain that have been roasted on a fire. 15 Since it is a grain offering,
put olive oil on it and sprinkle it with incense. 16 The priests will take a token portion of
the roasted grain mixed with olive oil, together with all the incense, and burn it as an
offering given to the LORD by fire.

Procedures for the Peace Offering

3 "If you want to present a peace offering from the herd, use either a bull or a cow.
The animal you offer to the LORD must have no physical defects. 2 Lay your hand on
the animal's head, and slaughter it at the entrance of the Tabernacle.* Aaron's sons, the
priests, will then sprinkle the animal's blood against the sides of the altar. 3 Part of this
peace offering must be presented to the LORD as an offering made by fire. This includes
the fat around the internal organs, 4 the two kidneys with the fat around them near the
loins, and the lobe of the liver, which is to be removed with the kidneys. 5 The sons of

3:2 Hebrew *Tent of Meeting;* also in 3:8, 13.

2:1 Exod 29:2; Lev 6:14-18; 24:7; Num 15:4-21
2:2 Lev 5:12-13; 6:15-18
2:3 Lev 10:12-13
2:4 Exod 29:2; Lev 7:12
2:9 Gen 8:21; Lev 2:2; 6:15
2:10 Lev 2:3
2:11 Lev 6:16-17
2:12 Lev 7:13; 23:9-14
2:13 Num 18:19; 2 Chr 13:5; Ezek 43:24; Mark 9:49
2:14 Lev 23:9-14; 2 Kgs 4:42
2:16 Lev 2:1-2
3:1 Lev 1:3; 7:11-21
3:2 Exod 29:11; Lev 1:4; 7:14
3:3 Exod 29:13, 22; Lev 3:9-11
3:5 Num 15:8-10

2:1ff The grain offering accompanied all burnt offerings and was a gift of thanks to God. It reminded the people that their food came from God and that they therefore owed their lives to him. Three kinds of grain offerings are listed: (1) fine flour with oil and incense, (2) baked cakes or wafers of fine flour and oil, and (3) roasted kernels of grain (corn) with oil and incense. The absence of yeast symbolized the absence of sin, and the oil symbolized God's presence. Part of the grain offering was burned on the altar as a gift to God, and the rest was eaten by the priests. The offerings helped support them in their work.

2:11 Why was no yeast allowed in the grain offerings? Yeast is a bacterial fungus or mold and is, therefore, an appropriate symbol for sin. It grows in bread dough just as sin grows in a life. A little yeast will affect the whole loaf, just as a little sin can ruin a whole life. Jesus continued this analogy by warning about the "yeast of the Pharisees and Sadducees" (Matthew 16:6; Mark 8:15).

2:13 The offerings were seasoned with salt as a reminder of the people's covenant (contract) with God. Salt is a good symbol of God's activity in a person's life because it penetrates, preserves, and aids in healing. God wants to be active in your life. Let him become part of you, penetrating every aspect of your life, preserving you from the evil all around, and healing you of your sins and shortcomings.

2:13 In Arab countries, an agreement was sealed with a gift of salt to show the strength and permanence of the contract. In Matthew 5:13 believers are called "the salt of the earth." Let the salt you use each day remind you that you are now one of God's covenant people, who actively help preserve and purify the world.

2:14, 15 Crushed heads of new grain mixed with oil and baked was typical food for the average person. This offering was a token presentation of a person's daily food. In this way, people acknowledged God as provider of their food. Even a poor person could fulfill this offering. God was pleased by the motivation and the dedication of the persons making it.

3:1ff A person gave a peace offering as an expression of gratitude and a means of establishing fellowship between himself and God. Because it symbolized peace with God, part of the offering could be eaten by the person presenting it.

Aaron will burn these on the altar on top of the burnt offering on the wood fire. It is an
offering made by fire, very pleasing to the LORD.
6 "If you present a peace offering to the LORD from the flock, you may bring either a
goat or a sheep. It may be either male or female, and it must have no physical defects.
7 If you bring a sheep as your gift, present it to the LORD 8 by laying your hand on its head
and slaughtering it at the entrance of the Tabernacle. The sons of Aaron will then sprinkle
the sheep's blood against the sides of the altar. 9 Part of this peace offering must be
presented to the LORD as an offering made by fire. This includes the fat of the entire tail
cut off near the backbone, the fat around the internal organs, 10 the two kidneys with the
fat around them near the loins, and the lobe of the liver, which is to be removed with the
kidneys. 11 The priest will burn them on the altar as food, an offering given to the LORD
by fire.
12 "If you bring a goat as your offering to the LORD, 13 lay your hand on its head, and
slaughter it at the entrance of the Tabernacle. Then the sons of Aaron will sprinkle the
goat's blood against the sides of the altar. 14 Part of this offering must be presented to the
LORD as an offering made by fire. This part includes the fat around the internal organs,
15 the two kidneys with the fat around them near the loins, and the lobe of the liver, which
is to be removed with the kidneys. 16 The priest will burn them on the altar as food, an
offering made by fire; these will be very pleasing to the LORD. Remember, all the fat
belongs to the LORD.
17 "You must never eat any fat or blood. This is a permanent law for you and all your
descendants, wherever they may live."

Procedures for the Sin Offering

4 Then the LORD said to Moses, 2 "Give the Israelites the following instructions for
dealing with those who sin unintentionally by doing anything forbidden by the
LORD's commands.
3 "If the high priest sins, bringing guilt upon the entire community, he must bring to
the LORD a young bull with no physical defects. 4 He must present the bull to the LORD
at the entrance of the Tabernacle,* lay his hand on the bull's head, and slaughter it there
in the LORD's presence. 5 The priest on duty will then take some of the animal's blood
into the Tabernacle, 6 dip his finger into the blood, and sprinkle it seven times before the
LORD in front of the inner curtain of the Most Holy Place. 7 The priest will put some of
the blood on the horns of the incense altar that stands in the LORD's presence in the
Tabernacle. The rest of the bull's blood must be poured out at the base of the altar of
burnt offerings at the entrance of the Tabernacle. 8 The priest must remove all the fat
around the bull's internal organs, 9 the two kidneys with the fat around them near the
loins, and the lobe of the liver. 10 Then he must burn them on the altar of burnt offerings,
just as is done with the bull or cow sacrificed as a peace offering. 11 But the rest of the
bull—its hide, meat, head, legs, internal organs, and dung—12 must be carried away to a
ceremonially clean place outside the camp, the place where the ashes are thrown. He will
burn it all on a wood fire in the ash heap.
13 "If the entire Israelite community does something forbidden by the LORD and the
matter escapes the community's notice, all the people will be guilty. 14 When they
discover their sin, the leaders of the community must bring a young bull for a sin offering
and present it at the entrance of the Tabernacle. 15 The leaders must then lay their hands
on the bull's head and slaughter it there before the LORD. 16 The priest will bring some
of its blood into the Tabernacle, 17 dip his finger into the blood, and sprinkle it seven times

3:6 Lev 3:1
3:12 Num 15:6-11
3:13 Lev 1:5
3:15-16 Lev 4:26; 7:23-25
3:17 Lev 7:26-27; 17:10; Deut 12:16; Acts 15:20
4:2 Lev 4:22; 22:14; Num 15:22-29
4:3 Lev 4:14; 9:2; Ezek 43:19
4:5 Lev 4:17; 16:14
4:7 Lev 8:15
4:8 Lev 3:3
4:11 Lev 6:11; Num 19:5; Heb 13:11
4:13 Num 15:23-26
4:14 Lev 4:3
4:15 Lev 8:14; Num 8:10-12
4:17 Lev 4:6

4:4 Hebrew *Tent of Meeting;* also in 4:5, 7, 14, 16, 18.

4:1ff Have you ever done something wrong without realizing it until later? Although your sin was unintentional, it was still sin. One of the purposes of God's commands was to make the Israelites aware of their unintentional sins so they would not repeat them and so they could be forgiven for them. Leviticus 4 and 5 mention some of these unintentional sins and the way the Israelites could be forgiven for them. As you read more of God's laws, keep in mind that they were meant to teach and guide the people. Let them help you become more aware of sin in your life.

4:3 The sin offering was for those who (1) committed a sin without realizing it or (2) committed a sin out of weakness or negligence as opposed to outright rebellion against God. Different animals were sacrificed for the different kinds of sin. The death of Jesus Christ was the final sin offering in the Bible (Hebrews 9:25-28 tells why).

before the LORD in front of the inner curtain. 18 He will then put some of the blood on the
horns of the incense altar that stands in the LORD's presence in the Tabernacle. The rest
of the blood must then be poured out at the base of the altar of burnt offerings at the
entrance of the Tabernacle. 19 The priest must remove all the animal's fat and burn it on **4:19**
the altar, 20 following the same procedure as with the sin offering for the priest. In this Lev 4:8
way, the priest will make atonement for the people, and they will be forgiven. 21 The **4:20** Num 15:25
priest must then take what is left of the bull outside the camp and burn it there, just as is **4:21**
done with the sin offering for the high priest. This is a sin offering for the entire Lev 4:12
community of Israel.

22 "If one of Israel's leaders does something forbidden by the LORD his God, he will **4:22**
be guilty even if he sinned unintentionally. 23 When he becomes aware of his sin, he must Lev 4:2, 13
bring as his offering a male goat with no physical defects. 24 He is to lay his hand on the **4:24**
goat's head and slaughter it before the LORD at the place where burnt offerings are Lev 6:25
slaughtered. This will be his sin offering. 25 Then the priest will dip his finger into the **4:25** Lev 4:7
blood of the sin offering, put it on the horns of the altar of burnt offerings, and pour out
the rest of the blood at the base of the altar. 26 He must burn all the goat's fat on the altar, **4:26**
just as is done with the peace offering. In this way, the priest will make atonement for Lev 4:19-20
the leader's sin, and he will be forgiven.

27 "If any of the citizens of Israel* do something forbidden by the LORD, they will be **4:27**
guilty even if they sinned unintentionally. 28 When they become aware of their sin, they Lev 4:2
must bring as their offering a female goat with no physical defects. It will be offered for **4:28** Lev 4:23
their sin. 29 They are to lay a hand on the head of the sin offering and slaughter it at the
place where burnt offerings are slaughtered. 30 The priest will then dip his finger into the **4:30**
blood, put the blood on the horns of the altar of burnt offerings, and pour out the rest of Lev 4:7
the blood at the base of the altar. 31 Those who are guilty must remove all the goat's fat, **4:31**
just as is done with the peace offering. Then the priest will burn the fat on the altar, and Gen 8:21 Exod 29:18
it will be very pleasing to the LORD. In this way, the priest will make atonement for them, Lev 2:2; 4:8; 6:15
and they will be forgiven.

32 "If any of the people bring a sheep as their sin offering, it must be a female with no **4:32**
physical defects. 33 They are to lay a hand on the head of the sin offering and slaughter Lev 4:28
it at the place where the burnt offerings are slaughtered. 34 The priest will then dip his
finger into the blood, put it on the horns of the altar of burnt offerings, and pour out the
rest of the blood at the base of the altar. 35 Those who are guilty must remove all the **4:35**
sheep's fat, just as is done with a sheep presented as a peace offering. Then the priest will Lev 3:5
burn the fat on the altar on top of the offerings given to the LORD by fire. In this way, the
priest will make atonement for them, and they will be forgiven.

Sins Requiring a Sin Offering

5 "If any of the people are called to testify about something they have witnessed, but **5:1** Prov 29:24
they refuse to testify, they will be held responsible and be subject to punishment. **5:2**
2 "Or if they touch something that is ceremonially unclean, such as the dead body of Lev 11:4-11, 24-39 Num 19:11-16
an animal that is ceremonially unclean—whether a wild animal, a domesticated animal, Deut 14:3-21
or an animal that scurries along the ground—they will be considered ceremonially
unclean and guilty, even if they are unaware of their defilement.
3 "Or if they come into contact with any source of human defilement, even if they don't

4:27 Hebrew *people of the land.*

5:4 Have you ever sworn to do or not do something and then realized how foolish your promise was? God's people are called to keep their word, even if they make promises that are tough to keep. Jesus was warning against swearing (in the sense of making vows or oaths) when he said, "Just say a simple, 'Yes, I will,' or 'No, I won't.' Your word is enough. To strengthen your promise with a vow shows that something is wrong" (Matthew 5:37). Our word should be enough. If we feel we have to strengthen it with an oath, something is wrong with our sincerity. The only promises we ought not to keep are promises that lead to sin. A wise and self-controlled person avoids making rash promises.

5:5 The entire system of sacrifices could not help a sinner unless he brought his offering with an attitude of repentance and a willingness to confess sin. Today, because of Christ's death on the cross, we do not have to sacrifice animals. But it is still vital to confess sin, because confession shows realization of sin, awareness of God's holiness, humility before God, and willingness to turn from this sin (Psalm 51:16, 17). Even Jesus' death will be of little value to us if we do not repent and follow him. It is like a vaccine for a dangerous disease—it won't help unless it enters the bloodstream.

realize they have been defiled, they will be considered guilty as soon as they become aware of it.

5:4 Num 30:6-8

4“Or if they make a rash vow of any kind, whether its purpose is for good or bad, they will be considered guilty even if they were not fully aware of what they were doing at the time.

5:5 Lev 16:21; Num 5:7; Josh 7:19
5:6 Lev 4:28, 32
5:7 Lev 12:8; Luke 2:24
5:8 Lev 1:15, 17
5:9 Lev 4:7; 7:2
5:10 Lev 1:14-17

5“When any of the people become aware of their guilt in any of these ways, they must confess their sin 6and bring to the LORD as their penalty a female from the flock, either a sheep or a goat. This will be a sin offering to remove their sin, and the priest will make atonement for them.

7“If any of them cannot afford to bring a sheep, they must bring to the LORD two young turtledoves or two young pigeons as the penalty for their sin. One of the birds will be a sin offering, and the other will be a burnt offering. 8They must bring them to the priest, who will offer one of the birds as the sin offering. The priest will wring its neck but without severing its head from the body. 9Then he will sprinkle some of the blood of the sin offering against the sides of the altar, and the rest will be drained out at the base of the altar. 10The priest will offer the second bird as a whole burnt offering, following all the procedures that have been prescribed. In this way, the priest will make atonement for those who are guilty, and they will be forgiven.

5:11 Lev 14:21; †Luke 2:24

11“If any of the people cannot afford to bring young turtledoves or pigeons, they must bring two quarts* of choice flour for their sin offering. Since it is a sin offering, they must not mix it with olive oil or put any incense on it. 12They must take the flour to the priest, who will scoop out a handful as a token portion. He will burn this flour on the altar just like any other offering given to the LORD by fire. This will be their sin offering. 13In this way, the priest will make atonement for those who are guilty, and they will be forgiven. The rest of the flour will belong to the priest, just as with the grain offering.”

Procedures for the Guilt Offering

5:15 Exod 30:13; Lev 6:6; 7:1-10; 22:14
5:16 Lev 6:5; 22:14

14Then the LORD said to Moses, 15“If any of the people sin by unintentionally defiling the LORD’s sacred property, they must bring to the LORD a ram from the flock as their guilt offering. The animal must have no physical defects, and it must be of the proper value in silver as measured by the standard sanctuary shekel.* 16They must then make restitution for whatever holy things they have defiled by paying for the loss, plus an added penalty of 20 percent. When they give their payments to the priest, he will make atonement for them with the ram sacrificed as a guilt offering, and they will be forgiven.

5:17 Lev 5:15

17“If any of them sin by doing something forbidden by the LORD, even if it is done unintentionally, they will be held responsible. When they become aware of their guilt, 18they must bring to the priest a ram from the flock as a guilt offering. The animal must have no physical defects, and it must be of the proper value. In this way, the priest will make atonement for those who are guilty, and they will be forgiven. 19This is a guilt offering, for they have been guilty of an offense against the LORD.”

Sins Requiring a Guilt Offering

6:2 Exod 22:7-15; Num 5:6; Col 3:9
6:3 Deut 22:1-3

6 And the LORD said to Moses, 2“Suppose some of the people sin against the LORD by falsely telling their neighbor that an item entrusted to their safekeeping has been lost or stolen. Or suppose they have been dishonest with regard to a security deposit, or they have taken something by theft or extortion. 3Or suppose they find a lost item and lie about it, or they deny something while under oath, or they commit any other similar sin. 4If they have sinned in any of these ways and are guilty, they must give back whatever they have taken by theft or extortion, whether a security deposit, or property

5:11 Hebrew *1/10 of an ephah* [2 liters]. **5:15** Each sanctuary shekel was about 0.4 ounces or 11 grams in weight.

5:14-19 The guilt offering was a way of taking care of sin committed unintentionally. It was for those who sinned in some way against “sacred property”—the Tabernacle or the priesthood—as well as for those who unintentionally sinned against someone. In either case, a ram with no defects had to be sacrificed, plus those harmed by the sin had to be compensated for their loss, plus a 20 percent penalty. Even though Christ’s death has made guilt offerings unnecessary for us today, we still need to make things right with those we hurt.

6:1-7 Here we discover that stealing involves more than just taking from someone. Finding something and not returning it or refusing to return something borrowed are other forms of stealing. These are sins against God and not just your neighbor, a stranger, or a large business. If you have gotten something deceitfully, then confess your sin to God, apologize to the owner, and return the stolen items—with interest.

entrusted to them, or a lost object that they claimed as their own, [5]or anything gained by **6:5-6** Lev 5:15-16
swearing falsely. When they realize their guilt, they must restore the principal amount Num 5:8
plus a penalty of 20 percent to the person they have harmed. [6]They must then bring a
guilt offering to the priest, who will present it before the LORD. This offering must be a
ram with no physical defects or the animal's equivalent value in silver.* [7]The priest will
then make atonement for them before the LORD, and they will be forgiven."

Further Instructions for the Burnt Offering

[8]Then the LORD said to Moses, [9]"Give Aaron and his sons the following instructions **6:9**
regarding the whole burnt offering. The burnt offering must be left on the altar until the Exod 29:38-42 Lev 6:12-13
next morning, and the altar fire must be kept burning all night. [10]The next morning, after Num 28:1-25
dressing in his special linen clothing and undergarments, the priest on duty must clean **6:10**
out the ashes of the burnt offering and put them beside the altar. [11]Then he must change Exod 28:39-43
back into his normal clothing and carry the ashes outside the camp to a place that is
ceremonially clean. [12]Meanwhile, the fire on the altar must be kept burning; it must **6:12**
never go out. Each morning the priest will add fresh wood to the fire and arrange the Lev 3:5
daily whole burnt offering on it. He must then burn the fat of the peace offerings on top
of this daily whole burnt offering. [13]Remember, the fire must be kept burning on the altar
at all times. It must never go out.

Further Instructions for the Grain Offering

[14]"These are the instructions regarding the grain offering. Aaron's sons must present this **6:14**
offering to the LORD in front of the altar. [15]The priest on duty will take a handful of the Lev 2:1
choice flour that has been mixed with olive oil and sprinkled with incense. He will burn **6:15**
this token portion on the altar, and it will be very pleasing to the LORD. [16]After burning Lev 2:1-2, 9
this handful, the rest of the flour will belong to Aaron and his sons for their food. It must, **6:16** Lev 10:12-15
however, be baked without yeast and eaten in a sacred place within the courtyard of the Num 18:10
Tabernacle.* [17]Remember, this flour may never be prepared with yeast. I have given it **6:17**
to the priests as their share of the offerings presented to me by fire. Like the sin offering Lev 2:11; 6:26, 29; 10:17
and the guilt offering, it is most holy. [18]Any of Aaron's male descendants, from **6:18**
generation to generation, may eat of the grain offering, because it is their regular share Lev 6:29
of the offerings given to the LORD by fire. Anyone or anything that touches this food will Num 18:10 1 Cor 9:13
become holy."

Procedures for the Ordination Offering

[19]And the LORD said to Moses, [20]"On the day Aaron and his sons are anointed, they must
bring to the LORD a grain offering of two quarts* of choice flour, half to be offered in the
morning and half to be offered in the evening. [21]It must be cooked on a griddle with olive
oil, and it must be well mixed and broken* into pieces. You must present this grain **6:21** Lev 2:5, 8; 7:9
offering, and it will be very pleasing to the LORD. [22]As the sons of the priests replace **6:22-23**
their fathers, they will be inducted into office by offering this same sacrifice on the day Exod 29:30
they are anointed. It is the LORD's regular share, and it must be completely burned up.
[23]All such grain offerings of the priests must be entirely burned up. None of the flour
may be eaten."

Further Instructions for the Sin Offering

[24]Then the LORD said to Moses, [25]"Give Aaron and his sons these further instructions **6:25**
regarding the sin offering. The animal given as a sin offering is most holy and must be Lev 4:24, 29
slaughtered in the LORD's presence at the place where the burnt offerings are slaughtered.
[26]The priest who offers the sacrifice may eat his portion in a sacred place within the
courtyard of the Tabernacle. [27]Anything or anyone who touches the sacrificial meat will **6:27** Exod 29:37

6:6 Or *and the animal must be of the proper value;* Hebrew lacks *in silver;* compare 5:15. **6:16** Hebrew *Tent of Meeting;* also in 6:26, 30. **6:20** Hebrew *1/10 of an ephah* [2 liters]. **6:21** The meaning of this Hebrew term is uncertain.

6:12, 13 While the previous offerings and sacrifices were ones that the people did, the section from 6:8—7:38 deals with priestly procedure. The burnt offering was presented in the morning and evening for the whole nation (see Exodus 29:38-43). The holy fire on the altar had to keep burning because God had started it. This represented God's eternal presence in the sacrificial system. It showed the people that only by God's gracious favor could their sacrifices be acceptable. God's fire is present in each believer's life today. He lights the fire when the Holy Spirit comes to live in us, and he tends it so that we will grow in grace as we walk with him. When we are aware that God lives in us, we have confidence to come to him for forgiveness and restoration. We can carry out our work with strength and enthusiasm.

become holy, and if the sacrificial blood splatters anyone's clothing, it must be washed
6:28 Lev 11:33; 15:12 — off in a sacred place. 28If a clay pot is used to boil the sacrificial meat, it must be broken.
6:29 Lev 6:18 — If a bronze kettle is used, it must be scoured and rinsed thoroughly with water. 29Only
males from a priest's family may eat of this offering, for it is most holy. 30If, however,
6:30 Lev 4:1, 18 — the blood of a sin offering has been taken into the Tabernacle to make atonement in the
Holy Place for the people's sins, none of that animal's meat may be eaten. It must be
completely burned up.

Further Instructions for the Guilt Offering

7:1 Lev 5:14–6:7 — **7** "These are the instructions for the guilt offering, which is most holy. 2The animal
7:2 Lev 1:11 — sacrificed as a guilt offering must be slaughtered where the burnt offerings are
slaughtered, and its blood sprinkled against the sides of the altar. 3The priest will then
7:3 Lev 3:3, 9 — offer all its fat on the altar, including the fat from the tail, the fat around the internal
organs, 4the two kidneys with the fat around them near the loins, and the lobe of the liver,
which is to be removed with the kidneys. 5The priests will burn these parts on the altar
7:6 Lev 6:18, 29; Num 18:10 — as an offering to the LORD made by fire. It is a guilt offering. 6All males from a priest's
family may eat the meat, and it must be eaten in a sacred place, for it is most holy.
7:7 Lev 14:13 — 7"For both the sin offering and the guilt offering, the meat of the sacrificed animal
belongs to the priest in charge of the atonement ceremony. 8In the case of the whole burnt
7:9 Lev 2:5, 8 — offering, the hide of the sacrificed animal also belongs to the priest. 9Any grain offering
that has been baked in an oven, prepared in a pan, or cooked on a griddle belongs to the
priest who presents it. 10All other grain offerings, whether flour mixed with olive oil or
dry flour, are to be shared among all the priests and their sons.

Further Instructions for the Peace Offering

7:11 Lev 3:1-17 — 11"These are the instructions regarding the different kinds of peace offerings that may
7:12 Lev 2:4; Num 6:15 — be presented to the LORD. 12If you present your peace offering as a thanksgiving offering,
the usual animal sacrifice must be accompanied by various kinds of bread—loaves,
wafers, and cakes—all made without yeast and soaked with olive oil. 13This peace
7:13 Lev 2:12; 23:17 — offering of thanksgiving must also be accompanied by loaves of yeast bread. 14One of
7:14 Num 18:8, 11, 19 — each kind of bread must be presented as a gift to the LORD. This bread will then belong
to the priest who sprinkles the altar with blood from the sacrificed animal. 15The animal's
7:15 Lev 22:29-30 — meat must be eaten on the same day it is offered. None of it may be saved for the next
morning.
7:16 Lev 19:6-8 — 16"However, if you bring an offering to fulfill a vow or as a freewill offering, the meat
may be eaten on that same day, and whatever is left over may be eaten on the second day.
7:17 Exod 12:10 — 17But anything left over until the third day must be completely burned up. 18If any of
the meat from this peace offering is eaten on the third day, it will not be accepted by the
LORD. It will have no value as a sacrifice, and you will receive no credit for bringing it
as an offering. By then, the meat will be contaminated; if you eat it, you will have to
answer for your sin.
7:19 Lev 11:47 — 19"Meat that touches anything ceremonially unclean may not be eaten; it must be
7:20 Gen 17:14; Lev 22:3-7; Num 19:13 — completely burned up. And as for meat that may be eaten, it may only be eaten by people
who are ceremonially clean. 20Anyone who is ceremonially unclean but eats meat from
a peace offering that was presented to the LORD must be cut off from the community. 21If
7:21 Lev 5:2-3 — anyone touches anything that is unclean, whether it is human defilement or an unclean
animal, and then eats meat from the LORD's sacrifices, that person must be cut off from
the community."

The Forbidden Blood and Fat

7:24 Exod 22:31; Lev 17:15 — 22Then the LORD said to Moses, 23"Give the Israelites these instructions: You must never
eat fat, whether from oxen or sheep or goats. 24The fat of an animal found dead or killed

---

7:11-18 The peace offering was divided into three kinds according to purpose: thanksgiving offering, vow offering, and freewill offering. A thanksgiving offering was appropriate whenever one wished to show thanks to God, as when recovering from a serious illness, or surviving a dangerous calamity (Psalm 107). A vow offering was given in fulfillment of a vow (2 Samuel 15:7, 8). The freewill offering, however, needed no special occasion or reason.

7:22-27 The fat portions were regarded as the best portions; therefore, it was appropriate to dedicate them only to God. Because blood was the river of life, and life was God's gift and his alone, blood had to be returned to God and not used by people.

by a wild animal may never be eaten, though it may be used for any other purpose.
25Anyone who eats fat from an offering given to the LORD by fire must be cut off from — 7:26
the community. 26Even in your homes, you must never eat the blood of any bird or — Gen 9:4; Lev 17:10-14
animal. 27Anyone who eats blood must be cut off from the community." — Acts 15:20, 29

A Portion for the Priests

28Then the LORD said to Moses, 29"Give these further instructions to the Israelites: — 7:29
When you present a peace offering to the LORD, bring part of it as a special gift to — Lev 3:1
the LORD. 30Present it to him with your own hands as an offering given to the LORD — 7:30
by fire. Bring the fat of the animal, together with the breast, and present it to the LORD — Exod 29:26-27
by lifting it up before him. 31Then the priest will burn the fat on the altar, but the — Lev 8:29; Num 6:20
breast will belong to Aaron and his sons. 32You are to give the right thigh of your — 7:31
peace offering to the priest as a gift. 33The right thigh must always be given to the — Lev 7:34
priest who sprinkles the blood and offers the fat of the peace offering. 34For I have — Num 18:11
designated the breast and the right thigh for the priests. It is their regular share of — 7:32
the peace offerings brought by the Israelites. 35This is their share. It has been set — Num 18:18; 7:34
apart for Aaron and his descendants from the offerings given to the LORD by fire from — Exod 29:22
the time they were appointed to serve the LORD as priests. 36The LORD commanded that — Lev 10:15
the Israelites were to give these portions to the priests as their regular share from the — 7:36
time of the priests' anointing. This regulation applies throughout the generations to — Exod 29:22-34; 40:13-15
come."

37These are the instructions for the whole burnt offering, the grain offering, the sin
offering, the guilt offering, the ordination offering, and the peace offering. 38The LORD — 7:38
gave these instructions to Moses on Mount Sinai when he commanded the Israelites to — Lev 26:46
bring their offerings to the LORD in the wilderness of Sinai.

2. Instructions for the priests

Ordination of the Priests

8 The LORD said to Moses, 2"Now bring Aaron and his sons, along with their special — 8:2
clothing, the anointing oil, the bull for the sin offering, the two rams, and the basket — Exod 28:1
of unleavened bread 3to the entrance of the Tabernacle.* Then call the entire community
of Israel to meet you there."

4So Moses followed the LORD's instructions, and all the people assembled at the
Tabernacle entrance. 5Moses announced to them, "The LORD has commanded what I am

8:3 Hebrew *Tent of Meeting;* also in 8:4, 31, 33, 35.

7:28-30 God told the people of Israel to bring their peace offerings personally, with their own hands. They were to take time and effort to express thanks to God. You are the only person who can express your thankfulness to God and to others. Do you leave it to others to express thanks for what people have done? Do you rely on the one leading the prayer to thank God for you? Take time yourself to express thanks both to God and to others who have helped and blessed you.

7:31-36 Part of the offering was designated for the priests. This food helped to care for the priests, who cared for God's house. The New Testament teaches that ministers should be paid by the people they serve (1 Corinthians 9:14). We should give generously to those who minister to us.

7:37 The ordination offering refers to the offering given at the ceremony when priests were inducted into office (8:22).

7:38 God gave his people many rituals and instructions to follow. All the rituals in Leviticus were meant to teach the people valuable lessons. But over time, the people became indifferent to the meanings of these rituals, and they began to lose touch with God. When your church appears to be conducting dry, meaningless rituals, try rediscovering the original meaning and purpose behind each. Your worship will be revitalized.

8:1ff Why did Aaron and his sons need to be cleansed and set apart? Although all the men from the tribe of Levi were dedicated for service to God, only Aaron's descendants could be priests. They alone had the honor and responsibility of performing the sacrifices. These priests had to cleanse and dedicate themselves before they could help the people do the same.

The ceremony described in Leviticus 8 and 9 was their ordination ceremony. Aaron and his sons were washed with water (8:6), clothed with special garments (8:7-9, 13), and anointed with oil (8:12). They placed their hands on a young bull as it was killed (8:14, 15), and on two rams as they were killed (8:18, 19, 22, 23). This showed that holiness came from God alone, not from the priestly role. Similarly, we are not spiritually cleansed because we have a religious position. Spiritual cleansing comes only from God. No matter how high our position or how long we have held it, we must depend on God for spiritual vitality.

8:2, 3 Why were priests needed in Israel? In Exodus 19:6, the Israelites were instructed to be a kingdom of priests; ideally they would all be holy and relate to God. But from the time of Adam's fall, sin has separated man and God, and people have needed mediators to help them find forgiveness. At first, the patriarchs—heads of households like Abraham and Job—were priests of the house or clan and made sacrifices for the family. When the Israelites left Egypt, the descendants of Aaron were chosen to serve as priests for the nation. The priests stood in the gap between God and man. They were the full-time spiritual leaders and overseers of offerings. The priestly system was a concession to people's inability, because of sin, to confront and relate to God individually and corporately. In Christ, this imperfect system was transformed. Jesus Christ himself is our High Priest. Now all believers can approach God through him.

8:6 Exod 29:3-4
8:8 Exod 28:30-31; Ezra 2:63
8:9 Exod 28:4, 36-38
8:10 Exod 30:26-33
8:11 Exod 29:37; Lev 16:14
8:12 Exod 28:41; 30:30; Lev 21:10-12
8:13 Exod 28:4, 39
8:14 Exod 29:10-14; Lev 4:4
8:15 Lev 4:7
8:17 Lev 4:11
8:18 Exod 29:15-19
8:22 Exod 29:31
8:23 Exod 29:20-21
8:25 Exod 29:22
8:26 Exod 29:23
8:27 Exod 29:24
8:28 Exod 29:25
8:29 Exod 29:26; Lev 7:31-34
8:30 Exod 29:21

now going to do!" 6 Then he presented Aaron and his sons and washed them with water.
7 He clothed Aaron with the embroidered tunic and tied the sash around his waist. He
dressed him in the robe of the ephod, along with the ephod itself, and attached the ephod
with its decorative sash. 8 Then Moses placed the chestpiece on Aaron and put the Urim
and the Thummim inside it. 9 He placed on Aaron's head the turban with the gold
medallion at its front, just as the LORD had commanded him.
10 Then Moses took the anointing oil and anointed the Tabernacle and everything in it,
thus making them holy. 11 He sprinkled the altar seven times, anointing it and all its
utensils and the washbasin and its pedestal, making them holy. 12 Then he poured some
of the anointing oil on Aaron's head, thus anointing him and making him holy for his
work. 13 Next Moses presented Aaron's sons and clothed them in their embroidered
tunics, their sashes, and their turbans, just as the LORD had commanded him.
14 Then Moses brought in the bull for the sin offering, and Aaron and his sons laid their
hands on its head 15 as Moses slaughtered it. Moses took some of the blood, and with his
finger he put it on the four horns of the altar to purify it. He poured out the rest of the
blood at the base of the altar. In this way, he set the altar apart as holy and made
atonement for it.* 16 He took all the fat around the internal organs, the lobe of the liver,
and the two kidneys and their fat, and he burned them all on the altar. 17 The rest of the
bull, including its hide, meat, and dung, was burned outside the camp, just as the LORD
had commanded Moses.
18 Then Moses presented the ram to the LORD for the whole burnt offering, and Aaron
and his sons laid their hands on its head 19 as Moses slaughtered it. Then Moses took the
ram's blood and sprinkled it against the sides of the altar. 20 Next he cut the ram into
pieces and burned the head, some of its pieces, and the fat on the altar. 21 After washing
the internal organs and the legs with water, Moses burned the entire ram on the altar as
a whole burnt offering. It was an offering given to the LORD by fire, very pleasing to the
LORD. All this was done just as the LORD had commanded Moses.
22 Next Moses presented the second ram, which was the ram of ordination. Aaron and
his sons laid their hands on its head 23 as Moses slaughtered it. Then Moses took some
of its blood and put it on the lobe of Aaron's right ear, the thumb of his right hand, and
the big toe of his right foot. 24 Next he presented Aaron's sons and put some of the blood
on the lobe of their right ears, the thumb of their right hands, and the big toe of their right
feet. He then sprinkled the rest of the blood against the sides of the altar.
25 Next he took the fat, including the fat from the tail, the fat around the internal organs,
the lobe of the liver, and the two kidneys with their fat, along with the right thigh. 26 On
top of these he placed a loaf of unleavened bread, a cake of unleavened bread soaked with
olive oil, and a thin wafer spread with olive oil. All these were taken from the basket of
bread made without yeast that was placed in the LORD's presence. 27 He gave all of these
to Aaron and his sons, and he presented the portions by lifting them up before the LORD.
28 Moses then took all the offerings back and burned them on the altar on top of the burnt
offering as an ordination offering. It was an offering given to the LORD by fire, very
pleasing to the LORD. 29 Then Moses took the breast and lifted it up in the LORD's presence.
This was Moses' share of the ram of ordination, just as the LORD had commanded him.
30 Next Moses took some of the anointing oil and some of the blood that was on the
altar, and he sprinkled them on Aaron and his clothing and on his sons and their clothing.
In this way, he made Aaron and his sons and their clothing holy.

8:15 Or *that atonement may be made on it.*

8:8 What were the Urim and Thummim? Little is known about them, but they were probably precious stones or flat objects that God used to give guidance to his people. The high priest kept them in a pocket attached to his chestpiece. Some scholars think the Urim may have been the *no* answer and the Thummim the *yes* answer. After a time of prayer for guidance, the priest would shake the stones and God would cause the proper one to fall out. Another view is that the Urim and Thummim were small flat objects, each with a *yes* side and a *no* side. The priest spilled both from his pouch. If both landed on their *yes* sides, God's answer was positive. Two *no* sides were negative. A *yes* and a *no* meant no reply. God had a specific purpose for using this method of guidance—he was teaching a nation the principles of following him. Our situation is not the same, however, so we must not invent ways like this for God to guide us.

8:12 What was the significance of anointing Aaron as high priest? The high priest had special duties that no other priest had. He alone could enter the Most Holy Place in the Tabernacle on the yearly Day of Atonement to atone for the sins of the nation. Therefore, he was in charge of all the other priests. The high priest was a picture of Jesus Christ, who is our High Priest (Hebrews 7:26-28).

31 Then Moses said to Aaron and his sons, "Boil the rest of the meat at the Tabernacle 8:31 Exod 29:31-32
entrance, and eat it along with the bread that is in the basket of ordination offerings, just
as I commanded you. 32 Any meat or bread that is left over must then be burned up. 33 Do 8:32 Exod 29:34
not leave the Tabernacle entrance for seven days, for that is the time it will take to 8:33 Exod 29:35
complete the ordination ceremony. 34 What has been done today was commanded by the
LORD in order to make atonement for you. 35 Remember, you must stay at the entrance 8:34 Heb 7:16
of the Tabernacle day and night for seven days, doing everything the LORD requires. If 8:35 Num 3:7; 9:19 Deut 11:1 1 Kgs 2:3 Ezek 48:11
you fail in this, you will die. This is what the LORD has said." 36 So Aaron and his sons
did everything the LORD had commanded through Moses.

The Priests Begin Their Work

9 After the ordination ceremony, on the eighth day, Moses called together Aaron and
his sons and the leaders of Israel. 2 He said to Aaron, "Take a young bull for a sin
offering and a ram for a whole burnt offering, both with no physical defects, and present
them to the LORD. 3 Then tell the Israelites to take a male goat for a sin offering for 9:3 Lev 4:3
themselves and a year-old calf and a year-old lamb for a whole burnt offering, each with
no physical defects. 4 Also tell them to take a bull* and a ram for a peace offering and 9:4 Exod 29:43
flour mixed with olive oil for a grain offering. Tell them to present all these offerings to
the LORD because the LORD will appear to them today."
5 So the people brought all of these things to the entrance of the Tabernacle,* just as
Moses had commanded, and the whole community came and stood there in the LORD's
presence. 6 Then Moses told them, "When you have followed these instructions from the 9:6 Lev 9:23
LORD, the glorious presence of the LORD will appear to you."
7 Then Moses said to Aaron, "Approach the altar and present your sin offering and 9:7 Heb 5:1-3; 7:27
your whole burnt offering to make atonement for yourself. Then present the offerings to
make atonement for the people, just as the LORD has commanded."
8 So Aaron went to the altar and slaughtered the calf as a sin offering for himself. 9 His 9:9 Lev 4:6-7
sons brought him the blood, and he dipped his finger into it and put it on the horns of the
altar. He poured out the rest of the blood at the base of the altar. 10 Then he burned on the
altar the fat, the kidneys, and the lobe of the liver from the sin offering, just as the LORD
had commanded Moses. 11 The meat and the hide, however, he burned outside the camp.
12 Next Aaron slaughtered the animal for the whole burnt offering. His sons brought him
the blood, and he sprinkled it against the sides of the altar. 13 They handed the animal to him
piece by piece, including the head, and he burned each part on the altar. 14 Then he washed
the internal organs and the legs and also burned them on the altar as a whole burnt offering.
15 Next Aaron presented the sacrifices for the people. He slaughtered the people's goat 9:15 Lev 4:27-31; 9:3
and presented it as their sin offering, just as he had done previously for himself. 16 Then 9:16 Lev 1:3, 10
he brought the whole burnt offering and presented it in the prescribed way. 17 He also
brought the grain offering, burning a handful of the flour on the altar, in addition to the 9:17 Lev 2:1-3; 3:5
regular morning burnt offering.
18 Then Aaron slaughtered the bull and the ram for the people's peace offering. His 9:18 Lev 3:1-11
sons brought him the blood, and he sprinkled it against the sides of the altar. 19 Then he
took the fat of the bull and the ram—the fat from the tail and from around the internal 9:19 Lev 3:9
organs—along with the kidneys and the lobe of the liver. 20 He placed these fat parts on
top of the breasts of these animals and then burned them on the altar. 21 Aaron then lifted 9:21 Lev 7:30, 32
up the breasts and right thighs as an offering to the LORD, just as Moses had commanded.
22 After that, Aaron raised his hands toward the people and blessed them. Then, after 9:22 Num 6:24-26

9:4 Or *cow;* also in 9:18, 19. **9:5** Hebrew *Tent of Meeting;* also in 9:23.

8:36 Aaron and his sons did "everything the LORD had commanded." Considering the many detailed lists of Leviticus, that was a remarkable feat. They knew what God wanted, how he wanted it done, and with what attitude it was to be carried out. This can serve as a model for how carefully we ought to obey God. God wants us to be thoroughly holy people, not a rough approximation of the way his followers should be.

9:22, 23 In 9:6 Moses said to the people, "When you have followed these instructions from the LORD, the glorious presence of the LORD will appear to you." Moses, Aaron, and the people then got to work and followed God's instructions. Soon after, the glory of the Lord appeared. Often we look for God's glorious acts without concern for following his instructions. Do you serve God in the daily routines of life, or do you wait for him to do a mighty act? If you depend on his glorious acts, you may find yourself sidestepping your everyday duty to obey.

9:23 Num 16:19, 42 presenting the sin offering, the whole burnt offering, and the peace offering, he stepped
down from the altar. 23 Next Moses and Aaron went into the Tabernacle, and when they
came back out, they blessed the people again, and the glorious presence of the LORD
9:24 1 Kgs 18:38 appeared to the whole community. 24 Fire blazed forth from the LORD's presence and
consumed the burnt offering and the fat on the altar. When the people saw all this, they
shouted with joy and fell face down on the ground.

The Sin of Nadab and Abihu

10:1 Exod 6:23 Num 3:2 **10** Aaron's sons Nadab and Abihu put coals of fire in their incense burners and
sprinkled incense over it. In this way, they disobeyed the LORD by burning before
10:2 Num 26:61 him a different kind of fire than he had commanded. 2 So fire blazed forth from the
LORD's presence and burned them up, and they died there before the LORD.

NADAB/ABIHU

Some brothers, like Cain and Abel or Jacob and Esau, get each other in trouble. Nadab and Abihu got in trouble together.

Although little is known of their early years, the Bible gives us an abundance of information about the environment in which they grew up. Born in Egypt, they were eyewitnesses of God's mighty acts of the Exodus. They saw their father, Aaron, their uncle, Moses, and their aunt, Miriam, in action many times. They had firsthand knowledge of God's holiness as few men have ever had, and for a while at least, they followed God wholeheartedly (Leviticus 8:36). But at a crucial moment they chose to treat with indifference the clear instructions from God. The consequence of their sin was fiery, instant, and shocking to all.

We are in danger of making the same mistake as these brothers when we treat lightly the justice and holiness of God. We must draw near to God while realizing that there is a proper fear of God. Don't forget that the opportunity to know God personally is based on his gracious invitation to an always unworthy people, not a gift to be taken for granted. Do your thoughts about God include a humble recognition of his great holiness?

Strengths and accomplishments
- Oldest sons of Aaron
- Primary candidates to become high priest after their father
- Involved with the original consecration of the Tabernacle
- Commended for doing "everything the LORD had commanded" (Leviticus 8:36)

Weakness and mistake
- Treated lightly God's direct commands

Lesson from their lives
- Sin has deadly consequences

Vital statistics
- Where: The Sinai peninsula
- Occupation: Priests-in-training
- Relatives: Father: Aaron. Uncle and Aunt: Moses and Miriam. Brothers: Eleazar and Ithamar

Key verses
"Aaron's sons Nadab and Abihu put coals of fire in their incense burners and sprinkled incense over it. In this way, they disobeyed the LORD by burning before him a different kind of fire than he had commanded. So fire blazed forth from the LORD's presence and burned them up, and they died there before the LORD" (Leviticus 10:1, 2).

The story of Nadab and Abihu is told in Leviticus 8—10. They are also mentioned in Exodus 24:1, 9; 28:1; Numbers 3:2-4; 26:60, 61.

9:24 As a display of his mighty power, God sent fire from the sky to consume Aaron's offering. The people fell to the ground in awe. Some people wonder if God really exists because they don't see his activity in the world. But God is at work in today's world just as he was in Moses' world. Where a large body of believers is active for him, God tends not to display his power in the form of mighty physical acts. Instead, he works to change the world through the work of these believers. When you realize that, you will begin to see acts of love and faith that are just as supernatural.

10:1 What was the different kind of fire that Nadab and Abihu offered before the Lord? The fire on the altar of burnt offering was never to go out (6:12, 13), implying that it was holy. It is possible that Nadab and Abihu brought coals of fire to the altar from another source, making the sacrifice unholy. It has also been suggested that the two priests gave an offering at an unprescribed time. Whatever explanation is correct, the point is that Nadab and Abihu abused their office as priests in a flagrant act of disrespect to God, who had just reviewed with them precisely how they were to conduct worship. As leaders, they had special responsibility to obey God. In their position, they could easily lead many people astray. If God has commissioned you to lead or teach others, be sure to stay close to him and follow his instructions.

10:2 Aaron's sons were careless about following the laws for sacrifices. In response, God destroyed them with a blast of fire. Performing the sacrifices was an act of obedience. Doing them correctly showed respect for God. It is easy for us to grow careless about obeying God, to live our way instead of God's. But if one way were just as good as another, God would not have commanded us to live his way. He always has good reasons for his commands, and we always place ourselves in danger when we consciously or carelessly disobey them.

3 Then Moses said to Aaron, "This is what the LORD meant when he said, 10:3 Exod 19:22 Ezek 38:16

'I will show myself holy
among those who are near me.
I will be glorified
before all the people.'"

And Aaron was silent.
4 Then Moses called for Mishael and Elzaphan, Aaron's cousins, the sons of Aaron's 10:4 Exod 6:18
uncle Uzziel. He said to them, "Come and carry the bodies of your relatives away from
the sanctuary to a place outside the camp." 5 So they came forward and carried them out
of the camp by their tunics as Moses had commanded.
6 Then Moses said to Aaron and his sons Eleazar and Ithamar, "Do not mourn by letting 10:6 Lev 21:1-15
your hair hang loose* or by tearing your clothes. If you do, you will die, and the LORD Num 1:53; 16:22
will be angry with the whole community of Israel. However, the rest of the Israelites, your Josh 7:1
relatives, may mourn for Nadab and Abihu, whom the LORD has destroyed by fire. 7 But 10:7 Lev 21:12
you are not to leave the entrance of the Tabernacle,* under penalty of death, for the anointing
oil of the LORD is upon you." So they did as Moses commanded.

Instructions for Priestly Conduct

8 Then the LORD said to Aaron, 9 "You and your descendants must never drink wine or 10:9 Ezek 44:21
any other alcoholic drink before going into the Tabernacle. If you do, you will die. This
is a permanent law for you, and it must be kept by all future generations. 10 You are to 10:10 Lev 11:47
distinguish between what is holy and what is ordinary, what is ceremonially unclean and Ezek 22:26
what is clean. 11 And you must teach the Israelites all the laws that the LORD has given 10:11
through Moses." Deut 33:10
12 Then Moses said to Aaron and his remaining sons, Eleazar and Ithamar, "Take what 10:12 Lev 21:22
is left of the grain offering after the handful has been presented to the LORD by fire. Make Num 3:2
sure there is no yeast in it, and eat it beside the altar, for it is most holy. 13 It must be eaten 10:13 Lev 16:16
in a sacred place, for it has been given to you and your descendants as your regular share
of the offerings given to the LORD by fire. These are the commands I have been given.
14 But the breast and thigh that were lifted up may be eaten in any place that is 10:14 Lev 7:28-36
ceremonially clean. These parts have been given to you and to your sons and daughters 10:15 Lev 7:30-34
as your regular share of the peace offerings presented by the people of Israel. 15 The thigh
and breast that are lifted up must be lifted up to the LORD along with the fat of the
offerings given by fire. Then they will belong to you and your descendants forever, just
as the LORD has commanded."
16 When Moses demanded to know what had happened to the goat of the sin offering, 10:16 Lev 9:3
he discovered that it had been burned up. As a result, he became very angry with Eleazar
and Ithamar, Aaron's remaining sons. 17 "Why didn't you eat the sin offering in the 10:17 Lev 6:24-30
sanctuary area?" he demanded. "It is a holy offering! It was given to you for removing
the guilt of the community and for making atonement for the people before the LORD.
18 Since the animal's blood was not taken into the Holy Place, you should have eaten the 10:18 Lev 6:30
meat in the sanctuary area as I ordered you."
19 Then Aaron answered Moses on behalf of his sons. "Today my sons presented both 10:19 Lev 9:8, 12

10:6 Or *by uncovering your heads.* **10:7** Hebrew *Tent of Meeting;* also in 10:9.

10:8-11 The priests were not to drink wine or other alcoholic beverages before going into the Tabernacle. If their senses were dulled by alcohol, they might repeat Nadab and Abihu's sin and bring something unholy into the worship ceremony. In addition, drinking would disqualify them to teach the people God's requirements of self-discipline. Drunkenness was associated with pagan practices and the Jewish priests were supposed to be distinctively different.

10:10, 11 This passage (along with 19:1, 2) shows the focus of Leviticus. The Ten Commandments recorded in Exodus 20 were God's fundamental laws. Leviticus explained and supplemented those laws with many other guidelines and principles that helped the Israelites put them into practice. The purpose of God's laws was to teach people how to distinguish right from wrong, the holy from the common. The nation who lived by God's laws would obviously be set apart, dedicated to his service.

10:16-20 The priest who offered the sin offering was supposed to eat a portion of the animal and then burn the rest (6:24-30). Moses was angry because Eleazar and Ithamar burned the sin offering but did not eat any of it. Aaron explained to Moses that his two sons did not feel it appropriate to eat the sacrifice after their two brothers, Nadab and Abihu, had just been killed for sacrificing wrongly. Moses then understood that Eleazar and Ithamar were not trying to disobey God. They were simply afraid and upset over what had just happened to their brothers.

their sin offering and their burnt offering to the LORD," he said. "This kind of thing has
also happened to me. Would the LORD have approved if I had eaten the sin offering
today?" 20And when Moses heard this, he approved.

3. Instructions for the people

Ceremonially Clean and Unclean Animals

11:1-23 //Deut 14:3-20 **11** Then the LORD said to Moses and Aaron, 2"Give the following instructions to the
Israelites: The animals you may use for food 3include those that have completely
11:4 Acts 10:14 divided hooves and chew the cud. 4You may not, however, eat the animals named here*
because they either have split hooves or chew the cud, but not both. The camel may not
be eaten, for though it chews the cud, it does not have split hooves. 5The same is true of
11:7 Isa 65:4; 66:3, 17 the rock badger* 6and the hare, so they also may never be eaten. 7And the pig may not
11:8 Heb 9:10 be eaten, for though it has split hooves, it does not chew the cud. 8You may not eat the
meat of these animals or touch their dead bodies. They are ceremonially unclean for you.
11:9-10 Deut 14:9-10 9"As for marine animals, you may eat whatever has both fins and scales, whether taken
from fresh water or salt water. 10You may not, however, eat marine animals that do not
have both fins and scales. You are to detest them, 11and they will always be forbidden to
you. You must never eat their meat or even touch their dead bodies. 12I repeat, any marine
animal that does not have both fins and scales is strictly forbidden to you.
11:13 Deut 14:12-19 13"These are the birds you must never eat because they are detestable for you: the
eagle, the vulture, the osprey, 14the buzzard, kites of all kinds, 15ravens of all kinds, 16the
ostrich, the nighthawk, the seagull, hawks of all kinds, 17the little owl, the cormorant,
the great owl, 18the white owl, the pelican, the carrion vulture, 19the stork, herons of all
kinds, the hoopoe, and the bat.
20"You are to consider detestable all swarming insects that walk along the ground.
21However, there are some exceptions that you may eat. These include insects that jump
11:22 Matt 3:4 Mark 1:6 with their hind legs: 22locusts of all varieties, crickets, bald locusts, and grasshoppers.
All these may be eaten. 23But you are to consider detestable all other swarming insects
that walk or crawl.
24"The following creatures make you ceremonially unclean. If you touch any of their
11:25 Lev 11:28, 40 Num 19:11-13 dead bodies, you will be defiled until evening. 25If you move the dead body of an unclean
animal, you must immediately wash your clothes, and you will remain defiled until
evening.
26"Any animal that has divided but unsplit hooves or that does not chew the cud is
unclean for you. If you touch the dead body of such an animal, you will be defiled until
evening. 27Of the animals that walk on all fours, those that have paws are unclean for
you. If you touch the dead body of such an animal, you will be defiled until evening. 28If
you pick up and move its carcass, you must immediately wash your clothes, and you will
remain defiled until evening.
29"Of the small animals that scurry or creep on the ground, these are unclean for you:
the mole, the mouse, the great lizard of all varieties, 30the gecko, the monitor lizard, the
common lizard, the sand lizard, and the chameleon. 31All these small animals are unclean
for you. If you touch the dead body of such an animal, you will be defiled until evening.
11:32 Lev 15:12 32If such an animal dies and falls on something, that object, whatever its use, will be
unclean. This is true whether the object is made of wood, cloth, leather, or sackcloth. It

11:4 The identification of some of the animals, birds, and insects in this chapter is uncertain. **11:5** Or *coney,* or *hyrax.*

11:8 God had strictly forbidden eating the meat of certain "unclean" animals; to make sure, he forbade even touching them. He wanted the people to be totally separated from those things he had forbidden. So often we flirt with temptation, rationalizing that at least we are technically keeping the commandment not to commit the sin. But God wants us to separate ourselves completely from all sin and tempting situations.

11:25 In order to worship, people need to be prepared. There were some acts of disobedience, some natural acts (such as childbirth, menstruation, or sex), or some accidents (such as touching a dead or diseased body) that would make a person ceremonially unclean and thus forbidden to participate in worship. This did not imply that they had sinned or were rejected by God, but it insured that all worship was done decently and in order. This chapter describes many of the intentional or accidental occurrences that would disqualify a person from worship until they were "cleansed" or straightened out. A person had to be *prepared* for worship. Similarly, we cannot live any way we want during the week and then rush into God's presence on Sunday. We should prepare ourselves through repentance and cleansing.

must be put into water, and it will remain defiled until evening. After that, it will be
ceremonially clean and may be used again.
33"If such an animal dies and falls into a clay pot, everything in the pot will be defiled, **11:33**
and the pot must be smashed. 34If the water used to cleanse an unclean object touches Lev 6:28
any food, all of that food will be defiled. And any beverage that is in such an unclean
container will be defiled. 35Any object on which the dead body of such an animal falls
will be defiled. If it is a clay oven or cooking pot, it must be smashed to pieces. It has
become defiled, and it will remain that way.
36"However, if the dead body of such an animal falls into a spring or a cistern, the
water will still be clean. But anyone who removes the dead body will be defiled. 37If the
dead body falls on seed grain to be planted in the field, the seed will still be considered
clean. 38But if the seed is wet when the dead body falls on it, the seed will be defiled.
39"If an animal that is permitted for eating dies and you touch its carcass, you will be **11:40**
defiled until evening. 40If you eat any of its meat or carry away its carcass, you must Lev 11:25; 17:15 Deut 14:21
wash your clothes. Then you will remain defiled until evening. Ezek 4:14; 44:31
41"Consider detestable any animal that scurries along the ground; such animals may **11:41**
never be eaten. 42This includes all animals that slither along on their bellies, as well as Lev 11:29
those with four legs and those with many feet. All such animals are to be considered
detestable. 43Never defile yourselves by touching such animals. 44After all, I, the LORD, **11:44-45**
am your God. You must be holy because I am holy. So do not defile yourselves by Exod 6:7; 19:6 Lev 19:2
touching any of these animals that scurry along the ground. 45I, the LORD, am the one 1 Thes 4:7 †1 Pet 1:16
who brought you up from the land of Egypt to be your God. You must therefore be holy
because I am holy.
46"These are the instructions regarding the land animals, the birds, and all the living
things that move through the water or swarm over the earth, 47so you can distinguish **11:47** Lev 10:10
between what is unclean and may not be eaten and what is clean and may be eaten." Ezek 22:26; 44:23

Purification after Childbirth

12 The LORD said to Moses, "Give these instructions to the Israelites: 2When a woman **12:2**
becomes pregnant and gives birth to a son, she will be ceremonially unclean for Lev 15:19; 18:19
seven days, just as she is defiled during her menstrual period. 3On the eighth day, the boy **12:3** Gen 17:12-14
must be circumcised. 4Then the woman must wait for thirty-three days until the time of her
purification from the blood of childbirth is completed. During this time of purification, she
must not touch anything that is holy. And she must not go to the sanctuary until her time of
purification is over. 5If a woman gives birth to a daughter, she will be ceremonially defiled
for two weeks, just as she is defiled during her menstrual period. She must then wait another
sixty-six days to be purified from the blood of childbirth.

11:44, 45 There is more to this chapter than eating right. These verses provide a key to understanding all the laws and regulations in Leviticus. God wanted his people to be *holy* (set apart, different, unique), just as he is holy. He knew they had only two options: to be separate and holy, or to compromise with their pagan neighbors and become corrupt. That is why he called them out of idolatrous Egypt and set them apart as a unique nation, dedicated to worshiping him alone and leading moral lives. That is also why he designed laws and restrictions to help them remain separate—both socially and spiritually—from the wicked pagan nations they would encounter in Canaan. Christians also are called to be holy (1 Peter 1:15). Like the Israelites, we should remain spiritually separate from the world's wickedness, even though unlike them, we rub shoulders with unbelievers every day. It is no easy task to be holy in an unholy world, but God doesn't ask you to accomplish this on your own. Through the death of his Son, "you are holy and blameless as you stand before him without a single fault" (Colossians 1:22).

11:47 The designations *clean* and *unclean* were used to define the kind of animals the Israelites could and could not eat. There were several reasons for this restricted diet: (1) To ensure the health of the nation. The forbidden foods were usually scavenging animals that fed on dead animals; thus disease could be transmitted through them. (2) To visibly distinguish Israel from other nations. The pig, for example, was a common sacrifice of pagan religions. (3) To avoid objectionable associations. The creatures that move about on the ground, for example, were reminiscent of serpents, which often symbolized sin.

12:1-4 Why was a woman considered "ceremonially unclean" after the wonderful miracle of birth? It was due to the bodily emissions and secretions occurring during and after childbirth. These were considered unclean and made the woman unprepared to enter the pure surroundings of the Tabernacle.

12:1-4 *Unclean* did not mean sinful or dirty. God created us male and female, and he ordered us to be fruitful and multiply (Genesis 1:27, 28). He did not change his mind and say that sex and procreation were now somehow unclean. Instead, he made a distinction between his worship and the popular worship of fertility gods and goddesses. Canaanite religions incorporated prostitution and immoral rites as the people begged their gods to make their crops, herds, and families increase. By contrast, Israel's religion avoided all sexual connotations. By keeping worship and sex entirely separate, God helped the Israelites avoid confusion with pagan rites. The Israelites worshiped God as their loving Creator and Provider, and they thanked him for bountiful crops and safe childbirth.

12:6 Luke 2:22 6"When the time of purification is completed for either a son or a daughter, the woman
must bring a year-old lamb for a whole burnt offering and a young pigeon or turtledove
for a purification offering. She must take her offerings to the priest at the entrance of the
Tabernacle.* 7The priest will then present them to the LORD and make atonement for her.
Then she will be ceremonially clean again after her bleeding at childbirth. These are the
instructions to be followed after the birth of a son or a daughter.
12:8 Lev 5:7 Luke 2:24 8"If a woman cannot afford to bring a sheep, she must bring two turtledoves or two
young pigeons. One will be for the whole burnt offering and the other for the purification
offering. The priest will sacrifice them, thus making atonement for her, and she will be
ceremonially clean."

Contagious Skin Diseases

13:2-3 Lev 14:56 Deut 24:8 **13** The LORD said to Moses and Aaron, 2"If some of the people notice a swelling or
a rash or a shiny patch on their skin that develops into a contagious skin disease,*
they must be brought to Aaron the priest or to one of his sons. 3The priest will then
examine the affected area of a person's skin. If the hair in the affected area has turned
white and appears to be more than skin-deep, then it is a contagious skin disease, and the
priest must pronounce the person ceremonially unclean.
4"But if the affected area of the skin is white but does not appear to be more than
skin-deep, and if the hair in the spot has not turned white, the priest will put the infected
person in quarantine for seven days. 5On the seventh day the priest will make another
examination. If the affected area has not changed or spread on the skin, then the priest
13:6 Lev 11:25 will put the person in quarantine for seven more days. 6The priest will examine the skin
again on the seventh day. If the affected area has faded and not spread, the priest will
pronounce the person ceremonially clean. It was only a temporary rash. So after washing
the clothes, the person will be considered free of disease. 7But if the rash continues to
spread after this examination and pronouncement by the priest, the infected person must
return to be examined again. 8If the priest notices that the rash has spread, then he must
pronounce this person ceremonially unclean, for it is a contagious skin disease.
9"Anyone who develops a contagious skin disease must go to the priest for an
13:10 Num 12:10 2 Kgs 5:27 examination. 10If the priest sees that some hair has turned white and an open sore appears
in the affected area, 11it is clearly a contagious skin disease, and the priest must pronounce
that person ceremonially unclean. In such cases, the person need not be quarantined for
further observation because it is clear that the skin is defiled by the disease.
12"Now suppose the priest discovers after his examination that a rash has broken out
all over someone's skin, covering the body from head to foot. 13In such cases, the priest
must examine the infected person to see if the disease covers the entire body. If it does,
he will pronounce the person ceremonially clean because the skin has turned completely
white. 14But if any open sores appear, the infected person will be pronounced ceremonially unclean. 15The priest must make this pronouncement as soon as he sees an open
13:16 Luke 5:12-14 sore because open sores indicate the presence of a contagious skin disease. 16However,
if the open sores heal and turn white like the rest of the skin, the person must return to
the priest. 17If, after another examination, the affected areas have indeed turned completely white, then the priest will pronounce the person ceremonially clean.
13:18 Exod 9:9 18"If anyone has had a boil on the skin that has started to heal, 19but a white swelling
or a reddish white spot remains in its place, that person must go to the priest to be
examined. 20If the priest finds the disease to be more than skin-deep, and if the hair in
the affected area has turned white, then the priest must pronounce that person ceremonially unclean. It is a contagious skin disease that has broken out in the boil. 21But if the
priest sees that there is no white hair in the affected area, and if it doesn't appear to be

12:6 Hebrew *Tent of Meeting.* **13:2** Traditionally rendered *leprosy.* The Hebrew word used throughout this passage is used to describe various skin diseases.

13:1ff Leprosy (here called "a contagious skin disease") is a name applied to several different diseases and was greatly feared in Bible times. Some of these diseases, unlike the disease we call leprosy or Hansen's disease today, were highly contagious. The worst of them slowly ruined the body and, in most cases, were fatal. Lepers were separated from family and friends and confined outside the camp. Since priests were responsible for the health of the camp, it was their duty to expel and readmit lepers. If someone's leprosy appeared to go away, only the priest could decide if that person was truly cured. Leprosy is often used in the Bible as an illustration of sin because sin is contagious and destructive and leads to separation.

more than skin-deep and has faded, then the priest is to put the person in quarantine for
seven days. 22If during that time the affected area spreads on the skin, the priest must
pronounce the person ceremonially unclean, because it is a contagious skin disease.
23But if the area grows no larger and does not spread, it is merely the scar from the boil,
and the priest will pronounce that person ceremonially clean.

24"If anyone has suffered a burn on the skin and the burned area changes color,
becoming either a shiny reddish white or white, 25then the priest must examine it. If the
hair in the affected area turns white and the problem appears to be more than skin-deep,
a contagious skin disease has broken out in the burn. The priest must then pronounce that
person ceremonially unclean, for it is clearly a contagious skin disease. 26But if the priest
discovers that there is no white hair in the affected area and the problem appears to be
no more than skin-deep and has faded, then the priest is to put the infected person in
quarantine for seven days. 27If at the end of that time the affected area has spread on the **13:27**
skin, the priest must pronounce that person ceremonially unclean, for it is clearly a Lev 13:5
contagious skin disease. 28But if the affected area has not moved or spread on the skin
and has faded, it is simply a scar from the burn. The priest must then pronounce the
person ceremonially clean.

29"If anyone, whether a man or woman, has an open sore on the head or chin, 30the
priest must examine the infection. If it appears to be more than skin-deep and fine
yellow hair is found in the affected area, the priest must pronounce the infected person
ceremonially unclean. The infection is a contagious skin disease of the head or chin.
31However, if the priest's examination reveals that the infection is only skin-deep and
there is no black hair in the affected area, then he must put the person in quarantine for
seven days. 32If at the end of that time the affected area has not spread and no yellow
hair has appeared, and if the infection does not appear to be more than skin-deep, 33the **13:33**
infected person must shave off all hair except the hair on the affected area. Then the Lev 14:9
priest must put the person in quarantine for another seven days, 34and he will examine **13:34**
the infection again on the seventh day. If it has not spread and appears to be no more Lev 14:8
than skin-deep, the priest must pronounce that person ceremonially clean. After washing clothes, that person will be clean. 35But if the infection begins to spread after the
person is pronounced clean, 36the priest must do another examination. If the infection
has spread, he must pronounce the infected person ceremonially unclean, even without
checking for yellow hair. 37But if it appears that the infection has stopped spreading
and black hair has grown in the affected area, then the infection has healed. The priest
will then pronounce the infected person ceremonially clean.

38"If anyone, whether a man or woman, has shiny white patches on the skin, 39the
priest must examine the affected area. If the patch is only a pale white, this is a harmless
skin rash, and the person is ceremonially clean.

40"If a man loses his hair and his head becomes bald, he is still ceremonially clean. **13:40**
41And if he loses hair on his forehead, he simply has a bald forehead; he is still clean. 2 Kgs 2:23 Isa 15:2
42However, if a reddish white infection appears on the front or the back of his head, Ezek 29:18 Amos 8:10
this is a contagious skin disease. 43The priest must examine him, and if he finds
swelling around the reddish white sore, 44the man is infected with a contagious skin
disease and is unclean. The priest must pronounce him ceremonially unclean because
of the infection. **13:45** Lam 4:15

45"Those who suffer from any contagious skin disease must tear their clothing and Ezek 24:17, 22 Mic 3:7
allow their hair to hang loose.* Then, as they go from place to place, they must cover **13:46**
their mouth and call out, 'Unclean! Unclean!' 46As long as the disease lasts, they will be Num 5:1-4; 12:14 2 Kgs 7:3; 15:5
ceremonially unclean and must live in isolation outside the camp. Luke 17:12

Treatment of Contaminated Clothing

47"Now suppose an infectious mildew* contaminates some woolen or linen clothing,
48some woolen or linen fabric, the hide of an animal, or anything made of leather. 49If the

13:45 Or *and uncover their heads.* **13:47** Traditionally rendered *leprosy.* The Hebrew term used throughout this passage is the same term used for the various skin diseases described in 13:1-46.

13:45, 46 A person with a contagious skin disease had to perform this strange ritual to protect others from coming too near. Because the disease described in Leviticus was contagious, it was important that people stay away from those who had it.

affected area in the clothing, the animal hide, the fabric, or the leather has turned bright green
or a reddish color, it is contaminated with an infectious mildew and must be taken to the
priest to be examined. 50After examining the affected spot, the priest will put it away for
13:51 seven days. 51On the seventh day the priest must inspect it again. If the affected area has
Lev 14:44 spread, the material is clearly contaminated by an infectious mildew and is unclean. 52The
priest must burn the linen or wool clothing or the piece of leather because it has been
contaminated by an infectious mildew. It must be completely destroyed by fire.
53"But if the priest examines it again and the affected spot has not spread in the
clothing, the fabric, or the leather, 54the priest will order the contaminated object to be
washed and then isolated for seven more days. 55Then the priest must inspect the object
again. If he sees that the affected area has not changed appearance after being washed,
even if it did not spread, the object is defiled. It must be completely burned up, whether
it is contaminated on the inside or outside. 56But if the priest sees that the affected area
has faded after being washed, he is to cut the spot from the clothing, the fabric, or the
leather. 57If the spot reappears at a later time, however, the mildew is clearly spreading,
and the contaminated object must be burned up. 58But if the spot disappears after the
object is washed, it must be washed again; then it will be ceremonially clean.
59"These are the instructions for dealing with infectious mildew in woolen or linen
clothing or fabric, or in anything made of leather. This is how the priest will determine
whether these things are ceremonially clean or unclean."

Cleansing from Skin Diseases

14:2 Matt 8:4 Mark 1:40-45 Luke 5:12-14; 17:12-14

14 And the LORD said to Moses, 2"The following instructions must be followed by
those seeking purification from a contagious skin disease.* Those who have been
healed must be brought to the priest, 3who will examine them at a place outside the camp.
14:3 Lev 13:46 If the priest finds that someone has been healed of the skin disease, 4he will perform a
purification ceremony, using two wild birds of a kind permitted for food, along with
14:4 Lev 14:6, 49-52 Num 19:6 some cedarwood, a scarlet cloth, and a hyssop branch. 5The priest will order one of the
birds to be slaughtered over a clay pot that is filled with fresh springwater. 6He will then
14:6 Ps 51:7 dip the living bird, along with the cedarwood, the scarlet cloth, and the hyssop branch,
into the blood of the slaughtered bird. 7The priest will also sprinkle the dead bird's blood
seven times over the person being purified, and the priest will pronounce that person to
be ceremonially clean. At the end of the ceremony, the priest will set the living bird free
so it can fly away into the open fields.
14:8 Lev 14:9 Num 8:7 8"The people being purified must complete the cleansing ceremony by washing their
clothes, shaving off all their hair, and bathing themselves in water. Then they will be
ceremonially clean and may return to live inside the camp. However, they must still
14:9 Lev 13:33; 14:8 Num 6:9 remain outside their tents for seven days. 9On the seventh day, they must again shave off
all their hair, including the hair of the beard and eyebrows, and wash their clothes and
bathe themselves in water. Then they will be pronounced ceremonially clean.
14:10 Lev 23:12-13 Num 6:10 Matt 8:4 Mark 1:44 Luke 5:14 10"On the next day, the eighth day, each person cured of the skin disease must bring
two male lambs and one female year-old lamb with no physical defects, along with five
quarts* of choice flour mixed with olive oil and three-fifths of a pint* of olive oil. 11Then
the officiating priest will present that person for cleansing, along with the offerings,
14:12 Exod 29:24 before the LORD at the entrance of the Tabernacle.* 12The priest will take one of the
lambs and the olive oil and offer them as a guilt offering by lifting them up before the
14:13 Lev 1:11-13; 6:1–7:10 LORD. 13He will then slaughter the lamb there in the sacred area at the place where sin
offerings and burnt offerings are slaughtered. As with the sin offering, the guilt offering
14:14 Exod 29:20 Lev 8:23-24 will be given to the priest. It is a most holy offering. 14The priest will then take some of
the blood from the guilt offering and put it on the tip of the healed person's right ear, on
the thumb of the right hand, and on the big toe of the right foot.
15"Then the priest will pour some of the olive oil into the palm of his own left hand.
16He will dip his right finger into the oil and sprinkle it seven times before the LORD.
17The priest will then put some of the oil remaining in his left hand on the tip of the
healed person's right ear, on the thumb of the right hand, and on the big toe of the right
foot, in addition to the blood of the guilt offering. 18The oil remaining in the priest's hand

14:2 Traditionally rendered *leprosy.* See note at 13:2. **14:10a** Hebrew *3/10 of an ephah* [5.4 liters]. **14:10b** Hebrew *1 log* [0.3 liters]; also in 14:21. **14:11** Hebrew *Tent of Meeting;* also in 14:23.

will then be poured over the healed person’s head. In this way, the priest will make
atonement before the LORD for the person being cleansed.
19 “Then the priest must offer the sin offering and again perform the atonement **14:19** Lev 14:12
ceremony for the person cured of the skin disease. After that, the priest will slaughter the
whole burnt offering 20 and offer it on the altar along with the grain offering. In this way, **14:20** Lev 14:8
the priest will make atonement for the person being cleansed, and the healed person will
be ceremonially clean.
21 “But anyone who cannot afford two lambs must bring one male lamb for a guilt **14:21** Lev 5:7, 11; 12:8
offering, along with two quarts* of choice flour mixed with olive oil as a grain offering
and three-fifths of a pint of olive oil. The guilt offering will be presented by lifting it up,
thus making atonement for the person being cleansed. 22 The person being cleansed must **14:22** Lev 5:7
also bring two turtledoves or two young pigeons, whichever the person can afford. One
of the pair must be used for a sin offering and the other for a whole burnt offering. 23 On **14:23** Lev 14:11
the eighth day, the person being cleansed must bring the offerings to the priest for the
cleansing ceremony to be performed in the LORD’s presence at the Tabernacle entrance.
24 The priest will take the lamb for the guilt offering, along with the olive oil, and lift
them up before the LORD as an offering to him. 25 Then the priest will slaughter the lamb **14:25** Lev 14:14
for the guilt offering and put some of its blood on the tip of the person’s right ear, on the
thumb of the right hand, and on the big toe of the right foot.
26 “The priest will also pour some of the olive oil into the palm of his own left hand.
27 He will dip his right finger into the oil and sprinkle some of it seven times before the
LORD. 28 The priest will then put some of the olive oil from his hand on the lobe of the
person’s right ear, on the thumb of the right hand, and on the big toe of the right foot, in
addition to the blood of the guilt offering. 29 The oil that is still in the priest’s hand will
then be poured over the person’s head. In this way, the priest will make atonement for
the person being cleansed.
30 “Then the priest will offer the two turtledoves or the two young pigeons, whichever
the person was able to afford. 31 One of them is for a sin offering and the other for a whole
burnt offering, to be presented along with the grain offering. In this way, the priest will
make atonement before the LORD for the person being cleansed. 32 These are the instructions for cleansing those who have recovered from a contagious skin disease but who
cannot afford to bring the sacrifices normally required for the ceremony of cleansing.”

Treatment of Contaminated Houses

33 Then the LORD said to Moses and Aaron, 34 “When you arrive in Canaan, the land I am **14:34** Gen 17:8; Num 32:22; Deut 7:1
giving you as an inheritance, I may contaminate some of your houses with an infectious
mildew.* 35 The owner of such a house must then go to the priest and say, ‘It looks like
my house has some kind of disease.’ 36 Before the priest examines the house, he must **14:35** Ps 91:10
have the house emptied so everything inside will not be pronounced unclean. Then the
priest will go in and inspect the house. 37 If he finds bright green or reddish streaks on
the walls of the house and the contamination appears to go deeper than the wall’s surface,
38 he will leave the house and lock it up for seven days. 39 On the seventh day the priest **14:39** Lev 13:5
must return for another inspection. If the mildew on the walls of the house has spread,
40 the priest must order that the stones from those areas be removed. The contaminated
material will then be thrown into an area outside the town designated as ceremonially
unclean. 41 Next the inside walls of the entire house must be scraped thoroughly and the
scrapings dumped in the unclean place outside the town. 42 Other stones will be brought
in to replace the ones that were removed, and the walls will be replastered.
43 “But if the mildew reappears after all these things have been done, 44 the priest must
return and inspect the house again. If he sees that the affected areas have spread, the walls
are clearly contaminated with an infectious mildew, and the house is defiled. 45 It must **14:45** Lev 14:41-45
be torn down, and all its stones, timbers, and plaster must be carried out of town to the

14:21 Hebrew *1/10 of an ephah* [2 liters]. **14:34** Traditionally rendered *leprosy.* See note at 13:47.

14:34, 35 This mildew was dry rot or mineral crystals affecting stone walls. There were specific cleansing procedures designated for mildewed clothing and buildings. These were fully required by the law (vv. 44-57). Why was mildew so dangerous? This fungus could spread rapidly and promote disease. It was therefore important to check its spread as soon as possible. In extreme cases, if the fungus had done enough damage, the clothing was burned or the house destroyed.

place designated as ceremonially unclean. [46]Anyone who enters the house while it is
closed will be considered ceremonially unclean until evening. [47]All who sleep or eat in
the house must wash their clothing.

[48]"But if the priest returns for his inspection and finds that the affected areas have not
reappeared after the fresh plastering, then he will pronounce the house clean because the
14:49 Lev 14:4 Num 19:6
infectious mildew is clearly gone. [49]To purify the house the priest will need two birds,
some cedarwood, a scarlet cloth, and a hyssop branch. [50]He will slaughter one of the birds
over a clay pot that is filled with fresh springwater. [51]Then he will dip the cedarwood, the
hyssop branch, the scarlet cloth, and the living bird into the blood of the slaughtered bird,
and he will sprinkle the house seven times. [52]After he has purified the house in this way,
[53]he will release the living bird in the open fields outside the town. In this way, the priest
will make atonement for the house, and it will be ceremonially clean.

[54]"These are the instructions for dealing with the various kinds of contagious skin
14:56 Lev 13:2
disease* and infectious mildew,* [55]whether in clothing, in a house, [56]in a swollen area
of skin, in a skin rash, or in a shiny patch of skin. [57]These instructions must be followed
when dealing with any contagious skin disease or infectious mildew, to determine when
something is ceremonially clean or unclean."

Bodily Discharges

15:2 Lev 22:4 Num 5:2

15 The LORD said to Moses and Aaron, [2]"Give these further instructions to the
Israelites: Any man who has a genital discharge* is ceremonially unclean because
of it. [3]This defilement applies whether the discharge continues or is stopped up. In either
case the man is unclean. [4]Any bedding on which he lies and anything on which he sits
will be defiled.

[5]"So if you touch the man's bedding, you will be required to wash your clothes and
bathe in water, and you will remain ceremonially defiled until evening. [6]If you sit where
the man with the discharge has sat, you will be required to wash your clothes and bathe in
water. You will then remain defiled until evening. [7]The same instructions apply if you
touch the man who has the unclean discharge. [8]And if he spits on you, you must undergo
the same procedure. [9]Any blanket on which the man rides will be defiled. [10]If you touch
or carry anything that was under him, you will be required to wash your clothes and bathe
in water, and you will remain defiled until evening. [11]If the man touches you without first
rinsing his hands, then you will be required to wash your clothes and bathe in water, and
15:12 Lev 6:28; 11:32-33
you will remain defiled until evening. [12]Any clay pot touched by the man with the
discharge must be broken, and every wooden utensil he touches must be rinsed with water.

15:13 Lev 15:28
[13]"When the man's discharge heals, he must count off a period of seven days. During
that time, he must wash his clothes and bathe in fresh springwater. Then he will be
ceremonially clean. [14]On the eighth day he must bring two turtledoves or two young
pigeons and present himself to the LORD at the entrance of the Tabernacle* and give his
15:15 Lev 14:30-31
offerings to the priest. [15]The priest will present the offerings there, one for a sin offering
and the other for a whole burnt offering. In this way, the priest will make atonement for
the man before the LORD for his discharge.

15:16 Lev 22:4 Deut 23:10-11
[16]"Whenever a man has an emission of semen, he must wash his entire body, and he
will remain ceremonially defiled until evening. [17]Any clothing or leather that comes in

14:54 Traditionally rendered *leprosy.* See notes at 13:2 and 13:47. **15:2** Hebrew *a discharge from his flesh;* also in 15:32. **15:14** Hebrew *Tent of Meeting;* also in 15:29.

14:54-57 God told the Israelites how to diagnose contagious skin diseases and mildew so they could avoid them or treat them. These laws were given for the people's health and protection. They helped the Israelites avoid diseases that were serious threats in that time and place. Although they wouldn't have understood the medical reasons for some of these laws, their obedience to them made them healthier. Many of God's laws must have seemed strange to the Israelites. His laws, however, helped them avoid not only physical contamination but also moral and spiritual infection.

The Word of God still provides a pattern for physically, spiritually, and morally healthy living. We may not always understand the wisdom of God's laws, but if we obey them, we will thrive. Does this mean we are to follow the Old Testament health and dietary restrictions? In general, the basic principles of health and cleanliness are still healthful practices, but it would be legalistic, if not wrong, to adhere to each specific restriction today. Some of these regulations were intended to mark the Israelites as different from the wicked people around them. Others were given to prevent God's people from becoming involved in pagan religious practices, one of the most serious problems of the day. Still others related to quarantines in a culture where exact medical diagnosis was impossible. Today, for example, physicians can diagnose the different forms of leprosy, and they know which ones are contagious. Treatment methods have greatly improved, and quarantine for leprosy is rarely necessary.

contact with the semen must be washed, and it will remain defiled until evening. 18After 15:18
having sexual intercourse, both the man and the woman must bathe, and they will remain 1 Sam 21:4
defiled until evening.
19"Whenever a woman has her menstrual period, she will be ceremonially unclean 15:19
for seven days. If you touch her during that time, you will be defiled until evening. Lev 12:2
20Anything on which she lies or sits during that time will be defiled. 21If you touch her
bed, you must wash your clothes and bathe in water, and you will remain defiled until
evening. 22The same applies if you touch an object on which she sits, 23whether it is
her bedding or any piece of furniture. 24If a man has sexual intercourse with her during 15:24
this time, her menstrual impurity will be transmitted to him. He will remain defiled for Lev 18:19; 20:18 Ezek 18:6
seven days, and any bed on which he lies will be defiled.
25"If the menstrual flow of blood continues for many days beyond the normal period, 15:25 Matt 9:20
or if she discharges blood unrelated to her menstruation, the woman will be ceremonially Mark 5:25
unclean as long as the discharge continues. 26Anything on which she lies or sits during Luke 8:43-44
that time will be defiled, just as it would be during her normal menstrual period. 27If you
touch her bed or anything on which she sits, you will be defiled. You will be required to
wash your clothes and bathe in water, and you will remain defiled until evening.
28"When the woman's menstrual discharge stops, she must count off a period of
seven days. After that, she will be ceremonially clean. 29On the eighth day, she must
bring two turtledoves or two young pigeons and present them to the priest at the
entrance of the Tabernacle. 30The priest will offer one for a sin offering and the other 15:30
for a whole burnt offering. In this way, the priest will make atonement for her before Lev 5:7; 14:22
the LORD for her menstrual discharge.
31"In this way, you will keep the people of Israel separate from things that will defile 15:31
them, so they will not die as a result of defiling my Tabernacle that is right there among Num 5:3; 19:13, 20
them. 32These are the instructions for dealing with a man who has been defiled by a
genital discharge or an emission of semen; 33for dealing with a woman during her
monthly menstrual period; for dealing with anyone, man or woman, who has had a
bodily discharge of any kind; and for dealing with a man who has had intercourse with
a woman during her period."

4. Instructions for the altar

The Day of Atonement

16 The LORD spoke to Moses after the death of Aaron's two sons, who died when they 16:1
burned a different kind of fire than the LORD had commanded.* 2The LORD said to Lev 10:1-2
Moses, "Warn your brother Aaron not to enter the Most Holy Place behind the inner curtain 16:2 Exod 25:21-22;
whenever he chooses; the penalty for intrusion is death. For the Ark's cover—the place of 30:10 Heb 9:25
atonement—is there, and I myself am present in the cloud over the atonement cover.
3"When Aaron enters the sanctuary area, he must follow these instructions fully. He 16:3
must first bring a young bull for a sin offering and a ram for a whole burnt offering. Lev 16:6-7
4Then he must wash his entire body and put on his linen tunic and the undergarments 16:4 Exod 28:39-43; 39:27-29 Ezek 44:17-18

16:1 Hebrew *when they approached the LORD's presence;* compare 10:1.

15:18 This verse is not implying that sex is dirty or disgusting. God created sex for the enjoyment of married couples as well as for continuing the race and continuing the covenant. Everything must be seen and done with a view toward God's love and control. Sex is not separate from spirituality and God's care. God is concerned about our sexual habits. We tend to separate our physical and spiritual lives, but there is an inseparable intertwining. God must be Lord over our whole selves—including our private lives.

15:32, 33 God is concerned about health, the dignity of the person, the dignity of the body, and the dignity of the sexual experience. His commands call the people to avoid unhealthy practices and promote healthy ones. To wash was the physical health response; to be purified or cleansed was the spiritual dignity response. This shows God's high regard for sex and sexuality. In our day, sex has been degraded by the media; it has become public domain, not private celebration. We are called to have a high regard for sex, both in good health and in purity.

16:1ff The Day of Atonement was the greatest day of the year for Israel. The Hebrew word for *atone* means "to cover." Old Testament sacrifices could not actually remove sins, only cover them. On this day, the people confessed their sins as a nation, and the high priest went into the Most Holy Place to make atonement for them. Sacrifices were made and blood was shed so that the people's sins could be "covered" until Christ's sacrifice on the cross would give people the opportunity to have their sin removed forever.

16:1-25 Aaron had to spend hours preparing himself to meet God. But we can approach God anytime (Hebrews 4:16). What a privilege! We are offered easier access to God than the high priests of Old Testament times! Still, we must never forget that God is holy nor let this privilege cause us to approach God carelessly. The way to God has been opened to us by Christ. But easy access to God does not eliminate our need to prepare our hearts as we draw near in prayer.

worn next to his body. He must tie the linen sash around his waist and put the linen turban
on his head. These are his sacred garments. 5 The people of Israel must then bring him
two male goats for a sin offering and a ram for a whole burnt offering.
6 "Aaron will present the bull as a sin offering, to make atonement for himself and his
family. 7 Then he must bring the two male goats and present them to the LORD at the
entrance of the Tabernacle.* 8 He is to cast sacred lots to determine which goat will be
sacrificed to the LORD and which one will be the scapegoat.* 9 The goat chosen to be
sacrificed to the LORD will be presented by Aaron as a sin offering. 10 The goat chosen
to be the scapegoat will be presented to the LORD alive. When it is sent away into the
wilderness, it will make atonement for the people.
11 "Then Aaron will present the young bull as a sin offering for himself and his family.
After he has slaughtered this bull for the sin offering, 12 he will fill an incense burner with
burning coals from the altar that stands before the LORD. Then, after filling both his hands
with fragrant incense, he will carry the burner and incense behind the inner curtain.
13 There in the LORD's presence, he will put the incense on the burning coals so that a
cloud of incense will rise over the Ark's cover—the place of atonement—that rests on
the Ark of the Covenant.* If he follows these instructions, he will not die. 14 Then he
must dip his finger into the blood of the bull and sprinkle it on the front of the atonement
cover and then seven times against the front of the Ark.
15 "Then Aaron must slaughter the goat as a sin offering for the people and bring its
blood behind the inner curtain. There he will sprinkle the blood on the atonement cover
and against the front of the Ark, just as he did with the bull's blood. 16 In this way, he will
make atonement for the Most Holy Place, and he will do the same for the entire
Tabernacle, because of the defiling sin and rebellion of the Israelites. 17 No one else is
allowed inside the Tabernacle while Aaron goes in to make atonement for the Most Holy
Place. No one may enter until he comes out again after making atonement for himself,
his family, and all the Israelites.
18 "Then Aaron will go out to make atonement for the altar that stands before the LORD
by smearing some of the blood from the bull and the goat on each of the altar's horns.
19 Then he must dip his finger into the blood and sprinkle it seven times over the altar. In
this way, he will cleanse it from Israel's defilement and return it to its former holiness.
20 "When Aaron has finished making atonement for the Most Holy Place, the

16:6 Lev 9:7; Heb 5:1-3; 7:27-28; 9:7
16:10 Isa 53:4-10
16:11 Heb 9:7
16:12 Exod 30:34-38; Num 16:18, 46
16:13 Exod 25:21; Lev 22:9
16:14 Lev 4:17
16:15 Heb 6:19; 9:3, 7, 12
16:16 Exod 29:36; 30:10; Heb 2:17
16:18 Lev 4:7, 25; Ezek 43:20
16:19 Lev 4:6; 16:14

16:7 Hebrew *Tent of Meeting;* also in 16:16, 17, 20, 23, 33. **16:8** Hebrew *azazel,* which in this context means "the goat of removal"; also in 16:10, 26. **16:13** Hebrew *on the Testimony,* referring to the terms of God's covenant with Israel, which were kept in the Ark.

OLD/NEW SYSTEMS OF SACRIFICE

Old System of Sacrifice	*New System of Sacrifice*
Was temporary (Hebrews 8:13)	Is permanent (Hebrews 7:21)
Aaron first high priest (Leviticus 16:32)	Jesus only High Priest (Hebrews 4:14)
From tribe of Levi (Hebrews 7:5)	From tribe of Judah (Hebrews 7:14)
Ministered on earth (Hebrews 8:4)	Ministers in heaven (Hebrews 8:1, 2)
Used blood of animals (Leviticus 16:15)	Uses blood of Christ (Hebrews 10:5–12)
Required many sacrifices (Leviticus 22:19)	Requires one sacrifice (Hebrews 9:28)
Needed perfect animals (Leviticus 22:19)	Needs a perfect life (Hebrews 5:9)
Required careful approach to Tabernacle (Leviticus 16:2)	Encourages confident approach to throne (Hebrews 4:16)
Looked forward to new system (Hebrews 10:1)	Sets aside old system (Hebrews 10:9)

16:5-28 This event with the two goats occurred on the Day of Atonement. The two goats represented the two ways God was dealing with the Israelites' sin: (1) He was forgiving their sin through the first goat, which was sacrificed, and (2) he was removing their guilt through the second goat, the scapegoat, that was sent into the wilderness. The same ritual had to be repeated every year. Jesus Christ's death replaced this system once and for all. We can have our sins forgiven and guilt removed by placing our trust in Christ (Hebrews 10:1-18).

16:12 An incense burner was a dish or shallow bowl that hung by a chain or was carried with tongs. Inside the burner were placed incense (a combination of sweet-smelling spices) and burning coals from the altar. On the Day of Atonement, the high priest entered the Most Holy Place carrying a smoking incense burner. The smoke shielded him from the Ark of the Covenant and the presence of God—otherwise he would die. Incense may also have had a very practical purpose. The sweet smell drew the people's attention to the morning and evening sacrifices and helped cover the sometimes foul smell.

Tabernacle, and the altar, he must bring the living goat forward. [21]He is to lay both of **16:21** Lev 5:5
his hands on the goat's head and confess over it all the sins and rebellion of the Israelites.
In this way, he will lay the people's sins on the head of the goat; then he will send it out
into the wilderness, led by a man chosen for this task. [22]After the man sets it free in the **16:22** Isa 53:12
wilderness, the goat will carry all the people's sins upon itself into a desolate land.
[23]"As Aaron enters the Tabernacle, he must take off the linen garments he wore when **16:23** Exod 28:42
he entered the Most Holy Place, and he must leave the garments there. [24]Then he must Lev 16:4
bathe his entire body with water in a sacred place, put on his garments, and go out to **16:24** Exod 29:3-9
sacrifice his own whole burnt offering and the whole burnt offering for the people. In
this way, he will make atonement for himself and for the people. [25]He must also burn all
the fat of the sin offering on the altar.
[26]"The man chosen to send the goat out into the wilderness as a scapegoat must wash
his clothes and bathe in water. Then he may return to the camp.
[27]"The bull and goat given as sin offerings, whose blood Aaron brought into the Most **16:27** Lev 4:12; 6:30
Holy Place to make atonement for Israel, will be carried outside the camp to be burned.
This includes the animals' hides, the internal organs, and the dung. [28]The man who does **16:28** Num 19:8, 10
the burning must wash his clothes and bathe himself in water before returning to the camp.
[29]"On the appointed day in early autumn,* you must spend the day fasting and not do **16:29** Lev 23:26-32
any work. This is a permanent law for you, and it applies to those who are Israelites by Num 29:7
birth, as well as to the foreigners living among you. [30]On this day, atonement will be
made for you, and you will be cleansed from all your sins in the LORD's presence. [31]It **16:31** Lev 23:32
will be a Sabbath day of total rest, and you will spend the day in fasting. This is a Ezra 8:21
permanent law for you. [32]In future generations, the atonement ceremony will be performed by the anointed high priest who serves in place of his ancestor Aaron. He will
put on the holy linen garments [33]and make atonement for the Most Holy Place, the
Tabernacle, the altar, the priests, and the entire community. [34]This is a permanent law **16:34** Lev 23:14, 21,
for you, to make atonement for the Israelites once each year." 30-31
Moses followed all these instructions that the LORD had given to him. Heb 9:7

Prohibitions against Eating Blood

17 Then the LORD said to Moses, [2]"Give Aaron and his sons and all the Israelites these
commands from the LORD: [3]If any Israelite sacrifices a bull* or a lamb or a goat
anywhere inside or outside the camp [4]and does not bring it to the entrance of the Taber- **17:4**
nacle* to present it as an offering to the LORD, that person will be guilty of a capital offense.* Deut 12:5-21
Such a person has shed blood and must be cut off from the community. [5]This rule will stop **17:5** Lev 3:1
the Israelites from sacrificing animals in the open fields. It will cause them to bring their Deut 12:4-7
sacrifices to the priest at the entrance of the Tabernacle, so he can present them to the LORD
as peace offerings. [6]That way the priest will be able to sprinkle the blood and burn the fat **17:6**
on the LORD's altar at the entrance of the Tabernacle, and it will be very pleasing to the LORD. Exod 29:18 Num 18:17
[7]The people must no longer be unfaithful to the LORD by offering sacrifices to evil spirits* **17:7**
out in the fields. This is a permanent law for them, to be kept generation after generation. Exod 22:20; 32:8 Deut 32:17
[8]"Give them this command as well, which applies both to Israelites and to the 2 Chr 11:15
foreigners living among you. If you offer a whole burnt offering or a sacrifice [9]and do 1 Cor 10:20
not bring it to the entrance of the Tabernacle to offer it to the LORD, you will be cut off **17:9**
from the community. Lev 17:4
[10]"And I will turn against anyone, whether an Israelite or a foreigner living among **17:10** Lev 3:17
you, who eats or drinks blood in any form. I will cut off such a person from the Deut 12:16, 23-25

16:29 Hebrew *On the tenth day of the seventh month.* This day of the Hebrew lunar calendar occurs in September or early October. **17:3** Or *cow.* **17:4a** Hebrew *Tent of Meeting;* also in 17:5, 6, 9. **17:4b** Hebrew *blood guilt.* **17:7** Or *goat idols.*

17:1ff Chapters 17—26 are sometimes called the "holiness code" because they focus on what it means to live a holy life. The central verse is 19:2, "You must be holy because I, the LORD your God, am holy."

17:3-9 Why were the Israelites prohibited from sacrificing outside the Tabernacle area? God had established specific times and places for sacrifices, and each occasion was permeated with symbolism. If people sacrificed on their own, they might easily add to or subtract from God's laws to fit their own lifestyles. Many pagan religions allowed every individual priest to set his own rules; God's command helped the Israelites resist the temptation to follow the pagan pattern. When the Israelites slipped into idolatry, it was because "the people did whatever seemed right in their own eyes" (Judges 17:6).

17:7 The "evil spirits" were objects of worship and sacrifice in ancient times, particularly in Egypt from which they had recently escaped. God did not want the people to make this kind of sacrifice in the wilderness or in the Promised Land, where they were heading.

17:11 Gen 9:4 Lev 17:14 Heb 9:22

community, [11]for the life of any creature is in its blood. I have given you the blood so
you can make atonement for your sins. It is the blood, representing life, that brings you
atonement. [12]That is why I said to the Israelites: 'You and the foreigners who live among
you must never eat or drink blood.'

17:13 Deut 12:16 Ezek 24:7

17:14 Gen 9:4 Lev 17:11

[13]"And this command applies both to Israelites and to the foreigners living among
you. If you go hunting and kill an animal or bird that is approved for eating, you must
drain out the blood and cover it with earth. [14]The life of every creature is in the blood.
That is why I have told the people of Israel never to eat or drink it, for the life of any bird
or animal is in the blood. So whoever eats or drinks blood must be cut off.

17:15 Exod 22:31 Lev 7:24 Deut 14:21

[15]"And this command also applies both to Israelites and the foreigners living among
you. If you eat from the carcass of an animal that died a natural death or was killed by a
wild animal, you must wash your clothes and bathe yourselves in water. Then you will
remain ceremonially unclean until evening; after that, you will be considered clean.
[16]But if you do not wash your clothes and bathe, you will be held responsible."

B. LIVING A HOLY LIFE (18:1—27:34)

After the sacrificial system for forgiving sins was in place, the people were instructed on how to live as forgiven people. Applying these standards to our lives helps us grow in obedience and live a life pleasing to God.

1. Standards for the people

Forbidden Sexual Practices

18:2 Exod 6:7 Lev 11:44

18:3 Exod 23:24 Lev 20:23

18:5 Ezek 20:11 Luke 10:28 †Rom 10:5 †Gal 3:12

18:7 Lev 20:11

18:8 Gen 35:22 Lev 20:10 Deut 27:20

18:9 Lev 20:17

18 Then the LORD said to Moses, [2]"Say this to your people, the Israelites: I, the LORD,
am your God. [3]So do not act like the people in Egypt, where you used to live, or like
the people of Canaan, where I am taking you. You must not imitate their way of life. [4]You
must obey all my regulations and be careful to keep my laws, for I, the LORD, am your God.
[5]If you obey my laws and regulations, you will find life through them. I am the LORD.
[6]"You must never have sexual intercourse with a close relative, for I am the LORD.
[7]Do not violate your father by having sexual intercourse with your mother. She is your
mother; you must never have intercourse with her. [8]Do not have sexual intercourse with
any of your father's wives, for this would violate your father.
[9]"Do not have sexual intercourse with your sister or half sister, whether she is your
father's daughter or your mother's daughter, whether she was brought up in the same family
or somewhere else.
[10]"Do not have sexual intercourse with your granddaughter, whether your son's
daughter or your daughter's daughter; that would violate you. [11]Do not have sexual

17:11-14 How does blood make atonement for sin? When offered with the right attitude, the sacrifice and the blood shed from it made forgiveness of sin possible. On the one hand, blood represented the sinner's life, infected by his sin and headed for death. On the other hand, the blood represented the innocent life of the animal that was sacrificed in place of the guilty person making the offering. The death of the animal (of which the blood was proof) fulfilled the penalty of death. God therefore granted forgiveness to the sinner. It is God who forgives based on the faith of the person doing the sacrificing.

17:14 Why was eating or drinking blood prohibited? The prohibition against eating blood can be traced all the way back to Noah (Genesis 9:4). God prohibited eating or drinking blood for several reasons: (1) To discourage pagan practices. Israel was to be separate and distinct from the foreign nations around them. Eating blood was a common pagan practice. It was often done in hopes of gaining the characteristics of the slain animal (strength, speed, etc.). God's people were to rely on him, not on ingested blood, for their strength. (2) To preserve the symbolism of the sacrifice. Blood symbolized the life of the animal that was sacrificed in the sinner's place. To drink it would change the symbolism of the sacrificial penalty and destroy the evidence of the sacrifice. (3) To protect the people from infection because many deadly diseases are transmitted through the blood. The Jews took this prohibition seriously, and that is why Jesus' hearers were so upset when Jesus told them to drink his blood (John 6:53-56). However, Jesus, as God himself and the last sacrifice ever needed for sins, was asking believers to identify with him completely. He wants us to take his life into us, and he wants to participate in our lives as well.

18:3 The Israelites moved from one idol-infested country to another. As God helped them form a new culture, he warned them to leave all aspects of their pagan background behind. He also warned them how easy it would be to slip into the pagan culture of Canaan, where they were going. Canaan's society and religions appealed to worldly desires, especially sexual immorality and drunkenness. The Israelites were to keep themselves pure and set apart for God. God did not want his people absorbed into the surrounding culture and environment. Society may pressure us to conform to its way of life and thought, but yielding to that pressure will (1) create confusion as to which side we should be on and (2) eliminate our effectiveness in serving God. Follow God, and don't let the culture around you mold your thoughts and actions.

18:6-18 Marrying relatives was prohibited by God for physical, social, and moral reasons. Children born to near relatives may experience serious health problems. Without these specific laws, sexual promiscuity would have been more likely, first in families, then outside. Improper sexual relations destroy family life.

intercourse with the daughter of any of your father's wives; she is your half sister. 12Do not have intercourse with your aunt, your father's sister, because she is your father's close relative. 13Do not have sexual intercourse with your aunt, your mother's sister, because she is your mother's close relative. 14And do not violate your uncle, your father's brother, by having sexual intercourse with his wife; she also is your aunt. 15Do not have sexual intercourse with your daughter-in-law; she is your son's wife. 16Do not have intercourse with your brother's wife; this would violate your brother.

17"Do not have sexual intercourse with both a woman and her daughter or marry both a woman and her granddaughter, whether her son's daughter or her daughter's daughter. They are close relatives, and to do this would be a horrible wickedness.

18"Do not marry a woman and her sister because they will be rivals. But if your wife dies, then it is all right to marry her sister.

19"Do not violate a woman by having sexual intercourse with her during her period of menstrual impurity.

20"Do not defile yourself by having sexual intercourse with your neighbor's wife.

21"Do not give any of your children as a sacrifice to Molech, for you must not profane the name of your God. I am the LORD.

22"Do not practice homosexuality; it is a detestable sin.

23"A man must never defile himself by having sexual intercourse with an animal, and a woman must never present herself to a male animal in order to have intercourse with it; this is a terrible perversion.

24"Do not defile yourselves in any of these ways, because this is how the people I am expelling from the Promised Land have defiled themselves. 25As a result, the entire land has become defiled. That is why I am punishing the people who live there, and the land will soon vomit them out. 26You must strictly obey all of my laws and regulations, and you must not do any of these detestable things. This applies both to you who are Israelites by birth and to the foreigners living among you.

27"All these detestable activities are practiced by the people of the land where I am taking you, and the land has become defiled. 28Do not give the land a reason to vomit you out for defiling it, as it will vomit out the people who live there now. 29Whoever does any of these detestable things will be cut off from the community of Israel. 30So be careful to obey my laws, and do not practice any of these detestable activities. Do not defile yourselves by doing any of them, for I, the LORD, am your God."

Holiness in Personal Conduct

19 The LORD also said to Moses, 2"Say this to the entire community of Israel: You must be holy because I, the LORD your God, am holy. 3Each of you must show respect for your mother and father, and you must always observe my Sabbath days of rest, for I, the LORD, am your God. 4Do not put your trust in idols or make gods of metal for yourselves. I, the LORD, am your God.

5"When you sacrifice a peace offering to the LORD, offer it properly so it will be accepted on your behalf. 6You must eat it on the same day you offer it or on the next day at the latest. Any leftovers that remain until the third day must be burned. 7If any of the offering is eaten on the third day, it will be contaminated, and I will not accept it. 8If you eat it on the third day, you will answer for the sin of profaning what is holy to the LORD and must be cut off from the community.

18:12 Lev 20:19
18:14 Lev 20:20
18:15 Lev 20:12; Ezek 22:11
18:16 Lev 20:21
18:17 Lev 20:14
18:19 Lev 15:24; 20:18
18:20 Exod 20:14; Lev 20:10; Matt 5:27-28; 1 Cor 6:9
18:21 Lev 19:12; 20:1-5; 21:6; Deut 12:31; 2 Kgs 23:10; Mal 1:12
18:22 Gen 19:5; Lev 20:13; Rom 1:27
18:23 Exod 22:19; Lev 20:15-16; Deut 27:21
18:24 Lev 18:3
18:25 Lev 20:22-23; Deut 9:5
18:26 Lev 18:2-3
19:2 Exod 19:6; Lev 11:44; †1 Pet 1:16
19:3 Exod 20:8, 12; Lev 11:44
19:4 Exod 20:23; Lev 26:1
19:6-7 Lev 7:16-18

18:6-27 Several detestable activities are listed here: (1) having sexual relations with close relatives, (2) committing adultery, (3) offering children as sacrifices, (4) having homosexual relations, and (5) having sexual relations with animals. These practices were common in pagan religions and cultures, and it is easy to see why God dealt harshly with those who began to follow them. Such practices lead to disease, deformity, and death. They disrupt family life and society and reveal a low regard for the value of oneself and of others. Society today takes some of these practices lightly, even trying to make them acceptable. But they are still sins in God's eyes. If you consider them acceptable, you are not judging by God's standards.

19:9, 10 This law was a protection for the poor and the foreigner and a reminder that God owned the land; the people were only caretakers. Laws such as this showed God's generosity and liberality. As people of God, the Israelites were to reflect his nature and characteristics in their attitudes and actions. Ruth and Naomi were two people who benefited from this merciful law (Ruth 2:2).

19:9, 10 God instructed the Hebrews to provide for those in need. He required that the people leave the edges of their fields unharvested, providing food for travelers and the poor. It is easy to ignore the poor or forget about those who have less than we do. But God desires generosity. In what ways can you leave the "edges of your fields" for those in need?

9“When you harvest your crops, do not harvest the grain along the edges of your fields, and do not pick up what the harvesters drop. 10It is the same with your grape crop—do not strip every last bunch of grapes from the vines, and do not pick up the grapes that fall to the ground. Leave them for the poor and the foreigners who live among you, for I, the LORD, am your God.

11“Do not steal.

“Do not cheat one another.

“Do not lie.

12“Do not use my name to swear a falsehood and so profane the name of your God. I am the LORD.

13“Do not cheat or rob anyone.

“Always pay your hired workers promptly.

14“Show your fear of God by treating the deaf with respect and by not taking advantage of the blind. I am the LORD.

15“Always judge your neighbors fairly, neither favoring the poor nor showing deference to the rich.

16“Do not spread slanderous gossip among your people.*

“Do not try to get ahead at the cost of your neighbor’s life, for I am the LORD.

17“Do not nurse hatred in your heart for any of your relatives.

“Confront your neighbors directly so you will not be held guilty for their crimes.

18“Never seek revenge or bear a grudge against anyone, but love your neighbor as yourself. I am the LORD.

19“You must obey all my laws.

“Do not breed your cattle with other kinds of animals. Do not plant your field with two kinds of seed. Do not wear clothing woven from two different kinds of fabric.

20“If a man has sexual intercourse with a slave girl who is committed to become someone else’s wife, compensation must be paid. But since she had not been freed at the time, the couple will not be put to death. 21The man, however, must bring a ram as a guilt offering and present it to the LORD at the entrance of the Tabernacle.* 22The priest will then make atonement for him before the LORD with the sacrificial ram of the guilt offering, and the man will be forgiven.

23“When you enter the land and plant fruit trees, leave the fruit unharvested for the first three years and consider it forbidden.* 24In the fourth year the entire crop will be devoted to the LORD as an outburst of praise. 25Finally, in the fifth year you may eat the fruit. In this way, its yield will be increased. I, the LORD, am your God.

26“Never eat meat that has not been drained of its blood.

“Do not practice fortune-telling or witchcraft.

27“Do not trim off the hair on your temples or clip the edges of your beards.

28“Never cut your bodies in mourning for the dead or mark your skin with tattoos, for I am the LORD.

29“Do not defile your daughter by making her a prostitute, or the land will be filled with promiscuity and detestable wickedness.

30“Keep my Sabbath days of rest and show reverence toward my sanctuary, for I am the LORD.

31“Do not rely on mediums and psychics, for you will be defiled by them. I, the LORD, am your God.

32“Show your fear of God by standing up in the presence of elderly people and showing respect for the aged. I am the LORD.

19:9 Lev 23:22; Deut 24:19-22
19:11 Exod 20:15-16
19:13 Exod 22:7-15, 21-27; 23:4-9; Deut 24:14-15; Mal 3:5; Jas 4:5
19:14 Deut 27:18
19:15 Exod 23:2-3, 6; Deut 1:17; Prov 24:23; Jas 2:1-4
19:16 Exod 23:1, 7; Ezek 22:9
19:17 Matt 17:17-18; 1 Jn 2:9, 11; 3:15
19:18 Deut 32:35; Ps 103:9; †Matt 19:19; 22:39; †Mark 12:31; †Luke 10:27; †Rom 13:9; †Gal 5:14; †Heb 2:8; †Jas 2:8
19:19 Deut 22:9-11
19:20 Deut 22:23-27
19:21 Lev 5:15
19:26 Deut 18:10-12
19:27 Lev 21:5
19:28 Lev 21:5; Deut 14:1; Jer 16:6; 41:5
19:29 Lev 21:9; Deut 23:17-18
19:30 Exod 20:8-11; Lev 26:2
19:31 Lev 20:6
19:32 1 Tim 5:1-2

19:16 Hebrew *Do not act as a merchant toward your own people.* **19:21** Hebrew *Tent of Meeting.* **19:23** Hebrew *consider it uncircumcised.*

19:10-35 “Do not . . .” Some people think the Bible is nothing but a book of don’ts. But Jesus neatly summarized all these rules when he said to love God with all your heart and your neighbor as yourself. He called these the greatest commandments (or rules) of all (Matthew 22:34-40). By carrying out Jesus’ simple commands, we find ourselves following all of God’s other laws as well.

19:32 People often find it easy to dismiss the opinions of the elderly and avoid taking time to visit with them. But the fact that God commanded the Israelites to show respect for the elderly shows how seriously we should take the responsibility of respecting those older than we are. Their wisdom gained from experience can save us from many pitfalls.

33“Do not exploit the foreigners who live in your land. 34They should be treated like 19:34 Lev 19:18
everyone else, and you must love them as you love yourself. Remember that you were
once foreigners in the land of Egypt. I, the LORD, am your God.
35“Do not use dishonest standards when measuring length, weight, or volume. 36Your 19:35 Deut 25:13-16
scales and weights must be accurate. Your containers for measuring dry goods or liquids 19:36 Deut 25:13-15 Prov 20:10
must be accurate.* I, the LORD, am your God, who brought you out of the land of Egypt.
37You must be careful to obey all of my laws and regulations, for I am the LORD.”

Punishments for Disobedience

20 The LORD said to Moses, 2“Give the Israelites these instructions, which apply to 20:2 Lev 18:21; 24:14-23
those who are Israelites by birth as well as to the foreigners living among you. If
any among them devote their children as burnt offerings to Molech, they must be stoned 20:3 Lev 18:21 Num 19:20 Ezek 5:11
to death by people of the community. 3I myself will turn against them and cut them off
from the community, because they have defiled my sanctuary and profaned my holy
name by giving their children to Molech. 4And if the people of the community ignore
this offering of children to Molech and refuse to execute the guilty parents, 5then I
myself will turn against them and cut them off from the community, along with all those 20:6 Lev 19:26, 31
who commit prostitution by worshiping Molech.
6“If any among the people are unfaithful by consulting and following mediums or 20:7 Lev 11:44-45 †1 Pet 1:16
psychics, I will turn against them and cut them off from the community. 7So set
yourselves apart to be holy, for I, the LORD, am your God. 8Keep all my laws and obey 20:9 Exod 21:17 Deut 27:16 †Matt 15:4
them, for I am the LORD, who makes you holy.
9“All who curse their father or mother must be put to death. They are guilty of a capital
offense. 20:10 Exod 20:14 Deut 22:22
10“If a man commits adultery with another man’s wife, both the man and the woman
must be put to death. 11If a man has intercourse with his father’s wife, both the man and 20:11 Lev 18:7-8 Deut 27:20
the woman must die, for they are guilty of a capital offense. 12If a man has intercourse
with his daughter-in-law, both must be put to death. They have acted contrary to nature 20:12 Lev 18:15
and are guilty of a capital offense.
13“The penalty for homosexual acts is death to both parties. They have committed a 20:13 Lev 18:22
detestable act and are guilty of a capital offense. 14If a man has intercourse with both a
woman and her mother, such an act is terribly wicked. All three of them must be burned 20:14 Lev 18:17 Deut 27:23
to death to wipe out such wickedness from among you.

19:36 Hebrew *Use an honest ephah* [a measure for dry goods] *and an honest hin* [a measure for liquids].

19:33, 34 How do you feel when you encounter foreigners, especially those who don’t speak your language? Are you impatient? Do you think or act as if they should go back where they came from? Are you tempted to take advantage of them? God says to treat foreigners as you’d treat fellow countrymen, to love them as you love yourself. In reality, we are all foreigners in this world because it is only our temporary home. View strangers, newcomers, and foreigners as opportunities to demonstrate God’s love.

20:1-3 Sacrificing children to the gods was a common practice in ancient religions. The Ammonites, Israel’s neighbors, made child sacrifice to Molech (their national god) a vital part of their religion. They saw this as the greatest gift they could offer to ward off evil or appease angry gods. God made it clear that this practice was detestable and strictly forbidden. In Old Testament times as well as New, his character made human sacrifice unthinkable. (1) Unlike the pagan gods, he is a God of love, who does not need to be appeased (Exodus 34:6). (2) He is a God of life, who prohibits murder and encourages practices that lead to health and happiness (Deuteronomy 30:15, 16). (3) He is God of the helpless, who shows special concern for children (Psalm 72:4). (4) He is a God of unselfishness, who instead of demanding blood gives his life for others (Isaiah 53:4, 5).

20:6 Everyone is interested in what the future holds, and we often look to others for guidance. But God warned about looking to the occult for advice. Mediums and psychics were outlawed because God was not the source of their information. At best, occult practitioners are fakes whose predictions cannot be trusted. At worst, they are in contact with evil spirits and are thus extremely dangerous. We don’t need to look to the occult for information about the future. God has given us the Bible so that we may obtain all the information we need—and the Bible’s teaching is trustworthy.

20:10-21 This list of commands against sexual sins includes extremely harsh punishments. Why? God had no tolerance for such acts for the following reasons: (1) They shatter the mutual commitment of married partners; (2) they destroy the sanctity of the family; (3) they twist people’s mental well-being; and (4) they spread disease. Sexual sin has always been widely available, but the glorification of sex between people who are not married to each other often hides deep tragedy and hurt behind the scenes. When society portrays sexual sins as attractive, it is easy to forget the dark side. God had good reasons for prohibiting sexual sins: He loves us and wants the very best for us.

20:10-21 The detestable acts listed here were very common in the pagan nations of Canaan; their religions were rampant with sex goddesses, temple prostitution, and other gross sins. The Canaanites’ immoral religious practices reflected a decadent culture that tended to corrupt whoever came in contact with it. By contrast, God was building a nation to make a positive influence on the world. He did not want the Israelites to adopt the Canaanites’ practices and slide into debauchery. So he prepared the people for what they would face in the Promised Land by commanding them to steer clear of sexual sins.

15“If a man has sexual intercourse with an animal, he must be put to death, and the
animal must be killed. 16If a woman approaches a male animal to have intercourse with
it, she and the animal must both be put to death. Both must die, for they are guilty of a
capital offense.

17“If a man has sexual intercourse with his sister, the daughter of either his father or his
mother, it is a terrible disgrace. Both of them must be publicly cut off from the community.
Since the man has had intercourse with his sister, he will suffer the consequences of his
guilt. 18If a man has intercourse with a woman suffering from a hemorrhage,* both of them
must be cut off from the community, because he exposed the source of her flow, and she
allowed him to do it.

19“If a man has sexual intercourse with his aunt, whether his mother’s sister or his
father’s sister, he has violated a close relative. Both parties are guilty of a capital offense.
20If a man has intercourse with his uncle’s wife, he has violated his uncle. Both the man
and woman involved are guilty of a capital offense and will die childless. 21If a man
marries his brother’s wife, it is an act of impurity. He has violated his brother, and the
guilty couple will remain childless.

22“You must carefully obey all my laws and regulations; otherwise the land to which
I am bringing you will vomit you out. 23Do not live by the customs of the people whom
I will expel before you. It is because they do these terrible things that I detest them so
much. 24But I have promised that you will inherit their land, a land flowing with milk
and honey. I, the LORD, am your God, who has set you apart from all other people.

25“You must therefore make a distinction between ceremonially clean and unclean
animals, and between clean and unclean birds. You must not defile yourselves by eating
any animal or bird or creeping creature that I have forbidden. 26You must be holy because
I, the LORD, am holy. I have set you apart from all other people to be my very own.

27“Men and women among you who act as mediums or psychics must be put to death
by stoning. They are guilty of a capital offense.”

2. Rules for priests

21 The LORD said to Moses, “Tell the priests to avoid making themselves ceremonially unclean by touching a dead relative 2unless it is a close relative—mother or
father, son or daughter, brother 3or virgin sister who was dependent because she had no
husband. 4As a husband among his relatives,* he must not defile himself.

5“The priests must never shave their heads, trim the edges of their beards, or cut their
bodies. 6They must be set apart to God as holy and must never dishonor his name. After
all, they are the ones who present the offerings to the LORD by fire, providing God with
his food, and they must remain holy.

7“The priests must not marry women defiled by prostitution or women who have been
divorced, for the priests must be set apart to God as holy. 8You must treat them as holy
because they offer up food to your God. You must consider them holy because I, the
LORD, am holy, and I make you holy. 9If a priest’s daughter becomes a prostitute, defiling
her father’s holiness as well as herself, she must be burned to death.

10“The high priest, who has had the anointing oil poured on his head and has been
ordained to wear the special priestly garments, must never let his hair hang loose* or tear
his clothing. 11He must never defile himself by going near a dead person, even if it is his
father or mother. 12He must not desecrate the sanctuary of his God by leaving it to attend
his parents’ funeral, because he has been made holy by the anointing oil of his God. I am
the LORD.

13“The high priest must marry a virgin. 14He must not marry a widow, a divorced
woman, or a woman defiled by prostitution. She must be a virgin from his own clan,

20:15 Lev 18:23; Deut 27:21
20:17 Lev 18:9
20:18 Lev 15:24; 18:19
20:19 Lev 18:12-13
20:20 Lev 18:14
20:21 Lev 18:16
20:22 Lev 18:28
20:23 Lev 18:1-3, 24-30
20:24 Exod 13:5; 33:1-3, 16
20:25 Lev 11:1-47; Deut 14:3-5
20:26 Lev 20:24
20:27 Lev 19:31
21:1 Lev 19:28; Ezek 44:25
21:2 Lev 21:11
21:5 Lev 19:27-28; Deut 14:1; Jer 16:6
21:6 Lev 10:3
21:7 Lev 21:14; Ezek 44:22
21:8 Lev 11:44
21:9 Lev 19:29; 20:14
21:10 Lev 10:6-7
21:11 Lev 19:28
21:12 Lev 10:7; Num 19:11-13
21:13 Ezek 44:22
21:14 Lev 21:7, 13

20:18 Or *a woman who is menstruating.* **21:4** The meaning of the Hebrew is uncertain. **21:10** Or *uncover his head.*

20:22, 23 God gave many rules to his people—but not without reason. He did not withhold good from them; he only prohibited those acts that would bring them to ruin. All of us understand God’s physical laws of nature. For example, jumping off a 10-story building means death because of the law of gravity. But some of us don’t understand how God’s spiritual laws work. God forbids us to do certain things because he wants to keep us from self-destruction. Next time you are drawn to a forbidden physical or emotional pleasure, remind yourself that its consequences might be suffering and separation from God, who is trying to help you.

15 that he may not dishonor his descendants among the members of his clan, because I,
the LORD, have made him holy."
16 Then the LORD said to Moses, 17 "Tell Aaron that in all future generations, his **21:17** Lev 21:6
descendants who have physical defects will not qualify to offer food to their God. 18 No
one who has a defect may come near to me, whether he is blind or lame, stunted or
deformed, 19 or has a broken foot or hand, 20 or has a humped back or is a dwarf, or has
a defective eye, or has oozing sores or scabs on his skin, or has damaged testicles.
21 Even though he is a descendant of Aaron, his physical defects disqualify him from **21:21** Lev 21:17-21
presenting offerings to the LORD by fire. Since he has a blemish, he may not offer food
to his God. 22 However, he may eat from the food offered to God, including the holy **21:22** 1 Cor 9:13
offerings and the most holy offerings. 23 Yet because of his physical defect, he must
never go behind the inner curtain or come near the altar, for this would desecrate my **21:23** Lev 21:17
holy places. I am the LORD who makes them holy."
24 So Moses gave these instructions to Aaron and his sons and to all the Israelites.

22 The LORD said to Moses, 2 "Tell Aaron and his sons to treat the sacred gifts that
the Israelites set apart for me with great care, so they do not profane my holy
name. I am the LORD. 3 Remind them that if any of their descendants are ceremonially **22:3** Lev 7:20-21
unclean when they approach the sacred food presented by the Israelites, they must be cut Num 19:13
off from my presence. I am the LORD!
4 "If any of the priests have a contagious skin disease* or any kind of discharge that **22:4** Lev 11:24, 28, 31,
makes them ceremonially unclean, they may not eat the sacred offerings until they 39-40; 14:1-32
have been pronounced clean. If any of the priests become unclean by touching a
corpse, or are defiled by an emission of semen, 5 or by touching a creeping creature **22:5** Lev 11:24-25,
that is unclean, or by touching someone who is ceremonially unclean for any reason, 41-44
6 they will remain defiled until evening. They must not eat any of the sacred offerings
until they have purified their bodies with water. 7 When the sun goes down, they will
be clean again and may eat the sacred offerings. After all, this food has been set aside
for them. 8 The priests may never eat an animal that has died a natural death or has **22:8** Exod 22:31
been torn apart by wild animals, for this would defile them. I am the LORD. 9 Warn all Lev 17:15
the priests to follow these instructions carefully; otherwise they will be subject to **22:9** Exod 28:43
punishment and die for violating them. I am the LORD who makes them holy. Lev 18:30
10 "No one outside a priest's family may ever eat the sacred offerings, even if the Num 18:1-7
person lives in a priest's home or is one of his hired servants. 11 However, if the priest **22:10** Exod 29:31-34
buys slaves with his own money, they may eat of his food. And if his slaves have Lev 22:13
children, they also may share his food. 12 If a priest's daughter marries someone outside **22:11** Gen 17:13
the priestly family, she may no longer eat the sacred offerings. 13 But if she becomes a Exod 12:44
widow or is divorced and has no children to support her, and she returns to live in her **22:13** Lev 22:10
father's home, she may eat her father's food again. But other than these exceptions, only
members of the priests' families are allowed to eat the sacred offerings.
14 "Anyone who eats the sacred offerings without realizing it must pay the priest for **22:14** Lev 5:15-16
the amount eaten, plus an added penalty of 20 percent. 15 No one may defile the sacred **22:15** Lev 19:8
offerings brought to the LORD by the Israelites 16 by allowing unauthorized people to
eat them. The negligent priest would bring guilt upon the people and require them to **22:16** Lev 22:9
pay compensation. I am the LORD, who makes them holy."

22:4 Traditionally rendered *leprosy.* See note at 13:2.

21:16-23 Was God unfairly discriminating against handicapped people when he said they were unqualified to offer sacrifices? Just as God demanded that no imperfect animals be used for sacrifice, he required that no handicapped priests offer sacrifices. This was not meant as an insult; rather, it had to do with the fact that the priest must match as closely as possible the perfect God he served. Of course, such perfection was not fully realized until Jesus Christ came. As Levites, the handicapped priests were protected and supported with food from the sacrifices. They were not abandoned but still performed many essential services within the Tabernacle.

22:1-9 Why were there so many specific guidelines for the priests? The Israelites would have been quite familiar with priests from Egypt. Egyptian priests were mainly interested in politics. They viewed religion as a way to gain power. Thus, the Israelites would have been suspicious of the establishment of a new priestly order. But God wanted his priests to serve him and the people. Their duties were religious—to help people draw near to God and worship him. They could not use their position to gain power because they were not allowed to own land or take money from anyone. All these guidelines reassured the people and helped the priests accomplish their purpose.

Worthy and Unworthy Offerings

17 And the LORD said to Moses, 18 "Give Aaron and his sons and all the Israelites these
instructions, which apply to those who are Israelites by birth as well as to the
foreigners living among you. If you offer a whole burnt offering to the LORD, whether
22:19 Lev 1:3
to fulfill a vow or as a freewill offering, 19 it will be accepted only if it is a male animal
with no physical defects. It may be either a bull, a ram, or a male goat. 20 Do not bring
22:20 Lev 1:3 Deut 15:21 Heb 9:14 1 Pet 1:19
an animal with physical defects, because it won't be accepted on your behalf.
21 "If you bring a peace offering to the LORD from the herd or flock, whether to
fulfill a vow or as a freewill offering, you must offer an animal that has no physical
defects of any kind. 22 An animal that is blind, injured, mutilated, or that has a growth,
an open sore, or a scab must never be offered to the LORD by fire on the altar. 23 If the
bull* or lamb is deformed or stunted, it may still be offered as a freewill offering, but
it may not be offered to fulfill a vow. 24 If an animal has damaged testicles or is
22:25 Lev 21:6, 17
castrated, it may never be offered to the LORD. 25 You must never accept mutilated or
defective animals from foreigners to be offered as a sacrifice to your God. Such
animals will not be accepted on your behalf because they are defective."
26 And the LORD said to Moses, 27 "When a bull or a ram or a male goat is born, it must
be left with its mother for seven days. From the eighth day on, it will be acceptable as an
22:28 Deut 22:6
offering given to the LORD by fire. 28 But you must never slaughter a mother animal and
her offspring on the same day, whether from the herd or the flock. 29 When you bring a
22:29 Lev 7:12
thanksgiving offering to the LORD, it must be sacrificed properly so it will be accepted on
22:30 Lev 7:15
your behalf. 30 Eat the entire sacrificial animal on the day it is presented. Don't leave any
of it until the second day. I am the LORD.
22:31 Lev 19:37
31 "You must faithfully keep all my commands by obeying them, for I am the LORD.
32 Do not treat my holy name as common and ordinary. I must be treated as holy by the
22:33 Lev 11:45
people of Israel. It is I, the LORD, who makes you holy. 33 It was I who rescued you from
Egypt, that I might be your very own God. I am the LORD."

3. Seasons and festivals

23:2 Lev 23:21 Num 29:39
23 The LORD said to Moses, 2 "Give the Israelites instructions regarding the LORD's
appointed festivals, the days when all of you will be summoned to worship me.
23:3 Exod 20:8-11; 23:12; 31:15 Deut 5:13-14
3 You may work for six days each week, but on the seventh day all work must come to a
complete stop. It is the LORD's Sabbath day of complete rest, a holy day to assemble for
worship. It must be observed wherever you live. 4 In addition to the Sabbath, the LORD has
established festivals, the holy occasions to be observed at the proper time each year.

Passover and the Festival of Unleavened Bread

23:5 Exod 12:3-20 Deut 16:1-8
5 "First comes the LORD's Passover, which begins at twilight on its appointed day in early
spring.* 6 Then the day after the Passover celebration,* the Festival of Unleavened Bread
23:6 Exod 12:14-20
begins. This festival to the LORD continues for seven days, and during that time all the
bread you eat must be made without yeast. 7 On the first day of the festival, all the people
must stop their regular work and gather for a sacred assembly. 8 On each of the next seven
days, the people must present an offering to the LORD by fire. On the seventh day, the
people must again stop all their regular work to hold a sacred assembly."

22:23 Or *cow;* also in 22:27. **23:5** Hebrew *on the fourteenth day of the first month.* This day of the Hebrew lunar calendar occurs in late March or early April. **23:6** Hebrew *On the fifteenth day of the same month.*

22:19-25 Animals with defects were not acceptable as sacrifices because they did not represent God's holy nature. Furthermore, the animal had to be without blemish in order to foreshadow the perfect, sinless life of Jesus Christ. When we give our best time, talent, and treasure to God rather than what is tarnished or common, we show the true meaning of worship and testify to God's supreme worth.

23:1ff Festivals played a major role in Israel's culture. Israel's festivals were different from those of any other nation because, being ordained by God, they were times of celebrating with him, not times of moral depravity. God wanted to set aside special days for the people to come together for rest, refreshment, and remembering with thanksgiving all he had done for them.

23:1-4 God established several national holidays each year for celebration, fellowship, and worship. Much can be learned about people by observing the holidays they celebrate and the way they celebrate them. Take note of your holiday traditions. What do they say about your values?

23:6 The Festival of Unleavened Bread reminded Israel of their escape from Egypt. For seven days they ate unleavened bread, just as they had eaten it back then (Exodus 12:14, 15). The symbolism of this bread made without yeast was important to the Israelites. First, because the bread was unique, it illustrated Israel's uniqueness as a nation. Second, because yeast was a symbol of sin, the bread represented Israel's moral purity. Third, the bread reminded them to obey quickly. Their ancestors left the yeast out of their dough so they could leave Egypt quickly without waiting for the dough to rise.

The Festival of Firstfruits

9Then the LORD told Moses 10to give these instructions to the Israelites: "When you arrive
in the land I am giving you and you harvest your first crops, bring the priest some grain
from the first portion of your grain harvest. 11On the day after the Sabbath, the priest will
lift it up before the LORD so it may be accepted on your behalf. 12That same day you must
sacrifice a year-old male lamb with no physical defects as a whole burnt offering to the
LORD. 13A grain offering must accompany it consisting of three quarts* of choice flour
mixed with olive oil. It will be an offering given to the LORD by fire, and it will be very
pleasing to him. Along with this sacrifice, you must also offer one quart* of wine as a drink
offering. 14Do not eat any bread or roasted grain or fresh kernels on that day until after you
have brought this offering to your God. This is a permanent law for you, and it must be
observed wherever you live.

23:10 Exod 23:19; 34:26
23:13 Lev 6:20

The Festival of Harvest

15"From the day after the Sabbath, the day the bundle of grain was lifted up as an offering,
count off seven weeks. 16Keep counting until the day after the seventh Sabbath, fifty days
later, and bring an offering of new grain to the LORD. 17From wherever you live, bring two
loaves of bread to be lifted up before the LORD as an offering. These loaves must be baked
from three quarts of choice flour that contains yeast. They will be an offering to the LORD
from the first of your crops. 18Along with this bread, present seven one-year-old lambs with
no physical defects, one bull, and two rams as burnt offerings to the LORD. These whole
burnt offerings, together with the accompanying grain offerings and drink offerings, will be
given to the LORD by fire and will be pleasing to him. 19Then you must offer one male goat
as a sin offering and two one-year-old male lambs as a peace offering.

20"The priest will lift up these offerings before the LORD, together with the loaves representing the first of your later crops. These offerings are holy to the LORD and will belong to
the priests. 21That same day, you must stop all your regular work and gather for a sacred
assembly. This is a permanent law for you, and it must be observed wherever you live.

22"When you harvest the crops of your land, do not harvest the grain along the edges
of your fields, and do not pick up what the harvesters drop. Leave it for the poor and the
foreigners living among you. I, the LORD, am your God."

23:15 Num 28:26-31; Deut 16:9-12
23:19 Lev 3:1; Num 28:30
23:20 Exod 29:24
23:22 Lev 19:9-10; Deut 24:19-21

The Festival of Trumpets

23The LORD told Moses 24to give these instructions to the Israelites: "On the appointed day
in early autumn,* you are to celebrate a day of complete rest. All your work must stop on
that day. You will call the people to a sacred assembly—the Festival of Trumpets—with
loud blasts from a trumpet. 25You must do no regular work on that day. Instead, you are to
present offerings to the LORD by fire."

23:24 Num 10:9-10; 29:1
23:25 Lev 23:7

The Day of Atonement

26Then the LORD said to Moses, 27"Remember that the Day of Atonement is to be celebrated
on the ninth day after the Festival of Trumpets.* On that day you must humble yourselves,
gather for a sacred assembly, and present offerings to the LORD by fire. 28Do no work during
that entire day because it is the Day of Atonement, when atonement will be made for you
before the LORD your God, and payment will be made for your sins. 29Anyone who does
not spend that day in humility will be cut off from the community. 30And I will destroy
anyone among you who does any kind of work on that day. 31You must do no work at all!
This is a permanent law for you, and it must be observed wherever you live. 32This will be
a Sabbath day of total rest for you, and on that day you must humble yourselves. This time

23:27 Lev 16:29-30
23:28 Lev 23:7
23:29 Gen 17:14
23:32 Lev 16:31

23:13a Hebrew *2/10 of an ephah* [3.6 liters]; also in 23:17. **23:13b** Hebrew *1/4 of a hin* [1 liter]. **23:24** Hebrew *On the first day of the seventh month.* This day of the Hebrew lunar calendar occurs in September or early October. **23:27** Hebrew *on the tenth day of the seventh month;* see 23:24 and the note there.

23:9-14 The Festival of Firstfruits required that the first crops harvested be offered to God. The Israelites could not eat the food from their harvest until they had made this offering. Today God still expects us to set aside his portion first, not last. Giving leftovers to God is no way to express thanks.

23:15-22 The Festival of Harvest was a festival praising God for a bountiful harvest.

23:23, 24 Most of the trumpets used were rams' horns, although some of the more special trumpets were made of beaten silver. Trumpets were blown to announce the beginning of each month as well as the start of festivals.

of rest and fasting will begin the evening before the Day of Atonement* and extend until
evening of that day."

The Festival of Shelters

[33]And the LORD said to Moses, [34]"Tell the Israelites to begin the Festival of Shelters on
the fifth day after the Day of Atonement.* This festival to the LORD will last for seven
days. [35]It will begin with a sacred assembly on the first day, and all your regular work
must stop. [36]On each of the seven festival days, you must present offerings to the LORD
by fire. On the eighth day, you must gather again for a sacred assembly and present
another offering to the LORD by fire. This will be a solemn closing assembly, and no
regular work may be done that day.
[37]"These are the LORD's appointed annual festivals. Celebrate them by gathering in
sacred assemblies to present all the various offerings to the LORD by fire—whole burnt
offerings and grain offerings, sacrificial meals and drink offerings—each on its proper
day. [38]These festivals must be observed in addition to the LORD's regular Sabbath days.
And these offerings must be given in addition to your personal gifts, the offerings you
make to accompany your vows, and any freewill offerings that you present to the LORD.
[39]"Now, on the first day of the Festival of Shelters,* after you have harvested all the
produce of the land, you will begin to celebrate this seven-day festival to the LORD.
Remember that the first day and closing eighth day of the festival will be days of total
rest. [40]On the first day, gather fruit from citrus trees,* and collect palm fronds and other
leafy branches and willows that grow by the streams. Then rejoice before the LORD your
God for seven days. [41]You must observe this seven-day festival to the LORD every year.
This is a permanent law for you, and it must be kept by all future generations. [42]During
the seven festival days, all of you who are Israelites by birth must live in shelters. [43]This
will remind each new generation of Israelites that their ancestors had to live in shelters
when I rescued them from the land of Egypt. I, the LORD, am your God."

23:33-34 Num 29:12-39; Deut 16:13-16; Ezra 3:4; Neh 8:14; Zech 14:16; John 7:2
23:35 Lev 23:7
23:36 Num 29:12-38
23:37 Lev 23:2
23:38 Num 29:39
23:40 Neh 8:15
23:43 Deut 13:31; Ps 78:1-8

23:32 Hebrew *the evening of the ninth day of the month;* see 23:24, 27 and the notes there. **23:34** Hebrew *on the fifteenth day of the seventh month;* see 23:24, 27 and the notes there. **23:39** Hebrew *on the fifteenth day of the seventh month;* see 23:24 and the note there. **23:40** Or *fruit from majestic trees.*

THE FESTIVALS
Besides enjoying one Sabbath day of rest each week, the Israelites also enjoyed 19 days when national holidays were celebrated.

Feast	*What It Celebrated*	*Its Importance*
Passover One day (Leviticus 23:5)	When God spared the lives of Israel's firstborn children in Egypt and freed the Hebrews from slavery	Reminded the people of God's deliverance
Unleavened Bread Seven days (Leviticus 23:6–8)	The exodus from Egypt	Reminded the people they were leaving the old life behind and entering a new way of living
Firstfruits One day (Leviticus 23:9–14)	The first crops of the barley harvest	Reminded the people how God provided for them
Pentecost (Harvest) One day (Leviticus 23:15–22)	The end of the barley harvest and beginning of the wheat harvest	Showed joy and thanksgiving over the bountiful harvest
Trumpets One day (Leviticus 23:23–25)	The beginning of the seventh month (civil new year)	Expressed joy and thanksgiving to God
Day of Atonement One day (Leviticus 23:26–32)	The removal of sin from the people and the nation	Restored fellowship with God
Shelters Seven days (Leviticus 23:33–43)	God's protection and guidance in the wilderness	Renewed Israel's commitment to God and trust in his guidance and protection

23:33-43 The Festival of Shelters, also called the Festival of Ingathering, was a special celebration involving the whole family (see 23:34; Exodus 23:16; Deuteronomy 16:13, 14). Like Passover, this festival taught family members of all ages about God's nature and what he had done for them and was a time of renewed commitment to God. Our families also need rituals of celebration to renew our faith and to pass it on to our children. In addition to Christmas and Easter, we should select other special days to commemorate God's goodness.

44 So Moses gave these instructions regarding the annual festivals of the LORD to the
Israelites.

Pure Oil and Holy Bread

24 The LORD said to Moses, 2 "Command the people of Israel to provide you with pure
olive oil for the lampstand, so it can be kept burning continually. 3 Aaron will set it
up outside the inner curtain of the Most Holy Place in the Tabernacle* and must arrange to
have the lamps tended continually, from evening until morning, before the LORD. This is a
permanent law for you, and it must be kept by all future generations. 4 The lamps on the
pure gold lampstand must be tended continually in the LORD's presence.

5 "You must bake twelve loaves of bread from choice flour, using three quarts* of flour
for each loaf. 6 Place the bread in the LORD's presence on the pure gold table, and arrange
the loaves in two rows, with six in each row. 7 Sprinkle some pure frankincense near each
row. It will serve as a token offering, to be burned in place of the bread as an offering
given to the LORD by fire. 8 Every Sabbath day this bread must be laid out before the
LORD on behalf of the Israelites as a continual part of the covenant. 9 The loaves of bread
belong to Aaron and his male descendants, who must eat them in a sacred place, for they
represent a most holy portion of the offerings given to the LORD by fire."

An Example of Just Punishment

10 One day a man who had an Israelite mother and an Egyptian father got into a fight with
one of the Israelite men. 11 During the fight, this son of an Israelite woman blasphemed
the LORD's name. So the man was brought to Moses for judgment. His mother's name
was Shelomith. She was the daughter of Dibri of the tribe of Dan. 12 They put the man
in custody until the LORD's will in the matter should become clear.

13 Then the LORD said to Moses, 14 "Take the blasphemer outside the camp, and tell all
those who heard him to lay their hands on his head. Then let the entire community stone
him to death. 15 Say to the people of Israel: Those who blaspheme God will suffer the
consequences of their guilt and be punished. 16 Anyone who blasphemes the LORD's
name must be stoned to death by the whole community of Israel. Any Israelite or
foreigner among you who blasphemes the LORD's name will surely die.

17 "Anyone who takes another person's life must be put to death.

18 "Anyone who kills another person's animal must pay it back in full—a live animal
for the animal that was killed.

19 "Anyone who injures another person must be dealt with according to the injury
inflicted—20 fracture for fracture, eye for eye, tooth for tooth. Whatever anyone does to
hurt another person must be paid back in kind.

21 "Whoever kills an animal must make full restitution, but whoever kills another
person must be put to death.

22 "These same regulations apply to Israelites by birth and foreigners who live among
you. I, the LORD, am your God."

23 After Moses gave all these instructions to the Israelites, they led the blasphemer
outside the camp and stoned him to death, just as the LORD had commanded Moses.

The Sabbath Year

25 While Moses was on Mount Sinai, the LORD said to him, 2 "Give these instructions
to the Israelites: When you have entered the land I am giving you as an inheritance,
the land itself must observe a Sabbath to the LORD every seventh year. 3 For six years you

24:3 Hebrew *the curtain of the Testimony in the Tent of Meeting.* 24:5 Hebrew *2/10 of an ephah* [3.6 liters].

23:44 Lev 23:37
24:2 Exod 27:20-21
24:4 Exod 25:31
24:5 Exod 25:30; 40:23 Lev 23:13 Heb 9:2
24:9 Lev 6:16-17 Matt 12:4
24:11 Exod 22:28 Job 1:11; 2:5 Isa 8:21
24:14 Lev 20:2, 27 Deut 13:9; 17:7; 21:21
24:15 Exod 22:28
24:17 Gen 9:5 Exod 21:12, 14 Num 35:30-31 Deut 19:11-12
24:18 Lev 24:21
24:20 Exod 21:24-25 Deut 19:21 Matt 5:38
24:21 Lev 24:17-18
24:22 Exod 12:49 Num 15:15-16, 29
25:2 Exod 23:11
25:3 Exod 23:10

23:44 Worship involves both celebration and confession. But in Israel's national holidays, the balance seems heavily tipped in favor of celebration—five joyous occasions to two solemn ones. The God of the Bible encourages joy! God does not intend for religion to be only meditation and introspection. He also wants us to celebrate. Serious reflection and immediate confession of sin is essential, of course. But this should be balanced by celebrating who God is and what he has done for his people.

24:14 This punishment for blasphemy (cursing God) seems extreme by modern standards. But it shows how seriously God expects us to take our relationship with him. Often we use his name in swearing, or we act as though he doesn't exist. We should be careful how we speak and act, treating God with reverence. Eventually he will have the last word.

24:17-22 This was a code for judges, not an endorsement of personal vengeance. In effect, it was saying that the punishment should fit the crime, but it should not go beyond.

25:1-7 The Sabbath year provided one year in seven for the fields to lay fallow (unplowed). This was good management of natural resources and reminded the people of God's control and provision for them.

may plant your fields and prune your vineyards and harvest your crops, [4]but during the
seventh year the land will enjoy a Sabbath year of rest to the LORD. Do not plant your crops
or prune your vineyards during that entire year. [5]And don't store away the crops that grow
naturally or process the grapes that grow on your unpruned vines. The land is to have a year
of total rest. [6]But you, your male and female slaves, your hired servants, and any foreigners
who live with you may eat the produce that grows naturally during the Sabbath year. [7]And
your livestock and the wild animals will also be allowed to eat of the land's bounty.

The Year of Jubilee

[8]"In addition, you must count off seven Sabbath years, seven years times seven, adding up
to forty-nine years in all. [9]Then on the Day of Atonement of the fiftieth year,* blow the
trumpets loud and long throughout the land. [10]This year will be set apart as holy, a time to
proclaim release for all who live there. It will be a jubilee year for you, when each of you
returns to the lands that belonged to your ancestors and rejoins your clan. [11]Yes, the fiftieth
year will be a jubilee for you. During that year, do not plant any seeds or store away any of
the crops that grow naturally, and do not process the grapes that grow on your unpruned
vines. [12]It will be a jubilee year for you, and you must observe it as a special and holy time.
You may, however, eat the produce that grows naturally in the fields that year. [13]In the Year
of Jubilee each of you must return to the lands that belonged to your ancestors.

[14]"When you make an agreement with a neighbor to buy or sell property, you must
never take advantage of each other. [15]When you buy land from your neighbor, the price
of the land should be based on the number of years since the last jubilee. The seller will
charge you only for the crop years left until the next Year of Jubilee. [16]The more the
years, the higher the price; the fewer the years, the lower the price. After all, the person
selling the land is actually selling you a certain number of harvests. [17]Show your fear of
God by not taking advantage of each other. I, the LORD, am your God.

[18]"If you want to live securely in the land, keep my laws and obey my regulations.
[19]Then the land will yield bumper crops, and you will eat your fill and live securely in
it. [20]But you might ask, 'What will we eat during the seventh year, since we are not
allowed to plant or harvest crops that year?' [21]The answer is, 'I will order my blessing
for you in the sixth year, so the land will produce a bumper crop, enough to support you
for three years. [22]As you plant the seed in the eighth year, you will still be eating the
produce of the previous year. In fact, you will eat from the old crop until the new harvest
comes in the ninth year.' [23]And remember, the land must never be sold on a permanent
basis because it really belongs to me. You are only foreigners and tenants living with me.

Redemption of Property

[24]"With every sale of land there must be a stipulation that the land can be redeemed at any
time. [25]If any of your Israelite relatives go bankrupt and are forced to sell some inherited
land, then a close relative, a kinsman redeemer, may buy it back for them. [26]If there is no
one to redeem the land but the person who sold it manages to get enough money to buy it
back, [27]then that person has the right to redeem it from the one who bought it. The price of
the land will be based on the number of years until the next Year of Jubilee. After buying it
back, the original owner may then return to the land. [28]But if the original owner cannot
afford to redeem it, then it will belong to the new owner until the next Year of Jubilee. In
the jubilee year, the land will be returned to the original owner.

[29]"Anyone who sells a house inside a walled city has the right to redeem it for a full
year after its sale. During that time, the seller retains the right to buy it back. [30]But if it
is not redeemed within a year, then the house within the walled city will become the
permanent property of the buyer. It will not be returned to the original owner in the Year

25:4 Lev 25:1, 20-23
25:5 2 Kgs 19:29
25:6 Lev 25:20-21
25:9 Num 10:10
25:10 Lev 25:8-16, 28-54; Isa 61:1; Jer 34:8, 15, 17; Luke 4:19
25:13 Lev 25:10, 24-31
25:14 Lev 25:17, 51-52
25:17 Lev 25:14-16
25:23 Exod 19:5; 1 Chr 29:15
25:25 Ruth 2:20; 4:4, 6; Jer 32:7
25:27 Lev 25:50-52
25:28 Lev 25:10, 13

25:9 Hebrew *on the tenth day of the seventh month, on the Day of Atonement;* see 23:27 and the note there.

25:8-17 The Year of Jubilee was meant to be celebrated every 50 years. It included canceling all debts, freeing all slaves, and returning to its original owners all land that had been sold. There is no indication in the Bible that the Year of Jubilee was ever carried out. If Israel had followed this practice faithfully, they would have been a society without permanent poverty.

25:23 The people would one day possess land in Canaan, but in God's plan, only God's ownership was absolute. He wanted his people to avoid greed and materialism. If you have the attitude that you are taking care of the Lord's property, you will make what you have more available to others. This is difficult to do if you have an attitude of ownership. Think of yourself as a manager of all that is under your care, not as an owner.

of Jubilee. 31 But a house in a village—a settlement without fortified walls—will be
treated like property in the open fields. Such a house may be redeemed at any time and
must be returned to the original owner in the Year of Jubilee.
32 "The Levites always have the right to redeem any house they have sold within the cities
belonging to them. 33 And any property that can be redeemed by the Levites—all houses within
the Levitical cities—must be returned in the Year of Jubilee. After all, the cities reserved for
the Levites are the only property they own in all Israel. 34 The strip of pastureland around **25:34**
each of the Levitical cities may never be sold. It is their permanent ancestral property. Num 35:2-5

Redemption of the Poor and Enslaved

35 "If any of your Israelite relatives fall into poverty and cannot support themselves, support **25:35**
them as you would a resident foreigner and allow them to live with you. 36 Do not demand Deut 15:7-11 Prov 21:26
an advance or charge interest on the money you lend them. Instead, show your fear of God **25:36**
by letting them live with you as your relatives. 37 Remember, do not charge your relatives Exod 22:25 Deut 23:19-20
interest on anything you lend them, whether money or food. 38 I, the LORD, am your God, **25:38**
who brought you out of Egypt to give you the land of Canaan and to be your God. Lev 11:45
39 "If any of your Israelite relatives go bankrupt and sell themselves to you, do not treat **25:39** Exod 21:2-11
them as slaves. 40 Treat them instead as hired servants or as resident foreigners who live Deut 15:12-18
with you, and they will serve you only until the Year of Jubilee. 41 At that time they and **25:40**
their children will no longer be obligated to you, and they will return to their clan and Lev 25:53
ancestral property. 42 The people of Israel are my servants, whom I brought out of the
land of Egypt, so they must never be sold as slaves. 43 Show your fear of God by treating **25:43**
them well; never exercise your power over them in a ruthless way. Col 4:11
44 "However, you may purchase male or female slaves from among the foreigners who
live among you. 45 You may also purchase the children of such resident foreigners,
including those who have been born in your land. You may treat them as your property,
46 passing them on to your children as a permanent inheritance. You may treat your slaves **25:46**
like this, but the people of Israel, your relatives, must never be treated this way. Lev 25:40, 53
47 "If a resident foreigner becomes rich, and if some of your Israelite relatives go bankrupt
and sell themselves to such a foreigner, 48 they still retain the right of redemption. They **25:48**
may be bought back by a close relative—49 an uncle, a nephew, or anyone else who is Neh 5:5 **25:49**
closely related. They may also redeem themselves if they can get the money. 50 The price Lev 25:26
of their freedom will be based on the number of years left until the next Year of **25:50**
Jubilee—whatever it would cost to hire a servant for that number of years. 51 If many years Job 7:1
still remain, they will repay most of what they received when they sold themselves. 52 If
only a few years remain until the Year of Jubilee, then they will repay a relatively small
amount for their redemption. 53 The foreigner must treat them as servants hired on a yearly **25:53**
basis. You must not allow a resident foreigner to treat any of your Israelite relatives Lev 25:40, 46
ruthlessly. 54 If any Israelites have not been redeemed by the time the Year of Jubilee **25:54**
arrives, then they and their children must be set free at that time. 55 For the people of Israel Lev 25:10, 13, 28
are my servants, whom I brought out of the land of Egypt. I, the LORD, am your God.

4. Receiving God's blessing

Blessings for Obedience

26 "Do not make idols or set up carved images, sacred pillars, or shaped stones to be **26:1** Exod 20:4; 34:17
worshiped in your land. I, the LORD, am your God. 2 You must keep my Sabbath **26:2**
days of rest and show reverence for my sanctuary. I am the LORD. Exod 20:8-11

25:35ff The Bible places great emphasis on assisting the poor and helpless, especially orphans, widows, and the handicapped. In Israelite society, no paid work was available to women; thus, a widow and her children had no livelihood. Neither was there work available for the seriously handicapped in this nation of farmers and shepherds. The poor were to be helped without charging any interest. Individual and family responsibility for the poor was crucial since there was no government aid.

25:35-37 God said that neglecting the poor was a sin. Permanent poverty was not allowed in Israel. Financially secure families were responsible to help and house those in need. Many times we do nothing, not because we lack compassion, but because we are overwhelmed by the size of the problem and don't know where to begin. God doesn't expect you to eliminate poverty, nor does he expect you to neglect your family while providing for others. He does, however, expect that when you see an individual in need, you will reach out with whatever help you can offer, including hospitality.

25:44 Why did God allow the Israelites to purchase slaves? Under Hebrew laws, slaves were treated differently from slaves in other nations. They were seen as human beings with dignity, and not as animals. Hebrew slaves, for example, took part in the religious festivals and rested on the Sabbath. Nowhere does the Bible condone slavery, but it recognizes its existence. God's laws offered many guidelines for treating slaves properly.

26:4 Lev 25:19; Deut 11:14-15
26:6 Ps 29:11
26:8 Deut 28:7; 32:30
26:9 Gen 17:6-7
26:10 Lev 25:22
26:11 Exod 29:45-46
26:12 Exod 6:7; †2 Cor 6:16
26:13 Exod 20:2
26:16 Deut 28:22, 33, 65-67; 32:25
26:17 Lev 26:36-37; Deut 28:25; Ps 106:41; Prov 28:1
26:18 Lev 26:21, 24, 28
26:19 Deut 28:23; Isa 25:11; 26:5
26:21 Lev 26:18
26:22 Deut 32:24
26:23 Jer 2:30; 5:3
26:25 Deut 28:21-22, 27-29; 32:35
26:26 Isa 3:1; 9:19-20; Ezek 4:16
26:29 Deut 28:53-57; 2 Kgs 6:26-30
26:30 1 Kgs 13:2; Isa 27:9
26:31 Ps 74:3; Isa 63:18

3 “If you keep my laws and are careful to obey my commands, 4 I will send the seasonal
rains. The land will then yield its crops, and the trees will produce their fruit. 5 Your
threshing season will extend until the grape harvest, and your grape harvest will extend
until it is time to plant grain again. You will eat your fill and live securely in your land.
6 “I will give you peace in the land, and you will be able to sleep without fear. I will
remove the wild animals from your land and protect you from your enemies. 7 In fact,
you will chase down all your enemies and slaughter them with your swords. 8 Five of you
will chase a hundred, and a hundred of you will chase ten thousand! All your enemies
will fall beneath the blows of your weapons.
9 “I will look favorably upon you and multiply your people and fulfill my covenant
with you. 10 You will have such a surplus of crops that you will need to get rid of the
leftovers from the previous year to make room for each new harvest. 11 I will live among
you, and I will not despise you. 12 I will walk among you; I will be your God, and you
will be my people. 13 I, the LORD, am your God, who brought you from the land of Egypt
so you would no longer be slaves. I have lifted the yoke of slavery from your neck so
you can walk free with your heads held high.

Punishments for Disobedience

14 “However, if you do not listen to me or obey my commands, 15 and if you break my
covenant by rejecting my laws and treating my regulations with contempt, 16 I will punish
you. You will suffer from sudden terrors, with wasting diseases, and with burning fevers,
causing your eyes to fail and your life to ebb away. You will plant your crops in vain because
your enemies will eat them. 17 I will turn against you, and you will be defeated by all your
enemies. They will rule over you, and you will run even when no one is chasing you!
18 “And if, in spite of this, you still disobey me, I will punish you for your sins seven
times over. 19 I will break down your arrogant spirit by making the skies above as
unyielding as iron and the earth beneath as hard as bronze. 20 All your work will be for
nothing, for your land will yield no crops, and your trees will bear no fruit.
21 “If even then you remain hostile toward me and refuse to obey, I will inflict you with
seven more disasters for your sins. 22 I will release wild animals that will kill your children
and destroy your cattle, so your numbers will dwindle and your roads will be deserted.
23 “And if you fail to learn a lesson from this and continue your hostility toward me,
24 then I myself will be hostile toward you, and I will personally strike you seven times
over for your sins. 25 I will send armies against you to carry out these covenant threats.
If you flee to your cities, I will send a plague to destroy you there, and you will be
conquered by your enemies. 26 I will completely destroy your food supply, so the bread
from one oven will have to be stretched to feed ten families. They will ration your food
by weight, and even if you have food to eat, you will not be satisfied.
27 “If after this you still refuse to listen and still remain hostile toward me, 28 then I will
give full vent to my hostility. I will punish you seven times over for your sins. 29 You will
eat the flesh of your own sons and daughters. 30 I will destroy your pagan shrines and cut
down your incense altars. I will leave your corpses piled up beside your lifeless idols, and
I will despise you. 31 I will make your cities desolate and destroy your places of worship,

---

26:1ff This chapter presents the two paths of obedience and disobedience that God set before the people (see also Deuteronomy 28). The people of the Old Testament were warned over and over against worshiping idols. We wonder how they could deceive themselves with these objects of wood and stone. Yet God could well give us the same warning, for we are prone to put idols before him. Idolatry is making anything more important than God, and our lives are full of that temptation. Money, looks, success, reputation, security—these are today's idols. As you look at these false gods that promise everything you want but nothing you need, does idolatry seem so far removed from your experience?

26:13 Imagine the joy of a slave set free. God took the children of Israel out of bitter slavery and gave them freedom and dignity. We, too, are set free when we accept Christ's payment that redeems us from sin's slavery. We no longer need to be bogged down in shame over our past sins; we can walk with dignity because God has forgiven us and forgotten them. But just as the Israelites were still in danger of returning to a slave mentality, we need to beware of the temptation to return to our former sinful patterns.

26:18 If the Israelites obeyed, there would be peace in the land. If they disobeyed, disaster would follow. God used sin's consequences to draw them to repentance, not to get back at them. Today, sin's consequences are not always so apparent. When calamity strikes us, we may not know the reason. It may be (1) the result of our own disobedience, (2) the result of someone else's sin, or (3) the result of natural disaster. Because we don't know, we should search our hearts and be sure we are at peace with God. His Spirit, like a great searchlight, will reveal those areas we need to deal with. Because calamity is not always the result of wrongdoing, we must guard against assigning or accepting blame for every tragedy we encounter. Misplaced guilt is one of Satan's favorite weapons against believers.

and I will take no pleasure in your offerings of incense. 32Yes, I myself will devastate your
land. Your enemies who come to occupy it will be utterly shocked at the destruction they
see. 33I will scatter you among the nations and attack you with my own weapons. Your land
will become desolate, and your cities will lie in ruins. 34Then at last the land will make up
for its missed Sabbath years as it lies desolate during your years of exile in the land of your
enemies. Then the land will finally rest and enjoy its Sabbaths. 35As the land lies in ruins,
it will take the rest you never allowed it to take every seventh year while you lived in it.
36"And for those of you who survive, I will demoralize you in the land of your enemies
far away. You will live there in such constant fear that the sound of a leaf driven by the
wind will send you fleeing. You will run as though chased by a warrior with a sword,
and you will fall even when no one is pursuing you. 37Yes, though no one is chasing you,
you will stumble over each other in flight, as though fleeing in battle. You will have no
power to stand before your enemies. 38You will die among the foreign nations and be
devoured in the land of your enemies. 39Those still left alive will rot away in enemy lands
because of their sins and the sins of their ancestors.
40"But at last my people will confess their sins and the sins of their ancestors for betraying
me and being hostile toward me. 41Finally, when I have given full expression to my hostility
and have brought them to the land of their enemies, then at last their disobedient hearts will
be humbled, and they will pay for their sins. 42Then I will remember my covenant with
Jacob, with Isaac, and with Abraham, and I will remember the land. 43And the land will
enjoy its years of Sabbath rest as it lies deserted. At last the people will receive the due
punishment for their sins, for they rejected my regulations and despised my laws.
44"But despite all this, I will not utterly reject or despise them while they are in exile in
the land of their enemies. I will not cancel my covenant with them by wiping them out. I,
the LORD, am their God. 45I will remember my ancient covenant with their ancestors,
whom I brought out of Egypt while all the nations watched. I, the LORD, am their God."
46These are the laws, regulations, and instructions that the LORD gave to the Israelites
through Moses on Mount Sinai.

Redeeming Gifts Offered to the LORD

27 The LORD said to Moses, 2"Give the following instructions to the Israelites: If you
make a special vow to dedicate someone to the LORD by paying the value of that
person, 3here is the scale of values to be used. A man between the ages of twenty and sixty
is valued at fifty pieces of silver*; 4a woman of that age is valued at thirty pieces of silver.
5A boy between five and twenty is valued at twenty pieces of silver; a girl of that age is valued
at ten pieces of silver. 6A boy between the ages of one month and five years is valued at five
pieces of silver; a girl of that age is valued at three pieces of silver. 7A man older than sixty
is valued at fifteen pieces of silver; a woman older than sixty is valued at ten pieces of silver. 8If
you desire to make such a vow but cannot afford to pay the prescribed amount, go to the priest
and he will evaluate your ability to pay. You will then pay the amount decided by the priest.
9"If your vow involves giving a clean animal—one that is acceptable as an offering to
the LORD—then your gift to the LORD will be considered holy. 10The animal should never

26:32 Jer 12:11; 18:16
26:33 Deut 28:64-68
26:34 Lev 26:43; 2 Chr 36:21
26:36 Ezek 21:7
26:38 Deut 4:25-27
26:39 Ezek 33:10
26:40 Jer 3:12-15; Luke 15:18; 1 Jn 1:9
26:42 Gen 12:1-3; 15:1-4, 13-16; 26:2-5; 28:13-15
26:43 Lev 26:34
26:44 Deut 4:29-31; Rom 11:2
26:45 Gen 17:7; Exod 6:6-8
26:46 Lev 27:34
27:3 Exod 30:13; Lev 5:15; 27:25
27:6 Num 3:46-48; 18:14-16
27:8 Lev 14:21-22
27:10 Lev 27:14-33

27:3 Hebrew *50 shekels of silver, according to the standard sanctuary shekel,* each about 0.4 ounces or 11 grams in weight. The term *shekels* also appears in 27:4, 5, 6, 7, 16.

26:33-35 In 2 Kings 17 and 25 the warning pronounced in these verses came true. The people persistently disobeyed, and eventually they were conquered and carried off to the lands of Assyria and Babylonia. The nation was held in captivity for 70 years, making up for all of the years that the Israelites did not observe the law of the Sabbath year (2 Chronicles 36:21).

26:40-45 These verses show what God meant when he said he is slow to anger (Exodus 34:6). Even if the Israelites chose to disobey and were scattered among their enemies, God would still give them the opportunity to repent and return to him. His purpose was not to destroy them, but to help them grow. Our day-to-day experiences and hardships are sometimes overwhelming; unless we can see that God's purpose is to bring about continual growth in us, we may despair. The hope we need is well expressed in Jeremiah 29:11, 12: "'For I know the plans I have for you,' says the LORD. 'They are plans for good and not for disaster, to give you a future and a hope. In those days when you pray, I will listen.'" To retain hope while we suffer shows we understand God's merciful ways of relating to his people.

27:1ff The Israelites were required to give or dedicate certain things to the Lord and to his service: the firstfruits of their harvests, firstborn animals, their firstborn sons, a tithe of their increase. Many wished to go beyond this and dedicate themselves or another family member, additional animals, a house, or a field to God. In these cases, it was possible to donate money instead of the actual person, animal, or property. Some people made rash or unrealistic vows. To urge them to think about it first, a 20 percent penalty was put on those items purchased back by money. This chapter explains how valuations were to be made and what to do if a donor later wished to buy back what had been donated to God.

27:9, 10 God taught the Israelites that when they made a vow to him, they must not go back on their promise even if it turned out to

be exchanged or substituted for another—neither a good animal for a bad one nor a bad animal
for a good one. But if such an exchange is in fact made, then both the original animal and
the substitute will be considered holy. 11 But if your vow involves an unclean animal—one
that is not acceptable as an offering to the LORD—then you must bring the animal to the
priest. 12 He will assess its value, and his assessment will be final. 13 If you want to redeem
the animal, you must pay the value set by the priest, plus 20 percent.

14 "If you dedicate a house to the LORD, the priest must come to assess its value. The
priest's assessment will be final. 15 If you wish to redeem the house, you must pay the value
set by the priest, plus 20 percent. Then the house will again belong to you.

16 "If you dedicate to the LORD a piece of your ancestral property, its value will be
assessed by the amount of seed required to plant it—fifty pieces of silver for an area that
produces* five bushels* of barley seed. 17 If the field is dedicated to the LORD in the Year
27:18 of Jubilee, then the entire assessment will apply. 18 But if the field is dedicated after the Year
Lev 25:14-16 of Jubilee, the priest must assess the land's value in proportion to the years left until the next
Year of Jubilee. 19 If you decide to redeem the dedicated field, you must pay the land's value
as assessed by the priest, plus 20 percent. Then the field will again belong to you. 20 But if
you decide not to redeem the field, or if the field is sold to someone else by the priests, it
27:21 can never be redeemed. 21 When the field is released in the Year of Jubilee, it will be holy,
Lev 25:8-54 a field specially set apart* for the LORD. It will become the property of the priests.
Num 18:14 Ezek 44:29 22 "If you dedicate to the LORD a field that you have purchased but which is not part of
your ancestral property, 23 the priest must assess its value based on the years until the next
Year of Jubilee. You must then give the assessed value of the land as a sacred donation to
27:24 the LORD. 24 In the Year of Jubilee the field will be released to the original owner from
Lev 25:28 **27:25** whom you purchased it. 25 All the value assessments must be measured in terms of the
Exod 30:13 Num 3:47; 18:16 standard sanctuary shekel.*
Ezek 45:12 26 "You may not dedicate to the LORD the firstborn of your cattle or sheep because the first-
27:26 born of these animals already belong to him. 27 However, if it is the firstborn of a ceremonially
Exod 13:2, 12 unclean animal, you may redeem it by paying the priest's assessment of its worth, plus 20
percent. If you do not redeem it, the priest may sell it to someone else for its assessed value.
27:28 28 "However, anything specially set apart by the LORD—whether a person, an animal,
Josh 6:17-19 or an inherited field—must never be sold or redeemed. Anything devoted in this way has
been set apart for the LORD as holy. 29 A person specially set apart by the LORD for
destruction cannot be redeemed. Such a person must be put to death.
27:30 30 "A tenth of the produce of the land, whether grain or fruit, belongs to the LORD and
Gen 28:22 Num 18:26 must be set apart to him as holy. 31 If you want to redeem the LORD's tenth of the fruit or
2 Chr 31:5-6 Neh 3:12 grain, you must pay its value, plus 20 percent. 32 The LORD also owns every tenth animal
Mal 3:8 counted off from your herds and flocks. They are set apart to him as holy. 33 The tenth
27:33 animal must not be selected on the basis of whether it is good or bad, and no substitutions
Lev 27:10 will be allowed. If any exchange is in fact made, then both the original animal and the
substituted one will be considered holy and cannot be redeemed."
27:34 Lev 26:46 34 These are the commands that the LORD gave to the Israelites through Moses on Mount
Sinai.

27:16a Or *requires.* **27:16b** Hebrew *1 homer* [182 liters]. **27:21** The Hebrew term used here refers to the complete consecration of things or people to the LORD, either by destroying them or by giving them as an offering; also in 27:28, 29. **27:25** Hebrew *measured according to the sanctuary shekel, 20 gerahs to each shekel.* Each sanctuary shekel was about 0.4 ounces or 11 grams in weight.

---

cost more than expected. (This applied to animals; humans could be redeemed or purchased back.) God takes our promises seriously. If you vow to give 10 percent of your income and suddenly some unexpected bills come along, your faithful stewardship will be costly. God, however, expects you to fulfill your vow even if it is difficult to do so.

27:14-25 Real estate could be given as a voluntary offering in much the same way that today people give property through a will or donate the proceeds from the sale of property to a church or Christian organizations.

27:28, 29 Things set apart for destruction applies to personal property or persons placed under God's ban, such as captured booty from idol worshipers or idols themselves. These were to be destroyed and could not be redeemed.

27:33 Many of the principles regarding sacrifices and tithes were intended to encourage inward attitudes as well as outward actions. If a person gives grudgingly, he shows that he has a stingy heart. God wants us to be cheerful givers (2 Corinthians 9:7), who give with gratitude to him.

27:34 The book of Leviticus is filled with the commands God gave his people at the foot of Mount Sinai. From these commands we can learn much about God's nature and character. At first glance, Leviticus seems irrelevant to our high-tech world. But digging a little deeper, we realize that the book still speaks to us today—God has not changed, and his principles are for all times. As people and society change, we need constantly to search for ways to apply the principles of God's law to our present circumstances. God was the same in Leviticus as he is today and will be forever (Hebrews 13:8).

NUMBERS

Joseph dies 1805 B.C. (1640 B.C.)	SLAVERY IN EGYPT	Exodus from Egypt 1446 (1280)	Ten Command-ments given 1445 (1279)	First census 1444 (1278)	First spy mission 1443 (1277)

VITAL STATISTICS

PURPOSE:
To tell the story of how Israel prepared to enter the Promised Land, how they sinned and were punished, and how they prepared to try again

AUTHOR:
Moses

TO WHOM WRITTEN:
The people of Israel

DATE WRITTEN:
1450–1410 B.C.

SETTING:
The vast desert of the Sinai region, as well as lands just south and east of Canaan

KEY VERSES:
"Not one of these people will ever enter that land. They have seen my glorious presence and the miraculous signs I performed both in Egypt and in the wilderness, but again and again they tested me by refusing to listen. They will never even see the land I swore to give their ancestors. None of those who have treated me with contempt will enter it" (14:22, 23).

KEY PEOPLE:
Moses, Aaron, Miriam, Joshua, Caleb, Eleazar, Korah, Balaam

KEY PLACES:
Mount Sinai, Promised Land (Canaan), Kadesh, Mount Hor, plains of Moab.

EVERY parent knows the shrill whine of a young child—a slow, high-pitched complaint that grates on the eardrums and aggravates the soul. The tone of voice is difficult to bear, but the real irritation is the underlying cause—discontentment and disobedience. As the "children" of Israel journeyed from the foot of Mount Sinai to the land of Canaan, they grumbled, whined, and complained at every turn. They focused on their present discomforts. Faith had fled, and they added an extra 40 years to their trip.

Numbers, which records the tragic story of Israel's unbelief, should serve as a dramatic lesson for all of God's people. God loves us and wants the very best for us. He can and should be trusted. Numbers also gives a clear portrayal of God's patience. Again and again he withholds judgment and preserves the nation. But his patience must not be taken for granted. His judgment will come. We must obey.

As Numbers begins, the nation of Israel was camped at the foot of Mount Sinai. The people had received God's laws and were preparing to move. A census was taken to determine the number of men fit for military service. Next, the people were set apart for God. God was making the people, both spiritually and physically, ready to receive their inheritance.

But then the complaining began. First, the people complained about the food. Next, it was over Moses' authority. God punished some people but spared the nation because of Moses' prayers. The nation then arrived at Kadesh, and spies were sent into Canaan to assess its strength. Ten returned with fearful stories of giants. Only Caleb and Joshua encouraged them to "go at once to take the land" (13:30). The minority report fell on deaf ears full of the ominous message of the majority. Because of their unbelief, God declared that the present generation would not live to see the Promised Land. Thus the "wanderings" began. During these wilderness wanderings there was a continuous pattern of grumbling, defiance, discipline, and death. How much better it would have been to have trusted God and entered his land! Then the terrible waiting began—waiting for the old generation to die off and waiting to see if the new generation could faithfully obey God.

Numbers ends as it begins, with preparation. This new generation of Israelites was numbered and sanctified. After defeating numerous armies, they settle the east side of the Jordan River. Then they faced their greatest test: to cross the river and possess the beautiful land God promised them.

The lesson is clear. God's people must trust him, moving ahead by *faith* if they are to claim his promised land.

WILDERNESS WANDERINGS	*Second census, Balaam prophesies 1407 (1241)*	*Joshua appointed, Canaan entered 1406 (1240)*	*Judges begin to rule 1375 (1220)*	*United kingdom under Saul 1050 (1045)*

THE BLUEPRINT

A. PREPARING FOR THE JOURNEY (1:1—10:10)
1. The first census of the nation
2. The role of the Levites
3. The purity of the camp
4. Receiving guidance for the journey

As part of their preparations, the Lord gave strict guidelines to the Israelites regarding purity in the camp. He wanted them to have a life-style distinct from the nations around them. He wanted them to be a holy people. Similarly, we should concern ourselves with purity in the church.

B. FIRST APPROACH TO THE PROMISED LAND (10:11—14:45)
1. The people complain
2. Miriam and Aaron oppose Moses
3. The scouts incite rebellion

The Israelites were prevented from entering the Promised Land because of their unbelief. Throughout history, God's people have continued to struggle with lack of faith.We must prevent unbelief from gaining a foothold in our lives, for it will keep us from enjoying the blessings that God has promised.

C. WANDERING IN THE WILDERNESS (15:1—21:35)
1. Additional regulations
2. Many leaders rebel against Moses
3. Duties of priests and Levites
4. The new generation

When the people complained against God and criticized Moses, they were severely punished. Over 14,000 people died as a result of rebellion against Moses. As a result of Korah's rebellion, Korah, Dathan, and Abiram and their households died, along with 250 false priests. Dissatisfaction and discontent, if allowed to remain in our lives, can easily lead to disaster. We should refrain from complaining and criticizing our leaders.

D. SECOND APPROACH TO THE PROMISED LAND (22:1—36:13)
1. The story of Balaam
2. The second census of the nation
3. Instructions concerning offerings
4. Vengeance on the Midianites
5. The Transjordan tribes
6. Camped on the plains of Moab

The Moabites and Midianites could not get Balaam to curse Israel, but they did get him to give advice on how to draw the Israelites to idol worship. Balaam knew what was right, but he gave in to the temptation of material rewards and sinned. Knowing what is right alone is never enough. We must also do what is right.

MEGATHEMES

THEME	EXPLANATION	IMPORTANCE
Census	Moses counted the Israelites twice. The first census organized the people into marching units to better defend themselves. The second prepared them to conquer the country east of the Jordan River.	People have to be organized, trained, and led to be effective in great movements. It is always wise to count the cost before setting out on some great undertaking. When we are aware of the obstacles before us, we can more easily avoid them. In God's work, we must remove barriers in our relationships with others so that our effectiveness is not diminished.
Rebellion	At Kadesh, 12 scouts were sent out into the land of Canaan to report on the fortifications of the enemies. When the scouts returned, 10 said that they should give up and go back to Egypt. As a result, the people refused to enter the land. Faced with a choice, Israel rebelled against God. Rebellion did not start with an uprising, but with griping and murmuring against Moses and God.	Rebellion against God is always a serious matter. It is not something to take lightly, for God's punishment for sin is often very severe. Our rebellion does not usually begin with all-out warfare, but in subtle ways—with griping and criticizing. Make sure your negative comments are not the product of a rebellious spirit.
Wandering	Because they rebelled, the Israelites wandered 40 years in the wilderness. This shows how severely God can punish sin. Forty years was enough time for all those who held on to Egypt's customs and values to die off. It gave time to train up a new generation in the ways of God.	God judges sin harshly because he is holy. The wanderings in the wilderness demonstrate how serious God considers flagrant disobedience of his commands. Purging our lives of sin is vital to God's purpose.

Canaan	Canaan is the Promised Land. It was the land God had promised to Abraham, Isaac, and Jacob—the land of the covenant. Canaan was to be the dwelling place of God's people, those set apart for true spiritual worship.	Although God's punishment for sin is often severe, he offers reconciliation and hope—his love is truly amazing. Just as God's love and law led Israel to the Promised Land, God desires to give purpose and destiny to our lives.

KEY PLACES IN NUMBERS

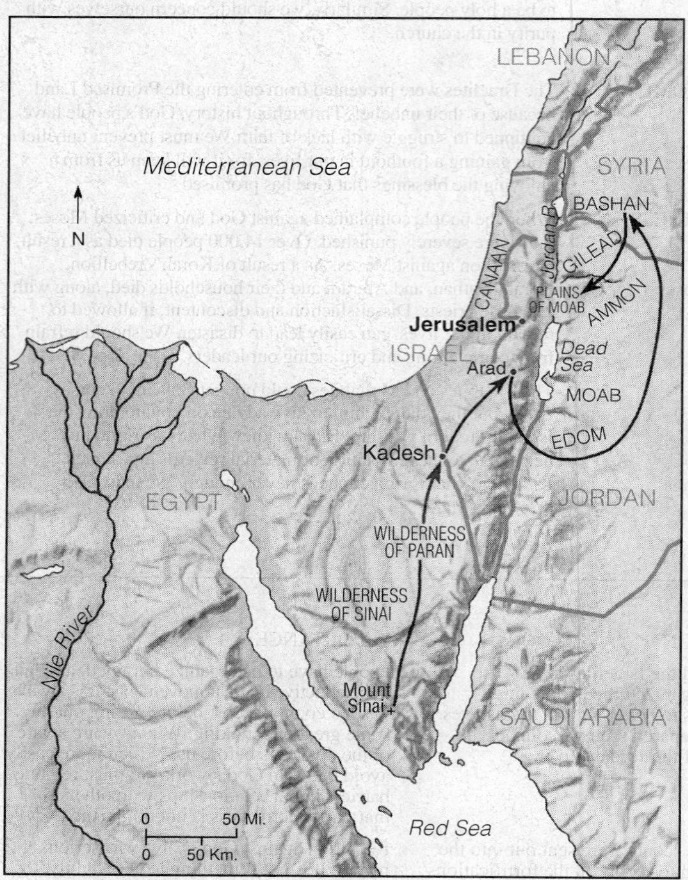

Modern names and boundaries are shown in gray.

1 Mount Sinai Numbers begins at Mount Sinai in the wilderness of Sinai with Moses taking a census of the men eligible for battle. As the battle preparations began, the people also prepared for the spiritual warfare they would face. The Promised Land was full of wicked people who would try to entice the Israelites to sin. God, therefore, taught Moses and the Israelites how to live right (1:1—12:15).

2 Wilderness of Paran After a full year at Mount Sinai, the Israelites broke camp and began their march toward the Promised Land by moving into the wilderness of Paran. From there, one leader from each tribe was sent to spy out the new land. After 40 days they returned, and all but Joshua and Caleb were too afraid to enter. Because of their lack of faith, the Israelites were made to wander in the wilderness for 40 years (12:16—19:22).

3 Kadesh With the years of wandering nearing an end, the Israelites set their sights once again on the Promised Land. Kadesh was the oasis where they spent most of their desert years. Miriam died here. And it was here that Moses angrily struck the rock, which kept him from entering the Promised Land (20).

4 Arad When the king there heard that Israel was on the move, he attacked, but he was soundly defeated. Moses then led the people southward and eastward around the Dead Sea (21:1–3).

5 Edom The Israelites wanted to travel through Edom, but the king of Edom refused them passage (20:14–22). So they traveled around Edom and became very discouraged. The people complained, and God sent poisonous snakes to punish them. Only by looking at a bronze snake on a pole could those bitten be healed (21:4–9).

6 Ammon Next, King Sihon of the Amorites refused Israel passage. When he attacked, Israel defeated his army and conquered the territory as far as the border of Ammon (21:21–32).

7 Bashan Moses sent spies to Bashan. King Og attacked, but he was also defeated (21:33–35).

8 Plains of Moab The people camped on the plains of Moab, east of the Jordan River across from Jericho. They were on the verge of entering the Promised Land (22:1).

9 Moab King Balak of Moab, terrified of the Israelites, called upon Balaam, a famous sorcerer, to curse Israel from the mountains above where the Israelites camped. But the Lord caused Balaam to bless them instead (22:2—24:25).

10 Gilead The tribes of Reuben and Gad decided to settle in the fertile country of Gilead east of the Jordan River because it was a good land for their sheep. But first they promised to help the other tribes conquer the land west of the Jordan River (32).

A. PREPARING FOR THE JOURNEY (1:1—10:10)

At Mount Sinai, the Israelites received specific directions for their life-style in the new land God would give to them. A census was taken and the second Passover was celebrated, marking one year of freedom from slavery in Egypt. The people were now prepared to continue their journey to the Promised Land. Just as the Lord prepared the Israelites, he prepares us for our journey through life.

1. The first census of the nation

1:1 Exod 40:2, 17
1:2 Exod 38:25-26; Num 26:2
1:4 Exod 18:21; Num 34:18
1:5 Gen 29:32; Rev 7:5
1:7 Ruth 4:20; 1 Chr 2:10
1:14 Num 2:14

1 One day in midspring,* during the second year after Israel's departure from Egypt,
the LORD spoke to Moses in the Tabernacle* in the wilderness of Sinai. He said,
2 "Take a census of the whole community of Israel by their clans and families. List the
names of all the men 3 twenty years old or older who are able to go to war. You and Aaron
are to direct the project, 4 assisted by one family leader from each tribe."
5 These are the tribes and the names of the leaders chosen for the task:

Tribe	*Leader*
Reuben	Elizur son of Shedeur
6 Simeon	Shelumiel son of Zurishaddai
7 Judah	Nahshon son of Amminadab
8 Issachar	Nethanel son of Zuar
9 Zebulun	Eliab son of Helon
10 Ephraim son of Joseph	Elishama son of Ammihud
Manasseh son of Joseph	Gamaliel son of Pedahzur
11 Benjamin	Abidan son of Gideoni
12 Dan	Ahiezer son of Ammishaddai
13 Asher	Pagiel son of Ocran
14 Gad	Eliasaph son of Deuel
15 Naphtali	Ahira son of Enan

1:16 Num 7:2; 16:2; 26:9
1:18 Num 1:1; Ezra 2:59
1:20 Num 26:5-11

16 These tribal leaders, heads of their own families, were chosen from among all the
people.
17 Now Moses and Aaron and the chosen leaders 18 called together the whole community of Israel on that very day.* All the people were registered according to their ancestry
by their clans and families. The men of Israel twenty years old or older were registered,
one by one, 19 just as the LORD had commanded Moses. So Moses counted the people
there in the wilderness of Sinai.
20-21 This is the number of men twenty years old or older who were able to go to war,
each listed according to his own clan and family*:

1:1a Hebrew *On the first day of the second month.* This day of the Hebrew lunar calendar occurs in April or early May. **1:1b** Hebrew *Tent of Meeting.* **1:18** Hebrew *on the first day of the second month;* see 1:1. **1:20-21a** In the Hebrew text, *number of men . . . family* is repeated in 1:22, 24, 26, 28, 30, 32, 34, 36, 38, 40, 42.

1:1 As the book of Numbers opens, the Israelites had been camped near Mount Sinai for more than a year. There they had received all the laws and regulations recorded in the book of Leviticus. They had been transformed into a new nation and equipped for their task. At this time, they were ready to move out and receive their land. In preparation, Moses and Aaron were told to number all the men who were able to serve in the army. This book is named for this census, or numbering, of the people.

1:1 The Tabernacle contained the sanctuary (or Holy Place) in one part, and the Most Holy Place with the Ark in another part. These two parts were separated by a curtain. God revealed himself to Moses in the Most Holy Place.

Exodus 33:7 mentions the "Tent of Meeting" as the place where Moses met with God before the Tabernacle was constructed. Many believe that the Tent of Meeting in Exodus served the same function as the Tabernacle described here.

1:2-15 Taking a census was long and tedious, but it was an important task. The fighting men had to be counted to determine Israel's military strength before entering the Promised Land. In addition, the tribes had to be organized to determine the amount of land each would need, as well as to provide genealogical records. Without such a census, the task of conquering and organizing the Promised Land would have been more difficult. Whenever we are at a crossroads, it is important to take inventory of our resources. We will serve more effectively if, before plunging in, we set aside time to take a "census" of all we have—possessions, relationships, spiritual condition, time, goals.

1:20-46 If there were 603,550 men, not counting the Levites or women and children, the total population must have numbered more than two million Israelites. How could such a large population grow from Jacob's family of 70 who moved down to Egypt? The book of Exodus tells us that the Israelites who descended from Jacob's family "multiplied so quickly that they soon filled the land" (Exodus 1:7). Because they remained in Egypt more than 400 years, they had plenty of time to grow into a large group of people. After leaving Egypt, they were able to survive in the wilderness because God miraculously provided the food and water they needed. The leaders of Moab were terrified because of the large number of Israelites (22:3).

	Tribe	*Number*
	Reuben (Jacob's* oldest son)	46,500
22-23	Simeon	59,300
24-25	Gad	45,650
26-27	Judah	74,600
28-29	Issachar	54,400
30-31	Zebulun	57,400
32-33	Ephraim son of Joseph	40,500
34-35	Manasseh son of Joseph	32,200
36-37	Benjamin	35,400
38-39	Dan	62,700
40-41	Asher	41,500
42-43	Naphtali	53,400

44 These were the men counted by Moses and Aaron and the twelve leaders of Israel, all listed according to their ancestral descent. 45 They were counted by families—all the men of Israel who were twenty years old or older and able to go to war. 46 The total number was 603,550.

47 But this total did not include the Levites. 48 For the LORD had said to Moses, 49 "Exempt the tribe of Levi from the census; do not include them when you count the rest of the Israelites. 50 You must put the Levites in charge of the Tabernacle of the Covenant,* along with its furnishings and equipment. They must carry the Tabernacle and its equipment as you travel, and they must care for it and camp around it. 51 Whenever the Tabernacle is moved, the Levites will take it down and set it up again. Anyone else who goes too near the Tabernacle will be executed. 52 Each tribe of Israel will have a designated camping area with its own family banner. 53 But the Levites will camp around the Tabernacle of the Covenant to offer the people of Israel protection from the LORD's fierce anger. The Levites are responsible to stand guard around the Tabernacle."

54 So the Israelites did everything just as the LORD had commanded Moses.

1:22 Num 26:12-14
1:24 Num 26:15-18
1:26 Num 26:19-22
1:28 Num 26:23-25
1:30 Num 26:26-27
1:32 Num 26:35-37
1:34 Num 26:28-34
1:36 Num 26:38-41
1:38 Num 26:42-43
1:40 Num 26:44-47
1:42 Num 26:48-50
1:44 Num 26:64
1:46 Num 2:32; 26:51
1:47 Num 2:33; 26:57
1:50 Num 3:25-37
1:51 Num 4:1-33
1:53 Num 1:50
1:52 Num 2:2

Organization for Israel's Camp

2

Then the LORD gave these instructions to Moses and Aaron: 2 "Each tribe will be assigned its own area in the camp, and the various groups will camp beneath their family banners. The Tabernacle* will be located at the center of these tribal compounds.

3-4 "The divisions of Judah, Issachar, and Zebulun are to camp toward the sunrise on the east side of the Tabernacle, beneath their family banners. These are the names of the tribes, their leaders, and the number of their available troops:

	Tribe	*Leader*	*Number*
	Judah	Nahshon son of Amminadab	74,600
5-6	Issachar	Nethanel son of Zuar	54,400
7-8	Zebulun	Eliab son of Helon	57,400

9 So the total of all the troops on Judah's side of the camp is 186,400. These three tribes are to lead the way whenever the Israelites travel to a new campsite.

10-11 "The divisions of Reuben, Simeon, and Gad are to camp on the south side of the Tabernacle, beneath their family banners. These are the names of the tribes, their leaders, and the number of their available troops:

	Tribe	*Leader*	*Number*
	Reuben	Elizur son of Shedeur	46,500
12-13	Simeon	Shelumiel son of Zurishaddai	59,300
14-15	Gad	Eliasaph son of Deuel*	45,650

2:2 Num 1:52
2:3 Num 10:14
2:5 Num 1:8
2:9 Num 10:14
2:10 Num 1:5
2:12 Num 1:6
2:14 Num 1:14

1:20-21b Hebrew *Israel's.* **1:50** Or *Tabernacle of the Testimony;* also in 1:53. **2:2** Hebrew *Tent of Meeting;* also in 2:17. **2:14-15** As in many Hebrew manuscripts, Samaritan Pentateuch, and Latin Vulgate (see also 1:14); most Hebrew manuscripts read *son of Reuel.*

2:2 The nation of Israel was organized according to tribes for several reasons. (1) It was an effective way to manage and govern a large group. (2) It made dividing the Promised Land easier. (3) It was part of their culture and heritage (people were not known by a last name, but by their family, clan, and tribe). (4) It made it easier to keep detailed genealogies, and genealogies were the only way to prove membership in God's chosen nation. (5) It made travel much more efficient. The people followed the tribe's standard (a kind of flag) and thus stayed together and kept from getting lost.

16 So the total of all the troops on Reuben's side of the camp is 151,450. These three
tribes will be second in line whenever the Israelites travel.
2:17 Num 1:53 — 17 "Then the Levites will set out from the middle of the camp with the Tabernacle. All
the tribes are to travel in the same order that they camp, each in position under the
appropriate family banner.
18-19 "The divisions of Ephraim, Manasseh, and Benjamin are to camp on the west side
of the Tabernacle, beneath their family banners. These are the names of the tribes, their
leaders, and the number of their available troops:

	Tribe	*Leader*	*Number*
	Ephraim	Elishama son of Ammihud	40,500
2:20 Num 1:10	20-21 Manasseh	Gamaliel son of Pedahzur	32,200
	22-23 Benjamin	Abidan son of Gideoni	35,400

2:24 Num 10:22 — 24 So the total of all the troops on Ephraim's side of the camp is 108,100, and they will
follow the Levites in the line of march.
2:25 Num 1:12 — 25-26 "The divisions of Dan, Asher, and Naphtali are to camp on the north side of the
Tabernacle, beneath their family banners. These are the names of the tribes, their leaders,
and the number of their available troops:

	Tribe	*Leader*	*Number*
	Dan	Ahiezer son of Ammishaddai	62,700
2:27 Num 1:13	27-28 Asher	Pagiel son of Ocran	41,500
	29-30 Naphtali	Ahira son of Enan	53,400

2:31 Num 10:25 — 31 So the total of all the troops on Dan's side of the camp is 157,600. They are to bring
2:32 Exod 38:26 Num 1:45-46 — up the rear whenever the Israelites move to a new campsite."
32 In summary, the troops of Israel listed by their families totaled 603,550. 33 The Levites
2:33 Num 1:47 — were exempted from this census by the LORD's command to Moses. 34 So the people of
Israel did everything just as the LORD had commanded Moses. Each clan and family set
up camp and marched under their banners exactly as the LORD had instructed them.

2. The role of the Levites

3:2 Num 26:60

Levites Appointed for Service

3:3 Exod 28:41 — **3** This is the family line of Aaron and Moses as it was recorded when the LORD spoke
to Moses on Mount Sinai: 2 Aaron's sons were Nadab (the firstborn), Abihu, Eleazar,
3:4 Lev 10:1-2 Num 26:61 — and Ithamar. 3 They were anointed and set apart to minister as priests. 4 But Nadab and
Abihu died in the LORD's presence in the wilderness of Sinai when they burned before

ARRANGEMENT OF TRIBES AROUND THE TABERNACLE WHILE IN THE DESERT

DAN
ASHER NAPHTALI
BENJAMIN — Merari (Son of Levi) — ISSACHAR
EPHRAIM — Gershon (Son of Levi) — TABERNACLE — Moses, Aaron, Sons of Aaron — JUDAH
MANASSEH — Kohath (Son of Levi) — ZEBULUN
GAD SIMEON
REUBEN

2:34 This must have been one of the biggest campsites the world has ever seen! It would have taken about 12 square miles to set up tents for just the 600,000 fighting men—not to mention the women and children. Moses must have had a difficult time managing such a group. In the early stages of the journey and at Mount Sinai, the people were generally obedient to both God and Moses. But when the people left Mount Sinai and traveled across the rugged wilderness, they began to complain, grumble, and disobey. Soon problems erupted, and Moses could no longer effectively manage the Israelites. The books of Exodus, Leviticus, and Numbers present a striking contrast between how much we can accomplish when we obey God and how little we can accomplish when we don't.

the LORD a different kind of fire than he had commanded. Since they had no sons, this
left only Eleazar and Ithamar to serve as priests with their father, Aaron.
[5]Then the LORD said to Moses, [6]"Call forward the tribe of Levi and present them to **3:6** Num 8:6-22; 18:2-6
Aaron the priest as his assistants. [7]They will serve Aaron and the whole community, **3:7**
performing their sacred duties in and around the Tabernacle.* [8]They will also maintain Num 3:11-12, 41;
all the furnishings of the sacred tent,* serving in the Tabernacle on behalf of all the 8:16-18
Israelites. [9]Assign the Levites to Aaron and his sons as their assistants. [10]Appoint Aaron **3:10**
and his sons to carry out the duties of the priesthood. Anyone else who comes too near Num 1:51
the sanctuary must be executed!"
[11]And the LORD said to Moses, [12]"I have chosen the Levites from among the Israelites **3:12**
as substitutes for all the firstborn sons of the people of Israel. The Levites are mine Num 3:45
[13]because all the firstborn sons are mine. From the day I killed all the firstborn sons of **3:13** Exod 13:2, 12, 15
the Egyptians, I set apart for myself all the firstborn in Israel of both men and animals. Num 8:17
They are mine; I am the LORD."

The Census of the Levites

[14]The LORD spoke again to Moses, there in the wilderness of Sinai. He said, [15]"Take a **3:15** Num 1:47
census of the tribe of Levi by its families and clans. Count every male who is one month
old or older." [16]So Moses counted them, just as the LORD had commanded.

[17]Levi had three sons, who were named Gershon, Kohath, and Merari.
[18]The clans descended from Gershon were named for two of his descendants, Libni
and Shimei.
[19]The clans descended from Kohath were named for four of his descendants, Amram,
Izhar, Hebron, and Uzziel.
[20]The clans descended from Merari were named for two of his descendants, Mahli
and Mushi.

These were the Levite clans, listed according to their family groups.
[21]The descendants of Gershon were composed of the clans descended from Libni and
Shimei. [22]There were 7,500 males one month old or older among these Gershonite clans.
[23]They were assigned the area to the west of the Tabernacle for their camp. [24]The leader
of the Gershonite clans was Eliasaph son of Lael. [25]These two clans were responsible to **3:25** Num 4:24-26
care for the tent of the Tabernacle with its layers of coverings, its entry curtains, [26]the
curtains of the courtyard that surrounded the Tabernacle and altar, the curtain at the
courtyard entrance, the cords, and all the equipment related to their use.
[27]The descendants of Kohath were composed of the clans descended from Amram, **3:27** 1 Chr 26:23
Izhar, Hebron, and Uzziel. [28]There were 8,600* males one month old or older among
these Kohathite clans. They were responsible for the care of the sanctuary. [29]They were **3:29** Exod 6:18
assigned the area south of the Tabernacle for their camp. [30]The leader of the Kohathite
clans was Elizaphan son of Uzziel. [31]These four clans were responsible for the care of
the Ark, the table, the lampstand, the altars, the various utensils used in the sanctuary, the
inner curtain, and all the equipment related to their use. [32]Eleazar the priest, Aaron's son,
was the chief administrator over all the Levites, with special responsibility for the
oversight of the sanctuary.
[33]The descendants of Merari were composed of the clans descended from Mahli and **3:33** Exod 6:19

3:7 Hebrew *around the Tent of Meeting, doing service at the Tabernacle.* **3:8** Hebrew *Tent of Meeting.* **3:28** Some Greek manuscripts read *8,300;* see total in 3:39.

3:4 See Leviticus 10:1, 2 for the story of Nadab and Abihu.

3:5-13 At the time of the first Passover, God instructed every Israelite family to dedicate its firstborn son to him (Exodus 13:2). They were set apart to assist Moses and Aaron in ministering to the people. This was only a temporary measure, however. Here God chose all the men from the tribe of Levi to replace the firstborn sons from every Israelite tribe (3:40-51 and 8:16). These men, called Levites, were set apart to care for the Tabernacle and minister to the people. All the priests had to belong to the tribe of Levi, but not all Levites were priests. The Levites were to be 25 years old before entering service. They probably received five years of on-the-job training before being admitted to full service at age 30.

3:10 Aaron and his descendants were appointed to the priesthood. There is a tremendous contrast between the priesthood of Aaron in the Old Testament and the priesthood of Christ in the New Testament. Aaron and his descendants were the only ones who could carry out the duties of the priests and approach God's dwelling place. Now that Christ is our High Priest—our intermediary with God—anyone who follows him is also called a priest (1 Peter 2:5, 9). Now all Christians may come into God's presence without fear because God's own Son encourages his followers to do so. We can put guilt behind us when we have a special relationship with God based on what Christ has done for us.

Mushi. 34There were 6,200 males one month old or older among these Merarite clans. 35They were assigned the area north of the Tabernacle for their camp. The leader of the Merarite clans was Zuriel son of Abihail. 36These two clans were responsible for the care of the frames supporting the Tabernacle, the crossbars, the pillars, the bases, and all the equipment related to their use. 37They were also responsible for the posts of the courtyard and all their bases, pegs, and cords.

3:38 Num 1:51; 3:10

38The area in front of the Tabernacle in the east toward the sunrise* was reserved for the tents of Moses and of Aaron and his sons, who had the final responsibility for the sanctuary on behalf of the people of Israel. Anyone other than a priest or Levite who came too near the sanctuary was to be executed.

3:39 Num 26:62

39So among the Levite clans counted by Moses and Aaron at the LORD's command, there were 22,000 males one month old or older.

Redeeming the Firstborn Sons

3:41 Num 3:12, 45

40Then the LORD said to Moses, "Now count all the firstborn sons in Israel who are one month old or older, and register each name. 41The Levites will be reserved for me as substitutes for the firstborn sons of Israel; I am the LORD. And the Levites' livestock are mine as substitutes for the firstborn livestock of the whole nation of Israel."

3:43 Num 3:39

42So Moses counted the firstborn sons of the people of Israel, just as the LORD had commanded. 43The total number of firstborn sons who were one month old or older was 22,273.

3:45 Lev 11:44

3:46 Exod 13:13, 15; Num 18:14-16

3:47 Exod 30:13; Lev 27:1-8

44Now the LORD said to Moses, 45"Take the Levites in place of the firstborn sons of the people of Israel. And take the livestock of the Levites as substitutes for the firstborn livestock of the people of Israel. The Levites will be mine; I am the LORD. 46To redeem the 273 firstborn sons of Israel who are in excess of the number of Levites, 47collect five pieces of silver for each person, each piece weighing the same as the standard sanctuary shekel.* 48Give the silver to Aaron and his sons as the redemption price for the extra firstborn sons."

3:50 Num 3:46-48

49So Moses collected redemption money for the firstborn sons of Israel who exceeded the number of Levites. 50The silver collected on behalf of these firstborn sons of Israel came to about thirty-four pounds in weight.* 51And Moses gave the redemption money to Aaron and his sons as the LORD had commanded.

Duties of the Kohathite Clan

4:3 Num 4:23; 8:24

4 Then the LORD said to Moses and Aaron, 2"Take a census of the clans and families of the Kohathite division of the Levite tribe. 3Count all the men between the ages of thirty and fifty who qualify to work in the Tabernacle.*

4:6 Num 4:25

4"The duties of the Kohathites at the Tabernacle will relate to the most sacred objects. 5When the camp moves, Aaron and his sons must enter the Tabernacle first to take down the inner curtain and cover the Ark of the Covenant* with it. 6Then they must cover the inner curtain with fine goatskin leather, and the goatskin leather with a dark blue cloth. Finally, they must put the carrying poles of the Ark in place.

4:7 Exod 37:10-16; Lev 24:5-8

7"Next they must spread a blue cloth over the table, where the Bread of the Presence is displayed, and place the dishes, spoons, bowls, cups, and the special bread on the cloth. 8They must spread a scarlet cloth over that, and finally a covering of fine goatskin leather on top of the scarlet cloth. Then they must insert the carrying poles into the table.

4:9 Exod 25:37-38

9"Next they must cover the lampstand with a dark blue cloth, along with its lamps, lamp snuffers, trays, and special jars of olive oil. 10The lampstand with its utensils must then be covered with fine goatskin leather, and the bundle must be placed on a carrying frame.

11"Aaron and his sons must also spread a dark blue cloth over the gold altar and cover this cloth with a covering of fine goatskin leather. Then they are to attach the carrying

3:38 Hebrew *toward the sunrise, in front of the Tent of Meeting.* **3:47** Hebrew *5 shekels* [2 ounces or 57 grams] *apiece, according to the sanctuary shekel, 20 gerahs to each shekel.* **3:50** Hebrew *1,365 shekels* [15.5 kilograms], *according to the sanctuary shekel.* **4:3** Hebrew *Tent of Meeting;* also in 4:4, 15, 23, 25, 28, 30, 31, 33, 35, 37, 39, 41, 43, 47. **4:5** Or *Ark of the Testimony.*

4:2ff The Kohathites, Gershonites (4:21), and Merarites (4:29) were families of Levites who were assigned special tasks in Israel's worship. For the jobs described in this chapter, a Levite had to be between 30 and 50 years old. He was expected to carry out his duties as described here in every detail. In fact, failure to do so would mean death (4:20). Worshiping our holy God must not be taken lightly.

poles to the altar. 12All the remaining utensils of the sanctuary must be wrapped in a dark
blue cloth, covered with fine goatskin leather, and placed on the carrying frame.
13"The ashes must be removed from the altar, and the altar must then be covered with
a purple cloth. 14All the altar utensils—the firepans, hooks, shovels, basins, and all the
containers—are to be placed on the cloth, and a covering of fine goatskin leather must
be spread over them. Finally, the carrying poles must be put in place. 15When Aaron and **4:15** Num 4:19-20
his sons have finished covering the sanctuary and all the sacred utensils, the Kohathites
will come and carry these things to the next destination. But they must not touch the
sacred objects, or they will die. So these are the objects of the Tabernacle that the
Kohathites must carry.
16"Eleazar son of Aaron the priest will be responsible for the oil of the lampstand, the **4:16** Exod 25:1-7; 30:22-34
fragrant incense, the daily grain offering, and the anointing oil. In fact, the supervision
of the entire Tabernacle and everything in it will be Eleazar's responsibility."
17Then the LORD said to Moses and Aaron, 18"Don't let the Kohathite clans be **4:17** Num 4:15
destroyed from among the Levites! 19This is what you must do so they will live and not
die when they approach the most sacred objects. Aaron and his sons must always go in
with them and assign a specific duty or load to each person. 20Otherwise they must not
approach the sanctuary and look at the sacred objects for even a moment, or they will die."

Duties of the Gershonite Clan

21And the LORD said to Moses, 22"Take a census of the clans and families of the
Gershonite division of the tribe of Levi. 23Count all the men between the ages of thirty **4:23** Num 4:3
and fifty who are eligible to serve in the Tabernacle.
24"The duties of the Gershonites will be in the areas of general service and carrying
loads. 25They must carry the curtains of the Tabernacle, the Tabernacle itself with its **4:25** Num 3:25-26
coverings, the outer covering of fine goatskin leather, and the curtain for the Tabernacle
entrance. 26They are also to carry the curtains for the courtyard walls that surround the
Tabernacle and altar, the curtain across the courtyard entrance, the necessary cords, and
all the altar's accessories. The Gershonites are responsible for transporting all these
items. 27Aaron and his sons will direct the Gershonites regarding their duties, whether it
involves moving or doing other work. They must assign the Gershonites the loads they
are to carry. 28So these are the duties assigned to the Gershonites at the Tabernacle. They
will be directly responsible to Ithamar son of Aaron the priest.

Duties of the Merarite Clan

29"Now take a census of the clans and families of the Merarite division of the Levite
tribe. 30Count all the men between the ages of thirty and fifty who are eligible to serve **4:30** Num 4:3
in the Tabernacle.
31"Their duties at the Tabernacle will consist of carrying loads. They will be required
to carry the frames of the Tabernacle, the crossbars, the pillars with their bases, 32the
posts for the courtyard walls with their bases, pegs, cords, accessories, and everything
else related to their use. You must assign the various loads to each man by name. 33So
these are the duties of the Merarites at the Tabernacle. They are directly responsible to
Ithamar son of Aaron the priest."

The Census of the Levites

34So Moses, Aaron, and the other leaders of the community counted the Kohathite
division by its clans and families. 35The count included all the men between thirty and **4:35** Num 3:3
fifty years of age who were eligible for service in the Tabernacle, 36and the total number
came to 2,750. 37So this was the total of all those from the Kohathite clans who were
eligible to serve at the Tabernacle. Moses and Aaron counted them, just as the LORD had
commanded through Moses.
38The Gershonite division was also counted by its clans and families. 39The count
included all the men between thirty and fifty years of age who were eligible for service
in the Tabernacle, 40and the total number came to 2,630. 41So this was the total of all

4:27, 28 The Gershonites could receive directions from any of Aaron's sons, but they were directly responsible to Ithamar only. The lines of authority and accountability were clearly communicated to all. As you function with others in service to God, make sure the lines of authority between you and those you work with are clearly understood. Good communication builds good relationships.

those from the Gershonite clans who were eligible to serve at the Tabernacle. Moses and
Aaron counted them, just as the LORD had commanded.
42 The Merarite division was also counted by its clans and families. 43 The count
included all the men between thirty and fifty years of age who were eligible for service
in the Tabernacle, 44 and the total number came to 3,200. 45 So this was the total of all
those from the Merarite clans who were eligible for service. Moses and Aaron counted
them, just as the LORD had commanded through Moses.
4:46 46 So Moses, Aaron, and the leaders of Israel counted all the Levites by their clans and
Num 1:19 families. 47 All the men between thirty and fifty years of age who were eligible for service
4:49 in the Tabernacle and for its transportation 48 numbered 8,580. 49 Each man was assigned
Num 1:47-49 his task and told what to carry, just as the LORD had commanded through Moses.
And so the census was completed, just as the LORD had commanded Moses.

3. The purity of the camp

5:2 Lev 13:3, 46; 15:2
5:3 Lev 26:12; 2 Cor 6:16

5 The LORD gave these instructions to Moses: 2 "Command the people of Israel to
remove anyone from the camp who has a contagious skin disease* or a discharge,
or who has been defiled by touching a dead person. 3 This applies to men and women
alike. Remove them so they will not defile the camp, where I live among you." 4 So
the Israelites did just as the LORD had commanded Moses and removed such people
from the camp.
5:5 5 Then the LORD said to Moses, 6 "Give these instructions to the people of Israel: If any
Lev 6:1-3 of the people—men or women—betray the LORD by doing wrong to another person, they
5:7 are guilty. 7 They must confess their sin and make full restitution for what they have done,
Lev 5:5, 16; 6:4-5; 16:21 adding a penalty of 20 percent and returning it to the person who was wronged. 8 But if
the person who was wronged is dead, and there are no near relatives to whom restitution
can be made, it belongs to the LORD and must be given to the priest, along with a ram
5:9 for atonement. 9 All the sacred gifts that the Israelites bring to a priest will belong to him.
Lev 6:17 10 Each priest may keep the sacred donations that he receives."

Protecting Marital Faithfulness

5:12 Num 5:19-21, 29 11 And the LORD said to Moses, 12 "Say to the people of Israel: 'Suppose a man's wife
goes astray and is unfaithful to her husband. 13 Suppose she sleeps with another man, but
5:15 there is no witness since she was not caught in the act. 14 If her husband becomes jealous
Ezek 29:16 and suspicious of his wife, even if she has not defiled herself, 15 the husband must bring
his wife to the priest with an offering of two quarts* of barley flour to be presented on
her behalf. Do not mix it with olive oil or frankincense, for it is a jealousy offering—an
offering of inquiry to find out if she is guilty.
16 "'The priest must then present her before the LORD. 17 He must take some holy water
in a clay jar and mix it with dust from the Tabernacle floor. 18 When he has presented her
before the LORD, he must unbind her hair and place the offering of inquiry—the jealousy
offering—in her hands to determine whether or not her husband's suspicions are
justified. The priest will stand before her, holding the jar of bitter water that brings a curse
to those who are guilty. 19 The priest will put the woman under oath and say to her, "If
no other man has slept with you, and you have not defiled yourself by being unfaithful,
may you be immune from the effects of this bitter water that causes the curse. 20 But if
5:21 you have gone astray while under your husband's authority and defiled yourself by
Josh 6:26 sleeping with another man"— 21 at this point the priest must put the woman under this
1 Sam 4:24 oath—"then may the people see that the LORD's curse is upon you when he makes you
Neh 10:29 infertile.* 22 Now may this water that brings the curse enter your body and make you

5:2 Traditionally rendered *leprosy.* The Hebrew word used here describes various skin diseases. **5:15** Hebrew *1/10 of an ephah* [2 liters]. **5:21** Hebrew *when he causes your thigh to waste away and your abdomen to swell.*

5:5-8 God included restitution, a unique concept for that day, as part of his law for Israel. When someone was robbed, the guilty person was required to restore the loss to the victim and pay an additional interest penalty. When we have wronged others, we ought to do more than apologize. We should look for ways to set matters right and, if possible, leave the victim even better off than when we harmed him or her. When we have been wronged, we should still seek restoration rather than striking out in revenge.

5:11-31 This test for adultery served to remove a jealous husband's suspicion. Trust between husband and wife had to be completely eroded for a man to bring his wife to the priest for this type of test. Today priests and pastors help restore marriages by counseling couples who have lost faith in each other. Whether justified or not, suspicion must be removed for a marriage to survive and trust to be restored.

infertile.*" And the woman will be required to say, "Yes, let it be so." [23]Then the priest
will write these curses on a piece of leather and wash them off into the bitter water. [24]He
will then make the woman drink the bitter water, so it may bring on the curse and cause
bitter suffering in cases of guilt.

[25]"'Then the priest will take the jealousy offering from the woman's hand, lift it up
before the LORD, and carry it to the altar. [26]He will take a handful as a token portion and **5:26** Lev 2:2
burn it on the altar. Then he will require the woman to drink the water. [27]If she has defiled **5:27** Jer 29:18; 42:18
herself by being unfaithful to her husband, the water that brings the curse will cause bitter
suffering. She will become infertile,* and her name will become a curse word among her
people. [28]But if she has not defiled herself and is pure, she will be unharmed and will
still be able to have children.

[29]"'This is the ritual law for dealing with jealousy. If a woman defiles herself by being **5:29** Num 5:11
unfaithful to her husband, [30]or if a man is overcome with jealousy and suspicion that his
wife has been unfaithful, the husband must present his wife before the LORD, and the
priest will apply this entire ritual law to her. [31]The husband will be innocent of any guilt
in this matter, but his wife will be held accountable for her sin.'"

Nazirite Laws

6 Then the LORD said to Moses, "Speak to the people of Israel and give them these **6:2** Judg 13:4-5; 16:17
instructions: [2]If some of the people, either men or women, take the special vow of Amos 2:11-12
a Nazirite, setting themselves apart to the LORD in a special way, [3]they must give up wine **6:3** Luke 1:15
and other alcoholic drinks. They must not use vinegar made from wine, they must not
drink other fermented drinks or fresh grape juice, and they must not eat grapes or raisins.
[4]As long as they are bound by their Nazirite vow, they are not allowed to eat or drink
anything that comes from a grapevine, not even the grape seeds or skins.

[5]"They must never cut their hair throughout the time of their vow, for they are holy **6:5** 1 Sam 1:11
and set apart to the LORD. That is why they must let their hair grow long. [6]And they may **6:6** Lev 21:1-3
not go near a dead body during the entire period of their vow to the LORD, [7]even if their Num 19:11-22
own father, mother, brother, or sister has died. They must not defile the hair on their head,
because it is the symbol of their separation to God. [8]This applies as long as they are set
apart to the LORD.

[9]"If their hair is defiled because someone suddenly falls dead beside them, they must **6:9** Num 6:18
wait for seven days and then shave their heads. Then they will be cleansed from their
defilement. [10]On the eighth day they must bring two turtledoves or two young pigeons to
the priest at the entrance of the Tabernacle.* [11]The priest will offer one of the birds for a **6:11** Lev 5:7; 12:6-8
sin offering and the other for a burnt offering. In this way, he will make atonement for the
guilt they incurred from the dead body. Then they must renew their vow that day and let **6:12** Lev 5:6
their hair begin to grow again. [12]The days of their vow that were completed before their
defilement no longer count. They must rededicate themselves to the LORD for the full term
of their vow, and each must bring a one-year-old male lamb for a guilt offering.

[13]"This is the ritual law of the Nazirites. At the conclusion of their time of separation **6:14** Lev 14:10
as Nazirites, they must each go to the entrance of the Tabernacle [14]and offer these
sacrifices to the LORD: a one-year-old male lamb without defect for a burnt offering, a
one-year-old female lamb without defect for a sin offering, a ram without defect for a **6:15** Num 15:1-7
peace offering, [15]a basket of bread made without yeast—cakes of choice flour mixed
with olive oil and wafers spread with olive oil—along with their prescribed grain
offerings and drink offerings. [16]The priest will present these offerings before the LORD:
first the sin offering and the burnt offering; [17]then the ram for a peace offering, along

5:22 Hebrew *enter your body so that your abdomen swells and your thigh wastes away.* **5:27** Hebrew *Her body will swell and her thigh will waste away.* **6:10** Hebrew *Tent of Meeting;* also in 6:13, 18.

6:1, 2 In Moses' day, a personal vow was as binding as a written contract. It was one thing to say you would do something, but it was considered much more serious when you made a solemn vow to do it. God instituted the Nazirite vow for people who wanted to devote some time exclusively to serving him. This vow could be taken for as little as 30 days or as long as a lifetime. It was voluntary, with one exception—parents could take the vow for their young children, making them Nazirites for life. The vow included three distinct restrictions: (1) He must abstain from wine and fermented drink; (2) the hair could not be cut, and the beard could not be shaved; (3) touching a dead body was prohibited. The purpose of the Nazirite vow was to raise up a group of leaders devoted completely to God. Samson, Samuel, and John the Baptist were probably Nazirites for life.

with the basket of bread made without yeast. The priest must also make the prescribed
grain offering and drink offering.
6:18 Num 6:9 — 18 “Then the Nazirites will shave their hair at the entrance of the Tabernacle and put it
on the fire beneath the peace-offering sacrifice. 19 After each Nazirite’s head has been
shaved, the priest will take for each of them the boiled shoulder of the ram, one cake made
without yeast, and one wafer made without yeast, and put them all into the Nazirite’s
6:20 Lev 7:28-34 — hands. 20 The priest will then lift the gifts up before the LORD in a gesture of offering. These
are holy portions for the priest, along with the breast and thigh pieces that were lifted up
before the LORD. After this ceremony the Nazirites may again drink wine.
21 “This is the ritual law of the Nazirites. If any Nazirites have vowed to give the LORD
anything else beyond what is required by their normal Nazirite vow, they must fulfill
their special vow exactly as they have promised.”

The Priestly Blessing

6:23 Deut 21:5; 1 Chr 23:13 — 22 Then the LORD said to Moses, 23 “Instruct Aaron and his sons to bless the people of
Israel with this special blessing:

6:24 Deut 28:3-6 — 24 ‘May the LORD bless you
and protect you.
6:25 Ps 80:3, 7, 19 — 25 May the LORD smile on you
and be gracious to you.
6:26 Pss 4:6; 29:11; 44:3 — 26 May the LORD show you his favor
and give you his peace.’

27 This is how Aaron and his sons will designate the Israelites as my people,* and I
myself will bless them.”

Offerings of Dedication

7:1 Exod 40:9-11 — 7 On the day Moses set up the Tabernacle, he anointed it and set it apart as holy, along
7:2 Num 1:2-16 — with all its furnishings and the altar with its utensils. 2 Then the leaders of Israel—the
tribal leaders who had organized the census—came and brought their offerings. 3 Together they brought six carts and twelve oxen. There was a cart for every two leaders and
an ox for each leader. They presented these to the LORD in front of the Tabernacle.
4 Then the LORD said to Moses, 5 “Receive their gifts and use these oxen and carts for the
7:7 Num 4:26 — work of the Tabernacle.* Distribute them among the Levites according to the work they
have to do.” 6 So Moses presented the carts and oxen to the Levites. 7 He gave two carts and
7:8 Num 4:33 — four oxen to the Gershonite division for their work, 8 and four carts and eight oxen to the
7:9 Num 4:5-15 — Merarite division for their work. All their work was done under the leadership of Ithamar
son of Aaron the priest. 9 But he gave none of the carts or oxen to the Kohathite division,
since they were required to carry the sacred objects of the Tabernacle on their shoulders.
10 The leaders also presented dedication gifts for the altar at the time it was anointed.
They each placed their gifts before the altar. 11 The LORD said to Moses, “Let each leader
bring his gift on a different day for the dedication of the altar.”

12 On the first day Nahshon son of Amminadab, leader of the tribe of Judah, presented
his offering.
7:13 Num 3:47 — 13 The offering consisted of a silver platter weighing about $3\frac{1}{4}$ pounds and a silver
basin of about $1\frac{3}{4}$ pounds.* These were both filled with grain offerings of choice
7:14 Exod 30:34 — flour mixed with olive oil. 14 He also brought a gold container weighing about four
ounces,* which was filled with incense. 15 He brought a young bull, a ram, and a

6:27 Hebrew *will put my name on the people of Israel.* **7:5** Hebrew *Tent of Meeting;* also in 7:89. **7:13** Hebrew *silver platter weighing 130 shekels* [1.5 kilograms] *and a silver basin weighing 70 shekels* [0.8 kilograms], *according to the sanctuary shekel;* also in 7:19, 25, 31, 37, 43, 49, 55, 61, 67, 73, 79, 85. **7:14** Hebrew *10 shekels* [114 grams]; also in 7:20, 26, 32, 38, 44, 50, 56, 62, 68, 74, 80, 86.

6:24-26 A blessing was one way of asking for God’s divine favor to rest upon others. The ancient blessing in these verses helps us understand what a blessing was supposed to do. Its five parts conveyed hope that God would (1) bless and protect them; (2) smile on them (be pleased); (3) be gracious (merciful and compassionate); (4) show his favor toward them (give his approval); (5) give peace. When you ask God to bless others or yourself, you are asking him to do these five things. The blessing you offer will not only help the one receiving it, it will also demonstrate love, encourage others, and provide a model of caring for others.

7:1ff After the Tabernacle was set up, anointed, and consecrated, the leaders of the 12 tribes brought gifts and offerings for its use and maintenance. All of the people participated—it was everyone’s Tabernacle.

one-year-old male lamb as a burnt offering; 16 a male goat for a sin offering; 17 and 7:16 Lev 4:3
two oxen, five rams, five male goats, and five one-year-old male lambs for a peace 7:17 Lev 3:1
offering. This was the offering brought by Nahshon son of Amminadab.

18 On the second day Nethanel son of Zuar, leader of the tribe of Issachar, presented his 7:18 Num 1:8
offering.
19 The offering consisted of a silver platter weighing about 3¼ pounds and a silver
basin of about 1¾ pounds. These were both filled with grain offerings of choice
flour mixed with olive oil. 20 He also brought a gold container weighing about four
ounces, which was filled with incense. 21 He brought a young bull, a ram, and a one-
year-old male lamb as a burnt offering; 22 a male goat for a sin offering; 23 and two
oxen, five rams, five male goats, and five one-year-old male lambs for a peace offering. This was the offering brought by Nethanel son of Zuar.

24 On the third day Eliab son of Helon, leader of the tribe of Zebulun, presented his
offering.
25 The offering consisted of a silver platter weighing about 3¼ pounds and a silver
basin of about 1¾ pounds. These were both filled with grain offerings of choice
flour mixed with olive oil. 26 He also brought a gold container weighing about four
ounces, which was filled with incense. 27 He brought a young bull, a ram, and a one-
year-old male lamb as a burnt offering; 28 a male goat for a sin offering; 29 and two 7:29 Lev 7:32
oxen, five rams, five male goats, and five one-year-old male lambs for a peace offering. This was the offering brought by Eliab son of Helon.

30 On the fourth day Elizur son of Shedeur, leader of the tribe of Reuben, presented his 7:30 Num 1:5
offering.
31 The offering consisted of a silver platter weighing about 3¼ pounds and a silver
basin of about 1¾ pounds. These were both filled with grain offerings of choice
flour mixed with olive oil. 32 He also brought a gold container weighing about four
ounces, which was filled with incense. 33 He brought a young bull, a ram, and a one-
year-old male lamb as a burnt offering; 34 a male goat for a sin offering; 35 and two 7:34 Heb 10:4
oxen, five rams, five male goats, and five one-year-old male lambs for a peace offering. This was the offering brought by Elizur son of Shedeur.

36 On the fifth day Shelumiel son of Zurishaddai, leader of the tribe of Simeon, 7:36 Num 1:6
presented his offering.
37 The offering consisted of a silver platter weighing about 3¼ pounds and a silver
basin of about 1¾ pounds. These were both filled with grain offerings of choice
flour mixed with olive oil. 38 He also brought a gold container weighing about four
ounces, which was filled with incense. 39 He brought a young bull, a ram, and a one-
year-old male lamb as a burnt offering; 40 a male goat for a sin offering; 41 and two
oxen, five rams, five male goats, and five one-year-old male lambs for a peace offering. This was the offering brought by Shelumiel son of Zurishaddai.

42 On the sixth day Eliasaph son of Deuel, leader of the tribe of Gad, presented his 7:42 Num 1:14
offering.
43 The offering consisted of a silver platter weighing about 3¼ pounds and a silver
basin of about 1¾ pounds. These were both filled with grain offerings of choice
flour mixed with olive oil. 44 He also brought a gold container weighing about four
ounces, which was filled with incense. 45 He brought a young bull, a ram, and a one-
year-old male lamb as a burnt offering; 46 a male goat for a sin offering; 47 and two
oxen, five rams, five male goats, and five one-year-old male lambs for a peace offering. This was the offering brought by Eliasaph son of Deuel.

48 On the seventh day Elishama son of Ammihud, leader of the tribe of Ephraim, 7:48 Num 1:10
presented his offering.
49 The offering consisted of a silver platter weighing about 3¼ pounds and a silver
basin of about 1¾ pounds. These were both filled with grain offerings of choice
flour mixed with olive oil. 50 He also brought a gold container weighing about four
ounces, which was filled with incense. 51 He brought a young bull, a ram, and a one-
year-old male lamb as a burnt offering; 52 a male goat for a sin offering; 53 and two 7:52 Heb 10:4

oxen, five rams, five male goats, and five one-year-old male lambs for a peace offering. This was the offering brought by Elishama son of Ammihud.

54 On the eighth day Gamaliel son of Pedahzur, leader of the tribe of Manasseh,
presented his offering.
55 The offering consisted of a silver platter weighing about 3¼ pounds and a silver
basin of about 1¾ pounds. These were both filled with grain offerings of choice
flour mixed with olive oil. 56 He also brought a gold container weighing about four
ounces, which was filled with incense. 57 He brought a young bull, a ram, and a one-
year-old male lamb as a burnt offering; 58 a male goat for a sin offering; 59 and two
oxen, five rams, five male goats, and five one-year-old male lambs for a peace offering. This was the offering brought by Gamaliel son of Pedahzur.

7:60 Num 1:11 60 On the ninth day Abidan son of Gideoni, leader of the tribe of Benjamin, presented
his offering.
61 The offering consisted of a silver platter weighing about 3¼ pounds and a silver
basin of about 1¾ pounds. These were both filled with grain offerings of choice
flour mixed with olive oil. 62 He also brought a gold container weighing about four
ounces, which was filled with incense. 63 He brought a young bull, a ram, and a one-
year-old male lamb as a burnt offering; 64 a male goat for a sin offering; 65 and two
oxen, five rams, five male goats, and five one-year-old male lambs for a peace offering. This was the offering brought by Abidan son of Gideoni.

7:66 Num 1:12 66 On the tenth day Ahiezer son of Ammishaddai, leader of the tribe of Dan, presented
his offering.
67 The offering consisted of a silver platter weighing about 3¼ pounds and a silver
basin of about 1¾ pounds. These were both filled with grain offerings of choice
flour mixed with olive oil. 68 He also brought a gold container weighing about four
7:70 ounces, which was filled with incense. 69 He brought a young bull, a ram, and a one-
Heb 10:4 year-old male lamb as a burnt offering; 70 a male goat for a sin offering; 71 and two
oxen, five rams, five male goats, and five one-year-old male lambs for a peace offering. This was the offering brought by Ahiezer son of Ammishaddai.

72 On the eleventh day Pagiel son of Ocran, leader of the tribe of Asher, presented his
offering.
73 The offering consisted of a silver platter weighing about 3¼ pounds and a silver
basin of about 1¾ pounds. These were both filled with grain offerings of choice
flour mixed with olive oil. 74 He also brought a gold container weighing about four
ounces, which was filled with incense. 75 He brought a young bull, a ram, and a one-
year-old male lamb as a burnt offering; 76 a male goat for a sin offering; 77 and two
oxen, five rams, five male goats, and five one-year-old male lambs for a peace offering. This was the offering brought by Pagiel son of Ocran.

7:78 Num 1:15 78 On the twelfth day Ahira son of Enan, leader of the tribe of Naphtali, presented his
offering.
79 The offering consisted of a silver platter weighing about 3¼ pounds and a silver
basin of about 1¾ pounds. These were both filled with grain offerings of choice
flour mixed with olive oil. 80 He also brought a gold container weighing about four
ounces, which was filled with incense. 81 He brought a young bull, a ram, and a one-
year-old male lamb as a burnt offering; 82 a male goat for a sin offering; 83 and two
oxen, five rams, five male goats, and five one-year-old male lambs for a peace offering. This was the offering brought by Ahira son of Enan.

7:84 Num 7:10 84 So this was the dedication offering for the altar, brought by the leaders of Israel at
the time it was anointed: twelve silver platters, twelve silver basins, and twelve gold
incense containers. 85 In all, the silver objects weighed about 60 pounds,* about 3¼
pounds for each platter and 1¾ pounds for each basin. 86 The weight of the donated gold
came to about three pounds,* about four ounces for each of the gold containers that were
filled with incense. 87 Twelve bulls, twelve rams, and twelve one-year-old male lambs
were donated for the burnt offerings, along with their prescribed grain offerings. Twelve

7:85 Hebrew *2,400 shekels* [27.4 kilograms]. **7:86** Hebrew *120 shekels* [1.4 kilograms].

male goats were brought for the sin offerings. 88 Twenty-four young bulls, sixty rams, **7:88**
sixty male goats, and sixty one-year-old male lambs were donated for the peace Num 7:1, 10
offerings. This was the dedication offering for the altar after it was anointed.
89 Whenever Moses went into the Tabernacle to speak with the LORD, he heard the voice **7:89** Exod 25:21-22;
speaking to him from between the two cherubim above the Ark's cover—the place of 33:9-11
atonement—that rests on the Ark of the Covenant.* The LORD spoke to him from there. Pss 80:1; 99:1

Preparing the Lamps

8 The LORD said to Moses, 2 "Tell Aaron that when he sets up the seven lamps in the **8:2**
lampstand, he is to place them so their light shines forward." 3 So Aaron did this. He set Exod 25:37
up the seven lamps so they reflected their light forward, just as the LORD had commanded
Moses. 4 The entire lampstand, from its base to its decorative blossoms, was made of beaten **8:4**
gold. It was built according to the exact design the LORD had shown Moses. Exod 25:18, 31-36, 40

The Levites Dedicated

5 Then the LORD said to Moses, 6 "Now set the Levites apart from the rest of the people
of Israel and make them ceremonially clean. 7 Do this by sprinkling them with the water **8:7**
of purification. And have them shave their entire body and wash their clothing. Then they Lev 14:8-9 Num 19:9, 17-18
will be ceremonially clean. 8 Have them bring a young bull and a grain offering of choice **8:8**
flour mixed with olive oil, along with a second young bull for a sin offering. 9 Then Num 15:3-12
assemble the whole community of Israel and present the Levites at the entrance of the **8:10**
Tabernacle.* 10 When you bring the Levites before the LORD, the people of Israel must Lev 3:2
lay their hands on them. 11 Aaron must present the Levites to the LORD as a special
offering from the people of Israel, thus dedicating them to the LORD's service.
12 "Next the Levites will lay their hands on the heads of the young bulls and present **8:12**
them to the LORD. One will be for a sin offering and the other for a burnt offering, to Exod 29:10-14
make atonement for the Levites. 13 Then have the Levites stand in front of Aaron and his
sons, and present them as a special offering to the LORD. 14 In this way, you will set the **8:14** Num 3:12
Levites apart from the rest of the people of Israel, and the Levites will belong to me.
15 After this, they may go in and out of the Tabernacle to do their work, because you have
purified them and presented them as a special offering.
16 "Of all the people of Israel, the Levites are reserved for me. I have claimed them for **8:16** Num 3:13
myself in place of all the firstborn sons of the Israelites; I have taken the Levites as their
substitutes. 17 For all the firstborn males among the people of Israel are mine, both people **8:17**
and animals. I set them apart for myself on the night I killed all the firstborn sons of the Exod 13:12-13
Egyptians. 18 Yes, I claim the Levites in place of all the firstborn sons of Israel. 19 And of **8:19** Num 1:53
all the Israelites, I have assigned the Levites to Aaron and his sons. They will serve in
the Tabernacle on behalf of the Israelites and make atonement for them so no plague will
strike them when they approach the sanctuary."
20 So Moses, Aaron, and the whole community of Israel dedicated the Levites, carefully
following all the LORD's instructions to Moses. 21 The Levites purified themselves and
washed their clothes, and Aaron presented them to the LORD as a special offering. He then
performed the rite of atonement over them to purify them. 22 From then on the Levites went
into the Tabernacle to perform their duties, helping Aaron and his sons. So they carried
out all the commands that the LORD gave Moses concerning the Levites.
23 The LORD also instructed Moses, 24 "This is the rule the Levites must follow: They **8:24** Num 4:3
must begin serving in the Tabernacle at the age of twenty-five, 25 and they must retire at

7:89 Or *Ark of the Testimony.* **8:9** Hebrew *Tent of Meeting;* also in 8:15, 19, 22, 24, 26.

7:89 Imagine hearing the very voice of God! Moses must have trembled at the sound. Yet we have God's words recorded for us in the Bible, and we should have no less reverence and awe for them. God sometimes spoke directly to his people to tell them the proper way to live. The Bible records these conversations to give us insights into God's character. How tragic when we take these very words of God lightly. Like Moses, we have the privilege of talking to God, but God answers us differently—through his written Word and the guidance of his Holy Spirit. To receive this guidance, we need to seek to know God as Moses did.

8:1-4 The lamps provided light for the priests as they carried out their duties. The light was also an expression of God's presence. Jesus said, "I am the light of the world" (John 8:12). The golden lampstand is still one of the major symbols of the Jewish faith.

8:25, 26 Why were the Levites supposed to retire at age 50? The reasons were probably more practical than theological. (1) Moving the Tabernacle and its furniture through the wilderness required strength. The younger men were more suited for the work of lifting the heavy articles. (2) The Levites over 50 did not stop working altogether. They were allowed to assist with various light duties in the Tabernacle. This helped the

the age of fifty. 26After retirement they may assist their fellow Levites by performing guard
duty at the Tabernacle, but they may not officiate in the service. This is how you will assign
duties to the Levites."

The Second Passover

9:1 Exod 40:2, 17
9:2 Exod 12:1-6

9 The LORD gave these instructions to Moses in early spring,* during the second year
after Israel's departure from Egypt, while he and the rest of the Israelites were in the
wilderness of Sinai: 2"Tell the Israelites to celebrate the Passover at the proper time, 3at
twilight on the appointed day in early spring.* Be sure to follow all my laws and
regulations concerning this celebration."

9:5 Josh 5:10
9:6 Num 19:11-22

4So Moses told the people to celebrate the Passover 5in the wilderness of Sinai as
twilight fell on the appointed day.* And they celebrated the festival there, just as the
LORD had commanded Moses. 6But some of the men had been ceremonially defiled by
touching a dead person, so they could not offer their Passover lambs that day. So they
came to Moses and Aaron that day 7and said, "We have become ceremonially unclean
by touching a dead person. But why should we be excluded from presenting the LORD's
offering at the proper time with the rest of the Israelites?"

9:8 Exod 18:15

8Moses answered, "Wait here until I have received instructions for you from the LORD."
9This was the LORD's reply: 10"Say to the Israelites: 'If any of the people now or in
future generations are ceremonially unclean at Passover time because of touching a dead
body, or if they are on a journey and cannot be present at the ceremony, they may still

9:11 Exod 12:8
9:12 Exod 12:10, 43, 46; †John 19:36

celebrate the LORD's Passover. 11They must offer the Passover sacrifice one month
later,* at twilight on the appointed day. They must eat the lamb at that time with bitter
herbs and bread made without yeast. 12They must not leave any of the lamb until the next
morning, and they must not break any of its bones. They must follow all the normal
regulations concerning the Passover.

9:13 Exod 12:15; Num 15:30-31
9:14 Exod 12:48-49

13"'But those who are ceremonially clean and not away on a trip, yet still refuse to
celebrate the Passover at the regular time, will be cut off from the community of Israel
for failing to present the LORD's offering at the proper time. They will suffer the
consequences of their guilt. 14And if foreigners living among you want to celebrate the
Passover to the LORD, they must follow these same laws and regulations. The same laws
apply both to you and to the foreigners living among you.'"

4. Receiving guidance for the journey

The Fiery Cloud

9:15 Exod 13:21-22; 40:2, 17, 34; Neh 9:12, 19; Ps 78:14

15The Tabernacle was set up, and on that day the cloud covered it.* Then from evening
until morning the cloud over the Tabernacle appeared to be a pillar of fire. 16This was

9:1 Hebrew *in the first month.* This month of the Hebrew lunar calendar usually occurs in March and April. **9:3** Hebrew *on the fourteenth day of the first month.* This day of the Hebrew lunar calendar occurs in late March or early April. **9:5** Hebrew *on the fourteenth day of the first month;* see note on 9:3. **9:11** Hebrew *on the fourteenth day of the second month.* This day of the Hebrew lunar calendar occurs in late April or early May. **9:15** Hebrew *covered the Tabernacle, the Tent of the Testimony.*

---

younger men assume more responsibilities, and it allowed the older men to be in a position to advise and counsel them.

9:2 This is the second Passover. The first was instituted in Egypt and recorded in Exodus 12. Passover and the Festival of Unleavened Bread were an eight-day religious observance (Leviticus 23:5, 6) commemorating the Israelites' escape from slavery in Egypt by God's power.

9:6-12 Several men came to Moses because of the predicament they faced: They were "unclean" because of contact with a dead body (or entering the home of a person who had died), and this prevented them from participating in the Passover meal. Notice that God did not adjust the requirements of the Passover. The standards of holiness were maintained, and the men were not allowed to participate. But God did make an exception and allowed the men to celebrate the Passover at a later date. This upheld the sacred requirements while allowing the men to participate in the feast—a duty for all Israelite men. Sometimes we face predicaments where the most obvious solution might cause us to compromise God's standards. Like Moses, we should use wisdom and prayer to reach a workable solution.

9:14 Sometimes we are tempted to excuse non-Christians from following God's guidelines for living. Christmas and Easter, for example, often have other meanings for them. We would not expect them to understand Lent. Yet foreigners at this time were expected to follow the same laws and ordinances as the Israelites. God did not have a separate set of standards for unbelievers, and he still does not today. The phrase "They must follow these same laws and regulations" emphasizes that non-Israelites were also subject to God's commands and promises. God singled out Israel for a special purpose—to be an example of how one nation could, and should, follow him. His aim, however, was to have all people obey and worship him.

9:15-22 A pillar of cloud by day and a pillar of fire by night guided and protected the Israelites as they traveled across the wilderness. Some have said this pillar may have been a burning bowl of pitch whose smoke was visible during the day and whose fire could be seen at night. However, a bowl of pitch would not have lifted itself up and moved ahead of the people, and the Bible is clear that the cloud and fire moved in accordance with the will of God. The cloud and the fire were not merely natural phenomena; they were the vehicle of God's presence and the visible evidence of his moving and directing his people.

the regular pattern—at night the cloud changed to the appearance of fire. 17When the
cloud lifted from over the sacred tent, the people of Israel followed it. And wherever the
cloud settled, the people of Israel camped. 18In this way, they traveled at the LORD's
command and stopped wherever he told them to. Then they remained where they were
as long as the cloud stayed over the Tabernacle. 19If the cloud remained over the
Tabernacle for a long time, the Israelites stayed for a long time, just as the LORD
commanded. 20Sometimes the cloud would stay over the Tabernacle for only a few days,
so the people would stay for only a few days. Then at the LORD's command they would
break camp. 21Sometimes the cloud stayed only overnight and moved on the next
morning. But day or night, when the cloud lifted, the people broke camp and followed.
22Whether the cloud stayed above the Tabernacle for two days, a month, or a year, the
people of Israel stayed in camp and did not move on. But as soon as it lifted, they broke
camp and moved on. 23So they camped or traveled at the LORD's command, and they did
whatever the LORD told them through Moses.

9:17 Exod 40:36-38; Num 10:11, 33-34
9:18 1 Cor 10:1
9:22 Exod 40:36-37

The Silver Trumpets

10 Now the LORD said to Moses, 2"Make two trumpets of beaten silver to be used
for summoning the people to assemble and for signaling the breaking of camp.
3When both trumpets are blown, the people will know that they are to gather before you
at the entrance of the Tabernacle.* 4But if only one is blown, then only the leaders of the
tribes of Israel will come to you.
5"When you sound the signal to move on, the tribes on the east side of the Tabernacle
will break camp and move forward. 6When you sound the signal a second time, the tribes
on the south will follow. You must sound short blasts to signal moving on. 7But when
you call the people to an assembly, blow the trumpets using a different signal. 8Only the
priests, Aaron's descendants, are allowed to blow the trumpets. This is a permanent law
to be followed from generation to generation.
9"When you arrive in your own land and go to war against your enemies, you must
sound the alarm with these trumpets so the LORD your God will remember you and
rescue you from your enemies. 10Blow the trumpets in times of gladness, too, sounding
them at your annual festivals and at the beginning of each month to rejoice over your
burnt offerings and peace offerings. The trumpets will remind the LORD your God of his
covenant with you. I am the LORD your God."

10:3 Jer 4:5
10:5 Num 10:14
10:7 Joel 2:1
10:8 Num 31:6; Josh 6:3-9; 2 Chr 5:11-12
10:9 Judg 2:18; Ps 106:4
10:10 Lev 23:24; Num 29:1; Ps 81:3-5

B. FIRST APPROACH TO THE PROMISED LAND (10:11—14:45)

As the Israelites approached the Promised Land, Moses sent leaders to scout out the land and its people. But the scouts returned with a discouraging report—"It is indeed a magnificent country. . . . But the people living there are powerful. . . . We can't go up against them!" Although Joshua and Caleb disagreed, the Israelites had already made up their minds and began to complain. As punishment for their lack of faith, God condemned them to wander in the wilderness for 40 years. Our obedience must be complete and timely.

1. The people complain

The Israelites Leave Sinai

11One day in midspring,* during the second year after Israel's departure from Egypt,
the cloud lifted from the Tabernacle of the Covenant.* 12So the Israelites set out from
the wilderness of Sinai and traveled on in stages until the cloud stopped in the
wilderness of Paran.
13When the time to move arrived, the LORD gave the order through Moses. 14The
tribes that camped with Judah headed the march with their banner, under the leadership

10:11 Exod 40:17
10:12 Gen 21:20-21; Num 12:16
10:13 Deut 1:6
10:14 Num 2:3-31

10:3 Hebrew *Tent of Meeting.* **10:11a** Hebrew *On the twentieth day of the second month.* This day of the Hebrew lunar calendar occurs in late April or early May. **10:11b** Or *Tabernacle of the Testimony.*

9:23 The Israelites traveled and camped as God guided. When you follow God's guidance, you know you are where God wants you, whether you're moving or staying in one place. You are physically somewhere right now. Instead of praying, "God, what do you want me to do next?" ask, "God, what do you want me to do while I'm right here?" Direction from God is not just for your next big move. He has a purpose in placing you where you are right now. Begin to understand God's purpose for your life by discovering what he wants you to do now!

10:1-10 The two silver trumpets were used to coordinate the tribes as they moved through the wilderness. To keep so many people in tight formations required clear communication and control. Trumpet blasts also reminded Israel of God's protection over them.

of Nahshon son of Amminadab. 15 The tribe of Issachar was led by Nethanel son of Zuar.
16 The tribe of Zebulun was led by Eliab son of Helon.
10:17 Num 4:21-23 17 Then the Tabernacle was taken down, and the Gershonite and Merarite divisions of
10:18 Num 2:10-16 the Levites were next in the line of march, carrying the Tabernacle with them. 18 Then
the tribes that camped with Reuben set out with their banner, under the leadership of
Elizur son of Shedeur. 19 The tribe of Simeon was led by Shelumiel son of Zurishaddai.
20 The tribe of Gad was led by Eliasaph son of Deuel.
10:21 Num 4:1-20 21 Next came the Kohathite division of the Levites, carrying the sacred objects from the
Tabernacle. When they arrived at the next camp, the Tabernacle would already be set up
10:22 Num 2:3-31 at its new location. 22 Then the tribes that camped with Ephraim set out with their banner,
under the leadership of Elishama son of Ammihud. 23 The tribe of Manasseh was led by
Gamaliel son of Pedahzur. 24 The tribe of Benjamin was led by Abidan son of Gideoni.
25 Last of all, the tribes that camped with Dan set out under their banner. They served
as the rear guard for all the tribal camps. The tribe of Dan headed this group, under the
leadership of Ahiezer son of Ammishaddai. 26 The tribe of Asher was led by Pagiel son
of Ocran. 27 The tribe of Naphtali was led by Ahira son of Enan.
28 This was the order in which the tribes marched, division by division.
10:29 Exod 2:18-21; 3:1; 18:12 Judg 1:16; 4:11 29 One day Moses said to his brother-in-law, Hobab son of Reuel the Midianite, "We
are on our way to the Promised Land. Come with us and we will treat you well, for the
LORD has given wonderful promises to Israel!"
30 But Hobab replied, "No, I will not go. I must return to my own land and family."
10:32 Ps 22:27-31 31 "Please don't leave us," Moses pleaded. "You know the places in the wilderness
where we should camp. 32 Come, be our guide and we will share with you all the good
10:33 Deut 1:33 things that the LORD does for us."
33 They marched for three days after leaving the mountain of the LORD, with the Ark
10:34 Num 9:15-23 of the LORD's covenant moving ahead of them to show them where to stop and rest. 34 As
10:35 Ps 68:1-2 they moved on each day, the cloud of the LORD hovered over them. 35 And whenever the
Ark set out, Moses would cry, "Arise, O LORD, and let your enemies be scattered! Let
10:36 Deut 1:10-11 them flee before you!" 36 And when the Ark was set down, he would say, "Return,
O LORD, to the countless thousands of Israel!"

The People Complain to Moses

11:1 Lev 10:1-2 Num 14:2; 16:35; 17:5 **11** The people soon began to complain to the LORD about their hardships; and when
the LORD heard them, his anger blazed against them. Fire from the LORD raged
among them and destroyed the outskirts of the camp. 2 The people screamed to Moses
11:3 Deut 9:22 for help; and when he prayed to the LORD, the fire stopped. 3 After that, the area was
known as Taberah—"the place of burning"—because fire from the LORD had burned
among them there.

ISRAEL'S DEPARTURE FROM SINAI
It has been two years since Israel left Egypt. Having received God's travel instructions through Moses, Israel set out from Mount Sinai into the wilderness of Paran on their way toward the Promised Land.

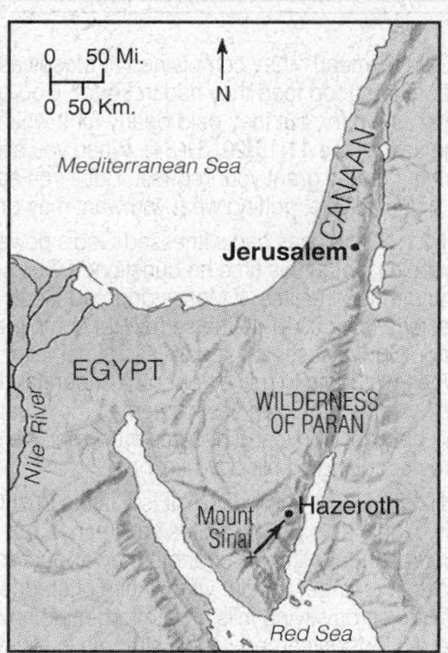

10:21 Those who travel, move, or face new challenges know what it is to be uprooted. Life is full of changes, and few things remain stable. The Israelites were constantly moving through the wilderness. They were able to handle change only because God's presence in the Tabernacle was always with them. The portable Tabernacle signified God and his people moving together. For us, stability does not mean lack of change, but moving with God in every circumstance.

10:29-32 By complimenting Hobab's wilderness skills, Moses let him know he was needed. People cannot know you appreciate them if you do not tell them they are important to you. Complimenting those who deserve it builds lasting relationships and helps people know they are valued. Think about those who have helped you this month. What can you do to let them know how much you need and appreciate them?

11:1, 6-15 The Israelites complained, and then Moses complained. But God responded positively to Moses and negatively to the rest of the people. Why? The people complained *to one another,* and nothing was accomplished. Moses took his complaint *to God,* who could solve any problem. Many of us are good at complaining to each other. We need to learn to take our problems to the One who can do something about them.

4 Then the foreign rabble who were traveling with the Israelites began to crave the **11:4** Exod 12:38
good things of Egypt, and the people of Israel also began to complain. "Oh, for some Lev 24:10-11
meat!" they exclaimed. 5 "We remember all the fish we used to eat for free in Egypt. And Ps 78:18; 1 Cor 10:6
we had all the cucumbers, melons, leeks, onions, and garlic that we wanted. 6 But now **11:6**
our appetites are gone, and day after day we have nothing to eat but this manna!" Num 21:5
7 The manna looked like small coriander seeds, pale yellow in color.* 8 The people **11:7** Exod 16:14, 31
gathered it from the ground and made flour by grinding it with hand mills or pounding
it in mortars. Then they boiled it in a pot and made it into flat cakes. These cakes tasted
like they had been cooked in olive oil. 9 The manna came down on the camp with the **11:9** Exod 16:13
dew during the night.
10 Moses heard all the families standing in front of their tents weeping, and the LORD **11:10** Ps 78:21
became extremely angry. Moses was also very aggravated. 11 And Moses said to the **11:11**
LORD, "Why are you treating me, your servant, so miserably? What did I do to deserve Exod 5:22
the burden of a people like this? 12 Are they my children? Am I their father? Is that why **11:12** Gen 26:3
you have told me to carry them in my arms—like a nurse carries a baby—to the land you Exod 13:4-5
swore to give their ancestors? 13 Where am I supposed to get meat for all these people? Isa 49:23
They keep complaining and saying, 'Give us meat!' 14 I can't carry all these people by **11:14** Exod 18:18
myself! The load is far too heavy! 15 I'd rather you killed me than treat me like this. Please Deut 1:12
spare me this misery!" **11:15** Exod 32:32

Moses Chooses Seventy Leaders

16 Then the LORD said to Moses, "Summon before me seventy of the leaders of Israel. **11:16** Exod 24:1, 9
Bring them to the Tabernacle* to stand there with you. 17 I will come down and talk to **11:17**
you there. I will take some of the Spirit that is upon you, and I will put the Spirit upon Exod 34:5-6
them also. They will bear the burden of the people along with you, so you will not have Num 11:25; 12:5
to carry it alone.
18 "And tell the people to purify themselves, for tomorrow they will have meat to eat. **11:18** Exod 19:10, 14-15
Tell them, 'The LORD has heard your whining and complaints: "If only we had meat to
eat! Surely we were better off in Egypt!" Now the LORD will give you meat, and you will
have to eat it. 19 And it won't be for just a day or two, or for five or ten or even twenty.
20 You will eat it for a whole month until you gag and are sick of it. For you have rejected
the LORD, who is here among you, and you have complained to him, "Why did we ever
leave Egypt?"'"
21 But Moses said, "There are 600,000 foot soldiers here with me, and yet you promise **11:21** Exod 12:37
them meat for a whole month! 22 Even if we butchered all our flocks and herds, would
that satisfy them? Even if we caught all the fish in the sea, would that be enough?"
23 Then the LORD said to Moses, "Is there any limit to my power? Now you will see **11:23** Isa 50:2
whether or not my word comes true!"

11:7 Hebrew *the color of gum resin.* **11:16** Hebrew *Tent of Meeting.*

11:4 The *rabble* refers to a mixed crowd of Egyptians and others who had followed Israel out of Egypt (Exodus 12:38).

11:4-6 Dissatisfaction comes when our attention shifts from what we have to what we don't have. The people of Israel didn't seem to notice what God was doing for them—setting them free, making them a nation, giving them a new land—because they were so wrapped up in what God wasn't doing for them. They could think of nothing but the delicious Egyptian food they had left behind. Somehow they forgot that the brutal whip of Egyptian slavery was the cost of eating that food. Before we judge the Israelites too harshly, it's helpful to think about what occupies our attention most of the time. Are we grateful for what God has given us, or are we always thinking about what we would like to have? We should not allow our unfulfilled desires to cause us to forget God's gifts of life, food, health, work, and friends.

11:4-9 Every morning the Israelites drew back their tent doors and witnessed a miracle. Covering the ground was pale yellow, fluffy manna—food from heaven. But soon that wasn't enough. Feeling it was their right to have more, they forgot what they already had. They didn't ask God to fill their need; instead, they demanded meat, and they stopped trusting God to care for them. "Give us meat!" they complained to Moses as they reminisced about the good food they had in Egypt. God gave them what they asked for, but they paid dearly for it when a plague struck the camp (see 11:18-20, 31-34). When you ask God for something, he may grant your request. But if you approach him with a sinful attitude, getting what you want may prove costly.

11:21, 22 Moses had witnessed God's power in spectacular miracles, yet at this time he questioned God's ability to feed the wandering Israelites. If Moses doubted God's power, how much easier it is for us to do the same. But completely depending upon God is essential, regardless of our level of spiritual maturity. When we begin to rely on our own understanding, we are in danger of ignoring God's assessment of the situation. By remembering his past works and his present power, we can be sure that we are not cutting off his potential help.

11:23 How strong is God? It is easy to trust God when we see his mighty acts (the Israelites saw many), but after a while, in the routine of daily life, his strength may appear to diminish. God doesn't change, but our view of him often does. The monotony of day-by-day living lulls us into forgetting how powerful God can be. As Moses learned, God's strength is always available.

24 So Moses went out and reported the LORD's words to the people. Then he gathered
11:25 Num 11:16-17 the seventy leaders and stationed them around the Tabernacle.* 25 And the LORD came
down in the cloud and spoke to Moses. He took some of the Spirit that was upon Moses
and put it upon the seventy leaders. They prophesied as the Spirit rested upon them, but
that was the only time this happened.
26 Two men, Eldad and Medad, were still in the camp when the Spirit rested upon
them. They were listed among the leaders but had not gone out to the Tabernacle, so they
prophesied there in the camp. 27 A young man ran and reported to Moses, "Eldad and
11:28 Josh 1:1; Mark 9:38-40 Medad are prophesying in the camp!" 28 Joshua son of Nun, who had been Moses'
personal assistant since his youth, protested, "Moses, my master, make them stop!"
29 But Moses replied, "Are you jealous for my sake? I wish that all the LORD's people
were prophets, and that the LORD would put his Spirit upon them all!" 30 Then Moses
returned to the camp with the leaders of Israel.

The LORD Sends Quail

11:31 Exod 16:13; Pss 78:26-33; 105:40 31 Now the LORD sent a wind that brought quail from the sea and let them fall into the
camp and all around it! For many miles in every direction from the camp there were quail
flying about three feet above the ground.* 32 So the people went out and caught quail all
that day and throughout the night and all the next day, too. No one gathered less than
11:33 Num 11:10 fifty bushels*! They spread the quail out all over the camp. 33 But while they were still

11:24 Hebrew *the tent;* also in 11:26. **11:31** Or *there were quail 3 feet* [2 cubits or 90 centimeters] *deep on the ground.* **11:32** Hebrew *10 homers* [1.8 kiloliters].

ISRAEL'S COMPLAINING

	Complaint	Sin	Result
11:1	About their hardships	Complained about their problems instead of praying to God about them	Thousands of people were destroyed when God sent a plague of fire to punish them
11:4	About the lack of meat	Lusted after things they didn't have	God sent quail; but as the people began to eat, God struck them with a plague that killed many
14:1–4	About being stuck in the wilderness, facing the giants of the Promised Land, and wishing to return to Egypt	Openly rebelled against God's leaders and failed to trust in his promises	All who complained were not allowed to enter the Promised Land, being doomed to wander in the wilderness until they died
16:3	About Moses' and Aaron's authority and leadership	Were greedy for more power and authority	The families, friends, and possessions of Korah, Dathan, and Abiram were swallowed up by the earth. Fire then burned up the 250 other men who rebelled
16:41	That Moses and Aaron caused the deaths of Korah and his conspirators	Blamed others for their own troubles	God began to destroy Israel with a plague. Moses and Aaron made atonement for the people, but 14,700 of them were killed
20:2, 3	About the lack of water	Refused to believe that God would provide as he had promised	Moses sinned along with the people. For this he was barred from entering the Promised Land
21:5	That God and Moses brought them into the wilderness	Failed to recognize that their problems were brought on by their own disobedience	God sent poisonous snakes that killed many people and seriously injured many others

11:26-29 This incident is similar to a story told in Mark 9:38-41. The disciples wanted Jesus to forbid others to drive out demons because they were not part of the disciples' group. But this type of narrow attitude was condemned by both Moses and Jesus. Beware of putting limits on God—he can work through whomever he chooses.

eating the meat, the anger of the LORD blazed against the people, and he caused a severe 11:34
plague to break out among them. 34 So that place was called Kibroth-hattaavah—"the Deut 9:22
graves of craving"—because they buried the people there who had craved meat from
Egypt. 35 From there the Israelites traveled to Hazeroth, where they stayed for some time. 11:35 Num 33:17

2. Miriam and Aaron oppose Moses

12 While they were at Hazeroth, Miriam and Aaron criticized Moses because he had 12:1 Exod 2:21; 15:20
married a Cushite woman. 2 They said, "Has the LORD spoken only through 12:2
Moses? Hasn't he spoken through us, too?" But the LORD heard them. Num 16:3
3 Now Moses was more humble than any other person on earth. 4 So immediately the 12:3 Matt 11:29
LORD called to Moses, Aaron, and Miriam and said, "Go out to the Tabernacle,* all three of
you!" And the three of them went out. 5 Then the LORD descended in the pillar of cloud and 12:5 Num 11:25
stood at the entrance of the Tabernacle.* "Aaron and Miriam!" he called, and they stepped
forward. 6 And the LORD said to them, "Now listen to me! Even with prophets, I the LORD 12:6 Gen 15:1;
communicate by visions and dreams. 7 But that is not how I communicate with my servant 31:10-11; 46:2
Moses. He is entrusted with my entire house. 8 I speak to him face to face, directly and not 1 Kgs 3:5
in riddles! He sees the LORD as he is. Should you not be afraid to criticize him?" 12:7 Ps 105:26
9 The LORD was furious with them, and he departed. 10 As the cloud moved from above Heb 3:2, 5
the Tabernacle, Miriam suddenly became white as snow with leprosy.* When Aaron saw 12:8
what had happened, 11 he cried out to Moses, "Oh, my lord! Please don't punish us for Exod 33:11, 19 Deut 34:10
this sin we have so foolishly committed. 12 Don't let her be like a stillborn baby, already 12:10
decayed at birth." Deut 24:9
13 So Moses cried out to the LORD, "Heal her, O God, I beg you!" 12:11 2 Sam 19:19
14 And the LORD said to Moses, "If her father had spit in her face, wouldn't she have 12:14
been defiled for seven days? Banish her from the camp for seven days, and after that she Lev 13:46
may return." Num 5:1-3 Deut 25:9
15 So Miriam was excluded from the camp for seven days, and the people waited until
she was brought back before they traveled again. 16 Then they left Hazeroth and camped
in the wilderness of Paran.

3. The scouts incite rebellion

Twelve Scouts Explore Canaan

13 The LORD now said to Moses, 2 "Send men to explore the land of Canaan, the land 13:2 Deut 1:22-25
I am giving to Israel. Send one leader from each of the twelve ancestral tribes." Josh 1:3
3 So Moses did as the LORD commanded him. He sent out twelve men, all tribal leaders

12:4 Hebrew *Tent of Meeting.* **12:5** Hebrew *the tent;* also in 12:10. **12:10** Or *with a contagious skin disease.* The Hebrew word used here can describe various skin diseases.

11:34 Craving or lusting is more than inappropriate sexual desire. It can be an unnatural or greedy desire for anything (sports, knowledge, possessions, influence over others). In this circumstance, God punished the Israelites for craving good food! Their desire was not wrong; the sin was in allowing that desire to turn into greed. They felt it was their right to have fine food, and they could think of nothing else. When you become preoccupied with something until it affects your perspective on everything else, you have moved from desire to lust.

12:1 Moses didn't have a Jewish wife because he lived with the Egyptians the first 40 years of his life, and he was in the wilderness the next 40 years. The woman is probably not Zipporah, his first wife, who was a Midianite (see Exodus 2:21). A Cushite was an Ethiopian. There is no explanation given for why Miriam objected to this woman.

12:1 People often argue over minor disagreements, leaving the real issue untouched. Such was the case when Miriam and Aaron criticized Moses. They represented the priests and the prophets, the two most powerful groups next to Moses. The real issue was their growing jealousy of Moses' position and influence. Since they could not find fault with the way Moses was leading the people, they chose to criticize his wife. Rather than face the problem squarely by dealing with their envy and pride, they chose to create a diversion from the real issue. When you are in a disagreement, stop and ask yourself if you are arguing over the real issue or if you have introduced a smoke screen by attacking someone's character. If you are unjustly criticized, remember that your critics may be afraid to face the real problem. Don't take this type of criticism personally. Ask God to help you identify the real issue and deal with it.

12:11 Aaron asked that he and Miriam not be punished for their sin. It is easy to look back at our mistakes and recognize their foolishness. It is much harder to recognize foolish plans while we are carrying them out because somehow then they seem appropriate. To get rid of foolish ideas before they turn into foolish actions requires eliminating our wrong thoughts and motives. Failing to do this caused Miriam and Aaron much grief.

12:14 Spitting in someone's face was considered the ultimate insult and a sign of shame imposed on wrongdoers. The religious leaders spat in Jesus' face to insult him (Matthew 26:67). God punished Miriam for her smug attitude not only toward Moses' authority but also God's. He struck her with leprosy, then ordered her out of the camp for a week. This punishment was actually quite lenient. A week was the length of time she would have been excluded if her father had spit in her face. How much more she deserved for wronging God! Once again, God was merciful while retaining effective discipline.

of Israel, from their camp in the wilderness of Paran. 4 These were the tribes and the
names of the leaders:

Tribe	Leader
Reuben	Shammua son of Zaccur
5 Simeon	Shaphat son of Hori
6 Judah	Caleb son of Jephunneh
7 Issachar	Igal son of Joseph
8 Ephraim	Hoshea son of Nun
9 Benjamin	Palti son of Raphu
10 Zebulun	Gaddiel son of Sodi
11 Manasseh son of Joseph	Gaddi son of Susi
12 Dan	Ammiel son of Gemalli
13 Asher	Sethur son of Michael
14 Naphtali	Nahbi son of Vophsi
15 Gad	Geuel son of Maki

13:8 Num 13:16

13:16 Num 13:8

13:17 Gen 12:9; 13:1 Num 13:21

16 These are the names of the men Moses sent to explore the land. By this time Moses
had changed Hoshea's name to Joshua.*
17 Moses gave the men these instructions as he sent them out to explore the land: "Go

13:16 *Hoshea* (see 13:8) means "salvation"; *Joshua* means "The LORD is salvation."

MIRIAM

Ask older brothers or sisters what their greatest trial in life is, and they will often answer, "My younger brother [or sister]!" This is especially true when the younger sibling is more successful than the older. The bonds of family loyalty can be strained to the breaking point.

When we first meet Miriam, she is involved in one of history's most unusual baby-sitting jobs. She is watching her infant brother float on the Nile River in a waterproof cradle. Miriam's quick thinking allowed Moses to be raised by his own mother. Her protective superiority, reinforced by that event, must have been hard to give up as she watched her little brother rise to greatness.

Eventually Moses' choice of a wife gave Miriam an opportunity to criticize. It was natural for her insecurity to break out over this issue. With Moses married, Miriam was clearly no longer the most important woman in his life. The real issue, however, was not the kind of woman Moses had married. It was the fact that he was now the most important man in Israel. "Has the LORD spoken only through Moses? Hasn't he spoken through us, too?" No mention is made of Moses' response, but God had a quick answer for Miriam and Aaron. Without denying their role in his plan, God clearly pointed out his special relationship with Moses. Miriam was stricken with leprosy, a deadly disease, as punishment for her insubordination. But Moses, true to his character, intervened for his sister so that God healed Miriam of her leprosy.

Before criticizing someone else, we need to pause long enough to discover our own motives. Failing to do this can bring disastrous results. What is often labeled "constructive criticism" may actually be destructive jealousy, since the easiest way to raise our own status is to bring someone else down. Are you willing to question your motives before you offer criticism? Does the critical finger you point need to be pointed first toward yourself?

Strengths and accomplishments
- Quick thinker under pressure
- Able leader
- Songwriter
- Prophet

Weaknesses and mistakes
- Was jealous of Moses' authority
- Openly criticized Moses' leadership

Lesson from her life
- The motives behind criticism are often more important to deal with than the criticism itself

Vital statistics
- Where: Egypt, Sinai peninsula
- Relatives: Brothers: Aaron and Moses

Key verses
"Then Miriam the prophet, Aaron's sister, took a tambourine and led all the women in rhythm and dance. And Miriam sang this song: 'I will sing to the LORD, for he has triumphed gloriously; he has thrown both horse and rider into the sea'" (Exodus 15:20, 21).

Miriam's story is told in Exodus 2; 15; and Numbers 12; 20. She is also mentioned in Deuteronomy 24:9; 1 Chronicles 6:3; Micah 6:4.

13:17-20 Moses decided what information was needed before the people could enter the Promised Land, and he took careful steps to get that information. When you are making decisions or assuming new responsibilities, remember these two important steps. Ask yourself what you need to know about the opportunity, and then obtain that knowledge. Common sense is a valuable aid in accomplishing God's purposes.

northward through the Negev into the hill country. 18See what the land is like and find
out whether the people living there are strong or weak, few or many. 19What kind of land
do they live in? Is it good or bad? Do their towns have walls or are they unprotected?
20How is the soil? Is it fertile or poor? Are there many trees? Enter the land boldly, and
bring back samples of the crops you see." (It happened to be the season for harvesting
the first ripe grapes.)
21So they went up and explored the land from the wilderness of Zin as far as Rehob,
near Lebo-hamath. 22Going northward, they passed first through the Negev and
arrived at Hebron, where Ahiman, Sheshai, and Talmai—all descendants of Anak—
lived. (The ancient town of Hebron was founded seven years before the Egyptian city
of Zoan.) 23When they came to what is now known as the valley of Eshcol, they cut
down a cluster of grapes so large that it took two of them to carry it on a pole between
them! They also took samples of the pomegranates and figs. 24At that time the
Israelites renamed the valley Eshcol—"cluster"—because of the cluster of grapes
they had cut there.

The Scouting Report

25After exploring the land for forty days, the men returned 26to Moses, Aaron, and the
people of Israel at Kadesh in the wilderness of Paran. They reported to the whole
community what they had seen and showed them the fruit they had taken from the
land. 27This was their report to Moses: "We arrived in the land you sent us to see, and
it is indeed a magnificent country—a land flowing with milk and honey. Here is some
of its fruit as proof. 28But the people living there are powerful, and their cities and
towns are fortified and very large. We also saw the descendants of Anak who are living
there! 29The Amalekites live in the Negev, and the Hittites, Jebusites, and Amorites
live in the hill country. The Canaanites live along the coast of the Mediterranean Sea*
and along the Jordan Valley."

13:20 Deut 1:25
13:21 Num 20:1; 27:14 Josh 19:28 Judg 1:31 Amos 6:14
13:22 Num 13:33 Josh 11:21; 15:14 Judg 1:20
13:23 Num 13:24; 32:9 Deut 1:24-25
13:26 Num 12:16; 13:3; 20:1; 32:8
13:27 Exod 13:5 Deut 1:25
13:28 Num 13:22-23
13:29 Num 14:43

13:29 Hebrew *the sea.*

13:25-29 God told the Israelites that the Promised Land was rich and fertile. Not only that, he promised that this bountiful land would be theirs. When the scouts reported back to Moses, they gave plenty of good reasons for entering the land, but they couldn't stop focusing on their fear. Talk of giants (descendants of Anak) and fortified cities made it easy to forget about God's promise to help. When facing a tough decision, don't let the negatives cause you to lose sight of the positives. Weigh both sides carefully. Don't let potential difficulties blind you to God's power to help and his promise to guide.

13:26 Although Kadesh was only an oasis in the wilderness, it was a crossroads in Israel's history. When the scouts returned to Kadesh from scouting the new land, the people had to decide either to enter the land or to retreat. They chose to retreat and were condemned to wander 40 years in the wilderness. It was also at Kadesh that Moses disobeyed God (20:7-12). For this, he, too, was denied entrance into the Promised Land. Aaron and Miriam died there, for they could not enter the new land either. Kadesh was near Canaan's southern borders, but because of the Israelites' lack of faith, they needed more than a lifetime to go from Kadesh to the Promised Land.

13:27 The Promised Land, also called the land of Canaan, was indeed magnificent, as the 12 scouts discovered. The Bible often calls it the land flowing with milk and honey. Although the land was relatively small—150 miles long and 60 miles wide—its lush hillsides were covered with fig, date, and nut trees. It was the land God had promised to Abraham, Isaac, and Jacob.

13:28 The "descendants of Anak" were a race of abnormally large people. The family of Goliath may have been descended from these people (see 2 Samuel 21:16-22).

13:28, 29 The fortified cities the scouts talked about were surrounded by high walls as much as 20 feet thick and 25 feet tall. Guards were often stationed on top, where there was a commanding view of the countryside. Some of the inhabitants, said the scouts, were formidable men—from seven to nine feet tall—so that the Israelites felt like grasshoppers next to them (13:33). The fortified cities and the giants struck fear into the hearts of most of the scouts.

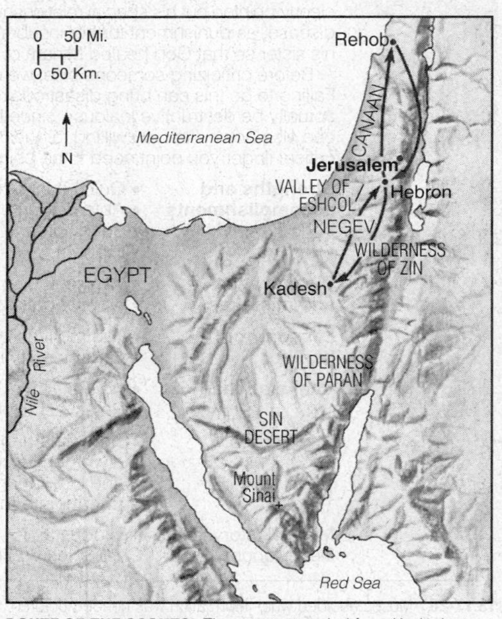

ROUTE OF THE SCOUTS The scouts traveled from Kadesh at the southernmost edge of the wilderness of Zin to Rehob at the northernmost edge and back, a round trip of about 500 miles.

30 But Caleb tried to encourage the people as they stood before Moses. "Let's go at
once to take the land," he said. "We can certainly conquer it!"
31 But the other men who had explored the land with him answered, "We can't go up
against them! They are stronger than we are!" 32 So they spread discouraging reports about
the land among the Israelites: "The land we explored will swallow up any who go to live
there. All the people we saw were huge. 33 We even saw giants* there, the descendants of
Anak. We felt like grasshoppers next to them, and that's what we looked like to them!"

The People Rebel

14 Then all the people began weeping aloud, and they cried all night. 2 Their voices
rose in a great chorus of complaint against Moses and Aaron. "We wish we had
died in Egypt, or even here in the wilderness!" they wailed. 3 "Why is the LORD taking
us to this country only to have us die in battle? Our wives and little ones will be carried
off as slaves! Let's get out of here and return to Egypt!" 4 Then they plotted among
themselves, "Let's choose a leader and go back to Egypt!"
5 Then Moses and Aaron fell face down on the ground before the people of Israel.
6 Two of the men who had explored the land, Joshua son of Nun and Caleb son of
Jephunneh, tore their clothing. 7 They said to the community of Israel, "The land we
explored is a wonderful land! 8 And if the LORD is pleased with us, he will bring us safely
into that land and give it to us. It is a rich land flowing with milk and honey, and he will
give it to us! 9 Do not rebel against the LORD, and don't be afraid of the people of the
land. They are only helpless prey to us! They have no protection, but the LORD is with
us! Don't be afraid of them!"
10 But the whole community began to talk about stoning Joshua and Caleb. Then the
glorious presence of the LORD appeared to all the Israelites from above the Tabernacle.*
11 And the LORD said to Moses, "How long will these people reject me? Will they never
believe me, even after all the miraculous signs I have done among them? 12 I will disown
them and destroy them with a plague. Then I will make you into a nation far greater and
mightier than they are!"

Moses Intercedes for the People

13 "But what will the Egyptians think when they hear about it?" Moses pleaded with the
LORD. "They know full well the power you displayed in rescuing these people from Egypt.
14 They will tell this to the inhabitants of this land, who are well aware that you are with this
people. They know, LORD, that you have appeared in full view of your people in the pillar
of cloud that hovers over them. They know that you go before them in the pillar of cloud
by day and the pillar of fire by night. 15 Now if you slaughter all these people, the nations

13:30 Num 14:6, 24
13:31 Deut 1:28
13:32 Num 14:36
13:33 Deut 1:28
14:2 Exod 15:24; 16:3 Num 11:1; 16:13; 20:4; 21:5
14:3 Exod 5:21; 16:3 Num 14:31 Deut 1:39
14:5 Num 16:22, 45
14:7 Num 13:27 Deut 1:25
14:8 Exod 3:8 Num 13:27
14:9 Deut 1:21, 29; 7:18; 9:7, 23-24
14:10 Exod 16:7, 10; 17:4; 24:16-17; 32:9-13 Lev 9:23
14:12 Exod 32:10 Lev 26:25 Deut 28:21
14:13 Exod 9:28; 32:12
14:14 Exod 13:21; 33:11 Deut 5:4
14:15 Exod 32:12

13:33 Hebrew *nephilim.* **14:10** Hebrew *Tent of Meeting.*

13:30-32 Imagine standing before a crowd and loudly voicing an unpopular opinion! Caleb was willing to take the unpopular stand to do as God had commanded. To be effective when you go against the crowd, you must (1) have the facts (Caleb had seen the land himself); (2) have the right attitude (Caleb trusted God's promise to give Israel the land); (3) state clearly what you believe (Caleb said, "We can certainly conquer it").

13:33—14:4 The negative opinion of 10 men caused a great rebellion among the people. Because it is human nature to accept opinion as fact, we must be especially careful when voicing our negative opinions. What we say may heavily influence the actions of those who trust us to give sound advice.

14:1-4 When the chorus of despair went up, everyone joined in. Their greatest fears were being realized. Losing their perspective, the people were caught up in the emotion of the moment, forgetting what they knew about God's character. What if the people had spent as much energy moving forward as they did moving back? They could have enjoyed their land—instead they never even entered it. When a cry of despair goes up around you, consider the larger perspective before you join in. You have better ways to use your energy than to complain.

14:5-9 With great miracles, God had led the Israelites out of slavery, through the desolate wilderness, and up to the very edge of the Promised Land. He had protected them, fed them, and fulfilled every promise. Yet when encouraged to take that last step of faith and enter the land, the people refused. After witnessing so many miracles, why did they stop trusting God? Why did they refuse to enter the Promised Land when that had been their goal since leaving Egypt? They were afraid. Often we do the same thing. We trust God to handle the smaller issues but doubt his ability to take care of the big problems, the tough decisions, the frightening situations. Don't stop trusting God just as you are ready to reach your goal. He brought you this far and won't let you down now. We can continue trusting God by remembering all he has done for us.

14:6 Tearing clothing was a customary way of showing deep sorrow, mourning, or despair. Joshua and Caleb were greatly distressed by the people's refusal to enter the land.

14:6-10 Two wise men, Joshua and Caleb, encouraged the people to act on God's promise and move ahead into the land. The people rejected their advice and even talked of stoning them. Don't be too quick to reject advice you don't like. Evaluate it carefully, comparing it to the teaching in God's Word. The advice may be God's message.

that have heard of your fame will say, 16 'The LORD was not able to bring them into the land
he swore to give them, so he killed them in the wilderness.'
17 "Please, Lord, prove that your power is as great as you have claimed it to be. For
you said, 18 'The LORD is slow to anger and rich in unfailing love, forgiving every kind
of sin and rebellion. Even so he does not leave sin unpunished, but he punishes the
children for the sins of their parents to the third and fourth generations.' 19 Please pardon
the sins of this people because of your magnificent, unfailing love, just as you have
forgiven them ever since they left Egypt."
20 Then the LORD said, "I will pardon them as you have requested. 21 But as surely as
I live, and as surely as the earth is filled with the LORD's glory, 22 not one of these people
will ever enter that land. They have seen my glorious presence and the miraculous signs
I performed both in Egypt and in the wilderness, but again and again they tested me by
refusing to listen. 23 They will never even see the land I swore to give their ancestors.
None of those who have treated me with contempt will enter it. 24 But my servant Caleb
is different from the others. He has remained loyal to me, and I will bring him into the
land he explored. His descendants will receive their full share of that land. 25 Now turn
around and don't go on toward the land where the Amalekites and Canaanites live.
Tomorrow you must set out for the wilderness in the direction of the Red Sea.*"

The LORD Punishes the Israelites

26 Then the LORD said to Moses and Aaron, 27 "How long will this wicked nation
complain about me? I have heard everything the Israelites have been saying. 28 Now tell
them this: 'As surely as I live, I will do to you the very things I heard you say. I, the
LORD, have spoken! 29 You will all die here in this wilderness! Because you complained
against me, none of you who are twenty years old or older and were counted in the census
30 will enter the land I swore to give you. The only exceptions will be Caleb son of
Jephunneh and Joshua son of Nun.
31 "'You said your children would be taken captive. Well, I will bring them safely into
the land, and they will enjoy what you have despised. 32 But as for you, your dead bodies
will fall in this wilderness. 33 And your children will be like shepherds, wandering in the
wilderness forty years. In this way, they will pay for your faithlessness, until the last of
you lies dead in the wilderness.
34 "'Because the men who explored the land were there for forty days, you must
wander in the wilderness for forty years—a year for each day, suffering the consequences
of your sins. You will discover what it is like to have me for an enemy.' 35 I, the LORD,

14:16 Deut 9:28; Josh 7:7
14:19 Exod 34:9; Ps 106:45
14:20 Ps 106:23; Mic 7:18-20
14:23 Num 26:65; 32:11
14:24 Num 32:12; Josh 14:6-15
14:25 Num 13:29
14:28 Num 14:21; Heb 3:17
14:29 Num 1:17-19; 26:2
14:30 Num 14:24, 38
14:31 Num 14:3
14:32 Num 26:64-65; 32:13; 1 Cor 10:5
14:33 Deut 2:7; 8:2

14:25 Hebrew *sea of reeds.*

14:17-20 Moses pleaded with God, asking him to forgive his people. His plea reveals several characteristics of God: (1) God is immensely patient; (2) God's love is one promise we can always count on; (3) God forgives again and again; (4) God is merciful, listening to and answering our requests. God has not changed since Moses' day. Like Moses, we can rely on God's love, patience, forgiveness, and mercy.

14:20-23 The people of Israel had a clearer view of God than any people before them, for they had both his laws and his physical presence. Their refusal to follow God after witnessing his miraculous deeds and listening to his words made the judgment against them more severe. Increased opportunity brings increased responsibility. As Jesus said: "Much is required from those to whom much is given" (Luke 12:48). How much greater is our responsibility to obey and serve God—we have the whole Bible, and we know God's Son, Jesus Christ.

14:22 God wasn't exaggerating when he said that the Israelites had "again and again" failed to trust and obey him. Here is a list of their failures: (1) lacking trust at the crossing of the Red Sea (Exodus 14:11, 12); (2) complaining over bitter water at Marah (Exodus 15:24); (3) complaining in the Sin Desert (Exodus 16:3); (4) collecting more than the daily quota of manna (Exodus 16:20); (5) collecting manna on the Sabbath (Exodus 16:27-29); (6) complaining over lack of water at Rephidim (Exodus 17:2, 3); (7) engaging in idolatry with a golden calf (Exodus 32:7-10); (8) complaining at Taberah (Numbers 11:1, 2); (9) more complaining over the lack of delicious food (Numbers 11:4); (10) failing to trust God and enter the Promised Land (Numbers 14:1-4).

14:24 The fulfillment of this verse is recorded in Joshua 14:6-15 when Caleb received his inheritance in the Promised Land. Caleb followed God with all his heart and was rewarded for his obedience. Are you wholehearted in your commitment to obey God?

14:34 God's judgment came in the form the people feared most. The people were afraid of dying in the wilderness, so God punished them by making them wander in the wilderness until they died. Now they wished they had the problem of facing the giants and the fortified cities of the Promised Land. Failing to trust God often brings even greater problems than those we originally faced. When we run from God, we inevitably run into problems.

14:35 Was this judgment—wandering 40 years in the wilderness—too harsh? Not compared to the instant death that God first threatened (14:12). Instead, God allowed the people to live. God had brought his people to the edge of the Promised Land, just as he said he would. He was ready to give them the rich land, but the people didn't want it (14:1, 2). By this time, God had put up with a lot. Again and again the people had refused to trust and obey him (14:22). The whole nation (except for Joshua, Caleb, Moses, and Aaron) showed contempt for and distrust of God. But God's punishment was not permanent. In 40 years, a new generation would have a chance to enter Canaan (Joshua 1–3).

have spoken! I will do these things to every member of the community who has
14:36 Num 13:4-16 conspired against me. They will all die here in this wilderness!"
36 Then the ten scouts who had incited the rebellion against the LORD by spreading
discouraging reports about the land 37 were struck dead with a plague before the LORD.
38 Of the twelve who had explored the land, only Joshua and Caleb remained alive.
14:39 Exod 33:4 39 When Moses reported the LORD's words to the Israelites, there was much sorrow
14:40 Deut 1:41-44 among the people. 40 So they got up early the next morning and set out for the hill country
of Canaan. "Let's go," they said. "We realize that we have sinned, but now we are ready
to enter the land the LORD has promised us."
41 But Moses said, "Why are you now disobeying the LORD's orders to return to the
wilderness? It won't work. 42 Do not go into the land now. You will only be crushed by
your enemies because the LORD is not with you. 43 When you face the Amalekites and
Canaanites in battle, you will be slaughtered. The LORD will abandon you because you
have abandoned the LORD."
14:44 Num 10:33; 31:6 44 But the people pushed ahead toward the hill country of Canaan, despite the fact that
14:45 Num 21:3; Judg 1:17 neither Moses nor the Ark of the LORD's covenant left the camp. 45 Then the Amalekites
and the Canaanites who lived in those hills came down and attacked them and chased
them as far as Hormah.

C. WANDERING IN THE WILDERNESS (15:1—21:35)

After their disobedience and unsuccessful attempt to enter the Promised Land, the Israelites were condemned to wander 40 years in the wilderness. Even in the midst of this punishment, the people continued to rebel, and thus God continued to punish them. But the hearts of the people remained hard and rebellious. Hard hearts toward God may bring similar calamity to us.

CALEB

The voice of the minority is not often given a hearing. Nevertheless, truth cannot be measured by numbers. On the contrary, it often stands against majority opinion. Truth remains unchanged because it is guaranteed by the character of God. God is truth; what he says is the last word. At times, a person must even stand alone on the side of truth.

Caleb was not so much a man of great faith as a man of faith in a great God! His boldness rested on his understanding of God, not on his confidence in Israel's abilities to conquer the land. He could not agree with the majority, for that would be to disagree with God.

We, on the other hand, often base our decisions on what everyone else is doing. Few of us are first-order cowards like the 10 scouts. We are more like the people of Israel, getting our cowardice secondhand. Our search for right and wrong usually starts with questions such as "What do the experts say?" or "What do my friends say?" The question we most often avoid is "What does God say?" The principles we learn as we study the Bible provide a dependable road map for life. They draw us into a personal relationship with the God whose Word is the Bible. The God who gave Caleb his boldness is the same God who offers us the gift of eternal life through his Son, Jesus. That's truth worth believing!

Strengths and accomplishments
- One of the scouts sent by Moses to survey the land of Canaan
- One of the only two adults who left Egypt and entered the Promised Land
- Voiced the minority opinion in favor of conquering the land
- Expressed faith in God's promises, in spite of apparent obstacles

Lessons from his life
- Majority opinion is not an accurate measurement of right and wrong
- Boldness based on God's faithfulness is appropriate
- For courage and faith to be effective, they must combine words and actions

Vital statistics
- Where: From Egypt to the Sinai peninsula to the Promised Land, specifically Hebron
- Occupations: Scout, soldier, shepherd

Key verse "But my servant Caleb is different from the others. He has remained loyal to me, and I will bring him into the land he explored. His descendants will receive their full share of that land" (Numbers 14:24).

Caleb's story is told in Numbers 13—14 and Joshua 14—15. He is also mentioned in Judges 1 and 1 Chronicles 4:15.

14:40-44 When the Israelites realized their foolish mistake, they were suddenly ready to return to God. But God didn't confuse their admission of guilt with true repentance because he knew their hearts. Sure enough, they soon went their own way again. Sometimes right actions or good intentions come too late. We must not only do what is right, but also do it at the right time. God wants complete and instant obedience.

1. Additional regulations

Laws concerning Offerings

15 The LORD told Moses to give these instructions to the people of Israel: 2"When you finally settle in the land I am going to give you, 3and you want to please the LORD with a burnt offering or any other offering given by fire, the sacrifice must be an animal from your flocks of sheep and goats or from your herds of cattle. When it is an ordinary burnt offering, a sacrifice to fulfill a vow, a freewill offering, or a special sacrifice at any of the annual festivals, 4whoever brings it must also give to the LORD a grain offering of two quarts* of choice flour mixed with one quart* of olive oil. 5For each lamb offered as a whole burnt offering, you must also present one quart of wine for a drink offering.

6"If the sacrifice is a ram, give three quarts* of choice flour mixed with two and a half pints* of olive oil, 7and give two and a half pints of wine for a drink offering. This sacrifice will be very pleasing to the LORD.

8"When you present a young bull as a burnt offering or a sacrifice in fulfillment of a special vow or as a peace offering to the LORD, 9then the grain offering accompanying it must include five quarts* of choice flour mixed with two quarts* of olive oil, 10plus two quarts of wine for the drink offering. This will be an offering made by fire, very pleasing to the LORD.

11"These are the instructions for what is to accompany each sacrificial bull, ram, lamb, or young goat. 12Each of you must do this with each offering you present. 13If you native Israelites want to present an offering by fire that is pleasing to the LORD, you must follow all these instructions. 14And if any foreigners living among you want to present an offering by fire, pleasing to the LORD, they must follow the same procedures. 15Native Israelites and foreigners are the same before the LORD and are subject to the same laws. This is a permanent law for you. 16The same instructions and regulations will apply both to you and to the foreigners living among you."

17The LORD also said to Moses at this time, 18"Give the people of Israel the following instructions: When you arrive in the land where I am taking you, 19you will eat from the crops that grow there. But you must set some aside as a gift to the LORD. 20Present a cake from the first of the flour you grind and set it aside as a gift, as you do with the first grain from the threshing floor. 21Throughout the generations to come, you are to present this offering to the LORD each year from the first of your ground flour.

22"But suppose some of you unintentionally fail to carry out all these commands that the LORD has given you through Moses. 23And suppose some of your descendants in the future fail to do everything the LORD has commanded through Moses. 24If the mistake was done unintentionally, and the community was unaware of it, the whole community must present a young bull for a burnt offering. It will be pleasing to the LORD, and it must be offered along with the prescribed grain offering and drink offering and with one male goat for a sin offering. 25With it the priest will make atonement for the whole community of Israel, and they will be forgiven. For it was an unintentional sin, and they have corrected it with their offering given to the LORD by fire and by their sin offering. 26The whole community of Israel will be forgiven, including the foreigners living among you, for the entire population was involved in the sin.

27"If the unintentional sin is committed by an individual, the guilty person must bring a one-year-old female goat for a sin offering. 28The priest will make atonement for the guilty person before the LORD, and that person will be forgiven. 29This same law applies both to native Israelites and the foreigners living among you.

30"But those who brazenly violate the LORD's will, whether native Israelites or foreigners, blaspheme the LORD, and they must be cut off from the community. 31Since they have treated the LORD's word with contempt and deliberately disobeyed his commands, they must be completely cut off and suffer the consequences of their guilt."

15:3 Lev 1:1; 2:1-16; 22:21; 23:37-38; 27:2
15:5 Num 15:5-10; 28:7
15:8 Lev 3:1; 7:11-18
15:10 Num 28:14
15:15 Num 9:14; 15:29
15:19 Josh 5:11-12
15:22 Lev 4:2
15:25 Lev 4:20
15:29 Num 15:15
15:30 Num 14:40-44; Deut 1:43; 17:13

15:4a Hebrew *1/10 of an ephah* [2 liters]. **15:4b** Hebrew *1/4 of a hin* [1 liter]; also in 15:5. **15:6a** Hebrew *2/10 of an ephah* [3.6 liters]. **15:6b** Hebrew *1/3 of a hin* [1.3 liters]; also in 15:7. **15:9a** Hebrew *3/10 of an ephah* [5.4 liters]. **15:9b** Hebrew *1/2 of a hin* [2 liters]; also in 15:10.

15:30, 31 God was willing to forgive those who made unintentional errors if they realized their mistakes quickly and corrected them. However, those who brazenly and deliberately sinned received a harsher judgment. Intentional sin grows out of an improper attitude toward God. A child who knowingly disobeys his parents challenges their authority and dares them to respond. Both the act and the attitude have to be dealt with.

Penalty for Breaking the Sabbath

15:32 Exod 31:14-15; 35:2-3
15:35 Lev 24:14, 23; Deut 21:21

32One day while the people of Israel were in the wilderness, they caught a man gathering
wood on the Sabbath day. 33He was apprehended and taken before Moses, Aaron, and the
rest of the community. 34They held him in custody because they did not know what to do
with him. 35Then the LORD said to Moses, "The man must be put to death! The whole
community must stone him outside the camp." 36So the whole community took the man
outside the camp and stoned him to death, just as the LORD had commanded Moses.

Tassels on Clothing

15:38 Lev 3:17; Num 10:8; Deut 22:12; Matt 23:5
15:40 Lev 11:44; Rom 12:1; Col 1:22; 1 Pet 1:15-16

37And the LORD said to Moses, 38"Say to the people of Israel: 'Throughout the generations
to come you must make tassels for the hems of your clothing and attach the tassels at each
corner with a blue cord. 39The tassels will remind you of the commands of the LORD, and
that you are to obey his commands instead of following your own desires and going your
own ways, as you are prone to do. 40The tassels will help you remember that you must obey
all my commands and be holy to your God. 41I am the LORD your God who brought you
out of the land of Egypt that I might be your God. I am the LORD your God!'"

2. Many leaders rebel against Moses

Korah, Dathan, and Abiram

16:1 Exod 6:21; Num 26:9; Deut 11:6; Jude 1:11
16:2 Num 1:16
16:3 Exod 19:6; Num 16:7; 35:34
16:4 Num 14:5
16:5 Lev 10:3; Num 17:5, 8; Ps 65:4
16:7 Num 16:3
16:10 Num 3:6-10
16:11 Exod 16:7; 1 Cor 10:10
16:13 Exod 16:3, 17; Num 11:5; 14:2-3; 20:3-4

16 One day Korah son of Izhar, a descendant of Kohath son of Levi, conspired with
Dathan and Abiram, the sons of Eliab, and On son of Peleth, from the tribe of
Reuben. 2They incited a rebellion against Moses, involving 250 other prominent leaders,
all members of the assembly. 3They went to Moses and Aaron and said, "You have gone
too far! Everyone in Israel has been set apart by the LORD, and he is with all of us. What
right do you have to act as though you are greater than anyone else among all these
people of the LORD?"
4When Moses heard what they were saying, he threw himself down with his face to the
ground. 5Then he said to Korah and his followers, "Tomorrow morning the LORD will
show us who belongs to him and who is holy. The LORD will allow those who are chosen
to enter his holy presence. 6You, Korah, and all your followers must do this: Take incense
burners, 7and burn incense in them tomorrow before the LORD. Then we will see whom
the LORD chooses as his holy one. You Levites are the ones who have gone too far!"
8Then Moses spoke again to Korah: "Now listen, you Levites! 9Does it seem a small
thing to you that the God of Israel has chosen you from among all the people of Israel to
be near him as you serve in the LORD's Tabernacle and to stand before the people to
minister to them? 10He has given this special ministry only to you and your fellow
Levites, but now you are demanding the priesthood as well! 11The one you are really
revolting against is the LORD! And who is Aaron that you are complaining about him?"
12Then Moses summoned Dathan and Abiram, the sons of Eliab, but they replied, "We
refuse to come! 13Isn't it enough that you brought us out of Egypt, a land flowing with

---

15:32-36 Stoning a man for gathering wood on the Sabbath seems like a severe punishment, and it was. This act was a deliberate sin, defying God's law against working on the Sabbath. Perhaps the man was trying to get ahead of everyone else, in addition to breaking the Sabbath.

15:39 The tassels were to remind people not to seek after their own lustful desires, but to seek the Lord. Idol worship is self-centered, focusing on what a person can get from serving an idol. Good luck, prosperity, long life, and success in battle were expected from the gods. So were power and prestige. The worship of God is the opposite. Believers are to be selfless rather than self-centered. Instead of expecting God to serve us, we are to serve him, expecting nothing in return. We serve God for who he is, not for what we get from him.

16:1-3 Korah and his associates had seen the advantages of the priesthood in Egypt. Egyptian priests had great wealth and political influence, something Korah wanted for himself. Korah may have assumed that Moses, Aaron, and his sons were trying to make the Israelite priesthood the same kind of political machine, and he wanted to be a part of it. He did not understand that Moses' main ambition was to serve God rather than to control others.

16:8-10 Moses saw through their charge to their true motivation—some of the Levites wanted the power of the priesthood. Like Korah, we often desire the special qualities God has given others. Korah had significant, worthwhile abilities and responsibilities of his own. In the end, however, his ambition for more caused him to lose everything. Inappropriate ambition is greed in disguise. Concentrate on finding the special purpose God has for you instead of wishing you were in someone else's shoes.

16:13, 14 One of the easiest ways to fall away from following God is to look at our present problems and exaggerate them. Dathan and Abiram did just that when they began to long for better food and more pleasant surroundings. Egypt, the place they had longed to leave, was now looking better and better—not because of slavery and taskmasters, of course, but because of its mouthwatering food! These two men and their followers had completely lost their perspective. When we take our eyes off God and start looking at ourselves and our problems, we begin to lose our perspective as well. Overrating problems can hinder our relationship with God. Don't let difficulties make you lose sight of God's direction for your life.

milk and honey, to kill us here in this wilderness, and that you now treat us like your subjects? 14What's more, you haven't brought us into the land flowing with milk and honey or given us an inheritance of fields and vineyards. Are you trying to fool us? We will not come."

15Then Moses became very angry and said to the LORD, "Do not accept their offerings! I have not taken so much as a donkey from them, and I have never hurt a single one of them." 16And Moses said to Korah, "Come here tomorrow and present yourself before the LORD with all your followers. Aaron will also be here. 17Be sure that each of your 250 followers brings an incense burner with incense on it, so you can present them before the LORD. Aaron will also bring his incense burner."

18So these men came with their incense burners, placed burning coals and incense on them, and stood at the entrance of the Tabernacle* with Moses and Aaron. 19Meanwhile, Korah had stirred up the entire community against Moses and Aaron, and they all assembled at the Tabernacle entrance. Then the glorious presence of the LORD appeared to the whole community, 20and the LORD said to Moses and Aaron, 21"Get away from these people so that I may instantly destroy them!"

22But Moses and Aaron fell face down on the ground. "O God, the God and source of all life," they pleaded. "Must you be angry with all the people when only one man sins?" 23And the LORD said to Moses, 24"Then tell all the people to get away from the tents of Korah, Dathan, and Abiram."

25So Moses got up and rushed over to the tents of Dathan and Abiram, followed closely by the Israelite leaders. 26"Quick!" he told the people. "Get away from the tents of these wicked men, and don't touch anything that belongs to them. If you do, you will be destroyed for their sins." 27So all the people stood back from the tents of Korah, Dathan, and Abiram. Then Dathan and Abiram came out and stood at the entrances of their tents with their wives and children and little ones.

28And Moses said, "By this you will know that the LORD has sent me to do all these things that I have done—for I have not done them on my own. 29If these men die a natural death, then the LORD has not sent me. 30But if the LORD performs a miracle and the ground opens up and swallows them and all their belongings, and they go down alive into the grave, then you will know that these men have despised the LORD."

31He had hardly finished speaking the words when the ground suddenly split open beneath them. 32The earth opened up and swallowed the men, along with their households and the followers who were standing with them, and everything they owned. 33So they went down alive into the grave, along with their belongings. The earth closed over them, and they all vanished. 34All of the people of Israel fled as they heard their screams, fearing that the earth would swallow them, too. 35Then fire blazed forth from the LORD and burned up the 250 men who were offering incense.

36And the LORD said to Moses, 37"Tell Eleazar son of Aaron the priest to pull all the incense burners from the fire, for they are holy. Also tell him to scatter the burning incense 38from the burners of these men who have sinned at the cost of their lives. He must then hammer the metal of the incense burners into a sheet as a covering for the altar, for these burners have become holy because they were used in the LORD's presence. The altar covering will then serve as a warning to the people of Israel."

39So Eleazar the priest collected the 250 bronze incense burners that had been used by the men who died in the fire, and they were hammered out into a sheet of metal to cover the altar. 40This would warn the Israelites that no unauthorized man—no one who was not a descendant of Aaron—should ever enter the LORD's presence to burn incense. If anyone did, the same thing would happen to him as happened to Korah and his followers. Thus, the LORD's instructions to Moses were carried out.

16:18 Hebrew *Tent of Meeting;* also in 16:19, 42, 43, 50.

16:14 Exod 22:5; Num 20:5
16:15 Gen 4:4; 1 Sam 12:3
16:19 Lev 9:6; Num 14:10; 16:42; 20:6
16:21 Exod 32:10
16:22 Gen 18:23-32
16:24 Num 16:45
16:26 Gen 19:12-17
16:28 Exod 3:12; 4:1-9; 7:9
16:32 Num 16:30; 26:10
16:35 Lev 10:2; Num 11:1-3; 26:10
16:40 Num 1:51; 3:10, 38

16:26 The Israelites were told not even to touch the belongings of the wicked rebels. In this case, doing so would have shown sympathy to their cause and agreement with their principles. Korah, Dathan, and Abiram were directly challenging Moses and God. Moses clearly stated what God intended to do to the rebels (16:28-30). He did this so that everyone would have to choose between following Korah or following Moses, God's chosen leader. When God asks us to make a fundamental choice between siding with wicked people or siding with him, we should not hesitate but commit ourselves to be 100 percent on the Lord's side.

16:27-35 Although the families of Dathan and Abiram were swallowed up, the sons of Korah were not wiped out (see 26:11).

16:41 Num 16:3
16:42 Exod 40:34; Num 14:10; 16:19
16:45 Num 16:21, 24
16:46 Lev 10:1, 6; Num 8:19; 18:5; 25:13; Deut 9:22
16:47 Num 16:36; 25:7-8, 13
16:49 Num 16:32-35; 25:9

41 But the very next morning the whole community began muttering again against
Moses and Aaron, saying, "You two have killed the LORD's people!" 42 As the people
gathered to protest to Moses and Aaron, they turned toward the Tabernacle and saw that
the cloud had covered it, and the glorious presence of the LORD appeared.
43 Moses and Aaron came and stood at the entrance of the Tabernacle, 44 and the LORD
said to Moses, 45 "Get away from these people so that I can instantly destroy them!" But
Moses and Aaron fell face down on the ground.
46 And Moses said to Aaron, "Quick, take an incense burner and place burning coals on
it from the altar. Lay incense on it and carry it quickly among the people to make atonement
for them. The LORD's anger is blazing among them—the plague has already begun."
47 Aaron did as Moses told him and ran out among the people. The plague indeed had
already begun, but Aaron burned the incense and made atonement for them. 48 He stood
between the living and the dead until the plague was stopped. 49 But 14,700 people died in
that plague, in addition to those who had died in the incident involving Korah. 50 Then
because the plague had stopped, Aaron returned to Moses at the entrance of the Tabernacle.

KORAH

Some notorious historical figures might have remained anonymous if they hadn't tried to grab on to more than they could hold. But by refusing to be content with what they had, and by trying to get more than they deserved, they ended up with nothing. Korah, one of the Israelite leaders, was such a person.

Korah was a Levite who assisted in the daily functions of the Tabernacle. Shortly after Israel's great rebellion against God (Numbers 13; 14), Korah instigated his own minirebellion. He recruited a grievance committee and confronted Moses and Aaron. Their list of complaints boils down to three statements: (1) You are no better than anyone else; (2) everyone in Israel has been chosen of the Lord; (3) we don't need to obey you. It is amazing to see how Korah twisted the first two statements—both true—to reach the wrong conclusion.

Moses would have agreed that he was no better than anyone else. He would also have agreed that all Israelites were God's chosen people. But Korah's application of these truths was wrong. Not all Israelites were chosen to lead. Korah's hidden claim was this: "I have as much right to lead as Moses does." His error cost him not only his job—a position of service that he enjoyed—but also his life.

Korah's story gives us numerous warnings: (1) Don't let desire for what someone else has make you discontented with what you already have. (2) Don't try to raise your own self-esteem by attacking someone else's. (3) Don't use part of God's Word to support what you want, rather than allowing its entirety to shape your wants. (4) Don't expect to find satisfaction in power and position; God may want to work through you in the position you are now in.

Strengths and accomplishments
- Popular leader; influential figure during the Exodus
- Mentioned among the chief men of Israel (Exodus 6)
- One of the first Levites appointed for special service in the Tabernacle

Weaknesses and mistakes
- Failed to recognize the significant position God had placed him in
- Forgot that his fight was against someone greater than Moses
- Allowed greed to blind his common sense

Lessons from his life
- There is sometimes a fine line between goals and greed
- If we are discontented with what we have, we may lose it without gaining anything better

Vital statistics
- Where: Egypt, Sinai peninsula
- Occupation: Levite (Tabernacle assistant)

Key verses
"Then Moses spoke again to Korah: 'Now listen, you Levites! Does it seem a small thing to you that the God of Israel has chosen you from among all the people of Israel to be near him as you serve in the LORD's Tabernacle and to stand before the people to minister to them? He has given this special ministry only to you and your fellow Levites, but now you are demanding the priesthood as well!'" (Numbers 16:8–10).

Korah's story is told in Numbers 16:1–40. He is also mentioned in Numbers 26:9; Jude 1:11.

16:41 Just one day after Korah and his followers were executed for grumbling and complaining against God, the Israelites started all over with more muttering and complaining. Their negative attitude only caused them to rebel even more and to bring about even greater trouble. It eroded their faith in God and encouraged thoughts of giving up and turning back. The path to open rebellion against God begins with dissatisfaction and skepticism, then moves to grumbling about both God and present circumstances. Next come bitterness and resentment, followed finally by rebellion and open hostility. If you are often dissatisfied, skeptical, complaining, or bitter—beware! These attitudes lead to rebellion and separation from God. Any choice to side against God is a step in the direction of letting go of him completely and making your own way through life.

The Budding of Aaron’s Staff

17 Then the LORD said to Moses, 2“Take twelve wooden staffs, one from each of Israel’s
ancestral tribes, and inscribe each tribal leader’s name on his staff. 3Inscribe Aaron’s
name on the staff of the tribe of Levi, for there must be one staff for the leader of each
ancestral tribe. 4Put these staffs in the Tabernacle in front of the Ark of the Covenant,* where
I meet with you. 5Buds will sprout on the staff belonging to the man I choose. Then I will
finally put an end to this murmuring and complaining against you.”

6So Moses gave the instructions to the people of Israel, and each of the twelve tribal
leaders, including Aaron, brought Moses a staff. 7Moses put the staffs in the LORD’s
presence in the Tabernacle of the Covenant.* 8When he went into the Tabernacle of the
Covenant the next day, he found that Aaron’s staff, representing the tribe of Levi, had
sprouted, blossomed, and produced almonds!

9When Moses brought all the staffs out from the LORD’s presence, he showed them to
the people. Each man claimed his own staff. 10And the LORD said to Moses: “Place
Aaron’s staff permanently before the Ark of the Covenant* as a warning to rebels. This
should put an end to their complaints against me and prevent any further deaths.” 11So
Moses did as the LORD commanded him.

12Then the people of Israel said to Moses, “We are as good as dead! We are ruined!
13Everyone who even comes close to the Tabernacle of the LORD dies. We are all doomed!”

17:4 Exod 25:22; Num 17:10
17:5 Num 16:5; 17:8
17:7 Num 18:2
17:8 Num 17:5; Heb 9:4
17:10 Num 17:4; Deut 9:7, 24
17:12 Isa 6:5
17:13 Num 1:51-53

3. Duties of priests and Levites

18 The LORD now said to Aaron: “You, your sons, and your relatives from the tribe
of Levi will be held responsible for any offenses related to the sanctuary. But you
and your sons alone will be held liable for violations connected with the priesthood.

2“Bring your relatives of the tribe of Levi to assist you and your sons as you perform
the sacred duties in front of the Tabernacle of the Covenant.* 3But as the Levites go about
their duties under your supervision, they must be careful not to touch any of the sacred
objects or the altar. If they do, both you and they will die. 4The Levites must join with
you to fulfill their responsibilities for the care and maintenance of the Tabernacle,* but
no one who is not a Levite may officiate with you.

5“You yourselves must perform the sacred duties within the sanctuary and at the altar. If
you follow these instructions, the LORD’s anger will never again blaze against the people of
Israel. 6I myself have chosen your fellow Levites from among the Israelites to be your
special assistants. They are dedicated to the LORD for service in the Tabernacle. 7But you
and your sons, the priests, must personally handle all the sacred service associated with the
altar and everything within the inner curtain. I am giving you the priesthood as your special
gift of service. Any other person who comes too near the sanctuary will be put to death.”

Support for the Priests and Levites

8The LORD gave these further instructions to Aaron: “I have put the priests in charge of
all the holy gifts that are brought to me by the people of Israel. I have given these
offerings to you and your sons as your regular share. 9You are allotted the portion of the
most holy offerings that is kept from the fire. From all the most holy offerings—including the grain offerings, sin offerings, and guilt offerings—that portion belongs to you
and your sons. 10You must eat it as a most holy offering. All the males may eat of it, and
you must treat it as most holy.

11“All the other offerings presented to me by the Israelites by lifting them up before
the altar also belong to you as your regular share. Any member of your family who is
ceremonially clean, male and female alike, may eat of these offerings.

18:1 Exod 28:38
18:2 Num 3:5-10
18:5 Num 16:46
18:6 Num 3:9, 12
18:7 Exod 29:9; Num 1:51; 3:10
18:8 Lev 7:28-34; Deut 12:6
18:9 Lev 2:1-16; 6:25-30
18:11 Lev 22:2-3, 11-13

17:4 Hebrew *in the Tent of Meeting before the Testimony.* **17:7** Or *Tabernacle of the Testimony;* also in 17:8. **17:10** Hebrew *before the Testimony.* **18:2** Or *Tabernacle of the Testimony.* **18:4** Hebrew *Tent of Meeting;* also in 18:6, 21, 22, 23, 31.

17:5, 10 After witnessing spectacular miracles, seeing the Egyptians punished by the plagues, and experiencing the actual presence of God, the Israelites still complained and rebelled. We wonder how they could be so blind and ignorant, and yet we often repeat this same pattern. We have centuries of evidence, the Bible in many translations, and the convincing results of archaeological and historical studies. But people today continue to disobey God and go their own way. Like the Israelites, we are more concerned about our physical condition than our spiritual condition. We can escape this pattern only by paying attention to all the signs of God’s presence that we have been given. Has God guided and protected you? Has he answered your prayers? Do you know people who have experienced remarkable blessings and healings? Do you know Bible stories about the way God has led his people? Focus your thoughts on what God has done, and rebellion will become unthinkable.

18:12 Exod 23:19 Deut 18:4
12“I also give you the harvest gifts brought by the people as offerings to the LORD—the
best of the olive oil, wine, and grain. 13All the firstfruits of the land that the people present
to the LORD belong to you. Any member of your family who is ceremonially clean may
eat this food.

18:14 Lev 27:28
14“Whatever is specially set apart for the LORD* also belongs to you.
15“The firstborn of every mother, whether human or animal, that is offered to the
LORD will be yours. But you must always redeem your firstborn sons and the firstborn
males of ritually unclean animals. 16Redeem them when they are one month old. The
redemption price is five pieces of silver, each piece weighing the same as the standard
sanctuary shekel.*

17“However, you may not redeem the firstborn of cattle, sheep, or goats. They are
holy and have been set apart for the LORD. Sprinkle their blood on the altar, and burn
their fat as an offering given by fire, very pleasing to the LORD. 18The meat of these
animals will be yours, just like the breast and right thigh that are presented by lifting

18:19 2 Chr 13:5
them up before the altar. 19Yes, I am giving you all these holy offerings that the people
of Israel bring to the LORD. They are for you and your sons and daughters, to be eaten
as your regular share. This is an unbreakable covenant* between the LORD and you and
your descendants.”

18:20 Deut 10:9; 18:2 Josh 13:33 Ezek 44:28
20And the LORD said to Aaron, “You priests will receive no inheritance of land or share
of property among the people of Israel. I am your inheritance and your share. 21As for

18:21 Lev 27:30-33
the tribe of Levi, your relatives, I will pay them for their service in the Tabernacle with
the tithes from the entire land of Israel.

18:23 Num 18:1, 20
22“From now on, Israelites other than the priests and Levites are to stay away from
the Tabernacle. If they come too near, they will be judged guilty and die. 23The Levites
must serve at the Tabernacle, and they will be held responsible for any offenses against
it. This is a permanent law among you. But the Levites will receive no inheritance of land
among the Israelites, 24because I have given them the Israelites’ tithes, which have been
set apart as offerings to the LORD. This will be the Levites’ share. That is why I said they
would receive no inheritance of land among the Israelites.”

18:26 Num 18:28 Neh 10:38
25The LORD also told Moses, 26“Say this to the Levites: ‘When you receive the tithes
from the Israelites, give a tenth of the tithes you receive—a tithe of the tithe—to the
LORD as a gift. 27The LORD will consider this to be your harvest offering, as though it
were the first grain from your own threshing floor or wine from your own winepress.

18:28 Num 18:21
28You must present one-tenth of the tithe received from the Israelites as a gift to the
LORD. From this you must present the LORD’s portion to Aaron the priest. 29Be sure to
set aside the best portions of the gifts given to you as your gifts to the LORD.’

18:31 Matt 10:10 Luke 10:7 1 Cor 9:13 1 Tim 5:18
30“Also say to the Levites: ‘When you present the best part, it will be considered as
though it came from your own threshing floor or winepress. 31You Levites and your
families may eat this food anywhere you wish, for it is your compensation for serving in

18:32 Lev 22:2, 15-16
the Tabernacle. 32You will not be considered guilty for accepting the LORD’s tithes if you
give the best portion to the priests. But be careful not to treat the holy gifts of the people
of Israel as though they were common. If you do, you will die.’”

The Water of Purification

19:2 Lev 22:20-25 Deut 21:3
19 The LORD said to Moses and Aaron, 2“Here is another ritual law required by the
LORD: Tell the people of Israel to bring you a red heifer that has no physical defects
and has never been yoked to a plow. 3Give it to Eleazar the priest, and it will be taken

19:4 Lev 4:6, 17; 16:14
outside the camp and slaughtered in his presence. 4Eleazar will take some of its blood
on his finger and sprinkle it seven times toward the front of the Tabernacle.* 5As Eleazar

19:6 Lev 14:4, 6, 49
watches, the heifer must be burned—its hide, meat, blood, and dung. 6Eleazar the priest

18:14 The Hebrew term used here refers to the complete consecration of things or people to the LORD, either by destroying them or by giving them as an offering. **18:16** Hebrew *5 shekels* [about 2 ounces or 57 grams] *of silver, according to the sanctuary shekel, 20 gerahs to each shekel.* **18:19** Hebrew *a covenant of salt.* **19:4** Hebrew *Tent of Meeting.*

18:25, 26 Even the Levites, who were ministers, had to tithe to support the Lord’s work. No one was exempt from returning to God a portion of what was received. Though the Levites owned no land and operated no great enterprises, they were to treat their income the same as everyone else did by giving a portion to care for the needs of the other Levites and of the Tabernacle. The tithing principle is still relevant. God expects all his followers to supply the material needs of those who devote themselves to meeting the spiritual needs of the community of faith.

must then take cedarwood, a hyssop branch, and scarlet thread and throw them into the
fire where the heifer is burning.
7"Then the priest must wash his clothes and bathe himself in water. Afterward he
may return to the camp, though he will remain ceremonially unclean until evening.
8The man who burns the animal must also wash his clothes and bathe in water, and he,
too, will remain unclean until evening. 9Then someone who is ceremonially clean will
gather up the ashes of the heifer and place them in a purified place outside the camp.
They will be kept there for the people of Israel to use in the water for the purification
ceremony. This ceremony is performed for the removal of sin. 10The man who gathers
up the ashes of the heifer must also wash his clothes, and he will remain ceremonially
unclean until evening. This is a permanent law for the people of Israel and any
foreigners who live among them.
11"All those who touch a dead human body will be ceremonially unclean for seven
days. 12They must purify themselves on the third and seventh days with the water of
purification; then they will be purified. But if they do not do this on the third and seventh
days, they will continue to be unclean even after the seventh day. 13All those who touch
a dead body and do not purify themselves in the proper way defile the LORD's Tabernacle
and will be cut off from the community of Israel. Since the water of purification was not
sprinkled on them, their defilement continues.
14"This is the ritual law that applies when someone dies in a tent: Those who enter
that tent, and those who were inside when the death occurred, will be ceremonially
unclean for seven days. 15Any container in the tent that was not covered with a lid is
also defiled. 16And if someone outdoors touches the corpse of someone who was killed
with a sword or who died a natural death, or if someone touches a human bone or a
grave, that person will be unclean for seven days.
17"To remove the defilement, put some of the ashes from the burnt purification
offering in a jar and pour fresh water over them. 18Then someone who is ceremonially
clean must take a hyssop branch and dip it into the water. That person must sprinkle
the water on the tent, on all the furnishings in the tent, and on anyone who was in the
tent, or anyone who has touched a human bone, or has touched a person who was
killed or who died naturally, or has touched a grave. 19On the third and seventh days
the ceremonially clean person must sprinkle the water on those who are unclean. Then
on the seventh day the people being cleansed must wash their clothes and bathe
themselves, and that evening they will be cleansed of their defilement.
20"But those who become defiled and do not purify themselves will be cut off from the
community, for they have defiled the sanctuary of the LORD. Since the water of purification has not been sprinkled on them, they remain defiled. 21This is a permanent law. Those
who sprinkle the water of purification must afterward wash their clothes, and anyone who

19:7 Lev 11:25; 16:26-28
19:9 Num 8:7; 19:13, 20-21
19:10 Num 19:7-8, 19
19:11 Lev 21:1
19:12 Num 19:17-19
19:13 Lev 7:20-21; 15:31; 20:3; 22:3
19:16 Num 19:11; 31:19
19:17 Num 19:9
19:19 Ezek 36:25-27 Heb 10:22
19:20 Num 19:13
19:21 Lev 11:25, 40; 16:26-28 Num 19:7

19:9, 10 What is the significance of the red heifer's ashes? When a person touched a dead body, he was considered unclean (i.e., unable to approach God in worship). This ritual purified the unclean person so that once again he could offer sacrifices and worship God. Death was the strongest of defilements because it was the final result of sin. Thus, a special sacrifice—a red heifer—was required. It had to be offered by someone who was not unclean. When it had been burned on the altar, its ashes were used to purify water for ceremonial cleansing—not so much literally as symbolically. The unclean person then washed himself, and often his clothes and belongings, with this purified water as an act of becoming clean again.

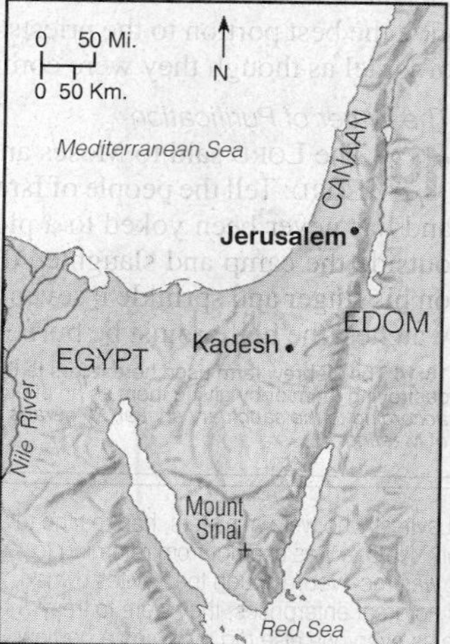

EVENTS AT KADESH
After wandering in the wilderness for 40 years, Israel arrived at Kadesh, where Miriam died. There was not enough water and the people complained bitterly. Moses struck a rock, and it gave enough water for everyone. The king of Edom refused Israel passage through his land, forcing them to travel around his country.

19:22 Lev 5:2-3; 7:21 touches the water of purification will remain defiled until evening. 22 Anything and anyone
that a defiled person touches will be ceremonially defiled until evening."

4. The new generation

Moses Strikes the Rock

20:1 Num 13:21 **20** In early spring* the people of Israel arrived in the wilderness of Zin and camped
at Kadesh. While they were there, Miriam died and was buried.
20:2 Exod 17:1 2 There was no water for the people to drink at that place, so they rebelled against
20:3 Exod 17:2 Num 14:2-3; 16:31-35 Moses and Aaron. 3 The people blamed Moses and said, "We wish we had died in the
LORD's presence with our brothers! 4 Did you bring the LORD's people into this wilder-
ness to die, along with all our livestock? 5 Why did you make us leave Egypt and bring
20:5 Num 16:14 us here to this terrible place? This land has no grain, figs, grapes, or pomegranates. And
there is no water to drink!"
6 Moses and Aaron turned away from the people and went to the entrance of the
Tabernacle,* where they fell face down on the ground. Then the glorious presence of
20:8 Exod 4:17, 20 the LORD appeared to them, 7 and the LORD said to Moses, 8 "You and Aaron must take
the staff and assemble the entire community. As the people watch, command the rock
over there to pour out its water. You will get enough water from the rock to satisfy all
the people and their livestock."

20:1 Hebrew *In the first month.* This month of the Hebrew lunar calendar usually occurs in March and April.
20:6 Hebrew *Tent of Meeting.*

ELEAZAR

An understudy must know the lead role completely and be willing to step into it at a moment's notice. Eleazar was an excellent understudy, well trained for his eventual leading role. However, his moments in the spotlight were painful. On one occasion, he watched his two older brothers burn to death for failing to take God's holiness seriously. Later, as his father was dying, he was made high priest, surely one of the most responsible—and therefore potentially most stressful—positions in Israel.

An understudy benefits from having both the script and a human model of the role. Ever since childhood, Eleazar had been able to observe Moses and Aaron. Now he could learn from watching Joshua. In addition, he had God's laws to guide him as he worked as priest and adviser to Joshua.

Strengths and accomplishments
- Succeeded his father, Aaron, as high priest
- Completed his father's work by helping lead the people into the Promised Land
- Teamed up with Joshua
- Acted as God's spokesman to the people

Lessons from his life
- Concentrating on our present challenges and responsibilities is the best way to prepare for what God has planned for our future
- God's desire is consistent obedience throughout our lives

Vital statistics
- Where: Wilderness of Sinai, Promised Land
- Occupations: Priest and high priest
- Relatives: Father: Aaron. Brothers: Nadab, Abihu, and Ithamar. Aunt and uncle: Miriam and Moses
- Contemporaries: Joshua, Caleb

Key verses "Then the LORD said to Moses and Aaron at Mount Hor on the border of the land of Edom, 'The time has come for Aaron to join his ancestors in death. . . . Now take Aaron and his son Eleazar up Mount Hor. There you will remove Aaron's priestly garments and put them on Eleazar, his son'" (Numbers 20:23–26).

Eleazar is mentioned in Exodus 6:23; Leviticus 10:16–20; Numbers 3:1–4; 4:16; 16:36–40; 20:25–29; 26:1–4, 63; 27:2, 15–23; 32:2; 34:17; Deuteronomy 10:6; Joshua 14:1; 17:4; 24:33.

20:1 It had been 37 years since Israel's first scouting mission into the Promised Land (Numbers 13–14) and 40 years since the Exodus from Egypt. The Bible is virtually silent about those 37 years of aimless wandering. The generation of those who had lived in Egypt had almost died off, and the new generation would soon be ready to enter the land. Moses, Aaron, Joshua, and Caleb were among the few who remained from those who had left Egypt. Once again they camped at Kadesh, the site of the first scouting mission that had ended in disaster. Moses hoped the people were ready for a fresh start.

20:3-5 After 37 years in the wilderness, the Israelites forgot that their wanderings were a result of their parents' and their own sin. They could not accept the fact that they brought their problems upon themselves, so they blamed Moses for their condition. Often our troubles result from our own disobedience or lack of faith. We cannot blame God for our sins. Until we face this reality, we will have little peace and no spiritual growth.

9 So Moses did as he was told. He took the staff from the place where it was kept before
the LORD. 10 Then he and Aaron summoned the people to come and gather at the rock.
"Listen, you rebels!" he shouted. "Must we bring you water from this rock?" 11 Then
Moses raised his hand and struck the rock twice with the staff, and water gushed out. So
all the people and their livestock drank their fill.
12 But the LORD said to Moses and Aaron, "Because you did not trust me enough to
demonstrate my holiness to the people of Israel, you will not lead them into the land I am
giving them!" 13 This place was known as the waters of Meribah,* because it was where the
people of Israel argued with the LORD, and where he demonstrated his holiness among them.

Edom Refuses Israel Passage

14 While Moses was at Kadesh, he sent ambassadors to the king of Edom with this message:

"This message is from your relatives, the people of Israel: You know all the
hardships we have been through, 15 and that our ancestors went down to Egypt. We
lived there a long time and suffered as slaves to the Egyptians. 16 But when we cried
out to the LORD, he heard us and sent an angel who brought us out of Egypt. Now
we are camped at Kadesh, a town on the border of your land. 17 Please let us pass
through your country. We will be careful not to go through your fields and
vineyards. We won't even drink water from your wells. We will stay on the king's
road and never leave it until we have crossed the opposite border."

18 But the king of Edom said, "Stay out of my land or I will meet you with an army!"
19 The Israelites answered, "We will stay on the main road. If any of our livestock drinks
your water, we will pay for it. We only want to pass through your country and nothing else."
20 But the king of Edom replied, "Stay out! You may not pass through our land." With
that he mobilized his army and marched out to meet them with an imposing force.
21 Because Edom refused to allow Israel to pass through their country, Israel was forced
to turn around.

20:11 Ps 78:16; Isa 48:21; 1 Cor 10:4
20:12 Lev 10:3; Num 20:24
20:13 Exod 17:7; Ps 95:8
20:14 Gen 36:31-39; Josh 2:10; 9:9
20:16 Exod 3:2-6; 14:19; 23:30
20:21 Num 21:4; Deut 2:8; Judg 11:18

20:13 *Meribah* means "arguing."

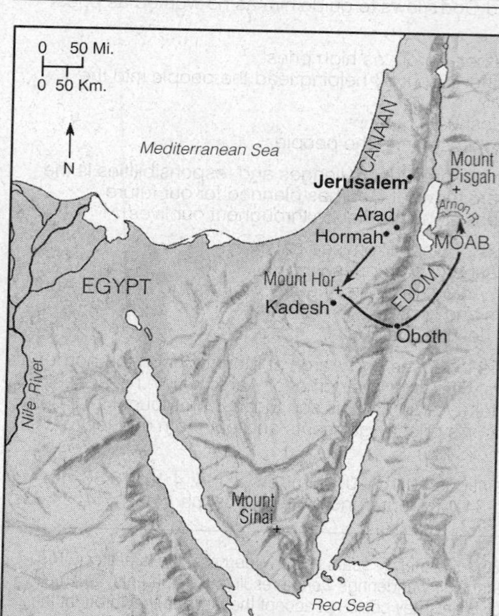

EVENTS IN THE WILDERNESS Israel next met resistance from the king of Arad but soundly defeated him. The next stop was Mount Hor (where Aaron had died); then they traveled south and east around Edom. After camping at Oboth, they moved toward the Arnon River and onto the plains of Moab near Mount Pisgah.

20:12 The Lord had told Moses to speak to the rock; however, Moses struck it, not once, but twice. God did the miracle; yet Moses was taking credit for it when he said, "Must we bring you water from this rock?" For this he was forbidden to enter the Promised Land. Was God's punishment of Moses too harsh? After all, the people had nagged him, slandered him, and rebelled against both him and God. Now they were at it again (20:5). But Moses was the leader and model for the entire nation. Because of this great responsibility to the people, he could not be let off lightly. By striking the rock, Moses disobeyed God's direct command and dishonored God in the presence of his people.

20:14 Two brothers became the ancestors of two nations. The Edomites descended from Esau, the Israelites from Jacob. Thus, the Edomites were "relatives" to the Israelites. Israel sent a brotherly message to Edom requesting passage through their land on the main road, a well-traveled trade route. Israel promised to stay on the road, thus harmlessly bypassing Edom's fields, vineyards, and wells. The Edomites refused, however, because they did not trust Israel's word. They were afraid that this great horde of people would either attack them or devour their crops (Deuteronomy 2:4, 5). Because brothers should not fight, God told the Israelites to turn back and travel by a different route to the Promised Land.

20:17 The king's road was an old caravan route. Long before this time it was used as a major public road.

20:21 Moses tried to negotiate and reason with the Edomite king. When nothing worked, he was left with two choices—force a conflict or avoid it. Moses knew there would be enough barriers in the days and months ahead. There was no point in adding another one unnecessarily. Sometimes conflict is unavoidable. Sometimes, however, it isn't worth the consequences. Open warfare may seem heroic, courageous, and even righteous, but it is not always the best choice. We should consider Moses' example and find another way to solve our problems, even if it is harder for us to do.

The Death of Aaron

22 The whole community of Israel left Kadesh as a group and arrived at Mount Hor.
23 Then the LORD said to Moses and Aaron at Mount Hor on the border of the land of
Edom, 24 "The time has come for Aaron to join his ancestors in death. He will not enter
the land I am giving the people of Israel, because the two of you rebelled against my
20:25 Num 3:4; 19:3-4 instructions concerning the waters of Meribah. 25 Now take Aaron and his son Eleazar
20:26 Num 20:24 up Mount Hor. 26 There you will remove Aaron's priestly garments and put them on
Eleazar, his son. Aaron will die there and join his ancestors."
27 So Moses did as the LORD commanded. The three of them went up Mount Hor
20:28 Num 33:38 together as the whole community watched. 28 At the summit, Moses removed the priestly
garments from Aaron and put them on Eleazar, Aaron's son. Then Aaron died there on
top of the mountain, and Moses and Eleazar went back down. 29 When the people
realized that Aaron had died, all Israel mourned for him thirty days.

Victory over the Canaanites

21:1 Num 33:40; Josh 12:14; Judg 1:16 **21** The Canaanite king of Arad, who lived in the Negev, heard that the Israelites were
approaching on the road to Atharim. So he attacked the Israelites and took some
of them as prisoners. 2 Then the people of Israel made this vow to the LORD: "If you will
21:3 Num 14:45 help us conquer these people, we will completely destroy* all their towns." 3 The LORD
heard their request and gave them victory over the Canaanites. The Israelites completely
destroyed them and their towns, and the place has been called Hormah* ever since.

The Bronze Snake

21:4 Deut 2:8 4 Then the people of Israel set out from Mount Hor, taking the road to the Red Sea* to
21:5 Num 11:5-6; 14:2-3; Ps 78:19 go around the land of Edom. But the people grew impatient along the way, 5 and they
began to murmur against God and Moses. "Why have you brought us out of Egypt to
die here in the wilderness?" they complained. "There is nothing to eat here and nothing
to drink. And we hate this wretched manna!"
21:6 Deut 8:15; 1 Cor 10:9 6 So the LORD sent poisonous snakes among them, and many of them were bitten and
died. 7 Then the people came to Moses and cried out, "We have sinned by speaking
21:7 Ps 78:34 against the LORD and against you. Pray that the LORD will take away the snakes." So
Moses prayed for the people.
21:8 Isa 14:29; John 3:14-15 8 Then the LORD told him, "Make a replica of a poisonous snake and attach it to the
top of a pole. Those who are bitten will live if they simply look at it!" 9 So Moses made

21:9 2 Kgs 18:4; John 3:14; 12:32

21:2 The Hebrew term used here refers to the complete consecration of things or people to the LORD, either by destroying them or by giving them as an offering; also in 21:3. **21:3** *Hormah* means "destruction." **21:4** Hebrew *sea of reeds.*

THE SNAKE IN THE WILDERNESS
Compare the texts for yourself: Numbers 21:7–9 and John 3:14, 15.

Israelites	*Christians*
Bitten by snakes	Bitten by sin
Little initial pain, then intense suffering	Little initial pain, then intense suffering
Physical death from snakes' poison	Spiritual death from sin's poison
Bronze snake lifted up in the wilderness	Christ lifted up on the cross
Looking to the snake spared one's life	Looking to Christ saves from eternal death

20:28 Aaron died just before entering the Promised Land, probably as punishment for his sin of rebellion (Exodus 32; Numbers 12:1-9). This was the first time that a new high priest was appointed. The priestly clothing was removed from Aaron and placed on his son Eleazar, following the commands recorded in the book of Leviticus.

21:5 In Psalm 78, we learn the sources of Israel's complaining: (1) Their spirits were not faithful to God (78:8); (2) they refused to obey God's law (78:10); (3) they forgot the miracles God had done for them (78:11). Our complaining often has its roots in one of these thoughtless actions and attitudes. If we can deal with the cause of our complaining, it will not take hold and grow in our lives.

21:6 God used poisonous snakes to punish the people for their unbelief and complaining. The wilderness where they traveled has a variety of snakes. Some hide in the sand and attack without warning. Both the Israelites and the Egyptians had a great fear of snakes. A bite by a poisonous snake often meant a slow death with intense suffering.

21:8, 9 When the bronze snake was hung on the pole, the Israelites didn't know the fuller meaning Jesus Christ would bring to this event (see John 3:14, 15). Jesus explained that just as the Israelites were healed of their sickness by looking at the snake on the pole, all believers today can be saved from the sickness of sin by looking to Jesus' death on the cross. It was not the snake that healed the people but their belief that God could heal them. This belief was demonstrated by their obedience to God's instructions. In the same way, we should continue to look to Christ (see Hebrews 12:2).

a snake out of bronze and attached it to the top of a pole. Whenever those who were bitten
looked at the bronze snake, they recovered!

Israel's Journey to Moab

10 The Israelites traveled next to Oboth and camped there. 11 Then they went on to
Iye-abarim, in the wilderness on the eastern border of Moab. 12 From there they traveled
to the valley of Zered Brook and set up camp. 13 Then they moved to the far side of the
Arnon River, in the wilderness adjacent to the territory of the Amorites. The Arnon is the
boundary line between the Moabites and the Amorites. 14 For this reason *The Book of the
Wars of the LORD* speaks of "the town of Waheb in the area of Suphah, and the ravines;
and the Arnon River 15 and its ravines, which extend as far as the settlement of Ar on the
border of Moab."

16 From there the Israelites traveled to Beer,* which is the well where the LORD said
to Moses, "Assemble the people, and I will give them water." 17 There the Israelites sang
this song:

"Spring up, O well!
Yes, sing about it!
18 Sing of this well,
which princes dug,
which great leaders hollowed out
with their scepters and staffs."

Then the Israelites left the wilderness and proceeded on through Mattanah, 19 Nahaliel,
and Bamoth. 20 Then they went to the valley in Moab where Pisgah Peak overlooks the
wasteland.*

Victory over Sihon and Og

21 The Israelites now sent ambassadors to King Sihon of the Amorites with this message:

22 "Let us travel through your land. We will stay on the king's road until we have
crossed your territory. We will not trample your fields or touch your vineyards or
drink your well water."

23 But King Sihon refused to let them cross his land. Instead, he mobilized his entire
army and attacked Israel in the wilderness, engaging them in battle at Jahaz. 24 But the
Israelites slaughtered them and occupied their land from the Arnon River to the Jabbok
River. They went only as far as the Ammonite border because the boundary of the
Ammonites was fortified.*

21:10 Num 33:43
21:15 Num 21:28; Deut 2:9
21:16 Judg 9:21
21:21 Deut 2:26-28; Judg 11:19-21
21:22 Num 20:17
21:23 Num 20:21; Deut 2:32; Judg 11:20
21:24 Deut 2:19, 31-37; Josh 12:1-2; 13:10

21:16 *Beer* means "well." **21:20** Or *overlooks Jeshimon.* **21:24** Or *because the terrain of the Ammonite frontier was rugged;* Hebrew *because the boundary of the Ammonites was strong.*

21:14 There is no existing record of *The Book of the Wars of the Lord.* Most likely, it was a collection of victory songs or poems.

21:27-30 Chemosh, the national god of Moab, was worshiped as a god of war. This false god, however, was no help to this nation when it fought against Israel. Israel's God was stronger than any of Canaan's war gods.

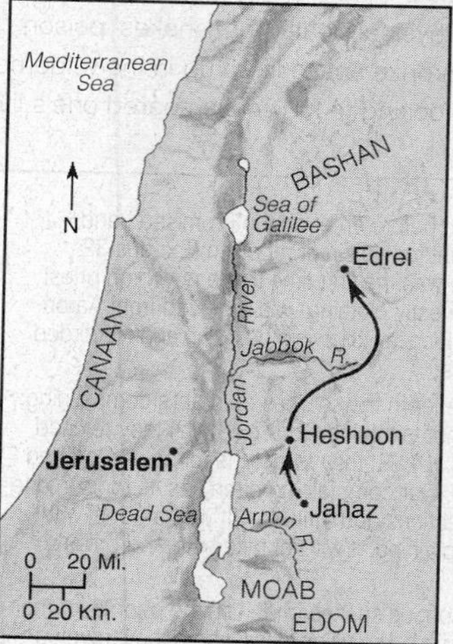

BATTLES WITH SIHON AND OG
King Sihon refused passage to the Israelites through his land, and he attacked Israel at Jahaz. Israel defeated him, occupying the land between the Arnon and Jabbok Rivers, including the capital city, Heshbon. As they moved north, they defeated King Og of Bashan at Edrei.

21:25 Amos 2:10
21:26 Ps 135:11

25 So Israel captured all the towns of the Amorites and settled in them, including the
city of Heshbon and its surrounding villages. 26 Heshbon had been the capital of King
Sihon of the Amorites. He had conquered a former Moabite king and seized all his land
as far as the Arnon River. 27 For this reason the ancient poets wrote this about him:

"Come to Heshbon, city of Sihon!
May it be restored and rebuilt.

21:28 Deut 2:9, 18; Jer 48:45-46

28 A fire flamed forth from Heshbon,
a blaze from the city of Sihon.
It burned the city of Ar in Moab;
it destroyed the rulers of the Arnon heights.

21:29 Judg 11:24; 1 Kgs 11:7, 33

29 Your destruction is certain, O people of Moab!
You are finished, O worshipers of Chemosh!
Chemosh has left his sons as refugees,
and his daughters as captives of Sihon, the Amorite king.
30 We have utterly destroyed them,
all the way from Heshbon to Dibon.
We have completely wiped them out
as far away as Nophah and Medeba.*"

21:32 Num 32:1, 35; Jer 48:32
21:33 Deut 3:3-4

31 So the people of Israel occupied the territory of the Amorites. 32 After Moses sent
men to explore the Jazer area, they captured all the towns in the region and drove out the
Amorites who lived there. 33 Then they turned and marched toward Bashan, but King Og
of Bashan and all his people attacked them at Edrei. 34 The LORD said to Moses, "Do not
be afraid of him, for I have given you victory over Og and his entire army, giving you
all his land. You will do the same to him as you did to King Sihon of the Amorites, who
ruled in Heshbon." 35 And Israel was victorious and killed King Og, his sons, and his
subjects; not a single survivor remained. Then Israel occupied their land.

D. SECOND APPROACH TO THE PROMISED LAND (22:1—36:13)

Now the old generation has died and a new generation stands poised at the border, ready to enter the Promised Land. Neighboring nations, however, cause Israel to begin worshiping other gods. Without Moses' quick action, the nation may never have entered Canaan. We must never let down our guard in resisting sin.

1. The story of Balaam

Balak Sends for Balaam

22:1 Num 33:48-49
22:2 Exod 15:15; Deut 2:25
22:4 Num 22:7; 25:15-18
22:5 Num 23:7; Deut 23:4

22 Then the people of Israel traveled to the plains of Moab and camped east of the
Jordan River, across from Jericho. 2 Balak son of Zippor, the Moabite king, knew
what the Israelites had done to the Amorites. 3 And when they saw how many Israelites
there were, he and his people were terrified. 4 The king of Moab said to the leaders of
Midian, "This mob will devour everything in sight, like an ox devours grass!"
So Balak, king of Moab, 5 sent messengers to Balaam son of Beor, who was living in
his native land of Pethor* near the Euphrates River.* He sent this message to request that
Balaam come to help him:

"A vast horde of people has arrived from Egypt. They cover the face of the earth
and are threatening me. 6 Please come and curse them for me because they are so

21:30 Or *until fire spread to Medeba.* The meaning of the Hebrew is uncertain. **22:5a** Or *who was at Pethor in the land of the Amavites.* **22:5b** Hebrew *the river.*

21:34 God assured Moses that Israel's enemy was conquered even before the battle began! God wants to give us victory over our enemies (which are usually problems related to sin rather than armed soldiers). But first we must believe that he can help us. Second, we must trust him to help us. Third, we must take the steps he shows us.

22:4-6 Balaam was a sorcerer, one called upon to place curses on others. Belief in curses and blessings was common in Old Testament times. Sorcerers were thought to have power with the gods. Thus, the king of Moab wanted Balaam to use his powers with the God of Israel to place a curse on Israel—hoping that, by magic, God would turn against his people. Neither Balaam nor Balak had any idea whom they were dealing with!

numerous. Then perhaps I will be able to conquer them and drive them from the
land. I know that blessings fall on the people you bless. I also know that the people
you curse are doomed."

7 Balak's messengers, officials of both Moab and Midian, set out and took money with 22:7
them to pay Balaam to curse Israel. They went to Balaam and urgently explained to him Num 23:23
what Balak wanted. 8 "Stay here overnight," Balaam said. "In the morning I will tell you
whatever the LORD directs me to say." So the officials from Moab stayed there with
Balaam.

9 That night God came to Balaam and asked him, "Who are these men with you?"

10 So Balaam said to God, "Balak son of Zippor, king of Moab, has sent me this
message: 11 'A vast horde of people has come from Egypt and has spread out over the
whole land. Come at once to curse them. Perhaps then I will be able to conquer them and
drive them from the land.' "

12 "Do not go with them," God told Balaam. "You are not to curse these people, for I 22:12
have blessed them!" Num 23:13-15

13 The next morning Balaam got up and told Balak's officials, "Go on home! The LORD
will not let me go with you."

14 So the Moabite officials returned to King Balak and reported, "Balaam refused to
come with us." 15 Then Balak tried again. This time he sent a larger number of even more
distinguished officials than those he had sent the first time. 16 They went to Balaam and
gave him this message:

"This is what Balak son of Zippor says: Please don't let anything stop you from
coming. 17 I will pay you well and do anything you ask of me. Just come and curse 22:17
these people for me!" Num 22:6

18 But Balaam answered them, "Even if Balak were to give me a palace filled with 22:18
silver and gold, I would be powerless to do anything against the will of the LORD my Num 23:26; 24:13
God. 19 But stay here one more night to see if the LORD has anything else to say to me."

20 That night God came to Balaam and told him, "Since these men have come for you, 22:20
get up and go with them. But be sure to do only what I tell you to do." Num 22:35; 23:12, 26

Balaam and His Donkey

21 So the next morning Balaam saddled his donkey and started off with the Moabite officials. 22:21
22 But God was furious that Balaam was going, so he sent the angel of the LORD to stand in 2 Pet 2:15
the road to block his way. As Balaam and two servants were riding along, 23 Balaam's
donkey suddenly saw the angel of the LORD standing in the road with a drawn sword in his
hand. The donkey bolted off the road into a field, but Balaam beat it and turned it back onto

---

22:9 Why would God speak through a sorcerer like Balaam? God wanted to give a message to the Moabites, and they had already chosen to employ Balaam. So Balaam was available for God to use, much as he used the wicked pharaoh to accomplish his will in Egypt (Exodus 10:1). Balaam entered into his prophetic role seriously, but his heart was mixed. He had some knowledge of God, but not enough to forsake his magic and turn wholeheartedly to God. Although this story leads us to believe he turned completely to God, later passages in the Bible show that Balaam couldn't resist the tempting pull of money and idolatry (31:16; 2 Peter 2:15; Jude 1:11).

22:20-23 God let Balaam go with Balak's messengers, but he was angry about Balaam's greedy attitude. Balaam claimed that he would not go against God just for money, but his resolve was beginning to slip. His greed for the wealth offered by the king blinded him so that he could not see how God was trying to stop him. Though we may know what God wants us to do, we can become blinded by the desire for money, possessions, or prestige. We can avoid Balaam's mistake by looking past the allure of fame or fortune to the long-range benefits of following God.

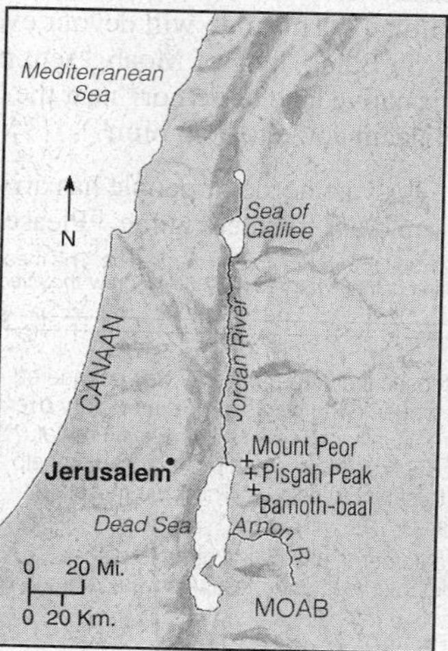

THE STORY OF BALAAM
At King Balak's request, Balaam traveled nearly 400 miles to curse Israel. Balak took Balaam to Bamoth-baal ("the high places of Baal"), then to Pisgah Peak, and finally to Mount Peor. Each place looked over the plains of Moab, where the Israelites were camped. But to the king's dismay, Balaam blessed, not cursed, Israel.

the road. 24 Then the angel of the LORD stood at a place where the road narrowed between
two vineyard walls. 25 When the donkey saw the angel of the LORD standing there, it tried
to squeeze by and crushed Balaam's foot against the wall. So Balaam beat the donkey again.
26 Then the angel of the LORD moved farther down the road and stood in a place so narrow
that the donkey could not get by at all. 27 This time when the donkey saw the angel, it lay
down under Balaam. In a fit of rage Balaam beat it again with his staff.
22:28 2 Pet 2:16 28 Then the LORD caused the donkey to speak. "What have I done to you that deserves
your beating me these three times?" it asked Balaam.
29 "Because you have made me look like a fool!" Balaam shouted. "If I had a sword
with me, I would kill you!"
22:30 2 Pet 2:16 30 "But I am the same donkey you always ride on," the donkey answered. "Have I ever
done anything like this before?"
"No," he admitted.
22:31 Josh 5:13-15 31 Then the LORD opened Balaam's eyes, and he saw the angel of the LORD standing
in the roadway with a drawn sword in his hand. Balaam fell face down on the ground
before him.
32 "Why did you beat your donkey those three times?" the angel of the LORD demanded.
"I have come to block your way because you are stubbornly resisting me. 33 Three times
the donkey saw me and shied away; otherwise, I would certainly have killed you by now
and spared the donkey."
22:34 1 Sam 15:24 34 Then Balaam confessed to the angel of the LORD, "I have sinned. I did not realize you
were standing in the road to block my way. I will go back home if you are against my going."

BALAAM

Balaam was one of those noteworthy Old Testament characters who, though not one of God's chosen people, was willing to acknowledge that Yahweh (the LORD) was indeed a powerful God. But he did not believe in the Lord as the only true God. His story exposes the deception of maintaining an outward facade of spirituality over a corrupt inward life. Balaam was a man ready to obey God's command as long as he could profit from doing so. This mixture of motives—obedience and profit—eventually led to Balaam's death. Although he realized the awesome power of Israel's God, his heart was occupied with the wealth he could gain in Moab. There he returned to die when the armies of Israel invaded.

Eventually, each of us lives through the same process. Who and what we are will somehow come to the surface, destroying any masks we may have put on to cover up our real selves. Efforts spent on keeping up appearances would be much better spent on finding the answer to sin in our lives. We can avoid Balaam's mistake by facing ourselves and realizing that God is willing to accept us, forgive us, and literally make us over from within. Don't miss this great discovery that eluded Balaam.

Strengths and accomplishments
- Widely known for his effective curses and blessings
- Obeyed God and blessed Israel, in spite of Balak's bribe

Weaknesses and mistakes
- Encouraged the Israelites to worship idols (Numbers 31:16)
- Returned to Moab and was killed in war

Lessons from his life
- Motives are just as important as actions
- Your treasure is where your heart is

Vital statistics
- Where: Lived near the Euphrates River, traveled to Moab
- Occupations: Sorcerer, prophet
- Relative: Father: Beor
- Contemporaries: Balak (king of Moab), Moses, Aaron

Key verses
"They have wandered off the right road and followed the way of Balaam son of Beor, who loved to earn money by doing wrong. But Balaam was stopped from his mad course when his donkey rebuked him with a human voice" (2 Peter 2:15, 16).

Balaam's story is told in Numbers 22:1—24:25. He is also mentioned in Numbers 31:7, 8, 16; Deuteronomy 23:4, 5; Joshua 24:9, 10; Nehemiah 13:2; Micah 6:5; 2 Peter 2:15, 16; Jude 11; Revelation 2:14.

22:27 Donkeys were all-purpose vehicles used for transportation, carrying loads, grinding grain, and plowing fields. They were usually highly dependable, which explains why Balaam became so angry when his donkey refused to move.

22:29 The donkey saved Balaam's life but made him look foolish in the process, so Balaam lashed out at the donkey. We sometimes strike out at blameless people who get in our way because we are embarrassed or our pride is hurt. Lashing out at others can be a sign that something is wrong with us. Don't allow your own hurt pride to lead you to hurt others.

35 But the angel of the LORD told him, "Go with these men, but you may say only what **22:35** Num 22:20
I tell you to say." So Balaam went on with Balak's officials. 36 When King Balak heard
that Balaam was on the way, he went out to meet him at a Moabite town on the Arnon
River at the border of his land.
37 "Did I not send you an urgent invitation? Why didn't you come right away?" Balak **22:37-38** Num 22:18
asked Balaam. "Didn't you believe me when I said I would reward you richly?"
38 Balaam replied, "I have come, but I have no power to say just anything. I will speak
only the messages that God gives me." 39 Then Balaam accompanied Balak to Kiriath-
huzoth, 40 where the king sacrificed cattle and sheep. He sent portions of the meat to
Balaam and the officials who were with him. 41 The next morning Balak took Balaam up **22:41** Num 21:28; 23:13
to Bamoth-baal. From there he could see the people of Israel spread out below him.

Balaam Blesses Israel

23 Balaam said to King Balak, "Build me seven altars here, and prepare seven young **23:1** Num 22:40
bulls and seven rams for a sacrifice." 2 Balak followed his instructions, and the
two of them sacrificed a young bull and a ram on each altar.
3 Then Balaam said to Balak, "Stand here by your burnt offerings, and I will go to see
if the LORD will respond to me. Then I will tell you whatever he reveals to me." So
Balaam went alone to the top of a hill, 4 and God met him there. Balaam said to him, "I
have prepared seven altars and have sacrificed a young bull and a ram on each altar."
5 Then the LORD gave Balaam a message for King Balak and said, "Go back to Balak **23:5** Num 22:20, 35; 23:16
and tell him what I told you."
6 When Balaam returned, the king was standing beside his burnt offerings with all the
officials of Moab. 7 This was the prophecy Balaam delivered: **23:7** Num 22:6

"Balak summoned me to come from Aram;
the king of Moab brought me from the eastern hills.
'Come,' he said, 'curse Jacob for me!
Come and announce Israel's doom.'
8 But how can I curse
those whom God has not cursed? **23:8** Num 22:12
How can I condemn
those whom the LORD has not condemned?
9 I see them from the cliff tops;
I watch them from the hills. **23:9** Num 22:41
I see a people who live by themselves,
set apart from other nations.
10 Who can count Jacob's descendants, as numerous as dust? **23:10** Gen 13:16 Ps 37:37 Isa 57:1
Who can count even a fourth of Israel's people?
Let me die like the righteous;
let my life end like theirs."

11 Then King Balak demanded of Balaam, "What have you done to me? I brought you
to curse my enemies. Instead, you have blessed them!"
12 But Balaam replied, "Can I say anything except what the LORD tells me?" **23:12** Num 22:20, 38

Balaam's Second Prophecy

13 Then King Balak told him, "Come with me to another place. There you will see only
a portion of the nation of Israel. Curse at least that many!" 14 So Balak took Balaam to
the plateau of Zophim on Pisgah Peak. He built seven altars there and offered a young
bull and a ram on each altar.
15 Then Balaam said to the king, "Stand here by your burnt offering while I go to meet
the LORD."

22:41 Bamoth-baal means the high places of Baal near Heshbon and Dibon. It was the first stopping point on the way to the high plains of Moab. From this vantage point, they could see the entire Israelite camp.

23:1-3 The number seven was sacred among many of the nations and religions at this time.

23:16 Num 22:38

16 So the LORD met Balaam and gave him a message. Then he said, "Go back to Balak
and give him this message."
17 So Balaam returned to the place where the king and the officials of Moab were
standing beside Balak's burnt offerings. "What did the LORD say?" Balak asked
eagerly.
18 This was the prophecy Balaam delivered:

"Rise up, Balak, and listen!
Hear me, son of Zippor.

23:19 1 Sam 15:29; Isa 40:8; 55:11

19 God is not a man, that he should lie.
He is not a human, that he should change his mind.
Has he ever spoken and failed to act?
Has he ever promised and not carried it through?

23:20 Isa 43:13

20 I received a command to bless;
he has blessed, and I cannot reverse it!

23:21 Exod 3:12; Deut 31:23

21 No misfortune is in sight for Jacob;
no trouble is in store for Israel.
For the LORD their God is with them;
he has been proclaimed their king.

23:22 Num 24:8

22 God has brought them out of Egypt;
he is like a strong ox for them.

23:23 Num 22:7

23 No curse can touch Jacob;
no sorcery has any power against Israel.
For now it will be said of Jacob,
'What wonders God has done for Israel!'

23:24 Gen 49:9

24 These people rise up like a lioness;
like a majestic lion they stand.
They refuse to rest
until they have feasted on prey,
drinking the blood of the slaughtered!"

25 Then Balak said to Balaam, "If you aren't going to curse them, at least don't bless
them!"

23:26 Num 22:38

26 But Balaam replied, "Didn't I tell you that I must do whatever the LORD tells me?"

Balaam's Third Prophecy

27 Then King Balak said to Balaam, "Come, I will take you to yet another place. Perhaps
it will please God to let you curse them from there."

23:28 Num 31:16; Josh 22:17

28 So Balak took Balaam to the top of Mount Peor, overlooking the wasteland.*
29 Balaam again told Balak, "Build me seven altars and prepare me seven young bulls
and seven rams for a sacrifice." 30 So Balak did as Balaam ordered and offered a young
bull and a ram on each altar.

24:1 Num 23:23, 38

24:2 Num 11:25-26; 1 Sam 10:10; 2 Chr 15:1

24

By now Balaam realized that the LORD intended to bless Israel, so he did not resort
to divination as he often did. Instead, he turned and looked out toward the
wilderness, 2 where he saw the people of Israel camped, tribe by tribe. Then the Spirit of
God came upon him, 3 and this is the prophecy he delivered:

24:3 Num 23:7-10, 18-24

"This is the prophecy of Balaam son of Beor,
the prophecy of the man whose eyes see clearly,

23:28 Or *overlooking Jeshimon.*

23:27 Balak took Balaam to several places to try to entice him to curse the Israelites. He thought a change of scenery might help change Balaam's mind. But changing locations won't change God's will. We must learn to face the source of our problems. Moving to escape problems only makes solving them more difficult. Problems rooted in us are not solved by a change of scenery. A change in location or job may only distract us from the need for us to change our heart.

24:1 Because Balaam was a sorcerer, he would look for omens or signs to help him tell the future. In this situation, however, it was clear that God himself was speaking, and so Balaam needed no other signs, real or imagined.

4 who hears the words of God,
who sees a vision from the Almighty,
who falls down with eyes wide open:
5 How beautiful are your tents, O Jacob;
how lovely are your homes, O Israel!
6 They spread before me like groves of palms,
like fruitful gardens by the riverside.
They are like aloes planted by the LORD,
like cedars beside the waters.
7 Water will gush out in buckets;
their offspring are supplied with all they need.
Their king will be greater than Agag;
their kingdom will be exalted.
8 God brought them up from Egypt,
drawing them along like a wild ox.
He devours all the nations that oppose him,
breaking their bones in pieces,
shooting them with arrows.
9 Like a lion, Israel crouches and lies down;
like a lioness, who dares to arouse her?
Blessed is everyone who blesses you, O Israel,
and cursed is everyone who curses you."

10 King Balak flew into a rage against Balaam. He angrily clapped his hands and
shouted, "I called you to curse my enemies! Instead, you have blessed them three times.
11 Now get out of here! Go back home! I had planned to reward you richly, but the LORD
has kept you from your reward."
12 Balaam told Balak, "Don't you remember what I told your messengers? I said,
13 'Even if Balak were to give me a palace filled with silver and gold, I am powerless to
do anything against the will of the LORD.' I told you that I could say only what the LORD
says! 14 Now I am returning to my own people. But first let me tell you what the Israelites
will do to your people in the future."

Balaam's Final Prophecies

15 This is the prophecy Balaam delivered:

"This is the message of Balaam son of Beor,
the prophecy of the man whose eyes see clearly,
16 who hears the words of God,
who has knowledge from the Most High,
who sees a vision from the Almighty,
who falls down with eyes wide open:
17 I see him, but not in the present time.
I perceive him, but far in the distant future.
A star will rise from Jacob;
a scepter will emerge from Israel.
It will crush the foreheads of Moab's people,
cracking the skulls of the people of Sheth.

24:4 Num 12:6; 22:20
24:6 Ps 45:8
24:7 1 Sam 15:8-9; Ps 145:11-13
24:8 Ps 45:5
24:9 Gen 12:3; 27:29; 49:9; Num 23:24
24:11 Num 22:17, 37
24:13 Num 22:18, 20
24:15 Gen 49:1; Num 24:3-4
24:17 Gen 49:10; Isa 15:1–16:4; Matt 2:2

24:7 Who was Agag? *Agag* was the title for the king of the Amalekites, just as *Pharaoh* was the ruler of Egypt. Saul, the first king of Israel, defeated Agag (1 Samuel 15:8). Balaam prophesied correctly the ruin of Israel's oldest enemy (Exodus 17:14-16).

24:11 Although Balaam's motives were not correct, in blessing Israel he acted with integrity. God's message had so filled him that Balaam spoke the truth. In so doing, he forfeited the reward that had lured him to speak in the first place. Staying true to God's Word may cost us promotions and advantages in the short run, but those who choose God over money will one day acquire heavenly wealth beyond measure (Matthew 6:19-21).

24:15-19 The star out of Jacob is often thought to refer to the coming Messiah. It was probably this prophecy that convinced the astrologers to travel to Israel to search for the baby Jesus (see Matthew 2:1, 2). It seems strange that God would use a sorcerer like Balaam to foretell the coming of the Messiah. But this teaches us that God can use anything or anyone to accomplish his plans. By using a sorcerer, God did not make sorcery acceptable; in fact, the Bible condemns it in several places (Exodus 22:18; 2 Chronicles 33:6; Revelation 18:23). Rather, God showed his ultimate sovereignty over good and evil.

24:18 Amos 9:12 18 Edom will be taken over,
and Seir, its enemy, will be conquered,
while Israel continues on in triumph.
24:19 Gen 49:10 19 A ruler will rise in Jacob
who will destroy the survivors of Ir."
24:20 Exod 17:14 20 Then Balaam looked over at the people of Amalek and delivered this prophecy:

"Amalek was the greatest of nations,
but its destiny is destruction!"

24:21 Gen 15:19 21 Then he looked over at the Kenites and prophesied:

"You are strongly situated;
your nest is set in the rocks.
24:22 Gen 10:22 22 But the Kenites will be destroyed
when Assyria* takes you captive."

23 Balaam concluded his prophecies by saying:

"Alas, who can survive when God does this?
24:24 Gen 10:4, 21 24 Ships will come from the coasts of Cyprus*;
they will oppress both Assyria and Eber,
but they, too, will be utterly destroyed."

25 Then Balaam and Balak returned to their homes.

Moab Seduces Israel

25:1 Num 33:49 Josh 2:1 **25** While the Israelites were camped at Acacia,* some of the men defiled themselves by
sleeping with the local Moabite women. 2 These women invited them to attend
sacrifices to their gods, and soon the Israelites were feasting with them and worshiping the
25:2 Exod 34:15-16 gods of Moab. 3 Before long Israel was joining in the worship of Baal of Peor, causing the
25:3 Num 25:5 Deut 4:3-4 LORD's anger to blaze against his people.
4 The LORD issued the following command to Moses: "Seize all the ringleaders and
execute them before the LORD in broad daylight, so his fierce anger will turn away from
the people of Israel." 5 So Moses ordered Israel's judges to execute everyone who had
joined in worshiping Baal of Peor.
25:6 Num 22:4 6 Just then one of the Israelite men brought a Midianite woman into the camp, right
before the eyes of Moses and all the people, as they were weeping at the entrance of the Taber-
25:7 Ps 106:30 nacle.* 7 When Phinehas son of Eleazar and grandson of Aaron the priest saw this, he
jumped up and left the assembly. Then he took a spear 8 and rushed after the man into his tent.
25:9 †1 Cor 10:8 Phinehas thrust the spear all the way through the man's body and into the woman's stomach.
So the plague against the Israelites was stopped, 9 but not before 24,000 people had died.
10 Then the LORD said to Moses, 11 "Phinehas son of Eleazar and grandson of Aaron

24:22 Hebrew *Asshur;* also in 24:24. **24:24** Hebrew *Kittim.* **25:1** Hebrew *Shittim.* **25:6** Hebrew *Tent of Meeting.*

25:1 This verse shows the great challenge Israel had to face. The most dangerous problem for Moses and Joshua was not Jericho's hostile army, but the ever-present temptation to compromise with the pagan Canaanite religions and cultures.

25:1, 2 The Bible doesn't say how the Israelite men got involved in sexual immorality. We do know that sacred prostitution was a common practice among Canaanite religions. At first, they didn't think about worshiping idols; they were just interested in sex. Before long they started attending local feasts and family celebrations that involved idol worship. Soon they were in over their heads, absorbed into the practices of the pagan culture. Their desire for fun and pleasure caused them to loosen their spiritual commitment. Have you relaxed your standards in order to justify your desires?

25:1-3 This combination of sexual sin and idolatry, it turns out, was Balaam's idea (see 31:16; Revelation 2:14), the same Balaam who had just blessed Israel and who appeared to be on their side. It is easy to see how the Israelites were misled, for Balaam seemed to say and do all the right things—at least for a while (22–24). Not until Balaam had inflicted great damage on them did the Israelites realize that he was greedy, used sorcery, and was deeply involved in pagan religious practices. We must be careful to weigh both the words and the deeds of those who claim to offer spiritual help.

25:3 Baal was the most popular god in Canaan, the land Israel was about to enter. Represented by a bull, symbol of strength and fertility, he was the god of the rains and harvest. The Israelites were continually attracted to Baal worship, in which prostitution played a large part, throughout their years in Canaan. Because Baal was so popular, his name was often used as a generic title for all the local gods.

25:6 That this man "brought a Midianite woman into the camp" meant that he took her into the inner room of his tent. Clearly the woman was brought into his tent for sex. Zimri (25:14) so disregarded the law of God that he brought that woman right into the camp.

the priest has turned my anger away from the Israelites by displaying passionate zeal
among them on my behalf. So I have stopped destroying all Israel as I had intended to
do in my anger. [12]So tell him that I am making my special covenant of peace with him.
[13]In this covenant, he and his descendants will be priests for all time, because he was
zealous for his God and made atonement for the people of Israel."

[14]The Israelite man killed with the Midianite woman was named Zimri son of Salu,
the leader of a family from the tribe of Simeon. [15]The woman's name was Cozbi; she
was the daughter of Zur, the leader of a Midianite clan.

[16]Then the LORD said to Moses, [17]"Attack the Midianites and destroy them, [18]because
they assaulted you with deceit by tricking you into worshiping Baal of Peor, and because
of Cozbi, the daughter of a Midianite leader, who was killed on the day of the plague at
Peor."

25:12 Num 16:46; Ps 106:30-31; Isa 54:10
25:15 Num 25:18; 31:8; Josh 13:21
25:16 Num 31:2
25:18 Num 23:28

2. The second census of the nation

26 After the plague had ended, the LORD said to Moses and to Eleazar son of Aaron, the
priest, [2]"Take a census of all the men of Israel who are twenty years old or older, to
find out how many of each family are of military age." [3]At that time the entire nation of
Israel was camped on the plains of Moab beside the Jordan River, across from Jericho.

So Moses and Eleazar the priest issued these census instructions to the leaders of Israel:
[4]"Count all the men of Israel twenty years old and older, just as the LORD commanded
Moses." This is the census record of all the descendants of Israel who came out of Egypt.

26:1 Num 25:6-9
26:2 Num 1:2-15

The Tribe of Reuben

[5]These were the clans descended from Reuben, Jacob's* oldest son:
The Hanochite clan, named after its ancestor Hanoch.
The Palluite clan, named after its ancestor Pallu.
[6] The Hezronite clan, named after its ancestor Hezron.
The Carmite clan, named after its ancestor Carmi.

[7]The men from all the clans of Reuben numbered 43,730.

[8]Pallu was the ancestor of Eliab, [9]and Eliab was the father of Nemuel, Dathan, and
Abiram. This Dathan and Abiram are the same community leaders who conspired with
Korah against Moses and Aaron, defying the LORD. [10]But the earth opened up and
swallowed them with Korah, and 250 of their followers were destroyed that day by fire
from the LORD. This served as a warning to the entire nation of Israel. [11]However, the
sons of Korah did not die that day.

26:5 Exod 6:14
26:9 Num 16:1
26:10 Num 16:32, 35, 38

The Tribe of Simeon

[12]These were the clans descended from the sons of Simeon:
The Nemuelite clan, named after its ancestor Nemuel.
The Jaminite clan, named after its ancestor Jamin.
The Jakinite clan, named after its ancestor Jakin.
[13] The Zerahite clan, named after its ancestor Zerah.
The Shaulite clan, named after its ancestor Shaul.

[14]The men from all the clans of Simeon numbered 22,200.

26:12 1 Chr 4:24-43

The Tribe of Gad

[15]These were the clans descended from the sons of Gad:
The Zephonite clan, named after its ancestor Zephon.
The Haggite clan, named after its ancestor Haggi.
The Shunite clan, named after its ancestor Shuni.

26:5 Hebrew *Israel's.*

25:10, 11 It is clear from Phinehas's story that some anger is proper and justified. Phinehas was angry because of his zeal for the Lord. But how can we know when our anger is appropriate and when it should be restrained? Ask these questions when you become angry: (1) Why am I angry? (2) Whose rights are being violated (mine or another's)? (3) Is the truth (a principle of God) being violated? If only your rights are at stake, it may be wiser to keep angry feelings under control. But if the truth is at stake, anger is often justified, although violence and retaliation are usually the wrong way to express it (Phinehas's case was unique). If we are becoming more and more like God, we should be angered by sin.

25:12, 13 Phinehas's act made atonement for the nation of Israel; in effect, what he did averted God's judgment. Because of this, his descendants would become the high priests of Israel. They continued so throughout the history of the Tabernacle and the Temple.

16 The Oznite clan, named after its ancestor Ozni.
The Erite clan, named after its ancestor Eri.
17 The Arodite clan, named after its ancestor Arodi.*
The Arelite clan, named after its ancestor Areli.

18 The men from all the clans of Gad numbered 40,500.

The Tribe of Judah

19 Judah had two sons, Er and Onan, who had died in the land of Canaan. 20 But the
following clans descended from Judah's surviving sons:
The Shelanite clan, named after its ancestor Shelah.
The Perezite clan, named after its ancestor Perez.
The Zerahite clan, named after its ancestor Zerah.

21 These were the subclans descended from the Perezites:
The Hezronites, named after their ancestor Hezron.
The Hamulites, named after their ancestor Hamul.

22 The men from all the clans of Judah numbered 76,500.

The Tribe of Issachar

26:23 1 Chr 7:1-5

23 These were the clans descended from the sons of Issachar:
The Tolaite clan, named after its ancestor Tola.
The Puite clan, named after its ancestor Puah.*
24 The Jashubite clan, named after its ancestor Jashub.
The Shimronite clan, named after its ancestor Shimron.

25 The men from all the clans of Issachar numbered 64,300.

The Tribe of Zebulun

26 These were the clans descended from the sons of Zebulun:
The Seredite clan, named after its ancestor Sered.
The Elonite clan, named after its ancestor Elon.
The Jahleelite clan, named after its ancestor Jahleel.

27 The men from all the clans of Zebulun numbered 60,500.

The Tribe of Manasseh

26:28 Gen 46:19-22

28 Two clans were descended from Joseph through Manasseh and Ephraim.

29 These were the clans descended from Manasseh:
The Makirite clan, named after its ancestor Makir.
The Gileadite clan, named after its ancestor Gilead, Makir's son.

30 These were the subclans descended from the Gileadites:
The Iezerites, named after their ancestor Iezer.
The Helekites, named after their ancestor Helek.
31 The Asrielites, named after their ancestor Asriel.
The Shechemites, named after their ancestor Shechem.
32 The Shemidaites, named after their ancestor Shemida.
The Hepherites, named after their ancestor Hepher.
33 Hepher's son, Zelophehad, had no sons, but his daughters' names were Mahlah, Noah, Hoglah, Milcah, and Tirzah.

34 The men from all the clans of Manasseh numbered 52,700.

The Tribe of Ephraim

26:35 1 Chr 7:20

35 These were the clans descended from the sons of Ephraim:
The Shuthelahite clan, named after its ancestor Shuthelah.
The Bekerite clan, named after its ancestor Beker.
The Tahanite clan, named after its ancestor Tahan.

26:17 As in Samaritan Pentateuch and Syriac version (see also Gen 46:16); Hebrew reads *Arod.* **26:23** As in Samaritan Pentateuch, Greek and Syriac versions, and Latin Vulgate (see also 1 Chr 7:1); Hebrew reads *The Punite clan, named after its ancestor Puvah.*

[36] This was the subclan descended from the Shuthelahites:
The Eranites, named after their ancestor Eran.

[37] The men from all the clans of Ephraim numbered 32,500.

These clans of Manasseh and Ephraim were all descendants of Joseph.

26:37 Num 1:33

The Tribe of Benjamin

[38] These were the clans descended from the sons of Benjamin:
The Belaite clan, named after its ancestor Bela.
The Ashbelite clan, named after its ancestor Ashbel.
The Ahiramite clan, named after its ancestor Ahiram.
[39] The Shuphamite clan, named after its ancestor Shupham.*
The Huphamite clan, named after its ancestor Hupham.

26:38 Gen 46:21; 1 Chr 8:1

[40] These were the subclans descended from the Belaites:
The Ardites, named after their ancestor Ard.*
The Naamites, named after their ancestor Naaman.

26:40 1 Chr 8:3

[41] The men from all the clans of Benjamin numbered 45,600.

The Tribe of Dan

[42] These were the clans descended from the sons of Dan:
The Shuhamite clan, named after its ancestor Shuham.

26:42 Gen 46:23-25

[43] All the clans of Dan were Shuhamite clans, and the men from these clans numbered 64,400.

The Tribe of Asher

[44] These were the clans descended from the sons of Asher:
The Imnite clan, named after its ancestor Imnah.
The Ishvite clan, named after its ancestor Ishvi.
The Beriite clan, named after its ancestor Beriah.

26:44 Gen 46:16-17

[45] These were the subclans descended from the Beriites:
The Heberites, named after their ancestor Heber.
The Malkielites, named after their ancestor Malkiel.

[46] Asher also had a daughter named Serah.

[47] The men from all the clans of Asher numbered 53,400.

The Tribe of Naphtali

[48] These were the clans descended from the sons of Naphtali:
The Jahzeelite clan, named after its ancestor Jahzeel.
The Gunite clan, named after its ancestor Guni.
[49] The Jezerite clan, named after its ancestor Jezer.
The Shillemite clan, named after its ancestor Shillem.

26:48 1 Chr 7:13

[50] The men from all the clans of Naphtali numbered 45,400.

The Census Results

[51] So the total number of Israelite men counted in the census numbered 601,730.
[52] Then the LORD said to Moses, [53] "Divide the land among the tribes in proportion to
their populations, as indicated by the census. [54] Give the larger tribes more land and the
smaller tribes less land, each group's inheritance reflecting the size of its population.
[55] Make sure you assign the land by lot, and define the inheritance of each ancestral tribe
by means of the census listings. [56] Each inheritance must be assigned by lot among the
larger and smaller tribal groups."

26:51 Num 1:43
26:54 Num 33:54
26:55 Num 33:54; 34:13

The Tribe of Levi

[57] This is the census record for the Levites who were counted according to their clans:
The Gershonite clan, named after its ancestor Gershon.

26:57 Gen 46:11; 1 Chr 6:1

26:39 As in some Hebrew manuscripts, Samaritan Pentateuch, Greek and Syriac versions, and Latin Vulgate; most Hebrew manuscripts read *Shephupham.* **26:40** As in Samaritan Pentateuch, some Greek manuscripts, and Latin Vulgate; Hebrew lacks *named after their ancestor Ard.*

The Kohathite clan, named after its ancestor Kohath.
The Merarite clan, named after its ancestor Merari.
26:58 Num 3:16-35 58The Libnites, the Hebronites, the Mahlites, the Mushites, and the Korahites were all
subclans of the Levites.
Now Kohath was the ancestor of Amram, 59and Amram's wife was named Jochebed.
26:60 Num 3:2 She also was a descendant of Levi, born among the Levites in the land of Egypt. Amram
and Jochebed became the parents of Aaron, Moses, and their sister, Miriam. 60To Aaron
26:61 Lev 10:1-2 Num 3:4 were born Nadab, Abihu, Eleazar, and Ithamar. 61But Nadab and Abihu died when they
burned before the LORD a different kind of fire than he had commanded.
26:62 Num 3:39 62The men from the Levite clans who were one month old or older numbered
23,000. But the Levites were not included in the total census figure of the people of
Israel because they were not given an inheritance of land when it was divided among
the Israelites.
63So these are the census figures of the people of Israel as prepared by Moses and
26:64 Num 14:20-43 Deut 2:14-15 Eleazar the priest on the plains of Moab beside the Jordan River, across from Jericho.
64Not one person that Moses and Aaron counted in this census had been among those
counted in the previous census taken in the wilderness of Sinai. 65For the LORD had said
of them, "They will all die in the wilderness." The only exceptions were Caleb son of
Jephunneh and Joshua son of Nun.

The Daughters of Zelophehad

27:1 Num 26:28-37; 36:1-4 **27** One day a petition was presented by the daughters of Zelophehad—Mahlah,
Noah, Hoglah, Milcah, and Tirzah. Their father, Zelophehad, was the son of
Hepher, son of Gilead, son of Makir, son of Manasseh, son of Joseph. 2These women
went and stood before Moses, Eleazar the priest, the tribal leaders, and the entire
community at the entrance of the Tabernacle.* 3"Our father died in the wilderness
without leaving any sons," they said. "But he was not among Korah's followers, who
rebelled against the LORD. He died because of his own sin. 4Why should the name of
our father disappear just because he had no sons? Give us property along with the rest
of our relatives."
27:7 Num 36:1-4 Josh 17:4 5So Moses brought their case before the LORD. 6And the LORD replied to Moses,
7"The daughters of Zelophehad are right. You must give them an inheritance of land
along with their father's relatives. Assign them the property that would have been given
to their father. 8Moreover announce this to the people of Israel: 'If a man dies and has
no sons, then give his inheritance to his daughters. 9And if he has no daughters, turn his
inheritance over to his brothers. 10If he has no brothers, give his inheritance to his
27:11 Num 35:29 father's brothers. 11But if his father has no brothers, pass on his inheritance to the nearest
relative in his clan. The Israelites must observe this as a general legal requirement, just
as the LORD commanded Moses.'"

27:12 Num 33:47 Deut 32:49 *Joshua Chosen to Lead Israel*

12One day the LORD said to Moses, "Climb to the top of the mountains east of the
27:13 Deut 32:50-51 river,* and look out over the land I have given the people of Israel. 13After you have
seen it, you will die as Aaron your brother did, 14for you both rebelled against my
27:14 Num 20:9-13 Deut 32:48-52 instructions in the wilderness of Zin. When the people of Israel rebelled, you failed

27:2 Hebrew *Tent of Meeting.* **27:12** Hebrew *the mountains of Abarim.*

26:64 A new census for a new generation. Thirty-eight years had elapsed since the first great census recorded in Numbers (see 1:1–2:33). During that time, every Israelite man and woman 20 years old and over—except Caleb, Joshua, and Moses—had died, and yet God's laws and the spiritual character of the nation were still intact. Numbers records some dramatic miracles. This is a quiet but powerful miracle often overlooked: A whole nation moved from one land to another, lost its entire adult population, yet managed to maintain its spiritual direction. Sometimes it may feel like God isn't working dramatic miracles in our lives. But God often works in quiet ways to bring about his long-range purposes.

27:3 "Died because of his own sin" means that he died a natural death. His death fell under the judgment of the entire nation for believing the faithless scouts.

27:3, 4 Up to this point, the Hebrew law gave sons alone the right to inherit. The daughters of Zelophehad, having no brothers, came to Moses to ask for their father's possessions. God told Moses that if a man died without sons, his inheritance would go to his daughters (27:8). But the daughters could keep it only if they married within their own tribe, probably so the territorial lines would remain intact (36:5-12).

to demonstrate my holiness to them at the waters." (These are the waters of Meribah at Kadesh* in the wilderness of Zin.)

15 Then Moses said to the LORD, 16 "O LORD, the God of the spirits of all living things, please appoint a new leader for the community. 17 Give them someone who will lead them into battle, so the people of the LORD will not be like sheep without a shepherd."

18 The LORD replied, "Take Joshua son of Nun, who has the Spirit in him, and lay your hands on him. 19 Present him to Eleazar the priest before the whole community, and publicly commission him with the responsibility of leading the people. 20 Transfer your authority to him so the whole community of Israel will obey him. 21 When direction from the LORD is needed, Joshua will stand before Eleazar the priest, who will determine the LORD's will by means of sacred lots.* This is how Joshua and the rest of the community of Israel will discover what they should do."

22 So Moses did as the LORD commanded and presented Joshua to Eleazar the priest and the whole community. 23 Moses laid his hands on him and commissioned him to his responsibilities, just as the LORD had commanded through Moses.

3. Instructions concerning offerings

The Daily Offerings

28 The LORD said to Moses, "Give these instructions to the people of Israel: 2 The offerings you present to me by fire on the altar are my food, and they are very pleasing to me. See to it that they are brought at the appointed times and offered according to my instructions.

3 "Say to them: When you present your daily whole burnt offerings to the LORD, you must offer two one-year-old male lambs with no physical defects. 4 One lamb will be sacrificed in the morning and the other in the evening. 5 With each lamb you must offer a grain offering of two quarts* of choice flour mixed with one quart* of olive oil. 6 This is the regular burnt offering ordained at Mount Sinai, an offering made by fire, very pleasing to the LORD. 7 Along with it you must present the proper drink offering, consisting of one quart of fermented drink with each lamb, poured out in the Holy Place as an offering to the LORD. 8 Offer the second lamb in the evening with the same grain offering and drink offering. It, too, is an offering made by fire, very pleasing to the LORD.

The Sabbath Offerings

9 "On the Sabbath day, sacrifice two one-year-old male lambs with no physical defects. They must be accompanied by a grain offering of three quarts* of choice flour mixed with olive oil, and a drink offering. 10 This is the whole burnt offering to be presented each Sabbath day, in addition to the regular daily burnt offering and its accompanying drink offering.

The Monthly Offerings

11 "On the first day of each month, present an extra burnt offering to the LORD of two

27:17 1 Kgs 22:17; Ezek 34:1-24; Zech 10:2; Matt 9:36; †Mark 6:34
27:18 Deut 34:9
27:20 Josh 1:16-17
27:21 Exod 28:30; 1 Sam 28:6
28:3 Exod 29:38-41
28:4 Lev 6:19-20
28:5 Num 15:3-12
28:7 Exod 29:42; Lev 23:13
28:11 Num 10:10; 28:19; Ezek 46:6-7

27:14 Hebrew *waters of Meribath-kadesh.* **27:21** Hebrew *of the Urim.* **28:5a** Hebrew *1/10 of an ephah* [2 liters]; also in 28:13, 21, 29. **28:5b** Hebrew *1/4 of a hin* [1 liter]; also in 28:7. **28:9** Hebrew *2/10 of an ephah* [3.6 liters]; also in 28:12, 20, 28.

27:15-17 Moses asked God to appoint a leader who was capable of directing both external and internal affairs—one who could lead them in battle but who would also care for their needs. The Lord responded by appointing Joshua. Many people want to be known as leaders. Some are very capable of reaching their goals, while others care deeply for the people in their charge. The best leaders are both goal-oriented and people-oriented.

27:15-21 Moses did not want to leave his work without making sure a new leader was ready to replace him. First, he asked God to help him find a replacement. Then, when Joshua was selected, Moses gave him a variety of tasks to ease the transition into his new position. Moses also clearly told the people that Joshua had the authority and the ability to lead the nation. His display of confidence in Joshua was good for both Joshua and the people. To minimize leadership gaps, anyone in a leadership position should train others to carry on the duties should he or she suddenly or eventually have to leave. While you have the opportunity, follow Moses' pattern: pray, select, develop, and commission.

28:1, 2 Offerings had to be brought regularly and presented according to prescribed rituals under the priests' supervision. Following these rituals took time, and this gave the people the opportunity to prepare their hearts for worship. Unless our hearts are ready, worship is meaningless. By contrast, God is delighted, and we get more from it, when our hearts are prepared to come before him in a spirit of thankfulness.

28:9, 10 Why were extra offerings made on the Sabbath day? The Sabbath was a special day of rest and worship commemorating both creation (Exodus 20:8-11) and the deliverance from Egypt (Deuteronomy 5:12-15). Because of the significance of this special day, it was only natural to offer extra sacrifices on it.

young bulls, one ram, and seven one-year-old male lambs, all with no physical
28:12 Num 15:4-12 defects. 12 These will be accompanied by grain offerings of choice flour mixed with
olive oil—five quarts* with each bull, three quarts with the ram, 13 and two quarts with
each lamb. This burnt offering must be presented by fire, and it will be very pleasing
to the LORD. 14 You must also give a drink offering with each sacrifice: two quarts* of
wine with each bull, two and a half pints* for the ram, and one quart* for each lamb.
Present this monthly burnt offering on the first day of each month throughout the
year.
28:15 Num 28:3 15 "Also, on the first day of each month you must offer one male goat for a sin offering
to the LORD. This is in addition to the regular daily burnt offering and its accompanying
drink offering.

Offerings for the Passover

28:16 Exod 12:6, 18 Lev 23:5-14 Deut 16:1-8 16 "On the appointed day in early spring,* you must celebrate the LORD's Passover. 17 On
the following day a joyous, seven-day festival will begin, but no bread made with yeast
may be eaten. 18 On the first day of the festival you must call a sacred assembly of the
28:19 Num 29:11 people. None of your regular work may be done on that day. 19 You must present as a
burnt offering to the LORD two young bulls, one ram, and seven one-year-old male
lambs, all with no physical defects. 20 These will be accompanied by grain offerings of
choice flour mixed with olive oil—five quarts with each bull, three quarts with the ram,
21 and two quarts with each of the seven lambs. 22 You must also offer a male goat as a
sin offering, to make atonement for yourselves. 23 You will present these offerings in
addition to your regular morning sacrifices. 24 On each of the seven days of the festival,
this is how you will prepare the food offerings to be presented by fire, very pleasing to
the LORD. These will be offered in addition to the regular whole burnt offerings and drink
offerings. 25 On the seventh day of the festival you must call another holy assembly of
the people. None of your regular work may be done on that day.

Offerings for the Festival of Harvest

28:26 Exod 23:16 Lev 23:9-22 Deut 16:9-12 26 "On the first day of the Festival of Harvest,* when you present the first of your new
grain to the LORD, you must call a holy assembly of the people. None of your regular
work may be done on that day. 27 A special whole burnt offering will be offered that day,
very pleasing to the LORD. It will consist of two young bulls, one ram, and seven
one-year-old male lambs. 28 These will be accompanied by grain offerings of choice flour
mixed with olive oil—five quarts with each bull, three quarts with the ram, 29 and two
quarts with each of the seven lambs. 30 Also, offer one male goat to make atonement for
28:31 Num 28:3 yourselves. 31 These special burnt offerings, along with their drink offerings, are in
addition to the regular daily burnt offering and its accompanying grain offering. Be sure
that all the animals you sacrifice have no physical defects.

Offerings for the Festival of Trumpets

29:1 Num 28:26 **29** "The Festival of Trumpets will be celebrated on the appointed day in early
autumn* each year. You must call a solemn assembly of all the people on that
day, and no regular work may be done. 2 On that day you must present a burnt offering,
very pleasing to the LORD. It will consist of one young bull, one ram, and seven
one-year-old male lambs, all with no physical defects. 3 These must be accompanied

28:12 Hebrew *3/10 of an ephah* [5.4 liters]; also in 28:20, 28. **28:14a** Hebrew *1/2 of a hin* [2 liters]. **28:14b** Hebrew *1/3 of a hin* [1.3 liters]. **28:14c** Hebrew *1/4 of a hin* [1 liter]. **28:16** Hebrew *On the fourteenth day of the first month.* This day of the Hebrew lunar calendar occurs in late March or early April. **28:26** Or *Festival of Weeks.* **29:1** Hebrew *on the first day of the seventh month.* This day of the Hebrew lunar calendar occurs in September or early October.

29:1ff God placed many holidays on Israel's calendar. The Festival of Trumpets was one of three great holidays celebrated in the seventh month (the Festival of Shelters and Day of Atonement were the other two). These holidays provided a time to refresh the mind and body and to renew one's commitment to God. If you feel tired or far from God, try taking a "spiritual holiday." Separate yourself from your daily routine and concentrate on renewing your commitment to God.

29:1, 2 The Festival of Trumpets demonstrated three important principles that we should follow in our worship today: (1) The people gathered together to celebrate and worship. There is an extra benefit to be gained from worshiping with other believers. (2) The normal daily routine was suspended, and no hard work was done. It takes time to worship, and setting aside the time allows us to adjust our attitudes before and reflect afterward. (3) The people gave God something of value by sacrificing animals as burnt offerings to him. We show our commitment to God when we give something of value to him. The best gift, of course, is ourselves.

by grain offerings of choice flour mixed with olive oil—five quarts* with the bull,
three quarts* with the ram, 4 and two quarts* with each of the seven lambs. 5 In
addition, you must sacrifice a male goat as a sin offering, to make atonement for
yourselves. 6 These special sacrifices are in addition to your regular monthly and **29:6** Num 28:3
daily burnt offerings, and they must be given with their prescribed grain offerings and
drink offerings. These offerings are given to the LORD by fire and are very pleasing
to him.

Offerings for the Day of Atonement

7 "Ten days later,* you must call another holy assembly of all the people. On that day, **29:7** Lev 16:29-34; 23:26-32
the Day of Atonement, the people must go without food, and no regular work may be
done. 8 You must present a burnt offering, very pleasing to the LORD. It will consist of
one young bull, one ram, and seven one-year-old male lambs, all with no physical
defects. 9 These offerings must be accompanied by the prescribed grain offerings of
choice flour mixed with olive oil—five quarts of choice flour with the bull, three
quarts of choice flour with the ram, 10 and two quarts of choice flour with each of the
seven lambs. 11 You must also sacrifice one male goat for a sin offering. This is in **29:11** Lev 16:1-35
addition to the sin offering of atonement and the regular daily burnt offering with its
grain offering, and their accompanying drink offerings.

Offerings for the Festival of Shelters

12 "Five days later,* you must call yet another holy assembly of all the people, and on **29:12** Lev 23:33-43; Deut 16:13-14
that day no regular work may be done. It is the beginning of the Festival of Shelters,
a seven-day festival to the LORD. 13 That day you must present a special whole burnt
offering by fire, very pleasing to the LORD. It will consist of thirteen young bulls, two
rams, and fourteen one-year-old male lambs, all with no physical defects. 14 Each of
these offerings must be accompanied by a grain offering of choice flour mixed with
olive oil—five quarts for each of the thirteen bulls, three quarts for each of the two
rams, 15 and two quarts for each of the fourteen lambs. 16 You must also sacrifice a
male goat as a sin offering, in addition to the regular daily burnt offering with its
accompanying grain offering and drink offering.

17 "On the second day of this seven-day festival, sacrifice twelve young bulls, two
rams, and fourteen one-year-old male lambs, all with no physical defects. 18 Each of
these offerings of bulls, rams, and lambs must be accompanied by the prescribed grain
offering and drink offering. 19 You must also sacrifice a male goat as a sin offering, in **29:19** Num 28:3, 11, 31
addition to the regular daily burnt offering with its accompanying grain offering and
drink offering.

20 "On the third day of the festival, sacrifice eleven young bulls, two rams, and
fourteen one-year-old male lambs, all with no physical defects. 21 Each of these offerings of bulls, rams, and lambs must be accompanied by the prescribed grain offering
and drink offering. 22 You must also sacrifice a male goat as a sin offering, in addition **29:22** Num 28:15
to the regular daily burnt offering with its accompanying grain offering and drink
offering.

23 "On the fourth day of the festival, sacrifice ten young bulls, two rams, and
fourteen one-year-old male lambs, all with no physical defects. 24 Each of these
offerings of bulls, rams, and lambs must be accompanied by the prescribed grain
offering and drink offering. 25 You must also sacrifice a male goat as a sin offering, in
addition to the regular daily burnt offering with its accompanying grain offering and
drink offering.

26 "On the fifth day of the festival, sacrifice nine young bulls, two rams, and
fourteen one-year-old male lambs, all with no physical defects. 27 Each of these
offerings of bulls, rams, and lambs must be accompanied by the prescribed grain
offering and drink offering. 28 You must also sacrifice a male goat as a sin offering, in
addition to the regular daily burnt offering with its accompanying grain offering and
drink offering.

29 "On the sixth day of the festival, sacrifice eight young bulls, two rams, and

29:3a Hebrew *3/10 of an ephah* [5.4 liters]; also in 29:9, 14. **29:3b** Hebrew *2/10 of an ephah* [3.6 liters]; also in 29:9, 14. **29:4** Hebrew *1/10 of an ephah* [2 liters]; also in 29:10, 15. **29:7** Hebrew *On the tenth day of the seventh month;* see 29:1 and the note there. **29:12** Hebrew *On the fifteenth day of the seventh month;* see 29:1, 7 and the notes there.

fourteen one-year-old male lambs, all with no physical defects. 30Each of these
offerings of bulls, rams, and lambs must be accompanied by the prescribed grain
offering and drink offering. 31You must also sacrifice a male goat as a sin offering, in
addition to the regular daily burnt offering with its accompanying grain offering and
drink offering.

32"On the seventh day of the festival, sacrifice seven young bulls, two rams, and
fourteen one-year-old male lambs, all with no physical defects. 33Each of these
offerings of bulls, rams, and lambs must be accompanied by the prescribed grain
offering and drink offering. 34You must also sacrifice one male goat as a sin offering,
in addition to the regular daily burnt offering with its accompanying grain offering
and drink offering.

29:35 Lev 23:36
35"On the eighth day of the festival, call all the people to another holy assembly. You
must do no regular work on that day. 36You must present a burnt offering, very pleasing
to the LORD. It will consist of one young bull, one ram, and seven one-year-old male
lambs, all with no physical defects. 37Each of these offerings must be accompanied by
the prescribed grain offering and drink offering. 38You must also sacrifice one male goat
as a sin offering, in addition to the regular daily burnt offering with its accompanying
grain offering and drink offering.

29:39 Lev 23:2 2 Chr 31:3 Ezra 3:5
39"You must present these offerings to the LORD at your annual festivals. These are
in addition to the sacrifices and offerings you present in connection with vows, or as
freewill offerings, burnt offerings, grain offerings, drink offerings, or peace offerings."

40So Moses gave all of these instructions to the people of Israel, just as the LORD had
commanded him.

Laws concerning Vows

30:2 Deut 23:21-25 Matt 5:23
30 Now Moses summoned the leaders of the tribes of Israel and told them, "This
is what the LORD has commanded: 2A man who makes a vow to the LORD or
makes a pledge under oath must never break it. He must do exactly what he said he
would do.

3"If a young woman makes a vow to the LORD or a pledge under oath while she is
still living at her father's home, 4and her father hears of the vow or pledge but says
nothing, then all her vows and pledges will stand. 5But if her father refuses to let her
fulfill the vow or pledge on the day he hears of it, then all her vows and pledges will
become invalid. The LORD will forgive her because her father would not let her fulfill
them.

6"Now suppose a young woman takes a vow or makes an impulsive pledge and later
marries. 7If her husband learns of her vow or pledge and raises no objections on the day
30:8 Gen 3:16
he hears of it, her vows and pledges will stand. 8But if her husband refuses to accept her
vow or impulsive pledge on the day he hears of it, he nullifies her commitments, and the
LORD will forgive her. 9If, however, a woman is a widow or is divorced, she must fulfill
all her vows and pledges no matter what.

10"Suppose a woman is married and living in her husband's home when she makes a
vow or pledge. 11If her husband hears of it and does nothing to stop her, her vow or
30:12 Eph 5:22 Col 3:18
pledge will stand. 12But if her husband refuses to accept it on the day he hears of it, her
vow or pledge will be nullified, and the LORD will forgive her. 13So her husband may
either confirm or nullify any vows or pledges she makes to deny herself. 14But if he says

---

30:1, 2 Moses reminded the people that their promises to God and others must be kept. In ancient times, people did not sign written contracts. A person's word was as binding as a signature. To make a vow even more binding, an offering was given along with it. No one was forced by law to make a vow; but once made, vows had to be fulfilled. Breaking a vow meant a broken trust and a broken relationship. Trust is still the basis of our relationships with God and others. A broken promise today is just as harmful as it was in Moses' day.

30:3-8 Under Israelite law, parents could overrule their children's vows. This helped young people avoid the consequences of making foolish promises or costly commitments. From this law comes an important principle for both parents and children. Young people still living at home should seek their parents' help when they make decisions. A parent's experience could save a child from a serious mistake. Parents, however, should exercise their authority with caution and grace. They should let children learn from their mistakes while protecting them from disaster.

nothing on the day he hears of it, then he is agreeing to it. 15If he waits more than a day
and then tries to nullify a vow or pledge, he will suffer the consequences of her guilt."
16These are the regulations the LORD gave Moses concerning relationships between
a man and his wife, and between a father and a young daughter who still lives at home.

4. Vengeance on the Midianites

31 Then the LORD said to Moses, 2"Take vengeance on the Midianites for leading 31:2
the Israelites into idolatry. After that, you will die and join your ancestors." Num 25:1, 16-17
3So Moses said to the people, "Choose some men to fight the LORD's war of
vengeance against Midian. 4From each tribe of Israel, send one thousand men into
battle." 5So they chose one thousand men from each tribe of Israel, a total of twelve
thousand men armed for battle. 6Then Moses sent them out, a thousand men from
each tribe, and Phinehas son of Eleazar the priest led them into battle. They carried 31:6
along the holy objects of the sanctuary and the trumpets for sounding the charge. Num 10:8-9
7They attacked Midian just as the LORD had commanded Moses, and they killed all 31:8
the men. 8All five of the Midianite kings—Evi, Rekem, Zur, Hur, and Reba—died in Josh 13:21-22
the battle. They also killed Balaam son of Beor with the sword.
9Then the Israelite army captured the Midianite women and children and seized their
cattle and flocks and all their wealth as plunder. 10They burned all the towns and villages
where the Midianites had lived. 11After they had gathered the plunder and captives, both
people and animals, 12they brought them all to Moses and Eleazar the priest, and to the
whole community of Israel, which was camped on the plains of Moab beside the Jordan
River, across from Jericho. 13Moses, Eleazar the priest, and all the leaders of the people
went to meet them outside the camp. 14But Moses was furious with all the military
commanders* who had returned from the battle.
15"Why have you let all the women live?" he demanded. 16"These are the very 31:16
ones who followed Balaam's advice and caused the people of Israel to rebel against Num 25:1-18
the LORD at Mount Peor. They are the ones who caused the plague to strike the LORD's 2 Pet 2:15-16
people. 17Now kill all the boys and all the women who have slept with a man. 18Only 31:17
the young girls who are virgins may live; you may keep them for yourselves. 19And Judg 21:10-12 Deut 7:2; 20:16-18
all of you who have killed anyone or touched a dead body must stay outside the camp
for seven days. You must purify yourselves and your captives on the third and seventh
days. 20Also, purify all your clothing and everything made of leather, goat hair, or
wood."
21Then Eleazar the priest said to the men who were in the battle, "The LORD has
given Moses this requirement of the law: 22Anything made of gold, silver, bronze,
iron, tin, or lead—23that is, metals that do not burn—must be passed through fire in
order to be made ceremonially pure. These metal objects must then be further purified
with the water of purification. But everything that burns must be purified by the water
alone. 24On the seventh day you must wash your clothes and be purified. Then you 31:24
may return to the camp." Lev 11:25; 14:9

Division of the Spoils

25And the LORD said to Moses, 26"You and Eleazar the priest and the family leaders
of each tribe are to make a list of all the plunder taken in the battle, including the

31:14 Hebrew *the commanders of thousands, and the commanders of hundreds;* also in 31:48, 52, 54.

31:1ff The Midianites were a nomadic people who descended from Abraham and his second wife, Keturah. The land of Midian lay far to the south of Canaan, but large bands of Midianites roamed many miles from their homeland, searching for grazing areas for their flocks. Such a group was near the Promised Land when the Israelites arrived. When Moses fled from Egypt (Exodus 2), he took refuge in the land of Midian. His wife and father-in-law were Midianites. Despite this alliance, the Israelites and Midianites were always bitter enemies.

31:14-16 Because Midianites were responsible for enticing Israel into Baal worship, God commanded Israel to destroy them (25:16-18). But Israel took the women as captives, rather than killing them, probably because of the tempting enticements of the Midianites' sinful life-style. When we discover sin in our lives, we must deal with it completely. When the Israelites later entered the Promised Land, it was their indifferent attitude to sin that eventually ruined them. Moses dealt with the sin promptly and completely. When God points out sin, move quickly to remove it from your life.

31:16 Balaam's story (22:1–24:25), taken alone, would lead us to believe that Balaam was an honest and God-fearing man. But here is the first of much biblical evidence that Balaam was not the good man he might appear to be. For more on Balaam, see the notes on 22:9 and 25:1-3 and Balaam's Profile in chapter 22.

31:25-30 Moses told the Israelites to give a portion of the war plunder to God. Another portion was to go to the people who

31:27 Josh 22:8
31:28 Num 18:21
31:29 Num 18:25-26

people and animals. 27 Then divide the plunder into two parts, and give half to the men who fought the battle and half to the rest of the people. 28 But first give the LORD his share of the captives, cattle, donkeys, sheep, and goats that belong to the army. Set apart one out of every five hundred as the LORD's share. 29 Give this share of their half to Eleazar the priest as an offering to the LORD. 30 Also take one of every fifty of the captives, cattle, donkeys, sheep, and goats in the half that belongs to the people of Israel. Give this share to the Levites in charge of maintaining the LORD's Tabernacle." 31 So Moses and Eleazar the priest did as the LORD commanded Moses.

32 The plunder remaining from the spoils that the fighting men had taken totaled 675,000 sheep, 33 72,000 cattle, 34 61,000 donkeys, 35 and 32,000 young girls.

36 So the half of the plunder given to the fighting men totaled 337,500 sheep, 37 of which 675 were the LORD's share; 38 36,000 cattle, of which 72 were the LORD's share; 39 30,500 donkeys, of which 61 were the LORD's share; 40 16,000 young girls, of whom 32 were the LORD's share. 41 Moses gave all the LORD's share to Eleazar the priest, just as the LORD had directed him.

42 The half of the plunder belonging to the people of Israel, which Moses had separated from the half belonging to the fighting men, 43 amounted to 337,500 sheep, 44 36,000 cattle, 45 30,500 donkeys, 46 and 16,000 young girls. 47 From the half-share given to the people, Moses took one of every fifty prisoners and animals and gave them to the Levites who maintained the LORD's Tabernacle. All this was done just as the LORD had commanded Moses.

31:49 Num 1:19

48 Then all the military commanders came to Moses 49 and said, "Sir, we have accounted for all the men who went out to battle under our command; not one of us is missing! 50 So we are presenting the items of gold we captured as an offering to the LORD from our share of the plunder—armbands, bracelets, rings, earrings, and necklaces. This will make atonement for our lives before the LORD."

31:53 Deut 20:14

51 So Moses and Eleazar the priest received the gold from all the military commanders, all kinds of jewelry and crafted objects. 52 In all, the gold that the commanders presented as a gift to the LORD weighed about 420 pounds.* 53 All the fighting men had taken some of the plunder for themselves. 54 So Moses and Eleazar the priest accepted the gifts from the military commanders and brought the gold to the Tabernacle* as a reminder to the LORD that the people of Israel belong to him.

5. The Transjordan tribes

32:1 Num 21:32
32:3 Num 32:33-42; Josh 13:17; Isa 15:4; 16:9

32 Now the tribes of Reuben and Gad owned vast numbers of livestock. So when they saw that the lands of Jazer and Gilead were ideally suited for their flocks and herds, 2 they came to Moses, Eleazar the priest, and the other leaders of the people. They said, 3 "Ataroth, Dibon, Jazer, Nimrah, Heshbon, Elealeh, Sebam, Nebo, and Beon—4 the LORD has conquered this whole area for the people of Israel. It is ideally suited for all our flocks and herds. 5 If we have found favor with you, please let us have this land as our property instead of giving us land across the Jordan River."

32:8 Num 13:2-26; 14:2; Deut 1:19-21
32:9 Num 13:23-24

6 "Do you mean you want to stay back here while your brothers go across and do all the fighting?" Moses asked the Reubenites and Gadites. 7 "Are you trying to discourage the rest of the people of Israel from going across to the land the LORD has given them? 8 This is what your ancestors did when I sent them from Kadesh-barnea to explore the land. 9 After they went up to the valley of Eshcol and scouted the land,

31:52 Hebrew *16,750 shekels* [191 kilograms]. **31:54** Hebrew *Tent of Meeting.*

remained behind. Similarly, the money we earn is not ours alone. Everything we possess comes directly or indirectly from God and ultimately belongs to him. We should return a portion to him and also share a portion with those in need.

31:48-50 After carefully accounting for all their men, the officers discovered that not one soldier had been lost in battle. At once they thanked God. After going through tough times, we should be quick to thank God for delivering us and protecting us from severe loss.

32:1ff Three tribes (Reuben, Gad, and the half-tribe of Manasseh) wanted to live east of the Jordan River (referred to as the Transjordan area) on land they had already conquered. Moses immediately assumed they had selfish motives and were trying to avoid helping the others fight for the land across the river. But Moses jumped to the wrong conclusion. In dealing with people, we must find out all the facts before making up our minds. We shouldn't automatically assume that their motives are wrong, even if their plans sound suspicious.

they discouraged the people of Israel from entering the land the LORD was giving
them. 10 Then the LORD was furious with them, and he vowed, 11 'Of all those I rescued
from Egypt, no one who is twenty years old or older will ever see the land I solemnly
promised to Abraham, Isaac, and Jacob, for they have not obeyed me completely.
12 The only exceptions are Caleb son of Jephunneh the Kenizzite and Joshua son of
Nun, for they have wholeheartedly followed the LORD.'
13 "The LORD was furious with Israel and made them wander in the wilderness for
forty years until the whole generation that sinned against him had died. 14 But here
you are, a brood of sinners, doing exactly the same thing! You are making the LORD
even angrier with Israel. 15 If you turn away from him like this and he abandons them
again in the wilderness, you will be responsible for destroying this entire nation!"
16 But they responded to Moses, "We simply want to build sheepfolds for our flocks
and fortified cities for our wives and children. 17 Then we will arm ourselves and lead
our fellow Israelites into battle until we have brought them safely to their inheritance.
Meanwhile, our families will stay in the fortified cities we build here, so they will be safe
from any attacks by the local people. 18 We will not return to our homes until all the
people of Israel have received their inheritance of land. 19 But we do not want any of the
land on the other side of the Jordan. We would rather live here on the east side where we
have received our inheritance."
20 Then Moses said, "If you keep your word and arm yourselves for the LORD's battles,
21 and if your troops cross the Jordan until the LORD has driven out his enemies, 22 then
you may return when the land is finally subdued before the LORD. You will have
discharged your duty to the LORD and to the rest of the people of Israel. And the land on
the east side of the Jordan will be your inheritance from the LORD. 23 But if you fail to
keep your word, then you will have sinned against the LORD, and you may be sure that
your sin will find you out. 24 Go ahead and build towns for your families and sheepfolds
for your flocks, but do everything you have said."
25 Then the people of Gad and Reuben replied, "We are your servants and will follow
your instructions exactly. 26 Our children, wives, flocks, and cattle will stay here in the
towns of Gilead. 27 But, sir, all who are able to bear arms will cross over to fight for the
LORD, just as you have said."
28 So Moses gave orders to Eleazar, Joshua, and the tribal leaders of Israel. 29 He said,
"If all the men of Gad and Reuben who are able to fight the LORD's battles cross the
Jordan with you, then when the land is conquered, you must give them the land of Gilead
as their property. 30 But if they refuse to cross over and march ahead of you, then they
must accept land with the rest of you in the land of Canaan."
31 The tribes of Gad and Reuben said again, "Sir, we will do as the LORD has commanded!

32:10 Num 14:28-30; Deut 1:34
32:12 Num 14:6, 24, 30; Deut 1:36; Josh 14:8-9
32:13 Num 14:31-39
32:15 Deut 30:17-18
32:17 Josh 4:12-13
32:18-19 Josh 13:8; 22:4
32:20 Deut 3:18
32:22 Deut 3:20; Josh 22:4
32:24 Num 30:2

32:16 A simple fold for livestock had four roughly built stone walls, high enough to keep wild animals out. Sometimes the top of the wall was lined with thorns to further discourage predators and thieves. The fold's single entrance made it easier for a shepherd to guard his flock. Often several shepherds used a single fold and took turns guarding the entrance. Mingling the animals was no problem since each flock responded readily to its own shepherd's voice. The three tribes who chose to remain east of the Jordan River wanted to build sheepfolds to protect their flocks, and cities to protect their families before the men crossed the river to help the rest of the tribes conquer the Promised Land.

32:16-19 The land on the east side of the Jordan had been conquered. The hard work was done by all of the tribes together. But the tribes of Reuben and Gad and the half-tribe of Manasseh did not stop after their land was cleared. They promised to keep working with the others until everyone's land was conquered. After others have helped you, do you make excuses to escape helping them? Finish the whole job, even those parts that may not benefit you directly.

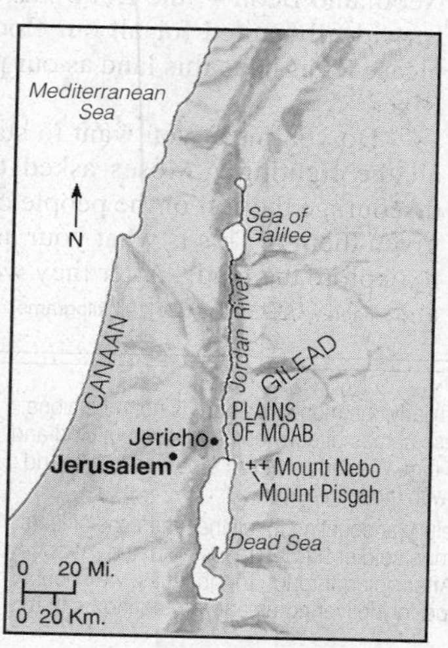

PREPARING TO ENTER THE PROMISED LAND
The Israelites had been camped in the plains of Moab, across from Jericho. From this position, they were ready to enter the Promised Land.

32 We will cross the Jordan into Canaan fully armed to fight for the LORD, but our inheritance of land will be here on this side of the Jordan."

32:33
Num 21:23-26; 34:14
Deut 3:8-17
Josh 12:1-6

33 So Moses assigned to the tribes of Gad, Reuben, and half the tribe of Manasseh son of Joseph the territory of King Sihon of the Amorites and the land of King Og of Bashan—the whole land with its towns and surrounding lands.

34 The people of Gad built the towns of Dibon, Ataroth, Aroer, 35 Atroth-shophan, Jazer, Jogbehah, 36 Beth-nimrah, and Beth-haran. These were all fortified cities with sheepfolds for their flocks.

37 The people of Reuben built the towns of Heshbon, Elealeh, Kiriathaim, 38 Nebo, Baal-meon, and Sibmah. They changed the names of some of the towns they conquered and rebuilt.

32:41
Deut 3:14
Josh 13:30
1 Chr 2:23

39 Then the descendants of Makir of the tribe of Manasseh went to Gilead and conquered it, and they drove out the Amorites, who were living there. 40 So Moses gave Gilead to the Makirites, descendants of Manasseh, and they lived there. 41 The people of Jair, another clan of the tribe of Manasseh, captured many of the towns in Gilead and changed the name of that region to the Towns of Jair.* 42 Meanwhile, a man named Nobah captured the town of Kenath and its surrounding villages, and he renamed that area Nobah after himself.

6. Camped on the plains of Moab

Remembering Israel's Journey

33 This is the itinerary the Israelites followed as they marched out of Egypt under the leadership of Moses and Aaron. 2 At the LORD's direction, Moses kept a written record of their progress. These are the stages of their march, identified by the different places they stopped along the way.

33:3
Exod 12:11-51

3 They set out from the city of Rameses on the morning after the first Passover celebration in early spring.* The people of Israel left defiantly, in full view of all the Egyptians. 4 Meanwhile, the Egyptians were burying all their firstborn sons, whom the LORD had killed the night before. The LORD had defeated the gods of Egypt that night with great acts of judgment!

33:5
Exod 13:20

5 After leaving Rameses, the Israelites set up camp at Succoth.

6 Then they left Succoth and camped at Etham on the edge of the wilderness.

33:7
Exod 14:2, 9

7 They left Etham and turned back toward Pi-hahiroth, opposite Baal-zephon, and camped near Migdol.

33:8
Exod 14:21-22

8 They left Pi-hahiroth and crossed the Red Sea* into the wilderness beyond. Then they traveled for three days into the Etham wilderness and camped at Marah.

33:9
Exod 15:27; 16:1

9 They left Marah and camped at Elim, where there are twelve springs of water and seventy palm trees.

10 They left Elim and camped beside the Red Sea.*

33:11
Exod 16:1; 17:1

11 They left the Red Sea and camped in the Sin* Desert.

12 They left the Sin Desert and camped at Dophkah.

13 They left Dophkah and camped at Alush.

33:14
Exod 17:1-8; 19:1

14 They left Alush and camped at Rephidim, where there was no water for the people to drink.

33:15
Exod 19:1

15 They left Rephidim and camped in the wilderness of Sinai.

33:16-17
Num 11:34-35

16 They left the wilderness of Sinai and camped at Kibroth-hattaavah.

17 They left Kibroth-hattaavah and camped at Hazeroth.

18 They left Hazeroth and camped at Rithmah.

32:41 Hebrew *Havvoth-jair.* **33:3** Hebrew *on the fifteenth day of the first month.* This day of the Hebrew lunar calendar occurs in late March or early April. **33:8** Hebrew *the sea.* **33:10** Hebrew *sea of reeds;* also in 33:11. **33:11** Not to be confused with the English word *sin.*

33:1ff Look at the map in the introduction to the book of Numbers to see the travels of the Israelites.

33:2 Moses recorded the Israelites' journeys as God instructed him, providing a record of their spiritual as well as geographic progress. Have you made spiritual progress lately? Recording your thoughts about God and lessons you have learned over a period of time can be a valuable aid to spiritual growth. A record of your spiritual pilgrimage will let you check up on your progress and avoid repeating past mistakes.

33:4 God "defeated the gods of Egypt" by sending the plagues. See the note on Exodus 10:22 for a further explanation.

19 They left Rithmah and camped at Rimmon-perez.
20 They left Rimmon-perez and camped at Libnah.
21 They left Libnah and camped at Rissah.
22 They left Rissah and camped at Kehelathah.
23 They left Kehelathah and camped at Mount Shepher.
24 They left Mount Shepher and camped at Haradah.
25 They left Haradah and camped at Makheloth.
26 They left Makheloth and camped at Tahath.
27 They left Tahath and camped at Terah.
28 They left Terah and camped at Mithcah.
29 They left Mithcah and camped at Hashmonah.
30 They left Hashmonah and camped at Moseroth. 33:30 Deut 10:6
31 They left Moseroth and camped at Bene-jaakan.
32 They left Bene-jaakan and camped at Hor-haggidgad.
33 They left Hor-haggidgad and camped at Jotbathah. 33:33 Deut 10:7
34 They left Jotbathah and camped at Abronah.
35 They left Abronah and camped at Ezion-geber.
36 They left Ezion-geber and camped at Kadesh in the wilderness of Zin. 33:36 Num 20:1
37 They left Kadesh and camped at Mount Hor, at the border of Edom. 38 While 33:38 Num 20:25-28
they were at the foot of Mount Hor, Aaron the priest was directed by the LORD to
go up the mountain, and there he died. This happened on a day in midsummer,*
during the fortieth year after Israel's departure from Egypt. 39 Aaron was 123 years
old when he died there on Mount Hor.
40 It was then that the Canaanite king of Arad, who lived in the Negev in the land 33:40 Num 21:1
of Canaan, heard that the people of Israel were approaching his land.
41 Meanwhile, the Israelites left Mount Hor and camped at Zalmonah.
42 Then they left Zalmonah and camped at Punon.
43 They left Punon and camped at Oboth. 33:43 Num 21:10-11
44 They left Oboth and camped at Iye-abarim on the border of Moab.
45 They left Iye-abarim* and camped at Dibon-gad.
46 They left Dibon-gad and camped at Almon-diblathaim.
47 They left Almon-diblathaim and camped in the mountains east of the river,* 33:47 Num 27:12
near Mount Nebo.
48 They left the mountains east of the river and camped on the plains of Moab 33:48 Num 22:1
beside the Jordan River, across from Jericho. 49 Along the Jordan River they
camped from Beth-jeshimoth as far as Abel-shittim on the plains of Moab. 33:49 Num 25:1
50 While they were camped near the Jordan River on the plains of Moab opposite
Jericho, the LORD said to Moses, 51 "Speak to the Israelites and tell them: 'When you
cross the Jordan River into the land of Canaan, 52 you must drive out all the people 33:52 Exod 23:24; 34:13
living there. You must destroy all their carved and molten images and demolish all Deut 7:2-5, 25-26
their pagan shrines. 53 Take possession of the land and settle in it, because I have given

33:38 Hebrew *on the first day of the fifth month.* This day of the Hebrew lunar calendar occurs in July or early August. **33:45** As in 33:44; Hebrew reads *Iyim,* another name for Iye-abarim. **33:47** Hebrew *the mountains of Abarim;* also in 33:48.

33:50-53 God told Moses that before the Israelites settled in the Promised Land they should drive out the wicked inhabitants and destroy their idols. In Colossians 3, Paul encourages us to live as Christians in the same manner: throwing away our old way of living and moving ahead into our new life of obedience to God and faith in Jesus Christ. Like the Israelites moving into the Promised Land, we can destroy the wickedness in our lives, or we can settle down and live with it. To move in and possess the new life, we must drive out the sinful thoughts and practices to make room for the new.

33:50-56 Why were the Israelites told to destroy the people living in Canaan? God had several compelling reasons for giving this command: (1) God was stamping out the wickedness of an extremely sinful group of nations. The Canaanites brought on their own punishment. Idol worship expressed their deepest evil desires. It ultimately led to the worship of Satan and the total rejection of God. (2) God was using Moses and Israel to judge Canaan for its sins in fulfillment of the prophecy in Genesis 9:25. (3) God wanted to remove all trace of pagan beliefs and practices from the land. He did not want his people to mix or compromise with idolatry in any way. The Israelites did not fully understand God's reasons, and they did not carry out his command. This eventually led them to compromise and corruption. In all areas of life, we should obey God's Word without question because we know he is just, even if we cannot fully understand his overall purposes.

33:54 Num 26:53-56 it to you to occupy. 54 You must distribute the land among the clans by sacred lot and
33:55 in proportion to their size. A larger inheritance of land will be allotted to each of the
Josh 23:13 larger clans, and a smaller inheritance will be allotted to each of the smaller clans. The
Ps 106:34-36 decision of the sacred lot is final. In this way, the land will be divided among your
ancestral tribes. 55 But if you fail to drive out the people who live in the land, those
who remain will be like splinters in your eyes and thorns in your sides. They will
harass you in the land where you live. 56 And I will do to you what I had planned to
do to them.'"

Boundaries of the Land

34:2 Gen 17:8 **34** Then the LORD said to Moses, 2 "Give these instructions to the Israelites: When
Deut 1:7-8 Ezek 47:15 you come into the land of Canaan, which I am giving you as your special
34:3 possession, these will be the boundaries. 3 The southern portion of your country will
Josh 15:1-4 extend from the wilderness of Zin, along the edge of Edom. The southern boundary will
34:4 begin on the east at the Dead Sea.* 4 It will then run south past Scorpion Pass* in the
Num 32:8 direction of Zin. Its southernmost point will be Kadesh-barnea, from which it will go to
Hazar-addar, and on to Azmon. 5 From Azmon the boundary will turn toward the brook
of Egypt and end at the Mediterranean Sea.*

34:6 Josh 15:4 6 "Your western boundary will be the coastline of the Mediterranean Sea.
34:7 7 "Your northern boundary will begin at the Mediterranean Sea and run eastward to
Ezek 47:15-17 Mount Hor, 8 then to Lebo-hamath, and on through Zedad 9 and Ziphron to Hazar-enan.
This will be your northern boundary.
34:10 10 "The eastern boundary will start at Hazar-enan and run south to Shepham, 11 then
Josh 15:5 34:11 down to Riblah on the east side of Ain. From there the boundary will run down along the
2 Kgs 23:33; 25:6 eastern edge of the Sea of Galilee,* 12 and then along the Jordan River to the Dead Sea.
Jer 52:9 These are the boundaries of your land."
34:13 13 Then Moses told the Israelites, "This is the territory you are to divide among
Josh 14:1-2 yourselves by sacred lot. The LORD commands that the land be divided up among the
34:14 nine and a half remaining tribes. 14 The families of the tribes of Reuben, Gad, and half
Num 32:33 the tribe of Manasseh have already received their inheritance of land 15 on the east side
of the Jordan River, across from Jericho."

Leaders to Divide the Land

16 And the LORD said to Moses, 17 "These are the men who are to divide the land among

34:3 Hebrew *Salt Sea;* also in 34:12. **34:4** Hebrew *the ascent of Akrabbim.* **34:5** Hebrew *the sea;* also in 34:6, 7.
34:11 Hebrew *sea of Kinnereth.*

THE BORDERS OF THE PROMISED LAND
The borders of the Promised Land stretched from the wilderness of Zin and Kadesh in the south to Lebo-hamath and Riblah in the north, and from the Mediterranean seacoast on the west to the Jordan River on the east. The land of Gilead was also included.

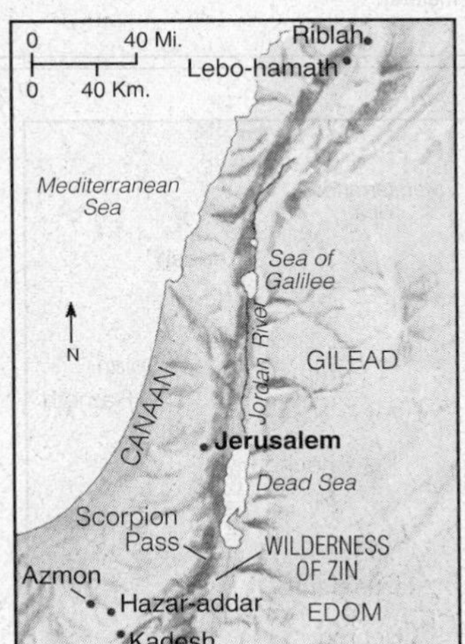

33:55 If you don't do the job right the first time, it often becomes much more difficult to accomplish. God warned that if the Israelites did not drive the wicked inhabitants out of the Promised Land, later these people would become a source of great irritation. That is exactly what happened. Just as the Israelites were hesitant to clear out all the wicked people, we are sometimes hesitant to clear out all the sin in our lives, either because we are afraid of it (as the Israelites feared the giants), or because it seems harmless and attractive (as sexual sin seemed). But Hebrews 12:1 tells us to throw off "the sin that so easily hinders our progress." We all have "idols" we don't want to let go of (a bad habit, an unhealthy relationship, a certain life-style). If we allow these idols to dominate us, they will cause serious problems later.

34:1ff The land was given by God as an inheritance; no tribe was to claim its own land. The boundaries declared by God are larger than the area actually occupied by the Hebrews. The boundaries correspond more to the land conquered by David and to the ideal territory portrayed by Ezekiel (Ezekiel 47–48). The size of the land portrays God's generosity. He always gives us more than we could ask or think.

34:16-29 In God's plan for settling the land, he (1) explained what to do, (2) communicated this clearly to Moses, and (3) assigned specific people to oversee the apportionment of the land. No plan is complete until each job is assigned and everyone understands his or her responsibilities. When you have a job to do, determine what must be done, give clear instructions, and put people in charge of each part.

the people: Eleazar the priest and Joshua son of Nun. [18]Also enlist one leader from each **34:18** Num 1:4, 16
tribe to help them with the task. [19]These are the tribes and the names of the leaders:

	Tribe	*Leader*
	Judah	Caleb son of Jephunneh
20	Simeon	Shemuel son of Ammihud
21	Benjamin	Elidad son of Kislon
22	Dan	Bukki son of Jogli
23	Manasseh son of Joseph	Hanniel son of Ephod
24	Ephraim son of Joseph	Kemuel son of Shiphtan
25	Zebulun	Elizaphan son of Parnach
26	Issachar	Paltiel son of Azzan
27	Asher	Ahihud son of Shelomi
28	Naphtali	Pedahel son of Ammihud

[29]These are the men the LORD has appointed to oversee the dividing of the land of
Canaan among the Israelites."

Towns for the Levites

35 While Israel was camped beside the Jordan on the plains of Moab, across from **35:2**
Jericho, the LORD said to Moses, [2]"Instruct the people of Israel to give to the Lev 25:32-34 Josh 14:3-4
Levites from their property certain towns to live in, along with the surrounding
pasturelands. [3]These towns will be their homes, and the surrounding lands will
provide pasture for their cattle, flocks, and other livestock. [4]The pastureland assigned
to the Levites around these towns will extend 1,500 feet* from the town walls in every
direction. [5]Measure off 3,000 feet* outside the town walls in every direction—east,
south, west, north—with the town at the center. This area will serve as the larger
pastureland for the towns. **35:6**
[6]"You must give the Levites six cities of refuge, where a person who has acciden- Josh 20:2-9; 21:3, 13, 21-38
tally killed someone can flee for safety. In addition, give them forty-two other towns. **35:7**
[7]In all, forty-eight towns with the surrounding pastureland will be given to the Josh 21:3-42
Levites. [8]These towns will come from the property of the people of Israel. The larger **35:8** Num 26:54
tribes will give more towns to the Levites, while the smaller tribes will give fewer.
Each tribe will give in proportion to its inheritance."

Cities of Refuge

[9]And the LORD said to Moses, [10]"Say this to the people of Israel: 'When you cross

35:4 Hebrew *1,000 cubits* [450 meters]. **35:5** Hebrew *2,000 cubits* [900 meters].

35:2, 3 The Levites were ministers. They were supported by the tithes of the people who gave them homes, flocks, and pasturelands. Likewise, we are responsible to provide for the needs of our ministers and missionaries so they can be free to do their God-ordained work.

35:6 Of the 48 cities given to the Levites, six were cities of refuge. These six cities were probably put under the Levites' supervision because they would be the most impartial judges. Such cities were needed because the ancient customs of justice called for revenge in the event of the death of a relative or loved one (2 Samuel 14:7). The Levites would hold a preliminary hearing outside the gates while the accused person was kept in the city until the time of his trial. If the killing was judged accidental, the person would stay in the city until the death of the high priest. At that time, he would be allowed to go free, and he could start a new life without worrying about avengers. If it was not accidental, the person would be delivered to the slain person's avengers. This system of justice shows how God's law and his mercy go hand in hand.

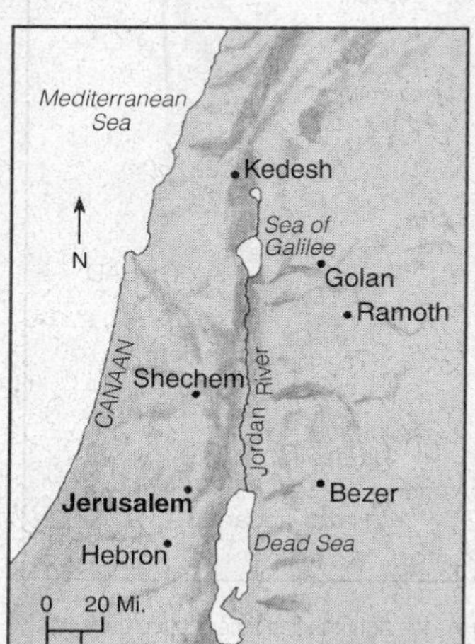

CITIES OF REFUGE
Six of the Levites' cities were designated as cities of refuge. They were spaced throughout the land and protected those who had accidentally committed a crime or who were awaiting trial.

35:11 Num 35:22-25
35:12 Josh 20:3

the Jordan into the land of Canaan, [11]designate cities of refuge for people to flee to if they have killed someone accidentally. [12]These cities will be places of protection from a dead person's relatives who want to avenge the death. The slayer must not be killed before being tried by the community. [13]Designate six cities of refuge for yourselves, [14]three on the east side of the Jordan River and three on the west in the land of Canaan. [15]These cities are for the protection of Israelites, resident foreigners, and traveling merchants. Anyone who accidentally kills someone may flee there for safety.

35:16 Exod 21:12-14 Lev 24:17

[16]"'But if someone strikes and kills another person with a piece of iron, it must be presumed to be murder, and the murderer must be executed. [17]Or if someone strikes and kills another person with a large stone, it is murder, and the murderer must be executed. [18]The same is true if someone strikes and kills another person with a wooden weapon. It must be presumed to be murder, and the murderer must be executed. [19]The victim's nearest relative is responsible for putting the murderer to death. When they meet, the avenger must execute the murderer. [20]So if in premeditated hostility someone pushes another person or throws a dangerous object and the person dies, it is murder. [21]Or if someone angrily hits another person with a fist and the person dies, it is murder. In such cases, the victim's nearest relative must execute the murderer when they meet.

[22]"'But suppose someone pushes another person without premeditated hostility, or throws something that unintentionally hits another person, [23]or accidentally drops a stone on someone, though they were not enemies, and the person dies. [24]If this should happen, the assembly must follow these regulations in making a judgment between the

PRIESTS IN ISRAEL'S HISTORY

Numbers 35:25–28 mentions the death of a high priest. Each new high priest had to come from the lineage of Aaron. Listed here are the ones whose stories are told elsewhere in the Bible.

Priest	*Importance*	*Reference*
Aaron	Moses' brother and first priest	Exodus 28:1–3
Eleazar	Watched two of his brothers die in a fire from God because they did not follow God's instructions. He obeyed God and became chief leader of the Tabernacle.	Leviticus 10 Numbers 3:32
Phinehas	Executed a young Israelite idol worshiper and his Midianite mistress to end a plague. He was then promised that his priestly line would never end.	Numbers 25:1–15
Ahitub	A priest during King Saul's reign	1 Samuel 14:3
Zadok	A faithful high priest under King David. He and Nathan anointed Solomon as the next king.	2 Samuel 8:17 1 Kings 1:38, 39
Ahimaaz	Carried the message of Absalom's death to King David but was apparently afraid to tell about it.	2 Samuel 18:19–29
Azariah	High priest under King Solomon	1 Kings 4:2
Azariah	High priest under Uzziah. He rebuked the king for burning incense himself.	2 Chronicles 26:17–21
	When Hezekiah became king, he reopened the Temple. Azariah again served as high priest.	2 Chronicles 26:17–21
Amariah	King Jehoshaphat appointed him to judge religious disputes.	2 Chronicles 19:11
Hilkiah	Found the Book of the Law during Josiah's reign	2 Kings 22:3–13 2 Chronicles 34:14–21
Azariah	Probably one of the first to return to Israel from Babylon	1 Chronicles 9:10, 11
Seraiah	The father of Ezra	Ezra 7:1–5

35:11-28 If anyone died because of violence, murder was assumed, but the murder suspect was not automatically assumed guilty. The cities of refuge assured the accused that justice would be served. But if that person left the city, then he or she would be assumed guilty and able to be killed by the avenging party. The people were to be intolerant of the sin yet impartial to the accused so as to have a fair trial. The cities of refuge represented God's concern for justice in a culture that did not always protect the innocent. It is unjust both to overlook wrongdoing and to jump to conclusions about guilt. When someone is accused of wrongdoing, stand up for justice, protect those not yet proven guilty, and listen carefully to all sides of the story.

slayer and the avenger, the victim's nearest relative. 25 They must protect the slayer from
the avenger, and they must send the slayer back to live in a city of refuge until the death
of the high priest.
26 "'But if the slayer leaves the city of refuge, 27 and the victim's nearest relative finds
him outside the city limits and kills him, it will not be considered murder. 28 The slayer
should have stayed inside the city of refuge until the death of the high priest. But after the
death of the high priest, the slayer may return to his own property. 29 These are permanent
laws for you to observe from generation to generation, wherever you may live.
30 "'All murderers must be executed, but only if there is more than one witness. No one
may be put to death on the testimony of only one witness. 31 Also, you must never accept a
ransom payment for the life of someone judged guilty of murder and subject to execution;
murderers must always be put to death. 32 And never accept a ransom payment from
someone who has fled to a city of refuge, allowing the slayer to return to his property before
the death of the high priest. 33 This will ensure that the land where you live will not be
polluted, for murder pollutes the land. And no atonement can be made for murder except
by the execution of the murderer. 34 You must not defile the land where you are going to
live, for I live there myself. I am the LORD, who lives among the people of Israel.'"

35:30 Deut 17:6-7; 19:15 Matt 18:16 2 Cor 13:1 Heb 10:28

35:34 Lev 18:25

Women Who Inherit Property

36 Then the heads of the clan of Gilead—descendants of Makir, son of Manasseh, son
of Joseph—came to Moses and the family leaders of Israel with a petition. 2 They
said, "Sir, the LORD instructed you to divide the land by sacred lot among the people of
Israel. You were told by the LORD to give the inheritance of our brother Zelophehad to his
daughters. 3 But if any of them marries a man from another tribe, their inheritance of land
will go with them to the tribe into which they marry. In this way, the total area of our tribal
land will be reduced. 4 Then when the Year of Jubilee comes, their inheritance of land will
be added to that of the new tribe, causing it to be lost forever to our ancestral tribe."
5 So Moses gave the Israelites this command from the LORD: "The men of the tribe of
Joseph are right. 6 This is what the LORD commands concerning the daughters of Zelophehad: Let them marry anyone they like, as long as it is within their own ancestral tribe. 7 None
of the inherited land may pass from tribe to tribe, for the inheritance of every tribe must
remain fixed as it was first allotted. 8 The daughters throughout the tribes of Israel who are
in line to inherit property must marry within their tribe, so that all the Israelites will keep
their ancestral property. 9 No inheritance may pass from one tribe to another; each tribe of
Israel must hold on to its allotted inheritance of land."
10 The daughters of Zelophehad did as the LORD commanded Moses. 11 Mahlah, Tirzah,
Hoglah, Milcah, and Noah all married cousins on their father's side. 12 They married into
the clans of Manasseh son of Joseph. Thus, their inheritance of land remained within their
ancestral tribe.
13 These are the commands and regulations that the LORD gave to the people of Israel
through Moses while they were camped on the plains of Moab beside the Jordan River,
across from Jericho.

36:1-2 Num 27:1-11

36:8 1 Chr 23:22

36:11 Num 26:33; 27:1

36:13 Lev 7:37; 27:34

36:1-9 Zelophehad had five daughters but no sons. After he died, his daughters appealed to Moses. Because the inheritance normally passed only through the male line, the family line of Zelophehad would have disappeared. God told Moses that if a man died without sons, then the inheritance would go to his daughters (27:8). But the question of marriage arose. If the daughters were to marry outside of their tribe, the land would belong to another tribe at the Year of Jubilee. So Moses commanded that in such cases the women should marry men in their own clan and tribe so that each tribe would retain its original inheritance. Later, when the tribes received their land under Joshua, the daughters of Zelophehad received their inheritance as God had instructed (Joshua 17:3-6).

We don't have to look far to find those who want to be considered "special cases" and "exceptions to the rule," but wise leaders will sort out those who have legitimate concerns and make sure that justice is done in these special situations.

36:13 The book of Numbers covers 39 years and closes with the Israelites poised near the banks of the Jordan River with the Promised Land in sight. The wanderings in the wilderness have come to an end, and the people are preparing for their next big move—the conquest of the land. The apostle Paul says that the events described in Numbers are examples that warn us and help us avoid the Israelites' mistakes (1 Corinthians 10:1-12). From their experiences we learn that unbelief is disastrous. We also learn not to long for the sinful pleasures of the past, to avoid complaining, and to stay away from all forms of compromise. If we choose to let God lead our lives, we should not ignore his message in the book of Numbers.

EIGHT WORDS FOR LAW
Hebrew law served as the personal and national guide for living under God's authority. It directed the moral, spiritual, and social life. Its purpose was to produce better understanding of God and greater commitment to him.

Word	*Meaning*	*Examples*	*Significance*
Torah	Direction, Guidance, Instruction	Exodus 24:12	Need for law in general; a command from a higher person to a lower
Mitswah	Commandment, Command	Genesis 26:5; Exodus 15:26; 20:2-17	God's specific instruction to be obeyed rather than a general law; used of the Ten Commandments
Mishpat	Regulations, Judgment, Ordinance	Genesis 18:19; Deuteronomy 16:18; 17:9	Refers to the civil, social, and sanitation laws
Eduth	Testimony, Truth	Exodus 25:22	Refers to God's law as he deals with his people
Huqqim	Statutes, Laws	Leviticus 18:4; Deuteronomy 4:1	Dealt with the royal pronouncements; mainly connected to worship and feasts
Piqqudim	Orders, Commandments	Psalms 19:8; 103:18	Used often in the psalms to describe God's orders and assignments
Dabar	Word, Terms	Exodus 34:28; Deuteronomy 4:13	Used to indicate divine oracles or revelations of God
Dath	Royal Edict, Public Law	Ezekiel 7:26; Daniel 6:8, 12	Refers to a public law or Jewish religious tradition

DEUTERONOMY

Joseph dies 1805 B.C. (1640 B.C.)	S L A V E R Y I N E G Y P T	Exodus from Egypt 1446 (1280)	Ten Commandments given 1445 (1279)
		WILDERNESS WANDERINGS	

VITAL STATISTICS

PURPOSE:
To remind the people of what God had done and encourage them to rededicate their lives to him

AUTHOR:
Moses (except for the final summary, which was probably written by Joshua after Moses' death)

TO WHOM WRITTEN:
Israel (the new generation entering the Promised Land)

DATE WRITTEN:
About 1407/6 B.C.

SETTING:
The east side of the Jordan River, in view of Canaan

KEY VERSE:
"Understand, therefore, that the LORD your God is indeed God. He is the faithful God who keeps his covenant for a thousand generations and constantly loves those who love him and obey his commands" (7:9).

KEY PEOPLE:
Moses, Joshua

KEY PLACE:
The Arabah in Moab

CLASS reunions, scrapbooks and photo albums, familiar songs, and old neighborhoods—like long-time friends they awaken our memories and stir our emotions. The past is a kaleidoscope of promises, failures, victories, and embarrassments. Sometimes we want to forget memories that are too painful. However, as the years pass, remembrances of unpleasant events usually fade into our subconscious. But there is a time to remember: Mistakes should not be repeated; commitments made must be fulfilled; and the memory of special events can encourage us and move us to action.

The book of Deuteronomy is written in the form of a treaty between a king and his vassal state typical of the second millenium B.C. It calls Israel to remember who God is and what he has done. Lacking faith, the old generation had wandered for 40 years and died in the wilderness. They left Egypt behind, but never knew the Promised Land. Then on the east bank of the Jordan River, Moses prepared the sons and daughters of that faithless generation to possess the land. After a brief history lesson emphasizing God's great acts on behalf of his people, Moses reviewed the law. Then he restated the covenant—God's contract with his people.

The lessons are clear. Because of what God has done, Israel should have hope and follow him; because of what he expects, they should listen and obey; because of who he is, they should love him completely. Learning these lessons will prepare them to possess the Promised Land.

As you hear the message of Deuteronomy, remember how God has expressed his kindness in your life, and then commit yourself anew to trust, love, and obey him.

THE BLUEPRINT

A. WHAT GOD HAS DONE FOR US: MOSES' FIRST ADDRESS (1:1—4:43)

Moses reviewed the mighty acts of God for the nation of Israel. Remembering God's special involvement in our lives gives us hope and encouragement for the future.

B. PRINCIPLES FOR GODLY LIVING: MOSES' SECOND ADDRESS (4:44—29:1)

1. The Ten Commandments
2. Love the Lord your God
3. Laws for proper worship
4. Laws for ruling the nation
5. Laws for human relationships
6. Consequences of obedience and disobedience

Obeying God's laws brought blessings to the Israelites and disobeying brought misfortune. This was part of the written agreement God made with his people. Although we are not part of this covenant, the principle holds true: Obedience and disobedience carry inevitable consequences in this life and the next.

Moses' death; Israelites enter Canaan 1406 (1240)	*Judges begin to rule 1375 (1220)*	*United kingdom under Saul 1050 (1045)*

C. A CALL FOR COMMITMENT TO GOD: MOSES' THIRD ADDRESS (29:2—30:20)

Moses called the people to commitment. God still calls us to be committed to love him with all our heart, soul, mind, and strength.

D. THE CHANGE IN LEADERSHIP: MOSES' LAST DAYS (31:1—34:12)

Although Moses made some serious mistakes, he had lived uprightly and carried out God's commands. Moses died with integrity. We too may make some serious mistakes, but that should not stop us from living with integrity and godly commitment.

MEGATHEMES

THEME	EXPLANATION	IMPORTANCE
History	Moses reviewed the mighty acts of God whereby he liberated Israel from slavery in Egypt. He recounted how God had helped them and how the people had disobeyed.	By reviewing God's promises and mighty acts in history, we can learn about his character. We come to know God more intimately through understanding how he has acted in the past. We can also avoid mistakes in our own lives through learning from Israel's past failures.
Laws	God reviewed his laws for the people. The legal contract between God and his people had to be renewed by the new generation about to enter the Promised Land.	Commitment to God and his truth cannot be taken for granted. Each generation and each person must respond afresh to God's call for obedience.
Love	God's faithful and patient love is portrayed more often than his punishment. God shows his love by being faithful to his people and his promises. In response, God desires love from the heart, not merely a legalistic keeping of his law.	God's love forms the foundation for our trust in him. We trust him because he loves us. Because God loves us, we should maintain justice and respect.
Choices	God reminded his people that in order to ratify his agreement, they must choose the path of obedience. A personal decision to obey would bring benefits to their lives; rebellion would bring severe calamity.	Our choices make a difference. Choosing to follow God benefits us and improves our relationships with others. Choosing to abandon God's ways brings harm to ourselves and others.
Teaching	God commanded the Israelites to teach their children his ways. They were to use ritual, instruction, and memorization to make sure their children understood God's principles and passed them on to the next generation.	Quality teaching for our children must be a priority. It is important to pass on God's truth to future generations in our traditions. But God desires that his truth be in our hearts and minds and not merely in our traditions.

A. WHAT GOD HAS DONE FOR US: MOSES' FIRST ADDRESS (1:1—4:43)

God has led his people out of Egypt and across the great wilderness. Now they stand ready to enter the Promised Land. But before the Israelites go into the land, Moses has some important advice to give them. He delivers his advice in three parts. In the first part, Moses reviews the history of God's previous care for the people of Israel. Through God's actions in the past, we can learn about the God we serve today.

The Command to Leave Sinai

1 This book records the words that Moses spoke to all the people of Israel while they **1:1** Deut 2:8, 24; 3:3;
were in the wilderness east of the Jordan River. They were camped in the Jordan 4:1, 44-46
Valley* near Suph, between Paran on one side and Tophel, Laban, Hazeroth, and
Di-zahab on the other. [2]Normally it takes only eleven days to travel from Mount Sinai*
to Kadesh-barnea, going by way of Mount Seir. [3]But forty years after the Israelites left
Mount Sinai, on a day in midwinter,* Moses gave these speeches to the Israelites, telling
them everything the LORD had commanded him to say. [4]This was after he had defeated **1:4** Num 21:24, 33
King Sihon of the Amorites, who had ruled in Heshbon, and King Og of Bashan, who
had ruled in Ashtaroth and Edrei.

[5]So Moses addressed the people of Israel while they were in the land of Moab east of
the Jordan River. He began to explain the law as follows: [6]"When we were at Mount **1:6** Num 10:11-13
Sinai, the LORD our God said to us, 'You have stayed at this mountain long enough. [7]It **1:7**
is time to break camp and move on. Go to the hill country of the Amorites and to all the Gen 15:18-21
neighboring regions—the Jordan Valley, the hill country, the western foothills,* the Josh 10:5, 40
Negev, and the coastal plain. Go to the land of the Canaanites and to Lebanon, and all
the way to the great Euphrates River. [8]I am giving all this land to you! Go in and occupy **1:8**
it, for it is the land the LORD swore to give to your ancestors Abraham, Isaac, and Jacob, Gen 12:7; 26:3
and to all their descendants.' Exod 33:1 Num 32:10-11

Moses Appoints Leaders from Each Tribe

[9]"At that time I told you, 'You are too great a burden for me to carry all by myself. [10]The **1:9** Exod 18:18, 24

1:1 Hebrew *the Arabah;* also in 1:7. **1:2** Hebrew *Horeb,* another name for Sinai; also in 1:6, 19. **1:3** Hebrew *on the first day of the eleventh month.* This day of the Hebrew lunar calendar occurs in January or early February.
1:7 Hebrew *the Shephelah.*

1:1, 2 The Israelites spent 40 years on a journey that should have lasted 11 days. It wasn't distance that stood between them and the Promised Land. It was the condition of their hearts. God's purpose went deeper than simply transporting a huge group of people to a new land. He was preparing them to live in obedience to him once they arrived. What good was the Promised Land if the Israelites were just as wicked as the nations already living there? The journey was a painful but necessary part of their preparation. Through it God taught the Israelites who he was: the living God, the Leader of their nation. He also taught them who they were: people who were fallen, sinful, prone to rebellion and doubt. He gave his rebellious people the law to help them understand how to relate to God and to other people. Your spiritual pilgrimage may be lengthy, and you may face pain, discouragement, and difficulties. But remember that God isn't just trying to keep you alive. He wants to prepare you to live in service and devotion to him.

1:1-5 The 40 years of wilderness wandering come to an end in this book. The events of Deuteronomy cover only a week or two of the 11th month of the 40th year (1:3). The 12th and last month was spent in mourning for Moses (34:8). Then the Israelites entered the Promised Land the first month of the 41st year after the Exodus (Joshua 4:19).

1:6, 7 Notice that Moses' summary of Israel's 40-year journey begins at Mount Sinai, not in Egypt. Why did Moses leave out the first part of the Exodus? Moses was not giving an itinerary—he was summarizing the nation's development. In Moses' mind the nation of Israel began at the base of Mount Sinai, not in Egypt, for it was at Mount Sinai that God gave his covenant to the people (Exodus 19, 20). Along with this covenant came knowledge and responsibility. After the people chose to follow God (and it was their choice), they had to know *how* to follow him. Therefore, God gave them a comprehensive set of laws and guidelines that stated how he wanted them to live (these are found in the books of Exodus, Leviticus, and Numbers). The people could no longer say they didn't know the difference between right and wrong. Now that the people had promised to follow God and knew how to follow him, they had a responsibility to do it. When God tells you to break camp and move out to face a challenge he gives you, will you be ready to obey?

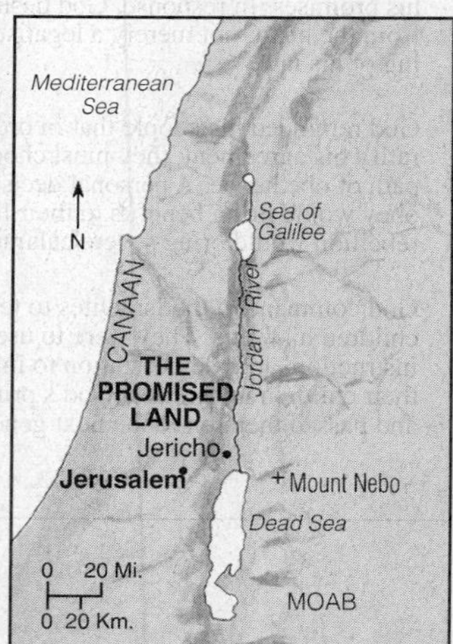

EVENTS IN DEUTERONOMY The book of Deuteronomy opens with Israel camped east of the Jordan River in the land of Moab. Just before the people crossed the river into the Promised Land, Moses delivered an inspirational speech indicating how they were to live.

1:9-13 It was a tremendous burden for Moses to lead the nation by himself. He could not accomplish the task single-handedly.

1:10 Gen 15:5; 22:17; Deut 10:22; 26:5; 28:62
1:11 Deut 1:8, 10
1:12 Exod 18:13-14
1:13 Exod 18:21-22; Num 11:16-17
1:16 Deut 16:18
1:17 Exod 18:25-26; Deut 10:17; 16:19; 24:17; Prov 24:23; Jas 2:1, 9
1:19 Deut 1:2; 8:15; 32:10
1:22-23 Num 13:1-3
1:24 Num 13:21-25
1:26 Num 14:1-3
1:27 Deut 9:28; Ps 106:25
1:28 Num 13:28, 33; Deut 9:1-2
1:29 Deut 3:22; 7:18
1:30 Exod 14:14; Deut 20:4
1:31 Deut 32:11; Acts 13:18

LORD your God has made you as numerous as the stars! 11 And may the LORD, the God
of your ancestors, multiply you a thousand times more and bless you as he promised!
12 But how can I settle all your quarrels and problems by myself? 13 Choose some men
from each tribe who have wisdom, understanding, and a good reputation, and I will
appoint them as your leaders.'

14 "You agreed that my plan was a good one. 15 So I took the wise and respected men
you had selected from your tribes and appointed them to serve as judges and officials
over you. Some were responsible for a thousand people, some for a hundred, some for
fifty, and some for ten. 16 I instructed the judges, 'You must be perfectly fair at all times,
not only to fellow Israelites, but also to the foreigners living among you. 17 When you
make decisions, never favor those who are rich; be fair to lowly and great alike. Don't
be afraid of how they will react, for you are judging in the place of God. Bring me any
cases that are too difficult for you, and I will handle them.' 18 And at that time I gave you
instructions about everything you were to do.

Scouts Explore the Land

19 "Then, just as the LORD our God directed us, we left Mount Sinai and traveled through
the great and terrifying wilderness, which you yourselves saw, and headed toward the
hill country of the Amorites. When we arrived at Kadesh-barnea, 20 I said to you, 'You
have now reached the land that the LORD our God is giving us. 21 Look! He has placed it
in front of you. Go and occupy it as the LORD, the God of your ancestors, has promised
you. Don't be afraid! Don't be discouraged!'

22 "But you responded, 'First, let's send out scouts to explore the land for us. They will
advise us on the best route to take and decide which towns we should capture.' 23 This
seemed like a good idea to me, so I chose twelve scouts, one from each of your tribes.
24 They crossed into the hills and came to the valley of Eshcol and explored it. 25 They
picked some of its fruit and brought it back to us. And they reported that the land the
LORD our God had given us was indeed a good land.

Israel Rebels against the LORD

26 "But you rebelled against the command of the LORD your God and refused to go in.
27 You murmured and complained in your tents and said, 'The LORD must hate us,
bringing us here from Egypt to be slaughtered by these Amorites. 28 How can we go on?
Our scouts have demoralized us with their report. They say that the people of the land
are taller and more powerful than we are, and that the walls of their towns rise high into
the sky! They have even seen giants there—the descendants of Anak!'

29 "But I said to you, 'Don't be afraid! 30 The LORD your God is going before you. He
will fight for you, just as you saw him do in Egypt. 31 And you saw how the LORD your
God cared for you again and again here in the wilderness, just as a father cares for his

---

Like nations, as organizations and churches grow, they become increasingly complex. Conflicting needs and quarrels arise. No longer can one leader make all the decisions. Like Moses, you may have a natural tendency to try to do all the work alone. You may be afraid or embarrassed to ask for help. Moses made a wise decision to share the leadership with others. Rather than trying to handle larger responsibilities alone, look for ways of sharing the load so that others may exercise their God-given gifts and abilities.

1:13-18 Moses identified some of the inner qualities of good leaders: (1) wisdom, (2) experience, and (3) understanding. These characteristics differ markedly from the ones that often help elect leaders today: good looks, wealth, popularity, willingness to do anything to get to the top. The qualities Moses identified should be evident in us as we lead, and we should look for them in those we elect to positions of leadership.

1:22 The scouts were sent into the land to determine not *whether* they should enter, but *where* they should enter. Upon returning, however, most of the scouts concluded that the land was not worth the obstacles. God would give the Israelites the power to conquer the land, but they were afraid of the risk and decided not to enter. God gives us the power to overcome our obstacles, but like the Israelites filled with fear and skepticism, we often let difficulties control our lives. Following God regardless of the difficulties is the way to have courageous, overcoming faith.

1:23-40 Moses retold the story of the scouting mission into the Promised Land (Numbers 13–14). When the scouts returned with reports of giants and walled cities, the people were afraid to move ahead and began to complain about their predicament. But the minority report of Joshua and Caleb pointed out that the land was fertile, the enemy was vulnerable, and God was on their side. We become fearful and immobile when we focus on the negative aspects of a situation. How much better it is to focus on the positive—God's direction and promises. When you are confronted with an important decision and know what you should do, move out in faith. Focus on the positives while trusting God to overcome the negatives. Problems don't have to rob you of the victory.

1:28 Canaan was a land with giants and imposing fortresses. The "descendants of Anak" may have been seven to nine feet tall. Many of the land's fortified cities had walls as high as 30 feet. The Israelites' fear was understandable but not justified, for the all-powerful God had already promised them victory.

child. Now he has brought you to this place.' [32]But even after all he did, you refused to
trust the LORD your God, [33]who goes before you looking for the best places to camp, 1:33 Exod 13:21
guiding you by a pillar of fire at night and a pillar of cloud by day. Num 9:15-23; 10:33-36
[34]"When the LORD heard your complaining, he became very angry. So he solemnly 1:34
swore, [35]'Not one of you from this entire wicked generation will live to see the good Num 14:23; 32:14
land I swore to give your ancestors, [36]except Caleb son of Jephunneh. He will see this 1:36 Num 14:24
land because he has followed the LORD completely. I will give to him and his descendants Josh 14:6
some of the land he walked over during his scouting mission.'
[37]"And the LORD was also angry with me because of you. He said to me, 'You will 1:37 Num 20:12; 27:18
never enter the Promised Land! [38]Instead, your assistant, Joshua son of Nun, will lead 1:38
the people into the land. Encourage him as he prepares to enter it. [39]I will give the land Num 34:16-28
to your innocent children. You were afraid they would be captured, but they will be the Deut 3:28; 31:7
ones who occupy it. [40]As for you, turn around now and go on back through the 1:39 Num 14:3, 31
wilderness toward the Red Sea.*' 1:40 Num 14:25
[41]"Then you confessed, 'We have sinned against the LORD! We will go into the land
and fight for it, as the LORD our God has told us.' So your men strapped on their weapons, 1:41 Num 14:40
thinking it would be easy to conquer the hill country.
[42]"But the LORD said to me, 'Tell them not to attack, for I will not go with them. If 1:42 Num 14:41-43
they do, they will be crushed by their enemies.' [43]This is what I told you, but you would 1:43
not listen. Instead, you again rebelled against the LORD's command and arrogantly went Num 14:44
into the hill country to fight. [44]But the Amorites who lived there came out against you 1:44 Num 14:45
like a swarm of bees. They chased and battered you all the way from Seir to Hormah.
[45]Then you returned and wept before the LORD, but he refused to listen. [46]So you stayed
there at Kadesh for a long time.

Remembering Israel's Wanderings

2 "Then we turned around and set out across the wilderness toward the Red Sea,* just 2:1 Num 21:4
as the LORD had instructed me, and we wandered around Mount Seir for a long time.
[2]Then at last the LORD said to me, [3]'You have been wandering around in this hill country
long enough; turn northward. [4]Give these orders to the people: "You will be passing 2:4
through the country belonging to your relatives the Edomites, the descendants of Esau, Exod 15:15 Num 20:14
who live in Seir. The Edomites will feel threatened, so be careful. [5]Don't bother them, 2:5
for I have given them all the hill country around Mount Seir as their property, and I will Deut 23:7
not give you any of their land. [6]Pay them for whatever food or water you use. [7]The LORD Josh 24:4
your God has blessed everything you have done and has watched your every step through 2:7 Deut 8:2; 29:5
this great wilderness. During these forty years, the LORD your God has been with you
and provided for your every need so that you lacked nothing."' [8]So we went past our 2:8
relatives, the descendants of Esau, who live in Seir, and avoided the road through the Num 20:20
Arabah Valley that comes up from Elath and Ezion-geber.
"Then as we traveled northward along the desert route through Moab, [9]the LORD 2:9 Gen 19:37
warned us, 'Do not bother the Moabites, the descendants of Lot, or start a war with them. Deut 2:18, 29
I have given them Ar as their property, and I will not give you any of their land.'"
[10](A numerous and powerful race of giants called the Emites had once lived in the 2:10
area of Ar. They were as tall as the Anakites, another race of giants. [11]Both the Emites Gen 14:5
and the Anakites are often referred to as the Rephaites, but the Moabites called them Num 13:22, 33
Emites. [12]In earlier times the Horites had lived at Mount Seir, but they were driven out 2:12 Gen 14:6
and displaced by the descendants of Esau. In a similar way the peoples in Canaan were Num 21:25, 35
driven from the land that the LORD had assigned to Israel.) Deut 2:22
[13]Moses continued, "Then the LORD told us to cross Zered Brook, and we did.

1:40 Hebrew *sea of reeds.* **2:1** Hebrew *sea of reeds.*

2:4-6 When the Israelites passed through Seir, God advised them to be careful. The Israelites were known as warriors, and the descendants of Esau—the Edomites—would be understandably nervous as the great crowd passed through their land. God warned the Israelites not to start a fight, to respect the Edomites' territory, and to pay for whatever they used. God wanted the Israelites to deal justly with these neighbors. We must also act justly in dealing with others. Recognize the rights of others, even your opponents. By behaving wisely and justly you may be able to establish or restore a relationship.

2:11 Both Moab and Ammon had removed a tall Anakim-like people usually known as the Rephaites, but called Emites by the Moabites and Zamzummites by the Ammonites (2:20). If our enemies seem overwhelming, we must remember that God can deliver us as he did the Israelites.

14 So thirty-eight years passed from the time we first arrived at Kadesh-barnea until
we finally crossed Zered Brook! For the LORD had vowed that this could not happen
until all the men old enough to fight in battle had died in the wilderness. 15 The LORD
had lifted his hand against them until all of them had finally died.
16 "When all the men of fighting age had died, 17 the LORD said to me, 18 'Today you
will cross the border of Moab at Ar 19 and enter the land of Ammon. But do not bother
the Ammonites, the descendants of Lot, or start a war with them. I have given the land
of Ammon to them as their property, and I will not give you any of their land.'"
20 (That area, too, was once considered the land of the Rephaites, though the Ammonites referred to them as Zamzummites. 21 They were a numerous and powerful race, as
tall as the Anakites. But the LORD destroyed them so the Ammonites could occupy their
land. 22 He had similarly helped the descendants of Esau at Mount Seir, for he destroyed
the Horites so they could settle there in their place. The descendants of Esau live there
to this day. 23 A similar thing happened when the Caphtorites from Crete* invaded and
destroyed the Avvites, who had lived in villages in the area of Gaza.)
24 Moses continued, "Then the LORD said, 'Now cross the Arnon Gorge! Look, I will help
you defeat Sihon the Amorite, king of Heshbon, and I will give you his land. Attack him
and begin to occupy the land. 25 Beginning today I will make all people throughout the earth
terrified of you. When they hear reports about you, they will tremble with dread and fear.'

Victory over Sihon of Heshbon

26 "Then from the wilderness of Kedemoth I sent ambassadors to King Sihon of Heshbon
with this proposal of peace: 27 'Let us pass through your land. We will stay on the main
road and won't turn off into the fields on either side. 28 We will pay for every bite of food
we eat and all the water we drink. All we want is permission to pass through your land.
29 The descendants of Esau at Mount Seir allowed us to go through their country, and so
did the Moabites, who live in Ar. Let us pass through until we cross the Jordan into the
land the LORD our God has given us.' 30 But King Sihon refused to allow you to pass
through, because the LORD your God made Sihon stubborn and defiant so he could help
you defeat them, as he has now done.
31 "Then the LORD said to me, 'Look, I have begun to hand King Sihon and his land
over to you. Begin now to conquer and occupy his land.' 32 Then King Sihon declared
war on us and mobilized his forces at Jahaz. 33 But the LORD our God handed him over
to us, and we crushed him, his sons, and all his people. 34 We conquered all his towns and
completely destroyed* everyone—men, women, and children. Not a single person was
spared. 35 We took all the livestock as plunder for ourselves, along with anything of value
from the towns we ransacked.
36 "The LORD our God helped us conquer Aroer on the edge of the Arnon Gorge, the town
in the gorge, and the whole area as far as Gilead. No town had walls too strong for us.
37 However, we stayed away from the Ammonites along the Jabbok River and the towns in
the hill country—all the places the LORD our God had commanded us to leave alone.

Victory over Og of Bashan

3 "Next we headed for the land of Bashan, where King Og and his army attacked us
at Edrei. 2 But the LORD told me, 'Do not be afraid of him, for I have given you
victory over Og and his army, giving you his entire land. Treat him just as you treated

2:14 Num 14:29-35; 26:64-65; Deut 2:7; 1 Cor 10:5
2:15 Ps 106:26; Jude 1:5
2:18 Num 21:15; Deut 2:9
2:20 Deut 2:11
2:23 Gen 10:13-14; 1 Chr 1:11-12; Jer 47:4; Amos 9:7
2:24 Num 21:13; Judg 11:18
2:25 Exod 15:14-16; 23:27; Deut 11:25; Josh 2:9
2:26 Num 21:21; Deut 20:10; Judg 11:19
2:29 Deut 2:8-9; 23:3
2:30 Exod 4:21; Num 21:23; Josh 11:20
2:33 Num 21:24-30; Deut 3:6; 29:7
2:35 Deut 3:7, 10
2:36 Ps 44:3
2:37 Deut 3:16
3:1 Num 21:33-35
3:2 Num 21:34

2:23 Hebrew *from Caphtor.* **2:34** The Hebrew term used here refers to the complete consecration of things or people to the LORD, either by destroying them or by giving them as an offering.

2:14, 15 Israel did not have to spend 40 years on the way to the Promised Land. God sentenced them to wilderness wanderings because they rejected his love, rebelled against his authority, ignored his commands for right living, and willfully broke their end of the agreement made in Exodus 19:8 and 24:3-8. In short, they disobeyed God. We often make life's journey more difficult than necessary by disobedience. Accept God's love, read and follow his commands in the Bible, and make a promise to stick with God whatever your situation. You will find that your life will be less complicated and more rewarding.

2:25 God told Moses he would make the enemy nations afraid of Israel. By worldly standards, Israel's army was not intimidating, but Israel had God on its side. Moses no longer had to worry about his enemies because his enemies were worried about him. God often goes before us in our daily battles, preparing the way and overcoming barriers. We need to follow him wholeheartedly and be alert to his leading.

3:1-3 The Israelites faced a big problem—the well-trained army of Og, king of Bashan. The Israelites hardly stood a chance. But they won because God fought for them. God can help his people regardless of the problems they face. No matter how insurmountable the obstacles may seem, remember that God is sovereign, and he will keep his promises.

King Sihon of the Amorites, who ruled in Heshbon.' 3So the LORD our God handed King
Og and all his people over to us, and we killed them all. 4We conquered all sixty of his
towns, the entire Argob region in his kingdom of Bashan. 5These were all fortified cities
with high walls and barred gates. We also took many unwalled villages at the same time.
6We completely destroyed* the kingdom of Bashan, just as we had destroyed King Sihon
of Heshbon. We destroyed* all the people in every town we conquered—men, women,
and children alike. 7But we kept all the livestock for ourselves and took plunder from all
the towns.

8"We now possessed all the land of the two Amorite kings east of the Jordan
River—from the Arnon Gorge to Mount Hermon. 9(Mount Hermon is called Sirion by
the Sidonians; the Amorites call it Senir.) 10We had now conquered all the cities on the
plateau, and all Gilead and Bashan as far as the towns of Salecah and Edrei, which were
part of Og's kingdom in Bashan. 11(Incidentally, King Og of Bashan was the last of the
giant Rephaites. His iron bed was more than thirteen feet long and six feet wide.* It can
still be seen in the Ammonite city of Rabbah.)

Land Division East of the Jordan

12"When we took possession of this land, I gave the territory beyond Aroer along the
Arnon Gorge, plus half of the hill country of Gilead with its towns, to the tribes of
Reuben and Gad. 13Then I gave the rest of Gilead and all of Bashan—Og's former
kingdom—to the half-tribe of Manasseh. (The Argob region of Bashan used to be known
as the land of the Rephaites. 14Jair, a leader from the tribe of Manasseh, acquired the
whole Argob region in Bashan all the way to the borders of the Geshurites and
Maacathites. Jair renamed this region after himself, calling it the Towns of Jair,* as it is
still known today.) 15I gave Gilead to the clan of Makir. 16And to the tribes of Reuben
and Gad I gave the area extending from Gilead to the middle of the Arnon Gorge, all the
way to the Jabbok River on the Ammonite frontier. 17They also received the Jordan
Valley, including the Jordan River and its eastern banks, all the way from the Sea of
Galilee down to the Dead Sea,* with the slopes of Pisgah on the east.

18"At that time I gave this command to the tribes that will live east of the Jordan:
'Although the LORD your God has given you this land as your property, all your fighting
men must cross the Jordan, armed and ready to protect your Israelite relatives. 19Your
wives, children, and numerous livestock, however, may stay behind in the towns I have
given you. 20When the LORD has given security to the rest of the Israelites, as he has to
you, and when they occupy the land the LORD your God is giving them across the Jordan
River, then you may return here to the land I have given you.'

Moses Forbidden to Enter the Land

21"At that time I said to Joshua, 'You have seen all that the LORD your God has done to
these two kings. He will do the same to all the kingdoms on the west side of the Jordan.
22Do not be afraid of the nations there, for the LORD your God will fight for you.'

23"At that time I pleaded with the LORD and said, 24'O Sovereign LORD, I am your
servant. You have only begun to show me your greatness and power. Is there any god in
heaven or on earth who can perform such great deeds as yours? 25Please let me cross the
Jordan to see the wonderful land on the other side, the beautiful hill country and the
Lebanon mountains.'

26"But the LORD was angry with me because of you, and he would not listen to me.
'That's enough!' he ordered. 'Speak of it no more. 27You can go to Pisgah Peak and view
the land in every direction, but you may not cross the Jordan River. 28But commission

3:6 The Hebrew term used here refers to the complete consecration of things or people to the LORD, either by destroying them or by giving them as an offering. **3:11** Hebrew *9 cubits* [4.1 meters] *long and 4 cubits* [1.8 meters] *wide.* **3:14** Hebrew *Havvoth-jair.* **3:17** Hebrew *from Kinnereth to the sea of the Arabah, the Salt Sea.*

3:3 Josh 9:10
3:4 1 Kings 4:13
3:6 Deut 2:33-34; 20:16
3:7 Deut 2:35
3:8 Num 32:33-42; Josh 12:1-6; 13:8-13
3:9 Deut 4:48; Josh 11:17; Ps 29:5-6
3:11 Deut 2:11, 20; 2 Sam 11:1; 12:26-27; Jer 49:2
3:12 Num 32:33-42; Deut 2:35-36; Josh 13:8-13
3:15 Num 32:40
3:17 Josh 13:27
3:18 Num 32:20; Josh 4:12-13
3:19 Num 32:16; Josh 1:14
3:22 Deut 1:29-30; 20:4
3:24 Ps 86:8
3:26 Deut 1:37; 31:2
3:27 Num 27:12; Deut 1:37
3:28 Num 27:18

3:21, 22 What encouraging news for Joshua, who was to lead his men against the persistent forces of evil in the Promised Land! Since God promised to help him win every battle, he had nothing to fear. Our battles may not be against godless armies, but they are just as real as Joshua's. Whether we are resisting temptation or battling fear, God has promised to fight with and for us as we obey him.

3:26-28 God had made it clear that Moses would not enter the Promised Land (Numbers 20:12). So God told Moses to commission Joshua as the new leader and encourage him in this new role. This is a good example to churches and organizations who must eventually replace their leaders. Good leaders prepare their people to function without them by discovering those with leadership potential, providing the training they need, and looking for ways to encourage them.

Joshua and encourage him, for he will lead the people across the Jordan. He will give
them the land you now see before you.' 29 So we stayed in the valley near Beth-peor.

Moses Urges Israel to Obey

4 "And now, Israel, listen carefully to these laws and regulations that I am about to
teach you. Obey them so that you may live, so you may enter and occupy the land
the LORD, the God of your ancestors, is giving you. 2 Do not add to or subtract from these
commands I am giving you from the LORD your God. Just obey them. 3 You saw what
the LORD did to you at Baal-peor, where the LORD your God destroyed everyone who
had worshiped the god Baal of Peor. 4 But all of you who were faithful to the LORD your
God are still alive today.

5 "You must obey these laws and regulations when you arrive in the land you are about
to enter and occupy. The LORD my God gave them to me and commanded me to pass them
on to you. 6 If you obey them carefully, you will display your wisdom and intelligence to
the surrounding nations. When they hear about these laws, they will exclaim, 'What other
nation is as wise and prudent as this!' 7 For what great nation has a god as near to them as
the LORD our God is near to us whenever we call on him? 8 And what great nation has laws
and regulations as fair as this body of laws that I am giving you today?

9 "But watch out! Be very careful never to forget what you have seen the LORD do for
you. Do not let these things escape from your mind as long as you live! And be sure to
pass them on to your children and grandchildren. 10 Tell them especially about the day
when you stood before the LORD your God at Mount Sinai,* where he told me, 'Summon
the people before me, and I will instruct them. That way, they will learn to fear me as
long as they live, and they will be able to teach my laws to their children.' 11 You came
near and stood at the foot of the mountain, while the mountain was burning with fire.
Flames shot into the sky, shrouded in black clouds and deep darkness. 12 And the LORD
spoke to you from the fire. You heard his words but didn't see his form; there was only
a voice. 13 He proclaimed his covenant, which he commanded you to keep—the Ten
Commandments—and wrote them on two stone tablets. 14 It was at that time that the
LORD commanded me to issue the laws and regulations you must obey in the land you
are about to enter and occupy.

A Warning against Idolatry

15 "But be careful! You did not see the LORD's form on the day he spoke to you from the
fire at Mount Sinai. 16 So do not corrupt yourselves by making a physical image in any
form—whether of a man or a woman, 17 an animal or a bird, 18 a creeping creature or a
fish. 19 And when you look up into the sky and see the sun, moon, and stars—all the

4:1 Lev 19:37; Deut 5:32-33; 8:1; 16:20; 30:16; Ezek 20:11; Rom 10:5
4:2 Deut 12:32; Prov 30:6; Matt 5:18
4:3 Num 25:1-9
4:5 Lev 26:46; 27:34
4:6 Ps 19:7-8; Prov 1:7-9
4:7 Ps 148:14
4:8 Ps 89:14-15
4:10 Exod 19:9, 16
4:11 Exod 19:18; Heb 12:18
4:13 Exod 31:18; 34:28; Deut 10:4
4:15 Exod 19:9, 18, 21
4:16 Exod 20:4-5; 32:8; Deut 9:12; 31:29
4:19 2 Kgs 17:16; Acts 7:43

4:10 Hebrew *Horeb,* another name for Sinai; also in 4:15.

4:2 What is meant by adding to or subtracting from God's commands? These laws were the word of God, and they were complete. How could any human being, with limited wisdom and knowledge, edit God's perfect laws? To add to the laws would make them a burden; to subtract from the laws would make them incomplete. Thus the laws were to remain unchanged. To presume to make changes in God's law is to assume a position of authority over God who gave the laws (Matthew 5:17-19; 15:3-9; Revelation 22:18, 19). The religious leaders at the time of Christ did exactly this; they elevated their own laws to the same level as God's. Jesus rebuked them for this (Matthew 23:1-4).

4:8 Do the laws God gave to the Israelites still apply to Christians today? God's laws are designed to guide all people toward life-styles that are healthy, upright, and devoted to God. Their purpose was to point out sin (or potential sin) and show the proper way to deal with that sin. The Ten Commandments, the heart of God's law, are just as applicable today as they were 3,000 years ago because they proclaim a life-style endorsed by God. They are the perfect expression of who God is and how he wants people to live.

But God gave other laws besides the Ten Commandments. Are these just as important? God never issued a law that didn't have a purpose. However, many of the laws we read in the Pentateuch were directed specifically to people of that time and culture. Although a specific law may not apply to us, the timeless truth or principle behind the law does.

For example, Christians do not practice animal sacrifice in worship. However, the principles behind the sacrifices—forgiveness for sin and thankfulness to God—still apply. The sacrifices pointed to the ultimate sacrifice made for us by Jesus Christ. The New Testament says that with the death and resurrection of Jesus Christ the Old Testament laws were fulfilled. This means that while the Old Testament laws help us recognize our sins and correct our wrongdoings, it is Jesus Christ who takes our sins away. Jesus is now our primary example to follow because he alone perfectly obeyed the law and modeled its true intent.

4:9 Moses wanted to make sure that the people did not forget all they had seen God do, so he urged parents to teach their children about God's great miracles. This helped parents remember God's faithfulness and provided the means for passing on from one generation to the next the stories recounting God's great acts. It is easy to forget the wonderful ways God has worked in the lives of his people. But you can remember God's great acts of faithfulness by telling your children, friends, or associates what you have seen him do.

forces of heaven—don't be seduced by them and worship them. The LORD your God
designated these heavenly bodies for all the peoples of the earth. 20 Remember that the
LORD rescued you from the burning furnace of Egypt to become his own people and
special possession; that is what you are today.
21 "But the LORD was very angry with me because of you. He vowed that I would never
cross the Jordan River into the good land the LORD your God is giving you as your special
possession. 22 Though you will cross the Jordan to occupy the land, I will die here on this
side of the river. 23 So be careful not to break the covenant the LORD your God has made
with you. You will break it if you make idols of any shape or form, for the LORD your God
has absolutely forbidden this. 24 The LORD your God is a devouring fire, a jealous God.
25 "In the future, when you have children and grandchildren and have lived in the land
a long time, do not corrupt yourselves by making idols of any kind. This is evil in the
sight of the LORD your God and will arouse his anger.
26 "Today I call heaven and earth as witnesses against you. If you disobey me, you will
quickly disappear from the land you are crossing the Jordan to occupy. You will live there
only a short time; then you will be utterly destroyed. 27 For the LORD will scatter you
among the nations, where only a few of you will survive. 28 There, in a foreign land, you
will worship idols made from wood and stone, gods that neither see nor hear nor eat nor
smell. 29 From there you will search again for the LORD your God. And if you search for
him with all your heart and soul, you will find him.
30 "When those bitter days have come upon you far in the future, you will finally return
to the LORD your God and listen to what he tells you. 31 For the LORD your God is
merciful—he will not abandon you or destroy you or forget the solemn covenant he made
with your ancestors.

There Is Only One God

32 "Search all of history, from the time God created people on the earth until now. Then
search from one end of the heavens to the other. See if anything as great as this has
ever happened before. 33 Has any nation ever heard the voice of God* speaking from
fire—as you did—and survived? 34 Has any other god taken one nation for himself by
rescuing it from another by means of trials, miraculous signs, wonders, war, awesome
power, and terrifying acts? Yet that is what the LORD your God did for you in Egypt,
right before your very eyes.
35 "He showed you these things so you would realize that the LORD is God and that
there is no other god. 36 He let you hear his voice from heaven so he could instruct you.
He let you see his great fire here on earth so he could speak to you from it. 37 Because he
loved your ancestors, he chose to bless their descendants and personally brought you out

4:20 1 Kgs 8:51; Jer 11:4
4:21 Num 20:12; Deut 1:37
4:23 Exod 20:4-5
4:24 Exod 24:17; 34:14; Heb 12:29
4:25 Deut 4:16; 31:29
4:26 Deut 7:4; 8:19; 31:29
4:27 Deut 28:64
4:28 Deut 28:36, 64; 29:17; Ps 115:4-8
4:29 Deut 6:5; 10:12; 30:1-3; 2 Chr 15:4
4:31 Deut 31:6, 8; Josh 1:5; Heb 13:5
4:32 Gen 1:27
4:33 Exod 20:22; Deut 5:24, 26
4:34 Exod 14:30; Deut 5:15; 6:21; 7:19; 33:29
4:35 Exod 8:10; 9:14; Deut 4:39; 1 Sam 2:2; †Mark 12:32
4:37 Deut 7:8

4:33 Or *voice of a god.*

4:19 God was not excusing the other nations for their idol worship. He was simply saying that while judgment might be delayed for those other nations, it would be swift and complete for Israel because Israel knew God's laws. We must remember that idol worship was not just keeping statues around the house—harmless lumps of clay, wood, or iron. It was the commitment to the other evil qualities, beliefs, and practices the idol represented (such as murder, prostitution, cruelty in war, self-centeredness) or to strengths and attributes of mankind, the animal kingdom, or the orderliness of stars that were revered without reference to God who created them. Because God had so clearly revealed himself in Israel's history, the Israelites had no excuse for worshiping anyone but the true God.

4:24 God is a devouring fire. Because he is morally perfect, he hates sin and cannot accept those who practice it. Moses' sin kept him from entering the Promised Land, and no sacrifice could remove that judgment. Sin kept us from entering God's presence, but Jesus Christ paid the penalty for our sin and removed God's judgment forever by his death. Trusting in Jesus Christ will save you from God's anger and allow you to begin a personal relationship with him.

4:24 Jealousy is a demand for someone else's exclusive affection or loyalty. Some jealousy is bad. It is destructive for a man to get upset when his wife talks to another man. But other jealousy is good. It is right for a man to demand that his wife treat him, and only him, as her husband. Usually we use the word *jealousy* only for the bad reaction. But God's kind of jealousy is appropriate and good. He is defending his word and his high honor. He makes a strong, exclusive demand on us: We must treat only the Lord—and no one else in all the universe—as God.

4:29 Do you want to know God? God promised the Israelites that they would find him when they searched with all their hearts and souls. God is knowable and wants to be known—but we have to want to know him. Acts of service and worship must be accompanied by sincere devotion of the heart. As Hebrews 11:6 says, "Anyone who wants to come to him must believe that there is a God and that he rewards those who sincerely seek him." God will reward those who pursue a relationship with him.

4:32 How tempted we are to look everywhere else but to God for our guidance and leadership! We trust medical doctors, financial advisers, and news commentators, but do we trust God? Get God's advice first (4:39, 40), and recognize his authority over every dimension of life.

4:38 Num 32:4 of Egypt with a great display of power. 38 He drove out nations far greater than you, so
he could bring you in and give you their land as a special possession, as it is today. 39 So
remember this and keep it firmly in mind: The LORD is God both in heaven and on earth,
4:40 Exod 23:26 and there is no other god! 40 If you obey all the laws and commands that I will give you
Deut 4:2; 5:16, 29, 33; 32:47 today, all will be well with you and your children. Then you will enjoy a long life in the
land the LORD your God is giving you for all time."

Eastern Cities of Refuge

4:41 Num 35:6 41 Then Moses set apart three cities of refuge east of the Jordan River, 42 where anyone who
Deut 19:1-13 had accidentally killed someone without having any previous hostility could flee for safety.
43 These were the cities: Bezer on the wilderness plateau for the tribe of Reuben; Ramoth in
Gilead for the tribe of Gad; Golan in Bashan for the tribe of Manasseh.

B. PRINCIPLES FOR GODLY LIVING: MOSES' SECOND ADDRESS (4:44—29:1)

After reviewing the history of Israel's journey, Moses recounts the Ten Commandments and the other laws given to the Israelites at Mount Sinai. He urges them to obey the law and reminds them of the consequences of disobeying God's laws. The Ten Commandments and all of God's laws point out to us where we fall short and show us how we should act as God's people.

Introduction to the Law

44 This is the law that Moses handed down to the Israelites. 45 These are the stipulations,
laws, and regulations that Moses gave to the people of Israel when they left Egypt, 46 and
as they camped in the valley near Beth-peor east of the Jordan River. (This land was
formerly occupied by the Amorites under King Sihon of Heshbon. He and his people had
been destroyed by Moses and the Israelites as they came up from Egypt. 47 Israel
conquered his land and that of King Og of Bashan—the two Amorite kings east of the
4:48 Deut 2:35-36 Jordan. 48 So Israel conquered all the area from Aroer at the edge of the Arnon Gorge to
Mount Sirion,* also called Mount Hermon. 49 And they took the eastern bank of the
Jordan Valley as far south as the Dead Sea,* below the slopes of Pisgah.)

1. The Ten Commandments

5 Moses called all the people of Israel together and said, "Listen carefully to all the
laws and regulations I am giving you today. Learn them and be sure to obey them!
5:2 Exod 19:5 Mal 4:4 2 "While we were at Mount Sinai,* the LORD our God made a covenant with us. 3 The
LORD did not make this covenant long ago with our ancestors, but with all of us who are
5:4 Num 14:14 alive today. 4 The LORD spoke to you face to face from the heart of the fire on the
5:5 Exod 19:16, 25 mountain. 5 I stood as an intermediary between you and the LORD, for you were afraid of
the fire and did not climb the mountain. He spoke to me, and I passed his words on to
you. This is what he said:

5:6 Exod 20:2-17 6 "'I am the LORD your God, who rescued you from slavery in Egypt.
5:7 Exod 20:3 7 "'Do not worship any other gods besides me.

4:48 As in Syriac version (see also 3:9); Hebrew reads *Mount Sion.* **4:49** Hebrew *took the Arabah on the east side of the Jordan as far as the sea of the Arabah.* **5:2** Hebrew *Horeb,* another name for Sinai.

4:40 Was Israel guaranteed prosperity for obeying God's laws? Yes—but we have to look carefully at what that means. God's laws were designed to make his chosen nation healthy, just, and merciful. When the people followed those laws, they prospered. This does not mean, however, that no sickness, no sadness, and no misunderstandings existed among them. Rather, it means that as a nation they prospered and that individuals' problems were handled as fairly as possible. Today God's promise of prosperity—his constant presence, comfort, and the resources to live as we should—extends to all believers. We will face trials; Jesus assured us of that. But we will avoid the misery that directly results from intentional sin, and we will know that a great treasure awaits us in heaven.

5:1 The people had entered into a covenant with God, and Moses commanded them to hear, learn, and follow his regulations. Christians also have entered into a covenant with God (through Jesus Christ) and should be responsive to what God expects. Moses' threefold command to the Israelites is excellent advice for all God's followers. *Listening* is absorbing and accepting information about God. *Learning* is understanding its meaning and implications. *Obeying* is putting into action all we have learned and understood. All three parts are essential to a growing relationship with God.

5:7 A *god* is whatever people put first in their lives. Some people literally worship other gods by joining cults or strange religions. In a more subtle way, many of us worship other gods by building our lives around something other than the one true God. If your greatest desire is for popularity, power, or money, you are devoting yourself to something other than God. To put God first, (1) recognize what is taking his place in your life; (2) renounce this substitute god as unworthy of your devotion; (3) ask God for forgiveness; (4) restructure your priorities so that love for God is the motive for everything you do; (5) examine yourself daily to be sure you are giving God first place.

8 “‘Do not make idols of any kind, whether in the shape of birds or animals or fish.
9 You must never worship or bow down to them, for I, the LORD your God, am a
jealous God who will not share your affection with any other god! I do not leave
unpunished the sins of those who hate me, but I punish the children for the sins of
their parents to the third and fourth generations. 10 But I lavish my love on those
who love me and obey my commands, even for a thousand generations.
11 “‘Do not misuse the name of the LORD your God. The LORD will not let you go
unpunished if you misuse his name.
12 “‘Observe the Sabbath day by keeping it holy, as the LORD your God has
commanded you. 13 Six days a week are set apart for your daily duties and regular
work, 14 but the seventh day is a day of rest dedicated to the LORD your God. On
that day no one in your household may do any kind of work. This includes you,
your sons and daughters, your male and female servants, your oxen and donkeys
and other livestock, and any foreigners living among you. All your male and female
servants must rest as you do. 15 Remember that you were once slaves in Egypt and
that the LORD your God brought you out with amazing power and mighty deeds.
That is why the LORD your God has commanded you to observe the Sabbath day.
16 “‘Honor your father and mother, as the LORD your God commanded you. Then you
will live a long, full life in the land the LORD your God will give you.
17 “‘Do not murder.
18 “‘Do not commit adultery.
19 “‘Do not steal.
20 “‘Do not testify falsely against your neighbor.
21 “‘Do not covet your neighbor’s wife. Do not covet your neighbor’s house or land,
male or female servant, ox or donkey, or anything else your neighbor owns.’

22 “The LORD spoke these words with a loud voice to all of you from the heart of the
fire, surrounded by clouds and deep darkness. This was all he said at that time, and he
wrote his words on two stone tablets and gave them to me. 23 But when you heard the
voice from the darkness, while the mountain was blazing with fire, all your tribal leaders
came to me. 24 They said, ‘The LORD our God has shown us his glory and greatness, and
we have heard his voice from the heart of the fire. Today we have seen God speaking to
humans, and yet we live! 25 But now, why should we die? If the LORD our God speaks to
us again, we will certainly die and be consumed by this awesome fire. 26 Can any living
thing hear the voice of the living God from the heart of the fire and yet survive? 27 You
go and listen to what the LORD our God says. Then come and tell us everything he tells
you, and we will listen and obey.’

5:8 Exod 20:4 Lev 26:1 Deut 4:16-17
5:9 Exod 34:7, 14
5:11 Deut 6:13; 10:20 Matt 5:33
5:12 Exod 20:8-11
5:15 Exod 20:11 Deut 15:15; 16:12
5:16 Exod 20:12; 21:17 †Matt 15:4; 19:9 †Mark 7:10; 10:9 †Luke 18:20 †Eph 6:2-3 Col 3:20
5:17 Exod 20:13 †Matt 5:21
5:18 Exod 20:14 †Mark 10:19 †Luke 18:20 †Rom 13:9 †Jas 2:11
5:19 Exod 20:15 †Matt 19:19 †Mark 10:19 †Luke 18:20 †Rom 13:9
5:20 †Matt 19:18 †Mark 10:19 †Luke 18:20
5:21 †Rom 7:7; 13:9
5:22 Exod 19:16-19 Deut 4:13
5:25 Exod 20:18-19 Deut 18:16 Heb 12:19
5:26 Exod 24:3

5:8, 9 How would you feel if someone took a picture of you, framed it, stared at it a lot, showed it to others, but completely ignored the real you? God does not want to be treated this way either. He wants a genuine relationship with us, not mere ritual. He wants us to know him. God knows that if we put anything other than him at the center of our lives, we will not reach our potential and become all that he wants us to be.

5:11 We are familar with the sin to be avoided in this commandment, that we should not misuse the name of the Lord by saying it in an empty or worthless way. But there is also a good work that is commanded: to use God’s name to praise him and ascribe to him glory. This is the opposite of misusing his name. While you might be able to keep yourself from swearing, how have you done at finding time to praise God and honor his name?

5:16 Obeying our parents is our main task when we are young, but honoring them should continue even beyond their death. One way to honor parents is to provide for them in times of financial need or when they are ill and unable to care for themselves. Perhaps the best way to honor them is to pass on their godly values to our children. Honoring involves all that sons and daughters do with their lives—the way they work and talk, the values they hold, and the morals they practice. What are you doing to show respect to your parents? Are you living in a way that brings honor to them?

5:17 “But I don’t murder people,” you may say. Good. That fulfills the letter of the law. But Jesus explained that hateful anger breaks this commandment (Matthew 5:21, 22). Have you ever been so angry with someone who mistreated you that for a moment you wished that person were dead? Have you ever fantasized that you could do someone in? Jesus’ teaching concerning this law demonstrates that we are capable of murder in our hearts. Even if we are legally innocent, we are all morally guilty of murder and need to ask God’s forgiveness. We need to commit ourselves to the opposite of hatred and anger—love and reconciliation.

5:21 To covet is to desire another person’s prosperity. We are not to set our desires on anything that belongs to someone else. Not only can such desires make us miserable, they can also lead us to other sins such as adultery and stealing. Envying others is a useless exercise because God is able to provide everything we really need, even if he does not always give us everything we want. To stop coveting, we need to practice being content with what we have. The apostle Paul emphasizes the significance of contentment in Philippians 4:11, 12. It’s a matter of perspective. Instead of thinking about what we don’t have, we should thank God for what he has given and strive to be content. After all, our most important possession is free and available to everyone—eternal life through Christ.

5:28 Deut 18:17
5:29 Deut 5:16, 33; Ps 81:13; Isa 48:18
5:31 Exod 24:12
5:32 Deut 17:20; Josh 1:7; 23:6
5:33 Exod 20:12; Deut 4:1, 40
6:2 Deut 4:9; 10:12
6:3 Exod 3:8, 17; Deut 5:33
6:4-5 Deut 4:35, 39; †Matt 22:37; †Mark 12:29-30; Luke 10:27; 1 Cor 8:4, 6
6:6 Deut 11:18

28"The LORD heard your request and said to me, 'I have heard what the people have
said to you, and they are right. 29Oh, that they would always have hearts like this, that
they might fear me and obey all my commands! If they did, they and their descendants
would prosper forever. 30Go and tell them to return to their tents. 31But you stay here
with me so I can give you all my commands, laws, and regulations. You will teach them
to the people so they can obey them in the land I am giving to them as their inheritance.'"
32So Moses told the people, "You must obey all the commands of the LORD your God,
following his instructions in every detail. 33Stay on the path that the LORD your God has
commanded you to follow. Then you will live long and prosperous lives in the land you
are about to enter and occupy.

2. Love the Lord your God

6 "These are all the commands, laws, and regulations that the LORD your God told me
to teach you so you may obey them in the land you are about to enter and occupy,
2and so you and your children and grandchildren might fear the LORD your God as long
as you live. If you obey all his laws and commands, you will enjoy a long life. 3Listen
closely, Israel, to everything I say. Be careful to obey. Then all will go well with you, and
you will have many children in the land flowing with milk and honey, just as the LORD,
the God of your ancestors, promised you.
4"Hear, O Israel! The LORD is our God, the LORD alone.* 5And you must love the
LORD your God with all your heart, all your soul, and all your strength. 6And you must

6:4 Or *The LORD our God is one LORD,* or *The LORD our God, the LORD is one,* or *The LORD is our God, the LORD is one.*

BROKEN COMMANDMENTS
The Ten Commandments were God's standards for right living. To obey them was to obey God. Yet throughout the Old Testament, we can see how each commandment was broken. As you read the stories, notice the tragic consequences that occurred as a result of violating God's law.

Ten Commandments	*Notable Violations*
"Do not worship any other gods besides me."	Solomon (1 Kings 11)
"Do not make idols of any kind. . . . You must never worship or bow down to them."	The golden calf-idol incident (Exodus 32); generations after Joshua (Judges 2:10–14; 2 Kings 21:1–15; Jeremiah 1:16)
"Do not misuse the name of the LORD your God."	Zedekiah (Ezekiel 17:15–21)
"Observe the Sabbath day by keeping it holy."	Judah (2 Chronicles 36:21)
"Honor your father and mother."	Eli's sons—Hophni and Phinehas (1 Samuel 2:12, 23–25)
"Do not murder."	Hazael (2 Kings 8:15)
"Do not commit adultery."	David (2 Samuel 11:2–5)
"Do not steal."	Ahab (1 Kings 21:1–19)
"Do not testify falsely against your neighbor."	Saul (1 Samuel 15:13–25)
"Do not covet your neighbor's wife. Do not covet your neighbor's house or land, . . . or anything else your neighbor owns."	Achan (Joshua 7:19–26)

5:29 God told Moses that he wanted the people to incline their hearts to fear him—to *want* to respect and obey him. There is a difference between doing something because it is required and doing something because we want to. God is not interested in forced religious exercises and rule keeping. He wants our hearts and lives completely dedicated to him. If we love him, obedience will follow.

6:3 For a nation that had wandered 40 years in a parched wilderness, a land flowing with milk and honey sounded like paradise. It brought to mind rich crops, rushing streams, gentle rains, and lush fields filled with livestock. The Israelites could have had all that 40 years earlier. Numbers 13 and 14 explain how the people missed their chance. Now Moses was determined to help the people avoid the same mistake by whetting their appetite for the beautiful land and then clearly explaining the conditions for entering the land.

6:4 Monotheism—belief in only one God—was a distinctive feature of Hebrew religion. Many ancient religions believed in many gods. But the God of Abraham, Isaac, and Jacob is the God of the whole earth, the only true God. This was an important insight for the nation of Israel because they were about to enter a land filled with people who believed in many gods. Both then and today, there are people who prefer to place their trust in many different "gods." But the day is coming when God will be recognized as the only one. He will be the king over the whole earth (Zechariah 14:9).

6:4-9 This passage provides the central theme of Deuteronomy. It sets a pattern that helps us relate the Word of God to our daily lives. We are to love God, think constantly about his commandments, teach his commandments to our children, and live each day by the guidelines in his Word. God emphasized the importance of parents' teaching the Bible to their children. The church and Christian schools cannot be used to escape from this responsibility. The Bible provides so many opportunities for object lessons and practical teaching that it would be a shame to study it only one day a week. Eternal truths are most effectively learned in the loving environment of a God-fearing home.

commit yourselves wholeheartedly to these commands I am giving you today. 7 Repeat
them again and again to your children. Talk about them when you are at home and when
you are away on a journey, when you are lying down and when you are getting up again.
8 Tie them to your hands as a reminder, and wear them on your forehead. 9 Write them on
the doorposts of your house and on your gates.

10 "The LORD your God will soon bring you into the land he swore to give your
ancestors Abraham, Isaac, and Jacob. It is a land filled with large, prosperous cities that
you did not build. 11 The houses will be richly stocked with goods you did not produce.
You will draw water from cisterns you did not dig, and you will eat from vineyards and
olive trees you did not plant. When you have eaten your fill in this land, 12 be careful not
to forget the LORD, who rescued you from slavery in the land of Egypt. 13 You must fear
the LORD your God and serve him. When you take an oath, you must use only his name.

14 "You must not worship any of the gods of neighboring nations, 15 for the LORD your
God, who lives among you, is a jealous God. His anger will flare up against you and wipe
you from the face of the earth. 16 Do not test the LORD your God as you did when you
complained at Massah. 17 You must diligently obey the commands of the LORD your
God—all the stipulations and laws he has given you. 18 Do what is right and good in the
LORD's sight, so all will go well with you. Then you will enter and occupy the good land
that the LORD solemnly promised to give your ancestors. 19 You will drive out all the
enemies living in your land, just as the LORD said you would.

20 "In the future your children will ask you, 'What is the meaning of these stipulations,
laws, and regulations that the LORD our God has given us?' 21 Then you must tell them,
'We were Pharaoh's slaves in Egypt, but the LORD brought us out of Egypt with amazing
power. 22 Before our eyes the LORD did miraculous signs and wonders, dealing terrifying
blows against Egypt and Pharaoh and all his people. 23 He brought us out of Egypt so he
could give us this land he had solemnly promised to give our ancestors. 24 And the LORD
our God commanded us to obey all these laws and to fear him for our own prosperity
and well-being, as is now the case. 25 For we are righteous when we obey all the
commands the LORD our God has given us.'

The Privilege of Holiness

7 "When the LORD your God brings you into the land you are about to enter and
occupy, he will clear away many nations ahead of you: the Hittites, Girgashites,
Amorites, Canaanites, Perizzites, Hivites, and Jebusites. These seven nations are all
more powerful than you. 2 When the LORD your God hands these nations over to you and
you conquer them, you must completely destroy* them. Make no treaties with them and

6:7 Deut 4:9; Eph 6:4
6:8 Exod 13:9
6:9 Deut 11:20
6:10 Deut 9:1; Josh 24:13
6:13 †Matt 4:10; Luke 4:8
6:15 Deut 4:24; 5:9
6:16 Exod 17:7; †Matt 4:7; †Luke 4:12
6:17 Deut 11:22
6:18 Deut 4:40
6:20 Exod 13:8, 14
6:24 Deut 6:17; 10:12
7:1 Deut 20:17; Acts 13:19
7:2 Exod 23:32

7:2 The Hebrew term used here refers to the complete consecration of things or people to the LORD, either by destroying them or by giving them as an offering; also in 7:26.

6:5 Jesus said that loving God with all of ourselves is the first and greatest commandment (Matthew 22:37-39). This command, combined with the command to love your neighbor (Leviticus 19:18), encompasses all the other Old Testament laws.

6:7 The Hebrews were extremely successful at making religion an integral part of life. The reason for their success was that religious education was life-oriented, not information-oriented. They used the context of daily life to teach about God. The key to teaching your children to love God is stated simply and clearly in these verses. If you want your children to follow God, you must make God a part of your everyday experiences. You must teach your children diligently to see God in all aspects of life, not just those that are church related.

6:10-13 Moses warned the people not to forget God when they entered the Promised Land and became prosperous. Prosperity, more than poverty, can dull our spiritual vision because it tends to make us self-sufficient and eager to acquire still more of everything—except God. The same thing can happen in our church. Once we become successful in terms of numbers, programs, and buildings, we can easily become self-sufficient and less sensitive to our need for God. This leads us to concentrate on self-preservation rather than thankfulness and service to God.

6:24 Does the phrase "for our own prosperity and well-being" mean that we can expect only good things and no suffering when we obey God? What is promised here is a right relationship with God for all those who love him with all their heart. It speaks of a good relationship with God and the ultimate benefit of knowing him. It is not blanket protection against poverty, adversity, or suffering. We can have this right relationship with God by obeying his command to love him with all that we are.

7:2 God told the Israelites to destroy their enemies totally. How can a God of love and mercy wipe out everyone, even children? Although God is loving and merciful, he is also just. These enemy nations were as much a part of God's creation as Israel was, and God does not allow evil to continue unchecked. God had punished Israel by keeping out of the Promised Land all those who had disobeyed. The command to destroy these nations was both a judgment (9:4-6) and a safety measure. On one hand, the people living in the land were being judged for their sin, and Israel was God's instrument of judgment—just as God would one day use other nations to judge Israel for its sin (2 Chronicles 36:17; Isaiah 10:12). On the other hand, God's command was designed to protect the nation of Israel from being ruined by the idolatry and immorality of its enemies. To think that God is too "nice" to judge sin would be to underestimate him.

7:3 Josh 23:12
show them no mercy. 3Do not intermarry with them, and don't let your daughters and
sons marry their sons and daughters. 4They will lead your young people away from me
to worship other gods. Then the anger of the LORD will burn against you, and he will
7:5 Exod 23:24
destroy you. 5Instead, you must break down their pagan altars and shatter their sacred
7:6 Exod 19:5-6; Deut 14:2; 26:18; 1 Pet 2:9
pillars. Cut down their Asherah poles and burn their idols. 6For you are a holy people,
who belong to the LORD your God. Of all the people on earth, the LORD your God has
chosen you to be his own special treasure.
7:7 Deut 4:37
7"The LORD did not choose you and lavish his love on you because you were larger
or greater than other nations, for you were the smallest of all nations! 8It was simply
because the LORD loves you, and because he was keeping the oath he had sworn to your
ancestors. That is why the LORD rescued you with such amazing power from your slavery
7:9 Exod 20:6; Deut 4:39; 5:9-10; 1 Cor 1:9; 1 Thes 5:24; 2 Tim 2:13
under Pharaoh in Egypt. 9Understand, therefore, that the LORD your God is indeed God.
He is the faithful God who keeps his covenant for a thousand generations and constantly
loves those who love him and obey his commands. 10But he does not hesitate to punish
and destroy those who hate him. 11Therefore, obey all these commands, laws, and
regulations I am giving you today.
7:12 Lev 26:3; Deut 28:1
12"If you listen to these regulations and obey them faithfully, the LORD your God will
keep his covenant of unfailing love with you, as he solemnly promised your ancestors.
7:13 Lev 26:9; Deut 28:4; 30:5-6
13He will love you and bless you and make you into a great nation. He will give you many
children and give fertility to your land and your animals. When you arrive in the land he
swore to give your ancestors, you will have large crops of grain, grapes, and olives, and
7:14 Exod 23:26
great herds of cattle, sheep, and goats. 14You will be blessed above all the nations of the
7:15 Exod 15:26; 23:26
earth. None of your men or women will be childless, and all your livestock will bear
young. 15And the LORD will protect you from all sickness. He will not let you suffer from
7:16 Exod 23:32; Deut 7:2
the terrible diseases you knew in Egypt, but he will bring them all on your enemies!
16"You must destroy all the nations the LORD your God hands over to you. Show
7:17 Num 33:53
them no mercy and do not worship their gods. If you do, they will trap you. 17Perhaps
you will think to yourselves, 'How can we ever conquer these nations that are so much
7:18 Num 14:9; Deut 1:21, 29
more powerful than we are?' 18But don't be afraid of them! Just remember what the
LORD your God did to Pharaoh and to all the land of Egypt. 19Remember the great
7:19 Deut 4:34
terrors the LORD your God sent against them. You saw it all with your own eyes! And
remember the miraculous signs and wonders, and the amazing power he used when he
brought you out of Egypt. The LORD your God will use this same power against the

DANGER IN PLENTY

"When you have eaten your fill in this land, be careful not to forget the LORD" (Deuteronomy 6:11, 12). It is often most difficult to follow God when life is easy—we can fall prey to temptation and fall away from God. Here are some notable examples of this truth.

Person	*Reference*	*Comment*
Adam	Genesis 3	Adam lived in a perfect world and had a perfect relationship with God. His needs were met; he had everything. But he fell to Satan's deception.
Noah	Genesis 9	Noah and his family had survived the Flood, and the whole world was theirs. They were prosperous, and life was easy. Noah shamed himself by becoming drunk and cursed his son Ham.
The nation of Israel	Judges 2	God had given Israel the Promised Land—rest at last with no more wandering. But as soon as brave and faithful Joshua died, they fell into the idolatrous practices of the Canaanites.
David	2 Samuel 11	David ruled well, and Israel was a dominant nation politically, economically, and militarily. In the midst of prosperity and success, he committed adultery with Bathsheba and had her husband, Uriah, murdered.
Solomon	1 Kings 11	Solomon truly had it all: power, wealth, fame, and wisdom. But his very abundance was the source of his downfall. He loved his pagan, idolatrous wives so much that he allowed himself and Israel to copy their detestable religious rites.

7:5 Asherah was a Canaanite mother goddess of the sea, associated with Baal.

7:6 How did Israel deserve to be chosen above all of the other nations at that time? It was not a matter of Israel's merit, but of God keeping his promise to their ancestors. Just as God chose the nation of Israel, he has chosen all believers today to be a part of his treasured possession. Similarly, it is not because of our merit that we have come to faith in Christ. Instead, God chose us out of his goodness and grace.

people you fear. [20]And then the LORD your God will send hornets* to drive out the few survivors still hiding from you!

[21]"No, do not be afraid of those nations, for the LORD your God is among you, and he is a great and awesome God. [22]The LORD your God will drive those nations out ahead of you little by little. You will not clear them away all at once, for if you did, the wild animals would multiply too quickly for you. [23]But the LORD your God will hand them over to you. He will throw them into complete confusion until they are destroyed. [24]He will put their kings in your power, and you will erase their names from the face of the earth. No one will be able to stand against you, and you will destroy them all.

[25]"You must burn their idols in fire, and do not desire the silver or gold with which they are made. Do not take it or it will become a snare to you, for it is detestable to the LORD your God. [26]Do not bring any detestable objects into your home, for then you will be set apart for destruction just like them. You must utterly detest such things, for they are set apart for destruction.

A Call to Remember and Obey

8 "Be careful to obey all the commands I am giving you today. Then you will live and multiply, and you will enter and occupy the land the LORD swore to give your ancestors. [2]Remember how the LORD your God led you through the wilderness for forty years, humbling you and testing you to prove your character, and to find out whether or not you would really obey his commands. [3]Yes, he humbled you by letting you go hungry and then feeding you with manna, a food previously unknown to you and your ancestors. He did it to teach you that people need more than bread for their life; real life comes by feeding on every word of the LORD. [4]For all these forty years your clothes didn't wear out, and your feet didn't blister or swell. [5]So you should realize that just as a parent disciplines a child, the LORD your God disciplines you to help you.

[6]"So obey the commands of the LORD your God by walking in his ways and fearing him. [7]For the LORD your God is bringing you into a good land of flowing streams and pools of water, with springs that gush forth in the valleys and hills. [8]It is a land of wheat and barley, of grapevines, fig trees, pomegranates, olives, and honey. [9]It is a land where food is plentiful and nothing is lacking. It is a land where iron is as common as stone, and copper is abundant in the hills. [10]When you have eaten your fill, praise the LORD your God for the good land he has given you.

7:20 Exod 23:28; Josh 24:12
7:21 Exod 29:45
7:22 Exod 23:28-30
7:24 Deut 11:25; Josh 1:5; 10:8; 23:9
7:25 Deut 7:2; 12:3; Josh 7:1, 21
7:26 Lev 27:28-29
8:1 Lev 26:3; Deut 4:1; 7:11
8:2 Exod 15:25; 2 Chr 32:31
8:3 Ps 78:24; †Matt 4:4; †Luke 4:4
8:4 Deut 29:5; Neh 9:21
8:5 Prov 3:11-12; Heb 12:6
8:7 Deut 11:10-12; Jer 2:7
8:8 Deut 32:13
8:10 Deut 6:11-12

7:20 Or *will spread panic,* or *will send a plague.* The meaning of the Hebrew is uncertain.

7:21-24 Moses told the Israelites that God would destroy Israel's enemies, but not all at once. God had the power to destroy those nations instantly, but he chose to do it in stages. In the same way and with the same power, God could miraculously and instantaneously change your life. Usually, however, he chooses to help you gradually, teaching you one lesson at a time. Rather than expecting instant spiritual maturity and solutions to all your problems, slow down and work one step at a time, trusting God to make up the difference between where you should be and where you are now. You'll soon look back and see that a miraculous transformation has occurred.

7:25, 26 Moses warned Israel against becoming ensnared by the idols of the defeated nations by desiring the silver or gold on them. We may think it's all right to be close to sin as long as we don't participate. "After all," we say, "I won't do anything wrong!" But being close can hurt us as we become attracted and finally give in. The only sure way to stay away from sin is to stay away!

8:3 Jesus quoted this verse when the devil tempted him to turn stones into bread (Matthew 4:4). Many people think that life is based on satisfying their appetites. If they can earn enough money to dress, eat, and play in high style, they think they are living "the good life." But such things do not satisfy our deepest longings. In the end they leave us empty and dissatisfied. Real life, according to Moses, comes from total commitment to God, the one who created life itself. It requires discipline, sacrifice, and hard work, and that's why most people never find it.

8:4 It's usually easy for us to take God's protection for granted. We seldom take notice or thank God when our car doesn't break down, our clothes don't rip, or our tools don't break. The people of Israel also failed to take notice, it seems, for they didn't even notice that in 40 years of wandering in the wilderness, their clothes didn't wear out and their feet didn't blister or swell. Thus, they did not remember to give thanks to God for these blessings. What has been working well for you? What has been giving you good service? What has been lasting for a long time without breaking down or apart? Remember to thank God for these quiet blessings.

8:10 This verse is traditionally cited as the reason we say grace before or after meals. Its purpose, however, was to warn the Israelites not to forget God when their needs and wants were satisfied. Let your table prayers serve as a constant reminder of the Lord's goodness to you and your duty to those who are less fortunate.

8:11-20 In times of plenty, we often take credit for our prosperity and become proud that our own hard work and cleverness have made us rich. It is easy to get so busy collecting and managing wealth that we push God right out of our lives. But it is God who gives us everything we have, and it is God who asks us to manage it for him.

8:11 Deut 4:9
8:12 Prov 30:9; Hos 13:6
8:15 Exod 17:6; Num 20:11; 21:6; Deut 1:19-21; 32:13; Pss 78:15; 114:8
8:16 Exod 16:15; Deut 8:2; John 6:30-31
8:18 Prov 10:22; Hos 2:8
8:19 Deut 4:26; 30:18
8:20 Ezek 5:15-17

[11]"But that is the time to be careful! Beware that in your plenty you do not forget the
LORD your God and disobey his commands, regulations, and laws. [12]For when you have
become full and prosperous and have built fine homes to live in, [13]and when your flocks
and herds have become very large and your silver and gold have multiplied along with
everything else, [14]that is the time to be careful. Do not become proud at that time and
forget the LORD your God, who rescued you from slavery in the land of Egypt. [15]Do not
forget that he led you through the great and terrifying wilderness with poisonous snakes
and scorpions, where it was so hot and dry. He gave you water from the rock! [16]He fed
you with manna in the wilderness, a food unknown to your ancestors. He did this to
humble you and test you for your own good. [17]He did it so you would never think that
it was your own strength and energy that made you wealthy. [18]Always remember that it
is the LORD your God who gives you power to become rich, and he does it to fulfill the
covenant he made with your ancestors.
[19]"But I assure you of this: If you ever forget the LORD your God and follow other
gods, worshiping and bowing down to them, you will certainly be destroyed. [20]Just as
the LORD has destroyed other nations in your path, you also will be destroyed for not
obeying the LORD your God.

Victory by God's Grace

9:1 Deut 11:23
9:3 Deut 4:24; Heb 12:29
9:4 Lev 18:23-30; Deut 7:24; 12:31; 18:9-14
9:6 Deut 9:13-14; 10:16; 31:27

9 "Hear, O Israel! Today you are about to cross the Jordan River to occupy the land
belonging to nations much greater and more powerful than you. They live in cities
with walls that reach to the sky! [2]They are strong and tall—descendants of the famous
Anakite giants. You've heard the saying, 'Who can stand up to the Anakites?' [3]But the
LORD your God will cross over ahead of you like a devouring fire to destroy them. He
will subdue them so that you will quickly conquer them and drive them out, just as the
LORD has promised.
[4]"After the LORD your God has done this for you, don't say to yourselves, 'The LORD
has given us this land because we are so righteous!' No, it is because of the wickedness
of the other nations that he is doing it. [5]It is not at all because you are such righteous,
upright people that you are about to occupy their land. The LORD your God will drive
these nations out ahead of you only because of their wickedness, and to fulfill the oath
he had sworn to your ancestors Abraham, Isaac, and Jacob. [6]I will say it again: The LORD
your God is not giving you this good land because you are righteous, for you are
not—you are a stubborn people.

Remembering the Gold Calf

9:7 Exod 14:11; Num 14:20-22

[7]"Remember how angry you made the LORD your God out in the wilderness. From the
day you left Egypt until now, you have constantly rebelled against him. [8]Remember how

---

OBEDIENCE
Deuteronomy 8:1 tells us to obey God's commandments. We do this by obeying God with . . .

OUR HEART	By loving him more than any relationship, activity, achievement, or possession
OUR WILL	By committing ourselves completely to him
OUR MIND	By seeking to know him and his Word, so his principles and values form the foundation of all we think and do
OUR BODY	By recognizing that our strengths, talents, and sexuality are given to us by God to be used for pleasure and fulfillment according to his rules, not ours
OUR FINANCES	By deciding that all of the resources we have ultimately come from God, and that we are to be managers of them and not owners
OUR FUTURE	By deciding to make service to God and man the main purpose of our life's work

---

9:2, 3 The Anakites were enormous people, some seven to nine feet tall. Goliath, probably a descendant of this race, was over nine feet tall (1 Samuel 17:4-7). Unfortunately, these great men used their stature as a means of intimidation rather than for noble causes. Their appearance alone frightened the Israelite scouts (Numbers 13:28), and their bad reputation may have been the deciding factor that kept the Israelites out of the land 40 years earlier (Numbers 13–14). Moses used all his persuasive power to convince his people that God could handle these bullies. He used the illustration of God as a devouring fire, for not even a giant could stand up to that.

angry you made the LORD at Mount Sinai,* where he was ready to destroy you. 9 That 9:8
was when I was on the mountain receiving the tablets of stone inscribed with the Exod 32:7
covenant that the LORD had made with you. I was there for forty days and forty nights, Ps 106:19-20
and all that time I ate nothing and drank no water. 10 The LORD gave me the covenant, 9:9
the tablets on which God himself had written all the words he had spoken to you from Exod 24:18 Deut 9:18
the fire on the mountain.

11 "At the end of the forty days and nights, the LORD handed me the two stone tablets
with the covenant inscribed on them. 12 Then the LORD said to me, 'Go down immediately 9:12
because the people you led out of Egypt have become corrupt. They have already turned Exod 32:7-8
from the way I commanded them to live and have cast an idol for themselves from gold.'

13 "The LORD said to me, 'I have been watching this people, and they are extremely 9:13
stubborn. 14 Leave me alone so I may destroy them and erase their name from under Exod 32:9
heaven. Then I will make a mighty nation of your descendants, a nation larger and more
powerful than they are.'

15 "So I came down from the fiery mountain, holding in my hands the two stone tablets 9:15
of the covenant. 16 There below me I could see the gold calf you had made in your terrible Exod 32:15
sin against the LORD your God. How quickly you had turned from the path the LORD had 9:16
commanded you to follow! 17 So I raised the stone tablets and dashed them to the ground. Exod 32:19
I smashed them before your very eyes. 18 Then for forty days and nights I lay prostrate
before the LORD, neither eating bread nor drinking water. I did this because you had sinned 9:18
by doing what the LORD hated, thus making him very angry. 19 How I feared for you, for Exod 34:8-9, 28 Deut 9:9; 10:10
the LORD was ready to destroy you. But again he listened to me. 20 The LORD was so angry 9:19
with Aaron that he wanted to destroy him. But I prayed for Aaron, and the LORD spared Exod 32:10-11
him. 21 I took your sin—the calf you had made—and I melted it in the fire and ground it †Heb 12:21
into fine dust. I threw the dust into the stream that cascades down the mountain. 9:21 Exod 32:20

22 "You also made the LORD angry at Taberah,* Massah,* and Kibroth-hattaavah.* 9:22
23 And at Kadesh-barnea the LORD sent you out with this command: 'Go up and take the Exod 17:7
land I have given you.' But you rebelled against the command of the LORD your God and Num 11:3, 34
refused to trust him or obey him. 24 Yes, you have been rebelling against the LORD as
long as I have known you. 9:24 Exod 32:9

25 "That is why I fell down and lay before the LORD for forty days and nights when he Deut 9:7; 31:27
was ready to destroy you. 26 I prayed to the LORD and said, 'O Sovereign LORD, do not 9:25
destroy your own people. They are your special possession, redeemed from Egypt by Deut 9:18
your mighty power and glorious strength. 27 Overlook the stubbornness and sin of these 9:26 Exod 32:11-13
people, but remember instead your servants Abraham, Isaac, and Jacob. 28 If you destroy 9:27
these people, the Egyptians will say, "The LORD destroyed them because he wasn't able Exod 32:9
to bring them to the land he had sworn to give them." Or they might say, "He destroyed
them because he hated them; he brought them into the wilderness to slaughter them."
29 But they are your people and your special possession, whom you brought from Egypt 9:29
by your mighty power and glorious strength.' Deut 4:34

New Tablets of Stone

10 "At that time the LORD said to me, 'Prepare two stone tablets like the first ones, 10:1
and make a sacred chest of wood to keep them in. Return to me on the mountain, Exod 25:10; 34:1
2 and I will write on the tablets the same words that were on the ones you smashed. Then 10:2
place the tablets in the sacred chest—the Ark of the Covenant.' Exod 25:16 Deut 4:13

3 "So I made a chest of acacia wood and cut two stone tablets like the first two, and I 10:3
took the tablets up the mountain. 4 The LORD again wrote the terms of the covenant—the Exod 34:4; 37:1
Ten Commandments—on them and gave them to me. They were the same words the LORD 10:4 Exod 34:28 Deut 4:13

9:8 Hebrew *Horeb*, another name for Sinai. **9:22a** *Taberah* means "place of burning." See Num 11:1-3. **9:22b** *Massah* means "place of testing." See Exod 17:1-7. **9:22c** *Kibroth-hattaavah* means "graves of craving." See Num 11:31-34.

9:18 From the record of this event in Exodus 32, it seems as though Moses acted immediately, grinding the golden calf into powder and forcing the people to drink water mixed with it. But evidently, Moses spent 40 days and nights interceding for the people.

9:23 Moses was reminding the people of the nation's unbelief 40 years earlier, when they were afraid to enter Canaan. The Israelites had not believed God would be able to help them in spite of all he had already done. They refused to follow because they looked only to their own limited resources instead of to God. Unbelief is the root of many sins and problems. When you feel lost, it may be because you're looking everywhere but to God for your help and guidance. (See Psalms 81:6-12; 95:8; 106:13-20; Hebrews 3.)

10:5 Exod 40:20
10:6 Num 20:25-26
10:8 Num 3:6; 18:1 Deut 18:5; 21:5; 31:9
10:9 Num 18:20, 24 Deut 18:2 Ezek 44:28
10:10 Deut 9:18

had spoken to you from the heart of the fire on the mountain as you were assembled below.
5 Then I came down and placed the tablets in the Ark of the Covenant, which I had made,
just as the LORD commanded me. And the tablets are still there in the Ark.
6 "The people of Israel set out from the wells of the people of Jaakan* and traveled to
Moserah, where Aaron died and was buried. His son Eleazar became the high priest in
his place. 7 Then they journeyed to Gudgodah, and from there to Jotbathah, a land with
brooks of water. 8 At that time the LORD set apart the tribe of Levi to carry the Ark of the
LORD's covenant, to minister before the LORD, and to pronounce blessings in his name.
These are still their duties. 9 That is why the Levites have no share or inheritance reserved
for them among the other Israelite tribes. The LORD himself is their inheritance, as the
LORD your God told them.
10 "As I said before, I stayed on the mountain in the LORD's presence for forty days
and nights, as I had done the first time. And once again the LORD yielded to my pleas
and didn't destroy you. 11 But the LORD said to me, 'Get up and lead the people into the
land I swore to give their ancestors, so they may take possession of it.'

A Call to Love and Obedience

10:12 Deut 6:5 Mic 6:8
10:16 Lev 26:41-42 Jer 4:4
10:17 Deut 1:17; 16:19 Ps 136:2
10:18 Exod 22:22-24 Pss 68:5; 103:6
10:19 Exod 22:21 Lev 19:34
10:20 Deut 5:11; 6:13
10:21 Exod 15:2
10:22 Gen 46:27 Deut 1:10

12 "And now, Israel, what does the LORD your God require of you? He requires you to
fear him, to live according to his will, to love and worship him with all your heart and
soul, 13 and to obey the LORD's commands and laws that I am giving you today for your
own good. 14 The highest heavens and the earth and everything in it all belong to the
LORD your God. 15 Yet the LORD chose your ancestors as the objects of his love. And he
chose you, their descendants, above every other nation, as is evident today. 16 Therefore,
cleanse your sinful hearts and stop being stubborn.
17 "The LORD your God is the God of gods and Lord of lords. He is the great God,
mighty and awesome, who shows no partiality and takes no bribes. 18 He gives justice to
orphans and widows. He shows love to the foreigners living among you and gives them
food and clothing. 19 You, too, must show love to foreigners, for you yourselves were
once foreigners in the land of Egypt. 20 You must fear the LORD your God and worship
him and cling to him. Your oaths must be in his name alone. 21 He is your God, the one
who is worthy of your praise, the one who has done mighty miracles that you yourselves
have seen. 22 When your ancestors went down into Egypt, there were only seventy of
them. But now the LORD your God has made you as numerous as the stars in the sky!

11:1 Lev 18:29-30 Deut 6:5-6; 10:12-13
11:2 Deut 5:24
11:4 Exod 14:28; 15:4 Deut 1:40

11 "You must love the LORD your God and obey all his requirements, laws, regulations, and commands. 2 Listen! I am not talking now to your children, who have
never experienced the discipline of the LORD your God or seen his greatness and
awesome power. 3 They weren't there to see the miraculous signs and wonders he
performed in Egypt against Pharaoh and all his land. 4 They didn't see what the LORD
did to the armies of Egypt and to their horses and chariots—how he drowned them in the
Red Sea* as they were chasing you, and how he has kept them devastated to this very

10:6 Or *set out from Beeroth of Bene-jaakan.* **11:4** Hebrew *sea of reeds.*

10:5 The tablets of the law were still in the Ark about 500 years later when Solomon put it in his newly built Temple (1 Kings 8:9). The Ark last appears in the Israelites' history during the reign of Josiah, about 300 years after Solomon (2 Chronicles 35:3).

10:12, 13 Often we ask, What does God expect of me? Here Moses gives a summary that is simple in form and easy to remember. Here are the essentials: (1) Fear God (have reverence for him). (2) Live according to his will. (3) Love him. (4) Worship him with all your heart and soul. (5) Obey his commands. How often we complicate faith with man-made rules, regulations, and requirements. Are you frustrated and burned out from trying hard to please God? Concentrate on his real requirements and find peace. Respect, follow, love, worship, and obey.

10:16-19 God required all male Israelites to be circumcised, but he wanted them to go beyond performing the surgery to understanding its meaning. They needed to submit to God inside, in their hearts, as well as outside, in their bodies. Then they could begin to imitate God's love and justice in their relationships with others. If our hearts are right with God, then our relationships with other people can be made right, too. When your heart has been cleansed and you have been reconciled to God, you will begin to see a difference in the way you treat others.

10:17 In saying that the Lord is God of gods and Lord of lords, Moses was distinguishing the true God from all the local gods worshiped throughout the land. Then Moses went a step further, calling God "mighty and awesome." He has such awesome power and justice that people cannot stand before him without his mercy. Fortunately, his mercy toward his people is unlimited. When we begin to grasp the extent of God's mercy toward us, we see what true love is and how deeply God loves us. Although our sins deserve severe judgment, God has chosen to show love and mercy to all who seek him.

10:20 "Your oaths must be in his name alone" means that God alone should have their allegiance.

day! 5They didn't see how the LORD cared for you in the wilderness until you arrived
here. 6They weren't there to see what he did to Dathan and Abiram (the sons of Eliab, a
descendant of Reuben) when the earth opened up and swallowed them, along with their
households and tents and every living thing that belonged to them. 7But you have seen
all the LORD's mighty deeds with your own eyes!

The Blessings of Obedience

8"Therefore, be careful to obey every command I am giving you today, so you may have
strength to go in and occupy the land you are about to enter. 9If you obey, you will enjoy
a long life in the land the LORD swore to give to your ancestors and to you, their
descendants—a land flowing with milk and honey! 10For the land you are about to enter
and occupy is not like the land of Egypt from which you came, where you planted your
seed and dug out irrigation ditches with your foot as in a vegetable garden. 11It is a land
of hills and valleys with plenty of rain—12a land that the LORD your God cares for. He
watches over it day after day throughout the year!

13"If you carefully obey all the commands I am giving you today, and if you love the
LORD your God with all your heart and soul, and if you worship him, 14then he will send
the rains in their proper seasons so you can harvest crops of grain, grapes for wine, and
olives for oil. 15He will give you lush pastureland for your cattle to graze in, and you
yourselves will have plenty to eat.

16"But do not let your heart turn away from the LORD to worship other gods. 17If you
do, the LORD's anger will burn against you. He will shut up the sky and hold back the
rain, and your harvests will fail. Then you will quickly die in that good land the LORD is
now giving you. 18So commit yourselves completely to these words of mine. Tie them
to your hands as a reminder, and wear them on your forehead. 19Teach them to your
children. Talk about them when you are at home and when you are away on a journey,
when you are lying down and when you are getting up again. 20Write them on the
doorposts of your house and on your gates, 21so that as long as the sky remains above
the earth, you and your children may flourish in the land the LORD swore to give your
ancestors.

22"Be careful to obey all the commands I give you; show love to the LORD your God
by walking in his ways and clinging to him. 23Then the LORD will drive out all the
nations in your land, though they are much greater and stronger than you. 24Wherever
you set your feet, the land will be yours. Your frontiers will stretch from the wilderness
in the south to Lebanon in the north, and from the Euphrates River in the east to the
Mediterranean Sea in the west.* 25No one will be able to stand against you, for the LORD
your God will send fear and dread ahead of you, as he promised you, wherever you go
in the whole land.

26"Today I am giving you the choice between a blessing and a curse! 27You will be
blessed if you obey the commands of the LORD your God that I am giving you today.
28You will receive a curse if you reject the commands of the LORD your God and turn
from his way by worshiping foreign gods.

29"When the LORD your God brings you into the land to possess it, you must

11:6 Num 16:31; 26:10-11
11:8 Deut 31:6-7, 23 Josh 1:6-7
11:9 Deut 4:40; 5:33; 9:5 Prov 10:27
11:11 Deut 8:7-9
11:13 Deut 4:29; 6:17; 10:12
11:14 Lev 26:4-5 Deut 28:12
11:15 Deut 6:10-12
11:16 Deut 8:19; 29:18
11:17 Deut 4:26; 28:24
11:18 Exod 13:9, 16
11:19 Deut 4:9; 6:7
11:22 Deut 6:17; 10:20
11:23 Deut 4:38; 7:1
11:24 Gen 15:8 Exod 23:31 Deut 1:7-8 Josh 1:3
11:25 Exod 23:27 Deut 7:24
11:26 Deut 30:1, 15-20
11:29 Deut 27:12-26 Josh 8:30-35

11:24 Hebrew *to the western sea.*

11:7 Israel had strong reasons to believe in God and obey his commands. They had witnessed a parade of mighty miracles that demonstrated God's love and care for them. Incredibly, they still had trouble remaining faithful. Because few of us have seen such dramatic miracles, it may seem even more difficult for us to obey God and remain faithful. But we have the Bible, the written record of God's acts throughout history. Reading God's Word gives us a panoramic view of both the miracles Israel saw and others they didn't see. The lessons from the past, the instructions for the present, and the glimpses into the future give us many opportunities to strengthen our faith in God.

11:26 What is God's curse? It is not a magician's spell. To understand it, we must remember the conditions of the covenant between God and Israel. Both parties had agreed to the terms. The blessings would benefit Israel if they kept their part of the covenant: They would receive the land, live there forever, have fruitful crops, and expel their enemies. The curse would fall on Israel only if they broke their agreement; then they would forfeit God's blessing and be in danger of crop failure, invasion, and expulsion from their land. Joshua later reviewed these blessings and curses with the entire nation (Joshua 8:34).

11:26 It is amazing that God set before the Israelites a choice between blessings and curses. It is even more amazing that most of them, through their disobedience, chose the curses. We have the same fundamental choice today. We can live for ourselves or live in service to God. To choose our own way is to travel on a dead-end road, but to choose God's way is to receive eternal life (John 5:24).

pronounce a blessing from Mount Gerizim and a curse from Mount Ebal. 30(These two
mountains are west of the Jordan River in the land of the Canaanites who live in the
Jordan Valley,* near the town of Gilgal. They are located toward the west, not far from
the oaks of Moreh.) 31For you are about to cross the Jordan to occupy the land the LORD
your God is giving you. When you are living in that land, 32you must be careful to obey
all the laws and regulations I am giving you today.

3. Laws for proper worship

The LORD's Chosen Place for Worship

12 "These are the laws and regulations you must obey as long as you live in the land
the LORD, the God of your ancestors, is giving you.
2"When you drive out the nations that live there, you must destroy all the places where
they worship their gods—high on the mountains, up on the hills, and under every green
tree. 3Break down their altars and smash their sacred pillars. Burn their Asherah poles
and cut down their carved idols. Erase the names of their gods from those places!
4"Do not worship the LORD your God in the way these pagan peoples worship their
gods. 5Rather, you must seek the LORD your God at the place he himself will choose
from among all the tribes for his name to be honored. 6There you will bring to the LORD
your burnt offerings, your sacrifices, your tithes, your special gifts, your offerings to
fulfill a vow, your freewill offerings, and your offerings of the firstborn animals of your
flocks and herds. 7There you and your families will feast in the presence of the LORD
your God, and you will rejoice in all you have accomplished because the LORD your God
has blessed you.
8"Today you are doing whatever you please, but that is not how it will be 9when you
arrive in the place of rest the LORD your God is giving you. 10You will soon cross the
Jordan River and live in the land the LORD your God is giving you as a special possession.
When he gives you rest and security from all your enemies, 11you must bring everything
I command you—your burnt offerings, your sacrifices, your tithes, your special gifts, and
your offerings to fulfill a vow—to the place the LORD your God will choose for his name
to be honored. 12You must celebrate there with your sons and daughters and all your
servants in the presence of the LORD your God. And remember the Levites who live in
your towns, for they will have no inheritance of land as their own. 13Be careful not to
sacrifice your burnt offerings just anywhere. 14You may do so only at the place the LORD
will choose within one of your tribal territories. There you must offer your burnt offerings
and do everything I command you.
15"But you may butcher animals for meat in any town, wherever you want, just as you
do now with gazelle and deer. You may eat as many animals as the LORD your God gives
you. All of you, whether ceremonially clean or unclean, may eat that meat. 16The only

11:30 Gen 12:6; Josh 4:19
11:31 Josh 1:11
12:1 Deut 4:9-10; 6:15
12:2 2 Kgs 17:10
12:5 Exod 20:24; Deut 26:2
12:6 Deut 14:22
12:7 Deut 12:12, 18; 14:26; 15:20
12:8 Judg 17:6
12:10 Josh 3:17; 11:23
12:12 Deut 10:9; 12:7, 18-19; 26:11
12:13 Deut 12:5
12:15 Deut 12:20-23; 14:3-5
12:16 Lev 17:10-12; Deut 15:23

11:30 Hebrew *the Arabah.*

12:2, 3 When taking over a nation, the Israelites were supposed to destroy every pagan altar and idol in the land. God knew it would be easy for them to change their beliefs if they started using those altars, so nothing was to remain that might tempt them to worship idols. We, too, should ruthlessly find and remove any centers of false worship in our lives. These may be activities, attitudes, possessions, relationships, places, or habits—anything that tempts us to turn our hearts from God and do wrong. We should never flatter ourselves by thinking we're too strong to be tempted. Israel learned that lesson.

12:12, 18 The Hebrews placed great emphasis on family worship. Whether offering a sacrifice or attending a great festival, the family was often together. This gave the children a healthy attitude toward worship, and it put extra meaning into it for the adults. Watching a family member confess his or her sin was just as important as celebrating a great holiday together. Although there are appropriate times to separate people by ages, some of the most meaningful worship can be experienced only when shared by old and young.

12:13, 14 While the pagans offered sacrifices to their gods, they offered them in many places. In contrast, the Israelites were only to offer sacrifices in the prescribed manner and in the prescribed places. This restriction was meant to ensure purity of worship for the nation of Israel. Later, they would neglect this injunction and offer sacrifices at the high places where pagan deities were worshiped. (See, for example, 2 Kings 23 where Josiah destroyed the other altars.) We should take steps to safeguard the purity of worship in our congregations. If we all individualized and customized worship to suit our own preferences, we would lose the benefit of worshiping as a body of believers.

12:16 Eating blood was forbidden for several reasons: (1) It was an integral part of the pagan practices of the land the Israelites were about to enter; (2) it represented life, which is sacred to God; (3) it was a symbol of the sacrifice that had to be made for sin. (For more on why eating blood was prohibited, see the note on Leviticus 17:14.)

restriction is that you are not to eat the blood. You must pour it out on the ground like
water.
17 “But your offerings must not be eaten at home—neither the tithe of your grain and **12:17**
new wine and olive oil, nor the firstborn of your flocks and herds, nor an offering to fulfill Deut 12:26;
a vow, nor your freewill offerings, nor your special gifts. 18 You must eat these in the 14:22-23 **12:18**
presence of the LORD your God at the place he will choose. Eat them there with your Deut 12:4-5, 26
children, your servants, and the Levites who live in your towns, celebrating in the presence
of the LORD your God in all you do. 19 Be very careful never to forget the Levites as long
as you live in your land.
20 “When the LORD your God enlarges your territory as he has promised, you may eat **12:20** Deut 11:24
meat whenever you want. 21 It might happen that the place the LORD your God chooses
for his name to be honored is a long way from your home. If so, you may butcher any of
the cattle or sheep the LORD has given you, and you may eat the meat at your home as I
have commanded you. 22 Anyone, whether ceremonially clean or unclean, may eat that
meat, just as you do now with gazelle and deer. 23 The only restriction is never to eat the
blood, for the blood is the life, and you must not eat the life with the meat. 24 Instead, **12:24**
pour out the blood on the ground like water. 25 Do not eat the blood; then all will go well Deut 4:40
with you and your children, because you will be doing what pleases the LORD. 26 Take **12:26**
your sacred gifts and your offerings given to fulfill a vow to the place the LORD chooses Num 5:9-10
to dwell. 27 You must offer the meat and blood of your burnt offerings on the altar of the Deut 12:17
LORD your God. The blood of your other sacrifices must be poured out beside the altar
of the LORD your God, but you may eat the meat. 28 Be careful to obey all my commands **12:28**
so that all will go well with you and your children, because you will be doing what Deut 4:40
pleases the LORD your God.
29 “When the LORD your God destroys the nations and you drive them out and occupy
their land, 30 do not be trapped into following their example in worshiping their gods. Do
not say, ‘How do these nations worship their gods? I want to follow their example.’
31 You must not do this to the LORD your God. These nations have committed many **12:31**
detestable acts that the LORD hates, all in the name of their gods. They have even burned Lev 18:21
their sons and daughters as sacrifices to their gods. 32 Carefully obey all the commands Deut 9:5; 18:10 Ps 106:37-38
I give you. Do not add to them or subtract from them. **12:32** Deut 4:2

A Warning against Idolatry

13 “Suppose there are prophets among you, or those who have dreams about the future, **13:1**
and they promise you signs or miracles, 2 and the predicted signs or miracles take Matt 24:24
place. If the prophets then say, ‘Come, let us worship the gods of foreign nations,’ 3 do not Mark 13:22 2 Thes 2:9
listen to them. The LORD your God is testing you to see if you love him with all your heart **13:3**
and soul. 4 Serve only the LORD your God and fear him alone. Obey his commands, listen Deut 6:5; 8:2, 16
to his voice, and cling to him. 5 The false prophets or dreamers who try to lead you astray **13:4** Deut 10:20
must be put to death, for they encourage rebellion against the LORD your God, who brought **13:5**
you out of slavery in the land of Egypt. Since they try to keep you from following the LORD Deut 13:9; 17:5;
your God, you must execute them to remove the evil from among you. 22:21
6 “Suppose your brother, son, daughter, beloved wife, or closest friend comes to you **13:6** Deut 17:2-7; 29:18

12:30, 31 God did not want the Israelites even to ask about the pagan religions surrounding them. Idolatry completely permeated the land of Canaan. It was too easy to get drawn into the subtle temptations of seemingly harmless practices. Sometimes curiosity can cause us to stumble. Knowledge of evil is harmful if the evil becomes too tempting to resist. To resist curiosity about harmful practices shows discretion and obedience.

13:1-3 Attractive leaders are not always led by God. Moses warned the Israelites against false prophets who encouraged worship of other gods. New ideas from inspiring people may sound good, but we must judge them by whether or not they are consistent with God's Word. When people claim to speak for God today, check them in these areas: Are they telling the truth? Is their focus on God? Are their words consistent with what you already know to be true? Some people speak the truth while directing you toward God, but others speak persuasively while directing you toward themselves. It is even possible to say the right words but still lead people in the wrong direction. God is not against new ideas, but he is for discernment. When you hear a new, attractive idea, examine it carefully before getting too excited. False prophets are still around today. The wise person will carefully test ideas against the truth of God's Word.

13:2-11 The Israelites were warned not to listen to false prophets or to anyone else who tried to get them to worship other gods—even if this person was a close friend or family member. The temptation to abandon God's commands often sneaks up on us. It may come not with a loud shout but in a whispering doubt. And whispers can be very persuasive, especially if they come from loved ones. But love for relatives should not take precedence over devotion to God. We can overcome whispered temptations by pouring out our hearts to God in prayer and by diligently studying his Word.

secretly and says, 'Let us go worship other gods'—gods that neither you nor your
ancestors have known. 7 They might suggest that you worship the gods of peoples who
live nearby or who come from the ends of the earth. 8 If they do this, do not give in or
listen, and have no pity. Do not spare or protect them. 9 You must put them to death! You
must be the one to initiate the execution; then all the people must join in. 10 Stone the
guilty ones to death because they have tried to draw you away from the LORD your God,
who rescued you from the land of Egypt, the place of slavery. 11 Then all Israel will hear
about it and be afraid, and such wickedness will never again be done among you.
12 "Suppose you hear in one of the towns the LORD your God is giving you 13 that some
worthless rabble among you have led their fellow citizens astray by encouraging them
to worship foreign gods. 14 In such cases, you must examine the facts carefully. If you
find it is true and can prove that such a detestable act has occurred among you, 15 you
must attack that town and completely destroy* all its inhabitants, as well as all the
livestock. 16 Then you must pile all the plunder in the middle of the street and burn it. Put
the entire town to the torch as a burnt offering to the LORD your God. That town must
remain a ruin forever; it may never be rebuilt. 17 Keep none of the plunder that has been
set apart for destruction. Then the LORD will turn from his fierce anger and be merciful
to you. He will have compassion on you and make you a great nation, just as he solemnly
promised your ancestors.
18 "The LORD your God will be merciful only if you obey him and keep all the
commands I am giving you today, doing what is pleasing to him.

Ceremonially Clean and Unclean Animals

14 "Since you are the people of the LORD your God, never cut yourselves or shave
the hair above your foreheads for the sake of the dead. 2 You have been set apart
as holy to the LORD your God, and he has chosen you to be his own special treasure from
all the nations of the earth.
3 "You must not eat animals that are ceremonially unclean. 4 These are the animals*
you may eat: the ox, the sheep, the goat, 5 the deer, the gazelle, the roebuck, the wild goat,
the ibex, the antelope, and the mountain sheep.
6 "Any animal that has split hooves and chews the cud may be eaten, 7 but if the animal
doesn't have both, it may not be eaten. So you may not eat the camel, the hare, or the rock
badger.* They chew the cud but do not have split hooves. 8 And the pig may not be eaten,
for though it has split hooves, it does not chew the cud. All these animals are ceremonially
unclean for you. You may not eat or even touch the dead bodies of such animals.
9 "As for marine animals, you may eat whatever has both fins and scales. 10 You may
not, however, eat marine animals that do not have both fins and scales. They are
ceremonially unclean for you.
11 "You may eat any bird that is ceremonially clean. 12 These are the birds you may not

13:8 Deut 7:2
13:9 Lev 24:13-14; Deut 13:5; 17:7
13:11 Deut 19:20
13:13 Deut 13:2
13:16 Deut 7:25-26; Josh 6:24
13:17 Exod 32:12; Num 25:4; Deut 7:13; 30:3
13:18 Deut 12:28
14:1 Lev 19:27-28; Jer 16:6
14:2 Exod 19:5
14:3-20 Lev 11:1-43
14:3 Ezek 4:14
14:4 Acts 10:14
14:12 Lev 11:3

13:15 The Hebrew term used here refers to the complete consecration of things or people to the LORD, either by destroying them or by giving them as an offering; also in 13:17. **14:4** The identification of some of the animals and birds listed in this chapter is uncertain. **14:7** Or *coney*, or *hyrax*.

13:12-16 A city that completely rejected God was to be destroyed so as not to lead the rest of the nation astray. But Israel was not to take action against a city until the rumor about its rejecting God was proven true. This guideline saved many lives when the leaders of Israel wrongly accused three tribes of falling away from their faith (Joshua 22). If we hear of friends who have wandered from the Lord or of entire congregations that have fallen away, we should check the facts and find the truth before doing or saying anything that could prove harmful. There are times, of course, when God wants us to take action—to rebuke a wayward friend, to discipline a child, to reject false teaching—but first we must be sure we have all the facts straight.

14:1 The actions described here refer to a cult of the dead. Many other religions today have some kind of worship of or service to the dead. But Christianity and Judaism are very different from other religions because they focus on serving God in this life. Don't let concern or worry over the dead distract you from the tasks that God has for you while you are still alive.

14:3-21 Why was Israel forbidden to eat certain foods? There are several reasons: (1) Predatory animals ate the blood of other animals, and scavengers ate dead animals. Because the people could not eat blood or animals they found dead, they could not eat animals that did these things either. (2) Some forbidden animals had bad associations in the Israelite culture just as bats, snakes, and spiders do for some people today. Some may have been used in pagan religious practices (Isaiah 66:17). To the Israelites, the unclean animals represented sin or unhealthy habits. (3) Perhaps some restrictions were given to Israel just to remind them continually that they were a different and separate people committed to God. Although we no longer must follow these laws about food (Acts 10:9-16), we can still learn from them the lesson that holiness is to be carried into all parts of life. We can't restrict holiness only to the spiritual side; we must be holy in the everyday practical part of life as well. Health practices, finances, use of leisure—all provide opportunities to put holy living into daily living.

eat: the eagle, the vulture, the osprey, 13 the buzzard, kites of all kinds, 14 ravens of all
kinds, 15 the ostrich, the nighthawk, the seagull, hawks of all kinds, 16 the little owl, the
great owl, the white owl, 17 the pelican, the carrion vulture, the cormorant, 18 the stork,
herons of all kinds, the hoopoe, and the bat.
19 "All flying insects are ceremonially unclean for you and may not be eaten. 20 But **14:19**
you may eat any winged creature that is ceremonially clean. Lev 11:20
21 "Do not eat anything that has died a natural death. You may give it to a foreigner **14:21** Exod 23:19; 34:26
living among you, or you may sell it to a foreigner. But do not eat it yourselves, for you Lev 17:15; 22:8
are set apart as holy to the LORD your God. Deut 14:2 Ezek 4:14
"Do not boil a young goat in its mother's milk.

The Giving of Tithes

22 "You must set aside a tithe of your crops—one-tenth of all the crops you harvest each **14:22**
year. 23 Bring this tithe to the place the LORD your God chooses for his name to be Deut 12:6, 17
honored, and eat it there in his presence. This applies to your tithes of grain, new wine, **14:23** Deut 4:10; 12:4
olive oil, and the firstborn males of your flocks and herds. The purpose of tithing is to **14:24**
teach you always to fear the LORD your God. 24 Now the place the LORD your God Deut 12:5, 21
chooses for his name to be honored might be a long way from your home. 25 If so, you
may sell the tithe portion of your crops and herds and take the money to the place the
LORD your God chooses. 26 When you arrive, use the money to buy anything you **14:26**
want—an ox, a sheep, some wine, or beer. Then feast there in the presence of the LORD Deut 12:7
your God and celebrate with your household. 27 And do not forget the Levites in your **14:27**
community, for they have no inheritance as you do. Num 18:20 Deut 12:12
28 "At the end of every third year bring the tithe of all your crops and store it in the **14:28**
nearest town. 29 Give it to the Levites, who have no inheritance among you, as well as to Deut 26:12 **14:29**
the foreigners living among you, the orphans, and the widows in your towns, so they can Deut 16:11; 24:19
eat and be satisfied. Then the LORD your God will bless you in all your work.

Release for Debtors

15 "At the end of every seventh year you must cancel your debts. 2 This is how it must **15:1**
be done. Creditors must cancel the loans they have made to their fellow Israelites. Deut 31:10-11
They must not demand payment from their neighbors or relatives, for the LORD's time **15:3**
of release has arrived. 3 This release from debt, however, applies only to your fellow Deut 23:20
Israelites—not to the foreigners living among you. 4 There should be no poor among you, **15:4**
for the LORD your God will greatly bless you in the land he is giving you as a special Deut 28:8
possession. 5 You will receive this blessing if you carefully obey the commands of the
LORD your God that I am giving you today. 6 The LORD your God will bless you as he **15:6**
has promised. You will lend money to many nations but will never need to borrow! You Deut 28:12-13
will rule many nations, but they will not rule over you!
7 "But if there are any poor people in your towns when you arrive in the land the LORD **15:7** Deut 15:11

14:21 This prohibition against cooking a young goat in its mother's milk may reflect a Canaanite fertility rite. Or it may just mean that the Israelites were not to take what was intended to promote life and use it to kill or destroy life. This commandment is also given in Exodus 23:19.

14:22, 23 The Bible makes the purpose of tithing very clear—to put God first in our lives. We are to give God the first and best of what we earn. For example, what we do first with our money shows what we value most. Giving the first part of our paycheck to God immediately focuses our attention on him. It also reminds us that all we have belongs to him. A habit of regular tithing can keep God at the top of our priority list and give us a proper perspective on everything else we have.

14:28, 29 The Bible supports an organized system of caring for the poor. God told his people to use their tithe every third year for those who were helpless, hungry, or poor. These regulations were designed to prevent the country from sinking under crushing poverty and oppression. It was everyone's responsibility to care for those less fortunate. Families were to help other family members, and towns were to help members of their community. National laws protected the rights of the poor, but helping the poor was also an active part of religious life. God counts on believers to provide for the needy, and we should use what God has given us to aid those less fortunate. Look beyond your regular giving and think of ways to help the needy. This will help you show your regard for God as Creator of all people, share God's goodness with others, and draw them to him. It is a practical and essential way to make faith work in everyday life.

15:7-11 God told the Israelites to help the poor among them when they arrived in the Promised Land. This was an important part of possessing the land. Many people conclude that people are poor through some fault of their own. This kind of reasoning makes it easy to close their hearts and hands to the needy. But we are not to invent reasons for ignoring the poor. We are to respond to their needs no matter who or what was responsible for their condition. Who are the poor in your community? How could your church help them? If your church does not have a program to identify the poor and assist in fulfilling their needs, why not help start one? What can you do to help someone in need?

15:9 Exod 22:22-23; Deut 15:1; 24:14-15; Job 34:28
15:10 2 Cor 9:5, 7
15:11 John 12:8

your God is giving you, do not be hard-hearted or tightfisted toward them. [8]Instead, be
generous and lend them whatever they need. [9]Do not be mean-spirited and refuse
someone a loan because the year of release is close at hand. If you refuse to make the
loan and the needy person cries out to the LORD, you will be considered guilty of sin.
[10]Give freely without begrudging it, and the LORD your God will bless you in everything
you do. [11]There will always be some among you who are poor. That is why I am
commanding you to share your resources freely with the poor and with other Israelites
in need.

Release for Hebrew Slaves

15:12 Exod 21:2; Lev 25:39; Jer 34:14
15:15 Deut 5:15; 16:12
15:16 Exod 21:5-6

[12]"If an Israelite man or woman voluntarily becomes your servant and serves you for six
years, in the seventh year you must set that servant free.
[13]"When you release a male servant, do not send him away empty-handed. [14]Give
him a generous farewell gift from your flock, your threshing floor, and your winepress.
Share with him some of the bounty with which the LORD your God has blessed you.
[15]Remember that you were slaves in the land of Egypt and the LORD your God redeemed
you! That is why I am giving you this command. [16]But suppose your servant says, 'I will
not leave you,' because he loves you and your family, and he is well off with you. [17]In
that case, take an awl and push it through his earlobe into the door. After that, he will be
your servant for life.
"You must do the same for your female servants.
[18]"Do not consider it a hardship when you release your servants. Remember that for
six years they have given you the services worth double the wages of hired workers, and
the LORD your God will bless you in all you do.

Sacrificing Firstborn Male Animals

15:19 Exod 13:2, 12; 34:19
15:20 Deut 12:7
15:21 Lev 22:19
15:22 Deut 12:15
15:23 Deut 12:16, 23-24

[19]"You must set aside for the LORD your God all the firstborn males from your flocks and
herds. Do not use the firstborn of your herds to work your fields, and do not shear the
firstborn of your flocks. [20]Instead, you and your family must eat these animals in the
presence of the LORD your God each year at the place he chooses. [21]But if this firstborn
animal has any defect, such as being lame or blind, or if anything else is wrong with it, you
must not sacrifice it to the LORD your God. [22]Instead, use it for food for your family at home.
Anyone may eat it, whether ceremonially clean or unclean, just as anyone may eat a gazelle
or deer. [23]But do not eat the blood. You must pour it out on the ground like water.

Passover and the Festival of Unleavened Bread

16:1-8 //Exod 12:14-20; //Lev 23:4-8; //Num 28:16-25
16:1 Exod 12:2; Num 28:16
16:2 Exod 12:5, 26
16:3 Exod 12:8, 15; 34:18
16:4 Exod 13:7; 34:25
16:6 Deut 12:5
16:7 2 Chr 35:13

16 "In honor of the LORD your God, always celebrate the Passover at the proper time
in early spring,* for that was when the LORD your God brought you out of Egypt
by night. [2]Your Passover sacrifice may be from either the flock or the herd, and it must
be sacrificed to the LORD your God at the place he chooses for his name to be honored.
[3]Eat it with bread made without yeast. For seven days eat only bread made without yeast,
as you did when you escaped from Egypt in such a hurry. Eat this bread—the bread of
suffering—so that you will remember the day you departed from Egypt as long as you
live. [4]Let no yeast be found in any house throughout your land for seven days. And do
not let any of the meat of the Passover lamb remain until the next morning.
[5]"The Passover must not be eaten in the towns that the LORD your God is giving you.
[6]It must be offered at the place the LORD your God will choose for his name to be
honored. Sacrifice it there as the sun goes down on the anniversary of your exodus from
Egypt. [7]Roast the lamb and eat it in the place the LORD your God chooses. Then go back
to your tents the next morning. [8]For the next six days you may not eat bread made with
yeast. On the seventh day the people must assemble before the LORD your God, and no
work may be done on that day.

16:1 Hebrew *in the month of Abib.* This month of the Hebrew lunar calendar usually occurs in March and April.

15:12-15 The Israelites were to release their servants after six years, sending them away with enough food so that they would be amply supplied until their needs could be met by some other means. This humanitarian act recognized that God created each person with dignity and worth. It also reminded the Israelites that they, too, had once been slaves in Egypt, and that their present freedom was a gift from God. We do not have servants such as these today, but God's instructions still apply to us: We must still be sure to treat our employees with respect and economic fairness.

The Festival of Harvest

9“Count off seven weeks from the beginning of your grain harvest. 10Then you must
celebrate the Festival of Harvest* to honor the LORD your God. Bring him a freewill
offering in proportion to the blessings you have received from him. 11It is a time to
celebrate before the LORD your God at the place he chooses for his name to be honored.
Celebrate with your whole family, all your servants, the Levites from your towns, and
the foreigners, orphans, and widows who live among you. 12Remember that you were
slaves in Egypt, so be careful to obey all these laws.

16:9-12 //Lev 23:15-22 //Num 28:26-31
16:9 Exod 23:16; 34:22 Lev 23:15 Num 28:26
16:11 Deut 12:7, 12; 14:29; 24:19

The Festival of Shelters

13“Another celebration, the Festival of Shelters, must be observed for seven days at the
end of the harvest season, after the grain has been threshed and the grapes have been
pressed. 14This festival will be a happy time of rejoicing with your family, your servants,
and with the Levites, foreigners, orphans, and widows from your towns. 15For seven
days celebrate this festival to honor the LORD your God at the place he chooses, for it is
the LORD your God who gives you bountiful harvests and blesses all your work. This
festival will be a time of great joy for all.

16“Each year every man in Israel must celebrate these three festivals: the Festival of
Unleavened Bread, the Festival of Harvest, and the Festival of Shelters. They must
appear before the LORD your God at the place he chooses on each of these occasions,
and they must bring a gift to the LORD. 17All must give as they are able, according to the
blessings given to them by the LORD your God.

16:13-17 //Lev 23:33-43 //Num 29:12-39
16:13 Lev 23:16, 40
16:16 Exod 23:14-17; 34:20, 22-24

4. Laws for ruling the nation

Justice for the People

18“Appoint judges and officials for each of your tribes in all the towns the LORD your
God is giving you. They will judge the people fairly throughout the land. 19You must
never twist justice or show partiality. Never accept a bribe, for bribes blind the eyes of
the wise and corrupt the decisions of the godly. 20Let true justice prevail, so you may
live and occupy the land that the LORD your God is giving you.

21“You must never set up an Asherah pole beside the altar of the LORD your God.
22And never set up sacred pillars for worship, for the LORD your God hates them.

16:18 Exod 18:21, 26 Deut 1:16
16:19 Exod 23:2-3 Lev 19:15
16:21 Exod 34:13 Deut 7:5

17 “Never sacrifice a sick or defective ox or sheep to the LORD your God, for he
detests such gifts.

2“Suppose a man or woman among you, in one of your towns that the LORD your God
is giving you, has done evil in the sight of the LORD your God and has violated the
covenant 3by serving other gods or by worshiping the sun, the moon, or any of the forces
of heaven, which I have strictly forbidden. 4When you hear about it, investigate the
matter thoroughly. If it is true that this detestable thing has been done in Israel, 5then that
man or woman must be taken to the gates of the town and stoned to death. 6But never
put a person to death on the testimony of only one witness. There must always be at least

17:1 Deut 15:21
17:2 Deut 13:6-11
17:4 Deut 13:12-14
17:5 Lev 24:14
17:6 Num 35:30 Deut 19:15

16:10 Or *Festival of Weeks;* also in 16:16.

16:16, 17 Three times a year every male was to make a journey to the sanctuary in the city that would be designated as Israel's religious capital. At these festivals, each participant was encouraged to give what he could in proportion to what God had given him. God does not expect us to give more than we can, but we will be blessed when we give cheerfully. For some, 10 percent may be a burden. For most of us, that would be far too little. Look at what you have and then give in proportion to what you have been given.

16:18-20 These verses anticipated a great problem the Israelites would face when they arrived in the Promised Land. Although they had Joshua as their national leader, they failed to complete the task and choose other spiritual leaders who would lead the tribes, districts, and cities with justice and God's wisdom. Because they did not appoint wise judges and faithful administrators, rebellion and injustice plagued their communities. It is a serious responsibility to appoint or elect wise and just officials. In your sphere of influence—home, church, school, job—are you ensuring that justice and godliness prevail? Failing to choose leaders who uphold justice can lead to much trouble, as Israel would discover.

17:1 The fact that this command was included probably indicates that some Israelites were sacrificing imperfect or deformed animals to God. Then, as now, it is difficult and expensive to offer God our best (i.e., the first part of what we earn). It is always tempting to shortchange God because we think we won't get caught. But our giving shows our real priorities. When we give God the leftovers, it is obvious that he is not at the center of our lives. Give God the honor of having first claim on your money, time, and talents.

17:6, 7 A person was not put to death on the testimony of only one witness. On the witness of two or three, a person could be condemned and then sentenced to death by stoning.

17:7 Lev 24:13-14; Deut 13:9; †1 Cor 5:13
17:8 Deut 12:5
17:11 Deut 25:1
17:14 Deut 11:31; Josh 21:43
17:16 1 Kgs 4:26; Ezek 17:15
17:17 2 Sam 5:13; 1 Kgs 11:3-4
17:18 Deut 31:9, 24
17:19 Deut 4:9-10; Josh 1:8
17:20 Deut 5:32
18:1 Deut 10:9; 1 Cor 9:13
18:2 Num 18:20

two or three witnesses. 7 The witnesses must throw the first stones, and then all the people
will join in. In this way, you will purge all evil from among you.
8 "Suppose a case arises in a local court that is too hard for you to decide—for instance,
whether someone is guilty of murder or only of manslaughter, or a difficult lawsuit, or a
case involving different kinds of assault. Take such cases to the place the LORD your God
will choose, 9 where the Levitical priests and the judge on duty will hear the case and
decide what to do. 10 The decision they make at the place the LORD chooses will always
stand. You must do exactly what they say. 11 After they have interpreted the law and
reached a verdict, the sentence they impose must be fully executed; do not modify it in
any way. 12 Anyone arrogant enough to reject the verdict of the judge or of the priest who
represents the LORD your God must be put to death. Such evil must be purged from Israel.
13 Then everyone will hear about it and be afraid to act so arrogantly.

Guidelines for a King

14 "You will soon arrive in the land the LORD your God is giving you, and you will conquer
it and settle there. Then you may begin to think, 'We ought to have a king like the other
nations around us.' 15 If this happens, be sure that you select as king the man the LORD your
God chooses. You must appoint a fellow Israelite, not a foreigner. 16 The king must not build
up a large stable of horses for himself, and he must never send his people to Egypt to buy
horses there, for the LORD has told you, 'You must never return to Egypt.' 17 The king must
not take many wives for himself, because they will lead him away from the LORD. And he
must not accumulate vast amounts of wealth in silver and gold for himself.
18 "When he sits on the throne as king, he must copy these laws on a scroll for himself
in the presence of the Levitical priests. 19 He must always keep this copy of the law with
him and read it daily as long as he lives. That way he will learn to fear the LORD his God
by obeying all the terms of this law. 20 This regular reading will prevent him from
becoming proud and acting as if he is above his fellow citizens. It will also prevent him
from turning away from these commands in the smallest way. This will ensure that he
and his descendants will reign for many generations in Israel.

Gifts for the Priests and Levites

18 "Remember that the Levitical priests and the rest of the tribe of Levi will not be
given an inheritance of land like the other tribes in Israel. Instead, the priests and
Levites will eat from the offerings given to the LORD by fire, for that is their inheritance.
2 They will have no inheritance of their own among the Israelites. The LORD himself is
their inheritance, just as he promised them.

The condemned person was taken outside the city gates, and the witnesses were the first to throw heavy stones down on him or her. Bystanders would then pelt the dying person with stones. This system would "purge all evil" by putting the idolater to death. At the same time, it protected the rights of accused persons two ways. First, by requiring several witnesses, it prevented any angry individual from giving false testimony. Second, by requiring the accusers to throw the first stones, it made them think twice about accusing unjustly. They were responsible to finish what they had started.

17:14-20 God was not encouraging Israel to appoint a king to rule their nation. He was actually against the idea because he was their King, and the people were to obey and follow him. But God knew that the people would one day demand a king for selfish reasons—they would want to be like the nations around them (1 Samuel 8). If they insisted on having a king, he wanted to make sure they chose the right person. That is why he included these instructions both for the people's benefit as they chose their king and for the king himself as he sought to lead the nation according to God's laws.

17:16, 17 Israel's kings did not heed this warning, and their behavior led to their downfall. Solomon had everything going for him, but when he became rich, built up a large army, and married many wives, his heart turned from God (1 Kings 11). Out of Solomon's sin came Israel's disobedience, division, and captivity.

17:18-20 The king was to be a man of God's Word. He was to (1) have a copy of the law made for his personal use, (2) keep it with him all the time, (3) read from it every day, and (4) obey it completely. Through this process he would learn respect for God, keep himself from feeling more important than others, and avoid neglecting God in times of prosperity. We can't know what God wants except through his Word, and his Word won't affect our lives unless we read and think about it regularly. With the abundant availability of the Bible today, it is not difficult to gain access to the source of the king's wisdom. What is more of a challenge is following its directives.

18:1-8 The priests and Levites served much the same function as our ministers today. Their duties included (1) teaching the people about God, (2) setting an example of godly living, (3) caring for the sanctuary and its workers, and (4) distributing the offerings. Because priests could not own property or pursue outside business interests, God made special arrangements so that people would not take advantage of them. Often churches take advantage of the men and women God has brought to lead them. For example, ministers may not be paid in accordance with their skills or the time they put in. Or pastors may be expected to attend every evening meeting, even if this continual absence is harmful to their families. As you look at your own church in light of God's Word, what ways do you see to honor the leaders God has given you?

3"These are the parts the priests may claim as their share from the oxen and sheep that
the people bring as offerings: the shoulder, the cheeks, and the stomach. 4You must also
give to the priests the first share of the grain, the new wine, the olive oil, and the wool at
shearing time. 5For the LORD your God chose the tribe of Levi out of all your tribes to
minister in the LORD's name forever.
6"Any Levite who so desires may come from any town in Israel, from wherever he is
living, to the place the LORD chooses. 7He may minister there in the name of the LORD
his God, just like his fellow Levites who are serving the LORD there. 8He may eat his
share of the sacrifices and offerings, even if he has a private source of income.

A Call to Holy Living

9"When you arrive in the land the LORD your God is giving you, be very careful not to
imitate the detestable customs of the nations living there. 10For example, never sacrifice
your son or daughter as a burnt offering.* And do not let your people practice fortune-telling
or sorcery, or allow them to interpret omens, or engage in witchcraft, 11or cast spells, or
function as mediums or psychics, or call forth the spirits of the dead. 12Anyone who does
these things is an object of horror and disgust to the LORD. It is because the other nations
have done these things that the LORD your God will drive them out ahead of you. 13You
must be blameless before the LORD your God. 14The people you are about to displace consult
with sorcerers and fortune-tellers, but the LORD your God forbids you to do such things.

True and False Prophets

15"The LORD your God will raise up for you a prophet like me from among your fellow
Israelites, and you must listen to that prophet. 16For this is what you yourselves requested
of the LORD your God when you were assembled at Mount Sinai.* You begged that you
might never again have to listen to the voice of the LORD your God or see this blazing
fire for fear you would die.
17"Then the LORD said to me, 'Fine, I will do as they have requested. 18I will raise up a
prophet like you from among their fellow Israelites. I will tell that prophet what to say, and
he will tell the people everything I command him. 19I will personally deal with anyone who
will not listen to the messages the prophet proclaims on my behalf. 20But any prophet who
claims to give a message from another god or who falsely claims to speak for me must die.'
21You may wonder, 'How will we know whether the prophecy is from the LORD or not?'
22If the prophet predicts something in the LORD's name and it does not happen, the LORD
did not give the message. That prophet has spoken on his own and need not be feared.

Cities of Refuge

19 "The LORD your God will soon destroy the nations whose land he is giving you,
and you will displace them and settle in their towns and homes. 2Then you must
set apart three cities of refuge in the land the LORD your God is giving you to occupy.
3Divide the land the LORD your God is giving you into three districts, with one of these

18:3 Lev 7:32; Num 18:11
18:4 Exod 22:29
18:5 Exod 28:1; Deut 10:8
18:6 Num 35:2-3
18:8 Lev 27:30; Num 18:21
18:9 Deut 9:5; 12:29-30
18:10 Exod 22:18; Lev 19:26, 31; 20:6; Deut 12:31; Jer 27:9-10
18:13 Gen 6:7-10; Matt 5:48
18:15 Luke 24:19; John 1:21, 24-25; †Acts 3:22; 7:37
18:16 Deut 5:23-27
18:18 †Acts 3:22
18:19 Deut 17:12; †Acts 3:22; Heb 12:25
18:20 Deut 13:1-4
18:22 Jer 28:9
19:1 Deut 6:10-12
19:2 Deut 4:41-42; Josh 20:2

18:10 Or *never make your son or daughter pass through the fire.* **18:16** Hebrew *Horeb,* another name for Sinai.

18:10 Child sacrifice and occult practices were strictly forbidden by God. These practices were common among pagan religions. Israel's own neighbors actually sacrificed their children to the god Molech (Leviticus 20:2-5). Other neighboring religions used supernatural means, such as contacting the spirit world, to foretell the future and gain guidance. Because of these wicked practices, God would drive out the pagan nations (Deuteronomy 18:12). The Israelites were to replace their evil practices with the worship of the one true God.

18:10-13 The Israelites were naturally curious about the occult practices of the Canaanite religions. But Satan is behind the occult, and God flatly forbade Israel to have anything to do with it. Today people are still fascinated by horoscopes, fortune-telling, witchcraft, and bizarre cults. Often their interest comes from a desire to know and control the future. But Satan is no less dangerous today than he was in Moses' time. In the Bible, God tells us all we need to know about what is going to happen. The information Satan offers is likely to be distorted or completely false. With the trustworthy guidance of the Holy Spirit through the Bible and the church, we don't need to turn to occult sources for faulty information.

18:15 Who is this prophet? Stephen used this verse to support his claim that Jesus Christ is God's Son, the Messiah (Acts 7:37). The coming of Jesus Christ to earth was not an afterthought, but part of God's original plan.

18:21, 22 As in the days of ancient Israel, some people today claim to have messages from God. God still speaks to his people, but we must be cautious before saying that someone is God's spokesman. How can we tell when people are speaking for the Lord? (1) We can see whether or not their prophecies come true—the ancient test for judging prophets. (2) We can check their words against the Bible. God never contradicts himself, so if someone says something contrary to the Bible, we can know that this is not God's word.

19:2, 3 The Israelites were told to build roads because these cities of refuge would have been ineffective if the roads that led to them were in disrepair. Many who came to the cities were literally running for their lives. A well-maintained road could have meant

cities in each district. Keep the roads to these cities in good repair so that anyone who
has killed someone can flee there for safety.
19:4 Num 35:9-34 4"If someone accidentally kills a neighbor without harboring any previous hatred, the
slayer may flee to any of these cities and be safe. 5For example, suppose someone goes
into the forest with a neighbor to cut wood. And suppose one of them swings an ax and
the ax head flies off the handle, killing the other person. In such cases, the slayer could
flee to one of the cities of refuge and be safe. 6If the distance to the nearest city of refuge
was too far, an enraged avenger might be able to chase down and kill the person who
caused the death. The slayer would die, even though there was no death sentence and the
first death had been an accident. 7That is why I am commanding you to set aside three
cities of refuge.
19:8 Deut 11:24 8"If the LORD your God enlarges your territory, as he solemnly promised your
19:9 Deut 6:5; 11:22 ancestors, and gives you all the land he promised them, 9you must designate three
additional cities of refuge. (He will give you this land if you obey all the commands I
19:10 Num 35:33; Deut 21:1-9 have given you—if you always love the LORD your God and walk in his ways.) 10That
way you will prevent the death of innocent people in the land the LORD your God is
giving you as a special possession, and you will not be held responsible for murder.
11"But suppose someone hates a neighbor and deliberately ambushes and murders that
neighbor and then escapes to one of the cities of refuge. 12In that case, the leaders of the
19:13 Deut 7:2 murderer's hometown must have the murderer brought back from the city of refuge and
handed over to the dead person's avenger to be killed. 13Do not feel sorry for that
19:14 Deut 27:17; Prov 23:10-11 murderer! Purge the guilt of murder from Israel so all may go well with you.

Concern for Justice

14"When you arrive in the land the LORD your God is giving you as a special possession,
19:15 Num 35:30; Deut 17:16; †Matt 18:16; †2 Cor 13:1 never steal someone's land by moving the boundary markers your ancestors set up to
mark their property.
15"Never convict anyone of a crime on the testimony of just one witness. The facts of
19:16 Exod 23:1 the case must be established by the testimony of two or three witnesses. 16If a malicious
witness comes forward and accuses someone of a crime, 17then both the accuser and
19:17 Deut 17:9; 21:5 accused must appear before the priests and judges who are on duty before the LORD.
19:19 †1 Cor 5:13; Prov 19:5 18They must be closely questioned, and if the accuser is found to be lying, 19the accuser
will receive the punishment intended for the accused. In this way, you will cleanse such
evil from among you. 20Those who hear about it will be afraid to do such an evil thing
19:21 Exod 21:24; Lev 24:20; †Matt 5:38 again. 21You must never show pity! Your rule should be life for life, eye for eye, tooth
for tooth, hand for hand, foot for foot.

20:1 Deut 3:22; 31:6-8

Regulations concerning War

20 "When you go out to fight your enemies and you face horses and chariots and an
20:2 Num 10:8; 31:6 army greater than your own, do not be afraid. The LORD your God, who brought you
20:3 Josh 23:10 safely out of Egypt, is with you! 2Before you go into battle, the priest will come forward to
speak with the troops. 3He will say, 'Listen to me, all you men of Israel! Do not be afraid

---

the difference between life and death. This involved continued maintenance, because these were dirt roads that could easily be washed away, covered by sand, or crisscrossed with deep ruts. It was important not only to initiate this system of justice but to provide the necessary means of maintaining it.

19:2-7 Every society must deal with the problem of murder. But how should society treat those who have innocently or accidentally killed someone? God had an answer for the Israelites. Since revenge was common and swift in Moses' day, God had the Israelites set apart several "cities of refuge." Anyone who claimed to have accidentally killed someone could flee to one of these cities until he could have a fair trial. If he was found innocent of intentional murder, he could remain in that city and be safe from those seeking revenge. This is a beautiful example of how God blended his justice and mercy toward his people. (For more information on cities of refuge, see the note on Numbers 35:6.)

19:12 The "avenger" was the nearest male relative to the person killed. He acted as the family protector (see Numbers 35:19).

19:21 This principle was for the judges to use, not a plan for personal vengeance. This attitude toward punishment may seem primitive, but it was actually a breakthrough for justice and fairness in ancient times when most nations used arbitrary methods to punish criminals. This guideline reflects a concern for evenhandedness and justice—ensuring that those who violated the law were not punished more severely than their particular crime deserved. In the same spirit of justice, a false witness was to receive the same punishment the accused person would have suffered. The principle of making the punishment fit the crime should still be observed today.

20:1 Just like the Israelites, we sometimes face overwhelming opposition. Whether at school, at work, or even at home, we can feel outnumbered and helpless. God bolstered the Israelites' confidence by reminding them that he was always with them and that he had already saved them from the potential danger. We, too, can feel secure when we consider that God is able to overcome even the most difficult odds.

as you go out to fight today! Do not lose heart or panic. 4For the LORD your God is going
with you! He will fight for you against your enemies, and he will give you victory!'
5"Then the officers of the army will address the troops and say, 'Has anyone just built 20:5 Neh 12:27
a new house but not yet dedicated it? If so, go home! You might be killed in the battle,
and someone else would dedicate your house! 6Has anyone just planted a vineyard but 20:6 Lev 19:23
not yet eaten any of its fruit? If so, go home! You might die in battle, and someone else
would eat from it! 7Has anyone just become engaged? Well, go home and get married! 20:7 Deut 24:5
You might die in the battle, and someone else would marry your fiancée.' 8Then the 20:8 Judg 7:3
officers will also say, 'Is anyone terrified? If you are, go home before you frighten
anyone else.' 9When the officers have finished saying this to their troops, they will
announce the names of the unit commanders.
10"As you approach a town to attack it, first offer its people terms for peace. 11If they 20:10 Luke 14:31-32
accept your terms and open the gates to you, then all the people inside will serve you in
forced labor. 12But if they refuse to make peace and prepare to fight, you must attack the
town. 13When the LORD your God hands it over to you, kill every man in the town. 14But 20:13 Num 31:7
you may keep for yourselves all the women, children, livestock, and other plunder. You 20:14 Josh 8:2
may enjoy the spoils of your enemies that the LORD your God has given you. 15But these
instructions apply only to distant towns, not to the towns of nations nearby.
16"As for the towns of the nations the LORD your God is giving you as a special 20:16 Exod 23:31 Deut 7:1-2
possession, destroy every living thing in them. 17You must completely destroy* the
Hittites, Amorites, Canaanites, Perizzites, Hivites, and Jebusites, just as the LORD your
God has commanded you. 18This will keep the people of the land from teaching you their 20:18 Deut 7:4; 9:5; 12:30
detestable customs in the worship of their gods, which would cause you to sin deeply
against the LORD your God.
19"When you are besieging a town and the war drags on, do not destroy the trees. Eat
the fruit, but do not cut down the trees. They are not enemies that need to be attacked!
20But you may cut down trees that you know are not valuable for food. Use them to make
the equipment you need to besiege the town until it falls.

5. Laws for human relationships

Cleansing for Unsolved Murder

21 "Suppose someone is found murdered in a field in the land the LORD your God is
giving you, and you don't know who committed the murder. 2In such cases, your
leaders and judges must determine which town is nearest the body. 3Then the leaders of
that town must select a young cow that has never been trained or yoked to a plow. 4They
must lead it to a valley that is neither plowed nor planted with a stream running through
it. There they must break the cow's neck. 5The Levitical priests must go there also, for 21:5 Deut 10:8; 17:9; 19:17
the LORD your God has chosen them to minister before him and to pronounce blessings
in the LORD's name. And they are to decide all lawsuits and punishments.
6"The leaders of the town nearest the body must wash their hands over the young cow 21:6 Matt 27:24
whose neck was broken. 7Then they must say, 'Our hands did not shed this blood, nor
did we see it happen. 8O LORD, forgive your people Israel whom you have redeemed. 21:8 Num 35:33-34 Jon 1:14
Do not charge your people Israel with the guilt of murdering an innocent person.' Then
they will be absolved of the guilt of this person's blood. 9By following these instructions 21:9 Deut 19:13
and doing what is right in the LORD's sight, you will cleanse the guilt of murder from
your community.

20:17 The Hebrew term used here refers to the complete consecration of things or people to the LORD, either by destroying them or by giving them as an offering.

20:13-18 How could a merciful and just God order the destruction of entire population centers? He did this to protect his people from idol worship, which was certain to bring ruin to Israel (20:18). In fact, because Israel did not completely destroy these evil people as God commanded, Israel was constantly oppressed by them and experienced greater bloodshed and destruction than if they had followed God's instructions in the first place.

20:20 Archaeologists have uncovered the remnants of many well-fortified cities in Canaan. Some had tall walls (up to 30 feet high), ramparts, moats, and towers. Accustomed to fighting on the open plains, the Israelites were going to have to learn new battle strategies to conquer these massive fortresses.

21:1-9 When a crime was committed and the criminal got away, the whole community was held responsible. In much the same way, if a city has a dangerous intersection and someone is killed there, the community may be held responsible for both damages and repairs. God was pointing to the need for the whole community to feel a keen sense of responsibility for what was going on around them and to move to correct any situations that were potentially harmful—physically, socially, or morally.

Marriage to a Captive Woman
21:10 Josh 21:44 10“Suppose you go to war against your enemies and the LORD your God hands them over
21:12 Lev 14:8-9 to you and you take captives. 11And suppose you see among the captives a beautiful
Num 6:9 woman, and you are attracted to her and want to marry her. 12If this happens, you may
21:13 take her to your home, where she must shave her head, cut her fingernails, 13and change
Ps 45:10 all her clothes. Then she must remain in your home for a full month, mourning for her
21:14 father and mother. After that you may marry her. 14But if you marry her and then decide
Gen 34:2 you do not like her, you must let her go free. You may not sell her or treat her as a slave,
for you have humiliated her.

Rights of the Firstborn
15“Suppose a man has two wives, but he loves one and not the other, and both have given
him sons. And suppose the firstborn son is the son of the wife he does not love. 16When
the man divides the inheritance, he may not give the larger inheritance to his younger
21:17 Gen 49:3 son, the son of the wife he loves. 17He must give the customary double portion to his
oldest son, who represents the strength of his father’s manhood and who owns the rights
of the firstborn son, even though he is the son of the wife his father does not love.

Dealing with a Rebellious Son
21:18 Prov 1:8 18“Suppose a man has a stubborn, rebellious son who will not obey his father or mother,
even though they discipline him. 19In such cases, the father and mother must take the
son before the leaders of the town. 20They must declare: ‘This son of ours is stubborn
21:21 and rebellious and refuses to obey. He is a worthless drunkard.’ 21Then all the men of
Lev 20:2, 27 the town must stone him to death. In this way, you will cleanse this evil from among you,
Num 15:35 and all Israel will hear about it and be afraid.

Various Regulations
21:22 22“If someone has committed a crime worthy of death and is executed and then hanged
Matt 26:65-66 **21:23** on a tree, 23the body must never remain on the tree overnight. You must bury the body
John 19:31 that same day, for anyone hanging on a tree is cursed of God. Do not defile the land the
†Gal 3:13 LORD your God is giving you as a special possession.

22:1 Exod 23:4 **22** “If you see your neighbor’s ox or sheep wandering away, don’t pretend not to see
it. Take it back to its owner. 2If it does not belong to someone nearby or you don’t
know who the owner is, keep it until the owner comes looking for it; then return it. 3Do
the same if you find your neighbor’s donkey, clothing, or anything else your neighbor
loses. Don’t pretend you did not see it.
4“If you see your neighbor’s ox or donkey lying on the road, do not look the other
way. Go and help your neighbor get it to its feet!
5“A woman must not wear men’s clothing, and a man must not wear women’s
22:6 clothing. The LORD your God detests people who do this.
Lev 22:28 6“If you find a bird’s nest on the ground or in a tree and there are young ones or eggs
in it with the mother sitting in the nest, do not take the mother with the young. 7You may
take the young, but let the mother go, so you may prosper and enjoy a long life.
8“Every new house you build must have a barrier around the edge of its flat rooftop.
That way you will not bring the guilt of bloodshed on your household if someone falls
from the roof.
22:9 Lev 19:19 9“Do not plant any other crop between the rows of your vineyard. If you do, you are
forbidden to use either the grapes from the vineyard or the produce of the other crop.

21:18-21 Disobedient and rebellious children were to be brought before the elders of the city and stoned to death. There is no biblical or archaeological evidence that this punishment was ever carried out, but the point was that disobedience and rebellion were not to be tolerated in the home or allowed to continue unchecked.

22:1-4 The Hebrews were to care for and return lost animals or possessions to their rightful owners. The way of the world, by contrast, is “Finders keepers, losers weepers.” To go beyond the finders-keepers rule by protecting and returning the property of others keeps us from being envious and greedy.

22:5 This verse commands men and women not to reverse their sexual roles. It is not a statement about clothing styles. Today role rejections are common—there are men who want to become women and women who want to become men. It’s not the clothing style that offends God, but using the style to act out a different sex role. God had a purpose in making us uniquely male and female.

22:8-11 These are practical laws, helpful for establishing good habits for everyday living. Verse 8: Since people used their flat roofs as porches, a guardrail was a wise safety precaution.

10“Do not plow with an ox and a donkey harnessed together.
11“Do not wear clothing made of wool and linen woven together.
12“You must put tassels on the four corners of your cloaks.

Regulations for Sexual Purity

13“Suppose a man marries a woman and, after sleeping with her, changes his mind about
her 14and falsely accuses her of having slept with another man. He might say, ‘I
discovered she was not a virgin when I married her.’ 15If the man does this, the woman’s
father and mother must bring the proof of her virginity to the leaders of the town. 16Her
father must tell them, ‘I gave my daughter to this man to be his wife, and now he has
turned against her. 17He has accused her of shameful things, claiming that she was not a
virgin when he married her. But here is the proof of my daughter’s virginity.’ Then they
must spread the cloth before the judges. 18The judges must then punish the man. 19They
will fine him one hundred pieces of silver,* for he falsely accused a virgin of Israel. The
payment will be made to the woman’s father. The woman will then remain the man’s
wife, and he may never divorce her.
20“But suppose the man’s accusations are true, and her virginity could not be proved.
21In such cases, the judges must take the girl to the door of her father’s home, and the
men of the town will stone her to death. She has committed a disgraceful crime in Israel
by being promiscuous while living in her parents’ home. Such evil must be cleansed from
among you.
22“If a man is discovered committing adultery, both he and the other man’s wife must
be killed. In this way, the evil will be cleansed from Israel.
23“Suppose a man meets a young woman, a virgin who is engaged to be married, and
he has sexual intercourse with her. If this happens within a town, 24you must take both
of them to the gates of the town and stone them to death. The woman is guilty because
she did not scream for help. The man must die because he violated another man’s wife.
In this way, you will cleanse the land of evil.
25“But if the man meets the engaged woman out in the country, and he rapes her, then
only the man should die. 26Do nothing to the young woman; she has committed no crime
worthy of death. This case is similar to that of someone who attacks and murders a
neighbor. 27Since the man raped her out in the country, it must be assumed that she
screamed, but there was no one to rescue her.
28“If a man is caught in the act of raping a young woman who is not engaged, 29he
must pay fifty pieces of silver* to her father. Then he must marry the young woman
because he violated her, and he will never be allowed to divorce her.
30“A man must not have intercourse with his father’s wife, for this would violate his
father.

Regulations concerning Worship

23 “If a man’s testicles are crushed or his penis is cut off, he may not be included in
the assembly of the LORD.
2“Those of illegitimate birth and their descendants for ten generations may not be
included in the assembly of the LORD.
3“No Ammonites or Moabites, or any of their descendants for ten generations, may
be included in the assembly of the LORD. 4These nations did not welcome you with food
and water when you came out of Egypt. Instead, they tried to hire Balaam son of Beor

22:10 2 Cor 6:14
22:12 Num 15:37-39; Matt 23:5
22:13 Deut 24:1
22:21 Deut 23:17-18
22:22 Lev 20:10; Ezek 16:38; John 8:5
22:23 Lev 19:20-22
22:28 Exod 22:16
22:30 Lev 18:8; 20:11; Deut 27:20
23:1 Lev 21:20; 22:24
23:3 Neh 13:1-2
23:4 Num 23:4, 7-10; 2 Pet 2:15; Jude 1:11

22:19 Hebrew *100 shekels of silver,* about 2.5 pounds or 1.1 kilograms in weight. **22:29** Hebrew *50 shekels of silver,* about 1.25 pounds or 570 grams in weight.

Verse 9: If you plant two different crops side by side, one of them will not survive, since the stronger, taller one will block the sunlight and take most of the vital nutrients from the soil. Verse 10: A donkey and an ox, due to differences in strength and size, cannot pull a plow evenly. Verse 11: Two different kinds of thread wear unevenly and wash differently. Combining them reduces the life of the garment. Don’t think of God’s laws as arbitrary restrictions. Look for the reasons behind the laws. They are made not just to teach or restrict but also to protect.

22:13-30 Why did God include all these laws about sexual sins? Instructions about sexual behavior would have been vital for three million people on a 40-year camping trip. But they would be equally important when they entered the Promised Land and settled down as a nation. Paul, in Colossians 3:5-8, recognizes the importance of strong rules about sex for believers because sexual sins have the power to disrupt and destroy the church. Sins involving sex are not innocent dabblings in forbidden pleasures, as is so often portrayed, but powerful destroyers of relationships. They confuse and tear down the climate of respect, trust, and credibility that is so essential for solid marriages and secure children.

from Pethor in Aram-naharaim* to curse you. 5(But the LORD your God would not listen
to Balaam. He turned the intended curse into a blessing because the LORD your God loves
you.) 6You must never, as long as you live, try to help the Ammonites or the Moabites
in any way.

23:7 Lev 19:34; Deut 10:19

7"Do not detest the Edomites or the Egyptians, because the Edomites are your
relatives, and you lived as foreigners among the Egyptians. 8The third generation of
Egyptians who came with you from Egypt may enter the assembly of the LORD.

Miscellaneous Regulations

9"When you go to war against your enemies, stay away from everything impure.
10"Any man who becomes ceremonially defiled because of a nocturnal emission must

23:11 Lev 15:16

leave the camp and stay away all day. 11Toward evening he must bathe himself, and at
sunset he may return to the camp.
12"Mark off an area outside the camp for a latrine. 13Each of you must have a spade
as part of your equipment. Whenever you relieve yourself, you must dig a hole with the

23:14 Lev 26:12

spade and cover the excrement. 14The camp must be holy, for the LORD your God moves
around in your camp to protect you and to defeat your enemies. He must not see any
shameful thing among you, or he might turn away from you.

23:15 1 Sam 30:15

15"If slaves should escape from their masters and take refuge with you, do not force
them to return. 16Let them live among you in whatever town they choose, and do not
oppress them.

23:17 Lev 18:22; 20:13; Deut 22:21

17"No Israelite man or woman may ever become a temple prostitute. 18Do not bring
to the house of the LORD your God any offering from the earnings of a prostitute, whether
a man or a woman, for both are detestable to the LORD your God.

23:19 Exod 22:25; Lev 25:36

19"Do not charge interest on the loans you make to a fellow Israelite, whether it is
money, food, or anything else that may be loaned with interest. 20You may charge

23:20 Deut 28:12

interest to foreigners, but not to Israelites, so the LORD your God may bless you in
everything you do in the land you are about to enter and occupy.

23:21 Num 30:1-2; Eccl 5:4; Matt 5:33

21"When you make a vow to the LORD your God, be prompt in doing whatever you
promised him. For the LORD your God demands that you promptly fulfill all your vows.
If you don't, you will be guilty of sin. 22However, it is not a sin to refrain from making
a vow. 23But once you have voluntarily made a vow, be careful to do as you have said,
for you have made a vow to the LORD your God.

23:25 Matt 12:1-2; Mark 2:23; Luke 6:1

24"You may eat your fill of grapes from your neighbor's vineyard, but do not take any
away in a basket. 25And you may pluck a few heads of your neighbor's grain by hand,
but you may not harvest it with a sickle.

24:1 Num 5:12-28; Deut 22:13-21; †Matt 5:31; 19:7; Mark 10:4-5

24

"Suppose a man marries a woman but later discovers something about her that is
shameful. So he writes her a letter of divorce, gives it to her, and sends her away.
2If she then leaves and marries another man 3and the second husband also divorces her
or dies, 4the former husband may not marry her again, for she has been defiled. That
would be detestable to the LORD. You must not bring guilt upon the land the LORD your
God is giving you as a special possession.

23:4 *Aram-naharaim* means "Aram of the two rivers," thought to have been located between the Euphrates and Balih Rivers in northwestern Mesopotamia.

23:17, 18 Prostitution was not overlooked in God's law—it was strictly forbidden. To forbid this practice may seem obvious to us, but it may not have been so obvious to the Israelites. Almost every other religion known to them included prostitution as an integral part of its worship services. Prostitution makes a mockery of God's original idea for sex, treating sex as an isolated physical act rather than an act of commitment to another. Outside of marriage, sex destroys relationships. Within marriage, if approached with the right attitude, it can be a relationship builder. God frequently had to warn the people against the practice of extramarital sex. Today we still need to hear his warnings.

23:24, 25 This commandment guarded against selfishly holding on to one's possessions. It also ensured that no one had to go hungry. It was not, however, an excuse for taking advantage of one's neighbor. The Pharisees did not interpret this appropriately when they accused Jesus and the disciples of harvesting on the Sabbath (Matthew 12:1, 2).

24:1-4 Some think this passage supports divorce, but that is not the case. It simply recognizes a practice that already existed in Israel. All four verses must be read to understand the point of the passage; it certainly is not suggesting that a man divorce his wife on a whim. Divorce was a permanent and final act for the couple. Once divorced and remarried to others, they could never be remarried to each other (24:4). This restriction was to prevent casual remarriage after a frivolous separation. The intention was to make people think twice before divorcing.

5 “A newly married man must not be drafted into the army or given any other special 24:5 Deut 20:7
responsibilities. He must be free to be at home for one year, bringing happiness to the
wife he has married.
6 “It is wrong to take a pair of millstones, or even just the upper millstone, as a pledge,
for the owner uses it to make a living.
7 “If anyone kidnaps a fellow Israelite and treats him as a slave or sells him, the
kidnapper must die. You must cleanse the evil from among you.
8 “Watch all contagious skin diseases* carefully and follow the instructions of the 24:8 Lev 13:1, 59
Levitical priests; obey the commands I have given them. 9 Remember what the LORD 24:9
your God did to Miriam as you were coming from Egypt. Num 12:10
10 “If you lend anything to your neighbor, do not enter your neighbor’s house to claim 24:10 Exod 22:24-26
the security. 11 Stand outside and the owner will bring it out to you. 12 If your neighbor is
poor and has only a cloak to give as security, do not keep the cloak overnight. 13 Return
the cloak to its owner by sunset so your neighbor can sleep in it and bless you. And the
LORD your God will count it as a righteous act.
14 “Never take advantage of poor laborers, whether fellow Israelites or foreigners 24:14 Lev 19:13
living in your towns. 15 Pay them their wages each day before sunset because they are 1 Tim 5:18
poor and are counting on it. Otherwise they might cry out to the LORD against you, and
it would be counted against you as sin.
16 “Parents must not be put to death for the sins of their children, nor the children for 24:16 2 Kgs 14:6
the sins of their parents. Those worthy of death must be executed for their own crimes. 2 Chr 25:4 Ezek 18:20
17 “True justice must be given to foreigners living among you and to orphans, and you 24:17
must never accept a widow’s garment in pledge of her debt. 18 Always remember that you Exod 22:21-22; 23:2-3
were slaves in Egypt and that the LORD your God redeemed you. That is why I have given Deut 1:17; 10:17
you this command. 24:18
19 “When you are harvesting your crops and forget to bring in a bundle of grain from Deut 5:15
your field, don’t go back to get it. Leave it for the foreigners, orphans, and widows. Then 24:19 Lev 19:9-10
the LORD your God will bless you in all you do. 20 When you beat the olives from your Deut 14:28-29
olive trees, don’t go over the boughs twice. Leave some of the olives for the foreigners, 24:20 Lev 19:10
orphans, and widows. 21 This also applies to the grapes in your vineyard. Do not glean
the vines after they are picked, but leave any remaining grapes for the foreigners,
orphans, and widows. 22 Remember that you were slaves in the land of Egypt. That is
why I am giving you this command.

25

“Suppose two people take a dispute to court, and the judges declare that one is 25:1 Deut 17:11
right and the other is wrong. 2 If the person in the wrong is sentenced to be flogged,
the judge will command him to lie down and be beaten in his presence with the number
of lashes appropriate to the crime. 3 No more than forty lashes may ever be given; more 25:3 2 Cor 11:24
than forty lashes would publicly humiliate your neighbor.

24:8 Traditonally rendered *leprosy.* The Hebrew word used here can describe various skin diseases.

24:5 Newly married couples were to remain together their first year. This was to avoid placing an excessive burden upon a new, unproven relationship and to give it a chance to mature and strengthen before confronting it with numerous responsibilities. A gardener starts a tiny seedling in a small pot and allows it to take root before planting it in the field. Let your marriage grow strong by protecting your relationship from too many outside pressures and distractions—especially in the beginning. And don’t expect or demand so much from newlyweds that they have inadequate time or energy to establish their marriage.

24:10-22 Throughout the Old Testament God told his people to treat the poor with justice. The powerless and poverty-stricken are often looked upon as incompetent or lazy when, in fact, they may be victims of oppression and circumstance. God says we must do all we can to help these needy ones. His justice did not permit the Israelites to insist on profits or quick payment from those who were less fortunate. Instead, his laws gave the poor every opportunity to better their situation, while providing humane options for those who couldn’t. None of us is completely isolated from the poor. God wants us to treat them fairly and do our part to see that their needs are met.

24:19-21 God’s people were instructed to leave some of their harvest in the fields so travelers and the poor could gather it. This second gathering, called gleaning, was a way for them to provide food for themselves. Years later, Ruth obtained food for herself and Naomi by gleaning behind the reapers in Boaz’s field, picking up the leftovers (Ruth 2:2). Because this law was being obeyed years after it was written, Ruth, a woman in Christ’s lineage, was able to find food.

25:1-3 At first glance these verses appear irrelevant today. But a closer look reveals some important principles about discipline. Are you responsible for the discipline of a child, a student, or an employee? Three important points will help you carry out your responsibility: (1) Let the punishment follow quickly after the offense; (2) let the degree of punishment reflect the seriousness of the offense; and (3) don’t overdo the punishment. Discipline that is swift, just, and restrained makes its point while preserving the dignity of the offender.

25:4 †1 Cor 9:9 †1 Tim 5:18 4“Do not keep an ox from eating as it treads out the grain.
5“If two brothers are living together on the same property and one of them dies without
25:5 †Matt 22:24 Mark 12:19 †Luke 20:28 a son, his widow must not marry outside the family. Instead, her husband’s brother must
marry her and fulfill the duties of a brother-in-law. 6The first son she bears to him will be
25:6 Ruth 4:5 counted as the son of the dead brother, so that his name will not be forgotten in Israel. 7But
if the dead man’s brother refuses to marry the widow, she must go to the town gate and
say to the leaders there, ‘My husband’s brother refuses to preserve his brother’s name in
Israel—he refuses to marry me.’ 8The leaders of the town will then summon him and try
to reason with him. If he still insists that he doesn’t want to marry her, 9the widow must
25:9-10 Ruth 4:7-8 walk over to him in the presence of the leaders, pull his sandal from his foot, and spit in
his face. She will then say, ‘This is what happens to a man who refuses to raise up a son
for his brother.’ 10Ever afterward his family will be referred to as ‘the family of the man
whose sandal was pulled off’!
25:12 Deut 7:2 11“If two Israelite men are fighting and the wife of one tries to rescue her husband by
grabbing the testicles of the other man, 12her hand must be cut off without pity.
25:13 Lev 19:35 Prov 11:1; 16:11 Ezek 45:10-11 13“You must use accurate scales when you weigh out merchandise, 14and you must
use full and honest measures. 15Yes, use honest weights and measures, so that you will
25:16 Prov 11:1 enjoy a long life in the land the LORD your God is giving you. 16Those who cheat with
dishonest weights and measures are detestable to the LORD your God.
25:17 Exod 17:8-16 17“Never forget what the Amalekites did to you as you came from Egypt. 18They
attacked you when you were exhausted and weary, and they struck down those who were
25:19 Deut 14:29 lagging behind. They had no fear of God. 19Therefore, when the LORD your God has
given you rest from all your enemies in the land he is giving you as a special possession,
you are to destroy the Amalekites and erase their memory from under heaven. Never
forget this!

Harvest Offerings and Tithes

26:2 Exod 22:29; 23:16, 19 **26** “When you arrive in the land the LORD your God is giving you as a special
possession and you have conquered it and settled there, 2put some of the first
produce from each harvest into a basket and bring it to the place the LORD your God
chooses for his name to be honored. 3Go to the priest in charge at that time and say to
him, ‘With this gift I acknowledge that the LORD your God has brought me into the land
26:5 Gen 43:1; 46:27 Deut 1:10; 10:22 he swore to give our ancestors.’ 4The priest will then take the basket from your hand and
set it before the altar of the LORD your God. 5You must then say in the presence of the
LORD your God, ‘My ancestor Jacob was a wandering Aramean who went to live in
Egypt. His family was few in number, but in Egypt they became a mighty and numerous
26:6 Exod 1:11-12 nation. 6When the Egyptians mistreated and humiliated us by making us their slaves,
7we cried out to the LORD, the God of our ancestors. He heard us and saw our hardship,
26:8 Deut 4:34 toil, and oppression. 8So the LORD brought us out of Egypt with amazing power,
26:9 Exod 3:8, 17 overwhelming terror, and miraculous signs and wonders. 9He brought us to this place
and gave us this land flowing with milk and honey! 10And now, O LORD, I have brought
you a token of the first crops you have given me from the ground.’ Then place the

---

25:4 What is the point of this Old Testament regulation? Oxen were often used to tread out the grain on a threshing floor. The animal was attached by poles to a large millstone. As it walked around the millstone, its hooves trampled the grain, separating the kernels from the chaff. At the same time, the millstone ground the grain into flour. To muzzle the ox would prevent it from eating while it was working. Paul used this illustration in the New Testament to argue that people productive in Christian work should not be denied its benefits—they should receive financial support (1 Corinthians 9:9-12; 1 Timothy 5:17, 18). The fact that a person is in Christian ministry doesn’t mean he or she should be unfairly paid. There is also a broader application: Don’t be stingy with those who work for you.

25:5-10 This law describes a “levirate” marriage, the marriage of a widow to the brother of her dead husband. The purpose of such a marriage was to carry on the dead man’s name and inheritance. Family ties were an important aspect of Israelite culture. The best way to be remembered was through your line of descendants. If a widow married someone outside the family, her first husband’s line would come to an end. Tamar fought for this right in Genesis 38.

26:5-10 This recitation of God’s dealings with his people helped the people remember what God had done for them. What is the history of your relationship with God? Can you put into clear and concise words what God has done for you? Find a friend with whom you can share your spiritual journey. Telling your stories to each other will help you clearly understand your personal spiritual history, as well as encouraging and inspiring you both. Note: *Wandering* can mean lost or dying. Also, Arameans were the people of northern Syria and among the ancestors of Abraham. This is also used as a reference to Jacob, who spent many years there (Genesis 29–31) and got his two wives in Aram.

produce before the LORD your God and worship him. 11Afterward go and celebrate 26:11
because of all the good things the LORD your God has given to you and your household. Deut 12:7, 12
Remember to include the Levites and the foreigners living among you in the celebration.
12"Every third year you must offer a special tithe of your crops. You must give these 26:12 Deut 14:28-29
tithes to the Levites, foreigners, orphans, and widows so that they will have enough to eat Heb 7:5, 9-10
in your towns. 13Then you must declare in the presence of the LORD your God, 'I have
taken the sacred gift from my house and have given it to the Levites, foreigners, orphans,
and widows, just as you commanded me. I have not violated or forgotten any of your
commands. 14I have not eaten any of it while in mourning; I have not touched it while I
was ceremonially unclean; and I have not offered any of it to the dead. I have obeyed the
LORD my God and have done everything you commanded me. 15Look down from your 26:15
holy dwelling place in heaven and bless your people Israel and the land you have given Zech 2:13
us—a land flowing with milk and honey—just as you solemnly promised our ancestors.'

A Call to Obey the LORD's Commands

16"Today the LORD your God has commanded you to obey all these laws and regulations. 26:16
You must commit yourself to them without reservation. 17You have declared today that Deut 4:29
the LORD is your God. You have promised to obey his laws, commands, and regulations 26:17 Ps 48:14
by walking in his ways and doing everything he tells you. 18The LORD has declared today 26:18
that you are his people, his own special treasure, just as he promised, and that you must Deut 7:6
obey all his commands. 19And if you do, he will make you greater than any other nation. 26:19
Then you will receive praise, honor, and renown. You will be a nation that is holy to the Deut 28:1
LORD your God, just as he promised."

6. Consequences of obedience and disobedience

The Altar on Mount Ebal

27 Then Moses and the leaders of Israel charged the people as follows: "Keep all
these commands that I am giving you today. 2When you cross the Jordan River 27:2 Josh 8:30-32
and enter the land the LORD your God is giving you, set up some large stones and coat
them with plaster. 3Then write all the terms of this law on them. I repeat, you will soon
cross the river to enter the land the LORD your God is giving you, a land flowing with
milk and honey, just as the LORD, the God of your ancestors, promised you. 4When you
cross the Jordan, set up these stones at Mount Ebal and coat them with plaster, as I am
commanding you today. 5Then build an altar there to the LORD your God, using natural
stones. 6Do not shape the stones with an iron tool. On the altar you must offer burnt
offerings to the LORD your God. 7Sacrifice peace offerings on it also, and feast there with
great joy before the LORD your God. 8On the stones coated with plaster, you must clearly
write all the terms of this law."
9Then Moses and the Levitical priests addressed all Israel as follows: "O Israel, be 27:9
quiet and listen! Today you have become the people of the LORD your God. 10So obey Deut 26:17
the LORD your God by keeping all these commands and laws that I am giving you today."

Curses from Mount Ebal

11That same day Moses gave this charge to the people: 12"When you cross the Jordan 27:12 Deut 11:26
River, the tribes of Simeon, Levi, Judah, Issachar, Joseph, and Benjamin must stand on Josh 8:33-35
Mount Gerizim to proclaim a blessing over the people. 13And the tribes of Reuben, Gad,
Asher, Zebulun, Dan, and Naphtali must stand on Mount Ebal to proclaim a curse.
14Then the Levites must shout to all the people of Israel:

15'Cursed is anyone who carves or casts idols and secretly sets them up. These 27:15 Exod 20:4, 23
idols, the work of craftsmen, are detestable to the LORD.' Lev 19:3-4
And all the people will reply, 'Amen.' Deut 4:16; 5:8

26:18 Moses said that because the Israelites were now God's people, they needed to start obeying God's commands.

27:5, 6 The Lord had specified an altar made of natural, uncut stones (fieldstones) so that the people would not begin worshiping the altars as idols. To use a chisel on a stone of the altar would be to profane it (Exodus 20:24-25). Additionally, because the Israelites did not have the capacity to work with iron at this time, using iron tools might mean using the cooperation and expertise of other nations.

27:9, 10 Moses was reviewing the law with the new generation of people. When we decide to believe in God, we must also decide to follow his ways. What we do shows what we really believe. Can people tell that you are a member of God's family?

27:16 Exod 21:17; Lev 20:9; Ezek 22:7

16 'Cursed is anyone who despises father or mother.'
And all the people will reply, 'Amen.'

27:17 Deut 19:14

17 'Cursed is anyone who steals property from a neighbor by moving a boundary
marker.'
And all the people will reply, 'Amen.'

27:18 Lev 19:14

18 'Cursed is anyone who leads a blind person astray on the road.'
And all the people will reply, 'Amen.'

27:19 Exod 22:21; Lev 19:33; Deut 10:18

19 'Cursed is anyone who is unjust to foreigners, orphans, and widows.'
And all the people will reply, 'Amen.'

27:20 Lev 18:8; 20:11; Deut 22:30

20 'Cursed is anyone who has sexual intercourse with his father's wife, for he has
violated his father.'
And all the people will reply, 'Amen.'

27:21 Exod 22:19; Lev 18:23; 20:15

21 'Cursed is anyone who has sexual intercourse with an animal.'
And all the people will reply, 'Amen.'

27:22 Lev 18:9; 20:17

22 'Cursed is anyone who has sexual intercourse with his sister, whether she is the
daughter of his father or his mother.'
And all the people will reply, 'Amen.'

27:23 Lev 18:17; 20:14

23 'Cursed is anyone who has sexual intercourse with his mother-in-law.'
And all the people will reply, 'Amen.'

27:24 Exod 21:12; Lev 24:17; Num 35:30

24 'Cursed is anyone who kills another person in secret.'
And all the people will reply, 'Amen.'

27:25 Exod 23:8; Deut 10:17

25 'Cursed is anyone who accepts payment to kill an innocent person.'
And all the people will reply, 'Amen.'

27:26 Deut 28:15; Gal 3:10

26 'Cursed is anyone who does not affirm the terms of this law by obeying them.'
And all the people will reply, 'Amen.'

Blessings for Obedience

28:1 Exod 15:26; 23:22; Lev 26:3; Deut 7:12; 11:13

28 "If you fully obey the LORD your God by keeping all the commands I am giving
you today, the LORD your God will exalt you above all the nations of the world.
2 You will experience all these blessings if you obey the LORD your God:

28:2 Jer 32:24 · 28:3 Ps 144:15 · 28:4 Gen 49:25 · 28:6 Ps 121:8

3 You will be blessed in your towns and in the country.
4 You will be blessed with many children and productive fields.
You will be blessed with fertile herds and flocks.
5 You will be blessed with baskets overflowing with fruit, and with kneading bowls
filled with bread.
6 You will be blessed wherever you go, both in coming and in going.

28:7 Lev 26:8, 17 · 28:8 Deut 15:4 · 28:9 Exod 19:5

7 "The LORD will conquer your enemies when they attack you. They will attack you
from one direction, but they will scatter from you in seven!
8 "The LORD will bless everything you do and will fill your storehouses with grain.
The LORD your God will bless you in the land he is giving you.
9 "If you obey the commands of the LORD your God and walk in his ways, the LORD

27:15-26 These curses were a series of oaths, spoken by the priests and affirmed by the people, by which the people promised to stay away from wrong actions. By saying *Amen,* "So be it," the people took responsibility for their actions. Sometimes looking at a list of curses like this gives us the idea that God has a bad temper and is out to crush anyone who steps out of line. But we need to see these restrictions not as threats, but as loving warnings about the plain facts of life. Just as we warn children to stay away from hot stoves and busy streets, God warns us to stay away from dangerous actions. The natural law of his universe makes it clear that wrongdoing toward others or God has tragic consequences. God is merciful enough to tell us this truth plainly. Motivated by love and not anger, his strong words help us avoid the serious consequences that result from neglecting God or wronging others. But God does not leave us with only curses or consequences. Immediately following these curses, we discover the great blessings (positive consequences) that come from living for God (28:1-14). These give us extra incentive to obey God's laws. While all these blessings may not come in our lifetime on earth, those who obey God will experience the fullness of his blessing when he establishes the new heaven and the new earth.

will establish you as his holy people as he solemnly promised to do. [10]Then all the
nations of the world will see that you are a people claimed by the LORD, and they will
stand in awe of you.

[11]"The LORD will give you an abundance of good things in the land he swore to give **28:11**
your ancestors—many children, numerous livestock, and abundant crops. [12]The LORD Deut 28:2-6, 8
will send rain at the proper time from his rich treasury in the heavens to bless all the work **28:12** Lev 26:4
you do. You will lend to many nations, but you will never need to borrow from them. Deut 11:14; 23:20
[13]If you listen to these commands of the LORD your God and carefully obey them, the **28:13** Deut 28:1, 44
LORD will make you the head and not the tail, and you will always have the upper hand.
[14]You must not turn away from any of the commands I am giving you today to follow **28:14** Deut 5:32-33
after other gods and worship them.

Curses for Disobedience

[15]"But if you refuse to listen to the LORD your God and do not obey all the commands **28:15** Lev 26:14
and laws I am giving you today, all these curses will come and overwhelm you: Josh 23:15-16

[16] You will be cursed in your towns and in the country.
[17] You will be cursed with baskets empty of fruit, and with kneading bowls empty of
bread.
[18] You will be cursed with few children and barren fields.
You will be cursed with infertile herds and flocks.
[19] You will be cursed wherever you go, both in coming and in going.

[20]"The LORD himself will send against you curses, confusion, and disillusionment in **28:20** Deut 8:11; 28:25
everything you do, until at last you are completely destroyed for doing evil and forsaking **28:21** Lev 26:25
me. [21]The LORD will send diseases among you until none of you are left in the land you Num 14:12
are about to enter and occupy. [22]The LORD will strike you with wasting disease, fever, Amos 4:10
and inflammation, with scorching heat and drought, and with blight and mildew. These **28:23** Lev 26:19
devastations will pursue you until you die. [23]The skies above will be as unyielding as
bronze, and the earth beneath will be as hard as iron. [24]The LORD will turn your rain into **28:24** Deut 11:17
sand and dust, and it will pour down from the sky until you are destroyed. 1 Kgs 17:1 Jer 14:1

[25]"The LORD will cause you to be defeated by your enemies. You will attack your **28:25**
enemies from one direction, but you will scatter from them in seven! You will be an 2 Chr 29:8 Isa 30:17
object of horror to all the kingdoms of the earth. [26]Your dead bodies will be food for the Jer 15:4
birds and wild animals, and no one will be there to chase them away. **28:26** Ps 79:2

[27]"The LORD will afflict you with the boils of Egypt and with tumors, scurvy, and the Jer 7:33; 16:4;
itch, from which you cannot be cured. [28]The LORD will strike you with madness, 19:7; 34:20
blindness, and panic. [29]You will grope around in broad daylight, just like a blind person **28:27**
groping in the darkness, and you will not succeed at anything you do. You will be Exod 9:9; 15:26 Deut 7:15
oppressed and robbed continually, and no one will come to save you. 1 Sam 5:6, 9, 12

[30]"You will be engaged to a woman, but another man will ravish her. You will build **28:29** Exod 10:21
a house, but someone else will live in it. You will plant a vineyard, but you will never Job 5:14
enjoy its fruit. [31]Your ox will be butchered before your eyes, but you won't get a single Isa 59:10
bite of the meat. Your donkey will be driven away, never to be returned. Your sheep will **28:30** Deut 20:6-7
be given to your enemies, and no one will be there to help you. [32]You will watch as your Job 31:10 Isa 65:22
sons and daughters are taken away as slaves. Your heart will break as you long for them, Amos 5:11
but nothing you do will help. [33]A foreign nation you have never heard about will eat the
crops you worked so hard to grow. You will suffer under constant oppression and harsh **28:34** Deut 28:28
treatment. [34]You will go mad because of all the tragedy around you. [35]The LORD will **28:35**
cover you from head to foot with incurable boils. Job 2:7

[36]"The LORD will exile you and the king you crowned to a nation unknown to you **28:36** 2 Kgs 17:4, 6;
and your ancestors. Then in exile you will worship gods of wood and stone! [37]You will 24:12, 14; 25:7, 11

28:23, 24 This curse is referring to a drought.

28:34 One of the curses for those who rejected God was that they would go mad from seeing all the tragedy around them. Do you ever feel that you will go crazy if you hear about one more rape, kidnapping, murder, or war? Much of the world's evil is a result of people's failure to acknowledge and serve God. When you hear bad news, don't groan helplessly as do unbelievers who have no hope for the future. Remind yourself that in spite of it all, God has ultimate control and will one day come back to make everything right.

28:36 This happened when Assyria and Babylonia took the Israelites captive to their lands (2 Kings 17:23; 25:11).

become an object of horror, a proverb and a mockery among all the nations to which the
LORD sends you.
38“You will plant much but harvest little, for locusts will eat your crops. 39You will
plant vineyards and care for them, but you will not drink the wine or eat the grapes, for
worms will destroy the vines. 40You will grow olive trees throughout your land, but you
will never use the olive oil, for the trees will drop the fruit before it is ripe. 41You will
have sons and daughters, but you will not keep them, for they will be led away into
captivity. 42Swarms of insects will destroy your trees and crops. 43The foreigners living
among you will become stronger and stronger, while you become weaker and weaker.
44They will lend money to you, not you to them. They will be the head, and you will be
the tail!
45“If you refuse to listen to the LORD your God and to obey the commands and laws
he has given you, all these curses will pursue and overtake you until you are destroyed.
46These horrors will serve as a sign and warning among you and your descendants
forever. 47Because you have not served the LORD your God with joy and enthusiasm for
the abundant benefits you have received, 48you will serve your enemies whom the LORD
will send against you. You will be left hungry, thirsty, naked, and lacking in everything.
They will oppress you harshly until you are destroyed.
49“The LORD will bring a distant nation against you from the end of the earth, and it
will swoop down on you like an eagle. It is a nation whose language you do not
understand, 50a fierce and heartless nation that shows no respect for the old and no pity
for the young. 51Its armies will devour your livestock and crops, and you will starve to
death. They will leave you no grain, new wine, olive oil, calves, or lambs, bringing about
your destruction. 52They will lay siege to your cities until all the fortified walls in your
land—the walls you trusted to protect you—are knocked down. They will attack all the
towns in the land the LORD your God has given you. 53The siege will be so severe that
you will eat the flesh of your own sons and daughters, whom the LORD your God has
given you. 54The most tenderhearted man among you will have no compassion for his
own brother, his beloved wife, and his surviving children. 55He will refuse to give them
a share of the flesh he is devouring—the flesh of one of his own children—because he
has nothing else to eat during the siege that your enemy will inflict on all your towns.
56The most tender and delicate woman among you—so delicate she would not so much
as touch her feet to the ground—will be cruel to the husband she loves and to her own
son or daughter. 57She will hide from them the afterbirth and the new baby she has borne,
so that she herself can secretly eat them. She will have nothing else to eat during the siege
and terrible distress that your enemy will inflict on all your towns.
58“If you refuse to obey all the terms of this law that are written in this book, and if you
do not fear the glorious and awesome name of the LORD your God, 59then the LORD will
overwhelm both you and your children with indescribable plagues. These plagues will be
intense and without relief, making you miserable and unbearably sick. 60He will bring
against you all the diseases of Egypt that you feared so much, and they will claim you. 61The
LORD will bring against you every sickness and plague there is, even those not mentioned
in this Book of the Law, until you are destroyed. 62Though you are as numerous as the stars
in the sky, few of you will be left because you would not listen to the LORD your God.
63“Just as the LORD has found great pleasure in helping you to prosper and multiply,
the LORD will find pleasure in destroying you, until you disappear from the land you are
about to enter and occupy. 64For the LORD will scatter you among all the nations from
one end of the earth to the other. There you will worship foreign gods that neither you
nor your ancestors have known, gods made of wood and stone! 65There among those
nations you will find no place of security and rest. And the LORD will cause your heart
to tremble, your eyesight to fail, and your soul to despair. 66Your lives will hang in doubt.
You will live night and day in fear, with no reason to believe that you will see the morning
light. 67In the morning you will say, ‘If only it were night!’ And in the evening you will

28:38 Lev 26:20; Isa 5:10; Mic 6:15
28:41 Deut 28:32
28:42 Deut 28:38
28:44 Deut 28:12-13
28:45 Deut 4:25-26
28:47 Deut 32:15
28:49 Isa 5:26; 7:18; Jer 5:15
28:52 Jer 10:17-18; Zeph 1:14-15
28:53 Lev 26:29; Jer 19:9; Lam 2:20; 4:10
28:60 Deut 28:21, 27
28:62 Deut 1:10
28:63 Jer 45:4
28:64 Lev 26:33; Deut 4:27; 32:17; Neh 1:8
28:65 Lam 1:3
28:66 Heb 10:27

28:64 This severe warning tragically came true when Israel was defeated and carried away into captivity by Assyria (722 B.C.), and Judah to Babylonia (586 B.C.). Later, in A.D. 70, Roman oppression forced many Jews to flee their homeland. Thus, the people were scattered throughout the various nations.

say, 'If only it were morning!' You will say this because of your terror at the awesome
horrors you see around you. 68 Then the LORD will send you back to Egypt in ships, a
journey I promised you would never again make. There you will offer to sell yourselves
to your enemies as slaves, but no one will want to buy you."

29 These are the terms of the covenant the LORD commanded Moses to make with
the Israelites while they were in the land of Moab, in addition to the covenant he
had made with them at Mount Sinai.*

C. A CALL FOR COMMITMENT TO GOD: MOSES' THIRD ADDRESS (29:2—30:20)

After reviewing God's laws, Moses calls for commitment, urging the people to honor the contract they had previously made with God. Knowing God's Word is not enough; we must obey it.

Moses Reviews the Covenant

2 Moses summoned all the Israelites and said to them, "You have seen with your own
eyes everything the LORD did in Egypt to Pharaoh and all his servants and his whole
country—3 all the great tests of strength, the miraculous signs, and the amazing wonders.
4 But to this day the LORD has not given you minds that understand, nor eyes that see,
nor ears that hear! 5 For forty years I led you through the wilderness, yet your clothes and
sandals did not wear out. 6 You had no bread or wine or other strong drink, but he gave
you food so you would know that he is the LORD your God. 7 When we came here, King
Sihon of Heshbon and King Og of Bashan came out to fight against us, but we defeated
them. 8 We took their land and gave it to the tribes of Reuben and Gad and to the half-tribe
of Manasseh as their inheritance.
9 "Therefore, obey the terms of this covenant so that you will prosper in everything
you do. 10 All of you—your tribal leaders, your judges, your officers, all the men of
Israel—are standing today before the LORD your God. 11 With you are your little ones,
your wives, and the foreigners living among you who chop your wood and carry your
water. 12 You are standing here today to enter into a covenant with the LORD your God.
The LORD is making this covenant with you today, and he has sealed it with an oath. 13 He
wants to confirm you today as his people and to confirm that he is your God, just as he
promised you, and as he swore to your ancestors Abraham, Isaac, and Jacob. 14 But you
are not the only ones with whom the LORD is making this covenant with its obligations.
15 The LORD your God is making this covenant with you who stand in his presence today
and also with all future generations of Israel.
16 "Surely you remember how we lived in the land of Egypt and how we traveled
through the lands of enemy nations as we left. 17 You have seen their detestable idols
made of wood, stone, silver, and gold. 18 The LORD made this covenant with you so that
no man, woman, family, or tribe among you would turn away from the LORD our God to
worship these gods of other nations, and so that no root among you would bear bitter and
poisonous fruit. 19 Let none of those who hear the warnings of this curse consider

29:1 Lev 27:34; Deut 1:1-5; 5:1
29:2 Exod 19:4
29:4 Isa 6:9-10; Acts 28:26; †Rom 11:8
29:5 Deut 8:2, 4
29:7 Num 21:21; Deut 1:2-5; 2:26
29:8 Num 32:31; Deut 3:12
29:9 Exod 19:5; Deut 4:6; Josh 1:7
29:11 Josh 9:21, 23, 27
29:13 Gen 17:7; Exod 6:7
29:14 Jer 31:31; Heb 8:7
29:17 Exod 20:23; Deut 4:28; 28:36
29:18 Deut 13:6; 32:32; Heb 12:15

29:1 Hebrew *Horeb,* another name for Sinai.

29:1ff At Mount Sinai, 40 years earlier, God and Israel had made a covenant (Exodus 19–20). Although there were many parts to the covenant (read the books of Exodus, Leviticus, and Numbers), its purpose can be summed up in two sentences: God promised to bless the Israelites by making them the nation through whom the rest of the world could know God. In return, the Israelites promised to love and obey God in order to receive physical and spiritual blessings. Here Moses reviewed this covenant. God was still keeping his part of the bargain (and he always would), but the Israelites were already neglecting their part. Moses restated the covenant to warn the people that if they did not keep their part of the agreement, they would experience severe discipline.

29:5 Just as the people of Israel did not notice God's care for them along their journey, we sometimes do not notice all of the ways that God takes care of us—that all of our daily needs have been supplied and we have been well fed and well clothed. Worse yet, we mistakenly take the credit ourselves for being good providers instead of recognizing God's hand in the process.

29:9 What is the best way to prosper in life? For the Israelites, their first step was to keep their part of the covenant. They were to love God with all of their heart, soul, and strength (6:4, 5). We, too, are to seek first the Kingdom of God and his righteousness (Matthew 6:33); then true success in life will follow as a blessing from the hand of God.

29:18 Moses cautioned that the day the Hebrews chose to turn from God, a root would be planted that would produce bitter and poisonous fruit (see Hebrews 12:15). When we decide to do what we know is wrong, we plant an evil seed that begins to grow out of control, eventually yielding a crop of sorrow and pain. But we can prevent those seeds of sin from taking root. If you have done something wrong, confess it to God and others immediately. If the seed never finds fertile soil, its bitter fruit will never ripen.

themselves immune, thinking, 'I am safe, even though I am walking in my own stubborn
29:20 Deut 9:14 2 Kgs 14:27 Pss 74:1; 80:4
way.' This would lead to utter ruin! 20The LORD will not pardon such people. His anger
and jealousy will burn against them. All the curses written in this book will come down
on them, and the LORD will erase their names from under heaven. 21The LORD will
separate them from all the tribes of Israel, to pour out on them all the covenant curses
recorded in this Book of the Law.
29:22 Jer 19:8
22"Then the generations to come, both your own descendants and the foreigners who
29:23 Gen 19:24 Isa 1:7; 34:9; 64:11
come from distant lands, will see the devastation of the land and the diseases the LORD
will send against it. 23They will find its soil turned into sulfur and salt, with nothing
29:24 1 Kgs 9:8 Jer 22:8-9
planted and nothing growing, not even a blade of grass. It will be just like Sodom and
Gomorrah, Admah and Zeboiim, which the LORD destroyed in his anger. 24The surrounding nations will ask, 'Why has the LORD done this to his land? Why was he so angry?'
29:25 2 Kgs 17:9 2 Chr 36:13
25"And they will be told, 'This happened because the people of the land broke the
covenant they made with the LORD, the God of their ancestors, when he brought them
out of the land of Egypt. 26They turned to serve and worship other gods that were foreign
29:27 Deut 29:20
to them, gods that the LORD had not designated for them. 27That is why the LORD's anger
burned against this land, bringing down on it all the curses recorded in this book. 28In
29:28 1 Kgs 14:15 Ezek 19:12
great anger and fury the LORD uprooted his people from their land and exiled them to
another land, where they still live today!'
29:29 John 5:39 Acts 1:7; 17:11
29"There are secret things that belong to the LORD our God, but the revealed things
belong to us and our descendants forever, so that we may obey these words of the law.

A Call to Return to the LORD

30:1 Lev 26:40-41 Deut 4:30; 11:26
30 "Suppose all these things happen to you—the blessings and the curses I have
listed—and you meditate on them as you are living among the nations to which the
30:2 Deut 4:29-30 Neh 1:9
LORD your God has exiled you. 2If at that time you return to the LORD your God, and you
and your children begin wholeheartedly to obey all the commands I have given you today,
30:3 Gen 28:15 Matt 23:37 John 12:51-52
3then the LORD your God will restore your fortunes. He will have mercy on you and gather
you back from all the nations where he has scattered you. 4Though you are at the ends of
the earth, the LORD your God will go and find you and bring you back again. 5He will return
30:4 Isa 43:6
you to the land that belonged to your ancestors, and you will possess that land again. He
will make you even more prosperous and numerous than your ancestors!
30:5 Deut 13:17 Jer 29:14; 30:3
6"The LORD your God will cleanse your heart and the hearts of all your descendants
so that you will love him with all your heart and soul, and so you may live! 7The LORD
30:7 Deut 7:15
your God will inflict all these curses on your enemies and persecutors. 8Then you will
30:9 Deut 15:10; 29:9
again obey the LORD and keep all the commands I am giving you today. 9The LORD your
God will make you successful in everything you do. He will give you many children and
numerous livestock, and your fields will produce abundant harvests, for the LORD will
30:10 Deut 4:29
delight in being good to you as he was to your ancestors. 10The LORD your God will
delight in you if you obey his voice and keep the commands and laws written in this
Book of the Law, and if you turn to the LORD your God with all your heart and soul.

30:11 Isa 45:19

The Choice of Life or Death

30:12-14 †Rom 10:6-8
11"This command I am giving you today is not too difficult for you to understand or
perform. 12It is not up in heaven, so distant that you must ask, 'Who will go to heaven

---

29:29 There are some secrets God has chosen not to reveal to us, possibly for the following reasons: (1) Our finite minds cannot fully understand the infinite aspects of God's nature and the universe (Ecclesiastes 3:11); (2) some things are unnecessary for us to know until we are more mature; (3) God is infinite and all-knowing, and we do not have the capacity to know everything he does. This verse shows that although God has not told us everything there is to know about obeying him, he has told us enough. Thus, disobedience comes from an act of the will, not a lack of knowledge. Through God's Word we know enough about him to be saved by faith and to serve him. We must not use the limitation of our knowledge as an excuse to reject his claim on our life.

30:1-6 Moses told the Hebrews that when they were ready to return to God, he would be ready to receive them. God's mercy is unbelievable. It goes far beyond what we can imagine. Even if the Jews deliberately walked away from him and ruined their lives, God would still take them back. God would give them inward spiritual renewal. God wants to forgive us and bring us back to himself, too. Some people will not learn this until their world has crashed in around them. Then the sorrow and pain seem to open their eyes to what God has been saying all along. Are you separated from God by sin? No matter how far you have wandered, God promises a fresh beginning if only you will turn to him.

30:11-14 God has called us to keep his commands, while reminding us that his laws are not hidden from us or beyond our reach. Have you ever said you would obey God if you knew what he wanted? Have you ever complained that obedience is too difficult for a mere human? These are unacceptable

and bring it down so we can hear and obey it?' [13]It is not beyond the sea, so far away
that you must ask, 'Who will cross the sea to bring it to us so we can hear and obey it?'
[14]The message is very close at hand; it is on your lips and in your heart so that you can
obey it.

[15]"Now listen! Today I am giving you a choice between prosperity and disaster, **30:15**
between life and death. [16]I have commanded you today to love the LORD your God and Deut 11:26 Jer 21:8
to keep his commands, laws, and regulations by walking in his ways. If you do this, you Matt 7:13-14
will live and become a great nation, and the LORD your God will bless you and the land **30:16**
you are about to enter and occupy. [17]But if your heart turns away and you refuse to listen, Deut 4:1; 6:5
and if you are drawn away to serve and worship other gods, [18]then I warn you now that **30:18** Deut 4:26
you will certainly be destroyed. You will not live a long, good life in the land you are
crossing the Jordan to occupy.

[19]"Today I have given you the choice between life and death, between blessings and **30:19**
curses. I call on heaven and earth to witness the choice you make. Oh, that you would Deut 4:26; 30:1
choose life, that you and your descendants might live! [20]Choose to love the LORD your **30:20**
God and to obey him and commit yourself to him, for he is your life. Then you will live Deut 10:20; 13:4
long in the land the LORD swore to give your ancestors Abraham, Isaac, and Jacob."

D. THE CHANGE IN LEADERSHIP: MOSES' LAST DAYS (31:1—34:12)

Realizing that he is about to die, Moses commissions Joshua, records the laws in a permanent form, and teaches a special song to the Israelites. Thus, Moses prepared the people for his departure. Similarly, we should not allow others to become dependent upon us for their spiritual growth but help them to become dependent upon God.

Joshua Becomes Israel's Leader

31 When Moses had finished saying* these things to all the people of Israel, [2]he said, **31:2**
"I am now 120 years old and am no longer able to lead you. The LORD has told Deut 34:7
me that I will not cross the Jordan River. [3]But the LORD your God himself will cross over **31:3**
ahead of you. He will destroy the nations living there, and you will take possession of Num 27:18
their land. Joshua is your new leader, and he will go with you, just as the LORD promised.
[4]The LORD will destroy the nations living in the land, just as he destroyed Sihon and Og,
the kings of the Amorites. [5]The LORD will hand over to you the people who live there,
and you will deal with them as I have commanded you. [6]Be strong and courageous! Do **31:6**
not be afraid of them! The LORD your God will go ahead of you. He will neither fail you Deut 20:1 Heb 13:5
nor forsake you."

[7]Then Moses called for Joshua, and as all Israel watched he said to him, "Be strong **31:7** Deut 1:38; 3:28
and courageous! For you will lead these people into the land that the LORD swore to give
their ancestors. You are the one who will deliver it to them as their inheritance. [8]Do not
be afraid or discouraged, for the LORD is the one who goes before you. He will be with
you; he will neither fail you nor forsake you."

Public Reading of the Law

[9]So Moses wrote down this law and gave it to the priests, who carried the Ark of the **31:9** Num 4:5-6 Deut 10:8
LORD's covenant, and to the leaders of Israel. [10]Then Moses gave them this command: **31:10**
"At the end of every seventh year, the Year of Release, during the Festival of Shelters, Deut 15:1

31:1 As in Dead Sea Scrolls and Greek version; Masoretic Text reads *Moses went and spoke.*

---

excuses. God's laws are written in the Bible and are clearly evident in the world around us. Obeying them is reasonable, sensible, and beneficial. The most difficult part of obeying God's laws is simply deciding to start now. Paul refers to this passage in Romans 10:5-8.

30:19, 20 Moses challenged Israel to choose life, to obey God, and therefore to continue to experience his blessings. God doesn't force his will on anyone. He lets us decide whether to follow him or reject him. This decision, however, is a life-or-death matter. God wants us to realize this, for he would like us all to choose life. Daily, in each new situation, we must affirm and reinforce this commitment.

31:10-13 The laws were to be read to the whole assembly so that everyone, including the children, could hear them. Every seven years the entire nation would gather together and listen as a priest read the law to them. There were no books, Bibles, or newsstands to spread God's word, so the people had to rely on word of mouth and an accurate memory. Memorization was an important part of worship because if everyone knew the law, ignorance would be no excuse for breaking it. To fulfill God's purpose and will in our lives, we need the content and substance of his Word in our hearts and minds. For the Hebrews, this process began in childhood. Teaching our children and new believers should be one of our top priorities. Our finest teachers, best resources, and most careful thought should be directed toward showing young believers how to follow God in all life's situations.

31:12 Deut 4:10

11 you must read this law to all the people of Israel when they assemble before the LORD
your God at the place he chooses. 12 Call them all together—men, women, children, and
the foreigners living in your towns—so they may listen and learn to fear the LORD your
God and carefully obey all the terms of this law. 13 Do this so that your children who have
not known these laws will hear them and will learn to fear the LORD your God. Do this
as long as you live in the land you are crossing the Jordan to occupy."

Israel's Disobedience Predicted

31:14 Num 27:13; Deut 34:5
31:15 Exod 33:9

14 Then the LORD said to Moses, "The time has come for you to die. Call Joshua and take
him with you to the Tabernacle,* and I will commission him there." So Moses and Joshua
went and presented themselves at the Tabernacle. 15 And the LORD appeared to them in
a pillar of cloud at the entrance to the sacred tent.

31:16 Deut 4:25; 32:50; Judg 2:11; 10:6
31:17 Judg 2:12-14

16 The LORD said to Moses, "You are about to die and join your ancestors. After you
are gone, these people will begin worshiping foreign gods, the gods of the land where
they are going. They will abandon me and break the covenant I have made with them.
17 Then my anger will blaze forth against them. I will abandon them, hiding my face from
them, and they will be destroyed. Terrible trouble will come down on them, so that they
will say, 'These disasters have come because God is no longer among us!' 18 At that time
I will hide my face from them on account of all the sins they have committed by
worshiping other gods.

31:20 Deut 6:10-12; 8:19; 11:16-17
31:21 Lev 26:41

19 "Now write down the words of this song, and teach it to the people of Israel. Teach
them to sing it, so it may serve as a witness against them. 20 For I will bring them into the
land I swore to give their ancestors—a land flowing with milk and honey. There they
will become prosperous; they will eat all the food they want and become well nourished.
Then they will begin to worship other gods; they will despise me and break my covenant.
21 Then great disasters will come down on them, and this song will stand as evidence
against them, for it will never be forgotten by their descendants. I know what these
people are like, even before they have entered the land I swore to give them." 22 So that
very day Moses wrote down the words of the song and taught it to the Israelites.

23 Then the LORD commissioned Joshua son of Nun with these words: "Be strong and
courageous! You must bring the people of Israel into the land I swore to give them. I will
be with you."

31:25 Deut 31:9
31:27 Deut 9:7, 24
31:28 Deut 30:19; 32:1
31:29 Deut 32:5

24 When Moses had finished writing down this entire body of law in a book, 25 he
gave these instructions to the Levites who carried the Ark of the LORD's covenant:
26 "Take this Book of the Law and place it beside the Ark of the Covenant of the LORD
your God, so it may serve as a witness against the people of Israel. 27 For I know how
rebellious and stubborn you are. Even now, while I am still with you, you have rebelled
against the LORD. How much more rebellious will you be after my death! 28 Now
summon all the leaders and officials of your tribes so that I can speak to them and call
heaven and earth to witness against them. 29 I know that after my death you will become
utterly corrupt and will turn from the path I have commanded you to follow. In the days
to come, disaster will come down on you, for you will make the LORD very angry by
doing what is evil in his sight."

31:14 Hebrew *Tent of Meeting;* also in 31:14b.

31:19-21 There is a place for music in Christian education and in the building up of all believers. Some people memorize classic hymns of the church to help them think of what is true, right, and good. Others find tapes to play when they are in the car or at home. In what creative ways can music be used to teach in your church? How might you maximize the benefit of music in your family?

31:23 Joshua had been appointed to take over the leadership of Israel and guide the people into the Promised Land (Moses could not enter the land due to his disobedience—Numbers 20:12). Joshua, first mentioned in Exodus 17:9, had been Moses' assistant for many years (Joshua 1:1). One of his key qualifications was his faith. As one of the 12 scouts to first enter Canaan, only he and Caleb believed that God could help Israel conquer the land (Numbers 13:1–14:30). Moses told Joshua to be strong and courageous twice in this chapter (31:7, 23). Indeed, this was a frightening task with three million people to care for, settle disputes for, and lead into battle. Finding courage would be Joshua's greatest test. He was strong and courageous because he knew God was with him and because he had faith that God would do all he had promised Israel.

31:27-29 Moses knew that the Israelites, in spite of all they had seen of God's work, were rebellious at heart. They deserved God's punishment, although they often received his mercy instead. We, too, are stubborn and rebellious by nature. Throughout our lives we struggle with sin. Repentance once a month or once a week is not enough. We must constantly turn from our sins to God and let him, in his mercy, save us.

The Song of Moses

30 So Moses recited this entire song to the assembly of Israel:

32 1 "Listen, O heavens, and I will speak!
Hear, O earth, the words that I say!
2 My teaching will fall on you like rain;
my speech will settle like dew.
My words will fall like rain on tender grass,
like gentle showers on young plants.
3 I will proclaim the name of the LORD;
how glorious is our God!
4 He is the Rock; his work is perfect.
Everything he does is just and fair.
He is a faithful God who does no wrong;
how just and upright he is!

5 "But they have acted corruptly toward him;
when they act like that, are they really his children?*
They are a deceitful and twisted generation.
6 Is this the way you repay the LORD,
you foolish and senseless people?
Isn't he your Father who created you?
Has he not made you and established you?
7 Remember the days of long ago;
think about the generations past.
Ask your father and he will inform you.
Inquire of your elders, and they will tell you.
8 When the Most High assigned lands to the nations,
when he divided up the human race,
he established the boundaries of the peoples
according to the number of angelic beings.*
9 For the people of Israel belong to the LORD;
Jacob is his special possession.

10 "He found them in a desert land,
in an empty, howling wasteland.
He surrounded them and watched over them;
he guarded them as his most precious possession.*
11 Like an eagle that rouses her chicks
and hovers over her young,
so he spread his wings to take them in
and carried them aloft on his pinions.
12 The LORD alone guided them;
they lived without any foreign gods.
13 He made them ride over the highlands;
he let them feast on the crops of the fields.
He nourished them with honey from the cliffs,
with olive oil from the hard rock.
14 He fed them curds from the herd and milk from the flock,
together with the fat of lambs and goats.

32:1 Deut 4:26; Isa 1:2
32:2 Ps 72:6; Isa 55:10
32:3 Gen 18:25; Exod 34:5-6; Deut 3:24
32:4 Gen 49:24; Deut 32:18; 2 Sam 22:2
32:5 Deut 4:25; 31:27; Matt 17:17
32:6 Deut 1:31; 32:28
32:7 Deut 7:18-19
32:9 1 Kgs 8:51; Jer 10:16
32:10 Ps 17:8
32:11 Exod 19:4; Pss 17:8; 18:10-18
32:12 Deut 4:36; Isa 43:12
32:13 Job 29:6; Ps 81:16
32:14 Ps 147:14

32:5 The meaning of the Hebrew is uncertain. **32:8** As in Dead Sea Scrolls, which read *of the sons of God,* and Greek version, which reads *of the angels of god;* Masoretic Text reads *of the sons of Israel.* **32:10** Hebrew *as the apple of his eye.*

32:1ff Moses was not only a great prophet but also a song leader. After three sermons, he changed the form of his message to singing. Sometimes reciting something in a different form makes it easier to remember. This song gives a brief history of Israel. It reminds the people of their mistakes, warns them to avoid repetition of those mistakes, and offers the hope that comes only in trusting God.

32:10, 11 The Israelites had no excuse for abandoning God. He had shielded them like a kindly shepherd. He had guarded them like a person protects the pupil (apple) of his eye. He had been the encircling protector, like a mother eagle who protects her young. The Lord alone had led them. And he alone leads us. Let us remember to trust in him.

He gave them choice rams and goats from Bashan,
together with the choicest wheat.
You drank the finest wine,
made from the juice of grapes.

32:15 Judg 10:6

15 But Israel* soon became fat and unruly;
the people grew heavy, plump, and stuffed!
Then they abandoned the God who had made them;
they made light of the Rock of their salvation.

32:16 Pss 78:58; 106:29

16 They stirred up his jealousy by worshiping foreign gods;
they provoked his fury with detestable acts.

32:17 Lev 17:7; 1 Cor 10:20

17 They offered sacrifices to demons, non-gods,
to gods they had not known before,
to gods only recently arrived,
to gods their ancestors had never feared.

32:18 Ps 106:21; Deut 8:11; 32:4

18 You neglected the Rock who had fathered you;
you forgot the God who had given you birth.

32:19 Lev 26:30; Ps 106:40

19 "The LORD saw this and was filled with loathing.
He was provoked to anger by his own sons and daughters.

32:20 Deut 32:5

20 He said, 'I will abandon them;
I will see to their end!
For they are a twisted generation,
children without integrity.

32:21 1 Kgs 16:13, 26; †Rom 10:19

21 They have roused my jealousy by worshiping non-gods;
they have provoked my fury with useless idols.
Now I will rouse their jealousy by blessing other nations;
I will provoke their fury by blessing the foolish Gentiles.

32:22 Lev 26:20; Ps 18:7-8

22 For my anger blazes forth like fire
and burns to the depths of the grave.*
It devours the earth and all its crops
and ignites the foundations of the mountains.

32:23 Deut 28:15-19; Ps 85:5

23 I will heap disasters upon them
and shoot them down with my arrows.

32:24 Deut 28:53; Ps 91:6

24 I will send against them wasting famine,
burning fever, and deadly disease.
They will be troubled by the fangs of wild beasts,
by poisonous snakes that glide in the dust.

32:25 2 Chr 36:17; Lam 1:20; 2:21; Ezek 7:15

25 Outside, the sword will bring death,
and inside, terror will strike
both young men and young women,
both infants and the aged.

32:26 Deut 4:27; 28:64

26 I decided to scatter them,*
so even the memory of them would disappear.
27 But I feared the taunt of the enemy,
that their adversaries might misunderstand and say,

32:15 Hebrew *Jeshurun,* a term of endearment for Israel. **32:22** Hebrew *of Sheol.* **32:26** As in Greek version; the meaning of the Hebrew is uncertain.

VARIETY IN WORSHIP
Israel's worship used all of the senses. They reinforced the meaning of the ceremony. Every sense can be used to worship God.

SIGHT	the beauty and symbolism of the Tabernacle; every color and hue had a meaning
HEARING	the use of music; there were instructions for the use of a variety of instruments, and the Bible records many songs
TOUCH	the head of the animal to be sacrificed was touched, symbolizing the fact that it was taking their place
SMELL	the sacrifices were burned, emitting a familiar aroma
TASTE	the festivals were celebrations and memorials—much of the food was symbolic

"Our power has triumphed!
It was not the LORD who did this!"'

28 "Israel is a nation that lacks sense;
the people are foolish, without understanding.
29 Oh, that they were wise and could understand this!
Oh, that they might know their fate!
30 How could one person chase a thousand of them,
and two people put ten thousand to flight,
unless their Rock had sold them,
unless the LORD had given them up?
31 But the rock of our enemies is not like our Rock,
as even they recognize.*
32 Their vine grows from the vine of Sodom,
from the vineyards of Gomorrah.
Their grapes are poison,
and their clusters are bitter.
33 Their wine is the venom of snakes,
the deadly poison of vipers.

34 "'I am storing up these things,
sealing them away within my treasury.
35 I will take vengeance; I will repay those who deserve it.
In due time their feet will slip.
Their day of disaster will arrive,
and their destiny will overtake them.'

36 "Indeed, the LORD will judge his people,
and he will change his mind about* his servants,
when he sees their strength is gone
and no one is left, slave or free.
37 Then he will ask, 'Where are their gods,
the rocks they fled to for refuge?
38 Where now are those gods,
who ate the fat of their sacrifices
and drank the wine of their offerings?
Let those gods arise and help you!
Let them provide you with shelter!
39 Look now; I myself am he!
There is no god other than me!
I am the one who kills and gives life;
I am the one who wounds and heals;
no one delivers from my power!
40 Now I raise my hand to heaven
and declare, "As surely as I live,
41 when I sharpen my flashing sword
and begin to carry out justice,
I will bring vengeance on my enemies
and repay those who hate me.
42 I will make my arrows drunk with blood,
and my sword will devour flesh—
the blood of the slaughtered and the captives,
and the heads of the enemy leaders."'

43 "Rejoice with him, O heavens,
and let all the angels of God worship him,*
for he will avenge the blood of his servants.

32:29 Deut 5:29
32:30 Lev 26:7-8; Deut 32:4, 18
32:32 Deut 29:18
32:35 Jer 23:12; Ezek 7:5; †Rom 12:19
32:36 Lev 26:44-45; Deut 30:2-3; †Heb 10:30
32:37 Jer 2:28
32:38 Num 25:1-2; Jer 11:12
32:39 1 Sam 2:6; Ps 50:22; Isa 41:4; 43:10
32:41 Isa 34:6-8; Jer 12:12; 46:10; 50:28-32
32:43 †Romans 15:10

32:31 The meaning of the Hebrew is uncertain. Greek version reads *our enemies are fools.* **32:36** Or *will take revenge for.* **32:43** As in Dead Sea Scrolls and Greek version; Masoretic Text reads *Rejoice with his people, O nations.*

He will take vengeance on his enemies
and cleanse his land and his people."

44 So Moses came with Joshua* son of Nun and recited all the words of this song to
the people. 45 When Moses had finished reciting these words to Israel, 46 he added: "Take
to heart all the words I have given you today. Pass them on as a command to your children
so they will obey every word of this law. 47 These instructions are not mere words—they
are your life! By obeying them you will enjoy a long life in the land you are crossing the
Jordan River to occupy."

32:46 Deut 4:9; Ezek 40:4; 44:5
32:47 Deut 4:40; 8:3; 30:20

Moses' Death Foretold

48 That same day the LORD said to Moses, 49 "Go to Moab, to the mountains east of the
river,* and climb Mount Nebo, which is across from Jericho. Look out across the land
of Canaan, the land I am giving to the people of Israel as their own possession. 50 Then
you must die there on the mountain and join your ancestors, just as Aaron, your brother,
died on Mount Hor and joined his ancestors. 51 For both of you broke faith with me
among the Israelites at the waters of Meribah at Kadesh* in the wilderness of Zin. You
failed to demonstrate my holiness to the people of Israel there. 52 So you will see the land
from a distance, but you may not enter the land I am giving to the people of Israel."

32:49 Num 27:12; Deut 3:27
32:50 Gen 25:8; Num 27:13
32:51 Num 20:12
32:52 Deut 1:37; 3:27

Moses Blesses the People

33 This is the blessing that Moses, the man of God, gave to the people of Israel before
his death:

2 "The LORD came from Mount Sinai
and dawned upon us* from Mount Seir;
he shone forth from Mount Paran
and came from Meribah-kadesh
with flaming fire at his right hand.*
3 Indeed, you love the people;
all your holy ones are in your hands.
They follow in your steps
and accept your instruction.
4 Moses charged us with the law,
the special possession of the assembly of Israel.*
5 The LORD became king in Israel*—
when the leaders of the people assembled,
when the tribes of Israel gathered."

6 Moses said this about the tribe of Reuben:*

"Let the tribe of Reuben live and not die out,
even though their tribe is small."

7 Moses said this about the tribe of Judah:

"O LORD, hear the cry of Judah
and bring them again to their people.

33:1 Josh 14:6
33:2 Exod 19:18, 20; Judg 5:4; Ps 68:8, 17; Dan 7:10; Hab 3:3; Gal 3:19
33:3 Deut 4:37; 6:1-9; 7:6; 14:2
33:4 Deut 4:2; Ps 119:111
33:5 Num 23:18-24; Ps 10:16
33:6 Gen 49:3
33:7 Gen 49:8-12

32:44 Hebrew *Hoshea,* a variant name for Joshua. **32:49** Hebrew *the mountains of Abarim.* **32:51** Hebrew *waters of Meribath-kadesh.* **33:2a** As in Greek and Syriac versions; Hebrew reads *upon them.* **33:2b** Or *came from myriads of holy ones, from the south, from his mountain slopes.* The meaning of the Hebrew is uncertain. **33:4** Hebrew *of Jacob.* **33:5** Hebrew *in Jeshurun,* a term of endearment for Israel. **33:6** Hebrew lacks *Moses said this about the tribe of Reuben.*

32:46, 47 Moses urged the people to think about God's word and teach it to their children. The Bible can sit on your bookshelf and gather dust, or you can make it a vital part of your life by regularly setting aside time to study it. When you discover the wisdom of God's message, you will want to apply it to your life and pass it on to your family and others. The Bible is not merely good reading—it's real help for real life.

33:6-25 Note the difference in blessings God gave each tribe. To one he gave the best land, to another strength, to another safety. Too often we see someone with a particular blessing and think that God must love that person more than others. Think rather that God draws out in all people their unique talents. All these gifts are needed to complete his plan. Don't be envious of the gifts others have. Instead, look for the gifts God has given you, and resolve to do the tasks he has uniquely qualified you to do.

Give them strength to defend their cause;
help them against their enemies!"

8 Moses said this about the tribe of Levi:

"O LORD, you have given the sacred lots*
to your faithful servants the Levites.
You put them to the test at Massah
and contended with them at the waters of Meribah.
9 The Levites obeyed your word
and guarded your covenant.
They were more loyal to you
than to their parents, relatives, and children.
10 Now let them teach your regulations to Jacob;
let them give your instructions to Israel.
They will present incense before you
and offer whole burnt offerings on the altar.
11 Bless the Levites, O LORD,
and accept all their work.
Crush the loins of their enemies;
strike down their foes so they never rise again."

12 Moses said this about the tribe of Benjamin:

"The people of Benjamin are loved by the LORD
and live in safety beside him.
He surrounds them continuously
and preserves them from every harm."

13 Moses said this about the tribes of Joseph:

"May their land be blessed by the LORD
with the choice gift of rain from the heavens,
and water from beneath the earth;
14 with the riches that grow in the sun,
and the bounty produced each month;
15 with the finest crops of the ancient mountains,
and the abundance from the everlasting hills;
16 with the best gifts of the earth and its fullness,
and the favor of the one who appeared in the burning bush.
May these blessings rest on Joseph's head,
crowning the brow of the prince among his brothers.
17 Joseph has the strength and majesty of a young bull;
his power is like the horns of a wild ox.
He will gore distant nations,
driving them to the ends of the earth.
This is my blessing for the multitudes of Ephraim
and the thousands of Manasseh."

18 Moses said this about the tribes of Zebulun and Issachar*:

"May the people of Zebulun prosper in their expeditions abroad.
May the people of Issachar prosper at home in their tents.
19 They summon the people to the mountain
to offer proper sacrifices there.
They benefit from the riches of the sea
and the hidden treasures of the sand."

20 Moses said this about the tribe of Gad:

33:8 Exod 17:7; Lev 8:8; Num 20:13, 24; Deut 6:16
33:9 Exod 32:27; Mal 2:5
33:10 Lev 10:11; 16:12-13; Deut 17:9; 31:9
33:12 Deut 12:10; 32:8
33:13 Gen 27:27-29; 49:22
33:16 Exod 3:2
33:17 Num 23:22; 24:8; 1 Kgs 22:11
33:18 Gen 49:13
33:19 Pss 4:5; 51:19
33:20 Gen 49:19

33:8 Hebrew *given your Thummim and Urim.* See Exod 28:30. **33:18** Hebrew lacks *and Issachar.*

"Blessed is the one who enlarges Gad's territory!
Gad is poised there like a lion
to tear off an arm or a head.

33:21 Num 32:1; 34:14 Josh 4:12; 22:1

21 The people of Gad took the best land for themselves;
a leader's share was assigned to them.
When the leaders of the people were assembled,
they carried out the LORD's justice
and obeyed his regulations for Israel."

33:22 Gen 49:16 Ezek 19:2-3

22 Moses said this about the tribe of Dan:

"Dan is a lion's cub,
leaping out from Bashan."

33:23 Gen 49:21

23 Moses said this about the tribe of Naphtali:

"O Naphtali, you are rich in favor
and full of the LORD's blessings;
may you possess the west and the south."

33:24 Gen 49:20 Job 29:6

24 Moses said this about the tribe of Asher:

"May Asher be blessed above other sons;
may he be esteemed by his brothers;
may he bathe his feet in olive oil.

33:25 Ps 147:13

25 May the bolts of your gates be of iron and bronze;
may your strength match the length of your days!"

33:26 Exod 15:11 Deut 4:35 Ps 68:33

26 "There is no one like the God of Israel.*
He rides across the heavens to help you,
across the skies in majestic splendor.

33:27 Gen 49:24 Deut 7:2 Josh 24:18 Ps 90:1

27 The eternal God is your refuge,
and his everlasting arms are under you.
He thrusts out the enemy before you;
it is he who cries, 'Destroy them!'

33:28 Gen 27:27-29, 37 Deut 33:12-13

28 So Israel will live in safety,
prosperous Jacob in security,
in a land of grain and wine,
while the heavens drop down dew.

33:26 Hebrew *of Jeshurun,* a term of endearment for Israel.

THE DEATH OF MOSES
Just before Moses died, he climbed Mount Nebo. Although he could not enter the Promised Land, God showed him its beauty from Mount Nebo's peak.

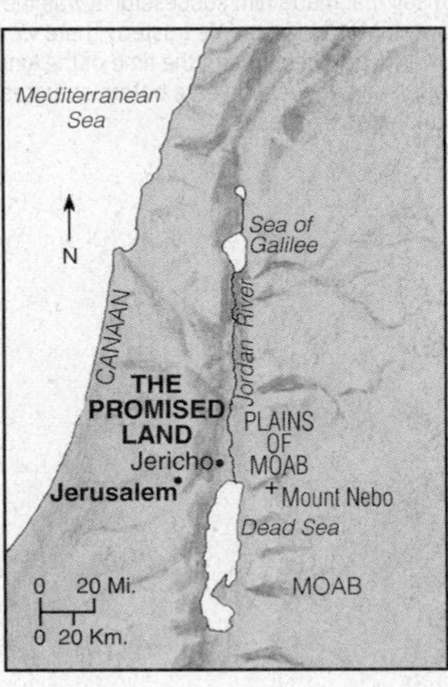

33:20, 21 The people of the tribe of Gad received the best of the new land because they obeyed God by punishing Israel's wicked enemies. Punishment is unpleasant for both the giver and the receiver, but it is a necessary part of growth. If you are in a position that sometimes requires you to correct others, don't hold back from fulfilling your task. Understand that realistic discipline is important to character development. Always strive to be both just and merciful, keeping in mind the best interests of the person who must receive the punishment.

33:24 Bathing feet in oil was a sign of prosperity.

33:27 Moses' song declares that God is our refuge, our only true security. How often we entrust our lives to other things—perhaps money, career, a noble cause, or a lifelong dream. But our only true refuge is the eternal God, who always holds out his arms to catch us when the shaky supports that we trust collapse and we fall. No storm can destroy us when we take refuge in him. Those without God, however, must forever be cautious. One mistake may wipe them out. Living for God in this world may look like risky business. But it is the godless who are on shaky ground. Because God is our refuge, we can dare to be bold.

29 How blessed you are, O Israel!
  Who else is like you, a people saved by the LORD?
He is your protecting shield
  and your triumphant sword!
Your enemies will bow low before you,
  and you will trample on their backs!"

The Death of Moses

34 Then Moses went to Mount Nebo from the plains of Moab and climbed Pisgah
Peak, which is across from Jericho. And the LORD showed him the whole land,
from Gilead as far as Dan; 2 all the land of Naphtali; the land of Ephraim and Manasseh;
all the land of Judah, extending to the Mediterranean Sea*; 3 the Negev; the Jordan Valley
with Jericho—the city of palms—as far as Zoar. 4 Then the LORD said to Moses, "This
is the land I promised on oath to Abraham, Isaac, and Jacob, and I told them I would give
it to their descendants. I have now allowed you to see it, but you will not enter the land."
5 So Moses, the servant of the LORD, died there in the land of Moab, just as the LORD
had said. 6 He was buried* in a valley near Beth-peor in Moab, but to this day no one
knows the exact place. 7 Moses was 120 years old when he died, yet his eyesight was
clear, and he was as strong as ever. 8 The people of Israel mourned thirty days for Moses
on the plains of Moab, until the customary period of mourning was over.
9 Now Joshua son of Nun was full of the spirit of wisdom, for Moses had laid his hands
on him. So the people of Israel obeyed him and did everything just as the LORD had
commanded Moses.
10 There has never been another prophet like Moses, whom the LORD knew face to
face. 11 The LORD sent Moses to perform all the miraculous signs and wonders in the land
of Egypt against Pharaoh, all his servants, and his entire land. 12 And it was through
Moses that the LORD demonstrated his mighty power and terrifying acts in the sight of
all Israel.

33:29 Gen 15:1; Deut 4:32; Pss 66:3; 115:11
34:1 Num 21:20; Deut 32:49, 52
34:2 Exod 23:31; Deut 11:24
34:4 Gen 12:7; 26:3
34:5 Num 12:7-8; Deut 32:50
34:6 Deut 3:29; 4:46; Jude 1:9
34:7 Deut 31:2
34:9 Num 27:18; Isa 11:2
34:10 Num 12:8
34:11-12 Deut 4:34

34:2 Hebrew *the western sea.* **34:6** Hebrew *He buried him,* that is, "The LORD buried him." Samaritan Pentateuch and some Greek manuscripts read *They buried him.*

34:4, 10 Moses was the only person who ever spoke with God face to face (Exodus 33:11; Numbers 12:8). He was called Israel's greatest prophet. Yet even this great man was not allowed to enter the Promised Land because he disobeyed God (Numbers 20:12). No matter how good we are or how much we've done for God, we sometimes disobey him. The result of our disobedience is that we will be disciplined. God disciplined Moses severely but still called him his friend. When you experience the sting of God's discipline, respond as Moses did. Don't turn away in anger, embarrassment, or resentment. Instead, turn toward God with love, openness, and a desire to do better.

34:10-12 Moses, the man who did not want to be sent to Egypt because he was "not a good speaker" (Exodus 4:10), delivered the three addresses to Israel that make up the book of Deuteronomy. God gave him the power to develop from a stuttering shepherd into a national leader and powerful orator. His courage, humility, and wisdom molded the Hebrew slaves into a nation. But Moses was one person who did not let success go to his head. In the end, God was still Moses' best friend. His love, respect, and awe for God had grown daily throughout his life. Moses knew that it was not any greatness in himself that made him successful; it was the greatness of the all-powerful God in whom he trusted. There were many great and powerful prophets during the time of the kings. But it would be more than a thousand years before one greater than Moses would appear—Jesus.

KEY PLACES IN JOSHUA

1 Acacia The story of Joshua begins with the Israelites camping at Acacia. The Israelites under Joshua were ready to enter and conquer Canaan. But before the nation moved out, Joshua received instructions from God (1:1–18).

2 Jordan River The entire nation prepared to cross this river, which was swollen from spring rains. After the spies returned from Jericho with a positive report, Joshua prepared the priests and people for a miracle. As the priests carried the Ark into the Jordan River, the water stopped flowing, and the entire nation crossed on dry ground into the Promised Land (2:1—4:24).

3 Gilgal After crossing the Jordan River, the Israelites camped at Gilgal, where they renewed their commitment to God and celebrated the Passover, the festival commemorating their deliverance from Egypt (see Exodus). As Joshua made plans for the attack on Jericho, an angel appeared to him (5:1–15).

4 Jericho The walled city of Jericho seemed a formidable enemy. But when Joshua followed God's plans, the great walls were no obstacle. The city was conquered with only the obedient marching of the people (6:1–27).

5 Ai Victory could not continue without obedience to God. That is why the disobedience of one man, Achan, brought defeat to the entire nation in the first battle against Ai. But once the sin was recognized and punished, God told Joshua to take heart and try Ai once again. This time the city was taken (7:1—8:29).

6 The Mountains of Ebal and Gerizim After the defeat of Ai, Joshua built an altar at Mount Ebal. Then the people divided themselves, half at the foot of Mount Ebal, half at the foot of Mount Gerizim. The priests stood between the mountains holding the Ark of the Covenant as Joshua read God's law to all the people (8:30–35).

7 Gibeon It was just after the Israelites reaffirmed their covenant with God that their leaders made a major mistake in judgment: They were tricked into making a peace treaty with the city of Gibeon. The Gibeonites pretended that they had traveled a long distance and asked the Israelites for a treaty. The leaders made the agreement without consulting God. The trick was soon discovered, but because the treaty had been made, Israel could not go back on its word. As a result, the Gibeonites saved their own lives, but they were forced to become Israel's slaves (9:1–27).

8 Valley of Aijalon The king of Jerusalem was very angry at Gibeon for making a peace treaty with the Israelites. He gathered armies from four other cities to attack the city. Gibeon summoned Joshua for help. Joshua took immediate action. Leaving Gilgal, he attacked the coalition by surprise. As the battle waged on and moved into the valley of Aijalon, Joshua prayed for the sun to stand still until the enemy could be destroyed (10:1–43).

9 Hazor Up north in Hazor, King Jabin mobilized the kings of the surrounding cities to unite and crush Israel. But God gave Joshua and Israel victory (11:1–23).

10 Shiloh After the armies of Canaan were conquered, Israel gathered at Shiloh to set up the Tabernacle. This movable building had been the nation's center of worship during their years of wandering. The seven tribes who had not received their land were given their allotments (18:1—19:51).

11 Shechem Before Joshua died he called the entire nation together at Shechem to remind them that it was God who had given them their land and that only with God's help could they keep it. The people vowed to follow God. As long as Joshua was alive, the land was at rest from war and trouble (24:1–33).

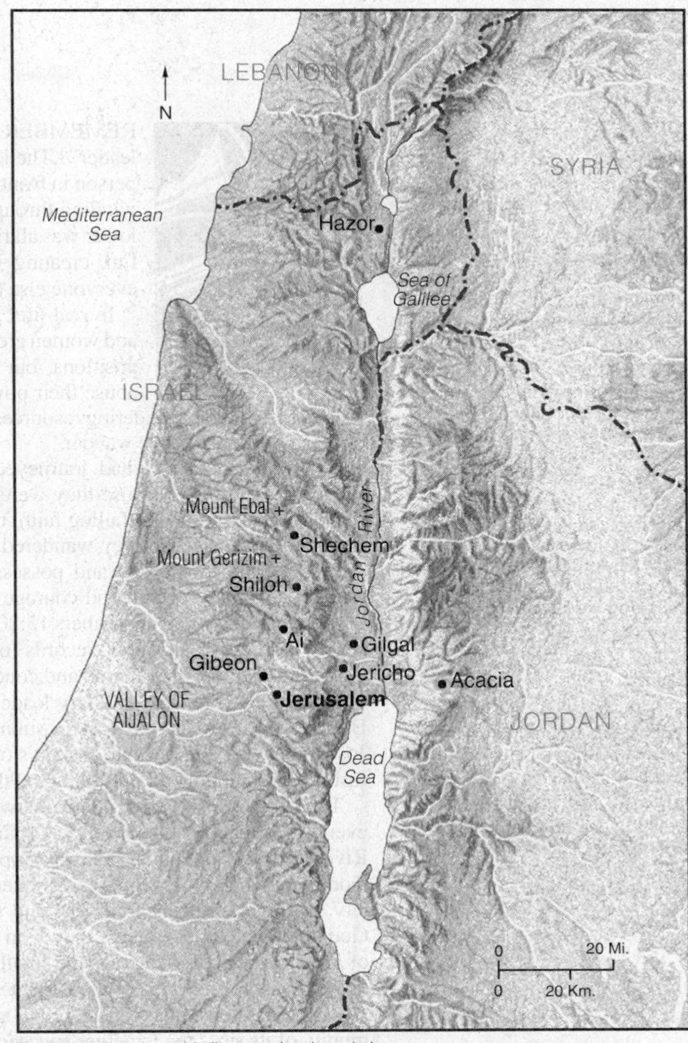

The broken lines (–·–·) indicate modern boundaries.

JOSHUA

Exodus from Egypt 1446 B.C. (1280 B.C.) | *Israelites enter Canaan 1406 (1240)* | *Judges begin to rule 1375 (1220)*

CONQUEST OF CANAAN

T H E D A Y S O F

VITAL STATISTICS

PURPOSE:
To give the history of Israel's conquest of the Promised Land

AUTHOR:
Joshua, except for the ending which may have been written by the high priest, Phinehas, an eyewitness to the events recounted there

SETTING:
Canaan, also called the Promised Land, which occupied the same general geographical territory of modern-day Israel

KEY VERSE:
"'Go through the camp and tell the people to get their provisions ready. In three days you will cross the Jordan River and take possession of the land the LORD your God has given you'" (1:11).

KEY PEOPLE:
Joshua, Rahab, Achan, Phinehas, Eleazar

KEY PLACES:
Jericho, Ai, Mount Ebal, Mount Gerizim, Gibeon, Gilgal, Shiloh, Shechem

SPECIAL FEATURE:
Out of over a million people, Joshua and Caleb were the only two who left Egypt and entered the Promised Land.

REMEMBER the childhood game "follow the leader"? The idea was to mimic the antics of the person in front of you in the line of boys and girls winding through the neighborhood. Being a follower was all right, but being leader was the most fun, creating imaginative routes and tasks for everyone else to copy.

In real life, great leaders are rare. Often, men and women are elected or appointed to leadership positions, but then falter or fail to act. Others abuse their power to satisfy their egos, crushing their subjects and squandering resources. But without faithful, ethical, and effective leaders, people wander.

For 40 years, Israel had journeyed a circuitous route through the wilderness, but *not* because they were following their leader. Quite the opposite was true—with failing faith, they had refused to obey God and to conquer Canaan. So they wandered. Finally, the new generation was ready to cross the Jordan and possess the land. Having distinguished himself as a man of faith and courage (he and Caleb gave the minority scout report recorded in Numbers 13:30—14:9), Joshua was chosen to be Moses' successor. This book records Joshua's leadership of the people of God as they finish their march and conquer the Promised Land.

Joshua was a brilliant military leader and a strong spiritual influence. But the key to his success was his submission to God. When God spoke, Joshua listened and obeyed. Joshua's obedience served as a model. As a result, Israel remained faithful to God throughout Joshua's lifetime.

The book of Joshua is divided into two main parts. The first narrates the events surrounding the conquest of Canaan. After crossing the Jordan River on dry ground, the Israelites camped near the mighty city of Jericho. God commanded the people to conquer Jericho by marching around the city 13 times, blowing trumpets, and shouting. Because they followed God's unique battle strategy, they won (chapter 6). After the destruction of Jericho, they set out against the small town of Ai. Their first attack was driven back because one of the Israelites (Achan) had sinned (chapter 7). After the men of Israel stoned Achan and his family—purging the community of its sin—the Israelites succeeded in capturing Ai (chapter 8). In their next battle against the Amorites, God even made the sun stand still to aid them in their victory (chapter 10). Finally, after defeating other assorted Canaanites led by Jabin and his allies (chapter 11), they possessed most of the land.

Part two of the book of Joshua records the assignment and settlement of the captured territory (chapters 13—22). The book concludes with Joshua's farewell address and his death (chapters 23, 24).

Joshua was committed to obeying God, and this book is about obedience. Whether conquering enemies or settling the land, God's people were required to do it God's way. In his final message to the people, Joshua underscored the importance of obeying God. "So be very careful to love the LORD your God" (23:11), and "choose today whom you will serve.... But as for me and my family, we will serve the LORD" (24:15). Read Joshua and make a fresh commitment to obey God today. Decide to follow your Lord wherever he leads and whatever it costs.

T H E J U D G E S	United kingdom under Saul 1050 (1045)	David becomes king 1010

THE BLUEPRINT

A. ENTERING THE PROMISED LAND (1:1—5:12)
1. Joshua leads the nation
2. Crossing the Jordan

Joshua demonstrated his faith in God as he took up the challenge to lead the nation. The Israelites reaffirmed their commitment to God by obediently setting out across the Jordan River to possess the land. As we live the Christian life, we need to cross over from the old life to the new, put off our selfish desires, and press on to possess all God has planned for us. Like Joshua and Israel, we need courageous faith to live the new life.

B. CONQUERING THE PROMISED LAND (5:13—12:24)
1. Joshua attacks the center of the land
2. Joshua attacks the southern kings
3. Joshua attacks the northern kings
4. Summary of conquests

Joshua and his army moved from city to city, cleansing the land of its wickedness by destroying every trace of idol worship. Conflict with evil is inevitable, and we should be as merciless as Israel in destroying sin in our lives.

C. DIVIDING THE PROMISED LAND (13:1—24:33)
1. The tribes receive their land
2. Special cities are set aside
3. Eastern tribes return home
4. Joshua's farewell to the leaders

Joshua urged the Israelites to continue to follow the Lord and worship him alone. The people had seen God deliver them from many enemies and miraculously provide for all their needs, but they were prone to wander from the Lord. Even though we may have experienced God at work in our lives, we, too, must continually renew our commitment to obey him above all other authority and to worship him alone.

MEGATHEMES

THEME	EXPLANATION	IMPORTANCE
Success	God gave success to the Israelites when they obeyed his master plan, not when they followed their own desires. Victory came when they trusted in him rather than in their military power, money, muscle, or mental capacity.	God's work done in God's way will bring his success. The standard for success, however, is not to be set by the society around us but by God's Word. We must adjust our minds to God's way of thinking in order to see his standard for success.
Faith	The Israelites demonstrated their faith by trusting God daily to save and guide them. By noticing how God fulfilled his promises in the past, they developed strong confidence that he would be faithful in the future.	Our strength to do God's work comes from trusting him. His promises reassure us of his love and that he will be there to guide us in the decisions and struggles we face. Faith begins with believing he can be trusted.
Guidance	God gave instructions to Israel for every aspect of their lives. His law guided their daily living, and his specific marching orders gave them victory in battle.	Guidance from God for daily living can be found in his Word. By staying in touch with God, we will have the needed wisdom to meet the great challenges of life.
Leadership	Joshua was an example of an excellent leader. He was confident in God's strength, courageous in the face of opposition, and willing to seek God's advice.	To be a strong leader like Joshua, we must be ready to listen and to move quickly when God instructs us. Once we have his instructions, we must be diligent in carrying them out. Strong leaders are led by God.
Conquest	God commanded his people to conquer the Canaanites and take all their land. Completing this mission would have fulfilled God's promise to Abraham and brought judgment on the evil people living there. Unfortunately, Israel never finished the job.	The Israelites were faithful in accomplishing their mission at first, but their commitment faltered. To love God means more than being enthusiastic about him. We must complete all the work he gives us and apply his instructions to every corner of our lives.

A. ENTERING THE PROMISED LAND (1:1—5:12)

After wandering for 40 years in the wilderness, a new generation is ready to enter Canaan. But first God prepares both Joshua and the nation by teaching them the importance of courageous and consistent faith. The nation then miraculously crosses the Jordan River to begin the long-awaited conquest of the Promised Land. Like Joshua, we, too, need faith to begin and continue living the Christian life.

1. Joshua leads the nation

The LORD's Charge to Joshua

1 After the death of Moses the LORD's servant, the LORD spoke to Joshua son of Nun, 1:2
Moses' assistant. He said, 2"Now that my servant Moses is dead, you must lead my Num 12:7 Deut 34:5
people across the Jordan River into the land I am giving them. 3I promise you what I 1:3
promised Moses: 'Everywhere you go, you will be on land I have given you—4from the Deut 11:24
Negev Desert in the south to the Lebanon mountains in the north, from the Euphrates
River on the east to the Mediterranean Sea* on the west, and all the land of the Hittites.'
5No one will be able to stand their ground against you as long as you live. For I will be 1:5
with you as I was with Moses. I will not fail you or abandon you. Deut 7:24; 31:6-8 Heb 13:5
6"Be strong and courageous, for you will lead my people to possess all the land I
swore to give their ancestors. 7Be strong and very courageous. Obey all the laws Moses 1:7
gave you. Do not turn away from them, and you will be successful in everything you do. Deut 5:29, 32; 28:14; 29:9
8Study this Book of the Law continually. Meditate on it day and night so you may be 1:8
sure to obey all that is written in it. Only then will you succeed. 9I command you—be Deut 17:8-9
strong and courageous! Do not be afraid or discouraged. For the LORD your God is with Ps 1:1-3 1:9
you wherever you go." Deut 31:6-8

Joshua's Charge to the Israelites

10Joshua then commanded the leaders of Israel, 11"Go through the camp and tell the 1:10
people to get their provisions ready. In three days you will cross the Jordan River and Deut 3:2-4, 15-17
take possession of the land the LORD your God has given you."
12Then Joshua called together the tribes of Reuben, Gad, and the half-tribe of 1:12 Num 32:20-22, 33

1:4 Hebrew *the Great Sea.*

1:1 As the book of Joshua opens, the Israelites are camped along the east bank of the Jordan River at the very edge of the Promised Land, and they are completing the mourning period for Moses, who has just died (Deuteronomy 34:7, 8). Thirty-nine years earlier (after spending a year at Mount Sinai receiving God's law), the Israelites had an opportunity to enter the Promised Land, but they failed to trust God to give them victory. As a result, God did not allow them to enter the land, but made them wander in the wilderness until the disobedient generation had all died.

During their wilderness wanderings, the Israelites obeyed God's laws. They also taught the new generation to obey God's laws so that they might enter the Promised Land (also called Canaan). As the children grew, they were often reminded that faith and obedience to God brought victory, while unbelief and disobedience brought tragedy. When the last of the older generation had died and the new generation had become adults, the Israelites prepared to make their long-awaited claim on the Promised Land.

1:1-5 Joshua succeeded Moses as Israel's leader. What qualifications did he have to become the leader of a nation? (1) God appointed him (Numbers 27:18-23). (2) He was one of only two living eyewitnesses to the Egyptian plagues and the Exodus from Egypt. (3) He was Moses' personal aide for 40 years. (4) Of the 12 scouts, only he and Caleb showed complete confidence that God would help them conquer the land.

1:2 Because Joshua had assisted Moses for many years, he was well prepared to take over the leadership of the nation. Changes in leadership are common in many organizations. At such times, a smooth transition is essential for the establishment of the new administration. This doesn't happen unless new leaders are trained. If you are currently in a leadership position, begin preparing someone to take your place. Then, when you leave or are promoted, operations can continue to run efficiently. If you want to be a leader, learn from others so that you will be prepared when the opportunity comes.

1:5 Joshua's new job consisted of leading more than two million people into a strange new land and conquering it. What a challenge—even for a man of Joshua's caliber! Every new job is a challenge. Without God it can be frightening. With God it can be a great adventure. Just as God was with Joshua, he is with us as we face our new challenges. We may not conquer nations, but every day we face tough situations, difficult people, and temptations. However, God promises that he will never abandon us or fail to help us. By asking God to direct us we can conquer many of life's challenges.

1:6-8 Many people think that prosperity and success come from having power, influential personal contacts, and a relentless desire to get ahead. But the strategy for gaining prosperity that God taught Joshua goes against such criteria. He said that to succeed Joshua must (1) be strong and courageous because the task ahead would not be easy, (2) obey God's law, and (3) constantly read and study the Book of the Law—God's Word. To be successful, follow God's words to Joshua. You may not succeed by the world's standards, but you will be a success in God's eyes—and his opinion lasts forever.

1:12-15 During the previous year, the tribes of Reuben and Gad and the half-tribe of Manasseh had asked Moses if they could settle just east of the Promised Land. The area was excellent pastureland for their large flocks. Moses agreed to give them the land on one condition—that they help their fellow tribes enter and conquer the Promised Land. Only after the land was conquered could they return to their homes. Now it was time for these three tribes to live up to their agreement.

1:13 Deut 3:18-20 Manasseh. He told them, 13"Remember what Moses, the servant of the LORD, commanded you: 'The LORD your God is giving you rest and has given you this land.' 14Your
wives, children, and cattle may remain here on the east side of the Jordan River, but your
warriors, fully armed, must lead the other tribes across the Jordan to help them conquer
1:15 Josh 22:1-4 their territory. Stay with them 15until the LORD gives rest to them as he has given rest to
you, and until they, too, possess the land the LORD your God is giving them. Only then
may you settle here on the east side of the Jordan River in the land that Moses, the servant
of the LORD, gave you."

1:16 Num 32:25 16They answered Joshua, "We will do whatever you command us, and we will go
1:17 Josh 1:5, 9 wherever you send us. 17We will obey you just as we obeyed Moses. And may the LORD
your God be with you as he was with Moses. 18Anyone who rebels against your word and
does not obey your every command will be put to death. So be strong and courageous!"

Rahab Protects the Spies

2:1 Num 25:1 Heb 11:31 Jas 2:25 **2** Then Joshua secretly sent out two spies from the Israelite camp at Acacia.* He
instructed them, "Spy out the land on the other side of the Jordan River, especially
around Jericho." So the two men set out and came to the house of a prostitute named
Rahab and stayed there that night.

2:1 Hebrew *Shittim.*

TAKE THE LAND
God told Joshua to lead the Israelites into the Promised Land (also called Canaan) and conquer it. This was not an act of imperialism or aggression but an act of judgment. Here are some of the earlier passages in the Bible where God promised to give this land to the Israelites and the reasons for doing so.

Genesis 12:1–3	God promised to bless Abraham and make his descendants into a great nation
Genesis 15:16	God would choose the right time for Israel to enter Canaan, because the nations living there then would be wicked and ripe for judgment (their sin would run its course)
Genesis 17:7, 8	God promised to give all the land of Canaan to Abraham's descendants
Exodus 33:1–3	God promised to help the Israelites drive out all the evil nations from Canaan
Deuteronomy 4:5–8	The Israelites were to be an example of right living to the whole world; this would not work if they intermingled with the wicked Canaanites
Deuteronomy 7:1–5	The Israelites were to utterly wipe out the Canaanites because of their wickedness and because of Israel's call to purity
Deuteronomy 12:2	The Israelites were to completely destroy the Canaanite altars so nothing would tempt them away from worshiping God alone

1:13 God was giving the people rest. This was wonderful news to these people who had been on the move for their entire lives. The people who had no land would be given a land of their own, and they would be able to settle and to "rest."

1:16 If everyone had tried to conquer the Promised Land his own way, chaos would have resulted. In order to complete the enormous task of conquering the land, everyone had to agree to the leader's plan and be willing to support and obey him. If we are going to complete the tasks God has given us, we must fully agree to his plan, pledge ourselves to obey it, and put his principles into action. Agreeing to God's plan means both knowing what the plan is (as found in the Bible) and carrying it out daily.

1:18 When God commissioned Joshua, he was told three times to be strong and courageous (see 1:6, 7, 9). Here, Joshua was given the same kind of encouragement from the people. Apparently, he took God's message to heart and found the strength and courage he needed in his relationship with God. The next time you are afraid to do what you know is right, remember that strength and courage are readily available from God.

2:1 Why did Joshua send the spies secretly? As far as he knew, he would be attacking a heavily fortified city using conventional warfare tactics. He needed strategic information about the city for the upcoming battle. But he also knew that this might draw criticism from the other leaders. After all, the last time spies were sent, the report they brought back caused disastrous problems (see Numbers 13:1–14:4). While he did not want to move ahead without information, he also did not want to cause the people to stumble and question his wisdom and ability to lead the nation.

2:1 Why would the spies stop at the house of Rahab, a prostitute? (1) It was a good place to gather information and have no questions asked in return. (2) Rahab's house was in an ideal location for a quick escape because it was built into the city wall (2:15). (3) God directed the spies to Rahab's house because he knew her heart was open to him and that she would be instrumental in the Israelite victory over Jericho. God often uses people with simple faith to accomplish his great purposes, no matter what kind of past they have had or how insignificant they seem to be. Rahab didn't allow her past to keep her from the new role God had for her.

[2]But someone told the king of Jericho, "Some Israelites have come here tonight to spy
out the land." [3]So the king of Jericho sent orders to Rahab: "Bring out the men who have
come into your house. They are spies sent here to discover the best way to attack us."
[4]Rahab, who had hidden the two men, replied, "The men were here earlier, but I didn't 2:4
know where they were from. [5]They left the city at dusk, as the city gates were about to close, 2 Sam 17:19
and I don't know where they went. If you hurry, you can probably catch up with them."
[6](But she had taken them up to the roof and hidden them beneath piles of flax.) [7]So the 2:6
king's men went looking for the spies along the road leading to the shallow crossing places Jas 2:25
of the Jordan River. And as soon as the king's men had left, the city gate was shut.
[8]Before the spies went to sleep that night, Rahab went up on the roof to talk with them.
[9]"I know the LORD has given you this land," she told them. "We are all afraid of you. 2:9
Everyone is living in terror. [10]For we have heard how the LORD made a dry path for you Exod 23:27
through the Red Sea* when you left Egypt. And we know what you did to Sihon and Og, Deut 2:25
Josh 9:24
the two Amorite kings east of the Jordan River, whose people you completely de- 2:10
stroyed.* [11]No wonder our hearts have melted in fear! No one has the courage to fight Exod 14:21
after hearing such things. For the LORD your God is the supreme God of the heavens Num 21:21
2:11
above and the earth below. [12]Now swear to me by the LORD that you will be kind to me Deut 4:39
and my family since I have helped you. Give me some guarantee that [13]when Jericho is 2:12
conquered, you will let me live, along with my father and mother, my brothers and Josh 2:18
sisters, and all their families."
[14]"We offer our own lives as a guarantee for your safety," the men agreed. "If you
don't betray us, we will keep our promise when the LORD gives us the land."
[15]Then, since Rahab's house was built into the city wall, she let them down by a rope 2:15
through the window. [16]"Escape to the hill country," she told them. "Hide there for three Josh 2:18, 21
days until the men who are searching for you have returned; then go on your way." 2:16
[17]Before they left, the men told her, "We can guarantee your safety [18]only if you leave Jas 2:25

2:10a Hebrew *sea of reeds.* **2:10b** The Hebrew term used here refers to the complete consecration of things or people to the LORD, either by destroying them or by giving them as an offering.

SPY MISSION TO JERICHO
Two spies left the Israelite camp at Acacia, crossed the Jordan River, and slipped into Jericho. The city was built around an oasis in the midst of a hot and desolate valley 840 feet below sea level. Jericho was the first major city the Israelites set out to conquer.

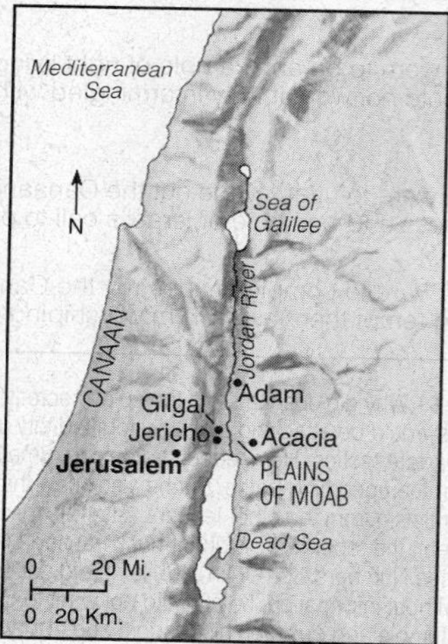

2:4, 5 Was Rahab justified in lying to save the lives of the spies? Although the Bible does not speak negatively about her lie, it is clear that lying is sin. In Hebrews 11:31, however, Rahab is commended for her faith in God. Her lie is not mentioned. Several explanations have been offered: (1) God forgave Rahab's lie because of her faith; (2) Rahab was simply deceiving the enemy, a normal and acceptable practice in wartime; (3) because Rahab was not a Jew, she could not be held responsible for keeping the moral standards set forth in God's law; (4) Rahab broke a lesser principle—telling the truth—to uphold a higher principle—protecting God's people.

There may have been another way to save the lives of the Israelite spies. But under the pressure of the moment, Rahab had to make a choice. Most of us will face dilemmas at one time or another. We may feel that there is no perfect solution to our problem. Fortunately, God does not demand that our judgment be perfect in all situations. He simply asks us to put our trust in him and to do the best we know how. Rahab did that and was commended for her faith.

2:6 Flax was harvested in the fields and piled high on the rooftops to dry. It was then made into yarn which was used to make linen cloth. Flax grows to a height of three or four feet. Stacked on the roof, it made an excellent hiding place for the spies.

2:8-13 Many would assume that Rahab—a pagan, a Canaanite, and a prostitute—would never be interested in God. Yet Rahab was willing to risk everything she had for a God she barely knew. We must not gauge a person's interest in God by his or her background, life-style, or appearance. We should let nothing get in the way of our telling people about God.

2:11 Rahab recognized something that many of the Israelites did not—the God of heaven is not an ordinary god! He is all-powerful. The people of Jericho were afraid because they had heard the news of God's extraordinary power in defeating the armies across the Jordan River. Today we can worship this same powerful, miracle-working God. He is powerful enough to destroy mighty, wicked armies, as he did in Jericho. He is also powerful enough to save us from certain death, as he did with Rahab.

2:15 In Joshua's day it was common to build houses on city walls. Many cities had two walls about 12 to 15 feet apart. Houses were built on wooden logs laid across the tops of the two walls. Rahab may have lived in such a house with a window that looked out over the outside wall.

this scarlet rope hanging from the window. And all your family members—your father,
mother, brothers, and all your relatives—must be here inside the house. 19 If they go out
into the street, they will be killed, and we cannot be held to our oath. But we swear that
no one inside this house will be killed—not a hand will be laid on any of them. 20 If you
betray us, however, we are not bound by this oath in any way."
21 "I accept your terms," she replied. And she sent them on their way, leaving the
scarlet rope hanging from the window.
22 The spies went up into the hill country and stayed there three days. The men who
were chasing them had searched everywhere along the road, but they finally returned
to the city without success. 23 Then the two spies came down from the hill country,
2:24 Josh 2:9; 6:2 crossed the Jordan River, and reported to Joshua all that had happened to them. 24 "The
LORD will certainly give us the whole land," they said, "for all the people in the land
are terrified of us."

2. Crossing the Jordan

3:1 Josh 2:1 **3** Early the next morning Joshua and all the Israelites left Acacia* and arrived at the
3:2 Josh 1:11 banks of the Jordan River, where they camped before crossing. 2 Three days later,
the Israelite leaders went through the camp 3 giving these instructions to the people:

3:1 Hebrew *Shittim.*

JOSHUA

One of the greatest challenges facing leaders is to replace themselves, training others to become leaders. Many outstanding accomplishments have been started by someone with great ability whose life or career ended before the vision became reality. The fulfillment of that dream then became the responsibility of that person's successor. Death is the ultimate deadline for leadership. One of the best tests of our leadership is our willingness and ability to train another for our position.

Moses made an excellent decision when he chose Joshua as his assistant. That choice was later confirmed by God himself when he instructed Moses to commission Joshua as his successor (Numbers 27:15–23). Joshua had played a key role in the exodus from Egypt. Introduced as the field general of Israel's army, he was the only person allowed to accompany Moses partway up the mountain when Moses received the law. Joshua and Caleb were the only 2 among the 12 scouts to bring back an encouraging report after being sent into the Promised Land the first time. Other references show him to have been Moses' constant shadow. His basic training was living with Moses—experiencing firsthand what it meant to lead God's people. This was modeling at its best!

Who is your Moses? Who is your Joshua? You are part of the chain of God's ongoing work in the world. You are modeling yourself after others, and others are patterning their lives after you. How important is God to those you want to be like? Do those who are watching you see God reflected in every area of your life? Ask God to lead you to a trustworthy Moses. Ask him to make you a good Joshua.

Strengths and accomplishments
- Moses' assistant and successor
- One of only two adults who experienced Egyptian slavery and lived to enter the Promised Land
- Led the Israelites into their God-given homeland
- Brilliant military strategist
- Faithful to ask God's direction in the challenges he faced

Lessons from his life
- Effective leadership is often the product of good preparation and encouragement
- The persons after whom we pattern ourselves will have a definite effect on us
- A person committed to God provides the best model for us

Vital statistics
- Where: Egypt, the wilderness of Sinai, and Canaan (the Promised Land)
- Occupations: Special assistant to Moses, warrior, leader
- Relative: Father: Nun
- Contemporaries: Moses, Caleb, Miriam, Aaron

Key verses
"So Moses did as the LORD commanded and presented Joshua to Eleazar the priest and the whole community. Moses laid his hands on him and commissioned him to his responsibilities, just as the LORD had commanded through Moses" (Numbers 27:22, 23).

Joshua is also mentioned in Exodus 17:9–14; 24:13; 32:17; 33:11; Numbers 11:28; 13; 14; 26:65; 27:18–23; 32:11–12, 28; 34:17; Deuteronomy 1:38; 3:21, 28; 31:3, 7, 14, 23; 34:9; the book of Joshua; Judges 2:6–9; and 1 Kings 16:34.

"When you see the Levitical priests carrying the Ark of the Covenant of the LORD your
God, follow them. 4 Since you have never traveled this way before, they will guide you.
Stay about a half mile* behind them, keeping a clear distance between you and the Ark.
Make sure you don't come any closer."
5 Then Joshua told the people, "Purify yourselves, for tomorrow the LORD will do 3:5
great wonders among you." Exod 19:10
6 In the morning Joshua said to the priests, "Lift up the Ark of the Covenant and lead Josh 7:13
the people across the river." And so they started out.
7 The LORD told Joshua, "Today I will begin to make you great in the eyes of all the 3:7
Israelites. Now they will know that I am with you, just as I was with Moses. 8 Give these Josh 4:14
instructions to the priests who are carrying the Ark of the Covenant: 'When you reach 3:8
the banks of the Jordan River, take a few steps into the river and stop.'" Josh 3:17
9 So Joshua told the Israelites, "Come and listen to what the LORD your God says.
10 Today you will know that the living God is among you. He will surely drive out the 3:10
Canaanites, Hittites, Hivites, Perizzites, Girgashites, Amorites, and Jebusites. 11 Think of Deut 7:1
it! The Ark of the Covenant, which belongs to the Lord of the whole earth, will lead you
across the Jordan River! 12 Now choose twelve men, one from each tribe. 13 The priests 3:12
will be carrying the Ark of the LORD, the Lord of all the earth. When their feet touch the Josh 4:2-4
water, the flow of water will be cut off upstream, and the river will pile up there in one 3:13
heap." Exod 15:8
14 When the people set out to cross the Jordan, the priests who were carrying the Ark of
the Covenant went ahead of them. 15 Now it was the harvest season, and the Jordan was 3:15
overflowing its banks. But as soon as the feet of the priests who were carrying the Ark 1 Chr 12:15
touched the water at the river's edge, 16 the water began piling up at a town upstream called 3:16
Adam, which is near Zarethan. And the water below that point flowed on to the Dead Sea* Pss 66:6; 74:15;
114:3, 5

3:4 Hebrew *about 2,000 cubits* [900 meters]. **3:16** Hebrew *the sea of the Arabah, the Salt Sea.*

3:2-4 The Ark of the Covenant was Israel's most sacred treasure. It was a symbol of God's presence and power. The Ark was a gold rectangular box with two cherubim (angels) facing each other on the lid. Inside the Ark were the tablets of the Ten Commandments Moses received from God, a jar of manna (the bread God miraculously sent from heaven during the wilderness wanderings), and Aaron's staff (the symbol of the high priest's authority). According to God's law, only the Levites could carry the Ark. The Ark was constructed at the same time as the Tabernacle (Exodus 37:1-9) and placed in the sanctuary's most sacred room.

3:5 Before entering the Promised Land, the Israelites were to perform a purification ceremony. This was often done before making a sacrifice or, as in this case, before witnessing a great act of God. God's law stated that a person could become unclean for many reasons—eating certain foods (Leviticus 11), childbirth (Leviticus 12), disease (Leviticus 13, 14), touching a dead person (Numbers 19:11-22). God used these various outward signs of uncleanness to illustrate man's inward uncleanness that comes as a result of sin. The purification ceremony pictured the importance of approaching God with a pure heart. Like the Israelites, we need God's forgiveness before we approach him.

3:9 Just before crossing over into the Promised Land, Joshua gathered the people to hear the words of the Lord. Their excitement was high. No doubt they wanted to rush on, but Joshua made them stop and listen. We live in a fast-paced age where everyone rushes just to keep up. It is easy to get caught up in our tasks, becoming too busy for what God says is most important—listening to his words. Before making your schedule, take time to focus on what God wants from all your activities. Knowing what God has said before you rush into your day may help you avoid foolish mistakes.

3:10 Why would God help the Israelites drive out these nations from their native land? God had punished Israel first for its disobedience. He then turned to the rest of the nations. Genesis 15:16 implies that the people of Canaan were wicked and deserved to be punished for their terrible sins. Israel was to be a vehicle for this punishment. More important was the fact that Israel, as a holy nation, could not live among such evil and idolatrous people. To do so would be to invite sin into their lives. The only way to prevent Israel from being infected by evil religions was to drive out those who practiced them. Israel, however, failed to drive everyone out as God had told them to do. It wasn't long before Israel—the nation God chose to be his holy people—began following the evil practices of the Canaanites.

3:13, 14 The Israelites were eager to enter the Promised Land, conquer nations, and live peacefully. But first they had to cross the flood-level waters of the Jordan River. God gave them specific instructions: In order to cross, the priests had to step into the water. What if these priests had been afraid to take that first step? Often God provides no solution to our problems until we trust him and move ahead with what we know we should do. What are the rivers, or obstacles, in your life? In obedience to God, take that first step into the water.

3:13-17 God had parted the waters of the Red Sea to let the people out of Egypt (Exodus 14), and here he parted the Jordan River to let them enter Canaan. These miracles showed Israel that God keeps his promises. God's presence among his people and his faithfulness to them made the entire journey from Egypt to the Promised Land possible. He was with them at the end of their wanderings just as he was with them in the beginning.

3:15, 16 The Israelites crossed the Jordan River in the spring, when it was overflowing its banks. God chose the time when the river was at its highest to demonstrate his power—parting the waters so that the entire nation could cross on dry ground. Some say that God used a natural occurrence (such as a landslide) to stop the waters of the Jordan; others say he did it by a direct miracle. In either case, God showed his great power by working a miracle of timing and location to allow his people to cross the river on dry ground. This testimony of God's supernatural power served to build the Israelites' hope in God and to give them a great reputation with their enemies, who greatly outnumbered them.

3:17 until the riverbed was dry. Then all the people crossed over near the city of Jericho.
Exod 14:21-22, 29 17 Meanwhile, the priests who were carrying the Ark of the LORD's covenant stood on dry
ground in the middle of the riverbed as the people passed by them. They waited there until
everyone had crossed the Jordan on dry ground.

Memorials to the Jordan Crossing

4:1 **4** When all the people were safely across the river, the LORD said to Joshua, 2 "Now
Deut 27:2 choose twelve men, one from each tribe. 3 Tell the men to take twelve stones from
4:2 where the priests are standing in the middle of the Jordan and pile them up at the place
Josh 3:12 where you camp tonight."
4 So Joshua called together the twelve men 5 and told them, "Go into the middle of the
Jordan, in front of the Ark of the LORD your God. Each of you must pick up one stone
and carry it out on your shoulder—twelve stones in all, one for each of the twelve tribes.
4:6 6 We will use these stones to build a memorial. In the future, your children will ask, 'What
Exod 12:26; 13:14 do these stones mean to you?' 7 Then you can tell them, 'They remind us that the Jordan
River stopped flowing when the Ark of the LORD's covenant went across.' These stones
will stand as a permanent memorial among the people of Israel."
4:8 8 So the men did as Joshua told them. They took twelve stones from the middle of the
Josh 4:20 Jordan River, one for each tribe, just as the LORD had commanded Joshua. They carried
them to the place where they camped for the night and constructed the memorial there.
4:9 9 Joshua also built another memorial of twelve stones in the middle of the Jordan, at
Gen 28:18 the place where the priests who carried the Ark of the Covenant were standing. The
memorial remains there to this day.
10 The priests who were carrying the Ark stood in the middle of the river until all of
the LORD's instructions, which Moses had given to Joshua, were carried out. Meanwhile,
4:12 the people hurried across the riverbed. 11 And when everyone was on the other side, the
Num 32:17 priests crossed over with the Ark of the LORD. 12 The armed warriors from the tribes of
Reuben, Gad, and the half-tribe of Manasseh led the Israelites across the Jordan, just as
Moses had directed. 13 These warriors—about forty thousand strong—were ready for
battle, and they crossed over to the plains of Jericho in the LORD's presence.
14 That day the LORD made Joshua great in the eyes of all the Israelites, and for the rest
of his life they revered him as much as they had revered Moses.
4:14-15 15 The LORD had said to Joshua, 16 "Command the priests carrying the Ark of the
Josh 3:7-8
4:18 Covenant* to come up out of the riverbed." 17 So Joshua gave the command. 18 And as
Josh 3:15 soon as the priests carrying the Ark of the LORD's covenant came up out of the riverbed,
the Jordan River flooded its banks as before.
4:19 19 The people crossed the Jordan on the tenth day of the first month—the month that
Josh 5:9 marked their exodus from Egypt.* They camped at Gilgal, east of Jericho. 20 It was there
at Gilgal that Joshua piled up the twelve stones taken from the Jordan River. 21 Then
Joshua said to the Israelites, "In the future, your children will ask, 'What do these stones
4:22 mean?' 22 Then you can tell them, 'This is where the Israelites crossed the Jordan on dry
Josh 3:17 ground.' 23 For the LORD your God dried up the river right before your eyes, and he kept
it dry until you were all across, just as he did at the Red Sea* when he dried it up until

4:16 Hebrew *Ark of the Testimony.* **4:19** Hebrew *the tenth day of the first month.* This day of the Hebrew lunar calendar occurs in late March or early April. **4:23** Hebrew *sea of reeds.*

4:1ff After the people safely crossed the river, what would be next? Conquering the land? Not yet. First, God directed them to build a memorial from 12 stones drawn from the river by 12 men, one from each tribe. This may seem like an insignificant step in their mission of conquering the land, but God did not want his people to plunge into their task unprepared. They were to focus on him and remember who was guiding them. As you are busy doing your God-given tasks, set aside quiet moments, times to build your own memorial to God's power. Too much activity may shift your focus away from God.

4:14 The Israelites revered Joshua for his role in leading them across the Jordan River. He, like Moses, would receive Israel's praises generation after generation. Although Israel was not a world power at that time, Joshua's reputation for handling his responsibilities God's way brought him greater glory than if he had been a hero in a "superpower" nation. Doing right is more important than doing well.

4:21-24 The memorial of 12 stones was to be a constant reminder of the day the Israelites crossed the Jordan River on dry ground. Their children would see the stones, hear the story, and learn about God. Do you have traditions—special dates or special places—to help your children learn about God's work in your life? Do you take time to tell them what God has done for you—forgiving and saving you, answering your prayers, supplying your needs? Retelling your story will help keep memories of God's faithfulness alive in your family.

we had all crossed over. 24 He did this so that all the nations of the earth might know the
power of the LORD, and that you might fear the LORD your God forever."

5 When all the Amorite kings west of the Jordan and all the Canaanite kings who
lived along the Mediterranean coast* heard how the LORD had dried up the Jordan
River so the people of Israel could cross, they lost heart and were paralyzed with
fear.

Israel Reestablishes Covenant Ceremonies

2 At that time the LORD told Joshua, "Use knives of flint to make the Israelites a
circumcised people again." 3 So Joshua made flint knives and circumcised the entire male
population of Israel at Gibeath-haaraloth.*

4 Joshua had to circumcise them because all the men who were old enough to bear arms
when they left Egypt had died in the wilderness. 5 Those who left Egypt had all been
circumcised, but none of those born after the Exodus, during the years in the wilderness,
had been circumcised. 6 The Israelites wandered in the wilderness for forty years until
all the men who were old enough to bear arms when they left Egypt had died. For they
had disobeyed the LORD, and the LORD vowed he would not let them enter the land he
had sworn to give us—a land flowing with milk and honey. 7 So Joshua circumcised their
sons who had not been circumcised on the way to the Promised Land—those who had
grown up to take their fathers' places. 8 After all the males had been circumcised, they
rested in the camp until they were healed.

9 Then the LORD said to Joshua, "Today I have rolled away the shame of your slavery
in Egypt." So that place has been called Gilgal* to this day.

10 While the Israelites were camped at Gilgal on the plains of Jericho, they celebrated
Passover on the evening of the fourteenth day of the first month—the month that marked
their exodus from Egypt.* 11 The very next day they began to eat unleavened bread and
roasted grain harvested from the land. 12 No manna appeared that day, and it was never
seen again. So from that time on the Israelites ate from the crops of Canaan.

4:24 1 Kgs 8:42-43; Ps 89:13
5:1 Num 13:29; Josh 2:9-11
5:2-3 Gen 17:9-10, 23
5:4 Deut 2:14
5:6 Num 14:29-35; 26:63-65; Deut 2:7
5:10 Exod 12:18; Josh 4:19
5:12 Exod 16:35

5:1 Hebrew *along the sea.* 5:3 *Gibeath-haaraloth* means "hill of foreskins." 5:9 *Gilgal* sounds like the Hebrew word *galal,* meaning "to roll." 5:10 Hebrew *the fourteenth day of the first month.* This day of the Hebrew lunar calendar occurs in late March or early April.

5:1 The Amorites and Canaanites were the two major groups living in Canaan at the time of Israel's invasion. The Canaanites worshiped a variety of gods, but Baal was their favorite. Canaanite culture was materialistic, and their religion, sensual. The Israelites continually turned to Baal after entering Canaan. The Amorite gods also infected Israel's worship and turned people away from worshiping the true God. Worshiping these false gods eventually brought about Israel's downfall.

5:1 The Israelites spent 39 years in the wilderness unnecessarily because they were terrified of the Canaanites. They underestimated God's ability. The Israelites' first attempt to enter the Promised Land had failed (Numbers 13–14). Here Israel saw that the Canaanites were terrified of their army. The Canaanites had heard about Israel's great victories through God (2:9-11), and they hoped that the Jordan River would slow Israel down or discourage them from entering Canaan. But news that the Israelites had crossed the Jordan on dry land caused any courage the Canaanites still had to melt away.

Don't underestimate God. If we are faithful to God, he will cause great opposition to disappear. God can change the attitudes of those who oppose him.

5:2, 3 The rite of circumcision marked Israel's position as God's covenant people. When God made the original covenant with Abraham, he required that each male be circumcised as a sign of cutting off the old life and beginning a new life with God (Genesis 17:13). Other cultures at that time used circumcision as a sign of entry into adulthood, but only Israel used it as a sign of following God. A man would only be circumcised once. "Again" here refers to the fact that many of the young men were uncircumcised at this time (see 5:5).

5:8, 9 Located about two miles northeast of Jericho, Gilgal was Israel's base camp and their temporary center of government and worship during their invasion of Canaan. Here the people renewed their commitment to God and covenant with him before attempting to conquer the new land. At Gilgal the angelic commander of the Lord's army appeared to Joshua with further instructions for battle and encouragement for the conquest (5:13-15). After the conquest, Gilgal continued to be an important place in Israel. It was here that Israel's first king, Saul, was crowned (1 Samuel 11:14, 15).

5:10 This joyous Passover was the first to be celebrated in the Promised Land and only the third celebrated by Israel since the Exodus from Egypt. The last time was at the foot of Mount Sinai, 39 years earlier. This celebration reminded Israel of God's mighty miracles that brought them out of Egypt. There they had to eat in fear and haste; here they ate in celebration of God's blessings and promises. (See Exodus 12 for a description of the night the angel "passed over" the Israelites' homes.)

5:11, 12 God had miraculously supplied manna to the hungry Israelites during their 40 years in the wilderness (Exodus 16:14-31). In the bountiful Promised Land they no longer needed this daily food supply because the land was ready for planting and harvesting. God had miraculously provided food for the Israelites while they were in the wilderness; here he provided food from the land itself. Prayer is not an alternative to preparation, and faith is not a substitute for hard work. God can and does provide miraculously for his people as needed, but he also expects them to use their God-given talents and resources to provide for themselves. If your prayers have gone unanswered, perhaps what you need is within your reach. Pray instead for the wisdom to see it and the energy and motivation to do it.

B. CONQUERING THE PROMISED LAND (5:13—12:24)

After crossing the Jordan River, the Israelites begin to conquer Canaan. Jericho is the first to fall. Then Israel suffers its first defeat because of one man's disobedience. After the people remove the sin from their community, they strike again—this time with success. Soon great kings attack from the north and south, but they are defeated because God is with Israel. Evil could not be tolerated in the Promised Land, nor can it be tolerated in our lives. We, like Israel, must ruthlessly remove sin from our lives before it takes control of us.

1. Joshua attacks the center of the land

The LORD's Commander Confronts Joshua

5:13 Gen 18:1-2; 32:24 Exod 23:23 Num 22:31
13 As Joshua approached the city of Jericho, he looked up and saw a man facing him with
sword in hand. Joshua went up to him and asked, "Are you friend or foe?"

5:14 Gen 17:3
14 "Neither one," he replied. "I am commander of the LORD's army."
At this, Joshua fell with his face to the ground in reverence. "I am at your command,"
Joshua said. "What do you want your servant to do?"
15 The commander of the LORD's army replied, "Take off your sandals, for this is holy
ground." And Joshua did as he was told.

The Fall of Jericho

6 Now the gates of Jericho were tightly shut because the people were afraid of the
6:2 Deut 7:24
Israelites. No one was allowed to go in or out. 2 But the LORD said to Joshua, "I have
given you Jericho, its king, and all its mighty warriors. 3 Your entire army is to march
6:4 Lev 25:9
around the city once a day for six days. 4 Seven priests will walk ahead of the Ark, each

---

RAHAB

Rahab was a prostitute in the city of Jericho. As a prostitute, she lived on the edge of society, one stop short of rejection. Her house, built right into the city wall, provided both lodging and favors to travelers. It was a natural place for the Israelite spies to stay, as they would be mistaken for Rahab's customers.

Stories about the Israelites had been circulating for some time, but now it was evident that the Israelites were about to invade. Living on the wall, Rahab felt especially vulnerable. Yet while she shared the general mood of fear with the rest of Jericho's population, she alone turned to the Lord for her salvation. Her faith gave her the courage to hide the spies and lie to the authorities. Rahab knew her position was dangerous; she could have been killed if she had been caught harboring the Israelites. Rahab took the risk, however, because she sensed that the Israelites relied on a God worth trusting. And God rewarded Rahab by promising safety for her and her family.

God works through people—like Rahab—whom we are inclined to reject. God remembers her because of her faith, not her profession. If at times you feel like a failure, remember that Rahab rose above her situation through her trust in God. You can do the same!

Strengths and accomplishments
- Relative of Boaz, and thus an ancestor of David and Jesus
- One of only two women listed in the Hall of Faith in Hebrews 11
- Resourceful, willing to help others at great cost to herself

Weakness and mistake
- She was a prostitute

Lesson from her life
- She did not let fear affect her faith in God's ability to deliver

Vital statistics
- Where: Jericho
- Occupations: Prostitute/innkeeper, later became a wife
- Relatives: Ancestor of David and Jesus (Matthew 1:5)
- Contemporary: Joshua

Key verse
"It was by faith that Rahab the prostitute did not die with all the others in her city who refused to obey God. For she had given a friendly welcome to the spies" (Hebrews 11:31).

Rahab's story is told in Joshua 2 and 6:22, 23. She is also mentioned in Matthew 1:5; Hebrews 11:31; and James 2:25.

5:14, 15 This was an angel of superior rank, the commander of the Lord's army. Some say he was an appearance of God in human form. As a sign of respect, Joshua took off his sandals. Although Joshua was Israel's leader, he was still subordinate to God, the absolute Leader. Awe and respect are the responses due to our holy God. How can we show respect for God? By our attitudes and actions. We should recognize God's power, authority, and deep love, and our actions must model our attitudes before others. Respect for God is just as important today as it was in Joshua's day, even though removing shoes is no longer our cultural way of showing it.

6:1 The city of Jericho, built thousands of years before Joshua was born, was one of the oldest cities in the world. In some places it had fortified walls up to 25 feet high and 20 feet thick.

carrying a ram's horn. On the seventh day you are to march around the city seven times,
with the priests blowing the horns. [5]When you hear the priests give one long blast on the
horns, have all the people give a mighty shout. Then the walls of the city will collapse,
and the people can charge straight into the city."

[6]So Joshua called together the priests and said, "Take up the Ark of the Covenant, and
assign seven priests to walk in front of it, each carrying a ram's horn." [7]Then he gave **6:7** Exod 14:15
orders to the people: "March around the city, and the armed men will lead the way in
front of the Ark of the LORD."

[8]After Joshua spoke to the people, the seven priests with the rams' horns started
marching in the presence of the LORD, blowing the horns as they marched. And the priests
carrying the Ark of the LORD's covenant followed behind them. [9]Armed guards marched **6:9** Isa 52:12
both in front of the priests and behind the Ark, with the priests continually blowing the
horns. [10]"Do not shout; do not even talk," Joshua commanded. "Not a single word from
any of you until I tell you to shout. Then shout!" [11]So the Ark of the LORD was carried
around the city once that day, and then everyone returned to spend the night in the camp.

[12]Joshua got up early the next morning, and the priests again carried the Ark of the
LORD. [13]The seven priests with the rams' horns marched in front of the Ark of the LORD, **6:13** Josh 6:4
blowing their horns. Armed guards marched both in front of the priests with the horns
and behind the Ark of the LORD. All this time the priests were sounding their horns. [14]On
the second day they marched around the city once and returned to the camp. They
followed this pattern for six days.

[15]On the seventh day the Israelites got up at dawn and marched around the city as they
had done before. But this time they went around the city seven times. [16]The seventh time
around, as the priests sounded the long blast on their horns, Joshua commanded the
people, "Shout! For the LORD has given you the city! [17]The city and everything in it must **6:17** Lev 27:28
be completely destroyed* as an offering to the LORD. Only Rahab the prostitute and the Deut 20:17
others in her house will be spared, for she protected our spies. [18]Do not take any of the **6:18** Deut 20:17
things set apart for destruction, or you yourselves will be completely destroyed, and you Josh 7:1, 25
will bring trouble on all Israel. [19]Everything made from silver, gold, bronze, or iron is **6:19**
sacred to the LORD and must be brought into his treasury." Num 31:21-23

[20]When the people heard the sound of the horns, they shouted as loud as they could. **6:20** Heb 11:30
Suddenly, the walls of Jericho collapsed, and the Israelites charged straight into the city **6:21**
from every side and captured it. [21]They completely destroyed everything in it—men and Deut 20:16
women, young and old, cattle, sheep, donkeys—everything.

6:17 The Hebrew term used here refers to the complete consecration of things or people to the LORD, either by destroying them or by giving them as an offering; also in 6:18, 21.

Soldiers standing guard on top of the walls could see for miles. Jericho was a symbol of military power and strength—the Canaanites considered it invincible.

Israel would attack this city first, and its destruction would put the fear of Israel into the heart of every person in Canaan. The Canaanites saw Israel's God as a nature god because he parted the Jordan and as a war god because he defeated Sihon and Og. But the Canaanites did not consider him a fortress god—one who could prevail against a walled city. The defeat of Jericho showed not only that Israel's God was superior to the Canaanite gods but also that he was invincible.

6:2-5 God told Joshua that Jericho was already delivered into his hands—the enemy was already defeated! What confidence Joshua must have had as he went into battle! Christians also fight against a defeated enemy. Our enemy, Satan, has been defeated by Christ (Romans 8:37-39; Hebrews 2:14, 15; 1 John 3:8). Although we still fight battles every day and sin runs rampant in the world, we have the assurance that the war has already been won. We do not have to be paralyzed by the power of a defeated enemy; we can overcome him through Christ's power.

6:3-5 Why did God give Joshua all these complicated instructions for the battle? Several answers are possible: (1) God was making it undeniably clear that the battle would depend upon him, and not upon Israel's weapons and expertise. This is why priests carrying the Ark, not soldiers, led the Israelites into battle. (2) God's method of taking the city accentuated the terror already felt in Jericho (2:9). (3) This strange military maneuver was a test of the Israelites' faith and their willingness to follow God completely. The blowing of the trumpets had a special significance. They had been instructed to blow the same trumpets used in the religious festivals in their battles to remind them that their victory would come from the Lord, not their own military might (Numbers 10:9).

6:21 Why did God demand that the Israelites destroy almost everyone and everything in Jericho? He was carrying out severe judgment against the wickedness of the Canaanites. This judgment, or *ban,* usually required that everything be destroyed (Deuteronomy 12:2, 3; 13:12-18). Because of their evil practices and intense idolatry, the Canaanites were a stronghold of rebellion against God. This threat to the right kind of living that God required had to be removed. If not, it would affect all Israel like a cancerous growth (as it did in the sad story told in the book of Judges). A few people and some items in Jericho were not destroyed, but these were special cases. Rahab and her household were saved because she had faith in God and because she helped the Israelite spies. The silver and gold and articles of bronze and iron were kept, not to enrich the people, but to beautify the Tabernacle and its services (6:24).

God's purpose in all this was to keep the people's faith and religion uncontaminated. He did not want the plunder to remind Israel of Canaanite practices.

6:22 Josh 2:14 Heb 11:31 22 Then Joshua said to the two spies, "Keep your promise. Go to the prostitute's house
and bring her out, along with all her family."
23 The young men went in and brought out Rahab, her father, mother, brothers, and all
the other relatives who were with her. They moved her whole family to a safe place near
the camp of Israel.
24 Then the Israelites burned the city and everything in it. Only the things made from
6:25 Josh 2:6 Heb 11:31 silver, gold, bronze, or iron were kept for the treasury of the LORD's house. 25 So Joshua
spared Rahab the prostitute and her relatives who were with her in the house, because she
had hidden the spies Joshua sent to Jericho. And she lives among the Israelites to this day.
6:26 1 Kgs 16:34 26 At that time Joshua invoked this curse:

"May the curse of the LORD fall on anyone
  who tries to rebuild the city of Jericho.
At the cost of his firstborn son,
  he will lay its foundation.
At the cost of his youngest son,
  he will set up its gates."

6:27 Josh 9:1 27 So the LORD was with Joshua, and his name became famous throughout the land.

Ai Defeats the Israelites

7:1 Josh 6:17-19 1 Chr 2:7 **7** But Israel was unfaithful concerning the things set apart for the LORD.* A man named
Achan had stolen some of these things, so the LORD was very angry with the Israelites.
Achan was the son of Carmi, of the family of Zimri,* of the clan of Zerah, and of the tribe
of Judah.
7:2 Gen 28:19 Josh 16:2 2 Joshua sent some of his men from Jericho to spy out the city of Ai, east of Bethel, near
Beth-aven. 3 When they returned, they told Joshua, "It's a small town, and it won't take more
than two or three thousand of us to destroy it. There's no need for all of us to go there."
4 So approximately three thousand warriors were sent, but they were soundly defeated.
7:5 Josh 2:11 The men of Ai 5 chased the Israelites from the city gate as far as the quarries,* and they
killed about thirty-six who were retreating down the slope. The Israelites were paralyzed
with fear at this turn of events, and their courage melted away.
7:6 Job 2:12; 42:6 Lam 2:10 Rev 18:19 6 Joshua and the leaders of Israel tore their clothing in dismay, threw dust on their
heads, and bowed down facing the Ark of the LORD until evening. 7 Then Joshua cried
7:7 Exod 5:22 out, "Sovereign LORD, why did you bring us across the Jordan River if you are going to

7:1a The Hebrew term used here refers to the complete consecration of things or people to the LORD, either by destroying them or by giving them as an offering; also in 7:11, 12, 13, 15. **7:1b** As in Greek version (see also 1 Chr 2:6); Hebrew reads *Zabdi.* Also in 7:17, 18. **7:5** Or *as far as Shebarim.*

God also wants us to be pure. He wants us to clean up our behavior when we begin a new life with him. We must not let the desire for personal gain distract us from our spiritual purpose. We must also reject any objects that are reminders of a life of rebellion against God. (For more information on how Israel handled its plunder, see the note on Numbers 31:25-30.)

6:26 This curse was fulfilled in 1 Kings 16:34 when a man, Hiel, rebuilt Jericho and consequently lost his oldest and youngest sons.

7:1 The things to be "set apart" refers to all the clothing, cattle, and other plunder that God said Israel should destroy when they conquered Jericho (see 6:17-19). It was not that they found a good use for something that was going to be thrown out anyway. This was a serious offense because it was in direct defiance of an explicit command of God (see Deuteronomy 20:16-18).

7:1ff Notice the results of Achan's sin: (1) Many men died (7:5); (2) Israel's army melted in fear (7:5); (3) Joshua questioned God (7:7-9); (4) God threatened to withdraw his presence from the people (7:12); (5) Achan and his family had to be destroyed (7:24-26).

When Israel eliminated the sin from their community, these were the results: (1) encouragement from God (8:1); (2) God's presence in battle (8:1); (3) God's guidance and promise of victory (8:2); (4) God's permission to keep the plunder and livestock from the battle for themselves (8:2). Throughout Israel's history, blessings came when the people got rid of their sin. You will also experience victory when you turn from your sin and follow God's plan wholeheartedly.

7:6 Joshua and the leaders tore their clothing and threw dust on their heads as signs of deep mourning before God. They were confused by their defeat at the small city of Ai after the spectacular Jericho victory, so they went before God in deep humility and sorrow to receive his instructions. When our lives fall apart, we also should turn to God for direction and help. Like Joshua and the leaders, we should humble ourselves so that we will be able to hear his words.

7:7 When Joshua first went against Ai (7:3), he did not consult God but relied on the strength of his army to defeat the small city. Only after Israel was defeated did they turn to God and ask what happened.

Too often we rely on our own skills and strength, especially when the task before us seems easy. We go to God only when the obstacles seem too great. However, only God knows what lies ahead. Consulting him, even when we are on a winning streak, may save us from grave mistakes or misjudgments. God may want us to learn lessons, remove pride, or consult others before he will work through us.

let the Amorites kill us? If only we had been content to stay on the other side! [8]Lord,
what am I to say, now that Israel has fled from its enemies? [9]For when the Canaanites **7:9**
and all the other people living in the land hear about it, they will surround us and wipe Exod 32:12 Deut 9:28
us off the face of the earth. And then what will happen to the honor of your great name?"
[10]But the LORD said to Joshua, "Get up! Why are you lying on your face like this?
[11]Israel has sinned and broken my covenant! They have stolen the things that I com- **7:11**
manded to be set apart for me. And they have not only stolen them; they have also lied Exod 14:15 1 Sam 15:24
about it and hidden the things among their belongings. [12]That is why the Israelites are
running from their enemies in defeat. For now Israel has been set apart for destruction.
I will not remain with you any longer unless you destroy the things among you that were
set apart for destruction.

[13]"Get up! Command the people to purify themselves in preparation for tomorrow.
For this is what the LORD, the God of Israel, says: Hidden among you, O Israel, are things
set apart for the LORD. You will never defeat your enemies until you remove these things.
[14]In the morning you must present yourselves by tribes, and the LORD will point out the
tribe to which the guilty man belongs. That tribe must come forward with its clans, and
the LORD will point out the guilty clan. That clan will then come forward, and the LORD
will point out the guilty family. Finally, each member of the guilty family must come one
by one. [15]The one who has stolen what was set apart for destruction will himself be
burned with fire, along with everything he has, for he has broken the covenant of the
LORD and has done a horrible thing in Israel."

Achan's Sin

[16]Early the next morning Joshua brought the tribes of Israel before the LORD, and the
tribe of Judah was singled out. [17]Then the clans of Judah came forward, and the clan of **7:17**
Zerah was singled out. Then the families of Zerah came before the LORD, and the family Num 26:20
of Zimri was singled out. [18]Every member of Zimri's family was brought forward person
by person, and Achan was singled out.
[19]Then Joshua said to Achan, "My son, give glory to the LORD, the God of Israel, by **7:19**
telling the truth. Make your confession and tell me what you have done. Don't hide it Jer 13:16 John 9:24
from me."
[20]Achan replied, "I have sinned against the LORD, the God of Israel. [21]For I saw a
beautiful robe imported from Babylon,* two hundred silver coins,* and a bar of gold
weighing more than a pound.* I wanted them so much that I took them. They are hidden
in the ground beneath my tent, with the silver buried deeper than the rest."
[22]So Joshua sent some men to make a search. They ran to the tent and found the stolen
goods hidden there, just as Achan had said, with the silver buried beneath the rest. [23]They
took the things from the tent and brought them to Joshua and all the Israelites. Then they
laid them on the ground in the presence of the LORD.
[24]Then Joshua and all the Israelites took Achan, the silver, the robe, the bar of gold, **7:24** Josh 15:7

7:21a Hebrew *Shinar.* **7:21b** Hebrew *200 shekels of silver,* about 5 pounds or 2.3 kilograms in weight.
7:21c Hebrew *50 shekels,* about 20 ounces or 570 grams in weight.

7:7-9 Imagine praying this way to God. This is not a formal church prayer; it is the prayer of a man who is afraid and confused by what is happening around him. Joshua poured out his real thoughts to God. Hiding your needs from God is ignoring the only one who can really help. God welcomes your honest prayers and wants you to express your true feelings to him. Any believer can become more honest in prayer by remembering that God is all-knowing and all-powerful and that his love is everlasting.

7:10-12 Why did Achan's sin bring judgment on the entire nation? Although it was one man's failure, God saw it as national disobedience to a national law. God needed the entire nation to be committed to the job they had agreed to do—conquer the land. Thus, when one person failed, everyone failed. If Achan's sin went unpunished, unlimited looting could break out. The nation as a whole had to take responsibility for preventing this undisciplined disobedience.

Achan's sin was not merely his keeping some of the captured goods (God allowed it in some cases), but his disobeying God's explicit command to destroy everything connected with Jericho. His sin was indifference to the evil and idolatry of the city, not just a desire for money and clothes. God would not protect Israel's army again until the sin was removed and the army returned to obeying him without reservation. God is not content with our doing what is right some of the time. He wants us to do what is right all the time. We are under his orders to eliminate any thoughts, practices, or possessions that hinder our devotion to him.

7:13 The Israelites had to undergo purification rites like those mentioned in 3:5 when they were preparing to cross the Jordan River. Such rites prepared the people to approach God and constantly reminded them of their sinfulness and his holiness.

7:24, 25 Achan underestimated God and didn't take his commands seriously (6:18). It may have seemed a small thing to Achan, but the effects of his sin were felt by the entire nation, especially his family. Like Achan, our actions affect more people than just ourselves. Beware of the temptation to rationalize your sins by saying they are too small or too personal to hurt anyone but you.

7:25 Josh 6:18
7:26 Isa 65:10 Hos 2:15

his sons, daughters, cattle, donkeys, sheep, tent, and everything he had, and they brought
them to the valley of Achor. [25]Then Joshua said to Achan, "Why have you brought
trouble on us? The LORD will now bring trouble on you." And all the Israelites stoned
Achan and his family and burned their bodies. [26]They piled a great heap of stones over
Achan, which remains to this day. That is why the place has been called the Valley of
Trouble* ever since. So the LORD was no longer angry.

The Israelites Defeat Ai

8:1 Deut 1:19-21 Josh 1:9; 6:2; 10:8
8:2 Deut 20:14 Josh 8:27

8 Then the LORD said to Joshua, "Do not be afraid or discouraged. Take the entire
army and attack Ai, for I have given to you the king of Ai, his people, his city, and
his land. [2]You will destroy them as you destroyed Jericho and its king. But this time
you may keep the captured goods and the cattle for yourselves. Set an ambush behind
the city."

[3]So Joshua and the army of Israel set out to attack Ai. Joshua chose thirty thousand
fighting men and sent them out at night [4]with these orders: "Hide in ambush close behind
the city and be ready for action. [5]When our main army attacks, the men of Ai will come
out to fight as they did before, and we will run away from them. [6]We will let them chase
us until they have all left the city. For they will say, 'The Israelites are running away from
us as they did before.' [7]Then you will jump up from your ambush and take possession
of the city, for the LORD your God will give it to you. [8]Set the city on fire, as the LORD
has commanded. You have your orders."

8:8 Judg 20:29-38

[9]So they left that night and lay in ambush between Bethel and the west side of Ai. But
Joshua remained among the people in the camp that night. [10]Early the next morning
Joshua roused his men and started toward Ai, accompanied by the leaders of Israel.
[11]They camped on the north side of Ai, with a valley between them and the city. [12]That
night Joshua sent five thousand men to lie in ambush between Bethel and Ai, on the west

7:26 Hebrew *valley of Achor.*

THE BATTLE FOR AI
During the night, Joshua sent one detachment of soldiers to the west of Ai to lie in wait. The next morning he led a second group north of Ai. When the army of Ai attacked, the Israelites to the north pretended to scatter, only to turn on the enemy as the men lying in ambush moved in and burned the city.

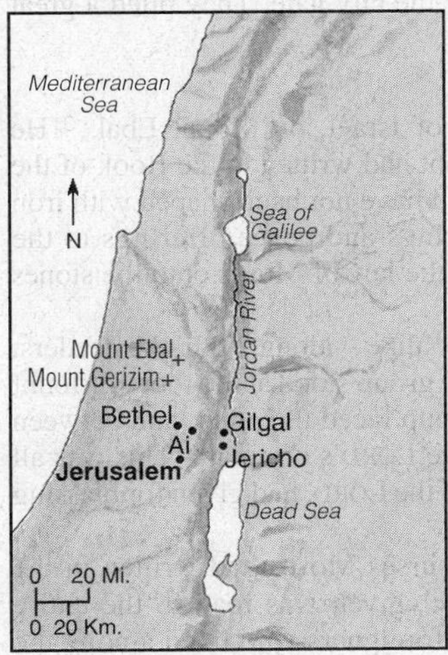

7:24-26 Why did Achan's entire family pay for his sin? The biblical record does not tell us if they were accomplices to his crime, but in the ancient world, the family was treated as a whole. Achan, as the head of his family, was like a tribal chief. If he prospered, the family prospered with him. If he suffered, so did they. Many Israelites had already died in battle because of Achan's sin. Now he was to be completely cut off from Israel.

Achan's entire family was to be stoned along with him so that no trace of the sin would remain in Israel. In our permissive and individualistic culture we have a hard time understanding such a decree, but in ancient cultures it was a common punishment. The punishment fit the crime: Achan had disobeyed God's command to destroy everything in Jericho; thus, everything that belonged to Achan had to be destroyed. Sin has drastic consequences, so we should take drastic measures to avoid it.

8:1 After Israel had been cleansed from Achan's sin, Joshua prepared to attack Ai again—this time to win. Joshua had learned some lessons that we can follow: (1) Confess your sins when God reveals them to you (7:19-21); (2) when you fail, refocus on God, deal with the problem, and move on (7:22-25; 8:1). God wants the cycle of sin, repentance, and forgiveness to strengthen us, not weaken us. The lessons we learn from our failures should make us better able to handle the same situation the second time around. Because God is eager to give us cleansing, forgiveness, and strength, the only way to lose is to give up. We can tell what kind of people we are by what we do on the second and third attempts.

8:2 Why did God allow the Israelites to keep the captured goods and cattle (livestock) this time? Israel's laws for handling the spoils of war covered two situations: (1) Cities like Jericho which were under God's *ban* (judgment for idolatry) could not be looted (see Deuteronomy 20:16-18). God's people were to be kept holy and separate from every influence of idolatry. (2) The distribution of captured goods from cities not under the ban was a normal part of warfare. It provided the army and the nation with the necessary food, flocks, and weapons needed to sustain itself in wartime. Ai was not under the ban. The conquering army needed the food and equipment. Because soldiers were not paid, the plunder was part of their incentive and reward for going to war.

8:3 The conquest of Ai was very important to the Israelites. Only 11 miles away from Jericho, Ai was a key stronghold for the Canaanites and a buffer fortress for Bethel (8:12). If the Canaanite kings got wind of an Israelite defeat at Ai, they could unite in a coordinated attack. They did not know that God had restored his power and protection to Joshua's troops. We must depend on God with absolute obedience to be sure of the victory he has promised.

side of the city. 13 So they stationed the main army north of the city and the ambush west of the city. Joshua himself spent that night in the valley.

14 When the king of Ai saw the Israelites across the valley, he and all his army hurriedly went out early the next morning and attacked the Israelites at a place overlooking the Jordan Valley.* But he didn't realize there was an ambush behind the city. 15 Joshua and the Israelite army fled toward the wilderness as though they were badly beaten, 16 and all the men in the city were called out to chase after them. In this way, they were lured away from the city. 17 There was not a man left in Ai or Bethel* who did not chase after the Israelites, and the city was left wide open.

18 Then the LORD said to Joshua, "Point your spear toward Ai, for I will give you the city." Joshua did as he was commanded. 19 As soon as Joshua gave the signal, the men in ambush jumped up and poured into the city. They quickly captured it and set it on fire.

20 When the men of Ai looked behind them, smoke from the city was filling the sky, and they had nowhere to go. For the Israelites who had fled in the direction of the wilderness now turned on their pursuers. 21 When Joshua and the other Israelites saw that the ambush had succeeded and that smoke was rising from the city, they turned and attacked the men of Ai. 22 Then the Israelites who were inside the city came out and started killing the enemy from the rear. So the men of Ai were caught in a trap, and all of them died. Not a single person survived or escaped. 23 Only the king of Ai was taken alive and brought to Joshua.

24 When the Israelite army finished killing all the men outside the city, they went back and finished off everyone inside. 25 So the entire population of Ai was wiped out that day—twelve thousand in all. 26 For Joshua kept holding out his spear until everyone who had lived in Ai was completely destroyed.* 27 Only the cattle and the treasures of the city were not destroyed, for the Israelites kept these for themselves, as the LORD had commanded Joshua. 28 So Ai* became a permanent mound of ruins, desolate to this very day.

29 Joshua hung the king of Ai on a tree and left him there until evening. At sunset the Israelites took down the body and threw it in front of the city gate. They piled a great heap of stones over him that can still be seen today.

The LORD's Covenant Renewed

30 Then Joshua built an altar to the LORD, the God of Israel, on Mount Ebal. 31 He followed the instructions that Moses the LORD's servant had written in the Book of the Law: "Make me an altar from stones that are uncut and have not been shaped with iron tools." Then on the altar they presented burnt offerings and peace offerings to the LORD. 32 And as the Israelites watched, Joshua copied the law of Moses onto the stones of the altar.*

33 Then all the Israelites—foreigners and citizens alike—along with the leaders, officers, and judges, were divided into two groups. One group stood at the foot of Mount Gerizim, the other at the foot of Mount Ebal. Each group faced the other, and between them stood the Levitical priests carrying the Ark of the LORD's covenant. This was all done according to the instructions Moses, the servant of the LORD, had given for blessing the people of Israel.

34 Joshua then read to them all the blessings and curses Moses had written in the Book of the Law. 35 Every command Moses had ever given was read to the entire assembly, including the women and children and the foreigners who lived among the Israelites.

8:14 Deut 1:1; Judg 20:34
8:18 Exod 14:16; 17:9-13; Josh 8:26
8:22 Deut 7:2
8:25 Deut 20:16-18
8:26 Exod 17:11-12
8:27 Josh 8:2
8:28 Deut 13:16
8:29 Deut 21:22-23
8:30 Deut 27:2-8
8:31 Exod 20:24-25; Deut 27:5-6
8:33 Deut 27:12-13
8:34 Deut 28:61; 31:11
8:35 Deut 31:12

8:14 Hebrew *the Arabah.* **8:17** Some manuscripts lack *or Bethel.* **8:26** The Hebrew term used here refers to the complete consecration of things or people to the LORD, either by destroying them or by giving them as an offering. **8:28** *Ai* means "ruin." **8:32** Or *onto stones.*

8:18, 19 The Lord gave Joshua the city. Yesterday's defeat became today's victory. Once sin is dealt with, forgiveness and victory lie ahead. With God's direction we need not stay discouraged or burdened with guilt. No matter how difficult a setback sin may bring, we must renew our efforts to carry out God's will.

8:30, 31 The altar was to be built out of uncut stones so it would be holy (see Exodus 20:25). This would prevent the people from worshiping altars like idols, or worshiping the craftsmanship of the workers rather than the great works of God.

8:32 It was most likely the Ten Commandments (recorded in Exodus 20) that Joshua copied on stones. These were the heart of all God's laws, and they are still relevant today.

2. Joshua attacks the southern kings

The Gibeonites Deceive Israel

9:1 Num 13:17, 29 Josh 3:10; 11:19 **9** Now all the kings west of the Jordan heard about what had happened. (These were
the kings of the Hittites, Amorites, Canaanites, Perizzites, Hivites, and Jebusites,
who lived in the hill country, in the western foothills,* and along the coast of the
Mediterranean Sea* as far north as the Lebanon mountains.) 2 These kings quickly
combined their armies to fight against Joshua and the Israelites.

9:3 Josh 10:2; 11:19 3 But when the people of Gibeon heard what had happened to Jericho and Ai, 4 they
resorted to deception to save themselves. They sent ambassadors to Joshua, loading
their donkeys with weathered saddlebags and old patched wineskins. 5 They put on
ragged clothes and worn-out, patched sandals. And they took along dry, moldy bread
for provisions. 6 When they arrived at the camp of Israel at Gilgal, they told Joshua and
the men of Israel, "We have come from a distant land to ask you to make a peace treaty
9:7 with us."

Exod 23:32 Josh 11:19 7 The Israelites replied to these Hivites, "How do we know you don't live nearby? For
if you do, we cannot make a treaty with you."

8 They replied, "We will be your servants."

9:9 "But who are you?" Joshua demanded. "Where do you come from?"

Josh 9:16-17 9 They answered, "We are from a very distant country. We have heard of the might of
9:10 Num 21:24, 33 the LORD your God and of all he did in Egypt. 10 We have also heard what he did to the
two Amorite kings east of the Jordan River—King Sihon of Heshbon and King Og of
Bashan (who lived in Ashtaroth). 11 So our leaders and our people instructed us, 'Prepare
for a long journey. Go meet with the people of Israel and declare our people to be their
servants, and ask for peace.'

12 "This bread was hot from the ovens when we left. But now, as you can see, it is dry
and moldy. 13 These wineskins were new when we filled them, but now they are old and
cracked. And our clothing and sandals are worn out from our long, hard trip."

9:14 Num 27:21 14 So the Israelite leaders examined their bread, but they did not consult the LORD.
15 Then Joshua went ahead and signed a peace treaty with them, and the leaders of Israel
ratified their agreement with a binding oath.

9:17 Josh 18:25-28; 15:9, 60 16 Three days later, the facts came out—these people of Gibeon lived nearby! 17 The
Israelites set out at once to investigate and reached their towns in three days. The names
of these towns were Gibeon, Kephirah, Beeroth, and Kiriath-jearim. 18 But the Israelites
did not attack the towns, for their leaders had made a vow to the LORD, the God of Israel.

The people of Israel grumbled against their leaders because of the treaty. 19 But the
leaders replied, "We have sworn an oath in the presence of the LORD, the God of Israel.
We cannot touch them. 20 We must let them live, for God would be angry with us if we
9:21 Deut 29:11 broke our oath. 21 Let them live. But we will make them chop the wood and carry the
water for the entire community."

So the Israelites kept their promise to the Gibeonites. 22 But Joshua called together the
Gibeonite leaders and said, "Why did you lie to us? Why did you say that you live in a
distant land when you live right here among us? 23 May you be cursed! From now on you
will chop wood and carry water for the house of my God."

9:1a Hebrew *the Shephelah.* **9:1b** Hebrew *the Great Sea.*

9:1-6 As the news about their victory became widespread, the Israelites experienced opposition in two forms: direct (kings in the area began to unite against them); and indirect (the Gibeonites resorted to deception). We can expect similar opposition as we obey God's commands. To guard against these pressures, we must rely on God and communicate daily with him. He will give us strength to endure the direct pressures and wisdom to see through the trickery.

9:14-17 When the leaders sampled these men's provisions, they saw that the bread was dry and moldy, the wineskins were cracked, and the clothes and sandals worn out. But they did not see through the deception. After the promise had been made and the treaty ratified, the facts came out—Israel's leaders had been deceived. God had specifically instructed Israel to make no treaties with the inhabitants of Canaan (Exodus 23:32; 34:12; Numbers 33:55; Deuteronomy 7:2; 20:17, 18). As a strategist, Joshua knew enough to talk to God before leading his troops into battle. But the peace treaty seemed innocent enough, so Joshua and the leaders made this decision on their own. By failing to seek God's guidance and rushing ahead with their own plans, they had to deal with angry people and an awkward alliance.

9:19, 20 Joshua and his advisers had made a mistake. But because they had given an oath to protect the Gibeonites, they would keep their word. The oath was not nullified by the Gibeonites' trickery. God had commanded that oaths be kept (Leviticus 5:4; 27:2, 28), and breaking an oath was serious. This encourages us not to take our promises lightly.

24 They replied, "We did it because we were told that the LORD your God instructed 9:24 Deut 7:1-2
his servant Moses to conquer this entire land and destroy all the people living in it. So
we feared for our lives because of you. That is why we have done it. 25 Now we are at
your mercy—do whatever you think is right."
26 Joshua did not allow the people of Israel to kill them. 27 But that day he made the 9:27 Deut 12:5
Gibeonites the woodchoppers and water carriers for the people of Israel and for the altar
of the LORD—wherever the LORD would choose to build it. That arrangement continues
to this day.

Israel Defeats the Southern Kings

10 Now Adoni-zedek, king of Jerusalem, heard that Joshua had captured and com- 10:1 Josh 8:22-28; 9:15
pletely destroyed* Ai and killed its king, just as he had destroyed the city of Jericho
and killed its king. He also learned that the Gibeonites had made peace with Israel and were
now their allies. 2 He and his people became very afraid when they heard all this because
Gibeon was a large city—as large as the royal cities and larger than Ai. And the Gibeonite
men were mighty warriors. 3 So King Adoni-zedek of Jerusalem sent messengers to several 10:3 2 Chr 11:9
other kings: Hoham of Hebron, Piram of Jarmuth, Japhia of Lachish, and Debir of Eglon.
4 "Come and help me destroy Gibeon," he urged them, "for they have made peace with
Joshua and the people of Israel." 5 So these five Amorite kings combined their armies for a 10:5 Num 13:29 Josh 9:2
united attack. They moved all their troops into place and attacked Gibeon.
6 The men of Gibeon quickly sent messengers to Joshua at Gilgal, "Don't abandon
your servants now!" they pleaded. "Come quickly and save us! For all the Amorite kings
who live in the hill country have come out against us with their armies."
7 So Joshua and the entire Israelite army left Gilgal and set out to rescue Gibeon. 8 "Do 10:8 Josh 1:5, 9
not be afraid of them," the LORD said to Joshua, "for I will give you victory over them.
Not a single one of them will be able to stand up to you."
9 Joshua traveled all night from Gilgal and took the Amorite armies by surprise. 10 The 10:10 Deut 7:23
LORD threw them into a panic, and the Israelites slaughtered them in great numbers at
Gibeon. Then the Israelites chased the enemy along the road to Beth-horon and attacked
them at Azekah and Makkedah, killing them along the way. 11 As the Amorites retreated
down the road from Beth-horon, the LORD destroyed them with a terrible hailstorm that
continued until they reached Azekah. The hail killed more of the enemy than the
Israelites killed with the sword.
12 On the day the LORD gave the Israelites victory over the Amorites, Joshua prayed to
the LORD in front of all the people of Israel. He said,

10:1 The Hebrew term used here refers to the complete consecration of things or people to the LORD, either by destroying them or by giving them as an offering; also in 10:28, 35, 37, 39, 40.

10:5-8 This alliance of enemy kings from the south actually helped Joshua and his army. Because the enemies had united to attack Gibeon, Joshua didn't have to spend the time and resources required to wage separate campaigns against each fortified city represented in the coalition. Joshua confidently confronted this coalition of armies and defeated them in a single battle because he trusted God to give Israel the victory.

10:6, 7 Joshua's response shows his integrity. After having been deceived by the Gibeonites, Joshua and the leaders could have been slow about their attempt to rescue them. Instead, they immediately responded to their call for help. How willing would you be to help someone who had deceived you, even though you had forgiven him or her? We should take our word just as seriously as Joshua did.

10:12-14 How did the sun stand still? Of course, in relation to the earth the sun always stands still—it is the earth that travels around the sun. But the terminology used in Joshua should not cause us to doubt the miracle. After all, we are not confused when someone tells us the sun rises or sets. The point is that the day was prolonged, not that God used a particular method to prolong it. Two explanations have been given for how this event occurred: (1) A slowing of the earth's normal rotation gave Joshua more time, as the original Hebrew language seems to indicate. (2) Some unusual refraction of the sun's rays gave additional hours of light. Regardless of God's chosen method, the Bible is clear that the day was prolonged by a miracle, and that God's intervention turned the tide of battle for his people.

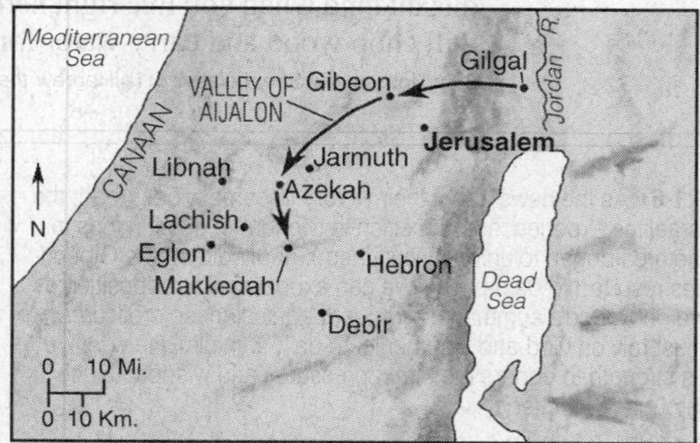

THE BATTLE FOR GIBEON Five Amorite kings conspired to destroy Gibeon. Israel came to the aid of the Gibeonites. The Israelites attacked the enemy armies outside of Gibeon and chased them through the valley of Aijalon as far as Makkedah and Azekah.

"Let the sun stand still over Gibeon,
and the moon over the valley of Aijalon."

10:13 2 Sam 1:18 Isa 38:8 13 So the sun and moon stood still until the Israelites had defeated their enemies.
Is this event not recorded in *The Book of Jashar**? The sun stopped in the middle of
10:14 Exod 14:14 Deut 1:30 the sky, and it did not set as on a normal day. 14 The LORD fought for Israel that day. Never
before or since has there been a day like that one, when the LORD answered such a request
from a human being.
10:15 Josh 10:6, 43 15 Then Joshua and the Israelite army returned to their camp at Gilgal.

Joshua Kills the Five Southern Kings

10:16 Josh 10:5 16 During the battle, the five kings escaped and hid in a cave at Makkedah. 17 When
Joshua heard that they had been found, 18 he issued this command: "Cover the opening
of the cave with large rocks and place guards at the entrance to keep the kings inside.
19 The rest of you continue chasing the enemy and cut them down from the rear. Don't
10:20 Deut 20:16 let them get back to their cities, for the LORD your God has given you victory over them."
20 So Joshua and the Israelite army continued the slaughter and wiped out the five
10:21 Josh 10:16 armies except for a tiny remnant that managed to reach their fortified cities. 21 Then the
Israelites returned safely to their camp at Makkedah. After that, no one dared to speak a
word against Israel.
10:22 Deut 7:24 22 Then Joshua said, "Remove the rocks covering the opening of the cave and bring
the five kings to me." 23 So they brought the five kings out of the cave—the kings of
Jerusalem, Hebron, Jarmuth, Lachish, and Eglon. 24 Joshua told the captains of his army,
"Come and put your feet on the kings' necks." And they did as they were told.
10:25 Josh 10:8 25 "Don't ever be afraid or discouraged," Joshua told his men. "Be strong and
10:26 Josh 8:29 courageous, for the LORD is going to do this to all of your enemies." 26 Then Joshua killed
each of the five kings and hung them on five trees until evening.
10:27 Deut 21:22-23 27 As the sun was going down, Joshua gave instructions for the bodies of the kings to
be taken down from the trees and thrown into the cave where they had been hiding. Then
they covered the opening of the cave with a large pile of stones, which remains to this
very day.

Israel Destroys the Southern Cities

28 That same day Joshua completely destroyed the city of Makkedah, killing everyone in
it, including the king. Not one person in the city was left alive. He killed the king of
10:29 Num 33:15-37 Josh 15:42 Makkedah as he had killed the king of Jericho. 29 Then Joshua and the Israelites went to
Libnah and attacked it. 30 There, too, the LORD gave them the city and its king. They
slaughtered everyone in the city and left no survivors. Then Joshua killed the king of
Libnah just as he had killed the king of Jericho.
31 From Libnah, Joshua and the Israelites went to Lachish and attacked it. 32 And the
LORD gave it to them on the second day. Here, too, the entire population was slaughtered, just as at Libnah. 33 During the attack on Lachish, King Horam of Gezer had
arrived with his army to help defend the city. But Joshua's men killed him and
destroyed his entire army.

10:13 Or *The Book of the Upright.*

10:13 *The Book of Jashar* (also mentioned in 2 Samuel 1:18) was probably a collection of historical events put to music. Many parts of the Bible contain quotations from previous books, songs, poems, or other spoken and written materials. Because God guided the writer of this book to select this material, his message comes with divine authority.

10:24 Placing a foot on the neck of a captive was a common military practice in the ancient Near East. It symbolized the victor's domination over his captives. These proud kings had boasted of their power. Now all Israel could see that God was superior to any earthly army.

10:25 With God's help, Israel won the battle against five Amorite armies. Such a triumph was part of God's daily business as he worked with his people for victory. Joshua told his men never to be afraid because God would give them similar victories over all their enemies. God has often protected us and won victories for us. The same God who empowered Joshua and who has led us in the past will help us with our present and future needs. Reminding ourselves of his help in the past will give us hope for the struggles that lie ahead.

10:32 Notice that in every Israelite victory, the text gives the credit to the Lord. All of Israel's victories came from God. When we are successful, the temptation is to take all the credit and glory as though we did it by ourselves, in our own strength. In reality, *God* gives us the victories, and he alone delivers us from our enemies. We should give him the credit and praise him for his goodness.

34 Then Joshua and the Israelite army went to Eglon and attacked it. 35 They captured
it in one day, and as at Lachish, they completely destroyed everyone in the city. 36 After
leaving Eglon, they attacked Hebron, 37 capturing it and all of its surrounding towns. And
just as they had done at Eglon, they completely destroyed the entire population. Not one
person was left alive. 38 Then they turned back and attacked Debir. 39 They captured the
city, its king, and all of its surrounding villages. And they killed everyone in it, leaving
no survivors. They completely destroyed Debir just as they had destroyed Libnah and
Hebron.
40 So Joshua conquered the whole region—the kings and people of the hill country,
the Negev, the western foothills,* and the mountain slopes. He completely destroyed
everyone in the land, leaving no survivors, just as the LORD, the God of Israel, had
commanded. 41 Joshua slaughtered them from Kadesh-barnea to Gaza and from Goshen
to Gibeon. 42 In a single campaign Joshua conquered all these kings and their land, for
the LORD, the God of Israel, was fighting for his people. 43 Then Joshua and the Israelite
army returned to their camp at Gilgal.

3. Joshua attacks the northern kings

11 When King Jabin of Hazor heard what had happened, he sent urgent messages to
the following kings: King Jobab of Madon; the king of Shimron; the king of
Acshaph; 2 all the kings of the northern hill country; the kings in the Jordan Valley* south
of Galilee*; the kings in the western foothills*; the kings of Naphoth-dor on the west;
3 the kings of Canaan, both east and west; the kings of the Amorites; the kings of the
Hittites; the kings of the Perizzites; the kings in the Jebusite hill country; and the Hivites
in the towns on the slopes of Mount Hermon, in the land of Mizpah.
4 All these kings responded by mobilizing their warriors and uniting to fight against
Israel. Their combined armies, along with a vast array of horses and chariots, covered
the landscape like the sand on the seashore. 5 They established their camp around the
water near Merom to fight against Israel.
6 Then the LORD said to Joshua, "Do not be afraid of them. By this time tomorrow they
will all be dead. Cripple their horses and burn their chariots."
7 So Joshua and his warriors traveled to the water near Merom and attacked suddenly.
8 And the LORD gave them victory over their enemies. The Israelites chased them as far
as Great Sidon and Misrephoth-maim, and eastward into the valley of Mizpah, until not
one enemy warrior was left alive. 9 Then Joshua crippled the horses and burned all the
chariots, as the LORD had instructed.
10 Joshua then turned back and captured Hazor and killed its king. (Hazor had at one

10:36 Josh 14:13; 15:13
10:40 Deut 1:7; 7:24; 20:16
10:41 Josh 11:16; 15:51
10:42 Josh 10:14
11:1 Josh 11:10
11:2 Josh 12:3
11:4 Josh 7:12
11:6 Josh 10:8; 2 Sam 8:4
11:10 Judg 4:2-3; 1 Sam 12:9; 1 Kgs 9:15; 2 Kgs 15:29

10:40 Hebrew *the Shephelah.* **11:2a** Hebrew *the Arabah;* also in 11:16. **11:2b** Hebrew *of Kinnereth.*
11:2c Hebrew *the Shephelah;* also in 11:16.

THE BATTLE FOR HAZOR
Kings from the north joined together to battle the Israelites who controlled the southern half of Canaan. They gathered by the water near Merom, but Joshua attacked them by surprise—the enemies' chariots were useless in the dense forests. Hazor, the largest Canaanite center in Galilee, was destroyed.

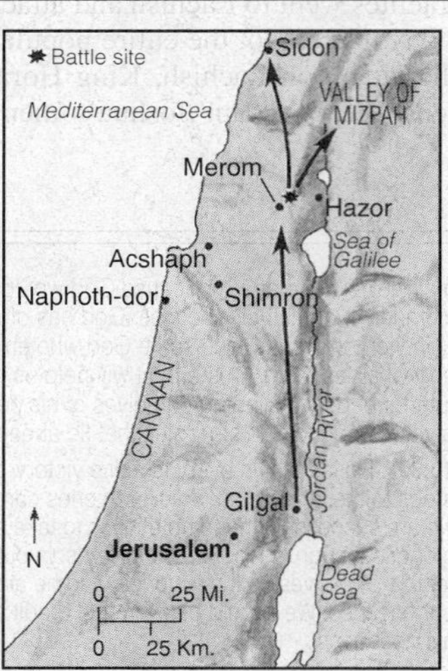

10:40-43 God had commanded Joshua to take the leadership in ridding the land of sin so God's people could occupy it. Joshua did his part thoroughly—leading the united army to weaken the inhabitants. When God orders us to stop sinning, we must not pause to debate, consider the options, negotiate a compromise, or rationalize. Instead, like Joshua, our response must be swift and complete. We must be ruthless in avoiding relationships and activities that can lead us into sin.

11:1-5 There were two kings of Hazor named Jabin. The other, apparently a weak ruler, is mentioned in Judges 4:2, 3. The Jabin of this story was quite powerful because he was able to build an alliance with dozens of kings. By all appearances, Jabin had a clear advantage over Joshua and his outnumbered forces. But those who honor God can be victorious regardless of the odds.

11:10-13 Victorious invaders usually kept captured cities intact, moving into them and making them centers of commerce and defense. For example, Moses predicted in Deuteronomy 6:10-12 that Israel would occupy cities they themselves had not built. Hazor, however, was burned. As a former capital of the land, it symbolized the wicked culture that Israel had come to destroy. In addition, its capture and destruction broke the backbone of the federation and weakened the will of the people to resist.

11:11 Deut 20:16-17 time been the capital of the federation of all these kingdoms.) 11 The Israelites completely
destroyed* every living thing in the city. Not a single person was spared. And then Joshua
burned the city.
12 Joshua slaughtered all the other kings and their people, completely destroying them,
11:14 Num 31:11-12 just as Moses, the servant of the LORD, had commanded. 13 However, Joshua did not burn
any of the cities built on mounds except Hazor. 14 And the Israelites took all the captured
11:15 Exod 34:11-12 goods and cattle of the ravaged cities for themselves, but they killed all the people. 15 As
the LORD had commanded his servant Moses, so Moses commanded Joshua. And Joshua
did as he was told, carefully obeying all of the LORD's instructions to Moses.

4. Summary of conquests

11:16 Josh 10:40 16 So Joshua conquered the entire region—the hill country, the Negev, the land of
Goshen, the western foothills, the Jordan Valley, and the mountains and lowlands of
11:17 Deut 7:24 Josh 12:7 Israel. 17 The Israelite territory now extended all the way from Mount Halak, which leads
up to Seir, to Baal-gad at the foot of Mount Hermon in the valley of Lebanon. Joshua
killed all the kings of those territories, 18 waging war for a long time to accomplish this.
11:19 Josh 9:3-15 19 No one in this region made peace with the Israelites except the Hivites of Gibeon. All
11:20 Exod 14:17 Deut 7:16 the others were defeated. 20 For the LORD hardened their hearts and caused them to fight
the Israelites instead of asking for peace. So they were completely and mercilessly
11:21 Num 13:33 Deut 9:1-2 Josh 14:12; 15:13 destroyed, as the LORD had commanded Moses.
21 During this period, Joshua destroyed all the descendants of Anak, who lived in the
hill country of Hebron, Debir, Anab, and the entire hill country of Judah and Israel. He
killed them all and completely destroyed their towns. 22 Not one was left in all the land
of Israel, though some still remained in Gaza, Gath, and Ashdod.
11:23 Deut 1:38; 12:9-10; 25:19 Heb 4:8 23 So Joshua took control of the entire land, just as the LORD had instructed Moses. He
gave it to the people of Israel as their special possession, dividing the land among the
tribes. So the land finally had rest from war.

Kings Defeated East of the Jordan

12:1 Num 32:33 Deut 3:8 Josh 11:1-3 **12** These are the kings east of the Jordan River who had been killed and whose land
was taken. Their territory extended from the Arnon Gorge to Mount Hermon and
included all the land east of the Jordan Valley.*
12:2 Num 21:23 Deut 2:36 2 King Sihon of the Amorites, who lived in Heshbon, was defeated. His kingdom
included Aroer, on the edge of the Arnon Gorge, and extended from the middle of the
Arnon Gorge to the Jabbok River, which serves as a boundary for the Ammonites. This
territory included half of the present area of Gilead, which lies north of the Jabbok
River. 3 Sihon also controlled the Jordan Valley as far north as the western shores of the
Sea of Galilee* and as far south as the Dead Sea,* from Beth-jeshimoth to the slopes
12:4 Num 21:33 Josh 13:12 of Pisgah.
4 King Og of Bashan, the last of the Rephaites, lived at Ashtaroth and Edrei. 5 He
12:5 Deut 3:10 ruled a territory stretching from Mount Hermon to Salecah in the north and to all of
Bashan in the east, and westward to the boundaries of the kingdoms of Geshur and
Maacah. His kingdom included the northern half of Gilead, the other portion of which

11:11 The Hebrew term used here refers to the complete consecration of things or people to the LORD, either by destroying them or by giving them as an offering; also in 11:12, 20, 21. **12:1** Hebrew *the Arabah;* also in 12:3, 8. **12:3a** Hebrew *sea of Kinnereth.* **12:3b** Hebrew *the sea of the Arabah, the Salt Sea.*

11:15 Joshua carefully obeyed all the instructions given by God. This theme of obedience is repeated frequently in the book of Joshua, partly because obedience is one aspect of life the individual believer can control. We can't always control our understanding because we may not have all the facts. We can't control what other people do or how they treat us. However, we can control our choice to obey God. Whatever new challenges we may face, the Bible contains relevant instructions that we can choose to ignore or choose to follow.

11:18 The conquest of much of the land of Canaan seems to have happened quickly (we can read about it in one sitting), but it actually took seven years. We often expect quick changes in our lives and quick victories over sin. But our journey with God is a lifelong process, and the changes and victories may take time. It is easy to grow impatient with God and feel like giving up hope because things are moving too slowly. When we are close to a situation, it is difficult to see progress. But when we look back, we can see that God never stopped working.

11:21, 22 The descendants of Anak were the tribes of giants the Israelite scouts described when they gave their negative report on the Promised Land (Numbers 13–14). This time the people did not let their fear of the giants prevent them from engaging in battle and claiming the land God had promised.

12:1ff Chapter 12 is a summary of the first half of the book of Joshua. It lists the kings and nations conquered by Joshua to both the east and the west of the Jordan River. As long as the people trusted and obeyed God, one evil nation after another fell in defeat.

was in the territory of King Sihon of Heshbon. 6 Moses, the servant of the LORD, and
the Israelites had destroyed the people of King Sihon and King Og. And Moses gave
their land to the tribes of Reuben, Gad, and the half-tribe of Manasseh.

Kings Defeated West of the Jordan

7 The following is a list of the kings Joshua and the Israelite armies defeated on the west **12:7** Josh 11:17
side of the Jordan, from Baal-gad in the valley of Lebanon to Mount Halak, which leads
up to Seir. (Joshua allotted this land to the tribes of Israel as their inheritance, 8 including **12:8** Josh 11:16
the hill country, the western foothills,* the Jordan Valley, the mountain slopes, the Judean
wilderness, and the Negev. The people who lived in this region were the Hittites, the
Amorites, the Canaanites, the Perizzites, the Hivites, and the Jebusites.) These are the
kings Israel defeated:

9 The king of Jericho **12:9** Josh 6:2; 8:29
The king of Ai, near Bethel

12:8 Hebrew *the Shephelah.*

THE CONQUERED LAND
Joshua displayed brilliant military strategy in the way he went about conquering the land of Canaan. He first captured the well-fortified Jericho to gain a foothold in Canaan and to demonstrate the awesome might of the God of Israel. Then he gained the hill country around Bethel and Gibeon. From there he subdued towns in the lowlands. Then his army conquered important cities in the north, such as Hazor. In all, Israel conquered land both east (12:1–6) and west (12:7–24) of the Jordan River; from Mount Hermon in the north to beyond the Negev to Mount Halak in the south. Thirty-one kings and their cities had been defeated. The Israelites had overpowered the Hittites, the Amorites, the Canaanites, the Perizzites, the Hivites, and the Jebusites. Other peoples living in Canaan were yet to be conquered.

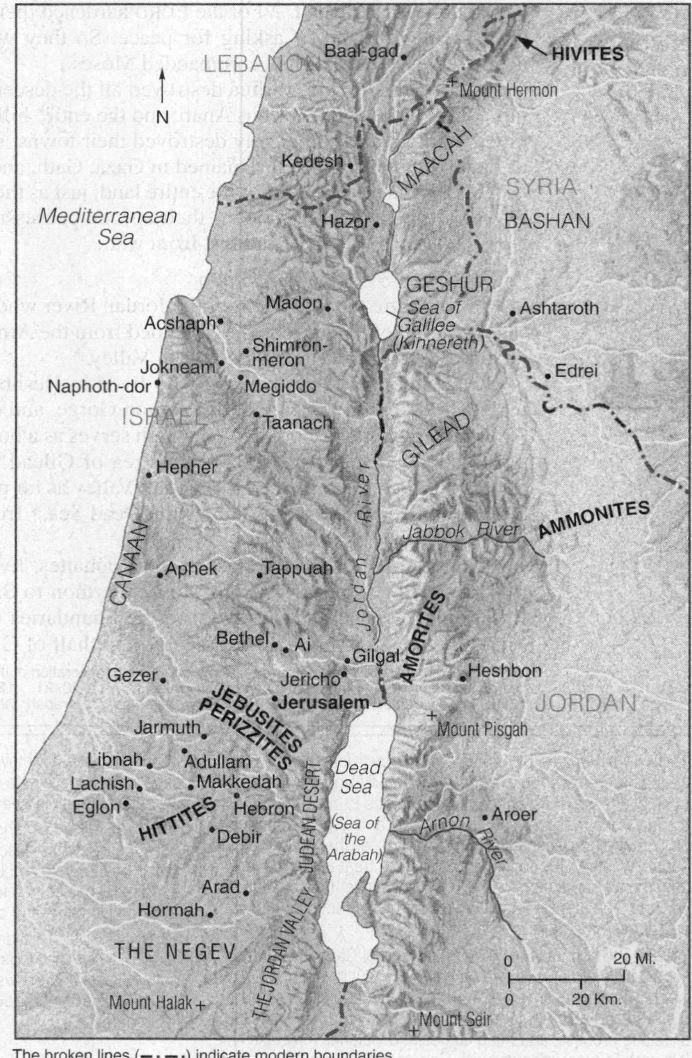

The broken lines (—·—) indicate modern boundaries.

10 The king of Jerusalem
The king of Hebron
11 The king of Jarmuth
The king of Lachish
12:12 Josh 10:33
12 The king of Eglon
The king of Gezer
12:13 Josh 10:3
13 The king of Debir
The king of Geder
12:24 Deut 7:24
14 The king of Hormah
The king of Arad
15 The king of Libnah
The king of Adullam
16 The king of Makkedah
The king of Bethel
17 The king of Tappuah
The king of Hepher
18 The king of Aphek
The king of Lasharon
19 The king of Madon
The king of Hazor
20 The king of Shimron-meron
The king of Acshaph
21 The king of Taanach
The king of Megiddo
22 The king of Kedesh
The king of Jokneam in Carmel
23 The king of Dor in the city of Naphoth-dor*
The king of Goyim in Gilgal*
24 The king of Tirzah.

In all, thirty-one kings and their cities were destroyed.

C. DIVIDING THE PROMISED LAND (13:1—24:33)

After seven years of battle, Israel gained control of the land, which was then divided and allotted to the tribes. Joshua dismisses the army, for it was now each tribe's responsibility to clear out the remaining enemies from their own areas. Joshua continues to encourage the people to remain faithful to God so they can remain in the land. The Promised Land was Israel's earthly inheritance. But Israel also had a spiritual inheritance in which we can share when we live a life of faithfulness to God.

1. The tribes receive their land

The Land Yet to Be Conquered

13:1 Josh 14:10
13:2 Judg 3:3

13 When Joshua was an old man, the LORD said to him, "You are growing old, and much
land remains to be conquered. 2 The people still need to occupy the land of the
Philistines and the Geshurites—3 territory that belongs to the Canaanites. This land extends

12:23a Hebrew *Naphath-dor,* a variant name for Naphoth-dor. **12:23b** Greek version reads *Goyim in Galilee.*

13–19 These chapters describe how the Promised Land was to be divided among the 12 tribes. First, the tribe of Levi was not to have any land because they were to spend all their energies serving the people, not their own interests (13:14; 21). Second, the tribes of Reuben and Gad and the half-tribe of Manasseh had already received land east of the Jordan River, which had been given to them by Moses (Numbers 32). Third, the tribes of Judah and Joseph (Ephraim and the other half-tribe of Manasseh) had received land that their ancestor Jacob had promised them 450 years earlier (Genesis 48:22; Joshua 15–17). The rest of the tribes divided up the remaining land by casting lots (chapter 18).

Through Jacob's original blessing of his sons (Genesis 49) and Moses' blessing of the 12 tribes (Deuteronomy 33), the type of land each tribe would receive was already known. The two blessings were prophetic, for although Joshua cast lots to determine the land to be given to each of the remaining tribes, the allotments came out just as Jacob and Moses had predicted.

13:1 Joshua was getting old—he was between 85 and 100 years of age at this time. God, however, still had work for him to do. Our culture often glorifies the young and strong and sets aside those who are older. Yet older people are filled with the wisdom that comes with experience. They are very capable of serving if given the chance and should be encouraged to do so. Believers are never allowed to retire from God's service. Those past retirement age should not assume that age alone disqualifies or excuses them from serving God.

from the stream of Shihor, which is on the boundary of Egypt, northward to the boundary
of Ekron, [4]and includes the five Philistine cities of Gaza, Ashdod, Ashkelon, Gath, and
Ekron. The land of the Avvites in the south also remains to be conquered. In the north, this
area has not yet been conquered: all the land of the Canaanites, including Mearah (which
belongs to the Sidonians), stretching northward to Aphek on the border of the Amorites;
[5]the land of the Gebalites and all of the Lebanon mountain area to the east, from Baal-gad
beneath Mount Hermon to Lebo-hamath; [6]and all the hill country from Lebanon to **13:6** Josh 11:8
Misrephoth-maim, including all the land of the Sidonians.

"I will drive these people out of the land for the Israelites. So be sure to give this land
to Israel as a special possession, just as I have commanded you. [7]Include all this territory
as Israel's inheritance when you divide the land among the nine tribes and the half-tribe
of Manasseh."

The Land Divided East of the Jordan

[8]Half the tribe of Manasseh and the tribes of Reuben and Gad had already received their **13:8** Josh 12:1-6
inheritance on the east side of the Jordan, for Moses, the servant of the LORD, had
previously assigned this land to them.

[9]Their territory extended from Aroer on the edge of the Arnon Gorge (including the **13:9** Num 32:34
town in the middle of the gorge) to the plain beyond Medeba, as far as Dibon. [10]It
also included all the towns of King Sihon of the Amorites, who reigned in Heshbon,
and extended as far as the borders of Ammon. [11]It included Gilead, the territory of
the kingdoms of Geshur and Maacah, all of Mount Hermon, all of Bashan as far as
Salecah, [12]and all the territory of King Og of Bashan, who had reigned in Ashtaroth **13:12** Num 21:24
and Edrei. King Og was the last of the Rephaites, for Moses had attacked them and
driven them out. [13]But the Israelites failed to drive out the people of Geshur and
Maacah, so they continue to live among the Israelites to this day.

An Inheritance for the Tribe of Levi

[14]Moses did not assign any land to the tribe of Levi. Instead, as the LORD had **13:14** Deut 18:1-2
promised them, their inheritance came from the offerings burned on the altar to the
LORD, the God of Israel.

The Land Given to the Tribe of Reuben

[15]Moses had assigned the following area to the families of the tribe of Reuben.

THE LAND YET TO BE CONQUERED Canaan was now controlled by the Israelites, although much land and several cities still needed to be conquered. Joshua told the people to include both conquered and unconquered lands in the territorial allotments (13:7). He was certain the people would complete the conquest as God had commanded.

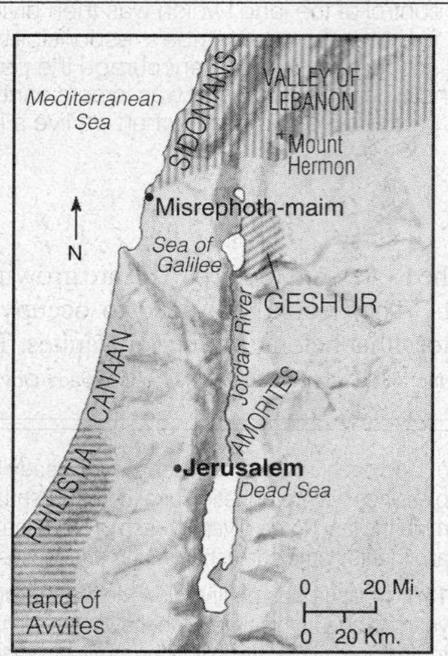

13:7 Much of the land was unconquered at this point, but God's plan was to go ahead and include it in the divisions among the tribes. God's desire was that it would eventually be conquered by the Israelites. God knows the future, and as he leads you he already knows about the victories that lie ahead. But just as the Israelites still had to go to battle and fight, we must still face the trials and fight the battles of our unconquered land.

What are our unconquered lands? They may be overseas missionary territories, new languages in which to translate the Bible, new missionary areas in our neighborhoods, interest groups or institutions that need redemptive work, unchallenged public problems or ethical issues, unconfessed sin in our lives, or underdeveloped talents and resources. What territory has God given you to conquer? This territory is your "Promised Land." Our inheritance will be a new heaven and a new earth (Revelation 21:1) if we fulfill the mission God has given us to do.

13:13 One reason the Israelites encountered so many problems as they settled the land was that they failed to *fully* conquer the land and drive out all its inhabitants. The cancerlike presence of the remaining pagan peoples of Canaan caused unending difficulties for the Israelites, as the book of Judges records. Just as they failed to remove completely the sin from the land, believers today often fail to remove completely the sin from their lives—with equally disastrous results. As a self-test, reread the Ten Commandments in Exodus 20:1-17. Ask yourself, Am I tolerating sinful practices or thoughts? Have I accepted half-measures as good enough? Do I condemn the faults of others but condone my own?

13:16 Josh 12:2 16 Their territory extended from Aroer on the edge of the Arnon Gorge (including
the town in the middle of the gorge) to the plain beyond Medeba. 17 It included
Heshbon and the other towns on the plain—Dibon, Bamoth-baal, Beth-baal-meon,
18 Jahaz, Kedemoth, Mephaath, 19 Kiriathaim, Sibmah, Zereth-shahar on the hill
above the valley, 20 Beth-peor, the slopes of Pisgah, and Beth-jeshimoth.
13:21-22 Num 31:8 21 The land of Reuben also included all the towns of the plain and the entire
kingdom of Sihon. Sihon was the Amorite king who had reigned in Heshbon and
was killed by Moses along with the chiefs of Midian—Evi, Rekem, Zur, Hur, and
Reba—princes living in the region who were allied with Sihon. 22 The Israelites
also killed Balaam the magician, the son of Beor. 23 The Jordan River marked the
western boundary for the tribe of Reuben. The towns and villages in this area were
given as an inheritance to the families of the tribe of Reuben.

The Land Given to the Tribe of Gad

24 Moses had assigned the following area to the families of the tribe of Gad.

25 Their territory included Jazer, all the towns of Gilead, and half of the land of
Ammon, as far as the town of Aroer just west of Rabbah. 26 It extended from Hesh-
13:27 Num 34:11 bon to Ramath-mizpeh and Betonim, and from Mahanaim to Lo-debar.* 27 In the
valley were Beth-haram, Beth-nimrah, Succoth, Zaphon, and the rest of the kingdom of King Sihon of Heshbon. The Jordan River was the western border, extending as far north as the Sea of Galilee.* 28 The towns and villages in this area were
given as an inheritance to the families of the tribe of Gad.

The Land Given to the Half-Tribe of Manasseh

29 Moses had assigned the following area to the families of the half-tribe of Manasseh.

13:30 Num 32:41 30 Their territory extended from Mahanaim, including all of Bashan, all the former
kingdom of King Og, and the sixty towns of Jair in Bashan. 31 It also included half of
Gilead and King Og's royal cities of Ashtaroth and Edrei. All this was given to the
descendants of Makir, who was Manasseh's son.

32 These are the allotments Moses had made while he was on the plains of Moab,
13:33 Num 18:20 Josh 13:14 across the Jordan River, east of Jericho. 33 But Moses gave no land to the tribe of Levi,
for the LORD, the God of Israel, had promised to be their inheritance.

13:26 Or *to the territory of Debir.* **13:27** Hebrew *sea of Kinnereth.*

13:15-23 There is often an interesting connection between the land a tribe received and the character of the tribe's founder. For example, because of Joseph's godly character (Genesis 49:22-26), the tribes descended from him—Ephraim and Manasseh—were given the richest, most fertile land in all of Canaan. Judah, who offered himself in exchange for his brother Benjamin's safety (Genesis 44:18-34), received the largest portion of land, which eventually became the southern kingdom and the seat of David's dynasty. Reuben, who slept with one of his father's wives (Genesis 49:4), was given desert land, the region described here.

13:29 The tribe of Manasseh was divided into two half-tribes. This occurred when many people from the tribe wanted to settle east of the Jordan River in an area that was especially suited for their flocks (Numbers 32:33). The rest of the tribe preferred to settle west of the Jordan River in the land of Canaan.

13:33 The tribe of Levi was dedicated to serving God. The Levites needed more time and mobility than a landowner could possibly have. Giving them land would mean saddling them with responsibilities and loyalties that would hinder their service to God. Instead, God arranged for the other tribes to meet the Levites' needs through donations. (See Numbers 35:2-4 for how the Levites were to receive cities within each tribal territory.)

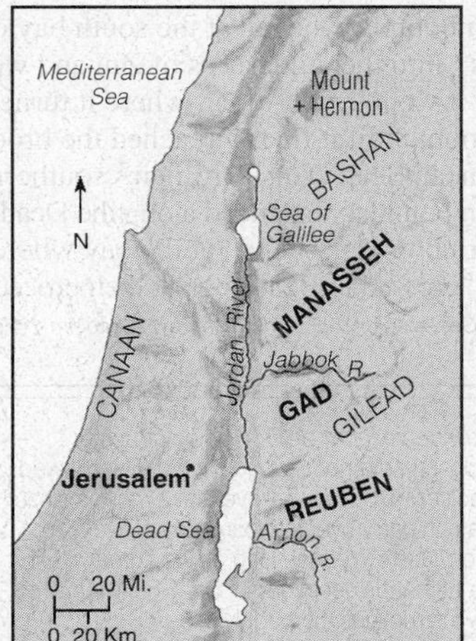

THE TRIBES EAST OF THE JORDAN
Joshua assigned territory to the tribes of Reuben, Gad, and the half-tribe of Manasseh on the east side of the Jordan where they had chosen to remain because of the wonderful livestock country (Numbers 32:1–5).

The Land Divided West of the Jordan

14 The remaining tribes of Israel inherited land in Canaan as allotted by Eleazar the 14:1 Num 34:16-29
priest, Joshua son of Nun, and the tribal leaders. 2 These nine and a half tribes
received their inheritance by means of sacred lots, in accordance with the LORD's
command through Moses. 3 Moses had already given an inheritance of land to the two 14:3 Num 32:33
and a half tribes on the east side of the Jordan River. 4 The tribe of Joseph had become Josh 13:14
two separate tribes—Manasseh and Ephraim. And the Levites were given no land at all,
only towns to live in and the surrounding pasturelands for their flocks and herds. 5 So the
distribution of the land was in strict accordance with the LORD's instructions to Moses.

Caleb Requests His Land

6 A delegation from the tribe of Judah, led by Caleb son of Jephunneh the Kenizzite, 14:6 Num 13:30; 14:6,
came to Joshua at Gilgal. Caleb said to Joshua, "Remember what the LORD said to 24, 30
Moses, the man of God, about you and me when we were at Kadesh-barnea. 7 I was
forty years old when Moses, the servant of the LORD, sent me from Kadesh-barnea to
explore the land of Canaan. I returned and gave from my heart a good report, 8 but my
brothers who went with me frightened the people and discouraged them from entering
the Promised Land. For my part, I followed the LORD my God completely. 9 So that 14:9 Deut 1:36
day Moses promised me, 'The land of Canaan on which you were just walking will
be your special possession and that of your descendants forever, because you wholeheartedly followed the LORD my God.'
10 "Now, as you can see, the LORD has kept me alive and well as he promised for all
these forty-five years since Moses made this promise—even while Israel wandered in
the wilderness. Today I am eighty-five years old. 11 I am as strong now as I was when
Moses sent me on that journey, and I can still travel and fight as well as I could then.
12 So I'm asking you to give me the hill country that the LORD promised me. You will 14:12 Num 13:33
remember that as scouts we found the Anakites living there in great, walled cities. But if
the LORD is with me, I will drive them out of the land, just as the LORD said."
13 So Joshua blessed Caleb son of Jephunneh and gave Hebron to him as an inheritance. 14 Hebron still belongs to the descendants of Caleb son of Jephunneh the Kenizzite
because he wholeheartedly followed the LORD, the God of Israel. 15 (Previously Hebron 14:15
had been called Kiriath-arba. It had been named after Arba, a great hero of the Anakites.) Josh 11:23
And the land had rest from war.

The Land Given to the Tribe of Judah

15 The land assigned to the families of the tribe of Judah reached southward to the 15:1 Num 34:3-4
border of Edom, with the wilderness of Zin being its southernmost point. Deut 32:51

2 The southern boundary began at the south bay of the Dead Sea,* 3 ran south of 15:3-4
Scorpion Pass* into the wilderness of Zin and went south of Kadesh-barnea to Num 34:4-5
Hezron. Then it went up to Addar, where it turned toward Karka. 4 From there it
passed to Azmon, until it finally reached the brook of Egypt, which it followed to
the Mediterranean Sea.* This was their* southern boundary.
5 The eastern boundary extended along the Dead Sea to the mouth of the Jordan River. 15:5-6
The northern boundary began at the bay where the Jordan River empties into Josh 18:15-19
the Dead Sea, 6 crossed to Beth-hoglah, then proceeded north of Beth-arabah to the

15:2 Hebrew *the Salt Sea;* also in 15:5. **15:3** Hebrew *Akrabbim.* **15:4a** Hebrew *the sea;* also in 15:11.
15:4b Hebrew *your.*

14:5 The land was divided exactly as God had instructed Moses years before. Joshua did not change a word. He followed God's commands precisely. Often we believe that *almost* is close enough, and this idea can carry over into our spiritual lives. For example, we may follow God's Word as long as we agree with it, but ignore it when the demands seem harsh. But God is looking for leaders who follow instructions thoroughly.

14:6-12 Caleb was faithful from the start. As one of the original scouts sent into the Promised Land (Numbers 13:30-33), he saw great cities and giants, yet he knew God would help the people conquer the land. Because of his faith, God promised him a personal inheritance of land (Numbers 14:24; Deuteronomy 1:34-36). Here, 45 years later, the land was given to him. His faith was still unwavering. Although his inherited land still had giants, Caleb knew the Lord would help him conquer them. Like Caleb, we must be faithful to God, not only at the start of our walk with him, but throughout our entire life. We must never allow ourselves to rest on our past accomplishments or reputations.

14:15 The Anakites were a race of giants who inhabited parts of the land before Joshua's conquest.

15:4 Notice that these boundaries and descriptions of the Promised Land are very specific. God was telling Israel exactly what to do, and he was giving them just what they needed. There was no excuse for disobedience.

stone of Bohan. (Bohan was Reuben's son.) 7 From that point it went through
the valley of Achor to Debir, turning north toward Gilgal, which is across from
the slopes of Adummim on the south side of the valley. From there the border extended
15:8 to the springs at En-shemesh and on to En-rogel. 8 The boundary then passed
Josh 15:63 through the valley of the son of Hinnom, along the southern slopes of the Jebusites,
where the city of Jerusalem is located. Then it went west to the top of the mountain
above the valley of Hinnom, and on up to the northern end of the valley of Rephaim.
15:9 9 From there the border extended from the top of the mountain to the spring at the
Josh 18:15 waters of Nephtoah,* and from there to the towns on Mount Ephron. Then it turned
toward Baalah (that is, Kiriath-jearim). 10 The border circled west of Baalah to
Mount Seir, passed along to the town of Kesalon on the northern slope of Mount
Jearim, and went down to Beth-shemesh and on to Timnah. 11 The boundary line
then proceeded to the slope of the hill north of Ekron, where it turned toward
Shikkeron and Mount Baalah. It passed Jabneel and ended at the Mediterranean Sea.
12 The western boundary was the shoreline of the Mediterranean Sea.*

These are the boundaries for the families of the tribe of Judah.

The Land Given to Caleb

15:13 13 The LORD instructed Joshua to assign some of Judah's territory to Caleb son of
Josh 14:13-15 **15:14** Jephunneh. So Caleb was given the city of Arba (that is, Hebron), which had been named
Num 13:33 Deut 9:2 after Anak's ancestor. 14 Caleb drove out the three Anakites—Sheshai, Ahiman, and
Josh 11:21-22 Talmai—descendants of Anak.
15 Then he fought against the people living in the town of Debir (formerly called
Kiriath-sepher). 16 Caleb said, "I will give my daughter Acsah in marriage to the one who
15:17 attacks and captures Kiriath-sepher." 17 Othniel, the son of Caleb's brother Kenaz, was
Judg 1:12-13; 3:9 the one who conquered it, so Acsah became Othniel's wife.
18 When Acsah married Othniel, she urged him* to ask her father for an additional field.
As she got down off her donkey, Caleb asked her, "What is it? What can I do for you?"
19 She said, "Give me a further blessing. You have been kind enough to give me land in
the Negev; please give me springs as well." So Caleb gave her the upper and lower springs.

The Towns Judah Inherited

20 This was the inheritance given to the families of the tribe of Judah.

15:21 21 The towns of Judah situated along the borders of Edom in the extreme south are
Gen 35:21 Kabzeel, Eder, Jagur, 22 Kinah, Dimonah, Adadah, 23 Kedesh, Hazor, Ithnan, 24 Ziph,
Telem, Bealoth, 25 Hazor-hadattah, Kerioth-hezron (that is, Hazor), 26 Amam, Shema,
Moladah, 27 Hazar-gaddah, Heshmon, Beth-pelet, 28 Hazar-shual, Beersheba, Bizio-
15:31 thiah, 29 Baalah, Iim, Ezem, 30 Eltolad, Kesil, Hormah, 31 Ziklag, Madmannah, San-
1 Sam 27:6 sannah, 32 Lebaoth, Shilhim, Ain, and Rimmon. In all, there were twenty-nine of
these towns with their surrounding villages.
15:33 33 The following towns situated in the western foothills* were also given to
Judg 13:25; 16:31 Judah: Eshtaol, Zorah, Ashnah, 34 Zanoah, En-gannim, Tappuah, Enam, 35 Jarmuth,
Adullam, Socoh, Azekah, 36 Shaaraim, Adithaim, Gederah, and Gederothaim. In all,
there were fourteen towns with their surrounding villages.
15:39 37 Also included were Zenan, Hadashah, Migdal-gad, 38 Dilean, Mizpeh, Joktheel,
Josh 10:3 39 Lachish, Bozkath, Eglon, 40 Cabbon, Lahmam, Kitlish, 41 Gederoth, Beth-dagon,
2 Kgs 14:19 Naamah, and Makkedah—sixteen towns with their surrounding villages. 42 Besides
these, there were Libnah, Ether, Ashan, 43 Iphtah, Ashnah, Nezib, 44 Keilah, Aczib,
and Mareshah—nine towns with their surrounding villages.
45 The territory of the tribe of Judah also included all the towns and villages of
Ekron. 46 From Ekron the boundary extended west and included the towns near

15:9 Or *the spring at Me-nephtoah.* **15:12** Hebrew *the Great Sea;* also in 15:47. **15:18** Some Greek manuscripts read *Othniel urged her.* **15:33** Hebrew *the Shephelah.*

15:16-19 Othniel became Israel's first judge after Joshua's death (Judges 1:13; 3:9-11). He played an important role in reforming Israel by chasing away an oppressive enemy army and bringing peace back to the land. Thus Caleb's legacy of faithfulness continued to the next generation.

15:19 Acsah asked Caleb for springs of water because her land was in the south and was very arid. Caleb probably granted her request as a wedding present (see 15:17).

Ashdod with their surrounding villages. 47It also included Ashdod with its towns 15:47
and villages and Gaza with its towns and villages, as far as the brook of Egypt and Num 34:6
along the coast of the Mediterranean Sea.
48Judah also received the following towns in the hill country: Shamir, Jattir,
Socoh, 49Dannah, Kiriath-sannah (that is, Debir), 50Anab, Eshtemoh, Anim,
51Goshen, Holon, and Giloh—eleven towns with their surrounding villages.
52Also included were the towns of Arab, Dumah, Eshan, 53Janim, Beth-tappuah,
Aphekah, 54Humtah, Kiriath-arba (that is, Hebron), and Zior—nine towns with
their surrounding villages.
55Besides these, there were Maon, Carmel, Ziph, Juttah, 56Jezreel, Jokdeam,
Zanoah, 57Kain, Gibeah, and Timnah—ten towns with their surrounding villages.
58In addition, there were Halhul, Beth-zur, Gedor, 59Maarath, Beth-anoth, and
Eltekon—six towns with their surrounding villages. 60There were also Kiriath-baal
(that is, Kiriath-jearim) and Rabbah—two towns with their surrounding villages.
61In the wilderness there were the towns of Beth-arabah, Middin, Secacah,
62Nibshan, the City of Salt, and En-gedi—six towns with their surrounding villages.

63But the tribe of Judah could not drive out the Jebusites, who lived in the city of 15:63
Jerusalem, so the Jebusites live there among the people of Judah to this day. Judg 1:21 2 Sam 5:6

The Inheritance of Ephraim and West Manasseh

16 The allotment to the descendants of Joseph extended from the Jordan River 16:1
near Jericho, east of the waters of Jericho, through the wilderness and into Josh 8:15; 18:12
the hill country of Bethel. 2From Bethel (that is, Luz)* it ran over to Ataroth in 16:2
the territory of the Arkites. 3Then it descended westward to the territory of the Josh 18:13
Japhletites as far as Lower Beth-horon, then to Gezer and on over to the Mediterranean Sea.*

The Land Given to Ephraim

4The families of Joseph's sons, Manasseh and Ephraim, received their inheritance.
5The following territory was given to the families of the tribe of Ephraim as their 16:5
inheritance. Josh 18:13

The eastern boundary of their inheritance began at Ataroth-addar. From there it ran
to Upper Beth-horon, 6then on to the Mediterranean Sea. The northern boundary began 16:6
at the Mediterranean, ran east past Micmethath, then curved eastward past Taanath- Josh 17:7
shiloh to the east of Janoah. 7From Janoah it turned southward to Ataroth and Naarah,
touched Jericho, and ended at the Jordan River. 8From Tappuah the border extended 16:8
westward, following the Kanah Ravine to the Mediterranean Sea. This is the inheri- Josh 17:8-9
tance given to the families of the tribe of Ephraim.
9Ephraim was also given some towns with surrounding villages in the territory of the 16:10
half-tribe of Manasseh. 10They did not drive the Canaanites out of Gezer, however, so Josh 15:63; 17:12-13
the people of Gezer live as slaves among the people of Ephraim to this day. Judg 1:29 1 Kgs 9:16

The Land Given to West Manasseh

17 The next allotment of land was given to the half-tribe of Manasseh, the descen- 17:1
dants of Joseph's older son. Gilead and Bashan on the east side of the Jordan had Josh 13:8
already been given to the family of Makir because he was a great warrior. (Makir was
Manasseh's oldest son and was the father of Gilead.) 2Land on the west side of the Jordan
was allotted to the remaining families within the tribe of Manasseh: Abiezer, Helek,
Asriel, Shechem, Hepher, and Shemida.

16:2 As in Greek version (also see 18:13); Hebrew reads *From Bethel to Luz.* **16:3** Hebrew *the sea;* also in 16:6, 8.

16:1ff Although Joseph was one of Jacob's 12 sons, he did not have a tribe named after him. This was because Joseph, as the oldest son of Jacob's wife Rachel, received a double portion of the inheritance. This double portion was given to Joseph's two sons, Ephraim and Manasseh, whom Jacob considered as his own (Genesis 48:5). The largest territory and the greatest influence in the northern half of Israel belonged to their tribes.

16:10 Occasionally this short phrase appears: "They did not drive out" the people of the land (see also 15:63; 17:12). This was contrary to God's explicit desire and command (13:1-6). The failure to remove completely the pagan people and their gods from the land would cause many problems for the nation. The book of Judges records many of these struggles.

17:3 Num 26:33; 27:1-7 3 However, Zelophehad son of Hepher, who was a descendant of Manasseh, Makir,
and Gilead, had no sons. Instead, he had five daughters. Their names were Mahlah,
Noah, Hoglah, Milcah, and Tirzah. 4 These women came to Eleazar the priest, Joshua
son of Nun, and the Israelite leaders and said, "The LORD commanded Moses to give
us an inheritance along with the men of our tribe."

So Joshua gave them an inheritance along with their uncles, as the LORD had
commanded. 5 As a result, Manasseh's inheritance came to ten parcels of land, in
17:6 Josh 13:30-31 addition to the land of Gilead and Bashan across the Jordan River, 6 because the
female descendants of Manasseh received an inheritance along with the male
descendants. (The land of Gilead was given to the rest of the male descendants of
Manasseh.)

7 The boundary of the tribe of Manasseh extended from the border of Asher to
Micmethath, which is east of Shechem. Then the boundary went south from
Micmethath to the people living near the spring of Tappuah. 8 (The land surround-
ing Tappuah belonged to Manasseh, but the town of Tappuah, on the border of
Manasseh's territory, belonged to the tribe of Ephraim.) 9 From the spring of
Tappuah, the border of Manasseh followed the northern side of the Kanah Ravine to
the Mediterranean Sea.* (Several towns in Manasseh's territory belonged to the
tribe of Ephraim.) 10 The land south of the ravine belonged to Ephraim, and the
land north of the ravine belonged to Manasseh, with the Mediterranean Sea forming
Manasseh's western border. North of Manasseh was the territory of Asher, and to
the east was the territory of Issachar.

17:11 1 Chr 7:29 11 The following towns within the territory of Issachar and Asher were given to
Manasseh: Beth-shan,* Ibleam, Dor (that is, Naphoth-dor),* Endor, Taanach, and
17:12 Judg 1:27-28 Megiddo, with their respective villages. 12 But the descendants of Manasseh were
unable to occupy these towns. They could not drive out the Canaanites who
continued to live there. 13 Later on, however, when the Israelites became strong
enough, they forced the Canaanites to work as slaves. But they did not drive them out
of the land.

17:14 Num 26:28-37 14 The descendants of Joseph came to Joshua and asked, "Why have you given us only
one portion of land when the LORD has given us so many people?"

15 Joshua replied, "If the hill country of Ephraim is not large enough for you, clear out
land for yourselves in the forest where the Perizzites and Rephaites live."

17:16 Judg 1:19; 4:3, 13 16 They said, "The hill country is not enough for us, and the Canaanites in the
lowlands around Beth-shan and the valley of Jezreel have iron chariots—they are too
strong for us."

17 Then Joshua said to the tribes of Ephraim and Manasseh, the descendants of
Joseph, "Since you are so large and strong, you will be given more than one portion.
18 The forests of the hill country will be yours as well. Clear as much of the land as you
wish and live there. And I am sure you can drive out the Canaanites from the valleys,
too, even though they are strong and have iron chariots."

17:9 Hebrew *the sea;* also in 17:10. **17:11a** Hebrew *Beth-shean,* a variant name for Beth-shan; also in 17:16. **17:11b** The meaning of the Hebrew here is uncertain.

17:3, 4 Although women did not traditionally inherit property in Israelite society, Moses put justice ahead of tradition and gave these five women the land they deserved (see Numbers 27:1-11). In fact, God told Moses to add a law that would help other women in similar circumstances inherit property as well. Joshua was now carrying out this law. It is easy to refuse to honor a reasonable request because "things have never been done that way before." But, like Moses and Joshua, it is best to look carefully at the purpose of the law and the merits of each case before deciding.

17:14, 15 Notice the two contrasting attitudes toward settling the Promised Land: Caleb took what God gave him and moved ahead to fulfill God's plan for him (14:12). He was confident that God would help him drive out the wicked inhabitants and that he would soon fully occupy his land (15:14, 15). In contrast, the two tribes of Joseph were given rich land and lots of it, but they were afraid to drive out the inhabitants and take full possession of it. Instead, they begged for more land. But Joshua asked them to prove their sincerity first by clearing the unclaimed forest areas. They agreed, but they failed to carry through (Judges 1:27).

The Allotments of the Remaining Land

18 Now that the land was under Israelite control, the entire Israelite assembly gathered at Shiloh and set up the Tabernacle.* 2But there remained seven tribes who had not yet been allotted their inheritance.

3Then Joshua asked them, "How long are you going to wait before taking possession of the remaining land the LORD, the God of your ancestors, has given to you? 4Select three men from each tribe, and I will send them out to survey the unconquered territory. They will return to me with a written report of their proposed divisions of the inheritance. 5The scouts will map the land into seven sections, excluding Judah's territory in the south and Joseph's territory in the north. 6Then I will cast sacred lots in the presence of the LORD our God to decide which section will be assigned to each tribe. 7However, the Levites will not receive any land. Their role as priests of the LORD is their inheritance. And the tribes of Gad, Reuben, and the half-tribe of Manasseh won't receive any more land, for they have already received their inheritance, which Moses, the servant of the LORD, gave them on the east side of the Jordan River."

8As the men who were mapping out the land started on their way, Joshua commanded them, "Go and survey the land. Then return to me with your written report, and I will assign the land to the tribes by casting sacred lots in the presence of the LORD here at Shiloh." 9The men did as they were told and mapped the entire territory into seven sections, listing the towns in each section. Then they returned to Joshua in the camp at Shiloh. 10There at Shiloh, Joshua cast sacred lots in the presence of the LORD to determine which tribe should have each section.

18:1 Josh 19:51 Judg 21:19 Jer 7:12
18:3 Judg 18:9
18:5 Josh 15:1; 16:1-4
18:7 Num 18:7, 20 Josh 13:33
18:8 Josh 18:1
18:10 Num 34:16-29 Josh 19:51

18:1 Hebrew *Tent of Meeting.*

18:1, 2 With most of the conquest behind them, Israel moved their religious center from Gilgal (see the note on 5:8, 9) to Shiloh. This was probably the first place where the Tabernacle was set up permanently. The Tent of Meeting was part of the Tabernacle and was where God lived among his people (Exodus 25:8). Its central location in the land made it easier for the people to attend the special worship services and yearly festivals.

The family of Samuel, a great priest and prophet, often traveled to Shiloh, and Samuel was taken there when he was a small boy (1 Samuel 1:3, 22). The Tabernacle remained in Shiloh through the period of the judges (about 300 years). Apparently the city was destroyed by the Philistines when the Ark of the Covenant was captured (1 Samuel 4–5). Shiloh never lived up to its reputation as Israel's religious center, for later references in the Bible point to the wickedness and idolatry in the city (Psalm 78:56-60; Jeremiah 7:12-15).

18:2ff Seven of the tribes had not yet been assigned their land. They gathered at Shiloh, where Joshua cast lots to determine which areas would be given to them. Using the sacred lottery, God would make the choice, not Joshua or any other human leader.

By this time, the Canaanites were, in most places, so weakened that they were no longer a threat. Instead of fulfilling God's command to destroy the remaining Canaanites, however, these seven tribes would often take the path of least resistance. As nomadic people, they may have been reluctant to settle down, preferring to depend economically on the people they were supposed to eliminate. Others may have feared the high cost of continued warfare. It was easier and more profitable to trade for goods than to destroy the suppliers and have to provide for themselves.

18:3-6 Joshua asked why some of the tribes were putting off the job of possessing the land. Often we delay doing jobs that seem large, difficult, boring, or disagreeable. But to continue putting them off shows lack of discipline, poor stewardship of time, and, in some cases, disobedience to God. Jobs we don't enjoy require concentration, teamwork, twice as much time, lots of encouragement, and accountability. Remember this when you are tempted to procrastinate.

18:8 Making decisions by casting lots was a common practice among the Hebrews. Little is known about the actual method used in Joshua's day. Dice may have been used. Another possibility is that two urns were used: one containing tribal names; the other, the divisions of the land. Drawing one name from each urn matched a tribe to a region. The Urim and Thummim (explained in the note on Leviticus 8:8) may also have been used. No matter how it was done, the process removed human choice from the decision-making process and allowed God to match tribes and lands as he saw fit.

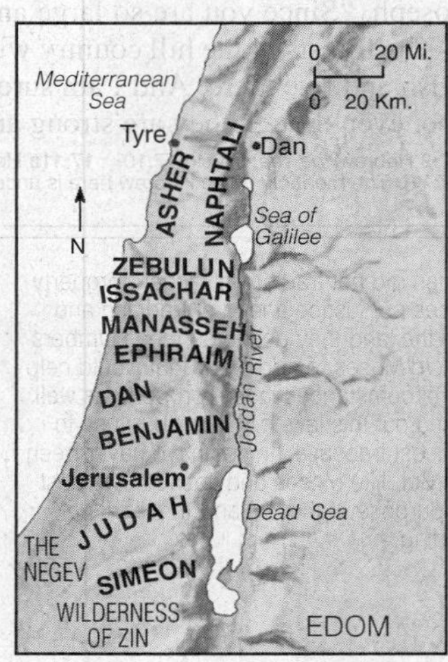

THE TRIBES WEST OF THE JORDAN
Judah, Ephraim, and the other half-tribe of Manasseh were the first tribes to receive land west of the Jordan because of their past acts of faith. The remaining seven tribes—Benjamin, Zebulun, Issachar, Asher, Naphtali, Simeon, and Dan—were slow to conquer and possess the land allotted to them.

The Land Given to Benjamin

11 The first allotment of land went to the families of the tribe of Benjamin. It lay between
the territory previously assigned to the tribes of Judah and Joseph.

12 The northern boundary began at the Jordan River, went north of the slope of Jericho, then west through the hill country and the wilderness of Beth-aven. 13 From
there the boundary went south to Luz (that is, Bethel) and proceeded down to Ataroth-addar to the top of the hill south of Lower Beth-horon.
18:14-15 Josh 15:5-9 14 The boundary then ran south along the western edge of the hill facing Beth-
horon, ending at the village of Kiriath-baal (that is, Kiriath-jearim), one of the
towns belonging to the tribe of Judah. This was the western boundary.
15 The southern boundary began at the outskirts of Kiriath-jearim. From there it
18:16 2 Kgs 23:10 ran westward* to the spring at the waters of Nephtoah,* 16 and down to the base of
the mountain beside the valley of the son of Hinnom, at the northern end of the
valley of Rephaim. From there it went down the valley of Hinnom, crossing south
18:17 Josh 15:7-8 of the slope where the Jebusites lived, and continued down to En-rogel. 17 From
En-rogel the boundary proceeded northeast to En-shemesh and on to Geliloth
(which is across from the slopes of Adummim). Then it went down to the stone of
Bohan. (Bohan was Reuben's son.) 18 From there it passed along the north side of
the slope overlooking the Jordan Valley.* The border then went down into the valley,
19 ran past the north slope of Beth-hoglah, and ended at the north bay of the Dead Sea,*
which is the southern end of the Jordan River.
20 The eastern boundary was the Jordan River.

This was the inheritance for the families of the tribe of Benjamin.

The Towns Given to Benjamin

21 These were the towns given to the families of the tribe of Benjamin.

Jericho, Beth-hoglah, Emek-keziz, 22 Beth-arabah, Zemaraim, Bethel, 23 Avvim,
18:24 Isa 10:29 Parah, Ophrah, 24 Kephar-ammoni, Ophni, and Geba—twelve towns with their
villages. 25 Also Gibeon, Ramah, Beeroth, 26 Mizpeh, Kephirah, Mozah, 27 Rekem,
18:28 Josh 15:8; 2 Sam 21:14 Irpeel, Taralah, 28 Zela, Haeleph, Jebus (that is, Jerusalem), Gibeah, and Kiriath-
jearim*—fourteen towns with their villages.

This was the inheritance given to the families of the tribe of Benjamin.

The Land Given to Simeon

19 The second allotment of land went to the families of the tribe of Simeon. Their
inheritance was surrounded by Judah's territory.

2 Simeon's inheritance included Beersheba, Sheba, Moladah, 3 Hazar-shual,
19:5 1 Sam 30:1 Balah, Ezem, 4 Eltolad, Bethul, Hormah, 5 Ziklag, Beth-marcaboth, Hazar-susah,
6 Beth-lebaoth, and Sharuhen—thirteen towns with their villages. 7 It also
included Ain, Rimmon, Ether, and Ashan—four towns with their villages,
8 including all the villages as far south as Baalath-beer (also known as Ramah
of the Negev).

This was the inheritance of the families of the tribe of Simeon. 9 Their inheritance came
from part of what had been given to Judah because Judah's territory was too large for
them. So the tribe of Simeon received an inheritance within the territory of Judah.

The Land Given to Zebulun

10 The third allotment of land went to the families of the tribe of Zebulun.

18:15a Or *it went to Ephron, and.* The meaning of the Hebrew is uncertain. **18:15b** Or *the spring at Me-nephtoah.* **18:18** Hebrew *the Arabah.* **18:19** Hebrew *Salt Sea.* **18:28** As in Greek version; Hebrew reads *Kiriath.*

18:11 The tribe of Benjamin was given a narrow strip of land that served as a buffer zone between Judah and Ephraim, the two tribes that would later dominate the land.

18:16 The valley of Hinnom became associated with the worship of Molech (the Ammonite god) in Jeremiah's time. These terrible rites involved the sacrifice of children. Later the valley was used for burning garbage and the corpses of criminals and animals. Thus, the name became a synonym for hell.

The boundary of Zebulun's inheritance started at Sarid. 11From there it went west, 19:11 Josh 21:34
going past Maralah, touching Dabbesheth, and proceeding to the brook east of
Jokneam. 12In the other direction, the boundary line went east from Sarid to the
border of Kisloth-tabor, and from there to Daberath and up to Japhia. 13Then it
continued east to Gath-hepher, Eth-kazin, and Rimmon and turned toward Neah.
14The northern boundary of Zebulun passed Hannathon and ended at the valley of
Iphtah-el. 15The towns in these areas included Kattath, Nahalal, Shimron, Idalah, and 19:15 Mic 5:2
Bethlehem—twelve towns with their surrounding villages.

16This was the inheritance of the families of the tribe of Zebulun.

The Land Given to Issachar

17The fourth allotment of land went to the families of the tribe of Issachar.

18Its boundaries included the following towns: Jezreel, Kesulloth, Shunem, 19:18 1 Sam 28:4
19Hapharaim, Shion, Anaharath, 20Rabbith, Kishion, Ebez, 21Remeth, En-gannim,
En-haddah, and Beth-pazzez. 22The boundary also touched Tabor, Shahazumah,
and Beth-shemesh, ending at the Jordan River—sixteen towns with their surrounding villages.

23This was the inheritance of the families of the tribe of Issachar.

The Land Given to Asher

24The fifth allotment of land went to the families of the tribe of Asher.

25Its boundaries included these towns: Helkath, Hali, Beten, Acshaph, 26Allam-
melech, Amad, and Mishal. The boundary on the west went from Carmel to Shihor-
libnath, 27turned east toward Beth-dagon, and ran as far as Zebulun in the valley of
Iphtah-el, running north to Beth-emek and Neiel. It then continued north to Cabul,
28Abdon,* Rehob, Hammon, Kanah, and as far as Greater Sidon. 29Then the bound- 19:28 Josh 11:8
ary turned toward Ramah and the fortified city of Tyre and came to the Mediterranean Sea* at Hosah. The territory also included Mehebel, Aczib, 30Ummah, Aphek,
and Rehob—twenty-two towns with their surrounding villages. 19:30 Josh 21:31

31This was the inheritance of the families of the tribe of Asher.

The Land Given to Naphtali

32The sixth allotment of land went to the families of the tribe of Naphtali.

33Its boundary ran from Heleph, from the oak at Zaanannim, and extended across
to Adami-nekeb, Jabneel, and as far as Lakkum, ending at the Jordan River. 34The
western boundary ran past Aznoth-tabor, then to Hukkok, and touched the bound- 19:34 Deut 33:23
ary of Zebulun in the south, the boundary of Asher on the west, and the Jordan
River* on the east. 35The fortified cities included in this territory were Ziddim, Zer, Hammath, Rakkath, Kinnereth, 36Adamah, Ramah, Hazor, 37Kedesh, Edrei, En-hazor,
38Yiron, Migdal-el, Horem, Beth-anath, and Beth-shemesh—nineteen cities with
their surrounding villages.

39This was the inheritance of the families of the tribe of Naphtali.

The Land Given to Dan

40The seventh and last allotment of land went to the families of the tribe of Dan.

41The towns within Dan's inheritance included Zorah, Eshtaol, Ir-shemesh, 42Shaa-
labbin, Aijalon, Ithlah, 43Elon, Timnah, Ekron, 44Eltekeh, Gibbethon, Baalath, 19:42 Judg 1:35
45Jehud, Bene-berak, Gath-rimmon, 46and Me-jarkon, also Rakkon along with the
territory across from Joppa.
47But the tribe of Dan had trouble taking possession of their land, so they fought 19:47 Judg 18:27-31

19:28 As in some Hebrew manuscripts (see also 21:30); most Hebrew manuscripts read *Ebron.* **19:29** Hebrew *the sea.* **19:34** Hebrew *and Judah at the Jordan River.*

19:47, 48 The tribe of Dan found that some of their land was difficult to conquer, so they chose to migrate to Laish, where they knew victory would be easier. Anyone can trust God when the going is easy. It is when everything looks impossible that our faith and courage are put to the test. Have faith that God is great enough to tackle your most difficult situations.

against the town of Laish.* They captured it, slaughtered its people, and settled
there. They renamed the city Dan after their ancestor.

48 This was the inheritance of the families of the tribe of Dan—these towns with their
villages.

The Land Given to Joshua

19:50 Josh 24:30 49 After all the land was divided among the tribes, the Israelites gave a special piece of
land to Joshua as his inheritance. 50 For the LORD had said he could have any town he
wanted. He chose Timnath-serah in the hill country of Ephraim. He rebuilt the town and
lived there.

19:51 Josh 14:1; 18:10 51 These are the territories that Eleazar the priest, Joshua son of Nun, and the tribal
leaders gave as an inheritance to the tribes of Israel by casting sacred lots in the presence
of the LORD at the entrance of the Tabernacle* at Shiloh. So the division of the land was
completed.

2. Special cities are set aside

The Cities of Refuge

20:2 Num 35:6-34 Deut 4:41; 19:2 **20** The LORD said to Joshua, 2 "Now tell the Israelites to designate the cities of refuge,
as I instructed Moses. 3 Anyone who kills another person unintentionally can run
to one of these cities and be protected from the relatives of the one who was killed, for
the relatives may seek to avenge the killing.

20:4 Ruth 4:1-2 4 "Upon reaching one of these cities, the one who caused the accidental death will
appear before the leaders at the city gate and explain what happened. They must allow
the accused to enter the city and live there among them. 5 If the relatives of the victim
come to avenge the killing, the leaders must not release the accused to them, for the death
was accidental. 6 But the person who caused the death must stay in that city and be tried
by the community and found innocent. Then the one declared innocent because the death
was accidental must continue to live in that city until the death of the high priest who
was in office at the time of the accident. After that, the one found innocent is free to return
home."

20:7 Josh 21:11, 32 1 Chr 6:76 Luke 1:39 7 The following cities were designated as cities of refuge: Kedesh of Galilee, in the hill
country of Naphtali; Shechem, in the hill country of Ephraim; and Kiriath-arba (that is,
20:8 Josh 21:27, 36, 38 Hebron), in the hill country of Judah. 8 On the east side of the Jordan River, across from
Jericho, the following cities were designated as cities of refuge: Bezer, in the wilderness
plain of the tribe of Reuben; Ramoth in Gilead, in the territory of the tribe of Gad; and
Golan in Bashan, in the land of the tribe of Manasseh. 9 These cities were set apart for

19:47 Hebrew *Leshem,* another name for Laish. **19:51** Hebrew *Tent of Meeting.*

19:49 There were several good reasons for establishing these well-set boundaries instead of turning the Promised Land into a single undivided nation. (1) The boundaries gave each tribe ownership of an area, promoting loyalty and unity that would strengthen each tribe. (2) The boundaries delineated areas of responsibility and privilege, which would help each tribe develop and mature. (3) The boundaries reduced conflicts that might have broken out if everyone had wanted to live in the choicest areas. (4) The boundaries fulfilled the promised inheritance to each tribe that began to be given as early as the days of Jacob (Genesis 48:21, 22).

20:6 A new nation in a new land needed a new government. Many years earlier God had told Moses how this government should function. One of the tasks God wanted the Israelites to do when they entered the Promised Land was to designate certain cities as "cities of refuge." These were to be scattered throughout the land. Their purpose was to prevent injustice, especially in cases of revenge. For example, if someone accidentally killed another person, he could flee to a city of refuge where he was safe until he could have a fair trial. The Levites were in charge of these cities. They were to ensure that God's principles of justice and fairness were kept. (For more on cities of refuge, see the notes on Numbers 35:6; 35:11-28.)

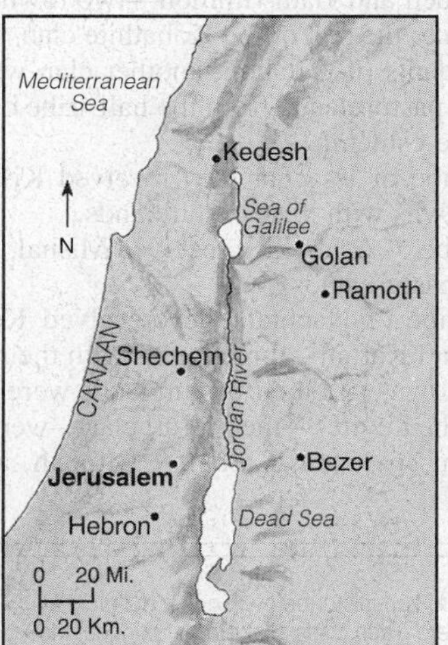

THE CITIES OF REFUGE
A city of refuge was just that—refuge for someone who committed an unintentional murder that would evoke revenge from the victim's friends and relatives. The six cities of refuge were spaced throughout the land so that a person was never too far from one.

Israelites as well as the foreigners living among them. Anyone who accidentally killed another person could take refuge in one of these cities. In this way, they could escape being killed in revenge prior to standing trial before the community.

The Towns Given to the Levites

21 Then the leaders of the tribe of Levi came to consult with Eleazar the priest, Joshua son of Nun, and the leaders of the other tribes of Israel. 2 They spoke to them at Shiloh in the land of Canaan, saying, "The LORD instructed Moses to give us towns to live in and pasturelands for our cattle." 3 So by the command of the LORD the Levites were given as their inheritance the following towns with their pasturelands.

21:1 Josh 14:1
21:2 Num 35:2

4 The descendants of Aaron, who were members of the Kohathite clan within the tribe of Levi, were given thirteen towns that were originally assigned to the tribes of Judah, Simeon, and Benjamin. 5 The other families of the Kohathite clan were allotted ten towns from the territories of Ephraim, Dan, and the half-tribe of Manasseh.

21:4-39 //1 Chr 6:54-80

6 The clan of Gershon received thirteen towns from the tribes of Issachar, Asher, Naphtali, and the half-tribe of Manasseh in Bashan.

7 The clan of Merari received twelve cities from the tribes of Reuben, Gad, and Zebulun.

8 So the Israelites obeyed the LORD's command to Moses and assigned these towns and pasturelands to the Levites by casting sacred lots.

9 The Israelites gave the following towns from the tribes of Judah and Simeon 10 to the descendants of Aaron, who were members of the Kohathite clan within the tribe of Levi, since the sacred lot fell to them first: 11 Kiriath-arba (that is, Hebron), in the hill country of Judah, along with its surrounding pasturelands. (Arba was an ancestor of Anak.) 12 But the fields beyond the city and the surrounding villages were given to Caleb son of Jephunneh.

21:11 Josh 15:13-14; 1 Chr 6:55

13 The following towns with their pasturelands were given to the descendants of Aaron the priest: Hebron (a city of refuge for those who accidentally killed someone), Libnah, 14 Jattir, Eshtemoa, 15 Holon, Debir, 16 Ain, Juttah, and Beth-shemesh—nine towns from these two tribes.

21:13 Josh 15:42, 54; 20:7; 1 Chr 6:55
21:15 Josh 15:49, 51; 1 Chr 6:58
21:16 Josh 15:10; 1 Chr 6:59

17 From the tribe of Benjamin the priests were given the following towns with their surrounding pasturelands: Gibeon, Geba, 18 Anathoth, and Almon—four towns. 19 So thirteen towns were given to the priests, the descendants of Aaron.

21:18 1 Chr 6:60

20 The rest of the Kohathite clan from the tribe of Levi was allotted these towns and pasturelands from the tribe of Ephraim: 21 Shechem (a city of refuge for those who accidentally killed someone), Gezer, 22 Kibzaim, and Beth-horon—four towns.

21:21 Josh 20:7

23 The following towns and pasturelands were allotted to the priests from the tribe of Dan: Eltekeh, Gibbethon, 24 Aijalon, and Gath-rimmon—four towns.

25 The half-tribe of Manasseh allotted the following towns with their pasturelands to the priests: Taanach and Gath-rimmon—two towns. 26 So ten towns with their pasturelands were given to the rest of the Kohathite clan.

27 The descendants of Gershon, another clan within the tribe of Levi, received two towns with their pasturelands from the half-tribe of Manasseh: Golan in Bashan (a city of refuge) and Be-eshterah.

28 From the tribe of Issachar they received Kishion, Daberath, 29 Jarmuth, and En-gannim—four towns with their pasturelands.

30 From the tribe of Asher they received Mishal, Abdon, 31 Helkath, and Rehob—four towns and their pasturelands.

32 From the tribe of Naphtali they received Kedesh in Galilee (a city of refuge), Hammoth-dor, and Kartan—three towns with their pasturelands.

21:32 Josh 20:7

33 So thirteen towns and their pasturelands were allotted to the clan of Gershon.

34 The rest of the Levites—the Merari clan—were given the following towns from the tribe of Zebulun: Jokneam, Kartah, 35 Dimnah, and Nahalal—four towns with their pasturelands.

21:2 The Levites were to minister before God on behalf of all the people, so they were given cities scattered throughout the land. Although Jerusalem was far away from the homes of many Israelites, almost no one lived more than a day's journey from a Levitical city.

21:36 Josh 20:8

36 From the tribe of Reuben they received Bezer, Jahaz,* 37 Kedemoth, and Mephaath—four towns with their pasturelands.
38 From the tribe of Gad they received Ramoth in Gilead (a city of refuge), Mahanaim,
39 Heshbon, and Jazer—four towns with their pasturelands. 40 So twelve towns were
allotted to the clan of Merari.

21:41 Num 35:7
21:43 Num 33:53; Deut 11:31; 17:14; 34:4
21:44 Exod 23:31; Deut 7:24

41 The total number of towns and pasturelands within Israelite territory given to the
Levites came to forty-eight. 42 Every one of these towns had pasturelands surrounding it.
43 So the LORD gave to Israel all the land he had sworn to give their ancestors, and they
conquered it and settled there. 44 And the LORD gave them rest on every side, just as he
had solemnly promised their ancestors. None of their enemies could stand against them,
for the LORD helped them conquer all their enemies. 45 All of the good promises that the
LORD had given Israel came true.

3. Eastern tribes return home

22:1 Num 32:20-22
22:2 Josh 1:12-18
22:4 Num 32:18; Deut 3:20
22:5 Deut 5:10; †Mark 12:32
22:7 Num 32:33; Josh 17:1-13

22 Then Joshua called together the tribes of Reuben, Gad, and the half-tribe of
Manasseh. 2 He told them, "You have done as Moses, the servant of the LORD,
commanded you, and you have obeyed every order I have given you. 3 You have not
deserted the other tribes, even though the campaign has lasted for such a long time. You
have been careful to obey the commands of the LORD your God up to the present day.
4 And now the LORD your God has given the other tribes rest, as he promised them. So
go home now to the land Moses, the servant of the LORD, gave you on the east side of
the Jordan River. 5 But be very careful to obey all the commands and the law that Moses
gave to you. Love the LORD your God, walk in all his ways, obey his commands, be
faithful to him, and serve him with all your heart and all your soul."
6 So Joshua blessed them and sent them home. 7 Now Moses had given the land of
Bashan to the half-tribe of Manasseh east of the Jordan. The other half of the tribe was
given land west of the Jordan. As Joshua sent them away, he blessed them 8 and said,
"Share with your relatives back home the great wealth you have taken from your
enemies. Share with them your large herds of cattle, your silver and gold, your bronze
and iron, and your clothing."

22:9 Deut 32:1, 26, 29

9 So the men of Reuben, Gad, and the half-tribe of Manasseh left the rest of Israel at
Shiloh in the land of Canaan. They started the journey back to their own land of Gilead,
the territory that belonged to them according to the LORD's command through Moses.

The Eastern Tribes Build a Memorial

10 But while they were still in Canaan, before they crossed the Jordan River, Reuben,
Gad, and the half-tribe of Manasseh built a very large altar near the Jordan River at a
place called Geliloth.

22:11 Deut 12:5

11 When the rest of Israel heard they had built the altar at Geliloth west of the Jordan

21:36 Hebrew *Jahzah,* a variant name for Jahaz.

21:43-45 God proved faithful in fulfilling every promise he had given to Israel. Fulfillment of some promises took several years, but "all of the good promises that the LORD had given Israel came true." His promises will be fulfilled according to his timetable, not ours, but we know that his word is sure. The more we learn of those promises God has fulfilled and continues to fulfill, the easier it is to hope for those yet to come. Sometimes we become impatient, wanting God to act in a certain way *now.* Instead, we should faithfully do what we know he wants us to do and trust him for the future.

22:2-4 Before the conquest had begun, these tribes were given land on the east side of the Jordan River. But before they could settle down, they had to first promise to help the other tribes conquer the land on the west side (Numbers 32:20-22). They had patiently and diligently carried out their promised duties. Joshua commended them for doing just that. At last they were permitted to return to their families and build their cities. Follow-through is vital in God's work. Beware of the temptation to quit early and leave God's work undone.

22:5 Here Joshua briefly restated the central message Moses gave the people in Deuteronomy: Obedience should be based on love for God. Although the Israelites had completed their military responsibility, Joshua reminded them of their spiritual responsibility. Sometimes we think so much about what we are to do that we neglect thinking about who we are to be. If we know we are God's children, we will love him and joyfully serve him. We must not let daily service take away from our love for God.

22:11-34 When the tribes of Reuben and Gad and the half-tribe of Manasseh built an altar near the Jordan River, the rest of Israel feared that these tribes were starting their own religion and rebelling against God. But before beginning an all-out war, Phinehas led a delegation to learn the truth, following the principle taught in Deuteronomy 13:12-18. He was prepared to negotiate rather than fight if a battle was not necessary. When he learned that the altar was for a memorial rather than for pagan sacrifice, war was averted and unity restored.

As nations and as individuals, we would benefit from a similar approach to resolving conflicts. Assuming the worst about the intentions of others only brings trouble. Israel averted the threat of civil war by asking before assaulting. Beware of reacting before you hear the whole story.

River, in the land of Canaan, 12 the whole assembly gathered at Shiloh and prepared to go
to war against their brother tribes. 13 First, however, they sent a delegation led by Phinehas **22:13**
son of Eleazar, the priest. They crossed the river to talk with the tribes of Reuben, Gad, Num 25:7, 11; 31:6
and the half-tribe of Manasseh. 14 In this delegation were ten high officials of Israel, one
from each of the ten tribes, and each a leader within the family divisions of Israel.
15 When they arrived in the land of Gilead, they said to the tribes of Reuben, Gad, and
the half-tribe of Manasseh, 16 "The whole community of the LORD demands to know why
you are betraying the God of Israel. How could you turn away from the LORD and build
an altar in rebellion against him? 17 Was our sin at Peor not enough? We are not yet fully **22:17**
cleansed of it, even after the plague that struck the entire assembly of the LORD. 18 And Num 25:1-9
yet today you are turning away from following the LORD. If you rebel against the LORD
today, he will be angry with all of us tomorrow. 19 If you need the altar because your land
is defiled, then join us on our side of the river, where the LORD lives among us in his
Tabernacle, and we will share our land with you. But do not rebel against the LORD or
draw us into your rebellion by building another altar for yourselves. There is only one
true altar of the LORD our God. 20 Didn't God punish all the people of Israel when Achan, **22:20**
a member of the clan of Zerah, sinned by stealing the things set apart for the LORD*? He Josh 7:1-6
was not the only one who died because of that sin."
21 Then the people of Reuben, Gad, and the half-tribe of Manasseh answered these
high officials: 22 "The LORD alone is God! The LORD alone is God! We have not built the **22:22**
altar in rebellion against the LORD. If we have done so, do not spare our lives this day. Deut 10:17
But the LORD knows, and let all Israel know, too, 23 that we have not built an altar for
ourselves to turn away from the LORD. Nor will we use it for our burnt offerings or grain
offerings or peace offerings. If we have built it for this purpose, may the LORD himself
punish us.
24 "We have built this altar because we fear that in the future your descendants will say
to ours, 'What right do you have to worship the LORD, the God of Israel? 25 The LORD
has placed the Jordan River as a barrier between our people and your people. You have
no claim to the LORD.' And your descendants may make our descendants stop worshiping
the LORD. 26 So we decided to build the altar, not for burnt sacrifices, 27 but as a memorial. **22:27**
It will remind our descendants and your descendants that we, too, have the right to Josh 24:27
worship the LORD at his sanctuary with our burnt offerings, sacrifices, and peace
offerings. Then your descendants will not be able to say to ours, 'You have no claim to
the LORD.' 28 If they say this, our descendants can reply, 'Look at this copy of the LORD's
altar that our ancestors made. It is not for burnt offerings or sacrifices; it is a reminder of
the relationship both of us have with the LORD.' 29 Far be it from us to rebel against the **22:29**
LORD or turn away from him by building our own altar for burnt offerings, grain Deut 12:13
offerings, or sacrifices. Only the altar of the LORD our God that stands in front of the
Tabernacle may be used for that purpose."
30 When Phinehas the priest and the high officials heard this from the tribes of Reuben,
Gad, and the half-tribe of Manasseh, they were satisfied. 31 Phinehas son of Eleazar, the **22:31**
priest, replied to them, "Today we know the LORD is among us because you have not Lev 26:11-12 2 Chr 15:2
sinned against the LORD as we thought. Instead, you have rescued Israel from being
destroyed by the LORD."
32 Then Phinehas son of Eleazar, the priest, and the ten high officials left the tribes
of Reuben and Gad in Gilead and returned to the land of Canaan to tell the Israelites
what had happened. 33 And all the Israelites were satisfied and praised God and spoke
no more of war against Reuben and Gad. 34 The people of Reuben and Gad named the **22:34**
Gen 31:47-49

22:20 The Hebrew term used here refers to the complete consecration of things or people to the LORD, either by destroying them or by giving them as an offering.

22:17 For the story of how Israel turned away from God and began to worship Baal at Peor, see Numbers 25:1-18.

22:20 For the story of Achan, a man who allowed greed to get the best of him, see chapter 7.

22:26-28 The tribes were concerned that, without some visible sign of unity between the people on the two sides of the Jordan, future generations might see conflict between them. The altar, patterned after the altar of the Lord, was to remind these people that they all worshiped the same God. Often we need to be reminded of the faith of our fathers. What actions demonstrate to your children your reliance on God and remind them of what he has done? Take the time to establish family traditions that will help your children remember.

altar "Witness,"* for they said, "It is a witness between us and them that the LORD is our God, too."

23:1 Josh 21:44
23:2 Josh 24:1
23:4 Exod 23:30
23:5 Num 33:53
23:6 Deut 5:32; Josh 1:7
23:7 Exod 20:5; 23:13; Ps 16:4
23:8 Deut 10:20
23:9 Deut 7:24
23:10 Lev 26:8; Deut 28:7
23:12 Deut 7:3-4; Ezra 9:2
23:13 Exod 23:33; 34:12; Deut 7:16
23:15 Lev 26:14-33; Deut 28:15
23:16 Deut 4:25-26

4. Joshua's farewell to the leaders

23 The years passed, and the LORD had given the people of Israel rest from all their enemies. Joshua, who was now very old, 2called together all the elders, leaders, judges, and officers of Israel. He said to them, "I am an old man now. 3You have seen everything the LORD your God has done for you during my lifetime. The LORD your God has fought for you against your enemies. 4I have allotted to you as an inheritance all the land of the nations yet unconquered, as well as the land of those we have already conquered—from the Jordan River to the Mediterranean Sea* in the west. 5This land will be yours, for the LORD your God will drive out all the people living there now. You will live there instead of them, just as the LORD your God promised you.

6"So be strong! Be very careful to follow all the instructions written in the Book of the Law of Moses. Do not deviate from them in any way. 7Make sure you do not associate with the other people still remaining in the land. Do not even mention the names of their gods, much less swear by them or worship them. 8But be faithful to the LORD your God as you have done until now.

9"For the LORD has driven out great and powerful nations for you, and no one has yet been able to defeat you. 10Each one of you will put to flight a thousand of the enemy, for the LORD your God fights for you, just as he has promised. 11So be very careful to love the LORD your God.

12"But if you turn away from him and intermarry with the survivors of these nations remaining among you, 13then know for certain that the LORD your God will no longer drive them out from your land. Instead, they will be a snare and a trap to you, a pain in your side and a thorn in your eyes, and you will be wiped out from this good land the LORD your God has given you.

14"Soon I will die, going the way of all the earth. Deep in your hearts you know that every promise of the LORD your God has come true. Not a single one has failed! 15But as surely as the LORD your God has given you the good things he promised, he will also bring disaster on you if you disobey him. He will completely wipe you out from this good land he has given you. 16If you break the covenant of the LORD your God by worshiping and serving other gods, his anger will burn against you, and you will quickly be wiped out from the good land he has given you."

24:1 Josh 23:2
24:2 Gen 11:27-32
24:3 Gen 12:1; 15:5; 21:3; 24:7

The LORD's Covenant Renewed

24 Then Joshua summoned all the people of Israel to Shechem, along with their elders, leaders, judges, and officers. So they came and presented themselves to God.

2Joshua said to the people, "This is what the LORD, the God of Israel, says: Your ancestors, including Terah, the father of Abraham and Nahor, lived beyond the Euphrates River,* and they worshiped other gods. 3But I took your ancestor Abraham from the land beyond the Euphrates and led him into the land of Canaan. I gave him many descendants

22:34 Hebrew *edh.* Some manuscripts lack this word. **23:4** Hebrew *the Great Sea.* **24:2** Hebrew *the river;* also in 24:3, 14, 15.

23:6-13 Joshua knew the nation's weak spots. Before dying, he called the people together and gave commands to help them where they were most likely to slip: (1) Follow all that is written in the Book of the Law of Moses without turning aside; (2) don't associate with the pagan nations or worship their gods; (3) don't intermarry with the pagan nations. These temptations were right in their backyard. Our associations and relationships can be temptations to us as well. It's wise to identify our weak spots before we break down. Then we can develop strategies to overcome these temptations instead of being overcome by them.

23:8 Joshua was dying, and so he called all the leaders of the nation together to give them his final words of encouragement and instruction. His whole message can be summarized in this verse: "Be faithful to the LORD your God." Joshua had been a living example of those words, and he wanted that to be his legacy. For what do you want to be remembered, and what do you want to pass on to your children and associates? You can leave them nothing better than the admonition to hold on to God and to the memory of a person who did.

23:12-16 This chilling prediction about the consequences of intermarriage with the Canaanite nations eventually became a reality. Numerous stories in the book of Judges show what Israel had to suffer because of failure to follow God wholeheartedly. God was supremely loving and patient with Israel, just as he is today. But we must not confuse his patience with us as approval of or indifference to our sin. Beware of demanding your own way because eventually you may get it—along with all its painful consequences.

through his son Isaac. [4]To Isaac I gave Jacob and Esau. To Esau I gave the hill country
of Seir, while Jacob and his children went down into Egypt.
[5]"Then I sent Moses and Aaron, and I brought terrible plagues on Egypt; and
afterward I brought you out as a free people. [6]But when your ancestors arrived at the
Red Sea,* the Egyptians chased after you with chariots and horses. [7]When you cried out
to the LORD, I put darkness between you and the Egyptians. I brought the sea crashing
down on the Egyptians, drowning them. With your very own eyes you saw what I did.
Then you lived in the wilderness for many years.
[8]"Finally, I brought you into the land of the Amorites on the east side of the Jordan.
They fought against you, but I gave you victory over them, and you took possession of
their land. [9]Then Balak son of Zippor, king of Moab, started a war against Israel. He
asked Balaam son of Beor to curse you, [10]but I would not listen to him. Instead, I made
Balaam bless you, and so I rescued you from Balak.
[11]"When you crossed the Jordan River and came to Jericho, the men of Jericho fought
against you. There were also many others who fought you, including the Amorites, the
Perizzites, the Canaanites, the Hittites, the Girgashites, the Hivites, and the Jebusites. But
I gave you victory over them. [12]And I sent hornets ahead of you to drive out the two
kings of the Amorites. It was not your swords or bows that brought you victory. [13]I gave
you land you had not worked for, and I gave you cities you did not build—the cities in
which you are now living. I gave you vineyards and olive groves for food, though you
did not plant them.
[14]"So honor the LORD and serve him wholeheartedly. Put away forever the idols your
ancestors worshiped when they lived beyond the Euphrates River and in Egypt. Serve
the LORD alone. [15]But if you are unwilling to serve the LORD, then choose today whom
you will serve. Would you prefer the gods your ancestors served beyond the Euphrates?
Or will it be the gods of the Amorites in whose land you now live? But as for me and my
family, we will serve the LORD."
[16]The people replied, "We would never forsake the LORD and worship other gods.
[17]For the LORD our God is the one who rescued us and our ancestors from slavery in the
land of Egypt. He performed mighty miracles before our very eyes. As we traveled
through the wilderness among our enemies, he preserved us. [18]It was the LORD who
drove out the Amorites and the other nations living here in the land. So we, too, will serve
the LORD, for he alone is our God."
[19]Then Joshua said to the people, "You are not able to serve the LORD, for he is a holy
and jealous God. He will not forgive your rebellion and sins. [20]If you forsake the LORD

24:4 Gen 25:25-26; 46:6-7; Deut 2:5
24:5 Exod 3:10; 4:14-17
24:6 Exod 14:2-31
24:7 Exod 14:19-31; Deut 1:46; 2:14
24:8 Num 21:21-35
24:9 Num 22:2-6
24:11 Exod 23:23; Deut 7:1; Josh 3:14-17
24:12 Exod 23:28; Deut 7:20; Ps 44:3, 6
24:13 Deut 6:10-11
24:14 Deut 10:12; 18:13; 1 Sam 12:24
24:15 Ruth 1:15; 1 Kgs 18:21
24:19 Exod 20:5; 23:21; 34:14; Lev 19:2; 20:7, 26
24:20 Deut 4:25-26; Josh 23:15; 1 Chr 28:9; Acts 7:42

24:6 Hebrew *sea of reeds.*

24:15 The people had to decide whether they would obey the Lord, who had proven his trustworthiness, or obey the local gods, which were only man-made idols. It's easy to slip into a quiet rebellion—going about life in your own way. But the time comes when you have to choose who or what will control you. The choice is yours. Will it be God, your own limited personality, or another imperfect substitute? Once you have chosen to be controlled by God's Spirit, reaffirm your choice every day.

24:15 In taking a definite stand for the Lord, Joshua again displayed his spiritual leadership. Regardless of what others decided, because Joshua had made a commitment to God, he was determined to set an example of living by that decision. The way we live shows others the strength of our commitment to serving God.

24:16-18, 21 All the people boldly claimed that they would never forsake the Lord. But they did not keep that promise. Very soon God would charge them with breaking their contract with him (Judges 2:2, 3). Talk is cheap. It is easy to say we will follow God, but it is much more important to live like it. Yet the nation followed God through Joshua's lifetime, a great tribute to Joshua's faith in God and powerful leadership.

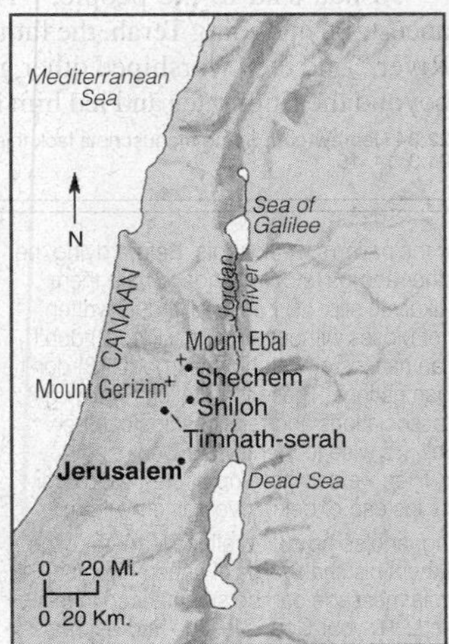

JOSHUA'S FINAL SPEECH
Joshua called all the Israelites to Shechem to hear his final words. He challenged the people to make a conscious choice to always serve God. Soon afterward, Joshua died and was buried in his hometown of Timnath-serah.

and serve other gods, he will turn against you and destroy you, even though he has been
so good to you."
21 But the people answered Joshua, saying, "No, we are determined to serve the
LORD!"
22 "You are accountable for this decision," Joshua said. "You have chosen to serve the
LORD."
"Yes," they replied, "we are accountable."
23 "All right then," Joshua said, "destroy the idols among you, and turn your hearts to
the LORD, the God of Israel."
24:24 Exod 19:8; 24:3, 7 Deut 5:27 — 24 The people said to Joshua, "We will serve the LORD our God. We will obey him
alone."
24:25 Exod 24:8 — 25 So Joshua made a covenant with the people that day at Shechem, committing them
to a permanent and binding contract between themselves and the LORD. 26 Joshua
recorded these things in the Book of the Law of God. As a reminder of their agreement,
he took a huge stone and rolled it beneath the oak tree beside the Tabernacle of the LORD.
24:27 Josh 22:27 — 27 Joshua said to all the people, "This stone has heard everything the LORD said to us.
It will be a witness to testify against you if you go back on your word to God."
28 Then Joshua sent the people away, each to his own inheritance.

Leaders Buried in the Promised Land

24:29 Judg 2:8 — 29 Soon after this, Joshua son of Nun, the servant of the LORD, died at the age of 110.
24:30 Josh 19:50 — 30 They buried him in the land he had inherited, at Timnath-serah in the hill country of
Ephraim, north of Mount Gaash.
31 Israel served the LORD throughout the lifetime of Joshua and of the leaders who
outlived him—those who had personally experienced all that the LORD had done for
Israel.
24:32 Gen 50:24-25 Exod 13:19 John 4:5 Acts 7:16 — 32 The bones of Joseph, which the Israelites had brought along with them when they
left Egypt, were buried at Shechem, in the parcel of ground Jacob had bought from the
sons of Hamor for one hundred pieces of silver.* This land was located in the territory
allotted to the tribes of Ephraim and Manasseh, the descendants of Joseph.
24:33 Josh 22:13 — 33 Eleazar son of Aaron also died. He was buried in the hill country of Ephraim, in the
town of Gibeah, which had been given to his son Phinehas.

24:32 Hebrew *100 kesitahs;* the value or weight of the kesitah is no longer known.

24:23 Joshua told the Israelites to throw away their foreign gods, or idols. To follow God requires destroying whatever gets in the way of worshiping him. We have our own form of idols—greed, wrong priorities, jealousies, prejudices—that get in the way of worshiping God. God is not satisfied if we merely hide these idols. We must completely remove them from our lives.

24:24-26 The covenant between Israel and God was that the people would worship and obey the Lord alone. Their purpose was to become a holy nation that would influence the rest of the world for God. The conquest of Canaan was a means to achieve this purpose, but Israel became preoccupied with the land and lost sight of the Lord God.

The same can happen in our lives. We can spend so much time on the means that we forget the end—to glorify God. Churches may make this mistake as well. For example, the congregation may pour all of its energies into a new facility, only to become self-satisfied or fearful of letting certain groups use it. If this happens, they have focused on the building and lost sight of its purpose—to bring others to God.

24:29-31 The book of Joshua opens with a new leader being handed a seemingly impossible task—to lead the nation in taking over the land of Canaan. By following God closely, Joshua led the people through military victories and faithful spiritual obedience. In 24:16 we read that the people were sure they would never forsake the Lord. The response of the whole nation during these many years is a tribute both to Joshua's leadership and to the God he faithfully served.

24:33 Joshua and Eleazar had died, but not before laying before the people the fundamentals of what it means to have faith in God. We are to fear and serve the Lord alone (24:14). This is based on a choice: to obey him instead of following other gods (24:15). We are incapable, however, of properly worshiping him because of our rebellion and sins (24:19). By choosing God as Lord, we enter into a covenant with him (24:25) whereby he promises not only to forgive and love us, but also to enable us by his Spirit to do his work here on earth. This covenant requires us to renounce the principles and practices of the culture around us that are hostile to God's plan (24:23). This is not to be done alone, but by binding ourselves together with others who have faith in God. (See Deuteronomy 30:15-20 for a similar message from Moses.)

JUDGES

Exodus from Egypt 1446 B.C. (1280 B.C.)	Israelites enter Canaan 1406 (1240)	Period of the judges begins 1375 (1220)	Othniel 1367–1327 (1202–1162)	Ehud 1309–1229 (1184–1104)	Deborah 1209–1169 (1192–1152)

VITAL STATISTICS

PURPOSE:
To show that God's judgment against sin is certain, and his forgiveness of sin and restoration to relationship are just as certain for those who repent

AUTHOR:
Possibly Samuel

SETTING:
The land of Canaan, later called Israel. God had helped the Israelites conquer Canaan, which had been inhabited by a host of wicked nations. But they were in danger of losing this Promised Land because they compromised their convictions and disobeyed God.

KEY VERSE:
"In those days Israel had no king, so the people did whatever seemed right in their own eyes" (17:6).

KEY PEOPLE:
Othniel, Ehud, Deborah, Gideon, Abimelech, Jephthah, Samson, Delilah

SPECIAL FEATURE:
Records Israel's first civil war

REAL heroes are hard to find these days. Modern research and the media have made the foibles and weaknesses of our leaders very apparent; we search in vain for men and women to emulate. The music, movie, and sports industries produce a steady stream of "stars" who shoot to the top and then quickly fade from view.

Judges is a book about heroes—12 men and women who delivered Israel from its oppressors. These judges were not perfect; in fact, they included an assassin, a sexually promiscuous man, and a person who broke all the laws of hospitality. But they were submissive to God, and God used them.

Judges is also a book about sin and its consequences. Like a minor cut or abrasion that becomes infected when left untreated, sin grows and soon poisons the whole body. The book of Joshua ends with the nation taking a stand for God, ready to experience all the blessings of the Promised Land. After settling in Canaan, however, the Israelites lost their spiritual commitment and motivation. When Joshua and the elders died, the nation experienced a leadership vacuum, leaving them without a strong central government. Instead of enjoying freedom and prosperity in the Promised Land, Israel entered the dark ages of her history.

Simply stated, the reason for this rapid decline was sin—individual and corporate. The first step away from God was incomplete obedience (1:11—2:5); the Israelites refused to eliminate the enemy completely from the land. This led to intermarriage and idolatry (2:6—3:7) and everyone doing "whatever seemed right" (17:6). Before long the Israelites became captives. Out of their desperation they begged God to rescue them. In faithfulness to his promise and out of his loving-kindness, God would raise up a judge to deliver his people, and for a time there would be peace. Then complacency and disobedience would set in, and the cycle would begin again.

The book of Judges spans a period of over 325 years, recording six successive periods of oppression and deliverance, and the careers of 12 deliverers. Their captors included the Mesopotamians, Moabites, Philistines, Canaanites, Midianites, and Ammonites. A variety of deliverers—from Othniel to Samson—were used by God to lead his people to freedom and true worship. God's deliverance through the judges is a powerful demonstration of his love and mercy toward his people.

As you read the book of Judges, take a good look at these heroes from Jewish history. Take note of their dependence on God and obedience to his commands. Observe Israel's repeated downward spiral into sin, refusing to learn from history and living only for the moment. But most of all, stand in awe of God's mercy as he delivers his people over and over again.

Gideon 1162–1122 (1146–1106)	Samuel born 1105 (1083)	Samson 1075–1055 (1083–1063)	Saul anointed king 1050 (1045)	David becomes king 1010

THE BLUEPRINT

A. THE MILITARY FAILURE OF ISRAEL (1:1—3:6) 1. Incomplete conquest of the land 2. Disobedience and defeat	The tribes had compromised God's command to drive out the inhabitants of the land. Incomplete removal of evil often means disaster in the end. We must beware of compromising with wickedness.
B. THE RESCUE OF ISRAEL BY THE JUDGES (3:7—16:31) 1. First period: Othniel 2. Second period: Ehud and Shamgar 3. Third period: Deborah and Barak 4. Fourth period: Gideon, Tola, and Jair 5. Fifth period: Jephthah, Ibzan, Elon, and Abdon 6. Sixth period: Samson	Repeatedly we see the nation of Israel sinning against God and God allowing suffering to come upon the land and the people. Sin always has its consequences. Where there is sin we can expect suffering to follow. Rather than living in an endless cycle of abandoning God and then crying out to him for rescue, we should seek to live a consistent life of faithfulness.
C. THE MORAL FAILURE OF ISRAEL (17:1—21:25) 1. Idolatry in the tribe of Dan 2. War against the tribe of Benjamin	Despite the efforts of Israel's judges, the people still would not turn wholeheartedly to God. They all did whatever they thought was best for themselves. The result was the spiritual, moral, and political decline of the nation. Our lives will also fall into decline and decay unless we live by the guidelines God has given us.

MEGATHEMES

THEME	EXPLANATION	IMPORTANCE
Decline/ Compromise	Whenever a judge died, the people faced decline and failure because they compromised their high spiritual purpose in many ways. They abandoned their mission to drive all the people out of the land, and they adopted the customs of the people living around them.	Society has many rewards to offer those who compromise their faith: wealth, acceptance, recognition, power, and influence. When God gives us a mission, it must not be polluted by a desire for approval from society. We must keep our eyes on Christ, who is our Judge and Deliverer.
Decay/Apostasy	Israel's moral downfall had its roots in the fierce independence that each tribe cherished. It led to everyone doing whatever seemed good in his own eyes. There was no unity in government or in worship. Law and order broke down. Finally, idol worship and man-made religion led to the complete abandoning of faith in God.	We can expect decay when we value anything more highly than God. If we value our own independence more than dedication to God, we have placed an idol in our hearts. Soon our lives become temples to that god. We must constantly regard God's first claim on our lives and all our desires.
Defeat/ Oppression	God used evil oppressors to punish the Israelites for their sin, to bring them to the point of repentance, and to test their allegiance to him.	Rebellion against God leads to disaster. God may use defeat to bring wandering hearts back to him. When all else is stripped away, we recognize the importance of serving only him.
Repentance	Decline, decay, and defeat caused the people to cry out to God for help. They vowed to turn from idolatry and to turn to God for mercy and deliverance. When they repented, God delivered them.	Idolatry gains a foothold in our hearts when we make anything more important than God. We must identify modern idols in our hearts, renounce them, and turn to God for his love and mercy.

Deliverance/ Heroes	Because Israel repented, God raised up heroes to deliver his people from their path of sin and the oppression it brought. He used many kinds of people to accomplish this purpose by filling them with his Holy Spirit.	God's Holy Spirit is available to all people. Anyone who is dedicated to God can be used for his service. Real heroes recognize the futility of human effort without God's guidance and power.

KEY PLACES IN JUDGES

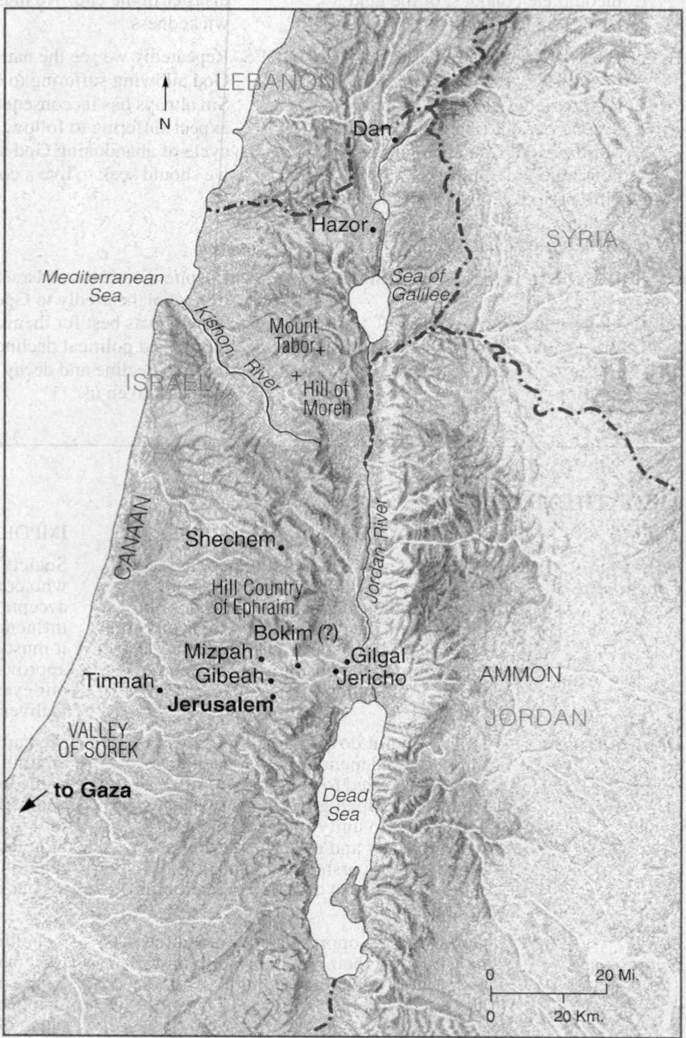

The broken lines (—·—) indicate modern boundaries.

1 Bokim The book of Judges opens with the Israelites continuing their conquest of the Promised Land. Their failure to obey God and destroy all the evil inhabitants soon comes back to haunt them in two ways: (1) the enemies reorganized and counterattacked, and (2) Israel turned away from God, adopting the evil and idolatrous practices of the inhabitants of the land. The angel of the Lord appeared at Bokim to inform the Israelites that their sin and disobedience had broken their agreement with God and would result in punishment through oppression (1:1—3:11).

2 Jericho The nation of Moab was one of the first to oppress Israel. Moab's king Eglon conquered much of Israel—including the city of Jericho—and forced the people to pay unreasonable taxes. The messenger chosen to deliver this tax money to King Eglon was named Ehud. But he had more than money to deliver, for he drew his hidden sword and killed the Moabite king. Ehud then escaped, only to return with an army that chased out the Moabites and freed Israel from its oppressors (3:12–31).

3 Hazor After Ehud's death, King Jabin of Hazor conquered Israel and oppressed the people for 20 years. Then Deborah became Israel's leader. She summoned Barak to fight Commander Sisera, the leader of King Jabin's army. Together Deborah and Barak led their army into battle against Jabin's forces in the land between Mount Tabor and the Kishon River and conquered them (4:1—5:31).

4 Hill of Moreh After 40 years of peace, the Midianites began to harass the Israelites by destroying their flocks and crops. When the Israelites finally cried out to God, he chose Gideon, a poor and humble farmer, to be their deliverer. After struggling with doubt and feelings of inferiority, Gideon took courage and knocked down his town's altar to Baal, causing a great uproar among the citizens. Filled with the Spirit of God, he attacked the vast army of Midian, which was camped near the hill of Moreh. With just a handful of men he sent the enemy running away in confusion (6:1—7:25).

5 Shechem Even great leaders make mistakes. Gideon's relations with a concubine in Shechem resulted in the birth

of a son named Abimelech. Abimelech turned out to be treacherous and power hungry—stirring up the people to proclaim him king. To carry out his plan, he went so far as to kill 69 of his 70 half brothers. Eventually some men of Shechem rebelled against Abimelech, but he gathered together an army and defeated them. His lust for power led him to ransack two other cities, but he was killed by a woman who dropped a millstone onto his head (8:28—9:57).

6 Land of Ammon Again Israel turned completely from God; so God turned from them. But when the Ammonites mobilized their army to attack, Israel threw away her idols and called upon God once again. Jephthah, a prostitute's son who had been run out of Israel, was asked to return and lead Israel's forces against the enemy. After defeating the Ammonites, Jephthah became involved in a war with the tribe of Ephraim over a misunderstanding (10:1—12:15).

7 Timnah Israel's next judge, Samson, was a miracle child promised by God to a barren couple. He was the one who would begin to free Israel from their next and most powerful oppressor, the Philistines. According to God's command, Samson was to be a Nazirite—one who took a vow to be set apart for special service to God. One of the stipulations of the vow was that Samson's hair could never be cut. But when Samson grew up, he did not always take his special responsibility to God seriously. He even fell in love with a Philistine girl in Timnah and asked to marry her. Before the wedding, Samson held a party for some men in the city, using a riddle to place a bet with them. The men, however, forced Samson's fiancée into giving the answer. Furious at being tricked, Samson paid his bet with the lives of 30 Philistines who lived in the nearby city of Ashkelon (13:1—14:20).

8 Valley of Sorek Samson killed thousands of Philistines with his incredible strength. The nation's leaders looked for a way to stop him. They got their chance when another Philistine woman stole Samson's heart. Her name was Delilah, and she lived in the valley of Sorek. In exchange for a great sum of money, Delilah deceived Samson into confiding in her the secret of his strength. One night while he slept, Delilah had his hair cut off. As a result, Samson fell helplessly into the hands of the enemy (15:1—16:20).

9 Gaza Samson was blinded and led captive to a prison in Gaza. There his hair began to grow again. After a while, the Philistines held a great festival to celebrate Samson's imprisonment and to humiliate him before the crowds. When he was brought out as the entertainment, he literally brought down the house when he pushed on the main pillars of the banquet hall and killed the thousands trapped inside. The prophecy that he would begin to free Israel from the Philistines had come true (16:21–31).

10 Hill Country of Ephraim In the hill country of Ephraim lived a man named Micah. Micah hired his own priest to perform priestly duties in the shrine which housed his collection of idols. He thought he was pleasing God with all his religiosity! Like many of the Israelites, Micah assumed that his own opinions of what was right would agree with God's (17:1–13).

11 Dan The tribe of Dan migrated north in order to find new territory. They sent spies ahead of them to scout out the land. One night the spies stopped at Micah's home. Looking for some assurance of victory, the spies stole Micah's idols and priest. Rejoining the tribe, they came upon the city of Laish and slaughtered the unarmed and innocent citizens, renaming the conquered city Dan. Micah's idols were then set up in the city and became the focal point of the tribe's worship for many years (18:1–31).

12 Gibeah The extent to which many people had fallen away from God became clear in Gibeah, a village in the territory of Benjamin. A man and his concubine were traveling north toward the hill country of Ephraim. They stopped for the night in Gibeah, thinking they would be safe. But some perverts in the city gathered around the home where they were staying and demanded that the man come out to have sexual relations with them. Instead, the man and his host pushed the concubine out the door. She was raped and abused all night. When the man found her lifeless body the next morning, he cut it into 12 pieces and sent the parts to each tribe of Israel. This tragic event demonstrated that the nation had sunk to its lowest spiritual level (19:1–30).

13 Mizpah The leaders of Israel came to Mizpah to decide how to punish the wicked men from the city of Gibeah. When the city leaders refused to turn the criminals over, the whole nation of Israel took vengeance upon both Gibeah and the tribe of Benjamin where the city was located. When the battle ended, the entire tribe had been destroyed except for a handful of men who took refuge in the hills. Israel had become morally depraved. The stage was now set for the much-needed spiritual renewal that would come under the prophet Samuel (20:1—21:25).

A. THE MILITARY FAILURE OF ISRAEL (1:1—3:6)

By faithfully obeying the Lord, Joshua led the Israelites to military victory. After his death, however, the tribes failed to clear the inhabitants from the land, so the Lord withdrew his promise to help drive the people out and bless the Israelites in battle. The new generation abandoned God and worshiped idols. This part of Judges shows what can happen when we neglect to teach our children to follow the Lord.

1. Incomplete conquest of the land

Judah and Simeon Conquer the Land

1 After Joshua died, the Israelites asked the LORD, "Which tribe should attack the
Canaanites first?" 1:1 Num 27:21
2 The LORD answered, "Judah, for I have given them victory over the land." 1:2
3 The leaders of Judah said to their relatives from the tribe of Simeon, "Join with us to Gen 49:8
fight against the Canaanites living in the territory allotted to us. Then we will help you 1:3 Judg 1:17
conquer your territory." So the men of Simeon went with Judah.
4 When the men of Judah attacked, the LORD gave them victory over the Canaanites 1:4
and Perizzites, and they killed ten thousand enemy warriors at the town of Bezek. 5 While Gen 13:7
at Bezek they encountered King Adoni-bezek and fought against him, and the Canaanites 1 Sam 11:8
and Perizzites were defeated. 6 Adoni-bezek escaped, but the Israelites soon captured him
and cut off his thumbs and big toes. 7 Adoni-bezek said, "I once had seventy kings with
thumbs and big toes cut off, eating scraps from under my table. Now God has paid me
back for what I did to them." They took him to Jerusalem, and he died there. 1:8
8 The men of Judah attacked Jerusalem and captured it, killing all its people and setting Josh 15:63

1:1 The people of Israel had finally entered and taken control of the land promised to their ancestors (Genesis 12:7; Exodus 3:16, 17). The book of Judges continues the story of this conquest that began in the book of Joshua. Through God's strength, the Israelites had conquered many enemies and overcome many difficulties, but their work was not yet finished. They had effectively met many political and military challenges, but facing spiritual challenges was more difficult. The unholy but attractive life-style of the Canaanites proved more dangerous than their military might. The Israelites gave in to the pressure and compromised their faith. If we attempt to meet life's challenges with human effort alone, we will find the pressures and temptations around us too great to resist.

1:1 Soon after Joshua died, Israel began to lose its firm grip on the land. Although Joshua was a great commander, the people missed his spiritual leadership even more than his military skill, for he had kept the people focused on God and his purposes. Joshua had been the obvious successor to Moses, but there was no obvious successor to Joshua. During this crisis of leadership, Israel had to learn that no matter how powerful and wise the current leader was, their real leader was God. We often focus our hope and confidence on some influential leader, failing to realize that in reality it is God who is in command. Acknowledge God as your commander in chief, and avoid the temptation of relying too heavily on human leaders, regardless of their spiritual wisdom.

1:1 The Canaanites were all the people who lived in Canaan (the Promised Land). They lived in city-states where each city had its own government, army, and laws. One reason Canaan was so difficult to conquer was that each city had to be defeated individually. There was no single king who could surrender the entire country into the hands of the Israelites.

Canaan's greatest threat to Israel was not its army, but its religion. Canaanite religion idealized evil traits: cruelty in war, sexual immorality, selfish greed, and materialism. It was a "me first, anything goes" society. Obviously, the religions of Israel and Canaan could not coexist.

1:2 The book of Joshua tells of a swift and thorough conquest of enemy armies and cities, while the book of Judges seems to suggest a more lengthy and gradual conquest. When the Israelites first entered the Promised Land (Joshua 1–12), they united as one army to crush the inhabitants until they were too weak to retaliate. Then, after the land was divided among the 12 tribes (Joshua 13–24), each tribe was responsible for driving out the remaining enemy from its own territory. The book of Judges tells of their failure to do this.

Some tribes were more successful than others. Under Joshua, they all began strong, but soon most were sidetracked by fear, weariness, lack of discipline, or pursuit of their own interests. As a result, their faith began to fade away, and "the people did whatever seemed right in their own eyes" (17:6). In order for our faith to survive, it must be practiced day by day. It must penetrate every aspect of our lives. Beware of starting out strong and then getting sidetracked from your real purpose—loving God and living for him.

1:6 The Israelites cut off the thumbs and big toes of Adoni-bezek to humiliate him and make him ineffective in battle. But according to God's instructions for conquering the Promised Land, he should have been killed.

1:8 Although the Israelites conquered Jerusalem, they did not occupy the city until the days of David (2 Samuel 5:6-10).

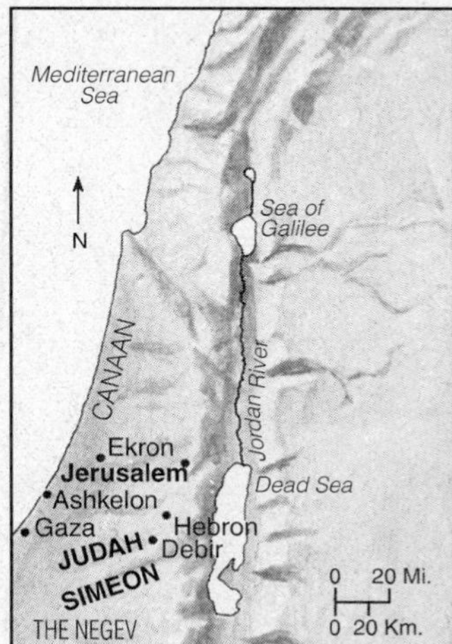

JUDAH FIGHTS FOR ITS LAND
The tribe of Judah wasted no time beginning their conquest of the territory allotted to them. With help from the tribe of Simeon, Jerusalem was conquered, as were the Canaanites in the Negev and along the coast. Hebron and Debir fell to Judah, and later Gaza, Ashkelon, and Ekron.

1:10-15 the city on fire. 9 Then they turned south to fight the Canaanites living in the hill country,
//Josh 15:13-19 the Negev, and the western foothills.* 10 Judah marched against the Canaanites in Hebron
(formerly called Kiriath-arba), defeating the forces of Sheshai, Ahiman, and Talmai.
11 From there they marched against the people living in the town of Debir (formerly
called Kiriath-sepher).

12 Then Caleb said, "I will give my daughter Acsah in marriage to the one who attacks
1:13 and captures Kiriath-sepher." 13 Othniel, the son of Caleb's younger brother Kenaz, was
Judg 3:9 the one who conquered it, so Acsah became Othniel's wife.

14 When Acsah married Othniel, she urged him* to ask her father for an additional field.
As she got down off her donkey, Caleb asked her, "What is it? What can I do for you?"

15 She said, "Give me a further blessing. You have been kind enough to give me land in
1:16 the Negev; please give me springs as well." So Caleb gave her the upper and lower springs.

Deut 34:3 16 When the tribe of Judah left Jericho,* the Kenites, who were descendants of Moses'
Judg 3:13; 4:11 father-in-law, traveled with them into the wilderness of Judah. They settled among the
1:17 people there, near the town of Arad in the Negev.

Num 21:3 17 Then Judah joined with Simeon to fight against the Canaanites living in Zephath,
and they completely destroyed* the town. So the town was named Hormah.* 18 In

1:9 Hebrew *the Shephelah.* **1:14** Greek version and Latin Vulgate read *he urged her.* **1:16** Hebrew *the city of palms.* **1:17a** The Hebrew term used here refers to the complete consecration of things or people to the LORD, either by destroying them or by giving them as an offering. **1:17b** *Hormah* means "destruction."

THE JUDGES OF ISRAEL

Judge	*Years of Judging*	*Memorable Act(s)*	*Reference*
OTHNIEL	40	He captured a powerful Canaanite city	Judges 3:7–11
EHUD	80	He killed Eglon and defeated the Moabites	Judges 3:12–30
SHAMGAR	unrecorded	He killed 600 Philistines with an ox goad	Judges 3:31
DEBORAH (w/Barak)	40	She defeated Sisera and the Canaanites and later sang a victory song with Barak	Judges 4, 5
GIDEON	40	He destroyed his family idols, used a fleece to determine God's will, raised an army of 10,000, and defeated 135,000 Midianites with 300 soldiers	Judges 6—8
TOLA	23	He judged Israel for 23 years	Judges 10:1, 2
JAIR	22	He had 30 sons	Judges 10:3–5
JEPHTHAH	6	He made a rash vow, defeated the Ammonites, and later battled jealous Ephraim	Judges 10:6—12:7
IBZAN	7	He had 30 sons and 30 daughters	Judges 12:8–10
ELON	10	unrecorded	Judges 12:11, 12
ABDON	8	He had 40 sons and 30 grandsons, each of whom had his own donkey	Judges 12:13–15
SAMSON	20	He was a Nazirite, killed a lion with his bare hands, burned the Philistine wheat fields, killed 1,000 Philistines with a donkey's jawbone, tore off an iron gate, was betrayed by Delilah, and destroyed thousands of Philistines in one last mighty act	Judges 13—16

1:12-15 This same event is recorded in Joshua 15:16-19. Caleb was one of the original men who scouted out the Promised Land (Numbers 13–14) and, with Joshua, encouraged the people to conquer it. For his faithfulness, he was given the land of his choice.

1:17 Why did God order the Israelites to drive the Canaanites from their land? Although the command seems cruel, the Israelites were under God's order to execute judgment on those wicked people. The other nations were to be judged for their sin as God had judged Israel by forcing them to wander for 40 years before they were allowed to enter the Promised Land. Over 700 years earlier, God had told Abraham that when the Israelites entered the Promised Land, the gross evil of the native people would be ready for judgment (Genesis 15:16). But God wasn't playing favorites with the Israelites because eventually they, too, would be severely punished for becoming as evil as the people they were ordered to drive out (2 Kings 17; 25; Jeremiah 6:18, 19; Ezekiel 8). God is not partial; all people are eligible for God's gracious forgiveness as well as for his firm justice.

addition, Judah captured the cities of Gaza, Ashkelon, and Ekron, along with their
surrounding territories.

Israel Fails to Conquer the Land

19The LORD was with the people of Judah, and they took possession of the hill country.
But they failed to drive out the people living in the plains because the people there had
iron chariots. 20The city of Hebron was given to Caleb as Moses had promised. And
Caleb drove out the people living there, who were descendants of the three sons of Anak.
21The tribe of Benjamin, however, failed to drive out the Jebusites, who were living in
Jerusalem. So to this day the Jebusites live in Jerusalem among the people of Benjamin.
22The descendants of Joseph attacked the town of Bethel, and the LORD was with
them. 23They sent spies to Bethel (formerly known as Luz), 24who confronted a man
coming out of the city. They said to him, "Show us a way into the city, and we will have
mercy on you." 25So he showed them a way in, and they killed everyone in the city
except for this man and his family. 26Later the man moved to the land of the Hittites,
where he built a city. He named the city Luz, and it is known by that name to this day.
27The tribe of Manasseh failed to drive out the people living in Beth-shan,* Taanach,
Dor, Ibleam, Megiddo, and their surrounding villages, because the Canaanites were
determined to stay in that region. 28When the Israelites grew stronger, they forced the
Canaanites to work as slaves, but they never did drive them out of the land.
29The tribe of Ephraim also failed to drive out the Canaanites living in Gezer, and so
the Canaanites continued to live there among them.
30The tribe of Zebulun also failed to drive out the Canaanites living in Kitron and
Nahalol, who continued to live among them. But they forced them to work as slaves.
31The tribe of Asher also failed to drive out the residents of Acco, Sidon, Ahlab, Aczib,
Helbah, Aphik, and Rehob. 32In fact, because they did not drive them out, the Canaanites
dominated the land where the people of Asher lived.
33The tribe of Naphtali also failed to drive out the residents of Beth-shemesh and
Beth-anath. Instead, the Canaanites dominated the land where they lived. Nevertheless,
the people of Beth-shemesh and Beth-anath were sometimes forced to work as slaves for
the people of Naphtali.
34As for the tribe of Dan, the Amorites forced them into the hill country and would
not let them come down into the plains. 35The Amorites were determined to stay in
Mount Heres, Aijalon, and Shaalbim, but when the descendants of Joseph became
stronger, they forced the Amorites to work as slaves. 36The boundary of the Amorites
ran from Scorpion Pass* to Sela and continued upward from there.

The LORD's Messenger Comes to Bokim

2 The angel of the LORD went up from Gilgal to Bokim with a message for the Israelites.
He told them, "I brought you out of Egypt into this land that I swore to give your
ancestors, and I said I would never break my covenant with you. 2For your part, you were

1:19 Josh 17:16; Judg 4:3
1:20 Josh 14:6-9; 15:14
1:21 Josh 15:63
1:22 Gen 28:19; Josh 14:3-4
1:24 Josh 2:12
1:25 Josh 6:25
1:27 Josh 17:11-13
1:29 Josh 16:10
1:34 Judg 18:1
1:36 Josh 15:3
2:1 Gen 17:7; Exod 20:2; Judg 6:11

1:27 Hebrew *Beth-shean,* a variant name for Beth-shan. **1:36** Hebrew *Akrabbim.*

1:19 Canaanite chariots pulled by horses were among the most sophisticated weapons of the day. Israelite foot soldiers were absolutely powerless when a speeding iron chariot bore down upon them. This is why Israel preferred to fight in the hills where chariots couldn't venture.

1:21ff Tribe after tribe failed to drive the evil Canaanites from their land. Why didn't they follow through and completely obey God's commands? (1) They had been fighting for a long time and were tired. Although the goal was in sight, they lacked the discipline and energy to reach it. (2) They were afraid the enemy was too strong—the iron chariots seemed invincible. (3) Since Joshua's death, power and authority had been decentralized to the tribal leaders, and the tribes were no longer unified in purpose. (4) Spiritual decay had infected them from within. They thought they could handle the temptation and be more prosperous by doing business with the Canaanites.

We, too, often fail to drive sin from our lives. Often we know what to do but just don't follow through. This results in a gradual deterioration of our relationship with God. In our battles, we may grow tired and want rest, but we need more than a break from our work. We need to know that God loves us and has given us a purpose for life. Victory comes from living according to his purpose.

2:1-3 This event marks a significant change in Israel's relationship with God. At Mount Sinai, God made a sacred and binding agreement with the Israelites called a covenant (Exodus 19:5-8). God's part was to make Israel a special nation (see the note on Genesis 12:1-3), to protect them, and to give them unique blessings for following him. Israel's part was to love God and obey his laws. But because they rejected and disobeyed God, the agreement to protect them was no longer in effect. But God wasn't going to abandon his people. They would receive wonderful blessings if they asked God to forgive them and sincerely followed him again.

2:2 Exod 23:32; 34:12-13 not to make any covenants with the people living in this land; instead, you were to destroy
their altars. Why, then, have you disobeyed my command? 3Since you have done this, I will
2:3 Num 33:55 no longer drive out the people living in your land. They will be thorns in your sides, and
their gods will be a constant temptation to you." 4When the angel of the LORD finished
2:5 Josh 7:26 speaking, the Israelites wept loudly. 5So they called the place "Weeping,"* and they offered
sacrifices to the LORD.

2. Disobedience and defeat

The Death of Joshua

2:6 Josh 24:28-31 6After Joshua sent the people away, each of the tribes left to take possession of the land
allotted to them. 7And the Israelites served the LORD throughout the lifetime of Joshua
and the leaders who outlived him—those who had seen all the great things the LORD had
done for Israel.
8Then Joshua son of Nun, the servant of the LORD, died at the age of 110. 9They buried
him in the land he had inherited, at Timnath-serah* in the hill country of Ephraim, north
of Mount Gaash.

Israel Disobeys God

2:10 Exod 5:2; 1 Sam 2:12 10After that generation died, another generation grew up who did not acknowledge the

2:5 Hebrew *Bokim.* **2:9** Hebrew *Timnath-heres,* a variant name for Timnath-serah.

WHY DID ISRAEL WANT TO WORSHIP IDOLS?

Worshiping God	*Worshiping idols*
long-range benefits	short-range benefits
gratification postponed	self-gratification immediate
morality required	sensuality approved
high ethical standards demanded	low ethical standards tolerated
neighbors' sins disapproved	neighbors' sins approved
unseen God worshiped	visible idols worshiped
unselfishness expected	selfishness condoned
business relations hindered	business relations improved
strict religious practices maintained	religious practices loosely regulated
changed life demanded	changed life not demanded
ethical stand expected	compromise and cooperation practiced
concern for others taught	no concern for others expected

The temptation to follow false gods because of short-term benefits, good feelings, easy "rules," or convenience was always present. *But the benefits were deceptive because the gods were false.* We worship God because he is the one and only true God.

Although God's agreement to help Israel conquer the land was no longer in effect, his promise to make Israel a nation through whom the whole world would be blessed (fulfilled in the Messiah's coming) remained valid. God still wanted the Israelites to be a holy people (just as he wants us to be holy), and he often used oppression to bring them back to him, just as he warned he would (Leviticus 26; Deuteronomy 28). The book of Judges records a number of instances where God allowed his people to be oppressed so that they would repent of their sins and return to him.

Too often people want God to fulfill his promises while excusing themselves from their responsibilities. Before you claim God's promises, ask, Have I done my part?

2:4 The people of Israel knew they had sinned, and they wept aloud, responding with deep sorrow. Because we have a tendency to sin, repentance is the true measure of spiritual sensitivity. Repentance means asking God to forgive us, and then abandoning our sinful ways. But we cannot do this sincerely unless we are truly sorry for our sinful actions. When we are aware that we have done wrong, we should admit it plainly to God rather than try to cover it up or hope we can get away with it.

2:7-9 The account of Joshua's death is found here and at the end of the book of Joshua (24:29). Either this account is a summary of what happened earlier, or the account in the book of Joshua omitted the events in the first chapter of Judges. (For more on Joshua, see his Profile in Joshua 3.)

2:10ff One generation died, and the next did not follow God. Judges 2:10–3:7 is a brief preview of the cycle of sin, judgment, and repentance that Israel experienced again and again. Each generation failed to teach the next generation to love and follow God. Yet this was at the very center of God's law (Deuteronomy 6:4-9). It is tempting to leave the job of teaching the Christian faith to the church or Christian school. Yet God says that the responsibility for this task belongs primarily to the family. Because children learn so much by our example, faith must be a family matter.

LORD or remember the mighty things he had done for Israel. 11 Then the Israelites did
what was evil in the LORD's sight and worshiped the images of Baal. 12 They abandoned
the LORD, the God of their ancestors, who had brought them out of Egypt. They chased
after other gods, worshiping the gods of the people around them. And they angered the
LORD. 13 They abandoned the LORD to serve Baal and the images of Ashtoreth. 14 This
made the LORD burn with anger against Israel, so he handed them over to marauders who
stole their possessions. He sold them to their enemies all around, and they were no longer
able to resist them. 15 Every time Israel went out to battle, the LORD fought against them,
bringing them defeat, just as he promised. And the people were very distressed.

God Rescues His People

16 Then the LORD raised up judges to rescue the Israelites from their enemies. 17 Yet
Israel did not listen to the judges but prostituted themselves to other gods, bowing
down to them. How quickly they turned away from the path of their ancestors, who
had walked in obedience to the LORD's commands. 18 Whenever the LORD placed a
judge over Israel, he was with that judge and rescued the people from their enemies
throughout the judge's lifetime. For the LORD took pity on his people, who were
burdened by oppression and suffering. 19 But when the judge died, the people returned
to their corrupt ways, behaving worse than those who had lived before them. They
followed other gods, worshiping and bowing down to them. And they refused to give
up their evil practices and stubborn ways.

20 So the LORD burned with anger against Israel. He said, "Because these people have
violated the covenant I made with their ancestors and have ignored my commands, 21 I will
no longer drive out the nations that Joshua left unconquered when he died. 22 I did this to
test Israel—to see whether or not they would obey the LORD as their ancestors did." 23 That
is why the LORD did not quickly drive the nations out or allow Joshua to conquer them all.

The Nations Left in Canaan

3 The LORD left certain nations in the land to test those Israelites who had not
participated in the wars of Canaan. 2 He did this to teach warfare to generations
of Israelites who had no experience in battle. 3 These were the nations: the Philistines

2:11 Judg 4:1; 6:1; 8:33; 10:6
2:12 Deut 31:16; 32:12 Judg 10:6 Ps 106:40
2:13 Judg 10:6
2:16 Ps 106:43-45
2:17 Ps 81:11-12
2:19 Judg 4:1; 8:33
2:21 Josh 23:13
3:1 Judg 1:1; 2:21-22
3:3 Josh 13:3

2:11-15 Baal was the god of storms and rains; therefore, he was thought to control vegetation and agriculture. Ashtoreth was the mother goddess of love, war, and fertility (she was also called Astarte or Ishtar). Temple prostitution and child sacrifice were a part of the worship of these Canaanite idols. This generation of Israelites abandoned the faith of their parents and began worshiping the gods of their neighbors. Many things can tempt us to abandon what we know is right. The desire to be accepted by our neighbors can lead us into behavior that is unacceptable to God. Don't be pressured into disobedience.

2:12-15 God often saved his harshest criticism and punishment for those who worshiped idols. Why were idols so bad in God's sight? To worship an idol violated the first two of the Ten Commandments (Exodus 20:3-6). The Canaanites had gods for almost every season, activity, or place. To them, the Lord was just another god to add to their collection of gods. Israel, by contrast, was to worship only the Lord. They could not possibly believe that God was the one true God and at the same time bow to an idol. Idol worshipers could not see their god as their creator because they created him. These idols represent sensual, carnal, and immoral aspects of human nature. God's nature is spiritual and moral. Adding the worship of idols to the worship of God could not be tolerated.

2:15, 16 Despite Israel's disobedience, God showed his great mercy by raising up judges to save the people from their oppressors. Mercy has been defined as "not giving a person what he or she deserves." This is exactly what God did for Israel and what he does for us. Our disobedience demands judgment! But God shows mercy toward us by providing an escape from sin's penalty through Jesus Christ, who alone saves us from sin. When we pray for forgiveness, we are asking for what we do not deserve. Yet when we take this step and trust in Christ's saving work on our behalf, we can experience God's forgiveness.

2:16-19 Throughout this period of history Israel went through seven cycles of (1) rebelling against God, (2) being overrun by enemy nations, (3) being delivered by a God-fearing judge, (4) remaining loyal to God under that judge, and (5) again forgetting God when the judge died. We tend to follow the same cycle—remaining loyal to God as long as we are near those who are devoted to him. But when we are on our own, the pressure to be drawn away from God increases. Determine to be faithful to God despite the difficult situations you encounter.

2:17 Why would the people of Israel turn away so quickly from their faith in God? Simply put, the Canaanite religion appeared more attractive to the sensual nature and offered more short-range benefits (sexual permissiveness and increased fertility in childbearing and farming). One of its most attractive features was that people could remain selfish and yet fulfill their religious requirements. They could do almost anything they wished and still be obeying at least one of the many Canaanite gods. Male and female prostitution was not only allowed but was encouraged as a form of worship.

Faith in the one true God, however, does not offer short-range benefits that appeal to our sinful human nature. The essence of sin is selfishness; the essence of God's way of life is selflessness. We must seek Christ's help to live God's way.

3:1-4 We learn from chapter 1 that these enemy nations were still in the land because the Israelites had failed to obey God and drive them out. Now God would allow the enemies to remain in order to "test" the Israelites; that is, to give them an opportunity to exercise faith and obedience. By now the

(those living under the five Philistine rulers), all the Canaanites, the Sidonians, and
the Hivites living in the hill country of Lebanon from Mount Baal-hermon to Lebo-
hamath. 4 These people were left to test the Israelites—to see whether they would obey
the commands the LORD had given to their ancestors through Moses.
5 So Israel lived among the Canaanites, Hittites, Amorites, Perizzites, Hivites, and
Jebusites, 6 and they intermarried with them. Israelite sons married their daughters, and
Israelite daughters were given in marriage to their sons. And the Israelites worshiped
their gods.

3:4 Deut 8:2; Judg 2:22
3:5 Ps 106:35
3:6 Exod 34:16; Deut 7:3-4

B. THE RESCUE OF ISRAEL BY THE JUDGES (3:7—16:31)

The Israelites began a series of cycles of sinning, worshiping idols, being punished, crying out for help, being rescued by a judge sent from God, obeying God for a while, then falling back into idolatry. They were conquered by Syria, Moab, Canaan, Midian, Ammon, and Philistia. They even faced the threat of civil war. Just as God sent help to the people when they cried out to him, he will deliver us when we call on him.

At first glance, Ehud's career as a judge in Israel may not seem relevant to us. He clearly lived in another time. He took radical and violent action to free his people. His murder of Eglon shocks us. His war on Moab was swift and deadly. His life is difficult to relate to. But our commitment to God's Word challenges us not to ignore this leader. As we read about his life, some questions come to mind: (1) When was the last time God showed me something wrong in my life and I took immediate and painful action to correct the error? (2) When was the last time I asked God to show me how he could use something unique about me (as he used Ehud's left-handedness)? (3) When was the last time I made a plan to obey God in some specific area of my life and then followed through on that plan? (4) When was the last time my life was an example to others of obedience to God?

The enemies we face are as real as Ehud's, but they are most often within ourselves. The battles we fight are not against other people but against the power of sin. We need God's help in doing battle against sin. We also need to remember that he has already won the war. He has defeated sin at the cross of his Son, Jesus. His help is the cause of each success, and his forgiveness is sufficient for each failure.

Strengths and accomplishments
- Second judge of Israel
- A man of direct action, a frontline leader
- Used a perceived weakness (left-handedness) to do a great work for God
- Led the revolt against Moabite domination and gave Israel 80 years of peace

Lessons from his life
- Some conditions call for radical action
- God responds to the cry of repentance
- God is ready to use our unique qualities to accomplish his work

Vital statistics
- Where: Born during the last years of the wilderness wanderings or during Israel's early years in the Promised Land
- Occupations: Messenger, judge
- Relative: Father: Gera
- Contemporary: Eglon of Moab

Key verse
"But when Israel cried out to the LORD for help, the LORD raised up a man to rescue them. His name was Ehud son of Gera, of the tribe of Benjamin, who was left-handed" (Judges 3:15).

His story is told in Judges 3:12–30.

younger generation that had not fought in the great battles of conquest was coming of age. It was their job to complete the conquest of the land. There were many obstacles yet to be overcome in their new homeland. How they would handle these obstacles would be a test of their faith.

Perhaps God has left obstacles in your life—hostile people, difficult situations, baffling problems—to allow you to develop faith and obedience.

3:5-7 The Israelites discovered that relationships affect faith. The men and women of the surrounding nations were attractive to the Israelites. Soon they intermarried, and the Israelites accepted their pagan gods. This was clearly prohibited by God (Exodus 34:15-17; Deuteronomy 7:1-4). By accepting these gods into their homes, the Israelites gradually began to accept the immoral practices associated with them. Most Israelites didn't start out determined to be idolaters; they just added the idols to the worship of God. But before long they found themselves absorbed in pagan worship.

A similar danger faces us. We want to befriend those who don't know God, but through those friendships we can become entangled in unhealthy practices. Friendships with unbelievers are important, but we must accept people without compromising or adopting their patterns of behavior.

1. First period: Othniel

Othniel Becomes Israel's Judge

7 The Israelites did what was evil in the LORD's sight. They forgot about the LORD their
God, and they worshiped the images of Baal and the Asherah poles. 8 Then the LORD 3:8 Judg 2:14
burned with anger against Israel, and he handed them over to King Cushan-rishathaim
of Aram-naharaim.* And the Israelites were subject to Cushan-rishathaim for eight
years. 3:9 Judg 1:13
9 But when Israel cried out to the LORD for help, the LORD raised up a man to rescue 3:10 Num 11:25-29; 24:2
them. His name was Othniel, the son of Caleb's younger brother, Kenaz. 10 The Spirit of Judg 6:34; 11:29
the LORD came upon him, and he became Israel's judge. He went to war against King 3:11
Cushan-rishathaim of Aram, and the LORD gave Othniel victory over him. 11 So there was Judg 5:31; 8:28
peace in the land for forty years. Then Othniel son of Kenaz died.

2. Second period: Ehud and Shamgar

Ehud Becomes Israel's Judge

12 Once again the Israelites did what was evil in the LORD's sight, so the LORD gave King 3:12 Judg 2:11
Eglon of Moab control over Israel. 13 Together with the Ammonites and Amalekites, 3:13
Eglon attacked Israel and took possession of Jericho.* 14 And the Israelites were subject Judg 1:16
to Eglon of Moab for eighteen years. 3:15
15 But when Israel cried out to the LORD for help, the LORD raised up a man to rescue Judg 20:16
them. His name was Ehud son of Gera, of the tribe of Benjamin, who was left-handed. 1 Chr 12:2
The Israelites sent Ehud to deliver their tax money to King Eglon of Moab. 16 So Ehud
made himself a double-edged dagger that was eighteen inches* long, and he strapped it
to his right thigh, keeping it hidden under his clothing. 17 He brought the tax money to
Eglon, who was very fat. 18 After delivering the payment, Ehud sent home those who had
carried the tax money.
19 But when Ehud reached the stone carvings near Gilgal, he turned back. He came
to Eglon and said, "I have a secret message for you." So the king commanded his

3:8 *Aram-naharaim* means "Aram of the two rivers," thought to have been located between the Euphrates and Balih Rivers in northwestern Mesopotamia. **3:13** Hebrew *the city of palms.* **3:16** Hebrew *1 cubit* [45 centimeters].

3:7 Baal was the most worshiped god of the Canaanites. Most often cast in the form of a bull, he symbolized strength and fertility and was considered the god of agriculture. Asherah was Baal's female consort, mother goddess of the sea, who was worshiped by means of wooden pillars that substituted for sacred trees. In times of famine, the Canaanites believed Baal was angry with them and was withholding rain as punishment. Archaeologists have uncovered many Baal idols in Israel. It is difficult to imagine the people of Israel trading worship of the Lord for worship of idols of wood, stone, and iron, but we do the same when we forsake worshiping God for other activities, hobbies, or priorities. Our idols are not made of wood or stone, but they are every bit as sinful.

3:9 Othniel was Israel's first judge. In 1:13 we read that he volunteered to lead an attack against a fortified city. Here he was to lead the nation back to God. Othniel had a rich spiritual heritage—his uncle was Caleb, a man with unwavering faith in God (Numbers 13:30; 14:24). Othniel's leadership brought the people back to God and freed them from oppression. But after Othniel's death, it didn't take the Israelites long to fall back into their neighbors' comfortable but sinful ways.

3:10 This phrase, "The Spirit of the LORD came upon him," was also spoken of the judges Gideon, Jephthah, and Samson, among others. It expresses a temporary and spontaneous increase of physical, spiritual, or mental strength. This was an extraordinary and supernatural occurrence to prepare a person for a special task. The Holy Spirit is available to all believers today, but he will come upon believers in an extraordinary way for special tasks. We should ask the Holy Spirit's help as we face our daily problems as well as life's major challenges.

3:12, 13 The Moabites, Ammonites, and Amalekites were nomadic tribes that lived near each other east and southeast of Canaan. These tribes were notorious raiders, possessing great military skill. This was the first time nations outside Canaan attacked the Israelites in their own land.

3:15-30 This is a strange story, but it teaches us that God can use us just the way he made us. Being left-handed in Ehud's day was considered a handicap. Many Benjaminites were left-handed (see 20:16). But God used Ehud's perceived weakness to give Israel victory. Let God use you the way you are to accomplish his work.

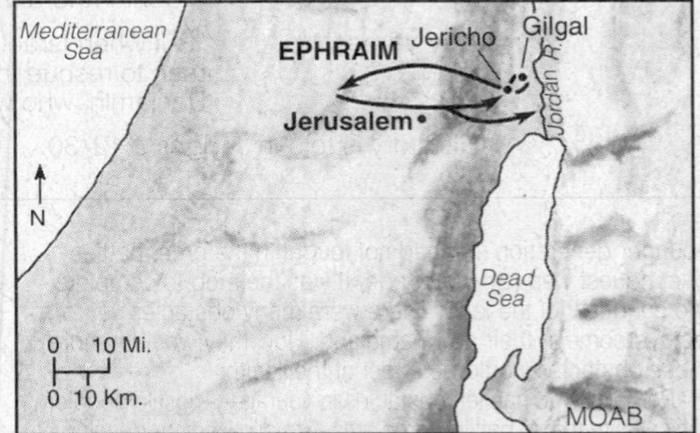

EHUD FREES ISRAEL FROM MOAB When King Eglon of Moab conquered part of Israel, he set up his throne in the city of Jericho. Ehud was chosen to take Israel's tribute there. After delivering Israel's tribute, Ehud killed King Eglon and escaped into the hill country of Ephraim. From there he gathered together an army to cut off any Moabites trying to escape across the Jordan River.

servants to be silent and sent them all out of the room. 20 Ehud walked over to Eglon
as he was sitting alone in a cool upstairs room and said, "I have a message for you
from God!" As King Eglon rose from his seat, 21 Ehud reached with his left hand,
pulled out the dagger strapped to his right thigh, and plunged it into the king's belly.
22 The dagger went so deep that the handle disappeared beneath the king's fat. So
Ehud left the dagger in, and the king's bowels emptied. 23 Then Ehud closed and
locked the doors and climbed down the latrine and escaped through the sewage
access.
3:24 24 After Ehud was gone, the king's servants returned and found the doors to the upstairs
1 Sam 24:3 room locked. They thought he might be using the latrine, 25 so they waited. But when the
king didn't come out after a long delay, they became concerned and got a key. And when
they opened the door, they found their master dead on the floor.
26 While the servants were waiting, Ehud escaped, passing the idols on his way to
Seirah. 27 When he arrived in the hill country of Ephraim, Ehud sounded a call to arms.
3:28 Judg 7:24; 12:5 Then he led a band of Israelites down from the hills. 28 "Follow me," he said, "for the
LORD has given you victory over Moab your enemy." So they followed him. And the
Israelites took control of the shallows of the Jordan River across from Moab, preventing
anyone from crossing. 29 They attacked the Moabites and killed about ten thousand of
their strongest and bravest warriors. Not one of them escaped. 30 So Moab was conquered
by Israel that day, and the land was at peace for eighty years.

Shamgar Becomes Israel's Judge

3:31 31 After Ehud, Shamgar son of Anath rescued Israel. He killed six hundred Philistines
Judg 5:6 with an ox goad.

3. Third period: Deborah and Barak

4:1 *Deborah Becomes Israel's Judge*
Judg 2:19 **4** After Ehud's death, the Israelites again did what was evil in the LORD's sight. 2 So
4:2 Josh 11:1 the LORD handed them over to King Jabin of Hazor, a Canaanite king. The com-
Ps 83:9 mander of his army was Sisera, who lived in Harosheth-haggoyim. 3 Sisera, who had nine

THE JUDGES' FUNCTIONS

Judges of Israel could be

saviors (deliverers) and redeemers (Gideon)	*or* mediators and administrators (Tola)
providers of rest and peace (Ehud and Jair)	*or* rude, petty dictators (Jephthah)
famous and powerful (Samson)	*or* hardworking yet unsung (Elon and Abdon)
leaders of the nation (Othniel and Deborah)	*or* local heroes (Shamgar and Ibzan)

Regardless of an individual judge's leadership style, each one demonstrated that God's judgment follows apostasy, while repentance brings restoration.

3:31 To kill 600 Philistines with an ox goad was quite a feat. An ox goad was a long stick with a small flat piece of iron on one side and a sharp point on the other. The sharp side was used to drive the oxen during the times of plowing, and the flat end was used to clean the mud off the plow. Eight-foot-long ancient ox goads have been found. In times of crisis they could easily have been used as spears, as in Shamgar's case. Ox goads are still used in the Middle East to drive oxen.

4:1 Israel sinned "in the LORD's sight." Our sins harm both ourselves and others, but all sin is ultimately against God because it disregards his commands and his authority over us. When confessing his sin, David prayed, "Against you, and you alone, have I sinned; I have done what is evil in your sight" (Psalm 51:4). Recognizing the seriousness of sin is the first step toward removing it from our lives.

4:2, 3 Nothing more is known about Jabin. Joshua had defeated a king by that name years earlier and burned the city of Hazor to the ground (Joshua 11:1-11). Either the city was rebuilt by this time, or Jabin was hoping to rebuild it.

This is the only time during the period of the judges when the Israelites' enemies came from within their land. The Israelites had failed to drive out all the Canaanites. These Canaanites had regrouped and were attempting to restore their lost power. If the Israelites had obeyed God in the first place and had driven the Canaanites from the land, this incident would not have happened.

4:2, 3 Chariots were the tanks of the ancient world. Made of iron or wood, they were pulled by one or two horses and were the most feared and powerful weapons of the day. Some chariots even had razor-sharp knives extending from the wheels designed to mutilate helpless foot soldiers. The Canaanite army had 900 iron chariots. Israel was not powerful enough to defeat such an invincible army. Therefore, Jabin and Sisera had no trouble oppressing the people—until a faithful woman named Deborah called upon God.

hundred iron chariots, ruthlessly oppressed the Israelites for twenty years. Then the
Israelites cried out to the LORD for help.
[4]Deborah, the wife of Lappidoth, was a prophet who had become a judge in Israel.
[5]She would hold court under the Palm of Deborah, which stood between Ramah and
Bethel in the hill country of Ephraim, and the Israelites came to her to settle their
disputes. [6]One day she sent for Barak son of Abinoam, who lived in Kedesh in the land **4:6** 1 Sam 12:11
of Naphtali. She said to him, "This is what the LORD, the God of Israel, commands you: Heb 11:32
Assemble ten thousand warriors from the tribes of Naphtali and Zebulun at Mount Tabor.
[7]I will lure Sisera, commander of Jabin's army, along with his chariots and warriors, to **4:7** Ps 83:9
the Kishon River. There I will give you victory over him."
[8]Barak told her, "I will go, but only if you go with me!"
[9]"Very well," she replied, "I will go with you. But since you have made this choice,
you will receive no honor. For the LORD's victory over Sisera will be at the hands of a
woman." So Deborah went with Barak to Kedesh. [10]At Kedesh, Barak called together **4:10**
the tribes of Zebulun and Naphtali, and ten thousand warriors marched up with him. Judg 5:18
Deborah also marched with them.
[11]Now Heber the Kenite, a descendant of Moses' brother-in-law* Hobab, had moved **4:11**
away from the other members of his tribe and pitched his tent by the Oak of Zaanannim, Josh 19:33 Judg 1:16
near Kedesh.
[12]When Sisera was told that Barak son of Abinoam had gone up to Mount Tabor, [13]he
called for all nine hundred of his iron chariots and all of his warriors, and they marched
from Harosheth-haggoyim to the Kishon River.
[14]Then Deborah said to Barak, "Get ready! Today the LORD will give you victory over
Sisera, for the LORD is marching ahead of you." So Barak led his ten thousand warriors
down the slopes of Mount Tabor into battle. [15]When Barak attacked, the LORD threw **4:15**
Sisera and all his charioteers and warriors into a panic. Then Sisera leaped down from Josh 10:10 Judg 7:21
his chariot and escaped on foot. [16]Barak chased the enemy and their chariots all the way **4:16**
to Harosheth-haggoyim, killing all of Sisera's warriors. Not a single one was left alive. Exod 14:28 Ps 83:9
[17]Meanwhile, Sisera ran to the tent of Jael, the wife of Heber the Kenite, because

4:11 Or *father-in-law.*

KING JABIN IS DEFEATED
Deborah traveled from her home between Ramah and Bethel to march with Barak and the Israelite army against Hazor. Sisera, commander of Hazor's army, assembled his men at Harosheth-haggoyim. In spite of Sisera's 900 chariots and expertly trained army, Israel was victorious.

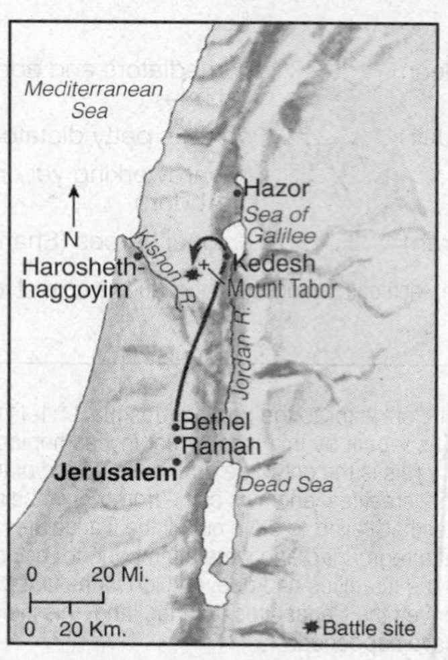

4:3 After 20 years of unbearable circumstances, the Israelites finally cried to the Lord for help. But God should be the first place we turn when we are facing struggles or dilemmas. The Israelites chose to go their own way and got into a mess. We often do the same. Trying to control our own lives without God's help leads to struggle and confusion. By contrast, when we stay in daily contact with the Lord, we are less likely to create painful circumstances for ourselves. This is a lesson the Israelites never fully learned. When struggles come our way, God wants us to come to him first, seeking his strength and guidance.

4:4ff The Bible records several women who held national leadership positions, and Deborah was an exceptional woman. Obviously she was the best person for the job, and God chose her to lead Israel. God can choose anyone to lead his people, young or old, man or woman. Don't let your prejudices get in the way of those God may have chosen to lead you.

4:6-8 Was Barak cowardly or just in need of support? We don't know Barak's character, but we see the character of a great leader in Deborah, who took charge as God directed. Deborah told Barak that God would be with him in battle, but that was not enough for Barak. He wanted Deborah to go with him. Barak's request shows that at heart he trusted human strength more than God's promise. A person of real faith steps out at God's command, even if he or she must do so alone.

4:9 How did Deborah command such respect? She was responsible for leading the people into battle, but more than that, she influenced them to live for God after the battle was over. Her personality drew people together and commanded the respect of even Barak, a military general. She was also a prophet, whose main role was to encourage the people to obey God. Those who lead must not forget about the spiritual condition of those being led. A true leader is concerned for persons, not just success.

4:11 Heber was Jael's husband (4:17). He was from the Kenite tribe, a longtime ally of Israel. But for some reason, Heber decided to side with Jabin, maybe because Jabin's army appeared to have the military advantage. It was probably Heber who told Sisera that the Israelites were camped near Mount Tabor (4:12; see map). Although Heber threw in his lot with Jabin and his forces, his wife, Jael, did not (4:21).

Heber's family was on friendly terms with King Jabin of Hazor. 18 Jael went out to meet
Sisera and said to him, "Come into my tent, sir. Come in. Don't be afraid." So he went
into her tent, and she covered him with a blanket.
4:19 Judg 5:25 19 "Please give me some water," he said. "I'm thirsty." So she gave him some milk to
drink and covered him again.
20 "Stand at the door of the tent," he told her. "If anybody comes and asks you if there
is anyone here, say no."
21 But when Sisera fell asleep from exhaustion, Jael quietly crept up to him with a
hammer and tent peg. Then she drove the tent peg through his temple and into the ground,
and so he died.
22 When Barak came looking for Sisera, Jael went out to meet him. She said, "Come,
and I will show you the man you are looking for." So he followed her into the tent and
found Sisera lying there dead, with the tent peg through his temple.
23 So on that day Israel saw God subdue Jabin, the Canaanite king. 24 And from that time
on Israel became stronger and stronger against King Jabin, until they finally destroyed him.

The Song of Deborah

5:1 Exod 15:1 **5** On that day Deborah and Barak son of Abinoam sang this song:

5:2 Ps 110:3 2 "When Israel's leaders take charge,
and the people gladly follow—
bless the LORD!

DEBORAH

Wise leaders are rare. They accomplish great amounts of work without direct involvement because they know how to work through other people. They are able to see the big picture that often escapes those directly involved, so they make good mediators, advisers, and planners. Deborah fit this description perfectly. She had all these leadership skills, and she had a remarkable relationship with God. The insight and confidence God gave this woman placed her in a unique position in the Old Testament. Deborah is among the outstanding women of history.

Her story shows that she was not power hungry. She wanted to serve God. Whenever praise came her way, she gave God the credit. She didn't deny or resist her position in the culture as a woman and wife, but she never allowed herself to be hindered by it either. Her story shows that God can accomplish great things through people who are willing to be led by him.

Deborah's life challenges us in several ways. She reminds us of the need to be available both to God and to others. She encourages us to spend our efforts on what we can do rather than on worrying about what we can't do. Deborah challenges us to be wise leaders. She demonstrates what a person can accomplish when God is in control.

Strengths and accomplishments
- Fourth and only female judge of Israel
- Special abilities as a mediator, adviser, and counselor
- When called on to lead, was able to plan, direct, and delegate
- Known for her prophetic power
- A writer of songs

Lessons from her life
- God chooses leaders by his standards, not ours
- Wise leaders choose good helpers

Vital statistics
- Where: Canaan
- Occupations: Prophet and judge
- Relative: Husband: Lappidoth
- Contemporaries: Barak, Jael, Jabin of Hazor, Sisera

Key verse
"Deborah, the wife of Lappidoth, was a prophet who had become a judge in Israel" (Judges 4:4).

Her story is told in Judges 4—5.

4:18-21 Sisera couldn't have been more pleased when Jael offered him her tent as a hiding place. First, because Jael was the wife of Heber, a man loyal to Sisera's forces (see the note on 4:11), he thought she certainly could be trusted. Second, because men were never allowed to enter a woman's tent, no one would think to look for Sisera there.

Even though her husband, Heber, was loyal to Sisera's forces, Jael certainly was not. Because women of that day were in charge of pitching the tents, Jael had no problem driving the tent peg into Sisera's head while he slept. Deborah's prediction was thus fulfilled: the honor of conquering Sisera went to a brave and resourceful woman (4:9).

5:1ff Music and singing were a cherished part of Israel's culture. Chapter 5 is a song, sung and possibly composed by Deborah and Barak. It sets to music the story of Israel's great victory recounted in chapter 4. This victory song was accompanied by joyous celebration. It proclaimed God's greatness by giving him credit for the victory. It was an excellent way to preserve and retell this wonderful story from generation to generation. (Other songs in the Bible are listed in the chart in Exodus 15.)

3 "Listen, you kings!
Pay attention, you mighty rulers!
For I will sing to the LORD.
I will lift up my song to the LORD, the God of Israel.

4 "LORD, when you set out from Seir
and marched across the fields of Edom,
the earth trembled
and the cloudy skies poured down rain.
5 The mountains quaked at the coming of the LORD.
Even Mount Sinai shook in the presence of the LORD, the God of Israel.

6 "In the days of Shamgar son of Anath, and in the days of Jael,
people avoided the main roads,
and travelers stayed on crooked side paths.
7 There were few people left in the villages of Israel—
until Deborah arose as a mother for Israel.
8 When Israel chose new gods,
war erupted at the city gates.
Yet not a shield or spear could be seen
among forty thousand warriors in Israel!
9 My heart goes out to Israel's leaders,
and to those who gladly followed.
Bless the LORD!

10 "You who ride on fine donkeys
and sit on fancy saddle blankets, listen!
And you who must walk along the road, listen!
11 Listen to the village musicians* gathered at the watering holes.
They recount the righteous victories of the LORD,
and the victories of his villagers in Israel.
Then the people of the LORD
marched down to the city gates.

12 "Wake up, Deborah, wake up!
Wake up, wake up, and sing a song!
Arise, Barak!
Lead your captives away, son of Abinoam!

13 "Down from Tabor marched the remnant against the mighty.
The people of the LORD marched down against mighty warriors.
14 They came down from Ephraim—a land that once belonged to the Amalekites,
and Benjamin also followed you.
From Makir the commanders marched down;
from Zebulun came those who carry the rod of authority.
15 The princes of Issachar were with Deborah and Barak.
They followed Barak, rushing into the valley.
But in the tribe of Reuben
there was great indecision.

5:4 Deut 33:2; Hab 3:6
5:5 Exod 19:18; Pss 97:5; 114:4; Isa 64:3
5:6 Judg 3:31; 4:17
5:8 Deut 32:17
5:10 Judg 10:4; 12:14
5:11 Gen 24:11; 1 Sam 12:7

5:11 The meaning of the Hebrew is uncertain.

5:1ff In victory, Barak and Deborah sang praises to God. Songs of praise focus our attention on God, give us an outlet for spiritual celebration, and remind us of God's faithfulness and character. Whether you are experiencing a great victory or a major dilemma, singing praises to God can have a positive effect on your attitude.

5:8 War was the inevitable result when Israel chose to follow false gods. Although God had given Israel clear directions, the people failed to put his words into practice. Without God at the center of their national life, pressure from the outside soon became greater than power from within, and they were an easy prey for their enemies. If you are letting a desire for recognition, craving for power, or love of money rule your life, you may find yourself besieged by enemies—stress, anxiety, illness, fatigue. Keep God at the center of your life, and you will have the power you need to fight these destroyers.

5:15-17 Four tribes—Reuben, Gilead (either Gad or Manasseh), Dan, and Asher—were accused of not lending a helping

5:16 Num 32:1-2, 24
16 Why did you sit at home among the sheepfolds—
to hear the shepherds whistle for their flocks?
In the tribe of Reuben
there was great indecision.
5:17 Josh 13:24-28
17 Gilead remained east of the Jordan.
And Dan, why did he stay home?
Asher sat unmoved at the seashore,
remaining in his harbors.
18 But Zebulun risked his life,
as did Naphtali, on the battlefield.

5:19 Josh 11:1-5 Judg 1:27
19 "The kings of Canaan fought at Taanach near Megiddo's springs,
but they carried off no treasures of battle.
20 The stars fought from heaven.
The stars in their orbits fought against Sisera.
5:21 Judg 4:7
21 The Kishon River swept them away—
that ancient river, the Kishon.
March on, my soul, with courage!
5:22 Job 39:19-25
22 Then the horses' hooves hammered the ground,
the galloping, galloping of Sisera's mighty steeds.
23 'Let the people of Meroz be cursed,' said the angel of the LORD.
'Let them be utterly cursed
because they did not come to help the LORD,
to help the LORD against the mighty warriors.'

5:24-25 Judg 4:17-19
24 "Most blessed is Jael,
the wife of Heber the Kenite.
May she be blessed above all women who live in tents.
25 Sisera asked for water,
and Jael gave him milk.
In a bowl fit for kings,
she brought him yogurt.
5:26-27 Judg 4:21-22
26 Then with her left hand she reached for a tent peg,
and with her right hand she reached for the workman's hammer.
She hit Sisera, crushing his head.
She pounded the tent peg through his head, piercing his temples.
27 He sank, he fell,
he lay dead at her feet.

28 "From the window Sisera's mother looked out.
Through the window she watched for his return, saying,
'Why is his chariot so long in coming?
Why don't we hear the sound of chariot wheels?'
29 A reply comes from her wise women,
and she repeats these words to herself:
5:30 Exod 15:9
30 'They are dividing the captured goods they found—
a woman or two for every man.
There are gorgeous robes for Sisera,
and colorful, beautifully embroidered robes for me.'

5:31 Pss 68:1-2; 92:9
31 "LORD, may all your enemies die as Sisera did!
But may those who love you rise like the sun at full strength!"

Then there was peace in the land for forty years.

---

hand in the battle. No reasons are given for their refusal to help their fellow Israelites, but they may be the same ones that stopped them from driving out the Canaanites in the first place: (1) lack of faith in God to help, (2) lack of effort, (3) fear of the enemy, and (4) fear of antagonizing those with whom they did business and thus from whom they prospered. This disobedience showed a lack of enthusiasm for God's plan.

4. Fourth period: Gideon, Tola, and Jair

Gideon Becomes Israel's Judge

6 Again the Israelites did what was evil in the LORD's sight. So the LORD handed them
over to the Midianites for seven years. 2 The Midianites were so cruel that the
Israelites fled to the mountains, where they made hiding places for themselves in caves
and dens. 3 Whenever the Israelites planted their crops, marauders from Midian, Amalek,
and the people of the east would attack Israel, 4 camping in the land and destroying crops
as far away as Gaza. They left the Israelites with nothing to eat, taking all the sheep, oxen,
and donkeys. 5 These enemy hordes, coming with their cattle and tents as thick as locusts,
arrived on droves of camels too numerous to count. And they stayed until the land was
stripped bare. 6 So Israel was reduced to starvation by the Midianites. Then the Israelites
cried out to the LORD for help.
7 When they cried out to the LORD because of Midian, 8 the LORD sent a prophet to the
Israelites. He said, "This is what the LORD, the God of Israel, says: I brought you up out
of slavery in Egypt 9 and rescued you from the Egyptians and from all who oppressed
you. I drove out your enemies and gave you their land. 10 I told you, 'I am the LORD your
God. You must not worship the gods of the Amorites, in whose land you now live.' But
you have not listened to me."
11 Then the angel of the LORD came and sat beneath the oak tree at Ophrah, which
belonged to Joash of the clan of Abiezer. Gideon son of Joash had been threshing wheat
at the bottom of a winepress to hide the grain from the Midianites. 12 The angel of the
LORD appeared to him and said, "Mighty hero, the LORD is with you!"
13 "Sir," Gideon replied, "if the LORD is with us, why has all this happened to us? And
where are all the miracles our ancestors told us about? Didn't they say, 'The LORD
brought us up out of Egypt'? But now the LORD has abandoned us and handed us over
to the Midianites."
14 Then the LORD turned to him and said, "Go with the strength you have and rescue
Israel from the Midianites. I am sending you!"
15 "But Lord," Gideon replied, "how can I rescue Israel? My clan is the weakest in the
whole tribe of Manasseh, and I am the least in my entire family!"
16 The LORD said to him, "I will be with you. And you will destroy the Midianites as
if you were fighting against one man."

6:1 Num 22:4; 25:15-18; 31:1-3 Judg 2:11
6:3 Isa 11:14
6:5 Judg 7:12
6:6 Deut 28:43
6:8 Exod 18:9 Judg 2:1-2
6:10 Josh 24:15
6:11 Judg 13:3 Heb 11:32
6:13 Deut 31:17 Ps 44:1
6:15 Exod 3:11

6:2 The Midianites were desert people descended from Abraham's second wife, Keturah (Genesis 25:1, 2). From this relationship came a nation that was always in conflict with Israel. Years earlier the Israelites, while still wandering in the wilderness, battled the Midianites and almost totally destroyed them (Numbers 31:1-20). Because of their failure to completely destroy them, however, the tribe repopulated. Here they were once again oppressing Israel.

6:6 Again the Israelites hit rock bottom before turning back to God. How much suffering they could have avoided if they had trusted him! Turning to God shouldn't be a last resort; we should look to him for help each day. This isn't to say life will always be easy. There will be struggles, but God will give us the strength to live through them. Don't wait until you're at the end of your rope. Call on God first in every situation.

6:11 The Old Testament records several appearances of the angel of the Lord: Genesis 16:7; 22:11; 31:11; Exodus 3:2; 14:19; Judges 2:1; 13:3; Zechariah 3:1-6. It is not known whether the same angel appeared in each case. The angel mentioned here appears to be separate from God in one place (6:12) and yet the same as God in another place (6:14). This has led some to believe that the angel was a special appearance of Jesus Christ prior to his mission on earth as recorded in the New Testament. It is also possible that as a special messenger from God, the angel had authority to speak for God. In either case, God sent a special messenger to deliver an important message to Gideon.

6:11 Threshing was the process of separating the grains of wheat from the useless outer shell called chaff. This was normally done in a large area, often on a hill, where the wind could blow away the lighter chaff when the farmer tossed the beaten wheat into the air. If Gideon had done this, however, he would have been an easy target for the bands of raiders who were overrunning the land. Therefore, he was forced to thresh his wheat in a winepress, a pit that was probably hidden from view and that would not be suspected as a place to find a farmer's crops.

6:13 Gideon questioned God about the problems he and his nation faced and about God's apparent lack of help. What he didn't acknowledge was the fact that the people had brought calamity upon themselves when they decided to disobey and neglect God. How easy it is to overlook personal accountability and blame our problems on God and others. Unfortunately, this does not solve our problems. It brings us no closer to God, and it escorts us to the very edge of rebellion and backsliding.

When problems come, the first place to look is within. Our first action should be confession to God of sins that may have created our problems.

6:14-16 "I will be with you," God told Gideon, and God promised to give him the strength he needed to overcome the opposition. In spite of this clear promise for strength, Gideon made excuses. Seeing only his limitations and weaknesses, he failed to see how God could work through him.

Like Gideon, we are called to serve God in specific ways. Although God promises us the tools and strength we need, we often make excuses. But reminding God of our limitations only implies that he does not know all about us or that he has made a mistake in evaluating our character. Don't spend time making excuses. Instead, spend it doing what God wants.

6:17 Isa 38:7 17 Gideon replied, "If you are truly going to help me, show me a sign to prove that it
is really the LORD speaking to me. 18 Don't go away until I come back and bring my
offering to you."

The LORD answered, "I will stay here until you return."
6:19 Gen 18:6-8 19 Gideon hurried home. He cooked a young goat, and with half a bushel* of flour he
baked some bread without yeast. Then, carrying the meat in a basket and the broth in a
pot, he brought them out and presented them to the angel, who was under the oak tree.

20 The angel of God said to him, "Place the meat and the unleavened bread on this
6:21 Lev 9:24 rock, and pour the broth over it." And Gideon did as he was told. 21 Then the angel of the
LORD touched the meat and bread with the staff in his hand, and fire flamed up from the
rock and consumed all he had brought. And the angel of the LORD disappeared.

6:22 Gen 13:21; 32:30 Exod 33:20 Judg 13:21-22 22 When Gideon realized that it was the angel of the LORD, he cried out, "Sovereign
LORD, I have seen the angel of the LORD face to face!"

23 "It is all right," the LORD replied. "Do not be afraid. You will not die." 24 And Gideon
built an altar to the LORD there and named it "The LORD Is Peace."* The altar remains
in Ophrah in the land of the clan of Abiezer to this day.

6:25 Exod 34:13 Deut 7:5 25 That night the LORD said to Gideon, "Take the second best bull from your father's
herd, the one that is seven years old. Pull down your father's altar to Baal, and cut down
the Asherah pole standing beside it. 26 Then build an altar to the LORD your God here on
this hill, laying the stones carefully. Sacrifice the bull as a burnt offering on the altar,

6:19 Hebrew *1 ephah* [18 liters]. **6:24** Hebrew *Yahweh Shalom.*

GOD USES COMMON PEOPLE

God uses all sorts of people to do his work—like you and me!

Person	*Known as*	*Task*	*Reference*
JACOB	A deceiver	To "father" the Israelite nation	Genesis 27
JOSEPH	A slave	To save his family	Genesis 39ff
MOSES	Shepherd in exile (and murderer)	To lead Israel out of bondage, to the Promised Land	Exodus 3
GIDEON	A farmer	To deliver Israel from Midian	Judges 6:11
JEPHTHAH	Son of a prostitute	To deliver Israel from the Ammonites	Judges 11:1
HANNAH	A homemaker	To be the mother of Samuel	1 Samuel 1
DAVID	A shepherd boy and last-born of the family	To be Israel's greatest king	1 Samuel 16
EZRA	A scribe	To lead the return to Judah and to write some of the Bible	Ezra, Nehemiah
ESTHER	A slave girl	To save her people from massacre	Esther
MARY	A peasant girl	To be the mother of Christ	Luke 1:27–38
MATTHEW	A tax collector	To be an apostle and Gospel writer	Matthew 9:9
LUKE	A Greek physician	To be a companion of Paul and a Gospel writer	Colossians 4:14
PETER	A fisherman	To be an apostle, a leader of the early church, and a writer of two New Testament letters	Matthew 4:18–20

6:22, 23 Why was Gideon afraid of seeing an angel? The Israelites believed that no one could see God and live (see God's words to Moses in Exodus 33:20). Evidently Gideon thought this also applied to angels.

6:25-30 After God called Gideon to be Israel's deliverer, he immediately asked him to tear down the altar of the pagan god Baal—an act that would test Gideon's faith and commitment. Canaanite religion was very political, so an attack on a god was often seen as an attack on the local government supporting that god. If caught, Gideon would face serious social problems and probable physical attack. (For more on Baal and Asherah, see the notes on 2:11-15 and 3:7.)

Gideon took a great risk by following God's higher law, which specifically forbids idol worship (Exodus 20:1-5). After learning what Gideon had done, the townspeople wanted to kill him. Many of those people were fellow Israelites. This shows how immoral God's people had become. God said in Deuteronomy 13:6-11 that idolaters must be stoned to death, but these Israelites wanted to stone Gideon for tearing down an idol and worshiping God! When you begin to accomplish something for God, you may be criticized by the very people who should support you.

using as fuel the wood of the Asherah pole you cut down." 27 So Gideon took ten of his
servants and did as the LORD had commanded. But he did it at night because he was
afraid of the other members of his father's household and the people of the town. He
knew what would happen if they found out who had done it.
28 Early the next morning, as the people of the town began to stir, someone discovered
that the altar of Baal had been knocked down and that the Asherah pole beside it was
gone. In their place a new altar had been built, and it had the remains of a sacrifice on it.
29 The people said to each other, "Who did this?" And after asking around and making a
careful search, they learned that it was Gideon, the son of Joash.
30 "Bring out your son," they shouted to Joash. "He must die for destroying the altar
of Baal and for cutting down the Asherah pole."
31 But Joash shouted to the mob, "Why are you defending Baal? Will you argue his
case? Whoever pleads his case will be put to death by morning! If Baal truly is a god, let
him defend himself and destroy the one who knocked down his altar!" 32 From then on
Gideon was called Jerubbaal, which means "Let Baal defend himself," because he
knocked down Baal's altar.
33 Soon afterward the armies of Midian, Amalek, and the people of the east formed an — 6:33 Josh 17:16
alliance against Israel and crossed the Jordan, camping in the valley of Jezreel. 34 Then the — 6:34 Judg 3:10
Spirit of the LORD took possession of Gideon. He blew a ram's horn as a call to arms, and
the men of the clan of Abiezer came to him. 35 He also sent messengers throughout Manas- — 6:35 Judg 7:23
seh, Asher, Zebulun, and Naphtali, summoning their warriors, and all of them responded.
36 Then Gideon said to God, "If you are truly going to use me to rescue Israel as you — 6:36 Judg 6:14
promised, 37 prove it to me in this way. I will put some wool on the threshing floor
tonight. If the fleece is wet with dew in the morning but the ground is dry, then I will
know that you are going to help me rescue Israel as you promised." 38 And it happened
just that way. When Gideon got up the next morning, he squeezed the fleece and wrung
out a whole bowlful of water.
39 Then Gideon said to God, "Please don't be angry with me, but let me make one more — 6:39 Gen 18:32
request. This time let the fleece remain dry while the ground around it is wet with dew."
40 So that night God did as Gideon asked. The fleece was dry in the morning, but the
ground was covered with dew.

GIDEON'S BATTLE In spite of Deborah and Barak's victory, the Canaanites still caused trouble in this fertile region. God appeared to Gideon at Ophrah and called him to defeat them. With only 300 fighting men, Gideon routed thousands of Midianites, chasing them to Zererah and Abel-meholah.

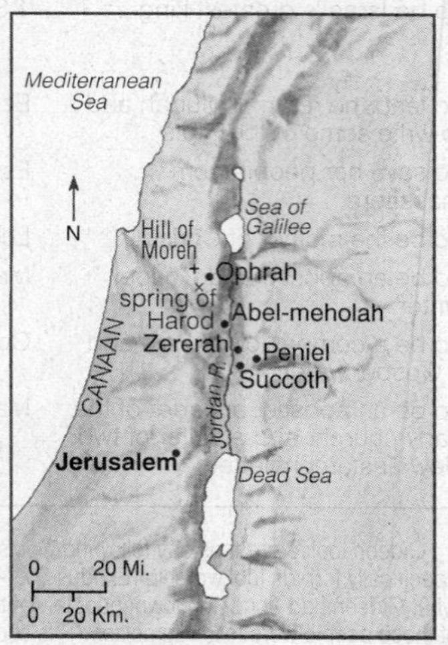

6:33 The armies of Midian and Amalek camped in the valley of Jezreel, the agricultural center for the area. Whoever controlled the valley's rich and fertile land controlled the people who lived in and around it. Because of the valley's vast resources, many major trade routes converged at the pass which led into it. This made it the site of many great battles. Gideon's men attacked the enemy armies from the hills, and the only escape route was through the pass toward the Jordan River. That is why Gideon urged some of his troops to take control of the river's crossing points (7:24).

6:37-39 Was Gideon testing God, or was he simply asking God for more encouragement? In either case, though his motive was right (to obey God and defeat the enemy), his method was less than ideal. Gideon seems to have known that his requests might displease God (6:39), and yet he demanded two miracles (6:37, 39), even after witnessing the miraculous fire from the rock (6:21). It is true that to make good decisions, we need facts. Gideon had all the facts, but still he hesitated. He delayed obeying God because he wanted even more proof.

Demanding extra signs was an indication of unbelief. Fear often makes us wait for more confirmation when we should be taking action. Visible signs are unnecessary if they only confirm what we already know is true.

Today the greatest means of God's guidance is his Word, the Bible. Unlike Gideon, we have God's complete, revealed Word. If you want to have more of God's guidance, don't ask for signs; study the Bible (2 Timothy 3:16, 17).

6:39 After seeing the miracle of the wet fleece, why did Gideon ask for another miracle? Perhaps he thought the results of the first test could have happened naturally. A thick fleece could retain moisture long after the sun had dried the surrounding ground. "Putting out fleeces" is a poor decision-making method. Those who do this put limitations on God. They ask him to fit their expectations. The results of such experiments are usually inconclusive and thus fail to make us any more confident about our choices. Don't let a "fleece" become a substitute for God's wisdom that comes through Bible study and prayer.

Gideon Defeats the Midianites

7 So Jerubbaal (that is, Gideon) and his army got up early and went as far as the spring
of Harod. The armies of Midian were camped north of them in the valley near the
hill of Moreh. 2 The LORD said to Gideon, "You have too many warriors with you. If I
let all of you fight the Midianites, the Israelites will boast to me that they saved

7:2
Deut 8:17-18
Isa 10:13
2 Cor 4:7

GIDEON

Most of us want to know God's plan for our lives, but we're not always sure how to find it. One common misunderstanding is the idea that God's guidance will come to us out of the blue, that it has nothing to do with what we're doing now. But if we're always looking around for God's next assignment, we run the risk of ruining whatever we're working on right now. Fortunately, the Bible points to a kind of guidance that does not put our current projects in jeopardy. In the Bible's descriptions of how God guided many people, we can see that often God's call came while people were completely immersed in the challenge of the moment. A good example of this kind of guidance is seen in Gideon's life.

Gideon had a limited vision, but he was committed to it. His challenge was to obtain food for his family even though hostile invaders were making the growing, gathering, and preparation of the food almost impossible. Gideon was resourceful. He put a winepress to double duty by turning it into a sunken threshing floor. It lacked ventilation to blow the chaff away, but at least it was hidden from the Midianites. Gideon was working in his threshing floor when God sent him a messenger with a challenge.

Gideon was surprised by what God told him to do. He did not want to jump into a task for which he was ill prepared. The angel had to overcome three objections before Gideon was convinced: (1) Gideon's feelings of responsibility for his family's welfare, (2) his doubts about the call itself, and (3) his feelings of inadequacy for the job. Once Gideon was convinced, however, he obeyed with zest, resourcefulness, and speed. He dedicated those personality traits to God, with whom he was now personally acquainted.

Gideon had his weak moments and failures, but he was still God's servant. If you can easily relate to Gideon's weakness, can you also see yourself being willing to serve? Remember Gideon as a man who obeyed God by giving his attention to the task at hand. Then give your full attention to believing God will prepare you for tomorrow when it comes.

Strengths and accomplishments
- Israel's fifth judge. A military strategist who was expert at surprise
- A member of the Hall of Faith in Hebrews 11
- Defeated the Midianite army
- Was offered a hereditary kingship by the men of Israel
- Though slow to be convinced, acted on his convictions

Weaknesses and mistakes
- Feared that his own limitations would prevent God from working
- Collected Midianite gold and made a symbol that became an evil object of worship
- Through a concubine, fathered a son who would bring great grief and tragedy to both Gideon's family and the nation of Israel
- Failed to establish the nation in God's ways; after he died they all went back to idol worship

Lessons from his life
- God calls in the middle of our present obedience. As we are faithful, he gives us more responsibility
- God expands and uses the abilities he has already built into us
- God uses us in spite of our limitations and failures
- Even those who make great spiritual progress can easily fall into sin if they don't consistently follow God

Vital statistics
- Where: Ophrah, valley of Jezreel, spring of Harod
- Occupations: Farmer, warrior, and judge
- Relatives: Father: Joash. Son: Abimelech
- Contemporaries: Zebah, Zalmunna

Key verses
" 'But Lord,' Gideon replied, 'how can I rescue Israel? My clan is the weakest in the whole tribe of Manasseh, and I am the least in my entire family!' The LORD said to him, 'I will be with you. And you will destroy the Midianites as if you were fighting against one man' " (Judges 6:15, 16).

His story is told in Judges 6—8. He is also mentioned in Hebrews 11:32.

7:2 Self-sufficiency is an enemy when it causes us to believe we can always do what needs to be done in our own strength. To prevent this attitude among Gideon's soldiers, God reduced their number from 32,000 to 300. With an army this small, there could be no doubt that victory was from God. The men could not take the credit. Like Gideon, we must recognize the danger of fighting in our own strength. We can be confident of victory only if we put our confidence in God and not ourselves.

themselves by their own strength. 3 Therefore, tell the people, 'Whoever is timid or afraid 7:3
may leave* and go home.'" Twenty-two thousand of them went home, leaving only ten Deut 20:8
thousand who were willing to fight.
4 But the LORD told Gideon, "There are still too many! Bring them down to the spring, 7:4
and I will sort out who will go with you and who will not." 5 When Gideon took his 1 Sam 14:6
warriors down to the water, the LORD told him, "Divide the men into two groups. In one
group put all those who cup water in their hands and lap it up with their tongues like
dogs. In the other group put all those who kneel down and drink with their mouths in the
stream." 6 Only three hundred of the men drank from their hands. All the others got down
on their knees and drank with their mouths in the stream. 7 The LORD told Gideon, "With
these three hundred men I will rescue you and give you victory over the Midianites. Send
all the others home." 8 So Gideon collected the provisions and rams' horns of the other
warriors and sent them home. But he kept the three hundred men with him.
Now the Midianite camp was in the valley just below Gideon. 9 During the night, the 7:9
LORD said, "Get up! Go down into the Midianite camp, for I have given you victory over Josh 2:24; 10:8;
them! 10 But if you are afraid to attack, go down to the camp with your servant Purah. 11:6
11 Listen to what the Midianites are saying, and you will be greatly encouraged. Then you
will be eager to attack."
So Gideon took Purah and went down to the outposts of the enemy camp. 12 The 7:12
armies of Midian, Amalek, and the people of the east had settled in the valley like a Josh 11:4
swarm of locusts. Their camels were like grains of sand on the seashore—too many to Judg 6:5; 8:10
count! 13 Gideon crept up just as a man was telling his friend about a dream. The man
said, "I had this dream, and in my dream a loaf of barley bread came tumbling down into
the Midianite camp. It hit a tent, turned it over, and knocked it flat!"
14 His friend said, "Your dream can mean only one thing—God has given Gideon son
of Joash, the Israelite, victory over all the armies united with Midian!"
15 When Gideon heard the dream and its interpretation, he thanked God. Then he
returned to the Israelite camp and shouted, "Get up! For the LORD has given you victory
over the Midianites!" 16 He divided the three hundred men into three groups and gave
each man a ram's horn and a clay jar with a torch in it. 17 Then he said to them, "Keep
your eyes on me. When I come to the edge of the camp, do just as I do. 18 As soon as my
group blows the rams' horns, those of you on the other sides of the camp blow your horns
and shout, 'For the LORD and for Gideon!'"
19 It was just after midnight, after the changing of the guard, when Gideon and the one
hundred men with him reached the outer edge of the Midianite camp. Suddenly, they
blew the horns and broke their clay jars. 20 Then all three groups blew their horns and
broke their jars. They held the blazing torches in their left hands and the horns in their
right hands and shouted, "A sword for the LORD and for Gideon!" 21 Each man stood at 7:21
his position around the camp and watched as all the Midianites rushed around in a panic, 2 Kgs 7:7
shouting as they ran. 22 When the three hundred Israelites blew their horns, the LORD
caused the warriors in the camp to fight against each other with their swords. Those who
were not killed fled to places as far away as Beth-shittah near Zererah and to the border
of Abel-meholah near Tabbath.
23 Then Gideon sent for the warriors of Naphtali, Asher, and Manasseh, who joined in

7:3 Hebrew *leave Mount Gilead.* The identity of Mount Gilead is uncertain in this context. It is perhaps used here as another name for Mount Gilboa.

7:10, 11 Facing overwhelming odds, Gideon was afraid. God understood his fear, but he didn't excuse Gideon from his task. Instead, he allowed Gideon to slip into the enemy camp and overhear a conversation that would give him courage (7:12-15). Are you facing a battle? God can give you the strength you need for any situation. And don't be startled by the way he helps you. Like Gideon, you must listen to God and be ready to take the first step. Only after you begin to obey God will you find the courage to move ahead.

7:12 Midianites were camel-riding marauders composed of five families linked to Abraham through Midian, the son of Abraham's second wife, Keturah. They inhabited the desert regions from the Dead Sea to the Red Sea.

7:13 An enemy soldier dreamed of a loaf of barley bread tumbling into camp. Barley grain had only half the value of wheat, and the bread made from it was considered inferior. In the same way, Israel's tiny band of men was considered inferior to the vast forces of Midian and Amalek. But God would make the underdog Israelites seem invincible.

7:21 Gideon's army simply watched as the army of Midian fell into panic, confusion, and disordered retreat. Not one man had to draw a sword to defeat the enemy. Gideon's small army could never have brought about such a victory in their own strength. God wanted to demonstrate to Israel that victory depends not on strength or numbers but on obedience and commitment to him.

7:24 Judg 3:27-28 the chase after the fleeing army of Midian. [24]Gideon also sent messengers throughout
the hill country of Ephraim, saying, "Come down to attack the Midianites. Cut them off
at the shallows of the Jordan River at Beth-barah." And the men of Ephraim did as they
7:25 Judg 8:4 Ps 83:11 Isa 10:26 were told. [25]They captured Oreb and Zeeb, the two Midianite generals, killing Oreb at
the rock of Oreb, and Zeeb at the winepress of Zeeb. And they continued to chase the
Midianites. Afterward the Israelites brought the heads of Oreb and Zeeb to Gideon, who
was by the Jordan.

Gideon Kills Zebah and Zalmunna

8:1 Judg 12:1 **8** Then the people of Ephraim asked Gideon, "Why have you treated us this way? Why
didn't you send for us when you first went out to fight the Midianites?" And they
argued heatedly with Gideon.
[2]But Gideon replied, "What have I done compared to you? Aren't the last grapes of
Ephraim's harvest better than the entire crop of my little clan of Abiezer? [3]God gave you
victory over Oreb and Zeeb, the generals of the Midianite army. What have I done
compared to that?" When the men of Ephraim heard Gideon's answer, they were no
longer angry.
[4]Gideon then crossed the Jordan River with his three hundred men, and though they
8:5 Gen 33:17 were exhausted, they continued to chase the enemy. [5]When they reached Succoth,
Gideon asked the leaders of the town, "Will you please give my warriors some food?
They are very tired. I am chasing Zebah and Zalmunna, the kings of Midian."
[6]But the leaders of Succoth replied, "You haven't caught Zebah and Zalmunna yet.
Catch them first, and then we will feed your warriors."
8:7 Judg 7:15 [7]So Gideon said, "After the LORD gives me victory over Zebah and Zalmunna, I will
return and tear your flesh with the thorns and briers of the wilderness."
8:8 Gen 32:30 1 Kgs 12:25 [8]From there Gideon went up to Peniel* and asked for food, but he got the same
answer. [9]So he said to the people of Peniel, "After I return in victory, I will tear down
this tower."
8:10 Isa 9:4 [10]By this time Zebah and Zalmunna were in Karkor with a remnant of 15,000
warriors—all that remained of the allied armies of the east—for 120,000 had already
been killed. [11]Gideon circled around by the caravan route east of Nobah and Jogbehah,
8:12 Ps 83:11 taking the Midianite army by surprise. [12]Zebah and Zalmunna, the two Midianite kings,
fled, but Gideon chased them down and captured all their warriors.
[13]After this, Gideon returned by way of Heres Pass. [14]There he captured a young man
from Succoth and demanded that he write down the names of all the seventy-seven rulers
8:15 Judg 8:6 and leaders in the town. [15]Gideon then returned to Succoth and said to the leaders, "Here
are Zebah and Zalmunna. When we were here before, you taunted me, saying, 'You
haven't caught Zebah and Zalmunna yet. Catch them first, and then we will feed your

8:8 Hebrew *Penuel,* a variant name for Peniel; also in 8:9, 17.

8:1-3 Ephraim's leaders felt left out because Gideon had not called them to join the battle but had left them in place to "clean up" the escaping Midianites ("the last grapes"), and so they angrily confronted him. Gideon assured the leaders of Ephraim that their accomplishment was even greater than his own clan's (Abiezer). His diplomatic explanation pointed out that this rear guard had managed to capture the enemy's generals, thus cutting off the leaders from their army. Not every necessary job is a highly visible leadership role. Much of the necessary labor of any effective enterprise is considered by many to be dirty work. But such work is vital to getting any big task done. Engineers and millionaires may design and finance an elegant building, but it is the bricklayers who get the work done. Pride causes us to want recognition. Are you content to be God's bricklayer, or do you resent the work God has given you?

8:5-9 The leaders of Succoth and Peniel refused to help Gideon, probably fearing Midian's revenge should he fail (Gideon's army was 300 men chasing 15,000). They should have realized that victory was certain because God was with Gideon. But they were so worried about saving themselves that they never thought about God's power to save.

Because of fear for ourselves, we may not recognize God's presence in other people and therefore miss God's victory. Then we must face the often bitter consequences of failing to join forces with those God has chosen to do his work. Because God will prevail with or without you, be quick to join others who are engaged in his work. Lend support with your time, money, talents, and prayer.

8:11 The Midianites were escaping into the desert area, where the tent-dwelling nomads lived. They didn't expect Gideon to follow them that far.

8:15-17 Gideon carried out the threats he had made in 8:7, 9. It is difficult to determine whether this act of revenge was justified or whether he should have left the punishment up to God. Gideon was God's appointed leader, but the officials of Succoth and Peniel refused to help him in any way because they feared the enemy. They showed neither faith nor respect for God or the man God had chosen to save them. We should help others because it is right, regardless of whether we will benefit personally.

exhausted warriors.'" 16Then Gideon took the leaders of the town and taught them a
lesson, punishing them with thorns and briers from the wilderness. 17He also knocked 8:17 Judg 8:8
down the tower of Peniel and killed all the men in the town.

18Then Gideon asked Zebah and Zalmunna, "The men you killed at Tabor—what
were they like?"

"Like you," they replied. "They all had the look of a king's son."

19"They were my brothers!" Gideon exclaimed. "As surely as the LORD lives, I
wouldn't kill you if you hadn't killed them."

20Turning to Jether, his oldest son, he said, "Kill them!" But Jether did not draw his
sword, for he was only a boy and was afraid.

21Then Zebah and Zalmunna said to Gideon, "Don't ask a boy to do a man's job! Do
it yourself!" So Gideon killed them both and took the royal ornaments from the necks of
their camels.

Gideon's Sacred Ephod

22Then the Israelites said to Gideon, "Be our ruler! You and your son and your grandson
will be our rulers, for you have rescued us from Midian."

23But Gideon replied, "I will not rule over you, nor will my son. The LORD will rule 8:23 1 Sam 12:12
over you! 24However, I have one request. Each of you can give me an earring out of the
treasures you collected from your fallen enemies." (The enemies, being Ishmaelites, all
wore gold earrings.)

25"Gladly!" they replied. They spread out a cloak, and each one threw in a gold earring
he had gathered. 26The weight of the gold earrings was forty-three pounds,* not
including the crescents and pendants, the royal clothing of the kings, or the chains around
the necks of their camels. 27Gideon made a sacred ephod from the gold and put it in 8:27 Exod 28:6
Ophrah, his hometown. But soon all the Israelites prostituted themselves by worshiping Judg 17:5
it, and it became a trap for Gideon and his family.

28That is the story of how Israel subdued Midian, which never recovered. Throughout
the rest of Gideon's lifetime—about forty years—the land was at peace.

29Then Gideon* son of Joash returned home. 30He had seventy sons, for he had many 8:30 Judg 9:2, 5
wives. 31He also had a concubine in Shechem, who bore him a son named Abimelech. 8:31
32Gideon died when he was very old, and he was buried in the grave of his father, Joash, Judg 9:1
at Ophrah in the land of the clan of Abiezer.

33As soon as Gideon was dead, the Israelites prostituted themselves by worshiping the 8:33
images of Baal, making Baal-berith their god. 34They forgot the LORD their God, who Judg 2:11
had rescued them from all their enemies surrounding them. 35Nor did they show any 8:34 Deut 4:9
loyalty to the family of Jerubbaal (that is, Gideon), despite all the good he had done for Judg 3:7
Israel.

8:26 Hebrew *1,700 shekels* [19.4 kilograms]. **8:29** Hebrew *Jerubbaal;* see 6:32.

8:20, 21 For a king to be killed by a boy was humiliating because it would look as though he was no match for a boy. The two men wanted to avoid that disgrace as well as the slower and more painful death that an inexperienced swordsman might inflict.

8:23 The people wanted to make Gideon their king, but Gideon stressed that the Lord was to rule over them. Despite his inconsistencies, Gideon never lost sight of the importance, for both a nation and an individual, of putting God first. Is God first in your life? If he is, he must affect every dimension of your life, not just what you do in church.

8:26, 27 Those who were very wealthy put ornaments on their camels as a way of displaying their riches. Women wore vast amounts of jewelry as well, often up to 15 pairs of earrings. Jewelry was also worn for good luck. After Gideon's rise to power, he seems to have become carried away with this accumulation of wealth. Eventually it led the Israelites to idolatry.

8:27 An ephod was a linen garment worn by priests over their chests. It was considered holy (Exodus 28:6-35; 39:2-24; Leviticus 8:7, 8). Gideon probably had good motives for making the ephod (a visible remembrance commemorating the victory). Unfortunately, the people began to worship the ephod as an idol. Sadly, many decisions that stem from good motives produce negative results. Perhaps no one stops to ask, "What might go wrong?" or "Is there a possibility of negative consequences?" In your plans and decisions, take time to anticipate how a good idea might lead to a potential problem.

8:31 This relationship between Gideon and a concubine produced a son who tore apart Gideon's family and caused tragedy for the nation. Gideon's story illustrates the fact that heroes in battle are not always heroes in daily life. Gideon led the nation but could not lead his family. No matter who you are, moral laxness will cause problems. Just because you have won a single battle with temptation does not mean you will automatically win the next one. We need to be constantly watchful against temptation. Sometimes Satan's strongest attacks come after a victory.

8:33 Baal-berith means "Baal (lord) of the covenant." Worship of the idol may have combined elements of both the Israelite and Canaanite religions.

Abimelech Rules over Shechem

9:1 Judg 8:31 **9** One day Gideon's* son Abimelech went to Shechem to visit his mother's brothers.
He said to them and to the rest of his mother's family, 2"Ask the people of Shechem
whether they want to be ruled by all seventy of Gideon's sons or by one man. And
remember, I am your own flesh and blood!"
3So Abimelech's uncles spoke to all the people of Shechem on his behalf. And after
listening to their proposal, they decided in favor of Abimelech because he was their
9:4 Judg 8:33 relative. 4They gave him seventy silver coins from the temple of Baal-berith, which he
9:5 Judg 6:11; 8:32 used to hire some soldiers who agreed to follow him. 5He took the soldiers to his father's
home at Ophrah, and there, on one stone, they killed all seventy of his half brothers. But

9:1 Hebrew *Jerubbaal's* (see 6:32); also in 9:2, 24.

ABIMELECH

People who desire power always outnumber those who are able to use power wisely once they have it. Perhaps this is because power has a way of taking over and controlling the person using it. This is especially true in cases of inherited but unmerited power. Abimelech's life shows us what happens when hunger for power corrupts judgment.

Abimelech's position in Gideon's family as the son of a concubine must have created great tension between him and Gideon's many other sons. One against 70: Such odds can either crush a person or make him ruthless. It is obvious which direction Abimelech chose. Gideon's position as warrior and judge had placed Abimelech in an environment of power; Gideon's death provided an opportunity for this son to seize power. Once the process began, the disastrous results were inevitable. A person's thirst for power is not satisfied when he gets power—it only becomes more intense. Abimelech's life was consumed by that thirst. Eventually, he could not tolerate any threat to his power.

By this time, ownership had changed: Abimelech no longer had power—power had him. One lesson we can learn from his life is that our goals control our actions. The amount of control is related to the importance of the goal. Abimelech's most important goal was to have power. His lust for power led him to wipe out not only his brothers but also whole cities that refused to submit to him. Nothing but death could stop his bloodthirsty drive to conquer. How ironic that he was fatally injured by a woman! The contrast between Abimelech and the godly people of the Bible is great. He wanted to control the nation; they were willing to be controlled by God.

Strengths and accomplishments
- The first self-declared king of Israel
- Qualified tactical planner and organizer

Weaknesses and mistakes
- Power hungry and ruthless
- Overconfident
- Took advantage of his father's position without imitating his character
- Had 69 of his 70 half brothers killed

Vital statistics
- Where: Shechem, Arumah, Thebez
- Occupations: Self-acclaimed king, judge, political troublemaker
- Relatives: Father: Gideon. Only surviving brother: Jotham

Key verses
"Thus, God punished Abimelech for the evil he had done against his father by murdering his seventy brothers. God also punished the men of Shechem for all their evil. So the curse of Jotham son of Gideon came true" (Judges 9:56, 57).

His story is told in Judges 8:31—9:57. He is also mentioned in 2 Samuel 11:21.

9:1-3 With Gideon dead, Abimelech wanted to take his father's place. (Jerubbaal is another name for Gideon; see 6:32.) To set his plan in motion he went to the city of Shechem, his mother's hometown, to drum up support. Here he felt kinship with the residents. These relatives were Canaanites and would be glad to unite against Israel. Shechem was an important city, a crossroads for trade routes and a natural link between the coastal plain and the Jordan Valley. Whoever controlled Shechem would dominate the countryside.

9:2-5 Israel's king was to be the Lord and not a man. But Abimelech wanted to usurp the position reserved for God alone. In his selfish quest, he killed all but one of his 70 half brothers. People with selfish desires often seek to fulfill them in ruthless ways. Examine your ambitions to see if they are self-centered or God-centered. Be sure you always fulfill your desires in ways that God would approve.

9:4 Politics played a major part in pagan religions such as the worship of Baal-berith. Governments often went so far as to hire temple prostitutes to bring in additional money. In many cases a religious system was set up and supported by the government so the offerings could fund community projects. Religion became a profit-making business. In Israel's religion, this was strictly forbidden. God's system of religion was designed to come from an attitude of the heart, not from calculated plans and business opportunities. It was also designed to serve people and help those in need, not to oppress the needy. Is your faith genuine and sincere, or is it based on convenience, comfort, and availability?

the youngest brother, Jotham, escaped and hid. [6]Then the people of Shechem and
Beth-millo called a meeting under the oak beside the pillar* at Shechem and made
Abimelech their king.

Jotham's Parable

[7]When Jotham heard about this, he climbed to the top of Mount Gerizim and shouted, 9:7 Deut 11:29; 27:12 John 4:20
"Listen to me, people of Shechem! Listen to me if you want God to listen to you! [8]Once
upon a time the trees decided to elect a king. First they said to the olive tree, 'Be our 9:8 2 Kgs 14:9 Ezek 17:3 Dan 4:10
king!' [9]But it refused, saying, 'Should I quit producing the olive oil that blesses both God
and people, just to wave back and forth over the trees?'

[10]"Then they said to the fig tree, 'You be our king!' [11]But the fig tree also refused,
saying, 'Should I quit producing my sweet fruit just to wave back and forth over the
trees?'

[12]"Then they said to the grapevine, 'You be our king!' [13]But the grapevine replied,
'Should I quit producing the wine that cheers both God and people, just to wave back
and forth over the trees?'

[14]"Then all the trees finally turned to the thornbush and said, 'Come, you be our
king!' [15]And the thornbush replied, 'If you truly want to make me your king, come and
take shelter in my shade. If not, let fire come out from me and devour the cedars of
Lebanon.'

[16]"Now make sure you have acted honorably and in good faith by making Abimelech
your king, and that you have done right by Gideon* and all of his descendants. Have you
treated my father with the honor he deserves? [17]For he fought for you and risked his life
when he rescued you from the Midianites. [18]But now you have revolted against my 9:18 Judg 8:31
father and his descendants, killing his seventy sons on one stone. And you have chosen
his slave woman's son, Abimelech, to be your king just because he is your relative. [19]If
you have acted honorably and in good faith toward Gideon and his descendants, then
may you find joy in Abimelech, and may he find joy in you. [20]But if you have not acted
in good faith, then may fire come out from Abimelech and devour the people of Shechem
and Beth-millo; and may fire come out from the people of Shechem and Beth-millo and
devour Abimelech!" [21]Then Jotham escaped and lived in Beer because he was afraid of
his brother Abimelech.

9:6 The meaning of the Hebrew is uncertain. **9:16** Hebrew *Jerubbaal* (see 6:32); also in 9:19, 28, 57.

ABIMELECH'S FALL
Gideon's illegitimate son killed 69 of his half brothers in Ophrah and returned to Shechem to be acclaimed king. But three years later, Shechem rebelled. From Arumah, Abimelech attacked Shechem, Beth-millo ("the pillar at Shechem"), and Thebez, where he was killed.

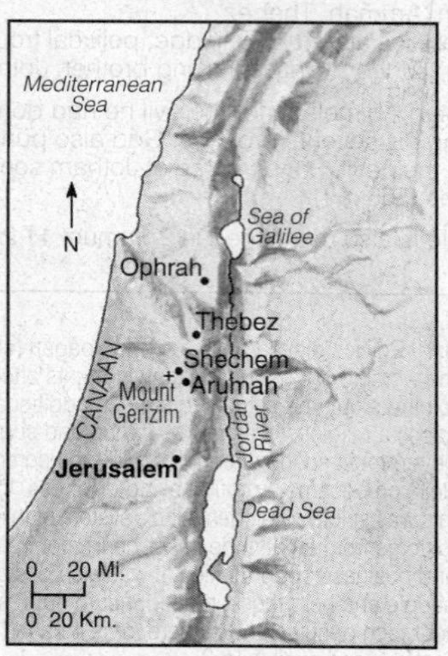

9:6 Abimelech was declared ruler of Israel at Shechem, the site of other key Bible events. It was one of Abraham's first stops upon arriving in Canaan (Genesis 12:6, 7). When Jacob lived there, two of his sons killed all the men in Shechem because the prince's son raped their sister (Genesis 34). Joseph's bones were buried in Shechem (Joshua 24:32); Israel renewed its covenant with God there (Joshua 24); and the kingdom of Israel split apart at this same city (1 Kings 12).

9:7-15 In Jotham's parable the trees represented Gideon's 70 sons, and the thornbush represented Abimelech. Jotham's point was this: A productive person would be too busy doing good to want to bother with power politics. A worthless person, on the other hand, would be glad to accept the honor—but he would destroy the people he ruled. Abimelech, like a thornbush, could offer Israel no real protection or security. Jotham's parable came true when Abimelech destroyed the city of Shechem (9:45), burned "the tower of Shechem" (the city of Beth-millo, 9:46-49), and was finally killed at Thebez (9:53, 54).

9:16 Jotham told the story about the trees in order to help the people set good priorities. He did not want them to appoint a leader of low character. As we serve in leadership positions, we should examine our motives. Do we just want praise, prestige, or power? In the parable, the good trees chose to be productive and to provide benefits to people. Make sure these are your priorities as you aspire to leadership.

Shechem's Revolt against Abimelech

9:23 1 Sam 16:14 22 After Abimelech had ruled over Israel for three years, 23 God stirred up trouble*
9:24 Num 35:33 Deut 27:25 between Abimelech and the people of Shechem, and they revolted. 24 In the events that
followed, God punished Abimelech and the men of Shechem for murdering Gideon's
seventy sons. 25 The people of Shechem set an ambush for Abimelech on the hilltops and
robbed everyone who passed that way. But someone warned Abimelech about their plot.
26 At that time Gaal son of Ebed moved to Shechem with his brothers and gained the
9:27 Judg 8:33 confidence of the people of Shechem. 27 During the annual harvest festival at Shechem,
held in the temple of the local god, the wine flowed freely, and everyone began cursing
Abimelech. 28 "Who is Abimelech?" Gaal shouted. "He's not a true descendant of
Shechem!* Why should we be Abimelech's servants? He's merely the son of Gideon,
and Zebul is his administrator. Serve the men of Hamor, who are Shechem's true
descendants. Why should we serve Abimelech? 29 If I were in charge, I would get rid of
Abimelech. I would say* to him, 'Get some more soldiers, and come out and fight!'"
30 But when Zebul, the leader of the city, heard what Gaal was saying, he was furious.
31 He sent messengers to Abimelech in Arumah,* telling him, "Gaal son of Ebed and his
brothers have come to live in Shechem, and now they are inciting the city to rebel against
9:33 1 Sam 10:7 you. 32 Come by night with an army and hide out in the fields. 33 In the morning, as soon
as it is daylight, storm the city. When Gaal and those who are with him come out against
you, you can do with them as you wish."
34 So Abimelech and his men went by night and split into four groups, stationing
themselves around Shechem. 35 Gaal was standing at the city gates when Abimelech and
his army came out of hiding. 36 When Gaal saw them, he said to Zebul, "Look, there are
people coming down from the hilltops!"
Zebul replied, "It's just the shadows of the hills that look like men."
9:37 Ezek 38:12 37 But again Gaal said, "No, people are coming down from the hills.* And another
group is coming down the road past the Diviners' Oak.*"
38 Then Zebul turned on him triumphantly. "Now where is that big mouth of yours?"
he demanded. "Wasn't it you that said, 'Who is Abimelech, and why should we be his
servants?' The men you mocked are right outside the city! Go out and fight them!"
39 Gaal then led the men of Shechem into battle against Abimelech, 40 but he was
defeated and ran away. Many of Shechem's warriors were killed, and the ground was
covered with dead bodies all the way to the city gate. 41 Abimelech stayed in Arumah,
and Zebul drove Gaal and his brothers out of Shechem.
42 The next day the people of Shechem went out into the fields to battle. When Abimelech
heard about it, 43 he divided his men into three groups and set an ambush in the fields. When
Abimelech saw the people coming out of the city, he and his men jumped up from their
hiding places and attacked them. 44 Abimelech and his group stormed the city gate to keep
the men of Shechem from getting back in, while Abimelech's other two groups cut them
9:45 Deut 29:23 down in the fields. 45 The battle went on all day before Abimelech finally captured the city.
He killed the people, leveled the city, and scattered salt all over the ground.
9:46 Judg 8:33 46 When the people who lived in the tower of Shechem heard what had happened, they
9:47 Ps 68:14 took refuge within the walls of the temple of Baal-berith.* 47 Someone reported to

9:23 Hebrew *sent a disturbing spirit.* 9:28 Hebrew *Who is Shechem?* 9:29 As in Greek version; Hebrew reads *And he said.* 9:31 Hebrew *Tormah;* see 9:41. 9:37a Or *the center of the land.* 9:37b Hebrew *Elon-meonenim.* 9:46 Hebrew *El-berith,* another name for Baal-berith; compare 9:4.

9:22-24 Abimelech was the opposite of what God wanted in a judge, but it was three years before God moved against him, fulfilling Jotham's parable. Those three years must have seemed like forever to Jotham. Why wasn't Abimelech punished sooner for his evil ways?

We are not alone when we wonder why evil seems to prevail (Job 10:3; 21:1-18; Jeremiah 12:1; Habakkuk 1:2-4, 12-17). God promises to deal with sin, but in his time, not ours. Actually it is good news that God doesn't punish *us* immediately because we all have sinned and deserve God's punishment. God, in his mercy, often spares us from immediate punishment and allows us time to turn from our sins and turn to him in repentance. Trusting God for justice means (1) we must first recognize our own sins and repent, and (2) we may face a difficult time of waiting for the wicked to be punished. But in God's time, all evil will be destroyed.

9:23 This "trouble" stirred up was not just an attitude of strife, it was a demon. It was not Satan himself, but one of the fallen angels under Satan's influence. God used this evil spirit to bring about judgment on Shechem. First Samuel 16:14 records how God judged Saul in a similar way.

9:45 To scatter salt over a conquered city was a ritual to symbolize the perpetual desolation of the city. It would not be rebuilt for 150 years.

Abimelech that the people were gathered together in the temple, 48so he led his forces
to Mount Zalmon. He took an ax and chopped some branches from a tree, and he put
them on his shoulder. "Quick, do as I have done!" he told his men. 49So each of them
cut down some branches, following Abimelech's example. They piled the branches
against the walls of the temple and set them on fire. So all the people who had lived in
the tower of Shechem died, about a thousand men and women.

50Then Abimelech attacked the city of Thebez and captured it. 51But there was a **9:50**
strong tower inside the city, and the entire population fled to it. They barricaded 2 Sam 11:21
themselves in and climbed up to the roof of the tower. 52Abimelech followed them to
attack the tower. But as he prepared to set fire to the entrance, 53a woman on the roof **9:53**
threw down a millstone that landed on Abimelech's head and crushed his skull. 54He said 2 Sam 11:21
to his young armor bearer, "Draw your sword and kill me! Don't let it be said that a
woman killed Abimelech!" So the young man stabbed him with his sword, and he died.
55When Abimelech's men saw that he was dead, they disbanded and returned to their
homes.

56Thus, God punished Abimelech for the evil he had done against his father by
murdering his seventy brothers. 57God also punished the men of Shechem for all their
evil. So the curse of Jotham son of Gideon came true.

Tola Becomes Israel's Judge

10 After Abimelech's death, Tola, the son of Puah and descendant of Dodo, came to
rescue Israel. He was from the tribe of Issachar but lived in the town of Shamir in
the hill country of Ephraim. 2He was Israel's judge for twenty-three years. When he died,
he was buried in Shamir.

Jair Becomes Israel's Judge

3After Tola died, a man from Gilead named Jair judged Israel for twenty-two years. 4His **10:4**
thirty sons rode around on thirty donkeys, and they owned thirty towns in the land of Gilead, Num 32:41
which are still called the Towns of Jair.* 5When Jair died, he was buried in Kamon.

5. Fifth period: Jephthah, Ibzan, Elon, and Abdon

The Ammonites Oppress Israel

6Again the Israelites did evil in the LORD's sight. They worshiped images of Baal and **10:6**
Ashtoreth, and the gods of Aram, Sidon, Moab, Ammon, and Philistia. Not only this, Judg 2:11-13 **10:7**
but they abandoned the LORD and no longer served him at all. 7So the LORD burned 1 Sam 12:9
with anger against Israel, and he handed them over to the Philistines and the Ammonites, 8who began to oppress them that year. For eighteen years they oppressed all the
Israelites east of the Jordan River in the land of the Amorites (that is, in Gilead). 9The
Ammonites also crossed to the west side of the Jordan and attacked Judah, Benjamin, **10:10**
and Ephraim. The Israelites were in great distress. 10Finally, they cried out to the Judg 3:9

10:4 Hebrew *Havvoth-jair.*

9:53 In times of battle, women were sometimes asked to join the men at the city wall to drop heavy objects on the soldiers below. A millstone would have been an ideal object for this purpose. It was a round stone about 18 inches in diameter with a hole in the center. Millstones were used to grind grain into flour. The grain was placed between two millstones. The top millstone was turned, crushing the grain.

Abimelech's death was especially humiliating: He was killed by a woman, not by fighting; and he was killed by a farm implement instead of a weapon. Abimelech, therefore, asked his armor bearer to stab him with his sword before he died from the blow of the millstone.

9:56, 57 Gideon, Abimelech's father, succeeded in military battles but sometimes failed in his personal struggles. Gideon was not condemned for taking a concubine (8:31), but the family problems that resulted from this relationship are clearly stated.

In the end, Abimelech killed 69 of his 70 half brothers, tore apart a nation, and then was killed himself. From Gideon's life we learn that no matter how much good we do for God's Kingdom, sin in our lives will still produce powerful, damaging consequences.

9:56, 57 Jotham's curse is found in 9:16-20.

10:1-5 In five verses we read about two men who judged Israel for a total of 45 years, yet all we know about them besides the length of their rules is that one had 30 sons who rode around on 30 donkeys. What are you doing for God that is worth noting? When your life is over, will people remember more than just what was in your bank account or the number of years you lived?

10:6 Baal and Ashtoreth are explained in the notes on 2:11-15 and 3:7. The gods of Aram and Sidon were very similar. The gods of Moab and Ammon were Chemosh and Molech. The Philistine gods were Dagon, Ashtoreth, Asherah, and Baal-zebul.

10:9, 10 Once again the Israelites suffered for many years before they gave up their sinful ways and called out to God for help (see 4:1-3; 6:1-6). Notice that when the Israelites were at the end of their rope they did not look to their pagan gods for help, but to the only one who was really able to help.

Is God your last resort? So much unnecessary suffering takes place because we don't call on God until we've used up all other resources. Rather than waiting until the situation becomes

LORD, saying, "We have sinned against you because we have abandoned you as our
God and have served the images of Baal."
10:11 Exod 14:30 Judg 3:13 [11]The LORD replied, "Did I not rescue you from the Egyptians, the Amorites, the
Ammonites, the Philistines, [12]the Sidonians, the Amalekites, and the Maonites? When
they oppressed you, you cried out to me, and I rescued you. [13]Yet you have abandoned
10:14 Deut 32:37 me and served other gods. So I will not rescue you anymore. [14]Go and cry out to the
gods you have chosen! Let them rescue you in your hour of distress!"
10:15 1 Sam 3:18 [15]But the Israelites pleaded with the LORD and said, "We have sinned. Punish us as
10:16 Deut 32:36 Josh 24:23 Jer 18:8 you see fit, only rescue us today from our enemies." [16]Then the Israelites put aside their
foreign gods and served the LORD. And he was grieved by their misery.
[17]At that time the armies of Ammon had gathered for war and were camped in Gilead,
preparing to attack Israel's army at Mizpah. [18]The leaders of Gilead said to each other,
"Whoever attacks the Ammonites first will become ruler over all the people of Gilead."

Jephthah Becomes Israel's Judge

11:1 1 Sam 12:11 Heb 11:32 **11** Now Jephthah from Gilead was a great warrior. He was the son of Gilead, but his
mother was a prostitute. [2]Gilead's wife also had several sons, and when these half
brothers grew up, they chased Jephthah off the land. "You will not get any of our father's

RASH VOWS

Ecclesiastes 5:2 says: "And don't make rash promises to God, for he is in heaven, and you are only here on earth. So let your words be few." Scripture records the vows of many men and women. Some of these vows proved to be rash and unwise, and others, though extreme, were kept to the letter by those who made them. Let us learn from the examples in God's Word not to make rash vows.

Person	*Vow*	*Result*	*Reference*
JACOB	To "choose" the true God and to give back a tenth to him if he kept him safe	God protected Jacob, who kept his vow to follow God	Genesis 28:20
JEPHTHAH	To offer to the Lord whoever came out to meet him after battle (it turned out to be his daughter)	He lost his daughter	Judges 11:30, 31
HANNAH	To give her son back to God if God would give her a son	When Samuel was born, she dedicated him to God	1 Samuel 1:9–11
SAUL	To kill anyone who ate before evening (Jonathan, his son, had not heard the command and broke it)	Saul would have killed Jonathan if soldiers had not intervened	1 Samuel 14:24–45
DAVID	To be kind to Jonathan's family	Mephibosheth, Jonathan's son, was treated royally by David	2 Samuel 9:7
ITTAI	To remain loyal to David	He became one of the great men in David's army	2 Samuel 15:21
MICAIAH	To say only what God told him to say	He was put in prison	1 Kings 22:14
JOB	That he was not rebelling against God	His fortunes were restored	Job 42:10
HEROD ANTIPAS	To give Herodias's daughter anything she requested	Herod was forced to order John the Baptist's death	Mark 6:22, 23
PAUL	To offer a sacrifice of thanksgiving in Jerusalem	He made the sacrifice despite the danger	Acts 18:18

desperate, turn to God first. He has the necessary resources to meet every kind of problem.

10:11-16 These verses show how difficult it can be to follow God over the long haul. The Israelites always seemed to forget God when all was well. But despite being rejected by his own people, God never failed to rescue them when they called out to him in repentance. God never fails to rescue us either. We act just like the Israelites when we put God outside our daily events instead of at the center of them. Just as a loving parent feels rejected when a child rebels, so God feels great rejection when we ignore or neglect him (1 Samuel 8:4-9; 10:17-19; John 12:44-50). We should strive to stay close to God rather than see how far we can go before judgment comes.

10:17, 18 The power of the Ammonite nation was at its peak during the period of the judges. The people were descendants of Ammon, conceived when Lot's daughter slept with her drunk father (Genesis 19:30-38). The land of Ammon was located just east of the Jordan River across from Jerusalem. South of Ammon lay the land of Moab, the nation conceived when Lot's other daughter slept with her father. Moab and Ammon were usually allies. It was a formidable task to defeat these nations.

11:1, 2 Jephthah, an illegitimate son of Gilead, was chased out of the country by his half brothers. He suffered as a result of another's decision and not for any wrong he had done. Yet in spite of his brothers' rejection, God used him. If you are suffering from unfair rejection, don't blame others and become discouraged. Remember how God used Jephthah despite his unjust circumstances, and realize that he is able to use you even if you feel rejected by some.

inheritance," they said, "for you are the son of a prostitute." 3So Jephthah fled from his
brothers and lived in the land of Tob. Soon he had a large band of rebels following him.
4At about this time, the Ammonites began their war against Israel. 5When the
Ammonites attacked, the leaders of Gilead sent for Jephthah in the land of Tob. They
said, 6"Come and be our commander! Help us fight the Ammonites!"
7But Jephthah said to them, "Aren't you the ones who hated me and drove me from
my father's house? Why do you come to me now when you're in trouble?"
8"Because we need you," they replied. "If you will lead us in battle against the
Ammonites, we will make you ruler over all the people of Gilead."
9Jephthah said, "If I come with you and if the LORD gives me victory over the
Ammonites, will you really make me ruler over all the people?"
10"The LORD is our witness," the leaders replied. "We promise to do whatever you
say."
11So Jephthah went with the leaders of Gilead, and he became their ruler and
commander of the army. At Mizpah, in the presence of the LORD, Jephthah repeated what
he had said to the leaders.
12Then Jephthah sent messengers to the king of Ammon, demanding to know why
Israel was being attacked. 13The king of Ammon answered Jephthah's messengers,
"When the Israelites came out of Egypt, they stole my land from the Arnon River to the
Jabbok River and all the way to the Jordan. Now then, give back the land peaceably."
14Jephthah sent this message back to the Ammonite king:

15"This is what Jephthah says: Israel did not steal any land from Moab or Ammon.
16When the people of Israel arrived at Kadesh on their journey from Egypt after
crossing the Red Sea,* 17they sent messengers to the king of Edom asking for permission to pass through his land. But their request was denied. Then they asked the
king of Moab for similar permission, but he wouldn't let them pass through either.
So the people of Israel stayed in Kadesh.
18"Finally, they went around Edom and Moab through the wilderness. They traveled along Moab's eastern border and camped on the other side of the Arnon River.
But they never once crossed the Arnon River into Moab.
19"Then Israel sent messengers to King Sihon of the Amorites, who ruled from
Heshbon, asking for permission to cross through his land to get to their destination.
20But King Sihon didn't trust Israel to pass through his land. Instead, he mobilized
his army at Jahaz and attacked them. 21But the LORD, the God of Israel, gave his
people victory over King Sihon. So Israel took control of all the land of the Amorites, who lived in that region, 22from the Arnon River to the Jabbok River, and
from the wilderness to the Jordan.
23"So you see, it was the LORD, the God of Israel, who took away the land from the
Amorites and gave it to Israel. Why, then, should we give it to you? 24You keep whatever your god Chemosh gives you, and we will keep whatever the LORD our God
gives us. 25Are you any better than Balak son of Zippor, king of Moab? Did he try to
make a case against Israel for disputed land? Did he go to war? No, of course not.

11:3 Judg 9:4; 2 Sam 10:6, 8
11:4 Judg 10:9
11:10 Gen 31:50
11:11 Judg 10:17
11:13 Num 21:24-26
11:16 Num 20:1-21
11:17 Num 20:14-21; Josh 24:9
11:18 Num 21:4; Deut 2:1-9, 18-19
11:19 Num 21:21-22
11:21 Deut 2:32-34
11:24 Num 21:27-30; 1 Kgs 11:7
11:25 Num 22:2

11:16 Hebrew *sea of reeds.*

11:3 Circumstances beyond his control forced Jephthah away from his people and into life as an outcast. Today, both believers and nonbelievers may drive away those who do not fit the norms dictated by our society, neighborhoods, or churches. Often, as in Jephthah's case, great potential is wasted because of prejudice—a refusal to look beyond ill-conceived stereotypes. Look around you to see if there are potential Jephthahs being kept out due to factors beyond their control. As a Christian, you know that everyone can have a place in God's family. Can you do anything to help these people gain acceptance for their character and abilities?

11:11 What does it mean that Jephthah repeated all his words before the Lord? Those making covenants in ancient times often made them at shrines so that they would be witnessed by deities. Often a written copy was also deposited at the shrine. This was much like a coronation ceremony for Jephthah.

11:14ff Jephthah sent messengers to the Ammonite king wanting to know why the Israelites in the land of Gilead were being attacked (11:12). The king replied that Israel had stolen this land and he wanted it back (11:13).

Jephthah sent another message to the king (11:14-27). In it he gave three arguments against the king's claim: (1) Gilead was never the king's land in the first place because Israel took it from the Amorites, not the Ammonites (11:16-22); (2) Israel should possess land given by Israel's God, and Ammon should possess land given by Ammon's god; (3) no one had contested Israel's ownership of the land since its conquest 300 years earlier (11:25, 26).

To Jephthah's credit, he tried to solve the problem without bloodshed. But the king of Ammon ignored his message and prepared his troops for battle.

11:26 Num 21:25 26 But now after three hundred years you make an issue of this! Israel has been living
here all this time, spread across the land from Heshbon to Aroer and in all the towns
along the Arnon River. Why have you made no effort to recover it before now? 27 I
have not sinned against you. Rather, you have wronged me by attacking me. Let the
LORD, who is judge, decide today which of us is right—Israel or Ammon."

28 But the king of Ammon paid no attention to Jephthah's message.

Jephthah's Vow

11:29 Judg 3:10 29 At that time the Spirit of the LORD came upon Jephthah, and he went throughout the
land of Gilead and Manasseh, including Mizpah in Gilead, and led an army against the
Ammonites. 30 And Jephthah made a vow to the LORD. He said, "If you give me victory

---

JEPHTHAH

It's hard not to admire people whose word can be depended on completely and whose actions are consistent with their words. For such people, talking is not avoiding action; it is the beginning of action. People like this can make excellent negotiators. They approach a conflict with the full intention of settling issues verbally, but they do not hesitate to use other means if verbal attempts fail. Jephthah was this kind of person.

In most of his conflicts, Jephthah's first move was to talk. In the war with the Ammonites, his strategy was negotiation. He clarified the issues so that everyone knew the cause of the conflict. His opponent's response determined his next action.

The fate of Jephthah's daughter is difficult to understand. We are not sure what Jephthah meant by his vow recorded in Judges 11:31. In any case, his vow was unnecessary. We do not know what actually happened to his daughter—whether she was burned as an offering or set apart as a virgin, thus denying Jephthah any hope of descendants since she was his only child. What we do know is that Jephthah was a person of his word, even when it was a word spoken in haste, and even when keeping his word cost him great pain.

How do you approach conflicts? There is a big difference between trying to settle a conflict through words and simply counterattacking someone verbally. How dependable are the statements you make? Do your children, friends, and fellow workers know you to be a person of your word? The measure of your trustworthiness is your willingness to take responsibility, even if you must pay a painful price because of something you said.

Strengths and accomplishments
- Listed in the Hall of Faith in Hebrews 11
- Controlled by God's Spirit
- Brilliant military strategist who negotiated before fighting

Weaknesses and mistakes
- Was bitter over the treatment he received from his half brothers
- Made a rash and foolish vow that was costly

Lesson from his life
- A person's background does not prevent God from working powerfully in his or her life

Vital statistics
- Where: Gilead
- Occupations: Warrior, judge
- Relative: Father: Gilead

Key verse "So Jephthah led his army against the Ammonites, and the LORD gave him victory" (Judges 11:32).

His story is told in Judges 11:1—12:7. He is also mentioned in 1 Samuel 12:11 and Hebrews 11:32.

11:27 Over the years, Israel had many judges to lead them. But Jephthah recognized the Lord as the people's true Judge, the only one who could really lead them and help them conquer the invading enemies.

11:30, 31 In God's law, a vow was a promise to God that should not be broken (Numbers 30:1, 2; Deuteronomy 23:21-23). It carried as much force as a written contract. Many people made vows in biblical times. Some, like Jephthah's, were very foolish.

11:30, 31 When Jephthah made his vow, did he stop to consider that a person, not a sheep or goat, might come out to meet him? Scholars are divided over the issue. Those who say Jephthah was considering human sacrifice use the following arguments: (1) He was from an area where pagan religion and human sacrifice were common. In his eyes, it may not have seemed like a sin. (2) Jephthah may not have had a background in religious law. Perhaps he was ignorant of God's command against human sacrifice.

Those who say Jephthah could not have been thinking about human sacrifice point to other evidence: (1) As leader of the people, Jephthah must have been familiar with God's laws; human sacrifice was clearly forbidden (Leviticus 18:21; 20:1-5). (2) No legitimate priest would have helped Jephthah carry out his vow if a person was to be the sacrifice.

Whatever Jephthah had in mind when he made the vow, did he or did he not sacrifice his daughter? Some think he did, because his vow was to make a burnt offering. Some think he did not, and they offer these two reasons: (1) If the girl was to die, she would not have spent her last two months in the hills. (2) God would not have honored a vow based on a wicked practice.

over the Ammonites, 31I will give to the LORD the first thing coming out of my house to
greet me when I return in triumph. I will sacrifice it as a burnt offering."
32So Jephthah led his army against the Ammonites, and the LORD gave him victory.
33He thoroughly defeated the Ammonites from Aroer to an area near Minnith—twenty
towns—and as far away as Abel-keramim. Thus Israel subdued the Ammonites.
34When Jephthah returned home to Mizpah, his daughter—his only child—ran out to **11:34** Exod 15:20
meet him, playing on a tambourine and dancing for joy. 35When he saw her, he tore his 1 Sam 18:6
clothes in anguish. "My daughter!" he cried out. "My heart is breaking! What a tragedy Jer 31:4
that you came out to greet me. For I have made a vow to the LORD and cannot take it **11:35** Num 30:2
back." Eccl 5:2, 4-5
36And she said, "Father, you have made a promise to the LORD. You must do to me **11:36** 2 Sam 18:19
what you have promised, for the LORD has given you a great victory over your enemies, Luke 1:38
the Ammonites. 37But first let me go up and roam in the hills and weep with my friends
for two months, because I will die a virgin."
38"You may go," Jephthah said. And he let her go away for two months. She and her
friends went into the hills and wept because she would never have children. 39When she
returned home, her father kept his vow, and she died a virgin. So it has become a custom
in Israel 40for young Israelite women to go away for four days each year to lament the
fate of Jephthah's daughter.

Ephraim Fights with Jephthah

12 Then the tribe of Ephraim mobilized its army and crossed over to Zaphon. They **12:1** Judg 8:1
sent this message to Jephthah: "Why didn't you call for us to help you fight
against Ammon? We are going to burn down your house with you in it!"
2"I summoned you at the beginning of the dispute, but you refused to come!" Jephthah
said. "You failed to help us in our struggle against Ammon. 3So I risked my life and went **12:3** 1 Sam 19:5
to battle without you, and the LORD gave me victory over the Ammonites. So why have Job 13:14
you come to fight me?"
4The leaders of Ephraim responded, "The men of Gilead are nothing more than rejects **12:4** Judg 3:28
from Ephraim and Manasseh." So Jephthah called out his army and attacked the men of
Ephraim and defeated them.
5Jephthah captured the shallows of the Jordan, and whenever a fugitive from Ephraim **12:5** Josh 2:7
tried to go back across, the men of Gilead would challenge him. "Are you a member of Judg 3:28; 7:24
the tribe of Ephraim?" they would ask. If the man said, "No, I'm not," 6they would tell
him to say "Shibboleth." If he was from Ephraim, he would say "Sibboleth," because

JEPHTHAH'S VICTORY
The Ephraimites mobilized an army because they were angry at not being included in the battle against Ammon. They planned to attack Jephthah at his home in Gilead. Jephthah captured the shallows of the Jordan at the Jabbok River and killed the Ephraimites who tried to cross.

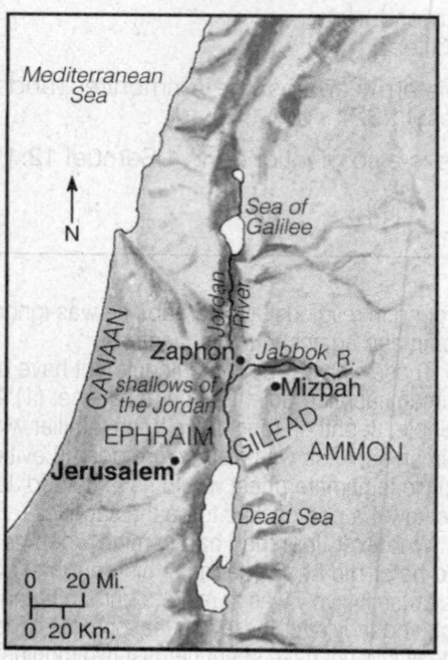

11:34, 35 Jephthah's rash vow brought him unspeakable grief. In the heat of emotion or personal turmoil it is easy to make foolish promises to God. These promises may sound very spiritual when we make them, but they may produce only guilt and frustration when we are forced to fulfill them. Making spiritual "deals" only brings disappointment. God does not want promises for the future, but obedience for today.

12:1ff Israel had just won a great battle, but instead of joy, there was pettiness and quarreling. The tribe of Ephraim was angry and jealous that they were not invited to join in the fighting (although Jephthah said he had invited them). The insults of the Ephraimites enraged Jephthah, who called out his troops and killed 42,000 men from Ephraim.

Jephthah usually spoke before he acted, but this time his revenge was swift. It cost Israel dearly, and it might have been avoided. Insulting others and being jealous are not right responses when we feel left out. But seeking revenge for an insult is just as wrong and very costly.

12:4-7 The men of the tribe of Ephraim caused Jephthah trouble just as they had Gideon (8:1-3). Jephthah captured the shallows of the Jordan, the boundary of Ephraim, and was able to defeat his countrymen as they crossed the river. He used a pronunciation test. *Shibboleth* is the word for "stream." The Ephraimites pronounced "sh" as "s," so Jephthah's army could easily identify them.

people from Ephraim cannot pronounce the word correctly. Then they would take him
and kill him at the shallows of the Jordan River. So forty-two thousand Ephraimites were
killed at that time.
12:7 Heb 11:32 7 Jephthah was Israel's judge for six years. When he died, he was buried in one of the
towns of Gilead.

Ibzan Becomes Israel's Judge

8 After Jephthah, Ibzan became Israel's judge. He lived in Bethlehem, 9 and he had thirty
sons and thirty daughters. He married his daughters to men outside his clan and brought
in thirty young women from outside his clan to marry his sons. Ibzan judged Israel for
seven years. 10 When he died, he was buried at Bethlehem.

Elon Becomes Israel's Judge

11 After him, Elon from Zebulun became Israel's judge. He judged Israel for ten years.
12 When he died, he was buried at Aijalon in Zebulun.

Abdon Becomes Israel's Judge

12:14 Judg 5:10 13 After Elon died, Abdon son of Hillel, from Pirathon, became Israel's judge. 14 He had
forty sons and thirty grandsons, who rode on seventy donkeys. He was Israel's judge for
eight years. 15 Then he died and was buried at Pirathon in Ephraim, in the hill country of
the Amalekites.

6. Sixth period: Samson

The Birth of Samson

13:1 Judg 2:11 **13** Again the Israelites did what was evil in the LORD's sight, so the LORD handed
13:2 Josh 19:41 them over to the Philistines, who kept them in subjection for forty years.
2 In those days, a man named Manoah from the tribe of Dan lived in the town of
13:3 Gen 16:7 Zorah. His wife was unable to become pregnant, and they had no children. 3 The angel
Judg 6:12 of the LORD appeared to Manoah's wife and said, "Even though you have been unable
13:4-5 to have children, you will soon become pregnant and give birth to a son. 4 You must not
Num 6:1-5 drink wine or any other alcoholic drink or eat any forbidden food. 5 You will become
Judg 13:14 pregnant and give birth to a son, and his hair must never be cut. For he will be dedicated
Luke 1:15 to God as a Nazirite from birth. He will rescue Israel from the Philistines."
13:6 1 Sam 2:27 6 The woman ran and told her husband, "A man of God appeared to me! He was like
one of God's angels, terrifying to look at. I didn't ask where he was from, and he didn't
tell me his name. 7 But he told me, 'You will become pregnant and give birth to a son.
You must not drink wine or any other alcoholic drink or eat any forbidden food. For
your son will be dedicated to God as a Nazirite from the moment of his birth until the
day of his death.'"
8 Then Manoah prayed to the LORD. He said, "Lord, please let the man of God come
back to us again and give us more instructions about this son who is to be born."
9 God answered his prayer, and the angel of God appeared once again to his wife as
she was sitting in the field. But her husband, Manoah, was not with her. 10 So she
quickly ran and told her husband, "The man who appeared to me the other day is here
again!"

12:8-15 There is little else known about these three judges or their importance. The large number of children and donkeys are an indication of the wealth of these men.

13:1 The Philistines lived on the west side of Canaan, along the Mediterranean seacoast. From Samson's day until the time of David they were the major enemy force in the land and a constant threat to Israel. The Philistines were fierce warriors; they had the advantage over Israel in numbers, tactical expertise, and technology. They knew the secret of making weapons out of iron (1 Samuel 13:19-22). But none of that mattered when God was fighting for Israel.

13:1ff Once again the cycle of sin, judgment, and repentance began (3:8, 9, 14, 15; 4:1-4; 6:1-14; 10:6–11:11). The Israelites would not turn to God unless they had been stunned by suffering, oppression, and death. This suffering was not caused by God, but resulted from the fact that the people ignored God, their Judge and Ruler. What will it take for you to follow God? The warnings in God's Word are clear: If we continue to harden our hearts against God, we can expect the same fate as Israel.

13:5 Samson was to be a Nazirite—a person who took a vow to be set apart for God's service. Samson's parents made the vow for him. A Nazirite vow was sometimes temporary, but in Samson's case, it was for life. As a Nazirite, Samson could not cut his hair, touch a dead body, or drink anything containing alcohol.

Although Samson often used poor judgment and sinned terribly, he accomplished much when he determined to be set apart for God. In this way he was like the nation Israel. As long as the Israelites remained set apart for God, the nation thrived. But they fell into terrible sin when they ignored God.

11 Manoah ran back with his wife and asked, "Are you the man who talked to my wife
the other day?"
"Yes," he replied, "I am."
12 So Manoah asked him, "When your words come true, what kind of rules should
govern the boy's life and work?"
13 The angel of the LORD replied, "Be sure your wife follows the instructions I gave **13:13**
her. 14 She must not eat grapes or raisins, drink wine or any other alcoholic drink, or eat Judg 13:4, 11
any forbidden food."
15 Then Manoah said to the angel of the LORD, "Please stay here until we can prepare **13:15**
a young goat for you to eat." Judg 6:19
16 "I will stay," the angel of the LORD replied, "but I will not eat anything. However,
you may prepare a burnt offering as a sacrifice to the LORD." (Manoah didn't realize it
was the angel of the LORD.)
17 Then Manoah asked the angel of the LORD, "What is your name? For when all this **13:17**
comes true, we want to honor you." Gen 32:29
18 "Why do you ask my name?" the angel of the LORD replied. "You wouldn't
understand if I told you."
19 Then Manoah took a young goat and a grain offering and offered it on a rock as a **13:19**
sacrifice to the LORD. And as Manoah and his wife watched, the LORD did an amazing Judg 6:20-21
thing. 20 As the flames from the altar shot up toward the sky, the angel of the LORD
ascended in the fire. When Manoah and his wife saw this, they fell with their faces to the
ground.
21 The angel did not appear again to Manoah and his wife. Manoah finally realized it
was the angel of the LORD, 22 and he said to his wife, "We will die, for we have seen **13:22**
God!" Gen 32:30 Judg 6:22
23 But his wife said, "If the LORD were going to kill us, he wouldn't have accepted our **13:24**
burnt offering and grain offering. He wouldn't have appeared to us and told us this 1 Sam 3:19 Luke 1:80
wonderful thing and done these miracles." Heb 11:32
24 When her son was born, they named him Samson. And the LORD blessed him as he **13:25**
grew up. 25 And in Mahaneh-dan, which is located between the towns of Zorah and Judg 3:10; 18:11-12
Eshtaol, the Spirit of the LORD began to take hold of him. 1 Sam 10:6, 10

Samson's Riddle

14 One day when Samson was in Timnah, he noticed a certain Philistine woman.
2 When he returned home, he told his father and mother, "I want to marry a young **14:2**
Philistine woman I saw in Timnah." Gen 21:21
3 His father and mother objected strenuously, "Isn't there one woman in our tribe or **14:3**
among all the Israelites you could marry? Why must you go to the pagan Philistines to Deut 7:3
find a wife?"

13:18 Why did the angel keep his name a secret? In those days people believed that if they knew someone's name, they knew his character and how to control him. By not giving his name, the angel was not allowing himself to be controlled by Manoah. He was also saying that his name was a mystery beyond understanding and too wonderful to imagine. Manoah asked the angel for an answer that he wouldn't have understood. Sometimes we ask God questions and then receive no answer. This may not be because God is saying no. We may have asked for knowledge beyond our ability to understand or accept.

13:19 Manoah sacrificed a grain offering to the Lord. A grain offering was grain, oil, and flour shaped into a cake and burned on the altar along with the *burnt offering* (the young goat). The grain offering, described in Leviticus 2, was offered to God as a sign of honor, respect, and worship. It was an acknowledgment that because the Israelites' food came from God, they owed their lives to him. With the grain offering, Manoah showed his desire to serve God and demonstrated his respect.

13:25 Samson's tribe, Dan, continued to wander in their inherited land (18:1), which was yet unconquered (Joshua 19:47, 48). Samson must have grown up with his warlike tribe's yearnings for a permanent and settled territory. Thus, his visits to the tribal army camp stirred his heart, and God's Spirit began preparing him for his role as judge and leader against the Philistines.

Perhaps there are things that stir your heart. These may indicate areas where God wants to use you. God uses a variety of means to develop and prepare us: hereditary traits, environmental influences, and personal experiences. As with Samson, this preparation often begins long before adulthood. Work at being sensitive to the Holy Spirit's leading and the tasks God has prepared for you. Your past may be more useful to you than you imagine.

14:3 Samson's parents objected to his marrying the Philistine woman for several reasons: (1) It was against God's law (Exodus 34:15-17; Deuteronomy 7:1-4). A stark example of what happened when the Israelites married pagans can be found in 3:5-7. (2) The Philistines were Israel's greatest enemies. Marriage to a hated Philistine would be a disgrace to Samson's family. But Samson's father gave in to Samson's demand and allowed the marriage, even though he had the right to refuse his son.

14:4 Josh 11:20

But Samson told his father, "Get her for me. She is the one I want." 4His father and
mother didn't realize the LORD was at work in this, creating an opportunity to disrupt the
Philistines, who ruled over Israel at that time.

5As Samson and his parents were going down to Timnah, a young lion attacked

14:6 Judg 13:25; 1 Sam 17:34-36

Samson near the vineyards of Timnah. 6At that moment the Spirit of the LORD powerfully took control of him, and he ripped the lion's jaws apart with his bare hands. He did
it as easily as if it were a young goat. But he didn't tell his father or mother about it.
7When Samson arrived in Timnah, he talked with the woman and was very pleased with
her.

8Later, when he returned to Timnah for the wedding, he turned off the path to look at
the carcass of the lion. And he found that a swarm of bees had made some honey in the
carcass. 9He scooped some of the honey into his hands and ate it along the way. He also
gave some to his father and mother, and they ate it. But he didn't tell them he had taken
the honey from the carcass of the lion.

10As his father was making final arrangements for the marriage, Samson threw a party

---

SAMSON

It is sad to be remembered for what one might have been. Samson had tremendous potential. Not many people have started life with credentials like his. Born as a result of God's plan in the lives of Manoah and his wife, Samson was to do a great work for God—to rescue Israel from the Philistines. To help him accomplish God's plan, he was given enormous physical strength.

Because Samson wasted his strength on practical jokes and getting out of scrapes, and because he eventually gave it up altogether to satisfy the woman he loved, we tend to see him as a failure. We remember him as the judge in Israel who spent his last days grinding grain in an enemy prison, and we say, "What wasted potential!"

Yes, Samson wasted his life. He could have strengthened his nation. He could have returned his people to the worship of God. He could have wiped out the Philistines. But even though he did none of those things, Samson still accomplished the purpose announced by the angel who visited his parents before his birth. In his final act, Samson began to rescue Israel from the Philistines.

Interestingly, the New Testament does not mention Samson's failures or his heroic feats of strength. In Hebrews 11:32, he is simply listed with others who "overthrew kingdoms, ruled with justice, and received what God had promised them," and in other ways were given superhuman aid. In the end, Samson recognized his dependence on God. When he died, God turned his failures and defeats into victory. Samson's story teaches us that it is never too late to start over. However badly we may have failed in the past, today is not too late for us to put our complete trust in God.

Strengths and accomplishments
- Dedicated to God from birth as a Nazirite
- Known for his feats of strength
- Listed in the Hall of Faith in Hebrews 11
- Began to free Israel from Philistine oppression

Weaknesses and mistakes
- Violated his vow and God's laws on many occasions
- Was controlled by sensuality
- Confided in the wrong people
- Used his gifts and abilities unwisely

Lessons from his life
- Great strength in one area of life does not make up for great weaknesses in other areas
- God's presence does not overwhelm a person's will
- God can use a person of faith in spite of his or her mistakes

Vital statistics
- Where: Zorah, Timnah, Ashkelon, Gaza, valley of Sorek
- Occupation: Judge
- Relative: Father: Manoah
- Contemporaries: Delilah, Samuel (who might have been born while Samson was a judge)

Key verse
"You will become pregnant and give birth to a son, and his hair must never be cut. For he will be dedicated to God as a Nazirite from birth. He will rescue Israel from the Philistines" (Judges 13:5).

His story is told in Judges 13—16. He is also mentioned in Hebrews 11:32.

14:6 "The Spirit of the LORD powerfully took control of him" refers to the unusual physical strength given him by the Spirit of the Lord. Samson did not seem to be affected in any other way than increased physical strength.

at Timnah, as was the custom of the day. 11 Thirty young men from the town were invited
to be his companions. 12 Samson said to them, "Let me tell you a riddle. If you solve my 14:12 Gen 29:27
riddle during these seven days of the celebration, I will give you thirty plain linen robes Ezek 17:2
and thirty fancy robes. 13 But if you can't solve it, then you must give me thirty linen
robes and thirty fancy robes."
"All right," they agreed, "let's hear your riddle."
14 So he said:

"From the one who eats came something to eat;
out of the strong came something sweet."

Three days later they were still trying to figure it out. 15 On the fourth* day they said 14:15 Judg 15:6; 16:5
to Samson's wife, "Get the answer to the riddle from your husband, or we will burn down
your father's house with you in it. Did you invite us to this party just to make us poor?"
16 So Samson's wife came to him in tears and said, "You don't love me; you hate me!
You have given my people a riddle, but you haven't told me the answer."
"I haven't even given the answer to my father or mother," he replied. "Why should I
tell you?" 17 So she cried whenever she was with him and kept it up for the rest of the
celebration. At last, on the seventh day, he told her the answer because of her persistent
nagging. Then she gave the answer to the young men.
18 So before sunset of the seventh day, the men of the town came to Samson with their
answer:

"What is sweeter than honey?
What is stronger than a lion?"

Samson replied, "If you hadn't plowed with my heifer, you wouldn't have found the
answer to my riddle!" 19 Then the Spirit of the LORD powerfully took control of him. He 14:19
went down to the town of Ashkelon, killed thirty men, took their belongings, and gave Judg 3:10
their clothing to the men who had answered his riddle. But Samson was furious about 14:20
what had happened, and he went back home to live with his father and mother. 20 So his John 3:29
wife was given in marriage to the man who had been Samson's best man at the wedding.

Samson's Vengeance on the Philistines

15 Later on, during the wheat harvest, Samson took a young goat as a present to his
wife. He intended to sleep with her, but her father wouldn't let him in. 2 "I really 15:2
thought you hated her," her father explained, "so I gave her in marriage to your best man. Judg 14:20
But look, her sister is more beautiful than she is. Marry her instead."
3 Samson said, "This time I cannot be blamed for everything I am going to do to you

14:15 As in Greek version; Hebrew reads *seventh.*

14:18 "If you hadn't plowed with my heifer" means "If you had not manipulated my wife." If they hadn't threatened his wife, they wouldn't have learned the answer to his riddle.

14:19 Samson impulsively used the special gift God gave him for selfish purposes. Today, God distributes abilities and skills throughout the church (1 Corinthians 12:1ff). The apostle Paul states that these gifts are to be used "to do his work and build up the church, the body of Christ" (Ephesians 4:12). To use these abilities for selfish purposes is to rob the church and fellow believers of strength. As you use the gifts God has given you, be sure you are helping others, not just yourself.

15:1ff Samson's reply in 15:11 tells the story of this chapter: "I only paid them back for what they did to me." Revenge is an uncontrollable monster. Each act of retaliation brings another. It is a boomerang that cannot be thrown without cost to the thrower. The revenge cycle can be halted only by forgiveness.

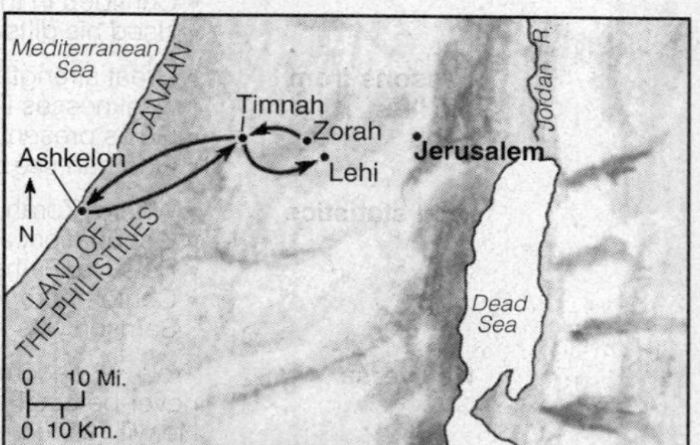

SAMSON'S VENTURES Samson grew up in Zorah and wanted to marry a Philistine girl from Timnah. Tricked at his own wedding feast, he went to Ashkelon and killed some Philistine men and stole their clothes to pay off a bet. Samson then let himself be captured and brought to Lehi, where he snapped his ropes and killed 1,000 people.

Philistines." 4 Then he went out and caught three hundred foxes. He tied their tails
together in pairs, and he fastened a torch to each pair of tails. 5 Then he lit the torches and
let the foxes run through the fields of the Philistines. He burned all their grain to the
ground, including the grain still in piles and all that had been bundled. He also destroyed
their grapevines and olive trees.

15:6 Judg 14:15

6 "Who did this?" the Philistines demanded.

"Samson," was the reply, "because his father-in-law from Timnah gave Samson's wife
to be married to his best man." So the Philistines went and got the woman and her father
and burned them to death.

7 "Because you did this," Samson vowed, "I will take my revenge on you, and I won't
stop until I'm satisfied!" 8 So he attacked the Philistines with great fury and killed many
of them. Then he went to live in a cave in the rock of Etam.

9 The Philistines retaliated by setting up camp in Judah and raiding the town of Lehi.
10 The men of Judah asked the Philistines, "Why have you attacked us?"

The Philistines replied, "We've come to capture Samson. We have come to pay him
back for what he did to us."

15:11 Judg 13:1; 14:4; 15:20

11 So three thousand men of Judah went down to get Samson at the cave in the rock of
Etam. They said to Samson, "Don't you realize the Philistines rule over us? What are
you doing to us?"

But Samson replied, "I only paid them back for what they did to me."

12 But the men of Judah told him, "We have come to tie you up and hand you over to
the Philistines."

"All right," Samson said. "But promise that you won't kill me yourselves."

13 "We will tie you up and hand you over to the Philistines," they replied. "We won't
kill you." So they tied him up with two new ropes and led him away from the rock.

15:14 Judg 14:19

14 As Samson arrived at Lehi, the Philistines came shouting in triumph. But the Spirit
of the LORD powerfully took control of Samson, and he snapped the ropes on his arms

15:15 Lev 26:8

as if they were burnt strands of flax, and they fell from his wrists. 15 Then he picked up
a donkey's jawbone that was lying on the ground and killed a thousand Philistines with
it. 16 And Samson said,

DELILAH

A person's greatest accomplishment may well be helping others accomplish great things. Likewise, a person's greatest failure may be preventing others from achieving greatness. Delilah played a minor role in Samson's life, but her effect was devastating, for she influenced him to betray his special calling from God. Motivated by greed, Delilah used her persistence to wear down Samson. His infatuation with her made Samson a vulnerable target. For all his physical strength, he was no match for her, and he paid a great price for giving in to her. Delilah is never mentioned again in the Bible. Her unfaithfulness to Samson brought ruin to him and to her people.

Are people helped by knowing you? Do they find that knowing you challenges them to be the best they can be? Even more important, does knowing you help their relationship with God? What do your demands for their time and attention tell them about your real care for them? Are you willing to be God's instrument in the lives of others?

Strength and accomplishment
- Persistent when faced with obstacles

Weaknesses and mistakes
- Valued money more than relationships
- Betrayed the man who trusted her

Lesson from her life
- We need to be careful to place our trust only in people who are trustworthy

Vital statistics
- Where: Valley of Sorek
- Contemporary: Samson

Key verses
"So day after day she nagged him until he couldn't stand it any longer. Finally Samson told her his secret" (Judges 16:16, 17).

Her story is told in Judges 16.

15:14-17 The Lord's strength came upon Samson, but he was proud and boasted only of his own strength. "With the jawbone of a donkey, I've killed a thousand men," he said. Pride can cause us to take credit for work we've done only because of God's strength.

"With the jawbone of a donkey,
I've made heaps on heaps!
With the jawbone of a donkey,
I've killed a thousand men!"

17 When he finished speaking, he threw away the jawbone; and the place was named
Jawbone Hill.*
18 Now Samson was very thirsty, and he cried out to the LORD, "You have accomplished this great victory by the strength of your servant. Must I now die of thirst and **15:19**
fall into the hands of these pagan people?" 19 So God caused water to gush out of a hollow Gen 45:27
in the ground at Lehi, and Samson was revived as he drank. Then he named that place 1 Sam 30:12 Isa 40:29
"The Spring of the One Who Cried Out,"* and it is still in Lehi to this day. **15:20**
20 Samson was Israel's judge for twenty years, while the Philistines ruled the land. Judg 13:1; 16:31 Heb 11:32

Samson Removes Gaza's Gates

16 One day Samson went to the Philistine city of Gaza and spent the night with a **16:1**
prostitute. 2 Word soon spread that Samson was there, so the men of Gaza gathered Josh 15:47
together and waited all night at the city gates. They kept quiet during the night, saying **16:2**
to themselves, "When the light of morning comes, we will kill him." Ps 118:10-12
3 But Samson stayed in bed only until midnight. Then he got up, took hold of the city
gates with its two posts, and lifted them, bar and all, right out of the ground. He put them
on his shoulders and carried them all the way to the top of the hill across from Hebron.

Samson and Delilah

4 Later Samson fell in love with a woman named Delilah, who lived in the valley of
Sorek. 5 The leaders of the Philistines went to her and said, "Find out from Samson what **16:5**
makes him so strong and how he can be overpowered and tied up securely. Then each of Judg 14:15
us will give you eleven hundred pieces* of silver."
6 So Delilah said to Samson, "Please tell me what makes you so strong and what it
would take to tie you up securely."
7 Samson replied, "If I am tied up with seven new bowstrings that have not yet been
dried, I will be as weak as anyone else."
8 So the Philistine leaders brought Delilah seven new bowstrings, and she tied Samson
up with them. 9 She had hidden some men in one of the rooms of her house, and she cried
out, "Samson! The Philistines have come to capture you!" But Samson snapped the
bowstrings as if they were string that had been burned in a fire. So the secret of his
strength was not discovered.
10 Afterward Delilah said to him, "You made fun of me and told me a lie! Now please
tell me how you can be tied up securely."

15:17 Hebrew *Ramath-lehi.* **15:19** Hebrew *En-hakkore.* **16:5** Hebrew *1,100 shekels,* about 28 pounds or 12.5 kilograms in weight.

15:18 Samson was physically and emotionally exhausted. After a great personal victory, his attitude declined quickly into self-pity—"Must I now die of thirst?" Emotionally, we are most vulnerable after a great effort or when faced with real physical needs. Severe depression often follows great achievements, so don't be surprised if you feel drained after a personal victory.

During these times of vulnerability, avoid the temptation to think that God owes you for your efforts. It was *his* strength that gave you victory. Concentrate on keeping your attitudes, actions, and words focused on God instead of yourself.

15:20 Apparently Samson was appointed Israel's judge after this victory over the Philistines.

16:5 The Philistines were ruled by five rulers, not just one. Each ruler ruled from a different city—Ashdod, Ashkelon, Ekron, Gath, or Gaza. Each of these cities was an important center for trade and commerce. Given Delilah's character, it is little wonder that she betrayed Samson when these rich and powerful men paid her a personal visit.

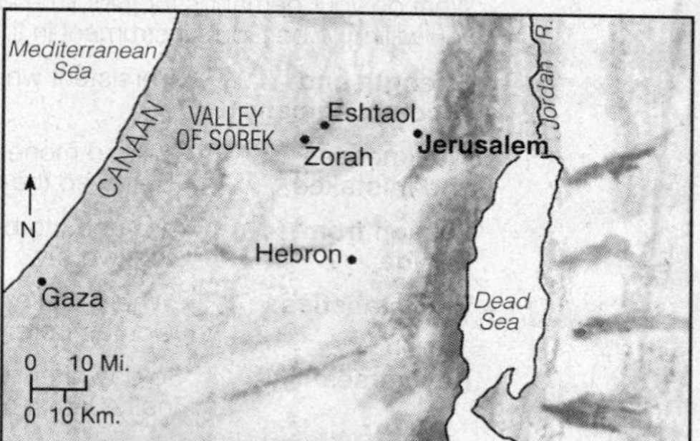

SAMSON AND DELILAH Samson was seduced by a Philistine woman named Delilah who lived in the valley of Sorek. She betrayed the secret of his strength to the Philistines, who captured him and led him away in chains to Gaza. There he died. His relatives buried him between Zorah and Eshtaol.

16:11 Judg 15:13
11 Samson replied, "If I am tied up with brand-new ropes that have never been used, I
will be as weak as anyone else."
12 So Delilah took new ropes and tied him up with them. The men were hiding in the
room as before, and again Delilah cried out, "Samson! The Philistines have come to
capture you!" But Samson snapped the ropes from his arms as if they were thread.
13 Then Delilah said, "You have been making fun of me and telling me lies! Won't you
please tell me how you can be tied up securely?"
Samson replied, "If you weave the seven braids of my hair into the fabric on your
loom and tighten it with the loom shuttle,* I will be as weak as anyone else."
So while he slept, Delilah wove the seven braids of his hair into the fabric 14 and
tightened it with the loom shuttle. Again she cried out, "Samson! The Philistines have
come to capture you!" But Samson woke up, pulled back the loom shuttle, and yanked
his hair away from the loom and the fabric.
16:15 Judg 14:16
15 Then Delilah pouted, "How can you say you love me when you don't confide in
me? You've made fun of me three times now, and you still haven't told me what makes
you so strong!" 16 So day after day she nagged him until he couldn't stand it any longer.
16:17 Num 6:2, 5; Judg 13:5
17 Finally, Samson told her his secret. "My hair has never been cut," he confessed, "for
I was dedicated to God as a Nazirite from birth. If my head were shaved, my strength
would leave me, and I would become as weak as anyone else."
18 Delilah realized he had finally told her the truth, so she sent for the Philistine leaders.
"Come back one more time," she said, "for he has told me everything." So the Philistine
leaders returned and brought the money with them. 19 Delilah lulled Samson to sleep with
his head in her lap, and she called in a man to shave off his hair, making his capture
16:20 1 Sam 16:14; 18:12
certain. And his strength left him. 20 Then she cried out, "Samson! The Philistines have
come to capture you!"
When he woke up, he thought, "I will do as before and shake myself free." But he
didn't realize the LORD had left him.
21 So the Philistines captured him and gouged out his eyes. They took him to Gaza,
where he was bound with bronze chains and made to grind grain in the prison. 22 But
before long his hair began to grow back.

16:13 As in Greek version; Hebrew lacks *on your loom and tighten it with the loom shuttle.*

16:15 Samson was deceived because he wanted to believe Delilah's lies. Although he could strangle a lion, he could not smother his burning lust and see Delilah for who she really was. How can you keep your desire for love and sexual pleasure from deceiving you? (1) You must decide what kind of a person you will love *before* passion takes over. Determine whether a person's character and faith in God are as desirable as his or her physical appearance. (2) Because most of the time you spend with your spouse will *not* involve sex, your companion's personality, temperament, and commitment to solve problems must be as gratifying as his or her kisses. (3) Be patient. The second look often reveals what is beneath the pleasant appearance and attentive touch.

16:16, 17 Delilah kept asking Samson for the secret of his strength until he finally grew tired of hearing her nagging and gave in. This was the second time that Samson allowed himself to be worn down by persistent nagging (14:17). What a pitiful excuse for disobedience. Don't allow anyone, no matter how attractive or persuasive, to talk you into doing wrong.

16:19 Delilah was a deceitful woman with honey on her lips and poison in her heart. Cold and calculating, she toyed with Samson, pretending to love him while looking for personal gain. How could Samson be so foolish? Four times Delilah took advantage of him. If he didn't realize what was happening after the first or second experience, surely he should have understood the situation by the fourth time! We think Samson is foolish, but how many times do we allow ourselves to be deceived by flattery and give in to temptation and wrong beliefs? Avoid falling prey to deceit by asking God to help you distinguish between deception and truth.

16:21 Samson, the mighty warrior, became a slave. Rather than kill him, the Philistines preferred to humiliate him by gouging out his eyes and making him grind grain. Samson now had plenty of time to wonder if Delilah's charms were worth spending the rest of his life in humiliation.

Although God did not completely abandon Samson (16:28-30), he allowed Samson's decision to stand, and the consequences of his decision followed naturally. We may choose to be close to God or to go our own way, but there are consequences resulting from our choice. Samson didn't choose to be captured, but he chose to be with Delilah, and he could not escape the consequences of his decision.

16:21 Blinded and without strength, Samson was taken to Gaza where he would spend the rest of his short life. Gaza was one of the five capital cities of the Philistines. Known for its many wells, Gaza was a vital stop along a great caravan route that connected Egypt to the south with Aram to the north. The Philistines probably showed off their prize captive, Samson, to many dignitaries passing through.

Ironically, it was in Gaza that Samson had earlier demonstrated his great strength by uprooting the city gates (16:1-3). Now he was an example of weakness.

Samson's Final Victory
23 The Philistine leaders held a great festival, offering sacrifices and praising their god, **16:23** 1 Sam 5:2
Dagon. They said, "Our god has given us victory over our enemy Samson!"
24 When the people saw him, they praised their god, saying, "Our god has delivered
our enemy to us! The one who killed so many of us is now in our power!"
25 Half drunk by now, the people demanded, "Bring out Samson so he can perform for
us!" So he was brought from the prison and made to stand at the center of the temple,
between the two pillars supporting the roof.
26 Samson said to the servant who was leading him by the hand, "Place my hands
against the two pillars. I want to rest against them." 27 The temple was completely filled
with people. All the Philistine leaders were there, and there were about three thousand
on the roof who were watching Samson and making fun of him.
28 Then Samson prayed to the LORD, "Sovereign LORD, remember me again. O God, **16:28** Judg 15:18
please strengthen me one more time so that I may pay back the Philistines for the loss of
my eyes." 29 Then Samson put his hands on the center pillars of the temple and pushed
against them with all his might. 30 "Let me die with the Philistines," he prayed. And the
temple crashed down on the Philistine leaders and all the people. So he killed more
people when he died than he had during his entire lifetime.
31 Later his brothers and other relatives went down to get his body. They took him back **16:31** Judg 15:21
home and buried him between Zorah and Eshtaol, where his father, Manoah, was buried.
Samson had been Israel's judge for twenty years.

C. THE MORAL FAILURE OF ISRAEL (17:1—21:25)

This section shows Israel falling into idolatry, moral decline, and petty fighting. Israel, the nation that was to set the example for spiritual living, had instead become morally depraved. When Israel did serve God, and that was seldom, it was often from selfish motives. Selfish obedience does not bring us far. Genuine obedience is motivated by a love and reverence for God himself.

1. Idolatry in the tribe of Dan

Micah's Idols

17 A man named Micah lived in the hill country of Ephraim. 2 One day he said to his
mother, "I heard you curse the thief who stole eleven hundred pieces* of silver
from you. Well, here they are. I was the one who took them."
"The LORD bless you for admitting it," his mother replied. 3 He returned the money to **17:3** Exod 20:4, 23; 34:17
her, and she said, "I now dedicate these silver coins to the LORD. In honor of my son, I
will have an image carved and an idol cast." 4 So his mother took two hundred of the
silver coins to a silversmith, who made them into an image and an idol. And these were
placed in Micah's house.
5 Micah set up a shrine, and he made a sacred ephod and some household idols. Then **17:5** Gen 31:19 Judg 8:27

17:2 Hebrew *1,100 shekels,* about 28 pounds or 12.5 kilograms in weight.

16:23, 24 Dagon was the chief god of the Philistines, the god of grain and harvest. Many temples were built to Dagon, and the worship there included human sacrifice. The temples were also the local entertainment centers. Just as people today crowd into theaters, Philistine townspeople crowded into the local temple. They sat on the flat temple roof and looked into the courtyard below. What they often saw was the torture and humiliation of prisoners.

Since the Philistines had control over the Israelites, they thought their god was stronger. But when the Ark of God was placed before Dagon in a similar temple, the idol fell over and broke into pieces (1 Samuel 5:1-7). God's strength goes beyond numbers or physical might.

16:28-30 In spite of Samson's past, God still answered his prayer and destroyed the pagan temple and worshipers. God still loved him. He was willing to hear Samson's prayer of confession and repentance and use him this final time. One of the effects of sin in our lives is to keep us from feeling like praying. But perfect moral behavior is not a condition for prayer. Don't let guilt feelings over sin keep you from your only means of restoration. No matter how long you have been away from God, he is ready to hear from you and restore you to a right relationship. Every situation can be salvaged if you are willing to turn again to him. If God could still work in Samson's situation, he can certainly make something worthwhile out of yours.

17:2 Micah and his mother seemed to be good and moral and may have sincerely desired to worship God, but they disobeyed God by following their own desires instead of doing what God wanted. The attitude that prevailed in Micah's day was this: "The people did whatever seemed right in their own eyes" (17:6). This is remarkably similar to today's prevailing attitudes. But God has given us standards. He has not left our conduct up to us and our opinions. We can avoid conforming to society's low standards by taking God's commands seriously and applying them to life. Independence and self-reliance are positive traits, but only within the framework of God's standards.

17:6 Deut 12:8 Judg 18:1; 19:1; 21:25
17:7 Judg 19:1 Ruth 1:1-2 Mic 5:2 Matt 2:1
17:10 Judg 18:19
17:12 Num 16:10 Judg 18:1-7

he installed one of his sons as the priest. 6 In those days Israel had no king, so the people
did whatever seemed right in their own eyes.
7 One day a young Levite from Bethlehem in Judah 8 arrived in that area of Ephraim,
looking for a good place to live. He happened to stop at Micah's house as he was
traveling through. 9 "Where are you from?" Micah asked him.
And he replied, "I am a Levite from Bethlehem in Judah, and I am looking for a place
to live."
10 "Stay here with me," Micah said, "and you can be a father and priest to me. I will
give you ten pieces* of silver a year, plus a change of clothes and your food." 11 The
Levite agreed to this and became like one of Micah's sons. 12 So Micah ordained the
Levite as his personal priest, and he lived in Micah's house. 13 "I know the LORD will
bless me now," Micah said, "because I have a Levite serving as my priest."

Idolatry in the Tribe of Dan

18:1 Josh 19:40-48 Judg 17:6; 19:1
18:2 Judg 13:25
18:4 Judg 17:10-12
18:7 Josh 19:47

18 Now in those days Israel had no king. And the tribe of Dan was trying to find a
place to settle, for they had not yet driven out the people who lived in the land
assigned to them. 2 So the men of Dan chose five warriors from among their clans, who
lived in the towns of Zorah and Eshtaol, to scout out a land for them to settle in.
When these warriors arrived in the hill country of Ephraim, they came to Micah's
home and spent the night there. 3 Noticing the young Levite's accent, they took him aside
and asked him, "Who brought you here, and what are you doing? Why are you here?"
4 He told them about his agreement with Micah and that he was Micah's personal priest.
5 Then they said, "Ask God whether or not our journey will be successful."
6 "Go in peace," the priest replied. "For the LORD will go ahead of you on your journey."
7 So the five men went on to the town of Laish, where they noticed the people living
carefree lives, like the Sidonians; they were peaceful and secure. The people were also
wealthy because their land was very fertile. And they lived a great distance from Sidon
and had no allies nearby.

17:10 Hebrew *10 shekels,* about 4 ounces or 114 grams in weight.

17:6 Today, as in Micah's day, everyone seems to put his or her own interests first. Time has not changed human nature. Most people still reject God's right way of living. The people in Micah's time replaced the true worship of God with a homemade version of worship. As a result, justice was soon replaced by revenge and chaos. Ignoring God's direction led to confusion and destruction. Anyone who has not submitted to God will end up doing whatever seems right at the time. This tendency is present in all of us. To know what is really right and to have the strength to do it, we need to draw closer to God and his Word.

17:7-12 Apparently the Israelites no longer supported the priests and Levites with their tithes because so many of the people no longer worshiped God. The young Levite in this story probably left his home in Bethlehem because the money he received from the people there was not enough to live on. But Israel's moral decay affected even the priests and Levites. This man accepted money (17:10, 11), idols (18:20), and position (17:12) in a way that was inconsistent with God's laws. While Micah revealed the religious downfall of individual Israelites, this priest illustrated the religious downfall of priests and Levites.

18:1 The Danites had been assigned enough land to meet their needs (Joshua 19:40-48). However, because they failed to trust God to help them conquer their territory, the Amorites forced them into the hill country and wouldn't let them settle in the plains (Judges 1:34). Rather than fight for their allotted territory, they preferred to look for new land in the north where resistance from the enemy wouldn't be so tough. It was while they were traveling north that some of their men passed Micah's home and stole some of his idols.

18:4-6 Priests and their assistants were all members of the tribe of Levi (Numbers 3:5-13). They were to serve the people, teach them how to worship God, and perform the rituals involved in the worship services both at the Tabernacle in Shiloh and in the designated cities throughout the land. But this disobedient priest showed disrespect for God because (1) he performed his duties in a house. Priestly duties were to be performed only in the Tabernacle or a designated city. This requirement was intended to prevent God's laws from being changed. (2) He carried idols with him (18:20). (3) He claimed to speak for God when God had not spoken through him (18:6).

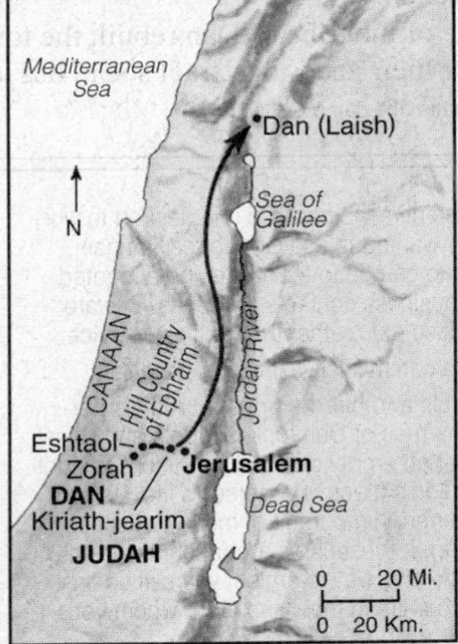

THE TRIBE OF DAN MOVES NORTH Troops from the tribe of Dan traveled from Zorah and Eshtaol into the hill country of Ephraim, where they persuaded Micah's priest to come with them. They continued north to Laish, where they ruthlessly butchered its citizens. The city was renamed Dan, and the priest's idols became the focus of their worship.

8 When the men returned to Zorah and Eshtaol, their relatives asked them, "What did
you find?"
9 The men replied, "Let's attack! We have seen the land, and it is very good. You should
not hesitate to go and take possession of it. 10 When you get there, you will find the people **18:10** Deut 8:9
living carefree lives. God has given us a spacious and fertile land, lacking in nothing!"
11 So six hundred warriors from the tribe of Dan set out from Zorah and Eshtaol.
12 They camped at a place west of Kiriath-jearim in Judah, which is called Mahaneh-dan*
to this day. 13 Then they went up into the hill country of Ephraim and came to the house
of Micah.
14 The five men who had scouted out the land around Laish said to the others, "There **18:14** Judg 17:5
is a shrine here with a sacred ephod, some household idols, a carved image, and a cast
idol. It's obvious what we ought to do." 15 So the five men went over to Micah's house,
where the young Levite lived, and greeted him kindly. 16 As the six hundred warriors
from the tribe of Dan stood just outside the gate, 17 the five spies entered the shrine and
took the carved image, the sacred ephod, the household idols, and the cast idol.
18 When the priest saw the men carrying all the sacred objects out of Micah's shrine,
he said, "What are you doing?"
19 "Be quiet and come with us," they said. "Be a father and priest to all of us. Isn't it **18:19** Judg 17:10
better to be a priest for an entire tribe of Israel than just for the household of one man?"
20 The young priest was quite happy to go with them, so he took along the sacred ephod,
the household idols, and the carved image. 21 They started on their way again, placing
their children, livestock, and possessions in front of them.
22 When the people from the tribe of Dan were quite a distance from Micah's home,
Micah and some of his neighbors came chasing after them. 23 They were shouting as they
caught up with them. The men of Dan turned around and said, "What do you want? Why
have you called these men together and chased after us like this?"
24 "What do you mean, What do I want?" Micah replied. "You've taken away all my
gods and my priest, and I have nothing left!"
25 The men of Dan said, "Watch what you say! Some of us are short-tempered, and
they might get angry and kill you and your family." 26 So the men of Dan went on their
way. When Micah saw that there were too many of them for him to attack, he turned
around and went home.
27 Then, with Micah's idols and his priest, the men of Dan came to the town of Laish, **18:27** Josh 19:47
whose people were peaceful and secure. They attacked and killed all the people and
burned the town to the ground. 28 There was no one to rescue the residents of the town, **18:28** 2 Sam 10:6
for they lived a great distance from Sidon and had no allies nearby. This happened in the
valley near Beth-rehob.

Then the people of the tribe of Dan rebuilt the town and lived there. 29 They renamed
the town Dan after their ancestor, Israel's son, but it had originally been called Laish.

18:12 *Mahaneh-dan* means "the camp of Dan."

18:11-26 Through this entire incident, no one desired to worship God; instead, they wanted to use God for selfish gain. Today some people go to church to feel better, be accepted, relieve guilt, and gain business contacts or friends. Beware of following God for selfish gain rather than selfless service.

18:14 An ephod was a ceremonial vest worn by a priest.

18:24 Micah made idols and hired a priest to run his personal religion. When the men of Dan took his idols and priest, nothing remained. What an empty spiritual condition! An idol is anything that takes God's place in a person's life. Some people invest all their energy in pursuit of money, success, possessions, or a career. If these idols are taken away, only an empty shell is left. The only way to protect yourself against such loss is to invest your life in the living God, whom you can never lose.

18:27 Did the tribe of Dan have the right to kill the citizens of Laish? No. God had commanded Israel to clean out and destroy certain cities because of their idolatry and wickedness, but Laish did not fall under that judgment. It was not within the assigned boundaries of Dan, and its people were peaceful in contrast to the warlike Canaanites. But the tribe of Dan had no regard for God's law. God's law said to destroy a city for idolatry (Deuteronomy 13:12-15). The Danites themselves were guilty of this sin. This story shows how far some of the tribes had wandered away from God.

18:27 Just because the Danites successfully defeated Laish doesn't mean their actions were right. Their idolatry showed that God was not guiding them. Today many justify their wrong actions by outward signs of success. They think that wealth, popularity, or lack of suffering is an indication of God's blessing. But many stories in the Bible indicate that evil and earthly success can go hand in hand (see, for example, 2 Kings 14:23-29). Success doesn't indicate God's approval. Don't allow personal success to become a measuring rod of whether or not you are pleasing God.

18:30 Exod 2:22; 18:3 30 Then they set up the carved image, and they appointed Jonathan son of Gershom, a
descendant of Moses,* as their priest. This family continued as priests for the tribe of
18:31 Josh 18:1 Dan until the Exile. 31 So Micah's carved image was worshiped by the tribe of Dan as
long as the Tabernacle of God remained at Shiloh.

2. War against the tribe of Benjamin

The Levite and His Concubine

19:1 Judg 18:1 **19** Now in those days Israel had no king. There was a man from the tribe of Levi
living in a remote area of the hill country of Ephraim. One day he brought home
a woman from Bethlehem in Judah to be his concubine. 2 But she was unfaithful to him
19:3 Gen 34:3; 50:21 and returned to her father's home in Bethlehem. After about four months, 3 her husband
took a servant and an extra donkey to Bethlehem to persuade her to come back. When
he arrived at her father's house, she took him inside, and her father welcomed him. 4 Her
father urged him to stay awhile, so he stayed three days, eating, drinking, and sleeping
there.

19:5 Gen 18:5 5 On the fourth day the man was up early, ready to leave, but the woman's father said,
"Have something to eat before you go." 6 So the two of them sat down together and had
something to eat and drink. Then the woman's father said, "Please stay the night and
enjoy yourself." 7 The man got up to leave, but his father-in-law kept urging him to stay,
so he finally gave in and stayed the night. 8 On the morning of the fifth day he was up
early again, ready to leave, and again the woman's father said, "Have something to eat;
then you can leave some time this afternoon." So they had another day of feasting.

9 That afternoon, as he and his concubine and servant were preparing to leave, his
father-in-law said, "Look, it's getting late. Stay the night and enjoy yourself. Tomorrow
19:10 Josh 15:8; 1 Chr 11:4-5 you can get up early and be on your way."

10 But this time the man was determined to leave. So he took his two saddled donkeys
19:11 Judg 19:19 and his concubine and headed in the direction of Jebus (that is, Jerusalem). 11 It was late
in the day when they reached Jebus, and the man's servant said to him, "It's getting too
late to travel; let's stay in this Jebusite city tonight."

12 "No," his master said, "we can't stay in this foreign city where there are no
Israelites. We will go on to Gibeah. 13 We will find a place to spend the night in either
Gibeah or Ramah." 14 So they went on. The sun was setting as they came to Gibeah, a

18:30 As in an ancient Hebrew tradition, some Greek manuscripts, and Latin Vulgate; Masoretic Text reads *of Manasseh.*

18:30, 31 The tribe of Dan had stolen Micah's idols, and now they set them up in Laish. Although the Danites were actually denying God by worshiping these images (Exodus 20:1-5), they probably assumed they were worshiping God through them (see the note on Exodus 32:4, 5). Worshiping images of God is *not* worshiping God, even if it resembles true worship in some ways. People repeat the same mistake today when they claim to be Christians without really believing in God's power or changing their conduct to conform to his expectations. Godliness cannot be merely a claim. It must be a reality in our motives and in our actions.

18:31 Shiloh was probably destroyed during the events reported in 1 Samuel 4 and 5, not long after the time described here. Because Shiloh was the religious center for Israel, all adult males were required to travel there for certain religious feasts. The tribe of Dan, however, set up idols and priests in the new territory they conquered. The fact that they were over 80 miles away from Shiloh may have been their excuse for not fulfilling the law's requirements. This act was a further demonstration of their disregard for God.

18:31 The true worship of God should have been maintained through the Levitical priests scattered throughout the land and the influence of the Tabernacle in Shiloh. This story shows how pagan influences and moral depravity had crept into every corner of Israelite culture. Although 300 years had passed since they entered the Promised Land, they still had not destroyed the idolatry and evil practices within it.

There may be a tendency in your life to allow "harmless" habits to have their own small corners, but they can become dominating forces. The values, attitudes, and practices you have adopted from the world's system can be exposed by applying the light of God's truth to them. Once you see them for what they are, you can begin to uproot them.

19:1–21:25 What is the significance of this tragic story? When the Israelites' faith in God disintegrated, their unity as a nation also disintegrated. They could have taken complete possession of the land if they had obeyed God and trusted him to keep his promises. But when they forgot him, they lost their purpose, and soon "the people did whatever seemed right in their own eyes" (21:25). When they stopped letting God lead them, they became no better than the evil people around them. When they made laws for their own benefit, they set standards far below God's. When you leave God out of your life, you may be shocked at what you are capable of doing (19:30).

19:1 Having concubines was an accepted part of Israelite society although this is not what God intended (Genesis 2:24). A concubine had most of the duties but only some of the privileges of a wife. Although she was legally attached to one man, she and her children usually did not have the inheritance rights of the legal wife and legitimate children. Her primary purpose was giving the man sexual pleasure, bearing additional children, and contributing more help to the household or estate. Concubines were often foreign prisoners of war. But they could also be Israelites, as was probably the case in this story.

town in the land of Benjamin, 15so they stopped there to spend the night. They rested in
the town square, but no one took them in for the night.
16That evening an old man came home from his work in the fields. He was from the **19:16** Ps 104:23
hill country of Ephraim, but he was living in Gibeah in the territory of Benjamin. 17When
he saw the travelers sitting in the town square, he asked them where they were from and
where they were going.
18"We have been in Bethlehem in Judah," the man replied. "We are on our way home **19:18** Judg 18:31
to a remote area in the hill country of Ephraim, and we're going to the Tabernacle of the
LORD. But no one has taken us in for the night, 19even though we have everything we
need. We have straw and fodder for our donkeys and plenty of bread and wine for
ourselves."
20"You are welcome to stay with me," the old man said. "I will give you anything you
might need. But whatever you do, don't spend the night in the square." 21So he took them **19:21** Gen 24:32-33
home with him and fed their donkeys. After they washed their feet, they had supper
together.
22While they were enjoying themselves, some of the wicked men in the town sur- **19:22** Gen 19:4-5
rounded the house. They began beating at the door and shouting to the old man, "Bring
out the man who is staying with you so we can have sex with him."
23The old man stepped outside to talk to them. "No, my brothers, don't do such an **19:23** Gen 34:7; 2 Sam 13:12
evil thing. For this man is my guest, and such a thing would be shameful. 24Here, take
my virgin daughter and this man's concubine. I will bring them out to you, and you can **19:24** Gen 19:8
do whatever you like to them. But don't do such a shameful thing to this man."
25But they wouldn't listen to him. Then the Levite took his concubine and pushed her
out the door. The men of the town abused her all night, taking turns raping her until
morning. Finally, at dawn, they let her go. 26At daybreak the woman returned to the
house where her husband was staying. She collapsed at the door of the house and lay
there until it was light.
27When her husband opened the door to leave, he found her there. She was lying face
down, with her hands on the threshold. 28He said, "Get up! Let's go!" But there was no **19:28** Judg 20:5
answer.* So he put her body on his donkey and took her home.
29When he got home, he took a knife and cut his concubine's body into twelve pieces. **19:29** 1 Sam 11:7
Then he sent one piece to each tribe of Israel. 30Everyone who saw it said, "Such a
horrible crime has not been committed since Israel left Egypt. Shouldn't we speak up **19:30** Judg 20:7
and do something about this?"

Israel's War with Benjamin

20 Then all the Israelites, from Dan to Beersheba and from the land of Gilead, came **20:1** 1 Sam 7:5
together in one large assembly and stood in the presence of the LORD at Mizpah.
2The leaders of all the people and all the tribes of Israel—400,000 warriors armed with
swords—took their positions in the assembly of the people of God. 3(Word soon reached

19:28 Greek version adds *for she was dead.*

19:24 Nowhere is the unwritten law of hospitality stronger than in the Middle East. Protecting a guest at any cost ranked at the top of a man's code of honor. But here the hospitality code turned to fanaticism. The rape and abuse of a daughter and companion were preferable to the *possibility* of a conflict between a guest and a neighbor. The two men were selfish (they didn't want to get hurt themselves); they lacked courage (they didn't want to face a conflict even when lives were at stake); and they disobeyed God's law (they allowed deliberate abuse and murder). What drastic consequences can result when social protocol carries more authority than moral convictions!

19:29, 30 Although this was a terrible way to spread the news, it effectively communicated the horror of the crime and called the people to action. Saul used a similar method in 1 Samuel 11:7. Ironically, the man who alerted Israel to the murder of his concubine was just as guilty for her death as the men who actually killed her.

19:30 The horrible crime described in this chapter wasn't Israel's worst offense. Even worse was the nation's failure to establish a government based upon God's moral principles, where the law of God was the law of the land. As a result, laws were usually unenforced and crime was ignored. Sexual perversion and lawlessness were by-products of Israel's disobedience to God. The Israelites weren't willing to speak up until events had gone too far.

Whenever we get away from God and his Word, all sorts of evil can follow. Our drifting away from God may be slow and almost imperceptible, with the ultimate results affecting a future generation. We must continually call our nation back to God and work toward the establishment of God's moral and spiritual reign in the heart of every person.

20:1 Dan was the northernmost city in Israel, and Beersheba, the southernmost. The two were often mentioned together as a reference to the entire nation.

the land of Benjamin that the other tribes had gone up to Mizpah.) The Israelites then
asked how this terrible crime had happened.
[4]The Levite, the husband of the woman who had been murdered, said, "My concubine
20:5 Judg 19:22, 25-26 and I came to Gibeah, a town in the land of Benjamin, to spend the night. [5]That night
some of the leaders of Gibeah surrounded the house, planning to kill me, and they raped
20:6-7 Judg 19:29-30 my concubine until she was dead. [6]So I cut her body into twelve pieces and sent the
pieces throughout the land of Israel, for these men have committed this terrible and
shameful crime. [7]Now then, the entire community of Israel must decide what should be
done about this!"
[8]And all the people stood up together and replied, "Not one of us will return home.
[9]Instead, we will draw lots to decide who will attack Gibeah. [10]One tenth of the men
from each tribe will be chosen to supply the warriors with food, and the rest of us will
take revenge on Gibeah* for this shameful thing they have done in Israel." [11]So all the
Israelites were united, and they gathered together to attack the town.
20:12 Deut 13:14 [12]The Israelites sent messengers to the tribe of Benjamin, saying, "What a terrible
thing has been done among you! [13]Give up these evil men from Gibeah so we can
20:13 1 Cor 5:13 execute them and purge Israel of this evil."
But the people of Benjamin would not listen. [14]Instead, they came from their towns
and gathered at Gibeah to fight the Israelites. [15]Twenty-six thousand of their warriors
armed with swords arrived in Gibeah to join the seven hundred warriors who lived there.
20:16 Judg 3:15 [16]Seven hundred of Benjamin's warriors were left-handed, each of whom could sling a
rock and hit a target within a hairsbreadth, without missing. [17]Israel had 400,000
warriors armed with swords, not counting Benjamin's warriors.
20:18 Num 27:21 Judg 1:1 [18]Before the battle the Israelites went to Bethel and asked God, "Which tribe should
lead the attack against the people of Benjamin?"
The LORD answered, "Judah is to go first."
[19]So the Israelites left early the next morning and camped near Gibeah. [20]Then they
advanced toward Gibeah to attack the men of Benjamin. [21]But Benjamin's warriors, who
were defending the town, came out and killed twenty-two thousand Israelites in the field
that day.
20:22 Josh 7:6-7 [22]But the Israelites took courage and assembled at the same place they had fought the
previous day. [23](For they had gone up to Bethel and wept in the presence of the LORD
until evening. Then they asked the LORD, "Should we fight against our relatives from
Benjamin again?" And the LORD said, "Go out and fight against them.")
[24]So they went out to fight against the warriors of Benjamin, [25]but the men of
Benjamin killed another eighteen thousand Israelites, all of whom were experienced with
a sword.
20:26 Judg 21:2-4 [26]Then all the Israelites went up to Bethel and wept in the presence of the LORD and
20:27 Judg 20:18 fasted until evening. They also brought burnt offerings and peace offerings to the LORD.
[27]And the Israelites went up seeking direction from the LORD. (In those days the Ark of
the Covenant of God was in Bethel, [28]and Phinehas son of Eleazar and grandson of
Aaron was the priest.) The Israelites asked the LORD, "Should we fight against our
relatives from Benjamin again or should we stop?"
The LORD said, "Go! Tomorrow I will give you victory over them."
[29]So the Israelites set an ambush all around Gibeah. [30]They went out on the third day

20:10 Hebrew *Geba,* in this case, a variant for Gibeah; also in 20:33.

20:13 Perhaps the leaders of the tribe of Benjamin had been given distorted facts about the serious crime in their territory, or perhaps they were too proud to admit that some of their people had stooped so low. In either case, they would not listen to the rest of Israel and hand over the accused criminals. They were more loyal to their own tribe than to God's law.

By covering for their kinsmen, the entire tribe of Benjamin sank to a level of immorality as low as that of the criminals. Through this act, we get a glimpse of how thoroughly the nation's moral fabric had unraveled. The time period of the judges ends in a bloody civil war that sets the stage for the spiritual renewal to come under Samuel (see 1 Samuel).

20:27, 28 This is the only place in Judges where the Ark of the Covenant is mentioned. This probably indicates how seldom the people consulted God.

Phinehas the high priest was also the high priest under Joshua (Joshua 22:13). The reference to Phinehas as high priest and the location of the Tabernacle in Bethel instead of Shiloh probably indicate that the events of this story occurred during the early years of the judges.

and assembled at the same place as before. 31 When the warriors of Benjamin came out **20:31**
to attack, they were drawn away from the town. And as they had done before, they began Josh 8:16
to kill the Israelites. About thirty Israelites died in the open fields and along the roads
leading to Bethel and Gibeah.
32 Then the warriors of Benjamin shouted, "We're defeating them as we did in the first
battle!" But the Israelites had agreed in advance to run away so that the men of Benjamin
would chase them along the roads and be drawn away from the town.
33 When the main group of Israelite warriors reached Baal-tamar, they turned and **20:33**
prepared to attack. Then the Israelites hiding in ambush west of Gibeah jumped up from Josh 8:19
where they were 34 and advanced against Benjamin from behind. The fighting was so **20:34** Josh 8:14
heavy that Benjamin didn't realize the impending disaster. 35 So the LORD helped Israel
defeat Benjamin, and that day the Israelites killed 25,100 of Benjamin's warriors, all of
whom were experienced with a sword. 36 Then the Benjaminites saw that they were **20:36**
beaten. Josh 8:15
The Israelites had retreated from Benjamin's warriors in order to give those hiding in
ambush more room to maneuver. 37 Then those who were in hiding rushed in from all **20:37-38**
sides and killed everyone in the town. 38 They sent up a large cloud of smoke from the Josh 8:19-20
town, 39 which was the signal for the Israelites to turn and attack Benjamin's warriors.
By that time Benjamin's warriors had killed about thirty Israelites, and they shouted,
"We're defeating them as we did in the first battle!" 40 But when the warriors of **20:40-41**
Benjamin looked behind them and saw the smoke rising into the sky from every part of Josh 8:20-21
the town, 41 the Israelites turned and attacked. At this point Benjamin's warriors realized
disaster was near and became terrified. 42 So they ran toward the wilderness, but the **20:42**
Israelites chased after them and killed them. 43 The Israelites surrounded the Benjamin- Josh 8:15, 24
ites and were relentless in chasing them down, finally overtaking them east of Gibeah.
44 Eighteen thousand of Benjamin's greatest warriors died in that day's battle. 45 The **20:45**
survivors fled into the wilderness toward the rock of Rimmon, but Israel killed five Judg 21:13
thousand of them along the road. They continued the chase until they had killed another
two thousand near Gidom.
46 So the tribe of Benjamin lost twenty-five thousand brave warriors that day, 47 leaving only six hundred men who escaped to the rock of Rimmon, where they lived for four
months. 48 Then the Israelites returned and slaughtered every living thing in all the
towns—the people, the cattle—everything. They also burned down every town they
came to.

Israel Provides Wives for Benjamin

21 The Israelites had vowed at Mizpah never to give their daughters in marriage to **21:1**
a man from the tribe of Benjamin. 2 And the people went to Bethel and sat in the Judg 21:7, 18 **21:2**
presence of God until evening, raising their voices and weeping bitterly. 3 "O LORD, God Judg 20:18, 26
of Israel," they cried out, "why has this happened? Now one of our tribes is missing!"
4 Early the next morning the people built an altar and presented their burnt offerings **21:4**
and peace offerings on it. 5 Then they said, "Was any tribe of Israel not represented Deut 12:5 2 Sam 24:25
when we held our council in the presence of the LORD at Mizpah?" At that time they
had taken a solemn oath in the LORD's presence, vowing that anyone who refused to
come must die.
6 The Israelites felt deep sadness for Benjamin and said, "Today we have lost one of
the tribes from our family; it is nearly wiped out. 7 How can we find wives for the few
who remain, since we have sworn by the LORD not to give them our daughters in
marriage?"

20:46-48 The effects of the horrible rape and murder should never have been felt outside the community where the crime happened. The local people should have brought the criminals to justice and corrected the laxness that originally permitted the crime. Instead, first the town and then the entire tribe defended this wickedness, even going to war over it.

To prevent unresolved problems from turning into major conflicts, firm action must be taken quickly, wisely, and forcefully *before* a situation gets out of hand.

20:48 The tribe of Benjamin eventually recovered from this slaughter. Saul, Israel's first king, was from this tribe (1 Samuel 9:21). So were Queen Esther (Esther 2:5-7) and the apostle Paul (Romans 11:1). But the tribe was always known for being smaller than the rest (as in Psalm 68:27).

8 So they asked, "Was anyone absent when we presented ourselves to the LORD at
Mizpah?" And they discovered that no one from Jabesh-gilead had attended. 9 For after
21:10 Num 31:17-18
they counted all the people, no one from Jabesh-gilead was present. 10 So they sent
twelve thousand warriors to Jabesh-gilead with orders to kill everyone there, including
women and children. 11 "This is what you are to do," they said. "Completely destroy*
all the males and every woman who is not a virgin." 12 Among the residents of Jabesh-
gilead they found four hundred young virgins who had never slept with a man, and they
brought them to the camp at Shiloh in the land of Canaan.
21:13 Deut 20:10
13 The Israelite assembly sent a peace delegation to the little remnant of Benjamin who
were living at the rock of Rimmon. 14 Then the men of Benjamin returned to their homes,
and the four hundred women of Jabesh-gilead who were spared were given to them as
wives. But there were not enough women for all of them.
15 The people felt sorry for Benjamin because the LORD had left this gap in the tribes
of Israel. 16 So the Israelite leaders asked, "How can we find wives for the few who
remain, since all the women of the tribe of Benjamin are dead? 17 There must be heirs for
the survivors so that an entire tribe of Israel will not be lost forever. 18 But we cannot give
them our own daughters in marriage because we have sworn with a solemn oath that
anyone who does this will fall under God's curse."
21:19 Josh 18:1 Judg 18:31 1 Sam 1:3
19 Then they thought of the annual festival of the LORD held in Shiloh, between
Lebonah and Bethel, along the east side of the road that goes from Bethel to Shechem.
20 They told the men of Benjamin who still needed wives, "Go and hide in the vineyards.
21:21 Exod 15:20 Judg 11:34
21 When the women of Shiloh come out for their dances, rush out from the vineyards,
and each of you can take one of them home to be your wife! 22 And when their fathers
and brothers come to us in protest, we will tell them, 'Please be understanding. Let them
have your daughters, for we didn't find enough wives for them when we destroyed
Jabesh-gilead. And you are not guilty of breaking the vow since you did not give your
daughters in marriage to them.'"
21:23 Judg 20:48
23 So the men of Benjamin did as they were told. They kidnapped the women who took
part in the celebration and carried them off to the land of their own inheritance. Then
they rebuilt their towns and lived in them. 24 So the assembly of Israel departed by tribes
and families, and they returned to their own homes.
25 In those days Israel had no king, so the people did whatever seemed right in their
own eyes.

21:11 The Hebrew term used here refers to the complete consecration of things or people to the LORD, either by destroying them or by giving them as an offering.

21:8-12 The Israelites moved from one mess to another. Because of a rash vow made in the heat of emotion (21:5), here they destroyed another town. The Israelites probably justified their action with the following arguments: (1) An oath could not be broken, and they had vowed that anyone who did not help them fight the tribe of Benjamin would be killed. (2) Because all the women from Benjamin had been killed, the few remaining men needed wives to prevent the tribe from disappearing. To spare the unmarried women from Jabesh-gilead seemed the right solution.

We do not know all the circumstances behind the brutal massacre at Jabesh-gilead, but it seems that the rest of Israel followed Benjamin's pattern. They put tribal loyalties above God's commands, and they justified wrong actions to correct past mistakes.

21:25 During the time of the judges, the people of Israel experienced trouble because everyone became his own authority and acted on his own opinions of right and wrong. This produced horrendous results. Our world is similar. Individuals, groups, and societies have made themselves the final authorities without reference to God. When people selfishly satisfy their personal desires at all costs, everyone pays the price.

It is the ultimate heroic act to submit all our plans, desires, and motives to God. Men like Gideon, Jephthah, and Samson are known for their heroism in battle. But their personal lives were far from heroic.

To be truly heroic, we must go into battle each day in our home, job, church, and society to make God's Kingdom a reality. Our weapons are the standards, morals, truths, and convictions we receive from God's Word. We will lose the battle if we gather the spoils of earthly treasures rather than seeking the treasures of heaven.

RUTH

VITAL STATISTICS

PURPOSE:
To show how three people remained strong in character and true to God even when the society around them was collapsing

AUTHOR:
Unknown. Some think it was Samuel, but internal evidence suggests that it was written after Samuel's death.

DATE WRITTEN:
Sometime after the period of the judges (1375–1050 B.C.)

SETTING:
A dark time in Israel's history when people lived to please themselves, not God (Judges 17:6)

KEY VERSE:
"But Ruth replied, 'Don't ask me to leave you and turn back. I will go wherever you go and live wherever you live. Your people will be my people, and your God will be my God'" (1:16).

KEY PEOPLE:
Ruth, Naomi, Boaz

KEY PLACES:
Moab, Bethlehem

WHEN someone says, "Let me tell you about my mother-in-law," we expect some kind of negative statement or humorous anecdote because the mother-in-law caricature has been a standard centerpiece of ridicule or comedy. The book of Ruth, however, tells a different story. Ruth loved her mother-in-law, Naomi. Recently widowed, Ruth begged to stay with Naomi wherever she went, even though it would mean leaving her homeland. In heartfelt words, Ruth said, "Your people will be my people, and your God will be my God" (1:16). Naomi agreed, and Ruth traveled with her to Bethlehem.

Not much is said about Naomi except that she loved and cared for Ruth. Obviously, Naomi's life was a powerful witness to the reality of God. Ruth was drawn to her—and to the God she worshiped. In the succeeding months, God led this young Moabite widow to a man named Boaz, whom she eventually married. As a result, she became the great-grandmother of David and an ancestor in the line of the Messiah. What a profound impact Naomi's life made!

The book of Ruth is also the story of God's grace in the midst of difficult circumstances. Ruth's story occurred during the time of the judges—a period of disobedience, idolatry, and violence. Even in times of crisis and deepest despair, there are those who follow God and through whom God works. No matter how discouraging or antagonistic the world may seem, there are always people who follow God. He will use anyone who is open to him to achieve his purposes. Ruth was a Moabite, and Boaz was a descendant of Rahab, a former prostitute from Jericho. Nevertheless, their offspring continued the family line through which the Messiah came into our world.

Read this book and be encouraged. God is at work in the world, and he wants to use you. God could use you, as he used Naomi, to bring family and friends to him.

THE BLUEPRINT

1. Ruth remains loyal to Naomi (1:1–22)
2. Ruth gleans in Boaz's field (2:1–23)
3. Ruth follows Naomi's plan (3:1–18)
4. Ruth and Boaz are married (4:1–22)

When we first meet Ruth, she is a destitute widow. We follow her as she joins God's people, gleans in the grainfields, and risks her honor at the threshing floor of Boaz. In the end, we see Ruth becoming the wife of Boaz. What a picture of how we come to faith in Christ. We begin with no hope and are rebellious aliens with no part in the kingdom of God. Then as we risk everything by putting our faith in Christ, God saves us, forgives us, rebuilds our lives, and gives us blessings that will last through eternity. Boaz's redeeming of Ruth is a picture of Christ redeeming us.

MEGATHEMES

THEME	EXPLANATION	IMPORTANCE
Faithfulness	Ruth's faithfulness to Naomi as a daughter-in-law and friend is a great example of love and loyalty. Ruth, Naomi, and Boaz are also faithful to God and his laws. Throughout the story we see God's faithfulness to his people.	Ruth's life was guided by faithfulness toward God and showed itself in loyalty toward the people she knew. To be loyal and loving in relationships, we must imitate God's faithfulness in our relationships with others.
Kindness	Ruth showed great kindness to Naomi. In turn, Boaz showed kindness to Ruth—a despised Moabite woman with no money. God showed his kindness to Ruth, Naomi, and Boaz by bringing them together for his purposes.	Just as Boaz showed his kindness by buying back land to guarantee Ruth and Naomi's inheritance, so Christ showed his kindness by dying for us to guarantee our eternal life. God's kindness should motivate us to love and honor him.
Integrity	Ruth showed high moral character by being loyal to Naomi, by her clean break from her former land and customs, and by her hard work in the fields. Boaz showed integrity in his moral standards, his honesty, and by following through on his commitments.	When we have experienced God's faithfulness and kindness, we should respond by showing integrity. Just as the values by which Ruth and Boaz lived were in sharp contrast to those of the culture portrayed in Judges, so our lives should stand out from the world around us.
Protection	We see God's care and protection over the lives of Naomi and Ruth. His supreme control over circumstances brings them safety and security. He guides the minds and activities of people to fulfill his purposes.	No matter how devastating our present situation may be, our hope is in God. His resources are infinite. We must believe that he can work in the life of any person—whether that person is a king or a stranger in a foreign land. Trust his protection.
Prosperity/Blessing	Ruth and Naomi came to Bethlehem as poor widows, but they soon became prosperous through Ruth's marriage to Boaz. Ruth became the great-grandmother of King David. Yet the greatest blessing was not the money, the marriage, or the child; it was the quality of love and respect between Ruth, Boaz, and Naomi.	We tend to think of blessings in terms of prosperity rather than the high-quality relationships God makes possible for us. No matter what our economic situation, we can love and respect the people God has brought into our lives. In so doing, we give and receive blessings. Love is the greatest blessing.

1. Ruth remains loyal to Naomi

Elimelech Moves His Family to Moab

1:1 Judg 2:16-18 **1** In the days when the judges ruled in Israel, a man from Bethlehem in Judah left the
country because of a severe famine. He took his wife and two sons and went to live
1:2 Gen 35:19 Judg 3:30 in the country of Moab. [2]The man's name was Elimelech, and his wife was Naomi. Their
two sons were Mahlon and Kilion. They were Ephrathites from Bethlehem in the land

1:1 The story of Ruth takes place sometime during the period of the rule of the judges. These were dark days for Israel, when "the people did whatever seemed right in their own eyes" (Judges 17:6; 21:25). But during those dark and evil times, there were still some who followed God. Naomi and Ruth are beautiful examples of loyalty, friendship, and commitment—to God and to each other.

1:1, 2 Moab was the land east of the Dead Sea. It was one of the nations that oppressed Israel during the period of the judges (Judges 3:12ff), so there was hostility between the two nations. The famine must have been quite severe in Israel for Elimelech to move his family there. They were called Ephrathites because Ephrath was an earlier name for Bethlehem. Even if Israel had already defeated Moab, there still would have been tensions between them.

of Judah. During their stay in Moab, 3Elimelech died and Naomi was left with her two
sons. 4The two sons married Moabite women. One married a woman named Orpah, and
the other a woman named Ruth. But about ten years later, 5both Mahlon and Kilion died.
This left Naomi alone, without her husband or sons.

Naomi and Ruth Return

6Then Naomi heard in Moab that the LORD had blessed his people in Judah by giving **1:6** Exod 4:31
them good crops again. So Naomi and her daughters-in-law got ready to leave Moab to
return to her homeland. 7With her two daughters-in-law she set out from the place where
she had been living, and they took the road that would lead them back to Judah.
8But on the way, Naomi said to her two daughters-in-law, "Go back to your mothers' **1:8** 2 Tim 1:16
homes instead of coming with me. And may the LORD reward you for your kindness to
your husbands and to me. 9May the LORD bless you with the security of another **1:9** Ruth 3:1
marriage." Then she kissed them good-bye, and they all broke down and wept.
10"No," they said. "We want to go with you to your people."
11But Naomi replied, "Why should you go on with me? Can I still give birth to other **1:11** Deut 25:5
sons who could grow up to be your husbands? 12No, my daughters, return to your
parents' homes, for I am too old to marry again. And even if it were possible, and I were
to get married tonight and bear sons, then what? 13Would you wait for them to grow up **1:13** Judg 2:15
and refuse to marry someone else? No, of course not, my daughters! Things are far more
bitter for me than for you, because the LORD himself has caused me to suffer."
14And again they wept together, and Orpah kissed her mother-in-law good-bye. But
Ruth insisted on staying with Naomi. 15"See," Naomi said to her, "your sister-in-law has
gone back to her people and to her gods. You should do the same."
16But Ruth replied, "Don't ask me to leave you and turn back. I will go wherever you **1:16** 2 Kgs 2:2

SETTING FOR THE STORY
Elimelech, Naomi, and their sons traveled from Bethlehem to Moab because of a famine. After her husband and sons died, Naomi returned to Bethlehem with her daughter-in-law Ruth.

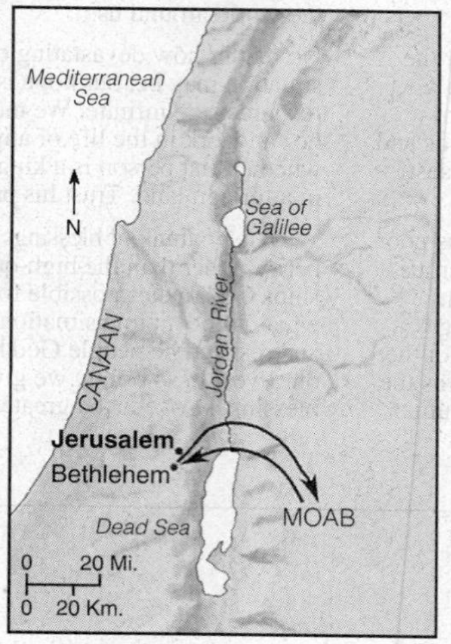

1:4, 5 Friendly relations with the Moabites were discouraged (Deuteronomy 23:3-6) but probably not forbidden, since the Moabites lived outside the Promised Land. Marrying a Canaanite (and all those living within the borders of the Promised Land), however, was against God's law (Deuteronomy 7:1-4). Moabites were not allowed to worship at the Tabernacle because they had not let the Israelites pass through their land during the Exodus from Egypt.

As God's chosen nation, Israel should have set the standards of high moral living for the other nations. Ironically it was Ruth, a Moabitess, whom God used as an example of genuine spiritual character. This shows just how bleak life had become in Israel during those days.

1:8, 9 There was almost nothing worse than being a widow in the ancient world. Widows were taken advantage of or ignored. They were almost always poverty stricken. God's law, therefore, provided that the nearest relative of the dead husband should care for the widow; but Naomi had no relatives in Moab, and she did not know if any of her relatives were alive in Israel.

Even in her desperate situation, Naomi had a selfless attitude. Although she had decided to return to Israel, she encouraged Ruth and Orpah to stay in Moab and start their lives over, even though this would mean hardship for her. Like Naomi, we must consider the needs of others and not just our own. As Naomi discovered, when you act selflessly, others are encouraged to follow your example.

1:11 Naomi's comment here ("sons who could grow up to be your husbands") refers to *levirate marriage,* the obligation of a dead man's brother to care for the widow (Deuteronomy 25:5-10). This law kept the widow from poverty and provided a way for the family name of the dead husband to continue.

Naomi, however, had no other sons for Ruth or Orpah to marry, so she encouraged them to remain in their homeland and remarry. Orpah agreed, which was her right. But Ruth was willing to give up the possibility of security and children in order to care for Naomi.

1:16 Ruth was a Moabitess, but that didn't stop her from worshiping the true God, nor did it stop God from accepting her worship and blessing her greatly. The Jews were not the only people God loved. God chose the Jews to be the people through whom the rest of the world would come to know him. This was fulfilled when Jesus Christ was born as a Jew. Through him, the entire world can come to know God. Acts 10:35 says that "in every nation he accepts those who fear him and do what is right." God accepts all who worship him; he works through people regardless of their race, sex, or nationality. The book of Ruth is a perfect example of God's impartiality. Although Ruth belonged to a race often despised by Israel, she was blessed because of her faithfulness. She became a great-grandmother of King David and a direct ancestor of Jesus. No one should feel disqualified to serve God because of race, sex, or national background. And God can use every circumstance to build his kingdom.

go and live wherever you live. Your people will be my people, and your God will be my
God. [17]I will die where you die and will be buried there. May the LORD punish me
1:18 Acts 21:14 severely if I allow anything but death to separate us!" [18]So when Naomi saw that Ruth
had made up her mind to go with her, she stopped urging her.
[19]So the two of them continued on their journey. When they came to Bethlehem, the
entire town was stirred by their arrival. "Is it really Naomi?" the women asked.
1:20 Exod 6:3; Job 6:4 [20]"Don't call me Naomi," she told them. "Instead, call me Mara,* for the Almighty
has made life very bitter for me. [21]I went away full, but the LORD has brought me home
1:21 Job 1:21 empty. Why should you call me Naomi when the LORD has caused me to suffer* and the
1:22 Exod 9:31 Almighty has sent such tragedy?"
[22]So Naomi returned from Moab, accompanied by her daughter-in-law Ruth, the
young Moabite woman. They arrived in Bethlehem at the beginning of the barley
harvest.

1:20 *Naomi* means "pleasant"; *Mara* means "bitter." **1:21** Or *has testified against me.*

RUTH & NAOMI

The stories of several people in the Bible are woven together so closely that they are almost inseparable. We know more about their relationship than we know about them as individuals. And in an age that worships individualism, their stories become helpful models of good relationships. Naomi and Ruth are beautiful examples of this blending of lives. Their cultures, family backgrounds, and ages were very different. As mother-in-law and daughter-in-law, they probably had as many opportunities for tension as for tenderness. And yet they were bound to each other.

They shared deep sorrow, great affection for each other, and an overriding commitment to the God of Israel. And yet as much as they depended on each other, they also gave each other freedom in their commitment to one another. Naomi was willing to let Ruth return to her family. Ruth was willing to leave her homeland to go to Israel. Naomi even helped arrange Ruth's marriage to Boaz although it would change their relationship.

God was at the center of their intimate communication. Ruth came to know the God of Israel through Naomi. The older woman allowed Ruth to see, hear, and feel all the joy and anguish of her relationship to God. How often do you feel that your thoughts and questions about God should be left out of a close relationship? How often do you share your unedited thoughts about God with your spouse or friends? Sharing openly about our relationship with God can bring depth and intimacy to our relationships with others.

Strengths and accomplishments
- A relationship where the greatest bond was faith in God
- A relationship of strong mutual commitment
- A relationship in which each person tried to do what was best for the other

Lesson from their lives
- God's living presence in a relationship overcomes differences that might otherwise create division and disharmony

Vital statistics
- Where: Moab, Bethlehem
- Occupation: Wives, widows
- Relatives: Elimelech, Mahlon, Kilion, Orpah, Boaz

Key verses
"But Ruth replied, 'Don't ask me to leave you and turn back. I will go wherever you go and live wherever you live. Your people will be my people, and your God will be my God. I will die where you die and will be buried there. May the LORD punish me severely if I allow anything but death to separate us!' " (Ruth 1:16, 17).

Their story is told in the book of Ruth. Ruth is also mentioned in Matthew 1:5.

1:20, 21 Naomi had experienced severe hardships. She had left Israel married and secure; she returned widowed and poor. Naomi changed her name to express the bitterness and pain she felt. Naomi was not rejecting God by openly expressing her pain. However, she seems to have lost sight of the tremendous resources she had in her relationship with Ruth and with God. When you face bitter times, God welcomes your honest prayers, but be careful not to overlook the love, strength, and resources that he provides in your present relationships. And don't allow bitterness and disappointment to blind you to your opportunities.

1:22 Bethlehem was about five miles southwest of Jerusalem. The town was surrounded by lush fields and olive groves. Its harvests were abundant.

Ruth and Naomi's return to Bethlehem was certainly part of God's plan because in this town David would be born (1 Samuel 16:1), and, as predicted by the prophet Micah (Micah 5:2), Jesus Christ would also be born there. This move, then, was more than mere convenience for Ruth and Naomi. It led to the fulfillment of Scripture.

1:22 Because Israel's climate is quite moderate, there are two harvests each year, in the spring and in the fall. The barley harvest took place in the spring, and it was during this time of hope and plenty that Ruth and Naomi returned to Bethlehem. Bethlehem was a farming community, and because it was the time of the harvest, there was plenty of leftover grain in the fields. This grain could be collected, or *gleaned,* and then made into food. (See the note on 2:2 for more information on gleaning.)

2. Ruth gleans in Boaz's field

2 Now there was a wealthy and influential man in Bethlehem named Boaz, who was 2:1 Ruth 1:2
a relative of Naomi's husband, Elimelech.
2One day Ruth said to Naomi, "Let me go out into the fields to gather leftover grain 2:2 Lev 19:9-10; 23:22
behind anyone who will let me do it."
And Naomi said, "All right, my daughter, go ahead." 3So Ruth went out to gather grain
behind the harvesters. And as it happened, she found herself working in a field that
belonged to Boaz, the relative of her father-in-law, Elimelech.
4While she was there, Boaz arrived from Bethlehem and greeted the harvesters. "The 2:4 Ps 129:8
LORD be with you!" he said. Luke 1:28
"The LORD bless you!" the harvesters replied.
5Then Boaz asked his foreman, "Who is that girl over there?"
6And the foreman replied, "She is the young woman from Moab who came back with 2:6 Ruth 1:22
Naomi. 7She asked me this morning if she could gather grain behind the harvesters.
She has been hard at work ever since, except for a few minutes' rest over there in the
shelter."
8Boaz went over and said to Ruth, "Listen, my daughter. Stay right here with us when
you gather grain; don't go to any other fields. Stay right behind the women working in
my field. 9See which part of the field they are harvesting, and then follow them. I have
warned the young men not to bother you. And when you are thirsty, help yourself to the
water they have drawn from the well."
10Ruth fell at his feet and thanked him warmly. "Why are you being so kind to me?" 2:10 1 Sam 25:23
she asked. "I am only a foreigner."
11"Yes, I know," Boaz replied. "But I also know about the love and kindness you have
shown your mother-in-law since the death of your husband. I have heard how you left 2:12 Ruth 1:16
your father and mother and your own land to live here among complete strangers. 12May
the LORD, the God of Israel, under whose wings you have come to take refuge, reward
you fully."
13"I hope I continue to please you, sir," she replied. "You have comforted me by
speaking so kindly to me, even though I am not as worthy as your workers."
14At lunchtime Boaz called to her, "Come over here and help yourself to some of our
food. You can dip your bread in the wine if you like." So she sat with his harvesters, and
Boaz gave her food—more than she could eat.
15When Ruth went back to work again, Boaz ordered his young men, "Let her gather
grain right among the sheaves without stopping her. 16And pull out some heads of barley

---

2:2 When the wheat and barley were ready to be harvested, harvesters were hired to cut down the stalks and tie them into bundles. Israelite law demanded that the corners of the fields not be harvested. In addition, any grain that was dropped was to be left for poor people, who picked it up (this was called *gleaning*) and used it for food (Leviticus 19:9; 23:22; Deuteronomy 24:19). The purpose of this law was to feed the poor and to prevent the owners from hoarding. This law served as a type of welfare program in Israel. Because she was a widow with no means of providing for herself, Ruth went into the fields to glean the grain.

2:2, 3 Ruth made her home in a foreign land. Instead of depending on Naomi or waiting for good fortune to happen, she took the initiative. She went to work. She was not afraid of admitting her need or working hard to supply it. When Ruth went out to the fields, God provided for her. If you are waiting for God to provide, consider this: He may be waiting for you to take the first step to demonstrate just how important your need is.

2:7 Ruth's task, though menial, tiring, and perhaps degrading, was done faithfully. What is your attitude when the task you have been given is not up to your true potential? The task at hand may be all you can do, or it may be the work God wants you to do. Or, as in Ruth's case, it may be a test of your character that can open up new doors of opportunity.

2:10-12 Ruth's life exhibited admirable qualities: She was hardworking, loving, kind, faithful, and brave. These qualities gained for her a good reputation, but only because she displayed them *consistently* in all areas of her life. Wherever Ruth went or whatever she did, her character remained the same.

Your reputation is formed by the people who watch you at work, in town, at home, in church. A good reputation comes by *consistently* living out the qualities you believe in—no matter what group of people or surroundings you are in.

2:15, 16 The characters in the book of Ruth are classic examples of good people in action. Boaz went far beyond the intent of the gleaners' law in demonstrating his kindness and generosity. Not only did he let Ruth glean in his field, he also told his workers to let some of the grain fall in her path. Out of his abundance, he provided for the needy. How often do you go beyond the accepted patterns of providing for those less fortunate? Do more than the minimum for others.

from the bundles and drop them on purpose for her. Let her pick them up, and don't give
her a hard time!"
[17] So Ruth gathered barley there all day, and when she beat out the grain that evening,
it came to about half a bushel.* [18] She carried it back into town and showed it to her
mother-in-law. Ruth also gave her the food that was left over from her lunch.
[19] "So much!" Naomi exclaimed. "Where did you gather all this grain today? Where
did you work? May the LORD bless the one who helped you!"
So Ruth told her mother-in-law about the man in whose field she had worked. And
she said, "The man I worked with today is named Boaz."
2:20 Ruth 3:9-10; 4:6 [20] "May the LORD bless him!" Naomi told her daughter-in-law. "He is showing his
kindness to us as well as to your dead husband.* That man is one of our closest relatives,
one of our family redeemers."
[21] Then Ruth said, "What's more, Boaz even told me to come back and stay with his
harvesters until the entire harvest is completed."
[22] "This is wonderful!" Naomi exclaimed. "Do as he said. Stay with his workers right
through the whole harvest. You will be safe there, unlike in other fields."
[23] So Ruth worked alongside the women in Boaz's fields and gathered grain with them
until the end of the barley harvest. Then she worked with them through the wheat harvest,
too. But all the while she lived with her mother-in-law.

2:17 Hebrew *about an ephah* [18 liters]. **2:20** Hebrew *to the living and to the dead.*

BOAZ

Heroes are easier to admire than to define. They are seldom conscious of their moments of heroism, and others may not recognize their acts as heroic. Heroes simply do the right thing at the right time, whether or not they realize the impact their action will have. Perhaps the one quality they share is a tendency to think of others before they think of themselves. Boaz was a hero.

In his dealings with other people, he was always sensitive to their needs. His words to his employees, relatives, and others were colored with kindness. He offered help openly, not grudgingly. When he discovered who Ruth was, he took several steps to help her because she had been faithful to his relative Naomi. When Naomi advised Ruth to request his protection, he was ready to marry her if the legal complications could be worked out.

Boaz not only did what was right; he also did it right away. Of course he could not foresee all that his actions would accomplish. He could not have known that the child he would have by Ruth would be an ancestor of both David and Jesus. He only met the challenge of taking the right action in the situation facing him.

We are faced with this challenge in our daily choices. Like Naomi's nearer relative, we are often more concerned with making the easy choice than with making the right one. Yet more often than not, the right choice is clear. Ask God to give you a special awareness in your choices today as well as renewed commitment to make the right ones.

Strengths and accomplishments
- A man of his word
- Sensitive to those in need, caring for his workers
- A keen sense of responsibility, integrity
- A successful and shrewd businessman

Lessons from his life
- It can be heroic to do what must be done and to do it right
- God often uses little decisions to carry out his big plan

Vital statistics
- Where: Bethlehem
- Occupation: Wealthy farmer
- Relatives: Elimelech, Naomi, Ruth

Key verse: "I have acquired Ruth, the Moabite widow of Mahlon, to be my wife. This way she can have a son to carry on the family name of her dead husband and to inherit the family property here in his hometown. You are all witnesses today" (Ruth 4:10).

His story is told in the book of Ruth. He is also mentioned in Matthew 1:5.

2:19, 20 Naomi had felt bitter (1:20, 21), but her faith in God was still alive, and she praised God for Boaz's kindness to Ruth. In her sorrows, she still trusted God and acknowledged his goodness. We may feel bitter about a situation, but we must never despair. Today is always a new opportunity for experiencing God's care. (For more on a family redeemer, see the note on 3:1-9.)

2:20 Though Ruth may not have always recognized God's guidance, he had been with her every step of the way. She went to glean and "just happened" to end up in the field owned by Boaz who "just happened" to be a close relative. This was more than mere coincidence. As you go about your daily tasks, God is working in your life in ways you may not even notice. We must not close the door on what God can do. Events do not occur by luck or coincidence. We should have faith that God is directing our lives for his purpose.

3. Ruth follows Naomi's plan

3 One day Naomi said to Ruth, "My daughter, it's time that I found a permanent home 3:1 Ruth 1:9
for you, so that you will be provided for. [2]Boaz is a close relative of ours, and he's 3:2
been very kind by letting you gather grain with his workers. Tonight he will be Deut 25:5-10
winnowing barley at the threshing floor. [3]Now do as I tell you—take a bath and put on
perfume and dress in your nicest clothes. Then go to the threshing floor, but don't let
Boaz see you until he has finished his meal. [4]Be sure to notice where he lies down; then
go and uncover his feet and lie down there. He will tell you what to do."
[5]"I will do everything you say," Ruth replied. [6]So she went down to the threshing
floor that night and followed the instructions of her mother-in-law.
[7]After Boaz had finished his meal and was in good spirits, he lay down beside the heap 3:7 Judg 19:6, 22
of grain and went to sleep. Then Ruth came quietly, uncovered his feet, and lay down. 2 Sam 13:28
[8]Around midnight, Boaz suddenly woke up and turned over. He was surprised to find a
woman lying at his feet! [9]"Who are you?" he demanded. 3:9
"I am your servant Ruth," she replied. "Spread the corner of your covering over me, Ruth 2:20
for you are my family redeemer."
[10]"The LORD bless you, my daughter!" Boaz exclaimed. "You are showing more
family loyalty now than ever by not running after a younger man, whether rich or poor.
[11]Now don't worry about a thing, my daughter. I will do what is necessary, for everyone 3:11
in town knows you are an honorable woman. [12]But there is one problem. While it is true Prov 12:4; 31:10
that I am one of your family redeemers, there is another man who is more closely related 3:12 Ruth 4:1
to you than I am. [13]Stay here tonight, and in the morning I will talk to him. If he is willing 3:13
to redeem you, then let him marry you. But if he is not willing, then as surely as the LORD Ruth 4:5
lives, I will marry you! Now lie down here until morning." Matt 22:24
[14]So Ruth lay at Boaz's feet until the morning, but she got up before it was light
enough for people to recognize each other. For Boaz said, "No one must know that a
woman was here at the threshing floor." [15]Boaz also said to her, "Bring your cloak and
spread it out." He measured out six scoops* of barley into the cloak and helped her put
it on her back. Then Boaz* returned to the town.

3:15a Hebrew *six measures,* an unknown quantity. **3:15b** Most Hebrew manuscripts read *he;* many Hebrew manuscripts, Syriac version, and Latin Vulgate read *she.*

3:1-9 As widows, Ruth and Naomi could only look forward to difficult times. (See the note on 1:8, 9 for more on a widow's life.) But when Naomi heard the news about Boaz, her hope for the future was renewed (2:20). Typical of her character, she thought first of Ruth, encouraging her to see if Boaz would take the responsibility of being the "family redeemer" (2:20).

A family redeemer was a relative who volunteered to take responsibility for the extended family. When a woman's husband died, the law (Deuteronomy 25:5-10) provided that she could marry a brother of her dead husband. But Naomi had no more sons. In such a case, the nearest relative to the deceased husband could become a family redeemer and marry the widow. The nearest relative did not have to marry the widow. If he chose not to, the next nearest relative could take his place. If no one chose to help the widow, she would probably live in poverty the rest of her life, because in Israelite culture the inheritance was passed on to the son or nearest male relative, not to the wife. To take the sting out of these inheritance rules, there were laws for gleaning and family redeemers.

We have a family redeemer in Jesus Christ, who though he was God, came to earth as a man in order to save us. By his death on the cross, he has redeemed us from sin and hopelessness and thereby purchased us to be his own possession (1 Peter 1:18, 19). This guarantees our eternal inheritance.

3:2 The threshing floor was the place where the grain was separated from the harvested wheat. The wheat stalks were crushed, either by hand or by oxen, and the valuable grain (inner kernels) separated from the worthless chaff (the outside shell). The floor was made from rock or soil and located outside the village, usually on an elevated site where the winds would blow away the lighter chaff when the crushed wheat was thrown into the air (or winnowed). Boaz spent the night beside the threshing floor for two reasons: (1) to prevent theft and (2) to wait for his turn to thresh grain. (Threshing was often done at night because daylight hours were spent harvesting.)

3:4 Naomi's advice seems strange, but she was not suggesting a seductive act. In reality, Naomi was telling Ruth to act in accordance with Israelite custom and law. It was common for a servant to lie at the feet of his master and even share a part of his covering. By observing this custom, Ruth would inform Boaz that he could be her family redeemer—that he could find someone to marry her or marry her himself. It was family business, nothing romantic. But the story later became beautifully romantic as Ruth and Boaz developed an unselfish love and deep respect for each other.

3:5 As a foreigner, Ruth may have thought that Naomi's advice was odd. But Ruth followed the advice because she knew Naomi was kind, trustworthy, and filled with moral integrity. Each of us knows a parent, older friend, or relative who is always looking out for our best interests. Be willing to listen to the advice of a person who is older and wiser than you are. The experience and knowledge of such a person can be invaluable. Imagine what Ruth's life would have been like had she ignored her mother-in-law.

3:12 Ruth and Naomi must have assumed that Boaz was their closest relative. Boaz, too, must have already considered marrying Ruth because his answer to her shows he had been thinking about it. He couldn't have considered marrying Naomi because she was probably too old to bear any more children (1:11, 12). One man in the city was a nearer relative than Boaz, and this man had the first right to take Ruth as his wife. If he chose not to, then Boaz could marry Ruth (3:13).

16When Ruth went back to her mother-in-law, Naomi asked, "What happened, my
daughter?"
Ruth told Naomi everything Boaz had done for her, 17and she added, "He gave me these
six scoops of barley and said, 'Don't go back to your mother-in-law empty-handed.'"
3:18 18Then Naomi said to her, "Just be patient, my daughter, until we hear what happens.
Ps 37:3-5 The man won't rest until he has followed through on this. He will settle it today."

4. Ruth and Boaz are married

4:1 **4** So Boaz went to the town gate and took a seat there. When the family redeemer he
Ruth 3:12 had mentioned came by, Boaz called out to him, "Come over here, friend. I want to
talk to you." So they sat down together. 2Then Boaz called ten leaders from the town and
4:3 Lev 25:25 asked them to sit as witnesses. 3And Boaz said to the family redeemer, "You know
Naomi, who came back from Moab. She is selling the land that belonged to our relative
4:4 Elimelech. 4I felt that I should speak to you about it so that you can redeem it if you wish.
Lev 25:25 Jer 32:7-8 If you want the land, then buy it here in the presence of these witnesses. But if you don't
want it, let me know right away, because I am next in line to redeem it after you."
The man replied, "All right, I'll redeem it."
4:5 5Then Boaz told him, "Of course, your purchase of the land from Naomi also requires
Deut 25:5-6 that you marry Ruth, the Moabite widow. That way, she can have children who will carry
on her husband's name and keep the land in the family."
6"Then I can't redeem it," the family redeemer replied, "because this might endanger
4:6 Lev 25:25 Ruth 3:12-13 my own estate. You redeem the land; I cannot do it."
4:7 7In those days it was the custom in Israel for anyone transferring a right of purchase to
remove his sandal and hand it to the other party. This publicly validated the transaction.
Deut 25:8-10 8So the other family redeemer drew off his sandal as he said to Boaz, "You buy the land."
9Then Boaz said to the leaders and to the crowd standing around, "You are witnesses
that today I have bought from Naomi all the property of Elimelech, Kilion, and Mahlon.
10And with the land I have acquired Ruth, the Moabite widow of Mahlon, to be my wife.
This way she can have a son to carry on the family name of her dead husband and to
inherit the family property here in his hometown. You are all witnesses today."
4:11 11Then the leaders and all the people standing there replied, "We are witnesses! May
Gen 29:25-30 the LORD make the woman who is now coming into your home like Rachel and Leah,
from whom all the nation of Israel descended! May you be great in Ephrathah and
4:12 famous in Bethlehem. 12And may the LORD give you descendants by this young woman
Gen 38:29; 46:12 who will be like those of our ancestor Perez, the son of Tamar and Judah."

The Descendants of Boaz

4:13 Gen 29:31; 33:5 13So Boaz married Ruth and took her home to live with him. When he slept with her, the
4:14 LORD enabled her to become pregnant, and she gave birth to a son. 14And the women of
Luke 1:58 the town said to Naomi, "Praise the LORD who has given you a family redeemer today!
May he be famous in Israel. 15May this child restore your youth and care for you in your

---

3:18 Naomi implied that Boaz would follow through with his promise at once. He obviously had a reputation for keeping his word and would not rest until his task was completed. Such reliable people stand out in any age and culture. Do others regard you as one who will do what you say? Keeping your word and following through on assignments should be high on anyone's priority list. Building a reputation for integrity, however, must be done one brick, one act, at a time.

4:1 Boaz knew he could find his relative at the town gate. This was the center of activity. No one could enter or leave the town without traveling through the gate. Merchants set up their temporary shops near the gate, which also served as "city hall." Here city officials gathered to transact business. Because there was so much activity, it was a good place to find witnesses (4:2) and an appropriate place for Boaz to make his transaction.

4:3 Boaz cleverly presented his case to the relative. First he brought in new information not yet mentioned in the story—Elimelech, Naomi's former husband, still had some property in the area that was now for sale. As the nearest relative, this man had the first right to buy the land, which he agreed to do (Leviticus 25:25). But then Boaz said that according to the law, if the relative bought the property he also had to marry the widow (probably because Mahlon, Ruth's former husband and Elimelech's son, had inherited the property). At this stipulation, the relative backed down. He did not want to complicate his inheritance. He may have feared that if he had a son through Ruth, some of his estate would transfer away from his family to the family of Elimelech. Whatever his reason, the way was now clear for Boaz to marry Ruth.

4:15 Ruth's love for her mother-in-law was known and recognized throughout the town. From the beginning of the book of Ruth to the end, her kindness toward others remained unchanged.

4:15 God brought great blessings out of Naomi's tragedy, even greater than "seven sons," or an abundance of heirs. Throughout her tough times, Naomi continued to trust God. And God, in his time, blessed her greatly. Even in our sorrow and calamity, God can bring great blessings. Be like Naomi, and don't turn your back on God when tragedy strikes. Instead of asking, "How can God allow this to happen to me?" trust him. He will be with you in the hard times.

old age. For he is the son of your daughter-in-law who loves you so much and who has been better to you than seven sons!"

4:15 Ruth 1:16-17; 2:11-12

16Naomi took care of the baby and cared for him as if he were her own. 17The
neighbor women said, "Now at last Naomi has a son again!" And they named him Obed.
He became the father of Jesse and the grandfather of David.
18This is their family line beginning with their ancestor Perez:

Perez was the father of Hezron.
19 Hezron was the father of Ram.
Ram was the father of Amminadab.
20 Amminadab was the father of Nahshon.
Nahshon was the father of Salmon.
21 Salmon was the father of Boaz.
Boaz was the father of Obed.
22 Obed was the father of Jesse.
Jesse was the father of David.

4:16, 17 To some, the book of Ruth may be just a nice story about a girl who was fortunate. But in reality, the events recorded in Ruth were part of God's preparations for the births of David and of Jesus, the promised Messiah. Just as Ruth was unaware of this larger purpose in her life, we will not know the full purpose and importance of our lives until we are able to look back from the perspective of eternity. We must make our choices with God's eternal values in mind. Taking moral shortcuts and living for short-range pleasures are not good ways to move ahead. Because of Ruth's faithful obedience, her life and legacy were significant even though she couldn't see all the results. Live in faithfulness to God, knowing that the significance of your life will extend beyond your lifetime. The rewards will outweigh any sacrifice you may have made.

NAMES OF GOD

Name of God	Meaning	Reference	Significance
Elohim	God	Genesis 1:1; Numbers 23:19; Psalm 19:1	Refers to God's power and might. He is the only supreme and true God.
Yahweh	The LORD	Genesis 2:4; Exodus 6:2,3	The proper name of the divine person.
El Elyon	God Most High	Genesis 14:17-20; Numbers 24:16; Psalm 7:17; Isaiah 14:13, 14	He is above all gods; nothing in life is more sacred.
El Roi	God Who Sees	Genesis 16:13	God oversees all creation and the affairs of people.
El Shaddai	God Almighty	Genesis 17:1; Psalm 91:1	God is all-powerful.
Yahweh Yireh	The LORD Will Provide	Genesis 22:13, 14	God will provide our real needs.
Yahweh Nissi	The LORD Is My Banner	Exodus 17:15	We should remember God for helping us.
Adonai	Lord	Deuteronomy 6:4	God alone is the head over all.
Yahweh Elohe Yisrael	LORD God of Israel	Judges 5:3; Psalm 59:5; Isaiah 17:6; Zephaniah 2:9	He is the God of the nation.
Yahweh Shalom	The LORD Is Peace	Judges 6:24	God gives us peace so we need not fear.
Qedosh Yisrael	Holy One of Israel	Isaiah 1:4	God is morally perfect
Yahweh Sabaoth	LORD of Hosts (*Hosts* refers to armies but also to all the heavenly powers.)	1 Samuel 1:3; Isaiah 6:1-3	God is our savior and protector.
El Olam	The Everlasting God	Isaiah 40:28-31	God is eternal. He will never die.
Yahweh Tsidkenu	The LORD Is Our Righteousness	Jeremiah 23:6; 33:16	God is our standard for right behavior. He alone can make us righteous.
Yahweh Shammah	The LORD Is There	Ezekiel 48:35	God is always present with us.
Attiq Yomin	Ancient of Days	Daniel 7:9, 13	God is the ultimate authority. He will one day judge all nations.

1 SAMUEL

Judges begn to rule 1375 B.C. (1220 B.C.)

Samuel born 1105 (1083)

Saul born 1080

VITAL STATISTICS

PURPOSE:
To record the life of Samuel, Israel's last judge; the reign and decline of Saul, the first king; and the choice and preparation of David, Israel's greatest king

AUTHOR:
Possibly Samuel, but also includes writings from the prophets Nathan and Gad (1 Chronicles 29:29)

SETTING:
The book begins in the days of the judges and describes Israel's transition from a theocracy (led by God) to a monarchy (led by a king)

KEY VERSES:
" 'Do as they say,' the LORD replied, 'for it is me they are rejecting, not you. They don't want me to be their king any longer. . . . Do as they ask, but solemnly warn them about how a king will treat them' " (8:7, 9).

KEY PEOPLE:
Eli, Hannah, Samuel, Saul, Jonathan, David

"RUNNERS, take your marks," the starter barks his signal, and the crowd turns quiet attention to the athletes walking toward the line. "Get set" . . . in position now, muscles tense, nervously anticipating the sound of the gun. It resounds! And the race begins. In any contest, the start is important, but the finish is even more crucial. Often a front-runner will lose strength and fade to the middle of the pack. And there is the tragedy of the brilliant beginner who sets the pace for a time, but does not even finish. He quits the race burned out, exhausted, injured.

First Samuel is a book of great beginnings . . . and tragic endings. It begins with Eli as high priest during the time of the judges. As a religious leader, Eli certainly must have begun his life with a close relationship to God. In his communication with Hannah, and in his training of her son Samuel, he demonstrated a clear understanding of God's purposes and call (chapters 1, 3). But his life ended in ignominy as his sacrilegious sons were judged by God and the sacred Ark of the Covenant fell into enemy hands (chapter 4). Eli's death marked the decline of the influence of the priesthood and the rise of the prophets in Israel.

Samuel was dedicated to God's service by his mother, Hannah. He became one of Israel's greatest prophets. He was a man of prayer who finished the work of the judges, began the school of the prophets, and anointed Israel's first kings. But even Samuel was not immune to finishing poorly. Like Eli's family, Samuel's sons turned away from God; they took bribes and perverted justice. The people rejected the leadership of the judges and priests and clamored for a king "like all the other nations have" (8:5).

Saul also started quickly. A striking figure, this handsome (9:2) and humble (9:21; 10:22) man was God's choice as Israel's first king (10:24). His early reign was marked by leadership (chapter 11) and bravery (14:46–48). But he disobeyed God (chapter 15), became jealous and paranoid (chapters 18, 19), and finally had his kingship taken away from him by God (chapter 16). Saul's life continued steadily downward. Obsessed with killing David (chapters 19—30), he consulted a medium (chapter 28) and finally committed suicide (chapter 31).

Among the events of Saul's life is another great beginner—David. A man who followed God (13:14; 16:7), David ministered to Saul (chapter 16), killed Goliath (chapter 17), and became a great warrior. But we'll have to wait until the book of 2 Samuel to see how David finished.

As you read 1 Samuel, note the transition from theocracy to monarchy; exult in the classic stories of David and Goliath, David and Jonathan, David and Abigail; and watch the rise of the influence of the prophets. But in the midst of reading all the history and adventure, determine to run your race as God's person from start to finish.

Samson becomes judge 1075 (1083)	Saul becomes king 1050 (1045)	David born 1040	David anointed; Goliath slain 1025	David becomes king over Judah 1010	David becomes king over all Israel 1003	Solomon becomes king 970	The kingdom is divided 930

THE BLUEPRINT

A. ELI AND SAMUEL
(1:1—7:17)
1. Samuel's birth and childhood
2. War with the Philistines

We see a vivid contrast between young Samuel and Eli's sons. Eli's sons were selfish, but Samuel was helpful. Eli's sons defrauded people, but Samuel grew in wisdom and gave the people messages from God. As an adult, Samuel became a prophet, priest, and judge over Israel. A person's actions reflect his character. This was true of Samuel and of Eli's sons. It is also true of us. Strive, like Samuel, to keep your heart pure before God.

B. SAMUEL AND SAUL
(8:1—15:35)
1. Saul becomes king of Israel
2. God rejects Saul for disobedience

Saul showed great promise. He was strong, tall, and modest. God's Spirit came upon him, and Samuel was his counselor. But Saul deliberately disobeyed God and became an evil king. We must not base our hopes or future on our potential. Instead, we must consistently obey God in all areas of life. God evaluates obedience, not potential.

C. SAUL AND DAVID
(16:1—31:13)
1. Samuel anoints David
2. David and Goliath
3. David and Jonathan become friends
4. Saul pursues David
5. Saul's defeat and death

David quickly killed Goliath but waited patiently for God to deal with Saul. Although David was anointed to be Israel's next king, he had to wait years to realize this promise. The difficult circumstances in life and the times of waiting often refine, teach, and prepare us for the future responsibilities God has for us.

MEGATHEMES

THEME	EXPLANATION	IMPORTANCE
King	Because Israel suffered from corrupt priests and judges, the people wanted a king. They wanted to be organized like the surrounding nations. Though it was against his original purpose, God chose a king for them.	Establishing a monarchy did not solve Israel's problems. What God desires is the genuine devotion of each person's mind and heart to him. No government or set of laws can substitute for the rule of God in your heart and life.
God's Control	Israel prospered as long as the people regarded God as their true king. When the leaders strayed from God's law, God intervened in their personal lives and overruled their actions. In this way, God maintained ultimate control over Israel's history.	God is always at work in this world, even when we can't see what he is doing. No matter what kinds of pressures we must endure or how many changes we must face, God is ultimately in control of our situation. Being confident of God's sovereignty, we can face the difficult situations in our lives with boldness.
Leadership	God guided his people using different forms of leadership: judges, priests, prophets, kings. Those whom he chose for these different offices, such as Eli, Samuel, Saul, and David, portrayed different styles of leadership. Yet the success of each leader depended on his devotion to God, not his position, leadership style, wisdom, age, or strength.	When Eli, Samuel, Saul, and David disobeyed God, they faced tragic consequences. Sin affected what they accomplished for God and how some of them raised their children. Being a real leader means letting God guide all aspects of your activities, values, and goals, including the way you raise your children.

Obedience	For God, "obedience is far better than sacrifice" (15:22). God wanted his people to obey, serve, and follow him with a whole heart rather than to maintain a superficial commitment based on tradition or ceremonial systems.	Although we are free from the sacrificial system of the Jewish law, we may still rely on outward observances to substitute for inward commitment. God desires that all our work and worship be motivated by genuine, heartfelt devotion to him.
God's Faithfulness	God faithfully kept the promises he made to Israel. He responded to his people with tender mercy and swift justice. In showing mercy, he faithfully acted in the best interest of his people. In showing justice, he was faithful to his word and perfect moral nature.	Because God is faithful, he can be counted on to be merciful toward us. Yet God is also just, and he will not tolerate rebellion against him. His faithfulness and unselfish love should inspire us to dedicate ourselves to him completely. We must never take his mercy for granted.

KEY PLACES IN 1 SAMUEL

1 Ramah Samuel was born in Ramah. Before his birth, Samuel's mother Hannah made a promise to God that she would dedicate her son to serve God alongside the priests in the Tabernacle at Shiloh (1:1—2:11).

2 Shiloh The focal point of Israel's worship was at Shiloh, where the Tabernacle and the Ark of the Covenant resided. Eli was the high priest, but his sons, Hophni and Phinehas, were evil men who took advantage of the people. Samuel, however, served God faithfully, and God blessed him as he grew (2:12—3:21).

3 Kiriath-jearim Israel was constantly at odds with the Philistines, and another battle was brewing. Hophni and Phinehas brought the Ark of the Covenant from Shiloh to the battlefield, believing that its mere presence would bring the Israelites victory. The Israelites were defeated by the Philistines at Ebenezer, and the Ark was captured. However, the Philistines soon found out that the Ark was not quite the great battle trophy they expected. For God sent plagues upon every Philistine city into which the Ark was brought. Finally, the Philistines sent it back to Kiriath-jearim in Israel (4:1—7:1).

4 Mizpah The Israelites' defeat made them realize that God was no longer blessing them. Samuel called the people together at Mizpah and asked them to fast and pray in sorrow for their sins. The assembly at Mizpah was a tempting target for the confident Philistines who advanced for an attack. But God intervened and routed their mighty army. Meanwhile, Samuel was judging cases throughout Israel. But as Samuel grew old, the people came to him at Ramah (his home base) demanding a king in order to be like the other nations. At Mizpah, Saul was chosen by sacred appointment to be Israel's

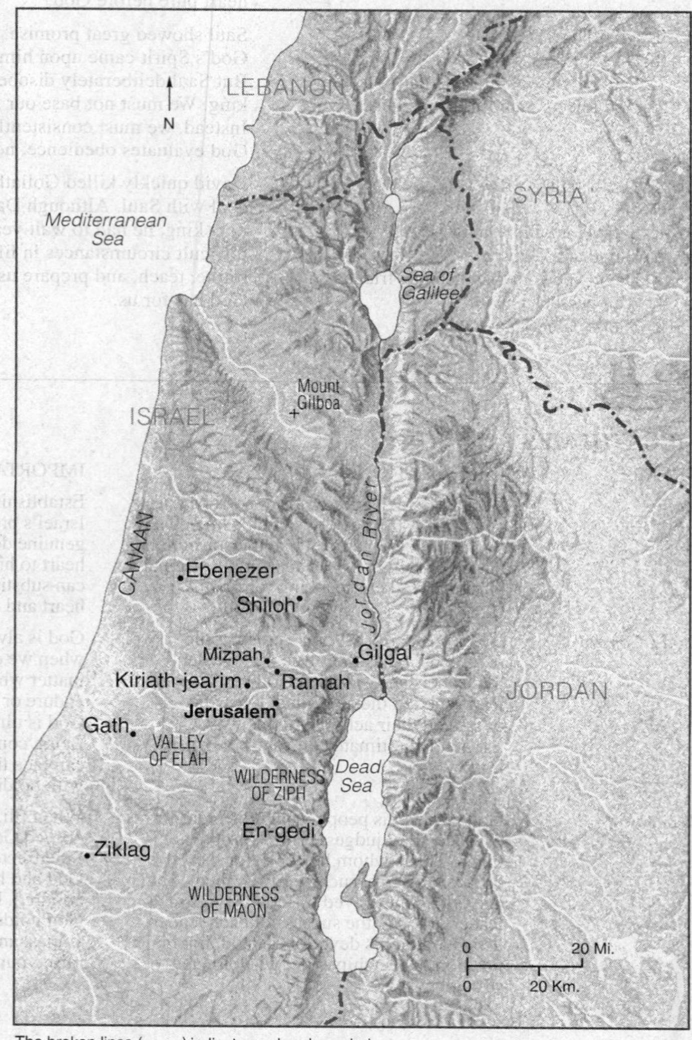

The broken lines (—·—·) indicate modern boundaries.

first king with the blessing, but not the approval, of God and Samuel (7:2—10:27).

5 Gilgal A battle with the Ammonites proved Saul's leadership abilities to the people of Israel. He protected the people of Jabesh-gilead and scattered the Ammonite army. Samuel and the people crowned Saul as king of Israel at Gilgal (11:1–15).

6 Valley of Elah Saul won many other battles, but over time he proved to be arrogant, sinful, and rebellious, so God finally rejected him as king. Unknown to Saul, a young shepherd and musician named David was anointed to be Israel's next king. But it would be many years before David sat upon the throne. Ironically, Saul hired David to play the harp in his palace. Saul grew to like David so much that he made him his personal armor bearer. In one particular battle with the Philistines in the valley of Elah, David killed Goliath, the Philistines' mightiest soldier. But this victory was the beginning of the end of Saul's love for David. The Israelites praised David more than Saul, causing Saul to become so jealous that he plotted to kill David (12:1—22:23).

7 The Wilderness Even anointed kings are not exempt from troubles. David literally ran for his life from King Saul, hiding with his band of followers in the wilderness of Ziph (where the men of Ziph constantly betrayed him), the wilderness of Maon, and the wilderness of En-gedi. Though he had opportunities to kill Saul, David refused to do so because Saul was God's anointed king (23:1—26:25).

8 Gath David moved his men and family to Gath, the Philistine city where King Achish lived. Saul then stopped chasing him. The Philistines seemed to welcome this famous fugitive from Israel (27:1–4).

9 Ziklag Desiring privacy in return for his pretended loyalty to King Achish, David asked for a city in which to house his men and family. Achish gave him Ziklag. From there David conducted raids against the cities of the Geshurites, Girzites, and Amalekites, making sure no one escaped to tell the tale (27:5–12). David later conquered the Amalekites after they raided Ziklag (30:1–31).

10 Mount Gilboa War with the Philistines broke out again in the north, near Mount Gilboa. Saul, who no longer relied on God, consulted a medium in a desperate attempt to contact Samuel for help. In the meantime, David was sent back to Ziklag because the Philistine commanders did not trust his loyalty in battle against Israel. The Philistines slaughtered the Israelites on Mount Gilboa, killing King Saul and his three sons, including David's loyal friend Jonathan. Without God, Saul led a bitter and misguided life. The consequences of his sinful actions affected not only him but hurt his family and the entire nation as well (28:1—31:13).

A. ELI AND SAMUEL (1:1—7:17)

Israel has been ruled by judges for over 200 years. Eli and Samuel are the last of those judges. Samuel is born near the end of Eli's life. He grows up in the Tabernacle as a priest-in-training under Eli and is well qualified to serve Israel as both a priest and a judge. Although the nation has fallen away from God, it is clear that God is preparing Samuel from the very beginning to lead the nation back to right living. God is always in control; he is able to bring his people back to him.

1. Samuel's birth and childhood

Elkanah and His Family

1:1 1 Chr 6:22-28, 33-38 **1** There was a man named Elkanah who lived in Ramah* in the hill country of
Ephraim. He was the son of Jeroham and grandson of Elihu, from the family of Tohu
1:2 Deut 21:15-17 and the clan of Zuph. [2]Elkanah had two wives, Hannah and Peninnah. Peninnah had
children, while Hannah did not.
1:3 Exod 34:23 Deut 12:4-7 Josh 18:1 Luke 2:41-42 [3]Each year Elkanah and his family would travel to Shiloh to worship and sacrifice
to the LORD Almighty at the Tabernacle. The priests of the LORD at that time were the
two sons of Eli—Hophni and Phinehas. [4]On the day Elkanah presented his sacrifice,
1:5 Gen 30:1-2 he would give portions of the sacrifice to Peninnah and each of her children. [5]But he
gave Hannah a special portion* because he loved her very much, even though the LORD

1:1 Hebrew *Ramathaim-zophim;* compare 1:19. **1:5** Or *a double portion.* The meaning of the Hebrew is uncertain.

1:1 The book of 1 Samuel begins in the days when the judges still ruled Israel, possibly during the closing years of Samson's life. Samuel was Israel's last judge and the first priest and prophet to serve during the time of a king. He was the best example of what a good judge should be, governing the people by God's word and not by his own impulses. Samuel was the man who anointed Saul as Israel's first king.

1:2 Although many great Old Testament leaders (such as Abraham, Jacob, and David) had more than one wife, this was not God's original intention for marriage. Genesis 2:24 states that in marriage, two people become one flesh. Why then did polygamy exist among God's people? First, it was to produce more offspring to help in a man's work and to assure the continuation of a man's family line. Numerous children were a symbol of status and wealth. Second, in societies where many young men were killed in battle, polygamy became an accepted way of supporting women who otherwise would have remained unmarried and, very likely, destitute. Nevertheless, polygamy often caused serious family problems, as we see in this story of Hannah and Peninnah.

1:3 The Tabernacle was located at Shiloh, the religious center of the nation (see Joshua 18:1). Three times a year all Israelite men were required to attend a religious feast held at the Tabernacle: the Passover with the Festival of Unleavened Bread, the Festival of Harvest, and the Festival of Shelters (Deuteronomy 16:16). Elkanah made this pilgrimage regularly to fulfill God's commands. (See Exodus 23:14-17 for the regulations concerning the pilgrimage, and see the note on Exodus 40:34 for more on the Tabernacle.)

had given her no children. [6]But Peninnah made fun of Hannah because the LORD had
closed her womb. [7]Year after year it was the same—Peninnah would taunt Hannah as
they went to the Tabernacle.* Hannah would finally be reduced to tears and would not
even eat.
[8]"What's the matter, Hannah?" Elkanah would ask. "Why aren't you eating? Why **1:8**
be so sad just because you have no children? You have me—isn't that better than having Ruth 4:15
ten sons?"

Hannah's Prayer for a Son

[9]Once when they were at Shiloh, Hannah went over to the Tabernacle* after supper to pray **1:9**
to the LORD. Eli the priest was sitting at his customary place beside the entrance. [10]Hannah 1 Sam 3:3
was in deep anguish, crying bitterly as she prayed to the LORD. [11]And she made this vow: **1:11**
"O LORD Almighty, if you will look down upon my sorrow and answer my prayer and give Gen 29:32
me a son, then I will give him back to you. He will be yours for his entire lifetime, and as a Num 6:1-6; 30:6-11
sign that he has been dedicated to the LORD, his hair will never be cut."* Judg 13:5; Luke 1:15
[12]As she was praying to the LORD, Eli watched her. [13]Seeing her lips moving but
hearing no sound, he thought she had been drinking. [14]"Must you come here drunk?" he **1:14**
demanded. "Throw away your wine!" Acts 2:13
[15]"Oh no, sir!" she replied, "I'm not drunk! But I am very sad, and I was pouring out **1:15**
my heart to the LORD. [16]Please don't think I am a wicked woman! For I have been Ps 42:4
praying out of great anguish and sorrow." Lam 2:19
[17]"In that case," Eli said, "cheer up! May the God of Israel grant the request you have **1:17**
asked of him." Ps 20:3-5

1:7 Hebrew *the house of the LORD;* also in 1:24. **1:9** Hebrew *the Temple of the LORD.* **1:11** Some manuscripts add *He will drink neither wine nor intoxicants.*

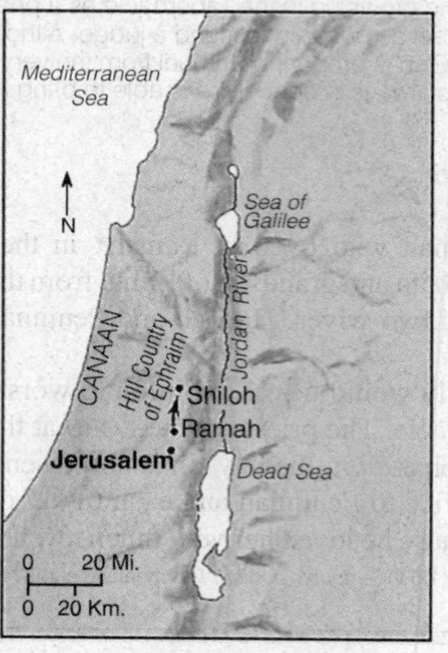

THE JOURNEY TO SHILOH
Each year Elkanah and his family traveled from their home at Ramah to Shiloh, where they worshiped and sacrificed at God's Tabernacle.

1:6 Hannah had been unable to conceive children, and in Old Testament times, a childless woman was considered a failure. Her barrenness was a social embarrassment for her husband. Children were a very important part of the society's economic structure. They were a source of labor for the family, and it was their duty to care for their parents in their old age. If a wife could not bear children, she was often obligated by ancient Middle Eastern custom to give one of her servant girls to her husband to bear children for her. Although Elkanah could have left Hannah (a husband was permitted to divorce a barren wife), he remained lovingly devoted to her despite social criticism and his rights under civil law.

1:7 Part of God's plan for Hannah involved postponing her years of childbearing. While Peninnah and Elkanah looked at Hannah's outward circumstances, God was moving ahead with his plan. Think of those in your world who are struggling with God's timing in answering their prayers and who need your love and help. By supporting those who are struggling, you may help them remain steadfast in their faith and confident in his timing to bring fulfillment to their lives.

1:8 Hannah knew her husband loved her, but even his encouragement could not comfort her. She could not keep from listening to Peninnah's jeers and letting Peninnah's words erode her self-confidence. Although we cannot keep others from unjustly criticizing us, we can choose how we will react to their hurtful words. Rather than dwelling upon our problems, we can enjoy the loving relationships God has given us. By so doing, we can exchange self-pity for hope.

1:10 Hannah had good reason to feel discouraged and bitter. She was unable to bear children; she shared her husband with a woman who ridiculed her (1:7); her loving husband could not solve her problem (1:8); and even the high priest misunderstood her motives (1:14). But instead of retaliating or giving up hope, Hannah prayed. She brought her problem honestly before God.

Each of us may face times of barrenness when nothing "comes to birth" in our work, service, or relationships. It is difficult to pray in faith when we feel so ineffective. But, as Hannah discovered, prayer opens the way for God to work (1:19, 20).

1:11 Be careful what you promise in prayer because God may take you up on it. Hannah so desperately wanted a child that she was willing to strike a bargain with God. God took her up on her promise, and to Hannah's credit, she did her part, even though it was painful (1:27, 28).

Although we are not in a position to barter with God, he may still choose to answer a prayer that has an attached promise. When you pray, ask yourself, Will I follow through on any promises I make to God if he grants my request? It is dishonest and dangerous to ignore a promise, especially to God. God keeps his promises, and he expects you to keep yours.

1:18 Ruth 2:13 18“Oh, thank you, sir!” she exclaimed. Then she went back and began to eat again,
and she was no longer sad.

Samuel's Birth and Dedication

1:19 Gen 21:1-2; 30:22 19The entire family got up early the next morning and went to worship the LORD once more.
Then they returned home to Ramah. When Elkanah slept with Hannah, the LORD remem-
bered her request, 20and in due time she gave birth to a son. She named him Samuel,* for
1:21 Luke 2:22 she said, “I asked the LORD for him.”
21The next year Elkanah, Peninnah, and their children went on their annual trip to offer a
sacrifice to the LORD. 22But Hannah did not go. She told her husband, “Wait until the baby is
weaned. Then I will take him to the Tabernacle and leave him there with the LORD permanently.”*
23“Whatever you think is best,” Elkanah agreed. “Stay here for now, and may the LORD
help you keep your promise.” So she stayed home and nursed the baby.
1:24 Num 15:8-10 24When the child was weaned, Hannah took him to the Tabernacle in Shiloh. They
brought along a three-year-old bull* for the sacrifice and half a bushel* of flour and some
wine. 25After sacrificing the bull, they took the child to Eli. 26“Sir, do you remember me?”
Hannah asked. “I am the woman who stood here several years ago praying to the LORD.

1:20 *Samuel* sounds like the Hebrew term for “asked of God” or “heard by God.” **1:22** Some manuscripts add *I will offer him as a Nazirite for all time.* **1:24a** As in Dead Sea Scrolls, Greek and Syriac versions; Masoretic Text reads *3 bulls.* **1:24b** Hebrew *and an ephah* [18 liters].

HANNAH

Hannah's prayer shows us that all we have and receive is on loan from God. Hannah might have had many excuses for being a possessive mother. But when God answered her prayer, she followed through on her promise to dedicate Samuel to God's service.

She discovered that the greatest joy in having a child is to give that child fully and freely back to God. She entered motherhood prepared to do what all mothers must eventually do—let go of their children.

When children are born, they are completely dependent upon their parents for all their basic necessities. This causes some parents to forget that those same children will grow toward independence within the span of a few short years. Being sensitive to the different stages of that healthy process will greatly strengthen family relationships; resisting or denying that process will cause great pain. We must gradually let go of our children in order to allow them to become mature, independent adults.

Strengths and accomplishments
- Mother of Samuel, Israel's greatest judge
- Fervent in worship; effective in prayer
- Willing to follow through on even a costly commitment

Weakness and mistake
- Struggled with her sense of self-worth because she was unable to have children

Lessons from her life
- God hears and answers prayer
- Our children are gifts from God
- God is concerned for the oppressed and afflicted

Vital statistics
- Where: Ephraim
- Occupation: Homemaker
- Relatives: Husband: Elkanah. Son: Samuel. Later, three other sons and two daughters
- Contemporary: Eli the priest

Key verses
“ ‘Sir, do you remember me?' Hannah asked. ‘I am the woman who stood here several years ago praying to the LORD. I asked the LORD to give me this child, and he has given me my request. Now I am giving him to the LORD, and he will belong to the LORD his whole life.' And they worshiped the Lord there” (1 Samuel 1:26–28).

Her story is told in 1 Samuel 1, 2.

1:18 Earlier Hannah had been discouraged to the point of being physically sick and unable to eat. At this point, she returned home well and happy. The change in her attitude may be attributed to three factors: (1) She honestly prayed to God (1:11); (2) she received encouragement from Eli (1:17); (3) she resolved to leave the problem with God (1:18). This is the antidote for discouragement: Tell God how you really feel and leave your problems with him. Then rely upon the support of good friends and counselors.

1:26-28 To do what she promised (1:11), Hannah gave up what she wanted most—her son—and presented him to Eli to serve in the house of the Lord. In dedicating her only son to God, Hannah was dedicating her entire life and future to God. Because Samuel's life was from God, Hannah was not really giving him up. Rather, she was returning him to God, who had given Samuel to Hannah in the first place. These verses illustrate the kinds of gifts we should give to God. Do your gifts cost you little (Sunday mornings, a comfortable tithe), or are they gifts of sacrifice? Are you presenting God with tokens, or are you presenting him with your entire life?

[27]I asked the LORD to give me this child, and he has given me my request. [28]Now I am giving him to the LORD, and he will belong to the LORD his whole life." And they* worshiped the LORD there.

Hannah's Prayer of Praise

2 Then Hannah prayed:

"My heart rejoices in the LORD!
  Oh, how the LORD has blessed me!
Now I have an answer for my enemies,
  as I delight in your deliverance.
2 No one is holy like the LORD!
  There is no one besides you;
  there is no Rock like our God.

3 "Stop acting so proud and haughty!
  Don't speak with such arrogance!
The LORD is a God who knows your deeds;
  and he will judge you for what you have done.
4 Those who were mighty are mighty no more;
  and those who were weak are now strong.
5 Those who were well fed are now starving;
  and those who were starving are now full.
The barren woman now has seven children;
  but the woman with many children will have no more.
6 The LORD brings both death and life;
  he brings some down to the grave but raises others up.
7 The LORD makes one poor and another rich;
  he brings one down and lifts another up.
8 He lifts the poor from the dust—
  yes, from a pile of ashes!
He treats them like princes,
  placing them in seats of honor.

"For all the earth is the LORD's,
  and he has set the world in order.
9 He will protect his godly ones,
  but the wicked will perish in darkness.
No one will succeed by strength alone.
10 Those who fight against the LORD will be broken.
He thunders against them from heaven;
  the LORD judges throughout the earth.

1:28 Or *he.*

2:1 Luke 1:46-55
2:2 Exod 15:11; Deut 4:35; 32:30-31; 2 Sam 22:32
2:3 1 Sam 16:7; 1 Kgs 8:39; Prov 8:13; 16:2; 24:11-12
2:4 Pss 37:15; 46:7-9
2:5 Ps 113:9; Jer 15:9
2:6 Deut 32:39
2:7 Deut 8:18; Job 1:21; 5:10-11; Ps 75:7
2:8 Job 36:7; 38:4-7; 42:10; Jas 2:5
2:9 Ps 91:11-12; Matt 8:12
2:10 Exod 15:6; 19:18; 1 Sam 7:10; Pss 18:13; 21:1, 7; 89:24; 96:13

1:28 Samuel was probably three years old—the customary age for weaning—when his mother left him at the Tabernacle. By saying, "I am giving him to the LORD," Hannah meant that she was dedicating Samuel to God for lifetime service. She did not, of course, forget her much-wanted son. She visited him regularly, and each year she brought him a robe just like Eli's (2:19). In later years, Samuel lived in Ramah (7:17), his parents' hometown (1:19, 20).

2:1-10 Hannah praised God for his answer to her prayer for a son. The theme of her poetic prayer is her confidence in God's sovereignty and her thankfulness for everything he had done. Mary, the mother of Jesus, modeled her own praise song, called the Magnificat, after Hannah's prayer (Luke 1:46-55). Like Hannah and Mary, we should be confident of God's ultimate control over the events in our lives, and we should be thankful for the ways God has blessed us. By praising God for all good gifts, we acknowledge his ultimate control over all the affairs of life.

2:2 Hannah praised God for being a Rock—firm, strong, and unchanging. In our fast-paced world, friends come and go, and circumstances change. It's difficult to find a solid foundation that will not change. Those who devote their lives to achievements, causes, or possessions have as their security that which is finite and changeable. The possessions that we work so hard to obtain will all pass away. But God is always present. Hope in him. He will never fail.

2:3 No doubt as Hannah said these words, she was thinking of Peninnah's arrogance and chiding. Hannah did not have to get even with Peninnah. She knew that God is all-knowing and that he will judge all sin and pride. Hannah wisely left judgment up to God. Resist the temptation to take justice into your own hands. God will weigh your deeds as well as the deeds of those who have wronged you.

2:10 Because we live in a world where evil abounds and a nuclear holocaust always threatens, we may forget that God is in control. Hannah saw God as (1) solid as a rock (2:2), (2) the one who knows what we do (2:3), (3) sovereign over all the affairs of people (2:4-8), and (4) the Supreme Judge who administers perfect justice (2:10). Remembering God's sovereign control helps us put both world and personal events in perspective.

He gives mighty strength to his king;
he increases the might of his anointed one."

2:11 1 Sam 3:1 11 Then Elkanah and Hannah returned home to Ramah without Samuel. And the boy
became the LORD's helper, for he assisted Eli the priest.

Eli's Wicked Sons

2:12 Jer 2:8; 9:3, 6 12 Now the sons of Eli were scoundrels who had no respect for the LORD 13 or for their
2:13 Lev 7:20, 28-36 duties as priests. Whenever anyone offered a sacrifice, Eli's sons would send over a
servant with a three-pronged fork. While the meat of the sacrificed animal was still
boiling, 14 the servant would stick the fork into the pot and demand that whatever it
2:15 Lev 3:2-5 brought it up be given to Eli's sons. All the Israelites who came to worship at Shiloh were
treated this way. 15 Sometimes the servant would come even before the animal's fat had
been burned on the altar. He would demand raw meat before it had been boiled so that it
could be used for roasting.
16 The man offering the sacrifice might reply, "Take as much as you want, but the fat
2:17 Mal 2:7-9 must first be burned." Then the servant would demand, "No, give it to me now, or I'll
take it by force." 17 So the sin of these young men was very serious in the LORD's sight,
for they treated the LORD's offerings with contempt.
2:18 1 Sam 2:11 18 Now Samuel, though only a boy, was the LORD's helper. He wore a linen tunic just
2:19 1 Sam 1:3 like that of a priest.* 19 Each year his mother made a small coat for him and brought it to
him when she came with her husband for the sacrifice. 20 Before they returned home, Eli
2:21 Gen 21:1 would bless Elkanah and his wife and say, "May the LORD give you other children to
1 Sam 3:19-21 take the place of this one she gave to the LORD.*" 21 And the LORD gave Hannah three
Luke 2:40 sons and two daughters. Meanwhile, Samuel grew up in the presence of the LORD.
2:22 Exod 38:8 22 Now Eli was very old, but he was aware of what his sons were doing to the
2:23 Num 15:30 people of Israel. He knew, for instance, that his sons were seducing the young women
Deut 1:17 who assisted at the entrance of the Tabernacle.* 23 Eli said to them, "I have been

2:18 Hebrew *He wore a linen ephod.* **2:20** As in Greek version; Hebrew reads *this one she requested of the LORD in prayer.* **2:22** Hebrew *Tent of Meeting.* Some manuscripts lack this entire sentence.

2:11, 18 Samuel assisted Eli the priest. In this role, Samuel's responsibilities would have included opening the Tabernacle doors each morning (3:15), cleaning the furniture, and sweeping the floors. As he grew older, Samuel would have assisted Eli in offering sacrifices. The fact that he was wearing a linen tunic (like the garments worn only by priests) shows that he was a priest-in-training. Because Samuel was Eli's helper, he was God's helper, too. When you serve others—even in carrying out ordinary tasks—you are serving God. Because ultimately we serve God, every job has dignity.

2:12ff The law stipulated that the needs of all the Levites were to be met through the people's tithes (Numbers 18:20-24; Joshua 13:14, 33). Because Eli's sons were priests, they were to be taken care of this way. But Eli's sons took advantage of their position to satisfy their lust for power, possessions, and control. Their contempt and arrogance toward both people and worship undermined the integrity of the whole priesthood.

Eli knew that his sons were evil, but he did little to correct or stop them, even when the integrity of God's sanctuary was threatened. As the high priest, Eli should have responded by executing his sons (Numbers 15:22-31). No wonder he chose not to confront the situation. But by ignoring their selfish actions, Eli let his sons ruin their own lives and the lives of many others. There are times when serious problems must be confronted, even if the process and consequences could be painful.

2:13, 14 This fork was a utensil used in the Tabernacle for offering sacrifices. Made of bronze (Exodus 27:3), it usually had three prongs to hook the meat that was to be offered on the altar. Eli's sons used the fork to take more meat from the pot than was due them.

2:13-17 What were Eli's sons doing wrong? They were taking parts of the sacrifices *before* they were offered to God on the altar. They were also eating meat before the fat was burned off. This was against God's laws (Leviticus 3:3-5). In effect, Eli's sons were treating God's offerings with contempt. Offerings were given to show honor and respect to God while seeking forgiveness for sins, but through their irreverence, Eli's sons were actually sinning while making the offerings. To add to their sins, they were also sleeping with the women who served there (2:22).

Like Eli's sons, some religious leaders look down on the faith of ordinary people and treat their offerings to God casually or even with contempt. God harshly judges those who lead his people astray or scorn what is devoted to him (Numbers 18:32).

2:18 Samuel wore a linen tunic (also called an ephod). *Ephods,* long sleeveless vests made of plain linen, were worn by all priests. The high priest's ephod carried special significance. It was embroidered with a variety of bright colors. Attached to it was the breastplate, a biblike garment with gold embroidered shoulder straps. Twelve precious gemstones were attached to the breastplate, each stone representing one of the tribes of Israel. A pouch on the ephod held the Urim and the Thummim, two small objects used to determine God's will in certain national matters.

2:21 God honored the desires of faithful Hannah. We never hear about Peninnah or her children again, but Samuel was used mightily by God. God also gave Hannah five children in addition to Samuel. God often blesses us in ways we do not expect. Hannah never expected to have a child at her age, much less six children! Don't resent God's timing. His blessings might not be immediate, but they will come if we are faithful to do what he says in his Word.

2:23-25 Eli's sons knew better, but they continued to disobey God deliberately by cheating, seducing, and robbing the people. Therefore, God planned to kill them. Any sin is wrong, but sin carried out deliberately and deceitfully is the worst kind. When we sin out of ignorance, we deserve punishment. But when we sin intentionally, the consequences will be more severe. Don't ignore God's warnings about sin. Abandon sin before it becomes a way of life.

hearing reports from the people about the wicked things you are doing. Why do
you keep sinning? 24 You must stop, my sons! The reports I hear among the LORD's
people are not good. 25 If someone sins against another person, God* can mediate for 2:25 Josh 11:20
the guilty party. But if someone sins against the LORD, who can intercede?" But Eli's
sons wouldn't listen to their father, for the LORD was already planning to put them to
death.
26 Meanwhile, as young Samuel grew taller, he also continued to gain favor with the 2:26 Luke 2:40, 52
LORD and with the people.

A Warning for Eli's Family

27 One day a prophet came to Eli and gave him this message from the LORD: "Didn't I 2:27 Judg 13:6
reveal myself to your ancestors when the people of Israel were slaves in Egypt? 28 I chose 2:28
your ancestor Aaron* from among all his relatives to be my priest, to offer sacrifices on Exod 28:1-4; 30:7-8
my altar, to burn incense, and to wear the priestly garments* as he served me. And I
assigned the sacrificial offerings to you priests. 29 So why do you scorn my sacrifices and 2:29
offerings? Why do you honor your sons more than me—for you and they have become Matt 10:37 Deut 12:5
fat from the best offerings of my people!
30 "Therefore, the LORD, the God of Israel, says: The terrible things you are doing 2:30
cannot continue! I had promised that your branch of the tribe of Levi* would always be Num 25:12-13 Ps 50:23
my priests. But I will honor only those who honor me, and I will despise those who Mal 2:7-9
despise me. 31 I will put an end to your family, so it will no longer serve as my priests. 2:31
All the members of your family will die before their time. None will live to a ripe old 1 Sam 4:11-18; 22:17-20
age. 32 You will watch with envy as I pour out prosperity on the people of Israel. But no
members of your family will ever live out their days. 33 Those who are left alive will live
in sadness and grief, and their children will die a violent death.* 34 And to prove that what 2:34
I have said will come true, I will cause your two sons, Hophni and Phinehas, to die on 1 Sam 4:11, 17 1 Kgs 13:3
the same day!
35 "Then I will raise up a faithful priest who will serve me and do what I tell him to
do. I will bless his descendants, and his family will be priests to my anointed kings
forever. 36 Then all of your descendants will bow before his descendants, begging for
money and food. 'Please,' they will say, 'give us jobs among the priests so we will have
enough to eat.'"

The LORD Speaks to Samuel

3 Meanwhile, the boy Samuel was serving the LORD by assisting Eli. Now in those 3:1 1 Sam 2:11
days messages from the LORD were very rare, and visions were quite uncommon. Ps 74:9
2 One night Eli, who was almost blind by now, had just gone to bed. 3 The lamp of God Amos 8:11

2:25 Or *the judges.* **2:28a** Hebrew *your father.* **2:28b** Hebrew *an ephod.* **2:30** Hebrew *that your house and your father's house.* **2:33** As in Dead Sea Scrolls, which read *die by the sword;* Masoretic Text reads *die like mortals.*

2:25 Does a loving God really will or want to put people to death? Consider the situation in the Tabernacle. A person made an offering in order to have his sins forgiven, and Eli's sons stole the offering and made a sham of the person's repentant attitude. God, in his love for Israel, could not permit this situation to continue. He allowed Eli's sons to die as a result of their own boastful presumption. They took the Ark into battle, thinking it would protect them. But God withdrew his protection, and the wicked sons of Eli were killed (4:10, 11).

2:29 Eli had a difficult time rearing his sons. He apparently did not take any strong disciplinary action with them when he became aware of their wrongdoing. But Eli was not just a father trying to handle his rebellious sons; he was the high priest ignoring the sins of priests under his jurisdiction. As a result, the Lord took the necessary disciplinary action that Eli would not.

Eli was guilty of honoring his sons above God by letting them continue in their sinful ways. Is there a situation in your life, family, or work that you allow to continue even though you know it is wrong? If so, you may become as guilty as those engaged in the wrong act.

2:31, 35, 36 For the fulfillment of this prediction see 1 Kings 2:26, 27. This is where Solomon removed Abiathar from his position, thus ending Eli's line. Then God raised up Zadok, a priest under David and then high priest under Solomon. Zadok's line was probably still in place as late as the days of Ezra.

3:1-5 Although God had spoken directly and audibly with Moses and Joshua, his word became rare during the three centuries of rule by judges. By Eli's time, no prophets were speaking God's messages to Israel. Why? Look at the attitude of Eli's sons. They either refused to listen to God or allowed greed to get in the way of any communication with him.

Listening and responding is vital in a relationship with God. Although God does not always use the sound of a human voice, he always speaks clearly through his Word. To receive his messages, we must be ready to listen and to act upon what he tells us. Like Samuel, be ready to say "Here I am" when God calls you to action.

3:2, 3 The Ark of God was kept in the Most Holy Place, the innermost room of the Tabernacle where only the high priest could enter once a year. In front of the Most Holy Place was the Holy Place, a small room where the other sacred furniture of the Tabernacle was kept (the altar of incense, the Bread of the Presence, the lampstand). Just outside the Holy Place was a court with small rooms where the priests were to stay. Samuel probably slept here with the other priests, only a few yards away from the Ark.

had not yet gone out, and Samuel was sleeping in the Tabernacle* near the Ark of God.
4 Suddenly, the LORD called out, "Samuel! Samuel!"
"Yes?" Samuel replied. "What is it?" 5 He jumped up and ran to Eli. "Here I am. What
do you need?"
"I didn't call you," Eli replied. "Go on back to bed." So he did.
6 Then the LORD called out again, "Samuel!"
Again Samuel jumped up and ran to Eli. "Here I am," he said. "What do you need?"
"I didn't call you, my son," Eli said. "Go on back to bed."
3:7 Amos 3:7
7 Samuel did not yet know the LORD because he had never had a message from the
LORD before. 8 So now the LORD called a third time, and once more Samuel jumped up
and ran to Eli. "Here I am," he said. "What do you need?"
Then Eli realized it was the LORD who was calling the boy. 9 So he said to Samuel,
"Go and lie down again, and if someone calls again, say, 'Yes, LORD, your servant is
listening.'" So Samuel went back to bed.
10 And the LORD came and called as before, "Samuel! Samuel!"
And Samuel replied, "Yes, your servant is listening."

3:3 Hebrew *the Temple of the LORD.*

ISRAELITES VERSUS PHILISTINES
The Israelites and Philistines were archenemies and constantly fought. Here are some of their confrontations, found in 1 and 2 Samuel. When the Israelites trusted God for the victory, they always won.

Location of the Battle	*Winner*	*Comments*	*Reference*
Aphek to Ebenezer	Philistines	The Ark was captured and Eli's sons killed	1 Samuel 4:1–11
Mizpah	Israelites	After the Ark was returned, the Philistines planned to attack again, but God confused them. Israel chased the Philistines back to Beth-car	1 Samuel 7:7–14
Geba	Israelites under Jonathan	One detachment destroyed	1 Samuel 13:3, 4
Gilgal	A standoff	The Israelites lost their nerve and hid	1 Samuel 13:6–17
Micmash	Israelites	Jonathan and his armor bearer said it didn't matter how many enemies there were. If God was with them, they would win. They began the battle, and the army completed it	1 Samuel 13:23—14:23
Valley of Elah	Israelites	David and Goliath	1 Samuel 17:1–58
?	Israelites	David killed 200 Philistines to earn a wife	1 Samuel 18:17–30
Keilah	Israelites under David	David protected the threshing floors from Philistine looters	1 Samuel 23:1–5
Aphek, Jezreel, to Mount Gilboa	Philistines	Saul and Jonathan killed	1 Samuel 29:1; 31:1–13
Baal-perazim	Israelites	The Philistines tried to capture King David	2 Samuel 5:17–25
Gath	Israelites	There was very little trouble with the Philistines after this defeat	2 Samuel 8:1
?	Israelites	Abishai saved David from a Philistine giant	2 Samuel 21:15–17
Gob	Israelites	Other giants were killed, including Goliath's brother	2 Samuel 21:18–22

3:8, 9 One would naturally expect an audible message from God to be given to the priest Eli and not to the child Samuel. Eli was older and more experienced, and he held the proper position. But God's chain of command is based on faith, not on age or position. In finding faithful followers, God may use unexpected channels. Be prepared for the Lord to work at any place, at any time, and through anyone he chooses.

11 Then the LORD said to Samuel, "I am about to do a shocking thing in Israel. 12 I am
going to carry out all my threats against Eli and his family. 13 I have warned him
continually that judgment is coming for his family, because his sons are blaspheming
God* and he hasn't disciplined them. 14 So I have vowed that the sins of Eli and his sons
will never be forgiven by sacrifices or offerings."

Samuel Speaks for the LORD

15 Samuel stayed in bed until morning, then got up and opened the doors of the
Tabernacle* as usual. He was afraid to tell Eli what the LORD had said to him. 16 But Eli
called out to him, "Samuel, my son."

"Here I am," Samuel replied.

17 "What did the LORD say to you? Tell me everything. And may God punish you if
you hide anything from me!" 18 So Samuel told Eli everything; he didn't hold anything
back. "It is the LORD's will," Eli replied. "Let him do what he thinks best."

19 As Samuel grew up, the LORD was with him, and everything Samuel said was wise
and helpful. 20 All the people of Israel from one end of the land to the other knew that
Samuel was confirmed as a prophet of the LORD. 21 The LORD continued to appear at
Shiloh and gave messages to Samuel there at the Tabernacle. 1 And Samuel's words went
out to all the people of Israel.

3:11 2 Kgs 21:12
3:12 1 Sam 2:27-36
3:14 1 Sam 2:25
3:18 Job 2:10; Isa 39:8
3:19 Gen 21:22; Judg 13:24
3:20 Judg 20:1

2. War with the Philistines

The Philistines Capture the Ark

4 At that time Israel was at war with the Philistines. The Israelite army was camped near
Ebenezer, and the Philistines were at Aphek. 2 The Philistines attacked and defeated the
army of Israel, killing four thousand men. 3 After the battle was over, the army of Israel
retreated to their camp, and their leaders asked, "Why did the LORD allow us to be defeated
by the Philistines?" Then they said, "Let's bring the Ark of the Covenant of the LORD from
Shiloh. If we carry it into battle with us, it* will save us from our enemies."

4 So they sent men to Shiloh to bring back the Ark of the Covenant of the LORD
Almighty, who is enthroned between the cherubim. Hophni and Phinehas, the sons of

4:1 1 Sam 7:12; 29:1
4:3 Num 10:35; Josh 7:7
4:4 2 Sam 6:2; Ps 80:1

3:13 As in Greek version; Hebrew reads *his sons have made themselves contemptible.* **3:15** Hebrew *the house of the LORD.* **4:3** Or *he.*

3:13 Eli had spent his entire life in service to God. His responsibility was to oversee all the worship in Israel. But in pursuing this great mission he neglected the responsibilities in his own home. Don't let your desire to do God's work cause you to neglect your family. If you do, your mission may degenerate into a quest for personal importance, and your family will suffer the consequences of your neglect.

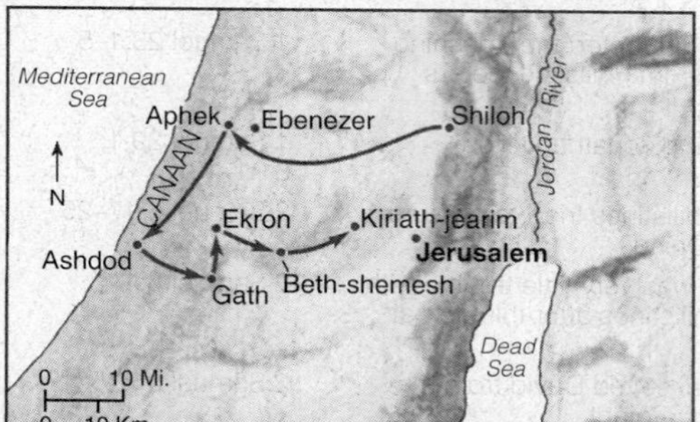

THE ARK'S TRAVELS Eli's sons took the Ark from Shiloh to the battlefield on the lower plains at Ebenezer and Aphek. The Philistines captured the Ark and took it to Ashdod, Gath, and Ekron. Plagues forced the people to send the Ark back to Israel, where it finally was taken by cattle-driven carts to Beth-shemesh and on to the home of Eleazar in Kiriath-jearim.

4:1 The Philistines, descendants of Noah's son Ham, settled along the southeastern Mediterranean coast between Egypt and Gaza. They were originally one of the "Sea Peoples" who had migrated to the Middle East in ships from Greece and Crete. By Samuel's time, these warlike people were well established in five of Gaza's cities in southwest Canaan and were constantly pressing inland against the Israelites. Throughout this time, the Philistines were Israel's major enemy.

4:3 The Ark of the Covenant contained the Ten Commandments given by God to Moses. The Ark was supposed to be kept in the Most Holy Place, a sacred part of the Tabernacle that only the high priest could enter once a year. Hophni and Phinehas desecrated the room by unlawfully entering it and removing the Ark.

The Israelites rightly recognized the great holiness of the Ark, but they thought that the Ark itself—the wood and metal box—was their source of power. They began to use it as a good luck charm, expecting it to protect them from their enemies. A symbol of God does not guarantee his presence and power. Their attitude toward the Ark came perilously close to idol worship. When the Ark was captured by their enemies, they thought that Israel's glory was gone (4:19-22) and that God had deserted them (7:1, 2). God uses his power according to his own wisdom and will. He responds to the faith of those who seek him.

4:4 "The LORD Almighty, who is enthroned between the cherubim," conveys that God's presence rested on the Ark of the Covenant between the two golden cherubim (or angels) attached to its lid. The people believed that the Ark would bring victory when Hophni and Phinehas carried it into battle.

4:5 Josh 6:5 Eli, helped carry the Ark of God to where the battle was being fought. 5When the Israelites saw the Ark of the Covenant of the LORD coming into the camp, their shout of joy was so loud that it made the ground shake!

6"What's going on?" the Philistines asked. "What's all the shouting about in the Hebrew camp?" When they were told it was because the Ark of the LORD had arrived,
4:7 Exod 14:25; 15:14 7they panicked. "The gods have* come into their camp!" they cried. "This is a disaster! We have never had to face anything like this before! 8Who can save us from these mighty gods of Israel? They are the same gods who destroyed the Egyptians
4:9 Judg 13:1 with plagues when Israel was in the wilderness. 9Fight as you never have before, Philistines! If you don't, we will become the Hebrews' slaves just as they have been ours!"

4:7 Or *A god has.*

Eli was one Old Testament person with a very modern problem. The recognition and respect he earned in public did not extend to his handling of his private affairs. He may have been an excellent priest, but he was a poor parent. His sons brought him grief and ruin. He lacked two important qualities needed for effective parental discipline: firm resolve and corrective action.

Eli responded to situations rather than solving them. But even his responses tended to be weak. God pointed out his sons' errors, but Eli did little to correct them. The contrast between God's dealing with Eli and Eli's dealing with his sons is clear—God gave warning, spelled out the consequences of disobedience, and then acted. Eli only warned. Children need to learn that their parents' words and actions go together. Both love and discipline must be spoken as well as acted out.

But Eli had another problem. He was more concerned with the symbols of his religion than with the God they represented. For Eli, the Ark of the Covenant had become a relic to be protected rather than a reminder of the Protector. His faith shifted from the Creator to the created.

It may be easier to worship things we can see, whether buildings, people, or Scripture itself, but such tangible things have no power in themselves. This book you hold is either merely a respectable religious relic, or it is the sharp and effective Word of God. Your attitude toward it is largely shaped by your relationship to the God from whom it comes. A relic or antique has to be carefully stored away; God's Word has to be used and obeyed. Which attitude accurately describes your approach to the Word of God?

Strengths and accomplishments
- Judged Israel for 40 years
- Spoke with Hannah, the mother of Samuel, and assured her of God's blessing
- Reared and trained Samuel, the greatest judge of Israel

Weaknesses and mistakes
- Failed to discipline his sons or correct them when they sinned
- Tended to react to situations rather than take decisive action
- Saw the Ark of the Covenant as a relic to be cherished rather than as a symbol of God's presence with Israel

Lessons from his life
- Parents need to discipline their children responsibly
- Life is more than simply reacting; it demands action
- Past victories cannot substitute for present trust

Vital statistics
- Where: Shiloh
- Occupations: High priest and judge of Israel
- Relatives: Sons: Hophni and Phinehas
- Contemporary: Samuel

Key verses
"Then the LORD said to Samuel, 'I am about to do a shocking thing in Israel. I am going to carry out all my threats against Eli and his family. I have warned him continually that judgment is coming for his family, because his sons are blaspheming God and he hasn't disciplined them. So I have vowed that the sins of Eli and his sons will never be forgiven by sacrifices or offerings.'" (1 Samuel 3:11–14).

His story is told in 1 Samuel 1—4. He is also mentioned in 1 Kings 2:26, 27.

4:5-8 The Philistines were afraid because they remembered stories about God's intervention for Israel when they left Egypt. But Israel had turned away from God and was clinging to only a form of godliness, a symbol of former victories.

People (and churches) often try to live on the memories of God's blessings. The Israelites wrongly assumed that because God had given them victory in the past, he would do it again, even though they had strayed far from him. Today, as in Bible times, spiritual victories come through a continually renewed relationship with God. Don't live off the past. Keep your relationship with God new and fresh.

10 So the Philistines fought desperately, and Israel was defeated again. The slaughter was great; thirty thousand Israelite men died that day. The survivors turned and fled to their tents. 11 The Ark of God was captured, and Hophni and Phinehas, the two sons of Eli, were killed.

4:10 Deut 28:15, 25
4:11 1 Sam 2:34; Ps 78:60-61

The Death of Eli

12 A man from the tribe of Benjamin ran from the battlefront and arrived at Shiloh later that same day. He had torn his clothes and put dust on his head to show his grief. 13 Eli was waiting beside the road to hear the news of the battle, for his heart trembled for the safety of the Ark of God. When the messenger arrived and told what had happened, an outcry resounded throughout the town. 14 "What is all the noise about?" Eli asked.

4:12 Josh 7:6; 2 Sam 1:2; Neh 9:1

The messenger rushed over to Eli, 15 who was ninety-eight years old and blind. 16 He said to Eli, "I have just come from the battlefront—I was there this very day."

4:15 Gen 27:1; 1 Sam 3:2

"What happened?" Eli demanded.

17 "Israel has been defeated," the messenger replied. "Thousands of Israelite troops are dead on the battlefield. Your two sons, Hophni and Phinehas, were killed, too. And the Ark of God has been captured."

4:17 1 Sam 22:18; Ps 78:61, 64

18 When the messenger mentioned what had happened to the Ark, Eli fell backward from his seat beside the gate. He broke his neck and died, for he was old and very fat. He had led Israel for forty years.

19 Eli's daughter-in-law, the wife of Phinehas, was pregnant and near her time of delivery. When she heard that the Ark of God had been captured and that her husband and father-in-law were dead, her labor pains suddenly began. 20 She died in childbirth, but before she passed away the midwives tried to encourage her. "Don't be afraid," they said. "You have a baby boy!" But she did not answer or respond in any way.

4:20 Gen 35:17-18

21 She named the child Ichabod—"Where is the glory?"—murmuring, "Israel's glory is gone." She named him this because the Ark of God had been captured and because her husband and her father-in-law were dead. 22 Then she said, "The glory has departed from Israel, for the Ark of God has been captured."

4:21 Ps 106:20

The Ark in Philistia

5 After the Philistines captured the Ark of God, they took it from the battleground at Ebenezer to the city of Ashdod. 2 They carried the Ark of God into the temple of Dagon and placed it beside the idol of Dagon. 3 But when the citizens of Ashdod went to see it the next morning, Dagon had fallen with his face to the ground in front of the Ark of the LORD! So they set the idol up again. 4 But the next morning the same thing happened—the idol had fallen face down before the Ark of the LORD again. This time his head and hands had broken off and were lying in the doorway. Only the trunk of his body was left intact. 5 That is why to this day neither the priests of Dagon nor anyone who enters the temple of Dagon will step on its threshold.

5:1 Josh 13:3; Judg 16:23; 1 Sam 4:1; Ps 78:61
5:3 Isa 19:1; 46:7
5:4 Ezek 6:6; Mic 1:7

4:11 This event fulfills the prophecy in 2:34 stating that Eli's sons, Hophni and Phinehas, would die "on the same day."

4:12 At this time, the city of Shiloh was Israel's religious center (Joshua 18:1; 1 Samuel 4:3). The Tabernacle was permanently set up there. Because Israel did not have a civil capital—a seat of national government—Shiloh was the natural place for a messenger to deliver the sad news from the battle. Many scholars believe that it was during this battle that Shiloh was destroyed (Jeremiah 7:12; 26:2-6; also see the note on 7:1).

4:18 Eli was Israel's judge and high priest. His death marked the end of the dark period of the judges when most of the nation ignored God. Although Samuel was also a judge, his career saw the transition from Israel's rule by judges to the nation's monarchy. He began the great revival that Israel would experience for the next century. The Bible does not say who became the next high priest (Samuel was not eligible because he was not a direct descendant of Aaron), but Samuel acted as high priest at this time by offering the important sacrifices throughout Israel.

4:19-22 This incident illustrates the spiritual darkness and decline of Israel. This young boy, Ichabod, was supposed to succeed his father, Phinehas, in the priesthood, but his father had been killed because he was an evil man who desecrated the Tabernacle. The terror of God's leaving his people overshadowed the joy of childbirth. When sin dominates our lives, even God-given joys and pleasures seem empty.

5:1ff Dagon was the chief god of the Philistines, whom they believed sent rain and assured a bountiful harvest. But the Philistines, like most of their pagan neighbors, worshiped many gods. The more gods they could have on their side, the more secure they felt. That was why they wanted the Ark, thinking that if it helped the Israelites, it could help them, too. But when the people living nearby began to get sick and die, the Philistines realized that the Ark was not a good omen. It was a source of greater power than they had ever seen—power they could not control.

5:6 Exod 9:3 1 Sam 6:4-5 6Then the LORD began to afflict the people of Ashdod and the nearby villages with a
plague of tumors.* 7When the people realized what was happening, they cried out, "We
can't keep the Ark of the God of Israel here any longer! He is against us! We will all be
5:8 Judg 16:18 destroyed along with our god Dagon." 8So they called together the rulers of the five
Philistine cities and asked, "What should we do with the Ark of the God of Israel?"
The rulers discussed it and replied, "Move it to the city of Gath." So they moved the
5:9 1 Sam 7:13; 12:15 Ark of the God of Israel to Gath. 9But when the Ark arrived at Gath, the LORD began
afflicting its people, young and old, with a plague of tumors, and there was a great panic.
5:10 Josh 13:3 10So they sent the Ark of God to the city of Ekron, but when the people of Ekron saw
it coming they cried out, "They are bringing the Ark of the God of Israel here to kill us,
too!" 11So the people summoned the rulers again and begged them, "Please send the Ark
of the God of Israel back to its own country, or it* will kill us all." For the plague from
God had already begun, and great fear was sweeping across the city. 12Those who didn't
die were afflicted with tumors; and there was weeping everywhere.

The Philistines Return the Ark

6:2 Gen 41:8 Exod 7:11 **6** The Ark of the LORD remained in Philistine territory seven months in all. 2Then the
Philistines called in their priests and diviners and asked them, "What should we do
about the Ark of the LORD? Tell us how to return it to its own land."
6:3 Lev 5:15-16 3"Send the Ark of the God of Israel back, along with a gift," they were told. "Send a
guilt offering so the plague will stop. Then, if the plague doesn't stop, you will know that
God didn't send the plague after all."
6:4 Josh 13:3 1 Sam 5:6, 11; 6:5 4"What sort of guilt offering should we send?" they asked.
And they were told, "Since the plague has struck both you and your five rulers, make
five gold tumors and five gold rats, just like those that have ravaged your land. 5Make
these things to show honor to the God of Israel. Perhaps then he will stop afflicting you,
6:6 Exod 8:15, 31-32; 12:31 your gods, and your land. 6Don't be stubborn and rebellious as Pharaoh and the
Egyptians were. They wouldn't let Israel go until God had ravaged them with dreadful
6:7 Deut 21:3 2 Sam 6:3 plagues. 7Now build a new cart, and find two cows that have just had calves. Make sure
the cows have never been yoked to a cart. Hitch the cows to the cart, but shut their calves
away from them in a pen. 8Put the Ark of the LORD on the cart, and beside it place a chest
6:9 Josh 15:10 1 Sam 6:3 containing the gold rats and gold tumors. Then let the cows go wherever they want. 9If
they cross the border of our land and go to Beth-shemesh, we will know it was the LORD
who brought this great disaster upon us. If they don't, we will know that the plague was
simply a coincidence and was not sent by the LORD at all."
10So these instructions were carried out. Two cows with newborn calves were hitched
to the cart, and their calves were shut up in a pen. 11Then the Ark of the LORD and the
chest containing the gold rats and gold tumors were placed on the cart. 12And sure

5:6 Greek version and Latin Vulgate read *tumors. And rats appeared in their land, and death and destruction were throughout the city.* **5:11** Or *he.*

5:6, 7 Although the Philistines had just witnessed a great victory by Israel's God over their god, Dagon, they didn't act upon that insight until they were afflicted with tumors (possibly bubonic plague). Similarly, today many people don't respond to biblical truth until they experience pain. Are you willing to listen to God for truth's sake, or do you turn to him only when you are hurting?

5:8 The Philistines were governed by five rulers. Each ruler lived in a different city—Gath, Ekron, Ashdod, Ashkelon, Gaza. The Ark was taken to three of these capital cities, and each time it brought great trouble and chaos to the citizens.

6:3 What was this guilt offering supposed to accomplish? This was a normal reaction to trouble in the Canaanite religion. The Philistines thought their problems were the result of their gods being angry. They recognized their guilt in taking the Ark and now were trying everything they could to placate Israel's God. The diviners (6:2) probably helped choose the gift they thought would placate Yahweh. But the offering consisted of images of tumors and rats, not the kind of guilt offering prescribed in God's laws (Leviticus 5:14–6:7; 7:1-10). How easy it is to design our own methods of acknowledging God rather than serving him in the way he requires.

6:7-12 The Philistine priests and diviners devised a test to see if God was really the one who had caused all their recent troubles. Two cows who had just given birth were hitched to a cart and sent toward Israel's border carrying the Ark of the Covenant. For a cow to leave her nursing calf, she would have to go against all her motherly instincts. Only God, who has power over the natural order, could cause this to happen. God sent the cows to Israel, not to pass the Philistines' test, but to show them his mighty power.

6:9 The Philistines acknowledged the existence of the Hebrew God, but only as one of many deities whose favor they sought. Thinking of God in this way made it easy for them to ignore his demand that people worship him alone. Many people "worship" God this way. They see God as just one ingredient in a successful life. But God is far more than an ingredient—he is the source of life itself. Are you a "Philistine," seeing God's favor as only an ingredient of the good life?

enough, the cows went straight along the road toward Beth-shemesh, lowing as they
went. The Philistine rulers followed them as far as the border of Beth-shemesh.
13 The people of Beth-shemesh were harvesting wheat in the valley, and when they
saw the Ark, they were overjoyed! 14 The cart came into the field of a man named
Joshua and stopped beside a large rock. So the people broke up the wood of the cart
for a fire and killed the cows and sacrificed them to the LORD as a burnt offering.
15 Several men of the tribe of Levi lifted the Ark of the LORD and the chest containing
the gold rats and gold tumors from the cart and placed them on the large rock. Many
burnt offerings and sacrifices were offered to the LORD that day by the people of
Beth-shemesh. 16 The five Philistine rulers watched all this and then returned to Ekron
that same day.
17 The five gold tumors that were sent by the Philistines as a guilt offering to the
LORD were gifts from the rulers of Ashdod, Gaza, Ashkelon, Gath, and Ekron. 18 The
five gold rats represented the five Philistine cities and their surrounding villages,
which were controlled by the five rulers. The large rock at Beth-shemesh, where they
set the Ark of the LORD, still stands in the field of Joshua as a reminder of what
happened there.

The Ark Moved to Kiriath-Jearim

19 But the LORD killed seventy men* from Beth-shemesh because they looked into the
Ark of the LORD. And the people mourned greatly because of what the LORD had done.
20 "Who is able to stand in the presence of the LORD, this holy God?" they cried out.
"Where can we send the Ark from here?" 21 So they sent messengers to the people at
Kiriath-jearim and told them, "The Philistines have returned the Ark of the LORD. Please
come here and get it!"

7 So the men of Kiriath-jearim came to get the Ark of the LORD. They took it to the
hillside home of Abinadab and ordained Eleazar, his son, to be in charge of it. 2 The
Ark remained in Kiriath-jearim for a long time—twenty years in all. During that time,
all Israel mourned because it seemed that the LORD had abandoned them.

Samuel Leads Israel to Victory

3 Then Samuel said to all the people of Israel, "If you are really serious about wanting to
return to the LORD, get rid of your foreign gods and your images of Ashtoreth. Determine

6:14 2 Sam 24:22
6:15 Josh 3:2-4
6:17 1 Sam 6:4
6:18 Deut 3:5
6:19 2 Sam 6:7
6:20 Lev 11:44-45; 2 Sam 6:9; Mal 3:2
6:21 Josh 15:9, 60
7:1 2 Sam 6:3-4
7:3 Deut 6:13; 13:4; Josh 24:14, 23; Judg 2:12-13; 10:16

6:19 As in a few Hebrew manuscripts; most Hebrew manuscripts and Greek version read *50,070 men.* Perhaps the text should be understood to read *the LORD killed 70 men and 50 oxen.*

6:19 Why were people killed for looking into the Ark? The Israelites had made an idol of the Ark. They had tried to harness God's power, to use it for their own purposes (victory in battle). But the Lord of the universe cannot be controlled by humans. To protect the Israelites from his power, he had warned them not even to look at the sacred sanctuary objects in the Most Holy Place or they would die (Numbers 4:20). Only Levites were allowed to move the Ark. Because of their disobedience, God carried out his promised judgment.

God could not allow the people to think they could use his power for their own ends. He could not permit them to disregard his warnings and come into his presence lightly. He did not want the cycle of disrespect, disobedience, and defeat to start all over again. God did not kill the men of Beth-shemesh to be cruel. He killed them because overlooking their presumptuous sin would encourage the whole nation of Israel to ignore God.

7:1 The Ark was taken to Kiriath-jearim, a city near the battlefield, for safekeeping, and Eleazar was given the task of caring for it. Why wasn't it taken back to the Tabernacle at Shiloh? Shiloh had probably been defeated and destroyed by the Philistines in an earlier battle (4:1-18; Jeremiah 26:2-6) because of the evil deeds of its priests (2:12-17). Apparently, the Tabernacle and its furniture were saved because we read that the Tabernacle was set up in Nob during Saul's reign (21:1-6) and in Gibeon during the reigns of David and Solomon (1 Chronicles 16:39; 21:29, 30; 2 Chronicles 1). Shiloh, however, is never again mentioned in the historical books of the Old Testament. Samuel's new home became Ramah (7:15-17; 8:4), his birthplace (further evidence of Shiloh's destruction).

7:2, 3 Israel mourned, and sorrow gripped the nation for 20 years. The Ark was put away like an unwanted box in an attic, and it seemed as if the Lord had abandoned his people. Samuel, now a grown man, roused them to action by saying that if they were truly sorry, they should do something about it. How easy it is for us to complain about our problems, even to God, while we refuse to act, change, and do what he requires. We don't even take the advice he has already given us. Do you ever feel as if God has abandoned you? Check to see if there is anything he has already told you to do. You may not receive new guidance from God until you have acted on his previous directions.

7:3 Samuel urged the Israelites to get rid of their foreign gods. Idols today are much more subtle than gods of wood and stone, but they are just as dangerous. Whatever holds first place in our lives or controls us is our god. Money, success, material goods, pride, or anything else can be an idol if it takes the place of God in our lives. The Lord alone is worthy of our service and worship, and we must let nothing rival him. If we have "foreign gods," we need to ask God to help us dethrone them, making the true God our first priority.

7:6 Judg 10:10; Neh 9:1; Lam 2:19
7:7 1 Sam 13:6; 17:11
7:8 1 Sam 12:19; Isa 37:4
7:9 Lev 22:26-27; Ps 99:6; Jer 15:1

to obey only the LORD; then he will rescue you from the Philistines." 4So the Israelites
destroyed their images of Baal and Ashtoreth and worshiped only the LORD.
5Then Samuel told them, "Come to Mizpah, all of you. I will pray to the LORD for
you." 6So they gathered there and, in a great ceremony, drew water from a well and
poured it out before the LORD. They also went without food all day and confessed that
they had sinned against the LORD. So it was at Mizpah that Samuel became Israel's judge.
7When the Philistine rulers heard that all Israel had gathered at Mizpah, they mobilized
their army and advanced. The Israelites were badly frightened when they learned that the
Philistines were approaching. 8"Plead with the LORD our God to save us from the Philistines!" they begged Samuel. 9So Samuel took a young lamb and offered it to the LORD as a
whole burnt offering. He pleaded with the LORD to help Israel, and the LORD answered.

SAMUEL

We often wonder about the childhoods of great people. We have little information about the early years of most of the people mentioned in the Bible. One delightful exception is Samuel; he came as a result of God's answer to Hannah's fervent prayer for a child. (In fact, the name *Samuel* comes from the Hebrew expression "heard of God.") God shaped Samuel from the start. Like Moses, Samuel was called to fill many different roles: judge, priest, prophet, counselor, and God's man at a turning point in the history of Israel. God worked through Samuel because Samuel was willing to be one thing: God's servant.

Samuel showed that those whom God finds faithful in small things will be trusted with greater things. He grew up assisting the high priest (Eli) in the Tabernacle until God directed him to other responsibilities. God was able to use Samuel because he was genuinely dedicated to God.

Samuel moved ahead because he was listening to God's directions. Too often we ask God to control our lives without making us give up the goals for which we strive. We ask God to help us get where *we* want to go. The first step in correcting this tendency is to turn over both the control and destination of our lives to him. The second step is to do what we *already know* God requires of us. The third step is to listen for further direction from his Word—God's map for life.

Strengths and accomplishments
- Used by God to assist Israel's transition from a loosely governed tribal people to a monarchy
- Anointed the first two kings of Israel
- Was the last and most effective of Israel's judges
- Is listed in the Hall of Faith in Hebrews 11

Weakness and mistake
- Was unable to lead his sons into a close relationship with God

Lessons from his life
- The significance of what people accomplish is directly related to their relationship with God
- The kind of person we are is more important than anything we might do

Vital statistics
- Where: Ephraim
- Occupations: Judge, prophet, priest
- Relatives: Mother: Hannah. Father: Elkanah. Sons: Joel and Abijah
- Contemporaries: Eli, Saul, David

Key verses
"As Samuel grew up, the LORD was with him, and everything Samuel said was wise and helpful. All the people of Israel from one end of the land to the other knew that Samuel was confirmed as a prophet of the LORD" (1 Samuel 3:19, 20).

His story is told in 1 Samuel 1—28. He is also mentioned in Psalm 99:6; Jeremiah 15:1; Acts 3:24; 13:20; Hebrews 11:32.

7:4 Baal was believed to be the son of El, chief deity of the Canaanites. Baal was regarded as the god of thunder and rain; thus he controlled vegetation and agriculture. Ashtoreth was a goddess of love and war (she was called Ishtar in Babylon and Astarte or Aphrodite in Greece). She represented fertility. The Canaanites believed that by the sexual union of Baal and Ashtoreth, the earth would be magically rejuvenated and made fertile.

7:5 Mizpah held special significance for the Israelite nation. It was there that the Israelites had gathered to mobilize against the tribe of Benjamin (Judges 20:1); Samuel was appointed to be leader (1 Samuel 7:6); and Saul, Israel's first king, was identified and presented to the people (10:17ff).

7:6 Pouring water on the ground "before the LORD" was a sign of repenting from sin, turning from idols, and determining to obey God alone.

7:6 Samuel became the last in the long line of Israel's judges (leaders). For a list of these judges, see the chart in Judges 1. A judge was both a political and a religious leader. God was Israel's true leader, while the judge was to be God's spokesperson to the people and administrator of justice throughout the land. While some of Israel's judges relied more on their own judgment than on God's, Samuel's obedience and dedication to God made him one of the greatest judges in Israel's history. (For more on Samuel as a judge, see the note on 4:18.)

[10]Just as Samuel was sacrificing the burnt offering, the Philistines arrived for battle.
But the LORD spoke with a mighty voice of thunder from heaven, and the Philistines were
thrown into such confusion that the Israelites defeated them. [11]The men of Israel chased
them from Mizpah to Beth-car, slaughtering them all along the way.
[12]Samuel then took a large stone and placed it between the towns of Mizpah and
Jeshanah.* He named it Ebenezer—"the stone of help"—for he said, "Up to this point the
LORD has helped us!" [13]So the Philistines were subdued and didn't invade Israel again for
a long time. And throughout Samuel's lifetime, the LORD's powerful hand was raised
against the Philistines. [14]The Israelite towns near Ekron and Gath that the Philistines had
captured were restored to Israel, along with the rest of the territory that the Philistines had
taken. And there was also peace between Israel and the Amorites in those days.
[15]Samuel continued as Israel's judge for the rest of his life. [16]Each year he traveled
around, setting up his court first at Bethel, then at Gilgal, and then at Mizpah. He judged
the people of Israel at each of these places. [17]Then he would return to his home at Ramah,
and he would hear cases there, too. And Samuel built an altar to the LORD at Ramah.

7:10 1 Sam 2:10; 2 Sam 22:14; Ps 18:14
7:12 Gen 35:13-15; Josh 4:9; 24:26
7:13 Judg 13:1; 1 Sam 13:5
7:15 1 Sam 7:6; 12:11
7:16 Gen 28:19; 1 Sam 7:5
7:17 1 Sam 1:1, 19; 2:11; 15:34

B. SAMUEL AND SAUL (8:1—15:35)

Samuel judges Israel well, saves them from the Philistines, and leads them back to God. But when he retires, the nation does not want another judge. Instead, they demand to be given a king in order to be like the nations around them. Although God is unhappy with their request, he tells Samuel to anoint Saul as Israel's first king. Saul is a skillful soldier who successfully leads the nation into many battles against their enemies. But in God's eyes Saul is a failure because he constantly disobeys and does things his own way. God eventually rejects Saul as king. Sometimes we want to go our own way rather than follow the ways of God. This will always end in ruin as it did for Saul.

1. Saul becomes king of Israel

Israel Requests a King

8 As Samuel grew old, he appointed his sons to be judges over Israel. [2]Joel and Abijah,
his oldest sons, held court in Beersheba. [3]But they were not like their father, for they
were greedy for money. They accepted bribes and perverted justice.
[4]Finally, the leaders of Israel met at Ramah to discuss the matter with Samuel.
[5]"Look," they told him, "you are now old, and your sons are not like you. Give us a king
like all the other nations have."

8:2 1 Kgs 19:3
8:3 Exod 23:6, 8; Deut 16:19
8:5 Deut 17:14-15; 1 Sam 12:2

7:12 As in Greek version; Hebrew reads *Shen.*

7:12 The Israelites had great difficulty with the Philistines, but God rescued them. In response, the people set up a stone as a memorial of God's great help and deliverance. During tough times, we may need to remember the crucial turning points in our past to help us through the present. Memorials can help us remember God's past victories and gain confidence and strength for the present.

7:14 In Joshua's time, the Amorites were a powerful tribe scattered throughout the hill country on both sides of the Jordan with a heavy concentration occupying the east side of the Jordan River opposite the Dead Sea. In the context of this verse, however, *Amorites* is another general name for all the inhabitants of Canaan who were not Israelites.

8:1-3 As an old man, Samuel appointed his sons to be judges over Israel in his place. But they turned out to be corrupt, much like Eli's sons (2:12). We don't know why Samuel's sons went wrong, but we do know that Eli was held responsible for his own sons' corruption (2:29-34).

It is impossible to know if Samuel was a bad parent. His children were old enough to be on their own. We must be careful not to blame ourselves for the sins of our children. On the other hand, parenthood is an awesome responsibility, and nothing is more important than molding and shaping our children's lives.

If your grown children are not following God, realize that you can't control them any longer. Don't blame yourself for something that is no longer your responsibility. But if your children are still in your care, know that what you do and teach can profoundly affect your children and lasts a lifetime.

8:4-9 Israel wanted a king for several reasons: (1) Samuel's sons were not fit to lead Israel. (2) The 12 tribes of Israel continually had problems working together because each tribe had its own leader and territory. It was hoped that a king would unite the tribes into one nation and one army. (3) The people wanted to be like the neighboring nations. This is exactly what God didn't want. Having a king would make it easy to forget that God was their real leader. It was not wrong for Israel to want a king; God had mentioned the possibility in Deuteronomy 17:14-20. Yet, in reality, the people were rejecting God as their leader. The Israelites wanted laws, an army, and a human monarch in the place of God. They wanted to run the nation through human strength, even though only God's strength could make them flourish in the hostile land of Canaan.

8:5, 6 The people clamored for a king, thinking that a new system of government would bring about a change in the nation. But because their basic problem was disobedience to God, their other problems would only continue under the new administration. What they needed was a unified faith, not a uniform rule.

Had the Israelites submitted to God's leadership, they would have thrived beyond their expectations (Deuteronomy 28:1). Our obedience is weak if we ask God to lead our family or personal life but continue to live by the world's standards and values. Faith in God must touch all the practical areas of life.

8:6 1 Sam 12:17; 15:11
8:7 Exod 16:8
8:9 1 Sam 8:11-18
8:11 Deut 17:16; 1 Sam 14:52; 2 Sam 15:1; 1 Kgs 1:5
8:12 1 Sam 22:7; 1 Kgs 4:7
8:14 1 Sam 22:7; 1 Kgs 21:7; Ezek 46:18
8:18 Job 27:9; Prov 1:25-28; Mic 3:4
8:19 Jer 44:16
8:22 1 Sam 8:7
9:1 1 Chr 8:33; 9:36-39
9:2 1 Sam 10:23-24; 2 Sam 14:25

6 Samuel was very upset with their request and went to the LORD for advice. 7 "Do as
they say," the LORD replied, "for it is me they are rejecting, not you. They don't want me
to be their king any longer. 8 Ever since I brought them from Egypt they have continually
forsaken me and followed other gods. And now they are giving you the same treatment.
9 Do as they ask, but solemnly warn them about how a king will treat them."

Samuel Warns against a Kingdom

10 So Samuel passed on the LORD's warning to the people. 11 "This is how a king will
treat you," Samuel said. "The king will draft your sons into his army and make them run
before his chariots. 12 Some will be commanders of his troops, while others will be slave
laborers. Some will be forced to plow in his fields and harvest his crops, while others
will make his weapons and chariot equipment. 13 The king will take your daughters from
you and force them to cook and bake and make perfumes for him. 14 He will take away
the best of your fields and vineyards and olive groves and give them to his own servants.
15 He will take a tenth of your harvest and distribute it among his officers and attendants.
16 He will want your male and female slaves and demand the finest of your cattle* and
donkeys for his own use. 17 He will demand a tenth of your flocks, and you will be his
slaves. 18 When that day comes, you will beg for relief from this king you are demanding,
but the LORD will not help you."

19 But the people refused to listen to Samuel's warning. "Even so, we still want a king,"
they said. 20 "We want to be like the nations around us. Our king will govern us and lead
us into battle."

21 So Samuel told the LORD what the people had said, 22 and the LORD replied, "Do as
they say, and give them a king." Then Samuel agreed and sent the people home.

Saul Meets Samuel

9 Kish was a rich, influential man from the tribe of Benjamin. He was the son of Abiel
and grandson of Zeror, from the family of Becorath and the clan of Aphiah. 2 His son
Saul was the most handsome man in Israel—head and shoulders taller than anyone else
in the land.

8:16 As in Greek version; Hebrew reads *young men.*

THE PROBLEMS WITH HAVING A KING

Problems (warned by Samuel)	*Reference*	*Fulfillment*
Drafting young men into the army	8:11, 12	14:52—"So whenever Saul saw a young man who was brave and strong, he drafted him into his army."
Having the young men "run ahead of him [the king's chariots]"	8:11	2 Samuel 15:1—"Absalom bought a chariot and horses, and he hired fifty footmen to run ahead of him."
Making slave laborers	8:12, 17	2 Chronicles 2:17, 18—Solomon assigned laborers to build the temple.
Taking the best of your fields and vineyards	8:14	1 Kings 21:5–16—Jezebel stole Naboth's vineyard.
Using your property for his personal gain	8:14–16	1 Kings 9:10–14—Solomon gave away 20 cities to Hiram of Tyre.
Demanding a tenth of your harvest and flocks	8:15, 17	1 Kings 12:1–16—Rehoboam was going to demand heavier taxation than Solomon.

8:19, 20 Samuel carefully explained all the negative consequences of having a king, but the Israelites refused to listen. When you have an important decision to make, weigh the positives and negatives carefully, considering everyone who might be affected by your choice. When you want something badly enough, it is difficult to see the potential problems. But don't discount the negatives. Unless you have a plan to handle each one, they will cause you great difficulty later.

8:19, 20 Israel was called to be a holy nation, separate from and unique among all others (Leviticus 20:26). The Israelites' motive in asking for a king was to be like the nations around them. This was in total opposition to God's original plan. It was not their desire for a king that was wrong, but their reasons for wanting a king.

Often we let others' values and actions dictate our attitudes and behavior. Have you ever made a wrong choice because you wanted to be like everyone else? Be careful that the values of your friends or "heroes" don't pull you away from what God says is right. When God's people want to be like unbelievers, they are heading for spiritual disaster.

[3]One day Kish's donkeys strayed away, and he told Saul, "Take a servant with you, 9:3 1 Sam 10:2, 14
and go look for them." [4]So Saul took one of his servants and traveled all through the hill
country of Ephraim, the land of Shalishah, the Shaalim area, and the entire land of
Benjamin, but they couldn't find the donkeys anywhere. [5]Finally, they entered the region 9:5 1 Sam 1:1
of Zuph, and Saul said to his servant, "Let's go home. By now my father will be more
worried about us than about the donkeys!"
[6]But the servant said, "I've just thought of something! There is a man of God who 9:6 Deut 33:1 1 Sam 3:19-20 2 Kgs 5:8
lives here in this town. He is held in high honor by all the people because everything he
says comes true. Let's go find him. Perhaps he can tell us which way to go."
[7]"But we don't have anything to offer him," Saul replied. "Even our food is gone, and 9:7 1 Kgs 14:3 2 Kgs 5:15; 8:8-9 Ezek 13:19
we don't have a thing to give him."
[8]"Well," the servant said, "I have one small silver piece.* We can at least offer it to
him and see what happens!" [9](In those days if people wanted a message from God, they 9:9 Exod 2:16 2 Sam 24:11 1 Chr 26:28
would say, "Let's go and ask the seer," for prophets used to be called seers.)
[10]"All right," Saul agreed, "let's try it!" So they started into the town where the man
of God was.
[11]As they were climbing a hill toward the town, they met some young women coming
out to draw water. So Saul and his servant asked, "Is the seer here today?"
[12]"Yes," they replied. "Stay right on this road. He is at the town gates. He has just 9:12 Luke 9:16 John 6:11
arrived to take part in a public sacrifice up on the hill. [13]Hurry and catch him before he
goes up the hill to eat. The guests won't start until he arrives to bless the food."
[14]So they entered the town, and as they passed through the gates, Samuel was
coming out toward them to climb the hill. [15]Now the LORD had told Samuel the 9:15 1 Sam 15:1 Acts 13:21
previous day, [16]"About this time tomorrow I will send you a man from the land of
Benjamin. Anoint him to be the leader of my people, Israel. He will rescue them from 9:16 Exod 3:7, 9
the Philistines, for I have looked down on my people in mercy and have heard their
cry."
[17]When Samuel noticed Saul, the LORD said, "That's the man I told you about! He 9:17 1 Sam 16:12
will rule my people."
[18]Just then Saul approached Samuel at the gateway and asked, "Can you please tell
me where the seer's house is?"
[19]"I am the seer!" Samuel replied. "Go on up the hill ahead of me to the place of
sacrifice, and we'll eat there together. In the morning I will tell you what you want to
know and send you on your way. [20]And don't worry about those donkeys that were lost 9:20 1 Sam 12:13
three days ago, for they have been found. And I am here to tell you that you and your
family are the focus of all Israel's hopes."

9:8 Hebrew *1/4 shekel of silver,* about 0.1 ounces or 3 grams in weight.

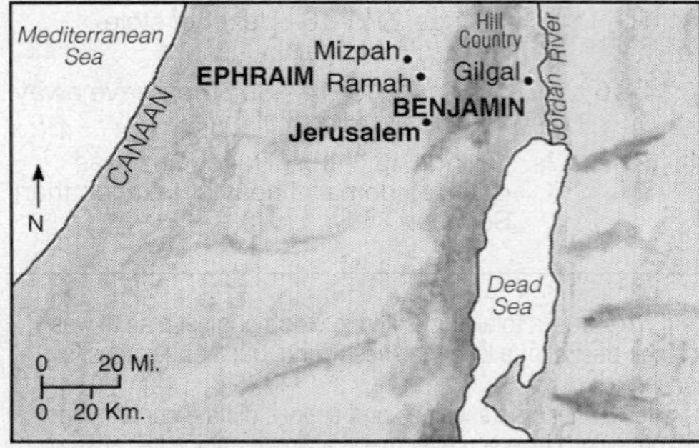

SAUL CHOSEN AS KING Saul and a servant searched for their lost donkeys in the hill country of Ephraim and the territory of Benjamin. They went to Ramah, looking for help from Samuel the prophet. While Saul was there, he found himself unexpectedly anointed by Samuel as Israel's first king. Samuel called Israel together at Mizpah to tell them God's choice for their king.

9:3 Saul was sent by his father on an important mission—to find their stray donkeys. Donkeys were all-purpose animals, the "pickup trucks" of Bible times. Used for transportation, hauling, and farming, they were considered necessities. Even the poorest family owned one. To own many donkeys was a sign of wealth, and to lose them was a disaster. Saul's father was wealthy, and his many donkeys were evidence of that wealth.

9:3ff Often we think that events "just happen" to us, but as we learn from this story about Saul, God may use common occurrences to lead us where he wants. It is important to evaluate all situations as potential "divine appointments" designed to shape our lives. Think of all the good and bad circumstances that have affected you lately. Can you see God's purpose in them? Perhaps he is building a certain quality in you or leading you to serve him in a new area.

9:6 The city where the servant said the prophet lived was probably Ramah, where Samuel moved after the Philistine battle near Shiloh (7:17). Saul's lack of knowledge about Samuel showed his ignorance of spiritual matters. Saul and Samuel even lived in the same territory—Benjamin.

9:21 Judg 20:46-48 1 Sam 15:17
21 Saul replied, "But I'm only from Benjamin, the smallest tribe in Israel, and my family
is the least important of all the families of that tribe! Why are you talking like this to me?"
22 Then Samuel brought Saul and his servant into the great hall and placed them at the
head of the table, honoring them above the thirty special guests. 23 Samuel then instructed
the cook to bring Saul the finest cut of meat, the piece that had been set aside for the guest
of honor. 24 So the cook brought it in and placed it before Saul. "Go ahead and eat it," Samuel
said. "I was saving it for you even before I invited these others!" So Saul ate with Samuel.
9:25 Deut 22:8 Acts 10:9-10
25 After the feast, when they had returned to the town, Samuel took Saul up to the roof
of the house and prepared a bed for him there.* 26 At daybreak the next morning, Samuel
called up to Saul, "Get up! It's time you were on your way." So Saul got ready, and he
and Samuel left the house together. 27 When they reached the edge of town, Samuel told
Saul to send his servant on ahead. After the servant was gone, Samuel said, "Stay here,
for I have received a special message for you from God."

Samuel Anoints Saul as King

10:1 1 Sam 9:16; 16:13; 26:9 2 Sam 1:14 2 Kgs 9:3, 6
10 Then Samuel took a flask of olive oil and poured it over Saul's head. He kissed Saul
on the cheek and said, "I am doing this because the LORD has appointed you to be
the leader of his people Israel.* 2 When you leave me today, you will see two men beside
10:2 Gen 35:19; 48:7
Rachel's tomb at Zelzah, on the border of Benjamin. They will tell you that the donkeys

9:25 As in Greek version; Hebrew reads *and talked with him there.* **10:1** Greek version reads *Israel. And you will rule over the LORD's people and save them from their enemies around them. This will be the sign to you that the LORD has appointed you to be leader over his inheritance.*

RELIGIOUS AND POLITICAL CENTERS OF ISRAEL

During the period of the judges, Israel may have had more than one capital. This may explain why the Scriptures overlap with reference to some cities.

GILGAL	Joshua 4:19; Judges 2:1; Hosea 4:15; Micah 6:5
SHILOH	Joshua 18:1–10; 19:51; Judges 18:31; 1 Samuel 1:3; Jeremiah 7:12–14
SHECHEM	Joshua 24:1
RAMAH	1 Samuel 7:17; 8:4
MIZPAH	Judges 11:11; 20:1; 1 Samuel 10:17
BETHEL	Judges 20:18, 26; 1 Samuel 10:3
GIBEAH (political center only)	1 Samuel 10:26
GIBEON (religious center only)	1 Kings 3:4; 2 Chronicles 1:2, 3
JERUSALEM	1 Kings 8:1ff; Psalm 51:16–19

Samuel called the Israelites together at Mizpah, where he would anoint Saul as their first king. Up to this point, the political seat of the nation seems to have been the religious center of the nation as well. Above are the cities which probably served as both the religious and political centers of Israel since the days of Joshua. Saul may have been the first Israelite leader to separate the nation's religious center (probably Mizpah at this time) from its political center (Gibeah—1 Samuel 11:4; 26:1). Politically, the nation grew strong for a while. But when Saul and his officials stopped seeking God's will, internal jealousies and strife soon began to decay the nation from within. When David became king, he brought the Ark of the Covenant back to Jerusalem, his capital. King Solomon then completely united the religious and political centers at Jerusalem.

9:21 "Why are you talking like this to me?" Saul's outburst reveals a problem he would face repeatedly—feeling inferior. Like a leaf tossed about by the wind, Saul vacillated between his feelings and his convictions. Everything he said and did was selfish because he was worried about himself. For example, Saul said his clan was "the least important" in the smallest tribe in Israel, but 9:1 says his father was "a rich, influential man." (The tribe of Benjamin was the smallest because they were nearly wiped out as punishment for their immorality—see Judges 19–21.) Saul didn't want to face the responsibility God had given him. Later, Saul kept some war plunder that he shouldn't have and then tried to blame his soldiers (15:21) while claiming that they had really taken it to sacrifice to God (15:15).

Although Saul had been called by God and had a mission in life, he struggled constantly with jealousy, insecurity, arrogance, impulsiveness, and deceit. He did not decide to be wholeheartedly committed to God. Because Saul would not let God's love give rest to his heart, he never became God's man.

10:1 When an Israelite king took office, he was not only crowned, he was anointed. The coronation was the political act of establishing the king as ruler; the anointing was the religious act of making the king God's representative to the people. A king was always anointed by a priest or prophet. The special anointing oil was a mixture of olive oil, myrrh, and other expensive spices. It was poured over the king's head to symbolize the presence and power of the Holy Spirit of God in his life. This anointing ceremony was to remind the king of his great responsibility to lead his people by God's wisdom and not his own.

have been found and that your father is worried about you and is asking, 'Have you seen my son?'

3 "When you get to the oak of Tabor, you will see three men coming toward you who are on their way to worship God at Bethel. One will be bringing three young goats, another will have three loaves of bread, and the third will be carrying a skin of wine. 4 They will greet you and offer you two of the loaves, which you are to accept.

5 "When you arrive at Gibeah of God,* where the garrison of the Philistines is located, you will meet a band of prophets coming down from the altar on the hill. They will be playing a harp, a tambourine, a flute, and a lyre, and they will be prophesying. 6 At that time the Spirit of the LORD will come upon you with power, and you will prophesy with them. You will be changed into a different person. 7 After these signs take place, do whatever you think is best, for God will be with you. 8 Then go down to Gilgal ahead of me and wait for me there seven days. I will join you there to sacrifice burnt offerings and peace offerings. When I arrive, I will give you further instructions."

Samuel's Signs Are Fulfilled

9 As Saul turned and started to leave, God changed his heart, and all Samuel's signs were fulfilled that day. 10 When Saul and his servant arrived at Gibeah, they saw the prophets coming toward them. Then the Spirit of God came upon Saul, and he, too, began to prophesy. 11 When his friends heard about it, they exclaimed, "What? Is Saul a prophet? How did the son of Kish become a prophet?" 12 But one of the neighbors responded, "It doesn't matter who his father is; anyone can become a prophet."* So that is the origin of the saying "Is Saul a prophet?"

13 When Saul had finished prophesying, he climbed the hill to the altar. 14 "Where in the world have you been?" Saul's uncle asked him.

"We went to look for the donkeys," Saul replied, "but we couldn't find them. So we went to the prophet Samuel to ask him where they were."

15 "Oh? And what did he say?" his uncle asked.

16 "He said the donkeys had been found," Saul replied. But Saul didn't tell his uncle that Samuel had anointed him to be king.

Saul Is Acclaimed King

17 Later Samuel called all the people of Israel to meet before the LORD at Mizpah. 18 And he gave them this message from the LORD, the God of Israel: "I brought you from Egypt and rescued you from the Egyptians and from all of the nations that were oppressing you. 19 But though I have done so much for you, you have rejected me and said, 'We want a king instead!' Now, therefore, present yourselves before the LORD by tribes and clans."

20 So Samuel called the tribal leaders together before the LORD, and the tribe of Benjamin was chosen.* 21 Then he brought each family of the tribe of Benjamin before

10:3 Gen 35:1, 3, 7
10:5 1 Sam 19:20; 2 Kgs 2:3, 5, 15; 1 Chr 25:1
10:6 Num 11:25, 29; Judg 3:10; 14:6; 1 Sam 19:23-24
10:8 1 Sam 7:16; 11:14-15; 13:7
10:9 1 Sam 10:6
10:10 1 Sam 10:5, 10
10:11 1 Sam 19:24; Amos 7:14-15; Matt 13:54-57
10:14 1 Sam 9:3
10:16 1 Sam 9:20
10:17 Judg 20:1; 1 Sam 7:5-6
10:18 Judg 6:8
10:19 1 Sam 8:5-7

10:5 Hebrew *Gibeath-elohim.* **10:12** Hebrew *responded, "Who is their father?"* **10:20** Hebrew *chosen by lot;* also in 10:21.

10:6 How could Saul be so filled with the Spirit and yet later commit such evil acts? Throughout the Old Testament, God's Spirit "came upon" a person temporarily so that God could use him or her for great acts. This happened frequently to Israel's judges when they were called by God to rescue the nation (Judges 3:8-10). This was not always a permanent, abiding influence, but sometimes a temporary manifestation of the Holy Spirit. Yet, at times in the Old Testament, the Spirit even came upon unbelievers to enable them to do unusual tasks (Numbers 24; 2 Chronicles 36:22, 23). The Holy Spirit gave the person power to do what God asked, but it did not always produce the other fruits of the Spirit, such as self-control. Saul, in his early years as king, was a different person (10:1-10) as a result of the Holy Spirit's work in him. But as Saul's power grew, so did his pride. After a while he refused to seek God; the Spirit left him (16:14), and his good attitude melted away.

10:10, 11 A prophet is someone who speaks God's words. While God told many prophets to predict certain events, what God wanted most was for them to instruct and inspire people to live in faithfulness to God. When Saul's friends heard inspired words coming from Saul, they exclaimed, "Is Saul a prophet?" This was an expression of surprise at worldly Saul's becoming religious. It is equivalent to "What? Has he got religion?"

10:19 Israel's true king was God, but the nation demanded another. Imagine wanting a human being instead of God as guide and leader! Throughout history, men and women have rejected God, and they continue to do it today. Are you rejecting God by pushing him aside and acknowledging someone or something else as your "king" or top priority? Learn from these stories of Israel's kings, and don't push God aside.

10:20 The Israelites chose their first king by casting lots or by using the Urim and Thummim, two plates or flat stones carried by the high priest. The fact that Saul was chosen may seem like luck, but it was really the opposite. God had instructed the Israelites to make the Urim and Thummim for the specific purpose of consulting him in times such as this (Exodus 28:30; Numbers 27:12-21). By using the Urim and Thummim, the Israelites were taking the decision out of their own hands and turning it over to God. Only the high priest could use the Urim and Thummim, which were designed to give only yes or no answers.

the LORD, and the family of the Matrites was chosen. And finally Saul son of Kish was
chosen from among them. But when they looked for him, he had disappeared! 22 So they
asked the LORD, "Where is he?"
10:23 1 Sam 9:2 And the LORD replied, "He is hiding among the baggage." 23 So they found him and
brought him out, and he stood head and shoulders above anyone else.
10:24 2 Sam 21:6 1 Kgs 1:25, 34, 39 2 Kgs 11:12 24 Then Samuel said to all the people, "This is the man the LORD has chosen as your
king. No one in all Israel is his equal!"
And all the people shouted, "Long live the king!"
10:25 Deut 17:15 1 Sam 8:11-18 25 Then Samuel told the people what the rights and duties of a king were. He wrote
them down on a scroll and placed it before the LORD. Then Samuel sent the people home
again.
26 When Saul returned to his home at Gibeah, a band of men whose hearts God had
10:27 1 Kgs 10:24-25 touched became his constant companions. 27 But there were some wicked men who
complained, "How can this man save us?" And they despised him and refused to bring
him gifts. But Saul ignored them.*

Saul Defeats the Ammonites

11:1 Judg 11:4-6; 21:8 1 Sam 12:12; 31:11 **11** About a month later,* King Nahash of Ammon led his army against the Israelite
city of Jabesh-gilead. But the citizens of Jabesh asked for peace. "Make a treaty
11:2 1 Sam 17:26 with us, and we will be your servants," they pleaded.
2 "All right," Nahash said, "but only on one condition. I will gouge out the right eye
of every one of you as a disgrace to all Israel!"
3 "Give us seven days to send messengers throughout Israel!" replied the leaders of
Jabesh. "If none of our relatives will come to save us, we will agree to your terms."
11:4 1 Sam 10:26; 30:4 4 When the messengers came to Gibeah, Saul's hometown, and told the people about

10:27 Dead Sea Scroll 4QSam[a] continues: *Nahash, king of the Ammonites, had been grievously oppressing the Gadites and Reubenites who lived east of the Jordan River. He gouged out the right eye of each of the Israelites living there, and he didn't allow anyone to come and rescue them. In fact, of all the Israelites east of the Jordan, there wasn't a single one whose right eye Nahash had not gouged out. But there were seven thousand men who had escaped from the Ammonites, and they had settled in Jabesh-gilead.* **11:1** As in Greek version; Hebrew lacks *About a month later.*

10:22 When the Israelites assembled to choose a king, Saul already knew he was the one (10:1). Instead of coming forward, however, he hid among the baggage. Often we hide from important responsibilities because we are afraid of failure, afraid of what others will think, or perhaps unsure about how to proceed. Prepare now to step up to your future responsibilities. Count on God's provision rather than your feelings of adequacy.

10:25 The kings of Israel, unlike kings of other nations, had specific regulations outlined for them (Deuteronomy 17:14-20). Pagan kings were considered gods; they made their own laws and answered to no one. By contrast, Israel's king had to answer to a higher authority—the Lord of heaven and earth. The Israelites now had a king like everyone else, just as they wanted. But Samuel, in his charge to both the king and the people, wanted to make sure that the rule of Israel's king would be different from that of his pagan counterparts. "Placed it before the LORD" means that Samuel put the scroll, as a witness to the agreement, in a special place at Mizpah.

10:26, 27 Some men became Saul's constant companions, while others despised him. Criticism will always be directed toward those who lead because they are out in front. At this time, Saul took no notice of those who seemed to be against him, although later he would become consumed with jealousy (19:1-3; 26:17-21). As you lead, listen to constructive criticism, but don't spend valuable time and energy worrying about those who may oppose you. Instead, focus your attention on those who are ready and willing to help.

11:1ff At this time, Israel was very susceptible to invasion by marauding tribes such as these Ammonites from east of the Jordan River. Saul's leadership in battle against this warlike tribe helped unify the nation and proved that he was a worthy military ruler. Saul's kingship was solidified when he saved the nation from disgrace and spared the people who had criticized him.

11:3 Why would Nahash give the city of Jabesh-gilead seven days to find an army to help them? Because Israel was still disorganized, Nahash was betting that no one would come to the city's aid. He was hoping to take the city without a fight and avoid a battle. He also may not have been prepared to attack the city because a siege against its walls could last weeks or months.

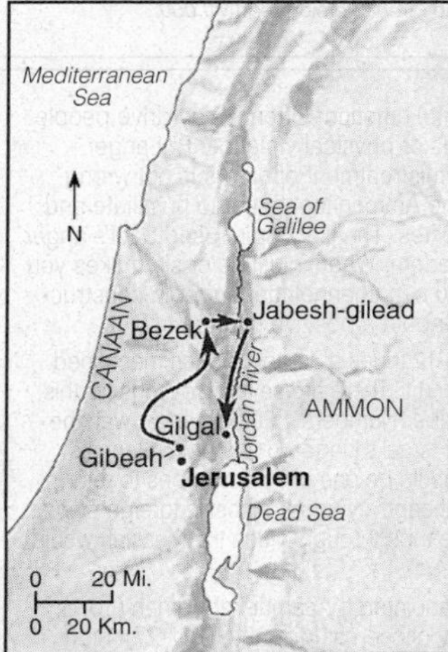

SAUL DEFEATS THE AMMONITES
The Ammonites prepared to attack Jabesh-gilead. The people of Jabesh sent messengers to Saul in Gibeah asking for help. Saul mobilized an army at Bezek and then attacked the Ammonites. After the battle, the Israelites returned to Gilgal to crown Saul as king.

their plight, everyone broke into tears. 5 Saul was plowing in the field, and when he **11:5** 1 Kgs 19:19
returned to town, he asked, "What's the matter? Why is everyone crying?" So they told
him about the message from Jabesh.
6 Then the Spirit of God came mightily upon Saul, and he became very angry. 7 He **11:6** Judg 3:10; 6:34 1 Sam 10:10
took two oxen and cut them into pieces and sent the messengers to carry them throughout
Israel with this message: "This is what will happen to the oxen of anyone who refuses **11:7** Judg 19:29; 20:1
to follow Saul and Samuel into battle!" And the LORD made the people afraid of Saul's **11:8** Judg 1:4-6
anger, and all of them came out together as one. 8 When Saul mobilized them at Bezek,
he found that there were 300,000 men of Israel, in addition to 30,000* from Judah.
9 So Saul sent the messengers back to Jabesh-gilead to say, "We will rescue you by
noontime tomorrow!" What joy there was throughout the city when that message
arrived!
10 The men of Jabesh then told their enemies, "Tomorrow we will come out to you, **11:10** 1 Sam 11:3
and you can do to us as you wish." 11 But before dawn the next morning, Saul arrived,
having divided his army into three detachments. He launched a surprise attack against **11:11** Judg 7:16
the Ammonites and slaughtered them the whole morning. The remnant of their army was
so badly scattered that no two of them were left together.
12 Then the people exclaimed to Samuel, "Now where are those men who said Saul **11:12** 1 Sam 10:27 Luke 19:27
shouldn't rule over us? Bring them here, and we will kill them!"
13 But Saul replied, "No one will be executed today, for today the LORD has rescued **11:13** Exod 14:13 1 Sam 19:5 2 Sam 19:22
Israel!"
14 Then Samuel said to the people, "Come, let us all go to Gilgal to reaffirm Saul's
kingship." 15 So they went to Gilgal, and in a solemn ceremony before the LORD they **11:14** 1 Sam 10:1, 8
crowned him king. Then they offered peace offerings to the LORD, and Saul and all the
Israelites were very happy.

Samuel's Farewell Address

12 Then Samuel addressed the people again: "I have done as you asked and given **12:1** 1 Sam 8:7, 9, 22
you a king. 2 I have selected him ahead of my own sons, and I stand here, an old, **12:2** 1 Sam 3:10, 19-20
gray-haired man. I have served as your leader since I was a boy. 3 Now tell me as I stand
before the LORD and before his anointed one—whose ox or donkey have I stolen? Have **12:3** Exod 23:8 Num 16:15 Deut 16:19
I ever cheated any of you? Have I ever oppressed you? Have I ever taken a bribe? Tell
me and I will make right whatever I have done wrong."
4 "No," they replied, "you have never cheated or oppressed us in any way, and you
have never taken even a single bribe."
5 "The LORD and his anointed one are my witnesses," Samuel declared, "that you can **12:5** Exod 22:4
never accuse me of robbing you."
"Yes, it is true," they replied.

11:8 Dead Sea Scrolls and Greek version read *70,000.*

11:6 Anger is a powerful emotion. Often it may drive people to hurt others with words or physical violence. But anger directed at sin and the mistreatment of others is not wrong. Saul was angered by the Ammonites' threat to humiliate and mistreat his fellow Israelites. The Holy Spirit used Saul's anger to bring justice and freedom. When injustice or sin makes you angry, ask God how you can channel that anger in constructive ways to help bring about a positive change.

11:8 Judah, one of the 12 tribes of Israel, is often mentioned separately from the other 11. There are several reasons for this. Judah was the largest tribe (Numbers 1:20-46), and it was the tribe from which most of Israel's kings would come (Genesis 49:8-12). Later, Judah would be one of the few tribes to return to God after a century of captivity under a hostile foreign power. Judah would also be the tribe through which the Messiah would come (Micah 5:2).

11:14 Saul had been anointed by Samuel at Ramah (10:1); then Saul was publically chosen at Mizpah (10:17-27); his defeat of the Ammonites confirmed his kingship in the people's minds; at this time, all the people confirmed his rule.

11:15 The Israelites offered peace offerings to God as they made Saul their first king. The instructions for giving these offerings are found in Leviticus 3. The peace offering was an expression of gratitude and thanksgiving to God, symbolizing the peace that comes to those who know him and who live in accordance with his commands. Although God did not want his people to have a human king, the people were demonstrating through their offerings that he was still their true King. Unfortunately, this attitude did not last, just as God had predicted (8:7-19).

12:1ff Samuel continued to serve the people as their priest, prophet, and judge, but Saul exercised more and more political and military control over the tribes (see 7:15).

12:1-3 In his farewell speech, Samuel asked the Israelites to point out any wrongs he had committed during his time as Israel's judge. By doing so, Samuel was reminding them that he could be trusted to tell the truth. He was also reminding them that having a king was their idea, not his. Samuel was setting the stage for the miraculous thunderstorm recorded in 12:16-19, so that the people could not blame him when God punished them for their selfish motives.

6“It was the LORD who appointed Moses and Aaron,” Samuel continued. “He brought
your ancestors out of the land of Egypt. 7Now stand here quietly before the LORD as I
remind you of all the great things the LORD has done for you and your ancestors.
8“When the Israelites were* in Egypt and cried out to the LORD, he sent Moses and
Aaron to rescue them from Egypt and to bring them into this land. 9But the people soon
forgot about the LORD their God, so he let them be conquered by Sisera, the general of
Hazor’s army, and by the Philistines and the king of Moab.
10“Then they cried to the LORD again and confessed, ‘We have sinned by turning away
from the LORD and worshiping the images of Baal and Ashtoreth. But we will worship
you and you alone if you will rescue us from our enemies.’ 11Then the LORD sent
Gideon,* Barak,* Jephthah, and Samuel* to save you, and you lived in safety.
12“But when you were afraid of Nahash, the king of Ammon, you came to me and said

12:6 Exod 6:26
12:7 Mic 6:4
12:8 Exod 2:23-25; 3:10; 4:14-16
12:9 Deut 32:18 Judg 3:7; 10:7; 13:1
12:10 Judg 10:10, 15-16
12:11 Judg 4:6; 6:32; 11:1
12:12 Judg 8:23-24

12:8 Hebrew *When Jacob was.* **12:11a** Hebrew *Jerubbaal,* another name for Gideon; see Judg 7:1. **12:11b** As in Greek and Syriac versions; Hebrew reads *Bedan.* **12:11c** Greek and Syriac versions read *Samson.*

SAUL

First impressions can be deceiving, especially when the image created by a person’s appearance is contradicted by his or her qualities and abilities. Saul presented the ideal visual image of a king, but the tendencies of his character often went contrary to God’s commands for a king. Saul was God’s chosen leader, but this did not mean he was capable of being king on his own.

During his reign, Saul had his greatest successes when he obeyed God. His greatest failures resulted from acting on his own. Saul had the raw materials to be a good leader—appearance, courage, and action. Even his weaknesses could have been used by God if Saul had recognized them and left them in God’s hands. His own choices cut him off from God and eventually alienated him from his own people.

From Saul we learn that while our strengths and abilities make us useful, it is our weaknesses that make us usable. Our skills and talents make us tools, but our failures and shortcomings remind us that we need a Craftsman in control of our lives. Whatever we accomplish on our own is only a hint of what God could do through our lives. Does he control your life?

Strengths and accomplishments
- First God-appointed king of Israel
- Known for his personal courage and generosity
- Stood tall, with a striking appearance

Weaknesses and mistakes
- His leadership abilities did not match the expectations created by his appearance
- Impulsive by nature, he tended to overstep his bounds
- Jealous of David, he tried to kill him
- He specifically disobeyed God on several occasions

Lessons from his life
- God wants obedience from the heart, not mere acts of religious ritual
- Obedience always involves sacrifice, but sacrifice is not always obedience
- God wants to make use of our strengths and weaknesses
- Weaknesses should help us remember our need for God’s guidance and help

Vital statistics
- Where: The land of Benjamin
- Occupation: King of Israel
- Relatives: Father: Kish. Sons: Jonathan and Ishbosheth. Wife: Ahinoam. Daughters: Merab and Michal

Key verses
“But Samuel replied, ‘What is more pleasing to the LORD: your burnt offerings and sacrifices or your obedience to his voice? Obedience is far better than sacrifice. Listening to him is much better than offering the fat of rams. Rebellion is as bad as the sin of witchcraft, and stubbornness is as bad as worshiping idols. So because you have rejected the word of the LORD, he has rejected you from being king’ ” (1 Samuel 15:22, 23).

His story is told in 1 Samuel 9—31. He is also mentioned in Acts 13:21.

12:10 “The images of Baal and the Ashtoreth” were pagan gods. See the note on 7:4 for more information.

12:12-15 God granted the nation’s request for a king, but his commands and requirements remained the same. God was to be their true King, and both Saul and the people were to be subject to his laws. No person is ever exempt from God’s laws. No human action is outside his jurisdiction. God is the true King of every area of life. We must recognize his kingship and pattern our relationships, work life, and home life according to his principles.

that you wanted a king to reign over you, even though the LORD your God was already your king. 13All right, here is the king you have chosen. Look him over. You asked for him, and the LORD has granted your request.

14"Now if you will fear and worship the LORD and listen to his voice, and if you do not rebel against the LORD's commands, and if you and your king follow the LORD your God, then all will be well. 15But if you rebel against the LORD's commands and refuse to listen to him, then his hand will be as heavy upon you as it was upon your ancestors.

16"Now stand here and see the great thing the LORD is about to do. 17You know that it does not rain at this time of the year during the wheat harvest. I will ask the LORD to send thunder and rain today. Then you will realize how wicked you have been in asking the LORD for a king!"

18So Samuel called to the LORD, and the LORD sent thunder and rain. And all the people were terrified of the LORD and of Samuel. 19"Pray to the LORD your God for us, or we will die!" they cried out to Samuel. "For now we have added to our sins by asking for a king."

20"Don't be afraid," Samuel reassured them. "You have certainly done wrong, but make sure now that you worship the LORD with all your heart and that you don't turn your back on him in any way. 21Don't go back to worshiping worthless idols that cannot help or rescue you—they really are useless! 22The LORD will not abandon his chosen people, for that would dishonor his great name. He made you a special nation for himself.

23"As for me, I will certainly not sin against the LORD by ending my prayers for you. And I will continue to teach you what is good and right. 24But be sure to fear the LORD and sincerely worship him. Think of all the wonderful things he has done for you. 25But if you continue to sin, you and your king will be destroyed."

12:13 1 Sam 8:5; 10:24; Hos 13:11
12:14 Josh 24:14, 20
12:15 Josh 24:20; Isa 1:2, 20
12:16 Exod 14:13, 21, 31
12:17 1 Sam 7:10; 8:6-7
12:20 Exod 32:30; Deut 11:16
12:21 Deut 11:16; Hab 2:18
12:22 Exod 32:12; Num 14:13; Deut 7:6; 31:6
12:23 1 Kgs 8:36; Rom 1:9; Col 1:9; 1 Thes 3:10
12:24 Deut 10:21
12:25 Josh 24:20; 1 Sam 31:1-5

2. God rejects Saul for disobedience

Continued War with Philistia

13 Saul was thirty* years old when he became king, and he reigned for forty-two years.* 2Saul selected three thousand special troops from the army of Israel and sent the rest of the men home. He took two thousand of the chosen men with him to Micmash and the hill country of Bethel. The other thousand went with Saul's son Jonathan to Gibeah in the land of Benjamin.

3Soon after this, Jonathan attacked and defeated the garrison of Philistines at Geba. The news spread quickly among the Philistines that Israel was in revolt, so Saul sounded the call to arms throughout Israel. 4He announced that the Philistine garrison at Geba had been destroyed, and he warned the people that the Philistines now hated the Israelites more than ever. So the entire Israelite army mobilized again and met Saul at Gilgal.

13:2 1 Sam 10:26
13:3 Judg 3:27; 6:34; 1 Sam 10:5; 2 Sam 2:28; 20:1

13:1a As in a few Greek manuscripts; the number is missing in the Hebrew. **13:1b** Hebrew *reigned . . . and two;* the number is incomplete in the Hebrew. Compare Acts 13:21.

12:17 The wheat harvest came near the end of the dry season during the months of May and June. Because rain rarely fell during this period, a great thunderstorm was considered a miraculous event. It was not a beneficial miracle, however, because rain during the wheat harvest could damage the crops and cause them to rot quickly. This unusual occurrence showed God's displeasure with Israel's demand for a king.

12:22 Why did God make Israel "his chosen people"? God did not choose them because they deserved it (Deuteronomy 7:7, 8), but in order that they might become his channel of blessing to all people through the Messiah (Genesis 12:1-3). Because God chose the people of Israel, he would never abandon them; but because they were his special nation, he would often punish them for their disobedience in order to bring them back to a right relationship with him.

12:23 Is failing to pray for others a sin? Samuel's words seem to indicate that it is. His actions illustrate two of God's people's responsibilities: (1) They should pray consistently for others (Ephesians 6:18), and (2) they should teach others the right way to God (2 Timothy 2:2). Samuel disagreed with the Israelites' demand for a king, but he assured them that he would continue to pray for them and teach them. We may disagree with others, but we shouldn't stop praying for them.

12:24 This is the second time in his farewell speech that Samuel reminded the people to take time to consider what great things God had done for them (see 12:7). Taking time for reflection allows us to focus our attention upon God's goodness and strengthens our faith. Sometimes we are so progress- and future-oriented that we fail to take time to recall all that God has already done. Remember what God has done for you so that you may move ahead with gratitude.

13:3, 4 Jonathan attacked and destroyed the Philistine outpost, but Saul took all the credit for it. Although this was normal in that culture, it didn't make his action right. Saul's growing pride started out small—taking credit for a battle that was won by his son. Left unchecked, his pride grew into an ugly obsession; thus, it destroyed him, tore his family apart, and threatened the well-being of the nation. Taking credit for the accomplishments of others indicates that pride is controlling your life. When you notice pride taking a foothold, take immediate steps to put it in check by giving credit to those who deserve it.

13:5 Josh 11:4 — 5 The Philistines mustered a mighty army of three thousand* chariots, six thousand
horsemen, and as many warriors as the grains of sand along the seashore! They camped at
13:6 Judg 6:2 — Micmash east of Beth-aven. 6 When the men of Israel saw the vast number of enemy troops,
they lost their nerve entirely and tried to hide in caves, holes, rocks, tombs, and cisterns.
7 Some of them crossed the Jordan River and escaped into the land of Gad and Gilead.

Saul's Disobedience and Samuel's Rebuke

13:8 1 Sam 10:8 — Meanwhile, Saul stayed at Gilgal, and his men were trembling with fear. 8 Saul waited
13:9 2 Sam 24:25, 1 Kgs 3:4 — there seven days for Samuel, as Samuel had instructed him earlier, but Samuel still didn't
come. Saul realized that his troops were rapidly slipping away. 9 So he demanded, "Bring
13:10 1 Sam 15:13 — me the burnt offering and the peace offerings!" And Saul sacrificed the burnt offering
himself. 10 Just as Saul was finishing with the burnt offering, Samuel arrived. Saul went
out to meet and welcome him, 11 but Samuel said, "What is this you have done?"

Saul replied, "I saw my men scattering from me, and you didn't arrive when you said
you would, and the Philistines are at Micmash ready for battle. 12 So I said, 'The
Philistines are ready to march against us, and I haven't even asked for the LORD's help!'
So I felt obliged to offer the burnt offering myself before you came."

13:13 1 Sam 15:23-24, 28; 2 Chr 16:9 — 13 "How foolish!" Samuel exclaimed. "You have disobeyed the command of the LORD
your God. Had you obeyed, the LORD would have established your kingdom over Israel
13:14 †Acts 13:22 — forever. 14 But now your dynasty must end, for the LORD has sought out a man after his
own heart. The LORD has already chosen him to be king over his people, for you have
not obeyed the LORD's command."

Israel's Military Disadvantage

13:15 1 Sam 14:2 — 15 Samuel then left Gilgal and went on his way, but the rest of the troops went with Saul
to meet the army. They went up from Gilgal to Gibeah in the land of Benjamin.* When

13:5 As in Greek and Syriac versions; Hebrew reads *30,000.* **13:15** As in Greek version; Hebrew reads *Samuel left Gilgal and went to Gibeah in the land of Benjamin.*

GLOOM AND DOOM

Reference	*Message*
3:11–14	Judgment will come to the house of Eli.
7:1–4	The nation must turn from idol worship.
8:10–22	Your kings will bring you nothing but trouble.
12:25	If you continue in sin, you will be destroyed by God.
13:13, 14	Saul's kingdom will not continue.
15:17–31	Saul, you have sinned before God.

It wasn't easy being a prophet. Most of the messages they had to give were very unpleasant to hear. They preached of repentance, judgment, impending destruction, sin, and, in general, how displeased God was over the behavior of his people. Prophets were not the most popular people in town (unless they were *false* prophets and said just what the people wanted to hear). But popularity was not the bottom line for true prophets of God—it was obedience to God and faithfully proclaiming his word. Samuel is a good example of a faithful prophet.

God has words for us to proclaim as well. And although his messages are loaded with "good news," there is also "bad news" to give. May we, like true prophets, faithfully deliver *all* God's words, regardless of their popularity or lack of it.

13:6 When we forget who is on our side or see only our own resources, we tend to panic at the sight of the opposition. The Israelites became terrified and hid when they saw the mighty Philistine army. They forgot that God was on their side and that he couldn't be defeated. As you face problems and temptations, focus your attention on God and his resources, trusting him to help you (Romans 8:31-37).

13:9 Rather than waiting for a priest, Saul offered the sacrifice himself. This was against God's laws (Deuteronomy 12:5-14) and against the specific instructions of Samuel (10:8). Under pressure from the approaching Philistines, he took matters into his own hands and disobeyed God. He was doing a good thing (offering a sacrifice to God before a crucial battle), but he did it in the wrong way. Like Saul, our true spiritual character is revealed under pressure. The methods we use to accomplish our goals are as important as the attainment of those goals.

13:11, 12 It is difficult to trust God when you feel your resources slipping away. When Saul felt that time was running out, he became impatient with God's timing. In thinking that the ritual was all he needed, he substituted the ritual for faith in God.

When faced with a difficult decision, don't allow impatience to drive you to disobey God. When you know what God wants, follow his plan regardless of the consequences. God often uses delays to test our obedience and patience.

13:12, 13 Saul had plenty of excuses for his disobedience. But Samuel zeroed in on the real issue: "You have disobeyed the command of the LORD your God." Like Saul, we often gloss over our mistakes and sins, trying to justify and spiritualize our actions because of our "special" circumstances. Our excuses, however, are nothing more than disobedience. God knows our true motives. He forgives, restores, and blesses only when we are honest about our sins. By trying to hide his sins behind excuses, Saul lost his kingship (13:14).

Saul counted the men who were still with him, he found only six hundred left! 16 Saul (13:16 Josh 18:24)
and Jonathan and the troops with them were staying at Geba, near Gibeah, in the land of
Benjamin. The Philistines set up their camp at Micmash. 17 Three raiding parties soon
left the camp of the Philistines. One went north toward Ophrah in the land of Shual,
18 another went west to Beth-horon, and the third moved toward the border above the (13:18 Neh 11:31-35)
valley of Zeboim near the wilderness.

19 There were no blacksmiths in the land of Israel in those days. The Philistines (13:19 Judg 5:8; 1 Sam 17:47; 2 Kgs 24:14; Jer 24:1)
wouldn't allow them for fear they would make swords and spears for the Hebrews. 20 So
whenever the Israelites needed to sharpen their plowshares, picks, axes, or sickles,* they
had to take them to a Philistine blacksmith. 21 (The schedule of charges was as follows:
a quarter of an ounce of silver* for sharpening a plowshare or a pick, and an eighth of
an ounce* for sharpening an ax, a sickle, or an ox goad.) 22 So none of the people of Israel
had a sword or spear, except for Saul and Jonathan.

23 The pass at Micmash had meanwhile been secured by a contingent of the Philistine (13:23 1 Sam 14:4; Isa 10:28)
army.

Jonathan's Daring Plan

14 One day Jonathan said to the young man who carried his armor, "Come on, let's
go over to where the Philistines have their outpost." But Jonathan did not tell his
father what he was doing. 2 Meanwhile, Saul and his six hundred men were camped on (14:2 1 Sam 13:15)
the outskirts of Gibeah, around the pomegranate tree at Migron. 3 (Among Saul's men (14:3 1 Sam 1:3; 22:11-12)
was Ahijah the priest, who was wearing the linen ephod. Ahijah was the son of Ahitub,
Ichabod's brother. Ahitub was the son of Phinehas and the grandson of Eli, the priest of
the LORD who had served at Shiloh.)

No one realized that Jonathan had left the Israelite camp. 4 To reach the Philistine
outpost, Jonathan had to go down between two rocky cliffs that were called Bozez and
Seneh. 5 The cliff on the north was in front of Micmash, and the one on the south was in
front of Geba. 6 "Let's go across to see those pagans," Jonathan said to his armor bearer. (14:6 Judg 7:4)
"Perhaps the LORD will help us, for nothing can hinder the LORD. He can win a battle
whether he has many warriors or only a few!"

13:20 As in Greek version; Hebrew reads *or plowshares.* **13:21a** Hebrew *1 pim* [8 grams]. **13:21b** Hebrew *1/3 of a shekel* [4 grams].

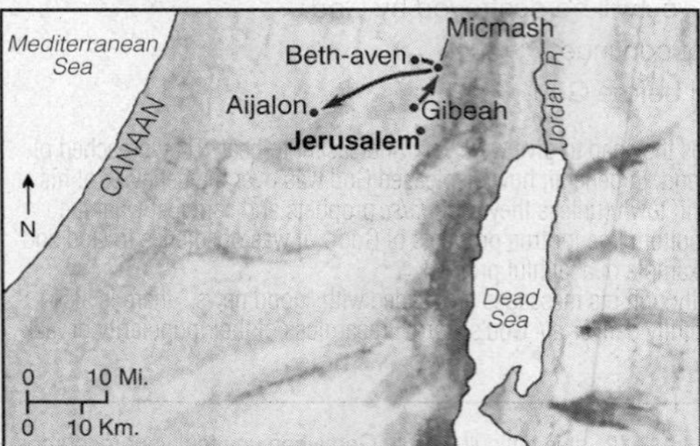

JONATHAN'S BRAVERY Jonathan, Saul's son, left the camp at Gibeah and crept to the Philistine camp at Micmash. With God's help, Jonathan and his armor bearer surprised the Philistines, who panicked and began killing each other! Saul's army heard the commotion and chased the Philistines as far as Beth-aven and Aijalon.

13:19-22 Israel was in no position to conquer anyone. The army had no iron weapons, and there were no facilities for turning their tools into weapons. In fact, if an Israelite wanted to sharpen his tools, he had to pay a Philistine blacksmith to do it because the Philistines had a carefully guarded monopoly on iron and blacksmithing. And they charged high prices for sharpening farm implements. The Philistines' tight control over the technology, along with their surprise raids, demoralized the Israelites and kept them in subjection.

Against such superiority, the Israelites were at a serious disadvantage. How could they hope to rout their oppressors? Only with God's help. God wanted to give Israel victory without swords so they would realize their true source of strength.

14:1ff In this chapter we read about the miserable job Saul did as leader: he had no communication with Jonathan (14:1, 17); he made a foolish curse (14:24); and he ignored the well-being of his own soldiers (14:31). Saul's poor leadership was not a result of personality traits but of decaying spiritual character. What we do is often a direct result of our spiritual condition. We cannot ignore the importance of spiritual character in effective leadership.

14:1 Why would Jonathan go alone to attack the Philistines? Jonathan may have been weary of the long, hopeless standoff in the battle; he trusted God to give the victory and wanted to act on that trust. He also knew that the number of Philistines was no problem for God. Perhaps he didn't tell his father about his mission because he thought Saul would not let him go.

14:6 Jonathan and his armor bearer weren't much of a force to attack the huge Philistine army. But while everyone else was afraid, they trusted God, knowing that the size of the enemy army would not restrict God's ability to help them. God honored the faith and brave action of these two men with a tremendous victory.

Have you ever felt surrounded by the "enemy" or faced overwhelming odds? God is never intimidated by the size of the enemy or the complexity of a problem. With him, there are always enough resources to resist the pressures and win the battle. If God has called you to action, then bravely commit what resources you have to God, and rely upon him to lead you to victory.

7“Do what you think is best,” the youth replied. “I'm with you completely, whatever you decide.”

8“All right then,” Jonathan told him. “We will cross over and let them see us. 9If they say to us, ‘Stay where you are or we'll kill you,’ then we will stop and not go up to them. 10But if they say, ‘Come on up and fight,’ then we will go up. That will be the LORD's sign that he will help us defeat them.”

11When the Philistines saw them coming, they shouted, “Look! The Hebrews are crawling out of their holes!” 12Then they shouted to Jonathan, “Come on up here, and we'll teach you a lesson!”

“Come on, climb right behind me,” Jonathan said to his armor bearer, “for the LORD will help us defeat them!” 13So they climbed up using both hands and feet, and the Philistines fell back as Jonathan and his armor bearer killed them right and left. 14They killed about twenty men in all, and their bodies were scattered over about half an acre.* 15Suddenly, panic broke out in the Philistine army, both in the camp and in the field, including even the outposts and raiding parties. And just then an earthquake struck, and everyone was terrified.

Israel Defeats the Philistines

16Saul's lookouts in Gibeah saw a strange sight—the vast army of Philistines began to melt away in every direction. 17“Find out who isn't here,” Saul ordered. And when they checked, they found that Jonathan and his armor bearer were gone. 18Then Saul shouted to Ahijah, “Bring the ephod here!” For at that time Ahijah was wearing the ephod in front of the Israelites.* 19But while Saul was talking to the priest, the shouting and confusion in the Philistine camp grew louder and louder. So Saul said to Ahijah, “Never mind; let's get going!”*

20Then Saul and his six hundred men rushed out to the battle and found the Philistines killing each other. There was terrible confusion everywhere. 21Even the Hebrews who had gone over to the Philistine army revolted and joined in with Saul, Jonathan, and the rest of the Israelites. 22Likewise, the men who were hiding in the hills joined the chase when they saw the Philistines running away. 23So the LORD saved Israel that day, and the battle continued to rage even out beyond Beth-aven.

Saul's Foolish Oath

24Now the men of Israel were worn out that day, because Saul had made them take an oath, saying, “Let a curse fall on anyone who eats before evening—before I have full revenge on my enemies.” So no one ate a thing all day, 25even though they found honeycomb on the ground in the forest. 26They didn't even touch the honey because they all feared the oath they had taken.

27But Jonathan had not heard his father's command, and he dipped a stick into a piece of honeycomb and ate the honey. After he had eaten it, he felt much better. 28But one of the men saw him and said, “Your father made the army take a strict oath that anyone who eats food today will be cursed. That is why everyone is weary and faint.”

29“My father has made trouble for us all!” Jonathan exclaimed. “A command like that only hurts us. See how much better I feel now that I have eaten this little bit of honey.

14:10 Gen 24:14; Judg 6:36
14:11 1 Sam 13:6
14:12 2 Sam 5:24
14:15 1 Sam 7:10; 2 Kgs 7:6
14:18 1 Sam 4:3; 23:9; 30:7
14:19 Num 27:21
14:20 Judg 7:21-22; 2 Chr 20:23
14:21 1 Sam 29:4
14:22 1 Sam 13:6; 31:7
14:23 Exod 14:30; 2 Chr 32:22
14:24 Josh 6:26
14:29 1 Kgs 18:18

14:14 Hebrew *half a yoke;* a “yoke” was the amount of land plowed by a pair of yoked oxen in one day. **14:18** As in some Greek manuscripts; Hebrew reads *“Bring the Ark of God.” For at that time the Ark of God was with the Israelites.* **14:19** Hebrew *Withdraw your hand.*

14:12 Jonathan did not have the authority to lead all the troops into battle, but he could start a small skirmish in one corner of the enemy camp. When he did, panic broke out among the Philistines; the Hebrews who had been drafted into the Philistine army revolted; and the men who were hiding in the hills regained their courage and returned to fight.

When you are facing a difficult situation that is beyond your control, ask yourself, What steps can I take now to work toward a solution? A few small steps may be just what is needed to begin the chain of events leading to eventual victory.

14:19 “Let's get going” refers to the use of the Urim and Thummim. These small objects were withdrawn from the linen ephod (vest) worn by the priest and used to determine God's will (see the note on 10:20). Saul was rushing the formalities of getting an answer from God so he could hurry and get into battle to take advantage of the confusion of the Philistines.

14:24 Saul made an oath without thinking through the implications. The results? (1) His men were too tired to fight; (2) they were so hungry they ate meat that still contained blood, which was against God's law (14:32); (3) Saul almost killed his own son (14:42-45).

Saul's impulsive oath sounded heroic, but it had disastrous side effects. If you are in the middle of a conflict, guard against impulsive statements that you may be forced to honor.

30 If the men had been allowed to eat freely from the food they found among our enemies,
think how many more we could have killed!"
31 But hungry as they were, they chased and killed the Philistines all day from
Micmash to Aijalon, growing more and more faint. 32 That evening they flew upon the
battle plunder and butchered the sheep, cattle, and calves, but they ate them without
draining the blood. 33 Someone reported to Saul, "Look, the men are sinning against the
LORD by eating meat that still has blood in it."
"That is very wrong," Saul said. "Find a large stone and roll it over here. 34 Then go
out among the troops and tell them, 'Bring the cattle and sheep here to kill them and drain
the blood. Do not sin against the LORD by eating meat with the blood still in it.'" So that
night all the troops brought their animals and slaughtered them there. 35 And Saul built
an altar to the LORD, the first one he had ever built.
36 Then Saul said, "Let's chase the Philistines all night and destroy every last one of
them."
His men replied, "We'll do whatever you think is best."
But the priest said, "Let's ask God first."
37 So Saul asked God, "Should we go after the Philistines? Will you help us defeat
them?" But God made no reply that day.
38 Then Saul said to the leaders, "Something's wrong! I want all my army commanders
to come here. We must find out what sin was committed today. 39 I vow by the name of
the LORD who rescued Israel that the sinner will surely die, even if it is my own son
Jonathan!" But no one would tell him what the trouble was. 40 Then Saul said, "Jonathan
and I will stand over here, and all of you stand over there." And the people agreed.
41 Then Saul prayed, "O LORD, God of Israel, please show us who is guilty and who
is innocent. Are Jonathan and I guilty, or is the sin among the others?"* And Jonathan
and Saul were chosen* as the guilty ones, and the people were declared innocent.
42 Then Saul said, "Now choose* between me and Jonathan." And Jonathan was
shown to be the guilty one.
43 "Tell me what you have done," Saul demanded of Jonathan.
"I tasted a little honey," Jonathan admitted. "It was only a little bit on the end of a
stick. Does that deserve death?"
44 "Yes, Jonathan," Saul said, "you must die! May God strike me dead if you are not
executed for this."
45 But the people broke in and said to Saul, "Should Jonathan, who saved Israel today,
die? Far from it! As surely as the LORD lives, not one hair on his head will be touched,

14:31 Josh 10:12
14:32 Gen 9:4; Lev 17:10; 1 Sam 15:19; Acts 15:20
14:35 1 Sam 7:12, 17
14:37 1 Sam 22:42; 28:5-6; 30:7-8
14:38 Josh 7:10-12
14:39 1 Sam 14:24-44; 2 Sam 12:15
14:41 Acts 1:24
14:43 Josh 7:19; 1 Sam 14:27
14:44 Ruth 1:17; 1 Sam 3:17; 14:39; 25:22
14:45 2 Sam 14:11; Luke 21:18; Acts 27:34

14:41a Greek version adds *If the fault is with me or my son Jonathan, respond with Urim; but if the men of Israel are at fault, respond with Thummim.* **14:41b** Hebrew *chosen by lot.* **14:42** Hebrew *draw lots.*

14:32-34 One of the oldest and strongest Hebrew food laws was the prohibition against eating meat containing the animal's blood (Leviticus 7:26, 27). This law began in Noah's day (Genesis 9:4) and was still observed by the early Christians (Acts 15:27-29). It was wrong to eat blood because blood represented life, and life belonged to God. (For a further explanation, see Leviticus 17:10-14.)

14:35, 36 After being king for several years, Saul finally built his first altar to God, but only as a last resort. Throughout Saul's reign he consistently approached God only after he had tried everything else. This was in sharp contrast to the priest, who suggested that God be consulted *first.* How much better if Saul had gone to God first, building an altar as his first official act as king. God is too great to be an afterthought. When we turn to him first, we will never have to turn to him as a last resort.

14:39 This is the second of Saul's foolish vows. Saul made the first of his two oaths (14:24-26) because he was overly anxious to defeat the Philistines and wanted to give his soldiers an incentive to finish the battle quickly. In the Bible, God never asked people to make oaths or vows, but if they did, he expected them to keep them (Leviticus 5:4; Numbers 30).

Saul's vow was not something God would have condoned, but still it was an oath. And Jonathan, although he didn't know about Saul's oath, was nevertheless guilty of breaking it. Like Jephthah (Judges 11), Saul made an oath that risked the life of his own child. Fortunately, the people intervened and spared Jonathan's life.

14:39 Saul had issued a ridiculous command and had driven his men to sin, but still he wouldn't back down even if he had to kill his son. When we make ridiculous statements, it is difficult to admit we are wrong. Sticking to the story, just to save face, only compounds the problem. It takes more courage to admit a mistake than to hold resolutely to an error.

14:43 Jonathan's spiritual character was in striking contrast to Saul's. Jonathan admitted what he had done; he did not try to make excuses. Even though he was unaware of Saul's oath, Jonathan was willing to accept the consequences of his actions. When you do wrong, even unintentionally, respond like Jonathan, not like Saul.

14:44, 45 Saul made another foolish statement, this time because he was more concerned about saving face than being right. To spare Jonathan's life would require him to admit he had acted foolishly, an embarrassment for a king. Saul was really more interested in protecting his image than in enforcing his vow. Fortunately, the people came to Jonathan's rescue. Don't be like Saul. Admit your mistakes, and show that you are more interested in doing what is right than in looking good.

for he has been used of God to do a mighty miracle today." So the people rescued
Jonathan, and he was not put to death. 46 Then Saul called back the army from chasing
the Philistines, and the Philistines returned home.

Saul's Military Successes

14:48 1 Sam 15:3, 7
47 Now when Saul had secured his grasp on Israel's throne, he fought against his enemies
in every direction—against Moab, Ammon, Edom, the kings of Zobah, and the Philis-
14:49 1 Sam 18:17, 20, 27; 19:11-12; 31:2 2 Sam 6:20 1 Chr 8:33; 10:2
tines. And wherever he turned, he was victorious. 48 He did great deeds and conquered
the Amalekites, saving Israel from all those who had plundered them.
49 Saul's sons included Jonathan, Ishbosheth,* and Malkishua. He also had two
14:50 2 Sam 2:8
daughters: Merab, who was older, and Michal. 50 Saul's wife was Ahinoam, the daughter
of Ahimaaz. The commander of Saul's army was his cousin Abner, his uncle Ner's son.
14:51 1 Sam 9:1
51 Abner's father, Ner, and Saul's father, Kish, were brothers; both were sons of Abiel.
14:52 1 Sam 8:11
52 The Israelites fought constantly with the Philistines throughout Saul's lifetime. So
whenever Saul saw a young man who was brave and strong, he drafted him into his army.

Saul Destroys the Amalekites

15:1 1 Sam 9:16; 10:1
15 One day Samuel said to Saul, "I anointed you king of Israel because the LORD told
me to. Now listen to this message from the LORD! 2 This is what the LORD
15:2 Exod 17:8-16 Num 24:20 Deut 25:17
Almighty says: 'I have decided to settle accounts with the nation of Amalek for opposing
Israel when they came from Egypt. 3 Now go and completely destroy* the entire
15:3 Deut 20:16-18 Josh 6:17-18
Amalekite nation—men, women, children, babies, cattle, sheep, camels, and donkeys.'"
4 So Saul mobilized his army at Telaim. There were 200,000 troops in addition to
15:6 Num 24:21-22 Judg 1:16; 4:11
10,000 men from Judah. 5 Then Saul went to the city of Amalek and lay in wait in the
valley. 6 Saul sent this message to the Kenites: "Move away from where the Amalekites
live or else you will die with them. For you were kind to the people of Israel when they
came up from Egypt." So the Kenites packed up and left.
15:7 Gen 16:7; 25:18 Exod 15:22 1 Sam 27:8
7 Then Saul slaughtered the Amalekites from Havilah all the way to Shur, east of
Egypt. 8 He captured Agag, the Amalekite king, but completely destroyed everyone else.
15:8 Num 24:7
9 Saul and his men spared Agag's life and kept the best of the sheep and cattle, the fat
15:9 1 Sam 15:15, 21
calves and lambs—everything, in fact, that appealed to them. They destroyed only what
was worthless or of poor quality.

The LORD Rejects Saul

15:11 Gen 6:6-7 Exod 32:9, 11, 14 2 Sam 24:16 Luke 6:12
10 Then the LORD said to Samuel, 11 "I am sorry that I ever made Saul king, for he has
not been loyal to me and has again refused to obey me." Samuel was so deeply moved
when he heard this that he cried out to the LORD all night.

14:49 Hebrew *Ishvi,* a variant name for Ishbosheth; also known as Eshbaal. **15:3** The Hebrew term used here refers to the complete consecration of things or people to the LORD, either by destroying them or by giving them as an offering; also in 15:8, 9, 15, 18, 20, 21.

14:47 Why was Saul so successful right after he had disobeyed God and been told that his reign would end (13:13, 14)? Sometimes ungodly people win battles. Victory is neither guaranteed nor limited to the righteous. God provides according to his will. God might have given Saul success for the sake of the people, not for Saul. He may have left Saul on the throne for a while to utilize his military talents so that David, Israel's next king, could spend more time focusing on the nation's spiritual battles. Regardless of God's reasons for delaying Saul's demise, his reign ended exactly the way God had foretold. The timing of God's plans and promises is known only to him. Our task is to commit our ways to God and then trust him for the outcome.

15:2, 3 Why did God command such utter destruction? The Amalekites were a band of guerrilla terrorists. They lived by attacking other nations and carrying off their wealth and their families. They were the first to attack the Israelites as they entered the Promised Land, and they continued to raid Israelite camps at every opportunity. God knew that the Israelites could never live peacefully in the Promised Land as long as the Amalekites existed. He also knew that their corrupt, idolatrous religious practices threatened Israel's relationship with him. The only way to protect the Israelites' bodies and souls was to utterly destroy the people of this warlike nation and all their possessions, including their idols.

15:9 Saul and his men did not destroy all the plunder from the battle as God commanded (15:3). The law of devoting something—setting it aside—entirely for destruction was well known to the Israelites. Anything under God's ban was to be completely destroyed (Deuteronomy 20:16-18). This was set up in order to prevent idolatry from taking hold in Israel because many of the valuables were idols. To break this law was punishable by death (Joshua 7). It showed disrespect and disregard for God because it directly violated his command.

When we gloss over sin in order to protect what we have or for material gain, we aren't being shrewd; we are disobeying God's law. Selective obedience is just another form of disobedience.

15:11 When God said he was sorry that he had made Saul king, was he saying he had made a mistake? God's comment was an expression of sorrow, not an admission of error (Genesis 6:5-7). An omniscient God cannot make a mistake; therefore, God did not change his mind. He did, however, change his attitude toward Saul when Saul changed. Saul's heart no longer belonged to God but to his own interests.

12Early the next morning Samuel went to find Saul. Someone told him, "Saul went to
Carmel to set up a monument to himself; then he went on to Gilgal."
13When Samuel finally found him, Saul greeted him cheerfully. "May the LORD bless
you," he said. "I have carried out the LORD's command!"
14"Then what is all the bleating of sheep and lowing of cattle I hear?" Samuel
demanded.
15"It's true that the army spared the best of the sheep and cattle," Saul admitted. "But
they are going to sacrifice them to the LORD your God. We have destroyed everything
else."
16Then Samuel said to Saul, "Stop! Listen to what the LORD told me last night!"
"What was it?" Saul asked.
17And Samuel told him, "Although you may think little of yourself, are you not the
leader of the tribes of Israel? The LORD has anointed you king of Israel. 18And the
LORD sent you on a mission and told you, 'Go and completely destroy the sinners, the
Amalekites, until they are all dead.' 19Why haven't you obeyed the LORD? Why did
you rush for the plunder and do exactly what the LORD said not to do?"
20"But I did obey the LORD," Saul insisted. "I carried out the mission he gave me.
I brought back King Agag, but I destroyed everyone else. 21Then my troops brought
in the best of the sheep and cattle and plunder to sacrifice to the LORD your God in
Gilgal."
22But Samuel replied, "What is more pleasing to the LORD: your burnt offerings and
sacrifices or your obedience to his voice? Obedience is far better than sacrifice. Listening
to him is much better than offering the fat of rams. 23Rebellion is as bad as the sin of
witchcraft, and stubbornness is as bad as worshiping idols. So because you have rejected
the word of the LORD, he has rejected you from being king."

Saul Pleads for Forgiveness

24Then Saul finally admitted, "Yes, I have sinned. I have disobeyed your instructions
and the LORD's command, for I was afraid of the people and did what they demanded.
25Oh, please, forgive my sin now and go with me to worship the LORD."
26But Samuel replied, "I will not return with you! Since you have rejected the LORD's
command, he has rejected you from being the king of Israel."
27As Samuel turned to go, Saul grabbed at him to try to hold him back and tore his
robe. 28And Samuel said to him, "See? The LORD has torn the kingdom of Israel from
you today and has given it to someone else—one who is better than you. 29And he who
is the Glory of Israel will not lie, nor will he change his mind, for he is not human that
he should change his mind!"

15:12 Josh 15:55
15:15 Gen 3:12-13; 1 Sam 15:9, 21
15:17 1 Sam 9:21; 10:22
15:19 1 Sam 14:32
15:21 1 Sam 15:9, 15
15:22 Pss 40:6-8; 51:16-17; Isa 1:11-15; Jer 7:22-23; Hos 6:6; Mic 6:7-8; Mark 12:33
15:23 Deut 18:10; 1 Sam 13:14
15:24 Num 22:34; 2 Sam 12:13; Ps 51:4; Isa 51:12-13
15:25 Exod 10:17
15:27 1 Kgs 11:30-31
15:28 1 Sam 28:17-18
15:29 Num 23:19; Ezek 24:14

15:12 Saul built a monument in honor of himself. What a contrast to Moses and Joshua, who gave all the credit to God.

15:13, 14 Saul thought he had won a great victory over the Amalekites, but God saw it as a great failure because Saul had disobeyed him and then lied to Samuel about the results of the battle. Saul may have thought his lie wouldn't be detected, or that what he did was not wrong. Saul was deceiving himself.

Dishonest people soon begin to believe the lies they construct around themselves. Then they lose the ability to tell the difference between truth and lies. By believing your own lies, you deceive yourself, you alienate yourself from God, and you lose credibility in all your relationships. In the long run, honesty wins out.

15:22, 23 This is the first of numerous places in the Bible where the theme "obedience is far better than sacrifice" is stated (Psalms 40:6-8; 51:16, 17; Proverbs 21:3; Isaiah 1:11-17; Jeremiah 7:21-23; Hosea 6:6; Micah 6:6-8; Matthew 12:7; Mark 12:33; Hebrews 10:8, 9). Was Samuel saying that sacrifice is unimportant? No, he was urging Saul to look at his reasons for making the sacrifice rather than at the sacrifice itself. A sacrifice was a ritual transaction between man and God that physically demonstrated a relationship between them. But if the person's heart was not truly repentant or if he did not truly love God, the sacrifice was a hollow ritual. Religious ceremonies or rituals are empty unless they are performed with an attitude of love and obedience. "Being religious" (going to church, serving on a committee, giving to charity) is not enough if we do not act out of devotion and obedience to God.

15:23 Rebellion and stubbornness are serious sins. They involve far more than being independent and strong-minded. Scripture equates them with witchcraft and idolatry, sins worthy of death (Exodus 22:18; Leviticus 20:6; Deuteronomy 13:12-15; 18:10; Micah 5:10-14).

Saul became both rebellious and stubborn, so it is little wonder that God finally rejected him and took away his kingdom. Rebellion against God is perhaps the most serious sin of all because as long as a person rebels, he or she closes the door to forgiveness and restoration with God.

15:26 Saul's excuses had come to an end. It was the time of reckoning. God wasn't rejecting Saul as a person; the king could still seek forgiveness and restore his relationship with God, but it was too late to get his kingdom back. If you do not act responsibly with what God has entrusted to you, eventually you will run out of excuses. All of us must one day give an account for our actions (Romans 14:12; Revelation 22:12).

15:30 Isa 29:13

30 Then Saul pleaded again, "I know I have sinned. But please, at least honor me before
the leaders and before my people by going with me to worship the LORD your God." 31 So
Samuel finally agreed and went with him, and Saul worshiped the LORD.

Samuel Executes King Agag

15:33 Gen 9:5-6; Judg 1:7
15:34 1 Sam 7:17; 11:4
15:35 1 Sam 16:1; 19:24

32 Then Samuel said, "Bring King Agag to me." Agag arrived full of smiles, for he
thought, "Surely the worst is over, and I have been spared!"* 33 But Samuel said, "As
your sword has killed the sons of many mothers, now your mother will be childless."
And Samuel cut Agag to pieces before the LORD at Gilgal. 34 Then Samuel went home
to Ramah, and Saul returned to his house at Gibeah. 35 Samuel never went to meet with
Saul again, but he mourned constantly for him. And the LORD was sorry he had ever
made Saul king of Israel.

C. SAUL AND DAVID (16:1—31:13)

While Saul is still on the throne, Samuel anoints David as Israel's next king. Young David then bravely conquers Goliath, the Philistine champion, and establishes a lifelong friendship with Jonathan, Saul's son. When Saul realizes that David will become king one day, he grows very jealous and tries to kill David on several occasions. David escapes into Philistine territory until Saul is killed in battle. When treated unjustly, we should not take matters into our own hands. God, who is faithful and just, sees all that is happening and will judge all evil.

1. Samuel anoints David

16:1 1 Sam 9:16; 13:13-14; 2 Kgs 9:1-2
16:2 1 Sam 20:28-29
16:3 Deut 17:14-15
16:4 1 Kgs 2:13; Luke 2:4
16:5 Gen 35:2; Exod 19:10

16 Finally, the LORD said to Samuel, "You have mourned long enough for Saul. I have
rejected him as king of Israel. Now fill your horn with olive oil and go to
Bethlehem. Find a man named Jesse who lives there, for I have selected one of his sons
to be my new king."

2 But Samuel asked, "How can I do that? If Saul hears about it, he will kill me."

"Take a heifer with you," the LORD replied, "and say that you have come to make a
sacrifice to the LORD. 3 Invite Jesse to the sacrifice, and I will show you which of his sons
to anoint for me."

4 So Samuel did as the LORD instructed him. When he arrived at Bethlehem, the leaders
of the town became afraid. "What's wrong?" they asked. "Do you come in peace?"

5 "Yes," Samuel replied. "I have come to sacrifice to the LORD. Purify yourselves and
come with me to the sacrifice." Then Samuel performed the purification rite for Jesse
and his sons and invited them, too.

16:6 1 Sam 17:13
16:7 1 Sam 9:2; 1 Kgs 8:39; 1 Chr 28:9; Luke 16:15
16:8 1 Sam 17:13
16:11 2 Sam 7:8

6 When they arrived, Samuel took one look at Eliab and thought, "Surely this is the
LORD's anointed!" 7 But the LORD said to Samuel, "Don't judge by his appearance or
height, for I have rejected him. The LORD doesn't make decisions the way you do! People
judge by outward appearance, but the LORD looks at a person's thoughts and intentions."

8 Then Jesse told his son Abinadab to step forward and walk in front of Samuel. But
Samuel said, "This is not the one the LORD has chosen." 9 Next Jesse summoned
Shammah, but Samuel said, "Neither is this the one the LORD has chosen." 10 In the same
way all seven of Jesse's sons were presented to Samuel. But Samuel said to Jesse, "The
LORD has not chosen any of these." 11 Then Samuel asked, "Are these all the sons you
have?"

15:32 Dead Sea Scrolls and Greek version read *Agag arrived hesitantly, for he thought, "Surely this is the bitterness of death."*

15:30 Saul was more concerned about what others would think of him than he was about the status of his relationship with God (15:24). He begged Samuel to go with him to worship as a public demonstration that Samuel still supported him. If Samuel had refused, the people probably would have lost all confidence in Saul.

16:5 Samuel "purified" Jesse and his sons to prepare them to come before God in worship or to offer a sacrifice. For more on this ceremony, see Genesis 35:2; Exodus 19:10, 14; and the note on Joshua 3:5.

16:7 Saul was tall and handsome; he was an impressive-looking man. Samuel may have been trying to find someone who looked like Saul to be Israel's next king, but God warned him against judging by appearance alone. When people judge by outward appearance, they may overlook quality individuals who lack the particular physical qualities society currently admires. Appearance doesn't reveal what people are really like or what their true value is.

Fortunately, God judges by faith and character, not appearances. And because only God can see on the inside, only he can accurately judge people. Most people spend hours each week maintaining their outward appearance; they should do even more to develop their inner character. While everyone can see your face, only you and God know what your heart really looks like. What steps are you taking to improve your heart's attitude?

"There is still the youngest," Jesse replied. "But he's out in the fields watching the sheep."
"Send for him at once," Samuel said. "We will not sit down to eat until he arrives."
12 So Jesse sent for him. He was ruddy and handsome, with pleasant eyes. And the
LORD said, "This is the one; anoint him."
13 So as David stood there among his brothers, Samuel took the olive oil he had
brought and poured it on David's head. And the Spirit of the LORD came mightily upon
him from that day on. Then Samuel returned to Ramah.

16:12 Gen 39:6; Exod 2:1-2; 1 Sam 9:17; Acts 7:20

David Serves in Saul's Court

14 Now the Spirit of the LORD had left Saul, and the LORD sent a tormenting spirit that
filled him with depression and fear. 15 Some of Saul's servants suggested a remedy. "It
is clear that a spirit from God is tormenting you," they said. 16 "Let us find a good
musician to play the harp for you whenever the tormenting spirit is bothering you. The
harp music will quiet you, and you will soon be well again."
17 "All right," Saul said. "Find me someone who plays well and bring him here."
18 One of the servants said to Saul, "The son of Jesse is a talented harp player. Not only
that; he is brave and strong and has good judgment. He is also a fine-looking young man,
and the LORD is with him."
19 So Saul sent messengers to Jesse to say, "Send me your son David, the shepherd."
20 Jesse responded by sending David to Saul, along with a young goat and a donkey
loaded down with food and wine. 21 So David went to Saul and served him. Saul liked
David very much, and David became one of Saul's armor bearers.
22 Then Saul sent word to Jesse asking, "Please let David join my staff, for I am very
pleased with him." 23 And whenever the tormenting spirit from God troubled Saul, David
would play the harp. Then Saul would feel better, and the tormenting spirit would go away.

16:14 Judg 9:3; 16:20; 1 Sam 11:6; 18:10-12; 19:9; 1 Kgs 22:22

16:18 1 Sam 3:19; 17:32-37

16:21 Gen 41:46

2. David and Goliath

Goliath Challenges the Israelites

17 The Philistines now mustered their army for battle and camped between Socoh in
Judah and Azekah at Ephes-dammim. 2 Saul countered by gathering his troops
near the valley of Elah. 3 So the Philistines and Israelites faced each other on opposite
hills, with the valley between them.

17:1 1 Sam 13:5; 1 Chr 11:13

17:2 1 Sam 21:9

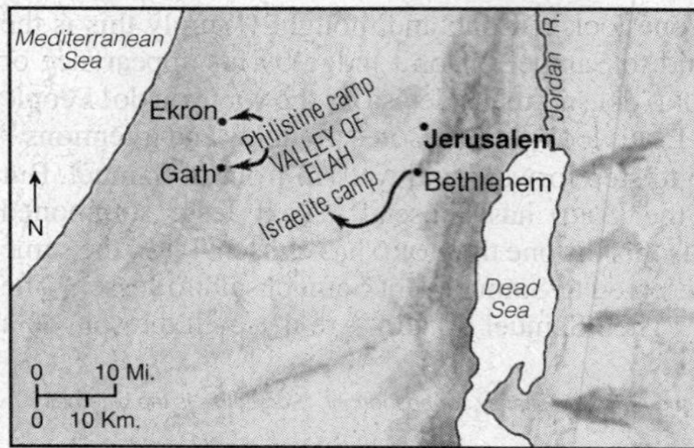

DAVID AND GOLIATH The armies of Israel and Philistia faced each other across the valley of Elah. David arrived from Bethlehem and offered to fight the giant Goliath. After David defeated Goliath, the Israelite army chased the Philistines to Ekron and Gath (Goliath's hometown).

16:13 David was anointed king, but it was done in secret; he was not publicly anointed until much later (2 Samuel 2:4; 5:3). Saul was still legally the king, but God was preparing David for his future responsibilities. The anointing oil poured over David's head stood for holiness. It was used to set people or objects apart for God's service. Each king and high priest of Israel was anointed with oil. This commissioned him as God's representative to the nation. Although God rejected Saul's kingship by not allowing any of his descendants to sit on Israel's throne, Saul himself remained in his position until his death.

16:14 What was this tormenting spirit the Lord sent? Perhaps Saul was simply depressed. Or perhaps the Holy Spirit had left Saul, and God allowed an evil spirit (a demon) to torment him as judgment for his disobedience (this would demonstrate God's power over the spirit world—1 Kings 22:19-23). Either way, Saul was driven to insanity, which led him to attempt to murder David.

16:15, 16 Harps were popular musical instruments in Saul's day, and their music is still known for its soothing qualities. The simplest harps were merely two pieces of wood fastened at right angles to each other. The strings were stretched across the wood to give the harp a triangular shape. Simple strings could be made of twisted grasses, but better strings were made of dried animal intestine. Harps could have up to 40 strings and were louder than the smaller three- or four-stringed instruments called lyres. David, known for his shepherding skills and bravery, was also an accomplished harpist and musician, who would eventually write many of the psalms found in the Bible.

16:19-21 When Saul asked David to be in his service, he obviously did not know that David had been secretly anointed king (16:12). Saul's invitation presented an excellent opportunity for the young man and future king to gain firsthand information about leading a nation ("David went back and forth between working for Saul and helping his father," 17:15).

Sometimes our plans—even the ones we think God has approved—have to be put on hold indefinitely. Like David, we can use this waiting time profitably. We can choose to learn and grow in our present circumstances, whatever they may be.

17:4 Josh 11:21-22 2 Sam 21:19 [4]Then Goliath, a Philistine champion from Gath, came out of the Philistine ranks to
face the forces of Israel. He was a giant of a man, measuring over nine feet* tall! [5]He
wore a bronze helmet and a coat of mail that weighed 125 pounds.* [6]He also wore bronze
leggings, and he slung a bronze javelin over his back. [7]The shaft of his spear was as
heavy and thick as a weaver's beam, tipped with an iron spearhead that weighed fifteen
pounds.* An armor bearer walked ahead of him carrying a huge shield.
[8]Goliath stood and shouted across to the Israelites, "Do you need a whole army to
settle this? Choose someone to fight for you, and I will represent the Philistines. We

17:4 Hebrew *6 cubits* [9 feet or 2.7 meters] *and 1 span* [9 inches or 23 centimeters]; Greek version reads *4 cubits* [6 feet or 1.8 meters] *and 1 span*, about 6.75 feet or 2 meters in length. **17:5** Hebrew *5,000 shekels* [57 kilograms]. **17:7** Hebrew *600 shekels* [6.8 kilograms].

DAVID

When we think of David, we think: shepherd, poet, giant-killer, king, ancestor of Jesus—in short, one of the greatest men in the Old Testament. But alongside that list stands another: betrayer, liar, adulterer, murderer. The first list gives qualities we all might like to have; the second, qualities that might be true of any one of us. The Bible makes no effort to hide David's failures. Yet he is remembered and respected for his heart for God. Knowing how much more we share in David's failures than in his greatness, we should be curious to find out what made God refer to David as "a man after my own heart" (Acts 13:22).

David, more than anything else, had an unchangeable belief in the faithful and forgiving nature of God. He was a man who lived with great zest. He sinned, but he was quick to confess his sins. His confessions were from the heart, and his repentance was genuine. David never took God's forgiveness lightly or his blessing for granted. In return, God never held back from David either his forgiveness or the consequences of his actions. David experienced the joy of forgiveness even when he had to suffer the consequences of his sins.

We tend to get these two reversed. Too often we would rather avoid the consequences than experience forgiveness. Another big difference between us and David is that while he sinned greatly, he did not sin repeatedly. He learned from his mistakes because he accepted the suffering they brought. Often we don't seem to learn from our mistakes or the consequences that result from those mistakes. What changes would it take for God to find this kind of obedience in you?

Strengths and accomplishments
- Greatest king of Israel
- Ancestor of Jesus Christ
- Listed in the Hall of Faith in Hebrews 11
- A man described by God himself as a man after his own heart

Weaknesses and mistakes
- Committed adultery with Bathsheba
- Arranged the murder of Uriah, Bathsheba's husband
- Directly disobeyed God in taking a census of the people
- Did not deal decisively with the sins of his children

Lessons from his life
- Willingness to honestly admit our mistakes is the first step in dealing with them
- Forgiveness does not remove the consequences of sin
- God greatly desires our complete trust and worship

Vital statistics
- Where: Bethlehem, Jerusalem
- Occupations: Shepherd, musician, poet, soldier, king
- Relatives: Father: Jesse. Wives: included Michal, Ahinoam, Bathsheba, Abigail. Sons: included Absalom, Amnon, Solomon, Adonijah. Daughters: included Tamar. Seven brothers
- Contemporaries: Saul, Jonathan, Samuel, Nathan

Key verses
"For you are God, O Sovereign LORD. Your words are truth, and you have promised these good things to me, your servant. And now, may it please you to bless me and my family so that our dynasty may continue forever before you. For when you grant a blessing to your servant, O Sovereign LORD, it is an eternal blessing!" (2 Samuel 7:28, 29).

His story is told in 1 Samuel 16—1 Kings 2. He is also mentioned in Amos 6:5; Matthew 1:1, 6; 22:43-45; Luke 1:32; Acts 13:22; Romans 1:3; Hebrews 11:32.

17:4-7 In the days of the Exodus, most of the Israelites had been afraid to enter the Promised Land because of the giants living there (Numbers 13:32, 33). King Og of Bashan needed a bed over 13 feet long (Deuteronomy 3:11). Now Goliath, over nine feet tall, taunted Israel's soldiers and appeared invincible to them. Saul, the tallest of the Israelites, may have been especially worried because he was obviously the best match for Goliath. In God's eyes, however, Goliath was no different than anyone else.

will settle this dispute in single combat! [9]If your man is able to kill me, then we will be your slaves. But if I kill him, you will be our slaves! [10]I defy the armies of Israel! Send me a man who will fight with me!" [11]When Saul and the Israelites heard this, they were terrified and deeply shaken.

Jesse Sends David to Saul's Camp

[12]Now David was the son of a man named Jesse, an Ephrathite from Bethlehem in the land of Judah. Jesse was an old man at that time, and he had eight sons in all. [13]Jesse's three oldest sons—Eliab, Abinadab, and Shammah—had already joined Saul's army to fight the Philistines. [14]David was the youngest of Jesse's sons. Since David's three oldest brothers were in the army, they stayed with Saul's forces all the time. [15]But David went back and forth between working for Saul and helping his father with the sheep in Bethlehem.

[16]For forty days, twice a day, morning and evening, the Philistine giant strutted in front of the Israelite army.

[17]One day Jesse said to David, "Take this half-bushel* of roasted grain and these ten loaves of bread to your brothers. [18]And give these ten cuts of cheese to their captain. See how your brothers are getting along, and bring me back a letter from them.*"

[19]David's brothers were with Saul and the Israelite army at the valley of Elah, fighting against the Philistines. [20]So David left the sheep with another shepherd and set out early the next morning with the gifts. He arrived at the outskirts of the camp just as the Israelite army was leaving for the battlefield with shouts and battle cries. [21]Soon the Israelite and Philistine forces stood facing each other, army against army. [22]David left his things with the keeper of supplies and hurried out to the ranks to greet his brothers. [23]As he was talking with them, he saw Goliath, the champion from Gath, come out from the Philistine ranks, shouting his challenge to the army of Israel.

[24]As soon as the Israelite army saw him, they began to run away in fright. [25]"Have you seen the giant?" the men were asking. "He comes out each day to challenge Israel. And have you heard about the huge reward the king has offered to anyone who kills him? The king will give him one of his daughters for a wife, and his whole family will be exempted from paying taxes!"

[26]David talked to some others standing there to verify the report. "What will a man get for killing this Philistine and putting an end to his abuse of Israel?" he asked them. "Who is this pagan Philistine anyway, that he is allowed to defy the armies of the living God?" [27]And David received the same reply as before: "What you have been hearing is true. That is the reward for killing the giant."

[28]But when David's oldest brother, Eliab, heard David talking to the men, he was angry. "What are you doing around here anyway?" he demanded. "What about those few sheep you're supposed to be taking care of? I know about your pride and dishonesty. You just want to see the battle!"

[29]"What have I done now?" David replied. "I was only asking a question!" [30]He walked over to some others and asked them the same thing and received the same answer. [31]Then David's question was reported to King Saul, and the king sent for him.

17:9 2 Sam 2:12-16
17:10 1 Sam 17:26, 45
17:12 Gen 35:19; Ruth 4:18-22; 1 Chr 2:13
17:13 1 Sam 16:6-9
17:15 1 Sam 16:19
17:17 1 Sam 25:18
17:18 Gen 37:13-14
17:20 1 Sam 26:5, 7
17:23 1 Sam 17:8-10
17:25 Josh 15:16; 1 Sam 18:17
17:26 1 Sam 11:2; 14:6; 2 Kgs 19:4
17:28 Gen 37:4, 8

17:17 Hebrew *ephah* [18 liters]. **17:18** Hebrew *and take their pledge.*

17:9 An army often avoided the high cost of battle by pitting its strongest warrior against the strongest warrior of the enemy. This avoided great bloodshed because the winner of the fight was considered the winner of the battle. Goliath had the definite advantage against David from a human standpoint. But Goliath didn't realize that in fighting David, he also had to fight God.

17:16 Why would this go on for 40 days without one side attacking the other? They were camped on opposite sides of a valley with steep walls. Whoever would rush down the valley and up the steep cliffs would be at a disadvantage at the beginning of the battle and probably suffer great casualties. Each side was waiting for the other to attack first.

17:26 What a difference perspective can make. Most of the onlookers saw only a giant. David, however, saw a mortal man defying almighty God. He knew he would not be alone when he faced Goliath; God would fight with him. He looked at his situation from God's point of view. Viewing impossible situations from God's point of view helps us put giant problems in perspective. Once we see clearly, we can fight more effectively.

17:28-32 Criticism couldn't stop David. While the rest of the army stood around, he knew the importance of taking action. With God to fight for him, there was no reason to wait. People may try to discourage you with negative comments or mockery, but continue to do what you know is right. By doing what is right, you will be pleasing God, whose opinion matters most.

David Kills Goliath

17:32
Deut 20:1
32“Don’t worry about a thing,” David told Saul. “I’ll go fight this Philistine!”
33“Don’t be ridiculous!” Saul replied. “There is no way you can go against this
Philistine. You are only a boy, and he has been in the army since he was a boy!”
34But David persisted. “I have been taking care of my father’s sheep,” he said.

17:35
Amos 3:12
“When a lion or a bear comes to steal a lamb from the flock, 35I go after it with a club
and take the lamb from its mouth. If the animal turns on me, I catch it by the jaw and
club it to death. 36I have done this to both lions and bears, and I’ll do it to this pagan

17:37
1 Sam 20:13
2 Tim 4:17
Philistine, too, for he has defied the armies of the living God! 37The LORD who saved
me from the claws of the lion and the bear will save me from this Philistine!”
Saul finally consented. “All right, go ahead,” he said. “And may the LORD be with
you!”
38Then Saul gave David his own armor—a bronze helmet and a coat of mail. 39David
put it on, strapped the sword over it, and took a step or two to see what it was like, for
he had never worn such things before. “I can’t go in these,” he protested. “I’m not used
to them.” So he took them off again. 40He picked up five smooth stones from a stream
and put them in his shepherd’s bag. Then, armed only with his shepherd’s staff and sling,
he started across to fight Goliath.

17:42
1 Sam 16:12
41Goliath walked out toward David with his shield bearer ahead of him, 42sneering in
contempt at this ruddy-faced boy. 43“Am I a dog,” he roared at David, “that you come

17:43
1 Sam 24:14
2 Sam 3:8; 9:8
1 Kgs 20:10
at me with a stick?” And he cursed David by the names of his gods. 44“Come over here,
and I’ll give your flesh to the birds and wild animals!” Goliath yelled.

17:45
2 Chr 32:8
Ps 124:8
Heb 11:32-34
45David shouted in reply, “You come to me with sword, spear, and javelin, but I come
to you in the name of the LORD Almighty—the God of the armies of Israel, whom you
have defied. 46Today the LORD will conquer you, and I will kill you and cut off your

17:46
Exod 7:5
Josh 4:24
1 Kgs 18:36
2 Kgs 19:19
Isa 37:20
head. And then I will give the dead bodies of your men to the birds and wild animals,
and the whole world will know that there is a God in Israel! 47And everyone will know
that the LORD does not need weapons to rescue his people. It is his battle, not ours. The
LORD will give you to us!”

17:47
1 Sam 14:6
2 Chr 14:11; 20:15
Ps 44:6
Hos 1:7
48As Goliath moved closer to attack, David quickly ran out to meet him. 49Reach-
ing into his shepherd’s bag and taking out a stone, he hurled it from his sling and hit
the Philistine in the forehead. The stone sank in, and Goliath stumbled and fell face

17:50
1 Sam 25:29
downward to the ground. 50So David triumphed over the Philistine giant with only a
stone and sling. And since he had no sword, 51he ran over and pulled Goliath’s sword
from its sheath. David used it to kill the giant and cut off his head.

SIMPLE OBJECTS

God often uses simple, ordinary objects to accomplish his tasks in the world. It is important only that they be dedicated to him for his use. What do you have that God can use? Anything and everything is a possible “instrument” for him.

Object	*Reference*	*Who Used It?*	*How Was It Used?*
a staff	Exodus 4:2–4	Moses	To work miracles before Pharaoh
horns	Joshua 6:3–5	Joshua	To flatten the walls of Jericho
a fleece	Judges 6:36–40	Gideon	To confirm God’s will
horns, jars, and torches	Judges 7:19–22	Gideon	To defeat the Midianites
jawbone	Judges 15:15	Samson	To kill 1,000 Philistines
small stone	1 Samuel 17:40	David	To kill Goliath
oil	2 Kings 4:1–7	Elisha	To demonstrate God’s power to provide
a river	2 Kings 5:9–14	Elisha	To heal a man of leprosy
linen loincloth	Jeremiah 13:1–11	Jeremiah	As an object lesson of God’s wrath
clay jar	Jeremiah 19:1–13	Jeremiah	As an object lesson of God’s wrath
iron griddle, water, and food	Ezekiel 4:1–17	Ezekiel	As an object lesson of judgment
five loaves and two fish	Mark 6:30–44	Jesus	To feed a crowd of over 5,000 people

Israel Routs the Philistines

When the Philistines saw that their champion was dead, they turned and ran. 52 Then the
Israelites gave a great shout of triumph and rushed after the Philistines, chasing them as
far as Gath* and the gates of Ekron. The bodies of the dead and wounded Philistines were
strewn all along the road from Shaaraim, as far as Gath and Ekron. 53 Then the Israelite
army returned and plundered the deserted Philistine camp. 54 (David took Goliath's head
to Jerusalem, but he stored the Philistine's armor in his own tent.)
55 As Saul watched David go out to fight Goliath, he asked Abner, the general of his
army, "Abner, whose son is he?"
"I really don't know," Abner said.
56 "Well, find out!" the king told him.
57 After David had killed Goliath, Abner brought him to Saul with the Philistine's head
still in his hand. 58 "Tell me about your father, my boy," Saul said.
And David replied, "His name is Jesse, and we live in Bethlehem."

17:52 Josh 15:11, 36

3. David and Jonathan become friends

Saul Becomes Jealous of David

18 After David had finished talking with Saul, he met Jonathan, the king's son. There
was an immediate bond of love between them, and they became the best of friends.
2 From that day on Saul kept David with him at the palace and wouldn't let him return
home. 3 And Jonathan made a special vow to be David's friend, 4 and he sealed the pact
by giving him his robe, tunic, sword, bow, and belt.
5 Whatever Saul asked David to do, David did it successfully. So Saul made him a
commander in his army, an appointment that was applauded by the fighting men and
officers alike. 6 But something happened when the victorious Israelite army was returning home after David had killed Goliath. Women came out from all the towns along the
way to celebrate and to cheer for King Saul, and they sang and danced for joy with
tambourines and cymbals.* 7 This was their song:

"Saul has killed his thousands,
and David his ten thousands!"

8 This made Saul very angry. "What's this?" he said. "They credit David with ten
thousands and me with only thousands. Next they'll be making him their king!" 9 So from
that time on Saul kept a jealous eye on David.
10 The very next day, in fact, a tormenting spirit from God overwhelmed Saul, and he
began to rave like a madman. David began to play the harp, as he did whenever this
happened. But Saul, who had a spear in his hand, 11 suddenly hurled it at David, intending
to pin him to the wall. But David jumped aside and escaped. This happened another time,
too, 12 for Saul was afraid of him, and he was jealous because the LORD had left him and

18:1 Gen 44:30; 2 Sam 1:26; 9:1
18:4 Gen 41:42; Esth 6:8
18:6 Exod 15:20; Judg 11:34; Pss 68:25; 149:3
18:7 1 Sam 21:11; 29:5
18:8 1 Sam 15:28-29
18:10 1 Sam 16:14
18:11 1 Sam 19:10

17:52 As in some Greek manuscripts; Hebrew reads *a valley.* **18:6** The type of instrument represented by the final word is uncertain.

17:55-58 Although David had played his harp many times in front of Saul, Saul's question to Abner seems to show he didn't know David very well. Perhaps, since David was scheduled to marry Saul's daughter if he was successful (17:25), Saul wanted to know more about his family. Or possibly Saul's unstable mental condition (16:14) may have prevented him from recognizing David.

18:1-4 When David and Jonathan met, they became close friends at once. Their friendship is one of the deepest and closest recorded in the Bible: (1) They based their friendship on commitment to God, not just each other; (2) they let nothing come between them, not even career or family problems; (3) they drew closer together when their friendship was tested; (4) they remained friends to the end.

Jonathan, the prince of Israel, later realized that David, and not he, would be the next king (23:17). But that did not weaken his love for David. Jonathan would much rather lose the throne of Israel than lose his closest friend.

18:8 Saul's appreciation for David turned to jealousy as people began to applaud David's exploits. In a jealous rage, Saul attempted to murder David by hurling his spear at him (18:11, 12).

Jealousy may not seem to be a major sin, but in reality, it is one step short of murder. Jealousy starts as you resent a rival; it leads to your wishing he or she were removed; then it manifests itself in your seeking ways to harm that person in word or action. Beware of letting jealousy get a foothold in your life.

18:10 The note on 16:14 explains what this evil spirit might have been.

18:11, 12 Saul tried to kill David because he was jealous of David's popularity, yet David continued to protect and comfort Saul. Perhaps people have been jealous of you and have even attacked you in some way. They may be intimidated by your strengths, which make them conscious of their own shortcomings. It would be natural to strike back or to avoid them. A better response is to befriend them (Matthew 5:43, 44) and to ask God for the strength to continue to love them, as David kept on loving Saul.

18:13 2 Sam 5:2
18:14 Gen 39:3-4

was now with David. 13 Finally, Saul banned him from his presence and appointed him
commander over only a thousand men, but David faithfully led his troops into battle.
14 David continued to succeed in everything he did, for the LORD was with him.
15 When Saul recognized this, he became even more afraid of him. 16 But all Israel and
Judah loved David because he was so successful at leading his troops into battle.

David Marries Saul's Daughter

18:17 1 Sam 17:25; 25:28

17 One day Saul said to David, "I am ready to give you my older daughter, Merab, as your
wife. But first you must prove yourself to be a real warrior by fighting the LORD's
battles." For Saul thought to himself, "I'll send him out against the Philistines and let
them kill him rather than doing it myself."

18:18 1 Sam 9:21; 2 Sam 7:18
18:19 Judg 7:22; 2 Sam 21:8
18:20 1 Sam 18:28

18 "Who am I, and what is my family in Israel that I should be the king's son-in-law?"
David exclaimed. "My father's family is nothing!" 19 So* when the time came for the
wedding, Saul gave Merab in marriage to Adriel, a man from Meholah.
20 In the meantime, Saul's daughter Michal had fallen in love with David, and Saul
was delighted when he heard about it. 21 "Here's another chance to see him killed by the
Philistines!" Saul said to himself. But to David he said, "I have a way for you to become
my son-in-law after all!"
22 Then Saul told his men to say confidentially to David, "The king really likes you,
and so do we. Why don't you accept the king's offer and become his son-in-law?"

18:23 Gen 29:20; 34:12

23 When Saul's men said these things to David, he replied, "How can a poor man from
a humble family afford the bride price for the daughter of a king?"
24 When Saul's men reported this back to the king, 25 he told them, "Tell David that all
I want for the bride price is one hundred Philistine foreskins! Vengeance on my enemies
is all I really want." But what Saul had in mind was that David would be killed in the
fight.

18:27 2 Sam 3:14

26 David was delighted to accept the offer. So before the time limit expired, 27 he and
his men went out and killed two hundred Philistines and presented all their foreskins to
the king. So Saul gave Michal to David to be his wife.
28 When the king realized how much the LORD was with David and how much Michal
loved him, 29 he became even more afraid of him, and he remained David's enemy for
the rest of his life. 30 Whenever the Philistine army attacked, David was more successful
against them than all the rest of Saul's officers. So David's name became very famous
throughout the land.

Saul Tries to Kill David

19:1 1 Sam 18:1-3
19:3 1 Sam 20:9, 13

19 Saul now urged his servants and his son Jonathan to assassinate David. But
Jonathan, because of his close friendship with David, 2 told him what his father
was planning. "Tomorrow morning," he warned him, "you must find a hiding place out
in the fields. 3 I'll ask my father to go out there with me, and I'll talk to him about you.
Then I'll tell you everything I can find out."

19:5 Deut 19:10-13; 1 Sam 11:13; 17:49-50; Ps 94:21

4 The next morning Jonathan spoke with his father about David, saying many good
things about him. "Please don't sin against David," Jonathan pleaded. "He's never done
anything to harm you. He has always helped you in any way he could. 5 Have you
forgotten about the time he risked his life to kill the Philistine giant and how the LORD
brought a great victory to Israel as a result? You were certainly happy about it then. Why
should you murder an innocent man like David? There is no reason for it at all!"

18:19 Or *But.*

18:15-18 While Saul's popularity made him proud and arrogant, David remained humble (18:23), even when the entire nation praised him. Although David succeeded in almost everything he tried and became famous throughout the land, he refused to use his popular support to his advantage against Saul. Don't allow popularity to twist your perception of your own importance. It's comparatively easy to be humble when you're not on center stage, but how will you react to praise and honor?

19:1, 2 Is it ever right to disobey your father, as Jonathan did here? It is clearly a principle of Scripture that when a father instructs a son to break God's laws, the son should obey God rather than man. This principle assumes that the son is old enough to be accountable and to see through any deception. A son's role is to be respectful, helpful, and obedient to his father (Ephesians 6:1-3), but not to follow commands or advice that violate God's laws.

6 So Saul listened to Jonathan and vowed, "As surely as the LORD lives, David will not be killed." 7 Afterward Jonathan called David and told him what had happened. Then he took David to see Saul, and everything was as it had been before.

8 War broke out shortly after that, and David led his troops against the Philistines. He attacked them with such fury that they all ran away.

9 But one day as Saul was sitting at home, the tormenting spirit from the LORD suddenly came upon him again. As David played his harp for the king, 10 Saul hurled his spear at David in an attempt to kill him. But David dodged out of the way and escaped into the night, leaving the spear stuck in the wall.

Michal Saves David's Life

11 Then Saul sent troops to watch David's house. They were told to kill David when he came out the next morning. But Michal, David's wife, warned him, "If you don't get away tonight, you will be dead by morning." 12 So she helped him climb out through a window, and he escaped. 13 Then she took an idol* and put it in his bed, covered it with blankets, and put a cushion of goat's hair at its head. 14 When the troops came to arrest David, she told them he was sick and couldn't get out of bed.

15 "Then bring him to me in his bed," Saul ordered, "so I can kill him as he lies there!" And he sent them back to David's house. 16 But when they came to carry David out, they discovered that it was only an idol in the bed with a cushion of goat's hair at its head.

17 "Why have you tricked me and let my enemy escape?" Saul demanded of Michal.

"I had to," Michal replied. "He threatened to kill me if I didn't help him."

18 So David got away and went to Ramah to see Samuel, and he told him all that Saul had done to him. Then Samuel took David with him to live at Naioth. 19 When the report reached Saul that David was at Naioth in Ramah, 20 he sent troops to capture him. But when they arrived and saw Samuel and the other prophets prophesying, the Spirit of God came upon Saul's men, and they also began to prophesy. 21 When Saul heard what had happened, he sent other troops, but they, too, prophesied! The same thing happened a third time! 22 Finally, Saul himself went to Ramah and arrived at the great well in Secu. "Where are Samuel and David?" he demanded.

"They are at Naioth in Ramah," someone told him. 23 But on the way to Naioth the Spirit of God came upon Saul, and he, too, began to prophesy! 24 He tore off his clothes and lay on the ground all day and all night, prophesying in the presence of Samuel. The people who were watching exclaimed, "What? Is Saul a prophet, too?"

Jonathan Helps David

20 David now fled from Naioth in Ramah and found Jonathan. "What have I done?" he exclaimed. "What is my crime? How have I offended your father that he is so determined to kill me?"

2 "That's not true!" Jonathan protested. "I'm sure he's not planning any such thing, for he always tells me everything he's going to do, even the little things. I know he wouldn't hide something like this from me. It just isn't so!"

3 Then David took an oath before Jonathan and said, "Your father knows perfectly well about our friendship, so he has said to himself, 'I won't tell Jonathan—why should I hurt him?' But I swear to you that I am only a step away from death! I swear it by the LORD and by your own soul!"

4 "Tell me what I can do!" Jonathan exclaimed.

5 David replied, "Tomorrow we celebrate the new moon festival. I've always eaten

19:7 1 Sam 16:21
19:9 1 Sam 16:14; 18:10-12
19:11 Judg 16:2; Ps 59:title, 3-4, 6
19:12 Josh 2:15; Acts 9:25
19:13 Judg 18:14, 17
19:18 1 Sam 7:17; 19:22-23
19:20 Num 11:24-25; 1 Sam 10:5-6, 10; Joel 2:28
19:23 1 Sam 10:13
19:24 1 Sam 10:10-12; 2 Sam 6:20; Mic 1:8
20:1 1 Sam 24:9
20:3 Deut 6:13; 2 Kgs 2:6-7
20:5 Num 10:10; 28:11-17; 1 Sam 19:2

19:13 Hebrew *teraphim;* also in 19:16.

19:20-24 This was the second time that Saul surprised everyone by joining a group of prophets and prophesying. The first time (chapter 10) happened right after he was anointed king and did not want to accept the responsibility. This time Saul was consumed with jealousy over David's growing popularity, but the Spirit of God immobilized him so he was unable to harm David. In both cases, Saul spoke God's words (he "prophesied"), although he was far from thinking God's thoughts.

20:5 At the beginning of each month, the Israelites gathered to celebrate the new moon festival. While this was mainly a time to be enjoyed, it was also a way to dedicate the next month to God. Other nations had celebrations during the full moon and worshiped the moon itself. The Israelites, however, celebrated their festival at the time of the new moon, when the moon was not visible in the sky. This was an added precaution against false worship. Nothing in the creation is to be worshiped—only the Creator.

20:6 1 Sam 16:2; 17:58
20:7 1 Sam 25:17
20:8 1 Sam 18:1-3; 2 Sam 1:26; 14:23
20:13 Ruth 1:17; 1 Sam 3:17; 14:44; 18:11-12; 1 Chr 28:20
20:15 2 Sam 9:1
20:16 1 Sam 25:22

with your father on this occasion, but tomorrow I'll hide in the field and stay there until
the evening of the third day. 6If your father asks where I am, tell him I asked permission
to go home to Bethlehem for an annual family sacrifice. 7If he says, 'Fine!' then you will
know all is well. But if he is angry and loses his temper, then you will know he was
planning to kill me. 8Show me this kindness as my sworn friend—for we made a
covenant together before the LORD—or kill me yourself if I have sinned against your
father. But please don't betray me to him!"
9"Never!" Jonathan exclaimed. "You know that if I had the slightest notion my father
was planning to kill you, I would tell you at once."
10Then David asked, "How will I know whether or not your father is angry?"
11"Come out to the field with me," Jonathan replied. And they went out there together.
12Then Jonathan told David, "I promise by the LORD, the God of Israel, that by this time
tomorrow, or the next day at the latest, I will talk to my father and let you know at once
how he feels about you. If he speaks favorably about you, I will let you know. 13But if
he is angry and wants you killed, may the LORD kill me if I don't warn you so you can
escape and live. May the LORD be with you as he used to be with my father. 14And may
you treat me with the faithful love of the LORD as long as I live. But if I die, 15treat my
family with this faithful love, even when the LORD destroys all your enemies."
16So Jonathan made a covenant with David,* saying, "May the LORD destroy all your
enemies!" 17And Jonathan made David reaffirm his vow of friendship again, for Jonathan loved David as much as he loved himself.
18Then Jonathan said, "Tomorrow we celebrate the new moon festival. You will be
missed when your place at the table is empty. 19The day after tomorrow, toward evening,
go to the place where you hid before, and wait there by the stone pile.* 20I will come out

20:16 Hebrew *with the house of David.* **20:19** Hebrew *the stone Ezel.* The meaning of the Hebrew is uncertain.

JONATHAN

Loyalty is one of life's most costly qualities; it is the most selfless part of love. To be loyal, you cannot live only for yourself. Loyal people not only stand by their commitments; they are willing to suffer for them. Jonathan is a shining example of loyalty. Sometimes he was forced to deal with conflicting loyalties: to his father, Saul, and to his friend David. His solution to that conflict teaches us both how to be loyal and what must guide loyalty. In Jonathan, truth always guided loyalty.

Jonathan realized that the source of truth was God, who demanded his ultimate loyalty. It was his relationship with God that gave Jonathan the ability to deal effectively with the complicated situations in his life. He was loyal to Saul because Saul was his father and the king. He was loyal to David because David was his friend. His loyalty to God guided him through the conflicting demands of his human relationships.

The conflicting demands of our relationships challenge us as well. If we attempt to settle these conflicts only at the human level, we will be constantly dealing with a sense of betrayal. But if we communicate to our friends that our ultimate loyalty is to God and his truth, many of our choices will be much clearer. The truth in his Word, the Bible, will bring light to our decisions. Do those closest to you know who has your greatest loyalty?

Strengths and accomplishments
- Brave, loyal, and a natural leader
- The closest friend David ever had
- Did not put his personal well-being ahead of those he loved
- Depended on God

Lessons from his life
- Loyalty is one of the strongest parts of courage
- An allegiance to God puts all other relationships in perspective
- Great friendships are costly

Vital statistics
- Occupation: Military leader
- Relatives: Father: Saul. Mother: Ahinoam. Brothers: Abinadab and Malkishua. Sisters: Merab and Michal. Son: Mephibosheth

Key verse
"How I weep for you, my brother Jonathan! Oh, how much I loved you! And your love for me was deep, deeper than the love of women!" (2 Samuel 1:26).

His story is told in 1 Samuel 13—31. He is also mentioned in 2 Samuel 9.

20:15 Jonathan asked David to keep a promise to treat his children kindly in the future. Years later David took great pains to fulfill this promise: he invited Jonathan's son Mephibosheth into his palace to live (2 Samuel 9).

and shoot three arrows to the side of the stone pile as though I were shooting at a target.
21 Then I will send a boy to bring the arrows back. If you hear me tell him, 'They're on
this side,' then you will know, as surely as the LORD lives, that all is well, and there is no
trouble. 22 But if I tell him, 'Go farther—the arrows are still ahead of you,' then it will
mean that you must leave immediately, for the LORD is sending you away. 23 And may **20:23**
the LORD make us keep our promises to each other, for he has witnessed them." Gen 31:49-50, 53
24 So David hid himself in the field, and when the new moon festival began, the king
sat down to eat. 25 He sat at his usual place against the wall, with Jonathan sitting opposite
him* and Abner beside him. But David's place was empty. 26 Saul didn't say anything **20:26**
about it that day, for he said to himself, "Something must have made David ceremonially Lev 7:20-21
unclean. Yes, that must be why he's not here." 27 But when David's place was empty 1 Sam 16:5
again the next day, Saul asked Jonathan, "Why hasn't the son of Jesse been here for
dinner either yesterday or today?"
28 Jonathan replied, "David earnestly asked me if he could go to Bethlehem. 29 He **20:28** 1 Sam 20:6
wanted to take part in a family sacrifice. His brother demanded that he be there, so I told
him he could go. That's why he isn't here."
30 Saul boiled with rage at Jonathan. "You stupid son of a whore!"* he swore at him.
"Do you think I don't know that you want David to be king in your place, shaming yourself
and your mother? 31 As long as that son of Jesse is alive, you'll never be king. Now go and
get him so I can kill him!"
32 "But what has he done?" Jonathan demanded. "Why should he be put to death?" **20:32**
33 Then Saul hurled his spear at Jonathan, intending to kill him. So at last Jonathan Matt 27:23
realized that his father was really determined to kill David. 34 Jonathan left the table in **20:33** 1 Sam 18:11;
fierce anger and refused to eat all that day, for he was crushed by his father's shameful 19:10-11
behavior toward David.
35 The next morning, as agreed, Jonathan went out into the field and took a young boy **20:36**
with him to gather his arrows. 36 "Start running," he told the boy, "so you can find the 1 Sam 20:20-21
arrows as I shoot them." So the boy ran, and Jonathan shot an arrow beyond him. 37 When
the boy had almost reached the arrow, Jonathan shouted, "The arrow is still ahead of you.
38 Hurry, hurry, don't wait." So the boy quickly gathered up the arrows and ran back to
his master. 39 He, of course, didn't understand what Jonathan meant; only Jonathan and
David knew. 40 Then Jonathan gave his bow and arrows to the boy and told him to take
them back to the city.
41 As soon as the boy was gone, David came out from where he had been hiding near
the stone pile.* Then David bowed to Jonathan with his face to the ground. Both of them
were in tears as they embraced each other and said good-bye, especially David. 42 At last **20:42** 1 Sam 20:14-15

20:25 As in Greek version; Hebrew reads *with Jonathan standing.* **20:30** Hebrew *You son of a perverse and rebellious woman.* **20:41** As in Greek version; Hebrew reads *near the south edge.*

20:26 Because the new moon festival involved making a sacrifice to God (Numbers 28:11-15), those attending the festival had to be ceremonially clean according to God's laws (Exodus 19:10; Leviticus 15; Numbers 19:11-22; also see the note on Joshua 3:5). This cleansing involved washing the body and clothes before approaching God to offer a sacrifice. The outward cleansing was a symbol of the inward desire for a purified heart and right relationship with God. Today our hearts are purified by faith in God through the death of Jesus Christ on our behalf (Hebrews 10:10, 22) and by reading and heeding God's Word (John 17:17).

20:31, 32 Saul was still trying to secure his throne for future generations even though he had already been told his dynasty would end with him (13:13, 14). Even worse, he was trying to do this by sinful human means because he knew he would get no help from God. Jonathan could have made a move to become the next king by killing his rival, but he bypassed this opportunity because of his love for both God and David (23:16-18).

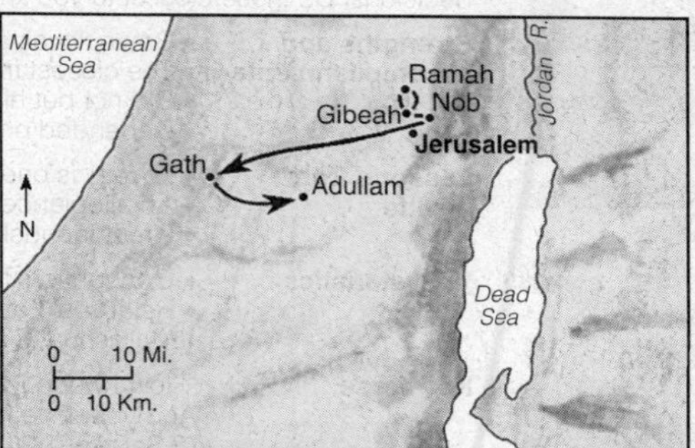

DAVID'S ESCAPE David learned of Saul's plans to kill him and fled to Samuel at Ramah. Returning to Gibeah to say good-bye to Jonathan, he then escaped to Nob, where he received food and a sword from the priest. He then fled to Gath in Philistine territory. When the Philistines became suspicious, he escaped to the cave of Adullam, where many men joined him.

Jonathan said to David, “Go in peace, for we have made a pact in the LORD’s name. We
have entrusted each other and each other’s children into the LORD’s hands forever.” Then
David left, and Jonathan returned to the city.

4. Saul pursues David

David Runs from Saul

21:1 1 Sam 16:4; 22:19 Neh 11:32
21 David went to the city of Nob to see Ahimelech the priest. Ahimelech trembled
when he saw him. “Why are you alone?” he asked. “Why is no one with you?”
2 “The king has sent me on a private matter,” David said. “He told me not to tell anyone
why I am here. I have told my men where to meet me later. 3 Now, what is there to eat?
Give me five loaves of bread or anything else you have.”
21:4 Exod 19:14-15 Lev 24:5-9 Matt 12:4
4 “We don’t have any regular bread,” the priest replied. “But there is the holy bread,
which I guess you can have if your young men have not slept with any women recently.”
5 “Don’t worry,” David replied. “I never allow my men to be with women when they
are on a campaign. And since they stay clean even on ordinary trips, how much more on
this one!”
21:6 Matt 12:3-4 Mark 2:25-28 Luke 6:3-4
6 So, since there was no other food available, the priest gave him the holy bread—the
Bread of the Presence that was placed before the LORD in the Tabernacle. It had just been
replaced that day with fresh bread.
21:7 1 Sam 22:9, 22 Ps 52:1
7 Now Doeg the Edomite, Saul’s chief herdsman, was there that day for ceremonial
purification.*
8 David asked Ahimelech, “Do you have a spear or sword? The king’s business was so
urgent that I didn’t even have time to grab a weapon!”
21:9 1 Sam 17:2, 50-51
9 “I only have the sword of Goliath the Philistine, whom you killed in the valley of
Elah,” the priest replied. “It is wrapped in a cloth behind the ephod. Take that if you want
it, for there is nothing else here.”
“There is nothing like it!” David replied. “Give it to me!”
21:10 1 Sam 27:2
10 So David escaped from Saul and went to King Achish of Gath. 11 But Achish’s
21:11 1 Sam 18:7; 29:5
officers weren’t happy about his being there. “Isn’t this David, the king of the land?”
they asked. “Isn’t he the one the people honor with dances, singing, ‘Saul has killed his
thousands, and David his ten thousands’?”
12 David heard these comments and was afraid of what King Achish might do to him.
21:13 Ps 34:title
13 So he pretended to be insane, scratching on doors and drooling down his beard.
14 Finally, King Achish said to his men, “Must you bring me a madman? 15 We already
have enough of them around here! Why should I let someone like this be my guest?”

21:7 Hebrew *was detained before the LORD.*

21:1ff This is the first time Ahimelech is mentioned. Either he was the Ahijah mentioned in 14:3, 18, or, more likely, he was Ahijah’s successor. In either case, Ahimelech had to go against the law to give the holy bread to David because the bread was supposed to be given only to the priests (Leviticus 24:5-9). But Ahimelech put David’s need and life ahead of religious ceremony and fed him the holy food. This upheld a higher law of love (Leviticus 19:18). Centuries later, Jesus would refer to this incident to show that God’s laws should not be applied without compassion. To do good and to save life is God’s greater law (Matthew 12:1-8; Luke 6:1-5).

21:2 David lied to protect himself from Saul (21:10). Some excuse this lie because a war was going on, and it is the duty of a good soldier to deceive the enemy. But nowhere is David’s lie condoned. In fact, the opposite is true because his lie led to the death of 85 priests (22:9-19). David’s small lie seemed harmless enough, but it led to tragedy. The Bible makes it very clear that lying is wrong (Leviticus 19:11). Lying, like every other sin, is serious in God’s sight and may lead to all sorts of harmful consequences. Don’t minimize or categorize sins. All sins must be avoided whether or not we can foresee their potential consequences.

21:5 The men’s bodies were ceremonially clean because they had not had sexual intercourse during this journey. Therefore, the priest allowed them to eat the holy bread.

21:6 Once a week on the Sabbath, a priest entered the Holy Place in the Tabernacle and placed 12 freshly baked loaves of bread on a small table. This bread, called the Bread of the Presence, symbolized God’s presence among his people as well as his loving care that met their physical needs. The bread that was replaced was to be eaten only by the priests on duty.

21:9 An ephod was a vest worn by the priest (see the note on 2:18 for a more detailed explanation). David didn’t know Goliath’s sword was there, probably because David was a young man when he killed the giant and he had spent much of his time at home.

21:10-15 Gath was one of the five major Philistine cities. Why did the Philistines accept their archenemy, David, into their camp? The Philistines may have been initially happy to accept a defector who was a high military leader. Any enemy of Saul would have been a friend of theirs. They could not have known that David had been anointed Israel’s next king (16:13). Soon, however, the Philistines became nervous about David’s presence. After all, he had slain thousands of their own people (18:7). David then protected himself by acting insane because it was the custom not to harm mentally unstable people.

David at the Cave of Adullam

22 So David left Gath and escaped to the cave of Adullam. Soon his brothers and 22:1-2
other relatives joined him there. 2Then others began coming—men who were in 2 Sam 23:13
trouble or in debt or who were just discontented—until David was the leader of about
four hundred men.

3Later David went to Mizpeh in Moab, where he asked the king, "Would you let my
father and mother live here under royal protection until I know what God is going to do
for me?" 4The king agreed, and David's parents stayed in Moab while David was living
in his stronghold.

5One day the prophet Gad told David, "Leave the stronghold and return to the land of 22:5
Judah." So David went to the forest of Hereth. 6The news of his arrival in Judah soon 2 Sam 24:11 1 Chr 21:9; 29:29
reached Saul. At the time, the king was sitting beneath a tamarisk tree on the hill at 2 Chr 29:25-26
Gibeah, holding his spear and surrounded by his officers. 22:6 Judg 4:5

7"Listen here, you men of Benjamin!" Saul shouted when he heard the news. "Has 1 Sam 14:2
David promised you fields and vineyards? Has he promised to make you commanders 22:7 1 Sam 8:12, 14
in his army? 8Is that why you have conspired against me? For not one of you has ever 1 Chr 12:16-18
told me that my own son is on David's side. You're not even sorry for me. Think of it! 22:8
My own son—encouraging David to try and kill me!" 1 Sam 23:21

9Then Doeg the Edomite, who was standing there with Saul's men, spoke up. "When 22:9 1 Sam 21:1, 7
I was at Nob," he said, "I saw David talking to Ahimelech the priest. 10Ahimelech 22:10
consulted the LORD to find out what David should do. Then he gave David food and the 1 Sam 21:6
sword of Goliath the Philistine."

The Slaughter of the Priests

11King Saul immediately sent for Ahimelech and all his family, who served as priests at
Nob. 12When they arrived, Saul shouted at him, "Listen to me, you son of Ahitub!"

"What is it, my king?" Ahimelech asked.

13"Why have you and David conspired against me?" Saul demanded. "Why did you
give him food and a sword? Why have you inquired of God for him? Why did you
encourage him to revolt against me and to come here and attack me?"

14"But sir," Ahimelech replied, "is there anyone among all your servants who is as 22:14 1 Sam 19:4-5;
faithful as David, your son-in-law? Why, he is the captain of your bodyguard and a 20:32
highly honored member of your household! 15This was certainly not the first time I had 22:15
consulted God for him! Please don't accuse me and my family in this matter, for I knew 2 Sam 5:19, 23
nothing of any plot against you."

16"You will surely die, Ahimelech, along with your entire family!" the king shouted.
17And he ordered his bodyguards, "Kill these priests of the LORD, for they are allies and 22:17 Exod 22:17
conspirators with David! They knew he was running away from me, but they didn't tell 1 Sam 14:45
me!" But Saul's men refused to kill the LORD's priests. 2 Kgs 10:25

22:2 Those in trouble, in debt, or discontented joined David, who himself was an outlaw. These people were outcasts themselves and could only improve their lot by helping David become king. David's control over this band of men again shows his resourcefulness and ability to lead and motivate others. It is difficult enough to build an army out of good men, but it takes even greater leadership to build one out of the kind of men that followed David. This group eventually formed the core of his military leadership and produced his "mightiest men" (2 Samuel 23:8ff).

22:7, 8 Apparently Saul's key officers were from the tribe of Benjamin, just as he was. David was from the neighboring tribe of Judah. Saul was appealing to tribal loyalty to maintain his hold on the throne.

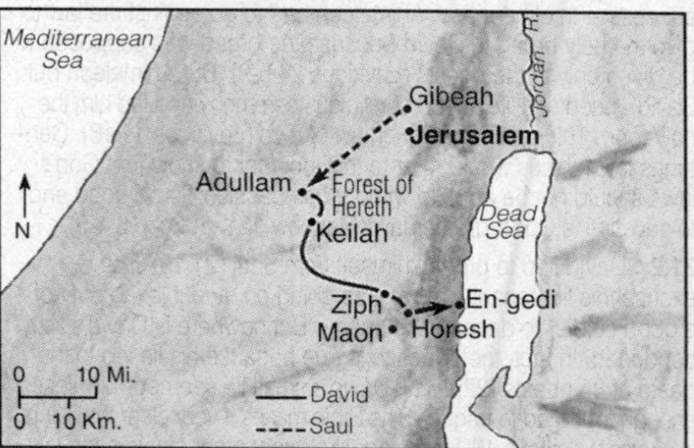

DAVID FLEES FROM SAUL David and his men attacked the Philistines at Keilah from the forest of Hereth. Saul came from Gibeah to attack David, but David escaped into the wilderness of Ziph. At Horesh he met Jonathan, who encouraged him. Then he fled into the wilderness of Maon and into the strongholds of En-gedi.

22:18 1 Sam 2:18, 30-33

18 Then the king said to Doeg, "You do it." So Doeg turned on them and killed them,
eighty-five priests in all, all still wearing their priestly tunics. 19 Then he went to Nob,
the city of the priests, and killed the priests' families—men and women, children and
babies, and all the cattle, donkeys, and sheep.

22:20 1 Sam 2:30-33; 23:6; 30:7; 1 Kgs 2:26-27
22:22 1 Sam 21:7

20 Only Abiathar, one of the sons of Ahimelech, escaped and fled to David. 21 When he
told David that Saul had killed the priests of the LORD, 22 David exclaimed, "I knew it!
When I saw Doeg there that day, I knew he would tell Saul. Now I have caused the death
of all your father's family. 23 Stay here with me, and I will protect you with my own life,
for the same person wants to kill us both."

David Protects the Town of Keilah

23:1 Josh 15:44; Neh 3:17
23:2 1 Sam 23:4, 12; 30:8; 2 Sam 5:19, 23
23:4 Josh 8:7; Judg 7:7
23:6 1 Sam 22:20

23 One day news came to David that the Philistines were at Keilah stealing grain
from the threshing floors. 2 David asked the LORD, "Should I go and attack them?"
"Yes, go and save Keilah," the LORD told him.
3 But David's men said, "We're afraid even here in Judah. We certainly don't want to
go to Keilah to fight the whole Philistine army!"
4 So David asked the LORD again, and again the LORD replied, "Go down to Keilah,
for I will help you conquer the Philistines."
5 So David and his men went to Keilah. They slaughtered the Philistines and took all
their livestock and rescued the people of Keilah. 6 Abiathar the priest went to Keilah with
David, taking the ephod with him to get answers for David from the LORD.
7 Saul soon learned that David was at Keilah. "Good!" he exclaimed. "We've got him
now! God has handed him over to me, for he has trapped himself in a walled city!"

23:9 1 Sam 22:20; 30:7

8 So Saul mobilized his entire army to march to Keilah and attack David and his men.
9 But David learned of Saul's plan and told Abiathar the priest to bring the ephod and ask
the LORD what he should do. 10 And David prayed, "O LORD, God of Israel, I have heard
that Saul is planning to come and destroy Keilah because I am here. 11 Will the men of
Keilah surrender me to him?* And will Saul actually come as I have heard? O LORD,
God of Israel, please tell me."

23:11 Some manuscripts lack the first sentence of 23:11.

22:18 Why would Saul have his own priests killed? Saul suspected a conspiracy among Jonathan, David, and the priests. His suspicion came from Doeg's report of seeing David talking to Ahimelech, the high priest, and receiving food and a weapon from him (22:9, 10). Saul's action showed his mental and emotional instability and how far he had strayed from God.

By destroying everything in Nob, Saul was placing the city under the ban (declaring it to be utterly destroyed) described in Deuteronomy 13:12-17, which was supposed to be used only in cases of idolatry and rebellion against God. But it was Saul, not the priests, who had rebelled against God.

22:18, 19 Why did God allow 85 innocent priests to be killed? Their deaths served to dramatize to the nation how a king could become an evil tyrant. Where were Saul's advisers? Where were the elders of Israel? Sometimes God allows evil to develop to teach us not to let evil systems flourish. Serving God is not a ticket to wealth, success, or health. God does not promise to protect good people from evil in this world, but he does promise that ultimately all evil will be abolished. Those who have remained faithful through their trials will experience great rewards in the age to come (Matthew 5:11, 12; Revelation 21:1-7; 22:1-21).

22:20 Abiathar escaped to David with an ephod (23:6), a priestly garment containing the Urim and Thummim, two objects David used to consult God. The ephod was probably the only symbol of the priesthood that survived Saul's raid and made it into David's camp (23:6). Saul destroyed Israel's priesthood, but when David became king, he installed Abiathar as the new high priest. Abiathar remained in that position during David's entire reign.

23:1 Threshing floors were open circular areas where the grain kernels were separated from their husks. (In order to separate the grain from the husk, farmers would toss their grain into the air. The wind would blow the husks away, leaving only the grain. This process is called *winnowing.*) By looting the threshing floors, the Philistines were robbing Keilah's citizens of all their food supplies. (For more on threshing, see the note on Ruth 3:2.)

23:2 Through the Urim and Thummim that Abiathar the priest brought (23:6), David sought the Lord's guidance *before* he took action. He listened to God's directions and then proceeded accordingly. Rather than trying to find God's will *after* the fact or having to ask God to undo the results of our hasty decisions, we should take time to discern God's will beforehand. We can hear him speak through the counsel of others, his Word, and the leading of his Spirit in our heart, as well as through circumstances.

23:6 An ephod was a sleeveless linen vest worn by priests. The high priest's ephod was brightly colored and had a breastplate with 12 gemstones, each stone representing one of the 12 tribes. The Urim and Thummim were kept in a pouch of the high priest's ephod. (See the note on 2:18 for a more detailed explanation of the ephod.)

23:7 When Saul heard that David was trapped in a walled city (one with gates and bars), he thought God was putting David at his mercy. Saul wanted to kill David so badly that he would have interpreted any sign as God's approval to move ahead with his plan. Had Saul known God better, he would have known what God wanted and would not have misread the situation as God's approval for murder.

Not every opportunity is sent from God. We may want something so much that we assume any opportunity to obtain it is of divine origin. As we see from Saul's case, however, this may not be true. An opportunity to do something against God's will can never be from God because God does not tempt us. When opportunities come your way, double-check your motives. Make sure you are following God's desires and not just your own.

And the LORD said, "He will come."
12 Again David asked, "Will these men of Keilah really betray me and my men to
Saul?"
And the LORD replied, "Yes, they will betray you."

David Hides in the Wilderness

13 So David and his men—about six hundred of them now—left Keilah and began 23:13 1 Sam 22:2; 25:13 2 Sam 15:20
roaming the countryside. Word soon reached Saul that David had escaped, so he didn't
go to Keilah after all. 14 David now stayed in the strongholds of the wilderness and in the 23:14 Josh 15:55 2 Chr 11:8
hill country of Ziph. Saul hunted him day after day, but God didn't let him be found.
15 One day near Horesh, David received the news that Saul was on the way to Ziph to
search for him and kill him. 16 Jonathan went to find David and encouraged him to stay
strong in his faith in God. 17 "Don't be afraid," Jonathan reassured him. "My father will 23:17 1 Sam 20:31; 24:20
never find you! You are going to be the king of Israel, and I will be next to you, as my
father is well aware." 18 So the two of them renewed their covenant of friendship before 23:18 1 Sam 18:3 2 Sam 9:2
the LORD. Then Jonathan returned home, while David stayed at Horesh.
19 But now the men of Ziph went to Saul in Gibeah and betrayed David to him. "We 23:19 1 Sam 26:1
know where David is hiding," they said. "He is in the strongholds of Horesh on the hill
of Hakilah, which is in the southern part of Jeshimon. 20 Come down whenever you're
ready, O king, and we will catch him and hand him over to you!"
21 "The LORD bless you," Saul said. "At last someone is concerned about me! 22 Go 23:21 1 Sam 22:8
and check again to be sure of where he is staying and who has seen him there, for I know
that he is very crafty. 23 Discover his hiding places, and come back with a more definite
report. Then I'll go with you. And if he is in the area at all, I'll track him down, even if
I have to search every hiding place in Judah!"
24 So the men of Ziph returned home ahead of Saul. Meanwhile, David and his men had 23:24 Josh 15:55
moved into the wilderness of Maon in the Arabah Valley south of Jeshimon. 25 When
David heard that Saul and his men were searching for him, he went even farther into the
wilderness to the great rock, and he remained there in the wilderness of Maon. But Saul
kept after him. 26 He and David were now on opposite sides of a mountain. Just as Saul 23:26 Ps 17:9
and his men began to close in on David and his men, 27 an urgent message reached
Saul that the Philistines were raiding Israel again. 28 So Saul quit the chase and returned to
fight the Philistines. Ever since that time, the place where David was camped has been 23:29 Josh 15:62 2 Chr 20:2
called the Rock of Escape.* 29 David then went to live in the strongholds of En-gedi.

David Spares Saul's Life

24 After Saul returned from fighting the Philistines, he was told that David had gone
into the wilderness of En-gedi. 2 So Saul chose three thousand special troops from 24:2 1 Sam 26:2
throughout Israel and went to search for David and his men near the rocks of the wild
goats. 3 At the place where the road passes some sheepfolds, Saul went into a cave to 24:3 Judg 3:24
relieve himself. But as it happened, David and his men were hiding in that very cave!
4 "Now's your opportunity!" David's men whispered to him. "Today is the day the 24:4 1 Sam 26:8, 11
LORD was talking about when he said, 'I will certainly put Saul into your power, to do
with as you wish.'" Then David crept forward and cut off a piece of Saul's robe.
5 But then David's conscience began bothering him because he had cut Saul's robe. 24:5 2 Sam 24:10
6 "The LORD knows I shouldn't have done it," he said to his men. "It is a serious thing 24:6 1 Sam 26:11

23:28 Hebrew *Sela-hammahlekoth.*

23:16-18 This may have been the last time David and Jonathan were together. As true friends they were more than just companions who enjoyed each other's company. They encouraged each other's faith in God and trusted each other with their deepest thoughts and closest confidences. These are the marks of true friendship.

24:3 David and his 600 men found the wilderness of En-gedi a good place to hide because of the many caves in the area. These caves were used by local people for housing and as tombs. For David's men they were places of refuge. These caves can still be seen today. Some are large enough to hold thousands of people.

24:4 Scripture does not record that God made any such statement to David or his men. The men were probably offering their own interpretation of some previous event such as David's anointing (16:13) or Jonathan's prediction that David would become king (23:17). When David's men saw Saul entering their cave, they wrongly assumed that this was an indication from God that they should act.

24:5, 6 David had great respect for Saul, in spite of the fact that Saul was trying to kill him. Although Saul was sinning and rebelling against God, David still respected the position he held as God's anointed king. David knew he would one day be king, and he also

24:7 1 Kgs 1:31
24:9 1 Sam 26:19
24:11 1 Sam 23:14, 23; 26:20
24:12 Gen 31:53; Judg 11:27
24:13 Matt 7:16-20
24:14 1 Sam 26:20
24:15 Ps 35:1
24:16 1 Sam 26:17
24:17 1 Sam 26:21; Matt 5:44
24:18 1 Sam 26:23
24:19 Ruth 2:12
24:20 1 Sam 13:14; 23:17
24:21 Gen 21:23; 1 Sam 20:14-17; 2 Sam 21:7
24:22 1 Sam 23:29

to attack the LORD's anointed one, for the LORD himself has chosen him." 7So David
sharply rebuked his men and did not let them kill Saul.
After Saul had left the cave and gone on his way, 8David came out and shouted after
him, "My lord the king!" And when Saul looked around, David bowed low before him.
9Then he shouted to Saul, "Why do you listen to the people who say I am trying to
harm you? 10This very day you can see with your own eyes it isn't true. For the LORD
placed you at my mercy back there in the cave, and some of my men told me to kill you,
but I spared you. For I said, 'I will never harm him—he is the LORD's anointed one.'
11Look, my father, at what I have in my hand. It is a piece of your robe! I cut it off, but
I didn't kill you. This proves that I am not trying to harm you and that I have not sinned
against you, even though you have been hunting for me to kill me. 12The LORD will
decide between us. Perhaps the LORD will punish you for what you are trying to do to
me, but I will never harm you. 13As that old proverb says, 'From evil people come evil
deeds.' So you can be sure I will never harm you. 14Who is the king of Israel trying to
catch anyway? Should he spend his time chasing one who is as worthless as a dead dog
or a flea? 15May the LORD judge which of us is right and punish the guilty one. He is my
advocate, and he will rescue me from your power!"
16Saul called back, "Is that really you, my son David?" Then he began to cry. 17And
he said to David, "You are a better man than I am, for you have repaid me good for evil.
18Yes, you have been wonderfully kind to me today, for when the LORD put me in a place
where you could have killed me, you didn't do it. 19Who else would let his enemy get
away when he had him in his power? May the LORD reward you well for the kindness
you have shown me today. 20And now I realize that you are surely going to be king, and
Israel will flourish under your rule. 21Now, swear to me by the LORD that when that
happens you will not kill my family and destroy my line of descendants!"
22So David promised, and Saul went home. But David and his men went back to their
stronghold.

LIFE OF DAVID VERSUS LIFE OF SAUL

Life of David	*Life of Saul*
David was God's kind of king (2 Samuel 7:8–16)	Saul was man's kind of king (1 Samuel 10:23, 24)
David was a man after God's heart (Acts 13:22)	Saul was a man after people's praise (1 Samuel 18:6–8)
David's kingship was eternal (through Jesus) (2 Samuel 7:29)	Saul's kingship was rejected (1 Samuel 15:23)
David was kind and benevolent (2 Samuel 9; 1 Chronicles 19:2)	Saul was cruel (1 Samuel 20:30–34; 22:11–19)
David was forgiving (1 Samuel 26)	Saul was unforgiving (1 Samuel 14:44; 18:9)
David repented (2 Samuel 12:13; 24:10)	When confronted, Saul lied (1 Samuel 15:10–31)
David was courageous (1 Samuel 17; 1 Chronicles 18)	Saul was fearful (1 Samuel 17:11; 18:12)
David was at peace with God (Psalms 4:8; 37:11)	Saul was separated from God (1 Samuel 16:14)

knew it was not right to strike down the man God had placed on the throne. If he assassinated Saul, he would be setting a precedent for his own opponents to remove him some day.

Romans 13:1-7 teaches that God has placed the government and its leaders in power. We may not know why, but, like David, we are to respect the positions and roles of those to whom God has given authority. There is one exception, however. Because God is our highest authority, we should not allow a leader to pressure us to violate God's law.

24:16-19 The means we use to accomplish a goal are just as important as the goal we are trying to accomplish. David's goal was to become king, so his men urged him to kill Saul when he had the chance. David's refusal was not an example of cowardice but of courage—the courage to stand against the group and do what he knew was right. Don't compromise your moral standards by giving in to group pressure or taking the easy way out.

24:21, 22 David kept his promise—he never took revenge on Saul's family or descendants. Most of Saul's sons were killed later, however, by the Philistines (31:2) and the Gibeonites (2 Samuel 21:1-14). David had promised to be kind to the descendants of Saul's son Jonathan (20:14, 15), and he kept this promise when he invited Mephibosheth to live in his palace (2 Samuel 9).

The Death of Samuel

25 Now Samuel died, and all Israel gathered for his funeral. They buried him near his home at Ramah.

Nabal Angers David

Then David moved down to the wilderness of Maon.* 2 There was a wealthy man from Maon who owned property near the village of Carmel. He had three thousand sheep and a thousand goats, and it was sheep-shearing time. 3 This man's name was Nabal, and his wife, Abigail, was a sensible and beautiful woman. But Nabal, a descendant of Caleb, was mean and dishonest in all his dealings.

4 When David heard that Nabal was shearing his sheep, 5 he sent ten of his young men to Carmel. He told them to deliver this message: 6 "Peace and prosperity to you, your family, and everything you own! 7 I am told that you are shearing your sheep and goats. While your shepherds stayed among us near Carmel, we never harmed them, and nothing was ever stolen from them. 8 Ask your own servants, and they will tell you this is true. So would you please be kind to us, since we have come at a time of celebration? Please give us any provisions you might have on hand." 9 David's young men gave this message to Nabal and waited for his reply.

10 "Who is this fellow David?" Nabal sneered. "Who does this son of Jesse think he is? There are lots of servants these days who run away from their masters. 11 Should I take my bread and water and the meat I've slaughtered for my shearers and give it to a band of outlaws who come from who knows where?" 12 So David's messengers returned and told him what Nabal had said.

13 "Get your swords!" was David's reply as he strapped on his own. Four hundred men started off with David, and two hundred remained behind to guard their equipment.

14 Meanwhile, one of Nabal's servants went to Abigail and told her, "David sent men from the wilderness to talk to our master, and he insulted them. 15 But David's men were very good to us, and we never suffered any harm from them. Nothing was stolen from us the whole time they were with us. 16 In fact, day and night they were like a wall of protection to us and the sheep. 17 You'd better think fast, for there is going to be trouble for our master and his whole family. He's so ill-tempered that no one can even talk to him!"

18 Abigail lost no time. She quickly gathered two hundred loaves of bread, two skins of wine, five dressed sheep, nearly a bushel* of roasted grain, one hundred raisin cakes, and two hundred fig cakes. She packed them on donkeys and said to her servants, 19 "Go on ahead. I will follow you shortly." But she didn't tell her husband what she was doing.

20 As she was riding her donkey into a mountain ravine, she saw David and his men coming toward her. 21 David had just been saying, "A lot of good it did to help this fellow. We protected his flocks in the wilderness, and nothing he owned was lost or stolen. But he has repaid me evil for good. 22 May God deal with me severely if even one man of his household is still alive tomorrow morning!"

Abigail Intercedes for Nabal

23 When Abigail saw David, she quickly got off her donkey and bowed low before him. 24 She fell at his feet and said, "I accept all blame in this matter, my lord. Please listen to what I have to say. 25 I know Nabal is a wicked and ill-tempered man; please don't pay any attention to him. He is a fool, just as his name suggests.* But I never even saw the messengers you sent.

25:1 Num 10:12; 13:3; Deut 34:8
25:2 Josh 15:55
25:3 Josh 15:13; 1 Sam 30:14
25:6 2 Chr 12:18
25:7 1 Sam 25:15
25:8 Neh 8:10
25:10 Judg 9:28
25:13 1 Sam 23:13
25:15 1 Sam 25:7
25:16 Exod 14:22
25:18 2 Sam 16:1; 1 Chr 12:40
25:19 Gen 32:16, 20
25:21 Ps 109:5
25:22 1 Sam 3:17; 1 Kgs 14:10

25:1 As in Greek version; Hebrew reads *Paran*. **25:18** Hebrew *5 seahs* [30 liters]. **25:25** The name *Nabal* means "fool."

25:1 Saul was king, but Samuel had been the nation's spiritual leader. As a young boy and an older man, Samuel was always careful to listen to (3:10; 9:14-17) and obey (3:21; 10:1, 2) the Lord. With Samuel gone, Israel would be without this spiritual leadership until David became king. (For more on Samuel, read his Profile in chapter 7.)

25:2-11 Nabal rudely refused David's request to feed his 600 men. If we sympathize with Nabal, it is because customs are so different today. First, simple hospitality demanded that travelers—any number of them—be fed. Nabal was very rich and could have easily afforded to meet David's request. Second, David wasn't asking for a handout. He and his men had been protecting Nabal's workforce, and part of Nabal's prosperity was due to David's vigilance. We should be generous with those who protect us and help us prosper, even if we are not obligated to do so by law or custom.

25:24 David was in no mood to listen when he set out for Nabal's property (25:13, 22). Nevertheless, he stopped to hear what Abigail had to say. If he had ignored her, he would have been guilty of taking vengeance into his own hands. No matter how right we think we are, we must always be careful to stop and listen to others. The extra time and effort can save us pain and trouble in the long run.

25:26 2 Sam 18:32
26“Now, my lord, as surely as the LORD lives and you yourself live, since the LORD
25:27 Gen 33:11
has kept you from murdering and taking vengeance into your own hands, let all your
1 Sam 30:26
enemies be as cursed as Nabal is. 27And here is a present I have brought to you and your
25:28
young men. 28Please forgive me if I have offended in any way. The LORD will surely
1 Sam 18:17; 22:11
reward you with a lasting dynasty, for you are fighting the LORD's battles. And you have
2 Sam 7:11, 16
not done wrong throughout your entire life.

25:29 1 Sam 20:1
29“Even when you are chased by those who seek your life, you are safe in the care
Jer 10:18
of the LORD your God, secure in his treasure pouch! But the lives of your enemies will
25:30 1 Sam 13:14
disappear like stones shot from a sling! 30When the LORD has done all he promised and
has made you leader of Israel, 31don't let this be a blemish on your record. Then you
won't have to carry on your conscience the staggering burden of needless bloodshed
and vengeance. And when the LORD has done these great things for you, please
remember me!”

25:32 Exod 18:10
32David replied to Abigail, “Praise the LORD, the God of Israel, who has sent you to
25:33 1 Sam 25:26
meet me today! 33Thank God for your good sense! Bless you for keeping me from
murdering the man and carrying out vengeance with my own hands. 34For I swear by
the LORD, the God of Israel, who has kept me from hurting you, that if you had not
hurried out to meet me, not one of Nabal's men would be alive tomorrow morning.”
25:35 Gen 19:21
35Then David accepted her gifts and told her, “Return home in peace. We will not kill
your husband.”

36When Abigail arrived home, she found that Nabal had thrown a big party and was
celebrating like a king. He was very drunk, so she didn't tell him anything about her
meeting with David until the next morning. 37The next morning when he was sober, she
told him what had happened. As a result he had a stroke,* and he lay on his bed paralyzed.
38About ten days later, the LORD struck him and he died.

25:37 Hebrew *his heart failed him.*

ABIGAIL

Some men don't deserve their wives. Abigail was probably the best woman Nabal could afford, and he got even more than he bargained for when he arranged to marry her. She was beautiful and more suited than he was to manage his wealth. But Nabal took this wife for granted.

In spite of his shortcomings, Nabal's household did what they could to keep him out of trouble. This loyalty must have been inspired by Abigail. Although her culture and her husband placed a low value on her, she made the most of her skills and opportunities. David was impressed with her abilities, and when Nabal died, he married her.

Abigail was an effective counselor to both of the men in her life, working hard to prevent them from making rash moves. By her swift action and skillful negotiation, she kept David from taking vengeance upon Nabal. She saw the big picture and left plenty of room for God to get involved.

Do you, like Abigail, look beyond the present crisis to the big picture? Do you use your skills to promote peace? Are you loyal without being blind? What challenge or responsibility do you face today that needs a person under God's control?

Strengths and accomplishments
- Sensible and capable
- A persuasive speaker, able to see beyond herself

Lessons from her life
- Life's tough situations can bring out the best in people
- One does not need a prestigious title to play a significant role

Vital statistics
- Where: Carmel
- Occupation: Homemaker
- Relatives: First husband: Nabal. Second husband: David. Son: Kileab (Daniel)
- Contemporaries: Saul, Michal, Ahinoam

Key verses
“David replied to Abigail, ‘Praise the LORD, the God of Israel, who has sent you to meet me today! Thank God for your good sense! Bless you for keeping me from murdering the man and carrying out vengeance with my own hands’ ” (1 Samuel 25:32, 33).

Her story is told in 1 Samuel 25—2 Samuel 2. She is also mentioned in 1 Chronicles 3:1.

25:36 Because Nabal was drunk, Abigail waited until morning to tell him what she had done. Abigail knew that Nabal, in his drunkenness, may not have understood her or may have reacted foolishly. When discussing difficult matters with people, especially family members, timing is everything. Ask God for wisdom to know the best time for confrontation and for bringing up touchy subjects.

David Marries Abigail

39 When David heard that Nabal was dead, he said, “Praise the LORD, who has paid 25:39
back Nabal and kept me from doing it myself. Nabal has received the punishment for 2 Sam 3:28-29
his sin.” Then David wasted no time in sending messengers to Abigail to ask her to
become his wife.
40 When the messengers arrived at Carmel, they told Abigail, “David has sent us to ask
if you will marry him.”
41 She bowed low to the ground and responded, “Yes, I am even willing to become a
slave to David's servants!” 42 Quickly getting ready, she took along five of her servant 25:42 Gen 24:61-67
girls as attendants, mounted her donkey, and went with David's messengers. And so she 25:43
became his wife. 43 David also married Ahinoam from Jezreel, making both of them his 1 Sam 27:2-3; 30:5
wives. 44 Saul, meanwhile, had given his daughter Michal, David's wife, to a man from 25:44 1 Sam 18:27
Gallim named Palti son of Laish. 2 Sam 3:14-15

David Spares Saul Again

26 Now some messengers from Ziph came back to Saul at Gibeah to tell him, 26:1
“David is hiding on the hill of Hakilah, which overlooks Jeshimon.” 2 So Saul 1 Sam 23:19 26:2
took three thousand of his best troops and went to hunt him down in the wilderness 1 Sam 13:2; 24:2
of Ziph. 3 Saul camped along the road beside the hill of Hakilah, near Jeshimon, where 26:3
David was hiding. But David knew of Saul's arrival, 4 so he sent out spies to watch 1 Sam 23:19
his movements.
5 David slipped over to Saul's camp one night to look around. Saul and his general, 26:5 1 Sam 14:50-51
Abner son of Ner, were sleeping inside a ring formed by the slumbering warriors. 6 “Will 26:6
anyone volunteer to go in there with me?” David asked Ahimelech the Hittite and 1 Chr 2:16
Abishai son of Zeruiah, Joab's brother.
“I'll go with you,” Abishai replied. 7 So David and Abishai went right into Saul's
camp and found him asleep, with his spear stuck in the ground beside his head. Abner
and the warriors were lying asleep around him. 8 “God has surely handed your enemy
over to you this time!” Abishai whispered to David. “Let me thrust that spear through 26:9
him. I'll pin him to the ground, and I won't need to strike twice!” 1 Sam 24:6
9 “No!” David said. “Don't kill him. For who can remain innocent after attacking the 2 Sam 1:14, 16
LORD's anointed one? 10 Surely the LORD will strike Saul down someday, or he will die 26:10 Deut 31:14
in battle or of old age. 11 But the LORD forbid that I should kill the one he has anointed! 1 Sam 25:38; 31:6
But I'll tell you what—we'll take his spear and his jug of water and then get out of here!” 26:12 Gen 2:21; 15:12
12 So David took the spear and jug of water that were near Saul's head. Then he and Isa 29:10

25:44 The story of David and Michal does not end here. (See 2 Samuel 3:12-16 for the next episode.)

26:5-9 Abishai showed great courage when he volunteered to go into Saul's camp with David. In the heat of emotion, Abishai wanted to kill Saul, but David restrained him. Although Abishai was only trying to protect David, his leader, David could not hurt Saul because of his respect for Saul's authority and position as God's anointed king. Abishai may have disagreed with David, but he also respected the one in authority over him. Eventually he became the greatest warrior in David's army (2 Samuel 23:18, 19).

26:8ff The strongest moral decisions are the ones we make before temptation strikes. David was determined to follow God, and this carried over into his decision not to murder God's anointed king, Saul, even when his men and the circumstances seemed to make it a feasible option. Who would you have been like in such a situation—David or David's men? To be like David and follow God, we must realize that we can't do wrong in order to execute justice. Even when our closest friends counsel us to do something that seems right, we must always put God's commands first.

26:9 Why did David refuse to kill Saul? God had placed Saul in power and had not yet removed him. David did not want to run ahead of God's timing. We are in similar situations when we have leaders in church or government who are unfaithful or incompetent. It may be easy for us to criticize or move against a leader oblivious to God's hidden purposes and timing. Determining not to do wrong, David left Saul's destiny in God's hands. While we should not ignore sin or sit back and allow evil leaders to carry on their wickedness, neither should we take actions that are against God's laws. We should work for righteousness while trusting God.

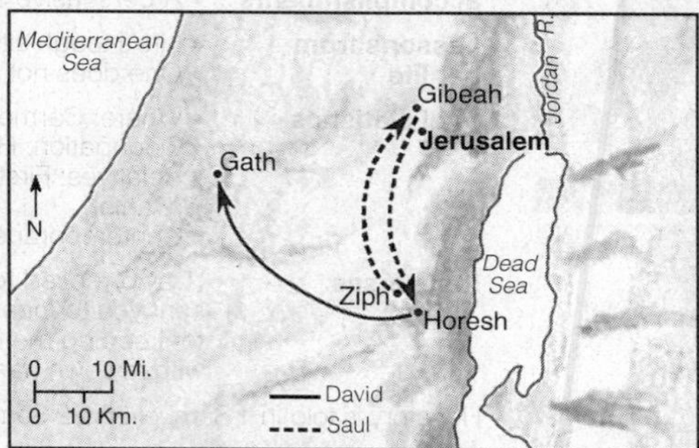

SAUL CHASES DAVID The men of Ziph again betrayed David to Saul, who was in his palace in Gibeah. Saul took 3,000 troops to the area around Horesh in order to find David. David could have killed Saul, but he refused. Saul, feeling foolish at David's kindness, returned to Gibeah, and David went to Gath.

Abishai got away without anyone seeing them or even waking up, because the LORD had
put Saul's men into a deep sleep. 13David climbed the hill opposite the camp until he was
at a safe distance. 14Then he shouted down to Abner and Saul, "Wake up, Abner!"
"Who is it?" Abner demanded.
15"Well, Abner, you're a great man, aren't you?" David taunted. "Where in all Israel
is there anyone as mighty? So why haven't you guarded your master the king when
someone came to kill him? 16This isn't good at all! I swear by the LORD that you and
your men deserve to die, because you failed to protect your master, the LORD's
anointed! Look around! Where are the king's spear and the jug of water that were
beside his head?"

26:17 1 Sam 24:16

17Saul recognized David's voice and called out, "Is that you, my son David?"
And David replied, "Yes, my lord the king. 18Why are you chasing me? What have I

26:19 1 Sam 24:9; 2 Sam 16:11

done? What is my crime? 19But now let my lord the king listen to his servant. If the LORD
has stirred you up against me, then let him accept my offering. But if this is simply a
human scheme, then may those involved be cursed by the LORD. For you have driven
me from my home, so I can no longer live among the LORD's people and worship as I

26:20 1 Sam 24:14

should. 20Must I die on foreign soil, far from the presence of the LORD? Why has the
king of Israel come out to search for a single flea? Why does he hunt me down like a
partridge on the mountains?"

26:21 1 Sam 15:24, 30; 24:17

21Then Saul confessed, "I have sinned. Come back home, my son, and I will no
longer try to harm you, for you valued my life today. I have been a fool and very, very
wrong."
22"Here is your spear, O king," David replied. "Let one of your young men come over

26:23 1 Sam 24:19

and get it. 23The LORD gives his own reward for doing good and for being loyal, and I
refused to kill you even when the LORD placed you in my power, for you are the LORD's

26:24 Ps 54:7

anointed one. 24Now may the LORD value my life, even as I have valued yours today.
May he rescue me from all my troubles."
25And Saul said to David, "Blessings on you, my son David. You will do heroic deeds
and be a great conqueror." Then David went away, and Saul returned home.

5. Saul's defeat and death

David among the Philistines

27 But David kept thinking to himself, "Someday Saul is going to get me. The best
thing for me to do is escape to the Philistines. Then Saul will stop hunting for me,
and I will finally be safe."

27:2 1 Sam 21:10; 2 Sam 2:2-3; 1 Kgs 2:39

2So David took his six hundred men and their families and went to live at Gath under
the protection of King Achish. 3David brought his two wives along with him—Ahinoam

27:3 1 Sam 25:43

of Jezreel and Abigail of Carmel, Nabal's widow. 4Word soon reached Saul that David
had fled to Gath, so he stopped hunting for him.

27:6 Josh 15:31; 19:5; Neh 11:28

5One day David said to Achish, "If it is all right with you, we would rather live in one
of the country towns instead of here in the royal city." 6So Achish gave him the town of

27:7 1 Sam 29:3

Ziklag (which still belongs to the kings of Judah to this day), 7and they lived there among
the Philistines for a year and four months.

26:15, 16 David could have killed Saul and Abner, but he would have disobeyed God and set into motion unknown consequences. Instead, he took a spear and water jug, showing that he could have killed the king but had not done it. And he made the point that he had great respect for both God and God's anointed king. When you need to make a point, look for creative, God-honoring ways to do so. It will have a more significant impact.

26:25 Saul had opportunities to kill David, but he never did. Why? First, every time David and Saul were face to face, David did something generous for Saul. The king did not want to respond to David's kindness with cruelty in front of all his men. Second, David had a large following in Israel. By killing him, Saul would risk his hold on the kingdom. Third, God had appointed David to become king of Israel and was protecting him.

27:4 Saul finally stopped pursuing David. His army was not strong enough to invade Philistine territory just to seek one man. Besides, the immediate threat to Saul's throne was gone while David was out of the country.

27:5-7 Gath was one of five principal cities in Philistia, and Achish was one of five co-rulers. David may have wanted to move out of this important city to avoid potential skirmishes or attacks upon his family. He may also have wanted to escape the close scrutiny of the Philistine officials. Achish let David move to Ziklag, where he lived until Saul's death (2 Samuel 2:1).

8 David and his men spent their time raiding the Geshurites, the Girzites, and the
Amalekites—people who had lived near Shur, along the road to Egypt, since ancient
times. 9 David didn't leave one person alive in the villages he attacked. He took the
sheep, cattle, donkeys, camels, and clothing before returning home to see King
Achish.
10 "Where did you make your raid today?" Achish would ask.
And David would reply, "Against the south of Judah, the Jerahmeelites, and the
Kenites."
11 No one was left alive to come to Gath and tell where he had really been. This
happened again and again while he was living among the Philistines. 12 Achish
believed David and thought to himself, "By now the people of Israel must hate him
bitterly. Now he will have to stay here and serve me forever!"

Saul Consults a Medium

28 About that time the Philistines mustered their armies for another war with
Israel. King Achish told David, "You and your men will be expected to join me
in battle."
2 "Very well!" David agreed. "Now you will see for yourself what we can do."
Then Achish told David, "I will make you my personal bodyguard for life."
3 Meanwhile, Samuel had died, and all Israel had mourned for him. He was buried in
Ramah, his hometown. And Saul had banned all mediums and psychics from the land
of Israel.
4 The Philistines set up their camp at Shunem, and Saul and the armies of Israel
camped at Gilboa. 5 When Saul saw the vast Philistine army, he became frantic with
fear. 6 He asked the LORD what he should do, but the LORD refused to answer him,
either by dreams or by sacred lots* or by the prophets. 7 Saul then said to his advisers,
"Find a woman who is a medium, so I can go and ask her what to do."
His advisers replied, "There is a medium at Endor."
8 So Saul disguised himself by wearing ordinary clothing instead of his royal robes.
Then he went to the woman's home at night, accompanied by two of his men.
"I have to talk to a man who has died," he said. "Will you call up his spirit for me?"
9 "Are you trying to get me killed?" the woman demanded. "You know that Saul
has expelled all the mediums and psychics from the land. Why are you setting a trap
for me?"

27:8 Exod 17:8; Josh 13:2-7, 13; 1 Sam 15:7-8
27:9 1 Sam 15:3
27:10 Judg 1:16; 4:11; 1 Sam 30:27-31; 1 Chr 2:9, 25
28:1-2 1 Sam 29:1-2
28:3 Lev 19:31; Deut 18:10; 1 Sam 15:23; 25:1
28:4 1 Sam 31:1, 3; 2 Sam 1:6
28:6 Exod 28:30
28:7 Ps 83:10; Acts 16:16
28:8 Isa 8:19
28:9 1 Sam 28:3

28:6 Hebrew *by Urim.*

27:8, 9 David probably conducted these guerrilla-style raids because these three tribes were known for their surprise attacks and cruel treatment of innocent people. These desert tribes were a danger, not just to the Philistines, but especially to the Israelites, the people David would one day lead.

27:10-12 Was David wrong in falsely reporting his activities to Achish? No doubt David was lying, but he may have felt his strategy was justified in a time of war against a pagan enemy. David knew he would one day be Israel's king. The Philistines were still his enemies, but this was an excellent place to hide from Saul. When Achish asked David to go into battle against Israel, David agreed, once again pretending loyalty to the Philistines (28:1ff). Whether he would have actually fought Saul's army we can't know, but we can be sure that his ultimate loyalty was to God and not to Achish or Saul.

28:1, 2 Achish's request put David in a difficult position. To refuse to help Achish fight the Israelites would give away David's loyalty to Israel and endanger the lives of his soldiers and family. But to fight his own people would hurt the very people he loved and would soon lead. David, however, never had to solve his dilemma because God protected him. The other Philistine leaders objected to his presence in battle; thus, he did not have to fight his countrymen.

28:3-8 It was Saul who had banned all mediums and psychics (those who consult with the dead) from Israel, but in desperation he turned to one for counsel. Although he had removed the sin of witchcraft from the land, he did not remove it from his heart. We may make a great show of denouncing sin, but if our hearts do not change, the sins will return. Knowing what is right and condemning what is wrong does not take the place of *doing* what is right.

28:5, 6 Casting lots meant using the Urim and Thummim to determine God's guidance in certain matters. (See the notes on 2:18 and 10:20 for further information on the use of the Urim and Thummim.)

28:5-7 Saul was overwhelmed at the sight of the Philistine army, and so he turned to the occult. Let life's difficulties and obstacles push you in God's direction and make you depend upon him. As we see from Saul's story, turning to anything or anyone else leads only to disaster.

28:7, 8 God had strictly forbidden the Israelites to have anything to do with divination, sorcery, witchcraft, mediums, spiritists, or anyone who consults the dead (Deuteronomy 18:9-14). In fact, sorcerers were to be put to death (Exodus 22:18). Occult practices were carried on in the name of pagan gods, and people turned to the occult for answers that God would not give.

Practitioners of the occult have Satan and demons as the source of their information; God does not reveal his will to them. Instead, he speaks through his own channels: the Bible, his Son Jesus Christ, and the Holy Spirit.

10 But Saul took an oath in the name of the LORD and promised, “As surely as the LORD
lives, nothing bad will happen to you for doing this.”
11 Finally, the woman said, “Well, whose spirit do you want me to call up?”
“Call up Samuel,” Saul replied.
12 When the woman saw Samuel, she screamed, “You’ve deceived me! You are Saul!”
13 “Don’t be afraid!” the king told her. “What do you see?”
“I see a god* coming up out of the earth,” she said.
28:14 1 Sam 15:27 14 “What does he look like?” Saul asked.
“He is an old man wrapped in a robe,” she replied. Saul realized that it was Samuel,
and he fell to the ground before him.
28:15 1 Sam 16:14 15 “Why have you disturbed me by calling me back?” Samuel asked.
“Because I am in deep trouble,” Saul replied. “The Philistines are at war with us, and
God has left me and won’t reply by prophets or dreams. So I have called for you to tell
me what to do.”
16 But Samuel replied, “Why ask me if the LORD has left you and has become your
28:17 1 Sam 15:28 enemy? 17 The LORD has done just as he said he would. He has taken the kingdom from
you and given it to your rival, David. 18 The LORD has done this because you did not obey
28:19 1 Sam 31:2, 6 his instructions concerning the Amalekites. 19 What’s more, the LORD will hand you and
the army of Israel over to the Philistines tomorrow, and you and your sons will be here
with me. The LORD will bring the entire army of Israel down in defeat.”
20 Saul fell full length on the ground, paralyzed with fright because of Samuel’s words.
28:21 Judg 12:3 He was also faint with hunger, for he had eaten nothing all day and all night. 21 When the
woman saw how distraught he was, she said, “Sir, I obeyed your command at the risk of
my life. 22 Now do what I say, and let me give you something to eat so you can regain
your strength for the trip back.”
28:23 2 Kgs 5:13 23 But Saul refused. The men who were with him also urged him to eat, so he finally
28:24 Gen 18:6-7 yielded and got up from the ground and sat on the couch. 24 The woman had been
fattening a calf, so she hurried out and killed it. She kneaded dough and baked
unleavened bread. 25 She brought the meal to Saul and his men, and they ate it. Then they
went out into the night.

The Philistines Reject David

29:1 Josh 12:18 1 Sam 4:1 2 Kgs 9:30 **29** The entire Philistine army now mobilized at Aphek, and the Israelites camped at
the spring in Jezreel. 2 As the Philistine rulers were leading out their troops in
29:2 1 Sam 28:2 groups of one hundred and one thousand, David and his men marched at the rear with
King Achish. 3 But the Philistine commanders demanded, “What are these Hebrews
29:3 1 Sam 27:1-7 1 Chr 12:19-20 doing here?”

28:13 Or *gods*.

THE BATTLE AT GILBOA
David pretended loyalty to Achish, but when war broke out with Israel, he was sent to Ziklag from Aphek. The Philistines defeated the Israelites at Mount Gilboa. David returned to Ziklag to find that the Amalekites had destroyed Ziklag. So David and his men pursued the Amalekite raiders and slaughtered them, recovering all that was taken.

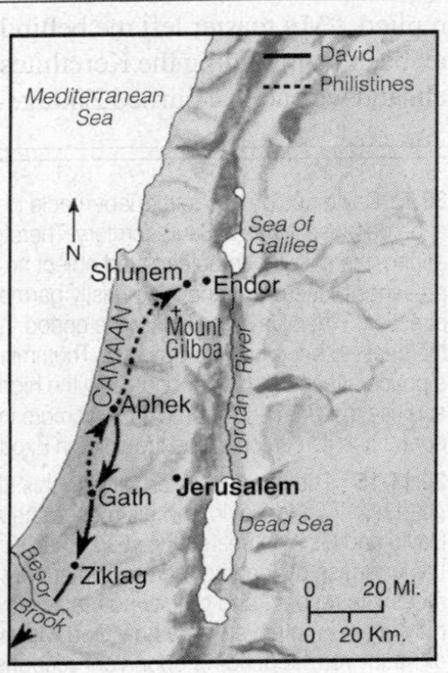

28:12 Did Samuel really come back from the dead at the medium’s call? The medium shrieked at the appearance of Samuel—she knew too well that the spirits she usually contacted were either contrived or satanic. Somehow Samuel’s appearance revealed to her that she was dealing with a power far greater than she had known. She did not call up Samuel by trickery or by the power of Satan; God brought Samuel back to give Saul a prediction regarding his fate, a message Saul already knew. This in no way justifies efforts to contact the dead or communicate with persons or spirits from the past. God is against all such practices (Galatians 5:19-21).

28:15 God did not answer Saul’s appeals because Saul had not followed God’s previous directions. Sometimes people wonder why their prayers are not answered. But if they don’t fulfill the responsibilities God has already given them, they should not be surprised when he does not give further guidance.

And Achish told them, "This is David, the man who ran away from King Saul of
Israel. He's been with me for years, and I've never found a single fault in him since he
defected to me."
4 But the Philistine commanders were angry. "Send him back!" they demanded. "He
can't go into the battle with us. What if he turns against us? Is there any better way
for him to reconcile himself with his master than by turning on us in battle? 5 Isn't this
the same David about whom the women of Israel sing in their dances, 'Saul has killed
his thousands, and David his ten thousands'?"
6 So Achish finally summoned David and his men. "I swear by the LORD," he told
them, "you are some of the finest men I've ever met. I think you should go with us, but
the other Philistine rulers won't hear of it. 7 Please don't upset them, but go back quietly."
8 "What have I done to deserve this treatment?" David demanded. "Why can't I fight
the enemies of my lord, the king?"
9 But Achish insisted, "As far as I'm concerned, you're as perfect as an angel of God.
But my commanders are afraid to have you with them in the battle. 10 Now get up early
in the morning, and leave with your men as soon as it gets light." 11 So David headed
back into the land of the Philistines, while the Philistine army went on to Jezreel.

David Destroys the Amalekites

30 Three days later, when David and his men arrived home at their town of Ziklag,
they found that the Amalekites had made a raid into the Negev and had burned
Ziklag to the ground. 2 They had carried off the women and children and everyone else
but without killing anyone. 3 When David and his men saw the ruins and realized what
had happened to their families, 4 they wept until they could weep no more. 5 David's
two wives, Ahinoam of Jezreel and Abigail, the widow of Nabal of Carmel, were
among those captured. 6 David was now in serious trouble because his men were very
bitter about losing their wives and children, and they began to talk of stoning him. But
David found strength in the LORD his God.
7 Then he said to Abiathar the priest, "Bring me the ephod!" So Abiathar brought it.
8 Then David asked the LORD, "Should I chase them? Will I catch them?"
And the LORD told him, "Yes, go after them. You will surely recover everything that
was taken from you!" 9 So David and his six hundred men set out, and they soon came to
Besor Brook. 10 But two hundred of the men were too exhausted to cross the brook, so
David continued the pursuit with his four hundred remaining troops. 11 Some of David's
troops found an Egyptian man in a field and brought him to David. They gave him some
bread to eat and some water to drink. 12 They also gave him part of a fig cake and two
clusters of raisins because he hadn't had anything to eat or drink for three days and nights.
It wasn't long before his strength returned.
13 "To whom do you belong, and where do you come from?" David asked him.
"I am an Egyptian—the slave of an Amalekite," he replied. "My master left me behind
three days ago because I was sick. 14 We were on our way back from raiding the Kerethites
in the Negev, the territory of Judah, and the land of Caleb, and we had just burned Ziklag."

29:4 1 Sam 19:21
29:5 1 Sam 18:7; 21:11
29:6 1 Sam 27:12; 29:3
29:9 2 Sam 14:17, 20; 19:27; 29:4
30:1 1 Sam 15:7; 27:6, 8
30:5 1 Sam 25:39, 42; 2 Sam 2:2
30:6 Exod 17:4; 1 Sam 23:16; Ps 18:2
30:7 1 Sam 23:9
30:8 1 Sam 23:2, 4
30:9 1 Sam 27:2
30:12 Judg 15:19
30:14 1 Sam 30:1; 2 Sam 1:1; 15:17-18; 1 Chr 18:17

29:4 The other Philistine commanders knew that David was the one who, as a young man, had killed their champion, Goliath (17:32-54), had killed hundreds of Philistine soldiers (18:27), and was the hero of Israelite victory songs (21:11). They were afraid that, in the heat of battle, David might turn against them. Although David was upset at this at first, God used the commanders' suspicion to keep him from having to fight against Saul and his countrymen.

30:6 Faced with the tragedy of losing their families, David's soldiers began to turn against him and even talked about killing him. Instead of planning a rescue, they looked for someone to blame. But David found his strength in God and began looking for a solution instead of a scapegoat. When facing problems, remember that it is useless to look for someone to blame or criticize. Instead, consider how you can help find a solution.

30:7 David couldn't go to the Tabernacle to ask the Lord for guidance because it was in Saul's territory. Therefore, he called for the ephod, the only Tabernacle-related object he possessed. In the presence of the priest and this priestly garment, he asked God for direction. When David called for the ephod, he was really asking the priest to bring him the Urim and Thummim, which were kept in a pouch attached to the ephod. Only the high priest could carry and use the Urim and Thummim. (For more information on the ephod and its contents, see the note on Exodus 39:1-21.)

30:11-15 The Amalekites cruelly left this slave to die, but God used him to lead David and his men to the Amalekite camp. David and his men treated the young man kindly, and he returned the kindness by leading them to the enemy. Treat those you meet with respect and dignity no matter how insignificant they may seem. You never know how God will use them to help you or haunt you, depending upon your response to them.

30:15 Deut 23:15
15“Will you lead me to them?” David asked.
The young man replied, “If you swear by God’s name that you will not kill me or give
me back to my master, then I will guide you to them.”
16So the Egyptian led them to the Amalekite encampment. When David and his
men arrived, the Amalekites were spread out across the fields, eating and drinking and
dancing with joy because of the vast amount of plunder they had taken from the
30:17 1 Sam 15:3
Philistines and the land of Judah. 17David and his men rushed in among them and
slaughtered them throughout that night and the entire next day until evening. None of
the Amalekites escaped except four hundred young men who fled on camels. 18David
got back everything the Amalekites had taken, and he rescued his two wives. 19Noth-
ing was missing: small or great, son or daughter, or anything else that had been taken.
David brought everything back. 20His troops rounded up all the flocks and herds and
drove them on ahead. “These all belong to David as his reward!” they said.
30:21 1 Sam 30:10-11
21When they reached Besor Brook and met the two hundred men who had been too
tired to go with them, David greeted them joyfully. 22But some troublemakers among
David’s men said, “They didn’t go with us, so they can’t have any of the plunder. Give
them their wives and children, and tell them to be gone.”
23But David said, “No, my brothers! Don’t be selfish with what the LORD has given
30:24 Num 31:27 Josh 22:7-8
us. He has kept us safe and helped us defeat the enemy. 24Do you think anyone will listen
to you when you talk like this? We share and share alike—those who go to battle and
30:26 Gen 33:11 1 Sam 25:27
those who guard the equipment.” 25From then on David made this a law for all of Israel,
and it is still followed.
26When he arrived at Ziklag, David sent part of the plunder to the leaders of Judah,
30:27 Josh 15:48
who were his friends. “Here is a present for you, taken from the LORD’s enemies,” he
30:28 Josh 13:16
said. 27The gifts were sent to the leaders of the following towns where David and his
men had been: Bethel, Ramoth-negev, Jattir, 28Aroer, Siphmoth, Eshtemoa, 29Racal,*
30:29 1 Sam 27:10
the towns of the Jerahmeelites, the towns of the Kenites, 30Hormah, Bor-ashan, Athach,
31Hebron, and all the other places they had visited.

The Death of Saul

31:1-13 //2 Sam 1:4-12 //1 Chr 10:1-12
31 Now the Philistines attacked Israel, forcing the Israelites to flee. Many were
31:1 1 Sam 28:4
slaughtered on the slopes of Mount Gilboa. 2The Philistines closed in on Saul and
his sons, and they killed three of his sons—Jonathan, Abinadab, and Malkishua. 3The
31:3 2 Sam 1:6, 10
fighting grew very fierce around Saul, and the Philistine archers caught up with him and
wounded him severely. 4Saul groaned to his armor bearer, “Take your sword and kill me
31:4 Judg 9:54
before these pagan Philistines run me through and humiliate me.” But his armor bearer

30:29 Greek version reads *Carmel.*

30:24, 25 David made a law that those who guarded the equipment were to be treated equally with those who fought in battle. Today it takes several people to provide the support services needed for every soldier in battle. In the church and other organizations, we need to treat those who provide support services equally with those on the front lines. Without bookkeepers, secretaries, trainers, and administrators, those with a public ministry would be unable to do their jobs. Are you on the front lines? Don’t forget those who are backing you up. Are you in the support group? Realize that your position, although it may be less glamorous or exciting, is vital to the work of the entire group.

31:3, 4 The Philistines had a well-earned reputation for torturing their captives. Saul no doubt knew about Samson’s fate (Judges 16:18-31) and did not want to risk physical mutilation or other abuse. When his armor bearer refused to kill him, he took his own life.

31:3, 4 Saul was tall, handsome, strong, rich, and powerful, but all of this was not enough to make him someone we should emulate. He was tall physically, but he was small in God’s eyes. He was handsome, but his sin made him ugly. He was strong, but his lack of faith made him weak. He was rich, but he was spiritually bankrupt. He could give orders to many, but he couldn’t command their respect or allegiance. Saul looked good on the outside, but he was decaying on the inside. A right relationship with God and a strong character are much more valuable than a good-looking exterior.

31:3, 4 Saul’s armor bearer faced a moral dilemma—should he carry out a sinful order from a man he was supposed to obey? He knew he should obey his master, the king, but he also knew murder was wrong. He decided not to kill Saul.

There is a difference between following an order with which you don’t agree and following one you know is wrong. It is never right or ethical to carry out a wrong act, no matter who gives the order or what the consequences for disobedience may be. What shapes your choice when you face a moral dilemma? Have the courage to follow God’s law above human commands.

31:4 Saul faced death the same way he faced life. He took matters into his own hands without thinking of God or asking for his guidance. If our lives aren’t the way we would like them to be now, we can’t assume that change will come more easily later. When nearing death, we will respond to God the same way we have been responding all along. Coming face to face with death only shows us what we are *really* like. How do you want to face death? Start facing life that way right now.

was afraid and would not do it. So Saul took his own sword and fell on it. 5 When his
armor bearer realized that Saul was dead, he fell on his own sword and died beside the
king. 6 So Saul, three of his sons, his armor bearer, and his troops all died together that
same day.
7 When the Israelites on the other side of the Jezreel Valley and beyond the Jordan saw
that their army had been routed and that Saul and his sons were dead, they abandoned
their towns and fled. So the Philistines moved in and occupied their towns.
8 The next day, when the Philistines went out to strip the dead, they found the bodies
of Saul and his three sons on Mount Gilboa. 9 So they cut off Saul's head and stripped
off his armor. Then they proclaimed the news of Saul's death in their pagan temple and
to the people throughout the land of Philistia. 10 They placed his armor in the temple of
the Ashtoreths, and they fastened his body to the wall of the city of Beth-shan.
11 But when the people of Jabesh-gilead heard what the Philistines had done to Saul,
12 their warriors traveled all night to Beth-shan and took the bodies of Saul and his sons
down from the wall. They brought them to Jabesh, where they burned the bodies. 13 Then
they took their remains and buried them beneath the tamarisk tree at Jabesh, and they
fasted for seven days.

31:9
Judg 16:23-24
2 Sam 1:20

31:10
Josh 17:11
Judg 2:12-14
1 Sam 7:3
2 Sam 21:12-14

31:11
1 Sam 11:1-13

31:12
2 Sam 2:4-7

31:10 To put Saul's armor in the Philistine temple gave credit to a pagan goddess for victory over Saul. Ashtoreth was a goddess of fertility and sex. Beth-shan was a town on the eastern slopes of Mount Gilboa, overlooking the Jordan Valley.

31:13 Consider the difference between the last judge of Israel and its first king. Saul, the king, was characterized by inconsistency, disobedience, and self-will. He did not have a heart for God. Samuel, the judge, was characterized by consistency, obedience, and a deep desire for God's will. He had a genuine desire for God.

When God called, Samuel said, "LORD, your servant is listening" (3:9). But when God, through Samuel, called Saul, Saul replied, "Why are you talking like this to me?" (9:21). Saul was dedicated to himself; Samuel was dedicated to God.

31:13 Saul's death was also the death of an ideal—Israel could no longer believe that having a king like the other nations would solve all their troubles. The real problem was not the form of government but the sinful king. Saul tried to please God by spurts of religiosity, but real spirituality takes a lifetime of consistent obedience.

Heroic spiritual lives are built by stacking days of obedience one on top of the other. Like a brick, each obedient act is small in itself, but in time the acts will pile up, and a huge wall of strong character will be built—a great defense against temptation. We should strive for consistent obedience each day.

KEY PLACES IN 2 SAMUEL

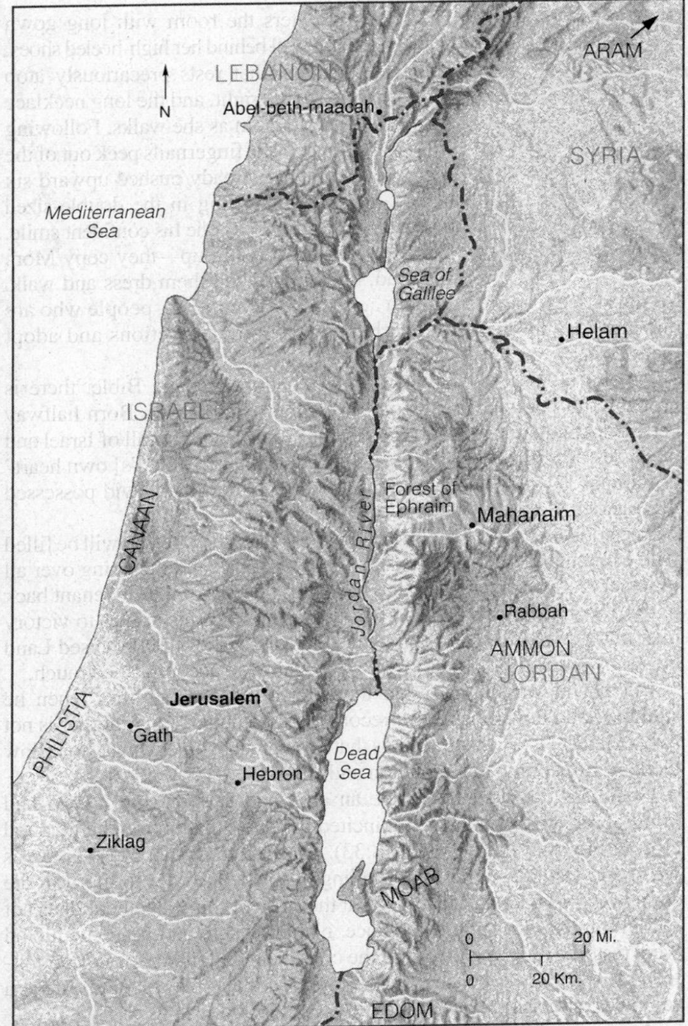

The broken lines (—·—) indicate modern boundaries.

1 Hebron After Saul's death, David moved from the Philistine city of Ziklag to Hebron, where the tribe of Judah crowned him king. But the rest of Israel's tribes backed Saul's son Ishbosheth and crowned him king at Mahanaim. As a result, there was war between Judah and the rest of the tribes of Israel until Ishbosheth was assassinated. Then all of Israel pledged loyalty to David as their king (1:1—5:5).

2 Jerusalem One of David's first battles as king occurred at the city of Zion (Jerusalem). David and his troops took the city by surprise, and it became his capital. It was here that David brought the Ark of the Covenant and made a special agreement with God (5:6—7:29).

3 Gath The Philistines were Israel's constant enemy, though they did give David sanctuary when he was hiding from Saul (1 Samuel 27). But when Saul died and David became king, the Philistines planned to defeat him. In a battle near Jerusalem, David and his troops routed the Philistines (5:17–25), but they were not completely subdued until David conquered their largest city (8:1).

4 Moab During the time of the judges, Moab controlled many cities in Israel and demanded heavy taxes (Judges 3:12–30). David conquered Moab and, in turn, levied tribute from them (8:2).

5 Edom Though the Edomites and the Israelites traced their ancestry back to the same man, Isaac (Genesis 25:19–23), they were long-standing enemies. David defeated Edom and forced them to pay tribute also (8:14).

6 Rabbah The Ammonites insulted David's delegation and turned a peacemaking mission into angry warfare. The Ammonites called troops from Aram, but David defeated this alliance first at Helam, then at Rabbah, the capital city (10:1—12:31).

7 Mahanaim David had victory in the field, but problems at home. His son Absalom incited a rebellion and crowned himself king at Hebron. David and his men fled to Mahanaim. Acting on bad advice, Absalom mobilized his army to fight David (13:1—17:29).

8 Forest of Ephraim The armies of Absalom and David fought in the Forest of Ephraim. Absalom's hair got caught in a tree, and Joab, David's general, found and killed him. With Absalom's death the rebellion died, and David was welcomed back to Jerusalem (18:1—19:43).

9 Abel-beth-maacah A man named Sheba also incited a rebellion against David. He fled to Abel-beth-maacah, but Joab and a small troop besieged the city. The citizens of Abel-beth-maacah killed Sheba themselves (20:1–26). David's victories laid the foundation for the peaceful reign of his son Solomon.

2 SAMUEL

Judges begin to rule 1375 B.C. (1220 B.C.)

Saul becomes king 1050 (1045)

VITAL STATISTICS

PURPOSES:
(1) to record the history of David's reign;
(2) to demonstrate effective leadership under God;
(3) to reveal that one person can make a difference;
(4) to show the personal qualities that please God;
(5) to depict David as an ideal leader of an imperfect kingdom, and to foreshadow Christ, who will be the ideal leader of a new and perfect kingdom (chapter 7)

AUTHOR:
Unknown. Some have suggested that Nathan's son Zabud may have been the author (1 Kings 4:5). The book also includes the writings of Nathan and Gad (1 Chronicles 29:29).

DATE WRITTEN:
930 B.C.; written soon after David's reign, 1050–970 B.C.

SETTING:
The land of Israel under David's rule

KEY VERSE:
"And David realized that the LORD had made him king over Israel and had made his kingdom great for the sake of his people Israel" (5:12).

KEY PEOPLE:
David, Joab, Bathsheba, Nathan, Absalom

SPECIAL FEATURES:
This book was named after the prophet who anointed David and guided him in living for God.

THE CHILD enters the room with long gown flowing, trailing well behind her high-heeled shoes. The wide-brimmed hat rests precariously atop her head, tilted to the right, and the long necklace swings like a pendulum as she walks. Following close is the "man." His fingernails peek out of the coat sleeves that are already pushed upward six inches. With feet shuffling in the double-sized boots, his unsteady steps belie his confident smile. Children at play, dressing up—they copy Mom and Dad, having watched them dress and walk. Models . . . everyone has them . . . people we emulate, people who are our ideals. Unconsciously, perhaps, we copy their actions and adopt their ideas.

Among all the godly role models mentioned in the Bible, there is probably no one who stands out more than King David. Born halfway between Abraham and Jesus, he became God's leader for all of Israel and the ancestor of the Messiah. David was "a man after [God's] own heart" (1 Samuel 13:14). What are the personal qualities that David possessed that pleased God?

The book of 2 Samuel tells David's story. As you read, you will be filled with excitement as he is crowned king over Judah and then king over all of Israel (5:1–5), praising God as he brings the Ark of the Covenant back to the Tabernacle (6:1–23) and exulting as he leads his armies to victory over all their enemies and completes the conquest of the Promised Land begun by Joshua (8—10). David was a man who accomplished much.

But David was human, and there were those dark times when he stumbled and fell into sin. The record of lust, adultery, and murder is not easy to read (11—13) and reveals that even great people who try to follow God are susceptible to temptation and sin.

Godliness does not guarantee an easy and carefree life. David had family problems—his own son incited the entire nation to rebellion and crowned himself king (14:1—18:33). And greatness can cause pride, as we see in David's sinful act of taking a census in order to glory in the strength of his nation (24:1–25). But the story of this fallen hero does not end in tragedy. Through repentance, his fellowship and peace with God were restored, but he had to face the consequences of the sins he committed (12—20). These consequences stayed with him the rest of his life as a reminder of his sinful deeds and his need for God.

As you read 2 Samuel, look for David's godlike characteristics—his faithfulness, patience, courage, generosity, commitment, honesty—as well as other God-honoring characteristics, such as modesty and penitence. Valuable lessons can be learned from his sins and from his repentance. You, like David, can become a person after God's own heart.

Saul dies; David is king over Judah 1010	David becomes king over all Israel 1003	David and Bathsheba sin 997(?)	Solomon born 991	David's census 980(?)	David dies; Solomon made king 970	The kingdom is divided 930

THE BLUEPRINT

A. DAVID'S SUCCESSES (1:1—10:19)
1. David becomes king over Judah
2. David becomes king over Israel
3. David conquers the surrounding nations

David took the fractured kingdom that Saul had left behind and built a strong, united power. Forty years later, David would turn this kingdom over to his son Solomon. David had a heart for God. He was a king who governed God's people by God's principles, and God blessed him greatly. We may not have David's earthly success, but following God is, ultimately, the most successful decision we can make.

B. DAVID'S STRUGGLES (11:1—24:25)
1. David and Bathsheba
2. Turmoil in David's family
3. National rebellion against David
4. The later years of David's rule

David sinned with Bathsheba and then tried to cover his sin by having her husband killed. Although he was forgiven for his sin, the consequences remained—he experienced trouble and distress, both with his family and with the nation. God is always ready to forgive, but we must live with the consequences of our actions. Covering up our sin will only multiply sin's painful consequences.

MEGATHEMES

THEME	EXPLANATION	IMPORTANCE
Kingdom Growth	Under David's leadership, Israel's kingdom grew rapidly. With the growth came many changes: from tribal independence to centralized government, from the leadership of judges to a monarchy, from decentralized worship to worship at Jerusalem.	No matter how much growth or how many changes we experience, God provides for us if we love him and highly regard his principles. God's work done in God's way never lacks God's supply of wisdom and energy.
Personal Greatness	David's popularity and influence increased greatly. He realized that the Lord was behind his success because he wanted to pour out his kindness on Israel. David regarded God's interests as more important than his own.	God graciously pours out his favor on us because of what Christ has done. God does not regard personal greatness as something to be used selfishly, but as an instrument to carry out his work among his people. The greatness we should desire is to love others as God loves us.
Justice	King David showed justice, mercy, and fairness to Saul's family, enemies, rebels, allies, and close friends alike. His just rule was grounded in his faith in and knowledge of God. God's perfect moral nature is the standard for justice.	Although David was the most just of all Israel's kings, he was still imperfect. His use of justice offered hope for a heavenly, ideal kingdom. This hope will never be satisfied in the heart of man until Christ, the Son of David, comes to rule in perfect justice forever.
Consequences of Sin	David abandoned his purpose as leader and king in time of war. His desire for prosperity and ease led him from triumph to trouble. Because David committed adultery with Bathsheba, he experienced consequences of his sin that destroyed both his family and the nation.	Temptation quite often comes when a person's life is aimless. We sometimes think that sinful pleasures and freedom from God's restraint will bring us a feeling of vitality; but sin creates a cycle of suffering that is not worth the fleeting pleasures it offers.
Feet of Clay	David not only sinned with Bathsheba, he murdered an innocent man. He neglected to discipline his sons when they got involved in rape and murder. This great hero showed a lack of character in some of his most important personal decisions. The man of iron had feet of clay.	Sin should never be considered as a mere weakness or flaw. Sin is fatal and must be eradicated from our lives. David's life teaches us to have compassion for all people, including those whose sinful nature leads them into sinful acts. It serves as a warning to us not to excuse sin in our own lives, even in times of success.

A. DAVID'S SUCCESSES (1:1—10:19)

After years of running from Saul, David was finally crowned king over the tribe of Judah. The rest of Israel, however, followed Ishbosheth, Saul's son. David did not attempt to take the tribes by force but placed the matter in God's hands. After a few years Ishbosheth was assassinated, and the rest of the tribes finally put their support behind David. David moved the capital to Jerusalem, defeated the surrounding nations, and even showed kindness to Saul's family. We may not understand why God seems to move slowly at times, but we must trust him and be faithful with what he has given us.

1. David becomes king over Judah

David Learns of Saul's Death

1 After the death of Saul, David returned from his victory over the Amalekites and
spent two days in Ziklag. 2 On the third day after David's return, a man arrived from
the Israelite battlefront. He had torn his clothes and put dirt on his head to show that he
was in mourning. He fell to the ground before David in deep respect.
3 "Where have you come from?" David asked.
"I escaped from the Israelite camp," the man replied.
4 "What happened?" David demanded. "Tell me how the battle went."
The man replied, "Our entire army fled. Many men are dead and wounded on the
battlefield, and Saul and his son Jonathan have been killed."
5 "How do you know that Saul and Jonathan are dead?" David demanded.
6 The young man answered, "I happened to be on Mount Gilboa. I saw Saul there
leaning on his spear with the enemy chariots closing in on him. 7 When he turned and
saw me, he cried out for me to come to him. 'How can I help?' I asked him. 8 And he said
to me, 'Who are you?' I replied, 'I am an Amalekite.' 9 Then he begged me, 'Come over
here and put me out of my misery, for I am in terrible pain and want to die.'
10 "So I killed him," the Amalekite told David, "for I knew he couldn't live. Then I
took his crown and one of his bracelets so I could bring them to you, my lord."
11 David and his men tore their clothes in sorrow when they heard the news. 12 They
mourned and wept and fasted all day for Saul and his son Jonathan, and for the LORD's
army and the nation of Israel, because so many had died that day. 13 Then David said to
the young man who had brought the news, "Where are you from?"
And he replied, "I am a foreigner, an Amalekite, who lives in your land."
14 "Were you not afraid to kill the LORD's anointed one?" David asked. 15 Then David

1:1 1 Sam 30:1, 17
1:2 1 Sam 4:12
1:4-12 //1 Sam 31:1-13 //1 Chr 10:1-12
1:4 1 Sam 4:16
1:6 1 Sam 28:4; 31:1-6
1:8 1 Sam 15:2-3; 30:1, 13, 17
1:11 Gen 37:29, 34
1:14 1 Sam 26:9-11
1:15 2 Sam 4:10, 12

1:1 David was a man who had great faith in God. He waited for God to fulfill his promises. The book of 1 Samuel tells of David's struggles as he waited to become king of Israel (Samuel had anointed David as king of Israel many years earlier). King Saul became jealous of David because the people were praising him for his accomplishments. Eventually, Saul's jealousy became so intense that he tried to kill David. As a result, David had to run and hide. For many years David hid from Saul in enemy territory and in the barren wilderness south and east of Jerusalem. David may have wondered when God's promise that he would be king would come true, but his struggles prepared him for the great responsibilities he would later face. The book of 2 Samuel tells how David was finally rewarded for his patience and consistent faith in God.

1:1 When Saul died, David and his men were still living in Ziklag, a Philistine city. Because Saul had driven him out of Israel, David had pretended to be loyal to Achish, a Philistine ruler (1 Samuel 27). There he was safe from Saul.

1:11, 12 "They mourned and wept and fasted all day." David and his men were visibly shaken over Saul's death. Their actions showed their genuine sorrow over the loss of their king, their friend Jonathan, and the other soldiers of Israel who died that day. They were not ashamed to grieve. Today, some people consider expressing emotions to be a sign of weakness. Those who wish to appear strong try to hide their feelings. But expressing our grief can help us deal with our intense sorrow when a loved one dies.

1:13 The man identified himself as an Amalekite from Saul's camp (1:2). He may have been an Amalekite under Israelite jurisdiction, but more likely he was a battlefield scavenger. Obviously the man was lying both about his identity and about what happened on the battlefield. (Compare his story with the account in 1 Samuel 31:3, 4.) Because he had Saul's crown with him, something the Philistines wouldn't have left behind, we can infer that he found Saul dead on the battlefield before the Philistines arrived (1 Samuel 31:8).

A life of deceit leads to disaster. The man lied to gain some personal reward for killing David's rival, but he misread David's character. If David had rewarded him for murdering the king, David would have shared his guilt. Instead, David had the messenger killed. Lying can bring disaster upon the liar, even for something he or she has not done.

1:13 The Amalekites were a fierce nomadic tribe that frequently conducted surprise raids on Canaanite villages. They had been Israel's enemies since Moses' time. David had just destroyed an Amalekite band of raiders who had burned his city and kidnapped its women and children (1 Samuel 30:1-20). This man was probably unaware of David's recent confrontations with Amalekites, or he may not have come. Instead, he incurred David's wrath by posing as an enemy of Israel and claiming to have killed God's chosen king.

1:15, 16 Why did David consider it a crime to kill the king, even though Saul was his enemy? David believed that God anointed Saul, and only God could remove him from office. If it became casual or commonplace to assassinate the king, the whole society would become chaotic. It was God's job, not David's, to judge Saul's sins (Leviticus 19:18). We must realize that God has placed rulers in authority over us, and we should respect their positions (Romans 13:1-7).

said to one of his men, "Kill him!" So the man thrust his sword into the Amalekite and
1:16 1 Sam 26:9 2 Sam 1:10 killed him. 16 "You die self-condemned," David said, "for you yourself confessed that
you killed the LORD's anointed one."

David's Song for Saul and Jonathan

1:17 2 Chr 35:27 17 Then David composed a funeral song for Saul and Jonathan. 18 Later he commanded
1:18 Josh 10:13 that it be taught to all the people of Judah. It is known as the Song of the Bow, and it is
recorded in *The Book of Jashar.**

1:19 2 Sam 3:38 19 Your pride and joy, O Israel, lies dead on the hills!
How the mighty heroes have fallen!
1:20 1 Sam 8:16; 31:8 Mic 1:10 20 Don't announce the news in Gath,
or the Philistines will rejoice.
Don't proclaim it in the streets of Ashkelon,
or the pagans will laugh in triumph.

1:21 1 Sam 31:1 Ezek 31:15 21 O mountains of Gilboa,
let there be no dew or rain upon you or your slopes.
For there the shield of the mighty was defiled;
the shield of Saul will no longer be anointed with oil.
22 Both Saul and Jonathan killed their strongest foes;
they did not return from battle empty-handed.

1:23 Judg 14:18 23 How beloved and gracious were Saul and Jonathan!
They were together in life and in death.
They were swifter than eagles;
they were stronger than lions.

24 O women of Israel, weep for Saul,
for he dressed you in fine clothing and gold ornaments.

1:25 2 Sam 1:19 25 How the mighty heroes have fallen in battle!
Jonathan lies dead upon the hills.
1:26 1 Sam 18:1 26 How I weep for you, my brother Jonathan!
Oh, how much I loved you!

1:18 Or *The Book of the Upright.*

CHARACTERS IN THE DRAMA
It can be confusing to keep track of all the characters introduced in the first few chapters of 2 Samuel. Here is some help.

Character	*Relation*	*Position*	*Whose Side?*
Joab	Son of Zeruiah, David's half sister	One of David's military leaders and, later, commander in chief	David's
Abner	Saul's cousin	Saul's commander in chief	Saul and Ishbosheth's, but made overtures to David
Abishai	Joab's brother	High officer in David's army—chief of "the Three"	Joab and David's
Asahel	Joab and Abishai's brother	High officer—one of David's 30 select warriors ("mighty men")	Joab and David's
Ishbosheth	Saul's son	Saul and Abner's selection as king	Saul's

1:17, 18 David was a talented musician. He played the harp (1 Samuel 16:23), he brought music into the worship services of the Temple (1 Chronicles 25), and he wrote many of the psalms. Here we are told that he wrote a lament in memory of Saul and his son Jonathan, David's closest friend. Music played an important role in Israel's history. (For other famous songs in the Bible, see the chart in Exodus 15.)

1:17-27 Saul had caused much trouble for David, but when he died, David composed a lament for the king and his son. David had every reason to hate Saul, but he chose not to. Instead, he chose to look at the good Saul had done and to ignore the times when Saul had attacked him. It takes courage to lay aside hatred and hurt and to respect the positive side of another person, especially an enemy.

1:26 By saying that Jonathan's love was "deeper than the love of women," David was not implying that he had a sexual relationship with Jonathan. Homosexual acts were absolutely forbidden in Israel. Leviticus 18:22 calls homosexuality "detestable," and Leviticus 20:13 decrees the death penalty for those who practice homosexuality. David was simply restating the deep brotherhood and faithful friendship he had with Jonathan. (For more on their friendship, see the note on 1 Samuel 18:1-4.)

And your love for me was deep,
deeper than the love of women!

27 How the mighty heroes have fallen!
Stripped of their weapons, they lie dead.

David Anointed King of Judah

2 After this, David asked the LORD, "Should I move back to Judah?"
And the LORD replied, "Yes."
Then David asked, "Which town should I go to?"
And the LORD replied, "Hebron."
2David's wives were Ahinoam from Jezreel and Abigail, the widow of Nabal from
Carmel. So David and his wives 3and his men and their families all moved to Judah, and
they settled near the town of Hebron. 4Then Judah's leaders came to David and crowned
him king over the tribe of Judah.
When David heard that the men of Jabesh-gilead had buried Saul, 5he sent them this
message: "May the LORD bless you for being so loyal to your king and giving him a
decent burial. 6May the LORD be loyal to you in return and reward you with his unfailing
love! And I, too, will reward you for what you have done. 7And now that Saul is dead, I
ask you to be my strong and loyal subjects like the people of Judah, who have anointed
me as their new king."

Ishbosheth Crowned King of Israel

8But Abner son of Ner, the commander of Saul's army, had already gone to Mahanaim
with Saul's son Ishbosheth.* 9There he proclaimed Ishbosheth king over Gilead, Jezreel,
Ephraim, Benjamin, the land of the Ashurites, and all the rest of Israel. 10Ishbosheth was
forty years old when he became king, and he ruled from Mahanaim for two years.
Meanwhile, the tribe of Judah remained loyal to David. 11David made Hebron his
capital, and he ruled as king of Judah for seven and a half years.

2:1 Josh 14:13-14; 1 Sam 23:2, 4, 9-12
2:2 1 Sam 25:39, 42-43
2:3 1 Chr 12:1
2:4 1 Sam 16:13; 31:11-13; 2 Sam 5:3-5
2:5 1 Sam 23:21; 24:19
2:6 Exod 34:5-6
2:8 1 Sam 14:50; 2 Sam 17:24

2:8 Also known as *Eshbaal.*

2:1 Although David knew he would become king (1 Samuel 16:13; 23:17; 24:20), and although the time seemed right now that Saul was dead, David still asked God if he should move back to Judah, the home territory of his tribe. Before moving ahead with what seems obvious, first bring the matter to God, who alone knows the best timing.

JOAB VERSUS ABNER
David was crowned king of Judah in Hebron; Ishbosheth was crowned king of Israel in Mahanaim. The opposing armies of Judah and Israel met at Gibeon for battle—Judah under Joab, Israel under Abner.

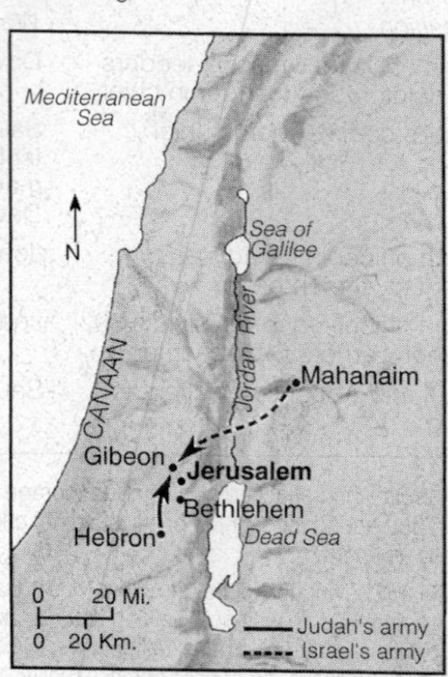

2:1 God told David to return to Hebron, where he would soon be crowned king of Judah. David made Hebron his capital because (1) it was the largest city in Judah at that time; (2) it was secure against attack; (3) it was located near the center of Judah's territory, an ideal location for a capital city; (4) many key trade routes converged at Hebron, making it difficult for supply lines to be cut off in wartime.

2:4 The men of Judah publicly anointed David as their king. David had been anointed king by Samuel years earlier (1 Samuel 16:13), but that ceremony had taken place in private. This one was like inaugurating a public official who has already been elected to office. The rest of Israel, however, didn't accept David's kingship for seven and a half years (2:10, 11).

2:4-7 David sent a message thanking the men of Jabesh-gilead who had risked their lives to bury Saul's body (1 Samuel 31:11-13). Saul had rescued Jabesh-gilead from certain defeat when Nahash the Ammonite surrounded the city (1 Samuel 11), so these citizens showed their gratitude and kindness. In his message, he also suggested that they follow Judah's lead and acknowledge him as their king. Jabesh-gilead was to the north in the land of Gilead, and David was seeking to gain support among the 10 remaining tribes who had not yet recognized him as king.

2:10, 11 David ruled over Judah for seven and a half years, while Ishbosheth reigned in Israel for only two years. The five-year gap may be due to Ishbosheth's not assuming the throne immediately after Saul's death. Because of constant danger from the Philistines in the northern part of Israel, five years may have passed before Ishbosheth could begin his reign. During that time, Abner, commander of his army, probably played a principal role in driving out the Philistines and leading the northern confederacy. Regardless of when Ishbosheth began to rule, his control was weak and limited. The Philistines still dominated the area, and Ishbosheth was intimidated by Abner (3:11).

War between Israel and Judah

2:12 Josh 10:12
2:13 2 Sam 8:16; 1 Chr 2:16; 11:5-6
2:17 2 Sam 3:1

[12]One day Abner led some of Ishbosheth's troops from Mahanaim to Gibeon. [13]About
the same time, Joab son of Zeruiah led David's troops from Hebron, and they met Abner
at the pool of Gibeon. The two groups sat down there, facing each other from opposite
sides of the pool. [14]Then Abner suggested to Joab, "Let's have a few of our warriors put
on an exhibition of hand-to-hand combat."
"All right," Joab agreed. [15]So twelve men were chosen from each side to fight against
each other. [16]Each one grabbed his opponent by the hair and thrust his sword into the
other's side so that all of them died. The place has been known ever since as the Field of
Swords.* [17]The two armies then began to fight each other, and by the end of the day
Abner and the men of Israel had been defeated by the forces of David.

2:16 Hebrew *Helkath-hazzurim.*

ABNER

The honest compliments of an opponent are often the best measure of someone's greatness. Although Abner and David frequently saw each other across battle lines, the Bible gives a glimpse of the respect they had for each other. As a young man, David had served under Abner. But later, Saul's campaign to kill David was carried out by Abner. After Saul's death, Abner temporarily upheld the power of the king's family. But the struggle between Abner and Saul's heir, Ishbosheth, brought about Abner's decision to support David's claim to the throne. It was during his efforts to unite the kingdom that Abner was murdered by Joab.

Several years earlier, in a battle between Ishbosheth's army under Abner and David's forces under Joab, Abner fled and was pursued by Joab's brother, Asahel. Abner told Asahel twice to stop following him. But the eager young soldier refused, so Abner killed him. Joab was determined to avenge his brother.

Abner realized Saul's family was doomed to defeat and that David would be the next king, so he decided to change sides. He hoped that in exchange for his delivering Saul's kingdom, David would make him commander in chief of his army. David's willingness to accept this proposal was probably another reason for Joab's action.

Abner lived by his wits and his will. To him, God was someone with whom he would cooperate if it suited his plans. Otherwise he did what seemed best for him at the time. We can identify with Abner's tendency to give God conditional cooperation. Obedience is easy when the instructions in God's Word fit in with our plans. But our allegiance to God is tested when his plans are contrary to ours. What action should you take today in obedience to God's Word?

Strengths and accomplishments
- Commander in chief of Saul's army and a capable military leader
- Held Israel together for several years under the weak king Ishbosheth
- Recognized and accepted God's plan to make David king over all Israel and Judah

Weaknesses and mistakes
- He had selfish motives in his effort to reunite Judah and Israel rather than godly conviction
- He slept with one of the royal concubines after Saul's death

Lesson from his life
- God requires more than conditional, halfhearted cooperation

Vital statistics
- Where: Territory of Benjamin
- Occupation: Commander of the armies under Saul and Ishbosheth
- Relatives: Father: Ner. Cousin: Saul. Son: Jaasiel
- Contemporaries: David, Asahel, Joab, Abishai

Key verse "Then King David said to the people, 'Do you not realize that a great leader and a great man has fallen today in Israel?' " (2 Samuel 3:38).

Abner's story is told in 1 Samuel 14:50—2 Samuel 4:12. He is also mentioned in 1 Kings 2:5, 32; 1 Chronicles 26:28; 27:16–22.

2:12ff With Israel divided, there was constant tension between north and south. David's true rival in the north, however, was not Ishbosheth but Abner. In this incident, Abner suggested hand-to-hand combat between the champions of his army and the champions of David's army, led by Joab. The fact that this confrontation occurred at the pool of Gibeon (located in Saul's home territory of Benjamin) suggests that Joab's men were pushing northward, gaining more territory. Abner may have suggested this confrontation in hopes of stopping Joab's advance.

Twelve men from each side were supposed to fight each other, and the side with the most survivors would be declared the winner. The confrontation between David and Goliath (1 Samuel 17) was a similar battle strategy—a way to avoid terrible bloodshed from an all-out war. In this case, however, all 24 champions were killed before either side could claim victory. Nothing was accomplished, and the civil war continued.

The Death of Asahel

18 Joab, Abishai, and Asahel, the three sons of Zeruiah, were among David's forces that 2:18 1 Chr 2:16; 11:26;
day. Asahel could run like a deer, 19 and he began chasing Abner. He was relentless and 12:8
single-minded in his pursuit. 20 When Abner looked back and saw him coming, he called
out, "Is that you, Asahel?"

"Yes, it is," he replied.

21 "Go fight someone else!" Abner warned. "Take on one of the younger men and strip
him of his weapons." But Asahel refused and kept right on chasing Abner.

22 Again Abner shouted to him, "Get away from here! I will never be able to face your 2:22 2 Sam 3:27
brother Joab if I have to kill you!" 23 But Asahel would not give up, so Abner thrust the
butt end of his spear through Asahel's stomach, and the spear came out through his back.
He stumbled to the ground and died there. And everyone who came by that spot stopped
and stood still when they saw Asahel lying there.

24 When Joab and Abishai found out what had happened, they set out after Abner.
The sun was just going down as they arrived at the hill of Ammah near Giah, along
the road to the wilderness of Gibeon. 25 Abner's troops from the tribe of Benjamin
regrouped there at the top of the hill to take a stand. 26 Abner shouted down to Joab, 2:26 Deut 32:42
"Must we always solve our differences with swords? Don't you realize the only thing
we will gain is bitterness toward each other? When will you call off your men from
chasing their Israelite brothers?"

27 Then Joab said, "God only knows what would have happened if you hadn't spoken,
for we would have chased you all night if necessary." 28 So Joab blew his trumpet, and
his men stopped chasing the troops of Israel.

29 All that night Abner and his men retreated through the Jordan Valley.* They crossed 2:29 Deut 3:17
the Jordan River, traveling all through the morning,* and they did not stop until they
arrived at Mahanaim.

30 Meanwhile, Joab and his men also returned home. When Joab counted his casualties, he discovered that only nineteen men were missing, in addition to Asahel. 31 But
three hundred and sixty of Abner's men, all from the tribe of Benjamin, had been killed.
32 Joab and his men took Asahel's body to Bethlehem and buried him there beside his 2:32 Gen 49:29
father. Then they traveled all night and reached Hebron at daybreak.

3 That was the beginning of a long war between those who had been loyal to Saul and 3:1 1 Kgs 14:30
those who were loyal to David. As time passed David became stronger and stronger, 3:2-5 //1 Chr 3:1-4
while Saul's dynasty became weaker and weaker.

David's Sons Born in Hebron

2 These were the sons who were born to David in Hebron: 3:2 1 Sam 25:43 2 Sam 13:1 1 Chr 3:1

The oldest was Amnon, whose mother was Ahinoam of Jezreel.
3 The second was Kileab, whose mother was Abigail, the widow of Nabal from Carmel. 3:3 1 Sam 25:42 1 Chr 3:2
The third was Absalom, whose mother was Maacah, the daughter of Talmai, king of Geshur.

2:29a Hebrew *the Arabah.* **2:29b** Or *continued on through the Bithron.* The meaning of the Hebrew is uncertain.

2:21-23 Abner repeatedly warned Asahel to turn back or risk losing his life, but Asahel refused to turn from his self-imposed duty. Persistence is a good trait if it is for a worthy cause. But if the goal is only personal honor or gain, persistence may be no more than stubbornness. Asahel's stubbornness not only cost him his life, but it also spurred unfortunate disunity in David's army for years to come (3:26, 27; 1 Kings 2:28-35). Before you decide to pursue a goal, make sure it is worthy of your devotion.

2:28 This battle ended with a victory for Joab's troops (2:17), but war in the divided nation continued until David was finally crowned king over all Israel (5:1-5).

3:1 The events recorded in chapter 2 led to a long war between David's followers and the troops loyal to Abner and Ishbosheth. Civil war rocked the country at great cost to both sides. This war occurred because Israel and Judah had lost sight of God's vision and purpose: to settle the land (Genesis 12:7), to drive out the Canaanites (Deuteronomy 7:1-4), and to obey God's laws (Deuteronomy 8:1). Instead of uniting to accomplish these goals, they fought each other. When you face conflict, step back from the hostilities and consider whether you and your enemy have common goals that are bigger than your differences. Appeal to those interests as you work for a settlement.

3:2-5 David suffered much heartache because of his many wives. Polygamy was a socially acceptable practice for kings at this time, although God specifically warned against it (Deuteronomy 17:14-17). Sadly, the numerous sons born to David's wives caused him great trouble. Rape (13:14), murder (13:28), rebellion (15:13), and greed (1 Kings 1:5, 6) all resulted from the jealous rivalries among the half brothers. Solomon, one of David's sons and his successor to the throne, also took many wives who eventually turned him away from God (1 Kings 11:3, 4).

3:4 1 Chr 3:2-3 4 The fourth was Adonijah, whose mother was Haggith.
The fifth was Shephatiah, whose mother was Abital.
3:5 1 Chr 3:3 5 The sixth was Ithream, whose mother was David's wife Eglah.

These sons were all born to David in Hebron.

Abner Joins Forces with David

6 As the war went on, Abner became a powerful leader among those who were loyal to
3:7 2 Sam 21:8-11 Saul's dynasty. 7 One day Ishbosheth,* Saul's son, accused Abner of sleeping with one
3:8 1 Sam 24:14; 2 Sam 9:8; 16:9 of his father's concubines, a woman named Rizpah. 8 Abner became furious. "Am I a
Judean dog to be kicked around like this?" he shouted. "After all I have done for you and
your father by not betraying you to David, is this my reward—that you find fault with
3:9 1 Sam 15:28 me about this woman? 9 May God deal harshly with me if I don't help David get all that
the LORD has promised him! 10 I should just go ahead and give David the rest of Saul's
kingdom. I should set him up as king over Israel as well as Judah, from Dan to
Beersheba." 11 Ishbosheth didn't dare say another word because he was afraid of what
Abner might do.

12 Then Abner sent messengers to David, saying, "Let's make an agreement, and I will
help turn the entire nation of Israel over to you."

3:13 1 Sam 18:20 13 "All right," David replied, "but I will not negotiate with you unless you bring back
my wife Michal, Saul's daughter, when you come."

3:14 1 Sam 18:25-27 14 David then sent this message to Ishbosheth, Saul's son: "Give me back my wife
3:15 1 Sam 25:44 Michal, for I bought her with the lives of one hundred Philistines." 15 So Ishbosheth took
3:16 2 Sam 16:5 Michal away from her husband Palti* son of Laish. 16 Palti followed along behind her as
far as Bahurim, weeping as he went. Then Abner told him, "Go back home!" So Palti
returned.

17 Meanwhile, Abner had consulted with the leaders of Israel. "For some time now,"
3:18 1 Sam 9:16; 15:28 he told them, "you have wanted to make David your king. 18 Now is the time! For the
LORD has said, 'I have chosen David to save my people from the Philistines and from all
3:19 1 Sam 10:20-21; 1 Chr 12:29 their other enemies.'" 19 Abner also spoke with the leaders of the tribe of Benjamin. Then
he went to Hebron to tell David that all the people of Israel and Benjamin supported him.

20 When Abner came to Hebron with his twenty men, David entertained them with a
3:21 1 Kgs 11:37 great feast. 21 Then Abner said to David, "Let me go and call all the people of Israel to
your side. They will make a covenant with you to make you their king. Then you will be
able to rule over everything your heart desires." So David sent Abner safely on his way.

Joab Murders Abner

3:22 1 Sam 27:8 22 But just after Abner left, Joab and some of David's troops returned from a raid,
bringing much plunder with them. 23 When Joab was told that Abner had just been there
3:24 1 Sam 29:3 visiting the king and had been sent away in safety, 24 he rushed to see the king. "What

3:7 Also known as *Eshbaal*. **3:15** As in 1 Sam 25:44; Hebrew reads *Paltiel*, a variant name for Palti.

3:6, 7 To sleep with any of the king's wives or concubines was to make a claim to the throne, and it was considered treason. Because Ishbosheth was a weak ruler, Abner was running the country; thus, he may have felt justified in sleeping with Saul's concubine. Ishbosheth, however, saw that Abner's power was becoming too great.

3:7 Ishbosheth may have been right to speak out against Abner's behavior, but he didn't have the moral strength to maintain his authority (3:11). Lack of moral backbone became the root of Israel's troubles over the next four centuries. Only 4 of the next 40 kings of Israel were called "good." It takes courage and strength to stand firm in your convictions and to confront wrongdoing in the face of opposition. When you believe something is wrong, do not let yourself be talked out of your position. Firmly attack the wrong and uphold the right.

3:8 By saying, "Am I a Judean dog?" Abner meant, "Am I a traitor for Judah?" He may have been refuting the accusation that he was trying to take over the throne, or he may have been angry that Ishbosheth scolded him after Abner had helped put him on the throne in the first place. Prior to this conversation, Abner realized that he could not keep David from eventually taking over Israel. Because he was angry at Ishbosheth, Abner devised a plan to turn over the kingdom of Israel to David.

3:13, 14 Michal had been married to David. Saul had arranged the marriage as a reward for David's acts of bravery (1 Samuel 17:25; 18:24-27). Later, however, in one of his jealous fits, Saul took Michal away from David and forced her to marry Palti (1 Samuel 25:44). Now David wanted his wife back before he would begin to negotiate peace with the northern tribes. Perhaps David still loved her (but see 6:20-23 for the tension in their relationship). More likely, he thought that marriage to Saul's daughter would strengthen his claim to rule all Israel and demonstrate that he had no animosity toward Saul's house. Palti was the unfortunate victim caught in the web of Saul's jealousy.

3:19 Because Saul, Ishbosheth, and Abner were all from the tribe of Benjamin, the support of the elders of that tribe meant that Abner was serious about his offer. There was a strong possibility of overcoming tribal jealousies and uniting the kingdom.

have you done?" he demanded. "What do you mean by letting Abner get away? 25 You
know perfectly well that he came to spy on you and to discover everything you are
doing!"

26 Joab then left David and sent messengers to catch up with Abner. They found him
at the pool of Sirah and brought him back with them. But David knew nothing about it.
27 When Abner arrived at Hebron, Joab took him aside at the gateway as if to speak with **3:27**
him privately. But then he drew his dagger and killed Abner in revenge for killing his 2 Sam 2:22-23; 20:8-10
brother Asahel. 1 Kgs 2:5

28 When David heard about it, he declared, "I vow by the LORD that I and my people **3:29**
are innocent of this crime against Abner. 29 Joab and his family are the guilty ones. May Lev 13:45-46 Deut 21:7-8
his family in every generation be cursed with a man who has open sores or leprosy* or 1 Kgs 2:31-33
who walks on crutches* or who dies by the sword or who begs for food!"

30 So Joab and his brother Abishai killed Abner because Abner had killed their brother **3:30** 2 Sam 2:23
Asahel at the battle of Gibeon.

David Mourns Abner's Death

31 Then David said to Joab and all those who were with him, "Tear your clothes and put **3:31** Gen 37:34
on sackcloth. Go into deep mourning for Abner." And King David himself walked behind Judg 11:35
the procession to the grave. 32 They buried Abner in Hebron, and the king and all the **3:32** Prov 24:17
people wept at his graveside. 33 Then the king sang this funeral song for Abner:

"Should Abner have died as fools die?
34 Your hands were not bound;
your feet were not chained.
No, you were murdered—
the victim of a wicked plot."

All the people wept again for Abner. 35 David had refused to eat anything the day of **3:35** 2 Sam 1:12; 12:17
the funeral, and now everyone begged him to eat. But David had made a vow, saying,
"May God kill me if I eat anything before sundown." 36 This pleased the people very
much. In fact, everything the king did pleased them! 37 So everyone in Judah and Israel
knew that David was not responsible for Abner's death.

38 Then King David said to the people, "Do you not realize that a great leader and a
great man has fallen today in Israel? 39 And even though I am the anointed king, these **3:39** 2 Sam 19:5-7
two sons of Zeruiah—Joab and Abishai—are too strong for me to control. So may the
LORD repay these wicked men for their wicked deeds."

3:29a Or *or a contagious skin disease.* The Hebrew word used here can describe various skin diseases. **3:29b** Or *who is effeminate;* Hebrew reads *who handles a spindle.*

3:26-29 Joab took revenge for the death of his brother instead of leaving justice to God. But that revenge backfired on him (1 Kings 2:31-34). God will repay those who deserve it (Romans 12:19). Refuse to rejoice when your enemies suffer, and don't try to get revenge. Seeking revenge will ruin your own peace of mind and increase the chances of further retaliation.

3:27 Abner killed Joab's brother Asahel in self-defense. Joab then killed Abner to avenge his brother's death and also to save his position of military leadership. People who killed in self-defense were supposed to be safe in cities of refuge (Numbers 35:22-25). Joab showed his disrespect for God's laws by killing Abner out of revenge in Hebron, a city of refuge (Joshua 20:7).

3:29 David was saying that Joab's descendants would be unclean, unhealthy, and in want. Why did David say such harsh words about Joab? David was upset over Abner's death for several reasons. (1) He was grieved over the loss of a skilled military officer. (2) He wanted to place the guilt of Abner's murder on Joab, not himself. (3) He was on the verge of becoming king over the entire nation, and utilizing Abner was the key to winning over the northern tribes. Abner's death could have revived the civil war. (4) Joab violated David's agreement to protect Abner. Joab's murderous act ruined David's plans, and David was especially angry that his own commander had committed the crime.

3:31 By walking behind the procession (that is, behind the casket), David was leading the mourning.

3:31ff David ordered Joab to mourn, possibly because few people were aware that Joab had committed the crime and because David did not want any further trouble. If this is true, David was thinking more about strengthening his kingdom than about justice.

3:39 Joab and Abishai were the two sons of Zeruiah David mentioned. David had an especially hard time controlling Joab because, although he was intensely loyal, he was strong willed, preferring to do things his own way. In exchange for his loyalty, however, David was willing to give him the flexibility he craved.

Joab's murder of Abner is an example of his fierce independence. While David opposed the murder, he allowed it to remain unpunished because (1) to punish Joab could cause the troops to rebel; (2) Joab was David's nephew, and any harsh treatment could cause family problems; (3) Joab was from the tribe of Judah, and David didn't want rebellion from his own tribe; (4) to get rid of Joab would mean losing a skilled and competent commander who had been invaluable in strengthening his army.

The Murder of Ishbosheth

4:1 2 Sam 3:27
4:2 Josh 9:17; 18:25
4:3 Neh 11:33
4:4 1 Sam 31:1-4; 2 Sam 9:3, 5-6; 1 Chr 8:34; 9:40

4 When Ishbosheth* heard about Abner's death at Hebron, he lost all courage, and his people were paralyzed with fear. 2Now there were two brothers, Baanah and Recab, who were captains of Ishbosheth's raiding parties. They were sons of Rimmon, who was a Benjaminite from Beeroth. The town of Beeroth is now part of Benjamin 3because the original people of Beeroth fled to Gittaim, where they still live as foreigners.

4(Saul's son Jonathan had a son named Mephibosheth,* who was crippled as a child. He was five years old when Saul and Jonathan were killed at the battle of Jezreel. When news of the battle reached the capital, the child's nurse grabbed him and fled. But she fell and dropped him as she was running, and he became crippled as a result.)

4:5 2 Sam 2:8
4:6 2 Sam 2:23

5One day Recab and Baanah, the sons of Rimmon from Beeroth, went to Ishbosheth's home around noon as he was taking a nap. 6The doorkeeper, who had been sifting wheat, became drowsy and fell asleep. So Recab and Baanah slipped past the doorkeeper, went into Ishbosheth's bedroom, and stabbed him in the stomach. Then they escaped. 7But before leaving, they cut off his head as he lay there on his bed. Taking his head with them, they fled across the Jordan Valley* through the night. 8They arrived at Hebron and presented Ishbosheth's head to David. "Look!" they exclaimed. "Here is the head of Ishbosheth, the son of your enemy Saul who tried to kill you. Today the LORD has given you revenge on Saul and his entire family!"

4:9 1 Kgs 1:29
4:10 2 Sam 1:1-2, 4, 15
4:11 Gen 9:5; Ps 9:12
4:12 2 Sam 1:15; 3:32

9But David said to Recab and Baanah, "As surely as the LORD lives, the one who saves me from my enemies, I will tell you the truth. 10Once before, someone told me, 'Saul is dead,' thinking he was bringing me good news. But I seized him and killed him at Ziklag. That's the reward I gave him for his news! 11Now what reward should I give the wicked men who have killed an innocent man in his own house and on his own bed? Should I not also demand your very lives?" 12So David ordered his young men to kill them, and they did. They cut off their hands and feet and hung their bodies beside the pool in Hebron. Then they took Ishbosheth's head and buried it in Abner's tomb in Hebron.

2. David becomes king over Israel

David Is Anointed King

5:1-3 //1 Chr 11:1-3
5:2 1 Sam 18:5, 14; 25:30

5 Then all the tribes of Israel went to David at Hebron and told him, "We are all members of your family. 2For a long time, even while Saul was our king, you were the one who really led Israel. And the LORD has told you, 'You will be the shepherd of

4:1 Also known as *Eshbaal.* **4:4** Also known as *Meribbaal.* **4:7** Hebrew *the Arabah.*

4:1 Ishbosheth was a man who took his courage from another man (Abner) rather than from God. When Abner died, Ishbosheth was left with nothing. In crisis and under pressure, he collapsed in fear. Fear can paralyze us, but faith and trust in God can overcome fear (2 Timothy 1:6-8; Hebrews 13:6). If we trust in God, we will be free to respond boldly to the events around us.

4:4 The rest of Mephibosheth's story is told in chapter 9; 16:1-4; and 19:24-30.

4:11 David called Ishbosheth an "innocent man." As Saul's son, Ishbosheth had reason to think he was in line for the throne. He was not wicked for wanting to be king; rather, he was simply too weak to stand against injustice. Although David knew Ishbosheth was not the strong leader needed to unite Israel, he had no intention of killing him. God had promised the kingdom to David, and he knew that God would fulfill his promise.

When David learned of Ishbosheth's death, he was angry. He had never harmed Saul, and he thought the assassins' method was cowardly. David wanted to unite Israel, not drive a permanent wedge between him and Ishbosheth's supporters. To show that he had nothing to do with the extermination of Saul's royal line, he ordered the assassins killed and gave Ishbosheth a proper burial. All the tribes of Israel, recognizing in David the strong leader they needed, pledged their loyalty to him. No doubt the Philistine threat and David's military reputation (1 Samuel 18:7) also helped unify the people.

DAVID DEFEATS THE PHILISTINES The Philistines camped in the valley of Rephaim. David defeated them at Baal-perazim, but they remained in the valley. He attacked again and chased them from Gibeon to Gezer.

my people Israel. You will be their leader.'" 3 So there at Hebron, David made a covenant
with the leaders of Israel before the LORD. And they anointed him king of Israel.
4 David was thirty years old when he began to reign, and he reigned forty years in all.
5 He had reigned over Judah from Hebron for seven years and six months, and from
Jerusalem he reigned over all Israel and Judah for thirty-three years.

David Captures Jerusalem

6 David then led his troops to Jerusalem to fight against the Jebusites. "You'll never get
in here," the Jebusites taunted. "Even the blind and lame could keep you out!" For the
Jebusites thought they were safe. 7 But David captured the fortress of Zion, now called
the City of David.
8 When the insulting message from the defenders of the city reached David, he told his
own troops, "Go up through the water tunnel into the city and destroy those 'lame' and
'blind' Jebusites. How I hate them." That is the origin of the saying, "The blind and the
lame may not enter the house."* 9 So David made the fortress his home, and he called it
the City of David. He built additional fortifications around the city, starting at the Millo*
and working inward. 10 And David became more and more powerful, because the LORD
God Almighty was with him.
11 Then King Hiram of Tyre sent messengers to David, along with carpenters and
stonemasons to build him a palace. Hiram also sent many cedar logs for lumber. 12 And
David realized that the LORD had made him king over Israel and had made his kingdom
great for the sake of his people Israel.
13 After moving from Hebron to Jerusalem, David married more wives and concubines, and he had many sons and daughters. 14 These are the names of David's sons who
were born in Jerusalem: Shimea,* Shobab, Nathan, Solomon, 15 Ibhar, Elishua, Nepheg,
Japhia, 16 Elishama, Eliada, and Eliphelet.

David Conquers the Philistines

17 When the Philistines heard that David had been anointed king of Israel, they mobilized
all their forces to capture him. But David was told they were coming and went into the
stronghold. 18 The Philistines arrived and spread out across the valley of Rephaim. 19 So David
asked the LORD, "Should I go out to fight the Philistines? Will you hand them over to me?"
The LORD replied, "Yes, go ahead. I will certainly give you the victory."

5:3 1 Sam 16:1, 13; 2 Sam 2:4; 3:21
5:4 Gen 41:46; 1 Kgs 2:11; 1 Chr 26:31-32; Luke 3:23
5:6-10 //1 Chr 11:4-9
5:7 1 Kgs 2:10
5:9 1 Kgs 9:15, 24
5:10 2 Sam 3:1
5:11-16 //1 Chr 3:5-9; 14:1-7
5:11 1 Kgs 5:10, 18; 1 Chr 14:1
5:12 Num 24:7
5:13 Deut 17:17; 1 Chr 3:9
5:14 1 Chr 3:5-8
5:17-25 //1 Chr 14:8-17
5:18 Josh 15:8; 18:16
5:19 1 Sam 23:2

5:8 The meaning of this saying is uncertain. **5:9** Or *the supporting terraces.* The meaning of the Hebrew is uncertain. **5:14** As in parallel text at 1 Chr 3:5; Hebrew reads *Shammua,* a variant name for Shimea.

5:3-5 This was the third time David was anointed king. First he was privately anointed by Samuel (1 Samuel 16:13). Then he was made king over the tribe of Judah (2:4). Finally he was crowned king over all Israel. David's life as an outlaw had looked bleak, but God's promise to make him king over all Israel was now being fulfilled. Although the kingdom would be divided again in less than 75 years, David's dynasty would reign over Judah, the southern kingdom, for over 400 years.

5:4, 5 David did not become king over all Israel until he was 37 years old, although he had been promised the kingdom many years earlier (1 Samuel 16:13). During those years, David had to wait patiently for the fulfillment of God's promise. If you feel pressured to achieve instant results and success, remember David's patience. Just as his time of waiting prepared him for his important task, a waiting period may help prepare you by strengthening your character.

5:6 The fortress of Zion (which became the city of Jerusalem) was located on a high ridge near the center of the united Israelite kingdom. It was considered neutral territory because it stood on the border of the territory of the tribes of Benjamin and Judah, and it was still occupied by the Jebusites, a Canaanite tribe that had never been expelled from the land (Judges 1:21). Because of its strategic advantages, David made Jerusalem his capital.

5:6, 7 The Jebusites had a clear military advantage, and they boasted of their security behind the impregnable walls of Zion. But they soon discovered that their walls would not protect them. David caught them by surprise by entering the city through the water tunnel.

Only in God are we truly safe and secure. Anything else is false security. Whether you are surrounded by mighty walls of stone, a comfortable home, or a secure job, no one can predict what tomorrow may bring. Our relationship with God is the only security that cannot be taken away.

5:12 "David realized that the LORD had made him king. . . ." Although the pagan kingdoms based their greatness on conquest, power, armies, and wealth, David knew that his greatness came only from God. To be great means keeping a close relationship with God personally and nationally. To do this, David had to keep his ambition under control. Although he was famous, successful, and well liked, he gave God first place in his life and served the people according to God's purposes. Do you seek greatness from God or from people? In the drive for success, remember to keep your ambition under God's control.

5:17 "The stronghold" is the mountain stronghold in the wilderness of Judah that David used when defending himself against Saul (see 23:14 and 1 Chronicles 12:8).

5:17 The Philistine oppression of Israel began in the days of Samson (Judges 13–16). The Philistines were still Israel's most powerful enemy although David was once considered a friend and ally (1 Samuel 27; 29). Because they occupied much of Israel's northern territory, they apparently did not bother David while he was king of Judah to the south. But when they learned that David was planning to unite all Israel, they tried to stop him.

5:20 1 Chr 14:11 20 So David went to Baal-perazim and defeated the Philistines there. "The LORD has
done it!" David exclaimed. "He burst through my enemies like a raging flood!" So David
named that place Baal-perazim (which means "the Lord who bursts through"). 21 The
Philistines had abandoned their idols there, so David and his troops confiscated them.
22 But after a while the Philistines returned and again spread out across the valley of
Rephaim. 23 And once again David asked the LORD what to do. "Do not attack them
straight on," the LORD replied. "Instead, circle around behind them and attack them near
5:24 Judg 4:14 the balsam trees. 24 When you hear a sound like marching feet in the tops of the balsam
trees, attack! That will be the signal that the LORD is moving ahead of you to strike down
5:25 Josh 12:12; 21:20-22 the Philistines." 25 So David did what the LORD commanded, and he struck down the
Philistines all the way from Gibeon* to Gezer.

The Ark Brought to Jerusalem

6:1-11 //1 Chr 13:1-14 **6** Then David mobilized thirty thousand special troops. 2 He led them to Baalah of
6:2 Lev 24:16 Judah* to bring home the Ark of God, which bears the name of the LORD Almighty,
who is enthroned between the cherubim. 3 They placed the Ark of God on a new cart and
6:3 Num 7:4-9; 1 Sam 6:7 brought it from the hillside home of Abinadab. Uzzah and Ahio, Abinadab's sons, were
guiding the cart 4 with the Ark of God on it, with Ahio walking in front. 5 David and all
6:5 1 Chr 13:7-8; 16:5 the people of Israel were celebrating before the LORD with all their might, singing songs*
and playing all kinds of musical instruments—lyres, harps, tambourines, castanets, and
cymbals.

5:25 As in Greek version (see also 1 Chr 14:16); Hebrew reads *Geba*. **6:2** *Baalah of Judah* is another name for Kiriath-jearim; compare 1 Chr 13:6. **6:5** As in Greek version (see also 1 Chr 13:8); Hebrew reads *cypress trees*.

CRITICIZING GOD'S LEADERS

It is dangerous to criticize God's leaders. Consider the consequences for these men and women.

Person/Situation	*Result*	*Reference*
Miriam: Mocked Moses because he had a Cushite wife	Stricken with leprosy	Numbers 12
Korah and followers: Led the people of Israel to rebel against Moses' leadership	Swallowed by the earth	Numbers 16
Michal: Despised David because he danced before the Lord	Remained childless	2 Samuel 6
Shimei: Cursed and threw stones at David	Executed at Solomon's order	2 Samuel 16 1 Kings 2
Youths: Mocked Elisha and laughed at his baldness	Killed by bears	2 Kings 2
Sanballat and Tobiah: Spread rumors and lies to stop the building of Jerusalem's walls	Frightened and humiliated	Nehemiah 2, 4, 6
Hananiah: Contradicted Jeremiah's prophecies with false predictions	Died two months later	Jeremiah 28
Bar-Jesus, a sorcerer: Lied about Paul in an attempt to turn the proconsul against him	Stricken with blindness	Acts 13

5:19 How could David get such a clear message from God? He may have prayed and been urged to action by the Holy Spirit. He may have asked God through a prophet. Most likely, however, he went to the high priest, who consulted God through the Urim and Thummim that God had told the Israelites to use for just such a purpose. (For more on the Urim and Thummim, see the notes on Leviticus 8:8 and 1 Samuel 10:20.)

5:19-25 David fought his battles the way God instructed him. In each instance he (1) asked if he should fight or not, (2) followed instructions carefully, and (3) gave God the glory. We can err in our "battles" by ignoring these steps and instead (1) do what we want without considering God's will, (2) do things our way and ignore advice in the Bible or from other wise people, and (3) take the glory ourselves or give it to someone else without acknowledging the help we received from God. All these responses are sinful.

5:25 After David became king, his first order of business was to subdue his enemies—a task the nation had failed to complete when they first entered the land (Judges 2:1-4). David knew this had to be done in order to (1) protect the nation, (2) unify the kingdom, and (3) prepare for building the Temple (which would unify religion under God and help abolish idolatrous influences).

6:3 The Ark of God was Israel's national treasure and was ordinarily kept in the Tabernacle. When the Ark was returned to Israel after a brief Philistine captivity (1 Samuel 4:1–7:2), it was kept in Abinadab's home for 20 years. David saw how God blessed Abinadab, and he wanted to bring the Ark to Jerusalem to ensure God's blessing on the entire nation. (See the notes on Exodus 37:1 and Joshua 3:2-4 for more information on the Ark.)

6 But when they arrived at the threshing floor of Nacon, the oxen stumbled, and Uzzah **6:6**
put out his hand to steady the Ark of God. 7 Then the LORD's anger blazed out against Num 4:15
Uzzah for doing this, and God struck him dead beside the Ark of God. 8 David was angry **6:7** 1 Sam 6:19
because the LORD's anger had blazed out against Uzzah. He named that place Perez-uzzah (which means "outbreak against Uzzah"). It is still called that today.
9 David was now afraid of the LORD and asked, "How can I ever bring the Ark of the
LORD back into my care?" 10 So David decided not to move the Ark of the LORD into the **6:10**
City of David. He took it instead to the home of Obed-edom of Gath. 11 The Ark of the 1 Chr 26:4-5
LORD remained there with the family of Obed-edom for three months, and the LORD
blessed him and his entire household.
12 Then King David was told, "The LORD has blessed Obed-edom's home and every- **6:12-19**
thing he has because of the Ark of God." So David went there and brought the Ark to the 1 Chr 15:25–16:3
City of David with a great celebration. 13 After the men who were carrying it had gone **6:12** 1 Kgs 8:1
six steps, they stopped and waited so David could sacrifice an ox and a fattened calf. **6:13**
14 And David danced before the LORD with all his might, wearing a priestly tunic.* 15 So 1 Kgs 8:5
David and all Israel brought up the Ark of the LORD with much shouting and blowing of **6:14** Exod 15:20
trumpets. 1 Sam 2:18, 28

Michal's Contempt for David

16 But as the Ark of the LORD entered the City of David, Michal, the daughter of Saul, **6:16** 1 Sam 18:27
looked down from her window. When she saw King David leaping and dancing before
the LORD, she was filled with contempt for him.
17 The Ark of the LORD was placed inside the special tent that David had prepared for **6:17**
it. And David sacrificed burnt offerings and peace offerings to the LORD. 18 When he had 1 Kgs 8:62-65 1 Chr 15:1
finished, David blessed the people in the name of the LORD Almighty. 19 Then he gave a 2 Chr 1:4
gift of food to every man and woman in Israel: a loaf of bread, a cake of dates,* and a
cake of raisins. Then everyone went home.
20 When David returned home to bless his family, Michal came out to meet him and
said in disgust, "How glorious the king of Israel looked today! He exposed himself to
the servant girls like any indecent person might do!"
21 David retorted to Michal, "I was dancing before the LORD, who chose me above **6:21**
your father and his family! He appointed me as the leader of Israel, the people of the 1 Sam 13:14
LORD. So I am willing to act like a fool in order to show my joy in the LORD. 22 Yes, and
I am willing to look even more foolish than this, but I will be held in honor by the girls
of whom you have spoken!" 23 So Michal, the daughter of Saul, remained childless
throughout her life.

6:14 Hebrew *a linen ephod.* **6:19** Or *a portion of meat.* The meaning of the Hebrew is uncertain.

6:6, 7 Uzzah was only trying to protect the Ark, so was God's anger against Uzzah just? According to Numbers 4:5-15, the Ark was to be moved only by the Levites, who were to carry it using the carrying poles—they were *never* to touch the Ark itself. To touch it was a capital offense under Hebrew law (Numbers 4:15). God's action was directed against both David and Uzzah. David placed the Ark on a cart, following the Philistines' example (1 Samuel 6:7, 8) rather than God's commands. Uzzah, though sincere in his desire to protect the Ark, had to face the consequences of the sin of touching it. Also, Uzzah may not have been a Levite. As David sought to bring Israel back into a relationship with God, God had to remind the nation dramatically that enthusiasm must be accompanied by obedience to his laws. The next time David tried to bring the Ark to Jerusalem, he was careful to handle it correctly (1 Chronicles 15:1-15).

6:8-12 David was angry that a well-meaning man had been killed and that his plans for a joyous return of the Ark had been spoiled (6:8). He undoubtedly knew that the fault was his own for transporting the Ark carelessly. After cooling down, he had the Ark put into temporary storage while he waited to see if the Lord would allow him to bring it to Jerusalem. This also gave David time to consider the right way to transport the Ark. The fact that God blessed the home of Obed-edom was a sign to David that he could try once again to move the Ark to Jerusalem.

6:14 David wore a priestly tunic, possibly because it was a religious celebration.

6:16ff Michal was David's first wife, but here she is called daughter of Saul, possibly to show how similar her attitude was to her father's. Her contempt for David probably did not start with David's grand entrance into the city. Perhaps she thought it was undignified to be so concerned with public worship at a time when it was so unimportant in the kingdom. Or maybe she thought it was not fitting for a king to display such emotion. She may have resented David's taking her from Palti (see the note on 3:13, 14). Whatever the reason, this contempt she felt toward her husband escalated into a difficult confrontation, and Michal ended up childless for life. Feelings of bitterness and resentment that go unchecked will destroy a relationship. Deal with your feelings before they escalate into open warfare.

6:17 Only a priest could place the sacrifices on the altar. Leviticus 1:2-13 indicates that anyone who was ceremonially clean could assist a priest in offering the sacrifice (see the notes on Joshua 3:5; 1 Samuel 20:26). So David probably offered these sacrifices to God with the aid of a priest. Solomon did the same (1 Kings 8:62-65).

7:1-17
//1 Chr 17:1-15
7:2
2 Sam 5:11
1 Kgs 1:22
1 Chr 29:29
7:5
1 Kgs 5:3, 5;
8:17-19
7:6
Exod 40:18, 34
1 Kgs 8:16

The LORD's Covenant Promise to David

7 When the king was settled in his palace and the LORD had brought peace to the land,
[2]David summoned Nathan the prophet. "Look!" David said. "Here I am living in
this beautiful cedar palace, but the Ark of God is out in a tent!"
[3]Nathan replied, "Go ahead and do what you have in mind, for the LORD is with you."
[4]But that same night the LORD said to Nathan,

[5]"Go and tell my servant David, 'This is what the LORD says: Are you the one to
build me a temple to live in? [6]I have never lived in a temple, from the day I brought
the Israelites out of Egypt until now. My home has always been a tent, moving

MICHAL

Sometimes love is not enough—especially if that love is little more than the strong emotional attraction that grows between a hero and an admirer. To Michal, Saul's daughter, the courageous young David must have seemed like a dream come true. Her feelings about this hero gradually became obvious to others, and eventually, her father heard about her love for David. He saw this as an opportunity to get rid of his rival for the people's loyalty. He promised Michal's hand in marriage in exchange for David's success in the impossible task of killing 100 Philistines. But David was victorious, and so Saul lost a daughter and saw his rival become even more popular with the people.

Michal's love for David did not have time to be tested by the realities of marriage. Instead, she became involved in saving David's life. Her quick thinking helped him escape, but it resulted in Saul's anger and her separation from David. Her father gave her to another man, Palti, but David eventually took her back.

Unlike her brother Jonathan, Michal did not have the kind of deep relationship with God that would have helped her through the difficulties in her life. Instead, she became bitter. She could not share David's joyful worship of God, so she hated it. As a result, she never bore David any children.

Beyond feeling sorry for her, we need to see Michal as a person mirroring our own tendencies. How quickly and easily we become bitter with life's unexpected turns. But bitterness cannot remove or change the bad things that have happened. Often bitterness only makes a bad situation worse. On the other hand, a willingness to respond to God gives him the opportunity to bring good out of the difficult situations. That willingness has two parts: asking God for his guidance and looking for that guidance in his Word.

Strengths and accomplishments
- Loved David and became his first wife
- Saved David's life
- Could think and act quickly when it was needed

Weaknesses and mistakes
- Lied under pressure
- Allowed herself to become bitter over her circumstances
- In her unhappiness, she hated David for loving God

Lessons from her life
- We are not as responsible for what happens to us as we are for how we respond to our circumstances
- Disobedience to God almost always harms us as well as others

Vital statistics
- Occupations: Daughter of one king, Saul, and wife of another, David
- Relatives: Parents: Saul and Ahinoam. Brothers: Abinadab, Jonathan, Malkishua. Sister: Merab. Husbands: David and Palti

Key verse "But as the Ark of the LORD entered the City of David, Michal, the daughter of Saul, looked down from her window. When she saw King David leaping and dancing before the LORD, she was filled with contempt for him" (2 Samuel 6:16).

Michal's story is told in 1 Samuel 14—2 Samuel 6. She is also mentioned in 1 Chronicles 15:29.

7:1ff This chapter records the covenant God made with David, promising to carry on David's line forever. This promise would be fully realized in the birth of Jesus Christ. Although the word *covenant* is not specifically stated here, it is used elsewhere to describe this occasion (23:5; Psalm 89:28, 34).

7:2 This is the first time Nathan the prophet is mentioned. God made certain that a prophet was living during the reign of each of the kings of Israel. The prophet's main tasks were to urge the people to follow God and to communicate God's laws and plans to the king. Most of the kings rejected the prophets God sent. But at least God had given them the opportunity to listen and obey. In earlier years, judges and priests had the role of prophets. Samuel served as judge, priest, and prophet, bridging the gap between the period of the judges and the monarchy.

7:5 In this message from Nathan, God is saying that he doesn't want David to build a temple for him. God told David that his job was to unify and lead Israel and to destroy its enemies. This huge task would require David to shed a great deal of blood. In 1 Chronicles 28:3, we learn that God did not want his Temple built by a warrior. Therefore, David made the plans and collected the materials so that his son Solomon could begin work on the Temple as soon as he became king (1 Kings 5–7). David accepted his part in God's plan and did not try to go beyond it. Sometimes God says no to our plans. When he does, we should utilize the other opportunities he gives us.

from one place to another. 7 And I have never once complained to Israel's leaders,
the shepherds of my people Israel. I have never asked them, "Why haven't you
built me a beautiful cedar temple?"'
8 "Now go and say to my servant David, 'This is what the LORD Almighty says: I
chose you to lead my people Israel when you were just a shepherd boy, tending
your sheep out in the pasture. 9 I have been with you wherever you have gone, and I
have destroyed all your enemies. Now I will make your name famous throughout
the earth! 10 And I have provided a permanent homeland for my people Israel, a secure place where they will never be disturbed. It will be their own land where
wicked nations won't oppress them as they did in the past, 11 from the time I appointed judges to rule my people. And I will keep you safe from all your enemies.
" 'And now the LORD declares that he will build a house for you—a dynasty of
kings! 12 For when you die, I will raise up one of your descendants, and I will make
his kingdom strong. 13 He is the one who will build a house—a temple—for my
name. And I will establish the throne of his kingdom forever. 14 I will be his father,
and he will be my son. If he sins, I will use other nations to punish him. 15 But my
unfailing love will not be taken from him as I took it from Saul, whom I removed
before you. 16 Your dynasty and your kingdom will continue for all time before me,
and your throne will be secure forever.'"
17 So Nathan went back to David and told him everything the LORD had said.

David's Prayer of Thanks

18 Then King David went in and sat before the LORD and prayed, "Who am I,
O Sovereign LORD, and what is my family, that you have brought me this far? 19 And
now, Sovereign LORD, in addition to everything else, you speak of giving me a lasting
dynasty! Do you deal with everyone this way,* O Sovereign LORD? 20 What more can
I say? You know what I am really like, Sovereign LORD. 21 For the sake of your
promise and according to your will, you have done all these great things and have
shown them to me.
22 "How great you are, O Sovereign LORD! There is no one like you—there is no
other God. We have never even heard of another god like you! 23 What other nation on
earth is like Israel? What other nation, O God, have you redeemed from slavery to be
your own people? You made a great name for yourself when you rescued your people
from Egypt. You performed awesome miracles and drove out the nations and gods that
stood in their way. 24 You made Israel your people forever, and you, O LORD, became
their God.
25 "And now, O LORD God, do as you have promised concerning me and my family.
Confirm it as a promise that will last forever. 26 And may your name be honored forever
so that all the world will say, 'The LORD Almighty is God over Israel!' And may the
dynasty of your servant David be established in your presence.
27 "O LORD Almighty, God of Israel, I have been bold enough to pray this prayer
because you have revealed that you will build a house for me—an eternal dynasty! 28 For
you are God, O Sovereign LORD. Your words are truth, and you have promised these
good things to me, your servant. 29 And now, may it please you to bless me and my family
so that our dynasty may continue forever before you. For when you grant a blessing to
your servant, O Sovereign LORD, it is an eternal blessing!"

7:7 Lev 26:11-12
7:8 1 Sam 16:10-11; Ps 78:70-71; †2 Cor 6:18
7:9 Ps 18:37-42
7:10 Ps 89:22; Isa 60:18
7:11 1 Sam 12:9-11; 25:28
7:12 1 Kgs 2:1; †Acts 2:30
7:13 1 Kgs 6:11-12; 8:19; Isa 9:7
7:14 Ps 89:26-27; †2 Cor 8:14; Heb 1:5-6
7:15 1 Sam 15:23; 16:14; Ps 89:33
7:16 1 Sam 25:28; Ps 89:36-37
7:18-29 ‖1 Chr 17:16-27
7:18 Exod 3:11; 1 Sam 18:18
7:19 1 Chr 17:17; Isa 55:8-9
7:20 1 Sam 16:7; John 21:17
7:22 Exod 10:2; Deut 3:24; 1 Sam 2:2; Ps 44:1
7:23 Deut 4:32; 9:26; 10:21
7:24 Gen 17:7-8; Exod 6:7; Deut 32:6; Ps 48:14
7:28 Exod 34:5-6; John 17:17
7:29 Num 6:23-27

7:19 The meaning of the Hebrew is uncertain.

7:8-16 David's request was good, but God said no. This does not mean that God rejected David. In fact, God was planning to do something even greater in David's life than allowing him the prestige of building the Temple. Although God turned down David's request, he promised to continue the house (or dynasty) of David forever. David's earthly dynasty ended four centuries later, but Jesus Christ, a direct descendant of David, was the ultimate fulfillment of this promise (Acts 2:22-36). Christ will reign for eternity—now in his spiritual kingdom and in heaven, and later, on earth, in the new Jerusalem (Luke 1:30-33; Revelation 21). Have you prayed with good intentions, only to have God say no? This is God's way of directing you to a greater purpose in your life. Accepting God's no requires as great a faith as carrying out his yes.

7:18ff This section records David's prayer expressing his humble acceptance of God's promise to extend his dynasty forever. David realized that these blessings were given to him and his descendants in order that Israel might benefit from them. They would help fulfill God's greater purpose and promises that through the nation the whole world would be blessed (Genesis 12:1-3).

3. David conquers the surrounding nations

David's Military Victories

8:1-14 //1 Chr 18:1-13 **8** After this, David subdued and humbled the Philistines by conquering Gath, their
8:2 1 Kgs 4:21 largest city.* 2 David also conquered the land of Moab. He made the people lie down
2 Kgs 3:4; 17:3 on the ground in a row, and he measured them off in groups with a length of rope. He
measured off two groups to be executed for every one group to be spared. The Moabites
who were spared became David's servants and brought him tribute money.
8:3 1 Sam 14:47 3 David also destroyed the forces of Hadadezer son of Rehob, king of Zobah, when
2 Sam 10:16, 19 Hadadezer marched out to strengthen his control along the Euphrates River. 4 David
8:4 Josh 11:6, 9 captured seventeen hundred charioteers* and twenty thousand foot soldiers. Then he
crippled all but one hundred of the chariot horses.
8:5 1 Kgs 11:23-25 5 When Arameans from Damascus arrived to help Hadadezer, David killed twenty-two
8:6 2 Sam 3:18 thousand of them. 6 Then he placed several army garrisons in Damascus, the Aramean
capital, and the Arameans became David's subjects and brought him tribute money. So
8:7 1 Kgs 10:16 the LORD gave David victory wherever he went. 7 David brought the gold shields of
8:8 Ezek 47:16 Hadadezer's officers to Jerusalem, 8 along with a large amount of bronze from Hadadezer's cities of Tebah* and Berothai.
9 When King Toi of Hamath heard that David had destroyed the army of Hadadezer,
10 he sent his son Joram to congratulate David on his success. Hadadezer and Toi had
long been enemies, and there had been many wars between them. Joram presented David
8:11 1 Kgs 7:51 with many gifts of silver, gold, and bronze. 11 King David dedicated all these gifts to the
LORD, along with the silver and gold he had set apart from the other nations he had
subdued—12 Edom,* Moab, Ammon, Philistia, and Amalek—and from Hadadezer son
of Rehob, king of Zobah.
8:13 2 Kgs 14:7 1 Chr 18:12 13 So David became very famous. After his return he destroyed eighteen thousand

8:1 Hebrew *by conquering Metheg-ammah,* a name which means "the bridle," possibly referring to the size of the city or the tribute money taken from it. Compare 1 Chr 18:1. **8:4** Greek version reads *1,000 chariots and 7,000 charioteers;* compare 1 Chr 18:4. **8:8** As in some Greek manuscripts (see also 1 Chr 18:8); Hebrew reads *Betah.* **8:12** As in a few Hebrew manuscripts and Greek and Syriac versions (see also 8:14; 1 Chr 18:11); most Hebrew manuscripts read *Aram.*

COVENANTS
A covenant is a legally binding obligation (promise). Throughout history God has made covenants with his people—he would keep his side if they would keep theirs. Here are seven covenants found in the Bible.

Name and Reference	*God's Promise*	*Sign*
In Eden Genesis 3:15	Satan and mankind will be enemies.	Pain of childbirth
Noah Genesis 9:8–17	God would never again destroy the earth with a flood.	Rainbow
Abraham Genesis 15:12–21; 17:1–14	Abraham's descendants would become a great nation if they obeyed God. God would be their God forever.	Smoking firepot and flaming torch
At Mount Sinai Exodus 19:5, 6	Israel would be God's special people, a holy nation. But they would have to keep their part of the covenant—obedience.	The Exodus
The Priesthood Numbers 25:10–13	Aaron's descendants would be priests forever.	The Aaronic priesthood
David 2 Samuel 7:13; 23:5	Salvation would come through David's line through the birth of the Messiah.	David's line continued, and the Messiah was born a descendant of David
New Covenant Hebrews 8:6–13	Forgiveness and salvation are available through faith in Christ.	Christ's resurrection

8:1-5 Part of God's covenant with David included the promise that the Israelites' enemies would be defeated and would no longer oppress them (7:10, 11). God fulfilled this promise by helping David defeat the opposing nations. Several enemies are listed in this chapter: (1) *The Moabites,* descendants of Lot who lived east of the Dead Sea. They posed a constant military and religious threat to Israel (Numbers 25:1-3; Judges 3:12-30; 1 Samuel 14:47). David seemed to have a good relationship with the Moabites at one time. (2) *King Hadadezer of Zobah.* His defeat at David's hands fulfilled God's promise to Abraham that Israel would control the land as far north as the Euphrates River (Genesis 15:18). (3) *The Edomites,* descendants of Esau (Genesis 36:1) who were also archenemies of Israel (see 2 Kings 8:20; Jeremiah 49:7-22; Ezekiel 25:12-14; and the note on Genesis 36:9).

8:6 The *tribute* was the tax levied on conquered nations. The tax helped to support Israel's government and demonstrated that the conquered nation was under Israel's control.

Edomites* in the Valley of Salt. 14 He placed army garrisons throughout Edom, and all
the Edomites became David's subjects. This was another example of how the LORD made
David victorious wherever he went.
15 David reigned over all Israel and was fair to everyone. 16 Joab son of Zeruiah was
commander of the army. Jehoshaphat son of Ahilud was the royal historian. 17 Zadok son
of Ahitub and Ahimelech son of Abiathar were the priests. Seraiah was the court
secretary. 18 Benaiah son of Jehoiada was captain of the king's bodyguard.* David's sons
served as priestly leaders.*

8:14 Gen 27:30, 37-40
8:15-18 //1 Chr 18:14-17
8:16 2 Sam 2:13; 1 Kgs 4:1, 4
8:18 2 Sam 20:7, 23; 1 Kgs 1:38, 44; 1 Chr 18:17

David's Kindness to Mephibosheth

9 One day David began wondering if anyone in Saul's family was still alive, for he
had promised Jonathan that he would show kindness to them. 2 He summoned a man
named Ziba, who had been one of Saul's servants. "Are you Ziba?" the king asked.
"Yes sir, I am," Ziba replied.
3 The king then asked him, "Is anyone still alive from Saul's family? If so, I want to
show God's kindness to them in any way I can."
Ziba replied, "Yes, one of Jonathan's sons is still alive, but he is crippled."
4 "Where is he?" the king asked.
"In Lo-debar," Ziba told him, "at the home of Makir son of Ammiel." 5 So David sent
for him and brought him from Makir's home. 6 His name was Mephibosheth*; he was
Jonathan's son and Saul's grandson. When he came to David, he bowed low in great fear
and said, "I am your servant."
7 But David said, "Don't be afraid! I've asked you to come so that I can be kind to you
because of my vow to your father, Jonathan. I will give you all the land that once
belonged to your grandfather Saul, and you may live here with me at the palace!"

9:1 1 Sam 20:14-17, 42
9:2 2 Sam 16:1-4; 19:17
9:3 1 Sam 20:14; 2 Sam 4:4
9:4 2 Sam 17:27-29
9:7 2 Sam 19:28; 2 Kgs 25:29

8:13 As in a few Hebrew manuscripts and Greek and Syriac versions (see also 8:14; 1 Chr 18:12); most Hebrew manuscripts read *Arameans*. **8:18a** Hebrew *of the Kerethites and Pelethites*. **8:18b** Hebrew *David's sons were priests;* compare parallel text at 1 Chr 18:17. **9:6** Also known as *Meribbaal*.

8:15 David pleased the people (3:36), not because he tried to please them, but because he tried to please God. Often those who try the hardest to become popular never make it. But the praise of people is not that important. Don't spend your time devising ways to become accepted in the public eye. Instead, strive to do what is right, and both God and people will respect your convictions.

DAVID'S ENEMIES
David wanted to complete the conquest of Canaan begun by Joshua. He defeated the Jebusites at Jerusalem and the Philistines in the vicinity of Gath. The Ammonites, Arameans, and Moabites became his subjects. He put garrisons in Edom and levied a tax upon them.

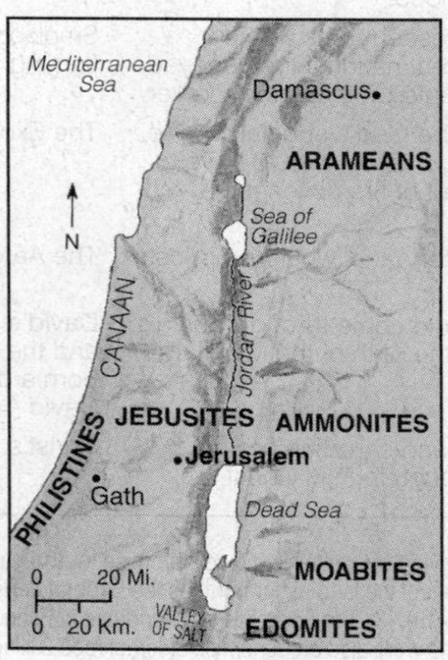

8:15 King David's reign was characterized by doing what was "fair to everyone." David was fair in interpreting the law, administering punishment with mercy, respecting people's rights, and recognizing people's duty toward God. Is it any wonder that almost everyone trusted and followed David? Why was it good for David to pursue justice? (1) It was God's command (Deuteronomy 16:18-20) and in keeping with his character (Deuteronomy 32:4). God's laws were meant to establish a just society. (2) It was in the nation's best interest because times would arise when each individual would need justice. Justice should characterize the way you relate to people. Make sure you are fair in the way you treat them.

9:1ff Most kings in David's day tried to wipe out the families of their rivals in order to prevent any descendants from seeking the throne. But David showed kindness to Mephibosheth, whose father was Jonathan and whose grandfather was King Saul. David was kind, partly because of his loyalty to God's previously anointed king (see the note on 1 Samuel 24:5, 6); partly for political reasons—to unite Judah and Israel (see the notes on 3:13, 14 and 3:29); and mainly because of his vow to show kindness to all of Jonathan's descendants (1 Samuel 20:14-17).

9:3 How Mephibosheth became crippled is recorded in 4:4. Mephibosheth was five years old when Saul and Jonathan died.

9:5, 6 Mephibosheth was afraid to visit the king, who wanted to treat him like a prince. Although Mephibosheth feared for his life and may have felt unworthy, that didn't mean he should refuse David's gifts. When God graciously offers us forgiveness of sins and a place in heaven, we may feel unworthy, but we will receive these gifts if we accept them. A reception even warmer than the one David gave Mephibosheth waits for all who receive God's gifts through trusting Jesus Christ, not because we deserve it, but because of God's promise (Ephesians 2:8, 9).

9:7 His treatment of Mephibosheth shows David's integrity as a leader who accepted his obligation to show love and mercy. His generous provision for Jonathan's son goes beyond any political benefit he might have received. Are you able to forgive those who have wronged you? Can you be generous with those less deserving? Each time we show compassion, our character is strengthened.

[8]Mephibosheth fell to the ground before the king. "Should the king show such kindness to a dead dog like me?" he exclaimed.

9:9 2 Sam 16:4; 19:29
9:10 2 Sam 19:28

[9]Then the king summoned Saul's servant Ziba and said, "I have given your master's grandson everything that belonged to Saul and his family. [10]You and your sons and servants are to farm the land for him to produce food for his family. But Mephibosheth will live here at the palace with me."

Ziba, who had fifteen sons and twenty servants, replied, [11]"Yes, my lord; I will do all that you have commanded." And from that time on, Mephibosheth ate regularly with David, as though he were one of his own sons. [12]Mephibosheth had a young son named Mica. And from then on, all the members of Ziba's household were Mephibosheth's servants. [13]And Mephibosheth, who was crippled in both feet, moved to Jerusalem to live at the palace.

David Defeats the Ammonites

10:1-19 //1 Chr 19:1-19

10 Some time after this, King Nahash of the Ammonites died, and his son Hanun became king. [2]David said, "I am going to show complete loyalty to Hanun because his father, Nahash, was always completely loyal to me." So David sent ambassadors to express sympathy to Hanun about his father's death.

But when David's ambassadors arrived in the land of Ammon, [3]Hanun's advisers said to their master, "Do you really think these men are coming here to honor your father? No! David has sent them to spy out the city so that they can come in and conquer it!"

10:4 Isa 15:2; 20:4 Jer 41:5

[4]So Hanun seized David's ambassadors and shaved off half of each man's beard, cut off their robes at the buttocks, and sent them back to David in shame. [5]When David heard what had happened, he sent messengers to tell the men to stay at Jericho until their beards grew out, for they were very embarrassed by their appearance.

10:6 Gen 34:30 2 Kgs 7:6

[6]Now the people of Ammon realized how seriously they had angered David, so they hired twenty thousand Aramean mercenaries from the lands of Beth-rehob and Zobah, one thousand from the king of Maacah, and twelve thousand from the land of Tob. [7]When David heard about this, he sent Joab and the entire Israelite army to fight them. [8]The Ammonite troops drew up their battle lines at the entrance of the city gates, while the Arameans from Zobah and Rehob and the men from Tob and Maacah positioned themselves to fight in the open fields.

[9]When Joab saw that he would have to fight on two fronts, he chose the best troops in his army. He placed them under his personal command and led them out to fight the Arameans in the fields. [10]He left the rest of the army under the command of his brother Abishai, who was to attack the Ammonites. [11]"If the Arameans are too strong for me, then come over and help me," Joab told his brother. "And if the Ammonites are too strong for you, I will come and help you. [12]Be courageous! Let us fight bravely to save our people and the cities of our God. May the LORD's will be done."

10:12 Deut 31:6 1 Sam 3:18 1 Cor 16:13

10:4, 5 In Israelite culture, all men wore full beards. It was a sign of maturity and authority. Thus when these ambassadors had their beards half shaved, they suffered great indignity. Cutting off their garments also exposed them to ridicule.

10:6 Because Hanun took the wrong advice, he suspected the motives of the ambassadors and humiliated them. Then he realized that David was angry and immediately marshaled his forces for battle. Hanun should have thought through the advice more carefully; but even if he had not, he should have tried to negotiate with David. Instead, he refused to admit any fault and got ready for war. Often we respond angrily and defensively rather than admitting our mistakes, apologizing, and trying to defuse the other person's anger. Instead of fighting, we should seek peace.

10:12 There must be a balance in life between our actions and our faith in God. Joab said, "Let us fight bravely." In other words, they should do what they could, using their minds to figure out the best techniques and using their resources. But he also said, "The LORD's will be done." He knew that the outcome was in God's hands. We should use our minds and our resources to obey God, while at the same time trusting God for the outcome.

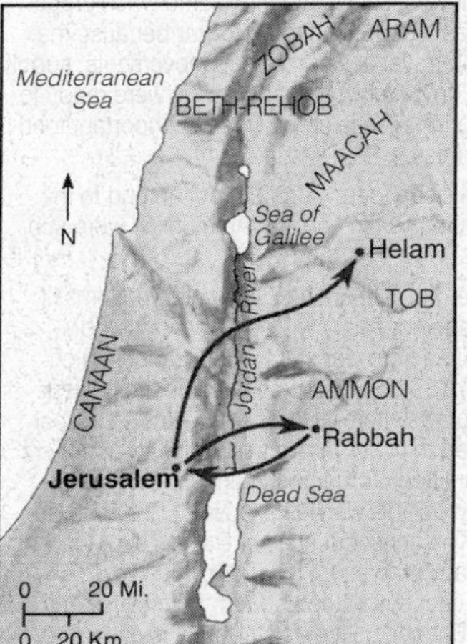

DAVID AND THE AMMONITES
Ammon gathered together its troops from the north; Joab brought the Israelite army to attack them near Rabbah. Joab returned to Jerusalem victorious, but the enemy recruited additional forces and regrouped at Helam. David himself led the next victorious attack.

[13]When Joab and his troops attacked, the Arameans began to run away. [14]And when 10:13
the Ammonites saw the Arameans running, they ran from Abishai and retreated into the 1 Kgs 20:13-21
city. After the battle was over, Joab returned to Jerusalem.
[15]The Arameans now realized that they were no match for Israel. So when they
regrouped, [16]they were joined by additional Aramean troops summoned by Hadadezer
from the other side of the Euphrates River.* These troops arrived at Helam under the
command of Shobach, the commander of all Hadadezer's forces. [17]When David heard
what was happening, he mobilized all Israel, crossed the Jordan River, and led the army
to Helam. The Arameans positioned themselves there in battle formation and then
attacked David. [18]But again the Arameans fled from the Israelites. This time David's 10:18
forces killed seven hundred charioteers and forty thousand horsemen,* including Sho- 1 Chr 19:17-18 10:19
bach, the commander of their army. [19]When Hadadezer and his Aramean allies realized 2 Sam 8:6
they had been defeated by Israel, they surrendered to them and became their subjects.
After that, the Arameans were afraid to help the Ammonites.

B. DAVID'S STRUGGLES (11:1—24:25)

After restoring the nation to peace and great military power, David's personal life becomes entangled in sin. He commits adultery with Bathsheba and then orders her husband killed in an attempted cover-up. David deeply regretted what he had done and sought God's forgiveness, but the child of his sinful act died. We may be forgiven by God for our sins, but we will often experience harsh consequences.

1. David and Bathsheba

David Sins with Bathsheba

11 The following spring, the time of year when kings go to war, David sent Joab and 11:1 2 Sam 12:26-29
the Israelite army to destroy the Ammonites. In the process they laid siege to the 1 Chr 20:1 Amos 1:14
city of Rabbah. But David stayed behind in Jerusalem.
[2]Late one afternoon David got out of bed after taking a nap and went for a stroll on the 11:2
roof of the palace. As he looked out over the city, he noticed a woman of unusual beauty Deut 22:8 1 Sam 9:25
taking a bath. [3]He sent someone to find out who she was, and he was told, "She is 11:3
Bathsheba, the daughter of Eliam and the wife of Uriah the Hittite." [4]Then David sent for 2 Sam 23:39
her; and when she came to the palace, he slept with her. (She had just completed the 1 Chr 3:5 11:4
purification rites after having her menstrual period.) Then she returned home. [5]When Lev 15:19; 18:20-28
Bathsheba discovered that she was pregnant, she sent a message to inform David. Ps 51:title
[6]So David sent word to Joab: "Send me Uriah the Hittite." [7]When Uriah arrived, David 11:5 Lev 20:10
asked him how Joab and the army were getting along and how the war was progressing. Deut 22:22
[8]Then he told Uriah, "Go on home and relax." David even sent a gift to Uriah after he had

10:16 Hebrew *the river.* **10:18** Some Greek manuscripts read *foot soldiers;* compare parallel text at 1 Chr 19:18.

11:1 Winter is the rainy season in Israel, the time when crops are planted. Spring was a good time to go to war because the roads were dry, making travel easier for troop movements, supply wagons, and chariots. In Israel, wheat and barley were ready to be harvested in the spring. These crops were an important food source for traveling armies.

11:1 This successful siege (see 12:26, 27) put an end to the Ammonites' power. From this time on, the Ammonites were subject to Israel.

11:1ff In the episode with Bathsheba, David allowed himself to fall deeper and deeper into sin. (1) David abandoned his purpose by staying home from war (11:1). (2) He focused on his own desires (11:2). (3) When temptation came, he looked into it instead of turning away from it (11:3). (4) He sinned deliberately (11:4). (5) He tried to cover up his sin by deceiving others (11:6-15). (6) He committed murder to continue the cover-up (11:15, 17). Eventually David's sin was exposed (12:9) and punished (12:10-14). (7) The consequences of David's sin were far-reaching, affecting many others (11:17; 12:11, 14, 15).

David could have chosen to stop and turn from evil at any stage along the way. But once sin gets started, it is difficult to stop (James 1:14, 15). The deeper the mess, the less we want to admit having caused it. It's much easier to stop sliding down a hill when you are near the top than when you are halfway down. The best solution is to stop sin before it starts.

11:3 See 1 Kings 1 for Bathsheba's Profile.

11:3, 4 As David looked from the roof of the palace, he saw a beautiful woman bathing, and he was filled with lust. David should have left the roof and fled the temptation. Instead, he entertained the temptation by inquiring about Bathsheba. The results were devastating.

To flee temptation, (1) ask God in earnest prayer to help you stay away from people, places, and situations that may tempt you. (2) Memorize and meditate on portions of Scripture that combat your specific weaknesses. At the root of most temptation is a real need or desire that God can fill, but we must trust in his timing. (3) Find another believer with whom you can openly share your struggles, and call this person for help when temptation strikes.

11:4 That Bathsheba had just completed the purification rites following menstruation means that she could not have already been pregnant by her own husband when David slept with her. Leviticus 15:19-30 gives more information on the purification rites Bathsheba had to perform.

left the palace. 9But Uriah wouldn't go home. He stayed that night at the palace entrance
with some of the king's other servants.
10When David heard what Uriah had done, he summoned him and asked, "What's
the matter with you? Why didn't you go home last night after being away for so long?"
11Uriah replied, "The Ark and the armies of Israel and Judah are living in tents,* and
11:11 2 Sam 7:2; 20:6 — Joab and his officers are camping in the open fields. How could I go home to wine and
dine and sleep with my wife? I swear that I will never be guilty of acting like that."
12"Well, stay here tonight," David told him, "and tomorrow you may return to the
army." So Uriah stayed in Jerusalem that day and the next. 13Then David invited him to
dinner and got him drunk. But even then he couldn't get Uriah to go home to his wife.
Again he slept at the palace entrance.

David Arranges for Uriah's Death

14So the next morning David wrote a letter to Joab and gave it to Uriah to deliver. 15The
letter instructed Joab, "Station Uriah on the front lines where the battle is fiercest. Then
11:14 1 Kgs 21:8-10 — pull back so that he will be killed." 16So Joab assigned Uriah to a spot close to the city
11:15 2 Sam 12:9 — wall where he knew the enemy's strongest men were fighting. 17And Uriah was killed
along with several other Israelite soldiers.
18Then Joab sent a battle report to David. 19He told his messenger, "Report all the
news of the battle to the king. 20But he might get angry and ask, 'Why did the troops go
so close to the city? Didn't they know there would be shooting from the walls? 21Wasn't
Gideon's son Abimelech killed* at Thebez by a woman who threw a millstone down on
him?' Then tell him, 'Uriah the Hittite was killed, too.'"
11:21 Judg 9:50-54 — 22So the messenger went to Jerusalem and gave a complete report to David. 23"The
enemy came out against us," he said. "And as we chased them back to the city gates, 24the
archers on the wall shot arrows at us. Some of our men were killed, including Uriah the
Hittite."
25"Well, tell Joab not to be discouraged," David said. "The sword kills one as well as
another! Fight harder next time, and conquer the city!"

11:11 Or *at Succoth.* **11:21** Hebrew *Was not Abimelech son of Jerubbesheth killed.*

DAVID'S FAMILY TROUBLES

David's many wives caused him much grief. And as a result of David's sin with Bathsheba, God said that murder would be a constant threat in his family, his family would rebel, and someone else would sleep with his wives. All this happened as the prophet Nathan had predicted. The consequences of sin affect not only us but those we know and love. Remember that the next time you are tempted to sin.

Wife	*Children*	*What Happened*
Michal (Saul's daughter)	She was childless	David gave her five nephews to the Gibeonites to be killed because of Saul's sins
Ahinoam (from Jezreel)	Amnon, David's firstborn	He raped Tamar, his half sister, and was later murdered by Absalom in revenge
Maacah (daughter of King Talmai of Geshur)	Absalom, third son Tamar, the only daughter mentioned by name	Absalom killed Amnon for raping Tamar and then fled to Geshur. Later he returned, only to rebel against David. He set up a tent on the roof and slept with 10 of his father's concubines there. His pride led to his death
Haggith	Adonijah, fourth son. He was very handsome, but it is recorded that he was never disciplined	He set himself up as king before David's death. His plot was exposed, and David spared his life, but his half brother Solomon later had him executed
Bathsheba	Unnamed son	Died in fulfillment of God's punishment for David and Bathsheba's adultery
Bathsheba	Solomon	Became the next king of Israel. Ironically, Solomon's many wives caused his downfall

---

11:15 David put both Bathsheba and Joab in difficult situations. Bathsheba knew it was wrong to commit adultery, but to refuse a king's request could mean punishment or death. Joab did not know why Uriah had to die, but it was obvious the king wanted him killed. We sometimes face situations with only two apparent choices, and both seem wrong. When that happens, we must not lose sight of what God wants. The answer may be to seek out more choices. By doing this, we are likely to find a choice that honors God.

11:25 David's response to Uriah's death seems flippant and insensitive. While he grieved deeply for Saul and Abner, his rivals (chapter 1; 3:31-39), he showed no grief for Uriah, a good man with strong spiritual character. Why? David had become callous to his own sin. The only way he could cover up his first sin (adultery) was to sin again, and soon he no longer felt guilty for what he had done. Feelings are not reliable guides for determining right and wrong. Deliberate, repeated sinning had dulled David's

26 When Bathsheba heard that her husband was dead, she mourned for him. 27 When
the period of mourning was over, David sent for her and brought her to the palace, and
she became one of his wives. Then she gave birth to a son. But the LORD was very
displeased with what David had done.

Nathan Rebukes David

12 So the LORD sent Nathan the prophet to tell David this story: "There were two men
in a certain town. One was rich, and one was poor. 2 The rich man owned many sheep
and cattle. 3 The poor man owned nothing but a little lamb he had worked hard to buy. He
raised that little lamb, and it grew up with his children. It ate from the man's own plate and
drank from his cup. He cuddled it in his arms like a baby daughter. 4 One day a guest arrived
at the home of the rich man. But instead of killing a lamb from his own flocks for food, he
took the poor man's lamb and killed it and served it to his guest."
5 David was furious. "As surely as the LORD lives," he vowed, "any man who would
do such a thing deserves to die! 6 He must repay four lambs to the poor man for the one
he stole and for having no pity."
7 Then Nathan said to David, "You are that man! The LORD, the God of Israel, says, 'I
anointed you king of Israel and saved you from the power of Saul. 8 I gave you his house
and his wives and the kingdoms of Israel and Judah. And if that had not been enough, I
would have given you much, much more. 9 Why, then, have you despised the word of
the LORD and done this horrible deed? For you have murdered Uriah and stolen his wife.
10 From this time on, the sword will be a constant threat to your family, because you have
despised me by taking Uriah's wife to be your own.
11 "'Because of what you have done, I, the LORD, will cause your own household to rebel
against you. I will give your wives to another man, and he will go to bed with them in public
view. 12 You did it secretly, but I will do this to you openly in the sight of all Israel.'"

David Confesses His Guilt

13 Then David confessed to Nathan, "I have sinned against the LORD."
Nathan replied, "Yes, but the LORD has forgiven you, and you won't die for this sin.
14 But you have given the enemies of the LORD great opportunity to despise and
blaspheme him, so your child will die."
15 After Nathan returned to his home, the LORD made Bathsheba's baby deathly ill.
16 David begged God to spare the child. He went without food and lay all night on the

11:26 Deut 34:8; 1 Sam 31:13
11:27 Ps 51:4-5
12:1 2 Sam 7:2, 17; Ps 51:title
12:5 1 Kgs 20:40
12:6 Exod 22:1
12:7 1 Sam 16:13; 1 Kgs 20:42
12:8 2 Sam 9:7
12:9 2 Sam 11:14, 27
12:10 2 Sam 13:28-29; 18:14; 1 Kgs 2:23
12:11 2 Sam 16:21-22
12:13 Lev 20:10; 24:17; Prov 28:13; Mic 7:18; Luke 18:13
12:14 Isa 52:5; Rom 2:23-24

---

sensitivity to God's laws and others' rights. The more you try to cover up a sin, the more insensitive you become toward it. Don't become hardened to sin, as David did. Confess your wrong actions to God before you forget they are sins.

12:1ff As a prophet, Nathan was required to confront sin, even the sin of a king. It took great courage, skill, and tact to speak to David in a way that would make him aware of his wrong actions. When you have to confront someone with unpleasant news, pray for courage, skill, and tact. If you want that person to respond constructively, think through what you are going to say. How you present your message may be as important as what you say. Season your words with wisdom.

12:5, 6 It was a year later, and by then David had become so insensitive to his own sins that he didn't realize he was the villain in Nathan's story. The qualities we condemn in others are often our own character flaws. Which friends, associates, or family members do you find easy to criticize and hard to accept? Instead of trying to change them, ask God to help you understand their feelings and see your own flaws more clearly. You may discover that in condemning others, you have been condemning yourself.

12:10-14 The predictions in these verses came true. Because David murdered Uriah and stole his wife, (1) murder was a constant threat in his family (13:26-30; 18:14, 15; 1 Kings 2:23-25); (2) his household rebelled against him (15:13); (3) his wives were given to another in public view (16:20-23); (4) his first child by Bathsheba died (12:18). If David had known the painful consequences of his sin, he might not have pursued the pleasures of the moment.

12:13 During this incident, David wrote Psalm 51, giving valuable insight into his character and offering hope for us as well. No matter how miserable guilt makes you feel or how terribly you have sinned, you can pour out your heart to God and seek his forgiveness as David did. There is forgiveness for us when we sin. David also wrote Psalm 32 to express the joy he felt after he was forgiven.

12:14 David confessed and repented of his sin (12:13), but God's judgment was that his child would die. The consequences of David's sin were irreversible. Sometimes an apology isn't enough. When God forgives us and restores our relationship with him, he doesn't eliminate all the consequences of our wrongdoing. We may be tempted to say, "If this is wrong, I can always apologize to God," but we must remember that we may set into motion events with irreversible consequences.

12:14 Why did this child have to die? This was not a judgment on the child for being conceived out of wedlock, but a judgment on David for his sin. David and Bathsheba deserved to die, but God spared their lives and took the child instead. God still had work for David to do in building the kingdom. Perhaps the child's death was a greater punishment for David than his own death would have been.

It is also possible that had the child lived, God's name would have been dishonored among Israel's pagan neighbors. What would they have thought of a God who rewards murder and adultery by giving a king a new heir? A baby's death is tragic, but despising God brings death to entire nations. While God readily forgave David's sin, he did not negate all its consequences.

12:17 2 Sam 3:35 bare ground. 17 The leaders of the nation pleaded with him to get up and eat with them,
but he refused. 18 Then on the seventh day the baby died. David's advisers were afraid to
tell him. "He was so broken up about the baby being sick," they said. "What will he do
to himself when we tell him the child is dead?"
19 But when David saw them whispering, he realized what had happened. "Is the baby
dead?" he asked.
"Yes," they replied. 20 Then David got up from the ground, washed himself, put on
lotions, and changed his clothes. Then he went to the Tabernacle and worshiped the
LORD. After that, he returned to the palace and ate. 21 His advisers were amazed. "We
don't understand you," they told him. "While the baby was still living, you wept and
refused to eat. But now that the baby is dead, you have stopped your mourning and are
eating again."
12:22 Isa 38:1-5 Jon 3:9 22 David replied, "I fasted and wept while the child was alive, for I said, 'Perhaps the
LORD will be gracious to me and let the child live.' 23 But why should I fast when he is
12:23 Gen 37:35 Job 7:9-10 dead? Can I bring him back again? I will go to him one day, but he cannot return to me."
24 Then David comforted Bathsheba, his wife, and slept with her. She became pregnant
12:24 1 Chr 22:9 and gave birth to a son, and they named him Solomon. The LORD loved the child 25 and
sent word through Nathan the prophet that his name should be Jedidiah—"beloved of
the LORD"—because the LORD loved him.

NATHAN

This prophet lived up to the meaning of his name, "He [God] has given." He was a necessary and helpful gift from God to David. He served as God's spokesman to David and proved himself a fearless friend and counselor, always willing to speak the truth, even when he knew great pain would result.

In confronting David's multiple sin of coveting, theft, adultery, and murder in his affair with Bathsheba, Nathan was able to help David see his own wrongdoing by showing that he would not have tolerated such actions from anyone else. David's repentance allowed Nathan to comfort him with the reality of God's forgiveness and at the same time remind him of the painful consequences his sin would bring.

Nathan's approach helps us judge our actions. How often do we make choices that we would condemn others for making? It is helpful to ask ourselves how God and others see our actions. Unfortunately, we have a huge capacity to lie to ourselves. God still provides two safeguards against self-deception: his Word and true friends. In each case, we get a view beyond ourselves. You are holding God's Word. Let it speak to you about yourself, even if the truth is painful. If you don't have a friend like Nathan, ask God for one. And ask God to use you as a suitable Nathan for someone else.

Strengths and accomplishments
- A trusted adviser to David
- A prophet of God
- A fearless but careful confronter
- One of God's controls in David's life

Weakness and mistake
- His eagerness to see David build a temple for God in Jerusalem made him speak without God's instruction

Lessons from his life
- We should not be afraid to tell the truth to those we care about
- A trustworthy companion is one of God's greatest gifts
- God cares enough to find a way to communicate to us when we are in the wrong

Vital statistics
- Occupations: Prophet, royal adviser
- Contemporaries: David, Bathsheba, Solomon, Zadok, Adonijah

Key verse
"So Nathan went back to David and told him everything the LORD had said" (2 Samuel 7:17).

Nathan's story is told in 2 Samuel 7—1 Kings 1. He is also mentioned in 1 Chronicles 17:15; 2 Chronicles 9:29; 29:25.

12:20-24 David did not continue to dwell on his sin. He returned to God, and God forgave him, opening the way to begin life anew. Even the name God gave Solomon, *Jedidiah* ("beloved of the LORD"; 12:25) was a reminder of God's grace. When we return to God, accept his forgiveness, and change our ways, he gives us a fresh start. To feel forgiven as David did, admit your sins to God and turn to him. Then move ahead with a new and fresh approach to life.

12:22, 23 Perhaps the most bitter experience in life is the death of one's child. For comfort in such difficult circumstances, see Psalms 16:9-11; 17:15; 139; Isaiah 40:11.

12:24 Solomon was the fourth son of David and Bathsheba (1 Chronicles 3:5). Therefore, several years passed between the death of their first child and Solomon's birth. Bathsheba may still have been grieving over the child's death.

David Captures Rabbah

26 Meanwhile, Joab and the Israelite army were successfully ending their siege of **12:26** Deut 3:11
Rabbah, the capital of Ammon. 27 Joab sent messengers to tell David, "I have fought 1 Chr 20:1-3
against Rabbah and captured its water supply.* 28 Now bring the rest of the army and
finish the job, so you will get credit for the victory instead of me."

29 So David led the rest of his army to Rabbah and captured it. 30 David removed the **12:29-31** //1 Chr 20:1-3
crown from the king's head,* and it was placed on David's own head. The crown was
made of gold and set with gems, and it weighed about seventy-five pounds.* David took
a vast amount of plunder from the city. 31 He also made slaves of the people of Rabbah
and forced them to labor with saws, picks, and axes, and to work in the brick kilns. That
is how he dealt with the people of all the Ammonite cities. Then David and his army
returned to Jerusalem.

2. Turmoil in David's family

The Rape of Tamar

13 David's son Absalom had a beautiful sister named Tamar. And Amnon, her half **13:1** 2 Sam 3:2-3
brother, fell desperately in love with her. 2 Amnon became so obsessed with Tamar 1 Chr 3:2, 9
that he became ill. She was a virgin, and it seemed impossible that he could ever fulfill
his love for her.

3 Now Amnon had a very crafty friend—his cousin Jonadab. He was the son of David's **13:3** 1 Sam 16:9
brother Shimea.* 4 One day Jonadab said to Amnon, "What's the trouble? Why should
the son of a king look so dejected morning after morning?"

So Amnon told him, "I am in love with Tamar, Absalom's sister."

5 "Well," Jonadab said, "I'll tell you what to do. Go back to bed and pretend you are
sick. When your father comes to see you, ask him to let Tamar come and prepare some
food for you. Tell him you'll feel better if she feeds you."

6 So Amnon pretended to be sick. And when the king came to see him, Amnon asked
him, "Please let Tamar come to take care of me and cook something for me to eat." 7 So
David agreed and sent Tamar to Amnon's house to prepare some food for him.

8 When Tamar arrived at Amnon's house, she went to the room where he was lying down
so he could watch her mix some dough. Then she baked some special bread for him. 9 But **13:9** Gen 45:1
when she set the serving tray before him, he refused to eat. "Everyone get out of here,"
Amnon told his servants. So they all left. 10 Then he said to Tamar, "Now bring the food
into my bedroom and feed it to me here." So Tamar took it to him. 11 But as she was feeding **13:11** Gen 39:12
him, he grabbed her and demanded, "Come to bed with me, my darling sister."

12 "No, my brother!" she cried. "Don't be foolish! Don't do this to me! You know what **13:12** Lev 20:17
a serious crime it is to do such a thing in Israel. 13 Where could I go in my shame? And
you would be called one of the greatest fools in Israel. Please, just speak to the king about
it, and he will let you marry me."

14 But Amnon wouldn't listen to her, and since he was stronger than she was, he raped
her. 15 Then suddenly Amnon's love turned to hate, and he hated her even more than he
had loved her. "Get out of here!" he snarled at her.

16 "No, no!" Tamar cried. "To reject me now is a greater wrong than what you have
already done to me."

12:27 Or *captured the city of water.* **12:30a** Greek version reads *removed the crown of Milcom;* compare 1 Kgs 11:5. Milcom, also called Molech, was the god of the Ammonites. **12:30b** Hebrew *1 talent* [34 kilograms]. **13:3** Hebrew *Shimeah* (also in 13:32), a variant name for Shimea; compare 1 Chr 2:13.

13:3-5 Amnon was encouraged by his cousin Jonadab to commit sexual sin. We may be more vulnerable to the advice of our relatives because we are close to them. However, we must make sure to evaluate every piece of advice by God's standards, even when it comes from relatives.

13:14, 15 Love and lust are very different. After Amnon raped his half sister, his "love" turned to hate. Although he had claimed to be in love, he was actually overcome by lust. Love is patient; lust requires immediate satisfaction. Love is kind; lust is harsh. Love does not demand its own way; lust does. You can read about the characteristics of real love in 1 Corinthians 13. Lust may feel like love at first, but when physically expressed, it results in self-disgust and hatred of the other person. If you just can't wait, what you feel is not true love.

13:16 Rape was strictly forbidden by God (Deuteronomy 22:28, 29). Why was sending Tamar away an even greater crime? By throwing her out, Amnon made it look as if Tamar had made a shameful proposition to him, and there were no witnesses on her behalf because he had gotten rid of the servants. His crime destroyed her chances of marriage—because she was no longer a virgin, she could not be given in marriage.

But Amnon wouldn't listen to her. 17 He shouted for his servant and demanded,
13:18 Gen 37:23
"Throw this woman out, and lock the door behind her!"
18 So the servant put her out. She was wearing a long, beautiful robe,* as was the
13:19 Gen 37:29; 2 Sam 1:11; Esth 4:1
custom in those days for the king's virgin daughters. 19 But now Tamar tore her robe and
put ashes on her head. And then, with her face in her hands, she went away crying.
20 Her brother Absalom saw her and asked, "Is it true that Amnon has been with you?
Well, don't be so upset. Since he's your brother anyway, don't worry about it." So Tamar
13:22 Gen 31:24; Lev 19:17-18; 1 Jn 2:9-11
lived as a desolate woman in Absalom's house. 21 When King David heard what had
happened, he was very angry. 22 And though Absalom never spoke to Amnon about it, he
hated Amnon deeply because of what he had done to his sister.

Absalom's Revenge on Amnon

13:23 1 Sam 25:17
23 Two years later, when Absalom's sheep were being sheared at Baal-hazor near
Ephraim, Absalom invited all the king's sons to come to a feast. 24 He went to the king
and said, "My sheep-shearers are now at work. Would the king and his servants please
come to celebrate the occasion with me?"
25 The king replied, "No, my son. If we all came, we would be too much of a burden
on you." Absalom pressed him, but the king wouldn't come, though he sent his thanks.
26 "Well, then," Absalom said, "if you can't come, how about sending my brother
Amnon instead?"
"Why Amnon?" the king asked. 27 But Absalom kept on pressing the king until he
finally agreed to let all his sons attend, including Amnon.
28 Absalom told his men, "Wait until Amnon gets drunk; then at my signal, kill him!
Don't be afraid. I'm the one who has given the command. Take courage and do it!" 29 So
13:29 2 Sam 18:9
at Absalom's signal they murdered Amnon. Then the other sons of the king jumped on
their mules and fled.
30 As they were on the way back to Jerusalem, this report reached David: "Absalom
has killed all your sons; not one is left alive!" 31 The king jumped up, tore his robe, and
13:31 2 Sam 12:16
fell prostrate on the ground. His advisers also tore their clothes in horror and sorrow.
32 But just then Jonadab, the son of David's brother Shimea, arrived and said, "No, not
13:32 2 Sam 13:3-5
all your sons have been killed! It was only Amnon! Absalom has been plotting this ever
since Amnon raped his sister Tamar. 33 No, your sons aren't all dead! It was only Amnon."
13:34 2 Sam 18:24
34 Meanwhile Absalom escaped.
Then the watchman on the Jerusalem wall saw a great crowd coming toward the city
from the west. He ran to tell the king, "I see a crowd of people coming from the
Horonaim road* along the side of the hill."
35 "Look!" Jonadab told the king. "There they are now! Your sons are coming, just as
I said." 36 They soon arrived, weeping and sobbing, and the king and his officials wept
13:37 2 Sam 3:3; 14:23, 32
bitterly with them. 37 And David mourned many days for his son Amnon.
Absalom fled to his grandfather, Talmai son of Ammihud, the king of Geshur. 38 He
13:39 2 Sam 12:19-23
stayed there in Geshur for three years. 39 And David, now reconciled to Amnon's death,
longed to be reunited with his son Absalom.*

Joab Arranges for Absalom's Return

14:2 2 Chr 11:5-10; Amos 1:1
14 Joab realized how much the king longed to see Absalom. 2 So he sent for a woman
from Tekoa who had a reputation for great wisdom. He said to her, "Pretend you
are in mourning; wear mourning clothes and don't bathe or wear any perfume. Act like

13:18 Or *a robe with sleeves,* or *an ornamented robe.* The meaning of the Hebrew is uncertain. **13:34** As in Greek version; Hebrew reads *from the road behind him.* **13:39** Or *no longer felt a need to go out after Absalom.*

13:20 Absalom tried to comfort Tamar and persuade her not to turn the incident into a public scandal. Secretly, he planned to take revenge against Amnon himself. This he did two years later (13:23-33). Absalom told Tamar the crime was only a family matter. But God's standards for moral conduct are not suspended when we deal with family matters.

13:21-24 David was angry with Amnon for raping Tamar, but David did not punish him. David probably hesitated because (1) he didn't want to cross Amnon, who was his firstborn son (1 Chronicles 3:1) and therefore next in line to be king, and (2) David was guilty of a similar sin himself in his adultery with Bathsheba. While David was unsurpassed as a king and military leader, he lacked skill and sensitivity as a husband and father.

13:37-39 Absalom fled to Geshur because King Talmai was his grandfather (1 Chronicles 3:2), and he would be welcomed.

a woman who has been in deep sorrow for a long time. 3Then go to the king and tell him
the story I am about to tell you." Then Joab told her what to say.

14:3 2 Sam 14:19

4When the woman approached the king, she fell with her face down to the floor in
front of him and cried out, "O king! Help me!"
5"What's the trouble?" the king asked.
"I am a widow," she replied. 6"My two sons had a fight out in the field. And since no
one was there to stop it, one of them was killed. 7Now the rest of the family is demanding,
'Let us have your son. We will execute him for murdering his brother. He doesn't deserve
to inherit his family's property.' But if I do that, I will have no one left, and my husband's
name and family will disappear from the face of the earth."

14:7 Num 35:19; Deut 19:12-13

8"Leave it to me," the king told her. "Go home, and I'll see to it that no one touches him."
9"Oh, thank you, my lord," she replied. "And I'll take the responsibility if you are
criticized for helping me like this."

14:9 Gen 43:9; 1 Sam 25:24

10"Don't worry about that!" the king said. "If anyone objects, bring them to me. I can
assure you they will never complain again!"
11Then she said, "Please swear to me by the LORD your God that you won't let anyone
take vengeance against my son. I want no more bloodshed."

14:11 Num 35:12, 19, 21; Deut 19:4-10; 1 Sam 14:45

"As surely as the LORD lives," he replied, "not a hair on your son's head will be
disturbed!"
12"Please let me ask one more thing of you!" she said.
"Go ahead," he urged. "Speak!"
13She replied, "Why don't you do as much for all the people of God as you have
promised to do for me? You have convicted yourself in making this decision, because
you have refused to bring home your own banished son. 14All of us must die eventually.
Our lives are like water spilled out on the ground, which cannot be gathered up again.
That is why God tries to bring us back when we have been separated from him. He does
not sweep away the lives of those he cares about—and neither should you!

14:13 2 Sam 13:37-39; 1 Kgs 20:40-42

14:14 Job 34:14-15; Heb 9:27

15"But I have come to plead with you for my son because my life and my son's life
have been threatened. I said to myself, 'Perhaps the king will listen to me 16and rescue
us from those who would cut us off from God's people. 17Yes, the king will give us peace
of mind again.' I know that you are like an angel of God and can discern good from evil.
May the LORD your God be with you."

14:17 1 Sam 29:9; 2 Sam 19:27

18"I want to know one thing," the king replied.
"Yes, my lord?" she asked.
19"Did Joab send you here?"
And the woman replied, "My lord the king, how can I deny it? Nobody can hide
anything from you. Yes, Joab sent me and told me what to say. 20He did it to place the
matter before you in a different light. But you are as wise as an angel of God, and you
understand everything that happens among us!"

14:19 2 Sam 14:3

21So the king sent for Joab and told him, "All right, go and bring back the young man
Absalom."
22Joab fell to the ground before the king and blessed him and said, "At last I know
that I have gained your approval, for you have granted me this request!"
23Then Joab went to Geshur and brought Absalom back to Jerusalem. 24But the king
gave this order: "Absalom may go to his own house, but he must never come into my
presence." So Absalom did not see the king.

14:23 2 Sam 13:37-39

Absalom Reconciled to David

25Now no one in Israel was as handsome as Absalom. From head to foot, he was the
perfect specimen of a man. 26He cut his hair only once a year, and then only because
it was too heavy to carry around. When he weighed it out, it came to five pounds!*
27He had three sons and one daughter. His daughter's name was Tamar, and she was
very beautiful.

14:27 2 Sam 13:1

14:26 Hebrew *200 shekels* [2.3 kilograms] *by the royal standard.*

14:11 The law provided for a way to avenge murder. Numbers 35:9-21 records how cities of refuge protected people from revenge and how blood avengers were to pursue murderers. This woman was asking for the king's protection against any claim against her.

14:28 2 Sam 14:24 28Absalom lived in Jerusalem for two years without getting to see the king. 29Then
Absalom sent for Joab to ask him to intercede for him, but Joab refused to come.
Absalom sent for him a second time, but again Joab refused to come. 30So Absalom said
to his servants, "Go and set fire to Joab's barley field, the field next to mine." So they
set his field on fire, as Absalom had commanded.
31Then Joab came to Absalom and demanded, "Why did your servants set my field
on fire?"
14:32 1 Sam 20:8 32And Absalom replied, "Because I wanted you to ask the king why he brought me
back from Geshur if he didn't intend to see me. I might as well have stayed there. Let
me see the king; if he finds me guilty of anything, then let him execute me."
14:33 Gen 33:4 Luke 15:20 33So Joab told the king what Absalom had said. Then at last David summoned his
estranged son, and Absalom came and bowed low before the king, and David kissed
him.

ABSALOM

A father's mistakes are often reflected in the lives of his children. In Absalom, David saw a bitter replay and amplification of many of his own past sins. God had predicted that David's family would suffer because of his sin against Bathsheba and Uriah. David's heart was broken as he realized that God's predictions were coming true. God forgave David, but he did not cancel the consequences of his sin. David was horrified as he saw his son's strengths run wild without the controls God had built into his own life.

By most casual evaluations, Absalom would have made an excellent king, and the people loved him. But he lacked the inner character and control needed in a good leader. His appearance, skill, and position did not make up for his lack of personal integrity.

David's sins took him away from God, but repentance brought him back. In contrast, Absalom sinned and kept on sinning. Although he relied heavily on the advice of others, he was not wise enough to evaluate the counsel he received.

Can you identify with Absalom? Do you find yourself on a fast track toward self-destruction? Absalom wasn't able to say, "I was wrong. I need forgiveness." God offers forgiveness, but we will not experience that forgiveness until we genuinely admit our sins and confess them to God. Absalom rejected his father's love and ultimately God's love. How often do you miss entering back into God's love through the door of forgiveness?

Strength and accomplishment
- Was handsome and charismatic like his father, David

Weaknesses and mistakes
- Avenged the rape of his sister Tamar by killing his half brother Amnon
- Plotted against his father to take away the throne
- Consistently listened to the wrong advice

Lessons from his life
- The sins of parents are often repeated and amplified in the children
- A smart man gets a lot of advice; a wise man evaluates the advice he gets
- Actions against God's plans will fail, sooner or later

Vital statistics
- Where: Hebron
- Occupation: Prince
- Relatives: Father: David. Mother: Maacah. Brothers: Amnon, Kileab, Solomon, and others. Sister: Tamar
- Contemporaries: Nathan, Jonadab, Joab, Ahithophel, Hushai

Key verse
"But while he was there, he sent secret messengers to every part of Israel to stir up a rebellion against the king. 'As soon as you hear the trumpets,' his message read, 'you will know that Absalom has been crowned king in Hebron' " (2 Samuel 15:10).

Absalom's story is told in 2 Samuel 3:3; 13—19.

14:27 By naming his daughter Tamar, Absalom was showing his love and respect for his sister Tamar. This was also a reminder to everyone of the Amnon/Tamar incident.

14:30 Already we can see the seeds of rebellion in Absalom. As an independent and scheming young man, he took matters into his own hands and killed his brother (13:22-29). Without his father or anyone else to keep him in check, he probably did whatever he wanted, as evidenced by his setting Joab's field on fire to get his attention (14:30). Undoubtedly his good looks also added to his self-centeredness (14:25). Children need discipline, especially those with natural abilities and beauty. Otherwise, like Absalom, they will grow up thinking they can do whatever they want whenever they want to.

14:33 David only made halfhearted efforts to correct his children. He did not punish Amnon for his sin against Tamar, nor did he deal decisively with Absalom's murder of Amnon. Such indecisiveness became David's undoing. When we ignore sin, we experience greater pain than if we deal with it immediately.

3. National rebellion against David

Absalom's Rebellion

15 After this, Absalom bought a chariot and horses, and he hired fifty footmen to run 15:1 1 Kgs 1:5
ahead of him. 2He got up early every morning and went out to the gate of the city.
When people brought a case to the king for judgment, Absalom would ask where they
were from, and they would tell him their tribe. 3Then Absalom would say, "You've really
got a strong case here! It's too bad the king doesn't have anyone to hear it. 4I wish I were 15:4 Judg 9:29
the judge. Then people could bring their problems to me, and I would give them justice!"
5And when people tried to bow before him, Absalom wouldn't let them. Instead, he took 15:5 2 Sam 14:33
them by the hand and embraced them. 6So in this way, Absalom stole the hearts of all 15:6 Rom 16:18
the people of Israel.
7After four years,* Absalom said to the king, "Let me go to Hebron to offer a sacrifice
to the LORD in fulfillment of a vow I made to him. 8For while I was at Geshur, I promised 15:8 Gen 28:20
to sacrifice to him in Hebron if he would bring me back to Jerusalem." 2 Sam 13:37-39
9"All right," the king told him. "Go and fulfill your vow."
So Absalom went to Hebron. 10But while he was there, he sent secret messengers to 15:10 1 Kgs 1:34
every part of Israel to stir up a rebellion against the king. "As soon as you hear the 2 Kgs 9:13
trumpets," his message read, "you will know that Absalom has been crowned king in
Hebron." 11He took two hundred men from Jerusalem with him as guests, but they knew
nothing of his intentions. 12While he was offering the sacrifices, he sent for Ahithophel, 15:12 Josh 15:51
one of David's counselors who lived in Giloh. Soon many others also joined Absalom, 2 Sam 17:14
and the conspiracy gained momentum. Ps 3:1

David Escapes from Jerusalem

13A messenger soon arrived in Jerusalem to tell King David, "All Israel has joined 15:13 Judg 9:3
Absalom in a conspiracy against you!"
14"Then we must flee at once, or it will be too late!" David urged his men. "Hurry! If 15:14 2 Sam 12:11
we get out of the city before he arrives, both we and the city of Jerusalem will be spared Ps 3:title
from disaster."
15"We are with you," his advisers replied. "Do what you think is best." 16So the king 15:16 2 Sam 16:21-22

15:7 As in Greek and Syriac versions; Hebrew reads *40 years.*

15:1ff David wrote several psalms during the days of Absalom's rebellion. Some of them are Psalms 39, 41, 55, 61, and 63.

ABSALOM'S REBELLION
Absalom crowned himself king in Hebron. David and his men fled from Jerusalem, crossed the Jordan, and went to Mahanaim. Absalom and his army followed, only to be defeated in the Forest of Ephraim, where Absalom was killed.

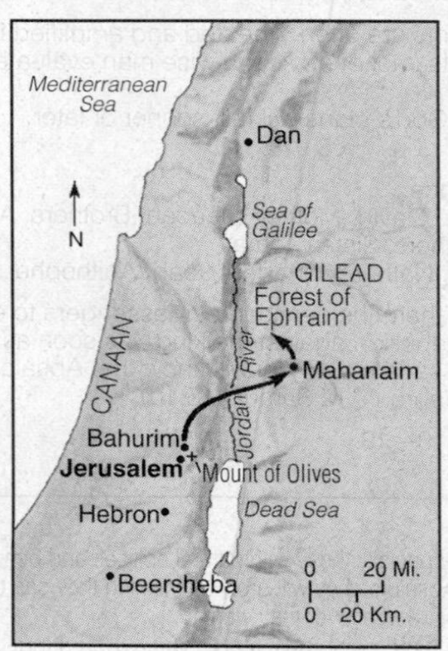

15:2 The city gate was like city hall and a shopping center combined. Because Jerusalem was the nation's capital, both local and national leaders met there daily to transact business and conduct government affairs. The city gate was the perfect spot for this because government and business transactions needed witnesses to be legitimate, and anyone entering or leaving the city had to enter through the gate. Merchants set up their tent-shops near the gate for the same reason. Absalom, therefore, went to the city gate to win the hearts of Israel's leaders as well as those of the common people.

15:5, 6 Absalom's political strategy was to steal the hearts of the people with his good looks, grand entrances, apparent concern for justice, and friendly embraces. Many were fooled and switched their allegiance. Later, however, Absalom proved to be an evil ruler.

We need to evaluate our leaders to make sure their charisma is not a mask covering graft, deception, or hunger for power. Make sure that underneath their style and charm, they are able to make good decisions and handle people wisely.

15:9 Absalom went to Hebron because it was his hometown (3:2, 3). Hebron was David's first capital as well, and there Absalom could expect to find loyal friends who would be proud of him.

15:14 Had David not escaped from Jerusalem, the ensuing fight might have killed him as well as many innocent inhabitants of the city. Some fights that we think necessary can be costly and destructive to those around us. In such cases, it may be wise to back down and save the fight for another day—even if doing so hurts our pride. It takes courage to stand and fight, but it also takes courage to back down for the sake of others.

15:14 Why couldn't David just crush this rebellion? There were several reasons he chose to flee: (1) The rebellion was widespread (15:10-13) and would not have been easily suppressed; (2) David did not want the city of Jerusalem to be destroyed; (3) David still cared for his son and did not want to hurt him. We know that David expected to return to Jerusalem soon because he left 10 of his concubines to take care of the palace (15:16).

and his household set out at once. He left no one behind except ten of his concubines to
keep the palace in order. [17]The king and his people set out on foot, and they paused at
the edge of the city [18]to let David's troops move past to lead the way. There were six
hundred Gittites who had come with David from Gath, along with the king's bodyguard.*

15:19 2 Sam 18:2

[19]Then the king turned to Ittai, the captain of the Gittites, and asked, "Why are you
coming with us? Go on back with your men to King Absalom, for you are a guest in
Israel, a foreigner in exile. [20]You arrived only yesterday, and now should I force you to
wander with us? I don't even know where we will go. Go on back and take your troops
with you, and may the LORD show you his unfailing love and faithfulness.*"

15:21 Ruth 1:16-17

[21]But Ittai said to the king, "I vow by the LORD and by your own life that I will go
wherever you go, no matter what happens—whether it means life or death."
[22]David replied, "All right, come with us." So Ittai and his six hundred men and their
families went along.

15:23 1 Kgs 15:13; 2 Chr 15:16; 29:16

[23]There was deep sadness throughout the land as the king and his followers passed
by. They crossed the Kidron Valley and then went out toward the wilderness.

15:24 Num 4:15; 1 Sam 4:4-5; 2 Sam 8:17; 20:25

[24]Abiathar and Zadok and the Levites took the Ark of the Covenant of God and set it
down beside the road. Then they offered sacrifices there until everyone had passed by.
[25]David instructed Zadok to take the Ark of God back into the city. "If the LORD sees
fit," David said, "he will bring me back to see the Ark and the Tabernacle again. [26]But
if he is through with me, then let him do what seems best to him."

15:25 1 Sam 3:18; Ps 43:3

15:27 2 Sam 17:17

[27]Then the king told Zadok the priest, "Look,* here is my plan. You and Abiathar*
should return quietly to the city with your son Ahimaaz and Abiathar's son Jonathan. [28]I
will stop at the shallows of the Jordan River* and wait there for a message from you. Let

15:28 2 Sam 17:16

15:18 Hebrew *the Kerethites and Pelethites.* **15:20** As in Greek version; Hebrew reads *and may unfailing love and faithfulness go with you.* **15:27a** As in Greek version; Hebrew reads *Are you a seer?* or *Do you see?* **15:27b** Hebrew lacks *and Abiathar;* compare 15:29. **15:28** Hebrew *at the crossing points of the wilderness.*

HIGHS AND LOWS OF DAVID'S LIFE

The Bible calls David a man after God's own heart (1 Samuel 13:14; Acts 13:22), but that didn't mean his life was free of troubles. David's life was full of highs and lows. Some of David's troubles were a result of his sins; some were a result of the sins of others. We can't always control our ups and downs, but we can trust God every day. We can be certain that he will help us through our trials, just as he helped David. In the end, he will reward us for our consistent faith.

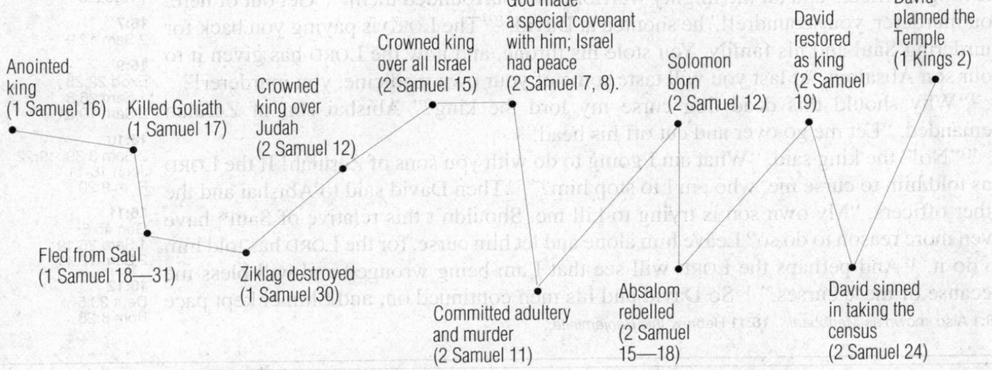

Anointed king (1 Samuel 16)
Killed Goliath (1 Samuel 17)
Fled from Saul (1 Samuel 18—31)
Ziklag destroyed (1 Samuel 30)
Crowned king over Judah (2 Samuel 12)
Crowned king over all Israel (2 Samuel 15)
God made a special covenant with him; Israel had peace (2 Samuel 7, 8).
Committed adultery and murder (2 Samuel 11)
Solomon born (2 Samuel 12)
Absalom rebelled (2 Samuel 15—18)
David restored as king (2 Samuel 19)
David sinned in taking the census (2 Samuel 24)
David planned the Temple (1 Kings 2)

15:17, 18 David had many loyal non-Israelites in his armed forces. The Gittites, from the Philistine city of Gath, were apparently friends David had acquired while hiding from Saul. "The king's bodyguard" is also translated "the Kerethites and Pelethites"; these men were also from Philistine territory. Although Israel was supposed to destroy wicked enemies, the nation was to welcome foreigners who came on friendly terms (Exodus 23:9; Deuteronomy 10:19) and to try to show them the importance of obeying God.

15:24, 25 The priests and Levites were also loyal to David.

15:27-37 David needed spies in Absalom's court to inform him of Absalom's decisions. By sending Hushai to Absalom as a supposed traitor to David, Hushai could offer advice contradictory to Ahithophel's advice. Ahithophel was Absalom's adviser (he was also Bathsheba's grandfather).

me know what happens in Jerusalem before I disappear into the wilderness." 29So Zadok
and Abiathar took the Ark of God back to the city and stayed there.
30David walked up the road that led to the Mount of Olives, weeping as he went. His 15:30 Esth 6:12
head was covered and his feet were bare as a sign of mourning. And the people who were Ezek 24:23
with him covered their heads and wept as they climbed the mountain. 31When someone 15:31 2 Sam 15:12;
told David that his adviser Ahithophel was now backing Absalom, David prayed, 16:23; 17:14, 23
"O LORD, let Ahithophel give Absalom foolish advice!"
32As they reached the spot at the top of the Mount of Olives where people worshiped 15:32 Josh 16:2
God, David found Hushai the Arkite waiting for him. Hushai had torn his clothing and
put dirt on his head as a sign of mourning. 33But David told him, "If you go with me,
you will only be a burden. 34Return to Jerusalem and tell Absalom, 'I will now be your 15:34 2 Sam 16:19; 19:35
adviser, just as I was your father's adviser in the past.' Then you can frustrate and counter 15:35
Ahithophel's advice. 35Zadok and Abiathar, the priests, are there. Tell them the plans that 2 Sam 17:15-16
are being made to capture me, 36and they will send their sons Ahimaaz and Jonathan to 15:36
find me and tell me what is going on." 37So David's friend Hushai returned to Jerusalem, 2 Sam 15:27 15:37
getting there just as Absalom arrived. 1 Chr 27:33

David and Ziba

16 David was just past the top of the hill when Ziba, the servant of Mephibosheth,* 16:1 2 Sam 9:1-13
caught up with him. He was leading two donkeys loaded with two hundred loaves
of bread, one hundred clusters of raisins, one hundred bunches of summer fruit, and a
skin of wine. 2"What are these for?" the king asked Ziba. 16:2
And Ziba replied, "The donkeys are for your people to ride on, and the bread and Judg 10:4 2 Sam 17:27-29
summer fruit are for the young men to eat. The wine is to be taken with you into the
wilderness for those who become faint." 16:3
3"And where is Mephibosheth?" the king asked him. 2 Sam 9:9-10;
"He stayed in Jerusalem," Ziba replied. "He said, 'Today I will get back the kingdom 19:26-27
of my grandfather Saul.'"
4"In that case," the king told Ziba, "I give you everything Mephibosheth owns."
"Thank you, sir," Ziba replied. "I will always do whatever you want me to do."

Shimei Curses David

5As David and his party passed Bahurim, a man came out of the village cursing them. It 16:5 Exod 22:28
was Shimei son of Gera, a member of Saul's family. 6He threw stones at the king and 1 Sam 17:43
the king's officers and all the mighty warriors who surrounded them. 7"Get out of here, 2 Sam 19:16-23 1 Kgs 2:8
you murderer, you scoundrel!" he shouted at David. 8"The LORD is paying you back for 16:7
murdering Saul and his family. You stole his throne, and now the LORD has given it to 2 Sam 12:9
your son Absalom. At last you will taste some of your own medicine, you murderer!" 16:9 Exod 22:28
9"Why should this dead dog curse my lord the king?" Abishai son of Zeruiah 1 Sam 26:8 2 Sam 19:21
demanded. "Let me go over and cut off his head!"
10"No!" the king said. "What am I going to do with you sons of Zeruiah! If the LORD 16:10 2 Sam 3:39; 19:22
has told him to curse me, who am I to stop him?" 11Then David said to Abishai and the John 18:11 Rom 9:20
other officers, "My own son is trying to kill me. Shouldn't this relative of Saul* have 16:11
even more reason to do so? Leave him alone and let him curse, for the LORD has told him Gen 45:5
to do it. 12And perhaps the LORD will see that I am being wronged and will bless me 1 Sam 26:19 2 Sam 12:11
because of these curses." 13So David and his men continued on, and Shimei kept pace 16:12 Deut 23:5
16:1 Also known as *Meribbaal.* **16:11** Hebrew *this Benjaminite.* Rom 8:28

16:3 Saul was Mephibosheth's grandfather. Most likely Ziba was lying, hoping to receive a reward from David. (See 19:24-30 for Mephibosheth's side of the story.) For the story of Mephibosheth, see chapter 9.

16:4 David believed Ziba's charge against Mephibosheth without checking into it or even being skeptical. Don't be hasty to accept someone's condemnation of another, especially when the accuser may profit from the other's downfall. David should have been skeptical of Ziba's comments until he checked them out for himself.

16:5-14 Shimei kept up a steady tirade against David. Although his curses were unjustified because David had had no part in Saul's death, David and his followers quietly tolerated the abuse. Maintaining your composure in the face of unjustified criticism can be a trying experience and an emotional drain, but if you can't stop criticism, it is best just to ignore it. Remember that God knows what you are enduring, and he will vindicate you if you are in the right.

with them on a nearby hillside, cursing as he went and throwing stones at David and
tossing dust into the air.
14 The king and all who were with him grew weary along the way, so they rested when
they reached the Jordan River.*

16:15
Ahithophel Advises Absalom

2 Sam 15:12, 37
15 Meanwhile, Absalom and his men arrived at Jerusalem, accompanied by Ahithophel.
16:16 1 Sam 10:24 2 Sam 15:33-34 2 Kgs 11:12
16 When David's friend Hushai the Arkite arrived, he went immediately to see Absalom.
"Long live the king!" he exclaimed. "Long live the king!"
17 "Is this the way you treat your friend David?" Absalom asked him. "Why aren't you
with him?"
18 "I'm here because I work for the man who is chosen by the LORD and by Israel,"
16:19 2 Sam 15:33-34
Hushai replied. 19 "And anyway, why shouldn't I serve you? I helped your father, and
now I will help you!"
20 Then Absalom turned to Ahithophel and asked him, "What should I do next?"
16:21 2 Sam 15:16
21 Ahithophel told him, "Go and sleep with your father's concubines, for he has left
them here to keep the house. Then all Israel will know that you have insulted him beyond
16:22 2 Sam 12:11; 20:3
hope of reconciliation, and they will give you their support." 22 So they set up a tent on
the palace roof where everyone could see it, and Absalom went into the tent to sleep with
his father's concubines.
16:23 2 Sam 15:12; 17:14, 23
23 Absalom followed Ahithophel's advice, just as David had done. For every word
Ahithophel spoke seemed as wise as though it had come directly from the mouth of God.

17

17:2 2 Sam 16:14 1 Kgs 22:31
Now Ahithophel urged Absalom, "Let me choose twelve thousand men to start out
after David tonight. 2 I will catch up to him while he is weary and discouraged. He
and his troops will panic, and everyone will run away. Then I will kill only the king, 3 and
I will bring all the people back to you as a bride returns to her husband. After all, it is
only this man's life that you seek.* Then all the people will remain unharmed and
peaceful." 4 This plan seemed good to Absalom and to all the other leaders of Israel.

Hushai Counters Ahithophel's Advice

17:5 2 Sam 15:32-34
5 But then Absalom said, "Bring in Hushai the Arkite. Let's see what he thinks about
this." 6 When Hushai arrived, Absalom told him what Ahithophel had said. Then he
asked, "What is your opinion? Should we follow Ahithophel's advice? If not, speak up."
17:7 2 Sam 16:21
7 "Well," Hushai replied, "this time I think Ahithophel has made a mistake. 8 You know
17:8 Hos 13:8
your father and his men; they are mighty warriors. Right now they are probably as
enraged as a mother bear who has been robbed of her cubs. And remember that your
father is an experienced soldier. He won't be spending the night among the troops. 9 He
has probably already hidden in some pit or cave. And when he comes out and attacks and
a few of your men fall, there will be panic among your troops, and everyone will start
17:10 Josh 2:9, 11
shouting that your men are being slaughtered. 10 Then even the bravest of them, though
they have the heart of a lion, will be paralyzed with fear. For all Israel knows what a
mighty man your father is and how courageous his warriors are.
17:11 1 Sam 3:20
11 "I suggest that you mobilize the entire army of Israel, bringing them from as far
away as Dan and Beersheba. That way you will have an army as numerous as the sand
on the seashore. And I think that you should personally lead the troops. 12 When we find
David, we can descend on him like the dew that falls to the ground, so that not one of his
17:13 Mic 1:6
men is left alive. 13 And if David has escaped into some city, you will have the entire army

16:14 As in Greek version (see also 17:16); Hebrew reads *when they reached their destination.* **17:3** As in Greek version; Hebrew reads *like the return of all is the man whom you seek.*

16:21, 22 This incident fulfilled Nathan's prediction that because of David's sin, another man would sleep with his wives (12:11, 12). (See the note on 3:6, 7 for the cultural significance of this act.)

16:23 Ahithophel was an adviser to Absalom. Most rulers had advisers to help them make decisions about governmental and political matters. They probably arranged the king's marriages as well because these were usually politically motivated unions. But God made Ahithophel's advice seem foolish, just as David had prayed (15:31).

17:11 Hushai appealed to Absalom through flattery, and Absalom's vanity became his own trap. Hushai predicted great glory for Absalom if he personally led the entire army against David. "Pride goes before destruction" (Proverbs 16:18) is an appropriate comment on Absalom's ambitions.

of Israel there at your command. Then we can take ropes and drag the walls of the city
into the nearest valley until every stone is torn down."
14 Then Absalom and all the leaders of Israel said, "Hushai's advice is better than
Ahithophel's." For the LORD had arranged to defeat the counsel of Ahithophel, which
really was the better plan, so that he could bring disaster upon Absalom!

Hushai Warns David to Escape

15 Then Hushai reported to Zadok and Abiathar, the priests, what Ahithophel had said
and what he himself had suggested instead. 16 "Quick!" he told them. "Find David and
urge him not to stay at the shallows of the Jordan River* tonight. He must go across
at once into the wilderness beyond. Otherwise he will die and his entire army with
him."
17 Jonathan and Ahimaaz had been staying at En-rogel so as not to be seen entering
and leaving the city. Arrangements had been made for a servant girl to bring them the
message they were to take to King David. 18 But a boy saw them leaving En-rogel to
go to David, and he told Absalom about it. Meanwhile, they escaped to Bahurim,
where a man hid them inside a well in his courtyard. 19 The man's wife put a cloth
over the top of the well with grain on it to dry in the sun; so no one suspected they
were there.
20 When Absalom's men arrived, they asked her, "Have you seen Ahimaaz and
Jonathan?"
She replied, "They were here, but they crossed the brook." Absalom's men looked for
them without success and returned to Jerusalem.
21 Then the two men crawled out of the well and hurried on to King David. "Quick!"
they told him, "cross the Jordan tonight!" And they told him how Ahithophel had advised
that he be captured and killed. 22 So David and all the people with him went across the
Jordan River during the night, and they were all on the other bank before dawn.
23 Meanwhile, Ahithophel was publicly disgraced when Absalom refused his advice.
So he saddled his donkey, went to his hometown, set his affairs in order, and hanged
himself. He died there and was buried beside his father.
24 David soon arrived at Mahanaim. By now, Absalom had mobilized the entire army
of Israel and was leading his troops across the Jordan River. 25 Absalom had appointed
Amasa as commander of his army, replacing Joab, who had been commander under
David. (Amasa was Joab's cousin. His father was Jether,* an Ishmaelite.* His mother,
Abigail daughter of Nahash, was the sister of Joab's mother, Zeruiah.) 26 Absalom and
the Israelite army set up camp in the land of Gilead.
27 When David arrived at Mahanaim, he was warmly greeted by Shobi son of Nahash
of Rabbah, an Ammonite, and by Makir son of Ammiel of Lo-debar, and by Barzillai the
Gileadite from Rogelim. 28 They brought sleeping mats, cooking pots, serving bowls,
wheat and barley flour, roasted grain, beans, lentils, 29 honey, butter, sheep, and cheese
for David and those who were with him. For they said, "You must all be very tired and
hungry and thirsty after your long march through the wilderness."

Absalom's Defeat and Death

18 David now appointed generals and captains to lead his troops. 2 One-third were
placed under Joab, one-third under Joab's brother Abishai son of Zeruiah, and
one-third under Ittai the Gittite. The king told his troops, "I am going out with you."
3 But his men objected strongly. "You must not go," they urged. "If we have to turn
and run—and even if half of us die—it will make no difference to Absalom's troops; they
will be looking only for you. You are worth ten thousand of us, and it is better that you
stay here in the city and send us help if we need it."
4 "If you think that's the best plan, I'll do it," the king finally agreed. So he stood at

17:14 2 Sam 15:31-34
17:15 2 Sam 15:35-36
17:16 2 Sam 15:28
17:17 Josh 15:7; 2 Sam 15:27, 35-36; 18:19
17:18 2 Sam 3:16; 16:5
17:19 Josh 2:4-6
17:20 Exod 1:19; Lev 19:11; 1 Sam 19:12-17
17:23 2 Sam 16:23; 2 Kgs 20:1; Matt 27:5
17:24 Gen 32:2; 2 Sam 2:8
17:25 2 Sam 19:13; 20:12; 1 Kgs 2:5; 1 Chr 2:12-16
17:27 2 Sam 9:4; 10:1-2; 12:26, 29; 1 Kgs 2:7
17:29 2 Sam 16:2
18:1 Exod 18:25; 1 Sam 22:7
18:2 1 Sam 11:11; 2 Sam 15:19-22
18:3 2 Sam 21:17
18:4 2 Sam 18:24

17:16 Hebrew *at the crossing points of the wilderness.* **17:25a** Hebrew *Ithra,* a variant name for Jether. **17:25b** As in some Greek manuscripts (see also 1 Chr 2:17); Hebrew reads *an Israelite.*

17:25 Joab and Amasa were David's nephews and Absalom's cousins. Because Joab had left Jerusalem with David (see 18:5, 10ff), Amasa took his place as commander of Israel's troops.

18:1 David took command as he had in former days. In recent years, his life had been characterized by indecisiveness and moral paralysis. At this time he began to take charge and do his duty.

the gate of the city as all the divisions of troops passed by. 5 And the king gave this
command to Joab, Abishai, and Ittai: "For my sake, deal gently with young Absalom."
And all the troops heard the king give this order to his commanders.
18:6 Josh 17:15 — 6 So the battle began in the forest of Ephraim, 7 and the Israelite troops were beaten
back by David's men. There was a great slaughter, and twenty thousand men laid down

REBELLION
The Bible records many rebellions. Many were against God's chosen leaders. They were doomed for failure. Others were begun by wicked men against wicked men. While these were sometimes successful, the rebel's life usually came to a violent end. Still other rebellions were made by good people against the wicked or unjust actions of others. This kind of rebellion is sometimes good in freeing the common people from oppression and giving them the freedom to turn back to God.

Who rebelled?	*Whom they rebelled against*	*What happened*	*Reference*
Adam and Eve	God	Expelled from Eden	Genesis 3
Israelites	God, Moses	Forced to wander in wilderness for 40 years	Numbers 14
Korah	Moses	Swallowed by the earth	Numbers 16
Israelites	God	God took away his special promise of protection	Judges 2
Absalom (David's son)	David	Killed in battle	2 Samuel 15–18
Sheba	David	Killed in battle	2 Samuel 20
Adonijah (David's son)	David, Solomon	Killed for treason	1 Kings 1, 2
Joab	David, Solomon	Supported Adonijah's kingship without seeking God's choice. Killed for treason	1 Kings 1, 2
Ten tribes of Israel	Rehoboam	The kingdom was divided. The 10 tribes forgot about God, sinned, and were eventually taken into captivity	1 Kings 12:16–20
Baasha, king of Israel	Nadab king of Israel	Overthrew the throne and became king. God destroyed his escendants	1 Kings 15:27–16:7
Zimri, king of Israel	Elah king of Israel	Overthrew the throne, but killed himself when his rule was not accepted	1 Kings 16:9–16
Jehu, king of Israel	Joram king of Israel Ahaziah king of Judah	Killed both kings. Later turned from God and his dynasty was wiped out	2 Kings 9, 10
Joash, king of Judah Jehoiada, a priest	Athaliah queen of Judah	Athaliah, a wicked queen, was overthrown. This was a "good" rebellion	2 Kings 11
Shallum, king of Israel	Zechariah king of Israel	Overthrew the throne, but then was assassinated	2 Kings 15:8–15
Menahem, king of Israel	Shallum king of Israel	Overthrew the throne, but then was invaded by Assyrian army	2 Kings 15:16–22
Hoshea, king of Israel	Assyria	The city of Samaria was destroyed, the nation of Israel taken into captivity	2 Kings 17
Zedekiah, king of Judah	Nebuchadnezzar king of Babylon	The city of Jerusalem was destroyed, the nation of Judah taken into captivity	2 Kings 24, 25

their lives that day. 8 The battle raged all across the countryside, and more men died
because of the forest than were killed by the sword.
9 During the battle, Absalom came unexpectedly upon some of David's men. He tried
to escape on his mule, but as he rode beneath the thick branches of a great oak, his head
got caught. His mule kept going and left him dangling in the air. 10 One of David's men
saw what had happened and told Joab, "I saw Absalom dangling in a tree."
11 "What?" Joab demanded. "You saw him there and didn't kill him? I would have
rewarded you with ten pieces of silver* and a hero's belt!"
12 "I wouldn't do it for a thousand pieces of silver,*" the man replied. "We all heard
the king say to you and Abishai and Ittai, 'For my sake, please don't harm young
Absalom.' 13 And if I had betrayed the king by killing his son—and the king would
certainly find out who did it—you yourself would be the first to abandon me."
14 "Enough of this nonsense," Joab said. Then he took three daggers and plunged them
into Absalom's heart as he dangled from the oak still alive. 15 Ten of Joab's young armor
bearers then surrounded Absalom and killed him. 16 Then Joab blew the trumpet, and his
men returned from chasing the army of Israel. 17 They threw Absalom's body into a deep
pit in the forest and piled a great heap of stones over it. And the army of Israel fled to
their homes.
18 During his lifetime, Absalom had built a monument to himself in the King's Valley,
for he had said, "I have no son to carry on my name." He named the monument after
himself, and it is known as Absalom's Monument to this day.

David Mourns Absalom's Death

19 Then Zadok's son Ahimaaz said, "Let me run to the king with the good news that the
LORD has saved him from his enemy Absalom."
20 "No," Joab told him, "it wouldn't be good news to the king that his son is dead. You
can be my messenger some other time, but not today."
21 Then Joab said to a man from Cush, "Go tell the king what you have seen." The man
bowed and ran off.
22 But Ahimaaz continued to plead with Joab, "Whatever happens, please let me go,
too."
"Why should you go, my son?" Joab replied. "There will be no reward for you."
23 "Yes, but let me go anyway," he begged.
Joab finally said, "All right, go ahead." Then Ahimaaz took a shortcut across the plain
of the Jordan and got to Mahanaim ahead of the man from Cush.
24 While David was sitting at the city gate, the watchman climbed to the roof of the
gateway by the wall. As he looked, he saw a lone man running toward them. 25 He
shouted the news down to David, and the king replied, "If he is alone, he has news."
As the messenger came closer, 26 the watchman saw another man running toward
them. He shouted down, "Here comes another one!"
The king replied, "He also will have news."
27 "The first man runs like Ahimaaz son of Zadok," the watchman said.
"He is a good man and comes with good news," the king replied.
28 Then Ahimaaz cried out to the king, "All is well!" He bowed low with his face to
the ground and said, "Blessed be the LORD your God, who has handed over the rebels
who dared to stand against you."
29 "What about young Absalom?" the king demanded. "Is he all right?"
Ahimaaz replied, "When Joab told me to come, there was a lot of commotion. But I
didn't know what was happening."
30 "Wait here," the king told him. So Ahimaaz stepped aside.

18:9 2 Sam 14:26
18:13 2 Sam 14:19-20
18:16 2 Sam 2:28; 20:22
18:17 Josh 7:26; 8:29
18:18 Gen 14:17; 1 Sam 15:12; 2 Sam 14:27
18:19 2 Sam 15:36
18:24 2 Sam 13:34; 19:8-10; 2 Kgs 9:17
18:27 1 Kgs 1:42
18:28 1 Sam 17:46; 25:23

18:11 Hebrew *10 shekels of silver,* about 4 ounces or 114 grams in weight. **18:12** Hebrew *1,000 shekels,* about 25 pounds or 11.4 kilograms in weight.

18:12-14 This man had caught Joab in his hypocrisy. He knew Joab would have turned on him for killing the man if the king had found out about it. Joab could not answer, but only dismissed him. Those about to do evil often do not take the time to consider what they are about to do. They don't care whether or not it is right or lawful. Don't rush into action without thinking. Consider whether what you are about to do is right or wrong.

18:29 Although he reached the city first, Ahimaaz was afraid to tell the king the truth about the death of his son Absalom.

31 Then the man from Cush arrived and said, "I have good news for my lord the king.
Today the LORD has rescued you from all those who rebelled against you."
32 "What about young Absalom?" the king demanded. "Is he all right?"
And the Cushite replied, "May all of your enemies, both now and in the future, be as
that young man is!"
33 The king was overcome with emotion. He went up to his room over the gateway
and burst into tears. And as he went, he cried, "O my son Absalom! My son, my son
Absalom! If only I could have died instead of you! O Absalom, my son, my son."

Joab Rebukes the King

19 Word soon reached Joab that the king was weeping and mourning for Absalom.
2 As the troops heard of the king's deep grief for his son, the joy of that day's
victory was turned into deep sadness. 3 They crept back into the city as though they were
ashamed and had been beaten in battle. 4 The king covered his face with his hands and
kept on weeping, "O my son Absalom! O Absalom, my son, my son!"

18:31 Judg 5:31
18:32 1 Sam 25:26
18:33 Exod 32:32; 2 Sam 19:4; Rom 9:1-3
19:1 2 Sam 18:5, 14
19:4 2 Sam 15:30; 18:33

Joab, the great military leader, had two brothers who were also famous soldiers: Abishai and Asahel. Joab proved to be the greatest leader of the three and was the commander of David's army throughout most of David's reign. There is no record that his troops ever lost a battle.

Joab was a fearless fighter like his brothers. Unlike them, he was also a brilliant and ruthless strategist. His plans usually worked, but he was seldom concerned about those hurt or killed by them. He did not hesitate to use treachery or murder to achieve his goals. His career is a story of great accomplishments and shameful acts. He conquered Jerusalem and the surrounding nations, defeated Abner, and reconciled Absalom and David. But he also murdered Abner, Amasa, and Absalom, took part in Uriah's murder, and plotted with Adonijah against Solomon. That plot led to his execution.

Joab set his own standards—he lived by them and died because of them. There is little evidence that Joab ever acknowledged God's standards. On one occasion he confronted David about the danger of taking a census without God's command, but this may have been little more than a move to protect himself. Joab's self-centeredness eventually destroyed him. He was loyal only to himself, even willing to betray his lifelong relationship with David to preserve his power.

Joab's life illustrates the disastrous results of having no source of direction outside oneself. Brilliance and power are self-destructive without God's guidance. Only God can give the direction we need. For that reason, he has made available his Word, the Bible, and he is willing to be personally present in the lives of those who admit their need for him.

Strengths and accomplishments
- Brilliant planner and strategist
- Fearless fighter and resourceful commander
- Confident leader who did not hesitate to confront even the king
- Helped reconcile David and Absalom
- Masterminded the conquest of Jerusalem

Weaknesses and mistakes
- Was repeatedly ruthless, violent, and vengeful
- Carried out David's scheme to have Uriah, Bathsheba's husband, killed
- Avenged his brother's murder by murdering Abner
- Killed Absalom against David's orders
- Plotted with Adonijah against David and Solomon

Lessons from his life
- Those who live by violence often die by violence
- Even brilliant leaders need guidance

Vital statistics
- Occupation: Commander in chief of David's army
- Relatives: Mother: Zeruiah. Brothers: Abishai, Asahel. Uncle: David
- Contemporaries: Saul, Abner, Absalom

Key verse
" 'Do as he said,' the king replied. 'Kill him there beside the altar and bury him. This will remove the guilt of his senseless murders from me and from my father's family' " (1 Kings 2:31).

Joab's story is told in 2 Samuel 2—1 Kings 2. He is also mentioned in 1 Chronicles 2:16; 11:5–9, 20, 26; 19:8–15; 20:1; 21:2–6; 26:28; and in the title of Psalm 60.

18:33 Why was David so upset over the death of his rebel son? (1) David realized that he, in part, was responsible for Absalom's death. Nathan the prophet had said that because David had killed Uriah, his own sons would rebel against him. (2) David was angry at Joab and his officers for killing Absalom against his wishes. (3) David truly loved his son, even though Absalom did nothing to deserve his love. It would have been kinder and more loving to deal with Absalom and his runaway ego when he was younger.

5 Then Joab went to the king's room and said to him, "We saved your life today and
the lives of your sons, your daughters, and your wives and concubines. Yet you act like
this, making us feel ashamed, as though we had done something wrong. 6 You seem to
love those who hate you and hate those who love you. You have made it clear today that
we mean nothing to you. If Absalom had lived and all of us had died, you would be
pleased. 7 Now go out there and congratulate the troops, for I swear by the LORD that if
you don't, not a single one of them will remain here tonight. Then you will be worse off
than you have ever been." 8 So the king went out and sat at the city gate, and as the news **19:8**
spread throughout the city that he was there, everyone went to him. 2 Sam 8:1; 15:2; 18:24

Meanwhile, the Israelites who supported Absalom had fled to their homes. 9 And **19:9**
throughout the tribes of Israel there was much discussion and argument going on. The 2 Sam 8:1-14; 15:14
people were saying, "The king saved us from our enemies, the Philistines, but Absalom
chased him out of the country. 10 Now Absalom, whom we anointed to rule over us, is
dead. Let's ask David to come back and be our king again."

11 Then King David sent Zadok and Abiathar, the priests, to say to the leaders of Judah, **19:11**
"Why are you the last ones to reinstate the king? For I have heard that all Israel is ready, 2 Sam 15:24
and only you are holding out. 12 Yet you are my relatives, my own tribe, my own flesh
and blood! Why are you the last ones to welcome me back?" 13 And David told them to **19:13**
tell Amasa, "Since you are my nephew, may God strike me dead if I do not appoint you 2 Sam 17:25
as commander of my army in place of Joab." 14 Then Amasa convinced all the leaders of
Judah, and they responded unanimously. They sent word to the king, "Return to us, and
bring back all those who are with you."

David's Return to Jerusalem

15 So the king started back to Jerusalem. And when he arrived at the Jordan River, the **19:15**
people of Judah came to Gilgal to meet him and escort him across the river. 16 Then Josh 5:8-9; 1 Sam 11:14-15
Shimei son of Gera the Benjaminite, the man from Bahurim, hurried across with the men **19:16**
of Judah to welcome King David. 17 A thousand men from the tribe of Benjamin were 2 Sam 16:5-13; 1 Kgs 2:8
with him, including Ziba, the servant of Saul, and Ziba's fifteen sons and twenty **19:17**
servants. They rushed down to the Jordan to arrive ahead of the king. 18 They all crossed 2 Sam 9:2
the ford and worked hard ferrying the king's household across the river, helping them in
every way they could.

David's Mercy to Shimei

As the king was about to cross the river, Shimei fell down before him. 19 "My lord the **19:19**
king, please forgive me," he pleaded. "Forget the terrible thing I did when you left 2 Sam 16:6-9
Jerusalem. 20 I know how much I sinned. That is why I have come here today, the very
first person in all Israel* to greet you."

21 Then Abishai son of Zeruiah said, "Shimei should die, for he cursed the LORD's **19:21**
anointed king!" Exod 22:28

22 "What am I going to do with you sons of Zeruiah!" David exclaimed. "This is not **19:22**
a day for execution but for celebration! I am once again the king of Israel!" 23 Then, 1 Sam 11:13; 2 Sam 16:9-10
turning to Shimei, David vowed, "Your life will be spared." **19:23** 1 Kgs 2:8

19:20 Hebrew *the house of Joseph.*

19:4-7 At times we must reprove those in authority over us. Joab knew he was risking the king's displeasure by confronting him, but he saw what had to be done. Joab told David that there would be dreadful consequences if he didn't commend the troops for their victory. Joab's actions are a helpful example to us when personal confrontation is necessary.

19:8 David sat at the city gate because that was where business was conducted and judgment rendered. His presence there showed that he was over his mourning and back in control.

19:8-10 Just a few days before, most of Israel was supporting the rebel ruler Absalom. Now the people wanted David back as their king. Because crowds are often fickle, there must be a higher moral code to follow than the pleasure of the majority. Following the moral principles given in God's Word will help you avoid being swayed by the popular opinions of the crowd.

19:13 David's appointment of Amasa was a shrewd political move. First, Amasa had been commander of Absalom's army; by making Amasa his commander, David would secure the allegiance of the rebel army. Second, by replacing Joab as commander in chief, David punished him for his previous crimes (3:26-29). Third, Amasa had a great deal of influence over the leaders of Judah (19:14). All of these moves would help to unite the kingdom.

19:19, 20 By admitting his wrong and asking David's forgiveness, Shimei was trying to save his own life. His plan worked for a while. This was a day of celebration, not execution. But we read in 1 Kings 2:8, 9 that David advised Solomon to execute Shimei.

19:21ff David showed tremendous mercy and generosity as he returned to Jerusalem. He spared Shimei, restored Mephibosheth, and rewarded faithful Barzillai. David's fairness sets a standard for government that will be fully realized in Christ's righteous rule in the coming Kingdom.

David's Kindness to Mephibosheth

19:24 2 Sam 9:5-10 [24]Now Mephibosheth,* Saul's grandson, arrived from Jerusalem to meet the king. He
had not washed his feet or clothes nor trimmed his beard since the day the king left
19:25 2 Sam 16:17 Jerusalem. [25]"Why didn't you come with me, Mephibosheth?" the king asked him.
19:26 2 Sam 9:2-3, 13 [26]Mephibosheth replied, "My lord the king, my servant Ziba deceived me. I told him,
'Saddle my donkey so that I can go with the king.' For as you know I am crippled. [27]Ziba
19:27 2 Sam 14:17, 20 has slandered me by saying that I refused to come. But I know that you are like an angel
19:28 2 Sam 9:7 of God, so do what you think is best. [28]All my relatives and I could expect only death
from you, my lord, but instead you have honored me among those who eat at your own
table! So how can I complain?"
[29]"All right," David replied. "My decision is that you and Ziba will divide your land
equally between you."
[30]"Give him all of it," Mephibosheth said. "I am content just to have you back again,
my lord!"

David's Kindness to Barzillai

19:31 2 Sam 17:27-29; 1 Kgs 2:7 [31]Barzillai the Gileadite now arrived from Rogelim to conduct the king across the
Jordan. [32]He was very old, about eighty, and very wealthy. He was the one who provided
food for the king during his stay in Mahanaim. [33]"Come across with me and live in
Jerusalem," the king said to Barzillai. "I will take care of you there."
19:35 Ps 90:10, 13 [34]"No," he replied, "I am far too old for that. [35]I am eighty years old today, and I can
no longer enjoy anything. Food and wine are no longer tasty, and I cannot hear the
musicians as they play. I would only be a burden to my lord the king. [36]Just to go across
19:37 1 Kgs 2:7; Jer 41:17 the river with you is all the honor I need! [37]Then let me return again to die in my own
town, where my father and mother are buried. But here is my son Kimham. Let him go
with you and receive whatever good things you want to give him."
[38]"Good," the king agreed. "Kimham will go with me, and I will do for him whatever
19:39 Gen 31:55; Ruth 1:14; 2 Sam 14:33 I would have done for you." [39]So all the people crossed the Jordan with the king. After
David had blessed and embraced him, Barzillai returned to his own home. [40]The king
then went on to Gilgal, taking Kimham with him. All the army of Judah and half the army
of Israel escorted him across the river.

An Argument over the King

[41]But the men of Israel complained to the king that the men of Judah had gotten to do
most of the work in helping him cross the Jordan. [42]"Why not?" the men of Judah
replied. "The king is one of our own tribe. Why should this make you angry? We have
charged him nothing. And he hasn't fed us or even given us gifts!"
19:43 2 Sam 5:1 [43]"But there are ten tribes in Israel," the others replied. "So we have ten times as much
right to the king as you do. Why did you treat us with such contempt? Remember, we
were the first to speak of bringing him back to be our king again." The argument
continued back and forth, and the men of Judah were very harsh in their replies.

The Revolt of Sheba

20:1 1 Sam 22:7-8; 1 Kgs 12:16; 2 Chr 10:16 **20** Then a troublemaker named Sheba son of Bicri, a Benjaminite, blew a trumpet
and shouted, "We have nothing to do with David. We want no part of this son of
Jesse. Come on, you men of Israel, let's all go home!" [2]So the men of Israel deserted
David and followed Sheba. But the men of Judah stayed with their king and escorted him
from the Jordan River to Jerusalem.
20:3 2 Sam 15:16; 16:21-22 [3]When the king arrived at his palace in Jerusalem, he instructed that the ten concubines he had left to keep house should be placed in seclusion. Their needs were to be
cared for, he said, but he would no longer sleep with them. So each of them lived like a
widow until she died.

19:24 Also known as *Meribbaal.*

19:24-30 David could not be certain if Mephibosheth or Ziba was in the right, and Scripture leaves the question unanswered. (For the whole story on Mephibosheth, see also 9:1-13 and 16:1-4.)

20:1 Although Israel was a united kingdom, it was still made up of 12 separate tribes. These tribes often had difficulty agreeing on the goals of the nation as a whole. Tribal jealousies had originally kept Israel from completely conquering the Promised Land (read the book of Joshua), and now tribal jealousies were threatening the stability of David's reign by giving Sheba an opportunity to rebel (20:1ff).

[4]Then the king instructed Amasa to mobilize the army of Judah within three days and **20:4**
to report back at that time. [5]So Amasa went out to notify the troops, but it took him longer 2 Sam 17:25; 19:13
than the three days he had been given. [6]Then David said to Abishai, "That troublemaker **20:6**
Sheba is going to hurt us more than Absalom did. Quick, take my troops and chase after 2 Sam 21:17
him before he gets into a fortified city where we can't reach him."
[7]So Abishai and Joab set out after Sheba with an elite guard from Joab's army and the **20:7**
king's own bodyguard.* [8]As they arrived at the great stone in Gibeon, Amasa met them, 2 Sam 8:18; 15:17-18
coming from the opposite direction. Joab was wearing his uniform with a dagger 1 Kgs 1:38
strapped to his belt. As he stepped forward to greet Amasa, he secretly slipped the dagger **20:8**
from its sheath. [9]"How are you, my cousin?" Joab said and took him by the beard with 2 Sam 2:18
his right hand as though to kiss him. [10]Amasa didn't notice the dagger in his left hand, **20:10**
and Joab stabbed him in the stomach with it so that his insides gushed out onto the 1 Kgs 2:5
ground. Joab did not need to strike again, and Amasa soon died. Joab and his brother
Abishai left him lying there and continued after Sheba.
[11]One of Joab's young officers shouted to Amasa's troops, "If you are for Joab and
David, come and follow Joab." [12]But Amasa lay in his blood in the middle of the road,
and Joab's officer saw that a crowd was gathering around to stare at him. So he pulled
him off the road into a field and threw a cloak over him. [13]With Amasa's body out of the
way, everyone went on with Joab to capture Sheba.
[14]Meanwhile, Sheba had traveled across Israel to mobilize his own clan of Bicri at the
city of Abel-beth-maacah. [15]When Joab's forces arrived, they attacked Abel-beth- **20:15**
maacah and built a ramp against the city wall and began battering it down. [16]But a wise Ezek 4:2
woman in the city called out to Joab, "Listen to me, Joab. Come over here so I can talk **20:16** 2 Sam 14:2
to you." [17]As he approached, the woman asked, "Are you Joab?"
"I am," he replied.
So she said, "Listen carefully to your servant."
"I'm listening," he said.
[18]Then she continued, "There used to be a saying, 'If you want to settle an argument, ask
advice at the city of Abel.' [19]I am one who is peace loving and faithful in Israel. But you are **20:19** Deut 20:10
destroying a loyal city. Why do you want to destroy what belongs to the LORD?" 2 Sam 14:15-16
[20]And Joab replied, "Believe me, I don't want to destroy your city! [21]All I want is a **20:21**
man named Sheba son of Bicri from the hill country of Ephraim, who has revolted Josh 24:33
against King David. If you hand him over to me, we will leave the city in peace." 2 Sam 20:2
"All right," the woman replied, "we will throw his head over the wall to you." [22]Then **20:22**
the woman went to the people with her wise advice, and they cut off Sheba's head and Eccl 9:13
threw it out to Joab. So he blew the trumpet and called his troops back from the attack,
and they all returned to their homes. Joab returned to the king at Jerusalem.

20:7 Hebrew *the Kerethites and Pelethites;* also in 20:23.

20:7-10 Once again Joab's murderous act went unpunished, just as it did when he killed Abner (3:26, 27). Eventually, however, justice caught up with him (1 Kings 2:28-35). It may seem that sin and treachery often go unpunished, but God's justice is not limited to this life's rewards. Even if Joab had died of old age, he would have to face the day of judgment.

20:16ff Joab's men were attacking the city, and it looked as if it would be destroyed. Though women in that society were usually quiet in public, this woman spoke out. She stopped Joab's attack, not with weapons, but with wise words and a plan of action. Often the courage to speak a few sensible words can prevent great disaster.

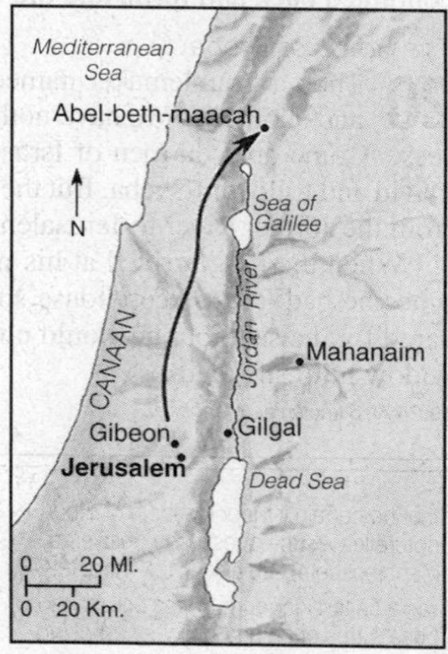

SHEBA'S REBELLION
After defeating Absalom, David returned to Jerusalem from Mahanaim. But Sheba incited a rebellion against David, so David sent Joab, Abishai, and a small army after him. Joab and his troops besieged Abel-beth-maacah, Sheba's hideout, until the people of Abel-beth-maacah killed Sheba themselves.

20:23 2 Sam 8:16-18 [23]Joab once again became the commander of David's army. Benaiah son of Jehoiada
20:25 2 Sam 2:35 was commander of the king's bodyguard. [24]Adoniram* was in charge of the labor force.
Jehoshaphat son of Ahilud was the royal historian. [25]Sheva was the court secretary.
Zadok and Abiathar were the priests. [26]Ira the Jairite was David's personal priest.

4. The later years of David's rule

David Avenges the Gibeonites

21:1 Gen 12:10; 26:1; 42:5 **21** There was a famine during David's reign that lasted for three years, so David
asked the LORD about it. And the LORD said, "The famine has come because Saul
and his family are guilty of murdering the Gibeonites."
21:2 Josh 9:15-20 [2]So King David summoned the Gibeonites. They were not part of Israel but were all
that was left of the nation of the Amorites. Israel had sworn not to kill them, but Saul, in
21:3 1 Sam 26:19 his zeal, had tried to wipe them out. [3]David asked them, "What can I do for you to make
amends? Tell me so that the LORD will bless his people again."
21:4 Num 35:33-34 [4]"Well, money won't do it," the Gibeonites replied. "And we don't want to see the
Israelites executed in revenge."

20:24 As in Greek version (see also 1 Kgs 4:6; 5:14); Hebrew reads *Adoram.*

ABISHAI

Most great leaders struggle with a few followers who try too hard. For David, Abishai was that kind of follower. His fierce loyalty to David had to be kept from becoming destructive—he was too willing to leap to his leader's defense. David never put down Abishai's eager loyalty. Instead, he patiently tried to direct its powerful energy. This approach, while not completely successful, saved David's life on at least one occasion. At three other times, however, Abishai would have killed for the king if David had not stopped him.

Abishai was an excellent soldier, but he was better at taking orders than giving them. When he wasn't carrying out David's orders, Abishai was usually under the command of his younger brother Joab. The two brothers helped each other accomplish great military feats as well as shameful acts of violence—Abishai helped Joab murder Abner and Amasa. When he was effective as a leader, he led mostly by example. But all too often he did not think before he acted.

We should be challenged by Abishai's admirable qualities of fearlessness and loyalty, but we should be warned by his tendency to act without thinking. It is not enough to be strong and effective; we must also have the self-control and wisdom that God can give us. We are to follow and obey with our hearts and our minds.

Strengths and accomplishments
- Known as one of the heroes among David's fighting men
- A fearless and willing volunteer, fiercely loyal to David
- Saved David's life

Weaknesses and mistakes
- Tended to act without thinking
- Helped Joab murder Abner and Amasa

Lessons from his life
- The most effective followers combine careful thought and action
- Blind loyalty can cause great evil

Vital statistics
- Occupation: Soldier
- Relatives: Mother: Zeruiah. Brothers: Joab and Asahel. Uncle: David

Key verses
"Abishai son of Zeruiah, the brother of Joab, was the leader of the Thirty. He once used his spear to kill three hundred enemy warriors in a single battle. It was by such feats that he became as famous as the Three. Abishai was the most famous of the Thirty and was their commander, though he was not one of the Three" (2 Samuel 23:18, 19).

Abishai's story is told in 2 Samuel 2:18—23:19. He is also mentioned in 1 Samuel 26:1–13; 1 Chronicles 2:16; 11:20; 18:12; 19:11, 15.

20:23 Benaiah was the captain of David's bodyguard and a famous member of that special group of mighty men called "the Thirty" (23:24). He remained loyal to David during Absalom's rebellion. Later he helped establish Solomon as king (1 Kings 1:32-40; 2:28-34) and eventually replaced Joab as commander of Israel's army (1 Kings 2:35).

21:1 Farmers relied heavily on spring and fall rains for their crops. If the rains stopped or came at the wrong time, or if the plants became insect infested, there would be drastic food shortages in the coming year. Agriculture at that time was completely dependent upon natural conditions. There were no irrigation sprinklers, fertilizers, or pesticides. Even moderate variations in rainfall or insect activity could destroy an entire harvest.

21:1ff The next four chapters are an appendix to the book. The events described are not presented in chronological order. They tell of David's exploits at various times during his reign.

21:1-14 Although the Bible does not record Saul's act of vengeance against the Gibeonites, it was apparently a serious crime making him guilty of their blood. Still, why were Saul's sons killed for the murders their father committed? In many Near Eastern cultures, including Israel's, an entire family was held guilty for the crime of the father because the family was considered an indissoluble unit. Saul broke the vow that the Israelites made to the

"What can I do then?" David asked. "Just tell me and I will do it for you."
5 Then they replied, "It was Saul who planned to destroy us, to keep us from having
any place at all in Israel. 6 So let seven of Saul's sons or grandsons be handed over to
us, and we will execute them before the LORD at Gibeon, on the mountain of the
LORD.*"

"All right," the king said, "I will do it." 7 David spared Jonathan's son Mephibosheth,*
who was Saul's grandson, because of the oath David and Jonathan had sworn before the
LORD. 8 But he gave them Saul's two sons Armoni and Mephibosheth, whose mother was
Rizpah daughter of Aiah. He also gave them the five sons of Saul's daughter Merab,*
the wife of Adriel son of Barzillai from Meholah. 9 The men of Gibeon executed them
on the mountain before the LORD. So all seven of them died together at the beginning of
the barley harvest.

10 Then Rizpah, the mother of two of the men, spread sackcloth on a rock and stayed
there the entire harvest season. She prevented vultures from tearing at their bodies
during the day and stopped wild animals from eating them at night. 11 When David
learned what Rizpah, Saul's concubine, had done, 12 he went to the people of Jabesh-
gilead and asked for the bones of Saul and his son Jonathan. (When Saul and Jonathan
had died in a battle with the Philistines, it was the people of Jabesh-gilead who had
retrieved their bodies from the public square of the Philistine city of Beth-shan.) 13 So
David brought the bones of Saul and Jonathan, as well as the bones of the men the
Gibeonites had executed. 14 He buried them all in the tomb of Kish, Saul's father, at the
town of Zela in the land of Benjamin. After that, God ended the famine in the land of
Israel.

Battles against Philistine Giants

15 Once again the Philistines were at war with Israel. And when David and his men were
in the thick of battle, David became weak and exhausted. 16 Ishbi-benob was a descendant of the giants*; his bronze spearhead weighed more than seven pounds,* and he was
armed with a new sword. He had cornered David and was about to kill him. 17 But
Abishai son of Zeruiah came to his rescue and killed the Philistine. After that, David's
men declared, "You are not going out to battle again! Why should we risk snuffing out
the light of Israel?"

18 After this, there was another battle against the Philistines at Gob. As they fought,
Sibbecai from Hushah killed Saph, another descendant of the giants. 19 In still another
battle at Gob, Elhanan son of Jair* from Bethlehem killed the brother of Goliath of
Gath.* The handle of his spear was as thick as a weaver's beam! 20 In another battle with
the Philistines at Gath, a huge man with six fingers on each hand and six toes on each
foot—a descendant of the giants—21 defied and taunted Israel. But he was killed by
Jonathan, the son of David's brother Shimea.* 22 These four Philistines were descended
from the giants of Gath, but they were killed by David and his warriors.

David's Song of Praise

22 David sang this song to the LORD after the LORD had rescued him from all his
enemies and from Saul. 2 These are the words he sang:

"The LORD is my rock, my fortress, and my savior;
3 my God is my rock, in whom I find protection.

21:5 2 Sam 21:1
21:6 Num 25:4; 1 Sam 10:24
21:7 1 Sam 18:1-3; 20:12-17; 23:18; 2 Sam 4:4
21:8 1 Sam 18:19; 2 Sam 3:7
21:10 Deut 21:23; 1 Sam 17:44
21:12 1 Sam 3:11-13
21:15-22 //1 Chr 20:4-8
21:16 Num 13:28
21:17 2 Sam 18:2; 20:6
21:18 1 Chr 11:29; 20:4-8; 27:11
21:19 1 Sam 17:4-7
21:22 1 Chr 20:8
22:1-51 //Ps 18:1-50
22:1 Exod 15:1; Ps 18:title
22:2 1 Sam 2:2; Pss 31:3; 71:3
22:3 Deut 33:29; Ps 3:3; Luke 1:69

21:6 As in Greek version (see also 21:9); Hebrew reads *at Gibeah of Saul, the chosen of the LORD.* **21:7** Also known as *Meribbaal.* **21:8** As in a few Hebrew and Greek manuscripts and Syriac version (see also 1 Sam 18:19); most Hebrew manuscripts read *Michal.* **21:16a** As in Greek version; Hebrew reads *a descendant of the Rephaites;* also in 21:18, 20, 22. **21:16b** Hebrew *300 shekels* [3.4 kilograms]. **21:19a** As in parallel text at 1 Chr 20:5; Hebrew reads *son of Jaare-oregim.* **21:19b** As in parallel text at 1 Chr 20:5; Hebrew reads *killed Goliath of Gath.* **21:21** As in parallel text at 1 Chr 20:7; Hebrew reads *Shimei,* a variant name for Shimea.

Gibeonites (Joshua 9:16-20). This was a serious offense against God's law (Numbers 30:1, 2). Either David was following the custom of treating the family as a unit, or Saul's sons were guilty of helping Saul kill the Gibeonites.

21:9, 10 The barley harvest was in late April and early May. Barley was similar to wheat but less suitable for breadmaking. Rizpah guarded the men's bodies during the entire harvest season, which lasted from April to October.

21:16-18 For more information on giants, see 1 Samuel 17:4-7 and the note on Genesis 6:4.

22:1ff David was a skilled musician who played his harp for Saul (1 Samuel 16:23), instituted the music programs in the Temple (1 Chronicles 25), and wrote more of the book of Psalms than anyone else. Writing a song like this was not unusual for David. This royal hymn of thanksgiving is almost identical to Psalm 18. (For other songs in the Bible, see the chart in Exodus 15.)

He is my shield, the strength of my salvation, and my stronghold,
my high tower, my savior, the one who saves me from violence.
4 I will call on the LORD, who is worthy of praise,
for he saves me from my enemies.

5 "The waves of death surrounded me;
the floods of destruction swept over me.
6 The grave* wrapped its ropes around me;
death itself stared me in the face.
7 But in my distress I cried out to the LORD;
yes, I called to my God for help.
He heard me from his sanctuary;
my cry reached his ears.

8 "Then the earth quaked and trembled;
the foundations of the heavens shook;
they quaked because of his anger.
9 Smoke poured from his nostrils;
fierce flames leaped from his mouth;
glowing coals flamed forth from him.
10 He opened the heavens and came down;
dark storm clouds were beneath his feet.
11 Mounted on a mighty angel,* he flew,
soaring* on the wings of the wind.
12 He shrouded himself in darkness,
veiling his approach with dense rain clouds.
13 A great brightness shone before him,
and bolts of lightning blazed forth.
14 The LORD thundered from heaven;
the Most High gave a mighty shout.
15 He shot his arrows and scattered his enemies;
his lightning flashed, and they were confused.
16 Then at the command of the LORD,
at the blast of his breath,
the bottom of the sea could be seen,
and the foundations of the earth were laid bare.

17 "He reached down from heaven and rescued me;
he drew me out of deep waters.
18 He delivered me from my powerful enemies,
from those who hated me and were too strong for me.
19 They attacked me at a moment when I was weakest,
but the LORD upheld me.
20 He led me to a place of safety;
he rescued me because he delights in me.
21 The LORD rewarded me for doing right;
he compensated me because of my innocence.

22:4 Pss 48:1; 96:4
22:5 Pss 69:14; 93:4 Jon 2:3
22:6 Ps 116:3-4
22:7 Pss 116:4; 120:1
22:8 Judg 5:4 Job 26:11 Ps 97:4
22:9 Deut 32:22 Heb 12:29
22:10 Exod 20:21 1 Kgs 8:12-13 Ps 97:2 Nah 1:3
22:12 Ps 104:3
22:14 Job 37:2 Ps 29:3
22:15 Deut 32:23 Josh 10:10 1 Sam 7:10
22:16 Exod 15:8 Nah 1:4
22:17 Ps 144:7
22:18 Ps 23:4
22:19 Ps 23:4
22:20 Pss 31:8; 118:5
22:21 1 Sam 26:23 Pss 24:4-5; 128:1

22:6 Hebrew *Sheol.* **22:11a** Hebrew *cherub.* **22:11b** As in some Hebrew manuscripts (see also Ps 18:10); other Hebrew manuscripts read *appearing.*

David reveals truths about God in his song of praise.	*David says, "The LORD is my . . ."*	Rock, Fortress, Savior, Protection, Shield, Strength of Salvation, Stronghold, High Tower, Light
	David names these characteristics of God. He is . . .	Saving, Worthy of praise, Hearing, Angry (against enemies), Rescuing, Rewarding, Seeing, Faithful, Showing (revealing) himself, Shrewd, Powerful, Strong, Perfect, Pure, Flawless, Shielding (us from enemies), Giving, Gentle, Preserving, Living

22 For I have kept the ways of the LORD;
I have not turned from my God to follow evil.
23 For all his laws are constantly before me;
I have never abandoned his principles.
24 I am blameless before God;
I have kept myself from sin.
25 The LORD rewarded me for doing right,
because of my innocence in his sight.

26 "To the faithful you show yourself faithful;
to those with integrity you show integrity.
27 To the pure you show yourself pure,
but to the wicked you show yourself hostile.
28 You rescue those who are humble,
but your eyes are on the proud to humiliate them.
29 O LORD, you are my light;
yes, LORD, you light up my darkness.
30 In your strength I can crush an army;
with my God I can scale any wall.

31 "As for God, his way is perfect.
All the LORD's promises prove true.
He is a shield for all who look to him for protection.
32 For who is God except the LORD?
Who but our God is a solid rock?
33 God is my strong fortress;
he has made my way safe.
34 He makes me as surefooted as a deer,
leading me safely along the mountain heights.
35 He prepares me for battle;
he strengthens me to draw a bow of bronze.
36 You have given me the shield of your salvation;
your help* has made me great.
37 You have made a wide path for my feet
to keep them from slipping.

38 "I chased my enemies and destroyed them;
I did not stop until they were conquered.
39 I consumed them; I struck them down so they could not get up;
they fell beneath my feet.
40 You have armed me with strength for the battle;
you have subdued my enemies under my feet.
41 You made them turn and run;
I have destroyed all who hated me.
42 They called for help, but no one came to rescue them.
They cried to the LORD, but he refused to answer them.
43 I ground them as fine as the dust of the earth;
I swept them into the gutter like dirt.

44 "You gave me victory over my accusers.
You preserved me as the ruler over nations;
people I don't even know now serve me.

22:22 Gen 18:19; Ps 128:1
22:23 Deut 6:6-9
22:24 Gen 6:9-10; 7:1; Eph 1:4
22:26 Matt 5:7
22:27 Lev 26:23-24; Matt 5:8
22:28 Exod 3:7-8; Ps 72:12-13; Isa 2:11-12, 17; 5:15
22:29 Ps 27:1
22:31 Deut 32:4; 2 Sam 22:3; Pss 12:6; 119:140; Prov 30:5; Matt 5:48
22:32 1 Sam 2:2
22:35 Ps 144:1
22:36 Eph 6:16-17
22:39 Mal 4:3
22:41 Exod 23:27
22:42 1 Sam 28:5-6; Isa 1:15
22:43 Isa 10:6; Mic 7:10
22:44 2 Sam 3:1; 8:1-14; 19:8-10; Isa 55:5

22:36 As in Dead Sea Scrolls; most Hebrew manuscripts read *your answering.*

22:22-24 David was not denying that he had ever sinned. Psalm 51 shows his tremendous anguish over his sin against Uriah and Bathsheba. But David understood God's faithfulness and was writing this hymn from God's perspective. He knew that God had made him clean again—"whiter than snow," (Psalm 51:7) with a "clean heart" (Psalm 51:10). Through the death and resurrection of Jesus Christ, we also are made clean and perfect. God replaces our sin with his purity, and he no longer sees our sin.

22:27 "To the wicked you show yourself hostile" means that to those who sin, God is a judge who will punish them for their sins. God destroys those who are evil.

22:45 Ps 66:3; Isa 55:5; 60:12
22:46 Mic 7:17
22:47 2 Sam 22:2, 32; Ps 89:26
22:48 1 Sam 24:12; 25:39; Pss 94:1; 144:2
22:49 Pss 44:5; 140:1, 4, 11
22:50 †Rom 15:9
22:51 2 Sam 7:12-16; Pss 89:20; 144:9-10

45 Foreigners cringe before me;
as soon as they hear of me, they submit.
46 They all lose their courage
and come trembling from their strongholds.

47 "The LORD lives! Blessed be my rock!
May God, the rock of my salvation, be exalted!
48 He is the God who pays back those who harm me;
he subdues the nations under me
49 and rescues me from my enemies.
You hold me safe beyond the reach of my enemies;
you save me from violent opponents.
50 For this, O LORD, I will praise you among the nations;
I will sing joyfully to your name.
51 You give great victories to your king;
you show unfailing love to your anointed,
to David and all his descendants forever."

David's Last Words

23:1 1 Sam 16:12-13; 2 Sam 7:8-9; Pss 78:70-72; 89:20
23:2 2 Pet 1:20-21

23 These are the last words of David:

"David, the son of Jesse, speaks—
David, the man to whom God gave such wonderful success,
David, the man anointed by the God of Jacob,
David, the sweet psalmist of Israel.

2 "The Spirit of the LORD speaks through me;
his words are upon my tongue.

DAVID'S MIGHTY MEN

One way to understand David's success is to notice the kind of men who followed him. During the time he was being hunted by Saul, David gradually built a fighting force of several hundred men. Some were relatives, others were outcasts of society, many were in trouble with the law. They all had at least one trait in common—complete devotion to David. Their achievements made them famous. Among these men were elite military groups like "the Three" and "the Thirty." They were true heroes.

Scripture gives the impression that these men were motivated to greatness by the personal qualities of their leader. David inspired them to achieve beyond their goals and meet their true potential. Likewise, the leaders we follow and the causes to which we commit ourselves will affect our lives. David's effectiveness was clearly connected with his awareness of God's leading. He was a good leader when he was following *his* Leader. Do you know whom the people you respect most are following? Your answer should help you decide whether they deserve your loyalty. Do you also recognize God's leading in your life? No one can lead you to excellence as your Creator can.

Strengths and accomplishments
- Able soldiers and military leaders
- Shared many special skills
- Though frequently outnumbered, were consistently victorious
- Loyal to David

Weakness and mistake
- Often had little in common beyond their loyalty to David and their military expertise

Lessons from their lives
- Greatness is often inspired by the quality and character of leadership
- Even a small force of able and loyal men can accomplish great feats

Vital statistics
- Where: They came from all over Israel (primarily Judah and Benjamin) and from some of the other surrounding nations as well
- Occupations: Various backgrounds—almost all were fugitives

Key verses
"So David left Gath and escaped to the cave of Adullam. Soon his brothers and other relatives joined him there. Then others began coming—men who were in trouble or in debt or who were just discontented—until David was the leader of about four hundred men" (1 Samuel 22:1, 2).

Their stories are told in 1 Samuel 22—2 Samuel 23:39. They are also mentioned in 1 Chronicles 11, 12.

3 The God of Israel spoke.
The Rock of Israel said to me:
'The person who rules righteously,
who rules in the fear of God,
4 he is like the light of the morning,
like the sunrise bursting forth in a cloudless sky,
like the refreshing rains that bring tender grass from the earth.'

5 "It is my family God has chosen!
Yes, he has made an everlasting covenant with me.
His agreement is eternal, final, sealed.
He will constantly look after my safety and success.
6 But the godless are like thorns to be thrown away,
for they tear the hand that touches them.
7 One must be armed to chop them down;
they will be utterly consumed with fire."

23:3 2 Sam 22:2, 32; 2 Chr 19:7, 9; Ps 72:1-3; Isa 11:1-5
23:4 Judg 5:31; Pss 72:6; 110:3
23:5 2 Sam 7:12; Ps 89:29; Isa 55:3
23:6 Matt 13:41-42

David's Mightiest Men

8These are the names of David's mightiest men. The first was Jashobeam the Hacmonite,*
who was commander of the Three—the three greatest warriors among David's men. He
once used his spear to kill eight hundred enemy warriors in a single battle.*
9Next in rank among the Three was Eleazar son of Dodai, a descendant of Ahoah. Once
Eleazar and David stood together against the Philistines when the entire Israelite army had
fled. 10He killed Philistines until his hand was too tired to lift his sword, and the LORD
gave him a great victory that day. The rest of the army did not return until it was time to
collect the plunder!
11Next in rank was Shammah son of Agee from Harar. One time the Philistines
gathered at Lehi and attacked the Israelites in a field full of lentils. The Israelite army
fled, 12but Shammah held his ground in the middle of the field and beat back the
Philistines. So the LORD brought about a great victory.
13Once during harvesttime, when David was at the cave of Adullam, the Philistine army
was camped in the valley of Rephaim. The Three (who were among the Thirty—an elite
group among David's fighting men) went down to meet him there. 14David was staying in
the stronghold at the time, and a Philistine detachment had occupied the town of Bethlehem.
15David remarked longingly to his men, "Oh, how I would love some of that good water
from the well in Bethlehem, the one by the gate." 16So the Three broke through the Philistine
lines, drew some water from the well, and brought it back to David. But he refused to drink
it. Instead, he poured it out before the LORD. 17"The LORD forbid that I should drink this!"
he exclaimed. "This water is as precious as the blood of these men who risked their lives to
bring it to me." So David did not drink it. This is an example of the exploits of the Three.

23:8 1 Chr 11:11-47
23:9 1 Chr 27:4
23:13 1 Sam 22:1; 2 Sam 5:18
23:14 1 Sam 22:4-5
23:16 Gen 35:13-14
23:17 Lev 17:10

David's Thirty Mighty Men

18Abishai son of Zeruiah, the brother of Joab, was the leader of the Thirty.* He once used
his spear to kill three hundred enemy warriors in a single battle. It was by such feats that
he became as famous as the Three. 19Abishai was the most famous of the Thirty* and
was their commander, though he was not one of the Three.

23:18 2 Sam 10:10, 14; 18:2; 1 Chr 11:20-21

23:8a As in parallel text at 1 Chr 11:11; Hebrew reads *Josheb-basshebeth the Tahkemonite.* **23:8b** As in some Greek manuscripts (see also 1 Chr 11:11); the Hebrew is uncertain, though it might be rendered *the Three. It was Adino the Eznite who killed eight hundred men at one time.* **23:18** As in a few Hebrew manuscripts and Syriac version; most Hebrew manuscripts read *the Three.* **23:19** As in Syriac version; Hebrew reads *the Three.*

23:3 In the style of a prophet, David spoke of a righteous ruler. This will be fulfilled in Jesus Christ when he returns to rule in perfect justice and peace. For similar prophecies, see Isaiah 11:1-10; Jeremiah 23:5, 6; 33:15-18; Zechariah 9:9, 10. For the fulfillment of some of these prophecies, see Matthew 4:14-16; Luke 24:25-27, 44-49; John 5:45-47; 8:28, 29.

23:8-39 These verses tell of some of the exploits that the special corps of David's army carried out. There were two elite groups of men: "the Thirty" and "the Three" (23:18, 23; 1 Chronicles 11:11-25). To become a member of such a group a man had to show unparalleled courage in battle as well as wisdom in leadership. "The Three" was the most elite group. The list of "the Thirty" actually contains 37 names, but it mentions some warriors known to be dead (Uriah, for example, in 23:39). Apparently, new members were appointed to replace those who had fallen in battle.

23:16 David poured out the water as an offering to God because he was so moved by the sacrifice it represented. When Hebrews offered sacrifices, they never consumed the blood. It represented life, and they poured it out before God. David would not drink this water that represented the lives of his soldiers. Instead, he offered it to God.

23:20 Josh 15:21 2 Sam 8:18; 20:23

20 There was also Benaiah son of Jehoiada, a valiant warrior from Kabzeel. He did
many heroic deeds, which included killing two of Moab's mightiest warriors. Another
time he chased a lion down into a pit. Then, despite the snow and slippery ground, he
caught the lion and killed it. 21 Another time, armed only with a club, he killed a great
Egyptian warrior who was armed with a spear. Benaiah wrenched the spear from the
Egyptian's hand and killed him with it. 22 These are some of the deeds that made Benaiah
almost as famous as the Three. 23 He was more honored than the other members of the
Thirty, though he was not one of the Three. And David made him commander of his
bodyguard.

23:24 2 Sam 2:18

24 Other members of the Thirty included:

Asahel, Joab's brother;
Elhanan son of Dodo from Bethlehem;

23:25 Judg 7:1

25 Shammah from Harod;
Elika from Harod;
26 Helez from Pelon*;
Ira son of Ikkesh from Tekoa;

23:27 Josh 21:18

27 Abiezer from Anathoth;
Sibbecai* from Hushah;

23:28 2 Kgs 25:27

28 Zalmon from Ahoah;
Maharai from Netophah;
29 Heled* son of Baanah from Netophah;
Ithai* son of Ribai from Gibeah (from the tribe of Benjamin);

23:30 Josh 24:30

30 Benaiah from Pirathon;
Hurai* from Nahale-gaash*;
31 Abi-albon the Arbathite;
Azmaveth from Bahurim;
32 Eliahba from Shaalbon;
the sons of Jashen;
33 Jonathan son of Shagee* from Harar;
Ahiam son of Sharar from Harar;

23:34 2 Sam 11:3; 15:12

34 Eliphelet son of Ahasbai from Maacah;
Eliam son of Ahithophel from Giloh;
35 Hezro from Carmel;
Paarai from Arba;
36 Igal son of Nathan from Zobah;
Bani from Gad;
37 Zelek from Ammon;
Naharai from Beeroth (Joab's armor bearer);

23:38 1 Chr 2:53

38 Ira from Jattir;
Gareb from Jattir;

23:39 2 Sam 11:3

39 Uriah the Hittite.

There were thirty-seven in all.

David Takes a Census

24:1-17 1 Chr 21:1-17

24:1 1 Chr 27:23

24 Once again the anger of the LORD burned against Israel, and he caused David to
harm them by taking a census. "Go and count the people of Israel and Judah," the
LORD told him.

24:2 Judg 20:1 2 Sam 3:9-10

2 So the king said to Joab, the commander of his army, "Take a census of all the people

23:26 As in parallel text at 1 Chr 11:27 (see also 1 Chr 27:10); Hebrew reads *from Palti.* **23:27** As in some Greek manuscripts (see also 1 Chr 11:29); Hebrew reads *Mebunnai.* **23:29a** As in some Hebrew manuscripts (see also 1 Chr 11:30); most Hebrew manuscripts read *Heleb.* **23:29b** As in parallel text at 1 Chr 11:31; Hebrew reads *Ittai.* **23:30a** As in some Greek manuscripts (see also 1 Chr 11:32); Hebrew reads *Hiddai.* **23:30b** Or *from the ravines of Gaash.* **23:33** As in parallel text at 1 Chr 11:34; Hebrew reads *Jonathan, Shammah;* some Greek manuscripts read *Jonathan son of Shammah.*

24:1 Did God cause David to sin? God does not cause people to sin, but he does allow sinners to reveal the sinfulness of their hearts by their actions. God presented the opportunity to David in order to deal with a disastrous national tendency, and he wanted this desire to show itself. First Chronicles 21:1 says Satan incited David to do it. Hebrew writers do not always distinguish between primary and secondary causes. So if God allowed Satan to tempt David, to them it is as if God did it.

in the land—from Dan in the north to Beersheba in the south—so that I may know how many people there are."

3But Joab replied to the king, "May the LORD your God let you live until there are a hundred times as many people in your kingdom as there are now! But why do you want to do this?"

4But the king insisted that they take the census, so Joab and his officers went out to count the people of Israel. 5First they crossed the Jordan and camped at Aroer, south of the town in the valley, in the direction of Gad. Then they went on to Jazer, 6then to Gilead in the land of Tahtim-hodshi* and to Dan-jaan and around to Sidon. 7Then they came to the stronghold of Tyre, and all the cities of the Hivites and Canaanites. Finally, they went south to Judah as far as Beersheba. 8Having gone through the entire land, they completed their task in nine months and twenty days and then returned to Jerusalem. 9Joab reported the number of people to the king. There were 800,000 men of military age in Israel and 500,000 in Judah.

Judgment for David's Sin

10But after he had taken the census, David's conscience began to bother him. And he said to the LORD, "I have sinned greatly and shouldn't have taken the census. Please forgive me, LORD, for doing this foolish thing."

11The next morning the word of the LORD came to the prophet Gad, who was David's seer. This was the message: 12"Go and say to David, 'This is what the LORD says: I will give you three choices. Choose one of these punishments, and I will do it.'"

13So Gad came to David and asked him, "Will you choose three* years of famine throughout the land, three months of fleeing from your enemies, or three days of severe plague throughout your land? Think this over and let me know what answer to give the LORD."

14"This is a desperate situation!" David replied to Gad. "But let us fall into the hands of the LORD, for his mercy is great. Do not let me fall into human hands."

15So the LORD sent a plague upon Israel that morning, and it lasted for three days. Seventy thousand people died throughout the nation. 16But as the death angel was preparing to destroy Jerusalem, the LORD relented and said to the angel, "Stop! That is enough!" At that moment the angel of the LORD was by the threshing floor of Araunah the Jebusite.

17When David saw the angel, he said to the LORD, "I am the one who has sinned and done wrong! But these people are innocent—what have they done? Let your anger fall against me and my family."

David Builds an Altar

18That day Gad came to David and said to him, "Go and build an altar to the LORD on the threshing floor of Araunah the Jebusite."

24:3 Deut 1:11
24:5 Num 21:32; 32:34-36; Josh 13:9, 16
24:6 Josh 19:28
24:9 Num 1:20-46; 1 Chr 21:5
24:10 1 Sam 24:5; 2 Sam 12:13
24:11 1 Sam 9:9; 22:5
24:13 1 Chr 21:12
24:14 Pss 51:1; 130:3-4, 7-8, 13
24:15 1 Chr 21:14; 27:24
24:16 Exod 12:23; 2 Kgs 19:35
24:17 2 Sam 7:8; Ps 74:1
24:18-25 //1 Chr 21:18-26

24:6 Greek version reads *to Gilead and to Kadesh in the land of the Hittites.* **24:13** As in Greek version (see also 1 Chr 21:12); Hebrew reads *seven.*

24:1-3 What was wrong with taking a census? A census was commanded in Numbers to prepare an army for conquering the Promised Land (Numbers 1:2; 26:2). A census amounted to a draft or conscription for the army. The land was now at peace, so there was no need to enlist troops. Israel had extended its borders and become a recognized power. David's sin was pride and ambition in counting the people so that he could glory in the size of his army, its power and defenses. By doing this, he put his faith in the size of his army rather than in God's ability to protect them regardless of their number. Even Joab knew a census was wrong, but David did not heed his advice. We sin in a similar way when we place our security in money, possessions, or the might of our nation.

24:12-14 Both David and the Israelites were guilty of sin (24:1). David's sin was pride, but the Bible does not say why God was angry with the people of Israel. Perhaps it was due to their support of the rebellions of Absalom (chapters 15–18) and Sheba (chapter 20), or perhaps they put their security in military and financial prosperity rather than in God, as David did. God dealt with the whole nation through David, who exemplified the national sin of pride.

God gave David three choices. Each was a form of punishment God had told the people they could expect if they disobeyed his laws (disease—Deuteronomy 28:20-22; famine—28:23, 24; war—28:25, 26). David wisely chose the form of punishment that came most directly from God. He knew how brutal and harsh men in war could be, and he also knew God's great mercy. When you sin greatly, turn back to God. To be punished by him is far better than to take your chances without him.

24:18 Many believe that this threshing floor where David built the altar is the location where Abraham nearly sacrificed his son Isaac (Genesis 22:1-18). After David's death, Solomon built the Temple on this spot. Centuries later, Jesus would teach and preach here.

[19]So David went to do what the LORD had commanded him. [20]When Araunah saw the
king and his men coming toward him, he came forward and bowed before the king with
24:21 Num 16:44-50 his face to the ground. [21]"Why have you come, my lord?" Araunah asked.
And David replied, "I have come to buy your threshing floor and to build an altar to
the LORD there, so that the LORD will stop the plague."
24:22 1 Sam 6:14; 1 Kgs 19:21 [22]"Take it, my lord, and use it as you wish," Araunah said to David. "Here are oxen
for the burnt offering, and you can use the threshing tools and ox yokes for wood to build
a fire on the altar. [23]I will give it all to you, and may the LORD your God accept your
sacrifice."
24:24 Gen 23:16 [24]But the king replied to Araunah, "No, I insist on buying it, for I cannot present burnt
offerings to the LORD my God that have cost me nothing." So David paid him fifty pieces
24:25 2 Sam 21:14 of silver* for the threshing floor and the oxen. [25]David built an altar there to the LORD
and offered burnt offerings and peace offerings. And the LORD answered his prayer, and
the plague was stopped.

24:24 Hebrew *50 shekels of silver,* about 20 ounces or 570 grams in weight.

24:25 The book of 2 Samuel describes David's reign. Since the Israelites first entered the Promised Land under Joshua, they had been struggling to unite the nation and drive out the wicked inhabitants. Now, after more than 400 years, Israel was finally at peace. David had accomplished what no leader before him, judge or king, had done. His administration was run on the principle of dedication to God and to the well-being of the people. Yet David also sinned. Despite his sins, however, the Bible calls David a man after God's own heart (1 Samuel 13:14; Acts 13:22) because when he sinned, he recognized it and confessed his sins to God. David committed his life to God and remained loyal to him throughout his lifetime. Psalms gives an even deeper insight into David's love for God.

1 KINGS

David becomes king 1010 B.C. | *Solomon becomes king 970* | *Temple completed 959* | *The kingdom divides 930* | *Shishak invades Jerusalem 925*

VITAL STATISTICS

PURPOSE:
To contrast the lives of those who live for God and those who refuse to do so through the history of the kings of Israel and Judah

AUTHOR:
Unknown. Possibly Jeremiah or a group of prophets

SETTING:
The once great nation of Israel turned into a land divided, not only physically, but also spiritually.

KEY VERSES:
"As for you, if you will follow me with integrity and godliness, as David your father did, always obeying my commands and keeping my laws and regulations, then I will establish the throne of your dynasty over Israel forever. For I made this promise to your father, David: 'You will never fail to have a successor on the throne of Israel'" (9:4, 5).

KEY PEOPLE:
David, Solomon, Rehoboam, Jeroboam, Elijah, Ahab, Jezebel

SPECIAL FEATURE:
The books of 1 and 2 Kings were originally one book.

"I DON'T CARE what anyone says, I'm going to do it!" he yells at his mother as he storms out of the house.

This is a familiar scene in our society. The words change, but the essential message is the same: A person is *not* open to advice because his mind is closed. Some advice may be sought, but it is heeded only if it reinforces the decision already made or is an easier path to take. It is human nature to reject help and to do things *our* way.

A much wiser approach is to seek, hear, and heed the advice of good counselors. Solomon, the world's wisest man, urges this in Proverbs (see 11:14; 15:22; 24:6). How ironic that his son and successor, Rehoboam, listened instead to foolish advice, with devastating results. At Rehoboam's inauguration, he was petitioned by the people to be a kind and generous ruler. The older men counseled him to "serve the people . . . and give them a favorable answer" (12:7). But Rehoboam agreed to the cruel words of his peers who urged him to be harsh. As a result, Rehoboam split the kingdom. Learn from Rehoboam's mistake. Commit yourself to seeking and following wise counsel.

The main events of 1 Kings are David's death, Solomon's reign, the division of the kingdom, and Elijah's ministry. As Solomon ascended the throne, David charged him to obey God's laws and to "follow all his ways" (2:3). This Solomon did; and when given the choice of gifts from God, he humbly asked for wisdom (3:9). As a result, Solomon's reign began with great success, including the construction of the Temple—his greatest achievement. Unfortunately, Solomon took many pagan wives and concubines who eventually turned his heart away from the Lord to their false gods (11:1–4).

Rehoboam succeeded Solomon and had the opportunity to be a wise, compassionate, and just king. Instead, he accepted the poor advice of his young friends and attempted to rule with an iron hand. But the people rebelled, and the kingdom split with 10 tribes in the north (Israel) ruled by Jeroboam, and only Judah and Benjamin remaining with Rehoboam. Both kingdoms wove a path through the reigns of corrupt and idolatrous kings with only the clear voice of the prophets continuing to warn and call the nation back to God.

Elijah is surely one of the greatest prophets, and chapters 17 through 22 feature his conflict with wicked Ahab and Jezebel in Israel. In one of the most dramatic confrontations in history, Elijah defeated the prophets of Baal at Mount Carmel. In spite of incredible opposition, Elijah stood for God and proves that *one plus God* is a majority. If God is on our side, no one can stand against us (Romans 8:31).

Asa becomes king of Judah 910	Elijah begins his ministry 875	Ahab becomes king of Israel 874	Jehoshaphat becomes king of Judah 872	Ben-hadad attacks Samaria 857	Ahab dies in battle 853

THE BLUEPRINT

A. THE UNITED KINGDOM (1:1—11:43)
1. Solomon becomes king
2. Solomon's wisdom
3. Solomon builds the Temple
4. Solomon's greatness and downfall

Solomon was a botanist, zoologist, architect, poet, and philosopher. He was the wisest king in the history of Israel, but his wives led to the introduction of false gods and false worship in Israel. It is good for us to have wisdom, but that is not enough. The highest goal in life is to obey the Lord. Patient obedience to God should characterize our lives.

B. THE DIVIDED KINGDOM (12:1—22:53)
1. Revolt of the northern tribes
2. Kings of Israel and Judah
3. Elijah's ministry
4. Kings of Israel and Judah

When the northern kingdom of Israel was being led by wicked kings, God raised up a prophet to proclaim his messages. Elijah single-handedly challenged the priesthood of the state religion and had them removed in one day. Through the dividing of the kingdom and the sending of Elijah, God dealt with the people's sin in powerful ways. Sin in our lives is graciously forgiven by God. However, the sin of an unrepentant person will be handled harshly. We must turn from sin and turn to God to be saved from judgment.

MEGATHEMES

THEME	EXPLANATION	IMPORTANCE
The King	Solomon's wisdom, power, and achievements brought honor to the Israelite nation and to God. All the kings of Israel and Judah were told to obey God and to govern according to his laws. But their tendency to abandon God's commands and to worship other gods led them to change the religion and government to meet their personal desires. This neglect of God's law led to their downfall.	Wisdom, power, and achievement do not ultimately come from any human source; they are from God. No matter what we lead or govern, we can't do well when we ignore God's guidelines. Whether or not we are leaders, effectiveness depends upon listening and obeying God's Word. Don't let your personal desires distort God's Word.
The Temple	Solomon's Temple was a beautiful place of worship and prayer. This sanctuary was the center of Jewish religion. It was the place of God's special presence and housed the Ark of the Covenant containing the Ten Commandments.	A beautiful house of worship doesn't always guarantee heartfelt worship of God. Providing opportunities for true worship doesn't ensure that it will happen. God wants to live in our hearts, not just meet us in a sanctuary.
Other Gods	Although the Israelites had God's law and experienced his presence among them, they became attracted to other gods. When this happened, their hearts became cold to God's law, resulting in the ruin of families and government, and eventually leading to the destruction of the nation.	Through the years, the people took on the false qualities of the false gods they worshiped. They became cruel, power-hungry, and sexually perverse. We tend to become what we worship. Unless we serve the true God, we will become slaves to whatever takes his place.
The Prophet's Message	The prophet's responsibility was to confront and correct any deviation from God's law. Elijah was a bolt of judgment against Israel. His messages and miracles were a warning to the evil and rebellious kings and people.	The Bible, the truth in sermons, and the wise counsel of believers are warnings to us. Anyone who points out how we deviate from obeying God's Word is a blessing to us. Changing our lives in order to obey God and get back on track often takes painful discipline and hard work.
Sin and Repentance	Each king had God's commands, a priest or prophet, and the lessons of the past to draw him back to God. All the people had the same resources. Whenever they repented and returned to God, God heard their prayers and forgave him.	God hears and forgives us when we pray—if we are willing to trust him and turn from sin. Our desire to forsake our sin must be heartfelt and sincere. Then he will give us a fresh start and a desire to live for him.

KEY PLACES IN 1 KINGS

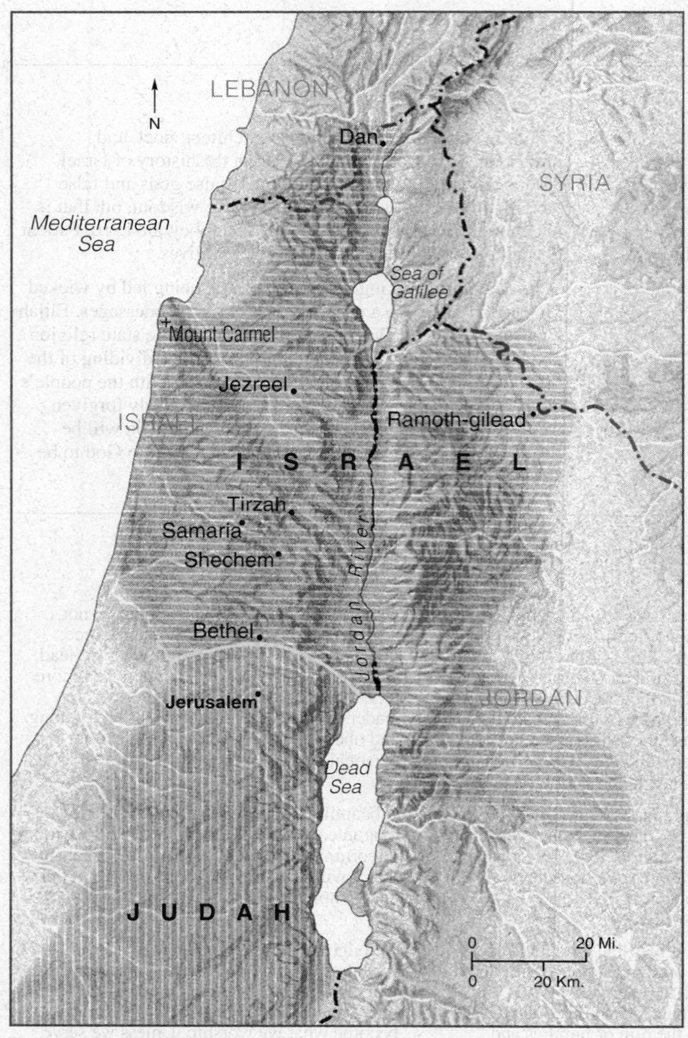

The broken lines (—·—) indicate modern boundaries.

Solomon, David's son, brought Israel into its golden age. His wealth and wisdom were acclaimed worldwide. But he ignored God in his later years (1:1—11:43).

1 Shechem After Solomon's death, Israel assembled at Shechem to inaugurate his son Rehoboam. However, Rehoboam foolishly angered the people by threatening even heavier burdens, causing a revolt (12:1–19).

2 Israel Jeroboam, leader of the rebels, was made king of Israel, now called the northern kingdom. Jeroboam made Shechem his capital city (12:20, 25).

3 Judah Only the tribes of Judah and part of Benjamin remained loyal to Rehoboam. These two tribes became the southern kingdom. Rehoboam returned to Judah from Shechem and prepared to force the rebels into submission, but a prophet's message halted these plans (12:21–24).

4 Jerusalem Jerusalem was the capital city of Judah. Its Temple, built by Solomon, was the focal point of Jewish worship. This worried Jeroboam. How could he keep his people loyal if they were constantly going to Rehoboam's capital to worship (12:26, 27)?

5 Dan Jeroboam's solution was to set up his own worship centers. Two golden calves were made and proclaimed to be Israel's gods. One was placed in Dan, and the people were told that they could go there instead of to Jerusalem to worship (12:28, 29).

6 Bethel The other golden calf was placed in Bethel. The people of the northern kingdom had two convenient locations for worship in their own country, but their sin displeased God. In Jerusalem, meanwhile, Rehoboam was also allowing idolatry to creep in. The two nations were constantly at war (12:29—15:26).

7 Tirzah Jeroboam had moved the capital city to Tirzah (1 Kings 14:17). Next, Baasha became king of Israel after assassinating Nadab (15:27—16:22).

8 Samaria Israel continued to gain and lose kings through plots, assassinations, and warfare. When Omri became king, he bought a hill on which he built a new capital city, Samaria. Omri's son, Ahab, became the most wicked king of Israel. His wife, Jezebel, worshiped Baal. Ahab erected a temple to Baal in Samaria (16:23–34).

9 Mount Carmel Great evil often brings great people who oppose it. Elijah challenged the prophets of Baal and Asherah at Mount Carmel, where he would prove that they were false prophets. There Elijah humiliated these prophets and then executed them (17:1—18:46).

10 Jezreel Elijah returned to Jezreel. But Queen Jezebel, furious at the execution of her prophets, vowed to kill Elijah. He ran for his life, but God cared for and encouraged him. During his travels he anointed the future kings of Aram and Israel, as well as Elisha, his own replacement (19:1–21).

11 Ramoth-gilead The king of Aram declared war on Israel and was defeated in two battles. But the Arameans occupied Ramoth-gilead. Ahab and Jehoshaphat joined forces to recover the city. In this battle, Ahab was killed. Jehoshaphat later died (20:1—22:53).

A. THE UNITED KINGDOM (1:1—11:43)

When Solomon is anointed king, he eliminates all opposition to the throne, builds the Temple, establishes a strong army, and becomes the richest and wisest king in the history of Israel. But his pagan wives lead him into idolatry, and as a result, he leads the nation into spiritual decline. No matter what position in life we attain, we are always ripe for a downfall and must never let our guard down against sin and temptation.

1. Solomon becomes king

David in His Old Age

1 Now King David was very old, and no matter how many blankets covered him, he could not keep warm. 2 So his advisers told him, "We will find a young virgin who will wait on you and be your nurse. She will lie in your arms and keep you warm." 3 So they searched throughout the country for a beautiful girl, and they found Abishag from Shunem and brought her to the king. 4 The girl was very beautiful, and she waited on the king and took care of him. But the king had no sexual relations with her.

1:3
Josh 19:18
1 Sam 28:4

Adonijah Claims the Throne

5 About that time David's son Adonijah, whose mother was Haggith, decided to make

1:5
2 Sam 3:4

Who joined Adonijah's conspiracy and who remained loyal to David?
Contrast the fate of those who rebelled and those who remained loyal to David, God's appointed leader. Adonijah, the leader of the conspiracy, met a violent death (2:25). Those who rebel against God's leaders rebel against God.

Joined Adonijah

JOAB (1:7)
Brilliant military general and commander of David's army. He continually demonstrated his belief that cold-blooded murder was as acceptable as a fairly fought battle. Solomon later had him executed.

ABIATHAR (1:7)
One of two high priests under David. He was a son of Ahimelech who had helped David, and David promised to protect him. Abiathar repaid David with his treachery. Solomon later had him banished, fulfilling the prophecy that Eli's priestly line would end (1 Samuel 2:31).

JONATHAN (1:42)
Abiathar's son. He helped David stop Absalom's rebellion (2 Samuel 17:17–22) but supported this rebellion by another of David's sons.

CHARIOTEERS (1:5)
Hired by Adonijah, apparently more loyal to money than to their king.

50 RUNNERS (1:5)
Recruited to give Adonijah a "royal" appearance.

Remained with David

ZADOK (1:8)
The other high priest under David. His loyalty gave him the privilege of crowning Solomon. He became the sole high priest under King Solomon.

BENAIAH (1:8)
Distinguished himself as a great warrior. Commanded a division of David's army—over 24,000 men. One of the Thirty, he was also placed in charge of David's bodyguard. Solomon later made him chief commander of the army.

NATHAN (1:8)
God's prominent prophet during David's reign. The Bible says he wrote a history of David and Solomon.

SHIMEI (1:8)
This man was probably the Shimei who was rewarded by Solomon and appointed district governor in Benjamin (4:18). (He was not the same person who cursed David at Bahurim and brought on his own death under Solomon.)

REI (1:8)
Only mentioned here. Possibly he was an army officer. The word means "and his friends."

DAVID'S BODYGUARD (1:8, 10)
David's army was highly organized with several different divisions of troops. It is enough to know that many of his leaders remained true to their king.

1:1 Israel was near the end of the golden years of David's reign. The book of 1 Kings begins with a unified kingdom, glorious and God-centered; it ends with a divided kingdom, degraded and idolatrous. The reason for Israel's decline appears simple to us—they failed to obey God. But we are vulnerable to the same forces that brought about Israel's decay—greed, jealousy, lust for power, weakening of marriage vows, and superficiality in our devotion to God. As we read about these tragic events in Israel's history, we must see ourselves in the mirror of their experiences.

1:4 David was about 70 years old. His health had deteriorated from years of hardship. Abishag served as his nurse and to help keep him warm. In times when polygamy was accepted and kings had harems, this action was not considered offensive.

1:5 Adonijah was David's fourth son and the logical choice to succeed him as king. David's first son, Amnon, had been killed by Absalom for having raped his sister (2 Samuel 13:20-33). His second son, Daniel, is mentioned only in the genealogy of 1 Chronicles 3:1 and had probably died by this time. David's third son, Absalom, died in an earlier rebellion (2 Samuel 18:1-18). Although many people expected Adonijah to be the next king (2:13-25), David (and God) had other plans (1:29, 30).

himself king in place of his aged father. So he provided himself with chariots and
horses* and recruited fifty men to run in front of him. 6 Now his father, King David,
had never disciplined him at any time, even by asking, "What are you doing?"
Adonijah was a very handsome man and had been born next after Absalom. 7 Adonijah 1:7
took Joab son of Zeruiah and Abiathar the priest into his confidence, and they agreed 1 Sam 22:20, 23 2 Sam 20:25
to help him become king. 8 But among those who remained loyal to David and refused 1 Kgs 2:22, 28
to support Adonijah were Zadok the priest, Benaiah son of Jehoiada, Nathan the 1:8 2 Sam 8:18; 12:1;
prophet, Shimei, Rei, and David's personal bodyguard. 20:25; 23:8-39
9 Adonijah went to the stone of Zoheleth* near the spring of En-rogel, where he
sacrificed sheep, oxen, and fattened calves. He invited all his brothers—the other sons
of King David—and all the royal officials of Judah. 10 But he did not invite Nathan the 1:10 2 Sam 12:24
prophet, or Benaiah, or the king's bodyguard, or his brother Solomon.
11 Then Nathan the prophet went to Bathsheba, Solomon's mother, and asked her, "Did
you realize that Haggith's son, Adonijah, has made himself king and that our lord David
doesn't even know about it? 12 If you want to save your own life and the life of your son
Solomon, follow my counsel. 13 Go at once to King David and say to him, 'My lord, 1:13
didn't you promise me that my son Solomon would be the next king and would sit upon 1 Chr 22:9-13
your throne? Then why has Adonijah become king?' 14 And while you are still talking
with him, I will come and confirm everything you have said."

1:5 Or *and charioteers.* **1:9** Or *to the Serpent's Stone;* Greek version supports reading *Zoheleth* as a proper name.

1:5 Adonijah decided to seize the throne without David's knowledge. He knew that Solomon, not he, was David's first choice to be the next king (1:17). This was why he did not invite Solomon and David's loyal advisers when he declared himself king (1:9, 10). But his deceptive plans to gain the throne were unsuccessful. The proud Adonijah was self-exalted and self-defeated.

1:6 God-fearing people like David and Samuel were used by God to lead nations; nevertheless they had problems in family relationships. God-fearing leaders cannot take for granted the spiritual well-being of their children. They are used to having others follow their orders, but they cannot expect their children to manufacture faith upon request. Moral and spiritual character takes years to build, and it requires constant attention and patient discipline.

David served God well as a king, but as a parent he often failed both God and his children. Don't let your service to God, even in leadership positions, take up so much of your time and energy that you neglect your other God-given responsibilities.

1:6 Because David had never interfered by opposing or even questioning his son, Adonijah did not know how to work within limits. The result was that he always wanted his own way, regardless of how it affected others. Adonijah did whatever he wanted and paid no respect to God's wishes. An undisciplined child may look cute to his or her parents, but an undisciplined adult destroys himself and others. As you set limits for your children, you make it possible for them to develop the self-restraint they will need in order to control themselves later. Discipline your children carefully while they are young, so that they will grow into self-disciplined adults.

1:7 See Joab's Profile in 2 Samuel 18 for a more complete picture of his life. For more information on Abiathar, see the note on 1 Samuel 22:20.

1:9 When Saul was anointed king, peace offerings were sacrificed as a reminder of the nation's covenant with God given at Mount Sinai. Adonijah wanted sacrifices offered, perhaps hoping to legitimize his takeover. But Adonijah was not God's choice to succeed David. Sealing an action with religious ceremony does not make it God's will.

1:11 For more on Bathsheba, David's wife, read 2 Samuel 11–12. As mother of the king, Bathsheba was highly influential in the royal palace.

1:11-14 When Nathan learned of Adonijah's conspiracy, he immediately tried to stop it. He was a man of both faith and action. He knew that Solomon should rightly be king, and he moved quickly when he saw someone else trying to take the throne. We often know what is right but don't act on it. Perhaps we don't want to get involved, or maybe we are fearful or lazy. Don't stop with prayer, good intentions, or angry feelings. Take the action needed to correct the situation.

1:13 The Bible does not record David's promise that Solomon would be Israel's next king, but it is clear that Solomon was the choice of both David (1:17, 30) and God (1 Chronicles 22:9, 10).

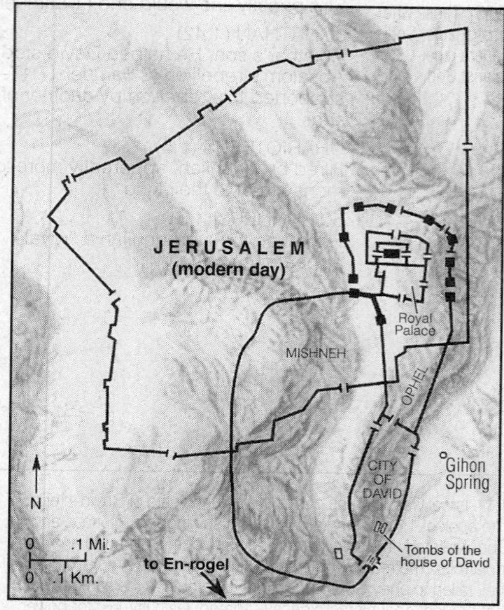

TWO CORONATIONS As David lay on his deathbed, his son Adonijah crowned himself king at En-rogel outside Jerusalem. When the news reached David, he declared that Solomon was to be the next ruler. Solomon was anointed at Gihon. It may have been more than coincidence that Gihon was not only within shouting distance of En-rogel but also closer to the royal palace.

15 So Bathsheba went into the king's bedroom. He was very old now, and Abishag was
taking care of him. 16 Bathsheba bowed low before him.
"What can I do for you?" he asked her.
17 She replied, "My lord, you vowed to me by the LORD your God that my son
Solomon would be the next king and would sit on your throne. 18 But instead, Adonijah
1:19 1 Kgs 1:9 has become the new king, and you do not even know about it. 19 He has sacrificed many
oxen, fattened calves, and sheep, and he has invited all your sons and Abiathar the priest
and Joab, the commander of the army. But he did not invite your servant Solomon. 20 And
now, my lord the king, all Israel is waiting for your decision as to who will become king
after you. 21 If you do not act, my son Solomon and I will be treated as criminals as soon
as you are dead."
22 While she was still speaking with the king, Nathan the prophet arrived. 23 The king's
advisers told him, "Nathan the prophet is here to see you."
Nathan went in and bowed low before the king. 24 He asked, "My lord, have you
1:25 1 Sam 10:24 1 Kgs 1:9 decided that Adonijah will be the next king and that he will sit on your throne? 25 Today
he has sacrificed many oxen, fattened calves, and sheep, and he has invited your sons to
attend the celebration. He also invited Joab, the commander of the army,* and Abiathar
the priest. They are feasting and drinking with him and shouting, 'Long live King

1:25 As in Greek version; Hebrew reads *invited the commanders of the army.*

BATHSHEBA

Bathsheba was the unlikely link between Israel's two most famous kings—David and Solomon. She was lover and wife to one, mother to the other. Her adultery with David almost brought an end to the family through which God planned to physically enter his world. Out of the ashes of that sin, however, God brought good. Eventually Jesus Christ, the salvation of mankind, was born to a descendant of David and Bathsheba.

David and Bathsheba's story shows that little wrong decisions often lead to big mistakes. It is likely that neither was where he or she should have been. Bathsheba may have been rash in bathing where she might be seen; David should have been at war with his army. Each decision contributed to the beginning of a very sad series of events.

Bathsheba must have been devastated by the chain of events—unfaithfulness to her husband, discovery of pregnancy, death of her husband, death of her child. We are told that David comforted her (2 Samuel 12:24), and she lived to see another son, Solomon, sit on the throne.

From her life we see that the little, day-to-day choices we make are very important. They prepare us to make the right choices when the big decisions come. The wisdom to make right choices in small and large matters is a gift from God. Understanding this should make us more conscious of the decisions we make and more willing to include God in our decision making. Have you asked for his help with today's decisions?

Strengths and accomplishments
- Became influential in the palace alongside her son Solomon
- Was the mother of Israel's wisest king and an ancestor of Jesus Christ

Weakness and mistake
- Committed adultery

Lessons from her life
- Although we may feel caught up in a chain of events, we are still responsible for the way we participate in those events
- A sin may seem like one small seed, but the harvest of consequences is beyond measure
- In the worst possible situations, God is still able to bring about good when people truly turn to him
- While we must live with the natural consequences of our sins, God's forgiveness of sin is total

Vital statistics
- Where: Jerusalem
- Occupations: Queen and queen mother
- Relatives: Father: Elim. Husbands: Uriah and David. Son: Solomon
- Contemporaries: Nathan, Joab, Adonijah

Key verses
"When Bathsheba heard that her husband was dead, she mourned for him. When the period of mourning was over, David sent for her and brought her to the palace, and she became one of his wives. Then she gave birth to a son. But the LORD was very displeased with what David had done" (2 Samuel 11:26, 27).

Her story is told in 2 Samuel 11—12 and 1 Kings 1— 2. A related passage is Psalm 51.

Adonijah!' 26But I myself, your servant, was not invited; neither were Zadok the priest,
Benaiah son of Jehoiada, nor Solomon. 27Has my lord really done this without letting
any of his servants know who should be the next king?"

David Makes Solomon King

28"Call Bathsheba," David said. So she came back in and stood before the king. 29And **1:28-53** //1 Chr 29:21-25
the king vowed, "As surely as the LORD lives, who has rescued me from every danger,
30today I decree that your son Solomon will be the next king and will sit on my throne, **1:29** 2 Sam 4:9
just as I swore to you before the LORD, the God of Israel."

31Then Bathsheba bowed low before him again and exclaimed, "May my lord King
David live forever!"

32Then King David ordered, "Call Zadok the priest, Nathan the prophet, and Benaiah
son of Jehoiada." When they came into the king's presence, 33the king said to them,
"Take Solomon and my officers down to Gihon Spring. Solomon is to ride on my
personal mule. 34There Zadok the priest and Nathan the prophet are to anoint him king **1:34** 1 Sam 10:1; 16:3, 12
over Israel. Then blow the trumpets and shout, 'Long live King Solomon!' 35When you 2 Sam 15:10
bring him back here, he will sit on my throne. He will succeed me as king, for I have
appointed him to be ruler over Israel and Judah."

36"Amen!" Benaiah son of Jehoiada replied. "May the LORD, the God of my lord the
king, decree it to be so. 37And may the LORD be with Solomon as he has been with you, **1:37** Josh 1:5, 17
and may he make Solomon's reign even greater than yours!" 1 Sam 20:13; 1 Kgs 1:47

38So Zadok the priest, Nathan the prophet, Benaiah son of Jehoiada, and the king's
bodyguard* took Solomon down to Gihon Spring, and Solomon rode on King David's
personal mule. 39There Zadok the priest took a flask of olive oil from the sacred tent and **1:39** 1 Kgs 1:34
poured it on Solomon's head. Then the trumpets were blown, and all the people shouted, 1 Chr 16:39; 29:22
"Long live King Solomon!" 40And all the people returned with Solomon to Jerusalem, Ps 89:20
playing flutes and shouting for joy. The celebration was so joyous and noisy that the earth **1:40** 1 Sam 10:5
shook with the sound.

41Adonijah and his guests heard the celebrating and shouting just as they were
finishing their banquet. When Joab heard the sound of trumpets, he asked, "What's going
on? Why is the city in such an uproar?"

42And while he was still speaking, Jonathan son of Abiathar the priest arrived. "Come **1:42** 2 Sam 18:26-27
in," Adonijah said to him, "for you are a good man. You must have good news."

43"Not at all!" Jonathan replied. "Our lord King David has just declared Solomon
king! 44The king sent him down to Gihon Spring with Zadok the priest, Nathan the
prophet, and Benaiah son of Jehoiada, protected by the king's bodyguard. They had him
ride on the king's own mule, 45and Zadok and Nathan have anointed him as the new king.
They have just returned, and the whole city is celebrating and rejoicing. That's what all
the noise is about. 46Moreover, Solomon is now sitting on the royal throne as king. 47All **1:47** 1 Kgs 1:37
the royal officials went to King David and congratulated him, saying, 'May your God
make Solomon's fame even greater than your own, and may Solomon's kingdom be even
greater than yours!' Then the king bowed his head in worship as he lay in his bed, 48and **1:48** 2 Sam 7:12
he spoke these words: 'Blessed be the LORD, the God of Israel, who today has chosen 1 Kgs 3:6
someone to sit on my throne while I am still alive to see it.'"

49Then all of Adonijah's guests jumped up in panic from the banquet table and quickly **1:49** 1 Kgs 2:28

1:38 Hebrew *the Kerethites and Pelethites;* also in 1:44.

1:39 The olive oil was used to anoint Israel's kings and high priests, as well as to dedicate certain objects to God. The sacred tent where the oil was kept was probably the tent David set up to shelter the Ark of the Covenant (2 Samuel 6:17). It was not the Tabernacle Moses carried in the wilderness; that Tabernacle was still at Gibeon (see the note on 1 Samuel 7:1 for more details). The recipe and uses for the sacred oil are found in Exodus 30:22-33. For more on anointing, see the notes on 1 Samuel 10:1 and 16:13.

1:49, 50 Sometimes it takes getting caught before someone is willing to give up his scheme. When Adonijah learned that his plans were doomed to fail, he ran in panic to the altar, the place of God's mercy and forgiveness. He went there, however, *after* his plans for treason were exposed. If Adonijah had first considered what God wanted, he might have avoided trouble. Don't wait until you have made a mess of your life before you run to God. Seek God's guidance *before* you act.

1:49-51 Both Adonijah and his commander, Joab, thought they would be safe by clutching the horns (or corner posts) of the sacred altar of burnt offering in the Tabernacle court. They hoped to place themselves under God's protection. Solomon granted Adonijah a reprieve, but later he had Joab killed right at the altar (2:28-34). This punishment was appropriate justice for a cold-blooded murderer such as Joab (Exodus 21:14).

went their separate ways. 50 Adonijah himself was afraid of Solomon, so he rushed to the
sacred tent and caught hold of the horns of the altar. 51 Word soon reached Solomon that
Adonijah had seized the horns of the altar and that he was pleading, "Let Solomon swear
today that he will not kill me!"
52 Solomon replied, "If he proves himself to be loyal, he will not be harmed.* But if
he does not, he will die." 53 So King Solomon summoned Adonijah, and they brought
him down from the altar. He came and bowed low before the king, and Solomon
dismissed him, saying, "Go on home."

David's Final Instructions to Solomon

2 As the time of King David's death approached, he gave this charge to his son
Solomon: 2 "I am going where everyone on earth must someday go. Take courage
and be a man. 3 Observe the requirements of the LORD your God and follow all his ways.
Keep each of the laws, commands, regulations, and stipulations written in the law of
Moses so that you will be successful in all you do and wherever you go. 4 If you do this,
then the LORD will keep the promise he made to me: 'If your descendants live as they
should and follow me faithfully with all their heart and soul, one of them will always sit
on the throne of Israel.'
5 "And there is something else. You know that Joab son of Zeruiah murdered my
two army commanders, Abner son of Ner and Amasa son of Jether. He pretended that
it was an act of war, but it was done in a time of peace,* staining his belt and sandals
with the blood of war. 6 Do with him what you think best, but don't let him die in
peace.
7 "Be kind to the sons of Barzillai from Gilead. Make them permanent guests of the
king, for they took care of me when I fled from your brother Absalom.
8 "And remember Shimei son of Gera, the Benjaminite from Bahurim. He cursed me
with a terrible curse as I was fleeing to Mahanaim. When he came down to meet me at
the Jordan River, I swore by the LORD that I would not kill him. 9 But that oath does not
make him innocent. You are a wise man, and you will know how to arrange a bloody
death for him."
10 Then David died and was buried in the City of David. 11 He had reigned over Israel
for forty years, seven of them in Hebron and thirty-three in Jerusalem. 12 Solomon
succeeded him as king, replacing his father, David, and he was firmly established on the
throne.

Solomon Establishes His Rule

13 One day Adonijah, whose mother was Haggith, came to see Bathsheba, Solomon's
mother. "Have you come to make trouble?" she asked him.

2:2 Josh 23:14
2:3 Deut 18:18-19; Josh 1:6-7; 23:14; 1 Chr 22:12
2:4 2 Sam 7:12-13, 25; 1 Kgs 8:25; 9:5
2:5 2 Sam 3:27; 20:10
2:7 2 Sam 17:27-29; 19:31-38
2:8 2 Sam 16:5-8; 19:18-23
2:10-12 //1 Chr 29:26-28
2:10 2 Sam 5:7; 1 Chr 29:28; Acts 2:29; 13:36
2:11 2 Sam 5:4-5
2:12 1 Chr 29:23; 2 Chr 1:1

1:52 Hebrew *not a hair on his head will be touched.* **2:5** Or *He murdered them during a time of peace as revenge for deaths they had caused in time of war.*

1:52, 53 While Adonijah feared for his life and expected the severest punishment, Solomon simply dismissed his brother and sent him home. As a new king, Solomon had the power to kill his rivals, something Adonijah would have done had his conspiracy succeeded. But Solomon acted as if he had nothing to prove, thus demonstrating his authority and power. Sometimes forgiving a personal attack shows more strength than lashing out in revenge. Trying to prove one's power and authority often proves only one's fear and self-doubt. Only after Adonijah made another attempt to secure royal power was Solomon forced to have him executed (2:13-25).

2:3, 4 David stressed to Solomon the need to make God and his laws the center of personal life and government in order to preserve the kingdom, as God had promised to do (2 Samuel 7). This promise from God had two parts. One part was conditional and depended upon the king's actions. The other part was unconditional.

God's conditional promise was that David and his descendants would remain in office as kings *only* when they honored and obeyed him. When David's descendants failed to do this, they lost the throne (2 Kings 25). God's unconditional promise was that David's line would go on forever. This was fulfilled in the birth of Jesus Christ, a descendant of David who was also the eternal Son of God (Romans 1:3, 4). David, whose life exemplified obedience, gave well-seasoned advice to his son, the next king. It would be up to Solomon to follow it.

2:5-7 Joab epitomizes those who are ruthless in accomplishing their goals. His strength was his only code, and winning the battle, his only law. He wanted to get power for himself and protect it. In contrast, Barzillai stands for those who are loyal to God and live by his standards. When offered glory, for example, he unselfishly asked that it be given to his son. Is your leadership self-serving or God-serving?

2:5-9 David had some harsh advice for Solomon concerning his enemies. This advice was designed to help the young king establish and secure his throne, and it was directed only toward blatant enemies—those who opposed God by opposing God's appointed king. Legally, David was asking Solomon to give his enemies the punishment they deserved. It was against both civil law and God's laws for Shimei to curse a king (Exodus 22:28).

2:10 David died at about age 70 (2 Samuel 5:4, 5). See David's Profile in 1 Samuel 17 for more on his life.

"No," he said, "I come in peace. [14]In fact, I have a favor to ask of you."

"What is it?" she asked.

[15]He replied, "As you know, the kingdom was mine; everyone expected me to be the next king. But the tables were turned, and everything went to my brother instead; for that is the way the LORD wanted it. [16]So now I have just one favor to ask of you. Please don't turn me down."

"What is it?" she asked.

[17]He replied, "Speak to King Solomon on my behalf, for I know he will do anything you request. Ask him to give me Abishag, the girl from Shunem, as my wife."

[18]"All right," Bathsheba replied. "I will speak to the king for you."

[19]So Bathsheba went to King Solomon to speak on Adonijah's behalf. The king rose from his throne to meet her, and he bowed down before her. When he sat down on his throne again, he ordered that a throne be brought for his mother, and she sat at his right hand.

[20]"I have one small request to make of you," she said. "I hope you won't turn me down."

"What is it, my mother?" he asked. "You know I won't refuse you."

[21]"Then let your brother Adonijah marry Abishag, the girl from Shunem," she replied.

[22]"How can you possibly ask me to give Abishag to Adonijah?" Solomon demanded. "You might as well be asking me to give him the kingdom! You know that he is my older brother, and that he has Abiathar the priest and Joab son of Zeruiah on his side." [23]Then King Solomon swore solemnly by the LORD: "May God strike me dead if Adonijah has not sealed his fate with this request. [24]The LORD has confirmed me and placed me on the throne of my father, David; he has established my dynasty as he promised. So as surely as the LORD lives, Adonijah will die this very day!" [25]So King Solomon ordered Benaiah son of Jehoiada to execute him, and Adonijah was put to death.

[26]Then the king said to Abiathar the priest, "Go back to your home in Anathoth. You deserve to die, but I will not kill you now, because you carried the Ark of the Sovereign LORD for my father, and you suffered right along with him through all his troubles." [27]So Solomon deposed Abiathar from his position as priest of the LORD, thereby fulfilling the decree the LORD had made at Shiloh concerning the descendants of Eli.

[28]Although he had not followed Absalom earlier, Joab had also joined Adonijah's revolt. When Joab heard about Adonijah's death, he ran to the sacred tent of the LORD and caught hold of the horns of the altar. [29]When news of this reached King Solomon, he sent Benaiah son of Jehoiada to execute him.

[30]Benaiah went into the sacred tent of the LORD and said to Joab, "The king orders you to come out!"

But Joab answered, "No, I will die here."

So Benaiah returned to the king and told him what Joab had said.

[31]"Do as he said," the king replied. "Kill him there beside the altar and bury him. This will remove the guilt of his senseless murders from me and from my father's family. [32]Then the LORD will repay him for the murders of two men who were more righteous and better than he. For my father was no party to the deaths of Abner son of Ner, commander of the army of Israel, and Amasa son of Jether, commander of the army of Judah. [33]May Joab and his descendants be forever guilty of these murders, and may the LORD grant peace to David and his descendants and to his throne forever."

2:17 1 Kgs 1:3
2:19 Ps 45:9
2:23 Ruth 1:17
2:25 2 Sam 8:18
2:26 Josh 21:17-18; 1 Sam 22:20; 26:16; 2 Sam 15:24; Jer 1:1
2:27 1 Sam 2:27-36
2:28 2 Sam 17:25; 1 Kgs 1:49-50
2:31 Exod 21:14; Num 35:33; Deut 19:13
2:32 Gen 9:5-6; Judg 9:24, 56-57; 2 Sam 3:27; 20:8-10; 2 Chr 21:13
2:33 2 Sam 3:29

2:15-22 This was not a case of thwarted love, although Adonijah probably hoped Bathsheba would think so. Although she was still a virgin, Abishag was considered part of David's harem. Adonijah wanted Abishag because possessing the king's harem was equivalent to claiming the throne. Absalom had done the same thing in his rebellion against David (2 Samuel 16:20-23). Solomon well understood what Adonijah was trying to do.

2:26, 27 As a young man, Abiathar was the only one to escape when King Saul massacred all the priests in the city of Nob (1 Samuel 22:11-23). Abiathar then became the high priest under David and remained loyal to David throughout his reign. When Abiathar supported Adonijah's wrongful claim to the throne after David's death (1:7), Solomon forced him to give up the priesthood, fulfilling the prophecy of 1 Samuel 2:27-36 that Eli's descendants would not continue to serve as priests.

2:31 Joab had spent his life trying to defend his position as David's commander. Twice David tried to replace him, and both times Joab treacherously killed his rivals before they could assume command (2 Samuel 3:17-30; 19:13; 20:4-10). Because Joab was in his service, David was ultimately responsible for these senseless deaths. But for political and military reasons (see the note on 2 Samuel 3:39), David decided not to publicly punish Joab. Instead, he put a curse on Joab and his family (2 Samuel 3:29). Solomon, in punishing Joab, was publicly declaring that David was not part of Joab's crimes, thus removing the guilt from David and placing it on Joab where it belonged.

34 So Benaiah son of Jehoiada returned to the sacred tent and killed Joab, and Joab was
2:35 1 Chr 29:22
buried at his home in the wilderness. 35 Then the king appointed Benaiah to command
the army in place of Joab, and he installed Zadok the priest to take the place of Abiathar.
2:36 2 Sam 16:5 1 Kgs 2:8
36 The king then sent for Shimei and told him, "Build a house here in Jerusalem and
live there. But don't step outside the city to go anywhere else. 37 On the day you cross
2:37 2 Sam 15:23
the Kidron Valley, you will surely die; your blood will be on your own head."
38 Shimei replied, "Your sentence is fair; I will do whatever my lord the king com-
2:39 1 Sam 27:2
mands." So Shimei lived in Jerusalem for a long time.
39 But three years later, two of Shimei's slaves escaped to King Achish of Gath. When
Shimei learned where they were, 40 he saddled his donkey and went to Gath to search for
them. When he had found them, he took them back to Jerusalem.
41 Solomon heard that Shimei had left Jerusalem and had gone to Gath and returned.
42 So he sent for Shimei and demanded, "Didn't I make you swear by the LORD and warn
you not to go anywhere else, or you would surely die? And you replied, 'The sentence
is fair; I will do as you say.' 43 Then why haven't you kept your oath to the LORD and
2:44 1 Sam 25:39 2 Sam 16:5-13
obeyed my command?"
44 The king also said to Shimei, "You surely remember all the wicked things you did to
2:45 2 Sam 7:13
my father, King David. May the LORD punish you for them. 45 But may I receive the LORD's
rich blessings, and may one of David's descendants always sit on this throne." 46 Then, at
2:46 1 Kgs 2:12 2 Chr 1:1
the king's command, Benaiah son of Jehoiada took Shimei outside and killed him.
So the kingdom was now firmly in Solomon's grip.

2. Solomon's wisdom

Solomon Asks for Wisdom

3:1 1 Kgs 7:8; 9:24
3 Solomon made an alliance with Pharaoh, the king of Egypt, and married one of his
3:2 Lev 17:3-5 Deut 12:13-14
daughters. He brought her to live in the City of David until he could finish building
his palace and the Temple of the LORD and the wall around the city. 2 At that time the
3:3 Deut 6:5
people of Israel sacrificed their offerings at local altars, for a temple honoring the name
3:4-15 //2 Chr 1:2-13
of the LORD had not yet been built.
3 Solomon loved the LORD and followed all the instructions of his father, David, except
3:4 1 Chr 16:39; 21:29
that Solomon, too, offered sacrifices and burned incense at the local altars. 4 The most
3:5 1 Kgs 9:2-3
important of these altars was at Gibeon, so the king went there and sacrificed one
thousand burnt offerings. 5 That night the LORD appeared to Solomon in a dream, and
3:6 2 Sam 7:8; 12:7
God said, "What do you want? Ask, and I will give it to you!"
6 Solomon replied, "You were wonderfully kind to my father, David, because he was

---

2:35 Abiathar the high priest and Joab the army commander were key men in David's kingdom. But when they conspired against Solomon, they were replaced with Zadok and Benaiah. Zadok, a descendant of Aaron, had been a prominent priest during David's reign, and he was also loyal to Solomon after David's death. He was put in charge of the Ark of the Covenant (2 Samuel 15:24ff). His descendants were in charge of the Temple until its destruction. At one time, Benaiah was one of David's mighty men (2 Samuel 23:20-23) and the captain of David's bodyguard.

2:46 Solomon ordered the executions of Adonijah, Joab, and Shimei; forced Abiathar out as priest; and then appointed new men to take their places. He did these things swiftly, securing his grip on the kingdom. By executing justice and tying up loose ends that could affect the future stability of his kingdom, Solomon was promoting peace, not bloodshed. He was a man of peace in two ways: He did not go to war, and he put an end to internal rebellion.

3:1 Marriage between royal families was a common practice in the ancient Near East because it secured peace. Although Solomon's marital alliances built friendships with surrounding nations, they were also the beginning of his downfall. These relationships became inroads for pagan ideas and practices. Solomon's foreign wives brought their gods to Jerusalem and eventually lured him into idolatry (11:1-6).

It is easy to minimize religious differences in order to encourage the development of a friendship, but seemingly small differences can have an enormous impact upon a relationship. God gives us standards to follow for all our relationships, including marriage. If we follow God's will, we will not be lured away from our true focus.

3:2, 3 God's laws said that the Israelites could make sacrifices only in specified places (Deuteronomy 12:13, 14). This was to prevent the people from instituting their own methods of worship and allowing pagan practices to creep into their worship. But many Israelites, including Solomon, made sacrifices in the surrounding hills. Solomon loved God, but this act was sin. It took the offerings out of the watchful care of priests and ministers loyal to God and opened the way for false teaching to be tied to these sacrifices. God appeared to Solomon to grant him wisdom, not during the sacrifice, but at night. God honored his prayer but did not condone the sacrifice.

3:6-9 When given a chance to have anything in the world, Solomon asked for wisdom—"an understanding mind"—in order to lead well and to make right decisions. We can ask God for this same wisdom (James 1:5). Notice that Solomon asked for understanding to carry out his job; he did not ask God to do the job for him. We should not ask God to do *for* us what he wants to do *through* us. Instead, we should ask God to give us the wisdom to know what to do and the courage to follow through on it.

honest and true and faithful to you. And you have continued this great kindness to him
today by giving him a son to succeed him. 7O LORD my God, now you have made me
king instead of my father, David, but I am like a little child who doesn't know his way
around. 8And here I am among your own chosen people, a nation so great they are too
numerous to count! 9Give me an understanding mind so that I can govern your people
well and know the difference between right and wrong. For who by himself is able to
govern this great nation of yours?"
10The Lord was pleased with Solomon's reply and was glad that he had asked for
wisdom. 11So God replied, "Because you have asked for wisdom in governing my
people and have not asked for a long life or riches for yourself or the death of your
enemies—12I will give you what you asked for! I will give you a wise and understanding
mind such as no one else has ever had or ever will have! 13And I will also give you what
you did not ask for—riches and honor! No other king in all the world will be compared
to you for the rest of your life! 14And if you follow me and obey my commands as your
father, David, did, I will give you a long life."
15Then Solomon woke up and realized it had been a dream. He returned to Jerusalem
and stood before the Ark of the Lord's covenant, where he sacrificed burnt offerings and
peace offerings. Then he invited all his officials to a great banquet.

Solomon Judges Wisely

16Some time later, two prostitutes came to the king to have an argument settled.
17"Please, my lord," one of them began, "this woman and I live in the same house. I gave
birth to a baby while she was with me in the house. 18Three days later, she also had a
baby. We were alone; there were only two of us in the house. 19But her baby died during
the night when she rolled over on it. 20Then she got up in the night and took my son from
beside me while I was asleep. She laid her dead child in my arms and took mine to sleep
beside her. 21And in the morning when I tried to nurse my son, he was dead! But when
I looked more closely in the morning light, I saw that it wasn't my son at all."
22Then the other woman interrupted, "It certainly was your son, and the living child
is mine."
"No," the first woman said, "the dead one is yours, and the living one is mine." And
so they argued back and forth before the king.
23Then the king said, "Let's get the facts straight. Both of you claim the living child
is yours, and each says that the dead child belongs to the other. 24All right, bring me a
sword." So a sword was brought to the king. 25Then he said, "Cut the living child in two
and give half to each of these women!"
26Then the woman who really was the mother of the living child, and who loved him
very much, cried out, "Oh no, my lord! Give her the child—please do not kill him!"
But the other woman said, "All right, he will be neither yours nor mine; divide him
between us!"
27Then the king said, "Do not kill him, but give the baby to the woman who wants
him to live, for she is his mother!"
28Word of the king's decision spread quickly throughout all Israel, and the people
were awed as they realized the great wisdom God had given him to render decisions with
justice.

3:7 1 Chr 22:9-13; 29:1 Jer 1:6-7
3:8 Gen 13:16; 15:5; 22:17 Exod 19:6 Deut 7:6
3:9 2 Sam 14:17 1 Kgs 3:12-13 2 Chr 1:10 Ps 72:1 Prov 2:3-5, 9 Jas 1:5
3:12 1 Kgs 4:29-31 1 Jn 5:14-15
3:13 1 Kgs 3:28; 4:20-24; 10:23
3:14 Ps 91:16 Prov 3:1-2, 16
3:15 1 Kgs 8:63, 65
3:26 Isa 49:15 Jer 31:20 Hos 11:8
3:28 1 Kgs 3:9-12; 4:29

3:11-14 Solomon asked for wisdom, not wealth, but God gave him riches and long life as well. While God does not promise riches to those who follow him, he gives us what we need if we put his kingdom, his interests, and his principles first (Matthew 6:31-33). Setting your sights on riches will only leave you dissatisfied because even if you get the riches you crave, you will still want something more. But if you put God and his work first, he will satisfy your deepest needs.

3:12 Solomon received "a wise and understanding mind" from God, but it was up to Solomon to apply that wisdom to all areas of his life. Solomon was obviously wise in governing the nation, but he was foolish in running his household. Wisdom is both the ability to discern what is best and the strength of character to act upon that knowledge. While Solomon remained wise all his life, he did not always act upon his wisdom (11:6).

3:16-28 Solomon's settlement of this dispute was a classic example of his wisdom. This wise ruling was verification that God had answered Solomon's prayer and given him an understanding mind. We have God's wisdom available to us as we pray and request it. But, like Solomon, we must put it into action. Applying wisdom to life demonstrates our understanding.

Solomon's Officials and Governors

4 So Solomon was king over all Israel, [2]and these were his high officials:

Azariah son of Zadok was the priest.

4:3 2 Sam 8:16

3 Elihoreph and Ahijah, the sons of Shisha, were court secretaries.
Jehoshaphat son of Ahilud was the royal historian.
4 Benaiah son of Jehoiada was commander of the army.
Zadok and Abiathar were the priests.
5 Azariah son of Nathan presided over the district governors.
Zabud son of Nathan, a priest, was a trusted adviser to the king.
6 Ahishar was manager of palace affairs.
Adoniram son of Abda was in charge of the labor force.

SOLOMON

Wisdom is only effective when it is put into action. Early in his life, Solomon had the sense to recognize his need for wisdom. But by the time Solomon asked for wisdom to rule his kingdom, he had already started a habit that would make his wisdom ineffective for his own life—he sealed a pact with Egypt by marrying Pharaoh's daughter. She was the first of hundreds of wives married for political reasons. In doing this, Solomon went against not only his father's last words but also against God's direct commands. His action reminds us how easy it is to know what is right and yet not do it.

It is clear that God's gift of wisdom to Solomon did not mean that he couldn't make mistakes. He had been given great possibilities as the king of God's chosen people, but with them came great responsibilities; unfortunately, he tended to pursue the former and neglect the latter. While becoming famous as the builder of the Temple and the palace, he became infamous as a leader who excessively taxed and worked his people. Visitors from distant lands came to admire this wise king, while his own people were gradually alienated from him.

Little is mentioned in the Bible about the last decade of Solomon's reign. Ecclesiastes probably records his last reflections on life. In that book we find a man proving through bitter experience that finding meaning in life apart from God is a vain pursuit. Security and contentment are found only in a personal relationship with God. The contentment we find in the opportunities and successes of this life is temporary. The more we expect our successes to be permanent, the more quickly they are gone. Be sure to balance your pursuit of life's possibilities with reliable fulfillment of your responsibilities.

Strengths and accomplishments
- Third king of Israel, David's chosen heir
- The wisest man who ever lived
- Author of Ecclesiastes and Song of Songs, as well as many of the proverbs and a couple of the psalms
- Built God's Temple in Jerusalem
- Diplomat, trader, collector, patron of the arts

Weaknesses and mistakes
- Sealed many foreign agreements by marrying pagan women
- Allowed his wives to affect his loyalty to God
- Excessively taxed his people and drafted them into a labor and military force

Lessons from his life
- Effective leadership can be nullified by an ineffective personal life
- Solomon failed to obey God, but did not learn the lesson of repentance until late in life
- Knowing what actions are required of us means little without the will to do those actions

Vital statistics
- Where: Jerusalem
- Occupation: King of Israel
- Relatives: Father: David. Mother: Bathsheba. Brothers: Absalom, Adonijah. Sister: Tamar. Son: Rehoboam

Key verse
" 'Wasn't this exactly what led King Solomon of Israel into sin?' I demanded. 'There was no king from any nation who could compare to him, and God loved him and made him king over all Israel. But even so he was led into sin by his foreign wives' " (Nehemiah 13:26).

Solomon's story is told in 2 Samuel 12:24—1 Kings 11:43. He is also mentioned in 1 Chronicles 28, 29; 2 Chronicles 1—10; Nehemiah 13:26; Psalm 72; and Matthew 6:29; 12:42.

4:1ff Solomon was well organized, with 11 high officials with specific responsibilities, 12 district governors, and a governor in charge of the district governors. Each person had a specific responsibility or territory to manage. This organization was essential to maintain the government's effectiveness: It was a wise move by a wise man. It is good stewardship to be well organized. Good organization helps people work together in harmony and ensures that the desired goal will be reached.

7 Solomon also had twelve district governors who were over all Israel. They were
responsible for providing food from the people for the king's household. Each of them
arranged provisions for one month of the year.
8 These are the names of the twelve governors:

Ben-hur, in the hill country of Ephraim.
9 Ben-deker, in Makaz, Shaalbim, Beth-shemesh, and Elon-bethhanan. **4:9** Judg 1:35
10 Ben-hesed, in Arubboth, including Socoh and all the land of Hepher. **4:10** Josh 12:17
11 Ben-abinadab, in Naphoth-dor.* (He was married to Taphath, one of Solomon's daughters.)
12 Baana son of Ahilud, in Taanach and Megiddo, all of Beth-shan* near Zarethan below Jezreel, and all the territory from Beth-shan to Abel-meholah and over to Jokmeam. **4:12** Josh 17:11
13 Ben-geber, in Ramoth-gilead, including the Towns of Jair (named for Jair son of Manasseh) in Gilead, and in the Argob region of Bashan, including sixty great fortified cities with gates barred with bronze. **4:13** Num 32:41 Deut 3:4
14 Ahinadab son of Iddo, in Mahanaim.
15 Ahimaaz, in Naphtali. (He was married to Basemath, another of Solomon's daughters.)
16 Baana son of Hushai, in Asher and in Aloth.
17 Jehoshaphat son of Paruah, in Issachar.
18 Shimei son of Ela, in Benjamin.
19 Geber son of Uri, in the land of Gilead,* including the territories of King Sihon of the Amorites and King Og of Bashan. **4:19** Deut 3:8-10

And there was one governor over the land of Judah.*

Solomon's Prosperity and Wisdom

20 The people of Judah and Israel were as numerous as the sand on the seashore. They **4:20** Gen 32:12
were very contented, with plenty to eat and drink. 21 King Solomon ruled all the
kingdoms from the Euphrates River* to the land of the Philistines, as far south as the **4:21** 2 Sam 8:2, 6
border of Egypt. The conquered peoples of those lands sent tribute money to Solomon 2 Chr 9:26
and continued to serve him throughout his lifetime. Ps 72:10-11
22 The daily food requirements for Solomon's palace were 150 bushels of choice
flour and 300 bushels of meal,* 23 ten oxen from the fattening pens, twenty pasture-
fed cattle, one hundred sheep or goats, as well as deer, gazelles, roebucks, and choice
fowl.
24 Solomon's dominion extended over all the kingdoms west of the Euphrates River, **4:24**
from Tiphsah to Gaza. And there was peace throughout the entire land. 25 Throughout the 1 Chr 22:9

4:25 Jer 23:5-6 Mic 4:4 Zech 3:10

4:11 Hebrew *Naphath-dor,* a variant name for Naphoth-dor. **4:12** Hebrew *Beth-shean,* a variant name for Beth-shan; also in 4:12b. **4:19a** Greek version reads *of Gad;* compare 4:13. **4:19b** As in some Greek manuscripts; Hebrew lacks *of Judah.* The meaning of the Hebrew is uncertain. **4:21** Hebrew *the river;* also in 4:24. **4:22** Hebrew *30 cors* [5.5 kiloliters] *of choice flour and 60 cors* [11 kiloliters] *of meal.*

4:20-25 Throughout most of his reign, Solomon applied his wisdom well because he sought God. The fruits of this wisdom were peace, security, and prosperity for the nation. Solomon's era is often looked upon as the ideal of what any nation can become when united in its trust in and obedience to God.

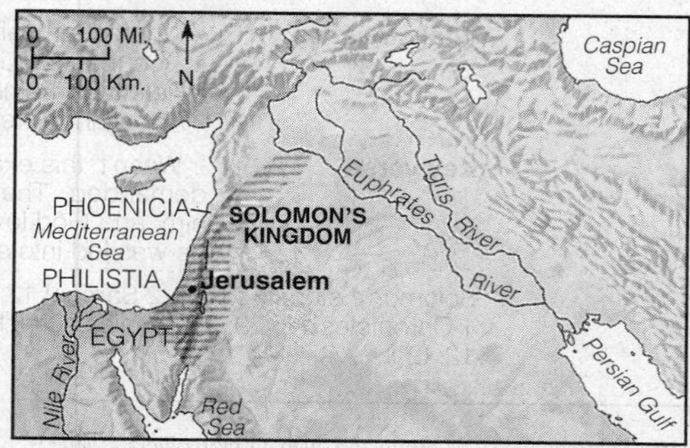

SOLOMON'S KINGDOM Solomon's kingdom spread from the Euphrates River in the north to the borders of Egypt. The entire land was at peace under his rule.

lifetime of Solomon, all of Judah and Israel lived in peace and safety. And from Dan to
Beersheba, each family had its own home and garden.
4:26 1 Kgs 10:26 2 Chr 1:14 26Solomon had four thousand* stalls for his chariot horses and twelve thousand
horses.* 27The district governors faithfully provided food for King Solomon and his
4:29 1 Kgs 3:12 court, each during his assigned month. 28They also brought the necessary barley and
straw for the royal horses in the stables.
4:30 Isa 19:11 Acts 7:22 29God gave Solomon great wisdom and understanding, and knowledge too vast to be
measured. 30In fact, his wisdom exceeded that of all the wise men of the East and the
4:31 1 Kgs 3:12 wise men of Egypt. 31He was wiser than anyone else, including Ethan the Ezrahite and
Heman, Calcol, and Darda—the sons of Mahol. His fame spread throughout all the
4:32 Prov 1:1 Eccl 12:9 Song 1:1 surrounding nations. 32He composed some 3,000 proverbs and wrote 1,005 songs. 33He
could speak with authority about all kinds of plants, from the great cedar of Lebanon to
the tiny hyssop that grows from cracks in a wall. He could also speak about animals,
4:34 1 Kgs 10:1 2 Chr 9:23 birds, reptiles, and fish. 34And kings from every nation sent their ambassadors to listen
to the wisdom of Solomon.

3. Solomon builds the Temple

Preparations for Building the Temple

5:1-16 //2 Chr 2:1-18 **5** King Hiram of Tyre had always been a loyal friend of David, so when he learned
that David's son Solomon was the new king of Israel, Hiram sent ambassadors to
5:1 2 Sam 5:11 1 Chr 14:1 congratulate him. 2Then Solomon sent this message back to Hiram:

3"You know that my father, David, was not able to build a Temple to honor the name
5:3 1 Chr 28:3 of the LORD his God because of the many wars he waged with surrounding nations.
He could not build until the LORD gave him victory over all his enemies. 4But now the
5:4 1 Kgs 4:24 1 Chr 22:9 LORD my God has given me peace on every side, and I have no enemies and all is
5:5 2 Sam 7:12-13 1 Chr 17:12 well. 5So I am planning to build a Temple to honor the name of the LORD my God, just
as he instructed my father that I should do. For the LORD told him, 'Your son, whom I
will place on your throne, will build the Temple to honor my name.' 6Now please command that cedars from Lebanon be cut for me. Let my men work alongside yours, and
I will pay your men whatever wages you ask. As you know, there is no one among us
who can cut timber like you Sidonians!"

7When Hiram received Solomon's message, he was very pleased and said, "Praise the
LORD for giving David a wise son to be king of the great nation of Israel." 8Then he sent
this reply to Solomon:

"I have received your message, and I will do as you have asked concerning the timber.
5:9 2 Chr 2:16 Ezra 3:7 Ezek 27:17 I can supply you with both cedar and cypress. 9My servants will bring the logs from
the Lebanon mountains to the Mediterranean Sea and build them into rafts. We will
float them along the coast to whatever place you choose. Then we will break the rafts
apart and deliver the timber to you. You can pay me with food for my household."

10So Hiram produced for Solomon as much cedar and cypress timber as he desired. 11In
return Solomon sent him an annual payment of 100,000 bushels* of wheat for his household
5:12 1 Kgs 3:12 and 110,000 gallons* of olive oil. 12So the LORD gave great wisdom to Solomon just as he
had promised. And Hiram and Solomon made a formal alliance of peace.
5:14 1 Kgs 4:6 13Then King Solomon enlisted thirty thousand laborers from all Israel. 14He sent them

4:26a As in some Greek manuscripts (see also 2 Chr 9:25); Hebrew reads *40,000.* **4:26b** Or *12,000 charioteers.* **5:11a** Hebrew *20,000 cors* [3,640 kiloliters]. **5:11b** As in Greek version, which reads *20,000 baths* [420 kiloliters] (see also 2 Chr 2:10); Hebrew reads *20 cors,* about 800 gallons or 3.6 kiloliters in volume.

4:32 The book of Proverbs records many of these 3,000 wise proverbs. Other biblical writings of Solomon include Psalms 72 and 127, and the books of Ecclesiastes and Song of Songs. Solomon's wisdom was known throughout the world.

5:2, 3 When David offered to build a Temple, God said no through the prophet Nathan (2 Samuel 7:1-17). God wanted a peacemaker, not a warrior, to build his house of prayer (1 Chronicles 28:2, 3).

5:13, 14 Solomon drafted three times the number of workers needed for the Temple project and then arranged their schedules so they didn't have to be away from home for long periods of time. This showed his concern for the welfare of his workers and the importance he placed on family life. The strength of a nation is in direct proportion to the strength of its families. Solomon wisely recognized that family should always be a top priority. As you structure your own work or arrange the schedules of others, watch for the impact of your plans on families.

to Lebanon in shifts, ten thousand every month, so that each man would be one month
in Lebanon and two months at home. Adoniram was in charge of this labor force.
15 Solomon also enlisted seventy thousand common laborers, eighty thousand stonecut-
ters in the hill country, 16 and thirty-six hundred* foremen to supervise the work. 17 At the **5:17** 2 Chr 22:2
king's command, the stonecutters quarried and shaped costly blocks of stone for the
foundation of the Temple. 18 Men from the city of Gebal helped Solomon's and Hiram's
builders prepare the timber and stone for the Temple.

Solomon Builds the Temple

6 It was in midspring,* during the fourth year of Solomon's reign, that he began the **6:1-29** //2 Chr 3:1-14
construction of the Temple of the LORD. This was 480 years after the people of Israel
were delivered from their slavery in the land of Egypt.
2 The Temple that King Solomon built for the LORD was 90 feet long, 30 feet wide,
and 45 feet high.* 3 The foyer at the front of the Temple was 30 feet wide, running across
the entire width of the Temple. It projected outward 15 feet from the front of the Temple. **6:4** Ezek 41:16
4 Solomon also made narrow, recessed windows throughout the Temple.
5 A complex of rooms was built against the outer walls of the Temple, all the way **6:5** Ezek 41:5-6
around the sides and rear of the building. 6 The complex was three stories high, the
bottom floor being 7½ feet wide, the second floor 9 feet wide, and the top floor 10½ feet
wide. The rooms were connected to the walls of the Temple by beams resting on ledges
built out from the wall. So the beams were not inserted into the walls themselves.
7 The stones used in the construction of the Temple were prefinished at the quarry, so **6:7** Exod 20:25 Deut 27:5-6
the entire structure was built without the sound of hammer, ax, or any other iron tool at
the building site.
8 The entrance to the bottom floor* was on the south side of the Temple. There were
winding stairs going up to the second floor, and another flight of stairs between the
second and third floors. 9 After completing the Temple structure, Solomon put in a ceiling **6:9** 1 Kgs 6:14, 38
made of beams and planks of cedar. 10 As already stated, there was a complex of rooms
on three sides of the building, attached to the Temple walls by cedar timbers. Each story
of the complex was 7½ feet high.
11 Then the LORD gave this message to Solomon: 12 "Concerning this Temple you are **6:12** 2 Sam 7:12-16 1 Kgs 9:4-5
building, if you keep all my laws and regulations and obey all my commands, I will fulfill
through you the promise I made to your father, David. 13 I will live among the people of **6:13** Exod 25:8 Deut 31:6 Josh 1:5
Israel and never forsake my people."

The Temple's Interior

14 So Solomon finished building the Temple. 15 The entire inside, from floor to ceiling,
was paneled with wood. He paneled the walls and ceilings with cedar, and he used
cypress for the floors. 16 He partitioned off an inner sanctuary—the Most Holy Place—at **6:16** Exod 26:33 Lev 16:1-2 2 Chr 3:8

5:16 As in some Greek manuscripts (see also 2 Chr 2:2, 18); Hebrew reads *3,300.* **6:1** Hebrew *in the month of Ziv, which is the second month.* This month of the Hebrew lunar calendar usually occurs in April and May. **6:2** Hebrew *60 cubits* [27 meters] *long, 20 cubits* [9 meters] *wide, and 30 cubits* [13.5 meters] *high.* In this chapter, the distance measures are calculated from the Hebrew cubit at a ratio of 18 inches or 45 centimeters per cubit. **6:8** As in Greek version; Hebrew reads *middle floor.*

5:18 Gebal, also called Byblos, was located north of what is now Beirut, near the cedar forest. These men were Phoenicians, probably skilled as shipbuilders, but employed for this project.

6:1ff For more information on the purpose of the Temple, see the note on 2 Chronicles 5:1ff.

6:3 The foyer was like a large porch.

6:4 These narrow, recessed windows were near the tops of the walls to help light the center of the Temple.

6:7 In honor of God, the Temple in Jerusalem was built without the sound of a hammer or any other tool at the building site. This meant that the stone had to be "prefinished" (cut and shaped) miles away at the quarry. The people's honor and respect for God extended to every aspect of constructing this house of worship. This detail is recorded not to teach us how to build a church, but to show us the importance of demonstrating care, concern, honor, and respect for God and his sanctuary.

6:13 This verse summarizes the Temple's main purpose. God promised that his eternal presence would never leave the Temple as long as one condition was met: The Israelites had to obey God's law. Knowing how many laws they had to follow, we may think this condition was difficult. But the Israelites' situation was much like ours today: They were not cut off from God for failing to keep some small subpoint of a law. Forgiveness was amply provided for all their sins, no matter how large or small. As you read the history of the kings, you will see that lawbreaking was the result, not the cause, of estrangement from God. The kings abandoned God in their hearts first and *then* failed to keep his laws. When we close our hearts to God, his power and presence soon leave us.

6:14 The concept of Solomon's Temple was more like a palace for God than a place of worship. As a dwelling place for God, it was fitting for it to be ornate and beautiful. It had small inside dimensions because most worshipers gathered outside.

the far end of the Temple. It was 30 feet deep and was paneled with cedar from floor to
ceiling. 17 The main room of the Temple, outside the Most Holy Place, was 60 feet long.
18 Cedar paneling completely covered the stone walls throughout the Temple, and the
paneling was decorated with carvings of gourds and open flowers.

19 Solomon prepared the inner sanctuary in the rear of the Temple, where the Ark of
the LORD's covenant would be placed. 20 This inner sanctuary was 30 feet long, 30 feet
wide, and 30 feet high. Solomon overlaid its walls and ceiling with pure gold. He also
overlaid the altar made of cedar.* 21 Then he overlaid the rest of the Temple's interior
with pure gold, and he made gold chains to protect the entrance to the Most Holy Place.
22 So he finished overlaying the entire Temple with gold, including the altar that belonged
to the Most Holy Place.

6:23 23 Within the inner sanctuary Solomon placed two cherubim made of olive wood, each
Exod 25:20; 37:1-9 15 feet tall. 24 The wingspan of each of the cherubim was 15 feet, each wing being 7½
2 Chr 3:10-12 feet long. 25 The two cherubim were identical in shape and size; 26 each was 15 feet tall.
27 Solomon placed them side by side in the inner sanctuary of the Temple. Their
outspread wings reached from wall to wall, while their inner wings touched at the center
of the room. 28 He overlaid the two cherubim with gold.

29 All the walls of the inner sanctuary and the main room were decorated with carvings
of cherubim, palm trees, and open flowers. 30 The floor in both rooms was overlaid with
gold.

31 For the entrance to the inner sanctuary, Solomon made double doors of olive wood
with five-sided doorposts. 32 These doors were decorated with carvings of cherubim,
palm trees, and open flowers, and the doors were overlaid with gold.

6:34 33 Then he made four-sided doorposts of olive wood for the entrance to the Temple.
Ezek 41:23-25 34 There were two folding doors of cypress wood, and each door was hinged to fold back
upon itself. 35 These doors were decorated with carvings of cherubim, palm trees, and
open flowers, and the doors were overlaid with gold.

6:36 36 The walls of the inner courtyard were built so that there was one layer of cedar
1 Kgs 7:12 beams after every three layers of hewn stone.

37 The foundation of the LORD's Temple was laid in midspring* of the fourth year of
Solomon's reign. 38 The entire building was completed in every detail by midautumn*
of the eleventh year of his reign. So it took seven years to build the Temple.

Solomon Builds His Palace

7:1 **7** Solomon also built a palace for himself, and it took him thirteen years to complete
1 Kgs 3:1; 9:10 the construction.
2 Chr 8:1

7:2 2 One of Solomon's buildings was called the Palace of the Forest of Lebanon. It was
1 Kgs 10:17 150 feet long, 75 feet wide, and 45 feet high.* The great cedar ceiling beams rested on
2 Chr 9:16 four rows of cedar pillars. 3 It had a cedar roof supported by forty-five rafters that rested
on three rows of pillars, fifteen in each row. 4 On each of the side walls there were three
rows of windows facing each other. 5 All the doorways were rectangular in frame; they
were in sets of three, facing each other.

6 He also built the Hall of Pillars, which was 75 feet long and 45 feet wide. There was
a porch at its front, covered by a canopy that was supported by pillars.

7:7 7 There was also the Hall of the Throne, also known as the Hall of Judgment, where
1 Kgs 6:9, 15-16 Solomon sat to hear legal matters. It was paneled with cedar from floor to ceiling.*
7:8 8 Solomon's living quarters surrounded a courtyard behind this hall; they were built the
1 Kgs 3:1 same way. He also built similar living quarters for Pharaoh's daughter, one of his wives.
2 Chr 8:11 9 All these buildings were built entirely from huge, costly blocks of stone, cut and
trimmed to exact measure on all sides. 10 Some of the huge foundation stones were

6:20 Or *overlaid the altar with cedar.* The meaning of the Hebrew is uncertain. **6:37** Hebrew *in the month of Ziv.* This month of the Hebrew lunar calendar usually occurs in April and May. **6:38** Hebrew *in the month of Bul, which is the eighth month.* This month of the Hebrew lunar calendar usually occurs in October and November. **7:2** Hebrew *100 cubits* [45 meters] *long, 50 cubits* [22.5 meters] *wide, and 30 cubits* [13.5 meters] *high.* In this chapter, the distance measures are calculated from the Hebrew cubit at a ratio of 18 inches or 45 centimeters per cubit. **7:7** As in Syriac version and Latin Vulgate; Hebrew reads *from floor to floor.*

7:1 That Solomon took longer to build his palace than to build the Temple is not a comment on his priorities. His palace project took longer because it was part of a huge civic building project including barracks and housing for his harem.

15 feet long, and some were 12 feet long. 11 The costly blocks of stone used in the walls
were also cut to measure, and cedar beams were also used. 12 The walls of the great **7:12**
courtyard were built so that there was one layer of cedar beams after every three layers 1 Kgs 6:36
of hewn stone, just like the walls of the inner courtyard of the LORD's Temple with its
entrance foyer.

Furnishings for the Temple

13 King Solomon then asked for a man named Huram* to come from Tyre, 14 for he was **7:13** 2 Chr 2:13-14
a craftsman skilled in bronze work. He was half Israelite, since his mother was a widow
from the tribe of Naphtali, and his father had been a foundry worker from Tyre. So he
came to work for King Solomon.

15 Huram cast two bronze pillars, each 27 feet tall and 18 feet in circumference. 16 For **7:15** 2 Kgs 25:17
the tops of the pillars he made capitals of molded bronze, each 7½ feet tall. 17 Each capital 2 Chr 3:15; 4:12
was decorated with seven sets of latticework and interwoven chains. 18 He also made two
rows of pomegranates that encircled the latticework to decorate the capitals over the
pillars. 19 The capitals on the columns inside the foyer were shaped like lilies, and they
were 6 feet tall. 20 Each capital on the two pillars had two hundred pomegranates in two **7:20** 2 Chr 3:16; 4:13
rows around them, beside the rounded surface next to the latticework. 21 Huram set the **7:21**
pillars at the entrance of the Temple, one toward the south and one toward the north. He 2 Chr 3:17
named the one on the south Jakin, and the one on the north Boaz.* 22 The capitals on the
pillars were shaped like lilies. And so the work on the pillars was finished.

23 Then Huram cast a large round tank, 15 feet across from rim to rim; it was called **7:23-26**
the Sea. It was 7½ feet deep and about 45 feet in circumference. 24 The Sea was encircled //2 Chr 4:2-5
just below its rim by two rows of decorative gourds. There were about six gourds per **7:23** 2 Kgs 25:13
foot* all the way around, and they had been cast as part of the tank.

25 The Sea rested on a base of twelve bronze oxen, all facing outward. Three faced
north, three faced west, three faced south, and three faced east. 26 The walls of the Sea
were about three inches* thick, and its rim flared out like a cup and resembled a lily
blossom. It could hold about 11,000 gallons* of water.

27 Huram also made ten bronze water carts, each 6 feet long, 6 feet wide, and 4½ feet **7:27**
tall. 28 They were constructed with side panels braced with crossbars. 29 Both the panels 2 Kgs 16:17
and the crossbars were decorated with carved lions, oxen, and cherubim. Above and
below the lions and oxen were wreath decorations. 30 Each of these carts had four bronze
wheels and bronze axles. At each corner of the carts were supporting posts for the bronze
basins; these supports were decorated with carvings of wreaths on each side. 31 The top
of each cart had a circular frame for the basin. It projected 1½ feet above the cart's top
like a round pedestal, and its opening was 2¼ feet across; it was decorated on the outside
with carvings of wreaths. The panels of the carts were square, not round. 32 Under the
panels were four wheels that were connected to axles that had been cast as one unit with
the cart. The wheels were 2¼ feet in diameter 33 and were similar to chariot wheels. The
axles, spokes, rims, and hubs were all cast from molten bronze.

34 There were supports at each of the four corners of the carts, and these, too, were cast
as one unit with the cart. 35 Around the top of each cart there was a rim 9 inches wide.*
The supports and side panels were cast as one unit with the cart. 36 Carvings of cherubim,
lions, and palm trees decorated the panels and supports wherever there was room, and
there were wreaths all around. 37 All ten water carts were the same size and were made
alike, for each was cast from the same mold.

38 Huram also made ten bronze basins, one for each cart. Each basin was 6 feet across **7:38-51**
and could hold 220 gallons* of water. 39 He arranged five water carts on the south side //2 Chr 4:6, 10–5:1

7:13 Hebrew *Hiram* (also in 7:40, 45); compare 2 Chr 2:13. This is not the same person mentioned in 5:1. **7:21** Jakin probably means "he establishes"; Boaz probably means "in him is strength." **7:24** Or *20 gourds per meter;* Hebrew reads *10 per cubit.* **7:26a** Hebrew *a handbreadth* [8 centimeters]. **7:26b** Hebrew *2,000 baths* [42 kiloliters]. **7:35** Hebrew *half a cubit wide* [22.5 centimeters]. **7:38** Hebrew *40 baths* [840 liters].

7:14 Huram was an expert craftsman. Solomon chose only the best.

7:23 The "Sea" was an enormous tank. Designed and used for the priests' ceremonial washings, it was placed in the Temple court near the altar of burnt offering. There the priests washed themselves before offering sacrifices or entering the Temple (Exodus 30:17-21).

7:27-39 These 10 "water carts" held basins of water. The basins were used for washing the various parts of the animal sacrifices. The basins were movable so they could be used where needed.

of the Temple and five on the north side. The Sea was placed at the southeast corner of
the Temple. 40 He also made the necessary pots, shovels, and basins.
So at last Huram completed everything King Solomon had assigned him to make for
the Temple of the LORD:

41 two pillars,
two bowl-shaped capitals on top of the pillars,
two networks of chains that decorated the capitals,
42 four hundred pomegranates that hung from the chains on the capitals (two rows of
pomegranates for each of the chain networks that were hung around the capitals
on top of the pillars),
43 the ten water carts holding the ten basins,
44 the Sea and the twelve oxen under it,
45 the pots, the shovels, and the basins.

All these utensils for the Temple of the LORD that Huram made for Solomon were made
of burnished bronze. 46 The king had them cast in clay molds in the Jordan Valley
7:47 1 Chr 22:3, 14
between Succoth and Zarethan. 47 Solomon did not weigh all the utensils because there
7:48 Exod 37:10-16
were so many; the weight of the bronze could not be measured.
48 So Solomon made all the furnishings of the Temple of the LORD:

the gold altar,
7:49 Exod 25:31; 37:14
the gold table for the Bread of the Presence,
49 the gold lampstands, five on the south and five on the north, in front of the Most
Holy Place,
the flower decorations, lamps, and tongs, all of gold,
7:50 2 Kgs 25:14-15
50 the cups, lamp snuffers, basins, dishes, and firepans, all of pure gold.
the doors for the entrances to the Most Holy Place and the main room of the
Temple, with their fronts overlaid with gold.

7:51 2 Sam 8:11 2 Chr 5:1
51 So King Solomon finished all his work on the Temple of the LORD. Then Solomon
brought all the gifts his father, David, had dedicated—the silver, the gold, and the other
utensils—and he stored them in the treasuries of the LORD's Temple.

The Ark Brought to the Temple

8:1-21 2 Chr 5:2–6:11
8 Solomon then summoned the leaders of all the tribes and families of Israel to
assemble in Jerusalem. They were to bring the Ark of the LORD's covenant from its
8:1 Num 7:2 2 Sam 5:7; 6:17
location in the City of David, also known as Zion, to its new place in the Temple. 2 They
all assembled before the king at the annual Festival of Shelters in early autumn.* 3 When
8:2 Lev 23:33-34 2 Chr 5:3; 7:8-10
all the leaders of Israel arrived, the priests picked up the Ark. 4 Then the priests and
Levites took the Ark of the LORD, along with the Tabernacle* and all its sacred utensils,
8:3 Num 7:9
and carried them up to the Temple. 5 King Solomon and the entire community of Israel
sacrificed sheep and oxen before the Ark in such numbers that no one could keep count!
8:5 2 Sam 6:13 2 Chr 1:5-6
6 Then the priests carried the Ark of the LORD's covenant into the inner sanctuary of
the Temple—the Most Holy Place—and placed it beneath the wings of the cherubim.
7 The cherubim spread their wings over the Ark, forming a canopy over the Ark and its

8:2 Hebrew *at the festival in the month Ethanim, which is the seventh month.* The Festival of Shelters began on the fifteenth day of the seventh month on the Hebrew lunar calendar. This occurs on our calendar in late September or early October. **8:4** Hebrew *Tent of Meeting.*

7:40-47 Huram's items of bronze would look strange in today's churches, but we use other articles to enhance worship. Stained-glass windows, crosses, pulpits, hymnbooks, and communion tables serve as aids to worship. While the instruments of worship may change, the purpose of worship should never change—to give honor and praise to God.

8:1ff Solomon gathered the people not just to dedicate the Temple, but to rededicate themselves to God's service. Solomon could well be speaking these words to us today: "And may you, his people, always be faithful to the LORD our God. May you always obey his laws and commands, just as you are doing today" (8:61).

8:1ff What was the difference between the Tabernacle and the Temple, and why did the Israelites change from one to the other? As a tent, the Tabernacle was a portable place of worship designed for the people as they were traveling toward the Promised Land. The Temple was a permanent place to worship God after the Israelites were at peace in their land. To bring the Ark of the Lord's covenant to the Temple signified God's actual presence there.

8:6 Cherubim are mighty angels.

carrying poles. 8These poles were so long that their ends could be seen from the front
entrance of the Temple's main room—the Holy Place—but not from outside it. They are
still there to this day. 9Nothing was in the Ark except the two stone tablets that Moses
had placed there at Mount Sinai,* where the LORD made a covenant with the people of
Israel as they were leaving the land of Egypt.
10As the priests came out of the inner sanctuary, a cloud filled the Temple of the LORD.
11The priests could not continue their work because the glorious presence of the LORD
filled the Temple.

Solomon Blesses the People

12Then Solomon prayed, "O LORD, you have said that you would live in thick darkness.
13But I have built a glorious Temple for you, where you can live forever!"
14Then the king turned around to the entire community of Israel standing before him
and gave this blessing: 15"Blessed be the LORD, the God of Israel, who has kept the
promise he made to my father, David. 16For he told my father, 'From the day I brought
my people Israel out of Egypt, I have never chosen a city among the tribes of Israel as
the place where a temple should be built to honor my name. But now I have chosen David
to be king over my people.'"
17Then Solomon said, "My father, David, wanted to build this Temple to honor the
name of the LORD, the God of Israel. 18But the LORD told him, 'It is right for you to want
to build the Temple to honor my name, 19but you will not be the one to do it. One of your
sons will build it instead.'
20"And now the LORD has done what he promised, for I have become king in my
father's place. I have built this Temple to honor the name of the LORD, the God of Israel.
21And I have prepared a place there for the Ark, which contains the covenant that the
LORD made with our ancestors when he brought them out of Egypt."

Solomon's Prayer of Dedication

22Then Solomon stood with his hands lifted toward heaven before the altar of the LORD
in front of the entire community of Israel. 23He prayed, "O LORD, God of Israel, there is
no God like you in all of heaven or earth. You keep your promises and show unfailing
love to all who obey you and are eager to do your will. 24You have kept your promise to
your servant David, my father. You made that promise with your own mouth, and today
you have fulfilled it with your own hands. 25And now, O LORD, God of Israel, carry out
your further promise to your servant David, my father. For you said to him, 'If your
descendants guard their behavior as you have done, they will always reign over Israel.'
26Now, O God of Israel, fulfill this promise to your servant David, my father.
27"But will God really live on earth? Why, even the highest heavens cannot contain
you. How much less this Temple I have built! 28Listen to my prayer and my request,
O LORD my God. Hear the cry and the prayer that your servant is making to you today.
29May you watch over this Temple both day and night, this place where you have said
you would put your name. May you always hear the prayers I make toward this place.
30May you hear the humble and earnest requests from me and your people Israel when
we pray toward this place. Yes, hear us from heaven where you live, and when you hear,
forgive.
31"If someone wrongs another person and is required to take an oath of innocence in
front of the altar at this Temple, 32then hear from heaven and judge between your
servants—the accuser and the accused. Punish the guilty party and acquit the one who
is innocent.

8:8 Exod 25:13-15; 37:4-5
8:9 Exod 24:7; 25:16; Deut 4:13-14; 10:2; Heb 9:4
8:10 Exod 40:34-35; 2 Chr 7:1-2
8:12 2 Chr 6:1; Ps 97:2
8:15 2 Sam 7:12-13; 1 Chr 22:10
8:16 Deut 12:4-5, 11; 1 Sam 16:1
8:17 2 Sam 7:2-3; 1 Chr 17:1-2
8:19 2 Sam 7:12-13; 1 Chr 17:11-12; 22:8-10
8:20 1 Chr 1:28
8:23 Deut 7:9; Neh 1:5; 9:32
8:25 2 Sam 7:25; 1 Kgs 2:4; 1 Chr 17:23
8:27 2 Chr 2:6; Ps 139:7-16; Isa 66:1; Jer 23:24; Acts 7:48-49
8:29 Deut 12:11; 2 Chr 7:12, 15-16
8:30 Neh 1:5-7
8:31 Exod 22:8-11; Lev 5:1
8:32 Deut 25:1

8:9 Hebrew *at Horeb,* another name for Sinai.

8:15-21 For 480 years after Israel's escape from Egypt, God did not ask them to build a temple for him. Instead, he emphasized the importance of his presence among them and their need for spiritual leaders. It is easy to think of a building as the focus of God's presence and power, but God chooses and uses *people* to do his work. He can use you more than he can use a building of wood and stone. Building or enlarging our place of worship may be necessary, but it should never take priority over developing spiritual leaders.

8:24 Solomon was referring to the promise God made to David in 2 Samuel 7:12-15 that one of David's sons would build the Temple.

8:27 In his prayer of dedication, Solomon declared that even the highest heavens cannot contain God. Isn't it amazing that, though the heavens can't contain God, he is willing to live in the hearts of those who love him? The God of the universe takes up residence in his people.

8:33
Lev 26:14-17, 40-42
Deut 28:25, 47-48
8:35
Lev 26:19
Deut 11:16-17
8:36
1 Sam 12:23
Ps 27:17
8:37
Lev 26:16, 25-26
Deut 28:21-23

33 "If your people Israel are defeated by their enemies because they have sinned
against you, and if they turn to you and call on your name and pray to you here in this
Temple, 34 then hear from heaven and forgive their sins and return them to this land you
gave their ancestors.
35 "If the skies are shut up and there is no rain because your people have sinned against
you, and then they pray toward this Temple and confess your name and turn from their
sins because you have punished them, 36 then hear from heaven and forgive the sins of
your servants, your people Israel. Teach them to do what is right, and send rain on your
land that you have given to your people as their special possession.
37 "If there is a famine in the land, or plagues, or crop disease, or attacks of locusts or

SOLOMON'S TEMPLE
960–586 B.C.
Solomon's Temple was a beautiful sight. It took over seven years to build and was a magnificent building containing gold, silver, bronze, and cedar. This house for God was without equal. The description is found in 2 Chronicles 2—4.

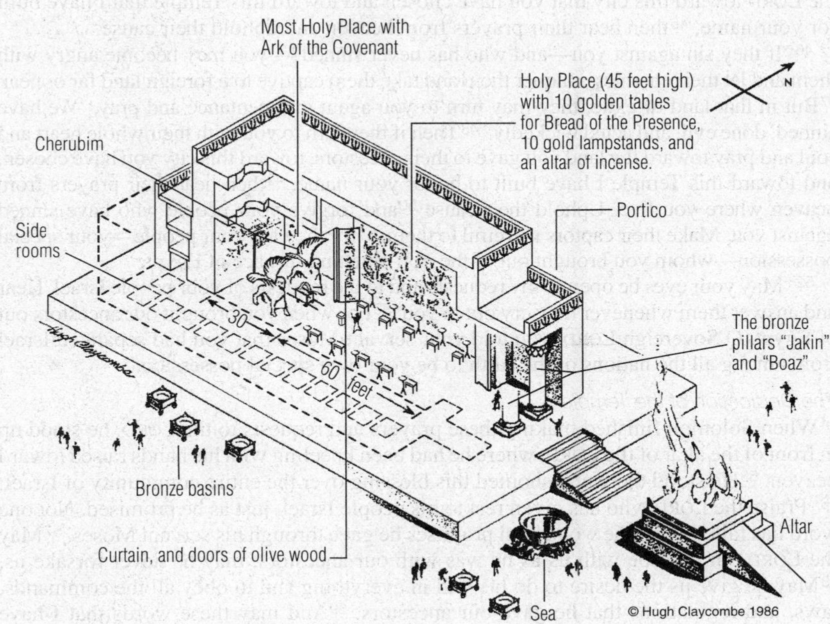

FURNISHINGS
Cherubim: represented heavenly beings, symbolized God's presence and holiness (gold-plated, 15 feet wide)
Ark of the Covenant: contained the law written on two tablets, symbolized God's presence with Israel (wood overlaid with gold)
Curtain: separated the Holy Place from the Most Holy Place (blue, purple, and crimson yarn and fine linen, with cherubim worked into it)
Doors: between Holy Place and Most Holy Place (wood overlaid with gold)
Golden tables (wood overlaid with gold), *gold lampstands* (with seven lamps on each stand), and *altar of incense* (wood overlaid with gold): instruments for priestly functions in the Holy Place
Bronze pillars: named Jakin (meaning "he establishes") and Boaz (meaning "in him is strength")—taken together they could mean "God provides the strength"
Altar: for burning of sacrifices (bronze)
Sea: for priests' washing (had 12,000-gallon capacity)
Bronze basins: for washing the sacrifices (water basins on wheeled bases)

This reconstruction uses known archaeological parallels to supplement the text, and assumes interior dimensions from 1 Kings 6:17–20.

8:33, 34 After Solomon's reign, the people continually turned away from God. The rest of the kingdom era is a vivid fulfillment of Solomon's description in these verses. As a result of the people's sin, God let them be overrun by enemies several times. Then, in desperation, they cried out to God for forgiveness, and God restored them.

caterpillars, or if your people's enemies are in the land besieging their towns—whatever
the trouble is—38and if your people offer a prayer concerning their troubles or sorrow,
raising their hands toward this Temple, 39then hear from heaven where you live, and
forgive. Give your people whatever they deserve, for you alone know the human heart.
40Then they will fear you and walk in your ways as long as they live in the land you gave
to our ancestors.
41"And when foreigners hear of you and come from distant lands to worship your
great name—42for they will hear of you and of your mighty miracles and your power—
and when they pray toward this Temple, 43then hear from heaven where you live, and
grant what they ask of you. Then all the people of the earth will come to know and fear
you, just as your own people Israel do. They, too, will know that this Temple I have built
bears your name.
44"If your people go out at your command to fight their enemies, and if they pray to
the LORD toward this city that you have chosen and toward this Temple that I have built
for your name, 45then hear their prayers from heaven and uphold their cause.
46"If they sin against you—and who has never sinned?—you may become angry with
them and let their enemies conquer them and take them captive to a foreign land far or near.
47But in that land of exile, they may turn to you again in repentance and pray, 'We have
sinned, done evil, and acted wickedly.' 48Then if they turn to you with their whole heart and
soul and pray toward the land you gave to their ancestors, toward this city you have chosen,
and toward this Temple I have built to honor your name, 49then hear their prayers from
heaven where you live. Uphold their cause 50and forgive your people who have sinned
against you. Make their captors merciful to them, 51for they are your people—your special
possession—whom you brought out of the iron-smelting furnace of Egypt.
52"May your eyes be open to my requests and to the requests of your people Israel. Hear
and answer them whenever they cry out to you. 53For when you brought our ancestors out
of Egypt, O Sovereign LORD, you told your servant Moses that you had separated Israel
from among all the nations of the earth to be your own special possession."

The Dedication of the Temple

54When Solomon finished making these prayers and requests to the LORD, he stood up
in front of the altar of the LORD, where he had been kneeling with his hands raised toward
heaven. 55He stood there and shouted this blessing over the entire community of Israel:
56"Praise the LORD who has given rest to his people Israel, just as he promised. Not one
word has failed of all the wonderful promises he gave through his servant Moses. 57May
the LORD our God be with us as he was with our ancestors; may he never forsake us.
58May he give us the desire to do his will in everything and to obey all the commands,
laws, and regulations that he gave our ancestors. 59And may these words that I have
prayed in the presence of the LORD be before him constantly, day and night, so that the
LORD our God may uphold my cause and the cause of his people Israel, fulfilling our
daily needs. 60May people all over the earth know that the LORD is God and that there is
no other god. 61And may you, his people, always be faithful to the LORD our God. May
you always obey his laws and commands, just as you are doing today."
62Then the king and all Israel with him offered sacrifices to the LORD. 63Solomon
sacrificed peace offerings to the LORD numbering 22,000 oxen and 120,000 sheep. And

8:39 1 Sam 2:3; 1 Chr 28:9; Jer 17:10; John 2:24-25
8:42 Deut 3:24
8:43 1 Sam 17:46
8:44 2 Chr 14:11
8:46 2 Kgs 17:6, 18; 25:21; Prov 20:9; 1 Jn 1:8-10
8:47 Lev 26:40-42; Ezra 9:5-7; Neh 1:6-7; Ps 106:6-7; Dan 9:5
8:48 Deut 4:29; 1 Sam 7:3-4
8:50 2 Chr 30:9; Ps 106:46
8:51 Exod 32:11-12; Deut 4:20; 9:26-29; Jer 11:4
8:53 Exod 19:5-6
8:56 Josh 21:45; 23:14-15; 2 Kgs 10:9-10
8:57 Josh 1:5; 1 Sam 12:22
8:58 Ps 119:36; Jer 31:33
8:60 Deut 4:35; 1 Sam 17:46; 1 Kgs 18:39
8:61 Deut 18:13; 1 Kgs 11:4; 2 Kgs 20:3
8:62-66 2 Chr 7:1-10

8:41-43 God chose Israel to be a blessing to the whole world (Genesis 12:1-3). This blessing found its fulfillment in Jesus—a descendant of Abraham and David (Galatians 3:8, 9)—who became the Messiah for all people, Jews and non-Jews. When the Israelites first entered the Promised Land, they were ordered to clear out several wicked nations; thus, we read in the Old Testament of many wars. But we should not conclude that war was Israel's first duty. After subduing the evil people, Israel was to become a light to the surrounding nations. Sadly, Israel's own sin and spiritual blindness prevented them from reaching out to the rest of the world with God's love. Jesus came to do what the nation of Israel failed to do.

8:46-53 Solomon, who seemed to have prophetic insight into the future captivities of his people (2 Kings 17; 25), asked God to be merciful to them when they cried out to him, to forgive them, and to return them to their homeland. Reference to their return is made in Ezra 1; 2; Nehemiah 1; 2.

8:56-60 Solomon praised the Lord and prayed for the people. His prayer can be a pattern for our prayers. He had five basic requests: (1) for God's presence (8:57); (2) for the desire to do God's will in everything (8:58); (3) for the desire and ability to obey God's decrees and commands (8:58); (4) for help with each day's needs (8:59); (5) for the spread of God's Kingdom to the entire world (8:60). These prayer requests are just as important today. When you pray for your church or family, you can make these same requests to God.

8:64 2 Chr 4:1 so the king and all Israel dedicated the Temple of the LORD. 64 That same day the king
dedicated the central area of the courtyard in front of the LORD's Temple. He offered
burnt offerings, grain offerings, and the fat of peace offerings there, because the bronze
altar in the LORD's presence was too small to handle so many offerings.
8:65 Gen 15:18 65 Then Solomon and all Israel celebrated the Festival of Shelters* in the presence of
the LORD their God. A large crowd had gathered from as far away as Lebo-hamath in the
north to the brook of Egypt in the south. The celebration went on for fourteen days in
all—seven days for the dedication of the altar and seven days for the Festival of
Shelters.* 66 After the festival was over,* Solomon sent the people home. They blessed
the king as they went, and they were all joyful and happy because the LORD had been
good to his servant David and to his people Israel.

4. Solomon's greatness and downfall

The LORD's Response to Solomon

9:1-9 //2 Chr 7:11-22 **9** So Solomon finished building the Temple of the LORD, as well as the royal palace.
9:1 1 Kgs 7:1-2; 2 Chr 8:6 He completed everything he had planned to do. 2 Then the LORD appeared to
Solomon a second time, as he had done before at Gibeon. 3 The LORD said to him, "I have
9:3 2 Kgs 20:5 heard your prayer and your request. I have set apart this Temple you have built so that
my name will be honored there forever. I will always watch over it and care for it. 4 As
9:4 1 Kgs 3:14; 11:4 for you, if you will follow me with integrity and godliness, as David your father did,
always obeying my commands and keeping my laws and regulations, 5 then I will
9:5 2 Sam 7:12 establish the throne of your dynasty over Israel forever. For I made this promise to your
father, David: 'You will never fail to have a successor on the throne of Israel.'
9:6 2 Sam 7:14-16; 1 Chr 28:9 6 "But if you or your descendants abandon me and disobey my commands and laws,
and if you go and worship other gods, 7 then I will uproot the people of Israel from this
9:7 Lev 18:24-29; Deut 4:26-27; 2 Kgs 17:23; Jer 7:4 land I have given them. I will reject this Temple that I have set apart to honor my name.
I will make Israel an object of mockery and ridicule among the nations. 8 And though this
Temple is impressive now, it will become an appalling sight for all who pass by. They
9:8 Deut 29:24-26; 2 Chr 7:21; Jer 22:8-9, 28 will scoff and ask, 'Why did the LORD do such terrible things to his land and to his
Temple?' 9 And the answer will be, 'Because his people forgot the LORD their God, who
brought their ancestors out of Egypt, and they worshiped other gods instead. That is why
9:9 Deut 29:25-28 the LORD has brought all these disasters upon them.'"

Solomon's Agreement with Hiram

9:10-28 2 Chr 8:1-18 10 Now at the end of the twenty years during which Solomon built the Temple of the LORD
and the royal palace, 11 Solomon gave twenty towns in the land of Galilee to King Hiram of

8:65a Hebrew *the festival;* see note on 8:2. **8:65b** Hebrew *seven days and seven days, fourteen days;* compare parallel text at 2 Chr 7:8-10. **8:66** Hebrew *On the eighth day,* probably referring to the day following the seven-day Festival of Shelters; compare parallel text at 2 Chr 7:9-10.

SOLOMON'S BUILDING PROJECTS
Solomon became known as one of the great builders in Israel's history. He built Hazor, Megiddo, and Gezer as fortress cities at key points during his reign. He also rebuilt the cities of lower Beth-horon, Baalath, and Tadmor.

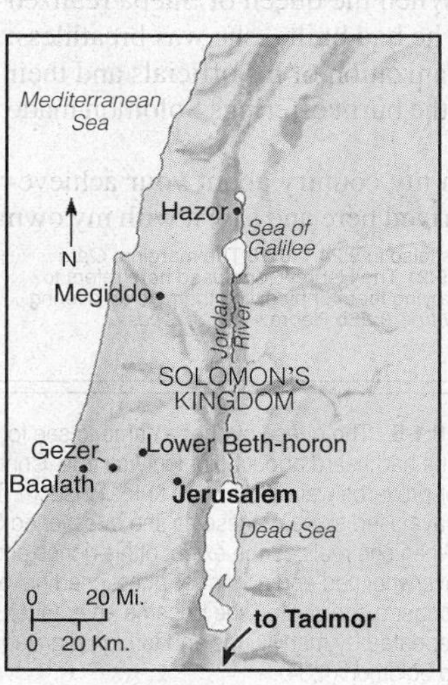

9:4-9 God appeared to Solomon a second time; the first was at Gibeon (3:4-15). For more on the conditions of God's great promise to David and his descendants, see the note on 2:3, 4.

9:11-14 Was Solomon being unfair to Hiram? It is not clear from these verses whether Solomon gave these towns to Hiram, or whether they were collateral until he could repay Hiram for the gold he had borrowed. Second Chronicles 8:1, 2 implies that the towns were returned to Solomon. In either case, Hiram probably preferred a piece of land on the coast more suitable for trade (the name he gave these cities, *Cabul,* sounds like the Hebrew word for "good-for-nothing"). In the end, Hiram was repaid many times over through his trade partnerships with Solomon (2 Chronicles 9:10, 21). Because Phoenicia was on friendly terms with Israel and dependent on it for grain and oil, Hiram's relationship with Solomon was more important than a feud over some cities.

Tyre as payment for all the cedar and cypress lumber and gold he had furnished for the construction of the buildings. 12 Hiram came from Tyre to see the towns Solomon had given him, but he was not at all pleased with them. 13 "What kind of towns are these, my brother?" he asked. "These towns are worthless!" So Hiram called that area Cabul—"worthless"—as it is still known today. 14 Hiram had sent Solomon nine thousand pounds* of gold.

Solomon's Many Achievements

15 This is the account of the forced labor that Solomon conscripted to build the LORD's Temple, the royal palace, the Millo,* the wall of Jerusalem, and the cities of Hazor, Megiddo, and Gezer. 16 (The king of Egypt had attacked and captured Gezer, killing the Canaanite population and burning it down. He gave the city to his daughter as a wedding gift when she married Solomon. 17 So Solomon rebuilt the city of Gezer.) He also built up the towns of Lower Beth-horon, 18 Baalath, and Tamar* in the desert, within his land. 19 He built towns as supply centers and constructed cities where his chariots and horses* could be kept. He built to his heart's content in Jerusalem and Lebanon and throughout the entire realm.

20 There were still some people living in the land who were not Israelites, including Amorites, Hittites, Perizzites, Hivites, and Jebusites. 21 These were descendants of the nations that Israel had not completely destroyed.* So Solomon conscripted them for his labor force, and they serve in the labor force to this day. 22 But Solomon did not conscript any of the Israelites for forced labor. Instead, he assigned them to serve as fighting men, government officials, officers in his army, commanders of his chariots, and charioteers. 23 He also appointed 550 of them to supervise the various projects.

24 After Solomon moved his wife, Pharaoh's daughter, from the City of David to the new palace he had built for her, he constructed the Millo.

25 Three times each year Solomon offered burnt offerings and peace offerings to the LORD on the altar he had built. He also burned incense to the LORD. And so he finished the work of building the Temple.

26 Later King Solomon built a fleet of ships at Ezion-geber, a port near Elath* in the land of Edom, along the shore of the Red Sea.* 27 Hiram sent experienced crews of sailors to sail the ships with Solomon's men. 28 They sailed to Ophir and brought back to Solomon some sixteen tons* of gold.

The Queen of Sheba's Visit

10 When the queen of Sheba heard of Solomon's reputation, which brought honor to the name of the LORD, she came to test him with hard questions. 2 She arrived in Jerusalem with a large group of attendants and a great caravan of camels loaded with spices, huge quantities of gold, and precious jewels. When she met with Solomon, they talked about everything she had on her mind. 3 Solomon answered all her questions; nothing was too hard for the king to explain to her. 4 When the queen of Sheba realized how wise Solomon was, and when she saw the palace he had built, 5 she was breathless. She was also amazed at the food on his tables, the organization of his officials and their splendid clothing, the cup-bearers and their robes, and the burnt offerings Solomon made at the Temple of the LORD.

6 She exclaimed to the king, "Everything I heard in my country about your achievements and wisdom is true! 7 I didn't believe it until I arrived here and saw it with my own

9:11 1 Kgs 5:4; 2 Chr 2:4
9:13 Josh 19:27
9:15 2 Sam 5:9
9:19 1 Kgs 4:26
9:21 Josh 15:63
9:22 Lev 25:39
9:24 1 Kgs 3:1; 7:8; 11:1, 27; 2 Chr 32:5
9:25 Exod 23:14-17; Deut 16:16
9:26 Num 33:35; 1 Kgs 22:48
9:27 1 Kgs 10:11
10:1-13 //2 Chr 9:1-12
10:1 2 Chr 9:1; Ps 72:10, 15; Matt 12:42

9:14 Hebrew *120 talents* [4 metric tons]. **9:15** Or *the supporting terraces;* also in 9:24. **9:18** The marginal *Qere* reading of the Masoretic Text reads *Tadmor.* **9:19** Or *and charioteers.* **9:21** The Hebrew term used here refers to the complete consecration of things or people to the LORD, either by destroying them or by giving them as an offering. **9:26a** As in Greek version (see also 2 Kgs 14:22; 16:6); Hebrew reads *Eloth.* **9:26b** Hebrew *sea of reeds.* **9:28** Hebrew *420 talents* [14 metric tons].

9:16 At this time Israel and Egypt were the major powers in the Near East. For many years Egypt had retained control of Gezer, even though it was in Israelite territory. In Solomon's time the Pharaoh gave the city to his daughter, whom Solomon married, putting Gezer under Israelite control. Intermarriage among royal families was common, but it was not endorsed by God (Deuteronomy 17:17).

10:1-5 The queen of Sheba came to see for herself if everything she had heard about Solomon was true. Contests using riddles or proverbs were often used to test wisdom. The queen may have used some of these as she questioned Solomon (10:1, 3). When she realized the extent of his riches and wisdom, she was overwhelmed and no longer questioned his power or wisdom. No longer a competitor, she became an admirer. Her experience was repeated by many kings and foreign dignitaries who paid honor to Solomon (4:34).

10:8 Prov 8:34
10:9 2 Sam 8:15; 23:3 1 Kgs 5:7 2 Chr 2:11
10:11 1 Kgs 9:27
10:14-29 //2 Chr 1:14-17; 9:13-28
10:16 1 Kgs 14:26-28 2 Chr 12:9-10
10:17 1 Kgs 7:2

eyes. Truly I had not heard the half of it! Your wisdom and prosperity are far greater than
what I was told. 8 How happy these people must be! What a privilege for your officials
to stand here day after day, listening to your wisdom! 9 The LORD your God is great
indeed! He delights in you and has placed you on the throne of Israel. Because the LORD
loves Israel with an eternal love, he has made you king so you can rule with justice and
righteousness."
10 Then she gave the king a gift of nine thousand pounds* of gold, and great quantities
of spices and precious jewels. Never again were so many spices brought in as those the
queen of Sheba gave to Solomon.
11 (When Hiram's ships brought gold from Ophir, they also brought rich cargoes of
almug wood and precious jewels. 12 The king used the almug wood to make railings for
the Temple of the LORD and the royal palace, and to construct harps and lyres for the
musicians. Never before or since has there been such a supply of beautiful almug wood.)
13 King Solomon gave the queen of Sheba whatever she asked for, besides all the other
customary gifts he had so generously given. Then she and all her attendants left and
returned to their own land.

Solomon's Wealth and Splendor

14 Each year Solomon received about twenty-five tons* of gold. 15 This did not include
the additional revenue he received from merchants and traders, all the kings of Arabia,
and the governors of the land.
16 King Solomon made two hundred large shields of hammered gold, each containing
over fifteen pounds* of gold. 17 He also made three hundred smaller shields of hammered
gold, each containing nearly four pounds* of gold. The king placed these shields in the
Palace of the Forest of Lebanon.
18 Then the king made a huge ivory throne and overlaid it with pure gold. 19 The throne

10:10 Hebrew *120 talents* [4 metric tons]. **10:14** Hebrew *666 talents* [23 metric tons]. **10:16** Hebrew *600 shekels* [6.8 kilograms]. **10:17** Hebrew *3 minas* [1.8 kilograms].

FRIENDS AND ENEMIES
Solomon's reputation brought acclaim and riches from many nations, but he disobeyed God, marrying pagan women and worshiping their gods. So God raised up enemies like Hadad from Edom and Rezon from Zobah (modern-day Syria). Jeroboam from Zeredah was another enemy who would eventually divide this mighty kingdom.

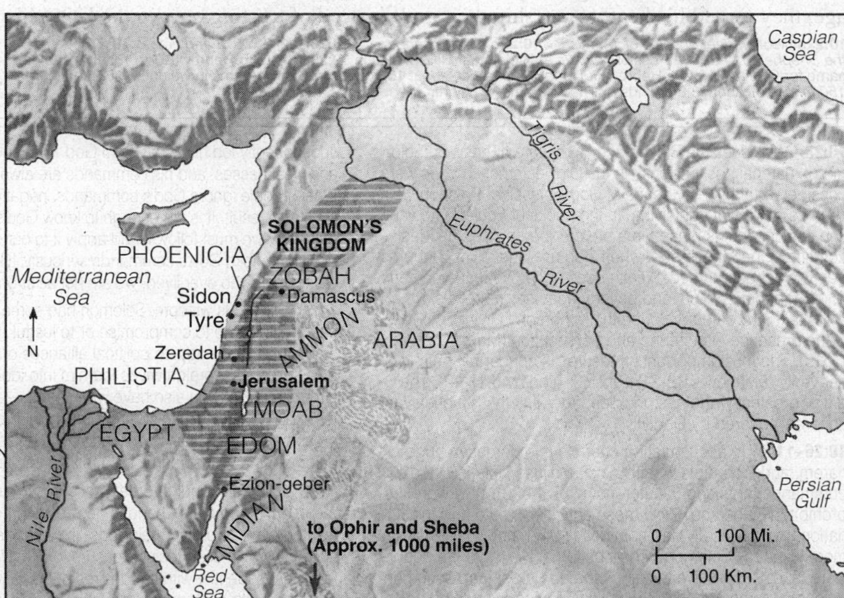

10:14ff When Solomon asked for wisdom, God promised him riches and honor as well (3:13). These verses show just how extensive his wealth became. Israel was no longer a second-rate nation, but at the height of its power and wealth. Solomon's riches became legendary. Great men came from many nations to listen to Israel's powerful king. Jesus would later refer to "Solomon in all his glory" (Matthew 6:29).

had six steps and a rounded back. On both sides of the seat were armrests, with the figure
of a lion standing on each side of the throne. 20Solomon made twelve other lion figures,
one standing on each end of each of the six steps. No other throne in all the world could
be compared with it!
21All of King Solomon's drinking cups were solid gold, as were all the utensils in the
Palace of the Forest of Lebanon. They were not made of silver because silver was
considered of little value in Solomon's day!
22The king had a fleet of trading ships* that sailed with Hiram's fleet. Once every
three years the ships returned, loaded down with gold, silver, ivory, apes, and peacocks.*
23So King Solomon became richer and wiser than any other king in all the earth. **10:23** 1 Kgs 3:12-13; 4:30
24People from every nation came to visit him and to hear the wisdom God had given him.
25Year after year, everyone who came to visit brought him gifts of silver and gold,
clothing, weapons, spices, horses, and mules.
26Solomon built up a huge force of chariots and horses. He had fourteen hundred
chariots and twelve thousand horses.* He stationed many of them in the chariot cities,
and some near him in Jerusalem. 27The king made silver as plentiful in Jerusalem as **10:27** 2 Chr 1:14-17;
stones. And valuable cedarwood was as common as the sycamore wood that grows in 9:25, 27
the foothills of Judah.* 28Solomon's horses were imported from Egypt* and from **10:28** 2 Chr 1:16; 9:28
Cilicia*; the king's traders acquired them from Cilicia at the standard price. 29At that **10:29**
time, Egyptian chariots delivered to Jerusalem could be purchased for 600 pieces of 2 Kgs 7:6-7
silver,* and horses could be bought for 150 pieces of silver.* Many of these were then
resold to the kings of the Hittites and the kings of Aram.

Solomon's Many Wives

11 Now King Solomon loved many foreign women. Besides Pharaoh's daughter, he **11:1**
married women from Moab, Ammon, Edom, Sidon, and from among the Hittites. Neh 13:23-27
2The LORD had clearly instructed his people not to intermarry with those nations, **11:2** Exod 23:31-33;
because the women they married would lead them to worship their gods. Yet Solomon 34:12-16
insisted on loving them anyway. 3He had seven hundred wives and three hundred Deut 7:3-4
concubines. And sure enough, they led his heart away from the LORD. 4In Solomon's old **11:3** 2 Sam 5:13-16
age, they turned his heart to worship their gods instead of trusting only in the LORD his

10:22a Hebrew *fleet of ships of Tarshish.* **10:22b** Or *and baboons.* **10:26** Or *12,000 charioteers.* **10:27** Hebrew *the Shephelah.* **10:28a** Possibly *Muzur,* a district near Cilicia; also in 10:29. **10:28b** Hebrew *Kue,* probably another name for Cilicia. **10:29a** Hebrew *600 shekels of silver,* about 15 pounds or 6.8 kilograms in weight. **10:29b** Hebrew *150 [shekels],* about 3.8 pounds or 1.7 kilograms in weight.

10:23 Why does the Bible place so much emphasis on Solomon's material possessions? In the Old Testament, riches were considered tangible evidence of God's blessing. Prosperity was seen as a proof of right living. In the books of Ecclesiastes and Job this concept is placed in a broader perspective. In ideal conditions, people prosper when God runs their lives, but prosperity is not guaranteed. Wealth does not prove that a person is living right before God, and poverty does not indicate sin.

In fact, a greater evidence that a person is living for God is the presence of suffering and persecution (Mark 10:29-31; 13:13). The most important "treasure" is not earthly but heavenly (Matthew 6:19-21; 19:21; 1 Timothy 6:17-19). The gift of greatest worth has no price tag—it is the gift of salvation freely offered by God.

10:26–11:3 In accumulating chariots and horses, a huge harem, and incredible wealth, Solomon was violating God's commands for a king (Deuteronomy 17:14-20). Why were they prohibited? God knew how these activities would hurt the nation both politically and spiritually (1 Samuel 8:11-18). The more luxurious Solomon's court became, the more the people were taxed. Excessive taxation created unrest, and soon conditions became ripe for a revolution. Having everything he wanted, Solomon forgot God and allowed pagan influences to enter his court through his pagan wives, thus accelerating the spiritual corruption of the nation.

11:2 Although Solomon had clear instructions from God *not* to marry women from foreign nations, he chose to disregard God's commands. He married not one, but many foreign women, who subsequently led him away from God. God knows our strengths and weaknesses, and his commands are always for our good. When people ignore God's commands, negative consequences inevitably result. It is not enough to know God's Word or even to believe it; we must follow it and apply it to our daily activities and decisions. Take God's commands seriously. Like Solomon, the wisest man who ever lived, we are not as strong as we may think.

11:3 For all his wisdom, Solomon had some weak spots. He could not say no to compromise or to lustful desires. Whether he married to strengthen political alliances or to gain personal pleasure, these foreign wives led him into idolatry. You may have strong faith, but you also have weak spots—and that is where temptation usually strikes. Strengthen and protect your weaker areas because a chain is only as strong as its weakest link. If Solomon, the wisest man, could fall, so can you.

11:4 Solomon handled great pressures in running the government, but he could not handle the pressure from his wives who wanted him to worship their gods. In marriage and close friendships, it is difficult to resist pressure to compromise. Our love leads us to identify with the desires of those we care about.

Faced with such pressure, Solomon at first *resisted* it, maintaining pure faith. Then he *tolerated* a more widespread practice of idolatry. Finally, he became involved in idolatrous worship, *rationalizing* away the potential danger to himself and to the kingdom. It is because we want to please and identify with our loved ones that God asks us not to marry those who do not share our commitment to him.

11:5 Judg 2:12-14; 10:6 1 Sam 7:3-4

11:7 Lev 20:2-5 Num 21:27-30 Judg 11:24 2 Kgs 23:10, 13

God, as his father, David, had done. 5 Solomon worshiped Ashtoreth, the goddess of the Sidonians, and Molech,* the detestable god of the Ammonites. 6 Thus, Solomon did what was evil in the LORD's sight; he refused to follow the LORD completely, as his father, David, had done. 7 On the Mount of Olives, east of Jerusalem, he even built a shrine for Chemosh, the detestable god of Moab, and another for Molech, the detestable god of the Ammonites. 8 Solomon built such shrines for all his foreign wives to use for burning incense and sacrificing to their gods.

11:9 1 Kgs 3:5; 9:2-3

11:10 1 Kgs 6:12; 9:61

11:11 1 Sam 2:30 1 Kgs 6:11-12; 11:31

11:12 2 Sam 7:15

9 The LORD was very angry with Solomon, for his heart had turned away from the LORD, the God of Israel, who had appeared to him twice. 10 He had warned Solomon specifically about worshiping other gods, but Solomon did not listen to the LORD's command. 11 So now the LORD said to him, "Since you have not kept my covenant and have disobeyed my laws, I will surely tear the kingdom away from you and give it to one of your servants. 12 But for the sake of your father, David, I will not do this while you are still alive. I will take the kingdom away from your son. 13 And even so, I will let him be king of one tribe, for the sake of my servant David and for the sake of Jerusalem, my chosen city."

Solomon's Enemies

11:15 2 Sam 8:13-14 1 Chr 18:12-13

14 Then the LORD raised up Hadad the Edomite, a member of Edom's royal family, to be an enemy against Solomon. 15 Years before, David had gone to Edom with Joab, his army commander, to bury some Israelites who had died in battle. While there, the Israelite army had killed nearly every male in Edom. 16 Joab and the army had stayed there for six months, killing them. 17 But Hadad and a few of his father's royal officials had fled. (Hadad was a very small child at the time.) 18 They escaped from Midian and went to Paran, where others joined them. Then they traveled to Egypt and went to Pharaoh, who gave them a home, food, and some land. 19 Pharaoh grew very fond of Hadad, and he gave him a wife—the sister of Queen Tahpenes. 20 She bore him a son, Genubath, who was brought up in Pharaoh's palace among Pharaoh's own sons.

11:21 1 Kgs 2:10, 34

21 When the news reached Hadad in Egypt that David and his commander Joab were both dead, he said to Pharaoh, "Let me return to my own country."

22 "Why?" Pharaoh asked him. "What do you lack here? How have we disappointed you that you want to go home?"

"Nothing is wrong," he replied. "But even so, I must return home."

11:23 2 Sam 8:3; 10:15-16

11:24 2 Sam 10:7-8, 18

23 God also raised up Rezon son of Eliada to be an enemy against Solomon. Rezon had fled from his master, King Hadadezer of Zobah, 24 and had become the leader of a gang of rebels. After David conquered Hadadezer, Rezon and his men fled to Damascus, where he became king. 25 Rezon was Israel's bitter enemy for the rest of Solomon's reign, and he made trouble, just as Hadad did. Rezon hated Israel intensely and continued to reign in Aram.

11:5 Hebrew *Milcom*, a variant name for Molech; also in 11:33.

11:5-8 Ashtoreth was a goddess that symbolized reproductive power—a mistress of the god Baal. Molech was the national god of the Ammonites and was called "detestable" because its worship rites included child sacrifice. Chemosh was the Moabites' national god. The Israelites were warned against worshiping all other gods in general and Molech in particular (Exodus 20:1-6; Leviticus 18:21; 20:1-5).

11:9, 10 Solomon didn't turn away from God all at once or in a brief moment. His spiritual coldness started with a minor departure from God's laws (3:1). Over the years, that little sin grew until it resulted in Solomon's downfall. A little sin can be the first step in turning away from God. It is not the sins we don't know about but the sins we excuse that cause us the greatest trouble. We must never let any sin go unchallenged. In your life, is an unchallenged sin spreading like a deadly cancer? Don't excuse it. Confess this sin to God and ask him for strength to resist temptation.

11:11-13 Solomon's powerful and glorious kingdom could have been blessed for all time; instead, it was approaching its end. Solomon had God's promises, guidance, and answers to prayer, and yet he allowed sin to remain all around him. Eventually it corrupted him so much that he was no longer interested in God. Psalm 127:1, written by Solomon, says, "Unless the LORD builds a house, the work of the builders is useless." Solomon had begun by laying the foundation with God, but he did not follow through in his later years. As a result, he lost everything. It is not enough to get off to a right start in building our marriage, career, or church on God's principles; we must remain faithful to God to the end (Mark 13:13). God must be in control of our lives from start to finish.

11:14-22 Edom was the kingdom southeast of the Dead Sea. David had added this nation to his empire (2 Samuel 8:13, 14). It was of strategic importance because it controlled the route to the Red Sea. Edom's revolt was disturbing the peace of Solomon's kingdom.

Jeroboam Rebels against Solomon

26Another rebel leader was Jeroboam son of Nebat, one of Solomon's own officials. He 11:26 2 Chr 13:6
came from the city of Zeredah in Ephraim, and his mother was Zeruah, a widow. 27This
is the story behind his rebellion. Solomon was rebuilding the Millo* and repairing the 11:27 1 Kgs 9:24
walls of the city of his father, David. 28Jeroboam was a very capable young man, and
when Solomon saw how industrious he was, he put him in charge of the labor force from
the tribes of Ephraim and Manasseh.*

29One day as Jeroboam was leaving Jerusalem, the prophet Ahijah from Shiloh met him 11:29 1 Kgs 12:15; 14:2
on the road, wearing a new cloak. The two of them were alone in a field, 30and Ahijah took
the new cloak he was wearing and tore it into twelve pieces. 31Then he said to Jeroboam, 11:30 1 Sam 15:27-28
"Take ten of these pieces, for this is what the LORD, the God of Israel, says: 'I am about to 11:31 1 Kgs 11:11-12
tear the kingdom from the hand of Solomon, and I will give ten of the tribes to you! 32But
I will leave him one tribe for the sake of my servant David and for the sake of Jerusalem,
which I have chosen out of all the tribes of Israel. 33For Solomon has abandoned me and 11:33 1 Kgs 11:5-8
worshiped Ashtoreth, the goddess of the Sidonians; Chemosh, the god of Moab; and
Molech, the god of the Ammonites. He has not followed my ways and done what is pleasing
in my sight. He has not obeyed my laws and regulations as his father, David, did.

34" 'But I will not take the entire kingdom from Solomon at this time. For the sake of
my servant David, the one whom I chose and who obeyed my commands and laws, I will
let Solomon reign for the rest of his life. 35But I will take the kingdom away from his 11:35 1 Kgs 12:16
son and give ten of the tribes to you. 36His son will have one tribe so that the descendants
of David my servant will continue to reign* in Jerusalem, the city I have chosen to be 11:36 1 Kgs 15:4; 2 Kgs 8:19; 2 Chr 21:7
the place for my name. 37And I will place you on the throne of Israel, and you will rule
over all that your heart desires. 38If you listen to what I tell you and follow my ways and 11:38 2 Sam 7:11, 27
do whatever I consider to be right, and if you obey my laws and commands, as my
servant David did, then I will always be with you. I will establish an enduring dynasty
for you as I did for David, and I will give Israel to you. 39But I will punish the
descendants of David because of Solomon's sin—though not forever.' "

40Solomon tried to kill Jeroboam, but he fled to King Shishak of Egypt and stayed 11:40 1 Kgs 14:25; 2 Chr 12:2
there until Solomon died.

41The rest of the events in Solomon's reign, including his wisdom, are recorded in *The* 11:41-43 //2 Chr 9:29-31
Book of the Acts of Solomon. 42Solomon ruled in Jerusalem over all Israel for forty years.
43When Solomon died, he was buried in the city of his father, David. Then his son
Rehoboam became the next king.

B. THE DIVIDED KINGDOM (12:1—22:53)

After Solomon's death, the northern tribes revolt, forming two separate nations. Each nation experiences disastrous consequences from having evil kings. Elijah appears on the scene, confronting these kings for their sin. God deals with sin in powerful ways. Although judgment may appear to be slow, God will judge evil harshly.

1. Revolt of the northern tribes

Rebellion against Rehoboam

12 Rehoboam went to Shechem, where all Israel had gathered to make him king. 12:1-24 //2 Chr 10:1–11:4
2When Jeroboam son of Nebat heard of Solomon's death, he returned from
Egypt,* for he had fled to Egypt to escape from King Solomon. 3The leaders of Israel 12:1 Judg 9:1, 6; 2 Chr 10:1

11:27 Or *the supporting terraces.* **11:28** Hebrew *from the house of Joseph.* **11:36** Hebrew *will continue to have a lamp.* **12:2** As in Greek version and Latin Vulgate (see also 2 Chr 10:2); Hebrew reads *he lived in Egypt.*

11:29-39 The prophet Ahijah predicted the division of the kingdom of Israel. After Solomon's death, 10 of Israel's 12 tribes would follow Jeroboam. The other two tribes, Judah and the area of Benjamin around Jerusalem, would remain loyal to David. Judah, the largest tribe, and Benjamin, the smallest, were often mentioned as one tribe because they shared the same border. Both Jeroboam and Ahijah were from Ephraim, the most prominent of the 10 rebel tribes. (For more on the divided kingdom, see the note on 12:20.)

11:41 Nothing is known of *The Book of the Acts of Solomon.* See also the note on 14:19.

12:1 Rehoboam was made king at Shechem, about 35 miles north of Jerusalem. It would have been normal to anoint the new king in Jerusalem, the capital city, but Rehoboam saw trouble brewing with Jeroboam and went north to try to maintain good relations with the northern tribes. He probably chose Shechem because it was an ancient location for making covenants (Joshua 24:1). When the kingdom divided, Shechem became the capital of the northern kingdom for a short time (12:25).

12:4 1 Sam 8:11-18 sent for Jeroboam, and the whole assembly of Israel went to speak with Rehoboam.
4“Your father was a hard master,” they said. “Lighten the harsh labor demands and heavy
12:5 1 Kgs 12:12 taxes that your father imposed on us. Then we will be your loyal subjects.”
5Rehoboam replied, “Give me three days to think this over. Then come back for my
answer.” So the people went away.
6Then King Rehoboam went to discuss the matter with the older men who had
counseled his father, Solomon. “What is your advice?” he asked. “How should I answer
these people?”
7The older counselors replied, “If you are willing to serve the people today and give
them a favorable answer, they will always be your loyal subjects.”
8But Rehoboam rejected the advice of the elders and instead asked the opinion of the
young men who had grown up with him and who were now his advisers. 9“What is your
advice?” he asked them. “How should I answer these people who want me to lighten the
burdens imposed by my father?”
10The young men replied, “This is what you should tell those complainers: ‘My little
finger is thicker than my father’s waist—if you think he was hard on you, just wait and
see what I’ll be like! 11Yes, my father was harsh on you, but I’ll be even harsher! My
father used whips on you, but I’ll use scorpions!’”
12:12 1 Kgs 12:5 12Three days later, Jeroboam and all the people returned to hear Rehoboam’s decision,
just as the king had requested. 13But Rehoboam spoke harshly to them, for he rejected
the advice of the older counselors 14and followed the counsel of his younger advisers.
He told the people, “My father was harsh on you, but I’ll be even harsher! My father
12:15 Deut 2:30 Judg 14:4 2 Chr 10:15 used whips on you, but I’ll use scorpions!” 15So the king paid no attention to the people’s
demands. This turn of events was the will of the LORD, for it fulfilled the LORD’s message
to Jeroboam son of Nebat through the prophet Ahijah from Shiloh.
12:16 2 Sam 20:1 16When all Israel realized that the king had rejected their request, they shouted,
“Down with David and his dynasty! We have no share in Jesse’s son! Let’s go home,
12:17 1 Kgs 11:13, 36 Israel! Look out for your own house, O David!” So the people of Israel returned home.
17But Rehoboam continued to rule over the Israelites who lived in the towns of Judah.

TRIBAL JEALOUSIES Although the kingdom of Israel was “united” under David and Solomon, the tensions between north and south were never resolved. The jealousy and animosity behind this civil war didn’t begin with Rehoboam and Jeroboam but had its roots in the days of the judges, when the people were more interested in tribal loyalty than in national unity. Note how easily tension arose between Ephraim, the most prominent tribe in the north, and Judah, the prominent tribe of the south.

- Ephraim claimed the promises in Genesis 48:17–22 and 49:22–26 for its leadership role.
- Joshua, who conquered the Promised Land, was an Ephraimite (Numbers 13:8).
- Samuel, Israel’s greatest judge, was from Ephraim (1 Samuel 1:1ff).
- Ephraim allied with Ishbosheth in revolt against David, who was from the tribe of Judah (2 Samuel 2:8–11).
- David, a shepherd from the tribe of Judah, became king over all Israel, including Ephraim, which no longer had a claim to leadership.
- Although David helped to smooth over the bad feelings, the heavy yoke under Solomon and Rehoboam led the northern tribes to the breaking point.

Such tension developed because Ephraim was the key tribe in the north. They resented Judah’s role in leadership under David and resented that the nation’s capital and center of worship were located in Jerusalem.

12:6-14 Rehoboam asked for advice, but he didn’t carefully evaluate what he was told. If he had, he would have realized that the advice offered by the elders was wiser than that of his peers. To evaluate advice, ask if it is realistic, workable, and consistent with biblical principles. Determine if the results of following the advice will be fair, make improvements, and give a positive solution or direction. Seek counsel from those more experienced and wiser. Advice is helpful only if it is consistent with God’s standards.

12:15-19 Both Jeroboam and Rehoboam did what was good for themselves, not what was good for their people. Rehoboam was harsh and did not listen to what the people said; Jeroboam established new places of worship to keep his people from traveling to Jerusalem, Rehoboam’s capital. Both actions backfired. Rehoboam’s move divided the nation, and Jeroboam’s turned the people from God. Good leaders put the best interests of the “followers” above their own. Making decisions only for yourself will backfire and cause you to lose more than if you had kept the welfare of others in mind.

[18]King Rehoboam sent Adoniram,* who was in charge of the labor force, to restore 12:18 2 Sam 20:24
order, but all Israel stoned him to death. When this news reached King Rehoboam, he
quickly jumped into his chariot and fled to Jerusalem. [19]The northern tribes of Israel 12:19 2 Kgs 17:21
have refused to be ruled by a descendant of David to this day.
[20]When the people of Israel learned of Jeroboam's return from Egypt, they called an 12:20 1 Kgs 11:13, 32
assembly and made him king over all Israel. So only the tribe of Judah remained loyal
to the family of David.

Shemaiah's Prophecy

[21]When Rehoboam arrived at Jerusalem, he mobilized the armies of Judah and Benja- 12:21 2 Chr 11:1
min—180,000 select troops—to fight against the army of Israel and to restore the
kingdom to himself. [22]But God said to Shemaiah, the man of God, [23]"Say to Rehoboam 12:22 2 Chr 11:2; 12:5-7
son of Solomon, king of Judah, and to all the people of Judah and Benjamin, [24]'This is
what the LORD says: Do not fight against your relatives, the Israelites. Go back home,
for what has happened is my doing!'" So they obeyed the message of the LORD and went
home, as the LORD had commanded.

Jeroboam Makes Gold Calves

[25]Jeroboam then built up the city of Shechem in the hill country of Ephraim, and it 12:25 Judg 8:8, 17
became his capital. Later he went and built up the town of Peniel.* [26]Jeroboam thought
to himself, "Unless I am careful, the kingdom will return to the dynasty of David. 12:27 Deut 12:4-6, 14
[27]When they go to Jerusalem to offer sacrifices at the Temple of the LORD, they will
again give their allegiance to King Rehoboam of Judah. They will kill me and make him
their king instead."
[28]So on the advice of his counselors, the king made two gold calves. He said to the 12:28 Exod 32:4; 2 Kgs 10:29; 2 Chr 11:15; Hos 8:4-7
people, "It is too much trouble for you to worship in Jerusalem. O Israel, these are the
gods who brought you out of Egypt!"
[29]He placed these calf idols at the southern and northern ends of Israel—in Bethel 12:29 Gen 28:19; Judg 18:27-31

12:18 As in some Greek manuscripts and Syriac version (see also 4:6; 5:14); Hebrew reads *Adoram.* **12:25** Hebrew *Penuel,* a variant name for Peniel.

THE KINGDOM DIVIDES

Rehoboam's threat of heavier burdens caused a rebellion and divided the nation. Rehoboam ruled the southern kingdom; Jeroboam ruled the northern kingdom. Jeroboam set up idols in Dan and Bethel to discourage worship in Jerusalem. At the same time Aram, Ammon, Moab, and Edom claimed independence from the divided nation.

12:20 This marks the beginning of the division of the kingdom that lasted for centuries. Ten of Israel's 12 tribes followed Jeroboam and called their new nation Israel (the northern kingdom). The other two tribes remained loyal to Rehoboam and called their nation Judah (the southern kingdom). The kingdom did not split overnight. It was already dividing as early as the days of the judges because of tribal jealousies, especially between Ephraim, the most influential tribe of the north, and Judah, the chief tribe of the south.

Before the days of Saul and David, the religious center of Israel was located, for the most part, in the territory of Ephraim. When Solomon built the Temple, he moved the religious center of Israel to Jerusalem. This eventually brought tribal rivalries to the breaking point. (For more information on tribal jealousies and how they affected Israel, see Judges 12:1ff; 2 Samuel 2:4ff; 19:41-43.)

12:28 All Jewish men were required to travel to the Temple three times each year (Deuteronomy 16:16), but Jeroboam set up his own worship centers and told his people it was too much trouble to travel all the way to Jerusalem. Those who obeyed Jeroboam were disobeying God. Some ideas, though practical, may include suggestions that lead you away from God. Don't let anyone talk you out of doing what is right by telling you that moral actions are not worth the effort. Do what God wants, no matter what the cost in time, energy, reputation, or resources.

12:28, 29 Calves were used as idols to symbolize fertility and strength. Pagan gods of the Canaanites were often depicted as standing on calves or bulls. Jeroboam shrewdly placed the golden calves in Bethel and Dan, strategic locations. Bethel was just 10 miles north of Jerusalem on the main road, enticing the citizens from the north to stop there instead of traveling the rest of the way to Jerusalem. Dan was the northernmost city in Israel, so people living in the north far from Jerusalem were attracted to its convenient location. As leader of the northern kingdom, Jeroboam wanted to establish his own worship centers; otherwise his people would make regular trips to Jerusalem, and his authority would be undermined. Soon this substitute religion had little in common with true faith in God.

12:30 2 Kgs 17:21
12:31 2 Kgs 17:32; 2 Chr 11:13-15

and in Dan. 30 This became a great sin, for the people worshiped them, traveling even
as far as Dan.
31 Jeroboam built shrines at the pagan high places and ordained priests from the rank
and file of the people—those who were not from the priestly tribe of Levi. 32 Jeroboam

JEROBOAM

Even clear warnings are hard to obey. The Bible is filled with stories of people who had direction from God and yet chose their own way. Their disobedience was rarely due to ignorance of what God wanted; rather, it grew out of stubborn selfishness. Jeroboam was a consistent example of this all-too-human trait.

During his construction activities, Solomon noticed young Jeroboam's natural leadership skills and made him a special project foreman. Shortly after this, God contacted Jeroboam through the prophet Ahijah. He told Jeroboam that God would punish David's dynasty by tearing the kingdom from Solomon's son and that Jeroboam would rule the 10 northern tribes. And God made it clear that the same fate would destroy the people of Jeroboam's family if they refused to obey God. Apparently Solomon heard about these events and tried to have Jeroboam killed. The future king escaped to Egypt, where he stayed until Solomon died.

When Rehoboam, Solomon's heir, took the throne, Jeroboam returned. He represented the people in demanding that the new king be more lenient than his father. Rehoboam's unwise choice to reject his people's request led to their rejecting him as king. Only Judah and the annexed tribe of Benjamin remained loyal to David's dynasty. The other 10 tribes made Jeroboam king.

Rather than seeing this fulfillment of God's promise as motivation to obey God, Jeroboam decided to do whatever he could to secure his position. He led his kingdom away from the God, who had allowed him to reign. God had already warned him of the consequences of this action—his family was eventually wiped out. And Jeroboam set into motion events that would lead to the destruction of the northern kingdom.

Sin's consequences are guaranteed in God's Word, but the timing of those consequences is hard to predict. When we do something directly opposed to God's commands and there isn't immediate disaster, we are often fooled into believing we got away with disobedience. But that is a dangerous assumption. Jeroboam's life should make us recognize our frequent need to admit our disobedience and ask God to forgive us.

Strengths and accomplishments
- An effective leader and organizer
- First king of the 10 tribes of Israel in the divided kingdom
- A charismatic leader with much popular support

Weaknesses and mistakes
- Erected idols in Israel to keep people away from the Temple in Jerusalem
- Appointed priests from outside the tribe of Levi
- Depended more on his own cunning than on God's promises

Lessons from his life
- Great opportunities are often destroyed by small decisions
- Careless efforts to correct another's errors often lead to the same errors
- Mistakes always occur when we attempt to take over God's role in a situation

Vital statistics
- Where: The northern kingdom of Israel
- Occupations: Project foreman, king of Israel
- Relatives: Father: Nebat. Mother: Zeruah. Sons: Abijah, Nadab
- Contemporaries: Solomon, Nathan, Ahijah, Rehoboam

Key verses "But even after this, Jeroboam did not turn from his evil ways. He continued to choose priests from the rank and file of the people. Anyone who wanted to could become a priest for the pagan shrines. This became a great sin and resulted in the destruction of Jeroboam's kingdom and the death of all his family" (1 Kings 13:33, 34).

Jeroboam's story is told in 1 Kings 11:26—14:20. He is also mentioned in 2 Chronicles 10—13.

12:30 Jeroboam and his advisers did not learn from Israel's previous disaster with a golden calf (Exodus 32). Perhaps they were ignorant of Scripture, or maybe they knew about the event and decided to ignore it. Study the Bible to become aware of God's acts in history, and then apply the important lessons to your life. If you learn from the past, you will not face disaster as a result of repeating others' mistakes (Isaiah 42:23; 1 Corinthians 10:11).

12:32, 33 In the days of Israel's founding fathers, the city of Bethel was a symbol of commitment to God because it was there that Jacob had rededicated himself to God (Genesis 28:16-22). But Jeroboam turned the city into Israel's chief religious center, intending it to compete with Jerusalem. Bethel's religion, however, centered on an idol, and this led to Israel's eventual downfall. Bethel developed a reputation as a wicked and idolatrous city. The prophets Hosea and Amos recognized the sins of Bethel and condemned the city for its godless ways (Hosea 4:15-17; 10:8; Amos 5:4-6).

also instituted a religious festival in Bethel, held on a day in midautumn,* similar to the annual Festival of Shelters in Judah. There at Bethel he himself offered sacrifices to the calves he had made. And it was at Bethel that he appointed priests for the pagan shrines he had made. 33 So on the appointed day in midautumn, a day that he himself had designated, Jeroboam offered sacrifices on the altar at Bethel. He instituted a religious festival for Israel, and he went up to the altar to burn incense.

12:32 Lev 23:33-34; Num 29:12

2. Kings of Israel and Judah

A Prophet Denounces Jeroboam

13 At the LORD's command, a man of God from Judah went to Bethel, and he arrived there just as Jeroboam was approaching the altar to offer a sacrifice. 2 Then at the LORD's command, he shouted, "O altar, altar! This is what the LORD says: A child named Josiah will be born into the dynasty of David. On you he will sacrifice the priests from the pagan shrines who come here to burn incense, and human bones will be burned on you." 3 That same day the man of God gave a sign to prove his message, and he said, "The LORD has promised to give this sign: This altar will split apart, and its ashes will be poured out on the ground."

4 King Jeroboam was very angry with the man of God for speaking against the altar. So he pointed at the man and shouted, "Seize that man!" But instantly the king's hand became paralyzed in that position, and he couldn't pull it back. 5 At the same time a wide crack appeared in the altar, and the ashes poured out, just as the man of God had predicted in his message from the LORD.

6 The king cried out to the man of God, "Please ask the LORD your God to restore my hand again!" So the man of God prayed to the LORD, and the king's hand became normal again.

7 Then the king said to the man of God, "Come to the palace with me and have something to eat, and I will give you a gift."

8 But the man of God said to the king, "Even if you gave me half of everything you own, I would not go with you. I would not eat any food or drink any water in this place. 9 For the LORD gave me this command: 'You must not eat any food or drink any water while you are there, and do not return to Judah by the same way you came.'" 10 So he left Bethel and went home another way.

11 As it happened, there was an old prophet living in Bethel, and his sons came home and told him what the man of God had done in Bethel that day. They also told him what he had said to the king. 12 The old prophet asked them, "Which way did he go?" So they told their father which road the man of God had taken. 13 "Quick, saddle the donkey," the old man said. And when they had saddled the donkey for him, 14 he rode after the man of God and found him sitting under an oak tree.

The old prophet asked him, "Are you the man of God who came from Judah?"

"Yes," he replied, "I am."

15 Then he said to the man of God, "Come home with me and eat some food."

16 "No, I cannot," he replied. "I am not allowed to eat any food or drink any water here in this place. 17 For the LORD gave me this command: 'You must not eat any food or drink any water while you are there, and do not return to Judah by the same way you came.'"

18 But the old prophet answered, "I am a prophet, too, just as you are. And an angel gave me this message from the LORD: 'Bring him home with you, and give him food to eat and water to drink.'" But the old man was lying to him. 19 So they went back together, and the man of God ate some food and drank some water at the prophet's home.

13:1 2 Kgs 23:17
13:2 2 Kgs 23:15-16, 20
13:6 Exod 8:8, 28; 9:28; Jer 37:3; Acts 8:24
13:7 1 Sam 9:7; 2 Kgs 5:15
13:8 Num 22:18
13:9 Num 22:18; 24:13
13:16 1 Kgs 13:8

12:32 Hebrew *on the fifteenth day of the eighth month* (also in 12:33). This day of the Hebrew lunar calendar occurs in late October or early November, exactly one month after the annual Festival of Shelters in Judah (see Lev 23:34).

13:2 Three hundred years later, this prophecy was fulfilled in every detail when Josiah killed the pagan priests at their own altars. The story is found in 2 Kings 23:1-20.

13:7-32 This prophet had been given strict orders from God not to eat or drink anything while on his mission (13:9). He died because he listened to a man who claimed to have a message from God, rather than to God himself. This prophet should have followed God's word instead of hearsay. Trust what God's Word says rather than what someone claims is true. And disregard what others claim are messages from God if their words contradict the Bible.

20 Then while they were sitting at the table, a message from the LORD came to the old
13:21 1 Sam 13:14
prophet. 21 He cried out to the man of God from Judah, "This is what the LORD says: You
have defied the LORD's message and have disobeyed the command the LORD your God
gave you. 22 You came back to this place and ate food and drank water where he told you
not to eat or drink. Because of this, your body will not be buried in the grave of your
ancestors."

23 Now after the man of God had finished eating and drinking, the prophet saddled
13:24 1 Kgs 20:36
his own donkey for him, 24 and the man of God started off again. But as he was traveling
along, a lion came out and killed him. His body lay there on the road, with the donkey
and the lion standing beside it. 25 People came by and saw the body lying in the road
and the lion standing beside it, and they went and reported it in Bethel, where the old
prophet lived.

26 When the old prophet heard the report, he said, "It is the man of God who disobeyed
the LORD's command. The LORD has fulfilled his word by causing the lion to attack and
kill him."

27 Then the prophet said to his sons, "Saddle a donkey for me." So they saddled a
donkey, 28 and he went out and found the body lying in the road. The donkey and lion
were still standing there beside it, for the lion had not eaten the body nor attacked the
donkey. 29 So the prophet laid the body of the man of God on the donkey and took it back
to the city to mourn over him and bury him. 30 He laid the body in his own grave, crying
out in grief, "Oh, my brother!"

13:31 2 Kgs 23:17-18
31 Afterward the prophet said to his sons, "When I die, bury me in the grave where the
13:32 1 Kgs 16:24
man of God is buried. Lay my bones beside his bones. 32 For the message the LORD told
him to proclaim against the altar in Bethel and against the pagan shrines in the towns of
13:33 1 Kgs 12:31; 2 Chr 13:9
Samaria will surely come true."

33 But even after this, Jeroboam did not turn from his evil ways. He continued to
13:34 1 Kgs 14:10; 15:29; 2 Kgs 17:21
choose priests from the rank and file of the people. Anyone who wanted to could become
a priest for the pagan shrines. 34 This became a great sin and resulted in the destruction
of Jeroboam's kingdom and the death of all his family.

Ahijah's Prophecy against Jeroboam

14:2 1 Sam 28:7-8; 2 Sam 14:2-3; 2 Chr 18:29
14 At that time Jeroboam's son Abijah became very sick. 2 So Jeroboam told his wife,
"Disguise yourself so that no one will recognize you as the queen. Then go to the
prophet Ahijah at Shiloh—the man who told me I would become king. 3 Take him a gift
14:3 1 Sam 9:7-8; 2 Kgs 4:42
of ten loaves of bread, some cakes, and a jar of honey, and ask him what will happen to
the boy."

14:4 1 Sam 3:2-3; 4:15
4 So Jeroboam's wife went to Ahijah's home at Shiloh. He was an old man now and
could no longer see. 5 But the LORD had told Ahijah, "Jeroboam's wife will come here,
pretending to be someone else. She will ask you about her son, for he is very sick. You
must give her the answer that I give you."

6 So when Ahijah heard her footsteps at the door, he called out, "Come in, wife of
Jeroboam! Why are you pretending to be someone else?" Then he told her, "I have
14:7 1 Kgs 11:28, 31
bad news for you. 7 Give your husband, Jeroboam, this message from the LORD, the
God of Israel: 'I promoted you from the ranks of the common people and made you
14:8 1 Kgs 11:33, 38; 15:5
ruler over my people Israel. 8 I ripped the kingdom away from the family of David and
gave it to you. But you have not been like my servant David, who obeyed my
commands and followed me with all his heart and always did whatever I wanted him

---

13:24, 25 Lions are mentioned frequently in the Old Testament. They were common enough to be a threat both to people and to their flocks. Samson (Judges 14:5, 6), David (1 Samuel 17:34-37), and Benaiah (2 Samuel 23:20) all faced lions. The fact that the lion and the donkey were standing by the prophet's body showed that this was a divine judgment. Normally, the lion would have attacked the donkey and/or devoured the man.

13:33, 34 Under penalty of death, God had forbidden anyone to be a priest who was not from the tribe of Levi (Numbers 3:10). Levites were assured of lifetime support from the tithe, so they did not have to spend time farming, worrying about tribal interests, or fearing for their financial future. Jeroboam's new priests were financed by the king and his fees. They had to mix priestly and secular duties, and they quickly fell into party politics. Because they didn't have job security, they were easily corrupted by bribes. Jeroboam's disobedience was the downfall of true religion in the northern kingdom.

to do. 9You have done more evil than all who lived before you. You have made other
gods and have made me furious with your gold calves. And since you have turned
your back on me, 10I will bring disaster on your dynasty and kill all your sons, slave
or free alike. I will burn up your royal dynasty as one burns up trash until it is all gone.
11I, the LORD, vow that the members of your family who die in the city will be eaten
by dogs, and those who die in the field will be eaten by vultures.' "
12Then Ahijah said to Jeroboam's wife, "Go on home, and when you enter the city,
the child will die. 13All Israel will mourn for him and bury him. He is the only member
of your family who will have a proper burial, for this child is the only good thing that
the LORD, the God of Israel, sees in the entire family of Jeroboam. 14And the LORD will
raise up a king over Israel who will destroy the family of Jeroboam. This will happen
today, even now! 15Then the LORD will shake Israel like a reed whipped about in a
stream. He will uproot the people of Israel from this good land that he gave their
ancestors and will scatter them beyond the Euphrates River,* for they have angered the
LORD by worshiping Asherah poles. 16He will abandon Israel because Jeroboam sinned
and made all of Israel sin along with him."
17So Jeroboam's wife returned to Tirzah, and the child died just as she walked through
the door of her home. 18When the people of Israel buried him, they mourned for him, as
the LORD had promised through the prophet Ahijah.
19The rest of the events of Jeroboam's reign, all his wars and how he ruled, are
recorded in *The Book of the History of the Kings of Israel*. 20Jeroboam reigned in Israel
twenty-two years. When Jeroboam died, his son Nadab became the next king.

Rehoboam Rules in Judah

21Meanwhile, Rehoboam son of Solomon was king in Judah. He was forty-one years
old when he became king, and he reigned seventeen years in Jerusalem, the city the
LORD had chosen from among all the tribes of Israel as the place to honor his name.
Rehoboam's mother was Naamah, an Ammonite woman. 22During Rehoboam's
reign, the people of Judah did what was evil in the LORD's sight, arousing his anger
with their sin, for it was even worse than that of their ancestors. 23They built pagan
shrines and set up sacred pillars and Asherah poles on every high hill and under every
green tree. 24There were even shrine prostitutes throughout the land. The people
imitated the detestable practices of the pagan nations the LORD had driven from the
land ahead of the Israelites.
25In the fifth year of King Rehoboam's reign, King Shishak of Egypt came up and
attacked Jerusalem. 26He ransacked the Temple of the LORD and the royal palace and
stole everything, including all the gold shields Solomon had made. 27Afterward Rehoboam made bronze shields as substitutes, and he entrusted them to the care of the palace

14:9 Exod 34:17; 2 Chr 11:15; Ps 50:17; Ezek 23:35
14:10 Deut 32:36; 1 Kgs 15:29; 21:22; 2 Kgs 9:8-9
14:11 1 Kgs 16:4-7; 21:24
14:12 1 Kgs 14:17
14:14 1 Kgs 15:27, 29
14:15 Deut 12:3-4; Ps 52:5
14:16 1 Kgs 12:30
14:17 1 Kgs 15:21, 33; 16:6-9
14:19 1 Kgs 14:29; 15:7, 23, 31; 16:4-7, 14, 20; 1 Chr 9:1
14:21, 25-31 //2 Chr 12:9-16
14:21 1 Kgs 11:32, 36; 2 Chr 12:13
14:22 Deut 32:21; 2 Chr 12:1, 14
14:23 Deut 12:2; 16:22; 2 Kgs 17:10; Jer 2:20; Ezek 16:24
14:24 Deut 23:17-18; 2 Kgs 23:7
14:25 2 Chr 12:2, 9
14:26 1 Kgs 10:16-17; 15:18

14:15 Hebrew *the river.*

14:10, 11 These disasters were practical applications to Israel of the specific teachings of Deuteronomy (see Deuteronomy 28:15-19, 36-68; 30:15-20). Ahijah is prophesying the downfall of Israel for its flagrant violation of God's commands.

14:14 Who was this king who would "destroy the family of Jeroboam"? His name was Baasha, and he would kill all of Jeroboam's descendants (15:27-30).

14:15 "Asherah poles" refers to idol worship. Wooden images were made for the worship of Asherah, a Canaanite mother-goddess.

14:19 Three books are mentioned in 1 and 2 Kings—*The Book of the History of the Kings of Israel* (14:19), *The Book of the History of the Kings of Judah* (14:29), and *The Book of the Acts of Solomon* (11:41). These historical records of Israel and Judah were the main sources of material God directed the author to use to write 1 and 2 Kings. No copies of these books have been found.

14:23 "Sacred pillars" were pillars of stone placed next to pagan altars. These pillars were supposed to represent deity.

14:25 When Rehoboam came to power, he inherited a mighty kingdom. Everything he could ever want was given to him. But apparently he did not recognize why he had so much or how it had been obtained. To teach Rehoboam a lesson, God allowed Shishak of Egypt to invade Judah and Israel. Egypt was no longer the world power it had once been, and Shishak, possibly resenting Solomon's enormous success, was determined to change that. Shishak's army was not strong enough to destroy Judah and Israel, but he weakened them so much that they were never the same again.

14:25, 26 Just five years after Solomon died, the Temple and palace were ransacked by foreign invaders. How quickly the glory, power, and money disappeared! When the people became spiritually corrupt and immoral (14:24), it was just a short time until they lost everything. Wealth, idol worship, and immorality had become more important to them than God. When God is gone from our lives, everything else becomes useless, no matter how valuable it seems.

guard officers. [28]Whenever the king went to the Temple of the LORD, the guards would
carry them along and then return them to the guardroom.
[29]The rest of the events in Rehoboam's reign and all his deeds are recorded in *The*
14:30 1 Kgs 12:21; 15:6 *Book of the History of the Kings of Judah.* [30]There was constant war between Rehoboam
and Jeroboam. [31]When Rehoboam died, he was buried among his ancestors in the City
of David. His mother was Naamah, an Ammonite woman. Then his son Abijam* became
the next king.

Abijam Rules in Judah

15:1-2 //2 Chr 13:1-2 **15** Abijam* began to rule over Judah in the eighteenth year of Jeroboam's reign in
Israel. [2]He reigned in Jerusalem three years. His mother was Maacah, the daughter
15:3 1 Kgs 11:4 of Absalom.* [3]He committed the same sins as his father before him, and his heart was
15:4 2 Chr 21:7 not right with the LORD his God, as the heart of his ancestor David had been. [4]But for
David's sake, the LORD his God allowed his dynasty to continue,* and he gave Abijam
15:5 2 Sam 11:2-27; 1 Kgs 9:4; 14:8 a son to rule after him in Jerusalem. [5]For David had done what was pleasing in the
LORD's sight and had obeyed the LORD's commands throughout his life, except in the
affair concerning Uriah the Hittite.
15:6-8 2 Chr 13:22–14:1 [6]There was war between Abijam and Jeroboam* throughout Abijam's reign. [7]The
rest of the events in Abijam's reign and all his deeds are recorded in *The Book of the*
History of the Kings of Judah. There was constant war between Abijam and Jeroboam.
[8]When Abijam died, he was buried in the City of David. Then his son Asa became the
next king.

Asa Rules in Judah

15:9-22 //2 Chr 14:2-3; 15:6–16:6 [9]Asa began to rule over Judah in the twentieth year of Jeroboam's reign in Israel. [10]He
reigned in Jerusalem forty-one years. His grandmother* was Maacah, the daughter of

14:31 Also known as *Abijah.* **15:1** Also known as *Abijah.* **15:2** Hebrew *Abishalom* (also in 15:10), a variant name for Absalom; compare 2 Chr 11:20. **15:4** Hebrew *gave him a lamp in Jerusalem.* **15:6** As in a few Hebrew manuscripts; most Hebrew manuscripts read *between Rehoboam and Jeroboam.* **15:10** Hebrew *his mother* (also in 15:13); compare 15:2.

THE APPEAL OF IDOLS

On the surface, the lives of the kings don't make sense. How could they run to idolatry so fast when they had God's word (at least some of it), prophets, and the example of David? Here are some of the reasons for the enticement of idols:

	The Appeal of Idols	*Modern Parallel*
POWER	The people wanted freedom from the authority of both God and the priests. They wanted their religion to fit their life-style, not their life-style to fit their religion.	People do not want to answer to a greater authority. Instead of having power *over* others, God wants us to have the Holy Spirit's power to *help* others.
PLEASURE	Idol worship exalted sensuality without responsibility or guilt. People acted out the vicious and sensuous personalities of the gods they worshiped, thus gaining approval for their degraded lives.	People deify pleasure, seeking it at the expense of everything else. Instead of seeking pleasure that leads to long-range disaster, God calls us to seek the kind of pleasure that leads to long-range rewards.
PASSION	Mankind was reduced to little more than animals. The people did not have to be viewed as unique individuals but could be exploited sexually, politically, and economically.	Like animals, people let physical drives and passion rule them. Instead of seeking passion that exploits others, God calls us to redirect our passions to areas that build others up.
PRAISE AND POPULARITY	The high and holy nature of God was replaced by gods who were more a reflection of human nature, thus more culturally suitable to the people. These gods no longer required sacrifice, just a token of appeasement.	Sacrifice is seen as self-inflicted punishment, making no sense. Success is to be sought at all costs. Instead of seeking praise for ourselves, God calls us to praise him and those who honor him.

As societies change, they often throw out norms and values no longer considered necessary or acceptable. Believers must be careful not to follow society's example if it discards God's Word. When society does that, only godlessness and evil remain.

15:5 See 2 Samuel 11 for the story of David and Uriah the Hittite.

15:9 See Asa's Profile in 2 Chronicles 15 for more information on this king.

Absalom. 11 Asa did what was pleasing in the LORD's sight, as his ancestor David had done. 12 He banished the shrine prostitutes from the land and removed all the idols his ancestors had made. 13 He even deposed his grandmother Maacah from her position as queen mother because she had made an obscene Asherah pole. He cut down the pole and burned it in the Kidron Valley. 14 Although the pagan shrines were not completely removed, Asa remained faithful to the LORD throughout his life. 15 He brought into the Temple of the LORD the silver and gold and the utensils that he and his father had dedicated.

16 There was constant war between King Asa of Judah and King Baasha of Israel. 17 King Baasha of Israel invaded Judah and fortified Ramah in order to prevent anyone from entering or leaving King Asa's territory in Judah. 18 Asa responded by taking all the silver and gold that was left in the treasuries of the LORD's Temple and the royal palace. He sent it with some of his officials to Ben-hadad son of Tabrimmon and grandson of Hezion, the king of Aram, who was ruling in Damascus, along with this message:

> 19 "Let us renew the treaty that existed between your father and my father. See, I am sending you a gift of silver and gold. Break your treaty with King Baasha of Israel so that he will leave me alone."

20 Ben-hadad agreed to King Asa's request and sent his armies to attack Israel. They conquered the towns of Ijon, Dan, Abel-beth-maacah, and all Kinnereth, with all the land of Naphtali. 21 As soon as Baasha of Israel heard what was happening, he abandoned his project of fortifying Ramah and withdrew to Tirzah. 22 Then King Asa sent an order throughout Judah, requiring that everyone, without exception, help to carry away the building stones and timbers that Baasha had been using to fortify Ramah. Asa used these materials to fortify the town of Geba in Benjamin and the town of Mizpah.

23 The rest of the events in Asa's reign, the extent of his power, and the names of the cities he built are recorded in *The Book of the History of the Kings of Judah.* In his old age his feet became diseased. 24 When Asa died, he was buried with his ancestors in the City of David. Then his son Jehoshaphat became the next king.

Nadab Rules in Israel

25 Nadab son of Jeroboam began to rule over Israel in the second year of King Asa's reign in Judah. He reigned in Israel two years. 26 But he did what was evil in the LORD's sight and followed the example of his father, continuing the sins of idolatry that Jeroboam had led Israel to commit.

27 Then Baasha son of Ahijah, from the tribe of Issachar, plotted against Nadab and assassinated him while he and the Israelite army were laying siege to the Philistine town of Gibbethon. 28 Baasha killed Nadab in the third year of King Asa's reign in Judah, and he became the next king of Israel. 29 He immediately killed all the descendants of King Jeroboam, so that not one of the royal family was left, just as the LORD had promised concerning Jeroboam by the prophet Ahijah from Shiloh. 30 This was done because Jeroboam had aroused the anger of the LORD, the God of Israel, by the sins he had committed and the sins he had led Israel to commit. 31 The rest of the events in Nadab's reign and all his deeds are recorded in *The Book of the History of the Kings of Israel.*

Baasha Rules in Israel

32 There was constant war between Asa and King Baasha of Israel. 33 Baasha began to rule over Israel in the third year of King Asa's reign in Judah. Baasha reigned in Tirzah twenty-four years. 34 But he did what was evil in the LORD's sight and followed the example of Jeroboam, continuing the sins of idolatry that Jeroboam had led Israel to commit.

15:11 2 Chr 14:2; 15:17
15:12 Deut 23:17-18; 1 Kgs 22:46; 2 Chr 15:2-5
15:13 1 Kgs 14:24; 2 Chr 15:16-18
15:14 1 Kgs 8:61; 22:43; 2 Kgs 12:3
15:17 Josh 18:25; 2 Chr 16:1-6
15:18 1 Kgs 14:26; 2 Kgs 12:17-18
15:19 2 Chr 16:7
15:22 Josh 18:24; 2 Chr 16:6
15:23-24 //2 Chr 16:11–17:1
15:25 1 Kgs 14:20
15:26 1 Kgs 12:28-33; 13:33; 14:16
15:27 Josh 19:44; 21:23-24
15:29 1 Kgs 14:9-16
15:31 1 Kgs 14:19
15:32 2 Chr 15:16

15:15 These gifts for the Temple were articles dedicated to God as sacred offerings that Abijah had taken in his war with Jeroboam (2 Chronicles 13:16, 17) and that Asa had taken when he defeated the Ethiopians (2 Chronicles 14:12, 13).

15:16 Baasha seized the throne from Nadab (15:27, 28), who had replaced his father, Jeroboam, as king.

15:29 See 1 Kings 14:12-14 for Ahijah's prediction of this event.

15:30 All the descendants of Jeroboam were killed because Jeroboam had led Israel into sin. Sin is always judged harshly, but the worst sinners are those who lead others into doing wrong. Jesus said it would be better if such people had millstones tied around their necks and were thrown into the sea (Mark 9:42). If you have taken the responsibility for leading others, remember the consequences of leading them astray. Teaching the truth is a responsibility that goes with the privilege of leadership.

16:1 1 Kgs 16:7; 2 Chr 19:2; 20:34
16:2 1 Sam 2:8; 1 Kgs 14:7-9
16:3 1 Kgs 14:10; 15:29; 21:21
16:4 1 Kgs 14:11
16:7 1 Kgs 16:1
16:9 2 Kgs 9:30-33
16:11 1 Kgs 15:29
16:13 Deut 32:21; 1 Kgs 15:30

16 This message from the LORD was delivered to King Baasha by the prophet Jehu
son of Hanani: 2"I lifted you out of the dust to make you ruler of my people Israel,
but you have followed the evil example of Jeroboam. You have aroused my anger by
causing my people to sin. 3So now I will destroy you and your family, just as I destroyed
the descendants of Jeroboam son of Nebat. 4Those of your family who die in the city
will be eaten by dogs, and those who die in the field will be eaten by the vultures."
5The rest of the events in Baasha's reign and the extent of his power are recorded in
The Book of the History of the Kings of Israel. 6When Baasha died, he was buried in
Tirzah. Then his son Elah became the next king.
7This message from the LORD had been spoken against Baasha and his family through
the prophet Jehu son of Hanani. It was delivered because Baasha had done what was evil
in the LORD's sight, arousing him to anger by his sins, just like the family of Jeroboam,
and also because Baasha had destroyed the family of Jeroboam.

Elah Rules in Israel

8Elah son of Baasha began to rule over Israel from Tirzah in the twenty-sixth year of
King Asa's reign in Judah. He reigned in Israel two years. 9Then Zimri, who commanded
half of the royal chariots, made plans to kill him. One day in Tirzah, Elah was getting
drunk at the home of Arza, the supervisor of the palace. 10Zimri walked in and struck
him down and killed him. This happened in the twenty-seventh year of King Asa's reign
in Judah. Then Zimri became the next king.
11Zimri immediately killed the entire royal family of Baasha, and he did not leave a
single male child. He even destroyed distant relatives and friends. 12So Zimri destroyed
the dynasty of Baasha as the LORD had promised through the prophet Jehu. 13This

KINGS TO DATE AND THEIR ENEMIES

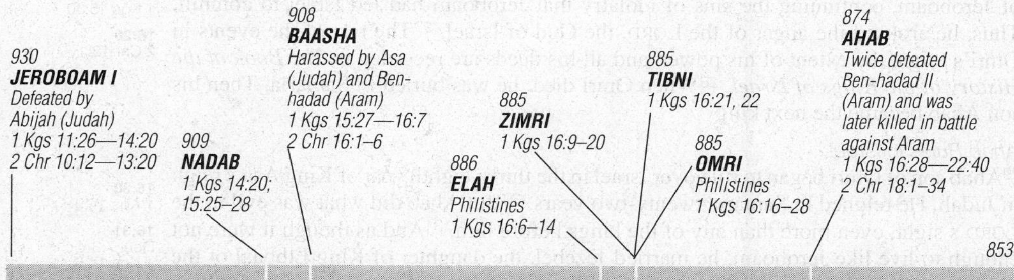

All dates are B.C.
For all the kings of Israel and Judah, see the chart at the end of 1 Kings.

16:1-7 God destroyed Jeroboam's descendants for their flagrant sins, and yet Baasha repeated the same mistakes. He did not learn from the example of those who went before him; he did not stop to think that his sin would be punished. Make sure you learn from your past, the experiences of others, and the lives of those whose stories are told in the Bible. Don't repeat mistakes.

happened because of the sins of Baasha and his son Elah and because of all the sins they
led Israel to commit, arousing the anger of the LORD, the God of Israel, with their idols.
14 The rest of the events in Elah's reign and all his deeds are recorded in *The Book of the*
History of the Kings of Israel.

Zimri Rules in Israel

15 Zimri began to rule over Israel from Tirzah in the twenty-seventh year of King Asa's
reign in Judah, but he reigned only seven days. When the army of Israel, which was
then engaged in attacking the Philistine town of Gibbethon, 16 heard that Zimri had
assassinated the king, they chose Omri, commander of the army, as their new king.
17 So Omri led the army of Israel away from Gibbethon to attack Tirzah, Israel's
capital. 18 When Zimri saw that the city had been taken, he went into the citadel of the
king's house and burned it down over himself and died in the flames. 19 For he, too,
had done what was evil in the LORD's sight and followed the example of Jeroboam,
continuing the sins of idolatry that Jeroboam had led Israel to commit. 20 The rest of
the events of Zimri's reign and his conspiracy are recorded in *The Book of the History*
of the Kings of Israel.

Omri Rules in Israel

21 But now the people of Israel were divided into two groups. Half the people tried to
make Tibni son of Ginath their king, while the other half supported Omri. 22 But Omri's
supporters defeated the supporters of Tibni son of Ginath. So Tibni was killed, and Omri
became the next king.

23 Omri began to rule over Israel in the thirty-first year of King Asa's reign in Judah.
He reigned twelve years in all, six of them in Tirzah. 24 Then Omri bought the hill now
known as Samaria from its owner, Shemer, for 150 pounds of silver.* He built a city on
it and called the city Samaria in honor of Shemer. 25 But Omri did what was evil in the
LORD's sight, even more than any of the kings before him. 26 He followed the example
of Jeroboam, continuing the sins of idolatry that Jeroboam had led Israel to commit.
Thus, he aroused the anger of the LORD, the God of Israel. 27 The rest of the events in
Omri's reign, the extent of his power, and all his deeds are recorded in *The Book of the*
History of the Kings of Israel. 28 When Omri died, he was buried in Samaria. Then his
son Ahab became the next king.

Ahab Rules in Israel

29 Ahab son of Omri began to rule over Israel in the thirty-eighth year of King Asa's reign
in Judah. He reigned in Samaria twenty-two years. 30 But Ahab did what was evil in the
LORD's sight, even more than any of the kings before him. 31 And as though it were not
enough to live like Jeroboam, he married Jezebel, the daughter of King Ethbaal of the
Sidonians, and he began to worship Baal. 32 First he built a temple and an altar for Baal
in Samaria. 33 Then he set up an Asherah pole. He did more to arouse the anger of the
LORD, the God of Israel, than any of the other kings of Israel before him.

34 It was during his reign that Hiel, a man from Bethel, rebuilt Jericho. When he laid
the foundations, his oldest son, Abiram, died. And when he finally completed it by setting
up the gates, his youngest son, Segub, died. This all happened according to the message
from the LORD concerning Jericho spoken by Joshua son of Nun.

16:24 Hebrew *for 2 talents* [68 kilograms] *of silver.*

16:14 1 Kgs 16:4-7, 20, 28, 30
16:18 1 Sam 31:4-5; 2 Sam 17:23
16:19 1 Kgs 12:28
16:20 1 Kgs 16:14, 27
16:24 1 Kgs 13:32
16:25 1 Kgs 14:9; Mic 6:16
16:26 1 Kgs 15:30
16:28 2 Chr 18:1
16:30 1 Kgs 14:9
16:31 Deut 7:3-4; 1 Kgs 11:5; 2 Kgs 10:18; 17:16
16:32 2 Kgs 10:21, 26-27
16:33 1 Kgs 21:19, 25; 2 Kgs 13:6
16:34 Josh 6:26

16:21, 22 Omri began his reign as political dissension brewed in Israel. After Zimri killed himself, the Israelite army chose Omri, their commander, as the next ruler. Tibni, Omri's chief rival to the throne, died, and Omri then began his evil reign. During his 12-year rule over Israel, he was a shrewd and capable leader. He organized the building of his new capital city, Samaria, while strengthening the nation politically and militarily. But he did not care about the nation's spiritual condition (Micah 6:16), and he purposely led Israel farther from God in order to put more power in his own hands.

16:24 Omri's new capital, Samaria, offered some political advantages. The city was his personal property, so he had total control over it. Samaria also commanded a hilltop position, which made it easy to defend. Omri died before completing the city. So his son, Ahab, completed it, building not only the beautiful ivory palace (1 Kings 22:39; Amos 3:13-15), but also a temple to the god Baal. Samaria served as the capital city for the rest of Israel's dynasties until it fell to the Assyrians in 722 B.C. (2 Kings 17:5).

16:31 Ahab's evil wife, Jezebel, came from the Phoenician city of Tyre where her father had been a high priest and eventually king. Jezebel worshiped the god Baal. In order to please her, Ahab built a temple and an altar for Baal (16:32), thus promoting idolatry and leading the entire nation into sin. (For more about Baal, see the note on 18:18.)

3. Elijah's ministry

Elijah Fed by Ravens

17:1 Judg 12:4 1 Kgs 22:14 Luke 4:25 Jas 5:17

17 Now Elijah, who was from Tishbe in Gilead, told King Ahab, "As surely as the
LORD, the God of Israel, lives—the God whom I worship and serve—there will
be no dew or rain during the next few years unless I give the word!"
[2]Then the LORD said to Elijah, [3]"Go to the east and hide by Kerith Brook at a place
east of where it enters the Jordan River. [4]Drink from the brook and eat what the ravens
bring you, for I have commanded them to bring you food."
[5]So Elijah did as the LORD had told him and camped beside Kerith Brook. [6]The ravens
brought him bread and meat each morning and evening, and he drank from the brook.
[7]But after a while the brook dried up, for there was no rainfall anywhere in the land.

The Widow at Zarephath

17:9 Obad 1:20 Luke 4:26

[8]Then the LORD said to Elijah, [9]"Go and live in the village of Zarephath, near the city
of Sidon. There is a widow there who will feed you. I have given her my instructions."

17:10 Gen 24:17 John 4:7

[10]So he went to Zarephath. As he arrived at the gates of the village, he saw a widow
gathering sticks, and he asked her, "Would you please bring me a cup of water?" [11]As
she was going to get it, he called to her, "Bring me a bite of bread, too."

17:12 2 Kgs 4:2-7

[12]But she said, "I swear by the LORD your God that I don't have a single piece of bread
in the house. And I have only a handful of flour left in the jar and a little cooking oil in
the bottom of the jug. I was just gathering a few sticks to cook this last meal, and then
my son and I will die."
[13]But Elijah said to her, "Don't be afraid! Go ahead and cook that 'last meal,' but bake
me a little loaf of bread first. Afterward there will still be enough food for you and your
son. [14]For this is what the LORD, the God of Israel, says: There will always be plenty of
flour and oil left in your containers until the time when the LORD sends rain and the crops
grow again!"
[15]So she did as Elijah said, and she and Elijah and her son continued to eat from
her supply of flour and oil for many days. [16]For no matter how much they used, there
was always enough left in the containers, just as the LORD had promised through
Elijah.

17:1 Elijah was the first in a long line of important prophets God sent to Israel and Judah. Israel, the northern kingdom, had no faithful kings throughout its history. Each king was wicked, actually leading the people in worshiping pagan gods. There were few priests left from the tribe of Levi (most had gone to Judah), and the priests appointed by Israel's kings were corrupt and ineffective. With no king or priests to bring God's word to the people, God called prophets to try to rescue Israel from its moral and spiritual decline. For the next 300 years these men and women would play vital roles in both nations, encouraging the people and leaders to turn back to God.

17:1 Those who worshiped Baal believed he was the god who brought the rains and bountiful harvests. So when Elijah walked into the presence of this Baal-worshiping king and told him there would be no rain for several years, Ahab was shocked. Ahab had built a strong military defense, but it would be no help against drought. He had many priests of Baal, but they could not bring rain. Elijah bravely confronted the man who led his people into evil, and he told of a power far greater than any pagan god—the Lord God of Israel. When rebellion and heresy were at an all-time high in Israel, God responded not only with words but with action.

17:10ff In a nation that was required by law to care for its prophets, it is ironic that God turned to ravens (unclean birds) and a widow (a foreigner from Jezebel's home territory) to care for Elijah. God has help where we least expect it. He provides for us in ways that go beyond our narrow definitions or expectations. No matter how bitter our trials or how seemingly hopeless our situation, we should look for God's caring touch. We may find his providence in some strange places!

17:13-16 When the widow of Zarephath met Elijah, she thought she was preparing her last meal. But a simple act of faith produced a miracle. She trusted Elijah and gave all she had to eat to him. Faith is the step between promise and assurance. Miracles seem so out of reach for our feeble faith. But every miracle, large or small, begins with an act of obedience. We may not see the solution until we take the first step of faith.

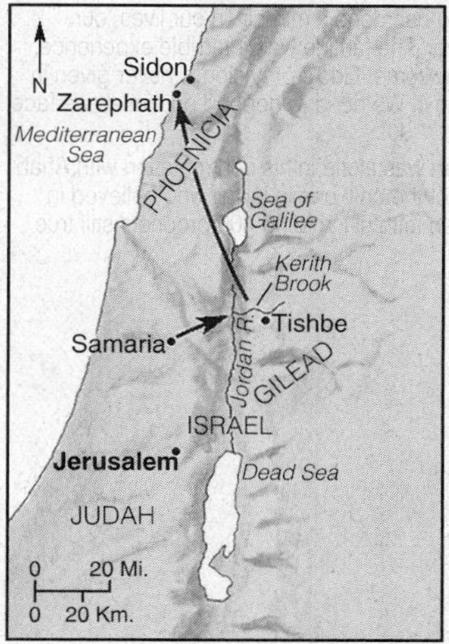

ELIJAH HIDES FROM AHAB
Elijah prophesied a drought and then hid from King Ahab by the Kerith Brook, where he was fed by ravens. When the brook dried up, God sent him to Zarephath in Phoenicia, where a widow and her son fed him and gave him lodging.

17 Some time later, the woman's son became sick. He grew worse and worse, and
finally he died. 18 She then said to Elijah, "O man of God, what have you done to me?
Have you come here to punish my sins by killing my son?"
19 But Elijah replied, "Give me your son." And he took the boy's body from her,
carried him up to the upper room, where he lived, and laid the body on his bed. 20 Then
Elijah cried out to the LORD, "O LORD my God, why have you brought tragedy on this
widow who has opened her home to me, causing her son to die?"
21 And he stretched himself out over the child three times and cried out to the LORD, **17:21** 2 Kgs 4:34; Acts 20:10-12
"O LORD my God, please let this child's life return to him." 22 The LORD heard Elijah's
prayer, and the life of the child returned, and he came back to life! 23 Then Elijah brought **17:23** Heb 11:35
him down from the upper room and gave him to his mother. "Look, your son is alive!"
he said.
24 Then the woman told Elijah, "Now I know for sure that you are a man of God, and **17:24** John 2:11; 3:1-2; 16:30
that the LORD truly speaks through you."

The Contest on Mount Carmel

18 After many months passed, in the third year of the drought, the LORD said to **18:1** Jas 5:17-18
Elijah, "Go and present yourself to King Ahab. Tell him that I will soon send rain!" **18:2** 1 Kgs 16:24
2 So Elijah went to appear before Ahab.
Meanwhile, the famine had become very severe in Samaria. 3 So Ahab summoned **18:3** 1 Kgs 18:16
Obadiah, who was in charge of the palace. (Now Obadiah was a devoted follower of the
LORD. 4 Once when Jezebel had tried to kill all the LORD's prophets, Obadiah had hidden
one hundred of them in two caves. He had put fifty prophets in each cave and had
supplied them with food and water.) 5 Ahab said to Obadiah, "We must check every
spring and valley to see if we can find enough grass to save at least some of my horses
and mules." 6 So they divided the land between them. Ahab went one way by himself,
and Obadiah went another way by himself.
7 As Obadiah was walking along, he saw Elijah coming toward him. Obadiah recognized
him at once and fell to the ground before him. "Is it really you, my lord Elijah?" he asked.
8 "Yes, it is," Elijah replied. "Now go and tell your master I am here."
9 "Oh, sir," Obadiah protested, "what harm have I done to you that you are sending me
to my death at the hands of Ahab? 10 For I swear by the LORD your God that the king has
searched every nation and kingdom on earth from end to end to find you. And each time
when he was told, 'Elijah isn't here,' King Ahab forced the king of that nation to swear
to the truth of his claim. 11 And now you say, 'Go and tell your master that Elijah is here'! **18:12** 2 Kgs 2:16; Ezek 3:12, 14; Acts 8:39
12 But as soon as I leave you, the Spirit of the LORD will carry you away to who knows
where. When Ahab comes and cannot find you, he will kill me. Yet I have been a true
servant of the LORD all my life. 13 Has no one told you, my lord, about the time when **18:13** 1 Kgs 18:3-4

17:17 Even when God has done a miracle in our lives, our troubles may not be over. The famine was a terrible experience, but the worst was yet to come. God's provision is never given in order to let us rest upon it. We need to depend on him as we face each new trial.

18:3, 4 Although Elijah was alone in his confrontation with Ahab and Jezebel, he was not the only one in Israel who believed in God. Obadiah had been faithful in hiding 100 prophets still true to the Lord.

THE SHOWDOWN AT CARMEL
In a showdown with the false prophets of Baal at Mount Carmel, Elijah set out to prove to evil Ahab that only the Lord is God. Elijah then killed the false prophets by the Kishon River and fled back to Jezreel.

Jezebel was trying to kill the LORD's prophets? I hid a hundred of them in two caves and
supplied them with food and water. 14 And now you say, 'Go and tell your master that
Elijah is here'! Sir, if I do that, I'm as good as dead!"
15 But Elijah said, "I swear by the LORD Almighty, in whose presence I stand, that I
will present myself to Ahab today."
18:17 Josh 7:25 16 So Obadiah went to tell Ahab that Elijah had come, and Ahab went out to meet him.
17 "So it's you, is it—Israel's troublemaker?" Ahab asked when he saw him.
18:18 1 Kgs 9:9; 21:25 18 "I have made no trouble for Israel," Elijah replied. "You and your family are the
troublemakers, for you have refused to obey the commands of the LORD and have

---

ELIJAH

Elijah's single-minded commitment to God shocks and challenges us. He was sent to confront, not comfort, and he spoke God's words to a king who often rejected his message just because he brought it. Elijah chose to carry out his ministry for God alone and paid for that decision by experiencing isolation from others who were also faithful to God.

It is interesting to think about the amazing miracles God accomplished through Elijah, but we would do well to focus on the relationship they shared. All that happened in Elijah's life began with the same miracle that is available to us—he responded to the miracle of being able to know God.

For example, after God worked an overwhelming miracle through Elijah in defeating the prophets of Baal, Queen Jezebel retaliated by threatening Elijah's life. And Elijah ran. He felt afraid, depressed, and abandoned. Despite God's provision of food and shelter in the wilderness, Elijah wanted to die. So God presented Elijah with an "audiovisual display" and a message he needed to hear. Elijah witnessed a windstorm, an earthquake, and fire. But the Lord was not in any of those powerful things. Instead, God displayed his presence in a gentle whisper.

Elijah, like us, struggled with his feelings even after this comforting message from God. So God confronted Elijah's emotions and commanded action. He told Elijah what to do next and informed him that part of his loneliness was based on ignorance: Seven thousand others in Israel were still faithful to God.

Even today, God often speaks through the gentle and obvious rather than the spectacular and unusual. God has work for us to do even when we feel fear and failure. And God always has more resources and people than we know about. Although we might wish to do amazing miracles for God, we should instead focus on developing a relationship with him. The real miracle of Elijah's life was his very personal relationship with God. And that miracle is available to us.

Strengths and accomplishments
- Was the most famous and dramatic of Israel's prophets
- Predicted the beginning and end of a three-year drought
- Was used by God to restore a dead child to his mother
- Represented God in a showdown with priests of Baal and Asherah
- Appeared with Moses and Jesus in the New Testament Transfiguration scene

Weaknesses and mistakes
- Chose to work alone and paid for it with isolation and loneliness
- Fled in fear from Jezebel when she threatened his life

Lessons from his life
- We are never closer to defeat than in our moments of greatest victory
- We are never as alone as we may feel; God is always there
- God speaks more frequently in persistent whispers than in shouts

Vital statistics
- Where: Gilead
- Occupation: Prophet
- Contemporaries: Ahab, Jezebel, Ahaziah, Obadiah, Jehu, Hazael

Key verses
"At the customary time for offering the evening sacrifice, Elijah the prophet walked up to the altar and prayed, 'O LORD, God of Abraham, Isaac, and Jacob, prove today that you are God in Israel and that I am your servant. Prove that I have done all this at your command. O LORD, answer me! Answer me so these people will know that you, O LORD, are God and that you have brought them back to yourself.'
"Immediately the fire of the LORD flashed down from heaven and burned up the young bull, the wood, the stones, and the dust. It even licked up all the water in the ditch!" (1 Kings 18:36–38).

Elijah's story is told in 1 Kings 17:1—2 Kings 2:11. He is also mentioned in 2 Chronicles 21:12–15; Malachi 4:5, 6; Matthew 11:14; 16:14; 17:3–13; 27:47–49; Luke 1:17; 4:25, 26; John 1:19–25; Romans 11:2–4; James 5:17, 18.

18:18 Instead of worshiping the true God, Ahab and his wife, Jezebel, worshiped Baal, the most popular Canaanite god. Baal idols were often made in the shape of a bull, representing strength and fertility and reflecting lust for power and sexual pleasure.

worshiped the images of Baal instead. 19Now bring all the people of Israel to Mount
Carmel, with all 450 prophets of Baal and the 400 prophets of Asherah, who are
supported by Jezebel."
20So Ahab summoned all the people and the prophets to Mount Carmel. 21Then Elijah
stood in front of them and said, "How long are you going to waver between two
opinions? If the LORD is God, follow him! But if Baal is God, then follow him!" But the
people were completely silent.
22Then Elijah said to them, "I am the only prophet of the LORD who is left, but Baal
has 450 prophets. 23Now bring two bulls. The prophets of Baal may choose whichever
one they wish and cut it into pieces and lay it on the wood of their altar, but without
setting fire to it. I will prepare the other bull and lay it on the wood on the altar, but not
set fire to it. 24Then call on the name of your god, and I will call on the name of the LORD.
The god who answers by setting fire to the wood is the true God!" And all the people
agreed.
25Then Elijah said to the prophets of Baal, "You go first, for there are many of you.
Choose one of the bulls and prepare it and call on the name of your god. But do not set
fire to the wood."
26So they prepared one of the bulls and placed it on the altar. Then they called on the
name of Baal all morning, shouting, "O Baal, answer us!" But there was no reply of any
kind. Then they danced wildly around the altar they had made.
27About noontime Elijah began mocking them. "You'll have to shout louder," he
scoffed, "for surely he is a god! Perhaps he is deep in thought, or he is relieving himself.
Or maybe he is away on a trip, or he is asleep and needs to be wakened!"
28So they shouted louder, and following their normal custom, they cut themselves
with knives and swords until the blood gushed out. 29They raved all afternoon until the
time of the evening sacrifice, but still there was no reply, no voice, no answer.
30Then Elijah called to the people, "Come over here!" They all crowded around him
as he repaired the altar of the LORD that had been torn down. 31He took twelve stones,
one to represent each of the tribes of Israel,* 32and he used the stones to rebuild the
LORD's altar. Then he dug a trench around the altar large enough to hold about three
gallons.* 33He piled wood on the altar, cut the bull into pieces, and laid the pieces on the
wood. Then he said, "Fill four large jars with water, and pour the water over the offering
and the wood." After they had done this, 34he said, "Do the same thing again!" And when
they were finished, he said, "Now do it a third time!" So they did as he said, 35and the
water ran around the altar and even overflowed the trench.
36At the customary time for offering the evening sacrifice, Elijah the prophet walked
up to the altar and prayed, "O LORD, God of Abraham, Isaac, and Jacob,* prove today
that you are God in Israel and that I am your servant. Prove that I have done all this at

18:19 Josh 19:26
18:21 Josh 24:15; 2 Kgs 17:41
18:22 1 Kgs 19:10, 14
18:24 1 Sam 7:8; 1 Kgs 18:38
18:26 Ps 115:4-5; Jer 10:5
18:28 Lev 19:28; Deut 14:1
18:30 1 Kgs 19:10, 14
18:31 2 Kgs 17:34
18:32 Col 3:17
18:33 Gen 22:9
18:36 Exod 3:6; 4:5; Num 16:28-32

18:31 Hebrew *each of the tribes of the sons of Jacob to whom the LORD had said, "Your name will be Israel."*
18:32 Hebrew *2 seahs* [12 liters] *of seed.* **18:36** Hebrew *and Israel.*

18:19 Ahab brought 850 pagan prophets to Mount Carmel to match wits and power with Elijah. Evil kings hated God's prophets because they spoke against sin and idolatry and undermined their control over the people. With the wicked kings' backing, many pagan prophets sprang up to counter the words of God's prophets. But Elijah showed the people that speaking a prophecy wasn't enough. One needed the power of the living God to fulfill it.

18:21 Elijah challenged the people to take a stand—to follow whoever was the true God. Why did so many people waver between the two choices? Perhaps some were not sure. Many, however, knew that the Lord was God, but they enjoyed the sinful pleasures and other benefits that came with following Ahab in his idolatrous worship. It is important to take a stand for the Lord. If we just drift along with whatever is pleasant and easy, we will someday discover that we have been worshiping a false god—ourselves.

18:29 Although the prophets of Baal raved all afternoon, no one answered them. Their god was silent because it was not real. The gods we may be tempted to follow are not idols of wood or stone, but they are just as false and dangerous because they cause us to depend on something other than God. Power, status, appearance, or material possessions can become our gods if we devote our lives to them. But when we reach times of crisis and desperately call out to these gods, there will only be silence. They can offer no true answers, no guidance, and no wisdom.

18:31 Using 12 stones to build the altar took courage. This would have angered some of the people because it was a silent reminder of the split between the tribes. While the 10 tribes of the north called themselves Israel, it was a name originally given to all 12 of the tribes together.

18:36-38 God flashed fire from heaven for Elijah, and he will help us accomplish what he commands us to do. The proof may not be as dramatic in our lives as in Elijah's, but God will make resources available to us in creative ways to accomplish his purposes. He will give us the wisdom to raise a family, the courage to take a stand for truth, or the means to provide help for someone in need. Like Elijah, we can have faith that whatever God commands us to do, he will provide what we need to carry it through.

your command. 37 O LORD, answer me! Answer me so these people will know that you,
18:38 Gen 15:17; Lev 9:24; 10:1; 2 Kgs 1:12; Job 1:16 — O LORD, are God and that you have brought them back to yourself."
38 Immediately the fire of the LORD flashed down from heaven and burned up the
young bull, the wood, the stones, and the dust. It even licked up all the water in the ditch!
39 And when the people saw it, they fell on their faces and cried out, "The LORD is God!
The LORD is God!"
18:40 Deut 13:5; 18:20; 2 Kgs 10:24 — 40 Then Elijah commanded, "Seize all the prophets of Baal. Don't let a single one
escape!" So the people seized them all, and Elijah took them down to the Kishon Valley
and killed them there.

Elijah Prays for Rain

41 Then Elijah said to Ahab, "Go and enjoy a good meal! For I hear a mighty rainstorm
coming!"
18:42 Jas 5:18 — 42 So Ahab prepared a feast. But Elijah climbed to the top of Mount Carmel and fell to
the ground and prayed. 43 Then he said to his servant, "Go and look out toward the sea."
The servant went and looked, but he returned to Elijah and said, "I didn't see
anything." Seven times Elijah told him to go and look, and seven times he went. 44 Finally
the seventh time, his servant told him, "I saw a little cloud about the size of a hand rising
from the sea."
Then Elijah shouted, "Hurry to Ahab and tell him, 'Climb into your chariot and go
back home. If you don't hurry, the rain will stop you!'"
45 And sure enough, the sky was soon black with clouds. A heavy wind brought a
18:46 2 Kgs 4:29 — terrific rainstorm, and Ahab left quickly for Jezreel. 46 Now the LORD gave special
strength to Elijah. He tucked his cloak into his belt and ran ahead of Ahab's chariot all
the way to the entrance of Jezreel.

Elijah Flees to Sinai

19:2 2 Kgs 6:31 — **19** When Ahab got home, he told Jezebel what Elijah had done and that he had
19:3 Gen 21:31 — slaughtered the prophets of Baal. 2 So Jezebel sent this message to Elijah: "May
the gods also kill me if by this time tomorrow I have failed to take your life like those
19:4 Num 11:5; Jer 20:14-18; Jon 4:3, 8 — whom you killed."
3 Elijah was afraid and fled for his life. He went to Beersheba, a town in Judah, and he
left his servant there. 4 Then he went on alone into the desert, traveling all day. He sat

PROPHETS—FALSE AND TRUE

False Prophets	*True Prophets*
Worked for political purposes to benefit themselves	Worked for spiritual purposes to serve God and the people
Held positions of great wealth	Owned little or nothing
Gave false messages	Spoke only true messages
Spoke only what the people wanted to hear	Spoke only what God told them to say—no matter how unpopular

The false prophets were an obstacle to bringing God's word to the people. They would bring messages that contradicted the words of the true prophets. They gave "messages" that appealed to the people's sinful nature and comforted their fears. False prophets told people what they wanted to hear. True prophets told God's truth.

18:46 Elijah ran the six miles back to the city in order to give Ahab a last chance to turn from his sin before joining Jezebel in Jezreel. His run also ensured that the correct story of what happened would reach Jezreel.

19:2 Jezebel was enraged about the death of her prophets because they had told her everything *she* wanted to hear, prophesying her future power and glory. Their job was to deify the king and queen and help perpetuate their kingdom. Jezebel was also angry because her supporters had been eliminated and her pride and authority damaged. The money she had invested in these prophets was now lost.

Elijah, who caused the prophets' deaths, was a constant thorn in Jezebel's side because he was always predicting gloom and doom. Because she could not control his actions, she vowed to kill him. As long as God's prophet was around, she could not carry out all the evil she wanted.

19:3ff Elijah experienced the depths of fatigue and discouragement just after his two great spiritual victories: the defeat of the prophets of Baal and the answered prayer for rain. Often discouragement sets in after great spiritual experiences, especially those requiring physical effort or involving great emotion. To lead him out of depression, God first let Elijah rest and eat. Then God confronted him with the need to return to his mission—to speak God's words in Israel. Elijah's battles were not over; there was still work for him to do. When you feel let down after a great spiritual experience, remember that God's purpose for your life is not yet over.

down under a solitary broom tree and prayed that he might die. "I have had enough,
LORD," he said. "Take my life, for I am no better than my ancestors."
5 Then he lay down and slept under the broom tree. But as he was sleeping, an angel
touched him and told him, "Get up and eat!" 6 He looked around and saw some bread
baked on hot stones and a jar of water! So he ate and drank and lay down again.
7 Then the angel of the LORD came again and touched him and said, "Get up and eat
some more, for there is a long journey ahead of you."
8 So he got up and ate and drank, and the food gave him enough strength to travel forty
days and forty nights to Mount Sinai,* the mountain of God. 9 There he came to a cave,
where he spent the night.

19:8 Exod 3:1; 4:27; 24:18; 34:28 Deut 9:9 Matt 4:2

The LORD Speaks to Elijah

But the LORD said to him, "What are you doing here, Elijah?"
10 Elijah replied, "I have zealously served the LORD God Almighty. But the people of
Israel have broken their covenant with you, torn down your altars, and killed every one
of your prophets. I alone am left, and now they are trying to kill me, too."
11 "Go out and stand before me on the mountain," the LORD told him. And as Elijah
stood there, the LORD passed by, and a mighty windstorm hit the mountain. It was such
a terrible blast that the rocks were torn loose, but the LORD was not in the wind. After the
wind there was an earthquake, but the LORD was not in the earthquake. 12 And after the
earthquake there was a fire, but the LORD was not in the fire. And after the fire there was
the sound of a gentle whisper. 13 When Elijah heard it, he wrapped his face in his cloak
and went out and stood at the entrance of the cave.
And a voice said, "What are you doing here, Elijah?"
14 He replied again, "I have zealously served the LORD God Almighty. But the people
of Israel have broken their covenant with you, torn down your altars, and killed every
one of your prophets. I alone am left, and now they are trying to kill me, too."
15 Then the LORD told him, "Go back the way you came, and travel to the wilderness of
Damascus. When you arrive there, anoint Hazael to be king of Aram. 16 Then anoint Jehu
son of Nimshi to be king of Israel, and anoint Elisha son of Shaphat from Abel-meholah

19:10 †Rom 11:2-4

19:11 Exod 19:16, 19-20; 24:12 Ezek 1:4

19:12 Job 4:16

19:13 Exod 3:6

19:15 2 Kgs 8:7-15

19:16 2 Kgs 2:9, 15; 9:1

19:8 Hebrew *Horeb,* another name for Sinai.

19:8 When Elijah fled to Mount Sinai, he was returning to the sacred place where God had met Moses and had given his laws to the people. Obviously, God gave Elijah special strength to travel this great distance—over 200 miles—without additional food. Like Moses before him and Jesus after him, Elijah fasted for 40 days and 40 nights (Deuteronomy 9:9; Matthew 4:1, 2). Centuries later, Moses, Elijah, and Jesus would meet together on a mountaintop (Luke 9:28-36).

19:10 Elijah thought he was the only person left who was still true to God. He had seen both the king's court and the priesthood become corrupt. After experiencing great victory at Mount Carmel, he had to run for his life. Lonely and discouraged, he forgot that others had remained faithful during the nation's wickedness. When you are tempted to think that you are the only one remaining faithful to a task, don't stop to feel sorry for yourself. Self-pity will dilute the good you are doing. Be assured that even if you don't know who they are, others are faithfully obeying God and fulfilling their duties.

19:11-13 Elijah knew that the sound of gentle whisper was God's voice. He realized that God doesn't reveal himself only in powerful, miraculous ways. To look for God only in something big (rallies, churches, conferences, highly visible leaders) may be to miss him because he is often found gently whispering in the quietness of a humbled heart. Are you listening for God? Step back from the noise and activity of your busy life, and listen humbly and quietly for his guidance. It may come when you least expect it.

19:15, 16 God asked Elijah to anoint three different people. The first was Hazael, as king of Aram. Elijah was told to anoint an enemy king because God was going to use Aram as his instrument to punish Israel for its sin. Aram brought Israel's *external* punishment.
Israel's *internal* punishment came from Jehu, the next man Elijah was to anoint. As king of Israel, Jehu would destroy those who worshiped the false god Baal (2 Kings 9–10).

The third person Elijah was told to anoint was Elisha, the prophet who would succeed him. Elisha's job was to work in Israel, the northern kingdom, to help point the people back to God. At this time, the southern kingdom was ruled by Jehoshaphat, a king devoted to God.

ELIJAH FLEES FROM JEZEBEL
After killing Baal's prophets, Elijah ran from the furious Queen Jezebel. He fled to Beersheba, then into the wilderness, and finally to Mount Horeb (Sinai). There, like Moses centuries earlier, he talked with God.

19:18
Hos 13:2
†Rom 11:4

to replace you as my prophet. 17Anyone who escapes from Hazael will be killed by Jehu,
and those who escape Jehu will be killed by Elisha! 18Yet I will preserve seven thousand
others in Israel who have never bowed to Baal or kissed him!"

The Call of Elisha

19:19
2 Kgs 2:8, 13-14

19So Elijah went and found Elisha son of Shaphat plowing a field with a team of oxen.
There were eleven teams of oxen ahead of him, and he was plowing with the twelfth
team. Elijah went over to him and threw his cloak across his shoulders and walked away
again. 20Elisha left the oxen standing there, ran after Elijah, and said to him, "First let
me go and kiss my father and mother good-bye, and then I will go with you!"

AHAB

The kings of Israel and Judah, both good and evil, had prophets sent by God to advise, confront, and aid them. King David had a faithful friend in God's prophet Nathan; Ahab could have had an equally faithful friend in Elijah. But while David listened to Nathan and was willing to repent of his sins, Ahab saw Elijah as his enemy. Why? Because Elijah always brought bad news to Ahab, and Ahab refused to acknowledge that it was his own constant disobedience to God and persistent idol worship, not Elijah's prophecies, that brought the evil on his nation. He blamed Elijah for bringing the prophecies of judgment, rather than taking his advice and changing his own evil ways.

Ahab was trapped by his own choices, and he was unwilling to take the right action. As king, he was responsible to God and his prophet Elijah, but he was married to an evil woman who drew him into idol worship. He was a childish man who brooded for days if unable to get his own way. He took his evil wife's advice, listened only to the "prophets" who gave good news, and surrounded himself with people who encouraged him to do whatever he wanted. But the value of advice cannot be judged by the number of people for or against it. Ahab consistently chose to follow the majority opinion of those who surrounded him, and that led to his death.

It may seem nice to have someone encourage us to do whatever we want because advice that goes against our wishes is difficult to accept. However, our decisions must be based on the quality of the advice, not on its attractiveness or the majority opinion of our peers. God encourages us to get advice from wise counselors, but how can we test the advice we receive? Advice that agrees with the principles in God's Word is reliable. We must always separate advice from our own desires, the majority opinion, or whatever seems best in our limited perspective, and weigh it against God's commands. He will never lead us to do what he has forbidden in his Word— even in principle. Unlike Ahab, we should trust godly counselors and have the courage to stand against those who would have us do otherwise.

Strengths and accomplishments
- Eighth king of Israel
- Capable leader and military strategist

Weaknesses and mistakes
- Was the most evil king of Israel
- Married Jezebel, a pagan woman, and allowed her to promote Baal worship
- Brooded about not being able to get a piece of land, and so his wife had its owner, Naboth, killed
- Was used to getting his own way and got depressed when he didn't

Lessons from his life
- The choice of a mate will have a significant effect on life—physically, spiritually, and emotionally
- Selfishness, left unchecked, can lead to great evil

Vital statistics
- Where: Northern kingdom of Israel
- Occupation: King
- Relatives: Wife: Jezebel. Father: Omri. Sons: Ahaziah, Joram
- Contemporaries: Elijah, Naboth, Jehu, Ben-hadad, Jehoshaphat

Key verses
"But Ahab did what was evil in the LORD's sight, even more than any of the kings before him. And as though it were not enough to live like Jeroboam, he married Jezebel, the daughter of King Ethbaal of the Sidonians, and he began to worship Baal. First he built a temple and an altar for Baal in Samaria. Then he set up an Asherah pole. He did more to arouse the anger of the LORD, the God of Israel, than any of the other kings of Israel before him" (1 Kings 16:30-33).

Ahab's story is told in 1 Kings 16:28—22:40. He is also mentioned in 2 Chronicles 18—22; Micah 6:16.

19:18 Kissing Baal meant kissing some object representing him to show loyalty to him.

19:19 The cloak was the most important article of clothing a person could own. It was used as protection against the weather, as bedding, as a place to sit, and as luggage. It could be given as a pledge for a debt or torn into pieces to show grief. Elijah put his cloak on Elisha's shoulders to show that he would become Elijah's successor. Later, when the transfer of authority was complete, Elijah left his cloak for Elisha (2 Kings 2:11-14).

Elijah replied, "Go on back! But consider what I have done to you."
21Elisha then returned to his oxen, killed them, and used the wood from the plow to
build a fire to roast their flesh. He passed around the meat to the other plowmen, and they
all ate. Then he went with Elijah as his assistant.

Ben-Hadad Attacks Samaria

20 Now King Ben-hadad of Aram mobilized his army, supported by the chariots and 20:1 1 Kgs 15:18
horses of thirty-two allied kings. They went to besiege Samaria, the Israelite 2 Kgs 6:24
capital, and launched attacks against it. 2Ben-hadad sent messengers into the city to relay 20:2 2 Chr 16:2
this message to King Ahab of Israel: "This is what Ben-hadad says: 3'Your silver and
gold are mine, and so are the best of your wives and children!'"
4"All right, my lord," Ahab replied. "All that I have is yours!"
5Soon Ben-hadad's messengers returned again and said, "This is what Ben-hadad
says: 'I have already demanded that you give me your silver, gold, wives, and children.
6But about this time tomorrow I will send my officials to search your palace and the
homes of your people. They will take away everything you consider valuable!'"
7Then Ahab summoned all the leaders of the land and said to them, "Look how this 20:7 2 Kgs 5:7
man is stirring up trouble! I already agreed when he sent the message demanding that I
give him my wives and children and silver and gold."
8"Don't give in to any more demands," the leaders and people advised.
9So Ahab told the messengers from Ben-hadad, "Say this to my lord the king: 'I will
give you everything you asked for the first time, but this last demand of yours I simply
cannot meet.'" So the messengers returned to Ben-hadad with the response.
10Then Ben-hadad sent this message to Ahab: "May the gods bring tragedy on me, and 20:10 1 Kgs 19:2
even worse than that, if there remains enough dust from Samaria to provide more than a 2 Kgs 6:31
handful for each of my soldiers."
11The king of Israel sent back this answer: "A warrior still dressing for battle should 20:11 Prov 27:1
not boast like a warrior who has already won."
12This reply of Ahab's reached Ben-hadad and the other kings as they were drinking
in their tents.* "Prepare to attack!" Ben-hadad commanded his officers. So they prepared
to attack the city.

Ahab's Victory over Ben-Hadad

13Then a prophet came to see King Ahab and told him, "This is what the LORD says: Do
you see all these enemy forces? Today I will hand them all over to you. Then you will
know that I am the LORD."
14Ahab asked, "How will he do it?"

20:12 Or *in Succoth;* also in 20:16.

19:21 By killing his oxen, Elisha made a strong commitment to follow Elijah. Without them, he could not return to his life as a wealthy farmer. This meal was more than a feast among farmers. It was an offering of thanks to the Lord who chose Elisha to be his prophet.

20:1ff With two evil and two good kings up to this point, the southern kingdom, Judah, wavered between godly and ungodly living. But the northern kingdom, Israel, had eight evil kings in succession. To punish both kingdoms for living their own way instead of following God, God allowed other nations to gain strength and become their enemies. Three main enemies threatened Israel and Judah during the next two centuries—Aram, Assyria, and Babylon. Aram, the first to rise to power, presented an immediate threat to Ahab and Israel.

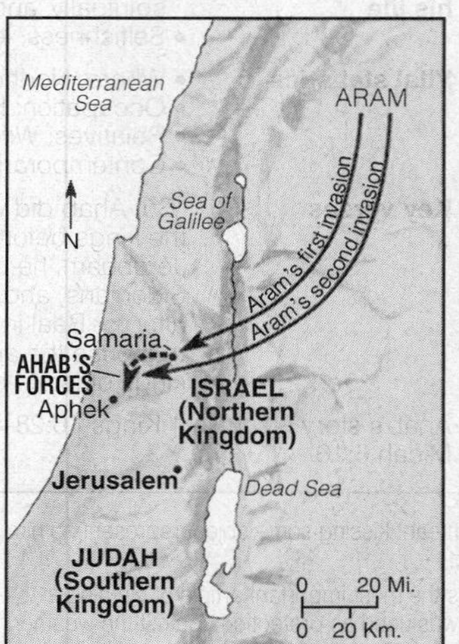

GOD DELIVERS AHAB
Despite Ahab's wickedness, God approached him in love. When Samaria was surrounded by Aramean forces, God miraculously delivered the city. But Ahab refused to give God credit. A year later, the Arameans attacked near Aphek. Again God gave Ahab victory, but again the king refused to acknowledge God's help.

And the prophet replied, "This is what the LORD says: The troops of the provincial
commanders will do it."
"Should we attack first?" Ahab asked.
"Yes," the prophet answered.
15So Ahab mustered the troops of the 232 provincial commanders. Then he called out
20:16 1 Kgs 16:9 the rest of his army of seven thousand men. 16About noontime, as Ben-hadad and the
thirty-two allied kings were still in their tents getting drunk, 17the troops of the provincial
commanders marched out of the city. As they approached, Ben-hadad's scouts reported
to him, "Some troops are coming from Samaria."
18"Take them alive," Ben-hadad commanded, "whether they have come for peace or
for war."
19But by now Ahab's provincial commanders had led the army out to fight. 20Each
Israelite soldier killed his Aramean opponent, and suddenly the entire Aramean army
panicked and fled. The Israelites chased them, but King Ben-hadad and a few others
escaped on horses. 21However, the other horses and chariots were destroyed, and the
Arameans were killed in a great slaughter.
20:22 2 Sam 11:1 22Afterward the prophet said to King Ahab, "Get ready for another attack by the king
of Aram next spring."

Ben-Hadad's Second Attack

23After their defeat, Ben-hadad's officers said to him, "The Israelite gods are gods of the
hills; that is why they won. But we can beat them easily on the plains. 24Only this time
replace the kings with field commanders! 25Recruit another army like the one you lost.
Give us the same number of horses, chariots, and men, and we will fight against them in
the plains. There's not a shadow of a doubt that we will beat them." So King Ben-hadad
20:26 2 Kgs 13:17 did as they suggested. 26The following spring he called up the Aramean army and
20:27 Judg 6:3-5; 1 Sam 13:5-8 marched out against Israel, this time at Aphek. 27Israel then mustered its army, set up
supply lines, and moved into the battle. But the Israelite army looked like two little flocks
of goats in comparison to the vast Aramean forces that filled the countryside!
28Then the man of God went to the king of Israel and said, "This is what the LORD
says: The Arameans have said that the LORD is a god of the hills and not of the plains.
So I will help you defeat this vast army. Then you will know that I am the LORD."
29The two armies camped opposite each other for seven days, and on the seventh day
20:30 1 Kgs 22:25; 2 Chr 18:24 the battle began. The Israelites killed 100,000 Aramean foot soldiers in one day. 30The
rest fled behind the walls of Aphek, but the wall fell on them and killed another 27,000.
20:31 Gen 37:34 Ben-hadad fled into the city and hid in a secret room. 31Ben-hadad's officers said to him,
"Sir, we have heard that the kings of Israel are very merciful. So let's humble ourselves
by wearing sackcloth and putting ropes on our heads. Then perhaps King Ahab will let
you live."
32So they put on sackcloth and ropes and went to the king of Israel and begged, "Your
servant Ben-hadad says, 'Please let me live!'"
The king of Israel responded, "Is he still alive? He is my brother!"
33The men were quick to grasp at this straw of hope, and they replied, "Yes, your
brother Ben-hadad!"
"Go and get him," the king of Israel told them. And when Ben-hadad arrived, Ahab
invited him up into his chariot!
20:34 1 Kgs 15:20 34Ben-hadad told him, "I will give back the towns my father took from your father,
and you may establish places of trade in Damascus, as my father did in Samaria."
Then Ahab said, "I will let you go under these conditions." So they made a treaty, and
Ben-hadad was set free.

20:23 Since the days of Joshua, Israel's soldiers had the reputation of being superior fighters in the hills but ineffective in the open plains and valleys because they did not use chariots in battle. Horse-drawn chariots, useless in hilly terrain and dense forests, could easily run down great numbers of foot soldiers on the plains. What Ben-hadad's officers did not understand was that it was God, not chariots, that made the difference in battle.

20:31 Sackcloth was coarse cloth usually made of goats' hair and was worn as a symbol of mourning for the dead or for natural disaster. Wearing ropes around the head may have been a symbol of putting oneself at another's disposal. In other words, Ahab could have hung them if he wished. Wearing ropes around the head, therefore, was a sign of submission.

A Prophet Condemns Ahab

35 Meanwhile, the LORD instructed one of the group of prophets to say to another man, **20:35** 1 Kgs 13:16-18
"Strike me!" But the man refused to strike the prophet. 36 Then the prophet told him, **20:36** 1 Kgs 13:24
"Because you have not obeyed the voice of the LORD, a lion will kill you as soon as you
leave me." And sure enough, when he had gone, a lion attacked and killed him.

37 Then the prophet turned to another man and said, "Strike me!" So he struck the
prophet and wounded him.

38 The prophet waited for the king beside the road, having placed a bandage over his **20:38** 1 Kgs 14:2
eyes to disguise himself. 39 As the king passed by, the prophet called out to him, "Sir, I **20:39** 2 Kgs 10:24
was in the battle, and a man brought me a prisoner. He said, 'Guard this man; if for any
reason he gets away, you will either die or pay a fine of seventy-five pounds* of silver!'
40 But while I was busy doing something else, the prisoner disappeared!"

"Well, it's your own fault," the king replied. "You have determined your own
judgment."

41 Then the prophet pulled the bandage from his eyes, and the king of Israel recognized
him as one of the prophets. 42 And the prophet told him, "This is what the LORD says:
Because you have spared the man I said must be destroyed,* now you must die in his
place, and your people will die instead of his people." 43 So the king of Israel went home **20:43** 1 Kgs 21:4
to Samaria angry and sullen.

Naboth's Vineyard

21 King Ahab had a palace in Jezreel, and near the palace was a vineyard owned by **21:1** 2 Kgs 9:21
a man named Naboth. 2 One day Ahab said to Naboth, "Since your vineyard is so
convenient to the palace, I would like to buy it to use as a vegetable garden. I will give
you a better vineyard in exchange, or if you prefer, I will pay you for it."

3 But Naboth replied, "The LORD forbid that I should give you the inheritance that was **21:3** Lev 25:23 Num 36:6-7 Ezek 46:18
passed down by my ancestors." 4 So Ahab went home angry and sullen because of
Naboth's answer. The king went to bed with his face to the wall and refused to eat!

5 "What in the world is the matter?" his wife, Jezebel, asked him. "What has made you
so upset that you are not eating?"

6 "I asked Naboth to sell me his vineyard or to trade it, and he refused!" Ahab told her.

7 "Are you the king of Israel or not?" Jezebel asked. "Get up and eat and don't worry **21:7** 1 Sam 8:14
about it. I'll get you Naboth's vineyard!"

8 So she wrote letters in Ahab's name, sealed them with his seal, and sent them to the **21:8** 2 Sam 11:14 2 Chr 32:17 Esth 3:12; 8:8
elders and other leaders of the city where Naboth lived. 9 In her letters she commanded:
"Call the citizens together for fasting and prayer and give Naboth a place of honor.
10 Find two scoundrels* who will accuse him of cursing God and the king. Then take him **21:10** Exod 22:28 Lev 24:15-16 Acts 6:11
out and stone him to death."

11 So the elders and other leaders followed the instructions Jezebel had written in the
letters. 12 They called for a fast and put Naboth at a prominent place before the people.
13 Then two scoundrels accused him before all the people of cursing God and the king.

20:39 Hebrew *1 talent* [34 kilograms]. **20:42** The Hebrew term used here refers to the complete consecration of things or people to the LORD, either by destroying them or by giving them as an offering. **21:10** Hebrew *two sons of Belial;* also in 21:13.

20:35, 36 The prophet needed a wound so he would look like an injured soldier and could effectively deliver his prophecy to Ahab. The first man was killed by a lion because he refused to obey the Lord's instructions through the prophet.

20:41, 42 It is difficult to explain why Ahab let Ben-hadad go, especially after all the trouble the Arameans had caused him. God helped Ahab destroy the Aramean army to prove to Ahab and to Aram that he alone was God. But Ahab failed to destroy the king, his greatest enemy. Ben-hadad was under God's judgment to die, and Ahab had no authority to let him live. For this, God told Ahab that he must now die instead. This prophet's message soon came true when Ahab was killed on the battlefield (22:35).

21:4 After hearing God's judgment (20:42), Ahab went home to pout. Driven by anger and rebellion against God, he had a fit of rage when Naboth refused to sell his vineyard. The same feelings that led him to a career of power grabbing drove him to resent Naboth. Rage turned to hatred and led to murder. Naboth, however, wanted to uphold God's laws: It was considered a duty to keep ancestral land in the family. This incident shows the cruel interplay between Ahab and Jezebel, two of the most wicked leaders in Israel's history.

21:13 Jezebel devised a scheme that appeared legal to get the land for her husband. Two witnesses were required to establish guilt, and the punishment for blasphemy was death by stoning. Those who twist the law and legal procedures to get what they want today may be more sophisticated in how they go about it, but they are still guilty of the same sin.

So he was dragged outside the city and stoned to death. 14 The city officials then sent
word to Jezebel, "Naboth has been stoned to death."
15 When Jezebel heard the news, she said to Ahab, "You know the vineyard Naboth
wouldn't sell you? Well, you can have it now! He's dead!" 16 So Ahab immediately went
down to the vineyard to claim it.
17 But the LORD said to Elijah, who was from Tishbe, 18 "Go down to meet King Ahab,
who rules in Samaria. He will be at Naboth's vineyard in Jezreel, taking possession of
it. 19 Give him this message: 'This is what the LORD says: Isn't killing Naboth bad
enough? Must you rob him, too? Because you have done this, dogs will lick your blood
outside the city just as they licked the blood of Naboth!'"
20 "So my enemy has found me!" Ahab exclaimed to Elijah.
"Yes," Elijah answered, "I have come because you have sold yourself to what is evil
in the LORD's sight. 21 The LORD is going to bring disaster to you and sweep you away.
He will not let a single one of your male descendants, slave or free alike, survive in Israel!
22 He is going to destroy your family as he did the family of Jeroboam son of Nebat and

21:19 1 Kgs 22:38; 2 Kgs 9:26
21:20 1 Kgs 18:17; Rom 7:14
21:21 1 Kgs 14:10; 2 Kgs 9:8
21:22 1 Kgs 14:16; 15:29; 16:3

JEZEBEL

The Bible is as honest about the lives of its heroes as it is about those who rejected God. Some Bible characters found out what God can do with failures when they turned to him. Many, however, neither admitted their failures nor turned to God.

Jezebel ranks as the most evil woman in the Bible. The Bible even uses her name as an example of people who completely reject God (Revelation 2:20, 21). Many pagan women married into Israel without acknowledging the God their husbands worshiped. They brought their religions with them. But no one was as determined as Jezebel to make all Israel worship *her* gods. To the prophet Elijah, she seemed to have succeeded. He felt he was the only one still faithful to God until God told him there were still 7,000 who had not turned from the faith. Jezebel's one outstanding "success" was in contributing to the cause of the eventual downfall of the northern kingdom—idolatry. God punished the northern tribes for their idolatry by having them carried off into captivity.

Jezebel held great power. She not only managed her husband, Ahab, but she also had 850 assorted pagan priests under her control. She was committed to her gods and to getting what she wanted. She believed that the king had the right to possess anything he wanted. When Naboth refused to sell Ahab his vineyard, Jezebel ruthlessly had Naboth killed and took ownership of the land. Jezebel's plan to wipe out worship of God in Israel led to painful consequences. Before she died, Jezebel suffered the loss of her husband in combat and her son at the hand of Jehu, who took the throne by force. She died in the defiant and scornful way she had lived.

When comparing Jezebel and Elijah, we have to admire each one's strength of commitment. The big difference was to *whom* they were committed. Jezebel was committed to herself and her false gods; Elijah was totally committed to the one true God. In the end, God proved Elijah right. To what or to whom are you most committed? How would God evaluate your commitment?

Weaknesses and mistakes
- Systematically eliminated the representatives of God in Israel
- Promoted and funded Baal worship
- Threatened to have Elijah killed
- Believed kings and queens could rightfully do or have anything they wanted
- Used her strong convictions to get her own way

Lessons from her life
- It is not enough to be committed or sincere. Where our commitment lies makes a great difference
- Rejecting God always leads to disaster

Vital statistics
- Where: Sidon, Samaria
- Occupation: Queen of Israel
- Relatives: Husband: Ahab. Father: Ethbaal. Sons: Joram, Ahaziah
- Contemporaries: Elijah, Jehu

Key verse
"No one else so completely sold himself to what was evil in the LORD's sight as did Ahab, for his wife, Jezebel, influenced him" (1 Kings 21:25).

Jezebel's story is told in 1 Kings 16:31—2 Kings 9:37. Her name is used as a synonym for great evil in Revelation 2:20.

21:19, 23 For the fulfillment of these verses, see 22:38 where dogs licked Ahab's blood, and 2 Kings 9:30–10:28 where Jezebel and the rest of Ahab's family were destroyed.

21:20 Ahab still refused to admit his sin against God. Instead, he accused Elijah of being his enemy. When we are blinded by envy and hatred, it is almost impossible to see our own sin.

the family of Baasha son of Ahijah, for you have made him very angry and have led all of Israel into sin. 23 The LORD has also told me that the dogs of Jezreel will eat the body of your wife, Jezebel, at the city wall. 24 The members of your family who die in the city will be eaten by dogs, and those who die in the field will be eaten by vultures."

25 No one else so completely sold himself to what was evil in the LORD's sight as did Ahab, for his wife, Jezebel, influenced him. 26 He was especially guilty because he worshiped idols just as the Amorites had done—the people whom the LORD had driven from the land ahead of the Israelites.

27 When Ahab heard this message, he tore his clothing, dressed in sackcloth, and fasted. He even slept in sackcloth and went about in deep mourning.

28 Then another message from the LORD came to Elijah, who was from Tishbe: 29 "Do you see how Ahab has humbled himself before me? Because he has done this, I will not do what I promised during his lifetime. It will happen to his sons; I will destroy all his descendants."

4. Kings of Israel and Judah

Jehoshaphat and Ahab

22 For three years there was no war between Aram and Israel. 2 Then during the third year, King Jehoshaphat of Judah went to visit King Ahab of Israel. 3 During the visit, Ahab said to his officials, "Do you realize that the Arameans are still occupying our city of Ramoth-gilead? And we haven't done a thing about it!" 4 Then he turned to Jehoshaphat and asked, "Will you join me in fighting against Ramoth-gilead?"

And Jehoshaphat replied to King Ahab, "Why, of course! You and I are brothers, and my troops are yours to command. Even my horses are at your service." 5 Then Jehoshaphat added, "But first let's find out what the LORD says."

6 So King Ahab summoned his prophets, about four hundred of them, and asked them, "Should I go to war against Ramoth-gilead or not?"

They all replied, "Go right ahead! The Lord will give you a glorious victory!"

7 But Jehoshaphat asked, "Isn't there a prophet of the LORD around, too? I would like to ask him the same question."

8 King Ahab replied, "There is still one prophet of the LORD, but I hate him. He never prophesies anything but bad news for me! His name is Micaiah son of Imlah."

"You shouldn't talk like that," Jehoshaphat said. "Let's hear what he has to say."

9 So the king of Israel called one of his officials and said, "Quick! Go and get Micaiah son of Imlah."

Micaiah Prophesies against Ahab

10 King Ahab of Israel and King Jehoshaphat of Judah, dressed in their royal robes, were sitting on thrones at the threshing floor near the gate of Samaria. All of Ahab's prophets were prophesying there in front of them. 11 One of them, Zedekiah son of Kenaanah, made some iron horns and proclaimed, "This is what the LORD says: With these horns you will gore the Arameans to death!"

12 All the other prophets agreed. "Yes," they said, "go up to Ramoth-gilead and be victorious, for the LORD will give you victory!"

13 Meanwhile, the messenger who went to get Micaiah said to him, "Look, all the prophets are promising victory for the king. Be sure that you agree with them and promise success."

14 But Micaiah replied, "As surely as the LORD lives, I will say only what the LORD tells me to say."

21:23 2 Kgs 9:10, 30-37
21:24 1 Kgs 14:11; 16:4-7
21:26 Gen 15:16; Lev 18:25-30; 2 Kgs 21:11
21:27 Gen 37:34; 2 Kgs 6:26-30
21:29 1 Kgs 22:38; 2 Kgs 9:25-37; 2 Chr 12:7; 34:27
22:1-28 //2 Chr 18:1-27
22:2 1 Kgs 15:24
22:3 Deut 4:43
22:4 2 Kgs 3:6-8
22:5 2 Kgs 3:11
22:7 2 Kgs 3:11
22:11 Deut 33:17; 2 Chr 18:10; Zech 1:18-21
22:14 Num 22:18; 24:13; 2 Chr 18:13

21:29 Ahab was more wicked than any other king of Israel (16:30; 21:25), but when he repented in deep humility, God took notice and reduced his punishment. The same Lord who was merciful to Ahab wants to be merciful to you. No matter how evil you have been, it is never too late to humble yourself, turn to God, and ask for forgiveness.

22:6 These 400 prophets may have been the 400 Asherah priests left alive by Elijah at Carmel, although 450 prophets of Baal were killed (see 18:19-40).

22:7 Jehoshaphat knew there was a difference between these pagan prophets and the "prophet of the LORD," so he asked if one was available. Evidently Jehoshaphat wanted to do what was right, although Ahab didn't. However, both kings disregarded God's message and listened only to the pagan prophets.

22:10 Threshing floors were placed in elevated areas to allow the wind to blow away the discarded hulls of grain.

[15]When Micaiah arrived before the king, Ahab asked him, "Micaiah, should we go to
war against Ramoth-gilead or not?"
And Micaiah replied, "Go right ahead! The LORD will give the king a glorious victory!"
[16]But the king replied sharply, "How many times must I demand that you speak only
the truth when you speak for the LORD?"
22:17 Num 27:17 1 Kgs 22:33-37 †Matt 9:36 Mark 6:34
[17]So Micaiah told him, "In a vision I saw all Israel scattered on the mountains, like
sheep without a shepherd. And the LORD said, 'Their master has been killed. Send them
home in peace.'"
[18]"Didn't I tell you?" the king of Israel said to Jehoshaphat. "He does it every time.
He never prophesies anything but bad news for me."
22:19 Isa 6:1 Dan 7:9-10
[19]Then Micaiah continued, "Listen to what the LORD says! I saw the LORD sitting on
his throne with all the armies of heaven around him, on his right and on his left. [20]And
the LORD said, 'Who can entice Ahab to go into battle against Ramoth-gilead so that he
can be killed there?' There were many suggestions, [21]until finally a spirit approached the
LORD and said, 'I can do it!'

KINGS TO DATE AND THEIR ENEMIES

ISRAEL

874 **AHAB** *Twice defeated Ben-hadad II (Aram) and was later killed in battle against Aram 1 Kgs 16:28—22:40 2 Chr 18:1–34*

853 **AHAZIAH** *1 Kgs 22:40— 2 Kgs 1:18 2 Chr 20:35–37*

852

JUDAH

910 **ASA** *Defeated Zerah (the Ethiopian) and harassed Baasha 1 Kgs 15:8–24 2 Chr 14:1—16:14 Co-regency 872–869*

869

872 **JEHOSHAPHAT** *Defeated by Ben-hadad II (Aram), gained miraculous victory over Moab and Ammon, and crushed a rebellion by Mesha (Moab) 1 Kgs 22:41–50 2 Chr 17:1—21:1 Co-regency 853–848*

853 848 841 **JEHORAM** *Lost dominion over Edom, assulted by Philistines and Arabs 2 Kgs 8:16–24 2 Chr 21:1–20*

All dates are B.C.
Solid section of the timeline indicates co-regency.
For all the kings of Israel and Judah, see the chart at the end of 1 Kings.

22:15, 16 Why did Micaiah tell Ahab to attack when he had previously vowed to speak only what God had told him? Perhaps he was speaking sarcastically, making fun of the messages from the pagan prophets by showing that they were telling the king only what he wanted to hear. Somehow, Micaiah's tone of voice let everyone know he was mocking the pagan prophets. When confronted, he predicted that the king would die and the battle would be lost. Although Ahab repented temporarily (21:27), he still maintained the system of false prophets. These false prophets would be instrumental in leading him to his own ruin.

22:19-22 The vision Micaiah saw was either a picture of a real incident in heaven or a parable of what was happening on earth, illustrating that the seductive influence of the false prophets would be part of God's judgment upon Ahab (22:23). Whether or not God sent an angel in disguise, he used the system of false prophets to snare Ahab in his sin. The lying spirit (22:22) symbolized the way of life for these prophets, who told the king only what he wanted to hear.

22:20-22 Does God allow angels to entice people to do evil? To understand evil one must first understand God. (1) God himself is good (Psalm 11:7). (2) God created a good world that fell because of man's sin (Romans 5:12). (3) Someday God will re-create the world, and it will be good again (Revelation 21:1). (4) God is stronger than evil (Matthew 13:41-43; Revelation 19:11-21). (5) God allows evil, and thus he has control over it. God did not create evil, and he offers help to those who wish to overcome it (Matthew 11:28-30). (6) God uses everything—both good and evil—for his good purposes (Genesis 50:20; Romans 8:28).

22“ ‘How will you do this?’ the LORD asked.
“And the spirit replied, ‘I will go out and inspire all Ahab’s prophets to speak lies.’
“ ‘You will succeed,’ said the LORD. ‘Go ahead and do it.’
23“So you see, the LORD has put a lying spirit in the mouths of your prophets. For the
LORD has determined disaster for you.”
24Then Zedekiah son of Kenaanah walked up to Micaiah and slapped him across the
face. “When did the Spirit of the LORD leave me to speak to you?” he demanded.
25And Micaiah replied, “You will find out soon enough when you find yourself hiding
in some secret room!”
26King Ahab of Israel then ordered, “Arrest Micaiah and take him back to Amon, the
governor of the city, and to my son Joash. 27Give them this order from the king: ‘Put this
man in prison, and feed him nothing but bread and water until I return safely from the
battle!’ ”
28But Micaiah replied, “If you return safely, the LORD has not spoken through me!”
Then he added to those standing around, “Take note of what I have said.”

The Death of Ahab

29So the king of Israel and King Jehoshaphat of Judah led their armies against Ramoth-
gilead. 30Now King Ahab said to Jehoshaphat, “As we go into battle, I will disguise
myself so no one will recognize me, but you wear your royal robes.” So Ahab disguised
himself, and they went into battle.
31Now the king of Aram had issued these orders to his thirty-two charioteers: “Attack
only the king of Israel!” 32So when the Aramean charioteers saw Jehoshaphat in his royal
robes, they went after him. “There is the king of Israel!” they shouted. But when
Jehoshaphat cried out, 33the charioteers realized he was not the king of Israel, and they
stopped chasing him.
34An Aramean soldier, however, randomly shot an arrow at the Israelite troops, and
the arrow hit the king of Israel between the joints of his armor. “Get me out of here!”
Ahab groaned to the driver of his chariot. “I have been badly wounded!” 35The battle
raged all that day, and Ahab was propped up in his chariot facing the Arameans. The
blood from his wound ran down to the floor of his chariot, and as evening arrived he
died. 36Just as the sun was setting, the cry ran through his troops: “It’s all over—return
home!” 37So the king died, and his body was taken to Samaria and buried there. 38Then
his chariot was washed beside the pool of Samaria, where the prostitutes bathed, and
dogs came and licked the king’s blood, just as the LORD had promised.
39The rest of the events in Ahab’s reign and the story of the ivory palace and the cities
he built are recorded in *The Book of the History of the Kings of Israel.* 40When Ahab
died, he was buried among his ancestors. Then his son Ahaziah became the next king.

Jehoshaphat Rules in Judah

41Jehoshaphat son of Asa began to rule over Judah in the fourth year of King Ahab’s
reign in Israel. 42He was thirty-five years old when he became king, and he reigned in
Jerusalem twenty-five years. His mother was Azubah, the daughter of Shilhi. 43Jehosha-

22:22 Judg 9:23; 2 Thes 2:11
22:23 Ezek 14:9
22:24 2 Chr 18:23
22:27 2 Chr 16:10; 18:25-27
22:28 Deut 18:22
22:29-36 //2 Chr 18:28-34
22:30 2 Chr 35:22
22:31 2 Chr 18:30
22:38 1 Kgs 21:19
22:39 Amos 3:15
22:41-50 //2 Chr 20:31–21:1
22:43 1 Kgs 15:14; 2 Kgs 12:3

The Bible shows us a God who hates all evil and will one day do away with it completely and forever (Revelation 20:10-15). God does not entice anyone to become evil. Those committed to evil, however, may be used by God to sin even more in order to hurry their deserved judgment (Exodus 11:10). We don’t need to understand every detail of how God works in order to have perfect confidence in his absolute power over evil and his total goodness toward us.

22:34 Ahab could not escape God’s judgment. The king of Aram sent 32 of his best chariot commanders with the sole purpose of killing Ahab. Thinking he could escape, Ahab tried a disguise, but a random arrow struck him while the chariots chased the wrong king—Jehoshaphat. It was foolish for Ahab to think he could escape by wearing a disguise. Sometimes people try to escape reality by disguising themselves—changing jobs, moving to a new town, even changing spouses. But God sees and evaluates the motives of each person. Any attempted disguise is futile.

22:35 Just as the prophet had predicted (20:42), Ahab was killed. See Ahab’s Profile in chapter 19 for more of Ahab’s sad story.

22:41-50 For more details on Jehoshaphat, see the other account of his reign in 2 Chronicles 17–20.

22:43 Just like his ancestors Solomon and Asa, Jehoshaphat followed God, but he didn’t remove the high places—the pagan shrines in the hills (2 Chronicles 20:33). It was against God’s laws to worship idols in the shrines (Numbers 33:52), and at first Jehoshaphat attempted to remove them (2 Chronicles 17:6). They were so popular, however, that this proved difficult. In spite of Jehoshaphat’s many contributions to the spiritual, moral, and material health of his country, he did not succeed in eradicating the hill shrines.

phat was a good king, following the example of his father, Asa. He did what was pleasing
in the LORD's sight. During his reign, however, he failed to remove all the pagan shrines,
and the people still offered sacrifices and burned incense there. 44 Jehoshaphat also made
peace with the king of Israel.

45 The rest of the events in Jehoshaphat's reign, the extent of his power, and the wars

22:46 Deut 23:17 1 Kgs 15:12

he waged are recorded in *The Book of the History of the Kings of Judah.* 46 He banished
from the land the rest of the shrine prostitutes, who still continued their practices from

22:47 2 Sam 8:14 2 Kgs 3:9

the days of his father, Asa. 47 There was no king in Edom at that time, only a deputy.

48 Jehoshaphat also built a fleet of trading ships* to sail to Ophir for gold. But the ships

22:48 1 Kgs 9:26-28

never set sail, for they were wrecked at Ezion-geber. 49 At that time Ahaziah son of Ahab
proposed to Jehoshaphat, "Let my men sail an expedition with your men." But Jehoshaphat refused the offer.

22:50 2 Chr 21:1

50 When Jehoshaphat died, he was buried with his ancestors in the City of David. Then
his son Jehoram became the next king.

Ahaziah Rules in Israel

51 Ahaziah son of Ahab began to rule over Israel in the seventeenth year of King

22:52 1 Kgs 15:26

Jehoshaphat's reign in Judah. He reigned in Samaria two years. 52 But he did what was
evil in the LORD's sight, following the example of his father and mother and the example
of Jeroboam son of Nebat, who had led Israel into the sin of idolatry. 53 He served Baal
and worshiped him, arousing the anger of the LORD, the God of Israel, just as his father
had done.

22:48 Hebrew *fleet of ships of Tarshish.*

22:52, 53 The book of 1 Kings begins with a nation united under David, the most devout king in Israel's history. The book ends with a divided kingdom and the death of Ahab, the most wicked king of all. What happened? The people forgot to acknowledge God as their ultimate leader; they appointed human leaders who ignored God; and then they conformed to the life-styles of these evil leaders. Occasional wrongdoing gradually turned into a way of life. Their blatant wickedness could be met only with judgment from God, who allowed enemy nations to arise and defeat Israel and Judah in battle as punishment for their sins. Failing to acknowledge God as our ultimate leader is the first step toward ruin.

DIVIDED KINGDOM OF ISRAEL

AHIJAH 934–909

ELIJAH 875–84

930
JEROBOAM I
(22 years)
Fortified a capital city (Shechem), set up two golden calf-idols, led the nation into sin, allowed anyone to be a priest
1 Kgs 11:26—14:34
2 Chr 10:12—13:20

909
NADAB
(2 years)
1 Kgs 15:25-28

908
BAASHA
(24 years)
Led people into idol worship
1 Kgs 15:27—16:7
2 Chr 16:1–6

886
ELAH
(2 years)
Continued idol worship
1 Kgs 16:6–14

885
ZIMRI
(7 days)
1 Kgs 16:9–20

885
TIBNI
(4 years)
1 Kgs 16:21–22

885
OMRI
(12 years)
Built the capital city of Samaria, had great military power, but continued to lead Israel into idolatry
1 Kgs 16:16–28

874
AHAB
(22 years)
Married Jezebel (a non-Jew and extremely wicked woman), worshipe Baal, and suffered three years of fam caused by his con sistent disobedier to God
1 Kgs 16:28—22.
2 Chr 18:1–34

CAPITAL: SHECHEM, THEN TIRZAH, THEN SAMARIA
THE NORTHERN KINGDOM OF ISRAEL (TEN TRIBES)

THE SOUTHERN KINGDOM OF JUDAH (TWO TRIBES)
CAPITAL: JERUSALEM

930
REHOBOAM
(17 years)
Built many fortified cities, strengthened the economy (despite the tribute paid to Egypt), followed God for three years, but then set up idols and shrines to foreign gods
1 Kgs 11:43—14:31
2 Chr 9:31—12:16

913
ABIJAH
(3 years)
Despite his wickedness, he called for God's help to win the battle against Israel
1 Kgs 14:31—15:8
2 Chr 13:1—14:1

910
ASA
(41 years)
Destroyed pagan altars and rebuilt altar of God, built fortified cities, gained much wealth from plunder of foreign conquest, removed the queen mother for worshiping Asherah, led the people to worship God with their hearts, provided peace on home soil, was greatly loved and given a beautiful funeral
1 Kgs 15:8–24
2 Chr 14:1—16:14

872
JEHOSHAPHAT
(25 years)
Arranged for the marr of his son to a daught Ahab (who made trou later on), had a strong military (kept troops i cities of Israel his fath had conquered), colle tribute from the Philis worshiped the Lord ar destroyed idols, estab lished education, and appointed judges and courts
1 Kgs 15:24; 22:41–5
2 Chr 17:1—21:1

All dates are B.C. The total years of reign sometimes includes years of co-regency.

ELISHA 848–797

JONAH 793–753(?)

853
AHAZIAH
(2 years)
Proposed a joint trade venture with Judah
1 Kgs 22:40—2 Kgs 1:18
2 Chr 20:35–37

852
JORAM
(12 years)
Suffered famine and war during most of his reign
2 Kgs 3:1—8:25
2 Chr 22:5–7

841
JEHU
(28 years)
Was responsible for the deaths of Joram (king of Israel), Ahaziah (king of Judah), and Jezebel (wicked mother of Joram); destroyed the priests and temples of Baal but did not consistently follow God
2 Kgs 9:1—10:36
2 Chr 22:7–12

814
JEHOAHAZ
(17 years)
Evil reign included worship of Asherah, usually called "detestable"
2 Kgs 13:1–9

798
JEHOASH
(16 years)
Even though he was evil, he recognized the authority of Elisha as a prophet of God
2 Kgs 13:10—14:16
2 Chr 25:17–24

793
JEROBOAM II
(41 years)
Very evil but politically powerful; his nation enjoyed economic prosperity and military peace
2 Kgs 14:16–29

853
JEHORAM
(8 years)
Married a wicked daughter of Ahab, compelled the people to worship idols, and killed all his brothers
2 Kgs 8:16–24
2 Chr 21:1–20

841
AHAZIAH
(1 year)
Friend of Joram of Israel
2 Kgs 8:24—9:29
2 Chr 22:1–10

841
ATHALIAH (QUEEN)
(6 years)
Killed all her grandchildren except Joash, who was hidden by his nurse for six years, and ravaged the Temple to furnish Baal's temple
2 Kgs 11:1–20
2 Chr 22:10—23:21

835
JOASH
(40 years)
Was crowned king at the age of seven by Jehoiada (the high priest), promoted peace and prosperity, repaired the Temple, and smashed the altars to Baal; but abandoned God after Jehoiada died, and even had Jehoiada's son killed
2 Kgs 11:2—12:21
2 Chr 22:11—24:27

796
AMAZIAH
(29 years)
Was basically good but did not completely wipe out idol worship; organized and mustered the army
2 Kgs 14:1–20
2 Chr 25:1–28

792
AZARIAH (UZZIAH)
(52 years)
Rebuilt a city named Elath, owned many farms and vineyards, constructed water reservoirs and fortified towers, reorganized the army (so powerful that his fame spread to Egypt), but violated God's laws for priestly function—so God struck him with leprosy
2 Kgs 15:1–17
2 Chr 26:1–23

HOSEA 753–715

AMOS 760–750

752
SHALLUM
(1 month)
2 Kgs 15:10–15

742
PEKAHIAH
(2 years)
Continued idol worship
2 Kgs 15:22–26

753
ZECHARIAH
(6 months)
Encouraged idol worship
2 Kgs 14:29—15:11

752
MENAHEM
(10 years)
Imposed heavy taxes and oppressed his people
2 Kgs 15:14–22

740
PEKAH
(8 years)
During his reign many of the people were taken captive to Assyria
2 Kgs 15:25–31
2 Chr 28:5–8

732
HOSHEA
(9 years)
Suffered heavy taxation by Assyria and eventual conquest—bringing about Israelite captivity and resettlement of foreigners in Israel
2 Kgs 15:30; 17:1–6

722
END OF THE NORTHERN KINGDOM—Israel taken to Assyria by Shalmaneser

ISRAEL

JUDAH

750
JOTHAM
(16 years)
Rebuilt the Upper Gate of the Temple, rebuilt walls and cities, but still permitted idol worship
2 Kgs 15:32–38
2 Chr 27:1–9

735
AHAZ
(16 years)
Sacrificed his own son to pagan gods, nailed the Temple doors shut
2 Kgs 16:1–20
2 Chr 28:1–27

715
HEZEKIAH
(29 years)
Was a devoted follower of God, reopened the Temple doors, purified the Temple, reinstated priests and their duties, organized an orchestra to aid worship, destroyed idols (including the bronze snake of Moses because people had begun to worship it), celebrated the Passover and even invited people who were living in the north to participate, constructed large public waterworks, was given 15 extra years of life, foolishly showed messengers the wealth in the Temple
2 Kgs 16:20; 18:1—20:21
2 Chr 29:1—32:33

697
MANASSEH
(55 years)
Rebuilt all the pagan shrines, sacrificed one [of] his own sons, practiced sorce[ry], set up an idol right in the Temple, murde[red] many of his ow[n] people, but repented durin[g] his Assyrian captivity
2 Kgs 21:1–18
2 Chr 33:1–20

MICAH 742–687

ISAIAH 740–681

586
END OF THE SOUTHERN KINGDOM—
carried off captive to Babylon by Nebuchadnezzar

642
AMON
(2 years)
2 Kgs 21:18–26
2 Chr 33:20–25

640
JOSIAH
(31 years)
Loved God with all his heart, repaired the Temple, found a lost scroll of the law (he promised to obey it, thus God delayed destruction for Judah until after his death), personally oversaw the major project of destroying idol shrines, reinstated the priests of God, celebrated the Passover with greater zeal than had been since Samuel's day, was greatly loved by his people
2 Kgs 21:26—23:30
2 Chr 33:25—35:27

609
JEHOAHAZ
(3 months)
Jailed and taken to Egypt, where he died
2 Kgs 23:30–34
2 Chr 36:1–4

609
JEHOIAKIM
(11 years)
Burned part of God's Word given to Jeremiah, was a puppet king for Egypt and then Babylon, watched gold and articles taken from the Temple to Babylon, saw first exile (in which Daniel was taken)
2 Kgs 23:34—24:6
2 Chr 36:5–8

598
JEHOIACHIN
(3 months)
Saw next exile to Babylon
2 Kgs 24:6–15; 25:27–30
2 Chr 36:8–10

597
ZEDEKIAH
(11 years)
Saw the Temple burned and Jerusalem destroyed, was tortured and carried away in the final exile to Babylon
2 Kgs 24:17—25:21
2 Chr 36:10–21

663–654

ZEPHANIAH 640–621

HULDAH 632

JEREMIAH 627–586

HABAKKUK 612–589

OBADIAH 598–580(?)

2 KINGS

Kingdom divides 930 B.C.	Ahab dies in battle 853	Elijah's ministry transfers to Elisha 848	Jehu becomes king of Israel 841	Joash becomes king of Judah 835	Elisha's ministry ends 797	Jeroboam II becomes king of Israel 793	Amos's ministry begins 760	Hosea's ministry begins 753

VITAL STATISTICS

PURPOSE:
To demonstrate the fate that awaits all who refuse to make God their true leader

AUTHOR:
Unknown. Possibly Jeremiah or a group of prophets

SETTING:
The once-united nation of Israel has been divided into two kingdoms, Israel and Judah, for over a century.

KEY VERSES:
"Again and again the LORD had sent his prophets and seers to warn both Israel and Judah: 'Turn from all your evil ways. Obey my commands and laws, which are contained in the whole law that I commanded your ancestors and which I gave you through my servants the prophets.' But the Israelites would not listen. They were as stubborn as their ancestors and refused to believe in the LORD their God" (17:13, 14).

KEY PEOPLE:
Elijah, Elisha, the woman from Shunem, Naaman, Jezebel, Jehu, Joash, Hezekiah, Sennacherib, Isaiah, Manasseh, Josiah, Jehoiakim, Zedekiah, Nebuchadnezzar

SPECIAL FEATURES:
The 17 prophetic books at the end of the Old Testament give great insights into the time period of 2 Kings.

SPARKLING as it crashes against boulders along its banks, the river swiftly cascades toward the sea. The current grabs, pushes, and tugs at leaves and logs, carrying them along for the ride. Here and there a sportsman is spotted in a kayak or a canoe, going with the flow. Gravity pulls the water, and the river pulls the rest . . . downward. Suddenly, a silver missile breaks the surface and darts upstream, and then another. Oblivious to the swirling opposition, the shining salmon swim against the stream. They must go upstream, and nothing will stop them from reaching their destination.

The current of society's river is flowing fast and furious, pulling downward everything in its way. It would be easy to float along with the current. But God calls us to swim against the flow. It will not be easy, and we may be alone, but it will be right.

In the book of 2 Kings, we read of evil rulers, rampant idolatry, and a complacent populace—certainly pulling downward. Despite the pressure to conform, to turn from the Lord and to serve only self, a minority of chosen people moved in the opposite direction, toward God. The Bethel prophets and others, as well as two righteous kings, spoke God's word and stood for him. As you read 2 Kings, watch these courageous individuals. Catch the strength and force of Elijah and Elisha and the commitment of Hezekiah and Josiah, and determine to be one who swims against the current!

Second Kings continues the history of Israel, halfway between the death of David and the death of the nation. Israel had been divided (1 Kings 12), and the two kingdoms had begun to slide into idolatry and corruption toward collapse and captivity. Second Kings relates the sordid stories of the 12 kings of the northern kingdom (called Israel) and the 16 kings of the southern kingdom (called Judah). For 130 years Israel endures the succession of evil rulers until they were conquered by Shalmaneser of Assyria and led into captivity in 722 B.C. (17:6). Of all the kings in both the north and south, only two—Hezekiah and Josiah—were called good. Because of their obedience to God and the spiritual revivals during their reigns, Judah stood for an additional 136 years until falling to Nebuchadnezzar and the Babylonians in 586 B.C.

Throughout this dark period, the Bible mentions 30 prophets who proclaimed God's message to the people and their leaders. Most notable of these fearless people of God are Elijah and Elisha. As Elijah neared the end of his earthly ministry, Elisha asked that he might become Elijah's rightful successor (2:9). Soon after, Elijah was taken to heaven in a whirlwind (2:11), and Elisha became God's spokesman to the northern kingdom. Elisha's life was filled with signs, proclamations, warnings, and miracles. Four of the most memorable are the flowing oil (4:1–7), the healing of the Shunammite woman's son (4:8–37), the healing of Naaman's leprosy (5:1–27), and the floating ax head (6:1–7).

Even in the midst of terrible situations, God will have his faithful minority, his remnant (19:31). He desires courageous men and women to proclaim his truth.

Micah's ministry begins 742	Isaiah's ministry begins 740	Israel (northern kingdom) falls 722	Hezekiah becomes king of Judah 715	Josiah becomes king of Judah 640	Jeremiah's ministry begins 627	Book of the Law found in the Temple 622	First captivity of Judah; Daniel taken 605	Second captivity of Judah; Ezekiel taken 597	Judah (southern kingdom) falls 586

THE BLUEPRINT

A. THE DIVIDED KINGDOM (1:1—17:41)
1. Elisha's ministry
2. Kings of Israel and Judah
3. Israel is exiled to Assyria

Although Israel had the witness and power of Elisha, the nation turned from God and was exiled to Assyria. Assyria filled the northern kingdom with people from other lands. There has been no return from this captivity—it was permanent. Such is the end of all who shut God out of their lives.

B. THE SURVIVING KINGDOM (18:1—25:30)
1. Kings of Judah
2. Judah is exiled to Babylon

The northern kingdom was destroyed, and prophets were predicting the same fate for Judah. What more could cause the nation to repent? Hezekiah and Josiah were able to stem the tide of evil. They both repaired the Temple and gathered the people for the Passover. Josiah eradicated idolatry from the land, but as soon as these good kings were gone, the people returned again to living their own way instead of God's way. Each individual must believe and live for God in his or her family, church, and nation.

MEGATHEMES

THEME	EXPLANATION	IMPORTANCE
Elisha	The purpose of Elisha's ministry was to restore respect for God and his message, and he stood firmly against the evil kings of Israel. By faith, with courage and prayer, he revealed not only God's judgment on sin but also his mercy, love, and tenderness toward faithful people.	Elisha's mighty miracles showed that God controls not only great armies but also events in everyday life. When we listen to and obey God, he shows us his power to transform any situation. God's care is for all who are willing to follow him. He can perform miracles in our lives.
Idolatry	Every evil king in both Israel and Judah encouraged idolatry. These false gods represented war, cruelty, power, and sex. Although they had God's law, priests, and prophets to guide them, these kings sought priests and prophets whom they could manipulate to their own advantage.	An idol is any idea, ability, possession, or person that we regard more highly than God. We condemn Israel and Judah for foolishly worshiping idols, but we also worship other gods—power, money, physical attractiveness. Those who believe in God must resist the lure of these attractive idols.
Evil Kings/ Good Kings	Only 20 percent of Israel and Judah's kings followed God. The evil kings were shortsighted. They thought they could control their nations' destinies by importing other religions, forming alliances with pagan nations, and enriching themselves. The good kings had to spend most of their time undoing the evil done by their predecessors.	Although the evil kings led the people into sin, the priests, princes, heads of families, and military leaders all had to cooperate with the evil plans and practices in order for them to be carried out. We cannot discharge our responsibility to obey God by blaming our leaders. We are responsible to know God's Word and obey it.
God's Patience	God told his people that if they obeyed him, they would live successfully; if they disobeyed, they would be judged and destroyed. God had been patient with the people for hundreds of years. He sent many prophets to guide them. And he gave ample warning of coming destruction. But even God's patience has limits.	God is patient with us. He gives us many chances to hear his message, to turn from sin, and to believe him. His patience does not mean he is indifferent to how we live, nor does it mean we can ignore his warnings. His patience should make us want to come to him now.
Judgment	After King Solomon's reign, Israel lasted 209 years before the Assyrians destroyed it; Judah lasted 345 years before the Babylonians took Jerusalem. After repeated warnings to his people, God used these evil nations as instruments for his justice.	The consequences of rejecting God's commands and purpose for our lives are severe. He will not ignore unbelief or rebellion. We must believe in him and accept Christ's sacrificial death on our behalf, or we will be judged also.

KEY PLACES IN 2 KINGS

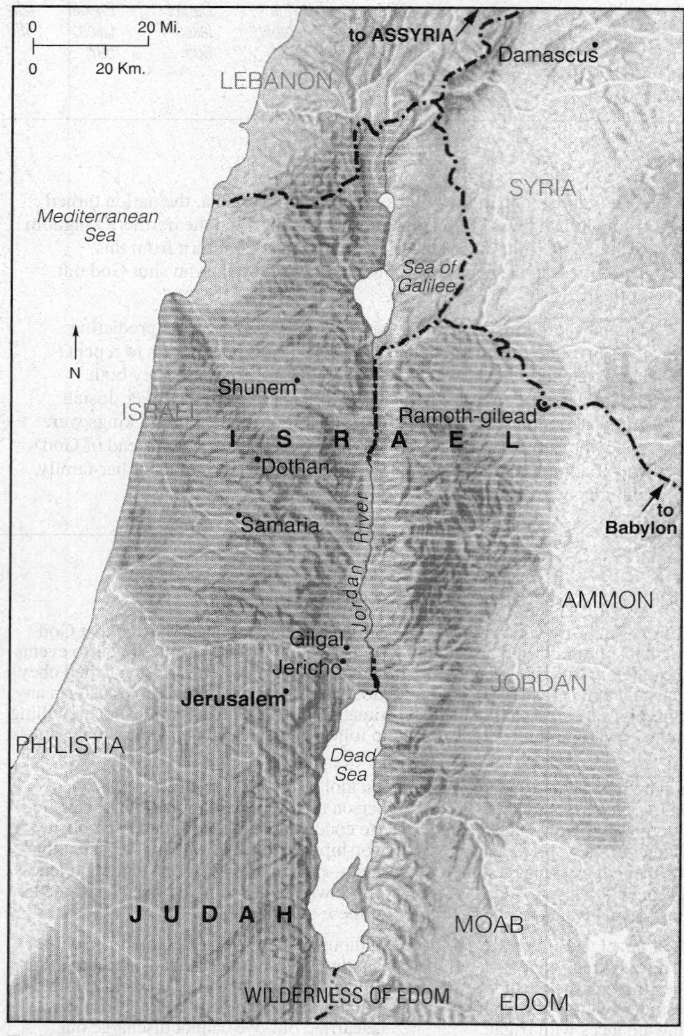

The broken lines (–·–·–) indicate modern boundaries.

The history of both Israel and Judah was much affected by the prophet Elisha's ministry. He served Israel for 50 years, fighting the idolatry of its kings and calling its people back to God.

1 Jericho Elijah's ministry had come to an end. He touched his cloak to the Jordan River, and he and Elisha crossed on dry ground. Elijah was taken by God in a whirlwind, and Elisha returned alone with the cloak. The prophets in Jericho realized that Elisha was Elijah's replacement (1:1—2:25).

2 Wilderness of Edom The king of Moab rebelled against Israel, so the nations of Israel, Judah, and Edom decided to attack from the wilderness of Edom but ran out of water. The kings consulted Elisha, who said God would send both water and victory (3:1–27).

3 Shunem Elisha cared for individuals and their needs. He helped a woman clear a debt by giving her a supply of oil to sell. For another family in Shunem, he raised a son from the dead (4:1–37).

4 Gilgal Elisha cared for the young prophets in Gilgal—he removed poison from a stew, made a small amount of food feed everyone, and even caused an ax head to float so it could be retrieved. It was to Elisha that Naaman, a commander in the Aramean army, came to be healed of leprosy (4:38—6:7).

5 Dothan Although he cured an Aramean commander's leprosy, Elisha was loyal to Israel. He knew the Aramean army's battle plans and kept Israel's king informed. The Aramean king tracked Elisha down in Dothan and surrounded the city, hoping to kill him. But Elisha prayed that the Arameans would be blinded; then he led the blinded army into Samaria, Israel's capital city (6:8–23).

6 Samaria But the Arameans didn't learn their lesson. They later besieged Samaria. Ironically, Israel's king thought it was Elisha's fault, but Elisha said food would be available in abundance the next day. True to Elisha's word, the Lord caused panic in the Aramean camp, and the enemy ran, leaving their supplies to Samaria's starving people (6:24—7:20).

7 Damascus Despite Elisha's loyalty to Israel, he obeyed God and traveled to Damascus, the capital of Aram. King Ben-hadad was sick, and he sent Hazael to ask Elisha if he would recover. Elisha knew the king would die and told this to Hazael. But Hazael then murdered Ben-hadad, making himself king. Later, Israel and Judah joined forces to fight this new Aramean threat (8:1–29).

8 Ramoth-gilead As Israel and Judah warred with Aram, Elisha sent a young prophet to Ramoth-gilead to anoint Jehu as Israel's next king. Jehu set out to destroy the wicked dynasties of Israel and Judah, killing kings Joram and Ahaziah, and wicked Queen Jezebel. He then destroyed King Ahab's family and all the Baal worshipers in Israel (9:1—11:1).

9 Jerusalem Power-hungry Athaliah became queen of Judah when her son Ahaziah was killed. She had all her grandsons killed except Joash, who was hidden by his aunt. Joash was crowned king at the age of seven and overthrew Athaliah. Meanwhile in Samaria, the Arameans continued to harass Israel. Israel's new king met with Elisha and was told that he would be victorious over Aram three times (11:2—13:19).

Following Elisha's death came a series of evil kings in Israel. Their idolatry and rejection of God caused their downfall. The Assyrian Empire captured Samaria and took most of the Israelites into captivity (13:20—17:41). Judah had a short reprieve because of a few good kings who destroyed idols and worshiped God. But many strayed from God. So Jerusalem fell to the next world power, Babylon (18:1—25:30).

A. THE DIVIDED KINGDOM (1:1—17:41)

Elisha begins his ministry to the northern kingdom after Elijah is taken away by a chariot of fire. Elisha performs many miracles and calls Israel to return to God, but they persist in their wickedness. Israel is defeated by Assyria, and the people of the northern kingdom are exiled, never to return. Such is the end of all those who ignore God's warnings and demand their own way in their desire to sin.

Elijah Confronts King Ahaziah

1:1 2 Sam 8:2 2 Kgs 3:5 **1** After King Ahab's death, the nation of Moab declared its independence from Israel.
2One day Israel's new king, Ahaziah, fell through the latticework of an upper
room at his palace in Samaria, and he was seriously injured. So he sent messengers to
1:2 2 Kgs 1:16; 8:7-10 Mark 3:22 the temple of Baal-zebub, the god of Ekron, to ask whether he would recover.
3But the angel of the LORD told Elijah, who was from Tishbe, "Go and meet the
1:3 1 Kgs 17:1 messengers of the king of Samaria and ask them, 'Why are you going to Baal-zebub, the
1:4 2 Kgs 1:16-17 god of Ekron, to ask whether the king will get well? Is there no God in Israel? 4Now,
therefore, this is what the LORD says: You will never leave the bed on which you are
lying, but you will surely die.'" So Elijah went to deliver the message.
5When the messengers returned to the king, he asked them, "Why have you returned
so soon?"
6They replied, "A man came up to us and told us to go back to the king with a message
from the LORD. He said, 'Why are you going to Baal-zebub, the god of Ekron, to ask
whether the king will get well? Is there no God in Israel? Now, since you have done this,
you will never leave the bed on which you are lying, but you will surely die.'"
7"Who was this man?" the king demanded. "What did he look like?"
1:8 Matt 3:4 Mark 1:6 8They replied, "He was a hairy man,* and he wore a leather belt around his waist."
"It was Elijah from Tishbe!" the king exclaimed. 9Then he sent an army captain with
fifty soldiers to arrest him. They found him sitting on top of a hill. The captain said to
him, "Man of God, the king has commanded you to come along with us."
1:10 1 Kgs 18:36-38 Job 1:16 Luke 9:54 10But Elijah replied to the captain, "If I am a man of God, let fire come down from
heaven and destroy you and your fifty men!" Then fire fell from heaven and killed
them all.
11So the king sent another captain with fifty men. The captain said to him, "Man of
God, the king says that you must come down right away."
12Elijah replied, "If I am a man of God, let fire come down from heaven and destroy
you and your fifty men!" And again the fire of God fell from heaven and killed them all.
13Once more the king sent a captain with fifty men. But this time the captain fell to
his knees before Elijah. He pleaded with him, "O man of God, please spare my life and
the lives of these, your fifty servants. 14See how the fire from heaven has destroyed the
first two groups. But now please spare my life!"

1:8 Or *He was wearing clothing made of hair.*

1:1 Because 1 and 2 Kings were originally one book, 2 Kings continues where 1 Kings ended. The once great nation of Israel was split in two because the people forgot God. The book begins with Elijah, a prophet of God, being carried away to heaven. It ends with the people of Israel and Judah being carried away into captivity. In 1 Kings, the beautiful Temple of God was built. In 2 Kings, it is desecrated and destroyed.

Our world is strikingly similar to the world described in 2 Kings. National and local governments do not seek God, and countries are tormented by war. Many people follow the false gods of technology, materialism, and war. True worship of God is rare on the earth.

In our chaotic and corrupt world, we can turn to examples such as David, Elijah, and Elisha, who were devoted to God's high honor and moral law and who brought about renewal and change in their society. More important, we can look to Jesus Christ, the perfect example. For nations to do God's will, they need individuals who will do God's work. If your heart is committed to God, he can work through you to accomplish the work he has called you to do.

1:2 Baal-zebub was not the same god as Baal, the Canaanite god worshiped by Ahab and Jezebel (1 Kings 16:31-33). Baal-zebub was another popular god whose temple was located in the city of Ekron. Because this god was thought to have the power of prophecy, King Ahaziah sent messengers to Ekron to learn of his fate. Supernatural power and mystery were associated with this god. Ahaziah's action showed the king's disrespect for God.

1:8 For more information on Elijah, see his Profile in 1 Kings 18.

1:13-15 Notice how the third captain went to Elijah. Although the first two captains called Elijah "man of God," they were not being genuine—God was not in their hearts. The third captain also called him "man of God," but he humbly begged for mercy. His attitude showed respect for God and his power and saved the lives of his men. Effective living begins with a right attitude toward God. Before religious words come to your mouth, make sure they are from your heart. Let respect, humility, and servanthood characterize your attitude toward God and others.

15 Then the angel of the LORD said to Elijah, "Don't be afraid. Go with him." So Elijah
got up and went to the king.
16 And Elijah said to the king, "This is what the LORD says: Why did you send
messengers to Baal-zebub, the god of Ekron, to ask whether you will get well? Is there
no God in Israel? Now, since you have done this, you will never leave the bed on which
you are lying, but you will surely die."
17 So Ahaziah died, just as the LORD had promised through Elijah. Since Ahaziah did
not have a son to succeed him, his brother Joram* became the next king. This took place
in the second year of the reign of Jehoram son of Jehoshaphat, king of Judah. 18 The rest
of the events in Ahaziah's reign are recorded in *The Book of the History of the Kings of
Israel.*

1. Elisha's ministry

Elijah Taken into Heaven

2 When the LORD was about to take Elijah up to heaven in a whirlwind, Elijah and
Elisha were traveling from Gilgal. 2 And Elijah said to Elisha, "Stay here, for the
LORD has told me to go to Bethel."
But Elisha replied, "As surely as the LORD lives and you yourself live, I will never
leave you!" So they went on together to Bethel.
3 The group of prophets from Bethel came to Elisha and asked him, "Did you know
that the LORD is going to take your master away from you today?"
"Quiet!" Elisha answered. "Of course I know it."
4 Then Elijah said to Elisha, "Stay here, for the LORD has told me to go to Jericho."
But Elisha replied again, "As surely as the LORD lives and you yourself live, I will
never leave you." So they went on together to Jericho.
5 Then the group of prophets from Jericho came to Elisha and asked him, "Did you
know that the LORD is going to take your master away from you today?"
"Quiet!" he answered again. "Of course I know it."
6 Then Elijah said to Elisha, "Stay here, for the LORD has told me to go to the Jordan
River."
But again Elisha replied, "As surely as the LORD lives and you yourself live, I will
never leave you." So they went on together.
7 Fifty men from the group of prophets also went and watched from a distance as Elijah
and Elisha stopped beside the Jordan River. 8 Then Elijah folded his cloak together and
struck the water with it. The river divided, and the two of them went across on dry
ground!
9 When they came to the other side, Elijah said to Elisha, "What can I do for you before
I am taken away?"
And Elisha replied, "Please let me become your rightful successor."*
10 "You have asked a difficult thing," Elijah replied. "If you see me when I am taken
from you, then you will get your request. But if not, then you won't."

1:17 Hebrew *Jehoram,* a variant name for Joram. **2:9** Hebrew *Let me inherit a double share of your spirit.*

1:15 2 Kgs 1:3; Isa 51:12; Jer 1:17; Ezek 2:6
1:17 2 Kgs 3:1; 8:16
2:1 Gen 5:23-24; 1 Kgs 19:16-21; Heb 11:5
2:6 Ruth 1:16; 2 Kgs 2:1-2
2:8 Exod 14:21; 1 Kgs 19:19

1:18 *The Book of the History of the Kings of Israel* and *The Book of the History of the Kings of Judah* (8:23) were history books. The inspired writer of 2 Kings selected facts from these books to retell the story of Israel and Judah from God's perspective. God directed the writer's thoughts and selection process to make sure that the truth, God's Word, would be written.

2:3 A "group of prophets from Bethel" was like a school, a gathering of disciples around a recognized prophet, such as Elijah or Elisha. These groups of prophets, located throughout the country, helped stem the tide of spiritual and moral decline in the nation begun under Jeroboam. The students at Bethel were eyewitnesses to the succession of the prophetic ministry from Elijah to Elisha.

2:8 Elijah's cloak was a symbol of his authority as a prophet.

2:9 Elisha asked to be Elijah's "rightful successor" (that is, he asked for a double portion of Elijah's spirit). Deuteronomy 21:17 helps explain Elisha's request. According to custom, the firstborn son received a double portion of the father's inheritance (see the note on Genesis 25:31). He was asking to be Elijah's successor, or heir, the one who would continue Elijah's work as leader of the prophets. But the decision to grant Elisha's request was up to God. Elijah only told him how he would know if his request had been granted.

2:9 God granted Elisha's request because Elisha's motives were pure. His main goal was not to be better or more powerful than Elijah, but to accomplish more for God. If our motives are pure, we don't have to be afraid to ask great things from God. When we ask God for great power or ability, we need to examine our desires and get rid of any selfishness we find. To have the Holy Spirit's help, we must be willing to ask.

2:11 2 Kgs 6:17 [11]As they were walking along and talking, suddenly a chariot of fire appeared, drawn
by horses of fire. It drove between them, separating them, and Elijah was carried by a
2:12 2 Kgs 13:14 whirlwind into heaven. [12]Elisha saw it and cried out, "My father! My father! The chariots
and charioteers of Israel!" And as they disappeared from sight, Elisha tore his robe in two.
[13]Then Elisha picked up Elijah's cloak and returned to the bank of the Jordan River.
2:14 2 Kgs 2:8 [14]He struck the water with the cloak and cried out, "Where is the LORD, the God of
Elijah?" Then the river divided, and Elisha went across.
[15]When the group of prophets from Jericho saw what happened, they exclaimed,
"Elisha has become Elijah's successor!"* And they went to meet him and bowed down
2:16 1 Kgs 18:12 Acts 8:39 before him. [16]"Sir," they said, "just say the word and fifty of our strongest men will
search the wilderness for your master. Perhaps the Spirit of the LORD has left him on
some mountain or in some valley."
"No," Elisha said, "don't send them." [17]But they kept urging him until he was
embarrassed, and he finally said, "All right, send them." So fifty men searched for three
days but did not find Elijah. [18]Elisha was still at Jericho when they returned. "Didn't I
tell you not to go?" he asked.

Elisha's First Miracles

[19]Now the leaders of the town of Jericho visited Elisha. "We have a problem, my lord,"
they told him. "This town is located in beautiful natural surroundings, as you can see.
But the water is bad, and the land is unproductive."

2:15 Hebrew *The spirit of Elijah rests upon Elisha.*

KINGS TO DATE AND THEIR ENEMIES

ISRAEL

853 ***AHAZIAH*** *1 Kgs 22:40–2 Kgs 1:18; 2 Chr 20:35–37*

852 ***JORAM*** *With Judah, defeated Mesha (Moab), and was miraculously delivered from Ben-hadad II (Aram); 2 Kgs 1:17; 3:1—8:25; 2 Chr 22:5–7*

841

JUDAH

872 ***JEHOSHAPHAT*** *Defeated by Ben-hadad II (Aram), gained miraculous victory over Moab and Ammon, and crushed a rebellion by Mesha (Moab); 2 Kgs 22:41–50; 2 Chr 17:1—21:1; Co-regency 853–848*

853 *848* *841* ***JEHORAM*** *Lost dominion over Edom, assaulted by Philistines and Arabs; 2 Kgs 8:16–24; 2 Chr 21:1–20*

All dates are B.C.
Solid section of the timeline indicates co-regency.
For all the kings of Israel and Judah, see the chart at the end of 1 Kings.

2:11 Elijah was taken to heaven without dying. He is the second person mentioned in Scripture to do so. Enoch was the first (Genesis 5:21-24). The other prophets may not have seen God take Elijah, or they may have had a difficult time believing what they saw. In either case, they wanted to search for Elijah (2:16-18). Finding no physical trace of him would confirm what had happened and strengthen their faith. The only other person taken to heaven in bodily form was Jesus after his resurrection from the dead (Acts 1:9).

2:13-25 These three incidents were testimonies to Elisha's commission as a prophet of God. They are recorded to demonstrate Elisha's new power and authority as Israel's chief prophet under God's ultimate power and authority.

2:14 When Elisha struck the water, it was not out of disrespect for God or Elijah. It was a plea by Elisha to God to confirm his appointment as Elijah's successor.

[20]Elisha said, "Bring me a new bowl with salt in it." So they brought it to him. [21]Then
he went out to the spring that supplied the town with water and threw the salt into it. And
he said, "This is what the LORD says: I have made this water wholesome. It will no longer
cause death or infertility.*" [22]And sure enough! The water has remained wholesome ever
since, just as Elisha said.
[23]Elisha left Jericho and went up to Bethel. As he was walking along the road, a group
of boys from the town began mocking and making fun of him. "Go away, you baldhead!"
they chanted. "Go away, you baldhead!" [24]Elisha turned around and looked at them, and
he cursed them in the name of the LORD. Then two bears came out of the woods and
mauled forty-two of them. [25]From there Elisha went to Mount Carmel and finally returned
to Samaria.

War between Israel and Moab

3 Ahab's son Joram* began to rule over Israel in the eighteenth year of King Jehoshaphat's reign in Judah. He reigned in Samaria twelve years. [2]He did what was evil in the
LORD's sight, but he was not as wicked as his father and mother. He at least tore down the
sacred pillar of Baal that his father had set up. [3]Nevertheless he continued in the sins of
idolatry that Jeroboam son of Nebat had led the people of Israel to commit.
[4]King Mesha of Moab and his people were sheep breeders. They used to pay the king
of Israel an annual tribute of 100,000 lambs and the wool of 100,000 rams. [5]But after
Ahab's death, the king of Moab rebelled against the king of Israel. [6]So King Joram
mustered the army of Israel and marched from Samaria. [7]On the way, he sent this
message to King Jehoshaphat of Judah: "The king of Moab has rebelled against me. Will
you help me fight him?"
And Jehoshaphat replied, "Why, of course! You and I are brothers, and my troops are

2:21 Exod 15:25-26; 2 Kgs 4:41; 6:6
2:25 1 Kgs 18:20
3:1 2 Kgs 1:17; 8:16
3:2 1 Kgs 16:30-32; 2 Kgs 10:25-26
3:3 1 Kgs 12:28; 14:16
3:4 2 Sam 8:2; Isa 16:1-2
3:5 2 Kgs 1:1
3:7 1 Kgs 22:4

2:21 Or *or make the land unproductive.* **3:1** Hebrew *Jehoram,* a variant name for Joram; also in 3:6.

2:23, 24 This mob of youths was from Bethel, the religious center of idolatry in the northern kingdom, and they were probably warning Elisha not to speak against their immorality as Elijah had done. They were not merely teasing Elisha about his baldness, but showing severe disrespect for Elisha's message and God's power. They may also have jeered because of their disbelief in the chariot of fire that had taken Elijah. When Elisha cursed them, he did not call out the bears himself. God sent them as a judgment for their callous unbelief.

WAR AGAINST MOAB
Moab's king rebelled against Israel. So Joram, Israel's king, and Jehoshaphat, Judah's king, attacked Moab. In the parched and rugged wilderness of Edom, the armies ran out of water, but Elisha promised that both water and victory would soon come.

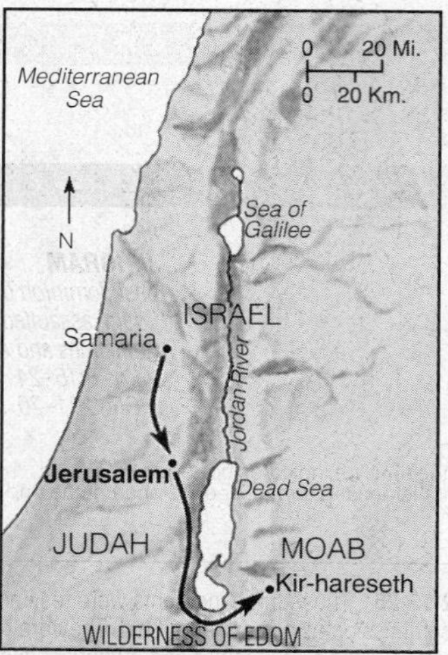

2:23, 24 These young men jeered at God's messenger and paid for it with their lives. Making fun of religious leaders has been a popular sport through the ages. To take a stand for God is to be different from the world and vulnerable to verbal abuse. When we are cynical and sarcastic toward religious leaders, we are in danger of mocking not just the person but also the spiritual message. While we are not to condone the sin that some leaders commit, we need to pray for them, not laugh at them. True leaders, those who follow God, need to be heard with respect and encouraged in their ministry.

3:1 Although 1:17 says that Jehoram was king of Judah, 3:1 says that Jehoshaphat was Judah's king. As a king grew older, it was common for his son to rule beside him. Jehoshaphat, nearing the end of his reign, appointed his son Jehoram to rule with him. Jehoram served as co-ruler with Jehoshaphat for five years (853–848 B.C.; he is mentioned again in 8:16-24). Joram, king of Israel, was Ahab's son and Ahaziah's brother (1:17). Both Ahab (1 Kings 16:29–22:40) and Ahaziah (1:2-18) served as kings of Israel before Joram.

3:3 The sins of Israel's kings are often compared to the sins of Jeroboam, the first ruler of the northern kingdom of Israel. His great sin was to institute idol worship throughout his kingdom, causing people to turn away from God (1 Kings 12:25-33). By ignoring God and allowing idol worship, Joram clung to Jeroboam's sins.

3:4, 5 Israel and Judah held some of the most fertile land and strategic positions in the ancient Near East. It is no wonder that neighboring nations like Moab envied them and constantly attempted to seize the land. Moab lay just southeast of Israel. The country had been under Israel's control for some time due to Ahab's strong military leadership. When Ahab died, Mesha, the Moabite king, took the opportunity to rebel. While Israel's next king, Ahaziah, did nothing about the revolt, his successor, Joram, decided to take action. He joined forces with Jehoshaphat, king of Judah, and went to fight the Moabites. Together, Israel and Judah brought the Moabites to the brink of surrender. But when they saw the Moabite king sacrifice his own son and successor (3:27), they withdrew even though they had won the battle. Moab fought many other battles with both Israel and Judah. Some of them, in fact, were recorded by Mesha (c. 840 B.C.), who carved his exploits on a plaque called the Moabite Stone (discovered in 1868).

yours to command. Even my horses are at your service." [8]Then Jehoshaphat asked,
"What route will we take?"

3:9 1 Kgs 22:47

"We will attack from the wilderness of Edom," Joram replied. [9]The king of Edom
and his troops joined them, and all three armies traveled along a roundabout route
through the wilderness for seven days. But there was no water for the men or their pack
animals.

[10]"What should we do?" the king of Israel cried out. "The LORD has brought the three
of us here to let the king of Moab defeat us."

3:11 1 Kgs 19:21; 22:7

[11]But King Jehoshaphat of Judah asked, "Is there no prophet of the LORD with us? If
there is, we can ask the LORD what to do."

One of King Joram's officers replied, "Elisha son of Shaphat is here. He used to be
Elijah's personal assistant.*"

[12]Jehoshaphat said, "Then the LORD will speak through him." So the kings of Israel,
Judah, and Edom went to consult with Elisha.

3:13 1 Kgs 22:6-11, 22-25

[13]"I want no part of you," Elisha said to the king of Israel. "Go to the pagan prophets
of your father and mother!"

But King Joram said, "No! For it was the LORD who called us three kings here to be
destroyed by the king of Moab!"

[14]Elisha replied, "As surely as the LORD Almighty lives, whom I serve, I would not

3:15 1 Sam 16:23

bother with you except for my respect for King Jehoshaphat of Judah. [15]Now bring me
someone who can play the harp."

While the harp was being played, the power of the LORD came upon Elisha, [16]and he
said, "This is what the LORD says: This dry valley will be filled with pools of water!
[17]You will see neither wind nor rain, says the LORD, but this valley will be filled with

3:11 Hebrew *He used to pour water on the hands of Elijah.*

MIRACLES OF ELIJAH & ELISHA

Baal, the false god worshiped by many Israelites, was the god of rain, fire, and farm crops. He also demanded child sacrifice. Elijah's and Elisha's miracles repeatedly show the power of the true God over the purported realm of Baal, as well as the value God places on the life of a child.

Miracle	*Reference*	*Factors*
ELIJAH		
1. Food brought by ravens	1 Kings 17:5, 6	Food
2. Widow's food multiplied	1 Kings 17:12-16	Flour and oil
3. Widow's son raised to life	1 Kings 17:17-24	Life of a child
4. Altar and sacrifice consumed	1 Kings 18:16-46	Fire and water
5. Ahaziah's soldiers consumed	2 Kings 1:9-14	Fire
6. Jordan River parted	2 Kings 2:6-8	Water
7. Transported to heaven	2 Kings 2:11, 12	Fire and wind
ELISHA		
1. Jordan River parted	2 Kings 2:13, 14	Water
2. Spring purified at Jericho	2 Kings 2:19-22	Water
3. Widow's oil multiplied	2 Kings 4:1-7	Oil
4. Dead boy raised to life	2 Kings 4:18-37	Life of a child
5. Poison in stew purified	2 Kings 4:38-41	Flour
6. Prophets' food multiplied	2 Kings 4:42-44	Bread and grain
7. Naaman healed of leprosy	2 Kings 5:1-14	Water
8. Gehazi became leprous	2 Kings 5:15-27	Words alone
9. Ax head floated	2 Kings 6:1-7	Water
10. Aramean army blinded	2 Kings 6:8-23	Elisha's prayer

3:9, 10 Edom was under Judah's control; thus, they marched with them, making three kings.

3:11-20 Jehoshaphat's request for "a prophet of the LORD" shows how true worship and religious experience in both Israel and Judah had declined. In David's day, both the high priest and the prophets gave the king advice. But most of the priests had left Israel (see the first note on 1 Kings 17:1), and God's prophets were seen as messengers of doom (1 Kings 22:18). This miracle predicted by Elisha affirmed God's power and authority and validated Elisha's ministry. In 2 Chronicles 18, King Jehoshaphat of Judah and King Ahab of Israel gave the prophet Micaiah a similar request. But they ignored God's advice—with disastrous results.

3:15 In Old Testament times music often accompanied prophecy (1 Chronicles 25:1).

water. You will have plenty for yourselves and for your cattle and your other animals.
18 But this is only a simple thing for the LORD, for he will make you victorious over the
army of Moab! 19 You will conquer the best of their cities, even the fortified ones. You
will cut down all their trees, stop up all their springs, and ruin all their good land with
stones."

20 And sure enough, the next day at about the time when the morning sacrifice was **3:20** Exod 29:39-40
offered, water suddenly appeared! It was flowing from the direction of Edom, and soon
there was water everywhere.

21 Meanwhile, when the people of Moab heard about the three armies marching
against them, they mobilized every man who could fight, young and old, and stationed
themselves along their border. 22 But when they got up the next morning, the sun was
shining across the water, making it look as red as blood. 23 "It's blood!" the Moabites
exclaimed. "The three armies have attacked and killed each other! Let's go and collect
the plunder!"

24 When they arrived at the Israelite camp, the army of Israel rushed out and attacked
the Moabites, who turned and ran. The army of Israel chased them into the land of Moab,
destroying everything as they went. 25 They destroyed the cities, covered their good land **3:25** Isa 16:7
with stones, stopped up the springs, and cut down the good trees. Finally, only Kir- Jer 48:31, 36
hareseth was left, but even that came under attack.*

26 When the king of Moab saw that he was losing the battle, he led seven hundred of
his warriors in a desperate attempt to break through the enemy lines near the king of
Edom, but they failed to escape. 27 So he took his oldest son, who would have been the **3:27** Mic 6:7
next king, and sacrificed him as a burnt offering on the wall. As a result, the anger against
Israel was great, so they withdrew and returned to their own land.

Elisha Helps a Poor Widow

4 One day the widow of one of Elisha's fellow prophets came to Elisha and cried **4:1** Lev 25:39-41, 48
out to him, "My husband who served you is dead, and you know how he feared Neh 5:2-5
the LORD. But now a creditor has come, threatening to take my two sons as slaves."

2 "What can I do to help you?" Elisha asked. "Tell me, what do you have in the **4:2** 1 Kgs 17:12
house?"

"Nothing at all, except a flask of olive oil," she replied.

3 And Elisha said, "Borrow as many empty jars as you can from your friends and
neighbors. 4 Then go into your house with your sons and shut the door behind you. Pour
olive oil from your flask into the jars, setting the jars aside as they are filled."

5 So she did as she was told. Her sons brought many jars to her, and she filled one after
another. 6 Soon every container was full to the brim!

"Bring me another jar," she said to one of her sons.

"There aren't any more!" he told her. And then the olive oil stopped flowing.

7 When she told the man of God what had happened, he said to her, "Now sell the olive **4:7** 1 Kgs 12:22
oil and pay your debts, and there will be enough money left over to support you and your
sons."

3:25 Hebrew *until only Kir-hareseth was left, with its stones, but the slingers surrounded and attacked it.*

3:20 The morning sacrifice was one of two sacrifices that the priests were required to offer each day.

4:1 Poor people and debtors were allowed to pay their debts by selling themselves or their children as slaves. God ordered rich people and creditors not to take advantage of these people during their time of extreme need (see Deuteronomy 15:1-18 for an explanation of these practices). This woman's creditor was not acting in the spirit of God's law. Elisha's kind deed demonstrates that God wants us to go beyond simply keeping the law. We must also show compassion.

4:1ff This chapter records four of God's miracles through Elisha: providing money for a poverty-stricken widow (4:1-7); raising a dead boy to life (4:32-37); purifying poisonous food (4:38-41); and providing food for 100 men (4:42-44). These miracles show God's tenderness and care for those who are faithful to him.

When reading the Old Testament, it is easy to focus on God's harsh judgment of the rebellious and to minimize his tender care for those who love and serve him. Seeing him at work providing for his followers helps us keep his severe justice toward the unrepentant in proper perspective.

4:6 The woman and her sons collected jars from their neighbors, pouring olive oil into them from their one flask. The olive oil was used for cooking, for lamps, and for fuel. The oil stopped flowing only when they ran out of containers. The number of jars they gathered was an indication of their faith. God's provision was as large as their faith and willingness to obey. Beware of limiting God's blessings by a lack of faith and obedience. God is able to do immeasurably more than all we ask or imagine (Ephesians 3:20).

Elisha and the Woman from Shunem
4:8 8 One day Elisha went to the town of Shunem. A wealthy woman lived there, and she
Josh 19:18 invited him to eat some food. From then on, whenever he passed that way, he would stop
there to eat.
9 She said to her husband, "I am sure this man who stops in from time to time is a holy
4:10 man of God. 10 Let's make a little room for him on the roof and furnish it with a bed, a
Matt 10:41 table, a chair, and a lamp. Then he will have a place to stay whenever he comes by."
Rom 12:13 11 One day Elisha returned to Shunem, and he went up to his room to rest. 12 He said
to his servant Gehazi, "Tell the woman I want to speak to her." When she arrived,
13 Elisha said to Gehazi, "Tell her that we appreciate the kind concern she has shown us.
Now ask her what we can do for her. Does she want me to put in a good word for her to
the king or to the commander of the army?"
"No," she replied, "my family takes good care of me."
14 Later Elisha asked Gehazi, "What do you think we can do for her?"
He suggested, "She doesn't have a son, and her husband is an old man."
4:15 15 "Call her back again," Elisha told him. When the woman returned, Elisha said to her
Gen 18:14 as she stood in the doorway, 16 "Next year at about this time you will be holding a son in
your arms!"
"No, my lord!" she protested. "Please don't lie to me like that, O man of God." 17 But
sure enough, the woman soon became pregnant. And at that time the following year she
had a son, just as Elisha had said.
18 One day when her child was older, he went out to visit his father, who was working
with the harvesters. 19 Suddenly he complained, "My head hurts! My head hurts!"
His father said to one of the servants, "Carry him home to his mother."
20 So the servant took him home, and his mother held him on her lap. But around
4:21 noontime he died. 21 She carried him up to the bed of the man of God, then shut the door
2 Kgs 4:32 and left him there. 22 She sent a message to her husband: "Send one of the servants and
a donkey so that I can hurry to the man of God and come right back."
23 "Why today?" he asked. "It is neither a new moon festival nor a Sabbath."
But she said, "It's all right." 24 So she saddled the donkey and said to the servant,
"Hurry! Don't slow down on my account unless I tell you to."
25 As she approached the man of God at Mount Carmel, Elisha saw her in the distance.
He said to Gehazi, "Look, the woman from Shunem is coming. 26 Run out to meet her
and ask her, 'Is everything all right with you, with your husband, and with your child?'"
"Yes," the woman told Gehazi, "everything is fine."
27 But when she came to the man of God at the mountain, she fell to the ground before
him and caught hold of his feet. Gehazi began to push her away, but the man of God said, "Leave
her alone. Something is troubling her deeply, and the LORD has not told me what it is."

THE FAMILY IN SHUNEM
Elisha often stayed with a kind family in Shunem. When the son suddenly died, his mother traveled to Mount Carmel to find Elisha. He returned with her and raised the boy from the dead. Elisha then went to his home in Gilgal.

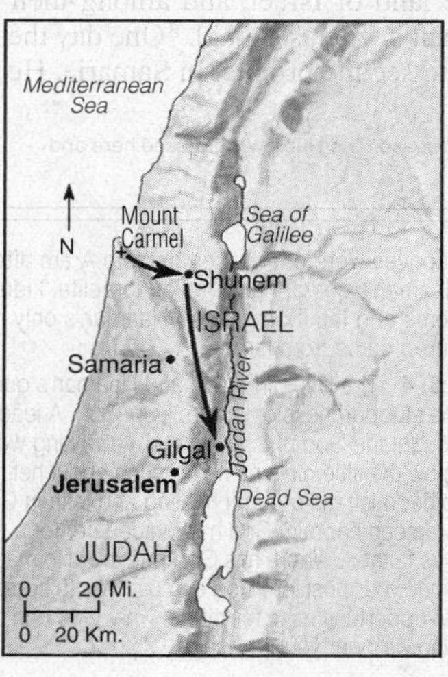

4:9 The Shunammite woman realized that Elisha was a man of God, and so she prepared a room for him to use whenever he was in town. She did this out of kindness and because she sensed a need, not for any selfish motives. Soon, however, her kindness would be rewarded far beyond her wildest dreams. How sensitive are you to those who pass by your home and flow through your life—especially those who teach and preach God's Word? What special needs do they have that you could meet? Look for ways to serve and help.

4:32-36 Elisha's prayer and method of raising the dead boy show God's personal care for hurting people. We must express genuine concern for others as we carry God's message to them. Only then will we faithfully represent our compassionate Father in heaven.

28 Then she said, "It was you, my lord, who said I would have a son. And didn't I tell you not to raise my hopes?"

29 Then Elisha said to Gehazi, "Get ready to travel; take my staff and go! Don't talk to anyone along the way. Go quickly and lay the staff on the child's face."

4:29 Exod 4:17; 7:19; 14:16 1 Kgs 18:46

30 But the boy's mother said, "As surely as the LORD lives and you yourself live, I won't go home unless you go with me." So Elisha returned with her.

31 Gehazi hurried on ahead and laid the staff on the child's face, but nothing happened. There was no sign of life. He returned to meet Elisha and told him, "The child is still dead."

32 When Elisha arrived, the child was indeed dead, lying there on the prophet's bed. 33 He went in alone and shut the door behind him and prayed to the LORD. 34 Then he lay down on the child's body, placing his mouth on the child's mouth, his eyes on the child's eyes, and his hands on the child's hands. And the child's body began to grow warm again! 35 Elisha got up and walked back and forth in the room a few times. Then he stretched himself out again on the child. This time the boy sneezed seven times and opened his eyes!

4:34 1 Kgs 17:21-23

36 Then Elisha summoned Gehazi. "Call the child's mother!" he said. And when she came in, Elisha said, "Here, take your son!" 37 She fell at his feet, overwhelmed with gratitude. Then she picked up her son and carried him downstairs.

4:37 Heb 11:35

Miracles during a Famine

38 Elisha now returned to Gilgal, but there was a famine in the land. One day as the group of prophets was seated before him, he said to his servant, "Put on a large kettle and make some stew for these men."

4:38 2 Kgs 2:1; 8:1

39 One of the young men went out into the field to gather vegetables and came back with a pocketful of wild gourds. He shredded them and put them into the kettle without realizing they were poisonous. 40 But after the men had eaten a bite or two they cried out, "Man of God, there's poison in this stew!" So they would not eat it.

41 Elisha said, "Bring me some flour." Then he threw it into the kettle and said, "Now it's all right; go ahead and eat." And then it did not harm them!

4:41 Exod 15:25 2 Kgs 2:21-22

42 One day a man from Baal-shalishah brought the man of God a sack of fresh grain and twenty loaves of barley bread made from the first grain of his harvest. Elisha said, "Give it to the group of prophets* so they can eat."

43 "What?" his servant exclaimed. "Feed one hundred people with only this?"

4:43 Luke 9:13 John 6:9, 12

But Elisha repeated, "Give it to the group of prophets so they can eat, for the LORD says there will be plenty for all. There will even be some left over!" 44 And sure enough, there was plenty for all and some left over, just as the LORD had promised.

4:44 Matt 14:16, 20

The Healing of Naaman

5 The king of Aram had high admiration for Naaman, the commander of his army, because through him the LORD had given Aram great victories. But though Naaman was a mighty warrior, he suffered from leprosy.*

5:1 Luke 4:27

2 Now groups of Aramean raiders had invaded the land of Israel, and among their captives was a young girl who had been given to Naaman's wife as a maid. 3 One day the girl said to her mistress, "I wish my master would go to see the prophet in Samaria. He would heal him of his leprosy."

5:2 2 Kgs 6:23

4:42 Hebrew *to the people;* also in 4:43. **5:1** Or *from a contagious skin disease.* The Hebrew word used here and throughout this passage can describe various skin diseases.

5:1 Leprosy, much like AIDS today, was one of the most feared diseases of the time. Some forms were extremely contagious and, in many cases, incurable. In its worst forms, leprosy led to death. Many lepers were forced out of the cities into quarantined camps. Because Naaman still held his post, he probably had a mild form of the disease, or perhaps it was still in the early stages. In either case, his life would have been tragically shortened by his disease. (For more about leprosy in Bible times, see the note on Leviticus 13:1ff.)

5:2 Aram was Israel's neighbor to the northeast, but the two nations were rarely on friendly terms. Under David, Aram paid tribute to Israel. In Elisha's day, Aram was growing in power and frequently conducted raids on Israel, trying to frustrate the people and bring about political confusion. Israelite captives were often taken back to Aram after successful raids. Naaman's servant girl was an Israelite, kidnapped from her home and family. Ironically, Naaman's only hope of being cured came from Israel.

5:3, 4 The little girl's faith and Naaman's quest contrast with the stubbornness of Israel's king (5:7). A leader in mighty Aram sought the God of Israel; Israel's own king would not. We don't know the little girl's name or much about her, but her brief word to her mistress brought healing and faith in God to a powerful Aramean captain. God had placed her for a purpose, and she was faithful. Where has God put you? No matter how humble or small your position, God can use you to spread his Word. Look for opportunities to tell others what God can do. There's no telling who will hear your message!

5:5 1 Sam 9:7-8

[4]So Naaman told the king what the young girl from Israel had said. [5]"Go and visit the
prophet," the king told him. "I will send a letter of introduction for you to carry to the
king of Israel." So Naaman started out, taking as gifts 750 pounds of silver, 150 pounds
of gold,* and ten sets of clothing. [6]The letter to the king of Israel said: "With this letter
I present my servant Naaman. I want you to heal him of his leprosy."

5:7 Gen 30:2; 37:29 1 Kgs 20:7

[7]When the king of Israel read it, he tore his clothes in dismay and said, "This man
sends me a leper to heal! Am I God, that I can kill and give life? He is only trying to find
an excuse to invade us again."
[8]But when Elisha, the man of God, heard about the king's reaction, he sent this
message to him: "Why are you so upset? Send Naaman to me, and he will learn that there
is a true prophet here in Israel."
[9]So Naaman went with his horses and chariots and waited at the door of Elisha's

5:10 John 9:7

house. [10]But Elisha sent a messenger out to him with this message: "Go and wash
yourself seven times in the Jordan River. Then your skin will be restored, and you will
be healed of leprosy."

5:5 Hebrew *10 talents* [340 kilograms] *of silver, 6,000 shekels* [68 kilograms] *of gold.*

ELISHA

Few "replacements" in Scripture were as effective as Elisha, who was Elijah's replacement as God's prophet to Israel. But Elisha had a great example to follow in the prophet Elijah. He remained with Elijah until the last moments of his teacher's life on earth. He was willing to follow and learn in order to gain power to do the work to which God had called him.

Both Elijah and Elisha concentrated their efforts on the particular needs of the people around them. The fiery Elijah confronted and exposed idolatry, helping to create an atmosphere where people could freely and publicly worship God. Elisha then moved in to demonstrate God's powerful, yet caring, nature to all who came to him for help. He spent less time in conflict with evil and more in compassionate care of people. The Bible records 18 encounters between Elisha and needy people.

Elisha saw more *in* life than most people because he recognized that with God there was more *to* life. He knew that all we are and have comes to us from God. The miracles that occurred during Elisha's ministry put people in touch with the personal and all-powerful God. Elijah would have been proud of his replacement's work.

We, too, have great examples to follow—both people in Scripture and those who have positively influenced our lives. We must resist the tendency to think about the limitations that our family background or environment creates for us. Instead, we should ask God to use us for his purposes—perhaps, like Elijah, to take a stand against great wrongs or, like Elisha, to show compassion for the daily needs of those around us. Ask him to use you as only he can.

Strengths and accomplishments
- Was Elijah's successor as a prophet of God
- Had a ministry that lasted over 50 years
- Had a major impact on four nations: Israel, Judah, Moab, and Aram
- Was a man of integrity who did not try to enrich himself at others' expense
- Did many miracles to help those in need

Lessons from his life
- In God's eyes, one measure of greatness is the willingness to serve the poor as well as the powerful
- An effective replacement not only learns from his master but also builds upon his master's achievements

Vital statistics
- Where: Prophesied to the northern kingdom
- Occupations: Farmer, prophet
- Relative: Father: Shaphat
- Contemporaries: Elijah, Ahab, Jezebel, Jehu

Key verse
"When they came to the other side, Elijah said to Elisha, 'What can I do for you before I am taken away?' And Elisha replied, 'Please let me become your rightful successor' " (2 Kings 2:9).

Elisha's story is told in 1 Kings 19:16—2 Kings 13:20. He is also mentioned in Luke 4:27.

5:9-15 Naaman, a great hero, was used to getting respect, and he was outraged when Elisha treated him like an ordinary person. A proud man, he expected royal treatment. To wash in a great river would be one thing, but the Jordan was small and dirty. To wash in the Jordan, Naaman thought, was beneath a man of his position. But Naaman had to humble himself and obey Elisha's commands in order to be healed.

Obedience to God begins with humility. We must believe that his way is better than our own. We may not always understand his ways of working, but by humbly obeying, we will receive his blessings. We must remember that (1) God's ways are best; (2) God wants our obedience more than anything else; (3) God can use anything to accomplish his purposes.

11 But Naaman became angry and stalked away. “I thought he would surely come out
to meet me!” he said. “I expected him to wave his hand over the leprosy and call on the
name of the LORD his God and heal me! 12 Aren’t the Abana River and Pharpar River of **5:12** Prov 14:17; 19:11
Damascus better than all the rivers of Israel put together? Why shouldn’t I wash in them
and be healed?” So Naaman turned and went away in a rage.
13 But his officers tried to reason with him and said, “Sir, if the prophet had told you
to do some great thing, wouldn’t you have done it? So you should certainly obey him
when he says simply to go and wash and be cured!” 14 So Naaman went down to the **5:14** Job 33:23-25
Jordan River and dipped himself seven times, as the man of God had instructed him. And Luke 4:27; 5:13
his flesh became as healthy as a young child’s, and he was healed!
15 Then Naaman and his entire party went back to find the man of God. They stood **5:15** 1 Sam 17:46-47
before him, and Naaman said, “I know at last that there is no God in all the world except
in Israel. Now please accept my gifts.”
16 But Elisha replied, “As surely as the LORD lives, whom I serve, I will not accept any **5:16** Gen 14:22-23
gifts.” And though Naaman urged him to take the gifts, Elisha refused. 2 Kgs 3:14
17 Then Naaman said, “All right, but please allow me to load two of my mules with **5:17** Exod 20:24
earth from this place, and I will take it back home with me. From now on I will never
again offer any burnt offerings or sacrifices to any other god except the LORD. 18 How- **5:18** 2 Kgs 7:2
ever, may the LORD pardon me in this one thing. When my master the king goes into the
temple of the god Rimmon to worship there and leans on my arm, may the LORD pardon
me when I bow, too.”
19 “Go in peace,” Elisha said. So Naaman started home again.

The Greed of Gehazi

20 But Gehazi, Elisha’s servant, said to himself, “My master should not have let this **5:20** 2 Kgs 4:11-12, 31, 36
Aramean get away without accepting his gifts. As surely as the LORD lives, I will chase
after him and get something from him.” 21 So Gehazi set off after him.
When Naaman saw him running after him, he climbed down from his chariot and went
to meet him. “Is everything all right?” Naaman asked.
22 “Yes,” Gehazi said, “but my master has sent me to tell you that two young prophets **5:22** 2 Kgs 5:5
from the hill country of Ephraim have just arrived. He would like 75 pounds* of silver
and two sets of clothing to give to them.”
23 “By all means, take 150 pounds* of silver,” Naaman insisted. He gave him two sets
of clothing, tied up the money in two bags, and sent two of his servants to carry the gifts
for Gehazi. 24 But when they arrived at the hill, Gehazi took the gifts from the servants
and sent the men back. Then he hid the gifts inside the house.
25 When he went in to his master, Elisha asked him, “Where have you been, Gehazi?”
“I haven’t been anywhere,” he replied.

5:22 Hebrew *1 talent* [34 kilograms]. **5:23** Hebrew *2 talents* [68 kilograms].

5:12 Naaman left in a rage because the cure for his disease seemed too simple. He was a hero, and he expected a heroic cure. Full of pride and self-will, he could not accept the simple cure of faith. Sometimes people react to God’s offer of forgiveness in the same way. Just to *believe* in Jesus Christ somehow doesn’t seem significant enough to bring eternal life. To obey God’s commands doesn’t seem heroic. What Naaman had to do to have his leprosy washed away is similar to what we must do to have our sin washed away—humbly accept God’s mercy. Don’t let your reaction to the way of faith keep you from the cure you need the most.

5:16 Elisha refused Naaman’s money to show that God’s favor cannot be purchased. Our money, like Naaman’s, is useless when we face death. No matter how much wealth we accumulate in this life, it will evaporate when we stand before God, our Creator. It will be our faith in Jesus Christ that saves us, not our bank accounts.

5:18, 19 How could Naaman be forgiven for bowing to a pagan idol? Naaman was not asking for permission to worship the god Rimmon, but to do his civil duty, helping the king get down and up as he bowed. Also known as Hadad, Rimmon, the god of Damascus, was believed to be a god of rain and thunder. Naaman, unlike most of his contemporaries, showed a keen awareness of God’s power. Instead of adding God to his nation’s collection of idols, he acknowledged that there was only one true God. He did not intend to worship other gods. His asking for pardon in this one area shows the marked contrast between Naaman and the Israelites, who were continually worshiping many idols.

5:20-27 Gehazi saw a perfect opportunity to get rich by selfishly asking for the reward Elisha had refused. Unfortunately, there were three problems with his plan: (1) He willingly accepted money that had been offered to someone else; (2) he wrongly implied that money could be exchanged for God’s free gift of healing and mercy; (3) he lied and tried to cover up his motives for accepting the money. Although Gehazi had been a helpful servant, personal gain had become more important to him than serving God.

This passage is not teaching that money is evil or that ministers should not get paid; instead, it is warning against greed and deceit. True service is motivated by love and devotion to God and seeks no personal gain. As you serve God, check your motives—you can’t serve both God and money (Matthew 6:24).

5:26 2 Kgs 5:16
5:27 Exod 4:6; Num 12:10

26 But Elisha asked him, "Don't you realize that I was there in spirit when Naaman
stepped down from his chariot to meet you? Is this the time to receive money and
clothing and olive groves and vineyards and sheep and oxen and servants? 27 Because
you have done this, you and your children and your children's children will suffer from
Naaman's leprosy forever." When Gehazi left the room, he was leprous; his skin was as
white as snow.

The Floating Ax Head

6:1 2 Kgs 2:3, 5, 7

6 One day the group of prophets came to Elisha and told him, "As you can see, this
place where we meet with you is too small. 2 Let's go down to the Jordan River,
where there are plenty of logs. There we can build a new place for us to meet."
"All right," he told them, "go ahead."
3 "Please come with us," someone suggested.
"I will," he said.
4 When they arrived at the Jordan, they began cutting down trees. 5 But as one of
them was chopping, his ax head fell into the river. "Ah, my lord!" he cried. "It was a
borrowed ax!"

6:6 Exod 15:25; 2 Kgs 2:21; 4:41

6 "Where did it fall?" the man of God asked. When he showed him the place, Elisha
cut a stick and threw it into the water. Then the ax head rose to the surface and floated.
7 "Grab it," Elisha said to him. And the man reached out and grabbed it.

Elisha Traps the Arameans

8 When the king of Aram was at war with Israel, he would confer with his officers and
say, "We will mobilize our forces at such and such a place."

6:9 1 Kgs 20:13, 28; 2 Kgs 6:12

9 But immediately Elisha, the man of God, would warn the king of Israel, "Do not go
near that place, for the Arameans are planning to mobilize their troops there." 10 So the
king of Israel would send word to the place indicated by the man of God, warning the
people there to be on their guard. This happened several times.
11 The king of Aram became very upset over this. He called in his officers and
demanded, "Which of you is the traitor? Who has been informing the king of Israel of
my plans?"
12 "It's not us, my lord," one of the officers replied. "Elisha, the prophet in Israel, tells
the king of Israel even the words you speak in the privacy of your bedroom!"

6:13 Gen 37:17

13 The king commanded, "Go and find out where Elisha is, and we will send troops to
seize him."
And the report came back: "Elisha is at Dothan." 14 So one night the king of Aram sent
a great army with many chariots and horses to surround the city. 15 When the servant of
the man of God got up early the next morning and went outside, there were troops,
horses, and chariots everywhere.

PEOPLE RAISED FROM THE DEAD
God is all-powerful. Nothing in life is beyond his control, not even death.

Elijah raised a boy from the dead	1 Kings 17:22
Elisha raised a boy from the dead	2 Kings 4:34–35
Elisha's bones raised a man from the dead	2 Kings 13:20–21
Jesus raised a boy from the dead	Luke 7:14, 15
Jesus raised a girl from the dead	Luke 8:52–56
Jesus raised Lazarus from the dead	John 11:38–44
Peter raised a woman from the dead	Acts 9:40, 41
Paul raised a man from the dead	Acts 20:9–20

6:1-7 The incident of the floating ax head is recorded to show God's care and provision for those who trust him, even in the insignificant events of everyday life. God is always present. Placed in the Bible between the healing of an Aramean general and the deliverance of Israel's army, this miracle also shows Elisha's personal contact with the students in the groups of the prophets. Although he had the respect of kings, Elisha never forgot to care for the faithful. Don't let the importance of your work drive out your concern for human need.

"Ah, my lord, what will we do now?" he cried out to Elisha.
16 "Don't be afraid!" Elisha told him. "For there are more on our side than on theirs!"
17 Then Elisha prayed, "O LORD, open his eyes and let him see!" The LORD opened his
servant's eyes, and when he looked up, he saw that the hillside around Elisha was filled
with horses and chariots of fire.
18 As the Aramean army advanced toward them, Elisha prayed, "O LORD, please make
them blind." And the LORD did as Elisha asked. 19 Then Elisha went out and told them,
"You have come the wrong way! This isn't the right city! Follow me, and I will take you
to the man you are looking for." And he led them to Samaria. 20 As soon as they had
entered Samaria, Elisha prayed, "O LORD, now open their eyes and let them see." And
the LORD did, and they discovered that they were in Samaria.
21 When the king of Israel saw them, he shouted to Elisha, "My father, should I kill
them?"
22 "Of course not!" Elisha told him. "Do we kill prisoners of war? Give them food and
drink and send them home again to their master."
23 So the king made a great feast for them and then sent them home to their king. After
that, the Aramean raiders stayed away from the land of Israel.

Ben-Hadad Besieges Samaria

24 Some time later, however, King Ben-hadad of Aram mobilized his entire army and
besieged Samaria. 25 As a result there was a great famine in the city. After a while even
a donkey's head sold for two pounds of silver, and a cup of dove's dung cost about two
ounces* of silver.
26 One day as the king of Israel was walking along the wall of the city, a woman called
to him, "Please help me, my lord the king!"
27 "If the LORD doesn't help you, what can I do?" he retorted. "I have neither food nor
wine to give you." 28 But then the king asked, "What is the matter?"
She replied, "This woman proposed that we eat my son one day and her son the next.
29 So we cooked my son and ate him. Then the next day I said, 'Kill your son so we can
eat him,' but she had hidden him."
30 When the king heard this, he tore his clothes in despair. And as the king walked
along the wall, the people could see that he was wearing sackcloth underneath next to

6:16 Exod 14:13; 2 Chr 32:7; Rom 8:31
6:17 2 Kgs 2:11-12
6:18 Gen 19:11
6:19 1 Kgs 20:1; 2 Kgs 3:1
6:21 1 Sam 24:4, 19; 26:8
6:22 Deut 20:11; 2 Kgs 5:13; 2 Chr 28:8-15; Rom 12:20
6:23 2 Kgs 5:2
6:24 1 Kgs 20:1
6:26 Lev 26:29; Deut 28:53-55
6:29 Lev 26:29; Deut 28:53

6:25 Hebrew *sold for 80 shekels* [0.9 kilograms] *of silver, and 1/4 of a cab* [0.3 liters] *of dove's dung cost 5 shekels* [57 grams]. *Dove's dung* may be a variety of wild vegetable.

ELISHA AND THE ARAMEANS
Elisha knew Aram's battle plans and kept Israel's king informed. The Aramean king tracked down Elisha at Dothan, but Elisha prayed that the Aramean army would be blinded. He then led the blind army into Samaria, Israel's capital city!

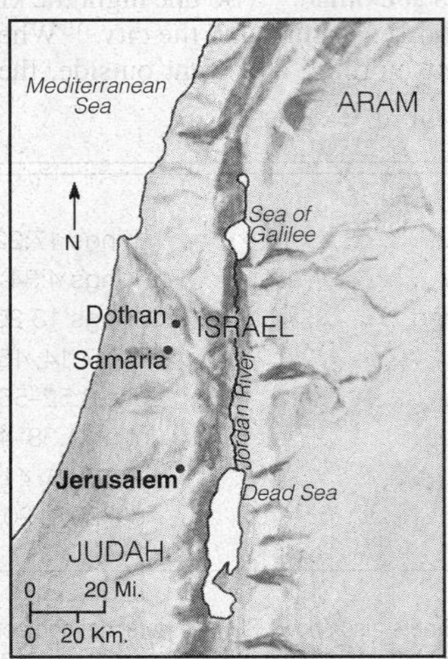

6:16, 17 Elisha's servant was no longer afraid when he saw God's mighty heavenly army. Faith reveals that God is doing more for his people than we can ever realize through sight alone. When you face difficulties that seem insurmountable, remember that spiritual resources are there even if you can't see them. Look through the eyes of faith, and let God show you his resources. If you don't see God working in your life, the problem may be your spiritual eyesight, not God's power.

6:21, 22 Elisha told the king not to kill the Arameans. The king was not to take credit for what God alone had done. In setting food and water before them, he was heaping "burning coals" on their heads (Proverbs 25:21, 22).

6:23 How long the Arameans stayed away from Israel is not known, but a number of years probably passed before the invasion recorded in 6:24 occurred. The Arameans must have forgotten the time their army was supernaturally blinded and sent home.

6:24 This was probably Ben-hadad II, whose father ruled Aram in the days of Baasha (1 Kings 15:18). Elisha constantly frustrated Ben-hadad II in his attempts to take control of Israel.

6:25 When a city like Samaria faced famine, it was no small matter. Although its farmers grew enough food to feed the people for a specific season, they did not have enough to maintain them in prolonged times of emergency when all supplies were cut off. This famine was so severe that mothers resorted to eating their children (6:26-30). Deuteronomy 28:49-57 predicted that this would happen when the people of Israel rejected God's leadership.

6:31 1 Kgs 19:2
his skin. 31“May God kill me if I don’t execute Elisha son of Shaphat this very day,”
6:32 1 Kgs 18:3-4, 14 Ezek 8:1; 14:1; 20:1
the king vowed.
32Elisha was sitting in his house at a meeting with the leaders of Israel when the king
sent a messenger to summon him. But before the messenger arrived, Elisha said to the
leaders, “A murderer has sent a man to kill me. When he arrives, shut the door and keep
him out. His master will soon follow him.”
6:33 Isa 8:21
33While Elisha was still saying this, the messenger arrived. And the king* said, “It is
the LORD who has brought this trouble on us! Why should I wait any longer for the
LORD?”

7 Elisha replied, “Hear this message from the LORD! This is what the LORD says: By
this time tomorrow in the markets of Samaria, five quarts of fine flour will cost only
half an ounce of silver,* and ten quarts of barley grain will cost only half an ounce of
silver.*”
7:2 Gen 7:11 2 Kgs 5:18 Mal 3:10
2The officer assisting the king said to the man of God, “That couldn’t happen even if
the LORD opened the windows of heaven!”
But Elisha replied, “You will see it happen, but you won’t be able to eat any of it!”

Lepers Visit the Enemy Camp

7:3 Lev 13:45-46 Num 5:1-4
3Now there were four men with leprosy* sitting at the entrance of the city gates. “Why
should we sit here waiting to die?” they asked each other. 4“We will starve if we stay
7:4 2 Kgs 6:24
here, and we will starve if we go back into the city. So we might as well go out and
surrender to the Aramean army. If they let us live, so much the better. But if they kill us,
we would have died anyway.”
7:6 2 Sam 5:24 2 Chr 12:2-3
5So that evening they went out to the camp of the Arameans, but no one was there!
6For the Lord had caused the whole army of Aram to hear the clatter of speeding
chariots and the galloping of horses and the sounds of a great army approaching. “The
7:7 Ps 48:4-6 Prov 28:1
king of Israel has hired the Hittites and Egyptians* to attack us!” they cried out. 7So
they panicked and fled into the night, abandoning their tents, horses, donkeys, and
everything else, and they fled for their lives.
8When the lepers arrived at the edge of the camp, they went into one tent after another,
eating, drinking wine, and carrying out silver and gold and clothing and hiding it.
9Finally, they said to each other, “This is not right. This is wonderful news, and we aren’t
sharing it with anyone! If we wait until morning, some terrible calamity will certainly
fall upon us. Come on, let’s go back and tell the people at the palace.”
10So they went back to the city and told the gatekeepers what had happened—that they
had gone out to the Aramean camp and no one was there! The horses and donkeys were

6:33 Hebrew *he.* **7:1a** Hebrew *1 seah* [6 liters] *of fine flour will cost 1 shekel* [11 grams]; also in 7:16, 18. **7:1b** Hebrew *2 seahs* [12 liters] *of barley grain will cost 1 shekel* [11 grams]; also in 7:16, 18. **7:3** Or *with a contagious skin disease.* The Hebrew word used here and throughout this passage can describe various skin diseases. **7:6** Possibly *and the people of Muzur,* a district near Cilicia.

6:31-33 Why did the king blame Elisha for the famine and troubles of the siege? Here are some possible reasons: (1) Some commentators say that Elisha must have told the king to trust God for deliverance. The king did this and even wore sackcloth (6:30), but at this point the situation seemed hopeless. Apparently the king thought Elisha had given him bad advice and not even God could help them. (2) For years there was conflict between the kings of Israel and the prophets of God. The prophets often predicted doom because of the kings’ evil, so the kings saw them as troublemakers. Thus, Israel’s king was striking out in frustration at Elisha. (3) The king may have remembered when Elijah helped bring an end to a famine (1 Kings 18:41-46). Knowing Elisha was a man of God, perhaps the king thought he could do any miracle he wanted and was angry that he had not come to Israel’s rescue.

7:1, 2 When Elisha prophesied God’s deliverance, the king’s officer said it couldn’t happen. The officer’s faith and hope were gone, but God’s words came true anyway (7:14-16)! Sometimes we become preoccupied with problems when we should be looking for opportunities. Instead of focusing on the negatives, develop an attitude of expectancy. To say that God *cannot* rescue someone or that a situation is *impossible* demonstrates a lack of faith.

7:3 According to the law, lepers were not allowed in the city but were to depend on charity outside the gate (Leviticus 13:45, 46; Numbers 5:1-4). Because of the famine and the presence of the Aramean army, their situation was desperate.

7:3-10 The lepers discovered the deserted camp and realized their lives had been spared. At first they kept the good news to themselves, forgetting their fellow citizens, who were starving in the city. The Good News about Jesus Christ must be shared, too, for no news is more important. We must not forget those who are dying without it. We must not become so preoccupied with our own faith that we neglect sharing it with those around us. Our “wonderful news,” like that of the lepers, will not “wait until morning.”

tethered and the tents were all in order, but there was not a single person around. 11 Then
the gatekeepers shouted the news to the people in the palace.

Israel Plunders the Camp

12 The king got out of bed in the middle of the night and told his officers, "I know what **7:12** Josh 8:6-12
has happened. The Arameans know we are starving, so they have left their camp and 2 Kgs 6:25-29
have hidden in the fields. They are expecting us to leave the city, and then they will take
us alive and capture the city."

13 One of his officers replied, "We had better send out scouts to check into this. Let
them take five of the remaining horses. If something happens to them, it won't be a
greater loss than if they stay here and die with the rest of us."

14 So two chariots with horses were prepared, and the king sent scouts to see what had
happened to the Aramean army. 15 They went all the way to the Jordan River, following
a trail of clothing and equipment that the Arameans had thrown away in their mad rush
to escape. The scouts returned and told the king about it. 16 Then the people of Samaria **7:16** 2 Kgs 7:1
rushed out and plundered the Aramean camp. So it was true that five quarts of fine flour
were sold that day for half an ounce of silver, and ten quarts of barley grain were sold
for half an ounce of silver, just as the LORD had promised. 17 The king appointed his **7:17** 2 Kgs 7:2
officer to control the traffic at the gate, but he was knocked down and trampled to death
as the people rushed out.

So everything happened exactly as the man of God had predicted when the king came
to his house. 18 The man of God had said to the king, "By this time tomorrow in the
markets of Samaria, five quarts of fine flour will cost half an ounce of silver, and ten
quarts of barley grain will cost half an ounce of silver." 19 The king's officer had replied, **7:19** 2 Kgs 7:2
"That couldn't happen even if the LORD opened the windows of heaven!" And the man
of God had said, "You will see it happen, but you won't be able to eat any of it!" 20 And
so it was, for the people trampled him to death at the gate!

The Woman from Shunem Returns Home

8 Elisha had told the woman whose son he had brought back to life, "Take your family **8:1** Gen 41:27
and move to some other place, for the LORD has called for a famine on Israel that Ps 105:16 Hag 1:11
will last for seven years." 2 So the woman did as the man of God instructed. She took her **8:2**
family and lived in the land of the Philistines for seven years. 2 Kgs 4:18, 31-35

3 After the famine ended she returned to the land of Israel, and she went to see the king
about getting back her house and land. 4 As she came in, the king was talking with Gehazi, **8:4**
the servant of the man of God. The king had just said, "Tell me some stories about the 2 Kgs 4:11-12; 5:20-27
great things Elisha has done." 5 And Gehazi was telling the king about the time Elisha **8:5**
had brought a boy back to life. At that very moment, the mother of the boy walked in to 2 Kgs 4:34-35
make her appeal to the king.

"Look, my lord!" Gehazi exclaimed. "Here is the woman now, and this is her son—the
very one Elisha brought back to life!"

6 "Is this true?" the king asked her. And she told him that it was. So he directed one of
his officials to see to it that everything she had lost was restored to her, including the
value of any crops that had been harvested during her absence.

Hazael Murders Ben-Hadad

7 Now Elisha went to Damascus, the capital of Aram, where King Ben-hadad lay sick. **8:7**
Someone told the king that the man of God had come. 8 When the king heard the news, 2 Kgs 6:24
he said to Hazael, "Take a gift to the man of God. Then tell him to ask the LORD if I will **8:8** 1 Kgs 14:3; 19:15
get well again."

9 So Hazael loaded down forty camels with the finest products of Damascus as a gift

---

7:19, 20 It is God, not worthless idols, who provides our daily food. Although our faith may be weak or very small, we must avoid becoming skeptical of God's provision. When our resources are low and our doubts are the strongest, remember God can open the floodgates of heaven.

8:1-6 This story must have happened before the events recorded in chapter 5, because the seven-year famine must have ended before Gehazi was struck with leprosy. This shows Elisha's long-term concern for this widow and contrasts his miraculous public ministry with his private ministry to this family. Elisha's life exemplifies the kind of concern we should have for others.

for Elisha. He went in to him and said, "Your servant Ben-hadad, the king of Aram, has sent me to ask you if he will recover."

10 And Elisha replied, "Go and tell him, 'You will recover.' But the LORD has shown me that he will actually die!" 11 Elisha stared at Hazael* with a fixed gaze until Hazael became uneasy. Then the man of God started weeping.

8:11 2 Kgs 2:17 Luke 19:41

8:12 2 Kgs 10:32-33; 12:17; 13:3; 15:16

12 "What's the matter, my lord?" Hazael asked him.

Elisha replied, "I know the terrible things you will do to the people of Israel. You will burn their fortified cities, kill their young men, dash their children to the ground, and rip open their pregnant women!"

8:13 1 Sam 17:43 2 Sam 9:8 1 Kgs 19:15

13 Then Hazael replied, "How could a nobody like me* ever accomplish such a great feat?"

But Elisha answered, "The LORD has shown me that you are going to be the king of Aram."

14 When Hazael went back, the king asked him, "What did Elisha tell you?"

And Hazael replied, "He told me that you will surely recover."

15 But the next day Hazael took a blanket, soaked it in water, and held it over the king's face until he died. Then Hazael became the next king of Aram.

2. Kings of Israel and Judah

Jehoram Rules in Judah

8:16-24 //2 Chr 21:5-20

8:17 2 Chr 21:5-10

16 Jehoram son of King Jehoshaphat of Judah began to rule over Judah in the fifth year of King Joram's reign in Israel. Joram was the son of Ahab. 17 Jehoram was thirty-two years old when he became king, and he reigned in Jerusalem eight years. 18 But Jehoram followed the example of the kings of Israel and was as wicked as King Ahab, for he had married one of Ahab's daughters. So Jehoram did what was evil in the LORD's sight.

8:19 2 Sam 7:12-15 1 Kgs 11:36

19 But the LORD was not willing to destroy Judah, for he had made a covenant with David and promised that his descendants would continue to rule forever.*

8:20 1 Kgs 22:47 2 Kgs 3:9, 26

8:22 Gen 27:39-40 Josh 21:13

20 During Jehoram's reign, the Edomites revolted against Judah and crowned their own king. 21 So Jehoram* went with all his chariots to attack the town of Zair.* The Edomites surrounded him and his charioteers, but he escaped at night under cover of darkness. Jehoram's army, however, deserted him and fled. 22 Edom has been independent from Judah to this day. The town of Libnah revolted about that same time.

8:24 2 Chr 21:20; 22:1

23 The rest of the events in Jehoram's reign and all his deeds are recorded in *The Book of the History of the Kings of Judah.* 24 When Jehoram died, he was buried with his ancestors in the City of David. Then his son Ahaziah became the next king.

Ahaziah Rules in Judah

8:25-29 //2 Chr 22:1-6

8:26 2 Kgs 11:1

25 Ahaziah son of Jehoram began to rule over Judah in the twelfth year of King Joram's reign in Israel. King Joram was the son of Ahab. 26 Ahaziah was twenty-two years old when he became king, and he reigned in Jerusalem one year. His mother was Athaliah,

8:11 Hebrew *He stared at him.* **8:13** Hebrew *a dog.* **8:19** Hebrew *promised to give a lamp to David and his descendants forever.* **8:21a** Hebrew *Joram,* a variant name for Jehoram; also in 8:23, 24. **8:21b** Greek version reads *Seir.*

8:12, 13 When Elisha told Hazael he would sin greatly, Hazael protested that he would never do that sort of thing. He did not acknowledge his personal potential for evil. In our enlightened society, it is easy to think we are above gross sin and can control our actions. We think that we would never sink so low. Instead, we should take a more biblical and realistic look at ourselves and admit our sinful potential. Then we will ask for God's strength to resist such evil.

8:12-15 Elisha's words about Hazael's treatment of Israel were partially fulfilled in 10:32, 33. Apparently Hazael had known he would be king because Elijah had anointed him (1 Kings 19:15). But he was impatient and, instead of waiting for God's timing, took matters into his own hands, killing Ben-hadad. God used Hazael as an instrument of judgment against the disobedient Israelites.

8:18 King Jehoshaphat arranged the marriage between Jehoram, his son, and Athaliah, the daughter of wicked Ahab and Jezebel. Athaliah followed the idolatrous ways of the northern kingdom, bringing Baal worship into Judah and starting the southern kingdom's decline. When Jehoram died, his son Ahaziah became king. Then, when Ahaziah was killed in battle, Athaliah murdered all her grandsons except Joash and made herself queen (11:1-3). Jehoram's marriage may have been politically advantageous, but spiritually it was deadly.

8:20-22 Although Judah and Edom shared a common border and a common ancestor (Isaac), the two nations fought continually. Edom had been a vassal state of the united kingdom of Israel and then the southern kingdom of Judah since the days of David (2 Samuel 8:13, 14). Here Edom rebelled against Jehoram and declared independence. Immediately Jehoram marched out to attack Edom, but his ambush failed. Thus, Jehoram lost some of his borderlands as punishment for his failure to honor God.

8:26 Ahaziah was the only remaining son of Jehoram of Judah. Although he was the youngest son, he took the throne because the rest of his brothers had been taken captive in a raid by the Philistines and Arabs (2 Chronicles 21:16, 17).

a granddaughter of King Omri of Israel. 27 Ahaziah followed the evil example of King 8:27 1 Kgs 16:30
Ahab's family, doing what was evil in the LORD's sight, because he was related by
marriage to the family of Ahab.
28 Ahaziah joined King Joram of Israel in his war against King Hazael of Aram at
Ramoth-gilead. When King Joram was wounded in the battle, 29 he returned to Jezreel to 8:29 2 Kgs 9:14-15
recover from his wounds. While Joram was there, King Ahaziah of Judah went to visit 2 Chr 22:5-6
him.

Jehu Anointed King of Israel

9 Meanwhile, Elisha the prophet had summoned a member of the group of prophets. "Get 9:1 1 Sam 10:1; 16:1
ready to go to Ramoth-gilead," he told him. "Take this vial of olive oil with you, 2 and 1 Kgs 1:39
find Jehu son of Jehoshaphat and grandson of Nimshi. Call him into a back room away from 2 Kgs 8:28
his friends, 3 and pour the oil over his head. Say to him, 'This is what the LORD says: I anoint 9:3 1 Kgs 19:16
you to be the king over Israel.' Then open the door and run for your life!"
4 So the young prophet did as he was told and went to Ramoth-gilead. 5 When he
arrived there, he found Jehu sitting in a meeting with the other army officers. "I have a
message for you, Commander," he said.
"For which one of us?" Jehu asked.
"For you, Commander," he replied.
6 So Jehu left the others and went into the house. Then the young prophet poured the 9:6 1 Kgs 19:16
oil over Jehu's head and said, "This is what the LORD, the God of Israel, says: I anoint
you king over the LORD's people, Israel. 7 You are to destroy the family of Ahab, your 9:7 Deut 32:35
master. In this way, I will avenge the murder of my prophets and all the LORD's servants 1 Sam 25:22
who were killed by Jezebel. 8 The entire family of Ahab must be wiped out—every male, 1 Kgs 18:3-4; 21:15, 21
slave and free alike, in Israel. 9 I will destroy the family of Ahab as I destroyed the 2 Kgs 10:17
families of Jeroboam son of Nebat and of Baasha son of Ahijah. 10 Dogs will eat Ahab's 9:9 1 Kgs 14:10;
wife, Jezebel, at the plot of land in Jezreel, and no one will bury her." Then the young 15:29; 16:3, 11
prophet opened the door and ran. 9:10 1 Kgs 21:23
11 Jehu went back to his fellow officers, and one of them asked him, "What did that 2 Kgs 9:35-36
crazy fellow want? Is everything all right?"
"You know the way such a man babbles on," Jehu replied.
12 "You're lying," they said. "Tell us." So Jehu told them what the man had said and
that at the LORD's command he had been anointed king over Israel. 9:13 2 Sam 15:10
13 They quickly spread out their cloaks on the bare steps and blew a trumpet, shouting, 1 Kgs 1:34, 39 Matt 21:8
"Jehu is king!"

JEHU TAKES OVER ISRAEL
Elisha sent a prophet to Ramoth-gilead to anoint Jehu as Israel's new king. Jehu immediately rode to Jezreel to find and kill King Joram of Israel and King Ahaziah of Judah. Jehu killed Joram; Ahaziah fled toward Beth-haggan, where he was wounded. He later died at Megiddo. Back in Jezreel, Jehu had Jezebel killed.

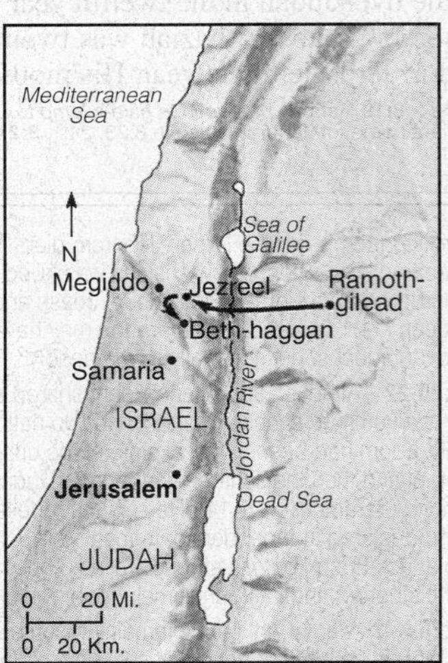

8:26, 27 Ahaziah's mother was Athaliah, daughter of Ahab and Jezebel, former king and queen of Israel, and granddaughter of Omri, Ahab's father and predecessor. The evil of Ahab and Jezebel spread to Judah through Athaliah.

8:29 Jezreel was the location of the summer palace of the kings of Israel.

9:3 Elijah had prophesied that many people would be killed when Jehu became king (1 Kings 19:16, 17). Thus Elisha advised the young prophet to get out of the area as soon as he delivered his message, before the slaughter began. Jehu's actions seem harsh, as he hunted down relatives and friends of Ahab (2 Chronicles 22:8, 9), but unchecked Baal worship was destroying the nation. If Israel was to survive, the followers of Baal had to be eliminated. Jehu fulfilled the need of the hour—justice.

9:7 Elisha's statement fulfilled Elijah's prophecy made 20 years earlier: All of Ahab's family would be killed (1 Kings 21:17-24). Jezebel's death, predicted by Elijah, is described in 9:30-37.

9:9 Ahab's dynasty would end as had those of Jeroboam and Baasha. Ahijah had prophesied the end of Jeroboam's dynasty (1 Kings 14:1-11), and this was fulfilled by Baasha (1 Kings 15:29). The prophet Jehu—not King Jehu—then foretold the end of Baasha's family (1 Kings 16:1-7), and this, too, was fulfilled (1 Kings 16:11, 12). The end of Ahab's family, therefore, was certain—Elijah had predicted it (1 Kings 21:17-24), and God brought it to pass.

Jehu Kills Joram and Ahaziah

9:14-15 2 Kgs 8:28-29 [14]So Jehu son of Jehoshaphat and grandson of Nimshi formed a conspiracy against King
Joram. (Now Joram had been with the army at Ramoth-gilead, defending Israel against
the forces of King Hazael of Aram. [15]But Joram* had been wounded in the fighting and
had returned to Jezreel to recover from his wounds.) So Jehu told the men with him,
"Since you want me to be king, don't let anyone escape to Jezreel to report what we have
done."
[16]Then Jehu got into a chariot and rode to Jezreel to find King Joram, who was lying
there wounded. King Ahaziah of Judah was there, too, for he had gone to visit him. [17]The
watchman on the tower of Jezreel saw Jehu and his company approaching, so he shouted
to Joram, "I see a company of troops coming!"
"Send out a rider to find out if they are coming in peace," King Joram shouted back.
[18]So a rider went out to meet Jehu and said, "The king wants to know whether you
are coming in peace."
Jehu replied, "What do you know about peace? Get behind me!"
The watchman called out to the king, "The rider has met them, but he is not returning."

9:15 Hebrew *Jehoram,* a variant name for Joram; also in 9:17, 21, 22, 23, 24.

JEHU

Jehu had the basic qualities that could have made him a great success. From a human perspective, in fact, he was a successful king. His family ruled the northern kingdom longer than any other. He was used by God as an instrument of punishment to Ahab's evil dynasty, and he fiercely attacked Baal worship. He came close to being God's kind of king, but he recklessly went beyond God's commands and failed to follow through on the obedient actions that began his reign. Within sight of victory, he settled for mediocrity.

Jehu was a man of immediate action but without ultimate purpose. His kingdom moved, but its destination was unclear. He eliminated one form of idolatry, Baal worship, only to uphold another by continuing to worship the golden calves Jeroboam had set up. He could have accomplished much for God if he had been obedient to the one who made him king. Even when he was carrying out God's directions, Jehu's style showed he was not fully aware of who was directing him.

As he did with Jehu, God gives each person strengths and abilities that will find their greatest usefulness only under his control. Outside that control, however, they don't accomplish what they could and often become tools for evil. One way to make sure this does not happen is to tell God of your willingness to be under his control. With his presence in your life, your natural strengths and abilities will be used to their greatest potential for the greatest good.

Strengths and accomplishments
- Took the throne from Ahab's family and destroyed his evil influence
- Founded the longest-lived dynasty of the northern kingdom
- Was anointed by Elijah and confirmed by Elisha
- Destroyed Baal worship

Weaknesses and mistakes
- Had a reckless outlook on life that made him bold and prone to error
- Worshiped Jeroboam's golden calves
- Was devoted to God only to the point that obedience served his own interests

Lessons from his life
- Fierce commitment needs control because it can result in recklessness
- Obedience involves both action and direction

Vital statistics
- Where: The northern kingdom of Israel
- Occupations: Commander in the army of Joram, king of Israel
- Relatives: Grandfather: Nimshi. Father: Jehoshaphat. Son: Jehoahaz
- Contemporaries: Elijah, Elisha, Ahab, Jezebel, Joram, Ahaziah

Key verse
"But Jehu did not obey the law of the LORD, the God of Israel, with all his heart. He refused to turn from the sins of idolatry that Jeroboam had led Israel to commit" (2 Kings 10:31).

Jehu's story is told in 1 Kings 19:16—2 Kings 10:36. He is also mentioned in 2 Kings 15:12; 2 Chronicles 22:7-9; Hosea 1:4, 5.

9:18, 19 The riders met Jehu and asked if he came in peace. But Jehu responded, "What do you know about peace?" Peace, properly understood, comes from God. It is not genuine except when rooted in belief in God and love for him. Jehu knew the men represented a disobedient, wicked king. Don't seek peace and friendship with those who are enemies of the good and the true. Lasting peace can come only from knowing God who gives it to us.

[19]So the king sent out a second rider. He rode up to them and demanded, "The king wants to know whether you come in peace."

Again Jehu answered, "What do you know about peace? Get behind me!"

[20]The watchman exclaimed, "The rider has met them, but he isn't returning either! It must be Jehu son of Nimshi, for he is driving so recklessly."

[21]"Quick! Get my chariot ready!" King Joram commanded.

Then King Joram of Israel and King Ahaziah of Judah rode out in their chariots to meet Jehu. They met him at the field that had belonged to Naboth of Jezreel. [22]King Joram demanded, "Do you come in peace, Jehu?"

Jehu replied, "How can there be peace as long as the idolatry and witchcraft of your mother, Jezebel, are all around us?"

[23]Then King Joram reined the chariot horses around and fled, shouting to King Ahaziah, "Treason, Ahaziah!" [24]Then Jehu drew his bow and shot Joram between the shoulders. The arrow pierced his heart, and he sank down dead in his chariot.

[25]Jehu said to Bidkar, his officer, "Throw him into the field of Naboth of Jezreel. Do you remember when you and I were riding along behind his father, Ahab? The LORD pronounced this message against him: [26]'I solemnly swear that I will repay him here on Naboth's property, says the LORD, for the murder of Naboth and his sons that I saw yesterday.' So throw him out on Naboth's field, just as the LORD said."

[27]When King Ahaziah of Judah saw what was happening, he fled along the road to Beth-haggan. Jehu rode after him, shouting, "Shoot him, too!" So they shot Ahaziah in his chariot at the Ascent of Gur, near Ibleam. He was able to go on as far as Megiddo, but he died there. [28]His officials took him by chariot to Jerusalem, where they buried him with his ancestors in the City of David. [29]Ahaziah's reign over Judah had begun in the eleventh year of King Joram's reign in Israel.

The Death of Jezebel

[30]When Jezebel, the queen mother, heard that Jehu had come to Jezreel, she painted her eyelids and fixed her hair and sat at a window. [31]When Jehu entered the gate of the palace, she shouted at him, "Have you come in peace, you murderer? You are just like Zimri, who murdered his master!"

[32]Jehu looked up and saw her at the window and shouted, "Who is on my side?" And two or three eunuchs looked out at him. [33]"Throw her down!" Jehu yelled. So they threw her out the window, and some of her blood spattered against the wall and on the horses. And Jehu trampled her body under his horses' hooves.

[34]Then Jehu went into the palace and ate and drank. Afterward he said, "Someone go and bury this cursed woman, for she is the daughter of a king." [35]But when they went out to bury her, they found only her skull, her feet, and her hands.

[36]When they returned and told Jehu, he stated, "This fulfills the message from the LORD, which he spoke through his servant Elijah from Tishbe: 'At the plot of land in Jezreel, dogs will eat Jezebel's flesh. [37]Her body will be scattered like dung on the field of Jezreel, so that no one will be able to recognize her.'"

Jehu Kills Ahab's Family

10 Now Ahab had seventy sons living in the city of Samaria. So Jehu wrote a letter and sent copies to Samaria, to the officials of the city,* to the leaders of the people, and to the guardians of King Ahab's sons. The letter said, [2]"The king's sons are with

9:20 2 Sam 18:27
9:21-29 1 Kgs 21:1; //2 Chr 22:7-9
9:22 1 Kgs 16:31; 18:19
9:23 2 Kgs 11:14
9:24 1 Kgs 22:34
9:25 1 Kgs 21:1, 19
9:26 1 Kgs 21:19
9:27 Josh 17:11; Judg 1:27; 2 Chr 22:7, 9
9:28 2 Kgs 23:30
9:29 2 Kgs 8:25, 28
9:30 Jer 4:30; Ezek 23:40
9:31 1 Kgs 16:9-20
9:34 1 Kgs 16:30-31
9:36 1 Kgs 21:23
9:37 Jer 8:2
10:1 1 Kgs 16:24-29

10:1 As in some Greek manuscripts and Latin Vulgate (see also 10:6); Hebrew reads *of Jezreel.*

9:26 Joram of Israel was wicked like his father and mother, Ahab and Jezebel; therefore, his body was thrown into the field that his parents had unlawfully taken. Jezebel had arranged the murder of Naboth, the previous owner, because he would not sell his vineyard—which Ahab wanted for a garden (1 Kings 21:1-24). Little did Ahab know that it would become a burial plot for his evil son.

9:31 Why did Jezebel refer to Zimri? Zimri was an army commander who, some 40 years earlier, had killed Elah and then had declared himself king of Israel (1 Kings 16:8-10). Jezebel was accusing Jehu of trying the same treachery.

9:35 Jezebel's skull, feet, and hands were all that remained of her evil life—no power, no money, no prestige, no royal finery, no family, no spiritual heritage. In the end, her life of luxury and treachery amounted to nothing. Power, health, and wealth may make you feel as if you can live forever. But death strips everyone of all external security. The time to set your life's course is now, while you still have time and before your heart becomes hardened. The end will come soon enough.

you, and you have at your disposal chariots, horses, a fortified city, and weapons. As soon
as you receive this letter, 3 select the best qualified of King Ahab's sons to be your king,
and prepare to fight for Ahab's dynasty."
4 But they were paralyzed with fear and said, "Two kings couldn't stand against this
10:5 Josh 9:8, 11 man! What can we do?" 5 So the palace and city administrators, together with the other
leaders and the guardians of the king's sons, sent this message to Jehu: "We are your
servants and will do anything you tell us. We will not make anyone king; do whatever
you think is best."
6 Jehu responded with a second letter: "If you are on my side and are going to obey
me, bring the heads of the king's sons to me at Jezreel at about this time tomorrow."
10:7 Judg 9:5 2 Kgs 11:1 Now the seventy sons of the king were being cared for by the leaders of Samaria,
where they had been raised since childhood. 7 When the letter arrived, the leaders killed
all seventy of the king's sons. They placed their heads in baskets and presented them to
Jehu at Jezreel. 8 A messenger went to Jehu and said, "They have brought the heads of
the king's sons."
So Jehu ordered, "Pile them in two heaps at the entrance of the city gate, and leave
them there until morning."
9 In the morning he went out and spoke to the crowd that had gathered around them.
10:10 1 Kgs 2:29 2 Kgs 9:7-10 "You aren't to blame," he told them. "I am the one who conspired against my master and
killed him. But who killed all these? 10 You can be sure that the message of the LORD that
was spoken concerning Ahab's family will not fail. The LORD declared through his
servant Elijah that this would happen." 11 Then Jehu killed all of Ahab's relatives living
in Jezreel and all his important officials, personal friends, and priests. So Ahab was left
without a single survivor.
12 Then Jehu set out for Samaria. Along the way, while he was at Beth-eked of the
10:13 2 Kgs 8:24, 29 2 Chr 22:8 Shepherds, 13 he met some relatives of King Ahaziah of Judah. "Who are you?" he asked
them.
And they replied, "We are relatives of King Ahaziah. We are going to visit the sons of
King Ahab and the queen mother."
14 "Take them alive!" Jehu shouted to his men. And they captured all forty-two of them
10:15 2 Kgs 10:23 Jer 35:6-19 and killed them at the well of Beth-eked. None of them escaped.
15 When Jehu left there, he met Jehonadab son of Recab, who was coming to meet him.
After they had greeted each other, Jehu said to him, "Are you as loyal to me as I am to you?"
"Yes, I am," Jehonadab replied.
"If you are," Jehu said, "then give me your hand." So Jehonadab put out his hand, and
10:17 2 Kgs 9:8 Jehu helped him into the chariot. 16 Then Jehu said, "Now come with me, and see how
devoted I am to the LORD." So Jehonadab rode along with him. 17 When Jehu arrived in
Samaria, he killed everyone who was left there from Ahab's family, just as the LORD had
promised through Elijah.

Jehu Kills the Priests of Baal

10:18 1 Kgs 16:31-32 18 Then Jehu called a meeting of all the people of the city and said to them, "Ahab hardly
worshiped Baal at all compared to the way I will worship him! 19 Summon all the prophets
and worshipers of Baal, and call together all his priests. See to it that every one of them
comes, for I am going to offer a great sacrifice to Baal. Any of Baal's worshipers who fail
to come will be put to death." But Jehu's plan was to destroy all the worshipers of Baal.

10:7 This fulfilled Elijah's prophecy that not one of Ahab's male descendants would survive (1 Kings 21:17-24).

10:11 In his zeal, Jehu went far beyond the Lord's command with this bloodbath. The prophet Hosea later announced punishment upon Jehu's dynasty for this senseless slaughter (Hosea 1:4, 5). Many times in history, "religious" people have mixed faith with personal ambition, power, or cruelty, without God's consent or blessing. To use God or the Bible to condone oppression is wrong. When people attack Christianity because of atrocities that "Christians" carried out, help them to see that these men and women were using faith for their own political ends and not following Christ.

10:15 Jehonadab was a man who, like Jehu, was zealous in following God. Jehonadab, however, demonstrated his zeal by separating himself and his family from the materialistic, idol-worshiping culture. He founded a group called the Recabites (named after his father Recab), who strove to keep their lives pure by living apart from society's pressures and temptations. Jeremiah 35 gives us an example of their dedication to God. Because of their dedication, God promised that they would always have descendants who would worship him.

20 Then Jehu ordered, "Prepare a solemn assembly to worship Baal!" So they did. 21 He **10:20**
sent messengers throughout all Israel summoning those who worshiped Baal. They all Exod 32:5
came and filled the temple of Baal from one end to the other. 22 And Jehu instructed the
keeper of the wardrobe, "Be sure that every worshiper of Baal wears one of these robes."
So robes were given to them.
23 Then Jehu went into the temple of Baal with Jehonadab son of Recab. Jehu said to
the worshipers of Baal, "Make sure that only those who worship Baal are here. Don't let
anyone in who worships the LORD!" 24 So they were all inside the temple to offer sacrifices
and burnt offerings. Now Jehu had surrounded the building with eighty of his men and
had warned them, "If you let anyone escape, you will pay for it with your own life."
25 As soon as Jehu had finished sacrificing the burnt offering, he commanded his **10:25** 1 Sam 22:17
guards and officers, "Go in and kill all of them. Don't let a single one escape!" So they 1 Kgs 18:40
killed them all with their swords, and the guards and officers dragged their bodies
outside. Then Jehu's men went into the fortress* of the temple of Baal. 26 They dragged **10:26**
out the sacred pillar used in the worship of Baal and destroyed it. 27 They broke down 1 Kgs 14:23 2 Kgs 3:2
the sacred pillar of Baal and wrecked the temple of Baal, converting it into a public toilet.
That is what it is used for to this day. 28 Thus, Jehu destroyed every trace of Baal worship
from Israel. 29 He did not, however, destroy the gold calves at Bethel and Dan, the great **10:29** 1 Kgs 12:28-30;
sin that Jeroboam son of Nebat had led Israel to commit. 13:33-34
30 Nonetheless the LORD said to Jehu, "You have done well in following my instruc- **10:30**
tions to destroy the family of Ahab. Because of this I will cause your descendants to be 2 Kgs 15:12
the kings of Israel down to the fourth generation." 31 But Jehu did not obey the law of
the LORD, the God of Israel, with all his heart. He refused to turn from the sins of
idolatry that Jeroboam had led Israel to commit.

The Death of Jehu

32 At about that time the LORD began to reduce the size of Israel's territory. King Hazael **10:32** 2 Kgs 8:12; 13:22;
conquered several sections of the country 33 east of the Jordan River, including all of 14:25
Gilead, Gad, Reuben, and Manasseh. He conquered the area from the town of Aroer by
the Arnon Gorge to as far north as Gilead and Bashan.
34 The rest of the events in Jehu's reign and all his deeds and achievements are
recorded in *The Book of the History of the Kings of Israel.* 35 When Jehu died, he was
buried with his ancestors in Samaria. Then his son Jehoahaz became the next king. 36 In
all, Jehu reigned over Israel from Samaria for twenty-eight years.

Athaliah Rules in Judah

11 When Athaliah, the mother of King Ahaziah of Judah, learned that her son was **11:1-21**
dead, she set out to destroy the rest of the royal family. 2 But Ahaziah's sister //2 Chr 22:10–23:21
Jehosheba, the daughter of King Jehoram,* took Ahaziah's infant son, Joash, and stole **11:2** 2 Kgs 12:1
him away from among the rest of the king's children, who were about to be killed.
Jehosheba put Joash and his nurse in a bedroom to hide him from Athaliah, so the child

10:25 Hebrew *city.* **11:2** Hebrew *Joram,* a variant name for Jehoram.

10:24 Israel was supposed to be intolerant of any religion that did not worship the true God. The religions of surrounding nations were evil and corrupt. They were designed to destroy life, not uphold it. Israel was God's special nation, chosen to be an example of what was right. But Israel's kings, priests, and elders first tolerated, then incorporated surrounding pagan beliefs, and thus became apathetic to God's way. We are to be completely intolerant of sin and remove it from our lives. We should be tolerant of people who hold differing views, but we should not condone beliefs or practices that lead people away from God's standards of living.

10:28, 29 Why did Jehu destroy the idols of Baal but not the gold calves in Bethel and Dan? Jehu's motives may have been more political than spiritual. (1) If Jehu had destroyed the gold calves, his people would have traveled to the Temple in Jerusalem, in the rival southern kingdom, and worshiped there (which is why Jeroboam set them up in the first place; see 1 Kings 12:25-33). (2) Baal worship was associated with the dynasty of Ahab, so it was politically advantageous to destroy Baal. The gold calves, on the other hand, had a longer history in the northern kingdom and were valued by all political factions. (3) Baal worship was anti-God, but the gold calves were thought by many to be visible representations of God himself, even though God's law stated clearly that such worship was idolatrous (Exodus 20:3-6). Like Jehu, it is easy for us to denounce the sins of others while excusing sin in our own lives.

10:30, 31 Jehu did much of what the Lord told him to, but he did not obey him with all his heart. He had become God's *instrument* for carrying out justice, but he had not become God's *servant.* As a result, he gave only lip service to God while permitting the worship of the gold calves. Check the condition of your heart toward God. We can be very active in our work for God and still not give the heartfelt obedience he desires.

11:1 This story is continued from 9:27, where Ahaziah, Athaliah's son, had been killed by Jehu. Athaliah's attempt to kill all of Ahaziah's sons was futile because God had promised that the Messiah would be born through David's descendants (2 Samuel 7).

was not murdered. [3]Joash and his nurse remained hidden in the Temple of the LORD for six years while Athaliah ruled over the land.

Revolt against Athaliah

11:4 2 Kgs 11:19 2 Chr 23:1

[4]In the seventh year of Athaliah's reign, Jehoiada the priest summoned the commanders, the Carite mercenaries, and the guards to come to the Temple of the LORD. He made a pact with them and made them swear an oath of loyalty there in the LORD's Temple; then he showed them the king's son.

11:5 1 Chr 9:25

[5]Jehoiada told them, "This is what you must do. A third of you who are on duty on the Sabbath are to guard the royal palace itself. [6]Another third of you are to stand guard at the Sur Gate. And the final third must stand guard behind the palace guard. These three groups will all guard the palace. [7]The other two units who are off duty on the Sabbath must stand guard for the king at the LORD's Temple. [8]Form a bodyguard for the king and keep your weapons in hand. Any unauthorized person who approaches you must be killed. Stay right beside the king at all times."

11:10 2 Sam 8:7 1 Chr 18:7-8

[9]So the commanders did everything just as Jehoiada the priest ordered. The commanders took charge of the men reporting for duty that Sabbath, as well as those who were going off duty. They brought them all to Jehoiada the priest, [10]and he supplied them with the spears and shields that had once belonged to King David and were stored in the Temple of the LORD. [11]The guards stationed themselves around the king, with their weapons ready. They formed a line from the south side of the Temple around to the north side and all around the altar.

11:12 Exod 25:16; 31:18 1 Sam 10:24

[12]Then Jehoiada brought out Joash, the king's son, and placed the crown on his head. He presented Joash with a copy of God's covenant and proclaimed him king. They anointed him, and all the people clapped their hands and shouted, "Long live the king!"

The Death of Athaliah

11:13 2 Chr 23:12

11:14 Gen 37:29 1 Kgs 1:39 2 Kgs 9:23

[13]When Athaliah heard all the noise made by the guards and the people, she hurried to the LORD's Temple to see what was happening. [14]And she saw the newly crowned king standing in his place of authority by the pillar, as was the custom at times of coronation. The officers and trumpeters were surrounding him, and people from all over the land were rejoicing and blowing trumpets. When Athaliah saw all this, she tore her clothes in despair and shouted, "Treason! Treason!"

[15]Then Jehoiada the priest ordered the commanders who were in charge of the troops, "Take her out of the Temple, and kill anyone who tries to rescue her. Do not kill her here in the Temple of the LORD." [16]So they seized her and led her out to the gate where horses enter the palace grounds, and she was killed there.

Jehoiada's Religious Reforms

11:17 Josh 24:25 2 Sam 5:3 2 Chr 15:12-14; 34:31

11:18 Deut 12:2-3 1 Kgs 18:40

[17]Then Jehoiada made a covenant between the LORD and the king and the people that they would be the LORD's people. He also made a covenant between the king and the people. [18]And all the people of the land went over to the temple of Baal and tore it down. They demolished the altars and smashed the idols to pieces, and they killed Mattan the priest of Baal in front of the altars.

11:19 2 Kgs 11:4

11:20 Prov 11:10

11:21 2 Chr 24:1-14

Jehoiada the priest stationed guards at the Temple of the LORD. [19]Then the commanders, the Carite mercenaries, the guards, and all the people of the land escorted the king from the Temple of the LORD. They went through the gate of the guards and into the palace, and the king took his seat on the royal throne. [20]So all the people of the land rejoiced, and the city was peaceful because Athaliah had been killed at the king's palace.

[21]Joash* was seven years old when he became king.

11:21 Hebrew *Jehoash,* a variant name for Joash.

11:2, 3 Jehosheba was the wife of Jehoiada, the high priest, so the Temple was a practical and natural place to hide baby Joash. Athaliah, who loved idolatry, would have had no interest in the Temple.

11:4 The Carites were mercenary troops possibly associated with the Philistines. Some scholars believe they settled in southern Palestine from Crete.

11:17 This covenant was, in fact, a recommitment to a very old covenant—the one set up in the book of Deuteronomy for the righteous rule of the nation. It was meant to function as a constitution for the people. This covenant, however, had been virtually ignored for over 100 years. Unfortunately, after Jehoiada's death, the reforms were discontinued.

11:21 If Joash became king at only seven years of age, who really ran the country? Although the answer is not spelled out in the Bible, Judah was probably run during the first seven years of Joash's reign by the king's mother, the high priest Jehoiada, and other advisers.

Joash Repairs the Temple

12 Joash* began to rule over Judah in the seventh year of King Jehu's reign in Israel.
He reigned in Jerusalem forty years. His mother was Zibiah, from Beersheba. 2All
his life Joash did what was pleasing in the LORD's sight because Jehoiada the priest
instructed him. 3Yet even so, he did not destroy the pagan shrines, and the people still
offered sacrifices and burned incense there.
4One day King Joash said to the priests, "Collect all the money brought as a sacred
offering to the LORD's Temple, whether it is a regular assessment, a payment of vows, or
a voluntary gift. 5Let the priests take some of that money to pay for whatever repairs are
needed at the Temple."
6But by the twenty-third year of Joash's reign, the priests still had not repaired the
Temple. 7So King Joash called for Jehoiada and the other priests and asked them, "Why
haven't you repaired the Temple? Don't use any more gifts for your own needs. From
now on, it must all be spent on getting the Temple into good condition." 8So the priests
agreed not to collect any more money from the people, and they also agreed not to
undertake the repairs of the Temple themselves.
9Then Jehoiada the priest bored a hole in the lid of a large chest and set it on the
right-hand side of the altar at the entrance of the Temple of the LORD. The priests
guarding the entrance put all of the people's contributions into the chest. 10Whenever the
chest became full, the court secretary and the high priest counted the money that had
been brought to the LORD's Temple and put it into bags. 11Then they gave the money to
the construction supervisors, who used it to pay the people working on the LORD's
Temple—the carpenters, the builders, 12the masons, and the stonecutters. They also used
the money to buy timber and cut stone for repairing the LORD's Temple, and they paid
any other expenses related to the Temple's restoration.
13The money brought to the Temple was not used for making silver cups, lamp
snuffers, basins, trumpets, or other articles of gold or silver for the Temple of the LORD.
14It was paid out to the workmen, who used it for the Temple repairs. 15No accounting
was required from the construction supervisors, because they were honest and faithful
workers. 16However, the money that was contributed for guilt offerings and sin offerings
was not brought into the LORD's Temple. It was given to the priests for their own use.

The End of Joash's Reign

17About this time King Hazael of Aram went to war against Gath and captured it. Then he
turned to attack Jerusalem. 18King Joash collected all the sacred objects that Jehoshaphat,
Jehoram, and Ahaziah, the previous kings of Judah, had dedicated, along with what he
himself had dedicated. He sent them all to Hazael, along with all the gold in the treasuries
of the LORD's Temple and the royal palace. So Hazael called off his attack on Jerusalem.
19The rest of the events in Joash's reign and all his deeds are recorded in *The Book of*

12:1-21 //2 Chr 24:1-14, 23-27
12:3 2 Kgs 14:4; 15:34-35
12:4 Exod 35:5-9, 22, 29; 2 Kgs 22:3-6; 1 Chr 29:3-9
12:9 Mark 12:41; Luke 21:1
12:13 1 Kgs 7:48-51
12:15 2 Kgs 22:7
12:17 2 Kgs 8:12; 10:32-33
12:18 1 Kgs 15:18; 2 Kgs 16:8; 18:15-16

12:1 Hebrew *Jehoash,* a variant name for Joash; also in 12:2, 4, 6, 7, 18.

12:2ff Joash didn't go far enough in removing sin from the nation, but he did much that was good and right. When we aren't sure if we've gone far enough in correcting our actions, we can ask: (1) Does the Bible expressly prohibit this action? (2) Does this action take me away from loving, worshiping, or serving God? (3) Does it make me its slave? (4) Is it bringing out the best in me, consistent with God's purpose? (5) Does it benefit other believers?

12:3 The Israelites were supposed to offer sacrifices to God only in designated areas under supervision of the priests, not just anywhere (Deuteronomy 12:13, 14). Making sacrifices on the hilltops (high places) copied pagan customs and encouraged other pagan practices to enter into their worship. By blending in these beliefs, people were custom-making their religion, and it led them far away from God. (For more information on these high places, see the note on 1 Kings 22:43.)

12:4, 5 The Temple needed repair because it had been damaged and neglected by previous evil leaders, especially Athaliah (2 Chronicles 24:7). The Temple was to be a holy place, set apart for worship of God. Thanks to Joash's fund-raising program, it could be restored. The dirt and filth that had collected inside over the years were cleaned out; joints were remortared; pagan idols and other traces of idol worship were removed; and the gold and bronze were polished. The neglected condition of the Temple reveals how far the people had strayed from God.

12:15 What a contrast between the workmen, who needed no accounting of their use of the money, and the priests, who couldn't be trusted to handle their funds well enough to set some aside for the Temple (12:8). As trained men of God, the Levites should have been responsible and concerned. After all, the Temple was their life's work. Though the priests were not dishonest, they did not have the commitment or energy needed to finish the work. Sometimes God's work is better accomplished by devoted laypeople. Don't let your lack of training or position stop you from contributing to God's Kingdom. Everyone's energy is needed to carry out God's work.

12:16 To read more about guilt and sin offerings, see Leviticus 4; 5; 6:24–7:10.

12:20 2 Sam 5:9; 2 Chr 24:25-27

the History of the Kings of Judah. 20 But his officers plotted against him and assassinated
him at Beth-millo on the road to Silla. 21 The assassins were Jozacar* son of Shimeath
and Jehozabad son of Shomer—both trusted advisers. Joash was buried with his ancestors in the City of David. Then his son Amaziah became the next king.

Jehoahaz Rules in Israel

13:2 1 Kgs 12:26-33
13:3 Judg 2:12-14; 2 Kgs 12:17

13 Jehoahaz son of Jehu began to rule over Israel in the twenty-third year of King
Joash's reign in Judah. He reigned in Samaria seventeen years. 2 But he did what
was evil in the LORD's sight. He followed the example of Jeroboam son of Nebat,
continuing the sins of idolatry that Jeroboam son of Nebat had led Israel to commit. 3 So
the LORD was very angry with Israel, and he allowed King Hazael of Aram and his son
Ben-hadad to defeat them time after time.

13:4 Exod 3:7-9; Num 21:7-9
13:5 Judg 2:18; Neh 9:27
13:6 1 Kgs 16:33

4 Then Jehoahaz prayed for the LORD's help, and the LORD heard his prayer. The LORD
could see how terribly the king of Aram was oppressing Israel. 5 So the LORD raised up
a deliverer to rescue the Israelites from the tyranny of the Arameans. Then Israel lived
in safety again as they had in former days. 6 But they continued to sin, following the evil
example of Jeroboam. They even set up an Asherah pole in Samaria. 7 Finally, Jehoahaz's
army was reduced to fifty mounted troops, ten chariots, and ten thousand foot soldiers.
The king of Aram had killed the others like they were dust under his feet.

8 The rest of the events in Jehoahaz's reign and all his deeds, including the extent of
his power, are recorded in *The Book of the History of the Kings of Israel.* 9 When
Jehoahaz died, he was buried in Samaria with his ancestors. Then his son Jehoash*
became the next king.

Jehoash Rules in Israel

13:12 2 Kgs 14:8, 15, 28

10 Jehoash son of Jehoahaz began to rule over Israel in the thirty-seventh year of King
Joash's reign in Judah. He reigned in Samaria sixteen years. 11 But he did what was evil
in the LORD's sight. He refused to turn from the sins of idolatry that Jeroboam son of
Nebat had led Israel to commit. 12 The rest of the events in Jehoash's reign and all his

12:21 As in Greek and Syriac versions; Hebrew reads *Jozabad;* compare parallel text at 2 Chr 24:26. **13:9** Hebrew *Joash,* a variant name for Jehoash; also in 13:10, 12, 13, 14, 25.

GOD OR IDOLS
Why did people continually turn to idols instead of to God?

Idols were:	*God is:*
Tangible	Intangible—no physical form
Morally similar—had human characteristics	Morally dissimilar—had divine characteristics
Comprehensible	Incomprehensible
Able to be manipulated	Not able to be manipulated
Worshiping idols involved:	*Worshiping God involved:*
Materialism	Sacrifice
Sexual immorality	Purity and commitment
Doing whatever a person wanted	Doing what God wants
Focusing on self	Focusing on others

12:20 The reasons for the officers' plot against Joash are listed in 2 Chronicles 24:17-26. Joash had begun to worship idols, had killed the prophet Zechariah, and had been conquered by the Arameans. When Joash turned away from God, his life began to unravel. The officers didn't kill Joash because he turned from God; they killed him because his kingdom was out of control. In the end he became an evil man and was killed by evil people.

13:4-6 The Lord heard Jehoahaz's prayer for help. God delayed his judgment on Israel when they turned to him for help, but they did not sustain their dependence on God for long. Although there were periodic breaks in their idol worship, there was rarely evidence of genuine faith. It is not enough to say no to sin; we must also say yes to a life of commitment to God. An occasional call for help is not a substitute for a daily life of trust in God.

13:5 Aram, which lay to the north of Israel, was always Israel's enemy. This was partly because Israel blocked most of Aram's trade from the south, and Aram cut off most of Israel's from the north. If one nation could conquer the other, all its trade routes would be open, and its economy would flourish. Israel and Aram were so busy fighting each other that they didn't notice the rapidly growing strength of the Assyrians to the far north. Soon both nations would be surprised (16:9; 17:6).

13:9, 10 Jehoash assumed the throne of Israel in 798 B.C. At that time the king of Judah, Joash, was nearing the end of his reign. In Hebrew, Jehoash and Joash were two forms of the same name. Thus, two kings with the same name, one in the south and one in the north, reigned at approximately the same time. While Joash of Judah began as a good king, Jehoash of Israel was evil.

deeds, including the extent of his power and his war with King Amaziah of Judah, are
recorded in *The Book of the History of the Kings of Israel.* 13 When Jehoash died, he was
buried with his ancestors in Samaria. Then his son Jeroboam II became the next king.

Elisha's Final Prophecy

14 When Elisha was in his last illness, King Jehoash of Israel visited him and wept over
him. "My father! My father! The chariots and charioteers of Israel!" he cried.
15 Elisha told him, "Get a bow and some arrows." And the king did as he was told.
16 Then Elisha told the king of Israel to put his hand on the bow, and Elisha laid his
own hands on the king's hands. 17 Then he commanded, "Open that eastern window,"
and he opened it. Then he said, "Shoot!" So he did.

Then Elisha proclaimed, "This is the LORD's arrow, full of victory over Aram, for you
will completely conquer the Arameans at Aphek. 18 Now pick up the other arrows and
strike them against the ground." So the king picked them up and struck the ground three
times. 19 But the man of God was angry with him. "You should have struck the ground
five or six times!" he exclaimed. "Then you would have beaten Aram until they were
entirely destroyed. Now you will be victorious only three times."
20 Then Elisha died and was buried.

Groups of Moabite raiders used to invade the land each spring. 21 Once when some
Israelites were burying a man, they spied a band of these raiders. So they hastily threw
the body they were burying into the tomb of Elisha. But as soon as the body touched
Elisha's bones, the dead man revived and jumped to his feet!
22 King Hazael of Aram had oppressed Israel during the entire reign of King Jehoahaz.
23 But the LORD was gracious to the people of Israel, and they were not totally destroyed.
He pitied them because of his covenant with Abraham, Isaac, and Jacob. And to this day
he still has not completely destroyed them or banished them from his presence.
24 King Hazael of Aram died, and his son Ben-hadad became the next king. 25 Then
Jehoash son of Jehoahaz recaptured from Ben-hadad son of Hazael the towns that Hazael
had taken from Jehoash's father, Jehoahaz. Jehoash defeated Ben-hadad on three occasions, and so recovered the Israelite towns.

13:14 2 Kgs 2:12
13:17 1 Kgs 20:26
13:20 2 Kgs 3:7; 24:2
13:21 Matt 27:52
13:22 2 Kgs 8:12
13:23 Gen 13:16; 17:2-5; 2 Kgs 14:27
13:25 2 Kgs 10:32-33; 14:25

Amaziah Rules in Judah

14 Amaziah son of Joash began to rule over Judah in the second year of the reign of
King Jehoash* of Israel. 2 Amaziah was twenty-five years old when he became
king, and he reigned in Jerusalem twenty-nine years. His mother was Jehoaddin, from
Jerusalem. 3 Amaziah did what was pleasing in the LORD's sight, but not like his ancestor
David. Instead, he followed the example of his father, Joash. 4 Amaziah did not destroy
the pagan shrines, where the people offered sacrifices and burned incense.
5 When Amaziah was well established as king, he executed the men who had assassinated his father. 6 However, he did not kill the children of the assassins, for he obeyed
the command of the LORD written in the Book of the Law of Moses: "Parents must not
be put to death for the sins of their children, nor the children for the sins of their parents.
Those worthy of death must be executed for their own crimes."*
7 It was Amaziah who killed ten thousand Edomites in the Valley of Salt. He also
conquered Sela and changed its name to Joktheel, as it is called to this day.

14:1-7 //2 Chr 25:1-4, 11-12
14:4 2 Kgs 12:3
14:5 2 Kgs 12:2
14:6 Deut 24:16; Jer 31:30; Ezek 18:4, 20
14:7 2 Sam 8:13; 1 Chr 18:12; 2 Chr 25:11; Isa 16:1

14:1 Hebrew *Joash,* a variant name for Jehoash; also in 14:13, 23, 27. **14:6** Deut 24:16.

13:14 Elisha was highly regarded for his prophetic powers and miracles on Israel's behalf. Jehoash called him "The chariots and charioteers of Israel!" This recalls the title Elisha gave to Elijah in 2:12. Jehoash feared Elisha's death because he ascribed the nation's well-being to Elisha rather than to God. Jehoash's fear reveals his lack of spiritual understanding. At least 43 years had passed since Elisha was last mentioned in Scripture (9:1), when he anointed Jehu king (841 B.C.). Jehoash's reign began in 798 B.C.

13:15-19 When Jehoash was told to strike the ground with the arrows, he did it only halfheartedly. As a result, Elisha told the king that his victory over Aram would not be complete. Receiving the full benefits of God's plan for our lives requires us to receive and obey God's commands fully. If we don't follow God's complete instructions, we should not be surprised that his full benefits and blessings are not present.

13:20, 21 Elisha was dead, but his good influence remained, even causing miracles. This demonstrated that Elisha was indeed a prophet of God. It also attested to God's power—no pagan idol ever raised anyone from the dead. This miracle served as one more reminder to Israel that it had rejected God's word as given through Elisha.

14:7 Sela was the ancient stronghold of Petra, a city carved into a rock cliff. It was not only a stronghold for Edom but also a wealthy outpost for trade with India.

14:8-22 //2 Chr 25:17–26:2 — 8 One day Amaziah sent this challenge to Israel's king Jehoash, the son of Jehoahaz
14:9 Judg 9:8-15 — and grandson of Jehu: "Come and meet me in battle!"
9 But King Jehoash of Israel replied to King Amaziah of Judah with this story: "Out
in the Lebanon mountains a thistle sent a message to a mighty cedar tree: 'Give your
daughter in marriage to my son.' But just then a wild animal came by and stepped on the
thistle, crushing it! 10 You have indeed destroyed Edom and are very proud about it. Be
content with your victory and stay at home! Why stir up trouble that will bring disaster
on you and the people of Judah?"
14:11 Josh 19:35-39 — 11 But Amaziah refused to listen, so King Jehoash of Israel mobilized his army against
King Amaziah of Judah. The two armies drew up their battle lines at Beth-shemesh in
Judah. 12 Judah was routed by the army of Israel, and its army scattered and fled for
14:13 2 Chr 25:23; Neh 8:16; 12:39 — home. 13 King Jehoash of Israel captured King Amaziah of Judah at Beth-shemesh and
marched on to Jerusalem. Then Jehoash ordered his army to demolish six hundred feet*
of Jerusalem's wall, from the Ephraim Gate to the Corner Gate. 14 He carried off all the
14:14 2 Kgs 12:18 — gold and silver and all the utensils from the Temple of the LORD, as well as from the
palace treasury. He also took hostages and returned to Samaria.
14:15 2 Kgs 13:12-13 — 15 The rest of the events in Jehoash's reign, including the extent of his power and his
war with King Amaziah of Judah, are recorded in *The Book of the History of the Kings*
of Israel. 16 When Jehoash died, he was buried with his ancestors in Samaria. Then his
son Jeroboam II became the next king.
14:17 2 Chr 25:25-28 — 17 King Amaziah of Judah lived on for fifteen years after the death of King Jehoash
of Israel. 18 The rest of the events in Amaziah's reign are recorded in *The Book of the*

14:13 Hebrew *400 cubits* [180 meters].

KINGS TO DATE AND THEIR ENEMIES

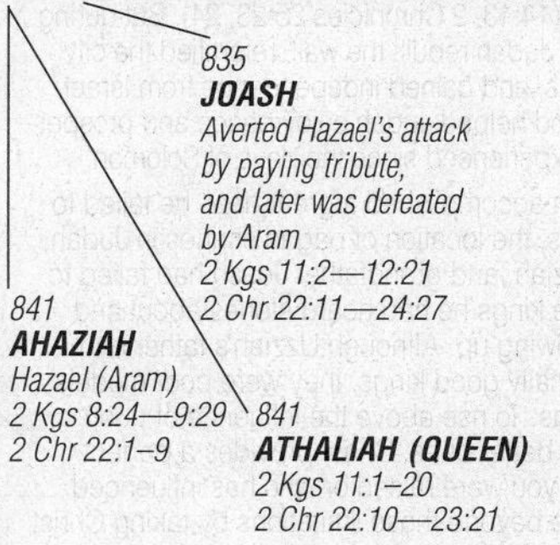

All dates are B.C.
Solid section of the timeline indicates co-regency.
For all the kings of Israel and Judah, see the chart at the end of 1 Kings.

14:9, 10 In this parable, Judah is compared to a small thistle. King Amaziah of Judah had become proud after defeating the Edomites. Here he was trying to pick a fight with Israel because he was sure his army was stronger. Jehoash tried to warn Amaziah not to attack by comparing his army to a thistle and Israel's army to a cedar tree. Amaziah had overrated his strength; his ambition was greater than his ability. He didn't listen to Jehoash and was soundly defeated.

14:13 A broken-down city wall disgraced the citizens and left them defenseless against future invasions.

History of the Kings of Judah. 19 There was a conspiracy against Amaziah's life in
Jerusalem, and he fled to Lachish. But his enemies sent assassins after him, and they
killed him there. 20 They brought him back to Jerusalem on a horse, and he was buried
with his ancestors in the City of David.

21 The people of Judah then crowned Amaziah's sixteen-year-old son, Uzziah,* as
their next king. 22 After his father's death, Uzziah rebuilt the town of Elath and restored
it to Judah.

14:19 2 Kgs 12:20
14:20 2 Kgs 9:28
14:21 2 Chr 26:23; Hos 1:1; Matt 1:9

Jeroboam II Rules in Israel

23 Jeroboam II, the son of Jehoash, began to rule over Israel in the fifteenth year of King
Amaziah's reign in Judah. Jeroboam reigned in Samaria forty-one years. 24 He did what
was evil in the LORD's sight. He refused to turn from the sins of idolatry that Jeroboam
son of Nebat had led Israel to commit. 25 Jeroboam II recovered the territories of Israel
between Lebo-hamath and the Dead Sea,* just as the LORD, the God of Israel, had
promised through Jonah son of Amittai, the prophet from Gath-hepher. 26 For the LORD
saw the bitter suffering of everyone in Israel, and how they had absolutely no one to help
them. 27 And because the LORD had not said he would blot out the name of Israel
completely, he used Jeroboam II, the son of Jehoash, to save them.

28 The rest of the events in the reign of Jeroboam II and all his deeds, including the
extent of his power, his wars, and how he recovered for Israel both Damascus and
Hamath, which had belonged to Judah,* are recorded in *The Book of the History of the*
Kings of Israel. 29 When Jeroboam II died, he was buried with his ancestors, the kings of
Israel. Then his son Zechariah became the next king.

14:23 2 Kgs 13:13; Amos 1:1
14:24 1 Kgs 15:30
14:25 Deut 3:17; 2 Kgs 13:25; Jon 1:1
14:26 Deut 32:36; 2 Kgs 13:4
14:27 2 Kgs 13:5, 23

Uzziah Rules in Judah

15 Uzziah* son of Amaziah began to rule over Judah in the twenty-seventh year of
the reign of King Jeroboam II of Israel. 2 He was sixteen years old when he became
king, and he reigned in Jerusalem fifty-two years. His mother was Jecoliah, from
Jerusalem. 3 He did what was pleasing in the LORD's sight, just as his father, Amaziah,
had done. 4 But he did not destroy the pagan shrines, where the people offered sacrifices
and burned incense. 5 The LORD struck the king with leprosy,* which lasted until the day
of his death; he lived in a house by himself. The king's son Jotham was put in charge of
the royal palace, and he governed the people of the land.

15:1 2 Kgs 14:21; 15:13, 17
15:5 Lev 13:46

14:21 Hebrew *Azariah,* a variant name for Uzziah. **14:25** Hebrew *the sea of the Arabah.* **14:28** Or *to Yaudi.*
15:1 Hebrew *Azariah,* a variant name for Uzziah; also in 15:6, 7, 8, 17, 23, 27. **15:5** Or *with a contagious skin disease.* The Hebrew word used here and throughout this passage can describe various skin diseases.

14:25 During this period of history, many prophets—such as Hosea, Amos, Jonah, Micah, and Isaiah—began collecting their prophecies and writing them under God's direction. They continued to preach about the worldwide significance of God's work as they looked forward to the future spiritual Kingdom. God would use Israel's moral and spiritual decline to prepare the way for the Messiah's coming. Because the kingdom and military power of Israel were stripped away, many people would be ready to turn to the Good News that Jesus would bring.

14:25 For more information about the prophet Jonah, see the book of Jonah.

14:28 Jeroboam II had no devotion to God, yet under his warlike policies and skillful administration, Israel enjoyed more national power and material prosperity than at any time since the days of Solomon. The prophets Amos and Hosea, however, tell us what was really happening within the kingdom (Hosea 13:4-8; Amos 6:11-14). Jeroboam's administration ignored policies of justice and fairness. As a result, the rich became richer, and the poor, poorer. The people became self-centered, relying more on their power, security, and possessions than on God. The poor were so oppressed that it was hard for them to believe God noticed their plight. Material prosperity is not always an indication of God's blessing. It can also be a result of self-centeredness. If you are experiencing prosperity, remember that God holds us accountable for how we attain success and how we use our wealth. Everything we have really belongs to him. We must use God's gifts with his interests in mind.

15:1 Uzziah was also known as Azariah. His story is given in greater detail in 2 Chronicles 26. He is also mentioned in Isaiah 1:1 and 6:1. Before the beginning of Uzziah's reign, Israel broke down 600 feet of Jerusalem's walls after defeating Judah and carrying off their king, Amaziah (14:13; 2 Chronicles 25:23, 24). But during Uzziah's 52-year reign, Judah rebuilt the wall, refortified the city with anti-siege weapons, and gained independence from Israel. Uzziah's devotion to God helped Judah enjoy peace and prosperity such as it had not experienced since the days of Solomon.

15:4 Although Uzziah accomplished a great deal, he failed to destroy the high places, the location of pagan shrines in Judah, just as his father, Amaziah, and grandfather Joash had failed to do. Uzziah imitated the kings he had heard stories about and had watched while growing up. Although Uzziah's father and grandfather were basically good kings, they were poor models in some important areas. To rise above the influence of poor models, we must seek better ones. Christ provides a perfect model. No matter how you were raised or who has influenced your life, you can move beyond those limitations by taking Christ as your example and consciously trying to live as he did.

15:5 For 10 years Jotham was the co-ruler with his father, Uzziah. A father and son would rule together for any of the following reasons: (1) The father was very old and needed help; (2) the father wanted to train his son in leading the nation; (3) the father was sick or exiled. There were many co-regents during the period of the kings—Asa/Jehoshaphat; Jehoshaphat/Jehoram; Azariah/Jotham; Jehoash/Jeroboam II; Hezekiah/Manasseh.

6 The rest of the events in Uzziah's reign and all his deeds are recorded in *The Book of*
the History of the Kings of Judah. 7 When Uzziah died, he was buried near his ancestors
in the City of David. Then his son Jotham became the next king.

Zechariah Rules in Israel

15:8 2 Kgs 14:29 8 Zechariah son of Jeroboam II began to rule over Israel in the thirty-eighth year of King
Uzziah's reign in Judah. He reigned in Samaria six months. 9 Zechariah did what was evil
in the LORD's sight, as his ancestors had done. He refused to turn from the sins of idolatry
15:10 Amos 7:9 that Jeroboam son of Nebat had led Israel to commit. 10 Then Shallum son of Jabesh
conspired against Zechariah, assassinated him in public,* and became the next king.
11 The rest of the events in Zechariah's reign are recorded in *The Book of the History of*
15:12 2 Kgs 10:30 *the Kings of Israel.* 12 So the LORD's message to Jehu came true: "Your descendants will
be kings of Israel down to the fourth generation."

Shallum Rules in Israel

15:13 2 Kgs 15:1, 8 13 Shallum son of Jabesh began to rule over Israel in the thirty-ninth year of King
Uzziah's reign in Judah. Shallum reigned in Samaria only one month. 14 Then Menahem
son of Gadi went to Samaria from Tirzah and assassinated him, and he became the next
king. 15 The rest of the events in Shallum's reign, including his conspiracy, are recorded
in *The Book of the History of the Kings of Israel.*

Menahem Rules in Israel

15:16 2 Kgs 8:12 Hos 13:16 16 At that time Menahem destroyed the town of Tappuah* and all the surrounding
countryside as far as Tirzah, because its citizens refused to surrender the town. He killed
the entire population and ripped open the pregnant women.
17 Menahem son of Gadi began to rule over Israel in the thirty-ninth year of King
15:18 2 Kgs 15:26 Uzziah's reign in Judah. He reigned in Samaria ten years. 18 But Menahem did what was
evil in the LORD's sight. During his entire reign, he refused to turn from the sins of
15:19 1 Chr 5:26 idolatry that Jeroboam son of Nebat had led Israel to commit. 19 Then King Tiglath-
pileser* of Assyria invaded the land. But Menahem paid him thirty-seven tons* of silver
to gain his support in tightening his grip on royal power. 20 Menahem extorted the money
from the rich of Israel, demanding that each of them pay twenty ounces* of silver in the
form of a special tax. So the king of Assyria turned from attacking Israel and did not stay
in the land. 21 The rest of the events in Menahem's reign and all his deeds are recorded
in *The Book of the History of the Kings of Israel.* 22 When Menahem died, his son
Pekahiah became the next king.

Pekahiah Rules in Israel

23 Pekahiah son of Menahem began to rule over Israel in the fiftieth year of King Uzziah's
reign in Judah. He reigned in Samaria two years. 24 But Pekahiah did what was evil in
the LORD's sight. He refused to turn from the sins of idolatry that Jeroboam son of Nebat
had led Israel to commit.
25 Then Pekah son of Remaliah, the commander of Pekahiah's army, conspired against
him. With fifty men from Gilead, Pekah assassinated the king, along with Argob and
Arieh, in the citadel of the palace at Samaria. Pekah then became the next king of Israel.

15:10 Or *at Ibleam.* **15:16** As in some Greek manuscripts; Hebrew reads *Tiphsah.* **15:19a** Hebrew *Pul,* another name for Tiglath-pileser. **15:19b** Hebrew *1,000 talents* [34 metric tons]. **15:20** Hebrew *50 shekels* [570 grams].

15:8 Zechariah was an evil king because he encouraged Israel to sin by worshiping idols. Sin in our lives is serious. But it is even more serious to encourage others to disobey God. We are responsible for the way we influence others. Beware of double sins: ones that not only hurt us but also hurt others by encouraging them to sin.

15:10 Zechariah was warned by the prophet Amos of his impending death and the subsequent end of Jeroboam's dynasty (Amos 7:9).

15:14 Ancient historical documents say that Menahem was the commander in chief of Jeroboam's army (see 14:23-29 for an account of Jeroboam II's reign). After Jeroboam's son was assassinated (15:8-10), Menahem probably saw himself, and not Shallum, as the rightful successor to Israel's throne.

15:18 Menahem, like the kings before him, led his people into sin: He "did what was evil in the LORD's sight." What a horrible epitaph for a leader! Leaders profoundly affect the people they serve. They can either encourage or discourage devotion to God both by their example and by the structure they give their organization. Good leaders put up no obstacles to faith in God or to right living.

15:19, 20 When King Tiglath-pileser took the throne of Assyria, the Assyrian Empire was becoming a world power, and the nations of Aram, Israel, and Judah were in decline. This is the first mention of Assyria in 2 Kings. Tiglath-pileser's invasion occurred in 743 B.C. Assyria made Israel a vassal state, and Menahem was forced to pay tribute to Assyria. This was the first of three Assyrian invasions (15:29 and 17:6 tell of the other ones).

26 The rest of the events in Pekahiah's reign and all his deeds are recorded in *The Book*
of the History of the Kings of Israel.

Pekah Rules in Israel

27 Pekah son of Remaliah began to rule over Israel in the fifty-second year of King
Uzziah's reign in Judah. He reigned in Samaria twenty years. 28 But Pekah did what was
evil in the LORD's sight. He refused to turn from the sins of idolatry that Jeroboam son
of Nebat had led Israel to commit. 29 During his reign, King Tiglath-pileser of Assyria
attacked Israel again, and he captured the towns of Ijon, Abel-beth-maacah, Janoah,
Kedesh, and Hazor. He also conquered the regions of Gilead, Galilee, and Naphtali, and
he took the people to Assyria as captives. 30 Then Hoshea son of Elah conspired against
Pekah and assassinated him. He began to rule over Israel in the twentieth year of Jotham
son of Uzziah. 31 The rest of the events in Pekah's reign and all his deeds are recorded in
The Book of the History of the Kings of Israel.

Jotham Rules in Judah

32 Jotham son of Uzziah began to rule over Judah in the second year of King Pekah's
reign in Israel. 33 He was twenty-five years old when he became king, and he reigned in
Jerusalem sixteen years. His mother was Jerusha, the daughter of Zadok.
34 Jotham did what was pleasing in the LORD's sight, just as his father Uzziah had done.
35 But he did not destroy the pagan shrines, where the people offered sacrifices and
burned incense. He was the one who rebuilt the upper gate of the Temple of the LORD.
36 The rest of the events in Jotham's reign and all his deeds are recorded in *The Book*
of the History of the Kings of Judah. 37 In those days the LORD began to send King Rezin
of Aram and King Pekah of Israel to attack Judah. 38 When Jotham died, he was buried
with his ancestors in the City of David. Then his son Ahaz became the next king.

Ahaz Rules in Judah

16 Ahaz son of Jotham began to rule over Judah in the seventeenth year of King
Pekah's reign in Israel. 2 Ahaz was twenty years old when he became king, and he
reigned in Jerusalem sixteen years. He did not do what was pleasing in the sight of the
LORD his God, as his ancestor David had done. 3 Instead, he followed the example of the
kings of Israel, even sacrificing his own son in the fire.* He imitated the detestable
practices of the pagan nations the LORD had driven from the land ahead of the Israelites.
4 He offered sacrifices and burned incense at the pagan shrines and on the hills and under
every green tree.
5 Then King Rezin of Aram and King Pekah of Israel declared war on Ahaz. They
besieged Jerusalem but did not conquer it. 6 At that time the king of Edom* recovered
the town of Elath for Edom.* He drove out the people of Judah and sent Edomites* to
live there, as they do to this day.
7 King Ahaz sent messengers to King Tiglath-pileser of Assyria with this message: "I
am your servant and your vassal.* Come up and rescue me from the attacking armies of
Aram and Israel." 8 Then Ahaz took the silver and gold from the Temple of the LORD and
the palace treasury and sent it as a gift to the Assyrian king. 9 So the Assyrians attacked
the Aramean capital of Damascus and led its population away as captives, resettling them
in Kir. They also killed King Rezin.

15:27 2 Kgs 15:32; 16:5; 2 Chr 28:6
15:29 2 Kgs 17:6
15:30 2 Kgs 12:20
15:32 2 Chr 27:1; Matt 1:9
15:33-38 //2 Chr 27:1-4, 7-9
15:34 2 Chr 26:4-5
15:36 2 Kgs 15:6; 16:19; 20:20
15:37 2 Kgs 16:5; Isa 7:1
16:1-20 //2 Chr 28:1-27
16:2 2 Kgs 14:3
16:3 Lev 18:21; Deut 12:31; 2 Kgs 17:17; 21:6
16:4 Deut 12:2
16:5 2 Kgs 15:37; 2 Chr 28:5; Isa 7:1-6
16:6 2 Kgs 14:22; 2 Chr 26:2
16:7 2 Kgs 15:29
16:8 2 Kgs 12:17-18; 18:15
16:9 Amos 1:3-5

16:3 Or *even making his son pass through the fire.* **16:6a** As in Latin Vulgate; Hebrew reads *Rezin king of Aram.* **16:6b** As in Latin Vulgate; Hebrew reads *Aram.* **16:6c** As in marginal *Qere* reading of the Masoretic Text, Greek version, and Latin Vulgate; Hebrew reads *Arameans.* **16:7** Hebrew *your son.*

15:30 Hoshea was Israel's last king.

15:32 A year after Pekah became king, Uzziah (also called Azariah) of Judah died, and Isaiah the prophet had a vision of God's holiness and Israel's future destruction. See Isaiah 6 for more details on what Isaiah saw.

15:34, 35 Much good can be said of Jotham and his reign as king of Judah, but he failed in a most important area: He didn't destroy the high places, although leaving them clearly violated the first commandment (Exodus 20:3). Like Jotham, we may live basically good lives and yet miss doing what is most important. A lifetime of doing good is not enough if we make the crucial mistake of not following God with all our hearts. A true follower of God puts God first in all areas of life.

16:3 Ahaz was so depraved that he sacrificed his own son to the pagan gods. This was a practice of the Canaanites, whom the Israelites were supposed to drive out of the land.

16:5 Israel and Aram were both under Assyria's control. They joined forces against Judah, hoping to force the southern kingdom to join their revolt against Assyria and strengthen their western alliance. But the plan backfired when King Ahaz of Judah unexpectedly asked Assyria to come to his aid (16:8, 9).

16:10 Isa 8:2 — 10 King Ahaz then went to Damascus to meet with King Tiglath-pileser of Assyria.
While he was there, he noticed an unusual altar. So he sent a model of the altar to
Uriah the priest, along with its design in full detail. 11 Uriah built an altar just like it
by following the king's instructions, and it was ready for the king when he returned
16:12 2 Chr 26:16, 19 — from Damascus. 12 When the king returned, he inspected the altar and made offerings
16:14 Exod 40:6; 1 Kgs 8:64 — on it. 13 The king presented a burnt offering and a grain offering, poured a drink
offering over it, and sprinkled the blood of peace offerings on it.
14 Then King Ahaz removed the old bronze altar from the front of the LORD's

KINGS TO DATE AND THEIR ENEMIES

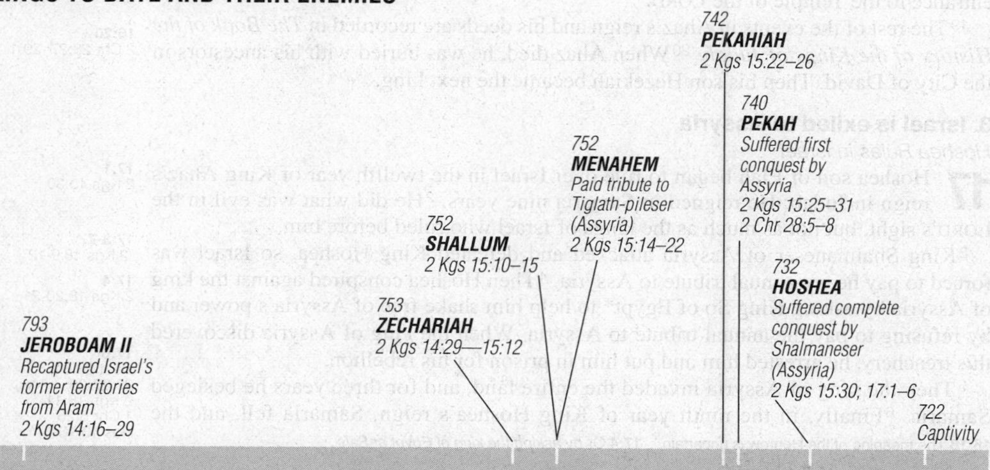

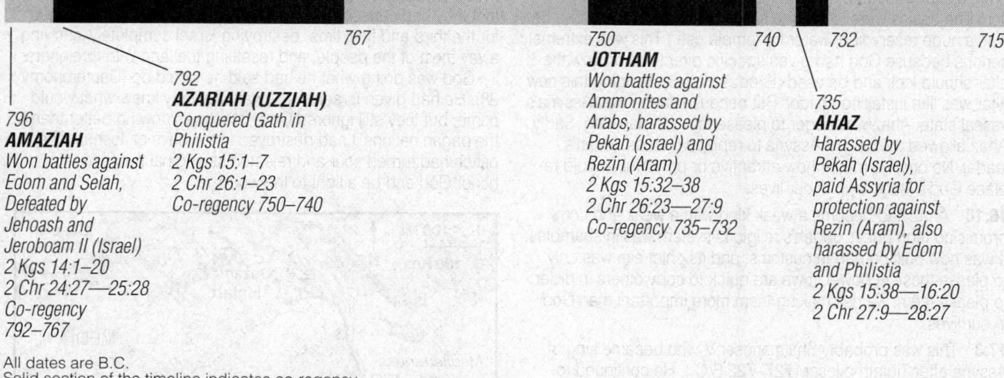

All dates are B.C.
Solid section of the timeline indicates co-regency.
For all the kings of Israel and Judah, see the chart at the end of 1 Kings.

16:10 Ahaz went to Damascus to express gratitude and loyalty to Tiglath-pileser. Because the Assyrians had captured Damascus, the capital of Aram (732 B.C.), Ahaz was afraid of a southern sweep. But he was relying more on money than on God to keep the powerful king out of his land, and his plan failed. Although Tiglath-pileser did not conquer Judah, he caused much trouble, and Ahaz regretted asking for his help (2 Chronicles 28:20, 21).

16:10-16 Evil King Ahaz copied pagan religious customs, changed the Temple services, and used the Temple altar for his personal benefit. In so doing, he demonstrated a callous disregard for God's commands. We condemn Ahaz for his action, but we act the same way if we try to mold God's message to fit our personal preferences. We must worship God for who he is, not what we would selfishly like him to be.

Temple, which had stood between the entrance and the new altar, and placed it on the
north side of the new altar. 15 He said to Uriah the priest, "Use the new altar for the 16:15 Exod 29:38-41
morning sacrifices of burnt offering, the evening grain offering, the king's burnt
offering and grain offering, and the offerings of the people, including their drink
offerings. The blood from the burnt offerings and sacrifices should be sprinkled over
the new altar. The old bronze altar will be only for my personal use." 16 Uriah the priest
did just as King Ahaz instructed him.
17 Then the king removed the side panels and basins from the portable water carts. He 16:17 1 Kgs 7:23, 25, 27
also removed the Sea from the backs of the bronze oxen and placed it on the stone
pavement. 18 In deference to the king of Assyria, he also removed the canopy that had
been constructed inside the palace for use on the Sabbath day,* as well as the king's outer
entrance to the Temple of the LORD.
19 The rest of the events in Ahaz's reign and his deeds are recorded in *The Book of the*
History of the Kings of Judah. 20 When Ahaz died, he was buried with his ancestors in 16:20 2 Chr 28:27; 29:1
the City of David. Then his son Hezekiah became the next king.

3. Israel is exiled to Assyria

Hoshea Rules in Israel

17 Hoshea son of Elah began to rule over Israel in the twelfth year of King Ahaz's 17:1 2 Kgs 15:30
reign in Judah. He reigned in Samaria nine years. 2 He did what was evil in the
LORD's sight, but not as much as the kings of Israel who ruled before him.
3 King Shalmaneser of Assyria attacked and defeated King Hoshea, so Israel was 17:3-7 //2 Kgs 18:9-12
forced to pay heavy annual tribute to Assyria. 4 Then Hoshea conspired against the king 17:4
of Assyria by asking King So of Egypt* to help him shake free of Assyria's power and 2 Kgs 18:20-21
by refusing to pay the annual tribute to Assyria. When the king of Assyria discovered
this treachery, he arrested him and put him in prison for his rebellion. 17:6
5 Then the king of Assyria invaded the entire land, and for three years he besieged Deut 28:64; 29:27-28
Samaria. 6 Finally, in the ninth year of King Hoshea's reign, Samaria fell, and the 2 Kgs 18:11 1 Chr 5:26 Hos 13:16

16:18 The meaning of the Hebrew is uncertain. **17:4** Or *by asking the king of Egypt at Sais.*

16:14-18 Ahaz replaced the altar of burnt offering with a replica of the pagan altar he had seen in Damascus. (The original bronze altar was not thrown out, but was kept for use in divination. The basins were where the sacrifices were washed. The Sea was a huge reservoir of water for temple use.) This was extremely serious because God had given specific directions on how the altar should look and be used (Exodus 27:1-8). Building this new altar was like installing an idol. But because Judah was Assyria's vassal state, Ahaz was eager to please the Assyrian king. Sadly, Ahaz allowed the king of Assyria to replace God as Judah's leader. No one, no matter how attractive or powerful, should replace God's leadership in our lives.

16:18 Ahaz had become a weak king with a weak and compromising high priest. Judah's religious system was in shambles. It was now built on pagan customs, and its chief aim was only to please those in power. If we are quick to copy others in order to please them, we risk making them more important than God in our lives.

17:3 This was probably Shalmaneser V, who became king of Assyria after Tiglath-pileser (727–722 B.C.). He continued to demand heavy tribute from Israel. Israel's king Hoshea decided to rebel against Assyria and join forces with King So of Egypt (17:4). This was not only foolish but also against God's commands. To destroy this conspiracy, Shalmaneser attacked and besieged Samaria for three years. But just before Samaria fell, Shalmaneser died. His successor, Sargon II, took credit for capturing the city, destroying the nation of Israel, and carrying away its people.

17:5, 6 This was Assyria's third and final invasion of Israel. (The first two invasions are recorded in 15:19 and 15:29.) The first wave was merely a warning to Israel—to avoid further attack, pay money, and not rebel. The people should have learned their lesson and returned to God. When they didn't, God allowed Assyria to invade again, this time carrying off some captives from the northern border. But the people still did not realize that they had caused their own troubles. Thus, Assyria invaded for the third and final time, destroying Israel completely, carrying away most of the people, and resettling the land with foreigners.

God was doing what he had said he would do (Deuteronomy 28). He had given Israel ample warning; they knew what would come, but they still ignored God. Israel was now no better than the pagan nations it had destroyed in the days of Joshua. The nation had turned sour and rejected its original purpose—to honor God and be a light to the world.

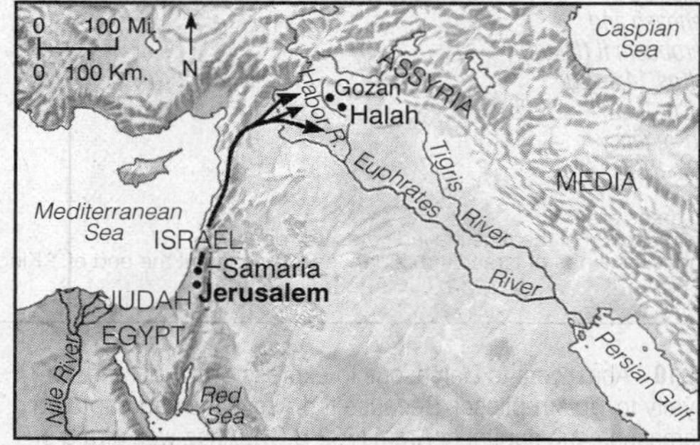

ISRAEL TAKEN CAPTIVE Finally the sins of Israel's people caught up with them. God allowed Assyria to defeat and disperse the people. They were led into captivity, swallowed up by the mighty, evil Assyrian Empire. Sin always brings discipline, and the consequences of that sin are sometimes irreversible.

people of Israel were exiled to Assyria. They were settled in colonies in Halah, along
the banks of the Habor River in Gozan, and among the cities of the Medes.

Samaria Falls to Assyria

7 This disaster came upon the nation of Israel because the people worshiped other
gods, sinning against the LORD their God, who had brought them safely out of their
slavery in Egypt. 8 They had imitated the practices of the pagan nations the LORD had
driven from the land before them, as well as the practices the kings of Israel had
introduced. 9 The people of Israel had also secretly done many things that were not
pleasing to the LORD their God. They built pagan shrines for themselves in all their
towns, from the smallest outpost to the largest walled city. 10 They set up sacred pillars
and Asherah poles at the top of every hill and under every green tree. 11 They burned
incense at the shrines, just like the nations the LORD had driven from the land ahead
of them. So the people of Israel had done many evil things, arousing the LORD's anger.
12 Yes, they worshiped idols, despite the LORD's specific and repeated warnings.
13 Again and again the LORD had sent his prophets and seers to warn both Israel and
Judah: "Turn from all your evil ways. Obey my commands and laws, which are
contained in the whole law that I commanded your ancestors and which I gave you
through my servants the prophets."
14 But the Israelites would not listen. They were as stubborn as their ancestors and
refused to believe in the LORD their God. 15 They rejected his laws and the covenant he
had made with their ancestors, and they despised all his warnings. They worshiped
worthless idols and became worthless themselves. They followed the example of the
nations around them, disobeying the LORD's command not to imitate them. 16 They
defied all the commands of the LORD their God and made two calves from metal. They
set up an Asherah pole and worshiped Baal and all the forces of heaven. 17 They even
sacrificed their own sons and daughters in the fire.* They consulted fortune-tellers and
used sorcery and sold themselves to evil, arousing the LORD's anger.
18 And because the LORD was angry, he swept them from his presence. Only the tribe
of Judah remained in the land. 19 But even the people of Judah refused to obey the
commands of the LORD their God. They walked down the same evil paths that Israel had
established. 20 So the LORD rejected all the descendants of Israel. He punished them by
handing them over to their attackers until they were destroyed. 21 For when the LORD tore
Israel away from the kingdom of David, they chose Jeroboam son of Nebat as their king.
Then Jeroboam drew Israel away from following the LORD and made them commit a
great sin. 22 And the people of Israel persisted in all the evil ways of Jeroboam. They did

17:7 Josh 23:15-16
17:8 Lev 18:3; Deut 18:9
17:9 2 Kgs 18:8
17:12 Exod 20:4
17:13 Neh 9:29-30; Jer 7:5-6; 18:11; Acts 7:51-52
17:14 Exod 32:9; 33:3
17:15 Exod 24:6-8; Deut 12:30-31; 29:25; 32:21
17:16 1 Kgs 12:28; 16:31
17:17 Lev 19:26; Deut 18:10-12; 2 Kgs 3:27; 16:3; 21:6
17:19 1 Kgs 14:22-24
17:21 1 Kgs 11:11, 31; 12:20

17:17 Or *They even made their sons and daughters pass through the fire.*

17:7-17 The Lord judged the people of Israel because they copied the evil customs of the surrounding nations, worshiping false gods, accommodating pagan customs, and following their own desires. It is not safe to create your own religion because people who do tend to live selfishly. And to live for yourself, as Israel learned, brings serious consequences from God. Sometimes it is difficult and painful to follow God, but consider the alternative. You can live for God or die for yourself. Determine to be God's person and do what he says regardless of the cost. What God thinks of you is infinitely more important than what those around you think. (See Romans 12:1, 2; 1 John 2:15-17.)

17:9 Ruin came upon Israel for both their public sins and their secret sins. Not only did they condone wickedness and idolatry in public, but they committed even worse sins in private. Secret sins are the ones we don't want others to know about because they are embarrassing or incriminating. Sins done in private are not secret to God, and secret defiance of him is just as damaging as open rebellion.

17:13-15 The people took on the characteristics of the idols and imitated the godless nations around them. Israel had forgotten the importance and benefits of obeying God's word. The king and the people were mired in wickedness. Time and again God had sent prophets to warn them about how far they had turned away from him and to call them to turn back.

God's patience and mercy are beyond our ability to understand. He will pursue us until we either respond to him or, by our own choice and hardness of heart, make ourselves unreachable. Then God's judgment is swift and sure. The only safe course is to turn to God before our stubbornness puts us out of his reach.

17:16 The "forces of heaven" refers to the Canaanite practice of worshiping the sun, moon, and constellations. These were Assyrian gods that were being added to their religion. (See also 21:1-6; 23:4, 5.)

17:17 Forms of witchcraft, fortune-telling, and black magic were forbidden by God (Deuteronomy 18:9-14). They were wrong because they sought power and guidance totally apart from God, his law, and his word. Isaiah echoed this law and prophesied of the complete destruction these occult practices would bring to those who participated in them (Isaiah 8:19-22).

17:23 Israel was taken into exile, just as God's prophets had warned. Whatever God predicts will come to pass. This, of course, is good news to those who trust and obey him—they can be confident of his promises; but it is bad news to those who ignore or disobey him. Both the promises and warnings God has given in his Word will surely come true.

not turn from these sins of idolatry [23]until the LORD finally swept them away, just as all his prophets had warned would happen. So Israel was carried off to the land of Assyria, where they remain to this day.

17:23
2 Kgs 18:11-12

WHO WERE

Who?	When? (B.C.)	Ministered during the reign of these kings	Main message	Significance
AHIJAH	934–909	Jeroboam I of Israel (1 Kings 11:29–39)	Israel would split in two, and God had chosen Jeroboam to lead the 10 tribes. Warned him to remain obedient to God.	We should not take lightly our God-given responsibilities. Jeroboam did and lost his kingdom.
ELIJAH	875–848	Ahab of Israel (1 Kings 17:1—2 Kings 2:11)	In fiery style, urged wicked Ahab to turn back to God. Proved on Mount Carmel who the one true God is (1 Kings 18).	Even giants of faith can't force sinners to change. But those who remain faithful to God have a great impact for him.
MICAIAH	865–853	Ahab of Israel Jehoshaphat of Judah (1 Kings 22:8; 2 Chronicles 18:28)	Ahab would be unsuccessful in fighting the Arameans.	It is foolish to move ahead with plans that are contrary to God's Word.
JEHU	853	Jehoshaphat of Judah (2 Chronicles 19:1–3)	Jehoshaphat should never have allied himself with wicked Ahab.	Partnerships with immoral people can lead us into trouble.
OBADIAH	855–840 (?)	Jehoram of Judah (The book of Obadiah)	God would judge the Edomites for taking advantage of God's people.	Pride is one of the most dangerous sins because it causes us to take advantage of others.
ELISHA	848–797	Joram, Jehu, Jehoahaz, and Jehoash, all of Israel (2 Kings 2:1—9:1; 13:10–21)	Expressed by his actions the importance of helping ordinary people in need.	God is concerned about the everyday needs of his people.
JOEL	835–796 (?)	Joash of Judah (The book of Joel)	Because a plague of locusts had come to punish the nation, called the people to turn back to God before an even greater judgment occurred.	While God judges all people for their sins, he gives eternal salvation only to those who have turned to him.
JONAH	793–753	Jeroboam II of Israel (2 Kings 14:25; the book of Jonah)	Warned Nineveh, the capital of Assyria, to repent of its sins.	God wants all nations to turn to him. His love reaches out to all peoples.
AMOS	760–750	Jeroboam II of Israel (The book of Amos)	Warned those who exploited or ignored the needy. (In Amos's day, Israel was an affluent and materialistic society.)	Believing in God is more than a personal matter. God calls all believers to work against injustices in society and to aid those less fortunate.
HOSEA	753–715	The last seven kings of Israel; Azariah (Uzziah), Jotham, Ahaz, and Hezekiah of Judah (The book of Hosea)	Condemned the people of Israel because they had sinned against God as an adulterous woman sins against her husband.	When we sin, we sever our relationship to God, breaking our commitment to him. While all must answer to God for their sins, those who seek God's forgiveness are spared from eternal judgment.

"Again and again the LORD had sent his prophets and seers to warn both Israel and Judah: 'Turn from all your evil ways. Obey my commands and laws . . .'" (2 Kings 17:13). Who were these prophets? Here are some of those who tried to turn their nations back to God. Predicting the future as revealed by God was just one part of a prophet's job; his main role was to preach God's word to the people—warning, instructing, and

Foreigners Settle in Israel

17:24
2 Kgs 18:34
Ezra 4:2, 10

[24]And the king of Assyria transported groups of people from Babylon, Cuthah, Avva,
Hamath, and Sepharvaim and resettled them in the towns of Samaria, replacing the

THESE PROPHETS?

Who?	*When? (B.C.)*	*Ministered during the reign of these kings*	*Main message*	*Significance*
MICAH	742–687	Jotham, Ahaz, and Hezekiah of Judah (The book of Micah)	Predicted the fall of both the northern and southern kingdoms. This was God's discipline on the people, actually showing how much he cared for them.	Choosing to live a life apart from God is making a commitment to sin. Sin leads to judgment and death. God alone shows us the way to eternal peace. His discipline often keeps us on the right path.
ISAIAH	740–681	Azariah (Uzziah), Jotham, Ahaz, Hezekiah, and Manasseh of Judah (The book of Isaiah)	Called the people back to a special relationship with God—although judgment through other nations was inevitable.	Sometimes we must suffer judgment and discipline before we are restored to God.
NAHUM	663–654	Manasseh of Judah (The book of Nahum)	The mighty empire of Assyria that oppressed God's people would soon tumble.	Those who do evil and oppress others will one day meet a bitter end.
ZEPHANIAH	640–621	Josiah of Judah (The book of Zephaniah)	A day would come when God, as Judge, would severely punish all nations; but afterward he would show mercy to his people.	We will all be judged for our disobedience to God, but if we remain faithful to him, he will show us mercy.
JEREMIAH	627–586	Josiah, Jehoahaz, Jehoiakim, Jehoiachin, Zedekiah of Judah (The book of Jeremiah)	Repentance would postpone Judah's coming judgment at the hands of Babylon.	Repentance is one of the greatest needs in our world of immorality. God's promises to the faithful shine brightly.
HABAKKUK	612–589	Josiah, Jehoahaz, Jehoiakim, Jehoiachin, Zedekiah of Judah (The book of Habakkuk)	Couldn't understand why God seemed to do nothing about the wickedness in society. Then realized that faith in God alone would one day supply the answer.	Instead of questioning the ways of God, we should realize that he is completely just, and we should have faith that he is in control and that one day evil will be utterly destroyed.
DANIEL	605–536	Prophesied as an exile in Babylon during the reigns of Nebuchadnezzar, Darius the Mede, and Cyrus of Persia (The book of Daniel)	Described both near and distant future events. Throughout it all, God is sovereign and triumphant.	We should spend less time wondering when these events will happen and more time learning how we should live *now* so we won't be victims of those events.
EZEKIEL	593–571	Prophesied as an exile in Babylon during the reign of Nebuchadnezzar (The book of Ezekiel)	Sent messages back to Jerusalem urging the people to turn back to God before they were all forced to join him in exile. After Jerusalem fell, he urged his fellow exiles to turn back to God so they could eventually return to their homeland.	God disciplines his people to draw them closer to him.

encouraging them to live as they ought. (The prophets Haggai, Zechariah, and Malachi were prophets to the people of Judah after they returned from exile. For more information, see the chart in Ezra 5.)

people of Israel. So the Assyrians took over Samaria and the other towns of Israel. 25But
since these foreign settlers did not worship the LORD when they first arrived, the LORD
sent lions among them to kill some of them.
26So a message was sent to the king of Assyria: "The people whom you have
resettled in the towns of Israel* do not know how to worship the God of the land. He
has sent lions among them to destroy them because they have not worshiped him
correctly."
27The king of Assyria then commanded, "Send one of the exiled priests from
Samaria back to Israel. Let him teach the new residents the religious customs of the
God of the land." 28So one of the priests who had been exiled from Samaria returned
to Bethel and taught the new residents how to worship the LORD.
29But these various groups of foreigners also continued to worship their own gods. **17:29** 1 Kgs 12:31; 13:32
In town after town where they lived, they placed their idols at the pagan shrines that
the people of Israel had built. 30Those from Babylon worshiped idols of their god
Succoth-benoth. Those from Cuthah worshiped their god Nergal. And those from
Hamath worshiped Ashima. 31The Avvites worshiped their gods Nibhaz and Tartak. **17:31** 2 Kgs 17:24; 19:37
And the people from Sepharvaim even burned their own children as sacrifices to
Adrammelech and Anammelech.
32These new residents worshiped the LORD, but they appointed from among **17:32** 1 Kgs 12:31
themselves priests to offer sacrifices at the pagan shrines. 33And though they worshiped the LORD, they continued to follow the religious customs of the nations from
which they came. 34And this is still going on among them today. They follow their **17:34** Gen 32:28; 35:10
former practices instead of truly worshiping the LORD and obeying the laws, regulations, instructions, and commands he gave the descendants of Jacob, whose name he
changed to Israel. 35For the LORD had made a covenant with the descendants of Jacob **17:35** Exod 20:5
and commanded them: "Do not worship any other gods or bow before them or serve
them or offer sacrifices to them. 36Worship only the LORD, who brought you out of
Egypt with such mighty miracles and power. You must worship him and bow before
him; offer sacrifices to him alone. 37Be careful to obey all the laws, regulations, **17:37** Deut 5:32
instructions, and commands that he wrote for you. You must not worship any other
gods. 38Do not forget the covenant I made with you, and do not worship other gods. **17:38** Deut 4:23; 6:10-12
39You must worship only the LORD your God. He is the one who will rescue you from
all your enemies."
40But the people would not listen and continued to follow their old ways. 41So while **17:41** Zeph 1:5
these new residents worshiped the LORD, they also worshiped their idols. And to this day Matt 6:24
their descendants do the same.

17:26 Hebrew *of Samaria;* also in 17:29.

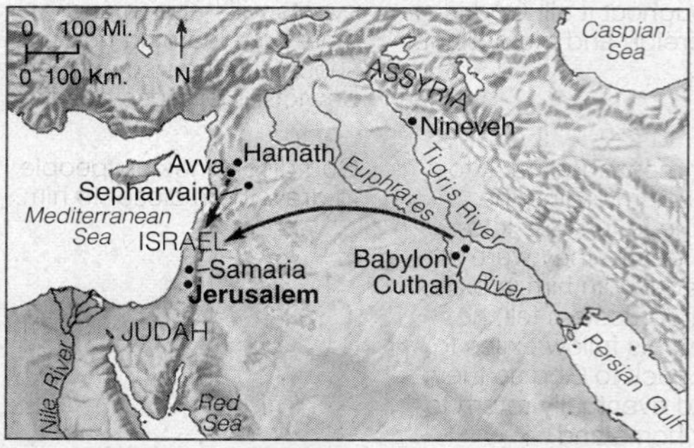

ISRAEL RESETTLED BY FOREIGNERS After the Israelites were deported, foreigners from the Assyrian Empire were sent to resettle the land. This policy helped Assyria keep peace in conquered territories.

17:24 Moving the Israelites out and moving foreigners in was Assyria's resettlement policy to prevent revolt. Spreading the captives across Assyria prevented their uniting, and repopulating Israel with foreign captives made it difficult for the remaining Israelites to unite as well. This mixture of peoples resettled in Israel came to be known as *Samaritans.* They were despised by the Jews, even through the time of Christ (John 4:9).

17:27-29 The new settlers in Israel worshiped God without giving up their pagan customs. They worshiped God to appease him rather than to please him, treating him as a good luck charm or just another idol to add to their collection. A similar attitude is common today. Many people claim to believe in God while refusing to give up attitudes and actions that God denounces. God cannot be added to the values we already have. He must come first, and his Word must shape all our actions and attitudes.

17:29-31 Israel was conquered because it had lost sight of the only true God and why it was important to follow him. When conquering the land, the Israelites were told to destroy the pagan influences that could lead them away from God. Their failure to do so brought about their ruin. Here they faced an even greater influx of gods from the many pagan peoples moving into the land.

B. THE SURVIVING KINGDOM (18:1—25:30)

After seeing their brothers and sisters carried away into exile, the people of Judah still lapse into sin. Hezekiah and Josiah begin many reforms, but this is not enough to permanently turn the nation back to God. Judah is defeated by the Babylonians, who exile many of them, but they are not scattered, and the land is not repopulated. Sometimes we do not learn from the examples of sin and foolishness around us.

1. Kings of Judah

Hezekiah Rules in Judah

18:1 2 Chr 28:27

18:2-4 //2 Chr 29:1-2; 31:1

18 Hezekiah son of Ahaz began to rule over Judah in the third year of King Hoshea's
reign in Israel. 2He was twenty-five years old when he became king, and he
reigned in Jerusalem twenty-nine years. His mother was Abijah,* the daughter of

18:2 As in parallel text at 2 Chr 29:1; Hebrew reads *Abi,* a variant name for Abijah.

HEZEKIAH

The past is an important part of today's actions and tomorrow's plans. The people and kings of Judah had a rich past, filled with God's action, guidance, and commands. But with each passing generation, they also had a growing list of tragedies that occurred when the people forgot that their God, who had cared for them in the past, also cared about the present and the future—and demanded their continued obedience. Hezekiah was one of the few kings of Judah who was constantly aware of God's acts in the past and his interest in the events of every day. The Bible describes him as a king who had a close relationship with God.

As a reformer, Hezekiah was most concerned with present obedience. Judah was filled with visual reminders of the people's lack of trust in God, and Hezekiah boldly cleaned house. Altars, idols, and pagan temples were destroyed. Even the bronze snake Moses had made in the wilderness was not spared because it had ceased to point the people to God and had also become an idol. The Temple in Jerusalem, whose doors had been nailed shut by Hezekiah's own father, was cleaned out and reopened. The Passover was reinstituted as a national holiday, and there was revival in Judah.

Although he had a natural inclination to respond to present problems, Hezekiah's life shows little evidence of concern about the future. He took few actions to preserve the effects of his sweeping reforms. His successful efforts made him proud. His unwise display of wealth to the Babylonian delegation got Judah included on Babylon's "Nations to Conquer" list. When Isaiah informed Hezekiah of the foolishness of his act, the king's answer displayed his persistent lack of foresight—he was thankful that any evil consequences would be delayed until after he died. And the lives of three kings who followed him—Manasseh, Amon, and Josiah—were deeply affected by both Hezekiah's accomplishments *and* his weaknesses.

The past affects your decisions and actions today, and these, in turn, affect the future. There are lessons to learn and errors to avoid repeating. Remember that part of the success of your past will be measured by what you do with it now and how well you use it to prepare for the future.

Strengths and accomplishments
- Was the king of Judah who instigated civil and religious reforms
- Had a personal, growing relationship with God
- Developed a powerful prayer life
- Noted as the patron of several chapters in the book of Proverbs (Proverbs 25:1)

Weaknesses and mistakes
- Showed little interest or wisdom in planning for the future and protecting for others the spiritual heritage he enjoyed
- Rashly showed all his wealth to messengers from Babylon

Lessons from his life
- Sweeping reforms are short-lived when little action is taken to preserve them for the future
- Past obedience to God does not remove the possibility of present disobedience
- Complete dependence on God yields amazing results

Vital statistics
- Where: Jerusalem
- Occupation: 13th king of Judah, the southern kingdom
- Relatives: Father: Ahaz. Mother: Abijah. Son: Manasseh
- Contemporaries: Isaiah, Hoshea, Micah, Sennacherib

Key verses
"Hezekiah trusted in the LORD, the God of Israel. There was never another king like him in the land of Judah, either before or after his time. He remained faithful to the LORD in everything, and he carefully obeyed all the commands the LORD had given Moses" (2 Kings 18:5, 6).

Hezekiah's story is told in 2 Kings 16:20—20:21; 2 Chronicles 28:27—32:33; Isaiah 36:1—39:8. He is also mentioned in Proverbs 25:1; Isaiah 1:1; Jeremiah 15:4; 26:18, 19; Hosea 1:1; Micah 1:1.

Zechariah. 3He did what was pleasing in the LORD's sight, just as his ancestor David had
done. 4He removed the pagan shrines, smashed the sacred pillars, and knocked down the
Asherah poles. He broke up the bronze serpent that Moses had made, because the people
of Israel had begun to worship it by burning incense to it. The bronze serpent was called
Nehushtan.*

5Hezekiah trusted in the LORD, the God of Israel. There was never another king like
him in the land of Judah, either before or after his time. 6He remained faithful to the
LORD in everything, and he carefully obeyed all the commands the LORD had given
Moses. 7So the LORD was with him, and Hezekiah was successful in everything he did.
He revolted against the king of Assyria and refused to pay him tribute. 8He also
conquered the Philistines as far distant as Gaza and its territory, from their smallest
outpost to their largest walled city.

9During the fourth year of Hezekiah's reign, which was the seventh year of King
Hoshea's reign in Israel, King Shalmaneser of Assyria attacked Israel and began a
siege on the city of Samaria. 10Three years later, during the sixth year of King
Hezekiah's reign and the ninth year of King Hoshea's reign in Israel, Samaria fell.
11At that time the king of Assyria deported the Israelites to Assyria and put them in
colonies in Halah, along the banks of the Habor River in Gozan, and among the cities
of the Medes. 12For they had refused to listen to the LORD their God. Instead, they
had violated his covenant—all the laws the LORD had given through his servant
Moses.

Assyria Invades Judah

13In the fourteenth year of King Hezekiah's reign, King Sennacherib of Assyria came
to attack the fortified cities of Judah and conquered them. 14King Hezekiah sent this
message to the king of Assyria at Lachish: "I have done wrong. I will pay whatever
tribute money you demand if you will only go away." The king of Assyria then
demanded a settlement of more than eleven tons of silver and about one ton of gold.*
15To gather this amount, King Hezekiah used all the silver stored in the Temple of the
LORD and in the palace treasury. 16Hezekiah even stripped the gold from the doors of
the LORD's Temple and from the doorposts he had overlaid with gold, and he gave it
all to the Assyrian king.

17Nevertheless the king of Assyria sent his commander in chief, his field commander,

18:4 *Nehushtan* sounds like the Hebrew terms that mean "snake," "bronze," and "unclean thing." **18:14** Hebrew *300 talents* [10 metric tons] *of silver and 30 talents* [1 metric ton] *of gold.*

18:4 Num 21:8-9; 2 Chr 31:1
18:5-7 //2 Chr 31:20-21
18:5 2 Kgs 19:10; 23:25
18:6 Deut 10:20
18:7 Gen 39:2-3; 1 Sam 18:14
18:8 2 Kgs 17:9; 2 Chr 28:18
18:9-12 //2 Kgs 17:3-7
18:12 1 Kgs 9:6; Dan 9:6, 10
18:13 2 Chr 32:1; Isa 36:1
18:15 1 Kgs 15:18-19; 2 Kgs 12:18
18:17-37 //2 Chr 32:9-19; //Isa 36:1-22

18:4 The bronze serpent had been made to cure the Israelites of the bite of poisonous snakes (Numbers 21:4-9). It demonstrated God's presence and power and reminded the people of his mercy and forgiveness. But it had become an object of worship instead of a reminder of *whom* to worship, so Hezekiah was forced to destroy it. We must be careful that aids to our worship don't become objects of worship themselves. Most objects are not made to be idols—they become idols by the way people use them.

18:5 "There was never another king like him. . . ." In dramatic contrast with his father, Ahaz, Hezekiah followed God more closely and sincerely than any other king of Judah or Israel. This statement refers to the kings after the division of the kingdom and so does not include David, considered the king most devoted to God.

18:7 Judah was sandwiched between two world powers, Egypt and Assyria. Both wanted to control Judah and Israel because they lay at the vital crossroads of all ancient Near East trade. The nation that controlled Judah would have a military and economic advantage over its rivals. When Hezekiah became king, Assyria controlled Judah. Acting with great courage, Hezekiah rebelled against this mighty empire to whom his father had submitted. He placed his faith in God's strength rather than his own, and he obeyed God's commands in spite of the obstacles and dangers that, from a purely human standpoint, looked overwhelming.

18:9-12 These verses flash back to the days just before Israel's destruction. Hezekiah reigned with his father, Ahaz, for 14 years (729–715 B.C.), by himself for 18 years (715–697 B.C.), and with his son Manasseh for 11 years (697–686 B.C.), a total of 43 years. The 29 years listed in 18:2 indicate only those years in which Hezekiah had complete control of the kingdom. While Hezekiah was on the throne, the nation of Israel to the north was destroyed (722 B.C.). Knowing Israel's fate probably caused Hezekiah to reform his own nation. (For more on Hezekiah, see 2 Chronicles 29–32 and Isaiah 36–39.)

18:13 This event occurred in 701 B.C., four years after Sennacherib had become Assyria's king. Sennacherib was the son of Sargon II, the king who had deported Israel's people into captivity (see the note on 17:3). To keep Assyria from attacking, the southern kingdom paid tribute annually. But when Sennacherib became king, Hezekiah stopped paying this money, hoping Assyria would ignore him. When Sennacherib and his army retaliated, Hezekiah realized his mistake and paid the tribute money (18:14), but Sennacherib attacked anyway (18:19ff). Although Sennacherib attacked Judah, he was not as war-hungry as the previous Assyrian kings, preferring to spend most of his time building and beautifying his capital city, Nineveh. With less frequent invasions, Hezekiah was able to institute many reforms and strengthen the nation.

18:17 Sending the commander in chief, the field commander, and the king's personal representative was like sending the vice president, secretary of state, and the head general of the army to speak to the enemy prior to a battle. All of these men were sent in an effort to impress and discourage the Israelites.

and his personal representative from Lachish with a huge army to confront King
Hezekiah in Jerusalem. The Assyrians stopped beside the aqueduct that feeds water into
18:18 the upper pool, near the road leading to the field where cloth is bleached. 18 They
2 Kgs 19:2 summoned King Hezekiah, but the king sent these officials to meet with them: Eliakim
Isa 22:15-16, 20 son of Hilkiah, the palace administrator, Shebna the court secretary, and Joah son of
Asaph, the royal historian.

Sennacherib Threatens Jerusalem

19 Then the Assyrian king's personal representative sent this message to King Hezekiah:

"This is what the great king of Assyria says: What are you trusting in that makes
you so confident? 20 Do you think that mere words can substitute for military skill
and strength? Which of your allies will give you any military backing against Assyria? 21 Will Egypt? If you lean on Egypt, you will find it to be a stick that breaks
beneath your weight and pierces your hand. The pharaoh of Egypt is completely unreliable!

22 "But perhaps you will say, 'We are trusting in the LORD our God!' But isn't he
the one who was insulted by King Hezekiah? Didn't Hezekiah tear down his
shrines and altars and make everyone in Judah worship only at the altar here in Jerusalem?

23 "I'll tell you what! My master, the king of Assyria, will strike a bargain with
you. If you can find two thousand horsemen in your entire army, he will give you
two thousand horses for them to ride on! 24 With your tiny army, how can you think
of challenging even the weakest contingent of my master's troops, even with the
help of Egypt's chariots and horsemen*? 25 What's more, do you think we have invaded your land without the LORD's direction? The LORD himself told us, 'Go and
destroy it!'"

18:26 26 Then Eliakim son of Hilkiah, Shebna, and Joah said to the king's representative,
Ezra 4:7 "Please speak to us in Aramaic, for we understand it well. Don't speak in Hebrew, for
Dan 2:4 the people on the wall will hear."

27 But Sennacherib's representative replied, "My master wants everyone in Jerusalem
to hear this, not just you. He wants them to know that if you do not surrender, this city
will be put under siege. The people will become so hungry and thirsty that they will eat
their own dung and drink their own urine."

28 Then he stood and shouted in Hebrew to the people on the wall, "Listen to this
message from the great king of Assyria! 29 This is what the king says: Don't let King
Hezekiah deceive you. He will never be able to rescue you from my power. 30 Don't let
him fool you into trusting in the LORD by saying, 'The LORD will rescue us! This city
will never be handed over to the Assyrian king.'

18:31 31 "Don't listen to Hezekiah! These are the terms the king of Assyria is offering: Make
Deut 8:7-9 peace with me—open the gates and come out. Then I will allow each of you to continue
1 Kgs 4:25 eating from your own garden and drinking from your own well. 32 Then I will arrange to
take you to another land like this one—a country with bountiful harvests of grain and
wine, bread and vineyards, olive trees and honey—a land of plenty. Choose life instead
of death!

"Don't listen to Hezekiah when he tries to mislead you by saying, 'The LORD will
18:33 2 Kgs 19:12 rescue us!' 33 Have the gods of any other nations ever saved their people from the king
18:34 of Assyria? 34 What happened to the gods of Hamath and Arpad? And what about the
2 Kgs 17:24; 19:13 gods of Sepharvaim, Hena, and Ivvah? Did they rescue Samaria from my power? 35 What
god of any nation has ever been able to save its people from my power? Name just one!
So what makes you think that the LORD can rescue Jerusalem?"

36 But the people were silent and did not answer because Hezekiah had told them not
to speak. 37 Then Eliakim son of Hilkiah, the palace administrator, Shebna the court
secretary, and Joah son of Asaph, the royal historian, went back to Hezekiah. They tore
their clothes in despair, and they went in to see the king and told him what the Assyrian
representative had said.

18:24 Or *and charioteers.*

Hezekiah Seeks the LORD's Help

19 When King Hezekiah heard their report, he tore his clothes and put on sackcloth and went into the Temple of the LORD to pray. 2And he sent Eliakim the palace administrator, Shebna the court secretary, and the leading priests, all dressed in sackcloth, to the prophet Isaiah son of Amoz. 3They told him, "This is what King Hezekiah says: This is a day of trouble, insult, and disgrace. It is like when a child is ready to be born, but the mother has no strength to deliver it. 4But perhaps the LORD your God has heard the Assyrian representative defying the living God and will punish him for his words. Oh, pray for those of us who are left!"

5After King Hezekiah's officials delivered the king's message to Isaiah, 6the prophet replied, "Say to your master, 'This is what the LORD says: Do not be disturbed by this blasphemous speech against me from the Assyrian king's messengers. 7Listen! I myself will move against him, and the king will receive a report from Assyria telling him that he is needed at home. Then I will make him want to return to his land, where I will have him killed with a sword.'"

8Meanwhile, the Assyrian representative left Jerusalem and went to consult his king, who had left Lachish and was attacking Libnah. 9Soon afterward King Sennacherib received word that King Tirhakah of Ethiopia* was leading an army to fight against him. Before leaving to meet the attack, he sent this message back to Hezekiah in Jerusalem:

> 10"This message is for King Hezekiah of Judah. Don't let this God you trust deceive you with promises that Jerusalem will not be captured by the king of Assyria. 11You know perfectly well what the kings of Assyria have done wherever they have gone. They have crushed everyone who stood in their way! Why should you be any different? 12Have the gods of other nations rescued them—such nations as Gozan, Haran, Rezeph, and the people of Eden who were in Tel-assar? The former kings of Assyria destroyed them all! 13What happened to the king of Hamath and the king of Arpad? What happened to the kings of Sepharvaim, Hena, and Ivvah?"

14After Hezekiah received the letter and read it, he went up to the LORD's Temple and spread it out before the LORD. 15And Hezekiah prayed this prayer before the LORD: "O LORD, God of Israel, you are enthroned between the mighty cherubim! You alone are God of all the kingdoms of the earth. You alone created the heavens and the earth. 16Listen to me, O LORD, and hear! Open your eyes, O LORD, and see! Listen to Sennacherib's words of defiance against the living God.

17"It is true, LORD, that the kings of Assyria have destroyed all these nations, just as the message says. 18And they have thrown the gods of these nations into the fire and burned them. But of course the Assyrians could destroy them! They were not gods at all—only idols of wood and stone shaped by human hands. 19Now, O LORD our God, rescue us from his power; then all the kingdoms of the earth will know that you alone, O LORD, are God."

19:1-13 //Isa 37:1-13
19:1 2 Chr 32:20-22
19:2 Isa 1:1
19:4 2 Sam 16:12; 2 Kgs 18:35; Isa 1:9
19:7 2 Kgs 19:37
19:8 2 Kgs 18:14
19:10 2 Kgs 18:5, 30
19:12 2 Kgs 17:6; 18:33; Isa 37:12
19:13 2 Kgs 18:34
19:14-19 //Isa 37:14-20
19:16 1 Kgs 8:29-30; 2 Chr 6:40
19:18 Isa 44:9-20; Acts 17:29
19:19 1 Kgs 8:42-43

Isaiah Predicts Judah's Deliverance

20Then Isaiah son of Amoz sent this message to Hezekiah: "This is what the LORD, the God of Israel, says: I have heard your prayer about King Sennacherib of Assyria. 21This is the message that the LORD has spoken against him:

19:20-37 //Isa 37:21-38
19:21 Lam 2:13

19:9 Hebrew *of Cush.*

19:1-7 Sennacherib, whose armies had captured all the fortified cities of Judah, sent a message to Hezekiah to surrender. Realizing the situation was hopeless, Hezekiah went to the Temple and prayed. God answered Hezekiah's prayer and delivered Judah by sending an army to attack the Assyrian camp, forcing Sennacherib to leave at once. Prayer should be our first response in any crisis. Don't wait until things are hopeless. Pray daily for his guidance. Our problems are God's opportunities.

19:2 Isaiah the prophet had been working for God since the days of Uzziah—40 years (Isaiah 6:1). Although Assyria was a world power, it could not conquer Judah as long as Isaiah counseled the kings. Isaiah prophesied during the reigns of Uzziah (Azariah), Jotham, Ahaz, and Hezekiah. Ahaz ignored Isaiah, but Hezekiah listened to his advice. To read his prophecies, see the book of Isaiah.

19:15 Cherubim are mighty angels.

19:15-19 Although Hezekiah came boldly to God, he did not take God for granted or approach him flippantly. Instead, Hezekiah acknowledged God's sovereignty and Judah's total dependence on him. Hezekiah's prayer provides a good model for us. We should not be afraid to approach God with our prayers, but we must come to him with respect for who he is and what he can do.

'The virgin daughter of Zion
despises you and laughs at you.
The daughter of Jerusalem
scoffs and shakes her head as you flee.

19:22 Exod 5:2 Isa 5:24; 30:10-15

22 'Whom do you think you have been insulting and ridiculing?
Against whom did you raise your voice?
At whom did you look in such proud condescension?
It was the Holy One of Israel!
23 By your messengers you have mocked the Lord.
You have said, "With my many chariots
I have conquered the highest mountains—
yes, the remotest peaks of Lebanon.
I have cut down its tallest cedars
and its choicest cypress trees.
I have reached its farthest corners
and explored its deepest forests.
24 I have dug wells in many a foreign land
and refreshed myself with their water.
I even stopped up the rivers of Egypt
so that my armies could go across!"

19:25 Isa 10:5-7; 45:5-7

25 'But have you not heard?
It was I, the LORD, who decided this long ago.
Long ago I planned what I am now causing to happen,
that you should crush fortified cities into heaps of rubble.

19:26 Ps 129:6-7

26 That is why their people have so little power
and are such easy prey for you.
They are as helpless as the grass,
as easily trampled as tender green shoots.
They are like grass sprouting on a housetop,
easily scorched by the sun.

19:27 Ps 139:1-4

27 'But I know you well—
your comings and goings and all you do.
I know the way you have raged against me.

19:28 2 Kgs 19:33 Ezek 29:4

28 And because of your arrogance against me,
which I have heard for myself,
I will put my hook in your nose
and my bridle in your mouth.
I will make you return
by the road on which you came.'"

19:29 Exod 3:12 2 Kgs 20:8-9 **19:30** 2 Chr 32:22-23 **19:31** Isa 9:7

29 Then Isaiah said to Hezekiah, "Here is the proof that the LORD will protect this city
from Assyria's king. This year you will eat only what grows up by itself, and next year
you will eat what springs up from that. But in the third year you will plant crops and
harvest them; you will tend vineyards and eat their fruit. 30 And you who are left in Judah,
who have escaped the ravages of the siege, will take root again in your own soil, and you
will flourish and multiply. 31 For a remnant of my people will spread out from Jerusalem,

---

19:21-34 God replied to Sennacherib's taunting words (18:19-25), indicting him for arrogance. Sennacherib believed his kingdom had grown because of his own efforts and strength. In reality, said God, he succeeded only because of what God had allowed and caused. It is arrogance to think we are solely responsible for our achievements. God, as Creator, rules over nations and people.

19:28 The Assyrians treated captives with cruelty. They tortured them for entertainment by blinding them, cutting them, or pulling off strips of their skin until they died. If they wished to make a captive a slave, they would often put a hook in his nose. God was saying that the Assyrians would be treated the way they had treated others.

19:31 As long as a tiny spark remains, a fire can be rekindled and fanned into a roaring blaze. Similarly, if just the smallest remnant of true believers retains the spark of faith, God can rebuild it into a strong nation. And if only a glimmer of faith remains in a heart, God can use it to restore blazing faith in that believer. If you feel that only a spark of faith remains in you, ask God to use it to rekindle a blazing fire of commitment to him.

a group of survivors from Mount Zion. The passion of the LORD Almighty will make this happen!

32“And this is what the LORD says about the king of Assyria: His armies will not enter Jerusalem to shoot their arrows. They will not march outside its gates with their shields and build banks of earth against its walls. 33The king will return to his own country by the road on which he came. He will not enter this city, says the LORD. 34For my own honor and for the sake of my servant David, I will defend it.”

19:33 2 Kgs 19:28
19:34 1 Kgs 11:12-13; 2 Kgs 20:6

35That night the angel of the LORD went out to the Assyrian camp and killed 185,000 Assyrian troops. When the surviving Assyrians* woke up the next morning, they found corpses everywhere. 36Then King Sennacherib of Assyria broke camp and returned to his own land. He went home to his capital of Nineveh and stayed there. 37One day while he was worshiping in the temple of his god Nisroch, his sons Adrammelech and Sharezer killed him with their swords. They then escaped to the land of Ararat, and another son, Esarhaddon, became the next king of Assyria.

19:35-37 //2 Chr 32:20-21
19:36 Jon 1:2
19:37 Gen 8:4; Ezra 4:2

Hezekiah's Sickness and Recovery

20 About that time Hezekiah became deathly ill, and the prophet Isaiah son of Amoz went to visit him. He gave the king this message: “This is what the LORD says: Set your affairs in order, for you are going to die. You will not recover from this illness.”

20:1-11 //2 Chr 32:24-26; //Isa 38:1-8

2When Hezekiah heard this, he turned his face to the wall and prayed to the LORD, 3“Remember, O LORD, how I have always tried to be faithful to you and do what is pleasing in your sight.” Then he broke down and wept bitterly.

20:3 2 Kgs 18:3-6

4But before Isaiah had left the middle courtyard, this message came to him from the LORD: 5“Go back to Hezekiah, the leader of my people. Tell him, ‘This is what the LORD, the God of your ancestor David, says: I have heard your prayer and seen your tears. I will heal you, and three days from now you will get out of bed and go to the Temple of the LORD. 6I will add fifteen years to your life, and I will rescue you and this city from the king of Assyria. I will do this to defend my honor and for the sake of my servant David.’”

20:5 2 Kgs 19:20; Ps 39:12
20:6 2 Kgs 19:34

7Then Isaiah said to Hezekiah's servants, “Make an ointment from figs and spread it over the boil.” They did this, and Hezekiah recovered!

8Meanwhile, Hezekiah had said to Isaiah, “What sign will the LORD give to prove that he will heal me and that I will go to the Temple of the LORD three days from now?”

9Isaiah replied, “This is the sign that the LORD will give you to prove he will do as he promised. Would you like the shadow on the sundial to go forward ten steps or backward ten steps?”

20:9 Isa 38:7-8

10“The shadow always moves forward,” Hezekiah replied. “Make it go backward instead.” 11So Isaiah asked the LORD to do this, and he caused the shadow to move ten steps backward on the sundial of Ahaz!

20:11 Josh 10:12-14

Envoys from Babylon

12Soon after this, Merodach-baladan son of Baladan, king of Babylon, sent Hezekiah his best wishes and a gift, for he had heard that Hezekiah had been very sick. 13Hezekiah welcomed the Babylonian envoys and showed them everything in his treasure-houses—the silver, the gold, the spices, and the aromatic oils. He also took them to see his armory and showed them all his other treasures—everything! There was nothing in his palace or kingdom that Hezekiah did not show them.

20:12-19 //Isa 39:1-8
20:13 2 Chr 32:27

19:35 Hebrew *When they.*

20:5, 6 Over a 100-year period of Judah's history (732–640 B.C.), Hezekiah was the only faithful king; but what a difference he made! Because of Hezekiah's faith and prayer, God healed him and saved his city from the Assyrians. You can make a difference, too, even if your faith puts you in the minority. Faith and prayer, if they are sincere and directed toward the one true God, can change any situation.

20:11 Egyptian sundials in this period were sometimes made in the form of miniature staircases so that the shadows moved up and down the steps.

20:12-19 Hezekiah had been a good and faithful king. But when Isaiah asked him what he had shown the messengers from Babylon, he replied, “I showed them everything I own—all my treasures.” From the account in 2 Chronicles 32:24-31, it appears that Hezekiah's prosperity, success, and deliverance from sickness had made him proud. Rather than giving credit to God for all his blessings, he tried to impress the foreigners. When God helps us, we must not use his blessings to impress others. A testimony of victory can quickly degenerate into vanity and self-congratulations.

14 Then Isaiah the prophet went to King Hezekiah and asked him, "What did those men want? Where were they from?"

Hezekiah replied, "They came from the distant land of Babylon."

15 "What did they see in your palace?" Isaiah asked.

"They saw everything," Hezekiah replied. "I showed them everything I own—all my treasures."

16 Then Isaiah said to Hezekiah, "Listen to this message from the LORD: 17 The time is coming when everything you have—all the treasures stored up by your ancestors—will be carried off to Babylon. Nothing will be left, says the LORD. 18 Some of your own descendants will be taken away into exile. They will become eunuchs who will serve in the palace of Babylon's king."

19 Then Hezekiah said to Isaiah, "This message you have given me from the LORD is good." But the king was thinking, "At least there will be peace and security during my lifetime."

20 The rest of the events in Hezekiah's reign, including the extent of his power and how he built a pool and dug a tunnel to bring water into the city, are recorded in *The Book of the History of the Kings of Judah.* 21 When Hezekiah died, his son Manasseh became the next king.

Manasseh Rules in Judah

21 Manasseh was twelve years old when he became king, and he reigned in Jerusalem fifty-five years. His mother was Hephzibah. 2 He did what was evil in the LORD's sight, imitating the detestable practices of the pagan nations whom the LORD had driven from the land ahead of the Israelites. 3 He rebuilt the pagan shrines his father, Hezekiah, had destroyed. He constructed altars for Baal and set up an Asherah pole, just as King Ahab of Israel had done. He also bowed before all the forces of heaven and worshiped them. 4 He even built pagan altars in the Temple of the LORD, the place where the LORD had said his name should be honored. 5 He built these altars for all the forces of heaven in both courtyards of the LORD's Temple. 6 Manasseh even sacrificed his own son in the fire.* He practiced sorcery and divination, and he consulted with mediums and psychics. He did much that was evil in the LORD's sight, arousing his anger.

7 Manasseh even took an Asherah pole he had made and set it up in the Temple, the very place where the LORD had told David and his son Solomon: "My name will be honored here forever in this Temple and in Jerusalem—the city I have chosen from

20:17 2 Kgs 24:13; 25:13-15 Jer 52:17-23
20:18 2 Kgs 24:12, 15 2 Chr 33:11
20:20-21 //2 Chr 32:32-33
20:21 2 Chr 32:33
21:1-10 //2 Chr 33:1-10
21:2 2 Kgs 16:3
21:3 Lev 18:25 Deut 12:31; 17:3 1 Kgs 16:29-33 2 Kgs 18:4
21:4 2 Sam 7:13
21:6 Lev 18:21; 19:26, 31 Deut 18:10 2 Kgs 16:3; 17:17
21:7 Deut 16:21 1 Kgs 9:3 2 Kgs 23:6

21:6 Or *even made his son pass through the fire.*

20:14 Babylon, a city that had rebelled against the Assyrian Empire, was destroyed by Sennacherib in 689 B.C. This story probably occurred shortly before that date. When Sennacherib died in 681 B.C., his son, Esarhaddon, foolishly rebuilt the city of Babylon. Assyria, whose rulers at that time were weak, allowed Babylon plenty of opportunity to become strong. As the Assyrian army marched off to conquer and oppress faraway lands, the city of Babylon grew and expanded into a small nation. After some years, Babylon was strong enough to rebel again. It eventually crushed Assyria (612 B.C.) and became the next world power.

20:19 Hezekiah was saying that it was good that these terrible events foretold by Isaiah wouldn't happen during his lifetime. Hezekiah's statement seems selfish, shortsighted, and proud. However, he knew that his nation would be punished for its sins, so he may have been acknowledging and thanking God for choosing not to destroy Judah during his lifetime.

20:20 The pool and the tunnel refer to a 1,777-foot tunnel built from the Upper Spring of Gihon to the Pool of Siloam (see 2 Chronicles 32:30). It was from a water source outside the wall of Jerusalem to a secure reservoir inside the city. This was done so the Assyrian army would not cut off the city's water supply.

21:1ff Manasseh followed the example of his grandfather Ahaz more than that of his father. He adopted the wicked practices of the Babylonians and Canaanites, including sacrificing his own son (21:6). He did not listen to the words of God's prophets but willfully led his people into sin. (See his Profile in 2 Chronicles 33 for more information about his life.)

21:6 Manasseh was an evil king, and he angered God with his sin. Listed among his sins are occult practices—sorcery and divination, and consulting mediums and psychics. These acts are strictly forbidden by God (Leviticus 19:31; Deuteronomy 18:9-13) because they demonstrate a lack of faith in him, involve sinful actions, and open the door to demonic influences. Today, many books, television shows, and games emphasize fortune-telling, séances, and other occult practices. Don't let desire to know the future or the belief that superstition is harmless lead you into condoning occult practices. They are counterfeits of God's power and have as their root a system of beliefs totally opposed to God.

21:7 Asherah was a Canaanite mother-goddess, a mistress of Baal. Her images were made of wood. In Exodus 34:13 and Deuteronomy 12:3, the Israelites were expressly forbidden to associate with Asherah practices in any way.

among all the other tribes of Israel. 8If the Israelites will obey my commands—the whole
law that was given through my servant Moses—I will not send them into exile from this
land that I gave their ancestors." 9But the people refused to listen, and Manasseh led
them to do even more evil than the pagan nations whom the LORD had destroyed when
the Israelites entered the land.

10Then the LORD said through his servants the prophets: 11"King Manasseh of Judah
has done many detestable things. He is even more wicked than the Amorites, who lived
in this land before Israel. He has led the people of Judah into idolatry. 12So this is what
the LORD, the God of Israel, says: I will bring such disaster on Jerusalem and Judah that
the ears of those who hear about it will tingle with horror. 13I will judge Jerusalem by
the same standard I used for Samaria and by the same measure I used for the family of
Ahab. I will wipe away the people of Jerusalem as one wipes a dish and turns it upside
down. 14Then I will reject even those few of my people who are left, and I will hand
them over as plunder for their enemies. 15For they have done great evil in my sight and
have angered me ever since their ancestors came out of Egypt."

16Manasseh also murdered many innocent people until Jerusalem was filled from one
end to the other with innocent blood. This was in addition to the sin that he caused the
people of Judah to commit, leading them to do evil in the LORD's sight.

17The rest of the events in Manasseh's reign and all his deeds, including the sins he
committed, are recorded in *The Book of the History of the Kings of Judah.* 18When
Manasseh died, he was buried in the palace garden, the garden of Uzza. Then his son
Amon became the next king.

Amon Rules in Judah

19Amon was twenty-two years old when he became king, and he reigned in Jerusalem
two years. His mother was Meshullemeth, the daughter of Haruz from Jotbah. 20He did
what was evil in the LORD's sight, just as his father, Manasseh, had done. 21He followed
the example of his father, worshiping the same idols that his father had worshiped. 22He
abandoned the LORD, the God of his ancestors, and he refused to follow the LORD's ways.

23Then Amon's own servants plotted against him and assassinated him in his palace.
24But the people of the land killed all those who had conspired against King Amon, and
they made his son Josiah the next king.

25The rest of the events in Amon's reign and all his deeds are recorded in *The Book of
the History of the Kings of Judah.* 26He was buried in his tomb in the garden of Uzza.
Then his son Josiah became the next king.

Josiah Rules in Judah

22 Josiah was eight years old when he became king, and he reigned in Jerusalem
thirty-one years. His mother was Jedidah, the daughter of Adaiah from Bozkath.
2He did what was pleasing in the LORD's sight and followed the example of his ancestor
David. He did not turn aside from doing what was right.

3In the eighteenth year of his reign, King Josiah sent Shaphan son of Azaliah and
grandson of Meshullam, the court secretary, to the Temple of the LORD. He told him,
4"Go up to Hilkiah the high priest and have him count the money the gatekeepers have
collected from the people at the LORD's Temple. 5Entrust this money to the men assigned
to supervise the Temple's restoration. Then they can use it to pay workers to repair the
Temple of the LORD. 6They will need to hire carpenters, builders, and masons. Also have
them buy the timber and the cut stone needed to repair the Temple. 7But there will be no
need for the construction supervisors to keep account of the money they receive, for they
are honest people."

21:8 2 Sam 7:10; 2 Kgs 18:11-12; 2 Chr 15:2
21:11 Gen 15:16; 1 Kgs 21:26; 2 Kgs 24:3-4
21:12 Jer 19:3
21:13 Isa 34:11; Amos 7:7-8
21:16 2 Kgs 24:3-4
21:17-18 //2 Chr 33:18-20
21:18 2 Kgs 21:26
21:22 2 Kgs 22:17
21:23 2 Kgs 12:20; 14:19
21:26 2 Kgs 21:18
22:1-20 //2 Chr 34:1-2, 8-28
22:1 Josh 15:39
22:3 2 Chr 34:8-9
22:4 2 Kgs 12:4
22:5 2 Kgs 12:11-14
22:7 2 Kgs 12:15

21:16 Tradition says that during Manasseh's massive slaughter, Isaiah was sawed in two when trying to hide in a hollow log (see Hebrews 11:37, 38). Other prophets may also have been killed at this time.

22:1, 2 In reading the biblical lists of kings, it is rare to find one who obeyed God completely. Josiah was such a person, and he was only eight years old when he began to reign. For 18 years he reigned obediently; then, when he was 26, he began the reforms based on God's laws. Children are the future leaders of our churches and our world. A person's major work for God may have to wait until he is an adult, but no one is ever too young to take God seriously and obey him. Josiah's early years laid the base for his later task of reforming Judah.

22:4 The gatekeepers controlled who entered the Temple and supervised the collection of the money.

Hilkiah Discovers God's Law

22:8 Deut 31:24-26 2 Chr 34:14-16

8Hilkiah the high priest said to Shaphan the court secretary, "I have found the Book of
the Law in the LORD's Temple!" Then Hilkiah gave the scroll to Shaphan, and he read it.
9Shaphan returned to the king and reported, "Your officials have given the money
collected at the Temple of the LORD to the workers and supervisors at the Temple."
10Shaphan also said to the king, "Hilkiah the priest has given me a scroll." So Shaphan
read it to the king.

22:11 Josh 7:6 · 22:12 2 Kgs 25:22; 2 Chr 34:20; Jer 26:24 · 22:13 Deut 29:23-28

11When the king heard what was written in the Book of the Law, he tore his clothes
in despair. 12Then he gave these orders to Hilkiah the priest, Ahikam son of Shaphan,
Acbor son of Micaiah, Shaphan the court secretary, and Asaiah the king's personal
adviser: 13"Go to the Temple and speak to the LORD for me and for the people and for
all Judah. Ask him about the words written in this scroll that has been found. The LORD's
anger is burning against us because our ancestors have not obeyed the words in this
scroll. We have not been doing what this scroll says we must do."

22:14 2 Chr 34:22 · 22:16 Dan 9:11

14So Hilkiah the priest, Ahikam, Acbor, Shaphan, and Asaiah went to the newer
Mishneh section* of Jerusalem to consult with the prophet Huldah. She was the wife of
Shallum son of Tikvah and grandson of Harhas, the keeper of the Temple wardrobe.
15She said to them, "The LORD, the God of Israel, has spoken! Go and tell the man who
sent you, 16'This is what the LORD says: I will destroy this city and its people, just as I
stated in the scroll you read. 17For my people have abandoned me and worshiped pagan
gods, and I am very angry with them for everything they have done. My anger is burning
against this place, and it will not be quenched.'

22:19 Lev 26:31; Jer 26:6

18"But go to the king of Judah who sent you to seek the LORD and tell him: 'This is
what the LORD, the God of Israel, says concerning the message you have just heard:
19You were sorry and humbled yourself before the LORD when you heard what I said
against this city and its people, that this land would be cursed and become desolate. You
tore your clothing in despair and wept before me in repentance. So I have indeed heard
you, says the LORD. 20I will not send the promised disaster against this city until after
you have died and been buried in peace. You will not see the disaster I am going to bring
on this place.'" So they took her message back to the king.

Josiah's Religious Reforms

23:1-3 //2 Chr 34:29-32 · 23:2 Deut 31:11 · 23:3 Deut 13:4; 2 Kgs 11:14, 17

23 Then the king summoned all the leaders of Judah and Jerusalem. 2And the king went
up to the Temple of the LORD with all the people of Judah and Jerusalem, and the
priests, and the prophets—all the people from the least to the greatest. There the king read
to them the entire Book of the Covenant that had been found in the LORD's Temple. 3The
king took his place of authority beside the pillar and renewed the covenant in the LORD's
presence. He pledged to obey the LORD by keeping all his commands, regulations, and laws
with all his heart and soul. In this way, he confirmed all the terms of the covenant that were
written in the scroll, and all the people pledged themselves to the covenant.

22:14 Or *the Second Quarter,* a newer section of Jerusalem.

22:8 This book may have been the entire Pentateuch (Genesis—Deuteronomy) or just the book of Deuteronomy. Because of the long line of evil kings, the record of God's laws had been lost. Josiah, who was about 26 years old at this time, wanted religious reform throughout the nation. When God's Word was found, drastic changes had to be made to bring the kingdom in line with God's commands. Today you have God's Word at your fingertips. How much change must you make in order to bring your life into line with God's Word?

22:11ff When Josiah heard the law, he tore his clothes in grief. He immediately instituted reforms. With just one reading of God's law, he changed the course of the nation. Today many people own Bibles, but few are affected by the truths found in God's Word. The Word of God should cause us, like Josiah, to take action immediately to reform our lives and bring them into harmony with God's will.

22:14 Huldah was a prophet, as were Miriam (Exodus 15:20) and Deborah (Judges 4:4). God freely selects his servants to carry out his will—rich or poor, male or female, king or slave (Joel 2:28-30). Huldah was obviously highly regarded by the people of her time.

22:19 When Josiah realized how corrupt his nation had become, he tore his clothes and wept before God. Then God had mercy on him. Josiah used the customs of his day to show his repentance. When we repent today, we are unlikely to tear our clothes, but weeping, fasting, and making restitution or apologies (if our sin has involved others) demonstrate our sincerity when we repent. The hardest part of repentance is changing the attitudes that originally produced the sinful behavior.

23:1, 2 For more about the importance and operation of the Temple, see 1 Kings 5–8 and 2 Chronicles 2–7.

4 Then the king instructed Hilkiah the high priest and the leading priests and the Temple gatekeepers to remove from the LORD's Temple all the utensils that were used to worship Baal, Asherah, and all the forces of heaven. The king had all these things burned outside Jerusalem on the terraces of the Kidron Valley, and he carried the ashes away to Bethel. 5 He did away with the pagan priests, who had been appointed by the previous kings of Judah, for they had burned incense at the pagan shrines throughout Judah and even in the vicinity of Jerusalem. They had also offered incense to Baal, and to the sun, the moon, the constellations, and to all the forces of heaven. 6 The king removed the Asherah pole from the LORD's Temple and took it outside Jerusalem to the Kidron Valley, where he burned it. Then he ground the pole to dust and threw the dust in the public cemetery. 7 He also tore down the houses of the shrine prostitutes that were inside the Temple of the LORD, where the women wove coverings for the Asherah pole.

8 Josiah brought back to Jerusalem all the priests of the LORD, who were living in other towns of Judah. He also defiled all the pagan shrines, where they had burned incense, from Geba to Beersheba. He destroyed the shrines at the entrance to the gate of Joshua, the governor of Jerusalem. This gate was located to the left of the city gate as one enters the city. 9 The priests who had served at the pagan shrines were not allowed to serve at the LORD's altar in Jerusalem, but they were allowed to eat unleavened bread with the other priests.

10 Then the king defiled the altar of Topheth in the valley of Ben-hinnom, so no one could ever again use it to sacrifice a son or daughter in the fire* as an offering to Molech. 11 He removed from the entrance of the LORD's Temple the horse statues that the former kings of Judah had dedicated to the sun. They were near the quarters of Nathan-melech the eunuch, an officer of the court. The king also burned the chariots dedicated to the sun.

12 Josiah tore down the altars that the kings of Judah had built on the palace roof above the upper room of Ahaz. The king destroyed the altars that Manasseh had built in the two courtyards of the LORD's Temple. He smashed them to bits and scattered the pieces in the Kidron Valley. 13 The king also desecrated the pagan shrines east of Jerusalem and south of the Mount of Corruption, where King Solomon of Israel had built shrines for Ashtoreth, the detestable goddess of the Sidonians; and for Chemosh, the detestable god of the Moabites; and for Molech,* the detestable god of the Ammonites. 14 He smashed the sacred pillars and cut down the Asherah poles. Then he desecrated these places by scattering human bones over them.

15 The king also tore down the altar at Bethel, the pagan shrine that Jeroboam son of Nebat had made when he led Israel into sin. Josiah crushed the stones to dust and burned the Asherah pole. 16 Then as Josiah was looking around, he noticed several tombs in the side of the hill. He ordered that the bones be brought out, and he burned them on the altar at Bethel to desecrate it. This happened just as the LORD had promised through the man of God as Jeroboam stood beside the altar at the festival. Then Josiah turned and looked up at the tomb of the man of God* who had predicted these things. 17 "What is that monument over there?" Josiah asked.

23:6 2 Chr 34:4
23:7 1 Kgs 14:24; 15:12; 22:46 Ezek 16:16
23:8 1 Kgs 15:22
23:9 Ezek 44:9-14
23:10 Lev 18:21 1 Kgs 11:7 Jer 7:31-32
23:12 2 Kgs 21:3-5 2 Chr 33:4-5 Jer 19:13 Zeph 1:5
23:13 1 Kgs 11:7 Jer 48:7
23:14 Deut 7:5, 25
23:15 1 Kgs 12:28-33
23:16 1 Kgs 13:2, 32
23:17 1 Kgs 13:1-2, 30-31

23:10 Or *to make a son or daughter pass through the fire.* **23:13** Hebrew *Milcom,* a variant name for Molech.
23:16 As in Greek version; Hebrew lacks *as Jeroboam stood beside the altar at the festival. Then Josiah turned and looked up at the tomb of the man of God.*

23:4-8 When Josiah realized the terrible state of Judah's religious life, he did something about it. It is not enough to say we believe what is right; we must respond with action, doing what faith requires. This is what James was emphasizing when he wrote, "Faith that does not result in good deeds is useless" (James 2:20). This means acting differently at home, school, work, and church. Simply talking about obedience is not enough.

23:6 This shameful Asherah pole had been set up in God's Temple by the evil King Manasseh (21:7). Asherah is most often identified as a sea goddess and the mistress of Baal. She was a chief goddess of the Canaanites. Her worship glorified sex and war and was accompanied by male prostitution.

23:11 These horses were used in processions honoring the sun.

23:13 The Mount of Olives is here called the Mount of Corruption because it had become a favorite spot to build pagan shrines. Solomon built a pagan shrine, and other kings built places of idol worship there, too. But God-fearing kings, such as Hezekiah and Josiah, destroyed these pagan worship centers. In New Testament times, Jesus often sat on the Mount of Olives and taught his disciples about serving only God (Matthew 24:3ff). For more background on Ashtoreth, Chemosh, and Molech, see the note on 1 Kings 11:5-8.

23:16-18 The prophecies mentioned in this passage appear in 1 Kings 13:21-32.

23:18 1 Kgs 13:11, 31
23:19 2 Chr 34:6-7
23:20 2 Kgs 11:18

And the people of the town told him, "It is the tomb of the man of God who came from
Judah and predicted the very things that you have just done to the altar at Bethel!"
18 Josiah replied, "Leave it alone. Don't disturb his bones." So they did not burn his
bones or those of the old prophet from Samaria.
19 Then Josiah demolished all the buildings at the pagan shrines in the towns of
Samaria, just as he had done at Bethel. They had been built by the various kings of Israel
and had made the LORD very angry. 20 He executed the priests of the pagan shrines on
their own altars, and he burned human bones on the altars to desecrate them. Finally, he
returned to Jerusalem.

Josiah Celebrates Passover

23:21 Deut 16:2-8

21 King Josiah then issued this order to all the people: "You must celebrate the Passover
to the LORD your God, as it is written in the Book of the Covenant." 22 There had not

JOSIAH

Josiah never knew his great-grandfather Hezekiah, but they were alike in many ways. Both had close, personal relationships with God. Both were passionate reformers, making valiant efforts to lead their people back to God. Both were bright flashes of obedience to God among kings with darkened consciences, who seemed bent on outdoing each other in disobedience and evil.

Although Josiah's father and grandfather were exceptionally wicked, his life is an example of God's willingness to provide ongoing guidance to those who set out to be obedient. At a young age, Josiah already understood that there was spiritual sickness in his land. Idols were sprouting in the countryside faster than crops. In a sense, Josiah began his search for God by destroying and cleaning up whatever he recognized as not belonging to the worship of the true God. In the process, God's Word was rediscovered. The king's intentions and the power of God's written revelation were brought together.

As the Book of God's Law was read to Josiah, he was shocked, frightened, and humbled. He realized what a great gap existed between his efforts to lead his people to God and God's expectations for his chosen nation. He was overwhelmed by God's holiness and immediately tried to expose his people to that holiness. The people did respond, but the Bible makes it clear that their renewed worship of God was much more out of respect for Josiah than out of personal understanding of their own guilt before God.

How would you describe your relationship with God? Are your feeble efforts at holiness based mostly on a desire to "go along" with a well-liked leader or popular opinion? Or are you, like Josiah, deeply humbled by God's Word, realizing the great gap between your life and the kind of life God expects, and realizing your deep need to be cleansed and renewed by him? Humble obedience pleases God. Good intentions, even reforms, are not enough. You must allow God's Word to truly humble you and change your life.

Strengths and accomplishments
- Was king of Judah
- Sought after God and was open to him
- Was a reformer like his great-grandfather Hezekiah
- Cleaned out the Temple and revived obedience to God's law

Weakness and mistake
- Became involved in a military conflict that he had been warned against

Lessons from his life
- God consistently responds to those with repentant and humble hearts
- Even sweeping outward reforms are of little lasting value if there are no changes in people's lives

Vital statistics
- Where: Jerusalem
- Occupation: 16th king of Judah, the southern kingdom
- Relatives: Father: Amon. Mother: Jedidah. Son: Jehoahaz
- Contemporaries: Jeremiah, Huldah, Hilkiah, Zephaniah

Key verse
"Never before had there been a king like Josiah, who turned to the LORD with all his heart and soul and strength, obeying all the laws of Moses. And there has never been a king like him since" (2 Kings 23:25).

Josiah's story is told in 2 Kings 21:24—23:30; 2 Chronicles 33:25—35:27. He is also mentioned in Jeremiah 1:1-3; 22:11, 18.

23:21-23 When Josiah rediscovered the Passover in the Book of the Covenant, he ordered everyone to observe the ceremonies exactly as prescribed. This Passover celebration was to have been a yearly holiday celebrated in remembrance of the entire nation's deliverance from slavery in Egypt (Exodus 12), but it had not been kept for many years. As a result, "there had not been a Passover celebration like that since the time when the judges ruled in Israel, throughout all the years of the kings of Israel and Judah." It is a common misconception that God is against celebration, wanting to take all the fun out of life. In reality, God wants to give us life in its fullness (John 10:10), and those who love him have the most to celebrate.

been a Passover celebration like that since the time when the judges ruled in Israel, **23:22** 2 Chr 35:18-19
throughout all the years of the kings of Israel and Judah. 23 This Passover was celebrated
to the LORD in Jerusalem during the eighteenth year of King Josiah's reign.

24 Josiah also exterminated the mediums and psychics, the household gods, and every **23:24** Lev 19:31
other kind of idol worship, both in Jerusalem and throughout the land of Judah. He did Deut 18:10-12
this in obedience to all the laws written in the scroll that Hilkiah the priest had found in 2 Kgs 21:6; 22:8
the LORD's Temple. 25 Never before had there been a king like Josiah, who turned to the **23:25** 2 Kgs 18:5
LORD with all his heart and soul and strength, obeying all the laws of Moses. And there
has never been a king like him since.

26 Even so, the LORD's anger burned against Judah because of all the great evils of **23:26** 2 Kgs 21:11-13;
King Manasseh, and he did not hold back his fierce anger from them. 27 For the LORD 22:15-16
had said, "I will destroy Judah just as I have destroyed Israel. I will banish the people **23:27** 2 Kgs 21:13-14
from my presence and reject my chosen city of Jerusalem and the Temple where my
name was to be honored."

28 The rest of the events in Josiah's reign and all his deeds are recorded in *The Book* **23:28-30** 2 Chr 35:20–36:1
of the History of the Kings of Judah.

29 While Josiah was king, Pharaoh Neco, king of Egypt, went to the Euphrates River **23:29** 2 Chr 35:20-24
to help the king of Assyria. King Josiah marched out with his army to fight him, but King **23:30**
Neco killed him when they met at Megiddo. 30 Josiah's officers took his body back in a 2 Chr 36:1-4
chariot from Megiddo to Jerusalem and buried him in his own tomb. Then the people
anointed his son Jehoahaz and made him the next king.

Jehoahaz Rules in Judah

31 Jehoahaz was twenty-three years old when he became king, and he reigned in Jerusalem **23:31-34** //2 Chr 36:2-4
three months. His mother was Hamutal, the daughter of Jeremiah from Libnah. 32 He did **23:31**
what was evil in the LORD's sight, just as his ancestors had done. 2 Kgs 24:18 Jer 22:11

33 Pharaoh Neco put Jehoahaz in prison at Riblah in the land of Hamath to prevent him
from ruling from Jerusalem. He also demanded that Judah pay 7,500 pounds of silver **23:33** 2 Kgs 23:29
and 75 pounds of gold* as tribute. 34 Pharaoh Neco then installed Eliakim, another of **23:34**
Josiah's sons, to reign in place of his father, and he changed Eliakim's name to 1 Chr 3:15 2 Chr 36:4-8
Jehoiakim. Jehoahaz was taken to Egypt as a prisoner, where he died. Jer 22:12 Ezek 19:3-4

2. Judah is exiled to Babylon

Jehoiakim Rules in Judah

35 In order to get the silver and gold demanded as tribute by Pharaoh Neco, Jehoiakim
collected a tax from the people of Judah, requiring them to pay in proportion to their wealth.

36 Jehoiakim was twenty-five years old when he became king, and he reigned in **23:36–24:6** //2 Chr 36:5-8
Jerusalem eleven years. His mother was Zebidah, the daughter of Pedaiah from Rumah. Jer 1:3; 26:21
37 He did what was evil in the LORD's sight, just as his ancestors had done.

23:33 Hebrew *100 talents* [3.4 metric tons] *of silver and 1 talent* [34 kilograms] *of gold.*

23:25 Josiah is remembered as Judah's most obedient king. His obedience followed this pattern: (1) He recognized sin; (2) he eliminated sinful practices; (3) he attacked the causes of sin. This approach for dealing with sin is still effective today. Not only must we remove sinful actions, we must also eliminate causes for sin—those situations, relationships, routines, and patterns of life that lead us to the door of temptation.

23:25 Both Josiah and Hezekiah (18:5) are praised for their reverence toward God. Hezekiah was said to be greatest in trusting God (faith), while Josiah is said to be greatest in following the law of God (obedience). May we follow their example through our trust in God and our obedient actions.

23:29 Pharaoh Neco of Egypt was marching through Judah to Assyria. Egypt and Assyria had formed an alliance to battle Babylon, which was threatening to become the dominant world power. Josiah may have thought that both nations would turn on him after the battle with Babylon, so he tried to stop Egypt's army from marching through his land. But Josiah was killed, his army was defeated, and the nation of Judah became a vassal state of Egypt (609 B.C.). A more detailed account of this story is found in 2 Chronicles 35:20-25.

23:31-34 The people appointed Jehoahaz, one of Josiah's sons, to be Judah's next king. But Neco was not happy with their choice, and he exiled Jehoahaz to Egypt, where he died. Neco then appointed Eliakim, another of Josiah's sons, king of Judah, changing his name to Jehoiakim. Jehoiakim was little more than a puppet ruler. In 605 B.C., Egypt was defeated by Babylon. Judah then became a vassal state of Babylon (24:1).

23:36, 37 Josiah followed God, but Jehoiakim, his son, was evil. He killed the prophet Uriah (Jeremiah 26:20-23) and was dishonest, greedy, and unjust with the people (Jeremiah 22:13-19). Jehoiakim also rebelled against Babylon, switching his allegiance to Egypt. This proved to be a crucial mistake. Nebuchadnezzar crushed Jehoiakim's rebellion and took him to Babylon (2 Chronicles 36:6), but he was eventually allowed to return to Jerusalem, where he died. The Bible does not record the cause of Jehoiakim's death.

24:1
2 Chr 36:6
Jer 25:1, 9

24:2
2 Kgs 13:20-21;
23:27

24:3
2 Kgs 18:25; 23:26

24:4
2 Kgs 21:16

24:6
Jer 22:19, 24-25

24:7
Jer 37:5, 7; 46:2

24:8-17
//2 Chr 36:9-10

24 During Jehoiakim's reign, King Nebuchadnezzar of Babylon invaded the land of
Judah. Jehoiakim surrendered and paid him tribute for three years but then
rebelled. 2 Then the LORD sent bands of Babylonian,* Aramean, Moabite, and Ammonite
raiders against Judah to destroy it, just as the LORD had promised through his prophets.
3 These disasters happened to Judah according to the LORD's command. He had decided
to remove Judah from his presence because of the many sins of Manasseh. 4 He had filled
Jerusalem with innocent blood, and the LORD would not forgive this.
5 The rest of the events in Jehoiakim's reign and all his deeds are recorded in *The Book
of the History of the Kings of Judah.* 6 When Jehoiakim died, his son Jehoiachin became
the next king. 7 The king of Egypt never returned after that, for the king of Babylon
occupied the entire area formerly claimed by Egypt—from the brook of Egypt to the
Euphrates River.

Jehoiachin Rules in Judah

8 Jehoiachin was eighteen years old when he became king, and he reigned in
Jerusalem three months. His mother was Nehushta, the daughter of Elnathan from

24:2 Or *Chaldean.*

KINGS TO DATE AND THEIR ENEMIES

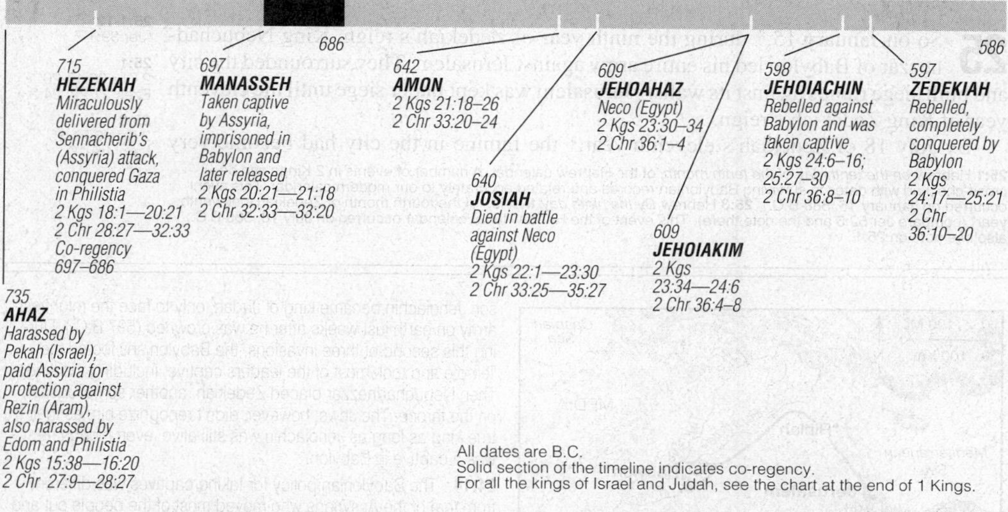

All dates are B.C.
Solid section of the timeline indicates co-regency.
For all the kings of Israel and Judah, see the chart at the end of 1 Kings.

23:37 Many good kings had children who did not follow God. Perhaps it was because of neglect or preoccupation with political and military affairs or because these kings delegated the religious education to others. No doubt many of the children simply rebelled at the way they were raised. Being a strong believer as a parent doesn't guarantee that your children will pick up your beliefs. Children must be taught about faith, and parents dare not leave that task for others to do. Make sure you practice, explain, and teach what you preach.

24:1 Babylon became the new world power after overthrowing Assyria in 612 B.C. and defeating Egypt at the battle of Carchemish in 605 B.C. After defeating Egypt, the Babylonians invaded Judah and brought it under their control. This was the first of three Babylonian invasions of Judah over the next 20 years. The other two invasions occurred in 597 and 586 B.C. With each invasion, captives were taken back to Babylon. Daniel was one of the captives taken during this first invasion (605 B.C.; Daniel 1:1-6).

24:1 For more information on Nebuchadnezzar, see his Profile in Daniel 3.

24:1-4 Nebuchadnezzar took control as king of Babylon in 605 B.C. Earlier that year Nebuchadnezzar had defeated the Egyptians led by Pharaoh Neco at Carchemish. Thus, Babylon took control of all Egypt's vassals (including Judah). Nebuchadnezzar invaded the land later in order to establish his rule by force.

Jerusalem. 9Jehoiachin did what was evil in the LORD's sight, just as his father had
done.
10During Jehoiachin's reign, the officers of King Nebuchadnezzar of Babylon came
up against Jerusalem and besieged it. 11Nebuchadnezzar himself arrived at the city
during the siege. 12Then King Jehoiachin, along with his advisers, nobles, and officials, **24:12**
and the queen mother, surrendered to the Babylonians. 2 Chr 36:10 Jer 24:1; 29:1-2

In the eighth year of Nebuchadnezzar's reign, he took Jehoiachin prisoner. 13As the **24:13**
LORD had said beforehand, Nebuchadnezzar carried away all the treasures from the 1 Kgs 7:48-50
LORD's Temple and the royal palace. They cut apart all the gold vessels that King 2 Kgs 20:17; 25:13-15
Solomon of Israel had placed in the Temple. 14King Nebuchadnezzar took ten thousand Isa 39:6
captives from Jerusalem, including all the princes and the best of the soldiers, craftsmen, **24:14** 2 Kgs 25:12
and smiths. So only the poorest people were left in the land. Jer 24:1; 52:28

15Nebuchadnezzar led King Jehoiachin away as a captive to Babylon, along with his
wives and officials, the queen mother, and all Jerusalem's elite. 16He also took seven
thousand of the best troops and one thousand craftsmen and smiths, all of whom were
strong and fit for war. 17Then the king of Babylon installed Mattaniah, Jehoiachin's **24:17** 2 Chr 36:10-13
uncle, as the next king, and he changed Mattaniah's name to Zedekiah. Jer 37:1

Zedekiah Rules in Judah

18Zedekiah was twenty-one years old when he became king, and he reigned in Jerusalem **24:18-20** //2 Chr 36:11-13
eleven years. His mother was Hamutal, the daughter of Jeremiah from Libnah. 19But //Jer 52:1-3
Zedekiah did what was evil in the LORD's sight, just as Jehoiakim had done. 20So the **24:20** 2 Chr 36:13
LORD, in his anger, finally banished the people of Jerusalem and Judah from his presence Jer 27:12; 38:17, 21-22; 39:1
and sent them into exile.

The Fall of Jerusalem

Then Zedekiah rebelled against the king of Babylon.

25 So on January 15,* during the ninth year of Zedekiah's reign, King Nebuchad- **25:1-12** //Jer 39:1-7
nezzar of Babylon led his entire army against Jerusalem. They surrounded the city **25:1**
and built siege ramps against its walls. 2Jerusalem was kept under siege until the eleventh 2 Chr 36:17-20 Ezek 21:22; 24:2
year of King Zedekiah's reign.
3By July 18 of Zedekiah's eleventh year,* the famine in the city had become very **25:3** 2 Kgs 6:24-25 Lam 4:9-10

25:1 Hebrew *on the tenth day of the tenth month,* of the Hebrew calendar. A number of events in 2 Kings can be cross-checked with dates in surviving Babylonian records and related accurately to our modern calendar. This event occurred on January 15, 588 B.C. **25:3** Hebrew *By the ninth day,* that is, "of the fourth month of Zedekiah's eleventh year" (compare Jer 52:6 and the note there). This event of the Hebrew lunar calendar occurred on July 18, 586 B.C.; also see note on 25:1.

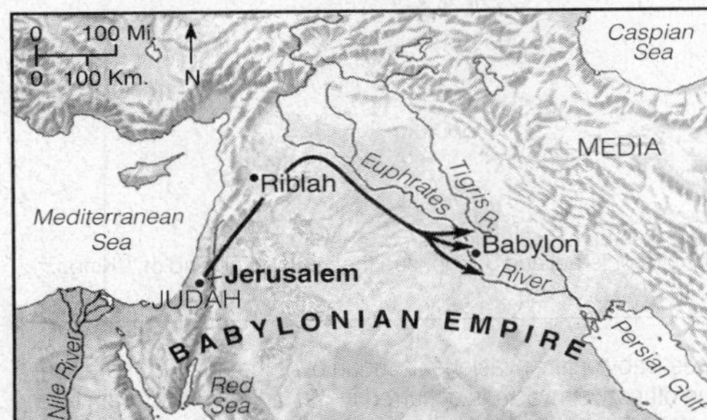

JUDAH EXILED Evil permeated Judah, and God's anger flared against his rebellious people. Babylon conquered Assyria and became the new world power. The Babylonian army marched into Jerusalem, burned the Temple, tore down the city's massive walls, and carried off the people into captivity.

24:10 Babylonian troops were already on the march to crush Jehoiakim's rebellion when he died. After Jehoiakim's death, his son Jehoiachin became king of Judah, only to face the mightiest army on earth just weeks after he was crowned (597 B.C.). During this second of three invasions, the Babylonians looted the Temple and took most of the leaders captive, including the king. Then Nebuchadnezzar placed Zedekiah, another son of Josiah, on the throne. The Jews, however, didn't recognize him as their true king as long as Jehoiachin was still alive, even though he was a captive in Babylon.

24:14 The Babylonian policy for taking captives was different from that of the Assyrians who moved most of the people out and resettled the land with foreigners (see the note on 17:24). The Babylonians took only the strong and skilled, leaving the poor and weak to rule the land, thus elevating them to positions of authority and winning their loyalty. The leaders were taken to Babylonian cities, where they were permitted to live together, find jobs, and become an important part of the society. This policy kept the Jews united and faithful to God throughout the captivity and made it possible for their return in the days of Zerubbabel and Ezra as recorded in the book of Ezra.

25:1 Judah was invaded by the Babylonians three times (24:1; 24:10; 25:1), just as Israel was invaded by the Assyrians three times. Once again, God demonstrated his mercy in the face of deserved judgment by giving the people repeated opportunities to repent.

severe, with the last of the food entirely gone. 4 Then a section of the city wall was broken
down, and all the soldiers made plans to escape from the city. But since the city was
surrounded by the Babylonians,* they waited for nightfall and fled through the gate
between the two walls behind the king's gardens. They made a dash across the fields, in
the direction of the Jordan Valley.*
5 But the Babylonians chased after them and caught the king on the plains of Jericho,
for by then his men had all abandoned him. 6 They brought him to the king of Babylon
at Riblah, where sentence was passed against him. 7 The king of Babylon made Zedekiah
watch as all his sons were killed. Then they gouged out Zedekiah's eyes, bound him in
bronze chains, and led him away to Babylon.

The Temple Destroyed

8 On August 14 of that year,* which was the nineteenth year of Nebuchadnezzar's reign,
Nebuzaradan, captain of the guard, an official of the Babylonian king, arrived in
Jerusalem. 9 He burned down the Temple of the LORD, the royal palace, and all the houses
of Jerusalem. He destroyed all the important buildings in the city. 10 Then the captain of
the guard supervised the entire Babylonian* army as they tore down the walls of
Jerusalem. 11 Nebuzaradan, captain of the guard, then took as exiles those who remained
in the city, along with the rest of the people and the troops who had declared their
allegiance to the king of Babylon. 12 But the captain of the guard allowed some of the
poorest people to stay behind in Judah to care for the vineyards and fields.
13 The Babylonians broke up the bronze pillars, the bronze water carts, and the bronze
Sea that were at the LORD's Temple, and they carried all the bronze away to Babylon.
14 They also took all the pots, shovels, lamp snuffers, dishes, and all the other bronze
utensils used for making sacrifices at the Temple. 15 Nebuzaradan, captain of the guard,
also took the firepans and basins, and all the other utensils made of pure gold or silver.
16 The bronze from the two pillars, the water carts, and the Sea was too great to be
weighed. These things had been made for the LORD's Temple in the days of King Solomon.
17 Each of the pillars was 27 feet* tall. The bronze capital on top of each pillar was 7½
feet* high and was decorated with a network of bronze pomegranates all the way around.
18 The captain of the guard took with him as prisoners Seraiah the chief priest, his
assistant Zephaniah, and the three chief gatekeepers. 19 And of the people still hiding in
the city, he took an officer of the Judean army, five of the king's personal advisers, the
army commander's chief secretary, who was in charge of recruitment, and sixty other
citizens. 20 Nebuzaradan the commander took them all to the king of Babylon at Riblah.
21 And there at Riblah, in the land of Hamath, the king of Babylon had them all put to
death. So the people of Judah were sent into exile from their land.

Gedaliah Governs in Judah

22 Then King Nebuchadnezzar appointed Gedaliah son of Ahikam and grandson of
Shaphan as governor over the people left in Judah. 23 When all the army commanders
and their men learned that the king of Babylon had appointed Gedaliah as governor, they
joined him at Mizpah. These included Ishmael son of Nethaniah, Johanan son of Kareah,
Seraiah son of Tanhumeth the Netophathite, and Jaazaniah son of the Maacathite, and all
their men.
24 Gedaliah vowed to them that the Babylonian officials meant them no harm. "Live

25:6 Jer 32:4
25:7 Jer 39:6-7; Ezek 12:13
25:8 Jer 52:12
25:9 2 Chr 36:19; Ps 74:3-8; Amos 2:5
25:10 Neh 1:3
25:11 2 Chr 36:20
25:12 2 Kgs 24:14; 2 Chr 24:14; Jer 40:7; 52:16
25:13 1 Kgs 7:15-22; 2 Chr 36:18
25:14 1 Kgs 7:47-50
25:17 1 Kgs 7:15-22
25:18 1 Chr 6:14; Ezra 7:1; Jer 29:25-26, 29
25:20 2 Kgs 23:33
25:21 Deut 28:64; 2 Kgs 23:27
25:22-26 //Jer 40:7-9; 41:1-3, 16-18
25:23 Jer 40:7-9

25:4a Or *the Chaldeans;* also in 25:5, 13, 25, 26. **25:4b** Hebrew *the Arabah.* **25:8** Hebrew *On the seventh day of the fifth month,* of the Hebrew calendar. This day was August 14, 586 B.C.; also see note on 25:1. **25:10** Or *Chaldean;* also in 25:24. **25:17a** Hebrew *18 cubits* [8.1 meters]. **25:17b** As in parallel texts at 1 Kgs 7:16, 2 Chr 3:15, and Jer 52:22, all of which read *5 cubits* [2.3 meters]; Hebrew reads *3 cubits,* which is 4.5 feet or 1.4 meters.

25:13 The bronze Sea was used to contain the huge reservoir of water for ritual cleansing for the priests. The bronze was so valuable that it was broken up and carried off to Babylon.

25:21 Judah, like Israel, was unfaithful to God. So God, as he had warned, allowed Judah to be destroyed and taken away (Deuteronomy 28). The book of Lamentations records the prophet Jeremiah's sorrow at seeing Jerusalem destroyed.

25:22 In place of the king (Zedekiah) who was deported to Babylon, Nebuchadnezzar appointed a governor (Gedaliah), who would faithfully administer the Babylonian policies.

25:22-30 This story shows that Israel's last hope of gaining back its land was gone—even the army commanders (now guerrilla rebels) had fled. Judah's earthly kingdom was absolutely demolished. But through prophets like Ezekiel and Daniel, who were also captives, God was able to keep his spiritual Kingdom alive in the hearts of many of the exiles.

in the land and serve the king of Babylon, and all will go well for you," he promised. 25:25
25 But in midautumn of that year,* Ishmael son of Nethaniah and grandson of Elishama, Jer 41:1-2
who was of the royal family, went to Mizpah with ten men and assassinated Gedaliah
and everyone with him, both Judeans and Babylonians.

26 Then all the people of Judah, from the least to the greatest, as well as the army 25:26 Jer 43:5-7
commanders, fled in panic to Egypt, for they were afraid of what the Babylonians would
do to them.

Hope for Israel's Royal Line

27 In the thirty-seventh year of King Jehoiachin's exile in Babylon, Evil-merodach 25:27
ascended to the Babylonian throne. He was kind to Jehoiachin and released him from 2 Kgs 24:12 Jer 52:31-34
prison on April 2 of that year.* 28 He spoke pleasantly to Jehoiachin and gave him
preferential treatment over all the other exiled kings in Babylon. 29 He supplied Jehoiachin with new clothes to replace his prison garb and allowed him to dine at the king's
table for the rest of his life. 30 The Babylonian king also gave him a regular allowance to
cover his living expenses until the day of his death.

25:25 Hebrew *in the seventh month,* of the Hebrew calendar. This month occurred in October and November 586 B.C.
25:27 Hebrew *on the twenty-seventh day of the twelfth month,* of the Hebrew calendar. This day was April 2, 561 B.C.; also see note on 25:1.

25:27 Evil-merodach, the son of Nebuchadnezzar, became king of the Babylonian Empire in 562 B.C., 24 years after the beginning of the general captivity and 37 years after Jehoiachin was removed from Jerusalem. The new king treated Jehoiachin with kindness, even allowing him to eat at his table (25:29). Evil-merodach was later killed in a plot by his brother-in-law, Nergal-sharezer, who succeeded him to the throne.

25:30 The book of 2 Kings opens with Elijah being carried to heaven—the destination awaiting those who follow God. But the book ends with the people of Judah being carried off to foreign lands as humiliated slaves—the result of failing to follow God.

Second Kings is an illustration of what happens when we make anything more important than God, when we make ruinous alliances, when our consciences become desensitized to right and wrong, and when we are no longer able to discern God's purpose for our lives. We may fail, like the people of Judah and Israel, but God's promises do not. He is always there to help us straighten out our lives and start over. And that is just what would happen in the book of Ezra. When the people acknowledged their sins, God was ready and willing to help them return to their land and start again.

KEY PLACES IN 1 CHRONICLES

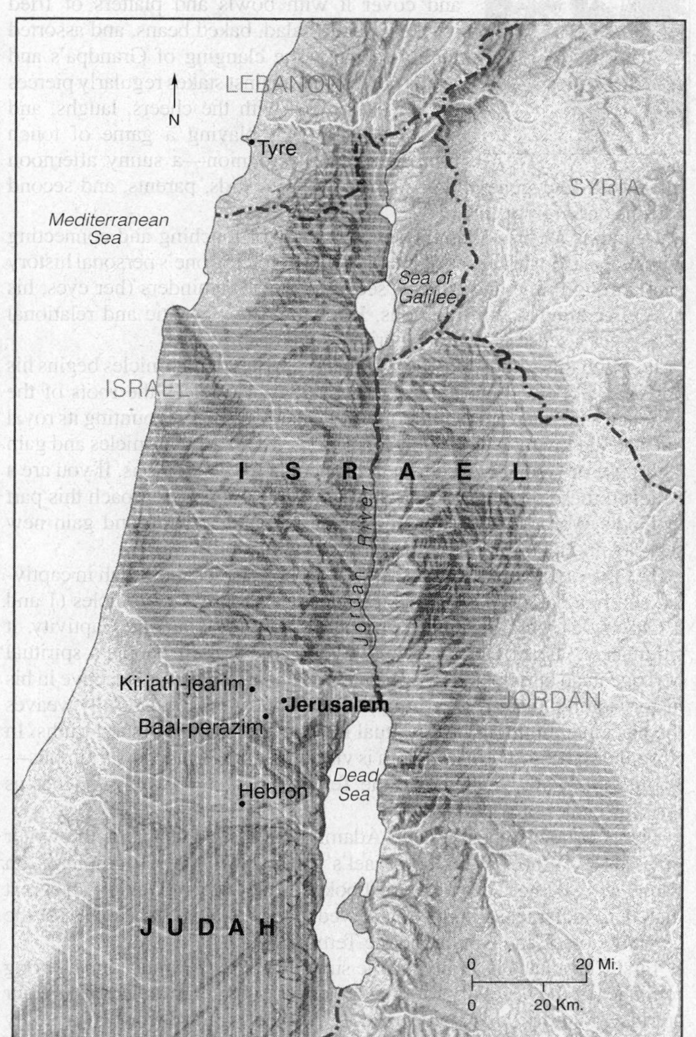

The broken lines (—·—) indicate modern boundaries.

1 Hebron Although David had been anointed king years earlier, his reign began when the leaders of Israel accepted him as king at Hebron (11:1–3).

2 Jerusalem David set out to complete the conquest of the land begun by Joshua. He attacked Jerusalem, captured it, and made it his capital (11:4—12:40).

3 Kiriath-jearim The Ark of the Covenant, which had been captured by the Philistines in battle and returned (1 Samuel 4—6), was in safekeeping in Kiriath-jearim. David summoned all Israel to this city to join in bringing the Ark to Jerusalem. Unfortunately, it was not moved according to God's instructions, and as a result, one man died. David left the Ark in the home of Obed-edom until he could discover how to transport it correctly (13:1–14).

4 Tyre David did much building in Jerusalem. King Hiram of Tyre sent workers and supplies to help build David's palace. Cedar, abundant in the mountains north of Israel, was a valuable and hardy wood for the beautiful buildings in Jerusalem (14:1—17:27).

5 Baal-perazim David was not very popular with the Philistines because he had slain Goliath, one of their greatest warriors (1 Samuel 17). When David began to rule over a united Israel, the Philistines set out to capture him. But as David and his army approached Jerusalem, they attacked the Philistines at Baal-perazim. His army defeated the mighty Philis- tines twice, causing all the surround- ing nations to fear David's power (14:11–17). After these battles, David moved the Ark to Jerusalem (this time in accordance with God's instructions for transporting the Ark). There was great celebration as the Ark was brought into Jerusalem (15:1—17:27). David spent the remainder of his life making preparations for the building of the Temple, a central place for the worship of God (18:1—29:30).

The genealogies of 1 Chronicles present an overview of Israel's history. The first nine chapters are filled with genealogies tracing the lineages of people from the Creation to the exile in Babylon. Saul's death is recorded in chapter 10. Chapter 11 begins the history of David's reign over Israel.

1 CHRONICLES

Saul becomes king 1050 B.C. (1045 B.C.)	Saul dies; David becomes king over Judah 1010	David becomes king over all Israel 1003	David captures Jerusalem 1000	David captures Rabbah 997(?)

VITAL STATISTICS

PURPOSE:
To unify God's people, to trace the Davidic line, and to teach that genuine worship ought to be the center of individual and national life

AUTHOR:
Ezra, according to Jewish tradition

TO WHOM WRITTEN:
All Israel

DATE WRITTEN:
Approximately 430 B.C., recording events that occurred from about 1000–960 B.C.

SETTING:
First Chronicles parallels 2 Samuel and serves as a commentary on it. Written after the Exile from a priestly point of view, 1 Chronicles emphasizes the religious history of Judah and Israel.

KEY VERSE:
"And David realized that the LORD had made him king over Israel and had made his kingdom very great for the sake of his people Israel" (14:2).

KEY PEOPLE:
David, Solomon

KEY PLACES:
Hebron, Jerusalem, the Temple

IN the wide shade of the ageless oak, a mother watches her toddler discover acorns, leaves, and dandelions. Nearby, her mother, aunt, and uncle spread the checkerboard cloth over park tables and cover it with bowls and platters of fried chicken, potato salad, baked beans, and assorted family recipes. The clanging of Grandpa's and Dad's horseshoes against stakes regularly pierces the air and mixes with the cheers, laughs, and shouts of teenagers playing a game of touch football. A family reunion—a sunny afternoon filled with four generations of miscellaneous kids, parents, and second cousins once removed.

Reunions are important. They are times for touching and connecting with others from branches of the family tree, tracing one's personal history back through time and culture, seeing physical reminders (her eyes, his nose), recalling warm traditions. Knowing one's genetic and relational path gives a sense of identity, heritage, and destiny.

It is with this same high purpose that the writer of Chronicles begins his unifying work with an extensive genealogy. He traces the roots of the nation in a literary family reunion from Adam onward, recounting its royal line and the loving plan of a personal God. We read 1 Chronicles and gain a glimpse of God at work through his people for generations. If you are a believer, these people are your ancestors, too. As you approach this part of God's Word, read their names with awe and respect, and gain new security and identity in your relationship with God.

The previous book, 2 Kings, ends with both Israel and Judah in captivity, surely a dark age for God's people. Then follows Chronicles (1 and 2 Chronicles were originally one book). Written after the Captivity, it summarizes Israel's history, emphasizing the Jewish people's spiritual heritage in an attempt to unify the nation. The chronicler is selective in his history telling. Instead of writing an exhaustive work, he carefully weaves the narrative, highlighting spiritual lessons and teaching moral truths. In Chronicles the northern kingdom is virtually ignored, David's triumphs—not his sins—are recalled, and the Temple is given great prominence as the vital center of national life.

First Chronicles begins with Adam, and for nine chapters, the writer gives us a "Who's Who" of Israel's history with special emphasis on David's royal line. The rest of the book tells the story of David—the great man of God, Israel's king—who served God and laid out the plans for the construction of and worship in the Temple.

First Chronicles is an invaluable supplement to 2 Samuel and a strong reminder of the necessity for tracing our roots and thus rediscovering our spiritual foundation. As you read 1 Chronicles, trace your own godly heritage, thank God for your spiritual forefathers, and recommit yourself to passing on God's truth to the next generation.

David's census 980(?)	Solomon becomes king 970	The kingdom divides 930

THE BLUEPRINT

A. THE GENEALOGIES OF ISRAEL (1:1—9:44)
1. Ancestry of the nation
2. The tribes of Israel
3. Returnees from exile in Babylon

The long list of names that follows presents a history of God's work in the world from Adam through Zerubbabel. Some of these names remind us of stories of great faith, and others, of tragic failure. About most of the people named, however, we know nothing. But those who died unknown to us are known by God. God will also remember us when we die.

B. THE REIGN OF DAVID (10:1—29:30)
1. David becomes king over all of Israel
2. David brings the Ark to Jerusalem
3. David's military exploits
4. David arranges for the building of the Temple

David loved the Lord and wanted to build a Temple to replace the Tabernacle, but God denied his request. David's greatest contribution to the Temple would not be the construction but the preparation. We may be unable to see the results of our labors for God in our lifetime, but David's example helps us understand that we serve God so *he* will see *his* results, not so we will see ours.

MEGATHEMES

THEME	EXPLANATION	IMPORTANCE
Israel's History	By retelling Israel's history in the genealogies and the stories of the kings, the writer laid down the true spiritual foundation for the nation. God kept his promises, and we are reminded of them in the historical record of his people, leaders, prophets, priests, and kings.	Israel's past formed a reliable basis for reconstructing the nation after the Exile. Because God's promises are revealed in the Bible, we can know God and trust him to keep his word. Like Israel, we should have no higher goal in life than devoted service to God.
God's People	By listing the names of people in Israel's past, God established Israel's true heritage. They were all one family in Adam, one nation in Abraham, one priesthood under Levi, and one kingdom under David. The national and spiritual unity of the people was important to the rebuilding of the nation.	God is always faithful to his people. He protects them in every generation and provides leaders to guide them. Because God has been at work throughout the centuries, his people can trust him to work in the present. You can rely on his presence today.
David, the King	The story of David's life and his relationship with God showed that he was God's appointed leader. David's devotion to God, the law, the Temple, true worship, the people, and justice sets the standard for what God's chosen king should be like.	Jesus Christ came to earth as a descendant of David. One day he will rule as King over all the earth. His strength and justice will fulfill God's ideal for the king. He is our hope. We can experience God's Kingdom now by giving Christ complete control of our lives.
True Worship	David brought the Ark of the Covenant to the Tabernacle at Jerusalem to restore true worship to the people. God gave the plans for building the Temple, and David organized the priests to make worship central to all Israel.	The Temple stood as the throne of God on earth, the place of true worship. God's true throne is in the hearts of his people. When we acknowledge him as the true King over our lives, true worship takes place.
The Priests	God ordained the priests and Levites to guide the people in faithful worship according to his law. By leading the people in worship according to God's design, the priests and Levites were an important safeguard to Israel's faith.	For true worship to remain central in our lives, God's people need to take a firm stand for the ways of God recorded in the Bible. Today, all believers are priests for one another, and we should encourage each other to faithful worship.

A. THE GENEALOGIES OF ISRAEL (1:1—9:44)

These genealogies are the official family records of the nation of Israel. They give us an overview of the history of God's work from Creation through the captivity of his people. These records served to teach the exiles returning from Babylon about their spiritual heritage as a nation and to inspire them to renew their faithfulness to God. Although these lists show the racial heritage of the Jews, they contain the spiritual heritage for every believer. We are a part of the community of faith that has existed from generation to generation since the dawn of man.

1. Ancestry of the nation

From Adam to Noah's Sons

1 The descendants of Adam were Seth, Enosh, 2 Kenan, Mahalalel, Jared, 3 Enoch,
Methuselah, Lamech, 4 and Noah.
The sons of Noah were* Shem, Ham, and Japheth.

1:1 Gen 5:1-32 Luke 3:36-38

Descendants of Japheth

5 The descendants of Japheth were Gomer, Magog, Madai, Javan, Tubal, Meshech,
and Tiras.
6 The descendants of Gomer were Ashkenaz, Riphath,* and Togarmah.
7 The descendants of Javan were Elishah, Tarshish, Kittim, and Rodanim.

1:5-7 //Gen 10:2-5

Descendants of Ham

8 The descendants of Ham were Cush, Mizraim,* Put, and Canaan.
9 The descendants of Cush were Seba, Havilah, Sabtah, Raamah, and Sabteca. The
descendants of Raamah were Sheba and Dedan. 10 Cush was also the ancestor of
Nimrod, who was known across the earth as a heroic warrior.
11 Mizraim was the ancestor of the Ludites, Anamites, Lehabites, Naphtuhites,
12 Pathrusites, Casluhites, and the Caphtorites, from whom the Philistines came.*
13 Canaan's oldest son was Sidon, the ancestor of the Sidonians. Canaan was also the
ancestor of the Hittites, 14 Jebusites, Amorites, Girgashites, 15 Hivites, Arkites,
Sinites, 16 Arvadites, Zemarites, and Hamathites.

1:8-16 //Gen 10:6-20

1:11 Gen 10:13-18

1:13 Gen 15:19-21

Descendants of Shem

17 The descendants of Shem were Elam, Asshur, Arphaxad, Lud, and Aram.
The descendants of Aram were* Uz, Hul, Gether, and Mash.*
18 Arphaxad was the father of Shelah. Shelah was the father of Eber. 19 Eber had two

1:17-23 //Gen 10:21-31; 11:10-27 Luke 3:36

1:19 Gen 11:16

1:4 As in Greek version (see also Gen 5:3-32); Hebrew lacks *The sons of Noah were.* **1:6** As in some Hebrew manuscripts and Greek version (see also Gen 10:3); most Hebrew manuscripts read *Diphath.* **1:8** Or *Egypt;* also in 1:11. **1:12** Hebrew *Casluhites, from whom the Philistines came, Caphtorites.* See Jer 47:4; Amos 9:7. **1:17a** As in one Hebrew manuscript and some Greek manuscripts (see also Gen 10:23); most Hebrew manuscripts lack *The descendants of Aram were.* **1:17b** As in parallel text at Gen 10:23; Hebrew reads *and Meshech.*

1:1 This record of names demonstrates that God is interested not only in nations but also in individuals. Although billions of people have lived since Adam, God knows and remembers the face and name of each person. Each of us is more than a name on a list; we are special persons whom God knows and loves. As we recognize and accept his love, we discover both our uniqueness as individuals and our solidarity with the rest of his family.

1:1ff This long list of names was compiled after the people of Judah, the southern kingdom, were taken captive to Babylon. As the exiles looked forward to the day when they would return to their homeland, one of their biggest fears was that the records of their heritage would be lost. The Jews placed great importance upon their heritage because each person wanted to be able to prove that he was a descendant of Abraham, the father of the Jewish people. Only then could he enjoy the benefits of the special blessings God promised to Abraham and his descendants (see the notes on Genesis 12:1-3 and 17:2-8 for what these special blessings were).

This list reconstructed the family tree for both Judah, the southern kingdom, and Israel, the northern kingdom, before their captivities and served as proof for those who claimed to be Abraham's descendants. (For more information about why the Bible includes genealogies, read the notes on Genesis 5:1ff, Matthew 1:1, and Luke 3:23-38.)

1:1ff There is more to this long genealogy than meets the eye. It holds importance for us today because it supports the Old Testament promise that Jesus the Messiah would be a descendant of Abraham and David. This promise is recorded in Genesis 12:1-3 and 2 Samuel 7:12, 13.

1:1, 4 Adam's story and Profile are found in Genesis 1–5. Noah's story and Profile are found in Genesis 6–9.

1:5-9 A biblical genealogy may skip several generations. These lists were not meant to be exhaustive, but to give adequate information about the various family lines.

1:10 Nimrod is also mentioned in Genesis 10:8, 9.

1:11, 12 The Philistines had been Israel's constant enemy from the days of the judges. King David finally weakened them, and by this time they were no longer a threat. (For more information on the Philistines, see the notes on Judges 13:1 and 1 Samuel 4:1.)

1:13-16 Canaan was the ancestor of the Canaanites, who inhabited the Promised Land (also called Canaan) before the Israelites entered under Joshua's leadership. God helped the Israelites drive out the Canaanites, a wicked and idolatrous people. The land's name was then changed to Israel. The book of Joshua tells that story.

sons. The first was named Peleg—"division"—for during his lifetime the people of
the world were divided into different language groups and dispersed. His brother's
name was Joktan.
20 Joktan was the ancestor of Almodad, Sheleph, Hazarmaveth, Jerah, 21 Hadoram,
Uzal, Diklah, 22 Obal,* Abimael, Sheba, 23 Ophir, Havilah, and Jobab. All these
were descendants of Joktan.

1:24 Gen 11:10-26; Luke 3:34-36

24 So this is the family line descended from Shem: Arphaxad, Shelah,* 25 Eber, Peleg,
Reu, 26 Serug, Nahor, Terah, 27 and Abram, later known as Abraham.

Descendants of Abraham

1:29-31 //Gen 25:12-16

28 The sons of Abraham were Isaac and Ishmael.
29 The sons of Ishmael were Nebaioth (the oldest), Kedar, Adbeel, Mibsam,
30 Mishma, Dumah, Massa, Hadad, Tema, 31 Jetur, Naphish, and Kedemah. These
were the sons of Ishmael.

1:32-33 //Gen 25:1-4

32 The sons of Keturah, Abraham's concubine, were Zimran, Jokshan, Medan, Midian,
Ishbak, and Shuah.
The sons of Jokshan were Sheba and Dedan.
33 The sons of Midian were Ephah, Epher, Hanoch, Abida, and Eldaah.
All these were sons of Abraham by his concubine Keturah.

Descendants of Isaac

1:34 Gen 25:25-26; 32:28; Matt 1:2

34 Abraham was the father of Isaac. The sons of Isaac were Esau and Israel.*

Descendants of Esau

1:35 Gen 36:4, 19

1:35-37 //Gen 36:10-14

35 The sons of Esau were Eliphaz, Reuel, Jeush, Jalam, and Korah.
36 The sons of Eliphaz were Teman, Omar, Zepho,* Gatam, Kenaz, and Amalek, who
was born to Timna.*
37 The sons of Reuel were Nahath, Zerah, Shammah, and Mizzah.

Original Peoples of Edom

1:38-42 //Gen 36:20-28

38 The sons of Seir were Lotan, Shobal, Zibeon, Anah, Dishon, Ezer, and Dishan.
39 The sons of Lotan were Hori and Heman.* Lotan's sister was named Timna.
40 The sons of Shobal were Alvan,* Manahath, Ebal, Shepho,* and Onam.
The sons of Zibeon were Aiah and Anah.
41 The son of Anah was Dishon.
The sons of Dishon were Hemdan,* Eshban, Ithran, and Keran.
42 The sons of Ezer were Bilhan, Zaavan, and Akan.*
The sons of Dishan* were Uz and Aran.

1:22 As in some Hebrew manuscripts and Syriac version (see also Gen 10:28); most Hebrew manuscripts read *Ebal.* **1:24** Some Greek manuscripts read *Arphaxad, Cainan, Shelah.* See notes on Gen 10:24; 11:12-13. **1:34** *Israel* is the name that God gave to Jacob. **1:36a** As in many Hebrew manuscripts and a few Greek manuscripts (see also Gen 36:11); most Hebrew manuscripts read *Zephi.* **1:36b** As in some Greek manuscripts (see also Gen 36:12); Hebrew reads *Kenaz, Timna, and Amalek.* **1:39** As in parallel text at Gen 36:22; Hebrew reads *and Homam.* **1:40a** As in many Hebrew manuscripts and a few Greek manuscripts (see also Gen 36:23); most Hebrew manuscripts read *Alian.* **1:40b** As in some Hebrew manuscripts (see also Gen 36:23); most Hebrew manuscripts read *Shephi.* **1:41** As in many Hebrew manuscripts and some Greek manuscripts (see also Gen 36:26); most Hebrew manuscripts read *Hamran.* **1:42a** As in many Hebrew and Greek manuscripts (see also Gen 36:27); most Hebrew manuscripts read *Jaakan.* **1:42b** Hebrew *Dishon;* compare 1:38 and parallel text at Gen 36:28.

1:19 At one time, everyone spoke a single language. But some people became proud of their accomplishments and gathered to build a monument to themselves—the tower of Babel. The building project was brought to an abrupt conclusion when God caused the people to speak different languages. Without the ability to communicate with one another, the people could not be unified. God showed them that their great efforts were useless without him. Pride in our achievements must not lead us to conclude that we no longer need God. This story is told in Genesis 11:1-9.

1:24-27 Abraham's story and Profile are found in Genesis 11:26–25:10.

1:28-31 Ishmael's story and Profile are found in Genesis 17 and 21.

1:34 Israel is another name for Jacob because Jacob's 12 sons became the nation of Israel. Esau's descendants became the nation of Edom, a constant enemy of Israel. To learn more about the lives of Isaac and his two sons, Jacob and Esau, read their stories and Profiles in Genesis 21–36 and 46–49.

1:36 Amalek, Esau's grandson, was the son of his father's concubine (Genesis 36:12). He was the ancestor of the wicked tribe known as the Amalekites, the first people to attack the Israelites on their way to the Promised Land. (For more about the Amalekites, read the note on Exodus 17:8.)

Rulers of Edom

43 These are the kings who ruled in Edom before there were kings in Israel*:

Bela son of Beor, who ruled from his city of Dinhabah.
44 When Bela died, Jobab son of Zerah from Bozrah became king.
45 When Jobab died, Husham from the land of the Temanites became king.
46 When Husham died, Hadad son of Bedad became king and ruled from the city of
Avith. He was the one who destroyed the Midianite army in the land of Moab.
47 When Hadad died, Samlah from the city of Masrekah became king.
48 When Samlah died, Shaul from the city of Rehoboth on the Euphrates River*
became king.
49 When Shaul died, Baal-hanan son of Acbor became king.
50 When Baal-hanan died, Hadad became king and ruled from the city of Pau.* His
wife was Mehetabel, the daughter of Matred and granddaughter of Me-zahab.
51 Then Hadad died.

The clan leaders of Edom were Timna, Alvah,* Jetheth, 52 Oholibamah, Elah, Pinon,
53 Kenaz, Teman, Mibzar, 54 Magdiel, and Iram. These were the clan leaders of
Edom.

Descendants of Israel

2 The sons of Israel* were Reuben, Simeon, Levi, Judah, Issachar, Zebulun, 2 Dan,
Joseph, Benjamin, Naphtali, Gad, and Asher.

Descendants of Judah

3 Judah had three sons through Bathshua, a Canaanite woman. Their names were Er,
Onan, and Shelah. But the oldest son, Er, was a wicked man, so the LORD killed
him. 4 Later Judah had twin sons through Tamar, his widowed daughter-in-law.
Their names were Perez and Zerah. So Judah had five sons in all.
5 The sons of Perez were Hezron and Hamul.
6 The sons of Zerah were Zimri, Ethan, Heman, Calcol, and Darda*—five in all.
7 Achan* son of Carmi, one of Zerah's descendants, brought disaster on Israel
by taking plunder that had been set apart for the LORD.*
8 The son of Ethan was Azariah.

From Judah's Grandson Hezron to David

9 The sons of Hezron were Jerahmeel, Ram, and Caleb.*
10 Ram was the father of Amminadab.
Amminadab was the father of Nahshon, a leader of Judah.
11 Nahshon was the father of Salmon.*
Salmon was the father of Boaz.

1:43-54 //Gen 36:31-43
1:45 Job 2:11
2:1-2 //Gen 35:23-26; 46:8-25; Exod 1:1-4; Num 1:2-15; Rev 7:4-8
2:3 Gen 38:2-10
2:4 Gen 38:13-30
2:5-15 //Ruth 4:18-22; Matt 1:3-6
2:7 Josh 7:1
2:10 Num 1:7

1:43 Or *before an Israelite king ruled over them.* **1:48** Hebrew *the river.* **1:50** As in many Hebrew manuscripts, some Greek manuscripts, Syriac version, and Latin Vulgate (see also Gen 36:39); most Hebrew manuscripts read *Pai.* **1:51** As in parallel text at Gen 36:40; Hebrew reads *Aliah.* **2:1** *Israel* is the name that God gave to Jacob. **2:6** As in many Hebrew manuscripts, some Greek manuscripts, and Syriac version (see also 1 Kgs 4:31); Hebrew reads *Dara.* **2:7a** Hebrew *Achar;* compare Josh 7:1. *Achar* means "disaster." **2:7b** The Hebrew term used here refers to the complete consecration of things or people to the LORD, either by destroying them or by giving them as an offering. **2:9** Hebrew *Kelubai,* a variant name for Caleb; compare 2:18. **2:11** As in Greek version (see also Ruth 4:21); Hebrew reads *Salma.*

1:43-54 Why are we given information in this genealogy about the descendants of Edom, who were Israel's enemies? Esau, ancestor of the Edomites, was Isaac's oldest son and thus a direct descendant of Abraham. As Abraham's first grandson, he deserved a place in the Jewish records. It was through Esau's marriages to pagan women, however, that the nation of Edom began. This genealogy shows the ancestry of enemy nations; they were *not* a part of the direct lineage of King David, and thus of the Messiah. This listing further identified Israel's special identity and role.

2:1, 2 The story of Israel's (Jacob's) sons is found in Genesis 29:32–50:26. Profiles of Reuben, Judah, and Joseph are found in the same section.

2:3 This long genealogy not only lists names but gives us insights into some of the people. Here, almost as an epitaph, the genealogy states that Er "was a wicked man, so the LORD killed him." Now, thousands of years later, this is all we know of the man. Each of us is forging a reputation, developing personal qualities by which we will be remembered. How would God summarize your life up to now? Some defiantly claim that how they live is their own business. But Scripture teaches that the way you live today will determine how you will be remembered by others and how you will be judged by God. What you do now *does* matter.

2:7 Achan is the man who kept for himself some of the plunder that was devoted to the Lord for destruction (see Joshua 7).

2:12 Boaz was Ruth's husband and an ancestor of both David and Jesus. Boaz's story and Profile are found in the book of Ruth.

2:12 Ruth 4:17 Matt 1:5
12 Boaz was the father of Obed.
Obed was the father of Jesse.

2:13 1 Sam 16:6
13 Jesse's first son was Eliab, his second was Abinadab, his third was Shimea, 14 his
fourth was Nethanel, his fifth was Raddai, 15 his sixth was Ozem, and his seventh
2:16 1 Sam 26:6 2 Sam 2:13
was David.
16 Their sisters were named Zeruiah and Abigail. Zeruiah had three sons named
2:17 2 Sam 17:25
Abishai, Joab, and Asahel. 17 Abigail married a man named Jether, an Ishmaelite,
and they had a son named Amasa.

Descendants of Hezron's Son Caleb

18 Hezron's son Caleb had two wives named Azubah and Jerioth. Azubah's sons were
named Jesher, Shobab, and Ardon. 19 After Azubah died, Caleb married Ephrathah,*
and they had a son named Hur. 20 Hur was the father of Uri. Uri was the father of
Bezalel.
21 When Hezron was sixty years old, he married Gilead's sister, the daughter of Makir.
They had a son named Segub. 22 Segub was the father of Jair, who ruled twenty-
three towns in the land of Gilead. 23 (Later Geshur and Aram captured the Towns
of Jair* and also took Kenath and its sixty surrounding villages.) All these were
descendants of Makir, the father of Gilead.
24 Soon after Hezron died in the town of Caleb-ephrathah, his wife Abijah gave birth
to a son named Ashhur (the father of* Tekoa).

Descendants of Hezron's Son Jerahmeel

25 The sons of Jerahmeel, the oldest son of Hezron, were Ram (the oldest), Bunah,
Oren, Ozem, and Ahijah. 26 Jerahmeel had a second wife named Atarah. She was
the mother of Onam.
27 The sons of Ram, the oldest son of Jerahmeel, were Maaz, Jamin, and Eker.
28 The sons of Onam were Shammai and Jada. The sons of Shammai were Nadab and
Abishur.
29 The sons of Abishur and his wife Abihail were Ahban and Molid.
30 The sons of Nadab were Seled and Appaim. Seled died without children, 31 but
Appaim had a son named Ishi. The son of Ishi was Sheshan. Sheshan had a
descendant named Ahlai.
32 Shammai's brother, Jada, had two sons named Jether and Jonathan. Jether died
without children, 33 but Jonathan had two sons named Peleth and Zaza. These were
all descendants of Jerahmeel.
34 Sheshan had no sons, though he did have daughters. He also had an Egyptian
servant named Jarha. 35 Sheshan gave one of his daughters to be the wife of Jarha,
and they had a son named Attai.

2:36 1 Chr 11:41
36 Attai was the father of Nathan.
Nathan was the father of Zabad.
37 Zabad was the father of Ephlal.
Ephlal was the father of Obed.
38 Obed was the father of Jehu.
Jehu was the father of Azariah.
39 Azariah was the father of Helez.
Helez was the father of Eleasah.
40 Eleasah was the father of Sismai.
Sismai was the father of Shallum.

2:19 Hebrew *Ephrath,* a variant name for Ephrathah; compare 2:50 and 4:4. **2:23** Or *captured Havvoth-jair.*
2:24 Or *the founder of;* also in 2:42, 45, 49-52 and perhaps other instances where the text reads *the father of.*

2:15 David is one of the best-known people of the Bible. He was certainly not perfect, but he exemplified what it means to seek God first in all areas of life. God called David "a man after my own heart" (Acts 13:22) because David's greatest desire was to serve and worship God. We can please God in the same way by making God our first consideration in all our desires and plans. David's story is found in 1 Samuel 16:1–1 Kings 2:10 and 1 Chronicles 10:14–29:30. David's Profile is found in 1 Samuel 17.

2:16 Joab's story is found in 2 Samuel 2; 3; 10–20; 24; 1 Kings 1–2; 1 Chronicles 11:4-9; 19–21. His Profile is found in 2 Samuel 18. Abishai's story is found in 1 Samuel 26; 2 Samuel 2; 3; 10; 15–21; 23; 1 Chronicles 18:12; 19. Abishai's Profile is found in 2 Samuel 21.

2:18 This is not the Caleb who spied out the Promised Land with Joshua. Caleb, the spy, is listed in 4:15.

41 Shallum was the father of Jekamiah.
Jekamiah was the father of Elishama.

Descendants of Hezron's Son Caleb

42 The oldest son of Caleb, the brother of Jerahmeel, was Mesha, the father of Ziph.
Caleb's second son was Mareshah, the father of Hebron.*
43 The sons of Hebron were Korah, Tappuah, Rekem, and Shema. 44 Shema was the
father of Raham. Raham was the father of Jorkeam. Rekem was the father of
Shammai. 45 The son of Shammai was Maon. Maon was the father of Beth-zur. **2:45** Josh 15:55
46 Caleb's concubine Ephah gave birth to Haran, Moza, and Gazez. Haran was the
father of Gazez.
47 The sons of Jahdai were Regem, Jotham, Geshan, Pelet, Ephah, and Shaaph.
48 Another of Caleb's concubines, Maacah, gave birth to Sheber and Tirhanah. 49 She
also gave birth to Shaaph (the father of Madmannah) and Sheva (the father of
Macbenah and Gibea). Caleb also had a daughter named Acsah. 50 These were all **2:50** 1 Chr 4:4
descendants of Caleb.

Descendants of Caleb's Son Hur

The sons of Hur, the oldest son of Caleb's wife Ephrathah, were Shobal (the father
of Kiriath-jearim), 51 Salma (the father of Bethlehem), and Hareph (the father of
Beth-gader).
52 The descendants of Shobal (the father of Kiriath-jearim) were Haroeh, half the
Manahathites, 53 and the families of Kiriath-jearim—the Ithrites, Puthites, Shu-
mathites, and Mishraites, from whom came the people of Zorah and Eshtaol.
54 The descendants of Salma were Bethlehem, the Netophathites, Atroth-beth-joab,
the other half of the Manahathites, the Zorites, 55 and the families of scribes living **2:55** 2 Kgs 10:15
at Jabez—the Tirathites, Shimeathites, and Sucathites. All these were Kenites who
descended from Hammath, the father of the family of Recab.*

Descendants of David

3 These were the sons who were born to David in Hebron: **3:1-4** //2 Sam 3:2-5
The oldest was Amnon, whose mother was Ahinoam of Jezreel. **3:1** 1 Sam 25:43
The second was Kileab,* whose mother was Abigail from Carmel.
2 The third was Absalom, whose mother was Maacah, the daughter of Talmai, king **3:2** 2 Sam 3:4; 13:20; 14:23
of Geshur.
The fourth was Adonijah, whose mother was Haggith.
3 The fifth was Shephatiah, whose mother was Abital.
The sixth was Ithream, whose mother was Eglah.

4 These six sons were born to David in Hebron, where he reigned seven and a half years. **3:4** 2 Sam 5:4-5

Then David moved the capital to Jerusalem, where he reigned another thirty-three
years. 5 The sons born to David in Jerusalem included Shimea, Shobab, Nathan, and **3:5-8** //2 Sam 5:14-16 //1 Chr 14:4-7
Solomon. Bathsheba,* the daughter of Ammiel, was the mother of these sons. 6 David
also had nine other sons: Ibhar, Elishua,* Elpelet,* 7 Nogah, Nepheg, Japhia, 8 Elishama,
Eliada, and Eliphelet.

2:42 The meaning of the Hebrew is uncertain. **2:55** Or *the founder of Beth-recab.* **3:1** As in parallel text at 2 Sam 3:3; Hebrew reads *Daniel.* **3:5** Hebrew *Bathshua,* a variant name for Bathsheba. **3:6a** As in some Hebrew and Greek manuscripts (see also 14:5-7 and 2 Sam 5:15); most Hebrew manuscripts read *Elishama.* **3:6b** Hebrew *Eliphelet;* compare parallel text at 14:5-7.

3:1 Abigail's story is found in 1 Samuel 25; her Profile is in 1 Samuel 25.

3:2 Absalom's story and Profile are found in 2 Samuel 13–18.

3:5 Bathsheba's story is found in 2 Samuel 11; 12; 1 Kings 1, and her Profile is in 1 Kings 1. The story of her son, Solomon, who became Israel's third king, is found in 1 Kings 1–11 and 2 Chronicles 1–9. Solomon's Profile is found in 1 Kings 4.

3:9 The tragic story of Tamar, David's daughter, is found in 2 Samuel 13; 14.

3:10-14 Many of Solomon's descendants ruled the nation of Judah. For Rehoboam's story and Profile, see 2 Chronicles 10–12. For Jehoshaphat's story and Profile, see 2 Chronicles 17–20. Azariah's (Uzziah's) story and Profile are found in 2 Chronicles 26. Hezekiah's story and Profile are in 2 Kings 18–20. For Josiah's story, see 2 Kings 22–23. His Profile is in 2 Kings 23.

3:15 Jehoiakim's story is found in Jeremiah 22–28; 35; 36. Zedekiah's story is found in Jeremiah 21–39.

3:19, 20 Zerubbabel was the leader of the first exiles to return from Babylon. His story and Profile are found in the book of Ezra.

3:9
2 Sam 13:1

[9]These were the sons of David, not including the sons of his concubines. David also
had a daughter named Tamar.

Descendants of Solomon

3:10
1 Kgs 15:1, 8, 24
2 Chr 13:1; 17:1

3:11
2 Kgs 8:24-25; 11:21
2 Chr 21:1; 22:11

3:15
2 Kgs 23:34

[10]The descendants of Solomon were Rehoboam, Abijah, Asa, Jehoshaphat, [11]Jehoram,*
Ahaziah, Joash, [12]Amaziah, Uzziah,* Jotham, [13]Ahaz, Hezekiah, Manasseh, [14]Amon,
and Josiah.
[15]The sons of Josiah were Johanan (the oldest), Jehoiakim (the second), Zedekiah (the
third), and Jehoahaz* (the fourth).
[16]Jehoiakim was succeeded by his son Jehoiachin; he, in turn, was succeeded by his
uncle Zedekiah.*

Descendants of Jehoiachin

[17]The sons of Jehoiachin,* who was taken prisoner by the Babylonians, were Shealtiel,
[18]Malkiram, Pedaiah, Shenazzar, Jekamiah, Hoshama, and Nedabiah.
[19]The sons of Pedaiah were Zerubbabel and Shimei.
The sons of Zerubbabel were Meshullam and Hananiah. He also had a daughter
named Shelomith. [20]His five other sons were Hashubah, Ohel, Berekiah, Hasadiah,
and Jushab-hesed.
[21]The sons of Hananiah were Pelatiah and Jeshaiah. Jeshaiah's son was Rephaiah.
Rephaiah's son was Arnan. Arnan's son was Obadiah. Obadiah's son was
Shecaniah.

3:22
Ezra 8:2-3

[22]Shecaniah's descendants were Shemaiah and his sons, Hattush, Igal, Bariah,
Neariah, and Shaphat—six in all.
[23]The sons of Neariah were Elioenai, Hizkiah, and Azrikam—three in all.
[24]The sons of Elioenai were Hodaviah, Eliashib, Pelaiah, Akkub, Johanan, Delaiah,
and Anani—seven in all.

2. The tribes of Israel

Other Descendants of Judah

4:1
Num 26:21
1 Chr 2:3

4 Some of the descendants of Judah were Perez, Hezron, Carmi, Hur, and Shobal.
[2]Shobal's son Reaiah was the father of Jahath. Jahath was the father of Ahumai
and Lahad. These were the families of the Zorathites.
[3]The descendants of* Etam were Jezreel, Ishma, Idbash, Hazzelelponi (his daughter),
[4]Penuel (the father of* Gedor), and Ezer (the father of Hushah). These were the
descendants of Hur (the firstborn of Ephrathah), the ancestor of Bethlehem.
[5]Ashhur (the father of Tekoa) had two wives, named Helah and Naarah. [6]Naarah gave
birth to Ahuzzam, Hepher, Temeni, and Haahashtari. [7]Helah gave birth to Zereth,
Izhar, Ethnan, [8]and Koz, who became the ancestor of Anub, Zobebah, and all the
families of Aharhel son of Harum.
[9]There was a man named Jabez who was more distinguished than any of his
brothers. His mother named him Jabez* because his birth had been so painful. [10]He
was the one who prayed to the God of Israel, "Oh, that you would bless me and
extend my lands! Please be with me in all that I do, and keep me from all trouble
and pain!" And God granted him his request.
[11]Kelub (the brother of Shuhah) was the father of Mehir. Mehir was the father of

3:11 Hebrew *Joram,* a variant name for Jehoram. **3:12** Hebrew *Azariah,* a variant name for Uzziah. **3:15** Hebrew *Shallum,* another name for Jehoahaz. **3:16** Hebrew *The descendants of Jehoiakim were his son Jeconiah* [a variant name for Jehoiachin] *and his son Zedekiah.* **3:17** Hebrew *Jeconiah,* a variant name for Jehoiachin. **4:3** As in Greek version; Hebrew reads *father of.* The meaning of the Hebrew is uncertain. **4:4** Or *the founder of;* also in 4:12, 14, 17-18, and perhaps other instances where the text reads *the father of.* **4:9** *Jabez* sounds like a Hebrew term meaning "distress" or "pain."

4:9, 10 Jabez is remembered for a prayer request rather than a heroic act. In his prayer, he asked God to (1) bless him, (2) help him in his work ("extend my lands"), (3) be with him in all he did, and (4) keep him from trouble and pain. Jabez acknowledged God as the true center of his work. When we pray for God's blessing, we should also ask him to take his rightful position as Lord over our work, our family time, and our recreation. Obeying him in daily responsibilities *is* heroic living.

4:10 Jabez prayed specifically to be protected from trouble and pain. We live in a fallen world filled with sin, and it is important to ask God to keep us safe from the unavoidable evil that comes our way. But we must also avoid evil motives, desires, and actions that begin within us. Therefore, not only must we seek God's protection from evil, but we must also ask God to guard our thoughts and actions. We can begin to utilize his protection by filling our mind with positive thoughts and attitudes.

Eshton. 12 Eshton was the father of Beth-rapha, Paseah, and Tehinnah. Tehinnah
was the father of Ir-nahash. These were the descendants of Recah.
13 The sons of Kenaz were Othniel and Seraiah. Othniel's sons were Hathath and Meon- **4:13** Josh 15:17
othai.* 14 Meonothai was the father of Ophrah. Seraiah was the father of Joab, the
founder of the Valley of Craftsmen,* so called because many craftsmen lived there.
15 The sons of Caleb son of Jephunneh were Iru, Elah, and Naam. The son of Elah was
Kenaz.
16 The sons of Jehallelel were Ziph, Ziphah, Tiria, and Asarel.
17 The sons of Ezrah were Jether, Mered, Epher, and Jalon. Mered married an Egyptian
woman, who became the mother of Miriam, Shammai, and Ishbah (the father of Eshtemoa). 18 Mered also married a woman of Judah, who became the mother of Jered
(the father of Gedor), Heber (the father of Soco), and Jekuthiel (the father of Zanoah).
Mered's Egyptian wife was named Bithiah, and she was an Egyptian princess.
19 Hodiah's wife was the sister of Naham. One of her sons was the father of Keilah the
Garmite, and another was the father of Eshtemoa the Maacathite.
20 The sons of Shimon were Amnon, Rinnah, Ben-hanan, and Tilon.
The descendants of Ishi were Zoheth and Ben-zoheth.

Descendants of Judah's Son Shelah

21 Shelah was one of Judah's sons. The descendants of Shelah were Er (the father of
Lecah), Laadah (the father of Mareshah), the families of linen workers at Beth-
ashbea, 22 Jokim, the people of Cozeba, Joash, and Saraph, who ruled over Moab
and Jashubi-lehem. These names all come from ancient records. 23 They were the
potters who lived in Netaim and Gederah. They all worked for the king.

Descendants of Simeon

24 The sons of Simeon were Nemuel, Jamin, Jarib, Zerah, and Shaul.
25 The descendants of Shaul were Shallum, Mibsam, and Mishma.
26 The descendants of Mishma were Hammuel, Zaccur, and Shimei.
27 Shimei had sixteen sons and six daughters, but none of his brothers had large
families. So Simeon's tribe never became as large as the tribe of Judah.
28 They lived in Beersheba, Moladah, Hazar-shual, 29 Bilhah, Ezem, Tolad,
30 Bethuel, Hormah, Ziklag, 31 Beth-marcaboth, Hazar-susim, Beth-biri, and Shaa- **4:28-33** //Josh 19:2-10
raim. These towns were under their control until the time of King David.
32 Their descendants also lived in Etam, Ain, Rimmon, Token, and Ashan—five
towns 33 and their surrounding villages as far away as Baalath.* This was their territory, and these names are recorded in their family genealogy.

34 Other descendants of Simeon included Meshobab, Jamlech, Joshah son of Amaziah,
35 Joel, Jehu son of Joshibiah, son of Seraiah, son of Asiel, 36 Elioenai, Jaakobah,
Jeshohaiah, Asaiah, Adiel, Jesimiel, Benaiah, 37 and Ziza son of Shiphi, son of
Allon, son of Jedaiah, son of Shimri, son of Shemaiah.

38 These were the names of some of the leaders of Simeon's wealthy clans, 39 who
traveled to the region of Gedor, in the east part of the valley, seeking pastureland for their
flocks. 40 They found lush pastures there, and the land was quiet and peaceful.
Some of Ham's descendants had been living in the region of Gedor. 41 But during the **4:40** Judg 18:7-10
reign of King Hezekiah of Judah, the leaders of Simeon invaded it and completely
destroyed* the homes of the descendants of Ham and of the Meunites. They killed everyone
who lived there and took the land for themselves, because they wanted its good pastureland
for their flocks. 42 Five hundred of these invaders from the tribe of Simeon went to Mount **4:42** Gen 36:8-9

4:13 As in some Greek manuscripts and Latin Vulgate; Hebrew lacks *and Meonothai.* **4:14** Or *Joab, the father of Ge-harashim.* **4:33** As in some Greek manuscripts (see also Josh 19:8); Hebrew reads *Baal.* **4:41** The Hebrew term used here refers to the complete consecration of things or people to the LORD, either by destroying them or by giving them as an offering.

4:13 Othniel was Israel's first judge. He reformed the nation and brought peace to the land. His story is found in Judges 1:9-15 and 3:5-11.

4:15 Caleb was one of the 12 scouts sent into the Promised Land by Moses. He and Joshua were the only two scouts to return with a positive report, believing in God's promise to help the Israelites conquer the land. Caleb's story is told in Numbers 13–14 and Joshua 14–15. His Profile is found in Numbers 14.

WHO'S WHO IN THE BIBLE
Here are some of the people mentioned in this genealogy who are also mentioned elsewhere in the Bible. The writer of Chronicles reproduced a thorough history of Israel in one list of people. Many of the people in this list have exciting stories that can be traced through the Bible. Look up some of the names here that intrigue you. You may be surprised at what you discover!

Name	Key Life Lesson	Reference
Adam (1:1)	Our sins have far greater implications than we realize.	Genesis 2, 3
Noah (1:4)	Great rewards come from obeying God.	Genesis 6—9
Abraham (1:27)	Faith alone makes one right in God's eyes.	Genesis 11:26—25:10
Isaac (1:28)	Seeking peace brings true respect.	Genesis 21—35
Esau (1:35)	It is never too late to put away bitterness and forgive.	Genesis 25:20—36:43
Amalek (1:36)	There are evil men and nations who seek to harm God's people.	Exodus 17:8–16
Israel (Jacob) (2:1)	While our sins may haunt us, God will honor our faith.	Genesis 25:20—50:13
Judah (2:3)	God can change the hearts of even the most wicked people.	Genesis 37—50
Tamar (2:4)	God works his purposes even through sinful events.	Genesis 38
Perez (2:5)	Your background does not matter to God.	Genesis 38:27–30
Boaz (2:12)	Those who are kind to others will receive kindness themselves.	The book of Ruth
Jesse (2:13)	Never take lightly the impact you may have on your children.	1 Samuel 16
David (2:15)	True greatness is having a heart for God.	The books of 1 and 2 Samuel
Joab (2:16)	Those who seek power die with nothing.	2 Samuel 2:13—1 Kings 2:34
Amnon (3:1)	Giving in to lust leads only to tragedy.	2 Samuel 13
Absalom (3:2)	Those seeking to oust a God-appointed leader will have a difficult battle.	2 Samuel 13—18
Adonijah (3:2)	God must determine what is rightfully ours.	1 Kings 1—2
Bathsheba (3:5)	One wrong act does not disqualify us from accomplishing things for God.	2 Samuel 11, 12; 1 Kings 1, 2
Solomon (3:5)	Man's wisdom is foolishness without God.	1 Kings 1—11
Reuben (5:1)	What is gained from a moment of passion is only perceived; what is lost is real and permanent.	Genesis 35:22; 37; 49:3, 4
Aaron (6:3)	Don't expect God's leaders to be perfect, but don't let them get away with sin either.	Exodus 4—Numbers 20
Nadab (6:3)	Pretending to be God's representative is dangerous business.	Leviticus 10
Eleazar (6:3)	Those who are consistent in their faith are the best models to follow.	Numbers 20:25–29; 26—34; Joshua 24:33
Korah (6:22)	Rebelling against God's leaders is rebelling against God and will always be unsuccessful.	Numbers 16
Joshua (7:27)	Real courage comes from God.	The book of Joshua
Saul (8:33)	Those who say they follow God but don't live like it waste their God-given potential.	1 Samuel 8—31
Jonathan (8:33)	True friends always think of the other person, not just themselves.	1 Samuel 14—31

Seir, led by Pelatiah, Neariah, Rephaiah, and Uzziel—all sons of Ishi. 43 They destroyed the
few Amalekites who had survived, and they have lived there ever since.

Descendants of Reuben

5 The oldest son of Israel* was Reuben. But since he dishonored his father by sleeping
with one of his father's concubines, his birthright was given to the sons of his brother
Joseph. For this reason, Reuben is not listed in the genealogy as the firstborn son. 2 It was
the descendants of Judah that became the most powerful tribe and provided a ruler for
the nation,* but the birthright belonged to Joseph.

3 The sons of Reuben, the oldest son of Israel, were Hanoch, Pallu, Hezron, and Carmi.
4 The descendants of Joel were Shemaiah, Gog, Shimei, 5 Micah, Reaiah, Baal, 6 and
Beerah.
Beerah was the leader of the Reubenites when they were taken into captivity by
King Tiglath-pileser* of Assyria.
7 Beerah's relatives are listed in their genealogy by their clans: Jeiel (the leader),
Zechariah, 8 and Bela son of Azaz, son of Shema, son of Joel.
These Reubenites lived in the area that stretches from Aroer to Nebo and Baal-
meon. 9 And since they had so many cattle in the land of Gilead, they spread eastward toward the edge of the desert that stretches to the Euphrates River.
10 During the reign of Saul, the Reubenites defeated the Hagrites in battle. Then
they moved into the Hagrite settlements all along the eastern edge of Gilead.

Descendants of Gad

11 Across from the Reubenites in the land of Bashan lived the descendants of Gad,
who were spread as far east as Salecah. 12 Joel was the leader in the land of Bashan,
and Shapham was second-in-command, along with Janai and Shaphat.
13 Their relatives, the leaders of seven other clans, were Michael, Meshullam, Sheba,
Jorai, Jacan, Zia, and Eber. 14 These were all descendants of Abihail son of Huri,
son of Jaroah, son of Gilead, son of Michael, son of Jeshishai, son of Jahdo, son of
Buz. 15 Ahi son of Abdiel, son of Guni, was the leader of their clans.

16 The Gadites lived in the land of Gilead, in Bashan and its villages, and throughout the
Sharon Plain. 17 All of these were listed in the genealogical records during the days of
King Jotham of Judah and King Jeroboam of Israel.

The Tribes East of the Jordan

18 There were 44,760 skilled warriors in the armies of Reuben, Gad, and the half-tribe of
Manasseh. They were all skilled in combat and armed with shields, swords, and bows.
19 They waged war against the Hagrites, the Jeturites, the Naphishites, and the Nodabites.
20 They cried out to God during the battle, and he answered their prayer because they
trusted in him. So the Hagrites and all their allies were defeated. 21 The plunder taken
from the Hagrites included 50,000 camels, 250,000 sheep, 2,000 donkeys, and 100,000
captives. 22 Many of the Hagrites were killed in the battle because God was fighting
against them. So they lived in their land until they were taken away into exile.

5:1 *Israel* is the name that God gave to Jacob. **5:2** Or *and from Judah came a prince.* **5:6** Hebrew *Tilgath-pilneser,* a variant name for Tiglath-pileser; also in 5:26.

4:43 1 Sam 15:7-8; 30:16-17
5:1 Gen 29:32; 35:22; 48:15-22; 49:4; 1 Chr 2:1
5:2 Gen 49:8-10, 12; Mic 5:2; Matt 2:6
5:3 Gen 46:9; Exod 6:14; Num 26:5
5:6 2 Kgs 15:19
5:7-8 Num 32:34; Josh 12:2
5:9 Josh 22:8-9
5:10 1 Chr 5:18-21
5:11 Josh 13:11, 24-28
5:16 1 Chr 27:29
5:17 2 Kgs 14:16, 28; 15:5, 32-33
5:18 Num 1:3
5:19 Gen 25:15; 1 Chr 1:31; 5:10
5:20 2 Chr 14:11-13; Ps 9:10
5:22 Josh 23:10; 2 Kgs 15:29; 17:6; 2 Chr 32:8

5:1 Reuben's sin of incest was recorded for all future generations to read. The purpose of this epitaph was not to smear Reuben's name, but to show that painful memories aren't the only results of sin. The real consequences of sin are ruined lives. As the oldest son, Reuben was the rightful heir to both a double portion of his father's estate and the leadership of Abraham's descendants, who had grown into a large tribe. But his sin stripped away his rights and privileges and destroyed his family. Before you give in to temptation, take a close look at the disastrous consequences sin may produce in your life and the lives of others.

5:2 This ruler from the tribe of Judah refers to David and his royal line and to Jesus the Messiah, David's greatest descendant.

5:18-22 The armies of Reuben, Gad, and Manasseh succeeded in battle because they trusted God. Although they had instinct and skill as soldiers, they prayed and sought God's direction. The natural and developed abilities God gives us are meant to be used for him, but they should never replace our dependence on him. When we trust in our own cleverness, skill, and strength rather than in God, we open the door for pride. When facing difficult situations, seek God's purpose and ask for his guidance and strength. Psalm 20:7 says, "Some nations boast of their armies and weapons, but we boast in the LORD our God."

5:22 The Exile mentioned here refers to the exile of the 10 northern tribes (the northern kingdom of Israel) to Assyria in 722 B.C. These tribes never returned to their homeland. This story is found in 2 Kings 15:29–17:41.

5:23 Deut 3:9 23 The half-tribe of Manasseh spread through the land from Bashan to Baal-hermon,
Senir, and Mount Hermon. They were very numerous. 24 These were the leaders of their
clans: Epher, Ishi, Eliel, Azriel, Jeremiah, Hodaviah, and Jahdiel. Each of these men had
5:25 Exod 34:15 2 Kgs 17:7 a great reputation as a warrior and leader. 25 But they were unfaithful and violated their
covenant with the God of their ancestors. They worshiped the gods of the nations that
5:26 2 Kgs 15:19, 29 God had destroyed. 26 So the God of Israel caused King Pul of Assyria (also known as
Tiglath-pileser) to invade the land and lead away the people of Reuben, Gad, and the
half-tribe of Manasseh as captives. The Assyrians exiled them to Halah, Habor, Hara,
and the Gozan River, where they remain to this day.

The Priestly Line

6:1 Gen 46:11 Exod 6:16-25 **6** The sons of Levi were Gershon, Kohath, and Merari.
2 The descendants of Kohath were Amram, Izhar, Hebron, and Uzziel.
6:3 Lev 10:1 3 The children of Amram were Aaron, Moses, and Miriam.
The sons of Aaron were Nadab, Abihu, Eleazar, and Ithamar.

4 Eleazar was the father of Phinehas.
Phinehas was the father of Abishua.
5 Abishua was the father of Bukki.
Bukki was the father of Uzzi.
6 Uzzi was the father of Zerahiah.
Zerahiah was the father of Meraioth.
7 Meraioth was the father of Amariah.
Amariah was the father of Ahitub.
6:8 Ezra 7:2 8 Ahitub was the father of Zadok.
Zadok was the father of Ahimaaz.
9 Ahimaaz was the father of Azariah.
Azariah was the father of Johanan.
10 Johanan was the father of Azariah, the high priest at the Temple built by Solomon in Jerusalem.
11 Azariah was the father of Amariah.
Amariah was the father of Ahitub.
12 Ahitub was the father of Zadok.
Zadok was the father of Shallum.
13 Shallum was the father of Hilkiah.
Hilkiah was the father of Azariah.
6:15 Neh 12:1 Hag 1:1, 14 Zech 6:11 14 Azariah was the father of Seraiah.
Seraiah was the father of Jehozadak, 15 who went into exile when the LORD sent the people of Judah and Jerusalem into captivity under Nebuchadnezzar.

The Levite Clans

16 The sons of Levi were Gershon,* Kohath, and Merari.
17 The descendants of Gershon included Libni and Shimei.
18 The descendants of Kohath included Amram, Izhar, Hebron, and Uzziel.
6:19 1 Chr 23:21 19 The descendants of Merari included Mahli and Mushi.

6:16 Hebrew *Gershom,* a variant name for Gershon (see 6:1); also in 6:17, 20, 43, 62, 71.

5:24, 25 As warriors and leaders, these men had established excellent reputations for their great skill and leadership qualities. But in God's eyes they failed in the most important quality—being faithful to God. If you try to measure up to society's standards for fame and success, you may neglect your true purpose—to please and obey God. In the end, God alone examines our hearts and determines our final standing.

6:1ff The tribe of Levi was set apart to serve God in the Tabernacle (Numbers 3–4), and later in the Temple (1 Chronicles 23–26). Aaron, Levi's descendant (6:3), became Israel's first high priest. God required all future priests to be descendants of Aaron. The rest of the Levites assisted the priests in various Tabernacle or Temple duties; they taught the people God's Word and encouraged them to obey it.

6:3 The people listed here played major roles in the drama of the Exodus. Aaron's story is found in the books of Exodus, Leviticus, and Numbers. His Profile is found in Exodus 32. Moses was one of the greatest prophets and leaders in Israel's history. His story is found in the books of Exodus, Leviticus, Numbers, and Deuteronomy. His Profile is found in Exodus 14. The story of Miriam, Moses and Aaron's sister, is found in Exodus 2; 15:20, 21; and Numbers 12; 20:1. Her Profile is found in Numbers 13. Nadab and Abihu were killed for disobeying God (Leviticus 10). Eleazar became Israel's high priest after Aaron (Numbers 20:24-28), and Ithamar played an important role in organizing the worship services of the Tabernacle (Numbers 4:28, 33; 7:8).

The following were the Levite clans, listed according to their ancestral descent:

20 The descendants of Gershon were Libni, Jahath, Zimmah, 21 Joah, Iddo, Zerah, and
Jeatherai.

22 The descendants of Kohath were Amminadab, Korah, Assir, 23 Elkanah, Abiasaph,*
Assir, 24 Tahath, Uriel, Uzziah, and Shaul.

25 The descendants of Elkanah were Amasai, Ahimoth, 26 Elkanah, Zophai, Nahath,
27 Eliab, Jeroham, Elkanah, and Samuel.* **6:27** 1 Sam 1:1, 20

28 The sons of Samuel were Joel* (the older) and Abijah (the second). **6:28** 1 Sam 8:2; 1 Chr 6:33

29 The descendants of Merari were Mahli, Libni, Shimei, Uzzah, 30 Shimea, Haggiah,
and Asaiah.

The Temple Musicians

31 David assigned the following men to lead the music at the house of the LORD after he **6:31** 2 Sam 6:17; 1 Chr 15:16-22, 27; 16:4-6
put the Ark there. 32 They ministered with music there at the Tabernacle* until Solomon
built the Temple of the LORD in Jerusalem. Then they carried on their work there,
following all the regulations handed down to them. 33 These are the men who served,
along with their sons:

Heman the musician was from the clan of Kohath. His genealogy was traced back
through Joel, Samuel, 34 Elkanah, Jeroham, Eliel, Toah, 35 Zuph, Elkanah, Mahath,
Amasai, 36 Elkanah, Joel, Azariah, Zephaniah, 37 Tahath, Assir, Abiasaph, Korah,
38 Izhar, Kohath, Levi, and Israel.*

39 Heman's first assistant was Asaph from the clan of Gershon.* Asaph's genealogy
was traced back through Berekiah, Shimea, 40 Michael, Baaseiah, Malkijah,
41 Ethni, Zerah, Adaiah, 42 Ethan, Zimmah, Shimei, 43 Jahath, Gershon, and Levi.

44 Heman's second assistant was Ethan from the clan of Merari. Ethan's genealogy
was traced back through Kishi, Abdi, Malluch, 45 Hashabiah, Amaziah, Hilkiah,
46 Amzi, Bani, Shemer, 47 Mahli, Mushi, Merari, and Levi.

48 Their relatives, also Levites, were appointed to various other tasks in the Tabernacle,
the house of God.

Aaron's Descendants

49 Only Aaron and his descendants served as priests. They presented the offerings on the
altar of burnt offering and the altar of incense, and they performed all the other duties
related to the Most Holy Place. They made atonement for Israel by following all the
commands that Moses, the servant of God, had given them.

50 The descendants of Aaron were Eleazar, Phinehas, Abishua, 51 Bukki, Uzzi, Zera- **6:50** 1 Chr 6:4-8
hiah, 52 Meraioth, Amariah, Ahitub, 53 Zadok, and Ahimaaz.

6:23 Hebrew *Ebiasaph,* a variant name for Abiasaph (also in 6:37); compare parallel text at Exod 6:24. **6:27** As in some Greek manuscripts (see also 6:33-34); Hebrew lacks *and Samuel.* **6:28** As in some Greek manuscripts and the Syriac version (see also 6:33 and 1 Sam 8:2); Hebrew lacks *Joel.* **6:32** Hebrew *the Tabernacle, the Tent of Meeting.* **6:38** *Israel* is the name that God gave to Jacob. **6:39** Hebrew lacks *from the clan of Gershon;* see 6:43.

6:28 When Samuel became God's leader and spokesman, Israel was on the brink of collapse. The last few chapters of the book of Judges give a vivid picture of the moral decay and the resulting decline of the nation. But with God's help, Samuel almost single-handedly brought the nation from ruin to revival. He unified the people by showing them that God was their common Leader and that any nation that focused on him would find and fulfill its true purpose. For the rest of Samuel's story, and to see how he set up rules for governing a nation based on spiritual principles, read the book of 1 Samuel and his Profile in chapter 7.

6:31 David did much to bring music into worship. He established songleaders and choirs to perform regularly at the Temple (chapter 25). As a young man, David was hired to play the harp for King Saul (1 Samuel 16:15-23). He also wrote many of the songs found in the book of Psalms.

6:31ff The builders and craftsmen had completed the Temple, and the priests and Levites had been given their responsibilities for taking care of it. Then it was time for another group of people—the musicians—to exercise their talents for God. Some of those who served with music are recorded here. You don't have to be an ordained minister to have an important place in the body of believers. Builders, craftsmen, worship assistants, choir members, and song leaders all have significant contributions to make. God has given you a unique combination of talents. Use them to serve and honor him.

6:49 Aaron and his descendants strictly followed the details of worship commanded by God through Moses. They did not choose only those commands they *wanted* to obey. Note what happened to Uzzah when important details in handling the Ark of the Covenant were neglected (13:6-10). We should not try to obey God selectively, choosing those commands we will obey and those we will ignore. God's Word has authority over every aspect of our lives, not just selected areas.

6:49 For more information on priests, see the note on Leviticus 8:1ff.

Territory for the Levites

6:54 Josh 21:4, 10 54 This is a record of the towns and territory assigned by means of sacred lots to the
6:55-56 Josh 14:13; 15:13 descendants of Aaron who were from the clan of Kohath. 55 This included Hebron and
its surrounding pasturelands in Judah, 56 but the fields and outlying areas were given to
Caleb son of Jephunneh. 57 So the descendants of Aaron were given the following towns,
each with its surrounding pasturelands: Hebron (a city of refuge), Libnah, Jattir, Eshte-
6:58 Josh 10:3 moa, 58 Holon,* Debir, 59 Ain,* Juttah,* and Beth-shemesh. 60 And from the territory of
Benjamin they were given Gibeon,* Geba, Alemeth, and Anathoth, each with its
6:61 Josh 21:5 1 Chr 6:66-70 pasturelands. So a total of thirteen towns was given to the descendants of Aaron. 61 The
remaining descendants of Kohath received ten towns from the territory of the half-tribe
of Manasseh by means of sacred lots.

62 The descendants of Gershon received by sacred lots thirteen towns from the
territories of Issachar, Asher, Naphtali, and from the Bashan area of Manasseh, east of
the Jordan.

6:63 Josh 21:7, 34-40 63 The descendants of Merari received by sacred lots twelve towns from the territories
of Reuben, Gad, and Zebulun.

6:64 Num 35:1-8 Josh 21:3, 41-42 1 Chr 6:57-60 64 So the people of Israel assigned all these towns and pasturelands to the Levites.
65 The towns in the territories of Judah, Simeon, and Benjamin, mentioned above, were
also assigned by means of sacred lots.

6:66 Josh 21:20-26 66 The descendants of Kohath received from the territory of Ephraim these towns, each
with its surrounding pasturelands: 67 Shechem (a city of refuge in the hill country of
Ephraim), Gezer, 68 Jokmeam, Beth-horon, 69 Aijalon, and Gath-rimmon. 70 The remaining descendants of Kohath were assigned these towns from the territory of the half-tribe
of Manasseh: Aner and Bileam, each with its pasturelands.

71 The descendants of Gershon received from the territory of the half-tribe of Manasseh
the town of Golan in Bashan with its pasturelands and Ashtaroth with its pasturelands.
72 From the territory of Issachar, they were given Kedesh, Daberath, 73 Ramoth, and Anem,
with their pasturelands. 74 From the territory of Asher, they received Mashal, Abdon,
75 Hukok, and Rehob, each with its pasturelands. 76 From the territory of Naphtali, they
were given Kedesh in Galilee, Hammon, and Kiriathaim, each with its pasturelands.

77 The remaining descendants of Merari received from the territory of Zebulun the
towns of Jokneam, Kartah,* Rimmono, and Tabor, each with its pasturelands. 78 From
the territory of Reuben, east of the Jordan River opposite Jericho, they received Bezer
(a desert town), Jahaz,* 79 Kedemoth, and Mephaath, each with its pasturelands. 80 And
from the territory of Gad, they received Ramoth in Gilead, Mahanaim, 81 Heshbon, and
Jazer, each with its pasturelands.

Descendants of Issachar

7:1 Gen 46:13 7 The four sons of Issachar were Tola, Puah, Jashub, and Shimron.
7:2 2 Sam 24:1-9 2 The sons of Tola were Uzzi, Rephaiah, Jeriel, Jahmai, Ibsam, and Shemuel. Each
of them was the leader of an ancestral clan. At the time of King David, the total number of men available for military service from these families was 22,600.
3 The son of Uzzi was Izrahiah. The sons of Izrahiah were Michael, Obadiah, Joel, and
Isshiah. These five became the leaders of clans. 4 The total number of men available

6:58 As in parallel text at Josh 21:15; Hebrew reads *Hilen.* **6:59a** As in parallel text at Josh 21:16; Hebrew reads *Ashan.* **6:59b** As in Syriac version (see also Josh 21:16); Hebrew lacks *Juttah.* **6:60** As in parallel text at Josh 21:17; Hebrew lacks *Gibeon.* **6:77** As in Greek version (see also Josh 21:34); Hebrew lacks *Jokneam, Kartah.* **6:78** Hebrew *Jahzah,* a variant name for Jahaz.

6:54 The tribe of Levi was not given a specific area of land as were the other tribes. Instead, the Levites were to live throughout the land in order to aid the people of *every* tribe in their worship of God. Thus, the Levites were given towns or pasturelands within the allotted areas of the other tribes (Joshua 13:14, 33).

6:57ff God had told the tribes to designate specific cities to be cities of refuge (Numbers 35). These cities were to provide refuge for a person who accidentally killed someone. This instruction may have seemed unimportant when it was given—the Israelites hadn't even entered the Promised Land. Sometimes God gives us instructions that do not seem relevant to us at the moment. But later we can see the importance of those instructions. Don't discard the lessons of the Bible because certain details seem irrelevant. Obey God now—in the future you will have a clearer understanding of the reasons for his instructions.

6:61 The Israelites cast lots in order to take the decision-making process out of man's hands and put it into God's hands. Casting lots was like drawing straws or throwing dice. Lots were cast only after seeking God's guidance in prayer. (For more information on casting lots, see the note on Joshua 18:8.)

for military service among their descendants was 36,000, for all five of them had
many wives and many sons.

5 The total number of men available for military service from all the clans of the tribe of
Issachar was 87,000. All of them were listed in their tribal genealogy.

Descendants of Benjamin

6 Three of Benjamin's sons were Bela, Beker, and Jediael. **7:6** 1 Chr 8:1-40
7 The sons of Bela were Ezbon, Uzzi, Uzziel, Jerimoth, and Iri. These five warriors were the
leaders of clans. The total number of men available for military service among their
descendants was 22,034. All of them were listed in their family genealogy.
8 The sons of Beker were Zemirah, Joash, Eliezer, Elioenai, Omri, Jeremoth, Abijah,
Anathoth, and Alemeth. 9 According to their family genealogy, there were 20,200
men available for military service among their descendants, in addition to their clan
leaders.
10 The son of Jediael was Bilhan. The sons of Bilhan were Jeush, Benjamin, Ehud,
Kenaanah, Zethan, Tarshish, and Ahishahar. 11 They were the leaders of the clans of
Jediael, and their descendants included 17,200 men available for military service.
12 The sons of Ir were Shuppim and Huppim. Hushim was the son of Aher.

Descendants of Naphtali

13 The sons of Naphtali were Jahzeel,* Guni, Jezer, and Shillem.* They were all **7:13** Gen 30:8
descendants of Jacob's wife Bilhah.

Descendants of Manasseh

14 The sons of Manasseh, born to his Aramean concubine, were Asriel and Makir. **7:14** Gen 50:23; Num 26:29-30
Makir was the father of Gilead.

15 Makir found wives for Huppim and Shuppim. Makir's sister was named
Maacah. One of his descendants was Zelophehad, who had only daughters.
16 Makir's wife, Maacah, gave birth to a son whom she named Peresh. His brother's
name was Sheresh. The sons of Peresh were Ulam and Rakem. 17 The son of
Ulam was Bedan. All these were considered Gileadites, descendants of Makir
son of Manasseh.
18 Makir's sister Hammoleketh gave birth to Ishhod, Abiezer, and Mahlah.
19 The sons of Shemida were Ahian, Shechem, Likhi, and Aniam.

Descendants of Ephraim

20 The descendants of Ephraim were Shuthelah, Bered, Tahath, Eleadah, Tahath, **7:20** Num 26:35-36
21 Zabad, and Shuthelah.

Ephraim's sons Ezer and Elead were killed trying to steal livestock from the local
farmers near Gath. 22 Their father, Ephraim, mourned for them a long time, and his
relatives came to comfort him. 23 Afterward Ephraim slept with his wife, and she
became pregnant and gave birth to a son. Ephraim named him Beriah* because of
the tragedy his family had suffered.

24 Ephraim had a daughter named Sheerah. She built the towns of Lower and **7:24** Josh 16:3, 5
Upper Beth-horon and Uzzen-sheerah.
25 Ephraim's line of descent was Rephah, Resheph, Telah, Tahan, 26 Ladan, Ammihud, **7:25-27** Exod 17:9-14; 24:13
Elishama, 27 Nun, and Joshua.

28 The descendants of Ephraim lived in the territory that included Bethel and its surrounding towns to the south, Naaran to the east, Gezer and its villages to the west, and Shechem
and its surrounding villages to the north as far as Ayyah and its towns. 29 Along the border **7:29** Josh 17:7-11
of Manasseh were the towns of Beth-shan,* Taanach, Megiddo, Dor, and their surrounding
villages. The descendants of Joseph son of Israel* lived in these towns.

7:13a As in parallel text at Gen 46:24; Hebrew reads *Jahziel,* a variant name for Jahzeel. **7:13b** As in some Hebrew and Greek manuscripts (see also Gen 46:24; Num 26:49); most Hebrew manuscripts read *Shallum.* **7:23** *Beriah* sounds like a Hebrew term meaning "tragedy" or "misfortune." **7:29a** Hebrew *Beth-shean,* a variant name for Beth-shan. **7:29b** *Israel* is the name that God gave to Jacob.

7:27 Joshua was one of Israel's great leaders, leading the people into the Promised Land. His story is told in the book of Joshua. His Profile is found in Joshua 2.

Descendants of Asher

7:30 Gen 46:17 Num 26:44-46

30 The sons of Asher were Imnah, Ishvah, Ishvi, and Beriah. They had a sister named
Serah.
31 The sons of Beriah were Heber and Malkiel (the father of Birzaith).
32 The sons of Heber were Japhlet, Shomer, and Hotham. They had a sister named Shua.
33 The sons of Japhlet were Pasach, Bimhal, and Ashvath.
34 The sons of Shomer were Ahi, Rohgah, Hubbah, and Aram.
35 The sons of his brother Helem* were Zophah, Imna, Shelesh, and Amal.
36 The sons of Zophah were Suah, Harnepher, Shual, Beri, Imrah, 37 Bezer, Hod,
Shamma, Shilshah, Ithran,* and Beera.
38 The sons of Jether were Jephunneh, Pispah, and Ara.
39 The sons of Ulla were Arah, Hanniel, and Rizia.

40 Each of these descendants of Asher was the head of an ancestral clan. They were all
skilled warriors and prominent leaders. There were 26,000 men available for military
service among the descendants listed in their tribal genealogy.

Descendants of Benjamin

8:1 Gen 46:21 1 Chr 7:6-12

8 The sons of Benjamin, in order of age, included Bela (the oldest), Ashbel, Aharah,
2 Nohah, and Rapha.
3 The sons of Bela were Addar, Gera, Abihud,* 4 Abishua, Naaman, Ahoah, 5 Gera,
Shephuphan, and Huram.
6 The sons of Ehud, leaders of the clans living at Geba, were driven out and moved to
Manahath. 7 Ehud's sons were Naaman, Ahijah, and Gera. Gera, the father of Uzza
and Ahihud, led them when they moved.
8 After Shaharaim divorced his wives Hushim and Baara, he had children in the land
of Moab. 9 Hodesh, his new wife, gave birth to Jobab, Zibia, Mesha, Malcam,
10 Jeuz, Sakia, and Mirmah. These sons all became the leaders of clans.

8:12 Ezra 2:33 Neh 6:2; 7:37; 11:35

8:13 Josh 10:12; 11:22

11 Shaharaim's wife Hushim had already given birth to Abitub and Elpaal. 12 The sons
of Elpaal were Eber, Misham, Shemed (who built Ono and Lod and their villages),
13 Beriah, and Shema. They were the leaders of the clans living in Aijalon, and they
drove out the inhabitants of Gath.

14 Ahio, Shashak, Jeremoth, 15 Zebadiah, Arad, Eder, 16 Michael, Ishpah, and Joha were
the sons of Beriah.
17 Zebadiah, Meshullam, Hizki, Heber, 18 Ishmerai, Izliah, and Jobab were the sons of
Elpaal.
19 Jakim, Zicri, Zabdi, 20 Elienai, Zillethai, Eliel, 21 Adaiah, Beraiah, and Shimrath were
the sons of Shimei.
22 Ishpan, Eber, Eliel, 23 Abdon, Zicri, Hanan, 24 Hananiah, Elam, Anthothijah, 25 Iphde-
iah, and Penuel were the sons of Shashak.
26 Shamsherai, Shehariah, Athaliah, 27 Jaareshiah, Elijah, and Zicri were the sons of Jeroham.

28 These were the leaders of the ancestral clans, and they were listed in their tribal
genealogy. They all lived in Jerusalem.

The Family of Saul

8:29 Josh 9:3

29 Jeiel* (the father of* Gibeon) lived in Gibeon. His wife's name was Maacah, 30 and
his oldest son was named Abdon. Jeiel's other sons were Zur, Kish, Baal, Ner,*
Nadab, 31 Gedor, Ahio, Zechariah,* 32 and Mikloth, who was the father of Shimeam.*
All these families lived near each other in Jerusalem.

7:35 Possibly another name for *Hotham;* compare 7:32. **7:37** Possibly another name for *Jether;* compare 7:38. **8:3** Possibly *Gera the father of Ehud;* compare 8:6. **8:29a** As in some Greek manuscripts (see also 9:35); Hebrew lacks *Jeiel.* **8:29b** Or *the founder of.* **8:30** As in some Greek manuscripts (see also 9:36); Hebrew lacks *Ner.* **8:31** As in parallel text at 9:37; Hebrew reads *Zeker,* a variant name for Zechariah.

8:8-10 These verses list Shaharaim's children by Hodesh after he had divorced his first two wives, Hushim and Baara. Divorce and polygamy are sometimes recorded in the Old Testament without critical comments. This does not mean that God takes divorce lightly. Malachi 2:15, 16 says to "remain loyal to the wife of your youth. 'For I hate divorce!' says the LORD, the God of Israel." Jesus explained that although divorce was allowed, it was not God's will: "Moses permitted divorce as a concession to your hard-hearted wickedness, but it was not what God had originally intended" (Matthew 19:8). Don't assume that God approves of an act because it isn't vigorously condemned in every related Bible reference.

33 Ner was the father of Kish. Kish was the father of Saul. Saul was the father of
Jonathan, Malkishua, Abinadab, and Eshbaal.
34 Jonathan was the father of Meribbaal. Meribbaal was the father of Micah. 35 Micah
was the father of Pithon, Melech, Tahrea,* and Ahaz.
36 Ahaz was the father of Jadah.*
Jadah was the father of Alemeth, Azmaveth, and Zimri.
Zimri was the father of Moza.
37 Moza was the father of Binea.
Binea was the father of Rephaiah.*
Rephaiah was the father of Eleasah.
Eleasah was the father of Azel.

38 Azel had six sons: Azrikam, Bokeru, Ishmael, Sheariah, Obadiah, and Hanan. These
were the sons of Azel.
39 Azel's brother Eshek had three sons: Ulam (the oldest), Jeush (the second), and
Eliphelet (the third). 40 The sons of Ulam were all skilled warriors and expert
archers. They had many sons and grandsons—150 in all.

All these were descendants of Benjamin.

9 All Israel was listed in the genealogical record in *The Book of the Kings of Israel.*

3. Returnees from exile in Babylon

The People in Jerusalem

The people of Judah were exiled to Babylon because they were unfaithful to the LORD.
2 The first to return to their property in their former towns were common people. With
them came some of the priests, Levites, and Temple assistants. 3 People from the tribes
of Judah, Benjamin, Ephraim, and Manasseh came and settled in Jerusalem.

4 One family that returned was that of Uthai son of Ammihud, son of Omri, son of
Imri, son of Bani, a descendant of Perez son of Judah.
5 Others returned from the Shilonite clan, including Asaiah (the oldest) and his sons.
6 From the Zerahite clan, Jeuel returned with his relatives.
In all, 690 families from the tribe of Judah returned.

7 From the tribe of Benjamin came Sallu son of Meshullam, son of Hodaviah, son of
Hassenuah; 8 Ibneiah son of Jeroham; Elah son of Uzzi, son of Micri; Meshullam
son of Shephatiah, son of Reuel, son of Ibnijah.
9 These men were all leaders of clans, and they were listed in their tribal genealogy. In
all, 956 families from the tribe of Benjamin returned.

The Returning Priests

10 Among the priests who returned were Jedaiah, Jehoiarib, Jakin, 11 Azariah son of

8:33 1 Sam 9:1; 14:49-50; 1 Chr 9:39-44
8:34 2 Sam 4:4
9:1 1 Chr 5:25
9:2 Ezra 2:43, 58, 70; 8:20; Neh 11:3-22
9:4 Gen 46:12
9:9 Neh 11:8
9:10 Neh 11:10-14

8:32 As in parallel text at 9:38; Hebrew reads *Shimeah,* a variant name for Shimeam. **8:35** As in parallel text at 9:41; Hebrew reads *Tarea,* a variant name for Tahrea. **8:36** As in parallel text at 9:42; Hebrew reads *Jehoaddah,* a variant name for Jadah. **8:37** As in parallel text at 9:43; Hebrew reads *Raphah,* a variant name for Rephaiah.

8:33 Saul, Israel's first king, was very inconsistent. His story is found in 1 Samuel 9–31, and his Profile is in 1 Samuel 12. Saul's son Jonathan was the opposite. Although Jonathan was the rightful heir to the throne, he realized that David was God's choice to be Israel's next king. Instead of being jealous, Jonathan was David's friend and even helped him escape from Saul's attempts at murder. Jonathan's story is told in 1 Samuel 14–31. His Profile is found in 1 Samuel 20.

9:1 Although not every person in Judah was unfaithful, the entire nation was carried away into captivity. Everyone was affected by the sin of a few. Even if we don't participate in a certain widespread wrongdoing, we will still be affected by those who do. It is not enough to say, "I didn't do it." We must speak out against the sins of our society.

9:1ff Chronologically, this chapter could be placed at the end of 2 Chronicles because it records the names of the exiles who returned from the Babylonian captivity. The writer included it here to show his concern for their need, as a nation, to return to what made them great in the first place—obedience to God.

9:10, 11 When we think of doing God's work, usually preaching, teaching, singing, and other kinds of up-front leadership come to mind. Azariah, however, was chief officer in charge of the house of God, and he was singled out for special mention. Whatever role you have in church, it is important to God. He appreciates your service and the attitude you have as you do it.

Hilkiah, son of Meshullam, son of Zadok, son of Meraioth, son of Ahitub. Azariah
was the chief officer of the house of God.
12 Other returning priests were Adaiah son of Jeroham, son of Pashhur, son of
Malkijah, and Maasai son of Adiel, son of Jahzerah, son of Meshullam, son of
Meshillemith, son of Immer.
13 In all, 1,760 priests returned. They were heads of clans and very able men. They were
responsible for ministering at the house of God.

The Returning Levites

9:14 14 The Levites who returned were Shemaiah son of Hasshub, son of Azrikam, son of
Neh 11:15-19 Hashabiah, a descendant of Merari; 15 Bakbakkar; Heresh; Galal; Mattaniah son of
Mica, son of Zicri, son of Asaph; 16 Obadiah son of Shemaiah, son of Galal, son of
Jeduthun; and Berekiah son of Asa, son of Elkanah, who lived in the area of
9:17 Netophah.
Ezek 46:1-2 17 The gatekeepers who returned were Shallum, Akkub, Talmon, Ahiman, and their
relatives. Shallum was the chief gatekeeper. 18 Prior to this time, they were
responsible for the King's Gate on the east side. These men served as gatekeepers
for the camps of the Levites. 19 Shallum was the son of Kore, a descendant of
Abiasaph,* from the clan of Korah. He and his relatives, the Korahites, were
responsible for guarding the entrance to the sanctuary, just as their ancestors had
guarded the Tabernacle in the camp of the LORD.
9:20 20 Phinehas son of Eleazar had been in charge of the gatekeepers in earlier times,
Num 25:7-13 and the LORD had been with him. 21 And later Zechariah son of Meshelemiah had
9:21 1 Chr 26:2, 14 been responsible for guarding the entrance to the Tabernacle.*

22 In all, there were 212 gatekeepers in those days, and they were listed by genealogies
in their villages. David and Samuel the seer had appointed their ancestors because they
were reliable men. 23 These gatekeepers and their descendants, by their divisions, were
responsible for guarding the entrance to the house of the LORD, the house that was
formerly a tent. 24 The gatekeepers were stationed on all four sides—east, west, north,
9:25 and south. 25 From time to time, their relatives in the villages came to share their duties
2 Kgs 11:5, 7 2 Chr 23:8 for seven-day periods.
26 The four chief gatekeepers, all Levites, were in an office of great trust, for they were
9:27 responsible for the rooms and treasuries at the house of God. 27 They would spend the
1 Chr 23:30-32 night around the house of God, since it was their duty to guard it. It was also their job to
open the gates every morning.
28 Some of the gatekeepers were assigned to care for the various utensils used in
9:29 worship. They checked them in and out to avoid any loss. 29 Others were responsible for
1 Chr 23:29 the furnishings, the items in the sanctuary, and the supplies such as choice flour, wine,
9:30 olive oil, incense, and spices. 30 But it was the priests who prepared the spices and
Exod 30:23-25 incense. 31 Mattithiah, a Levite and the oldest son of Shallum the Korahite, was entrusted
9:32 with baking the bread used in the offerings. 32 And some members of the clan of Kohath
Lev 24:5-8 were in charge of preparing the bread to be set on the table each Sabbath day.

9:19 Hebrew *Ebiasaph,* a variant name for Abiasaph; compare Exod 6:24. **9:21** Hebrew *Tent of Meeting.* **9:35** Or *the founder of.*

9:17, 18 Gatekeepers guarded the four main entrances to the Temple and opened the gates each morning for those who wanted to worship. In addition, they did other day-to-day chores to keep the Temple running smoothly—cleaning, preparing the offerings for sacrifice, and accounting for the gifts designated to the Temple (9:22-32).

Gatekeepers had to be reliable, honest, and trustworthy. The people in our churches who handle the offerings and care for the materials and functions of the building follow in a great tradition, and we should honor them for their reliability and service.

9:22-32 The priests put a great deal of time and care into worship. Not only did they perform rather complicated tasks (described in Leviticus 1–9); they also took care of many pieces of equipment. Everything relating to worship was carefully prepared and maintained so they and all the people could enter worship with their minds and hearts focused on God.

In our busy world, it is easy to rush into our one-hour-a-week worship services without preparing ourselves for worship beforehand. We reflect and worry about the week's problems; we pray about whatever comes into our minds; and we do not meditate on the words we are singing. But God wants our worship to be conducted "properly and in order" (1 Corinthians 14:40). Just as we prepare to meet a business associate or invited guests, we should carefully prepare to meet our King in worship.

33 The musicians, all prominent Levites, lived at the Temple. They were exempt from **9:33** 1 Chr 6:31-47;
other responsibilities there since they were on duty at all hours. 34 All these men lived in 25:1-31
Jerusalem. They were the heads of Levite families and were listed as prominent leaders Ps 134:1
in their tribal genealogy.

King Saul's Family Tree

35 Jeiel (the father of* Gibeon) lived in Gibeon. His wife's name was Maacah, 36 and **9:35** 1 Chr 8:29-32
his oldest son was named Abdon. Jeiel's other sons were Zur, Kish, Baal, Ner,
Nadab, 37 Gedor, Ahio, Zechariah, and Mikloth. 38 Mikloth was the father of
Shimeam. All these families lived near each other in Jerusalem.
39 Ner was the father of Kish. Kish was the father of Saul. Saul was the father of **9:39** 1 Chr 8:33-38
Jonathan, Malkishua, Abinadab, and Eshbaal.
40 Jonathan was the father of Meribbaal. Meribbaal was the father of Micah. 41 The **9:41** 1 Chr 8:35-37
sons of Micah were Pithon, Melech, Tahrea, and Ahaz.*
42 Ahaz was the father of Jadah.*
Jadah was the father of Alemeth, Azmaveth, and Zimri.
Zimri was the father of Moza.
43 Moza was the father of Binea.
Binea's son was Rephaiah.
Rephaiah's son was Eleasah.
Eleasah's son was Azel.
44 Azel had six sons, and their names were Azrikam, Bokeru, Ishmael, Sheariah,
Obadiah, and Hanan. These were the sons of Azel.

B. THE REIGN OF DAVID (10:1—29:30)

David becomes king over all Israel and captures the city of Jerusalem. God promises blessings to him and the nation, but David is not allowed to build the Temple. Instead, he begins to make preparations for its construction. Although stumbling and falling occasionally, David walks step by step with God, sincerely wanting to be obedient. Through David's successes and his failures, we learn the importance of giving our whole heart to God and letting him be the focus of our life, striving each day to be consistent in our obedience to his will.

1. David becomes king over all of Israel

The Death of King Saul

10 Now the Philistines attacked Israel, forcing the Israelites to flee. Many were slaugh- **10:1** 1 Sam 31:1-13
tered on the slopes of Mount Gilboa. 2 The Philistines closed in on Saul and his sons, **10:2** 1 Sam 31:2, 4
and they killed three of his sons—Jonathan, Abinadab, and Malkishua. 3 The fighting grew
very fierce around Saul, and the Philistine archers caught up with him and wounded him
severely. 4 Saul groaned to his armor bearer, "Take your sword and run me through before
these pagan Philistines come and humiliate me." But his armor bearer was afraid and would
not do it. So Saul took his own sword and fell on it. 5 When his armor bearer realized that
Saul was dead, he fell on his own sword and died. 6 So Saul and his three sons died there
together, bringing his dynasty to an end.
7 When the Israelites in the Jezreel Valley saw that their army had been routed and that
Saul and his sons were dead, they abandoned their towns and fled. So the Philistines
moved in and occupied their towns.
8 The next day when the Philistines went out to strip the dead, they found the bodies
of Saul and his sons on Mount Gilboa. 9 So they stripped off Saul's armor and cut off his **10:9** 1 Sam 31:9
head. Then they proclaimed the news of Saul's death before their idols and to the people

9:41 As in Syriac version and Latin Vulgate (see also 8:35); Hebrew lacks *and Ahaz.* **9:42** As in some Hebrew manuscripts and Greek version (see also 8:36); Hebrew reads *Jarah.*

9:33, 34 Worship was the primary focus of many Israelites, whose vocation centered on the house of the Lord. Worship (appreciating God for his nature and worth) should occupy the core of our lives and not just a few minutes once a week. We, too, can worship at any time if we stay aware of God's presence and guidance in all situations and if we maintain an attitude of serving him. Build your life around the worship of God rather than making worship just another activity in a busy schedule.

10:1 The chronology of chapters 1–9 covers Israelite history from Creation to the exile in Babylon (586 B.C.). At this point, the narrative goes back to the beginning of Israel's kingdom period, picking up with Israel's first king, Saul. First Chronicles begins with Saul's death. To learn about his reign, read 1 Samuel.

throughout the land of Philistia. 10 They placed his armor in the temple of their gods, and
they fastened his head to the wall in the temple of Dagon.
11 But when the people of Jabesh-gilead heard what the Philistines had done to Saul,
12 their warriors went out and brought the bodies of Saul and his three sons back to
Jabesh. Then they buried their remains beneath the oak tree at Jabesh, and they fasted
for seven days.
13 So Saul died because he was unfaithful to the LORD. He failed to obey the LORD's
command, and he even consulted a medium 14 instead of asking the LORD for guidance.
So the LORD killed him and turned his kingdom over to David son of Jesse.

10:13 Lev 19:31; 1 Sam 13:13-14; 15:23; 28:7
10:14 1 Sam 15:28; 1 Chr 12:23

David Becomes King of All Israel

11 Then all Israel went to David at Hebron and told him, "We are all members of your
family. 2 For a long time, even while Saul was our king, you were the one who
really led Israel. And the LORD your God has told you, 'You will be the shepherd of my
people Israel. You will be their leader.'" 3 So there at Hebron David made a covenant
with the leaders of Israel before the LORD. They anointed him king of Israel, just as the
LORD had promised through Samuel.

11:1-3 //2 Sam 5:1-3
11:2 2 Sam 5:2; 7:7
11:3 1 Sam 16:1-13

David Captures Jerusalem

4 Then David and all Israel went to Jerusalem (or Jebus, as it used to be called), where
the Jebusites, original inhabitants of the land, lived. 5 The people of Jebus said to David,
"You will never get in here!" But David captured the fortress of Zion, now called the
City of David.
6 David had said to his troops, "Whoever leads the attack against the Jebusites will
become the commander of my armies!" And Joab, the son of David's sister Zeruiah, led
the attack, so he became the commander of David's armies.
7 David made the fortress his home, and that is why it is called the City of David. 8 He

11:4-9 //2 Sam 5:6-10
11:4 Josh 15:8, 63; Judg 1:21
11:6 2 Sam 8:16

10:10 Dagon, the most important god of the Philistines, was believed to bring rain and provide rich harvests. The Philistines built temples to him when they settled in the grain-producing land of Canaan. In times of drought, people begged Dagon for pity, even to the point of sacrificing their children in his temples. In times of plenty, the temples were used for twisted forms of entertainment, such as the humiliation of captives (see Judges 16:23-30). But Dagon, like the other pagan gods, was powerless against the one true God (1 Samuel 5:1-7).

10:11, 12 The actions of the valiant warriors who brought back and buried the bodies of King Saul and his sons should encourage us to respect our God-given leaders. David showed respect for Saul's position, even when Saul was chasing him to kill him (1 Samuel 26). How easy it is to be critical of those in authority over us, focusing only on their weaknesses. We cannot excuse sin, but we should respect the positions of those in authority, whether at work, at church, or in government. First Thessalonians 5:12, 13 gives instructions for honoring church leaders. Romans 13:1ff gives instructions for relating to government leaders.

10:13, 14 Saul's unfaithfulness was both active and passive; he not only did wrong, but he also *failed to do right*. He actively disobeyed by attempting murder, ignoring God's instructions, and seeking guidance from a medium. He passively disobeyed by neglecting to ask God for guidance as he ran the kingdom. Obedience, too, is both passive and active. It is not enough just to avoid what is wrong; we need to actively pursue what is right.

10:13, 14 In the account in 1 Samuel 28, Saul asked the Lord for guidance but received no answer; this account implies that he did not ask God for help. The answer to this apparent contradiction lies in understanding Saul's motives and the timing of his request to God. His frantic requests came only when he had tried everything his own way. He never went to God unless there was nowhere else to turn. When he finally asked, God refused to answer. Saul sought God only when it suited him, and God rejected him for his constant stubbornness and rebellion.

10:14 Throughout much of Saul's reign, David was forced to hide from him (1 Samuel 19–30). During this time David had opportunities to kill Saul (1 Samuel 24; 26) and to assume the throne that God had promised him (1 Samuel 16:1-13). But David trusted in God's promise that he would be king in God's good timing. It was not up to David to decide when Saul's reign would end. During the battle, God ended Saul's reign just as he had promised.

10:14 Why does this verse say that the Lord killed Saul, when Saul took his own life (1 Samuel 31:3, 4)? God had rejected Saul because of his stubbornness and rebellion (1 Samuel 15:22-26) and had judged him for his sins (1 Samuel 28:16-19). God arranged a defeat in battle so that Saul would die and his kingdom would be taken from his family. If Saul had not taken his own life, the Philistine soldiers would have killed him.

11:1, 2 The details of how David came to power are given more completely in 2 Samuel. Chronicles emphasizes that *God* declared David to be the ruler although he used the efforts of many people, even some of Saul's own family. God is still sovereign over history, directing events to accomplish his will. The books of Chronicles demonstrate that no matter what people may do to try to hinder God's work, God still controls all events and works his will in them.

11:3, 4 David was king over Judah for seven and a half years before he captured Jerusalem. When David was finally anointed king over all Israel, 20 years had passed since Samuel had anointed him (1 Samuel 16:1-13). God's promises are worth waiting for, even when his timetable doesn't match our expectations or desires.

11:4 David chose Jerusalem as his capital for both political and military reasons. Jerusalem was near the center of the kingdom and, because it rested on a tribal border, was in neutral territory. Thus, its location decreased tribal jealousies. Jerusalem also sat on a high ridge, making it difficult to attack. (For more information on the city of Jerusalem, see the note on 2 Samuel 5:6.)

extended the city from the Millo* to the surrounding area, while Joab rebuilt the rest of
Jerusalem. 9And David became more and more powerful, because the LORD Almighty **11:9**
was with him. 2 Sam 3:1

David's Mightiest Men

10These are the leaders of David's mighty men. Together with all Israel, they determined **11:10**
to make David their king, just as the LORD had promised concerning Israel. 11Here is the 2 Sam 23:8-39 1 Chr 11:3
record of David's mightiest men: **11:11**
The first was Jashobeam the Hacmonite, who was commander of the Three—the three 2 Sam 23:8
greatest warriors among David's men.* He once used his spear to kill three hundred
enemy warriors in a single battle.
12Next in rank among the Three was Eleazar son of Dodai,* a descendant of Ahoah. **11:12** 1 Chr 27:4
13He was with David in the battle against the Philistines at Pas-dammim. The battle took **11:13**
place in a field full of barley, and the Israelite army fled. 14But Eleazar and David held 2 Sam 23:11-12
their ground in the middle of the field and beat back the Philistines. So the LORD saved
them by giving them a great victory.
15Once when David was at the rock near the cave of Adullam, the Philistine army was **11:15** 1 Chr 14:9
camped in the valley of Rephaim. The Three (who were among the Thirty—an elite group
among David's fighting men) went down to meet him there. 16David was staying in the **11:16** 1 Sam 10:5
stronghold at the time, and a Philistine detachment had occupied the town of Bethlehem.
17David remarked longingly to his men, "Oh, how I would love some of that good water
from the well in Bethlehem, the one by the gate." 18So the Three broke through the Philistine
lines, drew some water from the well, and brought it back to David. But David refused to
drink it. Instead, he poured it out before the LORD. 19"God forbid that I should drink this!"
he exclaimed. "This water is as precious as the blood of these men who risked their lives to
bring it to me." So David did not drink it. This is an example of the exploits of the Three.

David's Thirty Mighty Men

20Abishai, the brother of Joab, was the leader of the Thirty.* He once used his spear to
kill three hundred enemy warriors in a single battle. It was by such feats that he became
as famous as the Three. 21Abishai was the most famous of the Thirty and was their
commander, though he was not one of the Three.
22There was also Benaiah son of Jehoiada, a valiant warrior from Kabzeel. He did many **11:22**
heroic deeds, which included killing two of Moab's mightiest warriors. Another time he 2 Sam 8:18
chased a lion down into a pit. Then, despite the snow and slippery ground, he caught the
lion and killed it. 23Another time, armed with only a club, he killed an Egyptian warrior **11:23**
who was seven and a half feet* tall and whose spear was as thick as a weaver's beam. 1 Sam 17:7
Benaiah wrenched the spear from the Egyptian's hand and killed him with it. 24These are
some of the deeds that made Benaiah as famous as the Three. 25He was more honored than
the other members of the Thirty, though he was not one of the Three. And David made
him commander of his bodyguard.
26These were also included among David's mighty men:

Asahel, Joab's brother;
Elhanan son of Dodo from Bethlehem;

11:8 Or *the supporting terraces.* The meaning of the Hebrew is uncertain. **11:11** As in some Greek manuscripts (see also 2 Sam 23:8); Hebrew *commander of the Thirty,* or *commander of the captains.* **11:12** As in parallel text at 2 Sam 23:9 (see also 1 Chr 27:4); Hebrew reads *Dodo,* a variant name for Dodai. **11:20** As in Syriac version; Hebrew reads *the Three;* also in 11:21. **11:23** Hebrew *5 cubits* [2.3 meters].

11:9 David's power increased as a direct result of his consistent trust in God. In contrast, Saul's power decreased because he wanted all the credit for himself and ignored God (1 Samuel 15:17-26). Those who are concerned about building a name for themselves risk losing the very recognition they crave. Like David, we should be concerned for righteousness, honesty, and excellence and leave the results to God.

11:12-14 Eleazar's action changed the course of a battle. When everyone around him ran, he held his ground and was saved by the Lord. In any struggle, fear can keep us from taking a stand for God and from participating in God's victories. Face your fear head-on. If you are grounded in God, victory will come when you hold that ground.

11:15 The Thirty were the most courageous and highest-ranking officers of David's army.

11:15-19 These three men risked their lives just to serve and please David. David recognized that their devotion to him was inspired by their devotion to God, so he poured out the water as a drink offering, demonstrating that only God is worthy of such devotion. Just as these men gave of themselves to serve David, we should put aside our own interests to serve other Christians (Romans 12:10). When we serve others, we are also serving God.

27 Shammah from Harod;*
Helez from Pelon;
28 Ira son of Ikkesh from Tekoa;
Abiezer from Anathoth;
29 Sibbecai from Hushah;
Zalmon* from Ahoah;
30 Maharai from Netophah;
Heled son of Baanah from Netophah;
31 Ithai son of Ribai from Gibeah (from the tribe of Benjamin);
Benaiah from Pirathon;
32 Hurai from near Nahale-gaash*;
Abi-albon* the Arbathite;
33 Azmaveth from Bahurim*;
Eliahba from Shaalbon;
34 the sons of Jashen* from Gizon;
Jonathan son of Shagee from Harar;
35 Ahiam son of Sharar* from Harar;
Eliphal son of Ur;
36 Hepher from Mekerah;
Ahijah from Pelon;
37 Hezro from Carmel;
Paarai* son of Ezbai;
38 Joel, the brother of Nathan;
Mibhar son of Hagri;
39 Zelek from Ammon;
Naharai from Beeroth (Joab's armor bearer);
40 Ira from Jattir;
Gareb from Jattir;
41 Uriah the Hittite;
Zabad son of Ahlai;
42 Adina son of Shiza, the Reubenite leader who had thirty men with him;
43 Hanan son of Maacah;
Joshaphat from Mithna;
44 Uzzia from Ashtaroth;
Shama and Jeiel, the sons of Hotham, from Aroer;
45 Jediael son of Shimri;
Joha, his brother, from Tiz;
46 Eliel from Mahavah;
Jeribai and Joshaviah, the sons of Elnaam;
Ithmah from Moab;
47 Eliel and Obed;
Jaasiel from Zobah.

Warriors Join David's Army

12 The following men joined David at Ziklag while he was hiding from Saul son
of Kish. They were among the warriors who fought beside David in battle. 2All
of them were expert archers, and they could shoot arrows or sling stones with their
left hand as well as their right. They were all relatives of Saul from the tribe of

12:1 1 Sam 27:2-6
12:2 Judg 3:15; 20:16

11:27 As in parallel text at 2 Sam 23:25; Hebrew reads *Shammoth from Haror.* **11:29** As in parallel text at 2 Sam 23:28; Hebrew reads *Ilai.* **11:32a** Or *from the ravines of Gaash.* **11:32b** As in parallel text at 2 Sam 23:31; Hebrew reads *Abiel.* **11:33** As in parallel text at 2 Sam 23:31; Hebrew reads *Baharum.* **11:34** As in parallel text at 2 Sam 23:32; Hebrew reads *sons of Hashem.* **11:35** As in parallel text at 2 Sam 23:33; Hebrew reads *son of Sacar.* **11:37** As in parallel text at 2 Sam 23:35; Hebrew reads *Naarai.*

12:1 Ziklag was a city in Philistia to which David had escaped to hide from Saul. Achish, the Philistine ruler of the area, was happy to have a famous Israelite warrior defect to his land. He did not know, however, that David was only pretending loyalty. Achish gave the city of Ziklag to David, his family, and his army (1 Samuel 27:5-7). David's whereabouts were not a great secret, and many loyal followers joined him there.

12:1ff David surrounded himself with great warriors, the best of the Israelite army. What qualities made them worthy to be David's warriors and servants? (1) They had practiced long and hard to perfect their skills (with bow, sling, and spear); (2) they were mentally tough and determined ("fierce as lions," 12:8); (3) they were physically in shape ("as swift as deer," 12:8); (4) they were dedicated to serving God and David. Weak leaders are easily

Benjamin. 3 Their leader was Ahiezer son of Shemaah from Gibeah; his brother Joash
was second-in-command. These were the other warriors:

Jeziel and Pelet, sons of Azmaveth;
Beracah and Jehu from Anathoth;
4 Ishmaiah from Gibeon, a famous warrior and leader among the Thirty;
Jeremiah, Jahaziel, Johanan, and Jozabad from Gederah;
5 Eluzai, Jerimoth, Bealiah, Shemariah, and Shephatiah from Haruph;
6 Elkanah, Isshiah, Azarel, Joezer, and Jashobeam, who were Korahites;
7 Joelah and Zebadiah, sons of Jeroham from Gedor.

8 Some brave and experienced warriors from the tribe of Gad also defected to David
while he was at the stronghold in the wilderness. They were expert with both shield and
spear, as fierce as lions and as swift as deer on the mountains.

12:8 2 Sam 2:18

9 Ezer was their leader.
Obadiah was second.
Eliab was third.
10 Mishmannah was fourth.
Jeremiah was fifth.
11 Attai was sixth.
Eliel was seventh.
12 Johanan was eighth.
Elzabad was ninth.
13 Jeremiah was tenth.
Macbannai was eleventh.

14 These warriors from Gad were army commanders. The weakest among them could
take on a hundred regular troops, and the strongest could take on a thousand! 15 They
crossed the Jordan River during its seasonal flooding at the beginning of the year and
drove out all the people living in the lowlands on both the east and west banks.

12:14 Deut 32:30

12:15 Josh 3:15; 4:18

16 Others from Benjamin and Judah came to David at the stronghold. 17 David went
out to meet them and said, "If you have come in peace to help me, we are friends. But if
you have come to betray me to my enemies when I am innocent, then may the God of
our ancestors see and judge you."

18 Then the Spirit came upon Amasai, who later became a leader among the Thirty, and
he said,

12:18 Judg 3:10; 6:34; 1 Chr 2:17

"We are yours, David!
We are on your side, son of Jesse.
Peace and prosperity be with you,
and success to all who help you,
for your God is the one who helps you."

---

threatened by competent subordinates, but strong leaders surround themselves with the best. They are not intimidated by able and competent followers.

12:1-7 All the warriors mentioned here were from the tribe of Benjamin. Even members of Saul's own tribe (1 Samuel 9:1, 2) were deserting him to help David become king over all Israel. It was clear to them that God had chosen David to be Israel's next leader.

12:2 Archers and slingers had special weapons. The sling was unassuming in appearance but deadly in battle. A shallow leather pouch with a cord of leather or goats' hair attached to each side, the sling was whirled around the head. When one side was released, it sent a stone to its target. The bow and arrow had been in use for thousands of years. Arrowheads were made of stone, wood, or bone because the Philistines still had a monopoly on metalworking (1 Samuel 13:19, 20). Arrow shafts were made of reed or wood, and bowstrings were made of animal gut.

12:8 While the men of Benjamin were expert archers and slingers, the warriors of Gad were experts with the shield and spear. Israelite spears had wood shafts with spearheads of bone or stone and were often thrown through the air toward their mark. Philistine spears had bronze shafts and iron spearheads, and their shields were made of wood and overlaid with leather. Large shields were often carried by an armor bearer, whose main task was to protect the warrior.

12:18 How did the Holy Spirit work in Old Testament times? When there was an important job to be done, God chose a person to do it, and the Spirit gave that person the needed power and ability. The Spirit gave Bezalel artistic ability (Exodus 31:1-5), Jephthah military prowess (Judges 11:29), David power to rule (1 Samuel 16:13), and Zechariah an authoritative word of prophecy (2 Chronicles 24:20). Here the Holy Spirit came upon David's warriors. The Spirit came upon individuals in order to accomplish specific goals. Beginning at Pentecost, however, the Spirit came upon all believers, not only to empower them to do God's will, but also to dwell in them day by day (Acts 2:14-21).

So David let them join him, and he made them officers over his troops.
12:19 19 Some men from Manasseh defected from the Israelite army and joined David when
1 Sam 29:2-9 he went with the Philistines to fight against Saul. But as it turned out, the Philistine
leaders refused to let David and his men go with them. After much discussion, they sent
them back, for they said, "It will cost us our lives if David switches loyalties to Saul and
turns against us."
20 Here is a list of the men from Manasseh who defected to David as he was returning to
Ziklag: Adnah, Jozabad, Jediael, Michael, Jozabad, Elihu, and Zillethai. Each commanded
12:21 a thousand troops from the tribe of Manasseh. 21 They helped David chase down bands of
1 Sam 30:1 raiders, for they were all brave and able warriors who became commanders in his army.
12:22 22 Day after day more men joined David until he had a great army, like the army of God.
Josh 5:13-15 23 These are the numbers of armed warriors who joined David at Hebron. They were
12:23 2 Sam 2:3-4 all eager to see David become king instead of Saul, just as the LORD had promised.
1 Chr 10:14; 11:10

24 From the tribe of Judah, there were 6,800 warriors armed with shields and spears.
25 From the tribe of Simeon, there were 7,100 warriors.
26 From the tribe of Levi, there were 4,600 troops. 27 This included Jehoiada, leader of
12:28 the family of Aaron, who had 3,700 under his command. 28 This also included Zadok,
1 Chr 6:8 a young warrior, with twenty-two members of his family who were all officers.
12:29 29 From the tribe of Benjamin, Saul's relatives, there were 3,000 warriors. Most of the
2 Sam 2:8-9 Benjaminites had remained loyal to Saul until this time.
30 From the tribe of Ephraim, there were 20,800 warriors, each famous in his own clan.
31 From the half-tribe of Manasseh west of the Jordan, 18,000 men were sent for the
express purpose of helping David become king.
12:32 32 From the tribe of Issachar, there were 200 leaders of the tribe with their relatives.
Esth 1:13 All these men understood the temper of the times and knew the best course for
Ps 12:2 Israel to take.
33 From the tribe of Zebulun, there were 50,000 skilled warriors. They were fully
armed and prepared for battle and completely loyal to David.
34 From the tribe of Naphtali, there were 1,000 officers and 37,000 warriors armed
with shields and spears.
35 From the tribe of Dan, there were 28,600 warriors, all prepared for battle.
36 From the tribe of Asher, there were 40,000 trained warriors, all prepared for battle.
37 From the east side of the Jordan River—where the tribes of Reuben and Gad and the
half-tribe of Manasseh lived—there were 120,000 troops armed with every kind of
weapon.

12:38 38 All these men came in battle array to Hebron with the single purpose of making
2 Sam 5:1-3 1 Chr 12:33 David the king of Israel. In fact, all Israel agreed that David should be their king. 39 They
feasted and drank with David for three days, for preparations had been made by their
12:40 1 Sam 25:18 relatives for their arrival. 40 And people from as far away as Issachar, Zebulun, and
Naphtali brought food on donkeys, camels, mules, and oxen. Vast supplies of flour, fig
cakes, raisins, wine, olive oil, cattle, and sheep were brought to the celebration. There
was great joy throughout the land of Israel.

12:22 David "had a great army, like the army of God." Men were drawn to David by the reputation of his great warriors, the news of their victories, and their desire to see God's will done in making David king. People are often drawn to a great cause and the brave, determined people who support it. As believers, we have the greatest cause—the salvation of people. If we are brave, determined, and faithful, others will be drawn to work with us.

12:26-29 In Numbers 1:47-50, God said that the Levites were to be exempt from military service. Why then are they listed as part of David's army? Although they were exempt from the draft, they strongly supported David and volunteered their services to help install him as king.

12:32 The 200 leaders from the tribe of Issachar "understood the temper of the times." As a result, their knowledge and judgment provided needed help in making decisions for the nation. For leaders today, it is equally necessary to know what is happening in society in order to plan the best course of action for the church. Knowledge of current events, trends, and needs helps us understand people's thoughts and attitudes. This gives leaders information to help them make wise decisions for the church and make God's message relevant to people's lives.

12:40 The people were ready for change. They had suffered under Saul's leadership because of his disobedience to God (see 10:13). They were so overjoyed with David's coronation that they contributed lavishly to the celebration. It is right and proper to give generously for celebration and joyous worship. God is the author of joy, and he will join us in our celebrations.

2. David brings the Ark to Jerusalem

David Attempts to Move the Ark

13 David consulted with all his officials, including the generals and captains of his **13:1-4**
army. [2]Then he addressed the entire assembly of Israel as follows: “If you approve //2 Sam 6:1-11
and if it is the will of the LORD our God, let us send messages to all the Israelites
throughout the land, including the priests and Levites in their towns and pasturelands.
Let us invite them to come and join us. [3]It is time to bring back the Ark of our God, for **13:3**
we neglected it during the reign of Saul.” 1 Sam 7:1-2
[4]The whole assembly agreed to this, for the people could see it was the right thing to do.
[5]So David summoned all the people of Israel, from one end of the country to the other,* to **13:5** 1 Sam 6:21; 7:1
join in bringing the Ark of God from Kiriath-jearim. [6]Then David and all Israel went to 2 Sam 6:1
Baalah of Judah (also called Kiriath-jearim) to bring back the Ark of God, which bears the 1 Kgs 8:65 1 Chr 15:3
name of the LORD who is enthroned between the cherubim. [7]They transported the Ark of
God from the house of Abinadab on a new cart, with Uzzah and Ahio guiding it. [8]David **13:6** Josh 15:9
and all Israel were celebrating before God with all their might, singing and playing all kinds 2 Kgs 19:15
of musical instruments—lyres, harps, tambourines, cymbals, and trumpets. **13:7** 1 Sam 7:1
[9]But when they arrived at the threshing floor of Nacon,* the oxen stumbled, and **13:8**
Uzzah put out his hand to steady the Ark. [10]Then the LORD’s anger blazed out against 1 Chr 15:13-16
Uzzah, and he struck him dead because he had laid his hand on the Ark. So Uzzah died **13:9** 2 Sam 6:6
there in the presence of God. [11]David was angry because the LORD’s anger had blazed **13:10**
out against Uzzah. He named that place Perez-uzzah (which means “outbreak against Lev 10:2 1 Chr 15:13, 15
Uzzah”). It is still called that today.
[12]David was now afraid of God and asked, “How can I ever bring the Ark of God back **13:13**
into my care?” [13]So David decided not to move the Ark into the City of David. He took it 2 Chr 25:24-25

13:5 Hebrew *from the Shihor of Egypt to Lebo-hamath.* **13:9** As in parallel text at 2 Sam 6:6; Hebrew reads *Kidon.*

13:1 David took time to confer with all his officers. As king, he had ultimate authority and could have given orders on his own, but he chose to involve others in leadership. Perhaps this is why there was unanimous support for his decisions (13:1-5). When we are in charge, it is tempting to make unilateral decisions, pushing through our own opinions. But effective leaders listen carefully to others’ opinions, and they encourage others to participate in making decisions. Of course, we should always consult God first. We can run into big problems if we don’t talk to him (see the note on 13:10).

13:1ff The parallel account of moving the Ark (2 Samuel 5–6) shows that David’s building projects were completed *before* he brought the Ark to Jerusalem. The writer of Chronicles puts the moving of the Ark first in order to highlight David’s spiritual accomplishments and relationship to God.

13:3 The Ark of our God is also called the Ark of the Covenant. The most sacred object of the Hebrew faith, it was a large box containing the stone tablets on which God had written the Ten Commandments (Exodus 25:10-22). David had already made Jerusalem his political capital (11:4-9). At this time, David brought the Ark there in order to make Jerusalem the nation’s center for worship as well.

13:3 The Ark of God had been in Kiriath-jearim for many years. The neglect of the Ark symbolized Israel’s neglect of God. Bringing the Ark back to the center of Israel’s life reflected David’s desire to remind the nation of its true foundation—God. Neglecting those things that remind us of God—the Bible, the church, and contact with Christians—will cause us also to neglect God. We must keep God at the center of our lives.

13:6 Cherubim are mighty angels.

13:8 Worship in the Old Testament was more than a sober religious exercise. David’s exuberance as he worshiped God with dancing and music is approved in Scripture. Our worship should reflect a healthy balance: Sometimes we should be reflective and serious (see Exodus 19:14ff), and sometimes we should show enthusiasm and jubilation. What do you need—more serious reflection or more joyous celebration?

13:10 Why did Uzzah die? He touched the Ark, and that offense was punishable by death. God had given specific instructions about how the Ark was to be moved and carried (Numbers 4:5-15), and those instructions were ignored. The Levites were responsible to move the Ark (there is no record that Uzzah was a Levite), and it was to be carried on their shoulders with poles through its rings (Numbers 7:9). It was *never* to be touched. Bringing the Ark on a cart followed the Philistines’ example (1 Samuel 6:1ff). Uzzah, though sincere in his desire to protect the Ark, had to face the consequences of his sin, and David was reminded that his obedience to God’s laws was more important than his enthusiasm. Also David had “consulted with all his officials” (13:1), but he neglected to ask God. The advice of our friends and colleagues is no substitute for God’s direction.

13:10-14 Uzzah died instantly for touching the Ark, but God blessed Obed-edom’s home where the Ark was stored. This demonstrates the two-edged aspect of God’s power: He is perfectly loving and perfectly just. Great blessings come to those who obey his commands, but severe punishment comes to those who disobey him. This punishment may come swiftly or over time, but it will come. Sometimes we focus only on the blessings God gives us, while forgetting that when we sin, “It is a terrible thing to fall into the hands of the living God” (Hebrews 10:31). At other times, however, we concentrate so much on judgment that we miss his blessings. Don’t fall into a one-sided view of God. Along with God’s blessings comes the responsibility to live up to his demands for fairness, honesty, and justice.

13:11 David was angry at both God and himself. David knew that he had done something wrong in transporting the Ark, and he was angry that his plans for the joyous return of the Ark had ended in a man’s death. But David’s anger cooled, and he left the Ark in Obed-edom’s home until he could consider how to get it to Jerusalem. This allowed David to discover God’s instructions for transporting the Ark. The next trip would be carried out according to God’s commands.

13:14 1 Chr 26:4-5
instead to the home of Obed-edom of Gath. 14The Ark of God remained there with the
family of Obed-edom for three months, and the LORD blessed him and his entire household.

David's Palace and Family

14:1-7 //2 Sam 5:11-16 //1 Chr 3:5-8
14:1 2 Sam 5:11

14 Now King Hiram of Tyre sent messengers to David, along with stonemasons and
carpenters to build him a palace. Hiram also sent many cedar logs for lumber.
2And David realized that the LORD had made him king over Israel and had made his
kingdom very great for the sake of his people Israel.
3Then David married more wives in Jerusalem, and they had many sons and daughters.
14:4 1 Chr 3:5-9
4These are the names of David's sons who were born in Jerusalem: Shimea,* Shobab,
14:8-17 //2 Sam 5:17-25
Nathan, Solomon, 5Ibhar, Elishua, Elpelet, 6Nogah, Nepheg, Japhia, 7Elishama, Eliada,*
and Eliphelet.

David Conquers the Philistines

8When the Philistines heard that David had been anointed king over all Israel, they
mobilized all their forces to capture him. But David was told they were coming, so he
14:9 1 Chr 11:15; 14:13
and his men marched out to meet them. 9The Philistines had arrived in the valley of
Rephaim and raided it. 10So David asked God, "Should I go out to fight the Philistines?
Will you hand them over to me?"
The LORD replied, "Yes, go ahead. I will give you the victory."
11So David and his troops went to Baal-perazim and defeated the Philistines there.
"God has done it!" David exclaimed. "He used me to burst through my enemies like a
raging flood!" So that place was named Baal-perazim (which means "the Lord who
bursts through"). 12The Philistines had abandoned their idols* there, so David gave
orders to burn them up.
14:13 1 Chr 14:9
13But after a while, the Philistines returned and raided the valley again. 14And once
again David asked God what to do. "Do not attack them straight on," God replied.
"Instead, circle around behind them and attack them near the balsam trees. 15When you
hear a sound like marching feet in the tops of the balsam trees, attack! That will be the
signal that God is moving ahead of you to strike down the Philistines." 16So David did
what God commanded, and he struck down the Philistine army all the way from Gibeon
to Gezer.
14:17 Exod 15:14-16 Deut 2:25
17So David's fame spread everywhere, and the LORD caused all the nations to fear
David.

Preparing to Move the Ark

15:1 1 Chr 16:1; 17:1-5
15:2 Num 4:15 Deut 10:8

15 David now built several buildings for himself in the City of David. He also
prepared a place for the Ark of God and set up a special tent there to shelter it.
2Then he issued these instructions: "When we transport the Ark of God this time, no one
except the Levites may carry it. The LORD has chosen them to carry the Ark of the LORD
and to minister before him forever."

14:4 Hebrew *Shammua,* a variant name for Shimea; compare 3:5. **14:7** Hebrew *Beeliada,* a variant name for Eliada; compare 3:8 and parallel text at 2 Sam 5:16. **14:12** Hebrew *their gods;* compare parallel text at 2 Sam 5:21.

14:1 King Hiram also sent lumber and craftsmen to help Solomon build the Temple (2 Chronicles 2:1ff).

14:2 God gave David honor and success, but not simply for David's personal gain. David realized that God had prospered him for a special reason—for the sake of God's people! Often we are tempted to use our position or possessions only for our own good. Instead, we must remember that God has placed us where we are and given us all we have so that we may encourage others and give to those in need.

14:3 Accumulating wives and concubines in a harem was the custom of the day among Middle Eastern royalty, but it was not God's ideal (Genesis 2:24). David's marriages brought him greater power and influence, but they also caused strife, jealousy, and even murder within his family. (See the chart in 2 Samuel 11 for other consequences of polygamy.)

14:8-16 A map of this battle is in 2 Samuel 5.

14:10 Before David went to battle, he inquired of God first, asking for his presence and guidance. Too often we wait until we are in trouble before turning to God. By then the consequences of our actions are already unfolding. Do you ask for God's help only as a desperate last resort? Instead, go to him first! Like David, you may receive incredible help and avoid serious trouble.

14:12 David's quick and decisive action against idols helped unify his kingdom and focus the people on worshiping the one true God. He was obeying the law that said, "You must break down their pagan altars and shatter their sacred pillars. Cut down their Asherah poles and burn their idols" (Deuteronomy 7:5). Most of David's successors failed to destroy idols, and this led to unbelievable moral corruption in Israel.

14:12 Often the soldiers wanted to keep souvenirs from the battle (and 2 Samuel 5:21 states that some of the men kept some of these idols), but David ordered them to burn the idols. The only proper response to sin is to get rid of it completely. You cannot be a follower of God while continuing to hold on to parts of your life where God is not the center of your thoughts and actions. Eliminate whatever takes God's rightful place in your life, and follow him with complete devotion.

3 Then David summoned all the Israelites to Jerusalem to bring the Ark of the LORD
to the place he had prepared for it. 4 These are the priests* and Levites who were called
together:

5 There were 120 from the clan of Kohath, with Uriel as their leader.
6 There were 220 from the clan of Merari, with Asaiah as their leader.
7 There were 130 from the clan of Gershon,* with Joel as their leader.
8 There were 200 descendants of Elizaphan, with Shemaiah as their leader.
9 There were 80 descendants of Hebron, with Eliel as their leader.
10 There were 112 descendants of Uzziel, with Amminadab as their leader.

11 Then David summoned the priests, Zadok and Abiathar, and these Levite leaders:
Uriel, Asaiah, Joel, Shemaiah, Eliel, and Amminadab. 12 He said to them, "You are the
leaders of the Levite families. You must purify yourselves and all your fellow Levites,
so you can bring the Ark of the LORD, the God of Israel, to the place I have prepared for
it. 13 Because you Levites did not carry the Ark the first time, the anger of the LORD our
God burst out against us. We failed to ask God how to move it in the proper way." 14 So
the priests and the Levites purified themselves in order to bring the Ark of the LORD, the
God of Israel, to Jerusalem. 15 Then the Levites carried the Ark of God on their shoulders
with its carrying poles, just as the LORD had instructed Moses.

16 David also ordered the Levite leaders to appoint a choir of Levites who were
singers and musicians to sing joyful songs to the accompaniment of lyres, harps, and
cymbals. 17 So the Levites appointed Heman son of Joel, Asaph son of Berekiah, and
Ethan son of Kushaiah from the clan of Merari to direct the musicians. 18 The following
men were chosen as their assistants: Zechariah, Jaaziel, Shemiramoth, Jehiel, Unni,
Eliab, Benaiah, Maaseiah, Mattithiah, Eliphelehu, Mikneiah, and the gatekeepers,
Obed-edom and Jeiel.

19 Heman, Asaph, and Ethan were chosen to sound the bronze cymbals. 20 Zechariah,
Aziel, Shemiramoth, Jehiel, Unni, Eliab, Maaseiah, and Benaiah were chosen to play
the lyres.* 21 Mattithiah, Eliphelehu, Mikneiah, Obed-edom, Jeiel, and Azaziah were
chosen to play the harps.* 22 Kenaniah, the head Levite, was chosen as the choir leader
because of his skill.

23 Berekiah and Elkanah were chosen to guard the Ark. 24 Shebaniah, Joshaphat,
Nethanel, Amasai, Zechariah, Benaiah, and Eliezer—all of whom were priests—were
chosen to blow the trumpets as they marched in front of the Ark of God. Obed-edom and
Jehiah were chosen to guard the Ark.

15:3 2 Sam 6:12, 17; 1 Kgs 8:1; 1 Chr 13:5; 15:1, 12
15:4 1 Chr 6:16-30; 12:26
15:11 1 Sam 22:20-23; 1 Kgs 2:26, 35; 1 Chr 12:28
15:12 Exod 19:14-15; 2 Chr 35:6
15:13 1 Chr 13:7
15:15 Exod 25:14
15:16 1 Chr 13:8; 25:1
15:17 1 Chr 25:1
15:24 1 Chr 16:6

15:4 Hebrew *descendants of Aaron.* **15:7** Hebrew *Gershom,* a variant name for Gershon. **15:20** Hebrew adds *according to Alamoth,* which is probably a musical term. The meaning of the Hebrew is uncertain. **15:21** Hebrew adds *according to the Sheminith,* which is probably a musical term. The meaning of the Hebrew is uncertain.

15:12 The priests purified themselves so they would be prepared to carry the Ark. To *purify* literally means "to separate," to set apart for sacred purposes, to consecrate. The priests symbolically separated themselves from sin and evil. This was done by washing themselves and their clothing in a special ceremony (Numbers 8:5-8). While we are not required to carry out such ceremonies today, we can purify ourselves by reading God's Word and preparing our hearts to participate in worship.

15:13 David refers to the incident recorded in 13:8-11 and 2 Samuel 6:1-11. As the Ark was being brought back to Israel on an oxcart, the oxen stumbled. Uzzah, trying to steady the Ark with his hand, was killed instantly for touching it. The mistake was not in David's desire to move the Ark but in his method for its return. David either ignored or was unaware of the specific instructions in God's law about how the Ark was to be moved. Obviously he had discovered his mistake and was now preparing to correct it. This incident was a divine object lesson to all Israel that God governed the king and not the other way around. If David had been allowed to handle the Ark of God carelessly, what would that have said to the people about their faith?

15:13-15 When David's first attempt to move the Ark failed (13:8-14), he learned an important lesson: When God gives specific instructions, it is wise to follow them precisely. This time David saw to it that the Levites carried the Ark (Numbers 4:5-15). We may not fully understand the reasons behind God's instructions, but we do know that his wisdom is complete and his judgment infallible. The way to know God's instructions is to know his Word. But just as children do not understand the reasons for all their parents' instructions until they are older, we may not understand all of God's reasons in this life. It is far better to obey God first and then discover the reasons. We are never free to disobey God just because we don't understand.

15:16-25 The great musical procession was designed as a worthy accompaniment to this great occasion. It heightened the excitement, elevated the people's hearts and minds, and focused their attention on the event. It also helped seal it in their memory for years to come. Beginning any task by praising God can inspire us to give him our best. Develop the practice of giving praise to God, and you will experience greater joy and strength to face anything.

Moving the Ark to Jerusalem

15:25–16:3 //2 Sam 6:12-19
15:25 1 Chr 13:13
15:26 Num 23:1-4, 29

25 Then David and the leaders of Israel and the generals of the army went to the home
of Obed-edom to bring the Ark of the LORD's covenant up to Jerusalem with a great
celebration. 26 And because God was clearly helping the Levites as they carried the
Ark of the LORD's covenant, they sacrificed seven bulls and seven lambs. 27 David was
dressed in a robe of fine linen, as were the Levites who carried the Ark, the singers,
and Kenaniah the song leader. David was also wearing a priestly tunic.* 28 So all Israel
brought up the Ark of the LORD's covenant to Jerusalem with shouts of joy, the
blowing of horns and trumpets, the crashing of cymbals, and loud playing on harps
and lyres.

29 But as the Ark of the LORD's covenant entered the City of David, Michal, the
daughter of Saul, looked down from her window. When she saw King David dancing
and leaping for joy, she was filled with contempt for him.

16:1 1 Chr 15:1

16 So they brought the Ark of God into the special tent David had prepared for it,
and they sacrificed burnt offerings and peace offerings before God. 2 When he
had finished, David blessed the people in the name of the LORD. 3 Then he gave a gift
of food to every man and woman in Israel: a loaf of bread, a cake of dates,* and a cake
of raisins.

16:4 1 Chr 15:2

4 David appointed the following Levites to lead the people in worship before the
Ark of the LORD by asking for his blessings and giving thanks and praise to the LORD,
the God of Israel. 5 Asaph, the leader of this group, sounded the cymbals. His
assistants were Zechariah (the second), then Jeiel, Shemiramoth, Jehiel, Mattithiah,
Eliab, Benaiah, Obed-edom, and Jeiel. They played the harps and lyres. 6 The priests,
Benaiah and Jahaziel, played the trumpets regularly before the Ark of God's covenant.

David's Song of Praise

7 That day David gave to Asaph and his fellow Levites this song of thanksgiving to the
LORD:

16:8-22 //Ps 105:1-15
16:8 1 Kgs 8:43; 2 Kgs 19:19

8 Give thanks to the LORD and proclaim his greatness.
Let the whole world know what he has done.
9 Sing to him; yes, sing his praises.
Tell everyone about his miracles.
10 Exult in his holy name;
O worshipers of the LORD, rejoice!

16:11 Ps 24:6

11 Search for the LORD and for his strength,
and keep on searching.

16:12 Pss 78:43; 103:2

12 Think of the wonderful works he has done,
the miracles, and the judgments he handed down,
13 O children of Israel, God's servant,
O descendants of Jacob, God's chosen one.

16:14 Ps 48:10

14 He is the LORD our God.
His rule is seen throughout the land.

15:27 Hebrew *a linen ephod.* **16:3** Or *a portion of meat.* The meaning of the Hebrew is uncertain.

15:29 David was willing to look foolish in the eyes of some people in order to express his thankfulness to God fully and honestly. In contrast, Michal was so disgusted by his undignified actions that she could not rejoice in the Ark's return to Jerusalem. Worship had so deteriorated under the reign of her father, Saul, that it had become stilted and ritualistic. Michal could accept David as a military conqueror and as a king, but she could not accept his free and spontaneous expression of praise to God. Some devoted people may look foolish to us in their heartfelt expressions of worship, but we must accept them. In the same way, we should not be afraid to worship God with whatever expressions seem appropriate.

16:4 Certain Levites were appointed to give continual praise and thanks to God. Praise and thanksgiving should be a regular part of our routine, not reserved only for celebrations. Praise God continually, and you will find that you won't take his blessings for granted.

16:7-36 Four elements of true thanksgiving are found in this song (psalm): (1) *remembering* what God has done, (2) *telling* others about it, (3) *showing* God's glory to others, and (4) *offering* gifts of self, time, and resources. If you are truly thankful, your life will show it.

16:8ff Several parts of this psalm are parallel to songs in the book of Psalms: 16:8-22 with Psalm 105:1-15; 16:23-33 with Psalm 96; 16:34-36 with Psalm 106:1, 47, 48.

15 He always stands by his covenant*—
the commitment he made to a thousand generations.
16 This is the covenant he made with Abraham
and the oath he swore to Isaac.
17 He confirmed it to Jacob as a decree,
to the people of Israel as a never-ending treaty:
18 "I will give you the land of Canaan
as your special possession."
19 He said this when they were few in number,
a tiny group of strangers in Canaan.
20 They wandered back and forth between nations,
from one kingdom to another.
21 Yet he did not let anyone oppress them.
He warned kings on their behalf:
22 "Do not touch these people I have chosen,
and do not hurt my prophets."

23 Let the whole earth sing to the LORD!
Each day proclaim the good news that he saves.
24 Publish his glorious deeds among the nations.
Tell everyone about the amazing things he does.
25 Great is the LORD! He is most worthy of praise!
He is to be revered above all gods.
26 The gods of other nations are merely idols,
but the LORD made the heavens!
27 Honor and majesty surround him;
strength and beauty are in his dwelling.

28 O nations of the world, recognize the LORD,
recognize that the LORD is glorious and strong.
29 Give to the LORD the glory he deserves!
Bring your offering and come to worship him.
Worship the LORD in all his holy splendor.
30 Let all the earth tremble before him.
The world is firmly established and cannot be shaken.

31 Let the heavens be glad, and let the earth rejoice!
Tell all the nations that the LORD is king.
32 Let the sea and everything in it shout his praise!
Let the fields and their crops burst forth with joy!
33 Let the trees of the forest rustle with praise before the LORD!
For he is coming to judge the earth.

34 Give thanks to the LORD, for he is good!
His faithful love endures forever.

16:15 As in some Greek manuscripts (see also Ps 105:8); Hebrew reads *Remember his covenant forever.*

16:16 Gen 17:2; 22:16-18; 26:3
16:17 Gen 35:9-12
16:18 Gen 13:14-17
16:19 Gen 34:30 Deut 7:7
16:21 Gen 12:17; 20:3 Exod 7:15-18
16:22 Gen 20:7
16:23-33 //Ps 96:1-13
16:25 Pss 89:7; 144:3-6
16:26 Lev 19:4 Ps 102:25
16:29 Ps 29:2
16:31 Pss 93:1; 96:10 Isa 44:23; 49:13
16:32 Ps 98:7
16:34-36 //Ps 106:1, 47-48
16:34 Ezra 3:11 Pss 106:1; 136:1 Jer 33:11

16:15-18 This covenant was given to Abraham (Genesis 15:18-21) and then passed on to Isaac (Genesis 26:24, 25) and Jacob (Genesis 28:13-15). God promised to give the land of Canaan (present-day Israel) to their descendants. He also promised that the Messiah would come from their line.

16:25 The basis of praise is declaring God's character and attributes in the presence of others. When we recognize and affirm his goodness, we are holding up his perfect moral nature for all to see. Praise benefits us because it takes our mind off our problems and needs and focuses on God's power, mercy, majesty, and love.

16:29 Genuine praise also involves ascribing glory to God. Remember this in your worship and give God all the glory.

16:37 Asaph and his fellow Levites ministered in the Temple, doing each day whatever was needed. To carry out God's work is not merely to engage in religious exercises. It includes other necessary tasks. Even if you don't have the opportunity to teach or preach, God can use you in the ministry. What needs to be done—cleaning, serving, singing, planning, administering? Look for ways to minister each day.

16:39 David brought the Ark to Jerusalem although the Tabernacle was still at Gibeon. His plan was to reunite the Tabernacle and Ark in a new Temple at Jerusalem that would then become Israel's only worship center. The Temple, however, was not built until Solomon's time. In the meantime, Israel had two worship centers and two high priests (15:11), one at Gibeon and one at Jerusalem.

16:35
Ps 106:47-48

35 Cry out, "Save us, O God of our salvation!
Gather and rescue us from among the nations,
so we can thank your holy name
and rejoice and praise you."

16:36
Deut 27:15
1 Kgs 8:15, 56
Neh 8:6
Ps 72:18-19

36 Blessed be the LORD, the God of Israel,
from everlasting to everlasting!

And all the people shouted "Amen!" and praised the LORD.

Worship at Jerusalem and Gibeon

16:37
2 Chr 8:14
Ezra 3:4

37 David arranged for Asaph and his fellow Levites to minister regularly before the Ark
of the LORD's covenant, doing whatever needed to be done each day. 38 This group

16:38
1 Chr 13:13-14; 26:10

included Obed-edom (son of Jeduthun), Hosah, and sixty-eight other Levites as gatekeepers.

16:39
1 Kgs 3:4
1 Chr 15:11

39 Meanwhile, David stationed Zadok the priest and his fellow priests at the
Tabernacle of the LORD on the hill of Gibeon, where they continued to minister before

16:40
Exod 29:38-42
Num 28:1-8

the LORD. 40 They sacrificed the regular burnt offerings to the LORD each morning and
evening on the altar set aside for that purpose, obeying everything written in the law

16:41
1 Chr 6:33; 25:1-6
2 Chr 5:13

of the LORD, which he had given to Israel. 41 David also appointed Heman, Jeduthun,
and the others chosen by name to give thanks to the LORD, "for his faithful love

16:42
1 Chr 25:7
2 Chr 7:6; 29:27

endures forever." 42 They used their trumpets, cymbals, and other instruments to
accompany the songs of praise to God. And the sons of Jeduthun were appointed as
gatekeepers.
43 Then all the people returned to their homes, and David returned home to bless his
family.

The LORD's Covenant Promise to David

17:1-15
//2 Sam 7:1-17

17 Now when David was settled in his palace, he said to Nathan the prophet, "Here
I am living in this beautiful cedar palace, but the Ark of the LORD's covenant is
out in a tent!"
2 Nathan replied, "Go ahead with what you have in mind, for God is with you."
3 But that same night God said to Nathan,

17:4
1 Chr 28:2-3

4 "Go and tell my servant David, 'This is what the LORD says: You are not the one

17:5
Exod 40:2-3
2 Sam 7:6

to build me a temple to live in. 5 I have never lived in a temple, from the day I
brought the Israelites out of Egypt until now. My home has always been a tent, mov-

17:6
2 Sam 7:7

ing from one place to another. 6 And I never once complained to Israel's leaders,*
the shepherds of my people. I have never asked them, "Why haven't you built me
a beautiful cedar temple?"'
7 "Now go and say to my servant David, 'This is what the LORD Almighty
says: I chose you to lead my people Israel when you were just a shepherd boy,
tending your sheep out in the pasture. 8 I have been with you wherever you
have gone, and I have destroyed all your enemies. Now I will make your name
famous throughout the earth! 9 And I have provided a permanent homeland for
my people Israel, a secure place where they will never be disturbed. It will be
their own land where wicked nations won't oppress them as they did in the past,
10 from the time I appointed judges to rule my people. And I will subdue all your
enemies.
"'And now I declare that the LORD will build a house for you—a dynasty of
kings! 11 For when you die, I will raise up one of your sons, and I will make his

17:6 As in Greek version (see also 2 Sam 7:7); Hebrew reads *judges*.

17:1 David felt disturbed that the Ark, the symbol of God's presence, sat in a tent while he lived in a beautiful palace. David's desire was right, but his timing was wrong. God told David *not* to build a Temple (17:3, 4), and David was willing to abide by God's timing. If you live in comparative luxury while God's work, house, or ministers are lacking, perhaps God wants you to change the situation. Like David, take action to correct the imbalance, but be willing to move according to God's timing.

17:3-14 God did not want a warrior to build his Temple (28:3; 1 Kings 5:3), and David had shed much blood in unifying the nation. So the honor of building the Temple would go to David's son Solomon. David would pass on to Solomon a peaceful and united kingdom, ready to begin work on a beautiful Temple.

17:10 God promised to subdue David's enemies. Chapters 18–20 tell how God kept that promise.

kingdom strong. 12 He is the one who will build a house—a temple—for me. And I
will establish his throne forever. 13 I will be his father, and he will be my son. I will 17:13
not take my unfailing love from him as I took it from Saul, who ruled before you. 1 Chr 10:14 Heb 1:5
14 I will establish him over my dynasty and my kingdom for all time, and his throne
will be secure forever.'"

15 So Nathan went back to David and told him everything the LORD had said.

David's Prayer of Thanks

16 Then King David went in and sat before the LORD and prayed, "Who am I, O LORD 17:16-27
God, and what is my family, that you have brought me this far? 17 And now, O God, in //2 Sam 7:18-29
addition to everything else, you speak of giving me a lasting dynasty! You speak as 17:17
though I were someone very great,* O LORD God! 18 What more can I say about the way 2 Sam 7:19
you have honored me? You know what I am really like. 19 For my sake, O LORD, and 17:19
according to your will, you have done all these great things and have made them known. 2 Sam 7:21, 25 Isa 37:35

20 "O LORD, there is no one like you—there is no other God. We have never even heard
of another god like you! 21 What other nation on earth is like Israel? What other nation,
O God, have you redeemed from slavery to be your own people? You made a great name
for yourself when you rescued your people from Egypt. You performed awesome
miracles and drove out the nations that stood in their way. 22 You chose Israel to be your 17:22
people forever, and you, O LORD, have become their God. Exod 19:5-6

23 "And now, O LORD, do as you have promised concerning me and my family. May
it be a promise that will last forever. 24 And may your name be established and honored
forever so that all the world will say, 'The LORD Almighty is God over Israel!' And may
the dynasty of your servant David be established in your presence.

25 "O my God, I have been bold enough to pray this prayer because you have revealed
that you will build a house for me—an eternal dynasty! 26 For you are God, O LORD. And
you have promised these good things to me, your servant. 27 And now, it has pleased you
to bless me and my family so that our dynasty will continue forever before you. For when
you grant a blessing, O LORD, it is an eternal blessing!"

3. David's military exploits

David's Victories

18 After this, David subdued and humbled the Philistines by conquering Gath and its 18:1-13
surrounding towns. 2 David also conquered the land of Moab, and the Moabites //2 Sam 8:1-14
became David's subjects and brought him tribute money.

3 Then David destroyed the forces of King Hadadezer of Zobah, as far as Hamath,*
when Hadadezer marched out to strengthen his control along the Euphrates River.
4 David captured one thousand chariots, seven thousand charioteers, and twenty thousand foot soldiers. Then he crippled all but one hundred of the chariot horses.
5 When Arameans from Damascus arrived to help Hadadezer, David killed twenty-two

17:17 The meaning of the Hebrew is uncertain. **18:3** The meaning of the Hebrew is uncertain.

17:12-14 Why, after this eternal promise, were the Israelites eventually taken from the Promised Land into captivity? The promise to David had two parts. The first part was conditional: As long as David's descendants followed God's laws and honored him, they would continually be on the throne of Israel. The second part was unconditional: A son of David would occupy his throne forever. This was Jesus the Messiah. The first part of the promise was based on the faithful obedience of David's descendants. The second part would come true regardless of the way his descendants acted.

17:16-20 God told David that Solomon would be given the honor of building the Temple. David responded with deep humility, not resentment. This king who had conquered his enemies and was loved by his people said, "Who am I . . . that you have brought me this far?" David recognized that God was the *true* king. God has done just as much for us, and he plans to do even more! Like David, we should humble ourselves and give glory to God, saying, "O LORD, there is no one like you." When God chooses someone else to implement your ideas, will you respond with such humility?

17:16-27 David prayed by humbling himself (17:16-18), praising God (17:19, 20), recognizing God's blessings (17:21, 22), and accepting God's decisions, promises, and commands (17:23, 24). Sometimes we are quick to make requests to God and to tell him our troubles, but these other dimensions of prayer can deepen our spiritual life. Take time to praise God, to count his blessings, and to affirm your commitment to do what he has already said to do.

17:21 David's reference to Israel's exodus from Egypt would have had special significance to the original readers of 1 Chronicles, who were either beginning or had just completed a second great exodus back to Israel from captivity in Babylon. Remembering God's promises, mercy, and protection during the first exodus would have encouraged the exiles returning once again to Israel, just as God had promised.

18:2 In 2 Samuel 8:1, 2, it is recorded that David killed two-thirds of the people of Moab. His ancestor Ruth was originally from the land of Moab.

thousand of them. 6 Then he placed several army garrisons in Damascus, the Aramean
capital, and the Arameans became David's subjects and brought him tribute money. So
the LORD gave David victory wherever he went. 7 David brought the gold shields of
Hadadezer's officers to Jerusalem, 8 along with a large amount of bronze from Hadadezer's cities of Tebah* and Cun. Later Solomon melted the bronze and used it for the
Temple. He molded it into the bronze Sea, the pillars, and the various bronze utensils
used at the Temple.
9 When King Toi* of Hamath heard that David had destroyed the army of King
Hadadezer of Zobah, 10 he sent his son Joram* to congratulate David on his success.
Hadadezer and Toi had long been enemies, and there had been many wars between them.
18:11 Num 24:18-20 Joram presented David with many gifts of gold, silver, and bronze. 11 King David
dedicated all these gifts to the LORD, along with the silver and gold he had taken from
the other nations he had subdued—Edom, Moab, Ammon, Philistia, and Amalek.
12 Abishai son of Zeruiah destroyed eighteen thousand Edomites in the Valley of Salt.
13 He placed army garrisons throughout Edom, and all the Edomites became David's
subjects. This was another example of how the LORD made David victorious wherever
he went.
18:14-17 //2 Sam 8:15-18 14 David reigned over all Israel and was fair to everyone. 15 Joab son of Zeruiah was
18:15 1 Chr 11:6 commander of the army. Jehoshaphat son of Ahilud was the royal historian. 16 Zadok son
of Ahitub and Ahimelech* son of Abiathar were the priests. Seraiah* was the court
secretary. 17 Benaiah son of Jehoiada was captain of the king's bodyguard.* David's sons
served as the king's chief assistants.

David Defeats the Ammonites

19:1-19 //2 Sam 10:1-19 **19** Some time after this, King Nahash of the Ammonites died, and his son Hanun*
became king. 2 David said, "I am going to show complete loyalty to Hanun
because his father, Nahash, was always completely loyal to me." So David sent ambassadors to express sympathy to Hanun about his father's death.
But when David's ambassadors arrived in the land of Ammon, 3 Hanun's advisers said

18:8 Hebrew reads *Tibhath,* a variant name for Tebah; compare parallel text at 2 Sam 8:8. **18:9** As in parallel text at 2 Sam 8:9; Hebrew reads *Tou;* also in 18:10. **18:10** As in parallel text at 2 Sam 8:10; Hebrew reads *Hadoram,* a variant name for Joram. **18:16a** As in some Hebrew manuscripts, Syriac version, and Latin Vulgate (see also 2 Sam 8:17); most Hebrew manuscripts read *Abimelech.* **18:16b** As in parallel text at 2 Sam 8:17; Hebrew reads *Shavsha.* **18:17** Hebrew *of the Kerethites and Pelethites.* **19:1** Hebrew lacks *Hanun;* compare parallel text at 2 Sam 10:1.

18:6, 14 David was a victorious and fair ruler. We see in David's glowing success a hint of what Christ's reign will be like—complete victory and justice. If David's glory was great, how much greater will Christ's glory be! The great news for us is that we can be rightly related to Jesus Christ through faith. One day we will share in his glory as we reign with him.

18:9-11 When David received gifts from King Toi, he dedicated them to God, realizing that they had come from God and were to be used for him. It is easy to think that our financial and material blessings are the result of our own skill and hard work rather than coming from a loving God (James 1:17). What has God given you? Dedicate all your gifts and resources to him, and use them for his service. He will lead you in the method you should use. The first step is to be willing.

18:13 The list of battles in this chapter shows how God gave David victory after victory. Unbelieving people think that victory comes from their own skill plus a little luck. Just as David acknowledged God's role in his success, so should we. Don't take credit for the work God does.

19:1 The land of Ammon bordered Israel to the east. The nation had a sordid beginning: Its founding ancestor, Ben-ammi, was conceived through incest between Lot and his daughter (Genesis 19:30-38). The Ammonites, who were constant enemies of Israel, reached their greatest strength in the days of the judges. David was the first military leader of Israel to crush them. They were unable to cause further trouble for many years.

19:2, 3 Hanun misread David's intentions. He was overly suspicious and brought disaster upon himself. Because of past experiences, it is easy to be overly suspicious of others, questioning every move and second-guessing their motives. While we should be cautious and wise as we deal with others, we should not assume their every action is ill-intended.

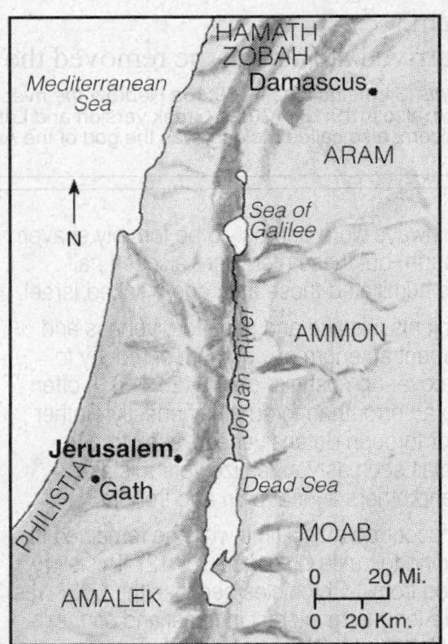

DAVID SUBDUES HIS ENEMIES
David expanded his kingdom as the Lord continued to give him victory. He subdued the Philistines by taking Gath, conquered Moab, won battles as far north as Zobah and Hamath (conquering Aram when they came to help these enemy nations), and subdued the other surrounding nations of Ammon and Amalek.

to him, "Do you really think these men are coming here to honor your father? No! David has sent them to spy out the land so that they can come in and conquer it!" 4So Hanun seized David's ambassadors and shaved their beards, cut off their robes at the buttocks, and sent them back to David in shame. 5When David heard what had happened, he sent messengers to tell the men to stay at Jericho until their beards grew out, for they were very embarrassed by their appearance.

6Now the people of Ammon realized how seriously they had angered David, so Hanun and the Ammonites sent thirty-eight tons* of silver to hire chariots and troops from Aram-naharaim, Aram-maacah, and Zobah. 7They also hired thirty-two thousand chariots and secured the support of the king of Maacah and his army. These forces camped at Medeba, where they were joined by the Ammonite troops that Hanun had recruited from his own towns. 8When David heard about this, he sent Joab and all his warriors to fight them. 9The Ammonite troops drew up their battle lines at the gate of the city, while the other kings positioned themselves to fight in the open fields.

19:7 Num 21:30 Josh 13:9, 16

10When Joab saw that he would have to fight on two fronts, he chose the best troops in his army. He placed them under his personal command and led them out to fight the Arameans in the fields. 11He left the rest of the army under the command of his brother Abishai, who was to attack the Ammonites. 12"If the Arameans are too strong for me, then come over and help me," Joab told his brother. "And if the Ammonites are too strong for you, I will help you. 13Be courageous! Let us fight bravely to save our people and the cities of our God. May the LORD's will be done."

14When Joab and his troops attacked, the Arameans began to run away. 15And when the Ammonites saw the Arameans running, they ran from Abishai and retreated into the city. Then Joab returned to Jerusalem.

19:14 2 Sam 10:14

16The Arameans now realized that they were no match for Israel, so they summoned additional Aramean troops from the other side of the Euphrates River.* These troops arrived under the command of Shobach,* the commander of all Hadadezer's forces. 17When David heard what was happening, he mobilized all Israel, crossed the Jordan River, and positioned his troops in battle formation. Then he engaged the enemy troops in battle, and they fought against him. 18But again the Arameans fled from the Israelites. This time David's forces killed seven thousand charioteers and forty thousand foot soldiers, including Shobach, the commander of their army. 19When the servants of Hadadezer realized they had been defeated by Israel, they surrendered to David and became his subjects. After that, the Arameans were no longer willing to help the Ammonites.

19:16 2 Sam 10:15-16

The Capture of Rabbah

20 The following spring, the time of year when kings go to war, Joab led the Israelite army in successful attacks against the towns and villages of the Ammonites. In the process they laid siege to the city of Rabbah and destroyed it. But David had stayed behind in Jerusalem.

20:1-3 //2 Sam 11:1; 12:29-31

2When David arrived at Rabbah, he removed the crown from the king's head,* and it

19:6 Hebrew *1,000 talents* [34 metric tons]. **19:16a** Hebrew *the river.* **19:16b** As in parallel text at 2 Sam 10:16; Hebrew reads *Shophach;* also in 19:18. **20:2a** Greek version and Latin Vulgate read *removed the crown of Milcom;* compare 1 Kgs 11:5. Milcom, also called Molech, was the god of the Ammonites.

19:4, 5 Israelite men always wore beards. To be forcibly shaven was embarrassing enough, but these men were also left half naked. Hanun's actions humiliated these men and insulted Israel.

19:6 Rather than admit his mistake and seek forgiveness and reconciliation, Hanun spent an enormous amount of money to cover up his error. His cover-up cost him dearly (20:1-3). It often costs more to cover up an error than to admit it honestly. Rather than compound an error through defensiveness, seek forgiveness and reconciliation as soon as you realize your mistake. You will save yourself and others a lot of pain and trouble.

20:1 David's adultery occurred at this time while he remained in Jerusalem instead of going to battle (2 Samuel 11–12). This story may have been excluded from 1 Chronicles because the book was written to focus on God's long-term interest in Israel and on the Temple as a symbol of God's presence among them. The story of David and Bathsheba did not fit this purpose. The story of Absalom's rebellion, which occurred between this chapter and the next, was probably omitted for the same reason (2 Samuel 15–18).

20:1 Kings went out to battle following the spring harvest. At this time, farm work eased off, and the armies could live off the land. During the winter, they plotted and planned future conquests. Then, when fair weather permitted, their armies went to war. But David ignored this opportunity. He stayed home and sent Joab out to lead the army. It was during this time of inactivity that he sinned with Bathsheba. Look for the "springs" in your life, the times when God wants you to respond, take the initiative, and move out to do his will. It is during these critical times that we may be most sensitive to temptation. Resolve to take the action God has prescribed. Don't give temptation a foothold in your inactivity.

20:1 Rabbah was the capital of the Ammonites and is the site of modern Amman in Jordan.

was placed on David's own head. The crown was made of gold and set with gems, and
it weighed about seventy-five pounds.* David took a vast amount of plunder from the
city. 3He also made slaves of the people of Rabbah and forced them to labor with saws,
picks, and axes.* That is how he dealt with the people of all the Ammonite cities. Then
David and his army returned to Jerusalem.

Battles against the Philistines

20:4-8 //2 Sam 21:15-22 4After this, war broke out with the Philistines at Gezer. As they fought, Sibbecai from
Hushah killed Saph,* a descendant of the giants,* and so the Philistines were subdued.
20:5 1 Sam 17:4-7 2 Sam 21:19 1 Chr 11:23 5During another battle with the Philistines, Elhanan son of Jair killed Lahmi, the brother
of Goliath of Gath. The handle of Lahmi's spear was as thick as a weaver's beam! 6In
another battle with the Philistines at Gath, a huge man with six fingers on each hand and
six toes on each foot—a descendant of the giants—7defied and taunted Israel. But he
was killed by Jonathan, the son of David's brother Shimea. 8These Philistines were
descendants of the giants of Gath, but they were killed by David and his warriors.

David Takes a Census

21:1-26 //2 Sam 24:1-25 **21** Satan rose up against Israel and caused David to take a census of the Israelites.
21:2 1 Chr 27:23-24 2David gave these orders to Joab and his commanders: "Take a census of all the
people in the land—from Beersheba in the south to Dan in the north—and bring me the
totals so I may know how many there are."

21:3 Deut 1:11 3But Joab replied, "May the LORD increase the number of his people a hundred times
over! But why, my lord, do you want to do this? Are they not all your servants? Why
must you cause Israel to sin?"

4But the king insisted that Joab take the census, so Joab traveled throughout Israel to
21:5 2 Sam 24:9 count the people. Then he returned to Jerusalem 5and reported the number of people to
21:6 1 Chr 27:24 David. There were 1,100,000 men of military age in Israel, and 470,000 in Judah. 6But
Joab did not include the tribes of Levi and Benjamin in the census because he was so
distressed at what the king had made him do.

Judgment for David's Sin

21:8 2 Sam 12:13 7God was very displeased with the census, and he punished Israel for it. 8Then David
said to God, "I have sinned greatly and shouldn't have taken the census. Please forgive
me for doing this foolish thing."

21:9 1 Sam 9:9 2 Sam 24:11 1 Chr 29:29 9Then the LORD spoke to Gad, David's seer. This was the message: 10"Go and say to
David, 'This is what the LORD says: I will give you three choices. Choose one of these
punishments, and I will do it.'"

11So Gad came to David and said, "These are the choices the LORD has given you.
21:12 2 Sam 24:13 12You may choose three years of famine, three months of destruction by your enemies,
or three days of severe plague as the angel of the LORD brings devastation throughout
the land of Israel. Think this over and let me know what answer to give the LORD."

20:2b Hebrew *1 talent* [34 kilograms]. **20:3** As in parallel text at 2 Sam 12:31; Hebrew reads *and saws.* **20:4a** As in parallel text at 2 Sam 21:18; Hebrew reads *Sippai.* **20:4b** Hebrew *descendant of the Rephaites;* also in 20:6, 8.

21:1 David's census brought disaster because, unlike the census taken in the book of Numbers (Numbers 1–2) that God had ordered, this census was taken so David could take pride in the strength of his army. In determining his military strength, he was beginning to trust more in military power than in God. There is a thin line between feeling confident because you are relying on God's power and becoming proud because you have been used by God for great purposes.

21:1 The Bible text says Satan *caused* David to take a census. Can Satan force people to do wrong? No, Satan only *tempted* David with the idea, but David *decided to act* on the temptation. Ever since the Garden of Eden, Satan has been tempting people to sin. David's census was not against God's law, but his reason for the census was wrong—pride in his mighty army. He forgot that his real strength came from God. Even Joab, not known for his high moral ideals, recognized the census as sin. From David's example we learn that an action that may not be wrong in itself can be sinful if it is motivated by greed, arrogance, or selfishness. Often our motives, not the action itself, contain the sin. We must constantly weigh our motives before we act.

21:1-3 David fell to Satan's temptation. God provided a way out in Joab's counsel, but David's curiosity was spurred on by arrogance. His faith was in his own strength rather than in God's. If we feel self-sufficient and put confidence in ourselves apart from God, we soon fall to Satan's schemes. Self-sufficiency pulls us away from God. When you are tempted, examine your inner desires to understand why the external temptation is so appealing. (See 1 Corinthians 10:13 for more about escaping temptation.)

21:8 When David realized his sin, he took full responsibility, admitted he was wrong, and asked God to forgive him. Many people want to add God and the benefits of Christianity to their lives without acknowledging their personal sin and guilt. But confession and repentance must come before receiving forgiveness. Like David, we must take full responsibility for our actions and confess them to God before we can expect him to forgive us and continue his work in us.

13“This is a desperate situation!” David replied to Gad. “But let me fall into the hands
of the LORD, for his mercy is very great. Do not let me fall into human hands.”
14So the LORD sent a plague upon Israel, and seventy thousand people died as a result.
15And God sent an angel to destroy Jerusalem. But just as the angel was preparing to destroy
it, the LORD relented and said to the death angel, “Stop! That is enough!” At that moment
the angel of the LORD was standing by the threshing floor of Araunah* the Jebusite.
16David looked up and saw the angel of the LORD standing between heaven and earth
with his sword drawn, stretched out over Jerusalem. So David and the leaders of Israel
put on sackcloth to show their distress and fell down with their faces to the ground. 17And
David said to God, “I am the one who called for the census! I am the one who has sinned
and done wrong! But these people are innocent—what have they done? O LORD my God,
let your anger fall against me and my family, but do not destroy your people.”

David Builds an Altar

18Then the angel of the LORD told Gad to instruct David to build an altar to the LORD at
the threshing floor of Araunah the Jebusite. 19So David obeyed the instructions the LORD
had given him through Gad. 20Araunah, who was busy threshing wheat at the time,
turned and saw the angel there. His four sons, who were with him, ran away and hid.
21When Araunah saw the king approaching, he left his threshing floor and bowed to the
ground before David.
22David said to Araunah, “Let me buy this threshing floor from you at its full price.
Then I will build an altar to the LORD there, so that he will stop the plague.”
23“Take it, my lord, and use it as you wish,” Araunah said to David. “Here are oxen
for the burnt offerings, and you can use the threshing tools for wood to build a fire on
the altar. And take the wheat for the grain offering. I will give it all to you.”
24But the king replied to Araunah, “No, I insist on paying what it is worth. I cannot
take what is yours and give it to the LORD. I will not offer a burnt offering that has cost
me nothing!” 25So David gave Araunah six hundred pieces of gold* in payment for the
threshing floor. 26David built an altar there to the LORD and sacrificed burnt offerings
and peace offerings. And when David prayed, the LORD answered him by sending fire
from heaven to burn up the offering on the altar. 27Then the LORD spoke to the angel,
who put the sword back into its sheath.
28When David saw that the LORD had answered his prayer, he offered sacrifices there
at Araunah's threshing floor. 29At that time, the Tabernacle of the LORD and the altar that
Moses made in the wilderness were located at the hill of Gibeon. 30But David was not
able to go there to inquire of God, because he was terrified by the drawn sword of the
angel of the LORD.

21:13 Pss 51:1; 130:4, 7
21:14 1 Chr 27:24
21:15 Exod 32:14; 1 Sam 15:11; Jon 3:10
21:16 1 Kgs 21:27
21:17 2 Sam 7:8; Ps 74:1
21:18 2 Chr 3:1
21:26 Lev 9:24; Judg 6:21
21:29 1 Kgs 3:4; 1 Chr 16:39

21:15 As in parallel text at 2 Sam 24:16; Hebrew reads *Ornan,* another name for Araunah; also in 21:18-28.
21:25 Hebrew *600 shekels of gold,* about 15 pounds or 6.8 kilograms in weight.

21:13, 14 Sin has a domino effect; once a sin is committed, a series of consequences follows. God will forgive our sin if we ask him, but the consequences of that sin have already been set in motion. David pled for mercy, and God responded by stopping the angel before his mission of death was complete. The consequences of David's sin, however, had already caused severe damage. God will always forgive our sins and will often intervene to make their bitter consequences less severe, but the scars will remain. Thinking through the possible consequences before we act can stop us and thus save us much sorrow and suffering.

21:14 Why did 70,000 innocent people die for David's sin? Our society places great emphasis upon the individual. In ancient times, however, the family leaders, tribal leaders, and kings represented the people they led, and all expected to share in their successes as well as in their failures and punishments. David deserved punishment for his sin, but his death could have resulted in political chaos and invasion by enemy armies, leaving hundreds of thousands dead. Instead, God graciously spared David's life. He also put a stop to the plague so that most of the people of Jerusalem were spared.

God made us to work together interdependently. Whether we think it is fair or not, the group usually suffers because of the sins of its leaders. Similarly, our actions always affect other people whether we want them to or not. We cannot fully know the mind of God in this severe judgment. We don't know where the prophets, the tribal leaders, and the other advisers were during this incident and whether or not they chose to go along with the king. We do know that putting confidence in military might alone is idolatry. To allow anything to take God's place is sinful, and it may cause disastrous consequences.

21:22-24 When David wanted to buy Araunah's land to build an altar, Araunah generously offered it as a gift. But David refused, saying, “I cannot take what is yours and give it to the LORD. I will not offer a burnt offering that has cost me nothing!” David wanted to offer an offering (or sacrifice) to God. An offering should cost the giver in terms of self, time, or money. To give sacrifically requires more than a token effort or gift. God wants us to give voluntarily, but he wants it to mean something. Giving to God what costs you nothing does not demonstrate commitment.

21:29–22:1 Gibeon was a Benjaminite city. After the defeat of Nob by Saul, who was a Benjaminite, Saul moved the Tabernacle to Gibeon. Gibeon was about two hours journey northwest of Jerusalem.

22:1 1 Chr 21:18-28; 2 Chr 3:1

22 Then David said, “This will be the location for the Temple of the LORD God and
the place of the altar for Israel’s burnt offerings!”

4. David arranges for the building of the Temple

Preparations for the Temple

22:2 1 Kgs 5:17-18; 9:20-21; 2 Chr 2:17

2 So David gave orders to call together the foreigners living in Israel, and he assigned
them the task of preparing blocks of stone for building the Temple of God. 3 David
provided large amounts of iron for the nails that would be needed for the doors in the

22:4 1 Kgs 5:6-10

gates and for the clamps, and more bronze than they could ever weigh. 4 He also provided

22:5 1 Kgs 3:7; 1 Chr 29:1

innumerable cedar logs, for the men of Tyre and Sidon had brought vast amounts of cedar
to David. 5 David said, “My son Solomon is still young and inexperienced, and the
Temple of the LORD must be a magnificent structure, famous and glorious throughout
the world. So I will begin making preparations for it now.” So David collected vast
amounts of building materials before his death.
6 Then David sent for his son Solomon and instructed him to build a Temple for the

22:7 2 Sam 7:2-3; 1 Chr 17:1-2

LORD, the God of Israel. 7 “I wanted to build a Temple to honor the name of the LORD
my God,” David told him. 8 “But the LORD said to me, ‘You have killed many men in the

22:8 1 Chr 28:3

great battles you have fought. And since you have shed so much blood before me, you
will not be the one to build a Temple to honor my name. 9 But you will have a son who

22:9 2 Sam 12:24-25; 1 Kgs 4:20, 25

will experience peace and rest. I will give him peace with his enemies in all the
surrounding lands. His name will be Solomon,* and I will give peace and quiet to Israel

22:10 2 Sam 7:13; 1 Chr 17:12

during his reign. 10 He is the one who will build a Temple to honor my name. He will be
my son, and I will be his father. And I will establish the throne of his kingdom over Israel
forever.’

22:11 1 Chr 22:16

11 “Now, my son, may the LORD be with you and give you success as you follow his
instructions in building the Temple of the LORD your God. 12 And may the LORD give you

22:12 1 Kgs 3:9-12; 2 Chr 1:10

wisdom and understanding, that you may obey the law of the LORD your God as you rule
over Israel. 13 For if you carefully obey the laws and regulations that the LORD gave to

22:13 Josh 1:6-9; 1 Chr 28:7

Israel through Moses, you will be successful. Be strong and courageous; do not be afraid
or lose heart!

22:14 1 Chr 22:3; 29:4

14 “I have worked hard to provide materials for building the Temple of the LORD—
nearly four thousand tons of gold, nearly forty thousand tons of silver,* and so much iron
and bronze that it cannot be weighed. I have also gathered lumber and stone for the walls,
though you may need to add more. 15 You have many skilled stonemasons and carpenters

22:16 1 Chr 22:11

and craftsmen of every kind available to you. 16 They are expert goldsmiths and
silversmiths and workers of bronze and iron. Now begin the work, and may the LORD be
with you!”

22:17 1 Chr 28:1-6

17 Then David ordered all the leaders of Israel to assist Solomon in this project. 18 “The

22:18 1 Chr 22:9; 23:25

LORD your God is with you,” he declared. “He has given you peace with the surrounding
nations. He has handed them over to me, and they are now subject to the LORD and his

22:19 1 Kgs 8:6, 21; 1 Chr 28:9; 2 Chr 5:7

people. 19 Now seek the LORD your God with all your heart. Build the sanctuary of the
LORD God so that you can bring the Ark of the LORD’s covenant and the holy vessels of
God into the Temple built to honor the LORD’s name.”

22:9 *Solomon* sounds like and is probably derived from the Hebrew word for “peace.” **22:14** Hebrew *100,000 talents* [3,400 metric tons] *of gold, 1,000,000 talents* [34,000 metric tons] *of silver.*

22:1 Out of David’s tragic mistake came the purchase of a plot of land that would become the site of God’s Temple, the symbol of God’s presence among his people. Every time the people would go to the Temple they would remember that God was their true King and that everyone, including their human king, was fallible and subject to sin. God can use our sins for good purposes if we are sorry for them and seek his forgiveness. When we confess our sins, the way is opened for God to bring good from a bad situation.

22:7-10 God told David he would not be the one to build the Temple. Instead, the task would be left to his son Solomon. David graciously accepted this no from God. He was not jealous of the fact that his son would have the honor of building God’s Temple but instead made preparations for Solomon to carry out his task. Similarly, we should take steps now to prepare the way for our children to find and fulfill God’s purpose. Sooner or later our children will have to make their own decisions, but we can help by supplying them with the proper tools: showing them how to pray and study God’s Word, the difference between right and wrong, and the importance of church involvement.

Duties of the Levites

23 When David was an old man, he appointed his son Solomon to be king over Israel.
[2]David summoned all the political leaders of Israel, together with the priests and
Levites, for the coronation ceremony. [3]All the Levites who were thirty years old or older
were counted, and the total came to thirty-eight thousand. [4]Then David said, "Twenty-
four thousand of them will supervise the work at the Temple of the LORD. Six thousand
are to serve as officials and judges. [5]Four thousand will work as gatekeepers, and another
four thousand will praise the LORD with the musical instruments I have made." [6]Then
David divided the Levites into divisions named after the clans descended from the three
sons of Levi—Gershon, Kohath, and Merari.

The Gershonites

[7]The Gershonite family units were defined by their lines of descent from Libni* and
Shimei, the sons of Gershon. [8]Three of the descendants of Libni were Jehiel (the
family leader), Zetham, and Joel. [9]These were the leaders of the family of Libni.
Three of the descendants of Shimei were Shelomoth, Haziel, and Haran. [10]Four other
descendants of Shimei were Jahath, Ziza,* Jeush, and Beriah. [11]Jahath was the
family leader, and Ziza was next. Jeush and Beriah were counted as a single family
because neither had many sons.

The Kohathites

[12]The descendants of Kohath included Amram, Izhar, Hebron, and Uzziel.
[13]The sons of Amram were Aaron and Moses. Aaron and his descendants were set
apart to dedicate the most holy things, to offer sacrifices in the LORD's presence, to
serve the LORD, and to pronounce blessings in his name forever.
[14]As for Moses, the man of God, his sons were included with the tribe of Levi.
[15]The sons of Moses were Gershom and Eliezer.
[16]The descendants of Gershom included Shebuel, the family leader.
[17]Eliezer had only one son, Rehabiah, the family leader. Rehabiah had numerous
descendants.
[18]The descendants of Izhar included Shelomith, the family leader.
[19]The descendants of Hebron included Jeriah (the family leader), Amariah (the second),
Jahaziel (the third), and Jekameam (the fourth).
[20]The descendants of Uzziel included Micah (the family leader) and Isshiah (the
second).

The Merarites

[21]The descendants of Merari included Mahli and Mushi.
The sons of Mahli were Eleazar and Kish. [22]Eleazar died with no sons, only daughters.
His daughters married their cousins, the sons of Kish.
[23]The three sons of Mushi were Mahli, Eder, and Jerimoth.

[24]These were the descendants of Levi by clans, the leaders of their family groups,
registered carefully by name. Each had to be twenty years old or older to qualify for
service in the house of the LORD. [25]For David said, "The LORD, the God of Israel, has
given us peace, and he will always live in Jerusalem. [26]Now the Levites will no longer
need to carry the Tabernacle and its utensils from place to place." [27]It was according to

23:7 Hebrew *Ladan* (also in 23:8-9), another name for Libni; compare 6:17. **23:10** As in Greek version and Latin Vulgate (see also 23:11); Hebrew reads *Zina.*

23:1 1 Chr 28:5; 29:22, 28
23:3 Num 4:3-49; 1 Chr 23:24
23:4 1 Chr 26:29; Ezra 3:8-9
23:5 1 Chr 15:16
23:6 1 Chr 6:1
23:13 Exod 6:20; 28:1; 30:6-10
23:14 Deut 33:1
23:21 1 Chr 6:19
23:24 Num 10:17, 21; 1 Chr 23:3
23:25 1 Chr 22:18
23:26 Num 4:5, 15; 7:9; Deut 10:8

23:1 For more information on Solomon's coronation and the attempts to seize his throne, see 1 Kings 1–2.

23:1ff Although David couldn't build the Temple, he could make preparations, and he took that job seriously. He not only gathered funds and materials for God's house but also planned much of the administration and arranged the worship services. The original readers of Chronicles were rebuilding the Temple after it had been destroyed by invading armies, and this information about its procedures was invaluable to them. The next five chapters demonstrate that organization is essential for smooth and effective service.

23:3 Why was this census acceptable when the other was not (chapter 21)? This census counted only the Levites—those set apart to serve God—and was used to organize the work in the Temple. The census was not based on pride or self-sufficiency, as was the previous census of fighting men.

23:14 All that is stated here about Moses is that he was "the man of God." What a profound description of a person! A man or woman of God is one whose life reflects God's presence, priorities, and power.

David's final instructions that all the Levites twenty years old or older were registered
for service.
28 The work of the Levites was to assist the priests, the descendants of Aaron, as they
served at the house of the LORD. They also took care of the courtyards and side rooms,
helped perform the ceremonies of purification, and served in many other ways in the
23:29 Lev 6:20-21; 19:35-36; 24:5-9 1 Chr 9:29, 32
house of God. 29 They were in charge of the sacred bread that was set out on the table,
the choice flour for the grain offerings, the wafers made without yeast, the cakes cooked
in olive oil, and the other mixed breads. They were also responsible to check all the
weights and measures. 30 And each morning and evening they stood before the LORD to
23:31 Lev 23:2-4 Isa 1:13-14
sing songs of thanks and praise to him. 31 They assisted with the burnt offerings that were
presented to the LORD on Sabbath days, at new moon celebrations, and at all the
appointed festivals. The proper number of Levites served in the LORD's presence at all
times, following all the procedures they had been given.
23:32 Num 1:53; 3:6-9, 38
32 And so, under the supervision of the priests, the Levites watched over the Tabernacle
and the Temple* and faithfully carried out their duties of service at the house of the
LORD.

Duties of the Priests

24:1 Exod 6:23
24:2 Lev 10:1-2

24 This is how Aaron's descendants, the priests, were divided into groups for service.
The sons of Aaron were Nadab, Abihu, Eleazar, and Ithamar. 2 But Nadab and
Abihu died before their father did, and they had no sons. So only Eleazar and Ithamar
were left to carry on as priests.

23:32 Hebrew *the Tent of Meeting and the sanctuary.*

DUTIES ASSIGNED IN THE TEMPLE
King David charged all these people to do their jobs "to honor the LORD's name" (1 Chronicles 22:17–19). God needs people of every talent—not just prophets and priests—to obey him.

Administrative Duties	Supervisors	1 Chronicles 23:4, 5
	Officials	1 Chronicles 23:4, 5
	Judges	1 Chronicles 23:4, 5
	Public administrators	1 Chronicles 26:29, 30
Ministerial Duties	Priests	1 Chronicles 24:1
	Prophets	1 Chronicles 25:1
	Assistants for sacrifices	1 Chronicles 23:29–31
	Assistants for purification ceremonies	1 Chronicles 23:28
Service Duties	Bakers of the sacred bread	1 Chronicles 23:29
	Those who checked the weights and measures	1 Chronicles 23:29
	Caretakers	1 Chronicles 23:28
Financial Duties	Those who cared for the treasuries	1 Chronicles 26:20
	Those who cared for the dedicated things	1 Chronicles 26:26–28
Artistic Duties	Musicians	1 Chronicles 25:6
	Singers	1 Chronicles 25:7
Protective Duties	Gatekeepers	1 Chronicles 26:12–18
Individual Assignments	Chief of the gatekeepers	1 Chronicles 9:19–21
	Recorder	1 Chronicles 24:6
	Seer	1 Chronicles 25:5
	Prophet under the king	1 Chroncles 25:2
	Chief officer of the treasuries	1 Chronicles 26:23, 24

23:28-32 Priests and Levites had different jobs in and around the Temple. Priests were authorized to perform the sacrifices. Levites were set apart to help the priests. They did the work of elders, deacons, custodians, assistants, musicians, moving men, and repairmen. Both priests and Levites came from the tribe of Levi, but priests also had to be descendants of Aaron, Israel's first high priest (Exodus 28:1-3). Priests and Levites were supported by Israel's tithes and by revenues from certain cities that had been given to them. Worship in the house of the Lord could not have taken place without the combined efforts of the priests and Levites. Their responsibilities were different, but they were equally important to God's plan. No matter what place of service you have in the church, you are important to the healthy functioning of the congregation.

24:1ff The Temple service was highly structured, but this did not hinder the Spirit of God. Rather, it provided an orderly context for worship. (Compare 1 Corinthians 14:40.) Sometimes we feel that planning and structure are unspiritual activities that may hinder spontaneity in worship. But order and structure can free us to respond to God. Order brings glory to God as we experience the joy, freedom, and calm that come when we have wisely planned in advance.

[3]With the help of Zadok, who was a descendant of Eleazar, and of Ahimelech, who was
a descendant of Ithamar, David divided Aaron's descendants into groups according to their
various duties. [4]Eleazar's descendants were divided into sixteen groups and Ithamar's into
eight, for there were more family leaders among the descendants of Eleazar.
[5]All tasks were assigned to the various groups by means of sacred lots so that no
preference would be shown, for there were many qualified officials serving God in the
sanctuary from among the descendants of both Eleazar and Ithamar. [6]Shemaiah son of
Nethanel, a Levite, acted as secretary and wrote down the names and assignments in the
presence of the king, Zadok the priest, Ahimelech son of Abiathar, and the family leaders
of the priests and Levites. The descendants of Eleazar and Ithamar took turns casting lots.

24:5 1 Chr 24:31
24:6 1 Chr 18:16

7 The first lot fell to Jehoiarib.
The second lot fell to Jedaiah.
8 The third lot fell to Harim.
The fourth lot fell to Seorim.
9 The fifth lot fell to Malkijah.
The sixth lot fell to Mijamin.
10 The seventh lot fell to Hakkoz.
The eighth lot fell to Abijah.
11 The ninth lot fell to Jeshua.
The tenth lot fell to Shecaniah.
12 The eleventh lot fell to Eliashib.
The twelfth lot fell to Jakim.
13 The thirteenth lot fell to Huppah.
The fourteenth lot fell to Jeshebeab.
14 The fifteenth lot fell to Bilgah.
The sixteenth lot fell to Immer.
15 The seventeenth lot fell to Hezir.
The eighteenth lot fell to Happizzez.
16 The nineteenth lot fell to Pethahiah.
The twentieth lot fell to Jehezkel.
17 The twenty-first lot fell to Jakin.
The twenty-second lot fell to Gamul.
18 The twenty-third lot fell to Delaiah.
The twenty-fourth lot fell to Maaziah.

24:7 Neh 12:6
24:10 Neh 12:4 Luke 1:5

[19]Each group carried out its duties in the house of the LORD according to the procedures
established by their ancestor Aaron in obedience to the commands of the LORD, the God
of Israel.

Family Leaders among the Levites

[20]These were the other family leaders descended from Levi:

From the descendants of Amram, the leader was Shebuel.*
From the descendants of Shebuel, the leader was Jehdeiah.
21 From the descendants of Rehabiah, the leader was Isshiah.
22 From the descendants of Izhar, the leader was Shelomith.*
From the descendants of Shelomith, the leader was Jahath.

24:20 Hebrew *Shubael* (also in 24:20b), a variant name for Shebuel; compare 23:16 and 26:24. **24:22** Hebrew *Shelomoth* (also in 24:22b), a variant name for Shelomith; compare 23:18.

24:3 This Ahimelech was the son of Abiathar and the grandson of another Ahimelech, one of the priests massacred by Saul (1 Samuel 22:11-18). Abiathar and Zadok were co–high priests under David: One was at Jerusalem where the Ark of God was kept, and one was at Gibeon serving at the Tabernacle. It appears from this verse and 18:16 that Ahimelech began to assume some of Abiathar's duties as his father grew old.

24:4 Eleazar's descendants were divided into 16 groups (as opposed to Ithamar's 8) for three reasons. (1) Eleazar had received the birthright since his two older brothers, Nadab and Abihu, had been killed (Leviticus 10). The birthright included a double portion of the father's estate. (2) His descendants were greater in number than Ithamar's. (3) His descendants had greater leadership ability. These 24 groups gave order to the functioning of the house of the Lord.

24:7-18 Each of these 24 groups of priests served two-week shifts each year at the house of the Lord. The rest of the time they served in their hometowns. This system was still in place in Jesus' day (Luke 1:5-9). Zechariah was a member of the Abijah division. During his shift at the Temple, an angel appeared to him and predicted that he would have a son, John.

24:23
1 Chr 23:19

23 From the descendants of Hebron, Jeriah was the leader,* Amariah was second-in-command, Jahaziel was third, and Jekameam was fourth.
24 From the descendants of Uzziel, the leader was Micah.
From the descendants of Micah, the leader was Shamir, 25 along with Isshiah, the brother of Micah.
From the descendants of Isshiah, the leader was Zechariah.
26 From the descendants of Merari, the leaders were Mahli and Mushi.
From the descendants of Jaaziah, the leader was Beno.
27 From the descendants of Merari through Jaaziah, the leaders were Beno, Shoham, Zaccur, and Ibri.
28 From the descendants of Mahli, the leader was Eleazar, though he had no sons.
29 From the descendants of Kish, the leader was Jerahmeel.
30 From the descendants of Mushi, the leaders were Mahli, Eder, and Jerimoth.

24:31
1 Chr 24:5-6

These were the descendants of Levi in their various families. 31 Like the descendants
of Aaron, they were assigned to their duties by means of sacred lots, without regard to age or rank. It was done in the presence of King David, Zadok, Ahimelech, and the family leaders of the priests and the Levites.

Duties of the Musicians

25:1
2 Kgs 3:15
1 Chr 6:33, 39; 15:16

25 David and the army commanders then appointed men from the families of Asaph, Heman, and Jeduthun to proclaim God's messages to the accompaniment of harps, lyres, and cymbals. Here is a list of their names and their work:

2 From the sons of Asaph, there were Zaccur, Joseph, Nethaniah, and Asarelah. They worked under the direction of their father, Asaph, who proclaimed God's messages by the king's orders.

24:23 Hebrew *From the descendants of Jeriah;* compare 23:19.

MUSIC IN BIBLE TIMES

Paul clearly puts forth the Christian's view that things are not good or bad in and of themselves (see Romans 14 and 1 Corinthians 14:7, 8, 26). The point should always be to worship the Lord or help others by means of the things of this world, including music. Music was created by God and can be returned to him in praise. Does the music you play or listen to have a negative or positive impact upon your relationship with God?

Highlights of Musical Use in Scripture	*Reference*
Jubal was father of all musicians	Genesis 4:21
Miriam and other women sang and danced to praise God	Exodus 15:1–21
The priest was to have bells on his robes	Exodus 28:34, 35
Jericho fell to the sound of horns	Joshua 6:4–20
Saul experienced the soothing effect of music	1 Samuel 16:14–23
The king's coronation was accompanied by music	1 Kings 1:39, 40
The Ark was accompanied by trumpeters	1 Chronicles 16:6
There were musicians for the king's court	Ecclesiastes 2:8
From David's time on, the use of music in worship was much more organized. Music for the temple became refined	1 Chronicles 15:16–24 1 Chronicles 16:4–7 2 Chronicles 5:11–14
Everything was to be used by everyone to praise the Lord	Psalm 150
In the New Testament, worship continued in the synagogues until the Christians became unwelcome there, so there was a rich musical heritage already established. The fact that music is mentioned less often in the New Testament does not mean it was less important.	
Jesus and the disciples sang a hymn	Matthew 26:30
Paul and Silas sang in jail	Acts 16:25
We are to sing to the Lord as a response to what he has done in our lives	Ephesians 5:19, 20 Colossians 3:16 James 5:13

25:1-7 There were many ways to contribute to the worship in the Tabernacle. Some proclaimed God's messages (25:1), some offered thanks and praise (25:3), and others played instruments (25:6, 7). God wants all his people to participate in worship. You may not be a master musician, a prophet, or a teacher, but God appreciates whatever you have to offer. Develop your special gifts to offer in service to God (Romans 12:3-8; 1 Corinthians 12:29-31).

3 Jeduthun had six sons: Gedaliah, Zeri, Jeshaiah, Shimei,* Hashabiah, and Mattithiah. **25:3** 1 Chr 16:41-42
They worked under the direction of their father, Jeduthun, who proclaimed God's
messages to the accompaniment of the harp, offering thanks and praise to the LORD.
4 Heman's sons were Bukkiah, Mattaniah, Uzziel, Shubael,* Jerimoth, Hananiah, **25:4** 2 Sam 24:11 1 Chr 21:9
Hanani, Eliathah, Geddalti, Romamti-ezer, Joshbekashah, Mallothi, Hothir, and
Mahazioth. 5 All these were the sons of Heman, the king's seer, for God had
honored him with fourteen sons and three daughters.

6 All these men were under the direction of their fathers as they made music at the **25:6** 1 Chr 15:16, 19
house of the LORD. Their responsibilities included the playing of cymbals, lyres, and
harps at the house of God. Asaph, Jeduthun, and Heman reported directly to the king.
7 They and their families were all trained in making music before the LORD, and each of **25:8** 1 Chr 26:13
them—288 in all—was an accomplished musician. 8 The musicians were appointed to
their particular term of service by means of sacred lots, without regard to whether they
were young or old, teacher or student.

9 The first lot fell to Joseph of the Asaph clan and twelve of his sons and relatives.*
The second lot fell to Gedaliah and twelve of his sons and relatives.
10 The third lot fell to Zaccur and twelve of his sons and relatives.
11 The fourth lot fell to Zeri* and twelve of his sons and relatives.
12 The fifth lot fell to Nethaniah and twelve of his sons and relatives.
13 The sixth lot fell to Bukkiah and twelve of his sons and relatives.
14 The seventh lot fell to Asarelah* and twelve of his sons and relatives.
15 The eighth lot fell to Jeshaiah and twelve of his sons and relatives.
16 The ninth lot fell to Mattaniah and twelve of his sons and relatives.
17 The tenth lot fell to Shimei and twelve of his sons and relatives.
18 The eleventh lot fell to Uzziel* and twelve of his sons and relatives.
19 The twelfth lot fell to Hashabiah and twelve of his sons and relatives.
20 The thirteenth lot fell to Shubael and twelve of his sons and relatives.
21 The fourteenth lot fell to Mattithiah and twelve of his sons and relatives.
22 The fifteenth lot fell to Jerimoth* and twelve of his sons and relatives.
23 The sixteenth lot fell to Hananiah and twelve of his sons and relatives.
24 The seventeenth lot fell to Joshbekashah* and twelve of his sons and relatives.
25 The eighteenth lot fell to Hanani and twelve of his sons and relatives.
26 The nineteenth lot fell to Mallothi and twelve of his sons and relatives.
27 The twentieth lot fell to Eliathah and twelve of his sons and relatives.
28 The twenty-first lot fell to Hothir and twelve of his sons and relatives.
29 The twenty-second lot fell to Geddalti* and twelve of his sons and relatives.
30 The twenty-third lot fell to Mahazioth and twelve of his sons and relatives.
31 The twenty-fourth lot fell to Romamti-ezer and twelve of his sons and relatives. **25:31** 1 Chr 9:33

Duties of the Gatekeepers

26 These are the divisions of the gatekeepers:

From the Korahites, there was Meshelemiah son of Kore, of the family of
Asaph. 2 The sons of Meshelemiah were Zechariah (the oldest), Jediael (the
second), Zebadiah (the third), Jathniel (the fourth), 3 Elam (the fifth), Jehohanan
(the sixth), and Eliehoenai (the seventh).

25:3 As in one Hebrew manuscript and some Greek manuscripts (see also 25:17); most Hebrew manuscripts lack *Shimei.* **25:4** Hebrew *Shebuel,* a variant name for Shubael; compare 25:20. **25:9** As in Greek version; Hebrew lacks *and twelve of his sons and relatives.* **25:11** Hebrew *Izri,* a variant name for Zeri; compare 25:3. **25:14** Hebrew *Jesharelah,* a variant name for Asarelah; compare 25:2. **25:18** Hebrew *Azarel,* a variant name for Uzziel; compare 25:4. **25:22** Hebrew *Jeremoth,* a variant name for Jerimoth; compare 25:4. **25:24** Hebrew *Joshbekasha,* a variant name for Joshbekashah; compare 25:4. **25:29** Hebrew *Giddalti,* a variant name for Geddalti; compare 25:4.

25:9-31 The musicians were divided into 24 groups to match the 24 groups of Levites (24:7-18). This division of labor gave order to the planning of Temple work, promoted excellence by making training easier, gave variety to worship because each group worked a term, and provided opportunities for many to be involved.

26:1 There were 4,000 gatekeepers (23:5). They were all Levites and did many other jobs as well. Some of their duties included (1) checking out the equipment and utensils used each day and making sure they were returned, (2) storing, ordering, and maintaining the food supplies for the priests and sacrifices, (3) caring for the furniture, (4) mixing the incense that was burned daily, and (5) accounting for the gifts brought. (For more on gatekeepers, see the note on 9:17, 18.)

4The sons of Obed-edom, also gatekeepers, were Shemaiah (the oldest), Jehozabad
(the second), Joah (the third), Sacar (the fourth), Nethanel (the fifth), 5Ammiel (the
sixth), Issachar (the seventh), and Peullethai (the eighth). God had richly blessed
Obed-edom.
6Obed-edom's son Shemaiah had sons with great ability who earned positions of
great authority in the clan. 7Their names were Othni, Rephael, Obed, and Elzabad.
Their relatives, Elihu and Semakiah, were also very capable men.
8All of these descendants of Obed-edom, including their sons and grandsons—
sixty-two of them in all—were very capable men, well qualified for their work.
9Meshelemiah's eighteen sons and relatives were also very capable men.

26:10 1 Chr 16:38

10Hosah, of the Merari clan, appointed Shimri as the leader among his sons, though
he was not the oldest. 11His other sons included Hilkiah (the second), Tebaliah
(the third), and Zechariah (the fourth). Hosah's sons and relatives, who served as
gatekeepers, numbered thirteen in all.

26:13 1 Chr 24:5, 31; 25:8

12These divisions of the gatekeepers were named for their family leaders, and like the
other Levites, they served at the house of the LORD. 13They were assigned by families
for guard duty at the various gates, without regard to age or training, for it was all decided
by means of sacred lots.
14The responsibility for the east gate went to Meshelemiah* and his group. The north
gate was assigned to his son Zechariah, a man of unusual wisdom. 15The south gate went
to Obed-edom, and his sons were put in charge of the storehouses. 16Shuppim and Hosah
were assigned the west gate and the gateway leading up to the Temple.* Guard duties were
divided evenly. 17Six Levites were assigned each day to the east gate, four to the north gate,
four to the south gate, and two to each of the storehouses. 18Six were assigned each day to
the west gate, four to the gateway leading up to the Temple, and two to the courtyard.*
19These were the divisions of the gatekeepers from the clans of Korah and Merari.

Treasurers and Other Officials

26:20 1 Chr 26:22, 24; 28:12

20Other Levites, led by Ahijah, were in charge of the treasuries of the house of God and
the storerooms. 21From the family of Libni* in the clan of Gershon, Jehiel* was the
leader. 22The sons of Jehiel, Zetham and his brother Joel, were in charge of the treasuries
of the house of the LORD.
23These are the leaders that descended from Amram, Izhar, Hebron, and Uzziel:

24From the clan of Amram, Shebuel was a descendant of Gershom son of Moses. He
was the chief officer of the treasuries. 25His relatives through Eliezer were
Rehabiah, Jeshaiah, Joram, Zicri, and Shelomoth.

26:26 2 Sam 8:11

26Shelomoth and his relatives were in charge of the treasuries that held all the
things dedicated to the LORD by King David, the family leaders, and the generals
and captains and other officers of the army. 27These men had dedicated some of the
plunder they had gained in battle to maintain the house of the LORD. 28Shelomoth
and his relatives also cared for the items dedicated to the LORD by Samuel the seer,
Saul son of Kish, Abner son of Ner, and Joab son of Zeruiah. All the other dedicated items were in their care, too.

26:29 1 Chr 23:4

29From the clan of Izhar came Kenaniah. He and his sons were appointed to serve as
public administrators and judges throughout Israel.

26:14 Hebrew *Shelemiah,* a variant name for Meshelemiah; compare 26:2. **26:16** Or *the gate of Shalleketh on the upper road* (also in 26:18). The meaning of the Hebrew is uncertain. **26:18** Or *the colonnade.* The meaning of the Hebrew is uncertain. **26:21a** Hebrew *Ladan,* another name for Libni; compare 6:17. **26:21b** Hebrew *Jehieli* (also in 26:22), a variant name for Jehiel; compare 23:8.

26:5 "God had richly blessed Obed-edom." The status of children in society has fluctuated throughout history; sometimes they are highly esteemed, and sometimes abused and cheated. But Scripture shows no such vacillation—children are called a gift from the Lord, and God never views them as a burden (Psalm 127:3-5; Mark 10:13-15).

26:27 War plunder rightfully belonged to the victorious army. These soldiers, however, gave their portion of all the plunder to the house of the Lord to express their dedication to God. Like these commanders, we should think of what we *can* give, rather than what we are obligated to give. Is your giving a matter of rejoicing rather than duty? Give as a response of joy and love for God.

30 From the clan of Hebron came Hashabiah. He and his relatives—seventeen hundred
capable men—were put in charge of the Israelite lands west of the Jordan River.
They were responsible for all matters related to the things of the LORD and the
service of the king in that area.
31 Also from the clan of Hebron came Jeriah,* who was the leader of the Hebronites according to the genealogical records. (In the fortieth year of David's reign, a
search was made in the records, and capable men from the clan of Hebron were
found at Jazer in the land of Gilead.) 32 There were twenty-seven hundred capable
men among the relatives of Jeriah. King David sent them to the east side of the Jordan River and put them in charge of the tribes of Reuben and Gad and the half-tribe
of Manasseh. They were responsible for all matters related to the things of God and
the service of the king.

26:30 1 Chr 27:17

26:31 1 Chr 23:19

Military Commanders and Divisions

27 This is the list of Israelite generals and captains, and their officers, who served the
king by supervising the army divisions that were on duty each month of the year.
Each division served for one month and had twenty-four thousand troops.
2 Jashobeam son of Zabdiel was commander of the first division, which was on duty
during the first month. There were twenty-four thousand troops in his division. 3 He
was a descendant of Perez and was in charge of all the army officers for the first
month.
4 Dodai, a descendant of Ahoah, was commander of the second division, which was on
duty during the second month. There were twenty-four thousand troops in his
division, and Mikloth was his chief officer.
5 Benaiah son of Jehoiada the priest was commander of the third division, which was
on duty during the third month. There were twenty-four thousand troops in his
division. 6 This was the Benaiah who commanded David's elite military group
known as the Thirty. His son Ammizabad was his chief officer.
7 Asahel, the brother of Joab, was commander of the fourth division, which was on
duty during the fourth month. There were twenty-four thousand troops in his
division. Asahel was succeeded by his son Zebadiah.
8 Shammah* the Izrahite was commander of the fifth division, which was on
duty during the fifth month. There were twenty-four thousand troops in his
division.
9 Ira son of Ikkesh from Tekoa was commander of the sixth division, which was
on duty during the sixth month. There were twenty-four thousand troops in his
division.
10 Helez, a descendant of Ephraim from Pelon, was commander of the seventh
division, which was on duty during the seventh month. There were twenty-four
thousand troops in his division.
11 Sibbecai, a descendant of Zerah from Hushah, was commander of the eighth
division, which was on duty during the eighth month. There were twenty-four
thousand troops in his division.
12 Abiezer from Anathoth in the territory of Benjamin was commander of the ninth
division, which was on duty during the ninth month. There were twenty-four
thousand troops in his division.
13 Maharai, a descendant of Zerah from Netophah, was commander of the tenth
division, which was on duty during the tenth month. There were twenty-four
thousand troops in his division.
14 Benaiah from Pirathon in Ephraim was commander of the eleventh division, which
was on duty during the eleventh month. There were twenty-four thousand troops in
his division.
15 Heled,* a descendant of Othniel from Netophah, was commander of the twelfth
division, which was on duty during the twelfth month. There were twenty-four
thousand troops in his division.

27:2 2 Sam 23:8 1 Chr 11:11-31

26:31 Hebrew *Jerijah,* a variant name for Jeriah; compare 23:19. **27:8** Hebrew *Shamhuth,* another name for Shammah; compare 11:27 and 2 Sam 23:25. **27:15** Hebrew *Heldai,* a variant name for Heled; compare 11:30 and 2 Sam 23:29.

Leaders of the Tribes

16 The following were the tribes of Israel and their leaders:

Tribe	Leader
Reuben	Eliezer son of Zicri
Simeon	Shephatiah son of Maacah
17 Levi	Hashabiah son of Kemuel
Aaron (the priests)	Zadok
18 Judah	Elihu (a brother of David)
Issachar	Omri son of Michael
19 Zebulun	Ishmaiah son of Obadiah
Naphtali	Jeremoth son of Azriel
20 Ephraim	Hoshea son of Azaziah
Manasseh (west)	Joel son of Pedaiah
21 Manasseh (east*)	Iddo son of Zechariah
Benjamin	Jaasiel son of Abner
22 Dan	Azarel son of Jeroham

27:17 1 Chr 12:28

These were the leaders of the tribes of Israel.

27:23 2 Sam 24:1
27:24 2 Sam 24:12-15; 1 Chr 21:1-7

23 When David took his census, he did not count those who were younger than twenty
years of age, because the LORD had promised to make the Israelites as numerous as the
stars in heaven. 24 Joab began the census but never finished it because the anger of God
broke out against Israel. The final total was never recorded in King David's official
records.

Officials of David's Kingdom

25 Azmaveth son of Adiel was in charge of the palace treasuries.
Jonathan son of Uzziah was in charge of the regional treasuries throughout the towns, villages, and fortresses of Israel.
26 Ezri son of Kelub was in charge of the field workers who farmed the king's lands.
27 Shimei from Ramah was in charge of the king's vineyards.
Zabdi from Shepham was responsible for the grapes and the supplies of wine.
27:28 1 Kgs 10:27; 2 Chr 1:15
28 Baal-hanan from Geder was in charge of the king's olive groves and sycamore-fig trees in the foothills of Judah.*
27:29 1 Chr 5:16
Joash was responsible for the supplies of olive oil.
29 Shitrai from Sharon was in charge of the cattle on the Sharon Plain.
Shaphat son of Adlai was responsible for the cattle in the valleys.
30 Obil the Ishmaelite was in charge of the camels.
27:31 1 Chr 5:10
Jehdeiah from Meronoth was in charge of the donkeys.
31 Jaziz the Hagrite was in charge of the king's sheep.
All these officials were overseers of King David's property.

27:33 2 Sam 15:12, 32, 37
27:34 1 Kgs 1:7; 1 Chr 11:6; 27:5

32 Jonathan, David's uncle, was a wise counselor to the king, a man of great insight, and
a scribe. Jehiel the Hacmonite was responsible to teach the king's sons. 33 Ahithophel was
the royal adviser. Hushai the Arkite was the king's friend. 34 Ahithophel was succeeded by
Jehoiada son of Benaiah and by Abiathar. Joab was commander of the Israelite army.

David's Instructions to Solomon

28:1 1 Chr 11:10-47; 23:2; 27:1-31

28 David summoned all his officials to Jerusalem—the leaders of the tribes, the
commanders of the twelve army divisions, the other generals and captains, the
overseers of the royal property and livestock, the palace officials, the mighty men,

27:21 Hebrew *in Gilead.* **27:28** Hebrew *the Shephelah.*

27:24 The book of the annals of King David was a historical document kept in the royal archives with other official records. It no longer exists. See 1 Kings 14:19.

27:33, 34 When Absalom rebelled against David, Ahithophel betrayed David and joined the rebellion. Hushai pretended loyalty to Absalom, and his advice caused Absalom's downfall (2 Samuel 15:31–17:23).

28:1 The last two chapters of 1 Chronicles present the transition from David to Solomon as king of Israel. The writer doesn't mention Adonijah's conspiracy or David's frailty (1 Kings 1–2). Instead, he focuses on the positive—God's plans for Israel and his promise to David's descendants.

and all the other warriors in the kingdom. [2]David rose and stood before them and **28:2** 1 Chr 17:1-2
addressed them as follows: "My brothers and my people! It was my desire to build a Ps 132:7
temple where the Ark of the LORD's covenant, God's footstool, could rest perma- Isa 66:1
nently. I made the necessary preparations for building it, [3]but God said to me, 'You **28:3**
must not build a temple to honor my name, for you are a warrior and have shed much 1 Chr 17:4; 22:8
blood.'
[4]"Yet the LORD, the God of Israel, has chosen me from among all my father's family **28:4** Gen 49:8-10
to be king over Israel forever. For he has chosen the tribe of Judah to rule, and from 1 Sam 16:1-6
among the families of Judah, he chose my father's family. And from among my father's 1 Chr 5:2; 17:23, 27
sons, the LORD was pleased to make me king over all Israel. [5]And from among my **28:5**
sons—for the LORD has given me many children—he chose Solomon to succeed me on 1 Chr 3:1-9; 14:3-7; 22:9-10
the throne of his kingdom of Israel. [6]He said to me, 'Your son Solomon will build my **28:6**
Temple and its courtyards, for I have chosen him as my son, and I will be his father. 2 Sam 7:13-14
[7]And if he continues to obey my commands and regulations as he does now, I will make **28:7**
his kingdom last forever.' [8]So now, with God as our witness, I give you this charge for 1 Chr 22:13
all Israel, the LORD's assembly: Be careful to obey all the commands of the LORD your
God, so that you may possess this good land and leave it to your children as a permanent
inheritance.
[9]"And Solomon, my son, get to know the God of your ancestors. Worship and serve **28:9**
him with your whole heart and with a willing mind. For the LORD sees every heart and 1 Kgs 8:61 2 Chr 15:2
understands and knows every plan and thought. If you seek him, you will find him. But Jer 29:13
if you forsake him, he will reject you forever. [10]So take this seriously. The LORD has **28:10**
chosen you to build a Temple as his sanctuary. Be strong, and do the work." 1 Chr 22:13
[11]Then David gave Solomon the plans for the Temple and its surroundings, including **28:11**
the treasuries, the upstairs rooms, the inner rooms, and the inner sanctuary where the Exod 25:17-22, 40
Ark's cover—the place of atonement—would be kept. [12]David also gave Solomon all **28:12**
the plans he had in mind* for the courtyards of the LORD's Temple, the outside rooms, 1 Chr 26:20, 28
the treasuries of God's Temple, and the rooms for the dedicated gifts. [13]The king also **28:13**
gave Solomon the instructions concerning the work of the various divisions of priests 1 Chr 23:6; 24:1
and Levites in the Temple of the LORD. And he gave specifications for the items in the
LORD's Temple which were to be used for worship and sacrifice.
[14]David gave instructions regarding how much gold and silver should be used to
make the necessary items. [15]He told Solomon the amount of gold needed for the gold **28:15**
lampstands and lamps, and the amount of silver for the silver lampstands and lamps, Exod 25:31
depending on how each would be used. [16]He designated the amount of gold for the
table on which the Bread of the Presence would be placed and the amount of silver for
other tables.
[17]David also designated the amount of gold for the solid gold meat hooks used to
handle the sacrificial meat and for the basins, pitchers, and dishes, as well as the
amount of silver for every dish. [18]Finally, he designated the amount of refined gold **28:18**
for the altar of incense and for the gold cherubim, whose wings were stretched out Exod 25:18-22; 30:1

28:12 Or *the plans of the spirit that was with him.*

28:5 The kingdom of Israel belonged to the Lord, not to David or anyone else. Israel's king, then, was God's deputy, commissioned to carry out God's will for the nation. Thus, God could choose the person he wanted as king without following customary lines of succession. David was not Saul's heir, and Solomon was not David's oldest son, but this did not matter because God appointed them.

28:8 David told Solomon to be careful to obey every one of God's commands to ensure Israel's prosperity and the continuation of David's descendants upon the throne. It was the king's solemn duty to study and obey God's laws. The teachings of Scripture are the keys to security, happiness, and justice, but you'll never discover them unless you search God's Word. If we ignore God's will and neglect his teaching, anything we attempt to build, even if it has God's name on it, will be headed for collapse. Get to know God's commands through regular Bible study, and find ways to apply them consistently.

28:9 "The LORD sees every heart." Nothing can be hidden from God. He sees and understands everything in our hearts. David found this out the hard way when God sent Nathan to expose David's sins of adultery and murder (2 Samuel 12). David told Solomon to be completely open with God and dedicated to him. It makes no sense to try to hide any thoughts or actions from an all-knowing God. This should cause us joy, not fear, because God knows even the worst about us and loves us anyway.

28:13 Some of the instructions about the work of the priests and Levites are in chapters 23 and 24.

28:19 1 Chr 28:11-12 over the Ark of the LORD's covenant. 19 "Every part of this plan," David told Solomon,
"was given to me in writing from the hand of the LORD.*"

28:20 Josh 1:5; 1 Chr 22:13; Heb 13:5 20 Then David continued, "Be strong and courageous, and do the work. Don't be afraid
or discouraged by the size of the task, for the LORD God, my God, is with you. He will
not fail you or forsake you. He will see to it that all the work related to the Temple of the
28:21 Exod 35:25-35; 36:1-2 LORD is finished correctly. 21 The various divisions of priests and Levites will serve in
the Temple of God. Others with skills of every kind will volunteer, and the leaders and
the entire nation are at your command."

Gifts for Building the Temple

29:1 1 Chr 22:5 **29** Then King David turned to the entire assembly and said, "My son Solomon,
whom God has chosen to be the next king of Israel, is still young and
inexperienced. The work ahead of him is enormous, for the Temple he will build is
29:2 1 Chr 22:2-5 not just another building—it is for the LORD God himself! 2 Using every resource at
my command, I have gathered as much as I could for building the Temple of my God.
Now there is enough gold, silver, bronze, iron, and wood, as well as great quantities
of onyx, other precious stones, costly jewels, and all kinds of fine stone and marble.
3 And now because of my devotion to the Temple of my God, I am giving all of my
own private treasures of gold and silver to help in the construction. This is in addition
29:4 1 Kgs 9:28; 1 Chr 22:14 to the building materials I have already collected for his holy Temple. 4 I am donating
more than 112 tons of gold* from Ophir and over 262 tons of refined silver* to be
used for overlaying the walls of the buildings 5 and for the other gold and silver work
to be done by the craftsmen. Now then, who will follow my example? Who is willing
to give offerings to the LORD today?"

29:6 1 Chr 27:1, 25; 28:1 6 Then the family leaders, the leaders of the tribes of Israel, the generals and captains
of the army, and the king's administrative officers all gave willingly. 7 For the construction of the Temple of God, they gave almost 188 tons of gold,* 10,000 gold coins,* about
29:8 1 Chr 23:8 375 tons of silver,* about 675 tons of bronze,* and about 3,750 tons of iron.* 8 They also
contributed numerous precious stones, which were deposited in the treasury of the house

28:19 Or *was written under the direction of the LORD.* **29:4a** Hebrew *3,000 talents* [102 metric tons] *of gold.* **29:4b** Hebrew *7,000 talents* [238 metric tons] *of silver.* **29:7a** Hebrew *5,000 talents* [170 metric tons] *of gold.* **29:7b** Hebrew *10,000 darics* [a Persian coin] *of gold,* about 185 pounds or 84 kilograms in weight. **29:7c** Hebrew *10,000 talents* [340 metric tons] *of silver.* **29:7d** Hebrew *18,000 talents* [612 metric tons] *of bronze.* **29:7e** Hebrew *100,000 talents* [3,400 metric tons] *of iron.*

PRINCIPLES TO LIVE BY

King David gave his son Solomon principles to guide him through life (see 1 Chronicles 28:9, 10). These same ideas are ones that any Christian parent would want to present to a child:

1. Get to know God personally.
2. Learn God's commands and discover what he wants you to do.
3. Worship God with wholehearted devotion.
4. Serve God with a willing mind.
5. Be faithful.
6. Don't become discouraged.

28:20 David advised Solomon not to be frightened about the size of his task as king and builder of the Temple. Fear can immobilize us. The size of a job, its risks, or the pressure of the situation can cause us to freeze and do nothing. One remedy for fear is found here: Don't focus on the fear; instead, get to work. Getting started is often the most difficult and frightening part of a job.

29:1 Solomon became king in 970 B.C.

29:1 It is possible to be obsessed with a church building to the neglect of the real church—the people of God. But the opposite response, neglecting the church building, is also wrong. David makes this point when he says that the Temple is "for the LORD God himself!" Although we should avoid wasteful extravagance, we must remember that every church building can be a visible witness for God. How can your church building be better used to tell the world about God?

29:3-5 David gave from his personal fortune to the Temple. He encouraged others to follow his example, and they willingly did. Both the Tabernacle (Exodus 35:5–36:7) and the Temple were built from the voluntary gifts of the people. Like David, we can acknowledge that all we have comes from God (29:14-16). We may not have David's wealth, but we can develop his willingness to give. It is not what we have that counts with God, but our willingness to give it.

29:6-9 These leaders displayed a right attitude toward their money by giving willingly to God's work. This attitude is described by Paul in 2 Corinthians 9:7: "You must each make up your own mind as to how much you should give. Don't give reluctantly or in response to pressure. For God loves the person who gives cheerfully." When we are generous because we are thankful, our attitude can inspire others. Give generously to God's work.

of the LORD under the care of Jehiel, a descendant of Gershon. 9 The people rejoiced over
the offerings, for they had given freely and wholeheartedly to the LORD, and King David
was filled with joy.

David's Prayer of Praise

10 Then David praised the LORD in the presence of the whole assembly: "O LORD, the
God of our ancestor Israel,* may you be praised forever and ever! 11 Yours, O LORD, is
the greatness, the power, the glory, the victory, and the majesty. Everything in the
heavens and on earth is yours, O LORD, and this is your kingdom. We adore you as the
one who is over all things. 12 Riches and honor come from you alone, for you rule over
everything. Power and might are in your hand, and it is at your discretion that people are
made great and given strength.

13 "O our God, we thank you and praise your glorious name! 14 But who am I, and who
are my people, that we could give anything to you? Everything we have has come from
you, and we give you only what you have already given us! 15 We are here for only a
moment, visitors and strangers in the land as our ancestors were before us. Our days on
earth are like a shadow, gone so soon without a trace.

16 "O LORD our God, even these materials that we have gathered to build a Temple
to honor your holy name come from you! It all belongs to you! 17 I know, my God,
that you examine our hearts and rejoice when you find integrity there. You know I
have done all this with good motives, and I have watched your people offer their gifts
willingly and joyously.

18 "O LORD, the God of our ancestors Abraham, Isaac, and Israel, make your people
always want to obey you. See to it that their love for you never changes. 19 Give my son
Solomon the wholehearted desire to obey all your commands, decrees, and principles,
and to build this Temple, for which I have made all these preparations."

20 Then David said to the whole assembly, "Give praise to the LORD your God!" And
the entire assembly praised the LORD, the God of their ancestors, and they bowed low
and knelt before the LORD and the king.

Solomon Named as King

21 The next day they brought a thousand bulls, a thousand rams, and a thousand male
lambs as burnt offerings to the LORD. They also brought drink offerings and many other
sacrifices on behalf of Israel. 22 They feasted and drank in the LORD's presence with great
joy that day.

And again they crowned David's son Solomon as their new king. They anointed him
before the LORD as their leader, and they anointed Zadok as their priest. 23 So Solomon
took the throne of the LORD in place of his father, David, and he prospered greatly, and
all Israel obeyed him. 24 All the royal officials, the army commanders, and the sons of
King David pledged their loyalty to King Solomon. 25 And the LORD exalted Solomon
so the entire nation of Israel stood in awe of him, and he gave Solomon even greater
wealth and honor than his father.

Summary of David's Reign

26 So David son of Jesse reigned over all Israel. 27 He ruled Israel for forty years in all,
seven years from Hebron and thirty-three years from Jerusalem. 28 He died at a ripe old

29:9 1 Kgs 8:61; 2 Cor 9:7
29:11 Rev 5:12-13
29:12 2 Chr 1:12; 20:6
29:15 Lev 25:23; Job 14:2, 10-12
29:17 1 Chr 28:9
29:19 1 Chr 28:9; Ps 72:1
29:20 Josh 22:33
29:21 1 Kgs 8:62-63
29:22 1 Kgs 1:33-34; 1 Chr 29:1
29:25 2 Chr 1:1, 12
29:26-28 //1 Kgs 2:10-12
29:26 1 Chr 18:14

29:10 *Israel* is the name that God gave to Jacob.

29:15 David contrasts God's everlasting nature with the fleeting lives of his people. Nothing lasts unless it is rooted in God's unchanging character. If our most impressive deeds fade to dust before God, where should we place our confidence? Only in a relationship with God can we find anything permanent. His love never fades, and nothing can take it away.

29:19 "Wholehearted desire to obey" means to be entirely dedicated to God. This is what David wished for Solomon—that he would desire, above all else, to serve God. Do you find it hard to do what God wants, or find it harder to *want* to do it? God can give you wholehearted devotion. If you believe in Jesus Christ, this is already happening in you. Paul wrote: "For God is working in you, giving you the desire to obey him and the power to do what pleases him" (Philippians 2:13).

29:21 Drink offerings of wine were poured out as sacrifices to God to acknowledge his role in providing for his people.

29:25 Solomon surpassed his father's wealth and splendor. David's legacy resulted from his vital relationship with the Lord, and he passed his spiritual values on to Solomon. Any money or power we leave to our children is far less valuable than the spiritual legacy we pass on. What spiritual inheritance will your children receive?

29:27 2 Sam 5:4-5
29:28 1 Chr 23:1 Acts 13:36

age, having enjoyed long life, wealth, and honor. Then his son Solomon ruled in his
place. 29 All the events of King David's reign, from beginning to end, are written in *The
Record of Samuel the Seer, The Record of Nathan the Prophet,* and *The Record of Gad
the Seer.* 30 These accounts include the mighty deeds of his reign and everything that
happened to him and to Israel and to all the surrounding kingdoms.

29:29 A seer was someone who received messages from God for the nation in visions or dreams.

29:30 First Chronicles vividly illustrates the importance of maintaining a relationship with God. The genealogies in chapters 1–9 emphasize the importance of a spiritual heritage. The second part of the book details the life of David. Few men or women in the Bible were as close to God as David was. His daily contact with God increased his capacity to worship and strengthened his desire to build God's Temple. David's life shows us the importance of staying close to God—through studying and obeying his Word and communicating with him daily. Second Chronicles, on the other hand, reveals how quickly our lives can deteriorate (spiritually, mentally, and socially) when we fail to stay well grounded in God.

2 CHRONICLES

Solomon becomes king 970 B.C.	Temple built 966–959	The kingdom divides 930	Asa becomes king of Judah 910	Jehoshaphat becomes king of Judah 872	Ahab killed in battle 853	Athaliah seizes the throne 841	Uzziah becomes king of Judah 792

VITAL STATISTICS

PURPOSE:
To unify the nation around true worship of God by showing his standard for judging kings. The righteous kings of Judah and the religious revivals under their rule are highlighted, and the sins of the evil kings are exposed.

AUTHOR:
Ezra, according to Jewish tradition

TO WHOM WRITTEN:
All Israel

DATE WRITTEN:
Approximately 430 B.C., recording events from the beginning of Solomon's reign (970 B.C.) to the beginning of the Babylonian captivity (586 B.C.)

SETTING:
Second Chronicles parallels 1 and 2 Kings and serves as their commentary. Originally 1 and 2 Chronicles were one book. It was written after the Exile from a priestly perspective, highlighting the importance of the Temple and the religious revivals in Judah. The northern kingdom, Israel, is virtually ignored in this history.

KEY VERSE:
"Then if my people who are called by my name will humble themselves and pray and seek my face and turn from their wicked ways, I will hear from heaven and will forgive their sins and heal their land" (7:14).

KEY PEOPLE:
Solomon, the queen of Sheba, Rehoboam, Asa, Jehoshaphat, Jehoram, Joash, Uzziah (Azariah), Ahaz, Hezekiah, Manasseh, Josiah

KEY PLACES:
Jerusalem, the Temple

SPECIAL FEATURES:
Includes a detailed record of the Temple's construction

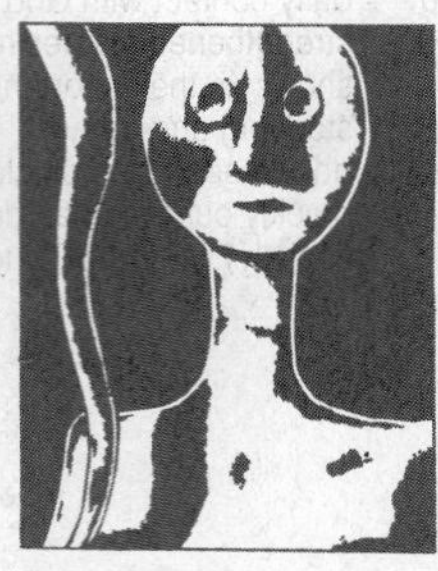

THE SLIDE clicks, and our eyes focus on the image flashed onto the screen in the darkened sanctuary. "This idol," explains the missionary, "is made of stone and is worshiped daily. The natives believe that this will guarantee good crops and healthy children." With condescending smiles, we wonder at their ignorance. How could anyone worship an object? Idols are for the naive and the superstitious! But after the presentation, we return home to *our* idols of wealth, prestige, or self-fulfillment. If we put anything in God's place, we worship it, despite what we profess with our lips.

Our experience parallels Israel's. They were chosen by God to represent him on earth. But too often they forgot the truth and their calling, stumbling blindly after idols as the neighboring nations did. Then prophets, priests, and judgment would push them abruptly back to the one true God. Second Chronicles relates this sordid history of Judah's corrupt and idolatrous kings. Here and there a good king would arise in Judah, and for a time there would be revival, but the downward spiral would continue—ending in chaos, destruction, and captivity.

The chronicler writes this volume to bring the people of Israel back to God by reminding them of their past. Only by following God would they prosper! As you read 2 Chronicles, you will catch a vivid glimpse of Judah's history (the history of Israel, the northern kingdom, is virtually ignored), and you will see the tragic results of idolatry. Learn the lessons of the past: Determine to get rid of any idols in your life and to worship God alone.

Second Chronicles continues the history of 1 Chronicles. David's son Solomon was inaugurated as king. Solomon built the magnificent Temple in Jerusalem, thus fulfilling his father's wish and last request (chapters 2—5). Solomon enjoyed a peaceful and prosperous reign of 40 years that made him world famous. After Solomon died, his son Rehoboam assumed the throne, and his immaturity divided the kingdom.

In Judah there were a few good kings and many evil ones. The writer of Chronicles faithfully records their achievements and failures, noting how each king measured up to God's standard for success. Clearly a good king obeyed God's laws, eliminated the places of idol worship, and made no alliances with other nations. Judah's good kings include Asa, Jehoshaphat, Uzziah (Azariah), Hezekiah, and Josiah. Of its many evil ones, Ahaz and Manasseh were perhaps the worst. Eventually the nation was conquered and taken captive, and the Temple was destroyed.

The writer's purpose was to reunite the nation around the true worship of God after the captivity. In these pages, he reminds the people of their past. He clearly broadcasts his message through one of the best-known verses in Scripture, "Then if my people who are called by my name will humble themselves and pray and seek my face and turn from their wicked ways, I will hear from heaven and will forgive their sins and heal their land" (7:14). As you read 2 Chronicles, listen to God's voice and obey him; and receive his redemptive, healing touch.

Israel (northern kingdom) falls 722	*Hezekiah becomes king of Judah 715*	*Sennacherib taunts Hezekiah 701*	*Josiah becomes king 640*	*Book of the Law found 622*	*Judah (southern kingdom) falls 586*	*Cyrus's decree 538*

THE BLUEPRINT

A. THE REIGN OF SOLOMON (1:1—9:31) 1. Solomon asks for wisdom 2. Solomon builds the Temple 3. Solomon dedicates the Temple 4. Solomon's riches and wisdom	Solomon achieved much in business and government, but most important, he was the man God used to build the glorious Temple. This beautiful building was the religious center of the nation. It symbolized the unity of all the tribes, the presence of God among them, and the nation's high calling. We may achieve great things in life, but we must not neglect any effort that will help nurture God's people or bring others into God's Kingdom. It is easy for us to get the wrong perspective on what's really important in life.
B. THE KINGDOM OF JUDAH (10:1—36:23) 1. The northern tribes revolt 2. History of apostasy and reform 3. Judah is exiled to Babylon	Throughout the reigns of 20 kings, the nation of Judah wavered between obedience to God and apostasy. The reigning king's response to God determined the spiritual climate of the nation and whether or not God would send judgment upon his people. Our personal history is shaped by our response to God. Just as Judah's failure to repent brought them captivity in Babylon, so the abuse of our high calling by sinful living will ultimately bring us catastrophe and destruction.

MEGATHEMES

THEME	EXPLANATION	IMPORTANCE
Temple	The Temple was the symbol of God's presence and the place set aside for worship and prayer. Built by Solomon from the plans God gave to David, the Temple was the spiritual center of the nation.	As Christians meet together to worship God, they experience the presence of God in a way that no individual believer can, for the dwelling place of God is the people of God. The body of Christ is God's temple.
Peace	As Solomon and his descendants were faithful to God, they experienced victory in battle, success in government, and peace with other nations. Peace was the result of the people being unified and loyal to God and his law.	Only God can bring true peace. God is greater than any enemy, army, or nation. Just as Israel's faithful response was key to her peace and survival as a nation, so our obedience to God as individuals and nations is vital to peace today.
Prayer	After Solomon died, David's kingdom was divided. When a king led the Israelites into idolatry, the nation suffered. When the king and his people prayed to God for deliverance and they turned from their sinful ways, God delivered them.	God still answers prayer today. We have God's promise that if we humble ourselves, seek him, turn from our sin, and pray, God will hear, heal, and forgive us. If we are alert, we can pray for God's guidance before we get into trouble.
Reform	Although idolatry and injustice were common, some kings turned to God and led the people in spiritual revival—renewing their commitment to God and reforming their society. Revival included the destruction of idols, obedience to the law, and the restoration of the priesthood.	We must constantly commit ourselves to obeying God. We are never secure in what others have done before us. Believers in each generation must dedicate themselves to the task of carrying out God's will in their own lives as well as in society.
National Collapse	In 586 B.C. the Babylonians completely destroyed Solomon's beautiful Temple. The formal worship of God was ended. The Israelites had abandoned God. As a result, God brought judgment upon his people, and they were carried off into captivity.	Although our disobedience may not be as blatant as Israel's, quite often our commitment to God is insincere and casual. When we forget that all our power, wisdom, and wealth come from God and not ourselves, we are in danger of the same spiritual and moral collapse that Israel experienced.

KEY PLACES IN 2 CHRONICLES

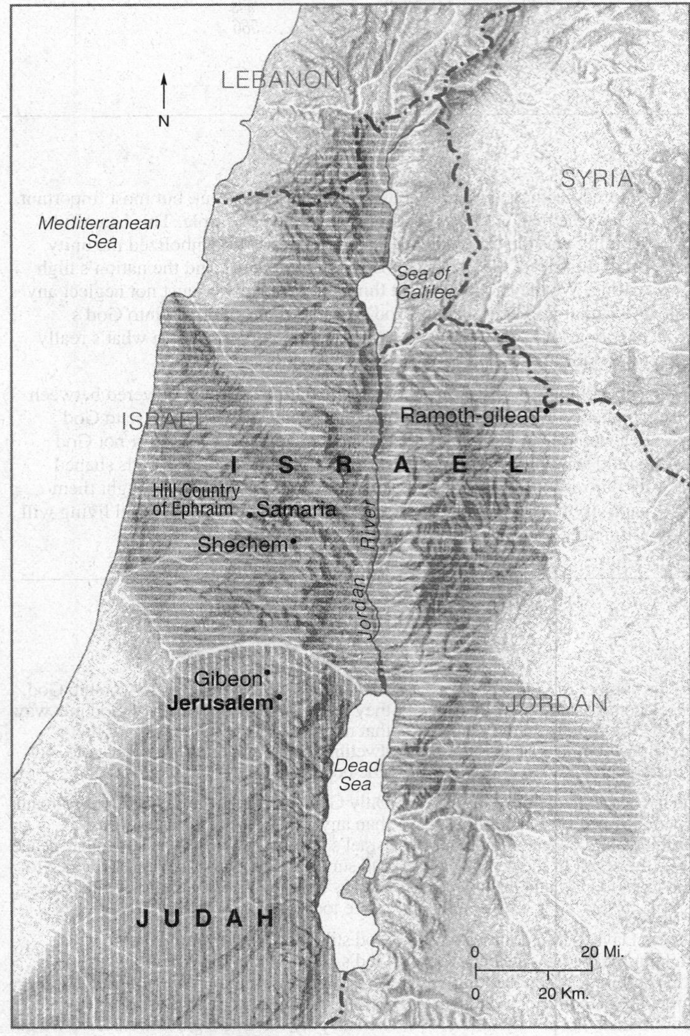

The broken lines (—·—·) indicate modern boundaries.

1 Gibeon David's son Solomon became king over Israel. He summoned the nation's leaders to a ceremony in Gibeon. Here God told Solomon to ask for whatever he desired. Solomon asked for wisdom and knowledge to rule Israel (1:1–12).

2 Jerusalem After the ceremony in Gibeon, Solomon returned to the capital city, Jerusalem. His reign began a golden age for Israel. Solomon implemented the plans for the Temple, which had been drawn up by his father, David. It was a magnificent construction. It symbolized Solomon's wealth and wisdom, which became known worldwide (1:13—9:31).

3 Shechem After Solomon's death, his son Rehoboam was ready to be crowned in Shechem. However, his promise of higher taxes and harder work for the people led to rebellion. Everyone but the tribes of Judah and Benjamin deserted Rehoboam and set up their own kingdom to the north called Israel. Rehoboam returned to Jerusalem as ruler over the southern kingdom called Judah (10:1—12:16). The remainder of 2 Chronicles records the history of Judah.

4 Hill Country of Ephraim Abijah became the next king of Judah, and soon war broke out between Israel and Judah. When the armies of the two nations arrived for battle in the hill country of Ephraim, Israel had twice as many troops as Judah. It looked like Judah's defeat was certain. But they cried out to God, and God gave them victory over Israel. In their history as separate nations, Judah had a few godly kings, who instituted reforms and brought the people back to God. Israel, however, had a succession of only evil kings (13:1–22).

5 Aram (Syria) Asa, a godly king, removed every trace of pagan worship from Judah and renewed the people's covenant with God in Jerusalem. But King Baasha of Israel built a fortress to control traffic into Judah. Instead of looking to God for guidance, Asa took the silver and gold from the Temple and sent it to the king of Aram, requesting his help against King Baasha. As a result, God became angry with Judah (14:1—16:14).

6 Samaria Although Jehoshaphat was a godly king, he allied himself with Israel's most evil king, Ahab. Ahab's capital was Samaria. Ahab wanted help fighting against Ramoth-gilead. Jehoshaphat wanted advice, but rather than listening to God's prophet who had promised defeat, he joined Ahab in battle (17:1—18:27).

7 Ramoth-gilead The alliance with Israel against Ramoth-gilead ended in defeat and Ahab's death. Shaken by his defeat, Jehoshaphat returned to Jerusalem and to God. But his son Jehoram was a wicked king, as was his son Ahaziah, and history repeated itself. Ahaziah formed an alliance with Israel's king Joram to do battle with the Arameans at Ramoth-gilead. This led to the death of both kings (18:28—22:9).

8 Jerusalem The rest of Judah's history recorded in 2 Chronicles centers on Jerusalem. Some kings caused Judah to sin by bringing idol worship into their midst. Others cleaned up the idol worship, reopened and restored the Temple, and in the case of Josiah, tried to follow God's laws as they were written by Moses. In spite of the few good influences, a series of evil kings sent Judah into a downward spiral that ended with the Babylonian Empire overrunning the country. The Temple was burned, the walls of the city were broken down, and the people were deported to Babylon.

A. THE REIGN OF SOLOMON (1:1—9:31)

In response to Solomon's request, God gives to Solomon great wisdom. Solomon launches great building programs, including the Temple, his greatest achievement. In the midst of the celebration dedicating the Temple, fire flashes down from heaven, and God's glory fills the Temple. God wants to live among his people and to be central in their lives. Today, our bodies are God's temple, the place where God, through his Holy Spirit, lives and reigns.

1. Solomon asks for wisdom

1 Solomon, the son of King David, now took firm control of the kingdom, for the
LORD his God was with him and made him very powerful. 2 He called together all
Israel—the generals and captains of the army, the judges, and all the political and clan
leaders. 3 Then Solomon led the entire assembly to the hill at Gibeon where God's
Tabernacle* was located. This was the Tabernacle that Moses, the LORD's servant, had
constructed in the wilderness. 4 David had already moved the Ark of God from Kiriath-
jearim to the special tent he had prepared for it in Jerusalem. 5 But the bronze altar made
by Bezalel son of Uri and grandson of Hur was still at Gibeon in front of the Tabernacle
of the LORD. So Solomon and the people gathered in front of it to consult the LORD.
6 There in front of the Tabernacle, Solomon went up to the bronze altar in the LORD's
presence and sacrificed a thousand burnt offerings on it.
7 That night God appeared to Solomon in a dream and said, "What do you want? Ask,
and I will give it to you!"
8 Solomon replied to God, "You have been so faithful and kind to my father, David,
and now you have made me king in his place. 9 Now, LORD God, please keep your
promise to David my father, for you have made me king over a people as numerous as
the dust of the earth! 10 Give me wisdom and knowledge to rule them properly, for who
is able to govern this great nation of yours?"
11 God said to Solomon, "Because your greatest desire is to help your people, and you
did not ask for personal wealth and honor or the death of your enemies or even a long
life, but rather you asked for wisdom and knowledge to properly govern my people, 12 I
will certainly give you the wisdom and knowledge you requested. And I will also give
you riches, wealth, and honor such as no other king has ever had before you or will ever
have again!" 13 Then Solomon returned to Jerusalem from the Tabernacle at the hill of
Gibeon, and he reigned over Israel.

1:3 Hebrew *Tent of Meeting;* also in 1:6, 13.

1:1 1 Kgs 2:12, 46; 1 Chr 29:25
1:2 1 Chr 28:1
1:3 Exod 36:8; 1 Kgs 3:4
1:4 1 Chr 15:25-28
1:5 Exod 31:9; 38:1-7
1:6 1 Kgs 3:4
1:7 1 Kgs 3:5-14
1:8 1 Chr 28:5
1:9 Gen 13:16; 22:17; 2 Sam 7:12-16
1:10 2 Sam 5:2; 1 Kgs 3:9
1:11 1 Kgs 3:11
1:12 1 Chr 29:25; 2 Chr 9:22
1:13 2 Chr 1:3

1:1 While the book of 1 Chronicles focuses mainly on David's life, 2 Chronicles focuses on the lives of the rest of the kings of Judah, the southern kingdom. Very little is mentioned about Israel, the northern kingdom, because (1) Chronicles was written for Judeans who had returned from captivity in Babylon, and (2) Judah represented David's family, from which the Messiah would come. Israel was in a state of constant turmoil, anarchy, and rebellion against God, but Judah, at least, made sporadic efforts to follow God.

1:1 More details about Solomon's rise to the throne can be read in 1 Kings 1–2. Solomon's Profile is found in 1 Kings 4.

1:2-5 The Tabernacle that Moses had built centuries earlier (Exodus 35–40) was still in operation although it had been moved several times. When Solomon became king, the Tabernacle was located at Gibeon, a town about six miles northwest of Jerusalem. All the Tabernacle furniture was kept at Gibeon except the Ark of God, which David had moved to Jerusalem (1 Chronicles 13; 15–16). David wanted the Ark, the symbol of God's presence, to reside in the city where he ruled the people. The Tabernacle at Gibeon, however, was still considered Israel's main religious center until Solomon built the Temple in Jerusalem.

1:10 Wisdom is the ability to make good decisions based on proper discernment and judgment. Knowledge, in this verse, refers to the practical know-how necessary for handling everyday matters. Solomon used his wisdom and knowledge not only to build the Temple from his father's plans but also to put the nation on firm economic footing.

1:10 God's offer to Solomon stretches the imagination: "Ask, and I will give it to you!" (1:7). But Solomon put the needs of his people first and asked for wisdom rather than riches. He realized that wisdom would be the most valuable asset he could have as king. Later he wrote, "Wisdom is more precious than rubies; nothing you desire can compare with her" (Proverbs 3:15). The same wisdom that was given to Solomon is available to us; the same God offers it. How can we acquire wisdom? First, we must ask God, who "will not resent your asking" (James 1:5). Second, we must devote ourselves wholeheartedly to studying and applying God's Word, the source of divine wisdom, to our life. (For more on Solomon's wisdom, read the notes on 1 Kings 3:6-9 and 3:12.)

1:11, 12 Solomon could have had anything, but he asked for wisdom to rule the nation. Because God approved of the way Solomon ordered his priorities, he gave Solomon wealth, riches, and honor as well. Jesus also spoke about priorities. He said that when we put God first, everything we really need will be given to us as well (Matthew 6:33). This does not guarantee that we will be wealthy and famous like Solomon, but it means that when we put God first, the wisdom he gives will enable us to have richly rewarding lives. When we have a purpose for living and learn to be content with what we have, we have greater wealth than we could ever imagine.

14Solomon built up a huge military force, which included fourteen hundred chariots
and twelve thousand horses.* He stationed many of them in the chariot cities, and some
near him in Jerusalem. 15During Solomon's reign, silver and gold were as plentiful in
Jerusalem as stones. And valuable cedarwood was as common as the sycamore wood
that grows in the foothills of Judah.* 16Solomon's horses were imported from Egypt*
and from Cilicia*; the king's traders acquired them from Cilicia at the standard price.
17At that time, Egyptian chariots delivered to Jerusalem could be purchased for 600
pieces of silver,* and horses could be bought for 150 pieces of silver.* Many of these
were then resold to the kings of the Hittites and the kings of Aram.

2. Solomon builds the Temple

Preparations for Building the Temple

2 Solomon now decided that the time had come to build a Temple for the LORD and a
royal palace for himself. 2He enlisted a force of seventy thousand common laborers,
eighty thousand stonecutters in the hill country, and thirty-six hundred foremen. 3Solo-
mon also sent this message to King Hiram* at Tyre:

"Send me cedar logs like the ones that were supplied to my father, David, when he
was building his palace. 4I am about to build a Temple to honor the name of the LORD
my God. It will be a place set apart to burn incense and sweet spices before him, to display the special sacrificial bread, and to sacrifice burnt offerings each morning and
evening, on the Sabbaths, at new moon celebrations, and at the other appointed festivals of the LORD our God. He has commanded Israel to do these things forever.
5"This will be a magnificent Temple because our God is an awesome God,
greater than any other. 6But who can really build him a worthy home? Not even the
highest heavens can contain him! So who am I to consider building a Temple for
him, except as a place to burn sacrifices to him?
7"So send me a master craftsman who can work with gold, silver, bronze, and
iron; someone who is expert at dyeing purple, scarlet, and blue cloth; and a skilled
engraver who can work with the craftsmen of Judah and Jerusalem who were
selected by my father, David. 8Also send me cedar, cypress, and almug* logs from

1:14 1 Kgs 4:26; 9:19; 10:26-29
1:15 1 Kgs 10:27
2:1 1 Kgs 5:5
2:2 1 Kgs 5:15-16; 2 Chr 2:18
2:3 1 Kgs 5:2-11; 1 Chr 14:1
2:4 Exod 25:30; 29:38-42; 30:7; Num 28:9-10
2:5 Exod 15:11; 1 Chr 16:25
2:6 1 Kgs 8:27; 2 Chr 6:18
2:7 Exod 31:3-5; 1 Chr 22:15; 2 Chr 2:13-15
2:8 2 Chr 9:10-11

1:14 Or *12,000 charioteers.* **1:15** Hebrew *the Shephelah.* **1:16a** Possibly *Muzur,* a district near Cilicia; also in 1:17. **1:16b** Hebrew *Kue,* probably another name for Cilicia. **1:17a** Hebrew *600 shekels of silver,* about 15 pounds or 6.8 kilograms in weight. **1:17b** Hebrew *150 shekels,* about 3.8 pounds or 1.7 kilograms in weight. **2:3** Hebrew *Huram,* a variant name for Hiram; also in 2:11, 12. **2:8** Hebrew *algum,* a variant name for almug; compare 9:10-11 and parallel text at 1 Kgs 10:11-12.

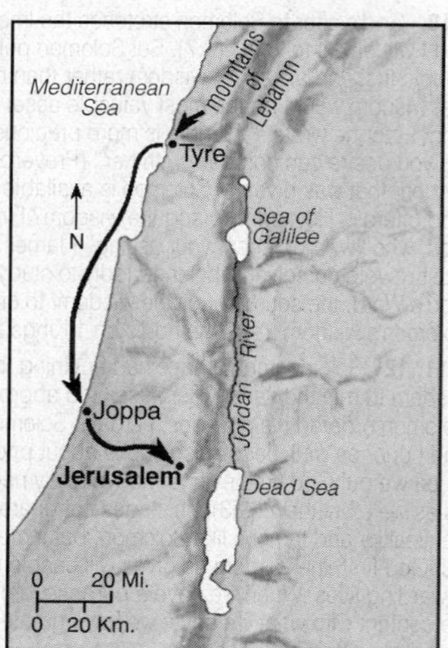

SHIPPING RESOURCES FOR THE TEMPLE Solomon asked King Hiram of Tyre to provide supplies and skilled workmen to help build God's Temple in Jerusalem. The plan was to cut the cedar logs in the mountains of Lebanon, float them by sea to Joppa, then bring them inland to Jerusalem by the shortest and easiest route.

2:1 David had wanted to build a Temple for God (2 Samuel 7). God denied his request because David had been a warrior, but God said that David's son Solomon would build the Temple. God allowed David to make the plans and preparations for the Temple (1 Chronicles 23–26; 28:11-19). David bought the land (2 Samuel 24:18-25; 1 Chronicles 22:1), gathered most of the construction materials (1 Chronicles 22:14-16), and received the plans from God (1 Chronicles 28:11, 12, 19). It was Solomon's responsibility to make the plans a reality. His job was made easier by his father's exhaustive preparations. God's work can be moved forward when the older generation paves the way for the younger.

2:3-12 Although Hiram was one of David's and Solomon's friendly allies, he was the ruler of a nation that worshiped many different gods. Hiram was happy to send materials for the Temple, and both David and Solomon used this occasion to testify about the one true God.

2:5, 6 We should try our best to build beautiful and helpful places of worship to be a testimony and credit to God. In so doing, however, we must remember that God cannot be contained in our building or beautiful setting. He is far greater than any building, so we must focus our praise on him and not merely on the place of worship.

2:7 Why use foreign craftsmen? The Israelites had great knowledge of agriculture but knew little about metalworking. So they found people who were experts in this area. It is not a sin to obtain secular expertise for God's work. He distributes talents as he chooses, and he often decides to give skill to non-Christians. When we hire secular contractors to build or repair our church buildings, we are recognizing that God gives gifts liberally. We may also be gaining an opportunity to tell the workers about God.

Lebanon, for I know that your men are without equal at cutting timber. I will send
my men to help them. 9An immense amount of timber will be needed, for the
Temple I am going to build will be very large and magnificent. 10I will pay your
2:10 1 Kgs 5:11 men 100,000 bushels of crushed wheat, 100,000 bushels of barley,* 110,000 gallons of wine, and 110,000 gallons of olive oil.*"

2:11 1 Kgs 10:9 2 Chr 9:8 11King Hiram sent this letter of reply to Solomon:

"It is because the LORD loves his people that he has made you their king! 12Blessed
2:12 2 Chr 2:1 Pss 33:6; 102:25 be the LORD, the God of Israel, who made the heavens and the earth! He has given
David a wise son, gifted with skill and understanding, who will build a Temple for
the LORD and a royal palace for himself.

13"I am sending you a master craftsman named Huram-abi. He is a brilliant man,
2:14 1 Kgs 7:14 14the son of a woman from Dan in Israel; his father is from Tyre. He is skillful at
making things from gold, silver, bronze, and iron. He also knows all about stonework, carpentry, and weaving. He is an expert in dyeing purple, blue, and scarlet
cloth and in working with linen. He is also an engraver and can follow any design
given to him. He will work with your craftsmen and those appointed by my lord
David, your father.

2:15 2 Chr 2:10 15"Send along the wheat, barley, olive oil, and wine that you mentioned. 16We
2:16 1 Kgs 5:8-9 will cut whatever timber you need from the Lebanon mountains and will float the
logs in rafts down the coast of the Mediterranean Sea to Joppa. From there you can
transport the logs up to Jerusalem."

2:17 1 Chr 22:2 17Solomon took a census of all foreigners in the land of Israel, like the census his
2:18 2 Chr 2:2 father had taken, and he counted 153,600. 18He enlisted 70,000 of them as common
laborers, 80,000 as stonecutters in the hill country, and 3,600 as foremen.

Solomon Builds the Temple

3 So Solomon began to build the Temple of the LORD in Jerusalem on Mount
3:1-14 1 Kgs 6:1-29 Moriah, where the LORD had appeared to Solomon's father, King David. The
3:1 1 Chr 21:18 Temple was built on the threshing floor of Araunah* the Jebusite, the site that David
had selected. 2The construction began in midspring,* during the fourth year of
Solomon's reign.

3The foundation for the Temple of God was ninety feet long and thirty feet wide.*
3:4 1 Kgs 6:3 4The foyer at the front of the Temple was thirty feet wide, running across the entire width
of the Temple. The inner walls of the foyer and the ceiling were overlaid with pure gold.
The roof of the foyer was thirty feet* high.

3:5 1 Kgs 6:17 5The main room of the Temple was paneled with cypress wood, overlaid with pure
gold, and decorated with carvings of palm trees and chains. 6The walls of the Temple

2:10a Hebrew *20,000 cors* [3,640 kiloliters] *of crushed wheat, 20,000 cors of barley.* **2:10b** Hebrew *20,000 baths* [420 kiloliters] *of wine, and 20,000 baths of olive oil.* **3:1** Hebrew reads *Ornan,* another name for Araunah; compare 2 Sam 24:16. **3:2** Hebrew *on the second day of the second month.* This day of the Hebrew lunar calendar occurs in April or early May. **3:3** Hebrew *60 cubits* [27 meters] *long and 20 cubits* [9 meters] *wide.* In this chapter, the distance measures are calculated from the Hebrew cubit at a ratio of 18 inches or 45 centimeters per cubit. **3:4** As in some Greek and Syriac manuscripts, which read *20 cubits* [9 meters]; Hebrew reads *120 cubits,* which is 180 feet or 54 meters.

2:8, 9 Israel did not have much wood, but Lebanon, a small nation on the seacoast, had some of the finest cedar forests in the ancient Near East. Lebanon also imported a great deal of food from Israel. Thus, the two kings made a trade agreement that was beneficial to both nations.

2:17, 18 Why would Solomon force foreigners living in Israel to do the work of slaves? These foreigners were descendants of the pagan nations that had not been driven out of the land in Joshua's day (Joshua 9:23-27; Judges 1:21-33; 1 Kings 9:20, 21). Scripture has specific laws about treating slaves fairly (Leviticus 25:39-55), so Solomon would not have treated them harshly as other nations might. Solomon's action was probably only in force during the construction of the Temple.

3:1 Solomon built a permanent Temple on Mount Moriah to replace the movable Tabernacle (now at Gibeon) that had accompanied Israel in the wilderness. Mount Moriah was also the place where God had stopped Abraham from sacrificing Isaac (Genesis 22:1-18). David purchased the land when it was a threshing floor (see 2 Samuel 24:15-25 and the note on 1 Chronicles 21:22-24).

3:1ff Why was the Temple decorated so ornately? Although no one can build God a worthy home (2:6), this Temple was going to be the best that humans could design. The care and craftsmanship were acts of worship in themselves. Although a simple chapel is an adequate place to pray and meet God, it is not wrong to want to make a beautiful place of worship.

were decorated with beautiful jewels and with pure gold from the land of Parvaim. 7All 3:7
the walls, beams, doors, and thresholds throughout the Temple were overlaid with gold, 1 Kgs 6:20-22,
and figures of cherubim were carved on the walls. 29-35
8The Most Holy Place was thirty feet wide, corresponding to the width of the Temple, 3:8
and it was also thirty feet deep. Its interior was overlaid with about twenty-three tons* Exod 26:33
of pure gold. 9They used gold nails that weighed about twenty ounces* each. The walls 1 Kgs 6:16 3:9
of the upper rooms were also overlaid with pure gold. 1 Chr 28:11
10Solomon made two figures shaped like cherubim and overlaid them with gold. 3:10
These were placed in the Most Holy Place. 11The total wingspan of the two cherubim 1 Kgs 6:23-28
standing side by side was 30 feet. One wing of the first figure was 7½ feet long, and it
touched the Temple wall. The other wing, also 7½ feet long, touched one of the wings of
the second figure. 12In the same way, the second figure had one wing 7½ feet long that
touched the opposite wall. The other wing, also 7½ feet long, touched the wing of the
first figure. 13So the wingspan of both cherubim together was 30 feet. They both stood
and faced out toward the main room of the Temple. 14Across the entrance of the Most 3:14
Holy Place, Solomon hung a curtain made of fine linen and blue, purple, and scarlet yarn, Exod 26:31
with figures of cherubim embroidered on it.
15For the front of the Temple, Solomon made two pillars that were 27 feet* tall, 3:15
each topped by a capital extending upward another 7½ feet. 16He made a network of 1 Kgs 7:15-20
interwoven chains and used them to decorate the tops of the pillars. He also made one
hundred decorative pomegranates and attached them to the chains. 17Then he set up 3:17
the two pillars at the entrance of the Temple, one to the south of the entrance and the 1 Kgs 7:21
other to the north. He named the one on the south Jakin, and the one on the north
Boaz.*

Furnishings for the Temple

4 Solomon also made a bronze altar 30 feet long, 30 feet wide, and 15 feet high.* 4:1 Exod 27:1-2
2Then he cast a large round tank, 15 feet across from rim to rim; it was called the 2 Kgs 16:14
Sea. It was 7½ feet deep and about 45 feet in circumference. 3The Sea was encircled 4:2
just below its rim by two rows of figures that resembled oxen. There were about six 1 Kgs 7:23-26
oxen per foot* all the way around, and they had been cast as part of the tank.
4The Sea rested on a base of twelve bronze oxen, all facing outward. Three faced
north, three faced west, three faced south, and three faced east. 5The walls of the Sea 4:5
were about three inches* thick, and its rim flared out like a cup and resembled a lily 1 Kgs 7:26
blossom. It could hold about 16,500 gallons* of water.
6He also made ten basins for water to wash the offerings, five to the south of the Sea 4:6
and five to the north. The priests used the Sea itself, and not the basins, for their own 1 Kgs 7:38, 40
washing.
7Solomon then cast ten gold lampstands according to the specifications that had been 4:7
given and put them in the Temple. Five were placed against the south wall, and five were Exod 25:31-40
placed against the north wall. 8He also built ten tables and placed them in the Temple, 1 Kgs 7:49 4:8
five along the south wall and five along the north wall. Then he molded one hundred 1 Kgs 7:48
gold basins.
9Solomon also built a courtyard for the priests and the large outer courtyard. He made 4:9
doors for the courtyard entrances and overlaid them with bronze. 10The Sea was placed 1 Kgs 6:36 4:10
near the southeast corner of the Temple. 1 Kgs 7:39

3:8 Hebrew *600 talents* [20.4 metric tons]. **3:9** Hebrew *50 shekels* [570 grams]. **3:15** As in Syriac version (see also 1 Kgs 7:15; 2 Kgs 25:17; Jer 52:21), which reads *18 cubits* [8.1 meters]; Hebrew reads *35 cubits,* which is 52.5 feet or 15.8 meters. **3:17** Jakin probably means "he establishes"; Boaz probably means "in him is strength." **4:1** Hebrew *20 cubits* [9 meters] *long, 20 cubits wide, and 10 cubits* [4.5 meters] *high.* In this chapter, the distance measures are calculated from the Hebrew cubit at a ratio of 18 inches or 45 centimeters per cubit. **4:3** Or *20 oxen per meter;* Hebrew reads *10 per cubit.* **4:5a** Hebrew *a handbreadth* [8 centimeters]. **4:5b** Hebrew *3,000 baths* [63 kiloliters].

3:10 Cherubim are angels.

4:6 Why was everything in the Temple built on such a grand scale? The great size and numbers were necessary to accommodate the huge crowds that would visit for the festivals, such as the Passover (30:13). The numerous daily sacrifices required many priests and much equipment.

4:7 The craftsmen followed God's specifications carefully—with spectacular results. When God gives specific instructions, they must be followed to the letter. There is a time to be creative and to put forth our own ideas, but not when the ideas add to, alter, or contradict any specific directions God has already given to us in the Bible. For best results in your spiritual life, carefully seek and follow God's instructions.

4:11
1 Kgs 7:40

11 Huram-abi also made the necessary pots, shovels, and basins.

So at last Huram-abi completed everything King Solomon had assigned him to make for the Temple of God:

4:12
1 Kgs 7:14;
20:27-43
2 Chr 2:13

4:13
1 Kgs 7:20

12 two pillars,
two bowl-shaped capitals on top of the pillars,
two networks of chains that decorated the capitals,
13 four hundred pomegranates that hung from the chains on the capitals (two rows of pomegranates for each of the chain networks that were hung around the capitals on top of the pillars),

4:14
1 Kgs 7:27

14 the water carts holding the basins,
15 the Sea and the twelve oxen under it,

4:16
1 Kgs 7:14

16 the pots, the shovels, the meat hooks, and all the related utensils.

4:17-18
1 Kgs 7:47

Huram-abi made all these things out of burnished bronze for the Temple of the LORD,
just as King Solomon had requested. 17 The king had them cast in clay molds in the
Jordan Valley between Succoth and Zarethan.* 18 Such great quantities of bronze were
used that its weight could not be determined.

19 So Solomon made all the furnishings for the Temple of God:

4:20
Exod 25:31-37

the gold altar;
the tables for the Bread of the Presence;
20 the lampstands and their lamps of pure gold to burn in front of the Most Holy Place as prescribed;
21 the flower decorations, lamps, and tongs, all of pure gold;

4:17 As in parallel text at 1 Kgs 7:46; Hebrew reads *Zeredah.*

CAREFUL OBEDIENCE

Solomon and his workers carefully followed God's instructions. As a result, the Temple work was blessed by God and completed in every detail. Here are a few examples of people in the Bible who did *not* carefully follow one of God's instructions, and the resulting consequences. It is not enough to obey God halfheartedly.

Who?	*God's Instruction*	*Disobedience*	*Result*
Adam and Eve	Don't eat fruit from the tree of the knowledge of good and evil (Genesis 2:16, 17)	Satan tempted them, and they ate (Genesis 3:1–6)	They were banished from the Garden of Eden; pain and death were inflicted on all mankind (Genesis 3:24; Romans 5:12)
Nadab and Abihu	Fire for the sacrifice must come from the proper source (Leviticus 6:12, 13)	They used unauthorized fire for their sacrifice (Leviticus 10:1)	They were struck dead (Leviticus 10:2)
Moses	"Command the rock over there to pour out its water" (Numbers 20:8)	He spoke to the rock, but also struck it with his staff (Numbers 20:11)	He was not allowed to enter the Promised Land (Numbers 20:12)
Saul	Completely destroy the evil Amalekites (1 Samuel 15:3)	He spared the king and kept some of the plunder (1 Samuel 15:8, 9)	God promised to end his reign (1 Samuel 15:16–26)
Uzzah	Only a priest can touch the holy furnishings and articles (Numbers 4:15)	He touched the Ark of the Covenant (2 Samuel 6:6)	He died instantly (2 Samuel 6:7)
Uzziah	Only the priests can offer incense in the Temple or Tabernacle sanctuary (Numbers 16:39, 40; 18:7)	He entered the Holy Place in the Temple where only priests were allowed to go (2 Chronicles 26:16–18)	He became a leper (2 Chronicles 26:19)

4:11-16 Pots, shovels, and basins—these are implements of worship unfamiliar to us. Although the articles we use to aid our worship have changed, the purpose of worship remains the same—to give honor and praise to God. We must never let our worship of God be overshadowed by things we use to help us worship him.

22 the lamp snuffers, basins, dishes, and firepans, all of pure gold;
the doors for the entrances to the Most Holy Place and the main room of the
Temple, overlaid with gold.

5 When Solomon had finished all the work related to building the Temple of the **5:1**
LORD, he brought in the gifts dedicated by his father, King David, including all 1 Kgs 7:51
the silver and gold and all the utensils. These were stored in the treasuries of the
Temple of God.

3. Solomon dedicates the Temple

The Ark Brought to the Temple

2 Solomon then summoned the leaders of all the tribes and families of Israel to assemble **5:2–6:11**
in Jerusalem. They were to bring the Ark of the LORD's covenant from its location in the //1 Kgs 8:1-21
City of David, also known as Zion, to its new place in the Temple. 3 They all assembled **5:2** 2 Sam 6:12
before the king at the annual Festival of Shelters in early autumn.* 4 When all the leaders 2 Chr 1:4
of Israel arrived, the Levites moved the Ark, 5 along with the special tent* and all its **5:4**
sacred utensils. The Levitical priests carried them all up to the Temple. 6 King Solomon 2 Chr 5:7
and the entire community of Israel sacrificed sheep and oxen before the Ark in such
numbers that no one could keep count!
7 Then the priests carried the Ark of the LORD's covenant into the inner sanctuary of
the Temple—the Most Holy Place—and placed it beneath the wings of the cherubim.
8 The cherubim spread their wings out over the Ark, forming a canopy over the Ark and
its carrying poles. 9 These poles were so long that their ends could be seen from the front **5:9**
entrance of the Temple's main room—the Holy Place—but not from outside it. They are 1 Kgs 8:8-9
still there to this day. 10 Nothing was in the Ark except the two stone tablets that Moses **5:10**
had placed there at Mount Sinai,* when the LORD made a covenant with the people of Deut 10:2-5 Heb 9:4
Israel after they left Egypt.

5:3 Hebrew *at the festival that is in the seventh month.* The Festival of Shelters began on the fifteenth day of the seventh month of the Hebrew lunar calendar. This occurs on our calendar in late September or early October. **5:5** Hebrew *Tent of Meeting.* **5:10** Hebrew *Horeb,* another name for Sinai.

4:22 All these details about the Temple demonstrated the care Israel gave to acts of worship (see the note on 3:1ff). The instructions also served as a manual to the original readers of 2 Chronicles, those who would rebuild a new Temple on its original site (Ezra 3:8–6:15) after Solomon's Temple was destroyed by the Babylonians (2 Kings 25).

5:1ff Why is there so much emphasis on the Temple in the Old Testament?

(1) *It was a symbol of religious authority.* The Temple was God's way of centralizing worship at Jerusalem in order to ensure that correct belief would be kept intact through many generations.

(2) *It was a symbol of God's holiness.* The Temple's beautiful atmosphere inspired respect and awe for God; it was the setting for many of the great visions of the prophets.

(3) *It was a symbol of God's covenant with Israel.* The Temple kept the people focused upon God's law (the tablets of the Ten Commandments were kept in the Temple) rather than on the kings' exploits. It was a place where God was especially present with his people.

(4) *It was a symbol of forgiveness.* The Temple's design, furniture, and customs were great object lessons for all the people, reminding them of the seriousness of sin, the penalty that sin incurred, and their need of forgiveness.

(5) *It prepared the people for the Messiah.* In the New Testament, Christ said he came to fulfill the law, not destroy it. Hebrews 8:1, 2 and 9:11, 12 use Temple customs to explain what Christ did when he died for us.

(6) *It was a testimony to human effort and creativity.* Inspired by the beauty of God's character, people devoted themselves to high achievements in engineering, science, and art in order to praise him.

(7) *It was a place of prayer.* In the Temple, people could spend time in prayer to God.

5:1-3 The Temple took seven years to build. First Kings 6:38 says that the Temple was completed in the eighth month (November) of Solomon's eleventh year as king (959 B.C.). Because 5:3 states that the dedication ceremonies were held in early autumn, they must have occurred either one month before or eleven months after the Temple's completion.

5:3 The Festival of Shelters celebrated God's protection of Israel as they wandered in the wilderness before entering the Promised Land. The purpose of this annual festival was to renew Israel's commitment to God and their trust in his guidance and protection. The festival beautifully coincided with the dedication of the Temple. As the people remembered the wanderings in the wilderness when their ancestors had lived in tents, they were even more thankful for the permanence of this glorious Temple.

5:9 Under God's inspiration, some books of the Bible were compiled and edited from other sources. Because 1 and 2 Chronicles cover many centuries, they were compiled from several sources by a single person. The phrase "they are still there to this day" (see also 1 Kings 8:8) was taken from material written before Judah's exile in 586 B.C. Although 1 and 2 Chronicles were compiled after the Exile and after Solomon's Temple was destroyed, the writer thought it best to leave this phrase in the narrative.

5:7-12 The priests came out of the Holy Place after having placed the Ark in the Most Holy Place of the Temple. The Holy Place is the outer room, where the Bread of the Presence, altar of incense, and lampstand were kept. Ordinarily the Most Holy Place could be entered only once a year by the high priest on the Day of Atonement. On this unique occasion, however, several priests had to enter the Most Holy Place to carry the Ark to its new resting place. The Levites praised God when these priests emerged from the Holy Place because they then knew God had accepted this new home for the Ark (5:13).

5:11 1 Chr 24:1-5
5:12 1 Chr 25:1-4; 2 Chr 7:6
5:13 1 Chr 16:34, 42; 2 Chr 7:3

11 Then the priests left the Holy Place. All the priests who were present had purified
themselves, whether or not they were on duty that day. 12 And the Levites who were
musicians—Asaph, Heman, Jeduthun, and all their sons and brothers—were dressed in
fine linen robes and stood at the east side of the altar playing cymbals, harps, and lyres.
They were joined by 120 priests who were playing trumpets. 13 The trumpeters and
singers performed together in unison to praise and give thanks to the LORD. Accompanied by trumpets, cymbals, and other instruments, they raised their voices and praised
the LORD with these words:

"He is so good!
His faithful love endures forever!"

5:14 1 Kgs 8:11

At that moment a cloud filled the Temple of the LORD. 14 The priests could not continue
their work because the glorious presence of the LORD filled the Temple of God.

Solomon Blesses the People

6:1 1 Kgs 8:12-50

6 Then Solomon prayed, "O LORD, you have said that you would live in thick
darkness. 2 But I have built a glorious Temple for you, where you can live forever!"
3 Then the king turned around to the entire community of Israel standing before him
and gave this blessing: 4 "Blessed be the LORD, the God of Israel, who has kept the
promise he made to my father, David. For he told my father, 5 'From the day I brought
my people out of Egypt, I have never chosen a city among the tribes of Israel as the place
where a temple should be built to honor my name. Nor have I chosen a king to lead my
people Israel. 6 But now I have chosen Jerusalem as that city, and David as that king.'"

6:6 1 Chr 28:4; 2 Chr 12:13
6:7 1 Chr 28:2
6:8 1 Kgs 5:3

7 Then Solomon said, "My father, David, wanted to build this Temple to honor the
name of the LORD, the God of Israel. 8 But the LORD told him, 'It is right for you to want
to build the Temple to honor my name, 9 but you will not be the one to do it. One of your
sons will build it instead.'
10 "And now the LORD has done what he promised, for I have become king in my
father's place. I have built this Temple to honor the name of the LORD, the God of Israel.
11 There I have placed the Ark, and in the Ark is the covenant that the LORD made with
the people of Israel."

6:11 2 Chr 5:7, 10

Solomon's Prayer of Dedication

6:12-40 //1 Kgs 8:22-53
6:12 Neh 8:4
6:14 Exod 15:11; Deut 3:24; 7:9
6:15 1 Chr 22:9-10
6:16 1 Kgs 2:4; 2 Chr 7:18

12 Then Solomon stood with his hands spread out before the altar of the LORD in front
of the entire community of Israel. 13 He had made a bronze platform 7½ feet long,
7½ feet wide, and 4½ feet high* and had placed it at the center of the Temple's outer
courtyard. He stood on the platform before the entire assembly, and then he knelt
down and lifted his hands toward heaven. 14 He prayed, "O LORD, God of Israel, there
is no God like you in all of heaven and earth. You keep your promises and show
unfailing love to all who obey you and are eager to do your will. 15 You have kept your
promise to your servant David, my father. You made that promise with your own
mouth, and today you have fulfilled it with your own hands. 16 And now, O LORD, God
of Israel, carry out your further promise to your servant David, my father. For you
said to him, 'If your descendants guard their behavior and obey my law as you have
done, they will always reign over Israel.' 17 Now, O LORD, God of Israel, fulfill this
promise to your servant David.

6:13 Hebrew *5 cubits* [2.3 meters] *long, 5 cubits wide, and 3 cubits* [1.4 meters] *high.*

5:13 The first service at the Temple began with honoring God and acknowledging his presence and goodness. In the same way, our worship should begin by acknowledging God's love. Praise God first; then you will be prepared to present your needs to him. Recalling God's love and mercy will inspire you to worship him daily. Psalm 107 is an example of how David recalled God's enduring love.

6:3 As the people received Solomon's blessing, they stood; as Solomon prayed, he knelt (6:13). Both standing and kneeling are acts of reverence. Acts of reverence make us feel more worshipful, and they let others see that we are honoring God. When you stand or kneel in church or at prayer, make these actions more than mere forms prescribed by tradition. Let them indicate your love for God.

6:12, 13 It was unusual for a king to kneel before someone else in front of his own people because kneeling meant submitting to a higher authority. Solomon demonstrated his great love and respect for God by kneeling before him. His action showed that he acknowledged God as the ultimate king and authority, and it encouraged the people to do the same.

18“But will God really live on earth among people? Why, even the highest heavens
cannot contain you. How much less this Temple I have built! 19Listen to my prayer and
my request, O LORD my God. Hear the cry and the prayer that your servant is making to
you. 20May you watch over this Temple both day and night, this place where you have
said you would put your name. May you always hear the prayers I make toward this
place. 21May you hear the humble and earnest requests from me and your people Israel
when we pray toward this place. Yes, hear us from heaven where you live, and when you
hear, forgive.

6:18 2 Chr 2:6
6:21 Mic 7:18

22“If someone wrongs another person and is required to take an oath of innocence in
front of the altar at this Temple, 23then hear from heaven and judge between your
servants—the accuser and the accused. Punish the guilty party, and acquit the one who
is innocent.

24“If your people Israel are defeated by their enemies because they have sinned
against you, and if they turn to you and call on your name and pray to you here in this
Temple, 25then hear from heaven and forgive their sins and return them to this land you
gave their ancestors.

26“If the skies are shut up and there is no rain because your people have sinned against
you, and then they pray toward this Temple and confess your name and turn from their
sins because you have punished them, 27then hear from heaven and forgive the sins of
your servants, your people Israel. Teach them to do what is right, and send rain on your
land that you have given to your people as their special possession.

6:26 1 Kgs 17:1

28“If there is a famine in the land, or plagues, or crop disease, or attacks of locusts or
caterpillars, or if your people's enemies are in the land besieging their towns—whatever
the trouble is—29and if your people offer a prayer concerning their troubles or sorrow,
raising their hands toward this Temple, 30then hear from heaven where you live, and
forgive. Give your people whatever they deserve, for you alone know the human heart.
31Then they will fear you and walk in your ways as long as they live in the land you gave
to our ancestors.

6:28 2 Chr 20:9
6:30 1 Sam 16:7; 1 Chr 28:9

32“And when foreigners hear of you and your mighty miracles, and they come from
distant lands to worship your great name and to pray toward this Temple, 33then hear
from heaven where you live, and grant what they ask of you. Then all the people of the
earth will come to know and fear you, just as your own people Israel do. They, too, will
know that this Temple I have built bears your name.

6:33 2 Chr 7:14

34“If your people go out at your command to fight their enemies, and if they pray to
you toward this city that you have chosen and toward this Temple that I have built for
your name, 35then hear their prayers from heaven and uphold their cause.

36“If they sin against you—and who has never sinned?—you may become angry with
them and let their enemies conquer them and take them captive to a foreign land far or
near. 37But in that land of exile, they may turn to you again in repentance and pray, ‘We
have sinned, done evil, and acted wickedly.’ 38Then if they turn to you with their whole

6:36 Job 15:14-16; Jas 3:2; 1 Jn 1:8-10

6:18 Solomon marveled that God would be willing to live on earth among sinful people. We marvel that God, through his Son, Jesus, lived among us in human form to reveal his eternal purposes to us. In doing so, God was reaching out to us in love. God wants us to reach out to him in return in order to know him and to love him with all our heart. Don't simply marvel at his power; take time to get to know him.

6:19-42 As Solomon led the people in prayer, he asked God to hear their prayers concerning a variety of situations: (1) crime (6:22, 23); (2) enemy attacks (6:24, 25); (3) drought (6:26, 27); (4) famine (6:28-31); (5) the influx of foreigners (6:32, 33); (6) war (6:34, 35); (7) sin (6:36-39). God is concerned with whatever we face, even the difficult consequences we bring upon ourselves. He wants us to turn to him in prayer. When you pray, remember that God hears you. Don't let the extremity of your situation cause you to doubt his care for you.

6:26 Why would Solomon assume that drought would come as a result of sin? Sin is not necessarily the direct cause of natural disasters today, but this was a special case. God had made a specific agreement with the Israelites that drought could be a consequence of their sins (Deuteronomy 28:20-24).

6:30 Have you ever felt far from God, separated by feelings of failure and personal problems? In his prayer, Solomon underscored the fact that God stands ready to hear his people, to forgive their sins, and to restore their relationship with him. God is waiting and listening for our confessions of guilt and our recommitment to obey him. He hears us when we pour out our needs and problems to him and is ready to forgive us and restore us to fellowship with him. Don't wait to experience his loving forgiveness.

6:36 "Who has never sinned?" The Bible makes it clear that no one is exempt from sin, not even God's appointed kings. Sin is a condition we all share, and we all should acknowledge it as Solomon did. When we realize we have sinned, we should quickly ask God for forgiveness and restoration. Knowing we have a tendency to sin should keep us close to God, seeking his guidance and strength. This truth is also mentioned in Psalm 14:3, Ecclesiastes 7:20, and Romans 3:23.

heart and soul and pray toward the land you gave to their ancestors, toward this city you
have chosen, and toward this Temple I have built to honor your name, 39 then hear their
prayers from heaven where you live. Uphold their cause and forgive your people who
have sinned against you.

6:40 2 Chr 7:15 Neh 1:6, 11 Ps 17:1 — 40 “O my God, be attentive to all the prayers made to you in this place. 41 And now,
O LORD God, arise and enter this resting place of yours, where your magnificent Ark has
been placed. May your priests, O LORD God, be clothed with salvation, and may your
6:41-42 //Ps 132:8-10 — saints rejoice in your goodness. 42 O LORD God, do not reject your anointed one.
Remember your unfailing love for your servant David.*”

The Dedication of the Temple

7:1-10 1 Kgs 8:62-66 — **7** When Solomon finished praying, fire flashed down from heaven and burned up the
7:1 1 Kgs 8:54; 18:24, 38 — burnt offerings and sacrifices, and the glorious presence of the LORD filled the
Temple. 2 The priests could not even enter the Temple of the LORD because the glorious
7:3 2 Chr 5:13; 20:21 — presence of the LORD filled it. 3 When all the people of Israel saw the fire coming down
and the glorious presence of the LORD filling the Temple, they fell face down on the
ground and worshiped and praised the LORD, saying,

“He is so good!
His faithful love endures forever!”

7:4 1 Kgs 8:62-63 — 4 Then the king and all the people offered sacrifices to the LORD. 5 King Solomon
offered a sacrifice of 22,000 oxen and 120,000 sheep. And so the king and all the people
7:6 1 Chr 15:16-21 2 Chr 5:12 — dedicated the Temple of God. 6 The priests took their assigned positions, and so did the
Levites who were singing, “His faithful love endures forever!” They accompanied the
singing with music from the instruments King David had made for praising the LORD.
On the other side of the Levites, the priests blew the trumpets, while all Israel stood.
7:7 1 Kgs 8:64-66 — 7 Solomon then dedicated the central area of the courtyard in front of the LORD’s
Temple so they could present burnt offerings and the fat from peace offerings there. He
did this because the bronze altar he had built could not handle all the burnt offerings,
grain offerings, and sacrificial fat.
7:8 1 Kgs 8:65 — 8 For the next seven days they celebrated the Festival of Shelters* with huge crowds
7:9 Lev 23:26 — gathered from all the tribes of Israel. They came from as far away as Lebo-hamath in the
north, to the brook of Egypt in the south. 9 On the eighth day they had a closing ceremony,
for they had celebrated the dedication of the altar for seven days and the Festival of
Shelters for seven days. 10 Then at the end of the celebration,* Solomon sent the people
home. They were all joyful and happy because the LORD had been so good to David and
Solomon and to his people Israel.

The LORD’s Response to Solomon

7:11-22 //1 Kgs 9:1-9 — 11 So Solomon finished building the Temple of the LORD, as well as the royal palace. He
completed everything he had planned to do. 12 Then one night the LORD appeared to
Solomon and said, “I have heard your prayer and have chosen this Temple as the place
7:13 2 Chr 6:26-28 — for making sacrifices. 13 At times I might shut up the heavens so that no rain falls, or I
might command locusts to devour your crops, or I might send plagues among you.

6:42 Or *Remember the faithfulness of your servant David.* **7:8** Hebrew *the festival* (also in 7:9); see note on 5:3. **7:10** Hebrew *Then on the twenty-seventh day of the seventh month.* This day of the Hebrew lunar calendar occurs in late September or early October.

7:1, 2 God sent fire from heaven to consume the offering and to begin the fire that was to burn continuously under the altar of burnt offering (see Leviticus 6:8-13). This perpetual fire symbolized God’s presence. God also sent fire when inaugurating the Tabernacle (Leviticus 9:22-24). This was the real dedication of the Temple because only God’s purifying power can make something holy.

7:4, 5 The Temple was dedicated to God, and Solomon and the people prepared to worship him. Dedication means setting apart a place, an object, or a person for an exclusive purpose. The purpose of this dedication was to set apart the Temple as a place to worship God. Today, our bodies are God’s temple (2 Corinthians 6:16). Solomon’s dedication of the Temple shows us that we should dedicate ourselves to carry out God’s special purpose (Ephesians 1:11, 12).

7:12 Months, maybe years, had passed since Solomon’s prayer of dedication (chapter 6). Several other building projects had been completed after the Temple (7:11; 8:1). Then after all this time, God told Solomon that he had heard Solomon’s prayer. How often do we look for immediate answers to our prayers and, when nothing happens, wonder if God has heard us? God does hear, and he will provide for us. We must trust that God will answer at the proper time.

[14]Then if my people who are called by my name will humble themselves and pray and
seek my face and turn from their wicked ways, I will hear from heaven and will forgive
their sins and heal their land. [15]I will listen to every prayer made in this place, [16]for I
have chosen this Temple and set it apart to be my home forever. My eyes and my heart
will always be here.

[17]"As for you, if you follow me as your father, David, did and obey all my commands,
laws, and regulations, [18]then I will not let anyone take away your throne. This is the same
promise I gave your father, David, when I said, 'You will never fail to have a successor
who rules over Israel.'

[19]"But if you abandon me and disobey the laws and commands I have given you, and
if you go and worship other gods, [20]then I will uproot the people of Israel from this land
of mine that I have given them. I will reject this Temple that I have set apart to honor my
name. I will make it a spectacle of contempt among the nations. [21]And though this
Temple is impressive now, it will become an appalling sight to all who pass by. They will
ask, 'Why has the LORD done such terrible things to his land and to his Temple?' [22]And
the answer will be, 'Because his people abandoned the LORD, the God of their ancestors,
who brought them out of Egypt, and they worshiped other gods instead. That is why he
brought all these disasters upon them.'"

4. Solomon's riches and wisdom

Solomon's Many Achievements

8 It was now twenty years since Solomon had become king, and the great building
projects of the LORD's Temple and his own royal palace were completed. [2]Solomon
now turned his attention to rebuilding the towns that King Hiram* had given him, and
he settled Israelites in them. [3]It was at this time, too, that Solomon fought against the
city of Hamath-zobah and conquered it. [4]He rebuilt Tadmor in the desert and built towns
in the region of Hamath as supply centers. [5]He fortified the cities of Upper Beth-horon
and Lower Beth-horon, rebuilding their walls and installing barred gates. [6]He also
rebuilt Baalath and other supply centers at this time and constructed cities where his
chariots and horses* could be kept. He built to his heart's content in Jerusalem and
Lebanon and throughout the entire realm.

[7]There were still some people living in the land who were not Israelites, including
Hittites, Amorites, Perizzites, Hivites, and Jebusites. [8]These were descendants of the
nations that Israel had not completely destroyed. So Solomon conscripted them for his
labor force, and they serve in the labor force to this day. [9]But Solomon did not conscript
any of the Israelites for forced labor. Instead, he assigned them to serve as fighting men,
officers in his army, commanders of his chariots, and charioteers. [10]King Solomon also
appointed 250 of them to supervise the various projects.

[11]Solomon moved his wife, Pharaoh's daughter, from the City of David to the new

7:14 2 Chr 6:37-39
7:15 2 Chr 6:20, 40
7:16 2 Chr 7:12
7:18 2 Chr 6:16
7:19 Lev 26:14, 33; Deut 28:15
7:20 Deut 28:37; 29:28; 1 Kgs 14:15
7:21 Deut 29:24-27
8:1-18 //1 Kgs 9:10-28
8:5 1 Chr 7:24; 2 Chr 14:7
8:8 1 Kgs 4:6; 9:21
8:11 1 Kgs 3:1; 7:8

8:2 Hebrew *Huram,* a variant name for Hiram; also in 8:18. **8:6** Or *and charioteers.*

7:14 In chapter 6, Solomon asked God to make provisions for the people when they sinned. God answered with four conditions for forgiveness: (1) Humble yourself by admitting your sins, (2) pray to God, asking for forgiveness, (3) seek God continually, and (4) turn from sinful behavior. True repentance is more than talk—it is changed behavior. Whether we sin individually, as a group, or as a nation, following these steps will lead to forgiveness. God will answer our earnest prayers.

7:17-22 God plainly set forth certain conditions for Solomon to meet if he wanted the kingdom to continue. If Solomon followed God, he and his descendants would prosper; if Solomon did not, he and the nation would be destroyed. In Deuteronomy 27 and 28, these conditions were outlined before all the people.

But sin is deceptively attractive, and Solomon eventually turned from God. As a result, his son and heir lost most of the kingdom. Following God brings benefits and rewards (not necessarily material). Turning away from God brings suffering, punishment, and ultimately destruction. Today, God's conditions are just as clear as they were in Solomon's day. Choose to obey God and live.

7:21, 22 Soon after Solomon's reign, the Temple was ransacked (12:9). It is difficult for us to imagine that such a great and wise king could become corrupted by idols—symbols of power, prosperity, and sexuality. But even today these idols lure us into their traps. When we allow any desire to rival God's proper place, we have taken the first step toward moral and spiritual decay.

8:11 Solomon married Pharaoh's daughter to secure a military alliance with Egypt. He did not let the woman live in David's palace, however, where the Ark of God had once been kept. This implies that Solomon knew his pagan marriage would not please God. Solomon married many other foreign women, and this was contrary to God's law (Deuteronomy 7:3, 4). These women worshiped false gods and were certain to contaminate Israel with their beliefs and practices. Eventually Solomon's pagan wives caused his downfall (1 Kings 11:1-11).

palace he had built for her. He said, "My wife must not live in King David's palace, for
the Ark of the LORD has been there, and it is holy ground."
8:12 2 Chr 4:1 [12]Then Solomon sacrificed burnt offerings to the LORD on the altar he had built in
8:13 Exod 23:14-17; 29:38-42 Num 28:3 front of the foyer of the Temple. [13]The number of sacrifices varied from day to day
according to the commands Moses had given. Extra sacrifices were offered on the
Sabbaths, on new moon festivals, and at the three annual festivals—the Passover
8:14 1 Chr 24:1; 25:1; 26:1 Neh 12:24, 36 celebration, the Festival of Harvest,* and the Festival of Shelters. [14]In assigning the
priests to their duties, Solomon followed the regulations of his father, David. He also
assigned the Levites to lead the people in praise and to assist the priests in their daily
duties. And he assigned the gatekeepers to their gates by their divisions, following the
commands of David, the man of God. [15]Solomon did not deviate in any way from
David's commands concerning the priests and Levites and the treasuries.
[16]So Solomon made sure that all the work related to building the Temple of the
LORD was carried out, from the day its foundation was laid to the day of its comple-
8:17 1 Kgs 9:26 2 Kgs 14:22 2 Chr 9:10, 13 tion.
[17]Later Solomon went to Ezion-geber and Elath,* ports in the land of Edom, along
8:18 2 Chr 9:10, 13 the shore of the Red Sea.* [18]Hiram sent him ships commanded by his own officers
and manned by experienced crews of sailors. These ships sailed to the land of
Ophir with Solomon's men and brought back to Solomon almost seventeen tons* of
gold.

The Queen of Sheba's Visit

9:1 1 Kgs 10:1-13 Matt 12:42 Luke 11:31 **9** When the queen of Sheba heard of Solomon's reputation, she came to Jerusalem
to test him with hard questions. She arrived with a large group of attendants and
a great caravan of camels loaded with spices, huge quantities of gold, and precious
jewels. [2]When she met with Solomon, they talked about everything she had on her
mind. Solomon answered all her questions; nothing was too hard for him to explain
to her. [3]When the queen of Sheba realized how wise Solomon was, and when she saw
the palace he had built, [4]she was breathless. She was also amazed at the food on his
tables, the organization of his officials and their splendid clothing, the cup-bearers
and their robes, and the burnt offerings Solomon made at the Temple of the LORD.
[5]She exclaimed to the king, "Everything I heard in my country about your achievements and wisdom is true! [6]I didn't believe it until I arrived here and saw it with my own
eyes. Truly I had not heard the half of it! Your wisdom is far greater than what I was told.
[7]How happy these people must be! What a privilege for your officials to stand here day
9:8 Deut 7:8 1 Chr 28:5; 29:23 2 Chr 2:11 after day, listening to your wisdom! [8]The LORD your God is great indeed! He delights
in you and has placed you on the throne to rule for him. Because God loves Israel so
much and desires this kingdom to last forever, he has made you king so you can rule with
justice and righteousness."
[9]Then she gave the king a gift of nine thousand pounds* of gold, and great quantities
of spices and precious jewels. Never before had there been spices as fine as those the
queen of Sheba gave to Solomon.
9:10 2 Chr 8:18 [10](When the crews of Hiram and Solomon brought gold from Ophir, they also brought

8:13 Or *Festival of Weeks.* **8:17a** As in Greek version (see also 2 Kgs 14:22; 16:6); Hebrew reads *Eloth.*
8:17b Hebrew *the sea.* **8:18** Hebrew *450 talents* [15.3 metric tons]. **9:9** Hebrew *120 talents* [4 metric tons].

8:15 Although Solomon carefully followed God's instructions for building the Temple and offering sacrifices (8:13), he paid no attention to what God said about marrying pagan women. His sin in marrying a foreign wife (8:11) began his slide away from God. No matter how good or spiritual we are in most areas of life, one unsurrendered area can begin a downfall. Guard carefully *every* area of your life, especially your relationships. Don't give sin any foothold.

9:1-8 The queen of Sheba had heard about Solomon's wisdom, but she was overwhelmed when she saw for herself the fruits of that wisdom. Although Solomon had married Pharaoh's daughter, he still sincerely tried to follow God at this stage in his life. When people get to know you and ask hard questions, will your responses reflect God? Your life can be a powerful witness; let others see God at work in you.

9:8 The queen of Sheba marveled at Solomon, claiming that God must love his people greatly to give them such a king. Israel greatly prospered during Solomon's reign, witnessing to God's power and love for his people. The good times show God's love and faithfulness, but hard times come to believers, too. Our perseverance and steadfast hope during those times will demonstrate our love and faithfulness to God.

rich cargoes of almug wood* and precious jewels. 11 The king used the almug wood to
make steps* for the Temple of the LORD and the royal palace, and to construct harps and
lyres for the musicians. Never before had there been such beautiful instruments in Judah.)
12 King Solomon gave the queen of Sheba whatever she asked for—gifts of greater
value than the gifts she had given him. Then she and all her attendants left and returned
to their own land.

Solomon's Wealth and Splendor

13 Each year Solomon received about 25 tons* of gold. 14 This did not include the **9:13-28** //1 Kgs 10:14-28
additional revenue he received from merchants and traders. All the kings of Arabia and //2 Chr 1:14-17
the governors of the land also brought gold and silver to Solomon.
15 King Solomon made two hundred large shields of hammered gold, each containing
over 15 pounds* of gold. 16 He also made three hundred smaller shields of hammered
gold, each containing about 7½ pounds* of gold. The king placed these shields in the
Palace of the Forest of Lebanon.
17 Then the king made a huge ivory throne and overlaid it with pure gold. 18 The throne
had six steps, and there was a footstool of gold attached to it. On both sides of the seat
were armrests, with the figure of a lion standing on each side of the throne. 19 Solomon
made twelve other lion figures, one standing on each end of each of the six steps. No
other throne in all the world could be compared with it!
20 All of King Solomon's drinking cups were solid gold, as were all the utensils in the
Palace of the Forest of Lebanon. They were not made of silver because silver was
considered of little value in Solomon's day!
21 The king had a fleet of trading ships* manned by the sailors sent by Hiram.* Once **9:21** 2 Chr 20:36-37
every three years the ships returned, loaded down with gold, silver, ivory, apes, and
peacocks.*
22 So King Solomon became richer and wiser than any other king in all the earth. **9:22** 1 Kgs 3:13
23 Kings from every nation came to visit him and to hear the wisdom God had given him. 2 Chr 1:12
24 Year after year, everyone who came to visit brought him gifts of silver and gold,
clothing, weapons, spices, horses, and mules.
25 Solomon had four thousand stalls for his chariot horses and twelve thousand **9:25** Deut 17:16
horses.* He stationed many of them in the chariot cities, and some near him in 1 Kgs 4:26; 10:26
Jerusalem. 26 He ruled over all the kings from the Euphrates River* to the land of the 2 Chr 1:14
Philistines and the border of Egypt. 27 The king made silver as plentiful in Jerusalem as **9:26** 1 Kgs 4:21, 24
stones. And valuable cedarwood was as common as the sycamore wood that grows in **9:27**
the foothills of Judah.* 28 Solomon's horses were imported from Egypt* and many 2 Chr 1:15-17
other countries. **9:28** 2 Chr 1:16

Summary of Solomon's Reign

29 The rest of the events of Solomon's reign, from beginning to end, are recorded in *The* **9:29-31**
Record of Nathan the Prophet and in *The Prophecy of Ahijah from Shiloh,* and also in //1 Kgs 11:41-43
The Visions of Iddo the Seer, concerning Jeroboam son of Nebat. 30 Solomon ruled in **9:30**
Jerusalem over all Israel for forty years. 31 When he died, he was buried in the city of his 1 Kgs 11:42-43 **9:31**
father, David. Then his son Rehoboam became the next king. 1 Kgs 2:10

B. THE KINGDOM OF JUDAH (10:1—36:23)

After Solomon's death, the northern tribes revolt, and we read little more about them in 2 Chronicles. The remainder of 2 Chronicles recounts the alternating periods of apostasy and reform in Judah. In the end, Judah would not turn from its sin, and the tragic result was a 70-year captivity in Babylon. Sin in our lives will also lead to judgment and devastation. Although God's judgment may seem slow, it is nevertheless certain.

9:10 Hebrew *algum wood* (also in 9:11); compare parallel text at 1 Kgs 10:11-12. **9:11** Or *gateways.* The meaning of the Hebrew is uncertain. **9:13** Hebrew *666 talents* [23 metric tons]. **9:15** Hebrew *600 shekels* [6.8 kilograms]. **9:16** Hebrew *300 shekels* [3.4 kilograms]. **9:21a** Hebrew *fleet of ships that could sail to Tarshish.* **9:21b** Hebrew *Huram,* a variant name for Hiram. **9:21c** Or *and baboons.* **9:25** Or *12,000 charioteers.* **9:26** Hebrew *the river.* **9:27** Hebrew *the Shephelah.* **9:28** Possibly *Muzur,* a district near Cilicia.

9:11 Almug wood was probably sandalwood, a smooth, red-colored wood that accepts a high polish. This beautiful wood was extremely expensive.

9:29 For the rest of Solomon's story, see 1 Kings 10:26–11:43. In his later years, Solomon turned away from God and led the nation into worshiping idols.

1. The northern tribes revolt

Israel Rebels against Rehoboam

10:1 1 Kgs 12:1-20 **10** Rehoboam went to Shechem, where all Israel had gathered to make him king.
10:2 1 Kgs 11:40 2 When Jeroboam son of Nebat heard of Solomon's death, he returned from Egypt,
for he had fled to Egypt to escape from King Solomon. 3 The leaders of Israel sent for
Jeroboam, and he and all Israel went together to speak with Rehoboam. 4 "Your father
was a hard master," they said. "Lighten the harsh labor demands and heavy taxes that
your father imposed on us. Then we will be your loyal subjects."
5 Rehoboam replied, "Come back in three days for my answer." So the people went
away.
6 Then King Rehoboam went to discuss the matter with the older men who had

---

REHOBOAM

Settling for cheap imitations in exchange for the real thing is a poor way to live. In every area of his life, Rehoboam consistently traded away what was real for what was counterfeit. Given wise and unwise counsel by his advisers at his coronation, he chose to grab for power and control rather than to take patiently the counsel of those older and wiser than he and treat his people with kindness. Although his position came from God, he chose to abandon God. These unwise decisions made him weaker rather than stronger. As a result, he was invaded by the Egyptians and stripped of the riches he inherited from David and Solomon. To replace them, he had cheap bronze copies made.

Throughout the early part of his reign, Rehoboam fluctuated between obeying God and going his own way. Outward appearances were kept up, but his inward attitudes were evil. Following in the tradition of David gave Rehoboam many opportunities for real greatness. Instead, he ended up with a divided and broken kingdom.

How much of real living have we traded away for the things that do not last? We trade healthy bodies for momentary excitement, personal integrity for fast-fading wealth, honesty for lies, God's wise guidance for our selfish ways. We sin when we willingly give little value to "the real thing" God has already given us.

Our counterfeit lives may fool some people, but they never fool God. Yet in spite of what he sees in us, God offers mercy. Are you a self-managed enterprise, counterfeit at best? Or have you placed yourself in God's care? Do the decisions you must make today need a second consideration in light of Rehoboam's example?

Strengths and accomplishments
- Fourth and last king of the united nation of Israel, but only for a short time
- Fortified his kingdom and achieved a measure of popularity

Weaknesses and mistakes
- Followed unwise advice and divided his kingdom
- Married foreign women, as his father, Solomon, had done
- Abandoned the worship of God and allowed idolatry to flourish

Lessons from his life
- Thoughtless decisions often lead to exchanging what is most valuable for something of far less value
- Every choice we make has real and long-lasting consequences

Vital statistics
- Where: Jerusalem
- Occupation: King of the united kingdom of Israel and later of the southern kingdom of Judah
- Relatives: Father: Solomon. Mother: Naamah. Son: Abijah. Wife: Maacah
- Contemporaries: Jeroboam, Shishak, Shemaiah

Key verse
"But when Rehoboam was firmly established and strong, he abandoned the law of the LORD, and all Israel followed him in this sin" (2 Chronicles 12:1).

Rehoboam's story is told in 1 Kings 11:43—14:31 and 2 Chronicles 9:31—13:7. He is also mentioned in Matthew 1:7.

10:1 The crowning of an Israelite king would normally have taken place in Jerusalem, the capital city. But Rehoboam saw that there was the possibility of trouble in the north; so to maintain his hold on the country, he chose Shechem, a city about 35 miles north of Jerusalem. Shechem was an ancient site for making covenants (Joshua 24:1).

10:1-15 Following bad advice can cause disaster. Rehoboam lost the chance to rule a peaceful, united kingdom because he rejected the advice of Solomon's older counselors, preferring the counsel of his peers. Rehoboam made two errors in seeking advice: (1) He did not give extra consideration to the suggestions of those who knew the situation better than he, and (2) he did not ask God for wisdom to discern which was the better option.

It is easy to follow the advice of our peers because they often feel as we do. But their view may be limited. It is important to listen carefully to those who have more experience than we do—they can see the bigger picture.

10:2, 3 Why was Jeroboam in Egypt? Ahijah the prophet had predicted that Israel would split in two and that Jeroboam would become king of the northern section. When Solomon learned of this prophecy, he tried to kill Jeroboam, and Jeroboam was forced to flee to Egypt (1 Kings 11:26-40).

counseled his father, Solomon. “What is your advice?” he asked. “How should I answer
these people?”
7 The older counselors replied, “If you are good to the people and show them kindness
and do your best to please them, they will always be your loyal subjects.”
8 But Rehoboam rejected the advice of the elders and instead asked the opinion of the
young men who had grown up with him and who were now his advisers. 9 “What is your
advice?” he asked them. “How should I answer these people who want me to lighten the
burdens imposed by my father?”
10 The young men replied, “This is what you should tell those complainers: ‘My little
finger is thicker than my father’s waist—if you think he was hard on you, just wait and
see what I’ll be like! 11 Yes, my father was harsh on you, but I’ll be even harsher! My
father used whips on you, but I’ll use scorpions!’”
12 Three days later, Jeroboam and all the people returned to hear Rehoboam’s decision,
just as the king had requested. 13 But Rehoboam spoke harshly to them, for he rejected
the advice of the older counselors 14 and followed the counsel of his younger advisers.
He told the people, “My father was harsh on you, but I’ll be even harsher! My father
used whips on you, but I’ll use scorpions!” 15 So the king paid no attention to the people’s **10:15**
demands. This turn of events was the will of God, for it fulfilled the prophecy of the 1 Kgs 11:29-39
LORD spoken to Jeroboam son of Nebat by the prophet Ahijah from Shiloh.
16 When all Israel realized that the king had rejected their request, they shouted, **10:16**
“Down with David and his dynasty! We have no share in Jesse’s son! Let’s go home, 2 Sam 20:1
Israel! Look out for your own house, O David!” So all Israel returned home. 17 But 2 Chr 10:19
Rehoboam continued to rule over the Israelites who lived in the towns of Judah.
18 King Rehoboam sent Adoniram,* who was in charge of the labor force, to restore **10:18**
order, but the Israelites stoned him to death. When this news reached King Rehoboam, 1 Kgs 4:6; 5:14
he quickly jumped into his chariot and fled to Jerusalem. 19 The northern tribes of Israel **10:19**
have refused to be ruled by a descendant of David to this day. 1 Kgs 12:19

Shemaiah’s Prophecy

11 When Rehoboam arrived at Jerusalem, he mobilized the armies of Judah and **11:1**
Benjamin—180,000 select troops—to fight against the army of Israel and to 1 Kgs 12:21-24
restore the kingdom to himself. 2 But the LORD said to Shemaiah, the man of God, 3 “Say **11:2**
to Rehoboam son of Solomon, king of Judah, and to all the Israelites in Judah and 2 Chr 12:5-7, 15
Benjamin: 4 ‘This is what the LORD says: Do not fight against your relatives. Go back **11:4**
home, for what has happened is my doing!’” So they obeyed the message of the LORD 2 Chr 10:15; 28:8-11
and did not fight against Jeroboam.

Rehoboam Fortifies Judah

5 Rehoboam remained in Jerusalem and fortified various cities for the defense of Judah. **11:5**
6 He built up Bethlehem, Etam, Tekoa, 7 Beth-zur, Soco, Adullam, 8 Gath, Mareshah, 2 Chr 8:2-6; 11:23

10:18 Hebrew *Hadoram,* a variant name for Adoniram; compare 1 Kgs 4:6; 5:14; 12:18.

10:14 Rehoboam must have gotten an unbalanced picture of leadership from his father, Solomon. Apparently Rehoboam saw only the difficulty of leading the nation, not the opportunities. He mentioned only the harsher aspects of Solomon’s rule, and he himself decided to be very harsh toward the people. As you discuss your responsibilities with your children, be sure that you temper words of complaint with words of joy. Otherwise you may sour their attitudes toward the work you do and those you serve.

10:16-19 In trying to have it all, Rehoboam lost almost everything. Motivated by greed and power, he pressed too hard and divided his kingdom. He didn’t need more money or power because he had inherited the richest kingdom in the world. He didn’t need more control because he was the king. His demands were based on selfishness rather than reason or spiritual discernment. Those who insist on having it all often wind up with little or nothing.

10:16-19 This is the beginning of the divided kingdom. The peaceful united kingdom under Solomon divided into two parts. Ten of the tribes followed Jeroboam and called their nation Israel, or the northern kingdom. The other two tribes, Judah and Benjamin, remained loyal to David’s line and accepted Rehoboam’s rule. They called their nation Judah, or the southern kingdom.

11:1 Rehoboam’s foolishness divided his kingdom, and he tried to reunite it by force. True unity, however, cannot be forced—it must be the free response of willing hearts. If you want the loyalty of employees, children, or anyone else in your charge, win their respect through love instead of trying to gain their submission through force.

11:4 Why would God support this rebellion? It was part of the nation’s punishment for turning away from God (1 Kings 11:11). It may also have been God’s way of saving Rehoboam’s smaller kingdom from defeat. In doing so, God preserved David’s line and kept intact his plan for the Messiah to be a descendant of David (see 2 Samuel 7:16). When we see division, especially in a church that splits, we wonder what God would have us do. God desires unity, but while we should always work toward reconciliation, we must recognize that only God knows the future. He may allow a division in order to fulfill his greater purposes.

Ziph, [9]Adoraim, Lachish, Azekah, [10]Zorah, Aijalon, and Hebron. These became the
fortified cities of Judah and Benjamin. [11]Rehoboam strengthened their defenses and
stationed commanders in them. In each of them, he stored supplies of food, olive oil, and
wine. [12]He also put shields and spears in these towns as a further safety measure. So only
Judah and Benjamin remained under his control.
[13]But all the priests and Levites living among the northern tribes of Israel sided with
11:14 Num 35:2-5 Rehoboam. [14]The Levites even abandoned their homes and property and moved to Judah
and Jerusalem, because Jeroboam and his sons would not allow them to serve the LORD
11:15 1 Kgs 12:31; 13:33 as priests. [15]Jeroboam appointed his own priests to serve at the pagan shrines, where they
worshiped the goat and calf idols he had made. [16]From all over Israel, those who sincerely
11:16 2 Chr 15:9 wanted to worship the LORD, the God of Israel, followed the Levites to Jerusalem, where
11:17 2 Chr 12:1 they could offer sacrifices to the LORD, the God of their ancestors. [17]This strengthened the
kingdom of Judah, and for three years they supported Rehoboam son of Solomon and
earnestly sought to obey the LORD as they had done during the reigns of David and
Solomon.

2. History of apostasy and reform

Rehoboam's Family

11:18 1 Sam 16:6 [18]Rehoboam married his cousin Mahalath, the daughter of David's son Jerimoth and of
Abihail, the daughter of Eliab. (Eliab was one of David's brothers, a son of Jesse.)
[19]Mahalath had three sons—Jeush, Shemariah, and Zaham.
[20]Later Rehoboam married another cousin, Maacah, the daughter of Absalom.
11:21 Deut 17:17 Maacah gave birth to Abijah, Attai, Ziza, and Shelomith. [21]Rehoboam loved Maacah
more than any of his other wives and concubines. In all, he had eighteen wives and sixty
11:22 Deut 21:15-17 concubines, and they gave birth to twenty-eight sons and sixty daughters. [22]Rehoboam
made Maacah's son Abijah chief among the princes, making it clear that he would be the
next king. [23]Rehoboam also wisely gave responsibilities to his other sons and stationed
them in the fortified cities throughout the land of Judah and Benjamin. He provided them
with generous provisions and arranged for each of them to have several wives.

Egypt Invades Judah

12:1 2 Chr 11:17 **12** But when Rehoboam was firmly established and strong, he abandoned the law of
12:3 2 Chr 16:8 Nah 3:9 the LORD, and all Israel followed him in this sin. [2]Because they were unfaithful
to the LORD, King Shishak of Egypt attacked Jerusalem in the fifth year of King
Rehoboam's reign. [3]He came with twelve hundred chariots, sixty thousand horsemen,
and a countless army of foot soldiers, including Libyans, Sukkites, and Ethiopians.*
12:4 2 Chr 11:5-12 [4]Shishak conquered Judah's fortified cities and then advanced to attack Jerusalem.
12:5 Deut 28:15 2 Chr 11:2; 15:2 [5]The prophet Shemaiah then met with Rehoboam and Judah's leaders, who had all
fled to Jerusalem because of Shishak. Shemaiah told them, "This is what the LORD says:
You have abandoned me, so I am abandoning you to Shishak."

12:3 Hebrew *and Cushites.*

11:13, 14 Before the nation split, the center of worship was in Jerusalem, and people flocked there for the three great annual religious festivals. During the rest of the year, other worship services and rituals were conducted in the tribal territories by priests and Levites who lived throughout the land. They offered sacrifices, taught God's laws, and encouraged the people to continue to follow God and avoid pagan influences.

After the nation split, Jeroboam, the new king of Israel, saw these priests and Levites as threats to his new government because they retained loyalty to Jerusalem, now the capital of Judah. So he appointed his own priests, effectively banning the Levites from their duties and forcing them to move to the southern kingdom. Jeroboam's pagan priests encouraged idol worship. With the absence of spiritual leaders, the new northern kingdom was in danger of abandoning God.

11:16 These people obeyed God rather than Jeroboam. By their actions, they preserved their integrity and strengthened the southern kingdom. In the future, most of the people in the northern kingdom would go along with the evil designs of the kings, hoping to benefit by cooperating. Don't follow their example and rationalize away God's teachings in order to gain earthly reward.

12:1, 2 Here "Israel" refers to Judah, the southern kingdom. During his first three years on the throne, Rehoboam made an attempt to obey God, and as a result, Judah prospered. But then, at his peak of popularity and power, he abandoned God. The result was destruction because God allowed Judah to be conquered by Egypt. How could this happen? Often it is more difficult to be a believer in good times than in bad. Tough times push us toward God; but easy times can make us feel self-sufficient and self-satisfied. When everything is going right, guard your faith closely.

12:2 A record of this invasion has been found on an Egyptian stone that says Shishak's army penetrated as far north as the Sea of Galilee, in the northern kingdom. Egypt was not the world power it had once been, and Shishak wanted to restore his nation to its former greatness. He was not strong enough to conquer both Israel and Judah, but he managed to destroy key cities in Judah in an effort to regain control of the trade routes and create dissension among the people.

6 The king and the leaders of Israel humbled themselves and said, "The LORD is right 12:6 Exod 9:27
in doing this to us!" Dan 9:14
7 When the LORD saw their change of heart, he gave this message to Shemaiah: "Since 12:7
the people have humbled themselves, I will not completely destroy them and will soon 1 Kgs 21:29 2 Chr 34:25-27
give them some relief. I will not use Shishak to pour out my anger on Jerusalem. 8 But Ps 78:38
they will become his subjects, so that they can learn how much better it is to serve me 12:8
than to serve earthly rulers." Deut 28:47-48
9 So King Shishak of Egypt came to Jerusalem and took away all the treasures of the 12:9-16 //1 Kgs 14:25-31
Temple of the LORD and of the royal palace, including all of Solomon's gold shields. 2 Chr 9:15-16
10 King Rehoboam later replaced them with bronze shields and entrusted them to the care
of the captain of his bodyguard. 11 Whenever the king went to the Temple of the LORD,
the guards would carry them along and then return them to the guardroom. 12 Because 12:12 2 Chr 12:6-7; 19:3
Rehoboam humbled himself, the LORD's anger was turned aside, and he did not destroy
him completely. And there was still goodness in the land of Judah.

Summary of Rehoboam's Reign

13 King Rehoboam firmly established himself in Jerusalem and continued to rule. He was 12:13 1 Kgs 14:21
forty-one years old when he became king, and he reigned seventeen years in Jerusalem,
the city the LORD had chosen from among all the tribes of Israel as the place to honor his
name. Rehoboam's mother was Naamah, a woman from Ammon. 14 But he was an evil 12:14
king, for he did not seek the LORD with all his heart. 2 Chr 19:3
15 The rest of the events of Rehoboam's reign, from beginning to end, are recorded in 12:15 1 Kgs 14:29
The Record of Shemaiah the Prophet and in *The Record of Iddo the Seer,* which are part 2 Chr 9:29; 12:5
of the genealogical record. Rehoboam and Jeroboam were continually at war with each 12:16
other. 16 When Rehoboam died, he was buried in the City of David. Then his son Abijah 2 Chr 11:20
became the next king.

Abijah's War with Jeroboam

13 Abijah began to rule over Judah in the eighteenth year of Jeroboam's reign in 13:1-2 //1 Kgs 15:1-2
Israel. 2 He reigned in Jerusalem three years. His mother was Maacah,* a daughter 2 Chr 11:20
of Uriel from Gibeah. 13:2 1 Kgs 15:6
Then war broke out between Abijah and Jeroboam. 3 Judah, led by King Abijah,
fielded 400,000 seasoned warriors, while Jeroboam mustered 800,000 courageous men 13:4
from Israel. 4 When the army of Judah arrived in the hill country of Ephraim, Abijah Josh 18:22
stood on Mount Zemaraim and shouted to Jeroboam and the Israelite army: "Listen to 13:5 Num 18:19
me! 5 Don't you realize that the LORD, the God of Israel, made an unbreakable covenant* 2 Sam 7:12-16
with David, giving him and his descendants the throne of Israel forever? 6 Yet Jeroboam 13:6 1 Kgs 11:26
son of Nebat, who was a mere servant of David's son Solomon, became a traitor to his 13:7
master. 7 Then a whole gang of scoundrels joined him, defying Solomon's son Rehoboam 2 Chr 12:13
when he was young and inexperienced and could not stand up to them. 8 Do you really 13:8 1 Kgs 12:28 2 Chr 11:15

13:2 As in most Greek manuscripts and Syriac version (see also 2 Chr 11:20-21; 1 Kgs 15:2); Hebrew reads *Micaiah.*
13:5 Hebrew *a covenant of salt.*

12:6-8 God lessened his judgment when Israel's leaders confessed their sins, humbled themselves, and recognized God's justice in punishing them. It's never too late to repent, even in the midst of punishment. Regardless of what we have done, God is willing to receive us back into fellowship. Are you struggling and alone because sin has broken your fellowship with God? Confession and humility will open the door to receiving God's mercy.

12:8 Subjection to other kings was the price Judah had to pay for disobeying God. The nation's leaders thought they could succeed in their own strength, but they were wrong. When we rebel against God, we always pay for it. When we leave God out of our lives, we lose more spiritually than we ever gain financially.

12:10, 11 How ironic that the pure gold of Solomon's Temple was replaced by cheaper bronze. Rehoboam tried to maintain the trappings and appearance of former glory, but he couldn't measure up. When God is no longer central in our lives, maintaining the appearance of a Christian life becomes superficial. Outer beauty must come from inner strength.

12:14 Rehoboam's story is tragic because he "did not seek the LORD with all his heart." It is dangerous to put off responding to God. God asks us for a firm commitment, and unless we respond by trusting him completely, we will find ourselves alienated from him.

13:1ff First Kings 15:3 says Abijah committed many sins, but the Chronicles account has only positive comments about him. For the most part, Abijah was, no doubt, a wicked king. The writer of Chronicles chose to highlight the little good he did in order to show that he was still under God's covenant promise to David. Because of Abijah's fiery speech to Jeroboam (13:4-12), he was spared the immediate consequences of his sin.

13:8 Jeroboam's army was cursed because of the gold calves they carried with them. It was as though they had put sin into a physical form so they could haul it around. Consider carefully the things you cherish. If you value anything more than God, it becomes your gold calf and will one day drag you down. Let go of anything that interferes with your relationship with God.

think you can stand against the kingdom of the LORD that is led by the descendants of
David? Your army is vast indeed, but with you are those gold calves that Jeroboam made
13:9 Exod 29:29-33; 2 Chr 11:14-15; Jer 2:11; 5:7
as your gods! [9]And you have chased away the priests of the LORD and the Levites and
have appointed your own priests, just like the pagan nations. You let anyone become a
priest these days! Whoever comes to be dedicated with a young bull and seven rams can
become a priest of these so-called gods of yours!
[10]"But as for us, the LORD is our God, and we have not abandoned him. Only the
descendants of Aaron serve the LORD as priests, and the Levites alone may help them in
13:11 Exod 25:30-39; 29:38; Lev 24:5-9; 2 Chr 2:4
their work. [11]They present burnt offerings and fragrant incense to the LORD every
morning and evening. They place the Bread of the Presence on the holy table, and they
light the gold lampstand every evening. We are following the instructions of the LORD
13:12 Num 10:8-9
our God, but you have abandoned him. [12]So you see, God is with us. He is our leader.
His priests blow their trumpets and lead us into battle against you. O people of Israel, do
not fight against the LORD, the God of your ancestors, for you will not succeed!"
[13]Meanwhile, Jeroboam had secretly sent part of his army around behind the men of
13:13 Josh 8:4-9
Judah to ambush them. [14]When Judah realized that they were being attacked from the
13:14 2 Chr 14:11
front and the rear, they cried out to the LORD for help. Then the priests blew the trumpets,
13:15 2 Chr 14:12
[15]and the men of Judah began to shout. At the sound of their battle cry, God defeated
Jeroboam and the Israelite army and routed them before Abijah and the army of Judah.
[16]The Israelite army fled from Judah, and God handed them over to Judah in defeat.
[17]Abijah and his army inflicted heavy losses on them; there were 500,000 casualties
among Israel's finest troops that day. [18]So Judah defeated Israel because they trusted in
13:18 2 Chr 14:11
the LORD, the God of their ancestors. [19]Abijah and his army pursued Jeroboam's troops
and captured some of his towns, including Bethel, Jeshanah, and Ephron, along with
their surrounding villages.
13:20 1 Sam 25:38; 1 Kgs 14:20
[20]So Jeroboam of Israel never regained his power during Abijah's lifetime, and finally
the LORD struck him down and he died. [21]By contrast, Abijah of Judah grew more and
13:22–14:1 1 Kgs 15:6-8; 2 Chr 9:20; 24:27
more powerful. He married fourteen wives and had twenty-two sons and sixteen
daughters. [22]The rest of the events of Abijah's reign, including his words and deeds, are
recorded in *The Commentary of Iddo the Prophet.*

Early Years of Asa's Reign

14:2-3 //1 Kgs 15:11-12
14 When Abijah died, he was buried in the City of David. Then his son Asa became
14:3 Exod 34:13
the next king. There was peace in the land for ten years, [2]for Asa did what was
pleasing and good in the sight of the LORD his God. [3]He removed the pagan altars and

---

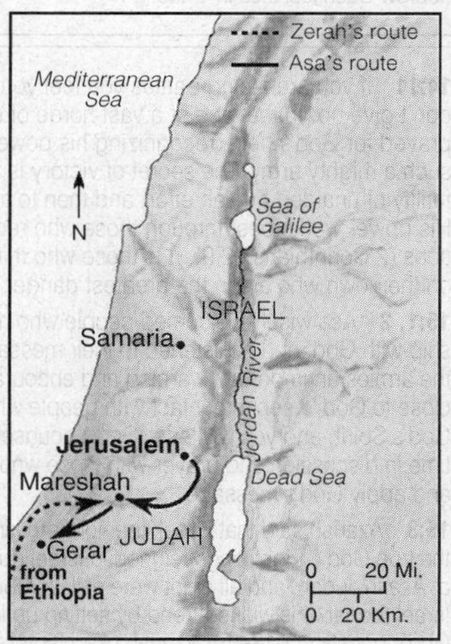

ASA'S BATTLES A huge army from Ethiopia under Zerah advanced toward Mareshah, greatly outnumbering King Asa's army. Asa sent his troops to meet them, and the battle took place in the valley north of Mareshah. Asa prayed to God, and the Ethiopians were defeated and chased as far as Gerar.

13:9 Abijah criticized Jeroboam's low standards in appointing priests. Anyone is qualified to represent a god that is worthless. To represent the Lord God Almighty, however, a person must live by God's standards. Those appointed to positions of responsibility in your church should not be selected merely because they volunteer, are influential, or are highly educated. Instead, they should demonstrate sound doctrine, dedication to God, and strong spiritual character (see 1 Timothy 3).

13:18, 19 Although outnumbered by Israel, Judah won this conflict by depending on God's help. Some kings in Judah's history focused on God, but not one Israelite king consistently followed God—all followed Jeroboam's idolatry or served Baal. As a result, Israel experienced God's punishment many years before Judah did.

Judah had an advantage: The Temple, with its sacrifices and the loyal priests and prophets, was in the southern kingdom. Many of Judah's kings were good, at least for parts of their reigns. Whenever an idolatrous king reigned, his rule was followed by that of a God-honoring king who reformed religious life. Also, the idolatrous kings usually served for a much shorter time than the good ones. The result was that true faith in God ran stronger and deeper in Judah than in Israel, but it was still not up to God's standards.

14:1-6 Asa's reign was marked by peace because he "did what was pleasing and good in the sight of the LORD his God." This refrain is often repeated in Chronicles—*obedience* to God leads to *peace* with God and others. In the case of Judah's kings, obedi-

the shrines. He smashed the sacred pillars and cut down the Asherah poles. [4]He
commanded the people of Judah to seek the LORD, the God of their ancestors, and to
obey his law and his commands. [5]Asa also removed the pagan shrines, as well as the
incense altars from every one of Judah's towns. So Asa's kingdom enjoyed a period of
peace. [6]During those peaceful years, he was able to build up the fortified cities throughout Judah. No one tried to make war against him at this time, for the LORD was giving
him rest from his enemies. [7]Asa told the people of Judah, "Let us build towns and fortify
them with walls, towers, gates, and bars. The land is ours because we sought the LORD
our God, and he has given us rest from our enemies." So they went ahead with these
projects and brought them to completion.

[8]King Asa had an army of 300,000 warriors from the tribe of Judah, armed with
large shields and spears. He also had an army of 280,000 warriors from the tribe of
Benjamin, armed with small shields and bows. Both armies were composed of
courageous fighting men.

[9]Once an Ethiopian* named Zerah attacked Judah with an army of a million men* and
three hundred chariots. They advanced to the city of Mareshah, [10]so Asa deployed his
armies for battle in the valley north of Mareshah.* [11]Then Asa cried out to the LORD his
God, "O LORD, no one but you can help the powerless against the mighty! Help us,
O LORD our God, for we trust in you alone. It is in your name that we have come against
this vast horde. O LORD, you are our God; do not let mere men prevail against you!"

[12]So the LORD defeated the Ethiopians* in the presence of Asa and the army of Judah,
and the enemy fled. [13]Asa and his army pursued them as far as Gerar, and so many
Ethiopians fell that they were unable to rally. They were destroyed by the LORD and his
army, and the army of Judah carried off vast quantities of plunder. [14]While they were at
Gerar, they attacked all the towns in that area, and terror from the LORD came upon the
people there. As a result, vast quantities of plunder were taken from these towns, too.
[15]They also attacked the camps of herdsmen and captured many sheep and camels before
finally returning to Jerusalem.

Asa's Religious Reforms

15 Then the Spirit of God came upon Azariah son of Oded, [2]and he went out to meet
King Asa as he was returning from the battle. "Listen to me, Asa!" he shouted.
"Listen, all you people of Judah and Benjamin! The LORD will stay with you as long as you
stay with him! Whenever you seek him, you will find him. But if you abandon him, he will
abandon you. [3]For a long time, Israel was without the true God, without a priest to teach
them, and without God's law. [4]But whenever you were in distress and turned to the LORD,

14:5 2 Chr 34:4, 7
14:6 2 Chr 11:5; 15:15
14:7 2 Chr 8:5
14:8 2 Chr 13:3
14:9 2 Chr 11:8; 12:2-3; 16:8
14:11 2 Chr 13:14, 18
14:12 2 Chr 13:15
14:13 Gen 10:19
14:14 2 Chr 17:10
15:1 2 Chr 20:14; 24:20
15:2 2 Chr 15:4, 15
15:3 Lev 10:8-11; 1 Kgs 12:28-33; 2 Chr 17:9
15:4 Deut 4:29

14:9a Hebrew *a Cushite.* **14:9b** Or *an army of thousands and thousands;* Hebrew reads *an army of a thousand thousands.* **14:10** Or *in the Zephathah Valley near Mareshah.* **14:12** Hebrew *Cushites;* also in 14:13.

---

ence to God led to national peace, just as God had promised centuries earlier. In our case, obedience may not always bring peace with our enemies, but it will bring peace with God and complete peace in his future Kingdom. Obeying God is the first step on the path to peace.

14:3-5 Simply attending worship services is not enough to secure God's peace. Like Asa, we must also actively remove anything that is offensive to God. Becoming more active in church attendance or doing good deeds will still leave us in turmoil if we have failed to eliminate sinful practices from our lives. We should continually ask God to help us remove any source of temptation from our lives.

14:7 Judah had peace with all her neighbors. Times of peace are not just for resting. They allow us to prepare for times of trouble. King Asa recognized the period of peace as the right time to build his defenses—the moment of attack would be too late. It is also difficult to withstand spiritual attack unless defenses are prepared beforehand. Decisions about how to face temptation must be made with cool heads long before we feel the heat of temptation. Build your defenses now before temptation strikes.

14:11 If you are facing battles you feel you can't possibly win, don't give up. In the face of a vast horde of enemy soldiers, Asa prayed for God's help, recognizing his powerlessness against such a mighty army. The secret of victory is first to admit the futility of unaided human effort and then to trust God to save. His power works best through those who recognize their limitations (2 Corinthians 12:9). It is those who think they can do it all on their own who are in the greatest danger.

15:1, 2 Asa wisely welcomed people who had a close relationship with God, and he listened to their messages. Azariah gave the armies an important warning and encouraged them to stay close to God. Keep in contact with people who are filled with God's Spirit, and you will learn God's counsel. Spend regular time in discussion and prayer with those who can help explain and apply God's message.

15:3 Azariah said that Israel, the northern kingdom, was "without the true God." Eight kings reigned in Israel during the 41-year rule of Asa in Judah, and all eight were evil. Jeroboam, the first ruler of Israel, began this wicked trend by setting up idols and expelling God's priests (11:13-15). Azariah used Israel's problems as an example of the evil that would come to the people of Judah if they turned away from God as their northern brothers and sisters had.

15:5 Judg 5:6 the God of Israel, and sought him out, you found him. [5]During those dark times, it was not
safe to travel. Problems troubled the nation on every hand. [6]Nation fought against nation,
15:6 Matt 24:7 and city against city, for God was troubling you with every kind of problem. [7]And now, you
15:7 Josh 1:7, 9 men of Judah, be strong and courageous, for your work will be rewarded."
[8]When Asa heard this message from Azariah the prophet,* he took courage and
15:8 2 Chr 4:1; 8:12; 13:19 removed all the idols in the land of Judah and Benjamin and in the towns he had captured
in the hill country of Ephraim. And he repaired the altar of the LORD, which stood in front
of the foyer of the LORD's Temple.
15:9 2 Chr 11:16 [9]Then Asa called together all the people of Judah and Benjamin, along with the people
of Ephraim, Manasseh, and Simeon who had settled among them. Many had moved to
Judah during Asa's reign when they saw that the LORD his God was with him. [10]The people
15:11 2 Chr 14:13-15 gathered at Jerusalem in late spring,* during the fifteenth year of Asa's reign. [11]On that day

15:8 As in Syriac version and Latin Vulgate (see also 15:1); Hebrew reads *from Oded the prophet.* **15:10** Hebrew *in the third month.* This month of the Hebrew lunar calendar usually occurs in May and June.

ASA

God does not condone the idea that "the end justifies the means." He is just and perfect in all his ways. People, on the other hand, are far from perfect. That a bond can exist between a loving and merciful Creator and his rebellious creation is as great a miracle as creation itself! As a king, Asa came very close to being good. He traveled a long way with God before getting off track. His sin was not so much deliberate disobedience as choosing the *easy* way rather than the *right* way.

When the odds seemed impossible in the battle with the Ethiopians, Asa recognized his need to depend on God. Following that victory, God's promise of peace based on obedience spurred the king and people to many years of right living. But Asa was to face a tougher test.

Years of animosity between Asa and Israel's king Baasha took an ugly turn. Baasha, king of the rival northern kingdom, was building a fort that threatened both the peace and the economy of Judah. Asa thought he saw a way out—he bribed King Ben-hadad of Aram to break his alliance with King Baasha. The plan worked brilliantly, but it wasn't God's way. When Asa was confronted by God's prophet Hanani, he flew into a rage, jailed Hanani, and took out his anger on his people. Asa rejected correction and refused to admit his error to God. His greatest failure was missing what God could have done with his life if he had been willing to be humble. His pride ruined the health of his reign. He stubbornly held on to his failure until his death.

Does this attitude sound familiar? Can you identify failures in your life that you have continued to rationalize rather than admit to God and accept his forgiveness for? The end does not justify the means. Such a belief leads to sin and failure. The stubborn refusal to admit a failure due to sin can become a big problem because it makes you spend time rationalizing rather than learning from your mistakes and moving on.

Strengths and accomplishments
- Obeyed God during the first 10 years of his reign
- Carried out a partially successful effort to abolish idolatry
- Deposed his idolatrous mother, Maacah
- Defeated Ethiopia's mighty army

Weaknesses and mistakes
- Responded with rage when confronted about his sin
- Made alliances with foreign nations and evil people

Lessons from his life
- God not only reinforces good, he confronts evil
- Efforts to follow God's plans and rules yield positive results
- How well a plan works is no measure of its rightness or approval by God

Vital statistics
- Where: Jerusalem
- Occupation: King of Judah
- Relatives: Mother: Maacah. Father: Abijah. Son: Jehoshaphat
- Contemporaries: Hanani, Ben-hadad, Zerah, Azariah, Baasha

Key verse
"The eyes of the LORD search the whole earth in order to strengthen those whose hearts are fully committed to him. What a fool you have been! From now on, you will be at war" (2 Chronicles 16:9).

Asa's story is told in 1 Kings 15:8–24 and 2 Chronicles 14—16. He is also mentioned in Jeremiah 41:9; Matthew 1:7.

15:7 Azariah encouraged the men of Judah to keep up the good work, "for your work will be rewarded." This is an inspiration for us, too. Recognition and reward are great motivators that have two dimensions: (1) *The temporal dimension.* Living by God's standards may result in acclaim here on earth. (2) *The eternal dimension.* Permanent recognition and reward will be given in the next life. Don't be discouraged if you feel your faith in God is going unrewarded here on earth. The best rewards are not in this life but in the life to come.

they sacrificed to the LORD some of the animals they had taken as plunder in the battle—
seven hundred oxen and seven thousand sheep and goats. 12Then they entered into a covenant
to seek the LORD, the God of their ancestors, with all their heart and soul. 13They agreed that
anyone who refused to seek the LORD, the God of Israel, would be put to death—whether
young or old, man or woman. 14They shouted out their oath of loyalty to the LORD with
trumpets blaring and horns sounding. 15All were happy about this covenant, for they had
entered into it with all their hearts. Eagerly they sought after God, and they found him.
And the LORD gave them rest from their enemies on every side.

16King Asa even deposed his grandmother Maacah from her position as queen mother
because she had made an obscene Asherah pole. He cut down the pole, broke it up, and
burned it in the Kidron Valley. 17Although the pagan shrines were not completely removed
from Israel, Asa remained fully committed to the LORD throughout his life. 18He brought
into the Temple of God the silver and gold and the utensils that he and his father had
dedicated. 19So there was no more war until the thirty-fifth year of Asa's reign.

15:12 2 Chr 23:16
15:13 Exod 22:20; Deut 13:6-9, 15
15:15 2 Chr 14:7
15:16-19 //1 Kgs 15:13-15; 2 Chr 14:2-5

Final Years of Asa's Reign

16 In the thirty-sixth year of Asa's reign, King Baasha of Israel invaded Judah and
fortified Ramah in order to prevent anyone from entering or leaving King Asa's
territory in Judah. 2Asa responded by taking the silver and gold from the treasuries of
the LORD's Temple and from the royal palace. He sent it to King Ben-hadad of Aram,
who was ruling in Damascus, along with this message:

> 3"Let us renew the treaty that existed between your father and my father. See, I am
> sending you a gift of silver and gold. Break your treaty with King Baasha of Israel
> so that he will leave me alone."

4Ben-hadad agreed to King Asa's request and sent his armies to attack Israel. They
conquered the towns of Ijon, Dan, Abel-beth-maacah,* and all the store cities in
Naphtali. 5As soon as Baasha of Israel heard what was happening, he abandoned his
project of fortifying Ramah. 6Then King Asa called out all the men of Judah to carry
away the building stones and timbers that Baasha had been using to fortify Ramah. Asa
used these materials to fortify the towns of Geba and Mizpah.

7At that time Hanani the seer came to King Asa and told him, "Because you have put
your trust in the king of Aram instead of in the LORD your God, you missed your chance
to destroy the army of the king of Aram. 8Don't you remember what happened to the
Ethiopians* and Libyans and their vast army, with all of their chariots and horsemen*?
At that time you relied on the LORD, and he handed them all over to you. 9The eyes of
the LORD search the whole earth in order to strengthen those whose hearts are fully
committed to him. What a fool you have been! From now on, you will be at war." 10Asa
became so angry with Hanani for saying this that he threw him into prison. At that time,
Asa also began to oppress some of his people.

Summary of Asa's Reign

11The rest of the events of Asa's reign, from beginning to end, are recorded in *The Book*

16:1-6 //1 Kgs 15:17-22
16:4 Exod 1:11
16:7 1 Kgs 16:1; 2 Chr 14:11; 19:2; 32:7-8
16:8 2 Chr 12:3; 13:16, 18; 14:9
16:9 2 Chr 15:17; Prov 15:3; Zech 4:10
16:11–17:1 //1 Kgs 15:23-24

16:4 As in parallel text at 1 Kgs 15:20; Hebrew reads *Abel-maim,* another name for Abel-beth-maacah.
16:8a Hebrew *Cushites.* **16:8b** Or *and charioteers.*

15:14, 15 Many people find it difficult to commit themselves to anything. They are tentative, indecisive, and afraid of responsibility. Asa and his people were different—they had clearly declared themselves for God. Their oath of allegiance was punctuated with shouts and trumpet blasts! This decisive and wholehearted commitment pleased God and resulted in peace for the nation. If you want peace, check to see if there is some area where you lack total commitment to God. Peace comes as a by-product of giving your life wholeheartedly to God.

15:16 The Ten Commandments tell us to honor our fathers and mothers, and yet Asa removed his mother from the throne. While honoring parents is God's command, maintaining loyalty to God is an even higher priority. Jesus warned that respect for parents should never keep us from following him (Luke 14:26). If you have unbelieving parents, you must respect and honor them, but you must make devotion to God an even higher priority.

16:7-10 Judah and Israel never learned! Although God had delivered them even when they were outnumbered (13:3ff; 14:9ff), they repeatedly sought help from pagan nations rather than from God. That Asa sought help from Aram was evidence of national spiritual decline. With help from God alone, Asa had defeated the Ethiopians in open battle. But his confidence in God had slipped, and now he sought only a human solution to his problem. When confronted by the prophet Hanani, Asa threw him in prison, revealing the true condition of his heart. It is not sin to use human means to solve our problems, but it is sin to trust them more than God, to think they are better than God's ways, or to leave God completely out of the problem-solving process.

16:12 Jer 17:5 *of the Kings of Judah and Israel.* 12 In the thirty-ninth year of his reign, Asa developed a
serious foot disease. Even when the disease became life threatening, he did not seek the
LORD's help but sought help only from his physicians. 13 So he died in the forty-first year
16:14 Gen 50:2; 2 Chr 21:19; John 19:39-40 of his reign. 14 He was buried in the tomb he had carved out for himself in the City of
David. He was laid on a bed perfumed with sweet spices and ointments, and at his funeral
the people built a huge fire in his honor.

Jehoshaphat Rules in Judah

17:1 1 Kgs 15:24 **17** Then Jehoshaphat, Asa's son, became the next king. He strengthened Judah to
stand against any attack from Israel. 2 He stationed troops in all the fortified cities
17:2 2 Chr 11:5; 15:8 of Judah, and he assigned additional garrisons to the land of Judah and to the towns of
Ephraim that his father, Asa, had conquered.
3 The LORD was with Jehoshaphat because he followed the example of his father's

---

JEHOSHAPHAT

Are children more likely to learn from their parents' mistakes or to simply repeat them? In the lives of the people in the Bible, we find that the effects of parental examples are powerful and long lasting. For much of his life, Jehoshaphat seems to have been a son who learned from his father Asa's mistakes and followed his positive actions. But on several occasions, his decisions reveal the negative aspects of his father's example.

When the challenges were obvious, like the need for religious education of the people or the threat of war with a vast army, Jehoshaphat turned to God for guidance and made the right choices. His dependence on God was consistent when the odds were clearly against him. It was in depending on God for the day-to-day plans and actions that Jehoshaphat was weak. He allowed his son to marry Athaliah, the daughter of the wicked Ahab and Jezebel of Israel, who did her best to be as evil as her parents. Jehoshaphat was almost killed when, without asking God, he made an alliance with Ahab. Later, he got involved in an unwise shipbuilding venture with Ahab's son, Ahaziah—a venture that was shipwrecked by God.

God's faithfulness when the issues are clear and the enemy overwhelming is more than enough reason to seek his guidance when the issues are unclear and the enemy unseen. Jehoshaphat knew this, yet he made little use of that knowledge.

We repeat Jehoshaphat's error when we relegate God to the background in the "easy" decisions of life. Then, when things get out of hand, we want him to get us out of the mess we got ourselves into. God wants us to give him not only the major decisions but also our daily lives—the things we are most often fooled into believing we can control. Perhaps there is nothing major facing you today. Have you paused long enough to give your day to God anyway?

Strengths and accomplishments
- A bold follower of God, he reminded the people of the early years of his father, Asa
- Carried out a national program of religious education
- Had many military victories
- Developed an extensive legal structure throughout the kingdom

Weaknesses and mistakes
- Failed to recognize the long-term results of his decisions
- Did not completely destroy idolatry in the land
- Became entangled with evil King Ahab through alliances
- Allowed his son Jehoram to marry Athaliah, Ahab's daughter
- Became Ahaziah's business partner in an ill-fated shipping venture

Vital statistics
- Where: Jerusalem
- Occupation: King of Judah
- Relatives: Father: Asa. Mother: Azubah. Son: Jehoram. Daughter-in-law: Athaliah
- Contemporaries: Ahab, Jezebel, Micaiah, Ahaziah, Jehu

Key verses
"Jehoshaphat was a good king, following the ways of his father, Asa. He did what was pleasing in the LORD's sight. During his reign, however, he failed to remove all the pagan shrines, and the people never fully committed themselves to following the God of their ancestors" (2 Chronicles 20:32, 33).

Jehoshaphat's story is told in 1 Kings 15:24—22:50 and 2 Chronicles 17:1—21:1. He is also mentioned in 2 Kings 3:1–14 and Joel 3:2, 12.

16:12 The criticism of Asa's visit to the physicians was not a general indictment of medicine. Asa's problem was that he completely ignored God's help. The medicine practiced at this time was a mixture of superstition and folk remedies. We should certainly avoid any medicinal treatments derived from occult sources. Asa's experience should encourage us to follow the New Testament practice of receiving prayer for our sickness (James 5:14) as we seek responsible medical help.

early years* and did not worship the images of Baal. 4He sought his father's God and
obeyed his commands instead of following the practices of the kingdom of Israel. 5So
the LORD established Jehoshaphat's control over the kingdom of Judah. All the people
of Judah brought gifts to Jehoshaphat, so he became very wealthy and highly esteemed.
6He was committed to the ways of the LORD. He knocked down the pagan shrines and
destroyed the Asherah poles.

7In the third year of his reign, Jehoshaphat sent out his officials to teach in all the
towns of Judah. These officials included Ben-hail, Obadiah, Zechariah, Nethanel, and
Micaiah. 8He sent Levites along with them, including Shemaiah, Nethaniah, Zebadiah,
Asahel, Shemiramoth, Jehonathan, Adonijah, Tobijah, and Tob-adonijah. He also sent
out the priests, Elishama and Jehoram. 9They took copies of the Book of the Law of the
LORD and traveled around through all the towns of Judah, teaching the people.

10Then the fear of the LORD fell over all the surrounding kingdoms so that none of
them declared war on Jehoshaphat. 11Some of the Philistines brought him gifts and silver
as tribute, and the Arabs brought seventy-seven hundred rams and seventy-seven
hundred male goats.

12So Jehoshaphat became more and more powerful and built fortresses and store cities
throughout Judah. 13He stored numerous supplies in Judah's towns and stationed an army
of seasoned troops at Jerusalem. 14His army was enrolled according to ancestral clans.

From Judah, there were 300,000 troops organized in units of one thousand, under the
command of Adnah. 15Next in command was Jehohanan, who commanded 280,000
troops. 16Next was Amasiah son of Zicri, who volunteered for the LORD's service,
with 200,000 troops under his command.

17From Benjamin, there were 200,000 troops equipped with bows and shields. They
were under the command of Eliada, a veteran soldier. 18Next in command was
Jehozabad, who commanded 180,000 armed men.

19These were the troops stationed in Jerusalem to serve the king, besides those Jehoshaphat stationed in the fortified cities throughout Judah.

Jehoshaphat and Ahab

18 Now Jehoshaphat enjoyed great riches and high esteem, and he arranged for his
son to marry the daughter of King Ahab of Israel. 2A few years later, he went to
Samaria to visit Ahab, who prepared a great banquet for him and his officials. They

17:4 1 Kgs 12:28
17:5 2 Chr 18:1
17:6 2 Chr 15:17
17:7 2 Chr 15:3; 19:8; 35:3
17:8 2 Chr 19:8
17:9 Deut 6:4-9
17:10 2 Chr 14:14
17:11 2 Chr 9:14; 26:8
17:16 Judg 5:2; 9 1 Chr 29:9
17:19 2 Chr 17:2
18:1-27 //1 Kgs 2:1-28
18:1 2 Chr 17:5

17:3 Some Hebrew manuscripts read *the example of his father, David.*

BATTLE WITH ARAM
King Jehoshaphat made an alliance with evil King Ahab of Israel. Together they decided to attack Ramoth-gilead and rout the Arameans who had occupied the city. But Jehoshaphat first wanted to seek the advice of a prophet. Ahab's prophets predicted victory, but Micaiah predicted defeat. The two kings were defeated, and Ahab was killed.

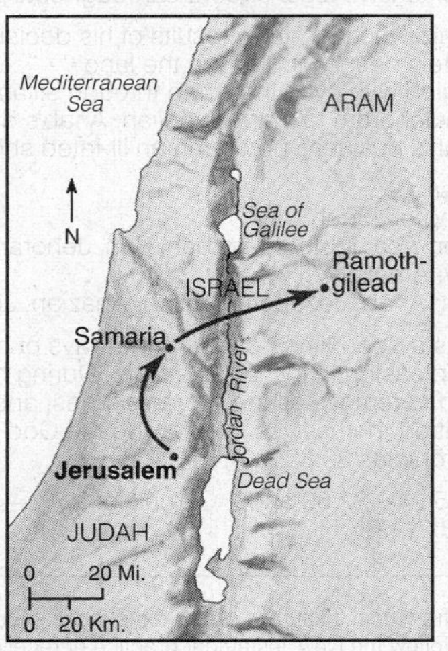

17:7-9 The people of Judah were biblically illiterate. They had never taken time to listen to and discuss God's law and understand how it could change them. Jehoshaphat realized that knowing God's commands was the first step to getting people to live as they should, so he initiated a nationwide religious education program. He reversed the religious decline that had occurred at the end of Asa's reign by putting God first in the people's minds and instilling in them a sense of commitment and mission. Because of this action, the nation began to follow God. Churches and Christian schools today need solid Christian education programs. Exposure to good Bible teaching through Sunday school, church, Bible study, and personal and family devotions is essential for living as God intended.

18:1ff Although Jehoshaphat was deeply committed to God, he arranged for his son to marry Athaliah, the daughter of wicked King Ahab of Israel, and then made a military alliance with him. Jehoshaphat's popularity and power made him attractive to the cunning and opportunistic Ahab. This alliance had three devastating consequences: (1) Jehoshaphat incurred God's anger (19:2); (2) when Jehoshaphat's grandson died, Athaliah seized the throne and almost destroyed all of David's descendants (22:10-12); (3) Athaliah brought the evil practices of Israel into Judah, which eventually led to the nation's downfall.

When believers in leadership positions become allied with unbelievers, values can be compromised and spiritual awareness dulled. The Bible often warns against teaming up with unbelievers (2 Corinthians 6:14). (See the note on 20:37 for more on alliances.)

18:2 1 Kgs 22:2-35 butchered great numbers of sheep and oxen for the feast. Then Ahab enticed Jehoshaphat
to join forces with him to attack Ramoth-gilead. 3"Will you join me in fighting against
Ramoth-gilead?" Ahab asked.
And Jehoshaphat replied, "Why, of course! You and I are brothers, and my troops are
yours to command. We will certainly join you in battle." 4Then Jehoshaphat added, "But
first let's find out what the LORD says."
5So King Ahab summoned his prophets, four hundred of them, and asked them,
"Should we go to war against Ramoth-gilead or not?"
They all replied, "Go ahead, for God will give you a great victory!"
6But Jehoshaphat asked, "Isn't there a prophet of the LORD around, too? I would like
to ask him the same question."
7King Ahab replied, "There is still one prophet of the LORD, but I hate him. He never
prophesies anything but bad news for me! His name is Micaiah son of Imlah."
"You shouldn't talk like that," Jehoshaphat said. "Let's hear what he has to say."
8So the king of Israel called one of his officials and said, "Quick! Go and get Micaiah
son of Imlah."

Micaiah Prophesies against Ahab

18:9 Ruth 4:1 9King Ahab of Israel and King Jehoshaphat of Judah, dressed in their royal robes, were
sitting on thrones at the threshing floor near the gate of Samaria. All of Ahab's prophets
were prophesying there in front of them. 10One of them, Zedekiah son of Kenaanah,
made some iron horns and proclaimed, "This is what the LORD says: With these horns
you will gore the Arameans to death!"
11All the other prophets agreed. "Yes," they said, "go up to Ramoth-gilead and be
victorious. The LORD will give you a glorious victory!"
12Meanwhile, the messenger who went to get Micaiah said to him, "Look, all the
prophets are promising victory for the king. Be sure that you agree with them and
promise success."
18:13 Num 22:18-20, 35 13But Micaiah replied, "As surely as the LORD lives, I will say only what my God tells
me to say."
14When Micaiah arrived before the king, Ahab asked him, "Micaiah, should we go to
war against Ramoth-gilead or not?"
And Micaiah replied, "Go right ahead! It will be a glorious victory!"
15But the king replied sharply, "How many times must I demand that you speak only
the truth when you speak for the LORD?"
18:16 Num 27:17 Ezek 34:4-8 Matt 9:36 †Mark 6:34 16So Micaiah told him, "In a vision I saw all Israel scattered on the mountains, like
sheep without a shepherd. And the LORD said, 'Their master has been killed. Send them
home in peace.'"
17"Didn't I tell you?" the king of Israel said to Jehoshaphat. "He does it every time.
He never prophesies anything but bad news for me."
18:18 Isa 6:1-5 Dan 7:9-10 18Then Micaiah continued, "Listen to what the LORD says! I saw the LORD sitting on
his throne with all the armies of heaven on his right and on his left. 19And the LORD said,
'Who can entice King Ahab of Israel to go into battle against Ramoth-gilead so that he
18:20 Job 1:6 can be killed there?' There were many suggestions, 20until finally a spirit approached the
LORD and said, 'I can do it!'

18:3-8 Evil kings did not like God's prophets bringing messages of doom (18:17; Jeremiah 5:13). Many, therefore, hired prophets who told them only what they wanted to hear (Isaiah 30:10, 11; Jeremiah 14:13-16; 23:16, 21, 30-36). These men were false prophets because they extolled the greatness of the king and predicted victory regardless of the real situation.

18:3-8 Wicked Ahab asked Jehoshaphat to join forces with him in battle (18:2, 3). Before making that commitment, Jehoshaphat rightly sought God's advice. However, when God gave his answer through the prophet Micaiah (18:16), Jehoshaphat ignored it (18:28). It does us no good to seek God's advice if we ignore it when it is given. Real love for God is shown, not by merely asking for direction, but by following that direction once it is given.

18:5-16 When you want to please or impress someone, it is tempting to lie to make yourself look good. Ahab's 400 prophets did just that, telling Ahab only what he wanted to hear. They were then rewarded for making Ahab happy. Micaiah, however, told the truth and got arrested (18:25, 26). Obeying God doesn't always protect us from evil consequences. Obedience may, in fact, provoke them. But it is better to suffer from man's displeasure than from God's wrath (Matthew 10:28). If you are ridiculed for being honest, remember that this can be a sign that you are indeed doing what is right in God's eyes (Matthew 5:10-12; Romans 8:17, 35-39).

"'How will you do this?' the LORD asked.
21 "And the spirit replied, 'I will go out and inspire all Ahab's prophets to speak lies.'
"'You will succeed,' said the LORD. 'Go ahead and do it.'
22 "So you see, the LORD has put a lying spirit in the mouths of your prophets. For the **18:22** Ezek 14:9
LORD has determined disaster for you."
23 Then Zedekiah son of Kenaanah walked up to Micaiah and slapped him across the **18:23** Jer 20:2; Mark 14:65; Acts 23:2
face. "When did the Spirit of the LORD leave me to speak to you?" he demanded.
24 And Micaiah replied, "You will find out soon enough, when you find yourself hiding
in some secret room!"
25 King Ahab of Israel then ordered, "Arrest Micaiah and take him back to Amon, the **18:25** 2 Chr 18:8; 34:8
governor of the city, and to my son Joash. 26 Give them this order from the king: 'Put this
man in prison, and feed him nothing but bread and water until I return safely from the **18:26** 2 Chr 16:10
battle!'"
27 But Micaiah replied, "If you return safely, the LORD has not spoken through me!" **18:27** Mic 1:2
Then he added to those standing around, "Take note of what I have said."

BIBLE

The Persecuted	*The Persecutors*	*Why the Persecution*	*Result*	*Reference*
Isaac	The Philistines	God was blessing Isaac, and they envied him	The Philistines could not subdue Isaac, so they made peace with him	Genesis 26:12–33
Moses	Israelites	The Israelites wanted water	God provided water, in answer to Moses' prayer	Exodus 17:1–7
David	Saul and others	David was becoming a powerful leader, threatening Saul's position as king	David endured the persecution and became king	1 Samuel 20—27 Psalms 31:13; 59:1–4
Priests of Nob	Saul and Doeg	Saul and Doeg thought the priests helped David escape	85 priests were killed	1 Samuel 22
Prophets	Jezebel	Jezebel didn't like to have her evil ways pointed out	Many prophets were killed	1 Kings 18:3, 4
Elijah	Ahab and Jezebel	Elijah confronted their sins	Elijah had to flee for his life	1 Kings 18:10—19:2
Micaiah	Ahab	Ahab thought Micaiah was stirring up trouble rather than prophesying from God	Micaiah was thrown into prison	2 Chronicles 18:12–26
Elisha	A king of Israel (Probably Joram)	The king thought Elisha had caused the famine	Elisha ignored the threatened persecution and prophesied the famine's end	2 Kings 6:31
Hanani	Asa	Hanani criticized Asa for trusting in Aram's help more than in God's help	Hanani was thrown in prison	2 Chronicles 16:7–10
Zechariah	Joash	Zechariah confronted the people of Judah for disregarding God's commands	Zechariah was executed	2 Chronicles 24:20–22
Uriah	Jehoiakim	Uriah confronted Jehoiakim about his evil ways	Uriah was butchered to death	Jeremiah 26:20–23
Jeremiah	Zedekiah	Zedekiah thought Jeremiah was a traitor for prophesying Jerusalem's fall	Jeremiah was thrown in prison, then into a muddy well	Jeremiah 37:1—38:13
Shadrach, Meshach, Abednego	Nebuchadnezzar	The three men refused to bow down to anyone but God	They were thrown into a fiery furnace, but God miraculously saved them	Daniel 3

18:22 God used the seductive influence of false prophets to judge Ahab. They were determined to tell Ahab what he wanted to hear. God confirmed their plans to lie as a means to remove Ahab from the throne. These prophets, supported by Ahab, snared him in his sin. Because he listened to them instead of God, he was killed in battle. The lying spirit is a picture of the prophets' entire way of life—telling the king only what he wanted to hear, not what he needed to hear. Leaders will only find trouble if they surround themselves with advisers whose only thought is to please them.

The Death of Ahab

18:28-34
//1 Kgs 22:29-36

28 So the king of Israel and King Jehoshaphat of Judah led their armies against Ramoth-
gilead. 29 Now King Ahab said to Jehoshaphat, "As we go into battle, I will disguise
myself so no one will recognize me, but you wear your royal robes." So Ahab disguised
himself, and they went into battle.
30 Now the king of Aram had issued these orders to his charioteers: "Attack only the
king of Israel!" 31 So when the Aramean charioteers saw Jehoshaphat in his royal robes,
they went after him. "There is the king of Israel!" they shouted. But Jehoshaphat cried out
to the LORD to save him, and God helped him by turning the attack away from him. 32 As
soon as the charioteers realized he was not the king of Israel, they stopped chasing him.
33 An Aramean soldier, however, randomly shot an arrow at the Israelite troops, and
the arrow hit the king of Israel between the joints of his armor. "Get me out of here!"
Ahab groaned to the driver of his chariot. "I have been badly wounded!" 34 The battle
raged all that day, and Ahab propped himself up in his chariot facing the Arameans until
evening. Then, just as the sun was setting, he died.

18:31
2 Chr 13:14-15

PERSECUTIONS

The Persecuted	*The Persecutors*	*Why the Persecution*	*Result*	*Reference*
Daniel	National leaders	Daniel was praying	Daniel was thrown into a den of lions, but God miraculously saved him	Daniel 6
Job	Satan	Satan wanted to prove that pain and suffering would make a person abandon God	Job remained faithful to God and was restored	Job 1:8–12; 2:3–7
John the Baptist	Herod and Herodias	John confronted King Herod's adultery	John was beheaded	Matthew 14:3–13
Jesus	Religious leaders	Jesus exposed their sinful motives	Jesus was crucified, but rose again from the dead to show his authority over all evil	Mark 7:1–16; Luke 22:63—24:7
Peter and John	Religious leaders	Peter and John preached that Jesus was God's Son and the only way to salvation	They were thrown into prison, but later released	Acts 4:1–31
Stephen	Religious leaders	Stephen exposed their guilt in crucifying Jesus	Stephen was stoned to death	Acts 6—7
The church	Paul and others	The Christians preached Jesus as the Messiah	Believers faced death, prison, torture, exile	Acts 8:1–3; 9:1–9
James	Herod Agrippa I	To please the Jewish leaders	James was executed	Acts 12:1–2
Peter	Herod Agrippa I	To please the Jewish leaders	Peter was thrown into prison	Acts 12:3–17
Paul	Jews, city officials	Paul preached about Jesus and confronted those who made money by manipulating others	Paul was stoned; thrown into prison	Acts 14:19; 16:16–24
Timothy	Unknown	Unknown	Timothy was thrown into prison	Hebrews 13:23
John	Probably the Romans	John told others about Jesus	John was sent into exile on a remote island	Revelation 1:9

Micaiah, like thousands of believers before and after him, was persecuted for his faith. The chart shows that persecution comes from a variety of people and is given in a variety of ways. Sometimes God protects us from it; sometimes he doesn't. But as long as we remain faithful to God *alone*, we must expect persecution (see also Luke 6:22; 2 Corinthians 6:4–10; 2 Timothy 2:9–12; Revelation 2:10). God also seems to have a special reward for those who endure such persecution (Revelation 6:9–11; 20:4).

18:31 Jehoshaphat's troubles began when he joined forces with the evil King Ahab. Almost at once he found himself the target for soldiers who mistakenly identified him as Ahab. He could have accepted this fate because he deserved it, but instead he cried out to God, who miraculously saved him. When we sin and the inevitable consequences follow, we may be tempted to give up. "I chose to sin," we may think, "it's my fault, and I must accept the consequences." While we may deserve what comes to us, that is no reason to avoid calling on God for urgent help. Had Jehoshaphat given up, he might have died. No matter how greatly you have sinned, you can still call upon God.

Jehoshaphat Appoints Judges

19 When King Jehoshaphat of Judah arrived safely home to Jerusalem, [2]Jehu son of 19:2 1 Kgs 16:1 2 Chr 18:1, 3; 20:34; 24:18
Hanani the seer went out to meet him. "Why should you help the wicked and love
those who hate the LORD?" he asked the king. "What you have done has brought the LORD's
anger against you. [3]There is some good in you, however, for you have removed the Asherah 19:3 2 Chr 12:12, 14; 17:6
poles throughout the land, and you have committed yourself to seeking God."
[4]So Jehoshaphat lived in Jerusalem, but he went out among the people, traveling from 19:4 Deut 16:18-20 2 Chr 15:8-13
Beersheba to the hill country of Ephraim, encouraging the people to return to the LORD,
the God of their ancestors. [5]He appointed judges throughout the nation in all the fortified 19:6 Lev 19:15 Deut 1:17
cities, [6]and he gave them these instructions: "Always think carefully before pronouncing
judgment. Remember that you do not judge to please people but to please the LORD. He 19:7 Gen 18:25 Deut 10:17-18; 32:4
will be with you when you render the verdict in each case that comes before you. [7]Fear
the LORD and judge with care, for the LORD our God does not tolerate perverted justice,
partiality, or the taking of bribes."
[8]Jehoshaphat appointed some of the Levites and priests and clan leaders in Israel to serve 19:8 2 Chr 17:8-9
as judges in Jerusalem for cases concerning both the law of the LORD and civil disputes.
[9]These were his instructions to them: "You must always act in the fear of the LORD, with
integrity and with undivided hearts. [10]Whenever a case comes to you from fellow citizens 19:10 Deut 17:8 2 Chr 19:2
in an outlying town, whether a murder case or some other violation of God's instructions,
commands, laws, or regulations, you must warn them not to sin against the LORD, so that
his anger will not come against you and them. Do this and you will not be guilty.
[11]"Amariah the high priest will have final say in all cases concerning the LORD. 19:11 1 Chr 28:20 2 Chr 19:8
Zebadiah son of Ishmael, a leader from the tribe of Judah, will have final say in all civil
cases. The Levites will assist you in making sure that justice is served. Take courage as
you fulfill your duties, and may the LORD be with those who do what is right."

War with Moab, Ammon, and Edom

20 After this, the armies of the Moabites, Ammonites, and some of the Meunites* 20:2 Gen 14:7
declared war on Jehoshaphat. [2]Messengers came and told Jehoshaphat, "A vast
army from Edom* is marching against you from beyond the Dead Sea.* They are already 20:3 1 Sam 7:6 2 Chr 19:3 Ezra 8:21
at Hazazon-tamar." (This was another name for En-gedi.) [3]Jehoshaphat was alarmed by
this news and sought the LORD for guidance. He also gave orders that everyone
throughout Judah should observe a fast. [4]So people from all the towns of Judah came to
Jerusalem to seek the LORD.
[5]Jehoshaphat stood before the people of Judah and Jerusalem in front of the new
courtyard at the Temple of the LORD. [6]He prayed, "O LORD, God of our ancestors, you 20:6 Deut 4:39 1 Chr 29:11

20:1 As in some Greek manuscripts (see also 26:7); Hebrew reads *Ammonites.* **20:2a** As in one Hebrew manuscript; most Hebrew manuscripts and ancient versions read *Aram.* **20:2b** Hebrew *the sea.*

18:33 Micaiah prophesied death for Ahab (18:16, 27), so Ahab disguised himself to fool the enemy. Apparently the disguise worked, but that didn't change the prophecy. A random Aramean arrow found a crack in his armor and killed him. God fulfills his will despite the defenses people try to erect. God can use anything, even an error, to bring his will to pass. This is good news for God's followers because we can trust him to work out his plans and keep his promises no matter how desperate our circumstances are.

19:5-10 Jehoshaphat delegated some of the responsibilities for ruling and judging the people, but he warned his appointees that they were accountable to God for the standards they used to judge others. Jehoshaphat's advice is helpful for all leaders: (1) Realize that you are judging for God (19:6); (2) be impartial and honest (19:7); (3) be faithful (19:9); (4) act only out of fear of God, not men (19:9). God holds us accountable for the authority we exercise.

19:8 Jehoshaphat appointed priests and Levites to help in administering civil laws. Many years earlier, Moses had chosen men who were capable, faithful, and honest to help him judge disputes among the people (Exodus 18:21, 22). Obviously the best kind of leader is one who always acts with reverence for God. Effective leaders get the job done; faithful leaders make sure the job is done in God's way and in God's time. They are careful to instill God's wisdom in future leaders and God's values in the entire community.

20:3 When the nation was faced with disaster, Jehoshaphat called upon the people to get serious with God by going without food (fasting) for a designated time. By separating themselves from the daily routine of food preparation and eating, they could devote that extra time to considering their sin and praying to God for help. Hunger pangs would reinforce their penitence and remind them of their weakness and their dependence upon God. Fasting still can be helpful today as we seek God's will in special situations.

20:6ff Jehoshaphat's prayer had several essential ingredients. (1) He committed the situation to God, acknowledging that only God could save the nation. (2) He sought God's favor because his people were God's people. (3) He acknowledged God's sovereignty over the current situation. (4) He praised God's glory and took comfort in his promises. (5) He professed complete dependence on God, not himself, for deliverance. To be God's kind of leader today, follow Jehoshaphat's example: Focus entirely on God's power rather than your own.

alone are the God who is in heaven. You are ruler of all the kingdoms of the earth. You
20:7 Isa 41:8
are powerful and mighty; no one can stand against you! 7 O our God, did you not drive
out those who lived in this land when your people arrived? And did you not give this
land forever to the descendants of your friend Abraham? 8 Your people settled here and
20:9 2 Chr 6:20, 28-30
built this Temple for you. 9 They said, 'Whenever we are faced with any calamity such
as war, disease, or famine, we can come to stand in your presence before this Temple
where your name is honored. We can cry out to you to save us, and you will hear us and
rescue us.'
20:10 Num 20:17-21; 2 Chr 20:1, 22
10 "And now see what the armies of Ammon, Moab, and Mount Seir are doing. You
would not let our ancestors invade those nations when Israel left Egypt, so they went
20:11 Ps 83:12
around them and did not destroy them. 11 Now see how they reward us! For they have
come to throw us out of your land, which you gave us as an inheritance. 12 O our God,
20:12 Judg 11:27; Pss 25:15; 121:1-2
won't you stop them? We are powerless against this mighty army that is about to attack
us. We do not know what to do, but we are looking to you for help."
13 As all the men of Judah stood before the LORD with their little ones, wives, and
20:14 2 Chr 15:1; 24:20
children, 14 the Spirit of the LORD came upon one of the men standing there. His name
20:15 Exod 14:13; 1 Sam 17:47; 2 Chr 32:7-8
was Jahaziel son of Zechariah, son of Benaiah, son of Jeiel, son of Mattaniah, a Levite
who was a descendant of Asaph. 15 He said, "Listen, King Jehoshaphat! Listen, all you
people of Judah and Jerusalem! This is what the LORD says: Do not be afraid! Don't be
discouraged by this mighty army, for the battle is not yours, but God's. 16 Tomorrow,
march out against them. You will find them coming up through the ascent of Ziz at the
20:17 Exod 14:13; 2 Chr 15:2
end of the valley that opens into the wilderness of Jeruel. 17 But you will not even need
to fight. Take your positions; then stand still and watch the LORD's victory. He is with
you, O people of Judah and Jerusalem. Do not be afraid or discouraged. Go out there
tomorrow, for the LORD is with you!"
18 Then King Jehoshaphat bowed down with his face to the ground. And all the people
of Judah and Jerusalem did the same, worshiping the LORD. 19 Then the Levites from the
clans of Kohath and Korah stood to praise the LORD, the God of Israel, with a very loud
shout.
20:20 Isa 7:9
20 Early the next morning the army of Judah went out into the wilderness of Tekoa. On
the way Jehoshaphat stopped and said, "Listen to me, all you people of Judah and
Jerusalem! Believe in the LORD your God, and you will be able to stand firm. Believe in
20:21 1 Chr 16:29, 34, 41; Ps 29:2
his prophets, and you will succeed." 21 After consulting the leaders of the people, the king
appointed singers to walk ahead of the army, singing to the LORD and praising him for
his holy splendor. This is what they sang:

"Give thanks to the LORD;
his faithful love endures forever!"

20:22 2 Chr 13:13; 20:10
22 At the moment they began to sing and give praise, the LORD caused the armies of
20:23 Judg 7:22; 1 Sam 14:20
Ammon, Moab, and Mount Seir to start fighting among themselves. 23 The armies of
Moab and Ammon turned against their allies from Mount Seir and killed every one
of them. After they had finished off the army of Seir, they turned on each other.
24 So when the army of Judah arrived at the lookout point in the wilderness, there were
dead bodies lying on the ground for as far as they could see. Not a single one of the
enemy had escaped. 25 King Jehoshaphat and his men went out to gather the plunder.
They found vast amounts of equipment, clothing,* and other valuables—more than they
could carry. There was so much plunder that it took them three days just to collect it all!
26 On the fourth day they gathered in the Valley of Blessing,* which got its name that day

20:25 As in some Hebrew manuscripts and Latin Vulgate; most Hebrew manuscripts read *corpses*. **20:26** Hebrew *valley of Beracah*.

20:15 As the enemy bore down on Judah, God spoke through Jahaziel: "Do not be afraid! . . . For the battle is not yours, but God's!" We may not fight an enemy army, but every day we battle temptation, pressure, and "rulers . . . of the unseen world" (Ephesians 6:12) who want us to rebel against God. Remember, as believers, we have God's Spirit in us. If we ask for God's help when we face struggles, God will fight for us. And God always triumphs.

How do we let God fight for us? (1) Realize that the battle is not ours, but God's; (2) Recognize human limitations and allow God's strength to work through our fears and weaknesses; (3) Make sure we are pursuing God's interests and not just our own selfish desires; (4) Ask God for help in our daily battles.

because the people praised and thanked the LORD there. It is still called the Valley of
Blessing today.
27 Then they returned to Jerusalem, with Jehoshaphat leading them, full of joy that the **20:27**
LORD had given them victory over their enemies. 28 They marched into Jerusalem to the Neh 12:43
music of harps, lyres, and trumpets and proceeded to the Temple of the LORD. 29 When
the surrounding kingdoms heard that the LORD himself had fought against the enemies
of Israel, the fear of God came over them. 30 So Jehoshaphat's kingdom was at peace, for **20:30** 2 Chr 14:6-7, 14;
his God had given him rest on every side. 15:15; 17:10

Summary of Jehoshaphat's Reign

31 So Jehoshaphat ruled over the land of Judah. He was thirty-five years old when he **20:31–21:1** //1 Kgs 22:41-50
became king, and he reigned in Jerusalem twenty-five years. His mother was Azubah, 2 Chr 17:6
the daughter of Shilhi. 32 Jehoshaphat was a good king, following the ways of his father,
Asa. He did what was pleasing in the LORD's sight. 33 During his reign, however, he failed **20:33** 2 Chr 17:6; 19:3
to remove all the pagan shrines, and the people never fully committed themselves to
following the God of their ancestors. 34 The rest of the events of Jehoshaphat's reign, **20:34** 1 Kgs 16:1, 7
from beginning to end, are recorded in *The Record of Jehu Son of Hanani,* which is 2 Chr 19:2
included in *The Book of the Kings of Israel.*
35 But near the end of his life, King Jehoshaphat of Judah made an alliance with King **20:35** 1 Kgs 22:48-49
Ahaziah of Israel, who was a very wicked man.* 36 Together they built a fleet of trading
ships* at the port of Ezion-geber. 37 Then Eliezer son of Dodavahu from Mareshah **20:36** 2 Chr 9:21
prophesied against Jehoshaphat. He said, "Because you have allied yourself with King
Ahaziah, the LORD will destroy your work." So the ships met with disaster and never put
out to sea.*

Jehoram Rules in Judah

21 When Jehoshaphat died, he was buried with his ancestors in the City of David. **21:1** 1 Kgs 22:50
Then his son Jehoram became the next king. 2 Jehoram's brothers—the other sons
of Jehoshaphat—were Azariah, Jehiel, Zechariah, Azariahu, Michael, and Shephatiah.
3 Their father had given each of them valuable gifts of silver, gold, and costly items, and **21:3**
also the ownership of some of Judah's fortified cities. However, Jehoram became king 2 Chr 11:5
because he was the oldest. 4 But when Jehoram had become solidly established as king,
he killed all his brothers and some of the other leaders of Israel.
5 Jehoram was thirty-two years old when he became king, and he reigned in Jerusalem **21:5-10** //2 Kgs 8:16-24
eight years. 6 But Jehoram followed the example of the kings of Israel and was as wicked **21:6**
as King Ahab, for he had married one of Ahab's daughters. So Jehoram did what was evil 1 Kgs 12:28-30
in the LORD's sight. 7 But the LORD was not willing to destroy David's dynasty, for he had 2 Chr 18:1
made a covenant with David and promised that his descendants would continue to rule **21:7** 2 Sam 7:12-17
forever.* 1 Kgs 11:13

20:35 Or *who made him do what was wrong.* **20:36** Hebrew *fleet of ships that could go to Tarshish.* **20:37** Hebrew *never set sail for Tarshish.* **21:7** Hebrew *promised to give a lamp to David and his descendants forever.*

20:33 This verse says that Jehoshaphat did not remove the pagan shrines, while 17:6 and 19:3 say he did remove them. Jehoshaphat destroyed most of the Baal and Asherah idols, but he did not succeed in wiping out the corrupt religions practiced at the shrines.

20:37 Jehoshaphat met disaster when he joined forces with wicked King Ahaziah. He did not learn from his disastrous alliance with Ahab (18:28-34) or from his father's alliance with Aram (16:2-9). The partnership stood on unequal footing because one man served the Lord and the other worshiped idols. We court disaster when we enter into partnership with unbelievers because our very foundations differ (2 Corinthians 6:14-18). While one serves the Lord, the other does not recognize God's authority. Inevitably, the one who serves God is faced with the temptation to compromise values. When that happens, spiritual disaster results.

Before entering into partnerships, ask: (1) What are my motives? (2) What problems am I avoiding by seeking this partnership? (3) Is this partnership the best solution, or is it only a quick solution to my problem? (4) Have I prayed or asked others to pray for guidance? (5) Are my partner and I really working toward the same goals? (6) Am I willing to settle for less financial gain in order to do what God wants?

21:6 Jehoram, the new king of Judah, married Athaliah, one of the daughters of King Ahab of Israel. She became the mother of Judah's next king, Ahaziah (22:2). Athaliah's mother was Jezebel, the most wicked woman Israel had ever known. Jehoram's marriage to Athaliah was Judah's downfall, for Athaliah brought her mother's wicked influence into Judah, causing the nation to forget God and turn to Baal worship (22:3).

21:7 God promised that a descendant of David would always sit on the throne (2 Samuel 7:8-16). What happened to this promise when the nation was destroyed and carried away? There were two parts to God's promise. (1) In the physical sense, as long as there was an actual throne in Judah, a descendant of David would sit upon it. But this part of the promise depended on the obedience of these kings. When they disobeyed, God was not bound to continue David's temporal line. (2) In the spiritual sense, this promise was completely fulfilled in the coming of Jesus the Messiah, a descendant of David, who would sit on the throne of David forever.

21:8
2 Chr 20:22-23;
21:10

8During Jehoram's reign, the Edomites revolted against Judah and crowned their own
king. 9So Jehoram went to attack Edom with his full army and all his chariots. The
Edomites surrounded him and his charioteers, but he escaped at night under cover of
darkness. 10Edom has been independent from Judah to this day. The town of Libnah
revolted about that same time, because Jehoram had abandoned the LORD, the God of his
ancestors. 11He had built pagan shrines in the hill country of Judah and had led the people
of Jerusalem and Judah to give themselves to pagan gods.

21:11
Lev 20:5
1 Kgs 11:7

21:12
2 Chr 14:2-5;
17:3-4

12Then Elijah the prophet wrote Jehoram this letter:

"This is what the LORD, the God of your ancestor David, says: You have not followed the good example of your father, Jehoshaphat, or your grandfather King Asa
of Judah. 13Instead, you have been as evil as the kings of Israel. You have led the
people of Jerusalem and Judah to worship idols, just as King Ahab did in Israel.
And you have even killed your own brothers, men who were better than you. 14So
now the LORD is about to strike you, your people, your children, your wives, and
all that is yours with a heavy blow. 15You yourself will be stricken with a severe
intestinal disease until it causes your bowels to come out."

21:13
1 Kgs 16:31-33
2 Chr 21:4, 6, 11

21:15
2 Chr 21:18-19

21:16
2 Chr 17:11; 22:1;
33:11

21:17
2 Chr 25:23

16Then the LORD stirred up the Philistines and the Arabs, who lived near the Ethiopians,* to attack Jehoram. 17They marched against Judah, broke down its defenses, and
carried away everything of value in the royal palace, including his sons and his wives.
Only his youngest son, Ahaziah,* was spared.

21:18
2 Chr 21:15

21:19
2 Chr 16:14

21:20
2 Chr 24:25; 28:27
Jer 22:18, 28

18It was after this that the LORD struck Jehoram with the severe intestinal disease. 19In
the course of time, at the end of two years, the disease caused his bowels to come out,
and he died in agony. His people did not build a great fire to honor him at his funeral as
they had done for his ancestors. 20Jehoram was thirty-two years old when he became
king, and he reigned in Jerusalem eight years. No one was sorry when he died. He was
buried in the City of David, but not in the royal cemetery.

Ahaziah Rules in Judah

22:1-6
//2 Kgs 8:25-29

22:1
2 Chr 21:16-17

22:2
2 Chr 21:6-7

22 Then the people of Jerusalem made Ahaziah, Jehoram's youngest son, their next
king. The marauding bands of Arabs had killed all the older sons. So Ahaziah son
of Jehoram reigned as king of Judah. 2Ahaziah was twenty-two* years old when he
became king, and he reigned in Jerusalem one year. His mother was Athaliah, a
granddaughter of King Omri of Israel. 3Ahaziah also followed the evil example of King
Ahab's family, for his mother encouraged him in doing wrong. 4He did what was evil in
the LORD's sight, just as Ahab had done. After the death of his father, members of Ahab's
family became his advisers, and they led him to ruin.

22:5
2 Kgs 8:28

22:7-9
//2 Kgs 9:21-29

5Following their evil advice, Ahaziah made an alliance with King Joram,* the son of
King Ahab of Israel. They went out to fight King Hazael of Aram at Ramoth-gilead, and
the Arameans wounded Joram in the battle. 6Joram returned to Jezreel to recover from
his wounds, and King Ahaziah* of Judah went to Jezreel to visit him. 7But this turned
out to be a fatal mistake, for God had decided to punish Ahaziah. It was during this visit
that Ahaziah went out with Joram to meet Jehu son of Nimshi, whom the LORD had
appointed to end the dynasty of Ahab.

22:8
2 Kgs 10:11-14

8While Jehu was executing judgment against the family of Ahab, he happened to meet

21:16 Hebrew *the Cushites.* **21:17** Hebrew *Jehoahaz,* a variant name for Ahaziah; compare 22:1. **22:2** As in some Greek manuscripts and Syriac version (see also 2 Kgs 8:26); Hebrew reads *forty-two.* **22:5** Hebrew *Jehoram,* a variant name for Joram; also in 22:6, 7. **22:6** Some Hebrew manuscripts, Greek and Syriac versions, and Latin Vulgate (see also 2 Kgs 8:29); most Hebrew manuscripts read *Azariah.*

21:8-11 Jehoram's reign was marked by sin and cruelty. He married a woman who worshiped idols; he killed his six brothers; he allowed and even promoted idol worship. Yet he was not killed in battle or by treachery—he died by a lingering and painful disease (21:18, 19). Punishment for sin is not always immediate or dramatic. But if we ignore God's laws, we will eventually suffer the consequences of our sin.

21:12 Chronicles mentions Elijah only here. Much more about this great prophet can be found in 1 Kings 17:1—2 Kings 2:11. Elijah's Profile is found in 1 Kings 18.

22:4, 5 Although it is wise to seek advice, we must also carefully weigh the advice we receive. Ahaziah had advisers, but they were wicked and led him to ruin. When you seek advice, listen carefully and use God's Word to "test everything. . . . Hold on to what is good" (1 Thessalonians 5:21).

22:7 Jehu's Profile and a more complete story of his reign are found in 2 Kings 9:1–10:36.

some of Judah's officials and Ahaziah's relatives* who were attending Ahaziah. So Jehu
killed them all. 9 Then Jehu's men searched for Ahaziah, and they found him hiding in **22:9**
the city of Samaria. They brought him to Jehu, who killed him. Ahaziah was given a 2 Kgs 9:27-28 2 Chr 17:4
decent burial because the people said, "He was the grandson of Jehoshaphat—a man who
sought the LORD with all his heart." None of the surviving members of Ahaziah's family
was capable of ruling the kingdom.

Athaliah Rules in Judah

10 When Athaliah, the mother of King Ahaziah of Judah, learned that her son was dead, **22:10–23:21**
she set out to destroy the rest of Judah's royal family. 11 But Ahaziah's sister Jehosheba,* 2 Kgs 11:1-21
the daughter of King Jehoram, took Ahaziah's infant son, Joash, and stole him away from
among the rest of the king's children, who were about to be killed. She put Joash and his
nurse in a bedroom. In this way, Jehosheba, the wife of Jehoiada the priest, hid the child
so that Athaliah could not murder him. 12 Joash remained hidden in the Temple of God
for six years while Athaliah ruled over the land.

Revolt against Athaliah

23 In the seventh year of Athaliah's reign, Jehoiada the priest decided to act. He got **23:1**
up his courage and made a pact with five army commanders: Azariah son of 2 Kgs 11:4-20
Jeroham, Ishmael son of Jehohanan, Azariah son of Obed, Maaseiah son of Adaiah, and
Elishaphat son of Zicri. 2 These men traveled secretly throughout Judah and summoned
the Levites and clan leaders in Judah's towns to come to Jerusalem. 3 They all gathered **23:3**
at the Temple of God, where they made a covenant with Joash, the young king. 2 Sam 7:12 2 Chr 21:7
Jehoiada said to them, "The time has come for the king's son to reign! The LORD has
promised that a descendant of David will be our king. 4 This is what you must do. When **23:4**
the priests and Levites come on duty on the Sabbath, a third of them will serve as 1 Chr 9:25
gatekeepers. 5 Another third will go over to the royal palace, and the final third will be at
the Foundation Gate. Everyone else should stay in the courtyards of the LORD's Temple.
6 Remember, only the priests and Levites on duty may enter the Temple of the LORD, for **23:6**
they are set apart as holy. The rest of the people must obey the LORD's instructions and Exod 25:16, 21 1 Sam 10:24
stay outside. 7 You Levites, form a bodyguard for the king and keep your weapons in 1 Chr 23:28-32
hand. Any unauthorized person who enters the Temple must be killed. Stay right beside
the king at all times."
8 So the Levites and the people did everything just as Jehoiada the priest ordered. The **23:8**
commanders took charge of the men reporting for duty that Sabbath, as well as those 1 Chr 24:1
who were going off duty. Jehoiada the priest did not let anyone go home after their shift
ended. 9 Then Jehoiada supplied the commanders with the spears and shields that had
once belonged to King David and were stored in the Temple of God. 10 He stationed the
guards around the king, with their weapons ready. They formed a line from the south side
of the Temple around to the north side and all around the altar.
11 Then Jehoiada and his sons brought out Joash, the king's son, and placed the crown
on his head. They presented Joash with a copy of God's laws and proclaimed him king.
Then they anointed him, and everyone shouted, "Long live the king!"

The Death of Athaliah

12 When Athaliah heard the noise of the people running and the shouts of praise to the
king, she hurried to the LORD's Temple to see what was happening. 13 And she saw the
newly crowned king standing in his place of authority by the pillar at the Temple

22:8 As in Greek version (see also 2 Kgs 10:13); Hebrew reads *and sons of the brothers of Ahaziah.* **22:11** As in parallel text at 2 Kgs 11:2; Hebrew reads *Jehoshabeath,* a variant name for Jehosheba.

23:1 After seven years of rule by Athaliah, the queen mother, Jehoiada the priest finally got up his courage and took action to get rid of the idolatrous ruler. To confront the king (or queen) with the demands of God's law was supposed to be the role of every priest in every generation. Tragically, many priests shied away from this duty, and thus only a few made a difference in the nation.

23:1 Although it could have cost him his life, this priest did what was right, restoring the Temple worship and anointing the new king. There are times when we must correct a wrong or speak out for what is right. When such a situation arises, gather up your courage and act.

23:12-15 Athaliah thought she had it made. After assuming the throne, she killed all potential heirs to it—so she thought. But even the best plans for evil go sour. When the truth was revealed, she was overthrown immediately. It is much safer to live according to the truth, even if it means not obtaining everything you want.

entrance. The officers and trumpeters were surrounding him, and people from all over
the land were rejoicing and blowing trumpets. Singers with musical instruments were
leading the people in a great celebration. When Athaliah saw all this, she tore her clothes
in despair and shouted, "Treason! Treason!"
14 Then Jehoiada the priest ordered the commanders who were in charge of the troops,
"Take her out of the Temple, and kill anyone who tries to rescue her. Do not kill her here
23:15 2 Chr 22:10; Neh 3:28 — in the Temple of the LORD." 15 So they seized her and led her out to the gate where horses
enter the palace grounds, and they killed her there.

Jehoiada's Religious Reforms

16 Then Jehoiada made a covenant between himself and the king and the people that they
23:17 Deut 13:9 — would be the LORD's people. 17 And all the people went over to the temple of Baal and
tore it down. They demolished the altars and smashed the idols, and they killed Mattan
the priest of Baal in front of the altars.
23:18 1 Chr 23:6, 25-31; 25:1; 2 Chr 5:5 — 18 Jehoiada now put the Levitical priests in charge of the Temple of the LORD,
following all the instructions given by David. He also commanded them to present burnt
offerings to the LORD, as prescribed by the law of Moses, and to sing and rejoice as David
23:19 1 Chr 9:22 — had instructed. 19 He stationed gatekeepers at the gates of the LORD's Temple to keep
those who were ceremonially unclean from entering.
23:20 2 Kgs 11:19 — 20 Then the commanders, nobles, rulers, and all the people escorted the king from the
Temple of the LORD. They went through the Upper Gate and into the palace, and they
seated the king on the royal throne. 21 So all the people of the land rejoiced, and the city
was peaceful because Athaliah had been killed.

Joash Repairs the Temple

24:1-14 //2 Kgs 12:1-16 — **24** Joash was seven years old when he became king, and he reigned in Jerusalem
24:1 2 Kgs 11:21 — forty years. His mother was Zibiah, from Beersheba. 2 Joash did what was pleasing
in the LORD's sight throughout the lifetime of Jehoiada the priest. 3 Jehoiada chose two
wives for Joash, and he had sons and daughters.
24:4 2 Chr 24:7 — 4 Some time later, Joash decided to repair and restore the Temple of the LORD. 5 He
summoned the priests and Levites and gave them these instructions: "Go at once to all
the towns of Judah and collect the required annual offerings, so that we can repair the
Temple of your God. Do not delay!" But the Levites did not act right away.
24:6 Exod 30:12-16 — 6 So the king called for Jehoiada the high priest and asked him, "Why haven't you
demanded that the Levites go out and collect the Temple taxes from the towns of Judah
and from Jerusalem? Moses, the servant of the LORD, levied this tax on the community
of Israel in order to maintain the Tabernacle of the Covenant.*"
24:7 2 Chr 21:17 — 7 Over the years, the followers of wicked Athaliah had broken into the Temple of God,
and they had used all the dedicated things from the Temple of the LORD to worship the
images of Baal. 8 So now Joash gave instructions for a chest to be made and set outside
24:9 2 Chr 24:6; 36:22 — the gate leading to the Temple of the LORD. 9 Then a proclamation was sent throughout
Judah and Jerusalem, telling the people to bring to the LORD the tax that Moses, the
servant of God, had required of the Israelites in the wilderness. 10 This pleased all the
leaders and the people, and they gladly brought their money and filled the chest with it.
24:11 2 Kgs 12:10 — 11 Whenever the chest became full, the Levites carried it to the king's officials. Then
the court secretary and an officer of the high priest counted the money and took the chest

24:6 Hebrew *Tent of the Testimony.*

23:15-17 Athaliah's life ended as her mother Jezebel's had—by execution. Her life of idolatry and treachery was cut short by God's judgment of her sin. By this time Judah had slipped so far away from God that Baal was worshiped in Jerusalem.

23:18 Jehoiada restored the Temple procedures and its worship services according to David's original plans, recorded in 1 Chronicles 24–25.

24:5 The Levites took their time carrying out the king's order, even though he told them not to delay. Offerings for keeping the Temple in order were not just the king's wish, but God's command (Exodus 30:11-16). The Levites, therefore, were not only disregarding the king but disregarding God. When it comes to following God's commands, a slow response may be little better than disobedience. Obey God willingly and immediately.

24:10 Evidently the Levites weren't convinced that the people would want to contribute to the rebuilding of the Temple (24:5), but the people were glad to give of what they had for this project. Don't underestimate people's desire to be faithful to God. When challenged to do God's work, they will often respond willingly and generously.

back to the Temple again. This went on day after day, and a large amount of money was
collected. [12]The king and Jehoiada gave the money to the construction supervisors, who
hired masons and carpenters to restore the Temple of the LORD. They also hired
metalworkers, who made articles of iron and bronze for the LORD's Temple.

[13]So the men in charge of the renovation worked hard, and they made steady progress.
They restored the Temple of God according to its original design and strengthened it.
[14]When all the repairs were finished, they brought the remaining money to the king and
Jehoiada. It was used to make utensils for the Temple of the LORD—utensils for worship
services and for burnt offerings, including ladles and other vessels made of gold and
silver. And the burnt offerings were sacrificed continually in the Temple of the LORD
during the lifetime of Jehoiada the priest.

[15]Jehoiada lived to a very old age, finally dying at 130. [16]He was buried among the kings
in the City of David, because he had done so much good in Israel for God and his Temple.

24:16 2 Chr 21:2, 20

Jehoiada's Reforms Reversed

[17]But after Jehoiada's death, the leaders of Judah came and bowed before King Joash
and persuaded the king to listen to their advice. [18]They decided to abandon the Temple
of the LORD, the God of their ancestors, and they worshiped Asherah poles and idols
instead! Then the anger of God burned against Judah and Jerusalem because of their sin.
[19]The LORD sent prophets to bring them back to him, but the people would not listen.

[20]Then the Spirit of God came upon Zechariah son of Jehoiada the priest. He stood
before the people and said, "This is what God says: Why do you disobey the LORD's
commands so that you cannot prosper? You have abandoned the LORD, and now he has
abandoned you!"

[21]Then the leaders plotted to kill Zechariah, and by order of King Joash himself, they
stoned him to death in the courtyard of the LORD's Temple. [22]That was how King Joash
repaid Jehoiada for his love and loyalty—by killing his son. Zechariah's last words as he
died were, "May the LORD see what they are doing and hold them accountable!"

24:18 Exod 34:12-14 Josh 22:30
24:19 Jer 7:25
24:20 Num 14:41 2 Chr 15:2; 20:14
24:21 Neh 9:26 Matt 23:35
24:22 Gen 9:5

The End of Joash's Reign

[23]At the beginning of the year, the Aramean army marched against Joash. They invaded
Judah and Jerusalem and killed all the leaders of the nation. Then they sent all the plunder
back to their king in Damascus. [24]Although the Arameans attacked with only a small army,
the LORD helped them conquer the much larger army of Judah. The people of Judah had
abandoned the LORD, the God of their ancestors, so judgment was executed against Joash.

[25]The Arameans withdrew, leaving Joash severely wounded. But his own officials
decided to kill him for murdering the son of Jehoiada the priest. They assassinated him
as he lay in bed. Then he was buried in the City of David, but not in the royal cemetery.
[26]The assassins were Jozacar,* the son of an Ammonite woman named Shimeath, and
Jehozabad, the son of a Moabite woman named Shomer.*

[27]The complete story about the sons of Joash, the prophecies about him, and the
record of his restoration of the Temple of God are written in *The Commentary on the
Book of the Kings.* When Joash died, his son Amaziah became the next king.

24:23-27 //2 Kgs 12:17-21
24:24 2 Chr 16:7-8
24:25 2 Kgs 12:20-21
24:27 2 Chr 13:22; 24:12

24:26a Hebrew *Zabad;* compare parallel text at 2 Kgs 12:21, and see note there. **24:26b** As in parallel text at 2 Kgs 12:21; Hebrew reads *Shimrith.*

24:18 If everything went so well in Judah when the people worshiped God, why did they turn away from him? Prosperity can be both a blessing and a curse. While it can be a sign of God's blessing to those who follow him, it carries with it the potential for moral and spiritual decline. Prosperous people are tempted to become self-sufficient and proud—to take God for granted. In our prosperity, we must not forget that God is the source of our blessings. See Deuteronomy 6:10-12; 8:11-14.

24:18-20 When King Joash and the nation of Judah abandoned God, God sent Zechariah to call them to repentance. Before dispensing judgment and punishment, God gave them another chance. In the same way, God does not abandon us or lash out in revenge when we sin. Instead, he aggressively pursues us through his Word, his Spirit in us, the words of others, and sometimes discipline. He does not intend to destroy us but to urge us to return to him. When you are moving away from God, remember that he is pursuing you. Stop and listen. Allow him to point out your sin so you can repent and follow him again.

24:19 God sent many prophets to Joash and the people to warn them that they were headed for destruction. Joel may have been one of these prophets. Read the book of Joel for more information about the political and spiritual climate of the times.

24:22 Zechariah asked God to call the people to account for their sins. He was not seeking revenge but pleading for justice. When we feel like despairing over the wickedness around us, we can rest assured that in the end, God will bring complete justice to the earth.

Amaziah Rules in Judah

25:1-4 //2 Kgs 14:1-6 **25** Amaziah was twenty-five years old when he became king, and he reigned in
25:2 2 Chr 25:14 Jerusalem twenty-nine years. His mother was Jehoaddin,* from Jerusalem.
2 Amaziah did what was pleasing in the LORD's sight, but not wholeheartedly.
3 When Amaziah was well established as king, he executed the men who had assassi-
25:4 Deut 24:16 nated his father. 4 However, he did not kill the children of the assassins, for he obeyed
the command of the LORD written in the Book of the Law of Moses: "Parents must not
be put to death for the sins of their children, nor the children for the sins of their parents.
Those worthy of death must be executed for their own crimes."*

25:1 As in parallel text at 2 Kgs 14:2; Hebrew reads *Jehoaddan,* a variant name for Jehoaddin. **25:4** Deut 24:16.

JOASH

All parents want their children to make the right decisions. But to do this, children must first learn to make *their own* decisions. Making bad ones helps them learn to make good ones. If parents make all the decisions for their children, they leave their children without the skills for wise decision making when they are on their own. This problem seriously affected Joash. He had great advice, but he never grew up. He became so dependent on what he was told that his effectiveness was limited to the quality of his advisers.

When Joash was one year old, his grandmother Athaliah decided to slaughter all her descendants in a desperate bid for power. Joash, the only survivor, was rescued and hidden by his aunt and uncle, Jehosheba and Jehoiada. Jehoiada's work as a priest made it possible to keep Joash hidden in the Temple for six years. At that point, Jehoiada arranged for the overthrow of Athaliah and the crowning of Joash. For many years following, Jehoiada made most of the kingdom's decisions for Joash. When the old priest died, he was buried in the royal cemetery as a tribute to his role.

But after Jehoiada's death, Joash didn't know what to do. He listened to counsel that led him into evil. Within a short time he even ordered the death of Jehoiada's son Zechariah. After a few months, Joash's army had been soundly defeated by the Arameans. Jerusalem was saved only because Joash stripped the Temple of its treasures as a bribe. Finally, the king's own officials assassinated him. In contrast to Jehoiada, Joash was not buried among the kings; he is not even listed in Jesus' genealogy in the New Testament.

As dependent as Joash was on Jehoiada, there is little evidence that he ever established a real dependence on the God Jehoiada obeyed. Like many children, Joash's knowledge of God was secondhand. It was a start, but the king needed his own relationship with God that would outlast and overrule the changes in the advice he received.

It would be easy to criticize Joash's failure were it not for the fact that we often fall into the same traps. How often have we acted on poor advice without considering God's Word?

Strengths and accomplishments
- Carried out extensive repairs on the Temple
- Was faithful to God as long as Jehoiada lived

Weaknesses and mistakes
- Allowed idolatry to continue among his people
- Used the Temple treasures to bribe King Hazael of Aram
- Killed Jehoiada's son Zechariah
- Allowed his advisers to lead the people away from God

Lessons from his life
- A good and hopeful start can be ruined by an evil end
- Even the best counsel is ineffective if it does not help us make wise decisions
- As helpful or hurtful as others may be, we are individually responsible for what we do

Vital statistics
- Where: Jerusalem
- Occupation: King of Judah
- Relatives: Father: Ahaziah. Mother: Zibiah. Grandmother: Athaliah. Aunt: Jehosheba. Uncle: Jehoiada. Son: Amaziah. Cousin: Zechariah
- Contemporaries: Jehu, Hazael

Key verses
"But after Jehoiada's death, the leaders of Judah came and bowed before King Joash and persuaded the king to listen to their advice. They decided to abandon the Temple of the LORD, the God of their ancestors, and they worshiped Asherah poles and idols instead! Then the anger of God burned against Judah and Jerusalem because of their sin" (2 Chronicles 24:17, 18).

Joash's story is told in 2 Kings 11:1—12:21 and 2 Chronicles 22:11—24:27.

25:2 Amaziah did what was right on the outside, but inside he often resented what he had to do. His obedience was at best half-hearted. When the prophet promised God's deliverance, Amaziah first complained about the money that had been lost (25:9). And he valued military success more than God's will. We must search our own hearts and root out any resistance to obeying God. Grudging compliance is not true obedience.

5Another thing Amaziah did was to organize the army, assigning leaders to each clan 25:5 Num 1:3 2 Chr 26:13
from Judah and Benjamin. Then he took a census and found that he had an army of
300,000 men twenty years old and older, all trained in the use of spear and shield. 6He also
paid about 7,500 pounds* of silver to hire 100,000 experienced fighting men from Israel.
7But a man of God came to the king and said, "O king, do not hire troops from Israel, 25:7 2 Kgs 4:9
for the LORD is not with Israel. He will not help those people of Ephraim! 8If you let 25:8 2 Chr 14:11; 20:6
them go with your troops into battle, you will be defeated no matter how well you fight.
God will overthrow you, for he has the power to help or to frustrate."
9Amaziah asked the man of God, "But what should I do about the silver I paid to hire
the army of Israel?"

The man of God replied, "The LORD is able to give you much more than this!" 10So
Amaziah discharged the hired troops and sent them back to Ephraim. This made them
angry with Judah, and they returned home in a great rage.
11Then Amaziah summoned his courage and led his army to the Valley of Salt, where 25:11-12 //2 Kgs 14:7
they killed ten thousand Edomite troops from Seir. 12They captured another ten thousand and
took them to the top of a cliff and threw them off, dashing them to pieces on the rocks below.
13Meanwhile, the hired troops that Amaziah had sent home raided several of the towns
of Judah between Samaria and Beth-horon, killing three thousand people and carrying
off great quantities of plunder.
14When King Amaziah returned from defeating the Edomites, he brought with him 25:14 2 Chr 28:23
idols taken from the people of Seir. He set them up as his own gods, bowed down in front 25:15 2 Chr 25:11-12
of them, and presented sacrifices to them! 15This made the LORD very angry, and he sent
a prophet to ask, "Why have you worshiped gods who could not even save their own
people from you?"
16But the king interrupted him and said, "Since when have I asked your advice? Be
quiet now before I have you killed!"

So the prophet left with this warning: "I know that God has determined to destroy you
because you have done this and have not accepted my counsel."
17After consulting with his advisers, King Amaziah of Judah sent this challenge to Israel's 25:17-28 //2 Kgs 14:8-20
king Jehoash,* the son of Jehoahaz and grandson of Jehu: "Come and meet me in battle!"
18But King Jehoash of Israel replied to King Amaziah of Judah with this story: "Out in 25:18 Judg 9:8-15
the Lebanon mountains, a thistle sent a message to a mighty cedar tree: 'Give your daughter
in marriage to my son.' But just then a wild animal came by and stepped on the thistle,
crushing it! 19You may be very proud of your conquest of Edom, but my advice is to stay 25:19 2 Chr 26:16; 32:25
home. Why stir up trouble that will bring disaster on you and the people of Judah?"
20But Amaziah would not listen, for God was arranging to destroy him for worshiping
the gods of Edom. 21So King Jehoash of Israel mobilized his army against King Amaziah
of Judah. The two armies drew up their battle lines at Beth-shemesh in Judah. 22Judah
was routed by the army of Israel, and its army scattered and fled for home. 23King 25:23 2 Chr 21:17; 22:1
Jehoash of Israel captured King Amaziah of Judah at Beth-shemesh and brought him
back to Jerusalem. Then Jehoash ordered his army to demolish six hundred feet* of
Jerusalem's wall, from the Ephraim Gate to the Corner Gate. 24He carried off all the gold 25:24 1 Chr 26:15

25:6 Hebrew *100 talents* [3.4 metric tons]. **25:17** Hebrew *Joash,* a variant name for Jehoash; also in 25:18, 21, 23, 25. **25:23** Hebrew *400 cubits* [180 meters].

25:9, 10 Amaziah made a financial agreement with Israelite soldiers, offering to pay them to fight for him (25:6). But before they could go to battle, Amaziah sent them home with their pay because of the prophet's warning. Although it cost him plenty, he wisely realized that the money was not worth the ruin the alliance could cause. How would you have reacted? Money must never stand in the way of making right decisions. The Lord's favor is priceless, worth more than any amount of money.

25:14 After the victory, Amaziah returned and sacrificed to idols. We are very susceptible to sin after great victories. It is then that we feel confident, relaxed, and ready to celebrate. If, in that excitement, we let our defenses down, Satan can attack with all sorts of temptations. When you win, watch out. After the mountain peaks come the valleys.

25:15 Amaziah made a foolish mistake by worshiping the gods of the nation he had just conquered. Impressed by the accomplishments of the Edomites, Amaziah worshiped their idols! How foolish to serve the gods of a defeated enemy. We make the same mistake as Amaziah when we run after money, power, or recognition. By recognizing the emptiness of these worldly pursuits, we can free ourselves from the desire to follow them.

25:18 In this parable, Judah is the thistle and Israel's army is the cedar. Amaziah was proud after defeating Edom. He wanted to defeat Israel, but Jehoash warned him not to attack. Amaziah had more ambition than ability, and he paid for it when he was soundly defeated. Don't let ambition and pride into your life, for they will cause you to forget God.

and silver and all the utensils from the Temple of God that had been in the care of
Obed-edom. He also seized the treasures of the royal palace, along with hostages, and
then returned to Samaria.
25:25 2 Kgs 14:17-22 25 King Amaziah of Judah lived on for fifteen years after the death of King Jehoash of
Israel. 26 The rest of the events of Amaziah's reign, from beginning to end, are recorded
in *The Book of the Kings of Judah and Israel.* 27 After Amaziah turned away from the
LORD, there was a conspiracy against his life in Jerusalem, and he fled to Lachish. But
his enemies sent assassins after him, and they killed him there. 28 They brought him back
to Jerusalem on a horse, and he was buried with his ancestors in the City of David.*

Uzziah Rules in Judah

26:1-4 //2 Kgs 14:21-22; 15:1-3 **26** The people of Judah then crowned Amaziah's sixteen-year-old son, Uzziah, as
their next king. 2 After his father's death, Uzziah rebuilt the town of Elath* and
restored it to Judah. 3 Uzziah was sixteen when he became king, and he reigned in
26:5 2 Chr 15:2; 24:2 Dan 1:17 Jerusalem fifty-two years. His mother was Jecoliah, from Jerusalem. 4 He did what was
pleasing in the LORD's sight, just as his father, Amaziah, had done. 5 Uzziah sought God
during the days of Zechariah, who instructed him in the fear of God. And as long as the
king sought the LORD, God gave him success.
26:6 Isa 14:29 6 He declared war on the Philistines and broke down the walls of Gath, Jabneh, and
Ashdod. Then he built new towns in the Ashdod area and in other parts of Philistia.

25:28 As in some Hebrew manuscripts and other ancient versions (see also 2 Kgs 14:20); most Hebrew manuscripts read *the city of Judah.* **26:2** As in Greek version (see also 2 Kgs 14:22; 16:6); Hebrew reads *Eloth.*

UZZIAH

We are never closer to failure than during our greatest successes. If we fail to recognize God's part in our achievements, they are no better than failures. Uzziah (also called Azariah) was a remarkably successful king. His achievements brought him fame. He was successful in war and peace, in planning and execution, in building and planting.

Uzziah overestimated his own importance in bringing about the great achievements he experienced. He did so many things well that a consuming pride gradually invaded his life like the leprous disease that finally destroyed his body. In trying to act like a priest, he took on a role that God did not mean for him to have. He had forgotten not only how much God had given him but also that God had certain roles for others that he needed to respect.

Uzziah's pride was rooted in his lack of thankfulness. We have no accounts of this king's ever showing appreciation to God for the marvelous gifts he received. Our accomplishments may not compare with Uzziah's, but we still owe a debt of thanksgiving to God for our very lives. If God is not getting the credit for your successes, shouldn't you start looking at your life differently?

Strengths and accomplishments
- Pleased God during his early years as king
- Successful warrior and city builder
- Skillful in organizing and delegating
- Reigned for 52 years

Weaknesses and mistakes
- Developed a prideful attitude due to his great success
- Tried to perform the priests' duties, in direct disobedience to God
- Failed to remove many of the symbols of idolatry in the land

Lessons from his life
- Lack of thankfulness to God can lead to pride
- Even successful people must acknowledge the role God has for others in their lives

Vital statistics
- Where: Jerusalem
- Occupation: King of Judah
- Relatives: Father: Amaziah. Mother: Jecoliah. Son: Jotham
- Contemporaries: Isaiah, Amos, Hosea, Jeroboam, Zechariah, Azariah

Key verses
"And he produced machines mounted on the walls of Jerusalem, designed by brilliant men to shoot arrows and hurl stones from the towers and the corners of the wall. His fame spread far and wide, for the LORD helped him wonderfully until he became very powerful.

But when he had become powerful, he also became proud, which led to his downfall. He sinned against the LORD his God by entering the sanctuary of the LORD's Temple and personally burning incense on the altar" (2 Chronicles 26:15, 16).

Uzziah's story is told in 2 Kings 15:1–7 (where he is called Azariah) and in 2 Chronicles 26:1–23. He is also mentioned in Isaiah 1:1; 6:1; 7:1; Hosea 1:1; Amos 1:1; Zechariah 14:5.

7God helped him not only with his wars against the Philistines, but also in his battles
with the Arabs of Gur* and in his wars with the Meunites. 8The Meunites* paid
annual tribute to him, and his fame spread even to Egypt, for he had become very
powerful.
9Uzziah built fortified towers in Jerusalem at the Corner Gate, at the Valley Gate, and
at the angle in the wall. 10He also constructed forts in the wilderness and dug many water
cisterns, because he kept great herds of livestock in the foothills of Judah* and on the
plains. He was also a man who loved the soil. He had many workers who cared for his
farms and vineyards, both on the hillsides and in the fertile valleys.
11Uzziah had an army of well-trained warriors, ready to march into battle, unit by
unit. This great army of fighting men had been mustered and organized by Jeiel, the
secretary of the army, and his assistant, Maaseiah. They were under the direction of
Hananiah, one of the king's officials. 12Twenty-six hundred clan leaders commanded
these regiments of seasoned warriors. 13The army consisted of 307,500 men, all elite
troops. They were prepared to assist the king against any enemy. 14Uzziah provided
the entire army with shields, spears, helmets, coats of mail, bows, and sling stones.
15And he produced machines mounted on the walls of Jerusalem, designed by brilliant
men to shoot arrows and hurl stones* from the towers and the corners of the wall. His
fame spread far and wide, for the LORD helped him wonderfully until he became very
powerful.

Uzziah's Sin and Punishment

16But when he had become powerful, he also became proud, which led to his downfall.
He sinned against the LORD his God by entering the sanctuary of the LORD's Temple and
personally burning incense on the altar. 17Azariah the high priest went in after him with
eighty other priests of the LORD, all brave men. 18They confronted King Uzziah and said,
"It is not for you, Uzziah, to burn incense to the LORD. That is the work of the priests
alone, the sons of Aaron who are set apart for this work. Get out of the sanctuary, for you
have sinned. The LORD God will not honor you for this!"
19Uzziah was furious and refused to set down the incense burner he was holding.
But as he was standing there with the priests before the incense altar in the LORD's
Temple, leprosy* suddenly broke out on his forehead. 20When Azariah and the other
priests saw the leprosy, they rushed him out. And the king himself was eager to get
out because the LORD had struck him. 21So King Uzziah had leprosy until the day he
died. He lived in isolation, excluded from the Temple of the LORD. His son Jotham
was put in charge of the royal palace, and he governed the people of the land.
22The rest of the events of Uzziah's reign, from beginning to end, are recorded by
the prophet Isaiah son of Amoz. 23So Uzziah died, and since he had leprosy, he was
buried nearby in a burial field belonging to the kings. Then his son Jotham became
the next king.

26:7 2 Chr 21:16
26:8 2 Chr 17:11
26:9 2 Chr 25:23; Neh 3:13; 21:13, 15
26:10 Gen 26:18-21
26:13 2 Chr 25:5
26:16 Deut 32:15; 1 Kgs 13:1-4; 2 Chr 25:19
26:17 1 Chr 6:10
26:18 Exod 30:7-8; Num 16:39-40
26:19 2 Kgs 5:25-27
26:21-23 //2 Kgs 15:5-7
26:22 Isa 1:1
26:23 2 Chr 21:20; 28:27; Isa 6:1

26:7 As in Greek version; Hebrew reads *Gur-baal.* **26:8** As in Greek version; Hebrew reads *Ammonites.* Compare 26:7. **26:10** Hebrew *the Shephelah.* **26:15** Or *designed by brilliant men to protect those who shot arrows and stones.* **26:19** Or *a contagious skin disease.* The Hebrew word used here and throughout this passage can describe various skin diseases.

26:15 These machines were similar to the catapults later used by the Romans and were capable of slinging stones or arrows a great distance.

26:16 After God gave Uzziah great prosperity and power, he became proud and corrupt. It is true that "pride goes before destruction" (Proverbs 16:18). If God has given you wealth, influence, popularity, and power, be thankful, but be careful. God hates pride. While it is normal to feel elation when we accomplish something, it is wrong to be disdainful of God or to look down on others. Check your attitudes and remember to give God the credit for what you have. Use your gifts in ways that please him.

26:17-21 When people have power, they often think they can live above the law. But even rulers are subject to God, as Uzziah discovered. No matter what your position in society, God expects you to honor, worship, and obey him.

26:21 For much of his life, Uzziah "did what was pleasing in the LORD's sight (26:4). But Uzziah turned away from God, and he was struck with leprosy and remained leprous until his death. He is remembered more for his arrogant act and subsequent punishment than for his great reforms. God requires lifelong obedience. Spurts of obedience are not enough. Only "those who endure to the end" will be rewarded (Mark 13:13). Be remembered for your consistent faith; otherwise you, too, may become more famous for your downfall than for your success.

26:23 This was the year that God called Isaiah to be a prophet (Isaiah 6:1).

Jotham Rules in Judah

27:1-9
//2 Kgs 15:33-38
27:2
2 Chr 26:16
27:3
2 Chr 33:14
Neh 3:26
27:4
2 Chr 11:5
27:6
2 Chr 26:5
27:7
2 Kgs 15:36
27:8
2 Chr 27:1

27 Jotham was twenty-five years old when he became king, and he reigned in Jerusalem sixteen years. His mother was Jerusha, the daughter of Zadok. 2He did what was pleasing in the LORD's sight, just as his father, Uzziah, had done. But unlike him, Jotham did not enter the Temple of the LORD. Nevertheless, the people continued in their corrupt ways.

3Jotham rebuilt the Upper Gate to the LORD's Temple and also did extensive rebuilding on the wall at the hill of Ophel. 4He built towns in the hill country of Judah and constructed fortresses and towers in the wooded areas. 5Jotham waged war against the Ammonites and conquered them. For the next three years, he received from them an annual tribute of 7,500 pounds* of silver, 50,000 bushels of wheat, and 50,000 bushels of barley.*

6King Jotham became powerful because he was careful to live in obedience to the LORD his God.

7The rest of the events of Jotham's reign, including his wars and other activities, are recorded in *The Book of the Kings of Israel and Judah.* 8He was twenty-five years old when he became king, and he reigned in Jerusalem sixteen years. 9When he died, he was buried in the City of David, and his son Ahaz became the next king.

Ahaz Rules in Judah

28:1-27
//2 Kgs 16:1-20
28:2
Exod 34:17
2 Chr 22:3
28:3
Lev 18:21
Josh 15:8
2 Chr 33:2, 6
28:4
2 Chr 28:25
28:5
2 Kgs 16:5
2 Chr 24:24
Isa 7:11
28:6
2 Kgs 16:5
28:8
Deut 28:25, 41
2 Chr 11:4
28:9
2 Chr 25:15
Ezra 9:6
Isa 47:6
Rev 18:5
28:10
Lev 25:39
28:11
2 Chr 28:8

28 Ahaz was twenty years old when he became king, and he reigned in Jerusalem sixteen years. He did not do what was pleasing in the sight of the LORD, as his ancestor David had done. 2Instead, he followed the example of the kings of Israel and cast images for the worship of Baal. 3He offered sacrifices in the valley of the son of Hinnom, even sacrificing his own sons in the fire.* He imitated the detestable practices of the pagan nations whom the LORD had driven from the land ahead of the Israelites. 4He offered sacrifices and burned incense at the pagan shrines and on the hills and under every green tree.

5That is why the LORD his God allowed the king of Aram to defeat Ahaz and to exile large numbers of his people to Damascus. The armies of Israel also defeated Ahaz and inflicted many casualties on his army. 6In a single day Pekah son of Remaliah, Israel's king, killed 120,000 of Judah's troops because they had abandoned the LORD, the God of their ancestors. 7Then Zicri, a warrior from Ephraim, killed Maaseiah, the king's son; Azrikam, the king's palace commander; and Elkanah, the king's second-in-command. 8The armies of Israel captured 200,000 women and children from Judah and took tremendous amounts of plunder, which they took back to Samaria.

9But a prophet of the LORD named Oded was there in Samaria when the army of Israel returned home. He went out to meet them and said, "The LORD, the God of your ancestors, was angry with Judah and let you defeat them. But you have gone too far, killing them without mercy, and all heaven is disturbed. 10And now you are planning to make slaves of these people from Judah and Jerusalem. What about your own sins against the LORD your God? 11Listen to me and return these captives you have taken, for they are your own relatives. Watch out, because now the LORD's fierce anger has been turned against you!"

12Then some of the leaders of Israel*—Azariah son of Jehohanan, Berekiah son of Meshillemoth, Jehizkiah son of Shallum, and Amasa son of Hadlai—agreed with this and confronted the men returning from battle. 13"You must not bring the prisoners here!" they declared. "We cannot afford to add to our sins and guilt. Our guilt is already great, and the LORD's fierce anger is already turned against Israel."

27:5a Hebrew *100 talents* [3.4 metric tons]. **27:5b** Hebrew *10,000 cors* [1,820 kiloliters] *of wheat, and 10,000 cors of barley.* **28:3** Or *even making his sons pass through the fire.* **28:12** Hebrew *Ephraim,* referring to the northern kingdom of Israel.

27:2 Jotham was generally a good king (27:6), but his people became corrupt. Those you lead will not always follow your example, but that should not affect the way you live for God. This sinfulness of Jotham's kingdom is vividly portrayed in Isaiah 1–5.

28:3 Imagine the monstrous evil of a religion that offers young children as sacrifices. God allowed the nation to be conquered in response to Ahaz's evil practices. Even today the practice hasn't abated. The sacrifice of children to the harsh gods of convenience, economy, and whim continues in sterile medical facilities in numbers that would astound the wicked Ahaz. If we are to allow children to come to Christ (Matthew 19:14), we must first allow them to come into the world.

14 So the warriors released the prisoners and handed over the plunder in the sight of all
the leaders and people. 15 Then the four men mentioned by name came forward and
distributed clothes from the plunder to the prisoners who were naked. They provided
clothing and sandals to wear, gave them enough food and drink, and dressed their wounds
with olive oil. They put those who were weak on donkeys and took all the prisoners back
to their own land—to Jericho, the city of palms. Then they returned to Samaria.

Ahaz Closes the Temple

16 About that time King Ahaz of Judah asked the king of Assyria for help against his
enemies. 17 The armies of Edom had again invaded Judah and taken captives. 18 And the
Philistines had raided towns located in the foothills of Judah* and in the Negev. They
had already captured Beth-shemesh, Aijalon, Gederoth, Soco with its villages, Timnah
with its villages, and Gimzo with its villages, and the Philistines had occupied these
towns. 19 The LORD was humbling Judah because of King Ahaz of Judah,* for he had
encouraged his people to sin and had been utterly unfaithful to the LORD. 20 So when
King Tiglath-pileser* of Assyria arrived, he oppressed King Ahaz instead of helping him.
21 Ahaz took valuable items from the LORD's Temple, the royal palace, and from the
homes of his officials and gave them to the king of Assyria as tribute. But even this did
not help him.

22 And when trouble came to King Ahaz, he became even more unfaithful to the LORD.
23 He offered sacrifices to the gods of Damascus who had defeated him, for he said,
"These gods helped the kings of Aram, so they will help me, too, if I sacrifice to them."
But instead, they led to his ruin and the ruin of all Israel. 24 The king took the utensils
from the Temple of God and broke them into pieces. He shut the doors of the LORD's
Temple so that no one could worship there and then set up altars to pagan gods in every
corner of Jerusalem. 25 He made pagan shrines in all the towns of Judah for offering
sacrifices to other gods. In this way, he aroused the anger of the LORD, the God of his
ancestors.

26 The rest of the events of Ahaz's reign and all his dealings, from beginning to end,
are recorded in *The Book of the Kings of Judah and Israel.* 27 When King Ahaz died, he
was buried in Jerusalem but not in the royal cemetery. Then his son Hezekiah became
the next king.

Hezekiah Rules in Judah

29 Hezekiah was twenty-five years old when he became the king of Judah, and he reigned
in Jerusalem twenty-nine years. His mother was Abijah, the daughter of Zechariah.
2 He did what was pleasing in the LORD's sight, just as his ancestor David had done.

Hezekiah Reopens the Temple

3 In the very first month of the first year of his reign, Hezekiah reopened the doors of the
Temple of the LORD and repaired them. 4 He summoned the priests and Levites to meet
him at the courtyard east of the Temple. 5 He said to them, "Listen to me, you Levites!
Purify yourselves, and purify the Temple of the LORD, the God of your ancestors.
Remove all the defiled things from the sanctuary. 6 Our ancestors were unfaithful and did
what was evil in the sight of the LORD our God. They abandoned the LORD and his
Temple; they turned their backs on him. 7 They also shut the doors to the Temple's foyer,
and they snuffed out the lamps. They stopped burning incense and presenting burnt
offerings at the sanctuary of the God of Israel. 8 That is why the LORD's anger has fallen

28:15 Deut 34:3; 2 Kgs 6:22; 2 Chr 28:12; Prov 25:21-22
28:16 2 Kgs 16:7
28:18 Ezek 16:57
28:19 2 Chr 21:2
28:20 1 Chr 5:26
28:21 2 Kgs 16:8-9
28:23 2 Chr 25:14; Jer 44:17-18
28:24 2 Kgs 16:17; 2 Chr 29:7; 30:14; 33:3-5
28:26 2 Kgs 16:19-20
28:27 2 Chr 24:25
29:1-2 //2 Kgs 18:2-3
29:2 2 Chr 28:1; 34:2
29:3 2 Chr 28:24; 29:7
29:5 2 Chr 29:15, 34; 35:6
29:6 Ezek 8:16
29:8 Deut 28:25; 2 Chr 24:18; 28:5; Jer 25:9, 18

28:18 Hebrew *the Shephelah.* **28:19** Hebrew *of Israel.* **28:20** Hebrew *Tilgath-pilneser,* a variant name for Tiglath-pileser.

28:22 Difficulties and struggles can devastate people, or they can stimulate growth and maturity. For Ahaz, deep troubles led to spiritual collapse. We do not need to respond like Ahaz. When facing problems or tragedy, we must remember that rough times give us a chance to grow (James 1:2-4). When you are facing trials, don't turn away from God; turn *to* him. See these times as opportunities for you to claim God's help.

29:1 Hezekiah's Profile is found in 2 Kings 18.

29:11 The Levites, chosen by God to serve in the Temple, had been kept from their duties by Ahaz's wickedness (28:24). But Hezekiah called them back into service, reminding them that the Lord had chosen them to minister.

We may not have to face a wicked king, but pressures or responsibilities can render us inactive and ineffective. When you have been given the responsibility to minister, don't neglect your duty. If you have become inactive in Christian service, either by choice or by circumstance, look for opportunities to minister (and listen to the "Hezekiahs") God will send your way. Then, like the Levites, be ready for action (29:12-15).

upon Judah and Jerusalem. He has made us an object of dread, horror, and ridicule, as
29:9 2 Chr 28:5-8, 17
you can so plainly see. 9 Our fathers have been killed in battle, and our sons and daughters
and wives are in captivity. 10 But now I will make a covenant with the LORD, the God of
29:10 2 Chr 23:16
Israel, so that his fierce anger will turn away from us. 11 My dear Levites, do not neglect
29:11 Num 3:6; 8:6, 14
your duties any longer! The LORD has chosen you to stand in his presence, to minister to
him, and to lead the people in worship and make offerings to him."
29:12 Num 3:19-20; 2 Chr 31:13
12 Then these Levites got right to work:

From the clan of Kohath: Mahath son of Amasai and Joel son of Azariah.
From the clan of Merari: Kish son of Abdi and Azariah son of Jehallelel.
From the clan of Gershon: Joah son of Zimmah and Eden son of Joah.
13 From the family of Elizaphan: Shimri and Jeiel.
From the family of Asaph: Zechariah and Mattaniah.
14 From the family of Heman: Jehiel and Shimei.
From the family of Jeduthun: Shemaiah and Uzziel.

29:15 1 Chr 23:28; 2 Chr 29:5; 30:12
15 These men called together their fellow Levites, and they purified themselves. Then
they began to purify the Temple of the LORD, just as the king had commanded. They were
29:16 2 Chr 15:16
careful to follow all the LORD's instructions in their work. 16 The priests went into the
sanctuary of the Temple of the LORD to cleanse it, and they took out to the Temple courtyard
all the defiled things they found. From there the Levites carted it all out to the Kidron Valley.
29:17 2 Chr 29:3
17 The work began on a day in early spring,* and in eight days they had reached the
foyer of the LORD's Temple. Then they purified the Temple of the LORD itself, which
took another eight days. So the entire task was completed in sixteen days.

The Temple Rededication

18 Then the Levites went to King Hezekiah and gave him this report: "We have purified
29:19 2 Chr 28:24
the Temple of the LORD, the altar of burnt offering with all its utensils, and the table of
the Bread of the Presence with all its utensils. 19 We have also recovered all the utensils
taken by King Ahaz when he was unfaithful and closed the Temple. They are now in front
of the altar of the LORD, purified and ready for use."
29:21 Lev 4:3-14
20 Early the next morning King Hezekiah gathered the city officials and went to the
Temple of the LORD. 21 They brought seven bulls, seven rams, seven lambs, and seven

29:17 Hebrew *on the first day of the first month.* This day of the Hebrew lunar calendar occurs in March or early April.

GREAT REVIVALS IN THE BIBLE

The Bible records several great revivals where people in great numbers turned to God and gave up their sinful ways of living. Each revival was characterized by a *leader* who recognized his nation's spiritual dryness. And in each case, the leader *took action* and was not afraid to make his desires known to the people.

Leader	*Reference*	*How the People Responded*
Moses	Exodus 32, 33	Accepted God's laws and built the Tabernacle
Samuel	1 Samuel 7:2–13	Promised to make God first in their lives by destroying their idols
David	2 Samuel 6	Brought the Ark of the Covenant to Jerusalem; praised God with singing and musical instruments
Jehoshaphat	2 Chronicles 20	Decided to trust in God alone to help them, and their discouragement turned to joy
Hezekiah	2 Chronicles 29—31	Purified the Temple; got rid of idols; brought tithes to God's house
Josiah	2 Chronicles 34, 35	Made a commitment to obey God's commands and remove sinful influences from their lives
Ezra	Ezra 9, 10 Haggai 1	Stopped associating with those who caused them to compromise their faith; renewed their commitment to God's commands; began rebuilding the Temple
Nehemiah (with Ezra)	Nehemiah 8—10	Fasted, confessed their sins, read God's Word publicly, and promised in writing to again serve God wholeheartedly

---

29:21 Throughout the Old Testament, the sacrifice was God's appointed way of approaching him and restoring a right relationship with him. The sin offering made by Hezekiah was a sacrifice given to God for forgiveness for unintentional sins. (For more information on why God required sacrifices and how they were carried out, see the notes in Leviticus 1.)

male goats as a sin offering for the kingdom, for the Temple, and for Judah. The king
commanded the priests, who were descendants of Aaron, to sacrifice the animals on the
altar of the LORD. 22 So they killed the bulls, and the priests took the blood and sprinkled
it on the altar. Next they killed the rams and sprinkled their blood on the altar. And finally,
they did the same with the lambs. 23 The male goats for the sin offering were then brought
before the king and the assembly of people, who laid their hands on them. 24 The priests
then killed the goats as a sin offering and sprinkled their blood on the altar to make
atonement for the sins of all Israel. The king had specifically commanded that this burnt
offering and sin offering should be made for all Israel.
25 King Hezekiah then stationed the Levites at the Temple of the LORD with cymbals,
harps, and lyres. He obeyed all the commands that the LORD had given to King David
through Gad, the king's seer, and the prophet Nathan. 26 The Levites then took their
positions around the Temple with the instruments of David, and the priests took their
positions with the trumpets. 27 Then Hezekiah ordered that the burnt offering be placed on
the altar. As the burnt offering was presented, songs of praise to the LORD were begun,
accompanied by the trumpets and other instruments of David, king of Israel. 28 The entire
assembly worshiped the LORD as the singers sang and the trumpets blew, until all the burnt
offerings were finished. 29 Then the king and everyone with him bowed down in worship.
30 King Hezekiah and the officials ordered the Levites to praise the LORD with the psalms
of David and Asaph the seer. So they offered joyous praise and bowed down in worship.
31 Then Hezekiah declared, "The dedication ceremony has come to an end. Now bring
your sacrifices and thanksgiving offerings to the Temple of the LORD." So the people
brought their sacrifices and thanksgiving offerings, and those whose hearts were willing
brought burnt offerings, too. 32 The people brought to the LORD seventy bulls, one
hundred rams, and two hundred lambs for burnt offerings. 33 They also brought six
hundred bulls and three thousand sheep as sacrifices. 34 But there were too few priests to
prepare all the burnt offerings, so their relatives the Levites helped them until the work
was finished and until more priests had been purified. For the Levites had been more
conscientious about purifying themselves than the priests. 35 There was an abundance of
burnt offerings, along with the usual drink offerings, and a great deal of fat from the
many peace offerings. So the Temple of the LORD was restored to service. 36 And
Hezekiah and all the people rejoiced greatly because of what God had done for the
people, for everything had been accomplished so quickly.

Preparations for Passover

30 King Hezekiah now sent word to all Israel and Judah, and he wrote letters of
invitation to Ephraim and Manasseh. He asked everyone to come to the Temple
of the LORD at Jerusalem to celebrate the Passover of the LORD, the God of Israel. 2 The
king, his officials, and all the community of Jerusalem decided to celebrate Passover in
midspring.* 3 Passover was normally celebrated one month earlier, in early spring,* but
not enough priests could be purified by that time, and the people had not yet assembled
at Jerusalem. 4 This plan for keeping the Passover seemed right to the king and all the

29:22 Lev 4:18
29:23 Lev 4:15
29:24 Lev 4:26
29:25 2 Sam 7:2; 24:11 1 Chr 25:6 2 Chr 8:14
29:26 1 Chr 23:5 2 Chr 5:12
29:27 2 Chr 23:18
29:29 2 Chr 20:18
29:31 Exod 35:5, 22 2 Chr 13:9
29:34 2 Chr 30:3; 35:11
29:35 Lev 3:16 Num 15:5-10 2 Chr 29:32
30:2 Num 9:10-11 2 Chr 30:13, 15
30:3 2 Chr 29:34

30:2 Hebrew *in the second month.* This month of the Hebrew lunar calendar usually occurs in April and May.
30:3 Hebrew *in the first month.* This month of the Hebrew lunar calendar usually occurs in March and April.

29:22 The blood sprinkled on the altar represented the innocence of the sacrificed animal taking the place of the guilt of the person making the offering. The animal died so the sinner could live. This ritual looked forward to the day when Jesus Christ, God's perfect Son, would sacrifice his innocent life on the cross in order that the sinful and guilty human race might be spared the punishment it deserves (Hebrews 10:1-14).

29:30 A seer was someone who received messages from God for the nation through visions or dreams.

29:31 A thanksgiving offering, one type of peace offering (see Leviticus 7:12-15), was given as an expression of gratitude to God. As a peace offering, it symbolized restored peace and fellowship with God.

30:1 The Passover celebration commemorated the time when God spared the lives of Israel's firstborn sons in Egypt. God had promised to send a plague to kill all the firstborn sons except in those homes where the blood of a slain lamb had been painted on the doorframes. The Israelites obeyed, and when the destroyer saw the blood, he "passed over" the house and did not harm anyone in it (Exodus 12:23). After this plague, Pharaoh freed the Israelites from slavery. This celebration was to be a yearly reminder of how God delivered his people. The careful preparations, both in the Temple and for the festival, show that this was not a temporary or impulsive revival, but a deep-seated change of heart and life.

30:2, 3 God's law had a provision that, under certain circumstances, the Passover could be celebrated one month later (Numbers 9:10, 11).

30:5 Judg 20:1

people. 5 So they sent a proclamation throughout all Israel, from Beersheba in the south
to Dan in the north, inviting everyone to come to Jerusalem to celebrate the Passover of
the LORD, the God of Israel. The people had not been celebrating it in great numbers as
prescribed in the law.

30:6 2 Chr 28:20; Esth 8:14; Job 9:25; Jer 51:31

6 At the king's command, messengers were sent throughout Israel and Judah. They
carried letters which said:

"O people of Israel, return to the LORD, the God of Abraham, Isaac, and Israel,* so
that he will return to the few of us who have survived the conquest of the Assyrian

30:7 2 Chr 29:8; Ezek 20:13, 18

kings. 7 Do not be like your ancestors and relatives who abandoned the LORD, the
God of their ancestors, and became an object of derision, as you yourselves can see.

30:8 Exod 3:29; 2 Chr 29:10

8 Do not be stubborn, as they were, but submit yourselves to the LORD. Come to his
Temple which he has set apart as holy forever. Worship the LORD your God so that

30:9 Exod 34:6-7; Deut 30:2; Mic 7:18

his fierce anger will turn away from you. 9 For if you return to the LORD, your relatives and your children will be treated mercifully by their captors, and they will be
able to return to this land. For the LORD your God is gracious and merciful. If you
return to him, he will not continue to turn his face from you."

Celebration of Passover

30:10 2 Chr 36:16

10 The messengers went from town to town throughout Ephraim and Manasseh and as
far as the territory of Zebulun. But most of the people just laughed at the messengers and

30:11 2 Chr 30:18, 21, 35

made fun of them. 11 However, some from Asher, Manasseh, and Zebulun humbled
themselves and went to Jerusalem. 12 At the same time, God's hand was on the people in
the land of Judah, giving them a strong desire to unite in obeying the orders of the king

30:13 2 Chr 30:2

and his officials, who were following the word of the LORD. 13 And so a huge crowd
assembled at Jerusalem in midspring* to celebrate Passover and the Festival of Unleav-

30:14 2 Chr 28:24; 29:16

ened Bread. 14 They set to work and removed the pagan altars from Jerusalem. They took
away all the incense altars and threw them into the Kidron Valley.

30:15 2 Chr 29:34; 30:2-3

15 On the appointed day in midspring,* the people slaughtered their Passover lambs.
Then the priests and Levites became ashamed, so they purified themselves and brought

30:16 2 Chr 35:10, 15

burnt offerings to the Temple of the LORD. 16 They took their places at the Temple
according to the regulations found in the law of Moses, the man of God. The Levites
brought the sacrificial blood to the priests, who then sprinkled it on the altar.

17 Since many of the people there had not purified themselves, the Levites had to

30:18 Exod 12:43-49; Num 9:6-10

slaughter their Passover lambs for them, to set them apart for the LORD. 18 Most of those
who came from Ephraim, Manasseh, Issachar, and Zebulun had not purified themselves.
But King Hezekiah prayed for them, and they were allowed to eat the Passover meal
anyway, even though this was contrary to God's laws. For Hezekiah said, "May the

30:6 *Israel* is the name that God gave to Jacob. **30:13** Hebrew *in the second month.* This month of the Hebrew lunar calendar usually occurs in April and May. **30:15** Hebrew *On the fourteenth day of the second month.* This day of the Hebrew lunar calendar occurs in late April or early May.

30:6-9 Hezekiah was a king dedicated to God and to the spiritual progress of the nation. He sent letters throughout Judah and Israel urging everyone to return to God. He told them not to be stubborn but to submit to the Lord. To submit means to obey him first, yielding our bodies, minds, wills, and emotions to him. His Holy Spirit must guide and renew every part of us. Only then will we be able to temper our stubborn selfishness.

30:10 The northern kingdom of Israel had recently been conquered by Assyria, and most of the people had been carried away to foreign lands. Hezekiah sent a proclamation to the few people who remained, inviting them to come to the Passover (30:1), but most responded with scorn and ridicule. People may mock you when you try to promote spiritual renewal and growth. Are you prepared to be ridiculed for your faith? When it comes your way, do not waver. Stand strong in your faith, as Hezekiah did, and God will honor you.

30:11 These people invited to the Passover scorned Hezekiah's messengers, but some accepted the invitation. Our efforts to tell others about God often meet with similar reactions. Many people will laugh at an invitation to accept Christ. But this must not stop us from reaching out. If you know and understand that rejecting the gospel is common, you can guard against feelings of personal rejection. Remember that the Holy Spirit convicts and convinces. Our task is to invite others to consider God's actions, his claims, and his promises.

30:14 Just as the priests had purified the Temple (29:4, 5), so the people cleared the city of pagan idols and then purified themselves to prepare for worship (30:17-19). Even the good kings of Judah found it difficult to get rid of the idols and altars in the pagan shrines (2 Kings 14:4; 2 Chronicles 20:33). Finally, Hezekiah, with the help of his people, completed this task.

30:15 The people were so zealous to celebrate the Passover and bring offerings to the Temple that the priests and Levites were ashamed they did not share the same enthusiasm. The zeal of common people's faith motivated the ministers to take action. Devout laypersons today can motivate professional church staff to rekindle their enthusiasm for God's work. Laypersons should never be shut out of church government or decision making. The church needs their good examples of faith.

LORD, who is good, pardon those [19]who decide to follow the LORD, the God of their
ancestors, even though they are not properly cleansed for the ceremony." [20]And the
LORD listened to Hezekiah's prayer and healed the people.
[21]So the people of Israel who were present in Jerusalem celebrated the Festival of
Unleavened Bread for seven days with great joy. Each day the Levites and priests sang
to the LORD, accompanied by loud instruments.* [22]Hezekiah encouraged the Levites for
the skill they displayed as they served the LORD. So for seven days the celebration
continued. Peace offerings were sacrificed, and the people confessed their sins to the
LORD, the God of their ancestors.
[23]The entire assembly then decided to continue the festival another seven days, so they
celebrated joyfully for another week. [24]King Hezekiah gave the people one thousand bulls
and seven thousand sheep for offerings, and the officials donated one thousand bulls and
ten thousand sheep. Meanwhile, many more priests purified themselves.
[25]The entire assembly of Judah rejoiced, including the priests, the Levites, all who
came from the land of Israel, the foreigners who came to the festival, and all those who
lived in Judah. [26]There was great joy in the city, for Jerusalem had not seen a celebration
like this one since the days of Solomon, King David's son. [27]Then the Levitical priests
stood and blessed the people, and God heard them from his holy dwelling in heaven.

Hezekiah's Religious Reforms

31 Now when the festival ended, the Israelites who attended went to all the towns of
Judah, Benjamin, Ephraim, and Manasseh, and they smashed the sacred pillars,
cut down the Asherah poles, and removed the pagan shrines and altars. After this, the
Israelites returned to their own towns and homes.
[2]Hezekiah then organized the priests and Levites into divisions to offer the burnt
offerings and peace offerings, and to worship and give thanks and praise to the LORD at
the gates of the Temple. [3]The king also made a personal contribution of animals for the
daily morning and evening burnt offerings, as well as for the weekly Sabbath festivals
and monthly new moon festivals, and for the other annual festivals as required in the law
of the LORD. [4]In addition, he required the people in Jerusalem to bring the prescribed
portion of their income to the priests and Levites, so they could devote themselves fully
to the law of the LORD.
[5]The people responded immediately and generously with the first of their crops and
grain, new wine, olive oil, honey, and all the produce of their fields. They brought a tithe
of all they owned. [6]The people who had moved to Judah from Israel, and the people of
Judah themselves, brought in the tithes of their cattle and sheep and a tithe of the things
that had been dedicated to the LORD their God, and they piled them up in great heaps.
[7]The first of these tithes was brought in late spring,* and the heaps continued to grow
until early autumn.* [8]When Hezekiah and his officials came and saw these huge piles,
they thanked the LORD and his people Israel!
[9]"Where did all this come from?" Hezekiah asked the priests and Levites.
[10]And Azariah the high priest, from the family of Zadok, replied, "Since the people

30:21 Exod 12:15; 13:6
30:22 2 Chr 32:6; Ezra 10:11
30:23 1 Kgs 8:65
30:24 2 Chr 29:34; 30:3; 35:7-8
30:25 2 Chr 30:11, 18
30:26 2 Chr 7:8-10
30:27 Num 6:23; Deut 26:15; 2 Chr 23:18; Ps 68:5
31:1 2 Kgs 18:4
31:2 1 Chr 23:28-31; 24:1
31:3 Num 28:1-29, 40; 2 Chr 35:7
31:4 Num 18:8
31:5 Neh 13:12
31:6 Lev 27:30; Deut 14:28
31:10 1 Chr 6:8-9; Mal 3:10

30:21 Or *sang to the LORD with all their strength.* **31:7a** Hebrew *in the third month.* This month of the Hebrew lunar calendar usually occurs in May and June. **31:7b** Hebrew *in the seventh month.* This month of the Hebrew lunar calendar usually occurs in September and October.

30:22 One important purpose of the peace offering was to express gratitude to God for health or for safety in times of crisis.

30:26 It had been more than 200 years since there had been such a celebration in Jerusalem.

31:1ff Why was idol worship so bad? The Israelites had access to the one true God, but they constantly fell into worshiping lifeless idols made of wood or stone. They put aside worshiping the Creator in order to worship the creation. We are just as guilty when God no longer holds first place in our lives. When we think more about wealth, pleasure, prestige, or material possessions than about God, we are actually worshiping them as gods. Because of idol worship, the people of Judah were eventually sent into captivity in foreign lands (36:14-17). We may not be sent into captivity, but discipline awaits all those who continually put earthly desires above spiritual priorities.

31:2-21 The priests had not been supported by the government during the evil kings' reigns. Now that the Temple was repaired, Hezekiah organized the priests and resumed the work of the Temple according to the plan originally set up by David (1 Chronicles 23:6-23; 24:3-19).

31:4-8 Hezekiah reinstated the practice of tithing—giving a tenth of one's income to the priests and Levites so they could be free to serve God and minister to the people. The people responded immediately and generously. God's work needs the support of God's people. Does God receive a regular percentage of your income? Generosity makes our giving delightful to us and to God (2 Corinthians 8; 9). How different the church would be today if all believers consistently followed this pattern.

began bringing their gifts to the LORD's Temple, we have had enough to eat and plenty
to spare, for the LORD has blessed his people."
31:11 1 Kgs 6:5, 8 [11]Hezekiah decided to have storerooms prepared in the Temple of the LORD, and this
was done. [12]Then all the gifts and tithes were faithfully brought to the Temple. Conaniah
the Levite was put in charge, assisted by his brother Shimei. [13]The supervisors under
them were Jehiel, Azaziah, Nahath, Asahel, Jerimoth, Jozabad, Eliel, Ismakiah, Mahath,
and Benaiah. These appointments were made by King Hezekiah and Azariah, the chief
official in the Temple of God.
[14]Kore son of Imnah the Levite, who was the gatekeeper at the East Gate, was put in
charge of distributing the freewill offerings of God, the gifts, and the things that had been
31:15 Josh 21:9-19; 2 Chr 29:12 dedicated to the LORD. [15]His faithful assistants were Eden, Miniamin, Jeshua, Shemaiah,
Amariah, and Shecaniah. They distributed the gifts among the families of priests in their
towns, by their divisions, dividing the gifts fairly among young and old alike. [16]They
also distributed the gifts to all males three years old or older, regardless of their place in
the genealogical records, who came daily to the LORD's Temple to perform their official
31:17 1 Chr 23:24 duties, by their divisions. [17]And they distributed gifts to the priests who were listed in
the genealogical records by families, and to the Levites twenty years old or older who
were listed according to their jobs and their divisions. [18]Food allotments were also given
to all the families listed in the genealogical records, including the little babies, the wives,
31:19 Lev 25:34; Num 35:2; 2 Chr 31:12-15 and the sons and daughters. For they had all been faithful in purifying themselves. [19]As
for the priests, the descendants of Aaron, who were living in the open villages around
the towns, men were appointed to distribute portions to every male among the priests
and to all the Levites listed in the genealogical records.
31:20-21 //2 Kgs 18:5-7 [20]In this way, King Hezekiah handled the distribution throughout all Judah, doing
what was pleasing and good in the sight of the LORD his God. [21]In all that he did in the
service of the Temple of God and in his efforts to follow the law and the commands,
Hezekiah sought his God wholeheartedly. As a result, he was very successful.

Assyria Invades Judah

32:1 Isa 36:1–37:38 **32** After Hezekiah had faithfully carried out this work, King Sennacherib of Assyria
invaded Judah. He laid siege to the fortified cities, giving orders for his army to
break through their walls. [2]When Hezekiah realized that Sennacherib also intended to

THE DAVIDIC DYNASTY

David (40 years, 1 Chr. 10—29)	Uzziah (Azariah) (52 years, 2 Chr. 26)
Solomon (40 years, 2 Chr. 1—9)	Jotham (16 years, 2 Chr. 27)
Rehoboam (17 years, 2 Chr. 10—12)	Ahaz (16 years, 2 Chr. 28)
Abijah (3 years, 2 Chr. 13)	Hezekiah (29 years, 2 Chr. 29—32)
Asa (41 years, 2 Chr. 14—16)	Manasseh (55 years, 2 Chr. 33:1–20)
Jehoshaphat (25 years, 2 Chr. 17—20)	Amon (2 years, 2 Chr. 33:21–25)
Jehoram (8 years, 2 Chr. 21)	Josiah (31 years, 2 Chr. 34—35)
Ahaziah (1 year, 2 Chr. 22:1–9)	Jehoahaz (3 months, 2 Chr. 36:1–4)
Athaliah (6 years, 2 Chr. 22:10—23:21)	Jehoiakim (11 years, 2 Chr. 36:5–8)
Joash (40 years, 2 Chr. 24)	Jehoiachin (3 months, 2 Chr. 36:9–10)
Amaziah (29 years, 2 Chr. 25)	Zedekiah (11 years, 2 Chr. 36:11–16)

The Lord promised David that his kingdom would endure and his throne would be established forever (2 Samuel 7:16). As a partial fulfillment of this promise, David and his descendants ruled Judah for over 400 years. Jesus Christ was a direct descendant of David and was the ultimate fulfillment of this promise (Acts 2:22–36).

31:20, 21 Because Hezekiah did "what was pleasing and good in the sight of the LORD his God," he led the people of Judah in spiritual renewal. His actions serve as a model of renewal for us: (1) He remembered God's compassion (30:9); (2) he kept going despite ridicule (30:10); (3) he aggressively removed evil influences from his life (30:14; 31:1); (4) he interceded for the people, asking for the Lord's pardon (30:15-20); (5) he was open to spontaneity in worship (30:23); (6) he contributed generously to God's work (31:3). If any of these are lacking in your life, consider how they might apply, and renew your commitment to God.

32:1 Assyria was a great empire by Hezekiah's time, controlling most of the Middle East. From a small strip of land located in present-day Iran and Iraq, it began to establish its power under Ashurnasirpal II (883–859 B.C.) and his son Shalmaneser III (859–824). Under Tiglath-pileser III (745–727), Assyria's boundaries extended to the borders of Israel, making it one of the largest empires in ancient history. Shalmaneser V destroyed the northern kingdom in 722, and his grandson Sennacherib (705–681) tried to bring Judah, the southern kingdom, under his control. Less than a century later, Assyria would lie in ruins (612).

attack Jerusalem, 3he consulted with his officials and military advisers, and they decided
to stop the flow of the springs outside the city. 4They organized a huge work crew to stop **32:4** 2 Kgs 20:20
the flow of the springs, cutting off the brook that ran through the fields. For they said, 2 Chr 32:30
"Why should the kings of Assyria come here and find plenty of water?"
5Then Hezekiah further strengthened his defenses by repairing the wall wherever it **32:5** 1 Kgs 9:24
was broken down and by adding to the fortifications and constructing a second wall 2 Kgs 25:4
outside the first. He also reinforced the Millo* in the City of David and manufactured 2 Chr 25:23
large numbers of weapons and shields. 6He appointed military officers over the people **32:6**
and asked them to assemble before him in the square at the city gate. Then Hezekiah 2 Chr 30:22
encouraged them with this address: 7"Be strong and courageous! Don't be afraid of the **32:7** 2 Kgs 6:16
king of Assyria or his mighty army, for there is a power far greater on our side! 8He may 1 Chr 22:13
have a great army, but they are just men. We have the LORD our God to help us and to **32:8**
fight our battles for us!" These words greatly encouraged the people. 2 Chr 20:17 Jer 17:5

Sennacherib Threatens Jerusalem

9Then King Sennacherib of Assyria, while still besieging the town of Lachish, sent **32:9-19** //2 Kgs 18:17-35
officials to Jerusalem with this message for Hezekiah and all the people in the city: //Isa 36:2-20

10"This is what King Sennacherib of Assyria says: What are you trusting in that
makes you think you can survive my siege of Jerusalem? 11Hezekiah has said, 'The
LORD our God will rescue us from the king of Assyria.' Surely Hezekiah is misleading you, sentencing you to death by famine and thirst! 12Surely you must realize **32:12** 2 Chr 31:1
that Hezekiah is the very person who destroyed all the LORD's shrines and altars.
He commanded Judah and Jerusalem to worship at only the one altar at the Temple
and to make sacrifices on it alone.
13"Surely you must realize what I and the other kings of Assyria before me have **32:13** 2 Kgs 18:33-35
done to all the people of the earth! Were any of the gods of those nations able to **32:14**
rescue their people from my power? 14Name just one time when any god, any- Isa 10:9-11
where, was able to rescue his people from me! What makes you think your God can
do any better? 15Don't let Hezekiah fool you! Don't let him deceive you like this! I
say it again—no god of any nation has ever yet been able to rescue his people from
me or my ancestors. How much less will your God rescue you from my power!"

32:5 Or *the supporting terraces.*

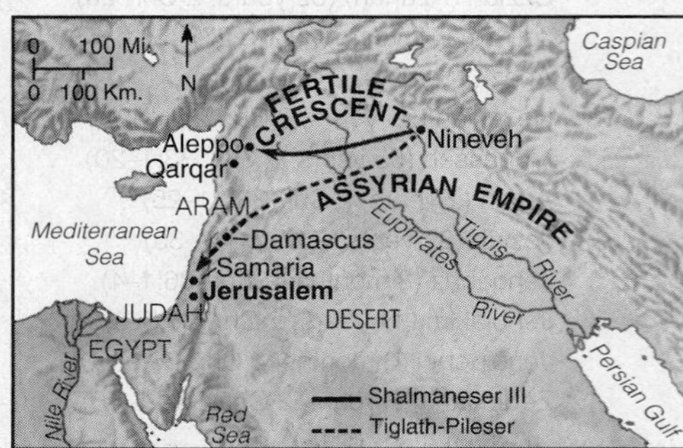

THE ASSYRIAN EMPIRE The mighty Assyrian Empire extended from the Persian Gulf, across the Fertile Crescent, and south to Egypt. Shalmaneser III extended the empire toward the Mediterranean Sea by conquering cities as far west as Qarqar. Tiglath-pileser extended the empire south into Aram, Israel, Judah, and Philistia. It was Shalmaneser V who destroyed Samaria, Israel's capital.

32:1 Sennacherib wanted to conquer these cities so he could force them to pay tribute. Forcing captured cities to pay tribute was a way for kings to build their income base. Often Assyria would require an oath of allegiance from a country, including the promise to pay taxes in the form of livestock, wine, battle equipment (horses, chariots, weapons), gold, silver, and anything else that pleased the invading king. Tribute was more important to Assyria than captives because captives cost money. Thus, captives were taken only in cases of extreme rebellion or to repopulate cities that had been destroyed.

32:1ff When Hezekiah was confronted with the frightening prospect of an Assyrian invasion, he made two important decisions. He did everything he could to deal with the situation, and he trusted God for the outcome. That is exactly what we must do when faced with difficult or frightening situations. Take all the steps you possibly can to solve the problem or improve the situation. But also commit the situation to God in prayer, trusting him for the solution.

32:3, 4 Cities had to be built near reliable water sources. Natural springs were some of Jerusalem's major sources of water. In a brilliant military move, Hezekiah plugged the springs outside the city and channeled the water through an underground tunnel (32:30); therefore, Jerusalem would have water even through a long siege. Hezekiah's tunnel has been discovered along with an inscription describing how it was built: Two groups of workers started digging underground, one in Jerusalem and one at the Gihon Spring, and they met in the middle.

32:7, 8 Hezekiah could see with eyes of faith. The number of his opponents meant nothing as long as he was on the Lord's side. Victory is "not by force nor by strength, but by my Spirit, says the LORD Almighty" (Zechariah 4:6). Hezekiah could confidently encourage his men because he had no doubt about where he stood with God. Are you on the Lord's side? You may never face an enemy army, but the battles you face every day can be won with God's strength.

32:17
2 Chr 32:14

16 And Sennacherib's officials further mocked the LORD God and his servant Hezekiah, heaping insult upon insult. 17 The king also sent letters scorning the LORD, the God
of Israel. He wrote, "Just as the gods of all the other nations failed to rescue their people
from my power, so the God of Hezekiah will also fail." 18 The Assyrian officials who
brought the letters shouted this in the Hebrew language to the people gathered on the
walls of the city, trying to terrify them so it would be easier to capture the city. 19 These
officials talked about the God of Jerusalem as though he were one of the pagan gods,
made by human hands.

32:20-21
//2 Kgs 19:35-37
//Isa 37:36-38

20 Then King Hezekiah and the prophet Isaiah son of Amoz cried out in prayer to God
in heaven. 21 And the LORD sent an angel who destroyed the Assyrian army with all its
commanders and officers. So Sennacherib returned home in disgrace to his own land.
And when he entered the temple of his god, some of his own sons killed him there with
a sword. 22 That is how the LORD rescued Hezekiah and the people of Jerusalem from
King Sennacherib of Assyria and from all the others who threatened them. So there was

32:23
2 Sam 8:10

peace at last throughout the land. 23 From then on King Hezekiah became highly
respected among the surrounding nations, and many gifts for the LORD arrived at
Jerusalem, with valuable presents for King Hezekiah, too.

Hezekiah's Sickness and Recovery

32:24-33
//2 Kgs 20:1-21
//Isa 37:21-38; 38:1-8

24 About that time, Hezekiah became deathly ill. He prayed to the LORD, who healed him
and gave him a miraculous sign. 25 But Hezekiah did not respond appropriately to the
kindness shown him, and he became proud. So the LORD's anger came against him and

32:25
2 Chr 24:18; 26:16

against Judah and Jerusalem. 26 Then Hezekiah repented of his pride, and the people of

32:26
Jer 26:18-19

Jerusalem humbled themselves. So the LORD's anger did not come against them during
Hezekiah's lifetime.
27 Hezekiah was very wealthy and held in high esteem. He had to build special treasury
buildings for his silver, gold, precious stones, and spices, and for his shields and other
valuable items. 28 He also constructed many storehouses for his grain, new wine, and olive

32:29
1 Chr 29:12

oil; and he made many stalls for his cattle and folds for his flocks of sheep and goats. 29 He
built many towns and acquired vast flocks and herds, for God had given him great wealth.

32:30
1 Kgs 1:33
2 Kgs 20:20

30 He blocked up the upper spring of Gihon and brought the water down through a tunnel
to the west side of the City of David. And so he succeeded in everything he did.

32:31
Deut 8:16
2 Kgs 20:12
2 Chr 32:24
Isa 38:7-8; 39:1

31 However, when ambassadors arrived from Babylon to ask about the remarkable
events that had taken place in the land, God withdrew from Hezekiah in order to test him
and to see what was really in his heart.

Summary of Hezekiah's Reign

32 The rest of the events of Hezekiah's reign and his acts of devotion are recorded in *The
Vision of the Prophet Isaiah Son of Amoz,* which is included in *The Book of the Kings of
Judah and Israel.* 33 When Hezekiah died, he was buried in the upper area of the royal
cemetery, and all Judah and Jerusalem honored him at his death. Then his son Manasseh
became the next king.

32:31 A test can bring out a person's true character. God tested Hezekiah to see what he was really like and to show him his own shortcomings and the attitude of his heart. God did not totally abandon Hezekiah, nor did he tempt him to sin or trick him. The test was meant to strengthen Hezekiah, develop his character, and prepare him for the tasks ahead. In times of success, most of us can live good lives. But pressure, trouble, or pain will quickly remove our thin veneer of goodness unless our strength comes from God. What are you like under pressure or when everything is going wrong? Do you give in or turn to God? Those who are consistently in touch with God don't have to worry about what pressure may reveal about them.

32:31 Babylon was slowly and quietly rising to become a world power. At the same time, the Assyrian Empire was slowly declining due to internal strife and a succession of weak kings. When Assyria was finally crushed in 612 B.C., Babylon, under Nebuchadnezzar, moved into its place of prominence. (For more information on Babylon, see the note on 2 Kings 20:14.)

32:31 Why did God leave Hezekiah to himself? After Hezekiah was healed of his sickness, he became proud. When ambassadors came to inquire about his miraculous healing, God stepped back to see how Hezekiah would respond. Unfortunately, Hezekiah's actions revealed his runaway pride. He pointed to his own accomplishments rather than to God (see 2 Kings 20:12-19). Pride is any attitude that elevates our effort or abilities above God's or treats with disdain his work in us. It causes us to congratulate ourselves for our successes and to look down on other people. God does not object to self-confidence, healthy self-esteem, or good feelings about our accomplishments. He objects to the foolish attitude of taking full credit for what he has done or for setting ourselves up as superior to others.

Manasseh Rules in Judah

33 Manasseh was twelve years old when he became king, and he reigned in Jerusalem fifty-five years. 2He did what was evil in the LORD's sight, imitating the
detestable practices of the pagan nations whom the LORD had driven from the land ahead
of the Israelites. 3He rebuilt the pagan shrines his father Hezekiah had destroyed. He
constructed altars for the images of Baal and set up Asherah poles. He also bowed before
all the stars of heaven and worshiped them. 4He even built pagan altars in the Temple of
the LORD, the place where the LORD had said his name should be honored forever. 5He
put these altars for the stars of heaven in both courtyards of the LORD's Temple.
6Manasseh even sacrificed his own sons in the fire* in the valley of the son of Hinnom.
He practiced sorcery, divination, and witchcraft, and he consulted with mediums and
psychics. He did much that was evil in the LORD's sight, arousing his anger.
7Manasseh even took a carved idol he had made and set it up in God's Temple, the
very place where God had told David and his son Solomon: "My name will be honored
here forever in this Temple and in Jerusalem—the city I have chosen from among all the
other tribes of Israel. 8If the Israelites will obey my commands—all the instructions,
laws, and regulations given through Moses—I will not send them into exile from this
land that I gave their ancestors." 9But Manasseh led the people of Judah and Jerusalem
to do even more evil than the pagan nations whom the LORD had destroyed when the
Israelites entered the land.
10The LORD spoke to Manasseh and his people, but they ignored all his warnings. 11So
the LORD sent the Assyrian armies, and they took Manasseh prisoner. They put a ring
through his nose, bound him in bronze chains, and led him away to Babylon. 12But while
in deep distress, Manasseh sought the LORD his God and cried out humbly to the God of
his ancestors. 13And when he prayed, the LORD listened to him and was moved by his
request for help. So the LORD let Manasseh return to Jerusalem and to his kingdom.
Manasseh had finally realized that the LORD alone is God!
14It was after this that Manasseh rebuilt the outer wall of the City of David, from west
of the Gihon Spring in the Kidron Valley to the Fish Gate, and continuing around the hill
of Ophel, where it was built very high. And he stationed his military officers in all of the
fortified cities of Judah. 15Manasseh also removed the foreign gods from the hills and
the idol from the LORD's Temple. He tore down all the altars he had built on the hill where
the Temple stood and all the altars that were in Jerusalem, and he dumped them outside
the city. 16Then he restored the altar of the LORD and sacrificed peace offerings and
thanksgiving offerings on it. He also encouraged the people of Judah to worship the
LORD, the God of Israel. 17However, the people still sacrificed at the pagan shrines, but
only to the LORD their God.
18The rest of the events of Manasseh's reign, his prayer to God, and the words the
seers spoke to him in the name of the LORD, the God of Israel, are recorded in *The Book*
of the Kings of Israel. 19Manasseh's prayer, the account of the way God answered him,
and an account of all his sins and unfaithfulness are recorded in *The Record of the Seers.**
It includes a list of the locations where he built pagan shrines and set up Asherah poles

33:1-10 //2 Kgs 21:1-10
33:2 2 Chr 28:3
33:3 Deut 16:21; 2 Kgs 23:5-6; 2 Chr 31:1
33:4 2 Chr 7:16; 28:24
33:5 2 Chr 4:9
33:6 Lev 19:31; 20:27; 2 Chr 28:3
33:8 2 Sam 7:10
33:11 Deut 28:36; 2 Chr 36:6
33:12 2 Chr 32:26
33:13 Ezra 8:23; Dan 4:25, 32
33:14 1 Kgs 1:33; 2 Chr 27:3; Neh 3:3
33:15 2 Chr 33:3-7
33:17 2 Chr 32:12
33:18-20 //2 Kgs 21:17-18
33:19 2 Chr 33:3, 13

33:6 Or *even made his sons pass through the fire.* **33:19** Or *The Record of Hozai.*

33:6 Sorcery is using power gained from evil spirits. Divination is predicting the future through omens.

33:11 Between 652 and 648 B.C., the city of Babylon rebelled against Assyria. The rebellion was crushed, but Assyria may have suspected that Manasseh supported it. That may explain why Manasseh was taken to Babylon for trial rather than to the Assyrian capital of Nineveh.

33:12, 13 In a list of corrupt kings, Manasseh would rank near the top. His life was a catalog of evil deeds including idol worship, sacrificing his own children, and Temple desecration. Eventually, however, he realized his sins and cried out to God for forgiveness. And God listened. If God can forgive Manasseh, surely he can forgive anyone. Are you burdened by overpowering guilt? Do you doubt that anyone could forgive what you have done? Take heart—until death, no one is beyond the reach of God's forgiveness.

33:17 Although the people worshiped God alone, they worshiped him in the wrong way. God had told them to make their sacrifices only in certain places (Deuteronomy 12:13, 14). This kept them from changing their way of worship and protected them against the dangerous influence of pagan religious practices. Unfortunately, the people continued to use these places of worship, not realizing that (1) they were adopting practices God opposed, and (2) these places were against God's law. They were mixing pagan beliefs with worship of God. Blending religious ideas leads to confusion about who God really is. We must take care that subtle secular influences do not distort our worship practices.

and idols before he repented. 20 When Manasseh died, he was buried at his palace. Then his son Amon became the next king.

Amon Rules in Judah

33:21-25
//2 Kgs 21:19-24

33:23
2 Chr 33:12, 19

33:24
2 Chr 25:27

21 Amon was twenty-two years old when he became king, and he reigned in Jerusalem two years. 22 He did what was evil in the LORD's sight, just as his father Manasseh had done. He worshiped and sacrificed to all the idols his father had made. 23 But unlike his father, he did not humble himself before the LORD. Instead, Amon sinned even more.

24 At last Amon's own officials plotted against him and assassinated him in his palace. 25 But the people of the land killed all those who had conspired against King Amon, and they made his son Josiah the next king.

Josiah Rules in Judah

34:1-2
//2 Kgs 22:1-2

34:2
2 Chr 29:2

34 Josiah was eight years old when he became king, and he reigned in Jerusalem thirty-one years. 2 He did what was pleasing in the LORD's sight and followed the example of his ancestor David. He did not turn aside from doing what was right.

34:3
1 Kgs 13:2
2 Chr 15:2; 33:17, 22

34:4
Exod 32:20
2 Kgs 23:4-5, 11

3 During the eighth year of his reign, while he was still young, Josiah began to seek the God of his ancestor David. Then in the twelfth year, he began to purify Judah and Jerusalem, destroying all the pagan shrines, the Asherah poles, and the carved idols and cast images. 4 He saw to it that the altars for the images of Baal and their incense altars were torn down. He also made sure that the Asherah poles, the carved idols, and

MANASSEH

Even a brief outline of King Manasseh's evil sickens us, and we wonder how God could ever forgive him. Not only did he intentionally offend God by desecrating Solomon's Temple with idols, but he also worshiped pagan gods and even sacrificed his children to them! Child sacrifice is a vile act of pagan idolatry, an act against both God and people. Such blatant sins require severe correction.

God showed justice to Manasseh in warning and punishing him. He showed mercy in responding to Manasseh's heartfelt repentance by forgiving and restoring him. Given the nature of Manasseh's rebellion, we are not surprised by God's punishment—defeat and exile at the hands of the Assyrians. But Manasseh's repentance and God's forgiveness are unexpected. Manasseh's life was changed. He was given a new start.

How far has God gone to get your attention? Have you ever, like Manasseh, come to your senses and cried out to God for help? Only your repentance and a prayer for a new attitude stand between you and God's complete forgiveness.

Strengths and accomplishments
- Despite the bitter consequences of his sins, he learned from them
- Humbly repented of his sins before God

Weaknesses and mistakes
- Challenged God's authority and was defeated
- Reversed many of the positive effects of his father Hezekiah's rule
- Sacrificed his children to idols

Lessons from his life
- God will go a long way to get someone's attention
- Forgiveness is limited, not by the amount of sin, but by our willingness to repent

Vital statistics
- Where: Jerusalem
- Occupation: King of Judah
- Relatives: Father: Hezekiah. Mother: Hephzibah. Son: Amon

Key verses
"But while in deep distress, Manasseh sought the LORD his God and cried out humbly to the God of his ancestors. And when he prayed, the LORD listened to him and was moved by his request for help. So the LORD let Manasseh return to Jerusalem and to his kingdom. Manasseh had finally realized that the LORD alone is God!" (2 Chronicles 33:12, 13).

Manasseh's story is told in 2 Kings 21:1–18 and 2 Chronicles 32:33—33:20. He is also mentioned in Jeremiah 15:4.

34:1 Josiah's Profile is found in 2 Kings 23.

34:3 In Josiah's day, boys were considered men at age 12. By 16, Josiah understood the responsibility of his office. Even at this young age, he showed greater wisdom than many of the older kings who came before him because he had decided to seek the Lord God and his wisdom. Don't let your age hinder you from serving God.

the cast images were smashed and scattered over the graves of those who had
sacrificed to them. [5]Then he burned the bones of the pagan priests on their own altars,
and so he purified Judah and Jerusalem.
[6]He did the same thing in the towns of Manasseh, Ephraim, and Simeon, even as far
as Naphtali. [7]He destroyed the pagan altars and the Asherah poles, and he crushed the
idols into dust. He cut down the incense altars throughout the land of Israel and then
returned to Jerusalem.
[8]In the eighteenth year of his reign, after he had purified the land and the Temple,
Josiah appointed Shaphan son of Azaliah, Maaseiah the governor of Jerusalem, and Joah
son of Joahaz, the royal historian, to repair the Temple of the LORD his God. [9]They gave
Hilkiah the high priest the money that had been collected by the Levites who served as
gatekeepers at the Temple of God. The gifts were brought by people from Manasseh,
Ephraim, and from all the remnant of Israel, as well as from all Judah, Benjamin, and the
people of Jerusalem. [10]He entrusted the money to the men assigned to supervise the
restoration of the LORD's Temple. Then they paid the workers who did the repairs and
renovation. [11]Thus, they hired carpenters and masons and purchased cut stone for the
walls and timber for the rafters and beams. They restored what earlier kings of Judah had
allowed to fall into ruin.
[12]The workers served faithfully under the leadership of Jahath and Obadiah,
Levites of the Merarite clan, and Zechariah and Meshullam, Levites of the Kohathite
clan. Other Levites, all of whom were skilled musicians, [13]were put in charge of
the laborers of the various trades. Still others assisted as secretaries, officials, and
gatekeepers.

34:5 1 Kgs 13:2; 2 Kgs 23:20
34:6 2 Kgs 23:15, 19
34:7 2 Chr 31:1
34:8-13 //2 Kgs 22:3-7
34:8 2 Chr 18:25
34:9 2 Chr 30:10, 18; 35:8
34:11 2 Chr 33:4-7
34:12 1 Chr 25:1
34:13 Neh 4:10

Hilkiah Discovers God's Law

[14]As Hilkiah the high priest was recording the money collected at the LORD's Temple,
he found the Book of the Law of the LORD as it had been given through Moses. [15]Hilkiah
said to Shaphan the court secretary, "I have found the Book of the Law in the LORD's
Temple!" Then Hilkiah gave the scroll to Shaphan.
[16]Shaphan took the scroll to the king and reported, "Your officials are doing
everything they were assigned to do. [17]The money that was collected at the Temple
of the LORD has been given to the supervisors and workmen." [18]Shaphan also said to
the king, "Hilkiah the priest has given me a scroll." So Shaphan read it to the king.
[19]When the king heard what was written in the law, he tore his clothes in
despair. [20]Then he gave these orders to Hilkiah, Ahikam son of Shaphan, Acbor
son of Micaiah,* Shaphan the court secretary, and Asaiah the king's personal
adviser: [21]"Go to the Temple and speak to the LORD for me and for all the remnant
of Israel and Judah. Ask him about the words written in this scroll that has been
found. The LORD's anger has been poured out against us because our ancestors
have not obeyed the word of the LORD. We have not been doing what this scroll
says we must do."
[22]So Hilkiah and the other men went to the newer Mishneh section* of Jerusalem
to consult with the prophet Huldah. She was the wife of Shallum son of Tikvah and
grandson of Harhas,* the keeper of the Temple wardrobe. [23]She said to them, "The
LORD, the God of Israel, has spoken! Go and tell the man who sent you, [24]'This is
what the LORD says: I will certainly destroy this city and its people. All the curses
written in the scroll you have read will come true. [25]For the people of Judah have

34:14-28 //2 Kgs 22:8-20
34:14 2 Chr 34:9
34:19 Josh 7:6
34:21 2 Chr 29:8
34:24 Deut 28:15-68; 2 Chr 36:14-20
34:25 2 Chr 33:3

34:20 As in parallel text at 2 Kgs 22:12; Hebrew reads *Abdon son of Micah.* **34:22a** Or *the Second Quarter,* a newer section of Jerusalem. **34:22b** As in parallel text at 2 Kgs 22:14; Hebrew reads *son of Tokhath, son of Hasrah.*

34:14, 15 The Book of the Law of the Lord that Hilkiah found was probably the book of Deuteronomy that had been lost during the reigns of the evil kings. Now that it was found, Josiah realized that drastic changes had to be made in order to bring the nation back in line with God's commands. This account is also recorded in 2 Kings 22:8-13.

34:19 It is human nature to treat sin lightly—to make excuses, blame somebody else, or minimize the harm done. Not so with Josiah. He was so appalled at the people's neglect of the law that he tore his clothing to express his grief. True understanding of our sins should lead to "sorrow" to "help us turn away from sin" (2 Corinthians 7:10). Are you always excusing your sin, blaming others, and pretending that it's not so bad? God does not take sin lightly, and he wants us to respond with true remorse as Josiah did.

abandoned me and worshiped pagan gods, and I am very angry with them for everything they have done. My anger will be poured out against this place, and nothing will be able to stop it.'

[26]"But go to the king of Judah who sent you to seek the LORD and tell him: 'This is what the LORD, the God of Israel, says concerning the message you have just heard: [27]You were sorry and humbled yourself before God when you heard what I said against this city and its people. You humbled yourself and tore your clothing in despair and wept before me in repentance. So I have indeed heard you, says the LORD. [28]I will not send the promised disaster against this city and its people until after you have died and been buried in peace. You will not see the disaster I am going to bring on this place.'" So they took her message back to the king.

34:27 2 Chr 12:7; 32:26

Josiah's Religious Reforms

34:29-32 //2 Kgs 23:1-3
34:30 Neh 8:1-3
34:31 2 Chr 23:16; 29:10

[29]Then the king summoned all the leaders of Judah and Jerusalem. [30]And the king went up to the Temple of the LORD with all the people of Judah and Jerusalem and the priests and the Levites—all the people from the greatest to the least. There the king read to them the entire Book of the Covenant that had been found in the LORD's Temple. [31]The king took his place of authority beside the pillar and renewed the covenant in the LORD's presence. He pledged to obey the LORD by keeping all his commands, regulations, and laws with all his heart and soul. He promised to obey all the terms of the covenant that were written in the scroll. [32]And he required everyone in Jerusalem and the people of Benjamin to make a similar pledge. As the people of Jerusalem did this, they renewed their covenant with God, the God of their ancestors.

34:33 2 Kgs 11:14; 23:3; 2 Chr 34:3-7

[33]So Josiah removed all detestable idols from the entire land of Israel and required everyone to worship the LORD their God. And throughout the rest of his lifetime, they did not turn away from the LORD, the God of their ancestors.

Josiah Celebrates Passover

35:1 Exod 12:6; Num 9:3; 2 Kgs 23:21-22
35:2 2 Chr 29:11
35:3 1 Chr 23:26; 2 Chr 17:8-9; Neh 8:7
35:4 1 Chr 9:10-13; 2 Chr 8:14
35:6 2 Chr 29:5, 15; 35:1

35 Then Josiah announced that the Passover of the LORD would be celebrated in Jerusalem on the appointed day in early spring.* The Passover lambs were slaughtered at twilight of that day. [2]Josiah also assigned the priests to their duties and encouraged them in their work at the Temple of the LORD. [3]He issued this order to the Levites, who had been set apart to serve the LORD and were teachers in Israel: "Since the Ark is now in Solomon's Temple and you do not need to carry it back and forth on your shoulders, spend your time serving the LORD your God and his people Israel. [4]Report for duty according to the family divisions of your ancestors, following the written instructions of King David of Israel and the instructions of his son Solomon. [5]Then stand in your appointed holy places and help the families assigned to you as they bring their offerings to the Temple. [6]Slaughter the Passover lambs, purify yourselves, and prepare to help those who come. Follow all the instructions that the LORD gave through Moses."

35:8 2 Chr 31:13

[7]Then Josiah contributed from his personal property thirty thousand lambs and young goats for the people's Passover offerings, and three thousand bulls. [8]The king's officials also made willing contributions to the people, priests, and Levites. Hilkiah, Zechariah, and Jehiel, the administrators of God's Temple, gave the priests twenty-six hundred lambs and young goats and three hundred bulls as

35:1 Hebrew *on the fourteenth day of the first month.* This day of the Hebrew lunar calendar occurs in late March or early April.

34:31 When Josiah read the book that Hilkiah discovered (34:14), he responded with repentance and humility and promised to follow God's commands as written in the book. The Bible is God's word to us, "full of living power" (Hebrews 4:12), but we cannot know what God wants us to do if we do not read it. And even reading God's Word is not enough; we must be willing to do what it says. There is not much difference between the book hidden in the Temple and the Bible hidden on the bookshelf. An unread Bible is as useless as a lost one.

35:3 In Moses' day, one of the duties of the Levites was to carry the Ark of the Covenant whenever Israel traveled. The Ark was now permanently housed in the Temple and would no longer be carried about in procession as it was in the wilderness. Josiah was telling the Levites that they were now free to take on other responsibilities (1 Chronicles 24).

Passover offerings. 9 The Levite leaders—Conaniah and his brothers Shemaiah **35:9**
and Nethanel, and Hashabiah, Jeiel, and Jozabad—gave five thousand lambs and 2 Chr 31:12
young goats and five hundred bulls to the Levites for their Passover offerings.
10 When everything was ready for the Passover celebration, the priests and the **35:10**
Levites took their places, organized by their divisions, according to the king's orders. 2 Chr 35:5
11 The Levites then slaughtered the Passover lambs and presented the blood to the **35:11**
priests, who sprinkled the blood on the altar while the Levites prepared the animals. 2 Chr 29:22, 34; 35:1, 6
12 They divided the burnt offerings among the people by their family groups, so they
could offer them to the LORD according to the instructions recorded in the Book of
Moses. They did the same with the bulls. 13 Then they roasted the Passover lambs as **35:13**
prescribed; and they boiled the holy offerings in pots, kettles, and pans, and brought Exod 12:8-9 Lev 6:25
them out quickly so the people could eat them.

14 Afterward the Levites prepared a meal for themselves and for the priests, because
the priests had been busy from morning till night offering the burnt offerings and the
fat portions. The Levites took responsibility for all these preparations. 15 The musi- **35:15**
cians, descendants of Asaph, were in their assigned places, following the orders given 1 Chr 25:1; 26:12-19
by David, Asaph, Heman, and Jeduthun, the king's seer. The gatekeepers guarded the
gates and did not need to leave their posts of duty, for their meals were brought to them
by their fellow Levites.

16 The entire ceremony for the LORD's Passover was completed that day. All the
burnt offerings were sacrificed on the altar of the LORD, as King Josiah had ordered.
17 All the Israelites present in Jerusalem celebrated Passover and the Festival of **35:17**
Unleavened Bread for seven days. 18 Never since the time of the prophet Samuel had Exod 12:15 2 Chr 30:21
there been such a Passover. None of the kings of Israel had ever kept a Passover as **35:18-19**
Josiah did, involving all the priests and Levites, all the people of Jerusalem, and //2 Kgs 23:21-23
people from all over Judah and Israel. 19 This Passover celebration took place in the
eighteenth year of Josiah's reign.

Josiah Dies in Battle

20 After Josiah had finished restoring the Temple, King Neco of Egypt led his army up **35:20–36:1**
from Egypt to do battle at Carchemish on the Euphrates River, and Josiah and his //2 Kgs 23:28-30

35:15 The Temple gatekeepers, who were all Levites, guarded the four main entrances to the Temple and opened the gates each morning. They also did other day-to-day chores, such as cleaning and preparing the offerings for sacrifice and accounting for the gifts given to the Temple. (For more on gatekeepers, see 1 Chronicles 26:1ff.)

35:17 The Festival of Unleavened Bread was a seven-day celebration beginning the day after Passover. Like Passover, it commemorated the Exodus from Egypt. For seven days the people ate bread without yeast, just as their ancestors did while leaving Egypt, because it could be made quickly in preparation for their swift departure (Exodus 12:14-20). This festival reminded the people that they had left slavery behind and had come to the land God promised them.

35:20 This event occurred in 609 B.C. Nineveh, the Assyrian capital, had been destroyed three years earlier by the Babylonians. The defeated Assyrians regrouped at Haran and Carchemish, but Babylon sent its army to destroy them once and for all. Pharaoh Neco, who wanted to make Egypt a world power, was worried about Babylon's growing strength, so he marched his army north through Judah to help the Assyrians at Carchemish. But King Josiah of Judah tried to prevent Neco from passing through his land on his way to Carchemish. Josiah was killed, and Judah became subject to Egypt. (2 Kings 23:25-30 helps explain the tragedy. Even though Josiah followed the Lord, God did not turn from his judgment on Judah because of Manasseh's sin and Israel's superficial repentance.) Neco went on to Carchemish and held off the Babylonians for four years, but in 605 he was soundly defeated, and Babylon moved into the spotlight as the dominant world power.

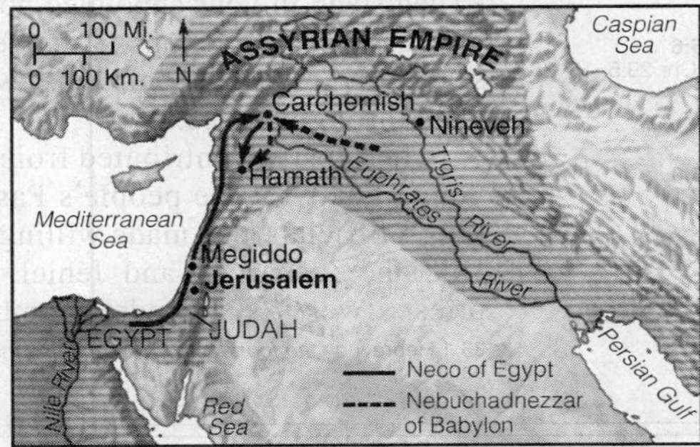

THE BATTLE AT CARCHEMISH A world war was brewing in 609 B.C. when Pharaoh Neco of Egypt set out for the city of Carchemish to join the Assyrians in an attempt to defeat the Babylonians, who were rising to great power. Neco marched his armies through Judah, where King Josiah tried to stop him at Megiddo, but was killed. The battle began at Carchemish in 605 B.C., and the Egyptians and Assyrians were soundly defeated, chased to Hamath, and defeated again. Babylon was now the new world power.

army marched out to fight him. 21 But King Neco sent ambassadors to Josiah with this message:

> "What do you want with me, king of Judah? I have no quarrel with you today! I only want to fight the nation with which I am at war. And God has told me to hurry! Do not interfere with God, who is with me, or he will destroy you."

35:22
Judg 5:19
2 Chr 18:29; 35:21

22 But Josiah refused to listen to Neco, to whom God had indeed spoken, and he would not turn back. Instead, he led his army into battle on the plain of Megiddo. He laid aside his royal robes so the enemy would not recognize him. 23 But the enemy archers hit King Josiah with their arrows and wounded him. He cried out to his men, "Take me from the battle, for I am badly wounded!"

35:25
Jer 22:10-13
Lam 4:20
Zech 12:11

24 So they lifted Josiah out of his chariot and placed him in another chariot. Then they brought him back to Jerusalem, where he died. He was buried there in the royal cemetery. And all Judah and Jerusalem mourned for him. 25 The prophet Jeremiah composed funeral songs for Josiah, and to this day choirs still sing these sad songs about his death. These songs of sorrow have become a tradition and are recorded in *The Book of Laments.* 26 The rest of the events of Josiah's reign and his acts of devotion done according to the written law of the LORD, 27 from beginning to end, are recorded in *The Book of the Kings of Israel and Judah.*

3. Judah is exiled to Babylon

Jehoahaz Rules in Judah

36:1
Jer 22:11

36:2-4
//2 Kgs 23:31-34

36:4
Jer 22:10, 12

36 Then the people of the land took Josiah's son Jehoahaz and made him the next king in Jerusalem. 2 Jehoahaz* was twenty-three years old when he became king, but he reigned only three months. 3 Then he was deposed by Neco, the king of Egypt, who demanded a tribute from Judah of 7,500 pounds of silver and 75 pounds of gold.* 4 The king of Egypt appointed Eliakim, the brother of Jehoahaz, as the next king of Judah and Jerusalem, and he changed Eliakim's name to Jehoiakim. Then Neco took Jehoahaz to Egypt as a prisoner.

Jehoiakim Rules in Judah

36:5-8
//2 Kgs 23:36–24:6

36:5
Jer 22:13-19

36:6
2 Chr 33:11
Jer 22:19-20

36:7
2 Kgs 24:13

5 Jehoiakim was twenty-five years old when he became king, and he reigned in Jerusalem eleven years. But he did what was evil in the sight of the LORD his God. 6 Then King Nebuchadnezzar of Babylon came to Jerusalem and captured it, and he bound Jehoiakim in chains and led him away to Babylon. 7 Nebuchadnezzar also took some of the treasures from the Temple of the LORD, and he placed them in his palace* in Babylon. 8 The rest of the events of Jehoiakim's reign, including all the evil things he did and everything

36:2 Hebrew *Joahaz,* a variant name for Jehoahaz; also in 36:4. **36:3** Hebrew *100 talents* [3.4 metric tons] *of silver and 1 talent* [34 kilograms] *of gold.* **36:7** Or *temple.*

EXILE TO BABYLON Despite Judah's few good kings and timely reforms, the people never truly changed. Their evil continued, and finally God used the Babylonian Empire, under Nebuchadnezzar, to conquer Judah, destroy Jerusalem, and take the people captive to Babylon.

35:21-24 Josiah ignored Neco's message because of who Neco was—king of a pagan nation. The mistaken assumption that Neco could not be part of God's larger plan cost Josiah his life. While not everyone who claims to have a message from God really does, God's messages may come in unexpected ways. God had spoken to pagan kings in the past (Genesis 12:17-20; 20:3-7; see also Daniel 4:1-3). Don't let prejudice or false assumptions blind you to God's message.

35:25 Though Jeremiah recorded these laments for the death of Josiah, they are not the same as the book of Lamentations.

36:6 Nebuchadnezzar was the son of the founder of the new Babylonian Empire. In 605 B.C., the year he became king, Nebuchadnezzar won the battle of Carchemish. That loss crushed Assyria (see the note on 35:20). (For more information about Nebuchadnezzar, read his Profile in Daniel 3.)

found against him, are recorded in *The Book of the Kings of Israel and Judah.* Then his
son Jehoiachin became the next king.

Jehoiachin Rules in Judah

9 Jehoiachin was eighteen* years old when he became king, but he reigned in Jerusalem only three months and ten days. Jehoiachin did what was evil in the LORD's sight.
10 In the spring of the following year, Jehoiachin was summoned to Babylon by King
Nebuchadnezzar. Many treasures from the Temple of the LORD were taken to Babylon
at that time. And Nebuchadnezzar appointed Jehoiachin's uncle,* Zedekiah, to be the
next king in Judah and Jerusalem.

Zedekiah Rules in Judah

11 Zedekiah was twenty-one years old when he became king, and he reigned in
Jerusalem eleven years. 12 He did what was evil in the sight of the LORD his God, and
he refused to humble himself in the presence of the prophet Jeremiah, who spoke for
the LORD. 13 He also rebelled against King Nebuchadnezzar, even though he had taken
an oath of loyalty in God's name. Zedekiah was a hard and stubborn man, refusing to
turn to the LORD, the God of Israel.
14 All the leaders of the priests and the people became more and more unfaithful.
They followed the pagan practices of the surrounding nations, desecrating the Temple
of the LORD in Jerusalem.
15 The LORD, the God of their ancestors, repeatedly sent his prophets to warn them,
for he had compassion on his people and his Temple. 16 But the people mocked these
messengers of God and despised their words. They scoffed at the prophets until the
LORD's anger could no longer be restrained and there was no remedy.

The Fall of Jerusalem

17 So the LORD brought the king of Babylon against them. The Babylonians* killed
Judah's young men, even chasing after them into the Temple. They had no pity on the
people, killing both young and old, men and women, healthy and sick. God handed
them all over to Nebuchadnezzar. 18 The king also took home to Babylon all the
utensils, large and small, used in the Temple of God, and the treasures from both the
LORD's Temple and the royal palace. He also took with him all the royal princes.
19 Then his army set fire to the Temple of God, broke down the walls of Jerusalem,
burned all the palaces, and completely destroyed everything of value.* 20 The few
who survived were taken away to Babylon, and they became servants to the king and
his sons until the kingdom of Persia came to power. 21 So the message of the LORD
spoken through Jeremiah was fulfilled. The land finally enjoyed its Sabbath rest, lying
desolate for seventy years, just as the prophet had said.

36:9-10 //2 Kgs 24:8-17
36:10 2 Sam 11:1; Jer 37:1
36:11-16 //2 Kgs 24:18-20; //Jer 52:1-3
36:12 2 Chr 33:23; Jer 21:3-7
36:13 2 Chr 30:8; Jer 52:3; Ezek 17:15
36:15 Jer 7:13; 25:3-4
36:16 2 Chr 30:10; Ezra 5:12; Prov 1:24-32; Jer 5:12-13
36:17-20 //2 Kgs 25:1-21; //Jer 52:4-27
36:18 2 Chr 36:7, 10
36:19 2 Kgs 25:9; Jer 52:13
36:20 2 Kgs 25:11; Jer 27:7
36:21 Lev 25:4; 26:33-34; Jer 29:10

36:9 As in one Hebrew manuscript, some Greek manuscripts, and Syriac version (see also 2 Kgs 24:8); most Hebrew manuscripts read *eight.* **36:10** As in parallel text at 2 Kgs 24:17; Hebrew reads *brother,* or *relative.* **36:17** Or *Chaldeans.* **36:19** Or *destroyed all the valuable Temple utensils.*

36:9, 10 In 2 Kings 24:8, Jehoiachin is listed as 18 years old. Many Hebrew manuscripts list him as 8 years old. The age given in 2 Kings 24:8 is most likely accurate because he had wives at that time (see 2 Kings 24:15).

36:16 God warned Judah about its sin and continually restored the people to his favor, only to have them turn away. Eventually the situation was beyond remedy. Beware of harboring sin in your heart. The day will come when remedy is no longer possible and God's judgment replaces his mercy. Sin often repeated, but never repented of, invites disaster.

36:21 Leviticus 26:27-45 strikingly predicts the captivity, telling how God's people would be torn from their land for disobeying him. One of the laws they had ignored stated that one year in every seven the land should lie fallow, resting from producing crops (Exodus 23:10, 11). The 70-year captivity allowed the land to rest, making up for all the years the Israelites had not observed this law. We know that God keeps all his promises—not only his promises of blessing, but also his promises of judgment.

36:22, 23 Cyrus made this proclamation 48 years after the Temple was destroyed (36:18, 19), in the year after he conquered Babylon. The book of Ezra tells the story of this proclamation and the return of the exiles to Judah.

36:22, 23 Second Chronicles focuses on the proper and improper worship of God as symbolized by the Jerusalem Temple. David planned the Temple; Solomon built it and then put on the greatest dedication service the world has ever seen. Worship in the Temple was superbly organized.

But several evil kings defiled the Temple and degraded worship so that the people revered idols more highly than God. Finally, King Nebuchadnezzar of Babylon destroyed the Temple (36:19). The kings were gone, the Temple was destroyed, and the people were removed. The nation was stripped to its very foundation. But fortunately there was a greater foundation—God himself. When everything in life seems stripped away from us, we, too, still have God—his Word, his presence, and his promises.

Cyrus Allows the Exiles to Return

36:22-23
//Ezra 1:1-3

36:22
Isa 44:28
Jer 25:12; 29:10

22 In the first year of King Cyrus of Persia,* the LORD fulfilled Jeremiah's prophecy
by stirring the heart of Cyrus to put this proclamation into writing and to send it
throughout his kingdom:

> 23 "This is what King Cyrus of Persia says: The LORD, the God of heaven, has
> given me all the kingdoms of the earth. He has appointed me to build him a
> Temple at Jerusalem in the land of Judah. All of you who are the LORD's people
> may return to Israel for this task. May the LORD your God be with you!"

36:22 The first year of Cyrus's reign was 538 B.C.

EZRA

Jerusalem destroyed; exiles go to Babylon 586 B.C.

Babylon overthrown by Cyrus 539

Exiles return to Jerusalem 538

Temple construction begins 536

Temple work halted 530

VITAL STATISTICS

PURPOSE:
To show God's faithfulness and the way he kept his promise to restore his people to their land

AUTHOR:
Not stated, but probably Ezra

DATE WRITTEN:
Around 450 B.C., recording events from about 538–450 B.C. (omitting 516–458 B.C.); possibly begun earlier in Babylon and finished in Jerusalem

SETTING:
Ezra follows 2 Chronicles as a history of the Jewish people, recording their return to the land after the captivity.

KEY VERSES:
"The Passover meal was eaten by the people of Israel who had returned from exile and by the others in the land who had turned from their immoral customs to worship the LORD, the God of Israel. They ate the Passover meal and celebrated the Festival of Unleavened Bread for seven days. There was great joy throughout the land because the LORD had changed the attitude of the king of Assyria toward them, so that he helped them to rebuild the Temple of God, the God of Israel" (6:21, 22).

KEY PEOPLE:
Cyrus, Zerubbabel, Haggai, Zechariah, Darius I, Artaxerxes I, Ezra

KEY PLACES:
Babylon, Jerusalem

SPECIAL FEATURES:
Ezra and Nehemiah were one book in the Hebrew Bible, and, with Esther, they comprise the post-captivity historical books. The post-captivity prophetic books are Haggai, Zechariah, and Malachi. Haggai and Zechariah should be studied with Ezra because they prophesied during the period of the reconstruction.

NAME the truly great men and women of your lifetime. Celebrities, including politicians, war heroes, sports figures, and maybe your parents and special friends come to mind. You remember them because of certain acts or character qualities. Now, name some biblical heroes—figures etched in your mind through countless sermons and church school lessons. This list undoubtedly includes many who served God faithfully and courageously. Does your list include Ezra? Far from being well known, this unheralded man of God deserves to be mentioned in any discussion of greatness.

Ezra was a priest, a scribe, and a great leader. His name means "help," and his whole life was dedicated to serving God and God's people. Tradition says that Ezra wrote most of 1 and 2 Chronicles, Ezra, Nehemiah, and Psalm 119 and that he led the council of 120 men who formed the Old Testament canon. The narrative of the book of Ezra is centered on God and his promise that the Jews would return to their land, as prophesied by Jeremiah (see the third note on 1:1). This message formed the core of Ezra's life. The last half of the book gives a very personal glimpse of Ezra. His knowledge of Scripture and his God-given wisdom were so obvious to the king that he appointed Ezra to lead the second emigration to Jerusalem, to teach the people God's Word, and to administer national life (7:14–26).

Ezra not only knew God's Word, he believed and obeyed it. Upon learning of the Israelites' sins of intermarriage and idolatry, Ezra fell in humility before God and prayed for the nation (9:1–15). Their disobedience touched him deeply (10:1). His response helped lead the people back to God.

Second Chronicles ends with Cyrus, king of Persia, asking for volunteers to return to Jerusalem to build a house for God. Ezra continues this account (1:1–3 is almost identical to 2 Chronicles 36:22, 23) as two caravans of God's people were returning to Jerusalem. Zerubbabel, the leader of the first trip, was joined by 42,360 pilgrims who journeyed homeward (chapter 2). After arriving, they began to build the altar and the Temple foundations (chapter 3). But opposition arose from the local inhabitants, and a campaign of accusations and rumors temporarily halted the project (chapter 4). During this time, the prophets Haggai and Zechariah encouraged the people (chapter 5). Finally, Darius decreed that the work should proceed unhindered (chapter 6).

After a 58-year gap, Ezra led a group of Jews from Persia. Armed with decrees and authority from Artaxerxes I, Ezra's task was to administer the affairs of the land (chapters 7, 8). Upon arriving, he learned of intermarriage between God's people and their pagan neighbors. He wept and prayed for the nation (chapter 9). Ezra's example of humble confession led to national revival (chapter 10). Ezra, a man of God and a true hero, was a model for Israel, and he is a fitting model for us.

Read Ezra, the book, and remember Ezra, the man—a humble, obedient helper. Commit yourself to serving God as he did, with your whole life.

Darius I becomes king of Persia 522	*Temple work resumed/ messages of Haggai, Zechariah 520*	*Temple completed 515*	*Ezra comes to Jerusalem 458*	*Nehemiah comes to Jerusalem 445*

THE BLUEPRINT

A. THE RETURN LED BY ZERUBBABEL (1:1—6:22)
   1. The first group of exiles returns to the land
   2. The people rebuild the Temple

Finally given the chance to return to their homeland, the people started to rebuild the Temple, only to be stopped by opposition from their enemies. God's work in the world is not without opposition. We must not get discouraged and quit, as the returning people did at first, but continue on boldly in the face of difficulties, as they did later with the encouragement from the prophets.

B. THE RETURN LED BY EZRA (7:1—10:44)
   1. The second group of exiles returns to the land
   2. Ezra opposes intermarriage

Ezra returned to Jerusalem almost 80 years after Zerubbabel, only to discover that the people had married pagan or foreign spouses. This polluted the religious purity of the people and endangered the future of the nation. Believers today must be careful not to threaten their walk with God by taking on the practices of unbelievers.

MEGATHEMES

THEME	EXPLANATION	IMPORTANCE
The Jews Return	By returning to the land of Israel from Babylon, the Jews showed their faith in God's promise to restore them as a people. They returned not only to their homeland but also to the place where their forefathers had promised to follow God.	God shows his mercy to every generation. He compassionately restores his people. No matter how difficult our present "captivity," we are never far from his love and mercy. He restores us when we return to him.
Rededication	In 536 B.C., Zerubbabel led the people in rebuilding the altar and laying the Temple foundation. They reinstated daily sacrifices and annual festivals, and rededicated themselves to a new spiritual worship of God.	In rededicating the altar, the people were recommitting themselves to God and his service. To grow spiritually, our commitment must be reviewed and renewed often. As we rededicate ourselves to God, our lives become altars to him.
Opposition	Opposition came soon after the altar was built and the Temple foundation laid. Enemies of the Jews used deceit to hinder the building for over six years. Finally, there was a decree to stop the building altogether. This opposition severely tested their wavering faith.	There will always be adversaries who oppose God's work. The life of faith is never easy. But God can overrule all opposition to his service. When we face opposition, we must not falter or withdraw, but keep active and patient.
God's Word	When the people returned to the land, they were also returning to the influence of God's Word. The prophets Haggai and Zechariah helped encourage them, while Ezra's preaching of Scripture built them up. God's Word gave them what they needed to do God's work.	We also need the encouragement and direction of God's Word. We must make it the basis for our faith and actions to finish God's work and fulfill our obligations. We must never waver in our commitment to hear and obey his Word.
Faith and Action	The urging of Israel's leaders motivated the people to complete the Temple. Over the years they had intermarried with idol-worshipers and adopted their pagan practices. Their faith, tested and revived, also led them to remove these sins from their lives.	Faith led them to complete the Temple and to remove sin from their society. As we trust God with our hearts and minds, we must also act by completing our daily responsibilities. It is not enough to say we believe; we must make the changes God requires.

A. THE RETURN LED BY ZERUBBABEL (1:1—6:22)

After 70 years in exile, the captives from Judah were allowed to return to their homeland. Nearly 50,000 people made this journey. Upon arrival they began to rebuild the Temple, but became discouraged by opposition. After encouragement from Haggai and Zechariah, they returned to the task and completed the Temple. The message of the prophets still speaks to us today, encouraging us to continue building up God's church.

1. The first group of exiles returns to the land

Cyrus Allows the Exiles to Return

1 In the first year of King Cyrus of Persia,* the LORD fulfilled Jeremiah's prophecy 1:1-3 //2 Chr 36:22-23
by stirring the heart of Cyrus to put this proclamation into writing and to send it 1:1
throughout his kingdom: Jer 25:11-12; 29:10-14

2 "This is what King Cyrus of Persia says: The LORD, the God of heaven, has given 1:2
me all the kingdoms of the earth. He has appointed me to build him a Temple at Isa 44:28; 45:1-13
Jerusalem in the land of Judah. 3 All of you who are his people may return to Jeru- 1:3
salem in Judah to rebuild this Temple of the LORD, the God of Israel, who lives in Dan 6:26
Jerusalem. And may your God be with you! 4 Those who live in any place where
Jewish survivors are found should contribute toward their expenses by supplying
them with silver and gold, supplies for the journey, and livestock, as well as a freewill offering for the Temple of God in Jerusalem."

5 Then God stirred the hearts of the priests and Levites and the leaders of the tribes of 1:5
Judah and Benjamin to return to Jerusalem to rebuild the Temple of the LORD. 6 And all their 2 Chr 36:22
neighbors assisted by giving them vessels of silver and gold, supplies for the journey, and
livestock. They gave them many choice gifts in addition to all the freewill offerings.

1:1 The first year of Cyrus's reign was 538 B.C.

1:1 The book of Ezra opens in 538 B.C., 48 years after Nebuchadnezzar destroyed Jerusalem, defeated the southern kingdom of Judah, and carried the Jews away to Babylon as captives (2 Kings 25; 2 Chronicles 36). Nebuchadnezzar died in 562, and because his successors were not strong, Babylon was overthrown by Persia in 539, just prior to the events recorded in this book. Both the Babylonians and the Persians had a relaxed policy toward their captives, allowing them to own land and homes and to take ordinary jobs. Many Jews such as Daniel, Mordecai, and Esther rose to prominent positions within the nation. King Cyrus of Persia went a step further: He allowed many groups of exiles, including the Jews, to return to their homelands. By doing this, he hoped to win their loyalty and thus provide buffer zones around the borders of his empire. For the Jews this was a day of hope, a new beginning.

1:1 Cyrus, king of Persia (539–530 B.C.), had already begun his rise to power in the Near East by unifying the Medes and Persians into a strong empire. As he conquered cities, he treated the inhabitants with mercy. Although not a servant of Yahweh, Cyrus was used by God to return the Jews to their homeland. Cyrus may have been shown the prophecy of Isaiah 44:28–45:6, written over a century earlier, which predicted that Cyrus himself would help the Jews return to Jerusalem. Daniel, a prominent government official (Daniel 5:29; 6:28), would have been familiar with the prophecy. The book of Daniel has more to say about Cyrus.

1:1 Jeremiah prophesied that the Jews would remain in captivity for 70 years (Jeremiah 25:11; 29:10). The 70-year period has been calculated two different ways: (1) from the first captivity in 605 B.C. (2 Kings 24:1) until the altar was rebuilt by the returned exiles in 537 (Ezra 3:1-6), or (2) from the destruction of the Temple in 586 until the exiles finished rebuilding it in 515. Many scholars prefer the second approach because the Temple was the focus and heartbeat of the nation. Without the Temple, the Jews did not consider themselves reestablished as a nation.

1:2 Cyrus was not a Jew, but God worked through him to return the exiled Jews to their homeland. Cyrus gave the proclamation allowing their return, and he gave them protection, money, and the Temple articles taken by Nebuchadnezzar. When you face difficult situations and feel surrounded, outnumbered, overpowered, or outclassed, remember that God's power is not limited to your resources. He is able to use anyone to carry out his plans.

1:2-4 This proclamation permitted the Jews to work together to accomplish the huge task of rebuilding the Temple. Some did the actual building, while others operated the supply lines. Significant ventures require teamwork, with certain people serving in the forefront and others providing support. Each function is vital to accomplishing the task. When you're asked to serve, do so faithfully as a team member, no matter who gets the credit.

1:5 Cyrus was king over the entire region that had once been Assyria and Babylon. Assyria had deported the Israelites from the northern kingdom (Israel) in 722 B.C. Babylon, the next world power, had taken Israelites captive from the southern kingdom (Judah) in 586 B.C. Therefore, when the Medo-Persian Empire came to power, King Cyrus's proclamation of freedom went to all the original 12 tribes, but only Judah and Benjamin responded and returned to rebuild God's Temple. The 10 tribes of the northern kingdom had been so fractured and dispersed by Assyria, and so much time had elapsed since their captivity, that many may have been unsure of their real heritage. Thus, they were unwilling to share in the vision of rebuilding the Temple.

1:5 God moved the hearts of the leaders, family heads, priests, and Levites and gave them a great desire to return to Jerusalem to rebuild the Temple. Major changes begin on the inside as God works on our attitudes, beliefs, and desires. These inner changes lead to faithful actions. After 48 years of captivity, the arrogant Jewish nation had been humbled. When the people's attitudes and desires changed, God ended their punishment and gave them another opportunity to go home and try again. Paul reminds us that "God is working in you, giving you the desire to obey him and the power to do what pleases him" (Philippians 2:13). Doing God's will begins with your desires. Are you willing to be humble, to be open to his opportunities, and to move at his direction? Ask God to give you the desire to follow him more closely.

1:5, 6 Many Jews chose to go to Jerusalem, but many more chose to remain in Babylon rather than return to their homeland.

1:7
2 Kgs 24:13; 25:13-16
2 Chr 36:7-18
Ezra 6:5
1:8
Ezra 5:14-16

7 King Cyrus himself brought out the valuable items which King Nebuchadnezzar had taken from the LORD's Temple in Jerusalem and had placed in the temple of his own gods. 8 Cyrus directed Mithredath, the treasurer of Persia, to count these items and present them to Sheshbazzar, the leader of the exiles returning to Judah.*
9 These were the items Cyrus donated:

gold trays . . . 30
silver trays . . . 1,000
silver censers* . . . 29
10 gold bowls . . . 30
silver bowls . . . 410
other items . . . 1,000

11 In all, 5,400 gold and silver items were turned over to Sheshbazzar to take back to Jerusalem when the exiles returned there from Babylon.

1:8 Hebrew *Sheshbazzar, the prince of Judah.* **1:9** The meaning of this Hebrew word is uncertain.

PROPHECIES FULFILLED BY THE RETURN OF ISRAEL FROM EXILE

Reference	*Prophecy*	*Approximate Date*	*Fulfillment Date*	*Significance*
Isaiah 44:28	Cyrus would be used by God to guarantee the return of a remnant. Jerusalem would be rebuilt and the Temple restored.	688 B.C.	538 B.C.	As God named Cyrus even before he was born, God knows what will happen—he is in control.
Jeremiah 25:12	Babylon would be punished for destroying Jerusalem and exiling God's people.	605 B.C.	539 B.C.	Babylon was conquered by Cyrus the Great. God may seem to allow evil to go unpunished, but consequences for wrongdoing are inevitable. God will punish evil.
Jeremiah 29:10	The people would spend 70 years in Babylon; then God would bring them back to their homeland.	594 B.C.	538 B.C.	The 70 years of captivity passed (see the third note on 1:1), and God provided the opportunity for Zerubbabel to lead the first group of captives home. God's plans may allow for hardship, but his desire is for our good.
Daniel 5:17–30	God had judged the Babylonian Empire. It would be given to the Medes and the Persians, forming a new world power.	539 B.C.	539 B.C.	Belshazzar was killed and Babylon was conquered the same night. God's judgment is accurate and swift. God knows the point of no return in each of our lives. Until then, he allows the freedom for us to repent and seek his forgiveness.

God, through his faithful prophets, predicted that the people of Judah would be taken into captivity because of their sinfulness. But he also predicted that they would return to Jerusalem and rebuild the city, the Temple, and the nation.

The journey back to Jerusalem was difficult, dangerous, and expensive, lasting over four months. Travel conditions were poor; Jerusalem and the surrounding countryside were in ruins; and the people living in the area were hostile.

Persian records indicate that many Jews in captivity had accumulated great wealth. Returning to Jerusalem would have meant giving up everything they had and starting over. Many people couldn't bring themselves to do that; they preferred wealth and security to the sacrifice that God's work would require. Their priorities were upside down (Mark 4:18, 19). We must not let our comfort, security, or material possessions prevent us from doing what God wants.

1:7 When King Nebuchadnezzar ransacked the Temple, he took many of the valuable furnishings with him. What he did not take, he burned (2 Chronicles 36:18, 19). Most of the captured items were made of solid gold (1 Kings 7:48-50), and Cyrus kindly returned them to the Jews for the Temple they would soon rebuild.

1:8 Either Sheshbazzar was the Babylonian name for Zerubbabel, one of the Jewish leaders during the first return (2:2; 3:8; 4:3), or he was a government official with responsibility for the returning party. The reasons Sheshbazzar may be identified with Zerubbabel are as follows: (1) Both were called governors (5:14; Haggai 1:1); (2) both laid the Temple foundation (3:8; 5:16); (3) Jews in exile were often given Babylonian names (see Daniel 1:7 where Daniel and his companions were given new names).

1:9-11 Every article of gold and silver was a witness to God's protection and care. Although many years had passed, God delivered these Temple articles back to his people. We may be discouraged by events in life, but we must never give up our hope in God's promises to us. The turning point may be just ahead.

Exiles Who Returned with Zerubbabel

2 Here is the list of the Jewish exiles of the provinces who returned from their captivity to Jerusalem and to the other towns of Judah. They had been deported to Babylon by King Nebuchadnezzar. 2 Their leaders were Zerubbabel, Jeshua, Nehemiah, Seraiah, Reelaiah, Mordecai, Bilshan, Mispar, Bigvai, Rehum, and Baanah. This is the number of the men of Israel who returned from exile:

2:1-70 //Neh 7:6-73
2:1 2 Kgs 24:14-16; 25:11; 2 Chr 36:20
2:2 Neh 7:7
2:5-6 Neh 7:10-11

3 The family of Parosh 2,172
4 The family of Shephatiah 372
5 The family of Arah 775
6 The family of Pahath-moab (descendants of Jeshua and Joab) 2,812
7 The family of Elam 1,254
8 The family of Zattu 945
9 The family of Zaccai 760
10 The family of Bani 642
11 The family of Bebai 623
12 The family of Azgad 1,222
13 The family of Adonikam 666
14 The family of Bigvai 2,056
15 The family of Adin 454
16 The family of Ater (descendants of Hezekiah) 98
17 The family of Bezai 323
18 The family of Jorah 112
19 The family of Hashum 223
20 The family of Gibbar 95
21 The people of Bethlehem 123
22 The people of Netophah 56
23 The people of Anathoth 128
24 The people of Beth-azmaveth* 42
25 The peoples of Kiriath-jearim,* Kephirah, and Beeroth 743
26 The peoples of Ramah and Geba 621
27 The people of Micmash 122
28 The peoples of Bethel and Ai 223
29 The citizens of Nebo 52
30 The citizens of Magbish 156
31 The citizens of Elam 1,254
32 The citizens of Harim 320
33 The citizens of Lod, Hadid, and Ono 725
34 The citizens of Jericho 345

2:24 As in parallel text at Neh 7:28; Hebrew reads *Azmaveth.* **2:25** As in some Hebrew manuscripts and Greek version (see also Neh 7:29); Hebrew reads *Kiriath-arim.*

2:2 The Nehemiah listed here is a different person from the one who rebuilt Jerusalem's walls 80 years later, and the Mordecai listed here is not the one who appears in the book of Esther.

2:2 This first list is made up of men who were leaders. The same list occurs in Nehemiah 7:7.

2:2-35 These people were from the tribes of Judah and Benjamin (1:5).

2:3-35 This list is the major group of those returning, divided by families (2:3-20) or by cities (2:21-35). Verse 36 begins listing priests, Levites, and other Temple servants.

THE JOURNEY HOME The vast Medo-Persian Empire included all the area on this map and more. A group of exiles began the long trip back to their homeland. Many exiles, however, preferred the comfort and security they had in Babylon to the dangerous trip back to Jerusalem, and so they decided to stay in Babylon.

[35] The citizens of Senaah 3,630

2:36 1 Chr 24:7-18

[36] These are the priests who returned from exile:
The family of Jedaiah (through the line of Jeshua) 973
[37] The family of Immer 1,052

2:38 1 Chr 9:12

[38] The family of Pashhur 1,247

2:39 1 Chr 24:8

[39] The family of Harim 1,017

2:40 Neh 12:24

[40] These are the Levites who returned from exile:
The families of Jeshua and Kadmiel (descendants of Hodaviah) 74
[41] The singers of the family of Asaph 128
[42] The gatekeepers of the families of Shallum, Ater, Talmon, Akkub, Hatita, and Shobai 139

2:43 1 Chr 9:2

[43] The descendants of the following Temple servants returned from exile:
Ziha, Hasupha, Tabbaoth,
[44] Keros, Siaha, Padon,
[45] Lebanah, Hagabah, Akkub,
[46] Hagab, Shalmai,* Hanan,
[47] Giddel, Gahar, Reaiah,
[48] Rezin, Nekoda, Gazzam,
[49] Uzza, Paseah, Besai,
[50] Asnah, Meunim, Nephusim,
[51] Bakbuk, Hakupha, Harhur,
[52] Bazluth, Mehida, Harsha,
[53] Barkos, Sisera, Temah,
[54] Neziah, and Hatipha.

2:55 Neh 7:57-60

[55] The descendants of these servants of King Solomon returned from exile:
Sotai, Sophereth,* Peruda,
[56] Jaalah, Darkon, Giddel,
[57] Shephatiah, Hattil, Pokereth-hazzebaim, and Ami.

[58] In all, the Temple servants and the descendants of Solomon's servants numbered 392.

[59] Another group returned to Jerusalem at this time from the towns of Tel-melah, Tel-

2:46 As in the marginal *Qere* reading of the Masoretic Text (see also Neh 7:48); Hebrew text reads *Shamlai.* **2:55** As in parallel text at Neh 7:57; Hebrew reads *Hassophereth.*

THE RETURN FROM EXILE

Year	Number of People Returned	Persian King	Jewish Leader	Main Accomplishment
538 B.C.	50,000	Cyrus	Zerubbabel	They rebuilt the Temple, but only after a 20-year struggle. The work was halted for several years but was finally finished.
458 B.C.	2,000 men and their families	Artaxerxes	Ezra	Ezra confronted the spiritual disobedience of the people, and they repented and established worship at the Temple. But the wall of Jerusalem remained in ruins.
445 B.C.	Small group	Artaxerxes	Nehemiah	The city was rebuilt, and a spiritual awakening followed. But the people still struggled with ongoing disobedience.

Babylon, the once-mighty nation that had destroyed Jerusalem and carried the people of Judah into captivity, had itself become a defeated nation. Persia was the new world power, and under its new foreign policy, captured peoples were allowed to return to their homelands. The people of Judah and Israel returned to their land in three successive waves.

2:59-63 Genealogies were very important credentials to the Hebrew people. If they could not prove they had descended from Abraham, they were not considered true Jews and were excluded from full participation in Jewish community life. In addition, some privileges were restricted to members of certain tribes. For example, only descendants of Levi (Abraham's great-grandson) could serve in the Temple.

harsha, Kerub, Addan, and Immer. However, they could not prove that they or their families
were descendants of Israel. 60This group consisted of the families of Delaiah, Tobiah, and
Nekoda—a total of 652 people.
61Three families of priests—Hobaiah, Hakkoz, and Barzillai—also returned to Jerusalem. (This Barzillai had married one of the daughters of Barzillai from Gilead and had
taken her family name.) 62But they had lost their genealogical records, so they were not
allowed to serve as priests. 63The governor would not even let them eat the priests' share
of food from the sacrifices until there was a priest who could consult the LORD about the
matter by means of sacred lots.*
64So a total of 42,360 people returned to Judah, 65in addition to 7,337 servants and
200 singers, both men and women. 66They took with them 736 horses, 245 mules, 67435
camels, and 6,720 donkeys.
68When they arrived at the Temple of the LORD in Jerusalem, some of the family
leaders gave generously toward the rebuilding of God's Temple on its original site, 69and
each leader gave as much as he could. The total of their gifts came to 61,000 gold coins,*
6,250 pounds* of silver, and 100 robes for the priests.
70So the priests, the Levites, the singers, the gatekeepers, the Temple servants, and
some of the common people settled in villages near Jerusalem. The rest of the people
returned to the other towns of Judah from which they had come.

2. The people rebuild the Temple

The Altar Is Rebuilt

3 Now in early autumn,* when the Israelites had settled in their towns, all the
people assembled together as one person in Jerusalem. 2Then Jeshua son of
Jehozadak* with his fellow priests and Zerubbabel son of Shealtiel with his family
began to rebuild the altar of the God of Israel so they could sacrifice burnt offerings
on it, as instructed in the law of Moses, the man of God. 3Even though the people were
afraid of the local residents, they rebuilt the altar at its old site. Then they immediately
began to sacrifice burnt offerings on the altar to the LORD. They did this each morning
and evening.
4They celebrated the Festival of Shelters as prescribed in the law of Moses, sacrificing

2:61 2 Sam 17:27
2:62 Num 3:10; 16:39-40; Ezra 2:59
2:63 Exod 28:30; Lev 2:3, 10
2:64 Neh 7:66-67
2:69 Ezra 8:25-34
2:70 Neh 7:73
3:1 Neh 7:73; 8:1
3:2 Lev 1:1-17; 6:8-13; 1 Chr 3:17-20; Ezra 2:2; Neh 12:1, 8; Hag 1:1; Zech 6:11
3:3 Num 28:1-8
3:4 Exod 23:16; Num 29:12; Neh 8:14
3:5 Exod 29:38, 42; Num 28:11-14

2:63 Hebrew *consult the Urim and Thummim about the matter.* **2:69a** Hebrew *61,000 darics of gold,* about 1,100 pounds or 500 kilograms in weight. **2:69b** Hebrew *5,000 minas* [3 metric tons]. **3:1** Hebrew *in the seventh month.* The year is not specific, so it may have been during Cyrus's first year (538 B.C.) or second year (537 B.C.). The seventh month of the Hebrew lunar calendar occurred in September/October 538 B.C. and October/November 537 B.C. **3:2** Hebrew *Jozadak,* a variant name for Jehozadak; also in 3:8.

2:63 The governor mentioned here was probably Zerubbabel. The sacred lots were probably the Urim and Thummim, two objects originally carried in the garment worn by the high priest. They were used to determine God's will in important matters. (For more on the Urim and Thummim, see the note on Leviticus 8:8.) The priests' share of food was their allotted portion of meat that was sacrificed on the altar.

2:68, 69 As the Temple reconstruction progressed, everyone contributed freewill offerings according to his or her ability. Some were able to give huge gifts and did so generously. Everyone's effort and cooperation were required, and the people gave as much as they could. Often we limit our giving to 10 percent of our income. The Bible, however, emphasizes that we should give from the heart *all* that we are able (2 Corinthians 8:12; 9:6). Let your gift be decided by God's call to give generously, not by the amount you have left over.

2:69 The money given was enough to start rebuilding the Temple. The people put what resources they had to their best use. They were enthusiastic and sincere, but this Temple would never match the splendor of Solomon's. The amount of money David gathered to start the building of Solomon's Temple was a thousand times more (1 Chronicles 22:14). Some people wept as they remembered the glorious Temple that had been destroyed (3:12).

3:2, 3 The Jews built the altar as one of their first official acts. It symbolized God's presence and protection. It also demonstrated their purpose as a nation and their commitment to serve God alone. Zerubbabel sacrificed burnt offerings as the law of Moses instructed (Leviticus 1–7). The sacrifices were essential because they demonstrated that the people were seeking God's guidance, rededicating themselves to living as he commanded, and daily asking him to forgive their sins.

3:3 The Jews were afraid they were going to be attacked by the surrounding people—a mixed group whose ancestors had been conquered by the Assyrians. Foreigners had been forced to resettle in the northern kingdom of Israel after Israel was defeated and her people taken captive in 722 B.C. (4:1, 2). This resettlement procedure was a common tactic of the Assyrians to prevent strong nationalistic uprisings by conquered peoples. Some of the resettled people in Israel had migrated south near Jerusalem, and they may have thought the returning exiles threatened their claim on the land.

3:4 The Festival of Shelters lasted seven days. During this time the people lived in temporary dwellings (tents, booths, lean-tos) as their ancestors had done years before as they journeyed through the wilderness on their way to the Promised Land. The festival reminded the people of God's past protection and guidance in the wilderness and of his continued love for them. The Festival of Shelters is described in detail in Leviticus 23:33-36.

3:5 Almost immediately after arriving in the new land, the returning exiles built an altar. The people began worshiping God through sacrifices even before the Temple foundation was laid. After many

the burnt offerings specified for each day of the festival. 5 They also offered the regular
burnt offerings and the offerings required for the new moon celebrations and the other
annual festivals to the LORD. Freewill offerings were also sacrificed to the LORD by the

ZERUBBABEL

Sometimes God's ownership of a project is recognized only after *our* best efforts have failed. It is dangerous to think that God is responsible for only insignificant details of a project, while we take charge of the larger aspects. Instead, it is God who is in control, and we only play a part in his overall plan. When God gives us important jobs to do, it isn't because he needs our help. Zerubbabel learned this lesson.

God's people had been exiled in Babylon for many years. Many had settled into comfortable life-styles there and wanted to stay. There were, however, almost 60,000 who had not forgotten Judah. When Babylon was defeated in 539 B.C., the Persian ruler, Cyrus, allowed the Jews to return to Jerusalem and rebuild their Temple. Zerubbabel led the first and largest group back to the Promised Land.

Zerubbabel's leadership was by right and recognition. Not only was he a descendant of David, he also had personal leadership qualities. When the people arrived in Judah, they were given time to establish living quarters and then were called to begin the work. They began not by laying the city walls or constructing government buildings, but by rebuilding the altar, worshiping God together, and celebrating a feast. Under Zerubbabel's leadership, they established a spiritual foundation for their building efforts.

The Temple foundation was then quickly completed, and another round of celebration followed. But soon two problems arose. A few old men remembered Solomon's glorious Temple and were saddened at how much smaller and less glorious this one was. Also, some enemies of the Jews tried to infiltrate the workforce and stop the building with political pressure. Fear caused the work to grind to a halt. The people went to their homes, and 16 years passed.

We do not know what Zerubbabel did during this time. His discouragement, following those first months of excitement and accomplishment, must have been deep. Those feelings eventually hardened into hopelessness. So God sent the prophets Haggai and Zechariah to be Zerubbabel's encouraging companions. They confronted the people's reluctance and comforted their fears. The work began once again with renewed energy and was completed in four years.

Zerubbabel, like many of us, knew how to start well but found it hard to keep going. His successes depended on the quality of encouragement he received. Zerubbabel let discouragement get the better of him. But when he let God take control, the work was finished. God is always in control. We must not let circumstances or lack of encouragement slow us from doing the tasks God has given us.

Strengths and accomplishments
- Led the first group of Jewish exiles back to Jerusalem from Babylon
- Completed the rebuilding of God's Temple
- Demonstrated wisdom in the help he accepted and refused
- Started his building project with worship as the focal point

Weaknesses and mistakes
- Needed constant encouragement
- Allowed problems and resistance to stop the rebuilding work

Lessons from his life
- A leader needs to provide not only the initial motivation for a project but the continued encouragement necessary to keep the project going
- A leader must find his/her own dependable source of encouragement
- God's faithfulness is shown in the way he preserved David's line

Vital statistics
- Where: Babylon, Jerusalem
- Occupation: Recognized leader of the exiles
- Relatives: Father: Shealtiel. Grandfather: Jehoiachin
- Contemporaries: Cyrus, Darius, Zechariah, Haggai

Key verses
"Then he said to me, 'This is what the LORD says to Zerubbabel: It is not by force nor by strength, but by my Spirit, says the LORD Almighty. Nothing, not even a mighty mountain, will stand in Zerubbabel's way; it will flatten out before him! Then Zerubbabel will set the final stone of the Temple in place, and the people will shout: "May God bless it! May God bless it!" ' " (Zechariah 4:6, 7).

Zerubbabel's story is told in Ezra 2:2—5:2. He is also mentioned in 1 Chronicles 3:19; Nehemiah 7:7; 12:1, 47; Haggai 1:1, 12, 14; 2:4, 21, 23; Zechariah 4:6–10; Matthew 1:12, 13; Luke 3:27.

years in captivity, they had learned their lesson—they knew that God does not offer special protection to people who ignore him. They had been carried off by the Babylonians when they were relatively strong; here they were few, weak, and surrounded by enemies. If ever they needed to rely on God's power, it was at this time. They realized the importance of obeying God from the heart, and not merely out of habit. If we want God's help when we undertake large tasks, we must make staying close to him our top priority.

people. 6 Fifteen days before the Festival of Shelters began,* the priests had begun to
sacrifice burnt offerings to the LORD. This was also before they had started to lay the
foundation of the LORD's Temple.

The People Rebuild the Temple

7 Then they hired masons and carpenters and bought cedar logs from the people of Tyre
and Sidon, paying them with food, wine, and olive oil. The logs were brought down from
the Lebanon mountains and floated along the coast of the Mediterranean Sea to Joppa,
for King Cyrus had given permission for this.
8 The construction of the Temple of God began in midspring,* during the second year
after they arrived in Jerusalem. The work force was made up of everyone who had returned
from exile, including Zerubbabel son of Shealtiel, Jeshua son of Jehozadak and his fellow
priests, and all the Levites. The Levites who were twenty years old or older were put in
charge of rebuilding the LORD's Temple. 9 The workers at the Temple of God were
supervised by Jeshua with his sons and relatives, and Kadmiel and his sons, all descendants of Hodaviah.* They were helped in this task by the Levites of the family of Henadad.
10 When the builders completed the foundation of the LORD's Temple, the priests put
on their robes and took their places to blow their trumpets. And the Levites, descendants
of Asaph, clashed their cymbals to praise the LORD, just as King David had prescribed.
11 With praise and thanks, they sang this song to the LORD:

"He is so good!
His faithful love for Israel endures forever!"

Then all the people gave a great shout, praising the LORD because the foundation of the
LORD's Temple had been laid.
12 Many of the older priests, Levites, and other leaders remembered the first Temple,
and they wept aloud when they saw the new Temple's foundation. The others, however,
were shouting for joy. 13 The joyful shouting and weeping mingled together in a loud
commotion that could be heard far in the distance.

3:7 1 Kgs 5:9-11; 2 Chr 2:10-16; Ezra 1:2; 6:3
3:8 Num 4:3; 1 Chr 23:24-32; Ezra 3:2; 4:2
3:9 Ezra 2:40
3:10 1 Chr 6:31; 25:1
3:11 1 Chr 16:34, 41; 2 Chr 7:3; Neh 12:24, 40; Ps 106:1
3:12 Hag 2:3

3:6 Hebrew *On the first day of the seventh month.* This day of the Hebrew lunar calendar occurs in September or October. The Festival of Shelters began on the fifteenth day of the seventh month. **3:8** Hebrew *in the second month.* This month of the Hebrew lunar calendar occurred in April and May 536 B.C. **3:9** Hebrew *sons of Judah* (i.e., *bene Yehudah*). *Bene* might also be read here as the proper name Binnui; *Yehudah* is probably another name for Hodaviah. Compare 2:40; Neh 7:43; 1 Esdras 5:58.

3:5 These sacrifices were originally set up under the law of Moses in Leviticus 1 and 6:8-13. The festivals are described in Leviticus 23. At the beginning of every month, they held a special observance (Numbers 10:10).

3:7 When Solomon built the first Temple (2 Chronicles 2), he also exchanged food and olive oil—plentiful resources in Israel—for wood, a resource Israel lacked. The wood came from Tyre and Sidon that time, too.

3:8 Why was the Lord's Temple begun first, even before the city wall? The Temple was used for spiritual purposes; the wall, for military and political purposes. God had always been the nation's protector, and the Jews knew that the strongest stone wall would not protect them if God was not with them. They knew that putting their spiritual lives in order was a far higher priority than assuring the national defense.

3:8 It took from September (3:1; September was the seventh month because the year began in March) to April just to *prepare* to build the Temple. The exiles took time to make plans because the project was important to them. Preparation may not feel heroic or spiritual, but it is vital to any project meant to be done well.

3:10, 11 David had given clear instructions concerning the use of music in worship services in the Temple (1 Chronicles 16; 25).

3:10, 11 Completing the foundation for the Temple required great effort on the part of all involved. But no one tried to get praise for himself and his own hard work. Instead, everyone praised God for what had been done. All good gifts come from God—talents, abilities, strength, and leadership. We should thank God for what has been done in and through us!

3:11 The Bible records many songs and musical events. For a list of such events, see the chart in Exodus 15.

3:12 Fifty years after its destruction, the Temple was being rebuilt (536 B.C.). Some of the older people remembered Solomon's Temple, and they wept because the new Temple would not be as glorious as the first one. But the beauty of the building was not nearly as important to God as were the attitudes of the builders and worshipers. God cares more about who we are than what we accomplish. Our world is always changing, and once-magnificent accomplishments decay and disappear. Seek to serve God wholeheartedly. Then you won't need to compare your work with anyone else's.

3:12 Because the new Temple was built on the foundation of Solomon's Temple, the two structures were not that different in size. But the old Temple was far more ornate and was surrounded by many buildings and a vast courtyard. Both Temples were constructed of imported cedarwood, but Solomon's was decorated with vast amounts of gold and precious stones. Solomon's Temple took over seven years to build; Zerubbabel's took about four years. Solomon's Temple was at the hub of a thriving city; Zerubbabel's was surrounded by ruins. No wonder the people wept.

3:13 The celebration after laying the Temple foundation was marked by contrasts of emotion—shouts of joy and sounds of weeping. Both were appropriate. The Holy Spirit can stimulate us both to rejoice over the goodness of his grace and to grieve over the sins that required him to correct us. When we come into the presence of almighty God, we may feel full of joy and thanksgiving, yet at the same time be sobered by our shortcomings.

Enemies Oppose the Rebuilding

4:1 Ezra 4:7-10
4:2 2 Kgs 17:32; 19:37
4:3 Ezra 1:1-4; 6:3-5; Neh 2:20
4:4 Ezra 3:3

4 The enemies of Judah and Benjamin heard that the exiles were rebuilding a Temple
to the LORD, the God of Israel. [2]So they approached Zerubbabel and the other
leaders and said, "Let us build with you, for we worship your God just as you do. We
have sacrificed to him ever since King Esarhaddon of Assyria brought us here."
[3]But Zerubbabel, Jeshua, and the other leaders of Israel replied, "You may have no
part in this work, for we have nothing in common. We alone will build the Temple for
the LORD, the God of Israel, just as King Cyrus of Persia commanded us."
[4]Then the local residents tried to discourage and frighten the people of Judah to keep
them from their work. [5]They bribed agents to work against them and to frustrate their
aims. This went on during the entire reign of King Cyrus of Persia and lasted until King
Darius of Persia took the throne.

Later Opposition under King Artaxerxes

4:6 Esth 1:1; Dan 9:1
4:7 2 Kgs 18:26; Isa 36:11; Dan 2:4
4:8 Ezra 5:6; 6:13

[6]Years later when Xerxes* began his reign, the enemies of Judah wrote him a letter of
accusation against the people of Judah and Jerusalem. [7]And even later, during the reign
of King Artaxerxes of Persia,* the enemies of Judah, led by Bishlam, Mithredath, and
Tabeel, sent a letter to Artaxerxes in the Aramaic language, and it was translated for the
king. [8]Rehum* the governor and Shimshai the court secretary wrote the letter, telling
King Artaxerxes about the situation in Jerusalem. [9]They greeted the king for all their
colleagues—the judges and local leaders, the people of Tarpel, the Persians, the Babylonians, and the people of Erech and Susa (that is, Elam). [10]They also sent greetings from

4:6 Hebrew *Ahasuerus,* another name for Xerxes. He reigned 486–465 B.C. **4:7** Artaxerxes reigned 465–424 B.C.
4:8 The original text of 4:8–6:18 is in Aramaic.

THE PERSIAN KINGS OF EZRA'S DAY

Name	*Date of Reign*	*Relationship to Israel*
Cyrus	559–530 B.C.	Conquered Babylon. Established a policy of returning exiles to their homelands. Sent Zerubbabel to Jerusalem, financed his project, and returned the gold and silver articles that Nebuchadnezzar had taken from the Temple. He probably knew Daniel.
Darius	522–486 B.C.	Supported construction of the Temple in Jerusalem.
Xerxes (Ahasuerus)	486–465 B.C.	Was Esther's husband. Allowed the Jews to protect themselves against Haman's attempt to eliminate their people.
Artaxerxes I	465–424 B.C.	Had Nehemiah as his cup-bearer. Allowed both Ezra and Nehemiah to return to Jerusalem.

4:1-3 The enemies of Judah and Benjamin were people who had been relocated in the northern kingdom when Assyria conquered Israel (see 2 Kings 17 and the note on 3:3). In an attempt to infiltrate and disrupt the project, these people offered to help in the rebuilding project. They wanted to keep a close eye on what the Jews were doing. They were hoping to keep Jerusalem from becoming strong again. The Jews, however, saw through their ploy. Such a partnership with unbelievers would have led God's people to compromise their faith.

4:1-6 Believers can expect opposition when they do God's work (2 Timothy 3:12). Unbelievers and evil spiritual forces are always working against God and his people. The opposition may offer compromising alliances (4:2), attempt to discourage and intimidate us (4:4, 5), or accuse us unjustly (4:6). If you expect these tactics, you won't be hindered by them. Move ahead with the work God has planned for you, and trust him to show you how to overcome the obstacles.

4:2 These enemies claimed to worship the same God as Zerubbabel and the rest of the Jews. In one sense, this was true; they worshiped God, but they also worshiped many other gods (see 2 Kings 17:27-29, 32-34, 41). In God's eyes, this was not worship—it was sin and rebellion. True worship involves devotion to God alone (Exodus 20:3-5). To these foreigners, God was just another "idol" to be added to their collection. Their real motive was to disrupt the Temple project. Believers today must beware of those who claim to be Christians but whose actions clearly reveal they are using Christianity to serve their own interests.

4:4, 5 Discouragement and fear are two of the greatest obstacles to completing God's work. Most often they come when you least expect them. Discouragement eats away at our motivation, and fear paralyzes us so we don't act at all. Recognize these common barriers. Remember that God's people in every age have faced these problems and with God's help have overcome them. By standing together with other believers, you can overcome fear and discouragement and complete God's will.

4:6-23 In these verses, Ezra summarizes the entire story of the opposition to building the Temple, the walls, and other important buildings in Jerusalem. Chronologically, 4:6 fits between chapters 6 and 7; 4:7-23 refers to the events between Ezra 7 and Nehemiah 1. Ezra grouped them here to highlight the persistent opposition to God's people over the years and God's ability to overcome it.

4:7 This letter sent to King Artaxerxes may have been inscribed on a clay tablet, a fragment of pottery, or sheets of parchment.

4:10 Ashurbanipal (669–627 B.C.) was the Assyrian king who completed the relocation of Israelite captives. He was the last of the strong Assyrian kings. After his death the nation quickly declined. Assyria was conquered by Babylon in 612.

the rest of the people whom the great and noble Ashurbanipal* had deported and
relocated in Samaria and throughout the neighboring lands of the province west of the
Euphrates River. 11This is a copy of the letter they sent him:

"To Artaxerxes, from your loyal subjects in the province west of the Euphrates
River.

12"Please be informed that the Jews who came here to Jerusalem from Babylon
are rebuilding this rebellious and evil city. They have already laid the foundation
for its walls and will soon complete them. 13But we wish you to know that if this
city is rebuilt and its walls are completed, it will be much to your disadvantage,
for the Jews will then refuse to pay their tribute, customs, and tolls to you.

14"Since we are loyal to you as your subjects and we do not want to see you dishonored in this way, we have sent you this information. 15We suggest that you search
your ancestors' records, where you will discover what a rebellious city this has been in
the past. In fact, it was destroyed because of its long history of sedition against the kings
and countries who attempted to control it. 16We declare that if this city is rebuilt and its
walls are completed, the province west of the Euphrates River will be lost to you."

17Then Artaxerxes made this reply:

"To Rehum the governor, Shimshai the court secretary, and their colleagues living
in Samaria and throughout the province west of the Euphrates River.

18"Greetings. The letter you sent has been translated and read to me. 19I have
ordered a search to be made of the records and have indeed found that Jerusalem
has in times past been a hotbed of insurrection against many kings. In fact, rebellion and sedition are normal there! 20Powerful kings have ruled over Jerusalem
and the entire province west of the Euphrates River and have received vast tribute,
customs, and tolls. 21Therefore, issue orders to have these people stop their work.
That city must not be rebuilt except at my express command. 22Do not delay, for
we must not permit the situation to get out of control."

23When this letter from King Artaxerxes was read to Rehum, Shimshai, and their
colleagues, they hurried to Jerusalem and forced the Jews to stop building.

The Rebuilding Resumes

24The work on the Temple of God in Jerusalem had stopped, and it remained at a standstill
until the second year of the reign of King Darius of Persia.*

5 At that time the prophets Haggai and Zechariah son of Iddo prophesied in the name
of the God of Israel to the Jews in Judah and Jerusalem. 2Zerubbabel son of Shealtiel
and Jeshua son of Jehozadak* responded by beginning the task of rebuilding the Temple
of God in Jerusalem. And the prophets of God were with them and helped them.

4:12 Ezra 5:3, 9
4:13 Ezra 4:20; 7:24; Neh 5:4
4:18 Neh 8:8
4:20 1 Kgs 4:21, 24; 1 Chr 18:3; Ezra 4:13
4:24 Hag 1:1, 15; Zech 1:1
5:1 Ezra 6:14; Hag 1:1; Zech 1:1
5:2 Ezra 3:2

4:10 Aramaic *Osnappar,* another name for Ashurbanipal. **4:24** The second year of Darius's reign was 520 B.C.
5:2 Aramaic *Jozadak,* a variant name for Jehozadak.

4:19, 20 Artaxerxes said that Jerusalem "has in times past been a hotbed of insurrection against many kings." By reading the historical records, he learned that mighty kings had come from Jerusalem, and he may have feared that another would arise if the city were rebuilt. Solomon had ruled a huge empire (1 Kings 4:21), and Jerusalem's kings had rebelled against mighty powers. For example, Zedekiah rebelled against Nebuchadnezzar despite his oath of loyalty (2 Chronicles 36:13). Artaxerxes did not want to aid the rebuilding of a rebellious city and nation.

4:23 Setbacks and standstills are painful and discouraging to God's workers. These exiles had received a double dose (see 4:1-5 and 4:6-22). Leaders should do everything to keep work from grinding to a halt; yet circumstances sometimes really are beyond our control. When you have been brought to a standstill, remember to still stand strong in the Lord.

4:24 Ezra resumes his chronological account here. It may have been 10 years since the Israelites had worked on the Temple. It did not begin again until 520 B.C., the second year of Darius's reign (5:1ff).

5:1 More details about the work and messages of Haggai and Zechariah are found in the books of the Bible that bear their names.

5:1, 2 "The prophets of God were with them and helped them." God sometimes sends prophets to encourage and strengthen his people. To accomplish this, Haggai and Zechariah not only preached but also got involved in the labor. In the church today God appoints prophetic voices to help us with our work (Ephesians 4:11-13). Their ministry should have the same effect upon us as Haggai's and Zechariah's had on Israel. "One who prophesies is helping others grow in the Lord, encouraging and comforting them" (1 Corinthians 14:3). In turn, we should encourage those who bring God's words to us.

5:3 Ezra 1:3; 5:6, 9, 17; 6:6, 13
5:4 Ezra 5:10
5:5 Ezra 7:6, 28; Ps 33:18

[3]But Tattenai, governor of the province west of the Euphrates, and Shethar-bozenai
and their colleagues soon arrived in Jerusalem and asked, "Who gave you permission to
rebuild this Temple and restore this structure?" [4]They also asked for a list of the names
of all the people who were working on the Temple. [5]But because their God was watching
over them, the leaders of the Jews were not prevented from building until a report was
sent to Darius and he returned his decision.

Tattenai's Letter to King Darius

5:6 Ezra 4:9

[6]This is the letter that Tattenai the governor, Shethar-bozenai, and the other officials of
the province west of the Euphrates River sent to King Darius:

[7]"Greetings to King Darius. [8]We wish to inform you that we went to the construction site of the Temple of the great God in the province of Judah. It is
being rebuilt with specially prepared stones, and timber is being laid in its
walls. The work is going forward with great energy and success. [9]We asked
the leaders, 'Who gave you permission to rebuild this Temple and restore this
structure?' [10]And we demanded their names so that we could tell you who the
leaders were.

5:11 1 Kgs 6:1-38; 2 Chr 3:1-2
5:12 2 Kgs 24:2, 10; 25:1, 8-11; 2 Chr 36:6-20

[11]"This was their answer: 'We are the servants of the God of heaven and earth,
and we are rebuilding the Temple that was built here many years ago by a great
king of Israel. [12]But because our ancestors angered the God of heaven, he aban-

THE POSTEXILIC PROPHETS

God used these men to confront and comfort his people after their return to their homeland from exile in Babylon.

Who?	*When?*	*Ministered to These Contemporary Leaders*	*Main Message*	*Significance*
Haggai	520 B.C.	Zerubbabel Joshua	• Encouraged the leaders and the people to continue rebuilding the Temple, which God would bless • Challenged the people's careless worship, which God would not bless	Disobedience and careless obedience of God's commands lead to judgment.
Zechariah	520 B.C.	Zerubbabel Joshua	• Emphasized God's command to rebuild his Temple • Gave the people another look at God's plan to bless the world through Israel and its coming king—the Messiah (9:9, 10)	Encouragement for today's effort sometimes requires that we remember God has a plan and purpose for tomorrow. Meanwhile the challenge is to live for him today.
Malachi	430 B.C.	The priests are the only leaders mentioned	• Confronted the people and priests with God's promises of judgment on those who reject him and God's blessing on those who live as he desires	God expects our obedience to him to affect our attitude toward him and our treatment of one another.

5:3-5 The non-Jews who lived nearby attempted to hinder the construction of the Temple. But while the legal debate went on and the decision was under appeal, the Jews continued to rebuild. When we are doing God's work, others may try to delay, confuse, or frustrate us, but we can proceed confidently. God will accomplish his purposes in our world, no matter who attempts to block them. Just as he watched over the Jewish elders, he watches over you. Concentrate on God's purpose, and don't be sidetracked by intrigues or slander.

5:11 While rebuilding the Temple, the workers were confronted by the Persia-appointed governor, demanding to know who gave permission for their construction project (5:3). This could have been intimidating, but, as we learn from the letter, they boldly replied, "We are the servants of the God of heaven and earth."

It is not always easy to speak up for our faith in an unbelieving world, but we must. The way to deal with pressure and intimidation is to recognize that we are workers for God. Our allegiance is to him first, people second. When we contemplate the reactions and criticisms of hostile people, we can become paralyzed with fear. If we try to offend no one or to please everyone, we won't be effective. God is our leader, and his rewards are most important. So don't be intimidated. Let others know by your words and actions whom you really serve.

doned them to King Nebuchadnezzar of Babylon,* who destroyed this Temple and
exiled the people to Babylonia. 13 However, King Cyrus of Babylon,* during the
first year of his reign, issued a decree that the Temple of God should be rebuilt.
14 King Cyrus returned the gold and silver utensils that Nebuchadnezzar had taken
from the Temple of God in Jerusalem and had placed in the temple of Babylon.
These items were taken from that temple and delivered into the safekeeping of a
man named Sheshbazzar, whom King Cyrus appointed as governor of Judah. 15 The
king instructed him to return the utensils to their place in Jerusalem and to rebuild
the Temple of God there as it had been before. 16 So this Sheshbazzar came and laid
the foundations of the Temple of God in Jerusalem. The people have been working
on it ever since, though it is not yet completed.'

17 "So now, if it pleases the king, we request that you search in the royal archives
of Babylon to discover whether King Cyrus ever issued a decree to rebuild God's
Temple in Jerusalem. And then let the king send us his decision in this matter."

5:13 Ezra 1:1-8
5:14 Ezra 1:7-8, 11; 5:16; 6:3-5 Dan 5:2
5:17 Ezra 6:1-2

Darius Approves the Rebuilding

6 So King Darius issued orders that a search be made in the Babylonian archives,
where treasures were stored. 2 But it was at the fortress at Ecbatana in the province
of Media that a scroll was found. This is what it said:

3 "Memorandum:

"In the first year of King Cyrus's reign, a decree was sent out concerning the Temple
of God at Jerusalem. It must be rebuilt on the site where Jews used to offer their sacrifices, retaining the original foundations. Its height will be ninety feet, and its width
will be ninety feet.* 4 Every three layers of specially prepared stones will be topped by

6:1 Ezra 5:17
6:3 Ezra 3:10
6:4 1 Kgs 6:36

5:12 Aramaic *Nebuchadnezzar the Chaldean.* **5:13** King Cyrus of Persia is here identified as the king of Babylon because Persia had conquered the Babylonian Empire. **6:3** Aramaic *Its height will be 60 cubits* [27 meters], *and its width will be 60 cubits.* It is commonly held that this verse should be emended to read: "Its height will be 45 feet, its length will be 90 feet, and its width will be 30 feet"; compare 1 Kgs 6:2. The emendation regarding the width is supported by the Syriac version.

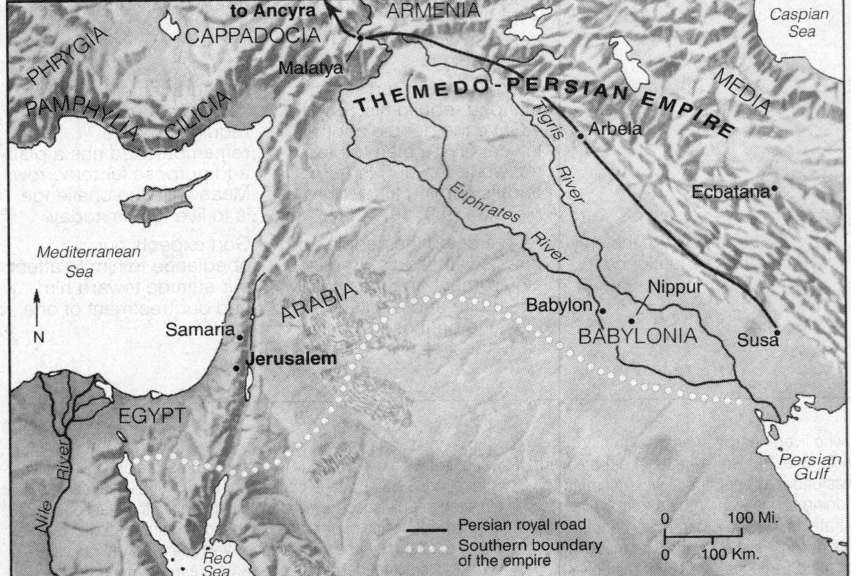

THE MEDO-PERSIAN EMPIRE
The Medo-Persian Empire included the lands of Media and Persia, much of the area shown on this map and more. The Jewish exiles were concentrated in the area around Nippur in the Babylonian province. The decree by King Cyrus that allowed the Israelites to return to their homeland and rebuild the Temple was discovered in the palace at Ecbatana.

5:13-17 Cyrus is called king of Persia in 1:1 and king of Babylon in 5:13. Because Persia had just conquered Babylon, Cyrus was king of both nations. Babylon is more important to this story because it was the location of the Hebrews' 70-year captivity. The Babylon in 5:17 may refer to the city of Babylon, which was the capital of the nation of Babylon.

6:1, 2 Many clay and papyrus documents recording business transactions and historical data have been discovered in this area (near present-day Syria). A great library and archives with thousands of such records have been discovered at Ebla in Syria.

a layer of timber. All expenses will be paid by the royal treasury. 5And the gold and
silver utensils, which were taken to Babylon by Nebuchadnezzar from the Temple of
God in Jerusalem, will be taken back to Jerusalem and put into God's Temple as they
were before."

6:6 Ezra 5:3; 6:13

6So King Darius sent this message:
"To Tattenai, governor of the province west of the Euphrates River, to Shethar-
bozenai, and to your colleagues and other officials west of the Euphrates:

"Stay away from there! 7Do not disturb the construction of the Temple of God. Let
it be rebuilt on its former site, and do not hinder the governor of Judah and the leaders of the Jews in their work. 8Moreover I hereby decree that you are to help these
leaders of the Jews as they rebuild this Temple of God. You must pay the full construction costs without delay from my taxes collected in your province so that the
work will not be discontinued. 9Give the priests in Jerusalem whatever is needed in
the way of young bulls, rams, and lambs for the burnt offerings presented to the
God of heaven. And without fail, provide them with the wheat, salt, wine, and olive

6:10 Ezra 7:23

oil that they need each day. 10Then they will be able to offer acceptable sacrifices to
the God of heaven and pray for me and my sons.

6:11 Ezra 7:26; Dan 2:5; 3:29

11"Those who violate this decree in any way will have a beam pulled from their
house. Then they will be tied to it and flogged, and their house will be reduced to a

6:12 Deut 12:4-5, 11; 1 Kgs 9:2-3

pile of rubble.* 12May the God who has chosen the city of Jerusalem as the place to
honor his name destroy any king or nation that violates this command and destroys
this Temple. I, Darius, have issued this decree. Let it be obeyed with all diligence."

The Temple's Dedication

6:13 Ezra 6:6

13Tattenai, governor of the province west of the Euphrates River, and Shethar-bozenai

6:14 Ezra 5:1-2; 6:12; 7:1, 7-9, 11; Zech 4:9

and their colleagues complied at once with the command of King Darius. 14So the Jewish
leaders continued their work, and they were greatly encouraged by the preaching of the
prophets Haggai and Zechariah son of Iddo. The Temple was finally finished, as had been
commanded by the God of Israel and decreed by Cyrus, Darius, and Artaxerxes, the
kings of Persia. 15The Temple was completed on March 12,* during the sixth year of
King Darius's reign.

6:16 1 Kgs 8:63; 2 Chr 7:5

16The Temple of God was then dedicated with great joy by the people of Israel, the
priests, the Levites, and the rest of the people who had returned from exile. 17During the

6:17 Ezra 8:35

dedication ceremony for the Temple of God, one hundred young bulls, two hundred
rams, and four hundred lambs were sacrificed. And twelve male goats were presented as

6:18 Num 3:6; 1 Chr 23:6; 2 Chr 35:4-5

a sin offering for the twelve tribes of Israel. 18Then the priests and Levites were divided
into their various divisions to serve at the Temple of God in Jerusalem, following all the
instructions recorded in the Book of Moses.

Celebration of Passover

6:19 Exod 12:6; Ezra 1:11

19On April 21* the returned exiles celebrated Passover. 20The priests and Levites had
purified themselves and were ceremonially clean. So they slaughtered the Passover

6:11 Aramaic *a dunghill.* **6:15** Aramaic *on the third day of the month Adar,* of the Hebrew calendar. This event occurred on March 12, 515 B.C.; also see note on 3:1. **6:19** Hebrew *On the fourteenth day of the first month,* of the Hebrew calendar. This event occurred on April 21, 515 B.C.; also see note on 3:1.

6:14 Ezra carefully pointed out that rebuilding the Temple was commanded first by God and then by the kings, who were his instruments. How ironic and wonderful that God's work was carried on by the discovery of a lost paragraph in a pagan library. All the opposition of powerful forces was stopped by a clause in a legal document. God's will is supreme over all rulers, all historical events, and all hostile forces. He can deliver us in ways we can't imagine. If we trust in his power and love, no opposition can stop us.

6:15 The Temple was completed in 515 B.C.

6:16-22 Feasting and celebration were in order at the great Temple dedication. This celebration was similar to the one that Solomon had when he dedicated the Temple in 1 Kings 8:63, although Solomon offered more than 200 times as many cattle and sheep. This Book of Moses was probably Leviticus. The priests and Levites were organized into groups in order to "serve at the Temple of God . . . following all the instructions recorded in the Book of Moses." There is a time to celebrate, but there is also a time to work. Both are proper and necessary when worshiping God, and both are pleasing to him.

6:19 The Passover was an annual celebration commemorating Israel's deliverance from Egypt. After a series of plagues failed to convince Pharaoh to free the Israelites, God said that he would send the destroying angel to kill the firstborn in every household. But the angel would pass over every home that had the blood of a specified type of lamb on the sides and top of the doorframe. See Exodus 12:1-30 for the story of this event and the establishment of the Passover celebration.

lamb for all the returned exiles, for the other priests, and for themselves. [21]The
Passover meal was eaten by the people of Israel who had returned from exile and by
the others in the land who had turned from their immoral customs to worship the
LORD, the God of Israel. [22]They ate the Passover meal and celebrated the Festival of
Unleavened Bread for seven days. There was great joy throughout the land because
the LORD had changed the attitude of the king of Assyria* toward them, so that he
helped them to rebuild the Temple of God, the God of Israel.

6:21 Exod 19:10, 14; Num 9:6-7, 10-14; Ezra 9:1-15; Neh 9:2; 10:28
6:22 Exod 12:15; Ezra 1:1; 7:27

B. THE RETURN LED BY EZRA (7:1—10:44)

Ezra returned to the land with a second group of exiles, 80 years after Zerubbabel. Ezra found the Temple rebuilt, but the lives of the people in shambles. Intermarriage with foreigners opposed to God threatened the spiritual future of the nation. So Ezra prayed for guidance and then followed through with action. Christians today must also strive to keep their lives pure, refusing to let the sinful allurements of the world around them compromise their life-style.

1. The second group of exiles returns to the land

Ezra Arrives in Jerusalem

7 Many years later, during the reign of King Artaxerxes of Persia, there was a man
named Ezra. He was the son* of Seraiah, son of Azariah, son of Hilkiah, [2]son of
Shallum, son of Zadok, son of Ahitub, [3]son of Amariah, son of Azariah, son* of
Meraioth, [4]son of Zerahiah, son of Uzzi, son of Bukki, [5]son of Abishua, son of Phinehas, son of Eleazar, son of Aaron the high priest. [6]This Ezra was a scribe, well versed
in the law of Moses, which the LORD, the God of Israel, had given to the people of
Israel. He came up to Jerusalem from Babylon, and the king gave him everything he
asked for, because the gracious hand of the LORD his God was on him. [7]Some of the
people of Israel, as well as some of the priests, Levites, singers, gatekeepers, and
Temple servants, traveled up to Jerusalem with him in the seventh year of King
Artaxerxes' reign.
[8]Ezra arrived in Jerusalem in August* of that year. [9]He had left Babylon on April 8*
and came to Jerusalem on August 4,* for the gracious hand of his God was on him.
[10]This was because Ezra had determined to study and obey the law of the LORD and to
teach those laws and regulations to the people of Israel.

7:1 1 Chr 6:9-14; Ezra 7:12, 21; 8:1-10:44; Neh 2:1; 8:1-18
7:6 Ezra 7:10-11, 21-29; Neh 8:9, 13
7:7 Ezra 8:1-20
7:9 Ezra 7:6
7:10 Neh 8:1

Artaxerxes' Letter to Ezra

[11]King Artaxerxes had presented a copy of this letter to Ezra, the priest and scribe who
studied and taught the commands and laws of the LORD to Israel:

[12]"Greetings* from Artaxerxes, the king of kings, to Ezra the priest, the teacher of
the law of the God of heaven.

7:12 Ezek 26:7; Dan 2:37, 47

6:22 King Cyrus of Persia is here identified as the king of Assyria because Persia had conquered the Babylonian Empire, which included the earlier Assyrian Empire. **7:1** Or *descendant;* see 1 Chr 6:14. **7:3** Or *descendant;* see 1 Chr 6:6-10. **7:8** Hebrew *in the fifth month.* This month of the Hebrew lunar calendar occurred in August and September 458 B.C. **7:9a** Hebrew *on the first day of the first month,* of the Hebrew calendar. This event occurred on April 8, 458 B.C.; also see note on 3:1. **7:9b** Hebrew *on the first day of the fifth month,* of the Hebrew calendar. This event occurred on August 4, 458 B.C.; also see note on 3:1. **7:12** The original text of 7:12-26 is in Aramaic.

6:22 There are many ways to pray for God's help. Have you ever considered that God would change the attitude of a person or group of people? God is infinitely powerful, his insight and wisdom transcend the laws of human nature. While you must always change your attitude as a first step, remember that he can change the attitude of others.

7:1 There is a gap of almost 60 years between the events of chapters six and seven. The story in the book of Esther occurred during this time, in the reign of Xerxes, who ruled from 486–465 B.C. Artaxerxes, his son, became king in 465, and Ezra returned to Jerusalem in 458.

7:6 Eighty years after the first exiles returned to Jerusalem (2:1), Ezra himself returned. This was his first trip, and it took four months. The Temple had been standing for about 58 years. Up to this point in the narrative, Ezra had remained in Babylon, probably compiling a record of the events that had taken place. Why did he have to ask the king if he could return? Ezra wanted to lead many Jews back to Jerusalem, and he needed a decree from the king stating that any Jew who wanted to return could do so. This decree would be like a passport in case they ran into opposition along the way. The king's generous decree showed that God was blessing Ezra (7:6, 28). It also indicated that Ezra was probably a prominent man in Artaxerxes' kingdom. He was willing to give up this position in order to return to his homeland and teach the Israelites God's laws.

7:6-10 Ezra demonstrates how a gifted Bible teacher can move God's people forward. He was effective because he was a well-versed student of the law of the Lord and because he was determined to obey those laws. He taught through both his speaking and his example. Like Ezra, we should determine both to study and to obey God's Word.

7:14 Ezra 7:15, 28

7:16 1 Chr 29:6; Ezra 8:25

7:17 Num 15:4-13; Deut 12:4-11

13“I decree that any of the people of Israel in my kingdom, including the priests
and Levites, may volunteer to return to Jerusalem with you. 14I and my Council of
Seven hereby instruct you to conduct an inquiry into the situation in Judah and Jerusalem, based on your God's law, which is in your hand. 15We also commission you
to take with you some silver and gold, which we are freely presenting as an offering
to the God of Israel who lives in Jerusalem.
16“Moreover you are to take any silver and gold which you may obtain from the
province of Babylon, as well as the freewill offerings of the people and the priests
that are presented for the Temple of their God in Jerusalem. 17These donations are
to be used specifically for the purchase of bulls, rams, lambs, and the appropriate

EZRA

It is not personal achievement but personal commitment to live for God that is important. Achievements are simply examples of what God can do through someone's life. The most effective leaders spoken of in the Bible had little awareness of the impact their lives had on others. They were too busy obeying God to keep track of their successes. Ezra fits that description.

About 80 years after the rebuilding of the Temple under Zerubbabel, Ezra returned to Judah with about 2,000 men and their families. He was given a letter from Artaxerxes instructing him to carry out a program of religious education. Along with the letter came significant power. But long before Ezra's mission began, God had shaped him in three important ways so that he would use the power well. First, as a scribe, Ezra dedicated himself to carefully studying God's Word. Second, he intended to apply and obey personally the commands he discovered in God's Word. Third, he was committed to teaching others God's Word and its application to life.

Knowing Ezra's priorities, it is not surprising to note his actions when he arrived in Jerusalem. The people had disobeyed God's command not to marry women of foreign nations. On a cold and rainy day, Ezra addressed the people and made it clear they had sinned. Because of the sins of many, all were under God's condemnation. Confession, repentance, and action were needed. The people admitted their sin and devised a plan to deal with the problem.

This initial effort on Ezra's part set the stage for what Nehemiah would later accomplish. Ezra continued his ministry under Nehemiah, and the two were used by God to start a spiritual movement that swept the nation following the rebuilding of Jerusalem.

Ezra achieved great things and made a significant impact because he had the right starting place for his actions and his life: God's Word. He studied it seriously and applied it faithfully. He taught others what he learned. He is, therefore, a great model for anyone who wants to live for God.

Strengths and accomplishments
- Committed to study, follow, and teach God's Word
- Led the second group of exiles from Babylon to Jerusalem
- May have written 1 and 2 Chronicles
- Concerned about keeping the details of God's commands
- Sent by King Artaxerxes to Jerusalem to evaluate the situation, set up a religious education system, and returned with a firsthand report
- Worked alongside Nehemiah during the last spiritual awakening recorded in the Old Testament

Lessons from his life
- A person's willingness to know and practice God's Word will have a direct effect on how God uses his/her life
- The starting place for serving God is a personal commitment to serve him today, even before knowing what that service will be

Vital statistics
- Where: Babylon, Jerusalem
- Occupations: Scribe among the exiles in Babylon, king's envoy, teacher
- Relative: Father: Seraiah
- Contemporaries: Nehemiah, Artaxerxes

Key verse “Ezra had determined to study and obey the law of the LORD and to teach those laws and regulations to the people of Israel” (Ezra 7:10).

Ezra's story is told in Ezra 7:1—10:16 and Nehemiah 8:1—12:36.

7:14 The Council of Seven was Artaxerxes' supreme court (see Esther 1:14).

7:14 When Nebuchadnezzar destroyed the Temple, he took a vast amount of plunder that may have included a copy of the Book of the Law (2 Chronicles 36:18). It is also possible that this book was brought by the Jews into exile and was confiscated and read by their conquerors. Foreign leaders who worshiped many gods liked to have records of the gods of other nations for military and political reasons.

grain offerings and drink offerings, all of which will be offered on the altar of the Temple of your God in Jerusalem. 18 Any money that is left over may be used in whatever way you and your colleagues feel is the will of your God. 19 But as for the utensils we are entrusting to you for the service of the Temple of your God, deliver them in full to the God of Jerusalem. 20 If you run short of money for anything necessary for your God's Temple or for any similar needs, you may requisition funds from the royal treasury.

21 "I, Artaxerxes the king, hereby send this decree to all the treasurers in the province west of the Euphrates River: 'You are to give Ezra whatever he requests of you, for he is a priest and teacher of the law of the God of heaven. 22 You are to give him up to 7,500 pounds* of silver, 500 bushels* of wheat, 550 gallons of wine, 550 gallons of olive oil,* and an unlimited supply of salt. 23 Be careful to provide whatever the God of heaven demands for his Temple, for why should we risk bringing God's anger against the realm of the king and his sons? 24 I also decree that no priest, Levite, singer, gatekeeper, Temple servant, or other worker in this Temple of God will be required to pay taxes of any kind.'

25 "And you, Ezra, are to use the wisdom God has given you to appoint magistrates and judges who know your God's laws to govern all the people in the province west of the Euphrates River. If the people are not familiar with those laws, you must teach them. 26 Anyone who refuses to obey the law of your God and the law of the king will be punished immediately by death, banishment, confiscation of goods, or imprisonment."

7:20 Ezra 6:4
7:21 Ezra 7:6
7:25 Exod 18:21-25; Deut 16:18; Ezra 7:6, 10
7:26 Ezra 6:11-12

Ezra Praises the LORD

27 Praise the LORD, the God of our ancestors, who made the king want to beautify the Temple of the LORD in Jerusalem! 28 And praise him for demonstrating such unfailing love to me by honoring me before the king, his council, and all his mighty princes! I felt encouraged because the gracious hand of the LORD my God was on me. And I gathered some of the leaders of Israel to return with me to Jerusalem.

7:27 Ezra 6:22
7:28 Ezra 9:9

Exiles Who Returned with Ezra

8 Here is a list of the family leaders and the genealogies of those who came with me from Babylon during the reign of King Artaxerxes:

2 From the family of Phinehas: Gershom.
From the family of Ithamar: Daniel.
3 From the family of David: Hattush son of Shecaniah.
From the family of Parosh: Zechariah and 150 other men.
4 From the family of Pahath-moab: Eliehoenai son of Zerahiah and 200 other men.
5 From the family of Zattu*: Shecaniah son of Jahaziel and 300 other men.
6 From the family of Adin: Ebed son of Jonathan and 50 other men.
7 From the family of Elam: Jeshaiah son of Athaliah and 70 other men.
8 From the family of Shephatiah: Zebadiah son of Michael and 80 other men.
9 From the family of Joab: Obadiah son of Jehiel and 218 other men.
10 From the family of Bani*: Shelomith son of Josiphiah and 160 other men.
11 From the family of Bebai: Zechariah son of Bebai and 28 other men.

8:1 Ezra 7:7
8:3 Ezra 2:3

7:22a Aramaic *100 talents* [3.4 metric tons]. **7:22b** Aramaic *100 cors* [18.2 kiloliters]. **7:22c** Aramaic *100 baths* [2.1 kiloliters] *of wine, 100 baths of olive oil.* **8:5** As in some Greek manuscripts (see also 1 Esdras 8:32); Hebrew lacks *Zattu.* **8:10** As in some Greek manuscripts (see also 1 Esdras 8:36); Hebrew lacks *Bani.*

7:24 Why did Artaxerxes exempt Temple workers from paying taxes? He recognized that the priests and Levites filled an important role in society as spiritual leaders, so he freed them of tax burdens. While the Bible does not teach tax exemption for religious employees, Artaxerxes, a pagan king, recognized and supported the principle. Today, churches have the responsibility to keep worldly burdens off the shoulders of spiritual workers.

7:27 In Ezra's doxology, he acknowledges that God "made the king want to beautify the Temple." God can change a king's heart (see Proverbs 21:1). When we face life's challenges, we often must work diligently and with extraordinary effort, realizing that God oversees all our work. Recognize his hand in your success, and remember to praise him for his help and protection.

7:27, 28 Ezra praised God for all that God had done for him and through him. Ezra had honored God throughout his life, and God chose to honor him. Ezra could have assumed that his own greatness and charisma had won over the king and his princes, but he gave the credit to God. We, too, should be grateful to God for our success and not think that we did it in our own power.

7:28 The speaker here is Ezra. He writes in the first person for the remainder of the book.

[12] From the family of Azgad: Johanan son of Hakkatan and 110 other men.
[13] From the family of Adonikam, who came later*: Eliphelet, Jeuel, Shemaiah, and
60 other men.
[14] From the family of Bigvai: Uthai, Zaccur, and 70 other men.

Ezra's Journey to Jerusalem

8:15 Ezra 7:7; 8:21, 31 [15] I assembled the exiles at the Ahava Canal, and we camped there for three days while
I went over the lists of the people and the priests who had arrived. I found that not one
Levite had volunteered to come along. [16] So I sent for Eliezer, Ariel, Shemaiah, Elnathan,
Jarib, Elnathan, Nathan, Zechariah, and Meshullam, who were leaders of the people. I
8:17 Ezra 2:43-54 also sent for Joiarib and Elnathan, who were very wise men. [17] I sent them to Iddo, the
8:18 leader of the Levites at Casiphia, to ask him and his relatives and the Temple servants to
Ezra 7:6 send us ministers for the Temple of God at Jerusalem. [18] Since the gracious hand of our
God was on us, they sent us a man named Sherebiah, along with eighteen of his sons and
brothers. He was a very astute man and a descendant of Mahli, who was a descendant of
Levi son of Israel.* [19] They also sent Hashabiah, together with Jeshaiah from the
8:20 Ezra 2:43 descendants of Merari, and twenty of his sons and brothers, [20] and 220 Temple servants.
The Temple servants were assistants to the Levites—a group of Temple workers first
8:21 instituted by King David. They were all listed by name.
2 Chr 20:3 Ezra 8:15, 31 [21] And there by the Ahava Canal, I gave orders for all of us to fast and humble
Ps 27:11 ourselves before our God. We prayed that he would give us a safe journey and protect
Isa 58:3, 5 us, our children, and our goods as we traveled. [22] For I was ashamed to ask the king for
8:22 2 Chr 15:2 soldiers and horsemen to accompany us and protect us from enemies along the way. After
Ezra 7:6, 9, 28 all, we had told the king, "Our God protects all those who worship him, but his fierce
8:23 2 Chr 33:13 anger rages against those who abandon him." [23] So we fasted and earnestly prayed that
our God would take care of us, and he heard our prayer.
[24] I appointed twelve leaders of the priests—Sherebiah, Hashabiah, and ten other
8:25 Ezra 7:15-16 priests—[25] to be in charge of transporting the silver, the gold, the gold bowls, and the
other items that the king, his council, his leaders, and the people of Israel had
presented for the Temple of God. [26] I weighed the treasure as I gave it to them and
found the totals to be as follows:

8:13 The meaning of the Hebrew for this phrase is uncertain. **8:18** *Israel* is the name that God gave to Jacob.

8:15 Ezra's progress back to Jerusalem was halted while he waited to recruit Levites. God had called these men to a special service, and yet few were willing to volunteer when their services were needed. God has gifted each of us with abilities so we can make a contribution to his kingdom work (Romans 12:4-8). Don't wait to be recruited, but look for opportunities to volunteer. Don't hinder God's work by holding back. "God has given gifts to each of you from his great variety of spiritual gifts. Manage them well so that God's generosity can flow through you" (1 Peter 4:10).

8:21 Ezra and the people traveled approximately 900 miles on foot. The trip took them through dangerous and difficult territory and lasted about four months. They prayed that God would give them a safe journey. Our journeys today may not be as difficult and dangerous as Ezra's, but we should recognize our need to ask God for guidance and protection.

8:21-23 Before making all the physical preparations for the journey, Ezra made spiritual preparations. Their prayers and fasting prepared them spiritually and showed their dependence on God for protection, their faith that God was in control, and their affirmation that they were not strong enough to make the trip without him. When we take time to put God first in any endeavor, we are preparing well for whatever lies ahead.

8:23 Ezra knew God's promises to protect his people, but he didn't take them for granted. He also knew that God's blessings are appropriated through prayer, so Ezra and the people humbled themselves by fasting and praying. And their prayers were answered. Fasting humbled them because going without food was a reminder of their complete dependence on God. Fasting also gave them more time to pray and meditate on God.

Too often we pray glibly and superficially. Serious prayer, by contrast, requires concentration. It puts us in touch with God's will and can really change us. Without serious prayer, we reduce God to a quick-service pharmacist with painkillers for our every ailment.

8:26 This was a large amount of treasure to transport, with or without a detachment of soldiers for protection.

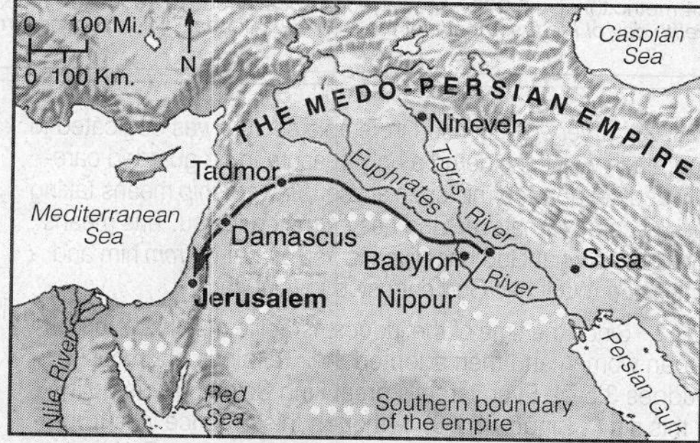

EZRA'S JOURNEY Ezra led a second group of exiles back to Judah and Jerusalem about 80 years after the first group. He traveled the dangerous route without military escort (8:22), but the people prayed and, under Ezra's godly leadership, arrived safely in Jerusalem after several months.

24 tons* of silver,
7,500 pounds* of silver utensils,
7,500 pounds* of gold,
27 20 gold bowls, equal in value to 1,000 gold coins,*
2 fine articles of polished bronze, as precious as gold.

28 And I said to these priests, "You and these treasures have been set apart as holy to 8:28 Lev 21:6-8; 22:2-3
the LORD. This silver and gold is a freewill offering to the LORD, the God of our Isa 52:11
ancestors. 29 Guard these treasures well until you present them, without an ounce lost, to 8:29
the leading priests, the Levites, and the leaders of Israel at the storerooms of the LORD's Ezra 8:33-34
Temple in Jerusalem." 30 So the priests and the Levites accepted the task of transporting
these treasures to the Temple of our God in Jerusalem.
31 We broke camp at the Ahava Canal on April 19* and started off to Jerusalem. And 8:31 Ezra 7:9
the gracious hand of our God protected us and saved us from enemies and bandits along 8:32
the way. 32 So at last we arrived safely in Jerusalem, where we rested for three days. Neh 2:11
33 On the fourth day after our arrival, the silver, gold, and other valuables were 8:33 Ezra 8:30
weighed at the Temple of our God and entrusted to Meremoth son of Uriah the priest and
to Eleazar son of Phinehas, along with Jozabad son of Jeshua and Noadiah son of
Binnui—both of whom were Levites. 34 Everything was accounted for by number and
weight, and the total weight was officially recorded.
35 Then the exiles who had returned from captivity sacrificed burnt offerings to the 8:35 Ezra 2:1; 6:17
God of Israel. They presented twelve oxen for the people of Israel, as well as ninety-six
rams and seventy-seven lambs. They also offered twelve goats as a sin offering. All this
was given as a burnt offering to the LORD. 36 The king's decrees were delivered to his 8:36
lieutenants and the governors of the province west of the Euphrates River, who then Ezra 7:21
cooperated by supporting the people and the Temple of God.

2. Ezra opposes intermarriage

Ezra's Prayer concerning Intermarriage

9 But then the Jewish leaders came to me and said, "Many of the people of Israel, and 9:1 Exod 23:28
even some of the priests and Levites, have not kept themselves separate from the Lev 18:24-30
other peoples living in the land. They have taken up the detestable practices of the Deut 20:17
Canaanites, Hittites, Perizzites, Jebusites, Ammonites, Moabites, Egyptians, and Amo- 9:2
rites. 2 For the men of Israel have married women from these people and have taken them Exod 34:16
as wives for their sons. So the holy race has become polluted by these mixed marriages.
To make matters worse, the officials and leaders are some of the worst offenders." 9:3 Neh 1:4
3 When I heard this, I tore my clothing, pulled hair from my head and beard, and sat 9:4
down utterly shocked. 4 Then all who trembled at the words of the God of Israel came Exod 29:38-39

8:26a Hebrew *650 talents* [22 metric tons]. **8:26b** Hebrew *100 talents* [3.4 metric tons]. **8:26c** Hebrew *100 talents* [3.4 metric tons]. **8:27** Hebrew *1,000 darics,* about 19 pounds or 8.6 kilograms in weight. **8:31** Hebrew *on the twelfth day of the first month,* of the Hebrew calendar. This event occurred on April 19, 458 B.C.; see note on 7:9a.

8:28, 29 Every object used in Temple service was dedicated to God; each was considered a holy treasure to be guarded carefully and set apart for his special use. *Stewardship* means taking special care of whatever God has entrusted to you. This means considering what God has given to you as being *from* him and *for* his use. What has God entrusted to your care?

9:1, 2 Since the time of the judges, Israelite men had married pagan women and then adopted their religious practices (Judges 3:5-7). Even Israel's great king Solomon was guilty of this sin (1 Kings 11:1-8). Although this practice was forbidden in God's law (Exodus 34:11-16; Deuteronomy 7:1-4), it happened in Ezra's day and again only a generation after him (Nehemiah 13:23-27). Opposition to mixed marriage was not racial prejudice because Jews and non-Jews of this area were of the same Semitic background. The reasons were strictly spiritual. A person who married a pagan was inclined to adopt that person's pagan beliefs and practices. If the Israelites were insensitive enough to disobey God in something as important as marriage, they wouldn't be strong enough to stand firm against their spouses' idolatry. Until the Israelites finally stopped this practice, idolatry remained a constant problem.

9:2 Some Israelites had married pagan spouses and lost track of God's purpose for them. The New Testament says that believers should not "team up with those who are unbelievers" (2 Corinthians 6:14). Such marriages cannot have unity in the most important issue in life—commitment and obedience to God. Because marriage involves two people becoming one, faith may become an issue, and one spouse may have to compromise beliefs for the sake of unity. Many people discount this problem only to regret it later. Don't allow emotion or passion to blind you to the importance of marrying someone with whom you can be united spiritually.

9:3-5 Tearing one's clothes and pulling hair from one's head or beard were signs of self-abasement or humility. They expressed sorrow for sin.

and sat with me because of this unfaithfulness of his people. And I sat there utterly appalled until the time of the evening sacrifice.

5At the time of the sacrifice, I stood up from where I had sat in mourning with my clothes torn. I fell to my knees, lifted my hands to the LORD my God. 6I prayed, "O my God, I am utterly ashamed; I blush to lift up my face to you. For our sins are piled higher than our heads, and our guilt has reached to the heavens. 7Our whole history has been one of great sin. That is why we and our kings and our priests have been at the mercy of the pagan kings of the land. We have been killed, captured, robbed, and disgraced, just as we are today.

8"But now we have been given a brief moment of grace, for the LORD our God has allowed a few of us to survive as a remnant. He has given us security in this holy place. Our God has brightened our eyes and granted us some relief from our slavery. 9For we were slaves, but in his unfailing love our God did not abandon us in our slavery. Instead, he caused the kings of Persia to treat us favorably. He revived us so that we were able to rebuild the Temple of our God and repair its ruins. He has given us a protective wall in Judah and Jerusalem.

10"And now, O our God, what can we say after all of this? For once again we have ignored your commands! 11Your servants the prophets warned us that the land we would possess was totally defiled by the detestable practices of the people living there. From one end to the other, the land is filled with corruption. 12You told us not to let our daughters marry their sons, and not to let our sons marry their daughters, and not to help those nations in any way. You promised that if we avoided these things, we would become a prosperous nation. You promised that we would enjoy the good produce of the land and leave this prosperity to our children as an inheritance forever.

13"Now we are being punished because of our wickedness and our great guilt. But we have actually been punished far less than we deserve, for you, our God, have allowed some of us to survive as a remnant. 14But now we are again breaking your commands and intermarrying with people who do these detestable things. Surely your anger will destroy us until even this little remnant no longer survives. 15O LORD, God of Israel, you are just. We stand before you in our guilt as nothing but an escaped remnant, though in such a condition none of us can stand in your presence."

The People Confess Their Sin

10 While Ezra prayed and made this confession, weeping and throwing himself to the ground in front of the Temple of God, a large crowd of people from Israel—men, women, and children—gathered and wept bitterly with him. 2Then Shecaniah son of Jehiel, a descendant of Elam, said to Ezra, "We confess that we have been unfaithful to our God, for we have married these pagan women of the land. But there is hope for Israel in spite of this. 3Let us now make a covenant with our God to divorce our pagan

9:5 Exod 9:29, 33
9:6 2 Chr 28:9; Rev 18:5
9:9 Exod 1:11-14; Neh 9:36-37; Ps 106:45-46
9:12 Deut 7:3
9:14 Deut 9:7-8, 13-14
9:15 Neh 9:33-34; Ps 130:3; Dan 9:7-11
10:1 2 Chr 20:9; Dan 9:4, 20
10:2 Ezra 9:2; 10:11; Neh 13:27
10:3 Deut 7:2-3

9:5-15 After learning about the sins of the people, Ezra fell to his knees in prayer. His heartfelt prayer provides a good perspective on sin. He recognized (1) that sin is serious (9:6); (2) that no one sins without affecting others (9:7); (3) that he was not sinless, although he didn't have a pagan wife (9:10ff); and (4) that God's love and mercy had spared the nation when they did nothing to deserve it (9:8, 9, 15). It is easy to view sin lightly in a world that sees sin as inconsequential, but we should view sin as seriously as Ezra did.

9:5-15 Ezra confessed the sins of his people. Although he had not sinned in the way his people had, he identified with their sins. With weeping, he expressed shame for sin, fear of the consequences, and desire that the people would come to their senses and repent. His prayer moved the people to tears (10:1). Ezra demonstrated the need for a holy community around the rebuilt Temple. We need a holy community in our local churches, too. Even when we sin in the worst imaginable way, we can turn to God with prayers of repentance.

9:9 Building a wall was not only a matter of civic pride or architectural beauty; it was essential for security and defense against robbers and marauders (see 9:7). God in his kindness had given them new life and protection.

9:15 Ezra recognized that if God gave the people the justice they deserved, they would not be able to stand before him. Often we cry out for justice when we feel abused and unfairly treated. In those moments, we forget the reality of our own sin and the righteous judgment we deserve. How fortunate we are that God gives us mercy and grace rather than only justice. The next time you ask God for fair treatment, pause to think what would happen if God gave you what you really deserve. Plead instead for his mercy.

10:3 Why were the men commanded to send away their wives and children? Although the measure was extreme, intermarriage to pagans was strictly forbidden (Deuteronomy 7:3, 4). Even the priests and Levites had intermarried, which could be compared today to a Christian marrying a devil worshiper. Although a severe solution, it only involved 113 of the approximately 29,000 families.

Ezra's strong act, though very difficult for some, was necessary to preserve Israel as a nation committed to God. Some of the exiles of the northern kingdom of Israel had lost both their spiritual and physical identity through intermarriage. Their pagan spouses had caused the people to worship idols. Ezra did not want this to happen to the exiles of the southern kingdom of Judah.

wives and to send them away with their children. We will follow the advice given by you
and by the others who respect the commands of our God. We will obey the law of God.
4Take courage, for it is your duty to tell us how to proceed in setting things straight, and **10:4** 1 Chr 28:10
we will cooperate fully."
5So Ezra stood up and demanded that the leaders of the priests and the Levites and all **10:5** Neh 5:12; 13:25
the people of Israel swear that they would do as Shecaniah had said. And they all swore
a solemn oath. 6Then Ezra left the front of the Temple of God and went to the room of **10:6** Deut 9:18
Jehohanan son of Eliashib. He spent the night* there, but he did not eat any food or drink.
He was still in mourning because of the unfaithfulness of the returned exiles. 7Then a
proclamation was made throughout Judah and Jerusalem that all the returned exiles
should come to Jerusalem. 8Those who failed to come within three days would, if the
leaders and elders so decided, forfeit all their property and be expelled from the assembly
of the exiles.
9Within three days, all the people of Judah and Benjamin had gathered in Jerusalem. **10:9** 1 Sam 12:17-18; Ezra 9:4; 10:3
This took place on December 19,* and all the people were sitting in the square before
the Temple of God. They were trembling both because of the seriousness of the matter
and because it was raining. 10Then Ezra the priest stood and said to them: "You have
sinned, for you have married pagan women. Now we are even more deeply under
condemnation than we were before. 11Confess your sin to the LORD, the God of your **10:11** Lev 26:40; Ezra 10:3
ancestors, and do what he demands. Separate yourselves from the people of the land and
from these pagan women."
12Then the whole assembly raised their voices and answered, "Yes, you are right; we
must do as you say!" 13Then they added, "This isn't something that can be done in a day
or two, for many of us are involved in this extremely sinful affair. This is the rainy season,
so we cannot stay out here much longer. 14Let our leaders act on behalf of us all. **10:14** 2 Chr 29:10; 30:8
Everyone who has a pagan wife will come at the scheduled time with the leaders and
judges of his city, so that the fierce anger of our God may be turned away from us
concerning this affair." 15Only Jonathan son of Asahel and Jahzeiah son of Tikvah
opposed this course of action, and Meshullam and Shabbethai the Levite supported them.
16So this was the plan that they followed. Ezra selected leaders to represent their
families, designating each of the representatives by name. On December 29,* the leaders
sat down to investigate the matter. 17By March 27 of the next year* they had finished
dealing with all the men who had married pagan wives.

Those Guilty of Intermarriage

18These are the priests who had married pagan wives:

From the family of Jeshua son of Jehozadak* and his brothers: Maaseiah, Eliezer,
Jarib, and Gedaliah. 19They vowed to divorce their wives, and they each **10:19** Lev 5:15
acknowledged their guilt by offering a ram as a guilt offering.
20From the family of Immer: Hanani and Zebadiah.
21From the family of Harim: Maaseiah, Elijah, Shemaiah, Jehiel, and Uzziah.
22From the family of Pashhur: Elioenai, Maaseiah, Ishmael, Nethanel, Jozabad, and
Elasah.

10:6 As in parallel text at 1 Esdras 9:2; Hebrew reads *He went.* **10:9** Hebrew *on the twentieth day of the ninth month,* of the Hebrew calendar. This event occurred on December 19, 458 B.C.; also see note on 7:9a. **10:16** Hebrew *On the first day of the tenth month,* of the Hebrew calendar. This event occurred on December 29, 458 B.C.; also see note on 7:9a. **10:17** Hebrew *By the first day of the first month,* of the Hebrew calendar. This event occurred on March 27, 457 B.C.; also see note on 7:9a. **10:18** Hebrew *Jozadak,* a variant name for Jehozadak.

10:3, 4, 11 Following Ezra's earnest prayer, the people confessed their sin to God. Then they asked for direction in restoring their relationship with God. True repentance does not end with words of confession—that would be mere lip service. It must lead to changed attitudes and behavior. When you sin and are truly sorry, confess this to God, ask his forgiveness, and accept his grace and mercy. Then, as an act of thankfulness for your forgiveness, make the needed corrections.

10:8 To forfeit one's property meant to be disinherited, to lose one's legal right to own land. This was to ensure that no pagan children would inherit Israel's land. In addition, the person who refused to come to Jerusalem would be expelled from the assembly of the exiles and not be allowed to worship in the Temple. The Jews considered this a horrible punishment.

10:11 As believers in Christ, all our sins are forgiven. His death cleansed us from all sin. Why do we then still confess our sins? Confession is more than appropriating Christ's forgiveness for what we have done wrong. Confession is agreeing with God that our thoughts, words, and actions are wrong and contrary to his will. It is recommitting ourselves to do his will and renouncing any acts of disobedience. We do not have to confess sins that were previously confessed. Confession involves turning away from all known sin and asking God for fresh power to live for him.

23 These are the Levites who were guilty: Jozabad, Shimei, Kelaiah (also called Kelita), Pethahiah, Judah, and Eliezer.

24 This is the singer who was guilty: Eliashib.

These are the gatekeepers who were guilty: Shallum, Telem, and Uri.

25 These are the other people of Israel who were guilty:

From the family of Parosh: Ramiah, Izziah, Malkijah, Mijamin, Eleazar, Hashabiah,* and Benaiah.
26 From the family of Elam: Mattaniah, Zechariah, Jehiel, Abdi, Jeremoth, and Elijah.
27 From the family of Zattu: Elioenai, Eliashib, Mattaniah, Jeremoth, Zabad, and Aziza.
28 From the family of Bebai: Jehohanan, Hananiah, Zabbai, and Athlai.
29 From the family of Bani: Meshullam, Malluch, Adaiah, Jashub, Sheal, and Jeremoth.
30 From the family of Pahath-moab: Adna, Kelal, Benaiah, Maaseiah, Mattaniah, Bezalel, Binnui, and Manasseh.
31 From the family of Harim: Eliezer, Ishijah, Malkijah, Shemaiah, Shimeon, 32 Benjamin, Malluch, and Shemariah.
33 From the family of Hashum: Mattenai, Mattattah, Zabad, Eliphelet, Jeremai, Manasseh, and Shimei.
34 From the family of Bani: Maadai, Amram, Uel, 35 Benaiah, Bedeiah, Keluhi, 36 Vaniah,
Meremoth, Eliashib, 37 Mattaniah, Mattenai, and Jaasu.
38 From the family of Binnui*: Shimei, 39 Shelemiah, Nathan, Adaiah, 40 Macnadebai,
Shashai, Sharai, 41 Azarel, Shelemiah, Shemariah, 42 Shallum, Amariah, and Joseph.
43 From the family of Nebo: Jeiel, Mattithiah, Zabad, Zebina, Jaddai, Joel, and Benaiah.

44 Each of these men had a pagan wife, and some even had children by these wives.*

10:44
Ezra 10:3

10:25 As in parallel text at 1 Esdras 9:26; Hebrew reads *Malkijah.* **10:37-38** As in Greek version; Hebrew reads *Jaasu, 38 Bani, Binnui.* **10:44** Or *and they sent them away with their children.* The meaning of the Hebrew is uncertain.

10:44 The book of Ezra opens with God's Temple in ruins and the people of Judah captive in Babylon. Ezra tells of the return of God's people, the rebuilding of the Temple, and the restoration of the sacrificial worship system. Similarly, God is able to restore and rebuild the lives of people today. No one is so far away from God that he or she cannot be restored. Repentance is all that is required. No matter how far we have strayed or how long it has been since we have worshiped God, he is able to restore our relationship to him and rebuild our lives.

NEHEMIAH

Jerusalem destroyed; exiles go to Babylon 586 B.C.

First exiles return to Jerusalem 538

Temple completed 515

VITAL STATISTICS

PURPOSE:
Nehemiah is the last of the Old Testament historical books. It records the history of the third return to Jerusalem after captivity, telling how the walls were rebuilt and the people were renewed in their faith.

AUTHOR:
Much of the book is written in the first person, suggesting Nehemiah as the author. Nehemiah probably wrote the book with Ezra serving as editor.

DATE WRITTEN:
Approximately 445–432 B.C.

SETTING:
Zerubbabel led the first return to Jerusalem in 538 B.C. In 458, Ezra led the second return. Finally, in 445, Nehemiah returned with the third group of exiles to rebuild the city walls.

KEY VERSES:
"So on October 2 the wall was finally finished—just fifty-two days after we had begun. When our enemies and the surrounding nations heard about it, they were frightened and humiliated. They realized that this work had been done with the help of our God" (6:15, 16).

KEY PEOPLE:
Nehemiah, Ezra, Sanballat, Tobiah

KEY PLACE:
Jerusalem

SPECIAL FEATURES:
The book shows the fulfillment of the prophecies of Zechariah and Daniel concerning the rebuilding of Jerusalem's walls.

"WHAT this church needs is . . . !" "I can't believe our government officials. If I were there I would . . . !" "Our schools are really in bad shape. Someone ought to do something!"

Gripers, complainers, self-proclaimed prophets, and "armchair quarterbacks" abound. It is easy to analyze, scrutinize, and *talk* about all the problems in the world. But what we really need are people who will not just discuss a situation but who will *do* something about it!

Nehemiah saw a problem and was distressed. Instead of complaining or wallowing in self-pity and grief, he took action. Nehemiah knew that God wanted him to motivate the Jews to rebuild Jerusalem's walls, so he left a responsible position in the Persian government to do what God wanted. Nehemiah knew God could use his talents to get the job done. From the moment he arrived in Jerusalem, everyone knew who was in charge. He organized, managed, supervised, encouraged, met opposition, confronted injustice, and kept going until the walls were built. Nehemiah was a man of action.

As the story begins, Nehemiah was talking with fellow Jews who reported that the walls and gates of Jerusalem were in disrepair. This was disturbing news, and rebuilding those walls became Nehemiah's burden. At the appropriate time, Nehemiah asked King Artaxerxes for permission to go to Jerusalem to rebuild its fallen walls. The king approved.

Armed with royal letters, Nehemiah traveled to Jerusalem. He organized the people into groups and assigned them to specific sections of the wall (chapter 3). The construction project was not without opposition, however. Sanballat, Tobiah, and others tried to halt the work with insults, ridicule, threats, and sabotage. Some of the workers became fearful; others became weary. In each case, Nehemiah employed a strategy to frustrate the enemies—prayer, encouragement, guard duty, consolidation (chapter 4). But a different problem arose—an internal one. Rich Jews were profiteering off the plight of their working countrymen. Hearing of their oppression and greed, Nehemiah confronted the extortioners face to face (chapter 5). Then, with the walls almost complete, Sanballat, Tobiah, and company tried one last time to stop Nehemiah. But Nehemiah stood firm, and the wall was finished in just 52 days. What a tremendous monument to God's love and faithfulness. Enemies and friends alike knew that God had helped (chapter 6).

After building the walls, Nehemiah continued to organize the people, taking a registration and appointing gatekeepers, Levites, and other officials (chapter 7). Ezra led the city in worship and Bible instruction (chapters 8, 9). This led to a reaffirmation of faith and religious revival as the people promised to serve God faithfully (chapters 10, 11).

Nehemiah closes with the listing of the clans and their leaders, the dedication of the new wall of Jerusalem, and the purging of sin from the land (chapters 12, 13). As you read this book, watch Nehemiah in action—and determine to be a person on whom God can depend to *act* for him in the world.

Xerxes becomes king of Persia 486	*Artaxerxes I becomes king of Persia 465*	*Ezra comes to Jerusalem 458*	*Nehemiah comes to Jerusalem; wall completed 445*	*Nehemiah returns to Babylon 433*	*Nehemiah goes back to Jerusalem 432*	*Malachi begins his ministry 430(?)*

THE BLUEPRINT

A. REBUILDING THE WALL (1:1—7:73) 1. Nehemiah returns to Jerusalem 2. Nehemiah leads the people	Nehemiah's life is an example of leadership and organization. Giving up a comfortable and wealthy position in Persia, he returned to the fractured homeland of his ancestors and rallied the people to rebuild Jerusalem's wall. In the face of opposition, he used wise defense measures to care for the people and to keep the project moving. To accomplish more for the sake of God's Kingdom, we must pray, persevere, and sacrifice, as did Nehemiah.
B. REFORMING THE PEOPLE (7:73—13:31) 1. Ezra renews the covenant 2. Nehemiah establishes policies	After the wall was rebuilt, Ezra read the law to the people, bringing about national repentance. Nehemiah and Ezra were very different people, yet God used them both to lead the nation. Remember, there is a place for you in God's work even if you're different from most other people. God uses each person in a unique way to accomplish his purposes.

MEGATHEMES

THEME	EXPLANATION	IMPORTANCE
Vision	Although the Jews completed the Temple in 515 B.C., the city walls remained in shambles for the next 70 years. These walls represented power, protection, and beauty to the city of Jerusalem. They were also desperately needed to protect the Temple from attack and to ensure the continuity of worship. God put the desire to rebuild the walls in Nehemiah's heart, giving him a vision for the work.	Does God have a vision for us? Are there "walls" that need to be built today? God still wants his people to be united and trained to do his work. As we recognize deep needs in our world, God can give us the vision and desire to "build." With that vision, we can mobilize others to pray and put together a plan of action.
Prayer	Both Nehemiah and Ezra responded to problems with prayer. When Nehemiah began his work, he recognized the problem, immediately prayed, and then acted on the problem.	Prayer is still God's mighty force in solving problems today. Prayer and action go hand in hand. Through prayer, God guides our preparation, teamwork, and diligent efforts to carry out his will.
Leadership	Nehemiah demonstrated excellent leadership. He was spiritually ready to heed God's call. He used careful planning, teamwork, problem solving, and courage to get the work done. Although he had tremendous faith, he never avoided the extra work necessary for good leadership.	Being God's leader is not just gaining recognition, holding a position, or being the boss. It requires planning, hard work, courage, and perseverance. Positive expectations are never a substitute for doing the difficult work. And in order to lead others, you need to listen for God's direction in your own life.
Problems	After the work began, Nehemiah faced scorn, slander, and threats from enemies, as well as fear, conflict, and discouragement from his own workers. Although these problems were difficult, they did not stop Nehemiah from finishing the work.	When difficulties come, there is a tendency for conflict and discouragement to set in. We must recognize that there are no triumphs without troubles. When problems arise, we must face them squarely and press on to complete God's work.
Repentance/ Revival	Although God had enabled them to build the wall, the work wasn't complete until the people rebuilt their lives spiritually. Ezra instructed the people in God's Word. As they listened, they recognized the sin in their lives, admitted it, and took steps to remove it.	Recognizing and admitting sin are not enough; revival must result in reform, or it is merely the expression of enthusiasm. God does not want halfhearted measures. We must not only remove sin from our lives but also ask God to move into the center of all we do.

A. REBUILDING THE WALL (1:1—7:73)

Despite the fact that the returned exiles had been in Jerusalem for many years, the walls of the city remained unrepaired, leaving its people defenseless and vulnerable. Upon hearing this news, Nehemiah seeks permission from the Persian king to go to Jerusalem. Arriving in Jerusalem, he mobilizes the people to begin rebuilding the wall. Faced with opposition, both from without and from within, Nehemiah perseveres until the project is complete and the city resettled. Seemingly impossible tasks can be accomplished when God is helping those who honor him and when their efforts are united.

1. Nehemiah returns to Jerusalem

Nehemiah's Concern for Jerusalem

1 These are the memoirs of Nehemiah son of Hacaliah.
In late autumn of the twentieth year of King Artaxerxes' reign,* I was at the fortress
of Susa. 2 Hanani, one of my brothers, came to visit me with some other men who had just
arrived from Judah. I asked them about the Jews who had survived the captivity and about
how things were going in Jerusalem. 3 They said to me, "Things are not going well for those
who returned to the province of Judah. They are in great trouble and disgrace. The wall of
Jerusalem has been torn down, and the gates have been burned."
4 When I heard this, I sat down and wept. In fact, for days I mourned, fasted, and
prayed to the God of heaven. 5 Then I said, "O LORD, God of heaven, the great and
awesome God who keeps his covenant of unfailing love with those who love him
and obey his commands, 6 listen to my prayer! Look down and see me praying night
and day for your people Israel. I confess that we have sinned against you. Yes, even
my own family and I have sinned! 7 We have sinned terribly by not obeying the
commands, laws, and regulations that you gave us through your servant Moses.
8 "Please remember what you told your servant Moses: 'If you sin, I will scatter you
among the nations. 9 But if you return to me and obey my commands, even if you are
exiled to the ends of the earth, I will bring you back to the place I have chosen for my
name to be honored.'

1:1 Neh 2:1; 10:1; Esth 1:2; Dan 8:2; Zech 7:1
1:2 Neh 7:2
1:3 Neh 2:3, 17; 7:6
1:4 Ezra 2:4; 9:3; 10:1
1:5 Exod 20:6; Neh 4:14; 9:32
1:6 2 Chr 29:6; Ezra 10:1; Dan 9:20
1:7 Deut 28:14; Dan 9:5
1:8 Lev 26:33
1:9 Deut 12:5; 30:2-4

1:1 Hebrew *In the month of Kislev of the twentieth year.* A number of dates in the book of Nehemiah can be cross-checked with dates in surviving Persian records and related accurately to our modern calendar. This month of the Hebrew lunar calendar occurred in November and December 446 B.C. The *twentieth year* probably refers to the reign of King Artaxerxes I; compare 2:1; 5:14.

1:1 Nehemiah wasn't the first of the exiles to return to Jerusalem. Zerubbabel had led the first group back in 538 B.C., more than 90 years earlier (Ezra 1–2). Ezra followed with a second group in 458 B.C. (Ezra 7), and here Nehemiah was ready to lead the third major return to Jerusalem (445 B.C.). When he arrived after a three-month journey, he saw the completed Temple and became acquainted with others who had returned to their homeland.

But Nehemiah also found a disorganized group of people and a defenseless city with no walls to protect it. Before the Exile, Israel had its own language, king, army, and identity. At this time it had none of these. What the Jews lacked most was leadership; there was no one to show them where to start and what direction to take as they tried to rebuild their city. As soon as Nehemiah arrived, he began a back-to-the-basics program. He helped care for the people's physical needs by setting up a fair system of government and rebuilding Jerusalem's walls. He also cared for their spiritual needs by rebuilding broken lives. Nehemiah is a model of committed, God-honoring leadership, and his book contains many useful lessons for today.

1:2-4 Nehemiah was concerned about Jerusalem because it was the Jews' holy city. As Judah's capital city, it represented Jewish national identity, and it was blessed with God's special presence in the Temple. Jewish history centered around the city from the time of Abraham's gifts to Melchizedek, king of Salem (Genesis 14:17-20), to the days when Solomon built the glorious Temple (1 Kings 7:51), and throughout the history of the kings. Nehemiah loved his homeland even though he had lived his whole life in Babylon. He wanted to return to Jerusalem to reunite the Jews and to remove the shame of Jerusalem's broken-down walls. This would bring glory to God and restore the reality and power of God's presence among his people.

1:4 Nehemiah broke down and wept when he heard that Jerusalem's walls still had not been rebuilt. Why did this upset him? Walls mean little in most present-day cities, but in Nehemiah's day they were essential. They offered safety from raids and symbolized strength and peace. Nehemiah also mourned for his people, the Jews, who had been stifled by a previous edict that kept them from rebuilding their walls (Ezra 4:6-23).

1:4 Nehemiah was deeply grieved about the condition of Jerusalem, but he didn't just brood about it. After his initial grief, he prayed, pouring his heart out to God (1:5-11), and he looked for ways to improve the situation. Nehemiah put all his resources of knowledge, experience, and organization into determining what should be done. When tragic news comes to you, first pray. Then seek ways to move beyond grief to specific action that helps those who need it.

1:5 God's "covenant of unfailing love" refers to God's promise to love the descendants of Abraham. It is also mentioned in Deuteronomy 7:7-9.

1:5ff Nehemiah fasted and prayed for several days, expressing his sorrow for Israel's sin and his desire that Jerusalem would again come alive with the worship of the one true God. Nehemiah demonstrated the elements of effective prayer: (1) praise, (2) thanksgiving, (3) repentance, (4) specific requests, and (5) commitment.

Heartfelt prayers like Nehemiah's can help clarify (1) any problem you may be facing, (2) God's great power to help you, and (3) the job you have to do. By the end of his prayer time, Nehemiah knew what action he had to take (1:11). When God's people pray, difficult decisions fall into proper perspective, and appropriate actions follow.

1:10 Exod 32:11 Deut 9:29 — 10“We are your servants, the people you rescued by your great power and might.
11O Lord, please hear my prayer! Listen to the prayers of those of us who delight in
1:11 Gen 40:21 Neh 1:6; 2:1 — honoring you. Please grant me success now as I go to ask the king* for a great favor. Put
it into his heart to be kind to me.”

In those days I was the king’s cup-bearer.

Nehemiah Goes to Jerusalem

2:1 Ezra 7:1 Neh 1:1, 11 — **2** Early the following spring,* during the twentieth year of King Artaxerxes’ reign, I
was serving the king his wine. I had never appeared sad in his presence before this
2:2 Prov 15:13 — time. 2So the king asked me, “Why are you so sad? You aren’t sick, are you? You look
like a man with deep troubles.”

2:3 Neh 1:3 Dan 2:4 — Then I was badly frightened, 3but I replied, “Long live the king! Why shouldn’t I be

1:11 Hebrew *stand before this man.* **2:1** Hebrew *In the month of Nisan.* This month of the Hebrew lunar calendar occurred in April and May 445 B.C.

HOW NEHEMIAH USED PRAYER

Reference	*Occasion*	*Summary of His Prayer*	*What Prayer Accomplished*	*Our Prayers*
1:4–11	After receiving the bad news about the state of Jerusalem’s walls	Recognized God’s holiness. Asked for a hearing. Confessed sin. Asked for specific help in approaching the king	Included God in Nehemiah’s plans and concerns. Prepared Nehemiah’s heart and gave God room to work	How often do you pour out your heart to God? How often do you give him a specific request to answer?
2:4	During his conversation with the king	“Here’s where you can help, God!”	Put the expected results in God’s hands	Giving God credit for what happens before it happens keeps us from taking more credit than we should.
4:4, 5	After being taunted and ridiculed by Tobiah and Sanballat	“They’re mocking you, God. You decide what to do with them.”	Expressed anger to God, but Nehemiah did not take matters into his own hands	We are prone to do exactly the opposite—take matters into our hands and not tell God how we feel.
4:9	After threats of attack by enemies	“We are in your hands, God. We’ll keep our weapons handy in case you want us to use them.”	Showed trust in God even while taking necessary precautions	Trusting God does not mean we do nothing. Action does not mean we do not trust.
6:9	Responding to threats	“O Lord God, please strengthen me!”	Showed Nehemiah’s reliance on God for emotional and mental stability	How often do you ask God for help when under pressure?
13:29	Reflecting on the actions of his enemies	Asked God to deal with the enemies and their evil plans	Took away the compulsion to get revenge, and entrusted justice to God	When did you last settle a desire for revenge by turning the matter over to God?
5:19; 13:14, 22, 31	Reflecting on his own efforts to serve God	“Remember me, God.”	Kept clear in Nehemiah’s mind his own motives for action	How many of your actions today will be done with the purpose of pleasing God?

1:11 Nehemiah was in a unique position to speak to the king. He was the trusted cup-bearer, who ensured the safety and quality of the king’s food and drink. Nehemiah was concerned, prayerful, and prepared as he looked for the right opportunity to tell the king about God’s people. Each of us is unique and capable of serving no matter what our position. Just as Nehemiah used his place as the king’s trusted servant to intercede for his people, we can use our present positions to serve God.

1:11 Nehemiah prayed for success in this venture, not just for the strength to cope with his problems (see also 2:20). Yet the success he prayed for was not for personal advantage, position, or acclaim. He requested success for God’s work. When God’s purposes are at work, don’t hesitate to ask for success.

2:2 The king noticed Nehemiah’s sad appearance. This frightened Nehemiah because it was dangerous to show sorrow before the king, who could execute anyone who displeased him. Anyone wearing mourning clothes was barred from the palace (Esther 4:2).

2:2, 3 Nehemiah wasn’t ashamed to admit his fear, but he refused to allow fear to stop him from doing what God had called him to do. When we allow fear to rule us, we make fear more powerful than God. Is there a task God wants you to do, but fear is holding you back? God is greater than all your fears. Recognizing why you are afraid is the first step in committing your fear to God. Realize that if God has called you to a task, he will help you accomplish it.

sad? For the city where my ancestors are buried is in ruins, and the gates have been
burned down."
4 The king asked, "Well, how can I help you?"
With a prayer to the God of heaven, 5 I replied, "If it please Your Majesty and if you — 2:4 Neh 1:4
are pleased with me, your servant, send me to Judah to rebuild the city where my
ancestors are buried."
6 The king, with the queen sitting beside him, asked, "How long will you be gone? — 2:6 Neh 13:6
When will you return?" So the king agreed, and I set a date for my departure.
7 I also said to the king, "If it please Your Majesty, give me letters to the governors of — 2:7 Ezra 7:21; 8:36
the province west of the Euphrates River, instructing them to let me travel safely through — Neh 2:9
their territories on my way to Judah. 8 And please send a letter to Asaph, the manager of — 2:8 Neh 7:2, 18
the king's forest, instructing him to give me timber. I will need it to make beams for the — Eccl 2:5-6
gates of the Temple fortress, for the city walls, and for a house for myself." And the king
granted these requests, because the gracious hand of God was on me.
9 When I came to the governors of the province west of the Euphrates River, I — 2:9 Ezra 8:22
delivered the king's letters to them. The king, I should add, had sent along army officers — Neh 2:7
and horsemen to protect me. 10 But when Sanballat the Horonite and Tobiah the Ammo- — 2:10
nite official heard of my arrival, they were very angry that someone had come who was — Neh 2:19; 4:1-3
interested in helping Israel.

2. Nehemiah leads the people

Nehemiah Inspects Jerusalem's Wall

11 Three days after my arrival at Jerusalem, 12 I slipped out during the night, taking only a few
others with me. I had not told anyone about the plans God had put in my heart for Jerusalem.

2:4 With little time to think, Nehemiah immediately prayed. Eight times in this book we read that he prayed spontaneously (2:4; 4:4-5, 9; 5:19; 6:14; 13:14, 22, 29). Nehemiah prayed at any time, even while talking with others. He knew that God is always in charge, is always present, and hears and answers every prayer. Nehemiah could confidently pray throughout the day because he had established an intimate relationship with God during times of extended prayer (1:4-7). If we want to reach God with our emergency prayers, we need to take time to cultivate a strong relationship with God through times of in-depth prayer.

2:6 The king asked Nehemiah how long he would be gone. The Bible does not record Nehemiah's immediate answer, but he ended up staying in Jerusalem 12 years (5:14; 13:6).

2:7, 8 After his prayer, Nehemiah asked the king for permission to go to Judah. As soon as he got a positive answer, he began asking for additional help. Sometimes when we have needs, we hesitate to ask the right people for help because we are afraid to approach them. Not Nehemiah! He went directly to the person who could help him the most. Don't be reluctant to ask those who are most able to help. They may be more interested and approachable than you think. God's answers to prayer may come as a result of our asking others.

2:8 Nehemiah had position, power, and many good organizational skills, but he acknowledged that God's gracious hand was upon him. He knew that without God's strength, his efforts would be in vain. Do you acknowledge God as your power source and the giver of your gifts?

2:9, 10, 19 When Nehemiah arrived in Judah, he was greeted with opposition. Opposition to the rebuilding of Jerusalem had been going on for 90 years by those who settled in the area when the Jews were taken captive. In every generation there are those who hate God's people and try to block God's purpose. When you attempt to do God's work, some will oppose you; some will even hope you fail. If you expect opposition, you will be prepared rather than surprised (1 John 3:13). Knowing that God is behind your task is the best incentive to move ahead in the face of opposition.

2:10 Sanballat was governor of Samaria, and Tobiah was probably governor of Transjordan under the Persians. Why were these government officials so concerned about the arrival of Nehemiah and his small band of exiles? There are several possible reasons. (1) When Zerubbabel first returned with his group (Ezra 1–2), his refusal to accept help from the Samaritans had caused bad relations. (2) Nehemiah was no ordinary exile; he was the king's personal adviser and cup-bearer, arriving in Jerusalem with the king's approval to build and fortify the city. If anyone could rebuild Jerusalem, he could. A rebuilt Jerusalem was a threat to the authority of the Samaritan officials who had been in charge of the land since Judah's exile. (3) This was the third group to return from exile. The increasing number of people in Jerusalem made Sanballat and Tobiah angry. They did not want returning exiles taking control of the land and threatening their secure position.

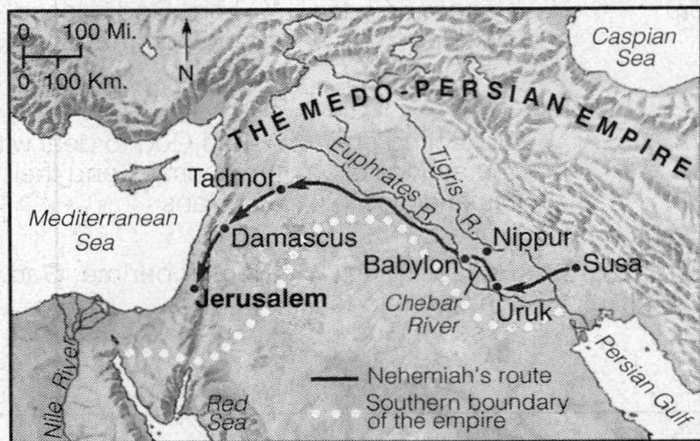

NEHEMIAH GOES TO JERUSALEM Nehemiah worked in Susa as a personal assistant for the king of the vast Medo-Persian Empire. When he heard that the rebuilding projects in Jerusalem were progressing slowly, he asked the king if he could go there to help his people complete the task of rebuilding their city's walls. The king agreed to let him go; so he left as soon as possible, traveling along much the same route Ezra had taken.

2:11-17 Nehemiah arrived quietly in Jerusalem and spent several days carefully observing and assessing the damage to the walls. Following this time of thoughtful consideration, he confidently presented his plan. Nehemiah demonstrated an excellent approach to problem solving. He got firsthand information and

2:13 Neh 1:3; 3:13
2:14 2 Kgs 20:20 Neh 3:15

We took no pack animals with us, except the donkey that I myself was riding. 13 I went out
through the Valley Gate, past the Jackal's Well,* and over to the Dung Gate to inspect the
broken walls and burned gates. 14 Then I went to the Fountain Gate and to the King's Pool,
but my donkey couldn't get through the rubble. 15 So I went up the Kidron Valley* instead,
inspecting the wall before I turned back and entered again at the Valley Gate.
16 The city officials did not know I had been out there or what I was doing, for I had not
yet said anything to anyone about my plans. I had not yet spoken to the religious and
political leaders, the officials, or anyone else in the administration. 17 But now I said to them,
"You know full well the tragedy of our city. It lies in ruins, and its gates are burned. Let us
rebuild the wall of Jerusalem and rid ourselves of this disgrace!" 18 Then I told them about
how the gracious hand of God had been on me, and about my conversation with the king.
They replied at once, "Good! Let's rebuild the wall!" So they began the good work.
19 But when Sanballat, Tobiah, and Geshem the Arab heard of our plan, they scoffed
contemptuously. "What are you doing, rebelling against the king like this?" they asked.
20 But I replied, "The God of heaven will help us succeed. We his servants will start
rebuilding this wall. But you have no stake or claim in Jerusalem."

2:17 Neh 1:3
2:18 2 Sam 2:7
2:19 Neh 6:6
2:20 Ezra 4:3 Neh 2:4

Rebuilding the Wall of Jerusalem

3:1 Neh 3:20, 32; 6:1; 7:1; 12:39; 13:28 Jer 31:38

3 Then Eliashib the high priest and the other priests started to rebuild at the Sheep
Gate. They dedicated it and set up its doors, building the wall as far as the Tower of

2:13 Or *Serpent's Well.* **2:15** Hebrew *the valley.*

---

carefully considered the situation. Then he presented a realistic strategy. Before jumping into a project, follow Nehemiah's example and plan ahead. Check your information to make sure your ideas will work—be realistic. Then you will be able to present your plan with confidence.

2:11-17 Nehemiah kept his mission a secret and surveyed the walls by moonlight to avoid unhealthy gossip about his arrival and to prevent enemies from being alerted to his plans. Only after planning carefully would he be ready to go public with his mission from God. A premature announcement could have caused rivalry among the Jews as to the best way to begin. In this case, Nehemiah didn't need tedious planning sessions; he needed one plan that would bring quick action.

2:17, 18 Spiritual renewal often begins with one person's vision. Nehemiah had a vision, and he shared it with enthusiasm, inspiring Jerusalem's leaders to rebuild the walls.

We frequently underestimate people and don't challenge them with our dreams for God's work in the world. When God plants an idea in your mind to accomplish something for him, share it with others and trust the Holy Spirit to impress them with similar thoughts. Don't regard yourself as the only one through whom God is working. Often God uses one person to express the vision and others to turn it into reality. When you encourage and inspire others, you put teamwork into action to accomplish God's goals.

2:19 Sanballat and Tobiah labeled the rebuilding of Jerusalem's walls as rebellion against the king, probably threatening to report the builders as traitors. These enemies also ridiculed Nehemiah, saying that the walls could never be rebuilt because the damage was too extensive. Nehemiah did not tell them he already had permission from the king to rebuild. Instead, he simply said he had God's approval—that was enough.

3:1 The high priest is the first person mentioned who pitched in and helped with the work. Spiritual leaders must lead not only by word but also by action. The Sheep Gate was the gate used to bring sheep into the city to the Temple for sacrifices. Nehemiah had the priests repair this gate and section of the wall, respecting the priests' area of interest and at the same time emphasizing the priority of worship.

3:1ff All the citizens of Jerusalem did their part on the huge job of rebuilding the city wall. Similarly, the work of the church requires every member's effort in order for the body of Christ to function effectively (1 Corinthians 12:12-27). The body needs you! Are you doing your part? Find a place to serve God, and start contributing whatever time, talent, and money are needed.

3:1ff Jerusalem was a large city, and because many roads converged there, it required many gates. The wall on each side of these heavy wooden gates was taller and thicker so soldiers could stand guard to defend the gates against attack. Sometimes two stone towers guarded the gate. In times of peace, the city gates were hubs of activity—city council was held there, and shopkeepers set up their wares at the entrance. Building the city walls and gates was not only a military priority but also a boost for trade and commerce.

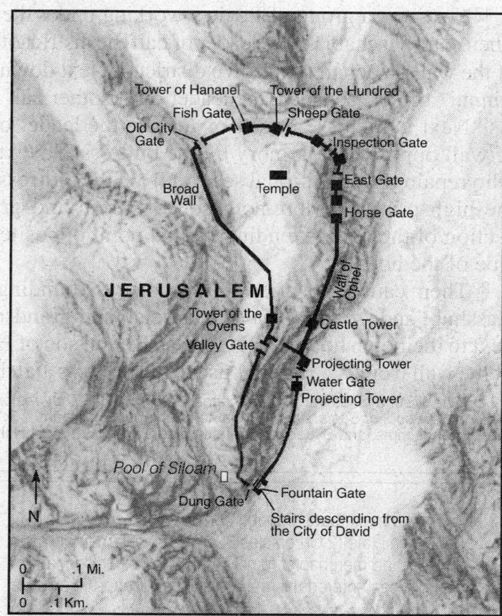

THE RESTORATION OF THE CITY WALLS Nehemiah takes us on a counterclockwise tour around Jerusalem (beginning with the Sheep Gate). He describes for us each section, gate, and tower on the wall and who worked to rebuild it.

the Hundred, which they dedicated, and the Tower of Hananel. 2People from the city of
Jericho worked next to them, and beyond them was Zaccur son of Imri.
3The Fish Gate was built by the sons of Hassenaah. They did the whole thing—laid
the beams, hung the doors, and put the bolts and bars in place. 4Meremoth son of Uriah
and grandson of Hakkoz repaired the next section of wall. Beside him were Meshullam
son of Berekiah and grandson of Meshezabel, and then Zadok son of Baana. 5Next were
the people from Tekoa, though their leaders refused to help.
6The Old City Gate* was repaired by Joiada son of Paseah and Meshullam son of
Besodeiah. They laid the beams, set up the doors, and installed the bolts and bars. 7Next
to them were Melatiah from Gibeon, Jadon from Meronoth, and people from Gibeon and
Mizpah, the headquarters of the governor of the province west of the Euphrates River.
8Next was Uzziel son of Harhaiah, a goldsmith by trade, who also worked on the wall.
Beyond him was Hananiah, a manufacturer of perfumes. They left out* a section of
Jerusalem as far as the Broad Wall.
9Rephaiah son of Hur, the leader of half the district of Jerusalem, was next to them on
the wall. 10Next Jedaiah son of Harumaph repaired the wall beside his own house, and
next to him was Hattush son of Hashabneiah. 11Then came Malkijah son of Harim and
Hasshub son of Pahath-moab, who repaired the Tower of the Ovens, in addition to
another section of the wall. 12Shallum son of Hallohesh and his daughters repaired the
next section. He was the leader of the other half of the district of Jerusalem.
13The people from Zanoah, led by Hanun, rebuilt the Valley Gate, hung its doors, and
installed the bolts and bars. They also repaired the fifteen hundred feet* of wall to the
Dung Gate.
14The Dung Gate was repaired by Malkijah son of Recab, the leader of the Beth-
hakkerem district. After rebuilding it, he hung the doors and installed the bolts and bars.
15Shallum son of Col-hozeh, the leader of the Mizpah district, repaired the Fountain
Gate. He rebuilt it, roofed it, hung its doors, and installed its bolts and bars. Then he
repaired the wall of the pool of Siloam* near the king's garden, and he rebuilt the wall
as far as the stairs that descend from the City of David. 16Next to him was Nehemiah son
of Azbuk, the leader of half the district of Beth-zur. He rebuilt the wall to a place opposite
the royal cemetery as far as the water reservoir and the House of the Warriors.
17Next was a group of Levites working under the supervision of Rehum son of Bani.
Then came Hashabiah, the leader of half the district of Keilah, who supervised the building
of the wall on behalf of his own district. 18Next down the line were his countrymen led by
Binnui* son of Henadad, the leader of the other half of the district of Keilah.
19Next to them, Ezer son of Jeshua, the leader of Mizpah, repaired another section
of wall opposite the armory by the buttress. 20Next to him was Baruch son of Zabbai,
who repaired an additional section from the buttress to the door of the home of Eliashib
the high priest. 21Meremoth son of Uriah and grandson of Hakkoz rebuilt another
section of the wall extending from a point opposite the door of Eliashib's house to the
side of the house.
22Then came the priests from the surrounding region. 23After them, Benjamin,
Hasshub, and Azariah son of Maaseiah and grandson of Ananiah repaired the sections
next to their own houses. 24Next was Binnui son of Henadad, who rebuilt another section
of the wall from Azariah's house to the buttress and the corner. 25Palal son of Uzai carried

3:2 Neh 7:36
3:3 Neh 12:39
3:6 Neh 12:39
3:8 Neh 3:31-32; 12:38
3:9 Neh 3:12, 17
3:11 Neh 12:38
3:12 Neh 3:9
3:13 Neh 2:13
3:14 Neh 2:13
3:15 2 Kgs 25:4-5 Neh 2:14; 12:37
3:16 2 Kgs 20:20 Neh 2:14; 3:9, 12, 17
3:19 2 Chr 26:9 Neh 3:15-16
3:20 Neh 3:1
3:22 Neh 12:28
3:24 Neh 3:19
3:25 Jer 32:2

3:6 Or *The Mishneh Gate,* or *The Jeshanah Gate.* **3:8** Or *They restored.* **3:13** Hebrew *1,000 cubits* [450 meters]. **3:15** Hebrew *pool of Shelah,* another name for the pool of Siloam. **3:18** As in a few Hebrew manuscripts, some Greek manuscripts, and Syriac version (see also 3:24; 10:9); most Hebrew manuscripts read *Bavvai.*

3:3 One of the main roads through Jerusalem entered the city through the Fish Gate (2 Chronicles 33:14). The fish market was near the gate, and merchants from Tyre, the Sea of Galilee, and other fishing areas entered this gate to sell their goods.

3:5 The leaders from Tekoa were lazy and wouldn't help. These men were the only ones who did not support the building project in Jerusalem. Every group, even churches, will have those who think they are too wise or important to work hard. Gentle encouragement doesn't seem to help. Sometimes the best policy is to ignore them. They may think they are getting away with something, but their inactivity will be remembered by all who worked hard.

3:12 Shallum's daughters helped with the difficult work of repairing the city walls. Rebuilding Jerusalem's walls was a matter of national emergency for the Jews, not just a civic beautification project. Nearly everyone was dedicated to the task and willing to work at it.

3:14 The Dung Gate was the gate through which the people carried their garbage to be burned in the valley of Hinnom.

on the work from a point opposite the buttress and the corner to the upper tower that
projects from the king's house beside the court of the guard. Next to him were Pedaiah
3:26 Neh 7:46; 8:1, 3; 11:21
son of Parosh 26 and the Temple servants living on the hill of Ophel, who repaired the
wall as far as the Water Gate toward the east and the projecting tower. 27 Then came the
3:27 Neh 3:5, 26
people of Tekoa, who repaired another section opposite the great projecting tower and
over to the wall of Ophel.
3:28 2 Kgs 11:16 2 Chr 23:15 Jer 31:40
28 The priests repaired the wall up the hill from the Horse Gate, each one doing the
section immediately opposite his own house. 29 Next Zadok son of Immer also rebuilt
the wall next to his own house, and beyond him was Shemaiah son of Shecaniah, the
gatekeeper of the East Gate. 30 Next Hananiah son of Shelemiah and Hanun, the sixth
3:31 Neh 3:1, 8, 32
son of Zalaph, repaired another section, while Meshullam son of Berekiah rebuilt the
wall next to his own house. 31 Malkijah, one of the goldsmiths, repaired the wall as far
3:32 Neh 3:1; 12:39
as the housing for the Temple servants and merchants, opposite the Inspection Gate.
Then he continued as far as the upper room at the corner. 32 The other goldsmiths and
merchants repaired the wall from that corner to the Sheep Gate.

Enemies Oppose the Rebuilding

4:1 Neh 2:10, 19
4 Sanballat was very angry when he learned that we were rebuilding the wall. He flew
into a rage and mocked the Jews, 2 saying in front of his friends and the Samarian
army officers, "What does this bunch of poor, feeble Jews think they are doing? Do they
think they can build the wall in a day if they offer enough sacrifices? Look at those
charred stones they are pulling out of the rubbish and using again!"
4:3 Neh 2:10
3 Tobiah the Ammonite, who was standing beside him, remarked, "That stone wall
would collapse if even a fox walked along the top of it!"
4:4 Pss 79:12; 123:3-4
4 Then I prayed, "Hear us, O our God, for we are being mocked. May their scoffing
fall back on their own heads, and may they themselves become captives in a foreign land!
4:5 Ps 69:27-28 Jer 18:23
5 Do not ignore their guilt. Do not blot out their sins, for they have provoked you to anger
here in the presence of* the builders."
6 At last the wall was completed to half its original height around the entire city, for
the people had worked very hard. 7 But when Sanballat and Tobiah and the Arabs,
Ammonites, and Ashdodites heard that the work was going ahead and that the gaps in
the wall were being repaired, they became furious. 8 They all made plans to come and

4:5 Or *for they have thrown insults in the face of.*

3:28 The Horse Gate was at the far eastern point of the wall, facing the Kidron Valley.

3:28 Each priest also repaired the wall in front of his own house, in addition to other sections. If each person was responsible for the part of the wall closest to his own house, (1) he would be more motivated to build it quickly and properly, (2) he wouldn't waste time traveling to more distant parts of the wall, (3) he would defend his own home if the wall were attacked, and (4) he would be able to make the building a family effort. Nehemiah blended self-interest with the group's objectives, helping everyone to feel that the wall project was his own. If you are part of a group working on a large project, make sure each person sees the importance and meaning of the job that he or she has to do. This will ensure high-quality work and personal satisfaction.

3:31 The Inspection Gate was in the northern part of the eastern wall.

4:1 Sanballat was governor of Samaria, the region just north of Judea, where Jerusalem was located. Sanballat may have hoped to become governor of Judea as well, but Nehemiah's arrival spoiled his plans. (For his other reasons for opposing Nehemiah, see the note on 2:10.) Sanballat tried to scare Nehemiah away or at least discourage him by scorn (4:2; 6:6), threats (4:8), and bluffs (6:7).

4:1, 2 Almost 300 years before Nehemiah's time, the northern kingdom of Israel was conquered, and most of the people were carried away captive (722 B.C.). Sargon of Assyria repopulated Israel with captives from other lands. These captives eventually intermarried with the few Israelites who remained in the land to form a mixed race of people who became known as Samaritans. The Jews who returned to Jerusalem and the southern region of Judea during the days of Ezra and Nehemiah would have nothing to do with Samaritans, whom they considered to be racially impure. Relations between both groups grew progressively worse—400 years later, the Jews and Samaritans hated each other (John 4:9).

4:1-5 Ridicule can cut deeply, causing discouragement and despair. Sanballat and Tobiah used ridicule to try to dissuade the Jews from building the wall. Instead of trading insults, however, Nehemiah prayed, and the work continued. When you are mocked for your faith or criticized for doing what you know is right, refuse to respond in the same way or to become discouraged. Tell God how you feel and remember his promise to be with you. This will give you encouragement and strength to carry on.

4:4, 5 Nehemiah is not praying for revenge but for God's justice to be carried out. His prayer is similar to many of David's (see the note on Psalm 7:1-6).

4:6 The work of rebuilding the wall progressed well because the people had set their hearts and minds on accomplishing the task. They did not lose faith or give up, but they persevered in the work. If God has called you to a task, determine to complete it, even if you face opposition or discouragement. The rewards of work well done will be worth the effort.

fight against Jerusalem and to bring about confusion there. [9]But we prayed to our God 4:9
and guarded the city day and night to protect ourselves. Neh 4:11
[10]Then the people of Judah began to complain that the workers were becoming tired.
There was so much rubble to be moved that we could never get it done by ourselves.
[11]Meanwhile, our enemies were saying, "Before they know what's happening, we will
swoop down on them and kill them and end their work."
[12]The Jews who lived near the enemy came and told us again and again, "They will
come from all directions and attack us!"* [13]So I placed armed guards behind the lowest 4:13
parts of the wall in the exposed areas. I stationed the people to stand guard by families, Neh 4:9, 17-18
armed with swords, spears, and bows.
[14]Then as I looked over the situation, I called together the leaders and the people and 4:14 Num 14:9
said to them, "Don't be afraid of the enemy! Remember the Lord, who is great and Deut 1:29-30
glorious, and fight for your friends, your families, and your homes!" 2 Sam 10:12
[15]When our enemies heard that we knew of their plans and that God had frustrated 4:15
them, we all returned to our work on the wall. [16]But from then on, only half my men 2 Sam 17:14
worked while the other half stood guard with spears, shields, bows, and coats of mail.
The officers stationed themselves behind the people of Judah [17]who were building the
wall. The common laborers carried on their work with one hand supporting their load
and one hand holding a weapon. [18]All the builders had a sword belted to their side. The
trumpeter stayed with me to sound the alarm.
[19]Then I explained to the nobles and officials and all the people, "The work is very
spread out, and we are widely separated from each other along the wall. [20]When you hear 4:20 Exod 14:14
the blast of the trumpet, rush to wherever it is sounding. Then our God will fight for us!" Deut 1:30
[21]We worked early and late, from sunrise to sunset. And half the men were always on
guard. [22]I also told everyone living outside the walls to move into Jerusalem. That way
they and their servants could go on guard duty at night as well as work during the day.
[23]During this time, none of us—not I, nor my relatives, nor my servants, nor the guards
who were with me—ever took off our clothes. We carried our weapons with us at all
times, even when we went for water.*

Nehemiah Defends the Oppressed

5 About this time some of the men and their wives raised a cry of protest against their 5:1 Lev 25:35
fellow Jews. [2]They were saying, "We have such large families. We need more Deut 15:7
money just so we can buy the food we need to survive." [3]Others said, "We have
mortgaged our fields, vineyards, and homes to get food during the famine." [4]And others 5:4
said, "We have already borrowed to the limit on our fields and vineyards to pay our taxes. Ezra 4:13; 7:24
[5]We belong to the same family, and our children are just like theirs. Yet we must sell our 5:5 Gen 37:27
children into slavery just to get enough money to live. We have already sold some of our Lev 25:39

4:12 The meaning of the Hebrew is uncertain. **4:23** Hebrew *Each his weapon the water.* The meaning of the Hebrew is uncertain.

4:9 Nehemiah constantly combined prayer with preparation and planning. His people trusted God and at the same time kept vigilant watch over what had been entrusted to them. Too often we pray without looking for what God wants us to do. We show God we are serious when we combine prayer with thought, preparation, and effort.

4:10-14 Accomplishing any large task is tiring. There are always pressures that foster discouragement—the task seems impossible, it can never be finished, or too many factors are working against us. The only cure for fatigue and discouragement is focusing on God's purposes. Nehemiah reminded the workers of their calling, their goal, and God's protection. If you are overwhelmed by an assignment, tired and discouraged, remember God's purpose for your life and his special purpose for the project.

4:16 The workers were spread out along the wall, so Nehemiah devised a plan of defense that would unite and protect his people—half the men worked while the other half stood guard. Christians need to help one another in the same way because we can become so afraid of possible dangers that we can't get anything done. By looking out for each other, we will be free to put forth our best efforts, confident that others are ready to offer help when needed. Don't cut yourself off from others; instead, join together for mutual benefit. You need them as much as they need you.

4:18-20 To further relieve the anxieties of the people, Nehemiah set up a communication system. The man who sounded the trumpet stayed with Nehemiah, and the people knew what to do if they heard it. We have no record that the trumpet was ever used, but simply knowing it would issue a warning when needed was reassuring. The promise of open, immediate communication helped the group accomplish its task.

4:23 Although the exact meaning of the Hebrew phrase "even when we went for water" is unclear (it has been translated, "in his right hand" or "at his right hand at night"), the point is that each man always had his weapon close at hand. The guards were prepared and took their responsibilities seriously.

5:1-5 Who were these bitterly resented Jews? They were either (1) Jews who had become wealthy in exile and brought this wealth with them to Jerusalem, or (2) descendants of Jews who had arrived almost a century earlier during the first return under Zerubbabel (Ezra 1–2) and had established lucrative businesses.

daughters, and we are helpless to do anything about it, for our fields and vineyards are
already mortgaged to others."

5:7 Exod 22:25 Lev 25:36

6 When I heard their complaints, I was very angry. 7 After thinking about the situation,
I spoke out against these nobles and officials. I told them, "You are oppressing your own
relatives by charging them interest when they borrow money!" Then I called a public
meeting to deal with the problem.

5:8 Lev 25:48

8 At the meeting I said to them, "The rest of us are doing all we can to redeem our
Jewish relatives who have had to sell themselves to pagan foreigners, but you are selling
them back into slavery again. How often must we redeem them?" And they had nothing
to say in their defense.

NEHEMIAH

God is in the business of working through his people to accomplish seemingly impossible tasks. God often shapes people with personality characteristics, experiences, and training that prepare them for his purpose, and usually the people have no idea what God has in store for them. God prepared and positioned Nehemiah to accomplish one of the Bible's "impossible" tasks.

Nehemiah was a common man in a unique position. He was secure and successful as cup-bearer to the Persian king Artaxerxes. Nehemiah had little power, but he had great influence. He was trusted by the king. He was also a man of God, concerned about the fate of Jerusalem.

Seventy years earlier, Zerubbabel had managed to rebuild God's Temple. Thirteen years had passed since Ezra had returned to Jerusalem and helped the people with their spiritual needs. Now Nehemiah was needed. Jerusalem's wall was still in ruins, and the news broke his heart. As he talked to God, a plan began to take form in Nehemiah's mind about his own role in the rebuilding of the city walls. He willingly left the security of his home and job in Persia to follow God on an "impossible" mission. And the rest is history.

From beginning to end, Nehemiah prayed for God's help. He never hesitated to ask God to remember him, closing his autobiography with these words: "Remember this in my favor, O my God." Throughout the "impossible" task, Nehemiah displayed unusual leadership. The wall around Jerusalem was rebuilt in record time, despite resistance. Even Israel's enemies grudgingly and fearfully admitted that God was with these builders. Not only that, but God worked through Nehemiah to bring about a spiritual awakening among the people of Judah.

You may not have Nehemiah's unique abilities or feel that you are in a position where you can do anything great for God, but there are two ways you can become useful to God. First, be a person who *talks* to God. Welcome him into your thoughts and share yourself with him—your concerns, feelings, and dreams. Second, be a person who *walks* with God. Put what you learn from his Word into action. God may have an "impossible" mission that he wants to do through you.

Strengths and accomplishments
- A man of character, persistence, and prayer
- Brilliant planner, organizer, and motivator
- Under his leadership, the wall around Jerusalem was rebuilt in 52 days
- As political leader, led the nation to religious reform and spiritual awakening
- Was calm in the face of opposition
- Was capable of being bluntly honest with his people when they were sinning

Lessons from his life
- The first step in any venture is to pray
- People under God's direction can accomplish impossible tasks
- There are two parts to real service for God: talking with him and walking with him

Vital statistics
- Where: Persia, Jerusalem
- Occupations: King's cup-bearer, city builder, governor of Judah
- Relative: Father: Hacaliah
- Contemporaries: Ezra, Artaxerxes, Tobiah, Sanballat

Key verse
"I told them about how the gracious hand of God had been on me, and about my conversation with the king. They replied at once, 'Good! Let's rebuild the wall!' So they began the good work" (Nehemiah 2:18).

Nehemiah's story is told in the book of Nehemiah.

5:7-9 Many of the returned exiles were suffering at the hands of some of their rich countrymen. These people would lend large sums of money; then, when the debtors missed a payment, they would take over their fields. Left with no means of income, the debtors were forced to sell their children into slavery, a common practice of this time. Nehemiah was angry with these Jews, who were taking advantage of their own people in order to enrich themselves. These practices violated the law set forth in Exodus 22:25.

9 Then I pressed further, "What you are doing is not right! Should you not walk in the 5:9
fear of our God in order to avoid being mocked by enemy nations? 10 I myself, as well Lev 25:48
as my brothers and my workers, have been lending the people money and grain, but now
let us stop this business of loans. 11 You must restore their fields, vineyards, olive groves,
and homes to them this very day. Repay the interest you charged on their money, grain,
wine, and olive oil."

12 Then they replied, "We will give back everything and demand nothing more from 5:12 Ezra 10:5
the people. We will do as you say." Then I called the priests and made the nobles and Neh 10:31
officials formally vow to do what they had promised.

13 I shook out the fold of my robe and said, "If you fail to keep your promise, may God 5:13
shake you from your homes and from your property!" Neh 8:6 Acts 18:6

The whole assembly responded, "Amen," and they praised the LORD. And the people
did as they had promised. 5:14

14 I would like to mention that for the entire twelve years that I was governor of Neh 1:1; 13:6
Judah—from the twentieth until the thirty-second year of the reign of King Artaxerxes*—neither I nor my officials drew on our official food allowance. 15 This was quite 5:15 Neh 5:9
a contrast to the former governors who had laid heavy burdens on the people, demanding
a daily ration of food and wine, besides a pound* of silver. Even their assistants took
advantage of the people. But because of my fear of God, I did not act that way. 16 I
devoted myself to working on the wall and refused to acquire any land. And I required
all my officials to spend time working on the wall. 17 I asked for nothing, even though I 5:17 1 Kgs 18:19
regularly fed 150 Jewish officials at my table, besides all the visitors from other lands!
18 The provisions required at my expense for each day were one ox, six fat sheep, and a 5:18
large number of domestic fowl. And every ten days we needed a large supply of all kinds 1 Kgs 4:22-23 2 Thes 3:8
of wine. Yet I refused to claim the governor's food allowance because the people were
already having a difficult time.

19 Remember, O my God, all that I have done for these people, and bless me for it. 5:19 Neh 13:14, 22, 31

Continued Opposition to Rebuilding

6 When Sanballat, Tobiah, Geshem the Arab, and the rest of our enemies found out 6:1
that I had finished rebuilding the wall and that no gaps remained—though we had Neh 3:1, 3
not yet hung the doors in the gates—2 Sanballat and Geshem sent me a message asking 6:2
me to meet them at one of the villages* in the plain of Ono. But I realized they were 1 Chr 8:12
plotting to harm me, 3 so I replied by sending this message to them: "I am doing a great
work! I cannot stop to come and meet with you."

5:14 That is, from 445 to 433 B.C. 5:15 Hebrew *40 shekels* [456 grams]. 6:2 As in Greek version; Hebrew reads *at Kephirim*.

5:9-11 God's concern for the poor is revealed in almost every book of the Bible. Here, Nehemiah insisted that fairness to the poor and oppressed was central to following God. The books of Moses clearly spelled out the Israelites' responsibility to care for the poor (Exodus 22:22-27; Leviticus 25:35-37; Deuteronomy 14:28, 29; 15:7-11). The way we help those in need ought to mirror God's love and concern.

5:10 Nehemiah told the rich Jews to stop charging interest on their loans to their needy brothers. God never intended people to profit from others' misfortune. In contrast to the values of this world, God says that caring for one another is more important than personal gain. When a Christian brother or sister suffers, we all suffer (1 Corinthians 12:26). We should help needy believers, not exploit them. The Jerusalem church was praised for working together to eliminate poverty (Acts 4:34, 35). Remember, "Whoever gives to the poor will lack nothing" (Proverbs 28:27). Make it a practice to help those in need around you.

5:13 This symbolic act was a curse. Nehemiah shook out the fold of his garment and pronounced that anyone who did not keep his promise would likewise be "shaken out and emptied," losing all he had.

5:14, 15 This comment by Nehemiah is a parenthetical statement, comparing his 12 years as governor with the unjust proceedings in the land before he arrived. The governor was appointed by the Persian king, not elected by the people.

5:16 Nehemiah led the entire construction project, but he also worked on the wall alongside the others. He was not a bureaucrat in a well-guarded office but a leader who got involved in the day-to-day work. He did not use his position to lord it over his people. A good leader keeps in touch with the work to be done. Those who lead best lead by what they *do* as well as by what they say.

6:1ff Sanballat and Tobiah were desperate. The wall was almost complete, and their efforts to stop its construction were failing. So they tried a new approach, centering their attacks on Nehemiah's character. They attacked him personally with rumors (6:6), deceit (6:10-13), and false reports (6:17). Personal attacks hurt, and when the criticism is unjustified, it is easy to despair. When you are doing God's work, you may receive attacks on your character. Follow Nehemiah's example by trusting God to accomplish the task and by overlooking unjustified insults.

6:2 The plain of Ono was about 20 miles northwest of Jerusalem. If Sanballat and Geshem could get Nehemiah to agree to meet them there, they could ambush him on the way.

[4]Four times they sent the same message, and each time I gave the same reply. [5]The fifth
6:6 Neh 2:19 time, Sanballat's servant came with an open letter in his hand, [6]and this is what it said:

"Geshem* tells me that everywhere he goes he hears that you and the Jews are
planning to rebel and that is why you are building the wall. According to his
reports, you plan to be their king. [7]He also reports that you have appointed prophets to prophesy about you in Jerusalem, saying, 'Look! There is a king in Judah!'
"You can be very sure that this report will get back to the king, so I suggest that
you come and talk it over with me."

[8]My reply was, "You know you are lying. There is no truth in any part of your story."
[9]They were just trying to intimidate us, imagining that they could break our resolve and
stop the work. So I prayed for strength to continue the work.
6:10 Jer 36:5 [10]Later I went to visit Shemaiah son of Delaiah and grandson of Mehetabel, who was
confined to his home. He said, "Let us meet together inside the Temple of God and bolt
the doors shut. Your enemies are coming to kill you tonight."
[11]But I replied, "Should someone in my position run away from danger? Should
someone in my position enter the Temple to save his life? No, I won't do it!" [12]I realized
that God had not spoken to him, but that he had uttered this prophecy against me because
6:13 Neh 6:6 Tobiah and Sanballat had hired him. [13]They were hoping to intimidate me and make me
sin by following his suggestion. Then they would be able to accuse and discredit me.

6:14 Neh 13:29 Ezek 13:17 [14]Remember, O my God, all the evil things that Tobiah and Sanballat have done.
And remember Noadiah the prophet and all the prophets like her who have tried to
intimidate me.

The Builders Complete the Wall

6:15 Neh 4:1-2 [15]So on October 2* the wall was finally finished—just fifty-two days after we had
6:16 Neh 2:10; 4:1, 7 begun. [16]When our enemies and the surrounding nations heard about it, they were
frightened and humiliated. They realized that this work had been done with the help of
our God.
[17]During those fifty-two days, many letters went back and forth between Tobiah and
the officials of Judah. [18]For many in Judah had sworn allegiance to him because his
father-in-law was Shecaniah son of Arah and because his son Jehohanan was married to
the daughter of Meshullam son of Berekiah. [19]They kept telling me what a wonderful
man Tobiah was, and then they told him everything I said. And Tobiah sent many
threatening letters to intimidate me.

6:6 Hebrew *Gashmu,* another name for Geshem. **6:15** Hebrew *on the twenty-fifth day of the month Elul,* of the Hebrew calendar. This event occurred on October 2, 445 B.C.; also see note on 1:1.

6:7 During these days, prophets such as Malachi proclaimed the coming of the Messiah (Malachi 3:1-3). Sanballat, with his usual flair for stirring up trouble, tried to turn Nehemiah's people against him by saying that Nehemiah was trying to set himself up as the king. Sanballat also tried to turn the local officials against Nehemiah by threatening to report to the king of Persia that Nehemiah was starting a revolt. The fact that Sanballat had an open, or unsealed, letter delivered to Nehemiah shows that he wanted to make sure the letter's contents were made public. But Sanballat's accusations were untrue and did not divert Nehemiah from his task.

6:9 When opposition builds up against you or God's work, it is tempting to pray, "God, get me out of this situation." But Nehemiah prayed for strength. He showed tremendous determination and character to remain steadfast in his responsibility. When we pray for strength, God always answers.

6:10 Shemaiah warned Nehemiah of danger and told him to hide in the Temple. Nehemiah wisely tested the message, exposing it as another trick of the enemy. People may misuse God's name by saying they know God's will when they have other motives. Examine self-proclaimed messengers from God to see if they stand up to the test of being consistent with what is revealed in God's Word.

6:10-13 Nehemiah did not have the full support of the people. Shemaiah (6:10), Noadiah (6:14), and many of the officials (6:17) were working against him. When Nehemiah was attacked personally, he refused to give in to fear and flee to the Temple. According to God's law, it would have been wrong for Nehemiah to go into the Temple to hide because he wasn't a priest (Numbers 18:22). If he had run for his life, he would have undermined the courage he was trying to instill in the people. Leaders are targets for attacks. Make it a practice to pray for those in authority (1 Timothy 2:1, 2). Request God to give them strength to stand against personal attacks and temptation. They need God-given courage to overcome fear.

6:15 Daniel, who was among the first group of captives taken from Jerusalem to Babylon (605 B.C.), predicted the rebuilding of the city (Daniel 9:25). Here his prophecy comes true. He, like Nehemiah, was a Jew who held a prominent position in the kingdom where he had been exiled (Daniel 5:29–6:3).

6:15 They said it couldn't be done. The job was too big, and the problems were too great. But God's men and women, joined together for special tasks, can solve huge problems and accomplish great goals. Don't let the size of a task or the length of time needed to accomplish it keep you from doing it. With God's help, it can be done.

7 After the wall was finished and I had hung the doors in the gates, the gatekeepers,
singers, and Levites were appointed. 2I gave the responsibility of governing Jerusalem to my brother Hanani, along with Hananiah, the commander of the fortress, for he
was a faithful man who feared God more than most. 3I said to them, "Do not leave the
gates open during the hottest part of the day.* And while the gatekeepers are still on duty,
have them shut and bar the doors. Appoint the residents of Jerusalem to act as guards,
everyone on a regular watch. Some will serve at their regular posts and some in front of
their own homes."

7:1 Neh 6:1, 15
7:2 Neh 1:2; 10:23

Nehemiah Registers the People

4At that time the city was large and spacious, but the population was small. And only a
few houses were scattered throughout the city. 5So my God gave me the idea to call
together all the leaders of the city, along with the ordinary citizens, for registration. I had
found the genealogical record of those who had first returned to Judah. This is what was
written there:
6"Here is the list of the Jewish exiles of the provinces who returned from their
captivity to Jerusalem and to the other towns of Judah. They had been deported to
Babylon by King Nebuchadnezzar. 7Their leaders were Zerubbabel, Jeshua, Nehemiah,
Seraiah,* Reelaiah,* Nahamani, Mordecai, Bilshan, Mispar,* Bigvai, Rehum,* and
Baanah. This is the number of men of Israel who returned from exile:

7:6-73 //Ezra 2:1-70
7:7 Ezra 2:2

8 The family of Parosh 2,172
9 The family of Shephatiah 372
10 The family of Arah 652
11 The family of Pahath-moab (descendants of Jeshua and Joab) 2,818
12 The family of Elam 1,254
13 The family of Zattu 845
14 The family of Zaccai 760
15 The family of Bani* 648
16 The family of Bebai 628
17 The family of Azgad 2,322
18 The family of Adonikam 667
19 The family of Bigvai 2,067
20 The family of Adin 655
21 The family of Ater (descendants of Hezekiah) 98
22 The family of Hashum 328
23 The family of Bezai 324
24 The family of Jorah* 112
25 The family of Gibbar* 95
26 The peoples of Bethlehem and Netophah 188
27 The people of Anathoth 128
28 The people of Beth-azmaveth 42

7:3 Or *Keep the gates of Jerusalem closed until the sun is hot.* **7:7a** As in parallel text at Ezra 2:2; Hebrew reads *Azariah.* **7:7b** As in parallel text at Ezra 2:2; Hebrew reads *Raamiah.* **7:7c** As in parallel text at Ezra 2:2; Hebrew reads *Mispereth.* **7:7d** As in parallel text at Ezra 2:2; Hebrew reads *Nehum.* **7:15** As in parallel text at Ezra 2:10; Hebrew reads *Binnui.* **7:24** As in parallel text at Ezra 2:18; Hebrew reads *Hariph.* **7:25** As in parallel text at Ezra 2:20; Hebrew reads *Gibeon.*

7:2 Faithfulness and fear of God were the key character traits that qualified these men to govern Jerusalem. Faithful people can be trusted to carry out their work; God-fearing people can be expected to do so in line with God's priorities. These men had both qualities. If you are in a position of selecting leaders, look for faithfulness and reverence as two of the most important qualifications. Although other qualities may seem more impressive, faithfulness and reverence pass the test of time.

7:3 City gates were usually opened at sunrise, enabling merchants to enter and set up their tent-stores. Nehemiah didn't want Jerusalem to be caught unprepared by an enemy attack, so he ordered the gates closed until well after sunrise when the people were sure to be awake and alert.

7:3 The wall was complete, but the work was not finished. Nehemiah assigned each family the task of protecting the section of wall next to their home. It is tempting to relax our guard and rest on past accomplishments after we have completed a large task. But we must continue to serve and to take care of all that God has entrusted to us. Following through after a project is completed is as vital as doing the project itself.

7:5ff Nehemiah found the genealogical record. Because this genealogy is almost identical to Ezra's (Ezra 2), most likely Ezra's list was stored in the Temple archives and was the one Nehemiah found.

29 The peoples of Kiriath-jearim, Kephirah, and Beeroth 743
30 The peoples of Ramah and Geba 621
31 The people of Micmash 122
32 The peoples of Bethel and Ai 123
33 The people of Nebo 52
34 The citizens of Elam 1,254
35 The citizens of Harim 320
36 The citizens of Jericho 345
37 The citizens of Lod, Hadid, and Ono 721
38 The citizens of Senaah 3,930

7:39 Ezra 2:36-39

39 "These are the priests who returned from exile:
The family of Jedaiah (through the line of Jeshua) 973
40 The family of Immer 1,052
41 The family of Pashhur 1,247
42 The family of Harim 1,017

7:43 Ezra 2:40-42

43 "These are the Levites who returned from exile:
The families of Jeshua and Kadmiel (descendants of Hodaviah*) 74
44 The singers of the family of Asaph 148
45 The gatekeepers of the families of Shallum, Ater, Talmon, Akkub,
Hatita, and Shobai 138

7:46 Ezra 2:43-54

46 "The descendants of the following Temple servants returned from exile:
Ziha, Hasupha, Tabbaoth,
47 Keros, Siaha,* Padon,
48 Lebanah, Hagabah, Shalmai,
49 Hanan, Giddel, Gahar,
50 Reaiah, Rezin, Nekoda,
51 Gazzam, Uzza, Paseah,
52 Besai, Meunim, Nephusim,*
53 Bakbuk, Hakupha, Harhur,
54 Bazluth,* Mehida, Harsha,
55 Barkos, Sisera, Temah,
56 Neziah, and Hatipha.

7:57 Ezra 2:55-57

57 "The descendants of these servants of King Solomon returned from exile:
Sotai, Sophereth, Peruda,*
58 Jaalah,* Darkon, Giddel,
59 Shephatiah, Hattil, Pokereth-hazzebaim, and Ami.*

60 "In all, the Temple servants and the descendants of Solomon's servants numbered 392.

61 "Another group returned to Jerusalem at this time from the towns of Tel-melah,
Tel-harsha, Kerub, Addan,* and Immer. However, they could not prove that they or their
families were descendants of Israel. 62 This group included the families of Delaiah,
Tobiah, and Nekoda—a total of 642 people.

7:63 Ezra 2:61

63 "Three families of priests—Hobaiah, Hakkoz, and Barzillai—also returned to
Jerusalem. (This Barzillai had married one of the daughters of Barzillai from Gilead and
had taken her family name.) 64 But they had lost their genealogical records, so they were

7:43 As in parallel text at Ezra 2:40; Hebrew reads *Hodevah.* **7:47** As in parallel text at Ezra 2:44; Hebrew reads *Sia.* **7:52** As in parallel text at Ezra 2:50; Hebrew reads *Nephushesim.* **7:54** As in parallel text at Ezra 2:52; Hebrew reads *Bazlith.* **7:57** As in parallel text at Ezra 2:55; Hebrew reads *Perida.* **7:58** As in parallel text at Ezra 2:56; Hebrew reads *Jaala.* **7:59** As in parallel text at Ezra 2:57; Hebrew reads *Amon.* **7:61** As in parallel text at Ezra 2:59; Hebrew reads *Addon.*

7:61 Genealogies were greatly valued because it was vitally important for a Jew to be able to prove that he or she was a descendant of Abraham and was, therefore, part of God's people (Genesis 12:1-3; 15; Exodus 19:5, 6; Deuteronomy 11:22-28). A lost genealogy put one's status as a Jew at risk.

7:64, 65 "Sacred lots" referred to the Urim and Thummim, a means of learning God's will (Exodus 28:30). If someone's name wasn't in the genealogies, he could still be admitted as a priest if the Urim and Thummim proved him to be a Jew and a Levite. It is not clear whether the Urim and Thummim were the originals that had survived the destruction of Jerusalem or if they were new. The "priests' share of food" was meat dedicated to God as part of the sacrifice. Only true priests could eat it.

not allowed to serve as priests. 65 The governor would not even let them eat the priests'
share of food from the sacrifices until there was a priest who could consult the LORD
about the matter by means of sacred lots.*
66 "So a total of 42,360 people returned to Judah, 67 in addition to 7,337 servants and
245 singers, both men and women. 68 They took with them 736 horses, 245 mules,*
69 435 camels, and 6,720 donkeys.
70 "Some of the family leaders gave gifts for the work. The governor gave to the
treasury 1,000 gold coins,* 50 gold basins, and 530 robes for the priests. 71 The other
leaders gave to the treasury a total of 20,000 gold coins* and some 2,750 pounds* of
silver for the work. 72 The rest of the people gave 20,000 gold coins, about 2,500 pounds*
of silver, and 67 robes for the priests.
73 "So the priests, the Levites, the gatekeepers, the singers, the Temple servants, along
with some of the people—that is to say, all Israel—settled in their own towns."

7:70 Neh 8:9
7:73 Ezra 3:1

B. REFORMING THE PEOPLE (7:73—13:31)

When Nehemiah arrived in Jerusalem he found more than just broken walls; he found broken lives. In response, Nehemiah gathers the people together to hear Ezra read God's law. The people repent and promise to change their lives by obeying God's words. No matter where we live, backsliding is an ever-present danger. We must constantly check our behavior against God's standards in the Bible so that we do not slide back into sinful ways of living.

1. Ezra renews the covenant

Ezra Reads the Law

Now in midautumn,* when the Israelites had settled in their towns, 1 all the people
assembled together as one person at the square just inside the Water Gate. They asked
Ezra the scribe to bring out the Book of the Law of Moses, which the LORD had given
for Israel to obey.

8:1 2 Chr 34:15; Ezra 7:6; Neh 3:26

8 2 So on October 8* Ezra the priest brought the scroll of the law before the assembly,
which included the men and women and all the children old enough to understand.
3 He faced the square just inside the Water Gate from early morning until noon and read
aloud to everyone who could understand. All the people paid close attention to the Book
of the Law. 4 Ezra the scribe stood on a high wooden platform that had been made for the
occasion. To his right stood Mattithiah, Shema, Anaiah, Uriah, Hilkiah, and Maaseiah.
To his left stood Pedaiah, Mishael, Malkijah, Hashum, Hashbaddanah, Zechariah, and
Meshullam. 5 Ezra stood on the platform in full view of all the people. When they saw
him open the book, they all rose to their feet.
6 Then Ezra praised the LORD, the great God, and all the people chanted, "Amen!
Amen!" as they lifted their hands toward heaven. Then they bowed down and worshiped
the LORD with their faces to the ground.
7 Now the Levites—Jeshua, Bani, Sherebiah, Jamin, Akkub, Shabbethai, Hodiah,
Maaseiah, Kelita, Azariah, Jozabad, Hanan, and Pelaiah—instructed the people who
were standing there. 8 They read from the Book of the Law of God and clearly explained

8:2 Lev 23:24; Deut 31:9-12
8:6 Gen 14:22; Exod 4:31; Neh 5:13; 1 Tim 2:8
8:7 Lev 10:11; Deut 33:10

7:65 Hebrew *consult the Urim and Thummim about the matter.* **7:68** As in some Hebrew manuscripts (see also Ezra 2:66); most Hebrew manuscripts lack this verse. **7:70** Hebrew *1,000 darics of gold,* about 19 pounds or 8.6 kilograms in weight. **7:71a** Hebrew *20,000 darics of gold,* about 375 pounds or 170 kilograms in weight; also in 7:72. **7:71b** Hebrew *2,200 minas* [1.3 metric tons]. **7:72** Hebrew *2,000 minas* [1.2 metric tons]. **7:73** Hebrew *in the seventh month.* This month of the Hebrew lunar calendar occurred in October and November 445 B.C. **8:2** Hebrew *on the first day of the seventh month,* of the Hebrew calendar. This event occurred on October 8, 445 B.C.; also see note on 1:1.

8:1 This is the first mention of Ezra in this book. He had arrived in Jerusalem from Babylon 13 years before Nehemiah (458 B.C., see Ezra 7:6-9).

8:1 Ezra and Nehemiah were contemporaries (8:9), although Ezra was probably much older. Nehemiah, as governor, was the political leader; and Ezra, as priest and scribe, was the religious leader. A scribe in these days was a combination lawyer, notary public, scholar, and consultant. Scribes were among the most educated people, so they were teachers. No doubt the Jews would have liked to set up the kingdom again as in the days of David, but this would have signaled rebellion against the king of Persia to whom they were subject. The best alternative was to divide the leadership between Nehemiah and Ezra.

8:1-5 The Book of the Law of Moses was probably the Pentateuch, the first five books of the Bible. The people listened attentively to Ezra as he read God's Word, and their lives were changed. Because we hear the Bible so often, we can become dulled to its words and immune to its teachings. Instead, we should *listen carefully* to every verse and ask the Holy Spirit to help us answer the question, How does this apply to *my* life?

8:9 Deut 12:7, 12 Neh 8:2
the meaning of what was being read, helping the people understand each passage. 9 Then
Nehemiah the governor, Ezra the priest and scribe, and the Levites who were interpreting
for the people said to them, "Don't weep on such a day as this! For today is a sacred day
before the LORD your God." All the people had been weeping as they listened to the
words of the law.
8:10 Deut 26:11-13 Esth 9:22
10 And Nehemiah* continued, "Go and celebrate with a feast of choice foods and sweet
drinks, and share gifts of food with people who have nothing prepared. This is a sacred
day before our Lord. Don't be dejected and sad, for the joy of the LORD is your strength!"
11 And the Levites, too, quieted the people, telling them, "Hush! Don't weep! For this
8:12 Neh 8:7-8, 10
is a sacred day." 12 So the people went away to eat and drink at a festive meal, to share
gifts of food, and to celebrate with great joy because they had heard God's words and
understood them.

The Festival of Shelters

13 On October 9* the family leaders and the priests and Levites met with Ezra to go over the
8:14 Lev 23:34, 40, 42
law in greater detail. 14 As they studied the law, they discovered that the LORD had
commanded through Moses that the Israelites should live in shelters during the festival to
be held that month.* 15 He had said that a proclamation should be made throughout their
towns and especially in Jerusalem, telling the people to go to the hills to get branches from
olive, wild olive, myrtle, palm, and fig trees. They were to use these branches to make
8:16 2 Kgs 14:13 Neh 8:1; 12:39 Jer 32:29
shelters in which they would live during the festival, as it was prescribed in the law.
16 So the people went out and cut branches and used them to build shelters on the roofs
of their houses, in their courtyards, in the courtyards of God's Temple, or in the squares
8:17 2 Chr 7:8; 8:13; 30:21
just inside the Water Gate and the Ephraim Gate. 17 So everyone who had returned from
captivity lived in these shelters for the seven days of the festival, and everyone was filled
8:18 Lev 23:36 Num 29:35 Deut 31:11
with great joy! The Israelites had not celebrated this way since the days of Joshua son of
Nun. 18 Ezra read from the Book of the Law of God on each of the seven days of the
festival. Then on October 15* they held a solemn assembly, as the law of Moses required.

The People Confess Their Sins

9:1 1 Sam 4:12 Ezra 8:23 Neh 8:2 Job 2:12
9 On October 31* the people returned for another observance. This time they fasted
and dressed in sackcloth and sprinkled dust on their heads. 2 Those of Israelite
descent separated themselves from all foreigners as they confessed their own sins and
9:2 Ezra 10:11 Neh 13:3
the sins of their ancestors. 3 The Book of the Law of the LORD their God was read aloud

9:3 Neh 8:4

8:10 Hebrew *he.* **8:13** Hebrew *On the second day,* of the seventh month of the Hebrew calendar. This event occurred on October 9, 445 B.C.; also see notes on 1:1 and 8:2. **8:14** Hebrew *in the seventh month.* This month of the Hebrew lunar calendar usually occurs in September and October. See Lev 23:39-43. **8:18** Hebrew *on the eighth day,* of the seventh month of the Hebrew calendar. This event occurred on October 15, 445 B.C.; also see notes on 1:1 and 8:2. **9:1** Hebrew *On the twenty-fourth day of that same month,* the seventh month of the Hebrew calendar. This event occurred on October 31, 445 B.C.; also see note on 1:1.

8:9 Ezra, not Nehemiah, was the official religious leader. It is significant that Nehemiah was a layman, not a member of the religious establishment or a prophet. He was motivated by his relationship with God, and he devoted his life to doing God's will in a secular world. Such people are crucial to God's work in all aspects of life. No matter what your work or role in life, view it as God's special calling to serve him.

8:9, 10 The people wept openly when they heard God's laws and realized how far they were from obeying them. But Ezra told them they should be filled with joy because the day was sacred. It was time to celebrate and to give gifts to those in need.

Celebration is not to be self-centered. Ezra connected celebration with giving. This gave those in need an opportunity to celebrate as well. Often when we celebrate and give to others (even when we don't feel like it), we are strengthened spiritually and filled with joy. Enter into celebrations that honor God, and allow him to fill you with his joy.

8:13ff After Ezra read God's laws to the people, they studied them further and then acted upon them. A careful reading of Scripture always calls for a response to these questions: What should we *do* with this knowledge? How should our lives change? We must *do* something about what we have learned if it is to have real significance for our lives.

8:14-17 During the seven-day Festival of Shelters, the people lived in booths made of branches. This practice was instituted as a reminder of their rescue from Egypt and the time spent in shelters in the wilderness (Leviticus 23:43). They were to think about God's protection and guidance during their years of wandering and the fact that God would still protect and guide them if they obeyed him. This was a time to remember their origins. It is helpful to remember our beginnings in order to appreciate where we are today. Think back on your life to see where God has led you. Then thank God for his continuing work to protect you and provide for your needs.

9:1 Fasting, wearing sackcloth, and putting dust on the head were public signs of sorrow and repentance.

9:2, 3 The Hebrews practiced open confession, admitting their sins to one another. Reading and studying God's Word should precede confession (see 8:18) because God can show us where we are sinning. Honest confession should precede worship, because we cannot have a right relationship with God if we hold on to certain sins.

to them for about three hours.* Then for three more hours they took turns confessing their sins and worshiping the LORD their God. 4 Some of the Levites were standing on the stairs, crying out to the LORD their God. Their names were Jeshua, Bani, Kadmiel, Shebaniah, Bunni, Sherebiah, Bani, and Kenani.

5 Then the leaders of the Levites—Jeshua, Kadmiel, Bani, Hashabneiah, Sherebiah, Hodiah, Shebaniah, and Pethahiah—called out to the people: "Stand up and praise the LORD your God, for he lives from everlasting to everlasting!"

Then they continued, "Praise his glorious name! It is far greater than we can think or say. 6 You alone are the LORD. You made the skies and the heavens and all the stars. You made the earth and the seas and everything in them. You preserve and give life to everything, and all the angels of heaven worship you.

7 "You are the LORD God, who chose Abram and brought him from Ur of the Chaldeans and renamed him Abraham. 8 When he had proved himself faithful, you made a covenant with him to give him and his descendants the land of the Canaanites, Hittites, Amorites, Perizzites, Jebusites, and Girgashites. And you have done what you promised, for you are always true to your word.

9 "You saw the sufferings and sorrows of our ancestors in Egypt, and you heard their cries from beside the Red Sea.* 10 You displayed miraculous signs and wonders against Pharaoh, his servants, and all his people, for you knew how arrogantly the Egyptians were treating them. You have a glorious reputation that has never been forgotten. 11 You divided the sea for your people so they could walk through on dry land! And then you hurled their enemies into the depths of the sea. They sank like stones beneath the mighty waters. 12 You led our ancestors by a pillar of cloud during the day and a pillar of fire at night so that they could find their way.

13 "You came down on Mount Sinai and spoke to them from heaven. You gave them regulations and instructions that were just, and laws and commands that were true. 14 You instructed them concerning the laws of your holy Sabbath. And you commanded them, through Moses your servant, to obey all your commands, laws, and instructions.

15 "You gave them bread from heaven when they were hungry and water from the rock when they were thirsty. You commanded them to go and take possession of the land you had sworn to give them. 16 But our ancestors were a proud and stubborn lot, and they refused to obey your commands.

17 "They refused to listen and did not remember the miracles you had done for them. Instead, they rebelled and appointed a leader to take them back to their slavery in Egypt! But you are a God of forgiveness, gracious and merciful, slow to become angry, and full of unfailing love and mercy. You did not abandon them, 18 even though they made an idol shaped like a calf and said, 'This is your god who brought you out of Egypt!' They sinned and committed terrible blasphemies. 19 But in your great mercy you did not abandon them to die in the wilderness. The pillar of cloud still led them forward by day, and the pillar of fire showed them the way through the night. 20 You sent your good Spirit to instruct them, and you did not stop giving them bread from heaven or water for their thirst. 21 For forty years you sustained them in the wilderness. They lacked nothing in all that time. Their clothes did not wear out, and their feet did not swell!

22 "Then you helped our ancestors conquer great kingdoms and many nations, and you placed your people in every corner of the land. They completely took over the land of King Sihon of Heshbon and the land of King Og of Bashan. 23 You made their descendants as numerous as the stars in the sky and brought them into the land you had promised to their ancestors. 24 They went in and took possession of the land. You subdued

9:4 Neh 8:7
9:6 Gen 1:1; Deut 6:4; 2 Kgs 19:15; Ps 103:20; Col 1:16-17
9:7 Gen 11:31; 12:1; 15:7; 17:5
9:8 Gen 15:6, 18-21; Josh 21:43-45
9:9 Exod 14:10-14
9:10 Exod 3:7; 5:2; 9:16
9:11 Exod 14:21; 15:1, 5, 10
9:12 Exod 13:21-22
9:13 Exod 19:11, 18-20; Ps 19:7-9
9:14 Exod 16:23; 20:8
9:15 Exod 16:4, 14-15; 17:6; Num 20:7-13; Deut 1:8, 21; Josh 1:2-4
9:16 Deut 31:27; Neh 9:10, 29
9:17 Exod 34:6-7; Num 14:4; Ps 78:11
9:18 Exod 32:4-8, 31
9:19 Neh 9:12, 27, 31
9:20 Num 11:17; Neh 9:15, 30; Isa 63:11-14
9:21 Deut 2:7
9:22 Num 21:21-35; Deut 2:26–3:11
9:23 Gen 15:5
9:24 Josh 18:1; 21:43

9:3 Hebrew *for a quarter of a day.* **9:9** Hebrew *sea of reeds.*

9:7-38 Many prayers and speeches in the Bible include a long summary of Israel's history because individuals did not have their own copies of the Bible as we do today. This summary of God's past works reminded the people of their great heritage and God's promises.

We should also remember our history to avoid repeating our mistakes so that we can serve God better. Reviewing our past helps us understand how to improve our behavior. It shows us the pattern to our spiritual growth. Learn from your past so that you will become the kind of person God wants you to be.

9:16-21 Seeing how God continued to be with his people shows that his patience is amazing! In spite of our repeated failings, pride, and stubbornness, he is always ready to pardon (9:17), and his Spirit is always ready to instruct (9:20). Realizing the extent of God's forgiveness helps us forgive those who fail us, even "seventy times seven" if necessary (Matthew 18:21, 22).

9:25 Num 13:27 Deut 3:5; 6:11; 32:15 1 Kgs 8:66
9:26 Judg 2:11 1 Kgs 14:9 2 Chr 36:16
9:27 Judg 2:14, 16, 18
9:28 Judg 3:11 Ps 106:43
9:29 Lev 18:5 Neh 9:26-30 Zech 7:11
9:30 2 Kgs 17:13 Neh 9:20
9:31 Neh 9:17 Jer 4:27
9:32 2 Kgs 15:19, 29; 17:3-6
9:33 Gen 18:25 Jer 12:1

whole nations before them. Even the kings and the Canaanites, who inhabited the land,
were powerless! Your people could deal with them as they pleased. [25]Our ancestors
captured fortified cities and fertile land. They took over houses full of good things, with
cisterns already dug and vineyards and olive groves and orchards in abundance. So they
ate until they were full and grew fat and enjoyed themselves in all your blessings.
[26]"But despite all this, they were disobedient and rebelled against you. They threw
away your law, they killed the prophets who encouraged them to return to you, and they
committed terrible blasphemies. [27]So you handed them over to their enemies. But in their
time of trouble they cried to you, and you heard them from heaven. In great mercy, you
sent them deliverers who rescued them from their enemies.
[28]"But when all was going well, your people turned to sin again, and once more you
let their enemies conquer them. Yet whenever your people cried to you again for help,
you listened once more from heaven. In your wonderful mercy, you rescued them
repeatedly! [29]You warned them to return to your law, but they became proud and
obstinate and disobeyed your commands. They did not follow your regulations, by which
people will find life if only they obey. They stubbornly turned their backs on you and
refused to listen. [30]In your love, you were patient with them for many years. You sent
your Spirit, who, through the prophets, warned them about their sins. But still they
wouldn't listen! So once again you allowed the pagan inhabitants of the land to conquer
them. [31]But in your great mercy, you did not destroy them completely or abandon them
forever. What a gracious and merciful God you are!
[32]"And now, our God, the great and mighty and awesome God, who keeps his
covenant of unfailing love, do not let all the hardships we have suffered be as nothing
to you. Great trouble has come upon us and upon our kings and princes and priests
and prophets and ancestors from the days when the kings of Assyria first triumphed
over us until now. [33]Every time you punished us you were being just. We have sinned

GOING HOME: TWO GREAT JOURNEYS OF ISRAEL

What about the Journeys?	*The Exodus*	*The Return from Exile*
Where were they?	Egypt (430 years)	Babylon (70 years)
How many?	About 1 million	60,000
How long did the journey take them?	40 years and 2 attempts	100 years and 3 journeys
Who led them?	Moses/Aaron/Joshua	Zerubbabel/Ezra/ Nehemiah
What was their purpose?	To reclaim the Promised Land	To rebuild the Temple and city of Jerusalem
What obstacles did they face?	Red Sea/Wilderness/Enemies	Ruins/Limited Resources/ Enemies
What failures did they experience?	Complaining/Disobedience/ Retreat—all of which turned a journey of a few weeks into a 40-year ordeal	Fear/Discouragement/ Apathy—all of which turned a project of a few months into one that required a century to complete
What successes did they have?	Eventually entered the Promised Land	Eventually rebuilt Jerusalem's Temple and wall
What lessons did they learn?	God will build his nation. God is both faithful and just. God will accomplish great acts to make his promises come true	God will preserve his nation. God will continue to have a chosen people, a home for them, and a plan to offer himself to them

9:28-31 Israel was devastated by times of intense rebellion and sin. Yet when the people repented and returned to God, he delivered them. God puts no limit on the number of times we can come to him to obtain mercy, but we must *come* in order to obtain it, recognizing our need and asking him for help. This miracle of grace should inspire us to say, "What a gracious and merciful God you are!" If there is a recurring problem or difficulty in your life, continue to ask God for help, and be willing and ready to make changes in your attitude and behavior that will correct that situation.

greatly, and you gave us only what we deserved. 34 Our kings, princes, priests, and
ancestors did not obey your law or listen to your commands and solemn warnings.
35 Even while they had their own kingdom, they did not serve you even though you **9:35**
showered your goodness on them. You gave them a large, fertile land, but they refused Deut 28:45-47
to turn from their wickedness.

36 "So now today we are slaves here in the land of plenty that you gave to our **9:36** Deut 28:48
ancestors! We are slaves among all this abundance! 37 The lush produce of this land **9:37**
piles up in the hands of the kings whom you have set over us because of our sins. They Deut 28:33
have power over us and our cattle. We serve them at their pleasure, and we are in great
misery.

38 "Yet in spite of all this,* we are making a solemn promise and putting it in writing. **9:38** Neh 10:1, 29
On this sealed document are the names of our princes and Levites and priests."

The People Agree to Obey

10 The document was ratified and sealed with the following names: **10:1** Neh 9:38

Nehemiah the governor, the son of Hacaliah.

The priests who signed were Zedekiah, 2 Seraiah, Azariah, Jeremiah, 3 Pashhur,
Amariah, Malkijah, 4 Hattush, Shebaniah, Malluch, 5 Harim, Meremoth, Obadiah,
6 Daniel, Ginnethon, Baruch, 7 Meshullam, Abijah, Mijamin, 8 Maaziah, Bilgai, and **10:8-9**
Shemaiah. These were the priests. Neh 12:1

9 The Levites who signed were Jeshua son of Azaniah, Binnui from the family of
Henadad, Kadmiel, 10 and their fellow Levites: Shebaniah, Hodiah, Kelita, Pelaiah,
Hanan, 11 Mica, Rehob, Hashabiah, 12 Zaccur, Sherebiah, Shebaniah, 13 Hodiah,
Bani, and Beninu.

14 The leaders who signed were Parosh, Pahath-moab, Elam, Zattu, Bani, 15 Bunni,
Azgad, Bebai, 16 Adonijah, Bigvai, Adin, 17 Ater, Hezekiah, Azzur, 18 Hodiah,
Hashum, Bezai, 19 Hariph, Anathoth, Nebai, 20 Magpiash, Meshullam, Hezir,
21 Meshezabel, Zadok, Jaddua, 22 Pelatiah, Hanan, Anaiah, 23 Hoshea, Hananiah,
Hasshub, 24 Hallohesh, Pilha, Shobek, 25 Rehum, Hashabnah, Maaseiah, 26 Ahiah,
Hanan, Anan, 27 Malluch, Harim, and Baanah.

28 The rest of the people—the priests, Levites, gatekeepers, singers, Temple servants,
and all who had separated themselves from the pagan people of the land in order to serve **10:28** Ezra 2:36-58
God, and who were old enough to understand— 29 now all heartily bound themselves Neh 9:2
with an oath. They vowed to accept the curse of God if they failed to obey the law of **10:29**
God as issued by his servant Moses. They solemnly promised to carefully follow all the Neh 5:12
commands, laws, and regulations of the LORD their Lord.

The Vow of the People

30 "We promise not to let our daughters marry the pagan people of the land, nor to let our **10:30** Exod 34:16 Deut 7:3

9:38 Or *Because of all this.*

9:35 Sometimes the very blessings God has showered on us make us forget him (9:28). We are often tempted to rely on wealth for security rather than on God. As you see what happened to the Israelites, look at your own life. Do your blessings make you thankful to God and draw you closer to him, or do they make you feel self-sufficient and forgetful of God?

9:36 The Israelites were in the strange position of being slaves in their own land, having to turn over a part of their resources each year to a foreign king. How ironic, since God had given the land to them.

9:38 This "solemn promise" between the people and God had six provisions. They agreed to (1) not marry non-Jewish neighbors (10:30), (2) observe the Sabbath (10:31), (3) observe every seventh year as a Sabbath year (10:31), (4) pay a Temple tax (10:32, 33), (5) supply wood for the burnt offerings in the Temple (10:34), and (6) give dues to the Temple (10:35-38). After years of decadence and exile, the people once again took seriously their responsibility to follow God and keep his laws wholeheartedly.

10:28ff The wall was completed, and the agreement God made with his people in the days of Moses was restored (Deuteronomy 8). This promise has principles that are important for us today. Our relationship with God must go far beyond church attendance and regular devotions. It should affect our relationships (10:30), our time (10:31), and our material resources (10:32-39). When you chose to follow God, you promised to serve him in this way. The Israelites had fallen away from their original commitment. We must keep our promise to God in times of adversity or prosperity.

10:30 If God's chosen people were going to witness for him in a pagan world, they needed united, God-fearing families. They also needed to avoid any enticements to worship the idols of the people who lived around them. This was why God prohibited marriage between Israelites and the pagan inhabitants of the land (Deuteronomy 7:3, 4). But Israelites and pagans often intermarried anyway, and the results were disastrous for the families and for the nation. Time after time, marrying foreigners led God's people into idolatry (1 Kings 11:1-11). Whenever the nation turned its back on God, it also lost its prosperity and influence for good.

10:31 Exod 23:10-11; Lev 25:1-7; Deut 15:1-2; Neh 13:15-22
10:32 Exod 30:11-16; Matt 17:24
10:33 Lev 23:1-44; 24:5
10:34 Neh 11:1; 13:31
10:35 Exod 23:19; Deut 26:2
10:36 Exod 13:2
10:37 Lev 23:17; 27:30; Neh 13:5, 9
10:38 Num 18:26; Neh 13:12-13
10:39 Deut 12:6; Neh 13:10-11
11:1 Neh 7:4; 10:34; 11:18; Isa 48:2

sons marry their daughters. 31 We further promise that if the people of the land should
bring any merchandise or grain to be sold on the Sabbath or on any other holy day, we
will refuse to buy it. And we promise not to do any work every seventh year and to cancel
the debts owed to us by other Jews.

32 "In addition, we promise to obey the command to pay the annual Temple tax of an
eighth of an ounce of silver,* so that there will be enough money to care for the Temple
of our God. 33 This will provide for the Bread of the Presence; for the regular grain
offerings and burnt offerings; for the offerings on the Sabbaths, the new moon celebrations, and the annual festivals; for the holy offerings; and for the sin offerings to make
atonement for Israel. It will also provide for the other items necessary for the work of
the Temple of our God.

34 "We have cast sacred lots to determine when—at regular times each year—the
families of the priests, Levites, and the common people should bring wood to God's
Temple to be burned on the altar of the LORD our God, as required in the law.

35 "We promise always to bring the first part of every harvest to the LORD's Temple—
whether it be a crop from the soil or from our fruit trees. 36 We agree to give to God our
oldest sons and the firstborn of all our herds and flocks, just as the law requires. We will
present them to the priests who minister in the Temple of our God. 37 We will store the
produce in the storerooms of the Temple of our God. We will bring the best of our flour
and other grain offerings, the best of our fruit, and the best of our new wine and olive
oil. And we promise to bring to the Levites a tenth of everything our land produces, for
it is the Levites who collect the tithes in all our rural towns. 38 A priest—a descendant of
Aaron—will be with the Levites as they receive these tithes. And a tenth of all that is
collected as tithes will be delivered by the Levites to the Temple of our God and placed
in the storerooms. 39 The people and the Levites must bring these offerings of grain, new
wine, and olive oil to the Temple and place them in the sacred containers near the
ministering priests, the gatekeepers, and the singers.

"So we promise together not to neglect the Temple of our God."

2. Nehemiah establishes policies

The People Occupy Jerusalem

11 Now the leaders of the people were living in Jerusalem, the holy city, at this time.
A tenth of the people from the other towns of Judah and Benjamin were chosen
by sacred lots to live there, too, while the rest stayed where they were. 2 And the people
commended everyone who volunteered to resettle in Jerusalem.

10:32 Hebrew *tax of 1/3 of a shekel* [4 grams].

10:31 God recognized that the lure of money would conflict with the need for a day of rest, so trade was forbidden inside the city on the Sabbath. By deciding to honor God first, the Israelites would be refusing to make money their god. Our culture often makes us choose between convenience and profit on the one hand, and putting God first on the other. Look at your work and worship habits: Is God really first?

10:31 Canceling all debts every seventh year was a part of the law (see Exodus 23:10, 11 and Deuteronomy 15:1, 2). The people were reciting and promising to obey God's law and keep the covenant.

10:32 The Temple had been rebuilt under Ezra's leadership about 70 years earlier (Ezra 6:14, 15). So the Temple tax, offerings, and festivals had been restored.

10:35 This practice was instituted at the time of the Exodus from Egypt (see the note on Exodus 13:12-14). The people needed to relearn the importance of dedicating the first part of their yield to God. Nehemiah was simply reinstating this practice from the early days of the nation (Exodus 13:1, 2; Numbers 3:40-51). Although this principle was not carried over to New Testament times, the concept of giving God the first portion of our time, treasure, and talent still remains. Do you give God your first and best or merely what is left over?

10:37-39 According to God's law, the people were to give a tenth of their produce to the Temple for the support of the Levites (those who cared for the Temple and the religious observances). A tenth of what the Levites received or produced went to the priests for their support. The principle at work was to ensure the support of the house of God and his workers. We must not overlook our responsibility to God's workers today.

11:1ff The exiles who returned were few in number compared to Jerusalem's population in the days of the kings. And because the walls had been rebuilt on their original foundations, the city seemed sparsely populated. Nehemiah asked one-tenth of the people from the outlying areas to move inside the city walls to keep large areas of the city from being vacant. Apparently these people did not want to move into the city. Only a few people volunteered (11:1, 2), and Nehemiah determined by sacred lot who among the remaining people would have to move.

Many of them may not have wanted to live in the city because (1) non-Jews attached a stigma to Jerusalem residents, often excluding them from trade because of their religious beliefs; (2) moving into the city meant rebuilding their homes and reestablishing their businesses, a major investment of time and money; (3) living in Jerusalem required stricter obedience to God's Word because of greater social pressure and proximity to the Temple.

3 Here is a list of the names of the provincial officials who came to Jerusalem. Most
of the people, priests, Levites, Temple servants, and descendants of Solomon's servants
continued to live in their own homes in the various towns of Judah, 4 but some of the
people from Judah and Benjamin resettled in Jerusalem.

From the tribe of Judah: Athaiah son of Uzziah, son of Zechariah, son of Amariah,
son of Shephatiah, son of Mahalalel, of the family of Perez; 5 and Maaseiah son
of Baruch, son of Col-hozeh, son of Hazaiah, son of Adaiah, son of Joiarib, son
of Zechariah, of the family of Shelah.* 6 There were also 468 descendants of Perez
who lived in Jerusalem—all outstanding men.

7 From the tribe of Benjamin: Sallu son of Meshullam, son of Joed, son of Pedaiah,
son of Kolaiah, son of Maaseiah, son of Ithiel, son of Jeshaiah; 8 and after him there
were Gabbai and Sallai, and a total of 928 relatives. 9 Their chief officer was Joel
son of Zicri, who was assisted by Judah son of Hassenuah, second-in-command
over the city.

10 From the priests: Jedaiah son of Joiarib; Jakin; 11 and Seraiah son of Hilkiah, son
of Meshullam, son of Zadok, son of Meraioth, son of Ahitub, the supervisor of the
Temple of God; 12 together with 822 of their associates, who worked at the Temple.
Also, there was Adaiah son of Jeroham, son of Pelaliah, son of Amzi, son of
Zechariah, son of Pashhur, son of Malkijah; 13 and 242 of his associates, who were
heads of their families. There were also Amashsai son of Azarel, son of Ahzai, son
of Meshillemoth, son of Immer; 14 and 128 of his outstanding associates. Their
chief officer was Zabdiel son of Haggedolim.

15 From the Levites: Shemaiah son of Hasshub, son of Azrikam, son of Hashabiah,
son of Bunni; 16 Shabbethai and Jozabad, who were in charge of the work outside
the Temple of God; 17 Mattaniah son of Mica, son of Zabdi, a descendant of
Asaph, who opened the thanksgiving services with prayer; Bakbukiah, who was
Mattaniah's assistant; and Abda son of Shammua, son of Galal, son of Jeduthun.
18 In all, there were 284 Levites in the holy city.

19 From the gatekeepers: Akkub, Talmon, and 172 of their associates, who guarded the gates.

20 The other priests, Levites, and the rest of the Israelites lived wherever their family
inheritance was located in any of the towns of Judah. 21 However, the Temple servants,
whose leaders were Ziha and Gishpa, all lived on the hill of Ophel.
22 The chief officer of the Levites in Jerusalem was Uzzi son of Bani, son of Hashabiah, son of Mattaniah, son of Mica, a descendant of Asaph, whose family served as
singers at God's Temple. 23 They were under royal orders, which determined their daily
activities.
24 Pethahiah son of Meshezabel, a descendant of Zerah son of Judah, was the king's
agent in all matters of public administration.
25 Some of the people of Judah lived in Kiriath-arba with its villages, Dibon with its
villages, and Jekabzeel with its villages.* 26 They also lived in Jeshua, Moladah, Beth-
pelet, 27 Hazar-shual, Beersheba with its villages, 28 Ziklag, and Meconah with its
villages. 29 They were also in En-rimmon, Zorah, Jarmuth, 30 Zanoah, and Adullam with
their villages. They were also in Lachish and its nearby fields and Azekah with its
surrounding villages. So the people of Judah were living all the way from Beersheba
to the valley of Hinnom.
31 Some of the people of Benjamin lived at Geba, Micmash, Aija, and Bethel with its
surrounding villages. 32 They were also in Anathoth, Nob, Ananiah, 33 Hazor, Ramah,
Gittaim, 34 Hadid, Zeboim, Neballat, 35 Lod, Ono, and the Valley of Craftsmen.* 36 Some
of the Levites who lived in Judah were sent to live with the tribe of Benjamin.

A History of the Priests and Levites

12 Here is the list of the priests and Levites who had returned with Zerubbabel son
of Shealtiel and Jeshua the high priest:

Seraiah, Jeremiah, Ezra,
2 Amariah, Malluch, Hattush,
3 Shecaniah, Harim,* Meremoth,

11:3-19
//1 Chr 9:2-34
Ezra 2:43-57
Neh 7:57-59; 11:20

11:16
1 Chr 26:29

11:18
Neh 11:1, 3

11:21
Neh 3:22

11:22
Ezra 6:8
Neh 11:9, 14, 17, 23

11:25
Josh 13:9, 17; 14:15; 15:31

12:1
Ezra 2:1-2

11:5 Hebrew *son of the Shilonite.* **11:35** Or *and Ge-harashim.* **12:3** Hebrew *Rehum;* compare 7:42; 12:15; Ezra 2:39.

4 Iddo, Ginnethon,* Abijah,
5 Miniamin, Moadiah,* Bilgah,
6 Shemaiah, Joiarib, Jedaiah,
7 Sallu, Amok, Hilkiah, and Jedaiah.

These were the leaders of the priests and their associates in the days of Jeshua.

12:8 Ezra 2:2 Neh 11:17

8 The Levites who had returned with them were Jeshua, Binnui, Kadmiel, Sherebiah,
Judah, and Mattaniah, who with his associates was in charge of the songs of thanksgiving. 9 Their associates, Bakbukiah and Unni, stood opposite them during the service.

10 Jeshua the high priest was the father of Joiakim.
Joiakim was the father of Eliashib.
Eliashib was the father of Joiada.
11 Joiada was the father of Johanan.*
Johanan was the father of Jaddua.

12 Now when Joiakim was high priest, the family leaders of the priests were as follows:

Meraiah was leader of the family of Seraiah.
Hananiah was leader of the family of Jeremiah.
13 Meshullam was leader of the family of Ezra.
Jehohanan was leader of the family of Amariah.
14 Jonathan was leader of the family of Malluch.*
Joseph was leader of the family of Shecaniah.*
15 Adna was leader of the family of Harim.
Helkai was leader of the family of Meremoth.*
16 Zechariah was leader of the family of Iddo.
Meshullam was leader of the family of Ginnethon.
17 Zicri was leader of the family of Abijah.
There was also a* leader of the family of Miniamin.
Piltai was leader of the family of Moadiah.
18 Shammua was leader of the family of Bilgah.
Jehonathan was leader of the family of Shemaiah.
19 Mattenai was leader of the family of Joiarib.
Uzzi was leader of the family of Jedaiah.
20 Kallai was leader of the family of Sallu.*
Eber was leader of the family of Amok.
21 Hashabiah was leader of the family of Hilkiah.
Nethanel was leader of the family of Jedaiah.

22 During the reign of Darius II of Persia,* a list was compiled of the family leaders of
the Levites and the priests in the days of the following high priests: Eliashib, Joiada,
Johanan, and Jaddua. 23 The heads of the Levite families were recorded in *The Book of
History* down to the days of Johanan, the grandson* of Eliashib.

12:24 Neh 11:17

24 These were the family leaders of the Levites: Hashabiah, Sherebiah, Jeshua, Binnui,* Kadmiel, and other associates, who stood opposite them during the ceremonies of
praise and thanksgiving, one section responding to the other, just as commanded by

12:25 1 Chr 26:15

David, the man of God. 25 This included Mattaniah, Bakbukiah, and Obadiah.

12:26 Neh 8:9

Meshullam, Talmon, and Akkub were the gatekeepers in charge of the storerooms at
the gates. 26 These all served in the days of Joiakim son of Jeshua, son of Jehozadak,*
and in the days of Nehemiah the governor and of Ezra the priest and scribe.

Dedication of Jerusalem's Wall

12:27 1 Chr 15:16, 28

27 During the dedication of the new wall of Jerusalem, the Levites throughout the land
were asked to come to Jerusalem to assist in the ceremonies. They were to take part in

12:4 As in some Hebrew manuscripts and Latin Vulgate (see also 12:16); most Hebrew manuscripts read *Ginnethoi.* **12:5** Hebrew *Mijamin, Maadiah;* compare 12:17. **12:11** Hebrew *Jonathan;* compare 12:22. **12:14a** As in Greek version (see also 10:4; 12:2); Hebrew reads *Malluchi.* **12:14b** As in many Hebrew manuscripts, some Greek manuscripts, and Syriac version (see also 12:3); most Hebrew manuscripts read *Shebaniah.* **12:15** As in some Greek manuscripts (see also 12:3); Hebrew reads *Meraioth.* **12:17** Hebrew lacks the name of this family leader. **12:20** Hebrew *Sallai;* compare 12:7. **12:22** Hebrew *Darius the Persian.* **12:23** Hebrew *son;* compare 12:10-11. **12:24** Hebrew *son of* (i.e., *ben*), which should probably be read here as the proper name Binnui; compare Ezra 3:9 and the note there. **12:26** Hebrew *Jozadak,* a variant name for Jehozadak.

the joyous occasion with their songs of thanksgiving and with the music of cymbals,
lyres, and harps. 28 The singers were brought together from Jerusalem and its surround- **12:28** 1 Chr 9:16
ing villages and from the villages of the Netophathites. 29 They also came from Beth-gil-
gal and the area of Geba and Azmaveth, for the singers had built their own villages
around Jerusalem. 30 The priests and Levites first dedicated themselves, then the people, **12:30** Neh 13:22, 30
the gates, and the wall.
31 I led the leaders of Judah to the top of the wall and organized two large choirs to **12:31** Neh 2:13; 3:13-14
give thanks. One of the choirs proceeded southward* along the top of the wall to the
Dung Gate. 32 Hoshaiah and half the leaders of Judah followed them, 33 along with
Azariah, Ezra, Meshullam, 34 Judah, Benjamin, Shemaiah, Jeremiah, 35 and some priests
who played trumpets. Then came Zechariah son of Jonathan, son of Shemaiah, son of
Mattaniah, son of Micaiah, son of Zaccur, a descendant of Asaph. 36 And finally came
Zechariah's colleagues Shemaiah, Azarel, Milalai, Gilalai, Maai, Nethanel, Judah, and
Hanani. They used the musical instruments prescribed by David, the man of God. Ezra
the scribe led this procession. 37 At the Fountain Gate they went straight up the steps on **12:37** Neh 2:14; 3:15, 26
the ascent of the city wall toward the City of David. They passed the house of David and
then proceeded to the Water Gate on the east.
38 The second choir went northward* around the other way to meet them. I followed **12:38** Neh 3:8, 11
them, with the other half of the people, along the top of the wall past the Tower of the
Ovens to the Broad Wall, 39 then past the Ephraim Gate to the Old City Gate,* past the **12:39** Neh 3:1, 3, 6, 25, 31-32; 8:16 Jer 31:38
Fish Gate and the Tower of Hananel, and went on to the Tower of the Hundred. Then we
continued on to the Sheep Gate and stopped at the Guard Gate.
40 The two choirs that were giving thanks then proceeded to the Temple of God, where
they took their places. So did I, together with the group of leaders who were with me.
41 We went together with the trumpet-playing priests—Eliakim, Maaseiah, Miniamin,
Micaiah, Elioenai, Zechariah, and Hananiah—42 and the singers—Maaseiah, Shemaiah,
Eleazar, Uzzi, Jehohanan, Malkijah, Elam, and Ezer. They played and sang loudly and
clearly under the direction of Jezrahiah the choir director.
43 Many sacrifices were offered on that joyous day, for God had given the people cause
for great joy. The women and children also participated in the celebration, and the joy of
the people of Jerusalem could be heard far away.

Provisions for Temple Worship

44 On that day men were appointed to be in charge of the storerooms for the gifts, the first **12:44** Neh 13:4-5, 12-13
part of the harvest, and the tithes. They were responsible to collect these from the fields
as required by the law for the priests and Levites, for all the people of Judah valued the
priests and Levites and their work. 45 They performed the service of their God and the **12:45** 1 Chr 25:1-8; 26:1-32
service of purification, as required by the laws of David and his son Solomon, and so did
the singers and the gatekeepers. 46 The custom of having choir directors to lead the choirs **12:46** 2 Chr 29:30
in hymns of praise and thanks to God began long ago in the days of David and Asaph.
47 So now, in the days of Zerubbabel and of Nehemiah, the people brought a daily supply **12:47** Num 18:21-29
of food for the singers, the gatekeepers, and the Levites. The Levites, in turn, gave a
portion of what they received to the priests, the descendants of Aaron.

Nehemiah's Various Reforms

13 On that same day, as the Book of Moses was being read, the people found a **13:1** Deut 23:3-5 Neh 13:23
statement which said that no Ammonite or Moabite should ever be permitted to
enter the assembly of God. 2 For they had not been friendly to the Israelites when they **13:2** Num 22:3-11

12:31 Hebrew *to the right.* **12:38** Hebrew *to the left.* **12:39** Or *the Mishneh Gate,* or *the Jeshanah Gate.*

12:35, 36 How could the priests have used musical instruments? David had instituted music as a part of worship in the Temple, and so his instruments had probably been stored there. Although Nebuchadnezzar destroyed the Temple, he took many Temple items back to Babylon with him (2 Chronicles 36:18). These were most likely preserved in Babylon and given back to the Israelites by Cyrus when they returned to their land (Ezra 1:7-11).

12:44 Further arrangements were made for supporting those who served at the Temple. The storerooms were administered by men who made sure the tithes and contributions were collected and distributed appropriately. These storerooms had to be large to hold all the grain presented by the people. This storeroom administration was an important responsibility.

12:44-47 The dedication of the city wall was characterized by joy, praise, and singing (12:24, 27-29, 35, 36, 40-43). Nehemiah repeatedly mentioned David, who began the custom of using choirs in worship. In David's day, Israel was a vigorous, God-fearing nation. These exiles who had returned wanted their rebuilt Jerusalem to be the hub of a renewed nation, strengthened by God; therefore, they dedicated themselves and their city to God.

left Egypt. Instead, they hired Balaam to curse them, though our God turned the curse
13:3 Neh 9:2; 10:28
into a blessing. 3When this law was read, all those of mixed ancestry were immediately
expelled from the assembly.

13:4 Neh 6:17-19; 12:44
4Before this had happened, Eliashib the priest, who had been appointed as supervisor
13:5 Num 18:21
of the storerooms of the Temple of our God and who was also a relative of Tobiah, 5had
converted a large storage room and placed it at Tobiah's disposal. The room had previously
been used for storing the grain offerings, frankincense, Temple utensils, and tithes of grain,
new wine, olive oil, and the special portion set aside for the priests. Moses had decreed
that these offerings belonged to the Levites, the singers, and the gatekeepers.

13:6 Ezra 6:22; Neh 5:14
6I was not in Jerusalem at that time, for I had returned to the king in the thirty-second
year of the reign of King Artaxerxes of Babylon,* though I later received his permission
13:7 Neh 13:5
to return. 7When I arrived back in Jerusalem and learned the extent of this evil deed of
Eliashib—that he had provided Tobiah with a room in the courtyards of the Temple of
13:9 2 Chr 29:5, 15-19
God— 8I became very upset and threw all of Tobiah's belongings from the room. 9Then
I demanded that the rooms be purified, and I brought back the utensils for God's Temple,
the grain offerings, and the frankincense.

13:10 Neh 10:37; 12:28-29
10I also discovered that the Levites had not been given what was due them, so they
and the singers who were to conduct the worship services had all returned to work their
fields. 11I immediately confronted the leaders and demanded, "Why has the Temple of
God been neglected?" Then I called all the Levites back again and restored them to their
13:12 Neh 10:37-39; 12:44
proper duties. 12And once more all the people of Judah began bringing their tithes of
grain, new wine, and olive oil to the Temple storerooms.

13:13 Neh 7:2
13I put Shelemiah the priest, Zadok the scribe, and Pedaiah, one of the Levites, in
charge of the storerooms. And I appointed Hanan son of Zaccur and grandson of
Mattaniah as their assistant. These men had an excellent reputation, and it was their job
to make honest distributions to their fellow Levites.

13:14 Neh 5:19; 13:22, 31
14Remember this good deed, O my God, and do not forget all that I have faithfully
done for the Temple of my God.

13:15 Exod 20:8-11; 34:21; Neh 13:21
15One Sabbath day I saw some men of Judah treading their winepresses. They were
also bringing in bundles of grain and loading them on their donkeys. And on that day
they were bringing their wine, grapes, figs, and all sorts of produce to Jerusalem to sell.
So I rebuked them for selling their produce on the Sabbath. 16There were also some men
from Tyre bringing in fish and all kinds of merchandise. They were selling it on the
Sabbath to the people of Judah—and in Jerusalem at that!

13:17 Neh 13:11, 15
17So I confronted the leaders of Judah, "Why are you profaning the Sabbath in this

13:6 The thirty-second year of Artaxerxes was 433 B.C.

13:3 "Those of mixed ancestry" refers to the Moabites and Ammonites, two nations who were bitter enemies of Israel (13:1). God's law clearly stated that these two peoples should never be allowed in the Temple (Deuteronomy 23:3-5). This had nothing to do with racial prejudice because God clearly loved all people, including foreigners (Deuteronomy 10:18). He allowed foreigners to make sacrifices (Numbers 15:15, 16), and he desires all nations to know and love him (Isaiah 42:6). But while God wants all to come to him, he warns believers to stay away from those bent on evil (Proverbs 24:1). The relationships established between Jews and pagans had caused their captivity in the first place. In their celebration and rededication, they had to show they were serious about following God's law.

13:6, 7 Nehemiah had to return to Babylon in 433 B.C., 12 years after he had arrived in Jerusalem. Either he was recalled by Artaxerxes, or he was fulfilling an agreement to return. It is not known exactly how long he remained in Babylon, but when he returned to Jerusalem (13:7), he found that one of his major opponents in rebuilding the wall, Tobiah, had been given his own room at the Temple. He was an Ammonite (4:3) and thus forbidden to enter the Temple. Eliashib the priest had married Tobiah's daughter, so Tobiah used his influence with his son-in-law to get this special room. Chapters 2, 4, and 6 tell about Tobiah's opposition to Nehemiah and Nehemiah's appropriate action.

13:10 Because the Levites were no longer supported, they had returned to their farms to support themselves, neglecting their Temple duties and the spiritual welfare of the people. Spiritual workers deserve their pay, and their support ought to be enough to care for their needs. They shouldn't have to suffer (or leave) because believers don't adequately assess and meet their needs.

13:16 Tyre was a large Phoenician city and port on the Mediterranean Sea.

13:17 God had commanded Israel not to work on the Sabbath, but to rest in remembrance of Creation and the Exodus (Exodus 20:8-11; Deuteronomy 5:12-15). The Sabbath rest, lasting from sunset Friday to sunset Saturday, was to be honored and observed by all Jews, servants, visiting foreigners, and even farm animals. Jerusalem's busy Sabbath trade directly violated God's law, so Nehemiah commanded that the city gates be shut and traders be sent home every Friday afternoon as the Sabbath hours approached.

evil way? 18 Wasn't it enough that your ancestors did this sort of thing, so that our God **13:18**
brought the present troubles upon us and our city? Now you are bringing even more Jer 17:21
wrath upon the people of Israel by permitting the Sabbath to be desecrated in this way!"
19 So I commanded that from then on the gates of the city should be shut as darkness fell **13:19**
every Friday evening,* not to be opened until the Sabbath ended. I also sent some of my Lev 23:32
own servants to guard the gates so that no merchandise could be brought in on the
Sabbath day. 20 The merchants and tradesmen with a variety of wares camped outside
Jerusalem once or twice. 21 But I spoke sharply to them and said, "What are you doing **13:21**
out here, camping around the wall? If you do this again, I will arrest you!" And that was Neh 13:15
the last time they came on the Sabbath. 22 Then I commanded the Levites to purify **13:22**
themselves and to guard the gates in order to preserve the holiness of the Sabbath. Neh 13:14, 31

Remember this good deed also, O my God! Have compassion on me according to
your great and unfailing love.

23 About the same time I realized that some of the men of Judah had married women from **13:23** Ezra 9:2
Ashdod, Ammon, and Moab. 24 Even worse, half their children spoke in the language of Neh 10:30
Ashdod or some other people and could not speak the language of Judah at all. 25 So I **13:25**
confronted them and called down curses on them. I beat some of them and pulled out their Deut 25:2 Neh 10:29-30;
hair. I made them swear before God that they would not let their children intermarry with 13:11, 17
the pagan people of the land.
26 "Wasn't this exactly what led King Solomon of Israel into sin?" I demanded. "There **13:26**
was no king from any nation who could compare to him, and God loved him and made 1 Kgs 3:13; 11:1-8 2 Chr 1:12
him king over all Israel. But even he was led into sin by his foreign wives. 27 How could **13:27**
you even think of committing this sinful deed and acting unfaithfully toward God by Ezra 10:2 Neh 13:23
marrying foreign women?"
28 One of the sons of Joiada* son of Eliashib the high priest had married a daughter of **13:28**
Sanballat the Horonite, so I banished him from my presence. Neh 2:10, 19

29 Remember them, O my God, for they have defiled the priesthood and the promises
and vows of the priests and Levites. **13:29** Num 25:13 Neh 6:14

30 So I purged out everything foreign and assigned tasks to the priests and Levites, **13:30**
making certain that each knew his work. 31 I also made sure that the supply of wood for Neh 10:30
the altar was brought at the proper times and that the first part of the harvest was collected **13:31** Neh 10:34; 13:14, 22
for the priests.

Remember this in my favor, O my God.

13:19 Hebrew *on the day before the Sabbath.* **13:28** Hebrew *Jehoiada,* a variant name for Joiada.

13:24 Ashdod was on the Mediterranean coast, in the region controlled by the Philistines. Ammon and Moab were across the Jordan to the east. These nations were abhorrent to those who knew Israel's history.

13:25 Nehemiah was filled with righteous indignation at the blatant way the Jews were breaking God's laws and disregarding the covenant they had previously reaffirmed (10:30). The people had promised not to allow their children to marry pagans. But during Nehemiah's absence, the people had been intermarrying, breaking their solemn promise with God. Nehemiah's severe treatment of these people shows the contrast between his great faithfulness to God and the people's neglect, disobedience, and disloyalty (see also Ezra 10:3).

13:26 Nehemiah used the example of Solomon's mistakes to teach his people. If one of the greatest kings of Israel fell because of the influence of unbelievers, others could too. Nehemiah saw this principle in Solomon's example: Your gifts and strengths won't be of much benefit if you fail to deal with your weaknesses. Although Solomon was a great king, his marriages to foreign women brought tragedy to the whole kingdom. A tendency to sin must be recognized and dealt with swiftly; otherwise, it may overpower you and bring you down. One of the strongest reasons for reading the Bible is to learn from the mistakes of God's people.

13:31 "Remember this in my favor" means "look favorably upon me for all that I have done."

13:31 Nehemiah's life story provides many principles of effective leadership that are still valid today: (1) *Have a clear purpose and keep evaluating it in light of God's will.* Nothing prevented Nehemiah from staying on track. (2) *Be straightforward and honest.* Everyone knew exactly what Nehemiah needed, and he spoke the truth even when it made his goal harder to achieve. (3) *Live above reproach.* The accusations against Nehemiah were empty and false. (4) *Be a person of constant prayer,* deriving power and wisdom from your contact with God. Everything Nehemiah did glorified God.

Leadership appears glamorous at times, but it is often lonely, thankless, and filled with pressures to compromise values and standards. Nehemiah was able to accomplish a huge task against incredible odds because he learned that there is no success without risk of failure, no reward without hard work, no opportunity without criticism, and no true leadership without trust in God. This book is about rebuilding the wall of a great city, but it is also about spiritual renewal, rebuilding a people's dependence on God. When we take our eyes off God, our lives begin to crumble.

ESTHER

Jerusalem destroyed/ exiles go to Babylon 586 B.C.	First exiles return to Jerusalem 538	Temple completed 515	Xerxes becomes king of Persia 486	Esther becomes queen 479	Haman's decree to destroy the Jews 474	First Festival of Purim 473

DRAMA, power, romance, intrigue—this is the stuff of which best-selling novels are made. But far from a modern piece of fiction, those words describe a true story, lived and written centuries ago. More than entertaining reading, it is a story of the profound interplay of God's sovereignty and human will. God prepared the place and the opportunity, and his people, Esther and Mordecai, chose to act.

The book of Esther begins with Queen Vashti refusing to obey an order from her husband, King Xerxes. She was subsequently banished, and the search began for a new queen. The king sent out a decree to gather together all the beautiful women in the empire and bring them into the royal harem. Esther, a young Jewish woman, was one of those chosen to be in the royal harem. King Xerxes was so pleased with Esther that he made her his queen.

Meanwhile, Mordecai, Esther's older cousin, became a government official and during his tenure foiled an assassination plot. But the ambitious and self-serving Haman was appointed second-in-command in the empire. When Mordecai refused to bow in reverence to him, Haman became furious and determined to destroy Mordecai and all the Jews along with him.

To accomplish his vengeful deed, Haman deceived the king and persuaded him to issue an edict condemning the Jews to death. Mordecai told Queen Esther about this edict, and she decided to risk her life to save her people. Esther asked King Xerxes and Haman to be her guests at a banquet. During the feast, the king asked Esther what she really wanted, and he promised to give her anything. Esther simply invited both men to another banquet the next day.

That night, unable to sleep, the king was flipping through some records in the royal archives when he read of the assassination plot that Mordecai thwarted. Surprised to learn that Mordecai had never been rewarded for this deed, the king asked Haman what should be done to properly thank a hero. Haman thought the king must be talking about him, and so he described a lavish reward. The king agreed, but to Haman's shock and utter humiliation, he learned that Mordecai was the person to be so honored.

During the second banquet, the king again asked Esther what she desired. She replied that someone had plotted to destroy her and her people, and she named Haman as the culprit. Immediately the king sentenced Haman to die on the gallows that he had built for Mordecai.

In the final act of this true-life drama, Mordecai was appointed to Haman's position, and the Jews were guaranteed protection throughout the land. To celebrate this historic occasion, the Festival of Purim was established.

Because of Queen Esther's courageous act, a whole nation was saved. Seeing her God-given opportunity, she seized it! Her life made a difference. Read Esther and watch for God at work in *your* life. Perhaps he has prepared you to act in "such a time as this" (4:14).

VITAL STATISTICS

PURPOSE:
To demonstrate God's sovereignty and his loving care for his people

AUTHOR:
Unknown. Possibly Mordecai (9:29). Some have suggested Ezra or Nehemiah because of the similarity of the writing style.

DATE WRITTEN:
Approximately 470 B.C. (Esther became queen in 479)

SETTING:
Although Esther follows Nehemiah in the Bible, its events are about 30 years prior to those recorded in Nehemiah. The story is set in the Persian Empire, and most of the action takes place in the king's palace in Susa, the Persian capital.

KEY VERSE:
"If you keep quiet at a time like this, deliverance for the Jews will arise from some other place, but you and your relatives will die. What's more, who can say but that you have been elevated to the palace for just such a time as this?" (4:14).

KEY PEOPLE:
Esther, Mordecai, King Xerxes I, Haman

KEY PLACE:
The king's palace in Susa, Persia

SPECIAL FEATURES:
Esther is one of only two books named for women (Ruth is the other). The book is unusual in that in the original version no name, title, or pronoun for God appears in it (see the note on 4:14). This caused some church fathers to question its inclusion in the canon. But God's presence is clear throughout the book.

THE BLUEPRINT

1. Esther becomes queen (1:1—2:23)
2. The Jews are threatened (3:1—4:17)
3. Esther intercedes for the Jews (5:1—8:17)
4. The Jews are delivered (9:1—10:3)

The book of Esther is an example of God's divine guidance and care over our lives. God's sovereignty and power are seen throughout this book. Although we may question certain circumstances in our lives, we must have faith that God is in control, working through both the pleasant and difficult times so that we can serve him effectively.

MEGATHEMES

THEME	EXPLANATION	IMPORTANCE
God's Sovereignty	The book of Esther tells of the circumstances that were essential to the survival of God's people in Persia. These "circumstances" were not the result of chance but of God's grand design. God is sovereign over every area of life.	With God in charge, we can take courage. He can guide us through the circumstances we face in our lives. We should expect God to display his power in carrying out his will. As we unite our life's purposes to God's purpose, we benefit from his sovereign care.
Racial Hatred	The Jews in Persia had been a minority since their deportation from Judah 100 years earlier. Haman was a descendant of King Agag, an enemy of the Jews. Lust for power and pride drove Haman to hate Mordecai, Esther's cousin. Haman convinced the king to kill all the Jews.	Racial hatred is always sinful. We must never condone it in any form. Every person on earth has intrinsic worth because God created people in his own image. Therefore, God's people must stand against racism whenever and wherever it occurs.
Deliverance	In February or March, the Jews celebrate the Festival of Purim, which symbolizes God's deliverance. *Purim* means "lots," such as those used by Haman to set the date for the extermination of all Jews from Persia. But God overruled, using Queen Esther to intercede on behalf of the Jews.	Because God is in control of history, he is never frustrated by any turn of events or human action. He is able to save us from the evil of this world and deliver us from sin and death. Because we trust God, we are not to fear what people may do to us; instead, we are to be confident in God's control.
Action	Faced with death, Esther and Mordecai set aside their own fear and took action. Esther risked her life by asking King Xerxes to save the Jews. They were not paralyzed by fear.	When outnumbered and powerless, it is natural for us to feel helpless. Esther and Mordecai resisted this temptation and acted with courage. It is not enough to know that God is in control; we must act with self-sacrifice and courage to follow God's guidance.
Wisdom	The Jews were a minority in a world hostile to them. It took great wisdom for Mordecai to survive. Serving as a faithful official of the king, Mordecai took steps to understand and work with the Persian law. Yet he did not compromise his integrity.	It takes great wisdom to survive in a non-believing world. In a setting which is for the most part hostile to Christianity, we can demonstrate wisdom by giving respect to what is true and good and by humbly standing against what is wrong.

1. Esther becomes queen

The King's Banquet

1 This happened in the days of King Xerxes,* who reigned over 127 provinces
stretching from India to Ethiopia.* 2At that time he ruled his empire from his throne

1:1a Hebrew *Ahasuerus,* another name for Xerxes; also throughout the book of Esther. 1:1b Hebrew *to Cush.*

1:1
Ezra 4:6
Esth 8:9-10
Dan 5:28; 8:2

1:2
Neh 1:1

1:1 Esther's story begins in 483 B.C., 103 years after Nebuchadnezzar had taken the Jews into captivity (2 Kings 25), 54 years after Zerubbabel led the first group of exiles back to Jerusalem (Ezra 1; 2), and 25 years before Ezra led the second group to Jerusalem (Ezra 7). Esther lived in the kingdom of Persia, the dominant kingdom in the Middle East after Babylon's fall in 539 B.C. Esther's parents must have been among those exiles who chose not to return to Jerusalem, even though Cyrus, the Persian king, had issued a decree allowing them to do so. The Jewish exiles had great freedom in Persia, and many remained because they had established themselves there or were fearful of the dangerous journey back to their homeland.

1:1 Xerxes the Great was Persia's fifth king (486–465 B.C.). He was proud and impulsive, as we see from the events in chapter 1. His winter palace was in Susa, where he held the banquet described in 1:3-7. Persian kings often held great banquets before going to war. In 481, Xerxes launched an attack against Greece. After his fleet won a great victory at Thermopylae, he was defeated at Salamis in 480 and had to return to Persia. Esther became queen in 479.

1:2 In this context, "fortress" means "palace."

1:3 Esth 2:18

at the fortress of Susa. 3In the third year of his reign, he gave a banquet for all his princes
and officials. He invited all the military officers of Media and Persia, as well as the
noblemen and provincial officials. 4The celebration lasted six months*—a tremendous
display of the opulent wealth and glory of his empire.

1:5 Esth 7:7-8
1:6 Ezek 23:41 Amos 6:4
1:7 Esth 2:18

5When it was all over, the king gave a special banquet for all the palace servants and
officials—from the greatest to the least. It lasted for seven days and was held at Susa in
the courtyard of the palace garden. 6The courtyard was decorated with beautifully woven
white and blue linen hangings, fastened by purple ribbons to silver rings embedded in
marble pillars. Gold and silver couches stood on a mosaic pavement of porphyry, marble,
mother-of-pearl, and other costly stones. 7Drinks were served in gold goblets of many
designs, and there was an abundance of royal wine, just as the king had commanded.
8The only restriction on the drinking was that no one should be compelled to take more
than he wanted. But those who wished could have as much as they pleased, for the king
had instructed his staff to let everyone decide this matter for himself.
9Queen Vashti gave a banquet for the women of the palace at the same time.

Queen Vashti Deposed

1:10 Judg 16:25 Dan 5:1-4

10On the seventh day of the feast, when King Xerxes was half drunk with wine, he told
Mehuman, Biztha, Harbona, Bigtha, Abagtha, Zethar, and Carcas, the seven eunuchs

1:4 Hebrew *180 days.*

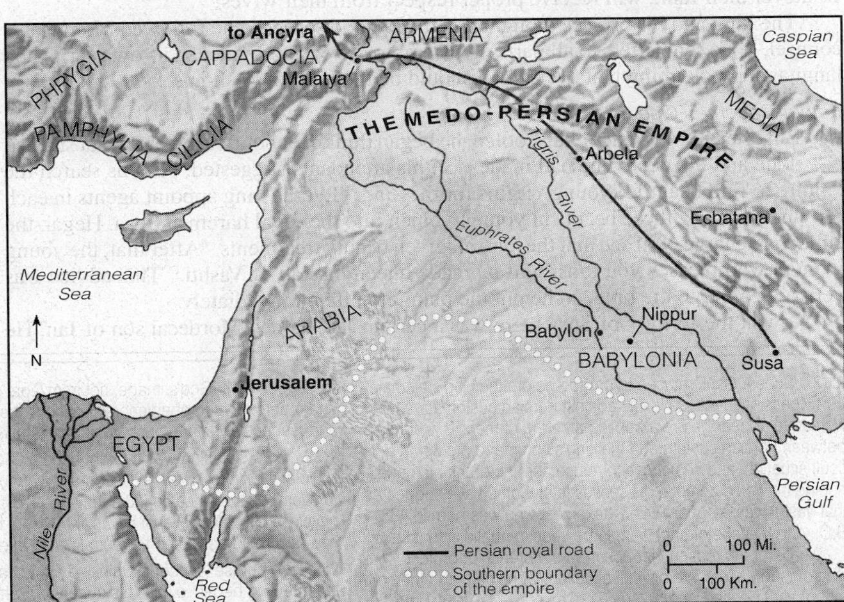

THE WORLD OF ESTHER'S DAY
Esther lived in the capital of the vast Medo-Persian Empire, which incorporated the provinces of Media and Persia, as well as the previous empires of Assyria and Babylon. Esther, a Jewess, was chosen by King Xerxes to be his queen. The story of how she saved her people takes place in the palace in Susa.

1:4 The celebration lasted 180 days (about six months) because its real purpose was to plan the battle strategy for invading Greece and to demonstrate that the king had sufficient wealth to carry it out. Waging war was not only for survival; it was a means of acquiring more wealth, territory, and power.

1:5-7 Persia was a world power, and the king, as the center of that power, was one of the wealthiest people in the world. Persian kings loved to flaunt their wealth, even wearing precious gemstones in their beards. Jewelry was a sign of rank for Persian men. Even soldiers wore great amounts of gold jewelry into battle.

1:9 Ancient Greek documents call Xerxes' wife Amestris, probably a Greek form of *Vashti.* Vashti was deposed in 483/482 B.C., but she is mentioned again in ancient records as the queen mother during the reign of her son, Artaxerxes, who succeeded Xerxes. Toward the end of Xerxes' reign, either Esther died or Vashti was able through her son to regain the influence she had lost.

1:10 Some advisers and government officials were castrated in order to prevent them from having children and then rebelling and trying to establish a dynasty of their own. A castrated official was called a eunuch.

1:10, 11 Xerxes made a rash, half-drunk decision, based purely on feelings. His self-restraint and practical wisdom were weakened by too much wine. Poor decisions are made when people don't think clearly. Base your decisions on careful thinking, not on the emotions of the moment. Impulsive decision making leads to severe complications.

who attended him, 11to bring Queen Vashti to him with the royal crown on her head. He
wanted all the men to gaze on her beauty, for she was a very beautiful woman. 12But
when they conveyed the king's order to Queen Vashti, she refused to come. This made
the king furious, and he burned with anger.
13He immediately consulted with his advisers, who knew all the Persian laws and 1:13
customs, for he always asked their advice. 14The names of these men were Carshena, 1 Chr 12:32
Shethar, Admatha, Tarshish, Meres, Marsena, and Memucan—seven high officials of Jer 10:7
Persia and Media. They were his closest associates and held the highest positions in the 1:14 2 Kgs 25:14
empire. 15"What must be done to Queen Vashti?" the king demanded. "What penalty
does the law provide for a queen who refuses to obey the king's orders, properly sent
through his eunuchs?"
16Memucan answered the king and his princes, "Queen Vashti has wronged not only
the king but also every official and citizen throughout your empire. 17Women everywhere will begin to despise their husbands when they learn that Queen Vashti has refused
to appear before the king. 18Before this day is out, the wife of every one of us, your
officials throughout the empire, will hear what the queen did and will start talking to their
husbands the same way. There will be no end to the contempt and anger throughout your
realm. 19So if it please the king, we suggest that you issue a written decree, a law of the 1:19 Esth 8:8
Persians and Medes that cannot be revoked. It should order that Queen Vashti be forever Dan 6:8-15, 17
banished from your presence and that you choose another queen more worthy than she.
20When this decree is published throughout your vast empire, husbands everywhere, 1:20
whatever their rank, will receive proper respect from their wives!" Eph 5:22 Col 3:18
21The king and his princes thought this made good sense, so he followed Memucan's
counsel. 22He sent letters to all parts of the empire, to each province in its own script and 1:22 Esth 3:12; 8:9-10
language, proclaiming that every man should be the ruler of his home.

Esther Becomes Queen

2 But after Xerxes' anger had cooled, he began thinking about Vashti and what she had 2:1
done and the decree he had made. 2So his attendants suggested, "Let us search the Esth 1:19-20; 7:10
empire to find beautiful young virgins for the king. 3Let the king appoint agents in each 2:3
province to bring these beautiful young women into the royal harem at Susa. Hegai, the Esth 1:1-3; 2:8-9,
eunuch in charge, will see that they are all given beauty treatments. 4After that, the young 15
woman who pleases you most will be made queen instead of Vashti." This advice was
very appealing to the king, so he put the plan into effect immediately.
5Now at the fortress of Susa there was a certain Jew named Mordecai son of Jair. He 2:5 Esth 3:2-6

1:12 Queen Vashti refused to parade before the king's all-male party, possibly because it was against Persian custom for a woman to appear before a public gathering of men. This conflict between Persian custom and the king's command put her in a difficult situation, and she chose to refuse her half-drunk husband, hoping he would come to his senses later. Some have suggested that Vashti was pregnant with Artaxerxes, who was born in 483 B.C., and that she did not want to be seen in public in that state.

Whatever the reason, her action was a breach of protocol that also placed Xerxes in a difficult situation. Once he made the command, as a Persian king he could not reverse it (see the note on 1:19). While preparing to invade Greece, Xerxes had invited important officials from all over his land to see his power, wealth, and authority. If it was perceived that he had no authority over his own wife, his military credibility would be damaged—the greatest criterion of success for an ancient king. In addition, King Xerxes was accustomed to getting what he wanted.

1:15 Middle Eastern kings often did not have close personal relationships with their wives. Xerxes demonstrates this because (1) he had a harem (2:3); (2) he showed no respect for Vashti's personhood (1:10-12); (3) Esther, when she became queen, did not see him for long periods of time (4:11).

1:16-21 Perhaps the men's thinking had been clouded by drinking. Obviously this law would not cause the women of the country to respect their husbands. Respect between men and women comes from mutual regard and appreciation for each other as those created in God's image, not from legal pronouncements and orders. Forced obedience is a poor substitute for the love and respect wives and husbands should have for each other.

1:19 A Persian king was thought to be a god by many of his people; therefore, when he issued a law or command, it stood forever (see the notes on 8:8 and Daniel 6:8). The law could never be canceled, even if it was ill-advised; but if necessary, a new law could be issued to neutralize the effects of the old law.

2:1 The phrase "he began thinking about Vashti" may mean that the king began to miss his queen and what she had done for him. But he also remembered that in his anger he had banished her from his presence with a decree that couldn't be rescinded.

2:3, 14-17 Persian kings collected not only vast amounts of jewelry but also great numbers of women. These young virgins were taken from their homes and were required to live in a separate building near the palace called a harem. Their sole purpose was to serve the king and to await his call for sexual pleasure. They rarely saw the king, and their lives were restricted and boring. If rejected, Esther would be one of many girls the king had seen once and forgotten. But Esther's presence and beauty pleased the king enough that he crowned her queen in place of Vashti. The queen held a more influential position than a concubine, and she was given more freedom and authority than others in the harem. But even as queen, Esther had few rights—especially because she had been chosen to replace a woman who had become too assertive.

2:6 2 Kgs 24:14-15 was from the tribe of Benjamin and was a descendant of Kish and Shimei. 6His family*
had been exiled from Jerusalem to Babylon by King Nebuchadnezzar, along with King
2:7-8 Esth 2:15 Jehoiachin* of Judah and many others. 7This man had a beautiful and lovely young
cousin, Hadassah, who was also called Esther. When her father and mother had died,
Mordecai adopted her into his family and raised her as his own daughter. 8As a result of
the king's decree, Esther, along with many other young women, was brought to the king's
2:9 Esth 2:3, 12 harem at the fortress of Susa and placed in Hegai's care. 9Hegai was very impressed with
Esther and treated her kindly. He quickly ordered a special menu for her and provided her
with beauty treatments. He also assigned her seven maids specially chosen from the king's
palace, and he moved her and her maids into the best place in the harem.

2:6a Hebrew *He.* **2:6b** Hebrew *Jeconiah,* a variant name for Jehoiachin.

MORDECAI

Following Jerusalem's last stand against Nebuchadnezzar, Mordecai's family was deported to Babylonia. He was probably born in Susa, a city that became one of Persia's capitals after Cyrus conquered Babylon, and inherited an official position among the Jewish captives that kept him around the palace even after the Babylonians were driven out. At one time, when he overheard plans to assassinate Xerxes, he reported the plot and saved the king's life.

Mordecai's life was filled with challenges that he turned into opportunities. When his aunt and uncle died, he adopted Esther, their daughter and his young cousin, probably because his own parents were dead and he felt responsible for her. Later, when she was drafted into Xerxes' harem and chosen to be queen, Mordecai continued to advise her. Shortly after this, he found himself in conflict with Xerxes' recently appointed second-in-command, Haman. Although willing to serve the king, Mordecai refused to worship the king's representative. Haman was furious with Mordecai. So he planned to have Mordecai and all the Jews killed. His plan became a law of the Medes and Persians, and it looked as though the Jews were doomed.

Mordecai, willing to be God's servant wherever he was, responded by contacting Esther and telling her that one reason God had allowed her to be queen might well be to save her people from this threat. But God had also placed *him* in the right place years earlier. God revealed to the king through his nighttime reading of historical documents that Mordecai had once saved his life, and the king realized he had never thanked Mordecai. The great honor then given to Mordecai ruined Haman's plan to hang him on the gallows. God had woven an effective counterstrategy against which Haman's plan could not stand.

Later, Mordecai instituted the Jewish Festival of Purim. He had a lengthy career of service to the king on behalf of the Jews. In Mordecai's life, God blended both character and circumstances to accomplish great things. He has not changed the way he works. God is using the situations you face each day to weave a pattern of godliness into your character. Pause and ask God to help you respond appropriately to the situations you find yourself in today.

Strengths and accomplishments
- Exposed an assassination plot against the king
- Cared enough to adopt his cousin
- Refused to bow to anyone except God
- Took Haman's place as second-in-command under Xerxes

Lessons from his life
- The opportunities we have are more important than the ones we wish we had
- We can trust God to weave together the events of life for our best, even though we may not be able to see the overall pattern
- The rewards for doing right are sometimes delayed, but they are guaranteed by God himself

Vital statistics
- Where: Susa, one of several capital cities in Persia
- Occupation: Jewish official who became second in rank to Xerxes
- Relatives: Adopted daughter: Esther. Father: Jair
- Contemporaries: Xerxes, Haman

Key verse
"Mordecai the Jew became the prime minister, with authority next to that of King Xerxes himself. He was very great among the Jews, who held him in high esteem, because he worked for the good of his people and was a friend at the royal court for all of them" (Esther 10:3).

Mordecai's story is told in the book of Esther.

2:5, 6 Mordecai was a Jew. The Jewish population had increased since their exile over 100 years earlier. They had been given great freedom and were allowed to run their own businesses and hold positions in government (2:19; Daniel 6:3).

2:6 The Bible implies that Mordecai was carried into exile from Jerusalem by Nebuchadnezzar. If this referred to Mordecai himself, he would have been over 100 years old at the time of this story. The Hebrew phrase translated "He had been exiled," referring to Mordecai, can also mean "His family had been exiled." It is likely that Mordecai's great-grandparents were carried into captivity rather than Mordecai himself.

[10]Esther had not told anyone of her nationality and family background, for Mordecai **2:10**
had told her not to. [11]Every day Mordecai would take a walk near the courtyard of the Esth 2:20
harem to ask about Esther and to find out what was happening to her.

[12]Before each young woman was taken to the king's bed, she was given the prescribed
twelve months of beauty treatments—six months with oil of myrrh, followed by six
months with special perfumes and ointments. [13]When the time came for her to go in to
the king, she was given her choice of whatever clothing or jewelry she wanted to enhance
her beauty. [14]That evening she was taken to the king's private rooms, and the next
morning she was brought to the second harem,* where the king's wives lived. There she
would be under the care of Shaashgaz, another of the king's eunuchs. She would live
there for the rest of her life, never going to the king again unless he had especially
enjoyed her and requested her by name.

[15]When it was Esther's turn* to go to the king, she accepted the advice of Hegai, the **2:15**
eunuch in charge of the harem. She asked for nothing except what he suggested, and she Esth 9:29
was admired by everyone who saw her. [16]When Esther was taken to King Xerxes at the
royal palace in early winter* of the seventh year of his reign, [17]the king loved her more **2:17** Esth 1:11
than any of the other young women. He was so delighted with her that he set the royal
crown on her head and declared her queen instead of Vashti. [18]To celebrate the occasion, **2:18** Esth 1:3-8
he gave a banquet in Esther's honor for all his princes and servants, giving generous gifts
to everyone and declaring a public festival for the provinces.

[19]Even after all the young women had been transferred to the second harem* and
Mordecai had become a palace official, [20]Esther continued to keep her nationality and
family background a secret. She was still following Mordecai's orders, just as she did **2:20** Esth 2:10
when she was living in his home.

Mordecai's Loyalty to the King

[21]One day as Mordecai was on duty at the palace, two of the king's eunuchs, Bigthana* **2:21** Esth 1:10; 6:2
and Teresh—who were guards at the door of the king's private quarters—became angry
at King Xerxes and plotted to assassinate him. [22]But Mordecai heard about the plot and **2:22** Esth 6:1-2
passed the information on to Queen Esther. She then told the king about it and gave
Mordecai credit for the report. [23]When an investigation was made and Mordecai's story **2:23** Esth 10:2
was found to be true, the two men were hanged on a gallows.* This was all duly recorded
in *The Book of the History of King Xerxes' Reign.*

2. The Jews are threatened

Haman's Plot against the Jews

3 Some time later, King Xerxes promoted Haman son of Hammedatha the Agagite to **3:1**
prime minister, making him the most powerful official in the empire next to the king Esth 3:10; 5:11
himself. [2]All the king's officials would bow down before Haman to show him respect **3:2** Esth 5:9

2:14 Or *to another part of the harem.* **2:15** Hebrew *the turn of Esther, the daughter of Abihail, who was Mordecai's uncle, who had adopted her.* **2:16** Hebrew *in the tenth month, the month of Tebeth.* A number of dates in the book of Esther can be cross-checked with dates in surviving Persian records and related accurately to our modern calendar. This month of the Hebrew lunar calendar occurred in December 479 B.C. and January 478 B.C. **2:19** The meaning of the Hebrew is uncertain. **2:21** Hebrew *Bigthan;* compare 6:2. **2:23** Or *on a pole.*

2:10 With virtually no rights and little access to the king, it was better for Esther not to reveal her identity. While boldness in stating our identity as God's people is our responsibility, at times a good strategy is to keep quiet until we have won the right to be heard. This is especially true when dealing with those in authority over us. But we can always let them see the difference God makes in our lives.

2:17 God placed Esther on the throne even before the Jews faced the possibility of complete destruction (3:5ff), so that when trouble came, a person would already be in the position to help. No human effort could thwart God's plan to send the Messiah to earth as a Jew. If you are changing jobs, position, or location and can't see God's purpose in your situation, understand that God is in control. He may be placing you in a position so you can help when the need arises.

3:2 Mordecai's determination came from his faith in God. He did not take a poll first to determine the safest or most popular course of action; he had the courage to stand alone. Doing what is right will not always make you popular. Those who do right will be in the minority, but to obey God is more important than to obey people (Acts 5:29).

3:2-4 Mordecai refused to kneel down before Haman. Jews did bow down to government authorities, at times, as a sign of respect (Genesis 23:7; 1 Samuel 24:8), but Haman's ancestors were ancient enemies of the Jews. Israel had been commanded by God to "destroy the Amalekites and erase their memory from under heaven" (Deuteronomy 25:17-19; see also Exodus 17:16). Mordecai was not about to kneel before wicked Haman and, by his act, acknowledge Haman as a god. Daniel's three friends had the same convictions (Daniel 3). We must worship God alone. We should never let any person, institution, or government take God's place. When people demand loyalties or duties from you that do not honor God, don't give in. It may be time to take a stand.

whenever he passed by, for so the king had commanded. But Mordecai refused to bow
down or show him respect.

3:3 Esth 3:2

3 Then the palace officials at the king's gate asked Mordecai, "Why are you disobeying
the king's command?" 4 They spoke to him day after day, but still he refused to comply
with the order. So they spoke to Haman about this to see if he would tolerate Mordecai's
conduct, since Mordecai had told them he was a Jew.

3:5 Esth 5:9
3:6 Ps 83:4
3:7 Ezra 6:15; Esth 9:24-26
3:8 Ezra 4:12-15; Acts 16:20-21

5 When Haman saw that Mordecai would not bow down or show him respect, he was
filled with rage. 6 So he decided it was not enough to lay hands on Mordecai alone. Since
he had learned that Mordecai was a Jew, he decided to destroy all the Jews throughout
the entire empire of Xerxes.
7 So in the month of April,* during the twelfth year of King Xerxes' reign, lots were
cast (the lots were called *purim*) to determine the best day and month to take action. And
the day selected was March 7, nearly a year later.*
8 Then Haman approached King Xerxes and said, "There is a certain race of people
scattered through all the provinces of your empire. Their laws are different from those
of any other nation, and they refuse to obey even the laws of the king. So it is not in the
king's interest to let them live. 9 If it please Your Majesty, issue a decree that they be
destroyed, and I will give 375 tons* of silver to the government administrators so they
can put it into the royal treasury."

3:7a Hebrew *in the first month, the month of Nisan.* This month of the Hebrew lunar calendar occurred in April and May 474 B.C.; also see note on 2:16. **3:7b** As in Greek version, which reads *the thirteenth day of the twelfth month, the month of Adar* (see also 3:13). Hebrew reads *in the twelfth month,* of the Hebrew calendar. The date selected was March 7, 473 B.C.; also see note on 2:16. **3:9** Hebrew *10,000 talents* [340 metric tons].

GOD BEHIND THE SCENES IN ESTHER

Although God's name is not mentioned in the Hebrew text of Esther, he makes himself known in these ways:

Indirect References	2:17	Esther, who worshiped God, became queen.
	4:14	God's existence and his power over the affairs of people are assumed.
	4:16	Fasting was a distinct spiritual activity usually connected with prayer.
Divine Incidents The book of Esther is filled with divine interventions	2:21, 23	Mordecai overhears a death plot and saves the king's life.
	6:1	Xerxes can't sleep and decides to read a history book.
	6:2	Xerxes reads the exact page needed for the moment, reminding him of an unpaid reward to Mordecai.
	7:9, 10	Haman's plan is exactly reversed—the intended victims are the victors.

Why was God's name hidden in the book of Esther? There were many gods in the Middle East and Persian Empire. Usually, their names were mentioned in official documents in order to control the peoples who worshiped those particular gods. The Jews were unique in being the people of one God. A story about them was naturally a story about God, for even the name "Jew" carried with it the connotation of one who worshiped Yahweh.

3:5, 6 Why did Haman want to destroy all Jews just because of one man's action? (1) Haman was an Agagite (3:1), a descendant of Agag, king of the Amalekites (1 Samuel 15:20). The Amalekites were ancient enemies of the Israelites (see Exodus 17:16; Deuteronomy 25:17-19). Haman's hatred was directed not just at Mordecai but at all the Jews. (2) As second-in-command in the Persian Empire (3:1), Haman loved his power and authority and the reverence shown him. The Jews, however, looked to God as their final authority, not to any man. Haman realized that the only way to fulfill his self-centered desires was to kill all those who disregarded his authority. His quest for personal power and his hatred of the Jewish race consumed him.

3:5, 6 Haman enjoyed the power and prestige of his position, and he was enraged when Mordecai did not respond with the expected reverential bow. Haman's anger was not directed just toward Mordecai, but toward what Mordecai stood for—the Jews' dedication to God as the only authority worthy of reverence. Haman's attitude was prejudiced: He hated a group of people because of a difference in belief or culture. Prejudice grows out of personal pride—considering oneself better than others. In the end, Haman was punished for his arrogant attitude (7:9, 10). God will harshly judge those who are prejudiced or whose pride causes them to look down on others.

3:7 Haman cast lots to determine the best day to carry out his decree. Little did he know that he was playing into the hands of God, for the day of death was set for almost a year away, giving Esther time to make her plea to the king. The Persian word for "lots" was *purim,* which became the name for the holiday celebrated by the Jews when they were delivered, not killed, on the day appointed by Haman.

3:9 Haman must have hoped to acquire this tremendous sum of money by plundering the homes and businesses of the Jews who would be killed through his decree.

10 The king agreed, confirming his decision by removing his signet ring from his finger **3:10**
and giving it to Haman son of Hammedatha the Agagite—the enemy of the Jews. Gen 41:42 Esth 8:2
11 "Keep the money," the king told Haman, "but go ahead and do as you like with these
people."
12 On April 17* Haman called in the king's secretaries and dictated letters to the **3:12**
princes, the governors of the respective provinces, and the local officials of each 1 Kgs 21:8 Esth 8:8-10
province in their own scripts and languages. These letters were signed in the name of
King Xerxes, sealed with his ring, 13 and sent by messengers into all the provinces of the **3:13**
empire. The letters decreed that all Jews—young and old, including women and chil- Esth 8:9-14; 9:2, 7-10, 17
dren—must be killed, slaughtered, and annihilated on a single day. This was scheduled
to happen nearly a year later on March 7.* The property of the Jews would be given to
those who killed them. 14 A copy of this decree was to be issued in every province and **3:14** Esth 4:8; 8:13-14
made known to all the people, so that they would be ready to do their duty on the
appointed day. 15 At the king's command, the decree went out by the swiftest messengers, **3:15** Esth 8:15
and it was proclaimed in the fortress of Susa. Then the king and Haman sat down to drink,
but the city of Susa fell into confusion.

Mordecai Requests Esther's Help

4 When Mordecai learned what had been done, he tore his clothes, put on sackcloth **4:1**
and ashes, and went out into the city, crying with a loud and bitter wail. 2 He stood 2 Sam 1:11 Esth 3:8-10
outside the gate of the palace, for no one was allowed to enter while wearing clothes of Ezek 27:30 Jon 3:4-9
mourning. 3 And as news of the king's decree reached all the provinces, there was great
mourning among the Jews. They fasted, wept, and wailed, and many people lay in
sackcloth and ashes.
4 When Queen Esther's maids and eunuchs came and told her about Mordecai, she
was deeply distressed. She sent clothing to him to replace the sackcloth, but he refused
it. 5 Then Esther sent for Hathach, one of the king's eunuchs who had been appointed
as her attendant. She ordered him to go to Mordecai and find out what was troubling
him and why he was in mourning. 6 So Hathach went out to Mordecai in the square in
front of the palace gate.
7 Mordecai told him the whole story and told him how much money Haman had **4:7** Esth 3:9
promised to pay into the royal treasury for the destruction of the Jews. 8 Mordecai gave **4:8**
Hathach a copy of the decree issued in Susa that called for the death of all Jews, and he Esth 3:14-15
asked Hathach to show it to Esther. He also asked Hathach to explain it to her and to urge
her to go to the king to beg for mercy and plead for her people. 9 So Hathach returned to
Esther with Mordecai's message.
10 Then Esther told Hathach to go back and relay this message to Mordecai: 11 "The **4:11**
whole world knows that anyone who appears before the king in his inner court without Esth 5:1-2; 6:4; 8:4 Dan 2:9
being invited is doomed to die unless the king holds out his gold scepter. And the king
has not called for me to come to him in more than a month." 12 So Hathach gave Esther's
message to Mordecai.
13 Mordecai sent back this reply to Esther: "Don't think for a moment that you will

3:12 Hebrew *On the thirteenth day of the first month,* of the Hebrew calendar. This event occurred on April 17, 474 B.C.; also see note on 2:16. **3:13** Hebrew *on the thirteenth day of the twelfth month, the month of Adar,* of the Hebrew calendar. The date selected was March 7, 473 B.C.; also see note on 2:16.

3:10-12 Officials in the ancient world used signet rings as personal signatures. The ring's surface had a raised imprint made of metal, wood, or bone; Xerxes' was probably made of silver or gold. Each individual had his own imprint. Letters were sealed by pressing the ring into soft wax, and official documents were certified by using the royal signet. By giving Haman his signet ring, Xerxes gave him his personal signature and with it the authority to do whatever he wished. Little did the king realize that his own ring would sign the death warrant for his queen, Esther.

4:11–5:2 Esther risked her life by coming before the king. Her courageous act gives us a model to follow in approaching a difficult or dangerous task. Like Esther, we can: (1) *Calculate the cost.* Esther realized her life was at stake. (2) *Set priorities.* She believed that the safety of the Jewish race was more important than her life. (3) *Prepare.* She gathered support and fasted. (4) *Determine a course of action and move ahead boldly.* She didn't think too long about it, allowing the interlude to lessen her commitment to what she had to do.

Do you have to face a hostile audience, confront a friend on a delicate subject, or talk to your family about changes to be made? Rather than dreading difficult situations or putting them off, take action with confidence by following Esther's inspiring example.

4:13 Although Esther was the queen and shared some of the king's power and wealth, she still needed God's protection and wisdom. No one is secure in his or her own strength in any political system. It is foolish to believe that wealth or position can make us impervious to danger. Deliverance only comes from God.

escape there in the palace when all other Jews are killed. [14]If you keep quiet at a time like this, deliverance for the Jews will arise from some other place, but you and your relatives will die. What's more, who can say but that you have been elevated to the palace for just such a time as this?"

4:16 2 Chr 20:3 Joel 2:2-17

[15]Then Esther sent this reply to Mordecai: [16]"Go and gather together all the Jews of Susa and fast for me. Do not eat or drink for three days, night or day. My maids and I will

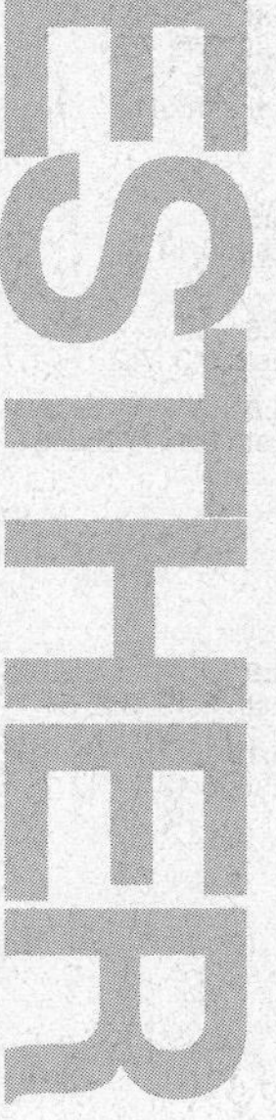

We treasure security, even though we know that security in this life carries no guarantees—possessions can be destroyed, beauty fades, relationships can be broken, death is inevitable. Real security, then, must be found beyond this life. Only when our security rests on God and his unchanging nature can we face the challenges that life is sure to bring our way.

Esther's beauty and character won Xerxes' heart, and he made her his queen. Even in her favored position, however, she would risk her life by attempting to see the king when he had not requested her presence. There was no guarantee that the king would even see her. Although she was queen, she was still not secure. But, cautiously and courageously, Esther decided to risk her life by approaching the king on behalf of her people.

She made her plans carefully. The Jews were asked to fast and pray with her before she went to the king. Then on the chosen day she went before him, and he *did* ask her to come forward and speak. But instead of issuing her request directly, she invited him and Haman to a banquet. He was astute enough to realize she had something on her mind; yet she conveyed the importance of the matter by insisting on a second banquet.

In the meantime, God was working behind the scenes. He caused Xerxes to read the historical records of the kingdom late one night, and the king discovered that Mordecai had once saved his life. Xerxes lost no time in honoring Mordecai for that act. During the second banquet, Esther told the king of Haman's plot against the Jews, and Haman was doomed. There is grim justice in Haman's death on the gallows he had built for Mordecai, and it seems fitting that the day on which the Jews were to be slaughtered became the day their enemies died. Esther's risk confirmed that God was the source of her security.

How much of your security lies in your possessions, position, or reputation? God has not placed you in your present position for your own benefit. He put you there *to serve him.* As in Esther's case, this may involve risking your security. Are you willing to let God be your ultimate security?

Strengths and accomplishments
- Her beauty and character won the heart of Persia's king
- She combined courage with careful planning
- She was open to advice and willing to act
- She was more concerned for others than for her own security

Lessons from her life
- Serving God often demands that we risk our own security
- God has a purpose for the situations in which he places us
- Courage, while often vital, does not replace careful planning

Vital statistics
- Where: Persian Empire
- Occupation: Xerxes' wife, queen of Persia
- Relatives: Cousin: Mordecai. Husband: Xerxes. Father: Abihail

Key verse
"Go and gather together all the Jews of Susa and fast for me. Do not eat or drink for three days, night or day. My maids and I will do the same. And then, though it is against the law, I will go in to see the king. If I must die, I am willing to die" (Esther 4:16).

Esther's story is told in the book of Esther.

4:13, 14 After the decree to kill the Jews was given, Mordecai and Esther could have despaired, decided to save only themselves, or just waited for God's intervention. Instead, they saw that God had placed them in their positions for a purpose, so they seized the moment and acted. When it is within our reach to save others, we must do so. In a life-threatening situation, don't withdraw, behave selfishly, wallow in despair, or wait for God to fix everything. Instead, ask God for his direction, and *act!* God may have placed you where you are "for just such a time as this."

4:14 God is not specifically mentioned in the book of Esther, but it is obvious that Mordecai expected God to deliver his people. While the book of Esther does not mention God directly, his presence fills the pages. Esther and Mordecai believed in God's care, and because they acted at the right time, God used them to save his people.

4:16 By calling for a fast, Esther was asking the Jews to pray for God's help on her dangerous mission. In the Old Testament, prayer always accompanied fasting (see Exodus 34:28; Deuteronomy 9:9; Ezra 8:21-23). An important function of a community of believers is mutual support in difficult times. When you are experiencing struggles, turn to fellow believers for support by sharing your trials with them and gaining strength from the bond that unites you. Ask them to pray for you. And when others need your support, give it willingly.

4:16 "Save your own skin" and "Watch out for number one" are mottoes that reflect our world's selfish outlook on life. Esther's attitude stands in bold contrast to this. She knew what she had to do, and she knew it could cost her her life. And yet she responded, "If I must die, I am willing to die." We should have the same commitment to do what is right despite the possible consequences. Do you try to save yourself by remaining silent rather than standing up for what is right? Decide to do what God wants, and trust him for the outcome.

do the same. And then, though it is against the law, I will go in to see the king. If I must
die, I am willing to die." 17So Mordecai went away and did as Esther told him.

3. Esther intercedes for the Jews

Esther's Request to the King

5 Three days later, Esther put on her royal robes and entered the inner court of the palace, **5:1** Esth 4:11, 16; 6:4
just across from the king's hall. The king was sitting on his royal throne, facing the
entrance. 2When he saw Queen Esther standing there in the inner court, he welcomed her, **5:2** Esth 4:11; 8:4
holding out the gold scepter to her. So Esther approached and touched its tip.
3Then the king asked her, "What do you want, Queen Esther? What is your request? **5:3** Esth 5:6; 7:2
I will give it to you, even if it is half the kingdom!" Mark 6:23
4And Esther replied, "If it please Your Majesty, let the king and Haman come today Luke 18:41
to a banquet I have prepared for the king."
5The king turned to his attendants and said, "Tell Haman to come quickly to a banquet, **5:5** Esth 6:14
as Esther has requested." So the king and Haman went to Esther's banquet.
6And while they were drinking wine, the king said to Esther, "Now tell me what you **5:6** Esth 5:3; 7:2
really want. What is your request? I will give it to you, even if it is half the kingdom!"
7Esther replied, "This is my request and deepest wish. 8If Your Majesty is pleased **5:8** Esth 6:14; 7:3; 8:5
with me and wants to grant my request, please come with Haman tomorrow to the
banquet I will prepare for you. Then tomorrow I will explain what this is all about."

Haman's Plan to Kill Mordecai

9What a happy man Haman was as he left the banquet! But when he saw Mordecai sitting **5:9**
at the gate, not standing up or trembling nervously before him, he was furious. 10How- Esth 2:19; 3:2, 5
ever, he restrained himself and went on home. Then he gathered together his friends and **5:10**
Zeresh, his wife, 11and boasted to them about his great wealth and his many children. He Esth 6:13
bragged about the honors the king had given him and how he had been promoted over
all the other officials and leaders.
12Then Haman added, "And that's not all! Queen Esther invited only me and the king
himself to the banquet she prepared for us. And she has invited me to dine with her and
the king again tomorrow!" 13Then he added, "But all this is meaningless as long as I see
Mordecai the Jew just sitting there at the palace gate."
14So Haman's wife, Zeresh, and all his friends suggested, "Set up a gallows* that **5:14**
stands seventy-five feet* tall, and in the morning ask the king to hang Mordecai on it. Esth 5:10; 6:4; 7:9-10
When this is done, you can go on your merry way to the banquet with the king." This
pleased Haman immensely, and he ordered the gallows set up.

The King Honors Mordecai

6 That night the king had trouble sleeping, so he ordered an attendant to bring the **6:1**
historical records of his kingdom so they could be read to him. 2In those records he Esth 2:21-23; 10:2 Dan 6:18
discovered an account of how Mordecai had exposed the plot of Bigthana and Teresh, **6:2**
two of the eunuchs who guarded the door to the king's private quarters. They had plotted Esth 2:21-22

5:14a Or *a pole.* **5:14b** Hebrew *50 cubits* [22.5 meters].

4:17–5:1 God was in control, yet Mordecai and Esther had to act. We cannot understand how both can be true at the same time, and yet they are. God chooses to work through those *willing* to act for him. We should pray as if all depended on God and act as if all depended on us. We should avoid two extremes: doing nothing, and feeling that we must do everything.

5:9 Hatred and bitterness are like weeds with long roots that grow in the heart and corrupt all of life. Haman was so consumed with hatred toward Mordecai that he could not even enjoy the honor of being invited to Esther's party. Hebrews 12:15 warns us to "watch out that no bitter root of unbelief rises up among you, for whenever it springs up, many are corrupted by its poison." Don't let hatred and its resulting bitterness build in your heart. Like Haman, you will find it backfiring against you (see 6:13; 7:9, 10). If the mere mention of someone's name provokes you to anger, confess your bitterness as sin. Ignoring bitterness, hiding it from others, or making superficial changes in behavior is not enough. If bitterness isn't completely removed, it will grow back, making matters worse.

5:14 Haman's family and friends, who were as arrogant as he, suggested that the gallows be 75 feet high, probably built on the city wall or some prominent building. They wanted to make sure that all the people of the city saw Mordecai's death and would be reminded of the consequences of disobeying Haman. Ironically, these high gallows allowed everyone to see Haman's death.

6:1, 2 Unable to sleep, the king decided to review the history of his reign, and his servants read to him about Mordecai's good deed. This seems coincidental, but God is *always* at work. God has been working quietly and patiently throughout your life as well. The events that have come together for good are not mere coincidence; they are the result of God's sovereign control over the course of people's lives (Romans 8:28).

to assassinate the king. 3“What reward or recognition did we ever give Mordecai for
this?” the king asked.
His attendants replied, “Nothing has been done.”
6:4 Esth 4:11; 5:14 4“Who is that in the outer court?” the king inquired. Now, as it happened, Haman had
just arrived in the outer court of the palace to ask the king to hang Mordecai from the
gallows* he had prepared.
5So the attendants replied to the king, “Haman is out there.”
6:6 Esth 6:7, 9, 11 “Bring him in,” the king ordered. 6So Haman came in, and the king said, “What
should I do to honor a man who truly pleases me?”
Haman thought to himself, “Whom would the king wish to honor more than me?” 7So
6:8 1 Kgs 1:33 he replied, “If the king wishes to honor someone, 8he should bring out one of the king’s
6:9 Gen 41:43 own royal robes, as well as the king’s own horse with a royal emblem on its head. 9Instruct
one of the king’s most noble princes to dress the man in the king’s robe and to lead him

6:4 Or *from the pole.*

HAMAN

The most arrogant people are often those who must measure their self-worth by the power or influence they think they have over others. Haman was an extremely arrogant leader. He recognized the king as his superior but could not accept anyone as an equal. When one man, Mordecai, refused to bow in submission to him, Haman wanted to destroy him. He became consumed with hatred for Mordecai. He was already filled with racial hatred for all the Jewish people because of the long-standing hatred between the Jews and Haman’s ancestors, the Amalekites. Mordecai’s dedication to God and his refusal to give homage to any human person challenged Haman’s self-centered religion. Haman saw the Jews as a threat to his power, and he decided to kill them all.

God was preparing Haman’s downfall and the protection of his people long before Haman came to power under Xerxes. Esther, a Jew, became queen, and Mordecai’s role in exposing an assassination plot indebted the king to him. Not only was Haman prevented from killing Mordecai; he also had to suffer the humiliation of publicly honoring him. Within hours, Haman died on the gallows he had built to hang Mordecai, and his plan to wipe out the Jews was thwarted. In contrast to Esther, who risked everything for God and won, Haman risked everything for an evil purpose and lost.

Our initial response to the story about Haman is to say that he got what he deserved. But the Bible leads us to ask deeper questions: How much of Haman is in me? Do I desire to control others? Am I threatened when others don’t appreciate me as I think they should? Do I want revenge when my pride is attacked? Confess these attitudes to God, and ask him to replace them with an attitude of forgiveness. Otherwise, God’s justice will settle the matter.

Strength and accomplishment
- Achieved great power, second in rank to Persia’s king Xerxes

Weaknesses and mistakes
- The desire to control others and receive honor was his highest goal
- Was blinded by arrogance and self-importance
- Planned to murder Mordecai and built a gallows for him
- Orchestrated the plan to slaughter God’s people throughout the empire

Lessons from his life
- Hatred will be punished
- God has an amazing record for making evil plans backfire on the planners
- Pride and self-importance will be punished
- An insatiable thirst for power and prestige is self-destructive

Vital statistics
- Where: Susa, the capital of Persia
- Occupation: Second in rank in the empire
- Relative: Wife: Zeresh
- Contemporaries: Xerxes, Mordecai, Esther

Key verses
“When Haman saw that Mordecai would not bow down or show him respect, he was filled with rage. So he decided it was not enough to lay hands on Mordecai alone. Since he had learned that Mordecai was a Jew, he decided to destroy all the Jews throughout the entire empire of Xerxes” (Esther 3:5, 6).

Haman’s story is told in the book of Esther.

6:7-9 Haman had wealth, but he craved something even his money couldn’t buy—respect. He could buy the trappings of success and power, but his lust for popularity had become an obsession. Don’t let your desire for approval, applause, and popularity drive you to immoral actions.

through the city square on the king's own horse. Have the prince shout as they go, 'This is
what happens to those the king wishes to honor!' "
10 "Excellent!" the king said to Haman. "Hurry and get the robe and my horse, and do
just as you have said for Mordecai the Jew, who sits at the gate of the palace. Do not fail
to carry out everything you have suggested."
11 So Haman took the robe and put it on Mordecai, placed him on the king's own horse,
and led him through the city square, shouting, "This is what happens to those the king
wishes to honor!" 12 Afterward Mordecai returned to the palace gate, but Haman hurried
home dejected and completely humiliated.
13 When Haman told his wife, Zeresh, and all his friends what had happened, they said,
"Since Mordecai—this man who has humiliated you—is a Jew, you will never succeed
in your plans against him. It will be fatal to continue to oppose him." 14 While they were
still talking, the king's eunuchs arrived to take Haman to the banquet Esther had
prepared.

6:12 2 Sam 15:30; Esth 7:8; Jer 14:3
6:13 Esth 5:10, 14
6:14 Esth 5:5-8

The King Executes Haman

7 So the king and Haman went to Queen Esther's banquet. 2 And while they were
drinking wine that day, the king again asked her, "Tell me what you want, Queen
Esther. What is your request? I will give it to you, even if it is half the kingdom!"
3 And so Queen Esther replied, "If Your Majesty is pleased with me and wants to grant
my request, my petition is that my life and the lives of my people will be spared. 4 For
my people and I have been sold to those who would kill, slaughter, and annihilate us. If
we had only been sold as slaves, I could remain quiet, for that would have been a matter
too trivial to warrant disturbing the king."
5 "Who would do such a thing?" King Xerxes demanded. "Who would dare touch
you?"
6 Esther replied, "This wicked Haman is our enemy." Haman grew pale with fright
before the king and queen. 7 Then the king jumped to his feet in a rage and went out into
the palace garden.
But Haman stayed behind to plead for his life with Queen Esther, for he knew that he
was doomed. 8 In despair he fell on the couch where Queen Esther was reclining, just as
the king returned from the palace garden. "Will he even assault the queen right here in
the palace, before my very eyes?" the king roared. And as soon as the king spoke, his
attendants covered Haman's face, signaling his doom.
9 Then Harbona, one of the king's eunuchs, said, "Haman has set up a gallows* that
stands seventy-five feet* tall in his own courtyard. He intended to use it to hang
Mordecai, the man who saved the king from assassination."
"Then hang Haman on it!" the king ordered. 10 So they hanged Haman on the gallows
he had set up for Mordecai, and the king's anger was pacified.

7:2 Esth 5:3, 6
7:3 Esth 5:7-8; 8:5
7:4 Esth 3:9; 4:7
7:6 Esth 3:10
7:8 Esth 1:6
7:9 Esth 5:14
7:10 Esth 9:25; Pss 7:16; 94:23

A Decree to Help the Jews

8 On that same day King Xerxes gave the estate of Haman, the enemy of the Jews, to
Queen Esther. Then Mordecai was brought before the king, for Esther had told the
king how they were related. 2 The king took off his signet ring—which he had taken back
from Haman—and gave it to Mordecai. And Esther appointed Mordecai to be in charge
of Haman's property.
3 Now once more Esther came before the king, falling down at his feet and begging

8:1 Esth 2:7; 7:6
8:2 Esth 3:10

7:9a Or *a pole;* also in 7:10. **7:9b** Hebrew *50 cubits* [22.5 meters].

6:10-13 Mordecai had exposed a plot to assassinate Xerxes—thus, he had saved the king's life (2:21-23). Although his good deed was recorded in the history books, Mordecai had gone unrewarded. But God was saving Mordecai's reward for the right time. Just as Haman was about to hang Mordecai unjustly, the king was ready to give the reward. Although God promises to reward our good deeds, we sometimes feel our "payoff" is too far away. Be patient. God steps in when it will do the most good.

7:6-10 Haman's hatred and evil plotting turned against him when the king discovered his true intentions. He was hanged on the gallows he had built for someone else. Proverbs 26:27 teaches that if you set a trap for others, you will get caught in it yourself. What happened to Haman shows the often violent results of setting any kind of trap for others.

7:8 A veil was placed over the face of someone condemned to death because Persian kings refused to look upon the face of a condemned person.

8:1-7 While we should not expect earthly rewards for being faithful to God, they often come. Esther and Mordecai were faithful, even to the point of risking their lives to save others. When they were willing to give up everything, God gave them a reward in proportion to their all-out commitment.

8:4 Esth 4:11; 5:2
8:5 Esth 3:13; 5:7-8; 7:3
8:6 Esth 3:13; 7:4; 9:1
8:7 Esth 7:10
8:8 Esth 1:19; 3:2, 12; 8:2, 9-10, 14 Dan 6:15
8:9 Esth 1:1, 2, 22; 3:12

him with tears to stop Haman's evil plot against the Jews. [4]Again the king held out the
gold scepter to Esther. So she rose and stood before him [5]and said, "If Your Majesty is
pleased with me and if he thinks it is right, send out a decree reversing Haman's orders
to destroy the Jews throughout all the provinces of the king. [6]For how can I endure to
see my people and my family slaughtered and destroyed?"
[7]Then King Xerxes said to Queen Esther and Mordecai the Jew, "I have given Esther
the estate of Haman, and he has been hanged on the gallows* because he tried to destroy
the Jews. [8]Now go ahead and send a message to the Jews in the king's name, telling them
whatever you want, and seal it with the king's signet ring. But remember that whatever
is written in the king's name and sealed with his ring can never be revoked."
[9]So on June 25* the king's secretaries were summoned. As Mordecai dictated, they
wrote a decree to the Jews and to the princes, governors, and local officials of all the
127 provinces stretching from India to Ethiopia.* The decree was written in the scripts
and languages of all the peoples of the empire, including the Jews. [10]Mordecai wrote

8:7 Or *on the pole.* **8:9a** Hebrew *on the twenty-third day of the third month, the month of Sivan,* of the Hebrew calendar. This event occurred on June 25, 474 B.C.; also see note on 2:16. **8:9b** Hebrew *to Cush.*

HOW GOD WORKS IN THE WORLD

God's Will	*What God wants done—he works through . . .*		
	Natural Order	*Miracles*	*Providence*
God's Action	God set into action through Creation a normal working of his universe. He also revealed his expectations of people through his Word and people's consciences.	God breaks into the natural order to respond to the expressed needs of people.	God overrules the natural order to accomplish an act that people may or may not have requested.
Examples from Esther	God gave Esther natural beauty.	God allowed Esther to speak to the king.	God allowed Mordecai to overhear a plot.
	Esther planned a way to save her people.	The people prayed and fasted.	Mordecai trusted God to accomplish what was impossible in human terms.
People's Will	*What people want done—we either . . .*		
	Plan	*Pray*	*Trust and Obey*
Action We Can Take	Can make plans based on the order and dependability of God's creation. Know and obey his words.	Can ask God to intervene in certain affairs while realizing that our knowledge and perspective are limited.	Can trust that God is in control even when circumstances seem to indicate that he is not.
	or . . .		
Mistakes We Can Make	*Disobey*	*Demand*	*Despair*
	Can violate the natural order, disobey God's commands.	Can assume that we understand what is needed and expect God to agree and answer our prayers that way.	Can assume God doesn't answer prayer or respond to our needs and live as though there is nothing but the natural order.

8:8 Haman's message had been sealed with the king's signet ring and could not be reversed, even by the king. It was part of the famed "law of the Medes and Persians." Now the king gave permission for whatever other decree Mordecai could devise that would offset the first, without actually canceling it.

in the name of King Xerxes and sealed the message with the king's signet ring. He
sent the letters by swift messengers, who rode horses especially bred for the king's
service.
11 The king's decree gave the Jews in every city authority to unite to defend their lives.
They were allowed to kill, slaughter, and annihilate anyone of any nationality or province
who might attack them or their children and wives, and to take the property of their
enemies. 12 The day chosen for this event throughout all the provinces of King Xerxes
was March 7 of the next year.* 13 A copy of this decree was to be recognized as law in
every province and proclaimed to all the people. That way the Jews would be ready on
that day to take revenge on their enemies. 14 So urged on by the king's command, the
messengers rode out swiftly on horses bred for the king's service. The same decree was
also issued at the fortress of Susa.
15 Then Mordecai put on the royal robe of blue and white and the great crown of gold,
and he wore an outer cloak of fine linen and purple. And the people of Susa celebrated
the new decree. 16 The Jews were filled with joy and gladness and were honored
everywhere. 17 In every city and province, wherever the king's decree arrived, the Jews
rejoiced and had a great celebration and declared a public festival and holiday. And many
of the people of the land became Jews themselves, for they feared what the Jews might
do to them.

8:11 Esth 3:13; 9:2, 10
8:12 Esth 3:13; 9:1
8:13 Esth 3:14

4. The Jews are delivered

The Victory of the Jews

9 So on March 7* the two decrees of the king were put into effect. On that day, the
enemies of the Jews had hoped to destroy them, but quite the opposite happened.
2 The Jews gathered in their cities throughout all the king's provinces to defend themselves against anyone who might try to harm them. But no one could make a stand
against them, for everyone was afraid of them. 3 And all the commanders of the
provinces, the princes, the governors, and the royal officials helped the Jews for fear of
Mordecai. 4 For Mordecai had been promoted in the king's palace, and his fame spread
throughout all the provinces as he became more and more powerful.
5 But the Jews went ahead on the appointed day and struck down their enemies with
the sword. They killed and annihilated their enemies and did as they pleased with those
who hated them. 6 They killed five hundred people in the fortress of Susa. 7 They also
killed Parshandatha, Dalphon, Aspatha, 8 Poratha, Adalia, Aridatha, 9 Parmashta, Arisai,
Aridai, and Vaizatha—10 the ten sons of Haman son of Hammedatha, the enemy of the
Jews. But they did not take any plunder.
11 That evening, when the king was informed of the number of people killed in the
fortress of Susa, 12 he called for Queen Esther and said, "The Jews have killed five
hundred people in the fortress of Susa alone and also Haman's ten sons. If they have done
that here, what has happened in the rest of the provinces? But now, what more do you
want? It will be granted to you; tell me and I will do it."
13 And Esther said, "If it please Your Majesty, give the Jews in Susa permission to do
again tomorrow as they have done today, and have the bodies of Haman's ten sons hung
from the gallows.*"

9:1 Esth 3:13; 8:11-12; 9:17
9:2 Esth 8:11, 17; 9:15-18
9:3 Esth 8:17, 36
9:5 Esth 3:13
9:10 Esth 5:11; 8:11
9:12 Esth 7:2
9:13 Esth 8:11

8:12 Hebrew *the thirteenth day of the twelfth month, the month of Adar,* of the Hebrew calendar. The date selected was March 7, 473 B.C.; also see note on 2:16. **9:1** Hebrew *on the thirteenth day of the twelfth month, the month of Adar,* of the Hebrew calendar. This event occurred on March 7, 473 B.C.; also see note on 2:16. **9:13** Or *the pole;* also in 9:14, 25.

8:12 This was the day set by Haman for the extermination of the Jews (3:13).

8:15-17 Everyone wants to be a hero and receive praise, honor, and wealth. But few are willing to pay the price. Mordecai served the government faithfully for years, bore Haman's hatred and oppression, and risked his life for his people. The price to be paid by God's heroes is long-term commitment. Are you ready and willing to pay the price?

9:5-16 Haman had decreed that on March 7 anyone could kill the Jews and take their property. Mordecai's decree could not reverse Haman's because no law signed by the king could be repealed. Instead, Mordecai had the king sign a new law giving Jews the right to fight back. When the dreaded day arrived, there was much fighting, but the Jews killed only those who wanted to kill them, and they did not take their enemies' possessions, even though they could have (8:11; 9:10, 16). There were no additional riots after the two-day slaughter, so obviously selfish gain or revenge was not a primary motive of the Jews. They simply wanted to defend themselves and their families from those who hated them.

9:11 Here the word *fortress* seems to refer to the fortified city of Susa. The king appears to be more concerned about Esther's wishes than the slaughter of his subjects.

[14]So the king agreed, and the decree was announced in Susa. They also hung the
9:15 Esth 9:10
bodies of Haman's ten sons from the gallows. [15]Then the Jews at Susa gathered
together on March 8* and killed three hundred more people, though again they took
no plunder.
9:16 Esth 9:2
[16]Meanwhile, the other Jews throughout the king's provinces had gathered together
to defend their lives. They gained relief from all their enemies, killing seventy-five
9:17-18 Esth 9:1-2, 21
thousand of those who hated them. But they did not take any plunder. [17]Throughout the
provinces this was done on March 7.* Then on the following day* they rested, celebrating their victory with a day of feasting and gladness. [18]But the Jews at Susa continued
killing their enemies on the second day also, and then rested on the third day,* making
9:19 Neh 8:10; Esth 9:20-31
that their day of feasting and gladness. [19]So to this day, rural Jews living in unwalled
villages celebrate an annual festival and holiday in late winter,* when they rejoice and
send gifts to each other.

The Festival of Purim

[20]Mordecai recorded these events and sent letters to the Jews near and far, throughout
all the king's provinces, [21]encouraging them to celebrate an annual festival on these two
days. [22]He told them to celebrate these days with feasting and gladness and by giving
gifts to each other and to the poor. This would commemorate a time when the Jews
gained relief from their enemies, when their sorrow was turned into gladness and their
mourning into joy.
[23]So the Jews adopted Mordecai's suggestion and began this annual custom.
9:24 Esth 3:1, 6-7
[24]Haman son of Hammedatha the Agagite, the enemy of the Jews, had plotted to crush
and destroy them on the day and month determined by casting lots (the lots were
9:25 Esth 3:6-15; 7:4-10; Ps 7:16
called *purim*). [25]But when Esther came before the king, he issued a decree causing
Haman's evil plot to backfire, and Haman and his sons were hanged on the gallows.
9:26 Esth 3:7; 9:20
[26](That is why this celebration is called Purim, because it is the ancient word for
casting lots.) So because of Mordecai's letter and because of what they had experi-
9:27 Esth 8:17; 9:20-21
enced, [27]the Jews throughout the realm agreed to inaugurate this tradition and to pass
it on to their descendants and to all who became Jews. They declared they would never
fail to celebrate these two prescribed days at the appointed time each year. [28]These
days would be remembered and kept from generation to generation and celebrated by
every family throughout the provinces and cities of the empire. These days would
never cease to be celebrated among the Jews, nor would the memory of what
happened ever die out among their descendants.
9:29 Esth 2:15; 9:20-21
[29]Then Queen Esther, the daughter of Abihail, along with Mordecai the Jew, wrote
another letter putting the queen's full authority behind Mordecai's letter to establish the
9:30 Esth 1:1
Festival of Purim. [30]In addition, letters wishing peace and security were sent to the Jews
9:31 Esth 4:3
throughout the 127 provinces of the empire of Xerxes. [31]These letters established the
Festival of Purim—an annual celebration of these days at the appointed time, decreed by
both Mordecai the Jew and Queen Esther. (The people decided to observe this festival,
just as they had decided for themselves and their descendants to establish the times of
fasting and mourning.) [32]So the command of Esther confirmed the practices of Purim,
and it was all written down in the records.

9:15 Hebrew *the fourteenth day of the month of Adar,* of the Hebrew calendar. This event occurred on March 8, 473 B.C.; also see note on 2:16. **9:17a** Hebrew *on the thirteenth day of the month of Adar,* of the Hebrew calendar. This event occurred on March 7, 473 B.C.; also see note on 2:16. **9:17b** Hebrew *on the fourteenth day,* of the Hebrew month of Adar. **9:18** Hebrew *killing their enemies on the thirteenth day and the fourteenth day, and then rested on the fifteenth day,* of the Hebrew month of Adar. **9:19** Hebrew *on the fourteenth day of the month of Adar.* This day of the Hebrew lunar calendar usually occurs in March.

9:19-22 People tend to have short memories when it comes to God's faithfulness. To help counter this, Mordecai wrote down these events and encouraged an annual holiday to commemorate the historic days of Purim. Jews still celebrate Purim today. Celebrations of feasting, gladness, and gift-giving are important ways to remember God's specific acts. Today the festivities of Christmas and Easter help us remember the birth and resurrection of Jesus Christ. Don't let the celebration or the exchanging of gifts hide the meaning of these great events.

9:29-31 Among Jews, women were expected to be quiet, to serve in the home, and to stay on the fringe of religious and political life. But Esther was a Jewish woman who broke through the cultural norms, stepping outside her expected role to risk her life to help God's people. Whatever your place in life, God can use you. Be open, available, and ready because God may use you to do what others are afraid to even consider.

The Greatness of Xerxes and Mordecai

10 King Xerxes imposed tribute throughout his empire, even to the distant coastlands. [2]His great achievements and the full account of the greatness of Mordecai, whom the king had promoted, are recorded in *The Book of the History of the Kings of Media and Persia.* [3]Mordecai the Jew became the prime minister, with authority next to that of King Xerxes himself. He was very great among the Jews, who held him in high esteem, because he worked for the good of his people and was a friend at the royal court for all of them.

10:1 Isa 24:15
10:2 Esth 2:23; 8:15; 9:4
10:3 Gen 41:43-44
Neh 2:10

10:3 Mordecai enjoyed a good reputation among the Jews because he was still their friend when he rose to a place of power. Corruption and abuse of authority often characterize those in power. But power used to lift the fallen and ease the burden of the oppressed is power used well. People placed by God in positions of power or political influence must not turn their backs on those in need.

10:3 No archaeological records of Mordecai's being prime minister and second-in-command have been discovered, but during this time there is a strange gap in ancient Persian records. The records indicate that another man held that position in 465 B.C., about seven years after Mordecai was first appointed. One tablet has been discovered naming Mardukaya as an official in the early years of Xerxes' reign; some believe this was Mordecai.

10:3 In the book of Esther, we clearly see God at work in the lives of individuals and in the affairs of a nation. Even when it looks as if the world is in the hands of evil people, God is still in control, protecting those who are his. Although we may not understand everything happening around us, we must trust in God's protection and retain our integrity by doing what we know is right. Esther, who risked her life by appearing before the king, became a heroine. Mordecai, who was effectively condemned to death, rose to become the second highest ranking official in the nation. No matter how hopeless our condition, or how much we would like to give up, we need not despair. God is in control of our world.

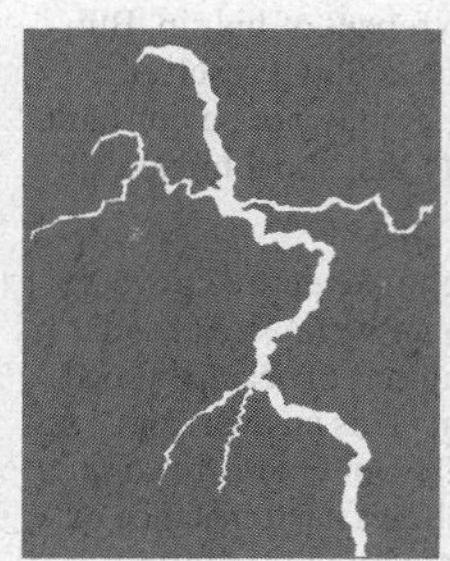

TREES snap like toothpicks or fly upward, wrenched from the earth. Whole rooftops sail, cars tumble like toys, houses collapse, and a wall of water obliterates the shore and inundates the land. A hurricane cuts and tears, and only solid foundations survive its unbridled fury. But those foundations can be used for rebuilding after the storm.

For any building, the foundation is critical. It must be deep enough and solid enough to withstand the weight of the building and other stresses. Lives are like buildings, and the quality of their foundation will determine the quality of the whole. Too often inferior materials are used, and when tests come, lives crumble.

Job was tested. With a life filled with prestige, possessions, and people, he was suddenly assaulted on every side, devastated, stripped down to his foundation. But his life was built on God, and he endured.

Job, the book, tells the story of Job, the man of God. It is a gripping drama of riches-to-rags-to-riches, a theological treatise about suffering and divine sovereignty and a picture of faith that endures. As you read Job, analyze your life and check your foundation. And may you be able to say that when all is gone but God, he is enough.

Job was a prosperous farmer living in the land of Uz. He had thousands of sheep, camels, and other livestock, a large family, and many servants. Suddenly, Satan the Accuser came before God claiming that Job was trusting God only because he was wealthy and everything was going well for him. And so the testing of Job's faith began.

Satan was allowed to destroy Job's children, servants, livestock, herdsmen, and home; but Job continued to trust in God. Next Satan attacked Job physically, covering him with painful sores. Job's wife told him to curse God and die (2:9), but Job suffered in silence.

Three of Job's friends, Eliphaz, Bildad, and Zophar, came to visit him. At first they silently grieved with Job. But when they began to talk about the reasons for Job's tragedies, they told him that sin had caused his suffering. They told him to confess his sins and turn back to God. But Job maintained his innocence.

Unable to convince Job of his sin, the three men fell silent (32:1). At this point, another voice—the young Elihu—entered the debate. Although his argument also failed to convince Job, it prepared the way for God to speak.

Finally, God spoke out of a mighty storm. Confronted with the great power and majesty of God, Job fell in humble reverence before God—speechless. God rebuked Job's friends, and the drama ended with Job restored to happiness and wealth.

It is easy to think that we have all the answers. In reality, only God knows exactly why things happen as they do, and we must submit to him as our Sovereign. As you read this book, emulate Job and decide to trust God no matter what happens.

VITAL STATISTICS

PURPOSE:
To demonstrate God's sovereignty and the meaning of true faith. It addresses the question Why do the righteous suffer?

AUTHOR:
Unknown, possibly Job. Some have suggested Moses, Solomon, or Elihu.

DATE WRITTEN:
Unknown. Records events that probably occurred during the time of the patriarchs, approximately 2000–1800 B.C.

SETTING:
The land of Uz, probably located northeast of Palestine, near desert land between Damascus and the Euphrates River

KEY VERSE:
"Then the LORD asked Satan, 'Have you noticed my servant Job? He is the finest man in all the earth—a man of complete integrity. He fears God and will have nothing to do with evil. And he has maintained his integrity, even though you persuaded me to harm him without cause'" (2:3).

KEY PEOPLE:
Job, Eliphaz the Temanite, Bildad the Shuhite, Zophar the Naamathite, Elihu the Buzite

SPECIAL FEATURES:
Job is the first of the poetic books in the Hebrew Bible. Some believe this was the first book of the Bible to be written. The book gives us insights into the work of Satan. Ezekiel 14:14, 20 and James 5:11 mention Job as a historical character.

THE BLUEPRINT

A. JOB IS TESTED (1:1—2:13)	Job, a wealthy and upright man, lost his possessions, his children, and his health. Job did not understand why he was suffering. Why does God allow his children to suffer? Although there is an explanation, we may not know it while we are here on earth. In the meantime, we must always be ready for testing in our lives.
B. THREE FRIENDS ANSWER JOB (3:1—31:40) 1. First round of discussion 2. Second round of discussion 3. Third round of discussion	Job's friends wrongly assumed that suffering always came as a result of sin. With this in mind, they tried to persuade Job to repent of his sin. But the three friends were wrong. Suffering is not always a direct result of personal sin. When we experience severe suffering, it may not be our fault, so we don't have to add to our pain by feeling guilty that some hidden sin is causing our trouble.
C. A YOUNG MAN ANSWERS JOB (32:1—37:24)	A young man named Elihu, who had been listening to the entire conversation, criticized the three friends for being unable to answer Job. He said that although Job was a good man, he had allowed himself to become proud, and God was punishing him in order to humble him. This answer was partially true because suffering does purify our faith. But God is beyond our comprehension, and we cannot know why he allows each instance of suffering to come into our lives. Our part is simply to remain faithful.
D. GOD ANSWERS JOB (38:1—41:34)	God himself finally answered Job. God is in control of the world, and only he understands why the good are allowed to suffer. This only becomes clear to us when we see God for who he is. We must courageously accept what God allows to happen in our lives and remain firmly committed to him.
E. JOB IS RESTORED (42:1–17)	Job finally learned that when nothing else was left, he had God, and that was enough. Through suffering, we learn that God is enough for our lives and our future. We must love God regardless of whether he allows blessing or suffering to come to us. Testing is difficult, but the result is often a deeper relationship with God. Those who endure the testing of their faith will experience God's great rewards in the end.

MEGATHEMES

THEME	EXPLANATION	IMPORTANCE
Suffering	Through no fault of his own, Job lost his wealth, children, and health. Even his friends were convinced that Job had brought this suffering upon himself. For Job, the greatest trial was not the pain or the loss; it was not being able to understand why God allowed him to suffer.	Suffering can be, but is not always, a penalty for sin. In the same way, prosperity is not always a reward for being good. Those who love God are not exempt from trouble. Although we may not be able to understand fully the pain we experience, it can lead us to rediscover God.
Satan's Attacks	Satan attempted to drive a wedge between Job and God by getting Job to believe that God's governing of the world was not just and good. Satan had to ask God for permission to take Job's wealth, children, and health away. Satan was limited to what God allowed.	We must learn to recognize but not fear Satan's attacks because Satan cannot exceed the limits that God sets. Don't let any experience drive a wedge between you and God. Although you can't control how Satan may attack, you can always choose how you will respond when it happens.
God's Goodness	God is all-wise and all-powerful. His will is perfect, yet he doesn't always act in ways that we understand. Job's suffering didn't make sense because everyone believed good people were supposed to prosper. When Job was at the point of despair, God spoke to him, showing him his great power and wisdom.	Although God is present everywhere, at times he may seem far away. This may cause us to feel alone and to doubt his care for us. We should serve God for who he is, not what we feel. He is never insensitive to our suffering. Because God is sufficient, we must hold on to him.
Pride	Job's friends were certain that they were correct in their judgment of him. God rebuked them for their pride and arrogance. Human wisdom is always partial and temporary, so undue pride in our own conclusions is sin.	We must be careful not to judge others who are suffering. We may be demonstrating the sin of pride. We must be cautious in maintaining the certainty of our own conclusions about how God treats us. When we congratulate ourselves for being right, we become proud.

Trusting	God alone knew the purpose behind Job's suffering, and yet he never explained it to Job. In spite of this, Job never gave up on God—even in the midst of suffering. He never placed his hope in his experience, his wisdom, his friends, or his wealth. Job focused on God.	Job showed the kind of trust we are to have. When everything is stripped away, we are to recognize that God is all we ever really had. We should not demand that God explain everything. God gives us himself, but not all the details of his plans. We must remember that this life, with all its pain, is not our final destiny.

A. JOB IS TESTED (1:1—2:13)

Job is portrayed as a wealthy man of upright character who loves God. Yet God allows Satan to destroy his flocks, his possessions, his children, and his health. Job refuses to give up on God, even though he does not understand why this is happening to him. We, too, must trust God when we do not understand the difficulties we face.

Prologue

1:1 Gen 6:9; 17:1; Exod 18:21; Job 28:28; 29:25; Jer 25:20; Lam 4:21; Ezek 14:14; Jas 5:11
1:2 Job 42:13
1:3 Job 42:12
1:5 Gen 8:20; 1 Kgs 21:10-11; Job 8:4; 42:8
1:6 Job 38:7
1:7 1 Pet 5:8

1 There was a man named Job who lived in the land of Uz. He was blameless, a man
of complete integrity. He feared God and stayed away from evil. 2He had seven sons
and three daughters. 3He owned seven thousand sheep, three thousand camels, five
hundred teams of oxen, and five hundred female donkeys, and he employed many
servants. He was, in fact, the richest person in that entire area.
4Every year when Job's sons had birthdays, they invited their brothers and sisters to
join them for a celebration. On these occasions they would get together to eat and drink.
5When these celebrations ended—and sometimes they lasted several days—Job would
purify his children. He would get up early in the morning and offer a burnt offering for
each of them. For Job said to himself, "Perhaps my children have sinned and have cursed
God in their hearts." This was Job's regular practice.

Job's First Test

6One day the angels* came to present themselves before the LORD, and Satan the
Accuser came with them. 7"Where have you come from?" the LORD asked Satan.

1:6 Hebrew *the sons of God.*

1:1 As we read the book of Job, we have information that the characters of the story do not. Job, the main character of the book, lost all he had through no fault of his own. As he struggled to understand why all this was happening to him, it became clear that he was not meant to know the reasons. He would have to face life with the answers and explanations held back. Only then would his faith fully develop.

We must experience life as Job did—one day at a time and without complete answers to all of life's questions. Will we, like Job, trust God no matter what? Or will we give in to the temptation to say that God doesn't really care?

1:1 The location of the land of Uz is uncertain. We only know that Uz had plentiful pastures and crops (1:3), was located near a desert (1:19), and was close enough to the Sabeans and Chaldeans to be raided (1:14-17). Uz is also mentioned in Jeremiah 25:19, 20. Most scholars believe Uz was located east of the Jordan River near Canaan (Israel), where the Jews (those to whom God first revealed himself) lived.

1:1ff As we see calamity and suffering in the book of Job, we must remember that we live in a fallen world where good behavior is not always rewarded and bad behavior is not always punished. When we see a notorious criminal prospering or an innocent child in pain, we say, "That's wrong." And it is. Sin has twisted justice and made our world unpredictable and ugly.

The book of Job shows a good man suffering for no apparent fault of his own. Sadly, our world is like that. But Job's story does not end in despair. Through Job's life we can see that faith in God is justified even when our situations look hopeless. Faith based on rewards or prosperity is hollow. To be unshakable, faith must be built on the confidence that God's ultimate purpose will come to pass.

1:5 It is not known for sure, but Job probably lived during the days of the patriarchs (Abraham, Isaac, Jacob) before God gave his written law or appointed priests to be religious leaders. During Job's day, the father was the family's religious leader. Because there were no priests to instruct him in God's laws, Job acted as the priest and offered sacrifices to God to ask for forgiveness for sins he and his family had committed. This demonstrated that Job did not consider himself sinless. Job did this out of conviction and love for God, not just because it was his role as head of the house. Do you carry out your spiritual duties because they are expected or spontaneously from a heart of devotion?

1:5 Job showed deep concern for the spiritual welfare of his children. Fearful that they might have sinned unknowingly, he offered sacrifices for them. Parents today can show the same concern by praying for their children. This means "sacrificing" some time each day to ask God to forgive them, to help them grow, to protect them, and to help them please him.

1:6 The Bible speaks of other heavenly councils where God and the angels plan their activities on earth and where angels are required to give account of themselves (i.e., 1 Kings 22:19-23). Because God is Creator of all angels—both of those who serve him and of those who rebelled—he has complete power and authority over them.

1:6, 7 Satan, originally an angel of God, became corrupt through his own pride. He has been evil since his rebellion against God (1 John 3:8). Satan considers God as his enemy. He tries to hinder God's work in people, but he is limited by God's power and can do only what he is permitted (Luke 22:31, 32; 1 Timothy 1:19, 20; 2 Timothy 2:23-26). Satan is called the enemy because he actively looks for people to attack with temptation (1 Peter 5:8, 9) and because he wants to make people hate God. He does this through lies and deception (Genesis 3:1-6). Job, a blameless and upright man who had been greatly blessed, was a perfect target for Satan. Any person who is committed to God should expect Satan's attacks. Satan, who hates God, also hates God's people.

And Satan answered the LORD, "I have been going back and forth across the earth,
watching everything that's going on."
8 Then the LORD asked Satan, "Have you noticed my servant Job? He is the finest man
in all the earth—a man of complete integrity. He fears God and will have nothing to do
with evil."
9 Satan replied to the LORD, "Yes, Job fears God, but not without good reason! 10 You
have always protected him and his home and his property from harm. You have made
him prosperous in everything he does. Look how rich he is! 11 But take away everything
he has, and he will surely curse you to your face!"
12 "All right, you may test him," the LORD said to Satan. "Do whatever you want with
everything he possesses, but don't harm him physically." So Satan left the LORD's
presence.
13 One day when Job's sons and daughters were dining at the oldest brother's house,
14 a messenger arrived at Job's home with this news: "Your oxen were plowing, with the
donkeys feeding beside them, 15 when the Sabeans raided us. They stole all the animals
and killed all the farmhands. I am the only one who escaped to tell you."
16 While he was still speaking, another messenger arrived with this news: "The fire of
God has fallen from heaven and burned up your sheep and all the shepherds. I am the
only one who escaped to tell you."
17 While he was still speaking, a third messenger arrived with this news: "Three bands
of Chaldean raiders have stolen your camels and killed your servants. I am the only one
who escaped to tell you."
18 While he was still speaking, another messenger arrived with this news: "Your sons
and daughters were feasting in their oldest brother's home. 19 Suddenly, a powerful wind
swept in from the desert and hit the house on all sides. The house collapsed, and all your
children are dead. I am the only one who escaped to tell you."
20 Job stood up and tore his robe in grief. Then he shaved his head and fell to the ground
before God. 21 He said,

1:8 Num 12:7; Josh 1:2, 7; Job 1:1; 7:8; 42:7-8
1:10 Job 29:2-6; 31:25
1:11 Job 2:5; 19:21
1:15 Job 6:19
1:16 Gen 19:24; Lev 10:2; Num 11:1-3
1:17 Gen 11:28, 31
1:20 Gen 37:29, 34
1:21 1 Sam 2:7-8; Job 2:10; Eccl 5:15; 1 Tim 6:7

1:6-12 From this conversation, we learn a great deal about Satan. (1) He is accountable to God. All angelic beings, good and evil, are compelled to present themselves before God (1:6). God knew that Satan was intent on attacking Job. (2) Satan can be at only one place at a time (1:6, 7). His demons aid him in his work; but as a created being, he is limited. (3) Satan cannot see into our minds or foretell the future (1:9-11). If he could, he would have known that Job would not break under pressure. (4) Because Satan can do nothing without God's permission (1:12), God's people can overcome his attacks through God's power. (5) God puts limitations on what Satan can do (1:12; 2:6). Satan's response to the Lord's question (1:7) tells us that Satan is real and active on earth. Knowing this about Satan should cause us to remain close to the one who is greater than Satan—God himself.

1:7ff Some people suggest that this dialogue was made up by the author of this book. Could this conversation between God and Satan really have happened? Other Bible passages tell us that Satan does indeed have access to God (see Revelation 12:10). He even went into God's presence to make accusations against Joshua the high priest (Zechariah 3:1, 2). If this conversation didn't take place, then the reasons for Job's suffering become meaningless, and the book of Job is reduced to fiction rather than fact.

1:8, 12 Job was a model of trust and obedience to God, yet God permitted Satan to attack him in an especially harsh manner. Although God loves us, believing and obeying him do not shelter us from life's calamities. Setbacks, tragedies, and sorrows strike Christians and non-Christians alike. But in our tests and trials, God expects us to express our faith to the world. How do you respond to your troubles? Do you ask God, "Why me?" or do you say, "Use me!"?

1:9 Satan attacked Job's motives, saying that Job was blameless and had integrity only because he had no reason to turn against God. Ever since he had started following God, everything had gone well for Job. Satan wanted to prove that Job worshiped God, not out of love, but because God had given him so much.

Satan accurately analyzed why many people trust God. They are fair-weather believers, following God only when everything is going well or for what they can get. Adversity destroys this superficial faith. But adversity strengthens real faith by causing believers to dig their roots deeper into God in order to withstand the storms. How deep does your faith go? Put the roots of your faith down deep into God so that you can withstand any storm you may face.

1:12 This conversation between God and Satan teaches us an important fact about God—he is fully aware of every attempt by Satan to bring suffering and difficulty upon us. While God may allow us to suffer for a reason beyond our understanding, he is never caught by surprise by our troubles and is always compassionate.

1:15-17 The Sabeans were from southwest Arabia, while the Chaldeans were from the region north of the Persian Gulf.

1:16 "The fire of God" was a poetic way to describe lightning (1 Kings 18:38; 2 Kings 1:10-14). In this case, it had to be unusually powerful to kill 7,000 sheep.

1:20-22 Job did not hide his overwhelming grief. He had not lost his faith in God; instead, his emotions showed that he was human and that he loved his family. God created our emotions, and it is not sinful or inappropriate to express them as Job did. If you have experienced a deep loss, a disappointment, or a heartbreak, admit your feelings to yourself and others, and grieve.

1:20-22 Job had lost his possessions and family in this first of Satan's tests, but he reacted rightly toward God by acknowledging God's sovereign authority over everything God had given him. Satan lost this first round. Job passed the test and proved that people can love God for who he is, not for what he gives.

"I came naked from my mother's womb,
and I will be stripped of everything when I die.
The LORD gave me everything I had,
and the LORD has taken it away.
Praise the name of the LORD!"

1:22 Job 2:10
22 In all of this, Job did not sin by blaming God.

Job's Second Test

2:1 Job 1:6-8
2 One day the angels* came again to present themselves before the LORD, and Satan
the Accuser came with them. 2 "Where have you come from?" the LORD asked Satan.
And Satan answered the LORD, "I have been going back and forth across the earth,
watching everything that's going on."

2:3 Job 27:5-6
3 Then the LORD asked Satan, "Have you noticed my servant Job? He is the finest man
in all the earth—a man of complete integrity. He fears God and will have nothing to do
with evil. And he has maintained his integrity, even though you persuaded me to harm
him without cause."
4 Satan replied to the LORD, "Skin for skin—he blesses you only because you bless

2:5 Job 1:11
him. A man will give up everything he has to save his life. 5 But take away his health, and
he will surely curse you to your face!"
6 "All right, do with him as you please," the LORD said to Satan. "But spare his life."

2:7 Deut 28:35; Job 7:5; 13:28
7 So Satan left the LORD's presence, and he struck Job with a terrible case of boils from
head to foot.

2:8 Job 42:6; Jer 6:26; Ezek 27:30; Jon 3:6; Matt 11:21
8 Then Job scraped his skin with a piece of broken pottery as he sat among the
ashes. 9 His wife said to him, "Are you still trying to maintain your integrity? Curse
God and die."

2:1 Hebrew *the sons of God.*

THE SOURCES OF SUFFERING

Sources	*Who Is Responsible*	*Who Is Affected*	*Needed Response*
My sin	I am	Myself and others	Repentance and confession to God
Others' sin	Person who sinned and others who allowed the sin	Probably many people, including those who sinned	Active resistance to the sinful behavior, while accepting the sinner
Avoidable physical (or natural) disaster	Persons who ignore the facts or refuse to take precautions	Most of those exposed to the cause	Prevent them if possible; be prepared if they can't be prevented
Unavoidable physical (or natural) disaster	God, Satan	Most of those present	Ongoing trust in God's faithfulness

When suffering or troubles happen, do they always come from Satan? In Job's story, his series of tragedies did come from Satan, but this is not always the case. The chart above demonstrates the four main causes of suffering. Any one of these or a combination of them may create suffering. If knowing why we are suffering will teach us to avoid the cause, then the causes are worth knowing. However, it is most important to know how to respond during suffering.

2:3-6 Can Satan persuade God to change his plans? At first God said he did not want Job harmed physically, but then he decided to allow it. Satan is unable to persuade God to go against his character: God is completely and eternally good. But God was willing to go along with Satan's plan because God knew the eventual outcome of Job's story. God cannot be fooled by Satan. Job's suffering was a test for Job, Satan, and us—not God.

2:4, 5 "Skin for skin" was Satan's comment concerning Job's response to the loss of his family. Satan still held to his opinion that Job was faithful only because of God's blessings. Satan believed that Job was willing to accept the loss of family and property as long as his own skin was safe. Satan's next step was to inflict physical suffering upon Job to prove his original accusation (1:9).

2:6 Again Satan had to seek permission from God to inflict pain upon Job. God limits Satan, and in this case he did not allow Satan to destroy Job.

2:9 Why was Job's wife spared when the rest of his family was killed? It is possible that her very presence caused Job even more suffering through either her chiding or her sorrow over all they had lost.

[10]But Job replied, “You talk like a godless woman. Should we accept only good things 2:10 Job 1:21-22
from the hand of God and never anything bad?” So in all this, Job said nothing wrong. Ps 39:1

Job's Three Friends Share His Anguish

[11]Three of Job's friends were Eliphaz the Temanite, Bildad the Shuhite, and Zophar the 2:12
Naamathite. When they heard of the tragedy he had suffered, they got together and Josh 7:6 Job 1:20
traveled from their homes to comfort and console him. [12]When they saw Job from a Lam 2:10
distance, they scarcely recognized him. Wailing loudly, they tore their robes and threw Ezek 27:30
dust into the air over their heads to demonstrate their grief. [13]Then they sat on the ground 2:13
with him for seven days and nights. And no one said a word, for they saw that his Gen 50:10
suffering was too great for words. Ezek 3:15

B. THREE FRIENDS ANSWER JOB (3:1—31:40)

Job agonizes over his situation. His three friends explain that he must be suffering because of some terrible sin he committed. They try to persuade Job to repent of his sin. When Job argues that he has not sinned enough to deserve such suffering, his friends respond with even harsher accusations. While there are elements of truth in the speeches of Job's three friends, they are based on wrong assumptions. We must be careful what we assume to be true in the lives of others. We cannot assume that suffering is their own fault or a result of their sin.

1. First round of discussion

Job's First Speech

3 At last Job spoke, and he cursed the day of his birth. [2]He said:
[3]“Cursed be the day of my birth, and cursed be the night when I was conceived. [4]Let 3:3 Jer 20:14
that day be turned to darkness. Let it be lost even to God on high, and let it be shrouded in
darkness. [5]Yes, let the darkness and utter gloom claim it for its own. Let a black cloud
overshadow it, and let the darkness terrify it. [6]Let that night be blotted off the calendar, never
again to be counted among the days of the year, never again to appear among the months.
[7]Let that night be barren. Let it have no joy. [8]Let those who are experts at cursing—those 3:8
who are ready to rouse the sea monster*—curse that day. [9]Let its morning stars remain dark. Job 41:1, 10, 25
Let it hope for light, but in vain; may it never see the morning light. [10]Curse it for its failure 3:9
to shut my mother's womb, for letting me be born to all this trouble. Job 41:18
[11]“Why didn't I die at birth as I came from the womb? [12]Why did my mother let me 3:11 Job 10:18-19

3:8 Hebrew *rouse Leviathan.*

2:10 Many people think that believing in God protects them from trouble, so when calamity comes, they question God's goodness and justice. But the message of Job is that you should not give up on God because he allows you to have bad experiences. Faith in God does not guarantee personal prosperity, and lack of faith does not guarantee troubles in this life. If this were so, people would believe in God simply to get rich. God is capable of rescuing us from suffering, but he may also allow suffering to come for reasons we cannot understand. It is Satan's strategy to get us to doubt God at exactly this moment. Here Job shows a perspective broader than seeking his own personal comfort. If we always knew why we were suffering, our faith would have no room to grow.

2:11 Eliphaz, Bildad, and Zophar were not only Job's friends, they were also known for their wisdom. In the end, however, their wisdom was shown to be narrow-minded and incomplete.

2:11 Upon learning of Job's difficulties, three of his friends came to sympathize with him and comfort him. Later we learn that their words of comfort were not helpful—but at least they came. While God rebuked them for what they said (42:7), he did not rebuke them for what they did—making the effort to come to someone who was in need. Unfortunately, when they came, they did a poor job of comforting Job because they were proud of their own advice and insensitive to Job's needs. When someone is in need, go to that person, but be sensitive about how you comfort him or her.

2:13 Why did the friends arrive and then just sit quietly? According to Jewish tradition, people who come to comfort someone in mourning should not speak until the mourner speaks. Often the best response to another person's suffering is silence. Job's friends realized that his pain was too deep to be healed with mere words, so they said nothing. (If only they had continued to sit quietly!) Often, we feel we must say something spiritual and insightful to a hurting friend. Perhaps what he or she needs most is just our presence, showing that we care. Pat answers and trite quotations say much less than empathetic silence and loving companionship.

3:1ff Job's response to his second test—physical affliction—contrasts greatly to his attitude after the first test (1:20-22). Job still did not curse God, but he cursed the day of his birth. He felt it would be better never to be born than to be forsaken by God. Job was struggling emotionally, physically, and spiritually; his misery was pervasive and deep. Never underestimate how vulnerable we are during times of suffering and pain. We must hold on to our faith even if there is no relief.

3:8 In Job's day, people were hired to pronounce curses. Job desires that the experts at cursing would call up the sea monster, Leviathan, to swallow up the day of Job's birth.

3:11 Job was experiencing extreme physical pain as well as grief over the loss of his family and possessions. He can't be blamed for wishing he were dead. Job's grief placed him at the crossroads of his faith, shattering many misconceptions about God (e.g., he makes you rich, always keeps you from trouble and pain, or protects your loved ones). Job was driven back to the basics of his faith in God. He had only two choices: (1) He could curse God and give up, or (2) he could trust God and draw strength from him to continue.

3:13 Job 14:10-15; live? Why did she nurse me at her breasts? [13]For if I had died at birth, I would be at peace
19:25-27 now, asleep and at rest. [14]I would rest with the world's kings and prime ministers, famous
for their great construction projects. [15]I would rest with wealthy princes whose palaces
were filled with gold and silver. [16]Why was I not buried like a stillborn child, like a baby
who never lives to see the light? [17]For in death the wicked cease from troubling, and the
weary are at rest. [18]Even prisoners are at ease in death, with no guards to curse them.
3:21 Rev 9:6 [19]Rich and poor are there alike, and the slave is free from his master.
3:23 [20]"Oh, why should light be given to the weary, and life to those in misery? [21]They
Job 19:6, 8, 12 Ps 88:8 long for death, and it won't come. They search for death more eagerly than for hidden
Lam 3:7 treasure. [22]It is a blessed relief when they finally die, when they find the grave. [23]Why

Children never tire of asking why. Yet the question produces a bitter taste the older we get. Children wonder about everything; adults wonder about suffering. We notice that the world seems to run by a system of cause and effect, yet there are some effects for which we can't find a clear cause, and some causes that don't lead to the expected effects. We would expect Job's wealth and family to give him a very happy life, and, for a while, they did. But the loss and pain he experienced shock us. The first two chapters of his story are more than we can bear. To those so quick to ask why at the smallest misfortune, Job's faithfulness seems incredible. But even Job had something to learn. We can learn with him.

Our age of "instant" everything has caused us to lose the ability to wait. We expect to learn patience instantly, and in our hurry, we miss the contradiction. Of all that we want now, relief from pain is at the top of our list. We want an instant cure for everything from toothaches to heartbreaks.

Although some pains have been cured, we still live in a world where many people suffer. Job was not expecting instant answers for the intense emotional and physical pain he endured. But in the end, what broke Job's patience was not the suffering, but not knowing *why* he suffered.

When Job expressed his frustration, his friends were ready with their answers. They believed that the law of cause and effect applied to all people's experiences. Their view of life boiled down to this: Good things happen to good people, and bad things happen to bad people. Because of this, they felt their role was to help Job admit to whatever sin was causing his suffering.

Job actually looked at life almost the same way as his friends. What he couldn't understand was why he was suffering so much when he was sure he had done nothing to deserve such punishment. The last friend, Elihu, did offer another explanation for the pain by pointing out that God might be allowing it to purify Job. But this was only partly helpful. When God finally spoke, he didn't offer Job an answer. Instead, he drove home the point that it is better to know God than to know answers.

Often we suffer consequences for bad decisions and actions. Job's willingness to repent and confess known wrongs is a good guideline for us. Sometimes suffering shapes us for special service to others. Sometimes suffering is an attack by Satan on our lives. And sometimes we don't know why we suffer. At those times, are we willing to trust God in spite of unanswered questions?

Strengths and accomplishments
- Was a man of faith, patience, and endurance
- Was known as a generous and caring person
- Was very wealthy

Weakness and mistake
- Allowed his desire to understand why he was suffering overwhelm him and make him question God

Lessons from his life
- Knowing God is better than knowing answers
- God is not arbitrary or uncaring
- Pain is not always punishment

Vital statistics
- Where: Uz
- Occupation: Wealthy landowner and livestock owner
- Relatives: Wife and first 10 children not named. Daughters from the second set of children: Jemimah, Keziah, Keren-happuch
- Contemporaries: Eliphaz, Bildad, Zophar, Elihu

Key verses
"For examples of patience in suffering, look at the prophets who spoke in the name of the Lord. We give great honor to those who endure under suffering. Job is an example of a man who endured patiently. From his experience we see how the Lord's plan finally ended in good, for he is full of tenderness and mercy" (James 5:10, 11).

Job's story is told in the book of Job. He is also referred to in Ezekiel 14:14, 20 and James 5:11.

is life given to those with no future, those destined by God to live in distress? 24I cannot
eat for sighing; my groans pour out like water. 25What I always feared has happened to
me. What I dreaded has come to be. 26I have no peace, no quietness. I have no rest;
instead, only trouble comes."

Eliphaz's First Response to Job

4 Then Eliphaz the Temanite replied to Job:
2"Will you be patient and let me say a word? For who could keep from speaking out?
3"In the past you have encouraged many a troubled soul to trust in God; you have
supported those who were weak. 4Your words have strengthened the fallen; you steadied
those who wavered. 5But now when trouble strikes, you faint and are broken. 6Does your
reverence for God give you no confidence? Shouldn't you believe that God will care for
those who are upright?
7"Stop and think! Does the innocent person perish? When has the upright person been
destroyed? 8My experience shows that those who plant trouble and cultivate evil will
harvest the same. 9They perish by a breath from God. They vanish in a blast of his anger.
10Though they are fierce young lions, they will all be broken and destroyed. 11The fierce
lion will starve, and the cubs of the lioness will be scattered.
12"This truth was given me in secret, as though whispered in my ear. 13It came in a
vision at night as others slept. 14Fear gripped me; I trembled and shook with terror. 15A
spirit* swept past my face. Its wind sent shivers up my spine. 16It stopped, but I couldn't
see its shape. There was a form before my eyes, and a hushed voice said, 17'Can a mortal
be just and upright before God? Can a person be pure before the Creator?'
18"If God cannot trust his own angels and has charged some of them with folly, 19how
much less will he trust those made of clay! Their foundation is dust, and they are crushed
as easily as moths. 20They are alive in the morning, but by evening they are dead, gone
forever without a trace. 21Their tent collapses; they die in ignorance.

4:15 Or *wind.*

3:24 Job 6:7; 33:20; Ps 42:3-4
3:26 Job 7:13-14
4:3 Job 29:21, 25
4:6 Job 1:1; Prov 3:26
4:7-8 Ps 37:25; Prov 22:8; Gal 6:7-8
4:9 Isa 30:33; 2 Thes 2:8
4:11 Job 5:4; Ps 34:10
4:12 Job 26:14; 33:15-18
4:17 Job 9:2; 35:10
4:18 Gen 2:7; 3:19; Job 15:15; 22:16
4:19 Job 10:9; 22:16
4:20 Job 14:2, 20; 20:7
4:21 Job 8:22

3:23-26 Job had been careful not to worship material possessions but to worship God alone. Here he was overwhelmed by calamities that mocked his caution, and he complained about trials that came despite his right living. All the principles by which he had lived were crumbling, and Job began to lose his perspective. Trials and grief, whether temporary or enduring, do not destroy the real purpose of life. Life is not given merely for happiness and personal fulfillment but for us to serve and honor God. The worth and meaning of life is not based on what we feel but on the one reality no one can take away—God's love for us. Don't assume that because God truly loves you, he will always prevent suffering. The opposite may be true. God's love cannot be measured or limited by how great or how little we may suffer. Romans 8:38, 39 teaches us that nothing can separate us from God's love.

4:1ff Eliphaz claimed to have been given secret knowledge through a special revelation from God (4:12-16), and that he had learned much from personal experience (4:8). He argued that suffering is a direct result of sin, so if Job would only confess his sin, his suffering would end. Eliphaz saw suffering as God's punishment, which should be welcomed in order to bring a person back to God. In some cases, of course, this may be true (Galatians 6:7, 8), but it was not true with Job. Although Eliphaz had many good and true comments, he made three wrong assumptions: (1) A good and innocent person never suffers; (2) those who suffer are being punished for their past sins; and (3) Job, because he was suffering, had done something wrong in God's eyes. (For more about Eliphaz, see the chart in chapter 29. Teman was a trading city in Edom, noted as a place of wisdom; see Jeremiah 49:7.)

4:7, 8 Part of what Eliphaz said is true, and part is false. It is true that those who promote sin and trouble eventually will be punished; it is false that anyone who is good and innocent will never suffer.

All the material recorded and quoted in the Bible is there by God's choice. Some is a record of what people said and did but is not an example to follow. The sins, the defeats, the evil thoughts, and misconceptions about God are all recorded in God's divinely inspired Word, but we should not follow those wrong examples just because they are in the Bible. The Bible gives us teachings and examples of what we *should* do as well as what we *should not* do. Eliphaz's comments are an example of what we should try to avoid—making false assumptions about others based on our own experiences.

4:12, 13 Although Eliphaz claimed that his vision was divinely inspired, it is doubtful that it came from God because later God criticized Eliphaz for misrepresenting him (42:7). Whatever the vision's source, it is summarized in 4:17. On the surface, this statement is completely true—a mere mortal cannot compare to God and should not try to question God's motives and actions. Eliphaz, however, took this thought and expounded on it later, expressing his own opinions. His conclusion (5:8) reveals a very shallow understanding of Job and his suffering. It is easy for teachers, counselors, and well-meaning friends to begin with a portion of God's truth but then go off on a tangent. Don't limit God to your perspective and finite understanding of life.

4:18, 19 Do angels really make errors? Remember that Eliphaz was speaking, not God, so we must be careful about building our knowledge of the spiritual world from Eliphaz's opinions. In addition, the word translated "folly" is used only here, and its meaning is unclear. We could save Eliphaz's credibility by saying he meant fallen angels, but this passage is not meant to teach about angels. Eliphaz was saying that sinful human beings are far beneath God and the angels. Eliphaz was right about God's greatness, but he did not understand God's greater purposes concerning suffering.

5:2 Prov 12:16; 27:3
5:3 Job 24:18; 31:30
5:5 Job 18:8-10
5:9 Job 9:10; 37:14, 16; 42:3
5:10 Job 36:27-29; 37:6-11 Ps 65:9
5:11 Job 22:29; 36:7
5:13 †1 Cor 3:19
5:14 Deut 28:29

Eliphaz's Response Continues

5 “You may cry for help, but no one listens. You may turn to the angels,* but they give
you no help. 2 Surely resentment destroys the fool, and jealousy kills the simple.
3 From my experience, I know that fools who turn from God may be successful for the
moment, but then comes sudden disaster. 4 Their children are abandoned far from help,
with no one to defend them. 5 Their harvests are stolen, and their wealth satisfies the thirst
of many others, not themselves! 6 But evil does not spring from the soil, and trouble does
not sprout from the earth. 7 People are born for trouble as predictably as sparks fly
upward from a fire.
8 “My advice to you is this: Go to God and present your case to him. 9 For he does great
works too marvelous to understand. He performs miracles without number. 10 He gives
rain for the earth. He sends water for the fields. 11 He gives prosperity to the poor and
humble, and he takes sufferers to safety. 12 He frustrates the plans of the crafty, so their
efforts will not succeed. 13 He catches those who think they are wise in their own

5:1 Hebrew *the holy ones.*

ADVICE FROM FRIENDS Overwhelmed by suffering, Job was not comforted but condemned by his friends. Each of their views represents a well-known way to understand suffering. God proves that each explanation given by Job's friends has less than the whole answer.

Who They Were	*Reference*	*How They Helped*	*Their Reasoning*	*Their Advice*	*Job's Response*	*God's Response*
Eliphaz the Temanite	Job 4, 5, 15, 22	They sat in silence with Job for seven days. (2:11–13)	Job is suffering because he has sinned.	Go to God and present your case to him. (5:8)	Stop assuming my guilt. (6:29)	God rebukes Job's friends. (42:7)
Bildad the Shuhite	Job 8, 18, 25		Job won't admit he sinned, so he's still suffering.	How long will you go on like this? (8:2)	I will say to God, . . . Tell me the charge you are bringing against me. (10:2)	
Zophar the Naamathite	Job 11, 20		Job's sin deserves even more suffering than he's experienced.	Get rid of your sins. (11:13,14)	I will be proved innocent. (13:18)	
Elihu the Buzite	Job 32—37		God is using suffering to mold and train Job.	Keep silent and I will teach you wisdom. (33:33)	No response	God does not directly address Elihu.
God	Job 38—41	Confronted Job with the need to be content even though he didn't know why he was suffering	Did not explain the reason for the pain	Do you still want to argue with the Almighty? (40:2)	I was talking about things I did not understand. (42:3–5)	

5:8 All three of Job's friends made the mistake of assuming that Job had committed some great sin that had caused his suffering. Neither they nor Job knew of Satan's conversation with God (1:6–2:6). It is human nature to blame people for their own troubles, but Job's story makes it clear that blame cannot always be attached to those whom trouble strikes.

5:13 Paul later quoted part of this verse (1 Corinthians 3:19)—the only time Job is clearly quoted in the New Testament. Although God rebuked Eliphaz for being wrong in his advice to Job (42:7), not all he said was in error. The part Paul quoted was correct—people are often caught in their own traps. This illustrates how Scripture must be used to explain and comment on itself. We must be familiar with the entire scope of God's Word to properly understand the difficult portions of it.

cleverness, so that their cunning schemes are thwarted. 14 They grope in the daylight as
though they were blind; they see no better in the daytime than at night. 15 He rescues the
poor from the cutting words of the strong. He saves them from the clutches of the
powerful. 16 And so at last the poor have hope, and the fangs of the wicked are broken.
17 "But consider the joy of those corrected by God! Do not despise the chastening of
the Almighty when you sin. 18 For though he wounds, he also bandages. He strikes, but
his hands also heal. 19 He will rescue you again and again so that no evil can touch you.
20 He will save you from death in time of famine, from the power of the sword in time of
war. 21 You will be safe from slander and will have no fear of destruction when it comes.
22 You will laugh at destruction and famine; wild animals will not terrify you. 23 You will
be at peace with the stones of the field, and its wild animals will be at peace with you.
24 You will know that your home is kept safe. When you visit your pastures, nothing will
be missing. 25 Your children will be many; your descendants will be as plentiful as grass!
26 You will live to a good old age. You will not be harvested until the proper time!
27 "We have found from experience that all this is true. Listen to my counsel, and apply
it to yourself."

Job's Second Speech: A Response to Eliphaz

6 Then Job spoke again:
2 "If my sadness could be weighed and my troubles be put on the scales, 3 they would
be heavier than all the sands of the sea. That is why I spoke so rashly. 4 For the Almighty
has struck me down with his arrows. He has sent his poisoned arrows deep within my spirit.
All God's terrors are arrayed against me. 5 Don't I have a right to complain? Wild donkeys
bray when they find no green grass, and oxen low when they have no food. 6 People
complain when there is no salt in their food. And how tasteless is the uncooked white of an
egg! 7 My appetite disappears when I look at it; I gag at the thought of eating it!
8 "Oh, that I might have my request, that God would grant my hope. 9 I wish he would
crush me. I wish he would reach out his hand and kill me. 10 At least I can take comfort
in this: Despite the pain, I have not denied the words of the Holy One. 11 But I do not
have the strength to endure. I do not have a goal that encourages me to carry on. 12 Do I
have strength as hard as stone? Is my body made of bronze? 13 No, I am utterly helpless,
without any chance of success.
14 "One should be kind to a fainting friend, but you have accused me without the
slightest fear of the Almighty. 15 My brother, you have proved as unreliable as a seasonal
brook that overflows its banks in the spring 16 when it is swollen with ice and melting
snow. 17 But when the hot weather arrives, the water disappears. The brook vanishes in
the heat. 18 The caravans turn aside to be refreshed, but there is nothing there to drink,
and so they perish in the desert. 19 With high hopes, the caravans from Tema and from
Sheba stop for water, 20 but finding none, their hopes are dashed. 21 You, too, have proved
to be of no help. You have seen my calamity, and you are afraid. 22 But why? Have I ever
asked you for a gift? Have I begged you to use any of your wealth on my behalf? 23 Have
I ever asked you to rescue me from my enemies? Have I asked you to save me from
ruthless people?

5:16 Ps 107:42
5:17 Ps 94:12; Heb 12:5-11
5:18 Deut 32:39; Isa 30:26; Hos 6:1
5:20 Pss 33:19; 144:10
5:23 Isa 11:6-9; 65:25
5:24 Job 8:6
5:26 Gen 15:15; Job 42:17; Prov 9:11
6:2 Job 31:6
6:3 Job 23:2
6:4 Job 16:13; 21:20; 30:15; Ps 38:2
6:5 Job 39:5-8
6:9 1 Kgs 19:4
6:10 Job 23:11
6:11 Job 21:4
6:13 Job 26:2-3
6:14 Job 1:5; 4:5
6:15 Jer 15:18
6:17 Job 24:19
6:19 Gen 25:15; Job 1:15; Isa 21:14
6:20 Jer 14:3

5:17 Eliphaz was correct—it is a joy to be disciplined (chastened) by God when we do wrong. Eliphaz's advice, however, did not apply to Job. As we know from the beginning of the book, Job's suffering was not a result of some great sin. We sometimes give people excellent advice only to learn that it does not apply to them and is therefore not very helpful. All who offer counsel from God's Word should take care to thoroughly understand a person's situation *before* giving advice.

5:17-26 Eliphaz's words in 5:17, 18 show a view of discipline that has been almost forgotten: Pain can help us grow. These are good words to remember when we face hardship and loss. Because Job did not understand why he suffered, his faith in God had a chance to grow. On the other hand, we must not make Eliphaz's mistake. God does not eliminate all hardship when we are following him closely, and good behavior is not always rewarded by prosperity. Rewards for good and punishment for evil are in God's hands and given out according to his timetable. Satan's ploy is to get us to doubt God's goodwill toward us.

6:6, 7 Job said that Eliphaz's advice was like eating the tasteless white of an egg. When people are going through severe trials, ill-advised counsel is distasteful. They may listen politely, but inside they are upset. Be slow to give advice to those who are hurting. They often need compassion more than they need advice.

6:8, 9 In his grief, Job wanted to give in, to be freed from his discomfort, and to die. But God did not grant Job's request. He had a greater plan for him. Our tendency, like Job's, is to want to give up and get out when the going gets rough. To trust God in the good times is commendable, but to trust him during the difficult times tests us to our limits and exercises our faith. In your struggles, large or small, trust that God is in control and that he will take care of you (Romans 8:28).

6:26 Job 8:2
6:27 Joel 3:3; Nah 3:10; 2 Pet 2:3
6:30 Job 12:11

[24]"All I want is a reasonable answer—then I will keep quiet. Tell me, what have I done
wrong? [25]Honest words are painful, but what do your criticisms amount to? [26]Do you
think your words are convincing when you disregard my cry of desperation? [27]You
would even send an orphan into slavery* or sell a friend. [28]Look at me! Would I lie to
your face? [29]Stop assuming my guilt, for I am righteous. Don't be so unjust. [30]Do you
think I am lying? Don't I know the difference between right and wrong?

7:1 Lev 25:50; Job 10:17; 14:6, 14
7:4 Deut 28:67; Job 7:13-14

7 "Is this not the struggle of all humanity? A person's life is long and hard, like that
of a hired hand, [2]like a worker who longs for the day to end, like a servant waiting
to be paid. [3]I, too, have been assigned months of futility, long and weary nights of misery.
[4]When I go to bed, I think, 'When will it be morning?' But the night drags on, and I toss
till dawn. [5]My skin is filled with worms and scabs. My flesh breaks open, full of pus.

Job Cries Out to God

7:7 Job 7:16; 9:25; Ps 78:39
7:8 Job 7:21; 20:9
7:10 Ps 103:16
7:13 Job 7:4; Ps 6:6

[6]"My days are swifter than a weaver's shuttle flying back and forth. They end without
hope. [7]O God, remember that my life is but a breath, and I will never again experience
pleasure. [8]You see me now, but not for long. Your eyes will be on me, but I will be dead.
[9]Just as a cloud dissipates and vanishes, those who die will not come back. [10]They are
gone forever from their home—never to be seen again.

[11]"I cannot keep from speaking. I must express my anguish. I must complain in my
bitterness. [12]Am I a sea monster that you place a guard on me? [13]If I think, 'My bed will
comfort me, and I will try to forget my misery with sleep,' [14]you shatter me with dreams.
You terrify me with visions. [15]I would rather die of strangulation than go on and on like
this. [16]I hate my life. I do not want to go on living. Oh, leave me alone for these few
remaining days.

7:17 Job 22:2; Heb 2:6
7:20 Job 35:3, 6
7:21 Job 10:9, 14

[17]"What are mere mortals, that you should make so much of us? [18]For you examine
us every morning and test us every moment. [19]Why won't you leave me alone—even
for a moment*? [20]Have I sinned? What have I done to you, O watcher of all humanity?
Why have you made me your target? Am I a burden to you? [21]Why not just pardon my
sin and take away my guilt? For soon I will lie down in the dust and die. When you look
for me, I will be gone."

Bildad's First Response to Job

8:3 Gen 18:25; Deut 32:4; 2 Chr 19:7; Job 34:10, 12; Rom 3:5

8 Then Bildad the Shuhite replied to Job:
[2]"How long will you go on like this? Your words are a blustering wind. [3]Does God
twist justice? Does the Almighty twist what is right? [4]Your children obviously sinned
against him, so their punishment was well deserved. [5]But if you pray to God and seek

6:27 Hebrew *even gamble over an orphan.* **7:19** Hebrew *long enough to swallow my spittle.*

6:29, 30 Job referred to his own righteousness, not because he was sinless, but because he had a right relationship with God. He was not guilty of the sins his friends accused him of (see chapter 31 for his summary of the life he had led). Another rendering of verse 29 could read, "My righteousness still stands." *Righteousness* is not the same as *sinlessness* (Romans 3:23). No one but Jesus Christ has ever been sinless—free from all wrong thoughts and actions. Even Job needed to make some changes in his attitude toward God, as we will see by the end of the book. Nevertheless Job was righteous (1:8). He carefully obeyed God to the best of his ability in all aspects of his life.

7:11 Job felt deep anguish and bitterness, and he spoke honestly to God about his feelings to let out his frustrations. If we express our feelings to God, we can deal with them without exploding in harsh words and actions, possibly hurting ourselves and others. The next time strong emotions threaten to overwhelm you, express them openly to God in prayer. This will help you gain an eternal perspective on the situation and give you greater ability to deal with it constructively.

7:12 Job stopped talking to Eliphaz and spoke directly to God. Although Job had lived a blameless life, he was beginning to doubt the value of living in such a way. By doing this, he was coming dangerously close to suggesting that God didn't care about him and was not being fair. Later God reproved Job for this attitude (38:2). Satan always exploits these thoughts to get us to forsake God. Our suffering, like Job's, may not be the result of our sin, but we must be careful not to sin as a result of our suffering.

7:20 Job referred to God as a watcher or observer of humanity. He was expressing his feeling that God seemed like an enemy to him—someone who mercilessly watched him squirm in his misery. We know that God does watch over everything that happens to us. We must never forget that he sees us with compassion, not merely with critical scrutiny. His eyes are eyes of love.

8:1ff Bildad was upset that Job still claimed innocence while questioning God's justice. The basis of Bildad's argument (the justice of God) was correct, but his idea of God's justice was not. Bildad's argument went like this: God could not be unjust, and God would not punish a just man; therefore, Job must be unjust. Bildad felt there were no exceptions to his theory. Like Eliphaz, Bildad wrongly assumed that people suffer only as a result of their sins. Bildad was even less sensitive and compassionate, saying that Job's children died because of *their* wickedness. (For more information about Bildad, see the chart in chapter 29.)

the favor of the Almighty, 6 if you are pure and live with complete integrity, he will rise
up and restore your happy home. 7 And though you started with little, you will end with
much.
8 "Just ask the former generation. Pay attention to the experience of our ancestors. 9 For
we were born but yesterday and know so little. Our days on earth are as transient as a
shadow. 10 But those who came before us will teach you. They will teach you from the
wisdom of former generations.
11 "Can papyrus reeds grow where there is no marsh? Can bulrushes flourish where
there is no water? 12 While they are still flowering, not ready to be cut, they begin to
wither. 13 Such is the fate of all who forget God. The hope of the godless comes to
nothing. 14 Everything they count on will collapse. They are leaning on a spiderweb.
15 They cling to their home for security, but it won't last. They try to hold it fast, but it
will not endure. 16 The godless seem so strong, like a lush plant growing in the sunshine,
its branches spreading across the garden. 17 Its roots grow down through a pile of rocks
to hold it firm. 18 But when it is uprooted, it isn't even missed! 19 That is the end of its
life, and others spring up from the earth to replace it.
20 "But look! God will not reject a person of integrity, nor will he make evildoers prosper.
21 He will yet fill your mouth with laughter and your lips with shouts of joy. 22 Those who
hate you will be clothed with shame, and the tent of the wicked will be destroyed."

Job's Third Speech: A Response to Bildad

9 Then Job spoke again:
2 "Yes, I know this is all true in principle. But how can a person be declared
innocent in the eyes of God? 3 If someone wanted to take God to court,* would it be
possible to answer him even once in a thousand times? 4 For God is so wise and so
mighty. Who has ever challenged him successfully?
5 "Without warning, he moves the mountains, overturning them in his anger. 6 He
shakes the earth from its place, and its foundations tremble. 7 If he commands it, the sun
won't rise and the stars won't shine. 8 He alone has spread out the heavens and marches
on the waves of the sea. 9 He made all the stars—the Bear, Orion, the Pleiades, and the
constellations of the southern sky. 10 His great works are too marvelous to understand.
He performs miracles without number.
11 Yet when he comes near, I cannot see him. When he moves on, I do not see him go.
12 If he sends death to snatch someone away, who can stop him? Who dares to ask him,
'What are you doing?' 13 And God does not restrain his anger. The mightiest forces
against him* are crushed beneath his feet.
14 "And who am I, that I should try to answer God or even reason with him? 15 Even
if I were innocent, I would have no defense. I could only plead for mercy. 16 And even if
I summoned him and he responded, he would never listen to me. 17 For he attacks me
without reason,* and he multiplies my wounds without cause. 18 He will not let me catch
my breath, but fills me instead with bitter sorrows. 19 As for strength, he has it. As for
justice, who can challenge him? 20 Though I am innocent, my own mouth would
pronounce me guilty. Though I am blameless, it* would prove me wicked.

9:3 Or *If God wanted to take a person to court.* **9:13** Hebrew *The helpers of Rahab,* the name of a mythical sea monster that represents chaos in ancient literature. **9:17** As in Syriac version; Hebrew reads *with a storm.* **9:20** Or *he.*

8:6 Job 22:27; Ps 7:6
8:7 Job 42:12
8:8 Deut 4:32; 32:7; Job 15:18
8:13 Ps 9:17
8:15 Job 27:18; Ps 49:11
8:16 Pss 37:35; 80:11
8:19 Job 20:5
8:21 Pss 126:1-2; 132:16
8:22 Job 8:15; Ps 132:18
9:2 Job 4:17; 25:4
9:5 Job 26:6-14
9:6 Isa 2:19, 21; 13:13; Hag 2:6; Heb 12:26
9:7 Isa 13:10
9:8 Gen 1:1; Pss 77:19; 104:2; Isa 40:22
9:11 Job 23:8-9
9:12 Job 10:7; 11:10; Isa 45:9
9:13 Job 26:12; Ps 89:10
9:15 Job 8:5; 10:15
9:17 Job 16:12, 14
9:18 Job 27:2
9:20 Job 9:15, 29

8:14, 15 Bildad wrongly assumed that Job was trusting in something other than God for security, so he pointed out that such supports will collapse. One of man's basic needs is security, and people will do almost anything to feel secure. Eventually, however, our money, possessions, knowledge, and relationships will fail or be gone. Only God can give lasting security. What have you trusted for your security? How lasting is it? If you have a secure foundation with God, feelings of insecurity will not undermine you.

9:1ff Bildad said nothing new to Job. Job knew that the wicked ultimately perish, but his situation confused him. Why, then, was *he* perishing? Job didn't think his life warranted such suffering, so he wanted his case presented before God (9:32-35). He recognized, however, that arguing with God would be futile and unproductive (9:4). Job didn't claim to be perfect (7:20, 21; 9:20), but he did claim to be good and faithful (6:29, 30). While Job showed impatience toward God, he did not reject or curse God.

9:9 The Bear, Orion, and Pleiades are constellations of stars.

9:20, 21 "Though I am innocent, my mouth would pronounce me guilty." Job was saying, "In spite of my good life, God is determined to condemn me." As his suffering continued, he became more impatient. Although Job remained loyal to God, he made statements he would later regret. In times of extended sickness or prolonged pain, it is natural for people to doubt, to despair, or to become impatient. During those times, people need someone to listen to them, to help them work through their feelings and frustrations. Your patience with their impatience will help them.

21“I am innocent, but it makes no difference to me—I despise my life. 22Innocent or
wicked, it is all the same to him. That is why I say, ‘He destroys both the blameless and
the wicked.’ 23He laughs when a plague suddenly kills the innocent. 24The whole earth
is in the hands of the wicked, and God blinds the eyes of the judges and lets them be
unfair. If not he, then who?

25“My life passes more swiftly than a runner. It flees away, filled with tragedy. 26It
disappears like a swift boat, like an eagle that swoops down on its prey. 27If I decided to
forget my complaints, if I decided to end my sadness and be cheerful, 28I would dread
all the pain he would send. For I know you will not hold me innocent, O God.
29Whatever happens, I will be found guilty. So what’s the use of trying? 30Even if I were
to wash myself with soap and cleanse my hands with lye to make them absolutely clean,
31you would plunge me into a muddy ditch, and I would be so filthy my own clothing
would hate me.

32“God is not a mortal like me, so I cannot argue with him or take him to trial. 33If
only there were a mediator who could bring us together, but there is none. 34The
mediator could make God stop beating me, and I would no longer live in terror of his
punishment. 35Then I could speak to him without fear, but I cannot do that in my own
strength.

Job Frames His Plea to God

10 “I am disgusted with my life. Let me complain freely. I will speak in the
bitterness of my soul. 2I will say to God, ‘Don’t simply condemn me—tell me
the charge you are bringing against me. 3What do you gain by oppressing me? Why
do you reject me, the work of your own hands, while sending joy and prosperity to
the wicked? 4Are your eyes only those of a human? Do you see things as people see
them? 5Is your lifetime merely human? Is your life so short 6that you are in a hurry
to probe for my guilt, to search for my sin? 7Although you know I am not guilty, no
one can rescue me from your power.

8“‘You formed me with your hands; you made me, and yet you completely destroy
me. 9Remember that I am made of dust—will you turn me back to dust so soon? 10You
guided my conception and formed me in the womb.* 11You clothed me with skin and
flesh, and you knit my bones and sinews together. 12You gave me life and showed me
your unfailing love. My life was preserved by your care.

13“‘Yet your real motive—I know this was your intent—14was to watch me, and if I
sinned, you would not forgive my iniquity. 15If I am guilty, too bad for me. And even if
I’m innocent, I am filled with shame and misery so that I can’t hold my head high. 16And
if I hold my head high, you hunt me like a lion and display your awesome power against
me. 17Again and again you witness against me. You pour out an ever-increasing volume
of anger upon me and bring fresh armies against me.

18“‘Why, then, did you bring me out of my mother’s womb? Why didn’t you let me
die at birth? 19Then I would have been spared this miserable existence. I would have
gone directly from the womb to the grave. 20I have only a little time left, so leave me
alone—that I may have a little moment of comfort 21before I leave for the land of
darkness and utter gloom, never to return. 22It is a land as dark as midnight, a land of
utter gloom where confusion reigns and the light is as dark as midnight.’”

10:10 Hebrew *You poured me out like milk and curdled me like cheese.*

9:22 Eccl 9:2-3
9:24 Job 12:6, 17; 16:11
9:25 Job 7:6-7
9:26 Hab 1:8
9:28 Job 3:25; 7:21; 10:14
9:29 Ps 37:33
9:30 Job 31:7; Jer 2:22
9:32 1 Sam 2:25; Rom 9:20
9:33 1 Sam 2:25
9:34 Ps 39:10
10:1 1 Kgs 19:4; Job 7:11, 16
10:2 Job 9:29
10:3 Job 9:22-24; 10:8; 19:6; 21:16; 22:18
10:4 1 Sam 16:7; Job 9:12; 36:26
10:8 Job 9:22; Ps 119:73
10:9 Job 4:19; 7:21; 33:6
10:12 Job 33:4
10:13 Job 23:13
10:14 Job 9:28
10:15 Job 6:29; Isa 3:11
10:16 Job 5:9
10:17 Job 7:1; 16:8
10:18 Job 3:11-13
10:20 Job 7:19; 14:1
10:21 Ps 23:4; 88:12

10:1 Job began to wallow in self-pity. When we face baffling affliction, our pain lures us toward feeling sorry for ourselves. At this point we are only one step from self-righteousness, where we keep track of life’s injustices and say, “Look what happened to me; how unfair it is!” We may feel like blaming God. Remember that life’s trials, whether allowed by God or sent by God, can be the means for development and refinement. When facing trials, ask, “What can I learn and how can I grow?” rather than “Who did this to me and how can I get out of it?”

10:13, 14 In frustration, Job jumped to the false conclusion that God was out to get him. Wrong assumptions lead to wrong conclusions. We dare not take our limited experiences and jump to conclusions about life in general. If you find yourself doubting God, remember that you don’t have all the facts. God wants only the very best for your life. Many people endure great pain, but ultimately they find some greater good came from it. When you’re struggling, don’t assume the worst.

10:20-22 Job was expressing the view of death common in Old Testament times, that the dead went to a joyless, dark place. There was no punishment or reward there, and no escape from it. (See the note on 19:25-27 for a broader picture of Job’s view of death.)

Zophar's First Response to Job

11 Then Zophar the Naamathite replied to Job:
2 “Shouldn't someone answer this torrent of words? Is a person proved innocent just by talking a lot? 3 Should I remain silent while you babble on? When you mock God, shouldn't someone make you ashamed? 4 You claim, ‘My teaching is pure,’ and ‘I am clean in the sight of God.’ 5 If only God would speak; if only he would tell you what he thinks! 6 If only he would tell you the secrets of wisdom, for true wisdom is not a simple matter. Listen! God is doubtless punishing you far less than you deserve!

7 “Can you solve the mysteries of God? Can you discover everything there is to know about the Almighty? 8 Such knowledge is higher than the heavens—but who are you? It is deeper than the underworld*—what can you know in comparison to him? 9 It is broader than the earth and wider than the sea. 10 If God comes along and puts a person in prison, or if he calls the court to order, who is going to stop him? 11 For he knows those who are false, and he takes note of all their sins. 12 An empty-headed person won't become wise any more than a wild donkey can bear human offspring*!

13 “If only you would prepare your heart and lift up your hands to him in prayer! 14 Get rid of your sins and leave all iniquity behind you. 15 Then your face will brighten in innocence. You will be strong and free of fear. 16 You will forget your misery. It will all be gone like water under the bridge. 17 Your life will be brighter than the noonday. Any darkness will be as bright as morning. 18 You will have courage because you will have hope. You will be protected and will rest in safety. 19 You will lie down unafraid, and many will look to you for help. 20 But the wicked will lose hope. They have no escape. Their hope becomes despair.”

Job's Fourth Speech: A Response to Zophar

12 Then Job spoke again:
2 “You really know everything, don't you? And when you die, wisdom will die with you! 3 Well, I know a few things myself—and you're no better than I am. Who doesn't know these things you've been saying? 4 Yet my friends laugh at me. I am a man who calls on God and receives an answer. I am a just and blameless man, yet they laugh at me. 5 People who are at ease mock those in trouble. They give a push to people who are stumbling. 6 But even robbers are left in peace, and those who provoke God—and God has them in his power—live in safety!

7 “Ask the animals, and they will teach you. Ask the birds of the sky, and they will tell you. 8 Speak to the earth, and it will instruct you. Let the fish of the sea speak to you. 9 They all know that the LORD has done this. 10 For the life of every living thing is in his hand, and the breath of all humanity. 11 Just as the mouth tastes good food, so the ear tests the words it hears. 12 Wisdom belongs to the aged, and understanding to those who have lived many years.

13 “But true wisdom and power are with God; counsel and understanding are his. 14 What he destroys cannot be rebuilt. When he closes in on someone, there is no escape. 15 If he holds back the rain, the earth becomes a desert. If he releases the waters, they flood the earth.

16 “Yes, strength and wisdom are with him; deceivers and deceived are both in his power. 17 He leads counselors away stripped of good judgment; he drives judges to

11:8 Hebrew *Sheol.* **11:12** Or *bear a tame colt.*

11:3 Job 17:2; 21:3
11:4 Job 6:10; 10:7
11:6 Job 22:5
11:7 Job 33:12-13; 36:26; 37:5
11:8 Job 22:12; 38:17
11:13 Pss 78:8; 88:9
11:15 Pss 27:3; 46:2
11:16 Job 22:11; Isa 65:16
11:17 Ps 37:6
11:19 Lev 26:6; Zeph 3:13
11:20 Deut 28:65; Job 6:9; 34:22
12:2 Job 17:10
12:4 Job 6:29; 17:6; 30:1, 9-10
12:6 Job 9:24; 21:7-9
12:9 Isa 41:20
12:11 Job 33:4; 34:3
12:12 Job 32:7
12:13 Job 9:4; 11:6
12:14 Job 19:10; 37:7; Isa 25:2
12:15 Gen 7:11-24; Deut 11:17; 1 Kgs 8:35
12:16 Job 13:7, 9

11:1ff Zophar is the third of Job's friends to speak, and the least courteous. Full of anger, he lashed out at Job, saying that Job deserved more punishment, not less. Zophar took the same position as Eliphaz (chapters 4–5) and Bildad (chapter 8)—that Job was suffering because of sin—but his speech was by far the most arrogant. Zophar was the kind of person who has an answer for everything; he was totally insensitive to Job's unique situation. (For more on Zophar, see the chart in chapter 28.)

11:11 By calling Job “false,” Zophar was accusing Job of hiding secret faults and sins. Although Zophar's assumption was wrong, he explained quite accurately that God knows and sees everything. We are often tempted by the thought “No one will ever know!” Perhaps we can hide some sin from others, but we can do *nothing* without God knowing about it. Because our very thoughts are known to God, of course he will notice our sins. Job understood this as well as Zophar did, but it didn't apply to his current dilemma.

12:1ff Job answered Zophar's argument with great sarcasm: “Wisdom will die with you!” He went on to say that his three friends didn't need to explain God to him—they were saying nothing he didn't already know (12:7-9; 13:1, 2). Job continued to maintain that his friends had completely misunderstood the reason for his suffering. Job did not know it either, but he was certain that his friends' reasons were both narrow-minded and incorrect. Once again Job appealed to God to give him an answer (13:3).

12:18 Ps 116:16
madness. [18]He removes the royal robe of kings. With ropes around their waist, they are
12:21 Job 12:18; 34:19 Ps 107:40
led away. [19]He leads priests away stripped of status; he overthrows the mighty. [20]He
silences the trusted adviser, and he removes the insight of the elders. [21]He pours disgrace
upon princes and confiscates weapons from the strong.
12:22 Dan 2:22 1 Cor 4:5
[22]"He floods the darkness with light; he brings light to the deepest gloom. [23]He raises
up nations, and he destroys them. He makes nations expand, and he abandons them. [24]He
12:23 Isa 9:3
takes away the understanding of kings, and he leaves them wandering in a wasteland
12:24 Job 12:20
without a path. [25]They grope in the darkness without a light. He makes them stagger like
drunkards.

Job Wants to Argue His Case with God

13 "Look, I have seen many instances such as you describe. I understand what you
13:3 Job 13:22; 23:4
are saying. [2]I know as much as you do. You are no better than I am. [3]Oh, how I
long to speak directly to the Almighty. I want to argue my case with God himself. [4]For
13:4 Ps 119:69 Jer 23:32
you are smearing me with lies. As doctors, you are worthless quacks. [5]Please be quiet!
That's the smartest thing you could do. [6]Listen to my charge; pay attention to my
13:5 Prov 17:28
arguments.
13:7 Job 27:4
[7]"Are you defending God by means of lies and dishonest arguments? [8]You should be
impartial witnesses, but will you slant your testimony in his favor? Will you argue God's
13:10 Job 32:21
case for him? [9]Be careful that he doesn't find out what you are doing! Or do you think
you can fool him as easily as you fool people? [10]No, you will be in serious trouble with
13:12 Job 15:3
him if even in your hearts you slant your testimony in his favor. [11]Doesn't his majesty
strike terror into your heart? Does not your fear of him seize you? [12]Your statements
13:13 Job 13:5
have about as much value as ashes. Your defense is as fragile as a clay pot.
13:15 Job 7:6; 27:5
[13]"Be silent now and leave me alone. Let me speak—and I will face the consequences.
[14]Yes, I will take my life in my hands and say what I really think. [15]God might kill me,
13:16 Job 34:21-23
but I cannot wait. I am going to argue my case with him. [16]But this is what will save me:
that I am not godless. If I were, I would be thrown from his presence.
13:18 Job 9:21; 23:4
[17]"Listen closely to what I am about to say. Hear me out. [18]I have prepared my case;
13:19 Isa 50:8
I will be proved innocent. [19]Who can argue with me over this? If you could prove me
wrong, I would remain silent until I die.

Job Asks How He Has Sinned

13:21 Job 9:34 Ps 39:10
[20]"O God, there are two things I beg of you, and I will be able to face you. [21]Remove
your hand from me, and don't terrify me with your awesome presence. [22]Now summon
13:24 Job 19:11; 33:10 Ps 13:1
me, and I will answer! Or let me speak to you, and you reply. [23]Tell me, what have I done
wrong? Show me my rebellion and my sin. [24]Why do you turn away from me? Why do
13:25 Lev 26:36
you consider me your enemy? [25]Would you terrify a leaf that is blown by the wind?
Would you chase a dry stalk of grass?
13:26 Ps 25:7
[26]"You write bitter accusations against me and bring up all the sins of my youth. [27]You
put my feet in stocks. You watch all my paths. You trace all my footprints. [28]I waste away
like rotting wood, like a moth-eaten coat.

14:1 Job 5:7 Eccl 2:23
14 "How frail is humanity! How short is life, and how full of trouble! [2]Like a flower,
we blossom for a moment and then wither. Like the shadow of a passing cloud,
we quickly disappear. [3]Must you keep an eye on such a frail creature and demand an

---

12:24, 25 Job affirmed that no leader has any real wisdom apart from God. No research or report can outweigh God's opinion. No scientific discovery or medical advance takes him by surprise. When we look for guidance for our decisions, we must recognize that God's wisdom is superior to any the world has to offer. Don't let earthly advisers dampen your desire to know God better.

13:4 Job compared his three friends to doctors who did not know what they were doing. They were like eye surgeons trying to perform open-heart surgery. Many of their ideas about God were true, but they did not apply to Job's situation. They were right to say that God is just. They were right to say God punishes sin. But they were wrong to assume that Job's suffering was a just punishment for his sin. They took a true principle and applied it wrongly, ignoring the vast differences in human circumstances. We must be careful and compassionate in how we apply biblical condemnations to others; we must be slow to judge.

14:1ff Life is short and full of trouble, Job laments in his closing remarks. Sickness, loneliness, disappointment, and death cause Job to say that life is not fair. Some understand verses 14 and 15 to mean that, even in his gloom, Job hoped for the resurrection of the dead. If this is true, then Job understood the one truth that could put his suffering in perspective. God's solution to believers who live in an unfair world is to guarantee life with him forever. No matter how unfair your present world seems, God offers the hope of being in his presence eternally. Have you accepted this offer?

accounting from me? 4 Who can create purity in one born impure? No one! 5 You have 14:4 Job 15:14; 25:4
decided the length of our lives. You know how many months we will live, and we are 14:5
not given a minute longer. 6 So give us a little rest, won't you? Turn away your angry Job 21:21
stare. We are like hired hands, so let us finish the task you have given us.
7 "If a tree is cut down, there is hope that it will sprout again and grow new branches.
8 Though its roots have grown old in the earth and its stump decays, 9 at the scent of water
it may bud and sprout again like a new seedling.
10 "But when people die, they lose all strength. They breathe their last, and then where 14:10 Job 13:19
are they? 11 As water evaporates from a lake and as a river disappears in drought, 14:11
12 people lie down and do not rise again. Until the heavens are no more, they will not Isa 19:5
wake up nor be roused from their sleep.
13 "I wish you would hide me with the dead and forget me there until your anger has 14:13
passed. But mark your calendar to think of me again! 14 If mortals die, can they live Isa 26:20
again? This thought would give me hope, and through my struggle I would eagerly wait 14:16 Job 10:6; 31:4;
for release. 15 You would call and I would answer, and you would yearn for me, your 34:21
handiwork. 16 For then you would count my steps, instead of watching for my sins. 17 My Prov 5:21
sins would be sealed in a pouch, and you would cover over my iniquity. 14:17 Deut 32:32-34
18 "But as mountains fall and crumble and as rocks fall from a cliff, 19 as water wears 14:19
away the stones and floods wash away the soil, so you destroy people's hope. 20 You Job 7:6
always overpower them, and then they pass from the scene. You disfigure them in death 14:20 Job 20:7; 34:20
and send them away. 21 They never know if their sons grow up in honor or sink to 14:21
insignificance. 22 They are absorbed in their own pain and grief." Eccl 9:5

2. Second round of discussion

Eliphaz's Second Response to Job

15 Then Eliphaz the Temanite replied:
2 "You are supposed to be a wise man, and yet you give us all this foolish talk. 15:4
You are nothing but a windbag. 3 It isn't right to speak so foolishly. What good do such Job 5:12-13
words do? 4 Have you no fear of God, no reverence for him? 5 Your sins are telling your 15:7 Job 38:4, 21
mouth what to say. Your words are based on clever deception. 6 But why should I Prov 8:25
condemn you? Your own mouth does! 15:8 Rom 11:34
7 "Were you the first person ever born? Were you born before the hills were made? 15:11
8 Were you listening at God's secret council? Do you have a monopoly on wisdom? Job 6:10
9 What do you know that we don't? What do you understand that we don't? 10 On our side 15:12 Job 36:13
are aged, gray-haired men much older than your father!
11 "Is God's comfort too little for you? Is his gentle word not enough? 12 What has 15:14 Prov 20:9
captured your reason? What has weakened your vision, 13 that you turn against God and Eccl 7:20
say all these evil things? 14 Can a mortal be pure? Can a human be just? 15 Why, God 15:15 Job 4:18; 25:5
doesn't even trust the angels*! Even the heavens cannot be absolutely pure in his sight. 15:16 Job 34:7
16 How much less pure is a corrupt and sinful person with a thirst for wickedness! Ps 14:1, 3
17 "If you will listen, I will answer you from my own experience. 18 And it is confirmed 15:18 Job 8:8

15:15 Hebrew *the holy ones.*

14:7-22 The Old Testament does not say much about the resurrection of the dead. This is not surprising because Jesus had not yet conquered death. Job's pessimism about death is understandable. What is remarkable is his budding hope (14:14). If only God would hide him with the dead and then bring him out again! If only he could die and live again! When we must endure suffering, we have an advantage over Job. We *know* that the dead will rise. Christ arose, and we have hope based on Christ's promise in John 14:19.

14:22 Job's profound speech in this chapter illustrates a great truth: To have a right set of doctrines is not enough. To know what to believe is not all that is required to please God. Truth untested by life's experiences may become static and stagnant. Suffering can bring a dynamic quality to life. Just as drought drives the roots of a tree deeper to find water, so suffering can drive us beyond superficial acceptance of truth to dependence on God for hope and life.

15:1ff With the first round of talks concluded, each friend, in the same order, pressed the argument further. Again Job answered each argument (chapters 15–31). This time Eliphaz was more rude, more intense, and more threatening, but he said nothing new. (See his first speech in chapters 4–5.) He began by saying that Job's words were empty and useless; then he restated his opinion that Job must be a great sinner. According to Eliphaz, the experience and wisdom of their ancestors were more valuable than Job's individual thoughts. Eliphaz assumed that his words were as true as God's. It is easy to spot his arrogance.

15:15, 16 "Even the heavens cannot be absolutely pure in his sight." Eliphaz was repeating his argument that anything created, whether angels or people, is not a sufficient basis for trust and hope. Only in God can we be sure. (See the note on 4:18, 19.)

by the experience of wise men who have heard the same thing from their fathers, 19 those to whom the land was given long before any foreigners arrived.

20 "Wicked people are in pain throughout their lives. 21 They are surrounded by terrors, and even on good days they fear the attack of the destroyer. 22 They dare not go out into the darkness for fear they will be murdered. 23 They wander abroad for bread, saying, 'Where is it?'* They know their ruin is certain. 24 That dark day terrifies them. They live in distress and anguish, like a king preparing for an attack. 25 For they have clenched their fists against God, defying the Almighty. 26 Holding their strong shields, they defiantly charge against him.

27 "These wicked people are fat and rich, 28 but their cities will be ruined. They will live in abandoned houses that are ready to tumble down. 29 They will not continue to be rich. Their wealth will not endure, and their possessions will no longer spread across the horizon.

30 "They will not escape the darkness. The flame will burn them up, and the breath of God will destroy everything they have. 31 Let them no longer trust in empty riches. They are only fooling themselves, for emptiness will be their only reward. 32 They will be cut down in the prime of life, and all they counted on will disappear. 33 They will be like a vine whose grapes are harvested before they are ripe, like an olive tree that sheds its blossoms so the fruit cannot form. 34 For the godless are barren. Their homes, enriched through bribery, will be consumed by fire. 35 They conceive trouble and evil, and their hearts give birth only to deceit."

Job's Fifth Speech: A Response to Eliphaz

16 Then Job spoke again:

2 "I have heard all this before. What miserable comforters you are! 3 Won't you ever stop your flow of foolish words? What have I said that makes you speak so endlessly? 4 I could say the same things if you were in my place. I could spout off my criticisms against you and shake my head at you. 5 But that's not what I would do. I would speak in a way that helps you. I would try to take away your grief. 6 But as it is, my grief remains no matter how I defend myself. And it does not help if I refuse to speak.

7 "O God, you have ground me down and devastated my family. 8 You have reduced me to skin and bones—as proof, they say, of my sins. 9 God hates me and tears angrily at my flesh. He gnashes his teeth at me and pierces me with his eyes. 10 People jeer and laugh at me. They slap my cheek in contempt. A mob gathers against me. 11 God has handed me over to sinners. He has tossed me into the hands of the wicked.

12 "I was living quietly until he broke me apart. He took me by the neck and dashed me to pieces. Then he set me up as his target. 13 His archers surrounded me, and his arrows pierced me without mercy. The ground is wet with my blood.* 14 Again and again he smashed me, charging at me like a warrior. 15 Here I sit in sackcloth. I have surrendered, and I sit in the dust. 16 My eyes are red with weeping; darkness covers my eyes. 17 Yet I am innocent, and my prayer is pure.

18 "O earth, do not conceal my blood. Let it cry out on my behalf. 19 Even now my witness is in heaven. My advocate is there on high. 20 My friends scorn me, but I pour out my tears to God. 21 Oh, that someone would mediate between God and me, as a person mediates between friends. 22 For soon I must go down that road from which I will never return.

15:21 Job 18:11; 20:21, 25
15:22 Job 15:30; 19:29; 27:14
15:25 Job 36:9
15:27 Pss 73:7; 119:70
15:29 Job 27:16-17
15:30 Job 4:9; 5:14; 22:20
15:31 Isa 59:4
15:32 Job 18:16; 22:16
15:34 Job 8:22
15:35 Ps 7:14; Isa 59:4
16:2 Job 13:4; 21:34
16:4 Pss 22:7; 109:25
16:6 Job 9:27-28
16:7 Job 7:3; 16:20; 19:13-15
16:8 Job 10:17; 19:20
16:9 Job 13:24; 33:10
16:12 Job 7:20; 9:17
16:13 Job 6:4; 19:12
16:14 Job 9:17; Joel 2:7
16:15 Gen 37:34; Job 30:19; Ps 69:11
16:16 Job 16:20; 24:17
16:17 Job 27:4; Jon 3:8
16:19 Job 19:25-27; 31:2

15:23 Greek version reads *He is appointed to be food for a vulture.* **16:13** Hebrew *my gall.*

16:1ff Job's friends were supposed to be comforting him in his grief. Instead, they condemned him for causing his own suffering. Job began his reply to Eliphaz by calling him and his friends "miserable comforters." Job's words reveal several ways to become a better comforter to those in pain: (1) Don't talk just for the sake of talking; (2) don't sermonize by giving pat answers; (3) don't accuse or criticize; (4) put yourself in the other person's place; and (5) offer help and encouragement. Try Job's suggestions, knowing that they are given by a person who needed great comfort. The best comforters are those who know something about personal suffering.

16:19 Job was afraid that God had abandoned him. Yet he appealed directly to God (his witness and advocate) and to God's knowledge of his innocence. A *witness* is someone who has seen what has happened, and an *advocate* is like a lawyer who speaks on behalf of the plaintiff. By using these terms, Job showed he had cast all his hope for any fair defense upon God in heaven because he would probably die before it happened on earth. In the New Testament we learn that Jesus Christ intercedes on our behalf (Hebrews 7:25; 1 John 2:1); therefore, we have nothing to fear.

Job Continues to Defend His Innocence

17 "My spirit is crushed, and I am near death. The grave is ready to receive me. 2 I
am surrounded by mockers. I watch how bitterly they taunt me.
3 "You must defend my innocence, O God, since no one else will stand up for me. 4 You
have closed their minds to understanding, but do not let them triumph. 5 They denounce
their companions for their own advantage, so let their children faint with hunger.
6 "God has made a mockery of me among the people; they spit in my face. 7 My eyes are
dim with weeping, and I am but a shadow of my former self. 8 The upright are astonished
when they see me. The innocent are aroused against the ungodly. 9 The righteous will move
onward and forward, and those with pure hearts will become stronger and stronger.
10 "As for all of you, come back and try again! But I will not find a wise man among
you. 11 My days are over. My hopes have disappeared. My heart's desires are broken.
12 They say that night is day and day is night; how they pervert the truth! 13 I might go to
the grave and make my bed in darkness. 14 And I might call the grave my father, and the
worm my mother and my sister. 15 But where then is my hope? Can anyone find it? 16 No,
my hope will go down with me to the grave. We will rest together in the dust!"

Bildad's Second Response to Job

18 Then Bildad the Shuhite replied:
2 "How long before you stop talking? Speak sense if you want us to answer! 3 Do
you think we are cattle? Do you think we have no intelligence? 4 You may tear your hair out
in anger, but will that cause the earth to be abandoned? Will it make rocks fall from a cliff?
5 "The truth remains that the light of the wicked will be snuffed out. The sparks of their
fire will not glow. 6 The light in their tent will grow dark. The lamp hanging above them
will be quenched. 7 The confident stride of the wicked will be shortened. Their own
schemes will be their downfall.
8 "The wicked walk into a net. They fall into a pit that's been dug in the path. 9 A trap
grabs them by the heel. A noose tightens around them. 10 A snare lies hidden in the
ground. A rope lies coiled on their path.
11 "Terrors surround the wicked and trouble them at every step. 12 Their vigor is
depleted by hunger, and calamity waits for them to stumble. 13 Disease eats their skin;
death devours their limbs. 14 They are torn from the security of their tent, and they are
brought down to the king of terrors. 15 The home of the wicked will disappear beneath a
fiery barrage of burning sulfur. 16 Their roots will dry up, and their branches will wither.
17 All memory of their existence will perish from the earth. No one will remember them.
18 They will be thrust from light into darkness, driven from the world. 19 They will have
neither children nor grandchildren, nor any survivor in their home country. 20 People in
the west are appalled at their fate; people in the east are horrified. 21 They will say, 'This
was the home of a wicked person, the place of one who rejected God.'"

Job's Sixth Speech: A Response to Bildad

19 Then Job spoke again:
2 "How long will you torture me? How long will you try to break me with your
words? 3 Ten times now you have meant to insult me. You should be ashamed of dealing

17:1 Ps 88:3-4
17:3 Ps 119:122
17:6 Job 30:9-10
17:9 Job 22:30
17:10 Job 12:2
17:11 Job 7:6
17:13 Job 3:13
17:14 Job 21:26
17:15 Job 7:6
17:16 Job 3:17; 21:33
18:3 Ps 73:22
18:5 Job 21:17
18:8 Job 22:10
18:11 Job 15:21; 18:18
18:14 Job 8:22; 15:21
18:16 Isa 5:24, Hos 9:1-16, Amos 2:9
18:17 Job 24:20, Ps 34:16, Prov 10:7
18:18 Job 5:14; 27:21-23
18:19 Job 27:14-15, Isa 14:22, Jer 22:30
18:20 Jer 50:27, Obad 1:12

17:10 Job's three friends had a reputation for being wise, but Job could not find wisdom in any of them. God backed up Job's claim in 42:7, when he condemned these men for their false portrayal of him. Obviously these men had a faulty view of wisdom. They assumed that because they were prosperous and successful, God must be pleased with the way they were living and thinking. Job, however, told his friends that they were starting with the wrong idea because earthly success and prosperity are not a reward for faith in God. Likewise, trouble and affliction do not prove faithlessness. The truly wise man knows that wisdom comes from God alone, not from human successes or failures. And the truly wise man never forsakes God. God's wisdom proved superior to Job and to all his friends.

17:15 Job was giving up hope of any future restoration of wealth and family and wrapping himself in thoughts of death and the rest from grief and pain it promised. The rewards that Job's friends described were all related to this present life. They were silent about the possibility of life after death. We must not evaluate life only in terms of this present world, because God promises a never-ending, wonderful future to those who are faithful to him.

18:1ff Bildad thought he knew how the universe should be run, and he saw Job as an illustration of the consequences of sin. Bildad rejected Job's side of the story because it did not fit in with his outlook on life. It is easy to condemn Bildad because his errors are obvious; unfortunately, however, we often act the same way when our ideas are threatened.

18:14 The "king of terrors" is a figure of speech referring to death. Bildad viewed death as a great devourer (18:13), but the Bible teaches that God has the power to devour even death (Psalm 49:15; Isaiah 25:8; 1 Corinthians 15:54-56).

19:5 Pss 35:26; 38:16
19:6 Job 18:8-10; 27:2 Ps 66:11
19:7 Hab 1:2
19:8 Lam 3:7, 9
19:9 Ps 89:39, 44 Lam 5:16
19:13 Pss 69:8; 88:8, 18
19:19 Pss 38:11; 55:12-13
19:20 Ps 102:5 Lam 4:8
19:22 Pss 16:11; 69:26
19:23 Isa 30:8 Jer 36:2
19:25 Ps 78:35 Isa 43:14 Jer 50:34
19:26 Matt 5:8 1 Cor 13:12 1 Jn 3:2
19:29 Ps 9:7 Eccl 12:14

with me so harshly. 4And even if I have sinned, that is my concern, not yours. 5You are
trying to overcome me, using my humiliation as evidence of my sin, 6but it is God who
has wronged me. I cannot defend myself, for I am like a city under siege.

7"I cry out for help, but no one hears me. I protest, but there is no justice. 8God has
blocked my way and plunged my path into darkness. 9He has stripped me of my honor
and removed the crown from my head. 10He has demolished me on every side, and I am
finished. He has destroyed my hope. 11His fury burns against me; he counts me as an
enemy. 12His troops advance. They build up roads to attack me. They camp all around
my tent.

13"My relatives stay far away, and my friends have turned against me. 14My neighbors
and my close friends are all gone. 15The members of my household have forgotten me. The
servant girls consider me a stranger. I am like a foreigner to them. 16I call my servant, but
he doesn't come; I even plead with him! 17My breath is repulsive to my wife. I am
loathsome to my own family. 18Even young children despise me. When I stand to speak,
they turn their backs on me. 19My close friends abhor me. Those I loved have turned against
me. 20I have been reduced to skin and bones and have escaped death by the skin of my teeth.

21"Have mercy on me, my friends, have mercy, for the hand of God has struck me.
22Why must you persecute me as God does? Why aren't you satisfied with my anguish?
23"Oh, that my words could be written. Oh, that they could be inscribed on a monument,
24carved with an iron chisel and filled with lead, engraved forever in the rock.

25"But as for me, I know that my Redeemer lives, and that he will stand upon the earth
at last. 26And after my body has decayed, yet in my body I will see God*! 27I will see
him for myself. Yes, I will see him with my own eyes. I am overwhelmed at the thought!

28"How dare you go on persecuting me, saying, 'It's his own fault'? 29I warn you, you
yourselves are in danger of punishment for your attitude. Then you will know that there
is judgment."

Zophar's Second Response to Job

20:3 Job 19:3
20:5 Job 8:12-13 Ps 37:35-36
20:6 Isa 14:13-14 Obad 1:3-4

20 Then Zophar the Naamathite replied:
2"I must reply because I am greatly disturbed. 3I have had to endure your
insults, but now my spirit prompts me to reply.

4"Don't you realize that ever since people were first placed on the earth, 5the triumph
of the wicked has been short-lived and the joy of the godless has been only temporary?
6Though the godless man's pride reaches to the heavens and though his head touches the

19:26 Or *without my body I will see God.*

19:3-5 It is easy to point out someone else's faults or sins. Job's friends accused him of sin to make him feel guilty, not to encourage or correct him. If we feel we must admonish someone, we should be sure we are confronting that person because we love him, not because we are annoyed, inconvenienced, or seeking to blame him.

19:6 Job felt that God was treating him as an enemy when, in fact, God was his friend and thought highly of him (1:8; 2:3). In his difficulty, Job pointed at the wrong person. It was Satan, not God, who was Job's enemy. Because they stressed ultimate causes, most Israelites believed that both good and evil came from God; they also thought people were responsible for their own destinies. But the evil power loose in this world accounts for much of the suffering we experience. In verse 7, Job continued to cry out to be heard by God.

19:25-27 At the heart of the book of Job comes his ringing affirmation of confidence: "I know that my Redeemer lives." In ancient Israel a *redeemer* was a family member who bought a slave's way to freedom or who took care of a widow (see the note on Ruth 3:1). What tremendous faith Job had, especially in light of the fact that he was unaware of the conference between God and Satan. Job thought that God had brought all these disasters upon him! Faced with death and decay, Job still expected to see God—and he expected to do so in his body. When the book of Job was written, Israel did not have a well-developed doctrine of the resurrection. Although Job struggled with the idea that God was presently against him, he firmly believed that in the end God would be on his side. This belief was so strong that Job became one of the first to talk about the resurrection of the body (see also Psalm 16:10; Isaiah 26:19; Daniel 12:2, 13).

19:26 Job said: "In my body I will see God." In Job's situation, it seemed unlikely to him that he would, in his body, see God. And that's just the point of Job's faith! He was confident that God's justice would triumph, even if it would take a miracle like resurrection to accomplish this.

20:1ff Zophar's speech again revealed his false assumption because he based his arguments purely on the idea that Job was an evil hypocrite. Zophar said that although Job had it good for a while, he didn't live righteously, so God took his wealth from him. According to Zophar, Job's calamities *proved* his wickedness.

20:6, 7 Although Zophar was wrong in directing this tirade against Job, he was correct in talking about the final end of evil people. At first, sin seems enjoyable and attractive. Lying, stealing, or oppressing others often brings temporary gain to those who practice these sins. Some live a long time with ill-gotten gain. But in the end, God's justice will prevail. What Zophar missed is that judgment for these sins may not come in the lifetime of the sinner. Punishment may be deferred until the last judgment, when sinners will be eternally cut off from God. We should not be impressed with the success and power of evil people. God's judgment on them is certain.

clouds, 7yet he will perish forever, thrown away like his own dung. Those who knew
him will ask, 'Where is he?' 8He will fade like a dream and not be found. He will vanish
like a vision in the night. 9Neither his friends nor his family will ever see him again.
10His children will beg from the poor, for he must give back his ill-gotten wealth. 11He
was just a young man, but his bones will lie in the dust.

12"He enjoyed the taste of his wickedness, letting it melt under his tongue. 13He savored
it, holding it long in his mouth. 14But suddenly, the food he has eaten turns sour within
him, a poisonous venom in his stomach. 15He will vomit the wealth he swallowed. God
won't let him keep it down. 16He will suck the poison of snakes. The viper will kill him.
17He will never again enjoy abundant streams of olive oil or rivers of milk and honey.
18His labors will not be rewarded. His wealth will bring him no joy. 19For he oppressed
the poor and left them destitute. He foreclosed on their homes. 20He was always greedy
but never satisfied. Of all the things he dreamed about, nothing remains. 21Nothing is left
after he finishes gorging himself; therefore, his prosperity will not endure.

22"In the midst of plenty, he will run into trouble, and disasters will destroy him.
23May God give him a bellyful of trouble. May God rain down his anger upon him. 24He
will try to escape, but God's arrow will pierce him. 25The arrow is pulled from his body,
and the arrowhead glistens with blood.* The terrors of death are upon him.

26"His treasures will be lost in deepest darkness. A wildfire will devour his goods,
consuming all he has left. 27The heavens will reveal his guilt, and the earth will give
testimony against him. 28A flood will sweep away his house. God's anger will descend
on him in torrents. 29This is the fate that awaits the wicked. It is the inheritance decreed
by God."

Job's Seventh Speech: A Response to Zophar

21 Then Job spoke again:
2"Listen closely to what I am saying. You can console me by listening to me.
3Bear with me, and let me speak. After I have spoken, you may mock me.

4"My complaint is with God, not with people. No wonder I'm so impatient. 5Look at
me and be stunned. Put your hand over your mouth in shock. 6When I think about what
I am saying, I shudder. My body trembles.

7"The truth is that the wicked live to a good old age. They grow old and wealthy.
8They live to see their children grow to maturity, and they enjoy their grandchildren.
9Their homes are safe from every fear, and God does not punish them. 10Their bulls
never fail to breed. Their cows bear calves without miscarriage. 11Their children skip
about like lambs in a flock of sheep. 12They sing with tambourine and harp. They make
merry to the sound of the flute. 13They spend their days in prosperity; then they go down
to the grave in peace. 14All this, even though they say to God, 'Go away. We want no
part of you and your ways. 15Who is the Almighty, and why should we obey him? What
good will it do us if we pray?' 16But their prosperity is not of their own doing, so I will
have nothing to do with that kind of thinking.

17"Yet the wicked get away with it time and time again. They rarely have trouble, and
God skips them when he distributes sorrows in his anger. 18Are they driven before the
wind like straw? Are they carried away by the storm? Not at all!

19"'Well,' you say, 'at least God will punish their children!' But I say that God should
punish the ones who sin, not their children! Let them feel their own penalty. 20Let their
own eyes see their destruction. Let them drink deeply of the anger of the Almighty. 21For
when they are dead, they will not care what happens to their family.

22"But who can teach a lesson to God, the supreme Judge? 23One person dies in
prosperity and security, 24the very picture of good health. 25Another person dies in bitter

20:8 Pss 73:20; 90:5
20:10 Job 5:4; 27:16-17
20:16 Deut 32:24, 33
20:17 Deut 32:13-14
20:20 Eccl 5:13-15
20:21 Job 15:29
20:23 Num 11:18-20, 33; Ps 78:30-31
20:24 Isa 24:18; Amos 5:19
20:25 Job 16:13; 18:11
20:26 Job 15:30; 18:18; Ps 21:9
20:27 Deut 31:28
20:28 Deut 28:31
20:29 Job 27:13; 31:2-3
21:4 Job 6:11; 7:11
21:5 Judg 18:19; Job 29:9; 40:4
21:6 Ps 55:5
21:7 Ps 73:3; Jer 12:1
21:8 Ps 17:14
21:9 Ps 73:5
21:13 Job 36:11
21:18 Pss 1:4; 35:5; 83:13; Isa 17:13
21:19 Exod 20:5
21:20 Isa 51:17; Jer 25:15; Ezek 18:4; Rev 14:10
21:22 Job 36:22; Ps 82:1; Isa 40:13-14; Rom 11:34

20:25 Hebrew *with gall.*

21:1ff Job refuted Zophar's idea that evil people never experience wealth and happiness, pointing out that in the real world the wicked do indeed prosper. God does as he wills to individuals (21:22-25), and people cannot use their circumstances to measure their own goodness or God's—they are sometimes (but not always) related. Success to Job's friends was based on outward performance; success to God, however, is based on a person's heart.

21:22 Although baffled by the reasons for his suffering, Job affirmed God's superior understanding by asking, "Who can teach a lesson to God?" The way you respond to your personal struggles shows your attitude toward God. Rather than becoming angry with God, continue to trust him, no matter what your circumstances may be. Although it is sometimes difficult to see, God *is* in control. We must commit ourselves to him so we will not resent his timing.

21:26 Job 3:13; 24:20
21:28 Job 1:3
21:30 Job 20:29; Prov 16:4; Rom 2:5; 2 Pet 2:9
21:33 Job 3:19, 22; 17:16; 24:24
21:34 Job 16:2

poverty, never having tasted the good life. 26 Both alike are buried in the same dust, both
eaten by the same worms.
27 "Look, I know your thoughts. I know the schemes you plot against me. 28 You will
tell me of rich and wicked people who came to disaster because of their sins. 29 But I tell
you to ask those who have been around, and they can tell you the truth. 30 Evil people are
spared in times of calamity and are allowed to escape. 31 No one rebukes them openly.
No one repays them for what they have done. 32 When they are carried to the grave, an
honor guard keeps watch at their tomb. 33 A great funeral procession goes to the cemetery.
Many pay their respects as the body is laid to rest and the earth gives sweet repose.
34 "How can you comfort me? All your explanations are wrong!"

3. Third round of discussion

Eliphaz's Third Response to Job

22:2 Job 35:7; Luke 17:10
22:6 Exod 22:26; Deut 24:6, 17; Ezek 18:16
22:7 Job 31:31; Matt 10:42
22:8 Job 9:24; 12:19
22:9 Job 6:27; 24:3, 21
22:13 Pss 10:11; 64:5; 94:7; Isa 29:15
22:16 Job 14:14; 15:32; Matt 9:26-27
22:17 Job 21:14-15
22:18 Job 12:6; 21:16
22:19 Pss 58:10; 107:42
22:20 Job 15:30
22:22 Job 6:10; 23:12; Prov 2:6
22:23 Job 8:5; 11:14; Isa 19:22; Zech 1:3
22:24 Job 31:24-25

22 Then Eliphaz the Temanite replied:
2 "Can a person's actions be of benefit to God? Can even a wise person be helpful
to him? 3 Is it any pleasure to the Almighty if you are righteous? Would it be any gain to
him if you were perfect? 4 Is it because of your reverence for him that he accuses and
judges you? 5 Not at all! It is because of your wickedness! Your guilt has no limit!
6 "For example, you must have lent money to your friend and then kept the clothing
he gave you as a pledge. Yes, you stripped him to the bone. 7 You must have refused water
for the thirsty and food for the hungry. 8 After all, you think the land belongs to the
powerful and that those who are privileged have a right to it! 9 You must have sent
widows away without helping them and crushed the strength of orphans. 10 That is why
you are surrounded by traps and sudden fears. 11 That is why you cannot see in the
darkness, and waves of water cover you.
12 "God is so great—higher than the heavens, higher than the farthest stars. 13 But you
reply, 'That's why God can't see what I am doing! How can he judge through the thick
darkness? 14 For thick clouds swirl about him, and he cannot see us. He is way up there,
walking on the vault of heaven.'
15 "Will you continue on the old paths where evil people have walked? 16 They were
snatched away in the prime of life, and the foundations of their lives were washed away
forever. 17 For they said to God, 'Leave us alone! What can the Almighty do for us?'
18 But they forgot that he had filled their homes with good things, so I will have nothing
to do with that kind of thinking.
19 "Now the righteous will be happy to see the wicked destroyed, and the innocent will
laugh them to scorn. 20 They will say, 'Surely our enemies have been destroyed. The last
of them have been consumed in the fire.'
21 "Stop quarreling with God! If you agree with him, you will have peace at last, and
things will go well for you. 22 Listen to his instructions, and store them in your heart. 23 If
you return to the Almighty and clean up your life, you will be restored. 24 Give up your
lust for money, and throw your precious gold into the river. 25 Then the Almighty himself
will be your treasure. He will be your precious silver!

21:29-33 If wicked people become wealthy despite their sin, why should we try to be good? The wicked may *seem* to get away with sin, but there is a higher Judge and a future judgment (Revelation 20:11-15). The final settlement of justice will come, not in this life, but in the next. What is important is how a person views God in prosperity or poverty, not the prosperity or poverty itself.

22:1ff This is Eliphaz's third and final speech to Job. When he first spoke to Job (chapters 4–5), he commended Job's good deeds and gently suggested that Job might need to repent of some sin. While he said nothing new in this speech, he did get more specific. He couldn't shake his belief that suffering is God's punishment for evil deeds, so he suggested several possible sins that Job might have committed. Eliphaz wasn't trying to destroy Job; at the end of his speech he promised that Job would receive peace and restoration if he would only admit his sin and repent.

22:12-14 Eliphaz declared that Job's view of God was too small, and he criticized Job for thinking that God was too far removed from earth to care about him. If Job knew of God's intense, personal interest in him, Eliphaz said, he wouldn't dare take his sins so lightly. Eliphaz had a point—some people do take sin lightly because they think God is far away and doesn't notice all we do. But his point did not apply to Job.

22:21-30 Several times Job's friends showed a partial knowledge of God's truth and character, but they had trouble accurately applying this truth to life. Such was the case with Eliphaz, who gave a beautiful summary of repentance. He was correct in saying that we must ask for God's forgiveness when we sin, but his statement did not apply to Job who had already sought God's forgiveness (7:20, 21; 9:20; 13:23) and had lived closely in touch with God all along.

26"Then you will delight yourself in the Almighty and look up to God. 27You will pray
to him, and he will hear you, and you will fulfill your vows to him. 28Whatever you
decide to do will be accomplished, and light will shine on the road ahead of you. 29If
someone is brought low and you say, 'Help him up,' God will save the downcast. 30Then
even sinners will be rescued by your pure hands."

Job's Eighth Speech: A Response to Eliphaz

23 Then Job spoke again:
2"My complaint today is still a bitter one, and I try hard not to groan aloud. 3If
only I knew where to find God, I would go to his throne and talk with him there. 4I would
lay out my case and present my arguments. 5Then I would listen to his reply and
understand what he says to me. 6Would he merely argue with me in his greatness? No,
he would give me a fair hearing. 7Fair and honest people can reason with him, so I would
be acquitted by my Judge.

8"I go east, but he is not there. I go west, but I cannot find him. 9I do not see him in
the north, for he is hidden. I turn to the south, but I cannot find him. 10But he knows
where I am going. And when he has tested me like gold in a fire, he will pronounce me
innocent.

11"For I have stayed in God's paths; I have followed his ways and not turned aside.
12I have not departed from his commands but have treasured his word in my heart.
13Nevertheless, his mind concerning me remains unchanged, and who can turn him from
his purposes? Whatever he wants to do, he does. 14So he will do for me all he has
planned. He controls my destiny. 15No wonder I am so terrified in his presence. When I
think of it, terror grips me. 16God has made my heart faint; the Almighty has terrified
me. 17Darkness is all around me; thick, impenetrable darkness is everywhere.

Job Asks Why the Wicked Are Not Punished

24 "Why doesn't the Almighty open the court and bring judgment? Why must the
godly wait for him in vain? 2Evil people steal land by moving the boundary
markers. They steal flocks of sheep, 3and they even take donkeys from the poor and
fatherless. A poor widow must surrender her valuable ox as collateral for a loan. 4The
poor are kicked aside; the needy must hide together for safety. 5Like the wild donkeys
in the desert, the poor must spend all their time just getting enough to keep body and soul
together. They go into the desert to search for food for their children. 6They harvest a
field they do not own, and they glean in the vineyards of the wicked. 7All night they lie
naked in the cold, without clothing or covering. 8They are soaked by mountain showers,
and they huddle against the rocks for want of a home.

9"The wicked snatch a widow's child from her breast; they take the baby as a pledge
for a loan. 10The poor must go about naked, without any clothing. They are forced to
carry food while they themselves are starving. 11They press out olive oil without being
allowed to taste it, and they tread in the winepress as they suffer from thirst. 12The groans
of the dying rise from the city, and the wounded cry for help, yet God does not respond
to their moaning.

13"Wicked people rebel against the light. They refuse to acknowledge its ways. They
will not stay in its paths. 14The murderer rises in the early dawn to kill the poor and
needy; at night he is a thief. 15The adulterer waits for the twilight, for he says, 'No one

22:26 Ps 37:4
22:27 Isa 58:9
22:29 Matt 23:12; 1 Pet 5:5
23:2 Job 6:2-3; 7:11
23:4 Job 13:18
23:6 Job 9:4
23:7 Job 13:3, 16
23:8 Job 9:11
23:10 Job 7:18; Pss 7:9; 11:5
23:11 Job 31:7; Pss 17:5; 44:18
23:12 Job 6:10
23:16 Deut 20:3; Jer 51:46
23:17 Job 10:18-19; 19:8
24:1 Isa 2:12; Jer 46:10
24:2 Deut 19:14; 27:17
24:3 Exod 22:26; Deut 24:17
24:4 Job 29:16; 30:25; Prov 14:31; Amos 8:4
24:5 Job 39:5-8; Ps 104:23
24:7 Exod 22:26; Job 22:26
24:8 Lam 4:5
24:14 Ps 10:8; Mic 2:1
24:15 Prov 7:9

23:1–24:25 Job continued his questioning, saying that his suffering would be more bearable if only he knew why it was happening. If there was sin for which he could repent, he would! He knew about the wicked and the fact that they would be punished; he knew God could vindicate him if he so chose. In all his examples of the wicked in the world, his overriding desire was for God to clear his name, prove his righteousness, and explain why he was chosen to receive all this calamity. Job tried to make his friends see that questions about God, life, and justice are not as simple as they assumed.

23:10 In chapter 22, Eliphaz had tried to condemn Job by identifying some secret sin that he may have committed. Here Job declares his confidence in his integrity and God's justice. We are always likely to have hidden sin in our lives, sin we don't even know about because God's standards are so high and our performance is so imperfect. If we are true believers, however, all our sins are forgiven because of what Christ did on the cross in our behalf (Romans 5:1; 8:1). The Bible also teaches that even if our hearts condemn us, God is greater than our hearts (1 John 3:20). His forgiveness and cleansing are sufficient; they overrule our nagging doubts. The Holy Spirit in us is our proof that we are forgiven in God's eyes even though we may *feel* guilty. If we, like Job, are truly seeking God, we can stand up to others' accusations as well as our own nagging doubts. If God has forgiven and accepted us, we are forgiven indeed.

24:16 Exod 22:2 Matt 6:19
24:17 Ps 91:5
24:19 Job 6:16-17; 21:13
24:20 Prov 10:7 Isa 49:15 Dan 4:14
24:23 Job 11:11; 12:6
24:24 Job 14:21 Ps 37:10
24:25 Job 6:28; 27:4
25:2 Job 9:4; 16:19; 31:2; 36:5; 37:23
25:4 Job 4:17; 9:2
25:5 Job 15:15; 31:26
25:6 Job 7:17
26:2 Ps 71:9
26:5 Job 3:13 Ps 88:10
26:8 Job 37:11 Prov 30:4
26:9 Job 22:14 Pss 97:2; 105:39
26:10 Job 38:1-11, 19-20, 24 Prov 8:29
26:13 Job 9:8 Isa 27:1

will see me then.' He masks his face so no one will know him. 16 They break into houses
at night and sleep in the daytime. They are not acquainted with the light. 17 The black
night is their morning. They ally themselves with the terrors of the darkness.
18 "But they disappear from the earth as quickly as foam is swept down a river.
Everything they own is cursed, so that no one enters their vineyard. 19 Death consumes
sinners just as drought and heat consume snow. 20 Even the sinner's own mother will
forget him. Worms will find him sweet to eat. No one will remember him. Wicked people
are broken like a tree in the storm. 21 For they have taken advantage of the childless who
have no protecting sons. They refuse to help the needy widows.
22 "God, in his power, drags away the rich. They may rise high, but they have no
assurance in life. 23 They may be allowed to live in security, but God is always watching
them. 24 And though they are great now, in a moment they will be gone like all others,
withered like heads of grain.
25 "Can anyone claim otherwise? Who can prove me wrong?"

Bildad's Third Response to Job

25 Then Bildad the Shuhite replied:
2 "God is powerful and dreadful. He enforces peace in the heavens. 3 Who is able
to count his heavenly army? Does his light not shine on all the earth? 4 How can a mere
mortal stand before God and claim to be righteous? Who in all the earth is pure? 5 God
is so glorious that even the moon and stars scarcely shine compared to him. 6 How much
less are mere people, who are but worms in his sight?"

Job's Ninth Speech: A Response to Bildad

26 Then Job spoke again:
2 "How you have helped the powerless! How you have saved a person who has
no strength! 3 How you have enlightened my stupidity! What wise things you have said!
4 Where have you gotten all these wise sayings? Whose spirit speaks through you?
5 "The dead tremble in their place beneath the waters. 6 The underworld* is naked in
God's presence. There is no cover for the place of destruction. 7 God stretches the
northern sky over empty space and hangs the earth on nothing. 8 He wraps the rain in his
thick clouds, and the clouds do not burst with the weight. 9 He shrouds his throne with
his clouds. 10 He created the horizon when he separated the waters; he set the boundaries
for day and night. 11 The foundations of heaven tremble at his rebuke. 12 By his power
the sea grew calm. By his skill he crushed the great sea monster.* 13 His Spirit made the
heavens beautiful, and his power pierced the gliding serpent.
14 "These are some of the minor things he does, merely a whisper of his power. Who
can understand the thunder of his power?"

26:6 Hebrew *Sheol.* **26:12** Hebrew *Rahab,* the name of a mythical sea monster that represents chaos in ancient literature.

24:18-21 Job suddenly seemed to be arguing on his friends' side. For this reason, some commentators think one of Job's friends said these words. But we shouldn't expect Job to present a unified argument. He was confused. He was not arguing that, in every case, God rewards the wicked and punishes the righteous; he was simply asserting that in his case, a righteous man was suffering.

25:1ff Bildad's final reply was weak. It ignored Job's examples of the prosperity of the wicked. Instead of attempting to refute Job, Bildad accused Job of pride because he was claiming that his suffering was not the result of sin. Job never claimed to be without sin, but only that his sin could not have caused his present trouble.

25:6 It is important to understand that Bildad, not God, was calling people worms. Human beings are created in God's image (Genesis 1:26, 27). Psalm 8:5 says that people are "a little lower than God." Bildad may have simply been using a poetic description to contrast our worth to the worth and power of God. To come to God, we need not crawl like worms. We can approach him boldly in faith (Hebrews 4:16).

26:1ff Job has the distinction of giving the longest speech in the book—six chapters—weaving together pictures of God's mystery and power in a beautiful poem of trust. Beginning by brushing off Bildad's latest reply as irrelevant (chapter 25), Job then told Bildad and his friends that they could not possibly know everything about God. Wisdom does not originate from this life or from the human mind—it comes from God (28:27, 28). Job then defended his upright and honest life. He had effectively sought to follow God's way of living. While admitting that he was not perfect, Job maintained that his motives were right.

26:2-4 With great sarcasm, Job attacked Bildad's comments. Job's friends' theological explanations failed to bring any relief because they were unable to turn their knowledge into helpful counsel. When dealing with people, it is more important to love and understand them than to analyze them or give advice. Compassion produces greater results than criticism or blame.

Job's Final Speech

27 Job continued speaking:
2"I make this vow by the living God, who has taken away my rights, by the Almighty who has embittered my soul. 3As long as I live, while I have breath from God, 4my lips will speak no evil, and my tongue will speak no lies. 5I will never concede that you are right; until I die, I will defend my innocence. 6I will maintain my innocence without wavering. My conscience is clear for as long as I live.

7"May my enemy be punished like the wicked, my adversary like evil men. 8For what hope do the godless have when God cuts them off and takes away their life? 9Will God listen to their cry when trouble comes upon them? 10Can they take delight in the Almighty? Can they call to God at any time?

11"I will teach you about God's power. I will not conceal anything that concerns the Almighty. 12But I don't need to, for you yourselves have seen all this; yet you are saying all these useless things to me.

13"This is what the wicked will receive from God; this is their inheritance from the Almighty. 14If they have a multitude of children, their children will die in war or starve to death. 15Those who survive will be brought down to the grave by a plague, with no one to mourn them, not even their wives.

16"Evil people may have all the money in the world, and they may store away mounds of clothing. 17But the righteous will wear that clothing, and the innocent will divide all that money. 18The houses built by the wicked are as fragile as a spiderweb, as flimsy as a shelter made of branches.

19"The wicked go to bed rich but wake up to find that all their wealth is gone. 20Terror overwhelms them, and they are blown away in the storms of the night. 21The east wind carries them away, and they are gone. It sweeps them away. 22It whirls down on them without mercy. They struggle to flee from its power. 23But everyone jeers at them and mocks them.

Job Speaks of Wisdom and Understanding

28 "People know how to mine silver and refine gold. 2They know how to dig iron from the earth and smelt copper from stone. 3They know how to put light into darkness and explore the farthest, darkest regions of the earth as they search for ore. 4They sink a mine shaft into the earth far from where anyone lives. They descend on ropes, swinging back and forth. 5Bread comes from the earth, but below the surface the earth is melted as by fire.

6"People know how to find sapphires and gold dust—7treasures that no bird of prey can see, no falcon's eye observe—8for they are deep within the mines. No wild animal has ever walked upon those treasures; no lion has set his paw there. 9People know how to tear apart flinty rocks and overturn the roots of mountains. 10They cut tunnels in the rocks and uncover precious stones. 11They dam up the trickling streams and bring to light the hidden treasures.

12"But do people know where to find wisdom? Where can they find understanding? 13No one knows where to find it, for it is not found among the living. 14'It is not here,' says the ocean. 'Nor is it here,' says the sea.

15"It cannot be bought for gold or silver. 16Its value is greater than all the gold of

27:2 Job 9:18; 16:11
27:4 Job 6:28; 33:3
27:6 Job 2:3; 13:18
27:8 Job 8:13; 11:20
27:9 Prov 1:27-28; Isa 1:15
27:13 Job 15:20; 20:29
27:14 Job 20:18-21
27:15 Ps 78:64
27:18 Job 8:15
27:19 Job 7:8, 21
27:20 Job 15:21; 20:8
27:21 Job 7:10; 21:18
27:22 Jer 13:14; Ezek 5:11; 24:14
27:23 Job 18:18; 20:8
28:5 Ps 104:14
28:9 Deut 8:15; 32:13
28:12 Job 28:23, 28

27:6 In the midst of all the accusations, Job was able to declare that his conscience was clear. Only God's forgiveness and the determination to live right before God can bring a clear conscience. How important Job's record became as he was being accused. Like Job, we can't claim sinless lives, but we *can* claim forgiven lives. When we confess our sins to God, he forgives us. Then we can live with clear consciences (1 John 1:9).

27:13-23 Job agreed with his friends that the end of the wicked will be disaster, but he did not agree that *he* was wicked and deserving of punishment. Most of the punishments Job listed never happened to him. So he wasn't including himself as one of the wicked. On the contrary, he continually pleaded for God to vindicate him.

28:13 Job stated that wisdom cannot be found among the living. It is natural for people who do not understand the importance of God's Word to seek wisdom here on earth. They look to philosophers and other leaders to give them direction for living. Yet Job said that wisdom is not found there. No leader or group of leaders can produce enough knowledge or insight to explain the totality of human experience. The ultimate interpretation of life, of who we are and where we are going, must come from outside and above our mortal life. When looking for guidance, seek God's wisdom as revealed in the Bible. To be lifted above and beyond the boundaries of life, we must know and trust the Lord of life.

28:16 Gold of Ophir was considered the finest gold available. Ophir may have been located in Africa, along the Arabian coast or in India. Wherever it was, it was a good distance from Israel, for it took Solomon's ships three years to make the voyage (1 Kings 9:28; 10:22).

28:17 Prov 8:10; 16:16
28:18 Prov 8:11
28:19 Prov 8:19
28:23 Prov 8:22-36
28:24 Ps 33:13-14; Prov 15:3
28:25 Job 12:15; 38:8-11; Ps 135:7
28:26 Job 37:3, 6, 11-12
28:28 Ps 111:10; Prov 1:7; 9:10

Ophir, greater than precious onyx stone or sapphires. 17 Wisdom is far more valuable than
gold and crystal. It cannot be purchased with jewels mounted in fine gold. 18 Coral and
valuable rock crystal are worthless in trying to get it. The price of wisdom is far above
pearls. 19 Topaz from Ethiopia* cannot be exchanged for it. Its value is greater than the
purest gold.
20 "But do people know where to find wisdom? Where can they find understanding?
21 For it is hidden from the eyes of all humanity. Even the sharp-eyed birds in the sky
cannot discover it. 22 But Destruction and Death say, 'We have heard a rumor of where
wisdom can be found.'
23 "God surely knows where it can be found, 24 for he looks throughout the whole
earth, under all the heavens. 25 He made the winds blow and determined how much rain
should fall. 26 He made the laws of the rain and prepared a path for the lightning. 27 Then,
when he had done all this, he saw wisdom and measured it. He established it and
examined it thoroughly. 28 And this is what he says to all humanity: 'The fear of the Lord
is true wisdom; to forsake evil is real understanding.' "

Job Speaks of His Former Blessings

29:1 Job 13:12; 27:1
29:2 Jer 31:28
29:3 Job 11:17
29:6 Deut 32:13; Ps 81:16
29:9 Job 21:5; 29:21
29:11 Job 4:3-4
29:12 Job 24:4, 9; 31:16-17, 21; 34:28

29
Job continued speaking:
2 "I long for the years gone by when God took care of me, 3 when he lighted the
way before me and I walked safely through the darkness. 4 In my early years, the
friendship of God was felt in my home. 5 The Almighty was still with me, and my
children were around me. 6 In those days my cows produced milk in abundance, and my
olive groves poured out streams of olive oil.
7 "Those were the days when I went to the city gate and took my place among the
honored leaders. 8 The young stepped aside when they saw me, and even the aged rose
in respect at my coming. 9 The princes stood in silence and put their hands over their
mouths. 10 The highest officials of the city stood quietly, holding their tongues in respect.
11 "All who heard of me praised me. All who saw me spoke well of me. 12 For I helped

28:19 Hebrew *from Cush.*

WHERE CAN WISDOM BE FOUND?
Job and his friends differed in their ideas of how people become wise.

Person	*His Source of Wisdom*	*Attitude toward God*
Eliphaz	Wisdom is learned by observing and experiencing life. He based his advice to Job on his confident, firsthand knowledge (4:7, 8; 5:3, 27).	"I have personally observed how God works and have figured him out."
Bildad	Wisdom is inherited from the past. Trustworthy knowledge is secondhand. He based his advice to Job on traditional proverbs and sayings that he frequently quoted (8:8, 9; 18:5–21).	"Those who have gone before us figured God out, and all we have to do is use that knowledge."
Zophar	Wisdom belongs to the wise. He based his advice on his wisdom that had no other source than himself (11:6; 20:1–29).	"The wise know what God is like, but there aren't many of us around."
Job	God is the source of wisdom, and the first step toward wisdom is to fear God (28:20–28).	"God reveals his wisdom to those who humbly trust him."

28:28 "The fear of the Lord" is a key theme in the wisdom literature of the Bible (Job through Song of Songs). It means to have respect and reverence for God and to be in awe of his majesty and power. This is the starting point to finding real wisdom (see Proverbs 1:7-9).

29:6 Milk and olive oil were symbols of material prosperity in an agricultural society. Job's flocks and olive trees were so plentiful that everything seemed to overflow.

29:7ff Job was walking a fine line between bragging about past accomplishments and recalling good deeds in order to answer the charges against him. Job's one weakness throughout his conversations is that he came dangerously close to pride. Pride is especially deceptive when we are doing right. But it separates us from God by making us think we're better than we really are. Then comes the tendency to trust our own opinions, which leads to other kinds of sin. While it is not wrong to recount past deeds, it is far better to recount God's blessings to us. This will help keep us from inadvertently falling into pride.

29:7-17 Because of this description of Job's work, many commentators believe that Job was a judge. In Job's day, a judge served as both a city councilman and a magistrate, helping to manage the community and settle disputes. In most cases, this was not a full-time position but a part-time post held on the basis of one's respect and standing in the area.

the poor in their need and the orphans who had no one to help them. [13]I helped those
who had lost hope, and they blessed me. And I caused the widows' hearts to sing for joy.
[14]All I did was just and honest. Righteousness covered me like a robe, and I wore justice
like a turban. [15]I served as eyes for the blind and feet for the lame. [16]I was a father to the
poor and made sure that even strangers received a fair trial. [17]I broke the jaws of godless
oppressors and made them release their victims.

[18]"I thought, 'Surely I will die surrounded by my family after a long, good life. [19]For
I am like a tree whose roots reach the water, whose branches are refreshed with the dew.
[20]New honors are constantly bestowed on me, and my strength is continually renewed.'

[21]"Everyone listened to me and valued my advice. They were silent as they waited for
me to speak. [22]And after I spoke, they had nothing to add, for my counsel satisfied them.
[23]They longed for me to speak as they longed for rain. They waited eagerly, for my
words were as refreshing as the spring rain. [24]When they were discouraged, I smiled at
them. My look of approval was precious to them. [25]I told them what they should do and
presided over them as their chief. I lived as a king among his troops and as one who
comforts those who mourn.

Job Speaks of His Anguish

30 "But now I am mocked by those who are younger than I, by young men whose
fathers are not worthy to run with my sheepdogs. [2]A lot of good they are to
me—those worn-out wretches! [3]They are gaunt with hunger and flee to the deserts and
the wastelands, desolate and gloomy. [4]They eat coarse leaves, and they burn the roots of
shrubs for heat. [5]They are driven from civilization, and people shout after them as if they
were thieves. [6]So now they live in frightening ravines and in caves and among the rocks.
[7]They sound like animals as they howl among the bushes; they huddle together for
shelter beneath the nettles. [8]They are nameless fools, outcasts of civilization.

[9]"And now their sons mock me with their vulgar song! They taunt me! [10]They despise
me and won't come near me, except to spit in my face. [11]For God has cut the cords of
my tent. He has humbled me, so they have thrown off all restraint. [12]These outcasts
oppose me to my face. They send me sprawling; they lay traps in my path. [13]They block
my road and do everything they can to hasten my calamity, knowing full well that I have
no one to help me. [14]They come at me from all directions. They rush upon me when I
am down. [15]I live in terror now. They hold me in contempt, and my prosperity has
vanished as a cloud before a strong wind.

[16]"And now my heart is broken. Depression haunts my days. [17]My weary nights are
filled with pain as though something were relentlessly gnawing at my bones. [18]With a
strong hand, God grabs my garment. He grips me by the collar of my tunic. [19]He has
thrown me into the mud. I have become as dust and ashes.

[20]"I cry to you, O God, but you don't answer me. I stand before you, and you don't
bother to look. [21]You have become cruel toward me. You persecute me with your great
power. [22]You throw me into the whirlwind and destroy me in the storm. [23]And I know
that you are sending me to my death—the destination of all who live.

[24]"Surely no one would turn against the needy when they cry for help. [25]Did I not
weep for those in trouble? Was I not deeply grieved for the needy? [26]So I looked for
good, but evil came instead. I waited for the light, but darkness fell. [27]My heart is
troubled and restless. Days of affliction have come upon me. [28]I walk in gloom, without

29:13 Job 31:19-20
29:14 Ps 132:9; Isa 59:17; 61:10; Eph 6:14
29:16 Prov 29:7
29:17 Ps 3:7
29:19 Jer 17:8; Hos 14:5
29:20 Gen 49:24; Ps 18:34
29:25 Job 1:3; 4:4; 16:5
30:1 Job 12:4
30:9 Job 12:4; 17:6; Ps 69:11-12
30:10 Num 12:14; Deut 25:9; Isa 50:6; Matt 26:67
30:11 Ruth 1:21; Ps 88:7
30:12 Pss 32:9; 140:4-5; Isa 3:5
30:15 Ps 55:3-5; Hos 13:3
30:16 Pss 22:14; 42:4
30:19 Ps 69:2, 14
30:20 Job 19:7
30:21 Job 16:9, 14
30:22 Job 9:17; 10:3
30:23 Job 3:19; 9:22; 10:8
30:26 Job 3:25-26; 19:8; Jer 8:15
30:28 Pss 38:6; 42:9; 43:2

30:1ff To suffer extreme loss, as Job did, was humiliating. But to face abuse at the hands of young upstarts added insult to injury. Job had lost his family, possessions, health, position, and good name. He was not even respected for suffering bravely. Unfortunately, young people sometimes mock and take advantage of older people and those who are limited in some way. Instead, they should realize that their own physical abilities and attributes are short-lived and that God loves all people equally.

31:1-4 Job had not only avoided committing the great sin of adultery; he had not even taken the first step toward that sin by looking at a woman with lust. Job said he was innocent of both outward and inward sins. In chapter 29, Job reviewed his good deeds. Here in chapter 31 he listed sins he had not committed—in his heart (31:1-12), against his neighbors (31:13-23), or against God (31:24-34).

31:24-28 Job affirmed that depending on wealth for happiness is idolatry and denies the God of heaven. We excuse our society's obsession with money and possessions as a necessary evil or "the way it works" in the modern world. But every society in every age has valued the power and prestige that money brings. True believers must purge themselves of the deep-seated desire for more power, prestige, and possessions. They must also not withhold their resources from neighbors near and far who have desperate physical needs.

sunlight. I stand in the public square and cry for help. 29 But instead, I am considered a brother to jackals and a companion to ostriches. 30 My skin has turned dark, and my bones burn with fever. 31 My harp plays sad music, and my flute accompanies those who weep.

Job's Final Protest of Innocence

31 "I made a covenant with my eyes not to look with lust upon a young woman. 2 What has God above chosen for us? What is our inheritance from the Almighty on high? 3 It is calamity for the wicked, misfortune for those who do evil. 4 He sees everything I do and every step I take.

5 "Have I lied to anyone or deceived anyone? 6 Let God judge me on the scales of justice, for he knows my integrity. 7 If I have strayed from his pathway, or if my heart has lusted for what my eyes have seen, or if I am guilty of any other sin, 8 then let someone else harvest the crops I have planted, and let all that I have planted be uprooted.

9 "If my heart has been seduced by a woman, or if I have lusted for my neighbor's wife, 10 then may my wife belong to another man; may other men sleep with her. 11 For lust is a shameful sin, a crime that should be punished. 12 It is a devastating fire that destroys to hell. It would wipe out everything I own.

13 "If I have been unfair to my male or female servants, if I have refused to hear their complaints, 14 how could I face God? What could I say when he questioned me about it? 15 For God created both me and my servants. He created us both.

16 "Have I refused to help the poor, or crushed the hopes of widows who looked to me for help? 17 Have I been stingy with my food and refused to share it with hungry orphans? 18 No, from childhood I have cared for orphans, and all my life I have cared for widows. 19 Whenever I saw someone who was homeless and without clothes, 20 did they not praise me for providing wool clothing to keep them warm? 21 If my arm has abused an orphan because I thought I could get away with it, 22 then let my shoulder be wrenched out of place! Let my arm be torn from its socket! 23 That would be better than facing the judgment sent by God. For if the majesty of God opposes me, what hope is there?

24 "Have I put my trust in money or felt secure because of my gold? 25 Does my happiness depend on my wealth and all that I own? 26 Have I looked at the sun shining in the skies, or the moon walking down its silver pathway, 27 and been secretly enticed in my heart to worship them? 28 If so, I should be punished by the judges, for it would mean I had denied the God of heaven.

29 "Have I ever rejoiced when my enemies came to ruin or become excited when harm came their way? 30 No, I have never cursed anyone or asked for revenge. 31 My servants have never let others go hungry. 32 I have never turned away a stranger but have opened my doors to everyone. 33 Have I tried to hide my sins as people normally do, hiding my guilt in a closet? 34 Have I feared the crowd and its contempt, so that I refused to acknowledge my sin and would not go outside?

35 "If only I had someone who would listen to me and try to see my side! Look, I will sign my name to my defense. Let the Almighty show me that I am wrong. Let my accuser write out the charges against me. 36 I would face the accusation proudly. I would treasure it like a crown. 37 For I would tell him exactly what I have done. I would come before him like a prince.

38 "If my land accuses me and all its furrows weep together, 39 or if I have stolen its crops or murdered its owners, 40 then let thistles grow on that land instead of wheat and weeds instead of barley."

Job's words are ended.

30:29 Mic 1:8
30:30 Ps 102:3
31:1 2 Sam 11:2-4; Matt 5:28
31:3 Job 4:22; 18:12; 21:30
31:4 2 Chr 16:9; Prov 5:21
31:6 Job 6:2-3; Isa 26:7
31:7 Lev 26:16; Job 9:30; 23:11
31:8 Lev 26:16; Job 20:18
31:10 Deut 28:30; Jer 8:10
31:11 Deut 22:24
31:13 Deut 24:14-15
31:16 Exod 22:22-24; Job 20:19
31:17 Job 22:7-9; 29:12
31:19 Job 22:6; 29:13
31:22 Job 38:15
31:23 Job 13:11; 31:3
31:24 Job 22:23-25; Mark 10:24
31:25 Ps 62:10
31:30 Job 5:3
31:31 Job 22:7
31:34 Prov 29:25
31:35 Job 19:7; 27:7; 30:20, 24, 28; 35:14; Ps 26:1
31:37 Job 1:3; 29:25; 31:4
31:38 Job 24:2, 6, 10-12
31:40 Isa 5:6

C. A YOUNG MAN ANSWERS JOB (32:1—37:24)

Young Elihu rebukes the three friends for being unable to give Job a reasonable answer for why he was suffering. But he only gives a partial answer to Job's question by saying that people cannot understand all that God allows but must trust him. This was the best answer that a human could give, yet it was incomplete. Often the best human answers are incomplete because we do not have all the facts.

31:33, 34 Job declared that he did not try to hide his sin as people often do. The fear that our sins will be discovered leads us to patterns of deception. We cover up with lies so that we will appear good to others. But we cannot hide from God. Do you try to keep people from seeing the real you? When you acknowledge your sins, you free yourself to receive forgiveness and a new life.

Elihu Responds to Job's Friends

32 Job's three friends refused to reply further to him because he kept insisting on his
innocence.
2 Then Elihu son of Barakel the Buzite, of the clan of Ram, became angry. He was
angry because Job refused to admit that he had sinned and that God was right in
punishing him. 3 He was also angry with Job's three friends because they had condemned
God* by their inability to answer Job's arguments. 4 Elihu had waited for the others to
speak because they were older than he. 5 But when he saw that they had no further reply,
he spoke out angrily.
6 Elihu son of Barakel the Buzite said, "I am young and you are old, so I held back and
did not dare to tell you what I think. 7 I thought, 'Those who are older should speak, for
wisdom comes with age.' 8 Surely it is God's Spirit within people, the breath of the
Almighty within them, that makes them intelligent. 9 But sometimes the elders are not
wise. Sometimes the aged do not understand justice. 10 So listen to me and let me express
my opinion.
11 "I have waited all this time, listening very carefully to your arguments, listening to
you grope for words. 12 I have listened, but not one of you has refuted Job or answered
his arguments. 13 And don't tell me, 'He is too wise for us. Only God can convince him.'
14 If Job had been arguing with me, I would not answer with that kind of logic! 15 You sit
there baffled, with no further response. 16 Should I continue to wait, now that you are
silent? Must I also remain silent? 17 No, I will say my piece. I will speak my mind. I surely
will. 18 For I am pent up and full of words, and the spirit within me urges me on. 19 I am
like a wine cask without a vent. My words are ready to burst out! 20 I must speak to find
relief, so let me give my answers. 21 I won't play favorites or try to flatter anyone. 22 And
if I tried, my Creator would soon do away with me.

Elihu Presents His Case against Job

33 "Listen, Job, to what I have to say. 2 Now that I have begun to speak, let me
continue. 3 I speak with all sincerity; I speak the truth. 4 For the Spirit of God has
made me, and the breath of the Almighty gives me life. 5 Answer me, if you can; make
your case and take your stand.
6 "Look, you and I are the same before God. I, too, was formed from clay. 7 So you
don't need to be afraid of me. I am not some great person to make you nervous and afraid.
8 "You have said it in my hearing. I have heard your very words. 9 You said, 'I am pure;
I am innocent; I have not sinned. 10 God is picking a quarrel with me, and he considers
me to be his enemy. 11 He puts my feet in the stocks and watches every move I make.'
12 "In this you are not right, and I will show you why. As you yourself have said, 'God
is greater than any person.' 13 So why are you bringing a charge against him? You say,
'He does not respond to people's complaints.' 14 But God speaks again and again, though
people do not recognize it. 15 He speaks in dreams, in visions of the night when deep

32:1 Job 10:7; 13:18; 31:6; 33:9
32:2 Gen 22:21
32:6 Job 15:10
32:8 Job 33:4; 38:36; Prov 2:6; 1 Cor 2:11
32:11 Prov 18:17
32:13 Jer 9:23
32:21 Lev 19:15; Job 13:8, 10; 34:19
33:3 Job 6:28; 27:4; 36:4
33:4 Job 10:3; 27:3; 32:8
33:5 Job 33:32
33:7 Job 13:22
33:10 Job 13:23-24
33:11 Job 13:27
33:13 Job 40:2; Isa 45:9
33:14 Job 40:5; Ps 62:11

32:3 As in ancient Hebrew scribal tradition; the Masoretic Text makes no reference to God.

32:1 If Job was really a good man, his three friends would have to drop their theory that suffering is always God's punishment for evil actions. Instead of considering another viewpoint, however, they cut off the discussion. They were convinced that Job had some hidden fault or sin, so there was no point in talking if Job would not confess it. But Job knew he had lived uprightly before God and others (chapter 29) and had avoided wrong thoughts and actions (chapter 31). He wasn't about to invent a sin to satisfy his friends!

32:2ff When Eliphaz, Bildad, and Zophar had nothing more to say, Elihu became the fourth person to speak to Job. This was the first and only time he spoke. Apparently he was a bystander and much younger than the others (32:6, 7), but he introduced a new viewpoint. While Job's three friends said he was suffering from some past sins, Elihu said Job's suffering would not go away until he realized his *present* sin. He maintained that Job wasn't suffering because of sin; he was sinning because of suffering. Elihu pointed out that Job's attitude had become arrogant as he tried to defend his innocence. Elihu also said that suffering is not meant to punish us as much as it is meant to correct and restore us, to keep us on the right path.

There is much truth in Elihu's speech. He was urging Job to look at his suffering from a different perspective and with a greater purpose in mind. While his speech is on a higher spiritual plateau than the others, Elihu still wrongly assumed that a correct response to suffering always brings healing and restoration (33:23-30) and that suffering is always in some way connected to sin (34:11).

32:7-9 "The breath of the Almighty within them, that makes them intelligent." It is not enough to recognize a great truth; it must be lived out each day. Elihu recognized the truth that God was the only source of real wisdom, but he did not use God's wisdom to help Job. While he recognized where wisdom came from, he did not seek to acquire it. Becoming wise is an ongoing, lifelong pursuit. Don't be content just to know about wisdom; make it part of your life.

33:16 Job 36:10, 15
33:18 Job 33:24, 28, 30
33:20 Job 3:24; 6:7; Ps 107:18
33:21 Job 16:8; 19:20; Ps 22:17
33:24 Isa 38:17
33:27 2 Sam 12:13; Luke 15:21; Rom 6:21
33:28 Job 22:28
33:29 Eph 1:11; Phil 2:13
33:33 Ps 34:11

sleep falls on people as they lie in bed. 16 He whispers in their ear and terrifies them with
his warning. 17 He causes them to change their minds; he keeps them from pride. 18 He
keeps them from the grave, from crossing over the river of death. 19 Or God disciplines
people with sickness and pain, with ceaseless aching in their bones. 20 They lose their
appetite and do not care for even the most delicious food. 21 They waste away to skin and
bones. 22 They are at death's door; the angels of death wait for them.

23 "But if a special messenger from heaven is there to intercede for a person, to declare
that he is upright, 24 God will be gracious and say, 'Set him free. Do not make him die,
for I have found a ransom for his life.' 25 Then his body will become as healthy as a
child's, firm and youthful again. 26 When he prays to God, he will be accepted. And God
will receive him with joy and restore him to good standing. 27 He will declare to his
friends, 'I sinned, but it was not worth it. 28 God rescued me from the grave, and now my
life is filled with light.'

29 "Yes, God often does these things for people. 30 He rescues them from the grave so
they may live in the light of the living. 31 Mark this well, Job. Listen to me, and let me
say more. 32 But if you have anything to say, go ahead. I want to hear it, for I am anxious
to see you justified. 33 But if not, then listen to me. Keep silent and I will teach you
wisdom!"

Elihu Accuses Job of Arrogance

34:3 Job 12:11
34:5 Job 27:2; 33:9
34:7 Job 15:16
34:9 Job 21:15; 35:3

34 Then Elihu said:
2 "Listen to me, you wise men. Pay attention, you who have knowledge. 3 'Just
as the mouth tastes good food, the ear tests the words it hears.' 4 So let us discern for
ourselves what is right; let us learn together what is good. 5 For Job has said, 'I am
innocent, but God has taken away my rights. 6 I am innocent, but they call me a liar. My
suffering is incurable, even though I have not sinned.'

7 "Has there ever been a man as arrogant as Job, with his thirst for irreverent talk? 8 He
seeks the companionship of evil people. He spends his time with wicked men. 9 He has
even said, 'Why waste time trying to please God?'

10 "Listen to me, you who have understanding. Everyone knows that God doesn't sin!

HOW SUFFERING AFFECTS US

Suffering is helpful when:	*Suffering is harmful when:*
We turn to God for understanding, endurance, and deliverance	We become hardened and reject God
We ask important questions we might not take time to think about in our normal routine	We refuse to ask any questions and miss any lessons that might be good for us
We are prepared by it to identify with and comfort others who suffer	We allow it to make us self-centered and selfish
We are open to being helped by others who are obeying God	We withdraw from the help others can give
We are ready to learn from a trustworthy God	We reject the fact that God can bring good out of calamity
We realize we can identify with what Christ suffered on the cross for us	We accuse God of being unjust and perhaps lead others to reject him
We are sensitized to the amount of suffering in the world	We refuse to be open to any changes in our lives

33:13 Being informed brings a sense of security. It's natural to want to know what's happening in our lives. Job wanted to know what was going on, why he was suffering. In previous chapters, we sense his frustration. Elihu claimed to have the answer for Job's biggest question, "Why doesn't God tell me what is happening?" Elihu told Job that God was trying to answer him, but he was not listening. Elihu misjudged God on this point. If God were to answer all our questions, we would not be adequately tested. What if God had said, "Job, Satan's going to test you and afflict you, but in the end you'll be healed and get everything back"? Job's greatest test was not the pain but that he did not know *why* he was suffering. Our greatest test may be that we must trust God's goodness even though we don't understand why our lives are going a certain way. We must learn to trust in *God,* who is good, and not in the goodness of life.

33:14-24 Elihu's point was that God had spoken again and again. He spoke in dreams and visions (33:15-18), through suffering (33:19-22), and by mediating angels (33:23, 24). Job already knew that. Elihu accused Job of not listening to God, which was not true.

The Almighty can do no wrong. 11 He repays people according to their deeds. He treats
people according to their ways. 12 There is no truer statement than this: God will not do
wrong. The Almighty cannot twist justice. 13 Who put the world in his care? Who has set
the whole world in place? 14 If God were to take back his spirit* and withdraw his breath,
15 all life would cease, and humanity would turn again to dust.
16 "Listen now and try to understand. 17 Could God govern if he hated justice? Are you
going to condemn the almighty Judge? 18 For he says to kings and nobles, 'You are
wicked and unjust.' 19 He doesn't care how great a person may be, and he doesn't pay
any more attention to the rich than to the poor. He made them all. 20 In a moment they
die. At midnight they all pass away; the mighty are removed without human hand.
21 "For God carefully watches the way people live; he sees everything they do. 22 No
darkness is thick enough to hide the wicked from his eyes. 23 For it is not up to mortals to
decide when to come before God in judgment. 24 He brings the mighty to ruin without asking
anyone, and he sets up others in their places. 25 He watches what they do, and in the night
he overturns them, destroying them. 26 He openly strikes them down for their wickedness.
27 For they turned aside from following him. They have no respect for any of his ways. 28 So
they cause the poor to cry out, catching God's attention. Yes, he hears the cries of the needy.
29 When he is quiet, who can make trouble? But when he hides his face, who can find him?
30 He prevents the godless from ruling so they cannot be a snare to the people.
31 "Why don't people say to God, 'I have sinned, but I will sin no more'? 32 Or 'I don't
know what evil I have done; tell me, and I will stop at once'?
33 "Must God tailor his justice to your demands? But you have rejected him! The choice
is yours, not mine. Go ahead, share your wisdom with us. 34 After all, bright people will tell
me, and wise people will hear me say, 35 'Job speaks without knowledge; his words lack
insight.' 36 Job, you deserve the maximum penalty for the wicked way you have talked.
37 For now you have added rebellion and blasphemy against God to your other sins."

Elihu Reminds Job of God's Justice

35 Then Elihu said:
2 "Do you think it is right for you to claim, 'I am righteous before God'? 3 Yet
you also ask, 'What's the use of living a righteous life? How will it benefit me?'
4 "I will answer you and all your friends, too. 5 Look up into the sky and see the clouds
high above you. 6 If you sin, what do you accomplish against him? Even if you sin again
and again, what effect will it have on him? 7 If you are good, is this some great gift to
him? What could you possibly give him? 8 No, your sins affect only people like yourself,
and your good deeds affect only other people.
9 "The oppressed cry out beneath the wrongs that are done to them. They groan
beneath the power of the mighty. 10 Yet they don't ask, 'Where is God my Creator, the
one who gives songs in the night? 11 Where is the one who makes us wiser than the
animals and birds?'
12 "And if they do cry out and God does not answer, it is because of their pride. 13 But
it is wrong to say God doesn't listen, to say the Almighty isn't concerned. 14 And it is
even more false to say he doesn't see what is going on. He will bring about justice if you
will only wait. 15 But do you cry out against him because he does not respond in anger?
16 Job, you have protested in vain. You have spoken like a fool."

36 Elihu continued speaking:
2 "Let me go on, and I will show you the truth of what I am saying. For I have
not finished defending God! 3 I will give you many illustrations of the righteousness of

34:11 Ps 62:12 Prov 24:12 Matt 16:27 Rom 2:6 2 Cor 5:10 Rev 22:12
34:15 Gen 3:19; 7:21 Job 9:22; 10:9
34:19 Deut 10:17 Acts 10:34 Rom 2:11 Gal 2:6 Eph 6:9 1 Pet 1:17
34:20 Exod 12:29
34:21 Prov 5:21; 15:3
34:22 Ps 139:11-12 Amos 9:2-3
34:27 1 Sam 15:11
34:28 Exod 22:23
34:29 Job 5:15; 20:5
34:30 Job 34:17
34:35 Job 35:16
34:36 Pss 17:3; 26:2
35:6 Prov 8:36 Jer 7:19
35:7 Prov 9:12 Luke 17:10 Rom 11:35
35:9 Exod 2:23
35:10 Pss 42:8; 149:5 Acts 16:25
35:11 Ps 94:12 Jer 32:33
35:12 Prov 1:28
35:13 Isa 1:15 Jas 4:3
35:14 Ps 37:5-6
36:3 Job 8:3; 37:23

34:14 Or *his Spirit.*

34:10-15 God doesn't sin and is never unjust, Elihu claimed. Throughout this book, Eliphaz, Bildad, Zophar, and Elihu all have elements of truth in their speeches. Unfortunately, the nuggets of truth are buried under layers of false assumptions and conclusions. Although we might have a wealth of Bible knowledge and life experiences, we must make sure our conclusions are consistent with all of God's Word, not just parts of it.

35:1ff Sometimes we wonder if being faithful to our convictions really does any good at all. Elihu spoke to this very point. His conclusion was that God is still concerned even though he doesn't intervene immediately in every situation. In the broad scope of time, God executes justice. We have his promise on that. Don't lose hope. Wait upon God. He notices your right living and your faith.

36:5 Pss 22:24; 69:33; 102:17
36:6 Job 5:15; 8:22; 34:26
36:7 Pss 33:18; 34:15; 113:8
36:9 Job 15:25
36:10 2 Kgs 17:3 Job 33:16; 36:21 Jon 3:8
36:12 Job 4:21; 15:22
36:15 Job 36:10
36:17 Job 22:5, 10-11
36:18 Job 33:24; 34:33 Jon 4:4, 9
36:20 Job 34:20, 25
36:21 Pss 31:6; 66:18

my Creator. 4I am telling you the honest truth, for I am a man of well-rounded
knowledge.
5"God is mighty, yet he does not despise anyone! He is mighty in both power and
understanding. 6He does not let the wicked live but gives justice to the afflicted. 7His
eyes never leave the innocent, but he establishes and exalts them with kings forever. 8If
troubles come upon them and they are enslaved and afflicted, 9he takes the trouble to
show them the reason. He shows them their sins, for they have behaved proudly. 10He
gets their attention and says they must turn away from evil.
11"If they listen and obey God, then they will be blessed with prosperity throughout
their lives. All their years will be pleasant. 12But if they refuse to listen to him, they will
perish in battle and die from lack of understanding. 13For the godless are full of
resentment. Even when he punishes them, they refuse to cry out to him for help. 14They
die young after wasting their lives in immoral living. 15But by means of their suffering,
he rescues those who suffer. For he gets their attention through adversity.
16"God has led you away from danger, giving you freedom. You have prospered in a
wide and pleasant valley. 17But you are too obsessed with judgment on the godless.
Don't worry, justice will be upheld. 18But watch out, or you may be seduced with wealth.
Don't let yourself be bribed into sin. 19Could all your wealth and mighty efforts keep
you from distress? 20Do not long for the cover of night, for that is when people will be
destroyed. 21Be on guard! Turn back from evil, for it was to prevent you from getting
into a life of evil that God sent this suffering.

Elihu Reminds Job of God's Power

36:26 Pss 90:2; 102:24, 27
36:27 Job 5:10; 37:6, 11 Ps 147:8

22"Look, God is all-powerful. Who is a teacher like him? 23No one can tell him what to
do. No one can say to him, 'You have done wrong.' 24Instead, glorify his mighty works,
singing songs of praise. 25Everyone has seen these things, but only from a distance.
26"Look, God is exalted beyond what we can understand. His years are without
number. 27He draws up the water vapor and then distills it into rain. 28The rain pours

GOD SPEAKS
On various occasions in the Old Testament, God chose to communicate audibly with individuals. God will always find a way to make contact with those who want to know him. Some of those occasions are listed here.

Whom He Spoke To	*What He Said*	*Reference*
Adam and Eve	Confronted them about sin	Genesis 3:8–13
Noah	Gave him directions about building the boat	Genesis 6:13–22; 7:1; 8:15–17
Abraham	Commanded him to follow God's leading and promised to bless him	Genesis 12:1–9
	Tested his obedience by commanding him to sacrifice his son	Genesis 22:1–14
Jacob	Permitted him to go to Egypt	Genesis 46:1–4
Moses	Sent him to lead the people out of Egypt	Exodus 3:1–10
	Gave him the Ten Commandments	Exodus 19:1—20:20
Moses, Aaron, Miriam	Pronounced judgment on a family conflict	Numbers 12:1–15
Joshua	Promised to be with him as he was with Moses	Joshua 1:1–9
Samuel	Chose him to be his spokesman	1 Samuel 3:1–18
Isaiah	Sent him to the people with his message	Isaiah 6:1–13
Jeremiah	Encouraged him to be his prophet	Jeremiah 1:4–10
Ezekiel	Sent him to Israel to warn them of coming judgment	Ezekiel 2:1–8

36:26 One theme in the poetic literature of the Bible is that God is incomprehensible; we cannot know him completely. We can have some knowledge about him, for the Bible is full of details about who God is, how we can know him, and how we can have an eternal relationship with him. But we can never know enough to answer all of life's questions (Ecclesiastes 3:11), to predict our own future, or to manipulate God for our own ends. Life always creates more questions than we have answers, and we must constantly go to God for fresh insights into life's dilemmas. (See 37:19-24.)

down from the clouds, and everyone benefits from it. 29 Can anyone really understand
the spreading of the clouds and the thunder that rolls forth from heaven? 30 See how he
spreads the lightning around him and how it lights up the depths of the sea. 31 By his
mighty acts he governs the people, giving them food in abundance. 32 He fills his hands
with lightning bolts. He hurls each at its target. 33 The thunder announces his presence;
the storm announces his indignant anger.*

37 My heart pounds as I think of this. It leaps within me. 2 Listen carefully to the
thunder of God's voice as it rolls from his mouth. 3 It rolls across the heavens, and
his lightning flashes out in every direction. 4 Then comes the roaring of the thunder—the
tremendous voice of his majesty. He does not restrain the thunder when he speaks. 5 God's
voice is glorious in the thunder. We cannot comprehend the greatness of his power.
6 "He directs the snow to fall on the earth and tells the rain to pour down. 7 Everyone
stops working at such a time so they can recognize his power. 8 The wild animals hide in
the rocks or in their dens. 9 The stormy wind comes from its chamber, and the driving
winds bring the cold. 10 God's breath sends the ice, freezing wide expanses of water. 11 He
loads the clouds with moisture, and they flash with his lightning. 12 The clouds turn
around and around under his direction. They do whatever he commands throughout the
earth. 13 He causes things to happen on earth, either as a punishment or as a sign of his
unfailing love.
14 "Listen, Job; stop and consider the wonderful miracles of God! 15 Do you know how
God controls the storm and causes the lightning to flash forth from his clouds? 16 Do you
understand how he balances the clouds with wonderful perfection and skill? 17 When you
are sweltering in your clothes and the south wind dies down and everything is still, 18 he
makes the skies reflect the heat like a giant mirror. Can you do that?
19 "You think you know so much, so teach the rest of us what to say to God. We are too
ignorant to make our own arguments. 20 Should God be told that I want to speak? Can we
speak when we are confused? 21 We cannot look at the sun, for it shines brightly in the sky
when the wind clears away the clouds. 22 Golden splendor comes from the mountain of
God. He is clothed in dazzling splendor. 23 We cannot imagine the power of the Almighty,
yet he is so just and merciful that he does not oppress us. 24 No wonder people everywhere
fear him. People who are truly wise show him reverence."

D. GOD ANSWERS JOB (38:1—41:34)

Instead of answering Job's question directly, God asks Job a series of questions which no human could possibly answer. Job responds by recognizing that God's ways are best. During difficult times, we, too, must humbly remember our position before the eternal, holy, incomprehensible God.

The LORD Challenges Job

38 Then the LORD answered Job from the whirlwind:
2 "Who is this that questions my wisdom with such ignorant words? 3 Brace
yourself, because I have some questions for you, and you must answer them.

36:29 Job 26:14; 37:11
36:31 Job 37:13; Acts 14:17
36:32 Job 37:11-12, 15
37:5 Job 5:9; 26:14; Rom 11:33
37:6 Job 36:27; 38:22
37:8 Job 38:40; Ps 104:21-22
37:9 Job 9:9
37:10 Job 38:29; Ps 147:17
37:11 Job 36:27, 29; 37:15
37:12 Ps 148:8; Isa 14:21; 27:6
37:13 Exod 9:18-19; 1 Kgs 18:45
37:18 Ps 104:2; Isa 44:24; 45:12; Jer 10:12
37:23 Isa 63:9
37:24 Job 5:13; Matt 10:28; 11:25; 1 Cor 1:26
38:2 Job 35:16; 42:3
38:3 Job 40:7; 42:4

36:33 Or *even the cattle know when a storm is coming.* The meaning of the Hebrew is uncertain.

37:2 Nothing can compare to God. His power and presence are awesome, and when he speaks, we must listen. Too often we presume to speak for God (as did Job's friends), to put words in his mouth, to take him for granted, or to interpret his silence to mean that he is absent or unconcerned. But God cares. He is in control, and he will speak. Be ready to hear his message—in the Bible, in your life through the Holy Spirit, and through circumstances and relationships.

37:21-24 Elihu concluded his speech with the tremendous truth that faith in God is far more important than Job's desire for an explanation for his suffering. He came so close to helping Job but then went down the wrong path. Significantly, it is here that God himself breaks into the discussion to draw the right conclusions from this important truth (38:1ff).

37:23 Elihu stressed God's sovereignty over all of nature as a reminder of his sovereignty over our lives. God is in control—he directs, preserves, and maintains his created order. Although we can't see it, God is divinely governing the moral and political affairs of people as well. By spending time observing the majestic and intricate parts of God's creation, we can be reminded of his power in every aspect of our lives.

38:1ff Out of a whirlwind, God spoke. Surprisingly, he didn't answer any of Job's questions; Job's questions were not at the heart of the issue. Instead, God used Job's ignorance of the earth's natural order to reveal his ignorance of God's moral order. If Job did not understand the workings of God's physical creation, how could he possibly understand God's mind and character? There is no standard or criterion higher than God himself by which to judge. God himself is the standard. Our only option is to submit to his authority and rest in his care.

38:4 Job 15:7
Ps 104:5
Prov 8:29; 30:4

38:7 Job 1:6

38:8 Gen 1:9

38:10 Gen 1:9
Ps 33:7
Prov 8:29
Jer 5:22

38:13 Job 37:3; 34:25-26

38:15 Num 15:30
Pss 10:15; 37:17

38:16 Gen 7:11; 8:2
Prov 8:24, 28

38:17 Job 28:24; 34:22
Ps 9:13

38:20 Job 26:10

38:21 Job 15:7

38:22 Exod 9:18
Isa 30:30
Ezek 13:11, 13
Rev 16:21

38:24 Job 26:10

38:26 Job 36:27

38:27 Ps 104:13-14

38:29 Job 37:10
Pss 104:13-14; 147:16-17

38:31 Job 9:9

4"Where were you when I laid the foundations of the earth? Tell me, if you know so
much. 5Do you know how its dimensions were determined and who did the surveying?
6What supports its foundations, and who laid its cornerstone 7as the morning stars sang
together and all the angels* shouted for joy?
8"Who defined the boundaries of the sea as it burst from the womb, 9and as I clothed
it with clouds and thick darkness? 10For I locked it behind barred gates, limiting its shores.
11I said, 'Thus far and no farther will you come. Here your proud waves must stop!'
12"Have you ever commanded the morning to appear and caused the dawn to rise in
the east? 13Have you ever told the daylight to spread to the ends of the earth, to bring an
end to the night's wickedness? 14For the features of the earth take shape as the light
approaches, and the dawn is robed in red. 15The light disturbs the haunts of the wicked,
and it stops the arm that is raised in violence.
16"Have you explored the springs from which the seas come? Have you walked about
and explored their depths? 17Do you know where the gates of death are located? Have
you seen the gates of utter gloom? 18Do you realize the extent of the earth? Tell me about
it if you know!
19"Where does the light come from, and where does the darkness go? 20Can you take
it to its home? Do you know how to get there? 21But of course you know all this! For
you were born before it was all created, and you are so very experienced!
22"Have you visited the treasuries of the snow? Have you seen where the hail is
made and stored? 23I have reserved it for the time of trouble, for the day of battle and
war. 24Where is the path to the origin of light? Where is the home of the east wind?
25"Who created a channel for the torrents of rain? Who laid out the path for the
lightning? 26Who makes the rain fall on barren land, in a desert where no one lives?
27Who sends the rain that satisfies the parched ground and makes the tender grass
spring up?
28"Does the rain have a father? Where does dew come from? 29Who is the mother of
the ice? Who gives birth to the frost from the heavens? 30For the water turns to ice as
hard as rock, and the surface of the water freezes.
31"Can you hold back the movements of the stars? Are you able to restrain the Pleiades
or Orion? 32Can you ensure the proper sequence of the seasons or guide the constellation
of the Bear with her cubs across the heavens? 33Do you know the laws of the universe
and how God rules the earth?

38:7 Hebrew *sons of God.*

GOD'S JUSTICE

Wrong View	*Correct View*
LAW OF FAIRNESS GOD	GOD JUSTICE
There is a law of fairness or justice that is higher and more absolute than God. It is binding even for God. God must act in response to that law in order to be fair. Our response is to appeal to that law.	God himself is the standard of justice. He uses his power according to his own moral perfection. Thus, whatever he does is fair, even if we don't understand it. Our response is to appeal directly to him.

38:22, 23 God said he was reserving the treasuries of the snow and hail for times of trouble. God used hail to help Joshua and the Israelites win a battle (Joshua 10:11). Just as armies keep weapons in the armory, God has all the forces of nature in his control. Sometimes he uses them to confound those opposed to him or his people. Job couldn't even begin to know all of God's resources.

38:22-35 God stated that he has all the forces of nature at his command and that he can unleash or restrain them at will. No one completely understands such common occurrences as rain or snow, and no one can command them—only God who created them has that power. God's point was that if Job could not explain such common events in nature, how could he possibly explain or question God? And if nature is beyond our grasp, God's moral purposes may not be what we imagine either.

38:31, 32 These are star constellations, and they are all under God's control.

34“Can you shout to the clouds and make it rain? 35Can you make lightning appear
and cause it to strike as you direct it? 36Who gives intuition and instinct? 37Who is wise
enough to count all the clouds? Who can tilt the water jars of heaven, 38turning the dry
dust to clumps of mud?

39“Can you stalk prey for a lioness and satisfy the young lions’ appetites 40as they lie
in their dens or crouch in the thicket? 41Who provides food for the ravens when their
young cry out to God as they wander about in hunger?

The LORD’s Challenge Continues

39 “Do you know when the mountain goats give birth? Have you watched as the wild
deer are born? 2Do you know how many months they carry their young? Are you
aware of the time of their delivery? 3They crouch down to give birth to their young and
deliver their offspring. 4Their young grow up in the open fields, then leave their parents
and never return.

5“Who makes the wild donkey wild? 6I have placed it in the wilderness; its home
is the wasteland. 7It hates the noise of the city, and it has no driver to shout at it. 8The
mountains are its pastureland, where it searches for every blade of grass.

9“Will the wild ox consent to being tamed? Will it stay in your stall? 10Can you
hitch a wild ox to a plow? Will it plow a field for you? 11Since it is so strong, can you
trust it? Can you go away and trust the ox to do your work? 12Can you rely on it to
return, bringing your grain to the threshing floor?

13“The ostrich flaps her wings grandly, but they are no match for the feathers of the
stork. 14She lays her eggs on top of the earth, letting them be warmed in the dust. 15She
doesn’t worry that a foot might crush them or that wild animals might destroy them. 16She
is harsh toward her young, as if they were not her own. She is unconcerned though they
die, 17for God has deprived her of wisdom. He has given her no understanding. 18But
whenever she jumps up to run, she passes the swiftest horse with its rider.

19“Have you given the horse its strength or clothed its neck with a flowing mane? 20Did
you give it the ability to leap forward like a locust? Its majestic snorting is something to
hear! 21It paws the earth and rejoices in its strength. When it charges to war, 22it is
unafraid. It does not run from the sword. 23The arrows rattle against it, and the spear and
javelin flash. 24Fiercely it paws the ground and rushes forward into battle when the
trumpet blows. 25It snorts at the sound of the bugle. It senses the battle even at a distance.
It quivers at the noise of battle and the shout of the captain’s commands.

26“Are you the one who makes the hawk soar and spread its wings to the south?
27Is it at your command that the eagle rises to the heights to make its nest? 28It lives
on the cliffs, making its home on a distant, rocky crag. 29From there it hunts its prey,
keeping watch with piercing eyes. 30Its nestlings gulp down blood, for it feeds on the
carcass of the slaughtered.”

40 Then the LORD said to Job, 2“Do you still want to argue with the Almighty? You
are God’s critic, but do you have the answers?”

Job Responds to the LORD

3Then Job replied to the LORD, 4“I am nothing—how could I ever find the answers? I

38:36 Job 32:8; Ps 51:6; Eccl 2:26
38:39 Ps 104:21
38:41 Ps 147:9; Luke 12:24
39:1 Deut 14:5; Ps 29:9
39:5 Job 6:5; 11:12; 24:5
39:6 Job 24:5; Jer 2:24
39:9 Num 23:22; Deut 33:17; Ps 92:10
39:16 Lam 4:3
39:20 Jer 8:16; Joel 2:5
39:21 Jer 8:6
39:27 Jer 49:16; Obad 1:4
39:29 Job 9:26
39:30 Matt 24:28; Luke 17:37
40:2 Job 9:3; 10:2; 13:3; 23:4; 31:35; 33:13
40:4 Job 21:5; 29:9

39:1ff God asked Job several questions about the animal kingdom in order to demonstrate how limited Job’s knowledge really was. God was not seeking answers from Job. Instead, he was getting Job to recognize and submit to God’s power and sovereignty. Only then could he hear what God was really saying to him.

40:2-5 How do you argue or criticize almighty God? Do you demand answers when things don’t go your way, you lose a job, someone close to you is ill or dies, finances are tight, you fail, or unexpected changes occur? The next time you are tempted to complain to God, consider how much he loves you. And remember Job’s reaction when he had his chance to speak. Are you worse off than Job or more righteous than he? Give God a chance to reveal his greater purposes for you, but remember that they may unfold over the course of your life and not at the moment you desire.

40:4 Throughout his time of suffering, Job longed to have an opportunity to plead his innocence before God. Here God appeared to Job and gave him that opportunity. But Job decided to remain quiet because it was no longer necessary for him to speak. God had shown Job that, as a limited human being, he had neither the ability to judge the God who created the universe nor the right to ask why. God’s actions do not depend on ours. He will do what he knows is best, regardless of what we think is fair. It is important to note, however, that God came to Job, demonstrating his love and care for him.

will put my hand over my mouth in silence. 5 I have said too much already. I have nothing
more to say."

The LORD Challenges Job Again

6 Then the LORD answered Job from the whirlwind:
7 "Brace yourself, because I have some questions for you, and you must answer
them. 8 Are you going to discredit my justice and condemn me so you can say you are
right? 9 Are you as strong as God, and can you thunder with a voice like his? 10 All
right then, put on your robes of state, your majesty and splendor. 11 Give vent to your
anger. Let it overflow against the proud. 12 Humiliate the proud with a glance;
walk on the wicked where they stand. 13 Bury them in the dust. Imprison them in
the world of the dead. 14 Then even I would praise you, for your own strength
would save you.
15 "Take a look at the mighty hippopotamus.* I made it, just as I made you. It eats grass
like an ox. 16 See its powerful loins and the muscles of its belly. 17 Its tail is as straight as
a cedar. The sinews of its thighs are tightly knit together. 18 Its bones are tubes of bronze.
Its limbs are bars of iron. 19 It is a prime example of God's amazing handiwork. Only its
Creator can threaten it. 20 The mountains offer it their best food, where all the wild
animals play. 21 It lies down under the lotus plants, hidden by the reeds. 22 The lotus plants
give it shade among the willows beside the stream. 23 It is not disturbed by raging rivers,
not even when the swelling Jordan rushes down upon it. 24 No one can catch it off guard
or put a ring in its nose and lead it away.

The LORD's Challenge Continues

41 "Can you catch a crocodile* with a hook or put a noose around its jaw? 2 Can you
tie it with a rope through the nose or pierce its jaw with a spike? 3 Will it beg you
for mercy or implore you for pity? 4 Will it agree to work for you? Can you make it be
your slave for life? 5 Can you make it a pet like a bird, or give it to your little girls to play
with? 6 Will merchants try to buy it? Will they sell it in their shops? 7 Will its hide be hurt
by darts, or its head by a harpoon? 8 If you lay a hand on it, you will never forget the
battle that follows, and you will never try it again!
9 "No, it is useless to try to capture it. The hunter who attempts it will be thrown
down. 10 And since no one dares to disturb the crocodile, who would dare to stand up
to me? 11 Who will confront me and remain safe*? Everything under heaven is mine.
12 "I want to emphasize the tremendous strength in the crocodile's limbs and
throughout its enormous frame. 13 Who can strip off its hide, and who can penetrate
its double layer of armor*? 14 Who could pry open its jaws? For its teeth are terrible!
15 The overlapping scales on its back make a shield. 16 They are close together so no
air can get between them. 17 They lock together so nothing can penetrate them.

40:5 Job 9:3, 15
40:6 Job 38:1
40:7 Job 38:3; 42:4
40:8 Job 10:3, 7; 13:18; 27:2, 6 Rom 3:4
40:9 Job 37:5
40:10 Pss 93:1; 104:1
40:11 Isa 2:12; 42:25 Dan 4:37 Nah 1:6, 8
40:12 Isa 13:11; 63:3
40:13 Isa 2:10-12
40:15 Job 40:19
40:19 Job 40:15; 41:33
41:1 Job 3:8 Pss 74:14; 104:26 Isa 27:1
41:2 2 Kgs 19:28 Isa 37:29
41:3 †Rom 11:35
41:10 Job 3:8
41:11 Exod 19:5 Deut 10:14 Pss 24:1; 50:12 Rom 11:35 1 Cor 10:26

40:15 Hebrew *at behemoth.* **41:1** Hebrew *Leviathan;* also throughout the following passage. **41:11** As in Greek version; Hebrew reads *confront me that I must pay.* **41:13** As in Greek version; Hebrew reads *its bridle.*

FOUR VIEWS OF SUFFERING

Satan's view	People believe in God only when they are prospering and not suffering. This is wrong.
The view of Job's three friends	Suffering is God's judgment for sin. This is not always true.
Elihu's view	Suffering is God's way to teach, discipline, and refine. This is true, but an incomplete explanation.
God's view	Suffering causes us to trust God for who he is, not what he does.

41:9-11 It is foolish for people to think they can stand up against God when they are afraid to confront even a crocodile. How much more powerful is God!

42:1ff Throughout the book, Job's friends had asked him to admit his sin and ask for forgiveness, and eventually Job did indeed repent. Ironically, Job's repentance was not the kind called for by his friends. He asked for forgiveness, not for committing secret sins, but for questioning God's sovereignty and justice. Job repented of his attitude and acknowledged God's great power and perfect justice. We sin when we angrily ask, "If God is in control, how could he let this happen?" Because we are locked into time, unable to see beyond today, we cannot know the reasons for everything that happens. Thus, we must often choose between doubt and trust. Will you trust God with your unanswered questions?

18“When it sneezes, it flashes light! Its eyes are like the red of dawn. 19Fire and sparks
leap from its mouth. 20Smoke streams from its nostrils like steam from a boiling pot on
a fire of dry rushes. 21Yes, its breath would kindle coals, for flames shoot from its mouth.
22“The tremendous strength in its neck strikes terror wherever it goes. 23Its flesh is
hard and firm, not soft and fat. 24Its heart is as hard as rock, as hard as a millstone.
25When it rises, the mighty are afraid, gripped by terror. 26No sword can stop it, nor spear
nor dart nor pointed shaft. 27To the crocodile, iron is nothing but straw, and bronze is
rotten wood. 28Arrows cannot make it flee. Stones shot from a sling are as ineffective as
straw. 29Clubs do no good, and it laughs at the swish of the javelins. 30Its belly is covered
with scales as sharp as glass. They tear up the ground as it drags through the mud.
31“The crocodile makes the water boil with its commotion. It churns the depths. 32The
water glistens in its wake. One would think the sea had turned white. 33There is nothing
else so fearless anywhere on earth. 34Of all the creatures, it is the proudest. It is the king
of beasts.”

41:18 Job 3:9
41:33 Job 40:19
41:34 Job 28:8

E. JOB IS RESTORED (42:1–17)

In response to God's speech, Job humbles himself. God rebukes his three friends for adding to Job's suffering by their false assumptions and critical attitudes. Job's material possessions and family are restored, and he receives even greater blessings than he had before. Those who persist in trusting God will be rewarded.

Job Responds to the LORD

42 Then Job replied to the LORD:
2“I know that you can do anything, and no one can stop you. 3You ask, ‘Who
is this that questions my wisdom with such ignorance?’ It is I. And I was talking about
things I did not understand, things far too wonderful for me.
4“You said, ‘Listen and I will speak! I have some questions for you, and you must
answer them.’
5“I had heard about you before, but now I have seen you with my own eyes. 6I take
back everything I said, and I sit in dust and ashes to show my repentance.”

42:2 Gen 18:14; Matt 19:26
42:3 Job 38:2; Pss 40:5; 131:1; 139:6
42:4 Job 38:3; 40:7
42:5 Job 26:14; Isa 6:5

Conclusion: The LORD Blesses Job

7After the LORD had finished speaking to Job, he said to Eliphaz the Temanite: “I am
angry with you and with your two friends, for you have not been right in what you said
about me, as my servant Job was. 8Now take seven young bulls and seven rams and go
to my servant Job and offer a burnt offering for yourselves. My servant Job will pray for
you, and I will accept his prayer on your behalf. I will not treat you as you deserve, for
you have not been right in what you said about me, as my servant Job was.”

42:7 Job 40:3-5; 42:1-6
42:8 Job 1:5; 22:30; Jas 5:16

JOB AND JESUS
The book of Job is intimately tied to the New Testament because Job's questions and problems are answered perfectly in Jesus Christ.

Subject/Reference in Job	*How Jesus Is the Answer*
Someone must help us approach God (9:32, 33)	1 Timothy 2:5
Is there life after death? (14:14)	John 11:25
There is one in heaven working on our behalf (16:19)	Hebrews 9:24
There is one who can save us from judgment (19:25)	Hebrews 7:24, 25
What is important in life? (21:715)	Matthew 16:26; John 3:16
Where do we find God? (23:3–5)	John 14:9

42:2-4 Job was quoting the Lord's earlier questions to him (38:2, 3). He openly and honestly faced God and admitted that he was the one who had been foolish. Are you using what you can't understand as an excuse for your lack of trust? Admit to God that you don't even have enough faith to trust him. True faith begins in such humility.

42:7, 8 God made it clear that Job's friends were wrong. The fact that God did not mention any specific sins shows that God confirmed Job's claim to have led a devout and obedient life. Job's friends had made the error of assuming that Job's suffering was caused by some great sin. They were judging Job without knowing what God was doing. We must be careful to avoid making judgments about a person because God may be working in ways we know nothing about.

42:8-10 After receiving much criticism, Job was still able to pray for his three friends. It is difficult to forgive someone who has accused us of wrongdoing, but Job did. Are you praying for those who have hurt you? Can you forgive them? Follow the actions of Job, whom God called a good man, and pray for those who have wronged you.

9 So Eliphaz the Temanite, Bildad the Shuhite, and Zophar the Naamathite did as the
LORD commanded them, and the LORD accepted Job's prayer.
42:10 Pss 14:7; 85:1-3; 126:1-6 10 When Job prayed for his friends, the LORD restored his fortunes. In fact, the LORD
gave him twice as much as before! 11 Then all his brothers, sisters, and former friends
42:11 Job 2:11; 19:13 came and feasted with him in his home. And they consoled him and comforted him
because of all the trials the LORD had brought against him. And each of them brought
him a gift of money* and a gold ring.
42:12 Job 1:3, 10; 8:7; 1 Tim 6:17 12 So the LORD blessed Job in the second half of his life even more than in the
beginning. For now he had fourteen thousand sheep, six thousand camels, one thousand
teams of oxen, and one thousand female donkeys. 13 He also gave Job seven more sons
and three more daughters. 14 He named his first daughter Jemimah, the second Keziah,
and the third Keren-happuch. 15 In all the land there were no other women as lovely as
the daughters of Job. And their father put them into his will along with their brothers.
16 Job lived 140 years after that, living to see four generations of his children and
42:17 Gen 15:15; 25:8 grandchildren. 17 Then he died, an old man who had lived a long, good life.

42:11 Hebrew *a kesitah;* the value or weight of the kesitah is no longer known.

WHEN WE SUFFER
Here are six questions to ask ourselves when we suffer, and what to do if the answer is yes.

Questions	*Our Response*
Am I being punished by God for sin?	Confess known sin.
Is Satan attacking me as I try to survive as a Christian?	Call on God for strength.
Am I being prepared for a special service, learning to be compassionate to those who suffer?	Resist self-pity. Ask God to open up doors of opportunity and help you discover others who suffer as you do.
Am I specifically selected for testing, like Job?	Accept help from the body of believers. Trust God to work his purpose through you.
Is my suffering a result of natural consequences for which I am not directly responsible?	Recognize that in a sinful world, both good and evil people will suffer. But the good person has a promise from God that his or her suffering will one day come to an end.
Is my suffering due to some unknown reason?	Don't draw inward from the pain. Proclaim your faith in God, know that he cares, and wait patiently for his aid.

42:10, 11 Would the message of the book of Job change if God had not restored to Job his former blessings? No. God is still sovereign. Jesus said that anyone who gives up something for the Kingdom of God will be repaid (Luke 18:29, 30). Our restoration may or may not be the same kind as Job's, which was both spiritual and material. Our complete restoration may not be in this life—but it *will* happen. God loves us, and he is just. He not only will restore whatever we have lost unjustly, but he also will give us more than we can imagine as we live with him in eternity. Cling tightly to your faith through all your trials, and you, too, will be rewarded by God—if not now, in the life to come.

42:17 The main question in the book of Job is timely: Why do believers experience troubles and suffering? Through a long debate, Job's supposedly wise friends were unable to answer this question. Job's friends made a serious error for which God rebuked them. They assumed that trouble comes only because people sin. People make the same mistake today when they assert that sickness or lack of material blessing is a sign of unconfessed sin or lack of faith. Though normally (but not always) following God leads to a happier life, and rebelling against God normally (but not always) leads to an unhappy life, *God is in control.* In our world invaded by sin, calamity and suffering come to good and bad alike.

This does not mean that God is indifferent, uncaring, unjust, or powerless to protect us. Bad things happen because we live in a fallen world, where both believers and unbelievers are hit with the tragic consequences of sin. God allows evil for a time although he turns it around for our good (Romans 8:28). We may have no answers as to why God allows evil, but we can be sure he is all-powerful and knows what he is doing. The next time you face trials and dilemmas, see them as opportunities to turn to God for strength. You will find a God who only desires to show his love and compassion to you. If you can trust him in pain, confusion, and loneliness, you will win the victory and eliminate doubt, one of Satan's greatest footholds in your life. Make God your foundation. You can never be separated from his love.

PSALMS

VITAL STATISTICS

PURPOSE:
To provide poetry for the expression of praise, worship, and confession to God

AUTHORS:
David wrote 73 psalms; Asaph wrote 12; the sons of Korah wrote 9; Solomon wrote 2; Heman (with the sons of Korah), Ethan, and Moses each wrote one; and 51 psalms are anonymous. The New Testament ascribes two of the anonymous psalms (Psalms 2 and 95) to David (see Acts 4:25; Hebrews 4:7).

DATE WRITTEN:
Between the time of Moses (approximately 1440 B.C.) and the Babylonian captivity (586 B.C.)

SETTING:
For the most part, the psalms were not intended to be narrations of historical events. However, they often parallel events in history, such as David's flight from Saul and his sin with Bathsheba.

KEY VERSE:
"Let everything that lives sing praises to the LORD! Praise the LORD!" (150:6).

KEY PERSON:
David

KEY PLACE:
God's holy Temple

"HI, how are you?" "Fine." Not exactly an "in-depth" discussion, this brief interchange is normal as friends and acquaintances pass and briefly touch each other with a cliché or two. Actually, clichés are a way of life, saturating sentences and permeating paragraphs. But if this is the essence of our communication, our relationships will stall on a superficial plateau. Facts and opinions also fill our verbiage. These words go deeper, but the true person still lies hidden beneath them. In reality, it is only when honest feelings and emotions are shared real people can be known, loved, and helped.

Often, patterns of superficial communication spill over into our talks with God. We easily slide through well-worn lines recited for decades, or we quickly toss a cliché or two at God and call it prayer. There is no doubt that God hears and understands these feeble attempts, but by limiting the depth of our communication, we become shallow in our relationship with him. But God knows us, and he wants to have genuine communication with us.

At the center of the Bible is the book of Psalms. This great collection of songs and prayers expresses the heart and soul of humanity. In them, the whole range of human experiences is expressed. There are no clichés in this book. Instead, David and the other writers honestly pour out their true feelings, reflecting a dynamic, powerful, and life-changing friendship with God. The psalmists confess their sins, express their doubts and fears, ask God for help in times of trouble, and praise and worship him.

As you read the book of Psalms, you will hear believers crying out to God from the depths of despair, and you will hear them singing to him in the heights of celebration. But whether the psalmists are despairing or rejoicing, you will always hear them sharing honest feelings with their God. Because of the honesty expressed by the psalmists, men and women throughout history have come, again and again, to the book of Psalms for comfort during times of struggle and distress. And with the psalmists, they have risen from the depths of despair to new heights of joy and praise as they also discovered the power of God's everlasting love and forgiveness. Let the honesty of the psalmists guide you into a deep and genuine relationship with God.

THE BLUEPRINT

BOOK I
PSALMS 1:1—41:13

While the psalms are not organized by topic, it is helpful to compare the dominant themes in each section of the Psalms to the five books of Moses. This first collection of psalms, mainly written by David, is similar to the book of Genesis. Just as Genesis tells how mankind was created, fell into sin, and was then promised redemption, many of these psalms discuss humans as blessed, fallen, and redeemed by God.

BOOK II PSALMS 42:1—72:20	This collection of psalms, mainly written by David and the sons of Korah, is similar to the book of Exodus. Just as Exodus describes the nation of Israel, many of these psalms describe the nation as ruined and then recovered. As God rescued the nation of Israel, he also rescues us. We do not have to work out solutions first, but we can go to God with our problems and ask him to help.
BOOK III PSALMS 73:1—89:52	This collection of psalms, mainly written by Asaph or Asaph's descendants, is similar to the book of Leviticus. Just as Leviticus discusses the Tabernacle and God's holiness, many of these psalms discuss the Temple and God's enthronement. Because God is almighty, we can turn to him for deliverance. These psalms praise God because he is holy, and his perfect holiness deserves our worship and reverence.
BOOK IV PSALMS 90:1—106:48	This collection of psalms, mainly written by unknown authors, is similar to the book of Numbers. Just as Numbers discusses the relationship of the nation of Israel to surrounding nations, these psalms often mention the relationship of God's overruling Kingdom to the other nations. Because we are citizens of the Kingdom of God, we can keep the events and troubles of earth in their proper perspective.
BOOK V PSALMS 107:1—150:6	This collection of psalms, mainly written by David, is similar to the book of Deuteronomy. Just as Deuteronomy was concerned with God and his Word, these psalms are anthems of praise and thanksgiving for God and his Word. Most of the psalms were originally set to music and used in worship. We can use these psalms today as they were used in the past, as a hymnbook of praise and worship. This is a book that ought to make our hearts sing.

MEGATHEMES

THEME	EXPLANATION	IMPORTANCE
Praise	Psalms are songs of praise to God as our Creator, Sustainer, and Redeemer. Praise is recognizing, appreciating, and expressing God's greatness.	Focusing our thoughts on God moves us to praise him. The more we know him, the more we can appreciate what he has done for us.
God's power	God is all-powerful; and he always acts at the right time. He is sovereign over every situation. God's power is shown by the ways he reveals himself in creation, history, and his Word.	When we feel powerless, God can help us. His strength can overcome the despair of any pain or trial. We can always pray that he will deliver, protect, and sustain us.
Forgiveness	Many psalms are intense prayers asking God for forgiveness. God forgives us when we confess our sin and turn from it.	Because God forgives us, we can pray to him honestly and directly. When we receive his forgiveness, we move from alienation to intimacy, from guilt to love.
Thankfulness	We are grateful to God for his personal concern, help, and mercy. Not only does he protect, guide, and forgive us, but his creation provides everything we need.	When we realize how we benefit from knowing God, we can fully express our thanks to him. By thanking him often, we develop spontaneity in our prayer life.
Trust	God is faithful and just. When we put our trust in him, he quiets our hearts. Because he has been faithful throughout history, we can trust him in times of trouble.	People can be unfair and friends may desert us. But we can trust God. Knowing God intimately drives away doubt, fear, and loneliness.

BOOK I
Psalms 1:1—41:13

In this book, the psalmists praise God for his justice, express confidence in God's compassion, recount the depravity of humanity, plead for vindication, ask God to deliver them from their enemies, speak of the blessedness of the forgiven sinner, and portray God as a shepherd. We should worship God with the same sense of adoration found in these psalms.

Theme: Life's two roads. The life of the faithful person is contrasted with the life of the faithless person.
Author: Anonymous

1 1 Oh, the joys of those
who do not follow the advice of the wicked,
or stand around with sinners,
or join in with scoffers.
2 But they delight in doing everything the LORD wants;
day and night they think about his law.
3 They are like trees planted along the riverbank,
bearing fruit each season without fail.
Their leaves never wither,
and in all they do, they prosper.
4 But this is not true of the wicked.
They are like worthless chaff, scattered by the wind.
5 They will be condemned at the time of judgment.
Sinners will have no place among the godly.
6 For the LORD watches over the path of the godly,
but the path of the wicked leads to destruction.

1:1 Pss 17:4; 26:5 Prov 4:14 Jer 15:17
1:2 Pss 25:5; 63:5-6; 119:13-16
1:3 Gen 39:3 Jer 17:7-8 Ezek 47:12
1:4 Job 21:18 Ps 35:5 Isa 17:13
1:5 Pss 5:5; 9:7-8; 89:5, 7
1:6 Neh 1:7 Pss 9:5-6; 11:6 John 10:14 2 Tim 2:19

1:1 The writer begins his psalm extolling the joys of obeying God and refusing to listen to those who discredit or ridicule him. Our friends and associates can have a profound influence on us, often in very subtle ways. If we insist on friendships with those who mock what God considers important, we might sin by becoming indifferent to God's will. This attitude is the same as mocking. Do your friends build up your faith, or do they tear it down? True friends should help you to draw closer to God, not hinder.

1:1ff God doesn't judge people on the basis of race, sex, or national origin. He judges them on the basis of their faith in him and their response to his revealed will. Those who diligently try to obey God's will are blessed. They are like healthy, fruit-bearing trees planted along a riverbank with strong roots (Jeremiah 17:7, 8), and God promises to watch over them. God's wisdom guides their lives. In contrast, those who don't trust and obey God have meaningless lives that blow away like dust.

There are only two paths of life before us—God's way of obedience or the way of rebellion and destruction. Be sure to choose God's path, because the path you choose determines how you will spend eternity.

1:2 You can learn how to follow God by thinking about his Word. This means spending time reading and thinking about what you have read. It means asking yourself how you should change so you're living as God wants. Knowing and thinking about God's Word are the first steps toward applying it to your everyday life. If you want to follow God more closely, you must know what he says.

1:2 This "law" means all of Scripture: the first five books of Moses, the Prophets, and the other writings. The more we know of the whole scope of God's Word, the more resources we will have to guide us in our daily decisions.

1:2, 3 There is simple wisdom in these two verses: The more we delight in obeying God, the more fruitful we are. On the other hand, the more we allow those who ridicule God to affect our thoughts and attitudes, the more we separate ourselves from our source of nourishment. We must have contact with unbelievers if we are to witness to them, but we must not join in or imitate their sinful behavior. If you want despair, spend time with mocking sinners; but if you want God's blessing, make friends with those who love God and his Word.

1:3 When Scripture says, "In all they do, they prosper," it does not mean immunity to failure or difficulties. Nor is it a guarantee of health, wealth, and happiness. What the Bible means by prosperity is this: When we apply God's wisdom, the fruit (results or by-products) we bear will be good and receive God's approval. Just as a tree soaks up water and bears luscious fruit, we also are to soak up God's Word, producing actions and attitudes that honor God. To achieve anything worthwhile, we must have God's Word in our hearts.

1:4 Chaff is the outer shell (or husk) that must be removed to get at the valuable kernels of grain inside. Chaff was removed by a process called threshing and winnowing. After the plants were cut, they were crushed, and then the pieces were thrown into the air. Chaff is very light and is carried away by even the slightest wind, while the good grain falls back to the earth. Chaff is a symbol of a faithless life that drifts along without direction. Good grain is a symbol of a faithful life that can be used by God. Unlike grain, however, we can choose the direction we will take.

Theme: God's ultimate rule. A psalm written to celebrate the coronation of an Israelite king, but also written for the coronation of Christ, the eternal King.
Author: David (see Acts 4:25, 26)

2:1 Pss 21:11; 46:6 Acts 4:25-26
2:2 Pss 48:4-6; 74:18, 23 John 1:41
2:3 Jer 5:5
2:4 Pss 37:12-13; 59:8

2

1 Why do the nations rage?
Why do the people waste their time with futile plans?
2 The kings of the earth prepare for battle;
the rulers plot together
against the LORD
and against his anointed one.
3 "Let us break their chains," they cry,
"and free ourselves from this slavery."

4 But the one who rules in heaven laughs.
The Lord scoffs at them.

REASONS TO READ PSALMS

When you want . . .	*Read*
to find comfort	Psalm 23
to meet God intimately	Psalm 103
to learn a new prayer	Psalm 136
to learn a new song	Psalm 92
to learn more about God	Psalm 24
to understand yourself more clearly	Psalm 8
to know how to come to God each day	Psalm 5
to be forgiven for your sins	Psalm 51
to feel worthwhile	Psalm 139
to understand why you should read the Bible	Psalm 119
to give praise to God	Psalm 145
to know that God is in control	Psalm 146
to give thanks to God	Psalm 136
to please God	Psalm 15
to know why you should worship God	Psalm 104

God's Word was written to be studied, understood, and applied, and the book of Psalms lends itself most directly to application. We understand the psalms best when we "stand under" them and allow them to flow over us like a rain shower. We may turn to Psalms looking for something, but sooner or later we will meet Someone. As we read and memorize the psalms, we will gradually discover how much they are already part of us. They put into words our deepest hurts, longings, thoughts, and prayers. They gently push us toward being what God designed us to be—people loving and living for him.

2:1ff Several psalms are called *messianic* because of their prophetic descriptions of Jesus the Messiah (Christ)—his life, death, resurrection, and future reign. David, who may have been the author of this psalm, was a shepherd, soldier, and king. We can see that he was also a prophet (Acts 2:29, 30) because this psalm describes the rebellion of the nations and the coming of Christ to establish his eternal reign. This psalm is often mentioned in the New Testament (see Acts 4:25, 26; 13:33; Hebrews 1:5, 6; 5:5; Revelation 2:26, 27; 12:5; 19:15).

2:1ff David may have written these words during a conspiracy against Israel by some of the surrounding pagan nations. Chosen and anointed by God, David knew that God would fulfill his promise to bring the Messiah into the world through his bloodline (2 Samuel 7:16; 1 Chronicles 17:11, 12).

2:3 People often think they will be free if they can get away from God. Yet we all inevitably serve somebody or something, whether a human king, an organization, or even our own selfish desires. Just as a fish is not free when it leaves the water and a tree is not free when it leaves the soil, we are not free when we leave the Lord. We can find the one sure route to freedom by wholeheartedly serving God the Creator. God can set you free to be the person he created you to be.

2:4 God laughs, not at the nations, but at their confused thoughts about power. It is the laughter of a father when his three-year-old boasts that he or she can outrun him or beat him in a wrestling match. The father knows the boundaries of power of his little child, and God knows the boundaries of power of the nations. Every nation is limited, but God is transcendent. If you have to choose between confidence in God and confidence in any nation, choose God!

2:4 God is all-powerful. He created the world and knew about the empires of the earth long before they came into being (Daniel 2:26-45). But pride and power cause nations and leaders to rebel against God and try to break free of him. Our world has many leaders who boast of their power, who rant and rave against God and his people, who promise to take over and form their own empires. But God laughs because any power they have comes from him, and he can also take it from them. We need not fear the boasts of tyrants—they are in God's hands.

5 Then in anger he rebukes them,
terrifying them with his fierce fury.
6 For the LORD declares, "I have placed my chosen king on the throne
in Jerusalem, my holy city.*"
7 The king proclaims the LORD's decree:
"The LORD said to me, 'You are my son.*
Today I have become your Father.*
8 Only ask, and I will give you the nations as your inheritance,
the ends of the earth as your possession.
9 You will break them with an iron rod
and smash them like clay pots.'"

10 Now then, you kings, act wisely!
Be warned, you rulers of the earth!
11 Serve the LORD with reverent fear,
and rejoice with trembling.
12 Submit to God's royal son, or he will become angry,
and you will be destroyed in the midst of your pursuits—
for his anger can flare up in an instant.

But what joy for all who find protection in him!

2:5 Pss 76:7; 78:49-50
2:6 Pss 3:4; 45:6; 48:1-2
2:7 †Acts 13:32-33 †Heb 1:5-6; 5:5
2:8 Pss 21:1-2; 22:27
2:9 Pss 28:5; 110:5-6 Rev 2:26-27; 12:5; 19:15
2:10 Prov 8:14-15
2:11 Pss 5:7; 119:119-120 Heb 12:28
2:12 Pss 5:11; 34:8, 22 John 5:23 Rom 9:33 Rev 6:16

Theme: Confidently trusting God for protection and peace.
Author: David

3

A psalm of David, regarding the time David fled from his son Absalom.

1 O LORD, I have so many enemies;
so many are against me.
2 So many are saying,
"God will never rescue him!"
*Interlude**
3 But you, O LORD, are a shield around me,
my glory, and the one who lifts my head high.
4 I cried out to the LORD,
and he answered me from his holy mountain.
Interlude
5 I lay down and slept.
I woke up in safety,
for the LORD was watching over me.

3:1 2 Sam 15:12 Ps 69:4
3:2 Pss 22:7-8; 71:11
3:3 Pss 5:12; 27:5-6; 28:7; 62:7
3:4 Pss 4:3; 34:4; 99:9
3:5 Lev 26:6 Pss 4:8; 139:17-18 Prov 3:24-26

2:6 Hebrew *on Zion, my holy mountain.* **2:7a** Or *Son;* also in 2:12. **2:7b** Or *Today I reveal you as my son.*
3:2 Hebrew *Selah.* The meaning of this word is uncertain, though it is probably a musical or literary term. It is rendered *Interlude* throughout the Psalms.

2:11, 12 We must surrender fully and submit to the Son. Christ is not only God's chosen King, he is also the rightful King of our hearts and lives. To be ready for his coming, we must submit to his leadership every day.

3:1, 2 David felt like he was in the minority. There may have been as many as 10,000 soldiers surrounding him at this time (3:6). Not only did David's enemies view life differently, they actively sought to harm him. As king, David could have trusted his army to defeat Absalom. Instead, he depended upon God's mercy (3:4); therefore, he was at peace with whatever outcome occurred, knowing that God's great purposes would prevail. We can overcome fear by trusting God for his protection in our darkest hour.

3:1-3 David was not sitting on his throne in a place of power, but he was running for his life from his rebellious son, Absalom, and a host of traitors. When circumstances go against us, it is tempting to think that God also is against us. But David reminds us that the opposite is true. When everything seems to go against us, God is still for us. If circumstance has turned against you, don't blame God—seek him!

3:2 The word *Interlude* is a translation of the Hebrew word *Selah* which occurs 71 times in Psalms and three times in Habakkuk (3:3, 9, 13). Though its precise use is unknown, it was most likely a musical sign. Three suggestions are: (1) It was a musical direction to the singers and orchestra to play *forte* or *crescendo.* (2) It was a signal to lift up the hands or voice in worship, or to the priest to give a benediction. (3) It was a phrase like "Amen" meaning "So be it," or "Hallelujah" meaning "Praise the Lord."

3:4 God's holy mountain was Mount Moriah in Jerusalem, the place where David's son Solomon would build the Temple (2 Chronicles 3:1). David knew that God could not be confined to any space, but he wrote poetically, expressing confidence that God would hear him when he prayed. God responds to us when we earnestly pray to him.

3:5 Sleep does not come easily during a crisis. David could have had sleepless nights when his son Absalom rebelled and gathered an army to kill him. But he slept peacefully, even during the rebellion. What made the difference? David cried out to the Lord, and the Lord heard him. The assurance of answered prayer

3:6 Pss 23:4; 27:3; 118:10-13

6 I am not afraid of ten thousand enemies
who surround me on every side.

7 Arise, O LORD!
Rescue me, my God!
Slap all my enemies in the face!
Shatter the teeth of the wicked!

3:8 Pss 28:8; 29:11 Isa 43:11 Jer 3:23

8 Victory comes from you, O LORD.
May your blessings rest on your people. *Interlude*

Theme: Rejoicing in God's protection and peace. We can place our confidence in God because he will listen when we call on him.
Author: David

4

For the choir director: A psalm of David, to be accompanied by stringed instruments.

4:1 Pss 3:4; 17:6; 18:6, 18-19; 25:16

1 Answer me when I call,
O God who declares me innocent.

PSALMS FROM DAVID'S LIFE
Of the more than 70 psalms attributed to David, at least 14 of them are connected with specific events in his life. From them we see an outline of a growing relationship with God. They are listed here, roughly in chronological order.

Event in David's Life	*Reference*	*Psalm*	*What David Learned about God*
When Saul sent men to David's home to kill him	1 Samuel 19	59	God is my refuge.
While running from Saul	1 Samuel 21	34	I will praise the Lord at all times.
While running from Saul	1 Samuel 21	56	When I am afraid, I put my trust in God.
While hiding in the cave of Adullam	1 Samuel 22	142	God is my refuge.
After learning that Doeg had murdered 85 priests and their families	1 Samuel 22	52	God will bring evil people down to everlasting ruin.
When the Ziphites tried to betray him	1 Samuel 23	54	God is my helper.
While hiding in a cave	1 Samuel 24	57	I will take refuge in the shadow of God's wings until the violent storm has passed.
While hiding in the wilderness of En-gedi	1 Samuel 24	63	My soul thirsts for God; his right hand holds me securely.
When Saul's pursuit was over	2 Samuel 22	18	To the faithful, God shows himself faithful.
After being confronted about his adultery with Bathsheba	2 Samuel 12	51	The sacrifices of God are a broken spirit; a broken and repentant heart he will not despise.
During Absalom's rebellion	2 Samuel 15	3	From the Lord comes deliverance.
During Absalom's rebellion	2 Samuel 15	7	He is a righteous God who searches minds and hearts and can bring to an end the violence of the wicked and make the righteous secure.

brings peace. It is easier to sleep well when we have full assurance that God is in control of circumstances. If you are lying awake at night worrying about circumstances you can't change, pour out your heart to God, and thank him that he is in control. Then sleep will come.

3:7 David's call for God to act reveals his desire for justice against his persecutors. David himself was slapped and insulted, and here he simply asked for equal treatment for his enemies. He did this, not out of personal revenge, but for the sake of God's justice. Verse 8 shows the humility behind David's words—he realized that faith in God's timing was the answer to his question about the success the wicked had unfairly achieved.

4:1ff This psalm may have been written as David was asking his enemies to reconsider their support of Absalom. Others see this psalm as a prayer for relief from a calamity such as a drought (see 4:7). It was probably written shortly after Psalm 3.

Take away my distress.
Have mercy on me and hear my prayer.

2 How long will you people ruin my reputation?
How long will you make these groundless accusations?
How long will you pursue lies? *Interlude*

3 You can be sure of this:
The LORD has set apart the godly for himself.
The LORD will answer when I call to him.

4 Don't sin by letting anger gain control over you.
Think about it overnight and remain silent. *Interlude*
5 Offer proper sacrifices,
and trust in the LORD.
6 Many people say, "Who will show us better times?"
Let the smile of your face shine on us, LORD.
7 You have given me greater joy
than those who have abundant harvests of grain and wine.

8 I will lie down in peace and sleep,
for you alone, O LORD, will keep me safe.

4:2 Pss 3:3; 31:6, 18; 69:7-10, 19-20
4:3 Pss 6:8-9; 17:6; 31:23; 50:5; 135:4
4:4 Pss 33:8; 77:6; 119:11; Eph 4:26
4:5 Pss 37:3, 5; 50:14; 51:19
4:6 Num 6:26; Job 7:7; 9:25; Ps 80:3, 7, 19
4:7 Ps 97:11-12; Acts 14:17
4:8 Lev 25:18; Deut 12:10; Job 11:19; Pss 3:5; 16:9

Theme: The lies of enemies. God is able to defend us from lies spoken against us.
Author: David

5

For the choir director: A psalm of David, to be accompanied by the flute.

1 O LORD, hear me as I pray;
pay attention to my groaning.
2 Listen to my cry for help, my King and my God,
for I will never pray to anyone but you.
3 Listen to my voice in the morning, LORD.
Each morning I bring my requests to you and wait expectantly.

4 O God, you take no pleasure in wickedness;
you cannot tolerate the slightest sin.
5 Therefore, the proud will not be allowed to stand in your presence,
for you hate all who do evil.
6 You will destroy those who tell lies.
The LORD detests murderers and deceivers.

5:1 Pss 54:2; 84:3
5:2 Ps 84:3
5:3 Pss 88:13; 130:5
5:4 Pss 11:5; 34:16; 92:15
5:5 Pss 1:5; 11:5; 45:7; 75:4
5:6 Pss 52:4-5; 55:23

4:3 The godly are those who are faithful and devoted to God. David knew that God would hear him when he called and would answer him. We, too, can be confident that God listens to our prayers and answers when we call on him. Sometimes we think that God will not hear us because we have fallen short of his high standards for holy living. But if we have trusted Christ for salvation, God has forgiven us, and he will listen to us. When you feel as though your prayers are bouncing off the ceiling, remember that as a believer you have been set apart by God and that he loves you. He hears and answers, although his answers may not be what you expect. Look at your problems in the light of God's power instead of looking at God in the shadow of your problems.

4:5 Worship in David's day included animal sacrifices by the priests in the Tabernacle. The animal's blood covered the sins of the one who offered the animal. There were specific rules for offering sacrifices, but more important to God than ceremony was the offerer's attitude of submission and obedience (1 Samuel 15:22, 23). Today, a "proper sacrifice," one that is pleasing to God, is still the same. He wants our obedience and our praise before our gifts (Hebrews 13:15). Offer God your sacrifice of total obedience and heartfelt praise.

4:7 Two kinds of joy are contrasted here—inward joy that comes from knowing and trusting God and happiness that comes as a result of pleasant circumstances. Inward joy is steady as long as we trust God; happiness is unpredictable. Inward joy defeats discouragement; happiness covers it up. Inward joy is lasting; happiness is temporary.

5:1-3 The secret of a close relationship with God is to pray to him earnestly *each morning.* In the morning, our minds are more free from problems, and then we can commit the whole day to God. Regular communication helps any friendship and is certainly necessary for a strong relationship with God. We need to communicate with him daily. Do you have a regular time to pray and read God's Word?

5:5 God cannot condone or excuse even the smallest sin. Therefore, we cannot excuse ourselves for sinning only a little bit. As we grow spiritually, our sensitivity to sin increases. What is your reaction to sin in your life? Are you insensitive, unconcerned, disappointed, or comfortable? As God makes us aware of sin, we must be intolerant toward it and be willing to change. All believers should strive to be more tolerant of people but less tolerant of the sin in others and in themselves.

5:7 Pss 69:13; 115:11, 13

7 Because of your unfailing love, I can enter your house;
with deepest awe I will worship at your Temple.

5:8 Pss 27:11; 31:1, 3

8 Lead me in the right path, O LORD,
or my enemies will conquer me.
Tell me clearly what to do,
and show me which way to turn.

5:9 †Rom 3:13; Luke 11:44

9 My enemies cannot speak one truthful word.
Their deepest desire is to destroy others.
Their talk is foul, like the stench from an open grave.
Their speech is filled with flattery.

5:10 Pss 9:16; 36:12; 107:10-11

10 O God, declare them guilty.
Let them be caught in their own traps.
Drive them away because of their many sins,
for they rebel against you.

5:11 Pss 2:12; 12:7; 33:1; 64:10; Isa 65:13

11 But let all who take refuge in you rejoice;
let them sing joyful praises forever.
Protect them,
so all who love your name may be filled with joy.

5:12 Pss 29:11; 32:7, 10

12 For you bless the godly, O LORD,
surrounding them with your shield of love.

Theme: Deliverance in trouble. God is able to rescue us.
Author: David

6

*For the choir director: A psalm of David, to be accompanied by an eight-stringed instrument.**

6:1 Pss 2:5; 38:1

1 O LORD, do not rebuke me in your anger
or discipline me in your rage.

6:2 Ps 22:14

2 Have compassion on me, LORD, for I am weak.
Heal me, LORD, for my body is in agony.

6:3 Pss 88:3; 90:13; John 12:27

3 I am sick at heart.
How long, O LORD, until you restore me?

6:4 Ps 17:13

4 Return, O LORD, and rescue me.
Save me because of your unfailing love.

6:5 Ps 30:9; Isa 38:18

5 For in death, who remembers you?
Who can praise you from the grave?

6:6 Pss 42:3; 69:3

6 I am worn out from sobbing.
Every night tears drench my bed;
my pillow is wet from weeping.

6:7 Ps 31:9

7 My vision is blurred by grief;
my eyes are worn out because of all my enemies.

8 Go away, all you who do evil,
for the LORD has heard my crying.

6:TITLE Hebrew *with stringed instruments; according to the sheminith.*

6:1ff This is the first of seven "penitential" psalms, in which the writer humbly realizes his predicament (usually the result of sin), expresses sorrow over it, and demonstrates a fresh commitment to remain close to God. We don't know the cause of David's pain, but whatever the cause, he sought God for the remedy.

6:1-3 David accepted God's punishment, but he begged God not to discipline him in anger. Jeremiah also asked God to correct him gently and not in anger (Jeremiah 10:24). David recognized that if God treated him with justice alone and not with mercy, he would be wiped out by God's wrath. Often we want God to show mercy to us and justice to everyone else. God in his kindness forgives us instead of giving us what we deserve.

6:6 Pouring out his heart with tears, David was completely honest with God. We can be honest with God even when we are filled with anger or despair because God knows us thoroughly and wants the very best for us. Anger may result in rash outward acts or turning inward in depression. But because we trust in our all-powerful God, we don't have to be victims of circumstance or be weighed down by the guilt of sin. Be honest with God, and he will help you turn your attention from yourself to him and his mercy.

9 The LORD has heard my plea;
the LORD will answer my prayer.
10 May all my enemies be disgraced and terrified.
May they suddenly turn back in shame.

6:10
Pss 71:24; 73:19

Theme: A request for justice against those who make slanderous comments. God is the perfect judge and will punish those who persecute the innocent.
Author: David

7

A psalm of David, which he sang to the LORD concerning Cush of the tribe of Benjamin.

1 I come to you for protection, O LORD my God.
Save me from my persecutors—rescue me!
2 If you don't, they will maul me like a lion,
tearing me to pieces with no one to rescue me.

3 O LORD my God, if I have done wrong
or am guilty of injustice,
4 if I have betrayed a friend
or plundered my enemy without cause,
5 then let my enemies capture me.
Let them trample me into the ground.
Let my honor be left in the dust. *Interlude*

6 Arise, O LORD, in anger!
Stand up against the fury of my enemies!
Wake up, my God, and bring justice!
7 Gather the nations before you.
Sit on your throne high above them.
8 The LORD passes judgment on the nations.
Declare me righteous, O LORD,
for I am innocent, O Most High!
9 End the wickedness of the ungodly,
but help all those who obey you.
For you look deep within the mind and heart,
O righteous God.

10 God is my shield,
saving those whose hearts are true and right.
11 God is a judge who is perfectly fair.
He is angry with the wicked every day.

12 If a person does not repent,
God* will sharpen his sword;
he will bend and string his bow.
13 He will prepare his deadly weapons
and ignite his flaming arrows.

7:12 Hebrew *he.*

7:1
Pss 11:1; 31:1, 14-15

7:2
Pss 17:12; 57:4

7:3
1 Sam 24:11

7:4
1 Sam 24:7; 26:9

7:6
Pss 3:7; 35:23; 94:2; 138:7

7:8
Pss 18:20; 35:24; 96:13

7:9
1 Chr 28:9
Pss 11:4-5; 34:21; 94:23
Jer 11:20
Rev 2:23

7:10
Pss 18:2, 30; 97:10-11; 125:4

7:11
Pss 50:6; 90:9

7:12
Deut 32:41
Ps 64:7
Ezek 33:9

7:13
Pss 18:14; 45:5; 64:7

7:1-6 Have you ever been falsely accused or so badly hurt that you wanted revenge? David wrote this psalm in response to the slanderous accusations of those who claimed he was trying to kill Saul and seize the throne (1 Samuel 24:9-11). Instead of taking matters into his own hands and striking back, David cried out to God for justice. The proper response to slander is prayer, not revenge, because God says, "I will take vengeance; I will repay those who deserve it" (Romans 12:19; see also Deuteronomy 32:35, 36; Hebrews 10:30). Instead of striking back, ask God to take your case, bring justice, and restore your reputation.

7:9 God looks "deep within the mind and heart." Nothing is hidden from God—this can be either terrifying or comforting. Our thoughts are an open book to him. Because he knows even our motives, we have no place to hide, no way to pretend we can get away with sin. But that very knowledge also gives us great comfort. We don't have to impress God or put up a false front. Instead, we can trust God to help us work through our weaknesses in order to serve him as he has planned. When we truly follow God, he rewards our efforts.

7:14 Job 15:35; Isa 59:4; Jas 1:15
7:15 Job 4:7-8; Ps 57:6
7:16 Esth 9:24-25; Ps 140:9, 11
7:17 Pss 9:2; 66:1-2, 4; 71:15-16

14 The wicked conceive evil;
they are pregnant with trouble
and give birth to lies.
15 They dig a pit to trap others
and then fall into it themselves.
16 They make trouble,
but it backfires on them.
They plan violence for others,
but it falls on their own heads.
17 I will thank the LORD because he is just;
I will sing praise to the name of the LORD Most High.

Theme: The greatness of God assures the worth of mankind. God, the all-powerful Creator, cares for his most valuable creation—people.
Author: David

8

*For the choir director: A psalm of David, to be accompanied by a stringed instrument.**

8:1 Pss 57:5, 11; 66:2; 113:4; 148:13
8:2 Matt 21:16
8:3 Pss 89:11; 136:9
8:4 Job 7:17; Ps 144:3; Heb 2:6-8
8:5 Pss 21:5; 82:6; 103:4
8:6 Gen 1:26, 28; †1 Cor 15:27

1 O LORD, our Lord, the majesty of your name fills the earth!
Your glory is higher than the heavens.
2 You have taught children and nursing infants
to give you praise.*
They silence your enemies
who were seeking revenge.
3 When I look at the night sky and see the work of your fingers—
the moon and the stars you have set in place—
4 what are mortals that you should think of us,
mere humans that you should care for us?*
5 For you made us only a little lower than God,*
and you crowned us with glory and honor.
6 You put us in charge of everything you made,
giving us authority over all things—

8:TITLE Hebrew *according to the gittith.* **8:2** As in Greek version; Hebrew reads *to show strength.* **8:4** Hebrew *what is man that you should think of him, the son of man that you should care for him?* **8:5** Or *a little lower than the angels;* Hebrew reads *Elohim.*

7:14-16 When allowed to run its course, evil destroys itself. Violent people become victims of violence, and liars become victims of others' deceit (9:15, 16). But in the process, innocent people are hurt. Sometimes God intervenes and stops evildoers in their tracks in order to protect his followers. At other times, for reasons known only to him, God allows evil to continue even though innocent people are hurt. It is during these times that we must ask God to protect us. Remember that God will execute final justice, although it may not be during our lifetime.

7:17 During a time of great evil and injustice, David was grateful that God is just and fair (see also 7:11). When we wonder if anyone is honest or fair, we can be assured that God will continue to bring justice and fairness when we involve him in our activities. If you ever feel that you are being treated unfairly, ask the one who is always fair and just to be with you. Then thank him for his presence (see Isaiah 42:1-6).

8:1ff Portions of this psalm are quoted in the New Testament and applied to Christ (1 Corinthians 15:27; Hebrews 2:6-8). God became human—lower than God—in the person of Jesus (8:5), and he will raise all who belong to him when he comes to reign over the new heaven and new earth. Jesus is the only person who perfectly reflects God's image (Galatians 2:20; Colossians 1:15).

8:2 Children are able to trust and praise God without doubts or reservations. As we get older, many of us find this more and more difficult to do. Ask God to give you childlike faith, removing any barriers to having a closer walk with him.

8:3, 4 To respect God's majesty, we must compare ourselves to his greatness. When we look at creation, we often feel small by comparison. To feel small is a healthy way to get back to reality, but God does not want us to dwell on our smallness. Humility means proper respect for God, not self-depreciation.

8:3-5 When we look at the vast expanse of creation, we wonder how God could be concerned for people who constantly disappoint him. Yet God created us only a little lower than himself or the angels! The next time you question your worth as a person, remember that God considers you highly valuable. We have great worth because we bear the stamp of the Creator. (See Genesis 1:26, 27 for the extent of worth God places on all people.) Because God has already declared how valuable we are to him, we can be set free from feelings of worthlessness.

8:6 God gave human beings tremendous authority—to be in charge of the whole earth. But with great authority comes great responsibility. If we own a pet, we have the legal authority to do with it as we wish, but we also have the responsibility to feed and care for it. How do you treat God's creation? Use your resources wisely because God holds you accountable as stewards.

7 the sheep and the cattle
and all the wild animals,
8 the birds in the sky, the fish in the sea,
and everything that swims the ocean currents.

9 O LORD, our Lord, the majesty of your name fills the earth!

Theme: God never ignores our cries for help.
Author: David, probably written after a victory over the Philistines

9

For the choir director: A psalm of David, to be sung to the tune "Death of the Son."

1 I will thank you, LORD, with all my heart;
I will tell of all the marvelous things you have done.
2 I will be filled with joy because of you.
I will sing praises to your name, O Most High.

3 My enemies turn away in retreat;
they are overthrown and destroyed before you.
4 For you have judged in my favor;
from your throne, you have judged with fairness.

5 You have rebuked the nations and destroyed the wicked;
you have wiped out their names forever.
6 My enemies have met their doom;
their cities are perpetual ruins.
Even the memory of their uprooted cities is lost.

7 But the LORD reigns forever,
executing judgment from his throne.
8 He will judge the world with justice
and rule the nations with fairness.

9 The LORD is a shelter for the oppressed,
a refuge in times of trouble.
10 Those who know your name trust in you,
for you, O LORD, have never abandoned anyone who searches for you.

11 Sing praises to the LORD who reigns in Jerusalem.*
Tell the world about his unforgettable deeds.
12 For he who avenges murder cares for the helpless.
He does not ignore those who cry to him for help.

13 LORD, have mercy on me.
See how I suffer at the hands of those who hate me.
Snatch me back from the jaws of death.

9:1 Pss 26:7; 86:12
9:2 Pss 66:2, 4; 92:1; 104:34
9:3 Pss 27:2; 56:9
9:4 Pss 47:8; 140:12; 1 Pet 2:23
9:5 Pss 69:28; 119:21
9:6 Pss 34:16; 40:15
9:7 Pss 10:16; 89:14-15
9:8 Ps 96:13
9:9 Pss 18:2; 37:39; 59:9, 16-17
9:10 Pss 37:28; 91:14; 94:14
9:11 Pss 76:2; 105:1
9:12 Gen 9:5-6; Ps 72:14
9:13 Pss 30:3; 38:19; 86:13

9:11 Hebrew *Zion;* also in 9:14.

9:1ff Praise is expressing to God our appreciation and understanding of his worth. It is saying thank you for each aspect of his divine nature. Our inward attitude becomes outward expression. When we praise God, we help ourselves by expanding our awareness of who he is. In each psalm you read, look for an attribute or characteristic of God for which you can thank him.

9:4 God upholds our just cause; he is our vindicator (one who clears us from criticism and justifies us before others). In this life, we may face many injustices: (1) We may be falsely accused and misunderstood by friends and enemies; (2) we may not be truly appreciated by others for the love we show; (3) the true value of our work and service may not be duly rewarded; (4) our ideas may be ignored. But God is to be praised, for he sees and remembers all the good we do, and it is up to him to decide the timing and the appropriateness of our rewards. If we do not trust him to vindicate us, then we will be susceptible to hatred and self-pity. If we do trust him, we can experience God's peace and be free from the worry of how others perceive us and treat us.

9:10 God will never abandon those who seek him. God's promise does not mean that if we trust in him we will escape loss or suffering; it means that God himself will never leave us no matter what we face.

9:11 God does not live only in Jerusalem (or Zion, another name for Mount Moriah, the hill on which the Temple was built); he is everywhere all the time. The focal point of Israelite worship, however, came to be Jerusalem and its beautiful Temple. God was present in the Tabernacle (Exodus 25:8, 9) and in the Temple built by Solomon (2 Chronicles 7:16). From this central place of worship, the Jews were to tell the world about the one true God.

9:13, 14 All of us want God to help us when we are in trouble, but often for different reasons. Some want God's help so that

9:14
Pss 13:5; 20:5; 35:9; 51:12; 106:2

14 Save me, so I can praise you publicly at Jerusalem's gates,
so I can rejoice that you have rescued me.

9:15
Pss 7:15; 35:8

15 The nations have fallen into the pit they dug for others.
They have been caught in their own trap.
16 The LORD is known for his justice.
The wicked have trapped themselves in their own snares. *Quiet Interlude**

9:17
Pss 49:14; 50:22

17 The wicked will go down to the grave.*
This is the fate of all the nations who ignore God.

9:18
Pss 9:12; 62:5; 71:5

18 For the needy will not be forgotten forever;
the hopes of the poor will not always be crushed.

9:19
Num 10:35
2 Chr 14:11

19 Arise, O LORD!
Do not let mere mortals defy you!
Let the nations be judged in your presence!

9:20
Ps 62:9

20 Make them tremble in fear, O LORD.
Let them know they are merely human. *Interlude*

Theme: Why do the wicked succeed? Although God may seem to be hidden at times, we can be assured that he is aware of every injustice.
Author: Anonymous, but probably David. Many ancient manuscripts combine Psalms 9 and 10, and Psalm 9 was written by David.

10

10:1
Pss 13:1; 22:1; 55:1

1 O LORD, why do you stand so far away?
Why do you hide when I need you the most?

10:2
Pss 7:15; 9:16; 73:6, 8

2 Proud and wicked people viciously oppress the poor.
Let them be caught in the evil they plan for others.

10:3
Pss 49:6; 94:3-4

3 For they brag about their evil desires;
they praise the greedy and curse the LORD.

10:4
Pss 14:1; 36:1-2

4 These wicked people are too proud to seek God.
They seem to think that God is dead.

10:5
Pss 28:5; 52:7

5 Yet they succeed in everything they do.
They do not see your punishment awaiting them.
They pour scorn on all their enemies.

10:6
Pss 30:6-7; 49:11

6 They say to themselves, "Nothing bad will ever happen to us!
We will be free of trouble forever!"

10:7
Pss 59:12; 73:8; 140:3
†Rom 3:14

7 Their mouths are full of cursing, lies, and threats.
Trouble and evil are on the tips of their tongues.

10:8
Pss 11:2; 94:6-7

8 They lurk in dark alleys,
murdering the innocent who pass by.

9:16 Hebrew *Higgaion Selah.* The meaning of this phrase is uncertain. **9:17** Hebrew *to Sheol.*

---

they will be successful and other people will like them. Others want God's help so that they will be comfortable and feel good about themselves. David, however, wanted help from God so that justice would be restored to Israel and so that he could show others God's power. When you call to God for help, consider your motive. Is it to save yourself pain and embarrassment or to bring God glory and honor?

9:18 The world may ignore the plight of the needy, crushing any earthly hope they may have. But God, the champion of the weak, promises that this will not be the case forever. Wicked nations, which forget the Lord and refuse to help their people, will be judged by God. He knows our needs, he knows our tendency to despair, and he has promised to care for us (see also 9:9, 12). Even when others forget us, he will remember.

10:1 "Why do you hide when I need you the most?" To the psalmist, God seemed far away. But even though the writer had honest doubts, he did not stop praying or conclude that God no longer cared. He was not complaining but simply asking God to hurry to his aid. It is during those times when we feel most alone or oppressed that we need to keep praying, telling God about our troubles.

10:4-6 Some people succeed in everything they do, and they brag that no one, not even God, can keep them down. We may wonder why God allows these people to amass great wealth while they despise him as they do. But why are we upset when the wicked prosper? Are we angry about the damage they are doing or just jealous of their success? To answer these questions, we must gain the right perspective on wickedness and wealth. The wicked will surely be punished because God hates their evil deeds. Wealth is only temporary. It is not necessarily a sign of God's approval on a person's life; nor is lack of it a sign of God's disapproval. Don't let wealth become your obsession. See Proverbs 30:7, 8 for a prayer you can pray.

They are always searching
for some helpless victim.
9 Like lions they crouch silently,
waiting to pounce on the helpless.
Like hunters they capture their victims
and drag them away in nets.
10 The helpless are overwhelmed and collapse;
they fall beneath the strength of the wicked.
11 The wicked say to themselves, "God isn't watching!
He will never notice!"

12 Arise, O LORD!
Punish the wicked, O God!
Do not forget the helpless!
13 Why do the wicked get away with cursing God?
How can they think, "God will never call us to account"?
14 But you do see the trouble and grief they cause.
You take note of it and punish them.
The helpless put their trust in you.
You are the defender of orphans.

15 Break the arms of these wicked, evil people!
Go after them until the last one is destroyed!
16 The LORD is king forever and ever!
Let those who worship other gods be swept from the land.

17 LORD, you know the hopes of the helpless.
Surely you will listen to their cries and comfort them.
18 You will bring justice to the orphans and the oppressed,
so people can no longer terrify them.

10:9 Pss 10:2; 17:12; 59:3; 140:5
10:11 Ps 10:4
10:12 Pss 9:12; 17:7
10:14 Pss 9:12; 22:9-11; 37:5
10:15 Pss 37:17; 140:11
10:16 Deut 8:20 Ps 29:10
10:17 1 Chr 29:18 Pss 9:18; 34:15; 145:19
10:18 Pss 9:9; 74:21; 146:9 Isa 29:20

Theme: God's rule provides stability in the midst of panic. Because we can trust him, we can face our problems.
Author: David

11

For the choir director: A psalm of David.

1 I trust in the LORD for protection.
So why do you say to me,
"Fly to the mountains for safety!
2 The wicked are stringing their bows
and setting their arrows in the bowstrings.
They shoot from the shadows at those who do right.
3 The foundations of law and order have collapsed.
What can the righteous do?"

11:1 Ps 121:1-2
11:2 Pss 7:12; 64:3-4
11:3 Ps 82:5

10:11 There is an incompatibility between blind arrogance and the presence of God in our hearts. The proud person depends on himself rather than on God. This causes God's guiding influences to leave his life. When God's presence is welcome, there is no room for pride because he makes us aware of our true selves.

10:14 God sees and takes note of each evil deed, encourages us, and listens to our cries (10:17). He is always with us. We can face the wicked because we do not face them alone. God is by our side.

11:1-4 David was forced to flee for safety several times. Being God's anointed king did not make him immune to injustice and hatred from others. This psalm may have been written when he was being hunted by Saul (1 Samuel 18–31) or during the days of Absalom's rebellion (2 Samuel 15–18). In both instances, David fled, but not as if all was lost. He knew God was in control. While David wisely avoided trouble, he did not fearfully run away from his troubles.

11:1-4 David seems to be speaking to those who are advising him to run from his enemies. David's faith contrasts dramatically with the fear of the advisers who tell him to flee. Faith in God keeps us from losing hope and helps us resist fear. David's advisers were afraid because they saw only frightening circumstances and crumbling foundations. David was comforted and optimistic because he knew God was greater than anything his enemies could bring against him (7:10; 16:1; 31:2, 3).

11:4 Pss 34:15-16; 103:19

4 But the LORD is in his holy Temple;
the LORD still rules from heaven.
He watches everything closely,
examining everyone on earth.

11:5 Gen 22:1 Pss 5:5; 34:19

5 The LORD examines both the righteous and the wicked.
He hates everyone who loves violence.

11:6 Jer 4:11-12 Ezek 38:22

6 He rains down blazing coals on the wicked,
punishing them with burning sulfur and scorching winds.

11:7 Pss 7:9-11; 17:15; 33:5

7 For the LORD is righteous, and he loves justice.
Those who do what is right will see his face.

Theme: The proud and lying words of people versus the true and pure words of God. A call for protection against those who try to manipulate us.
Author: David

12

*For the choir director: A psalm of David, to be accompanied by an eight-stringed instrument.**

12:1 Mic 7:1-2

1 Help, O LORD, for the godly are fast disappearing!
The faithful have vanished from the earth!

12:2 Pss 28:3; 41:6 Jer 9:8 Rom 16:18

2 Neighbors lie to each other,
speaking with flattering lips and insincere hearts.

12:3 Pss 55:21; 73:8-9

3 May the LORD bring their flattery to an end
and silence their proud tongues.
4 They say, "We will lie to our hearts' content.
Our lips are our own—who can stop us?"

12:5 Pss 3:7; 34:6; 35:10

5 The LORD replies, "I have seen violence done to the helpless,
and I have heard the groans of the poor.
Now I will rise up to rescue them,
as they have longed for me to do."

12:6 Pss 19:8-10; 119:140 Prov 30:5

6 The LORD's promises are pure,
like silver refined in a furnace,
purified seven times over.

12:7 Pss 37:28; 97:10

7 Therefore, LORD, we know you will protect the oppressed,
preserving them forever from this lying generation,

12:8 Ps 55:10-11

8 even though the wicked strut about,
and evil is praised throughout the land.

12:TITLE Hebrew *according to the sheminith.*

11:4 When the foundations are shaking and you wish you could hide, remember that God is still in control. His power is not diminished by any turn of events. Nothing happens without his knowledge and permission. When you feel like running away—run to God. He will restore justice and goodness on the earth in his good time.

11:5 God does not preserve believers from difficult circumstances, but he examines (or tests) both the righteous and the wicked. For some, God's tests become a refining fire, while for others, they become an incinerator for destruction. Don't ignore or defy the tests and challenges that come your way. Use them as opportunities for you to grow.

12:1 Living for God in a deceitful world can be a difficult and lonely battle. At one time the great prophet Elijah felt so lonely he wanted to die. But God told him that there were 7,000 other faithful servants (1 Kings 19:4, 14, 18). We are never alone in our battle against evil. When you feel alone, seek out other believers for strength and support.

12:2-4 We may be tempted to believe that lies are relatively harmless, even useful at times. But God does not overlook lies, flattery, deception, or boasting. Each of these sins originates from a bad attitude that is eventually expressed in our speech. The tongue can be our greatest enemy because, though small, it can do great damage (James 3:5, 6). Be careful how you use yours.

12:5 God cares for the weak and the needy. Here he promises to protect the downtrodden and confront their oppressors. We should identify with God's attitude. His work is not done until we care for the needs of the poor.

12:6 Sincerity and truth are extremely valuable because they are so rare. Many people are deceivers, liars, flatterers; they think they will get what they want by deception. As a king, David certainly faced his share of such people, who hoped to win his favor and gain advancement through flattery. When we feel as though sincerity and truth have nearly gone out of existence, we have one hope—the word of God. God's words are as flawless as refined silver. So listen carefully when he speaks.

Theme: Praying for relief from despair. We must continue to trust God even when he doesn't answer us immediately.
Author: David

13 *For the choir director: A psalm of David.*

[1] O LORD, how long will you forget me? Forever?
How long will you look the other way?
[2] How long must I struggle with anguish in my soul,
with sorrow in my heart every day?
How long will my enemy have the upper hand?

[3] Turn and answer me, O LORD my God!
Restore the light to my eyes, or I will die.
[4] Don't let my enemies gloat, saying, "We have defeated him!"
Don't let them rejoice at my downfall.

[5] But I trust in your unfailing love.
I will rejoice because you have rescued me.
[6] I will sing to the LORD
because he has been so good to me.

13:1 Job 13:24; Pss 44:24; 89:46
13:2 Ps 42:4-5, 9
13:3 Ezra 9:8; Job 33:29-30; Ps 5:1
13:4 Pss 25:2; 38:16
13:5 Pss 9:14; 52:8
13:6 Ps 116:7

Theme: Only the fool denies God. How foolish it must seem to God when people say there is no God.
Author: David

14 *For the choir director: A psalm of David.*

[1] Only fools say in their hearts,
"There is no God."
They are corrupt, and their actions are evil;
no one does good!

[2] The LORD looks down from heaven
on the entire human race;
he looks to see if there is even one with real understanding,
one who seeks for God.
[3] But no, all have turned away from God;
all have become corrupt.
No one does good,
not even one!

14:1-7 //Ps 53:1-6
14:1 Pss 10:4; 53:1; †Rom 3:10-12
14:2 Pss 33:13-15; 102:19
14:3 Pss 58:3; 143:2

13:1 Sometimes all we need to do is talk over a problem with a friend to help put it in perspective. In this psalm, the phrase "how long" occurs four times in the first two verses, indicating the depth of David's distress. David expressed his feelings to God and found strength. By the end of his prayer, he was able to express hope and trust in God. Through prayer we can express our feelings and talk our problems out with God. He helps us regain the right perspective, and this gives us peace (Habakkuk 3:17-19).

13:1-5 David frequently claimed that God was slow to act on his behalf. We often feel this same impatience. It seems that evil and suffering go unchecked, and we wonder when God is going to stop them. David affirmed that he would continue to trust God no matter how long he had to wait for God's justice to be realized. When you feel impatient, remember David's steadfast faith in God's unfailing love.

14:1-3 The true atheist is either foolish or wicked—foolish because he ignores the evidence that God exists or wicked because he refuses to live by God's truths. We become atheists in practice when we rely more on ourselves than on God. The fool mentioned here is someone who is aggressively perverse in his actions. To speak in direct defiance of God is utterly foolish according to the Bible.

14:3 No one but God is perfect; all of us stand guilty before him (see Romans 3:23) and need his forgiveness. No matter how well we perform or how much we achieve compared to others, none of us can boast of his or her goodness when compared to God's standard. God not only expects us to obey his guidelines, but he wants us to love him with all our heart. No one except Jesus Christ has done that perfectly. Because we all fall short, we must turn to Christ to save us (Romans 10:9-11). Have you asked him to save you?

14:3, 4 David applies these observations to his enemies when he says the evildoers "eat up my people like bread" (17:4). "All have turned away from God; all have become corrupt. No one does good, not even one!" By contrast, David said, "You have scrutinized me and found nothing amiss" (17:3).

There is a clear distinction between those who worship God and those who refuse to worship him. David worshiped God, and under his leadership Israel obeyed God and prospered. Several hundred years later, however, Israel forgot God, and it became difficult to distinguish between God's followers and those who worshiped idols. When Isaiah called Israel to repentance, he, like David, spoke of people who had gone astray (Isaiah 53:6). But Isaiah was talking about the Israelites themselves. Paul quoted Psalm 14 in Romans 3:10-12. He made the image of straying sheep even more general, referring to all people. The whole human race—Jew and Gentile alike—has turned away from God.

14:4 Isa 64:7

4 Will those who do evil never learn?
They eat up my people like bread;
they wouldn't think of praying to the LORD.

14:5 Pss 73:15; 112:2

5 Terror will grip them,
for God is with those who obey him.

14:6 Pss 9:9; 40:17

6 The wicked frustrate the plans of the oppressed,
but the LORD will protect his people.

14:7 Job 42:10 Pss 53:6; 85:1-2

7 Oh, that salvation would come from Mount Zion to rescue Israel!
For when the LORD restores his people,
Jacob will shout with joy, and Israel will rejoice.

Theme: Guidelines for living a blameless life.
Author: David

15

A psalm of David.

15:1 Pss 24:3; 27:5-6

1 Who may worship in your sanctuary, LORD?
Who may enter your presence on your holy hill?

15:2 Ps 24:4 Eph 4:25

2 Those who lead blameless lives
and do what is right,
speaking the truth from sincere hearts.

15:3 Exod 23:1 Ps 28:3

3 Those who refuse to slander others
or harm their neighbors
or speak evil of their friends.

15:4 Judg 11:35 Acts 28:10

4 Those who despise persistent sinners,
and honor the faithful followers of the LORD
and keep their promises even when it hurts.

TROUBLES AND COMPLAINTS IN PSALMS

We can relate to the psalms because they express our feelings. We all face troubles, as did the psalm writers hundreds of years ago, and we often respond as they did. In Psalm 3, David told God how he felt about the odds against him. But within three verses, the king realized that God's presence and care made the odds meaningless. This experience is repeated in many of the psalms. Usually, the hope and confidence in God outweigh the fear and suffering; sometimes they do not. Still, the psalm writers consistently poured out their thoughts and emotions to God. When they felt abandoned by God, they told him so. When they were impatient with how slowly God seemed to be answering their prayers, they also told him so. Because they recognized the difference between themselves and God, they were free to be men and to be honest with their Creator. That is why so many of the dark psalms end in the light. The psalmists started by expressing their feelings and ended up remembering to whom they were speaking!

Although we have much in common with the psalmists, we may differ in two ways: We might not tell God what we are really thinking and feeling; therefore, we also might not recognize, even faintly, who is listening to our prayers!

Notice this pattern as you read Psalms, and put the psalmists' insights to the test. You may well find that your awareness and appreciation of God will grow as you are honest with him. (See Psalms 3; 6; 13; 31; 37; 64; 77; 102; 121; 142.)

14:5 If "God is with those who obey him," then those who attack God's followers may be attacking God. To attack God is utterly futile (see 2:4, 5, 10-12). Thus, while we may feel we are losing the battle, there can be absolutely no doubt that our ultimate victory is in God.

15:1 *Sanctuary* and *holy hill* are interchangeable words describing the focal point of Israelite worship—the dwelling place of God. In Hebrew poetry the repeating pattern is found more in the thought than in the sound or rhythm.

15:1ff God calls his people to be morally upright, and, in this psalm, he gives us 10 standards to determine how we are doing. We live among evil people whose standards and morals are eroding. Our standards for living should not come from our evil society but from God. For other references where righteous conduct is summarized, see Isaiah 33:15; 56:1; Micah 6:8; Habakkuk 2:4; and Mark 12:29-31.

15:3, 4 Words are powerful, and how you use them reflects on your relationship with God. Perhaps nothing so identifies Christians as their ability to control their speech—speaking the truth, refusing to slander, and keeping oaths (promises). Watch what you say. (See James 3:1-12 for more on the importance of controlling your tongue.)

5 Those who do not charge interest on the money they lend,
and who refuse to accept bribes to testify against the innocent.

Such people will stand firm forever.

15:5 Exod 22:25; 23:8 Deut 16:19

Theme: The joys and benefits of a life lived in companionship with God. We enjoy these benefits now and eternally.
Author: David

16

A psalm of David.

1 Keep me safe, O God,
for I have come to you for refuge.

16:1 Pss 7:1; 17:8

2 I said to the LORD, "You are my Master!
All the good things I have are from you."
3 The godly people in the land
are my true heroes!
I take pleasure in them!
4 Those who chase after other gods will be filled with sorrow.
I will not take part in their sacrifices
or even speak the names of their gods.

16:2 Ps 73:25
16:3 Pss 101:6; 119:63
16:4 Exod 23:13 Josh 23:7 Pss 32:10; 106:37-38

5 LORD, you alone are my inheritance, my cup of blessing.
You guard all that is mine.
6 The land you have given me is a pleasant land.
What a wonderful inheritance!

16:6 Ps 78:55 Jer 3:19

7 I will bless the LORD who guides me;
even at night my heart instructs me.
8 I know the LORD is always with me.
I will not be shaken, for he is right beside me.

16:7 Pss 73:24; 77:6
16:8 Pss 27:8; 73:23; 110:5; 123:1-2

9 No wonder my heart is filled with joy,
and my mouth* shouts his praises!
My body rests in safety.
10 For you will not leave my soul among the dead*
or allow your godly one* to rot in the grave.

16:10 Pss 49:15; 86:13 †Acts 2:25-28; 13:35

16:9 As in Greek version; Hebrew reads *glory.* **16:10a** Hebrew *in Sheol.* **16:10b** Or *your Holy One.*

15:5 God was against the Jews' charging interest or making a profit on loans to needy, fellow Jews (see also Exodus 22:25; Leviticus 25:35-37), although charging interest on loans to foreigners was allowed (Deuteronomy 23:20). Interest was also allowable for business purposes, as long as it wasn't exorbitant (Proverbs 28:8).

15:5 Some people are so obsessed with money that they will change their God-given standards and life-style to get it. If money is a controlling force in your life, it must be curbed, or it will harm others and destroy your relationship with God.

16:7, 8 It is human nature to make our own plans and *then* ask God to bless them. Instead, we should seek God's will first. By constantly thinking about the Lord and his way of living, we will gain insights that will help us make right decisions and live the way God desires. Communicating with God allows him to counsel us and give us wisdom.

16:8 By saying that he "will not be shaken," David was talking about the unique sense of security felt by believers. God does not exempt believers from the day-to-day circumstances of life. Believers and unbelievers alike experience pain, trouble, and failure at times (Matthew 5:45). Unbelievers have a sense of hopelessness about life and confusion over their true purpose on earth. Those who seek God, however, can move ahead, confident in knowing what is right in God's eyes. They know that God will keep them from straying off his chosen path.

16:8-11 This psalm is often called a messianic psalm because it is quoted in the New Testament as referring to the resurrection of Jesus Christ. Both Peter and Paul quoted from this psalm when speaking of Christ's bodily resurrection (see Acts 2:25-28, 31; 13:35-37).

16:9 David's heart was glad—he had found the secret to joy. True joy is far deeper than happiness; we can feel joy in spite of our deepest troubles. Happiness is temporary because it is based on external circumstances, but joy is lasting because it is based on God's presence within us. As we contemplate his daily presence, we will find contentment. As we understand the future he has for us, we will experience joy. Don't base your life on circumstances, but on God.

16:10 David stated confidently that God would not leave him in the grave. Many people fear death because they can neither control nor understand it. As believers, we can be assured that God will not forget us when we die. He will bring us to life again to live with him forever. This provides *real* security. For other passages about resurrection, see Job 19:25, 26; Isaiah 26:19; Daniel 12:2, 13; Mark 13:27; 1 Corinthians 15:12-58; 1 Thessalonians 4:13-18; Revelation 20:11–21:4.

16:11
Ps 36:7-8

11 You will show me the way of life,
granting me the joy of your presence
and the pleasures of living with you forever.

Theme: A plea for justice in the face of false accusations and persecution. David urges us to realize the true goal of life—to know God—and the true reward of life—to see God one day.
Author: David, written while he was being persecuted by Saul

17

A prayer of David.

17:1
Pss 61:1; 88:2; 142:6

1 O LORD, hear my plea for justice.
Listen to my cry for help.
Pay attention to my prayer,
for it comes from an honest heart.

17:2
Pss 98:8-9; 99:4; 103:6

2 Declare me innocent,
for you know those who do right.

17:3
Job 23:10
Pss 26:1-2; 39:1; 66:10
Jer 50:20

3 You have tested my thoughts and examined my heart in the night.
You have scrutinized me and found nothing amiss,
for I am determined not to sin in what I say.

17:4
Pss 10:5-11; 119:9, 101

4 I have followed your commands,
which have kept me from going along with cruel and evil people.

17:5
Pss 18:36; 37:30-31; 44:18

5 My steps have stayed on your path;
I have not wavered from following you.

6 I am praying to you because I know you will answer, O God.
Bend down and listen as I pray.
7 Show me your unfailing love in wonderful ways.
You save with your strength
those who seek refuge from their enemies.

17:8
Deut 32:10
Ruth 2:12
Pss 36:7; 91:1, 4

8 Guard me as the apple of your eye.
Hide me in the shadow of your wings.
9 Protect me from wicked people who attack me,
from murderous enemies who surround me.

17:10
1 Sam 2:3
Pss 31:18; 73:7-8

10 They are without pity.
Listen to their boasting.

17:11
Pss 37:14; 88:17

11 They track me down, surround me,
and throw me to the ground.

17:12
Pss 7:2; 10:9

12 They are like hungry lions, eager to tear me apart—
like young lions in hiding, waiting for their chance.

17:13
Ps 22:20

13 Arise, O LORD!
Stand against them and bring them to their knees!
Rescue me from the wicked with your sword!

17:14
Ps 73:3-7

14 Save me by your mighty hand, O LORD,
from those whose only concern is earthly gain.

17:3 Was David saying he was sinless? Far from a proud assumption of purity, David's claim was an understanding of his relationship with God. In Psalms 32 and 51, David freely acknowledged his own sins. Nevertheless his relationship with God was one of close fellowship and constant repentance and forgiveness. His claim to goodness, therefore, was based on his continual seeking after God.

17:8 Just as we protect the pupils ("apples") of our eyes, so God will protect us. We must not conclude, however, that we have somehow missed God's protection if we experience troubles. God's protection has far greater purposes than helping us avoid pain; it is to make us better servants for him. God also protects us by guiding us through painful circumstances, not only by helping us escape them.

17:8 The "shadow of your wings" is a figure of speech symbolizing God's protection. He guards us just as a mother bird protects her young by covering them with her wings. Moses used a similar metaphor in Deuteronomy 32:11.

17:13-15 We deceive ourselves when we measure our happiness or contentment in life by the amount of wealth we possess. When we put riches at the top of our value system, we let power, pleasure, and financial security overshadow the eternal value of our relationship with God. We think we will be happy or content when we get riches, only to discover that they don't really satisfy, and the pleasures fade away. The true measurement of happiness or contentment is found in God's love and in doing his will. You will find true happiness if you put your relationship with God above earthly riches.

May they have their punishment in full.
May their children inherit more of the same,
and may the judgment continue to their children's children.

15 But because I have done what is right, I will see you.
When I awake, I will be fully satisfied,
for I will see you face to face.

17:15 Pss 4:6-7; 16:11; 140:13

Theme: Gratitude for deliverance and victory. The only sure way to be delivered from surrounding evil is to call upon God for help and strength.
Author: David

18

For the choir director: A psalm of David, the servant of the LORD. He sang this song to the LORD on the day the LORD rescued him from all his enemies and from Saul.

18:title //2 Sam 22:1-51

1 I love you, LORD; you are my strength.
2 The LORD is my rock, my fortress, and my savior;
my God is my rock, in whom I find protection.
He is my shield, the strength of my salvation, and my stronghold.
3 I will call on the LORD, who is worthy of praise,
for he saves me from my enemies.

4 The ropes of death surrounded me;
the floods of destruction swept over me.
5 The grave* wrapped its ropes around me;
death itself stared me in the face.
6 But in my distress I cried out to the LORD;
yes, I prayed to my God for help.
He heard me from his sanctuary;
my cry reached his ears.

7 Then the earth quaked and trembled;
the foundations of the mountains shook;
they quaked because of his anger.
8 Smoke poured from his nostrils;
fierce flames leaped from his mouth;
glowing coals flamed forth from him.
9 He opened the heavens and came down;
dark storm clouds were beneath his feet.
10 Mounted on a mighty angel,* he flew,
soaring on the wings of the wind.
11 He shrouded himself in darkness,
veiling his approach with dense rain clouds.
12 The brilliance of his presence broke through the clouds,
raining down hail and burning coals.

18:1 Ps 59:17
18:2 1 Sam 2:2; Pss 19:14; 28:1; 59:9, 11; 71:3; 75:10; 144:2
18:3 Num 10:9; Pss 34:6; 96:4
18:4 Pss 69:1-2; 116:3; 124:2-5
18:5 Ps 116:3
18:6 Pss 3:4; 34:15
18:7 Ps 114:4, 6-7
18:9 Exod 20:21; Pss 97:2; 144:5
18:10 Pss 80:1; 99:1
18:12 Pss 97:2; 104:1-2

18:5 Hebrew *Sheol.* **18:10** Hebrew *a cherub.*

17:15 The word *awake* shows that David believed in life after death. Although belief in resurrection was not widespread in Old Testament times, several verses show that it was partially understood. Some of these are Job 19:25-27; Psalms 16:10; 49:15; 139:17, 18; Isaiah 26:19; and Daniel 12:2, 13.

18:1ff This psalm is almost a duplicate of 2 Samuel 22. It may have been written toward the end of David's life when there was peace. God is praised for his glorious works and blessings through the years.

18:2, 3 God's protection of his people is limitless and can take many forms. David characterized God's care with five military symbols. God is like (1) a *rock* that can't be moved by any who would harm us, (2) a *fortress* or place of safety where the enemy can't follow, (3) a *shield* that comes between us and harm, (4) *strength* of salvation, a symbol of might and power, (5) a *stronghold* high above our enemies. If you need protection, look to God.

18:10 One of the functions of these "mighty angels" (also called cherubim) was to serve as guardians. These angels guarded the entrances to both the tree of life (Genesis 3:24) and the Most Holy Place (Exodus 26:31-33). Two angels of hammered gold were part of the Ark of the Covenant (Exodus 25:18-22). The living creatures carrying God's throne in Ezekiel 1 may have been cherubim.

18:13 Pss 29:3; 104:7-8

13 The LORD thundered from heaven;
the Most High gave a mighty shout.*

18:14 Ps 144:6

14 He shot his arrows and scattered his enemies;
his lightning flashed, and they were greatly confused.

18:15 Exod 15:8 Ps 106:9

15 Then at your command, O LORD,
at the blast of your breath,
the bottom of the sea could be seen,
and the foundations of the earth were laid bare.

18:16 Ps 144:7

16 He reached down from heaven and rescued me;
he drew me out of deep waters.

18:17 Ps 35:10

17 He delivered me from my powerful enemies,
from those who hated me and were too strong for me.

18:18 Pss 16:8; 59:16

18 They attacked me at a moment when I was weakest,
but the LORD upheld me.

18:19 Pss 31:8; 37:23; 41:1, 11; 118:5

19 He led me to a place of safety;
he rescued me because he delights in me.

18:20 Pss 7:8; 24:4

20 The LORD rewarded me for doing right;
he compensated me because of my innocence.

18:21 2 Chr 34:33 Pss 37:34; 119:33, 102-103

21 For I have kept the ways of the LORD;
I have not turned from my God to follow evil.
22 For all his laws are constantly before me;
I have never abandoned his principles.
23 I am blameless before God;
I have kept myself from sin.
24 The LORD rewarded me for doing right,
because of the innocence of my hands in his sight.

18:25 Ps 62:12 Matt 5:7

25 To the faithful you show yourself faithful;
to those with integrity you show integrity.
26 To the pure you show yourself pure,
but to the wicked you show yourself hostile.

18:27 Pss 72:12; 101:5 Prov 6:16-19

27 You rescue those who are humble,
but you humiliate the proud.

18:28 Job 18:6 Ps 27:1

28 LORD, you have brought light to my life;
my God, you light up my darkness.

18:29 Ps 118:10-12 2 Cor 12:9

29 In your strength I can crush an army;
with my God I can scale any wall.

18:30 Pss 12:6; 19:7

30 As for God, his way is perfect.
All the LORD's promises prove true.
He is a shield for all who look to him for protection.

18:31 Deut 32:31, 39 Pss 62:2; 86:8-10

31 For who is God except the LORD?
Who but our God is a solid rock?

18:13 As in Greek version (see also 2 Sam 22:14); Hebrew adds *raining down hail and burning coals.*

18:13 The "Most High" was an important designation for David to make. Pagan idol worship was deeply rooted in the land, and each region had its own deity. But these images of wood and stone were powerless. David was placing the Lord alone in a superior category: He is by far the Most High.

18:16 Do your troubles, like "deep waters," threaten to drown you? David, helpless and weak, knew that God alone had rescued him from his enemies when he was defenseless. When you wish that God would quickly rescue you from your troubles, remember that he can either deliver you or be your support as you go through them (18:18). Either way, his protection is best for you. When you feel like you're drowning in troubles, ask God to help you, hold you steady, and protect you. In his care, you are never helpless.

18:30 Some people think that belief in God is a crutch for weak people who cannot make it on their own. God is indeed a shield to protect us when we are too weak to face certain trials by ourselves, but he does not want us to remain weak. He strengthens, protects, and guides us in order to send us back into an evil world to fight for him. And then he continues to work with us because the strongest person on earth is infinitely weaker than God and needs his help. David was not a coward; he was a mighty warrior who, even with all his armies and weapons, knew that only God could ultimately protect and save him.

32 God arms me with strength;
he has made my way safe.
33 He makes me as surefooted as a deer,
leading me safely along the mountain heights.
34 He prepares me for battle;
he strengthens me to draw a bow of bronze.
35 You have given me the shield of your salvation.
Your right hand supports me;
your gentleness has made me great.
36 You have made a wide path for my feet
to keep them from slipping.

37 I chased my enemies and caught them;
I did not stop until they were conquered.
38 I struck them down so they could not get up;
they fell beneath my feet.
39 You have armed me with strength for the battle;
you have subdued my enemies under my feet.
40 You made them turn and run;
I have destroyed all who hated me.
41 They called for help, but no one came to rescue them.
They cried to the LORD, but he refused to answer them.
42 I ground them as fine as dust carried by the wind.
I swept them into the gutter like dirt.

43 You gave me victory over my accusers.
You appointed me as the ruler over nations;
people I don't even know now serve me.
44 As soon as they hear of me, they submit;
foreigners cringe before me.
45 They all lose their courage
and come trembling from their strongholds.

46 The LORD lives! Blessed be my rock!
May the God of my salvation be exalted!
47 He is the God who pays back those who harm me;
he subdues the nations under me
48 and rescues me from my enemies.
You hold me safe beyond the reach of my enemies;
you save me from violent opponents.
49 For this, O LORD, I will praise you among the nations;
I will sing joyfully to your name.
50 You give great victories to your king;
you show unfailing love to your anointed,
to David and all his descendants forever.

18:32 Isa 45:5
18:33 Deut 32:13; Hab 3:19
18:35 Pss 33:20; 63:8; 119:117
18:36 Pss 31:8; 66:9
18:37 Ps 44:5
18:38 Pss 36:12; 47:3
18:40 Pss 21:12; 94:23
18:41 Ps 50:22
18:42 Ps 83:13
18:43 2 Sam 3:1; Ps 89:27; Isa 55:5
18:44 Ps 66:3
18:47 Pss 47:3; 94:1-2; 144:2
18:48 Pss 3:7; 27:5-6
18:49 Ps 108:1; †Rom 15:9
18:50 Pss 21:1; 28:8; 89:4

18:32-34 God promises to give us strength to meet challenges, but he doesn't promise to eliminate them. If he gave us no rough roads to walk, no mountains to climb, and no battles to fight, we would not grow. He does not leave us alone with our challenges, however. Instead, he stands beside us, teaches us, and strengthens us to face them.

18:40-42 David was a merciful man. He spared the lives of Saul (1 Samuel 24:1-8), Nabal (1 Samuel 25:21-35), and Shimei (2 Samuel 16:5-12) and showed great kindness to Mephibosheth (2 Samuel 9). In asking God to destroy his enemies, David was simply asking him to give the wicked the punishment they deserved.

18:43-45 David's great power had become legendary. God gave him victory in every battle. The book of 2 Samuel records victories over the Jebusites (5:6-10), the Philistines (5:17-25; 8:1), Hadadezer of Zobah (8:3, 4), the Arameans (8:5, 6; 10), the Edomites (8:13, 14), and the Ammonites (12:26-31). In addition, the king of Tyre sent supplies and workmen to help David build his palace (5:11). But David did not attribute his victories to himself. He fully realized that the purpose of his position was to bless God's people (1 Chronicles 14:2).

Theme: Both God's creation and his word reveal his greatness.
Author: David

19

For the choir director: A psalm of David.

19:1 Gen 1:6-8 Rom 1:19-20

1 The heavens tell of the glory of God.
The skies display his marvelous craftsmanship.

19:2 Ps 74:16

2 Day after day they continue to speak;
night after night they make him known.
3 They speak without a sound or a word;
their voice is silent in the skies;*

19:4 †Rom 10:18

4 yet their message has gone out to all the earth,
and their words to all the world.

The sun lives in the heavens
where God placed it.
5 It bursts forth like a radiant bridegroom
after his wedding.
It rejoices like a great athlete
eager to run the race.

19:6 Ps 113:3

6 The sun rises at one end of the heavens
and follows its course to the other end.
Nothing can hide from its heat.

19:7 Pss 23:3; 36:9; 111:7; 119:14, 98-100, 160

7 The law of the LORD is perfect,
reviving the soul.
The decrees of the LORD are trustworthy,
making wise the simple.

19:8 Pss 12:6; 119:128

8 The commandments of the LORD are right,
bringing joy to the heart.
The commands of the LORD are clear,
giving insight to life.

19:9 Ps 119:138, 142

9 Reverence for the LORD is pure,
lasting forever.
The laws of the LORD are true;
each one is fair.

19:10 Ps 119:127

10 They are more desirable than gold,
even the finest gold.
They are sweeter than honey,
even honey dripping from the comb.

19:11 Ps 17:4 Prov 29:18-19

11 They are a warning to those who hear them;
there is great reward for those who obey them.

19:3 Or *There is no speech or language where their voice is not heard.*

19:1ff In this psalm, David meditates on God's creation, God's Word, his own sinfulness, and God's forgiveness. As God reveals himself through nature (19:1-6), we learn about his power and our finiteness. As God reveals himself through Scripture (19:7-11), we learn about his holiness and our sinfulness. As God reveals himself through daily experiences (19:12-14), we learn about his gracious forgiveness that frees us from guilt.

19:1-6 We are surrounded by fantastic displays of God's craftsmanship—the heavens give dramatic evidence of his existence, his power, his love, his care. To say that the universe happened by chance is absurd. Its design, intricacy, and orderliness point to a personally involved Creator. As you look at God's handiwork in nature and the heavens, thank him for such magnificent beauty and the truth it reveals about the Creator.

19:3, 4 The apostle Paul referred to this psalm when he explained that everyone knows about God because nature proclaims God's existence and power (Romans 1:19, 20). This does not cancel the need for missions because the message of God's salvation found in his Word, the Bible, must still be told to the ends of the earth. While nature points to the existence of God, the Bible tells us about God's plan of salvation. God's people must explain to others how they can have a relationship with God. Although most people believe in a Creator because of the evidence of nature around them, they need to know about his love, mercy, and grace. What are you doing to take God's message to the world?

19:7-11 When we think of the law, we often think of something that keeps us from having fun. But here we see the opposite: God's laws revive us, make us wise, bring joy to the heart, give insight, warn us, and reward us. God's laws are guidelines and lights for our path, rather than chains on our hands and feet. They point at danger to warn us, then point at success to guide us.

[12] How can I know all the sins lurking in my heart?
Cleanse me from these hidden faults.
[13] Keep me from deliberate sins!
Don't let them control me.
Then I will be free of guilt
and innocent of great sin.

[14] May the words of my mouth and the thoughts of my heart
be pleasing to you,
O LORD, my rock and my redeemer.

19:12 Pss 51:1-2; 90:8; 139:23-24
19:13 Pss 25:11; 32:2
19:14 Pss 18:2; 104:34

Theme: A prayer for victory in battle. Such a prayer can help us prepare for any great challenge. David knew that trust should be placed in the Lord more than in human power.
Author: David. The events in 2 Samuel 10 may have prompted this prayer.

20

For the choir director: A psalm of David.

[1] In times of trouble, may the LORD respond to your cry.
May the God of Israel* keep you safe from all harm.
[2] May he send you help from his sanctuary
and strengthen you from Jerusalem.*
[3] May he remember all your gifts
and look favorably on your burnt offerings. *Interlude*

[4] May he grant your heart's desire
and fulfill all your plans.
[5] May we shout for joy when we hear of your victory,
flying banners to honor our God.
May the LORD answer all your prayers.

[6] Now I know that the LORD saves his anointed king.
He will answer him from his holy heaven
and rescue him by his great power.
[7] Some nations boast of their armies and weapons,*
but we boast in the LORD our God.
[8] Those nations will fall down and collapse,
but we will rise up and stand firm.

[9] Give victory to our king, O LORD!
Respond to our cry for help.

20:1 Ps 46:7, 11
20:2 Pss 3:4; 110:2; 119:28
20:3 Ps 51:19; Acts 10:4
20:4 Pss 21:2; 145:19
20:5 1 Sam 1:17; Pss 9:14; 60:4
20:6 Pss 28:8; 41:11; Isa 58:9
20:7 2 Chr 32:8; Ps 33:16-17
20:9 Ps 17:6

Theme: Praising God after victory in battle. When God answers our prayers for victory, we must quickly and openly thank him for his help.
Author: David

21

For the choir director: A psalm of David.

[1] How the king rejoices in your strength, O LORD!
He shouts with joy because of your victory.

21:1 Ps 59:16-17

20:1 Hebrew *of Jacob.* **20:2** Hebrew *Zion.* **20:7** Hebrew *chariots and horses.*

19:12, 13 Many Christians are plagued by guilt. They worry that they may have committed a sin unknowingly, done something good with selfish intentions, failed to put their whole heart into a task, or neglected what they should have done. Guilt can play an important role in bringing us to Christ and in keeping us behaving properly, but it should not cripple us or make us fearful. God fully and completely forgives us—even for those sins we do unknowingly.

19:14 Would you change the way you live if you knew that every word and thought would be examined by God first? David asks that God approve his words and thoughts as though they were offerings brought to the altar. As you begin each day, determine that God's love will guide what you say and how you think.

20:6-8 As long as there have been armies and weapons, nations have boasted of their power, but such power does not last. Throughout history, empires and kingdoms have risen to great power only to vanish in the dust. David, however, knew that the true might of his nation was not in weaponry but in worship, not in firepower but in God's power. Because God alone can preserve a nation or an individual, be sure your confidence is in God, who gives eternal victory. Whom do you trust?

21:1-6 David described all that he had as gifts from God: his heart's desire, success and prosperity, a crown of finest gold,

21:2 Ps 37:4

2 For you have given him his heart's desire;
you have held back nothing that he requested. *Interlude*

21:3 Ps 59:10

3 You welcomed him back with success and prosperity.
You placed a crown of finest gold on his head.

21:4 Pss 61:6; 91:16; 133:3

4 He asked you to preserve his life,
and you have granted his request.
The days of his life stretch on forever.

21:5 Pss 8:5; 96:6

5 Your victory brings him great honor,
and you have clothed him with splendor and majesty.
6 You have endowed him with eternal blessings.
You have given him the joy of being in your presence.

21:7 Pss 112:6; 125:1

7 For the king trusts in the LORD.
The unfailing love of the Most High will keep him from stumbling.

21:8 Isa 10:10

21:9 Lam 2:2 Mal 4:1

8 You will capture all your enemies.
Your strong right hand will seize all those who hate you.
9 You will destroy them as in a flaming furnace
when you appear.
The LORD will consume them in his anger;
fire will devour them.
10 You will wipe their children from the face of the earth;
they will never have descendants.

21:11 Ps 2:1-3

11 Although they plot against you,
their evil schemes will never succeed.

21:12 Pss 7:12-13; 18:40

12 For they will turn and run
when they see your arrows aimed at them.

21:13 Pss 59:16; 81:1

13 We praise you, LORD, for all your glorious power.
With music and singing we celebrate your mighty acts.

Theme: A prayer that carries us from great suffering to great joy. Despite apparent rejection by his friends and God, David believed that God would lead him out of despair. He looked forward to that future day when God would rule over the entire earth.
Author: David

22

For the choir director: A psalm of David, to be sung to the tune "Doe of the Dawn."

22:1 †Matt 27:46 †Mark 15:34

22:2 Pss 42:3; 88:1

1 My God, my God! Why have you forsaken me?
Why do you remain so distant?
Why do you ignore my cries for help?
2 Every day I call to you, my God, but you do not answer.
Every night you hear my voice, but I find no relief.

long life, splendor and majesty, eternal blessings, joy. We, too, must look upon all we have—position, family, wealth, talent—as gifts from God. Only then will we use them to give glory back to him.

21:7 A good leader trusts the Lord and depends upon his unfailing love. Too often leaders trust in their own cleverness, popular support, or military power. But God is above all these "gods." If you aspire to leadership, keep the Lord God at the center of your life and depend on him. His wisdom is the best strength you can have.

21:7 Because David trusted in God, God would not let him stumble (be removed from the throne). When we trust in God, we have permanence and stability. We may lose a great deal—families, jobs, material possessions—but we cannot be shaken from God's favor. He will be our foundation of solid rock. He will never leave or desert us.

21:11 When you see people succeeding with evil acts, remember that they will not succeed forever. Their power is only temporary, and God's very presence can send them scattering in a moment. God, according to his plan and purpose, will intervene for his people and give the wicked the judgment they deserve. We should not be dismayed when we see the temporary advantage God's enemies seem to have.

22:1 David gave an amazingly accurate description of the suffering the Messiah would endure hundreds of years later. David was obviously enduring some great trial, but through his suffering, he, like the Messiah to come, gained victory. Jesus, the Messiah, quoted this verse while hanging on the cross carrying our burden of sin (Matthew 27:46). It was not a cry of doubt, but an urgent appeal to God.

3 Yet you are holy.
The praises of Israel surround your throne.
4 Our ancestors trusted in you,
and you rescued them.
5 You heard their cries for help and saved them.
They put their trust in you and were never disappointed.

6 But I am a worm and not a man.
I am scorned and despised by all!
7 Everyone who sees me mocks me.
They sneer and shake their heads, saying,
8 "Is this the one who relies on the LORD?
Then let the LORD save him!
If the LORD loves him so much,
let the LORD rescue him!"

9 Yet you brought me safely from my mother's womb
and led me to trust you when I was a nursing infant.
10 I was thrust upon you at my birth.
You have been my God from the moment I was born.

11 Do not stay so far from me,
for trouble is near,
and no one else can help me.
12 My enemies surround me like a herd of bulls;
fierce bulls of Bashan have hemmed me in!
13 Like roaring lions attacking their prey,
they come at me with open mouths.
14 My life is poured out like water,
and all my bones are out of joint.
My heart is like wax,
melting within me.
15 My strength has dried up like sunbaked clay.
My tongue sticks to the roof of my mouth.
You have laid me in the dust and left me for dead.

16 My enemies surround me like a pack of dogs;
an evil gang closes in on me.
They have pierced my hands and feet.
17 I can count every bone in my body.
My enemies stare at me and gloat.
18 They divide my clothes among themselves
and throw dice* for my garments.

19 O LORD, do not stay away!
You are my strength; come quickly to my aid!
20 Rescue me from a violent death;
spare my precious life from these dogs.
21 Snatch me from the lions' jaws,
and from the horns of these wild oxen.

22:3 Pss 99:9; 107:6; 148:14
22:6 Job 25:6; Ps 31:11; Isa 41:14; 49:7
22:7 Isa 53:3; Matt 27:39; Mark 15:29-30
22:8 Matt 27:43
22:9 Pss 71:5-6, 12; 72:12
22:10 Isa 46:3
22:11 Ps 72:12
22:13 Job 16:10; Ps 17:12
22:14 Job 30:16; Ps 31:9-10
22:15 Pss 38:10; 104:29; †John 19:28
22:16 Ps 59:6-7; Matt 27:35; John 20:25
22:18 †Matt 27:35; †Mark 15:24; Luke 23:34; John 19:23-24
22:19 Pss 22:11; 70:5
22:20 Pss 35:17; 37:14
22:21 Pss 34:4; 118:5; 120:1

22:18 Hebrew *cast lots.*

22:6 When others despise us and heap scorn upon us, they treat us as less than human. After much degradation, we, like David, may begin to feel like worms. When we feel the sting of rejection, we must keep in mind the hope and victory that God promises us (22:22ff).

22:9-11 God's loving concern does not begin on the day we are born and conclude on the day we die. It reaches back to those days before we were born and reaches ahead along the unending path of eternity. Our only sure help comes from a God whose concern for us reaches beyond our earthly existence. How can anyone reject such love?

22:12 The land of Bashan, located east of the Sea of Galilee, was known for its strong and well-fed cattle (Amos 4:1). Because of its grain fields, it was often called the breadbasket of Palestine.

22:22 †Heb 2:12

[22] Then I will declare the wonder of your name to my brothers and sisters.
I will praise you among all your people.

22:23 Pss 33:8; 86:12; 135:19-20

[23] Praise the LORD, all you who fear him!
Honor him, all you descendants of Jacob!
Show him reverence, all you descendants of Israel!

22:24 Pss 27:9; 31:22 Heb 5:7

[24] For he has not ignored the suffering of the needy.
He has not turned and walked away.
He has listened to their cries for help.

22:25 Pss 35:18; 40:9-10

[25] I will praise you among all the people;
I will fulfill my vows in the presence of those who worship you.

22:26 Pss 40:16; 69:32; 107:9

[26] The poor will eat and be satisfied.
All who seek the LORD will praise him.
Their hearts will rejoice with everlasting joy.
[27] The whole earth will acknowledge the LORD and return to him.
People from every nation will bow down before him.

22:28 Ps 47:6-8

[28] For the LORD is king!
He rules all the nations.

[29] Let the rich of the earth feast and worship.
Let all mortals—those born to die—bow down in his presence.

CHRIST IN THE PSALMS

Both the Jewish and Christian faiths have long believed that many psalms referred as much to the promised Messiah as they did to events at the time. Because the Messiah was to be a descendant of David, it was expected that many of the royal psalms would apply to him. Christians noted how many of the passages seemed to describe in detail events from Christ's life and death. Jesus himself frequently quoted from Psalms. Almost everything that happened at the Crucifixion and most of Jesus' words during his final hours were prophesied in Psalms.

The following is a list of the main references in Psalms pertaining to Christ.

Reference in Psalms	*Reference to Christ*	*Fulfillment in the New Testament*
2:7	The Messiah will be God's Son	Hebrews 1:5, 6
16:8–10	He will rise from the dead	Luke 24:5–7
22:1–21	He will experience agony on the cross	Matthew 26, 27
22:18	Evil men cast lots for his clothing	Matthew 27:35; John 19:23, 24
22:15	He thirsts while on the cross	John 19:28
22:22	He will declare God's name	Hebrews 2:12
34:20	His bones would not be broken	John 19:36, 37
40:6–8	He came to do God's will	Hebrews 10:5–7
41:9	His close friend would betray him	Luke 22:48
45:6, 7	His throne will last forever	Hebrews 1:8, 9
68:18	He ascended into heaven	Ephesians 4:8–10
69:9	He is zealous for God	John 2:17
69:21	He was offered vinegar for his thirst on the cross	Matthew 27:48
89:3, 4, 35, 36	He will be a descendant of David	Luke 1:31–33
96:13	He will return to judge the world	1 Thessalonians 1:10
110:1	He is David's son and David's Lord	Matthew 22:44
110:4	He is the eternal priest-king	Hebrews 6:20
118:22	He is rejected by many but accepted by God	1 Peter 2:7, 8

22:22 David would praise God among the people because his private deliverance deserved a public testimony. God may wonderfully deliver us in the quiet moments when we are hurting, and we must be prepared to offer public praise for his care.

[30] Future generations will also serve him.
Our children will hear about the wonders of the Lord.
[31] His righteous acts will be told to those yet unborn.
They will hear about everything he has done.

22:30 Ps 102:18, 28

Theme: God is seen as a caring shepherd and a dependable guide. We must follow God and obey his commands. He is our only hope for eternal life and security.
Author: David

23

A psalm of David.

[1] The LORD is my shepherd;
I have everything I need.
[2] He lets me rest in green meadows;
he leads me beside peaceful streams.
[3] He renews my strength.
He guides me along right paths,
bringing honor to his name.

[4] Even when I walk
through the dark valley of death,*
I will not be afraid,
for you are close beside me.
Your rod and your staff
protect and comfort me.

[5] You prepare a feast for me
in the presence of my enemies.
You welcome me as a guest,
anointing my head with oil.
My cup overflows with blessings.
[6] Surely your goodness and unfailing love will pursue me
all the days of my life,
and I will live in the house of the LORD
forever.

23:4 Or *the darkest valley.*

23:1 John 10:11; 1 Pet 2:25
23:2 Pss 5:8; 46:4; Ezek 34:14; Rev 7:17
23:3 Pss 5:8; 19:7; 85:13
23:4 Pss 27:1; 107:14
23:5 Pss 16:5; 78:19; 92:10
23:6 Pss 25:6-7, 10; 27:4-6

22:30, 31 Unborn generations are depending on our faithfulness today. As we teach our children about the Lord, so they will teach their children and their children's children. If we fail to tell our children about the Lord, we may well be breaking the chain of God's influence in generations to come. We must view our children and all the young people we meet as God's future leaders. If we are faithful in opportunities today, we may well be affecting the future.

22:30, 31 If we want our children to serve the Lord, they must hear about him from us. It is not enough to rely on the church or those with more knowledge to provide all their Christian education. We must reinforce the lessons of the Bible in our homes.

23:1 In describing the Lord as a shepherd, David wrote out of his own experience because he had spent his early years caring for sheep (1 Samuel 16:10, 11). Sheep are completely dependent on the shepherd for provision, guidance, and protection. The New Testament calls Jesus the good shepherd (John 10:11); the great Shepherd (Hebrews 13:20); and the head Shepherd (1 Peter 5:4). As the Lord is the good shepherd, so we are his sheep—not frightened, passive animals, but obedient followers, wise enough to follow one who will lead us in the right places and in right ways. This psalm does not focus on the animal-like qualities of sheep but on the discipleship qualities of those who follow. When you recognize the good shepherd, follow him!

23:2, 3 When we allow God, our shepherd, to guide us, we have contentment. When we choose to sin and go our own way, however, we cannot blame God for the environment we create for ourselves. Our shepherd knows the "green meadows" and "peaceful streams" that will restore us. We will reach these places only by following him obediently. Rebelling against the shepherd's leading is actually rebelling against our own best interests. We must remember this the next time we are tempted to go our own way rather than the shepherd's way.

23:4 Death casts a frightening shadow over us because we are entirely helpless in its presence. We can struggle with other enemies—pain, suffering, disease, injury—but strength and courage cannot overcome death. It has the final word. Only one person can walk with us through death's dark valley and bring us safely to the other side—the God of life, our shepherd. Because life is uncertain, we should follow this shepherd who offers us eternal comfort.

23:5, 6 In ancient Near Eastern culture, at a banquet it was customary to anoint a person with fragrant oil as a lotion. Hosts were also expected to protect their guests at all costs. God offers the protection of a host even when enemies surround us. In the final scene of this psalm, we see that believers will dwell with God. God, the perfect shepherd and host, promises to guide and protect us throughout our life and to bring us into his house forever.

Theme: Everything belongs to God—the glorious eternal King. Let us worship him and welcome his glorious reign.
Author: David

24

A psalm of David.

24:1 Ps 89:11 †1 Cor 10:26

1 The earth is the LORD's, and everything in it.
The world and all its people belong to him.
2 For he laid the earth's foundation on the seas
and built it on the ocean depths.

24:3 Pss 15:1; 65:4

3 Who may climb the mountain of the LORD?
Who may stand in his holy place?

24:4 Job 17:9 Pss 51:10; 73:1 Matt 5:8

4 Only those whose hands and hearts are pure,
who do not worship idols
and never tell lies.

24:5 Deut 11:26-27

5 They will receive the LORD's blessing
and have right standing with God their savior.

24:6 Ps 27:8

6 They alone may enter God's presence
and worship the God of Israel.* *Interlude*

7 Open up, ancient gates!
Open up, ancient doors,
and let the King of glory enter.

24:8 Exod 15:3, 6 Ps 76:3-6

8 Who is the King of glory?
The LORD, strong and mighty,
the LORD, invincible in battle.

24:6 Hebrew *of Jacob.*

PSALMS TO LEARN AND LOVE

Almost everyone, whether religious or not, has heard Psalm 23 because it is quoted so frequently. Many other psalms are also familiar because they are quoted in music, in literature, or in the words of the worship service.

The psalms we know and love are the ones that come into our minds when we need them. They inspire us, comfort us, correct us just when we need a word from the Lord. If you want to begin memorizing psalms, start with some of these favorites. Memorize the whole psalm or just the verses that speak most directly to you. Or read the psalm aloud several times a day until it is part of you.

Psalms to bring us into God's presence	29; 95:1–7a; 96; 100
Psalms about goodness	1; 19; 24; 133; 136; 139
Psalms of praise	8; 97; 103; 107; 113; 145; 150
Psalms of repentance and forgiveness	32:1–5; 51; 103
Psalms for times of trouble	3; 14; 22; 37:1–11; 42; 46; 53; 116:1–7
Psalms of confidence and trust	23; 40:1–4; 91; 119:11; 121; 127

24:1 Because "the earth is the LORD's," all of us are stewards, or caretakers. We should be committed to the proper management of this world and its resources, but we are not to become devoted to anything created or act as sole proprietors because this world will pass away (1 John 2:17).

24:1ff This psalm may have been written to celebrate moving the Ark of the Covenant from Obed-edom's house to Jerusalem (2 Samuel 6:10-12). Tradition says that this psalm was sung on the first day of each week in the Temple services. Verses 1-6 tell who is worthy to join in such a celebration of worship.

24:4 This refers to all lies, especially those told under oath. How greatly God values honesty! Dishonesty comes easily, especially when complete truthfulness could cost us something, make us uncomfortable, or put us in an unfavorable light. Dishonest communication hinders relationships. Without honesty, a relationship with God is impossible. If we lie to others, we will begin to deceive ourselves. God cannot hear us or speak to us if we are building a wall of self-deception.

24:7-10 Who is this King of glory? The King of glory, identified here also as the Lord Almighty, is the Messiah himself, eternal, holy, and mighty. This psalm is not only a battle cry for the church, but it also looks forward to Christ's future entry into the new Jerusalem to reign forever (Revelation 19:11-21).

24:7-10 This psalm, often set to music, was probably used in corporate worship. It may have been reenacted many times at the Temple. The people outside would call out to the Temple gates to open up and let the King of glory in. From inside, the priests or another group would ask, "Who is the King of glory?" Outside, the people would respond in unison, "The LORD, strong and mighty, the LORD, invincible in battle," proclaiming his great power and strength. The exchange was then repeated (24:9, 10), and the Temple gates would swing open, symbolizing the people's desire to have God's presence among them. This would have been an important lesson for children who were participating.

9 Open up, ancient gates!
Open up, ancient doors,
and let the King of glory enter.
10 Who is the King of glory?
The LORD Almighty—
he is the King of glory. *Interlude*

24:9 Zech 9:9; Matt 21:5
24:10 Josh 5:14

Theme: A prayer for defense, guidance, and pardon. As we trust in God, he grants these same requests for us.
Author: David

25

A psalm of David.

1 To you, O LORD, I lift up my soul.
2 I trust in you, my God!
Do not let me be disgraced,
or let my enemies rejoice in my defeat.
3 No one who trusts in you will ever be disgraced,
but disgrace comes to those who try to deceive others.

4 Show me the path where I should walk, O LORD;
point out the right road for me to follow.
5 Lead me by your truth and teach me,
for you are the God who saves me.
All day long I put my hope in you.

6 Remember, O LORD, your unfailing love and compassion,
which you have shown from long ages past.
7 Forgive the rebellious sins of my youth;
look instead through the eyes of your unfailing love,
for you are merciful, O LORD.

8 The LORD is good and does what is right;
he shows the proper path to those who go astray.
9 He leads the humble in what is right,
teaching them his way.
10 The LORD leads with unfailing love and faithfulness
all those who keep his covenant and obey his decrees.

11 For the honor of your name, O LORD,
forgive my many, many sins.
12 Who are those who fear the LORD?
He will show them the path they should choose.

25:3 Pss 37:9; 40:1; Isa 49:23
25:4 Pss 5:8; 86:11
25:5 Pss 24:5; 40:1
25:6 Ps 103:17
25:7 Job 13:26; Ps 51:1
25:8 Ps 86:5
25:9 Pss 23:3; 32:8
25:10 Pss 40:11; 103:17-18
25:11 Pss 79:9; 92:15
25:12 Ps 31:19

25:2 Seventy-two psalms—almost half the book—speak about enemies. Enemies are those who oppose not only us, but also God's way of living. We can view temptations—money, success, prestige, lust—as our enemies. And our greatest enemy is Satan. David asked God to keep his enemies from overcoming him because they opposed what God stood for. If his enemies succeeded, David feared that many would think that living for God was futile. David did not question his own faith—he knew that God would triumph. But he didn't want his enemies' success to be an obstacle to the faith of others.

25:4 David expressed his desire for guidance. How do we receive God's guidance? The first step is to *want* to be guided and to realize that God's primary guidance system is in his Word, the Bible. Psalm 119 tells of the endless knowledge found in God's Word. By reading it and constantly learning from it, we will gain the wisdom to perceive God's direction for our lives. We may be tempted to demand answers from God, but David asked for direction. When we are willing to seek God, learn from his Word, and obey his commands, then we will receive his specific guidance.

25:8-11 We are bombarded today with relentless appeals to go in various directions. Television advertising alone places hundreds of options before us, in addition to appeals made by political parties, cults, false religions, and dozens of other groups. Numerous organizations, including Christian organizations, seek to motivate us to support a cause. Add to that the dozens of decisions we must make concerning our job, our family, our money, and our society, and we become desperate for someone to show us the right way. If you find yourself pulled in several directions, remember that God teaches the humble his way.

25:12 To fear the Lord is to recognize God's attributes: He is holy, almighty, righteous, pure, all-knowing, all-powerful, and all-wise. When we regard God correctly, we gain a clearer picture of ourselves: sinful, weak, frail, and needy. When we recognize who God is and who we are, we will fall at his feet in humble respect. Only then will he show us how to choose his way.

25:13 Pss 37:11; 69:36

13 They will live in prosperity,
and their children will inherit the Promised Land.

25:14 Prov 3:32 John 7:17

14 Friendship with the LORD is reserved for those who fear him.
With them he shares the secrets of his covenant.

25:15 Pss 31:4; 123:2; 141:8

15 My eyes are always looking to the LORD for help,
for he alone can rescue me from the traps of my enemies.

25:16 Ps 69:16

16 Turn to me and have mercy on me,
for I am alone and in deep distress.

25:17 Pss 40:12; 107:6

17 My problems go from bad to worse.
Oh, save me from them all!

25:18 Pss 31:7; 103:3

18 Feel my pain and see my trouble.
Forgive all my sins.

25:19 Pss 3:1; 9:13

19 See how many enemies I have,
and how viciously they hate me!

25:20 Pss 25:2; 86:2

20 Protect me! Rescue my life from them!
Do not let me be disgraced, for I trust in you.

25:21 Pss 25:3; 41:12

21 May integrity and honesty protect me,
for I put my hope in you.

22 O God, ransom Israel
from all its troubles.

Theme: Declaring loyalty to God. If we are genuinely committed to God, we can stand up to opposition and examination.
Author: David, possibly written during the days of Absalom's rebellion

26

A psalm of David.

26:1 Pss 7:8; 13:5 Heb 10:23

1 Declare me innocent, O LORD,
for I have acted with integrity;
I have trusted in the LORD without wavering.

26:2 Pss 7:9; 139:23

2 Put me on trial, LORD, and cross-examine me.
Test my motives and affections.

26:3 Pss 1:2; 48:9

3 For I am constantly aware of your unfailing love,
and I have lived according to your truth.

26:4 Ps 1:1

4 I do not spend time with liars
or go along with hypocrites.

26:5 Pss 1:1; 31:6; 139:21

5 I hate the gatherings of those who do evil,
and I refuse to join in with the wicked.

25:14 "Friendship with the LORD is reserved for those who fear him." God offers intimate and lasting friendship to those who revere him, who hold him in highest honor. What relationship could ever compare with having the Lord of all creation for a friend? Your everlasting friendship with God will grow as you revere him.

25:16, 17 Do life's problems always seem to go from bad to worse? God is the only one who can reverse this downward spiral. He can take our problems and turn them into glorious victories. There is one necessary requirement—we, like David, must cry out, "Turn to me and have mercy on me." When you are willing to do that, God can turn the worst into something wonderful. The next step is yours—God has already made his offer.

25:21 If ever two powerful forces were needed to preserve us along life's way, they are integrity and honesty. The psalmist asks for these to protect him step by step. Honesty makes us learn God's requirements and strive to fulfill them. Integrity—being what we say we are—keeps us from claiming to be honest while living as if we do not know God. Honesty says, "This is the Shepherd's way," and integrity says, "I will walk consistently in it."

26:1-3 By saying that he was "innocent," David was not claiming to be sinless—that is impossible for any human being to achieve. But he was consistently in fellowship with God, clearing his record when he sinned by asking for forgiveness. Here he pleads with God to clear his name of the false charges made against him by his enemies. We also can ask God to examine us, trusting him to forgive our sins and clear our record according to his mercy.

26:4, 5 Should we stay away from unbelievers? No. Although there are some places Christians should avoid, Jesus demonstrated that we must go among unbelievers to help them. But there is a difference between being *with* unbelievers and being *one of* them. Trying to be one of them harms our witness for God. Ask yourself about the people you enjoy: If I am with them often, will I become less obedient to God in outlook or action? If the answer is yes, carefully monitor how you spend your time with these people and what effect it has on you.

6 I wash my hands to declare my innocence.
I come to your altar, O LORD,
7 singing a song of thanksgiving
and telling of all your miracles.
8 I love your sanctuary, LORD,
the place where your glory shines.

9 Don't let me suffer the fate of sinners.
Don't condemn me along with murderers.
10 Their hands are dirty with wicked schemes,
and they constantly take bribes.

11 But I am not like that; I do what is right.
So in your mercy, save me.
12 I have taken a stand,
and I will publicly praise the LORD.

26:6 Ps 43:3-4
26:7 Ps 9:1
26:8 Ps 27:4
26:9 Ps 28:3
26:11 Pss 26:1; 44:26; 69:18
26:12 Pss 22:22; 27:11; 40:2

Theme: God offers help for today and hope for the future. Unwavering confidence in God is our antidote for fear and loneliness.
Author: David

27

A psalm of David.

1 The LORD is my light and my salvation—
so why should I be afraid?
The LORD protects me from danger—
so why should I tremble?

2 When evil people come to destroy me,
when my enemies and foes attack me,
they will stumble and fall.
3 Though a mighty army surrounds me,
my heart will know no fear.
Even if they attack me,
I remain confident.

4 The one thing I ask of the LORD—
the thing I seek most—
is to live in the house of the LORD all the days of my life,
delighting in the LORD's perfections
and meditating in his Temple.
5 For he will conceal me there when troubles come;
he will hide me in his sanctuary.
He will place me out of reach on a high rock.
6 Then I will hold my head high,
above my enemies who surround me.

27:1 Pss 18:28; 118:6, 14
27:3 Pss 3:6-7; 14:4
27:4 Pss 23:6; 26:8
27:5 Pss 17:8; 31:20
27:6 Pss 13:6; 107:22

26:8 God's sanctuary in this verse can mean either the Tabernacle in Gibeon (the one constructed in the days of Moses; see Exodus 40:35) or the temporary dwelling David built to house the Ark of the Covenant (2 Samuel 6:17). David exclaimed how he loved to worship God at this place. We should worship God with the same love and reverence as David did.

26:12 Too often we complain about our problems to anyone who will listen and praise God only in private. How much better it would be for us to complain privately and to praise God publicly.

27:1 Fear is a dark shadow that envelops us and ultimately imprisons us within ourselves. Each of us has been a prisoner of fear at one time or another—fear of rejection, misunderstanding, uncertainty, sickness, or even death. But we can conquer fear by using the bright liberating light of the Lord, who brings salvation. If we want to dispel the darkness of fear, let us remember with the psalmist that "the LORD is my light and my salvation."

27:4 By the "house of the LORD" and "his Temple," David could be referring to the Tabernacle in Gibeon, to the sanctuary he had put up to house the Ark of the Covenant, or to the Temple that his son Solomon was to build. David probably had the Temple in mind because he made many of the plans for it (1 Chronicles 22). But David may also have used the word *Temple* to mean "the presence of the LORD." His greatest desire was to live in God's presence each day of his life. Sadly, this is not the greatest desire of many who claim to be believers. But those who desire to live in God's presence each day will be able to enjoy that relationship forever.

At his Tabernacle I will offer sacrifices with shouts of joy,
singing and praising the LORD with music.

27:7 Pss 13:3; 37:12

7 Listen to my pleading, O LORD.
Be merciful and answer me!

27:8 Ps 105:4

8 My heart has heard you say, "Come and talk with me."
And my heart responds, "LORD, I am coming."

27:9 Pss 6:1; 40:17; 69:17; 94:14

9 Do not hide yourself from me.
Do not reject your servant in anger.
You have always been my helper.
Don't leave me now; don't abandon me,
O God of my salvation!

27:10 Isa 40:11; 49:15

10 Even if my father and mother abandon me,
the LORD will hold me close.

27:11 Pss 5:8; 25:4; 86:11

11 Teach me how to live, O LORD.
Lead me along the path of honesty,
for my enemies are waiting for me to fall.

27:12 Ps 35:11; Matt 26:60; Acts 9:1

12 Do not let me fall into their hands.
For they accuse me of things I've never done
and breathe out violence against me.

27:13 Pss 116:9; 142:5; Isa 38:11; Jer 11:19

13 Yet I am confident that I will see the LORD's goodness
while I am here in the land of the living.

27:14 Pss 31:24; 37:34

14 Wait patiently for the LORD.
Be brave and courageous.
Yes, wait patiently for the LORD.

Theme: Prayer when surrounded by trouble or wickedness. God is our only real source of safety. Prayer is our best help when trials come our way because it keeps us in communion with God.
Author: David

28

A psalm of David.

28:1 Pss 18:2; 35:22; 83:1; 88:4

1 O LORD, you are my rock of safety.
Please help me; don't refuse to answer me.
For if you are silent,
I might as well give up and die.

28:2 Ps 141:2; Lam 2:19; 1 Tim 2:18

2 Listen to my prayer for mercy
as I cry out to you for help,
as I lift my hands toward your holy sanctuary.

28:3 Pss 26:9-10; 55:21; 62:4; Jer 9:8

3 Don't drag me away with the wicked—
with those who do evil—

27:10 Many have had the sad experience of being abandoned by father or mother. Broken homes, differences of belief, addiction to drugs or alcohol, even psychological isolation can leave children crippled by this loss. Even as adults, the pain may linger. God can take that place in our life, fill that void, and heal that hurt. He can direct us to adults who may take the role of father or mother for us. His love is sufficient for all our needs.

27:13 The "land of the living" simply means "this life." David was obviously going through a trial, but he was confident that in this present life, God would see him through it.

27:14 David knew from experience what it meant to wait for the Lord. He had been anointed king at age 16 but didn't become king until he was 30. During the interim, he was chased through the wilderness by jealous King Saul. David had to wait on God for the fulfillment of his promise to reign. Later, after becoming king, he was chased by his rebellious son, Absalom.

Waiting for God is not easy. Often it seems that he isn't answering our prayers or doesn't understand the urgency of our situation. That kind of thinking implies that God is not in control or is not fair. But God is worth waiting for. Lamentations 3:24-26 calls us to hope in and wait for the Lord because often God uses times of waiting to refresh, renew, and teach us. Make good use of your waiting times by discovering what God may be trying to teach you in them.

28:3-5 It's easy to pretend friendship. Wicked people often put on a show of kindness or friendship in order to gain their own ends. David, in his royal position, may have met many who pretended friendship only to meet their own goals. David knew that God would punish them eventually, but he prayed that their punishment would come swiftly. True believers should be straightforward and sincere in all their relationships.

those who speak friendly words to their neighbors
while planning evil in their hearts.
4 Give them the punishment they so richly deserve!
Measure it out in proportion to their wickedness.
Pay them back for all their evil deeds!
Give them a taste of what they have done to others.
5 They care nothing for what the LORD has done
or for what his hands have made.
So he will tear them down like old buildings,
and they will never be rebuilt!

6 Praise the LORD!
For he has heard my cry for mercy.
7 The LORD is my strength, my shield from every danger.
I trust in him with all my heart.
He helps me, and my heart is filled with joy.
I burst out in songs of thanksgiving.

8 The LORD protects his people
and gives victory to his anointed king.
9 Save your people!
Bless Israel, your special possession!
Lead them like a shepherd,
and carry them forever in your arms.

28:4 Ps 62:12; 2 Tim 4:14; Rev 18:6
28:5 Isa 5:12
28:6 Ps 116:1
28:7 Pss 13:5-6; 16:9; 40:3; 59:17
28:8 Ps 20:6
28:9 Deut 9:29; 32:9; Pss 33:12; 80:1; Isa 40:11

Theme: God reveals his great power in nature. We can trust God to give us both the peace and the strength to weather the storms of life.
Author: David

29

A psalm of David.

1 Give honor to the LORD, you angels;
give honor to the LORD for his glory and strength.
2 Give honor to the LORD for the glory of his name.
Worship the LORD in the splendor of his holiness.

3 The voice of the LORD echoes above the sea.
The God of glory thunders.
The LORD thunders over the mighty sea.
4 The voice of the LORD is powerful;
the voice of the LORD is full of majesty.
5 The voice of the LORD splits the mighty cedars;
the LORD shatters the cedars of Lebanon.
6 He makes Lebanon's mountains skip like a calf
and Mount Hermon* to leap like a young bull.
7 The voice of the LORD strikes with lightning bolts.
8 The voice of the LORD makes the desert quake;
the LORD shakes the desert of Kadesh.
9 The voice of the LORD twists mighty oaks*
and strips the forests bare.
In his Temple everyone shouts, "Glory!"

29:1 1 Chr 16:28-29; Ps 96:7-9
29:2 Ps 110:3
29:4 Pss 68:33; 104:3
29:5 Ps 104:16; Isa 2:13
29:6 Deut 3:9; Ps 114:4
29:8 Num 13:26
29:9 Ps 26:8

29:6 Hebrew *Sirion*, another name for Mount Hermon. **29:9** Or *causes the deer to writhe in labor.*

29:5, 6 The cedars of Lebanon were giant trees that could grow to 120 feet in height and 30 feet in circumference. A voice that could split the cedars of Lebanon would be a truly powerful voice—the voice of God. All that was impressive to people was under God's complete control.

29:10 Gen 6:17 Ps 10:16

10 The LORD rules over the floodwaters.
The LORD reigns as king forever.

29:11 Pss 28:8; 37:11; 68:35 Isa 40:29

11 The LORD gives his people strength.
The LORD blesses them with peace.

Theme: A celebration of God's deliverance. Earthly security is uncertain, but God is always faithful.
Author: David

30

A psalm of David, sung at the dedication of the Temple.

30:1 Pss 25:2; 35:19, 24; 118:28; 145:1

1 I will praise you, LORD, for you have rescued me.
You refused to let my enemies triumph over me.

30:2 Pss 6:2; 88:13

2 O LORD my God, I cried out to you for help,
and you restored my health.

30:3 Pss 28:1; 86:13

3 You brought me up from the grave, O LORD.
You kept me from falling into the pit of death.

30:4 Pss 97:12; 149:1

4 Sing to the LORD, all you godly ones!
Praise his holy name.

30:5 Pss 54:7-8; 103:9; 118:1

5 His anger lasts for a moment,
but his favor lasts a lifetime!
Weeping may go on all night,
but joy comes with the morning.

30:6 Pss 10:6; 143:7

6 When I was prosperous I said,
"Nothing can stop me now!"

30:7 Ps 104:29

7 Your favor, O LORD, made me as secure as a mountain.
Then you turned away from me, and I was shattered.

8 I cried out to you, O LORD.
I begged the Lord for mercy, saying,

30:9 Ps 6:5

9 "What will you gain if I die,
if I sink down into the grave?
Can my dust praise you from the grave?
Can it tell the world of your faithfulness?

30:10 Pss 4:1; 27:7, 9

10 Hear me, LORD, and have mercy on me.
Help me, O LORD."

30:11 Ps 6:8 Jer 31:4, 13

11 You have turned my mourning into joyful dancing.
You have taken away my clothes of mourning and clothed me with joy,

30:12 Pss 44:8; 57:8; 108:1

12 that I might sing praises to you and not be silent.
O LORD my God, I will give you thanks forever!

29:10, 11 Throughout history, God has revealed his power through mighty miracles over nature, such as the great Flood (Genesis 6–9). He promises to continue to reveal his power. Paul urged us to understand how great God's power is (Ephesians 1:18-23). The same power that raised Christ from the dead is available to help us with our daily problems. When you feel weak and limited, don't despair. Remember that God can give you strength. The same power that controls creation and raises the dead is available to you.

30:1ff David may have written this psalm when he dedicated Araunah's threshing floor (which became the future site of the Temple), after God stopped the great plague he had used to discipline David (1 Chronicles 21:1–22:6). The serious illness mentioned in 30:2, 3 may refer to an illness David experienced or to the plague itself.

30:5 Like a shot given by a doctor, the discomfort of God's anger lasts only a moment, but the good effects go on for a long time. Let God's anger be a sharp pain that warns you to turn from sin.

30:6, 7 Security had made David feel invincible. Although he knew that his riches and power had come from God, they had gone to his head, making him proud. Wealth, power, and fame have an intoxicating effect on people, making them feel self-reliant, self-secure, and independent of God. But this false security can be easily shattered. Don't be trapped by the false security of prosperity. Depend on God for your security, and you won't be shaken when worldly possessions disappear.

Theme: In times of stress, depending upon God requires complete commitment.
Author: David, although some say Jeremiah

31

For the choir director: A psalm of David.

1 O LORD, I have come to you for protection;
don't let me be put to shame.
Rescue me, for you always do what is right.
2 Bend down and listen to me;
rescue me quickly.
Be for me a great rock of safety,
a fortress where my enemies cannot reach me.
3 You are my rock and my fortress.
For the honor of your name, lead me out of this peril.
4 Pull me from the trap my enemies set for me,
for I find protection in you alone.
5 I entrust my spirit into your hand.
Rescue me, LORD, for you are a faithful God.

6 I hate those who worship worthless idols.
I trust in the LORD.
7 I am overcome with joy because of your unfailing love,
for you have seen my troubles,
and you care about the anguish of my soul.
8 You have not handed me over to my enemy
but have set me in a safe place.

9 Have mercy on me, LORD, for I am in distress.
My sight is blurred because of my tears.
My body and soul are withering away.
10 I am dying from grief;
my years are shortened by sadness.
Misery* has drained my strength;
I am wasting away from within.
11 I am scorned by all my enemies
and despised by my neighbors—
even my friends are afraid to come near me.
When they see me on the street,
they turn the other way.
12 I have been ignored as if I were dead,
as if I were a broken pot.
13 I have heard the many rumors about me,
and I am surrounded by terror.

31:1-4 //Ps 71:1-3
31:1 Pss 25:2; 143:1
31:2 Pss 71:3; 86:1; 102:2
31:3 Pss 18:2; 23:2-3
31:4 Ps 25:15
31:5 Luke 23:46 Acts 7:59
31:6 Jon 2:8-9
31:7 Pss 10:14; 90:14
31:8 Deut 32:30
31:9 Pss 6:7; 32:3; 38:3-4; 39:11; 63:1; 69:17; 102:1, 3-4
31:10 Pss 13:2; 38:13; 39:11
31:11 Pss 38:11; 88:8, 18 Isa 53:4
31:12 Ps 88:5
31:13 Ps 41:7 Jer 20:10 Matt 27:1

31:10 Or *Sin.*

31:1 David called upon God to deliver him. He wanted God to stop those who were unjustly causing trouble. Therefore, David made his request based upon what he knew of God's name, or character. Because God is righteous and loving, he loves to deliver his people.

31:1-6 We say we have faith in God, but do we really trust him? David's words, "I entrust my spirit into your hand," convey his complete trust in God. Jesus used this phrase as he was dying on the cross—showing his absolute dependence on God the Father (Luke 23:46). Stephen repeated these words as he was being stoned to death (Acts 7:59), confident that in death he was simply passing from God's earthly care to God's eternal care. We should commit our possessions, our families, and our vocations to God. But first and foremost, we should commit *ourselves* completely to him.

31:6 Why did David suddenly bring up the subject of idol worship? He wanted to contrast his total devotion to God with the diluted worship offered by many Israelites. Pagan religious rituals were never completely banished from Israel and Judah, despite the efforts of David and a few other kings. Obviously a person who clung to idols could not commit his spirit into God's hands. When we put today's idols (wealth, material possessions, success) first in our lives, we cannot expect God's Spirit to guide us. God is our highest authority and requires our first allegiance.

31:9-13 In describing his own feelings, David writes of the helplessness and hopelessness everyone feels when hated or rejected. But adversity is easier to accept when we recognize our true relationship with the sovereign God (31:14-18). Although our enemies may seem to have the upper hand, they are ultimately the helpless and hopeless ones. Those who know God will be victorious in the end (31:23). We can have courage today because God will preserve us.

My enemies conspire against me,
plotting to take my life.

31:14
Pss 140:6; 143:9

[14] But I am trusting you, O LORD,
saying, "You are my God!"

31:15
Job 24:1
Ps 143:9

[15] My future is in your hands.
Rescue me from those who hunt me down relentlessly.

31:16
Num 6:24-26
Ps 6:4

[16] Let your favor shine on your servant.
In your unfailing love, save me.

31:17
1 Sam 2:9
Ps 25:2-3, 20

[17] Don't let me be disgraced, O LORD,
for I call out to you for help.
Let the wicked be disgraced;
let them lie silent in the grave.

31:18
1 Sam 2:3
Pss 94:4; 120:2

[18] May their lying lips be silenced—
those proud and arrogant lips that accuse the godly.

31:19
Ps 5:11
Isa 64:14
Rom 11:22

[19] Your goodness is so great!
You have stored up great blessings for those who honor you.
You have done so much for those who come to you for protection,
blessing them before the watching world.

31:20
Job 5:21
Pss 27:5; 31:13

[20] You hide them in the shelter of your presence,
safe from those who conspire against them.
You shelter them in your presence,
far from accusing tongues.

31:21
Ps 17:7

[21] Praise the LORD,
for he has shown me his unfailing love.
He kept me safe when my city was under attack.

31:22
Pss 66:19;
116:11-12; 145:19
Lam 3:54-56

[22] In sudden fear I had cried out,
"I have been cut off from the LORD!"
But you heard my cry for mercy
and answered my call for help.

31:23
Deut 32:40-41
Ps 37:28

[23] Love the LORD, all you faithful ones!
For the LORD protects those who are loyal to him,
but he harshly punishes all who are arrogant.

31:24
Ps 27:14

[24] So be strong and take courage,
all you who put your hope in the LORD!

Theme: Forgiveness brings true joy. Only when we ask God to forgive our sins will he give us real happiness and relief from guilt.
Author: David

32

A psalm of David.

[1] Oh, what joy for those
whose rebellion is forgiven,
whose sin is put out of sight!

32:2
Ps 85:2
†Rom 4:7-8

[2] Yes, what joy for those
whose record the LORD has cleared of sin,
whose lives are lived in complete honesty!

31:14, 15 In saying, "My future is in your hands," David was expressing his belief that all of life's circumstances are under God's control. Knowing that God loves and cares for us enables us to keep steady in our faith regardless of our circumstances. It keeps us from sinning foolishly by taking matters into our own hands or resenting God's timetable.

32:1ff Read this psalm in conjunction with Psalm 51—both are penitential psalms. Here David expresses the joy of forgiveness. God had forgiven him for the sins he had committed against Bathsheba and Uriah (2 Samuel 11–12). This is another of the penitential (repentance) psalms where the writer confesses his sin to God.

32:1, 2 God *wants* to forgive sinners. Forgiveness has always been part of his loving nature. He announced this to Moses (Exodus 34:6, 7); he revealed it to David; and he dramatically showed it to the world through Jesus Christ. These verses convey several aspects of God's forgiveness: He forgives rebellion, puts sin out of sight, clears our record of sin. Paul quoted these verses in Romans 4:7, 8 and showed that we can have this joyous experience of forgiveness through faith in Christ.

3 When I refused to confess my sin,
I was weak and miserable,
and I groaned all day long.
4 Day and night your hand of discipline was heavy on me.
My strength evaporated like water in the summer heat. *Interlude*

5 Finally, I confessed all my sins to you
and stopped trying to hide them.
I said to myself, "I will confess my rebellion to the LORD."
And you forgave me! All my guilt is gone. *Interlude*

6 Therefore, let all the godly confess their rebellion to you while there is time,
that they may not drown in the floodwaters of judgment.
7 For you are my hiding place;
you protect me from trouble.
You surround me with songs of victory. *Interlude*

8 The LORD says, "I will guide you along the best pathway for your life.
I will advise you and watch over you.
9 Do not be like a senseless horse or mule
that needs a bit and bridle to keep it under control."

10 Many sorrows come to the wicked,
but unfailing love surrounds those who trust the LORD.
11 So rejoice in the LORD and be glad, all you who obey him!
Shout for joy, all you whose hearts are pure!

32:3 Pss 31:10; 39:2
32:4 Job 33:7; Pss 22:15; 39:10
32:5 Lev 26:40; Job 31:33; Ps 38:18; 1 Jn 1:9
32:6 Pss 69:13; 144:7; Isa 43:2
32:7 Exod 15:1; Pss 31:20; 40:3; 121:7
32:8 Pss 25:8; 33:18-19
32:10 Ps 16:4; Prov 16:20; Rom 2:9-10

Theme: Because God is Creator, Lord, Savior, and Deliverer, he is worthy of our trust and praise. Because he is faithful and his word is dependable, we can rejoice and sing, giving thanks and praise.
Author: Anonymous

33

1 Let the godly sing with joy to the LORD,
for it is fitting to praise him.
2 Praise the LORD with melodies on the lyre;
make music for him on the ten-stringed harp.
3 Sing new songs of praise to him;
play skillfully on the harp and sing with joy.

4 For the word of the LORD holds true,
and everything he does is worthy of our trust.
5 He loves whatever is just and good,
and his unfailing love fills the earth.

6 The LORD merely spoke,
and the heavens were created.
He breathed the word,
and all the stars were born.

33:1 Pss 32:11; 147:1
33:2 Ps 92:3
33:3 Pss 96:1; 98:1; Rev 5:9
33:4 Ps 19:8
33:5 Pss 11:7; 119:64
33:6 Gen 1:6-7; Ps 148:5; Heb 11:3

32:5 What is confession? To confess our sin is to agree with God, acknowledging that he is right to declare what we have done as sinful and that we are wrong to desire or to do it. It is to affirm our intention of forsaking that sin in order to follow him more faithfully.

32:8, 9 God describes some people as being like horses or mules that have to be controlled by bits and bridles. Rather than letting God guide them step by step, they stubbornly leave God only one option. If God wants to keep them useful for him, he must use discipline and punishment. God longs to guide us with love and wisdom rather than punishment. He offers to teach us the *best* way to go. Accept the advice written in God's Word, and don't let your stubbornness keep you from obeying God.

33:2, 3 David, who some believe wrote this psalm, was an accomplished harpist (1 Samuel 16:15-23). He frequently spoke about musical instruments throughout his psalms. He undoubtedly composed music for many of the psalms, and he commissioned musicians for Temple worship (1 Chronicles 25).

33:4 All God's words are true and trustworthy. The Bible is reliable because, unlike people, God does not lie, forget, change his words, or leave his promises unfulfilled. We can trust the Bible because it contains the words of a holy, trustworthy, and unchangeable God.

33:6-9 This is a poetic summary of the first chapter of Genesis. God is not just the coordinator of natural forces; he is the Lord of creation, the almighty God. Because he is all-powerful, we should revere him in all we do.

33:7 Exod 15:8

7 He gave the sea its boundaries
and locked the oceans in vast reservoirs.

33:8 Pss 67:7; 96:9

8 Let everyone in the world fear the LORD,
and let everyone stand in awe of him.

33:9 Gen 1:3 Ps 148:5

9 For when he spoke, the world began!
It appeared at his command.

33:10 Isa 8:9-10; 19:3

10 The LORD shatters the plans of the nations
and thwarts all their schemes.
11 But the LORD's plans stand firm forever;
his intentions can never be shaken.

33:12 Exod 19:5 Ps 144:15

12 What joy for the nation whose God is the LORD,
whose people he has chosen for his own.

13 The LORD looks down from heaven
and sees the whole human race.
14 From his throne he observes
all who live on the earth.
15 He made their hearts,
so he understands everything they do.

33:16 Pss 44:6; 147:10

16 The best-equipped army cannot save a king,
nor is great strength enough to save a warrior.

33:17 Ps 20:7 Prov 21:31

17 Don't count on your warhorse to give you victory—
for all its strength, it cannot save you.

33:18 Ps 34:15

18 But the LORD watches over those who fear him,
those who rely on his unfailing love.

33:19 Ps 37:19

19 He rescues them from death
and keeps them alive in times of famine.

33:20 Ps 115:9 Isa 8:17

20 We depend on the LORD alone to save us.
Only he can help us, protecting us like a shield.
21 In him our hearts rejoice,
for we are trusting in his holy name.

CONFESSION, REPENTANCE, AND FORGIVENESS IN PSALMS

Over the centuries, many believers, overcome by an awareness of their own sins, have found in the words of the penitential (confession) psalms a ray of hope. The psalmists shared with God the depth of their sorrow and repentance, as well as the height of joy at being forgiven. They rejoiced in the knowledge that God would respond to confession and repentance with complete forgiveness. We who live on the other side of the cross of Christ can rejoice even more because we understand more. God has shown us that he is willing to forgive because his judgment on sin was satisfied by Christ's death on the cross.

As you read these psalms, note the pattern followed by the psalmists in responding to God: (1) They recognized their sinfulness and tendency to do wrong; (2) they realized that sin was rebellion against God himself; (3) they admitted their sins to God; (4) they trusted in God's willingness to forgive; and (5) they accepted his forgiveness. Use these psalms as a reminder of how easy it is to drift away from God and fall into sin, and what is needed to reestablish that fellowship.

Selected psalms that emphasize these themes are 6; 14; 31; 32; 38; 41; 51; 102; 130; 143.

33:11 "The LORD's plans stand firm forever." Are you frustrated by inconsistencies you see in others or even in yourself? God is completely trustworthy—his intentions never change. There is a promise that whatever is good and perfect comes to us from the Creator who never changes (James 1:17). When you wonder if there is anyone whom you can trust, remember that God is completely consistent. Let him counsel you.

33:16, 17 *Warhorse* refers to military strength. Because God rules and overrules every nation, leaders should never put their trust in their physical power. Military might is not the basis for our hope. Our hope is in God and in his gracious offer to save us if we will trust in him.

33:18, 19 This is not an ironclad guarantee that all believers will be delivered from death and starvation. Thousands of Christian saints have been beaten to death, whipped, fed to lions, or executed (Romans 8:35, 36; Hebrews 11:32-40). God can (and often does) miraculously deliver his followers from pain and death; although sometimes, for purposes known only to him, he chooses not to. When faced with these harsh realities, we must focus on the wise judgments of God. The writer was pleading for God's watchful care and protection. In times of crisis, we can place our hope in God.

22 Let your unfailing love surround us, LORD,
for our hope is in you alone.

Theme: God pays attention to those who call on him. Whether God offers escape from trouble or help in times of trouble, we can be certain that he always hears and acts on behalf of those who love him.
Author: David, after pretending to be insane in order to escape from King Achish (1 Samuel 21:10-15)

34

A psalm of David, regarding the time he pretended to be insane in front of Abimelech, who sent him away.

1 I will praise the LORD at all times.
I will constantly speak his praises.
2 I will boast only in the LORD;
let all who are discouraged take heart.
3 Come, let us tell of the LORD's greatness;
let us exalt his name together.

4 I prayed to the LORD, and he answered me,
freeing me from all my fears.
5 Those who look to him for help will be radiant with joy;
no shadow of shame will darken their faces.
6 I cried out to the LORD in my suffering, and he heard me.
He set me free from all my fears.
7 For the angel of the LORD guards all who fear him,
and he rescues them.

8 Taste and see that the LORD is good.
Oh, the joys of those who trust in him!
9 Let the LORD's people show him reverence,
for those who honor him will have all they need.
10 Even strong young lions sometimes go hungry,
but those who trust in the LORD will never lack any good thing.

11 Come, my children, and listen to me,
and I will teach you to fear the LORD.
12 Do any of you want to live
a life that is long and good?

34:1 Ps 71:6; Eph 5:20
34:2 Jer 9:24
34:3 Luke 1:46
34:4 †1 Pet 3:10-12
34:5 Pss 25:31; 36:9
34:7 Ps 2:12; Dan 6:22
34:8 1 Pet 2:3
34:9 Pss 23:1; 31:23
34:10 Ps 84:11
34:11 Ps 111:10
34:12 1 Pet 3:10-12

34:1ff God promises great blessings to his people, but many of these blessings require our active participation. He will set us free from our fears (34:4, 6), guard and rescue us (34:7), show us goodness (34:8), supply our needs (34:9), listen when we call to him (34:15), and redeem us (34:22), but we must do our part. We can appropriate his blessings when we seek him (34:4, 10); cry out to him (34:6, 17); trust him (34:8); fear him (34:7); reverence him (34:9); refrain from lying (34:13); turn from evil, do good and seek peace (34:14); are brokenhearted (34:18); and serve him (34:22).

34:8 "Taste and see" does not mean, "Check out God's credentials." Instead, it is a warm invitation: "Try this; I know you'll like it." When we take that first step of obedience in following God, we cannot help discovering that he is good and kind. When we begin the Christian life, our knowledge of God is partial and incomplete. As we trust him daily, we experience how good he is.

34:9 You say you belong to the Lord, but do you show reverence to him? To revere the Lord means to show deep respect and honor to him. We demonstrate true reverence by our humble attitude and genuine worship. Reverence was shown by Abraham (Genesis 17:2-4), Moses (Exodus 3:5, 6), and the Israelites (Exodus 19:16-24). Their reactions to God's presence varied, but all deeply respected him.

34:9, 10 At first we may question David's statement because we seem to lack many good things. This is not a blanket promise that all Christians will have everything they want. Instead, this is David's praise for God's goodness—all those who call upon God in their need will be answered, sometimes in unexpected ways.

Remember, God knows what we need, and our deepest needs are spiritual. Many Christians, even though they face unbearable poverty and hardship, still have enough spiritual nourishment to live for God. David was saying that if you have God, you have all you really need. God is enough.

If you feel you don't have everything you need, ask: (1) Is this really a need? (2) Is this really good for me? (3) Is this the best time for me to have what I desire? Even if you answer yes to all three questions, God may allow you to go without to help you grow more dependent on him. He may want you to learn that you need *him* more than you need your immediate desires met.

34:13 Jas 1:26; 1 Pet 2:22
34:14 Ps 37:27; Rom 14:18-19; Heb 12:14
34:15 Job 36:7; Ps 33:18-19
34:16 Pss 9:6; 109:15
34:18 Pss 51:17; 145:18; Isa 57:15
34:19 Ps 71:20; Prov 24:16
34:21 Ps 94:23
34:22 1 Kgs 1:29; Ps 71:23

13 Then watch your tongue!
Keep your lips from telling lies!
14 Turn away from evil and do good.
Work hard at living in peace with others.

15 The eyes of the LORD watch over those who do right;
his ears are open to their cries for help.
16 But the LORD turns his face against those who do evil;
he will erase their memory from the earth.

17 The LORD hears his people when they call to him for help.
He rescues them from all their troubles.
18 The LORD is close to the brokenhearted;
he rescues those who are crushed in spirit.

19 The righteous face many troubles,
but the LORD rescues them from each and every one.
20 For the LORD protects them from harm—
not one of their bones will be broken!

21 Calamity will surely overtake the wicked,
and those who hate the righteous will be punished.
22 But the LORD will redeem those who serve him.
Everyone who trusts in him will be freely pardoned.

Theme: A prayer to God for help against those who try to inflict injury for no reason. When our enemies are unjust and lie about us, even when we do good to them, we can appeal to God who is always just.
Author: David, possibly written when he was being hunted by Saul (1 Samuel 24)

35

A psalm of David.

35:1 Ps 56:1-2; Isa 49:25
35:2 Ps 91:4
35:3 Ps 62:2

1 O LORD, oppose those who oppose me.
Declare war on those who are attacking me.
2 Put on your armor, and take up your shield.
Prepare for battle, and come to my aid.
3 Lift up your spear and javelin
and block the way of my enemies.
Let me hear you say,
"I am your salvation!"

34:11-14 The Bible often connects the fear of the Lord (love and reverence for him) with obedience. "Fear God and obey his commands" (Ecclesiastes 12:13); "All those who love me will do what I say" (John 14:23). David said that a person who fears the Lord doesn't lie, turns from evil, does good, and promotes peace. Reverence is much more than sitting quietly in church. It includes obeying God in the way we speak and the way we treat others.

34:14 Somehow we think that peace should come to us with no effort. But David explained that we are to work hard at peace. Paul echoed this thought in Romans 12:18. A person who wants peace cannot be argumentative and contentious. Because peaceful relationships come from our efforts at peacemaking, work hard at living in peace with others each day.

34:18, 19 We often wish we could escape troubles—the pain of grief, loss, sorrow, and failure, or even the small daily frustrations that constantly wear us down. God promises to be "close to the brokenhearted" and to be our source of power, courage, and wisdom, helping us through our problems. Sometimes he chooses to deliver us from those problems. When trouble strikes, don't get frustrated with God. Instead, admit that you need God's help and thank him for being by your side.

34:20 This is a prophecy about Christ when he was crucified. Although it was the Roman custom to break the legs of the victim to speed death, not one of Jesus' bones was broken (John 19:32-37). In addition to the prophetic meaning, David was pleading for God's protection in times of crisis.

35:1ff This is one of the "imprecatory" (cursing) psalms that call upon God to deal with enemies. These psalms sound extremely harsh, but we must remember: (1) David could not understand why he was forced to flee from men who were unjustly seeking to kill him. He was God's anointed king over a nation called to annihilate the evil people of the land. (2) David's call for justice was sincere; it was not a cover for his own personal vengeance. He truly wanted God's perfect ideal for his nation. (3) David did not say that *he* would take revenge, but he gave the matter to God. These are merely his suggestions. (4) These psalms use hyperbole (or overstatement). They were meant to motivate others to take a strong stand against sin and evil.

Cruelty may be far removed from some people's experience, but it is a daily reality to others. God promises to help the persecuted and to bring judgment on unrepentant sinners. When we pray for justice to be done, we are praying as David did. When Christ returns, the wicked will be punished.

4 Humiliate and disgrace those trying to kill me;
turn them back in confusion.
5 Blow them away like chaff in the wind—
a wind sent by the angel of the LORD.
6 Make their path dark and slippery,
with the angel of the LORD pursuing them.
7 Although I did them no wrong,
they laid a trap for me.
Although I did them no wrong,
they dug a pit for me.
8 So let sudden ruin overtake them!
Let them be caught in the snare they set for me!
Let them fall to destruction in the pit they dug for me.

9 Then I will rejoice in the LORD.
I will be glad because he rescues me.
10 I will praise him from the bottom of my heart:
"LORD, who can compare with you?
Who else rescues the weak and helpless from the strong?
Who else protects the poor and needy from those who want to rob them?"

11 Malicious witnesses testify against me.
They accuse me of things I don't even know about.
12 They repay me with evil for the good I do.
I am sick with despair.
13 Yet when they were ill,
I grieved for them.
I even fasted and prayed for them,
but my prayers returned unanswered.
14 I was sad, as though they were my friends or family,
as if I were grieving for my own mother.
15 But they are glad now that I am in trouble;
they gleefully join together against me.
I am attacked by people I don't even know;
they hurl slander at me continually.
16 They mock me with the worst kind of profanity,
and they snarl at me.

17 How long, O Lord, will you look on and do nothing?
Rescue me from their fierce attacks.
Protect my life from these lions!
18 Then I will thank you in front of the entire congregation.
I will praise you before all the people.
19 Don't let my treacherous enemies
rejoice over my defeat.
Don't let those who hate me without cause
gloat over my sorrow.
20 They don't talk of peace;
they plot against innocent people
who are minding their own business.

35:4 Pss 40:14; 70:2-3
35:5 Job 21:18; Pss 1:4; 83:13; Isa 29:5
35:6 Ps 73:18; Jer 23:12
35:7 Pss 9:15; 69:4; 109:3
35:8 Ps 9:15; Isa 47:11; 1 Thes 5:3
35:9 Isa 61:10; Luke 1:47
35:10 Exod 15:11-12; Pss 18:17; 37:14
35:11 Ps 27:12
35:12 Ps 38:20; John 10:32
35:13 Job 30:25; Ps 69:10; Jer 18:20
35:16 Lam 2:16
35:17 Pss 13:1; 22:20-21; Hab 1:13
35:18 Ps 22:23, 25
35:19 Pss 13:4; 38:16, 19; 69:4; †John 15:25

35:13 David was sad when his prayers seemed "unanswered." When our deliverance is delayed, it is easy to assume that God hasn't answered our prayers. God hears every prayer, but he answers according to his wisdom. Don't let the absence of an immediate answer cause you to doubt or resent God. Instead, let it be an occasion to deepen your faith.

35:21-23 David cried out to God to defend him when people wrongly accused him. If you are unjustly accused, your natural reaction may be to lash out in revenge or to give a detailed defense of your every move. Instead, ask God to fight the battle for you. He will clear your name in the eyes of those who really matter.

35:21
Pss 22:13; 40:15

21 They shout that they have seen me doing wrong.
"Aha," they say. "Aha!
With our own eyes we saw him do it!"

35:22
Exod 3:7
Ps 10:14

22 O LORD, you know all about this.
Do not stay silent.
Don't abandon me now, O Lord.
23 Wake up! Rise to my defense!
Take up my case, my God and my Lord.

35:24
Pss 9:4; 43:1

24 Declare me "not guilty," O LORD my God, for you give justice.
Don't let my enemies laugh about me in my troubles.

35:25
Ps 56:1
Lam 2:16

25 Don't let them say, "Look! We have what we wanted!
Now we will eat him alive!"

35:26
Pss 38:16; 40:14

26 May those who rejoice at my troubles
be humiliated and disgraced.
May those who triumph over me
be covered with shame and dishonor.

35:27
Pss 40:16; 70:4; 149:4-5

27 But give great joy to those
who have stood with me in my defense.
Let them continually say, "Great is the LORD,
who enjoys helping his servant."

35:28
Ps 51:14-15

28 Then I will tell everyone of your justice and goodness,
and I will praise you all day long.

Theme: God's faithfulness, justice, and love are contrasted with the sinful hearts of men and women. In spite of our fallen condition, God pours out his love on those who know him.
Author: David

36

For the choir director: A psalm of David, the servant of the LORD.

36:1
†Rom 3:18

1 Sin whispers to the wicked, deep within their hearts.
They have no fear of God to restrain them.
2 In their blind conceit,
they cannot see how wicked they really are.

36:3
Ps 10:7
Jer 4:22

3 Everything they say is crooked and deceitful.
They refuse to act wisely or do what is good.

36:4
Prov 4:16
Isa 65:2
Mic 2:1

4 They lie awake at night, hatching sinful plots.
Their course of action is never good.
They make no attempt to turn from evil.

36:5
Pss 57:10; 103:11; 108:4

5 Your unfailing love, O LORD, is as vast as the heavens;
your faithfulness reaches beyond the clouds.

36:6
Job 11:8
Pss 104:14-15; 145:16-17
Rom 11:33

6 Your righteousness is like the mighty mountains,
your justice like the ocean depths.
You care for people and animals alike, O LORD.

36:7
Ruth 2:12
Pss 91:4; 139:17-18

7 How precious is your unfailing love, O God!
All humanity finds shelter
in the shadow of your wings.

36:8
Ps 46:4
Isa 25:6
Rev 22:1

8 You feed them from the abundance of your own house,
letting them drink from your rivers of delight.

36:1 Because the wicked have no fear of God, nothing restrains them from sinning. They plunge ahead as if nothing will happen to them. But God is just and is only delaying their punishment. This knowledge should hold us back from sinning. Let the fear of God do its work in you to keep you from sin. In your gratitude for God's love, don't ignore his justice.

36:5-8 In contrast to evil people and their wicked plots that end in failure, God is faithful, righteous, and just. His love is as vast as the heavens; his faithfulness reaches beyond the clouds; his righteousness is as solid as mighty mountains; and his judgments are as full of wisdom as the oceans are with water. We need not fear evil people because we know God loves us, judges evil, and will care for us throughout eternity.

9 For you are the fountain of life,
the light by which we see.

10 Pour out your unfailing love on those who love you;
give justice to those with honest hearts.
11 Don't let the proud trample me;
don't let the wicked push me around.
12 Look! They have fallen!
They have been thrown down, never to rise again.

36:9
1 Pet 2:9

36:12
Ps 140:10

Theme: Trust in the Lord and wait patiently for him to act. This psalm vividly contrasts the wicked person with the righteous.
Author: David

37

A psalm of David.

1 Don't worry about the wicked.
Don't envy those who do wrong.
2 For like grass, they soon fade away.
Like springtime flowers, they soon wither.

3 Trust in the LORD and do good.
Then you will live safely in the land and prosper.
4 Take delight in the LORD,
and he will give you your heart's desires.

5 Commit everything you do to the LORD.
Trust him, and he will help you.
6 He will make your innocence as clear as the dawn,
and the justice of your cause will shine like the noonday sun.

7 Be still in the presence of the LORD,
and wait patiently for him to act.
Don't worry about evil people who prosper
or fret about their wicked schemes.

8 Stop your anger!
Turn from your rage!
Do not envy others—
it only leads to harm.
9 For the wicked will be destroyed,
but those who trust in the LORD will possess the land.

10 In a little while, the wicked will disappear.
Though you look for them, they will be gone.

37:1
Ps 73:3
Prov 3:31

37:2
Job 14:2
Ps 90:5-6

37:3
Deut 30:20
Ps 62:8
Isa 40:11

37:4
Ps 145:19
Isa 58:14

37:5
Ps 55:22
Prov 16:3
1 Pet 5:7

37:6
Isa 58:8, 10
Mic 7:9

37:7
Pss 40:1; 62:5
Jer 12:1

37:8
Eph 4:31
Col 3:8

37:9
Ps 25:13
Isa 60:21

37:10
Job 24:24

36:9 "Fountain of life" is a vivid image of fresh, cleansing water that gives life to the spiritually thirsty. This same picture is used in Jeremiah 2:13, where God is called the "fountain of living water." Jesus spoke of himself as living water that could quench thirst forever and give eternal life (John 4:14).

37:1 We should never envy evil people, even though some may be extremely popular or excessively rich. No matter how much they have, it will fade and vanish like grass that withers and dies. Those who follow God live differently from the wicked and, in the end, will have treasures in heaven. What an unbeliever gets on earth may last a lifetime, but what you get from following God lasts forever.

37:4, 5 David calls us to take delight in the Lord and to commit everything we have and do to him. But how do we do this? To *delight* in someone means to experience great pleasure and joy in his or her presence. This happens only when we know that person well. Thus, to delight in the Lord, we must know him better. Knowledge of God's great love for us will indeed give us delight.

To *commit* ourselves to the Lord means entrusting everything—our lives, families, jobs, possessions—to his control and guidance. To commit ourselves to the Lord means to trust in him (37:5), believing that he can care for us better than we can ourselves. We should be willing to wait patiently (37:7) for him to work out what is best for us.

37:8, 9 Anger, rage, and envy are very destructive emotions. They reveal a lack of faith that God loves us and is in control. We should not worry; instead, we should trust in God, giving ourselves to him for his use and safekeeping. When you dwell on your problems, you will become anxious and angry. But if you concentrate on God and his goodness, you will find peace. Where do you focus your attention?

37:11 Matt 5:3, 5

11 Those who are gentle and lowly will possess the land;
they will live in prosperous security.

37:12 Ps 35:16

12 The wicked plot against the godly;
they snarl at them in defiance.

37:13 Ps 2:4

13 But the Lord just laughs,
for he sees their day of judgment coming.

37:14 Pss 11:2; 35:10

14 The wicked draw their swords
and string their bows
to kill the poor and the oppressed,
to slaughter those who do right.

37:15 Pss 9:16; 46:9

15 But they will be stabbed through the heart with their own swords,
and their bows will be broken.

37:16 Prov 15:16; 16:8

16 It is better to be godly and have little
than to be evil and possess much.

37:17 Job 38:15 Ps 10:15

17 For the strength of the wicked will be shattered,
but the LORD takes care of the godly.

18 Day by day the LORD takes care of the innocent,
and they will receive a reward that lasts forever.

37:19 Job 5:20 Ps 33:18-19

19 They will survive through hard times;
even in famine they will have more than enough.

37:20 Pss 68:2; 73:27; 102:3

20 But the wicked will perish.
The LORD's enemies are like flowers in a field—
they will disappear like smoke.

21 The wicked borrow and never repay,
but the godly are generous givers.

37:22 Job 5:3 Prov 3:33

22 Those blessed by the LORD will inherit the land,
but those cursed by him will die.

37:23 1 Sam 2:9 Pss 40:2; 147:11

23 The steps of the godly are directed by the LORD.
He delights in every detail of their lives.

37:24 Pss 145:14; 147:6 Prov 24:15-16

24 Though they stumble, they will not fall,
for the LORD holds them by the hand.

37:25 Isa 41:17 Heb 13:5

25 Once I was young, and now I am old.
Yet I have never seen the godly forsaken,
nor seen their children begging for bread.

37:26 Pss 37:21; 147:13

26 The godly always give generous loans to others,
and their children are a blessing.

37:27 Ps 34:14

27 Turn from evil and do good,
and you will live in the land forever.

37:11 Being gentle and lowly hardly seems the proper demeanor to deal with enemies. God's warfare, however, must be carried out with calm faith, humility before God, and hope in his deliverance. Jesus also promises a sure reward for those with humble attitudes (Matthew 5:5).

37:21 You can tell a lot about a person's character by the way he or she handles money. The wicked person steals under the guise of borrowing. The righteous person gives generously to the needy. The wicked person, therefore, focuses on himself, while the righteous person looks to the welfare of others.

37:23, 24 The person in whom God delights is one who follows God, trusts him, and tries to do his will. God watches over and makes firm every step that person takes. If you would like to have God direct your way, then seek his advice before you step out.

37:25 Because children starve today, as they did in David's time, what did David mean by these words? The children of the righteous need not go hungry because other believers should help them in their time of need. In David's day, Israel obeyed God's laws, which ensured that the poor were treated fairly and mercifully. As long as Israel was obedient, there was enough food for everyone. When Israel forgot God, the rich took care of themselves only, and the poor suffered (Amos 2:6, 7).

When we see a Christian brother or sister suffering today, we can respond in one of three ways: (1) We can say, as Job's friends did, that the afflicted person brought this on himself. (2) We can say that this is a test to help the person develop more patience and trust in God. (3) We can help the person in need. David would approve of only the last option. Although many governments today have their own programs for helping those in need, this is no excuse for ignoring the poor and needy within our reach.

28 For the LORD loves justice,
and he will never abandon the godly.

He will keep them safe forever,
but the children of the wicked will perish.
29 The godly will inherit the land
and will live there forever.

30 The godly offer good counsel;
they know what is right from wrong.
31 They fill their hearts with God's law,
so they will never slip from his path.

32 Those who are evil spy on the godly,
waiting for an excuse to kill them.
33 But the LORD will not let the wicked succeed
or let the godly be condemned when they are brought before the judge.

34 Don't be impatient for the LORD to act!
Travel steadily along his path.
He will honor you, giving you the land.
You will see the wicked destroyed.

35 I myself have seen it happen—
proud and evil people thriving like mighty trees.
36 But when I looked again, they were gone!
Though I searched for them, I could not find them!

37 Look at those who are honest and good,
for a wonderful future lies before those who love peace.
38 But the wicked will be destroyed;
they have no future.

39 The LORD saves the godly;
he is their fortress in times of trouble.
40 The LORD helps them,
rescuing them from the wicked.
He saves them,
and they find shelter in him.

37:28 Pss 11:7; 21:10
37:29 Ps 37:9, 18
37:31 Pss 37:23; 40:8; Isa 51:7
37:32 Pss 10:8; 37:14
37:33 2 Pet 2:9
37:34 Pss 27:14; 37:9
37:35 Job 5:3
37:37 Isa 57:1-2
37:38 Pss 1:1; 73:19
37:39 Pss 3:8; 9:9

Theme: Sorrow for sin brings hope. God alone is the true source of healing and protection for those who confess their sins to him.
Author: David

38

A psalm of David, to bring us to the LORD's remembrance.

1 O LORD, don't rebuke me in your anger!
Don't discipline me in your rage!
2 Your arrows have struck deep,
and your blows are crushing me.

3 Because of your anger, my whole body is sick;
my health is broken because of my sins.

38:1 Ps 6:1
38:2 Job 6:4; Ps 32:4
38:3 Pss 6:2; 31:9-10; Isa 1:5-6

37:34 It is difficult to wait patiently for God to act when we want change right away. But God promises that if we submit to his timing, he will honor us. Peter said, "So humble yourselves under the mighty power of God, and in his good time he will honor you" (1 Peter 5:6). Be patient, steadily doing the work God has given you to do, and allow God to choose the best time to change your circumstances.

38:1 As a child might cry to his father, so David cried to God. David was not saying, "Don't punish me," but, "Don't punish me while you are angry." He acknowledged that he deserved to be punished, but he asked that God temper his discipline with mercy. Like children, we are free to ask for mercy, but we should not deny that we deserve punishment.

38:1ff This is called a penitential psalm because David expressed sorrow for his sin (38:18). He stated that his sin led to health problems (38:1-8) and separated him from God and others, causing extreme loneliness (38:9-14). He then confessed his sin and repented (38:15-22).

38:2-4 David saw his anguish as judgment from God for his sins. Although God does not always send physical illness to

38:4 Ezra 9:6

4 My guilt overwhelms me—
it is a burden too heavy to bear.

38:5 Ps 69:5

5 My wounds fester and stink
because of my foolish sins.

38:6 Pss 35:14; 42:9

6 I am bent over and racked with pain.
My days are filled with grief.

38:7 Ps 102:3-4

7 A raging fever burns within me,
and my health is broken.

38:8 Job 3:24; Ps 22:1

8 I am exhausted and completely crushed.
My groans come from an anguished heart.

38:9 Pss 6:6; 10:17

9 You know what I long for, Lord;
you hear my every sigh.

38:10 Pss 6:7; 31:10

10 My heart beats wildly, my strength fails,
and I am going blind.

11 My loved ones and friends stay away, fearing my disease.
Even my own family stands at a distance.

38:12 Pss 35:20; 54:3; 140:5

12 Meanwhile, my enemies lay traps for me;
they make plans to ruin me.
They think up treacherous deeds all day long.

13 But I am deaf to all their threats.
I am silent before them as one who cannot speak.

14 I choose to hear nothing,
and I make no reply.

38:15 Pss 17:6; 37:9

15 For I am waiting for you, O LORD.
You must answer for me, O Lord my God.

38:16 Pss 13:4; 35:26

16 I prayed, "Don't let my enemies gloat over me
or rejoice at my downfall."

38:17 Ps 13:2

17 I am on the verge of collapse,
facing constant pain.

38:18 2 Cor 7:9-10

18 But I confess my sins;
I am deeply sorry for what I have done.

38:19 Pss 18:17; 35:19

19 My enemies are many;
they hate me though I have done nothing against them.

38:20 Ps 35:12; 1 Jn 3:12

20 They repay me evil for good
and oppose me because I stand for the right.

38:21 Pss 22:19; 35:22

21 Do not abandon me, LORD.
Do not stand at a distance, my God.

38:22 Pss 27:1; 40:13, 17

22 Come quickly to help me, O Lord my savior.

Theme: Apart from God, life is fleeting and empty. This is an appeal for God's mercy because life is so brief.
Author: David

39

For Jeduthun, the choir director: A psalm of David.

39:1 Pss 34:13; 141:3; Jas 3:2, 5-12

1 I said to myself, "I will watch what I do
and not sin in what I say.

punish us for sin, this verse and others in Scripture (Acts 12:21-23; 1 Corinthians 11:30-32) indicate that he does in certain circumstances. Our sin can have physical or mental side effects that can cause great suffering. Sometimes God has to punish his children in order to bring them back to himself (Hebrews 12:5-11). When we repent of our sin, God promises to forgive us. He delivers us from sin's eternal consequences, although he does not promise to undo all of sin's earthly consequences.

38:13, 14 It is extremely difficult to be silent when others tear us down, because we want to protect our reputation. We find it difficult to do nothing while they assault something so precious to us. But we don't need to lash out in revenge or justify our position; we can trust God to protect our reputation. Jesus was silent before his accusers (Luke 23:9, 10); he left his case in God's hands (1 Peter 2:21-24). That is a good place to leave our case, too!

I will curb my tongue
when the ungodly are around me."
2 But as I stood there in silence—
not even speaking of good things—
the turmoil within me grew to the bursting point.
3 My thoughts grew hot within me
and began to burn,
igniting a fire of words:
4 "LORD, remind me how brief my time on earth will be.
Remind me that my days are numbered,
and that my life is fleeing away.
5 My life is no longer than the width of my hand.
An entire lifetime is just a moment to you;
human existence is but a breath." *Interlude*

6 We are merely moving shadows,
and all our busy rushing ends in nothing.
We heap up wealth for someone else to spend.

7 And so, Lord, where do I put my hope?
My only hope is in you.
8 Rescue me from my rebellion,
for even fools mock me when I rebel.
9 I am silent before you; I won't say a word.
For my punishment is from you.
10 Please, don't punish me anymore!
I am exhausted by the blows from your hand.
11 When you discipline people for their sins,
their lives can be crushed like the life of a moth.
Human existence is as frail as breath. *Interlude*

12 Hear my prayer, O LORD!
Listen to my cries for help!
Don't ignore my tears.
For I am your guest—
a traveler passing through,
as my ancestors were before me.
13 Spare me so I can smile again
before I am gone and exist no more.

39:2 Ps 38:13-16
39:4 Pss 78:39; 90:12; 103:14-15
39:5 Job 14:2 Pss 62:9; 89:47; 144:4
39:6 Ps 127:2 Luke 12:20 1 Pet 1:24
39:8 Pss 51:9; 79:4, 9
39:9 2 Sam 16:10 Job 2:10
39:10 Job 9:34 Ps 32:4
39:11 Job 13:27-28 Ps 90:7 2 Pet 2:16
39:12 Ps 102:1 Heb 11:13 1 Pet 2:11
39:13 Job 10:20; 14:6

39:1-3 David resolved to keep his tongue from sin; that is, he decided not to complain to other people about God's treatment of him. David certainly had reason to complain. David was the anointed king of Israel, but he had to wait many years before taking the throne. Then one of his sons tried to kill him and become king instead. But when David could not keep still any longer, he took his complaints directly to God. We all have complaints about our job, money, or situation, but complaining to others may make them think that God cannot take care of us. It may also look as if we blame God for our troubles. Instead, like David, we should take our complaints directly to God.

39:4 Life is short no matter how long we live. If there is something important we want to do, we must not put it off for a better day. Ask yourself If I had only six months to live, what would I do? Tell someone that you love him or her? Deal with an undisciplined area in your life? Tell someone about Jesus? Because life is short, don't neglect what is truly important.

39:5, 6 The brevity of life is a theme throughout the books of Psalms, Proverbs, and Ecclesiastes. Jesus also spoke about it (Luke 12:20). It is ironic that people spend so much time securing their lives on earth but take little or no thought about where they will spend eternity. David realized that amassing riches and busily accomplishing worldly tasks would make no difference in eternity. Few people understand that their only hope is in the Lord. (For other verses on the brevity of life, see Ecclesiastes 2:18 and James 4:14.)

39:10 What did David mean when he asked God to stop punishing him with "blows" from his hand? It may be a picture of the difficulties David was facing that caused him to feel as if he were being struck. Just as a loving father carefully disciplines his children, so God corrects us (Hebrews 12:5-9).

Theme: Doing God's will sometimes means waiting patiently. While we wait, we can love God, serve others, and tell others about him.
Author: David

40

For the choir director: A psalm of David.

40:1 Pss 27:14; 34:15
40:2 Pss 27:5; 69:1-2 Jer 38:6
40:3 Pss 32:7; 33:3; 64:9
40:4 Job 37:24 Ps 84:12
40:5 Job 5:9 Pss 136:4; 139:17-18 Isa 55:8
40:6-8 1 Sam 15:22 Jer 7:22-23 Mic 6:6-8 †Heb 10:5-7
40:8 Ps 37:31 2 Cor 3:3 John 4:34 Rom 7:22
40:9 Pss 22:25; 119:13
40:10 Ps 89:1 Acts 20:20, 27
40:11 Pss 43:3; 61:7

1 I waited patiently for the LORD to help me,
and he turned to me and heard my cry.
2 He lifted me out of the pit of despair,
out of the mud and the mire.
He set my feet on solid ground
and steadied me as I walked along.
3 He has given me a new song to sing,
a hymn of praise to our God.
Many will see what he has done and be astounded.
They will put their trust in the LORD.

4 Oh, the joys of those who trust the LORD,
who have no confidence in the proud,
or in those who worship idols.
5 O LORD my God, you have done many miracles for us.
Your plans for us are too numerous to list.
If I tried to recite all your wonderful deeds,
I would never come to the end of them.

6 You take no delight in sacrifices or offerings.
Now that you have made me listen, I finally understand—
you don't require burnt offerings or sin offerings.
7 Then I said, "Look, I have come.
And this has been written about me in your scroll:
8 I take joy in doing your will, my God,
for your law is written on my heart."

9 I have told all your people about your justice.
I have not been afraid to speak out,
as you, O LORD, well know.
10 I have not kept this good news hidden in my heart;
I have talked about your faithfulness and saving power.
I have told everyone in the great assembly
of your unfailing love and faithfulness.

11 LORD, don't hold back your tender mercies from me.
My only hope is in your unfailing love and faithfulness.

40:1-3 Waiting for God to help us is not easy, but David received four benefits from waiting: God (1) lifted him out of his despair, (2) set his feet on solid ground, (3) steadied him as he walked, and (4) put a new song of praise in his mouth. Often blessings cannot be received unless we go through the trial of waiting.

40:6 The religious ritual of David's day involved sacrificing animals in the Tabernacle. David said these acts were meaningless unless done for the right reasons. Today we often make rituals of going to church, taking Communion, or paying tithes. These activities are also empty if our reasons for doing them are selfish. God doesn't want these sacrifices and offerings without an attitude of devotion to him. The prophet Samuel told Saul, "Obedience is far better than sacrifice" (1 Samuel 15:22). Make sure that you give God the obedience and lifelong service he desires from you.

40:7, 8 "I take joy in doing your will, my God." Jesus portrayed this attitude of obeying and serving God (John 4:34; 5:30). He came as the prophets foretold, proclaiming the Good News of God's righteousness and forgiveness of sins. In Hebrews 10:5-10, verses 6-8 are applied to Jesus.

40:9, 10 David said he would speak of God's faithfulness and salvation to those around him. When we realize the impact of God's righteousness on our lives, we cannot keep it hidden. We want to tell other people what God has done for us. If God's faithfulness has changed your life, don't be timid. It is natural to share a good bargain with others or recommend a skillful doctor, so it should also be natural to share what God has done for us.

40:10 When we think of faithfulness, a friend or a spouse may come to mind. Friends who are faithful accept and love us, even when we are unlovable. Faithful people keep their promises, whether of support or made in marriage vows. God's faithfulness is like human faithfulness, only perfect. His love is absolute, and his promises are irrevocable. He loves us in spite of our constant bent toward sin, and he keeps all the promises he has made to us, even when we break our promises to him.

12 For troubles surround me—
too many to count!
They pile up so high
I can't see my way out.
They are more numerous than the hairs on my head.
I have lost all my courage.

13 Please, LORD, rescue me!
Come quickly, LORD, and help me.
14 May those who try to destroy me
be humiliated and put to shame.
May those who take delight in my trouble
be turned back in disgrace.
15 Let them be horrified by their shame,
for they said, "Aha! We've got him now!"

16 But may all who search for you
be filled with joy and gladness.
May those who love your salvation
repeatedly shout, "The LORD is great!"

17 As for me, I am poor and needy,
but the Lord is thinking about me right now.
You are my helper and my savior.
Do not delay, O my God.

40:12 Pss 18:5; 38:4; 73:26; 116:3

40:13-17 //Ps 70:1-5

40:14 Pss 35:4, 26; 70:2-3

40:16 Pss 35:27; 70:4

40:17 Pss 40:5; 70:5

Theme: A prayer for God's mercy when feeling sick or abandoned. When we're sick or when everyone deserts us, God remains at our side.
Author: David

41

For the choir director: A psalm of David.

1 Oh, the joys of those who are kind to the poor.
The LORD rescues them in times of trouble.
2 The LORD protects them
and keeps them alive.
He gives them prosperity
and rescues them from their enemies.
3 The LORD nurses them when they are sick
and eases their pain and discomfort.

4 "O LORD," I prayed, "have mercy on me.
Heal me, for I have sinned against you."
5 But my enemies say nothing but evil about me.
"How soon will he die and be forgotten?" they ask.
6 They visit me as if they are my friends,
but all the while they gather gossip,
and when they leave, they spread it everywhere.
7 All who hate me whisper about me,
imagining the worst for me.
8 "Whatever he has, it is fatal," they say.
"He will never get out of that bed!"
9 Even my best friend, the one I trusted completely,
the one who shared my food,
has turned against me.

41:1 Pss 37:19; 82:3-4 Prov 14:21

41:2 Pss 27:12; 37:22, 28

41:4 Pss 5:4; 6:2; 51:4; 103:3

41:5 Ps 38:12

41:6 Ps 12:2

41:7 Ps 56:5

41:9 Job 19:19 Ps 55:12-13, 20 Jer 20:10 †Mark 14:22-25 †John 13:18

41:1 The Bible often speaks of God's care for the weak, poor, and needy, and of his blessing on those who share this concern. God wants our generosity to reflect his own free giving. As he has blessed us, we should bless others.

41:9 This verse, a prophecy of Christ's betrayal, is referred to in John 13:18. Judas, one of Jesus' 12 disciples, had spent three years learning from Jesus, traveling and eating with him (Mark 3:14-19), and handling the finances for the group. Eventually this "best friend" betrayed Jesus (Matthew 26:14-16, 20-25).

41:10 Ps 3:3

41:11 Pss 25:2; 37:23; 147:11

41:12 Job 36:7 Pss 18:32; 21:6; 37:17

41:13 Pss 72:18-19; 106:48

10 LORD, have mercy on me.
Make me well again, so I can pay them back!
11 I know that you are pleased with me,
for you have not let my enemy triumph over me.
12 You have preserved my life because I am innocent;
you have brought me into your presence forever.

13 Bless the LORD, the God of Israel,
who lives forever from eternal ages past.
Amen and amen!

BOOK II
Psalms 42:1—72:20

These psalms include a prayer for rescue, a call to worship, a confession of sin, an encouragement to trust God, a psalm for those hurt by friends, a prayer for those who have been slandered, and a missionary psalm. These psalms can help us retain a sense of wonder in our worship.

Theme: A thirst for God. When you feel lonely or depressed, meditate on God's kindness and love.
Author: The sons of Korah, who were Temple musicians and assistants

42

For the choir director: A psalm of the descendants of Korah.

42:1 Ps 63:1

42:2 Pss 43:4; 84:2; 143:6 Jer 10:10 Rom 9:26

42:3 Pss 79:10; 80:5 Joel 2:17

42:4 Job 30:16 Pss 62:8; 100:4 Isa 30:29

42:5 Pss 38:6; 44:3; 77:3 Lam 3:24

42:6 Ps 61:2 †Mark 14:34

1 As the deer pants for streams of water,
so I long for you, O God.
2 I thirst for God, the living God.
When can I come and stand before him?
3 Day and night, I have only tears for food,
while my enemies continually taunt me, saying,
"Where is this God of yours?"

4 My heart is breaking
as I remember how it used to be:
I walked among the crowds of worshipers,
leading a great procession to the house of God,
singing for joy and giving thanks—
it was the sound of a great celebration!

5 Why am I discouraged?
Why so sad?
I will put my hope in God!
I will praise him again—
my Savior and 6 my God!

Now I am deeply discouraged,
but I will remember your kindness—

41:13 Psalms is divided into five books, and each one ends with a doxology or an expression of praise to God. The first book of the psalms, chapters 1 through 41, takes us on a journey through suffering, sorrow, and great joy. It teaches us about God's eternal love and care for us and how we should trust him even in the day-to-day experiences of life.

42:1ff Psalms 42–49 were written by the descendants of Korah. Korah was a Levite who led a rebellion against Moses (Numbers 16:1-35). He was killed, but his descendants remained faithful to God and continued to serve God in the Temple. David appointed men from the clan of Korah to serve as choir leaders (1 Chronicles 6:31-38), and they continued to be Temple musicians for hundreds of years (2 Chronicles 20:18, 19).

42:1, 2 As the life of a deer depends upon water, so our lives depend upon God. Those who seek him and long to understand him find eternal life. Feeling separated from God, this psalmist wouldn't rest until he restored his relationship with God because he knew that his very life depended on it.

42:4, 5 The writer of this psalm was discouraged because he was exiled to a place far from Jerusalem and could not worship in the Temple. During these God-given holidays, the nation was to remember all that God had done for them. Many of these festivals are explained in the chart in Leviticus 23.

42:5, 6 Depression is one of the most common emotional ailments. One antidote for depression is to meditate on the record of God's goodness to his people. This will take your mind off the present situation as you focus your thoughts on God's ability to help you rather than on your inability to help yourself. When you feel depressed, take advantage of this psalm's antidepressant: Read the Bible's accounts of God's goodness, and meditate on them.

from Mount Hermon, the source of the Jordan,
from the land of Mount Mizar.
7 I hear the tumult of the raging seas
as your waves and surging tides sweep over me.

42:7 Ps 88:7 Jon 2:3

8 Through each day the LORD pours his unfailing love upon me,
and through each night I sing his songs,
praying to God who gives me life.

42:8 Job 35:10 Pss 16:7; 57:3; 77:6; 149:4-5

9 "O God my rock," I cry,
"Why have you forsaken me?
Why must I wander in darkness,
oppressed by my enemies?"

42:9 Pss 17:9; 18:2; 38:6

10 Their taunts pierce me like a fatal wound.
They scoff, "Where is this God of yours?"

11 Why am I discouraged?
Why so sad?
I will put my hope in God!
I will praise him again—
my Savior and my God!

Theme: Hope in a time of discouragement. In the face of discouragement, our only hope is in God. **Author:** The sons of Korah (Temple assistants). Psalms 42 and 43 are one psalm in many Hebrew manuscripts.

43

1 O God, take up my cause!
Defend me against these ungodly people.
Rescue me from these unjust liars.

43:1 1 Sam 24:15 Pss 26:1; 35:24

2 For you are God, my only safe haven.
Why have you tossed me aside?
Why must I wander around in darkness,
oppressed by my enemies?

43:2 Pss 28:7; 42:9; 44:9

3 Send out your light and your truth;
let them guide me.
Let them lead me to your holy mountain,
to the place where you live.

43:3 Pss 36:9; 42:4-5; 84:1

4 There I will go to the altar of God,
to God—the source of all my joy.
I will praise you with my harp,
O God, my God!

43:4 Pss 26:6; 33:2

5 Why am I discouraged?
Why so sad?
I will put my hope in God!
I will praise him again—
my Savior and my God!

43:3 The "holy mountain" is Mount Zion, in Jerusalem, the city that David named as Israel's capital. The Temple was built there as the place for the people to meet God in worship and prayer.

43:3, 4 The psalmist asked God to send his light and truth to guide him to the holy mountain, the Temple, where he would meet God. God's truth (see 1 John 2:27) provides the right path to follow, and God's light (see 1 John 1:5) provides the clear vision to follow it. If you feel surrounded by darkness and uncertainty, follow God's light and truth. He will guide you.

Theme: A plea for victory by the battle-weary and defeated. When it seems that God has let you down, don't despair. Instead, remember God's past deliverance and be confident that he will restore you.
Author: The sons of Korah (Temple assistants)

44 *For the choir director: A psalm of the descendants of Korah.*

44:1 Exod 12:26-27

1 O God, we have heard it with our own ears—
our ancestors have told us
of all you did in other days,
in days long ago:

44:2 Pss 78:55; 80:8

2 You drove out the pagan nations
and gave all the land to our ancestors;
you crushed their enemies,
setting our ancestors free.

44:3 Deut 4:37 Josh 24:12 Ps 77:15

3 They did not conquer the land with their swords;
it was not their own strength that gave them victory.
It was by your mighty power that they succeeded;
it was because you favored them and smiled on them.

44:4 Ps 74:12

4 You are my King and my God.
You command victories for your people.*

44:5 Ps 60:12

5 Only by your power can we push back our enemies;
only in your name can we trample our foes.
6 I do not trust my bow;
I do not count on my sword to save me.

44:7 Pss 53:5; 136:24

7 It is you who gives us victory over our enemies;
it is you who humbles those who hate us.

44:8 Pss 30:12; 34:2

8 O God, we give glory to you all day long
and constantly praise your name. *Interlude*

44:9 Pss 43:2; 60:10; 74:1

9 But now you have tossed us aside in dishonor.
You no longer lead our armies to battle.

44:10 Josh 7:8, 12 Ps 89:41

10 You make us retreat from our enemies
and allow them to plunder our land.

44:11 Deut 4:27; 26:64 Ps 106:27 Ezek 20:23-24

11 You have treated us like sheep waiting to be slaughtered;
you have scattered us among the nations.

44:12 Isa 52:3-4

12 You sold us—your precious people—for a pittance.
You valued us at nothing at all.

44:13 Pss 79:4; 80:6

13 You have caused all our neighbors to mock us.
We are an object of scorn and derision to the nations around us.

44:14 Ps 109:25 Jer 24:9

14 You have made us the butt of their jokes;
we are scorned by the whole world.
15 We can't escape the constant humiliation;
shame is written across our faces.
16 All we hear are the taunts of our mockers.
All we see are our vengeful enemies.

44:4 Hebrew *for Jacob.*

44:1ff This psalm may have been sung at an occasion like the one in 2 Chronicles 20:18, 19, where the faithful Jehoshaphat was surrounded by enemies and the Levites sang to the Lord before the battle.

44:1-3 "You drove out the pagan nations" refers to the conquest of Canaan (the Promised Land) described in the book of Joshua. God gave the land to the Israelites; they were supposed to enter and drive out anyone who was wicked and opposed to God. Israel was told to settle the land and to be a witness to the world of God's power and love. Surrounded by enemies, the psalmist remembered what God had done for his people and took heart. We can have this same confidence in God when we feel attacked.

44:6, 7 In whom or in what do you trust? Only God is trustworthy. He will never let you down.

44:9-22 Israel had been defeated despite their faith (44:17) and obedience (44:18) to God. The psalmist could not understand why God allowed this to happen, but he did not give up hope of discovering the answer (44:17-22). Although he felt his suffering was undeserved, he revealed the real reason for it: He suffered because he was *committed to the Lord.* Paul quoted the psalmist's complaint (Romans 8:36) to show that we must always be ready to face death for the cause of Christ. Thus, our suffering may not be a punishment but a battle scar that demonstrates our loyalty.

17 All this has happened despite our loyalty to you.
We have not violated your covenant.
18 Our hearts have not deserted you.
We have not strayed from your path.
19 Yet you have crushed us in the desert.
You have covered us with darkness and death.

20 If we had turned away from worshiping our God
or spread our hands in prayer to foreign gods,
21 God would surely have known it,
for he knows the secrets of every heart.
22 For your sake we are killed every day;
we are being slaughtered like sheep.

23 Wake up, O Lord! Why do you sleep?
Get up! Do not reject us forever.
24 Why do you look the other way?
Why do you ignore our suffering and oppression?
25 We collapse in the dust,
lying face down in the dirt.
26 Rise up! Come and help us!
Save us because of your unfailing love.

44:17 Pss 78:7, 51; 119:61, 83, 109, 141, 153, 176
44:18 Job 23:11; Ps 119:51, 157
44:19 Job 3:5; Pss 51:8; 94:5
44:20 Pss 78:11; 81:9
44:22 Isa 53:7; †Rom 8:36
44:23 Pss 7:6; 77:7; 78:65
44:24 Job 13:24; Pss 42:9; 88:14
44:25 Ps 119:25

Theme: A poem to the king (possibly Solomon) on the occasion of his wedding. While this psalm was written for a historic occasion, it is also seen as a prophecy about Christ and his bride, the church, who will praise him throughout all generations.
Author: The sons of Korah (Temple assistants)

45

For the choir director: A psalm of the descendants of Korah, to be sung to the tune "Lilies." A love song.

1 My heart overflows with a beautiful thought!
I will recite a lovely poem to the king,
for my tongue is like the pen of a skillful poet.

2 You are the most handsome of all.
Gracious words stream from your lips.
God himself has blessed you forever.
3 Put on your sword, O mighty warrior!
You are so glorious, so majestic!
4 In your majesty, ride out to victory,
defending truth, humility, and justice.
Go forth to perform awe-inspiring deeds!
5 Your arrows are sharp,
piercing your enemies' hearts.
The nations fall before you,
lying down beneath your feet.

6 Your throne, O God,* endures forever and ever.
Your royal power is expressed in justice.

45:1 Ezra 7:6
45:2 Ps 21:6; Luke 4:22
45:3 Isa 9:6
45:4 Rev 6:2
45:5 Ps 120:4; Isa 5:28
45:6 Pss 93:2; 98:8-9; †Heb 1:8-9

45:6 Or *Your divine throne.*

44:22-26 The writer cried out to God to save his people because of his unfailing love. Nothing can separate us from God's love, not even death (Romans 8:36-39). When you fear for your life, ask God for deliverance, and remember that even death cannot separate you from him.

44:23-25 The psalmist's words suggest that he did not believe God had left him. God was still in control, but he seemed to be asleep, and the psalmist wondered why. In the New Testament, the disciples wondered why Jesus was asleep when they needed his help during a storm (Mark 4:35-41). In both cases, of course, God was ready to help, but he wanted first to build faith in his followers.

45:1ff This is called a messianic psalm because it prophetically describes the Messiah's future relationship to the church, his body of believers. Verse 2 expresses God's abundant blessing on his Messiah; verses 6-8 find their ultimate fulfillment in Christ (Hebrews 1:8, 9). The church is described as the bride of Christ in Revelation 19:7, 8; 21:9; 22:17.

45:7 Pss 11:7; 21:6; 33:5

7 You love what is right and hate what is wrong.
Therefore God, your God, has anointed you,
pouring out the oil of joy on you more than on anyone else.

45:8 Song 1:3; 4:13-14

8 Your robes are perfumed with myrrh, aloes, and cassia.
In palaces decorated with ivory,
you are entertained by the music of harps.

45:9 1 Kgs 2:19; 9:28 Song 6:8 Isa 13:12

9 Kings' daughters are among your concubines.
At your right side stands the queen,
wearing jewelry of finest gold from Ophir!

45:10 Deut 21:13

10 Listen to me, O royal daughter; take to heart what I say.
Forget your people and your homeland far away.
11 For your royal husband delights in your beauty;
honor him, for he is your lord.

45:12 Pss 22:29; 72:10-11

12 The princes of Tyre* will shower you with gifts.
People of great wealth will entreat your favor.

45:13 Isa 61:10

13 The bride, a princess, waits within her chamber,
dressed in a gown woven with gold.

45:14 Song 1:4 Ezek 16:9-13

14 In her beautiful robes, she is led to the king,
accompanied by her bridesmaids.
15 What a joyful, enthusiastic procession
as they enter the king's palace!

16 Your sons will become kings like their father.
You will make them rulers over many lands.

45:17 Ps 138:4 Mal 1:11

17 I will bring honor to your name in every generation.
Therefore, the nations will praise you forever and ever.

Theme: God is always there to help, providing refuge, security, and peace. God's power is complete and his ultimate victory is certain. He will not fail to rescue those who love him.
Author: The sons of Korah (Temple assistants)

46

For the choir director: A psalm of the descendants of Korah, to be sung by soprano voices. A song.*

46:1 Deut 4:7 Pss 9:9; 14:6; 62:7-8; 145:18

1 God is our refuge and strength,
always ready to help in times of trouble.

46:2 Pss 18:7; 23:4; 82:5

2 So we will not fear, even if earthquakes come
and the mountains crumble into the sea.
3 Let the oceans roar and foam.
Let the mountains tremble as the waters surge! *Interlude*

46:4 Ps 87:3 Isa 60:14 Rev 3:12; 22:1

4 A river brings joy to the city of our God,
the sacred home of the Most High.

45:12 Hebrew *The daughter of Tyre.* **46:TITLE** Hebrew *according to alamoth.*

45:8, 9 Myrrh is a fragrant gum of an Arabian tree, generally used in perfumes. Aloes, a spice, may have come from sandalwood, a close-grained and fragrant wood often used for storage boxes or chests (see also Proverbs 7:14-17; Song of Songs 4:13, 14). Cassia was probably made from flowers of the cinnamon tree. These expensive fragrances were appropriate for a king's wedding. The location of Ophir is unknown but believed to be in either Arabia or Africa. It was famous as a source of gold.

45:13-17 This beautiful section of poetry pictures Christ's bride, the church, with the richest blessings as she unites forever with him (see Revelation 19:6-8; 21:2).

46–48 Psalms 46–48 are hymns of praise, celebrating deliverance from some great foe. Psalm 46 may have been written when the Assyrian army invaded the land and surrounded Jerusalem (2 Kings 18:13–19:37).

46:1-3 The fear of mountains or cities suddenly crumbling into the sea as the result of an earthquake or a nuclear blast haunts many people today. But the psalmist says that even if the world ends, we need not fear. In the face of utter destruction, the writer expressed a quiet confidence in God's ability to save him. It seems impossible to consider the end of the world without becoming consumed by fear, but the Bible is clear—God is our refuge even in the midst of total destruction. He is not merely a temporary retreat; he is our eternal refuge and can provide strength in any circumstance.

46:4, 5 Many great cities have rivers flowing through them, sustaining people's lives by making agriculture possible and facilitating trade with other cities. Jerusalem had no river, but it had God, who, like a river, sustained the people's lives. As long as God lived among the people, the city was invincible. But when the people abandoned him, God no longer protected them, and Jerusalem fell to the Babylonian army.

5 God himself lives in that city; it cannot be destroyed.
God will protect it at the break of day.
6 The nations are in an uproar,
and kingdoms crumble!
God thunders,
and the earth melts!

7 The LORD Almighty is here among us;
the God of Israel* is our fortress. *Interlude*

8 Come, see the glorious works of the LORD:
See how he brings destruction upon the world
9 and causes wars to end throughout the earth.
He breaks the bow and snaps the spear in two;
he burns the shields with fire.

10 "Be silent, and know that I am God!
I will be honored by every nation.
I will be honored throughout the world."

11 The LORD Almighty is here among us;
the God of Israel is our fortress. *Interlude*

46:5 Isa 12:6; 41:14 Ezek 43:7 Luke 1:54
46:6 Ps 2:1 Mic 1:4
46:7 Num 14:9 2 Chr 13:12 Ps 9:9
46:8 Ps 66:5 Isa 61:4 Jer 51:43
46:9 Isa 2:4; 9:5 Mic 4:3
46:10 Ps 100:3 Isa 2:11, 17

Theme: God is still King of the world. All nations of the earth will eventually recognize his lordship.
Author: The sons of Korah (Temple assistants)

47

For the choir director: A psalm of the descendants of Korah.

1 Come, everyone, and clap your hands for joy!
Shout to God with joyful praise!
2 For the LORD Most High is awesome.
He is the great King of all the earth.
3 He subdues the nations before us,
putting our enemies beneath our feet.
4 He chose the Promised Land as our inheritance,
the proud possession of Jacob's descendants, whom he loves. *Interlude*

5 God has ascended with a mighty shout.
The LORD has ascended with trumpets blaring.
6 Sing praise to God, sing praises;
sing praise to our King, sing praises!

7 For God is the King over all the earth.
Praise him with a psalm!
8 God reigns above the nations,
sitting on his holy throne.
9 The rulers of the world have gathered together.
They join us in praising the God of Abraham.
For all the kings of the earth belong to God.
He is highly honored everywhere.

47:1 Pss 98:8-9; 106:47
47:2 Deut 7:21
47:3 Ps 18:47
47:4 1 Pet 1:4
47:5 Pss 68:18, 25, 33; 98:6
47:6 Pss 68:4; 89:18
47:7 1 Cor 14:15
47:8 1 Chr 16:31
47:9 Pss 72:11; 89:18; 97:9 Isa 49:7, 23 Rom 4:11-12

46:7 Hebrew *of Jacob;* also in 46:11.

46:10 War and destruction are inevitable, but so is God's final victory. At that time, all will stand quietly before the Lord Almighty. How proper, then, for us to be still now, reverently honoring him and his power and majesty. Take time each day to be still and to exalt God.

47:1ff This psalm may have been written about the same event as Psalm 46—the Assyrian invasion of Judah by Sennacherib (2 Kings 18:13–19:37).

47:2 The Lord Most High is awesome beyond words, but this didn't keep Bible writers from trying to describe him. And it shouldn't keep us from talking about him either. We can't describe God completely, but we can tell others what he has done for us. Don't let the indescribable aspects of God's greatness prevent you from telling others what you know about him.

47:9 Abraham was the father of the Israelite nation. The one true God was sometimes called the "God of Abraham" (Exodus 3:6; 1 Kings 18:36). In a spiritual sense, God's promises to Abraham apply to all who believe in God, Jew or Gentile (Romans 4:11, 12; Galatians 3:7-9). Thus, the God of Abraham is our God, too.

Theme: God's presence is our joy, security, and salvation. God is praised as the defender of Jerusalem, the holy city of the Jews. He is also our defender and guide forever.
Author: The sons of Korah (Temple assistants)

48

A psalm of the descendants of Korah. A song.

1 How great is the LORD,
and how much we should praise him
in the city of our God,
which is on his holy mountain!
2 It is magnificent in elevation—
the whole earth rejoices to see it!
Mount Zion, the holy mountain,*
is the city of the great King!
3 God himself is in Jerusalem's towers.
He reveals himself as her defender.
4 The kings of the earth joined forces
and advanced against the city.
5 But when they saw it, they were stunned;
they were terrified and ran away.
6 They were gripped with terror,
like a woman writhing in the pain of childbirth
7 or like the mighty ships of Tarshish
being shattered by a powerful east wind.

8 We had heard of the city's glory,
but now we have seen it ourselves—
the city of the LORD Almighty.
It is the city of our God;
he will make it safe forever. *Interlude*

9 O God, we meditate on your unfailing love
as we worship in your Temple.
10 As your name deserves, O God,
you will be praised to the ends of the earth.
Your strong right hand is filled with victory.

48:1 1 Chr 16:25; Pss 87:1; 96:4; 145:3; Zech 8:3
48:2 Ps 50:2; Lam 2:15; Matt 5:35
48:3 Ps 46:7
48:4 2 Sam 10:6-19
48:5 Exod 15:15
48:6 Isa 13:8
48:7 Jer 18:17
48:8 Ps 87:5
48:9 Pss 26:3; 40:10
48:10 Josh 7:9; Isa 41:10; Mal 1:11

48:2 Or *Mount Zion, in the far north;* Hebrew reads *Mount Zion, the heights of Zaphon.*

PSALMS THAT HAVE INSPIRED HYMNS

Psalm 23	The King of Love My Shepherd Is My Shepherd Shall Supply My Need The Lord Is My Shepherd
Psalm 46	A Mighty Fortress Is Our God
Psalm 61	Hiding in Thee (O safe to the Rock that is higher than I . . .)
Psalm 87	Glorious Things of Thee Are Spoken
Psalm 90	O God, Our Help in Ages Past
Psalm 100	All People That on Earth Do Dwell Before Jehovah's Awful Throne
Psalm 103	Praise to the Lord, the Almighty
Psalm 104	O Worship the King, All Glorious Above
Psalm 126	Bringing in the Sheaves

48:2 Why is Mount Zion—Jerusalem—"the city of the great King"? Because the Temple was located in Jerusalem, the city was seen as the center of God's presence in the world. The Bible pictures Jerusalem as the place where believers will gather in the last days (Isaiah 2:2ff) and as the spiritual home of all believers, where God will live among them (Revelation 21:2, 3).

48:8 Because Jerusalem has been destroyed several times since this psalm was written, the phrase God "will make it safe forever" may refer prophetically to the new Jerusalem, where God will judge all nations and live with all believers (Revelation 21).

11 Let the people on Mount Zion rejoice.
Let the towns of Judah be glad,
for your judgments are just.

12 Go, inspect the city of Jerusalem.*
Walk around and count the many towers.

13 Take note of the fortified walls,
and tour all the citadels,
that you may describe them
to future generations.

14 For that is what God is like.
He is our God forever and ever,
and he will be our guide until we die.

48:11
Ps 97:8

48:13
Pss 78:5-7; 122:7

48:14
Ps 23:4
Isa 58:11

Theme: Trusting in worldly possessions is futile. You cannot take possessions with you when you die, and they cannot buy forgiveness from sin.
Author: The sons of Korah (Temple assistants)

49

For the choir director: A psalm of the descendants of Korah.

1 Listen to this, all you people!
Pay attention, everyone in the world!

2 High and low,
rich and poor—listen!

3 For my words are wise,
and my thoughts are filled with insight.

4 I listen carefully to many proverbs
and solve riddles with inspiration from a harp.

5 There is no need to fear when times of trouble come,
when enemies are surrounding me.

6 They trust in their wealth
and boast of great riches.

7 Yet they cannot redeem themselves from death*
by paying a ransom to God.

8 Redemption does not come so easily,
for no one can ever pay enough

9 to live forever
and never see the grave.

49:1
Pss 33:8; 78:1

49:3
Pss 37:30; 119:130

49:4
Num 12:8
2 Kgs 3:15
Ps 78:2

49:5
Pss 23:4; 27:1

49:6
Ps 52:7
Mark 10:24

49:7
Job 36:18
Matt 25:8-9

49:8
Matt 16:26

49:9
Pss 22:29; 89:48

48:12 Hebrew *Zion.* **49:7** Or *no one can redeem the life of another.*

48:11 The people of Judah were from Israel's largest tribe, which settled in the southern part of Canaan, where Jerusalem was located (Joshua 15:1-12). David was from Judah, and he made Jerusalem his capital and the center of the nation's worship. Jesus was also a member of the tribe of Judah. The psalmist was saying that the day would come when God would bring justice to the land, and God's people would get the respect they deserved.

48:12, 13 After an enemy army had unsuccessfully besieged Jerusalem, it was important for the people to make a tour of the city, inspecting its defenses and praising God for the protection it had offered. In times of great joy or after God has brought us through some great trial, we ought to inspect our defenses to make sure that the foundations—faith in God, knowledge of his Word, and the fellowship and prayers of the body of believers—remain strong (Ephesians 2:20-22). Then we should praise God for his protection!

48:14 We often pray for God's guidance as we struggle with decisions. What we need is both a map that gives us directions and a constant companion who has an intimate knowledge of the way and will make sure we interpret the map correctly. The Bible is such a map, and the Holy Spirit is our the constant companion and guide. As you make your way through life, use both the map and your Guide.

49:1ff The futility of worldliness—riches, pride, fame—resounds from this psalm. Comparable in form to the book of Ecclesiastes, this psalm is one of the few written more to instruct than to give praise.

49:7, 8, 15 In the slave market of the ancient world, a slave had to be redeemed (someone had to pay the price) in order to go free. In Mark 10:45, Ephesians 1:7, and Hebrews 9:12, we learn that Jesus paid such a price so that we could be set free from slavery to sin in order to begin a new life with him.

There is no way for a person to buy eternal life with God. God alone can redeem a soul. Don't count on wealth and physical comforts to keep you happy because you will never have enough wealth to keep from dying.

49:10 Ps 39:6 Luke 12:20-21

49:11 Deut 3:14 Pss 10:6; 64:6

49:13 Jer 17:11

49:14 Ps 9:17 Dan 7:18 Mal 4:3 1 Cor 6:2 Rev 2:26

49:15 Ps 16:10-11

49:16 Ps 37:7

49:17 Ps 17:14 1 Tim 6:7

49:18 Ps 10:3 Luke 12:19

49:19 Job 33:29-30

49:20 Ps 49:12

10 Those who are wise must finally die,
just like the foolish and senseless,
leaving all their wealth behind.
11 The grave is their eternal home,
where they will stay forever.
They may name their estates after themselves,
but they leave their wealth to others.
12 They will not last long despite their riches—
they will die like the animals.
13 This is the fate of fools,
though they will be remembered as being so wise. *Interlude*
14 Like sheep, they are led to the grave,
where death will be their shepherd.
In the morning the godly will rule over them.
Their bodies will rot in the grave,
far from their grand estates.
15 But as for me, God will redeem my life.
He will snatch me from the power of death. *Interlude*
16 So don't be dismayed when the wicked grow rich,
and their homes become ever more splendid.
17 For when they die, they carry nothing with them.
Their wealth will not follow them into the grave.
18 In this life they consider themselves fortunate,
and the world loudly applauds their success.
19 But they will die like all others before them
and never again see the light of day.
20 People who boast of their wealth don't understand
that they will die like the animals.

Theme: The contrast between true and false faith. God desires sincere thanks, trust, and praise.
Author: Asaph, one of David's chief musicians

50

A psalm of Asaph.

50:1 Josh 22:22 Ps 113:3

50:2 Deut 33:2 Pss 48:2; 80:1

50:3 Ps 18:12-13 Dan 7:10

50:4 Deut 4:26; 32:1 Isa 1:2

1 The mighty God, the LORD, has spoken;
he has summoned all humanity from east to west!
2 From Mount Zion, the perfection of beauty,
God shines in glorious radiance.
3 Our God approaches with the noise of thunder.
Fire devours everything in his way,
and a great storm rages around him.
4 Heaven and earth will be his witnesses
as he judges his people:

49:10-14 The rich and poor have one similarity: When they die, they leave all they own here on earth. At the moment of death (and all of us will face that moment), both rich and poor are naked and empty-handed before God. The only riches we have at that time are those we have already invested in our eternal heritage. At the time of death, each of us will wish we had invested less on earth, where we must leave it, and more in heaven, where we will retain it forever. To have treasure in heaven, we must place our faith in God, pledge ourselves to obey him, and utilize our resources for the good of his Kingdom. This is a good time to check up on your investments and see where you have invested the most. Then do whatever it takes to place your investments where they really count.

50:1ff God judges people for treating him lightly. First, he speaks to the superficially religious people who bring their sacrifices but are only going through the motions (50:1-15). They do not honor God with true praise and thankfulness. Second, he chides wicked, hard-hearted people for their evil words and immoral lives (50:16-22). He asks the superficially religious for genuine thanksgiving and trust, and he warns the evil people to consider their deeds, lest he destroy them in his anger.

50:1-4 Asaph begins his psalm by describing God's final judgment of people on earth. Surprisingly, we read that God's great fury is leveled against his own people (or at least those who claim to be his). God's judgment must first begin with his own children (1 Peter 4:17).

5 "Bring my faithful people to me—
those who made a covenant with me by giving sacrifices."
6 Then let the heavens proclaim his justice,
for God himself will be the judge. *Interlude*

7 "O my people, listen as I speak.
Here are my charges against you, O Israel:
I am God, your God!
8 I have no complaint about your sacrifices
or the burnt offerings you constantly bring to my altar.
9 But I want no more bulls from your barns;
I want no more goats from your pens.
10 For all the animals of the forest are mine,
and I own the cattle on a thousand hills.
11 Every bird of the mountains
and all the animals of the field belong to me.
12 If I were hungry, I would not mention it to you,
for all the world is mine and everything in it.
13 I don't need the bulls you sacrifice;
I don't need the blood of goats.
14 What I want instead is your true thanks to God;
I want you to fulfill your vows to the Most High.
15 Trust me in your times of trouble,
and I will rescue you,
and you will give me glory."

16 But God says to the wicked:
"Recite my laws no longer,
and don't pretend that you obey me.
17 For you refuse my discipline
and treat my laws like trash.
18 When you see a thief, you help him,
and you spend your time with adulterers.
19 Your mouths are filled with wickedness,
and your tongues are full of lies.
20 You sit around and slander a brother—
your own mother's son.
21 While you did all this, I remained silent,
and you thought I didn't care.
But now I will rebuke you,
listing all my charges against you.
22 Repent, all of you who ignore me,
or I will tear you apart,
and no one will help you.
23 But giving thanks is a sacrifice that truly honors me.
If you keep to my path,
I will reveal to you the salvation of God."

50:5 Exod 24:7 Pss 30:4; 37:28
50:6 Pss 75:7; 96:13; 97:6
50:8 Ps 40:6, 8
50:9 Ps 69:31
50:10 Ps 104:24
50:12 Exod 19:5
50:13 Hos 6:6
50:14 Deut 23:21 Hos 14:2 Rom 12:1 Heb 13:15
50:16 Isa 29:13
50:17 Neh 9:26 Rom 2:21-22
50:18 Rom 1:32 1 Tim 5:22
50:19 Pss 10:7; 36:3
50:20 Matt 10:21
50:21 Ps 90:8 Eccl 8:11 Isa 42:14
50:22 Job 8:13 Pss 7:2; 9:17
50:23 Pss 50:14; 85:13; 91:16

50:5-9 God's perfect moral nature demands that the penalty for sin be death; however, a person could offer an animal to God as a substitute for himself, symbolizing the person's faith in the merciful, forgiving God. But the people were offering sacrifices and forgetting their significance! The very act of sacrifice showed that they had once agreed to follow God wholeheartedly. But at this time their hearts were not in it. We may fall into the same pattern when we participate in religious activities, tithe, or attend church out of habit or conformity rather than out of heartfelt love and obedience. God wants righteousness, not empty ritual. (See the note on 40:6.)

50:16-22 Some people glibly recite God's laws but are filled with deceit and evil. They claim his promises but refuse to obey him. This is sin, and God will judge people for it. We, too, are hypocrites when we are not what we claim to be. To let this inconsistency remain shows that we are not true followers of God.

50:21 Just because God is silent does not mean he is condoning sin or is indifferent to it. Instead, he is withholding deserved punishment, giving time for people to repent (2 Peter 3:9). God takes no pleasure in the death of the wicked and wants them to turn from evil (Ezekiel 33:11). But his silence does not last forever—a time of punishment will surely come.

Theme: David's plea for mercy, forgiveness, and cleansing. God wants our hearts to be right with him.
Author: David

51

For the choir director: A psalm of David, regarding the time Nathan the prophet came to him after David had committed adultery with Bathsheba.

51:1 Ps 4:1 Acts 3:19
51:2 Jer 33:8 Acts 22:16 Heb 9:13-14 1 Jn 1:7, 9
51:3 Isa 59:12
51:4 Gen 20:6 Luke 15:21 †Rom 3:4
51:5 Ps 58:3 Job 14:4 Eph 2:3
51:7 Exod 12:22 Isa 1:18
51:8 Ps 35:10
51:9 Jer 16:17
51:10 Ps 78:37 Matt 5:8 Acts 15:9 Eph 2:10
51:11 Eph 4:30
51:13 Ps 22:27

1 Have mercy on me, O God,
because of your unfailing love.
Because of your great compassion,
blot out the stain of my sins.
2 Wash me clean from my guilt.
Purify me from my sin.

3 For I recognize my shameful deeds—
they haunt me day and night.
4 Against you, and you alone, have I sinned;
I have done what is evil in your sight.
You will be proved right in what you say,
and your judgment against me is just.

5 For I was born a sinner—
yes, from the moment my mother conceived me.
6 But you desire honesty from the heart,
so you can teach me to be wise in my inmost being.

7 Purify me from my sins,* and I will be clean;
wash me, and I will be whiter than snow.
8 Oh, give me back my joy again;
you have broken me—
now let me rejoice.
9 Don't keep looking at my sins.
Remove the stain of my guilt.
10 Create in me a clean heart, O God.
Renew a right spirit within me.
11 Do not banish me from your presence,
and don't take your Holy Spirit from me.
12 Restore to me again the joy of your salvation,
and make me willing to obey you.
13 Then I will teach your ways to sinners,
and they will return to you.

51:7 Hebrew *Purify me with the hyssop branch.*

51:1-7 David was truly sorry for his adultery with Bathsheba and for murdering her husband to cover it up. He knew that his actions had hurt many people. But because David repented of those sins, God mercifully forgave him. No sin is too great to be forgiven! Do you feel that you could never come close to God because you have done something terrible? God can and will forgive you of any sin. While God forgives us, however, he does not always erase the natural consequences of our sin. David's life and family were never the same as a result of what he had done (see 2 Samuel 12:1-23).

51:4 Although David had sinned with Bathsheba, David said that he had sinned against God. When someone steals, murders, or slanders, it is against someone else—a victim. According to the world's standards, extramarital sex between two consenting adults is acceptable if nobody gets hurt. But people *do* get hurt—in David's case, a man was murdered, and a baby died. All sin hurts us and others, but ultimately it offends God because sin in any form is rebellion against God's way of living. When you are tempted to do wrong, remember that you will be sinning against God. That may help you stay on the right track.

51:10 Because we are born sinners (51:5), our natural inclination is to please ourselves rather than God. David followed that inclination when he took another man's wife. Like David, we must ask God to cleanse us from within (51:7), filling our hearts and spirits with new thoughts and desires. Right conduct can come only from a clean heart and spirit. Ask God to create a pure heart and spirit in you.

51:12 Do you ever feel stagnant in your faith, as though you are just going through the motions? Has sin ever driven a wedge between you and God, making him seem distant? David felt this way. He had sinned with Bathsheba and had just been confronted by Nathan the prophet. In his prayer he cried, "Restore to me again the joy of your salvation." God wants us to be close to him and to experience his full and complete life. But sin that remains unconfessed makes such intimacy impossible. Confess your sin to God. You may still have to face some earthly consequences, as David did, but God will give back the joy of your relationship with him.

51:13 When God forgives our sin and restores our fellowship with him, we want to reach out to others who need this forgiveness and reconciliation. The more you have felt God's forgiveness, the more you will desire to tell others about it.

14 Forgive me for shedding blood, O God who saves;
then I will joyfully sing of your forgiveness.
15 Unseal my lips, O Lord,
that I may praise you.

16 You would not be pleased with sacrifices,
or I would bring them.
If I brought you a burnt offering,
you would not accept it.
17 The sacrifice you want is a broken spirit.
A broken and repentant heart, O God,
you will not despise.

18 Look with favor on Zion and help her;
rebuild the walls of Jerusalem.
19 Then you will be pleased with worthy sacrifices
and with our whole burnt offerings;
and bulls will again be sacrificed on your altar.

51:14 2 Sam 12:9; Pss 9:14; 25:5; 71:15
51:16 1 Sam 15:22; Ps 40:6
51:17 Ps 34:18
51:18 Isa 51:3
51:19 Pss 4:5; 66:13, 15

Theme: God will judge the evildoer. Our anger must not block our confidence in God's ability to defeat evil.
Author: David

52

For the choir director: A psalm of David, regarding the time Doeg the Edomite told Saul that Ahimelech had given refuge to David.

1 You call yourself a hero, do you?
Why boast about this crime of yours,
you who have disgraced God's people?
2 All day long you plot destruction.
Your tongue cuts like a sharp razor;
you're an expert at telling lies.
3 You love evil more than good
and lies more than truth. *Interlude*

4 You love to say things that harm others,
you liar!
5 But God will strike you down once and for all.
He will pull you from your home
and drag you from the land of the living. *Interlude*

6 The righteous will see it and be amazed.
They will laugh and say,
7 "Look what happens to mighty warriors
who do not trust in God.
They trust their wealth instead
and grow more and more bold in their wickedness."

8 But I am like an olive tree,
thriving in the house of God.

52:1 Ps 94:4
52:2 Pss 5:9; 57:4; 59:7
52:3 Pss 36:4; 58:3; Jer 9:4-5
52:4 Ps 120:3
52:5 Ps 27:13; Prov 2:22; Isa 22:18-19
52:6 Job 22:19; Pss 37:34; 40:3
52:8 Pss 13:5; 128:3; Jer 11:16

51:17 God wants a broken spirit and a broken and repentant heart. You can never please God by outward actions—no matter how good—if your heart attitude is not right. Are you sorry for your sin? Do you genuinely intend to stop? God is pleased by this kind of repentance.

52:1 This psalm was written about Doeg the Edomite, who had betrayed Ahimelech and David and then killed God's priests (see 1 Samuel 21:7; 22:9-23). Doeg thought he was a great hero—even boasting about his deed. In reality, his deed was evil, an offense to God. It is easy to mistake "accomplishment" for goodness. Just because something is done well or thoroughly doesn't mean it is good (for example, someone may be a great gambler or a skillful liar). Measure all you do by the rule of God's Word, not by how proficiently you do it.

52:8 With God by his side, David compared himself to an olive tree, thriving in the house of God. Not only is an olive tree a thriving tree, it is one of the longest-living trees. David was contrasting God's eternal protection of his faithful servants with the sudden destruction of the wicked (52:5-7).

I trust in God's unfailing love
forever and ever.

52:9 Pss 30:12; 54:6

9 I will praise you forever, O God,
for what you have done.
I will wait for your mercies
in the presence of your people.

Theme: All have sinned. Because of sin, no person can find God on his own. Only God can save us.
Author: David

53

For the choir director: A meditation of David.

53:1-6 //Ps 14:1-7

1 Only fools say in their hearts,
"There is no God."
They are corrupt, and their actions are evil;
no one does good!

53:2 Ps 33:13-15

2 God looks down from heaven
on the entire human race;
he looks to see if there is even one with real understanding,
one who seeks for God.

53:3 Rom 3:10, 12

3 But no, all have turned away from God;
all have become corrupt.
No one does good,
not even one!

53:4 Jer 4:22

4 Will those who do evil never learn?
They eat up my people like bread;
they wouldn't think of praying to God.

53:5 Lev 26:17, 36; Ps 44:7; Prov 28:1; Jer 6:30; 8:1-2; Ezek 6:5

5 But then terror will grip them,
terror like they have never known before.
God will scatter the bones of your enemies.
You will put them to shame, for God has rejected them.

53:6 Ps 14:7

6 Oh, that salvation would come from Mount Zion to rescue Israel!
For when God restores his people,
Jacob will shout with joy, and Israel will rejoice.

Theme: A call for God to overcome enemies. God is our helper, even in times of hurt and betrayal.
Author: David

54

For the choir director: A meditation of David, regarding the time the Ziphites came and said to Saul, "We know where David is hiding." To be accompanied by stringed instruments.

54:1 2 Chr 20:6; Ps 20:1

1 Come with great power, O God, and rescue me!
Defend me with your might.
2 O God, listen to my prayer.
Pay attention to my plea.

54:3 1 Sam 20:1; Pss 36:1; 40:14; 86:14; 140:1, 4

3 For strangers are attacking me;
violent men are trying to kill me.
They care nothing for God. *Interlude*

53:1 Echoing the message of Psalm 14, this psalm proclaims the foolishness of atheism (see also Romans 3:10). People may say there is no God in order to cover up their sin, to have an excuse to continue in sin, and/or to ignore the Judge in order to avoid the judgment. "Fools" do not necessarily lack intelligence; many atheists and unbelievers are highly educated. Fools are people who reject God, the only one who can save them.

54:3, 4 Many of David's psalms follow the pattern found in these two verses—a transition from prayer to praise. David was not afraid to come to God and express his true feelings and needs. Thus, his spirit was lifted, and he praised God, his helper, protector, and friend.

4 But God is my helper.
The Lord is the one who keeps me alive!
5 May my enemies' plans for evil be turned against them.
Do as you promised and put an end to them.

6 I will sacrifice a voluntary offering to you;
I will praise your name, O LORD,
for it is good.
7 For you will rescue me from my troubles
and help me to triumph over my enemies.

54:4
Ps 37:17, 24, 40

54:6
Ps 50:14

54:7
Pss 34:6; 59:10

Theme: Expressing deep dismay over the treachery of a close friend. When friends hurt us, the burden is too difficult to carry alone.
Author: David

55 *For the choir director: A psalm of David, to be accompanied by stringed instruments.*

1 Listen to my prayer, O God.
Do not ignore my cry for help!
2 Please listen and answer me,
for I am overwhelmed by my troubles.
3 My enemies shout at me,
making loud and wicked threats.
They bring trouble on me,
hunting me down in their anger.

4 My heart is in anguish.
The terror of death overpowers me.
5 Fear and trembling overwhelm me.
I can't stop shaking.
6 Oh, how I wish I had wings like a dove;
then I would fly away and rest!
7 I would fly far away
to the quiet of the wilderness. *Interlude*
8 How quickly I would escape—
far away from this wild storm of hatred.

9 Destroy them, Lord, and confuse their speech,
for I see violence and strife in the city.
10 Its walls are patrolled day and night against invaders,
but the real danger is wickedness within the city.
11 Murder and robbery are everywhere there;
threats and cheating are rampant in the streets.

12 It is not an enemy who taunts me—
I could bear that.
It is not my foes who so arrogantly insult me—
I could have hidden from them.

55:1
Pss 27:9; 61:1

55:2
1 Sam 1:16
Pss 77:3; 86:6-7
Isa 38:14

55:3
2 Sam 16:7-8
Pss 17:9; 71:11

55:4
Ps 116:3

55:5
Job 21:6

55:6
Job 3:13

55:8
Isa 4:6

55:9
Jer 6:7

55:11
Pss 5:9; 10:7

55:12-13
Ps 41:9

54:5 David said that God repays evil to his enemies. Proverbs 26:27 warns that those who cause trouble will reap trouble. What we have intended for others may blow up in our own face. To be honest and straightforward before God and others is simpler, easier, and safer in the long run.

55:1ff This psalm was most likely written during the time of Absalom's rebellion and Ahithophel's betrayal (2 Samuel 15–17). Some say verses 12-14 are messianic because they also describe Judas's betrayal of Christ (Matthew 26:14-16, 20-25).

55:6-8 Even those who are especially close to God, as David was, have moments when they want to escape from their problems and pressures.

55:9-11 The city that was supposed to be holy was plagued by internal problems: violence, strife, wickedness, murder, robbery, threats, and cheating. External enemies, though a constant threat, were not nearly as dangerous as the corruption inside. Even today, churches often look to defend themselves against troubles from the sinful world while failing to see that their own sins are causing their troubles.

55:12-14 Nothing hurts more than a wound from a friend. There may be times when friends lovingly confront you in order to help you. Real friends stick by you in times of trouble and bring healing, love, acceptance, and understanding. What kind of friend are you? Don't betray those you love.

13 Instead, it is you—my equal,
my companion and close friend.

55:14 Ps 42:4

14 What good fellowship we enjoyed
as we walked together to the house of God.

55:15 Num 16:30, 33; Ps 64:7

15 Let death seize my enemies by surprise;
let the grave* swallow them alive,
for evil makes its home within them.

55:16 Ps 57:2-3

16 But I will call on God,
and the LORD will rescue me.

55:17 Pss 5:3; 88:13; 141:2; Dan 6:10; Acts 3:1

17 Morning, noon, and night
I plead aloud in my distress,
and the LORD hears my voice.

55:18 Ps 103:4

18 He rescues me and keeps me safe
from the battle waged against me,
even though many still oppose me.

55:19 Pss 36:1; 90:2; 93:2

19 God, who is king forever,
will hear me and will humble them. *Interlude*
For my enemies refuse to change their ways;
they do not fear God.

55:20 Num 30:2; Pss 7:3-4; 89:34

20 As for this friend of mine, he betrayed me;
he broke his promises.

55:21 Pss 12:2; 28:3; Prov 5:3-4

21 His words are as smooth as cream,
but in his heart is war.
His words are as soothing as lotion,
but underneath are daggers!

55:22 Pss 37:5; 112:6; 1 Pet 5:7

22 Give your burdens to the LORD,
and he will take care of you.
He will not permit the godly to slip and fall.

55:23 Pss 5:6; 56:3-4; 73:18

23 But you, O God, will send the wicked
down to the pit of destruction.
Murderers and liars will die young,
but I am trusting you to save me.

Theme: Trusting in God's care in the midst of fear. When all seems dark, one truth still shines bright: When God is for us, those against us will never succeed.
Author: David

56

For the choir director: A psalm of David, regarding the time the Philistines seized him in Gath. To be sung to the tune "Dove on Distant Oaks."

56:1 Pss 17:9; 35:1, 25

1 O God, have mercy on me.
The enemy troops press in on me.
My foes attack me all day long.
2 My slanderers hound me constantly,
and many are boldly attacking me.

55:15 Hebrew *let Sheol.*

55:17 Praying morning, noon, and night is certainly an excellent way to maintain correct priorities throughout every day. Daniel followed this pattern (Daniel 6:10), as did Peter (Acts 10:9, 10). The prayers of God's people are effective against the overwhelming evil in the world.

55:22 God wants us to give our burdens to him, but often we continue to bear them ourselves even when we say we are trusting in him. Trust the same strength that sustains you to carry your cares also.

56:1ff This was probably written on the same occasion as Psalm 34, when David fled from Saul to Philistine territory. He had to pretend insanity before Achish when some servants grew suspicious of him (1 Samuel 21:10-15).

3 But when I am afraid,
I put my trust in you.
4 O God, I praise your word.
I trust in God, so why should I be afraid?
What can mere mortals do to me?

5 They are always twisting what I say;
they spend their days plotting ways to harm me.
6 They come together to spy on me—
watching my every step, eager to kill me.
7 Don't let them get away with their wickedness;
in your anger, O God, throw them to the ground.

8 You keep track of all my sorrows.
You have collected all my tears in your bottle.
You have recorded each one in your book.

9 On the very day I call to you for help,
my enemies will retreat.
This I know: God is on my side.*
10 O God, I praise your word.
Yes, LORD, I praise your word.
11 I trust in God, so why should I be afraid?
What can mere mortals do to me?

12 I will fulfill my vows to you, O God,
and offer a sacrifice of thanks for your help.
13 For you have rescued me from death;
you have kept my feet from slipping.
So now I can walk in your presence, O God,
in your life-giving light.

56:3 Pss 11:1; 56:10-11
56:4 Ps 118:6; Heb 13:6
56:5 Ps 41:7; 2 Pet 3:15-16
56:6 Pss 17:11; 59:3
56:7 Pss 36:12; 55:23
56:8 Pss 39:12; 139:3; Mal 3:16
56:9 Pss 41:11; 118:6; Rom 8:31
56:12 Ps 50:14-15
56:13 Job 33:30; Pss 33:19; 86:13; 116:8-9

Theme: God's faithful help and love in times of trouble. When we face trials, God will quiet our hearts and give us confidence.
Author: David

57

For the choir director: A psalm of David, regarding the time he fled from Saul and went into the cave. To be sung to the tune "Do Not Destroy!"

1 Have mercy on me, O God, have mercy!
I look to you for protection.
I will hide beneath the shadow of your wings
until this violent storm is past.

2 I cry out to God Most High,
to God who will fulfill his purpose for me.
3 He will send help from heaven to save me,
rescuing me from those who are out to get me. *Interlude*
My God will send forth his unfailing love and faithfulness.

57:1 Ruth 2:12; Pss 36:7; 91:4; Isa 26:20
57:2 Pss 2:12; 138:8
57:3 Pss 18:16; 25:10; 56:2; 144:5, 7

56:9 Or *By this I will know that God is on my side.*

56:3, 4 David stated, "What can mere mortals do to me?" How much harm can people do to us? They can inflict pain, suffering, and death. But no person can rob us of our souls or our future beyond this life. How much harm can we do to ourselves? The worst thing we can do is to reject God and lose our eternal life. Jesus said, "Don't be afraid of those who want to kill you. They can only kill your body; they cannot touch your soul" (Matthew 10:28). Instead, we should fear God, who controls this life and the next.

56:8 Even in our deepest sorrow, God cares! Jesus reminded us further of how much God understands us—even the hairs on our head are all numbered (Matthew 10:30). Often we waver between faith and fear. When you feel so discouraged that you are sure no one understands, remember that God knows every problem and sees every tear.

57:1ff This psalm was probably written when David was hiding in a cave from Saul (see 1 Samuel 22–24).

57:4
Pss 58:6; 64:3
Prov 30:13-14

4 I am surrounded by fierce lions
who greedily devour human prey—
whose teeth pierce like spears and arrows,
and whose tongues cut like swords.

57:5
Ps 108:5

5 Be exalted, O God, above the highest heavens!
May your glory shine over all the earth.

57:6
Pss 10:9; 35:7; 140:5
Prov 26:27

6 My enemies have set a trap for me.
I am weary from distress.
They have dug a deep pit in my path,
but they themselves have fallen into it. *Interlude*

57:7-11
//Ps 108:1-5

7 My heart is confident in you, O God;
no wonder I can sing your praises!

57:8
Pss 16:9; 30:12; 150:3

8 Wake up, my soul!
Wake up, O harp and lyre!
I will waken the dawn with my song.
9 I will thank you, Lord, in front of all the people.
I will sing your praises among the nations.

57:10
Ps 36:5

10 For your unfailing love is as high as the heavens.
Your faithfulness reaches to the clouds.

11 Be exalted, O God, above the highest heavens.
May your glory shine over all the earth.

Theme: A prayer for God's justice. When no justice can be found, rejoice in knowing that justice will triumph because there is a God who will judge with complete fairness.
Author: David, at a time when men in authority were twisting justice

58

For the choir director: A psalm of David, to be sung to the tune "Do Not Destroy!"

58:1
Ps 82:2

1 Justice—do you rulers know the meaning of the word?
Do you judge the people fairly?

58:2
Ps 94:20
Mal 3:15

2 No, all your dealings are crooked;
you hand out violence instead of justice.

58:3
Ps 53:3
Isa 48:8

3 These wicked people are born sinners;
even from birth they have lied and gone their own way.

58:4
Deut 32:33
Pss 81:11; 140:3

4 They spit poison like deadly snakes;
they are like cobras that refuse to listen,
5 ignoring the tunes of the snake charmers,
no matter how skillfully they play.

58:6
Job 4:10
Ps 3:7

6 Break off their fangs, O God!
Smash the jaws of these lions, O LORD!

58:7
Josh 7:5
Pss 64:3; 112:10

7 May they disappear like water into thirsty ground.
Make their weapons useless in their hands.*

58:7 Or *Let them be trodden down and wither like grass.* The meaning of the Hebrew is uncertain.

57:4 At times we may be surrounded by people who gossip about us or criticize us. Verbal cruelty can damage us as badly as physical abuse. Rather than answering with hateful words, we, like David, can talk with God about the problem.

57:7 David's firm faith in God contrasted sharply with his enemies' loud lying and boasting. When confronted with verbal attacks, the best defense is simply to be quiet and praise God, realizing that our confidence is in his love and faithfulness (57:10). In times of suffering, don't turn inward to self-pity or outward to revenge, but turn upward to God.

58:1ff This is called an imprecatory psalm (see the note on 35:1ff). It is a cry for justice so intense that it seems, at first glance, to be a call for revenge.

58:1ff The Old Testament is filled with references to justice—it is a key topic in the psalms. Unfortunately, many judges and rulers in ancient times took justice into their own hands. They had complete authority with no accountability and the power to make their own laws. When earth's judges are corrupt, there is little hope of justice in this life. But God loves justice, and those who obey him will experience perfect justice in eternity.

8 May they be like snails that dissolve into slime,
like a stillborn child who will never see the sun.
9 God will sweep them away, both young and old,
faster than a pot heats on an open flame.

10 The godly will rejoice when they see injustice avenged.
They will wash their feet in the blood of the wicked.
11 Then at last everyone will say,
"There truly is a reward for those who live for God;
surely there is a God who judges justly here on earth."

58:8 Job 3:16
58:9 Job 27:21; Ps 118:12; Prov 10:25
58:10 Pss 32:11; 64:10; 68:22-23; 91:8
58:11 Pss 9:8; 18:20; Luke 6:23, 35

Theme: Prayer and praise for God's saving help. God's constant love is our place of safety in a wicked world.
Author: David

59

For the choir director: A psalm of David, regarding the time Saul sent soldiers to watch David's house in order to kill him. To be sung to the tune "Do Not Destroy!"

1 Rescue me from my enemies, O God.
Protect me from those who have come to destroy me.
2 Rescue me from these criminals;
save me from these murderers.

3 They have set an ambush for me.
Fierce enemies are out there waiting,
though I have done them no wrong, O LORD.
4 Despite my innocence, they prepare to kill me.
Rise up and help me! Look on my plight!
5 O LORD God Almighty, the God of Israel,
rise up to punish hostile nations.
Show no mercy to wicked traitors. *Interlude*

6 They come at night,
snarling like vicious dogs
as they prowl the streets.
7 Listen to the filth that comes from their mouths,
the piercing swords that fly from their lips.
"Who can hurt us?" they sneer.

8 But LORD, you laugh at them.
You scoff at all the hostile nations.
9 You are my strength; I wait for you to rescue me,
for you, O God, are my place of safety.
10 In his unfailing love, my God will come and help me.
He will let me look down in triumph on all my enemies.

11 Don't kill them, for my people soon forget such lessons;
stagger them with your power, and bring them to their knees,
O Lord our shield.

59:1 Pss 20:1; 143:9
59:2 Pss 14:4; 28:3; 94:16; 139:19
59:3 Pss 7:3-4; 56:6; 69:4
59:4 Ps 35:19, 23
59:5 Pss 9:5; 84:8; Jer 18:23
59:7 Job 22:13; Pss 10:11; 73:11; 94:47
59:8 Pss 2:4; 37:13
59:9 Ps 9:9
59:10 Ps 54:7
59:11 Deut 4:9; Pss 106:27; 144:6

58:11 Of all people, our national leaders should be just and fair. When they are unjust and unfair, people suffer. The rich get richer, the poor get poorer, politicians wrest power from the people, national morality deteriorates, and God is ignored. When right triumphs at last, "the godly will rejoice" (58:10). Be assured that there will be a day of accountability and that God judges fairly. Be careful never to side with injustice, lest you find yourself standing before an angry Judge.

59:7, 8 Vile men curse God as if he cannot hear or will not respond. But God scoffs at them. Evil people live as if God cannot see them or will not punish them. But God watches patiently until that day when their deeds will rise up to accuse them. As believers we must be careful not to follow the same foolish practices as evil people. We must remember that God hears and sees all we do.

59:10 David was hunted by those whose love had turned to jealousy, and this was driving them to try to murder him. Trusted friends, and even his son, had turned against him. What changeable love! But David knew that God's love for him was *changeless.* "His unfailing love continues forever" (100:5). God's mercy to all who trust him is just as permanent as his mercy to David. When the love of others fails or disappoints us, we can rest in God's enduring love.

59:12
Ps 10:7
Prov 12:13
Zeph 3:11

12 Because of the sinful things they say,
because of the evil that is on their lips,
let them be captured by their pride,
their curses, and their lies.

59:13
Pss 83:18; 104:35

13 Destroy them in your anger!
Wipe them out completely!
Then the whole world will know
that God reigns in Israel.* *Interlude*

59:14
Ps 59:6

14 My enemies come out at night,
snarling like vicious dogs
as they prowl the streets.
15 They scavenge for food
but go to sleep unsatisfied.*

59:16
Pss 21:13; 46:1; 101:1

16 But as for me, I will sing about your power.
I will shout with joy each morning because of your unfailing love.
For you have been my refuge,
a place of safety in the day of distress.

59:17
Ps 59:9-10

17 O my Strength, to you I sing praises,
for you, O God, are my refuge,
the God who shows me unfailing love.

Theme: Real help comes from God alone. When a situation seems out of control, we can trust God to do mighty things.
Author: David, when Israel was away at war with Aram in the north, and Edom invaded Judah from the south (2 Samuel 8)

60

For the choir director: A psalm of David useful for teaching, regarding the time David fought Aram-naharaim and Aram-zobah, and Joab returned and killed twelve thousand Edomites in the Valley of Salt. To be sung to the tune "Lily of the Testimony."

60:1
Pss 44:9; 79:5; 80:3

1 You have rejected us, O God, and broken our defenses.
You have been angry with us; now restore us to your favor.

60:2
2 Chr 7:14
Ps 18:7

2 You have shaken our land and split it open.
Seal the cracks before it completely collapses.

60:3
Ps 66:12

3 You have been very hard on us,
making us drink wine that sent us reeling.

60:4
Pss 11:12; 13:2

4 But you have raised a banner for those who honor you—
a rallying point in the face of attack. *Interlude*

60:5-12
//Ps 108:6-13

5 Use your strong right arm to save us,
and rescue your beloved people.

60:6
Gen 33:17
Josh 17:7
Ps 89:35

6 God has promised this by his holiness*:
"I will divide up Shechem with joy.
I will measure out the valley of Succoth.

60:6
Gen 49:10
Deut 33:17
Josh 13:31

7 Gilead is mine,
and Manasseh is mine.
Ephraim will produce my warriors,
and Judah will produce my kings.

59:13 Hebrew *in Jacob.* **59:15** Or *and growl if they don't get enough.* **60:6** Or *in his sanctuary.*

60:1ff This psalm gives us information about David's reign not found in the books of 1 and 2 Samuel or 1 and 2 Chronicles. Although the setting of the psalm is found in 2 Samuel 8, that passage makes no reference to the fact that David's forces had met stiff resistance (60:1-3) and apparently even a temporary defeat (60:9, 10). The closer we get to God, the more our enemies will attack us because we threaten their evil and selfish way of living.

60:3 Instead of the wine of blessing, God had given them the cup of his judgment. God's rejection was intended to bring them back to himself.

60:6-10 God said the cities and territories of Israel were his, and he knew the future of each of the nations. When the world seems out of control, we must remind ourselves that God owns the cities and knows the future of every nation. God is in control. With God's help, we will gain the victory.

8 Moab will become my lowly servant,
and Edom will be my slave.
I will shout in triumph over the Philistines."

9 But who will bring me into the fortified city?
Who will bring me victory over Edom?
10 Have you rejected us, O God?
Will you no longer march with our armies?
11 Oh, please help us against our enemies,
for all human help is useless.
12 With God's help we will do mighty things,
for he will trample down our foes.

60:8 2 Sam 8:1-2, 14
60:9 Ps 44:9
60:10 Ps 60:1
60:11 Ps 146:3
60:12 Num 24:15-19; Pss 44:5; 118:16

Theme: Prayer for security and assurance. Wherever we are, we can trust that God will be there to answer our cries for help.
Author: David, written when he was forced to escape during the days of Absalom's rebellion (2 Samuel 15—18), or after he had narrowly escaped one of Saul's efforts to kill him while hiding in the wilderness

61

For the choir director: A psalm of David, to be accompanied by stringed instruments.

1 O God, listen to my cry!
Hear my prayer!
2 From the ends of the earth,
I will cry to you for help,
for my heart is overwhelmed.
Lead me to the towering rock of safety,
3 for you are my safe refuge,
a fortress where my enemies cannot reach me.
4 Let me live forever in your sanctuary,
safe beneath the shelter of your wings! *Interlude*
5 For you have heard my vows, O God.
You have given me an inheritance reserved for those who fear your name.

6 Add many years to the life of the king!
May his years span the generations!
7 May he reign under God's protection forever.
Appoint your unfailing love and faithfulness to watch over him.

8 Then I will always sing praises to your name
as I fulfill my vows day after day.

61:1 Pss 64:1; 86:6
61:2 Pss 18:2; 77:3
61:3 Ps 62:7; Prov 18:10
61:4 Pss 17:8; 23:6; 27:4; 91:4
61:5 Pss 56:12; 86:11; Mal 2:5; 4:2
61:7 Pss 40:11; 41:12
61:8 Pss 30:4; 65:1; 71:22

Theme: Placing all hope in God. Knowing that God is in control allows us to wait patiently for him to rescue us. True relief does not come when the problem is resolved because more problems are on the way! True relief comes from an enduring hope in God's ultimate salvation. Only then will all trials be resolved.
Author: David, written during the days of Absalom's rebellion (2 Samuel 15—18)

62

For Jeduthun, the choir director: A psalm of David.

1 I wait quietly before God,
for my salvation comes from him.

62:1 Pss 33:20; 37:39

60:8 David mentioned the enemy nations that surrounded Israel: Moab lay directly to the east, Edom to the south, and Philistia to the west. At the time this psalm was written, David was fighting Aram to the north. Although he was surrounded by enemies, David believed that God would help him triumph.

61:1, 2 David must have been far from home when he wrote this psalm. Fortunately, God is not limited to any geographic location. Even when we are among strange people and surroundings, God never abandons us. His all-surpassing strength is always with us.

61:8 David made a vow to praise God each day. David continually praised God through both the good and difficult times of his life. Do you find something to praise God for each day? As you do, you will find your heart elevated from daily distractions to lasting confidence.

62:2
Pss 59:17; 89:26

2 He alone is my rock and my salvation,
my fortress where I will never be shaken.

62:3
Pss 28:3; 55:21
Isa 30:13

3 So many enemies against one man—
all of them trying to kill me.
To them I'm just a broken-down wall
or a tottering fence.

62:4
Pss 4:2; 28:3

4 They plan to topple me from my high position.
They delight in telling lies about me.
They are friendly to my face,
but they curse me in their hearts. *Interlude*

5 I wait quietly before God,
for my hope is in him.
6 He alone is my rock and my salvation,
my fortress where I will not be shaken.

62:7
Pss 46:1; 85:9

7 My salvation and my honor come from God alone.
He is my refuge, a rock where no enemy can reach me.

62:8
Pss 42:4; 52:8
Lam 2:19

8 O my people, trust in him at all times.
Pour out your heart to him,
for God is our refuge. *Interlude*

62:9
Isa 40:15

9 From the greatest to the lowliest—
all are nothing in his sight.
If you weigh them on the scales,
they are lighter than a puff of air.

62:10
Ps 49:6
Isa 30:12-13; 61:8
Mark 10:24
Luke 12:15
1 Tim 6:10

10 Don't try to get rich
by extortion or robbery.
And if your wealth increases,
don't make it the center of your life.

62:11
Job 13:14

11 God has spoken plainly,
and I have heard it many times:
Power, O God, belongs to you;

62:12
Job 34:11
Matt 16:27
†Rom 2:6

12 unfailing love, O Lord, is yours.
Surely you judge all people
according to what they have done.

Theme: A desire for God's presence, provision, and protection. No matter where we are, our desire should be for God because only he satisfies fully.
Author: David

63

A psalm of David, regarding a time when David was in the wilderness of Judah.

63:1
Pss 42:2; 84:2

1 O God, you are my God;
I earnestly search for you.
My soul thirsts for you;
my whole body longs for you
in this parched and weary land
where there is no water.

62:3-6 David expressed his feelings to God and then reaffirmed his faith. Prayer can release our tensions in times of emotional stress. Trusting God to be our rock, salvation, and fortress (62:2) will change our entire outlook on life. No longer must we be held captive by resentment toward others when they hurt us. When we are resting in God's strength, nothing can shake us.

62:9-12 It is tempting to use honor, power, wealth, or prestige to measure people. We may even think that such people are really getting ahead in life. But on God's scales, these people are "lighter than a puff of air." What, then, can tilt the scales when God weighs us? Trusting God and working for him (62:12). Wealth, honor, power, or prestige add nothing to our value in God's eyes; only the faithful work we do for him has eternal value.

63:1ff Psalms 61, 62, and 63 were probably written when David was seeking refuge during Absalom's rebellion (2 Samuel 15–18).

2 I have seen you in your sanctuary
and gazed upon your power and glory.
3 Your unfailing love is better to me than life itself;
how I praise you!
4 I will honor you as long as I live,
lifting up my hands to you in prayer.
5 You satisfy me more than the richest of foods.
I will praise you with songs of joy.

6 I lie awake thinking of you,
meditating on you through the night.
7 I think how much you have helped me;
I sing for joy in the shadow of your protecting wings.
8 I follow close behind you;
your strong right hand holds me securely.

9 But those plotting to destroy me will come to ruin.
They will go down into the depths of the earth.
10 They will die by the sword
and become the food of jackals.

11 But the king will rejoice in God.
All who trust in him will praise him,
while liars will be silenced.

63:2 Ps 27:4
63:3 Ps 69:16
63:4 Pss 28:2; 104:33
63:5 Pss 36:8; 71:23
63:6 Pss 4:4; 16:7; 42:8
63:8 Ps 18:35
63:9 Pss 40:14; 55:15
63:11 Deut 6:13 Isa 45:23

Theme: A complaint against conspiracy. When others conspire against us, we can ask God for protection because he knows everything.
Author: David

64

For the choir director: A psalm of David.

1 O God, listen to my complaint.
Do not let my enemies' threats overwhelm me.
2 Protect me from the plots of the wicked,
from the scheming of those who do evil.
3 Sharp tongues are the swords they wield;
bitter words are the arrows they aim.
4 They shoot from ambush at the innocent,
attacking suddenly and fearlessly.
5 They encourage each other to do evil
and plan how to set their traps.
"Who will ever notice?" they ask.
6 As they plot their crimes, they say,
"We have devised the perfect plan!"
Yes, the human heart and mind are cunning.

7 But God himself will shoot them down.
Suddenly, his arrows will pierce them.

64:2 Pss 56:6; 59:2
64:3 Ps 140:3
64:4 Pss 10:8; 11:2
64:5 Ps 140:5
64:6 Ps 49:11
64:7 Ps 7:12-13

63:1-5 Hiding from his enemies in the barren wilderness of Judah, David was intensely lonely. He longed for a friend he could trust to ease his loneliness. No wonder he cried out, "O God, . . . my soul thirsts for you . . . in this parched and weary land." If you are lonely or thirsty for something lasting in your life, remember David's prayer. God alone can satisfy our deepest longings!

64:1ff Evil can come in the form of a conspiracy or an ambush because Satan wants to catch us unprepared. He tempts us in our weakest areas when we least expect it. But God himself will strike down our enemies (64:7), whether they are physical or spiritual. Wickedness is widespread and affects us in many ways, but the final victory already belongs to God and to those who trust and believe in him.

64:1, 2 We may believe that God hears only certain requests from us. While it is true that we should offer praise, confession, and respectful petitions, it is true also that God is willing to listen to *anything* we want to tell him. David expressed himself honestly, knowing that God would hear his voice. God will always listen to us, and he fully understands us.

64:3-10 Words spoken against us are among the most painful attacks we may have to face. If we trust in God, however, these attacks need not cause any lasting damage.

64:8 Ps 9:3 Prov 18:6-7

8 Their own words will be turned against them, destroying them.
All who see it happening will shake their heads in scorn.
9 Then everyone will stand in awe,
proclaiming the mighty acts of God,
realizing all the amazing things he does.

64:10 Pss 11:1; 25:20; 32:11

10 The godly will rejoice in the LORD
and find shelter in him.
And those who do what is right
will praise him.

Theme: God provides abundantly. We can be thankful to God for his many blessings.
Author: David

65

For the choir director: A psalm of David. A song.

65:1 Pss 86:9; 116:18

1 What mighty praise, O God,
belongs to you in Zion.
We will fulfill our vows to you,

65:2 Isa 66:23

2 for you answer our prayers,
and to you all people will come.

65:3 Pss 38:4; 40:12 Heb 9:14

3 Though our hearts are filled with sins,
you forgive them all.

65:4 Pss 4:3; 33:12; 36:8

4 What joy for those you choose to bring near,
those who live in your holy courts.
What joys await us
inside your holy Temple.

65:5 Pss 45:4; 48:10

5 You faithfully answer our prayers with awesome deeds,
O God our savior.
You are the hope of everyone on earth,
even those who sail on distant seas.

65:6 Pss 93:1; 95:4

6 You formed the mountains by your power
and armed yourself with mighty strength.

65:7 Ps 89:9 Isa 17:12-13 Matt 8:26

7 You quieted the raging oceans
with their pounding waves
and silenced the shouting of the nations.

65:8 Ps 139:9-10

8 Those who live at the ends of the earth
stand in awe of your wonders.
From where the sun rises to where it sets,
you inspire shouts of joy.

65:9 Pss 46:4; 104:13-14, 24

9 You take care of the earth and water it,
making it rich and fertile.
The rivers of God will not run dry;
they provide a bountiful harvest of grain,
for you have ordered it so.

65:1, 2 In Old Testament times, vows were taken seriously and fulfilled completely. No one had to make a vow, but once made, it was binding (Deuteronomy 23:21-23). The vow that is being fulfilled here is the promise to praise God for his answers to prayer.

65:3 Although we may feel overwhelmed by the multitude of our sins, God will forgive them all if we ask sincerely. Do you feel as though God could never forgive you, that your sins are too many, or that some of them are too great? The good news is that God can and will forgive them all. Nobody is beyond redemption, and nobody is so full of sin that he or she cannot be forgiven.

65:4 Access to God, the joy of living in the Temple courts, was a great honor. God had chosen a special group of Israelites from the tribe of Levi to serve as priests in the Tabernacle (Numbers 3:5-51). They were the only ones who could enter the sacred rooms where God's presence resided. Because of Jesus' death on the cross, believers today have access to God's presence in every place and at any time.

65:6-13 This harvest psalm glorifies God the Creator as reflected in the beauty of nature. Nature helps us understand something of God's character. The Jews believed that God's care of nature was a sign of his love and provision for them. Nature shows God's generosity—giving us more than we need or deserve. God's abundant generosity should make us grateful to him and generous to others.

10 You drench the plowed ground with rain,
melting the clods and leveling the ridges.
You soften the earth with showers
and bless its abundant crops.
11 You crown the year with a bountiful harvest;
even the hard pathways overflow with abundance.
12 The wilderness becomes a lush pasture,
and the hillsides blossom with joy.
13 The meadows are clothed with flocks of sheep,
and the valleys are carpeted with grain.
They all shout and sing for joy!

65:12 Job 38:26-27
65:13 Pss 98:8; 144:13; Isa 30:23; 55:12

Theme: God answers prayer. Individually and as a body of believers, we should praise and worship God.
Author: Anonymous, written after a great victory in battle

66

For the choir director: A psalm. A song.

1 Shout joyful praises to God, all the earth!
2 Sing about the glory of his name!
Tell the world how glorious he is.
3 Say to God, "How awesome are your deeds!
Your enemies cringe before your mighty power.
4 Everything on earth will worship you;
they will sing your praises,
shouting your name in glorious songs." *Interlude*

5 Come and see what our God has done,
what awesome miracles he does for his people!
6 He made a dry path through the Red Sea,*
and his people went across on foot.
Come, let us rejoice in who he is.
7 For by his great power he rules forever.
He watches every movement of the nations;
let no rebel rise in defiance. *Interlude*

8 Let the whole world bless our God
and sing aloud his praises.
9 Our lives are in his hands,
and he keeps our feet from stumbling.
10 You have tested us, O God;
you have purified us like silver melted in a crucible.
11 You captured us in your net
and laid the burden of slavery on our backs.
12 You sent troops to ride across our broken bodies.
We went through fire and flood.
But you brought us to a place of great abundance.

13 Now I come to your Temple with burnt offerings
to fulfill the vows I made to you—

66:3 Pss 18:44; 47:2
66:4 Pss 22:27; 67:4
66:5 Ps 46:8
66:6 Exod 14:21; Ps 105:43
66:7 Pss 11:4; 140:8; 145:13
66:9 Ps 30:3
66:10 Ps 17:3; Zech 13:9; 1 Pet 1:6-7
66:11 Lam 1:13
66:12 Ps 18:19; Isa 43:2; 51:23
66:13 Ps 22:25; Eccl 5:4

66:6 Hebrew *the sea.*

66:5-7 The writer was remembering the famous story about God's rescue of the Israelites by parting the Red Sea. God saved the Israelites then, and he continues to save his people today.

66:10-12 Just as fire purifies silver in the smelting process, trials refine our character. They bring us a new and deeper wisdom, helping us discern truth from falsehood and giving us the discipline to do what we know is right. Above all, these trials help us realize that life is a gift from God to be cherished, not a right to be taken for granted.

66:13-15 People sometimes make bargains with God, saying, "If you heal me [or get me out of this mess], I'll obey you for the rest of my life." However, soon after they recover, the vow is forgotten and the old life-style is resumed. This writer made a promise to God, but he remembered the promise and was prepared to carry it out. God always keeps his promises and wants us to follow his example. Be careful to follow through on whatever you promise to do.

66:14 Ps 18:6

14 yes, the sacred vows you heard me make
when I was in deep trouble.

66:15 Num 6:14 Ps 51:19

15 That is why I am sacrificing burnt offerings to you—
the best of my rams as a pleasing aroma.
And I will sacrifice bulls and goats. *Interlude*

66:16 Ps 34:11; 71:15, 24

16 Come and listen, all you who fear God,
and I will tell you what he did for me.
17 For I cried out to him for help,
praising him as I spoke.

66:18 Job 36:21 Ps 18:41 Isa 1:15 Jas 4:3

18 If I had not confessed the sin in my heart,
my Lord would not have listened.
19 But God did listen!
He paid attention to my prayer.

66:19 Ps 116:1-2

66:20 Pss 22:24; 68:35

20 Praise God, who did not ignore my prayer
and did not withdraw his unfailing love from me.

Theme: Joy comes from spreading the news about God around the world.
Author: Anonymous, possibly written for one of the harvest festivals

67

For the choir director: A psalm, to be accompanied by stringed instruments. A song.

67:1 Num 6:25 Pss 4:6; 80:3, 7, 19

1 May God be merciful and bless us.
May his face shine with favor upon us. *Interlude*

67:2 Acts 18:25 Tit 2:11

2 May your ways be known throughout the earth,
your saving power among people everywhere.

67:3 Ps 66:4

3 May the nations praise you, O God.
Yes, may all the nations praise you.

67:4 Ps 96:10, 13

4 How glad the nations will be, singing for joy,
because you govern them with justice
and direct the actions of the whole world. *Interlude*
5 May the nations praise you, O God.
Yes, may all the nations praise you.

67:6 Lev 26:4 Ps 22:27 Ezek 34:27

6 Then the earth will yield its harvests,
and God, our God, will richly bless us.
7 Yes, God will bless us,
and people all over the world will fear him.

67:7 Ps 33:8

Theme: Remembering God's glory and power. Times and cultures change, but God is always majestically present as defender and provider.
Author: David

68

For the choir director: A psalm of David. A song.

68:1 Num 10:35

1 Arise, O God, and scatter your enemies.
Let those who hate God run for their lives.

66:18 Our confession of sin must be continual because we continue to do wrong. But true confession requires us to listen to God and to want to stop doing what is wrong. David confessed his sin and prayed, "Cleanse me from these hidden faults. Keep me from deliberate sins" (19:12, 13). When we *refuse* to repent or when we harbor and cherish certain sins, we place a wall between us and God. We may not be able to remember *every* sin we have ever committed, but our attitude should be one of confession and obedience.

67:2 Could the psalmist have looked across the years to see the gospel go throughout the earth? This psalm surely speaks of the fulfillment of the great commission (Matthew 28:18-20), when Jesus commanded that the gospel be taken to all nations. Count yourself among that great crowd of believers worldwide who know the Savior; praise him for his Good News; and share that gospel so that the harvest will be abundant.

68:1ff This psalm begins just like Moses' cry in Numbers 10:35 as the Israelites followed the Ark of the Covenant. It undoubtedly brought to mind the time when David led a joyous procession and brought the Ark from the house of Obed-edom to Jerusalem (2 Samuel 6:11-15).

2 Drive them off like smoke blown by the wind.
Melt them like wax in fire.
Let the wicked perish in the presence of God.
3 But let the godly rejoice.
Let them be glad in God's presence.
Let them be filled with joy.

4 Sing praises to God and to his name!
Sing loud praises to him who rides the clouds.
His name is the LORD—
rejoice in his presence!

5 Father to the fatherless, defender of widows—
this is God, whose dwelling is holy.
6 God places the lonely in families;
he sets the prisoners free and gives them joy.
But for rebels, there is only famine and distress.

7 O God, when you led your people from Egypt,
when you marched through the wilderness, *Interlude*
8 the earth trembled, and the heavens poured rain
before you, the God of Sinai,
before God, the God of Israel.
9 You sent abundant rain, O God,
to refresh the weary Promised Land.
10 There your people finally settled,
and with a bountiful harvest, O God,
you provided for your needy people.

11 The Lord announces victory,
and throngs of women shout the happy news.
12 Enemy kings and their armies flee,
while the women of Israel divide the plunder.
13 Though they lived among the sheepfolds,
now they are covered with silver and gold,
as a dove is covered by its wings.
14 The Almighty scattered the enemy kings
like a blowing snowstorm on Mount Zalmon.

15 The majestic mountains of Bashan
stretch high into the sky.
16 Why do you look with envy, O rugged mountains,
at Mount Zion, where God has chosen to live,
where the LORD himself will live forever?

68:2 Ps 37:20 Isa 9:18 Hos 13:3 Mic 1:4

68:4 Pss 40:3; 68:33

68:5 Deut 10:18; 26:15

68:7 Exod 13:21

68:8 Exod 19:18 Judg 5:4-5

68:9 Deut 11:11

68:11 Exod 15:20

68:13 Gen 49:14

68:14 Josh 10:10

68:15 Ps 36:6

68:3-6 With shouts of praise and the sound of trumpets, David and his people took the holy Ark toward Mount Zion (2 Samuel 6:15). It was a time to sing praises to the Lord, whose presence brings great joy. Only in God is there hope for orphans, widows, prisoners, and all other lonely people. If you are lonely or disadvantaged, join David in praise, and discover great joy from loving and praising God.

68:4-6 David praised God for his protection and provision. When we see God's true majesty, our response should be to praise him. This was a song of faith because many of these benefits had not yet come true in David's time. It should also be our song of faith. We must continue to trust God because, in time, he will fulfill all his promises.

68:8 Mount Sinai had a prominent role in Israelite history. It was at Mount Sinai that God met Moses and commissioned him to lead Israel out of Egypt (Exodus 3:1-10). It was to Mount Sinai that the nation of Israel returned to receive God's laws (Exodus 19:1-3), and God's presence made the entire mountain tremble (Exodus 19:18). This sacred mountain was a constant reminder of God's words and promises.

68:13 The dove is a symbol of God's beloved Israel, who is so protected and blessed that it has taken silver and gold from its enemies, even though it stayed in camp.

68:15, 16 Bashan, the land northeast of Israel, was the home of mighty mountains, including Mount Hermon, the tallest and most awesome mountain in the region. God's choice of Mount Zion, a foothill by comparison, for the site of the Temple led the psalmist to write poetically of the envy of the mountains of Bashan.

68:17 Deut 33:2 Dan 7:10

17 Surrounded by unnumbered thousands of chariots,
the Lord came from Mount Sinai into his sanctuary.

68:18 †Eph 4:8 1 Tim 1:13

18 When you ascended to the heights,
you led a crowd of captives.
You received gifts from the people,
even from those who rebelled against you.
Now the LORD God will live among us here.

68:19 Pss 55:22; 65:5 Isa 46:4

19 Praise the Lord; praise God our savior!
For each day he carries us in his arms. *Interlude*

68:20 Ps 56:13

20 Our God is a God who saves!
The Sovereign LORD rescues us from death.

68:21 Ps 110:6 Hab 3:13

21 But God will smash the heads of his enemies,
crushing the skulls of those who love their guilty ways.

68:22 Amos 9:1-3

22 The Lord says, "I will bring my enemies down from Bashan;
I will bring them up from the depths of the sea.

68:23 1 Kgs 21:19 Ps 58:10 Jer 15:3

23 You, my people, will wash your feet in their blood,
and even your dogs will get their share!"

68:24 Pss 63:2; 77:13

24 Your procession has come into view, O God—
the procession of my God and King
as he goes into the sanctuary.

68:25 Exod 15:20 Judg 11:34 1 Chr 13:8

25 Singers are in front, musicians are behind;
with them are young women playing tambourines.

68:26 Deut 33:28 Pss 22:22-23; 26:12

26 Praise God, all you people of Israel;
praise the LORD, the source of Israel's life.
27 Look, the little tribe of Benjamin leads the way.
Then comes a great throng of rulers from Judah
and all the rulers of Zebulun and Naphtali.

68:28 Pss 29:11; 44:4

28 Summon your might, O God.
Display your power, O God, as you have in the past.

68:29 Ps 72:10

29 The kings of the earth are bringing tribute
to your Temple in Jerusalem.

68:30 Ps 89:10

30 Rebuke these enemy nations—
these wild animals lurking in the reeds,
this herd of bulls among the weaker calves.
Humble those who demand tribute from us.*
Scatter the nations that delight in war.

68:31 Isa 19:19-21; 45:14

31 Let Egypt come with gifts of precious metals;
let Ethiopia* bow in submission to God.

68:32 Ps 102:21-22

32 Sing to God, you kingdoms of the earth.
Sing praises to the Lord. *Interlude*

68:33 Deut 10:14 Pss 18:10; 29:4

33 Sing to the one who rides across the ancient heavens,
his mighty voice thundering from the sky.

68:30 Or *Humble them until they submit, bringing pieces of silver as tribute.* **68:31** Hebrew *Cush.*

68:17 This psalm celebrates the final stages of a journey that began at Mount Sinai with the construction of the Ark of the Covenant and finally ended at Mount Zion (site of the sanctuary), the chosen dwelling place of God among his people. It may describe the moving of the Ark of the Covenant into Jerusalem.

68:18 This verse, quoted in Ephesians 4:8, is applied to the ministry of the ascended Christ. It celebrates his victory over evil. It assures all of us who believe in Christ that by trusting him, we can overcome evil.

68:19-21 God sets his people free and crushes his enemies. Salvation is freedom from sin and death. Those who refuse to turn to God will be crushed by sin and death. They will be trapped by the sin they loved and destroyed by the death they feared. How much better it will be for those who love God and fear the consequences of sin.

34 Tell everyone about God's power.
His majesty shines down on Israel;
his strength is mighty in the heavens.
35 God is awesome in his sanctuary.
The God of Israel gives power and strength to his people.

Praise be to God!

68:35
Deut 10:17
Pss 29:11; 47:2

Theme: A cry of distress in a sea of trouble. We may have to suffer severely for our devotion to God, but that should cause us to look forward with joy to the day when evil and injustice will be gone forever.
Author: David

69

For the choir director: A psalm of David, to be sung to the tune "Lilies."

1 Save me, O God,
for the floodwaters are up to my neck.
2 Deeper and deeper I sink into the mire;
I can't find a foothold to stand on.
I am in deep water,
and the floods overwhelm me.
3 I am exhausted from crying for help;
my throat is parched and dry.
My eyes are swollen with weeping,
waiting for my God to help me.
4 Those who hate me without cause
are more numerous than the hairs on my head.
These enemies who seek to destroy me
are doing so without cause.
They attack me with lies,
demanding that I give back what I didn't steal.

5 O God, you know how foolish I am;
my sins cannot be hidden from you.
6 Don't let those who trust in you stumble because of me,
O Sovereign LORD Almighty.
Don't let me cause them to be humiliated,
O God of Israel.
7 For I am mocked and shamed for your sake;
humiliation is written all over my face.
8 Even my own brothers pretend they don't know me;
they treat me like a stranger.

9 Passion for your house burns within me,
so those who insult you are also insulting me.
10 When I weep and fast before the LORD,
they scoff at me.

69:2
Jon 2:3

69:3
Pss 6:6; 119:82, 123
Isa 38:14

69:4
Pss 35:11; 59:3
†John 15:25

69:5
Ps 44:21

69:6
2 Sam 12:14

69:8
Pss 31:11; 38:11

69:9
†John 2:17
†Rom 15:13

68:34, 35 When we consider all God has done for us, we should feel an overwhelming sense of awe as we kneel before the Lord in his sanctuary. Nature surrounds us with countless signs of God's wonderful power. His unlimited power and unspeakable majesty leave us breathless in his presence. How fortunate we are that God cares for us.

69:1ff This is one of the most quoted psalms in the New Testament, and it is often applied to the ministry and suffering of Jesus. Verse 4, like John 15:25, speaks of Jesus' many enemies. The experience of being scorned by his brothers (69:8) is expressed in John 7:5. Verse 9 portrays David's zeal for God; Christ showed great zeal when he threw the money changers out of the Temple (John 2:14-17). Paul quoted part of 69:9 in Romans 15:3. Christ's great suffering is portrayed in 69:20, 21 (Matthew 27:24; Mark 15:23; Luke 23:36; John 19:28-30). Verses 22 through 28 are quoted in Romans 11:9, 10; and Peter applied 69:25 to Judas (Acts 1:20).

69:3 David cried out until he was physically exhausted, with a parched throat and eyes swollen from weeping. Yet he still trusted God to save him. When devastated by death or tragedy, we need not collapse or despair because we can turn to God and ask him to save us and help us. The tears will still come, but we will not be crying in vain.

[11] When I dress in sackcloth to show sorrow,
they make fun of me.

69:12
Job 30:9

[12] I am the favorite topic of town gossip,
and all the drunkards sing about me.

69:13
Ps 32:6
Isa 49:8
2 Cor 6:2

[13] But I keep right on praying to you, LORD,
hoping this is the time you will show me favor.
In your unfailing love, O God,
answer my prayer with your sure salvation.

69:14
Ps 144:7

[14] Pull me out of the mud;
don't let me sink any deeper!
Rescue me from those who hate me,
and pull me from these deep waters.

69:15
Num 16:33
Ps 124:4-5

[15] Don't let the floods overwhelm me,
or the deep waters swallow me,
or the pit of death devour me.

69:16
Pss 25:16; 51:1; 63:3

[16] Answer my prayers, O LORD,
for your unfailing love is wonderful.
Turn and take care of me,
for your mercy is so plentiful.
[17] Don't hide from your servant;
answer me quickly, for I am in deep trouble!

69:18
Pss 49:15; 119:134

[18] Come and rescue me;
free me from all my enemies.

69:19
Ps 22:6-7
Isa 53:3

[19] You know the insults I endure—
the humiliation and disgrace.
You have seen all my enemies
and know what they have said.
[20] Their insults have broken my heart,
and I am in despair.
If only one person would show some pity;
if only one would turn and comfort me.

69:21
†Matt 27:48
†John 19:29

[21] But instead, they give me poison for food;
they offer me sour wine to satisfy my thirst.

[22] Let the bountiful table set before them become a snare,
and let their security become a trap.

69:23
†Rom 11:9-10

[23] Let their eyes go blind so they cannot see,
and let their bodies grow weaker and weaker.
[24] Pour out your fury on them;
consume them with your burning anger.

69:25
Matt 23:38
Luke 13:35
†Acts 1:20

[25] May their homes become desolate
and their tents be deserted.

69:26
2 Chr 28:9
Isa 53:4

[26] To those you have punished, they add insult to injury;
they scoff at the pain of those you have hurt.

69:28
Exod 32:32-33
Luke 10:20
Rev 3:5; 13:8; 20:15

[27] Pile their sins up high,
and don't let them go free.
[28] Erase their names from the Book of Life;
don't let them be counted among the righteous.

69:13 What problems David faced! He was scoffed at, mocked, insulted, humiliated, and made the object of citywide gossip. But still he prayed. When we are completely beaten down, we are tempted to turn from God, give up, and quit trusting him. When your situation seems hopeless, determine that no matter how bad things become you will continue to pray. God will hear your prayer, and he will rescue you. When others reject us, we need God most. Don't turn from your most faithful friend.

69:28 The "Book of Life" is God's list of those who are in right relationship to him and who remain faithful (1:3; 7:9; 11:7; 34:12; 37:17, 29; 55:22; 75:10; 92:12-14; 140:13). This term in the New Testament refers to those who will receive eternal life (see Philippians 4:3; Revelation 3:5; 13:8; 20:15).

29 I am suffering and in pain.
Rescue me, O God, by your saving power.

30 Then I will praise God's name with singing,
and I will honor him with thanksgiving.
31 For this will please the LORD more than sacrificing an ox
or presenting a bull with its horns and hooves.
32 The humble will see their God at work and be glad.
Let all who seek God's help live in joy.
33 For the LORD hears the cries of his needy ones;
he does not despise his people who are oppressed.

34 Praise him, O heaven and earth,
the seas and all that move in them.
35 For God will save Jerusalem*
and rebuild the towns of Judah.
His people will live there
and take possession of the land.
36 The descendants of those who obey him will inherit the land,
and those who love him will live there in safety.

69:30 Pss 28:7; 50:14-15
69:31 Ps 50:13-14
69:32 Pss 22:26; 34:2
69:34 Ps 148:1-13
69:35 Ps 147:2; Isa 44:26
69:36 Ps 25:13

Theme: An urgent prayer for help. It can be your prayer when you're short on time and long on need.
Author: David

70

For the choir director: A psalm of David, to bring us to the LORD's remembrance.

1 Please, God, rescue me!
Come quickly, LORD, and help me.
2 May those who try to destroy me
be humiliated and put to shame.
May those who take delight in my trouble
be turned back in disgrace.
3 Let them be horrified by their shame,
for they said, "Aha! We've got him now!"
4 But may all who search for you
be filled with joy and gladness.
May those who love your salvation
repeatedly shout, "God is great!"
5 But I am poor and needy;
please hurry to my aid, O God.
You are my helper and my savior;
O LORD, do not delay!

70:1-5 //Ps 40:13-17
70:2 Ps 35:4, 26

69:35 Hebrew *Zion.*

69:32 Most people want lasting joy and will try almost anything to obtain it, from scrambling for more money to being involved in sexual escapades. The only genuine source of happiness is God, and we receive lasting joy only by seeking him. How are you trying to find happiness? Seek God and live as he directs you (Matthew 6:33, 34), and true joy will soon follow.

70:1-5 When others disappoint and threaten us, we feel empty, as though a vital part of ourselves has been stolen. When others break the trust we have placed in them, they also break our spirits. At those empty, broken moments, we must join the psalmist in begging God to rush to our aid. He alone can fill our lives with his joy (70:4). With the psalmist we should cry out, "O LORD, do not delay!"

70:4 This short psalm (similar in content to 40:13-17) was David's plea for God to come quickly with his help. Yet even in his moment of panic, he did not forget praise. Praise is important because it helps us remember who God is. Often our prayers are filled with requests for ourselves and others, and we forget to thank God for what he has done and to worship him for who he is. Don't take God for granted and treat him as a vending machine. Even when David was afraid, he praised God.

Theme: God's constant help—from childhood to old age. Our lives are a testimony of what God has done for us.
Author: Anonymous

71:1 Pss 25:2-3; 31:1-3

71

1 O LORD, you are my refuge;
never let me be disgraced.

71:2 Pss 17:6; 31:1

2 Rescue me! Save me from my enemies, for you are just.
Turn your ear to listen and set me free.

71:3 Deut 33:27 Ps 18:2

3 Be to me a protecting rock of safety,
where I am always welcome.
Give the order to save me,
for you are my rock and my fortress.

4 My God, rescue me from the power of the wicked,
from the clutches of cruel oppressors.

71:5 Ps 22:9-11 Jer 17:7, 13, 17

5 O Lord, you alone are my hope.
I've trusted you, O LORD, from childhood.

71:6 Pss 22:9-10; 34:1 Isa 46:3

6 Yes, you have been with me from birth;
from my mother's womb you have cared for me.
No wonder I am always praising you!

71:7 Ps 61:3

7 My life is an example to many,
because you have been my strength and protection.
8 That is why I can never stop praising you;
I declare your glory all day long.

71:9 Ps 92:14

9 And now, in my old age, don't set me aside.
Don't abandon me when my strength is failing.

71:10 Matt 27:1

10 For my enemies are whispering against me.
They are plotting together to kill me.

71:11 Pss 3:2; 7:2

11 They say, "God has abandoned him.
Let's go and get him,
for there is no one to help him now."

71:12 Ps 22:9-11

12 O God, don't stay away.
My God, please hurry to help me.

71:13 Ps 35:4, 26

13 Bring disgrace and destruction on those who accuse me.
May humiliation and shame cover
those who want to harm me.

14 But I will keep on hoping for you to help me;
I will praise you more and more.

71:15 Pss 35:28; 40:5

15 I will tell everyone about your righteousness.
All day long I will proclaim your saving power,
for I am overwhelmed by how much you have done for me.

71:16 Pss 51:14; 106:2

16 I will praise your mighty deeds, O Sovereign LORD.
I will tell everyone that you alone are just and good.

17 O God, you have taught me from my earliest childhood,
and I have constantly told others about the wonderful things you do.

71:18 Pss 22:31; 78:4, 6

18 Now that I am old and gray,
do not abandon me, O God.

71:1ff The psalmist was old and saw his life as an "example," a solemn sign or testimony to others of all God had done for him (71:7, 18). Remembering our lifetime of blessings will help us to see the consistency of God's grace throughout the years, trust him for the future, and share with others the benefits of following him.

71:14 As we face the sunset years, we recognize that God has been our constant help in the past. As physical powers wane, we need God even more, and we realize he is still our constant help. We must never despair, but keep on expecting his help no matter how severe our limitations. Hope in him helps us to keep going, to keep serving him.

71:18 A person is never too old to serve God, never too old to pray. Though age may stop us from certain physical activities, it need not end our desire to tell others (especially children) about all we have seen God do in our many years of life.

Let me proclaim your power to this new generation,
 your mighty miracles to all who come after me.

19 Your righteousness, O God, reaches to the highest heavens.
 You have done such wonderful things.
 Who can compare with you, O God?
20 You have allowed me to suffer much hardship,
 but you will restore me to life again
 and lift me up from the depths of the earth.
21 You will restore me to even greater honor
 and comfort me once again.

22 Then I will praise you with music on the harp,
 because you are faithful to your promises, O God.
I will sing for you with a lyre,
 O Holy One of Israel.
23 I will shout for joy and sing your praises,
 for you have redeemed me.
24 I will tell about your righteous deeds
 all day long,
for everyone who tried to hurt me
 has been shamed and humiliated.

71:19 Deut 3:24; Pss 35:10; 57:10; Luke 1:49
71:20 Pss 23:4; 60:3; 119:25; Hos 6:2
71:22 Pss 33:2; 89:18; 147:7
71:23 Pss 5:11; 103:4
71:24 Pss 35:28; 71:13

Theme: The perfect king. In this psalm, a king asks God to help his son rule the nation justly and wisely. It looks forward to the endless reign of the Messiah, who alone can rule with perfect justice and whose citizens will enjoy perfect peace.
Author: Solomon

72

A psalm of Solomon.

1 Give justice to the king, O God,
 and righteousness to the king's son.
2 Help him judge your people in the right way;
 let the poor always be treated fairly.
3 May the mountains yield prosperity for all,
 and may the hills be fruitful,
 because the king does what is right.
4 Help him to defend the poor,
 to rescue the children of the needy,
 and to crush their oppressors.
5 May he live* as long as the sun shines,
 as long as the moon continues in the skies.
 Yes, forever!
6 May his reign be as refreshing as the springtime rains—
 like the showers that water the earth.
7 May all the godly flourish during his reign.
 May there be abundant prosperity until the end of time.
8 May he reign from sea to sea,
 and from the Euphrates River* to the ends of the earth.
9 Desert nomads will bow before him;
 his enemies will fall before him in the dust.
10 The western kings of Tarshish and the islands
 will bring him tribute.
The eastern kings of Sheba and Seba
 will bring him gifts.

72:1 1 Kgs 3:9; Ps 24:5
72:2 Ps 82:3; Isa 9:7; 11:2-5
72:3 Isa 9:5-6; Mic 4:3-4; Zech 9:10
72:4 Isa 11:4
72:5 Ps 89:36-37
72:6 Deut 32:2; Ps 65:10; Hos 6:3
72:7 Ps 92:12
72:8 Exod 23:31; Zech 9:10
72:9 Isa 49:23; Mic 7:17
72:10 Pss 45:12; 68:29; Isa 42:4, 10; 60:6

72:5 As in Greek version; Hebrew reads *May they fear you.* **72:8** Hebrew *the river.*

72:1, 2 What qualities do we want most in our leaders? God desires all who rule under him to be just and righteous. Think how the world would change if world leaders would commit themselves to these two qualities. Let us pray that they will (see 1 Timothy 2:1, 2).

72:11 Pss 86:9; 138:4 Isa 49:23

11 All kings will bow before him,
and all nations will serve him.

72:12 Job 29:12

12 He will rescue the poor when they cry to him;
he will help the oppressed, who have no one to defend them.
13 He feels pity for the weak and the needy,
and he will rescue them.

72:14 Ps 116:15

14 He will save them from oppression and from violence,
for their lives are precious to him.

72:15 Isa 60:6

15 Long live the king!
May the gold of Sheba be given to him.
May the people always pray for him
and bless him all day long.

72:16 Job 5:25 Ps 114:16

16 May there be abundant crops throughout the land,
flourishing even on the mountaintops.
May the fruit trees flourish as they do in Lebanon,
sprouting up like grass in a field.

72:17 Gen 12:3; 22:18 Ps 89:36

17 May the king's name endure forever;
may it continue as long as the sun shines.
May all nations be blessed through him
and bring him praise.

72:18 Exod 15:11 Pss 41:13; 77:14

18 Bless the LORD God, the God of Israel,
who alone does such wonderful things.

72:19 Num 14:20-21 Neh 9:5

19 Bless his glorious name forever!
Let the whole earth be filled with his glory.
Amen and amen!

20 (This ends the prayers of David son of Jesse.)

BOOK III
Psalms 73:1—89:52

These psalms celebrate the sovereignty of God, God's hand in history, God's faithfulness, and God's covenant with David. These psalms remind us that our worship of the almighty God should be continual.

Theme: The temporary prosperity of the wicked and the lasting rewards of the righteous. We should live holy lives and trust God for our future rewards.
Author: Asaph, a leader of one of the Temple choirs (see 1 Chronicles 25:1)

73

A psalm of Asaph.

73:1 Pss 24:3-4; 51:10 Matt 5:8

1 Truly God is good to Israel,
to those whose hearts are pure.

73:2 Ps 94:18

2 But as for me, I came so close to the edge of the cliff!
My feet were slipping, and I was almost gone.

72:12-14 God cares for the poor, oppressed, weak, and needy because they are precious to him. If God feels so strongly about these needy ones and loves them so deeply, how can we ignore their plight? Examine what you are doing to reach out with God's love. Are you ignoring their plight or are you meeting their needs?

72:17 Solomon, David's son, reigned in Israel's golden age. He built the magnificent Temple, and the land rested in peace. This psalm, though written by Solomon, looks beyond Solomon's reign to that of Jesus the Messiah, whose kingdom extends "to the ends of the earth" (72:8) and is greater than any human empire. This will be fulfilled when Christ returns to reign forever (Revelation 11:15). When we anticipate his worldwide rule, it fills our hearts with hope.

72:19, 20 Book 2 ends with "Amen and amen," as did Psalm 41, which closed Book 1. This last verse does not mean that David wrote this psalm but that he wrote most of the psalms in Book 2.

73:1ff Asaph was the leader of one of David's levitical choirs. He collected Psalms 73–83 but may not have written all of them. In this psalm, Asaph explains that until he entered God's sanctuary, he could not understand the justice in allowing the wicked to thrive while the righteous endured hardship. But when he saw that one day justice would be done, he acknowledged God's wisdom.

73:1-20 Two strong themes wind their way through these verses: (1) The wicked prosper, leaving godly people wondering why they bother to be good, and (2) the wealth of the wicked

3 For I envied the proud
when I saw them prosper despite their wickedness.
4 They seem to live such a painless life;
their bodies are so healthy and strong.
5 They aren't troubled like other people
or plagued with problems like everyone else.
6 They wear pride like a jeweled necklace,
and their clothing is woven of cruelty.
7 These fat cats have everything
their hearts could ever wish for!
8 They scoff and speak only evil;
in their pride they seek to crush others.
9 They boast against the very heavens,
and their words strut throughout the earth.
10 And so the people are dismayed and confused,
drinking in all their words.
11 "Does God realize what is going on?" they ask.
"Is the Most High even aware of what is happening?"
12 Look at these arrogant people—
enjoying a life of ease while their riches multiply.

13 Was it for nothing that I kept my heart pure
and kept myself from doing wrong?
14 All I get is trouble all day long;
every morning brings me pain.

15 If I had really spoken this way,
I would have been a traitor to your people.
16 So I tried to understand why the wicked prosper.
But what a difficult task it is!
17 Then one day I went into your sanctuary, O God,
and I thought about the destiny of the wicked.
18 Truly, you put them on a slippery path
and send them sliding over the cliff to destruction.
19 In an instant they are destroyed,
swept away by terrors.
20 Their present life is only a dream
that is gone when they awake.
When you arise, O Lord,
you will make them vanish from this life.

21 Then I realized how bitter I had become,
how pained I had been by all I had seen.
22 I was so foolish and ignorant—
I must have seemed like a senseless animal to you.
23 Yet I still belong to you;
you are holding my right hand.

73:3 Ps 37:1, 7; Jer 12:1
73:5 Job 21:9-10
73:6 Ps 109:18
73:7 Job 15:27-28; Ps 17:10
73:8 Pss 1:1; 17:10; Jude 1:16
73:11 Job 22:13
73:12 Ps 49:6; Jer 49:31; Ezek 23:42
73:13 Job 21:15; 34:9; Ps 26:6
73:14 Pss 38:5-6; 118:18
73:16 Eccl 8:16-17
73:17 Pss 27:4; 77:13
73:19 Num 16:21; Isa 47:11
73:22 Eccl 3:18

looks so inviting that faithful people may wish they could trade places. But these two themes come to unexpected ends, for the wealth of the wicked suddenly loses its power at death, and the rewards for the godly suddenly take on eternal value. What seemed like wealth is now waste, and what seemed worthless now lasts forever. Don't wish you could trade places with evil people to get their wealth. One day they will wish they could trade places with you and have your eternal wealth.

73:20 Asaph realized that the rich who put their hope, joy, and confidence in their wealth live in a dreamworld. A dream exists only in the mind of the dreamer. Don't let your life's goals be so unreal that you awaken too late and miss the reality of God's truth. Happiness and hope can be a reality, but only when they are based on God, not on riches. Because reality is in God, we should get as close to him as we can in order to be realistic about life.

73:23, 24 Asaph declares his confidence in God's presence and guidance. From birth to death, we are continually in God's grip. But far more, we have the hope of the resurrection. Though our courage and strength may fail, we know that one day we will be raised to life to serve him forever. He is our security, and we must cling to him.

73:24 Pss 32:8; 48:14

24 You will keep on guiding me with your counsel,
leading me to a glorious destiny.
25 Whom have I in heaven but you?
I desire you more than anything on earth.

73:26 Pss 16:5; 38:10

26 My health may fail, and my spirit may grow weak,
but God remains the strength of my heart;
he is mine forever.

73:27 Exod 34:15 Ps 37:20

27 But those who desert him will perish,
for you destroy those who abandon you.

73:28 Pss 40:5; 71:7 Heb 10:22

28 But as for me, how good it is to be near God!
I have made the Sovereign LORD my shelter,
and I will tell everyone about the wonderful things you do.

Theme: A plea for God to help his people defend his cause and remember his promises. When we feel devastated or forgotten, we can ask God for help, knowing that he hears.
Author: Asaph (or one of his descendants, since many believe this to have been written after Jerusalem's fall in 586 B.C.)

74

A psalm of Asaph.

74:1 Deut 29:20 Pss 44:9; 89:46

1 O God, why have you rejected us forever?
Why is your anger so intense against the sheep of your own pasture?

74:2 Deut 32:6, 9 Ps 68:16

2 Remember that we are the people you chose in ancient times,
the tribe you redeemed as your own special possession!
And remember Jerusalem,* your home here on earth.

74:3 Ps 79:1 Isa 61:4

3 Walk through the awful ruins of the city;
see how the enemy has destroyed your sanctuary.
4 There your enemies shouted their victorious battle cries;
there they set up their battle standards.

74:5 Jer 46:22

5 They chopped down the entrance
like woodcutters in a forest.
6 With axes and picks,
they smashed the carved paneling.

74:7 2 Kgs 25:9

7 They set the sanctuary on fire, burning it to the ground.
They utterly defiled the place that bears your holy name.

74:8 Ps 83:4

8 Then they thought, "Let's destroy everything!"
So they burned down all the places where God was worshiped.

74:9 Lev 24:16 Ps 78:43

9 We see no miraculous signs
as evidence that you will save us.
All the prophets are gone;
no one can tell us when it will end.

74:10 Ps 44:16

10 How long, O God, will you allow our enemies to mock you?
Will you let them dishonor your name forever?

74:11 Ps 59:13

11 Why do you hold back your strong right hand?
Unleash your powerful fist and deliver a deathblow.

74:2 Hebrew *Mount Zion.*

74:1, 2 God's anger against Israel had grown hot during the many years of their sin and idolatry. His patience endured for generations, but at last it was set aside for judgment. If you fall into sin but quickly seek God's forgiveness, his mercy may come quickly and his anger may leave quickly. If you persist in sinning against him, don't be surprised when his patience runs out.

74:8 When enemy armies defeated Israel, they sacked and burned Jerusalem, trying to wipe out every trace of God. This has often been the response of people who hate God. Today many are trying to eliminate God from our society and particularly from our schools. Do what you can to maintain a Christian influence, but don't become discouraged when others appear to make great strides in removing all traces of God. They cannot eliminate his presence among believers.

74:10-18 From our perspective, God sometimes seems slow to intervene on our behalf. But what might appear slow to us is good timing from God's perspective. It's easy to become impatient while waiting for God to act, but we must never give up on him. When God is silent and you are in deep anguish, follow the method in this psalm. Review the great acts of God throughout biblical history; then review what he has done for you. This will remind you that God is at work, not only in history, but also in your life today.

12 You, O God, are my king from ages past,
bringing salvation to the earth.
13 You split the sea by your strength
and smashed the sea monster's heads.
14 You crushed the heads of Leviathan
and let the desert animals eat him.
15 You caused the springs and streams to gush forth,
and you dried up rivers that never run dry.
16 Both day and night belong to you;
you made the starlight* and the sun.
17 You set the boundaries of the earth,
and you make both summer and winter.

18 See how these enemies scoff at you, LORD.
A foolish nation has dishonored your name.
19 Don't let these wild beasts destroy your doves.
Don't forget your afflicted people forever.

20 Remember your covenant promises,
for the land is full of darkness and violence!
21 Don't let the downtrodden be constantly disgraced!
Instead, let these poor and needy ones give praise to your name.

22 Arise, O God, and defend your cause.
Remember how these fools insult you all day long.
23 Don't overlook these things your enemies have said.
Their uproar of rebellion grows ever louder.

74:12 Ps 44:4
74:13 Exod 14:21
74:15 Exod 14:21-22; 17:5-6
74:16 Gen 1:14-18 Ps 136:7-8
74:17 Gen 8:22 Acts 17:26
74:18 Deut 32:6 Pss 39:8; 74:10
74:20 Gen 17:7 Ps 106:45
74:21 Ps 35:10 Isa 41:17
74:22 Ps 43:1
74:23 Ps 65:7

Theme: Because God is the final judge, the tables will be turned upon the wicked. When arrogant people threaten our security, we can be confident that God will ultimately overrule and destroy them.
Author: Asaph

75 *For the choir director: A psalm of Asaph, to be sung to the tune "Do Not Destroy!" A song.*

1 We thank you, O God!
We give thanks because you are near.
People everywhere tell of your mighty miracles.

2 God says, "At the time I have planned,
I will bring justice against the wicked.
3 When the earth quakes and its people live in turmoil,
I am the one who keeps its foundations firm. *Interlude*

4 "I warned the proud, 'Stop your boasting!'
I told the wicked, 'Don't raise your fists!
5 Don't lift your fists in defiance at the heavens
or speak with rebellious arrogance.'"

6 For no one on earth—from east or west,
or even from the wilderness—
can raise another person up.

75:1 Pss 44:1; 71:17
75:3 1 Sam 2:8 Ps 46:6
75:5 Ps 94:4

74:16 Or *moon;* Hebrew reads *light.*

74:13, 14 "The sea monster" recalls the Lord's words to Egypt (Ezekiel 32:2ff). "Leviathan" refers to the Canaanite seven-headed serpent, Lotan. In their legends, Baal defeated these creatures. This psalm praised God for doing in reality what the Canaanite gods could only do in legends.

75:2 God will act when he is ready. Children have difficulty grasping the concept of time. "It's not time yet" is not a reason they easily understand because they only comprehend the present. As limited human beings, we can't understand God's perspective about time. We want everything now, unaware that God's timing is better. When God is ready, he will do what needs to be done, not what we would like him to do. We may be as impatient as children, but we must not doubt the wisdom of God's timing. Wait for God to reveal his plan. Don't take matters into your own hands.

75:7 1 Sam 2:7
7 It is God alone who judges;
he decides who will rise and who will fall.
75:8 Ps 11:6
8 For the LORD holds a cup in his hand;
it is full of foaming wine mixed with spices.
He pours the wine out in judgment,
and all the wicked must drink it,
draining it to the dregs.

75:9 Ps 40:10
9 But as for me, I will always proclaim what God has done;
I will sing praises to the God of Israel.*

75:10 Pss 89:17; 148:14
10 For God says, "I will cut off the strength of the wicked,
but I will increase the power of the godly."

Theme: A call for God to punish evildoers. Even people's angry revolts will be used by God to bring glory to himself.
Author: Asaph

76 *For the choir director: A psalm of Asaph, to be accompanied by stringed instruments. A song.*

1 God is well known in Judah;
his name is great in Israel.
76:2 Pss 48:2-3; 132:13; 135:21
2 Jerusalem* is where he lives;
Mount Zion is his home.
76:3 Ps 46:9
3 There he breaks the arrows of the enemy,
the shields and swords and weapons of his foes. *Interlude*

4 You are glorious and more majestic
than the everlasting mountains.*
76:5 Isa 10:12
5 The mightiest of our enemies have been plundered.
They lie before us in the sleep of death.
No warrior could lift a hand against us.
76:6 Exod 15:1, 21 Ps 78:53
6 When you rebuked them, O God of Jacob,
their horses and chariots stood still.

76:7 Ps 89:7 Nah 1:6 Rev 6:17
7 No wonder you are greatly feared!
Who can stand before you when your anger explodes?
76:8 1 Chr 16:30
8 From heaven you sentenced your enemies;
the earth trembled and stood silent before you.
76:9 Pss 9:7-9; 72:4
9 You stand up to judge those who do evil, O God,
and to rescue the oppressed of the earth. *Interlude*

76:10 Exod 9:16 Rom 9:17
10 Human opposition only enhances your glory,
for you use it as a sword of judgment.*

11 Make vows to the LORD your God, and fulfill them.
Let everyone bring tribute to the Awesome One.
12 For he breaks the spirit of princes
and is feared by the kings of the earth.

75:9 Hebrew *of Jacob.* **76:2** Hebrew *Salem,* another name for Jerusalem. **76:4** As in Greek version; Hebrew reads *than mountains filled with beasts of prey.* **76:10** The meaning of the Hebrew is uncertain.

75:8 The cup of wine represents God's judgment that is coming against the wicked. God will pour out his fury on his enemies, and they will be forced to drink it. Drinking the cup of God's judgment is a picture used frequently in Scripture (Isaiah 51:17, 22; Jeremiah 25:15; 49:12; Habakkuk 2:16; Revelation 14:10; 16:19; 18:6). It gives the impression of taking a dose of one's own medicine. To drink it down "to the dregs" means to be punished completely.

76:1ff This psalm praises God for his awesome power. It was most likely written to celebrate the defeat of Sennacherib's army after he invaded Judah (see 2 Kings 18:13-19, 37).

76:10 How can wrath bring praise to God? Hostility to God and his people gives God the opportunity to do great deeds. For example, the pharaoh of Egypt refused to free the Hebrew slaves (Exodus 5:1, 2) and thus allowed God to work mighty miracles for his people (Exodus 11:9). God turns the tables on evildoers and brings glory to himself from the foolishness of those who deny him or revolt against him. God's wrath expressed in judgment brings praise from those who have been delivered.

Theme: We are comforted through the hard times by remembering God's help in the past. Recalling God's miracles and previous works can give us courage to continue.
Author: Asaph

77

For Jeduthun, the choir director: A psalm of Asaph.

1 I cry out to God without holding back.
Oh, that God would listen to me!
2 When I was in deep trouble,
I searched for the Lord.
All night long I pray, with hands lifted toward heaven, pleading.
There can be no joy for me until he acts.
3 I think of God, and I moan,
overwhelmed with longing for his help. *Interlude*

4 You don't let me sleep.
I am too distressed even to pray!
5 I think of the good old days, long since ended,
6 when my nights were filled with joyful songs.
I search my soul and think about the difference now.
7 Has the Lord rejected me forever?
Will he never again show me favor?
8 Is his unfailing love gone forever?
Have his promises permanently failed?
9 Has God forgotten to be kind?
Has he slammed the door on his compassion? *Interlude*

10 And I said, "This is my fate,
that the blessings of the Most High have changed to hatred."
11 I recall all you have done, O LORD;
I remember your wonderful deeds of long ago.
12 They are constantly in my thoughts.
I cannot stop thinking about them.

13 O God, your ways are holy.
Is there any god as mighty as you?
14 You are the God of miracles and wonders!
You demonstrate your awesome power among the nations.
15 You have redeemed your people by your strength,
the descendants of Jacob and of Joseph by your might. *Interlude*

16 When the Red Sea* saw you, O God,
its waters looked and trembled!
The sea quaked to its very depths.
17 The clouds poured down their rain;
the thunder rolled and crackled in the sky.
Your arrows of lightning flashed.
18 Your thunder roared from the whirlwind;
the lightning lit up the world!
The earth trembled and shook.

77:2 Job 11:13; Pss 50:15; 88:9; Isa 26:9, 16
77:3 Pss 43:5; 61:2; 142:2-3
77:5 Ps 143:5
77:6 Pss 4:4; 42:8
77:8 Ps 89:49
77:9 Ps 25:6
77:10 Ps 31:22
77:11 Exod 15:11; Ps 86:8
77:13 Exod 15:11; Pss 73:17; 86:8
77:15 Exod 6:6; Deut 9:29
77:16 Exod 14:21
77:17 Ps 68:33
77:18 Judg 5:4

77:16 Hebrew *the waters.*

77:1-12 Asaph cried out to God for courage during a time of deep distress. The source of Asaph's distress (77:4) was his doubt (77:7-9). He said, "I cry out to God." But in 77:13-20, the *I* is gone. As Asaph expressed his requests to God, his focus changed from thinking of himself to worshiping God: "You are the God of miracles and wonders!" (77:14). Only after he put aside his doubts about God's holiness and care for him (77:13, 14) did he eliminate his distress (77:20). As we pray to God, he shifts our focus from ourselves to him.

77:11, 12 Memories of God's miracles and faithfulness sustained Israel through their difficulties. They knew that God was capable and trustworthy. When you meet new trials, review how good God has been to you, and this will strengthen your faith.

77:16 This statement refers to the miraculous parting of the Red Sea. This great event is mentioned many times in the Old Testament (Exodus 14:21, 22; Joshua 24:6; Nehemiah 9:9; Psalm 74:13; 106:9; 136:13-15). The story of this incredible miracle was handed down from generation to generation, reminding the Israelites of God's power, protection, and love.

77:19 Hab 3:15

77:20 Exod 6:26; 13:21 Ps 78:52 Isa 63:11-13

19 Your road led through the sea,
your pathway through the mighty waters—
a pathway no one knew was there!
20 You led your people along that road like a flock of sheep,
with Moses and Aaron as their shepherds.

Theme: Lessons from history. Asaph retells the history of the Jewish nation from the time of slavery in Egypt to David's reign. It was told over and over to each generation so they would not forget God and make the same mistakes as their ancestors.
Author: Asaph

78

A psalm of Asaph.

78:2 †Matt 13:34-35

78:3 Ps 44:1

78:4 Deut 11:19 Ps 22:30

78:5 Deut 6:4-9

78:6 Deut 11:19 Ps 102:18

78:7 Deut 4:2, 9 Josh 22:5

78:8 Exod 32:9 Ezek 20:18

1 O my people, listen to my teaching.
Open your ears to what I am saying,
2 for I will speak to you in a parable.
I will teach you hidden lessons from our past—
3 stories we have heard and know,
stories our ancestors handed down to us.
4 We will not hide these truths from our children
but will tell the next generation about the glorious deeds of the LORD.
We will tell of his power and the mighty miracles he did.
5 For he issued his decree to Jacob;
he gave his law to Israel.
He commanded our ancestors
to teach them to their children,
6 so the next generation might know them—
even the children not yet born—
that they in turn might teach their children.
7 So each generation can set its hope anew on God,
remembering his glorious miracles
and obeying his commands.
8 Then they will not be like their ancestors—
stubborn, rebellious, and unfaithful,
refusing to give their hearts to God.

78:10 2 Kgs 18:12

78:11 Ps 106:13

78:12 Exod 7:12 Num 13:22 Isa 19:11

78:13 Exod 14:21; 15:18

9 The warriors of Ephraim, though fully armed,
turned their backs and fled when the day of battle came.
10 They did not keep God's covenant,
and they refused to live by his law.
11 They forgot what he had done—
the wonderful miracles he had shown them,
12 the miracles he did for their ancestors in Egypt, on the plain of Zoan.
13 For he divided the sea before them and led them through!
The water stood up like walls beside them!

78:1ff The people of Israel rebelled and were not faithful to God (78:8). They forgot about the miracles God had done (78:11, 12) and put God to the test by making demands of him (78:18). They lied to him, tried to flatter him (78:36), and continued to turn away from him even after he did great works on their behalf (78:42-56). This is recorded in God's Word so that we can avoid the same errors. In 1 Corinthians 10:5-12, Paul used this classic story of Israel's unfaithfulness to warn the early Christians to be faithful.

78:5 God commanded that the stories of his mighty acts in Israel's history and his laws be passed on from parents to children. This shows the purpose and importance of religious education: To help each generation obey God and set its hope on him. It is important to keep children from repeating the same mistakes as their ancestors. What are you doing to pass on the history of God's work to the next generation?

78:9, 10 Ephraim was the most prominent tribe of Israel from the days of Moses to Saul's time. The Tabernacle was set up in its territory. There is no other biblical record of Ephraim's soldiers turning back from battle, so this is probably a metaphor referring to Ephraim's failure to provide strong leadership during those years. When David became king, the tribe of Judah gained prominence. Because of David's faith and obedience, God chose Jerusalem in Judah to be the place for the new Temple and rejected Ephraim (78:67). This caused tension between the two tribes. This psalm may have been written because of that tension in order to demonstrate once again why God chose Judah. God works through those who are faithful to him.

14 In the daytime he led them by a cloud,
and at night by a pillar of fire.
15 He split open the rocks in the wilderness
to give them plenty of water, as from a gushing spring.
16 He made streams pour from the rock,
making the waters flow down like a river!

17 Yet they kept on with their sin,
rebelling against the Most High in the desert.
18 They willfully tested God in their hearts,
demanding the foods they craved.
19 They even spoke against God himself, saying,
"God can't give us food in the desert.
20 Yes, he can strike a rock so water gushes out,
but he can't give his people bread and meat."
21 When the LORD heard them, he was angry.
The fire of his wrath burned against Jacob.
Yes, his anger rose against Israel,
22 for they did not believe God
or trust him to care for them.
23 But he commanded the skies to open—
he opened the doors of heaven—
24 and rained down manna for them to eat.
He gave them bread from heaven.
25 They ate the food of angels!
God gave them all they could hold.
26 He released the east wind in the heavens
and guided the south wind by his mighty power.
27 He rained down meat as thick as dust—
birds as plentiful as the sands along the seashore!
28 He caused the birds to fall within their camp
and all around their tents.
29 The people ate their fill.
He gave them what they wanted.
30 But before they finished eating this food they had craved,
while the meat was yet in their mouths,
31 the anger of God rose against them,
and he killed their strongest men;
he struck down the finest of Israel's young men.
32 But in spite of this, the people kept on sinning.
They refused to believe in his miracles.
33 So he ended their lives in failure
and gave them years of terror.
34 When God killed some of them, the rest finally sought him.
They repented and turned to God.
35 Then they remembered that God was their rock,
that their redeemer was the Most High.
36 But they followed him only with their words;
they lied to him with their tongues.
37 Their hearts were not loyal to him.
They did not keep his covenant.
38 Yet he was merciful and forgave their sins
and didn't destroy them all.

78:14 Exod 13:21
78:15 Exod 17:5-6; †1 Cor 10:4
78:16 Num 20:8, 10-11
78:17 Heb 3:16
78:18 Num 11:4-5; †1 Cor 10:9-10
78:19 Exod 16:3; Num 21:5
78:20 Num 20:11
78:21 Num 11:1
78:22-23 Heb 3:18
78:23 Mal 3:10
78:24 Exod 16:4; †John 6:30-31
78:26 Num 11:31
78:27 Exod 16:13; Ps 105:40
78:29 Num 11:19-20
78:31 Num 11:33-34
78:32 Num 14:10-11
78:33 Num 14:29, 34-35
78:34 Hos 5:15
78:35 Deut 9:26; 32:4
78:36 Exod 32:7-8; Ezek 33:31
78:38 Exod 34:5-6; Num 14:18-20

78:36, 37 Over and over the children of Israel claimed that they would follow God, but then they turned away from him. The problem was that they followed God with words and not with their hearts; thus, their repentance was empty. Talk is cheap. God wants our conduct to back up our spiritual claims and promises.

Many a time he held back his anger
and did not unleash his fury!

78:39 Job 7:7, 16; Jas 4:14

39 For he remembered that they were merely mortal,
gone in a moment like a breath of wind, never to return.

40 Oh, how often they rebelled against him in the desert
and grieved his heart in the wilderness.

78:41 2 Kgs 19:22

41 Again and again they tested God's patience
and frustrated the Holy One of Israel.

78:42 Judg 8:34

42 They forgot about his power
and how he rescued them from their enemies.

78:43 Exod 7:3

43 They forgot his miraculous signs in Egypt,
his wonders on the plain of Zoan.

78:44 Exod 7:20; Ps 105:29

44 For he turned their rivers into blood,
so no one could drink from the streams.

78:45 Exod 8:6, 24; Ps 105:30-31

45 He sent vast swarms of flies to consume them
and hordes of frogs to ruin them.

78:46 Exod 10:14

46 He gave their crops to caterpillars;
their harvest was consumed by locusts.

78:47 Exod 9:23-25; Ps 105:32

47 He destroyed their grapevines with hail
and shattered their sycamores with sleet.

78:48 Exod 9:19

48 He abandoned their cattle to the hail,
their livestock to bolts of lightning.

78:49 Exod 15:7

49 He loosed on them his fierce anger—
all his fury, rage, and hostility.
He dispatched against them
a band of destroying angels.

50 He turned his anger against them;
he did not spare the Egyptians' lives
but handed them over to the plague.

78:51 Exod 12:29-30; Ps 105:36

51 He killed the oldest son in each Egyptian family,
the flower of youth throughout the land of Egypt.*

78:52 Ps 77:20

52 But he led his own people like a flock of sheep,
guiding them safely through the wilderness.

78:53 Exod 14:19-20, 27-28

53 He kept them safe so they were not afraid;
but the sea closed in upon their enemies.

78:54 Exod 15:17

54 He brought them to the border of his holy land,
to this land of hills he had won for them.

78:55 Josh 23:4-5; Pss 44:1-2; 105:10-11

55 He drove out the nations before them;
he gave them their inheritance by lot.
He settled the tribes of Israel into their homes.

56 Yet though he did all this for them,
they continued to test his patience.
They rebelled against the Most High
and refused to follow his decrees.

57 They turned back and were as faithless as their parents had been.
They were as useless as a crooked bow.

78:58 Lev 26:1; Deut 32:16, 21

58 They made God angry by building altars to other gods;
they made him jealous with their idols.

78:59 Lev 26:30; Deut 32:19

59 When God heard them, he was very angry,
and he rejected Israel completely.

78:60 1 Sam 4:11

60 Then he abandoned his dwelling at Shiloh,
the Tabernacle where he had lived among the people.

78:61 1 Sam 4:17

61 He allowed the Ark of his might to be captured;
he surrendered his glory into enemy hands.

78:51 Hebrew *in the tents of Ham.*

62 He gave his people over to be butchered by the sword,
because he was so angry with his own people—his special possession.
63 Their young men were killed by fire;
their young women died before singing their wedding songs.
64 Their priests were slaughtered,
and their widows could not mourn their deaths.
65 Then the Lord rose up as though waking from sleep,
like a mighty man aroused from a drunken stupor.
66 He routed his enemies
and sent them to eternal shame.
67 But he rejected Joseph's descendants;
he did not choose the tribe of Ephraim.
68 He chose instead the tribe of Judah,
Mount Zion, which he loved.
69 There he built his towering sanctuary,
as solid and enduring as the earth itself.
70 He chose his servant David,
calling him from the sheep pens.
71 He took David from tending the ewes and lambs
and made him the shepherd of Jacob's descendants—
God's own people, Israel.
72 He cared for them with a true heart
and led them with skillful hands.

78:62 Judg 20:21 1 Sam 4:10
78:63 Num 11:1 Jer 7:34; 16:9
78:64 1 Sam 22:18
78:65 Isa 42:13
78:66 1 Sam 5:6
78:68 Ps 87:1-2
78:69 1 Kgs 6:1-38
78:70 1 Sam 16:10-12
78:71 2 Sam 5:2; 7:8 1 Chr 11:2
78:72 1 Kgs 9:4

Theme: When outraged by injustice, cry out to God, not against him. In times of disaster, our mood may be anger, but our trust must remain in God.
Author: Asaph (or one of his descendants), probably written after the Babylonians had leveled Jerusalem (see 2 Kings 25)

79

A psalm of Asaph.

1 O God, pagan nations have conquered your land, your special possession.
They have defiled your holy Temple
and made Jerusalem a heap of ruins.
2 They have left the bodies of your servants
as food for the birds of heaven.
The flesh of your godly ones
has become food for the wild animals.
3 Blood has flowed like water all around Jerusalem;
no one is left to bury the dead.
4 We are mocked by our neighbors,
an object of scorn and derision to those around us.

5 O LORD, how long will you be angry with us? Forever?
How long will your jealousy burn like fire?
6 Pour out your wrath on the nations that refuse to recognize you—
on kingdoms that do not call upon your name.

79:1 Ps 74:2-7 Jer 26:18 Lam 1:10
79:2 Deut 28:26 Jer 7:33; 16:4
79:3 Jer 14:16
79:4 Ps 44:13
79:5 Ps 74:1, 9-10 Zeph 3:8
79:6 Jer 10:25 2 Thes 1:8

78:71, 72 Although David had been on the throne when this psalm was written, he is called a shepherd and not a king. Shepherding, a common profession in biblical times, was a highly responsible job. The flocks were completely dependent upon shepherds for guidance, provision, and protection. David had spent his early years as a shepherd (1 Samuel 16:10, 11). This was a training ground for the future responsibilities God had in store for him. When he was ready, God took him from caring for sheep to caring for Israel, God's people. Don't treat your present situation lightly or irresponsibly; it may be God's training ground for your future.

79:6 According to the Old Testament, God's wrath and judgment often fell on entire nations because of the sins of people within those nations. Here Asaph pled for judgment on kingdoms that refused to acknowledge God's authority. Ironically, Asaph's own nation of Judah was being judged by God for refusing to do this very thing (2 Chronicles 36:14-20). These were people who had sworn allegiance to God but were now rejecting him. This made their judgment even worse.

79:7 Ps 53:4

7 For they have devoured your people Israel,*
making the land a desolate wilderness.

79:8 Pss 106:6; 142:6 Isa 26:5; 64:9

8 Oh, do not hold us guilty for our former sins!
Let your tenderhearted mercies quickly meet our needs,
for we are brought low to the dust.

79:9 2 Chr 14:11 Jer 14:7

9 Help us, O God of our salvation!
Help us for the honor of your name.
Oh, save us and forgive our sins
for the sake of your name.

79:10 Ps 115:2

10 Why should pagan nations be allowed to scoff,
asking, "Where is their God?"
Show us your vengeance against the nations,
for they have spilled the blood of your servants.
11 Listen to the moaning of the prisoners.
Demonstrate your great power by saving those condemned to die.

79:12 Gen 4:15 Ps 74:10, 18, 22

12 O Lord, take sevenfold vengeance on our neighbors
for the scorn they have hurled at you.

79:13 Pss 74:1; 95:7; 100:3 Isa 43:21

13 Then we your people, the sheep of your pasture,
will thank you forever and ever,
praising your greatness from generation to generation.

79:7 Hebrew *Jacob.*

PRAYER IN THE BOOK OF PSALMS

Prayer is human communication with God. Psalms could be described as a collection of song-prayers. Probably the most striking feature of these prayers is their unedited honesty. The words often express our own feelings—feelings that we would prefer no one, much less God, ever knew. Making these psalms our prayers can teach us a great deal about how God wants us to communicate with him. Too often we give God a watered-down version of our feelings, hoping we won't offend him or make him curious about our motives. As we use the psalms to express our feelings, we learn that honesty, openness, and sincerity are valuable to God.

Following are several types of prayers with examples from Psalms. Note that the psalm writers communicated with God in a variety of ways for a variety of reasons. Each of us is invited to communicate with God. Using the psalms will enrich your personal prayer life.

Prayers of:	*Psalms:*
Praise to God	100; 113; 117
Thanksgiving by a community	67; 75; 136
Thanksgiving by an individual	18; 30; 32
Request by the community	79; 80; 123
Request by an individual	3; 55; 86
Sorrow by the community	44; 74; 137
Sorrow by an individual	5; 6; 120
Anger	35; 109; 140
Confession	6; 32; 51
Faith	11; 16; 23

79:10 In the end, God's glory will be evident to all people, but in the meantime, we must endure suffering with patience and allow God to strengthen our character through it. For reasons that we do not know, God sometimes allows pagan people to scoff at believers. We should be prepared for criticism, jokes, and unkind remarks because God does not place us beyond the attacks of scoffers.

Theme: A prayer for revival and restoration after experiencing destruction. God is our only hope for salvation.
Author: Asaph (or one of his descendants), probably written after the northern kingdom of Israel was defeated and its people deported to Assyria

80

For the choir director: A psalm of Asaph, to be sung to the tune "Lilies of the Covenant."

1 Please listen, O Shepherd of Israel,
you who lead Israel* like a flock.
O God, enthroned above the cherubim,
display your radiant glory
2 to Ephraim, Benjamin, and Manasseh.
Show us your mighty power.
Come to rescue us!

3 Turn us again to yourself, O God.
Make your face shine down upon us.
Only then will we be saved.

4 O LORD God Almighty,
how long will you be angry and reject our prayers?
5 You have fed us with sorrow
and made us drink tears by the bucketful.
6 You have made us the scorn of neighboring nations.
Our enemies treat us as a joke.

7 Turn us again to yourself, O God Almighty.
Make your face shine down upon us.
Only then will we be saved.
8 You brought us from Egypt as though we were a tender vine;
you drove away the pagan nations and transplanted us into your land.
9 You cleared the ground for us,
and we took root and filled the land.
10 The mountains were covered with our shade;
the mighty cedars were covered with our branches.
11 We spread our branches west to the Mediterranean Sea,
our limbs east to the Euphrates River.*
12 But now, why have you broken down our walls
so that all who pass may steal our fruit?
13 The boar from the forest devours us,
and the wild animals feed on us.

14 Come back, we beg you, O God Almighty.
Look down from heaven and see our plight.
Watch over and care for this vine
15 that you yourself have planted,
this son you have raised for yourself.
16 For we are chopped up and burned by our enemies.
May they perish at the sight of your frown.
17 Strengthen the man you love,
the son of your choice.

80:1 Hebrew *Joseph.* **80:11** Hebrew *west to the sea, . . . east to the river.*

80:1 Exod 25:22; Pss 23:1; 77:20
80:2 Ps 35:23
80:3 Num 6:24-26; Pss 31:16; 60:1; Lam 5:21
80:4 Pss 79:5; 84:8
80:5 Pss 42:3; 102:9
80:6 Pss 44:13; 79:4
80:8 2 Chr 20:7; Ps 44:2; Isa 5:2, 7; Jer 2:21; 11:17; Ezek 17:6, 23; Amos 9:15
80:9 Exod 23:28; Isa 5:2; Hos 14:5
80:11 Ps 72:8
80:12 Ps 89:40; Isa 5:5
80:13 Jer 5:6
80:16 2 Chr 36:19; Pss 39:11; 76:6; Jer 52:13
80:17 Ps 89:21

80:1 Cherubim are mighty angels.

80:3, 7, 19 Three times the writer calls on God to "turn us again to yourself." Before God can turn us to himself, we must turn away from sin. Repentance involves humbling ourselves and turning to God to receive his forgiveness. As we turn to God, he helps us see ourselves, including our sin, more clearly. Then, as we see our sin, we must repeat the process of repentance. Only then can we constantly be restored to fellowship with God.

80:17 "The son of your choice" is probably not the Messiah but Israel, whom God calls elsewhere his "firstborn son" (Exodus 4:22). The psalmist is making a plea that God would restore his mercy to Israel, the people he chose to bring his message into the world.

80:18 Ps 71:20 Isa 50:5

[18] Then we will never forsake you again.
Revive us so we can call on your name once more.

[19] Turn us again to yourself, O LORD God Almighty.
Make your face shine down upon us.
Only then will we be saved.

Theme: A holiday hymn. This hymn celebrates the Exodus from Egypt—God's goodness versus Israel's waywardness. God is our deliverer in spite of our wanderings.
Author: Asaph, probably written to be used during the Feasts of Shelters

81

*For the choir director: A psalm of Asaph, to be accompanied by a stringed instrument.**

81:1 Pss 46:1; 59:16; 66:1; 95:1-2
81:2 Pss 108:2; 144:9; 149:3
81:3 Lev 23:24 Num 10:10
81:5 Exod 11:4
81:6 Isa 9:4; 10:27
81:7 Exod 2:23; 17:5-7; 19:19 Pss 50:15; 95:8
81:8 Ps 50:7
81:9 Exod 20:3 Isa 43:12
81:10 Exod 20:2 Pss 78:25; 103:5
81:11 Exod 32:1
81:12 Acts 7:42 Rom 1:24, 26

[1] Sing praises to God, our strength.
Sing to the God of Israel.*
[2] Sing! Beat the tambourine.
Play the sweet lyre and the harp.
[3] Sound the trumpet for a sacred feast
when the moon is new,
when the moon is full.
[4] For this is required by the laws of Israel;
it is a law of the God of Jacob.
[5] He made it a decree for Israel*
when he attacked Egypt to set us free.

I heard an unknown voice that said,
[6] "Now I will relieve your shoulder of its burden;
I will free your hands from their heavy tasks.
[7] You cried to me in trouble, and I saved you;
I answered out of the thundercloud.
I tested your faith at Meribah,
when you complained that there was no water. *Interlude*

[8] "Listen to me, O my people, while I give you stern warnings.
O Israel, if you would only listen!
[9] You must never have a foreign god;
you must not bow down before a false god.
[10] For it was I, the LORD your God,
who rescued you from the land of Egypt.
Open your mouth wide, and I will fill it with good things.

[11] "But no, my people wouldn't listen.
Israel did not want me around.
[12] So I let them follow their blind and stubborn way,
living according to their own desires.

81:TITLE Hebrew *according to the gittith.* **81:1** Hebrew *of Jacob.* **81:5** Hebrew *for Joseph.*

81:1-5 Israel's holidays reminded the nation of God's great miracles. They were times of rejoicing and times to renew one's strength for life's daily struggles. At Christmas, do your thoughts revolve mostly around presents? Is Easter only a warm anticipation of spring and Thanksgiving only a good meal? Remember the spiritual origins of these special days, and use them as opportunities to worship God for his goodness to you, your family, and your nation.

81:2-4 David instituted music for the Temple worship services (1 Chronicles 25). Music and worship go hand in hand. Worship involves the whole person, and music helps lift a person's thoughts and emotions to God. Through music we can reflect upon our needs and shortcomings as well as celebrate God's greatness.

81:11, 12 God let the Israelites go on blindly, stubbornly, and selfishly, when they should have been obeying and following God's desires. God sometimes lets us continue in our stubbornness to bring us to our senses. He does not keep us from rebelling because he wants us to learn the consequences of sin. He uses these experiences to turn people away from greater sin to faith in him.

13 But oh, that my people would listen to me!
Oh, that Israel would follow me, walking in my paths!
14 How quickly I would then subdue their enemies!
How soon my hands would be upon their foes!
15 Those who hate the LORD would cringe before him;
their desolation would last forever.
16 But I would feed you with the best of foods.
I would satisfy you with wild honey from the rock."

81:13 Deut 5:29; Isa 48:18; Jer 7:23
81:14 Ps 47:3; Amos 1:8
81:16 Deut 32:13-14

Theme: A fair judge. God will judge the wicked who have unfairly treated others.
Author: Asaph

82

A psalm of Asaph.

1 God presides over heaven's court;
he pronounces judgment on the judges:
2 "How long will you judges hand down unjust decisions?
How long will you shower special favors on the wicked? *Interlude*
3 "Give fair judgment to the poor and the orphan;
uphold the rights of the oppressed and the destitute.
4 Rescue the poor and helpless;
deliver them from the grasp of evil people.
5 But these oppressors know nothing;
they are so ignorant!
And because they are in darkness,
the whole world is shaken to the core.
6 I say, 'You are gods
and children of the Most High.
7 But in death you are mere men.
You will fall as any prince,
for all must die.'"
8 Rise up, O God, and judge the earth,
for all the nations belong to you.

82:1 Exod 21:6; Ps 58:11; Isa 3:13
82:2 Deut 1:17; Ps 58:1-2; Prov 18:5
82:3 Deut 24:17
82:4 Job 29:12
82:6 †John 10:34
82:7 Pss 49:12; 83:11
82:8 Pss 2:8; 12:5; Rev 11:15

Theme: Combatting God's enemies. This psalm is a prayer for God to do whatever it takes to convince the world that he is indeed God. Someday all will recognize and admit that God is in charge.
Author: Asaph (or one of his descendants)

83

A psalm of Asaph. A song.

1 O God, don't sit idly by,
silent and inactive!
2 Don't you hear the tumult of your enemies?
Don't you see what your arrogant enemies are doing?
3 They devise crafty schemes against your people,
laying plans against your precious ones.
4 "Come," they say, "let us wipe out Israel as a nation.
We will destroy the very memory of its existence."
5 This was their unanimous decision.
They signed a treaty as allies against you—

83:1 Pss 28:1; 109:1
83:2 Pss 2:1; 81:15; Isa 17:12
83:3 Pss 27:5; 31:20
83:4 Esth 3:5-6
83:5 Ps 2:2

81:13-16 God had provided in his covenant that he would restore his people if they would listen to him and return to him (Exodus 23:22-27; Leviticus 26:3-13; Deuteronomy 7:12-26; 28:1-14).

82:6 This psalm calls the rulers and judges of Israel "gods" and "children of the Most High." They were called gods because they represented God in executing judgment. John 10:34-36 records Jesus using this passage to defend his claims to be God. His argument was as follows: If God would call mere people "gods," why was it blasphemous for him, the true Son of God, to declare himself equal with God?

83:5-8 This alliance against God may refer to the gathering of certain kings to fight against Jehoshaphat and the people of Judah (2 Chronicles 20). The psalm's author is called Asaph, but it could

83:6 Gen 25:12-16; 2 Chr 20:1, 10; Ps 137:7
83:7 1 Sam 4:1; 15:22; Chr 20:10; Ezek 27:2-3, 9
83:9 Judg 4:22-23
83:11 Judg 7:25; 8:21
83:12 2 Chr 20:11; Ps 132:13
83:14 Deut 32:22; Isa 9:18
83:15 Job 9:17; Ps 58:9
83:16 Ps 109:29
83:18 Ps 59:13; Isa 45:21

6 these Edomites and Ishmaelites,
Moabites and Hagrites,
7 Gebalites, Ammonites, and Amalekites,
and people from Philistia and Tyre.
8 Assyria has joined them, too,
and is allied with the descendants of Lot. *Interlude*

9 Do to them as you did to the Midianites
or as you did to Sisera and Jabin at the Kishon River.
10 They were destroyed at Endor,
and their decaying corpses fertilized the soil.
11 Let their mighty nobles die as Oreb and Zeeb did.
Let all their princes die like Zebah and Zalmunna,
12 for they said, "Let us seize for our own use
these pasturelands of God!"

13 O my God, blow them away like whirling dust,
like chaff before the wind!
14 As a fire roars through a forest
and as a flame sets mountains ablaze,
15 chase them with your fierce storms;
terrify them with your tempests.
16 Utterly disgrace them
until they submit to your name, O LORD.
17 Let them be ashamed and terrified forever.
Make them failures in everything they do,
18 until they learn that you alone are called the LORD,
that you alone are the Most High, supreme over all the earth.

Theme: God's living presence is our greatest joy. His radiant presence helps us grow in strength, grace, and glory.
Author: The sons of Korah (Temple assistants)

84

*For the choir director: A psalm of the descendants of Korah, to be accompanied by a stringed instrument.**

84:1 Ps 27:4
84:2 Pss 42:1-2; 63:1
84:3 Ps 43:4

1 How lovely is your dwelling place,
O LORD Almighty.
2 I long, yes, I faint with longing
to enter the courts of the LORD.
With my whole being, body and soul,
I will shout joyfully to the living God.
3 Even the sparrow finds a home there,
and the swallow builds her nest

84:TITLE Hebrew *according to the gittith.*

be Asaph or one of his descendants. A descendant of Asaph named Jahaziel prophesied victory for Judah in the battle against Jehoshaphat (2 Chronicles 20:13-17) and exclaimed, "The battle is not yours, but God's" (2 Chronicles 20:15). God is "the Most High, supreme over all the earth" (83:18), and the enemies of Israel were considered God's enemies.

83:6 The Hagrites may have been the descendants of Hagar (Genesis 21:8-21).

83:8-11 The "descendants of Lot" refers to the Moabites and Ammonites (Genesis 19:36-38). Sisera was the commander of the army of the oppressive Canaanite king Jabin. He was killed by a woman (see Judges 4 for the complete story). (For the story of Oreb and Zeeb, see Judges 7:25; for Zebah and Zalmunna, see Judges 8:21.)

83:13-18 Surrounding Judah were pagan nations that sought Judah's downfall. The psalmist prayed that God would blow these nations away like chaff before the wind until they recognized that the Lord is above all rulers of the earth. Sometimes we must be humbled by adversity before we will look up and see the Lord; we must be defeated before we can have the ultimate victory. Wouldn't it be better to seek the Lord in times of prosperity than to wait until his judgment is upon us?

84:1, 4 The writer longed to get away from the bustling world to meet God inside his dwelling place, his holy Temple. We can meet God anywhere, at any time. But we know that going into a church building can help us step aside from the busy mainstream of life so we can quietly meditate and pray. We find joy and strength not only in the prayers, music, lessons, and sermons but also in fellowshiping with other believers in a special place.

and raises her young—
at a place near your altar,
O LORD Almighty, my King and my God!
4 How happy are those who can live in your house,
always singing your praises. *Interlude*

5 Happy are those who are strong in the LORD,
who set their minds on a pilgrimage to Jerusalem.
6 When they walk through the Valley of Weeping,*
it will become a place of refreshing springs,
where pools of blessing collect after the rains!
7 They will continue to grow stronger,
and each of them will appear before God in Jerusalem.*

8 O LORD God Almighty, hear my prayer.
Listen, O God of Israel.* *Interlude*

9 O God, look with favor upon the king, our protector!
Have mercy on the one you have anointed.

10 A single day in your courts
is better than a thousand anywhere else!
I would rather be a gatekeeper in the house of my God
than live the good life in the homes of the wicked.
11 For the LORD God is our light and protector.
He gives us grace and glory.
No good thing will the LORD withhold
from those who do what is right.
12 O LORD Almighty,
happy are those who trust in you.

84:4 Ps 65:4
84:5 Ps 81:1
84:6 Ps 107:35
84:7 Deut 16:16; 2 Chr 3:18; Isa 40:31
84:8 Pss 59:5; 81:1
84:9 Gen 15:1; 2 Sam 19:21; Ps 115:9-11
84:10 1 Chr 23:5; Ps 27:4
84:11 Ps 2:12
84:12 Ps 2:12; Isa 60:19-20; Rev 21:23

Theme: From reverence to restoration. Reverence leads to forgiveness, restoring our love and joy for God.
Author: The sons of Korah (Temple assistants)

85

For the choir director: A psalm of the descendants of Korah.

1 LORD, you have poured out amazing blessings on your land!
You have restored the fortunes of Israel.*
2 You have forgiven the guilt of your people—
yes, you have covered all their sins. *Interlude*

3 You have withdrawn your fury.
You have ended your blazing anger.
4 Now turn to us again, O God of our salvation.
Put aside your anger against us.
5 Will you be angry with us always?
Will you prolong your wrath to distant generations?
6 Won't you revive us again,
so your people can rejoice in you?

85:1 Jer 30:18; Ezek 39:25; Joel 3:1
85:2 Num 14:19; Ps 32:1; Jer 31:34
85:3 Exod 32:12; Deut 13:17; Ps 78:38
85:4 Ps 80:3, 7
85:5 Pss 74:1; 79:5; 80:4
85:6 Ps 149:2

84:6 Hebrew *valley of Baca.* **84:7** Hebrew *Zion.* **84:8** Hebrew *of Jacob.* **85:1** Hebrew *of Jacob.*

84:5-7 The pilgrimage to the Temple passed through the barren Valley of Weeping. No specific valley has been identified. The "weeping" may have been a symbolic reference to the times of struggles and tears through which people must pass on their way to meet God. Growing strong in God's presence is often preceded by a journey through barren places in our lives. The person who loves to spend time with God will see his or her adversity as an opportunity to reexperience God's faithfulness. If you are walking through your own Valley of Weeping today, be sure your pilgrimage leads toward God, not away from him.

84:11 God does not promise to give us everything *we* think is good, but he will not withhold what is permanently good. He will give us the means to walk along his paths, but we must do the walking. When we obey him, he will not hold anything back that will help us serve him.

85:6, 7 The psalmist was asking God to revive his people, bringing them back to spiritual life. God is capable of reviving both churches and individuals. He can pour out his love on us, renewing our love for him. If you need revival in your church, family, or personal spiritual life, ask God to give you a fresh touch of his love.

7 Show us your unfailing love, O LORD,
and grant us your salvation.

85:8
Pss 29:11; 78:57

8 I listen carefully to what God the LORD is saying,
for he speaks peace to his people, his faithful ones.
But let them not return to their foolish ways.

85:9
Pss 34:18; 84:11
Isa 46:13
John 1:14

9 Surely his salvation is near to those who honor him;
our land will be filled with his glory.

85:10
Ps 72:3
Prov 3:3
Isa 32:17

10 Unfailing love and truth have met together.
Righteousness and peace have kissed!

85:11
Isa 45:8

11 Truth springs up from the earth,
and righteousness smiles down from heaven.

85:12
Ps 84:11
Jas 1:17

12 Yes, the LORD pours down his blessings.
Our land will yield its bountiful crops.
13 Righteousness goes as a herald before him,
preparing the way for his steps.

Theme: Devoted trust in times of deep trouble
Author: David

86

A prayer of David.

86:1
Pss 17:6; 40:17

1 Bend down, O LORD, and hear my prayer;
answer me, for I need your help.

86:2
Pss 4:3; 25:20

2 Protect me, for I am devoted to you.
Save me, for I serve you and trust you.
You are my God.
3 Be merciful, O Lord,
for I am calling on you constantly.

86:4
Ps 25:1

4 Give me happiness, O Lord,
for my life depends on you.

86:5
Pss 103:8; 130:4

5 O Lord, you are so good, so ready to forgive,
so full of unfailing love for all who ask your aid.

86:6
Ps 55:1

6 Listen closely to my prayer, O LORD;
hear my urgent cry.

86:7
Ps 50:14-15
Rev 15:4

7 I will call to you whenever trouble strikes,
and you will answer me.

86:8
Exod 15:11
Deut 3:24

8 Nowhere among the pagan gods is there a god like you, O Lord.
There are no other miracles like yours.

86:9
Isa 66:23
Rev 15:3-4

9 All the nations—and you made each one—
will come and bow before you, Lord;
they will praise your great and holy name.

86:10
Deut 32:39
Isa 44:6, 8
Mark 12:29
1 Cor 8:4

10 For you are great and perform great miracles.
You alone are God.

86:11
Ps 25:5
Jer 32:39

11 Teach me your ways, O LORD,
that I may live according to your truth!
Grant me purity of heart,
that I may honor you.

86:7 Sometimes our trouble or pain is so great that all we can do is cry out to God for protection (86:2). And often, when there is no relief in sight, all we can do is acknowledge the greatness of God and wait for better days ahead. The conviction that God answers prayer will sustain us in such difficult times.

86:8-10 "Nowhere among the pagan gods is there a god like you." The God of the Bible is unique! He is alive and able to do mighty deeds for those who love him. All human-created deities are powerless because they are merely inventions of the mind, not living beings. The Lord alone is "worthy . . . to receive glory and honor and power" (Revelation 4:11). Although people believe in many gods, you need never fear that God is only one among many or that you may be worshiping the wrong God. The Lord alone is God.

12 With all my heart I will praise you, O Lord my God.
I will give glory to your name forever,
13 for your love for me is very great.
You have rescued me from the depths of death*!

14 O God, insolent people rise up against me;
violent people are trying to kill me.
And you mean nothing to them.
15 But you, O Lord, are a merciful and gracious God,
slow to get angry,
full of unfailing love and truth.
16 Look down and have mercy on me.
Give strength to your servant;
yes, save me, for I am your servant.
17 Send me a sign of your favor.
Then those who hate me will be put to shame,
for you, O LORD, help and comfort me.

86:12 Ps 111:1
86:13 Ps 30:3
86:14 Ps 54:3
86:16 Ps 68:35
86:17 Pss 112:10; 118:13; 119:122

Theme: The city of God, where all believers will one day gather.
Author: The sons of Korah (Temple assistants)

87

A psalm of the descendants of Korah. A song.

1 On the holy mountain stands the city founded by the LORD.
2 He loves the city of Jerusalem
more than any other city in Israel.*
3 O city of God,
what glorious things are said of you! *Interlude*

4 I will record Egypt* and Babylon among those who know me—
also Philistia and Tyre, and even distant Ethiopia.*
They have all become citizens of Jerusalem!
5 And it will be said of Jerusalem,*
"Everyone has become a citizen here."
And the Most High will personally bless this city.
6 When the LORD registers the nations,
he will say, "This one has become a citizen of Jerusalem." *Interlude*

7 At all the festivals, the people will sing,
"The source of my life is in Jerusalem!"

87:1 Ps 78:68-69; Isa 28:16
87:2 Ps 78:67
87:3 Pss 46:4; 48:8; Isa 60:1
87:4 Pss 45:12; 68:31; Isa 19:23-25
87:5 Ps 48:8
87:6 Isa 4:2-4
87:7 Pss 30:11; 36:9

Theme: When there is no relief in sight. God understands even our deepest misery.
Author: Heman, one of the sons of Korah (possibly the same man mentioned in 1 Chronicles 15:19; 16:41; 25:4-5 as a musician and the king's seer)

88

For the choir director: A psalm of the descendants of Korah, to be sung to the tune "The Suffering of Affliction." A psalm of Heman the Ezrahite. A song.

1 O LORD, God of my salvation,
I have cried out to you day and night.

88:1 Pss 22:2; 24:5; Luke 18:7

86:13 Hebrew *of Sheol.* **87:2** Hebrew *He loves the gates of Zion more than all the dwellings of Jacob.* **87:4a** Hebrew *Rahab,* the name of a mythical sea monster that represents chaos in ancient literature. The name is used here as a poetic name for Egypt. **87:4b** Hebrew *Cush.* **87:5** Hebrew *Zion.*

86:17 It is right to pray for a sign of God's goodness. As David found, it may be just what we need. But let us not overlook the signs he has already given: the support of family and friends, the fellowship of other Christians, the light of each new day. And we can be confident that he knows our situation no matter how desperate it becomes, and he cares.

87:1ff Zion (the holy mountain, Jerusalem) and its Temple here represent the future community of all believers. This psalm looks ahead to the Holy City of God described in Revelation 21:10-27. The honor of living there will be granted to all whose names are recorded in the Lamb's Book of Life (Revelation 21:27). It is God's grace that forms and sustains this wonderful community. How could anyone refuse God's offer to be part of this celebration?

88:1ff Have you ever felt as though you have hit bottom? The psalmist is so low that he even despairs of life itself. Although everything is bad and getting worse, he is able to tell it all to

88:2 Pss 18:6; 86:1
2 Now hear my prayer;
listen to my cry.

88:3 Pss 107:18; 116:3
3 For my life is full of troubles,
and death draws near.

88:4 Ps 28:1
4 I have been dismissed as one who is dead,
like a strong man with no strength left.

88:5 Ps 31:12; Isa 53:8
5 They have abandoned me to death,
and I am as good as dead.
I am forgotten,
cut off from your care.

88:6 Pss 32:4; 42:7; 69:15; 143:3; Lam 3:55
6 You have thrust me down to the lowest pit,
into the darkest depths.

88:7 Ps 42:7
7 Your anger lies heavy on me;
wave after wave engulfs me. *Interlude*

88:8 Job 19:19; 30:10; Ps 31:11
8 You have caused my friends to loathe me;
you have sent them all away.
I am in a trap with no way of escape.

88:9 Job 11:13; Pss 6:7; 22:2
9 My eyes are blinded by my tears.
Each day I beg for your help, O LORD;
I lift my pleading hands to you for mercy.

88:10 Ps 6:5
10 Of what use to the dead are your miracles?
Do the dead get up and praise you? *Interlude*

11 Can those in the grave declare your unfailing love?
In the place of destruction, can they proclaim your faithfulness?

88:12 Job 10:20-21
12 Can the darkness speak of your miracles?
Can anyone in the land of forgetfulness talk about your righteousness?

88:13 Pss 5:3; 119:147
13 O LORD, I cry out to you.
I will keep on pleading day by day.

88:14 Job 13:24; Ps 13:1
14 O LORD, why do you reject me?
Why do you turn your face away from me?

88:15 Job 6:4
15 I have been sickly and close to death since my youth.
I stand helpless and desperate before your terrors.

16 Your fierce anger has overwhelmed me.
Your terrors have cut me off.

88:17 Ps 22:12, 16
17 They swirl around me like floodwaters all day long.
They have encircled me completely.

88:18 Job 19:13; Pss 31:11; 38:11
18 You have taken away my companions and loved ones;
only darkness remains.

Theme: God's promise to preserve David's descendants. God's promise is fulfilled in Jesus Christ, who will reign for eternity. The love and kindness promised to David is ours in Christ.
Author: Ethan (a Levite leader and possibly one of the head musicians in the Temple, 1 Chronicles 15:17, 19), or one of his descendants

89

A psalm of Ethan the Ezrahite.

89:1 Pss 40:10; 59:16
1 I will sing of the tender mercies of the LORD forever!
Young and old will hear of your faithfulness.

God. This is one of the few psalms that gives no answer or expression of hope. Don't think that you must always be cheerful and positive. Grief and depression take time to heal. No matter how low we feel, we can always take our problems to God and express our anguish to him.

88:13, 14 When writing this, the psalmist was close to death, perhaps debilitated by disease, and forsaken by friends. But he could still pray. Perhaps you are not so afflicted, but you know someone who is. Consider being a prayer companion for that person. This psalm can be a prayer you can lift to God on his or her behalf.

89:1ff This psalm was written to describe the glorious reign of David. God had promised to make David the mightiest king on earth and to keep his descendants on the throne forever (2 Samuel 7:8-16). But Jerusalem was destroyed, and kings no longer reign there. So these verses can only look forward, prophetically, to the future reign of Jesus Christ, David's descendant. Verse 27 is a prophecy concerning David's never-ending dynasty, which will reach its fulfillment and highest expression in Christ's future reign over the world (see Revelation 22:5).

2 Your unfailing love will last forever.
Your faithfulness is as enduring as the heavens.

3 The LORD said, "I have made a solemn agreement with David, my chosen servant.
I have sworn this oath to him:
4 'I will establish your descendants as kings forever;
they will sit on your throne from now until eternity.'" *Interlude*

5 All heaven will praise your miracles, LORD;
myriads of angels will praise you for your faithfulness.
6 For who in all of heaven can compare with the LORD?
What mightiest angel is anything like the LORD?
7 The highest angelic powers stand in awe of God.
He is far more awesome than those who surround his throne.
8 O LORD God Almighty!
Where is there anyone as mighty as you, LORD?
Faithfulness is your very character.

9 You are the one who rules the oceans.
When their waves rise in fearful storms, you subdue them.
10 You are the one who crushed the great sea monster.*
You scattered your enemies with your mighty arm.
11 The heavens are yours, and the earth is yours;
everything in the world is yours—you created it all.
12 You created north and south.
Mount Tabor and Mount Hermon praise your name.
13 Powerful is your arm!
Strong is your hand!
Your right hand is lifted high in glorious strength.
14 Your throne is founded on two strong pillars—righteousness and justice.
Unfailing love and truth walk before you as attendants.
15 Happy are those who hear the joyful call to worship,
for they will walk in the light of your presence, LORD.
16 They rejoice all day long in your wonderful reputation.
They exult in your righteousness.
17 You are their glorious strength.
Our power is based on your favor.
18 Yes, our protection comes from the LORD,
and he, the Holy One of Israel, has given us our king.

19 You once spoke in a vision to your prophet and said,
"I have given help to a warrior.
I have selected him from the common people to be king.
20 I have found my servant David.
I have anointed him with my holy oil.
21 I will steady him,
and I will make him strong.

89:10 Hebrew *Rahab,* the name of a mythical sea monster that represents chaos in ancient literature.

89:2 Ps 36:5
89:3 2 Sam 7:16; Ps 132:11; Isa 9:7; Luke 1:31-33
89:4 2 Sam 7:16; Isa 9:7; Luke 1:33
89:6 Pss 29:1; 96:4
89:7 Pss 47:2; 96:4
89:8 Pss 35:10; 71:19
89:9 Pss 65:7; 107:29
89:10 Ps 18:14
89:11 Gen 1:1; 1 Chr 29:11; Ps 24:1
89:12 Josh 12:1; 19:22
89:13 Ps 118:16
89:14 Pss 97:2; 98:6
89:15 Num 10:10
89:17 Pss 44:3; 75:10; 148:14
89:18 Pss 47:9; 71:22
89:19 2 Sam 17:10; 1 Kgs 11:34
89:20 1 Sam 16:13; †Acts 13:22

89:5 In the courts of heaven, a host of angels praise the Lord. This scene is one of majesty and grandeur to show that God is beyond compare. His power and purity place him high above nature and angels. See Deuteronomy 33:2, Luke 2:13, and Hebrews 12:22 for more about angels.

89:12 Mount Tabor, though low in elevation (1,900 feet), was the scene of Deborah's victory in Judges 4. Mount Hermon (9,000 feet) was tall and majestic.

89:14, 15 Righteousness, justice, love, and truth are the foundation of God's throne; they are fundamental aspects of the way God rules. As God's ambassadors, we should deal with people similarly. Make sure your actions flow out of righteousness, justice, love, and faithfulness, because any unfair, unloving, or dishonest action cannot come from God.

89:17, 24 David is promised to have God's power to accomplish God's will. Without God's help, we are weak and powerless, inadequate for even the simplest spiritual tasks. But when we are filled with God's Spirit, his power flows through us and our accomplishments will exceed our expectations.

89:22 2 Sam 7:10-11
89:23 2 Sam 7:9
89:26 2 Sam 7:14; 1 Chr 22:10
89:27 Pss 2:7; 72:11; Rev 19:1, 5, 16
89:29 1 Kgs 2:4; Isa 9:7; Jer 33:17
89:30 2 Sam 7:14
89:33 2 Sam 7:15
89:34 Num 23:19; Jer 33:20-21
89:36 Ps 72:5
89:38 1 Chr 28:9
89:39 Ps 78:59; Lam 2:7; 5:16
89:40 Ps 80:12; Lam 2:2, 5
89:42 Pss 13:2; 80:6
89:43 Ps 44:10
89:44 Ezek 28:7
89:45 Ps 44:15-16

22 His enemies will not get the best of him,
nor will the wicked overpower him.
23 I will beat down his adversaries before him
and destroy those who hate him.
24 My faithfulness and unfailing love will be with him,
and he will rise to power because of me.
25 I will extend his rule from the Mediterranean Sea in the west
to the Tigris and Euphrates rivers in the east.*
26 And he will say to me, 'You are my Father,
my God, and the Rock of my salvation.'
27 I will make him my firstborn son,
the mightiest king on earth.
28 I will love him and be kind to him forever;
my covenant with him will never end.
29 I will preserve an heir for him;
his throne will be as endless as the days of heaven.
30 But if his sons forsake my law
and fail to walk in my ways,
31 if they do not obey my decrees
and fail to keep my commands,
32 then I will punish their sin with the rod,
and their disobedience with beating.
33 But I will never stop loving him,
nor let my promise to him fail.
34 No, I will not break my covenant;
I will not take back a single word I said.
35 I have sworn an oath to David,
and in my holiness I cannot lie:
36 His dynasty will go on forever;
his throne is as secure as the sun,
37 as eternal as the moon,
my faithful witness in the sky!" *Interlude*

38 But now you have rejected him.
Why are you so angry with the one you chose as king?
39 You have renounced your covenant with him,
for you have thrown his crown in the dust.
40 You have broken down the walls protecting him
and laid in ruins every fort defending him.
41 Everyone who comes along has robbed him
while his neighbors mock.
42 You have strengthened his enemies against him
and made them all rejoice.
43 You have made his sword useless
and have refused to help him in battle.
44 You have ended his splendor
and overturned his throne.
45 You have made him old before his time
and publicly disgraced him. *Interlude*

89:25 Hebrew *I will set his hand on the sea, his right hand on the rivers.*

89:34-37 In light of Israel's continual disobedience throughout history, this is an amazing promise. God promised that David's descendants would always sit on the throne (89:29), but that if the people disobeyed, they would be punished (89:30-32). Yet, even through their disobedience and punishment, God would never break faith with them (89:33). Israel *did* disobey, evil ran rampant, the nation was divided, exile came—but through it all, a remnant of God's people remained faithful. Centuries later, the Messiah arrived, the eternal King from David's line, just as God had promised. All that God promises, he fulfills. He will not take back even one word of what he says. God can also be trusted to save us as he promised he would (Hebrews 6:13-18). God is completely reliable.

46 O LORD, how long will this go on?
Will you hide yourself forever?
How long will your anger burn like fire?
47 Remember how short my life is,
how empty and futile this human existence!
48 No one can live forever; all will die.
No one can escape the power of the grave. *Interlude*

49 Lord, where is your unfailing love?
You promised it to David with a faithful pledge.
50 Consider, Lord, how your servants are disgraced!
I carry in my heart the insults of so many people.
51 Your enemies have mocked me, O LORD;
they mock the one you anointed as king.

52 Blessed be the LORD forever!
Amen and amen!

89:46 Pss 13:1; 79:5
89:47 Job 7:7; 14:1; Ps 39:5-6; Eccl 1:2; 2:11
89:48 Ps 22:29; Heb 11:5
89:49 2 Sam 7:15
89:51 Ps 74:9-10, 18, 22
89:52 Pss 41:13; 106:48

BOOK IV
Psalms 90:1—106:48

These psalms include a prayer of Moses, a psalm about oppressors, and a psalm praising God as our King. These psalms remind us that we should remember our place and be submissive before the almighty God.

Theme: God's eternal nature is contrasted with people's frailty. Our time on earth is limited and we are to use it wisely, not living for the moment, but with our eternal home in mind.
Author: Moses, making this the oldest of the psalms

90

A prayer of Moses, the man of God.

1 Lord, through all the generations
you have been our home!
2 Before the mountains were created,
before you made the earth and the world,
you are God, without beginning or end.

3 You turn people back to dust, saying,
"Return to dust!"
4 For you, a thousand years are as yesterday!
They are like a few hours!
5 You sweep people away like dreams that disappear
or like grass that springs up in the morning.
6 In the morning it blooms and flourishes,
but by evening it is dry and withered.
7 We wither beneath your anger;
we are overwhelmed by your fury.
8 You spread out our sins before you—
our secret sins—and you see them all.
9 We live our lives beneath your wrath.
We end our lives with a groan.

10 Seventy years are given to us!
Some may even reach eighty.

90:1 Deut 33:27; Ezek 11:16; Rev 21:3
90:2 Gen 1:1; Ps 102:24-25, 27; Prov 8:22-26
90:3 Job 34:14-15
90:4 Ps 39:5; 2 Pet 3:8
90:5 Job 14:2; 20:8; Isa 40:6; Matt 6:30
90:6 Ps 92:7
90:9 Ps 78:33
90:10 Ps 78:39; Eccl 12:2-7

90:4 Moses reminds us that a thousand years are like a day to the Lord. God is not limited by time. It's easy to get discouraged when years pass and the world doesn't get better. We sometimes wonder if God is able to see the future. But don't assume that God has our limitations. God is completely unrestricted by time. Because he is eternal, we can depend on him.

90:8 God knows all our sins as if they were spread out before him, even the secret ones. We don't need to cover up our sins before him because we can talk openly and honestly with him. But while he knows all that terrible information about us, God still loves us and wants to forgive us. This should encourage us to come to him rather than frighten us into covering up our sin.

But even the best of these years are filled with pain and trouble;
soon they disappear, and we are gone.

90:11 Ps 76:7
11 Who can comprehend the power of your anger?
Your wrath is as awesome as the fear you deserve.

90:12 Ps 39:4
12 Teach us to make the most of our time,
so that we may grow in wisdom.

90:13 Deut 32:36
13 O LORD, come back to us!
How long will you delay?
Take pity on your servants!

90:14 Pss 36:8; 103:5 Jer 31:14
14 Satisfy us in the morning with your unfailing love,
so we may sing for joy to the end of our lives.

90:15 Pss 31:10; 86:4
15 Give us gladness in proportion to our former misery!
Replace the evil years with good.

90:16 Ps 44:1
16 Let us see your miracles again;
let our children see your glory at work.

90:17 Ps 27:4 Isa 26:12
17 And may the Lord our God show us his approval
and make our efforts successful.
Yes, make our efforts successful!

Theme: God's protection in the midst of danger. God doesn't promise a world free from danger, but he does promise his help whenever we face danger.
Author: Anonymous

91

91:1 Isa 25:4; 32:2
1 Those who live in the shelter of the Most High
will find rest in the shadow of the Almighty.

91:2 Pss 18:2; 142:5 Jer 16:19
2 This I declare of the LORD:
He alone is my refuge, my place of safety;
he is my God, and I am trusting him.

91:3 2 Chr 20:9 Ps 124:7
3 For he will rescue you from every trap
and protect you from the fatal plague.

91:4 Pss 35:2; 57:1; 63:7 Isa 51:1-6
4 He will shield you with his wings.
He will shelter you with his feathers.
His faithful promises are your armor and protection.

91:5 Job 5:19-23 Ps 23:4
5 Do not be afraid of the terrors of the night,
nor fear the dangers of the day,

91:6 Job 5:22
6 nor dread the plague that stalks in darkness,
nor the disaster that strikes at midday.
7 Though a thousand fall at your side,
though ten thousand are dying around you,
these evils will not touch you.

91:8 Ps 37:34
8 But you will see it with your eyes;
you will see how the wicked are punished.

9 If you make the LORD your refuge,
if you make the Most High your shelter,

91:10 Prov 12:21
10 no evil will conquer you;
no plague will come near your dwelling.

90:12 Realizing that life is short helps us use the little time we have more wisely and for eternal good. Take time to number your days by asking, What do I want to see happen in my life before I die? What small step could I take toward that purpose today?

90:17 Because our days are numbered, we want our work to count, to be effective and productive. We desire to see God's eternal plan revealed now and for our work to reflect his permanence. If we feel dissatisfied with this life and all its imperfections, we must remember our desire to see our work established is placed there by God (see the note on Ecclesiastes 3:11). But our desire can only be satisfied in eternity. Until then we must apply ourselves to loving and serving God.

91:1-6 God is a shelter, a refuge when we are afraid. The writer's faith in almighty God as protector would carry him through all the dangers and fears of life. This should be a picture of our trust—trading all our fears for faith in him, no matter how intense our fears. To do this we must "live" and "rest" with him (91:1). By entrusting ourselves to his protection and pledging our daily devotion to him, we will be kept safe.

[11] For he orders his angels
to protect you wherever you go.
[12] They will hold you with their hands
to keep you from striking your foot on a stone.
[13] You will trample down lions and poisonous snakes;
you will crush fierce lions and serpents under your feet!

[14] The LORD says, "I will rescue those who love me.
I will protect those who trust in my name.
[15] When they call on me, I will answer;
I will be with them in trouble.
I will rescue them and honor them.
[16] I will satisfy them with a long life
and give them my salvation."

91:11 Ps 34:7; †Matt 4:6; †Luke 4:9-11
1:13 Judg 14:6; Luke 10:19
91:15 1 Sam 2:30; Ps 50:15; John 12:26

Theme: Be thankful and faithful every day. This psalm was used in Temple services on the Sabbath.
Author: Anonymous

92

A psalm to be sung on the LORD's Day. A song.

[1] It is good to give thanks to the LORD,
to sing praises to the Most High.
[2] It is good to proclaim your unfailing love in the morning,
your faithfulness in the evening,
[3] accompanied by the harp and lute
and the harmony of the lyre.
[4] You thrill me, LORD, with all you have done for me!
I sing for joy because of what you have done.

[5] O LORD, what great miracles you do!
And how deep are your thoughts.
[6] Only an ignorant person would not know this!
Only a fool would not understand it.
[7] Although the wicked flourish like weeds,
and evildoers blossom with success,
there is only eternal destruction ahead of them.
[8] But you are exalted in the heavens.
You, O LORD, continue forever.
[9] Your enemies, LORD, will surely perish;
all evildoers will be scattered.

[10] But you have made me as strong as a wild bull.
How refreshed I am by your power!
[11] With my own eyes I have seen the downfall of my enemies;
with my own ears I have heard the defeat of my wicked opponents.
[12] But the godly will flourish like palm trees
and grow strong like the cedars of Lebanon.
[13] For they are transplanted into the LORD's own house.
They flourish in the courts of our God.

92:3 1 Sam 10:5; 1 Chr 13:8; Neh 12:27
92:5 Pss 36:6; 40:5; 139:17; Rom 11:33
92:6 Ps 73:22
92:7 Ps 37:38
92:9 Pss 37:20; 68:1
92:10 Pss 23:5; 45:7; 75:10
92:11 Ps 54:7

91:11 One of the functions of angels is to watch over believers (Hebrews 1:14). There are examples of guardian angels in Scripture (1 Kings 19:5; Daniel 6:22; Matthew 18:10; Luke 16:22; Acts 12:7), although there is no indication that one angel is assigned to each believer. Angels can also be God's messengers (Matthew 2:13; Acts 27:23, 24). Angels are not visible, except on special occasions (Numbers 22:31; Luke 2:9). Verses 11 and 12 were quoted by Satan when he tempted Jesus (Matthew 4:6; Luke 4:10, 11). It is comforting to know that God watches over us even in times of great stress and fear.

92:1, 2 During the Thanksgiving holiday, we focus on our blessings and express our gratitude to God for them. But thanks should be on our lips every day. We can never say thank you enough to parents, friends, leaders, and especially to God. When thanksgiving becomes an integral part of your life, you will find that your attitude toward life will change. You will become more positive, gracious, loving, and humble.

92:12, 13 Palm trees are known for their long life. To flourish like palm trees means to stand tall and to live long. The cedars of Lebanon grew to 120 feet in height and up to 30 feet in circumference; thus, they were solid, strong, and immovable. The psalmist saw believers as upright, strong, and unmoved by the winds of circumstance. Those who place their faith firmly in God can have this strength and vitality.

92:14 Isa 37:31 John 15:2
14 Even in old age they will still produce fruit;
they will remain vital and green.
92:15 Rom 9:14
15 They will declare, "The LORD is just!
He is my rock!
There is nothing but goodness in him!"

Theme: God's unchanging and almighty nature. His creation reminds us of his great power.
Author: Anonymous

93:1 Pss 65:6; 96:10; 97:1; 99:1; 104:1 Isa 51:9

93

1 The LORD is king! He is robed in majesty.
Indeed, the LORD is robed in majesty and armed with strength.
The world is firmly established;
it cannot be shaken.
93:2 Lam 5:19
2 Your throne, O LORD, has been established from time immemorial.
You yourself are from the everlasting past.
93:3 Ps 98:7-8
3 The mighty oceans have roared, O LORD.
The mighty oceans roar like thunder;
the mighty oceans roar as they pound the shore.
93:4 Ps 65:7
4 But mightier than the violent raging of the seas,
mightier than the breakers on the shore—
the LORD above is mightier than these!
93:5 Ps 19:7 1 Cor 3:17
5 Your royal decrees cannot be changed.
The nature of your reign, O LORD, is holiness forever.

Theme: God will keep his people from the severe punishment awaiting the wicked. Since God is holy and just, we can be certain that the wicked will not prevail.
Author: Anonymous

94:1 Deut 32:35 Isa 35:4 Nah 1:2 Rom 12:19

94

1 O LORD, the God to whom vengeance belongs,
O God of vengeance, let your glorious justice be seen!
2 Arise, O judge of the earth.
Sentence the proud to the penalties they deserve.
3 How long, O LORD?
How long will the wicked be allowed to gloat?
94:4 Pss 31:18; 52:1
4 Hear their arrogance!
How these evildoers boast!
5 They oppress your people, LORD,
hurting those you love.
94:6 Isa 10:2
6 They kill widows and foreigners
and murder orphans.
7 "The LORD isn't looking," they say,
"and besides, the God of Israel* doesn't care."

8 Think again, you fools!
When will you finally catch on?

94:7 Hebrew *of Jacob.*

92:14 Honoring God is not limited to young people who seem to have unlimited strength and energy. Even in old age, devout believers can produce spiritual fruit. There are many faithful older people who continue to have a fresh outlook and can teach us from a lifetime of experience of serving God. Seek out an elderly friend or relative who can tell you about his or her experiences with the Lord and challenge you to new heights of spiritual growth.

93:1ff Jewish tradition claims that the next seven psalms (93–99) anticipated some of the works of the Messiah. Psalm 93 is said to have been used in postcaptivity Temple services and may have been written during Sennacherib's invasion (2 Kings 18:13–19:37).

93:5 The key to God's eternal reign is his holiness. God's glory is seen not only in his strength but in his perfect moral character as well. God will never do anything that is not morally perfect. This reassures us that we can trust him, yet it places a demand on us. Our desire to be holy (dedicated to God and morally clean) is our only suitable response. We must never use unholy means to reach a holy goal because God says, "You must be holy because I, the LORD your God, am holy" (Leviticus 19:1, 2).

9 Is the one who made your ears deaf?
Is the one who formed your eyes blind?
10 He punishes the nations—won't he also punish you?
He knows everything—doesn't he also know what you are doing?
11 The LORD knows people's thoughts,
that they are worthless!

12 Happy are those whom you discipline, LORD,
and those whom you teach from your law.
13 You give them relief from troubled times
until a pit is dug for the wicked.
14 The LORD will not reject his people;
he will not abandon his own special possession.
15 Judgment will come again for the righteous,
and those who are upright will have a reward.

16 Who will protect me from the wicked?
Who will stand up for me against evildoers?
17 Unless the LORD had helped me,
I would soon have died.
18 I cried out, "I'm slipping!"
and your unfailing love, O LORD, supported me.
19 When doubts filled my mind,
your comfort gave me renewed hope and cheer.

20 Can unjust leaders claim that God is on their side—
leaders who permit injustice by their laws?
21 They attack the righteous
and condemn the innocent to death.
22 But the LORD is my fortress;
my God is a mighty rock where I can hide.
23 God will make the sins of evil people fall back upon them.
He will destroy them for their sins.
The LORD our God will destroy them.

Theme: An invitation to worship God
Author: Anonymous

95

1 Come, let us sing to the LORD!
Let us give a joyous shout to the rock of our salvation!
2 Let us come before him with thanksgiving.
Let us sing him psalms of praise.
3 For the LORD is a great God,
the great King above all gods.
4 He owns the depths of the earth,
and even the mightiest mountains are his.
5 The sea belongs to him, for he made it.
His hands formed the dry land, too.

6 Come, let us worship and bow down.
Let us kneel before the LORD our maker,
7 for he is our God.
We are the people he watches over,
the sheep under his care.

Oh, that you would listen to his voice today!

94:9 Exod 4:11; Prov 20:12
94:10 Ps 44:2
94:11 †1 Cor 3:20
94:12 Deut 8:5; Ps 9:15; Heb 12:5-6
94:14 1 Sam 12:22; Rom 11:2
94:15 Isa 42:3; Mic 7:9
94:16 Num 10:35; Isa 28:21; 33:10
94:17 Ps 124:1-2
94:19 Isa 57:18; 66:13
94:20 Ps 58:2
94:21 Exod 23:7; Matt 27:4
94:22 Pss 39:9; 71:7
94:23 Pss 7:16; 140:9, 11
95:2 Mic 6:6-8
95:4 Ps 135:5-6
95:5 Gen 1:9-10
95:7-11 †Heb 3:7-11, 15; 4:7

94:12, 13 At times, God must discipline us to help us. This is similar to a loving parent disciplining his child. The discipline is not very enjoyable to the child, but it is essential to teach him or her right from wrong. The Bible says that "no discipline is enjoyable while it is happening—it is painful! But afterward there will be a quiet harvest of right living for those who are trained in this way" (Hebrews 12:11). When you feel God's hand of correction, accept it as proof of his love. Realize that God is urging you to follow his paths instead of stubbornly going your own way.

95:8 Num 20:13 Deut 6:16

95:9 Num 14:22

95:10 Acts 7:36; 13:18 Heb 3:10, 17

95:11 Deut 1:35 †Heb 4:3, 5

8 The LORD says, "Don't harden your hearts as Israel did at Meribah,
as they did at Massah in the wilderness.
9 For there your ancestors tried my patience;
they courted my wrath though they had seen my many miracles.
10 For forty years I was angry with them, and I said,
'They are a people whose hearts turn away from me.
They refuse to do what I tell them.'
11 So in my anger I made a vow:
'They will never enter my place of rest.'"

Theme: How to praise God. We can sing about him, tell others about him, worship him, give him glory, bring offerings to him, and live holy lives.
Author: Possibly David because this psalm closely resembles David's hymn of praise in 1 Chronicles 16:23-36

96:1-13 //1 Chr 16:23-33

96:2 Ps 71:15

96:3 Ps 145:12

96:5 1 Chr 16:26 Isa 42:5

96:6 Ps 104:1

96:8 Pss 79:9; 115:1

96

1 Sing a new song to the LORD!
Let the whole earth sing to the LORD!
2 Sing to the LORD; bless his name.
Each day proclaim the good news that he saves.
3 Publish his glorious deeds among the nations.
Tell everyone about the amazing things he does.
4 Great is the LORD! He is most worthy of praise!
He is to be revered above all the gods.
5 The gods of other nations are merely idols,
but the LORD made the heavens!
6 Honor and majesty surround him;
strength and beauty are in his sanctuary.

7 O nations of the world, recognize the LORD;
recognize that the LORD is glorious and strong.
8 Give to the LORD the glory he deserves!
Bring your offering and come to worship him.

JUSTICE IN THE BOOK OF PSALMS

Justice is a major theme in Psalms. The psalmists praise God because he is just; they plead for him to intervene and bring justice where there is oppression and wickedness; they condemn the wicked who trust in their wealth; they extol the righteous who are just toward their neighbors.

Justice in Psalms is more than honesty. It is active intervention on behalf of the helpless, especially the poor. The psalmists do not merely wish the poor could be given what they need, but they plead with God to destroy those nations that are subverting justice and oppressing God's people.

Here are some examples of psalms that speak about justice. As you read them, ask yourself, Who is my neighbor? Does my life-style—my work, my play, my buying habits, my giving—help or hurt people who have less than I do? What one thing could I do this week to help a helpless person?

Selected psalms that emphasize this theme are 7; 9; 15; 37; 50; 72; 75; 82; 94; 145.

95:8 A hardened heart is as useless as a hardened lump of clay or a hardened loaf of bread. Nothing can restore it and make it useful. The psalmist warns against hardening our hearts as Israel did in the wilderness by continuing to resist God's will (Exodus 17:7). They were so convinced that God couldn't deliver them that they simply lost their faith in him. When people become so stubbornly set in their ways that their hearts are hardened, they find it impossible to turn to God. This does not happen all at once; it is the result of a series of choices to disregard God's will. If you resist God long enough, God may toss you aside like hardened bread, useless and worthless.

95:8 *Meribah* means "quarreling," and *Massah* means "testing." These refer to the incident at Rephidim (Exodus 17:1-7) when the Israelites complained to Moses because they had no water (see also Numbers 20:1-13).

95:11 What keeps us from God's ultimate blessings (entering his "rest")? Ungrateful hearts (95:2), not worshiping or submitting to him (95:6), hardening our hearts (95:8), testing God because of stubborn doubts (95:9). In Hebrews 4:5-11, we are warned not to harden our hearts, but to reject the glamour of sin and anything else that would lead us away from God.

96:1-4 The psalmist sings out his praises to God, overwhelmed by all that God has done. As we reflect on God's majesty and his goodness to us, we cannot help telling others about him. Witnessing comes naturally when our hearts are full of appreciation for what he has done. God has chosen to use us to "publish his glorious deeds among the nations." Praise for our great God overflows from his creation and should overflow from our lips. How well are you doing at telling others about God's greatness?

9 Worship the LORD in all his holy splendor.
Let all the earth tremble before him.
10 Tell all the nations that the LORD is king.
The world is firmly established and cannot be shaken.
He will judge all peoples fairly.

11 Let the heavens be glad, and let the earth rejoice!
Let the sea and everything in it shout his praise!
12 Let the fields and their crops burst forth with joy!
Let the trees of the forest rustle with praise
13 before the LORD!
For the LORD is coming!
He is coming to judge the earth.
He will judge the world with righteousness
and all the nations with his truth.

96:9 1 Chr 16:29; 2 Chr 20:21
96:10 Pss 58:11; 67:4; 93:1
96:11 Pss 97:1; 98:7; Isa 49:13
96:12 Isa 35:1; 44:23; 55:12-13

Theme: God, our awesome conqueror, is righteous and just.
Author: Anonymous

97

1 The LORD is king! Let the earth rejoice!
Let the farthest islands be glad.
2 Clouds and darkness surround him.
Righteousness and justice are the foundation of his throne.
3 Fire goes forth before him
and burns up all his foes.
4 His lightning flashes out across the world.
The earth sees and trembles.
5 The mountains melt like wax before the LORD,
before the Lord of all the earth.
6 The heavens declare his righteousness;
every nation sees his glory.
7 Those who worship idols are disgraced—
all who brag about their worthless gods—
for every god must bow to him.
8 Jerusalem* has heard and rejoiced,
and all the cities of Judah are glad
because of your justice, LORD!
9 For you, O LORD, are most high over all the earth;
you are exalted far above all gods.
10 You who love the LORD, hate evil!
He protects the lives of his godly people
and rescues them from the power of the wicked.
11 Light shines on the godly,
and joy on those who do right.
12 May all who are godly be happy in the LORD
and praise his holy name!

97:8 Hebrew *Zion.*

97:1 Ps 96:10-11
97:2 Exod 19:9; Deut 4:11; 1 Kgs 8:12; Pss 18:11; 89:14
97:3 Heb 12:29
97:5 Josh 3:11; Amos 9:5
97:6 Ps 50:6
97:7 Jer 10:14; †Heb 1:6
97:8 Exod 18:11; Zeph 3:14
97:9 Exod 18:11; Pss 83:18; 95:3
97:10 Dan 3:28; Rom 12:9
97:11 Job 22:28
97:12 Ps 32:11

97:2 The clouds and darkness that surround God symbolize his unapproachable holiness and the inability of people to find him on their own. If he were uncovered, no one could stand before his blazing holiness and glory.

97:7 People worship all kinds of images and idols. Although God reveals himself and his love through nature and the Bible, there are many who decide to ignore or reject him and pursue goals they believe are more important. The Bible makes it clear that these people are idol worshipers because they give their highest loyalty to something other than God. One day we will stand before God in all his glory and power. Then we will see all our goals and accomplishments for what they really are. How foolish our earthly pursuits will seem then!

97:10 A sincere desire to please God will result in an alignment of your desires with God's desires. You will love what God loves and hate what God hates. If you love the Lord, you will hate evil. If you do not despise the actions of people who take advantage of others, if you admire people who only look out for themselves, or if you envy those who get ahead using any means to accomplish their ends, then your primary desire in life is not to please God. Learn to love God's ways and hate evil in every form—not only the obvious sins but also the socially acceptable ones.

Theme: A song of joy and victory. Because God is victorious over evil, all those who follow him will be victorious with him when he judges the earth.
Author: Anonymous

98 *A psalm.*

98:1 Exod 15:6 Isa 52:10

1 Sing a new song to the LORD,
for he has done wonderful deeds.
He has won a mighty victory
by his power and holiness.

98:2 Luke 1:54, 72 Rom 3:25

2 The LORD has announced his victory
and has revealed his righteousness to every nation!

98:3 Luke 1:54

3 He has remembered his promise to love and be faithful to Israel.
The whole earth has seen the salvation of our God.

98:4 Ps 100:1

4 Shout to the LORD, all the earth;
break out in praise and sing for joy!
5 Sing your praise to the LORD with the harp,
with the harp and melodious song,

98:6 Num 10:10 2 Chr 15:14

6 with trumpets and the sound of the ram's horn.
Make a joyful symphony before the LORD, the King!

98:7 Pss 24:1; 96:11

7 Let the sea and everything in it shout his praise!
Let the earth and all living things join in.
8 Let the rivers clap their hands in glee!
Let the hills sing out their songs of joy

98:9 Ps 96:10, 13

9 before the LORD.
For the LORD is coming to judge the earth.
He will judge the world with justice,
and the nations with fairness.

Theme: Praise for God's fairness and holiness. Because God is perfectly just and fair, we can trust him completely.
Author: Anonymous

99

99:1 Exod 25:22 1 Sam 4:4

1 The LORD is king!
Let the nations tremble!
He sits on his throne between the cherubim.
Let the whole earth quake!
2 The LORD sits in majesty in Jerusalem,*
supreme above all the nations.

99:3 Deut 28:58 Josh 24:19 1 Sam 2:2

3 Let them praise your great and awesome name.
Your name is holy!

99:4 Ps 17:2

4 Mighty king, lover of justice,
you have established fairness.
You have acted with justice
and righteousness throughout Israel.*

99:2 Hebrew *Zion.* **99:4** Hebrew *Jacob.*

98:1ff This is a psalm of praise anticipating the coming of God to rule his people. Jesus fulfilled this anticipation when he came to save all people from their sins (98:2, 3), and he will come again to judge the world (98:8, 9). God is both perfectly loving and perfectly just. He is merciful when he punishes, and he overlooks no sin when he loves. Praise him for his promise to save you and to return again.

99:1 Cherubim are mighty angels that comprise one of several ranks of angels. (For more on angels, see the note on 91:11.)

99:3 Everyone should praise God's great and awesome name because his name symbolizes his nature, his personage, and his reputation. But the name of God is often used so carelessly in conversation that we have lost sight of its holiness. How easy it is to treat God lightly in everyday life. If you claim him as your Father, live worthy of the family name. Respect God's name and give him praise by both your *words* and your *life.*

5 Exalt the LORD our God!
Bow low before his feet, for he is holy!

6 Moses and Aaron were among his priests;
Samuel also called on his name.
They cried to the LORD for help,
and he answered them.
7 He spoke to them from the pillar of cloud,
and they followed the decrees and principles he gave them.
8 O LORD our God, you answered them.
You were a forgiving God,
but you punished them when they went wrong.

9 Exalt the LORD our God
and worship at his holy mountain in Jerusalem,
for the LORD our God is holy!

99:6 Exod 15:25; 1 Sam 7:9
99:7 Exod 33:9; Num 12:5
99:8 Num 14:20

Theme: An invitation to enter joyfully into God's presence. His faithfulness extends to our generation and beyond.
Author: Anonymous

100

A psalm of thanksgiving.

1 Shout with joy to the LORD, O earth!
2 Worship the LORD with gladness.
Come before him, singing with joy.
3 Acknowledge that the LORD is God!
He made us, and we are his.
We are his people, the sheep of his pasture.

4 Enter his gates with thanksgiving;
go into his courts with praise.
Give thanks to him and bless his name.
5 For the LORD is good.
His unfailing love continues forever,
and his faithfulness continues to each generation.

100:1 Ps 98:4
100:2 Deut 12:11-12; 28:47
100:3 1 Kgs 18:39; Ezek 34:30-31; Mark 14:27; John 10:11
100:4 Pss 95:2; 96:2
100:5 Pss 25:8; 119:90

Theme: A prayer for help to walk a blameless path. To live with integrity, both our efforts and God's help are necessary.
Author: David

101

A psalm of David.

1 I will sing of your love and justice.
I will praise you, LORD, with songs.

101:1 Pss 89:1; 145:7

99:5 God's holiness is terribly frightening for sinners, but a wonderful comfort for believers. God is morally perfect and is set apart from people and sin. He has no weaknesses or shortcomings. For sinners, this is frightening because all their inadequacies and evil are exposed by the light of God's holiness. God cannot tolerate, ignore, or excuse sin. For believers, God's holiness gives comfort because, as we worship him, we are lifted from the mire of sin. As we believe in him, we are made holy.

99:6 The Bible records several instances where Moses, Aaron, and Samuel cried out to God for help (Exodus 15:25; 17:4; Numbers 11:11-15; 12:13; 14:13ff; 16:44-48; 1 Samuel 7:5, 9; 15:11).

100:3 God is our Creator; we did not create ourselves. Many people live as though they are the creator and center of their own little world. This mind-set leads to greed, and if everything should be taken away, a loss of hope itself. But when we realize that God created us and gives us all we have, we will want to give to others as God gave to us (2 Corinthians 9:8). Then, even if all is lost, we still have God and all he gives us.

100:4 God alone is worthy of being worshiped. What is your attitude toward worship? Do you willingly and joyfully come into God's presence, or are you just going through the motions, reluctantly going to church? This psalm tells us to remember God's goodness and dependability, and then to worship with thanksgiving and praise!

101:1ff David may have written this psalm early in his reign as king as he set down the standards he wanted to follow. David knew that to lead a blameless life he would need God's help (101:2). We can lead blameless lives if we avoid (1) looking at wickedness ("I will refuse to look at anything vile and vulgar," 101:3), (2) evil thoughts ("perverse ideas," 101:4), (3) slander (101:5), and (4) pride (101:5). While avoiding these wrongs, we must also let God's Word show us the standards by which to live.

2 I will be careful to live a blameless life—
when will you come to my aid?
I will lead a life of integrity
in my own home.

101:3 Deut 15:9

3 I will refuse to look at
anything vile and vulgar.
I hate all crooked dealings;
I will have nothing to do with them.

101:4 Prov 11:20

4 I will reject perverse ideas
and stay away from every evil.

101:5 Ps 50:20 Prov 6:16-19

5 I will not tolerate people who slander their neighbors.
I will not endure conceit and pride.

101:6 Ps 119:1

6 I will keep a protective eye on the godly,
so they may dwell with me in safety.
Only those who are above reproach
will be allowed to serve me.
7 I will not allow deceivers to serve me,
and liars will not be allowed to enter my presence.

101:8 Pss 46:4; 75:10; 118:10-12

8 My daily task will be to ferret out criminals
and free the city of the LORD from their grip.

Theme: The cure for distress. Because God is living, eternal, and unchanging, we can trust him to help his people in this generation just as he helped his people in past generations.
Author: Anonymous

102 *A prayer of one overwhelmed with trouble, pouring out problems before the* LORD.

102:1 Exod 2:23 1 Sam 9:16

1 LORD, hear my prayer!
Listen to my plea!

102:2 Ps 69:17

2 Don't turn away from me
in my time of distress.
Bend down your ear
and answer me quickly when I call to you,

102:3 Ezra 10:6 Job 30:30 Jas 4:14

3 for my days disappear like smoke,
and my bones burn like red-hot coals.
4 My heart is sick, withered like grass,
and I have lost my appetite.

102:5 Lam 4:8

5 Because of my groaning,
I am reduced to skin and bones.
6 I am like an owl in the desert,
like a lonely owl in a far-off wilderness.

102:7 Ps 77:4

7 I lie awake,
lonely as a solitary bird on the roof.

102:8 2 Sam 16:5 Isa 65:15 Luke 23:11 Acts 26:11

8 My enemies taunt me day after day.
They mock and curse me.
9 I eat ashes instead of my food.
My tears run down into my drink

101:6 David said that he would keep his "eye on the godly." In other words, he would choose as models and as friends those who were godly and truthful. Our friends and associates can have a profound influence on our life. Make sure to keep your eyes on those who are faithful to God and his Word.

102:3, 4 The psalmist felt so bad that he lost his appetite. When we face sickness and despair, our days pass blindly, and we don't care about even our basic needs. In these times, God alone is our comfort and strength. Even when we are too weak to fight, we can lean on him. It is often when we recognize our weaknesses that God's greatest strength becomes available.

102:6, 7 These birds are pictures of loneliness and desolation. At times we may need to be alone, and solitude may comfort us. But we must be careful not to spurn those who reach out to us. Don't reject help and conversation. Suffering silently is neither Christian nor particularly healthy. Instead, accept graciously the support and help from family and friends.

10 because of your anger and wrath.
For you have picked me up and thrown me out.
11 My life passes as swiftly as the evening shadows.
I am withering like grass.

12 But you, O LORD, will rule forever.
Your fame will endure to every generation.
13 You will arise and have mercy on Jerusalem*—
and now is the time to pity her,
now is the time you promised to help.
14 For your people love every stone in her walls
and show favor even to the dust in her streets.
15 And the nations will tremble before the LORD.
The kings of the earth will tremble before his glory.
16 For the LORD will rebuild Jerusalem.
He will appear in his glory.
17 He will listen to the prayers of the destitute.
He will not reject their pleas.

18 Let this be recorded for future generations,
so that a nation yet to be created will praise the LORD.
19 Tell them the LORD looked down
from his heavenly sanctuary.
He looked to the earth from heaven
20 to hear the groans of the prisoners,
to release those condemned to die.
21 And so the LORD's fame will be celebrated in Zion,
his praises in Jerusalem,
22 when multitudes gather together
and kingdoms come to worship the LORD.

23 He has cut me down in midlife,
shortening my days.
24 But I cried to him, "My God, who lives forever,
don't take my life while I am still so young!
25 In ages past you laid the foundation of the earth,
and the heavens are the work of your hands.
26 Even they will perish, but you remain forever;
they will wear out like old clothing.
You will change them like a garment,
and they will fade away.
27 But you are always the same;
your years never end.
28 The children of your people
will live in security.
Their children's children
will thrive in your presence."

102:13 Hebrew *Zion;* also in 102:16.

102:12 Exod 3:15 Lam 5:19
102:13 Isa 60:10 Zech 1:12
102:15 1 Kgs 8:41-42
102:16 Isa 60:1-2
102:17 Neh 1:6
102:18 Deut 31:19 1 Cor 10:11
102:19 Deut 26:15
102:21 Isa 49:22; 23 Zech 8:20-23
102:22 Ps 86:9
102:24 Isa 38:10
102:25-27 Gen 1:1 †Heb 1:10-12
102:26 Matt 24:35 2 Pet 3:10 Rev 20:11
102:27 Mal 3:6 Jas 1:17

102:16-22 Christ's future reign on earth will encompass two events mentioned in these verses. Jerusalem (Zion) will be restored, and the entire world will worship God (Revelation 11:15; 21:1-27).

102:25-27 The writer of this psalm felt rejected and tossed aside because of his great troubles (102:9, 10). Problems and heartaches can overwhelm us and cause us to feel that God has rejected us. But God our Creator is eternally with us and will keep all his promises, even though we may feel alone. The world will perish, but God will remain. Hebrews 1:10-12 quotes these verses to show that Jesus Christ, God's Son, was also present and active at the creation of the world.

Theme: God's great love for us. What God does for us tells us what he is really like.
Author: David

103

A psalm of David.

103:1 Pss 33:21; 104:1

1 Praise the LORD, I tell myself;
with my whole heart, I will praise his holy name.
2 Praise the LORD, I tell myself,
and never forget the good things he does for me.

103:3 Exod 34:7; Jer 30:17

3 He forgives all my sins
and heals all my diseases.

103:4 Ps 49:15

4 He ransoms me from death
and surrounds me with love and tender mercies.

103:5 Isa 40:31

5 He fills my life with good things.
My youth is renewed like the eagle's!
6 The LORD gives righteousness
and justice to all who are treated unfairly.

103:7 Exod 33:13

7 He revealed his character to Moses
and his deeds to the people of Israel.

103:8 Num 14:18; Neh 1:3; 9:17; Joel 2:13; Jon 4:2

8 The LORD is merciful and gracious;
he is slow to get angry and full of unfailing love.

103:9 Ps 30:5; Isa 57:16; Jer 3:5

9 He will not constantly accuse us,
nor remain angry forever.

103:10 Lam 3:22

10 He has not punished us for all our sins,
nor does he deal with us as we deserve.

103:11 Ps 36:5

11 For his unfailing love toward those who fear him
is as great as the height of the heavens above the earth.

103:12 Isa 38:17; Heb 9:26

12 He has removed our rebellious acts
as far away from us as the east is from the west.

103:13 Mal 3:17

13 The LORD is like a father to his children,
tender and compassionate to those who fear him.

103:14 Gen 3:19; Eccl 12:7; Isa 29:16

14 For he understands how weak we are;
he knows we are only dust.

103:15 Jas 1:10-11; 1 Pet 1:24

15 Our days on earth are like grass;
like wildflowers, we bloom and die.
16 The wind blows, and we are gone—
as though we had never been here.
17 But the love of the LORD remains forever
with those who fear him.
His salvation extends to the children's children

103:18 Deut 7:9

18 of those who are faithful to his covenant,
of those who obey his commandments!
19 The LORD has made the heavens his throne;
from there he rules over everything.

103:1ff David's praise focused on God's glorious deeds. It is easy to complain about life, but David's list gives us plenty for which to praise God: He forgives our sins, heals our diseases, redeems us from death, crowns us with love and compassion, satisfies our desires, and gives righteousness and justice. We receive all of these without deserving any of them. No matter how difficult your life's journey, you can always count your blessings—past, present, and future. When you feel as though you have nothing for which to praise God, read David's list.

103:7 God's law was given first to Moses and the people of Israel. God's law presents a clear picture of God's nature and will. It was God's training manual to prepare his people to serve him and to follow his ways. Review the Ten Commandments (Exodus 20) and the history of how they were given, asking God to show you his will and his ways through them.

103:12 East and west can never meet. This is a symbolic portrait of God's forgiveness: When he forgives our sin, he separates it from us and doesn't even remember it. We need never wallow in the past, for God forgives and forgets. We tend to dredge up the ugly past, but God has wiped our record clean. If we are to follow God, we must model his forgiveness. When we forgive another, we must also forget the sin. Otherwise we have not truly forgiven.

103:13, 14 We are fragile, but God's care is eternal. Too often we focus on God as judge and lawgiver, ignoring his compassion and concern for us. When God examines our lives, he remembers our human condition. Our weakness should never be used as a justification for sin. His mercy takes everything into account. God will deal with you compassionately. Trust him.

20 Praise the LORD, you angels of his,
you mighty creatures who carry out his plans,
listening for each of his commands.
21 Yes, praise the LORD, you armies of angels
who serve him and do his will!
22 Praise the LORD, everything he has created,
everywhere in his kingdom.
As for me—I, too, will praise the LORD.

103:20 Matt 6:10 Heb 1:14

Theme: Appreciating God through his creation. He not only creates, but maintains his creation. The Lord's care is the source of our joy.
Author: Anonymous

104

1 Praise the LORD, I tell myself;
O LORD my God, how great you are!
You are robed with honor and with majesty;
2 you are dressed in a robe of light.
You stretch out the starry curtain of the heavens;
3 you lay out the rafters of your home in the rain clouds.
You make the clouds your chariots;
you ride upon the wings of the wind.
4 The winds are your messengers;
flames of fire are your servants.

5 You placed the world on its foundation
so it would never be moved.
6 You clothed the earth with floods of water,
water that covered even the mountains.
7 At the sound of your rebuke, the water fled;
at the sound of your thunder, it fled away.
8 Mountains rose and valleys sank
to the levels you decreed.
9 Then you set a firm boundary for the seas,
so they would never again cover the earth.

10 You make the springs pour water into ravines,
so streams gush down from the mountains.
11 They provide water for all the animals,
and the wild donkeys quench their thirst.
12 The birds nest beside the streams
and sing among the branches of the trees.
13 You send rain on the mountains from your heavenly home,
and you fill the earth with the fruit of your labor.
14 You cause grass to grow for the cattle.
You cause plants to grow for people to use.
You allow them to produce food from the earth—
15 wine to make them glad,
olive oil as lotion for their skin,
and bread to give them strength.

104:2 Dan 7:9
104:3 Ps 18:10 Amos 9:6
104:4 2 Kgs 2:11; 6:17 †Heb 1:7
104:5 Job 38:4
104:6 Gen 1:2
104:7 Pss 18:15; 29:3
104:9 Job 38:10-11 Jer 5:22
104:10 Isa 41:18
104:12 Matt 8:20
104:14 Gen 1:29 Job 28:5
104:15 Judg 9:13; 19:5, 8 Prov 31:6 Eccl 10:19 Luke 7:46

103:20-22 Everything everywhere is to praise the Lord: all his angels and all his works! Praising God means remembering all he has done for us (103:2), fearing him and obeying his commands (103:17, 18), and doing his will (103:21). Does your life praise the Lord?

104:1ff This psalm is a poetic summary of God's creation of the world as found in the first chapter of Genesis. What God created each day is mentioned by the psalmist as a reason to praise God. On day one, God created light (104:1, 2; Genesis 1:3); day two, the heavens and the waters (104:2, 3; Genesis 1:6); day three, land and vegetation (104:6-18; Genesis 1:9-13); day four, the sun, moon, and stars (104:19-23; Genesis 1:14-16); day five, fish and birds (104:25, 26; Genesis 1:20-23); and on day six, animals, people, and food to sustain them (104:21-24, 27-30; Genesis 1:24-31). God's act of creation deserves the praise of all people.

104:5 The earth is built on God's foundations, and he guarantees its permanence. "It would never be moved" by anyone other than God. Even though one day the heavens and the earth will be destroyed (2 Peter 3:10), he will create a new heaven and a new earth that will last forever (Isaiah 65:17; Revelation 21:1). The same power that undergirds the world also provides a firm foundation for believers.

16 The trees of the LORD are well cared for—
the cedars of Lebanon that he planted.
104:17 Lev 11:19
17 There the birds make their nests,
and the storks make their homes in the firs.
104:18 Lev 11:5 Prov 30:26
18 High in the mountains are pastures for the wild goats,
and the rocks form a refuge for rock badgers.*
104:19 Gen 1:14
19 You made the moon to mark the seasons
and the sun that knows when to set.
104:20 Isa 45:7; 56:9
20 You send the darkness, and it becomes night,
when all the forest animals prowl about.
21 Then the young lions roar for their food,
but they are dependent on God.
104:22 Job 37:8
22 At dawn they slink back
into their dens to rest.
104:23 Gen 3:19
23 Then people go off to their work;
they labor until the evening shadows fall again.

104:24 Pss 40:5; 65:9 Jer 10:12; 51:15
24 O LORD, what a variety of things you have made!
In wisdom you have made them all.
The earth is full of your creatures.
25 Here is the ocean, vast and wide,
teeming with life of every kind,
both great and small.
104:26 Job 41:1
26 See the ships sailing along,
and Leviathan, which you made to play in the sea.
104:27 Ps 136:25
27 Every one of these depends on you
to give them their food as they need it.
28 When you supply it, they gather it.
You open your hand to feed them, and they are satisfied.

104:18 Or *coneys,* or *hyraxes.*

HOW GOD IS DESCRIBED IN PSALMS

Most of the psalms speak to God or about God. Because they were composed in a variety of situations, various facets of God's character are mentioned. Here is a sample of God's characteristics as understood and experienced by the psalm writers. As you read these psalms, ask yourself if this is the God you know.

God is . . .	*Reference*
All-knowing and ever present	Psalm 139
Beautiful and desirable	Psalms 27; 36; 45
Creator	Psalms 8; 104; 148
Good and generous	Psalms 34; 81; 107
Great and sovereign	Psalms 33; 89; 96
Holy	Psalms 66; 99; 145
Loving and faithful	Psalms 23; 42; 51
Merciful and forgiving	Psalms 32; 111; 130
Powerful	Psalms 76; 89; 93
Willing to reveal his will, law, and direction	Psalms 1; 19; 119
Righteous and just	Psalms 71; 97; 113
Spirit	Psalms 104; 139; 143

104:24 Creation is filled with stunning variety, revealing the rich creativity, goodness, and wisdom of our loving God. As you observe your natural surroundings, thank God for his creativity. Take a fresh look at people, seeing each one as God's unique creation, with his or her own special talents, abilities, and gifts.

104:26 Here *Leviathan* simply means a large and active sea creature.

104:28-30 Psalm 105 expresses God's sovereignty in history; this psalm tells of his sovereignty over all creation. God has supreme, unlimited power over the entire universe. He creates; he preserves; he governs. As we understand God's power, we realize that he is sufficient to handle our life.

29 But if you turn away from them, they panic.
When you take away their breath, they die
and turn again to dust.
30 When you send your Spirit, new life is born
to replenish all the living of the earth.

31 May the glory of the LORD last forever!
The LORD rejoices in all he has made!
32 The earth trembles at his glance;
the mountains burst into flame at his touch.
33 I will sing to the LORD as long as I live.
I will praise my God to my last breath!
34 May he be pleased by all these thoughts about him,
for I rejoice in the LORD.
35 Let all sinners vanish from the face of the earth;
let the wicked disappear forever.
As for me—I will praise the LORD!

Praise the LORD!

104:29 Gen 3:19
104:30 Ezek 37:9
104:31 Gen 1:31
104:32 Exod 19:18; Judg 5:5
104:35 Pss 37:10; 89:13; 104:1

Theme: God's mighty deeds in bringing Israel to the Promised Land. Remembering his miracles encourages us to keep living close to him.
Author: David

105

1 Give thanks to the LORD and proclaim his greatness.
Let the whole world know what he has done.
2 Sing to him; yes, sing his praises.
Tell everyone about his miracles.
3 Exult in his holy name;
O worshipers of the LORD, rejoice!
4 Search for the LORD and for his strength,
and keep on searching.
5 Think of the wonderful works he has done,
the miracles and the judgments he handed down,
6 O children of Abraham, God's servant,
O descendants of Jacob, God's chosen one.
7 He is the LORD our God.
His rule is seen throughout the land.
8 He always stands by his covenant—
the commitment he made to a thousand generations.
9 This is the covenant he made with Abraham
and the oath he swore to Isaac.
10 He confirmed it to Jacob as a decree,
to the people of Israel as a never-ending treaty:
11 "I will give you the land of Canaan
as your special possession."

105:1-15 //1 Chr 16:8-22
105:2 Ps 98:5
105:3 Ps 33:21
105:4 Ps 27:8
105:5 1 Chr 16:13
105:7 Isa 26:9
105:8 Gen 22:16-18; Deut 7:9; Luke 1:72
105:10 Gen 28:13-15; Josh 23:4
105:11 Gen 13:15; 15:18

104:29 Today many people are arrogant enough to think they don't need God. But our every breath depends on the life he has breathed into us (Genesis 2:7; 3:19; Job 33:4; 34:14, 15; Daniel 5:23). Not only do we depend on God for our very life, but he wants the best for us. We should also desire to learn more of his plans for us each day.

105:1ff The first 15 verses of this psalm are also found in 1 Chronicles 16:8-22, where they are sung as part of the celebration of David's bringing the Ark of the Covenant to Jerusalem. Three other psalms are also hymns recounting Israel's history: 78, 106, and 136.

105:4, 5 If God seems far away, persist in your search for him. God rewards those who sincerely look for him (Hebrews 11:6). Jesus promised, "Everyone who seeks, finds" (Matthew 7:7). The psalmist suggested a valuable way to find God—become familiar with the way he has helped his people in the past. The Bible records the history of God's people. In searching its pages we will discover a loving God who is waiting for us to find him.

105:6-11 The nation Israel, the people through whom God revealed his laws to everyone, is descended from Abraham. God chose Abraham and promised that his descendants would live in the land of Canaan (now called Israel) and that they would be too numerous to count (Genesis 17:6-8). Abraham's son was Isaac; Isaac's son was Jacob. These three men are considered the patriarchs or founders of Israel. God blessed them because of their faith (see Hebrews 11:8-21).

105:12 Gen 34:30 Heb 11:9

12 He said this when they were few in number,
a tiny group of strangers in Canaan.
13 They wandered back and forth between nations,
from one kingdom to another.

105:14 Gen 12:17; 20:7; 35:5

14 Yet he did not let anyone oppress them.
He warned kings on their behalf:
15 "Do not touch these people I have chosen,
and do not hurt my prophets."

105:16 Lev 26:26 Isa 3:1 Ezek 4:16

16 He called for a famine on the land of Canaan,
cutting off its food supply.

105:17 Gen 37:28, 36 Acts 7:9

17 Then he sent someone to Egypt ahead of them—
Joseph, who was sold as a slave.
18 There in prison, they bruised his feet with fetters
and placed his neck in an iron collar.

105:19 Ps 66:10

19 Until the time came to fulfill his word,
the LORD tested Joseph's character.

105:20 Gen 41:14

20 Then Pharaoh sent for him and set him free;
the ruler of the nation opened his prison door.
21 Joseph was put in charge of all the king's household;
he became ruler over all the king's possessions.
22 He could instruct the king's aides as he pleased
and teach the king's advisers.

23 Then Israel arrived in Egypt;
Jacob lived as a foreigner in the land of Ham.

105:24 Exod 1:7, 9

24 And the LORD multiplied the people of Israel
until they became too mighty for their enemies.

105:25 Exod 1:8 Acts 7:19

25 Then he turned the Egyptians against the Israelites,
and they plotted against the LORD's servants.

105:26 Exod 3:10 Num 16:5

26 But the LORD sent Moses his servant,
along with Aaron, whom he had chosen.

105:27 Ps 78:43-51

27 They performed miraculous signs among the Egyptians,
and miracles in the land of Ham.

105:28 Exod 10:22 Ps 99:7

28 The LORD blanketed Egypt in darkness,
for they had defied his commands to let his people go.

105:29 Exod 7:20

29 He turned the nation's water into blood,
poisoning all the fish.

105:30 Exod 8:6

30 Then frogs overran the land;
they were found even in the king's private rooms.

105:31 Exod 8:16, 21

31 When he spoke, flies descended on the Egyptians,
and gnats swarmed across Egypt.

HISTORY IN THE BOOK OF PSALMS

For the original hearers, the historical psalms were vivid reminders of God's past acts on behalf of Israel. These history songs were written for passing on important lessons to succeeding generations. They celebrated the many promises God had made and faithfully kept; they also recounted the faithlessness of the people.

We cannot read this ancient history without reflecting on how consistently God's people failed to learn from the past. They repeatedly turned from fresh examples of God's faithfulness and forgiveness only to plunge back into sin. God can use these psalms to remind us how often we do exactly the same thing: Having every reason to live for God, we choose instead to live for everything but God. If we paid more attention to "his story," we wouldn't make so many mistakes in our own stories.

Selected historical psalms include: 68; 78; 95; 105; 106; 111; 114; 135; 136; 149.

105:23-25 Did God cause the Egyptians to hate the Israelites? God is not the author of evil, but the Bible writers don't always distinguish between God's ultimate action and the intermediate steps. Thus, by God blessing the Israelites, the Egyptians came to hate them (Exodus 1:8-22). Because God caused the Israelites' blessing, he is also said to have caused the Egyptians' hatred. God used their animosity as a means to lead the Israelites out of Egypt.

32 Instead of rain, he sent murderous hail,
and flashes of lightning overwhelmed the land.
33 He ruined their grapevines and fig trees
and shattered all the trees.
34 He spoke, and hordes of locusts came—
locusts beyond number.
35 They ate up everything green in the land,
destroying all the crops.
36 Then he killed the oldest child in each Egyptian home,
the pride and joy of each family.

37 But he brought his people safely out of Egypt, loaded with silver and gold;
there were no sick or feeble people among them.
38 Egypt was glad when they were gone,
for the dread of them was great.
39 The LORD spread out a cloud above them as a covering
and gave them a great fire to light the darkness.
40 They asked for meat, and he sent them quail;
he gave them manna—bread from heaven.
41 He opened up a rock, and water gushed out
to form a river through the dry and barren land.
42 For he remembered his sacred promise
to Abraham his servant.
43 So he brought his people out of Egypt with joy,
his chosen ones with rejoicing.
44 He gave his people the lands of pagan nations,
and they harvested crops that others had planted.
45 All this happened so they would follow his principles
and obey his laws.

Praise the LORD!

105:32 Exod 9:23
105:36 Exod 12:29-30
105:37 Exod 12:33
105:39 Neh 9:12; Isa 4:5
105:40 Num 11:31; John 6:31
105:41 Exod 17:6; Ps 78:15; 1 Cor 10:4
105:43 Exod 15:1
105:44 Josh 13:7
105:45 Deut 4:40

Theme: A song of national repentance as the people return from captivity. God patiently delivers us, in spite of our forgetfulness and self-willed rebellion.
Author: Anonymous

106

1 Praise the LORD!

Give thanks to the LORD, for he is good!
His faithful love endures forever.
2 Who can list the glorious miracles of the LORD?
Who can ever praise him half enough?
3 Happy are those who deal justly with others
and always do what is right.

4 Remember me, too, LORD, when you show favor to your people;
come to me with your salvation.
5 Let me share in the prosperity of your chosen ones.
Let me rejoice in the joy of your people;
let me praise you with those who are your heritage.

106:1 1 Chr 16:34, 41; Pss 100:5; 105:1
106:3 Ps 15:2
106:4 Ps 44:3
106:5 Pss 1:3; 105:3; 118:15

105:45 God's purpose for saving the Israelites was that they would "follow his principles and obey his laws." Too often we use our lives and freedom to please ourselves, but we should honor God. That is God's purpose for our lives and why he gave us his Word.

106:1ff While Psalm 105 is a summary of God's faithfulness, Psalm 106 is a summary of humanity's sinfulness. Psalm 105 covers events up to the exodus from Egypt (Exodus 5–14), and Psalm 106 covers events from the Exodus up to what appears to be the Babylonian captivity (2 Kings 25).

106:2 If we ever stopped to list all the mighty acts or miracles in the Bible, we would be astounded. They cover every aspect of life. The more we think about what God has done, the more we can appreciate the miracles he has done for us individually—birth, personal development, salvation, specific guidance, healing, loving friends and family—the list goes on and on. If you think you have never seen a miracle, look closer. You will see God's power and loving intervention on your behalf. God still performs great miracles!

106:6 2 Chr 30:7 Ezra 9:7 Neh 1:7 Zech 1:4

6 Both we and our ancestors have sinned.
We have done wrong! We have acted wickedly!

106:7 Judg 3:7

7 Our ancestors in Egypt
were not impressed by the LORD's miracles.
They soon forgot his many acts of kindness to them.
Instead, they rebelled against him at the Red Sea.*

106:8 Ezek 20:9

8 Even so, he saved them—
to defend the honor of his name
and to demonstrate his mighty power.

106:9 Exod 14:21 Isa 63:11-13

9 He commanded the Red Sea* to divide, and a dry path appeared.
He led Israel across the sea bottom that was as dry as a desert.
10 So he rescued them from their enemies
and redeemed them from their foes.

106:11 Exod 15:5

11 Then the water returned and covered their enemies;
not one of them survived.
12 Then at last his people believed his promises.
Then they finally sang his praise.

13 Yet how quickly they forgot what he had done!
They wouldn't wait for his counsel!

106:14 Num 11:4

14 In the wilderness, their desires ran wild,
testing God's patience in that dry land.

106:15 Num 16:32 Pss 78:29-31; 106:17

15 So he gave them what they asked for,
but he sent a plague along with it.

106:16 Num 16:1-3

16 The people in the camp were jealous of Moses
and envious of Aaron, the LORD's holy priest.

106:17 Deut 11:6

17 Because of this, the earth opened up;
it swallowed Dathan
and buried Abiram and the other rebels.

106:18 Num 16:35

18 Fire fell upon their followers;
a flame consumed the wicked.

106:19 Acts 7:41

19 The people made a calf at Mount Sinai*;
they bowed before an image made of gold.

106:20 Jer 2:11 Rom 1:23

20 They traded their glorious God
for a statue of a grass-eating ox!

106:21 Deut 10:21

21 They forgot God, their savior,
who had done such great things in Egypt—

106:22 Ps 105:27

22 such wonderful things in that land,
such awesome deeds at the Red Sea.

106:23 Exod 32:10-14

23 So he declared he would destroy them.
But Moses, his chosen one, stepped between the LORD and the people.
He begged him to turn from his anger and not destroy them.

106:24 Jer 3:19

24 The people refused to enter the pleasant land,
for they wouldn't believe his promise to care for them.
25 Instead, they grumbled in their tents
and refused to obey the LORD.

106:26 Heb 3:11

26 Therefore, he swore
that he would kill them in the wilderness,

106:7 Hebrew *at the sea, the sea of reeds.* **106:9** Hebrew *sea of reeds;* also in 106:22. **106:19** Hebrew *at Horeb,* another name for Sinai.

106:13-15 In the wilderness, the Israelites were so intent on getting the food and water *they* wanted that they became blind to what God wanted. They were more concerned about immediate physical gratification than lasting spiritual satisfaction. They did not want what was best for them, and they refused to trust in God's care and provision (Numbers 11:18-33). If you complain enough, God may give you what you ask for, even if it is not the best for you. If you're not getting what you want, perhaps God knows it is not in your best interest. Trust in his care and provision.

106:23 Moses served as the people's intercessor. This refers to the time when the Lord wanted to destroy the people for worshiping the gold calf (Exodus 32:7-14).

27 that he would scatter their descendants among the nations,
exiling them to distant lands.

28 Then our ancestors joined in the worship of Baal at Peor;
they even ate sacrifices offered to the dead!
29 They angered the LORD with all these things,
so a plague broke out among them.
30 But Phinehas had the courage to step in,
and the plague was stopped.
31 So he has been regarded as a righteous man
ever since that time.

32 At Meribah, too, they angered the LORD,
causing Moses serious trouble.
33 They made Moses angry,*
and he spoke foolishly.

34 Israel failed to destroy the nations in the land,
as the LORD had told them to.
35 Instead, they mingled among the pagans
and adopted their evil customs.
36 They worshiped their idols,
and this led to their downfall.
37 They even sacrificed their sons
and their daughters to the demons.
38 They shed innocent blood,
the blood of their sons and daughters.
By sacrificing them to the idols of Canaan,
they polluted the land with murder.
39 They defiled themselves by their evil deeds,
and their love of idols was adultery in the LORD's sight.

40 That is why the LORD's anger burned against his people,
and he abhorred his own special possession.
41 He handed them over to pagan nations,
and those who hated them ruled over them.
42 Their enemies crushed them
and brought them under their cruel power.
43 Again and again he delivered them,
but they continued to rebel against him,
and they were finally destroyed by their sin.
44 Even so, he pitied them in their distress
and listened to their cries.
45 He remembered his covenant with them
and relented because of his unfailing love.
46 He even caused their captors
to treat them with kindness.

106:28 Hos 9:10
106:30 Num 25:7-13
106:32 Ps 78:40
106:34 Judg 1:21, 27-36
106:37 Num 35:33; 2 Kgs 17:17
106:39 Hos 4:12
106:40 Judg 2:12-14
106:41 Neh 9:27
106:43 Judg 6:6; Ps 81:12
106:45 Lev 26:42
106:46 2 Chr 30:9; Ezra 9:9

106:33 Hebrew *They embittered his spirit.*

106:34-39 Israel constantly turned away from God. How could they turn from God and worship the idols of the land after the great miracles they saw? We also have seen God's great miracles but sometimes find ourselves enticed by the world's gods: power, money, convenience, fame, sex, and pleasure. As Israel forgot God, so we are susceptible to forgetting him and giving in to the pressures of an evil world. Remember all that God has done for you so that you won't be drawn away from him by the world's pleasures.

106:40-42 God allowed trouble to come to the Israelites in order to help them. Our troubles can be helpful because they (1) humble us, (2) wean us from the allurements of the world and drive us back to God, (3) vitalize our prayers, (4) allow us to experience more of God's faithfulness, (5) make us more dependent upon God, (6) encourage us to submit to God's purpose for our lives, and (7) make us more compassionate toward others in trouble.

106:44-46 This is a beautiful picture of God's great love for his people who deserved only judgment. Fortunately, God's compassion and mercy toward us are not limited by our faithfulness to him. God was merciful to us in sending his Son to die for our sins. If he did this while we were captive to sin, how much more merciful will he be now that we are his children?

106:47-48
//1 Chr 16:34-36

47 O LORD our God, save us!
Gather us back from among the nations,
so we can thank your holy name
and rejoice and praise you.

48 Blessed be the LORD, the God of Israel,
from everlasting to everlasting!
Let all the people say, "Amen!"

Praise the LORD!

BOOK V
Psalms 107:1—150:6

These psalms praise God's works, recount the blessings of righteous living, thank God for deliverance, and praise God for his wonderful word. These psalms remind us that the best sacrifice we can offer to God is a faithful and obedient life.

Theme: Thankfulness to God should constantly be on the lips of those whom he has saved. This psalm was written to celebrate the Jews' return from their exile in Babylon.
Author: Anonymous

107:1 Ps 106:1
107:2 Isa 35:9-10
107:3 Neh 1:9; Ps 106:47; Ezek 20:34
107:4 Josh 5:6
107:7 Jer 31:9
107:9 Matt 5:6; Luke 1:53
107:10 Mic 7:8; Luke 1:79
107:11 Num 15:31
107:12 Ps 22:11

107

1 Give thanks to the LORD, for he is good!
His faithful love endures forever.
2 Has the LORD redeemed you? Then speak out!
Tell others he has saved you from your enemies.
3 For he has gathered the exiles from many lands,
from east and west, from north and south.

4 Some wandered in the desert,
lost and homeless.
5 Hungry and thirsty,
they nearly died.
6 "LORD, help!" they cried in their trouble,
and he rescued them from their distress.
7 He led them straight to safety,
to a city where they could live.
8 Let them praise the LORD for his great love
and for all his wonderful deeds to them.
9 For he satisfies the thirsty
and fills the hungry with good things.

10 Some sat in darkness and deepest gloom,
miserable prisoners in chains.
11 They rebelled against the words of God,
scorning the counsel of the Most High.
12 That is why he broke them with hard labor;
they fell, and no one helped them rise again.
13 "LORD, help!" they cried in their trouble,
and he saved them from their distress.

107:1ff This psalm speaks of four different types of people in distress and how God rescues them: wanderers (107:4-9), prisoners (107:10-16), the distressed (107:17-20), and the storm-tossed (107:23-30). No matter how extreme our calamity, God is able to help us. He is loving and kind to those who are distressed.

107:1, 2 "Has the LORD redeemed you? Then speak out!" God has done so much for us, and we have so much for which to thank him (see Psalm 103). He wants us to tell everyone all that he has done. These verses are not so much a mandate to witness as a declaration that when we live in God's presence, we will not be able to keep this glorious experience to ourselves (see also Acts 1:8; 2 Corinthians 5:18-20). What has God done for you? Is there someone you can tell?

107:4-9 Lost, hungry, thirsty, and exhausted, these wanderers typify the Israelites in exile. But they also typify anyone who has not found the satisfaction that comes from knowing God. Anyone who recognizes his or her own lostness can receive the offer of Jesus to satisfy these needs. Jesus is the way (John 14:6), the bread from heaven (John 6:33, 35), the living water (John 4:10-14), and the giver of rest (Matthew 11:28-30). Have you received his life-giving offer?

14 He led them from the darkness and deepest gloom;
he snapped their chains.
15 Let them praise the LORD for his great love
and for all his wonderful deeds to them.
16 For he broke down their prison gates of bronze;
he cut apart their bars of iron.

17 Some were fools in their rebellion;
they suffered for their sins.
18 Their appetites were gone,
and death was near.
19 "LORD, help!" they cried in their trouble,
and he saved them from their distress.
20 He spoke, and they were healed—
snatched from the door of death.
21 Let them praise the LORD for his great love
and for all his wonderful deeds to them.
22 Let them offer sacrifices of thanksgiving
and sing joyfully about his glorious acts.

23 Some went off in ships,
plying the trade routes of the world.
24 They, too, observed the LORD's power in action,
his impressive works on the deepest seas.
25 He spoke, and the winds rose,
stirring up the waves.
26 Their ships were tossed to the heavens
and sank again to the depths;
the sailors cringed in terror.
27 They reeled and staggered like drunkards
and were at their wits' end.
28 "LORD, help!" they cried in their trouble,
and he saved them from their distress.
29 He calmed the storm to a whisper
and stilled the waves.
30 What a blessing was that stillness
as he brought them safely into harbor!
31 Let them praise the LORD for his great love
and for all his wonderful deeds to them.
32 Let them exalt him publicly before the congregation
and before the leaders of the nation.

33 He changes rivers into deserts,
and springs of water into dry land.
34 He turns the fruitful land into salty wastelands,
because of the wickedness of those who live there.
35 But he also turns deserts into pools of water,
the dry land into flowing springs.
36 He brings the hungry to settle there
and build their cities.
37 They sow their fields, plant their vineyards,
and harvest their bumper crops.
38 How he blesses them!
They raise large families there,
and their herds of cattle increase.

107:14 Ps 116:16; Acts 12:7
107:16 Isa 45:1-2
107:17 Isa 65:6-7; Ezek 24:23
107:18 Job 33:19-22; Pss 9:13; 88:3
107:20 2 Kgs 20:5; Matt 8:8
107:22 Lev 7:12; Pss 9:11; 50:14; 73:28; 118:17
107:25 Ps 93:3-4
107:26 Ps 22:14
107:29 Matt 8:26; Luke 8:24
107:32 Ps 22:22, 25; Isa 25:1
107:34 Gen 19:24-25
107:35 Isa 35:6-7; 41:18
107:37 2 Kgs 19:29; Amos 9:14
107:38 Gen 12:2; Exod 1:7

107:32 Those who have never truly suffered may not appreciate God as much as those who have matured under hardship. Those who have seen God work in times of distress have a deeper insight into his loving-kindness. If you have experienced great trials, you have the potential for great praise.

39 When they decrease in number and become impoverished
through oppression, trouble, and sorrow,
40 the LORD pours contempt on their princes,
causing them to wander in trackless wastelands.
41 But he rescues the poor from their distress
and increases their families like vast flocks of sheep.
42 The godly will see these things and be glad,
while the wicked are stricken silent.
43 Those who are wise will take all this to heart;
they will see in our history the faithful love of the LORD.

107:42 Job 22:19 Ps 52:6 Rom 3:19
107:43 Ps 64:9 Jer 9:12 Hos 14:9

Theme: Victory in God's strength. With God's help, we can do more than we think.
Author: David

108

A psalm of David. A song.

1 My heart is confident in you, O God;
no wonder I can sing your praises!
Wake up, my soul!
2 Wake up, O harp and lyre!
I will waken the dawn with my song.
3 I will thank you, LORD, in front of all the people.
I will sing your praises among the nations.
4 For your unfailing love is higher than the heavens.
Your faithfulness reaches to the clouds.
5 Be exalted, O God, above the highest heavens.
May your glory shine over all the earth.

6 Use your strong right arm to save me,
and rescue your beloved people.
7 God has promised this by his holiness*:
"I will divide up Shechem with joy.
I will measure out the valley of Succoth.
8 Gilead is mine,
and Manasseh is mine.
Ephraim will produce my warriors,
and Judah will produce my kings.
9 Moab will become my lowly servant,
and Edom will be my slave.
I will shout in triumph over the Philistines."

10 But who will bring me into the fortified city?
Who will bring me victory over Edom?
11 Have you rejected us, O God?
Will you no longer march with our armies?
12 Oh, please help us against our enemies,
for all human help is useless.
13 With God's help we will do mighty things,
for he will trample down our foes.

108:1-5 //Ps 57:7-11
108:4 Ps 113:4
108:6-13 //Ps 60:5-12
108:11 Ps 44:9

108:7 Or *in his sanctuary.*

108:1ff The conclusions from two previous psalms have been put together to make this psalm. The first five verses are quoted from Psalm 57:7-11, and the next eight verses (108:6-13) are from Psalm 60:5-12.

108:9 Moab, Edom, and Philistia were Israel's enemies to the east, south, and west, respectively. They despised the Israelites and Israel's God.

108:13 Do our prayers end with requests for help to make it through stressful situations? David prayed not merely for rescue, but for victory. With God's help we can claim more than mere survival, we can claim victory! Look for ways God can use your distress as an opportunity to show his mighty power.

Theme: Righteous indignation against liars and slanderers. We can tell God our true feelings and desires.
Author: David

109

For the choir director: A psalm of David.

1 O God, whom I praise,
don't stand silent and aloof
2 while the wicked slander me
and tell lies about me.
3 They are all around me with their hateful words,
and they fight against me for no reason.
4 I love them, but they try to destroy me—
even as I am praying for them!
5 They return evil for good,
and hatred for my love.

6 Arrange for an evil person to turn on him.
Send an accuser to bring him to trial.
7 When his case is called for judgment,
let him be pronounced guilty.
Count his prayers as sins.
8 Let his years be few;
let his position be given to someone else.
9 May his children become fatherless,
and may his wife become a widow.
10 May his children wander as beggars;
may they be evicted from their ruined homes.
11 May creditors seize his entire estate,
and strangers take all he has earned.
12 Let no one be kind to him;
let no one pity his fatherless children.
13 May all his offspring die.
May his family name be blotted out in a single generation.
14 May the LORD never forget the sins of his ancestors;
may his mother's sins never be erased from the record.
15 May these sins always remain before the LORD,
but may his name be cut off from human memory.
16 For he refused all kindness to others;
he persecuted the poor and needy,
and he hounded the brokenhearted to death.
17 He loved to curse others;
now you curse him.
He never blessed others;
now don't you bless him.
18 Cursing is as much a part of him as his clothing,
or as the water he drinks,
or the rich food he eats.
19 Now may his curses return and cling to him like clothing;
may they be tied around him like a belt.

109:1 Ps 83:1
109:2 Pss 52:4; 120:2
109:3 Ps 69:4
109:4 Ps 38:20
109:5 John 7:7
109:6 Zech 3:1
109:7 Prov 28:9
109:8 †Acts 1:20
109:9 Exod 22:24
109:11 Isa 1:7
109:12 Isa 9:17
109:14 Neh 4:5; Isa 65:6-7
109:15 Jer 16:17
109:16 Ps 37:32
109:17 Matt 7:2
109:18 Ps 73:6
109:19 Ezek 7:27

109:1ff David endured many false accusations (1 Samuel 22:7-13; 2 Samuel 15:3, 4), as did Christ centuries later (Matthew 26:59-61; 27:39-44). Verse 8 is quoted in Acts 1:20 as being fulfilled in Judas's death.

109:4 David was angry at being attacked by evil people who slandered him and lied. Yet David remained a friend and a man of prayer. While we must hate evil and work to overcome it, we must love everyone, including those who do evil, because God loves them. We are called to hate the sin, but love the person. Only through God's strength will we be able to follow David's example.

109:6-20 This is another of the imprecatory psalms, a call for God to judge the wicked. (For an explanation of imprecatory psalms, see the note on 35:1ff.) David was not taking vengeance into his own hands; he was asking that God be swift in his promised judgment of evil people. David's words depict the eventual doom of all God's enemies.

109:20
Isa 3:11
2 Tim 4:14

20 May those curses become the LORD's punishment for my accusers
who are plotting against my life.

109:21
Ps 25:11
Ezek 36:22

21 But deal well with me, O Sovereign LORD,
for the sake of your own reputation!
Rescue me because you are so faithful and good.

109:22
Ps 40:17
Prov 18:14

22 For I am poor and needy,
and my heart is full of pain.
23 I am fading like a shadow at dusk;
I am falling like a grasshopper that is brushed aside.

109:24
Heb 12:12

24 My knees are weak from fasting,
and I am skin and bones.
25 I am an object of mockery to people everywhere;
when they see me, they shake their heads.

109:26
Ps 119:86

26 Help me, O LORD my God!
Save me because of your unfailing love.
27 Let them see that this is your doing,
that you yourself have done it, LORD.

109:28
2 Sam 16:11-12

28 Then let them curse me if they like,
but you will bless me!
When they attack me, they will be disgraced!
But I, your servant, will go right on rejoicing!

109:29
Job 8:22
Ps 35:26

29 Make their humiliation obvious to all;
clothe my accusers with disgrace.

109:30
Ps 35:18

30 But I will give repeated thanks to the LORD,
praising him to everyone.

109:31
Pss 16:8; 37:33

31 For he stands beside the needy,
ready to save them from those who condemn them.

Theme: The credentials for the Messiah. Jesus is the Messiah.
Author: David

110

A psalm of David.

110:1
†Matt 22:44
†Mark 12:36; 14:62
†Luke 20:42
†Acts 2:34
†Heb 1:13

1 The LORD said to my Lord,
"Sit in honor at my right hand
until I humble your enemies,
making them a footstool under your feet."

110:2
Ps 45:6
Dan 7:13-14

2 The LORD will extend your powerful dominion from Jerusalem*;
you will rule over your enemies.

110:3
Judg 5:2
Ps 96:9

3 In that day of battle,
your people will serve you willingly.
Arrayed in holy garments,
your vigor will be renewed each day like the morning dew.

110:4
†Heb 5:6; 7:21, 17

4 The LORD has taken an oath and will not break his vow:
"You are a priest forever in the line of Melchizedek."

110:2 Hebrew *Zion.*

110:1 This is one of the most-quoted psalms in the New Testament because of its clear references to the Messiah. In Matthew 22:41-45, Jesus recited the words of this verse and applied them to himself. Verses 1 and 6 look forward to Christ's final and total destruction of the wicked (Revelation 6–9); 110:2 prophesies Christ's reign on the earth (Revelation 20:1-7); 110:3, 4 tell of Christ's priestly work for his people (Hebrews 5–8); and 110:5, 6 look forward to the final battle on earth when Christ will overcome the forces of evil (Revelation 19:11-21).

110:1-7 Many people have a vague belief in God but refuse to accept Jesus as anything more than a great human teacher. But the Bible does not allow that option. Both the Old and New Testaments proclaim the deity of the one who came to save and to reign. Jesus explained that this psalm spoke of the Messiah as greater than David, Israel's greatest king (Mark 12:35-37). Peter used this psalm to show that Jesus, the Messiah, sits at God's right hand and is Lord over all (Acts 2:32-35). You can't straddle the fence, calling Jesus "just a good teacher," because the Bible clearly calls him Lord.

110:4 For more about Melchizedek, see his Profile in Genesis 16. As a priest like Melchizedek, Christ will never abuse his divine position, and his reign will be forever. Jesus is more fully described as our High Priest in Hebrews 5.

5 The Lord stands at your right hand to protect you.
He will strike down many kings in the day of his anger.
6 He will punish the nations
and fill them with their dead;
he will shatter heads
over the whole earth.
7 But he himself will be refreshed from brooks along the way.
He will be victorious.

110:5 Pss 2:5, 12; 16:8 Rom 2:5 Rev 6:17

Theme: All that God does is good. Reverence for God is the beginning of wisdom.
Author: Anonymous

111

1 Praise the LORD!

I will thank the LORD with all my heart
as I meet with his godly people.
2 How amazing are the deeds of the LORD!
All who delight in him should ponder them.
3 Everything he does reveals his glory and majesty.
His righteousness never fails.
4 Who can forget the wonders he performs?
How gracious and merciful is our LORD!
5 He gives food to those who trust him;
he always remembers his covenant.
6 He has shown his great power to his people
by giving them the lands of other nations.
7 All he does is just and good,
and all his commandments are trustworthy.
8 They are forever true,
to be obeyed faithfully and with integrity.
9 He has paid a full ransom for his people.
He has guaranteed his covenant with them forever.
What a holy, awe-inspiring name he has!
10 Reverence for the LORD is the foundation of true wisdom.
The rewards of wisdom come to all who obey him.

Praise his name forever!

111:1 Pss 92:5; 138:1
111:2 Ps 92:5
111:3 Pss 96:6; 145:5
111:4 Pss 86:15; 103:8
111:5 Matt 6:31-33
111:7 Ps 19:7-9 Rev 15:3-4
111:8 Isa 40:8 Matt 5:18
111:9 Ps 99:3 Luke 1:68
111:10 Prov 1:7, 9; 3:4-5; 9:10

Theme: The advantages of having faith in God. God guards the minds and actions of those who follow his commands.
Author: Anonymous

112

1 Praise the LORD!

Happy are those who fear the LORD.
Yes, happy are those who delight in doing what he commands.
2 Their children will be successful everywhere;
an entire generation of godly people will be blessed.

112:1 Ps 119:16
112:2 Ps 25:13

111–118 Psalms 111–118 are called hallelujah psalms. *Hallelujah* means "praise the LORD" and expresses the uplifting and optimistic tone of these songs.

111:9 The ransom here pictures the rescue by God of the Israelites from Egypt and the future return from captivity in Babylon (see Deuteronomy 7:8; Jeremiah 31:11). *Ransom* means "to free from captivity by paying a price". All people were being held in slavery by sin until Jesus paid the price to free us—giving his life as a perfect sacrifice. Before Jesus offered himself as a sacrifice for sin, people were not permitted into God's presence (the Most Holy Place); now, all believers can freely approach God's throne through prayer and have God in their lives through the Holy Spirit.

111:10 The only way to become truly wise is to fear (revere) God. This same thought is expressed in Proverbs 1:7-9. Too often people want to skip this step, thinking they can become wise by life experience and academic knowledge alone. But if we do not acknowledge God as the source of wisdom, then our foundation for making wise decisions is shaky, and we are prone to mistakes and foolish choices.

112:1 Many blessings are available to us—honor, prosperity, security, freedom from fear (112:2-9)—if we *fear* the Lord and *delight* in obeying his commands. If you expect God's blessings, you must revere him and gladly obey him.

112:3 Prov 3:16-17; 8:18
3 They themselves will be wealthy,
and their good deeds will never be forgotten.

112:4 Job 11:17 Ps 97:11
4 When darkness overtakes the godly, light will come bursting in.
They are* generous, compassionate, and righteous.

112:5 Ps 37:21, 26
5 All goes well for those who are generous,
who lend freely and conduct their business fairly.

112:6 Pss 15:5; 55:22
6 Such people will not be overcome by evil circumstances.
Those who are righteous will be long remembered.

112:7 Ps 56:4
7 They do not fear bad news;
they confidently trust the LORD to care for them.

112:8 Ps 56:10-11
8 They are confident and fearless
and can face their foes triumphantly.

112:9 Ps 148:14 †2 Cor 9:9
9 They give generously to those in need.
Their good deeds will never be forgotten.
They will have influence and honor.

112:10 Matt 8:12 Luke 13:28
10 The wicked will be infuriated when they see this.
They will grind their teeth in anger;
they will slink away, their hopes thwarted.

Theme: The scope of God's care. God's great mercy is demonstrated by his concern for the poor and the oppressed.
Author: Anonymous

113

113:1 Ps 135:1
1 Praise the LORD!

Yes, give praise, O servants of the LORD.
Praise the name of the LORD!

113:2 Dan 2:20
2 Blessed be the name of the LORD
forever and ever.

113:3 Ps 50:1
3 Everywhere—from east to west—
praise the name of the LORD.

113:4 Pss 8:1; 97:9; 99:2
4 For the LORD is high above the nations;
his glory is far greater than the heavens.

113:5 Pss 89:6; 103:19
5 Who can be compared with the LORD our God,
who is enthroned on high?

113:6 Ps 11:4 Isa 57:15
6 Far below him are the heavens and the earth.
He stoops to look,

113:7 1 Sam 2:8
7 and he lifts the poor from the dirt
and the needy from the garbage dump.

113:8 Job 36:7
8 He sets them among princes,
even the princes of his own people!

113:9 1 Sam 2:5 Ps 68:6 Isa 54:1
9 He gives the barren woman a home,
so that she becomes a happy mother.

Praise the LORD!

112:4 Greek version reads *The LORD is.*

112:5 Generosity can cure two problems that having money can create. The rich person may abuse others in the desire to accumulate wealth. Generosity will eliminate that abuse. Also, the fear of losing money can be a snare. Generosity shows that we have placed our trust in God, not in our money, for justice and security.

112:7, 8 We all want to live without fear; our heroes are fearless people who take on all dangers and overcome them. The psalmist teaches us that *fear* of God can lead to a *fearless* life. To fear God means to respect and revere him as the almighty Lord. When we trust God completely to take care of us, we will find that our other fears—even of death itself—will subside.

113:5-9 In God's eyes, a person's value has no relationship to his or her wealth or position on the social ladder. Many people who have excelled in God's work began in poverty or humble beginnings. God supersedes the social orders of this world, often choosing his future leaders and ambassadors from among social outcasts. Do you treat the unwanted in society as though they have value? Demonstrate by your actions that all people are valuable and useful in God's eyes.

Theme: The mighty God who delivered Israel from Egypt. We can celebrate God's great work in our life.
Author: Anonymous

114 1 When the Israelites escaped from Egypt—
when the family of Jacob left that foreign land—
2 the land of Judah became God's sanctuary,
and Israel became his kingdom.

3 The Red Sea* saw them coming and hurried out of their way!
The water of the Jordan River turned away.
4 The mountains skipped like rams,
the little hills like lambs!
5 What's wrong, Red Sea, that made you hurry out of their way?
What happened, Jordan River, that you turned away?
6 Why, mountains, did you skip like rams?
Why, little hills, like lambs?

7 Tremble, O earth, at the presence of the Lord,
at the presence of the God of Israel.*
8 He turned the rock into pools of water;
yes, springs of water came from solid rock.

114:1 Exod 13:3
114:2 Exod 19:6; 29:45-46 Ps 78:68-69
114:3 Exod 14:21 Josh 3:13-14, 16
114:4 Ps 29:5-6 Hab 3:6
114:5 Hab 3:8
114:7 Ps 96:9
114:8 Exod 17:5-6 Deut 8:15

Theme: God is alive. He is thinking about us and caring for us, and we should put him first in our life.
Author: Anonymous

115 1 Not to us, O LORD, but to you goes all the glory
for your unfailing love and faithfulness.
2 Why let the nations say,
"Where is their God?"
3 For our God is in the heavens,
and he does as he wishes.
4 Their idols are merely things of silver and gold,
shaped by human hands.
5 They cannot talk, though they have mouths,
or see, though they have eyes!
6 They cannot hear with their ears,
or smell with their noses,
7 or feel with their hands,
or walk with their feet,
or utter sounds with their throats!
8 And those who make them are just like them,
as are all who trust in them.

115:1 Ps 29:2 Isa 48:11 Ezek 36:22, 32
115:2 Pss 42:3; 79:10; 96:8
115:3 Pss 103:19; 135:6 Dan 4:35
115:4-11 //Ps 135:15-20
115:5 Jer 10:25
115:8 Ps 135:18

114:3 Hebrew *the sea;* also in 114:5. **114:7** Hebrew *of Jacob.*

114:7 When God gave the law at Mount Sinai, the mountain trembled in God's presence. Even with our great technology, the seas, rivers, and mountains still present us with formidable challenges. But to God, who controls nature, they are as nothing. When observing the power of an ocean wave or the majesty of a mountain peak, think of God's greatness and glory, which are far more awesome than the natural wonders you can see. To tremble at God's presence means to recognize God's complete power and authority and our frailty by comparison.

115–118 Psalms 115–118 were traditionally sung at the Passover meal, commemorating Israel's escape from slavery in Egypt (Exodus 11–12).

115:1 The psalmist asked that God's name, not the nation's, be glorified. Too often we ask God to glorify his name *with* ours. For example, we may pray for help to do a good job so that our work will be noticed. Or we may ask that a presentation go well so we will get applause. There is nothing wrong with looking good or impressing others; the problem comes when we want to look good no matter what happens to God's reputation in the process. Before you pray, ask yourself, Who will get the credit if God answers my prayer?

115:4-8 When the psalms were written, many people worshiped idols—statues of wood, stone, or metal. They took pride in what they could see and had contempt for what they couldn't see. Today, we still may value tangible objects (home, clothing, possessions) rather than intangible realities (spiritual growth, salvation, giving to those in need, spending time with loved ones). Those who spend their time obtaining tangible objects are as foolish and empty as the idols themselves. (For more on the foolishness of idols, see Isaiah 44:9-20.)

115:9 Pss 33:20; 62:8

9 O Israel, trust the LORD!
He is your helper; he is your shield.
10 O priests of Aaron, trust the LORD!
He is your helper; he is your shield.

115:11 Pss 103:11; 135:20

11 All you who fear the LORD, trust the LORD!
He is your helper; he is your shield.

115:12 Ps 98:3

12 The LORD remembers us,
and he will surely bless us.
He will bless the people of Israel
and the family of Aaron, the priests.

115:13 Ps 128:1, 4

13 He will bless those who fear the LORD,
both great and small.

115:14 Deut 1:11

14 May the LORD richly bless
both you and your children.

115:15 Gen 1:1; 14:19

15 May you be blessed by the LORD,
who made heaven and earth.

115:16 Pss 8:6; 89:11

16 The heavens belong to the LORD,
but he has given the earth to all humanity.

115:17 Pss 6:5; 31:17

17 The dead cannot sing praises to the LORD,
for they have gone into the silence of the grave.

115:18 Ps 113:2

18 But we can praise the LORD
both now and forever!

Praise the LORD!

Theme: Praise for being saved from certain death. Worship is a thankful response and not a repayment for what God has done.
Author: Anonymous

116

116:1 Pss 18:1; 66:19

1 I love the LORD because he hears
and answers my prayers.

116:2 Pss 17:6; 31:2

2 Because he bends down and listens,
I will pray as long as I have breath!

116:3 Ps 18:4-6

3 Death had its hands around my throat;
the terrors of the grave* overtook me.
I saw only trouble and sorrow.

116:4 Pss 22:20; 118:5

4 Then I called on the name of the LORD:
"Please, LORD, save me!"

116:5 Exod 34:6

5 How kind the LORD is! How good he is!
So merciful, this God of ours!

116:6 Ps 142:6 Prov 1:4

6 The LORD protects those of childlike faith;
I was facing death, and then he saved me.

116:7 Ps 13:6 Matt 11:29

7 Now I can rest again,
for the LORD has been so good to me.

116:8 Pss 49:15; 56:13

8 He has saved me from death,
my eyes from tears,
my feet from stumbling.
9 And so I walk in the LORD's presence
as I live here on earth!

116:3 Hebrew *of Sheol.*

115:12 "The LORD remembers us," says the psalm writer. What a fantastic truth! There are many times when we feel isolated, alone, and abandoned, even by God. In reality, he sees, understands, and thinks about us. When depressed by problems or struggling with self-worth, be encouraged that God keeps you in his thoughts. If he thinks about you, surely his help is near.

116:1, 2 God is so responsive that you can always reach him. He bends down and listens to your voice. This writer's love for the Lord had grown because he had experienced answers to his prayers. If you are discouraged, remember that God is near, listening carefully to every prayer and answering each one in order to give you his best.

10 I believed in you, so I prayed,
"I am deeply troubled, LORD."
11 In my anxiety I cried out to you,
"These people are all liars!"
12 What can I offer the LORD
for all he has done for me?
13 I will lift up a cup symbolizing his salvation;
I will praise the LORD's name for saving me.
14 I will keep my promises to the LORD
in the presence of all his people.
15 The LORD's loved ones are precious to him;
it grieves him when they die.
16 O LORD, I am your servant;
yes, I am your servant, the son of your handmaid,
and you have freed me from my bonds!
17 I will offer you a sacrifice of thanksgiving
and call on the name of the LORD.
18 I will keep my promises to the LORD
in the presence of all his people,
19 in the house of the LORD,
in the heart of Jerusalem.

Praise the LORD!

116:10 †2 Cor 4:13
116:12 2 Chr 32:25; 1 Thes 3:9
116:14 Pss 22:25; 50:14
116:15 Ps 72:14

Theme: Another reason for praise—God's love for the whole world. We should praise God for his unlimited love.
Author: Anonymous

117

1 Praise the LORD, all you nations.
Praise him, all you people of the earth.
2 For he loves us with unfailing love;
the faithfulness of the LORD endures forever.

Praise the LORD!

117:1 †Rom 15:11
117:2 Ps 100:5

Theme: Confidence in God's eternal love. God's love is unchanging in the midst of changing situations. This gives us security.
Author: Anonymous

118

1 Give thanks to the LORD, for he is good!
His faithful love endures forever.
2 Let the congregation of Israel repeat:
"His faithful love endures forever."
3 Let Aaron's descendants, the priests, repeat:
"His faithful love endures forever."
4 Let all who fear the LORD repeat:
"His faithful love endures forever."
5 In my distress I prayed to the LORD,
and the LORD answered me and rescued me.

118:1 Ps 136:1-26
118:2 Ps 115:9
118:5 Pss 18:19; 120:1

116:15 God stays close to us even in death. When someone we love is nearing death, we may become angry and feel abandoned. But believers (the Lord's loved ones) are precious to God, and he carefully chooses the time when they will be called into his presence. Let this truth provide comfort when you've lost a loved one. God sees, and each life is valuable to him (see Jesus' statement in Matthew 10:29).

117:1, 2 Not only is Psalm 117 the shortest chapter in the Bible, it is also the middle chapter. Paul quotes from this psalm in Romans 15:11 to show that God's salvation is for *all* people, not just the Jews.

117:1, 2 Have you ever said, "I can't think of anything God has done for me. How can I praise him?" This psalm gives two reasons for praising God: his unfailing love toward us and his faithfulness that endures forever. If he did nothing else for us, he would still be worthy of our highest praise.

118:6 Job 19:27 †Heb 13:6

6 The LORD is for me, so I will not be afraid.
What can mere mortals do to me?

118:7 Ps 54:7

7 Yes, the LORD is for me; he will help me.
I will look in triumph at those who hate me.

118:8 2 Chr 32:7-8 Isa 57:13

8 It is better to trust the LORD
than to put confidence in people.
9 It is better to trust the LORD
than to put confidence in princes.

118:10 Ps 18:40

10 Though hostile nations surrounded me,
I destroyed them all in the name of the LORD.
11 Yes, they surrounded and attacked me,
but I destroyed them all in the name of the LORD.

118:12 Deut 1:44

12 They swarmed around me like bees;
they blazed against me like a roaring flame.
But I destroyed them all in the name of the LORD.
13 You did your best to kill me, O my enemy,
but the LORD helped me.

118:14 Exod 15:2 Isa 12:2

14 The LORD is my strength and my song;
he has become my victory.

118:15 Ps 89:13 Luke 1:51

15 Songs of joy and victory are sung in the camp of the godly.
The strong right arm of the LORD has done glorious things!
16 The strong right arm of the LORD is raised in triumph.
The strong right arm of the LORD has done glorious things!
17 I will not die, but I will live
to tell what the LORD has done.

118:18 Jer 31:18 1 Cor 11:32 2 Cor 6:9

18 The LORD has punished me severely,
but he has not handed me over to death.

118:19 Isa 26:2

19 Open for me the gates where the righteous enter,
and I will go in and thank the LORD.
20 Those gates lead to the presence of the LORD,
and the godly enter there.
21 I thank you for answering my prayer
and saving me!

118:22 Matt 21:42 Mark 12:10-11 †Luke 20:17 †Acts 4:11 †1 Pet 2:7

22 The stone rejected by the builders
has now become the cornerstone.

118:23 †Matt 21:42 †Mark 12:11

23 This is the LORD's doing,
and it is marvelous to see.
24 This is the day the LORD has made.
We will rejoice and be glad in it.

118:25 Ps 122:6-7

25 Please, LORD, please save us.
Please, LORD, please give us success.

118:26 †Matt 21:9 †Mark 11:9 †Luke 13:35; 19:38 †John 12:13

26 Bless the one who comes in the name of the LORD.
We bless you from the house of the LORD.

118:8 Pilots put confidence in their planes. Commuters place confidence in trains, cars, or buses. Each day we must put our confidence in something or someone. If you are willing to trust a plane or car to get you to your destination, are you willing to trust God to guide you here on earth and to your eternal destination? Do you trust him more than any human being? How futile it is to trust anything or anyone more than God.

118:22, 23 Jesus referred to this verse when he spoke of being rejected by his own people (Matthew 21:42; Mark 12:10, 11; Luke 20:17). Although he was rejected, Jesus is now the "cornerstone," the most important part of the church (Acts 4:11; Ephesians 2:20; 1 Peter 2:6, 7). The cornerstone is the foundation stone, holding the structure together.

118:24 There are days when the last thing we want to do is rejoice. Our mood is down, our situation is out of hand, and our sorrow or guilt is overwhelming. We can relate to the writers of the psalms who often felt this way. But no matter how low the psalmists felt, they were always honest with God. And as they talked to God, their prayers ended in praise. When you don't feel like rejoicing, tell God how you truly feel. You will find that God will give you a reason to rejoice. God has given you this day to live and to serve him—be glad!

27 The LORD is God, shining upon us.
Bring forward the sacrifice and put it on the altar.
28 You are my God, and I will praise you!
You are my God, and I will exalt you!

29 Give thanks to the LORD, for he is good!
His faithful love endures forever.

118:27 Isa 25:1; 1 Pet 2:9
118:28 Exod 15:2; Isa 25:1

Theme: God's word is true and wonderful. Stay true to God and his word no matter how bad the world becomes. Obedience to God's laws is the only way to achieve real happiness.
Author: Anonymous, some suggest Ezra the priest

119

1 Happy are people of integrity,
who follow the law of the LORD.
2 Happy are those who obey his decrees
and search for him with all their hearts.
3 They do not compromise with evil,
and they walk only in his paths.
4 You have charged us
to keep your commandments carefully.
5 Oh, that my actions would consistently
reflect your principles!
6 Then I will not be disgraced
when I compare my life with your commands.
7 When I learn your righteous laws,
I will thank you by living as I should!
8 I will obey your principles.
Please don't give up on me!

9 How can a young person stay pure?
By obeying your word and following its rules.
10 I have tried my best to find you—
don't let me wander from your commands.
11 I have hidden your word in my heart,
that I might not sin against you.
12 Blessed are you, O LORD;
teach me your principles.
13 I have recited aloud
all the laws you have given us.

119:1 Prov 11:20; 13:6
119:2 Deut 4:29; 10:12; 11:13; 30:2
119:4 Deut 4:13
119:5 2 Chr 7:17; Prov 4:26
119:8 Ps 71:9, 18
119:9 1 Kgs 8:25; 2 Chr 6:16
119:11 Luke 2:19, 51
119:13 Ps 40:9

119 This psalm is a Hebrew acrostic poem; there are 22 stanzas, one for each letter of the Hebrew alphabet. The 8 verses within each stanza begin with the Hebrew letter of its section.

119:1ff This is both the longest psalm and the longest chapter in the Bible. It may have been written by Ezra after the Temple was rebuilt (Ezra 6:14, 15) as a repetitive meditation on the beauty of God's Word and how it helps us stay pure and grow in faith. Psalm 119 has 22 carefully constructed sections, each corresponding to a different letter in the Hebrew alphabet and each verse beginning with the letter of its section. Almost every verse mentions God's Word. Such repetition was common in the Hebrew culture. People did not have personal copies of the Scriptures to read as we do, so God's people memorized his Word and passed it along orally. The structure of this psalm allowed for easy memorization. Remember, God's Word, the Bible, is the only sure guide for living a pure life.

119:9 We are drowning in a sea of impurity. Everywhere we look we find temptation to lead impure lives. The psalmist asked a question that troubles us all: How do we stay pure in a filthy environment? We cannot do this on our own but must have counsel and strength more dynamic than the tempting influences around us. Where can we find that strength and wisdom? By reading God's Word and doing what it says.

119:11 Hiding (keeping) God's Word in our heart is a deterrent to sin. This alone should inspire us to memorize Scripture. But memorization alone will not keep us from sin; we must also put God's Word to work in our life, making it a vital guide for everything we do.

119:12-24 Most of us chafe under rules, for we think they restrict us from doing what we want. At first glance, then, it may seem strange to hear the psalmist talk of rejoicing in following God's laws as much as in having great riches. But God's laws were given to free us to be all he wants us to be. They restrict us from doing what might cripple us and keep us from being our best. God's guidelines help us follow his path and avoid paths that lead to destruction.

14 I have rejoiced in your decrees
as much as in riches.

119:15 Isa 58:2

15 I will study your commandments
and reflect on your ways.
16 I will delight in your principles
and not forget your word.

17 Be good to your servant,
that I may live and obey your word.
18 Open my eyes to see
the wonderful truths in your law.
19 I am but a foreigner here on earth;

119:19 1 Chr 29:15 Heb 11:13

I need the guidance of your commands.
Don't hide them from me!
20 I am overwhelmed continually

119:20 Ps 42:1-2

with a desire for your laws.
21 You rebuke those cursed proud ones

119:21 Deut 27:26 Ps 37:22

who wander from your commands.
22 Don't let them scorn and insult me,
for I have obeyed your decrees.
23 Even princes sit and speak against me,
but I will meditate on your principles.
24 Your decrees please me;
they give me wise advice.

119:25 Ps 44:25

25 I lie in the dust, completely discouraged;
revive me by your word.
26 I told you my plans, and you answered.
Now teach me your principles.
27 Help me understand the meaning of your commandments,
and I will meditate on your wonderful miracles.
28 I weep with grief;

119:28 Ps 22:14 1 Pet 5:10

encourage me by your word.
29 Keep me from lying to myself;
give me the privilege of knowing your law.
30 I have chosen to be faithful;
I have determined to live by your laws.

119:31 Deut 11:22

31 I cling to your decrees.
LORD, don't let me be put to shame!

119:32 1 Kgs 4:29 Isa 60:5 2 Cor 6:11

32 If you will help me,
I will run to follow your commands.

119:33 1 Chr 22:12 Ezek 44:24

33 Teach me, O LORD,
to follow every one of your principles.
34 Give me understanding and I will obey your law;
I will put it into practice with all my heart.

119:35 Pss 25:4; 112:1

35 Make me walk along the path of your commands,
for that is where my happiness is found.

119:19 The psalmist said that he is a "foreigner here on earth," and so he needed guidance. Almost any long trip requires a map or guide. As we travel through life, the Bible should be our road map, pointing out safe routes, obstacles to avoid, and our final destination. We must recognize ourselves as pilgrims, travelers here on earth who need to study God's map to learn the way. If we ignore the map, we will wander aimlessly through life and risk missing our real destination.

119:27, 28 Our lives are cluttered with rule books, but the authors never come with us to help us follow the rules. But God does. That is the uniqueness of our Bible. God not only provides the rules and guidelines but comes with us personally each day to strengthen us so that we can live according to those rules. All we must do is invite him and respond to his direction.

36 Give me an eagerness for your decrees;
do not inflict me with love for money!
37 Turn my eyes from worthless things,
and give me life through your word.*
38 Reassure me of your promise,
which is for those who honor you.
39 Help me abandon my shameful ways;
your laws are all I want in life.
40 I long to obey your commandments!
Renew my life with your goodness.

41 LORD, give to me your unfailing love,
the salvation that you promised me.
42 Then I will have an answer for those who taunt me,
for I trust in your word.
43 Do not snatch your word of truth from me,
for my only hope is in your laws.
44 I will keep on obeying your law
forever and forever.
45 I will walk in freedom,
for I have devoted myself to your commandments.
46 I will speak to kings about your decrees,
and I will not be ashamed.
47 How I delight in your commands!
How I love them!
48 I honor and love your commands.
I meditate on your principles.

49 Remember your promise to me,
for it is my only hope.
50 Your promise revives me;
it comforts me in all my troubles.
51 The proud hold me in utter contempt,
but I do not turn away from your law.
52 I meditate on your age-old laws;
O LORD, they comfort me.
53 I am furious with the wicked,
those who reject your law.
54 Your principles have been the music of my life
throughout the years of my pilgrimage.
55 I reflect at night on who you are, O LORD,
and I obey your law because of this.
56 This is my happy way of life:
obeying your commandments.

57 LORD, you are mine!
I promise to obey your words!
58 With all my heart I want your blessings.
Be merciful just as you promised.

119:36 Luke 12:15; Heb 13:5
119:37 Ps 71:20; Isa 33:15
119:38 2 Sam 7:25
119:40 Ps 102:39
119:44 Acts 26:1-2
119:46 Matt 10:18; Acts 26:1-2
119:50 Rom 15:14
119:51 Job 23:11; Jer 20:7
119:52 Ps 103:18
119:53 Exod 32:19; Neh 13:25
119:55 Pss 42:8; 63:6; 92:2; Acts 16:25
119:57 Deut 33:9; Ps 16:5
119:58 Ps 41:4

119:37 Some manuscripts read *in your ways.*

119:36 In today's world, people most often covet financial gain. Money represents power, influence, and success. For many people, money is a god. They think about little else. True, money can buy certain comforts and offer some security. But far more valuable than wealth is obedience to God because it is a heavenly treasure rather than an earthly one (Luke 12:33). We should do what God wants, regardless of the financial implications. Make the psalmist's prayer your own, asking God to turn your heart toward his statutes and not toward making money; it's in your own best interest in the long run.

119:44-46 The psalmist talks about keeping the laws and yet being free. Contrary to what we often expect, obeying God's laws does not inhibit or restrain us. Instead, it frees us to be what God designed us to be. By seeking God's salvation and forgiveness, we have freedom from sin and the resulting oppressive guilt. By living God's way, we have freedom to fulfill God's plan for our life.

119:59 Mark 14:72 Luke 15:17

59 I pondered the direction of my life,
and I turned to follow your statutes.
60 I will hurry, without lingering,
to obey your commands.

119:61 Ps 140:5

61 Evil people try to drag me into sin,
but I am firmly anchored to your law.
62 At midnight I rise to thank you
for your just laws.

119:63 Ps 101:6

63 Anyone who fears you is my friend—
anyone who obeys your commandments.

119:64 Ps 33:5

64 O LORD, the earth is full of your unfailing love;
teach me your principles.

65 You have done many good things for me, LORD,
just as you promised.

119:66 Phil 1:9

66 I believe in your commands;
now teach me good judgment and knowledge.

119:67 Jer 31:18-19 Heb 12:5-11

67 I used to wander off until you disciplined me;
but now I closely follow your word.

119:68 Deut 30:5 Pss 86:5; 125:4

68 You are good and do only good;
teach me your principles.
69 Arrogant people have made up lies about me,
but in truth I obey your commandments with all my heart.

119:70 Ps 17:10 Isa 6:10 Jer 5:28

70 Their hearts are dull and stupid,
but I delight in your law.
71 The suffering you sent was good for me,
for it taught me to pay attention to your principles.

119:72 Prov 8:10-11, 19

72 Your law is more valuable to me
than millions in gold and silver!

119:73 Job 31:15 Ps 139:15-16

73 You made me; you created me.
Now give me the sense to follow your commands.

119:74 Ps 35:27

74 May all who fear you find in me a cause for joy,
for I have put my hope in your word.

119:75 Heb 12:10

75 I know, O LORD, that your decisions are fair;
you disciplined me because I needed it.
76 Now let your unfailing love comfort me,
just as you promised me, your servant.
77 Surround me with your tender mercies so I may live,
for your law is my delight.

119:78 Jer 50:32

78 Bring disgrace upon the arrogant people who lied about me;
meanwhile, I will concentrate on your commandments.
79 Let me be reconciled
with all who fear you and know your decrees.
80 May I be blameless in keeping your principles;
then I will never have to be ashamed.

81 I faint with longing for your salvation;
but I have put my hope in your word.

119:82 Isa 38:14 Lam 2:11

82 My eyes are straining to see your promises come true.
When will you comfort me?

119:83 Job 30:30

83 I am shriveled like a wineskin in the smoke, exhausted with waiting.
But I cling to your principles and obey them.

119:84 Ps 39:4 Rev 6:10

84 How long must I wait?
When will you punish those who persecute me?

119:85 Pss 35:19; 57:6 Jer 18:22

85 These arrogant people who hate your law
have dug deep pits for me to fall into.
86 All your commands are trustworthy.
Protect me from those who hunt me down without cause.

87 They almost finished me off,
but I refused to abandon your commandments.
88 In your unfailing love, spare my life;
then I can continue to obey your decrees.

89 Forever, O LORD,
your word stands firm in heaven.
90 Your faithfulness extends to every generation,
as enduring as the earth you created.
91 Your laws remain true today,
for everything serves your plans.
92 If your law hadn't sustained me with joy,
I would have died in my misery.
93 I will never forget your commandments,
for you have used them to restore my joy and health.
94 I am yours; save me!
For I have applied myself to obey your commandments.
95 Though the wicked hide along the way to kill me,
I will quietly keep my mind on your decrees.
96 Even perfection has its limits,
but your commands have no limit.

97 Oh, how I love your law!
I think about it all day long.
98 Your commands make me wiser than my enemies,
for your commands are my constant guide.
99 Yes, I have more insight than my teachers,
for I am always thinking of your decrees.
100 I am even wiser than my elders,
for I have kept your commandments.
101 I have refused to walk on any path of evil,
that I may remain obedient to your word.
102 I haven't turned away from your laws,
for you have taught me well.
103 How sweet are your words to my taste;
they are sweeter than honey.
104 Your commandments give me understanding;
no wonder I hate every false way of life.

105 Your word is a lamp for my feet
and a light for my path.
106 I've promised it once, and I'll promise again:
I will obey your wonderful laws.
107 I have suffered much, O LORD;
restore my life again, just as you promised.
108 LORD, accept my grateful thanks
and teach me your laws.
109 My life constantly hangs in the balance,
but I will not stop obeying your law.
110 The wicked have set their traps for me along your path,
but I will not turn from your commandments.

119:89 Isa 40:8; Matt 24:35; 1 Pet 1:25
119:90 Pss 89:1-2; 104:2-4; 148:6
119:91 Jer 31:35
119:95 Ps 40:14; Isa 32:7
119:98 Deut 4:6
119:100 Job 32:7-9
119:102 Deut 17:20; Josh 23:6
119:103 Ps 19:10
119:108 Hos 14:2; Heb 13:15
119:110 Pss 91:3; 140:5

119:97-104 God's Word makes us wise—wiser than our enemies and wiser than any teachers who ignore it. True wisdom goes beyond amassing knowledge; it is *applying* knowledge in a life-changing way. Intelligent or experienced people are not necessarily wise. Wisdom comes from allowing God's teachings to guide us.

119:105 To walk safely in the woods at night we need a light so we don't trip over tree roots or fall into holes. In this life, we walk through a dark forest of evil. But the Bible can be our light to show us the way ahead so we won't stumble as we walk. It reveals the entangling roots of false values and philosophies. Study the Bible so you will be able to see your way clear enough to stay on the right path.

119:111 Deut 33:4

111 Your decrees are my treasure;
they are truly my heart's delight.
112 I am determined to keep your principles,
even forever, to the very end.

119:113 1 Kgs 18:21 Jas 1:8; 4:8
119:114 Pss 31:20; 61:4
119:115 Pss 6:8; 139:19 Matt 7:23
119:116 Pss 25:2, 20; 31:1, 17 Rom 5:5; 9:33 Phil 1:20
119:117 Ps 12:5 Prov 29:25
119:119 Isa 1:22, 25 Ezek 22:18-19
119:120 Job 4:14 Hab 3:16
119:121 2 Sam 8:15 Job 29:14

113 I hate those who are undecided about you,
but my choice is clear—I love your law.
114 You are my refuge and my shield;
your word is my only source of hope.
115 Get out of my life, you evil-minded people,
for I intend to obey the commands of my God.
116 LORD, sustain me as you promised, that I may live!
Do not let my hope be crushed.
117 Sustain me, and I will be saved;
then I will meditate on your principles continually.
118 But you have rejected all who stray from your principles.
They are only fooling themselves.
119 All the wicked of the earth are the scum you skim off;
no wonder I love to obey your decrees!
120 I tremble in fear of you;
I fear your judgments.

121 Don't leave me to the mercy of my enemies,
for I have done what is just and right.
122 Please guarantee a blessing for me.
Don't let those who are arrogant oppress me!
123 My eyes strain to see your deliverance,
to see the truth of your promise fulfilled.

119:124 Pss 51:1; 106:45; 109:26
119:126 Jer 18:23 Ezek 31:11
119:128 Ps 19:8

124 I am your servant;
deal with me in unfailing love,
and teach me your principles.
125 Give discernment to me, your servant;
then I will understand your decrees.
126 LORD, it is time for you to act,
for these evil people have broken your law.
127 Truly, I love your commands
more than gold, even the finest gold.
128 Truly, each of your commandments is right.
That is why I hate every false way.

119:130 Prov 6:23

129 Your decrees are wonderful.
No wonder I obey them!
130 As your words are taught, they give light;
even the simple can understand them.
131 I open my mouth, panting expectantly,
longing for your commands.
132 Come and show me your mercy,
as you do for all who love your name.

119:113 Undecided people cannot make up their minds between good and evil. But when it comes to obeying God, there is no middle ground; you must take a stand. Either you are obeying him or you are not. Either you are doing what he wants or you are undecided. Choose to obey God, and say with the psalmist, "I love your law."

119:125 The psalmist asked God for discernment. Faith comes alive when we apply Scripture to our daily tasks and concerns. We need discernment so we can understand, and we need the desire to apply Scripture where we need help. The Bible is like medicine: It goes to work only when we apply it to the affected areas. As you read the Bible, be alert for lessons, commands, or examples that you can put into practice.

133 Guide my steps by your word,
so I will not be overcome by any evil.
134 Rescue me from the oppression of evil people;
then I can obey your commandments.
135 Look down on me with love;
teach me all your principles.
136 Rivers of tears gush from my eyes
because people disobey your law.

137 O LORD, you are righteous,
and your decisions are fair.
138 Your decrees are perfect;
they are entirely worthy of our trust.
139 I am overwhelmed with rage,
for my enemies have disregarded your words.
140 Your promises have been thoroughly tested;
that is why I love them so much.
141 I am insignificant and despised,
but I don't forget your commandments.
142 Your justice is eternal,
and your law is perfectly true.
143 As pressure and stress bear down on me,
I find joy in your commands.
144 Your decrees are always fair;
help me to understand them, that I may live.

145 I pray with all my heart; answer me, LORD!
I will obey your principles.
146 I cry out to you; save me,
that I may obey your decrees.
147 I rise early, before the sun is up;
I cry out for help and put my hope in your words.
148 I stay awake through the night,
thinking about your promise.
149 In your faithful love, O LORD, hear my cry;
in your justice, save my life.
150 Those lawless people are coming near to attack me;
they live far from your law.
151 But you are near, O LORD,
and all your commands are true.
152 I have known from my earliest days
that your decrees never change.

153 Look down upon my sorrows and rescue me,
for I have not forgotten your law.
154 Argue my case; take my side!
Protect my life as you promised.
155 The wicked are far from salvation,
for they do not bother with your principles.
156 LORD, how great is your mercy;
in your justice, give me back my life.
157 Many persecute and trouble me,
yet I have not swerved from your decrees.
158 I hate these traitors
because they care nothing for your word.
159 See how I love your commandments, LORD.
Give back my life because of your unfailing love.
160 All your words are true;
all your just laws will stand forever.

119:133 Ps 19:13
119:134 Ps 142:6
119:135 Num 6:25; Ps 67:1
119:136 Jer 9:1, 18; 14:17; Lam 3:48
119:137 Ezra 9:15; Jer 12:1; Dan 9:7, 14
119:139 Ps 69:9
119:140 Ps 12:6
119:141 Ps 22:6
119:144 Ps 19:9
119:146 Ps 3:7
119:147 Ps 108:2
119:151 Ps 34:18; Isa 50:8
119:152 Luke 21:33
119:154 Ps 35:1; Mic 7:9
119:156 2 Sam 24:14
119:158 Ps 139:21; Isa 24:16
119:160 Ps 139:17

119:161 1 Sam 26:18

161 Powerful people harass me without cause,
but my heart trembles only at your word.

119:162 1 Sam 30:16 Isa 9:3

162 I rejoice in your word
like one who finds a great treasure.

119:163 Ps 31:6 Prov 13:5

163 I hate and abhor all falsehood,
but I love your law.
164 I will praise you seven times a day
because all your laws are just.

119:165 Prov 3:23 1 Jn 2:10

165 Those who love your law have great peace
and do not stumble.

119:166 Gen 49:18

166 I long for your salvation, LORD,
so I have obeyed your commands.
167 I have obeyed your decrees,
and I love them very much.

119:168 Ps 139:3 Prov 5:21

168 Yes, I obey your commandments and decrees,
because you know everything I do.

119:169 Ps 18:6

169 O LORD, listen to my cry;
give me the discerning mind you promised.

119:170 Pss 22:20; 31:2; 140:6

170 Listen to my prayer;
rescue me as you promised.

119:171 Isa 2:3 Mic 4:2

171 Let my lips burst forth with praise,
for you have taught me your principles.

119:172 Ps 51:14

172 Let my tongue sing about your word,
for all your commands are right.

119:173 Josh 24:22 Ps 37:24 Luke 10:42

173 Stand ready to help me,
for I have chosen to follow your commandments.
174 O LORD, I have longed for your salvation,
and your law is my delight.

119:175 Isa 55:3

175 Let me live so I can praise you,
and may your laws sustain me.

119:176 Isa 53:6 Luke 15:4

176 I have wandered away like a lost sheep;
come and find me,
for I have not forgotten your commands.

Theme: A prayer for deliverance from false accusers. All believers must live with the tension of being in the world but not belonging to it.
Author: Anonymous, some suggest Hezekiah

120

A song for the ascent to Jerusalem.

120:1 Pss 18:6; 66:14; 102:2

1 I took my troubles to the LORD;
I cried out to him, and he answered my prayer.

120:2 Ps 52:4 Prov 12:22

2 Rescue me, O LORD, from liars
and from all deceitful people.
3 O deceptive tongue, what will God do to you?
How will he increase your punishment?

120:4 Pss 45:15; 140:10

4 You will be pierced with sharp arrows
and burned with glowing coals.

119:160 One of God's characteristics is truthfulness. He embodies perfect truth; therefore, his Word cannot lie. It is true and dependable for guidance and help (see John 17:14-17). The Bible is completely true and trustworthy.

119:165 Modern society longs for peace of mind. Here is clear-cut instruction on how to attain this: If we love God and obey his laws, we will have "great peace." Trust in God, who alone stands above the pressures of daily life and gives us full assurance.

120–134 Psalms 120–134 are called "pilgrim psalms" or "songs of ascent." They were sung by those who journeyed (and thus "ascended") to the Temple for the annual festivals. Each psalm is a "step" along the journey. Psalm 120 begins the journey in a distant land in hostile surroundings; Psalm 122 pictures the pilgrims arriving in Jerusalem; and the rest of the psalms move toward the Temple, mentioning various characteristics of God.

5 How I suffer among these scoundrels of Meshech!
It pains me to live with these people from Kedar!
6 I am tired of living here
among people who hate peace.
7 As for me, I am for peace;
but when I speak, they are for war!

120:5 Gen 10:2; 25:13 Jer 2:10; 49:28

120:7 Pss 55:21; 109:4

Theme: We can depend upon God for help. Pilgrims must travel through lonely country to their destination; they are protected, not by anything created, but by the Creator of everything.
Author: Anonymous, some suggest Hezekiah

121

A song for the ascent to Jerusalem.

1 I look up to the mountains—
does my help come from there?
2 My help comes from the LORD,
who made the heavens and the earth!

3 He will not let you stumble and fall;
the one who watches over you will not sleep.
4 Indeed, he who watches over Israel
never tires and never sleeps.

5 The LORD himself watches over you!
The LORD stands beside you as your protective shade.
6 The sun will not hurt you by day,
nor the moon at night.
7 The LORD keeps you from all evil
and preserves your life.
8 The LORD keeps watch over you as you come and go,
both now and forever.

121:2 Pss 115:15; 124:8

121:3 Pss 66:9; 127:1

121:5 Ps 91:4

121:6 Isa 49:10 Rev 7:16

121:7 Ps 91:10-12

Theme: Stepping into the presence of God. What Jerusalem was for the Israelites, the church is to the believer.
Author: David

122

A song for the ascent to Jerusalem. A psalm of David.

1 I was glad when they said to me,
"Let us go to the house of the LORD."
2 And now we are standing here
inside your gates, O Jerusalem.
3 Jerusalem is a well-built city,
knit together as a single unit.
4 All the people of Israel—the LORD's people—
make their pilgrimage here.

122:1 Isa 2:3 Zech 8:21

122:3 Ps 48:13

122:4 Deut 16:16

120:5, 6 Meshech was a nation far to the north of Israel; Kedar a nation to the southeast. Both were known for being warlike and barbarian. Because the psalmist couldn't have been in two places at one time, he was lamenting that he felt far from home and surrounded by pagan people.

120:7 Peacemaking is not always popular. Some people prefer to fight for what they believe in. The glory of battle is in the hope of winning, but someone must be a loser. The glory of peacemaking is that it may actually produce two winners. Peacemaking is God's way, so we should carefully and prayerfully attempt to be peacemakers.

121:1ff This song expresses assurance and hope in God's protection day and night. He not only made the hills but heaven and earth as well. We should never trust a lesser power than God himself. But not only is he all-powerful, he also watches over us. Nothing diverts or deters him. We are safe. We never outgrow our need for God's untiring watch over our life.

122:1 Going to God's house can be a chore or a delight. For the psalmist, it was a delight. As a pilgrim attending one of the three great religious festivals, he rejoiced to worship with God's people in God's house. We may find worship a chore if we have unconfessed sin or if our love for God has cooled. But if we are close to God and enjoy his presence, we will be eager to worship and praise him. Our attitude toward God will determine our view of worship.

They come to give thanks to the name of the LORD
as the law requires.

122:5 Deut 17:8; 2 Chr 19:8

5 Here stand the thrones where judgment is given,
the thrones of the dynasty of David.

122:6 Ps 102:14

6 Pray for the peace of Jerusalem.
May all who love this city prosper.

122:7 Isa 62:6

7 O Jerusalem, may there be peace within your walls
and prosperity in your palaces.

122:8 Ps 133:1

8 For the sake of my family and friends, I will say,
"Peace be with you."

122:9 Neh 2:10

9 For the sake of the house of the LORD our God,
I will seek what is best for you, O Jerusalem.

Theme: Look to God for mercy. We are encouraged to be attentive to God's leading.
Author: Anonymous, some suggest Hezekiah

123

A song for the ascent to Jerusalem.

123:1 Pss 11:4; 141:8

1 I lift my eyes to you,
O God, enthroned in heaven.

123:2 Mal 1:6

2 We look to the LORD our God for his mercy,
just as servants keep their eyes on their master,
as a slave girl watches her mistress for the slightest signal.

123:3 Neh 4:4; Pss 4:1; 51:1; 79:4; 119:22

3 Have mercy on us, LORD, have mercy,
for we have had our fill of contempt.

123:4 Ps 79:4

4 We have had our fill of the scoffing of the proud
and the contempt of the arrogant.

Theme: God delivers us from those who seek to destroy us. God is on the side of those who seek him.
Author: David, probably written after his defeat of the Philistines (2 Samuel 5:17-25)

124

A song for the ascent to Jerusalem. A psalm of David.

124:1 Pss 94:17; 129:1

1 If the LORD had not been on our side—
let Israel now say—
2 if the LORD had not been on our side
when people rose up against us,

124:3 Pss 56:1; 57:3

3 they would have swallowed us alive
because of their burning anger against us.

124:4 Pss 18:16; 69:2

4 The waters would have engulfed us;
a torrent would have overwhelmed us.
5 Yes, the raging waters of their fury
would have overwhelmed our very lives.

6 Blessed be the LORD,
who did not let their teeth tear us apart!

122:5 The "thrones where judgment is given" are the courts of justice by the town gate. In Bible times, the elders in a town sat to hear cases and administer justice at the gate (Ruth 4:1, 2). Sometimes the king himself would sit at the gate to meet his subjects and make legal decisions (2 Samuel 19:8). Speeches and prophecies were also made at the city gate (Nehemiah 8:1; Jeremiah 17:19, 20).

122:6-9 The psalmist was not praying for his own peace and prosperity but for that of his brothers and friends in Jerusalem. This is intercessory prayer, prayer on behalf of others. Too often we are quick to pray for our own needs and desires but neglect interceding for others. Will you intercede for someone in need today?

122:6-9 The peace sought in these verses is much more than the mere absence of conflict. It suggests completeness, health, justice, prosperity, and protection. The world cannot provide this peace. Real peace comes from faith in God, because he alone embodies all the characteristics of peace. To find peace of mind and peace with others, you must find peace with God.

123:1ff The psalmist lifted his eyes to God, waiting and watching for God to send his mercy. The more he waited, the more he cried out to God because he knew that the evil and proud offered no help—they had only contempt for God.

7 We escaped like a bird from a hunter's trap.
The trap is broken, and we are free!
8 Our help is from the LORD,
who made the heavens and the earth.

124:7
Pss 91:3; 141:10
Prov 6:5
124:8
Gen 1:1
Ps 121:2

Theme: God is our Protector. The mountains around Jerusalem symbolize God's protection for his people.
Author: Anonymous, some suggest Hezekiah

125

A song for the ascent to Jerusalem.

1 Those who trust in the LORD are as secure as Mount Zion;
they will not be defeated but will endure forever.
2 Just as the mountains surround and protect Jerusalem,
so the LORD surrounds and protects his people, both now and forever.
3 The wicked will not rule the godly,
for then the godly might be forced to do wrong.
4 O LORD, do good to those who are good,
whose hearts are in tune with you.
5 But banish those who turn to crooked ways, O LORD.
Take them away with those who do evil.
And let Israel have quietness and peace.

125:1
Ps 46:5
125:2
Ps 121:8
Zech 2:5
125:3
1 Sam 24:10
Prov 22:8
Isa 14:5
125:4
Pss 7:10; 94:15; 119:68
125:5
Gal 6:16

Theme: God does great things. His power not only releases us from sin's captive hold but brings us back to him.
Author: Anonymous, possibly written to celebrate the exiles' return from captivity (Ezra 1)

126

A song for the ascent to Jerusalem.

1 When the LORD restored his exiles to Jerusalem,*
it was like a dream!
2 We were filled with laughter,
and we sang for joy.
And the other nations said,
"What amazing things the LORD has done for them."
3 Yes, the LORD has done amazing things for us!
What joy!

4 Restore our fortunes, LORD,
as streams renew the desert.
5 Those who plant in tears
will harvest with shouts of joy.
6 They weep as they go to plant their seed,
but they sing as they return with the harvest.

126:1
Jer 29:14
126:2
Job 8:21
Ps 51:14
126:3
Isa 25:9
126:4
Isa 35:6; 43:19
126:5
Ps 80:5
Gal 6:9

126:1 Hebrew *Zion.*

124:7, 8 Do you ever feel trapped by overwhelming odds? With God, there is always a way out because he is the Creator of all that exists. No problem is beyond his ability to solve; no circumstance is too difficult for him. We can turn to the Creator for help in our time of need, for he is on our side. God will provide a way out; we need only trust him and look for it. David compared this to a bird escaping the hunter's trap.

125:1 Have you ever known people who were drawn to every new fad or idea? Such people are unstable and therefore unreliable. The secret to stability is to trust in God, because he never changes. He cannot be shaken by the changes in our world, and he endures forever. The fads and ideas of our world, and our world itself, will not.

125:3 Although the psalmist wrote, "The wicked will not rule the godly," often Israel had to put up with evil rulers. The psalmist was expressing what will ultimately happen when God executes his final judgment. Human sinfulness often ruins God's ideal on earth, but that doesn't mean God has lost control. Evil prevails only as long as God allows.

126:5, 6 God's ability to restore life is beyond our understanding. Forests burn down and are able to grow back. Broken bones heal. Even grief is not a permanent condition. Our tears can be seeds that will grow into a harvest of joy because God is able to bring good out of tragedy. When burdened by sorrow, know that your times of grief will end and that you will again find joy. We must be patient as we wait. God's great harvest of joy is coming!

Theme: Life without God is senseless. All of life's work—building a home, establishing a career, and raising a family—must have God as the foundation.
Author: Solomon

127 *A song for the ascent to Jerusalem. A psalm of Solomon.*

127:1 Ps 78:69

1 Unless the LORD builds a house,
the work of the builders is useless.
Unless the LORD protects a city,
guarding it with sentries will do no good.

127:2 Gen 3:17 Job 11:18-19 Eccl 5:12

2 It is useless for you to work so hard
from early morning until late at night,
anxiously working for food to eat;
for God gives rest to his loved ones.

127:3 Deut 28:4

3 Children are a gift from the LORD;
they are a reward from him.
4 Children born to a young man
are like sharp arrows in a warrior's hands.
5 How happy is the man whose quiver is full of them!
He will not be put to shame when he confronts his accusers at the city gates.

Theme: God, the true head of the home. [This is called the marriage prayer because it was often sung at Israelite marriages.] God will reward your devotion to him with inner peace.
Author: Anonymous, some suggest Hezekiah

128 *A song for the ascent to Jerusalem.*

128:1 Pss 112:1; 119:3

1 How happy are those who fear the LORD—
all who follow his ways!

128:2 Eccl 8:12

2 You will enjoy the fruit of your labor.
How happy you will be! How rich your life!

128:3 Ps 52:8

3 Your wife will be like a fruitful vine,
flourishing within your home.
And look at all those children!
There they sit around your table
as vigorous and healthy as young olive trees.
4 That is the LORD's reward
for those who fear him.

128:5 Pss 122:9; 134:3

5 May the LORD continually bless you from Zion.
May you see Jerusalem prosper as long as you live.

128:6 Gen 48:11

6 May you live to enjoy your grandchildren.
And may Israel have quietness and peace.

127:1 Families establish homes and sentries guard cities, but both these activities are futile unless God is in them. A family without God can never experience the spiritual bond God brings to relationships. A city without God will crumble from evil and corruption on the inside. Don't make the mistake of leaving God out of your life. If you do, all your accomplishments will be futile. Make God your highest priority, and let him do the building.

127:2 God is not against human effort. Hard work honors God (Proverbs 31:10-29). But working to the exclusion of rest or to the neglect of family may be a cover-up for an inability to trust God to provide for our needs. We all need adequate rest and times of spiritual refreshment. On the other hand, this verse is not an excuse to be lazy (Proverbs 18:9). Be careful to maintain a balance: Work while trusting God, and also rest while trusting him.

127:3-5 Too often children are seen as liabilities rather than assets. But the Bible calls children "a gift from the LORD," a reward. We can learn valuable lessons from their inquisitive minds and trusting spirits. Those who view children as a distraction or nuisance should instead see them as an opportunity to shape the future. We dare not treat children as an inconvenience when God values them so highly.

128:1ff The psalmist wrote that a good family life is a reward for following God. The values outlined in God's Word include love, service, honesty, integrity, and prayer. These help all relationships, and they are especially vital to home life. Is your home life heavenly or hectic? Reading and obeying God's Word is a good place to start to make your family all that it should be.

Theme: Confidence in times of persecution. God will bring us through the tough times.
Author: Anonymous, some suggest Hezekiah

129

A song for the ascent to Jerusalem.

1 From my earliest youth my enemies have persecuted me—
let Israel now say—
2 from my earliest youth my enemies have persecuted me,
but they have never been able to finish me off.
3 My back is covered with cuts,
as if a farmer had plowed long furrows.
4 But the LORD is good;
he has cut the cords used by the ungodly to bind me.

5 May all who hate Jerusalem*
be turned back in shameful defeat.
6 May they be as useless as grass on a rooftop,
turning yellow when only half grown,
7 ignored by the harvester,
despised by the binder.
8 And may those who pass by refuse to give them this blessing:
"The LORD's blessings be upon you;
we bless you in the LORD's name."

129:1 Exod 1:11; Jer 22:21; Hos 2:15; 11:1
129:2 Jer 15:20; Matt 16:18
129:4 Ps 119:127
129:5 Ps 71:13; Mic 4:11
129:6 2 Kgs 19:26; Ps 37:2
129:8 Ruth 2:4; Ps 118:26

Theme: Assurance of the Lord's forgiveness. God will surely forgive us if we confess our sins to him.
Author: Anonymous, some suggest Hezekiah

130

A song for the ascent to Jerusalem.

1 From the depths of despair, O LORD,
I call for your help.
2 Hear my cry, O Lord.
Pay attention to my prayer.

3 LORD, if you kept a record of our sins,
who, O Lord, could ever survive?
4 But you offer forgiveness,
that we might learn to fear you.

5 I am counting on the LORD;
yes, I am counting on him.
I have put my hope in his word.

130:1 Pss 42:7; 69:2
130:2 2 Chr 6:40; Pss 28:2; 64:1
130:3 Pss 76:7; 86:5
130:4 Exod 34:7
130:5 Ps 40:1; Isa 8:17

129:5 Hebrew *Zion.*

129:2 The people of Israel were persecuted from their earliest days but never destroyed completely. The same is true of the church. Christians have faced times of severe persecution, but the church has never been destroyed. As Jesus said to Peter, "Now I say to you that you are Peter, and upon this rock I will build my church, and all the powers of hell will not conquer it" (Matthew 16:18). When you face persecution and discrimination, take courage—the church will never be destroyed.

129:3 This verse foreshadowed Jesus' unjust punishment before his death. He endured horrible lashes from the whip of his tormentors, which indeed made "furrows" on his back (John 19:1).

130:1, 2 In the depths of despair, the psalmist cried out to God. Despair makes us feel isolated and distant from God, but this is precisely when we need God most. Despair over sin should not lead to self-pity, causing us to think more about ourselves than God. Instead, it should lead to confession and then to God's mercy, forgiveness, and redemption. When we feel overwhelmed by a problem, feeling sorry for ourselves will only increase feelings of hopelessness; but crying out to God will turn our attention to the only one who can really help.

130:3, 4 Keeping a record of sins (or holding a grudge) is like building a wall between you and another person, and it is nearly impossible to talk openly while the wall is there. God doesn't keep a record of our sins; when he forgives, he forgives completely, tearing down any wall between us and him. Therefore, we fear (revere) God, yet we can talk to him about anything. When you pray, realize that God is holding nothing against you. His lines of communication are completely open.

130:6 Ps 63:6

6 I long for the Lord
more than sentries long for the dawn,
yes, more than sentries long for the dawn.

130:7 Pss 103:4; 131:3

7 O Israel, hope in the LORD;
for with the LORD there is unfailing love
and an overflowing supply of salvation.

130:8 Luke 1:68

8 He himself will free Israel
from every kind of sin.

Theme: Trust and contentment. Quiet trust in God is the basis for our contentment.
Author: David

131

A song for the ascent to Jerusalem. A psalm of David.

131:1 Rom 12:16

1 LORD, my heart is not proud;
my eyes are not haughty.
I don't concern myself with matters too great
or awesome for me.

131:2 Ps 62:1

2 But I have stilled and quieted myself,
just as a small child is quiet with its mother.
Yes, like a small child is my soul within me.

131:3 Ps 130:7

3 O Israel, put your hope in the LORD—
now and always.

Theme: Honor God and he will honor you. The psalmist reflects upon that great day when the Ark of the Covenant was brought to Jerusalem and praises God for his promise to perpetuate David's line.
Author: Anonymous

132

A song for the ascent to Jerusalem.

1 LORD, remember David
and all that he suffered.

132:2 Gen 49:24 Isa 49:26 Acts 7:46

2 He took an oath before the LORD.
He vowed to the Mighty One of Israel,*
3 "I will not go home;
I will not let myself rest.

132:4 Prov 6:4

4 I will not let my eyes sleep
nor close my eyelids in slumber

132:5 Acts 7:46

5 until I find a place to build a house for the LORD,
a sanctuary for the Mighty One of Israel."

132:6 Gen 35:19 1 Sam 7:1; 17:12

6 We heard that the Ark was in Ephrathah;
then we found it in the distant countryside of Jaar.

132:7 1 Chr 28:2 Pss 5:7; 99:5

7 Let us go to the dwelling place of the LORD;
let us bow low before him.

132:8-10 //2 Chr 6:41-42

132:8 Num 10:35 Ps 78:61

8 Arise, O LORD, and enter your sanctuary,
along with the Ark, the symbol of your power.

132:9 Job 29:14 Ps 149:5

9 Your priests will be agents of salvation;
may your loyal servants sing for joy.

132:2 Hebrew *of Jacob;* also in 132:5.

131:1, 2 Pride results from overvaluing ourselves above others. It leads to restlessness because it makes us dissatisfied with what we have and concerned about what everyone else is doing. It keeps us always hungering for more attention and adoration. By contrast, humility puts others first and allows us to be content with God's leading in our lives. Such contentment gives us security so that we no longer have to prove ourselves to others. Let humility and trust affect your perspective and give you the strength and freedom to serve God and others.

132:2-5 This refers to David's desire to build the Temple. When David became king, he built a beautiful palace, but he was troubled that the Ark of the Covenant, the symbol of God's presence among his people (Exodus 25:10-22), remained in a tent (2 Samuel 6:17; 7:1-17). This so bothered David that he couldn't sleep until he corrected the situation. He began to lay the plans for the Temple to house the Ark. (Eventually the Temple was built by his son Solomon.) We must live so close to God that we become restless until God's will is accomplished through us.

10 For the sake of your servant David,
do not reject the king you chose for your people.
11 The LORD swore to David
a promise he will never take back:
"I will place your descendants on your throne.
12 If your descendants obey the terms of my covenant
and follow the decrees that I teach them,
then your royal line will never end."

13 For the LORD has chosen Jerusalem*;
he has desired it as his home.
14 "This is my home where I will live forever," he said.
"I will live here, for this is the place I desired.
15 I will make this city prosperous
and satisfy its poor with food.
16 I will make its priests the agents of salvation;
its godly people will sing for joy.
17 Here I will increase the power of David;
my anointed one will be a light for my people.
18 I will clothe his enemies with shame,
but he will be a glorious king."

132:11 2 Sam 7:12-16; 2 Chr 6:16; †Acts 2:30
132:12 Luke 1:32
132:13 Ps 78:68
132:14 Matt 23:21
132:15 Ps 107:9

Theme: The joy of harmonious relationships.
Author: David

133

A song for the ascent to Jerusalem. A psalm of David.

1 How wonderful it is, how pleasant,
when brothers live together in harmony!
2 For harmony is as precious as the fragrant anointing oil
that was poured over Aaron's head,
that ran down his beard
and onto the border of his robe.
3 Harmony is as refreshing as the dew from Mount Hermon
that falls on the mountains of Zion.
And the LORD has pronounced his blessing,
even life forevermore.

133:2 Exod 30:25, 30; Lev 8:12
133:3 Deut 4:48; 28:8

132:13 Hebrew *Zion.*

132:11, 12 The promise that David's sons would sit on Israel's throne forever is found in 2 Samuel 7:8-29. This promise had two parts: (1) David's descendants would perpetually rule over Israel as long as they followed God, and (2) David's royal line would never end. The first part was conditional: As long as the kings obeyed God ("obey the terms of my covenant"), their dynasty continued. The second part of the promise was unconditional: It was fulfilled in Jesus Christ, a descendant of David, who reigns forever.

132:17, 18 The "increase" of David's power refers to one of his mighty descendants. David's son Solomon was indeed a glorious king (1 Kings 3:10-14); but these verses look ahead even further to another descendant of David, Jesus the Messiah (Matthew 1:17). The power, might, and glory of the Messiah will last forever.

133:1-3 David stated that unity is pleasant and precious. Unfortunately, unity is not always found in the church, as it should be. People disagree and cause division over unimportant issues. Some delight in causing tension by discrediting others. Unity is important because (1) it makes the church a positive example to the world and helps draw others to the Lord; (2) it helps us cooperate as a body of believers as God meant us to, giving us a foretaste of heaven; (3) it renews and revitalizes ministry because there is less tension to sap our energy.

Living in unity does not mean that we will agree on everything; there will be many opinions just as there are many notes in a musical chord. But we must agree on our purpose in life—to work together for God. Our outward expression of unity will reflect our inward unity of purpose.

133:2 Expensive oil was used by Moses to anoint Aaron as the first high priest of Israel (Exodus 29:7) and to dedicate all the priests to God's service. Brotherly unity, like the anointing oil, shows that we are dedicated to serving God wholeheartedly.

133:3 Mount Hermon is the tallest mountain in Palestine, located northeast of the Sea of Galilee.

Theme: Worship God and experience the joy of his blessings.
Author: Anonymous, some suggest Hezekiah

134

A song for the ascent to Jerusalem.

134:1 Deut 10:8; 1 Chr 9:33; 2 Chr 29:11

1 Oh, bless the LORD, all you servants of the LORD,
you who serve as night watchmen in the house of the LORD.

134:2 Ps 28:2; 1 Tim 2:8

2 Lift your hands in holiness,
and bless the LORD.

134:3 Pss 124:8; 128:5

3 May the LORD, who made heaven and earth,
bless you from Jerusalem.*

Theme: A hymn of praise. This psalm contrasts the greatness of God with the powerlessness of idols. Pagans worship idols while God's people worship the living God.
Author: Anonymous

135

1 Praise the LORD!
Praise the name of the LORD!
Praise him, you who serve the LORD,

135:2 Ps 116:19

2 you who serve in the house of the LORD,
in the courts of the house of our God.

135:3 Pss 68:4; 100:5

3 Praise the LORD, for the LORD is good;
celebrate his wonderful name with music.

135:4 Exod 19:5; Deut 7:6; 10:15; 1 Pet 2:9

4 For the LORD has chosen Jacob for himself,
Israel for his own special treasure.

135:5 Pss 48:1; 97:9

5 I know the greatness of the LORD—
that our Lord is greater than any other god.

135:6 Ps 115:3

6 The LORD does whatever pleases him
throughout all heaven and earth,
and on the seas and in their depths.

135:7 Job 38:25-26; Jer 51:16; Zech 10:1

7 He causes the clouds to rise over the earth.
He sends the lightning with the rain
and releases the wind from his storehouses.

135:8 Ps 78:51

8 He destroyed the firstborn in each Egyptian home,
both people and animals.

135:9 Deut 6:22

9 He performed miraculous signs and wonders in Egypt;
Pharaoh and all his people watched.

135:10 Ps 136:17-21

10 He struck down great nations
and slaughtered mighty kings—

135:11 Num 21:33-35; Josh 12:7-24

11 Sihon king of the Amorites,
Og king of Bashan,
and all the kings of Canaan.

135:12 Ps 78:55

12 He gave their land as an inheritance,
a special possession to his people Israel.

135:13 Exod 3:15; Ps 102:12

13 Your name, O LORD, endures forever;
your fame, O LORD, is known to every generation.

135:14 Deut 32:36; Ps 106:45

14 For the LORD will vindicate his people
and have compassion on his servants.

134:3 Hebrew *Zion.*

134:1-3 This psalm is about a very small group—the Levites who served as Temple watchmen. Singing this psalm, the last of the "songs of ascent" (Psalms 120–134), the worshipers would ascend the hill where the Temple sat and see the watchmen who protected it day and night. They saw the watchmen's work as an act of praise to God, done reverently and responsibly. Make your job or your responsibility in the church an act of praise by doing it with reverence to God. Honor him by the quality of your work and the attitude of service you bring to it.

135:4 That the descendants of Jacob (Israel) were a chosen people reflects God's commission to the nation in Deuteronomy 7:6-8 and in Peter's sermon to the church in 1 Peter 2:9. God treasures us. He gives love and mercy to all those who believe in him.

[15] Their idols are merely things of silver and gold,
shaped by human hands.
[16] They cannot talk, though they have mouths,
or see, though they have eyes!
[17] They cannot hear with their ears
or smell with their noses.
[18] And those who make them are just like them,
as are all who trust in them.

[19] O Israel, praise the LORD!
O priests of Aaron, praise the LORD!
[20] O Levites, praise the LORD!
All you who fear the LORD, praise the LORD!
[21] The LORD be praised from Zion,
for he lives here in Jerusalem.

Praise the LORD!

135:15-20 //Ps 115:4-11
135:20 Ps 118:4

Theme: The never-ending story of God's love. God deserves our praise because his endless love never fails.
Author: Anonymous

136

[1] Give thanks to the LORD, for he is good!
His faithful love endures forever.
[2] Give thanks to the God of gods.
His faithful love endures forever.
[3] Give thanks to the Lord of lords.
His faithful love endures forever.

[4] Give thanks to him who alone does mighty miracles.
His faithful love endures forever.
[5] Give thanks to him who made the heavens so skillfully.
His faithful love endures forever.
[6] Give thanks to him who placed the earth on the water.
His faithful love endures forever.
[7] Give thanks to him who made the heavenly lights—
His faithful love endures forever.
[8] the sun to rule the day,
His faithful love endures forever.
[9] and the moon and stars to rule the night.
His faithful love endures forever.

[10] Give thanks to him who killed the firstborn of Egypt.
His faithful love endures forever.
[11] He brought Israel out of Egypt.
His faithful love endures forever.
[12] He acted with a strong hand and powerful arm.
His faithful love endures forever.
[13] Give thanks to him who parted the Red Sea.*
His faithful love endures forever.
[14] He led Israel safely through,
His faithful love endures forever.

136:1 1 Chr 16:41; 2 Chr 20:21; Ps 107:1
136:2 Deut 10:17
136:4 Ps 72:18
136:5 Prov 3:19
136:6 Ps 24:2
136:7 Ps 74:16
136:8 Gen 1:16
136:10 Exod 12:29; Ps 78:51
136:11 Exod 12:51; 13:3; Deut 9:29
136:12 Deut 4:34; Ps 44:3
136:13 Exod 14:21; Ps 78:13
136:14 Ps 106:9

136:13 Hebrew *sea of reeds;* also in 136:15.

135:15-18 Those who worshiped idols were as blind and insensitive as the idols themselves. They couldn't see or hear what God had to say. In subtle, imperceptible ways we become like the idols we worship. If the true God is your God, you will become more like him as you worship him. What are your goals? What takes priority in your life? Choose carefully because you will take on the characteristics of whatever you worship.

136:1ff Repeated throughout this psalm is the phrase "His faithful love endures forever." This psalm may have been a responsive reading, with the congregation saying these words in unison after each sentence. The repetition made this important lesson sink in. God's love includes aspects of love, kindness, mercy, and faithfulness. We never have to worry that God will run out of love because it flows from a well that will never run dry.

136:16 Exod 13:18 Deut 8:15
136:17 Ps 135:10-12
136:21 Josh 12:1
136:22 Ps 105:6 Isa 41:8; 45:4
136:23 Pss 9:12; 106:45
136:24 Judg 6:9
136:25 Pss 104:27; 145:15
136:26 2 Chr 36:23 Ezra 5:11

15 but he hurled Pharaoh and his army into the sea.
His faithful love endures forever.
16 Give thanks to him who led his people through the wilderness.
His faithful love endures forever.

17 Give thanks to him who struck down mighty kings.
His faithful love endures forever.
18 He killed powerful kings—
His faithful love endures forever.
19 Sihon king of the Amorites,
His faithful love endures forever.
20 and Og king of Bashan.
His faithful love endures forever.
21 God gave the land of these kings as an inheritance—
His faithful love endures forever.
22 a special possession to his servant Israel.
His faithful love endures forever.

23 He remembered our utter weakness.
His faithful love endures forever.
24 He saved us from our enemies.
His faithful love endures forever.
25 He gives food to every living thing.
His faithful love endures forever.
26 Give thanks to the God of heaven.
His faithful love endures forever.

Theme: A person in exile weeps over the bitterness of captivity. Our sorrow can make it difficult to imagine singing joyful songs again.
Author: Anonymous

137:1 Neh 1:4 Ezek 1:1, 3
137:2 Ezek 26:13
137:3 2 Chr 29:27 Neh 12:46
137:6 Ezek 3:26
137:7 Jer 49:7-22 Ezek 25:12-14 Obad 1:10-14

137

1 Beside the rivers of Babylon, we sat and wept
as we thought of Jerusalem.*
2 We put away our lyres,
hanging them on the branches of the willow trees.
3 For there our captors demanded a song of us.
Our tormentors requested a joyful hymn:
"Sing us one of those songs of Jerusalem!"
4 But how can we sing the songs of the LORD
while in a foreign land?

5 If I forget you, O Jerusalem,
let my right hand forget its skill upon the harp.
6 May my tongue stick to the roof of my mouth
if I fail to remember you,
if I don't make Jerusalem my highest joy.

7 O LORD, remember what the Edomites did
on the day the armies of Babylon captured Jerusalem.
"Destroy it!" they yelled.
"Level it to the ground!"

137:1 Hebrew *Zion;* also in 137:3.

137:7 The Edomites were related to the Israelites, both nations having descended from Isaac and his father, Abraham. Although Israel shared its southern border with Edom, there was bitter hatred between the two nations. The Edomites did not come to help when the city of Jerusalem was besieged by the Babylonian army. In fact, they rejoiced when the city was destroyed (Jeremiah 49:7-22; Joel 3:19; Obadiah 1:1-21).

8 O Babylon, you will be destroyed.
Happy is the one who pays you back
for what you have done to us.
9 Happy is the one who takes your babies
and smashes them against the rocks!

137:8 Isa 13:1-22; 47:1-15 Jer 50:1-46; 51:1-64

Theme: Thanksgiving for answered prayer. God works out his plans for our lives and will bring us through the difficulties we face.
Author: David

138

A psalm of David.

1 I give you thanks, O LORD, with all my heart;
I will sing your praises before the gods.
2 I bow before your holy Temple as I worship.
I will give thanks to your name
for your unfailing love and faithfulness,
because your promises are backed
by all the honor of your name.
3 When I pray, you answer me;
you encourage me by giving me the strength I need.
4 Every king in all the earth will give you thanks, O LORD,
for all of them will hear your words.
5 Yes, they will sing about the LORD's ways,
for the glory of the LORD is very great.
6 Though the LORD is great, he cares for the humble,
but he keeps his distance from the proud.
7 Though I am surrounded by troubles,
you will preserve me against the anger of my enemies.
You will clench your fist against my angry enemies!
Your power will save me.
8 The LORD will work out his plans for my life—
for your faithful love, O LORD, endures forever.
Don't abandon me, for you made me.

138:1 Pss 95:3; 96:4; 111:1
138:2 Ps 5:7 Isa 42:21
138:3 Pss 28:7; 46:1; 118:5
138:4 Ps 102:15
138:6 Pss 101:5; 113:4-7 Prov 3:34 Jas 4:6
138:7 Exod 15:12 Ezra 9:8-9 Pss 20:6; 23:4; 71:20
138:8 Job 10:3 Pss 27:9; 71:9 Phil 1:6

Theme: God is all-seeing, all-knowing, all-powerful, and everywhere present. God knows us, God is with us, and his greatest gift is to allow us to know him.
Author: David

139

For the choir director: A psalm of David.

1 O LORD, you have examined my heart
and know everything about me.
2 You know when I sit down or stand up.
You know my every thought when far away.

139:1 Ps 44:21
139:2 Ps 94:11

137:8, 9 God destroyed Babylon and its offspring for their proud assault against God and his Kingdom. The Medes and Persians destroyed Babylon in 539 B.C. Many of those who were oppressed lived to see the victory. The phrase about the infants is harsh because the psalmist is crying out for judgment: "Treat the Babylonians the way they treated us."

138:1 "Before the gods" may mean in the presence of subordinate heavenly beings (angels), or, more likely, it may be a statement ridiculing the kings or gods of the pagan nations. God is supreme in the whole earth.

138:1-3 Thanksgiving should be an integral part of our praise to God. This theme is woven throughout the Psalms. As we praise and thank God for material and spiritual blessings, we should also thank him for answered prayer. Remember when you asked God for protection, strength, comfort, patience, love, or other special needs, and he supplied them. Beware of taking God's provision and answered prayer for granted.

138:8 Every person dreams and makes plans for the future. Then they work hard to see those dreams and plans come true. But to make the most of life, we must include God's plan in our plans. He alone knows what is best for us; he alone can fulfill his purpose for us. As you make plans and dream dreams, talk with God about them.

139:1-5 Sometimes we don't let people get to know us completely because we are afraid they will discover something about us that they won't like. But God already knows everything about us, even to the number of hairs on our heads (Matthew 10:30), and still he accepts and loves us. God is with us through every situation, in every trial—protecting, loving, guiding. He knows and loves us completely.

139:3 Job 14:16

3 You chart the path ahead of me
and tell me where to stop and rest.
Every moment you know where I am.

139:4 Heb 4:13

4 You know what I am going to say
even before I say it, LORD.

139:5 Ps 34:7

5 You both precede and follow me.
You place your hand of blessing on my head.

139:6 Job 42:3 Rom 11:33

6 Such knowledge is too wonderful for me,
too great for me to know!

139:7 Jer 23:24

7 I can never escape from your spirit!
I can never get away from your presence!

139:8 Prov 15:11 Amos 9:2-4

8 If I go up to heaven, you are there;
if I go down to the place of the dead,* you are there.
9 If I ride the wings of the morning,
if I dwell by the farthest oceans,

139:10 Ps 23:2-3

10 even there your hand will guide me,
and your strength will support me.

139:11 Job 22:13

11 I could ask the darkness to hide me
and the light around me to become night—

139:12 Job 34:22 Dan 2:22 1 Jn 1:5

12 but even in darkness I cannot hide from you.
To you the night shines as bright as day.
Darkness and light are both alike to you.

139:13 Ps 119:73

13 You made all the delicate, inner parts of my body
and knit me together in my mother's womb.

139:8 Hebrew *to Sheol.*

ANGER AND VENGEANCE IN THE BOOK OF PSALMS

Several psalms shock those familiar with New Testament teachings. The psalmists didn't hesitate to demand God's justice and make vivid suggestions on how he might carry it out. Apparently, no subject was unsuitable for discussion with God, but our tendency is to avoid the subjects of anger and vengeance in the book of Psalms.

To understand the words of anger and vengeance, we need to understand several things:

(1) The judgments asked for are to be carried out by God and are written out of intense personal and national suffering. The people are unable or unwilling to take revenge themselves and are asking God to intervene. Because few of us have suffered intense cruelty on a personal or national level, we find it difficult to grasp these outbursts.

(2) These writers were intimately aware of God's justice. Some of their words are efforts to vividly imagine what God might allow to happen to those who had harmed his people.

(3) If we dared to write down our thoughts while being unjustly attacked or suffering cruelty, we might be shocked at our own bold desire for vengeance. We would be surprised at how much we have in common with these men of old. The psalmists did not have Jesus' command to pray for one's enemies, but they did point to the right place to start. We are challenged to pay back good for evil, but until we respond to this challenge, we will not know how much we need God's help in order to forgive others.

(4) There is a helpful parallel between the psalms of anger and the psalms of vengeance. The "angry" psalms are intense and graphic, but they are directed at God. He is boldly told how disappointing it is when he turns his back on his people or acts too slowly. But while these thoughts and feelings were sincerely expressed, we know from the psalms themselves that these passing feelings were followed by renewed confidence in God's faithfulness. It is reasonable to expect the same of the "vengeance" psalms. We read, for example, David's angry outburst against Saul's pursuit in Psalm 59, yet we know that David never took personal revenge on Saul. The psalmists freely spoke their minds to God, having confidence that he could sort out what was meant and what was felt. Pray with that same confidence—God can be trusted with your heart.

Selected psalms that emphasize these themes are 10; 23; 28; 35; 59; 69; 109; 137; 139; 140.

139:7 God is omnipresent—he is present everywhere. Because this is so, you can never escape from his Spirit. This is good news to those who know and love God, because no matter what we do or where we go, we can never be far from God's comforting presence (see Romans 8:35-39).

139:13-15 God's character goes into the creation of every person. When you feel worthless or even begin to hate yourself, remember that God's Spirit is ready and willing to work within you. We should have as much respect for ourselves as our Maker has for us.

14 Thank you for making me so wonderfully complex!
Your workmanship is marvelous—and how well I know it.
15 You watched me as I was being formed in utter seclusion,
as I was woven together in the dark of the womb.
16 You saw me before I was born.
Every day of my life was recorded in your book.
Every moment was laid out
before a single day had passed.

17 How precious are your thoughts about me,* O God!
They are innumerable!
18 I can't even count them;
they outnumber the grains of sand!
And when I wake up in the morning,
you are still with me!

19 O God, if only you would destroy the wicked!
Get out of my life, you murderers!
20 They blaspheme you;
your enemies take your name in vain.
21 O LORD, shouldn't I hate those who hate you?
Shouldn't I despise those who resist you?
22 Yes, I hate them with complete hatred,
for your enemies are my enemies.

23 Search me, O God, and know my heart;
test me and know my thoughts.
24 Point out anything in me that offends you,
and lead me along the path of everlasting life.

139:15 Job 10:8-10 Eccl 11:5
139:16 Job 14:5 Ps 56:8
139:17 Ps 40:5
139:19 Isa 11:4
139:20 Exod 20:7 Deut 5:11
139:23 Ps 26:2
139:24 Pss 5:8; 16:11; 143:10

Theme: Prayer for protection against those who slander or threaten you. Deliverance begins with concentrating on our future life with God.
Author: David

140

For the choir director: A psalm of David.

1 O LORD, rescue me from evil people.
Preserve me from those who are violent,
2 those who plot evil in their hearts
and stir up trouble all day long.
3 Their tongues sting like a snake;
the poison of a viper drips from their lips. *Interlude*
4 O LORD, keep me out of the hands of the wicked.
Preserve me from those who are violent,
for they are plotting against me.
5 The proud have set a trap to catch me;
they have stretched out a net;
they have placed traps all along the way. *Interlude*

140:1 Ps 17:13
140:2 Ps 56:6 Prov 6:14 Isa 59:4
140:3 Rom 3:13 Jas 3:8
140:4 Ps 71:4
140:5 Job 18:9 Pss 35:7; 57:6

139:17 Or *How precious to me are your thoughts.*

139:21-24 David's hatred for his enemies came from his zeal for God. David regarded his enemies as God's enemies, so his hatred was a desire for God's righteous justice and not for personal vengeance. Is it all right to be angry at people who hate God? Yes, but we must remember that it is God who will deal with them, not us. If we truly love God, then we will be deeply hurt if someone hates him. David asked God to search his heart and mind and point out any wrong motives that may have been behind his strong words. But while we seek justice against evil, we must also pray that God's enemies will turn to him before he judges them (see Matthew 5:44).

139:23, 24 David asked God to search for sin and point it out, even to the level of testing his thoughts. This is exploratory surgery for sin. How are we to recognize sin unless God points it out? Then, when God shows us, we can repent and be forgiven. Make this verse your prayer. If you ask the Lord to search your heart and your thoughts and to reveal your sin, you will be continuing on "the path of everlasting life."

140:6 Esth 9:25 Ps 112:10
6 I said to the LORD, "You are my God!"
Listen, O LORD, to my cries for mercy!
140:7 Pss 28:8; 144:10
7 O Sovereign LORD, my strong savior,
you protected me on the day of battle.
140:8 Ps 112:10
8 LORD, do not give in to their evil desires.
Do not let their evil schemes succeed, O God. *Interlude*
140:9 Ps 7:16
9 Let my enemies be destroyed
by the very evil they have planned for me.
140:10 Pss 11:6; 21:19; 36:10 Matt 3:10
10 Let burning coals fall down on their heads,
or throw them into the fire,
or into deep pits from which they can't escape.
140:11 Ps 34:21
11 Don't let liars prosper here in our land.
Cause disaster to fall with great force on the violent.
140:12 Pss 9:4; 35:10
12 But I know the LORD will surely help those they persecute;
he will maintain the rights of the poor.
140:13 Pss 16:11; 17:15; 97:12
13 Surely the godly are praising your name,
for they will live in your presence.

Theme: A prayer for help when facing temptation. David asks God to protect him and to give him wisdom in accepting criticism. Be open to honest criticism—God may be speaking to you through others.
Author: David

141
A psalm of David.

141:1 Ps 70:5
1 O LORD, I am calling to you. Please hurry!
Listen when I cry to you for help!
141:2 Exod 29:41; 30:8 Dan 9:21 Rev 5:8; 8:3-4
2 Accept my prayer as incense offered to you,
and my upraised hands as an evening offering.
141:3 Ps 39:1 Prov 13:3; 21:23
3 Take control of what I say, O LORD,
and keep my lips sealed.
141:4 Ps 119:36 Prov 23:6 Mal 3:15
4 Don't let me lust for evil things;
don't let me participate in acts of wickedness.
Don't let me share in the delicacies
of those who do evil.
141:5 Pss 23:5; 35:14 Prov 9:8; 19:25; 27:6 Gal 6:1
5 Let the godly strike me!
It will be a kindness!
If they reprove me, it is soothing medicine.
Don't let me refuse it.
But I am in constant prayer
against the wicked and their deeds.

140:12 To whom can the poor turn when they are persecuted? They lack the money to get professional help and so are usually unable to defend themselves. But there is always someone on their side—the Lord will stand by them and ultimately bring about justice. This should be a comfort for us all. No matter what our situation may be, the Lord is with us. But this truth should also call us to live responsibly with others. As God's people, we are required to defend the rights of the powerless.

141:3 James wrote that "the tongue is a small thing, but what enormous damage it can do" (James 3:5). On the average, a person opens his or her mouth approximately 700 times a day to speak. David wisely asked God to keep him from speaking evil—even as he underwent persecution. Jesus himself was silent before his accusers (Matthew 26:63). Knowing the power of the tongue, we would do well to ask God to guard what we say so that our words will bring honor to his name.

141:4 Evil acts begin with evil desires. It isn't enough to ask God to keep you away from temptation, make you stronger, or change your circumstances. You must ask him to change you on the inside—at the level of your desires.

141:5 David says that being rebuked by a godly person is a kindness. Nobody really likes criticism, but everybody can benefit from it when it is given wisely and taken humbly. David suggested how to accept criticism: (1) Don't refuse it, (2) consider it a kindness, and (3) keep quiet (don't fight back). Putting these suggestions into practice will help you control how you react to criticism, making it productive rather than destructive, no matter how it was originally intended.

6 When their leaders are thrown down from a cliff,
they will listen to my words and find them pleasing.
7 Even as a farmer breaks up the soil and brings up rocks,
so the bones of the wicked will be scattered without a decent burial.

8 I look to you for help, O Sovereign LORD.
You are my refuge; don't let them kill me.
9 Keep me out of the traps they have set for me,
out of the snares of those who do evil.
10 Let the wicked fall into their own snares,
but let me escape.

141:7 Ps 53:5
141:8 Ps 11:1
141:9 Ps 91:3
141:10 Ps 35:8

Theme: A prayer when overwhelmed and desperate. When we feel cornered by our enemies, only God can keep us safe.
Author: David

142

A psalm of David, regarding his experience in the cave. A prayer.

1 I cry out to the LORD;
I plead for the LORD's mercy.
2 I pour out my complaints before him
and tell him all my troubles.
3 For I am overwhelmed,
and you alone know the way I should turn.
Wherever I go,
my enemies have set traps for me.
4 I look for someone to come and help me,
but no one gives me a passing thought!
No one will help me;
no one cares a bit what happens to me.
5 Then I pray to you, O LORD.
I say, "You are my place of refuge.
You are all I really want in life.
6 Hear my cry,
for I am very low.
Rescue me from my persecutors,
for they are too strong for me.
7 Bring me out of prison
so I can thank you.
The godly will crowd around me,
for you treat me kindly."

142:1 Pss 30:8; 77:1
142:3 Ps 140:5
142:4 Ps 88:8, 18; Jer 30:17
142:5 Ps 91:2, 9
142:6 Pss 18:17; 79:8
142:7 Ps 13:6

Theme: A prayer in the midst of hopelessness and depression. Our prayers should fit into what we know is consistent with God's character and plans.
Author: David

143

A psalm of David.

1 Hear my prayer, O LORD;
listen to my plea!
Answer me because you are faithful and righteous.
2 Don't bring your servant to trial!
Compared to you, no one is perfect.
3 My enemy has chased me.
He has knocked me to the ground.
He forces me to live in darkness like those in the grave.

143:1 Ps 140:6
143:2 1 Kgs 8:46; Job 14:3; 22:4
143:3 Lam 3:6

142:6 Have you ever felt that no one cared what happened to you? David had good reason to feel that way, and he wrote, "Hear my cry, for I am very low." Through prayer we can pull out of our tailspin and be reminded that God cares for us deeply.

142:7 This psalm was written when David was hiding from Saul in caves like the ones at Adullam (1 Samuel 22) or En-gedi (1 Samuel 24). These may have seemed like prisons to him because of the confinement.

143:4 Lam 3:11

4 I am losing all hope;
I am paralyzed with fear.

143:5 Ps 77:5, 10-11

5 I remember the days of old.
I ponder all your great works.
I think about what you have done.

143:6 Ps 63:1

6 I reach out for you.
I thirst for you as parched land thirsts for rain. *Interlude*

143:7 Pss 69:17; 88:4

7 Come quickly, LORD, and answer me,
for my depression deepens.
Don't turn away from me,
or I will die.

143:8 Ps 32:8

8 Let me hear of your unfailing love to me in the morning,
for I am trusting you.
Show me where to walk,
for I have come to you in prayer.

143:9 Ps 59:1

9 Save me from my enemies, LORD;
I run to you to hide me.

143:10 Neh 9:20 Pss 23:3; 119:12

10 Teach me to do your will,
for you are my God.
May your gracious Spirit lead me forward
on a firm footing.

11 For the glory of your name, O LORD, save me.
In your righteousness, bring me out of this distress.

143:12 Pss 52:5; 116:16

12 In your unfailing love, cut off all my enemies
and destroy all my foes,
for I am your servant.

Theme: Rejoicing in God's care. Whether in times of prosperity or adversity, blessed are those whose God is the Lord.
Author: David

144

A psalm of David.

144:1 Ps 18:2

1 Bless the LORD, who is my rock.
He gives me strength for war
and skill for battle.

144:2 Ps 84:9

2 He is my loving ally and my fortress,
my tower of safety, my deliverer.
He stands before me as a shield, and I take refuge in him.
He subdues the nations* under me.

144:3 Ps 8:4

3 O LORD, what are mortals that you should notice us,
mere humans that you should care for us?

144:4 Job 8:9; 14:2 Pss 39:11; 109:23

4 For we are like a breath of air;
our days are like a passing shadow.

144:5 Ps 18:9 Isa 64:1

5 Bend down the heavens, LORD, and come down.
Touch the mountains so they billow smoke.

144:2 Some manuscripts read *my people.*

143:7 David was losing hope, caught in paralyzing fear and deep depression. At times we feel caught in deepening depression, and we are unable to pull ourselves out. At those times we can come to the Lord and, like David, express our true feelings. Then we will find help as we remember his works (143:5), reach out to him in prayer (143:6), trust him (143:8), and seek to do his will (143:10).

143:10 David's prayer was to be taught to do God's will, not his own. A prayer for guidance is self-centered if it doesn't recognize God's power to redirect our life. Asking God to restructure our priorities awakens our minds and stirs our will.

144:3, 4 Life is short. David reminds us that it is "like a breath" and that our "days are like a passing shadow." James says that our life is "like the morning fog—it's here a little while, then it's gone" (James 4:14). Because life is short, live for God while you have the time. Don't waste your life by selecting an inferior purpose that has no lasting value. Only God can make your life worthwhile, purposeful, and meaningful.

6 Release your lightning bolts and scatter your enemies!
Release your arrows and confuse them!
7 Reach down from heaven and rescue me;
deliver me from deep waters,
from the power of my enemies.
8 Their mouths are full of lies;
they swear to tell the truth, but they lie.

9 I will sing a new song to you, O God!
I will sing your praises with a ten-stringed harp.
10 For you grant victory to kings!
You are the one who rescued your servant David.
11 Save me from the fatal sword!
Rescue me from the power of my enemies.
Their mouths are full of lies;
they swear to tell the truth, but they lie.

12 May our sons flourish in their youth
like well-nurtured plants.
May our daughters be like graceful pillars,
carved to beautify a palace.
13 May our farms be filled
with crops of every kind.
May the flocks in our fields multiply by the thousands,
even tens of thousands,
14 and may our oxen be loaded down with produce.
May there be no breached walls, no forced exile,
no cries of distress in our squares.
15 Yes, happy are those who have it like this!
Happy indeed are those whose God is the LORD.

144:6 Hab 3:11 Zech 9:14
144:7 Pss 18:44; 69:1, 14
144:8 Deut 32:40 Pss 12:2; 41:6 Isa 44:20
144:9 Ps 40:3
144:10 2 Sam 18:7 Ps 140:7
144:11 Ps 12:2 Isa 44:20
144:12 Ps 92:12-14 Prov 3:9-10 Song 4:4; 7:4
144:14 2 Kgs 25:11 Isa 24:11 Jer 14:2

Theme: A time will come when all people will join together in recognizing and worshiping God. Because God is full of love, he satisfies all who trust in him.
Author: David

145

A psalm of praise of David.

1 I will praise you, my God and King,
and bless your name forever and ever.
2 I will bless you every day,
and I will praise you forever.
3 Great is the LORD! He is most worthy of praise!
His greatness is beyond discovery!

4 Let each generation tell its children
of your mighty acts.
5 I will meditate* on your majestic, glorious splendor
and your wonderful miracles.
6 Your awe-inspiring deeds will be on every tongue;
I will proclaim your greatness.
7 Everyone will share the story of your wonderful goodness;
they will sing with joy of your righteousness.

8 The LORD is kind and merciful,
slow to get angry, full of unfailing love.
9 The LORD is good to everyone.
He showers compassion on all his creation.
10 All of your works will thank you, LORD,
and your faithful followers will bless you.

145:5 Some manuscripts read *They will speak.*

145:3 Rom 11:33
145:4 Isa 38:19
145:5 Ps 119:27
145:6 Deut 10:21; 32:3
145:7 Ps 51:14 Isa 63:7
145:8 Exod 34:6
145:9 Ps 100:5 Nah 1:7 Matt 19:17 Mark 10:18
145:10 Pss 19:1; 68:26

[11] They will talk together about the glory of your kingdom;
they will celebrate examples of your power.
145:12 Ps 105:1 Isa 2:10, 19, 21
[12] They will tell about your mighty deeds
and about the majesty and glory of your reign.
145:13 2 Pet 1:11
[13] For your kingdom is an everlasting kingdom.
You rule generation after generation.

The LORD is faithful in all he says;
he is gracious in all he does.*
[14] The LORD helps the fallen
and lifts up those bent beneath their loads.
145:15 Ps 104:27
[15] All eyes look to you for help;
you give them their food as they need it.
[16] When you open your hand,
you satisfy the hunger and thirst of every living thing.

[17] The LORD is righteous in everything he does;
he is filled with kindness.
145:18 Deut 4:7 John 4:24
[18] The LORD is close to all who call on him,
yes, to all who call on him sincerely.
145:19 Ps 10:17 Prov 15:29
[19] He fulfills the desires of those who fear him;
he hears their cries for help and rescues them.
145:20 Pss 31:23; 37:38
[20] The LORD protects all those who love him,
but he destroys the wicked.
145:21 Pss 71:8; 150:6
[21] I will praise the LORD,
and everyone on earth will bless his holy name
forever and forever.

Theme: The help of people versus the help of God. Help from people is temporal and unstable, but help from God is lasting and complete.
Author: Anonymous

146:1 Ps 103:1

146

[1] Praise the LORD!

Praise the LORD, I tell myself.
146:2 Pss 63:4; 104:33
[2] I will praise the LORD as long as I live.
I will sing praises to my God even with my dying breath.

145:13 The last two lines of 145:13 are not found in many of the ancient manuscripts.

PRAISE IN THE BOOK OF PSALMS

Most of the psalms are prayers, and most of the prayers include praise to God. Praise expresses admiration, appreciation, and thanks. Praise in the book of Psalms is often directed to God, and just as often the praise is shared with others. Considering all that God has done and does for us, what could be more natural than outbursts of heartfelt praise?

As you read Psalms, note the praise given to God, not only for what he does—his creation, his blessings, his forgiveness—but also for who he is—loving, just, faithful, forgiving, patient. Note also those times when the praise of God is shared with others and they, too, are encouraged to praise him. In what ways have you recently praised God or told others all that he has done for you?

Selected psalms that emphasize this theme are 8; 19; 30; 65; 84; 96; 100; 136; 145; 150.

145:14 Sometimes our burdens seem more than we can bear, and we wonder how we can go on. David stands at this bleak intersection of life's road and meditates on the Lord, the great burden bearer. God is able to lift us up because (1) his greatness is beyond discovery (145:3); (2) he does mighty acts for each generation (145:4); (3) he is full of glorious splendor and majesty (145:5); (4) he does awe-inspiring deeds (145:5, 6); (5) he is righteous (145:7); (6) he is kind, merciful, patient, loving, and compassionate (145:8, 9); (7) he rules over an everlasting Kingdom (145:13); (8) he is our source of all our daily needs (145:15, 16); (9) he is righteous and kind in all his dealings (145:17); (10) he remains close to those who call on him (145:18); (11) he hears our cries and rescues us (145:19, 20). If you are bending under a burden and feel that you are about to fall, turn to God for help. He is ready to lift you up and bear your burden.

146–150 These last five psalms overflow with praise. Each begins and ends with "Praise the LORD." They show us where, why, and how to praise God. What does praise do? (1) Praise takes our mind off our problems and shortcomings and helps us focus on God. (2) Praise leads us from individual meditation to corporate worship. (3) Praise causes us to consider and appreciate God's character. (4) Praise lifts our perspective from the earthly to the heavenly.

3 Don't put your confidence in powerful people;
there is no help for you there.
4 When their breathing stops, they return to the earth,
and in a moment all their plans come to an end.
5 But happy are those who have the God of Israel* as their helper,
whose hope is in the LORD their God.
6 He is the one who made heaven and earth,
the sea, and everything in them.
He is the one who keeps every promise forever,
7 who gives justice to the oppressed
and food to the hungry.
The LORD frees the prisoners.
8 The LORD opens the eyes of the blind.
The LORD lifts the burdens of those bent beneath their loads.
The LORD loves the righteous.
9 The LORD protects the foreigners among us.
He cares for the orphans and widows,
but he frustrates the plans of the wicked.

10 The LORD will reign forever.
O Jerusalem,* your God is King in every generation!

Praise the LORD!

146:3 Ps 60:11
146:4 Pss 33:10; 104:29 Eccl 12:7
146:5 Ps 71:5
146:6 Acts 14:15
146:7 Ps 68:6
146:8 Matt 9:30 John 9:7
146:9 Exod 22:21 Lev 19:34 Deut 10:18
146:10 Ps 10:16

Theme: What gives God joy? Although God created everything, his greatest joy comes from our genuine worship and trust.
Author: Anonymous, written when the exiles returned to Jerusalem

147

1 Praise the LORD!

How good it is to sing praises to our God!
How delightful and how right!
2 The LORD is rebuilding Jerusalem
and bringing the exiles back to Israel.
3 He heals the brokenhearted,
binding up their wounds.
4 He counts the stars
and calls them all by name.
5 How great is our Lord! His power is absolute!
His understanding is beyond comprehension!
6 The LORD supports the humble,
but he brings the wicked down into the dust.

7 Sing out your thanks to the LORD;
sing praises to our God, accompanied by harps.
8 He covers the heavens with clouds,
provides rain for the earth,
and makes the green grass grow in mountain pastures.

147:1 Pss 33:1; 135:3
147:2 Isa 11:12; 56:8 Ezek 39:28
147:4 Gen 15:5 Isa 40:26
147:5 Ps 98:1 Isa 40:28
147:8 Job 5:10; 26:8; 38:26

146:5 Hebrew *of Jacob.* **146:10** Hebrew *Zion.*

146:3-8 The psalmist portrays powerful people as inadequate saviors, making false promises they cannot deliver (146:3). God is the hope and the help of the needy. Jesus affirms his concern for the poor and afflicted in Luke 4:18-21; 7:21-23. He does not separate the physical needs from spiritual needs but attends to both. While God, not the government, is the hope of the needy, *we* are his instruments to help here on earth.

146:9 God's plans frustrate the "plans of the wicked" because his values are the opposite of society's. Jesus turned society's values upside down when he proclaimed that "many who seem to be important now will be the least important then, and those who are considered least here will be the greatest then" (Matthew 19:30). "If you try to keep your life for yourself, you will lose it. But if you give up your life for me, you will find true life" (Matthew 16:25). Don't be surprised when others don't understand your Christian values; but don't give in to theirs.

147:5 Sometimes we feel as if we don't understand ourselves—what we want, how we feel, what's wrong with us, or what we should do about it. But God's understanding has no limit, and therefore he understands us fully. If you feel troubled and don't understand yourself, remember that God understands you perfectly. Take your mind off yourself and focus on God. Seek to become more and more like him. The more you learn about God and his ways, the better you will understand yourself.

147:9 Job 38:41 Ps 104:27
147:10 1 Sam 16:7 Ps 33:17

9 He feeds the wild animals,
and the young ravens cry to him for food.
10 The strength of a horse does not impress him;
how puny in his sight is the strength of a man.
11 Rather, the LORD's delight is in those who honor him,
those who put their hope in his unfailing love.

12 Praise the LORD, O Jerusalem!
Praise your God, O Zion!

147:13 Neh 3:3; 7:3 Ps 37:26
147:14 Deut 32:14 Isa 54:13; 60:17-18
147:15 Job 37:12 Ps 104:4

13 For he has fortified the bars of your gates
and blessed your children within you.
14 He sends peace across your nation
and satisfies you with plenty of the finest wheat.
15 He sends his orders to the world—
how swiftly his word flies!
16 He sends the snow like white wool;
he scatters frost upon the ground like ashes.
17 He hurls the hail like stones.
Who can stand against his freezing cold?
18 Then, at his command, it all melts.
He sends his winds, and the ice thaws.

147:19 Deut 33:3-4 Mal 4:4
147:20 Deut 4:7-8 Ps 79:6 Jer 10:25

19 He has revealed his words to Jacob,
his principles and laws to Israel.
20 He has not done this with any other nation;
they do not know his laws.

Praise the LORD!

Theme: Let all creation praise and worship the Lord.
Author: Anonymous

148:1 Ps 102:19 †Matt 21:9 †Luke 19:38
148:2 Ps 103:20-21

148

1 Praise the LORD!

Praise the LORD from the heavens!
Praise him from the skies!
2 Praise him, all his angels!
Praise him, all the armies of heaven!
3 Praise him, sun and moon!
Praise him, all you twinkling stars!

148:4 Gen 1:7 Deut 10:14
148:5 Gen 1:1
148:6 Job 38:33

4 Praise him, skies above!
Praise him, vapors high above the clouds!
5 Let every created thing give praise to the LORD,
for he issued his command, and they came into being.
6 He established them forever and forever.
His orders will never be revoked.

148:7 Gen 1:21 Ps 74:13 Hab 3:10

7 Praise the LORD from the earth,
you creatures of the ocean depths,
8 fire and hail, snow and storm,
wind and weather that obey him,

147:10, 11 We may spend a lot of effort trying to sharpen our skills or become physically fit. There is nothing wrong with doing so, and, in fact, our gifts can be used to glorify God. But when we use our gifts with no regard for God, they are indeed worth little. It is our honor and trust that God desires. When he has those, then he will use our gifts and strengths in ways far greater than we can imagine.

147:19, 20 The nation of Israel (the descendants of Jacob) was special to God because to its people God brought his laws, and through its people he sent his Son, Jesus Christ. Now any individual who follows God is just as special to him. In fact, the Bible says that the real nation of Israel is not a specific people or geographic place but the community of all who believe in and obey God (see Galatians 3:28, 29).

148:5-14 All creation is like a majestic symphony or a great choir composed of many harmonious parts that together offer up songs of praise to the Lord. Each part (independent, yet part of the whole) is caught up and carried along in swelling tides of praise. This is a picture of how we as believers should praise God—individually, yet as part of the great choir of believers worldwide. Are you singing your part well in the worldwide choir of praise?

9 mountains and all hills,
fruit trees and all cedars,
10 wild animals and all livestock,
reptiles and birds,
11 kings of the earth and all people,
rulers and judges of the earth,
12 young men and maidens,
old men and children.
13 Let them all praise the name of the LORD.
For his name is very great;
his glory towers over the earth and heaven!
14 He has made his people strong,
honoring his godly ones—
the people of Israel who are close to him.

Praise the LORD!

148:9 Isa 44:23; 49:13; 55:12
148:13 Pss 8:1; 113:4 Rev 5:12
148:14 Deut 10:21 1 Sam 2:1 Eph 2:17

Theme: A victory celebration. We have the assurance that God truly enjoys his people.
Author: Anonymous

149

1 Praise the LORD!

Sing to the LORD a new song.
Sing his praises in the assembly of the faithful.
2 O Israel, rejoice in your Maker.
O people of Jerusalem,* exult in your King.
3 Praise his name with dancing,
accompanied by tambourine and harp.
4 For the LORD delights in his people;
he crowns the humble with salvation.
5 Let the faithful rejoice in this honor.
Let them sing for joy as they lie on their beds.
6 Let the praises of God be in their mouths,
and a sharp sword in their hands—
7 to execute vengeance on the nations
and punishment on the peoples,
8 to bind their kings with shackles
and their leaders with iron chains,
9 to execute the judgment written against them.
This is the glory of his faithful ones.

Praise the LORD!

149:1 Pss 33:3; 89:5
149:2 Judg 8:23 Ps 47:6
149:3 Exod 15:20
149:4 Ps 35:27
149:5 Job 35:10 Ps 32:16
149:6 Ps 66:17
149:8 Nah 3:10
149:9 Ps 148:14 Ezek 28:26

Theme: A closing hymn of praise. God's creation praises him everywhere in every way. We should join this rejoicing song of praise.
Author: Anonymous

150

1 Praise the LORD!

Praise God in his heavenly dwelling;
praise him in his mighty heaven!
2 Praise him for his mighty works;
praise his unequaled greatness!
3 Praise him with a blast of the trumpet;
praise him with the lyre and harp!

150:1 Pss 19:1; 73:17; 102:19
150:2 Deut 3:24
150:3 Ps 98:6

149:2 Hebrew *Zion.*

149:3-5 Although the Bible invites us to praise God, we often aren't sure how to go about it. Here, several ways are suggested: by singing, dancing, or playing musical instruments. God enjoys his people, and we should enjoy praising him.

149:6, 7 The sharp sword symbolizes the completeness of judgment that will be executed by the Messiah when he returns to punish all evildoers (Revelation 1:16).

150:4
Isa 38:20

4 Praise him with the tambourine and dancing;
praise him with stringed instruments and flutes!

150:5
1 Chr 13:8; 15:16

5 Praise him with a clash of cymbals;
praise him with loud clanging cymbals.

150:6
Ps 145:21

6 Let everything that lives sing praises to the LORD!

Praise the LORD!

WHERE TO GET HELP IN THE BOOK OF PSALMS

When you feel . . .

Afraid: 3; 4; 27; 46; 49; 56; 91; 118
Alone: 9; 10; 12; 13; 27; 40; 43
"Burned out": 6; 63
Cheated: 41
Confused: 10; 12; 73
Depressed: 27; 34; 42; 43; 88; 143
Distressed: 13; 25; 31; 40; 107
Elated: 19; 96
Guilty: 19; 32; 38; 51
Hateful: 11
Impatient: 13; 27; 37; 40
Insecure: 3; 5; 12; 91
Insulted: 41; 70
Jealous: 37
Like quitting: 29; 43; 145
Lost: 23; 139
Overwhelmed: 25; 69; 142
Penitent/Sorry: 32; 51; 66
Proud: 14; 30; 49
Purposeless: 14; 25; 39; 49; 90
Sad: 13
Self-confident: 24
Tense: 4
Thankful: 118; 136; 138
Threatened: 3; 11; 17
Tired/Weak: 6; 13; 18; 28; 29; 40; 86
Trapped: 7; 17; 42; 88; 142
Unimportant: 8; 90; 139
Vengeful: 3; 7; 109
Worried: 37
Worshipful: 8; 19; 27; 29; 150

When you're facing . . .

Atheists: 10; 14; 19; 52; 53; 115
Competition: 133
Criticism: 35; 56; 120
Danger: 11
Death: 6; 71; 90
Decisions: 1; 119
Discrimination: 54
Doubts: 34; 37; 94
Evil people: 10; 35; 36; 49; 52; 109; 140
Enemies: 3; 25; 35; 41; 56; 59
Heresy: 14
Hypocrisy: 26; 28; 40; 50
Illness: 6; 139
Lies: 5; 12; 120
Old age: 71; 92
Persecution: 1; 3; 7; 56
Poverty: 9; 10; 12
Punishment: 6; 38; 39
Slander/Insults: 7; 15; 35; 43; 120
Slaughter: 6; 46; 83
Sorrow: 23; 34
Success: 18; 112; 127; 128
Temptation: 38; 141
Troubles: 34; 55; 86; 102; 142; 145
Verbal cruelty: 35; 120

When you want . . .

Acceptance: 139
Answers: 4; 17
Confidence: 46; 71
Courage: 11; 42
Fellowship with God: 5; 16; 25; 27; 37; 133
Forgiveness: 32; 38; 40; 51; 69; 86; 103; 130
Friendship: 16
Godliness: 15; 25
Guidance: 1; 5; 15; 19; 25; 32; 48
Healing: 6; 41
Hope: 16; 17; 18; 23; 27
Humility: 19; 147
Illumination: 19
Integrity: 24; 25
Joy: 9; 16; 28; 126
Justice: 2; 7; 14; 26; 37; 49; 58; 82
Knowledge: 2; 8; 18; 19; 25; 29; 97; 103
Leadership: 72
Miracles: 60; 111
Money: 15; 16; 17; 49
Peace: 3; 4
Perspective: 2, 11
Prayer: 5; 17; 27; 61
Protection: 3; 4; 7; 16; 17; 18; 23; 27; 31; 91; 121; 125
Provision: 23
Rest: 23; 27
Salvation: 26; 37; 49; 126
Stability: 11; 33; 46
Vindication: 9; 14; 28; 35; 109
Wisdom: 1; 16; 19; 64; 111

150:3-5 Music and song were an integral part of Old Testament worship. David introduced music into the Tabernacle and Temple services (1 Chronicles 16:4-7). The music must have been loud and joyous as evidenced by the list of instruments and the presence of choirs and song leaders. Music was also important in New Testament worship (Ephesians 5:19; Colossians 3:16).

150:6 How could the message be more clear? The writer was telling the individual listeners to praise God. What a fitting way to end this book of praise—with a direct encouragement for *you* to praise God, too. Remember to praise him every day!

150:6 In a way, the book of Psalms parallels our spiritual journey through life. It begins by presenting us with two roads: the way to life and the way to death. If we choose God's way to life, we still face both blessings and troubles, joy and grief, successes and obstacles. Throughout it all, God is at our side, guiding, encouraging, comforting, and caring. As the wise and faithful person's life draws to an end, it becomes clear that God's road is the right road. Knowing this will cause us to praise God for leading us in the right direction and for assuring us of a place in the perfect world he has in store for those who have faithfully followed him.

PROVERBS

VITAL STATISTICS

PURPOSE:
To teach people how to attain wisdom and discipline and a prudent life, and how to do what is right and just and fair (see 1:2, 3)—in short, to apply divine wisdom to daily life and to provide moral instruction

AUTHOR:
Solomon wrote most of this book, with Agur and Lemuel contributing some of the later sections.

DATE WRITTEN:
Solomon wrote and compiled most of these proverbs early in his reign.

SETTING:
This is a book of wise sayings, a textbook for teaching people how to live godly lives through the repetition of wise thoughts.

KEY VERSE:
"Fear of the LORD is the beginning of knowledge. Only fools despise wisdom and discipline" (1:7).

SPECIAL FEATURES:
The book uses varied literary forms: poems, brief parables, pointed questions, and couplets. Other literary devices include antithesis, comparison, and personification.

ALPHABET letters, vowels, and consonants formed into words, sentences, paragraphs, and books—spoken, signed, whispered, written, and printed. From friendly advice to impassioned speeches and from dusty volumes to daily tabloids, messages are sent and received, with each sender trying to impart knowledge . . . and wisdom.

Woven into human fabric is the desire to learn and understand. Our mind sets us apart from animals, and we analyze, conceptualize, theorize, discuss, and debate everything from science to the supernatural. We build schools, institutes, and universities, where learned professors can teach us about the world and about life.

Knowledge is good, but there is a vast difference between "knowledge" (having the facts) and "wisdom" (applying those facts to life). We may amass knowledge, but without wisdom our knowledge is useless. We must learn how to *live out* what we know.

The wisest man who ever lived, Solomon, left us a legacy of written wisdom in three volumes—Proverbs, Ecclesiastes, and Song of Songs. In these books, under the inspiration of the Holy Spirit, he gives practical insights and guidelines for life.

In the first of these three volumes, Solomon passes on his practical advice in the form of proverbs. A proverb is a short, concise sentence that conveys moral truth. The book of Proverbs is a collection of these wise statements. The main theme of Proverbs, as we might expect, is the nature of true wisdom. Solomon writes, "Fear of the LORD is the beginning of knowledge. Only fools despise wisdom and discipline" (1:7). He then proceeds to give hundreds of practical examples of how to live according to godly wisdom.

Proverbs covers a wide range of topics, including youth and discipline, family life, self-control and resisting temptation, business matters, words and the tongue, knowing God, marriage, seeking the truth, wealth and poverty, immorality, and, of course, wisdom. These proverbs are short poems (usually in couplet form), containing a holy mixture of common sense and timely warnings. Although they are not meant to teach doctrine, a person who follows their advice will walk closely with God. The word *proverb* comes from a Hebrew word that means "to rule or to govern," and these sayings, reminders, and admonitions provide profound advice for governing our life.

As you read Proverbs, understand that knowing God is the key to wisdom. Listen to the thoughts and lessons from the world's wisest man, and apply these truths to your life. Don't just read these proverbs; act on them!

THE BLUEPRINT

A. WISDOM FOR YOUNG PEOPLE (1:1—9:18)	Solomon instructed the young people of his day like a father giving advice to his child. While many of these proverbs are directed toward young people, the principles supporting them are helpful to all believers, male and female, young and old. Anyone beginning his or her journey to discover more of wisdom will benefit greatly from these wise sayings.
B. WISDOM FOR ALL PEOPLE (10:1—24:34)	Solomon wanted to impart wisdom to all people, regardless of their age, sex, or position in society. These short, wise sayings give us practical wisdom for daily living. We should study them diligently and integrate them into our life.
C. WISDOM FOR THE LEADERS (25:1—31:31)	In addition to the proverbs that Solomon collected, the men of Hezekiah collected many proverbs that Solomon and others wrote. While most of these are general in nature, many are directed specifically to the king and those who dealt with the king. These are particularly useful for those who are leaders or aspire to be leaders.

MEGATHEMES

THEME	EXPLANATION	IMPORTANCE
Wisdom	God wants his people to be wise. Two kinds of people portray two contrasting paths of life. The fool is the wicked, stubborn person who hates or ignores God. The wise person seeks to know and love God.	When we choose God's way, he grants us wisdom. His Word, the Bible, leads us to live right, have right relationships, and make right decisions.
Relationships	Proverbs gives us advice for developing our personal relationships with friends, family members, and co-workers. In every relationship, we must show love, dedication, and high moral standards.	To relate to people, we need consistency, tact, and discipline to use the wisdom God gives us. If we don't treat others according to the wisdom God gives, our relationships will suffer.
Speech	What we say shows our real attitude toward others. How we talk reveals what we're really like. Our speech is a test of how wise we have become.	To be wise in our speech we need to use self-control. Our words should be honest and well chosen.
Work	God controls the final outcome of all we do. We are accountable to carry out our work with diligence and discipline, not laziness.	Because God evaluates how we live, we should work purposefully. We must never be lax or self-satisfied in using our skills.
Success	Although people work very hard for money and fame, God views success as having a good reputation, moral character, and the spiritual devotion to obey him.	A successful relationship with God counts for eternity. Everything else is perishable. All our resources, time, and talents come from God. We should strive to use them wisely.

A. WISDOM FOR YOUNG PEOPLE (1:1—9:18)

Proverbs begins with a clear statement of its purpose—to impart wisdom for godly living. The first few chapters are Solomon's fatherly advice to young people. Although most of the material in this section is directed toward young people, all who seek wisdom will greatly benefit from these wise words. This is where one can discover the source of wisdom, the value of wisdom, and the benefits of wisdom.

The Purpose of Proverbs

1 These are the proverbs of Solomon, David's son, king of Israel.
2 The purpose of these proverbs is to teach people wisdom and discipline, and to
help them understand wise sayings. 3 Through these proverbs, people will receive
instruction in discipline, good conduct, and doing what is right, just, and fair. 4 These
proverbs will make the simpleminded clever. They will give knowledge and purpose to
young people.
5 Let those who are wise listen to these proverbs and become even wiser. And let those
who understand receive guidance 6 by exploring the depth of meaning in these proverbs,
parables, wise sayings, and riddles.
7 Fear of the LORD is the beginning of knowledge. Only fools despise wisdom and
discipline.

A Father's Exhortation: Acquire Wisdom

8 Listen, my child,* to what your father teaches you. Don't neglect your mother's
teaching. 9 What you learn from them will crown you with grace and clothe you with
honor.
10 My child, if sinners entice you, turn your back on them! 11 They may say, "Come
and join us. Let's hide and kill someone! Let's ambush the innocent! 12 Let's swallow
them alive as the grave swallows its victims. Though they are in the prime of life, they
will go down into the pit of death. 13 And the loot we'll get! We'll fill our houses with
all kinds of things! 14 Come on, throw in your lot with us; we'll split our loot with
you."
15 Don't go along with them, my child! Stay far away from their paths. 16 They rush to
commit crimes. They hurry to commit murder. 17 When a bird sees a trap being set, it
stays away. 18 But not these people! They set an ambush for themselves; they booby-trap
their own lives! 19 Such is the fate of all who are greedy for gain. It ends up robbing them
of life.

1:8 Hebrew *my son;* also in 1:10, 15.

1:1 1 Kgs 4:32; Prov 25:1; Eccl 1:1; 12:9
1:3 Prov 2:9; 19:20
1:4 Prov 2:10-11; 8:5, 12
1:5 Prov 9:9; 14:6; Eccl 9:1
1:7 Prov 9:10; 15:33; Eccl 12:13
1:8-9 Prov 6:20
1:10 Ps 1:1; Prov 7:21; 13:20
1:11 Prov 1:18
1:15 Pss 1:1; 119:101; Prov 4:14
1:16 Isa 59:7; †Rom 3:15-17
1:19 Prov 15:27

1:1 What the book of Psalms is to prayer and devotional life, the book of Proverbs is to everyday life. Proverbs gives practical suggestions for effective living. This book is not just a collection of homey sayings; it contains deep spiritual insights drawn from experience. A *proverb* is a short, wise, easy-to-remember saying that calls a person to action. It doesn't argue about basic spiritual and moral beliefs; it assumes we already hold them. The book of Proverbs focuses on God—his character, works, and blessings—and it tells how we can live in close relationship to him.

1:1 Solomon, the third king of Israel, son of the great king David, reigned during Israel's golden age. When God said he would give him whatever he wanted, he asked for an understanding mind (1 Kings 3:5-14). God was pleased with this request. He not only made Solomon wise but also gave him great riches and power and an era of peace. Solomon built the glorious Temple in Jerusalem (1 Kings 6) and wrote most of the book of Proverbs. His Profile is found in 1 Kings 4.

1:6 Riddles were thought-provoking questions.

1:7 One of the most annoying types of people is a know-it-all, a person who has a dogmatic opinion about everything, is closed to anything new, resents discipline, and refuses to learn. Solomon calls this kind of person a fool. Don't be a know-it-all. Instead, be open to the advice of others, especially those who know you well and can give valuable insight and counsel. Learn how to learn from others. Remember, only God knows it all.

1:7-9 In this age of information, knowledge is plentiful, but wisdom is scarce. Wisdom means far more than simply knowing a lot. It is a basic attitude that affects every aspect of life. The foundation of knowledge is to fear the Lord—to honor and respect God, to live in awe of his power, and to obey his Word. Faith in God should be the controlling principle for your understanding of the world, your attitudes, and your actions. Trust in God—he will make you truly wise.

1:8 Our actions speak louder than our words. This is especially true in the home. Children learn values, morals, and priorities by observing how their parents act and react every day. If parents exhibit a deep reverence for and dependence on God, the children will catch these attitudes. Let them see your reverence for God. Teach them right living by giving worship an important place in your family life and by reading the Bible together.

1:10-19 Sin is enticing because it offers a quick route to prosperity and makes us feel like one of the crowd. But when we go along with others and refuse to listen to the truth, our own appetites become our masters, and we'll do anything to satisfy them. Sin, even when attractive, is deadly. We must learn to make choices, not on the basis of flashy appeal or short-range pleasure, but in view of the long-range effects. Sometimes this means steering clear of people who want to entice us into activities that we know are wrong. We can't be friendly with sin and expect our lives to remain unaffected.

1:23
Joel 2:28

1:24
Isa 65:12; 66:4

1:25
2 Chr 36:16
Ps 107:11

1:28
Job 27:9
Ps 18:41
Ezek 8:18
Zech 7:13

1:29
Job 21:14

1:30
Ps 81:11

1:31
Job 4:8

1:32
Jer 2:19

1:33
Pss 23:4; 25:13

Wisdom Shouts in the Streets

20 Wisdom shouts in the streets. She cries out in the public square. 21 She calls out to the
crowds along the main street, and to those in front of city hall. 22 "You simpletons!" she
cries. "How long will you go on being simpleminded? How long will you mockers relish
your mocking? How long will you fools fight the facts? 23 Come here and listen to me!
I'll pour out the spirit of wisdom upon you and make you wise.

24 "I called you so often, but you didn't come. I reached out to you, but you paid no
attention. 25 You ignored my advice and rejected the correction I offered. 26 So I will
laugh when you are in trouble! I will mock you when disaster overtakes you— 27 when
calamity overcomes you like a storm, when you are engulfed by trouble, and when
anguish and distress overwhelm you.

28 "I will not answer when they cry for help. Even though they anxiously search for
me, they will not find me. 29 For they hated knowledge and chose not to fear the LORD.
30 They rejected my advice and paid no attention when I corrected them. 31 That is why
they must eat the bitter fruit of living their own way. They must experience the full terror
of the path they have chosen. 32 For they are simpletons who turn away from me—to
death. They are fools, and their own complacency will destroy them. 33 But all who listen
to me will live in peace and safety, unafraid of harm."

2:1
Prov 3:1; 4:10

2:4
Prov 3:14
Matt 13:44

2:6
Job 32:8
Jas 1:5

The Benefits of Wisdom

2 My child,* listen to me and treasure my instructions. 2 Tune your ears to wisdom,
and concentrate on understanding. 3 Cry out for insight and understanding. 4 Search
for them as you would for lost money or hidden treasure. 5 Then you will understand
what it means to fear the LORD, and you will gain knowledge of God. 6 For the LORD

2:1 Hebrew *My son.*

UNDERSTANDING PROVERBS
Most often, proverbs are written in the form of couplets. These are constructed in three ways:

Type	*Description*	*Key Word(s)*	*Examples*
Contrasting	Meaning and application come from the differences or contrast between the two statements of the proverb.	"but"	10:3; 14:11, 18
Comparing	Meaning and application come from the similarities or comparison between the two statements of the proverb.	"as/so" "better/than" "like"	15:16, 17; 25:25
Complementing	Meaning and application come from the way the second statement complements the first.	"and"	11:16; 14:10, 17

1:19 Being "greedy for gain" is one of Satan's surest traps. It begins when he plants the suggestion that we can't live without some possession or more money. Then that desire fans its own fire until it becomes an all-consuming obsession. Ask God for wisdom to recognize any greedy desire before it destroys you. God will help you overcome it.

1:20 The picture of Wisdom calling aloud in the streets is a personification—a literary device to make wisdom come alive for us. Wisdom is not a living being; it is the mind of God revealed. By reading about Jesus Christ's earthly ministry, we can see Wisdom in action. In order to understand how to become wise, we need to heed Wisdom calling and instructing us in the book of Proverbs (see the chart in chapter 15). For New Testament calls to wisdom, see 2 Timothy 1:7 and James 1:5. Make sure you don't reject God's offer of wisdom to you.

1:22 In the book of Proverbs, a "simpleton" or a fool is not someone with a *mental* deficiency but someone with a *character* deficiency (such as rebellion, laziness, or anger). The fool is not stupid, but he or she is unable to tell right from wrong or good from bad.

1:23-28 God is more than willing to pour out his heart and make known his thoughts to us. To receive his advice, we must be willing to listen, refusing to let pride stand in our way. Pride is thinking more highly of our own wisdom and desires than of God's. If we think we know better than God or feel we have no need of God's direction, we have fallen into foolish and disastrous pride.

1:31, 32 Many proverbs point out that the "bitter fruit of living their own way" will be the consequence people will experience in this life. Faced with either choosing God's wisdom or persisting in rebellious independence, many decide to go it alone. The problems such people create for themselves will destroy them. Don't ignore God's advice even if it is painful for the present. It will keep you from greater pain in the future.

2:3-6 Wisdom comes in two ways: It is a God-given gift and also the result of an energetic search. Wisdom's starting point is God and his revealed Word, the source of "knowledge and understanding" (2:6). In that sense, wisdom is his gift to us. But he gives it only to those who earnestly seek it. But because God's wisdom is hidden from the rebellious and foolish, it takes effort to find it and use it. The pathway to wisdom is strenuous. When we are on the path, we discover that true wisdom is God's and that he will guide us and reward our sincere and persistent search.

2:6, 7 God gives wisdom and victory to the godly but not to those drifting through life or acting irresponsibly with his gifts and resources. If we are faithful to him and keep our purpose in life clearly in mind, he will keep us from pride and greed.

grants wisdom! From his mouth come knowledge and understanding. 7 He grants a
treasure of good sense to the godly. He is their shield, protecting those who walk with
integrity. 8 He guards the paths of justice and protects those who are faithful to him.
9 Then you will understand what is right, just, and fair, and you will know how to find
the right course of action every time. 10 For wisdom will enter your heart, and knowledge
will fill you with joy. 11 Wise planning will watch over you. Understanding will keep you
safe.
12 Wisdom will save you from evil people, from those whose speech is corrupt.
13 These people turn from right ways to walk down dark and evil paths. 14 They rejoice
in doing wrong, and they enjoy evil as it turns things upside down. 15 What they do is
crooked, and their ways are wrong.
16 Wisdom will save you from the immoral woman, from the flattery of the adulterous
woman. 17 She has abandoned her husband and ignores the covenant she made before
God. 18 Entering her house leads to death; it is the road to hell.* 19 The man who visits
her is doomed. He will never reach the paths of life.
20 Follow the steps of good men instead, and stay on the paths of the righteous. 21 For
only the upright will live in the land, and those who have integrity will remain in it. 22 But
the wicked will be removed from the land, and the treacherous will be destroyed.

Trusting in the LORD

3 My child,* never forget the things I have taught you. Store my commands in your heart,
2 for they will give you a long and satisfying life. 3 Never let loyalty and kindness get
away from you! Wear them like a necklace; write them deep within your heart. 4 Then you
will find favor with both God and people, and you will gain a good reputation.
5 Trust in the LORD with all your heart; do not depend on your own understanding.
6 Seek his will in all you do, and he will direct your paths.
7 Don't be impressed with your own wisdom. Instead, fear the LORD and turn your
back on evil. 8 Then you will gain renewed health and vitality.
9 Honor the LORD with your wealth and with the best part of everything your land
produces. 10 Then he will fill your barns with grain, and your vats will overflow with the
finest wine.

2:8 1 Sam 2:9
2:9 Prov 8:20
2:10 Prov 14:33; 22:18
2:11 Ps 82:5; Prov 6:22
2:14 Prov 10:23; Hab 1:15
2:16 Prov 6:24; 23:27
2:17 Mal 2:14-15
2:18 Prov 7:27
2:21 Ps 37:9, 29; Prov 10:30
2:22 Deut 28:63; Ps 37:38
3:1 Exod 20:6; Deut 30:16
3:3 Prov 6:21; 7:3; 2 Cor 3:3
3:4 1 Sam 2:26; Jer 9:23-24; Luke 2:52
3:6 1 Chr 28:9; Prov 16:3
3:9 Exod 23:19; Isa 43:23; Mal 3:10

2:18 Hebrew *to the spirits of the dead.* **3:1** Hebrew *My son;* also in 3:11, 21.

2:9, 10 We gain wisdom through a constant process of growing. First, we must trust and honor God. Second, we must realize that the Bible reveals God's wisdom to us. Third, we must make a lifelong series of right choices and avoid moral pitfalls. Fourth, when we make sinful choices or mistakes, we must learn from our errors and recover. People don't develop all aspects of wisdom at once. For example, some people have more insight than discretion; others have more knowledge than common sense. But we can pray for all aspects of wisdom and take the steps to develop them in our life.

2:16, 17 An *adulterous woman* is seductive or a prostitute. Two of the most difficult sins to resist are pride and sexual immorality. Both are seductive. Pride says, "I deserve it"; sexual desire says, "I need it." In combination, their appeal is deadly. In fact, says Solomon, only by relying on God's strength can we overcome them. Pride appeals to the empty head; sexual enticement to the empty heart. By looking to God, we can fill our heads with his wisdom and our hearts with his love. Don't be fooled—remember what God says about who you are and what you were meant to be. Ask him for strength to resist these temptations.

3:3 Loyalty and kindness are important character qualities. Both involve actions as well as attitudes. A loyal person acts responsibly. A kind person works for justice for others. Thoughts and words are not enough—our life reveals whether we are truly loyal and kind. Do your actions measure up to your attitudes?

3:5, 6 When we have an important decision to make, we sometimes feel that we can't trust anyone—not even God. But God knows what is best for us. He is a better judge of what we want than we are! We must trust him completely in every choice we make. We should not omit careful thinking or belittle our God-given ability to reason; but we should not trust our own ideas to the exclusion of all others. We must not be wise in our own eyes but be willing to listen to and be corrected by God's Word and wise counselors. Bring your decisions to God in prayer; use the Bible as your guide; and then follow God's leading. He will direct your paths by both guiding and protecting you.

3:6 To receive God's guidance, said Solomon, we must seek God's will in all we do. This means turning every area of life over to him. About a thousand years later, Jesus emphasized this same truth (Matthew 6:33). Examine your values and priorities. What is important to you? In what areas have you not acknowledged him? You may already acknowledge God in many areas of your life, but the areas where you attempt to restrict or ignore him will cause you grief. Make him a vital part of everything you do; then he will guide you because you will be working to accomplish his purposes.

3:9, 10 This refers to the practice of giving to God the first and best portion of the harvest (Deuteronomy 26:9-11). Many people give God their leftovers. If they can afford to donate anything after the bills are paid, they do so. These people may be sincere and contribute willingly, but they are not obeying what God says. God wants the first part of our income. This demonstrates that God, not possessions, has first place in our life and that our resources belong to him (we are only managers). Giving to God helps us conquer greed, helps us properly manage God's resources, and opens us up to receive God's special blessings.

3:11 Job 5:17 †Heb 12:5-6
3:13 Job 28:17
3:14 Prov 8:10, 19
3:16 Ps 21:4 Prov 3:2; 8:18; 16:7; 22:4
3:18 Gen 2:9 Prov 11:30 Rev 2:7
3:20 Gen 7:11

11 My child, don't ignore it when the LORD disciplines you, and don't be discouraged
when he corrects you. 12 For the LORD corrects those he loves, just as a father corrects a
child* in whom he delights.
13 Happy is the person who finds wisdom and gains understanding. 14 For the profit of
wisdom is better than silver, and her wages are better than gold. 15 Wisdom is more
precious than rubies; nothing you desire can compare with her. 16 She offers you life in
her right hand, and riches and honor in her left. 17 She will guide you down delightful
paths; all her ways are satisfying. 18 Wisdom is a tree of life to those who embrace her;
happy are those who hold her tightly.
19 By wisdom the LORD founded the earth; by understanding he established the
heavens. 20 By his knowledge the deep fountains of the earth burst forth, and the clouds
poured down rain.

3:12 Hebrew *a son.*

PEOPLE CALLED "WISE" IN THE BIBLE
The special description "wise" is used for 12 significant people in the Bible. They can be helpful models in our own pursuit of wisdom.

The Person	*Their Role*	*Reference*	*How They Practiced Wisdom*
Joseph	Wise leader	Acts 7:10	Prepared for a major famine; helped rule Egypt
Moses	Wise leader	Acts 7:20–22	Learned all the Egyptian wisdom, then graduated to God's lessons in wisdom to lead Israel out of Egypt
Bezalel	Wise artist	Exodus 31:1–5	Designed and supervised the construction of the Tabernacle and its utensils in the wilderness
Joshua	Wise leader	Deuteronomy 34:9	Learned by observing Moses, obeyed God, led the people into the Promised Land
David	Wise leader	2 Samuel 14:20	Never let his failures keep him from the source of wisdom—reverence for God
Abigail	Wise wife	1 Samuel 25:3	Managed her household well in spite of a surly and mean husband
Solomon	Wise leader	1 Kings 3:5–14; 4:29–34	Knew what to do even though he often failed to put his own wisdom into action
Daniel	Wise counselor	Daniel 5:11, 12	Known as a man in touch with God; a solver of complex problems with God's help
Astrologers	Wise learners	Matthew 2:1–12	Not only received special knowledge of God's visit to earth but checked it out personally
Stephen	Wise leader	Acts 6:8–10	Organized the distribution of food to the Grecian widows; preached the gospel to the Jews
Paul	Wise messenger	2 Peter 3:15, 16	Spent his life communicating God's love to all who would listen
Christ	Wise youth Wise Savior Wisdom of God	Luke 2:40, 52; 1 Corinthians 1:20–25	Not only lived a perfect life but died on the cross to save us and make God's wise plan of eternal life available to us

3:11, 12 *Discipline* means "to teach and to train." *Discipline* sounds negative to many people because some disciplinarians are not loving. God, however, is the source of all love. He doesn't punish us because he enjoys inflicting pain but because he is deeply concerned about our development. He knows that in order to become morally strong and good, we must learn the difference between right and wrong. His loving discipline enables us to do that.

3:11, 12 It's difficult to know when God has been disciplining us until we look back on the situation later. Not every calamity comes directly from God, of course. But if we rebel against God and refuse to repent when God has identified some sin in our life, he may use guilt, crises, or bad experiences to bring us back to him. Sometimes, however, difficult times come even when there is no flagrant sin in our life. Then our response should be patience, integrity, and confidence that God will show us what to do.

3:16, 17 Proverbs contains many strong statements about the benefits of wisdom, including long life, wealth, honor, and peace. If you aren't experiencing them, does this mean you are short on wisdom? Not necessarily. Instead of guarantees, these statements are general principles. In a perfect world, wise behavior would always lead to these benefits. Even in our troubled world, living wisely usually results in obvious blessings—but not always. Sometimes sin intervenes, and some blessings must be delayed until Jesus returns to establish his eternal Kingdom. That is why we must "live by believing and not by seeing" (2 Corinthians 5:7). We can be sure that wisdom ultimately leads to blessing.

21 My child, don't lose sight of good planning and insight. Hang on to them, 22 for they
fill you with life and bring you honor and respect. 23 They keep you safe on your way and
keep your feet from stumbling. 24 You can lie down without fear and enjoy pleasant
dreams. 25 You need not be afraid of disaster or the destruction that comes upon the wicked,
26 for the LORD is your security. He will keep your foot from being caught in a trap.

27 Do not withhold good from those who deserve it when it's in your power to help
them. 28 If you can help your neighbor now, don't say, "Come back tomorrow, and then
I'll help you."

29 Do not plot against your neighbors, for they trust you. 30 Don't make accusations
against someone who hasn't wronged you.

31 Do not envy violent people; don't copy their ways. 32 Such wicked people are an
abomination to the LORD, but he offers his friendship to the godly.

33 The curse of the LORD is on the house of the wicked, but his blessing is on the home
of the upright.

34 The LORD mocks at mockers, but he shows favor to the humble.

35 The wise inherit honor, but fools are put to shame!

A Father's Wise Advice

4 My children,* listen to me. Listen to your father's instruction. Pay attention and
grow wise, 2 for I am giving you good guidance. Don't turn away from my teaching.
3 For I, too, was once my father's son, tenderly loved by my mother as an only child.

4 My father told me, "Take my words to heart. Follow my instructions and you will
live. 5 Learn to be wise, and develop good judgment. Don't forget or turn away from my
words. 6 Don't turn your back on wisdom, for she will protect you. Love her, and she will
guard you. 7 Getting wisdom is the most important thing you can do! And whatever else
you do, get good judgment. 8 If you prize wisdom, she will exalt you. Embrace her and
she will honor you. 9 She will place a lovely wreath on your head; she will present you
with a beautiful crown."

10 My child,* listen to me and do as I say, and you will have a long, good life. 11 I will
teach you wisdom's ways and lead you in straight paths. 12 If you live a life guided by
wisdom, you won't limp or stumble as you run. 13 Carry out my instructions; don't
forsake them. Guard them, for they will lead you to a fulfilled life.

14 Do not do as the wicked do or follow the path of evildoers. 15 Avoid their haunts.
Turn away and go somewhere else, 16 for evil people cannot sleep until they have done
their evil deed for the day. They cannot rest unless they have caused someone to stumble.
17 They eat wickedness and drink violence!

3:21 Prov 3:2; 4:21
3:22 Deut 32:47
3:24 Job 5:21; 11:19 Ps 3:5 Prov 1:33; 6:22
3:27 Deut 24:15 Rom 13:8
3:30 Rom 12:18
3:31 Ps 37:1
3:33 Deut 11:28 Mal 2:2
3:34 Jas 4:6 †1 Pet 5:5
4:1 Prov 1:8
4:6 Prov 2:11 2 Thes 2:10
4:7 Prov 23:23
4:8 Prov 3:18
4:10 Prov 2:1; 9:11; 10:27; 22:4
4:12 Ps 91:11
4:13 Prov 3:18, 22 John 6:63
4:14 Ps 1:1 Prov 1:15
4:16 Ps 36:4 Mic 2:1

4:1 Hebrew *My sons.* **4:10** Hebrew *My son;* also in 4:20.

3:27, 28 Withholding good is inconsiderate and unfair, whether it is repaying a loan, returning a tool, or fulfilling a promise. Withholding destroys trust and creates a great inconvenience for the other person. Be as eager to do good as you are to have good done to you.

4:3, 4 One of the greatest responsibilities of parents is to encourage their children to become wise. Here Solomon tells how his father, David, encouraged him to seek wisdom when he was young (see 1 Kings 2:1-9 and 1 Chronicles 28–29 for David's charge to his son). This encouragement may have prompted Solomon to ask God for an understanding mind above everything else (1 Kings 3:9). Wisdom can be passed on from parents to children, from generation to generation. Ultimately, of course, all wisdom comes from God; parents can only urge their children to turn to him. If your parents never taught you in this way, you can learn from the Scriptures and then create a legacy of wisdom as you teach your own children.

4:5-7 If you want wisdom, you must decide to go after it. It takes resolve—a determination not to abandon the search once you begin, no matter how difficult the road may become. This is not a once-in-a-lifetime step but a daily process of choosing between two paths—the wicked (4:14-17, 19) and the righteous (4:18). Nothing else is more important or more valuable.

4:7 David taught Solomon as a young boy that seeking God's wisdom was the most important choice he could make. Solomon learned the lesson well. When God appeared to the new king to fulfill any request, Solomon chose wisdom above all else. We should also make God's wisdom our first choice. We don't have to wait for God to appear to us. We can boldly ask him for wisdom today through prayer. James 1:5 assures us that God will grant our request.

4:13-17 Even friends can make you fall. It is difficult for people to accept the fact that friends and acquaintances may lure them to do wrong. Young people want to be accepted, so they would never confront or criticize a friend for wrong plans or actions. Many other people can't see how their friends' actions could lead to trouble. While we should be accepting of others, we need a healthy skepticism about human behavior. When you feel yourself being heavily influenced, proceed with caution. Don't let your friends cause you to fall into sin.

4:18 2 Sam 23:4; Dan 12:3
4:19 Job 18:5; Isa 59:9-10
4:22 Prov 3:8, 22
4:23 Luke 6:45
4:26 †Heb 12:13
4:27 Deut 5:32; 28:14

18 The way of the righteous is like the first gleam of dawn, which shines ever brighter
until the full light of day. 19 But the way of the wicked is like complete darkness. Those
who follow it have no idea what they are stumbling over.
20 Pay attention, my child, to what I say. Listen carefully. 21 Don't lose sight of my
words. Let them penetrate deep within your heart, 22 for they bring life and radiant health
to anyone who discovers their meaning.
23 Above all else, guard your heart, for it affects everything you do.*
24 Avoid all perverse talk; stay far from corrupt speech.
25 Look straight ahead, and fix your eyes on what lies before you. 26 Mark out a straight
path for your feet; then stick to the path and stay safe. 27 Don't get sidetracked; keep your
feet from following evil.

Avoid Immoral Women

5:1 Prov 4:20
5:3 Ps 55:21; Prov 5:20; 7:5
5:4 Ps 57:4; Eccl 7:26
5:5 Prov 2:18; 7:27
5:6 2 Pet 2:14
5:8 Prov 7:25; 9:14

5 My son, pay attention to my wisdom; listen carefully to my wise counsel. 2 Then you
will learn to be discreet and will store up knowledge.
3 The lips of an immoral woman are as sweet as honey, and her mouth is smoother than
oil. 4 But the result is as bitter as poison, sharp as a double-edged sword. 5 Her feet go
down to death; her steps lead straight to the grave.* 6 For she does not care about the path
to life. She staggers down a crooked trail and doesn't even realize where it leads.
7 So now, my sons, listen to me. Never stray from what I am about to say: 8 Run from
her! Don't go near the door of her house! 9 If you do, you will lose your honor and hand
over to merciless people everything you have achieved in life. 10 Strangers will obtain
your wealth, and someone else will enjoy the fruit of your labor. 11 Afterward you will

4:23 Hebrew *for from it flow the springs of life.* **5:5** Hebrew *to Sheol.*

WISDOM: APPLIED TRUTH
The book of Proverbs tells us about people who have wisdom and enjoy its benefits.

Reference	*The Person Who Has Wisdom*	*Benefits of Wisdom*
Proverbs 3, 4 A father's instructions	Is loving Is faithful Trusts in the Lord Puts God first Turns away from evil Knows right from wrong Listens and learns Does what is right	Long, prosperous life Favor with God and people Reputation for good judgment Success Health, vitality Riches, honor, pleasure, peace Protection
Proverbs 8:9 Wisdom speaks	Possesses knowledge and discretion Hates pride, arrogance, and evil behavior Respects and fears God Gives good advice and has common sense Loves correction and is teachable Knows God	Riches, honor Justice Righteousness Life God's favor Constant learning Understanding

4:23-27 Our heart—our feelings of love and desire—dictates to a great extent how we live because we always find time to do what we enjoy. Solomon tells us to guard our heart above all else, making sure we concentrate on those desires that will keep us on the right path. Make sure your affections lead you in the right direction. Put boundaries on your desires: Don't go after everything you see. Look straight ahead, keep your eyes fixed on your goal, and don't get sidetracked on detours that lead to sin.

5:3 This "immoral woman" is a prostitute. Proverbs includes many warnings against illicit sex for several reasons. First, a prostitute's charm is used as an example of any temptation to do wrong or to leave the pursuit of wisdom. Second, sexual immorality of any kind was and still is extremely dangerous. It destroys family life. It erodes a person's ability to love. It degrades human beings and turns them into objects. It can lead to disease. It can result in unwanted children. Third, sexual immorality is against God's law.

5:3-8 Any person should be on guard against those who use flattery and smooth talk (lips that "are sweet as honey") that would lead him or her into sin. The best advice is to take a detour and even avoid conversation with such people.

5:11-13 At the end of your life, it will be too late to ask for advice. When desire is fully activated, people don't want advice—they want satisfaction. The best time to learn the dangers and foolishness of going after forbidden sex (or anything else that is harmful) is long before the temptation comes. Resistance is easier if the decision has already been made. Don't wait to see what happens. Prepare for temptation by deciding *now* how you will act when you face it.

groan in anguish when disease consumes your body, [12]and you will say, "How I hated
discipline! If only I had not demanded my own way! [13]Oh, why didn't I listen to my
teachers? Why didn't I pay attention to those who gave me instruction? [14]I have come
to the brink of utter ruin, and now I must face public disgrace."

[15]Drink water from your own well—share your love only with your wife.* [16]Why
spill the water of your springs in public, having sex with just anyone?* [17]You should
reserve it for yourselves. Don't share it with strangers.

[18]Let your wife be a fountain of blessing for you. Rejoice in the wife of your youth.
[19]She is a loving doe, a graceful deer. Let her breasts satisfy you always. May you always
be captivated by her love. [20]Why be captivated, my son, with an immoral woman, or
embrace the breasts of an adulterous woman?

[21]For the LORD sees clearly what a man does, examining every path he takes. [22]An
evil man is held captive by his own sins; they are ropes that catch and hold him. [23]He
will die for lack of self-control; he will be lost because of his incredible folly.

Lessons for Daily Life

6 My child,* if you co-sign a loan for a friend or guarantee the debt of someone you
hardly know—[2]if you have trapped yourself by your agreement and are caught by
what you said—[3]quick, get out of it if you possibly can! You have placed yourself at
your friend's mercy. Now swallow your pride; go and beg to have your name erased.
[4]Don't put it off. Do it now! Don't rest until you do. [5]Save yourself like a deer escaping
from a hunter, like a bird fleeing from a net.

[6]Take a lesson from the ants, you lazybones. Learn from their ways and be wise!
[7]Even though they have no prince, governor, or ruler to make them work, [8]they labor
hard all summer, gathering food for the winter. [9]But you, lazybones, how long will you
sleep? When will you wake up? I want you to learn this lesson: [10]A little extra sleep, a
little more slumber, a little folding of the hands to rest—[11]and poverty will pounce on
you like a bandit; scarcity will attack you like an armed robber.

[12]Here is a description of worthless and wicked people: They are constant liars,
[13]signaling their true intentions to their friends by making signs with their eyes and feet
and fingers. [14]Their perverted hearts plot evil. They stir up trouble constantly. [15]But they
will be destroyed suddenly, broken beyond all hope of healing.

[16]There are six things the LORD hates—no, seven things he detests:

[17] haughty eyes,
a lying tongue,
hands that kill the innocent,

5:12 Prov 1:22, 25
5:16 Prov 5:18
5:18 Eccl 9:9; Mal 2:14
5:19 Song 4:5; 7:3
5:20 Prov 2:16; 5:3
5:21 Job 14:16; Ps 119:168
5:22 Num 32:23
5:23 Job 4:21; 36:12
6:1 Prov 11:15; 17:18; 20:16; 22:26; 27:13
6:5 Pss 91:3; 124:7
6:6 Prov 10:26; 13:4; 30:24-25
6:10 Prov 24:33
6:12 Prov 4:27; 8:13; 10:27
6:13 Ps 35:19; Prov 10:10
6:14 Prov 6:19; Mic 2:1
6:15 2 Chr 36:16; Prov 24:22; Jer 19:11
6:16-19 Gen 6:5; Prov 1:16; 6:14; 19:5, 9; 21:4; 24:2; 28:17; Isa 1:15

5:15 Hebrew *Drink water from your own cistern, flowing water from your own well.* **5:16** Hebrew *Why spill your springs in public, your streams in the streets?* **6:1** Hebrew *My son.*

5:15 "Drink water from your own well" is a picture of faithfulness in marriage. It means to enjoy the spouse God has given you. In desert lands, water is precious, and a well is a family's most important possession. In Old Testament times, it was considered a crime to steal water from someone else's well, just as it was a crime to have intercourse with another man's wife. In both cases, the offender is endangering the health and security of family.

5:15-21 In contrast to much of what we read, see, and hear today, this passage urges couples to look to each other for lifelong satisfaction and companionship. Many temptations entice husbands and wives to leave their spouses when marriage becomes dull and find excitement and pleasures elsewhere. But God designed marriage and sanctified it, and only within this covenant relationship can we find real love and fulfillment. Don't let God's best for you be wasted on the illusion of greener pastures somewhere else. Instead, rejoice with your spouse as you give yourselves to God and to each other.

5:18-20 God never intended marriage to become boring, lifeless, pleasureless, and dull. Sex is a gift God gives to married people for their mutual enjoyment. Real happiness comes when we decide to find pleasure in the spouse God has given us and to commit ourselves to meeting his or her needs. The real danger is in doubting that God knows and cares for us. We then may resent his timing and carelessly pursue sexual pleasure without his blessing.

5:19 See Song of Songs, chapter 4, for parallels to this frank expression of the joys of sexual pleasure in marriage.

6:1-5 These verses are not a plea against generosity, but against overextending one's financial resources and acting in irresponsible ways that could lead to poverty. It is important to maintain a balance between generosity and good stewardship. God wants us to help our friends and the needy, but he does not promise to cover the costs of every unwise commitment we make. We should also act responsibly so that our family does not suffer.

6:6-11 Those last few moments of sleep are delicious; we savor them as we resist beginning another workday. But Proverbs warns against giving in to the temptation of laziness, of sleeping instead of working. This does not mean we should never rest: God gave the Jews the Sabbath, a weekly day of rest and restoration. But we should not rest when we should be working. The ant is used as an example because it utilizes its energy and resources economically. If laziness turns us from our responsibilities, poverty may soon bar us from the legitimate rest we should enjoy. (See also the chart in chapter 27.)

18 a heart that plots evil,
feet that race to do wrong,
19 a false witness who pours out lies,
a person who sows discord among brothers.

20 My son, obey your father's commands, and don't neglect your mother's teaching.
21 Keep their words always in your heart. Tie them around your neck. 22 Wherever you
walk, their counsel can lead you. When you sleep, they will protect you. When you wake
up in the morning, they will advise you. 23 For these commands and this teaching are a
lamp to light the way ahead of you. The correction of discipline is the way to life.
24 These commands and this teaching will keep you from the immoral woman, from
the smooth tongue of an adulterous woman. 25 Don't lust for her beauty. Don't let her
coyness seduce you. 26 For a prostitute will bring you to poverty, and sleeping with
another man's wife may cost you your very life. 27 Can a man scoop fire into his lap
and not be burned? 28 Can he walk on hot coals and not blister his feet? 29 So it is with
the man who sleeps with another man's wife. He who embraces her will not go
unpunished.
30 Excuses might be found for a thief who steals because he is starving. 31 But if he is
caught, he will be fined seven times as much as he stole, even if it means selling
everything in his house to pay it back.
32 But the man who commits adultery is an utter fool, for he destroys his own soul.
33 Wounds and constant disgrace are his lot. His shame will never be erased. 34 For the
woman's husband will be furious in his jealousy, and he will have no mercy in his day
of vengeance. 35 There is no compensation or bribe that will satisfy him.

Another Warning about Immoral Women

7 Follow my advice, my son; always treasure my commands. 2 Obey them and live!
Guard my teachings as your most precious possession.* 3 Tie them on your fingers
as a reminder. Write them deep within your heart.
4 Love wisdom like a sister; make insight a beloved member of your family. 5 Let them
hold you back from an affair with an immoral woman, from listening to the flattery of
an adulterous woman.

7:2 Hebrew *as the apple of your eye.*

6:21 Prov 3:3
6:22 Prov 3:23
6:23 Ps 119:105; Prov 13:9
6:24 Prov 2:16; 5:3
6:25 2 Kgs 9:30; Matt 5:28
6:26 Prov 5:9-10; 29:3
6:29 Prov 16:5; Ezek 18:6
6:31 Ezek 22:1-4
6:32 Prov 7:7, 22-23; 9:14, 16
6:34 Prov 11:4; 27:4; Song 8:6
7:1 Prov 2:1; 4:1
7:2 Deut 32:10; Prov 4:4; 9:11
7:3 Deut 6:8; Prov 3:3; 6:21
7:5 Prov 6:24

STRATEGY FOR EFFECTIVE LIVING

Begins with	God's wisdom	Respecting and appreciating who God is; reverence and awe in recognizing the almighty God
Requires	Moral application	Trusting in God and his Word; allowing his Word to speak to us personally; willing to obey
Requires	Practical application	Acting on God's direction in daily devotions
Results in	Effective living	Experiencing what God does with our obedience

6:20-23 It is natural and good for children, as they grow toward adulthood, to become increasingly independent of their parents. Young adults, however, should take care not to turn a deaf ear to their parents—to reject their advice just when it is needed most. If you are struggling with a decision or looking for insight, check with your parents or other older adults who know you well. Their years of experience may have given them the wisdom you seek.

6:25 Regard lust as a warning sign of danger ahead. When you notice that you are attracted to a person of the opposite sex or preoccupied with thoughts of him or her, your desires may lead you to sin. Ask God to help you change your desires before you are drawn into sin.

6:25-35 Some people argue that it is all right to break God's law against sexual sin if nobody gets hurt. In truth, somebody always gets hurt. In the case of adultery, spouses are devastated; children are scarred. Even if the partners escape disease and unwanted pregnancy, they may lose their ability to fulfill commitments, to feel sexual desire, to trust, and to be entirely open with another person. God's laws are not arbitrary. They do not forbid good, clean fun; rather, they warn us against destroying ourselves through unwise actions or running ahead of God's timetable.

6 I was looking out the window of my house one day 7 and saw a simpleminded young
man who lacked common sense. 8 He was crossing the street near the house of an
immoral woman. He was strolling down the path by her house 9 at twilight, as the day
was fading, as the dark of night set in. 10 The woman approached him, dressed seduc-
tively and sly of heart. 11 She was the brash, rebellious type who never stays at home.
12 She is often seen in the streets and markets, soliciting at every corner.

13 She threw her arms around him and kissed him, and with a brazen look she said,
14 "I've offered my sacrifices and just finished my vows. 15 It's you I was looking for! I
came out to find you, and here you are! 16 My bed is spread with colored sheets of finest
linen imported from Egypt. 17 I've perfumed my bed with myrrh, aloes, and cinnamon.
18 Come, let's drink our fill of love until morning. Let's enjoy each other's caresses, 19 for
my husband is not home. He's away on a long trip. 20 He has taken a wallet full of money
with him, and he won't return until later in the month."

21 So she seduced him with her pretty speech. With her flattery she enticed him. 22 He
followed her at once, like an ox going to the slaughter or like a trapped stag, 23 awaiting
the arrow that would pierce its heart. He was like a bird flying into a snare, little knowing
it would cost him his life.

24 Listen to me, my sons, and pay attention to my words. 25 Don't let your hearts stray
away toward her. Don't wander down her wayward path. 26 For she has been the ruin of
many; numerous men have been her victims. 27 Her house is the road to the grave.* Her
bedroom is the den of death.

Wisdom Calls for a Hearing

8 Listen as wisdom calls out! Hear as understanding raises her voice! 2 She stands on
the hilltop and at the crossroads. 3 At the entrance to the city, at the city gates, she
cries aloud, 4 "I call to you, to all of you! I am raising my voice to all people. 5 How naive
you are! Let me give you common sense. O foolish ones, let me give you understanding.
6 Listen to me! For I have excellent things to tell you. Everything I say is right, 7 for I
speak the truth and hate every kind of deception. 8 My advice is wholesome and good.
There is nothing crooked or twisted in it. 9 My words are plain to anyone with understanding, clear to those who want to learn.

10 "Choose my instruction rather than silver, and knowledge over pure gold. 11 For
wisdom is far more valuable than rubies. Nothing you desire can be compared with it.

12 "I, Wisdom, live together with good judgment. I know where to discover knowledge
and discernment. 13 All who fear the LORD will hate evil. That is why I hate pride,
arrogance, corruption, and perverted speech. 14 Good advice and success belong to me.
Insight and strength are mine. 15 Because of me, kings reign, and rulers make just laws.
16 Rulers lead with my help, and nobles make righteous judgments.

17 "I love all who love me. Those who search for me will surely find me. 18 Unending
riches, honor, wealth, and justice are mine to distribute. 19 My gifts are better than the
purest gold, my wages better than sterling silver! 20 I walk in righteousness, in paths of
justice. 21 Those who love me inherit wealth, for I fill their treasuries.

7:27 Hebrew *to Sheol.*

7:7 Prov 1:22; 6:32
7:8 Prov 7:12
7:9 Job 24:15
7:10 Gen 38:14-15
7:11 Prov 9:13
7:12 Prov 23:28
7:16 Prov 31:22; Ezek 27:7
7:21 Prov 5:3; 6:24
7:23 Eccl 9:12
7:24 Prov 4:1
7:25 Prov 5:8
7:27 Prov 2:18; 9:18
8:1 Prov 1:20-21
8:4 Ps 19:7
8:9 Prov 3:13; 14:6
8:11 Prov 3:14-15; 16:16; 20:15
8:13 Prov 3:7; 6:12; 15:9
8:17 1 Sam 2:30; Ps 91:14; Prov 2:4-5; 4:6; John 14:21
8:18 Ps 112:3; Prov 3:16; 22:4; Matt 6:33; Jas 2:5
8:20 Pss 23:3; 25:4
8:21 Prov 3:19

7:6-23 Although this advice is directed toward young men, young women should heed it as well. The person who has no purpose in life is simpleminded (7:7). Without aim or direction, an empty life is unstable, vulnerable to many temptations. Even though the young man in this passage doesn't know where he is going, the immoral woman knows where she wants him. Notice her strategies: She is dressed to allure men (7:10); her approach is bold (7:13); she invites him over to her place (7:16-18); she cunningly answers his every objection (7:19, 20); she persuades him with smooth talk (7:21); she traps him (7:23). To combat temptation, make sure your life is full of God's Word and wisdom (7:4). Recognize the strategies of temptation, and run away from them—fast.

7:25-27 There are definite steps you can take to avoid sexual sins. First, guard your mind. Don't read books, look at pictures, or encourage fantasies that stimulate the wrong desires. Second, keep away from settings and friends that tempt you to sin. Third, don't think only of the moment—focus on the future. Today's thrill may lead to tomorrow's ruin.

8:1ff Wisdom's call is contrasted to the call of the immoral woman in chapter 7. Wisdom is portrayed as a woman who guides us (8:1-13) and makes us succeed (8:14-21). Wisdom was present at the Creation and works with the Creator (8:22-31). God approves of those who listen to Wisdom's counsel (8:32-35). Those who hate wisdom love death (8:36). Wisdom should affect every aspect of our entire life, from beginning to end. Be sure to open all corners of your life to God's direction and guidance.

8:13 The more a person fears and respects God, the more he or she will hate evil. Love for God and love for sin cannot coexist. Harboring secret sins means that you are tolerating evil within yourself. Make a clean break with sin and commit yourself completely to God.

22“The LORD formed me from the beginning, before he created anything else. 23I was
appointed in ages past, at the very first, before the earth began. 24I was born before the
oceans were created, before the springs bubbled forth their waters. 25Before the mountains and the hills were formed, I was born—26before he had made the earth and fields
and the first handfuls of soil.
27“I was there when he established the heavens, when he drew the horizon on the
oceans. 28I was there when he set the clouds above, when he established the deep
fountains of the earth. 29I was there when he set the limits of the seas, so they would not
spread beyond their boundaries. And when he marked off the earth’s foundations, 30I
was the architect at his side. I was his constant delight, rejoicing always in his presence.
31And how happy I was with what he created—his wide world and all the human family!
32“And so, my children,* listen to me, for happy are all who follow my ways. 33Listen
to my counsel and be wise. Don’t ignore it.
34“Happy are those who listen to me, watching for me daily at my gates, waiting for
me outside my home! 35For whoever finds me finds life and wins approval from the
LORD. 36But those who miss me have injured themselves. All who hate me love death.”

9 Wisdom has built her spacious house with seven pillars. 2She has prepared a great
banquet, mixed the wines, and set the table. 3She has sent her servants to invite
everyone to come. She calls out from the heights overlooking the city. 4“Come home
with me,” she urges the simple. To those without good judgment, she says, 5“Come, eat
my food, and drink the wine I have mixed. 6Leave your foolish ways behind, and begin
to live; learn how to be wise.”
7Anyone who rebukes a mocker will get a smart retort. Anyone who rebukes the
wicked will get hurt. 8So don’t bother rebuking mockers; they will only hate you. But
the wise, when rebuked, will love you all the more. 9Teach the wise, and they will be
wiser. Teach the righteous, and they will learn more.
10Fear of the LORD is the beginning of wisdom. Knowledge of the Holy One results
in understanding.

8:22 Job 28:27; Ps 104:24
8:23 John 17:5, 24
8:24 Job 38:16
8:25 Ps 90:2
8:27 Job 26:10; Prov 3:19
8:29 Job 38:6, 10; Ps 104:9; Job 38:6
8:34 Ps 27:4; Jas 1:22
8:35 John 17:3
9:1 Eph 2:20-22; 1 Pet 2:5
9:3 Prov 1:20; 8:1-2; Matt 22:3
9:5 Song 5:1; Isa 55:1; John 6:27
9:7 Prov 23:9
9:10 Job 28:28; Ps 111:10; Prov 1:7

8:32 Hebrew *my sons.*

THINGS GOD HATES
The book of Proverbs notes 14 types of people and actions that God hates. Let these be guidelines of what we are *not* to be and do!

Violent people	Proverbs 3:31
Haughtiness, lying, murdering, scheming, eagerness to do evil, a false witness, stirring up dissension	Proverbs 6:16–19
Those who are untruthful	Proverbs 12:22
The sacrifice of the wicked	Proverbs 15:8
The way of the wicked	Proverbs 15:9
The thoughts of the wicked	Proverbs 15:26
Those who are proud	Proverbs 16:5
Those who judge unjustly	Proverbs 17:15

8:22-31 God says wisdom is primary and fundamental. It is the foundation on which all life is built. Paul and John may have alluded to some of Solomon’s statements about wisdom to describe Christ’s presence at the creation of the world (Colossians 1:15-17; 2:2, 3; Revelation 3:14).

9:1 The seven pillars are figurative; they do not represent seven principles of wisdom. In the Bible, the number seven represents completeness and perfection. This verse poetically states that wisdom lacks nothing—it is complete and perfect.

9:1ff Wisdom and Folly (foolishness) are portrayed in this chapter as rival young women, each preparing a feast and inviting people to it. But Wisdom is a responsible woman of character, while Folly is a prostitute serving stolen food. Wisdom appeals to the mind; Folly to the senses. It is easier to excite the senses, but the pleasures of Folly are temporary. By contrast, the satisfaction that Wisdom brings lasts forever.

9:1-5 The banquet described in this chapter has some interesting parallels to the banquet Jesus described in one of his parables (Luke 14:15-24). Many may intend to go, but they never make it because they get sidetracked by other activities that seem more important at the time. Don’t let anything become more important than your search for God’s wisdom.

9:7-10 Are you a mocker or a wise person? You can tell by the way you respond to criticism. Instead of replying with a quick put-down or clever retort when rebuked, listen to what is being said. Learn from your critics; this is the path to wisdom. Wisdom begins with knowing God. He gives insight into living because he created life. To know God you must not just know the facts about him; you must have a personal relationship with him. Do you really want to be wise? Get to know God better and better. (See James 1:5 and 2 Peter 1:2-4 for more on how to become wise.)

11 Wisdom will multiply your days and add years to your life. 12 If you become wise,
you will be the one to benefit. If you scorn wisdom, you will be the one to suffer.

Folly Calls for a Hearing

13 The woman named Folly is loud and brash. She is ignorant and doesn't even know it.
14 She sits in her doorway on the heights overlooking the city. 15 She calls out to men
going by who are minding their own business. 16 "Come home with me," she urges the
simple. To those without good judgment, she says, 17 "Stolen water is refreshing; food
eaten in secret tastes the best!" 18 But the men don't realize that her former guests are
now in the grave.*

9:11 Prov 3:2, 16; 9:6; 10:27
9:13 Prov 5:4; 7:11
9:16 Prov 9:4
9:17 Prov 20:17
9:18 Prov 7:27

B. WISDOM FOR ALL PEOPLE (10:1—24:34)

These short couplets are what we commonly recognize as proverbs. They cover a wide range of topics. The first section was written by Solomon. The next two sections were written by others but collected by Solomon. These sayings give people practical wisdom for godly living at every stage of life.

The Proverbs of Solomon

10 The proverbs of Solomon:
A wise child* brings joy to a father; a foolish child brings grief to a mother.
2 Ill-gotten gain has no lasting value, but right living can save your life.
3 The LORD will not let the godly starve to death, but he refuses to satisfy the craving
of the wicked.
4 Lazy people are soon poor; hard workers get rich.
5 A wise youth works hard all summer; a youth who sleeps away the hour of opportunity brings shame.
6 The godly are showered with blessings; evil people cover up their harmful intentions.
7 We all have happy memories of the godly, but the name of a wicked person rots away.
8 The wise are glad to be instructed, but babbling fools fall flat on their faces.
9 People with integrity have firm footing, but those who follow crooked paths will slip
and fall.
10 People who wink at wrong cause trouble, but a bold reproof promotes peace.*
11 The words of the godly lead to life; evil people cover up their harmful intentions.
12 Hatred stirs up quarrels, but love covers all offenses.
13 Wise words come from the lips of people with understanding, but fools will be
punished with a rod.
14 Wise people treasure knowledge, but the babbling of a fool invites trouble.
15 The wealth of the rich is their fortress; the poverty of the poor is their calamity.
16 The earnings of the godly enhance their lives, but evil people squander their money
on sin.
17 People who accept correction are on the pathway to life, but those who ignore it will
lead others astray.

10:2 Ps 49:6-7; Eccl 2:4
10:3 Pss 34:9-10; 37:25; Matt 6:33
10:4 Prov 13:4
10:7 Ps 9:5-6
10:8 Prov 9:8; Matt 7:24
10:9 Ps 23:4; Isa 33:15-16; Matt 10:26
10:11 Prov 13:14; 18:4; 37:30
10:12 1 Cor 13:4-7; †1 Pet 4:8
10:13 Prov 10:31; 26:3
10:14 Prov 9:19; 13:3; Jas 3:2, 5
10:15 Ps 52:7; Prov 18:11; 19:7
10:17 Prov 6:23

9:18 Hebrew *in Sheol.* **10:1** Hebrew *son;* also in 10:1b. **10:10** As in Greek version; Hebrew reads *but babbling fools fall flat on their faces.*

9:14-17 There is something hypnotic and intoxicating about wickedness. One sin leads to another; sinful behavior seems more exciting than the Christian life. That is why many people put aside all thought of Wisdom's sumptuous banquet (9:1-5) in order to eat the stolen food of Folly. Don't be deceived—sin is dangerous. Before reaching for forbidden fruit, take a long look at what happens to those who eat it. (See the chart in chapter 21.)

10:2 Some people bring unhappiness on themselves by choosing ill-gotten gain. For example, craving satisfaction, they may do something that destroys their chances of ever achieving happiness. God's principles for right living bring lasting happiness, because they guide us into long-term right behavior in spite of our ever changing feelings.

10:3 Proverbs is full of verses contrasting the godly (righteous) person with the wicked. These statements are not intended to apply universally to all people in every situation. For example, some good people do go hungry. Rather, they are intended to communicate the general truth that the life of the person who seeks God is better in the long run than the life of the wicked person—a life that leads to ruin. These statements are not ironclad promises but general truths. In addition, a proverb like this assumes a just government that cares for the poor and needy—the kind of government Israel was intended to have (see Deuteronomy 24:17-22). A corrupt government often thwarts the plans of godly men and women.

10:4, 5 Every day has 24 hours filled with opportunities to grow, serve, and be productive. Yet it is so easy to waste time, letting life slip from our grasp. Refuse to be a lazy person, sleeping or frittering away the hours meant for productive work. See time as God's gift, and seize your opportunities to live diligently for him.

18 To hide hatred is to be a liar; to slander is to be a fool.
19 Don't talk too much, for it fosters sin. Be sensible and turn off the flow!
20 The words of the godly are like sterling silver; the heart of a fool is worthless.
21 The godly give good advice, but fools are destroyed by their lack of common sense.
22 The blessing of the LORD makes a person rich, and he adds no sorrow with it.
23 Doing wrong is fun for a fool, while wise conduct is a pleasure to the wise.
24 The fears of the wicked will all come true; so will the hopes of the godly.
25 Disaster strikes like a cyclone, whirling the wicked away, but the godly have a
lasting foundation.
26 Lazy people are a pain to their employer. They are like smoke in the eyes or vinegar
that sets the teeth on edge.
27 Fear of the LORD lengthens one's life, but the years of the wicked are cut short.
28 The hopes of the godly result in happiness, but the expectations of the wicked are
all in vain.
29 The LORD protects the upright but destroys the wicked.
30 The godly will never be disturbed, but the wicked will be removed from the land.
31 The godly person gives wise advice, but the tongue that deceives will be cut off.
32 The godly speak words that are helpful, but the wicked speak only what is corrupt.

11

1 The LORD hates cheating, but he delights in honesty.
2 Pride leads to disgrace, but with humility comes wisdom.
3 Good people are guided by their honesty; treacherous people are destroyed by their
dishonesty.
4 Riches won't help on the day of judgment, but right living is a safeguard against death.
5 The godly are directed by their honesty; the wicked fall beneath their load of sin.
6 The godliness of good people rescues them; the ambition of treacherous people traps
them.

10:19 Job 11:2; Eccl 5:3; Jas 3:2
10:22 Gen 24:35; 26:12; Deut 8:18; Prov 8:21
10:24 Ps 145:19; Prov 1:27; 15:8; Matt 5:6
10:25 Ps 15:1-5; Matt 7:24-25
10:27 Ps 55:23; Prov 3:2; 9:11
10:28 Job 11:20
10:30 Ps 37:29
10:32 Prov 6:12; Eccl 12:10
11:1 Deut 25:13-16; Prov 16:11
11:2 Prov 16:18; 18:12; 29:23
11:4 Prov 10:2; Ezek 7:19
11:5 Prov 3:6; 5:22

GOD'S ADVICE ABOUT MONEY

Proverbs gives some practical instruction on the use of money, although sometimes it is advice we would rather not hear. It's more comfortable to continue in our habits than to learn how to use money more wisely. The advice includes

Be generous in giving.	11:24, 25; 22:9
Place people's needs ahead of profit.	11:26
Be cautious of countersigning for another.	17:18; 22:26, 27
Don't accept bribes.	17:23
Help the poor.	19:17; 21:13
Store up for the future.	21:20
Be careful about borrowing.	22:7

Other verses to study include 11:15; 20:16; 25:14; 27:13.

10:18 By hating another person you may become a liar or a fool. If you try to conceal your hatred, you end up lying. If you slander the other person and are proven wrong, you are a fool. The only way out is to admit your hateful feelings to God. Ask him to change your heart, to help you love instead of hate.

10:20 Words from a good person are valuable ("sterling silver"). A lot of poor advice is worth less than a little good advice. It is easy to get opinions from people who will tell us only what they think will please us, but such advice is not helpful. Instead, we should look for those who will speak the truth, even when it hurts. Think about the people to whom you go for advice. What do you expect to hear from them?

10:22 God supplies most people with the personal and financial abilities to respond to the needs of others. If we all realized how God has blessed us, and if we all used our resources to do God's will, hunger and poverty would be wiped out. Wealth is a blessing only if we use it in the way God intended.

10:24 The wicked person dreads death. Those who do not believe in God usually fear death, and with good reason. By contrast, believers desire eternal life and God's salvation—their hopes will be rewarded. This verse offers a choice: You can have either your fears or your hopes come true. You make that choice by rejecting God and living your own way or by accepting God and following him.

11:4 "The day of judgment" refers to when we die or to the time when God settles accounts with all people. On judgment day, each of us will stand alone, accountable for all our deeds. At that time, no amount of riches will buy reconciliation with God. Only our love for God and obedience to him will count.

7 When the wicked die, their hopes all perish, for they rely on their own feeble strength.

8 God rescues the godly from danger, but he lets the wicked fall into trouble.

9 Evil words destroy one's friends; wise discernment rescues the godly.

10 The whole city celebrates when the godly succeed; they shout for joy when the godless die.

11 Upright citizens bless a city and make it prosper, but the talk of the wicked tears it apart.

12 It is foolish to belittle a neighbor; a person with good sense remains silent.

13 A gossip goes around revealing secrets, but those who are trustworthy can keep a confidence.

14 Without wise leadership, a nation falls; with many counselors, there is safety.

15 Guaranteeing a loan for a stranger is dangerous; it is better to refuse than to suffer later.

16 Beautiful women obtain wealth, and violent men get rich.

17 Your own soul is nourished when you are kind, but you destroy yourself when you are cruel.

18 Evil people get rich for the moment, but the reward of the godly will last.

19 Godly people find life; evil people find death.

20 The LORD hates people with twisted hearts, but he delights in those who have integrity.

21 You can be sure that evil people will be punished, but the children of the godly will go free.

22 A woman who is beautiful but lacks discretion is like a gold ring in a pig's snout.

23 The godly can look forward to happiness, while the wicked can expect only wrath.

24 It is possible to give freely and become more wealthy, but those who are stingy will lose everything.

25 The generous prosper and are satisfied; those who refresh others will themselves be refreshed.

26 People curse those who hold their grain for higher prices, but they bless the one who sells to them in their time of need.

27 If you search for good, you will find favor; but if you search for evil, it will find you!

28 Trust in your money and down you go! But the godly flourish like leaves in spring.

29 Those who bring trouble on their families inherit only the wind. The fool will be a servant to the wise.

11:7
Prov 10:28

11:10
Prov 28:12

11:13
Lev 19:16
Prov 19:11; 20:19
1 Tim 5:13

11:14
Prov 15:22; 20:18; 24:6

11:15
Prov 6:1; 27:13

11:16
Prov 31:28, 30

11:17
Matt 5:7; 25:34-36

11:18
Hos 10:12
Gal 6:8-9

11:19
Prov 10:16; 19:23; 21:16
Rom 6:23
Jas 1:15

11:20
Prov 13:6

11:21
Prov 16:5

11:23
Prov 10:28
Rom 2:8-9

11:25
Matt 5:7
2 Cor 9:6-7

11:26
Job 29:13

11:27
Ps 7:15

11:28
Pss 1:2-3; 92:12
Jer 17:7-8
Mark 10:24-25
1 Tim 6:17

11:29
Prov 14:19; 15:27

11:7, 8 These verses, like 10:3, contrast two paths in life but are not intended to apply universally to all people in all circumstances. God's people are not excluded from problems or struggles. If a person follows God's wisdom, however, God can rescue him or her from trouble. But a wicked person will fall into his or her own traps. Even if good people suffer, they can be sure they will ultimately be rescued from eternal death.

11:9 The mouth can be used either as a weapon or a tool, hurting relationships or building them up. Sadly, it is often easier to destroy than to build, and most people have received more destructive comments than those that build up. Every person you meet today is either a demolition site or a construction opportunity. Your words will make a difference. Will they be weapons for destruction or tools for construction?

11:14 A good leader needs and uses wise counselors. One person's perspective and understanding is severely limited; he or she may not have all the facts or may be blinded by bias, emotions, or wrong impressions. To be a wise leader at home, at church, or at work, seek the counsel of others and be open to their advice. Then, after considering all the facts, make your decision. (See the chart in chapter 29.)

11:19 Godly people find life because they live life more fully each day. They also find life because people usually live longer when they live right, with proper diet, exercise, and rest. In addition, they need not fear death because eternal life is God's gift to them (John 11:25). By contrast, evil people not only find eternal death but also miss out on real life on earth.

11:22 Physical attractiveness without discretion soon wears thin. We are to seek those character strengths that help us make wise decisions, not just those that make us look good. Not everyone who looks good is pleasant to live or work with. While taking good care of our body and appearance is not wrong, we also need to develop our ability to think and make wise decisions.

11:24, 25 These two verses present a paradox: We become richer by being generous. The world says to hold on to as much as possible, but God blesses those who give freely of their possessions, time, and energy. When we give, God supplies us with more so that we can give more. In addition, giving helps us gain a right perspective on our possessions. We realize they were never really ours to begin with, but they were given to us by God to be used to help others. What then do we gain by giving? Freedom from enslavement to our possessions, the joy of helping others, and God's approval.

11:29 One of the greatest resources God gives us is the family. Families provide acceptance, encouragement, guidance, and counsel. Bringing trouble on your family—whether through anger or through an exaggerated desire for independence—is foolish because you cut yourself off from all they provide. In your family, strive for healing, communication, and understanding.

11:30 Jas 5:20
11:31 †1 Pet 4:18
12:1 Prov 1:5; 9:9; 25:12
12:3 Ps 15:1-5; Prov 10:25; 11:5
12:4 Prov 14:1; 31:10; 1 Cor 11:7
12:5 Prov 16:23; Matt 12:34; 15:18
12:7 Isa 3:10-11; Matt 7:24-27
12:8 Eccl 8:1
12:9 Luke 14:11
12:10 Gen 33:13
12:11 Prov 9:6; 14:24

30 The godly are like trees that bear life-giving fruit, and those who save lives are wise.
31 If the righteous are rewarded here on earth, how much more true that the wicked and
the sinner will get what they deserve!

12

1 To learn, you must love discipline; it is stupid to hate correction.
2 The LORD approves of those who are good, but he condemns those who plan
wickedness.
3 Wickedness never brings stability; only the godly have deep roots.
4 A worthy wife is her husband's joy and crown; a shameful wife saps his strength.
5 The plans of the godly are just; the advice of the wicked is treacherous.
6 The words of the wicked are like a murderous ambush, but the words of the godly
save lives.
7 The wicked perish and are gone, but the children of the godly stand firm.
8 Everyone admires a person with good sense, but a warped mind is despised.
9 It is better to be a nobody with a servant than to be self-important but have no food.
10 The godly are concerned for the welfare of their animals, but even the kindness of
the wicked is cruel.
11 Hard work means prosperity; only fools idle away their time.
12 Thieves are jealous of each other's loot, while the godly bear their own fruit.
13 The wicked are trapped by their own words, but the godly escape such trouble.

TEACHING AND LEARNING

Good teaching comes from good learning—and Proverbs has more to say to students than to teachers. Proverbs is concerned with the learning of wisdom. The book makes it clear that there are no good alternatives to learning wisdom. We are either becoming wise learners or refusing to learn and becoming foolish failures. Proverbs encourages us to make the right choice.

Wise Learners	*Proverb(s)*	*Foolish Failures*
Quietly accept instruction and criticism	10:8; 23:12; 25:12	Ignore instruction
Love discipline	12:1	Hate correction
Listen to advice	12:15; 21:11; 24:6	Think they need no advice
Accept parents' discipline	13:1	Mock parents
Lead others to life	10:17	Lead others astray
Receive honor	13:18	End in poverty and shame
Profit from constructive rebuke	15:31, 32; 29:1	Self-destruct by refusing rebuke

Advice to Teachers:
Help people avoid traps (13:14), use pleasant words (16:21), and speak at the right time (15:23; 18:20).

11:30 A godly person is a model of a meaningful life. Like a tree attracts people to its shade, a godly person's sense of purpose attracts others who want to know how they, too, can find meaning. Gaining wisdom yourself can be the first step in leading people to God.

11:31 Contrary to popular opinion, no one sins and gets away with it. The righteous are rewarded for their faith. The wicked are punished for their sins. Don't think for a moment that "it won't matter" or "nobody will know" or "we won't get caught" (see also 1 Peter 4:18).

12:1 If you don't want to learn, years of schooling will teach you very little. But if you want to be taught, there is no end to what you can learn. This includes being willing to accept discipline and correction and to learn from the wisdom of others. A person who refuses constructive criticism has a problem with pride. Such a person is unlikely to learn very much.

12:3 To have deep roots and to be stable means to be successful. Real success comes only to those who do what is right. Their efforts stand the test of time. Then, what kind of success does wickedness bring? We may know people who cheated to pass the course or to get a larger tax refund—is this not success? And what about the person who ignores his family commitments and mistreats his workers but gets ahead in business? These apparent successes are only temporary. They are bought at the expense of character. Cheaters grow more and more dishonest, and those who hurt others become callous and cruel. In the long run, evil behavior does not lead to success; it leads only to more evil. Real success maintains personal integrity. If you are not a success by God's standards, you have not achieved true success. (See the chart in chapter 19.)

12:13 Evil people twist the facts to support their claims. Those who do this will eventually be trapped by their own lies. But for those who always tell the truth, the facts—plain and unvarnished—give an unshakable defense. If you find that you always have to defend yourself to others, maybe you are not being honest. (See the chart in chapter 20.)

14 People can get many good things by the words they say; the work of their hands also
gives them many benefits.
15 Fools think they need no advice, but the wise listen to others.
16 A fool is quick-tempered, but a wise person stays calm when insulted.
17 An honest witness tells the truth; a false witness tells lies.
18 Some people make cutting remarks, but the words of the wise bring healing.
19 Truth stands the test of time; lies are soon exposed.
20 Deceit fills hearts that are plotting evil; joy fills hearts that are planning peace!
21 No real harm befalls the godly, but the wicked have their fill of trouble.
22 The LORD hates those who don't keep their word, but he delights in those who do.
23 Wise people don't make a show of their knowledge, but fools broadcast their folly.
24 Work hard and become a leader; be lazy and become a slave.
25 Worry weighs a person down; an encouraging word cheers a person up.
26 The godly give good advice to their friends;* the wicked lead them astray.
27 Lazy people don't even cook the game they catch, but the diligent make use of
everything they find.
28 The way of the godly leads to life; their path does not lead to death.

13 A wise child* accepts a parent's discipline; a young mocker refuses to listen.
2 Good people enjoy the positive results of their words, but those who are
treacherous crave violence.
3 Those who control their tongue will have a long life; a quick retort can ruin
everything.
4 Lazy people want much but get little, but those who work hard will prosper and be
satisfied.
5 Those who are godly hate lies; the wicked come to shame and disgrace.
6 Godliness helps people all through life, while the evil are destroyed by their wickedness.
7 Some who are poor pretend to be rich; others who are rich pretend to be poor.
8 The rich can pay a ransom, but the poor won't even get threatened.
9 The life of the godly is full of light and joy, but the sinner's light is snuffed out.
10 Pride leads to arguments; those who take advice are wise.

12:14 Isa 3:10
12:15 Prov 14:12; 16:2
12:19 Job 20:5; Zech 1:4
12:21 Ps 121:7; Prov 1:33; 1 Pet 3:13
12:22 Eccl 5:2; Isa 19:21
12:25 Prov 15:13; 17:22; 18:15
12:27 Prov 10:4; 13:4
12:28 Ezek 18:9, 20; Rom 5:21
13:1 Prov 10:1; 15:12
13:3 Prov 18:7, 21; 20:19; 21:23; Jas 3:2
13:5 Prov 3:35
13:7 Prov 11:24; Luke 12:20-21; 2 Cor 6:10; Jas 2:5
13:9 Job 18:5; 29:3; Prov 4:18; 24:20

12:26 Or *The godly are cautious in friendship,* or *the godly are freed from evil.* The meaning of the Hebrew is uncertain. **13:1** Hebrew *son.*

12:16 When someone annoys or insults you, it is natural to retaliate. But this solves nothing and only encourages trouble. Instead, answer slowly and quietly. Your positive response will achieve positive results. Proverbs 15:1 says, "A gentle answer turns away wrath."

12:19 Truth is always timely; it applies today and in the future. Because it is connected with God's changeless character, it is also changeless. Think for a moment about the centuries that have passed since these proverbs were written. Consider the countless hours that have been spent carefully studying every sentence of Scripture. The Bible has withstood the test of time. Because God is truth, you can trust his Word to guide you.

12:21 This is a general, but not universal, truth. Although harm does befall the godly, they are able to see opportunities in their problems and move ahead. The wicked, without God's wisdom, are ill-equipped to handle their problems. (See the notes on 3:16, 17; 10:3; 11:7, 8 for more about general truths that are not intended as universal statements.)

12:23 Wise people have a quiet confidence. Insecure or unstable people feel the need to prove themselves, but wise people don't have to prove anything. They know they are capable, so they can get on with their work. Beware of showing off. If you are modest, people may not notice you at first, but they will respect you later.

12:27 The diligent make wise use of their possessions and resources; the lazy waste them. Waste has become a way of life for many who live in a land of plenty. Waste is poor stewardship. Make good use of everything God has given you, and prize it.

12:28 For many, death is a darkened door at the end of life, a passageway to an unknown and feared destiny. But for God's people, death is a bright pathway to a new and better life. So why do we fear death? Is it fear of the pain we expect, the separation from loved ones, or the unknown? God can help us deal with those fears. He has shown us that death is not final but just another step in the eternal life we received when we followed him.

13:3 You have not mastered self-control if you do not control what you say. Words can cut and destroy. James recognized this truth when he stated, "The tongue is a small thing, but what enormous damage it can do" (James 3:5). If you want to be self-controlled, begin with your tongue. Stop and think before you react or speak. If you can control this small but powerful member, you can control the rest of your body. (See the chart in chapter 26.)

13:6 Godly living safeguards your life. Every choice for good sets into motion other opportunities for good. Evil choices follow the same pattern, but in the opposite direction. Each decision you make to obey God's Word will bring a greater sense of order to your life, while each decision to disobey will bring confusion and destruction. The right choices you make reflect your integrity. Obedience brings the greatest safeguard and security.

13:10 "I was wrong" or "I need advice" are difficult phrases to utter because they require humility. Pride is an ingredient in every quarrel. It stirs up conflict and divides people. Humility, by contrast, heals. Guard against pride. If you find yourself constantly arguing, examine your life for pride. Be open to the advice of others, ask for help when you need it, and be willing to admit your mistakes.

[11]Wealth from get-rich-quick schemes quickly disappears; wealth from hard work
grows.

13:13 2 Chr 36:16

[12]Hope deferred makes the heart sick, but when dreams come true, there is life and
joy.

13:14 Ps 18:5 Prov 10:11

[13]People who despise advice will find themselves in trouble; those who respect it will
succeed.

13:15 Ps 111:10 Prov 3:4

[14]The advice of the wise is like a life-giving fountain; those who accept it avoid the
snares of death.

13:16 Prov 12:23

[15]A person with good sense is respected; a treacherous person walks a rocky road.
[16]Wise people think before they act; fools don't and even brag about it!

13:17 Prov 25:13

[17]An unreliable messenger stumbles into trouble, but a reliable messenger brings
healing.

13:18 Prov 15:5, 32

[18]If you ignore criticism, you will end in poverty and disgrace; if you accept criticism,
you will be honored.

13:20 Prov 2:20

[19]It is pleasant to see dreams come true, but fools will not turn from evil to attain them.

13:21 Ps 32:10 Prov 11:31 Isa 3:10; 47:11

[20]Whoever walks with the wise will become wise; whoever walks with fools will
suffer harm.
[21]Trouble chases sinners, while blessings chase the righteous!

13:22 Ezra 9:12 Ps 37:25 Prov 28:8

[22]Good people leave an inheritance to their grandchildren, but the sinner's wealth
passes to the godly.

13:24 Prov 19:18; 22:15; 23:13

[23]A poor person's farm may produce much food, but injustice sweeps it all away.
[24]If you refuse to discipline your children, it proves you don't love them; if you love
your children, you will be prompt to discipline them.

13:25 Ps 34:10 Prov 10:3

[25]The godly eat to their hearts' content, but the belly of the wicked goes hungry.

14:1 Prov 31:10-27

14 A wise woman builds her house; a foolish woman tears hers down with her own
hands.

14:2 Prov 19:1

[2]Those who follow the right path fear the LORD; those who take the wrong path
despise him.

14:3 Prov 12:6

[3]The talk of fools is a rod for their backs,* but the words of the wise keep them out
of trouble.

14:3 Hebrew *a rod of pride.*

13:13 God created us, knows us, and loves us. It only makes sense, then, to listen to his instructions and do what he says. The Bible is his unfailing word to us. It is like an owner's manual for a car. If you obey God's instructions, you will "run right" and find his kind of power to live. If you ignore them, you will have breakdowns, accidents, and failures.

13:17 In Solomon's day, a king had to rely on messengers for information about his country. These messengers had to be trustworthy. Inaccurate information could lead to bloodshed. Reliable communication is still vital. If the message received is different from the message sent, marriages, businesses, and diplomatic relations can all break down. It is important to choose your words well and to avoid reacting until you clearly understand what the other person means.

13:19 Whether a "dream come true" is good or bad depends on the nature of the dream or desire. It is pleasant to achieve worthwhile goals, but not all goals are worth pursuing. When you set your heart on something, you may lose your ability to assess it objectively. With your desire blinding your judgment, you may proceed with an unwise relationship, a wasteful purchase, or a poorly conceived plan. Faithfulness is a virtue, but stubbornness is not.

13:20 The old saying "A rotten apple spoils the barrel" is often applied to friendships, and with good reason. Our friends and associates affect us, sometimes profoundly. Be careful whom you choose as your closest friends. Spend time with people you want to be like—because you and your friends will surely grow to resemble each other.

13:20 When most people need advice, they go to their friends first because friends accept them and usually agree with them. But that is why they may not be able to help them with difficult problems. Our friends are so much like us that they may not have any answers we haven't already heard. Instead, we should seek out older and wiser people to advise us. Wise people have experienced a lot in life—and have succeeded. They are not afraid to tell the truth. Who are the wise, godly people who can warn you of the pitfalls ahead?

13:23 The poor are often victims of an unjust society. A poor man's soil may be good, but unjust laws may rob him of his own produce. This proverb does not take poverty lightly or wink at injustice; it simply describes what often occurs. We should do what we can to fight injustice of every sort. Our efforts may seem inadequate; but it is comforting to know that in the end God's justice will prevail.

13:24 It is not easy for a loving parent to discipline a child, but it is necessary. The greatest responsibility that God gives parents is the nurture and guidance of their children. Lack of discipline puts parents' love in question because it shows a lack of concern for the character development of their children. Disciplining children averts long-range disaster. Without correction, children grow up with no clear understanding of right and wrong and with little direction to their lives. Don't be afraid to discipline your children. It is an act of love. Remember, however, that your efforts cannot make your children wise; they can only encourage your children to seek God's wisdom above all else!

[4]An empty stable stays clean, but no income comes from an empty stable.
[5]A truthful witness does not lie; a false witness breathes lies.
[6]A mocker seeks wisdom and never finds it, but knowledge comes easily to those with understanding.
[7]Stay away from fools, for you won't find knowledge there.
[8]The wise look ahead to see what is coming, but fools deceive themselves.
[9]Fools make fun of guilt, but the godly acknowledge it and seek reconciliation.
[10]Each heart knows its own bitterness, and no one else can fully share its joy.
[11]The house of the wicked will perish, but the tent of the godly will flourish.
[12]There is a path before each person that seems right, but it ends in death.
[13]Laughter can conceal a heavy heart; when the laughter ends, the grief remains.
[14]Backsliders get what they deserve; good people receive their reward.
[15]Only simpletons believe everything they are told! The prudent carefully consider their steps.
[16]The wise are cautious* and avoid danger; fools plunge ahead with great confidence.
[17]Those who are short-tempered do foolish things, and schemers are hated.
[18]The simpleton is clothed with folly, but the wise person is crowned with knowledge.
[19]Evil people will bow before good people; the wicked will bow at the gates of the godly.
[20]The poor are despised even by their neighbors, while the rich have many "friends."
[21]It is sin to despise one's neighbors; blessed are those who help the poor.
[22]If you plot evil, you will be lost; but if you plan good, you will be granted unfailing love and faithfulness.
[23]Work brings profit, but mere talk leads to poverty!
[24]Wealth is a crown for the wise; the effort of fools yields only folly.
[25]A truthful witness saves lives, but a false witness is a traitor.
[26]Those who fear the LORD are secure; he will be a place of refuge for their children.
[27]Fear of the LORD is a life-giving fountain; it offers escape from the snares of death.
[28]A growing population is a king's glory; a dwindling nation is his doom.
[29]Those who control their anger have great understanding; those with a hasty temper will make mistakes.
[30]A relaxed attitude lengthens life; jealousy rots it away.
[31]Those who oppress the poor insult their Maker, but those who help the poor honor him.
[32]The wicked are crushed by their sins, but the godly have a refuge when they die.
[33]Wisdom is enshrined in an understanding heart; wisdom is not* found among fools.
[34]Godliness exalts a nation, but sin is a disgrace to any people.
[35]A king rejoices in servants who know what they are doing; he is angry with those who cause trouble.

14:5 Prov 6:19; 12:17 Rev 3:14
14:7 Prov 23:9
14:8 Prov 15:28
14:11 Prov 12:7
14:12 Prov 16:25 Rom 6:21
14:13 Eccl 2:1-2
14:14 Prov 1:31; 12:14, 21
14:16 Prov 22:3
14:17 Prov 14:29
14:19 1 Sam 2:36 Prov 11:29
14:20 Prov 19:4, 7
14:21 Ps 41:1 Prov 11:12
14:22 Prov 12:2 Gal 6:7
14:25 Prov 14:5
14:26 Prov 19:23
14:27 Prov 13:14
14:29 Prov 16:32; 19:11 Jas 1:19
14:31 Ps 12:5 Prov 14:21; 17:5; 22:2, 16
14:32 2 Cor 1:9
14:35 Matt 24:45

14:16 Hebrew *The wise fear.* **14:33** As in Greek version; Hebrew lacks *not.*

14:4 When a farmer has no oxen, the stable will be clean, but he will be unable to make a living. The only way to keep your life free of people problems is to keep it free of people. But if your life is empty of people, it is useless; and if you live only for yourself, your life loses its meaning. Instead of avoiding people, we should serve others, share our faith, and work for justice. Is your life clean but empty? Or does it give evidence of your serving God wholeheartedly?

14:6 We all know mockers, people who scoff at every word of instruction or advice. They never find wisdom because they don't seek it seriously. Wisdom comes to those who apply God's Word to their lives and seek out godly counselors. If the wisdom you need does not come easily to you, perhaps your attitude is the barrier.

14:12 The "path . . . that seems right" may offer many options and require few sacrifices. Easy choices, however, should make us take a second look. Is this solution attractive because it allows me to be lazy? because it doesn't ask me to change my life-style? because it requires no moral restraints? The right choice often requires hard work and self-sacrifice. Don't be enticed by apparent shortcuts that seem right but end in death.

14:29 A nasty and quick temper can be like a fire out of control. It can burn us and everyone else in its path. Anger divides people. It pushes us into hasty decisions that only cause bitterness and guilt. Yet anger, in itself, is not wrong. Anger can be a legitimate reaction to injustice and sin. When you feel yourself getting angry, look for the cause. Are you reacting to an evil situation that you are going to set right? Or are you responding selfishly to a personal insult? Pray that God will help you control a quick temper, channeling your feelings into effective action and conquering selfish anger through humility and repentance.

14:31 God has a special concern for the poor. He insists that people who have material goods should be generous with those who are needy. Providing for the poor is not just a suggestion in the Bible; it is a command that may require a change of attitude (see Leviticus 23:22; Deuteronomy 15:7, 8; Psalms 113:5-9; 146:5-9; Isaiah 58:7; 2 Corinthians 9:9; James 2:1-9).

15:1
Judg 8:1-3
1 Sam 25:10-13
Prov 15:18; 25:10

15:2
Prov 12:23; 13:16
Eccl 12:10

15:3
Job 31:4; 34:21
Heb 4:13

15:6
Prov 8:21

15:8
Isa 1:11

15 A gentle answer turns away wrath, but harsh words stir up anger.
[2]The wise person makes learning a joy; fools spout only foolishness.
[3]The LORD is watching everywhere, keeping his eye on both the evil and the good.
[4]Gentle words bring life and health; a deceitful tongue crushes the spirit.
[5]Only a fool despises a parent's discipline; whoever learns from correction is wise.
[6]There is treasure in the house of the godly, but the earnings of the wicked bring
trouble.
[7]Only the wise can give good advice; fools cannot do so.
[8]The LORD hates the sacrifice of the wicked, but he delights in the prayers of the
upright.

WISDOM AND FOOLISHNESS
The wise and the foolish are often contrasted in Proverbs. The characteristics, reputation, and results of each are worth knowing if wisdom is our goal.

	The Wise	*The Foolish*	*Reference*
Characteristics	Give good advice	Lack common sense	10:21
	Enjoy wisdom	Enjoy foolishness	10:23
	Consider their steps	Gullible	14:15
		Avoid the wise	15:12
	Hungry for truth	Feed on foolishness	15:14
	Value wisdom above riches		16:16
	Receive life	Receive punishment	16:22
	Respond to correction	Respond to punishment	17:10
	Pursue wisdom	Pursue illusive dreams	17:24
		Blame failure on God	19:3
	Profit from correction	An example to others	19:25
		Are proud and arrogant	21:24
		Despise wise advice	23:9
		Make truth useless	26:7
		Repeat their folly	26:11
	Trust in wisdom	Trust in themselves	28:26
	Control their anger	Unleash their anger	29:11
Reputation	Admired as counselors	Punished as servants	10:13
	Crowned with knowledge	Inherit folly	14:18
		Cause strife and quarrels	22:10
		Receive no honor	26:1
	Keep peace	Stir up anger	29:8
Results	Stay on straight paths	Go the wrong way	15:21
		Lash out when discovered in folly	17:12
		Endangered by their words	18:6, 7
	Their wisdom conquers others' strength		21:22
	Avoid wicked paths	Walk a troublesome path	22:5
	Have great advice		24:5
		Will never be chosen as counselors	24:7
		Must be guided by hardship	26:3
		Persist in foolishness	27:22

15:1 Have you ever tried to argue in a whisper? It is equally hard to argue with someone who insists on answering gently. On the other hand, a rising voice and harsh words almost always trigger an angry response. To turn away wrath and seek peace, choose gentle words.

15:3 At times it seems that God has let evil run rampant in the world, and we wonder if he even notices it. But God sees everything clearly—both the evil actions and the evil intentions lying behind them (15:11). He is not an indifferent observer. He cares and is active in our world. Right now, his work may be unseen and unfelt, but don't give up. One day he will wipe out evil and punish the evildoers, just as he will establish the good and reward those who do his will.

9The LORD despises the way of the wicked, but he loves those who pursue godliness.
10Whoever abandons the right path will be severely punished; whoever hates correction will die.
11Even the depths of Death and Destruction* are known by the LORD. How much
more does he know the human heart!
12Mockers don't love those who rebuke them, so they stay away from the wise.
13A glad heart makes a happy face; a broken heart crushes the spirit.
14A wise person is hungry for truth, while the fool feeds on trash.
15For the poor, every day brings trouble; for the happy heart, life is a continual feast.
16It is better to have little with fear for the LORD than to have great treasure with
turmoil.
17A bowl of soup with someone you love is better than steak with someone you hate.
18A hothead starts fights; a cool-tempered person tries to stop them.
19A lazy person has trouble all through life; the path of the upright is easy!
20Sensible children bring joy to their father; foolish children despise their mother.
21Foolishness brings joy to those who have no sense; a sensible person stays on the
right path.
22Plans go wrong for lack of advice; many counselors bring success.
23Everyone enjoys a fitting reply; it is wonderful to say the right thing at the right
time!
24The path of the wise leads to life above; they leave the grave* behind.
25The LORD destroys the house of the proud, but he protects the property of widows.
26The LORD despises the thoughts of the wicked, but he delights in pure words.
27Dishonest money brings grief to the whole family, but those who hate bribes will
live.
28The godly think before speaking; the wicked spout evil words.
29The LORD is far from the wicked, but he hears the prayers of the righteous.
30A cheerful look brings joy to the heart; good news makes for good health.
31If you listen to constructive criticism, you will be at home among the wise.
32If you reject criticism, you only harm yourself; but if you listen to correction, you
grow in understanding.
33Fear of the LORD teaches a person to be wise; humility precedes honor.

16 We can gather our thoughts, but the LORD gives the right answer.
2People may be pure in their own eyes, but the LORD examines their motives.

15:11 1 Sam 16:7 2 Chr 6:30 Job 26:6 Acts 1:24
15:12 Prov 9:7; 13:1; 19:25; 24:9
15:13 Prov 17:22 Eccl 8:1
15:14 Prov 18:15
15:16 Ps 37:16 Prov 16:8 1 Tim 6:6
15:17 Prov 17:1
15:18 Prov 14:29; 16:28; 26:21 Eccl 10:4
15:20 Prov 10:1; 29:3; 30:17
15:21 Eph 5:15
15:25 Pss 68:5; 146:9 Prov 14:11
15:27 Exod 23:8 Deut 16:19 Prov 28:25
15:28 Prov 10:19, 32 1 Pet 3:15
15:29 Ps 145:18-19
15:31 Prov 15:5
15:33 Prov 1:7
16:2 Prov 21:2

15:11 Hebrew *Sheol and Abaddon.* **15:24** Hebrew *Sheol.*

15:14 What we feed our mind is just as important as what we feed our body. The kinds of books we read, the people we talk with, the music we listen to, and the films we watch are all part of our mental diet. Be discerning because what you feed your mind influences your total health and well-being. Thus, a strong desire to discover knowledge is a mark of wisdom.

15:15 Our attitudes color our whole personality. We cannot always choose what happens to us, but we can choose our attitude toward each situation. The secret to a happy heart is filling our mind with thoughts that are true, pure, and lovely, with thoughts that dwell on the good things in life (Philippians 4:8). This was Paul's secret as he faced imprisonment, and it can be ours as we face the struggles of daily living. Look at your attitudes and then examine what you allow to enter your mind and what you choose to dwell on. You may need to make some changes.

15:17-19 The "path of the upright" doesn't always seem easy (15:19), but look at the alternatives. Hatred (15:17), dissension (15:18), and laziness (15:19) cause problems that the upright person does not have to face. By comparison, his or her life is a smooth, level road because it is built on a solid foundation of love for God.

15:22 People with tunnel vision, those who are locked into one way of thinking, are likely to miss the right road because they have closed their minds to any new options. We need the help of those who can enlarge our vision and broaden our perspective. Seek out the advice of those who know you and have a wealth of experience. Build a network of advisers. Then be open to new ideas, and be willing to weigh their suggestions carefully. Your plans will be stronger and more likely to succeed.

15:28 The godly weigh their answers; the wicked don't think before speaking because they don't care about the effects of their words. It is important to have something to say, but it is equally important to think about it first. Do you carefully plan your words, or do you pour out your thoughts without concern for their impact?

16:1 This verse can be understood to mean that the final outcome of the plans we make is in God's hands. If this is so, why make plans? In doing God's will, there must be partnership between our efforts and God's control. He wants us to use our minds, to seek the advice of others, and to plan. Nevertheless, the results are up to him. Planning, then, helps us act God's way. As you live for him, ask for guidance as you plan, and then act on your plan as you trust in him.

16:2 People can rationalize anything if they have no standards for judging right and wrong. We can always prove that we are right. Before putting any plan into action, ask yourself these three questions: (1) Is this plan in harmony with God's truth? (2) Will it work under real-life conditions? (3) Is my attitude pleasing to God?

16:3 Pss 37:5; 55:22 Prov 3:6
16:4 Job 38:23 Eccl 3:11 Isa 43:7
16:5 Prov 6:16-17; 8:13; 11:21
16:9 Ps 37:23 Prov 16:1; 19:21; 20:24 Jer 10:23
16:10 1 Kgs 3:28
16:11 Prov 11:1
16:13 Prov 14:35
16:16 Prov 8:10, 19

3 Commit your work to the LORD, and then your plans will succeed.
4 The LORD has made everything for his own purposes, even the wicked for punishment.
5 The LORD despises pride; be assured that the proud will be punished.
6 Unfailing love and faithfulness cover sin; evil is avoided by fear of the LORD.
7 When the ways of people please the LORD, he makes even their enemies live at peace with them.
8 It is better to be poor and godly than rich and dishonest.
9 We can make our plans, but the LORD determines our steps.
10 The king speaks with divine wisdom; he must never judge unfairly.
11 The LORD demands fairness in every business deal; he sets the standard.
12 A king despises wrongdoing, for his rule depends on his justice.
13 The king is pleased with righteous lips; he loves those who speak honestly.
14 The anger of the king is a deadly threat; the wise do what they can to appease it.
15 When the king smiles, there is life; his favor refreshes like a gentle rain.
16 How much better to get wisdom than gold, and understanding than silver!
17 The path of the upright leads away from evil; whoever follows that path is safe.

HOW GOD IS DESCRIBED IN PROVERBS

Proverbs is a book about wise living. It often focuses on a person's response and attitude toward God, who is the source of wisdom. And a number of proverbs point out aspects of God's character. Knowing God helps us on the way to wisdom.

God . . .	is aware of all that happens (15:3)
	knows the heart of all people (15:11; 16:2; 21:2)
	controls all things (16:33; 21:30)
	is a place of safety (18:10)
	rescues good people from danger (11:8, 21)
	condemns the wicked (11:31)
	delights in our prayers (15:8, 29)
	loves those who obey him (15:9; 22:12)
	cares for poor and needy (15:25; 22:22, 23)
	purifies hearts (17:3)
	hates evil (17:5; 21:27; 28:9)
Our response should be . . .	to fear and reverence God (10:27; 14:26, 27; 15:16; 16:6; 19:23; 28:14
	to obey God's Word (13:13; 19:16)
	to please God (21:3)
	to trust in God (22:17–19; 29:25)

16:3 There are different ways to fail to commit whatever we do to the Lord. Some people commit their work only superficially. They say the project is being done for the Lord, but in reality they are doing it for themselves. Others give God temporary control of their interests, only to take control back the moment things stop going the way they expect. Still others commit a task fully to the Lord but put forth no effort themselves, and then they wonder why they do not succeed. We must maintain a delicate balance: trusting God as if everything depended on him, while working as if everything depended on us. Think of a specific effort in which you are involved right now. Have you committed it to the Lord?

16:4 This verse doesn't mean that God created some people to be wicked, but rather that God uses even the activities of wicked people for his good purposes (see Genesis 50:20). God is infinite, and we are finite. No matter how great our intellects, we will never be able to understand him completely. But we can accept by faith that he is all-powerful, all-loving, and perfectly good. We can believe that he is not the cause of evil (James 1:13, 17); and we can trust that there are no loose ends in his system of judgment. Evil is a temporary condition in the universe. One day God will destroy it.

16:5 Pride is the inner voice that whispers, "My way is best." It is resisting God's leadership and believing that you are able to live without his help. Whenever you find yourself wanting to do it your way or looking down on other people, you are being controlled by pride. Only when you eliminate pride can God help you become all he meant you to be. (See the chart in chapter 19.)

16:7 We want other people to like us, and sometimes we will do almost anything to win their approval. But God tells us to put our energy into pleasing him instead. Our effort to be peacemakers will usually make us more attractive to those around us, even our enemies. But even if it doesn't, we haven't lost anything. We are still pleasing God, the only one who truly matters.

16:11 Whether we buy or sell, make a product or offer a service, we know what is fair and honest and what is unfair and dishonest. Sometimes we feel pressure to be dishonest in order to advance ourselves or gain more profit. But if we want to obey God, there is no middle ground: God demands honesty in every business transaction. No amount of rationalizing can justify a dishonest business practice. Honesty and fairness are not always easy, but they are what God demands. Ask him for discernment and courage to be consistently honest and fair.

18 Pride goes before destruction, and haughtiness before a fall.
19 It is better to live humbly with the poor than to share plunder with the proud.
20 Those who listen to instruction will prosper; those who trust the LORD will be happy.
21 The wise are known for their understanding, and instruction is appreciated if it's
well presented.
22 Discretion is a life-giving fountain to those who possess it, but discipline is wasted
on fools.
23 From a wise mind comes wise speech; the words of the wise are persuasive.
24 Kind words are like honey—sweet to the soul and healthy for the body.
25 There is a path before each person that seems right, but it ends in death.
26 It is good for workers to have an appetite; an empty stomach drives them on.
27 Scoundrels hunt for scandal; their words are a destructive blaze.
28 A troublemaker plants seeds of strife; gossip separates the best of friends.
29 Violent people deceive their companions, leading them down a harmful path.
30 With narrowed eyes, they plot evil; without a word, they plan their mischief.
31 Gray hair is a crown of glory; it is gained by living a godly life.
32 It is better to be patient than powerful; it is better to have self-control than to
conquer a city.
33 We may throw the dice, but the LORD determines how they fall.

16:18 Jer 49:16
16:19 Isa 57:15
16:20 Pss 2:12; 34:8 Jer 17:7
16:21 Prov 16:23
16:23 Ps 37:30 Prov 15:18, 28
16:24 Prov 4:22; 15:26; 17:22; 24:13
16:25 Prov 14:12
16:27 Prov 6:14, 18 Jas 3:6
16:29 Prov 1:10
16:31 Prov 20:29
16:32 Prov 19:11

17

A dry crust eaten in peace is better than a great feast with strife.
2 A wise slave will rule over the master's shameful sons and will share their
inheritance.
3 Fire tests the purity of silver and gold, but the LORD tests the heart.
4 Wrongdoers listen to wicked talk; liars pay attention to destructive words.
5 Those who mock the poor insult their Maker; those who rejoice at the misfortune
of others will be punished.
6 Grandchildren are the crowning glory of the aged; parents are the pride of their
children.
7 Eloquent speech is not fitting for a fool; even less are lies fitting for a ruler.
8 A bribe seems to work like magic for those who give it; they succeed in all they do.

17:1 Prov 15:17
17:3 1 Chr 29:17 Ps 26:2
17:5 Job 31:29 Prov 14:31; 24:17
17:6 Gen 48:11 Prov 13:22
17:8 Prov 21:14 Isa 1:23 Amos 5:12

16:18 Proud people take little account of their weaknesses and do not anticipate stumbling blocks. They think they are above the frailties of common people. In this state of mind they are easily tripped up. Ironically, proud people seldom realize that pride is their problem, although everyone around them is well aware of it. Ask someone you trust whether self-satisfaction has blinded you to warning signs. He or she may help you avoid a fall.

16:22 For centuries people sought a fountain of youth, a spring that promised to give eternal life and vitality. It was never found. But God's wisdom is a life-giving fountain that can make a person happy, healthy, and alive forever. How? When we live by God's Word, he washes away the deadly effects of sin (see Titus 3:4-8), and the hope of eternal life with him gives us a joyful perspective on our present life. The fountain of youth was only a dream, but the life-giving fountain is reality. The choice is yours. You can be enlightened by God's wisdom, or you can be dragged down by the weight of your own foolishness.

16:31 The Hebrews believed that a long life was a sign of God's blessing; therefore, gray hair and old age were good. While young people glory in their strength, old people can rejoice in their years of experience and practical wisdom. Gray hair is not a sign of disgrace to be covered over; it is a crown of splendor. As you deal with older people, treat them with respect.

16:32 Self-control is superior to conquest. Success in business, school, or home life can be ruined by a person who loses control of his or her temper. So it is a great personal victory to control your temper. When you feel yourself ready to explode, remember that losing control may cause you to forfeit what you want the most.

17:3 It takes intense heat to purify gold and silver. Similarly, it often takes the heat of trials for the Christian to be purified. Through trials, God shows us what is in us and clears out anything that gets in the way of complete trust in him. Peter says, "These trials are only to test your faith, to show that it is strong and pure. It is being tested as fire tests and purifies gold—and your faith is far more precious to God than mere gold" (1 Peter 1:7). So when tough times come your way, realize that God wants to use them to refine your faith and purify your heart.

17:5 Few acts are as cruel as making fun of the less fortunate, but many people do this because it makes them feel good to be better off or more successful than someone else. Mocking the poor is mocking the God who made them. We also ridicule God when we mock the weak, those who are different, or anyone else. When you catch yourself putting others down just for fun, stop and think about who created them.

17:8 Solomon is not condoning bribery (see 17:15, 23), but he is making an observation about the way the world operates. Bribes may get people what they want, but the Bible clearly condemns using them (Exodus 23:8; Proverbs 17:23; Matthew 28:11-15).

17:9
Prov 10:12
Jas 5:20
17:12
Prov 29:9
Hos 13:8
17:13
Ps 109:5
Jer 18:20
17:15
Exod 23:7
Isa 5:23
17:17
Ruth 1:16
Prov 18:24
17:18
Prov 6:1; 11:15; 22:26
17:19
Prov 13:2; 16:18; 29:22-23
17:20
Jas 3:8
17:21
Prov 10:1; 17:25
17:22
Prov 15:13
17:23
Exod 23:8
17:24
Eccl 2:14
17:25
Prov 10:1
17:27
Prov 10:19
Jas 1:19

9 Disregarding another person's faults preserves love; telling about them separates close friends.

10 A single rebuke does more for a person of understanding than a hundred lashes on the back of a fool.

11 Evil people seek rebellion, but they will be severely punished.

12 It is safer to meet a bear robbed of her cubs than to confront a fool caught in folly.

13 If you repay evil for good, evil will never leave your house.

14 Beginning a quarrel is like opening a floodgate, so drop the matter before a dispute breaks out.

15 The LORD despises those who acquit the guilty and condemn the innocent.

16 It is senseless to pay tuition to educate a fool who has no heart for wisdom.

17 A friend is always loyal, and a brother is born to help in time of need.

18 It is poor judgment to co-sign a friend's note, to become responsible for a neighbor's debts.

19 Anyone who loves to quarrel loves sin; anyone who speaks boastfully* invites disaster.

20 The crooked heart will not prosper; the twisted tongue tumbles into trouble.

21 It is painful to be the parent of a fool; there is no joy for the father of a rebel.

22 A cheerful heart is good medicine, but a broken spirit saps a person's strength.

23 The wicked accept secret bribes to pervert justice.

24 Sensible people keep their eyes glued on wisdom, but a fool's eyes wander to the ends of the earth.

25 A foolish child* brings grief to a father and bitterness to a mother.

26 It is wrong to fine the godly for being good or to punish nobles for being honest!

27 A truly wise person uses few words; a person with understanding is even-tempered.

28 Even fools are thought to be wise when they keep silent; when they keep their mouths shut, they seem intelligent.

17:19 Or *who builds up defenses;* Hebrew reads *who makes a high gate.* **17:25** Hebrew *son.*

HUMILITY AND PRIDE

Results of . . .	*Humility*	*Pride*	
	Leads to wisdom	Leads to disgrace	11:2
	Takes advice	Produces arguments	13:10
	Leads to honor		15:33
		Leads to punishment	16:5
		Leads to destruction	16:18
	Ends in honor	Ends in downfall	18:12
	Brings one to honor	Brings one to humiliation	29:23

Proverbs is direct and forceful in rejecting pride. The proud attitude heads the list of seven things God hates (6:16, 17). The harmful results of pride are constanty contrasted with humility and its benefits.

17:9 This proverb is saying that we should be willing to disregrad the faults of others. Covering over offenses is necessary to any relationship. It is tempting, especially in an argument, to bring up all the mistakes the other person has ever made. Love, however, keeps its mouth shut—difficult though that may be. Try never to bring anything into an argument that is unrelated to the topic being discussed. As we grow to be like Christ, we will acquire God's ability to forget the confessed sins of the past.

17:17 What kind of friend are you? There is a vast difference between knowing someone well and being a true friend. The greatest evidence of genuine friendship is loyalty (see 1 Corinthians 13:7)—being available to help in times of distress or personal struggle. Too many people are fair-weather friends. They stick around when the friendship helps them and leave when they're not getting anything out of the relationship. Think of your friends and assess your loyalty to them. Be the kind of true friend the Bible encourages.

17:22 To be cheerful is to be ready to greet others with a welcome, a word of encouragement, an enthusiasm for the task at hand, and a positive outlook on the future. Such people are as welcome as pain-relieving medicine.

17:24 While there is something to be said for having big dreams, this proverb points out the folly of chasing fantasies (having eyes that "wander to the ends of the earth," see 12:11). How much better to align your goals with God's, being the kind of person he wants you to be! Such goals (wisdom, honesty, patience, love) may not seem exciting, but they will determine your eternal future. Take time to think about your dreams and goals, and make sure they cover the really important areas of life.

17:27, 28 This proverb highlights several benefits of keeping quiet: (1) It is the best policy if you have nothing worthwhile to say; (2) it allows you the opportunity to listen and learn; (3) it gives you something in common with those who are wiser. Make sure you pause to think and to listen so that when you do speak, you will have something important to say.

18 A recluse is self-indulgent, snarling at every sound principle of conduct.
[2]Fools have no interest in understanding; they only want to air their own opinions.
[3]When the wicked arrive, contempt, shame, and disgrace are sure to follow.
[4]A person's words can be life-giving water; words of true wisdom are as refreshing as
a bubbling brook.
[5]It is wrong for a judge to favor the guilty or condemn the innocent.
[6]Fools get into constant quarrels; they are asking for a beating.
[7]The mouths of fools are their ruin; their lips get them into trouble.
[8]What dainty morsels rumors are—but they sink deep into one's heart.
[9]A lazy person is as bad as someone who destroys things.
[10]The name of the LORD is a strong fortress; the godly run to him and are safe.
[11]The rich think of their wealth as an impregnable defense; they imagine it is a high
wall of safety.
[12]Haughtiness goes before destruction; humility precedes honor.
[13]What a shame, what folly, to give advice before listening to the facts!
[14]The human spirit can endure a sick body, but who can bear it if the spirit is crushed?
[15]Intelligent people are always open to new ideas. In fact, they look for them.
[16]Giving a gift works wonders; it may bring you before important people!
[17]Any story sounds true until someone sets the record straight.
[18]Casting lots can end arguments and settle disputes between powerful opponents.
[19]It's harder to make amends with an offended friend than to capture a fortified city.
Arguments separate friends like a gate locked with iron bars.
[20]Words satisfy the soul as food satisfies the stomach; the right words on a person's
lips bring satisfaction.
[21]Those who love to talk will experience the consequences, for the tongue can kill or
nourish life.
[22]The man who finds a wife finds a treasure and receives favor from the LORD.
[23]The poor plead for mercy; the rich answer with insults.
[24]There are "friends" who destroy each other, but a real friend sticks closer than a brother.

18:2 Prov 12:23
18:4 Prov 20:5
18:6 Prov 10:14; 13:3
18:8 Prov 10:14
18:10 2 Sam 22:2; Pss 18:2; 61:3; 91:2
18:11 Prov 10:15
18:12 Prov 11:2; 16:18; 29:23
18:13 Prov 20:25; John 7:51
18:15 Prov 15:14
18:16 Gen 32:20; 1 Sam 25:27
18:18 Prov 16:33
18:20 Prov 12:14
18:21 Prov 13:3; Matt 12:37
18:22 Prov 12:4; 19:14; 31:10-31
18:23 2 Chr 10:13; Prov 19:7; Jas 2:3

19 It is better to be poor and honest than to be a fool and dishonest.
[2]Zeal without knowledge is not good; a person who moves too quickly may go
the wrong way.

19:1 Prov 20:7; 28:6

18:8 It is as hard to refuse to listen to gossip as it is to turn down a delicious dessert. Taking just one morsel of either one creates a taste for more. You can resist rumors the same way a determined dieter resists candy—never even open the box. If you don't nibble on the first bite of gossip, you can't take the second and the third.

18:11 In imagining that their wealth is their strongest defense, rich people are sadly mistaken. Money cannot provide safety—there are too many ways for it to lose its power. The government may cease to back it; thieves may steal it; inflation may rob it of all value. But God never loses his power. He is always dependable. Where do you look for security and safety—uncertain wealth or God who is always faithful?

18:13, 15, 17 In these concise statements, there are three basic principles for making sound decisions: (1) Get the facts before answering; (2) be open to new ideas; (3) make sure you hear both sides of a story before judging. All three principles center around seeking additional information. This is difficult work, but the only alternative is prejudice—judging before getting the facts.

18:22 This verse states that it is good to be married. Today's emphasis on individual freedom is misguided. Strong individuals are important, but so are strong marriages. God created marriage for our enjoyment, and he pronounced it good. This is one of many passages in the Bible that show marriage as a joyful and good creation of God (Genesis 2:21-25; Proverbs 5:15-19; John 2:1-11).

18:23 This verse does not condone insulting the poor; it is simply recording an unfortunate fact of life. It is wrong for rich people to treat the less fortunate with contempt and arrogance, and God will judge such actions severely (see 14:31).

18:24 Loneliness is everywhere—many people feel cut off and alienated from others. Being in a crowd just makes people more aware of their isolation. We all need friends who will stick close, listen, care, and offer help when it is needed—in good times and bad. It is better to have one such friend than dozens of superficial acquaintances. Instead of wishing you could find a true friend, seek to become one. There are people who need your friendship. Ask God to reveal them to you, and then take on the challenge of being a true friend.

19:1 A blameless life is far more valuable than wealth, but most people don't act as if they believe this. Afraid of not getting everything they want, they will pay any price to increase their wealth—cheating on their taxes, stealing from stores or employers, withholding tithes, refusing to give. But when we know and love God, we realize that a lower standard of living—or even poverty—is a small price to pay for personal integrity. Do your actions show that you sacrifice your integrity to increase your wealth? What changes do you need to make in order to get your priorities straight?

19:2 We often move hastily through life, rushing headlong into the unknown. Many people marry without knowing what to expect of their partner or of married life. Others try illicit sex or drugs without considering the consequences. Some plunge into jobs without evaluating whether or not they are suitable to that line of work. Don't rush into the unknown. Be sure you understand what you're getting into and where you want to go before you take the first step. And if it still seems unknown, be sure you are following God.

19:3 Isa 8:21
19:5 Exod 23:1; Deut 19:16-19
19:7 Ps 38:11; Prov 18:23
19:8 Prov 16:20
19:10 Eccl 10:6-7
19:11 Prov 14:29; 16:32
19:12 Gen 27:28; Prov 16:14-15
19:13 Prov 17:25; 21:9
19:14 2 Cor 12:14
19:15 Prov 6:9; 16:26
19:16 Luke 10:28; 11:28
19:17 Deut 15:7; Prov 14:31; 28:27; Luke 6:38
19:18 Prov 13:24
19:21 Ps 33:10-11; Prov 16:1, 9

3 People ruin their lives by their own foolishness and then are angry at the LORD.
4 Wealth makes many "friends"; poverty drives them away.
5 A false witness will not go unpunished, nor will a liar escape.
6 Many beg favors from a prince; everyone is the friend of a person who gives gifts!
7 If the relatives of the poor despise them, how much more will their friends avoid
them. The poor call after them, but they are gone.
8 To acquire wisdom is to love oneself; people who cherish understanding will prosper.
9 A false witness will not go unpunished, and a liar will be destroyed.
10 It isn't right for a fool to live in luxury or for a slave to rule over princes!
11 People with good sense restrain their anger; they earn esteem by overlooking wrongs.
12 The king's anger is like a lion's roar, but his favor is like dew on the grass.
13 A foolish child* is a calamity to a father; a nagging wife annoys like a constant dripping.
14 Parents can provide their sons with an inheritance of houses and wealth, but only
the LORD can give an understanding wife.
15 A lazy person sleeps soundly—and goes hungry.
16 Keep the commandments and keep your life; despising them leads to death.
17 If you help the poor, you are lending to the LORD—and he will repay you!
18 Discipline your children while there is hope. If you don't, you will ruin their lives.
19 Short-tempered people must pay their own penalty. If you rescue them once, you
will have to do it again.
20 Get all the advice and instruction you can, and be wise the rest of your life.
21 You can make many plans, but the LORD's purpose will prevail.
22 Loyalty makes a person attractive. And it is better to be poor than dishonest.
23 Fear of the LORD gives life, security, and protection from harm.
24 Some people are so lazy that they won't even lift a finger to feed themselves.

19:13 Hebrew *son;* also in 19:27.

HOW TO SUCCEED IN GOD'S EYES

Proverbs notes two significant by-products of wise living: success and good reputation. Several verses also point out what causes failure and poor reputation.

Qualities that promote success and a good reputation	
Godliness (righteousness)	10:7; 12:3; 28:12
Hating what is false	13:5
Committing all work to the Lord	16:3
Using words with restraint; being even-tempered	17:27, 28
Loving wisdom and understanding	19:8
Humility and fear of the Lord	22:4
Willingness to confess and forsake sin	28:13
Qualities that prevent success and cause a bad reputation	
Wickedness	10:7; 12:3; 28:12
Seeking honor	25:27
Hatred	26:24–26
Praising oneself	27:2
Concealing sin	28:13

Other verses dealing with one's reputation are 11:10, 16; 14:3; 19:10; 22:1; 23:17, 18; 24:13, 14.

19:8 Is it good to love yourself? Yes, when your soul is at stake! This proverb does not condone the self-centered person, who loves and protects his or her selfish interests and will do anything to serve them. Instead, it encourages those who really care about themselves to seek wisdom.

19:16 The commandments we are told to obey are those found in God's Word, such as the Ten Commandments (Exodus 20) and other passages of instruction. To obey what God teaches in the Bible is self-preserving. To disobey is self- destructive.

19:17 Here God identifies with the poor as Jesus does in Matthew 25:31-46. As our Creator, God values all of us, whether we are poor or rich. When we help the poor, we honor both the Creator and his creation. God accepts our help as if we had offered it directly to him.

19:23 Those who fear the Lord receive "protection from harm" because of their healthy habits, their beneficial life-style, and sometimes through God's direct intervention. Nevertheless the fear of the Lord does not always protect us from trouble in this life: Evil things still happen to people who love God. This verse is not a universal promise but a general guideline. It describes what would happen if this world were sinless, and what will happen in the new earth, when faithful believers will be under God's protection forever. (See the note on 3:16, 17 for more about this concept.)

[25]If you punish a mocker, the simpleminded will learn a lesson; if you reprove the wise, they will be all the wiser.
[26]Children who mistreat their father or chase away their mother are a public disgrace and an embarrassment.
[27]If you stop listening to instruction, my child, you have turned your back on knowledge.
[28]A corrupt witness makes a mockery of justice; the mouth of the wicked gulps down evil.
[29]Mockers will be punished, and the backs of fools will be beaten.

19:25 Prov 9:7-8; 21:11
19:26 Prov 20:20; 28:24
19:28 Job 15:16
19:29 Prov 9:12; 10:13; 26:3

20

Wine produces mockers; liquor leads to brawls. Whoever is led astray by drink cannot be wise.
[2]The king's fury is like a lion's roar; to rouse his anger is to risk your life.
[3]Avoiding a fight is a mark of honor; only fools insist on quarreling.
[4]If you are too lazy to plow in the right season, you will have no food at the harvest.
[5]Though good advice lies deep within a person's heart, the wise will draw it out.
[6]Many will say they are loyal friends, but who can find one who is really faithful?
[7]The godly walk with integrity; blessed are their children after them.
[8]When a king judges, he carefully weighs all the evidence, distinguishing the bad from the good.
[9]Who can say, "I have cleansed my heart; I am pure and free from sin"?
[10]The LORD despises double standards of every kind.
[11]Even children are known by the way they act, whether their conduct is pure and right.
[12]Ears to hear and eyes to see—both are gifts from the LORD.
[13]If you love sleep, you will end in poverty. Keep your eyes open, and there will be plenty to eat!
[14]The buyer haggles over the price, saying, "It's worthless," then brags about getting a bargain!
[15]Wise speech is rarer and more valuable than gold and rubies.
[16]Be sure to get collateral from anyone who guarantees the debt of a stranger. Get a deposit if someone guarantees the debt of a foreigner.*
[17]Stolen bread tastes sweet, but it turns to gravel in the mouth.
[18]Plans succeed through good counsel; don't go to war without the advice of others.
[19]A gossip tells secrets, so don't hang around with someone who talks too much.
[20]If you curse your father or mother, the lamp of your life will be snuffed out.
[21]An inheritance obtained early in life is not a blessing in the end.
[22]Don't say, "I will get even for this wrong." Wait for the LORD to handle the matter.
[23]The LORD despises double standards; he is not pleased by dishonest scales.
[24]How can we understand the road we travel? It is the LORD who directs our steps.

20:1 Prov 31:4 Isa 5:22; 56:12
20:3 Prov 14:29; 16:32; 19:11
20:6 Matt 6:2 Luke 18:8, 11
20:7 Pss 37:26; 112:2
20:9 2 Chr 6:36 Job 14:4
20:10 Prov 11:1; 20:23
20:11 Matt 7:16
20:12 Exod 4:11
20:13 Prov 6:9-10; 19:15; 24:32-33
20:18 Prov 15:22; 24:6 Luke 14:31
20:19 Prov 11:13
20:20 Exod 21:17 Lev 20:9 Matt 15:4
20:22 Ps 27:14 Prov 24:28-29 Matt 5:39 Rom 12:17
20:23 Prov 11:1; 20:10

20:16 An alternate reading in the Hebrew text is *the debt of an adulterous woman;* compare 27:13.

19:25 There is a great difference between the person who learns from criticism and the person who refuses to accept correction. How we respond to criticism determines whether or not we grow in wisdom. The next time someone criticizes you, listen carefully to all that is said. You might learn something.

20:3 A person who is truly confident of his or her strength does not need to parade it. A truly brave person does not look for chances to prove it. A resourceful woman can find a way out of a fight. A man of endurance will avoid retaliating. Foolish people find it impossible to avoid strife. Men and women of character can. What kind of person are you?

20:4 You've heard similar warnings: If you don't study, you'll fail the test; if you don't save, you won't have money when you need it. God wants us to anticipate future needs and prepare for them. We can't expect him to come to our rescue when we cause our own problems through lack of planning and action. He provides for us, but he also expects us to be responsible.

20:9 No one is without sin. As soon as we confess our sin and repent, sinful thoughts and actions begin to creep back into our life. We all need ongoing cleansing, moment by moment. Thank God he provides forgiveness by his mercy when we ask for it. Make confession and repentance a regular part of your talks with God. Rely on him moment by moment for the cleansing you need.

20:23 "Dishonest scales" refers to the loaded scales a merchant might use in order to cheat customers. Dishonesty is a difficult sin to avoid. It is easy to cheat if we think no one is looking. But dishonesty affects the very core of a person. It makes him untrustworthy and untrusting. It eventually makes him unable to know himself or relate to others. Don't take dishonesty lightly. Even the smallest portion of dishonesty contains enough of the poison of deceit to kill your spiritual life. If there is any dishonesty in your life, tell God about it now.

20:24 We are often confused by the events around us. Some things we will never understand until years later when we look back and see how God was working. This proverb counsels us to not worry if we don't understand everything as it happens. Instead, we should trust that God knows what he's doing, even if his timing or design is not clear to us. See Psalm 37:23 for a reassuring promise of God's direction in your life.

20:25 Eccl 5:4-5
20:26 Prov 20:8, 30
20:27 1 Cor 2:11
20:28 Prov 29:14
20:29 Prov 16:31

25 It is dangerous to make a rash promise to God before counting the cost.
26 A wise king finds the wicked, lays them out like wheat, then runs the crushing wheel
over them.
27 The LORD's searchlight penetrates the human spirit,* exposing every hidden
motive.
28 Unfailing love and faithfulness protect the king; his throne is made secure
through love.
29 The glory of the young is their strength; the gray hair of experience is the splendor
of the old.
30 Physical punishment cleanses away evil;* such discipline purifies the heart

20:27 Or *The human spirit is the LORD's searchlight.* **20:30** The meaning of the Hebrew is uncertain.

HONESTY AND DISHONESTY
Proverbs tells us plainly that God despises all forms of dishonesty. Not only does God hate dishonesty, but we are told that it works against us—others no longer trust us, and we cannot even enjoy our dishonest gains. It is wiser to be honest because "the godly escape such trouble" (12:13).

Others' Opinions
Leaders value those who speak honestly 16:13
Most people will appreciate truth in the end more than flattery 28:23

Quality of Life
The godly person's plans are just 12:5
Truthful witnesses do not lie; false witnesses breathe lies 14:5
Truthful witnesses save lives 14:25
The children of the righteous are blessed 20:7

Short-Term Results
Ill-gotten gain has no lasting value 10:2
The righteous are rescued from trouble 11:8
The evil are trapped by their own words 12:13
Fraudulent gain is sweet for a while 20:17

Long-Term Results
Good people are guided by their honesty 11:3
Truthful lips endure 12:19
Riches gained quickly don't las 20:21
Riches gained dishonestly don't last 21:6
The honest are kept safe 28:18

God's Opinion
God delights in honesty 11:1
God delights in those who are truthful 12:22
God despises double standards 20:10
God is pleased when we do what is right and just 21:3

20:25 This proverb points out the danger of making a vow rashly and then reconsidering it. God takes vows seriously and requires that they be carried out (Deuteronomy 23:21-23). We often have good intentions when making a vow because we want to show God that we are determined to please him. Jesus, however, says it is better not to make promises to God because he knows how difficult they are to keep (Matthew 5:33-37). If you still feel it is important to make a vow, make sure that you weigh the consequences of breaking that vow. (In Judges 11, Jephthah made a rash promise to sacrifice the first thing he saw on his return home. As it happened, he saw his daughter first.) It is better not to make promises than to make them and then later not keep them. It is best to count the cost beforehand and then to fulfill them. (For a list of other Bible people who made rash vows, see the chart in Judges 11.)

21:1 In Solomon's day, kings possessed absolute authority and were often considered to be like gods. This proverb shows that God has ultimate authority over world rulers. Although they may not have realized it, the earth's most powerful kings have always been under God's control. (See Isaiah 10:5-8 for an example of a king who was used for God's purposes.)

21:2 People may mistakenly think they are doing right, but God sees the motives of their hearts. We often have to make choices in areas where the right action is difficult to discern. We can help ourselves make such decisions by trying to identify our motives first and then asking, Would God be pleased with my real reasons for doing this? God is not pleased when we do good deeds only to receive something in return.

21

21 The king's heart is like a stream of water directed by the LORD; he turns it
wherever he pleases.
2 People may think they are doing what is right, but the LORD examines the heart.
3 The LORD is more pleased when we do what is just and right than when we give him
sacrifices.
4 Haughty eyes, a proud heart, and evil actions are all sin.
5 Good planning and hard work lead to prosperity, but hasty shortcuts lead to
poverty.
6 Wealth created by lying is a vanishing mist and a deadly trap.*
7 Because the wicked refuse to do what is just, their violence boomerangs and destroys
them.
8 The guilty walk a crooked path; the innocent travel a straight road.
9 It is better to live alone in the corner of an attic than with a contentious wife in a
lovely home.
10 Evil people love to harm others; their neighbors get no mercy from them.
11 A simpleton can learn only by seeing mockers punished; a wise person learns from
instruction.

21:1 Ezra 6:21, 22
21:2 Prov 16:2; 24:11-12; Luke 16:15
21:3 Prov 15:8; Isa 1:11; Mic 6:6-8
21:4 Prov 6:17; 30:13; Luke 11:34
21:5 Prov 10:4; 28:22
21:6 Prov 10:2; 13:11
21:10 Prov 2:14
21:11 Prov 19:25

21:6 As in Greek version; Hebrew reads *mist for those who seek death.* **21:12** Or *The righteous man.*

RIGHTEOUSNESS

Proverbs often compares the lifestyles of the wicked and the righteous, and makes a strong case for living by God's pattern. The advantages of righteous living and the disadvantages of wicked living are pointed out. The kind of person we decide to be will affect every area of our lives.

	Righteous	*Wicked*	*Reference*
Outlook on life	Hopeful	Fearful	10:24
	Concerned about the welfare of God's creation	Even their kindness is cruel	12:10
	Understand justice	Don't understand justice	28:5
Response to life	Showered with blessings	Covered with violence	10:6
		Plot evil	16:30
	Give thought to their ways	Put up a bold front	21:29
	Persevere against evil	Brought down by calamity	24:15, 16
		Hate the honest	29:10
How they are seen by others	Are respected	Do not endure	13:15
		Lead others into sin	16:29
	Conduct is upright	Conduct is devious	21:8
	Are not to desire the company of godless people	Plot violence	24:1, 2
	Others are glad when they succeed	Others hide when they rise to power	28:12
	Care for the poor	Unconcerned about the poor	29:7
	Despise the wicked	Despise the godly	29:27
Quality of life	Stand firm	Swept away	10:25
	Delivered by godliness	Trapped by evil desires	11:6

21:3 Sacrifices are not bribes to make God overlook our character faults. If our personal and business dealings are not characterized by justice, no amount of generosity when the offering plate is passed will make up for it.

21:5 Faithful completion of one's work is a great accomplishment. Being a diligent worker does not come naturally to some people; it is a result of strong character. Don't look for shortcuts that result in inefficiency. Work hard as if in the service of God.

21:11, 12 It is usually better to learn from the mistakes of others than from our own. We can do this by listening to their advice. Take counsel from others instead of plunging ahead and learning the hard way.

21:13 Matt 18:30-34 Luke 16:19-31 Jas 2:13 1 Jn 3:17
21:16 Ps 49:14
21:17 Prov 23:19-21
21:18 Prov 11:8 Isa 43:3-4
21:20 Job 20:15, 18 Prov 8:21
21:21 Matt 5:6
21:22 2 Sam 5:6-9 Eccl 9:15-16
21:23 Prov 12:13; 13:3 Jas 3:2

12 The Righteous One* knows what is going on in the homes of the wicked; he will
bring the wicked to disaster.
13 Those who shut their ears to the cries of the poor will be ignored in their own time
of need.
14 A secret gift calms anger; a secret bribe pacifies fury.
15 Justice is a joy to the godly, but it causes dismay among evildoers.
16 The person who strays from common sense will end up in the company of the
dead.
17 Those who love pleasure become poor; wine and luxury are not the way to riches.
18 Sometimes the wicked are punished to save the godly, and the treacherous for the
upright.
19 It is better to live alone in the desert than with a crabby, complaining wife.
20 The wise have wealth and luxury, but fools spend whatever they get.
21 Whoever pursues godliness and unfailing love will find life, godliness, and
honor.
22 The wise conquer the city of the strong and level the fortress in which they trust.
23 If you keep your mouth shut, you will stay out of trouble.
24 Mockers are proud and haughty; they act with boundless arrogance.

AND WICKEDNESS

	Righteous	*Wicked*	*Reference*
Quality of life (cont.)	No real harm befalls them	Constant trouble befalls them	12:21
	Income results in treasure	Income results in trouble	15:6
	Avoid evil		16:17
		Fall into constant trouble	17:20
	Are bold as lions	Are fearful constantly	28:1
	Will be safe	Will suddenly fall	28:18
Short-term results	Walk securely	Will be found out	10:9
	Chased by blessings	Chased by trouble	13:21
Long-term results	God protects them	God destroys them	10:29
	Evil people will bow to them	Will bow to the righteous	14:19
		Will be punished for rebellion	17:11
Eternal expectations	Never uprooted	Will not remain	10:30
	Earn a sure reward	Earn deceptive wages	11:18
	Attain life	Go to death	11:19
	End only in good	End only in wrath	11:23
	Will stand firm	Will perish	12:7
	Have a refuge when they die	Crushed by their sins	14:32
God's opinion of them	Delights in the good	Detests the perverse	11:20

21:13 We should work to meet the needs of the poor and protect their rights for someday we may be in need of such services ourselves.

21:20 This proverb is about saving for the future. Easy credit has many people living on the edge of bankruptcy. The desire to keep up appearances and to accumulate more drives them to spend every penny they earn, and they stretch their credit to the limit. But anyone who spends all he has is spending more than he can afford. A wise person puts money aside for hard times. God approves of foresight and restraint. God's people need to examine their life-styles to see whether their spending is God-pleasing or merely self-pleasing.

25 The desires of lazy people will be their ruin, for their hands refuse to work. 26 They
are always greedy for more, while the godly love to give!
27 God loathes the sacrifice of an evil person, especially when it is brought with ulterior
motives.
28 A false witness will be cut off, but an attentive witness will be allowed to speak.
29 The wicked put up a bold front, but the upright proceed with care.
30 Human plans, no matter how wise or well advised, cannot stand against the LORD.
31 The horses are prepared for battle, but the victory belongs to the LORD.

22 Choose a good reputation over great riches, for being held in high esteem is better
than having silver or gold.
2 The rich and the poor have this in common: The LORD made them both.
3 A prudent person foresees the danger ahead and takes precautions; the simpleton goes
blindly on and suffers the consequences.
4 True humility and fear of the LORD lead to riches, honor, and long life.
5 The deceitful walk a thorny, treacherous road; whoever values life will stay away.
6 Teach your children to choose the right path, and when they are older, they will
remain upon it.
7 Just as the rich rule the poor, so the borrower is servant to the lender.
8 Those who plant seeds of injustice will harvest disaster, and their reign of terror will
end.
9 Blessed are those who are generous, because they feed the poor.
10 Throw out the mocker, and fighting, quarrels, and insults will disappear.
11 Anyone who loves a pure heart and gracious speech is the king's friend.
12 The LORD preserves knowledge, but he ruins the plans of the deceitful.
13 The lazy person is full of excuses, saying, "If I go outside, I might meet a lion in the
street and be killed!"
14 The mouth of an immoral woman is a deep pit; those living under the LORD's
displeasure will fall into it.

21:25 Prov 13:4
21:27 Prov 15:8
21:30 Isa 8:9; 14:27; Acts 5:38-39
21:31 Ps 20:7; Isa 31:1-3; 1 Cor 15:57
22:2 Job 31:15; Prov 14:31
22:3 Prov 14:16; 27:12
22:4 Prov 3:16; 4:4
22:6 Eph 6:4
22:7 Jas 2:6
22:8 Job 4:8
22:9 Prov 19:17; Luke 14:13; 2 Cor 9:6
22:11 Ps 24:4; Prov 14:35; Matt 5:8
22:13 Rom 12:11
22:14 Prov 5:3; 26:13; Eccl 7:26

21:27 The kind of worship ("sacrifice") described in this proverb is no better than a bribe. How do people try to bribe God? They may go to church, tithe, or volunteer, not because of their love and devotion to God, but because they hope God will bless them in return. But God has made it very clear that he desires obedience and love more than religious ritual (see 21:3; 1 Samuel 15:22). God does not want our sacrifices of time, energy, and money alone; he wants our heart—our complete love and devotion. We may be able to bribe people (21:14), but we cannot bribe God.

21:31 This proverb refers to preparing for battle. All our preparation for any task is useless without God. But even with God's help we still must do our part and prepare. His control of the outcome does not negate our responsibilities. God may want you to produce a great book, but you must learn to write. God may want to use you in foreign missions, but you must learn the language. God will accomplish his purposes, and he will be able to use you if you have done your part by being well prepared.

22:4 This is a general observation that would have been especially applicable to an obedient Israelite living in Solomon's God-fearing kingdom. Nevertheless some have been martyrs at a young age, and some have given away all their wealth for the sake of God's Kingdom. The book of Proverbs describes life the way it should be. It does not dwell on the exceptions. (For more on this concept, see the note on 3:16, 17.)

22:6 In the process of helping our children "choose the right path," we must discern differing paths for each child. It is natural to want to bring up all our children alike or train them the same way. This verse implies that parents should discern the individuality and special strengths that God has given each one. While we should not condone or excuse self-will, each child has natural inclinations that parents can develop. By talking to teachers, other parents, and grandparents, we can better discern and develop the individual capabilities of each child.

22:6 Many parents want to make all the choices for their child, but this hurts him or her in the long run. When parents teach a child how to make decisions, they don't have to watch every step he or she takes. They know their children will remain on the right path because they have made the choice themselves. Train your children to choose the right way.

22:7 Does this mean we should never borrow? No, but it warns us never to take on a loan without carefully examining our ability to repay it. A loan we can handle is enabling; a loan we can't handle is enslaving. The borrower must realize that until the loan is repaid, he is a servant to the individual or institution that made it.

22:12 "Knowledge" refers to those who have knowledge, those who live right and speak the truth. It takes discipline, determination, and hard work to live God's way, but God protects and rewards those who make the commitment to follow him. The unfaithful may seem to have an easier time of it, but in the long run their plans fail and their lives amount to nothing. Don't resist God and expect lasting success.

22:13 This proverb refers to an excuse a lazy person might use to avoid going to work. The excuse sounds silly to us, but that's often how our excuses sound to others. Don't rationalize laziness. Take your responsibilities seriously and get to work.

22:15 Prov 13:24; 23:14
22:16 Prov 14:31; 28:3

15 A youngster's heart is filled with foolishness, but discipline will drive it away.
16 A person who gets ahead by oppressing the poor or by showering gifts on the rich
will end in poverty.

Thirty Sayings of the Wise

22:17 Prov 5:1

17 Listen to the words of the wise; apply your heart to my instruction. 18 For it is good to
keep these sayings deep within yourself, always ready on your lips. 19 I am teaching you
today—yes, you—so you will trust in the LORD. 20 I have written thirty sayings for you,
filled with advice and knowledge. 21 In this way, you may know the truth and bring an
accurate report to those who sent you.

22:22 Zech 7:10; Mal 3:5

22 Do not rob the poor because they are poor or exploit the needy in court. 23 For the
LORD is their defender. He will injure anyone who injures them.

22:24 Prov 29:22

24 Keep away from angry, short-tempered people, 25 or you will learn to be like them
and endanger your soul.

22:26 Prov 6:1-5

26 Do not co-sign another person's note or put up a guarantee for someone else's loan.
27 If you can't pay it, even your bed will be snatched from under you.

22:28 Deut 19:14; 27:17

28 Do not steal your neighbor's property by moving the ancient boundary markers set
up by your ancestors.

22:29 1 Kgs 10:8; 11:28

29 Do you see any truly competent workers? They will serve kings rather than ordinary
people.

23:2 Prov 23:20
23:4 Prov 15:27; 28:20; Matt 6:19; 1 Tim 6:9
23:6 Ps 141:4; Prov 1:15; 4:14; 23:1
23:10 Deut 19:14; Prov 22:28; Jer 22:3; Zech 7:10
23:12 Prov 22:17

23 When dining with a ruler, pay attention to what is put before you. 2 If you are a
big eater, put a knife to your throat, 3 and don't desire all the delicacies—deception may be involved.
4 Don't weary yourself trying to get rich. Why waste your time? 5 For riches can
disappear as though they had the wings of a bird!
6 Don't eat with people who are stingy; don't desire their delicacies. 7 "Eat and drink,"
they say, but they don't mean it. They are always thinking about how much it costs. 8 You
will vomit up the delicious food they serve, and you will have to take back your words
of appreciation for their "kindness."
9 Don't waste your breath on fools, for they will despise the wisest advice.
10 Don't steal the land of defenseless orphans by moving the ancient boundary
markers, 11 for their Redeemer is strong. He himself will bring their charges against you.
12 Commit yourself to instruction; attune your ears to hear words of knowledge.

22:15 Young children often do foolish and dangerous things simply because they don't understand the consequences. Wisdom and common sense are not transferred by a parent's good example alone. Just as God trains and corrects us to make us better, so parents must discipline their children to help them learn the difference between right and wrong. To see how God corrects us, read 3:11, 12.

22:22, 23 This proverb is a message of hope to people who must live and work under unjust authoritarian leaders. It is also a warning to those who enjoy ruling with an iron hand. Sometimes God intervenes and directly destroys tyrants. More often, he uses other rulers to overthrow them or their own oppressed people to rebel against them. If you are in a position of authority at church, work, or home, remember what happens to tyrants. Leadership through kindness is more effective and longer lasting than leadership by force.

22:24, 25 People tend to become like those with whom they spend a lot of time. Even the negative characteristics sometimes rub off. The Bible exhorts us to be cautious in our choice of companions. Choose people with characteristics you would like to develop in your own life.

22:28 In Joshua 13–21, the land was divided, and the boundaries were marked out for each tribe. Moses had already warned the people that when they reached the Promised Land they shouldn't cheat their neighbors by moving any of the markers to give themselves more land and their neighbors less (Deuteronomy 19:14; 27:17).

23:1-3 The point of this proverb is to be careful when eating with an important or influential person because he or she may try to bribe you. No good will come from the meal.

23:4, 5 We have all heard of people who have won millions of dollars and then lost everything. Even the average person can spend an inheritance—or a paycheck—with lightning speed and have little to show for it. Don't spend your time chasing fleeting earthly treasures. Instead, store up treasures in heaven, for such treasures will never be lost. (See Luke 12:33, 34 for Jesus' teaching.)

23:6-8 In graphic language, the writer warns us not to envy the life-styles of those who have become rich by being stingy and miserly, and not to gain their favor by fawning over them. Their "friendship" is phony—they will just use you for their own gain.

23:10, 11 The term *redeemer* referred to someone who bought back a family member who had fallen into slavery or who accepted the obligation to marry the widow of a family member (Ruth 4:3-10). God is also called a Redeemer (Exodus 6:6; Job 19:25). (For an explanation of ancient boundary markers, see the note on 22:28.)

23:12 The people most likely to gain knowledge are those who are willing to listen. It is a sign of strength, not weakness, to pay attention to what others have to say. People who are eager to listen continue to learn and grow throughout their lives. If we refuse to become set in our ways, we can always expand the limits of our knowledge.

[13]Don't fail to correct your children. They won't die if you spank them. [14]Physical
discipline may well save them from death.*
[15]My child,* how I will rejoice if you become wise. [16]Yes, my heart will thrill when
you speak what is right and just.
[17]Don't envy sinners, but always continue to fear the LORD. [18]For surely you have a
future ahead of you; your hope will not be disappointed.
[19]My child, listen and be wise. Keep your heart on the right course. [20]Do not carouse
with drunkards and gluttons, [21]for they are on their way to poverty. Too much sleep
clothes a person with rags.
[22]Listen to your father, who gave you life, and don't despise your mother's experience
when she is old. [23]Get the truth and don't ever sell it; also get wisdom, discipline, and
discernment. [24]The father of godly children has cause for joy. What a pleasure it is to
have wise children.* [25]So give your parents joy! May she who gave you birth be happy.
[26]O my son, give me your heart. May your eyes delight in my ways of wisdom. [27]A
prostitute is a deep pit; an adulterous woman is treacherous.* [28]She hides and waits like
a robber, looking for another victim who will be unfaithful to his wife.
[29]Who has anguish? Who has sorrow? Who is always fighting? Who is always
complaining? Who has unnecessary bruises? Who has bloodshot eyes? [30]It is the one
who spends long hours in the taverns, trying out new drinks. [31]Don't let the sparkle and
smooth taste of wine deceive you. [32]For in the end it bites like a poisonous serpent; it
stings like a viper. [33]You will see hallucinations, and you will say crazy things. [34]You
will stagger like a sailor tossed at sea, clinging to a swaying mast. [35]And you will say,
"They hit me, but I didn't feel it. I didn't even know it when they beat me up. When will
I wake up so I can have another drink?"

24 Don't envy evil people; don't desire their company. [2]For they spend their days
plotting violence, and their words are always stirring up trouble.
[3]A house is built by wisdom and becomes strong through good sense. [4]Through
knowledge its rooms are filled with all sorts of precious riches and valuables.
[5]A wise man is mightier than a strong man,* and a man of knowledge is more powerful
than a strong man. [6]So don't go to war without wise guidance; victory depends on having
many counselors.
[7]Wisdom is too much for a fool. When the leaders gather, the fool has nothing to say.
[8]A person who plans evil will get a reputation as a troublemaker. [9]The schemes of a
fool are sinful; everyone despises a mocker.

23:13 Prov 13:24; 19:18; 1 Cor 5:5
23:15 Prov 15:20; 27:11; 29:3
23:17 Pss 37:1; 73:3; Prov 24:1, 14, 19
23:19 Prov 23:29
23:21 Prov 21:17
23:22 Prov 1:8; 30:17
23:23 Prov 4:7; 18:15; Matt 13:44
23:24 Prov 10:1
23:26 Prov 3:1; 4:4
23:29 Isa 5:11, 22
23:31 Song 7:9
23:35 Isa 56:12
24:1 Pss 1:1; 37:1; Prov 1:15; 23:17
24:2 Ps 10:7; Jer 22:17
24:5 Prov 21:22
24:6 Prov 11:14; 20:18
24:7 Prov 14:6; 17:16
24:8 Prov 6:14; 14:22; Rom 1:30

23:14 Hebrew *from Sheol.* **23:15** Hebrew *My son;* also in 23:19. **23:24** Hebrew *a wise son.* **23:27** Hebrew *is a narrow well.* **24:5** As in Greek version; Hebrew reads *A wise man is strength.*

23:13, 14 The stern tone of discipline here is offset by the affection expressed in verse 15. However, many parents are reluctant to discipline their children at all. Some fear that they will forfeit their relationship, their children will resent them, or they will stifle their children's development. But correction won't kill children, and it may prevent them from foolish moves that will.

23:17, 18 How easy it is to envy those who get ahead, unhampered by responsibility to God's laws. For a time they do seem to prosper without paying any attention to what God wants, but they have no future. To those who follow him, God promises a hope and a wonderful future, even if they don't realize it in this life.

23:29, 30 The soothing comfort of alcohol is only temporary. Real relief comes from dealing with the cause of the anguish and sorrow and turning to God for peace. Don't lose yourself in alcohol; find yourself in God.

23:29-35 Israel was a wine-producing country. In the Old Testament, winepresses bursting with new wine were considered a sign of blessing (3:10). Wisdom is even said to have set her table with wine (9:2, 5). But the Old Testament writers were alert to the dangers of wine. It dulls the senses; it limits clear judgment (31:1-9); it lowers the capacity for control (4:17); it destroys a person's efficiency (21:17). To make wine an end in itself, a means of self-indulgence, or as an escape from life is to misuse it and invite the consequences of the drunkard.

24:5 The athlete who has wisdom—who assesses the situation and plans strategies—has an advantage over a physically stronger but unwise opponent. We exercise regularly and eat well to build our strength, but do we take equal pains to develop wisdom and knowledge? Because wisdom is a vital part of strength, it pays to attain it.

24:6 In any major decision we make concerning college, marriage, career, children, etc., it is not a sign of weakness to ask for advice. Instead, it is foolish not to ask for it. Find good advisers before making any big decision. They can help you expand your alternatives and evaluate your choices.

24:8 Plotting to do evil can be as wrong as doing it because what you think determines what you will do. Left unchecked, wrong desires will lead us to sin. God wants pure hearts, free from sin, and planning evil brings sinful thoughts into our mind. Should you say, "Then I might as well go ahead and do it because I've already planned it"? No. You have sinned in your attitude, but you have not yet harmed other people. Stop in your tracks and ask God to forgive you and put you on a different path.

10 If you fail under pressure, your strength is not very great.
11 Rescue those who are unjustly sentenced to death; don't stand back and let them die.
12 Don't try to avoid responsibility by saying you didn't know about it. For God knows
all hearts, and he sees you. He keeps watch over your soul, and he knows you knew! And
he will judge all people according to what they have done.
13 My child,* eat honey, for it is good, and the honeycomb is sweet to the taste. 14 In
the same way, wisdom is sweet to your soul. If you find it, you will have a bright future,
and your hopes will not be cut short.
15 Do not lie in wait like an outlaw at the home of the godly. And don't raid the house
where the godly live. 16 They may trip seven times, but each time they will rise again.
But one calamity is enough to lay the wicked low.
17 Do not rejoice when your enemies fall into trouble. Don't be happy when they
stumble. 18 For the LORD will be displeased with you and will turn his anger away from
them.
19 Do not fret because of evildoers; don't envy the wicked. 20 For the evil have no
future; their light will be snuffed out.
21 My child, fear the LORD and the king, and don't associate with rebels. 22 For you will
go down with them to sudden disaster. Who knows where the punishment from the LORD
and the king will end?

More Sayings of the Wise

23 Here are some further sayings of the wise:
It is wrong to show favoritism when passing judgment. 24 A judge who says to the
wicked, "You are innocent," will be cursed by many people and denounced by the
nations. 25 But blessings are showered on those who convict the guilty.
26 It is an honor to receive an honest reply.
27 Develop your business first before building your house.
28 Do not testify spitefully against innocent neighbors; don't lie about them. 29 And
don't say, "Now I can pay them back for all their meanness to me! I'll get even!"
30 I walked by the field of a lazy person, the vineyard of one lacking sense. 31 I saw
that it was overgrown with thorns. It was covered with weeds, and its walls were broken
down. 32 Then, as I looked and thought about it, I learned this lesson: 33 A little extra
sleep, a little more slumber, a little folding of the hands to rest—34 and poverty will
pounce on you like a bandit; scarcity will attack you like an armed robber.

24:10 Job 4:5; Heb 12:3
24:11 Ps 82:4; Isa 58:6-7
24:12 †Rom 2:6
24:13 Ps 19:10; Prov 25:16
24:14 Prov 2:10
24:15 Ps 10:9-12
24:17 Ps 35:15; Rom 11:18-21
24:19 Job 15:31; Prov 13:9; 24:1
24:21 Rom 13:4; 1 Pet 2:17
24:24 Prov 17:15
24:28 Prov 25:18
24:29 Prov 20:22; Matt 5:39
24:30 Prov 6:6-11
24:32 Prov 6:10; 12:24; 23:21

C. WISDOM FOR THE LEADERS (25:1—31:31)

These proverbs were collected by Hezekiah's aides. The first section was written by Solomon, and the next two sections were written by others. While we all can learn from these proverbs, many were originally directed toward the king or those who dealt with the king. These are particularly helpful for those who are leaders or aspire to become leaders. The book ends with a description of a truly good wife, who is an example of godly wisdom.

24:13 Hebrew *My son;* also in 24:21.

24:10 Times of trouble can be useful. They can show you who you really are—what kind of character you have developed. In addition, they can help you grow stronger. When Jeremiah questioned God because of the trouble he faced, God asked how he ever expected to face big challenges if the little ones tired him out (Jeremiah 12:5). Don't complain about your problems. The trouble you face today is training you to be strong for the more difficult situations you will face in the future.

24:17, 18 David, Solomon's father, refused to gloat over the death of his lifelong enemy, Saul (see 2 Samuel 1). On the other hand, the nation of Edom rejoiced over Israel's defeat and was punished by God for their attitude (Obadiah 1:12). To gloat over others' misfortune is to make yourself the avenger and to put yourself in the place of God, who alone is the real Judge of all the earth (see Deuteronomy 32:35).

24:26 People often think that they should bend the truth to avoid hurting a friend. But one who gives an honest, straightforward answer is a true friend.

24:27 We should carry out our work in its proper order. If a farmer builds his house in the spring, he will miss the planting season and go a year without food. If a businessman invests his money in a house while his business is struggling to grow, he may lose both. It is possible to work hard and still lose everything if the timing is wrong or the resources to carry it out are not in place.

24:29 Here is a reverse version of the Golden Rule (see Luke 6:31). Revenge is the way the world operates, but it is not God's way.

More Proverbs of Solomon

25 These are more proverbs of Solomon, collected by the advisers of King Hezekiah
of Judah.
2 It is God's privilege to conceal things and the king's privilege to discover them.
3 No one can discover the height of heaven, the depth of the earth, or all that goes on
in the king's mind!
4 Remove the dross from silver, and the sterling will be ready for the silversmith.
5 Remove the wicked from the king's court, and his reign will be made secure by
justice.
6 Don't demand an audience with the king or push for a place among the great. 7 It
is better to wait for an invitation than to be sent to the end of the line, publicly
disgraced!
Just because you see something, 8 don't be in a hurry to go to court. You might go down
before your neighbors in shameful defeat. 9 So discuss the matter with them privately.
Don't tell anyone else, 10 or others may accuse you of gossip. Then you will never regain
your good reputation.
11 Timely advice is as lovely as golden apples in a silver basket.
12 Valid criticism is as treasured by the one who heeds it as jewelry made from finest gold.
13 Faithful messengers are as refreshing as snow in the heat of summer. They revive
the spirit of their employer.
14 A person who doesn't give a promised gift is like clouds and wind that don't bring rain.
15 Patience can persuade a prince, and soft speech can crush strong opposition.
16 Do you like honey? Don't eat too much of it, or it will make you sick!
17 Don't visit your neighbors too often, or you will wear out your welcome.
18 Telling lies about others is as harmful as hitting them with an ax, wounding them
with a sword, or shooting them with a sharp arrow.
19 Putting confidence in an unreliable person is like chewing with a toothache or
walking on a broken foot.
20 Singing cheerful songs to a person whose heart is heavy is as bad as stealing
someone's jacket in cold weather or rubbing salt in a wound.
21 If your enemies are hungry, give them food to eat. If they are thirsty, give them water
to drink. 22 You will heap burning coals on their heads, and the LORD will reward you.
23 As surely as a wind from the north brings rain, so a gossiping tongue causes anger!
24 It is better to live alone in the corner of an attic than with a contentious wife in a
lovely home.
25 Good news from far away is like cold water to the thirsty.
26 If the godly compromise with the wicked, it is like polluting a fountain or muddying
a spring.

25:1 Prov 1:1
25:2 Deut 29:29
25:3 Ezra 6:1; Rom 11:33
25:4 Ezek 22:18; Mal 3:2-3
25:8 Prov 17:14
25:11 Prov 15:23
25:12 Prov 15:31; 20:12
25:13 Prov 13:17
25:15 Prov 15:1; Eccl 10:4
25:16 Prov 25:27
25:18 Ps 57:4; Prov 12:18; 24:28; Jer 9:8
25:19 Job 6:15
25:21 Exod 23:4-5; 2 Kgs 6:22; 2 Chr 28:15; Matt 5:44; Rom 12:20
25:23 Prov 13:3; 26:20
25:24 Prov 21:9
25:25 Prov 15:30
25:26 Ezek 32:2; 34:18

25:1 Hezekiah's story is told in 2 Kings 18–20; 2 Chronicles 29–32; and Isaiah 36–39. He was one of the few kings of Judah who honored the Lord. By contrast, his father, Ahaz, actually nailed the Temple door shut. Hezekiah restored the Temple, destroyed idol worship centers, and earned the respect of surrounding nations, many of whom brought gifts to God because of him. It is not surprising that Hezekiah had these proverbs copied and read, for "in all that he did in the service of the Temple of God and in his efforts to follow the law and the commands, Hezekiah sought his God wholeheartedly. As a result, he was very successful" (2 Chronicles 31:21).

25:6, 7 Jesus made this proverb into a parable (see Luke 14:7-11). We should not seek honor for ourselves. It is better to quietly and faithfully accomplish the work God has given us to do. As others notice the quality of our life, then they will draw attention to us.

25:13 It is often difficult to find people you can really trust. A faithful employee ("messenger") is punctual, responsible, honest, and hardworking. This person is invaluable as he or she helps take some of the pressure off his or her employer. Find out what your employer needs from you to make his or her job easier, and do it.

25:14 Most churches, missions organizations, and Christian groups depend on the gifts of people to keep their ministries going. But many who promise to give fail to follow through. The Bible is very clear about the effect this has on those involved in the ministry. If you make a pledge, keep your promise.

25:18 Lying about someone is vicious. Its effects can be as permanent as those of a wound. The next time you are tempted to pass on a bit of gossip, imagine yourself wounding the victim of your remarks with a sword. This image may shock you into silence.

25:21, 22 God's form of retaliation is most effective and yet difficult to do. Paul quotes this proverb in Romans 12:19-21. In Matthew 5:44, Jesus encourages us to pray for those who hurt us. By returning good for evil, we are acknowledging God as the balancer of all accounts and trusting him to be the judge.

25:26 To compromise with the wicked means setting aside your standards of right and wrong. No one is helped by someone who compromises with the wicked.

25:27
Prov 25:16; 27:2
25:28
2 Chr 32:5
Prov 16:32
26:1
1 Sam 12:17
26:2
Num 23:8
2 Sam 16:12
26:3
Ps 32:9
Prov 10:13
26:4
Prov 23:9; 29:9

27 Just as it is not good to eat too much honey, it is not good for people to think about
all the honors they deserve.
28 A person without self-control is as defenseless as a city with broken-down walls.

26 Honor doesn't go with fools any more than snow with summer or rain with
harvest.
2 Like a fluttering sparrow or a darting swallow, an unfair curse will not land on its
intended victim.
3 Guide a horse with a whip, a donkey with a bridle, and a fool with a rod to his back!
4 When arguing with fools, don't answer their foolish arguments, or you will become
as foolish as they are.
5 When arguing with fools, be sure to answer their foolish arguments, or they will
become wise in their own estimation.
6 Trusting a fool to convey a message is as foolish as cutting off one's feet or drinking
poison!
7 In the mouth of a fool, a proverb becomes as limp as a paralyzed leg.
8 Honoring a fool is as foolish as tying a stone to a slingshot.
9 A proverb in a fool's mouth is as dangerous as a thornbush brandished by a drunkard.

THE FOUR TONGUES
What we say probably affects more people than any other action we take. It is not surprising, then, to find that Proverbs gives special attention to words and how they are used. Four common speech patterns are described in Proverbs. The first two should be copied, while the last two should be avoided.

The Controlled Tongue	Those with this speech pattern think before speaking, know when silence is best, and give wise advice.	10:19; 11:12, 13; 12:16; 13:3; 15:1, 4, 28; 16:23; 17:14, 27, 28; 21:23; 24:26
The Caring Tongue	Those with this speech pattern speak truthfully while seeking to encourage.	10:32; 12:18, 25; 15:23; 16:24; 25:15; 27:9
The Conniving Tongue	Those with this speech pattern are filled with wrong motives, gossip, slander, and a desire to twist truth.	6:12–14; 8:13; 16:28; 18:8; 25:18; 26:20–28
The Careless Tongue	Those with this speech pattern are filled with lies, curses, quick-tempered words—which can lead to rebellion and destruction.	10:18, 32; 11:9; 12:16, 18; 15:4; 17:9, 14, 19; 20:19; 25:23

Other verses about our speech include 10:11, 20, 31; 12:6, 17–19; 13:2; 14:3; 19:5, 28; 25:11; 27:2, 5, 14, 17; 29:9.

25:27 Dwelling on the honors you deserve can only be harmful. It can make you bitter, discouraged, or angry, and it will not bring you the rewards that you think should be yours. Pining for what you should have received may make you miss the satisfaction of knowing you did your best.

25:28 Even though city walls restricted the inhabitants' movements, people were happy to have them. Without walls, they would have been vulnerable to attack by any passing group of marauders. Self-control limits us, to be sure, but it is necessary. An out-of-control life is open to all sorts of attacks by the enemy. Think of self-control as a wall for defense and protection.

26:2 "An unfair curse will not land" means that it has no effect.

26:4, 5 These two verses seem to be in contradiction. But the writer is saying that we shouldn't take foolish people seriously and try to reason with their empty arguments. This will only make them proud and determined to win the argument. In some situations, you ought not to even try to answer fools, for there is no way you can penetrate their closed minds. You may, in fact, be stooping to their level if you do choose to answer. Fools will abuse you, and you will be tempted to abuse them in return. There are other situations where your common sense tells you to answer in order to expose their pride and folly.

26:7 Some people are so blind that they won't get much wisdom from reading these proverbs. Only those who want to be wise have the receptive attitude needed to make the most of them. If we want to learn from God, he will respond and pour out his heart to us (1:23).

26:8 Sometimes when someone in a group causes discord or dissension, the leader tries to make him loyal and productive by giving him a place of privilege or responsibility. This usually doesn't work. In fact, it is like tying the stone to the sling—it won't go anywhere and will swing back and hurt you. The dissenter's new power may be just what he needs to manipulate the group.

26:9 Normally the first prick of a thorn alerts us, so we remove the thorn before it damages us. A drunk person, however, may not feel the thorn, and so it will work its way into his flesh. Similarly, a fool may not feel the sting of a proverb because he does not see how it applies to his life. Instead of taking its point to heart, a fool will apply it to his church, his employer, his spouse, or whomever he is rebelling against. The next time you find yourself saying, "So-and-so should really pay attention to that," stop and ask yourself, Is there a message in it for me?

10 An employer who hires a fool or a bystander is like an archer who shoots recklessly.
11 As a dog returns to its vomit, so a fool repeats his folly.
12 There is more hope for fools than for people who think they are wise.
13 The lazy person is full of excuses, saying, "I can't go outside because there might be a lion on the road! Yes, I'm sure there's a lion out there!"
14 As a door turns back and forth on its hinges, so the lazy person turns over in bed.
15 Some people are so lazy that they won't lift a finger to feed themselves.
16 Lazy people consider themselves smarter than seven wise counselors.
17 Yanking a dog's ears is as foolish as interfering in someone else's argument.
18 Just as damaging as a mad man shooting a lethal weapon 19 is someone who lies to a friend and then says, "I was only joking."
20 Fire goes out for lack of fuel, and quarrels disappear when gossip stops.
21 A quarrelsome person starts fights as easily as hot embers light charcoal or fire lights wood.
22 What dainty morsels rumors are—but they sink deep into one's heart.
23 Smooth* words may hide a wicked heart, just as a pretty glaze covers a common clay pot.
24 People with hate in their hearts may sound pleasant enough, but don't believe them.
25 Though they pretend to be kind, their hearts are full of all kinds of evil. 26 While their hatred may be concealed by trickery, it will finally come to light for all to see.
27 If you set a trap for others, you will get caught in it yourself. If you roll a boulder down on others, it will roll back and crush you.
28 A lying tongue hates its victims, and flattery causes ruin.

27

Don't brag about tomorrow, since you don't know what the day will bring.
2 Don't praise yourself; let others do it!
3 A stone is heavy and sand is weighty, but the resentment caused by a fool is heavier than both.
4 Anger is cruel, and wrath is like a flood, but who can survive the destructiveness of jealousy?
5 An open rebuke is better than hidden love!
6 Wounds from a friend are better than many kisses from an enemy.
7 Honey seems tasteless to a person who is full, but even bitter food tastes sweet to the hungry.
8 A person who strays from home is like a bird that strays from its nest.
9 The heartfelt counsel of a friend is as sweet as perfume and incense.
10 Never abandon a friend—either yours or your father's. Then in your time of need, you won't have to ask your relatives for assistance. It is better to go to a neighbor than to a relative who lives far away.
11 My child,* how happy I will be if you turn out to be wise! Then I will be able to answer my critics.

26:23 As in Greek version; Hebrew reads *Burning.* **27:11** Hebrew *My son.*

26:11 Exod 8:15 †2 Pet 2:22
26:12 Prov 3:7; 29:20
26:13 Prov 22:13
26:14 Prov 6:9
26:17 Prov 3:30; 20:3
26:18 Prov 24:12, 28 Isa 50:11
26:20 Prov 16:28; 22:10; 24:28
26:21 Prov 15:18; 29:22
26:22 Prov 18:8
26:23 Luke 11:39
26:24 Ps 41:6 Prov 12:20
26:27 Ps 7:15
26:28 Prov 28:23
27:1 Luke 12:19-20 Jas 4:13-16
27:2 Prov 25:27 2 Cor 10:12, 18
27:4 Prov 6:34
27:5 Prov 25:12
27:6 Ps 141:5 Matt 26:49
27:10 1 Kgs 12:6 2 Chr 10:6-8 Prov 17:17; 18:24
27:11 Prov 10:1; 23:15

26:13-16 If a person is not willing to work, he or she can find endless excuses to avoid it. But laziness is more dangerous than a prowling lion. The less you do, the less you want to do, and the more useless you become. To overcome laziness, take a few small steps toward change. Set a concrete, realistic goal. Figure out the steps needed to reach it, and follow those steps. Pray for strength and persistence. To keep your excuses from making you useless, stop making useless excuses.

26:17 Yanking the ears of a dog is a good way to get bitten, and interfering in arguments is a good way to get hurt. Many times both arguers will turn on the person who interferes. It is best simply to keep out of arguments that are none of your business. If you must become involved, try to wait until the arguers have stopped fighting and cooled off a bit. Then maybe you can help them mend their differences and their relationship.

26:20 Talking about every little irritation and piece of gossip only keeps the fires of anger going. Refusing to discuss them cuts the fuel line and makes the fires die out. Does someone continually irritate you? Decide not to complain about the person, and see if your irritation dies from lack of fuel.

27:6 Who would prefer a friend's wounds to an enemy's kisses? Anyone who considers the source. A friend who has your best interests at heart may have to give you unpleasant advice at times, but you know it is for your own good. An enemy, by contrast, may whisper sweet words and happily send you on your way to ruin. We tend to hear what we want to hear, even if an enemy is the only one who will say it. A friend's advice, no matter how painful, is much better.

27:12 Prov 22:3

[12]A prudent person foresees the danger ahead and takes precautions. The simpleton
goes blindly on and suffers the consequences.

27:13 Prov 20:16

[13]Be sure to get collateral from anyone who guarantees the debt of a stranger. Get a
deposit if someone guarantees the debt of an adulterous woman.
[14]If you shout a pleasant greeting to your neighbor too early in the morning, it will be
counted as a curse!

27:15 Prov 19:13

[15]A nagging wife is as annoying as the constant dripping on a rainy day. [16]Trying
to stop her complaints is like trying to stop the wind or hold something with greased
hands.
[17]As iron sharpens iron, a friend sharpens a friend.

27:18 Luke 12:42-44; 1 Cor 9:7; 2 Tim 2:6

[18]Workers who tend a fig tree are allowed to eat its fruit. In the same way, workers
who protect their employer's interests will be rewarded.
[19]As a face is reflected in water, so the heart reflects the person.

27:20 Prov 30:15; Eccl 1:8-11; Hab 2:5

[20]Just as Death and Destruction* are never satisfied, so human desire is never
satisfied.

27:20 Hebrew *Sheol and Abaddon.*

DILIGENCE AND LAZINESS

Proverbs makes it clear that diligence—being willing to work hard and do one's best at any job given to him or her—is a vital part of wise living. We work hard, not to become rich, famous, or admired (although those may be by-products), but to serve God with our very best during our lives.

The Diligent	*The Lazy*	*Reference*
Become rich	Are soon poor	10:4
Gather crops early	Sleep during harvest	10:5
	Are an annoyance	10:26
Are prosperous	Are idle	12:11
Hard work returns rewards		12:14
Will become leaders	Will become slaves	12:24
Make good use of resources	Waste good resources	12:27
Are fully satisfied	Want much but get little	13:4
Bring profit	Experience poverty	14:23
Have an easy path	Have trouble all through life	15:19
	Are like those who destroy	18:9
	Go hungry	19:15
	Won't feed themselves	19:24
	Won't plow in season	20:4
Stay awake and have food to spare	Love sleep and grow poor	20:13
Make careful plans	Make hasty shortcuts	21:5
	Love pleasure and become poor	21:17
Love to give	Desire things but refuse to work for them	21:25, 26
	Are full of excuses for not working	22:13
Will serve before kings		22:29
	Sleep too much, which leads to poverty	24:30–34
Reap abundance through hard work	Experience poverty because of laziness	28:19

27:15, 16 Quarrelsome nagging, a steady stream of unwanted advice, is a form of torture. People nag because they think they're not getting through, but nagging hinders communication more than it helps. When tempted to engage in this destructive habit, stop and examine your motives. Are you more concerned about yourself—getting your way, being right—than about the person you are pretending to help? If you are truly concerned about other people, think of a more effective way to get through to them. Surprise them with words of patience and love, and see what happens.

27:17 There is a mental sharpness that comes from being around good people. And a meeting of minds can help people see their ideas with new clarity, refine them, and shape them into brilliant insights. This requires partners who can challenge each other and stimulate thought—people who focus on the idea without involving their egos in the discussion; people who know how to attack the thought and not the thinker. Two friends who bring their ideas together can help each other become sharper.

27:18 With all the problems and concerns a leader has, it can be easy to overlook the very people who most deserve attention—faithful employees or volunteers (those who tend the fig trees). The people who stand behind you, who work hard and help you get the job done, deserve to share in your success. Be sure that in all your planning, organizing, and working, you don't forget the people who are helping you the most.

21 Fire tests the purity of silver and gold, but a person is tested by being praised.
22 You cannot separate fools from their foolishness, even though you grind them like
grain with mortar and pestle.
23 Know the state of your flocks, and put your heart into caring for your herds, 24 for
riches don't last forever, and the crown might not be secure for the next generation. 25 After
the hay is harvested, the new crop appears, and the mountain grasses are gathered in,
26 your sheep will provide wool for clothing, and your goats will be sold for the price of a
field. 27 And you will have enough goats' milk for you, your family, and your servants.

27:21 Prov 17:3; Zech 13:9; Luke 6:26
27:22 Prov 23:35; 26:11; Jer 5:3
27:23 Ezek 34:12; John 10:3

28

28 The wicked run away when no one is chasing them, but the godly are as bold as
lions.
2 When there is moral rot within a nation, its government topples easily. But with wise
and knowledgeable leaders, there is stability.
3 A poor person who oppresses the poor is like a pounding rain that destroys the crops.
4 To reject the law is to praise the wicked; to obey the law is to fight them.
5 Evil people don't understand justice, but those who follow the LORD understand
completely.
6 It is better to be poor and honest than rich and crooked.
7 Young people who obey the law are wise; those who seek out worthless companions
bring shame to their parents.
8 A person who makes money by charging interest will lose it. It will end up in the
hands of someone who is kind to the poor.
9 The prayers of a person who ignores the law are despised.
10 Those who lead the upright into sin will fall into their own trap, but the honest will
inherit good things.
11 Rich people picture themselves as wise, but their real poverty is evident to the poor.
12 When the godly succeed, everyone is glad. When the wicked take charge, people go
into hiding.
13 People who cover over their sins will not prosper. But if they confess and forsake
them, they will receive mercy.
14 Blessed are those who have a tender conscience,* but the stubborn are headed for
serious trouble.

28:14 Hebrew *those who fear.*

28:1 Lev 26:17, 36
28:2 1 Kgs 16:8-28; 2 Kgs 15:8-15
28:3 Matt 18:28
28:4 Rom 1:32; Eph 5:11
28:5 Ps 92:6-7
28:6 Prov 19:1
28:7 Prov 23:20
28:8 Exod 22:25; Deut 23:19-20
28:9 Pss 66:18; 109:7
28:10 Prov 26:27; Heb 6:12
28:12 Eccl 10:5-6
28:13 Ps 32:1-11; 1 Jn 1:6-9
28:14 Rom 2:5

27:21 Praise tests a person, just as high temperatures test metal. How does praise affect you? Do you work to get it? Do you work harder after you've gotten it? Your attitude toward praise tells a lot about your character. People of high integrity are not swayed by praise. They are attuned to their inner convictions, and they do what they should whether or not they are praised for it.

27:23-27 Because life is uncertain, we should be all the more diligent in preparing for the future. We should act with foresight, giving responsible attention to our home, our family, and our career. We should be responsible stewards, like a farmer with his lands and herds. Thinking ahead is a duty, not an option, for God's people.

28:2 For a government or a society to endure, it needs wise, informed leaders—and these are hard to find. Each person's selfishness quickly affects others. A selfish employee who steals from his company ruins its productivity. A selfish driver who drinks before taking the wheel makes the state highways unsafe. A selfish spouse who has an adulterous affair often breaks up several families. When people live for themselves with little concern for how their actions affect others, the resulting moral rot contaminates the entire nation. Are you part of the problem or the solution?

28:5 Because justice is part of God's character, a person who follows God treats others justly. Justice begins with concern for what is happening to others. A Christian cannot be indifferent to human suffering because God isn't. And we certainly must not contribute to human suffering through selfish business practices or unfair government policies. Be sure you are more concerned for justice than for the bottom line.

28:9 God does not listen to our prayers if we intend to go back to our sin as soon as we get off our knees. When we forsake our sin and follow him, however, he willingly listens—no matter how bad our sin has been. What closes his ears is not the depth of our sin but our secret intention to do it again.

28:11 Rich people often think they are wonderful; depending on no one, they take credit for all they do. But that's a hollow self-esteem. Through dependence on God in their struggles, the poor may develop a richness of spirit that no amount of wealth can provide. The rich man can lose all his material wealth, while no one can take away the poor man's character. Don't be jealous of the rich; money may be all they will ever have.

28:13 It is human nature to hide our sins or overlook our mistakes. But it is hard to learn from a mistake you don't acknowledge making. And what good is a mistake if it doesn't teach you something? To learn from an error you need to admit it, confess it, analyze it, and make adjustments so that it doesn't happen again. Everybody makes mistakes, but only fools repeat them.

28:13 Something in each of us strongly resists admitting we are wrong. That is why we admire people who openly and graciously admit their mistakes and sins. These people have a strong self-image. They do not always have to be right to feel good about themselves. Be willing to reconsider—to admit you are wrong and to change your plans when necessary. And remember, the first step toward forgiveness is confession.

15 A wicked ruler is as dangerous to the poor as a lion or bear attacking them.
16 Only a stupid prince will oppress his people, but a king will have a long reign if he
hates dishonesty and bribes.
17 A murderer's tormented conscience will drive him into the grave. Don't protect him!
18 The honest will be rescued from harm, but those who are crooked will be destroyed.
19 Hard workers have plenty of food; playing around brings poverty.
20 The trustworthy will get a rich reward. But the person who wants to get rich quick
will only get into trouble.
21 Showing partiality is never good, yet some will do wrong for something as small as
a piece of bread.
22 A greedy person tries to get rich quick, but it only leads to poverty.
23 In the end, people appreciate frankness more than flattery.
24 Robbing your parents and then saying, "What's wrong with that?" is as serious as
committing murder.
25 Greed causes fighting; trusting the LORD leads to prosperity.
26 Trusting oneself is foolish, but those who walk in wisdom are safe.
27 Whoever gives to the poor will lack nothing. But a curse will come upon those who
close their eyes to poverty.
28 When the wicked take charge, people hide. When the wicked meet disaster, the
godly multiply.

28:15 Prov 19:12; Matt 2:16; 1 Pet 5:8
28:16 Eccl 10:16; Isa 3:12
28:17 Gen 9:6; Exod 21:14
28:19 Prov 12:11
28:20 Matt 25:21
28:21 Ezek 13:19
28:24 Prov 19:26; 20:20
28:26 Prov 3:5
28:27 Prov 11:24; 19:17

29

29 Whoever stubbornly refuses to accept criticism will suddenly be broken beyond
repair.
2 When the godly are in authority, the people rejoice. But when the wicked are in
power, they groan.
3 The man who loves wisdom brings joy to his father, but if he hangs around with
prostitutes, his wealth is wasted.
4 A just king gives stability to his nation, but one who demands bribes destroys it.

29:1 1 Sam 2:25; 2 Chr 36:16
29:2 Esth 8:15-16; Prov 11:10; 28:12
29:3 Prov 6:26; 10:1; Luke 15:13

LEADERSHIP
Since many of the proverbs came from King Solomon, it is natural to expect some of his interest to be directed toward leadership.
Other verses to study: 24:27; 25:13; 27:18.

Qualities of a good leader	*Reference*
Works hard	12:24
Doesn't penalize people for integrity	17:26
Listens before answering	18:13
Open to new ideas	18:15
Listens to both sides of the story	18:17
Stands up under pressure	24:10
Stands up under praise	27:21
What happens without good leadership	
Fools are honored	26:8
A wicked ruler is dangerous	28:15
People despair	29:2
A wicked ruler has wicked advisers	29:12

28:17, 18 A sinner's conscience will drive him into either guilt, resulting in repentance, or to death itself because of a refusal to repent. It is no act of kindness to try to make him feel better; the more guilt he feels, the more likely he is to turn to God and repent. If we interfere with the natural consequences of his act, we may make it easier for him to continue in sin.

28:26 For many people, the rugged individualist is a hero. We admire the bold, self-directed men and women who know what they want and fight for it. They are self-reliant, neither giving nor asking advice. What a contrast to God's way. A person can't know the future or predict the consequences of his or her choices with certainty. And so the totally self-reliant person is doomed to failure. The wise person depends on God.

28:27 God wants us to identify with the needy, not ignore them. The second part of this proverb could be restated positively: "Those who open their eyes to poor people will be blessed." If we help others when they are in trouble, they will do whatever they can to return the favor (see 11:24, 25). Paul promises that God will supply all our needs (Philippians 4:19); he usually does this through other people. What can you do today to help God supply someone's need?

5 To flatter people is to lay a trap for their feet.
6 Evil people are trapped by sin, but the righteous escape, shouting for joy.
7 The godly know the rights of the poor; the wicked don't care to know.
8 Mockers can get a whole town agitated, but those who are wise will calm anger.
9 If a wise person takes a fool to court, there will be ranting and ridicule but no satisfaction.
10 The bloodthirsty hate the honest, but the upright seek out the honest.
11 A fool gives full vent to anger, but a wise person quietly holds it back.
12 If a ruler honors liars, all his advisers will be wicked.
13 The poor and the oppressor have this in common—the LORD gives light to the eyes
of both.
14 A king who is fair to the poor will have a long reign.
15 To discipline and reprimand a child produces wisdom, but a mother is disgraced by
an undisciplined child.
16 When the wicked are in authority, sin increases. But the godly will live to see the
tyrant's downfall.
17 Discipline your children, and they will give you happiness and peace of mind.
18 When people do not accept divine guidance, they run wild. But whoever obeys the
law is happy.
19 For a servant, mere words are not enough—discipline is needed. For the words may
be understood, but they are not heeded.
20 There is more hope for a fool than for someone who speaks without thinking.
21 A servant who is pampered from childhood will later become a rebel.
22 A hot-tempered person starts fights and gets into all kinds of sin.
23 Pride ends in humiliation, while humility brings honor.
24 If you assist a thief, you are only hurting yourself. You will be punished if you report
the crime, but you will be cursed if you don't.
25 Fearing people is a dangerous trap, but to trust the LORD means safety.
26 Many seek the ruler's favor, but justice comes from the LORD.
27 The godly despise the wicked; the wicked despise the godly.

The Sayings of Agur

30 The message of Agur son of Jakeh. An oracle.*
I am weary, O God; I am weary and worn out, O God.* 2 I am too ignorant to
be human, and I lack common sense. 3 I have not mastered human wisdom, nor do I know
the Holy One.
4 Who but God goes up to heaven and comes back down? Who holds the wind in his

29:5 Ps 5:9
29:7 Ps 41:1; Prov 31:8-9
29:8 Prov 11:11; 16:14
29:10 1 Jn 3:2
29:12 1 Kgs 12:14
29:13 Ps 13:3
29:14 Ps 72:4; Prov 16:12
29:16 Ps 37:34-38
29:18 Exod 32:25; Pss 1:1-2; 119:2-3
29:20 Prov 26:12; Jas 1:19
29:23 Prov 15:33; 22:4; Dan 4:30; Matt 23:12; Jas 4:6
29:24 Lev 5:1
29:25 Gen 12:11-13; Luke 12:4
29:26 Isa 49:4
29:27 Pss 69:4; 139:21-22; Matt 10:22; 24:9
30:2 Job 42:3-6; Ps 49:10
30:4 Exod 15:10; Job 26:8; 38:8-9; Isa 45:18; Rev 19:12

30:1a Or *son of Jakeh from Massa.* **30:1b** The Hebrew can also be translated *The man declares this to Ithiel, to Ithiel and to Ucal.*

29:13 "The LORD gives light to the eyes of both" means that everyone depends on God for sight. Both the oppressor and the poor have the gift of sight from the same God. God sees and judges both, and his judgment falls on those whose greed or power drives them to oppress the poor.

29:15 Parents of young children often weary of disciplining them. They feel like all they do is nag, scold, and punish. When you're tempted to give up and let your children do what they want, or when you wonder if you've ruined every chance for a loving relationship with them, remember that kind, firm correction helps them learn, and learning makes them wise. Consistent, loving discipline will ultimately teach them to discipline themselves.

29:16 When the wicked are in leadership, sin prevails. In any organization—whether a church, a business, a family, or a government—the climate comes from the top. The people become like their leaders. What kind of climate are you setting for the people you lead?

29:18 "Divine guidance" refers to words from God received by prophets. Where there is ignorance of God, crime and sin run rampant. Public morality depends on the knowledge of God, but it also depends on keeping God's laws. In order for nations and individuals to function well, people must know God's ways and keep his rules.

29:24 This proverb is saying that a thief's accomplice won't tell the truth when under oath. Thus, by his perjury, he will hurt himself.

29:25 Fear of people can hamper everything you try to do. In extreme forms, it can make you afraid to leave your home. By contrast, fear of God—respect, reverence, and trust—is liberating. Why fear people who can do no eternal harm? Instead, trust God who can turn the harm intended by others into good for those who trust him.

30:1 The origin of these sayings is not clear. Nothing is known about Agur except that he was a wise teacher who may have come from Lemuel's kingdom (see the note on 31:1).

30:2-4 Because God is infinite, certain aspects of his nature will always remain a mystery. Compare these questions with the questions God asked Job (Job 38–41).

30:4 Some scholars feel that the son referred to is the Son of God, the preincarnate being of the Messiah who, before the foundation of the earth, participated in the Creation. Colossians 1:16, 17 teaches that through Christ the world was created.

fists? Who wraps up the oceans in his cloak? Who has created the whole wide world?
What is his name—and his son's name? Tell me if you know!
5 Every word of God proves true. He defends all who come to him for protection. 6 Do
not add to his words, or he may rebuke you, and you will be found a liar. 7 O God, I beg
two favors from you before I die. 8 First, help me never to tell a lie. Second, give me
neither poverty nor riches! Give me just enough to satisfy my needs. 9 For if I grow rich,
I may deny you and say, "Who is the LORD?" And if I am too poor, I may steal and thus
insult God's holy name.

10 Never slander a person to his employer. If you do, the person will curse you, and
you will pay for it.

11 Some people curse their father and do not thank their mother. 12 They feel pure, but
they are filthy and unwashed. 13 They are proud beyond description and disdainful.
14 They devour the poor with teeth as sharp as swords or knives. They destroy the needy
from the face of the earth.

15 The leech has two suckers that cry out, "More, more!"* There are three other
things—no, four!—that are never satisfied:
16 the grave,
the barren womb,
the thirsty desert,
the blazing fire.

17 The eye that mocks a father and despises a mother will be plucked out by ravens of
the valley and eaten by vultures.

18 There are three things that amaze me—no, four things I do not understand:
19 how an eagle glides through the sky,
how a snake slithers on a rock,
how a ship navigates the ocean,
how a man loves a woman.
20 Equally amazing is how an adulterous woman can satisfy her sexual appetite, shrug
her shoulders, and then say, "What's wrong with that?"

21 There are three things that make the earth tremble—no, four it cannot endure:
22 a slave who becomes a king,
an overbearing fool who prospers,
23 a bitter woman who finally gets a husband,
a servant girl who supplants her mistress.

24 There are four things on earth that are small but unusually wise:
25 Ants—they aren't strong,
but they store up food for the winter.
26 Rock badgers*—they aren't powerful,
but they make their homes among the rocky cliffs.
27 Locusts—they have no king,
but they march like an army in ranks.
28 Lizards—they are easy to catch,
but they are found even in kings' palaces.

30:5 Pss 3:3; 12:6; 18:30; 84:11 Prov 2:7-8
30:6 Deut 4:2; 12:32 Rev 22:18
30:8 Matt 6:11
30:9 Deut 8:12; 31:20 Neh 9:25 Hos 13:6
30:10 Eccl 7:21
30:11 Exod 21:17 Prov 20:20
30:14 Job 29:17 Ps 14:4
30:15 Prov 27:20
30:17 Gen 9:22
30:20 Prov 5:6
30:26 Prov 6:6

30:15 Hebrew *two daughters who cry out, "Give, give!"* **30:26** Or *coneys,* or *hyraxes.*

30:7-9 Having too much money can be dangerous, but so can having too little. Being poor can, in fact, be hazardous to spiritual as well as physical health. On the other hand, being rich is not the answer. As Jesus pointed out, rich people have trouble getting into God's Kingdom (Matthew 19:23, 24). Like Paul, we can learn how to live whether we have little or plenty (Philippians 4:12), but our lives are more likely to be effective if we have "neither poverty nor riches."

30:13 This phrase refers to prideful and haughty people who look down on others. Verses 11-14 contain a fourfold description of arrogance.

30:15ff "Three things . . . no, four" is a poetic way of saying the list is not complete. The writer of these proverbs is observing the world with delighted interest. Verses 15-31 are an invitation to look at nature from the perspective of a keen observer.

30:24-28 Ants can teach us about preparation; badgers about wise building; locusts about cooperation and order; and lizards about fearlessness.

29 There are three stately monarchs on the earth—no, four:
30 the lion, king of animals, who won't turn aside for anything,
31 the strutting rooster,
the male goat,
a king as he leads his army.

32 If you have been a fool by being proud or plotting evil, don't brag about it—cover
your mouth with your hand in shame.

33 As the beating of cream yields butter, and a blow to the nose causes bleeding, so
anger causes quarrels.

The Sayings of King Lemuel

31 These are the sayings of King Lemuel, an oracle* that his mother taught him.
2 O my son, O son of my womb, O son of my promises, 3 do not spend your
strength on women, on those who ruin kings.

4 And it is not for kings, O Lemuel, to guzzle wine. Rulers should not crave liquor.
5 For if they drink, they may forget their duties and be unable to give justice to those who
are oppressed. 6 Liquor is for the dying, and wine for those in deep depression. 7 Let them
drink to forget their poverty and remember their troubles no more.

8 Speak up for those who cannot speak for themselves; ensure justice for those who
are perishing. 9 Yes, speak up for the poor and helpless, and see that they get justice.

A Wife of Noble Character

10 Who can find a virtuous and capable wife? She is worth more than precious rubies.
11 Her husband can trust her, and she will greatly enrich his life. 12 She will not hinder
him but help him all her life.

13 She finds wool and flax and busily spins it. 14 She is like a merchant's ship; she
brings her food from afar. 15 She gets up before dawn to prepare breakfast for her
household and plan the day's work for her servant girls. 16 She goes out to inspect a field
and buys it; with her earnings she plants a vineyard.

17 She is energetic and strong, a hard worker. 18 She watches for bargains; her lights
burn late into the night. 19 Her hands are busy spinning thread, her fingers twisting fiber.

20 She extends a helping hand to the poor and opens her arms to the needy.

21 She has no fear of winter for her household because all of them have warm* clothes.
22 She quilts her own bedspreads. She dresses like royalty in gowns of finest cloth.

23 Her husband is well known, for he sits in the council meeting with the other civic
leaders.

24 She makes belted linen garments and sashes to sell to the merchants.

25 She is clothed with strength and dignity, and she laughs with no fear of the future.
26 When she speaks, her words are wise, and kindness is the rule when she gives

30:32 Job 21:5; 40:4; Mic 7:16
30:33 Prov 10:12; 29:22
31:2 1 Sam 1:11; Isa 49:15
31:3 Deut 17:17; 1 Kgs 11:1; Prov 5:9
31:4 Prov 20:1; Eccl 10:16-17; Isa 5:22-23; Hos 4:11
31:5 Deut 16:19; Prov 17:15
31:6 Job 3:20; Isa 38:15
31:8 Job 29:12-17; Ps 82:3-5
31:9 Lev 19:15; Isa 1:17
31:10 Ruth 3:11; Prov 12:4; 19:14
31:13 1 Tim 2:9-10
31:15 Rom 12:11
31:20 Eph 4:28
31:26 Prov 10:31

31:1 Or *of Lemuel, king of Massa.* **31:21** As in Greek version; Hebrew *scarlet.*

31:1 Little is known about Lemuel except that he was a king who received wise teachings from his mother. His name means "devoted to God." Some believe that Lemuel and Agur were both from the kingdom of Massa in northern Arabia.

31:4-7 Drunkenness might be understandable among dying people in great pain, but it is inexcusable for national leaders. Alcohol clouds the mind and can lead to injustice and poor decisions. People in leadership who anesthetize themselves with alcohol will eventually compromise their principles.

31:10-31 Proverbs has a lot to say about women. How fitting that the book ends with a picture of a woman of strong character, great wisdom, many skills, and great compassion.

Some people have the mistaken idea that the ideal woman in the Bible is retiring, servile, and entirely domestic. Not so! This woman is an excellent wife and mother. She is also a manufacturer, importer, manager, realtor, farmer, seamstress, upholsterer, and merchant. Her strength and dignity do not come from her amazing achievements, however. They are a result of her reverence for God. In our society, where physical appearance counts for so much, it may surprise us to realize that her appearance is never mentioned. Her attractiveness comes entirely from her character.

The woman described in this chapter has outstanding abilities. Her family's social position is high. In fact, she may not be one woman at all—she may be a composite portrait of ideal womanhood. Do not see her as a model to imitate in every detail; your days are not long enough to do everything she does! See her instead as an inspiration to be all you can be. We can't be just like her, but we can learn from her industry, integrity, and resourcefulness.

31:27 Prov 19:15

instructions. 27 She carefully watches all that goes on in her household and does not
have to bear the consequences of laziness.
28 Her children stand and bless her. Her husband praises her: 29 "There are many
virtuous and capable women in the world, but you surpass them all!"

31:30 Prov 22:4

30 Charm is deceptive, and beauty does not last; but a woman who fears the LORD will
be greatly praised. 31 Reward her for all she has done. Let her deeds publicly declare her
praise.

31:31 The book of Proverbs begins with the command to fear the Lord (1:7) and ends with the picture of a woman who fulfills this command. Her qualities are mentioned throughout the book: hard work, fear of God, respect for spouse, foresight, encouragement, care for others, concern for the poor, wisdom in handling money. These qualities, when coupled with fear of God, lead to enjoyment, success, honor, and worth. Proverbs is practical for us because it shows how to become wise, make good decisions, and live according to God's ideal.

ECCLESIASTES

VITAL STATISTICS

PURPOSE:
To spare future generations the bitterness of learning through their own experience that life is meaningless apart from God

AUTHOR:
Solomon

TO WHOM WRITTEN:
Solomon's subjects in particular, and all people in general

DATE WRITTEN:
Probably around 935 B.C., late in Solomon's life

SETTING:
Solomon was looking back on his life, much of which was lived apart from God

KEY VERSE:
"Here is my final conclusion: Fear God and obey his commands, for this is the duty of every person" (12:13).

THE MOLDED bunny lies in the basket, surrounded by green paper "grass." With Easter morning eyes wide with anticipation, the little boy carefully lifts the chocolate figure and bites into one of the long ears. But the sweet taste fades quickly, and the child looks again at the candy in his hand. It's hollow!

Empty, futile, hollow, nothing—the words have a ring of disappointment and disillusionment. Yet this is the life experience of many. Grasping the sweet things—possessions, experience, power, and pleasure—they find nothing inside. Life is empty, meaningless—and they sink into despair.

Almost 3,000 years ago, Solomon spoke of this human dilemma; but the insights and applications of his message are relevant to our time. Ecclesiastes, Solomon's written sermon, is an analysis of life's experiences and a critical essay about life's true meaning. In this profound book, Solomon takes us on a reflective journey through his life, explaining how everything he had tried, tested, or tasted had been "meaningless"—useless, irrational, pointless, foolish, and empty—an exercise in futility. And remember, these words are from one who "had it all"—tremendous intellect, power, and wealth. After this biographical tour, Solomon made his triumphant conclusion: "Fear God and obey his commands, for this is the duty of every person. God will judge us for everything we do, including every secret thing, whether good or bad" (12:13, 14).

When Solomon became king, he asked God for wisdom (2 Chronicles 1:7–12), and he became the wisest man in the world (1 Kings 4:29–34). He studied, taught, judged, and wrote. Kings and leaders from other nations came to Jerusalem to learn from him. But with all of his practical insight on life, Solomon failed to heed his own advice, and he began a downward spiral. Near the end of his life, Solomon looked back with an attitude of humility and repentance. He took stock of his life, hoping to spare his readers the bitterness of learning through personal experience that everything apart from God is empty, hollow, and meaningless.

Although the tone of Ecclesiastes is negative and pessimistic, we must not conclude that the only chapter worth reading and applying is the last one, where he draws his conclusions. In reality, the entire book is filled with practical wisdom (how to accomplish things in the world and stay out of trouble) and spiritual wisdom (how to find and know eternal values). Solomon had a very honest approach to life. All of his remarks relating to the futility of life are there for a purpose: to lead us to seek fulfillment and happiness in God alone. He was not trying to destroy all hope, but to direct our hopes to the only one who can truly fulfill them and give our life meaning. Solomon affirms the value of knowledge, relationships, work, and pleasure, but only *in their proper place.* All of these temporal things in life must be seen in light of the eternal.

Read Ecclesiastes and learn about life. Hear the stern warnings and dire predictions, and commit yourself to remember your Creator now (12:1).

THE BLUEPRINT

1. Solomon's personal experience (1:1—2:26) 2. Solomon's general observations (3:1—5:20) 3. Solomon's practical counsel (6:1—8:17) 4. Solomon's final conclusion (9:1—12:14)	Ecclesiastes shows that certain paths in life lead to emptiness. This profound book also helps us discover true purpose in life. Such wisdom can spare us from the emptiness that results from a life without God. Solomon teaches that people will not find meaning in life through knowledge, money, pleasure, work, or popularity. True satisfaction comes from knowing that what we are doing is part of God's purpose for our life. This is a book that can help free us from our scramble for power, approval, and money, and draw us closer to God.

MEGATHEMES

THEME	EXPLANATION	IMPORTANCE
Searching	Solomon searched for satisfaction almost as though he was conducting a scientific experiment. Through this process, he discovered that life without God is a long and fruitless search for enjoyment, meaning, and fulfillment. True happiness is not in our power to attain because we always want more than we can have. In addition, there are circumstances beyond our control that can snatch away our possessions or attainments.	People are still searching. Yet the more they try to get, the more they realize how little they really have. No pleasure or happiness is possible without God. Without him, satisfaction is a lost search. Above everything we should strive to know and love God. He gives wisdom, knowledge, and joy.
Emptiness	Solomon shows how empty it is to pursue the pleasures that this life has to offer rather than seek to have a relationship with the eternal God. The search for pleasure, wealth, and success is ultimately disappointing. Nothing in the world can fill the emptiness and satisfy the deep longings in our restless hearts.	The cure for emptiness is to center on God. His love also can fill the emptiness of human experience. Fear God throughout your life, and fill your life with serving God and others rather than with selfish pleasures.
Work	Solomon tried to shake people's confidence in their own efforts, abilities, and wisdom and to direct them to faith in God as the only sound basis for living. Without God, there is no lasting reward or benefit in hard work.	Work done with the wrong attitude will leave us empty. But work accepted as an assignment from God can be seen as a gift. Examine what you expect from your efforts. God gives you abilities and opportunities to work so that you can use your time well.
Death	The certainty of death makes all human achievements futile. God has a plan for each one of us that goes beyond life and death. The reality of aging and dying reminds each individual of the end to come when God will judge each person's life.	Because life is short, we need wisdom that is greater than this world can offer. We need the words of God so we can live right. If we listen to him, his wisdom spares us the bitterness of futile human experience and gives us a hope that goes beyond death.
Wisdom	Human wisdom doesn't contain all the answers. Knowledge and education have their limits. To understand life and make right choices, we need the wisdom that can be found only in God's Word—the Bible.	When we realize that God will evaluate all that we do, we should learn to live wisely, remembering that he is present each day, and learn to obey his guidelines for living. But in order to have God's wisdom, we must first get to know and honor him.

1. Solomon's personal experience

1 These are the words of the Teacher,* King David's son, who ruled in Jerusalem.

Everything Is Meaningless

2 "Everything is meaningless," says the Teacher, "utterly meaningless!"
3 What do people get for all their hard work? 4 Generations come and go, but
nothing really changes. 5 The sun rises and sets and hurries around to rise again. 6 The
wind blows south and north, here and there, twisting back and forth, getting nowhere.
7 The rivers run into the sea, but the sea is never full. Then the water returns again to
the rivers and flows again to the sea. 8 Everything is so weary and tiresome! No matter
how much we see, we are never satisfied. No matter how much we hear, we are not
content.
9 History merely repeats itself. It has all been done before. Nothing under the sun is
truly new. 10 What can you point to that is new? How do you know it didn't already exist
long ago? 11 We don't remember what happened in those former times. And in future
generations, no one will remember what we are doing now.

The Futility of Wisdom

12 I, the Teacher, was king of Israel, and I lived in Jerusalem. 13 I devoted myself to search
for understanding and to explore by wisdom everything being done in the world. I soon
discovered that God has dealt a tragic existence to the human race. 14 Everything under
the sun is meaningless, like chasing the wind. 15 What is wrong cannot be righted. What
is missing cannot be recovered.
16 I said to myself, "Look, I am wiser than any of the kings who ruled in Jerusalem
before me. I have greater wisdom and knowledge than any of them." 17 So I worked hard
to distinguish wisdom from foolishness. But now I realize that even this was like chasing
the wind. 18 For the greater my wisdom, the greater my grief. To increase knowledge only
increases sorrow.

1:1 Eccl 1:12; 7:27; 12:8-10
1:2 Pss 39:5-6; 62:9; 144:4; Rom 8:20
1:3 Eccl 2:11; 3:9; 5:16
1:4 Pss 104:5; 119:90
1:6 John 3:8
1:8 Prov 27:20; Eccl 4:8
1:9 Eccl 2:12; 3:15
1:11 Eccl 2:16; 9:5
1:12 Eccl 1:1; 7:27; 12:8-10
1:13 Eccl 7:25; 8:17
1:14 Eccl 2:11; 4:4; 6:9
1:16 1 Kgs 3:12; 4:30; 10:23
1:17 Eccl 2:12; 7:25
1:18 Eccl 12:12

1:1 Hebrew *Koheleth;* this term is rendered "the Teacher" throughout this book.

1:1 The author, Solomon (the "king of Israel," see 1:12), referred to himself as the Teacher, or leader of the assembly. He was both assembling people to hear a message and gathering wise sayings (proverbs). Solomon, one person in the Bible who had everything (wisdom, power, riches, honor, reputation, God's favor), is the one who discussed the ultimate emptiness of all that this world has to offer. He tried to destroy people's confidence in their own efforts, abilities, and righteousness and direct them to commitment to God as the only reason for living.

1:1-11 Solomon had a purpose for writing skeptically and pessimistically. Near the end of his life, he looked back over everything he had done, and most of it seemed meaningless. A common belief was that only good people prospered and that only the wicked suffered, but that hadn't proven true in his experience. Solomon wrote this book after he had tried everything and achieved much, only to find that nothing apart from God made him happy. He wanted his readers to avoid these same senseless pursuits. If we try to find meaning in our accomplishments rather than in God, we will never be satisfied, and everything we pursue will become meaningless.

1:2 Solomon's kingdom, Israel, was in its golden age, but Solomon wanted the people to understand that success and prosperity don't last long (Psalm 103:14-16; Isaiah 40:6-8; James 4:14). All human accomplishments will one day disappear, and we must keep this in mind in order to live wisely. If we don't, we will become either proud and self-sufficient when we succeed or sorely disappointed when we fail. Solomon's goal was to show that earthly possessions and accomplishments are ultimately meaningless. Only the pursuit of God brings real satisfaction. We should honor God in all we say, think, and do.

1:8-11 Many people feel restless and dissatisfied. They wonder: (1) If I am in God's will, why am I so tired and unfulfilled? (2) What is the meaning of life? (3) When I look back on it all, will I be happy with my accomplishments? (4) Why do I feel burned out, disillusioned, dry? (5) What is to become of me? Solomon tests our faith, challenging us to find true and lasting meaning in God alone. As you take a hard look at your life, as Solomon did his, you will see how important serving God is over all other options. Perhaps God is asking you to rethink your purpose and direction in life, just as Solomon did in Ecclesiastes.

1:12-15 "What is wrong cannot be righted. What is missing cannot be recovered" refers to the ultimate perplexity and confusion that come to us because of all the unanswered questions in life. Solomon, writing about his own life, discovered that neither his accomplishments nor his wisdom could make him truly happy. True wisdom is found in God, and true happiness comes from pleasing him.

1:16-18 The more you understand, the greater your pain and difficulty. For example, the more you know, the more imperfection you see around you; and the more you observe, the more evil becomes evident. As you set out with Solomon to find the meaning of life, you must be ready to feel more, think more, question more, hurt more, and do more. Are you ready to pay the price for wisdom?

1:16-18 Solomon highlights two kinds of wisdom in the book of Ecclesiastes: (1) human knowledge, reasoning, or philosophy, and (2) the wisdom that comes from God. In these verses Solomon is talking about human knowledge. When human knowledge ignores God, it only highlights our problems because it can't provide answers without God's eternal perspective and solution.

2:1 Eccl 7:4, 6; 8:15
2:2 Prov 14:15
2:3 Judg 9:13; Eccl 6:12; 8:15; 12:13
2:4 1 Kgs 7:1-12; Song 8:10-11
2:5 Neh 2:8; Song 4:16; 5:1
2:6 Neh 2:14; 3:15-16
2:7 Gen 14:14; 15:3; 1 Kgs 4:23
2:8 1 Kgs 9:28; 10:10, 14
2:9 1 Chr 29:25; Eccl 1:16
2:11 Eccl 1:3, 14; 2:22; 3:9; 5:16
2:12 Eccl 1:9-10, 17; 7:25
2:13 Eccl 7:11-12, 19
2:14 Ps 49:10; Eccl 9:2-3
2:18 Pss 39:6; 49:10; Eccl 2:11

The Futility of Pleasure

2 I said to myself, "Come now, let's give pleasure a try. Let's look for the 'good things'
in life." But I found that this, too, was meaningless. 2"It is silly to be laughing all
the time," I said. "What good does it do to seek only pleasure?" 3After much thought, I
decided to cheer myself with wine. While still seeking wisdom, I clutched at foolishness.
In this way, I hoped to experience the only happiness most people find during their brief
life in this world.
4I also tried to find meaning by building huge homes for myself and by planting
beautiful vineyards. 5I made gardens and parks, filling them with all kinds of fruit trees.
6I built reservoirs to collect the water to irrigate my many flourishing groves. 7I bought
slaves, both men and women, and others were born into my household. I also owned
great herds and flocks, more than any of the kings who lived in Jerusalem before me. 8I
collected great sums of silver and gold, the treasure of many kings and provinces. I hired
wonderful singers, both men and women, and had many beautiful concubines. I had
everything a man could desire!
9So I became greater than any of the kings who ruled in Jerusalem before me. And
with it all, I remained clear-eyed so that I could evaluate all these things. 10Anything I
wanted, I took. I did not restrain myself from any joy. I even found great pleasure in hard
work, an additional reward for all my labors. 11But as I looked at everything I had
worked so hard to accomplish, it was all so meaningless. It was like chasing the wind.
There was nothing really worthwhile anywhere.

The Wise and the Foolish

12So I decided to compare wisdom and folly, and anyone else would come to the same
conclusions I did. 13Wisdom is of more value than foolishness, just as light is better than
darkness. 14For the wise person sees, while the fool is blind. Yet I saw that wise and foolish
people share the same fate. 15Both of them die. Just as the fool will die, so will I. So of what
value is all my wisdom? Then I said to myself, "This is all so meaningless!" 16For the wise
person and the fool both die, and in the days to come, both will be forgotten.

The Futility of Work

17So now I hate life because everything done here under the sun is so irrational.
Everything is meaningless, like chasing the wind. 18I am disgusted that I must leave the

---

2:1ff Solomon conducted his search for life's meaning as an experiment. He first tried pursuing pleasure. He undertook great projects, bought slaves and herds and flocks, amassed wealth, acquired singers, added many concubines to his harem, and became the greatest person in Jerusalem. But none of these gave him satisfaction: "But as I looked at everything I had worked so hard to accomplish, it was all so meaningless. It was like chasing the wind. There was nothing really worthwhile anywhere" (2:11). Some of the pleasures Solomon sought were wrong, and some were worthy; but even the worthy pursuits were futile when he pursued them as an end in themselves. We must look beyond our activities to the reasons we do them and the purpose they fulfill. Is your goal in life to search for meaning or to pursue God, who gives meaning?

2:4-6 Solomon had built houses, a Temple, a kingdom, a family (see 1 Kings 3–11). In the course of history, they all would be ruined. In Psalm 127:1, Solomon wrote, "Unless the LORD builds a house, the work of the builders is useless. Unless the LORD protects a city, guarding it with sentries will do no good." This book is part of Solomon's testimony as to what happens to a kingdom or family that forgets God. As you examine your projects or goals, what is your starting point, your motivation? Without God as your foundation, all you are living for is meaningless.

2:11 Solomon summarized his many attempts at finding life's meaning as "chasing the wind." We feel the wind as it passes, but we can't catch hold of it or keep it. In all our accomplishments, even the big ones, our good feelings are only temporary. Security and self-worth are found, not in these accomplishments, but far beyond them in the love of God. Think about what you consider worthwhile in your life—where you place your time, energy, and money. Will you one day look back and decide that these, too, were a "chasing the wind"?

2:16 Solomon realized that wisdom alone cannot guarantee eternal life. Wisdom, riches, and personal achievement matter very little after death—and everyone must die. We must not build our life on perishable pursuits, but on the solid foundation of God. Then even if everything we have is taken away, we still will have God, who is all we really need anyway. This is the point of the book of Job (see the introduction to Job).

2:16 Is death the ultimate equalizer of all people, no matter what they attained in life? While this appears to be true from an earthly perspective, God makes it clear (as Solomon later points out in 12:14) that what we do here has a great impact upon our eternal reward.

2:18-23 Solomon continues to show that hard work bears no lasting fruit for those who work solely to earn money and gain possessions. Not only will everything be left behind at death, but it may be left to those who have done nothing to earn it. In addition, it may not be well cared for, and all that was gained may be lost. In fact, Solomon's son, who inherited his throne, was often foolish—see 1 Kings 12. Hard work done with proper motives (caring for your family, serving God) is not wrong. We must work to survive, and, more important, we are responsible for the physical and spiritual well-being of those under our care. But the fruit of hard work done to glorify only ourselves will be passed on to those who may later lose or spoil it all. Such toil often leads to grief, while serving God leads to everlasting joy. Do you know the real reason you are working so hard?

fruits of my hard work to others. 19And who can tell whether my successors will be wise
or foolish? And yet they will control everything I have gained by my skill and hard work.
How meaningless!
20So I turned in despair from hard work. It was not the answer to my search for
satisfaction in this life. 21For though I do my work with wisdom, knowledge, and skill,
I must leave everything I gain to people who haven't worked to earn it. This is not only
foolish but highly unfair. 22So what do people get for all their hard work? 23Their days
of labor are filled with pain and grief; even at night they cannot rest. It is all utterly
meaningless.
24So I decided there is nothing better than to enjoy food and drink and to find
satisfaction in work. Then I realized that this pleasure is from the hand of God. 25For
who can eat or enjoy anything apart from him? 26God gives wisdom, knowledge, and
joy to those who please him. But if a sinner becomes wealthy, God takes the wealth away
and gives it to those who please him. Even this, however, is meaningless, like chasing
the wind.

2. Solomon's general observations

A Time for Everything

3 1 There is a time for everything,
a season for every activity under heaven.
2 A time to be born and a time to die.
A time to plant and a time to harvest.
3 A time to kill and a time to heal.
A time to tear down and a time to rebuild.
4 A time to cry and a time to laugh.
A time to grieve and a time to dance.
5 A time to scatter stones and a time to gather stones.
A time to embrace and a time to turn away.
6 A time to search and a time to lose.
A time to keep and a time to throw away.
7 A time to tear and a time to mend.
A time to be quiet and a time to speak up.
8 A time to love and a time to hate.
A time for war and a time for peace.

9What do people really get for all their hard work? 10I have thought about this in
connection with the various kinds of work God has given people to do. 11God has made
everything beautiful for its own time. He has planted eternity in the human heart, but

2:21 Eccl 2:18; 4:4
2:22 Eccl 1:3
2:23 Job 5:7; 14:1; Ps 127:2; Eccl 1:18
2:24 Eccl 2:3; 3:12, 22; 5:18; 6:12; 8:15; 9:7
2:26 Job 27:16-17; 32:8; Eccl 1:14
3:1 Eccl 3:17; 8:6
3:2 Heb 9:27
3:4 Exod 15:20; Ps 126:2; Rom 12:15
3:7 Amos 5:13
3:8 Ps 101:3
3:9 Eccl 1:3; 2:11; 5:16
3:10 Eccl 1:13; 2:26
3:11 Gen 1:31; Job 5:9; Eccl 8:17; Rom 11:33

2:24-26 Is Solomon recommending we make life a big, irresponsible party? No, he is encouraging us to take pleasure in what we're doing now and to enjoy life because it comes from God's hand. True enjoyment in life comes only as we follow God's guidelines for living. Without him, satisfaction is a lost search. Those who really know how to enjoy life are the ones who take life each day as a gift from God, thanking him for it and serving him in it. Those without God will have no relief from toil and no direction to guide them through life's complications.

3:1–5:20 Solomon's point in this section is that God has a plan for all people. Thus, he provides cycles of life, each with its work for us to do. Although we may face many problems that seem to contradict God's plan, these should not be barriers to believing in him, but rather opportunities to discover that, without God, life's problems have no lasting solutions!

3:1-8 Timing is important. All the experiences listed in these verses are appropriate at certain times. The secret to peace with God is to discover, accept, and appreciate God's perfect timing. The danger is to doubt or resent God's timing. This can lead to despair, rebellion, or moving ahead without his advice.

3:8 When is there a time for hating? We shouldn't hate evil people, but we should hate what they do. We should also hate it when people are mistreated, when children are starving, and when God is being dishonored. In addition, we must hate the sin in our life—this is God's attitude (see Psalm 5:5).

3:9-13 Your ability to find satisfaction in your work depends to a large extent upon your attitude. You will become dissatisfied if you lose the sense of purpose God intended for your work. We can enjoy our work if we (1) remember that God has given us work to do (3:10), and (2) realize that the fruit of our labor is a gift from him (3:13). See your work as a way to serve God.

3:11 God has "planted eternity in the human heart." This means that we can never be completely satisfied with earthly pleasures and pursuits. Because we are created in God's image, (1) we have a spiritual thirst, (2) we have eternal value, and (3) nothing but the eternal God can truly satisfy us. He has built in us a restless yearning for the kind of perfect world that can only be found in his perfect rule. He has given us a glimpse of the perfection of his creation. But it is only a glimpse; we cannot see into the future or comprehend everything. So we must trust him now and do his work on earth.

3:12 Eccl 2:24
3:13 Eccl 5:19
3:14 Eccl 5:7; 7:18; 8:12-13; 12:13
3:15 Eccl 1:9; 6:10

even so, people cannot see the whole scope of God's work from beginning to end. 12 So
I concluded that there is nothing better for people than to be happy and to enjoy
themselves as long as they can. 13 And people should eat and drink and enjoy the fruits
of their labor, for these are gifts from God.
14 And I know that whatever God does is final. Nothing can be added to it or taken
from it. God's purpose in this is that people should fear him. 15 Whatever exists today
and whatever will exist in the future has already existed in the past. For God calls each
event back in its turn.*

The Injustices of Life

3:17 Gen 18:25; Pss 96:13; 98:9; Matt 16:27; Rom 2:6-10; 2 Thes 1:6-9
3:18 Pss 49:12, 20; 73:22
3:20 Gen 3:19; Ps 103:14; Eccl 12:7
3:22 Eccl 2:18, 24; 6:12; 8:7; 10:14

16 I also noticed that throughout the world there is evil in the courtroom. Yes, even the
courts of law are corrupt! 17 I said to myself, "In due season God will judge everyone,
both good and bad, for all their deeds."
18 Then I realized that God allows people to continue in their sinful ways so he can test
them. That way, they can see for themselves that they are no better than animals. 19 For
humans and animals both breathe the same air,* and both die. So people have no real
advantage over the animals. How meaningless! 20 Both go to the same place—the dust
from which they came and to which they must return. 21 For who can prove that the
human spirit goes upward and the spirit of animals goes downward into the earth? 22 So
I saw that there is nothing better for people than to be happy in their work. That is why
they are here! No one will bring them back from death to enjoy life in the future.

4:1 Isa 5:7; Lam 1:9
4:2 Job 3:11-26; Eccl 2:17
4:4 Eccl 1:14; 2:21
4:5 Prov 6:10; 24:33; Isa 9:20
4:6 Prov 15:16-17; 16:8

4

Again I observed all the oppression that takes place in our world. I saw the tears of
the oppressed, with no one to comfort them. The oppressors have great power, and
the victims are helpless. 2 So I concluded that the dead are better off than the living. 3 And
most fortunate of all are those who were never born. For they have never seen all the evil
that is done in our world.
4 Then I observed that most people are motivated to success by their envy of their
neighbors. But this, too, is meaningless, like chasing the wind.
5 Foolish people refuse to work and almost starve. 6 They feel it is better to be lazy and
barely survive than to work hard, especially when in the long run everything is so futile.

The Advantages of Companionship

4:8 Prov 27:20; Eccl 1:8; 2:21

7 I observed yet another example of meaninglessness in our world. 8 This is the case of a
man who is all alone, without a child or a brother, yet who works hard to gain as much

3:15 Hebrew *For God calls the past to account.* **3:19** Or *both have the same spirit.*

3:12 To be happy and do good are worthy goals for life, but we can pursue them in the wrong way. God wants us to enjoy life. When we have the proper view of God, we discover that real pleasure is found in enjoying whatever we have as gifts from God, not in what we accumulate.

3:14 What is the purpose of life? It is that we should fear the all-powerful God. To *fear* God means to respect and stand in awe of him because of who he is. Purpose in life starts with *whom* we know, not what we know or how good we are. It is impossible to fulfill your God-given purpose unless you revere God and give him first place in your life.

3:16 There is evil and corruption in the place where there should be justice. It even affects the legal system. Solomon asked how God's plan can be perfect when there is so much injustice and oppression in the world (4:1). He concluded that God does not ignore injustice but will bring it to an end at his appointed time (12:13, 14).

3:16ff Solomon reflects on several apparent contradictions in God's control of the world: (1) There is evil and corruption where there should be justice (3:16, 17); (2) people created in God's image die just like the animals (3:18-21); (3) no one comforts the oppressed (4:1-3); (4) many people are motivated by envy (4:4-6); (5) people are lonely (4:7-12); (6) recognition for accomplishments is temporary (4:13-16). It is easy to use such contradictions as excuses to not believe in God. But Solomon used them to show how we can honestly look at life's problems and still keep our faith. This life is not all there is, yet even in this life we should not pass judgment on God because we don't know everything. God's plan is for us to live forever with him. So live with eternal values in view, realizing that all contradictions will one day be cleared up by the Creator himself (12:14).

3:19-22 Our bodies can't live forever in their present state. In that sense, humans and animals are alike. But Solomon acknowledged that God has given people the hope of eternity (see the note on 3:11), and that we will undergo judgment in the next life (3:17; 12:7, 14)—making us different from animals. Because we have eternity planted in our heart, we have a unique purpose in God's overall plan. Yet we cannot discover God's purpose for our life by our own efforts—only through building a relationship with him and seeking his guidance. Are you now living as God wants? Do you see life as a gift from him?

4:4-6 Some people are lazy while others are workaholics. The lazy person, seeing the futility of dashing about for success, idles away his time and hurts both himself and those who depend on him. The workaholic is often driven by envy, greed, and a constant desire to stay ahead of everyone else. Both extremes are foolish and irresponsible. The answer is to work hard but with moderation. Take time to enjoy the other gifts God has given, and realize that it is God who gives out the assignments and the rewards, not us.

wealth as he can. But then he asks himself, "Who am I working for? Why am I giving
up so much pleasure now?" It is all so meaningless and depressing.
9 Two people can accomplish more than twice as much as one; they get a better return
for their labor. 10 If one person falls, the other can reach out and help. But people who
are alone when they fall are in real trouble. 11 And on a cold night, two under the same
blanket can gain warmth from each other. But how can one be warm alone? 12 A person
standing alone can be attacked and defeated, but two can stand back-to-back and
conquer. Three are even better, for a triple-braided cord is not easily broken.

The Futility of Political Power

13 It is better to be a poor but wise youth than to be an old and foolish king who refuses
all advice. 14 Such a youth could come from prison and succeed. He might even become
king, though he was born in poverty. 15 Everyone is eager to help such a youth, even to
help him take the throne. 16 He might become the leader of millions and be very popular.
But then the next generation grows up and rejects him! So again, it is all meaningless,
like chasing the wind.

The Importance of Fearing God

5 As you enter the house of God, keep your ears open and your mouth shut! Don't be
a fool who doesn't realize that mindless offerings to God are evil. 2 And don't make
rash promises to God, for he is in heaven, and you are only here on earth. So let your
words be few.
3 Just as being too busy gives you nightmares, being a fool makes you a blabbermouth.
4 So when you make a promise to God, don't delay in following through, for God takes
no pleasure in fools. Keep all the promises you make to him. 5 It is better to say nothing
than to promise something that you don't follow through on. 6 In such cases, your mouth
is making you sin. And don't defend yourself by telling the Temple messenger that the
promise you made was a mistake. That would make God angry, and he might wipe out
everything you have achieved.
7 Dreaming all the time instead of working is foolishness. And there is ruin in a flood
of empty words. Fear God instead.

The Futility of Wealth

8 If you see a poor person being oppressed by the powerful and justice being miscarried
throughout the land, don't be surprised! For every official is under orders from higher
up, and matters of justice only get lost in red tape and bureaucracy. 9 Even the king milks
the land for his own profit!*
10 Those who love money will never have enough. How absurd to think that wealth
brings true happiness! 11 The more you have, the more people come to help you spend
it. So what is the advantage of wealth—except perhaps to watch it run through your
fingers!

5:9 The meaning of the Hebrew is uncertain.

4:11 1 Kgs 1:1-4
4:13 Eccl 7:19; 9:15
4:14 Gen 41:14, 41-43
4:16 Eccl 1:14
5:1 Exod 3:5; 30:18-20; 1 Sam 15:22; Prov 15:8; 21:27
5:2 Prov 10:19; 20:25; Matt 6:7
5:4 Num 30:2; Pss 50:14; 66:13-14; 76:11
5:5 Prov 20:25; Acts 5:4
5:6 Lev 4:2, 22; Num 15:25
5:7 Eccl 3:14; 12:13
5:8 Ps 12:5; Eccl 4:1; Ezek 18:18; 1 Pet 4:12
5:10 Eccl 2:10-11
5:11 Eccl 2:9

4:9-12 There are advantages to cooperating with others. Life is designed for companionship, not isolation, for intimacy, not loneliness. Some people prefer isolation, thinking they cannot trust anyone. We are not here on earth to serve ourselves, however, but to serve God and others. Don't isolate yourself and try to go it alone. Seek companions; be a team member.

4:13-16 Advancement or getting to the top is meaningless. Position, popularity, and prestige are poor goals for a life's work. Although many seek them, they are shadows without substance. Many people seek recognition for their accomplishments; but people are fickle, changing quickly and easily. How much better to seek God's approval. His love never changes.

5:1 When we enter the house of God, we should have the attitude of being open and ready to listen to God, not to dictate to him what we think he should do.

5:4, 5 Solomon warns his readers about making foolish promises to God. In Israelite culture, making vows was a serious matter. Vows were voluntary, but once made, they were unbreakable (Deuteronomy 23:21-23). It is foolish to make a vow you cannot keep or to play games with God by only partially fulfilling your vow (Proverbs 20:25). It's better not to vow than to make a vow to God and break it. If you make a vow, keep it. (See the note on Matthew 5:33ff.)

5:10, 11 We always want more than we have. Solomon observed that those who spend their lives obsessively seeking after money never find the happiness it promises. Wealth attracts freeloaders and thieves, causes sleeplessness and fear, and ultimately ends in loss because it must be left behind (Mark 10:23-25; Luke 12:16-21). No matter how much you earn, if you try to create happiness by accumulating wealth, you will never have enough. Money in itself is not wrong, but loving money leads to all sorts of sin. Whatever your financial situation, don't depend on money to make you happy. Instead, use what you have for the Lord.

5:12 Prov 3:24

12 People who work hard sleep well, whether they eat little or much. But the rich are
always worrying and seldom get a good night's sleep.

5:13 Eccl 6:2

13 There is another serious problem I have seen in the world. Riches are sometimes
hoarded to the harm of the saver, 14 or they are put into risky investments that turn sour,
and everything is lost. In the end, there is nothing left to pass on to one's children.

5:15 Job 1:21; Ps 49:17; 1 Tim 6:7

15 People who live only for wealth come to the end of their lives as naked and empty-
handed as on the day they were born.

5:16 Prov 11:29; Eccl 1:3; 2:11; 3:9

16 And this, too, is a very serious problem. As people come into this world, so they
depart. All their hard work is for nothing. They have been working for the wind, and
everything will be swept away. 17 Throughout their lives, they live under a cloud—frustrated, discouraged, and angry.

5:17 Eccl 2:23

5:18 Eccl 2:10, 24

18 Even so, I have noticed one thing, at least, that is good. It is good for people to eat
well, drink a good glass of wine, and enjoy their work—whatever they do under the
sun—for however long God lets them live. 19 And it is a good thing to receive wealth
from God and the good health to enjoy it. To enjoy your work and accept your lot in
life—that is indeed a gift from God. 20 People who do this rarely look with sorrow on the
past, for God has given them reasons for joy.

5:19 2 Chr 1:12; Eccl 3:13; 6:2

3. Solomon's practical counsel

6:1 Eccl 5:13

6:2 1 Kgs 3:13; Pss 17:14; 73:7

6 There is another serious tragedy I have seen in our world. 2 God gives great wealth
and honor to some people and gives them everything they could ever want, but then
he doesn't give them the health to enjoy it. They die, and others get it all! This is
meaningless—a sickening tragedy.

6:3 Job 3:16; Eccl 4:3; Isa 14:20; Matt 26:24

3 A man might have a hundred children and live to be very old. But if he finds no
satisfaction in life and in the end does not even get a decent burial, I say he would have
been better off born dead. 4 I realize that his birth would have been meaningless and
ended in darkness. He wouldn't even have had a name, 5 and he would never have seen
the sun or known of its existence. Yet he would have had more peace than he has in
growing up to be an unhappy man. 6 He might live a thousand years twice over but not
find contentment. And since he must die like everyone else—well, what's the use?

6:6 Eccl 2:14

6:7 Prov 16:26

7 All people spend their lives scratching for food, but they never seem to have enough.
8 Considering this, do wise people really have any advantage over fools? Do poor people
gain anything by being wise and knowing how to act in front of others?

6:8 Eccl 2:15

6:9 Eccl 1:14; 11:9

9 Enjoy what you have rather than desiring what you don't have. Just dreaming about
nice things is meaningless; it is like chasing the wind.

The Future—Determined and Unknown

6:10 Gen 3:17-19; Job 9:32; 40:2; Eccl 1:9; 3:15; Isa 45:9

10 Everything has already been decided. It was known long ago what each person would
be. So there's no use arguing with God about your destiny.
11 The more words you speak, the less they mean. So why overdo it?
12 In the few days of our empty lives, who knows how our days can best be spent? And
who can tell what will happen in the future after we are gone?

6:11 Hos 12:1

5:19, 20 God wants us to view what we have (whether it is much or little) with the right perspective—our possessions are a gift from God. Although they are not the source of joy, they are a reason to rejoice because every good thing comes from God. We should focus more on the Giver than the gift. We can be content with what we have when we realize that in God we have everything we need.

6:1–8:15 In this section, Solomon shows that having the right attitude about God can help us deal with present injustices. Prosperity is not always good, and adversity is not always bad. But God is always good; if we live as he wants us to, we will be content.

6:1-6 This person has died without being able to enjoy his wealth and honor. Even if he had lived a long life, it is ultimately meaningless in itself because all that he has accumulated is left behind. Everyone dies, and both rich and poor end up in the grave. Many people work hard to prolong life and improve their physical condition. Yet people spend little time or effort on their spiritual health. How shortsighted it is to work hard to extend this life and not take the time to prepare for eternity.

6:10 God knows and directs everything that happens, and he is in complete control over our lives, even though at times it may not seem like it. How foolish it is for us to contend with our Creator, who knows us completely and can see the future. (See also Jeremiah 18:6; Romans 9:19-24.)

6:12 Solomon is stating the profound truth that we cannot predict what the future holds. The only one who knows what will happen after we're gone is God. No human knows the future, so each day must be lived for its own value. Solomon is arguing against the notion that human beings can take charge of their own destiny. In all our plans we should look up to God, not just ahead to the future.

Wisdom for Life

7 A good reputation is more valuable than the most expensive perfume. In the same
way, the day you die is better than the day you are born.
2 It is better to spend your time at funerals than at festivals. For you are going to die,
and you should think about it while there is still time.
3 Sorrow is better than laughter, for sadness has a refining influence on us.
4 A wise person thinks much about death, while the fool thinks only about having a
good time now.
5 It is better to be criticized by a wise person than to be praised by a fool! 6 Indeed, a
fool's laughter is quickly gone, like thorns crackling in a fire. This also is meaningless.
7 Extortion turns wise people into fools, and bribes corrupt the heart.
8 Finishing is better than starting. Patience is better than pride.
9 Don't be quick-tempered, for anger is the friend of fools.
10 Don't long for "the good old days," for you don't know whether they were any better
than today.
11 Being wise is as good as being rich; in fact, it is better. 12 Wisdom or money can get
you almost anything, but it's important to know that only wisdom can save your life.
13 Notice the way God does things; then fall into line. Don't fight the ways of God, for
who can straighten out what he has made crooked?
14 Enjoy prosperity while you can. But when hard times strike, realize that both come
from God. That way you will realize that nothing is certain in this life.

The Limits of Human Wisdom

15 In this meaningless life, I have seen everything, including the fact that some good
people die young and some wicked people live on and on. 16 So don't be too good or too
wise! Why destroy yourself? 17 On the other hand, don't be too wicked either—don't be
a fool! Why should you die before your time? 18 So try to walk a middle course—but
those who fear God will succeed either way.
19 A wise person is stronger than the ten leading citizens of a town!
20 There is not a single person in all the earth who is always good and never sins.
21 Don't eavesdrop on others—you may hear your servant laughing at you. 22 For you
know how often you yourself have laughed at others.
23 All along I have tried my best to let wisdom guide my thoughts and actions. I said

7:1 Prov 22:1
7:2 Ps 90:12
7:3 2 Cor 7:10
7:5 Ps 141:5; Prov 6:23; 13:18; 15:31-32; 25:12
7:7 Exod 23:8; Deut 16:19; Prov 17:23
7:8 Prov 14:29; 16:32; Gal 5:22; Eph 4:2
7:9 Prov 14:17; Jas 1:19
7:12 Prov 3:18; 8:35
7:13 Eccl 1:15; 3:11; 8:17
7:14 Deut 8:5; 26:11; Eccl 3:22; 9:7; 11:9
7:15 Eccl 6:12; 8:12-14; 9:9
7:18 Eccl 3:14; 5:7; 8:12-13
7:20 1 Kgs 8:46; 2 Chr 6:36; Ps 143:2; Prov 20:9; Rom 3:23

7:1-4 This seems to contradict Solomon's previous advice to eat, drink, and find satisfaction in one's work—to enjoy what God has given. We are to enjoy what we have while we can but realize that adversity also strikes. Adversity reminds us that life is short, teaches us to live wisely, and refines our character. Christianity and Judaism see value in suffering and sorrow. The Greeks and Romans despised it; Eastern religions seek to live above it; but Christians and Jews see it as a refining fire. Most would agree that we learn more about God from difficult times than from happy times. Do you try to avoid sorrow and suffering at all cost? See your struggles as great opportunities to learn from God.

7:2, 4 Many people avoid thinking about death, refuse to face it, and are reluctant to attend funerals. Solomon is not encouraging us to think morbidly, but he knows that it is helpful to think clearly about death. It reminds us that there is still time for change, time to examine the direction of our life, and time to confess our sins and find forgiveness from God. Because everyone will eventually die, it makes sense to plan ahead to experience God's mercy rather than his justice.

7:7 Money talks, and it can confuse those who would otherwise judge fairly. We hear about bribes given to judges, police officers, and witnesses. Bribes are given to hurt those who tell the truth and help those who oppose it. The person who is involved in extortion or takes a bribe is indeed a fool, no matter how wise he thought he was beforehand. It is said that everyone has a price, but those who are truly wise cannot be bought at any price.

7:8 To finish what we start takes hard work, wisdom, self-discipline, and patience. Anyone with vision can start a big project. But vision without wisdom often results in unfinished projects and goals.

7:14 God allows both good times and bad times to come to everyone. He blends them in our lives in such a way that we can't predict the future or count on human wisdom and power. We usually give ourselves the credit for the good times. Then in bad times, we tend to blame God without thanking him for the good that comes out of it. When life appears certain and controllable, don't let self-satisfaction or complacency make you too comfortable, or God may allow bad times to drive you back to him. When life seems uncertain and uncontrollable, don't despair—God is in control and will bring good results out of tough times.

7:16-18 How can a person be too good or too wise? This is a warning against pride—legalism or false righteousness. Solomon was saying that some people become so good or wise *in their own eyes* that they become deluded by their own religious acts. They are so rigid or narrow in their views that they lose their sensitivity to the true reason for being good—to honor God. Balance is important. God created us to be whole people who seek his righteousness and goodness. Thus, we should avoid both extremes of legalism and immorality.

7:23-25 Solomon, the wisest man in the world, confessed how difficult it had been to act and think wisely. He emphasized that no matter how much we know, there are always mysteries we will never understand. So thinking you have wisdom is a sure sign that you don't.

7:24 Deut 30:11-14 Job 11:7; 37:23 Rom 11:33
7:25 Eccl 1:17
7:26 Prov 5:4; 6:23-24; 7:23; 22:14
7:28 1 Kgs 11:3
7:29 Gen 1:27

to myself, "I am determined to be wise." But it didn't really work. 24 Wisdom is always
distant and very difficult to find. 25 I searched everywhere, determined to find wisdom
and to understand the reason for things. I was determined to prove to myself that
wickedness is stupid and that foolishness is madness.
26 I discovered that a seductive woman is more bitter than death. Her passion is a trap,
and her soft hands will bind you. Those who please God will escape from her, but sinners
will be caught in her snare.
27 "This is my conclusion," says the Teacher. "I came to this result after looking into
the matter from every possible angle. 28 Just one out of every thousand men I interviewed
can be said to be upright, but not one woman! 29 I discovered that God created people to
be upright, but they have each turned to follow their own downward path."

8:1 Exod 34:29-30 Deut 28:50
8:2 Exod 22:11 2 Sam 21:7 Ezek 17:18
8:4 Dan 4:35
8:5 Exod 1:17-21 Prov 12:21
8:6 Eccl 3:1, 17, 22
8:8 Deut 20:5-8 Ps 49:7-9
8:9 Eccl 4:1, 16; 5:8
8:11 Exod 34:6 Ps 86:15 Rom 2:4-5 2 Pet 3:9
8:12 Deut 4:40 Ps 37:11 Prov 1:33 Isa 3:10
8:13 Isa 3:11
8:14 Job 21:7 Ps 73:3, 12 Jer 12:1 Mal 3:15

8 How wonderful to be wise, to be able to analyze and interpret things. Wisdom lights
up a person's face, softening its hardness.

Obedience to the King

2 Obey the king because you have vowed before God to do this. 3 Don't try to avoid doing
your duty, and don't take a stand with those who plot evil. For the king will punish those
who disobey him. 4 The king's command is backed by great power. No one can resist or
question it. 5 Those who obey him will not be punished. Those who are wise will find a
time and a way to do what is right. 6 Yes, there is a time and a way for everything, even
as people's troubles lie heavily upon them.
7 Indeed, how can people avoid what they don't know is going to happen? 8 None of
us can hold back our spirit from departing. None of us has the power to prevent the day
of our death. There is no escaping that obligation, that dark battle. And in the face of
death, wickedness will certainly not rescue those who practice it.

The Wicked and the Righteous

9 I have thought deeply about all that goes on here in the world, where people have the power
to hurt each other. 10 I have seen wicked people buried with honor. How strange that they
were the very ones who frequented the Temple and are praised* in the very city where they
committed their crimes! 11 When a crime is not punished, people feel it is safe to do wrong.
12 But even though a person sins a hundred times and still lives a long time, I know that those
who fear God will be better off. 13 The wicked will never live long, good lives, for they do
not fear God. Their days will never grow long like the evening shadows.
14 And this is not all that is meaningless in our world. In this life, good people are often
treated as though they were wicked, and wicked people are often treated as though they
were good. This is so meaningless!
15 So I recommend having fun, because there is nothing better for people to do in this
world than to eat, drink, and enjoy life. That way they will experience some happiness
along with all the hard work God gives them.

8:10 As in some Hebrew manuscripts and Greek version; many Hebrew manuscripts read *and are forgotten.*

7:27, 28 Did Solomon think women were not capable of being upright (wise and good)? No, because in the book of Proverbs he personified wisdom as a responsible woman. The point of Solomon's statement is not that women are unwise, but that hardly anyone, man or woman, is upright before God. In his search, Solomon found that goodness and wisdom were almost as scarce among men as among women, even though men were given a religious education program in his culture and women were not. In effect, the verse is saying, "I have found only one in a thousand people who is wise in God's eyes. No, I have found even fewer than that!"

8:1 Wisdom is the ability to see life from God's perspective and then to know the best course of action to take. Most people would agree that wisdom is a valuable asset, but how can we acquire it? Proverbs 9:10 teaches that the fear of the Lord (respect and honor) is the beginning of wisdom. Wisdom comes from knowing and trusting God; it is not merely the way to find God. Knowing God will lead to understanding and then to sharing this knowledge with others.

8:10 This verse probably refers to how we quickly forget the evil done by some people after they have died. Returning from the cemetery, we praise them in the very city where they did their evil deeds.

8:11 If God doesn't punish us immediately for sin, we must not assume that he doesn't care or that sin has no consequences. When a young child does something wrong and is not punished, it is much easier for the child to repeat the act. Remember, God knows every wrong we commit, and one day we will have to answer for all that we have done (12:14).

8:15 Solomon recommends the remedy for life's unanswered questions: joy and contentment. We must accept each day with its measure of work, food, and pleasure. Let us learn to enjoy what God has given to refresh and strengthen us so we may continue his work.

16 In my search for wisdom, I tried to observe everything that goes on all across the
earth. I discovered that there is ceaseless activity, day and night. 17 This reminded me that
no one can discover everything God has created in our world, no matter how hard they
work at it. Not even the wisest people know everything, even if they say they do.

4. Solomon's final conclusion

Death Comes to All

9 This, too, I carefully explored: Even though the actions of godly and wise people
are in God's hands, no one knows whether or not God will show them favor in this
life. 2 The same destiny ultimately awaits everyone, whether they are righteous or
wicked, good or bad,* ceremonially clean or unclean, religious or irreligious. Good
people receive the same treatment as sinners, and people who take oaths are treated like
people who don't.

3 It seems so tragic that one fate comes to all. That is why people are not more careful
to be good. Instead, they choose their own mad course, for they have no hope. There is
nothing ahead but death anyway. 4 There is hope only for the living. For as they say, "It
is better to be a live dog than a dead lion!"

5 The living at least know they will die, but the dead know nothing. They have no
further reward, nor are they remembered. 6 Whatever they did in their lifetime—loving,
hating, envying—is all long gone. They no longer have a part in anything here on earth.
7 So go ahead. Eat your food and drink your wine with a happy heart, for God approves
of this! 8 Wear fine clothes, with a dash of cologne!

9 Live happily with the woman you love through all the meaningless days of life that
God has given you in this world. The wife God gives you is your reward for all your
earthly toil. 10 Whatever you do, do well. For when you go to the grave, there will be no
work or planning or knowledge or wisdom.

11 I have observed something else in this world of ours. The fastest runner doesn't
always win the race, and the strongest warrior doesn't always win the battle. The wise
are often poor, and the skillful are not necessarily wealthy. And those who are educated
don't always lead successful lives. It is all decided by chance, by being at the right place
at the right time.

12 People can never predict when hard times might come. Like fish in a net or birds in
a snare, people are often caught by sudden tragedy.

Thoughts on Wisdom and Folly

13 Here is another bit of wisdom that has impressed me as I have watched the way our
world works. 14 There was a small town with only a few people living in it, and a great

8:16 Eccl 1:13-14

9:1 Deut 33:3; Eccl 9:6; 10:14

9:2 Job 9:22; Eccl 2:14; 3:19; 6:6; 7:2

9:3 Eccl 1:17; 8:11; 9:2

9:5 Job 14:21; Ps 88:12; Isa 26:14

9:7 Eccl 2:24

9:8 Ps 23:5; Rev 3:4

9:9 Eccl 6:12; 7:15

9:10 Gen 37:35; Job 21:13; Rom 12:11; Col 3:23

9:11 Deut 8:17-18; 1 Sam 6:9; 2 Chr 20:15; Ps 76:5; Amos 2:14-15; Zech 4:6

9:12 Isa 24:18; Hos 9:8; Luke 21:34-35

9:2 As in Greek and Syriac versions, and Latin Vulgate; Hebrew lacks *or bad*.

8:16, 17 Even if he had access to all the world's wisdom, the wisest man would know very little. No one can fully comprehend God and all that he has done, and there are always more questions than answers. But the unknown should not cast a shadow over our joy, faith, or work because we know that someone greater is in control and that we can put our trust in him. Don't let what you don't know about the future destroy the joy God wants to give you today.

9:2 "The same destiny ultimately awaits everyone" means that all will die.

9:5, 10 When Solomon says the dead know nothing and that there is no work, planning, knowledge, or wisdom after death, he is not contrasting life with afterlife, but life with death. After you die, you can't change what you have done. Resurrection to a new life after death was a vague concept for Old Testament believers. It was only made clear after Jesus rose from the dead.

9:7-10 Considering the uncertainties of the future and the certainty of death, Solomon recommends enjoying life as God's gift. He may have been criticizing those who put off all present pleasures in order to accumulate wealth, much like those who get caught up in today's rat race. Solomon asks, "What is your wealth really worth, anyway?" Because the future is so uncertain, we should enjoy God's gifts while we are able.

9:9 Solomon also wrote a proverb about marriage. "The man who finds a wife finds a treasure and receives favor from the LORD" (Proverbs 18:22). How sad it would be to be married and not appreciate or enjoy the companion God has given you.

9:10, 11 It isn't difficult to think of cases where the fastest and the strongest don't win, the wise are poor, and the skillful are unrewarded with wealth or honor. Some people see such examples and call life unfair, and they are right. The world is finite, and sin has twisted life, making it what God did not intend. Solomon is trying to reduce our expectations. The book of Proverbs emphasizes how life would go if everyone acted fairly; Ecclesiastes explains what usually happens in our sinful and imperfect world. We must keep our perspective. Don't let the inequities of life keep you from earnest, dedicated work. We serve God, not people (see Colossians 3:23).

9:13-18 Our society honors wealth, attractiveness, and success above wisdom. Yet wisdom is a greater asset than strength, although it is often overlooked. Even though it is more effective, wisdom from people who are poor often goes unheeded. From this parable we can learn to appreciate wisdom, no matter whom it comes from.

king came with his army and besieged it. 15 There was a poor, wise man living there who knew how to save the town, and so it was rescued. But afterward no one thought any more about him. 16 Then I realized that though wisdom is better than strength, those who are wise will be despised if they are poor. What they say will not be appreciated for long. 17 But even so, the quiet words of a wise person are better than the shouts of a foolish king. 18 A wise person can overcome weapons of war, but one sinner can destroy much that is good.

10

Dead flies will cause even a bottle of perfume to stink! Yes, an ounce of foolishness can outweigh a pound of wisdom and honor.

2 The hearts of the wise lead them to do right, and the hearts of the foolish lead them to do evil. 3 You can identify fools just by the way they walk down the street!

4 If your boss is angry with you, don't quit! A quiet spirit can overcome even great mistakes.

5 There is another evil I have seen as I have watched the world go by. Kings and rulers make a grave mistake 6 if they give foolish people great authority, and if they fail to give people of proven worth their rightful place of dignity. 7 I have even seen servants riding like princes—and princes walking like servants.

8 When you dig a well, you may fall in. When you demolish an old wall, you could be bitten by a snake. 9 When you work in a quarry, stones might fall and crush you! When you chop wood, there is danger with each stroke of your ax! Such are the risks of life.

10 Since a dull ax requires great strength, sharpen the blade. That's the value of wisdom; it helps you succeed.

11 It does no good to charm a snake after it has bitten you.

12 It is pleasant to listen to wise words, but the speech of fools brings them to ruin. 13 Since fools base their thoughts on foolish premises, their conclusions will be wicked madness.

14 Foolish people claim to know all about the future and tell everyone the details! But who can really know what is going to happen?

15 Fools are so exhausted by a little work that they have no strength for even the simplest tasks.

16 Destruction is certain for the land whose king is a child* and whose leaders feast in the morning. 17 Happy is the land whose king is a nobleman and whose leaders feast only to gain strength for their work, not to get drunk.

18 Laziness lets the roof leak, and soon the rafters begin to rot.

19 A party gives laughter, and wine gives happiness, and money gives everything!

20 Never make light of the king, even in your thoughts. And don't make fun of a rich man, either. A little bird may tell them what you have said.

10:16 Or *whose king is a servant.*

9:15 2 Sam 20:22
9:16 Prov 21:22
9:17 Eccl 7:5; 10:12
9:18 Josh 7:1-26; 2 Kgs 21:2-17
10:1 Exod 30:25
10:3 Prov 13:16; 18:2
10:4 1 Sam 25:24-33; Prov 25:15; Eccl 8:3
10:6 Esth 3:1; Prov 28:12; 29:2
10:7 Esth 6:8; Prov 19:10
10:8 Ps 7:15; Prov 26:27; Amos 5:19
10:11 Ps 58:45; Jer 8:17
10:12 Prov 10:14, 32; 22:11
10:14 Prov 15:2; Eccl 3:22; 5:3; 6:12; 7:14; 8:7
10:16 Isa 3:4-5, 12; 5:11
10:18 Prov 24:30-34
10:19 Judg 9:13; Ps 104:15; Eccl 2:3; 7:12
10:20 Exod 22:28; 2 Kgs 6:12; Luke 12:3; Acts 23:5

10:4 This proverb has implications for employer/employee relationships. Employees should ride out the temper tantrums of their employer. If we quietly do our work and don't get upset, the employer will probably get over his or her anger and calm down.

10:5-7 By describing these circumstances that aren't fair or don't make sense, Solomon is saying that wealth alone can't bring justice. Solomon continues to build to his conclusion that everything we have (from wisdom to riches) is nothing without God. But when God uses what little we have, it becomes all we could ever want or need.

10:10 Trying to do anything without the necessary skills or tools is like chopping wood with a dull ax. If your tool is dull, you should sharpen it to do a better job. Similarly, if you lack skills, you should sharpen them through training and practice. "Sharpening the blade" means recognizing where a problem exists, acquiring or honing the skills (or tools) to do the job better, and then going out and doing it. Find the areas of your life where your "ax" is dull, and sharpen your skills so you can be more effective for God's work.

10:16-18 When the Israelites had immature and irresponsible leaders, their nation fell. The books of 1 and 2 Kings describe the decline of the kingdoms when the leaders were concerned only about themselves. These verses pinpoint the basic problems of these leaders—selfishness and laziness.

10:19 Government leaders, businesses, families, even churches get trapped into thinking money is the answer to every problem. We throw money at our problems. But just as the thrill of wine is only temporary, the soothing effect of the last purchase soon wears off, and we have to buy more. Scripture recognizes that money is necessary for survival, but it warns against the love of money (see Matthew 6:24; 1 Timothy 6:10; Hebrews 13:5). Money is dangerous because it deceives us into thinking that wealth is the easiest way to get everything we want. The love of money is sinful because we trust money rather than God to solve our problems. Those who pursue its empty promises will one day discover that they have nothing because they are spiritually bankrupt.

Generosity and Diligence

11 Give generously, for your gifts will return to you later. 2 Divide your gifts among
many, for you do not know what risks might lie ahead.
3 When the clouds are heavy, the rains come down.
When a tree falls, whether south or north, there it lies.
4 If you wait for perfect conditions, you will never get anything done.
5 God's ways are as hard to discern as the pathways of the wind, and as mysterious as
a tiny baby being formed in a mother's womb.
6 Be sure to stay busy and plant a variety of crops, for you never know which will
grow—perhaps they all will.

Advice for Old and Young

7 Light is sweet; it's wonderful to see the sun! 8 When people live to be very old, let them
rejoice in every day of life. But let them also remember that the dark days will be many.
Everything still to come is meaningless.
9 Young man, it's wonderful to be young! Enjoy every minute of it. Do everything you
want to do; take it all in. But remember that you must give an account to God for
everything you do. 10 So banish grief and pain, but remember that youth, with a whole
life before it, still faces the threat of meaninglessness.

12 Don't let the excitement of youth cause you to forget your Creator. Honor him in
your youth before you grow old and no longer enjoy living. 2 It will be too late
then to remember him, when the light of the sun and moon and stars is dim to your old
eyes, and there is no silver lining left among the clouds. 3 Your limbs will tremble with
age, and your strong legs will grow weak. Your teeth will be too few to do their work,
and you will be blind, too. 4 And when your teeth are gone, keep your lips tightly closed
when you eat! Even the chirping of birds will wake you up. But you yourself will be deaf
and tuneless, with a quavering voice. 5 You will be afraid of heights and of falling,
white-haired and withered, dragging along without any sexual desire. You will be
standing at death's door. And as you near your everlasting home, the mourners will walk
along the streets.
6 Yes, remember your Creator now while you are young, before the silver cord of life
snaps and the golden bowl is broken. Don't wait until the water jar is smashed at the
spring and the pulley is broken at the well. 7 For then the dust will return to the earth, and
the spirit will return to God who gave it.

11:1 Deut 15:7-11; Prov 19:17; Isa 32:20; Matt 10:42; 2 Cor 9:8; Gal 6:9; Heb 6:10
11:5 Ps 139:13-16; Eccl 1:15; 3:10; John 3:8
11:9 Num 15:39; Ps 81:12; Acts 21:25; Rom 14:10
11:10 2 Cor 7:1; 2 Tim 2:22
12:1 Deut 8:18; 2 Sam 19:35; Neh 4:14; Pss 63:6; 119:55; Eccl 11:8
12:2 Isa 13:10; Ezek 32:7-8; Joel 3:5; Matt 24:29
12:7 Gen 3:19; Job 34:14; Ps 104:29; Eccl 3:20-21; Isa 57:16; Zech 12:1; Luke 23:46; Acts 7:59

11:1-5 In these verses Solomon summarizes that life involves both risk and opportunity. Because life has no guarantees, we must be prepared. "Give generously" because life has opportunities and we must seize them. Solomon does not support a stingy, despairing attitude. Just because life is uncertain does not mean we should do nothing. We need a spirit of trust and adventure, facing life's risks and opportunities with God-directed enthusiasm and faith.

11:4 Waiting for perfect conditions will mean inactivity. This practical insight is especially applicable to our spiritual life. If we wait for the perfect time and place for personal Bible reading, we will never begin. If we wait for a perfect church, we will never join. If we wait for the perfect ministry, we will never serve. Take steps now to grow spiritually. Don't wait for conditions that may never exist.

11:7, 8 Solomon is no dreary pessimist in 11:7–12:14. He encourages us to rejoice in every day but to remember that eternity is far longer than a person's life span. Psalm 90:12 says, "Teach us to make the most of our time, so that we may grow in wisdom." The wise person does not just think about the moment and its impact; he or she takes the long-range view toward eternity. Approach your decisions from God's perspective—consider their impact 10 years from now and into eternity. Live with the attitude that although our life is short, we will live with God forever.

11:9, 10 We often hear people say, "It doesn't matter." But many of your choices will be irreversible—they will stay with you for a lifetime. What you do when you're young *does* matter. Enjoy life now, but don't do anything physically, morally, or spiritually that will prevent you from enjoying life when you are old.

12:1 A life without God can produce bitterness, loneliness, and hopelessness in old age. A life centered around God is fulfilling and can be richer and more bearable when we are faced with disabilities, sickness, or handicaps. Being young is exciting. But the excitement of youth can become a barrier to closeness with God if it makes young people focus on passing pleasures instead of eternal values. Make your strength available to God when it is still yours—during your youthful years. Don't waste it on evil or meaningless activities that become bad habits and make you callous. Seek God now.

12:6-8 The silver cord, golden bowl, water jar, and pulley symbolize life's fragility. How easily death comes to us; how swiftly and unexpectedly we may return to the dust from which we came. Therefore, we should recognize life as a precious resource to be used wisely and not squandered frivolously.

12:7, 8 Stripped of the life-giving spirit breathed into us by God, our bodies return to dust. Stripped of God's purpose, our work is in vain. Stripped of God's love, our service is futile. We must put God first over all we do and in all we do because without him we have nothing. Knowing that life is futile without God motivates the wise person to seek God first.

12:8 Eccl 1:2

8"All is meaningless," says the Teacher, "utterly meaningless."

Concluding Thoughts

12:9 1 Kgs 4:32

12:11 Ezra 9:8 Isa 22:23 Acts 2:37

12:13 Deut 4:2; 6:2; 10:12 Eccl 3:14; 8:5 Mic 6:8

12:14 Matt 10:26 Rom 2:16 1 Cor 4:5

9Because the Teacher was wise, he taught the people everything he knew. He collected
proverbs and classified them. 10Indeed, the Teacher taught the plain truth, and he did so
in an interesting way.

11A wise teacher's words spur students to action and emphasize important truths. The
collected sayings of the wise are like guidance from a shepherd.

12But, my child,* be warned: There is no end of opinions ready to be expressed.
Studying them can go on forever and become very exhausting!

13Here is my final conclusion: Fear God and obey his commands, for this is the duty
of every person. 14God will judge us for everything we do, including every secret thing,
whether good or bad.

12:12 Hebrew *my son.*

12:12 There is no end of opinions about life and philosophies about how we should live that could be read and studied forever. It is not wrong to study these opinions, but because our life on earth is so short, we should make the best use of time by learning the important truths in God's Word. They affect this life and eternity. Wise students of the Bible will understand and do what it says.

12:13, 14 In his conclusion, Solomon presents his antidotes for the two main ailments presented in this book. Those who lack purpose and direction in life should fear God and obey his commands. Those who think life is unfair should remember that God will review every person's life to determine how he or she has responded to him, and he will bring every deed into judgment. Have you committed your life to God? Does your life measure up to his standards?

12:13, 14 The book of Ecclesiastes cannot be interpreted correctly without reading these final verses. No matter what the mysteries and apparent contradictions of life are, we must work toward the single purpose of knowing God.

In Ecclesiastes, Solomon shows us that we should enjoy life, but this does not exempt us from obeying God's commands. We should search for purpose and meaning in life, but they cannot be found in human endeavors. We should acknowledge the evil, foolishness, and injustice in life yet maintain a positive attitude and strong faith in God.

All people will have to stand before God and be judged for what they have done in this life. We will not be able to use the inequities of life as an excuse for failing to live properly. We need to (1) recognize that human effort apart from God is futile; (2) put God first—now; (3) receive everything good as a gift from God; and (4) realize that God will judge every person's life, whether good or evil. How strange that people spend their lives striving for the joy that God gives freely, as a gift.

SONG OF SONGS

VITAL STATISTICS

PURPOSE:
To tell of the love between a bridegroom (King Solomon) and his bride, to affirm the sanctity of marriage, and to picture God's love for his people

AUTHOR: Solomon

DATE WRITTEN:
Probably early in Solomon's reign

SETTING:
Israel—the Shulammite woman's garden and the king's palace

KEY VERSE:
"I am my lover's, and my lover is mine. He grazes among the lilies!" (6:3).

KEY PEOPLE:
King Solomon, the Shulammite woman, and friends

SATURATED with stories of sexual escapades, secret rendezvous, and extramarital affairs, today's media teach that immorality means freedom, perversion is natural, and commitment is old-fashioned. Sex, created by God and pronounced good in Eden, has been twisted, exploited, and turned into an urgent, illicit, casual, and self-gratifying activity. Love has turned into lust, giving into getting, and lasting commitment into "no strings attached."

In reality, sexual intercourse, the physical and emotional union of male and female, should be a holy means of celebrating love, producing children, and experiencing pleasure, protected by the commitment of marriage.

God thinks sex is important, and Scripture contains numerous guidelines for its use and warnings about its misuse. And sex is always mentioned in the context of a loving relationship between husband and wife. Perhaps the highlight of this is Song of Songs, the intimate story of a man and a woman, their love, courtship, and marriage. Solomon probably wrote this "song" in his youth, before being overtaken by his own obsession with women, sex, and pleasure.

A moving story, drama, and poem, Song of Songs features the love dialogue between a simple Jewish maiden (the young woman) and her lover (Solomon, the king). They describe in intimate detail their feelings for each other and their longings to be together. Throughout the dialogue, sex and marriage are put in their proper, God-given perspective.

There has been much debate over the meaning of this song. Some say it is an allegory of God's love for Israel and/or for the church. Others say it is a literal story about married love. But in reality, it is both—a historical story with two layers of meaning. On one level, we learn about love, marriage, and sex; and on the other level, we see God's overwhelming love for his people. As you read Song of Songs, remember that you are loved by God, and commit yourself to seeing life, sex, and marriage from his point of view.

THE BLUEPRINT

1. The wedding day (1:1—2:7)
2. Memories of courtship (2:8—3:5)
3. Memories of engagement (3:6—5:1)
4. A troubling dream (5:2—6:3)
5. Praising the bride's beauty (6:4—7:9)
6. The bride's tender appeal (7:10—8:4)
7. The power of love (8:5–14)

Song of Songs is a wedding song honoring marriage. The most explicit statements on sex in the Bible can be found in this book. It has often been criticized down through the centuries because of its sensuous language. The purity and sacredness of love represented here, however, are greatly needed in our day in which distorted attitudes about love and marriage are commonplace. God created sex and intimacy, and they are holy and good when enjoyed within marriage. A husband and wife honor God when they love and enjoy each other.

MEGATHEMES

THEME	EXPLANATION	IMPORTANCE
Sex	Sex is God's gift to his creatures. He endorses sex but restricts its expression to those committed to each other in marriage.	God wants sex to be motivated by love and commitment, not lust. It is for mutual pleasure, not selfish enjoyment.
Love	As the relationship developed, the beauty and wonder of a romance unfolded between Solomon and his bride. The intense power of love affected the hearts, minds, and bodies of the two lovers.	Because love is such a powerful expression of feeling and commitment between two people, it is not to be regarded casually. We are not to manipulate others into loving us, and love should not be prematurely encouraged in a relationship.
Commitment	The power of love requires more than the language of feeling to protect it. Sexual expression is such an integral part of our selfhood that we need the boundary of marriage to safeguard our love. Marriage is the celebration of daily commitment to each other.	While romance keeps a marriage interesting, commitment keeps romance from dwindling away. The decision to commit yourself to your spouse alone *begins* at the marriage altar. It must be maintained day by day.
Beauty	The two lovers praise the beauty they see in each other. The language they use shows the spontaneity and mystery of love. Praise should not be limited to physical beauty; beautiful personality and moral purity should also be praised.	Our love for someone makes him or her appear beautiful to us. As you consider marriage, don't just look for physical attractiveness in a person. Look for the inner qualities that don't fade with time—spiritual commitment, integrity, sensitivity, and sincerity.
Problems	Over time, feelings of loneliness, indifference, and isolation came between Solomon and his bride. During those times, love grew cold, and barriers were raised.	Through careful communication, lovers can be reconciled, commitment can be renewed, and romance refreshed. Don't let walls come between you and your partner. Take care of problems while they are still small.

1. The wedding day

1:1 1 Kgs 4:32
1:2 Song 1:4; 4:10
1:3 Eccl 7:1; Song 4:10; John 12:3
1:4 Ps 45:14-15

1 This is Solomon's song of songs, more wonderful than any other.
*Young Woman:** 2"Kiss me again and again, for your love is sweeter than wine.
3How fragrant your cologne, and how pleasing your name! No wonder all
the young women love you! 4Take me with you. Come, let's run! Bring me
into your bedroom, O my king.*"

1:1 The headings identifying the speakers are not in the original text, though the Hebrew usually gives clues by means of the gender of the person speaking. **1:4** Or *The king has brought me into his bedroom.*

1:1 Solomon, a son of King David, became king and was chosen by God to build the Temple in Jerusalem. God gave him extraordinary wisdom. Much of his reign was characterized by wisdom and reverence for God, although toward the end of his life he became proud and turned from God. Read about Solomon in 1 Kings 1–11 and 1 Chronicles 28—2 Chronicles 9. Solomon wrote more than 3,000 proverbs (see the book of Proverbs) and over 1,000 songs, one of which is this book, Song of Songs. His Profile is found in 1 Kings 4.

1:1ff Solomon frequently visited the various parts of his kingdom. One day, as he visited some royal vineyards in the north, his royal entourage came by surprise upon a beautiful peasant woman tending the vines. Embarrassed, she ran from them. But Solomon could not forget her. Later, disguised as a shepherd, he returned to the vineyards and won her love. Then he revealed his true identity and asked her to return to Jerusalem with him. Solomon and his beloved are being married in the palace as this book begins.

The Song of Songs is a series of seven poems, not necessarily in chronological order, describing the first meeting of Solomon and the peasant woman, their engagement, their wedding, their wedding night, and the growth of their marriage after the wedding.

Young Women of Jerusalem: “How happy we are for him! We praise his love even
more than wine.”
Young Woman: 5“I am dark and beautiful, O women of Jerusalem, tanned as the dark
tents of Kedar. Yes, even as the tents of Solomon!
6“Don’t look down on me, you fair city girls, just because my complexion is
so dark. The sun has burned my skin. My brothers were angry with me and sent
me out to tend the vineyards in the hot sun. Now see what it has done to me!*
7“Tell me, O my love, where are you leading your flock today? Where will
you rest your sheep at noon? For why should I wander like a prostitute* among
the flocks of your companions?”
Young Man: 8“If you don’t know, O most beautiful woman, follow the trail of my
flock to the shepherds’ tents, and there feed your young goats. 9What a lovely
filly you are, my beloved one!* 10How lovely are your cheeks, with your earrings setting them afire! How stately is your neck, accented with a long string
of jewels. 11We will make earrings of gold for you and beads of silver.”
Young Woman: 12“The king is lying on his couch, enchanted by the fragrance of my
perfume. 13My lover is like a sachet of myrrh lying between my breasts. 14He is
like a bouquet of flowers in the gardens of En-gedi.”
Young Man: 15“How beautiful you are, my beloved, how beautiful! Your eyes are soft
like doves.”
Young Woman: 16“What a lovely, pleasant sight you are, my love, as we lie here on
the grass, 17shaded by cedar trees and spreading firs.”

2 *Young Woman:* “I am the rose of Sharon, the lily of the valley.”
Young Man: 2“Yes, compared to other women, my beloved is like a lily among thorns.”
Young Woman: 3“And compared to other youths, my lover is like the finest apple tree
in the orchard. I am seated in his delightful shade, and his fruit is delicious to eat.
4He brings me to the banquet hall, so everyone can see how much he loves me.
5Oh, feed me with your love—your ‘raisins’ and your ‘apples’—for I am utterly
lovesick! 6His left hand is under my head, and his right hand embraces me.
7“Promise me, O women of Jerusalem, by the swift gazelles and the deer of
the wild, not to awaken love until the time is right.*

1:6 Ps 69:8; Song 8:11
1:7 Song 2:16; 3:1-4; 8:13
1:8 Song 5:9; 6:1
1:9 2 Chr 1:16-17
1:10 Gen 24:53; Song 5:13
1:12 Song 4:13-14; Mark 14:3
1:13 Ps 45:8; John 19:39
1:14 1 Sam 23:29; Song 4:13
1:15 Song 1:16; 2:10, 13; 4:1
1:17 1 Kgs 6:9-10; 2 Chr 3:5; Jer 22:14; Ezek 41:16
2:3 Song 8:5
2:4 Ps 63:2-5; Song 1:4
2:6 Prov 4:8; Song 8:3
2:7 Gen 49:21; Song 3:5; 5:8; 8:14; Hab 3:19

1:6 Hebrew *My own vineyard I have neglected.* **1:7** Hebrew *like a veiled woman.* **1:9** Hebrew *I compare you, my beloved, to a mare among Pharaoh’s chariots.* **2:7** Or *not to awaken love until it is ready.*

1:1ff There are three characters or groups of characters in this book: the girl (the “young woman”), Solomon (the “young man”), and “young women of Jerusalem.” The girl who caught Solomon’s attention may have been from Shunem, a farming community about 60 miles north of Jerusalem. Her tanned skin indicates that she probably worked outside in the vineyards (1:6); thus, she may not have been from the upper class. The young women of Jerusalem include either members of Solomon’s harem or workers in the palace.

1:1-4 This vivid description of a love relationship begins with a picture of love itself. Love is “sweeter than wine”; it makes the lovers rejoice. Acts 10:9-16 teaches that what God has created and cleansed we should not misuse or call common. We can enjoy love. God created it as a gift to us and a delight for all our senses.

1:5 Kedar was a nomadic community in northern Arabia. It was known for its tents that were woven from black goats’ hair.

1:6 The vineyard mentioned here was apparently owned by Solomon (because he came to visit it) and leased to the girl’s brothers, who made her take care of the vineyards in the hot sun. Thus, she could not take care of her own skin. When she was brought to Jerusalem, the young girl was embarrassed about her tanned complexion because the girls in the city had fair, delicate skin that was considered much more beautiful. But Solomon loved her dark skin.

1:7 The girl felt insecure at being different from the women of Jerusalem (1:6) and at being alone while her lover was away (1:7). She longed for the security of his presence. The basis of true love is commitment; so in a relationship where there is genuine love, there is never any fear of deceit, manipulation, or exploitation.

1:14 En-gedi was an oasis hidden at the base of rugged limestone cliffs west of the Dead Sea. It was known for its fruitful palm trees and fragrant balsam oil. The terrain surrounding En-gedi was some of the most desolate in Palestine, and it had an extremely hot desert climate. The henna blossoms in En-gedi would have appeared all the more beautiful because of their stark surroundings; thus, the girl was complimenting Solomon’s looks, saying that he stood out among all the men.

1:16, 17 The lover and his beloved describe their woodland surroundings as a wedding bedroom.

2:1 The rose of Sharon and lily of the valley were flowers commonly found in Israel. Perhaps the girl was saying, “I’m not so special; I’m just an ordinary flower,” to which Solomon replied, “Oh no, you are extraordinary—a lily among thorns.” Solomon used the language of love. There is nothing more vital than encouraging and appreciating the person you love. Be sure to tell your spouse, “I love you” every day, and show that love by your actions.

2:7 Feelings of love can create emotions that overpower reason. Young people are too often in a hurry to develop an intimate relationship based on their strong feelings. But feelings aren’t enough to support a lasting relationship. This verse encourages us not to force romance lest the feelings of love grow faster than the commitment needed to make love last. Patiently wait for feelings of love and commitment to develop together.

2:8 Song 2:17; Isa 52:7
2:9 Judg 5:28; Prov 6:5; Song 2:17; 3:5; 8:14
2:12 Gen 15:9; Ps 74:19
2:13 Matt 24:32
2:14 Song 5:2; 6:9; Jer 48:28
2:16 Song 4:5; 6:2-3; 7:10
2:17 Song 2:8-9; 4:6

2. Memories of courtship

8“Ah, I hear him—my lover! Here he comes, leaping on the mountains and
bounding over the hills. 9My lover is like a swift gazelle or a young deer. Look,
there he is behind the wall! Now he is looking in through the window, gazing
into the room.
10“My lover said to me, ‘Rise up, my beloved, my fair one, and come away.
11For the winter is past, and the rain is over and gone. 12The flowers are springing up, and the time of singing birds has come, even the cooing of turtledoves.
13The fig trees are budding, and the grapevines are in blossom. How delicious
they smell! Yes, spring is here! Arise, my beloved, my fair one, and come away.’”
Young Man: 14“My dove is hiding behind some rocks, behind an outcrop on the cliff. Let
me see you; let me hear your voice. For your voice is pleasant, and you are lovely.”
Young Women of Jerusalem: 15“Quick! Catch all the little foxes before they ruin the
vineyard of your love, for the grapevines are all in blossom.”
Young Woman: 16“My lover is mine, and I am his. He feeds among the lilies! 17Before
the dawn comes and the shadows flee away, come back to me, my love. Run like
a gazelle or a young stag on the rugged mountains.*”

3:1 Song 1:7; 5:6
3:2 Jer 5:1
3:3 Song 5:7
3:4 Song 8:2
3:5 Song 2:7; 8:2

3 *Young Woman:* “One night as I lay in bed, I yearned deeply for my lover, but he
did not come. 2So I said to myself, ‘I will get up now and roam the city, searching for him in all its streets and squares.’ But my search was in vain. 3The watchmen stopped me as they made their rounds, and I said to them, ‘Have you seen
him anywhere, this one I love so much?’ 4A little while later I found him and
held him. I didn’t let him go until I had brought him to my childhood home, into
my mother’s bedroom, where I had been conceived.
5“Promise me, O women of Jerusalem, by the swift gazelles and the deer of
the wild, not to awaken love until the time is right.*”

3:6 Exod 13:21-22; Song 1:13; 4:12-14; Rev 5:8; 18:13
3:8 Pss 45:3; 91:5; Jer 50:9

3. Memories of engagement

Young Women of Jerusalem: 6“Who is this sweeping in from the deserts like a cloud of
smoke along the ground? Who is it that smells of myrrh and frankincense and every
other spice? 7Look, it is Solomon’s carriage, with sixty of Israel’s mightiest men
surrounding it. 8They are all skilled swordsmen and experienced warriors. Each
one wears a sword on his thigh, ready to defend the king against an attack during
the night.
9“King Solomon has built a carriage for himself from wood imported from
Lebanon’s forests. 10Its posts are of silver, its canopy is gold, and its seat is
upholstered in purple cloth. Its interior was a gift of love from the young women
of Jerusalem.”

2:17 Or *on the hills of Bether.* **3:5** Or *not to awaken love until it is ready.*

2:8–3:5 In this section Solomon’s beloved reflects on her courtship with Solomon, remembering the first day they met and recalling one of her dreams about their being together.

2:12, 13 The lovers celebrated their joy in the creation and in their love. God created the world, the beauty of nature, and the gift of love and sex, and gave us senses to enjoy them. Never let problems, conflicts, or the ravages of time ruin your ability to enjoy God’s gifts. Take time to enjoy the world God has created.

2:15 “The little foxes” are an example of the kinds of problems that can disturb or destroy a relationship. The lovers wanted anything that could potentially cause problems between them to be removed. It is often the “little foxes” that cause the biggest problems in marriage. These irritations must not be minimized or ignored but identified so that, together, the couple can deal with them.

3:1-4 Many scholars agree that in these verses the girl was recalling a dream that caused her to become so concerned about her lover’s whereabouts that she arose in the middle of the night to search for him. When you love someone, you will do all you can to ensure the safety of that person and care for his or her needs, even at a cost to your personal comfort. This is demonstrated most often in small actions—getting your spouse a glass of water, leaving work early to attend some function your child is involved in, or sacrificing your personal comfort to tend to the needs of a friend.

3:6–5:1 Here the scene changes. Some believe that the wedding procession is described in 3:6-11, the wedding night in 4:1–5:1, and the consummation of the marriage in 4:16–5:1. Another possible explanation is that the period of Solomon’s engagement to the girl is being remembered. In the previous section (2:8–3:5), Solomon and the girl fell in love. In this section, Solomon returns to the girl in all his royal splendor (3:6-11), expresses his great love for her (4:1-5), and then proposes (4:7-15). The girl accepts (4:16), and Solomon responds to her acceptance (5:1).

3:7, 9 Solomon’s carriage was probably a covered and curtained couch for a single passenger that was carried on the shoulders of men.

Young Woman: 11 "Go out to look upon King Solomon, O young women of Jerusalem.* See the crown with which his mother crowned him on his wedding day,
the day of his gladness."

4 *Young Man:* "How beautiful you are, my beloved, how beautiful! Your eyes behind
your veil are like doves. Your hair falls in waves, like flocks of goats frisking across
the slopes of Gilead. 2 Your teeth are as white as sheep, newly shorn and washed.
They are perfectly matched; not one is missing. 3 Your lips are like a ribbon of scarlet. Oh, how beautiful your mouth! Your cheeks behind your veil are like pomegranate halves—lovely and delicious. 4 Your neck is as stately as the tower of David,
jeweled with the shields of a thousand heroes. 5 Your breasts are like twin fawns of a
gazelle, feeding among the lilies. 6 Before the dawn comes and the shadows flee
away, I will go to the mountain of myrrh and to the hill of frankincense. 7 You are so
beautiful, my beloved, so perfect in every part.
8 "Come with me from Lebanon, my bride. Come down* from the top of
Mount Amana, from Mount Senir and Mount Hermon, where lions have their
dens and panthers prowl. 9 You have ravished my heart, my treasure, my bride. I
am overcome by one glance of your eyes, by a single bead of your necklace.
10 How sweet is your love, my treasure, my bride! How much better it is than
wine! Your perfume is more fragrant than the richest of spices. 11 Your lips, my
bride, are as sweet as honey. Yes, honey and cream are under your tongue. The
scent of your clothing is like that of the mountains and the cedars of Lebanon.
12 "You are like a private garden, my treasure, my bride! You are like a spring
that no one else can drink from, a fountain of my own. 13 You are like a lovely orchard bearing precious fruit, with the rarest of perfumes: 14 nard and saffron, calamus and cinnamon, myrrh and aloes, perfume from every incense tree, and every
other lovely spice. 15 You are a garden fountain, a well of living water, as refreshing as the streams from the Lebanon mountains."
Young Woman: 16 "Awake, north wind! Come, south wind! Blow on my garden and
waft its lovely perfume to my lover. Let him come into his garden and eat its
choicest fruits."

5 *Young Man:* "I am here in my garden, my treasure, my bride! I gather my myrrh
with my spices and eat my honeycomb with my honey. I drink my wine with my
milk."
Young Women of Jerusalem: "Oh, lover and beloved, eat and drink! Yes, drink deeply
of this love!"

3:11 Hebrew *Zion.* **4:8** Or *Look down.*

3:11 Isa 62:5
4:1 Song 1:15; 5:12; 6:5, 7
4:3 Song 5:13, 16; 6:7
4:4 Neh 3:19; Song 7:4
4:5 Song 2:16; 6:2-3; 7:3
4:8 Deut 3:9; 1 Kgs 4:33; 2 Kgs 5:12; 1 Chr 5:23; Isa 62:5
4:9 Gen 41:42; Ezek 16:11
4:11 Gen 27:27; Prov 24:13-14; Hos 14:6
4:12 Gen 29:3; Prov 5:15-18
4:14 Exod 30:23; John 19:39
4:15 Zech 14:8; John 4:10, 14; 7:38
4:16 Song 1:13; 2:3; 5:1; 6:2
5:1 Prov 9:5; Song 1:13; 4:9; 6:2; Isa 55:1; John 3:29

4:1-7 We feel like awkward onlookers when we read this intensely private and intimate exchange. In the ecstasy of their love, the lovers praised each other using beautiful imagery. Their words may seem strange to readers from a different culture, but their intense feelings of love and admiration are universal. Communicating love and expressing admiration in both words and actions can enhance every marriage.

4:12 In comparing his bride to a private garden, Solomon was praising her virginity. Virginity, considered old-fashioned by many in today's culture, has always been God's plan for unmarried people—and with good reason. Sex without marriage is cheap. It cannot compare with the joy of giving yourself completely to the one who is totally committed to you in marriage.

4:15 Solomon's bride was as refreshing to him as a fountain. Could your spouse say the same about you? Sometimes the familiarity that comes with marriage causes us to forget the overwhelming feelings of love and bliss we shared at the beginning. Many marriages could use a course in "refreshing." Do you refresh your spouse, or are you a burden of complaints, sorrows, and problems? Partners in marriage should continually work at refreshing each other by an encouraging word, an unexpected gift, a change of pace, a surprise call or note, or even the withholding of a discussion of some problem until the proper time. Your spouse needs you to be a haven of refreshment because the rest of the world usually isn't.

5:2ff This new section tells how the couple's marriage grew and matured in spite of problems. Some time had passed since the wedding, and the girl felt as though some indifference had developed in their relationship. She had become cool to her husband's advances, and by the time she changed her mind and responded to him, he had left. Her self-centeredness and impatience, though brief, caused separation. But she quickly moved to correct the problem by searching for her husband (5:6-8).

5:2-8 It is inevitable that, with the passing of time and the growth of familiarity, a marriage will start to lose its initial sparkle. Glances and touches no longer produce the same emotional response. Conflicts and pressures may creep in, causing you to lose your tenderness toward your spouse. The world is not a haven for lovers; in fact, external stress often works against the marriage relationship. But you and your spouse can learn to be a haven for

4. A troubling dream

Young Woman: 2"One night as I was sleeping, my heart awakened in a dream. I heard
the voice of my lover. He was knocking at my bedroom door. 'Open to me, my
darling, my treasure, my lovely dove,' he said, 'for I have been out in the night.
My head is soaked with dew, my hair with the wetness of the night.'
3"But I said, 'I have taken off my robe. Should I get dressed again? I have
washed my feet. Should I get them soiled?'
4"My lover tried to unlatch the door, and my heart thrilled within me. 5I
jumped up to open it. My hands dripped with perfume, my fingers with lovely
myrrh, as I pulled back the bolt. 6I opened to my lover, but he was gone. I
yearned for even his voice! I searched for him, but I couldn't find him anywhere.
I called to him, but there was no reply. 7The watchmen found me as they were
making their rounds; they struck and wounded me. The watchman on the wall
tore off my veil.
8"Make this promise to me, O women of Jerusalem! If you find my beloved
one, tell him that I am sick with love."
Young Women of Jerusalem: 9"O woman of rare beauty, what is it about your loved
one that brings you to tell us this?"
Young Woman: 10"My lover is dark and dazzling, better than ten thousand others!
11His head is the finest gold, and his hair is wavy and black. 12His eyes are like
doves beside brooks of water; they are set like jewels. 13His cheeks are like
sweetly scented beds of spices. His lips are like perfumed lilies. His breath is like
myrrh. 14His arms are like round bars of gold, set with chrysolite. His body is
like bright ivory, aglow with sapphires. 15His legs are like pillars of marble set in
sockets of the finest gold, strong as the cedars of Lebanon. None can rival him.
16His mouth is altogether sweet; he is lovely in every way. Such, O women of
Jerusalem, is my lover, my friend."

5:2 Song 2:14; 4:9; 6:9
5:3 Gen 19:2; Luke 11:7
5:5 Song 5:13
5:6 Prov 1:28; Song 3:1; 5:2; 6:1
5:7 Song 3:3
5:8 Song 2:5, 7; 3:5
5:9 Song 1:8; 6:1
5:10 1 Sam 16:12; Ps 45:2
5:12 Song 1:15; 4:1
5:13 Song 2:1; 5:5; 6:2
5:14 Exod 24:10; 28:18; Job 28:16; Isa 54:11; Ezek 1:16
5:15 1 Kgs 4:33; Song 7:4
5:16 2 Sam 1:23; Song 7:9

6 *Young Women of Jerusalem:* "O rarest of beautiful women, where has your lover
gone? We will help you find him."
Young Woman: 2"He has gone down to his garden, to his spice beds, to graze and
to gather the lilies. 3I am my lover's, and my lover is mine. He grazes among
the lilies!"

5. Praising the bride's beauty

Young Man: 4"O my beloved, you are as beautiful as the lovely town of Tirzah. Yes, as
beautiful as Jerusalem! You are as majestic as an army with banners! 5Look away,
for your eyes overcome me! Your hair, as it falls across your face, is like a flock of
goats frisking down the slopes of Gilead. 6Your teeth are white like freshly washed
ewes, perfectly matched and not one missing. 7Your cheeks behind your veil are
like pomegranate halves—lovely and delicious. 8There may be sixty wives, all
queens, and eighty concubines and unnumbered virgins available to me. 9But I
would still choose my dove, my perfect one, the only beloved daughter of her

6:2 Song 1:7; 2:1; 4:16; 5:1, 13
6:3 Song 2:16; 4:5; 7:10
6:4 1 Kgs 14:17; Pss 48:2; 50:2
6:5 Song 4:1
6:8 1 Kgs 11:3
6:9 Gen 30:13; Song 2:14; 5:2

---

each other. If intimacy and passion decline, remember that they can be renewed and regenerated. Take time to remember the commitment you made, those first thrills, the excitement of sex, and your spouse's strengths. When you focus on the positives, reconciliation and renewal can result.

5:7 The girl was alone outside during the night. In Old Testament times, she would have been looked upon as a criminal or a prostitute and treated as such. This image symbolizes the pain she felt at being separated from her lover.

5:16 The girl calls Solomon her "friend." In a healthy marriage, lovers are also good friends. Too often people are driven into marriage by the exciting feelings of love and passion before they take the time to develop a deep friendship. This involves listening, sharing, and showing understanding for the other's likes and dislikes. Friendship takes time, but it makes a love relationship much deeper and far more satisfying.

6:3 The girl said that she and her lover belonged to each other—they had given themselves to each other unreservedly. No matter how close we may be to our parents or our best friends, it is only in marriage that we realize complete union of mind, heart, and body.

6:4 Tirzah was a city about 35 miles northeast of Jerusalem. Its name means "pleasure" or "beauty." Jeroboam made Tirzah the first capital of the divided northern kingdom (1 Kings 14:17). "Majestic as an army with banners" means that his beloved must have had awe-inspiring beauty, like a mighty army readying for battle.

6:8, 9 Solomon did indeed have many queens (wives) and concubines (1 Kings 11:3). Polygamy, though not condoned, was common in Old Testament days. Solomon said that his love for this woman had not diminished since their wedding night, even though many other women were available to him.

mother! The young women are delighted when they see her; even queens and concubines sing her praises! 10‘Who is this,’ they ask, ‘arising like the dawn, as fair as
the moon, as bright as the sun, as majestic as an army with banners?’
11“I went down into the grove of nut trees and out to the valley to see the new
growth brought on by spring. I wanted to see whether the grapevines were budding yet, or whether the pomegranates were blossoming. 12Before I realized it, I
found myself in my princely bed with my beloved one.*”
Young Women of Jerusalem: 13“Return, return to us, O maid of Shulam. Come back,
come back, that we may see you once again.”
Young Man: “Why do you gaze so intently at this young woman of Shulam, as she
moves so gracefully between two lines of dancers?*”

7 *Young Man:* “How beautiful are your sandaled feet, O queenly maiden. Your
rounded thighs are like jewels, the work of a skilled craftsman. 2Your navel is
as delicious as a goblet filled with wine. Your belly is lovely, like a heap of
wheat set about with lilies. 3Your breasts are like twin fawns of a gazelle.
4Your neck is as stately as an ivory tower. Your eyes are like the sparkling
pools in Heshbon by the gate of Bath-rabbim. Your nose is as fine as the tower
of Lebanon overlooking Damascus. 5Your head is as majestic as Mount Carmel, and the sheen of your hair radiates royalty. A king is held captive in your
queenly tresses.
6“Oh, how delightful you are, my beloved; how pleasant for utter delight!
7You are tall and slim like a palm tree, and your breasts are like its clusters of
dates. 8I said, ‘I will climb up into the palm tree and take hold of its branches.’
Now may your breasts be like grape clusters, and the scent of your breath like
apples. 9May your kisses be as exciting as the best wine, smooth and sweet, flowing gently over lips and teeth.*”

6. The bride’s tender appeal

Young Woman: 10“I am my lover’s, the one he desires. 11Come, my love, let us go out
into the fields and spend the night among the wildflowers.* 12Let us get up early
and go out to the vineyards. Let us see whether the vines have budded, whether
the blossoms have opened, and whether the pomegranates are in flower. And
there I will give you my love. 13There the mandrakes give forth their fragrance,
and the rarest fruits are at our doors, the new as well as old, for I have stored
them up for you, my lover.”

8 *Young Woman:* “Oh, if only you were my brother, who nursed at my mother’s
breast. Then I could kiss you no matter who was watching, and no one would
criticize me. 2I would bring you to my childhood home, and there you would
teach me. I would give you spiced wine to drink, my sweet pomegranate
wine. 3Your left hand would be under my head and your right hand would
embrace me.
4“I want you to promise, O women of Jerusalem, not to awaken love until the
time is right.*”

6:10 Job 31:26; Song 6:4; Matt 17:2; Rev 1:16
6:11 Song 4:13; 7:12
6:13 Gen 32:2; Judg 21:21; 2 Sam 17:24
7:1ff Ps 45:13
7:3 Song 4:5
7:4 Num 21:26; Song 4:4
7:5 Isa 35:2
7:6 Song 1:15-16
7:8 Song 2:5
7:9 Prov 23:31; Song 5:16
7:10 Ps 45:11; Song 2:16; 6:3
7:12 Song 6:11
7:13 Gen 30:14; Song 2:3; 4:13, 16
8:2 Song 3:4
8:3 Song 2:6
8:4 Song 2:7; 3:5

6:12 Or *among the royal chariots of my people,* or *among the chariots of Amminadab.* The meaning of the Hebrew is uncertain. **6:13** Or *as you would at the movements of two armies?* or *as you would at the dance of Mahanaim?* The meaning of the Hebrew is uncertain. **7:9** As in Greek and Syriac versions and Latin Vulgate; Hebrew reads *over lips of sleepers.* **7:11** Or *in the villages.* **8:4** Or *not to awaken love until it is ready.*

7:4, 5 Heshbon was the ancient capital of the Amorites. Bath-rabbim may have been a gate of Heshbon. The “tower of Lebanon” may have been a watchtower (evidently a prominent one and seen as very beautiful). Some suggest that this refers to the Lebanon mountain range. Mount Carmel overlooks the Mediterranean Sea and Palestine.

7:10-13 As a marriage matures, there should be more love and freedom between marriage partners. Here the girl takes the initiative in lovemaking. Many cultures have stereotypes of the roles men and women play in lovemaking, but the security of true love gives both marriage partners the freedom to initiate acts of love and express their true feelings.

7:13 Mandrakes were a somewhat rare plant often thought to increase fertility. Mandrakes are also mentioned in Genesis 30:14-17.

8:1 In the ancient Near East, it was improper to show public affection except between family members. The girl is wishing that she could freely show affection to her lover, even in public.

7. The power of love

8:5 Song 2:3; 3:6

Young Women of Jerusalem: 5“Who is this coming up from the desert, leaning on her
lover?”
Young Woman: “I aroused you under the apple tree, where your mother gave you
birth, where in great pain she delivered you. 6Place me like a seal over your
heart, or like a seal on your arm. For love is as strong as death, and its jealousy is
as enduring as the grave. Love flashes like fire, the brightest kind of flame.
7Many waters cannot quench love; neither can rivers drown it. If a man tried to
buy love with everything he owned, his offer would be utterly despised.”
The Young Woman's Brothers: 8“We have a little sister too young for breasts. What
will we do if someone asks to marry her? 9If she is chaste, we will strengthen
and encourage her. But if she is promiscuous, we will shut her off from men.*”
Young Woman: 10“I am chaste, and I am now full breasted. And my lover is content
with me.
11“Solomon has a vineyard at Baal-hamon, which he rents to some farmers
there. Each of them pays one thousand pieces of silver* for its use. 12But as for
my own vineyard, O Solomon, you can take my thousand pieces of silver. And I
will give two hundred pieces of silver* to those who care for its vines.”
Young Man: 13“O my beloved, lingering in the gardens, how wonderful that your companions can listen to your voice. Let me hear it, too!”
Young Woman: 14“Come quickly, my love! Move like a swift gazelle or a young deer
on the mountains of spices.”

8:6 Prov 6:34; Isa 49:16; Jer 22:24; Hag 2:23
8:8 Ezek 16:7
8:9 1 Kgs 6:15
8:11 Eccl 2:4; Song 1:6; 2:3; 8:12; Isa 7:23; Matt 21:33
8:13 Song 1:7; 2:14
8:14 Song 2:7, 9, 17; 4:6

8:9 Hebrew *If she is a wall, we will build battlements of silver on her; but if she is a door, we will surround her with panels of cedar.* **8:11** Hebrew *1,000 shekels of silver,* about 25 pounds or 11.4 kilograms in weight; also in 8:12. **8:12** Hebrew *200 [shekels],* about 5 pounds or 2.3 kilograms in weight.

8:6, 7 In this final description of their love, the girl includes some of its significant characteristics (see also 1 Corinthians 13). Love is as strong as death; it cannot be killed by time or disaster; and it cannot be bought for any price because it is freely given. Love is priceless, and even the richest king cannot buy it. Love must be accepted as a gift from God and then shared within the guidelines God provides. Accept the love of your spouse as God's gift, and strive to make your love a reflection of the perfect love that comes from God himself.

8:8, 9 The girl was reflecting on the days when she was younger and under the care of her brothers, who wondered how to help her prepare for marriage. They decided that if she was chaste, standing firm against sexual temptation, they would praise her. But if she was promiscuous and given over to immorality, they would take steps to guard her from doing something foolish. In 8:10, she testifies that she has been persistent in her morality and thus has found favor in Solomon's eyes.

8:11, 12 Solomon could demand rent from the tenants for his vineyard, but the girl had her own vineyard, and it was her right to assign it. But she willingly gave Solomon its fruit. In a good marriage, there is no private property, for everything is shared between the partners. This is the only time Baal-hamon is mentioned in the Bible, and its location is unknown.

8:14 The love between Solomon and his bride did not diminish in intensity after their wedding night. The lovers relied on each other and kept no secrets from each other. Devotion and commitment were the keys to their relationship, just as they are in our relationships to our spouses and to God. The faithfulness of our marital love should reflect God's perfect faithfulness to us.

Paul shows how marriage represents Christ's relationship to his church (Ephesians 5:22-33), and John pictures the Second Coming as a great marriage feast for Christ and his bride, his faithful followers (Revelation 19:7, 8; 21:1, 2). Many theologians have thought that Song of Songs is an allegory showing Christ's love for his church. It might be even better to say that it is a love poem about a real human love relationship, and that all loving, committed marriages are a reflection of God's love.

ISAIAH

Amos becomes a prophet 760 B.C.	Hosea becomes a prophet 753	Micah becomes a prophet 742	Isaiah becomes a prophet 740	Ahaz becomes king of Judah 735	Hoshea becomes king of Israel 732	Israel falls to the Assyrians 722	Hezekiah becomes king of Judah 715

VITAL STATISTICS

PURPOSE:
To call the nation of Judah back to God and to tell of God's salvation through the Messiah

AUTHOR:
The prophet Isaiah son of Amoz

DATE WRITTEN:
The events of chapters 1—39 occurred during Isaiah's ministry, so they were probably written about 700 B.C. Chapters 40—66, however, may have been written near the end of his life, about 681 B.C.

SETTING:
Isaiah is speaking and writing mainly in Jerusalem

KEY VERSE:
"But he was wounded and crushed for our sins. He was beaten that we might have peace. He was whipped, and we were healed!" (53:5).

KEY PEOPLE:
Isaiah; his two sons, Shear-jashub and Maher-shalal-hash-baz

SPECIAL FEATURES:
The book of Isaiah contains both prose and poetry and uses personification (attributing personal qualities to divine beings or inanimate objects). Also, many of the prophecies in Isaiah contain predictions that foretell a soon-to-occur event and a distant future event at the same time.

SLOWLY he rose, and the crowd fell silent. Those at the back leaned forward, straining to hear. The atmosphere was electric. He spoke, and his carefully chosen words flew like swift arrows and found their mark. The great man, a spokesman for God, was warning—and condemning. The crowd became restless—shifting positions, clenching fists, and murmuring. Some agreed with his message, nodding their heads and weeping softly. But most were angry, and they began to shout back insults and threats.

Such was the life of a prophet.

The "office" of prophet was instituted during the days of Samuel, the last of the judges. Prophets stood with the priests as God's special representatives. The prophet's role was to speak for God, confronting the people and their leaders with God's commands and promises. Because of this confrontational stance and the continuing tendency of people to disobey God, true prophets usually were not very popular. But though their message often went unheeded, they faithfully and forcefully proclaimed the truth.

The book of Isaiah is the first of the writings of the prophets in the Bible; and Isaiah, the author, is generally considered to be the greatest prophet. He was probably reared in an aristocratic home and was married to a prophet. In the beginning of his ministry he was well liked. But, like most prophets, he soon became unpopular because his messages were so difficult to hear. He called the people to turn from their lives of sin and warned them of God's judgment and punishment. Isaiah had an active ministry for 60 years before he was executed during Manasseh's reign (according to tradition). As God's special messenger to Judah, Isaiah prophesied during the reigns of several of its rulers. Many of those messages are recorded in his book: Uzziah and Jotham, chapters 1—6; Ahaz, chapters 7—14; and Hezekiah, chapters 15—39.

The first half of the book of Isaiah (chapters 1—39) contains scathing denunciations and pronouncements as he calls Judah, Israel, and the surrounding nations to repent of their sins. However, the last 27 chapters (40—66) are filled with consolation and hope as Isaiah unfolds God's promise of future blessings through his Messiah.

As you read Isaiah, imagine this strong and courageous man of God, fearlessly proclaiming God's word, and listen to his message in relation to your own life—*return, repent, and be renewed.* Then trust in God's *redemption* through Christ and *rejoice.* Your Savior has come, and he's coming again!

Sennacherib surrounds Jerusalem 701	Manasseh becomes king of Judah 697	Isaiah's ministry ends 681	Josiah becomes king of Judah 640

THE BLUEPRINT

A. WORDS OF JUDGMENT (1:1—39:8)
1. The sins of Israel and Judah
2. Judgment against heathen nations
3. God's purpose in judgment
4. Jerusalem's true and false hopes
5. Events during the reign of Hezekiah

The 39 chapters in the first half of Isaiah generally carry the message of judgment for sin. Isaiah brings the message of judgment to Judah, Israel, and the surrounding pagan nations. The people of Judah had a form of godliness, but in their hearts they were corrupt. Isaiah's warnings were intended to purify the people by helping them understand God's true nature and message. However, they ignored the repeated warnings that Isaiah brought. We need to heed the prophetic voice and not repeat their error.

B. WORDS OF COMFORT (40:1—66:24)
1. Israel's release from captivity
2. The future Redeemer
3. The future kingdom

The 27 chapters in the second half of Isaiah generally bring a message of forgiveness, comfort, and hope. This message of hope looks forward to the coming of the Messiah. Isaiah speaks more about the Messiah than does any other Old Testament prophet. He describes the Messiah as both a suffering Servant and a sovereign Lord. The fact that the Messiah was to be both a suffering Servant and a sovereign Lord could not be understood clearly until New Testament times. Based on what Jesus Christ has done, God freely offers forgiveness to all who turn to him in faith. This is God's message of comfort to us because those who heed it find eternal peace and fellowship with him.

MEGATHEMES

THEME	EXPLANATION	IMPORTANCE
Holiness	God is highly exalted above all his creatures. His moral perfection stands in contrast to evil people and nations. God is perfect and sinless in all his motives and actions, so he is in perfect control of his power, judgment, love, and mercy. His holy nature is our yardstick for morality.	Because God is without sin, he alone can help us with our sin. It is only right that we regard him as supreme in power and moral perfection. We must never treat God as common or ordinary. He alone deserves our devotion and praise. He is always truthful, fair, and just.
Punishment	Because God is holy, he requires his people to treat others justly. He promised to punish Israel, Judah, and other nations for faithless immorality and idolatry. True faith had degenerated into national pride and empty religious rituals.	We must trust in God alone and fulfill his commands. We cannot forsake justice nor give in to selfishness. If we harden our heart against his message, punishment will surely come to us.
Salvation	Because God's judgment is coming, we need a Savior. No man or nation can be saved without God's help. Christ's perfect sacrifice for our sins is foretold and portrayed in Isaiah. All who trust God can be freed from their sin and restored to him.	Christ died to save us from our sin. We cannot save ourselves. He is willing to save all those who turn from their sin and come to him. Salvation is from God alone. No amount of good works can earn it.
Messiah	God will send the Messiah to save his people. He will set up his own Kingdom as the faithful Prince of Peace, who rules with righteousness. He will come as sovereign Lord, but he will do so as a servant who will die to take away sins.	Our trust must be in the Messiah, not in ourselves or in any nation or power. There is no hope unless we believe in him. Trust Christ fully and let him rule in your life as your sovereign Lord.
Hope	God promises comfort, deliverance, and restoration in his future Kingdom. The Messiah will rule over his faithful followers in the age to come. Hope is possible because Christ is coming.	We can be refreshed because there is compassion for those who repent. No matter how bleak our situation or how evil the world is, we must continue to be God's faithful people who hope for his return.

A. WORDS OF JUDGMENT (1:1—39:8)

Isaiah begins by bringing a message of divine judgment for both Israel and Judah. Although the advance of the Assyrians poses a problem for Judah, God foretells the destruction of Assyria and other evil surrounding nations through the prophet Isaiah. This section ends with the Assyrian invasion being held off, demonstrating the clear unfolding of God's plan and promises for the nation at this time.

1. The sins of Israel and Judah

1 These visions concerning Judah and Jerusalem came to Isaiah son of Amoz during
the reigns of Uzziah, Jotham, Ahaz, and Hezekiah—all kings of Judah.

A Message for Rebellious Judah

2Hear, O heavens! Listen, O earth! This is what the LORD says: "The children I raised
and cared for have turned against me. 3Even the animals—the donkey and the ox—know
their owner and appreciate his care, but not my people Israel. No matter what I do for
them, they still do not understand."
4Oh, what a sinful nation they are! They are loaded down with a burden of guilt. They
are evil and corrupt children who have turned away from the LORD. They have despised
the Holy One of Israel, cutting themselves off from his help.
5Why do you continue to invite punishment? Must you rebel forever? Your head is
injured, and your heart is sick. 6You are sick from head to foot—covered with bruises,
welts, and infected wounds—without any ointments or bandages. 7Your country lies in
ruins, and your cities are burned. As you watch, foreigners plunder your fields and
destroy everything they see. 8Jerusalem* stands abandoned like a watchman's shelter in
a vineyard or field after the harvest is over. It is as helpless as a city under siege. 9If the
LORD Almighty had not spared a few of us, we would have been wiped out as completely
as Sodom and Gomorrah.
10Listen to the LORD, you leaders of Israel! Listen to the law of our God, people of
Israel. You act just like the rulers and people of Sodom and Gomorrah. 11"I am sick of
your sacrifices," says the LORD. "Don't bring me any more burnt offerings! I don't want

1:1 2 Kgs 15:1, 13; 16:1; 18:1
1:2 Deut 32:1; Isa 65:2; Jer 3:22; Mic 1:2
1:3 Jer 8:7; 9:3, 6
1:4 Song 2:7, 9, 17; 4:6; Isa 1:28; 5:24; 14:20
1:5 Isa 31:6; 33:24
1:7 Lev 26:33; Jer 44:6
1:9 Isa 10:20-22; 11:11, 16; †Rom 9:29
1:10 Ezek 16:46; Rev 11:8
1:11 Jer 6:20; Mal 1:10

1:8 Hebrew *The daughter of Zion.*

1:1 Isaiah was a prophet during the time when the original nation of Israel had been divided into two kingdoms—Israel in the north and Judah in the south. The northern kingdom had sinned greatly against God, and the southern kingdom was headed in the same direction—perverting justice, oppressing the poor, turning from God to idols, and looking for military aid from pagan nations rather than from God. Isaiah came primarily as a prophet to Judah, but his message was also for the northern kingdom. Sometimes "Israel" refers to both kingdoms. Isaiah lived to see the destruction and captivity of the northern kingdom in 722 B.C. Thus, his ministry began with warning the northern kingdom.

1:2-4 Here "Israel" means the southern kingdom, Judah. The people of Judah were sinning greatly and had turned against God. God brought charges against them through Isaiah because they had rebelled and had forsaken the Lord. By these acts, they had broken their moral and spiritual covenant with God (see Deuteronomy 28). By breaking their agreement, they were bringing God's punishment upon themselves. First God gave them prosperity, but they didn't serve him. Then God sent them warnings, but they refused to listen. Finally, he would bring the fire of his judgment (see 1:7).

1:4-9 As long as the people of Judah continued to sin, they cut themselves off from God's help and isolated themselves. When you feel lonely and separated from God, remember that God does not abandon you. Our sins cut us off from him. The only sure cure for this kind of loneliness is to restore a meaningful relationship with God by confessing your sins, obeying his instructions, and communicating regularly with him (see Psalm 140:13; Isaiah 1:16-19; 1 John 1:9).

1:7 Was this destruction taking place at that time? Judah was attacked many times during Isaiah's lifetime. To be plundered by foreigners was the worst kind of judgment. This verse could be a picture of the results of these invasions or a prediction of the coming invasion of Israel by Assyria. But most likely it pointed to Babylon's future invasion of Judah and the fall of Jerusalem in 586 B.C. as well.

1:9 Sodom and Gomorrah were two cities that God completely destroyed for their great wickedness (Genesis 19:1-25). They are mentioned elsewhere in the Bible as examples of God's judgment against sin (Jeremiah 50:40; Ezekiel 16:46-63; Matthew 11:23, 24; Jude 1:7). Some survivors from Judah were spared by God because they were faithful.

1:10 Isaiah compared the rulers and people of Judah to the rulers and people of Sodom and Gomorrah. To hear what God wanted to say, the people had to listen and be willing to obey. When we can't hear God's message, perhaps we are not listening carefully, or we are not truly willing to do what he says.

1:10-14 God was unhappy with their sacrifices, but he was not revoking the system of sacrifices he had initiated with Moses. Instead, God was calling for sincere faith and devotion. The leaders were carefully making the traditional sacrifices and offerings at holy celebrations, but they were still unfaithful to God in their hearts. Sacrifices were to be an outward sign of their faith in God, but the outward signs became empty because no faith existed. Why, then, did they continue to offer sacrifices? Like many people today, they had come to place more faith in the rituals of their religion than in the God they worshiped. Examine your own religious practices: Do they spring from your faith in the living God? God does not take pleasure in our outward expressions if our inward faith is missing (see Deuteronomy 10:12-16; 1 Samuel 15:22, 23; Psalm 51:16-19; Hosea 6:6).

the fat from your rams or other animals. I don't want to see the blood from your offerings
of bulls and rams and goats. 12Why do you keep parading through my courts with your
worthless sacrifices? 13The incense you bring me is a stench in my nostrils! Your
celebrations of the new moon and the Sabbath day, and your special days for fasting—
even your most pious meetings—are all sinful and false. I want nothing more to do with
them. 14I hate all your festivals and sacrifices. I cannot stand the sight of them! 15From
now on, when you lift up your hands in prayer, I will refuse to look. Even though you
offer many prayers, I will not listen. For your hands are covered with the blood of your
innocent victims. 16Wash yourselves and be clean! Let me no longer see your evil deeds.
Give up your wicked ways. 17Learn to do good. Seek justice. Help the oppressed. Defend
the orphan. Fight for the rights of widows.
18"Come now, let us argue this out," says the LORD. "No matter how deep the stain of
your sins, I can remove it. I can make you as clean as freshly fallen snow. Even if you
are stained as red as crimson, I can make you as white as wool. 19If you will only obey
me and let me help you, then you will have plenty to eat. 20But if you keep turning away
and refusing to listen, you will be destroyed by your enemies. I, the LORD, have spoken!"

Unfaithful Jerusalem

21See how Jerusalem, once so faithful, has become a prostitute. Once the home of justice
and righteousness, she is now filled with murderers. 22Once like pure silver, you have
become like worthless slag. Once so pure, you are now like watered-down wine. 23Your
leaders are rebels, the companions of thieves. All of them take bribes and refuse to defend
the orphans and the widows.
24Therefore, the Lord, the LORD Almighty, the Mighty One of Israel, says, "I will pour
out my fury on you, my enemies! 25I will turn against you. I will melt you down and
skim off your slag. I will remove all your impurities. 26Afterward I will give you good
judges and wise counselors like the ones you used to have. Then Jerusalem will again be
called the Home of Justice and the Faithful City."
27Because the LORD is just and righteous, the repentant people of Jerusalem* will be
redeemed. 28But all sinners will be completely destroyed, for they refuse to come to the LORD.

1:13 1 Chr 23:31
1:14 Isa 43:24
1:15 Isa 59:2; Mic 3:4
1:16 Ps 26:6; Isa 52:11; Jer 25:5
1:17 Jer 22:3
1:18 Ps 51:7; Isa 43:26; 44:22; Rev 7:14
1:19 Deut 30:15-16
1:21 Jer 2:20
1:23 Exod 23:8; Jer 5:28; Ezek 22:7; Mic 7:3
1:24 Isa 35:4; 49:26
1:25 Ezek 22:19-22; Mal 3:3
1:26 Isa 33:5; Zech 8:3
1:28 Ps 9:5; 2 Thes 1:8-9

1:27 Hebrew *Zion.*

ISAIAH served as a prophet to Judah from 740–681 B.C.

Climate of the times	Society was in a great upheaval. Under King Ahaz and King Manasseh, the people reverted to idolatry, and there was even child sacrifice.
Main message	Although judgment from other nations was inevitable, the people could still have a special relationship with God.
Importance of message	Sometimes we must suffer judgment and discipline before we are restored to God.
Contemporary prophets	Hosea (753–715 B.C.), Micah (742–687 B.C.)

1:13 New moon celebrations and Sabbaths refer to monthly offerings (Numbers 28:11-14) and weekly and special annual Sabbaths on the Day of Atonement and Festival of Shelters (Leviticus 16:31, 23-34). For all the festivals, see the chart in Leviticus 23. Although the people did not feel sorry for their sins, they continued to offer sacrifices for forgiveness. Gifts and sacrifices mean nothing to God when they come from someone with a corrupt heart. God wants us to love him, trust him, and turn from our sin; after that, he will be pleased with our "sacrifices" of time, money, or service.

1:18 Crimson was the color of a deep-red permanent dye, and its deep stain was virtually impossible to remove from clothing. The bloodstained hands of the murderers are probably in view here (see 1:15, 21). The stain of sin seems equally permanent, but God can remove sin's stain from our life as he promised to do for the Israelites. We don't have to go through life permanently soiled. God's Word assures us that if we are willing and obedient, Christ will forgive and remove our most indelible stains (Psalm 51:1-7).

1:21, 22 Jerusalem here represents all of Judah. God compares the actions of his people to a prostitute. The people had turned from the worship of the true God to worshiping idols. Their faith was worthless, impure, and diluted. Idolatry, outward or inward, is spiritual adultery, breaking our commitment to God in order to love something else. Jesus described the people of his day as adulterous, even though they were religiously strict. As the church, we are the "bride" of Christ (Revelation 19:7), and, by faith, we can be clothed in his righteousness. Has your faith become impure? Ask God to restore you. Keep your devotion to him strong and pure.

1:25 God promised to refine his people similar to the way that metal is purged with lye in a smelting pot. This process involves melting the metal and skimming off the impure dross until the worker can see his own image in the liquid metal. We must be willing to submit to God, allowing him to remove our sin so that we might reflect his image.

29 Shame will cover you when you think of the times you offered sacrifices to idols
in your groves of sacred oaks. You will blush when you think of all the sins you
committed in your sacred gardens. 30 You will wither away like an oak or garden
without water. 31 The strongest among you will disappear like burning straw. Your evil
deeds are the spark that will set the straw on fire, and no one will be able to put it out.

The LORD's Future Reign

2 This is another vision that Isaiah son of Amoz saw concerning Judah and
Jerusalem:
2 In the last days, the Temple of the LORD in Jerusalem will become the most
important place on earth. People from all over the world will go there to worship.
3 Many nations will come and say, "Come, let us go up to the mountain of the LORD,
to the Temple of the God of Israel.* There he will teach us his ways, so that we may
obey him." For in those days the LORD's teaching and his word will go out from
Jerusalem.
4 The LORD will settle international disputes. All the nations will beat their swords into
plowshares and their spears into pruning hooks. All wars will stop, and military training
will come to an end. 5 Come, people of Israel, let us walk in the light of the LORD!

A Warning of Judgment

6 The LORD has rejected the people of Israel because they have made alliances with
foreigners from the East who practice magic and divination, just like the Philistines.
7 Israel has vast treasures of silver and gold and many horses and chariots. 8 The land
is filled with idols. The people bow down and worship these things they have made.
9 So now everyone will be humbled and brought low. The LORD cannot simply ignore
their sins!
10 Crawl into caves in the rocks. Hide from the terror of the LORD and the glory of his
majesty. 11 The day is coming when your pride will be brought low and the LORD alone
will be exalted. 12 In that day the LORD Almighty will punish the proud, bringing them
down to the dust. 13 He will cut down the tall cedars of Lebanon and the mighty oaks of

2:3 Hebrew *of Jacob;* also in 2:5, 6.

1:29 Isa 57:15; 65:3
1:31 Isa 5:24; 33:11-14; 66:24; Matt 3:12
2:1-4 //Mic 4:1-3
2:3 Isa 51:4-5; Luke 29:47
2:4 Isa 32:17-18; Hos 2:18
2:5 Isa 58:1; 60:1-2; 1 Jn 1:5, 7
2:6 Deut 31:17; 2 Kgs 1:2; 16:7-8
2:7 Deut 17:16
2:10 2 Thes 1:9; Rev 6:15-16
2:12 Job 40:11-12; Mal 4:1
2:13 Isa 10:33-34; Zech 11:2

1:29, 30 Throughout history, the oak tree has been a symbol of strength, but the people were worshiping "sacred oaks." Ezekiel mentions that groves of oak trees were used as places for idol worship (Ezekiel 6:13). Are you devoted to symbols of strength and power that rival God's place in your life? Does your commitment to any of your interests border on worship? Make God your first loyalty; everything else will fade in time and burn away under his scrutiny.

1:31 A spark set to tinder ignites a quick, devouring fire. God compares the evil deeds of powerful people to a roaring fire that will devour them. Our life can be destroyed quickly by a small but deadly spark of evil. What potential "fire hazards" do you need to remove?

2:2 The Temple was built on the mountain of the Lord, Mount Moriah, highly visible to all the people of Jerusalem. For more on the significance of the Temple, see the note on 2 Chronicles 5:1ff. In the last days the Temple will attract the nations, not because of its architecture and prominence, but because of God's presence and influence.

2:2-4 God gave Isaiah the gift of seeing into the future. At this time, God showed Isaiah what would eventually happen to Jerusalem. Revelation 21 depicts the glorious fulfillment of this prophecy in the new Jerusalem, where only those whose names are written in the Lamb's book of life will be allowed to enter. God made a covenant (promise) with his people and will never break it. God's faithfulness gives us hope for the future.

2:4, 5 This describes a wonderful future of peace when instruments of war will be converted to instruments of farming, and we will be taught God's laws and obey them. Although we know that eventually God will remove all sin, which leads to war, conflicts, and other problems, we should not wait for him to act before we begin to obey him. We should walk in his light now, just as Judah was told to do. Though our eternal reward awaits us, we already can enjoy many benefits of obedience now as we apply God's Word to our life.

2:6 The people were following practices of the Assyrian Empire. *Divination* meant claiming to know and control the future by the power of demons or by interpreting omens. These practices were forbidden by God (see Leviticus 19:26; Deuteronomy 18:10, 14). The Philistines worshiped Dagon, Ashtoreth, and Baal-zebub. During the more sinful periods of their history, the people of Israel worshiped these pagan gods along with Yahweh and even gave them Hebrew names.

2:8, 9 Under the reign of evil kings, idol worship flourished in both Israel and Judah. A few good kings in Judah stopped it during their reigns. Although very few people worship carved or molded images today, worshiping people or objects that symbolize power continues. We pay homage to cars, homes, sports stars, celebrities, money, etc. Idol worship is evil because (1) it insults God when we worship something he created rather than worshiping him; (2) it keeps us from knowing and serving God when we put our confidence in anything other than him; (3) it causes us to rely on our own efforts rather than on God. (See also Deuteronomy 27:15.)

2:12 The "day" of the Lord Almighty is the day of judgment, the time when God will judge both evil and good. That day will come, and we will want a proper relationship with God when it does. God alone must be exalted (2:11, 17) as the first step toward developing that relationship with him.

Bashan. 14 He will level the high mountains and hills. 15 He will break down every high
tower and wall. 16 He will destroy the great trading ships* and all the small boats in the
harbor. 17 The arrogance of all people will be brought low. Their pride will lie in the dust.
The LORD alone will be exalted! 18 Idols will be utterly abolished and destroyed.
19 When the LORD rises to shake the earth, his enemies will crawl with fear into holes
in the ground. They will hide in caves in the rocks from the terror of the LORD and the
glory of his majesty. 20 They will abandon their gold and silver idols to the moles and
bats. 21 They will crawl into caverns and hide among the jagged rocks at the tops of cliffs.
In this way, they will try to escape the terror of the LORD and the glory of his majesty as
he rises to shake the earth.
22 Stop putting your trust in mere humans. They are as frail as breath. How can they
be of help to anyone?

Judgment against Judah

3 The Lord, the LORD Almighty, will cut off the supplies of food and water from
Jerusalem and Judah. 2 He will destroy all the nation's leaders—the heroes, soldiers,
judges, prophets, diviners, elders, 3 army officers, honorable citizens, advisers, skilled
magicians, and expert enchanters. 4 Then he will appoint children to rule over them, and
anarchy will prevail. 5 People will take advantage of each other—man against man,
neighbor fighting neighbor. Young people will revolt against authority, and nobodies will
sneer at honorable people.
6 In those days a man will say to his brother, "Since you have a cloak, you be our
leader! Take charge of this heap of ruins!"
7 "No!" he will reply. "I can't help. I don't have any extra food or clothes. Don't ask
me to get involved!"
8 Judah and Jerusalem will lie in ruins because they speak out against the LORD and
refuse to obey him. They have offended his glorious presence among them. 9 The very
look on their faces gives them away and displays their guilt. They sin openly like the
people of Sodom. They are not one bit ashamed. How terrible it will be for them! They
have brought about their own destruction.
10 But all will be well for those who are godly. Tell them, "You will receive a wonderful
reward!" 11 But say to the wicked, "Your destruction is sure. You, too, will get what you
deserve. Your well-earned punishment is on the way."
12 Children oppress my people, and women rule over them. O my people, can't you
see what fools your rulers are? They are leading you down a pretty garden path to
destruction.

2:16 Hebrew *every ship of Tarshish.*

2:16 1 Kgs 10:22; Isa 23:1, 14
2:18 Isa 21:9; Mic 1:7; Heb 12:26
2:19 Ps 18:7; Hag 2:6-7
2:20 Isa 30:22
2:22 Pss 8:4; 144:3-4; Jer 17:5; Jas 4:14
3:1 Ezek 4:16
3:2 Lev 26:26; Isa 9:14-15
3:4 Eccl 10:16
3:5 Isa 9:19; Jer 9:3-8; Mic 7:3-6
3:7 Ezek 34:4
3:8 Isa 1:7; 6:11; 9:17; 65:3, 5
3:9 Gen 13:13; Prov 8:36
3:10 Deut 28:1-14
3:11 Deut 28:15-68
3:12 Isa 9:16

2:15-17 High towers were part of a city or nation's defenses. This phrase refers to security based on military fortresses. "Great trading ships" picture economic prosperity; and "the small boats in the harbor" are pleasure vessels. Nothing can compare with or rival the place God must have in our hearts and minds. To place our hope elsewhere is nothing but false pride. Place your confidence in God alone.

2:19 See Revelation 6:15-17 for a description of the dread in God's enemies on the day of his wrath.

2:22 "As frail as breath" refers to our mortality. People are very limited when compared to God. They can be unreliable, selfish, and shortsighted. Yet we entrust our life and future more readily to mortal human beings than to the all-knowing God. Beware of people who want you to trust them instead of God. Remember that only God is completely reliable. He is perfect, and he loves us with an unfailing love (Psalm 100:5).

3:1-3 Jerusalem besieged, her leaders destroyed—this unhappy picture would soon become a reality. Disobedience would bring serious affliction and great destruction, as God had warned (Deuteronomy 28).

3:2 Isaiah was not condoning diviners, magicians, and enchanters by including them in this list. He was showing how far the nation had sunk. See the note on 2:6.

3:4-9 This section describes what happens when a nation loses its leadership.

3:9-11 The people would be proud of their sins, parading them out in the open. But sin is self-destructive. In today's world, sinful living often appears glamorous, exciting, and clever. But sin is wrong, regardless of how society perceives it, and, in the long run, sin will make us miserable and destroy us. God tries to protect us by warning us about the harm we will cause ourselves by sinning. Those who are proud of their sins will receive the punishment from God they deserve. Having rejected God's path to life (see Psalm 1), they had only one alternative—the path to destruction.

3:10, 11 In the middle of this gloomy message, God gives hope: Eventually the righteous will receive God's reward, and the wicked will receive their punishment. It is disheartening to see the wicked prosper, while we struggle to obey God and follow his plan. But let us keep holding on to God's truth and take heart! God will bring about justice in the end, and he will reward those who have been faithful.

13 The LORD takes his place in court. He is the great prosecuting attorney, presenting
his case against his people! 14 The leaders and the princes will be the first to feel the
LORD's judgment. "You have ruined Israel, which is my vineyard. You have taken
advantage of the poor, filling your barns with grain extorted from helpless people.
15 How dare you grind my people into the dust like that!" demands the Lord, the LORD
Almighty.

A Warning for Jerusalem's Women

16 Next the LORD will judge the women of Jerusalem,* who walk around with their noses
in the air, with tinkling ornaments on their ankles. Their eyes rove among the crowds,
flirting with the men. 17 The Lord will send a plague of scabs to ornament their heads.
Yes, the LORD will make them bald for all to see!

18 The Lord will strip away their artful beauty—their ornaments, headbands, and
crescent necklaces; 19 their earrings, bracelets, and veils of shimmering gauze. 20 Gone
will be their scarves, ankle chains, sashes, perfumes, and charms; 21 their rings,
jewels, 22 party clothes, gowns, capes, and purses; 23 their mirrors, linen garments,
head ornaments, and shawls. 24 Instead of smelling of sweet perfume, they will stink.
They will wear ropes for sashes, and their well-set hair will fall out. They will wear
rough sackcloth instead of rich robes. Their beauty will be gone. Only shame will be
left to them.

25 The men of the city will die in battle. 26 The gates of Jerusalem* will weep and
mourn. The city will be like a ravaged woman, huddled on the ground.

4 In that day few men will be left alive. Seven women will fight over each of them and
say, "Let us all marry you! We will provide our own food and clothing. Only let us
be called by your name so we won't be mocked as old maids."

A Promise of Restoration

2 But in the future, Israel—the branch of the LORD—will be lush and beautiful, and
the fruit of the land will be the pride of its people. 3 All those whose names are written
down, who have survived the destruction of Jerusalem, will be a holy people. 4 The
Lord will wash the moral filth from the women of Jerusalem.* He will cleanse
Jerusalem of its bloodstains by a spirit of judgment that burns like fire. 5 Then the
LORD will provide shade for Jerusalem* and all who assemble there. There will be a
canopy of smoke and cloud throughout the day and clouds of fire at night, covering
the glorious land. 6 It will be a shelter from daytime heat and a hiding place from
storms and rain.

3:13 Isa 66:16; Hos 4:1; Mic 6:2
3:14 Pss 10:9; 14:4; Ezek 18:12; 20:35-36
3:16 Isa 4:4
3:18 Judg 8:21
3:24 Esth 2:12; Isa 15:3; 22:12; 1 Pet 3:3
3:25 Isa 1:20; 65:12
3:26 Jer 14:2; Lam 2:10
4:1 Isa 13:12; 54:4
4:2 Isa 11:1-5; 52:13; 53:2; Jer 23:5-6; Zech 3:8; 6:12
4:3 Isa 28:5; 52:1; Luke 10:20
4:5 Num 9:15-23
4:6 Ps 27:5; Isa 25:4; 32:1-2

3:16 Hebrew *the daughters of Zion.* **3:26** Hebrew *Zion.* **4:4** Hebrew *from the daughters of Zion.* **4:5** Hebrew *Mount Zion.*

3:14 The leaders and princes were responsible to help people, but instead they stole from the poor. Because they were unjust, Isaiah said the leaders would be the first to receive God's judgment. Leaders will be held accountable for how they lead. If you are in a position of leadership, you must lead according to God's just commands. Corruption will bring God's wrath, especially if others follow your example.

3:14 Why is justice so important in the Bible? (1) Justice is part of God's nature; it is the way he runs the universe. (2) It is a natural desire in every person. Even as sinners, we all want justice for ourselves. (3) When government and church leaders are unjust, the poor and powerless suffer. Thus, they are hindered from worshiping God. (4) God holds the poor in high regard. They are the ones most likely to turn to him for help and comfort. Injustice, then, attacks God's children. When we do nothing to help the oppressed, we are, in fact, joining with the oppressor. Because we follow a just God, we must uphold justice.

3:16-26 The women of Judah had placed their emphasis on clothing and jewelry rather than on God. They dressed to be noticed, to gain approval, and to be fashionable. Yet they ignored the real purpose for their lives. Instead of being concerned about the oppression around them (3:14, 15), they were self-serving and self-centered. People who abuse their possessions will end up with nothing. These verses are not an indictment against clothing and jewelry, but a judgment on those who use them lavishly while remaining blind to the needs of others. When God blesses you with money or position, don't flaunt it. Use what you have to help others, not impress them.

4:2-4 The "branch of the LORD" probably refers to the Messiah, although some believe it refers to Judah. The point is that during the distress predicted by Isaiah, some people will be protected by God's loving grace. Those protected will be set apart to God when Messiah rules the earth (Jeremiah 23:5, 6; Zechariah 6:12, 13). Their distinctive mark will be their holiness, not wealth or prestige. This holiness comes from a sincere desire to obey God and from wholehearted devotion to him. Evil will not always continue as it does now. The time will come when God will put an end to all evil, and his faithful followers will share in his glorious reign.

A Song about the LORD's Vineyard

5:1
Ps 80:8-9
Jer 12:10
Matt 21:33
Mark 12:1
Luke 20:9

5 Now I will sing a song for the one I love about his vineyard:

My beloved has a vineyard
on a rich and fertile hill.

5:2
Jer 2:21
Matt 21:19
Mark 11:13
Luke 13:6

2 He plowed the land, cleared its stones,
and planted it with choice vines.
In the middle he built a watchtower
and carved a winepress in the nearby rocks.
Then he waited for a harvest of sweet grapes,
but the grapes that grew were wild and sour.
3 "Now, you people of Jerusalem and Judah,
you have heard the case; you be the judges.

5:4
Jer 7:25-26
Matt 23:37

4 What more could I have done
to cultivate a rich harvest?
Why did my vineyard give me wild grapes
when I expected sweet ones?

5:5
Ps 80:12
Lam 1:15
Luke 21:24
Rev 11:2

5 Now this is what I am going to do to my vineyard:
I will tear down its fences
and let it be destroyed.
I will break down its walls
and let the animals trample it.

5:6
Isa 24:13
Jer 14:1-22; 25:11

6 I will make it a wild place.
I will not prune the vines or hoe the ground.
I will let it be overgrown with briers and thorns.
I will command the clouds
to drop no more rain on it."

7 This is the story of the LORD's people.
They are the vineyard of the LORD Almighty.
Israel and Judah are his pleasant garden.
He expected them to yield a crop of justice,
but instead he found bloodshed.
He expected to find righteousness,
but instead he heard cries of oppression.

Judah's Guilt and Judgment

5:8
Jer 22:13-17
Mic 2:2

5:9
Isa 6:11-12
Matt 23:38

5:10
Hag 1:6; 2:16

5:11
Prov 23:29-30
Isa 28:1, 3, 7-8

5:12
Ps 28:5

8 Destruction is certain for you who buy up property so others have no place to live. Your
homes are built on great estates so you can be alone in the land. 9 But the LORD Almighty
has sealed your awful fate. With my own ears I heard him say, "Many beautiful homes
will stand deserted, the owners dead or gone. 10 Ten acres* of vineyard will not produce
even six gallons* of wine. Ten measures of seed will yield only one measure* of grain."
11 Destruction is certain for you who get up early to begin long drinking bouts that last
late into the night. 12 You furnish lovely music and wine at your grand parties; the harps,
lyres, tambourines, and flutes are superb! But you never think about the LORD or notice

5:10a Hebrew *A ten yoke,* that is, the area of land plowed by ten teams of oxen in one day. **5:10b** Hebrew *a bath* [21 liters]. **5:10c** Hebrew *A homer* [5 bushels or 182 liters] *of seed will yield only an ephah* [0.5 bushels or 18.2 liters].

5:1-7 The lesson of the song of the vineyard shows that God's chosen nation was to bear fruit—to carry out his work, to uphold justice. It did bear fruit, but the fruit was bad. This passage uses plays on words: the Hebrew words for *justice* and *bloodshed* sound very much alike, as do those for *righteousness* and *oppression.* Jesus said, "The way to identify a tree or a person is by the kind of fruit that is produced" (Matthew 7:20). Have you examined your own "fruit" lately? Is it good or bad—useful or wild?

5:8-25 In this section, God condemns six sins: (1) exploiting others (5:8-10); (2) drunkenness (5:11, 12); (3) taking pride in sin (5:18, 19); (4) confusing moral standards (5:20); (5) being conceited (5:21); (6) perverting justice (5:22-24). Because of these sins, God punished Israel with destruction by Assyria (5:25-30). A similar fate was awaiting Judah if they didn't turn from these sins.

5:11-13 These people spent many hours drinking and partying, but Isaiah predicted that eventually many would die of hunger and thirst. Ironically, our pleasures—if they do not have God's blessing—may destroy us. Leaving God out of our life allows sin to come in. God wants us to enjoy life (1 Timothy 6:17) but to avoid those activities that could lead us away from him.

what he is doing. 13 So I will send my people into exile far away because they do not
know me. The great and honored among them will starve, and the common people will
die of thirst.
14 The grave* is licking its chops in anticipation of Jerusalem, this delicious morsel.
Her great and lowly will be swallowed up, with all her drunken crowds. 15 In that day
the arrogant will be brought down to the dust; the proud will be humbled. 16 But the
LORD Almighty is exalted by his justice. The holiness of God is displayed by his
righteousness. 17 In those days flocks will feed among the ruins; lambs and kids* will
pasture there.
18 Destruction is certain for those who drag their sins behind them, tied with
cords of falsehood. 19 They even mock the Holy One of Israel and say, "Hurry up
and do something! Quick, show us what you can do. We want to see what you have
planned."
20 Destruction is certain for those who say that evil is good and good is evil; that dark
is light and light is dark; that bitter is sweet and sweet is bitter.
21 Destruction is certain for those who think they are wise and consider themselves to
be clever.
22 Destruction is certain for those who are heroes when it comes to drinking, who boast
about all the liquor they can hold. 23 They take bribes to pervert justice. They let the
wicked go free while punishing the innocent.
24 Therefore, they will all disappear like burning straw. Their roots will rot and
their flowers wither, for they have rejected the law of the LORD Almighty. They
have despised the word of the Holy One of Israel. 25 That is why the anger of the LORD
burns against his people. That is why he has raised his fist to crush them. The hills
tremble, and the rotting bodies of his people are thrown as garbage into the streets.
But even then the LORD's anger will not be satisfied. His fist is still poised to
strike!
26 He will send a signal to the nations far away. He will whistle to those at the ends
of the earth, and they will come racing toward Jerusalem. 27 They will not get tired or
stumble. They will run without stopping for rest or sleep. Not a belt will be loose, not
a sandal thong broken. 28 Their arrows will be sharp and their bows ready for battle.
Sparks will fly from their horses' hooves as the wheels of their chariots spin like the
wind. 29 Roaring like lions, they will pounce on their prey. They will seize my people
and carry them off into captivity, and no one will be there to rescue them. 30 The
enemy nations will growl over their victims like the roaring of the sea. A cloud of
darkness and sorrow will hover over Israel. The clouds will blot out the light.

5:14 Hebrew *Sheol.* **5:17** As in Greek version; Hebrew reads *strangers.*

5:13 Isa 1:3; 3:3; Hos 4:6
5:14 Prov 30:16
5:15 Isa 2:11
5:16 Isa 33:5, 10
5:17 Isa 29:23; Zeph 2:6
5:18 Jer 23:10-14
5:19 2 Pet 3:3-4
5:20 Prov 17:15; Matt 6:22-23; Luke 11:34-35
5:21 Prov 3:7; Rom 12:16; 1 Cor 3:18-20
5:22 Isa 5:11; 56:12; Hab 2:15
5:23 Ps 94:21; Mic 3:11; Jas 5:6
5:24 Isa 9:18-19; 30:12
5:25 2 Kgs 22:13, 17; Isa 9:12, 17, 21; 10:4; 66:15
5:26 Isa 13:2-3
5:27 Joel 2:7-8
5:28 Ps 7:12-13; Jer 4:13
5:29 Isa 42:22; Zeph 3:3
5:30 Isa 8:22; 17:12; Jer 4:23-28; 6:23; Joel 2:10

5:13 The nation's heroes—the "great and honored"—would suffer the same humiliation as the common people. Why? Because they lived by their own values rather than God's. Many of today's media and sports heroes are idolized because of their ability to live as they please. Are your heroes those who defy God or those who defy the world in order to serve God?

5:18, 19 Some people drag their sins around with them. Some do so arrogantly, but for others, their sins have become a burden that wears them out. Are you dragging around a cartload of sins that you refuse to give up? Before you find yourself worn out and useless, turn to the one who promises to take away your burden of sin and replace it with a purpose for living that is a joy to fulfill (see Matthew 11:28-30).

5:20 When people see no distinction between good and evil, destruction soon follows. It is easy for people to say, "No one can decide for anyone else what is really right or wrong." They may think getting drunk can't hurt them, extramarital sex isn't really wrong, or money doesn't control them. But when they make excuses for their actions, they break down the distinction between right and wrong. If people do not take God's Word, the Bible, as their standard, soon all moral choices become fuzzy. Without God, they are headed for a breakdown and much suffering.

5:24 The people suffered because they rejected God's law. It is sad to see so many people today searching for meaning in life while spurning God's Word. We can avoid the error of Israel and Judah by making reading the Bible a high priority in our life.

5:26-30 This passage describes what God would do if the people disobeyed him (Deuteronomy 28). Assyria began to torment Israel during the reign of Ahaz (735–715 B.C.). This powerful aggressor destroyed the northern kingdom in 722 B.C. and scattered the people throughout its own empire. Sin has consequences. Although this judgment was not immediate, eventually Israel was punished.

6:1
2 Kgs 15:7
Isa 1:1
John 12:41

6:2
Rev 4:8

6:3
Ps 72:19
Rev 4:8

Isaiah's Cleansing and Call

6 In the year King Uzziah died, I saw the Lord. He was sitting on a lofty throne, and the
train of his robe filled the Temple. 2 Hovering around him were mighty seraphim, each
with six wings. With two wings they covered their faces, with two they covered their feet,
and with the remaining two they flew. 3 In a great chorus they sang, "Holy, holy, holy is the
LORD Almighty! The whole earth is filled with his glory!" 4 The glorious singing shook the
Temple to its foundations, and the entire sanctuary was filled with smoke.

ISAIAH

Trees and prophets share at least one important characteristic—both are planted for the future. Yet seedlings are often overlooked and prophets often ignored. Isaiah is one of the best examples of this. The people of his time could have been rescued by his words. Instead, they refused to believe him. With the passing of centuries, however, Isaiah's words have cast a shadow on all of history.

Isaiah was active as a prophet during the reigns of five kings, but he did not set out to be a prophet. By the time King Uzziah died, Isaiah may have been established as a scribe in the royal palace in Jerusalem. It was a respectable career, but God had other plans for his servant. Isaiah's account of God's call leaves little doubt about what motivated the prophet for the next half century. His vision of God was unforgettable.

The encounter with God permanently affected Isaiah's character. He reflected the God he represented. Isaiah's messages—some comforting, some confronting—are so dissimilar that some have guessed they came from different authors. Isaiah's testimony is that the messages came from the only one capable of being perfect in justice as well as in mercy—God himself.

When he called Isaiah as a prophet, God did not encourage him with predictions of great success. God told Isaiah that the people would not listen. But he was to speak and write his messages anyway because eventually some *would* listen. God compared his people to a tree that would have to be cut down so that a new tree could grow from the old stump (Isaiah 6:13).

We who are part of that future can see that many of the promises God gave through Isaiah have been fulfilled in Jesus Christ. We also gain the hope of knowing that God is active in all of history, including our own.

Strengths and accomplishments
- Considered the greatest Old Testament prophet
- Quoted at least 50 times in the New Testament
- Had powerful messages of both judgment and hope
- Carried out a consistent ministry even though there was little positive response from his listeners
- His ministry spanned the reigns of five kings of Judah

Lessons from his life
- God's help is needed in order to comfort people while effectively confronting sin
- One result of experiencing forgiveness is the desire to share that forgiveness with others
- God is purely and perfectly holy, just, and loving

Vital statistics
- Where: Jerusalem
- Occupations: Scribe, prophet
- Relatives: Father: Amoz. Sons: Shear-jashub, Maher-shalal-hash-baz
- Contemporaries: Uzziah, Jotham, Ahaz, Hezekiah, Manasseh, Micah

Key verse
"Then I heard the Lord asking, 'Whom should I send as a messenger to my people? Who will go for us?' And I said, 'Lord, I'll go! Send me' " (Isaiah 6:8).

Isaiah's story is told in 2 Kings 19:2—20:19. He is also mentioned in 2 Chronicles 26:22; 32:20, 32; Matthew 3:3; 8:17; 12:17–21; John 12:38–41; Romans 10:16, 20, 21.

6:1 The year that King Uzziah died was approximately 740 B.C. He remained leprous until he died because he tried to take over the high priest's duties (2 Chronicles 26:18-21). Although Uzziah was generally a good king with a long and prosperous reign, many of his people turned away from God.

6:1ff Isaiah's vision was his commission to be God's messenger to his people. Isaiah was given a difficult mission. He had to tell people who believed they were blessed by God that God was going to destroy them instead because of their disobedience.

6:1ff Isaiah's lofty view of God in 6:1-4 gives us a sense of God's greatness, mystery, and power. Isaiah's example of recognizing his sinfulness before God encourages us to confess our sin. His picture of forgiveness reminds us that we, too, are forgiven. When we recognize how great our God is, how sinful we are, and the extent of God's forgiveness, we receive power to do his work. How does your concept of the greatness of God measure up to Isaiah's?

6:1-3 The throne, the attending seraphim or angels, and the threefold *holy* all stressed God's holiness. Seraphim were a type of angel whose name is derived from the word for "burn," perhaps indicating their purity as God's ministers. In a time when moral and spiritual decay had peaked, it was important for Isaiah to see God in his holiness. *Holiness* means "morally perfect, pure, and set apart from all sin." We also need to discover God's holiness. Our daily frustrations, society's pressures, and our shortcomings narrow our view of God. We need the Bible's view of God as high and lifted up to empower us to deal with our problems and concerns. God's moral perfection, properly seen, will purify us from sin, cleanse our mind of our problems, and enable us to worship and to serve.

5 Then I said, "My destruction is sealed, for I am a sinful man and a member of a sinful
race. Yet I have seen the King, the LORD Almighty!"
6 Then one of the seraphim flew over to the altar, and he picked up a burning coal with
a pair of tongs. 7 He touched my lips with it and said, "See, this coal has touched your
lips. Now your guilt is removed, and your sins are forgiven."
8 Then I heard the Lord asking, "Whom should I send as a messenger to my people?
Who will go for us?"
And I said, "Lord, I'll go! Send me."
9 And he said, "Yes, go. But tell my people this: 'You will hear my words, but you will
not understand. You will see what I do, but you will not perceive its meaning.' 10 Harden
the hearts of these people. Close their ears, and shut their eyes. That way, they will not
see with their eyes, hear with their ears, understand with their hearts, and turn to me for
healing."
11 Then I said, "Lord, how long must I do this?"
And he replied, "Until their cities are destroyed, with no one left in them. Until their
houses are deserted and the whole country is an utter wasteland. 12 Do not stop until the
LORD has sent everyone away to distant lands and the entire land of Israel lies deserted.
13 Even if only a tenth—a remnant—survive, it will be invaded again and burned. Israel
will remain a stump, like a tree that is cut down, but the stump will be a holy seed that
will grow again."

A Message for Ahaz

7 During the reign of Ahaz son of Jotham and grandson of Uzziah, Jerusalem was
attacked by King Rezin of Aram and King Pekah of Israel, the son of Remaliah. The
city withstood the attack, however, and was not taken.
2 The news had come to the royal court: "Aram is allied with Israel* against us!"
So the hearts of the king and his people trembled with fear, just as trees shake in a
storm.
3 Then the LORD said to Isaiah, "Go out to meet King Ahaz, you and your son
Shear-jashub.* You will find the king at the end of the aqueduct that feeds water into

6:5 Jer 9:3-8; 51:57 Luke 5:8
6:7 Isa 40:2 Jer 1:9 1 Jn 1:7
6:9 †Matt 13:15 †Luke 8:10 Acts 26:19 Rom 11:8
6:10 Jer 5:21 †Mark 4:12 †John 12:40 †Acts 28:26-27
6:11 Lev 26:31 Mic 3:12
6:12 Jer 4:29
6:13 Ezra 9:2 Job 14:7
7:1 2 Kgs 15:25, 37; 16:1
7:2 Isa 7:13; 8:12

7:2 Hebrew *Ephraim,* referring to the northern kingdom of Israel; also in 7:5, 8, 9, 17. **7:3** *Shear-jashub* means "A remnant will return."

6:5-8 Seeing the Lord and listening to the praise of the angels, Isaiah realized that he was sinful before God, with no hope of measuring up to God's standard of holiness. When Isaiah's lips were touched with a live burning coal, however, he was told that his sins were forgiven. It wasn't the coal that cleansed him, but God. In response, Isaiah submitted himself entirely to God's service. No matter how difficult his task would be, he said, "Lord, I'll go! Send me." The painful cleansing process was necessary before Isaiah could fulfill the task to which God was calling him. Before we accept God's call to speak for him to those around us, we must be cleansed as Isaiah was, confessing our sins and submitting to God's control. Letting God purify us may be painful, but we must be purified so that we can truly represent God, who is pure and holy.

6:8 The more clearly Isaiah saw God (6:5), the more aware Isaiah became of his own powerlessness and inadequacy to do anything of lasting value without God. But he was willing to be God's spokesman. When God calls, will you also say, "Send me"?

6:9-13 God told Isaiah that the people would listen but not learn from his message because their hearts had become hardened beyond repentance. God's patience with their chronic rebellion was finally exhausted. His judgment was to abandon them to their rebellion and hardness of heart. Why did God send Isaiah if he knew the people wouldn't listen? Although the nation itself would not repent and would reap judgment, some individuals would listen. In 6:13 God explains his plan for a remnant (holy seed) of faithful followers. God is merciful even when he judges. We can gain encouragement from God's promise to preserve his people. If we are faithful to him, we can be sure of his mercy.

6:11-13 When would the people listen? Only after they had come to the end and had nowhere to turn but to God. This would happen when the land was destroyed by invading armies and the people taken into captivity. The "tenth" refers either to those who remained in the land after the captivity or to those who returned from Babylon to rebuild the land. Each group was about a tenth of the total population. When will we listen to God? Must we, like Judah, go through calamities before we will listen to God's words? Consider what God may be telling you, and obey him before time runs out.

7:1 The year was 734 B.C. Ahaz, king of Judah in Jerusalem, was about to be attacked by an alliance of the northern kingdom of Israel and Aram. He was frightened by the prospect of the possible end of his reign and by the invading armies that killed many people or took them as captives (2 Chronicles 28:5-21). But, as Isaiah predicted, the kingdom of Judah did not come to an end at this time. The sign of Immanuel would be a sign of deliverance.

7:3 *Shear-jashub* means "a remnant will return." God told Isaiah to give his son this name as a reminder of his plan for mercy. From the beginning of God's judgment he planned to restore a remnant of his people. Shear-jashub was a reminder to the people of God's faithfulness to them.

7:3 The "aqueduct" may have been the site of the Gihon Spring, located east of Jerusalem. The Gihon Spring was the main source of water for the holy city and was also the spring that emptied into Hezekiah's famous water tunnel (2 Chronicles 32:30). The field where the cloth is bleached was a well-known place where clothing or newly woven cloth was laid in the sun to dry and whiten (see 36:2).

7:4 Exod 14:13; Isa 10:24; 30:15; 35:4; Lam 3:26
7:7 Isa 8:10
7:8 Isa 17:1-3
7:9 2 Chr 20:20; Isa 30:12-14
7:11 2 Kgs 19:29; Isa 37:30; 38:7-8
7:14 Isa 8:8, 10; †Matt 1:23
7:15 Isa 8:4; 17:3
7:17 1 Kgs 12:16-17; Isa 10:5-6
7:18 Isa 5:26
7:19 Jer 16:16

the upper pool, near the road leading to the field where cloth is bleached. 4 Tell him
to stop worrying. Tell him he doesn't need to fear the fierce anger of those two
burned-out embers, King Rezin of Aram and Pekah son of Remaliah.
5 "Yes, the kings of Aram and Israel are coming against you. They are saying, 6 'We
will invade Judah and throw its people into panic. Then we will fight our way into
Jerusalem and install the son of Tabeel as Judah's king.'
7 "But this is what the Sovereign LORD says: This invasion will never happen,
8 because Aram is no stronger than its capital, Damascus. And Damascus is no stronger
than its king, Rezin. As for Israel, within sixty-five years it will be crushed and
completely destroyed. 9 Israel is no stronger than its capital, Samaria. And Samaria is
no stronger than its king, Pekah son of Remaliah. You do not believe me? If you want
me to protect you, learn to believe what I say."

The Sign of Immanuel

10 Not long after this, the LORD sent this message to King Ahaz: 11 "Ask me for a sign,
Ahaz, to prove that I will crush your enemies as I have promised. Ask for anything
you like, and make it as difficult as you want."
12 But the king refused. "No," he said, "I wouldn't test the LORD like that."
13 Then Isaiah said, "Listen well, you royal family of David! You aren't satisfied to
exhaust my patience. You exhaust the patience of God as well! 14 All right then, the
Lord himself will choose the sign. Look! The virgin* will conceive a child! She will
give birth to a son and will call him Immanuel—'God is with us.' 15 By the time this
child is old enough to eat curds and honey, he will know enough to choose what is
right and reject what is wrong. 16 But before he knows right from wrong, the two kings
you fear so much—the kings of Israel and Aram—will both be dead.
17 "The LORD will bring a terrible curse on you, your nation, and your family. You
will soon experience greater terror than has been known in all the years since Solomon's empire was divided into Israel and Judah. The mighty king of Assyria will come
with his great army!"
18 In that day the LORD will whistle for the army of Upper Egypt and for the army
of Assyria. They will swarm around you like flies. Like bees, they will sting and kill.
19 They will come in vast hordes, spreading across the whole land. They will settle in

7:14 Or *young woman.*

7:4–8:15 Isaiah predicted the breakup of Israel's alliance with Aram (7:4-9). Because of this alliance, Israel would be destroyed; Assyria would be the instrument God would use to destroy them (7:8-25) and to punish Judah. But God would not let Assyria destroy Judah (8:1-15). They would be spared because God's gracious plans cannot be thwarted.

7:8 Ahaz, one of Judah's worst kings, refused God's help, and instead, he tried to buy aid from the Assyrians with silver and gold from the Temple (2 Kings 16:8). When the Assyrians came, they brought further trouble instead of help. In 722 B.C., Samaria, the capital of Israel, the northern kingdom, fell to the Assyrian armies, thus ending the northern kingdom.

7:12 Ahaz appeared righteous by saying he would not test God with a sign ("I wouldn't test the LORD like that"). In fact, God had told him to ask, but Ahaz didn't really want to know what God would say. Often we use some excuse, such as not wanting to bother God, to keep us from communicating with him. Don't let anything keep you from hearing and obeying God.

7:14-16 *Virgin* is translated from a Hebrew word used for an unmarried woman who is old enough to be married, one who is sexually mature (see Genesis 24:43; Exodus 2:8; Psalm 68:25; Proverbs 30:19; Song of Songs 1:3; 6:8). Some have compared this young woman to Isaiah's young wife and newborn son (8:1-4). This is not likely because she had a child, Shear-jashub, and her second child was not named Immanuel. Some believe that Isaiah's first wife may have died, and so this is his second wife. It is more likely that this prophecy had a double fulfillment. (1) A young woman from the house of Ahaz who was not married would marry and have a son. Before three years passed (one year for pregnancy and two for the child to be old enough to talk), the two invading kings would be destroyed. (2) Matthew 1:23 quotes Isaiah 7:14 to show a further fulfillment of this prophecy in that a virgin named Mary conceived and bore a son, Immanuel, the Christ.

7:18 Flies and bees are symbols of God's judgment (see Exodus 23:28). Egypt and Assyria did not at this time devastate Judah. Hezekiah followed Ahaz as king, and he honored God; therefore, God held back his hand of judgment. Two more evil kings reigned before Josiah, of whom it was said that no other king turned so completely to the Lord (2 Kings 23:25). However, Judah's doom had been sealed by the extreme evil of Josiah's father, Amon. During Josiah's reign, Egypt marched against the Assyrians. Josiah then declared war on Egypt, although God told him not to. After Josiah was killed (2 Chronicles 35:20-27), only weak kings reigned in Judah. The Egyptians carried off Josiah's son, Jehoahaz, after three months. The next king, Jehoiakim, was taken by Nebuchadnezzar to Babylon. Egypt and Assyria had dealt death blows to Judah.

the fertile areas and also in the desolate valleys, caves, and thorny places. 20 In that
day the Lord will take this "razor"—these Assyrians you have hired to protect
you—and use it to shave off everything: your land, your crops, and your people.*
21 When they finally stop plundering, a farmer will be fortunate to have a cow and two
sheep left. 22 The few people still left in the land will live on curds and wild honey
because that is all the land will produce. 23 In that day the lush vineyards, now worth as
much as a thousand pieces of silver,* will become patches of briers and thorns. 24 The
entire land will be one vast brier patch, a hunting ground overrun by wildlife. 25 No one
will go to the fertile hillsides where the gardens once grew, for briers and thorns will
cover them. Cattle, sheep, and goats will graze there.

The Coming Assyrian Invasion

8 Again the LORD said to me, "Make a large signboard and clearly write this name on
it: Maher-shalal-hash-baz.*" 2 I asked Uriah the priest and Zechariah son of Jebere-
kiah, both known as honest men, to testify that I had written it before the child was
conceived.
3 Then I slept with my wife, and she became pregnant and had a son. And the LORD
said, "Call him Maher-shalal-hash-baz. 4 This name prophesies that within a couple of
years, before this child is old enough to say 'Papa' or 'Mama,' the king of Assyria will
invade both Damascus and Samaria and carry away their riches."
5 Then the LORD spoke to me again and said, 6 "The people of Judah have rejected
my gentle care* and are rejoicing over what will happen to King Rezin and King Pekah.
7 Therefore, the Lord will overwhelm them with a mighty flood from the Euphrates
River*—the king of Assyria and all his mighty armies. 8 This flood will overflow all its
channels and sweep into Judah. It will submerge Immanuel's land from one end to the
other.
9 "The Assyrians will cry, 'Do your best to defend yourselves, but you will be
shattered! Listen all you nations. Prepare for battle—and die! Yes, die! 10 Call your
councils of war, develop your strategies, prepare your plans of attack—and then die! For
God is with us!*'"

A Call to Trust the LORD

11 The LORD has said to me in the strongest terms: "Do not think like everyone else does.
12 Do not be afraid that some plan conceived behind closed doors will be the end of you.
13 Do not fear anything except the LORD Almighty. He alone is the Holy One. If you fear
him, you need fear nothing else. 14 He will keep you safe. But to Israel and Judah he will
be a stone that causes people to stumble and a rock that makes them fall. And for the
people of Jerusalem he will be a trap that entangles them. 15 Many of them will stumble
and fall, never to rise again. Many will be captured."

7:20 Isa 8:7; 10:5, 15; 24:1 Ezek 5:1-4
7:21 Jer 39:10
8:1 Isa 30:8 Hab 2:2
8:2 2 Kgs 16:10-11, 15-16
8:4 Isa 7:8-9, 16
8:6 Isa 7:1; 30:12
8:7 Isa 17:12-13 Amos 8:8; 9:5
8:8 Isa 7:14; 10:6; 30:28
8:9 Dan 2:34-35
8:12 Isa 7:2 †1 Pet 3:13-15
8:13 Num 20:12 Isa 5:16; 29:23
8:14 Ezek 11:16 Luke 2:34 †Rom 9:33 †1 Pet 2:8
8:15 Luke 20:18 Rom 9:32

7:20 Hebrew *shave off the head, the hair of the legs, and the beard.* **7:23** Hebrew *1,000 shekels of silver,* about 25 pounds or 11.4 kilograms in weight. **8:1** *Maher-shalal-hash-baz* means "Swift to plunder and quick to spoil." **8:6** Hebrew *rejected the gently flowing waters of Shiloah.* **8:7** Hebrew *the river.* **8:10** Hebrew *Immanuel!*

7:20 Hiring Assyria to save them would be Judah's downfall (2 Kings 16:7, 8). To "shave" Judah's hair was symbolic of total humiliation. Numbers 6:9 explains that after being defiled, a person who had been set apart for the Lord had to shave his head as part of the cleansing process. Shaving bodily hair was an embarrassment—an exposure of nakedness. For a Hebrew man to have his beard shaved was humiliating (2 Samuel 10:4, 5).

7:21-25 Judah's rich farmland would be trampled until it became pastureland, fit only for grazing. No longer would it be a place of agricultural abundance, "a land flowing with milk and honey" (Exodus 3:8), but a land with only briers and thorns.

8:1-4 These verses predict the fall of Israel and Aram. Aram fell to Assyria in 732 B.C., and Israel followed in 722 B.C. Isaiah put his message on a large scroll in a public place. God was warning all his people.

8:6-8 Because the people of Judah rejected God's kindness, choosing instead to seek help from other nations, God would punish them. We see two distinct attributes of God—his love and his wrath. To ignore his love and guidance results in sin and invites his wrath. We must recognize the consequences of our choices. God wants to protect us from bad choices, but he still gives us the freedom to make them.

8:7, 8 The heart of the Assyrian Empire was located between the Tigris and Euphrates Rivers. This flood is a poetic way of describing the overwhelming force of the Assyrian army.

8:9 To "be shattered" means to lose courage by the pressure of sudden fear.

8:11-15 Isaiah, along with most of the prophets, was viewed as a traitor because he did not support Judah's national policies. He called the people to commit themselves first to God and then to the king. He even predicted the overthrow of the government.

8:17 Deut 31:17; Isa 30:18; 54:8; Hab 2:3
8:18 †Heb 2:13
8:19 Lev 20:6; 1 Sam 28:8; 2 Kgs 21:6; Isa 19:3; 30:2
8:20 Mic 3:6; Luke 16:29
8:22 Isa 5:30; Jer 13:16; Amos 5:18, 20; Zeph 1:14-15

16 I will write down all these things as a testimony of what the LORD will do. I will
entrust it to my disciples, who will pass it down to future generations. 17 I will wait for
the LORD to help us, though he has turned away from the people of Israel.* My only hope
is in him. 18 I and the children the LORD has given me have names* that reveal the plans
the LORD Almighty has for his people. 19 So why are you trying to find out the future by
consulting mediums and psychics? Do not listen to their whisperings and mutterings.
Can the living find out the future from the dead? Why not ask your God?
20 "Check their predictions against my testimony," says the LORD. "If their predictions
are different from mine, it is because there is no light or truth in them. 21 My people will
be led away as captives, weary and hungry. And because they are hungry, they will rage
and shake their fists at heaven and curse their king and their God. 22 Wherever they look,
there will be trouble and anguish and dark despair. They will be thrown out into the
darkness."

Hope in the Messiah

9:1 2 Kgs 15:29; 2 Chr 16:4
9:2 †Matt 4:15-16
9:3 Isa 26:15; 35:10; 66:10
9:4 Isa 49:26
9:6 Deut 10:17; Neh 9:32; Isa 7:14; 26:3, 12; Matt 28:18; 1 Cor 15:25

9 Nevertheless, that time of darkness and despair will not go on forever. The land of
Zebulun and Naphtali will soon be humbled, but there will be a time in the future
when Galilee of the Gentiles, which lies along the road that runs between the Jordan and
the sea, will be filled with glory. 2 The people who walk in darkness will see a great
light—a light that will shine on all who live in the land where death casts its shadow.
3 Israel will again be great, and its people will rejoice as people rejoice at harvesttime.
They will shout with joy like warriors dividing the plunder. 4 For God will break the
chains that bind his people and the whip that scourges them, just as he did when he
destroyed the army of Midian with Gideon's little band. 5 In that day of peace, battle gear
will no longer be issued. Never again will uniforms be bloodstained by war. All such
equipment will be burned.
6 For a child is born to us, a son is given to us. And the government will rest on his
shoulders. These will be his royal titles: Wonderful Counselor,* Mighty God, Everlasting

8:17 Hebrew *the house of Jacob.* 8:18 *Isaiah* means "The LORD will save"; *Shear-jashub* means "A remnant will return"; and *Maher-shalal-hash-baz* means "Swift to plunder and quick to spoil." 9:6 Or *Wonderful, Counselor.*

NAMES FOR MESSIAH

Wonderful Counselor	He is exceptional, distinguished, and without peer, the one who gives the right advice.
Mighty God	He is God himself.
Everlasting Father	He is timeless; he is God our Father.
Prince of Peace	His government is one of justice and peace.

Isaiah uses four names in 9:6 to describe the Messiah. These names have special meaning to us.

8:16 Because some people faithfully passed on these words from generation to generation, we have the book of Isaiah today. Each of us needs to accept the responsibility to pass on God's Word to our children and grandchildren, encouraging them to love the Bible, read it, and learn from it. Then they will faithfully pass it on to their children and grandchildren.

8:17 Isaiah decided to wait for the Lord, though God had "turned away from the people of Israel." Many of the prophecies God gave through the prophets would not come true for 700 years; others still haven't been fulfilled. Are you willing to accept the Lord's timing, not yours?

8:19 The people would consult mediums and psychics, seeking answers from dead people instead of consulting the living God. God alone knows the future, and only he is eternal. We can trust God to guide us.

8:21 After rejecting God's plan for them, the people of Judah would blame God for their trials. People continually blame God for their self-induced problems. How do you respond to the unpleasant results of your own choices? Where do you fix the blame? Instead of blaming God, look for ways to grow through your bad choices and failures.

9:1 In our gloom and despair, we fear that our sorrows and troubles will never end. But we can take comfort in this certainty: Although the Lord may not always spare us from troubles, if we follow him wholeheartedly, he will lead us safely through them.

9:1-7 This child, who would become their deliverer, is the Messiah, Jesus. Matthew quotes these verses in describing Christ's ministry (Matthew 4:15, 16). The territories of Zebulun and Naphtali represent the northern kingdom as a whole. These were also the territories where Jesus grew up and often ministered; this is why they would see "a great light."

9:2 The apostle John also referred to Jesus as the "light" (John 1:9). Jesus referred to himself as "the light of the world" (John 8:12).

9:2-6 In a time of great darkness, God promised to send a light who would shine on everyone living in the shadow of death. He is both "Wonderful Counselor" and "Mighty God." This message of hope was fulfilled in the birth of Christ and the establishment of his eternal Kingdom. He came to deliver all people from their slavery to sin.

Father, Prince of Peace. 7His ever expanding, peaceful government will never end. He
will rule forever with fairness and justice from the throne of his ancestor David. The
passionate commitment of the LORD Almighty will guarantee this!

The LORD's Anger against Israel

8The Lord has spoken out against that braggart Israel, 9and the people of Israel* and
Samaria will soon discover it. In their pride and arrogance they say, 10"Our land lies in
ruins now, but we will rebuild it better than before. We will replace the broken bricks
with cut stone, the fallen sycamore trees with cedars." 11The LORD will reply to their
bragging by bringing Rezin's enemies, the Assyrians, against them—12along with
Arameans from the east and Philistines from the west. With bared fangs, they will devour
Israel. But even then the LORD's anger will not be satisfied. His fist is still poised to
strike. 13For after all this punishment, the people will still not repent and turn to the LORD
Almighty.

14Therefore, in a single day, the LORD will destroy both the head and the tail, the palm
branch and the reed. 15The leaders of Israel are the head, and the lying prophets are the
tail. 16For the leaders of the people have led them down the path of destruction. 17That
is why the Lord has no joy in the young men and no mercy on even the widows and
orphans. For they are all hypocrites, speaking wickedness with lies. But even then the
LORD's anger will not be satisfied. His fist is still poised to strike.

18This wickedness is like a brushfire. It burns not only briers and thorns but the
forests, too. Its burning sends up vast clouds of smoke. 19The land is blackened by the
fury of the LORD Almighty. The people are fuel for the fire, and no one spares anyone
else. 20They fight against their own neighbors to steal food, but they will still be hungry.
In the end they will even eat their own children.* 21Manasseh will feed on Ephraim,
Ephraim will feed on Manasseh, and both will devour Judah. But even then the LORD's
anger will not be satisfied. His fist is still poised to strike.

10 Destruction is certain for the unjust judges, for those who issue unfair laws. 2They
deprive the poor, the widows, and the orphans of justice. Yes, they rob widows
and fatherless children! 3What will you do when I send desolation upon you from a
distant land? To whom will you turn for help? Where will your treasures be safe? 4I will
not help you. You will stumble along as prisoners or lie among the dead. But even then
the LORD's anger will not be satisfied. His fist is still poised to strike.

Judgment against Assyria

5"Destruction is certain for Assyria, the whip of my anger. Its military power is a club
in my hand. 6Assyria will enslave my people, who are a godless nation. It will plunder
them, trampling them like dirt beneath its feet. 7But the king of Assyria will not know
that it is I who sent him. He will merely think he is attacking my people as part of his
plan to conquer the world. 8He will say, 'Each of my princes will soon be a king, ruling
a conquered land. 9We will destroy Calno just as we did Carchemish. Hamath will fall

9:7 Dan 2:44; Luke 1:32-33
9:9 Isa 7:8-9
9:12 Ps 79:7
9:13 Jer 5:3; Hos 7:10
9:14 Isa 19:15; Rev 18:8
9:16 Matt 15:14
9:17 Amos 8:13; Matt 12:34
9:18 Mal 4:1
9:19 Joel 2:3; Mic 7:2, 6
9:20 Isa 8:21-22; 49:26
9:21 Isa 5:25; 11:13
10:1 Ps 94:20
10:2 Isa 1:23; 5:23
10:4 Isa 34:3; 66:16
10:5 Jer 51:20
10:7 Gen 50:20; Mic 4:11-12; Acts 2:23-24
10:9 2 Kgs 16:9; 2 Chr 35:20; Amos 6:2

9:9 Hebrew *of Ephraim,* referring to the northern kingdom of Israel. **9:20** Or *eat their own arms.*

9:8-10 Pride made Israel think it would recover and rebuild in its own strength. Even though God made the people of Israel a nation and gave them the land they occupied, they put their trust in themselves rather than in him. Too often we take pride in our accomplishments, forgetting that it is God who has given us our resources and abilities. We may even become proud of our unique status as Christians. God is not pleased with *any* pride or trust in ourselves because it cuts off our contact with him.

9:21 Ephraim and Manasseh were tribes in the northern kingdom descended from Joseph's two sons. They fought a civil war because of their selfishness and wickedness (see Judges 12:4).

10:1 God will judge unjust judges and those who make unfair laws. Those who oppress others will be oppressed themselves. It is not enough to live in a land founded on justice; each individual must deal justly with the poor and the powerless. Don't pass your responsibility off onto your nation or even your church. You are accountable to God for what you do.

10:7 Although Assyria did not know it was part of God's plan, God used this nation to judge his people. God accomplishes his plans in history despite people or nations who reject him. He did not merely set the world in motion and let it go! Because our all-powerful, sovereign God is still in control today, we have security even in a rapidly changing world.

10:9 Calno, Carchemish, Hamath, Arpad, Samaria, and Damascus were cities conquered by Assyria. Assured of great victories that would enlarge their empire, the king of Assyria gave an arrogant speech. Already Assyria had conquered several cities and thought Judah would be defeated along with the others. Little did he know that they were under the mightier hand of God.

10:10 2 Kgs 19:17-18
10:12 2 Kgs 19:31; Jer 50:18
10:13 2 Kgs 19:22-24; Isa 37:24-27; Ezek 28:4; Dan 4:30
10:15 Isa 10:5; 29:16; Jer 51:20; Rom 9:20-21
10:17 Isa 27:4; 30:33; 31:9; 33:12; 37:23; Jer 4:4
10:19 Isa 21:17
10:20 Isa 17:7-8
10:22 Isa 28:22; †Rom 9:27-28
10:24 Exod 5:14-16
10:25 Isa 17:14
10:26 Exod 14:16, 27; Judg 7:25; Isa 37:36-38
10:27 Isa 14:25

before us as Arpad did. And we will destroy Samaria just as we did Damascus. 10 Yes,
we have finished off many a kingdom whose gods were far greater than those in
Jerusalem and Samaria. 11 So when we have defeated Samaria and her gods, we will
destroy Jerusalem with hers.'"
12 After the Lord has used the king of Assyria to accomplish his purposes in Jerusalem,
he will turn against the king of Assyria and punish him—for he is proud and arrogant.
13 He boasts, "By my own power and wisdom I have won these wars. By my own strength
I have captured many lands, destroyed their kings, and carried off their treasures. 14 By
my greatness I have robbed their nests of riches and gathered up kingdoms as a farmer
gathers eggs. No one can even flap a wing against me or utter a peep of protest."
15 Can the ax boast greater power than the person who uses it? Is the saw greater than
the person who saws? Can a whip strike unless a hand is moving it? Can a cane walk by
itself?
16 Listen now, king of Assyria! Because of all your evil boasting, the Lord, the LORD
Almighty, will send a plague among your proud troops, and a flaming fire will ignite
your glory. 17 The LORD, the Light of Israel and the Holy One, will be a flaming fire that
will destroy them. In a single night he will burn those thorns and briers, the Assyrians.
18 Assyria's vast army is like a glorious forest, yet it will be destroyed. The LORD will
completely destroy Assyria's warriors, and they will waste away like sick people in a
plague. 19 Only a few from all that mighty army will survive—so few that a child could
count them!

Hope for the LORD's People

20 Then at last those left in Israel and Judah* will trust the LORD, the Holy One of Israel.
They will no longer depend on the Assyrians, who would destroy them. 21 A remnant of
them will return* to the Mighty God. 22 But though the people of Israel are as numerous
as the sand on the seashore, only a few of them will return at that time. The LORD has
rightly decided to destroy his people. 23 Yes, the Lord, the LORD Almighty, has already
decided to consume them.
24 So this is what the Lord, the LORD Almighty, says: "My people in Jerusalem,* do
not be afraid of the Assyrians when they oppress you just as the Egyptians did long ago.
25 It will not last very long. In a little while my anger against you will end, and then my
anger will rise up to destroy them."
26 The LORD Almighty will beat them with his whip, as he did when Gideon triumphed
over the Midianites at the rock of Oreb, or when the LORD's staff was raised to drown
the Egyptian army in the sea. 27 In that day the LORD will end the bondage of his people.
He will break the yoke of slavery and lift it from their shoulders.*

10:20 Hebrew *and the house of Jacob.* **10:21** Hebrew *Shear-jashub;* see 7:3; 8:18. **10:24** Hebrew *Zion.* **10:27** As in Greek version; Hebrew reads *The yoke will be broken, for you have grown so fat.*

10:10 Samaria and Jerusalem were filled with idols that were powerless against the Assyrian military machine. Only the God of the universe could and would overthrow Assyria, but not until he had used the Assyrians for his purposes.

10:12 The predicted punishment of the Assyrians took place in 701 B.C., when 185,000 Assyrian soldiers were slain by the angel of the Lord (37:36, 37). Later, the Assyrian Empire fell to Babylon, never to rise again as a world power.

10:12 The Assyrians were haughty. Proud of the victories God permitted, they thought they had accomplished everything in their own power. Our perspective can also become distorted by pride in our accomplishments. If we do not acknowledge God to be in control of our life, working out his purposes, we are bound to fail.

10:15 No instrument or tool accomplishes its purposes without a greater power. The Assyrians were a tool in God's hands, but they failed to recognize it. When a tool boasts of greater power than the one who uses it, it is in danger of being discarded. We are useful only to the extent that we allow God to use us.

10:17 Assyria's downfall came in 612 B.C. when Nineveh, the capital city, was destroyed. Assyria had been God's instrument of judgment against Israel, but it, too, would be judged for its wickedness. No one escapes God's judgment against sin, not even the most powerful of nations (Psalm 2).

10:20, 21 Once Assyria's army was destroyed, a small group of God's people would stop relying on Assyria and start trusting God. This remnant would be but a fraction of Israel's former population: see Ezra 2:64, 65 for the small number who returned to Judah (see also 11:10-16).

10:20, 21 Those who remained faithful to God despite the horrors of the invasion are called the remnant. The key to being a part of the remnant was *faith.* Being a descendant of Abraham, living in the Promised Land, having trusted God at one time—none of these were good enough. Are you relying on your Christian heritage, the rituals of worship, or past experience to qualify you for belonging to God's family? The key to being a true Christian is faith in God.

28 Look, the mighty armies of Assyria are coming! They are now at Aiath, now at Migron. They are storing some of their equipment at Micmash. 29 They are crossing the pass and are staying overnight at Geba. Fear strikes the city of Ramah. All the people of Gibeah—the city of Saul—are running for their lives. 30 Well may you scream in terror, you people of Gallim! Shout out a warning to Laishah, for the mighty army comes. Poor Anathoth, what a fate is yours! 31 There go the people of Madmenah, all fleeing. And the citizens of Gebim are preparing to run. 32 But the enemy stops at Nob for the rest of that day. He shakes his fist at Mount Zion in Jerusalem.

33 But look! The Lord, the LORD Almighty, will chop down the mighty tree! He will destroy all that vast army of Assyria—officers and high officials alike. 34 The Mighty One will cut down the enemy as an ax cuts down the forest trees in Lebanon.

A Branch from David's Line

11 Out of the stump of David's family* will grow a shoot—yes, a new Branch bearing fruit from the old root. 2 And the Spirit of the LORD will rest on him—the Spirit of wisdom and understanding, the Spirit of counsel and might, the Spirit of knowledge and the fear of the LORD. 3 He will delight in obeying the LORD. He will never judge by appearance, false evidence, or hearsay. 4 He will defend the poor and the exploited. He will rule against the wicked and destroy them with the breath of his mouth. 5 He will be clothed with fairness and truth.

6 In that day the wolf and the lamb will live together; the leopard and the goat will be at peace. Calves and yearlings will be safe among lions, and a little child will lead them all. 7 The cattle will graze among bears. Cubs and calves will lie down together. And lions will eat grass as the livestock do. 8 Babies will crawl safely among poisonous snakes. Yes, a little child will put its hand in a nest of deadly snakes and pull it out unharmed. 9 Nothing will hurt or destroy in all my holy mountain. And as the waters fill the sea, so the earth will be filled with people who know the LORD.

10 In that day the heir to David's throne* will be a banner of salvation to all the world. The nations will rally to him, for the land where he lives will be a glorious place. 11 In that day the Lord will bring back a remnant of his people for the second time, returning them to the land of Israel from Assyria, Lower Egypt, Upper Egypt, Ethiopia,* Elam, Babylonia,* Hamath, and all the distant coastlands.

12 He will raise a flag among the nations for Israel to rally around. He will gather the scattered people of Judah from the ends of the earth. 13 Then at last the jealousy between Israel* and Judah will end. They will not fight against each other anymore. 14 They will join forces to swoop down on Philistia to the west. Together they will

10:28 1 Sam 13:2, 5; 14:2; 17:22
10:29 Josh 18:25; 21:17; 1 Sam 10:26
10:30 Josh 21:18; 1 Sam 25:44
10:32 Isa 19:16; Zech 2:9
10:33 Ezek 31:2-3; Amos 2:9
11:1 Jer 23:5; Rev 5:5
11:2 Isa 61:1; Matt 3:16; John 1:32; Eph 1:17
11:3 John 2:24-25; 7:24
11:4 Isa 30:28; 2 Thes 2:8
11:6 Isa 65:25
11:9 Job 5:23; Ezek 34:25; Hos 2:18; Hab 2:14
11:10 Luke 2:32; John 3:14-15; †Rom 15:12
11:11 Isa 60:9; 66:19; Zech 10:10
11:12 Isa 11:10; Zeph 3:10
11:13 Jer 3:18; Ezek 37:16-17, 22

11:1 Hebrew *the line of Jesse.* Jesse was King David's father. **11:10** Hebrew *the root of Jesse.* **11:11a** Hebrew *Pathros, Cush.* **11:11b** Hebrew *Shinar.* **11:13** Hebrew *Ephraim,* referring to the northern kingdom of Israel.

10:28-34 The way these cities are listed approximates the route the Assyrians would take in their invasion of Judah in 701 B.C. They would go from Aiath (probably Ai) at the northern border to Nob (only two miles from Jerusalem).

11:1-9 Assyria would be like a tree cut down at the height of its power (10:33, 34), never to rise again. Judah (the royal line of David) would be like a tree chopped down to a stump. But from that stump a new shoot would grow—the Messiah. He would be greater than the original tree and would bear much fruit. The Messiah is the fulfillment of God's promise that a descendant of David would rule forever (2 Samuel 7:16).

11:3-5 God will judge with fairness and truth. How we long for fair treatment from others, but do we give it? We hate those who base their judgments on appearance, false evidence, or hearsay, but are we quick to judge others using those standards? Only Christ can be the perfectly fair judge. Only as he governs our hearts can we learn to be as fair in our treatment of others as we expect others to be toward us.

11:4, 5 Judah had become corrupt and was surrounded by hostile, foreign powers. The nation desperately needed a revival of righteousness, justice, and faithfulness. They needed to turn from selfishness and show justice to the poor and the oppressed. The righteousness that God values is more than refraining from sin. It is actively turning toward others and offering them the help they need.

11:6-10 A golden age is yet to come, a time of peace when children will play with formerly dangerous animals. Not all of this was fulfilled at Christ's first coming. For example, nature has not returned to its intended balance and harmony (see Romans 8:9-22). Such perfect tranquility is possible only when Christ reigns over the earth.

11:11 When will this remnant of God's people be returned to their land? Old Testament prophecy is often applied both to the near future and the distant future. Judah would soon be exiled to Babylon, and a remnant would return to Jerusalem in 537 B.C. at Cyrus's decree. In the ages to come, however, God's people would be dispersed throughout the world. These locations represent the four corners of the known world—Hamath in the north, Egypt in the south, Assyria and Babylonia in the east, the islands of the sea in the west. Ultimately God's people will be regathered when Christ comes to reign over the earth.

11:14 Edom, Moab, and Ammon were three countries bordering Judah (along with Philistia). They were the nations who, when Judah was defeated, rejoiced and took their land.

attack and plunder the nations to the east. They will occupy all the lands of Edom,
Moab, and Ammon.
15 The LORD will make a dry path through the Red Sea.* He will wave his hand over
the Euphrates River,* sending a mighty wind to divide it into seven streams that can
easily be crossed. 16 He will make a highway from Assyria for the remnant there, just as
he did for Israel long ago when they returned from Egypt.

Songs of Praise for Salvation

12 In that day you will sing:

"Praise the LORD!
He was angry with me,
but now he comforts me.
2 See, God has come to save me.
I will trust in him and not be afraid.
The LORD GOD is my strength and my song;
he has become my salvation."

3 With joy you will drink deeply from the fountain of salvation! 4 In that wonderful day
you will sing:

"Thank the LORD!
Praise his name!
Tell the world what he has done.
Oh, how mighty he is!
5 Sing to the LORD,
for he has done wonderful things.
Make known his praise around the world.
6 Let all the people of Jerusalem* shout his praise with joy!
For great is the Holy One of Israel who lives among you."

2. Judgment against heathen nations

A Message about Babylon

13 Isaiah son of Amoz received this message concerning the destruction of Babylon:
2 "See the flags waving as the enemy attacks. Cheer them on, O Israel! Wave to
them as they march against Babylon to destroy the palaces of the high and mighty. 3 I,
the LORD, have assigned this task to these armies, and they will rejoice when I am
exalted. I have called them to satisfy my anger."
4 Hear the noise on the mountains! Listen, as the armies march! It is the noise and the
shout of many nations. The LORD Almighty has brought them here to form an army.
5 They came from countries far away. They are the LORD's weapons; they carry his anger
with them and will destroy the whole land. 6 Scream in terror, for the LORD's time has
arrived—the time for the Almighty to destroy. 7 Every arm is paralyzed with fear. Even
the strongest hearts melt 8 and are afraid. Fear grips them with terrible pangs, like those
of a woman about to give birth. They look helplessly at one another as the flames of the
burning city reflect on their faces. 9 For see, the day of the LORD is coming—the terrible

11:15 Isa 51:10
11:16 Exod 14:26-29; Isa 19:23
12:1 Isa 40:1
12:2 Ps 118:14; Isa 26:3; 62:11
12:3 Jer 2:13; John 4:10; 7:37-38
12:4 Ps 145:4
12:5 Ps 98:1; Isa 44:23
12:6 Isa 54:1; Zeph 3:14, 15-17
13:1 Jer 50:1-51
13:2 Isa 45:1-3
13:3 Joel 3:11
13:5 Isa 5:26
13:6 Isa 34:2, 8; Ezek 30:3; Amos 5:18
13:7 Ezek 21:7
13:8 Isa 21:3; 26:17
13:9 Isa 66:15-16

11:15a Hebrew *sea of Egypt.* **11:15b** Hebrew *the river.* **12:6** Hebrew *Zion.*

11:15, 16 Isaiah is talking about a new or second exodus when God will bring his scattered people back to Judah, and the Messiah will come to rule the world. The Lord dried up the Red Sea so the Israelites could walk through it on their way to the Promised Land (Exodus 14). He dried up the Jordan River so the nation could cross into the land (Joshua 3). God will again provide the way of return for his people.

12:1ff This chapter is a hymn of praise—another graphic description of the people's joy when Jesus Christ comes to reign over the earth. Even now we need to express our gratitude to God, thanking him, praising him, and telling others about him. From the depths of our gratitude, we must praise him. And we should share the Good News with others.

13:1ff Chapters 1–12 speak of judgment against the southern kingdom and, to a lesser extent, against the northern kingdom. Chapters 13–23 are about the judgment on other nations. Chapter 13 is an oracle or message from God concerning Babylon. Long before Babylon became a world power and threatened Judah, Isaiah spoke of its destruction. Babylon was the rallying point of rebellion against God after the Flood (Genesis 11). Revelation 17 and 18 use Babylon as a symbol of God's enemies. At the time of this oracle, Babylon was still part of the Assyrian Empire. Isaiah communicated a message of challenge and hope to God's people, telling them not to rely on other nations but to rely on God alone. And he let them know that their greatest enemies would receive from God the punishment they deserved.

day of his fury and fierce anger. The land will be destroyed and all the sinners with it.
10 The heavens will be black above them. No light will shine from stars or sun or moon.
11 "I, the LORD, will punish the world for its evil and the wicked for their sin. I will
crush the arrogance of the proud and the haughtiness of the mighty. 12 Few will be left
alive when I have finished my work. People will be as scarce as gold—more rare than
the gold of Ophir. 13 For I will shake the heavens, and the earth will move from its place.
I, the LORD Almighty, will show my fury and fierce anger."
14 Everyone will run until exhausted, rushing back to their own lands like hunted deer,
wandering like sheep without a shepherd. 15 Anyone who is captured will be run through
with a sword. 16 Their little children will be dashed to death right before their eyes. Their
homes will be sacked and their wives raped by the attacking hordes. 17 For I will stir up
the Medes against Babylon, and no amount of silver or gold will buy them off. 18 The
attacking armies will shoot down the young people with arrows. They will have no mercy
on helpless babies and will show no compassion for the children.
19 Babylon, the most glorious of kingdoms, the flower of Chaldean culture, will be
devastated like Sodom and Gomorrah when God destroyed them. 20 Babylon will never
rise again. Generation after generation will come and go, but the land will never again
be lived in. Nomads will refuse to camp there, and shepherds will not allow their sheep
to stay overnight. 21 Wild animals of the desert will move into the ruined city. The houses
will be haunted by howling creatures. Ostriches will live among the ruins, and wild goats
will come there to dance. 22 Hyenas will howl in its fortresses, and jackals will make their
dens in its palaces. Babylon's days are numbered; its time of destruction will soon arrive.

A Taunt for Babylon's King

14 But the LORD will have mercy on the descendants of Jacob. Israel will be his
special people once again. He will bring them back to settle once again in their
own land. And people from many different nations will come and join them there and
become a part of the people of Israel.* 2 The nations of the world will help the LORD's
people to return, and those who come to live in their land will serve them. Those who
captured Israel will be captured, and Israel will rule over its enemies.
3 In that wonderful day when the LORD gives his people rest from sorrow and fear,
from slavery and chains, 4 you will taunt the king of Babylon. You will say, "The mighty
man has been destroyed. Yes, your insolence is ended. 5 For the LORD has crushed your
wicked power and broken your evil rule. 6 You persecuted the people with unceasing
blows of rage and held the nations in your angry grip. Your tyranny was unrestrained.
7 But at last the land is at rest and is quiet. Finally it can sing again! 8 Even the trees of
the forest—the cypress trees and the cedars of Lebanon—sing out this joyous song:
'Your power is broken! No one will come to cut us down now!'
9 "In the place of the dead* there is excitement over your arrival. World leaders and
mighty kings long dead are there to see you. 10 With one voice they all cry out, 'Now you
are as weak as we are! 11 Your might and power are gone; they were buried with you. All
the pleasant music in your palace has ceased. Now maggots are your sheet and worms
your blanket.'

14:1 Hebrew *the house of Jacob.* **14:9** Hebrew *Sheol;* also in 14:15.

13:10 Matt 24:29 †Mark 13:24-25
13:11 Dan 5:22-23
13:12 Isa 6:11-12
13:13 Hag 2:6
13:14 1 Kgs 22:17 Matt 9:36
13:15 Jer 51:3-4
13:16 Ps 137:8-9 Hos 10:14
13:17 Jer 51:11
13:18 2 Chr 36:17
13:19 Gen 19:24 Rev 18:11-16, 19
13:20 Jer 51:37-43
13:21 Isa 34:11-15 Zeph 2:14
14:1 Ps 102:13 Isa 41:8-9; 49:13, 15 Zech 2:11-12
14:2 Isa 45:14 Dan 7:18, 27
14:3 Ezra 9:8-9 Jer 30:10
14:4 Hab 2:6
14:6 Isa 47:6
14:7 Ps 98:1-9
14:8 Isa 55:12
14:10 Ezek 32:21
14:11 Isa 5:14

13:12 Ophir was known for its rare and valuable gold. It is thought to have been located on the southwestern coast of Arabia.

13:20 Even before Babylon became a world power, Isaiah prophesied that, though it would shine for a while, Babylon's destruction would be so complete that the land would never again be inhabited. Babylon, in present-day Iraq, still lies in utter ruin, buried under mounds of dirt and sand.

14:1 A prominent theme in Isaiah is that non-Israelites would join the returning Israelites (56:6, 7; 60:10; 61:5). God's intention was that through his faithful people all the world would be blessed (Genesis 12:3). Through the family of David, the whole world could be saved by Christ. We must not limit God's love to our own people. God loves the whole world.

14:4-11 These verses could have both present and future significance in reference to Babylon. The historical city and empire would be permanently destroyed. Babylon has also been used as a picture of all those who oppose God. Thus, in the end times, all who oppose God will be destroyed, and all evil will be removed from the earth forever.

14:5, 6 Power fades quickly. God permitted Babylon to have temporary power for a purpose—to punish his wayward people. When the purpose ended, so did the power. Beware of placing confidence in human power because one day it will fade, no matter how strong it appears now.

12 "How you are fallen from heaven, O shining star, son of the morning! You have
been thrown down to the earth, you who destroyed the nations of the world. 13 For
you said to yourself, 'I will ascend to heaven and set my throne above God's stars.
I will preside on the mountain of the gods far away in the north. 14 I will climb to
the highest heavens and be like the Most High.' 15 But instead, you will be brought
down to the place of the dead, down to its lowest depths. 16 Everyone there will
stare at you and ask, 'Can this be the one who shook the earth and the kingdoms of
the world? 17 Is this the one who destroyed the world and made it into a wilderness?
Is this the king who demolished the world's greatest cities and had no mercy on his
prisoners?'

18 "The kings of the nations lie in stately glory in their graves, 19 but your body is
thrown from the grave like a discarded branch. Like a corpse trampled underfoot, you
will be dumped into a mass grave with those killed in battle. You will descend to the
pit. 20 You will not be given a proper burial, for you have destroyed your nation and
slaughtered your people. Your son will not succeed you as king. 21 Kill the children of
this sinner! Do not let them rise and conquer the land or rebuild the cities of the
world."

22 This is what the LORD Almighty says: "I, myself, have risen against him! I will
destroy his children and his children's children, so they will never sit on his throne.
23 I will make Babylon into a desolate land, a place of porcupines, filled with swamps
and marshes. I will sweep the land with the broom of destruction. I, the LORD
Almighty, have spoken!"

A Message about Assyria

24 The LORD Almighty has sworn this oath: "It will all happen as I have planned. It
will come about according to my purposes. 25 I will break the Assyrians when they are
in Israel; I will trample them on my mountains. My people will no longer be their
slaves. 26 I have a plan for the whole earth, for my mighty power reaches throughout
the world. 27 The LORD Almighty has spoken—who can change his plans? When his
hand moves, who can stop him?"

A Message about Philistia

28 This message came to me the year King Ahaz died:

29 Do not rejoice, you Philistines, that the king who attacked you is dead. For even
though that whip is broken, his son will be worse than his father ever was. From that
snake a poisonous snake will be born, a fiery serpent to destroy you! 30 I will feed the
poor in my pasture; the needy will lie down in peace. But as for you, I will wipe you
out with famine. I will destroy the few who remain.

31 Weep, you Philistine cities, for you are doomed! Melt in fear, for everyone will
be destroyed. A powerful army is coming out of the north. Each soldier rushes forward
ready to fight. 32 What should we tell the enemy messengers? Tell them that the LORD
has built Jerusalem,* and that the poor of his people will find refuge in its walls.

14:12 Luke 10:18; Rev 9:1
14:13 Ezek 28:2; †Luke 10:15
14:14 2 Thes 2:4
14:15 †Matt 11:23; †Luke 10:15
14:17 Isa 45:13; Joel 2:3
14:19 Isa 5:25
14:20 Job 18:19; Ps 21:10
14:21 Exod 20:5; Isa 13:16
14:23 Isa 13:6; 34:11
14:24 Job 23:13; Isa 46:11
14:26 Exod 15:12; Isa 23:9
14:27 Isa 43:13; Dan 4:31, 35
14:28 2 Kgs 16:20
14:29 2 Chr 26:6; Jer 47:1-7
14:31 Isa 3:26; Jer 1:14
14:32 Ps 87:1, 5; Isa 25:4

14:32 Hebrew *Zion.*

14:12 "Shining star, son of the morning" could be names used to worship the kings of Assyria and Babylon. More likely, it means that they will fade like the morning star when the sun rises.

14:12-14 There are several interpretations for the fallen one in these verses. (1) He is Satan, because the person here is too powerful to be any human king. Although Satan may fit verses 12-14, he does not fit well with the rest of the chapter. (2) This could be Sennacherib or Nebuchadnezzar, kings with supreme power. Their people looked upon them as gods. These kings wanted to rule the world. (3) This could refer to both Satan and a great human king, possibly Nebuchadnezzar, because Babylon is pictured as the seat of evil in Revelation 17–18. Pride was Satan's sin as well as Babylon's. Common to all three viewpoints is the truth that pride willfully opposes God and will result in judgment. Israel made the mistake of being too proud to depend on God, and we are vulnerable to that same mistake.

14:24-27 This prophecy came true as Isaiah predicted (see 2 Kings 19 and Isaiah 37:21-38).

14:28-31 Isaiah received this message from the Lord in 715 B.C., the year that King Ahaz of Judah died. "The king who attacked you" (14:29) was not Ahaz but Shalmaneser V or Sargon of Assyria. The "powerful army" from the north (14:31) refers to the soldiers of Sargon of Assyria.

A Message about Moab

15 This message came to me concerning Moab:
In one night your cities of Ar and Kir will be destroyed. 2 Your people in Dibon
will mourn at their temples and shrines, weeping for the fate of Nebo and Medeba. They
will shave their heads in sorrow and cut off their beards. 3 They will wear sackcloth as
they wander the streets. From every home will come the sound of weeping. 4 The cries
from the cities of Heshbon and Elealeh will be heard far away, even in Jahaz! The bravest
warriors of Moab will cry out in utter terror.
5 My heart weeps for Moab. Its people flee to Zoar and Eglath-shelishiyah. Weeping,
they climb the road to Luhith. Their crying can be heard all along the road to Horonaim.
6 Even the waters of Nimrim are dried up! The grassy banks are scorched, and the tender
plants are gone. 7 The desperate refugees take only the possessions they can carry and
flee across the Ravine of Willows. 8 The whole land of Moab is a land of weeping from
one end to the other—from Eglaim to Beer-elim. 9 The stream near Dibon* runs red with
blood, but I am still not finished with Dibon! Lions will hunt down the survivors, both
those who try to run and those who remain behind.

16 Moab's refugees at Sela send lambs to Jerusalem* as a token of alliance with the
king of Judah. 2 The women of Moab are left like homeless birds at the shallow
crossings of the Arnon River. 3 "Help us," they cry. "Defend us against our enemies.
Protect us from their relentless attack. Do not betray us. 4 Let our outcasts stay among
you. Hide them from our enemies until the terror is past."
When oppression and destruction have ceased and enemy raiders have disappeared,
5 then David's throne will be established by love. From that throne a faithful king will
reign, one who always does what is just and right.
6 Is this Moab, the proud land we have heard so much about? Its pride and insolence
are all gone now! 7 The entire land of Moab weeps. Yes, you people of Moab, mourn for
the delicacies of Kir-hareseth. 8 Weep for the abandoned farms of Heshbon and the
vineyards at Sibmah. The wine from those vineyards used to make the rulers of the
nations drunk. Moab was once like a spreading grapevine. Her tendrils spread out as far
as Jazer and trailed out into the desert. Her shoots once reached as far as the Dead Sea.*
9 But now the enemy has completely destroyed that vine. So I wail and lament for Jazer
and the vineyards of Sibmah. My tears will flow for Heshbon and Elealeh, for their
summer fruits and harvests have all been destroyed.
10 Gone now is the gladness; gone is the joy of harvest. The happy singing in the
vineyards will be heard no more. The treading out of grapes in the winepresses has
ceased forever. I have ended all their harvest joys. 11 I will weep for Moab. My sorrow
for Kir-hareseth* will be very great. 12 On the hilltops the people of Moab will pray in
anguish to their idols, but it will do them no good. They will cry to the gods in their
temples, but no one will come to save them.
13 The LORD has already said this about Moab in the past. 14 But now the LORD says,

15:1 Jer 48:1; Ezek 25:8-11
15:2 Lev 21:5; Jer 48:37
15:3 Jer 48:38
15:5 Jer 48:5
15:6 Jer 48:34; Joel 1:10-12
15:7 Jer 48:36
15:9 2 Kgs 17:25; Jer 50:17
16:1 2 Kgs 3:4; 14:7; Isa 42:11
16:2 Num 21:13-14
16:4 Isa 9:4; 54:14
16:6 Jer 48:29; Zeph 2:8, 10
16:7 2 Kgs 3:25; 1 Chr 16:3; Jer 48:31
16:8 Num 32:38; Isa 15:4; Jer 48:32
16:9 Jer 48:32
16:10 Job 24:11; Isa 24:7-8; Jer 48:33; Amos 5:17
16:11 Isa 15:5; 63:15
16:12 1 Kgs 18:26-29; Jer 48:35

15:9 As in Dead Sea Scrolls, some Greek manuscripts, and Latin Vulgate; Masoretic Text reads *Dimon;* also in 15:9b.
16:1 Hebrew *to the daughter of Zion.* **16:8** Hebrew *the sea.* **16:11** Hebrew *Kir-heres,* a variant name for Kir-hareseth.

15:1 Moab was east of the Dead Sea. The Moabites were descendants of Lot through his incestuous relationship with his older daughter (Genesis 19:31-37). Moab had always been Israel's enemy. They oppressed Israel and invaded their land (Judges 3:12-14), fought against Saul (1 Samuel 14:47) and against David (2 Samuel 8:2, 11, 12). Moab would be punished for treating Israel harshly.

16:1ff Attacked by the Assyrians, Moabite refugees would flee to Sela, which lay in the country of Edom to the south. Desperate Moabites, seeking Judah's protection, would send a tribute of lambs to Jerusalem. Jerusalem would be a safe refuge for a while. Isaiah advised Judah to accept these refugees as a sign of compassion during the enemy's time of devastation.

16:10 The treading out of grapes (squeezing the juice from grapes by mashing them with bare feet) was the climax of the harvest season, a time of great joy in the vineyards. But the joy of harvest would soon be ended because the people in their pride ignored God and rebelled against him.

16:12 When the people of Moab experienced God's wrath, they sought their own idols and gods. Nothing happened, however, because there was no one there to save them. We may seek our own ways of escaping daily troubles—work, friends, pleasure, or even some man-made religious idea. But our only hope lies in God, the only one who can hear and help us.

16:13, 14 Tiglath-pileser III invaded Moab in 732 B.C.; Sennacherib invaded Moab the same year that he invaded Judah, 701 B.C. The earlier event occurred three years after Isaiah's prediction, marking Isaiah as a true prophet. In these events, the people of Israel saw prophecy fulfilled before their very eyes.

"Within three years, without fail, the glory of Moab will be ended, and few of its people will be left alive."

A Message about Damascus and Israel

17 This message came to me concerning Damascus:

"Look, Damascus will disappear! It will become a heap of ruins. 2The cities of Aroer will be deserted. Sheep will graze in the streets and lie down unafraid. There will be no one to chase them away. 3The fortified cities of Israel* will also be destroyed, and the power of Damascus will end. The few left in Aram will share the fate of Israel's departed glory," says the LORD Almighty.

4"In that day the glory of Israel* will be very dim, for poverty will stalk the land. 5Israel will be abandoned like the grainfields in the valley of Rephaim after the harvest. 6Only a few of its people will be left, like the stray olives left on the tree after the harvest. Only two or three remain in the highest branches, four or five out on the tips of the limbs. Yes, Israel will be stripped bare of people," says the LORD, the God of Israel.

7Then at last the people will think of their Creator and have respect for the Holy One of Israel. 8They will no longer ask their idols for help or worship what their own hands have made. They will never again bow down to their Asherah poles or burn incense on the altars they built.

9Their largest cities will be as deserted as overgrown thickets. They will become like the cities the Amorites abandoned when the Israelites came here so long ago. 10Why? Because you have turned from the God who can save you—the Rock who can hide you. You may plant the finest imported grapevines, 11and they may grow so well that they blossom on the very morning you plant them, but you will never pick any grapes from them. Your only harvest will be a load of grief and incurable pain.

12Look! The armies rush forward like waves thundering toward the shore. 13But though they roar like breakers on a beach, God will silence them. They will flee like chaff scattered by the wind or like dust whirling before a storm. 14In the evening Israel waits in terror, but by dawn its enemies are dead. This is the just reward of those who plunder and destroy the people of God.

A Message about Ethiopia

18 Destruction is certain for the land of Ethiopia,* which lies at the headwaters of the Nile. Its winged sailboats glide along the river, 2and ambassadors are sent in fast boats down the Nile. Go home, swift messengers! Take a message to your land divided by rivers, to your tall, smooth-skinned people, who are feared far and wide for their conquests and destruction.

3When I raise my battle flag on the mountain, let all the world take notice. When I blow the trumpet, listen! 4For the LORD has told me this: "I will watch quietly from my

17:1 Isa 10:9; 25:2; Mic 1:6
17:2 Mic 4:4; Zeph 2:6
17:3 Isa 8:4; Hos 9:11
17:4 Isa 10:3, 16
17:5 Jer 51:33
17:6 Deut 4:27; Isa 24:13; 27:12
17:7 Isa 10:20; Hos 6:1
17:8 Exod 34:13; Isa 27:9; 30:22
17:10 Deut 32:4, 18; Isa 30:29; 62:11
17:11 Hos 10:13
17:12 Jer 6:23
17:13 Ps 1:4; Isa 29:5
17:14 2 Kgs 19:35; Isa 41:11-12
18:1 Ezek 30:4, 6, 9; Zeph 2:12; 3:10
18:2 2 Chr 12:2-4
18:3 Ps 49:1; Mic 1:2
18:4 Isa 26:21

17:3 Hebrew *of Ephraim,* referring to the northern kingdom of Israel. **17:4** Hebrew *of Jacob.* **18:1** Hebrew *Cush.*

17:1ff The northern kingdom and Aram made an alliance to fight against Assyria. But Tiglath-pileser III captured Damascus, the capital of Aram, in 732 B.C. and annexed the northern kingdom to the Assyrian Empire. Ahaz, king of Judah, paid tribute to Tiglath-pileser III (2 Kings 16:1-14).

17:7-11 God's message to Damascus was that it would be completely destroyed. The Arameans had turned from the God who could save them, depending instead on their idols and their own strength. No matter how successful they were, God's judgment was sure. Often we depend on the trappings of success (expensive cars, pastimes, clothes, homes) to give us fulfillment. But God says we will reap grief and pain if we have depended on temporal things to give us eternal security. If we don't want the same treatment Damascus received, we must turn from these false allurements and trust in God.

17:8 The Asherah poles were images of Asherah, a Canaanite goddess who was the female consort of Baal. Queen Jezebel may have brought the worship of Asherah into the northern kingdom. The cult encouraged immoral sexual practices and attracted many people. The Bible warns against worshiping Asherah poles (Deuteronomy 12:3; 16:21), and Manasseh was condemned for putting up an Asherah pole in the Temple (2 Kings 21:7). Unlike these pagan gods, our God does not try to attract the greatest number of people but instead seeks the greatest good for all people.

18:1ff This prophecy was probably given in the days of Hezekiah (2 Kings 19; 20). The king of Ethiopia had heard that Assyria's great army was marching south toward them. He sent messengers up the Nile asking the surrounding nations to form an alliance. Judah was also asked to join, but Isaiah told the messengers to return home because Judah needed only God's help to repel the Assyrians. Isaiah prophesied that Assyria would be destroyed at the proper time (37:21-38).

18:3 This is a signal of the doom of Ethiopia and Assyria's victory over Ethiopia (see 20:1-6).

dwelling place—as quietly as the heat rises on a summer day, or as the dew forms on an
autumn morning during the harvest."
5 Even before you begin your attack, while your plans are ripening like grapes, the
LORD will cut you off as though with pruning shears. He will snip your spreading
branches. 6 Your mighty army will be left dead in the fields for the mountain birds and
wild animals to eat. The vultures will tear at corpses all summer. The wild animals will
gnaw at bones all winter.
7 But the time will come when the LORD Almighty will receive gifts from this land
divided by rivers, from this tall, smooth-skinned people, who are feared far and wide for
their conquests and destruction. They will bring the gifts to the LORD Almighty in
Jerusalem,* the place where his name dwells.

A Message about Egypt

19 This message came to me concerning Egypt:
Look! The LORD is advancing against Egypt, riding on a swift cloud. The idols
of Egypt tremble. The hearts of the Egyptians melt with fear.
2 "I will make the Egyptians fight against each other—brother against brother, neighbor
against neighbor, city against city, province against province. 3 The Egyptians will lose
heart, and I will confuse their plans. They will plead with their idols for wisdom. They will
call on spirits, mediums, and psychics to show them which way to turn. 4 I will hand Egypt
over to a hard, cruel master, to a fierce king," says the Lord, the LORD Almighty.
5 The waters of the Nile will fail to rise and flood the fields. The riverbed will be
parched and dry. 6 The canals of the Nile will dry up, and the streams of Egypt will
become foul with rotting reeds and rushes. 7 All the greenery along the riverbank will
wither and blow away. All the crops will dry up, and everything will die. 8 The fishermen
will weep for lack of work. Those who fish with hooks and those who use nets will all
be unemployed. 9 The weavers will have no flax or cotton, for the crops will fail. 10 The
weavers and all the workers will be sick at heart.
11 What fools are the counselors of Zoan! Their best counsel to the king of Egypt is
stupid and wrong. Will they still boast of their wisdom? Will they dare tell Pharaoh about
their long line of wise ancestors? 12 What has happened to your wise counselors,
Pharaoh? If they are so wise, let them tell you what the LORD Almighty is going to do to
Egypt. 13 The wise men from Zoan are fools, and those from Memphis* are deluded. The
leaders of Egypt have ruined the land with their foolish counsel. 14 The LORD has sent a
spirit of foolishness on them, so all their suggestions are wrong. They cause the land of
Egypt to stagger like a sick drunkard. 15 Nobody in Egypt, whether rich or poor,
important or unknown, can offer any help.
16 In that day the Egyptians will be as weak as women. They will cower in fear beneath
the upraised fist of the LORD Almighty. 17 Just to speak the name of Israel will strike deep
terror in their hearts, for the LORD Almighty has laid out his plans against them.
18 In that day five of Egypt's cities will follow the LORD Almighty. They will even
begin to speak the Hebrew language.* One of these will be Heliopolis, the City of the
Sun. 19 In that day there will be an altar to the LORD in the heart of Egypt, and there will
be a monument to the LORD at its border. 20 It will be a sign and a witness to the LORD
Almighty in the land of Egypt. When the people cry to the LORD for help against those
who oppress them, he will send them a savior who will rescue them.

18:5 Ezek 17:6-10
18:6 Isa 56:9; Ezek 39:17-20
18:7 Zech 14:16-17
19:1 Josh 2:11; Ps 104:3; Jer 43:12; Matt 26:64
19:2 Judg 7:22; Matt 10:21, 36
19:3 Isa 8:19
19:4 Isa 20:4; Ezek 29:19
19:5 Jer 51:36; Ezek 30:12
19:6 Exod 7:18
19:9 Prov 7:16; Ezek 27:17
19:11 Gen 41:38-39; 1 Kgs 4:30; Acts 7:22
19:12 Rom 9:17
19:13 Jer 2:16
19:14 Isa 3:12
19:16 Jer 51:30; Heb 10:31
19:17 Dan 4:35
19:18 Isa 45:23; 65:16
19:19 Gen 28:18; Josh 22:10, 26-27
19:20 Isa 43:3, 11; 45:15, 21; 49:25

18:7 Hebrew *on Mount Zion.* **19:13** Hebrew *Noph.* **19:18** Hebrew *the language of Canaan.*

19:1 Egypt, the nation where God's people were enslaved for about 400 years (Exodus 1), was hated by the people of Israel. Yet Judah was considering an alliance with Egypt against Assyria (2 Kings 18:17ff). But Isaiah warned against this alliance because God would destroy Assyria in his time.

19:11-15 Egypt was noted for its wisdom, but here its wise men and counselors were deceived and foolish. True wisdom can come only from God. We must ask him for wisdom to guide our decisions, or we will also be uncertain and misdirected. Are you confused about something in your life now? Ask God for wisdom to deal with it.

19:19, 23 After Egypt's chastening, it would turn from idols and worship the one true God. Even more amazing is Isaiah's prophecy that the two chief oppressors of Israel, Egypt and Assyria, would unite in worship. This prophecy will come true "in that day," the future day when Christ comes to reign.

19:20 When Egypt calls to God for help, he will send a savior to deliver them. Our Savior, Jesus Christ, is available to all who call upon him. We, too, can pray and receive his saving power (John 1:12).

19:21 Isa 56:7
19:22 Deut 32:39; Isa 27:13; 45:14; Heb 12:11
19:23 Isa 11:16
19:25 Hos 2:23

21 In that day the LORD will make himself known to the Egyptians. Yes, they will know
the LORD and will give their sacrifices and offerings to him. They will make promises to
the LORD and keep them. 22 The LORD will strike Egypt in a way that will bring healing.
For the Egyptians will turn to the LORD, and he will listen to their pleas and heal them.
23 In that day Egypt and Assyria will be connected by a highway. The Egyptians and
Assyrians will move freely between their lands, and they will worship the same God.
24 And Israel will be their ally. The three will be together, and Israel will be a blessing to
them. 25 For the LORD Almighty will say, "Blessed be Egypt, my people. Blessed be
Assyria, the land I have made. Blessed be Israel, my special possession!"

A Message about Egypt and Ethiopia

20:1 1 Sam 5:1; 2 Kgs 18:17
20:2 1 Sam 19:24; Mic 1:8
20:3 Isa 8:18; 43:3
20:4 Isa 19:4; 47:2-3
20:5 Jer 9:23-24
20:6 Isa 10:3; 30:3-5, 7; Matt 23:33

20 In the year when King Sargon of Assyria captured the Philistine city of Ashdod,
2 the LORD told Isaiah son of Amoz, "Take off all your clothes, including your
sandals." Isaiah did as he was told and walked around naked and barefoot.
3 Then the LORD said, "My servant Isaiah has been walking around naked and barefoot
for the last three years. This is a sign—a symbol of the terrible troubles I will bring upon
Egypt and Ethiopia.* 4 For the king of Assyria will take away the Egyptians and
Ethiopians* as prisoners. He will make them walk naked and barefoot, both young and
old, their buttocks uncovered, to the shame of Egypt. 5 How dismayed will be the
Philistines, who counted on the power of Ethiopia and boasted of their allies in Egypt!
6 They will say, 'If this can happen to Egypt, what chance do we have? For we counted
on Egypt to protect us from the king of Assyria.'"

A Message about Babylon

21:1 Isa 13:20-22; Zech 9:14
21:2 Isa 33:1; Jer 49:34
21:3 Ps 48:6; 1 Thes 5:3

21 This message came to me concerning the land of Babylonia*:
Disaster is roaring down on you from the desert, like a whirlwind sweeping in
from the Negev. 2 I see an awesome vision: I see you plundered and destroyed. Go ahead,
you Elamites and Medes, take part in the siege. Babylon will fall, and the groaning of all
the nations she enslaved will end. 3 My stomach aches and burns with pain. Sharp pangs
of horror are upon me, like the pangs of a woman giving birth. I grow faint when I hear

20:3 Hebrew *Cush;* also in 20:5. **20:4** Hebrew *Cushites.* **21:1** Hebrew *the desert of the sea.*

ALLIANCES TODAY

Government	We rely on government legislation to protect the moral decisions we want made, but legislation cannot change people's hearts.
Science	We enjoy the benefits of science and technology. We look to scientific predictions and analysis before we look to the Bible.
Education	We act as though education and degrees can guarantee our future and success without considering what God plans for our future.
Medical care	We regard medicine as the way to prolong life and preserve its quality—quite apart from faith and moral living.
Financial systems	We place our faith in financial "security"—making as much money as we can for ourselves—forgetting that, while being wise with our money, we must trust God for our needs.

Isaiah warned Judah not to ally with Egypt (20:5; 30:1, 2; 31:1). He knew that trust in any nation or any military might was futile. Judah's only hope was to trust in God. Although we don't consciously put our hope for deliverance in political alliances in quite the same way, we often put our hope in other forces.

19:22 Egypt is but one Gentile nation that will bow before the Lord. Philippians 2:10, 11 says that *every* knee will bow and every tongue will confess that Jesus Christ is Lord. So we shouldn't be surprised that Egyptians and Assyrians are part of the "every." Each of us is part of that "every," too. We may bow now in devotion, or later in submission.

19:23-25 In Jesus Christ, former enemies may unite in love. In Christ, people and nations that are poles apart politically will bow at his feet as brothers and sisters. Christ breaks down every barrier that threatens relationships (see Ephesians 2:13-19).

20:1ff Sargon II was king of Assyria from 722–705 B.C., and this event happened in 711 B.C. Isaiah graphically reminds Judah that they should not count on foreign alliances to protect them.

20:2 God's command to Isaiah to walk about naked for three years was a humiliating experience. God was using Isaiah to demonstrate the humiliation that Egypt and Ethiopia would experience at the hands of Assyria. But the message was really for Judah: Don't put your trust in foreign governments, or you will experience this kind of shame and humiliation from your captors.

20:2 God asked Isaiah to do something that seemed shameful and illogical. At times, God may ask us to do things we don't understand. We must obey God in complete faith, for he will never ask us to do something wrong.

21:1ff Some scholars say this prophecy was fulfilled at Babylon's fall in 539 B.C. (see Daniel 5). But others say this was a prophecy of Babylon's revolt against Assyria around 700 B.C.

what God is planning; I am blinded with dismay. 4My mind reels; my heart races. The
sleep I once enjoyed at night is now a faint memory. I lie awake, trembling.
5Look! They are preparing a great feast. They are spreading rugs for people to sit on.
Everyone is eating and drinking. Quick! Grab your shields and prepare for battle! You
are being attacked!
6Meanwhile, the Lord said to me, "Put a watchman on the city wall to shout out what
he sees. 7Tell him to sound the alert when he sees chariots drawn by horses and warriors
mounted on donkeys and camels."
8Then the watchman* called out, "Day after day I have stood on the watchtower, my
lord. Night after night I have remained at my post. 9Now at last—look! Here come the
chariots and warriors!" Then the watchman said, "Babylon is fallen! All the idols of
Babylon lie broken on the ground!"
10O my people, threshed and winnowed, I have told you everything the LORD Almighty, the God of Israel, has said.

A Message about Edom

11This message came to me concerning Edom*:
Someone from Edom* keeps calling to me, "Watchman, how much longer until
morning? When will the night be over?"
12The watchman replies, "Morning is coming, but night will soon follow. If you wish
to ask again, then come back and ask."

A Message about Arabia

13This message came to me concerning Arabia:
O caravans from Dedan, hide in the deserts of Arabia. 14O people of Tema, bring food
and water to these weary refugees. 15They have fled from drawn swords and sharp
arrows and the terrors of war. 16"But within a year,"* says the Lord, "all the glory of
Kedar will come to an end. 17Only a few of its courageous archers will survive. I, the
LORD, the God of Israel, have spoken!"

A Message about Jerusalem

22 This message came to me concerning Jerusalem*:
What is happening? Why is everyone running to the rooftops? 2The whole city
is in a terrible uproar. What do I see in this reveling city? Bodies are lying everywhere,
killed by famine and disease.* 3All your leaders flee. They surrender without resistance.
The people try to slip away, but they are captured, too. 4Leave me alone to weep; do not
try to comfort me. Let me cry for my people as I watch them being destroyed.

21:4 Deut 28:67
21:5 Jer 51:39, 57
21:7 Isa 21:9
21:8 Hab 2:1
21:9 Isa 46:1; Jer 50:2; Rev 14:8
21:10 Jer 51:33
21:11 Gen 32:3
21:13 Jer 49:28
21:14 Gen 25:15; Job 6:9
21:16 Ps 120:5; Isa 16:14
22:1 Jer 21:13; Joel 3:12, 14
22:2 Isa 23:7; Jer 14:18; Lam 2:20
22:3 Isa 21:15
22:4 Jer 9:1

21:8 As in Dead Sea Scrolls and Syriac version; Masoretic Text reads *a lion.* **21:11a** Hebrew *Dumah,* which means "silence" or "stillness." It is a wordplay on the word *Edom.* **21:11b** Hebrew *Seir,* another name for Edom. **21:16** Hebrew *Within a year, like the years of a hired hand.* Some ancient manuscripts read *Within three years,* as in 16:14. **22:1** Hebrew *concerning the Valley of Vision.* **22:2** Hebrew *killed, but not by sword and not in battle.*

21:5 If the prophecy refers to the fall of Babylon in 539 B.C., this may picture the feast in Daniel 5.

21:6, 7 Watchmen on the city walls often appear in prophetic visions of destruction. They are the first to see trouble coming. The prophet Habakkuk was a watchman (Habakkuk 2:1). The vision of the chariots and warriors could represent the Medes and Persians attacking Babylon in 539 B.C.

21:8, 9 Babylon was not only a great and powerful city, it was also filled with horrible sin (idolatry, witchcraft, and temple prostitution). Babylon was, and remains, a symbol of all that stands against God. Despite all its glory and power, Babylon would be destroyed, along with all its idols. They would give no help in time of trouble.

21:10 Threshing and winnowing were two steps in ancient Israel's farming process. The heads of wheat (often used to symbolize Israel) were first trampled to break open the seeds and expose the valued grain inside (threshing). The seeds were then thrown into the air, and the worthless chaff blew away while the grain fell back to the ground (winnowing). Israel would experience this same kind of process: The sinful, rebellious people (worthless chaff) would be taken away, but God would keep the good "grain" to replenish Israel.

21:11 Edom had been a constant enemy of God's people. It rejoiced when Israel fell to the Assyrians, and this sealed Edom's doom (34:8ff; 63:4). Seir was another name for Edom because the hill country of Seir was given to Esau and his descendants (see Joshua 24:4). Obadiah foretells, in great detail, the destruction of Edom.

21:13ff The places listed here are all in Arabia. They are border cities that controlled the trade routes throughout the land. This is Isaiah's prediction of disaster.

22:1-13 "The Valley of Vision" refers to the city of Jerusalem, where God revealed himself. Jerusalem would be attacked unless God's people returned to him. Instead, they used every means of protection possible except asking God for help. They wanted to trust in their ingenuity, their weapons, and even their pagan neighbors (see 2 Chronicles 32 for the description of a siege of Jerusalem).

22:4 Isaiah had warned his people, but they did not repent; thus, they experienced God's judgment. Because of his care for them, Isaiah was hurt by their punishment and mourned for them. Sometimes people we care for ignore our attempts to help, so they suffer the very grief we wanted to spare them. At times like

5 Oh, what a day of crushing trouble! What a day of confusion and terror the Lord,
the LORD Almighty, has brought upon the Valley of Vision! The walls of Jerusalem
have been broken, and cries of death echo from the mountainsides. 6 Elamites are the
archers; Arameans drive the chariots. The men of Kir hold up the shields. 7 They fill
your beautiful valleys and crowd against your gates. 8 Judah's defenses have been
stripped away. You run to the armory for your weapons. 9 You inspect the walls of
Jerusalem* to see what needs to be repaired. You store up water in the lower pool.
10 You check the houses and tear some down to get stone to fix the walls. 11 Between
the city walls, you build a reservoir for water from the old pool. But all your feverish
plans are to no avail because you never ask God for help. He is the one who planned
this long ago.

12 The Lord, the LORD Almighty, called you to weep and mourn. He told you to shave
your heads in sorrow for your sins and to wear clothes of sackcloth to show your
remorse. 13 But instead, you dance and play; you slaughter sacrificial animals, feast on
meat, and drink wine. "Let's eat, drink, and be merry," you say. "What's the difference,
for tomorrow we die." 14 The LORD Almighty has revealed to me that this sin will never
be forgiven you until the day you die. That is the judgment of the Lord, the LORD
Almighty.

A Message for Shebna

15 Furthermore, the Lord, the LORD Almighty, told me to confront Shebna, the palace
administrator, and to give him this message: 16 "Who do you think you are, building
a beautiful tomb for yourself in the rock? 17 For the LORD is about to seize you and
hurl you away. He is going to send you into captivity, you strong man! 18 He will
crumple you up into a ball and toss you away into a distant, barren land. There you
will die, and there your glorious chariots will remain, broken and useless. You are a
disgrace to your master.

19 "Yes, I will drive you out of office," says the LORD. "I will pull you down from your
high position. 20 And then I will call my servant Eliakim son of Hilkiah to replace you.
21 He will have your royal robes, your title, and your authority. And he will be a father to
the people of Jerusalem and Judah. 22 I will give him the key to the house of David—the
highest position in the royal court. He will open doors, and no one will be able to shut
them; he will close doors, and no one will be able to open them. 23 He will bring honor
to his family name, for I will drive him firmly in place like a tent stake. 24 He will be
loaded down with responsibility, and he will bring honor to even the lowliest members
of his family."

25 The LORD Almighty says: "When that time comes, I will pull out the stake that
seemed so firm. It will come out and fall to the ground. Everything it supports will fall
with it. I, the LORD, have spoken!"

22:5 Isa 37:3; Lam 2:2
22:6 Isa 21:2
22:8 1 Kgs 7:2; 10:17
22:11 2 Kgs 20:20; 25:4
22:12 Isa 32:11; Joel 1:13; Mic 1:16
22:13 Isa 5:11, 22; 56:12; †1 Cor 15:32
22:14 Isa 65:7, 20
22:16 2 Chr 16:14; Matt 27:60
22:18 Job 18:18; Isa 17:13
22:19 Ezek 17:24
22:20 Isa 36:3
22:21 Gen 45:8
22:23 Job 36:7; Zech 10:4
22:25 Esth 9:24-25; Isa 46:11

22:9 Hebrew *the city of David.*

---

that we grieve because of our concern. God expects us to be involved with others, and this may sometimes require us to suffer with them.

22:6, 7 Elam and Kir were under Assyrian rule. The entire Assyrian army, including its vassals, joined in the attack against Jerusalem.

22:8-11 The leaders did what they could to prepare for war: They got weapons, inspected the walls, and stored up water in a reservoir. But all their work was pointless because they never asked God for help. Too often we take steps that, although good in themselves, really won't give us the help we need. We must get the weapons and inspect the walls, but God must guide the work.

22:13, 14 The people said, "Let's eat, drink, and be merry," because they had given up hope. Attacked on every side (22:7), they should have repented (22:12), but they chose to feast instead. The root problem was that Judah did not trust God's power or his promises (see 56:12; 1 Corinthians 15:32). Today we still see people living without hope. There are two common responses to hopelessness: despair and self-indulgence. But we need not act as if we had no hope. As we face difficulties, our proper response should be to trust God and his promises.

22:15-25 Shebna, a high court steward or official, was just as materialistic as the rest of the people in Jerusalem (22:13). He may have been in the group favoring an alliance with foreigners, thus ignoring Isaiah's advice. The Lord revealed that Shebna would lose his position and be replaced by Eliakim (22:20). Eliakim would be the "tent stake" driven firmly in place (22:23). Unfortunately, Eliakim too would fall (22:25).

A Message about Tyre

23 This message came to me concerning Tyre:
Weep, O ships of Tarshish, returning home from distant lands! Weep for your
harbor at Tyre because it is gone! The rumors you heard in Cyprus* are all true. 2 Mourn
in silence, you people of the coast and you merchants of Sidon. Your traders crossed the
sea, 3 sailing over deep waters. They brought you grain from Egypt* and harvests from
along the Nile. You were the merchandise mart of the world.
4 But now you are put to shame, city of Sidon, fortress on the sea. For the sea says,
"Now I am childless; I have no sons or daughters." 5 When Egypt hears the news about
Tyre, there will be great sorrow. 6 Flee now to Tarshish! Wail, you people who live by the
sea! 7 How can this silent ruin be all that is left of your once joyous city? What a history
was yours! Think of all the colonists you sent to distant lands.
8 Who has brought this disaster on Tyre, empire builder and chief trader of the
world? 9 The LORD Almighty has done it to destroy your pride and show his contempt
for all human greatness. 10 Come, Tarshish, sweep over your mother Tyre like the
flooding Nile, for the city is defenseless. 11 The LORD holds out his hand over the seas.
He shakes the kingdoms of the earth. He has spoken out against Phoenicia* and
depleted its strength. 12 He says, "Never again will you rejoice, O daughter of Sidon.
Once you were a lovely city, but you will never again be strong. Even if you flee to
Cyprus, you will find no rest."
13 Look at the land of Babylonia*—the people of that land are gone! The Assyrians
have handed Babylon over to the wild beasts. They have built siege ramps against its
walls, torn down its palaces, and turned it into a heap of rubble.
14 Wail, O ships of Tarshish, for your home port is destroyed! 15 For seventy years,
the length of a king's life, Tyre will be forgotten. But then the city will come back to
life and sing sweet songs like a prostitute. 16 Long absent from her lovers, she will
take a harp, walk the streets, and sing her songs, so that she will again be remembered.
17 Yes, after seventy years the LORD will revive Tyre. But she will be no different
than she was before. She will return again to all her evil ways around the world.
18 But in the end her businesses will give their profits to the LORD. Her wealth will
not be hoarded but will be used to provide good food and fine clothing for the LORD's
priests.

3. God's purpose in judgment

Destruction of the Earth

24 Look! The LORD is about to destroy the earth and make it a vast wasteland. See
how he is scattering the people over the face of the earth. 2 Priests and laypeople,
servants and masters, maids and mistresses, buyers and sellers, lenders and borrowers,
bankers and debtors—none will be spared. 3 The earth will be completely emptied and
looted. The LORD has spoken!

23:1 Josh 19:29; Ezek 26:1-28
23:2 Isa 47:5
23:3 Ezek 27:3-23
23:4 Gen 10:15, 19; Jer 47:4
23:5 Josh 2:9-11
23:7 Isa 32:13
23:9 Isa 5:13; Dan 4:37
23:11 Isa 50:2; Zech 9:3-4
23:12 Rev 18:22
23:13 Isa 13:21
23:15 Jer 25:11
23:18 Isa 60:5-9; Zech 14:20
24:2 Lev 25:36-37; Deut 23:19-20

23:1 Hebrew *Kittim;* also in 23:12. **23:3** Hebrew *from Shihor,* a branch of the Nile River. **23:11** Hebrew *Canaan.* **23:13** Or *Chaldea.*

23:1ff Isaiah's prophecies against other nations began in the east with Babylon (chapter 13) and ended in the west with Tyre in Phoenicia. Tyre was one of the most famous cities of the ancient world. A major trading center with a large seaport, Tyre was very wealthy and very evil. Tyre was rebuked by Jeremiah (Jeremiah 25:22, 27; 47:4), Ezekiel (Ezekiel 26–28), Joel (Joel 3:4-8), Amos (Amos 1:9, 10), and Zechariah (Zechariah 9:3, 4). This is another warning against political alliances with unstable neighbors.

23:5 Why would Egypt experience "great sorrow" when Tyre fell? Egypt depended on Tyre's shipping expertise to promote and carry their products around the world. Egypt would lose an important trading partner with the fall of Tyre.

23:9 God would destroy Tyre because he hated its people's pride. Pride separates people from God, and he will not tolerate it. As we examine our life, we must remember that all true accomplishment comes as a result of our Creator's help. We have no reason to take pride in ourselves.

23:15, 16 Some scholars believe this is a literal 70 years; some say it is symbolic of a long period of time. If it is literal, this may have occurred between 700 and 630 B.C. during the Assyrian captivity of Israel, or it may have been during the 70-year captivity of the Jews in Babylon (605–536 B.C.). During the 70 years, the Jews would forget about Tyre. But when they returned from captivity, they would once again trade with Tyre.

24–27 These four chapters are often called "Isaiah's Apocalypse." They discuss God's judgment on the entire world for its sin. Isaiah's prophecies were first directed to Judah, then to Israel, then to the surrounding nations, and finally to the whole world. These chapters describe the last days when God will judge the whole world. At that time he will finally and permanently remove evil.

24:5 Gen 3:17 Num 35:33
24:6 Isa 34:5 Zech 5:3-4
24:7 Joel 1:10, 12
24:8 Jer 16:9
24:9 Isa 5:11, 22
24:10 Gen 1:2
24:11 Isa 32:13
24:13 Isa 17:6
24:14 Isa 12:6; 52:8
24:15 Isa 42:4, 10, 12 Jer 5:1
24:16 Isa 11:12; 28:5
24:18 Gen 7:10-12 Ps 46:2
24:19 Num 16:31-32
24:20 Isa 19:14; 43:27; 66:24
24:21 Ps 76:12
24:23 Mic 4:7 Heb 12:22 Rev 21:23
25:1 Exod 15:2 Ps 40:5 Eph 1:11
25:2 Isa 17:1
25:4 Isa 32:2
25:5 Jer 51:54-56

4 The earth dries up, the crops wither, the skies refuse to rain. 5 The earth suffers for
the sins of its people, for they have twisted the instructions of God, violated his laws,
and broken his everlasting covenant. 6 Therefore, a curse consumes the earth and its
people. They are left desolate, destroyed by fire. Few will be left alive.
7 All the joys of life will be gone. The grape harvest will fail, and there will be no wine.
The merrymakers will sigh and mourn. 8 The clash of tambourines will be stilled; the
happy cries of celebration will be heard no more. The melodious chords of the harp will
be silent. 9 Gone are the joys of wine and song; strong drink now turns bitter in the mouth.
10 The city writhes in chaos; every home is locked to keep out looters. 11 Mobs gather
in the streets, crying out for wine. Joy has reached its lowest ebb. Gladness has been
banished from the land. 12 The city is left in ruins, with its gates battered down.
13 Throughout the earth the story is the same—like the stray olives left on the tree or the
few grapes left on the vine after harvest, only a remnant is left.
14 But all who are left will shout and sing for joy. Those in the west will praise the
LORD's majesty. 15 In eastern lands, give glory to the LORD. In the coastlands of the sea,
praise the name of the LORD, the God of Israel. 16 Listen to them as they sing to the LORD
from the ends of the earth. Hear them singing praises to the Righteous One!
But my heart is heavy with grief. I am discouraged, for evil still prevails, and treachery
is everywhere. 17 Terror and traps and snares will be your lot, you people of the earth.
18 Those who flee in terror will fall into a trap, and those who escape the trap will step
into a snare.
Destruction falls on you from the heavens. The world is shaken beneath you. 19 The
earth has broken down and has utterly collapsed. Everything is lost, abandoned, and
confused. 20 The earth staggers like a drunkard. It trembles like a tent in a storm. It falls
and will not rise again, for its sins are very great.
21 In that day the LORD will punish the fallen angels in the heavens and the proud rulers
of the nations on earth. 22 They will be rounded up and put in prison until they are tried
and condemned. 23 Then the LORD Almighty will mount his throne on Mount Zion. He
will rule gloriously in Jerusalem, in the sight of all the leaders of his people. There will
be such glory that the brightness of the sun and moon will seem to fade away.

Praise for Judgment and Salvation

25 O LORD, I will honor and praise your name, for you are my God. You do such
wonderful things! You planned them long ago, and now you have accomplished
them. 2 You turn mighty cities into heaps of ruins. Cities with strong walls are turned to
rubble. Beautiful palaces in distant lands disappear and will never be rebuilt. 3 Therefore,
strong nations will declare your glory; ruthless nations will revere you.
4 But to the poor, O LORD, you are a refuge from the storm. To the needy in distress,
you are a shelter from the rain and the heat. For the oppressive acts of ruthless people
are like a storm beating against a wall, 5 or like the relentless heat of the desert. But you
silence the roar of foreign nations. You cool the land with the shade of a cloud. So the
boastful songs of ruthless people are stilled.

24:4, 5 Not only the people suffered from their sins; even the land suffered the effects of evil and lawbreaking. Today we see the results of sin in our own land: pollution, crime, addiction, poverty. Sin affects every aspect of society so extensively that even those faithful to God suffer. We cannot blame God for these conditions because sin has brought them about. The more we who are believers renounce sin, speak against immoral practices, and share God's Word with others, the more we slow our society's deterioration. We must not give up: Sin is rampant, but we can make a difference.

24:14-16 The believers who are left behind after God judges Judah will sing to the glory of God's righteousness. Isaiah grieved because of his world's condition. We, too, can become depressed by the evil all around us. At those times we need to hold on to God's promises for the future and look forward to singing praises to him when he restores heaven and earth.

24:21 "The fallen angels in the heavens" refer to spiritual forces opposed to God. Nobody, not even the fallen angels, will escape due punishment.

25:1 Isaiah exalted and praised God because he realized that God completes his plans as promised. God also fulfills his promises to you. Think of the prayers he has answered, and praise him for his goodness and faithfulness.

25:4 The poor suffered because ruthless people oppressed them. But God is concerned for the poor and is a refuge for them. When we are disadvantaged or oppressed, we can turn to God for comfort and help. Jesus states that the Kingdom of God belongs to the poor (Luke 6:20).

6 In Jerusalem,* the LORD Almighty will spread a wonderful feast for everyone around
the world. It will be a delicious feast of good food, with clear, well-aged wine and choice
beef. 7 In that day he will remove the cloud of gloom, the shadow of death that hangs
over the earth. 8 He will swallow up death forever! The Sovereign LORD will wipe away
all tears. He will remove forever all insults and mockery against his land and people. The
LORD has spoken!
9 In that day the people will proclaim, "This is our God. We trusted in him, and he
saved us. This is the LORD, in whom we trusted. Let us rejoice in the salvation he brings!"
10 For the LORD's good hand will rest on Jerusalem.
Moab will be crushed like trampled straw and left to rot. 11 God will push down Moab's
people as a swimmer pushes down water with his hands. He will end their pride and all their
evil works. 12 The high walls of Moab will be demolished and ground to dust.

25:6 Isa 2:2-4
25:8 Ps 69:9; Isa 65:19; †1 Cor 15:54-55; 1 Pet 4:14; Rev 21:4
25:9 Isa 30:18; 35:1-2, 10; 40:9
25:11 Isa 16:6
25:12 Isa 26:5

A Song of Praise to the LORD

26 In that day, everyone in the land of Judah will sing this song:
Our city is now strong!
We are surrounded by the walls of God's salvation.
2 Open the gates to all who are righteous;
allow the faithful to enter.
3 You will keep in perfect peace all who trust in you,
whose thoughts are fixed on you!
4 Trust in the LORD always,
for the LORD GOD is the eternal Rock.
5 He humbles the proud
and brings the arrogant city to the dust.
Its walls come crashing down!
6 The poor and oppressed trample it underfoot.

7 But for those who are righteous,
the path is not steep and rough.
You are a God of justice,
and you smooth out the road ahead of them.
8 LORD, we love to obey your laws;
our heart's desire is to glorify your name.
9 All night long I search for you;
earnestly I seek for God.
For only when you come to judge the earth
will people turn from wickedness and do what is right.

26:1 Isa 12:1; 60:18
26:2 Isa 45:25
26:3 Isa 57:19
26:4 Isa 50:10
26:6 Isa 29:19
26:7 Ps 25:4-5; Isa 42:16
26:8 Isa 12:4
26:9 Pss 63:1; 77:2; Hos 5:15

25:6 Hebrew *On this mountain;* also in 25:10.

25:6 Here is a marvelous prophecy of "everyone around the world"—Gentiles and Jews together—at God's messianic feast, celebrating the overthrow of evil and the joy of eternity with God. It shows that God intended his saving message to go out to the whole world, not just to the Jews. During the feast, God will end death forever (25:7, 8). The people who participate in this great feast will be those who have been living by faith. That is why they say, "This is our God. We trusted in him, and he saved us" (25:9). See also chapter 55 for another presentation of this great feast.

25:8 When the Lord speaks, he does what he says. It is comforting to know that God's plans and activities are closely tied to his word. When we pray according to God's will (as expressed in the Bible) and claim his promises (as recorded in the Bible), he hears us and answers our requests.

25:8 Part of this verse is quoted in 1 Corinthians 15:54 to describe Christ's victory over death. God's ultimate victory is seen when death, our ultimate enemy, is defeated (see also Hosea 13:14). Another part of this verse is quoted in Revelation 21:4, which describes the glorious scene of God's presence with his people.

25:10 Moab was a symbol of all who oppose God and are rebellious to the end. Moab was Israel's enemy for years (see the note on 15:1).

26:1ff People will praise God on the day of the Lord when Christ establishes his Kingdom (see chapter 12). Chapter 26 is a psalm of trust, praise, and meditation. Once more, God revealed the future to Isaiah.

26:3 We can never avoid strife in the world around us, but when we fix our thoughts on God, we can know perfect peace even in turmoil. As we focus our mind on God and his Word, we become steady and stable. Supported by God's unchanging love and mighty power, we are not shaken by the surrounding chaos (see Philippians 4:7). Do you want peace? Keep your thoughts on God and your trust in him.

26:7, 8 At times the "path" of the righteous doesn't seem smooth, and it isn't easy to do God's will, but we are never alone when we face tough times. God is there to help us, to comfort us, and to lead us. God does this by giving us a purpose (keeping our mind centered on him, 26:3) and giving us provisions as we travel. God provides us with relationships of family, friends, and mentors. God gives us wisdom to make decisions and faith to trust him. Don't despair; stay on God's path.

26:10 Isa 22:12-13 John 5:37-38

10 Your kindness to the wicked does not make them do good.
They keep doing wrong and take no notice of the LORD's majesty.

26:11 Isa 9:7; 10:17; 66:15, 24

11 O LORD, they do not listen when you threaten.
They do not see your upraised fist.
Show them your eagerness to defend your people.
Perhaps then they will be ashamed.
Let your fire consume your enemies.

12 LORD, you will grant us peace,
for all we have accomplished is really from you.

26:13 Isa 2:8

13 O LORD our God, others have ruled us,
but we worship you alone.

26:14 Hab 2:19

14 Those we served before are dead and gone.
Never again will they return!
You attacked them and destroyed them,
and they are long forgotten.

26:15 Isa 54:2

15 We praise you, LORD!
You have made our nation great;
you have extended our borders!

26:16 Hos 5:15

16 LORD, in distress we searched for you.
We were bowed beneath the burden of your discipline.

26:17 John 16:21

17 We were like a woman about to give birth,
writhing and crying out in pain.
When we are in your presence, LORD,

26:18 Isa 33:11

18 we, too, writhe in agony,
but nothing comes of our suffering.
We have done nothing to rescue the world;
no one has been born to populate the earth.

26:19 Ezek 37:1-14 Dan 12:2 Eph 5:14

19 Yet we have this assurance:
Those who belong to God will live;
their bodies will rise again!
Those who sleep in the earth
will rise up and sing for joy!
For God's light of life will fall like dew
on his people in the place of the dead!

Restoration for Israel

20 Go home, my people, and lock your doors! Hide until the LORD's anger against your
enemies has passed. 21 Look! The LORD is coming from heaven to punish the people of
the earth for their sins. The earth will no longer hide those who have been murdered.
They will be brought out for all to see.

26:21 Job 16:18 Mic 1:3 Jude 1:14

26:10 Even wicked people receive God's benefits, but that doesn't teach them to do what is right. Sometimes God's judgment teaches us more than God's good gifts. If you have been enriched by God's goodness and grace, respond to him with your grateful devotion.

26:16-19 The people realized the pain of being away from God's presence, and yet they were assured that they would live again. God turned his back on his people when they disobeyed, but a small number never lost hope and continued to seek him. No matter how difficult times may be, we have hope when we keep our trust in him. Can you wait patiently for God to act?

26:19 Some people say there is no life after death. Others believe that there is, but it is not physical life. But Isaiah tells us that our bodies shall rise again. According to 1 Corinthians 15:50-53, all the dead believers will arise with new imperishable bodies—bodies like the one Jesus had when he was resurrected (see Philippians 3:21). Isaiah 26:19 is not the only Old Testament verse to speak about the resurrection; see also Job 19:26; Psalm 16:10; Daniel 12:2, 13.

26:20, 21 When God comes to judge the earth, the guilty will find no place to hide. Jesus said that the hidden will be made known because his truth, like a light shining in a dark corner, will reveal it (Matthew 10:26). Instead of trying to hide your shameful thoughts and actions from God, confess them to him and receive his forgiveness.

27 In that day the LORD will take his terrible, swift sword and punish Leviathan, the swiftly moving serpent, the coiling, writhing serpent, the dragon of the sea.

2“In that day we will sing of the pleasant vineyard. 3I, the LORD, will watch over it and tend its fruitful vines. Each day I will water them; day and night I will watch to keep enemies away. 4My anger against Israel will be gone. If I find briers and thorns bothering her, I will burn them up. 5These enemies will be spared only if they surrender and beg for peace and protection.”

6The time is coming when my people will take root. Israel will bud and blossom and fill the whole earth with her fruit! 7Has the LORD punished Israel in the same way he has punished her enemies? No, for he devastated her enemies, 8but he has punished Israel only a little. He has exiled her from her land as though blown away in a storm from the east. 9The LORD did this to purge away Israel's* sin. When he has finished, all the pagan altars will be crushed to dust. There won't be an Asherah pole or incense altar left standing. 10Israel's fortified cities will be silent and empty, the houses abandoned, the streets covered with grass. Cattle will graze there, chewing on twigs and branches.

11The people are like the dead branches of a tree, broken off and used for kindling beneath the cooking pots. Israel is a foolish and stupid nation, for its people have turned away from God. Therefore, the one who made them will show them no pity or mercy. 12Yet the time will come when the LORD will gather them together one by one like handpicked grain. He will bring them to his great threshing floor—from the Euphrates River* in the east to the brook of Egypt in the west. 13In that day the great trumpet will sound. Many who were dying in exile in Assyria and Egypt will return to Jerusalem to worship the LORD on his holy mountain.

4. Jerusalem's true and false hopes

A Message about Samaria

28 Destruction is certain for the city of Samaria—the pride and joy of the drunkards of Israel*! It sits in a rich valley, but its glorious beauty will suddenly disappear. Destruction is certain for that city—the pride of a people brought low by wine. 2For the Lord will send the mighty Assyrian army against it. Like a mighty hailstorm and a torrential rain, they will burst upon it and dash it to the ground. 3The proud city of Samaria—the pride and joy of the drunkards of Israel—will be trampled beneath its enemies' feet. 4It sits in a fertile valley, but its glorious beauty will suddenly disappear. It will be greedily snatched up, as an early fig is hungrily picked and eaten.

5Then at last the LORD Almighty will himself be Israel's crowning glory. He will be the pride and joy of the remnant of his people. 6He will give a longing for justice to their judges. He will give great courage to their warriors who stand at the gates.

7Now, however, Israel is being led by drunks! The priests and prophets reel and

27:1 Job 3:8; Ps 74:14
27:2 Ps 80:8
27:3 John 10:28
27:4 2 Sam 23:6; Isa 33:12
27:5 Job 22:21; Isa 25:4
27:6 Isa 35:1-2; 37:31
27:7 Isa 10:12, 17
27:9 Isa 17:8; Dan 11:35; Rom 1:27
27:11 Deut 32:18, 28; Isa 43:1, 7
27:12 Deut 30:3-4; Isa 11:11
27:13 Zech 14:16; Matt 24:31; Rev 11:15
28:2 Isa 8:7; 30:28; Nah 1:8
28:4 Hos 9:10; Nah 3:12
28:5 Isa 41:16; 62:3
28:6 2 Chr 32:6-8; Isa 11:2; 25:4; 32:15
28:7 Hab 2:15-16

27:9 Hebrew *Jacob's.* **27:12** Hebrew *the river.* **28:1** Hebrew *of Ephraim,* referring to the northern kingdom of Israel; also in 28:3.

27:1 "That day" is a reference to the end of the evil world as we know it. In ancient Aramean (Ugaritic) literature, Leviathan was a seven-headed monster, the enemy of God's created order. Thus, Isaiah is comparing God's slaughter of the wicked to the conquering of a great enemy. Although evil is a powerful foe, God will crush it and abolish it from the earth forever.

27:2-6 The trampled vineyard of chapter 5 will be restored in God's new earth. God will protect and care for the vineyard, his people. It will no longer produce worthless fruit but will produce enough good fruit for the whole world. Gentiles will come to know God through Israel.

27:9 Only God can take away sin, but to be driven out of the land was considered the penalty that would purify God's people. Deuteronomy 28:49-52, 64 explains God's warning about these consequences.

27:11 Isaiah compares the state of Israel's spiritual life with dry twigs that are broken off and used to make fires. Trees in Scripture often represent spiritual life. The trunk is the channel of strength from God; the branches are the people who serve him. Tree branches sometimes waver and blow in the wind. Like Israel, they may dry up from internal rottenness and become useless for anything except building a fire. What kind of branch are you? If you are withering spiritually, check to see if you are firmly attached to God.

27:12 To "thresh" means to "judge." God's purpose in judging the earth is not vengeance, but purging. He wants to correct us and bring us back to him. God does not punish us for our sin just to make us suffer, but to make those who are faithful better equipped for fruitful service.

28:1 Samaria, the capital city of the northern kingdom of Israel, represents the entire kingdom, ruled by a line of evil kings. When Israel split into two kingdoms after Solomon's reign, Jerusalem ended up in the southern kingdom. Leaders in the northern kingdom, wishing to stay entirely separate from their relatives to the south, set up idols to keep the people from going to the Temple in Jerusalem to worship (see 1 Kings 12). Thus, the people in the northern kingdom were led into idolatry. Isaiah gave this message to Israel to warn them that destruction was certain. It was also meant to encourage Judah to repent before being punished, as the northern kingdom would be only a few years later.

28:8 Jer 48:26
28:9 Heb 5:12-13
28:10 Neh 9:30
28:11 Isa 33:19; †1 Cor 14:21
28:12 Jer 6:16; Matt 11:28-29
28:13 Matt 21:44
28:14 Isa 28:22; 29:20
28:15 Isa 28:18
28:16 Ps 118:22; Matt 21:42; Acts 4:11; †Rom 9:33; 10:11; Eph 2:20; †1 Pet 2:6
28:17 Isa 61:8; Amos 7:7-9
28:18 Isa 28:15
28:19 Ps 88:15; Isa 50:4
28:21 2 Sam 5:20; Luke 19:41-44
28:22 Isa 10:22-23; 28:14; †Rom 9:28
28:27 Amos 1:3
28:29 Rom 11:33

stagger from beer and wine. They make stupid mistakes as they carry out their responsibilities. 8 Their tables are covered with vomit; filth is everywhere. 9 They say, "Who
does the LORD think we are? Why does he speak to us like this? Are we little children,
barely old enough to talk? 10 He tells us everything over and over again, a line at a time,
in very simple words!*"

11 Since they refuse to listen, God will speak to them through foreign oppressors who
speak an unknown language! 12 God's people could have rest in their own land if they
would only obey him, but they will not listen. 13 So the LORD will spell out his message
for them again, repeating it over and over, a line at a time, in very simple words. Yet they
will stumble over this simple, straightforward message. They will be injured, trapped,
and captured.

14 Therefore, listen to this message from the LORD, you scoffing rulers in Jerusalem.
15 You boast that you have struck a bargain to avoid death and have made a deal to dodge
the grave.* You say, "The Assyrians can never touch us, for we have built a strong refuge
made of lies and deception." 16 Therefore, this is what the Sovereign LORD says: "Look!
I am placing a foundation stone in Jerusalem.* It is firm, a tested and precious cornerstone that is safe to build on. Whoever believes need never run away again.*

17 "I will take the measuring line of justice and the plumb line of righteousness to
check the foundation wall you have built. Your refuge looks strong, but since it is made
of lies, a hailstorm will knock it down. Since it is made of deception, the enemy will
come like a flood to sweep it away. 18 I will cancel the bargain you made to avoid death,
and I will overturn your deal to dodge the grave. When the terrible enemy floods in, you
will be trampled into the ground. 19 Again and again that flood will come, morning after
morning, day and night, until you are carried away."

This message will bring terror to your people. 20 For you have no place of refuge—the
bed you have made is too short to lie on. The blankets are too narrow to cover you. 21 The
LORD will come suddenly and in anger, as he did against the Philistines at Mount Perazim
and against the Amorites at Gibeon. He will come to do a strange, unusual thing: He will
destroy his own people! 22 So scoff no more, or your punishment will be even greater.
For the Lord, the LORD Almighty, has plainly told me that he is determined to crush you.

23 Listen to me; listen as I plead! 24 Does a farmer always plow and never sow? Is he
forever cultivating the soil and never planting it? 25 Does he not finally plant his seeds
for dill, cummin, wheat, barley, and spelt, each in its own section of his land? 26 The
farmer knows just what to do, for God has given him understanding. 27 He doesn't thresh
all his crops the same way. A heavy sledge is never used on dill; rather, it is beaten with
a light stick. A threshing wheel is never rolled on cummin; instead, it is beaten softly with
a flail. 28 Bread grain is easily crushed, so he doesn't keep on pounding it. He threshes it
under the wheels of a cart, but he doesn't pulverize it. 29 The LORD Almighty is a
wonderful teacher, and he gives the farmer great wisdom.

28:10 The Hebrew text for this verse may simply be childish sounds that have no meaning, or perhaps a childish mimicking of the prophet's words. Also in 28:13. **28:15** Hebrew *Sheol;* also in 28:18. **28:16a** Hebrew *in Zion.* **28:16b** Greek version reads *Anyone who believes in him will not be disappointed.*

28:9-14 These verses characterize the people's reaction to Isaiah. In effect, they were saying, "He's speaking to us like a schoolteacher speaks to small children. We don't need to be taught. We'll make up our own minds." For this attitude, Isaiah prophesied that the Assyrians would teach them in a way they would like even less.

28:15 Judah was afraid of the Assyrians. Instead of trusting God, the Judeans turned to other sources for security. God accused them of making a deal with the grave, referring to the state of being dead. This passage may refer to Hezekiah's alliance with Pharaoh Tirhakah against Assyria (2 Kings 19:9; Isaiah 37:9). God would cancel this agreement—Egypt would be of no help when Assyria attacked. Is it worth selling out what you believe in for temporary protection against an enemy? If you want lasting protection, turn to the only one able to deliver you from *eternal* death—God.

28:16 If you're building anything, you need a firm base. Isaiah speaks of a foundation stone, a *cornerstone,* that will be laid in Zion. This cornerstone is the Messiah, the foundation on whom we build our lives. Is your life built on the flimsy base of your own successes or dreams? Or is it set on a firm foundation (see Psalm 118:22; 1 Peter 2:8)?

28:21 God fought on Joshua's side at the valley of Gibeon (Joshua 10:1-14) and on David's side at Mount Perazim (2 Samuel 5:20). But here he would fight *against* Israel, his own people, in these same places.

28:23-29 The farmer uses special tools to plant and harvest tender herbs so he will not destroy them. He takes into account how fragile they are. In the same way God takes all our individual circumstances and weaknesses into account. He deals with each of us sensitively. We should follow his example when we deal with others. Different people require different treatment. Be sensitive to the needs of those around you and the special treatment they may need.

A Message about Jerusalem

29 "Destruction is certain for Ariel,* the City of David. Year after year you offer your
many sacrifices. 2Yet I will bring disaster upon you, and there will be much
weeping and sorrow. For Jerusalem will become as her name Ariel means—an altar
covered with blood. 3I will be your enemy, surrounding Jerusalem and attacking its
walls. I will build siege towers around it and will destroy it. 4Your voice will whisper
like a ghost from the earth where you will lie buried.
5"But suddenly, your ruthless enemies will be driven away like chaff before the wind.
6In an instant, I, the LORD Almighty, will come against them with thunder and earthquake
and great noise, with whirlwind and storm and consuming fire. 7All the nations fighting
against Jerusalem* will vanish like a dream! Those who are attacking her walls will
vanish like a vision in the night. 8A hungry person dreams of eating but is still hungry.
A thirsty person dreams of drinking but is still faint from thirst when morning comes. In
the same way, your enemies will dream of a victorious conquest over Jerusalem,* but all
to no avail."
9Are you amazed and incredulous? Do you not believe it? Then go ahead and be blind
if you must. You are stupid, but not from wine! You stagger, but not from beer! 10For the
LORD has poured out on you a spirit of deep sleep. He has closed the eyes of your
prophets and visionaries. 11All these future events are a sealed book to them. When you
give it to those who can read, they will say, "We can't read it because it is sealed."
12When you give it to those who cannot read, they will say, "Sorry, we don't know how
to read."
13And so the Lord says, "These people say they are mine. They honor me with their
lips, but their hearts are far away. And their worship of me amounts to nothing more than
human laws learned by rote.* 14Because of this, I will do wonders among these
hypocrites. I will show that human wisdom is foolish and even the most brilliant people
lack understanding."
15Destruction is certain for those who try to hide their plans from the LORD, who try
to keep him in the dark concerning what they do! "The LORD can't see us," you say to
yourselves. "He doesn't know what is going on!" 16How stupid can you be? He is the
Potter, and he is certainly greater than you. You are only the jars he makes! Should the
thing that was created say to the one who made it, "He didn't make us"? Does a jar ever
say, "The potter who made me is stupid"?
17Soon—and it will not be very long—the wilderness of Lebanon will be a fertile field
once again. And the fertile fields will become a lush and fertile forest. 18In that day deaf
people will hear words read from a book, and blind people will see through the gloom
and darkness. 19The humble will be filled with fresh joy from the LORD. Those who are
poor will rejoice in the Holy One of Israel. 20Those who intimidate and harass will be
gone, and all those who plot evil will be killed. 21Those who make the innocent guilty
by their false testimony will disappear. And those who use trickery to pervert justice and
tell lies to tear down the innocent will be no more.
22That is why the LORD, who redeemed Abraham, says to the people of Israel,* "My
people will no longer pale with fear or be ashamed. 23For when they see their many

29:1 2 Sam 5:9
29:2 Lam 2:5
29:3 Luke 19:43-44
29:4 Isa 8:19
29:5 Isa 17:13-14; 41:15-16; 1 Thes 5:3
29:6 Matt 24:7; Mark 13:8; Luke 21:11; Rev 11:13, 19; 16:18
29:7 Zech 12:9
29:8 Isa 54:17
29:9 Isa 21:22; 51:17
29:10 †Rom 11:8; 2 Thes 2:9-12
29:11 Dan 12:4; Matt 13:11
29:13 Ezek 33:31; Mark 7:6-7
29:14 Isa 44:25; †1 Cor 1:19
29:15 Ps 10:11, 13; Isa 47:10
29:16 Isa 45:9; †Rom 9:20-21
29:18 Isa 32:3
29:19 Isa 14:30, 32; Matt 5:5; Jas 2:5
29:21 Amos 5:10, 12
29:22 Isa 41:8

29:1 *Ariel* sounds like a Hebrew term that means "hearth" or "altar." **29:7** Hebrew *Ariel.* **29:8** Hebrew *Mount Zion.*
29:13 Greek version reads *Their worship is a farce, for they merely teach human commands and teachings.*
29:22 Hebrew *of Jacob;* also in 29:23.

29:1 *Ariel* is a special name for Jerusalem, David's city. It may mean "lion of God" (Jerusalem is strong as a lion) or "altar hearth" (Jerusalem is the place of the altar in the Temple; see 29:2; Ezekiel 43:15, 16).

29:13, 14 The people claimed to be close to God, but they were disobedient and merely went through the motions; therefore, God would bring judgment upon them. Religion had become routine instead of real. Jesus quoted Isaiah's condemnation of Israel's hypocrisy when he spoke to the Pharisees, the religious leaders of his day (Matthew 15:7-9; Mark 7:6, 7). We are all capable of hypocrisy. Often we slip into routine patterns when we worship, and we neglect to give God our love and devotion. If we want to be called God's people, we must be obedient and worship him honestly and sincerely.

29:15 Thinking God couldn't see them and didn't know what was happening, the people of Jerusalem tried to hide their plans from him. How strange that so many people think they can hide from God. In Psalm 139 we learn that God has examined us and knows everything about us. Would you be embarrassed if your best friends knew your personal thoughts? Remember that God knows all of them.

29:17-24 The world described here, under Christ's rule, will be far different from the one we live in today. There will be no more violence or gloom. This new world will be characterized by joy, understanding, justice, and praise to God.

29:24 Isa 30:21; 41:20

children and material blessings, they will recognize the holiness of the Holy One of
Israel. They will stand in awe of the God of Israel. 24Those in error will then believe the
truth, and those who constantly complain will accept instruction.

Judah's Worthless Treaty with Egypt

30:1 Isa 8:11-12
30:2 Isa 8:19; 31:1
30:3 Isa 36:6; Jer 42:18, 22
30:5 Isa 31:3; Jer 2:36
30:6 Deut 8:15
30:7 Isa 51:9

30 "Destruction is certain for my rebellious children," says the LORD. "You make
plans that are contrary to my will. You weave a web of plans that are not from
my Spirit, thus piling up your sins. 2For without consulting me, you have gone down
to Egypt to find help. You have put your trust in Pharaoh for his protection. 3But in
trusting Pharaoh, you will be humiliated and disgraced. 4For though his power
extends to Zoan and Hanes, 5it will all turn out to your shame. He will not help you
even one little bit."

6Look at the animals moving slowly across the terrible desert to Egypt—donkeys and
camels loaded with treasure to pay for Egypt's aid. On through the wilderness they go,
where lions and poisonous snakes live. All this, and Egypt will give you nothing in
return. 7Egypt's promises are worthless! I call her the Harmless Dragon.*

A Warning for Rebellious Judah

30:8 Isa 8:1
30:9 Isa 24:5; 28:15; 30:1
30:10 1 Kgs 22:8, 13; Jer 6:14; Ezek 13:7; Amos 2:12; 2 Tim 4:3-4
30:11 Job 21:14
30:12 Isa 5:24; 59:13
30:13 Isa 26:21; 29:5
30:14 Ps 2:9; Jer 19:10-11
30:15 Isa 7:4; 28:12; 32:17
30:16 Isa 31:1, 3
30:17 Deut 28:25; 32:30

8Now go and write down these words concerning Egypt. They will then stand until the
end of time as a witness to Israel's unbelief. 9For these people are stubborn rebels who
refuse to pay any attention to the LORD's instructions.

10They tell the prophets, "Shut up! We don't want any more of your reports." They
say, "Don't tell us the truth. Tell us nice things. Tell us lies. 11Forget all this gloom. We
have heard more than enough about your 'Holy One of Israel.' We are tired of listening
to what he has to say."

12This is the reply of the Holy One of Israel: "Because you despise what I tell you and
trust instead in oppression and lies, 13calamity will come upon you suddenly. It will be
like a bulging wall that bursts and falls. In an instant it will collapse and come crashing
down. 14You will be smashed like a piece of pottery—shattered so completely that there
won't be a piece left that is big enough to carry coals from a fireplace or a little water
from the well."

15The Sovereign LORD, the Holy One of Israel, says, "Only in returning to me and
waiting for me will you be saved. In quietness and confidence is your strength. But you
would have none of it. 16You said, 'No, we will get our help from Egypt. They will give
us swift horses for riding into battle.' But the only swiftness you are going to see is the
swiftness of your enemies chasing you! 17One of them will chase a thousand of you. Five
of them will make all of you flee. You will be left like a lonely flagpole on a distant
mountaintop."

30:7 Hebrew *Rahab who sits still.* Rahab is the name of a mythical sea monster that represents chaos in ancient literature. The name is used here as a poetic name for Egypt.

30:1 The rebellious children are the people of Judah (see 1:2), those who have rebelled against God. The negotiations for an alliance were underway, and Isaiah condemned their twisted plans. The people of Judah sought advice from everyone but God. When we are driven by fear, we tend to search everywhere for comfort, advice, and relief, hoping to find an easy way out of our troubles. Instead, we should consult God. Although he gives emergency help in a crisis, he prefers to be our guide throughout our life. By reading his Word and actively seeking to do his will, we can maintain our bond with him who provides stability no matter what the crisis.

30:2ff Hezekiah had been seeking a defensive alliance with Egypt against Sennacherib of Assyria (see 2 Kings 18:21).

30:6 This oracle is directed to those who carried bribes to Egypt through the desert in the Negev region.

30:7 This Harmless Dragon (also calld Rahab) was a mythological female sea monster associated with Leviathan (see the note on 27:1; also Job 9:13; 26:12). It was a name associated with Egypt, where hippopotamuses, perhaps a likeness to Rahab, sat on the Nile River and did nothing.

30:10, 11 Some people in Judah may have sought refuge in Egypt. In their desire to find security, they wanted to hear only good news. They did not welcome the truth from God's prophets. Often the truth makes us uncomfortable. We prefer lies and illusions when they make us feel more secure. It is much better to face reality than to live a lie. Don't settle for something that makes you feel comfortable but is not true.

30:15 God warned Judah that turning to Egypt and other nations for military might could not save them. Only God could do that. They must wait for him in "quietness and confidence." No amount of fast talking or hasty activity could speed up God's grand design. We have nothing to say to God but thank you. Salvation comes from God alone. Because he has saved us, we can trust him and be peacefully confident that he will give us strength to face our difficulties. We should lay aside our well-laid plans and allow him to act.

Blessings for the LORD's People

18 But the LORD still waits for you to come to him so he can show you his love and
compassion. For the LORD is a faithful God. Blessed are those who wait for him to help
them.
19 O people of Zion, who live in Jerusalem, you will weep no more. He will be gracious
if you ask for help. He will respond instantly to the sound of your cries. 20 Though the
Lord gave you adversity for food and affliction for drink, he will still be with you to teach
you. You will see your teacher with your own eyes, 21 and you will hear a voice say, "This
is the way; turn around and walk here." 22 Then you will destroy all your silver idols and
gold images. You will throw them out like filthy rags. "Ugh!" you will say to them.
"Begone!"
23 Then the LORD will bless you with rain at planting time. There will be wonderful
harvests and plenty of pastureland for your cattle. 24 The oxen and donkeys that till the
ground will eat good grain, its chaff having been blown away by the wind. 25 In that day,
when your enemies are slaughtered, there will be streams of water flowing down every
mountain and hill. 26 The moon will be as bright as the sun, and the sun will be seven
times brighter—like the light of seven days! So it will be when the LORD begins to heal
his people and cure the wounds he gave them.
27 Look! The LORD is coming from far away, burning with anger, surrounded by a
thick, rising smoke. His lips are filled with fury; his words consume like fire. 28 His anger
pours out like a flood on his enemies, sweeping them all away. He will sift out the proud
nations. He will bridle them and lead them off to their destruction.
29 But the people of God will sing a song of joy, like the songs at the holy festivals.
You will be filled with joy, as when a flutist leads a group of pilgrims to Jerusalem—the
mountain of the LORD—to the Rock of Israel. 30 And the LORD will make his majestic
voice heard. With angry indignation he will bring down his mighty arm on his enemies.
It will descend with devouring flames, with cloudbursts, thunderstorms, and huge
hailstones, bringing their destruction. 31 At the LORD's command, the Assyrians will be
shattered. He will strike them down with his rod. 32 And as the LORD strikes them, his
people will keep time with the music of tambourines and harps. 33 Topheth—the place
of burning—has long been ready for the Assyrian king; it has been piled high with wood.
The breath of the LORD, like fire from a volcano, will set it ablaze.

The Futility of Relying on Egypt

31 Destruction is certain for those who look to Egypt for help, trusting their cavalry
and chariots instead of looking to the LORD, the Holy One of Israel. 2 In his
wisdom, the LORD will send great disaster; he will not change his mind. He will rise
against those who are wicked, and he will crush their allies, too. 3 For these Egyptians
are mere humans, not God! Their horses are puny flesh, not mighty spirits! When the
LORD clenches his fist against them, they will stumble and fall among those they are
trying to help. They will all fall down and die together.
4 But the LORD has told me this: "When a lion, even a young one, kills a sheep, it pays
no attention to the shepherd's shouts and noise. It just goes right on eating. In the same
way, the LORD Almighty will come and fight on Mount Zion. He will not be frightened
away! 5 The LORD Almighty will hover over Jerusalem as a bird hovers around its nest.
He will defend and save the city; he will pass over it and rescue it."

30:18 Isa 25:9; 2 Pet 3:9, 15
30:19 Isa 25:8; 65:24
30:20 Ps 80:5
30:21 Isa 35:8-9
30:22 Exod 32:2, 4
30:23 Ps 65:9-13
30:24 Matt 3:12
30:25 Isa 41:18
30:26 Isa 33:24; Hos 6:1-2; Rev 21:23; 22:5
30:27 Isa 66:15
30:28 2 Kgs 19:28; Isa 8:7-8; 2 Thes 2:8
30:31 Isa 31:8
30:32 1 Sam 18:6; Jer 31:4
30:33 Gen 19:24; Isa 34:9
31:1 Ps 20:7; Isa 10:17; Hos 11:9; Hab 1:12
31:2 Num 23:19; Jer 44:29; Rom 16:27
31:3 Jer 15:6; Ezek 28:9
31:4 Deut 32:11; Isa 42:13
31:5 Ps 91:4

30:20 The Lord gave his people adversity for food and affliction for drink, but he promised to be with them, teach them, and guide them during hard times. God expects a lot from us, and many times following him can be painful; but he always acts out of his love for us. Next time you go through a difficult time, try to appreciate the experience and grow from it, learning what God wants to teach you. God may be showing you his love by patiently walking with you through adversity.

30:21 When the people of Jerusalem left God's path, he would correct them. He will do the same for us. But when we hear his voice of correction, we must be willing to follow it!

31:1 It was wrong for Judah to look to other nations for military help. (1) They were trusting in human beings instead of God. Judah sought protection from those who had far less power than God. Both Egypt and Judah would fall as a result of their arrogance. (2) They were serving their own interests instead of God's, and thus they did not even consult him. They violated God's stipulation in Deuteronomy 17:16. (3) They did not want to pay the price of looking to God and repenting of their sinful ways. When we have problems, it is good to seek help, but we must never bypass God or his previous directions to us.

31:6 Isa 55:7; Jer 3:10, 14, 22
31:7 Isa 2:20
31:8 Isa 10:12; 14:2
31:9 Isa 13:2

6 Therefore, my people, though you are such wicked rebels, come and return to the LORD. 7 I know the glorious day will come when every one of you will throw away the gold idols and silver images that your sinful hands have made.

8 "The Assyrians will be destroyed, but not by the swords of men. The sword of God will strike them, and they will panic and flee. The strong young Assyrians will be taken away as captives. 9 Even their generals will quake with terror and flee when they see the battle flags," says the LORD, whose flame burns brightly in Jerusalem.

Israel's Ultimate Deliverance

32:1 Jer 23:5; Ezek 37:24; Zech 9:9
32:2 Isa 25:4; 35:6
32:4 Isa 29:24
32:5 1 Sam 25:25
32:6 Isa 10:2, 6; 59:7, 13
32:7 Jer 5:26-28; Mic 7:3
32:8 2 Cor 9:6-11
32:9 Isa 28:23; 47:8
32:10 Isa 5:5-6
32:11 Isa 22:12; 47:2
32:13 Isa 5:5-6, 10, 17
32:15 Ps 107:35; Isa 11:2; Joel 2:28
32:17 Isa 2:4; Rom 14:17; Jas 3:18
32:18 Hos 2:18-23
32:20 Isa 30:23

32 Look, a righteous king is coming! And honest princes will rule under him. 2 He will shelter Israel from the storm and the wind. He will refresh her as a river in the desert and as the cool shadow of a large rock in a hot and weary land. 3 Then everyone who can see will be looking for God, and those who can hear will listen to his voice. 4 Even the hotheads among them will be full of sense and understanding. Those who stammer in uncertainty will speak out plainly.

5 In that day ungodly fools will not be heroes. Wealthy cheaters will not be respected as outstanding citizens. 6 Everyone will recognize ungodly fools for what they are. They spread lies about the LORD; they deprive the hungry of food and give no water to the thirsty. 7 The smooth tricks of evil people will be exposed, including all the lies they use to oppress the poor in the courts. 8 But good people will be generous to others and will be blessed for all they do.

9 Listen, you women who lie around in lazy ease. Listen to me, and I will tell you of your reward. 10 In a short time—in just a little more than a year—you careless ones will suddenly begin to care. For your fruit crop will fail, and the harvest will never take place. 11 Tremble, you women of ease; throw off your unconcern. Strip off your pretty clothes, and wear sackcloth in your grief. 12 Beat your breasts in sorrow for your bountiful farms that will soon be gone, and for those fruitful vines of other years. 13 For your land will be overgrown with thorns and briers. Your joyful homes and happy cities will be gone. 14 The palace and the city will be deserted, and busy towns will be empty. Herds of donkeys and goats will graze on the hills where the watchtowers are, 15 until at last the Spirit is poured down upon us from heaven. Then the wilderness will become a fertile field, and the fertile field will become a lush and fertile forest. 16 Justice will rule in the wilderness and righteousness in the fertile field. 17 And this righteousness will bring peace. Quietness and confidence will fill the land forever.

18 My people will live in safety, quietly at home. They will be at rest. 19 Even though the forest will be destroyed and the city torn down, 20 God will greatly bless his people. Wherever they plant seed, bountiful crops will spring up. Their flocks and herds will graze in green pastures.

31:7 Someday these people would throw their idols away, recognizing that they were nothing but man-made objects. Idols such as money, fame, or success are seductive. Instead of contributing to our spiritual development, they rob us of our time, energy, and devotion that ought to be directed toward God. At first our idols seem exciting and promise to take us places, but in the end we will find that we have become their slaves. We need to recognize their worthlessness now, before they rob us of our freedom.

32:1 Having suffered much injustice from evil rulers, many in Judah were hungry for a strong king who would rule with justice. This "righteous King" will be Christ. Judah would be destroyed and taken into captivity. But one day, God's Son, a King unlike any other king, will reign in righteousness and rule with justice.

32:5, 6 When the righteous King comes, people's motives will become transparent. Fools will not be regarded as heroes. Those who have opposed God's standards of living will be unable to maintain their deception. In the blazing light of the holy Savior, sin cannot disguise itself and appear good. Christ's revealing light shines into the darkest corners of our hearts, showing sin clearly for what it is. When King Jesus reigns in your heart, there is no place for sin, no matter how well hidden you may think it is.

32:9-13 The people turned their backs on God and concentrated on their own pleasures. This warning is not just to the women of Jerusalem (see 3:16–4:1) but to all who sit back in their thoughtless complacency, enjoying crops, clothes, land, and cities while an enemy approaches. Wealth and luxury bring false security, lulling us into thinking all is well when disaster is around the corner. By abandoning God's purpose for our life, we also abandon his help.

32:15-17 God acts from above to change people's condition here on earth. Only when God's Spirit is among us can we achieve true peace and fruitfulness (Ezekiel 36:22-38; Galatians 5:22, 23). This will happen in the end times. We can also have God's Spirit with us now, for he is available to all believers through Christ (John 15:26). But the outpouring mentioned here happens when the worldwide Kingdom of God is established for all eternity (see Joel 2:28, 29).

A Message about Assyria

33 Destruction is certain for you Assyrians,* who have destroyed everything around
you but have never felt destruction yourselves. You expect others to respect their
promises to you, while you betray your promises to them. Now you, too, will be betrayed
and destroyed!
2But LORD, be merciful to us, for we have waited for you. Be our strength each day
and our salvation in times of trouble. 3The enemy runs at the sound of your voice. When
you stand up, the nations flee! 4Just as locusts strip the fields and vines, so Jerusalem
will strip the fallen army of Assyria!
5Though the LORD is very great and lives in heaven, he will make Jerusalem* his
home of justice and righteousness. 6In that day he will be your sure foundation,
providing a rich store of salvation, wisdom, and knowledge. The fear of the LORD is the
key to this treasure.
7But now your ambassadors weep in bitter disappointment, for Assyria has refused
their petition for peace. 8Your roads are deserted; no one travels them anymore. The
Assyrians have broken their peace pact and care nothing for the promises they made
before witnesses.* They have no respect for anyone. 9All the land of Israel is in trouble.
Lebanon has been destroyed. The plain of Sharon is now a wilderness. Bashan and
Carmel have been plundered.
10But the LORD says: "I will stand up and show my power and might. 11You Assyrians
will gain nothing by all your efforts. Your own breath will turn to fire and kill you. 12Your
people will be burned up completely, like thorns cut down and tossed in a fire. 13Listen
to what I have done, you nations far away! And you that are near, acknowledge my
might!"
14The sinners among my people* shake with fear. "Which one of us," they cry, "can
live here in the presence of this all-consuming fire?" 15The ones who can live here are
those who are honest and fair, who reject making a profit by fraud, who stay far away
from bribes, who refuse to listen to those who plot murder, who shut their eyes to all
enticement to do wrong. 16These are the ones who will dwell on high. The rocks of the
mountains will be their fortress of safety. Food will be supplied to them, and they will
have water in abundance.
17Your eyes will see the king in all his splendor, and you will see a land that stretches
into the distance. 18You will think back to this time of terror when the Assyrian officers
outside your walls counted your towers and estimated how much plunder they would get
from your fallen city. 19But soon they will all be gone. These fierce, violent people with
a strange, unknown language will disappear.
20Instead, you will see Zion as a place of worship and celebration. You will see
Jerusalem, a city quiet and secure. 21The LORD will be our Mighty One. He will be like
a wide river of protection that no enemy can cross. 22For the LORD is our judge, our
lawgiver, and our king. He will care for us and save us. 23The enemies' sails hang loose
on broken masts with useless tackle. Their treasure will be divided by the people of God.

33:1 Jer 25:12-14; Hab 2:8
33:2 Isa 25:9; 40:10
33:3 Jer 25:30-31
33:5 Ps 97:9
33:6 Ps 112:1-3; Isa 51:6
33:7 2 Kgs 18:18, 37
33:9 Isa 10:34; 24:4; 35:2
33:10 Ps 12:5; Isa 2:19
33:11 Isa 26:18
33:12 2 Sam 23:6-7; Isa 10:17
33:13 Isa 49:1
33:14 Isa 1:28; 30:27; Heb 12:29
33:15 Ps 24:3-4; Isa 58:6-11
33:16 Isa 25:4; 49:10
33:17 Isa 6:5
33:18 1 Cor 1:20
33:19 Deut 28:49-50
33:20 Ps 46:5
33:21 Isa 48:18
33:22 Isa 49:25-26; Zech 9:9; Jas 4:12

33:1 Hebrew *for you, O destroyer . . . O betrayer.* The Hebrew text does not specifically name Assyria as the object of this prophecy. **33:5** Hebrew *Zion.* **33:8** As in Dead Sea Scrolls; Masoretic Text reads *care nothing for the cities.* **33:14** Hebrew *in Zion.*

33:1 Assyria continually broke its promises but demanded that others keep theirs. It is easy to put ourselves in the same selfish position, demanding our rights while ignoring the rights of others. Broken promises shatter trust and destroy relationships. Determine to keep your promises; at the same time, ask forgiveness for past promises you have broken. Treat others with the same fairness that you demand for yourself.

33:2 These are the words of the righteous remnant who were waiting for God to deliver them from their oppression.

33:4 See 2 Kings 19:20-37 and Isaiah 37:21-38 for a description of the victory over Assyria described here.

33:5 When Christ's Kingdom is established, Jerusalem will be the home of justice and righteousness because the Messiah will reign there. As a light to the world, the new Jerusalem will be the holy city (Revelation 21:2).

33:9 These fruitful, productive areas would become deserts. Lebanon was known for its huge cedars. Sharon was very fertile. Bashan was very productive in grain and cattle. Carmel was thickly forested.

33:14-16 These sinners realized that they could not live in the presence of the holy God, for he is like a fire that consumes evil. Only those who walk uprightly and speak what is right can live with God. Isaiah gives examples of how to demonstrate our righteousness and uprightness: We can reject gain from extortion and bribes, refuse to listen to plots of wrong actions, and shut our eyes to evil. If we are fair and honest in our relationships, we will dwell with God, and he will supply our needs.

Even the lame will win their share! 24The people of Israel will no longer say, "We are
sick and helpless," for the LORD will forgive their sins.

A Message for the Nations

34 Come here and listen, O nations of the earth. Let the world and everything in it
hear my words. 2For the LORD is enraged against the nations. His fury is against
all their armies. He will completely destroy* them, bringing about their slaughter. 3Their
dead will be left unburied, and the stench of rotting bodies will fill the land. The
mountains will flow with their blood. 4The heavens above will melt away and disappear
like a rolled-up scroll. The stars will fall from the sky, just as withered leaves and fruit
fall from a tree.

5And when my sword has finished its work in the heavens, then watch. It will fall upon
Edom, the nation I have completely destroyed. 6The sword of the LORD is drenched with
blood. It is covered with fat as though it had been used for killing lambs and goats and
rams for a sacrifice. Yes, the LORD will offer a great sacrifice in the rich city of Bozrah.
He will make a mighty slaughter in Edom. 7The strongest will die—veterans and young
men, too. The land will be soaked with blood and the soil enriched with fat. 8For it is the
day of the LORD's vengeance, the year when Edom will be paid back for all it did to
Israel.* 9The streams of Edom will be filled with burning pitch, and the ground will be
covered with fire.

10This judgment on Edom will never end; the smoke of its burning will rise forever.
The land will lie deserted from generation to generation. No one will live there anymore.
11It will be haunted by the horned owl, the hawk, the screech owl, and the raven.* For
God will bring chaos and destruction to that land. 12It will be called the Land of Nothing,
and its princes soon will all be gone. 13Thorns will overrun its palaces; nettles will grow
in its forts. The ruins will become a haunt for jackals and a home for ostriches. 14Wild
animals of the desert will mingle there with hyenas, their howls filling the night. Wild
goats will bleat at one another among the ruins, and night creatures will come there to
rest. 15There the owl will make her nest and lay her eggs. She will hatch her young and
cover them with her wings. And the vultures will come, each one with its mate.

16Search the book of the LORD, and see what he will do. He will not miss a single
detail. Not one of these birds and animals will be missing, and none will lack a mate, for
the LORD has promised this. His Spirit will make it all come true. 17He has surveyed and
divided the land and deeded it over to those creatures. They will possess it forever, from
generation to generation.

Hope for Restoration

35 Even the wilderness will rejoice in those days. The desert will blossom with
flowers. 2Yes, there will be an abundance of flowers and singing and joy! The
deserts will become as green as the mountains of Lebanon, as lovely as Mount Carmel's
pastures and the plain of Sharon. There the LORD will display his glory, the splendor of
our God.

33:24 Mic 7:18-19; 1 Jn 1:7-9
34:1 Deut 32:1
34:2 Isa 26:20-21
34:3 Ezek 14:19; 35:6
34:4 Joel 2:31; †Matt 24:29; †Mark 13:24-25; 2 Pet 3:10; Rev 6:12-14
34:5 Isa 24:6
34:6 Isa 63:1
34:7 Pss 22:21; 68:30
34:8 Isa 13:6; 63:4
34:9 Deut 29:23
34:10 Isa 1:31; Ezek 29:11; Mal 1:3-4; Rev 14:11; 19:3
34:11 Lam 2:8
34:13 Jer 9:11; 10:22
34:14 Isa 13:21
34:15 Deut 14:13
34:16 Isa 40:5
34:17 Jer 13:25
35:1 Isa 41:18-19; 51:3; 55:12-13
35:2 Isa 25:9; 60:13; 66:10, 14

34:2 The Hebrew term used here refers to the complete consecration of things or people to the LORD, either by destroying them or by giving them as an offering; also in 34:5. **34:8** Hebrew *to Zion.* **34:11** The identification of some of these birds is uncertain.

34:5 The Edomites shared a common ancestry with Israel. The Israelites were descended from Jacob; the Edomites from Jacob's twin brother, Esau. Edom was always Israel's bitter enemy. The destruction of Edom mentioned here is a picture of the ultimate end of all who oppose God and his people.

34:16 Isaiah referred to the prophecies that God commanded him to write down as the "book of the LORD." Whoever lived to see the time of Edom's destruction would have only to look up these prophecies to find agreement between what happened and what was predicted. Prophecy predicts and history reveals what has been in God's mind for all time.

35:1ff In chapters 1–34, Isaiah has delivered a message of judgment on all nations, including Israel and Judah, for rejecting God. Although there have been glimpses of relief and restoration for the remnant of faithful believers, the climate of wrath, fury, judgment, and destruction has prevailed. Now Isaiah breaks through with a vision of beauty and encouragement. God is just as thorough in his mercy as he is severe in his judgment. God's complete moral perfection is revealed by his hatred of all sin, and this leads to judgment. This same moral perfection is revealed in his love for all he has created. This leads to mercy for those who have sinned but who have sincerely loved Jesus and put their trust in him.

35:1ff This chapter is a beautiful picture of the final Kingdom in which God will establish his justice and destroy all evil. This is the world the redeemed can anticipate after the judgment when creation itself will rejoice in God. Chapter 34 spoke of great distress when God will judge all people for their actions. Chapter 35 pictures the days when life will be peaceful at last and everything will be made right. Carmel and Sharon were regions of thick vegetation and fertile soil. They were symbols of productivity and plenty.

3 With this news, strengthen those who have tired hands, and encourage those who have weak knees. 4 Say to those who are afraid, "Be strong, and do not fear, for your God is coming to destroy your enemies. He is coming to save you." 5 And when he comes, he will open the eyes of the blind and unstop the ears of the deaf. 6 The lame will leap like a deer, and those who cannot speak will shout and sing! Springs will gush forth in the wilderness, and streams will water the desert. 7 The parched ground will become a pool, and springs of water will satisfy the thirsty land. Marsh grass and reeds and rushes will flourish where desert jackals once lived.

8 And a main road will go through that once deserted land. It will be named the Highway of Holiness. Evil-hearted people will never travel on it. It will be only for those who walk in God's ways; fools will never walk there. 9 Lions will not lurk along its course, and there will be no other dangers. Only the redeemed will follow it. 10 Those who have been ransomed by the LORD will return to Jerusalem,* singing songs of everlasting joy. Sorrow and mourning will disappear, and they will be overcome with joy and gladness.

35:3 Job 4:3-4; Heb 12:12
35:4 Ps 145:19
35:5 John 9:6-7
35:6 Luke 11:14; John 7:38; Acts 3:7-8
35:8 Matt 7:13-14
35:9 Isa 51:10
35:10 Rev 21:4

5. Events during the reign of Hezekiah

Assyria Invades Judah

36 In the fourteenth year of King Hezekiah's reign, King Sennacherib of Assyria came to attack the fortified cities of Judah and conquered them. 2 Then the king of Assyria sent his personal representative with a huge army from Lachish to confront King Hezekiah in Jerusalem. The Assyrians stopped beside the aqueduct that feeds water into the upper pool, near the road leading to the field where cloth is bleached.

3 These are the officials who went out to meet with them: Eliakim son of Hilkiah, the palace administrator, Shebna the court secretary, and Joah son of Asaph, the royal historian. 4 Then the Assyrian king's personal representative sent this message to King Hezekiah:

"This is what the great king of Assyria says: What are you trusting in that makes you so confident? 5 Do you think that mere words can substitute for military skill and strength? Which of your allies will give you any military backing against Assyria? 6 Will Egypt? If you lean on Egypt, you will find it to be a stick that breaks beneath your weight and pierces your hand. The Pharaoh of Egypt is completely unreliable!

7 "But perhaps you will say, 'We are trusting in the LORD our God!' But isn't he the one who was insulted by King Hezekiah? Didn't Hezekiah tear down his shrines and altars and make everyone in Judah worship only at the altar here in Jerusalem?

8 "I'll tell you what! My master, the king of Assyria, will strike a bargain with you. If you can find two thousand horsemen in your entire army, he will give you two thousand horses for them to ride on! 9 With your tiny army, how can you think of challenging even the weakest contingent of my master's troops, even with the help of Egypt's

36:1-22 //2 Kgs 18:13-37; //2 Chr 32:9-19
36:3 Isa 22:15, 20
36:4 2 Kgs 18:19
36:5 2 Kgs 18:7
36:6 Ps 146:3; Ezek 29:6-7
36:7 Deut 12:2-5; 2 Kgs 18:4-5
36:9 Isa 20:5

35:10 Hebrew *Zion.*

35:8-10 This "Highway of Holiness" is the way that righteous pilgrims will take from the desert of suffering to Zion (Jerusalem). It is found only by following God. Only the redeemed will travel God's highway; they will be protected from wicked travelers and harmful animals. God is preparing a way for his people to travel to his home, and he will walk with us. God doesn't simply point the way; he is always beside us as we go.

36:4-6 Chapter 19 describes Isaiah's prophecy of judgment upon Egypt, while chapters 30 and 31 pronounce woe on those from Judah who would ally themselves with Egypt in the face of Assyria's impending attack. Sennacherib of Assyria was taunting Judah for trusting in Egypt. Even the Assyrians knew that Egypt could not help Judah.

36:5 Hezekiah put great trust in Pharaoh's promise to help Israel against the Assyrians, but promises are only as good as the credibility of the person making them. It was Pharaoh's word against God's. How quickly we seek human advice while we neglect God's eternal promises. When choosing between God's Word and someone else's, whose will you believe?

36:7 The Assyrian king's personal representative claimed that Hezekiah had insulted God by tearing down his altars and making the people worship only in Jerusalem. But Hezekiah's reform sought to eliminate idol worship (which occurred mainly on high hills) so that the people worshiped only the true God. Either the Assyrians didn't know about the religion of the true God, or they wanted to deceive the people into thinking they had angered a powerful god.

In the same way, Satan tries to confuse or deceive us. People don't necessarily need to be sinful to be ineffective for God; they need only be confused about what God wants. To avoid Satan's deceit, study God's Word carefully and regularly. When you know what God says, you will not fall for Satan's lies.

36:10 1 Kgs 13:18 chariots and horsemen*? 10What's more, do you think we have invaded your land
without the LORD's direction? The LORD himself told us, 'Go and destroy it!'"

36:11 Ezra 4:7 Dan 2:4 11Then Eliakim, Shebna, and Joah said to the king's representative, "Please speak to
us in Aramaic, for we understand it well. Don't speak in Hebrew, for the people on the
wall will hear."

12But Sennacherib's representative replied, "My master wants everyone in Jerusalem
to hear this, not just you. He wants them to know that if you do not surrender, this city
will be put under siege. The people will become so hungry and thirsty that they will eat
their own dung and drink their own urine."

36:13 2 Chr 32:18 13Then he stood and shouted in Hebrew to the people on the wall, "Listen to this
36:14 Isa 37:10 message from the great king of Assyria! 14This is what the king says: Don't let King
Hezekiah deceive you. He will never be able to rescue you. 15Don't let him fool you into
trusting in the LORD by saying, 'The LORD will rescue us! This city will never be handed
over to the Assyrian king.'

36:16 Zech 3:10 16"Don't listen to Hezekiah! These are the terms the king of Assyria is offering: Make
peace with me—open the gates and come out. Then I will allow each of you to continue
eating from your own garden and drinking from your own well. 17Then I will arrange to
take you to another land like this one—a country with bountiful harvests of grain and
wine, bread and vineyards—a land of plenty.

18"Don't let Hezekiah mislead you by saying, 'The LORD will rescue us!' Have the

36:9 Or *and charioteers.*

ASSYRIA ADVANCES
As Sennacherib beautified his capital city, Nineveh, Hezekiah withheld tribute and prepared for battle. The Assyrians advanced toward their rebellious western border, attacking swiftly down the Mediterranean coast. From Lachish, Sennacherib threatened to take Jerusalem, but Isaiah knew his threats would die with him on his return to Nineveh.

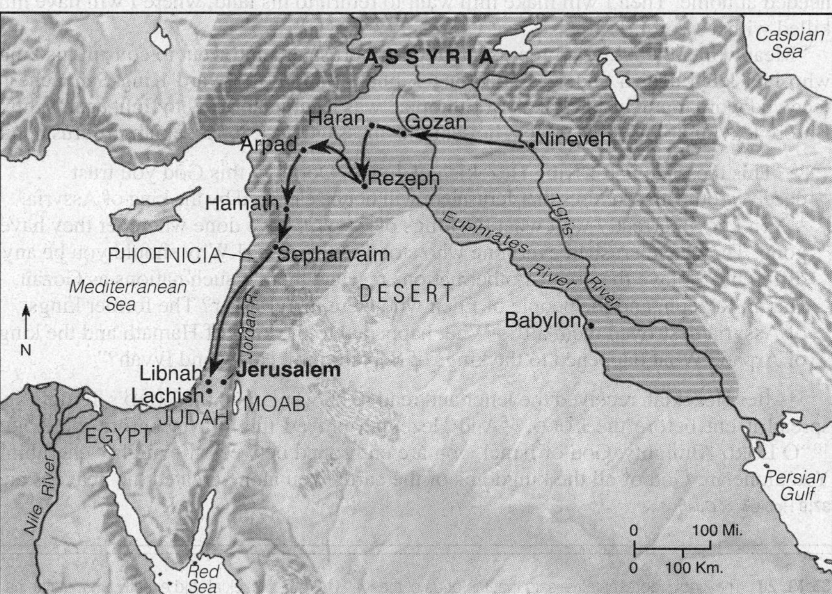

36:10 Sennacherib continued his demoralization campaign by sending his personal representative to try to convince the people of Judah that God had turned against them. The Assyrians hoped to convince the people of Judah to surrender without fighting. But Isaiah had already said that the Assyrians *would not* destroy Jerusalem, so the people did not need to be afraid of them (10:24-27; 29:5-8).

36:11 Aramaic was an international language at this time. See also 22:15-25 for Isaiah's prophecies concerning Eliakim and Shebna.

36:17 Sennacherib's representative tried yet another ploy to demoralize the people. He appealed to the starving city under siege by offering to take them to a land with plenty of food if they surrendered. The Assyrian policy for dealing with conquered nations was to resettle the inhabitants and then to move other conquered peoples into the recently conquered area. This provided manpower for their armies and prevented revolts in conquered territories.

gods of any other nations ever saved their people from the king of Assyria? 19 What happened to the gods of Hamath and Arpad? And what about the gods of Sepharvaim? Did they rescue Samaria from my power? 20 What god of any nation has ever been able to save its people from my power? Name just one! So what makes you think that the LORD can rescue Jerusalem?"

21 But the people were silent and did not answer because Hezekiah had told them not to speak. 22 Then Eliakim son of Hilkiah, the palace administrator, Shebna the court secretary, and Joah son of Asaph, the royal historian, went back to Hezekiah. They tore their clothes in despair, and they went in to see the king and told him what the Assyrian representative had said.

Hezekiah Seeks the LORD's Help

37 When King Hezekiah heard their report, he tore his clothes and put on sackcloth and went into the Temple of the LORD to pray. 2 And he sent Eliakim the palace administrator, Shebna the court secretary, and the leading priests, all dressed in sackcloth, to the prophet Isaiah son of Amoz. 3 They told him, "This is what King Hezekiah says: This is a day of trouble, insult, and disgrace. It is like when a child is ready to be born, but the mother has no strength to deliver it. 4 But perhaps the LORD your God has heard the Assyrian representative defying the living God and will punish him for his words. Oh, pray for those of us who are left!"

5 After King Hezekiah's officials delivered the king's message to Isaiah, 6 the prophet replied, "Say to your master, 'This is what the LORD says: Do not be disturbed by this blasphemous speech against me from the Assyrian king's messengers. 7 Listen! I myself will make sure that the king will receive a report from Assyria telling him that he is needed at home. Then I will make him want to return to his land, where I will have him killed with a sword.'"

8 Meanwhile, the Assyrian representative left Jerusalem and went to consult his king, who had left Lachish and was attacking Libnah. 9 Soon afterward King Sennacherib received word that King Tirhakah of Ethiopia* was leading an army to fight against him. Before leaving to meet the attack, he sent this message back to Hezekiah in Jerusalem:

> 10 "This message is for King Hezekiah of Judah. Don't let this God you trust deceive you with promises that Jerusalem will not be captured by the king of Assyria. 11 You know perfectly well what the kings of Assyria have done wherever they have gone. They have crushed everyone who stood in their way! Why should you be any different? 12 Have the gods of other nations rescued them—such nations as Gozan, Haran, Rezeph, and the people of Eden who were in Tel-assar? The former kings of Assyria destroyed them all! 13 What happened to the king of Hamath and the king of Arpad? What happened to the kings of Sepharvaim, Hena, and Ivvah?"

14 After Hezekiah received the letter and read it, he went up to the LORD's Temple and spread it out before the LORD. 15 And Hezekiah prayed this prayer before the LORD: 16 "O LORD Almighty, God of Israel, you are enthroned between the mighty cherubim! You alone are God of all the kingdoms of the earth. You alone created the heavens and

36:19 2 Kgs 17:6; Isa 10:9-11; 37:11-13; Jer 49:23
36:20 1 Kgs 20:23, 28
37:1-13 //2 Kgs 19:1-13
37:3 Isa 22:5; 26:17-18
37:4 Isa 1:9; 10:20-22
37:6 Isa 7:4; 35:4
37:8 Isa 20:5
37:11 Isa 10:9-11
37:12 Gen 11:31; 2 Kgs 17:6; Acts 7:2
37:14-20 //2 Kgs 19:14-19
37:16 Exod 25:22; Pss 80:1; 86:10; Jer 10:12

37:9 Hebrew *of Cush.*

36:19, 20 The king's representative said that the gods of the other cities he had conquered had not been able to save their people, so how could the God of Jerusalem save them? The Lord was supposedly the God of Samaria (the northern kingdom), and it fell. But the Lord was the God of Samaria in name only because the people were not worshiping him. That is why prophets foretold the fall of Samaria. But for the Lord's own sake and for the sake of David, the Lord would rescue Jerusalem from the Assyrian army (37:35).

37:3 Judah is compared to a woman who is trying to give birth to a child but is too weak to deliver. When the situation seemed hopeless, Hezekiah didn't give up. Instead, he asked the prophet Isaiah to pray that God would help his people. No matter how bad your circumstances seem, don't despair. Turn to God.

37:4 Hezekiah did exactly what Isaiah had been calling the people to do (chapters 1–35). He turned to God and watched him come to Judah's aid. Turning to God means believing that God is there and that he is able to help you.

37:8-10 Although the answer to Hezekiah's prayer was already in motion because Tirhakah was poised to attack, Hezekiah did not know it. He persisted in prayer and faith even though he could not see the answer coming. When we pray, we must have faith that God has already prepared the best answer. Our task is to ask in faith and wait in humility.

37:16 Cherubim are mighty angels. The phrase "enthroned between the mighty cherubim" refers to the atonement cover on the Ark of the Covenant, which symbolized God's holiness, power, and sovereignty.

the earth. 17 Listen to me, O LORD, and hear! Open your eyes, O LORD, and see! Listen
to Sennacherib's words of defiance against the living God.

37:18 2 Kgs 15:29; 1 Chr 5:26
37:19 Isa 17:8; 26:14
37:20 1 Kgs 18:36-37; Isa 33:22; Ezek 36:23

18 "It is true, LORD, that the kings of Assyria have destroyed all these nations, just as
the message says. 19 And they have thrown the gods of these nations into the fire and
burned them. But of course the Assyrians could destroy them! They were not gods at
all—only idols of wood and stone shaped by human hands. 20 Now, O LORD our God,
rescue us from his power; then all the kingdoms of the earth will know that you alone,
O LORD, are God."

Isaiah Predicts Judah's Deliverance

21 Then Isaiah son of Amoz sent this message to Hezekiah: "This is what the LORD, the
God of Israel, says: This is my answer to your prayer concerning King Sennacherib of
Assyria. 22 This is the message that the LORD has spoken against him:

37:22 Lam 2:13; Zeph 3:14

'The virgin daughter of Zion
despises you and laughs at you.
The daughter of Jerusalem
scoffs and shakes her head as you flee.

37:23 Isa 5:15, 21; Ezek 39:7; Hab 1:12

23 'Whom do you think you have been insulting and ridiculing?
Against whom did you raise your voice?
At whom did you look in such proud condescension?
It was the Holy One of Israel!

37:24 Isa 14:8

24 By your messengers you have mocked the Lord.
You have said, "With my many chariots
I have conquered the highest mountains—
yes, the remotest peaks of Lebanon.
I have cut down its tallest cedars
and its choicest cypress trees.
I have reached its farthest corners
and explored its deepest forests.
25 I have dug wells in many a foreign land
and refreshed myself with their water.
I even stopped up the rivers of Egypt
so that my armies could go across!"

37:26 Isa 25:2; Acts 2:23; 4:27-28

26 'But have you not heard?
It was I, the LORD, who decided this long ago.
Long ago I planned what I am now causing to happen,
that you should crush fortified cities into heaps of rubble.

37:27 Ps 129:6; Isa 40:7

27 That is why their people have so little power
and are such easy prey for you.
They are as helpless as the grass,
as easily trampled as tender green shoots.
They are like grass sprouting on a housetop,
easily scorched by the sun.

37:28 Ps 139:1

28 'But I know you well—
your comings and goings and all you do.
I know the way you have raged against me.

37:29 Isa 30:28; Ezek 38:4

29 And because of your arrogance against me,
which I have heard for myself,
I will put my hook in your nose
and my bridle in your mouth.
I will make you return
by the road on which you came.'"

37:29 This was a common torture the Assyrians used on their captives. They were often led away with hooks in their noses or bits in their mouths to humiliate them. The Lord was threatening to do to the Assyrians what they had done to others.

30 Then Isaiah said to Hezekiah, "Here is the proof that the LORD will protect this city
from Assyria's king. This year you will eat only what grows up by itself, and next year you
will eat what springs up from that. But in the third year you will plant crops and harvest
them; you will tend vineyards and eat their fruit. 31 And you who are left in Judah, who have
escaped the ravages of the siege, will take root again in your own soil, and you will flourish
and multiply. 32 For a remnant of my people will spread out from Jerusalem, a group of
survivors from Mount Zion. The passion of the LORD Almighty will make this happen!
33 "And this is what the LORD says about the king of Assyria: His armies will not enter
Jerusalem to shoot their arrows. They will not march outside its gates with their shields
and build banks of earth against its walls. 34 The king will return to his own country by
the road on which he came. He will not enter this city, says the LORD. 35 For my own
honor and for the sake of my servant David, I will defend it."
36 That night the angel of the LORD went out to the Assyrian camp and killed 185,000
Assyrian troops. When the surviving Assyrians* woke up the next morning, they found
corpses everywhere. 37 Then King Sennacherib of Assyria broke camp and returned to
his own land. He went home to his capital of Nineveh and stayed there. 38 One day while
he was worshiping in the temple of his god Nisroch, his sons Adrammelech and Sharezer
killed him with their swords. They then escaped to the land of Ararat, and another son,
Esarhaddon, became the next king of Assyria.

Hezekiah's Sickness and Recovery

38 About that time Hezekiah became deathly ill, and the prophet Isaiah son of Amoz
went to visit him. He gave the king this message: "This is what the LORD says:
Set your affairs in order, for you are going to die. You will not recover from this illness."
2 When Hezekiah heard this, he turned his face to the wall and prayed to the LORD,
3 "Remember, O LORD, how I have always tried to be faithful to you and do what is
pleasing in your sight." Then he broke down and wept bitterly.
4 Then this message came to Isaiah from the LORD: 5 "Go back to Hezekiah and tell
him, 'This is what the LORD, the God of your ancestor David, says: I have heard your
prayer and seen your tears. I will add fifteen years to your life, 6 and I will rescue you
and this city from the king of Assyria. Yes, I will defend this city.
7 "'And this is the sign that the LORD will give you to prove he will do as he promised:
8 I will cause the sun's shadow to move ten steps backward on the sundial of Ahaz!'" So
the shadow on the sundial moved backward ten steps.

Hezekiah's Poem of Praise

9 When King Hezekiah was well again, he wrote this poem about his experience:

10 I said, "In the prime of my life,
must I now enter the place of the dead?
Am I to be robbed of my normal years?"
11 I said, "Never again will I see the LORD GOD
while still in the land of the living.
Never again will I see my friends
or laugh with those who live in this world.
12 My life has been blown away
like a shepherd's tent in a storm.

37:30 Lev 25:5, 11
37:31 Isa 10:20; 27:6
37:32 2 Kgs 19:31
37:35 2 Kgs 20:6; Isa 48:9, 11
37:36 2 Kgs 19:35; Isa 10:12, 33-34
37:37 Gen 10:11; Jon 3:3; Zeph 2:13
37:38 Gen 8:4
38:1-8 //2 Kgs 20:1-11; //2 Chr 32:24-26
38:3 2 Kgs 18:5-6; Neh 13:14; Ps 6:6-8
38:5 2 Kgs 18:2, 13
38:6 Isa 31:5
38:7 Isa 7:11, 14
38:8 2 Kgs 20:9-11
38:10 Pss 102:24; 107:18
38:11 Ps 27:13
38:12 Job 4:20; 2 Cor 5:1

37:36 Hebrew *When they.*

37:35 God would defend Jerusalem for the sake of his own honor and for David's sake in remembrance of his promise to David. The Assyrians had insulted God. They would not be his instrument to punish Jerusalem. What Jerusalem could not possibly do, God would do for it. God is prepared to do the impossible if we trust him enough to ask.

37:38 The death of Sennacherib was prophesied by Isaiah in 10:12, 33, 34 and in 37:7. His death is also recorded in 2 Kings 19.

38:1ff The events of chapters 38 and 39 happened before those of chapters 36 and 37.

38:1-5 When Isaiah went to Hezekiah, who was extremely ill, and told him of his impending death, Hezekiah immediately turned to God. God responded to his prayer, allowing Hezekiah to live another 15 years. If you have a desperate need in your life, bring it to the Lord. In response to fervent prayer, God may change the course of your life, too.

38:1-6 According to 2 Chronicles 32:24-26, Hezekiah had a problem with pride even after this double miracle of healing and deliverance. Eventually he and his subjects humbled themselves, so God's judgment was put off for several more generations.

It has been cut short,
as when a weaver cuts cloth from a loom.
Suddenly, my life was over.

38:13 Job 10:16

13 I waited patiently all night,
but I was torn apart as though by lions.
Suddenly, my life was over.

38:14 Ps 119:123 Ezek 7:16

14 Delirious, I chattered like a swallow or a crane,
and then I moaned like a mourning dove.
My eyes grew tired of looking to heaven for help.
I am in trouble, Lord. Help me!"

38:15 Job 7:11

15 But what could I say?
For he himself had sent this sickness.
Now I will walk humbly throughout my years
because of this anguish I have felt.

38:16 Pss 39:13; 119:71, 75

16 Lord, your discipline is good,
for it leads to life and health.
You have restored my health
and have allowed me to live!

38:17 Isa 43:25 Jer 31:34 Jon 2:6

17 Yes, it was good for me to suffer this anguish,
for you have rescued me from death
and have forgiven all my sins.

38:18 Ps 6:5

18 For the dead cannot praise you;
they cannot raise their voices in praise.
Those who go down to destruction
can no longer hope in your faithfulness.

38:19 Pss 78:5-7; 119:175

19 Only the living can praise you as I do today.
Each generation can make known your faithfulness to the next.

38:20 Pss 33:1-3; 116:17-19; 146:2

20 Think of it—the LORD has healed me!
I will sing his praises with instruments
every day of my life
in the Temple of the LORD.

38:21 2 Kgs 20:7-8

21 Isaiah had said to Hezekiah's servants, "Make an ointment from figs and spread it
over the boil, and Hezekiah will recover."
22 And Hezekiah had asked, "What sign will prove that I will go to the Temple of the
LORD three days from now?"

Envoys from Babylon

39:1-8 //2 Kgs 20:12-19

39 Soon after this, Merodach-baladan son of Baladan, king of Babylon, sent Hezekiah his best wishes and a gift. He had heard that Hezekiah had been very sick
and that he had recovered. 2 Hezekiah welcomed the Babylonian envoys and showed
them everything in his treasure-houses—the silver, the gold, the spices, and the aromatic
oils. He also took them to see his armory and showed them all his other treasures—everything! There was nothing in his palace or kingdom that Hezekiah did not show them.

39:2 2 Kgs 18:15-16 2 Chr 32:25, 31

38:16-18 Hezekiah realized that his prayer brought deliverance and forgiveness. His words "the dead cannot praise you" may reveal that he was unaware of the blessedness of the future life for those who trust in God (57:1, 2), or he may have meant that dead bodies cannot praise God. In either case, Hezekiah knew that God had spared his life, so in his poem Hezekiah praises God. Hezekiah recognized the good that came from his bitter experience. The next time you have difficult struggles, pray for God's help to gain something beneficial from them.

38:19 Hezekiah spoke of the significance of passing the joy of the Lord from generation to generation. The heritage of our faith has come to us because of faithful men and women who have carried God's message to us across the centuries. Do you share with your children or other young people the excitement of your relationship with God?

39:1ff Merodach-baladan, a Babylonian prince, was planning a revolt against Assyria and was forming an alliance. He probably hoped to convince Hezekiah to join this alliance against Assyria. Hezekiah, feeling honored by this attention and perhaps feeling some sympathy for their proposal, showed the Babylonian envoys his treasures. But Isaiah warned the king not to trust Babylon. Someday they would turn on Judah and devour Jerusalem's wealth.

3 Then Isaiah the prophet went to King Hezekiah and asked him, “What did those men 39:3 Jer 5:15
want? Where were they from?”
Hezekiah replied, “They came from the distant land of Babylon.”
4 “What did they see in your palace?” asked Isaiah.
“They saw everything,” Hezekiah replied. “I showed them everything I own—all my
treasures.”
5 Then Isaiah said to Hezekiah, “Listen to this message from the LORD Almighty: 6 The 39:5 1 Sam 13:13-14; 15:16
time is coming when everything you have—all the treasures stored up by your ances-
tors—will be carried off to Babylon. Nothing will be left, says the LORD. 7 Some of your 39:6 2 Kgs 24:13 Jer 20:5
own descendants will be taken away into exile. They will become eunuchs who will
serve in the palace of Babylon’s king.” 39:7 Dan 1:2-7
8 Then Hezekiah said to Isaiah, “This message you have given me from the LORD is
good.” But the king was thinking, “At least there will be peace and security during my 39:8 2 Chr 34:28
lifetime.”

B. WORDS OF COMFORT (40:1—66:24)

Isaiah now speaks of events that will occur after the Captivity. This includes the decree by Cyrus to release the remnant captives and allow them to return to Jerusalem after he conquered Babylon. But Isaiah also foretells the coming of the suffering Servant, Jesus Christ, and describes his life and death with incredible detail. Isaiah also speaks about the coming of the new heavens and earth, when God's people will be completely restored. Because all believers will participate in this new world to come, we can have confident hope in the future.

1. Israel's release from captivity

Comfort for God's People

40 “Comfort, comfort my people,” says your God. 2 “Speak tenderly to Jerusalem. 40:1 †Luke 2:25 2 Cor 1:4
Tell her that her sad days are gone and that her sins are pardoned. Yes, the LORD
has punished her in full for all her sins.” 40:2 Zech 9:12
3 Listen! I hear the voice of someone shouting, “Make a highway for the LORD through 40:3 Mal 3:1 †Matt 3:3 †Mark 1:3 †John 1:23
the wilderness. Make a straight, smooth road through the desert for our God. 4 Fill the
valleys and level the hills. Straighten out the curves and smooth off the rough spots.
5 Then the glory of the LORD will be revealed, and all people will see it together. The
LORD has spoken!” 40:4 Ezek 17:24
6 A voice said, “Shout!”
I asked, “What should I shout?” 40:5 Hab 2:14 †Luke 3:4-6
“Shout that people are like the grass that dies away. Their beauty fades as quickly as

---

39:4-7 What was so wrong about showing these Babylonians around? Hezekiah failed to see that the Babylonians would become his next threat and that they, not the Assyrians, would conquer his city. When Isaiah told him that Babylon would someday carry it all away, this was an amazing prophecy because Babylon was struggling for independence under Assyria. Hezekiah's prideful display of his earthly treasures brought its own consequences (2 Kings 25; Daniel 1:1, 2). His response (39:8) may seem a bit shortsighted, but he simply was expressing gratitude for the blessing from God that peace would reign during his lifetime and that God's judgment would not be more severe.

39:8 Hezekiah, one of Judah's most faithful kings, worked hard throughout his reign to stamp out idol worship and to purify the worship of the true God at the Jerusalem Temple. Nevertheless he knew his kingdom was not pure. Powerful undercurrents of evil invited destruction, and only God's miraculous interventions preserved Judah from its enemies. Here Hezekiah was grateful that God would preserve peace during his reign. As soon as Hezekiah died, the nation rushed back to its sinful ways under the leadership of Manasseh, Hezekiah's son. He actually rebuilt the centers of idolatry his father had destroyed.

40:1ff The book of Isaiah makes a dramatic shift at this point. The following chapters discuss the majesty of God, who is coming to rule the earth and judge all people. God will reunite Israel and Judah and restore them to glory. Instead of warning the people of impending judgment, Isaiah here comforts them. Chapter 40 refers to the restoration after the Exile. Cyrus is the instrument of their deliverance from Babylon. Isaiah also foretells a time when "Babylon"—the future evil world system—will be destroyed and the persecution of God's people will end.

40:1, 2 Judah still had 100 years of trouble before Jerusalem would fall, then 70 years of exile. So God tells Isaiah to speak tenderly and to comfort Jerusalem.

The seeds of comfort may take root in the soil of adversity. When your life seems to be falling apart, ask God to comfort you. You may not escape adversity, but you may find God's comfort as you face it. Sometimes, however, the only comfort we have is in the knowledge that someday we will be with God. Appreciate the comfort and encouragement found in his Word, his presence, and his people.

40:3-5 Preparing a straight, smooth road means removing obstacles and rolling out the red carpet for the coming of the Lord. The desert is a picture of life's trials and sufferings. We are not immune to these, but our faith need not be hindered by them. Isaiah told people to prepare to see God work. John the Baptist used these words as he challenged the people to prepare for the coming Messiah (Matthew 3:3).

40:6-8 People are compared here to grass and flowers that wither away. We are mortal, but God's Word is eternal and unfailing. Public opinion changes and is unreliable, but God's Word is constant. Only in God's eternal Word will we find lasting solutions to our problems and needs.

the beauty of flowers in a field. 7 The grass withers, and the flowers fade beneath the
breath of the LORD. And so it is with people. 8 The grass withers, and the flowers fade,
but the word of our God stands forever."
9 Messenger of good news, shout to Zion from the mountaintops! Shout louder to
Jerusalem—do not be afraid. Tell the towns of Judah, "Your God is coming!" 10 Yes, the
Sovereign LORD is coming in all his glorious power. He will rule with awesome strength.
See, he brings his reward with him as he comes. 11 He will feed his flock like a shepherd.
He will carry the lambs in his arms, holding them close to his heart. He will gently lead
the mother sheep with their young.
12 Who else has held the oceans in his hand? Who has measured off the heavens with
his fingers? Who else knows the weight of the earth or has weighed out the mountains
and the hills? 13 Who is able to advise the Spirit of the LORD? Who knows enough to be
his teacher or counselor? 14 Has the LORD ever needed anyone's advice? Does he need
instruction about what is good or what is best? 15 No, for all the nations of the world are
nothing in comparison with him. They are but a drop in the bucket, dust on the scales.
He picks up the islands as though they had no weight at all. 16 All Lebanon's forests do
not contain sufficient fuel to consume a sacrifice large enough to honor him. All
Lebanon's sacrificial animals would not make an offering worthy of our God. 17 The
nations of the world are as nothing to him. In his eyes they are less than nothing—mere
emptiness and froth.
18 To whom, then, can we compare God? What image might we find to resemble him?
19 Can he be compared to an idol formed in a mold, overlaid with gold, and decorated
with silver chains? 20 Or is a poor person's wooden idol better? Can God be compared to
an idol that must be placed on a stand so it won't fall down?
21 Have you never heard or understood? Are you deaf to the words of God—the words
he gave before the world began? Are you so ignorant? 22 It is God who sits above the circle
of the earth. The people below must seem to him like grasshoppers! He is the one who
spreads out the heavens like a curtain and makes his tent from them. 23 He judges the great
people of the world and brings them all to nothing. 24 They hardly get started, barely taking
root, when he blows on them and their work withers. The wind carries them off like straw.
25 "To whom will you compare me? Who is my equal?" asks the Holy One.
26 Look up into the heavens. Who created all the stars? He brings them out one after
another, calling each by its name. And he counts them to see that none are lost or have
strayed away.
27 O Israel, how can you say the LORD does not see your troubles? How can you say
God refuses to hear your case? 28 Have you never heard or understood? Don't you know
that the LORD is the everlasting God, the Creator of all the earth? He never grows faint
or weary. No one can measure the depths of his understanding. 29 He gives power to those
who are tired and worn out; he offers strength to the weak. 30 Even youths will become
exhausted, and young men will give up. 31 But those who wait on the LORD will find new
strength. They will fly high on wings like eagles. They will run and not grow weary. They
will walk and not faint.

40:7 Jas 1:10-11
40:8 Matt 5:18; †1 Pet 1:24-25
40:10 Isa 59:16; Rev 22:12
40:11 Ezek 34:12-14, 23; John 10:11, 14-16
40:12 Isa 48:13
40:13 †Rom 11:34; †1 Cor 2:16
40:14 Col 2:3
40:15 Isa 17:13
40:18 Exod 8:10; Isa 46:5; Mic 7:18
40:19 Ps 115:4-8; Hab 2:18-19
40:20 Isa 46:7
40:21 Isa 51:13; Rom 1:19
40:22 Ps 104:2
40:23 Ps 107:40; Jer 25:18-27
40:24 Isa 17:13
40:26 Ps 147:4; Isa 42:5
40:27 Job 34:5-6; Isa 54:8
40:28 Pss 90:2; 147:5; Rom 11:33
40:29 Jer 31:25
40:30 Jer 9:21
40:31 2 Cor 4:8-10, 16; Heb 12:3

40:11 God is often pictured as a shepherd, gently caring for and guiding his flock. He is powerful (40:10), yet careful and gentle. He is called a shepherd (Psalm 23); the good shepherd (John 10:11, 14); the great Shepherd (Hebrews 13:20); and the head Shepherd (1 Peter 5:4). Note that the shepherd is caring for the most defenseless members of his society: children and those caring for them. This reinforces the prophetic theme that the truly powerful nation is not the one with a strong military, but rather the one that relies on God's caring strength.

40:12-31 Isaiah describes God's power to create, his provision to sustain, and his presence to help. God is almighty and all-powerful; but even so, he cares for each of us personally. No person or thing can be compared to God (40:25). We describe God as best we can with our limited knowledge and language, but we only limit our understanding of him and his power when we compare him to what we experience on earth. What is your concept of God, especially as revealed in his Son, Jesus Christ? Don't limit his work in your life by underestimating him.

40:29-31 Even the strongest people get tired at times, but God's power and strength never diminish. He is never too tired or too busy to help and listen. His strength is our source of strength. When you feel all of life crushing you and you cannot go another step, remember that you can call upon God to renew your strength.

40:31 Waiting on the Lord is the patient expectation that God will fulfill his promises in his Word and strengthen us to rise above life's difficulties. It means to completely trust in God.

God's Help for Israel

41 “Listen in silence before me, you lands beyond the sea. Bring your strongest
arguments. Come now and speak. The court is ready for your case.
2“Who has stirred up this king from the east, who meets victory at every step? Who,
indeed, but the LORD? He gives him victory over many nations and permits him to
trample their kings underfoot. He puts entire armies to the sword. He scatters them in the
wind with his bow. 3He chases them away and goes on safely, though he is walking over
unfamiliar ground. 4Who has done such mighty deeds, directing the affairs of the human
race as each new generation marches by? It is I, the LORD, the First and the Last. I alone
am he.”
5The lands beyond the sea watch in fear. Remote lands tremble and mobilize for war.
6They encourage one another with the words, “Be strong!” 7The craftsmen rush to make
new idols. The carver hurries the goldsmith, and the molder helps at the anvil. “Good,”
they say. “It's coming along fine.” Carefully they join the parts together, then fasten the
thing in place so it won't fall over.
8“But as for you, Israel my servant, Jacob my chosen one, descended from my friend
Abraham, 9I have called you back from the ends of the earth so you can serve me. For I
have chosen you and will not throw you away. 10Don't be afraid, for I am with you. Do
not be dismayed, for I am your God. I will strengthen you. I will help you. I will uphold
you with my victorious right hand.
11“See, all your angry enemies lie there, confused and ashamed. Anyone who opposes
you will die. 12You will look for them in vain. They will all be gone! 13I am holding you
by your right hand—I, the LORD your God. And I say to you, ‘Do not be afraid. I am here
to help you. 14Despised though you are, O Israel, don't be afraid, for I will help you. I
am the LORD, your Redeemer. I am the Holy One of Israel.’ 15You will be a new threshing
instrument with many sharp teeth. You will tear all your enemies apart, making chaff of
mountains. 16You will toss them in the air, and the wind will blow them all away; a
whirlwind will scatter them. And the joy of the LORD will fill you to overflowing. You
will glory in the Holy One of Israel.
17“When the poor and needy search for water and there is none, and their tongues are
parched from thirst, then I, the LORD, will answer them. I, the God of Israel, will never
forsake them. 18I will open up rivers for them on high plateaus. I will give them fountains
of water in the valleys. In the deserts they will find pools of water. Rivers fed by springs
will flow across the dry, parched ground. 19I will plant trees—cedar, acacia, myrtle,
olive, cypress, fir, and pine—on barren land. 20Everyone will see this miracle and
understand that it is the LORD, the Holy One of Israel, who did it.
21“Can your idols make such claims as these? Let them come and show what they can
do!” says the LORD, the King of Israel.* 22“Let them try to tell us what happened long

41:21 Hebrew *the King of Jacob.*

41:1 Hab 2:20; Zech 2:13
41:2 2 Chr 36:23; Isa 46:11
41:4 Isa 44:7; 48:12; Rev 1:8, 17-18; 22:13
41:5 Josh 5:1; Ezek 26:15-16
41:6 Joel 3:9-11
41:8 Isa 51:2; Jas 2:23
41:9 Deut 7:6; Isa 11:11
41:10 Deut 31:6; Ps 89:13; Rom 8:31
41:11 Isa 29:5, 7-8
41:12 Job 20:7-9
41:13 Isa 45:1
41:14 Isa 43:14
41:15 Mic 4:13
41:16 Isa 35:10
41:17 Isa 30:19; 42:16; 44:3
41:18 Ps 107:35; Isa 30:25
41:19 Isa 55:13
41:20 Job 12:7-9
41:22 Isa 43:9; 45:21

41:1ff The “king from the east” is Cyrus II of Persia, who would be king within a century and a half (he is also mentioned by name in 44:28). He conquered Babylon in 539 B.C. and was responsible for the decree releasing the exiled Jews to return to Jerusalem. God could even use a pagan ruler to protect and care for Israel, because God is in control of all world empires and politics.

41:4 Each generation gets caught up in its own problems, but God's plan embraces all generations. When your great-grandparents lived, God worked personally in the lives of his people. When your great-grandchildren live, God will still work personally in the lives of his people. He is the only one who sees 100 years from now as clearly as 100 years ago. When you are concerned about the future, talk with God, who knows the generations of the future as well as he knows the generations of the past.

41:8-10 God chose Israel through Abraham because he wanted to, not because the people deserved it (Deuteronomy 7:6-8; 9:4-6). Although God chose the Israelites to represent him to the world, they failed to do this; so God punished them and sent them into captivity. Now all believers are God's chosen people, and all share the responsibility of representing him to the world. One day God will bring all his faithful people together. We need not fear because (1) God is with us (“I am with you”), (2) God has established a relationship with us (“I am your God”), and (3) God gives us assurance of his strength, help, and victory over sin and death. Are you aware of all the ways God has helped you?

41:21-24 Israel was surrounded by many nations whose gods supposedly had special powers, such as helping crops grow and providing victory in war. These gods, however, failed to deliver. A god with limited or no power at all is not really a god. When we are tempted to put our trust in something other than the living God—money, career, family, or even military power—we should stop and ask some serious questions. Will it come through? Will it unfailingly provide what I am looking for? God delivers. When he makes a promise, he keeps it. He is completely trustworthy.

41:23 Jer 10:5 John 13:19
41:24 1 Cor 8:4
41:25 Jer 50:3 Mic 7:10
41:26 Isa 44:7 Hab 2:18-19
41:27 Isa 40:9
41:29 Jer 5:13

ago or what the future holds. 23Yes, that's it! If you are gods, tell what will occur in the
days ahead. Or perform a mighty miracle that will fill us with amazement and fear. Do
something, whether good or bad! 24But no! You are less than nothing and can do nothing
at all. Anyone who chooses you becomes filthy, just like you!
25"But I have stirred up a leader from the north and east. He will come against the
nations and call on my name, and I will give him victory over kings and princes. He will
trample them as a potter treads on clay.
26"Who but I have told you this would happen? Who else predicted this, making you
admit that he was right? No one else said a word! 27I was the first to tell Jerusalem,
'Look! Help is on the way!' 28Not one of your idols told you this. Not one gave any
answer when I asked. 29See, they are all foolish, worthless things. Your idols are all as
empty as the wind.

The LORD's Chosen Servant

42:1-4 †Matt 12:18-21
42:1 Isa 11:2; 53:11 Matt 3:17; 12:18
42:3 Ps 72:2, 4
42:4 Isa 24:15; 66:19
42:5 Job 33:4 Ps 104:2 Isa 45:18 Acts 17:25
42:6 Jer 23:5-6 Luke 2:32
42:7 Isa 35:5; 61:1
42:8 Exod 3:15; 20:3-5

42 "Look at my servant, whom I strengthen. He is my chosen one, and I am pleased
with him. I have put my Spirit upon him. He will reveal justice to the nations. 2He
will be gentle—he will not shout or raise his voice in public. 3He will not crush those
who are weak or quench the smallest hope. He will bring full justice to all who have been
wronged. 4He will not stop until truth and righteousness prevail throughout the earth.
Even distant lands beyond the sea will wait for his instruction."
5God, the LORD, created the heavens and stretched them out. He created the earth and
everything in it. He gives breath and life to everyone in all the world. And it is he who says,
6"I, the LORD, have called you to demonstrate my righteousness. I will guard and support
you, for I have given you to my people as the personal confirmation of my covenant with
them. And you will be a light to guide all nations to me. 7You will open the eyes of the blind
and free the captives from prison. You will release those who sit in dark dungeons.
8"I am the LORD; that is my name! I will not give my glory to anyone else. I will not
share my praise with carved idols. 9Everything I prophesied has come true, and now I
will prophesy again. I will tell you the future before it happens."

A Song of Praise to the LORD

42:10 Ps 33:3

10 Sing a new song to the LORD!
Sing his praises from the ends of the earth!
Sing, all you who sail the seas,
all you who live in distant coastlands.
11 Join in the chorus, you desert towns;
let the villages of Kedar rejoice!

THE SERVANT IN ISAIAH

The nation Israel is called the servant:	41:8; 42:19; 43:10; 44:1, 2, 21; 45:4; 48:20
The Messiah is called the Servant:	42:1–17; 49:3, 5–7; 50:10; 52:13; 53:11

The nation was given a mission to serve God, to be custodian of his word, and to be a light to the Gentile nations. Because of sin and rebellion, they failed. God sent his Son, Christ, as Messiah to fulfill his mission on earth.

42:1-4 These verses are quoted in Matthew 12:18-21 with reference to Christ. The chosen servant reveals a character of gentleness, encouragement, justice, and truth. When you feel broken and bruised or burned out in your spiritual life, God won't step on you or toss you aside as useless but will gently pick you up. God's loving attributes are desperately needed in the world today. Through God's Spirit, we can show such sensitivity to people around us, reflecting God's goodness and honesty to them.

42:1-9 Sometimes called the Servant Song, these verses are about the Servant-Messiah, not the servant Cyrus (described in chapter 41). Israel and the Messiah are both often called *servant.* Israel, as God's servant, was to help bring the world to a knowledge of God. The Messiah, Jesus, would fulfill this task and show God himself to the world.

42:6, 7 Part of Christ's mission on earth was to demonstrate God's righteousness and to be a light for the Gentiles (to all nations). Through Christ, all people have the opportunity to share in his mission. God calls us to be servants of his Son, demonstrating God's righteousness and bringing his light. What a rare privilege it is to help the Messiah fulfill his mission! But we must seek his righteousness (Matthew 6:33) before we demonstrate it to others and let his light shine in us before we can be lights ourselves (Matthew 5:16; 2 Corinthians 4:6).

42:10 Look at all the Lord will do for us and through us (42:6-9)! Majestic works prompt majestic responses. Do you really appreciate the good things that God does for you and through you? If so, let your praise to him reflect how you really feel.

Let the people of Sela sing for joy;
shout praises from the mountaintops!
12 Let the coastlands glorify the LORD;
let them sing his praise.
13 The LORD will march forth like a mighty man;
he will come out like a warrior, full of fury.
He will shout his thundering battle cry,
and he will crush all his enemies.
14 He will say, "I have long been silent;
yes, I have restrained myself.
But now I will give full vent to my fury;
I will gasp and pant like a woman giving birth.
15 I will level the mountains and hills
and bring a blight on all their greenery.
I will turn the rivers into dry land
and will dry up all the pools.
16 I will lead blind Israel down a new path,
guiding them along an unfamiliar way.
I will make the darkness bright before them
and smooth out the road ahead of them.
Yes, I will indeed do these things;
I will not forsake them.
17 But those who trust in idols,
calling them their gods—
they will be turned away in shame.

Israel's Failure to See and Listen

18 "Oh, how deaf and blind you are toward me! Why won't you listen? Why do you refuse
to see? 19 Who in all the world is as blind as my own people, my servant? Who is as deaf as
my messengers? Who is as blind as my chosen people, the servant of the LORD? 20 You see
and understand what is right but refuse to act on it. You hear, but you don't really listen."
21 The LORD has magnified his law and made it truly glorious. Through it he had planned
to show the world that he is righteous. 22 But what a sight his people are, for they have
been robbed, enslaved, imprisoned, and trapped. They are fair game for all and have no
one to protect them. 23 Will not even one of you apply these lessons from the past and see
the ruin that awaits you? 24 Who allowed Israel to be robbed and hurt? Was it not the LORD?
It was the LORD whom we sinned against, for the people would not go where he sent them,
nor would they obey his law. 25 That is why he poured out such fury on them and destroyed
them in battle. They were set on fire and burned, but they still refused to understand.

The Savior of Israel

43 But now, O Israel, the LORD who created you says: "Do not be afraid, for I have
ransomed you. I have called you by name; you are mine. 2 When you go through
deep waters and great trouble, I will be with you. When you go through rivers of

42:13 Isa 59:17; 66:14-16
42:14 Isa 57:11
42:15 Ezek 38:19-20
42:16 Ps 94:14; Isa 40:4; Luke 1:78-79; Eph 5:8
42:17 Ps 97:7; Isa 44:9, 11
42:18 Isa 35:5
42:19 Isa 44:26
42:20 Jer 6:10
42:22 Isa 24:18
42:24 Isa 10:5; 48:18
42:25 Isa 5:25; Hos 7:9
43:2 Deut 31:6, 8; Isa 8:7; Dan 3:25, 27

42:19, 20 How could Israel and Judah be God's servants and yet be so blind? How could they be so close to God and see so little? Jesus condemned the religious leaders of his day for the same disregard of God (John 9:39-41). Yet do we not fail in the same way? Sometimes partial blindness—seeing but not understanding, or knowing what is right but not doing it—can be worse than not seeing at all.

42:23 We may condemn our predecessors for their failures, but we are twice as guilty if we repeat the same mistakes that we recognize as failures. Often we are so ready to direct God's message at others that we can't see how it touches our own life. Make sure you are willing to take your own advice as you teach or lead.

43:1ff Chapter 42 ends with God's sorrow over the spiritual decay of his people. In chapter 43, God says that despite the people's spiritual failure, he will show them mercy, bring them back from captivity, and restore them. He would give them an outpouring of love, not wrath. Then the world would know that God alone had done this.

43:1-4 God created the people of Israel, and they were special to him. God redeemed them and called them by name to be those who belong to him. God protected Israel in times of trouble. We are important to God, too. If we claim to belong to God, we must never do anything that would bring shame to him.

43:2 Going through rivers of difficulty will either cause you to drown or force you to grow stronger. If you go in your own strength, you are more likely to drown. If you invite the Lord to go with you, he will protect you.

43:3 Exod 20:2 Isa 43:11
43:4 Isa 63:9
43:5 Isa 49:12 Jer 30:10-11
43:6 Ps 107:3 2 Cor 6:17-18
43:7 Ps 100:3 Isa 46:13 Eph 2:10
43:8 Ezek 12:2
43:9 Isa 41:22, 26
43:11 Hos 13:4
43:12 Ps 81:9
43:13 Job 9:12 Ps 90:2
43:14 Isa 41:14
43:16 Exod 14:21-22 Josh 3:15-16 Ps 77:19
43:17 Ps 76:5-6
43:18 Jer 16:14
43:19 Deut 8:15 2 Cor 5:17 Rev 21:5
43:20 Isa 41:17-18 †2 Pet 2:9
43:22 Mic 6:3
43:23 Exod 30:34 Mal 1:6-8
43:24 Jer 6:20 Mal 2:17
43:25 Isa 55:7 Jer 31:34 Ezek 36:22

difficulty, you will not drown! When you walk through the fire of oppression, you will not be burned up; the flames will not consume you. [3]For I am the LORD, your God, the Holy One of Israel, your Savior. I gave Egypt, Ethiopia,* and Seba as a ransom for your freedom. [4]Others died that you might live. I traded their lives for yours because you are precious to me. You are honored, and I love you.

[5]"Do not be afraid, for I am with you. I will gather you and your children from east and west [6]and from north and south. I will bring my sons and daughters back to Israel from the distant corners of the earth. [7]All who claim me as their God will come, for I have made them for my glory. It was I who created them."

[8]Bring out the people who have eyes but are blind, who have ears but are deaf. [9]Gather the nations together! Which of their idols has ever foretold such things? Can any of them predict something even a single day in advance? Where are the witnesses of such predictions? Who can verify that they spoke the truth?

[10]"But you are my witnesses, O Israel!" says the LORD. "And you are my servant. You have been chosen to know me, believe in me, and understand that I alone am God. There is no other God; there never has been and never will be. [11]I am the LORD, and there is no other Savior. [12]First I predicted your deliverance; I declared what I would do, and then I did it—I saved you. No foreign god has ever done this before. You are witnesses that I am the only God," says the LORD. [13]"From eternity to eternity I am God. No one can oppose what I do. No one can reverse my actions."

The LORD's Promise of Victory

[14]The LORD your Redeemer, the Holy One of Israel, says: "For your sakes I will send an invading army against Babylon. And the Babylonians* will be forced to flee in those ships they are so proud of. [15]I am the LORD, your Holy One, Israel's Creator and King. [16]I am the LORD, who opened a way through the waters, making a dry path through the sea. [17]I called forth the mighty army of Egypt with all its chariots and horses. I drew them beneath the waves, and they drowned, their lives snuffed out like a smoldering candlewick.

[18]"But forget all that—it is nothing compared to what I am going to do. [19]For I am about to do a brand-new thing. See, I have already begun! Do you not see it? I will make a pathway through the wilderness for my people to come home. I will create rivers for them in the desert! [20]The wild animals in the fields will thank me, the jackals and ostriches, too, for giving them water in the wilderness. Yes, I will make springs in the desert, so that my chosen people can be refreshed. [21]I have made Israel for myself, and they will someday honor me before the whole world.

[22]"But, my dear people, you refuse to ask for my help. You have grown tired of me! [23]You have not brought me lambs for burnt offerings. You have not honored me with sacrifices, though I have not burdened and wearied you with my requests for grain offerings and incense. [24]You have not brought me fragrant incense or pleased me with the fat from sacrifices. Instead, you have burdened me with your sins and wearied me with your faults.

[25]"I—yes, I alone—am the one who blots out your sins for my own sake and will never think of them again. [26]Let us review the situation together, and you can present

43:3 Hebrew *Cush.* **43:14** Or *Chaldeans.*

43:3 God gave other nations to Persia in exchange for returning the Jews to their homeland. Egypt, Ethiopia, and parts of Arabia (Seba) had attacked Persia, and the Persians defeated them.

43:5, 6 Isaiah was speaking primarily of Israel's return from Babylon. But there is a broader meaning: All God's people will be regathered when Christ comes to rule in peace over the earth.

43:10, 11 Israel's task was to be a witness (44:8), telling the world who God is and what he had done. Believers today share the responsibility of being God's witnesses. Do people know what God is like through your words and example? They cannot see God directly, but they can see him reflected in you.

43:15-21 This section pictures a new exodus for a people once again oppressed, as the Israelites had been as slaves in Egypt before the Exodus. They would cry to God, and again he would hear and deliver them. A new exodus would take place through a new wilderness. The past miracles were nothing compared to what God would do for his people in the future.

43:22-24 A sacrifice required both giving up a valuable animal and pleading with God for forgiveness. But the people presented God with sins instead of sacrifices. Can you imagine bringing the best of your sins to God's altar? This ironic picture shows the depths to which Israel had sunk. What do you present to God—your sins or a plea for his forgiveness?

43:25 How tempting it is to remind someone of a past offense! But when God forgives our sins, he totally forgets them. We never have to fear that he will remind us of them later. Because God forgives our sins, we need to forgive others.

your case if you have one. 27From the very beginning, your ancestors sinned against
me—all your leaders broke my laws. 28That is why I have disgraced your priests and
assigned Israel a future of complete destruction* and shame.

44

"But now, listen to me, Jacob my servant, Israel my chosen one. 2The LORD who
made you and helps you says: O Jacob, my servant, do not be afraid. O Israel,* my
chosen one, do not fear. 3For I will give you abundant water to quench your thirst and to moisten
your parched fields. And I will pour out my Spirit and my blessings on your children. 4They
will thrive like watered grass, like willows on a riverbank. 5Some will proudly claim, 'I
belong to the LORD.' Others will say, 'I am a descendant of Jacob.' Some will write the
LORD's name on their hands and will take the honored name of Israel as their own.

The Foolishness of Idols

6"This is what the LORD, Israel's King and Redeemer, the LORD Almighty, says: I am
the First and the Last; there is no other God. 7Who else can tell you what is going to
happen in the days ahead? Let them tell you if they can and thus prove their power. Let
them do as I have done since ancient times. 8Do not tremble; do not be afraid. Have I
not proclaimed from ages past what my purposes are for you? You are my witnesses—is
there any other God? No! There is no other Rock—not one!"

9How foolish are those who manufacture idols to be their gods. These highly valued
objects are really worthless. They themselves are witnesses that this is so, for their idols
neither see nor know. No wonder those who worship them are put to shame. 10Who but
a fool would make his own god—an idol that cannot help him one bit! 11All who worship
idols will stand before the LORD in shame, along with all these craftsmen—mere
humans—who claim they can make a god. Together they will stand in terror and shame.

12The blacksmith stands at his forge to make a sharp tool, pounding and shaping it
with all his might. His work makes him hungry and thirsty, weak and faint. 13Then the
wood-carver measures and marks out a block of wood, takes the tool, and carves the
figure of a man. Now he has a wonderful idol that cannot even move from where it is
placed! 14He cuts down cedars; he selects the cypress and the oak; he plants the cedar in
the forest to be nourished by the rain. 15And after his care, he uses part of the wood to
make a fire to warm himself and bake his bread. Then—yes, it's true—he takes the rest
of it and makes himself a god for people to worship! He makes an idol and bows down
and praises it! 16He burns part of the tree to roast his meat and to keep himself warm.
17Then he takes what's left and makes his god: a carved idol! He falls down in front of
it, worshiping and praying to it. "Rescue me!" he says. "You are my god!"

18Such stupidity and ignorance! Their eyes are closed, and they cannot see. Their
minds are shut, and they cannot think. 19The person who made the idol never stops to
reflect, "Why, it's just a block of wood! I burned half of it for heat and used it to bake
my bread and roast my meat. How can the rest of it be a god? Should I bow down to
worship a chunk of wood?" 20The poor, deluded fool feeds on ashes. He is trusting
something that can give him no help at all. Yet he cannot bring himself to ask, "Is this
thing, this idol that I'm holding in my hand, a lie?"

Restoration for Jerusalem

21"Pay attention, O Israel, for you are my servant. I, the LORD, made you, and I will not
forget to help you. 22I have swept away your sins like the morning mists. I have scattered
your offenses like the clouds. Oh, return to me, for I have paid the price to set you free."

43:27 Isa 51:2
43:28 Ezek 5:15
44:1 Jer 30:10
44:2 Deut 32:15
44:3 Isa 61:9; Joel 2:28
44:6 Isa 41:21; 45:5-6, 21; Rev 1:8, 17
44:7 Isa 41:22
44:8 Deut 4:35, 39; Isa 30:29
44:9 Ps 97:7
44:10 Jer 10:5; Hab 2:18; Acts 19:26
44:12 Isa 40:19; 41:6
44:13 Ps 115:5-7; Isa 41:7
44:15 2 Chr 25:14
44:17 1 Kgs 18:26, 28; Isa 45:20
44:18 Ps 81:12; Isa 6:9-10; 29:10; Jer 10:8, 14
44:19 Deut 27:15
44:20 Ps 102:9; Hos 4:12
44:21 Isa 44:1-2; 46:8
44:22 Ps 51:1, 9; Isa 55:7; Acts 3:19; 1 Pet 1:18-19

43:28 The Hebrew term used here refers to the complete consecration of things or people to the LORD, either by destroying them or by giving them as an offering. **44:2** Hebrew *Jeshurun,* a term of endearment for Israel.

44:5 The time will come when Israel will be proud of belonging to God. If we are truly God's, we should be unashamed and delighted to let everyone know about our relationship with him (44:8).

44:9-20 Here Isaiah describes how people make their own gods. How absurd to make a god from the same tree that gives firewood. What are the gods we make—money, fame, or power? We deceive ourselves if we expect them to empower our life.

44:21 God said that we should serve our Creator (17:7; 40:28; 43:15; 45:9). Idolaters do the opposite—serving or worshiping what they have made rather than the one who made them. Our Creator paid the price to set us free from our sins against him. By contrast, no idol ever created anybody, and no idol can redeem us from our sins.

44:23 Pss 69:34; 98:7-8
23 Sing, O heavens, for the LORD has done this wondrous thing. Shout, O earth! Break
forth into song, O mountains and forests and every tree! For the LORD has redeemed
Jacob and is glorified in Israel.
44:24 Isa 40:22
24 The LORD, your Redeemer and Creator, says: "I am the LORD, who made all things.
44:25 1 Cor 1:20, 27
I alone stretched out the heavens. By myself I made the earth and everything in it. 25 I am
the one who exposes the false prophets as liars by causing events to happen that are
contrary to their predictions. I cause wise people to give bad advice, thus proving them
44:26 Jer 32:15, 44
to be fools. 26 But I carry out the predictions of my prophets! When they say Jerusalem
will be saved and the towns of Judah will be lived in once again, it will be done! 27 When
44:27 Isa 50:2
I speak to the rivers and say, 'Be dry!' they will be dry. 28 When I say of Cyrus, 'He is
44:28 2 Chr 36:22-23; Isa 14:32
my shepherd,' he will certainly do as I say. He will command that Jerusalem be rebuilt
and that the Temple be restored."

Cyrus, the LORD's Chosen One

45:1 Ps 73:23; Jer 51:11, 20, 24
45 This is what the LORD says to Cyrus, his anointed one, whose right hand he will
empower. Before him, mighty kings will be paralyzed with fear. Their fortress
45:2 Ps 107:16; Isa 40:4; Jer 51:30
gates will be opened, never again to shut against him. 2 This is what the LORD says: "I
will go before you, Cyrus, and level the mountains.* I will smash down gates of bronze
and cut through bars of iron. 3 And I will give you treasures hidden in the darkness—secret
45:3 Isa 49:1; Jer 41:8
riches. I will do this so you may know that I am the LORD, the God of Israel, the one who
calls you by name.
45:4 Isa 43:1; Acts 17:23
4 "And why have I called you for this work? It is for the sake of Jacob my servant,
Israel my chosen one. I called you by name when you did not know me. 5 I am the LORD;
45:5 Ps 18:39; Isa 44:8
there is no other God. I have prepared you, even though you do not know me, 6 so all the
world from east to west will know there is no other God. I am the LORD, and there is no
45:6 Mal 1:11
other. 7 I am the one who creates the light and makes the darkness. I am the one who sends
good times and bad times. I, the LORD, am the one who does these things. 8 Open up,
45:7 Ps 104:20; Amos 3:6
O heavens, and pour out your righteousness. Let the earth open wide so salvation and
righteousness can sprout up together. I, the LORD, created them.
45:8 Pss 72:6; 85:11; Isa 61:11
9 "Destruction is certain for those who argue with their Creator. Does a clay pot ever
argue with its maker? Does the clay dispute with the one who shapes it, saying, 'Stop,
45:9 †Rom 9:20-21
you are doing it wrong!' Does the pot exclaim, 'How clumsy can you be!' 10 How terrible

45:2 As in Dead Sea Scrolls and Greek version; Masoretic Text reads *the swellings.*

TODAY'S IDOLATRY

Isaiah tells us, "Who but a fool would make his own god—an idol that cannot help him one bit!" We think of idols as statues of wood or stone, but in reality an idol is anything natural that is given sacred value and power. If your answer to any of the following questions is anything or anyone other than God, you may need to check out who or what you are worshiping.

- Who created me?
- Whom do I ultimately trust?
- Whom do I look to for ultimate truth?
- Whom do I look to for security and happiness?
- Who is in charge of my future?

44:25, 26 False prophets were people who claimed to bring messages from the gods. Because God is truth, he is the standard for all teachings. We can always trust his Word as absolute truth. His Word is completely accurate, and against it we can measure all other teachings. If you are unsure about a teaching, test it against God's Word. God condemned the false prophets because they gave advice opposite to his.

44:28 Isaiah, who prophesied from about 740–681 B.C., called Cyrus by name almost 150 years before he ruled (559–530 B.C.)! Later historians said that Cyrus read this prophecy and was so moved that he carried it out. Isaiah also predicted that Jerusalem would fall more than 100 years before it happened (586 B.C.) and that the Temple would be rebuilt about 200 years before it happened. It is clear these prophecies came from God, who knows the future.

45:1-8 This is the only place in the Bible where a Gentile ruler is said to be "anointed." God is the power over all rulers, and he anoints whom he chooses for his special tasks. Cyrus's kingdom spread across 2,000 miles (the largest of any empire then known), including the territories of both the Assyrian and the Babylonian Empires. Why did God anoint Cyrus? Because God had a special task for him to do for Israel. Cyrus would allow God's city, Jerusalem, to be rebuilt, and he would set the exiles free without expecting anything in return. Few kings of Israel or Judah had done as much for God's people as Cyrus would.

45:7 God is ruler over light and darkness, over good times and bad times. Our lives are sprinkled with both types of experiences, and both are needed for us to grow spiritually. When good times come, thank God and use your prosperity for him. When bad times come, don't resent them, but ask what you can learn from this refining experience to make you a better servant of God.

it would be if a newborn baby said to its father and mother, 'Why was I born? Why did
you make me this way?'"
11 This is what the LORD, the Creator and Holy One of Israel, says: "Do you question
what I do? Do you give me orders about the work of my hands? 12 I am the one who made
the earth and created people to live on it. With my hands I stretched out the heavens. All
the millions of stars are at my command. 13 I will raise up Cyrus to fulfill my righteous
purpose, and I will guide all his actions. He will restore my city and free my captive
people—and not for a reward! I, the LORD Almighty, have spoken!"

Future Conversion of Gentiles

14 This is what the LORD says: "The Egyptians, Ethiopians,* and Sabeans will be subject
to you. They will come to you with all their merchandise, and it will all be yours. They
will follow you as prisoners in chains. They will fall to their knees in front of you and
say, 'God is with you, and he is the only God.'"
15 Truly, O God of Israel, our Savior, you work in strange and mysterious ways. 16 All
who make idols will be humiliated and disgraced. 17 But the LORD will save the people of
Israel with eternal salvation. They will never again be humiliated and disgraced throughout everlasting ages. 18 For the LORD is God, and he created the heavens and earth and put
everything in place. He made the world to be lived in, not to be a place of empty chaos.
"I am the LORD," he says, "and there is no other. 19 I publicly proclaim bold promises.
I do not whisper obscurities in some dark corner so no one can understand what I mean.
And I did not tell the people of Israel* to ask me for something I did not plan to give. I,
the LORD, speak only what is true and right.
20 "Gather together and come, you fugitives from surrounding nations. What fools
they are who carry around their wooden idols and pray to gods that cannot save!
21 Consult together, argue your case, and state your proofs that idol worship pays. Who
made these things known long ago? What idol ever told you they would happen? Was it
not I, the LORD? For there is no other God but me—a just God and a Savior—no, not
one! 22 Let all the world look to me for salvation! For I am God; there is no other. 23 I
have sworn by my own name, and I will never go back on my word: Every knee will
bow to me, and every tongue will confess allegiance to my name."
24 The people will declare, "The LORD is the source of all my righteousness and
strength." And all who were angry with him will come to him and be ashamed. 25 In the
LORD all the generations of Israel will be justified, and in him they will boast.

Babylon's False Gods

46 The idols of Babylon, Bel and Nebo, are being hauled away on ox carts. But look!
The beasts are staggering under the weight! 2 Both the idols and the ones carrying
them are bowed down. The gods cannot protect the people, and the people cannot protect
the gods. They go off into captivity together.
3 "Listen to me, all you who are left in Israel. I created you and have cared for you
since before you were born. 4 I will be your God throughout your lifetime—until your
hair is white with age. I made you, and I will care for you. I will carry you along and
save you.
5 "To whom will you compare me? Who is my equal? 6 Some people pour out their
silver and gold and hire a craftsman to make a god from it. Then they bow down and

45:11 Ezek 39:7
45:12 Neh 9:6; Jer 27:5
45:13 2 Chr 36:22-23; Isa 52:3
45:14 Isa 14:1-2; 49:23; 1 Cor 14:25
45:16 Isa 44:11
45:17 Isa 51:6; Rom 11:26
45:18 Gen 1:2, 26; Ps 115:16; Isa 42:5
45:19 2 Chr 15:2; Isa 43:12; Jer 29:13-14
45:20 Isa 44:18-19; 46:6-7; Jer 10:5
45:21 Isa 43:3, 11; 44:7; †Mark 12:32
45:22 Num 21:8-9; Isa 52:10; Mic 7:7
45:23 †Rom 14:11; Phil 2:10-11
45:25 Isa 53:11
46:1 Isa 21:9; Jer 50:2; 51:44
46:2 Jer 43:12-13
46:3 Isa 10:21-22
46:4 Ps 71:18
46:5 Isa 40:18, 25
46:6 Isa 44:12-17

45:14 Hebrew *Cushites.* **45:19** Hebrew *of Jacob.*

45:14 The Sabeans were people from Seba in southern Arabia.

45:17 Until this time, Israel had anticipated temporal salvation—God would save them from their enemies. Here Isaiah tells of everlasting salvation with God.

45:18, 19 God's promises are public, and their fulfillment is sure. So why do we ever doubt him? We never have to be uncertain when we have a God of truth and righteousness.

45:22 Salvation is for all nations, not just the Israelites. Many times it seems as though Israel had an inside track on salvation. But God makes it clear that his people include *all* those who follow him. Israel was to be the means through which the whole world would come to know God. Jesus, the Messiah, fulfilled Israel's role and gave all people the opportunity to follow God. (See also Romans 11:11; Galatians 3:28; Ephesians 3:6; Philippians 2:10.)

46:1-4 Cyrus would carry out God's judgment against Babylon. Bel was the chief deity of the Babylonians; Nebo was the god of science and learning. These gods, however, needed animals and people to carry them around and could not even save themselves from being taken into captivity. They had no power at all. In contrast, our God created us and cares for us. His love is so enduring that he will care for us throughout our lifetime and even through death.

46:7 Isa 40:20; Jer 10:5
46:9 Isa 41:26-27; 42:9
46:10 Acts 5:39
46:11 Num 23:19
46:12 Zech 7:11-12
46:13 Isa 51:5; 61:3

worship it! 7They carry it around on their shoulders, and when they set it down, it stays
there. It cannot even move! And when someone prays to it, there is no answer. It has no
power to get anyone out of trouble.
8"Do not forget this, you guilty ones. 9And do not forget the things I have done
throughout history. For I am God—I alone! I am God, and there is no one else like me.
10Only I can tell you what is going to happen even before it happens. Everything I plan
will come to pass, for I do whatever I wish. 11I will call a swift bird of prey from the
east—a leader from a distant land who will come and do my bidding. I have said I would
do it, and I will. 12Listen to me, you stubborn, evil people! 13For I am ready to set things
right, not in the distant future, but right now! I am ready to save Jerusalem* and give my
glory to Israel.

Prediction of Babylon's Fall

47:1 Jer 48:18
47:2 Gen 24:65; 1 Cor 11:5
47:3 Isa 63:4
47:5 Lam 2:10; Dan 2:37
47:6 Deut 28:50; Zech 1:15
47:7 Isa 42:25; Rev 18:7
47:8 Isa 22:13; 32:9, 11; Rev 18:7

47 "Come, Babylon, unconquered one, sit in the dust. For your days of glory, pomp,
and honor have ended. O daughter of Babylonia,* never again will you be the
lovely princess, tender and delicate. 2Take heavy millstones and grind the corn. Remove
your veil and strip off your robe. Expose yourself to public view. 3You will be naked and
burdened with shame. I will take vengeance against you and will not negotiate."
4Our Redeemer, whose name is the LORD Almighty, is the Holy One of Israel.
5"O daughter of Babylonia, sit now in darkness and silence. Never again will you be
known as the queen of kingdoms. 6For I was angry with my chosen people and began
their punishment by letting them fall into your hands. But you, Babylon, showed them
no mercy. You have forced even the elderly to carry heavy burdens. 7You thought, 'I will
reign forever as queen of the world!' You did not care at all about my people or think
about the consequences of your actions.
8"You are a pleasure-crazy kingdom, living at ease and feeling secure, bragging as if
you were the greatest in the world! You say, 'I'm self-sufficient and not accountable to

46:13 Hebrew *Zion.* **47:1** Or *Chaldea;* also in 47:5.

MAJOR IDOLS MENTIONED IN THE BIBLE

Name	Where they were worshiped	What they stood for	What the worship included
Bel (Marduk)	Babylon	Weather, war, sun god	Prostitution, child sacrifice
Nebo (son of Marduk)	Babylon	Learning, astronomy, science	
Ashtoreth (Asherah)	Canaan	Goddess of love, childbirth, and fertility	Prostitution
Chemosh	Moab		Child sacrifice
Molech	Ammon	National god	Child sacrifice
Baal	Canaan	Rain, harvest, symbolized strength and fertility	Prostitution
Dagon	Philistia	Harvest, grain, success in farming	Child sacrifice

46:8-11 Israel was tempted to waver between the Lord God and pagan gods. Isaiah affirms the sole lordship of God. God is unique in his knowledge and in his control of the future. His consistent purpose is to carry out what he has planned. When we are tempted to pursue anything that promises pleasure, comfort, peace, or security apart from God, we must remember our commitment to God.

46:13 Much of the book of Isaiah speaks of a future deliverance when we will all live with God in perfect peace. God offers not only this future hope but also help for our present needs. His righteousness is near us, and we do not have to wait for his salvation.

47:1ff Here Isaiah predicted the fall of Babylon more than 150 years before it happened. At this time, Babylon had not yet emerged as the mightiest force on earth, the proud empire that would destroy Judah and Jerusalem. But the Babylonians, Judah's captors, would become captives themselves in 539 B.C. God, not Babylon, has the ultimate power. He used Babylon to punish his sinful people; he would use Medo-Persia to destroy Babylon and free his people.

47:8, 9 Caught up in the pursuit of power and pleasure, Babylon believed in its own greatness and claimed to be the *only* power on earth. Babylon felt completely secure, and Nebuchadnezzar, its king, exalted himself as a "god." But the true God taught Nebuchadnezzar a powerful lesson by taking everything away from him (Daniel 4:28-37). Our society is addicted to pleasure and power, but these can quickly vanish. Look at your own life and ask yourself how you can be more responsible with the talents and possessions God has given you. How can you use your life for God's honor rather than your own?

anyone! I will never be a widow or lose my children.' 9Well, those two things will come
upon you in a moment: widowhood and the loss of your children. Yes, these calamities
will come upon you, despite all your witchcraft and magic.
10"You felt secure in all your wickedness. 'No one sees me,' you said. Your 'wisdom'
and 'knowledge' have caused you to turn away from me and claim, 'I am self-sufficient
and not accountable to anyone!' 11So disaster will overtake you suddenly, and you won't
be able to charm it away. Calamity will fall upon you, and you won't be able to buy your
way out. A catastrophe will arise so fast that you won't know what hit you.
12"Call out the demon hordes you have worshiped all these years. Ask them to help
you strike terror into the hearts of people once again. 13You have more than enough
advisers, astrologers, and stargazers. Let them stand up and save you from what the
future holds. 14But they are as useless as dried grass burning in a fire. They cannot even
save themselves! You will get no help from them at all. Their hearth is not a place to sit
for warmth. 15And all your friends, those with whom you have done business since
childhood, will slip away and disappear, unable to help.

God's Stubborn People

48 "Listen to me, O family of Jacob, who are called by the name of Israel and born
into the family of Judah. Listen, you who take oaths in the name of the LORD
and call on the God of Israel. You don't follow through on any of your promises, 2even
though you call yourself the holy city and talk about depending on the God of Israel,
whose name is the LORD Almighty. 3Time and again I warned you about what was
going to happen in the future. Then suddenly I took action, and all my predictions
came true.
4"I know how stubborn and obstinate you are. Your necks are as unbending as iron.
You are as hardheaded as bronze. 5That is why I told you ahead of time what I was going
to do. That way, you could never say, 'My idols did it. My wooden image and metal god
commanded it to happen!' 6You have heard my predictions and seen them fulfilled, but
you refuse to admit it. Now I will tell you new things I have not mentioned before, secrets
you have not yet heard. 7They are brand new, not things from the past. So you cannot
say, 'We knew that all the time!'
8"Yes, I will tell you of things that are entirely new, for I know so well what traitors
you are. You have been rebels from your earliest childhood, rotten through and through.
9Yet for my own sake and for the honor of my name, I will hold back my anger and not
wipe you out. 10I have refined you but not in the way silver is refined. Rather, I have
refined you in the furnace of suffering. 11I will rescue you for my sake—yes, for my own
sake! That way, the pagan nations will not be able to claim that their gods have conquered
me. I will not let them have my glory!

Freedom from Babylon

12"Listen to me, O family of Jacob, Israel my chosen one! I alone am God, the First and
the Last. 13It was my hand that laid the foundations of the earth. The palm of my right
hand spread out the heavens above. I spoke, and they came into being.

47:9 Isa 13:16; 1 Thes 5:2-3; Rev 18:8, 10, 23
47:10 Ps 52:7; Isa 5:21; Ezek 8:12
47:11 Jer 51:8, 43
47:13 Isa 8:19
47:14 Jer 51:30, 32, 58; Nah 1:10
47:15 Rev 18:11
48:1 Isa 45:23
48:2 Rom 2:17
48:3 Josh 21:45; Isa 42:9
48:4 Ezek 2:4
48:5 Jer 44:15-18
48:6 Isa 43:19
48:8 Deut 9:7, 24; Ps 58:3
48:9 Ps 103:8-10
48:10 1 Kgs 8:51; Ezek 22:18-22
48:11 Deut 32:26-27; Ps 106:8; Isa 42:8
48:12 Rev 1:17
48:13 Ps 102:25

47:12-15 The people of Babylon sought advice and help from astrologers and stargazers. But like the idols of wood or gold, astrologers could not even deliver themselves from what was to come from the hand of God. Why rely on those who are powerless? The helpless cannot help us. Alternatives to God are destined to fail. If you want help, find it in God, who has proven his power in creation and in history.

48:1 The people of Judah felt confident because they lived in Jerusalem, the city with God's Temple. They depended on their heritage, their city, and their Temple—but this was false security because they did not depend on God. Do you feel secure because you go to church or live in a Christian country? Heritage, buildings, or nations cannot give us a relationship with God; we must truly depend on him personally, with all our hearts and minds.

48:9-11 There was nothing in the people's actions, attitudes, or accomplishments to compel God to love and to save them. But for his own sake, to show who he is and what he can do, he saved them. God does not save us because we are good but because he loves us and because of his forgiving nature.

48:10 Do you find it easy to complain when your life becomes complicated or difficult? Why would a loving God allow all kinds of unpleasant experiences to come to his children? This verse shows us plainly that God tests us in the "furnace of suffering." Rather than complain, our response should be to turn to God in faith for the strength to endure and rejoice in our sufferings (see Romans 5:3; James 1:2-4). For without the testing, we would never know what we are capable of doing, nor would we grow. And without the refining, we will not become more pure and more like Christ. What kinds of adversity are you currently facing?

48:14 Jer 50:21-29
48:15 Isa 41:2; 45:1-2
48:16 Isa 45:19
48:17 Ps 32:8; Isa 41:14
48:18 Deut 5:29; 32:29; Ps 119:165; Amos 5:24
48:19 Gen 12:17
48:20 Isa 52:9; Jer 31:10
48:21 Ps 78:15-16; Matt 1:20-21

14“Have any of your idols ever told you this? Come, all of you, and listen: ‘The LORD
has chosen Cyrus as his ally. He will use him to put an end to the empire of Babylon,
destroying the Babylonian* armies.’ 15I have said it: I am calling Cyrus! I will send him
on this errand and will help him succeed. 16Come closer and listen. I have always told
you plainly what would happen so you would have no trouble understanding.”

And now the Sovereign LORD and his Spirit have sent me with this message: 17“The
LORD, your Redeemer, the Holy One of Israel, says: I am the LORD your God, who
teaches you what is good and leads you along the paths you should follow. 18Oh, that
you had listened to my commands! Then you would have had peace flowing like a gentle
river and righteousness rolling like waves. 19Then you would have become as numerous
as the sands along the seashore—too many to count! There would have been no need for
your destruction.”

20Yet even now, be free from your captivity! Leave Babylon and the Babylonians,*
singing as you go! Shout to the ends of the earth that the LORD has redeemed his servants,
the people of Israel.* 21They were not thirsty when he led them through the desert. He
divided the rock, and water gushed out for them to drink.

22“But there is no peace for the wicked,” says the LORD.

2. The future Redeemer

The LORD's Servant Commissioned

49:2 Isa 51:16; Heb 4:12; Rev 1:16
49:5 Isa 12:2
49:6 Ps 37:28; †Acts 13:47; 26:23
49:7 Ps 22:6-8; Isa 53:3

49 Listen to me, all of you in far-off lands! The LORD called me before my birth; from
within the womb he called me by name. 2He made my words of judgment as sharp as a
sword. He has hidden me in the shadow of his hand. I am like a sharp arrow in his quiver.

3He said to me, “You are my servant, Israel, and you will bring me glory.”

4I replied, “But my work all seems so useless! I have spent my strength for nothing and
to no purpose at all. Yet I leave it all in the LORD's hand; I will trust God for my reward.”

5And now the LORD speaks—he who formed me in my mother's womb to be his
servant, who commissioned me to bring his people of Israel back to him. The LORD has
honored me, and my God has given me strength. 6He says, “You will do more than
restore the people of Israel to me. I will make you a light to the Gentiles, and you will
bring my salvation to the ends of the earth.”

7The LORD, the Redeemer and Holy One of Israel, says to the one who is despised and
rejected by a nation, to the one who is the servant of rulers: “Kings will stand at attention
when you pass by. Princes will bow low because the LORD has chosen you. He, the
faithful LORD, the Holy One of Israel, chooses you.”

Promises of Israel's Restoration

49:8 Ps 69:13; Isa 26:3; 42:7; 44:26; 2 Cor 6:2
49:9 Luke 4:18

8This is what the LORD says: “At just the right time, I will respond to you. On the day of
salvation, I will help you. I will give you as a token and pledge to Israel. This will prove
that I will reestablish the land of Israel and reassign it to its own people again. 9Through
you I am saying to the prisoners of darkness, ‘Come out! I am giving you your freedom!’

48:14 Or *Chaldean.* **48:20a** Or *the Chaldeans.* **48:20b** Hebrew *his servant, Jacob.*

48:14, 15 That the Lord would choose Cyrus as his “ally” must have shocked his audience. How could the Lord choose a pagan king, an enemy? But it was Cyrus whom God would use to free his people from their captivity in Babylon. Cyrus's mission was to set Israel free by conquering Babylon, then to decree that all Jews could return to their homeland. Who but a prophet of God could predict such an inconceivable but true story almost 200 years before it happened?

48:17, 18 Like a loving parent, God teaches and guides us. We should listen to him because peace and righteousness come to us as we obey his Word. Refusing to pay attention to God's commands invites punishment and threatens that peace and righteousness.

48:20 Do you see the captives leaving Babylon many years later? No wonder they are shouting with joy, as their ancestors shouted joyfully after they crossed the Red Sea, free from slavery at last! What is holding you captive? Be free! The Lord has redeemed his servants from slavery to sin. When you let him free you from your captivity, you will feel like shouting with joy.

48:22 Many people cry out for comfort, security, and relief, but they haven't taken the first steps to turn away from sin and open the channels to God. They have not repented and trusted in him. If you want true peace, seek God first. Then he will give you his peace.

49:1-7 Before the Servant, the Messiah, was born, God had chosen him to bring the light of the gospel (the message of salvation) to the world (see Acts 13:47). Christ offered salvation to all nations, and his apostles began the missionary movement to take this gospel to the ends of the earth. Missionary work today continues Jesus' great commission (Matthew 28:18-20), taking the light of the gospel to all nations.

They will be my sheep, grazing in green pastures and on hills that were previously bare.
10 They will neither hunger nor thirst. The searing sun and scorching desert winds will
not reach them anymore. For the LORD in his mercy will lead them beside cool waters.
11 And I will make my mountains into level paths for them. The highways will be raised
above the valleys. 12 See, my people will return from far away, from lands to the north
and west, and from as far south as Egypt.*"
13 Sing for joy, O heavens! Rejoice, O earth! Burst into song, O mountains! For the
LORD has comforted his people and will have compassion on them in their sorrow.
14 Yet Jerusalem* says, "The LORD has deserted us; the Lord has forgotten us."
15 "Never! Can a mother forget her nursing child? Can she feel no love for a child she
has borne? But even if that were possible, I would not forget you! 16 See, I have written
your name on my hand. Ever before me is a picture of Jerusalem's walls in ruins. 17 Soon
your descendants will come back, and all who are trying to destroy you will go away.
18 Look and see, for all your children will come back to you. As surely as I live," says the
LORD, "they will be like jewels or bridal ornaments for you to display.
19 "Even the most desolate parts of your abandoned land will soon be crowded with
your people. Your enemies who enslaved you will be far away. 20 The generations born
in exile will return and say, 'We need more room! It's crowded here!' 21 Then you will
think to yourself, 'Who has given me all these descendants? For most of my children
were killed, and the rest were carried away into exile. I was left here all alone. Who bore
these children? Who raised them for me?'"
22 This is what the Sovereign LORD says: "See, I will give a signal to the godless
nations. They will carry your little sons back to you in their arms; they will bring your
daughters on their shoulders. 23 Kings and queens will serve you. They will care for all
your needs. They will bow to the earth before you and lick the dust from your feet. Then
you will know that I am the LORD. Those who wait for me will never be put to shame."
24 Who can snatch the plunder of war from the hands of a warrior? Who can demand
that a tyrant* let his captives go? 25 But the LORD says, "The captives of warriors will be
released, and the plunder of tyrants will be retrieved. For I will fight those who fight you,
and I will save your children. 26 I will feed your enemies with their own flesh. They will
be drunk with rivers of their own blood. All the world will know that I, the LORD, am
your Savior and Redeemer, the Mighty One of Israel.*"

50 The LORD asks, "Did I sell you as slaves to my creditors? Is that why you are not
here? Is your mother gone because I divorced her and sent her away? No, you went
away as captives because of your sins. And your mother, too, was taken because of your
sins. 2 Was I too weak to save you? Is that why the house is silent and empty when I come
home? Is it because I have no power to rescue? No, that is not the reason! For I can speak
to the sea and make it dry! I can turn rivers into deserts covered with dying fish. 3 I am the
one who sends darkness out across the skies, bringing it to a state of mourning."

The LORD's Obedient Servant

4 The Sovereign LORD has given me his words of wisdom, so that I know what to say to
all these weary ones. Morning by morning he wakens me and opens my understanding
to his will. 5 The Sovereign LORD has spoken to me, and I have listened. I do not rebel

49:10 Ps 23:2; Rev 7:16
49:11 Isa 40:4
49:12 Isa 43:5-6
49:13 Isa 54:7-8, 10; †Luke 2:25; Rev 12:12
49:16 Song 8:6; Isa 62:6
49:18 Isa 45:23; †Rom 14:11
49:19 Ps 56:1-2; Isa 1:7; Zech 10:10
49:20 Isa 54:1-3
49:21 Lam 1:1
49:22 Isa 11:10, 12; 14:2
49:23 Pss 25:3; 72:9; Isa 60:14, 16
49:25 Jer 50:33-34
49:26 Isa 14:4; Ezek 39:7
50:1 Deut 32:30; Isa 59:2; Jer 3:8
50:2 Gen 18:14; Exod 14:21; Josh 3:16
50:3 Rev 6:12
50:4 Ps 5:3; Jer 31:25
50:5 Matt 26:39; John 8:29; 14:31; Acts 26:19

49:12 As in Dead Sea Scrolls, which read *from the region of Aswan*, which is in southern Egypt. Masoretic Text reads *from the region of Sinim.* **49:14** Hebrew *Zion.* **49:24** As in Dead Sea Scrolls, Syriac version, and Latin Vulgate (also see 49:25); Masoretic Text reads *a righteous person.* **49:26** Hebrew *of Jacob.*

49:14, 15 The people of Israel felt that God had forsaken them in Babylon; but Isaiah pointed out that God would never forget them, as a loving mother would not forget her little child. When we feel that God has forsaken us, we must ask if we have forsaken and forgotten God (see Deuteronomy 31:6).

49:24, 25 God would prove to the world that he is God by doing the impossible—causing warriors to set their captives free; and these warriors would even return the plunder they had taken from the captives! God had done this before at the Exodus and would do it again when the exiles returned to Israel. Never should we doubt that God will fulfill his promises. He will even do the impossible to make them come true.

50:1, 2 God promised to fight for Israel, but Israel sold itself into sin. Israel had caused its own problems. The people of Israel forgot God and trusted in other countries to help them. God did not reject Israel, but Israel rejected God.

50:10, 11 If we walk by our own light and reject God's, we become self-sufficient, and the result of self-sufficiency is torment. When we place confidence in our own intelligence, appearance, or accomplishments instead of in God, we risk torment later when these strengths fade.

or turn away. 6I give my back to those who beat me and my cheeks to those who pull out
my beard. I do not hide from shame, for they mock me and spit in my face.
7Because the Sovereign LORD helps me, I will not be dismayed. Therefore, I have set
my face like a stone, determined to do his will. And I know that I will triumph. 8He who
gives me justice is near. Who will dare to oppose me now? Where are my enemies? Let
them appear! 9See, the Sovereign LORD is on my side! Who will declare me guilty? All
my enemies will be destroyed like old clothes that have been eaten by moths!
10Who among you fears the LORD and obeys his servant? If you are walking in
darkness, without a ray of light, trust in the LORD and rely on your God. 11But watch out,
you who live in your own light and warm yourselves by your own fires. This is the
reward you will receive from me: You will soon lie down in great torment.

A Call to Trust the LORD

51 "Listen to me, all who hope for deliverance—all who seek the LORD! Consider
the quarry from which you were mined, the rock from which you were cut! 2Yes,
think about your ancestors Abraham and Sarah, from whom you came. Abraham was
alone when I called him. But when I blessed him, he became a great nation."
3The LORD will comfort Israel* again and make her deserts blossom. Her barren
wilderness will become as beautiful as Eden—the garden of the LORD. Joy and gladness
will be found there. Lovely songs of thanksgiving will fill the air.
4"Listen to me, my people. Hear me, Israel, for my law will be proclaimed, and my justice
will become a light to the nations. 5My mercy and justice are coming soon. Your salvation
is on the way. I will rule the nations. They will wait for me and long for my power. 6Look
up to the skies above, and gaze down on the earth beneath. For the skies will disappear like
smoke, and the earth will wear out like a piece of clothing. The people of the earth will die
like flies, but my salvation lasts forever. My righteous rule will never end!
7"Listen to me, you who know right from wrong and cherish my law in your hearts. Do
not be afraid of people's scorn or their slanderous talk. 8For the moth will destroy them as
it destroys clothing. The worm will eat away at them as it eats wool. But my righteousness
will last forever. My salvation will continue from generation to generation."
9Wake up, LORD! Robe yourself with strength! Rouse yourself as in the days of old
when you slew Egypt, the dragon of the Nile.* 10Are you not the same today, the one
who dried up the sea, making a path of escape when you saved your people? 11Those
who have been ransomed by the LORD will return to Jerusalem,* singing songs of
everlasting joy. Sorrow and mourning will disappear, and they will be overcome with
joy and gladness.
12"I, even I, am the one who comforts you. So why are you afraid of mere humans,
who wither like the grass and disappear? 13Yet you have forgotten the LORD, your
Creator, the one who put the stars in the sky and established the earth. Will you remain
in constant dread of human oppression? Will you continue to fear the anger of your

50:6 Matt 26:67; Mark 15:19; Luke 22:63
50:7 Ezek 3:8-9
50:8 Rom 8:33-34
50:10 Eph 5:8
51:1 Gen 17:15-17
51:2 Gen 12:1; Heb 11:11
51:3 Gen 2:8; Isa 41:19
51:4 Ps 78:1; Isa 42:4
51:5 Isa 46:13
51:6 Ps 102:25-26; Matt 24:35; 2 Pet 3:10
51:7 Ps 37:30-31; Matt 5:11; Acts 5:40-41
51:8 Isa 14:11
51:9 Deut 4:34
51:10 Exod 14:21-22; Isa 63:11-12
51:11 Isa 61:7; Rev 7:17; 21:4; 22:3
51:12 Ps 118:6; 1 Pet 1:24
51:13 Deut 8:11; Job 9:8

51:3 Hebrew *Zion;* also in 51:16. **51:9** Hebrew *slew Rahab the dragon.* Rahab is the name of a mythical sea monster that represents chaos in ancient literature. The name is used here as a poetic name for Egypt.
51:11 Hebrew *Zion.*

51:1, 2 The faithful remnant may have felt alone because they were few. But God reminded them of their ancestors, the source of their spiritual heritage—Abraham and Sarah. Abraham was only one person, but much came from his faithfulness. If the faithful few would remain faithful, even more could come from them. If we Christians, even a faithful few, remain faithful, think what God can do through us!

51:7 Isaiah encouraged those who follow God's laws. He gave them hope when they faced people's reproach or insults because of their faith. We need not fear when people insult us for our faith because God is with us and truth will prevail. If people make fun of you or dislike you because you believe in God, remember that they are not against you personally but against God. God will deal with them; you should concentrate on loving and obeying him.

51:9, 10 God had performed many powerful miracles in founding Israel, perhaps none more exciting than making a dry path through the middle of the Red Sea (see Exodus 14). Our God is the same God who made that road through the sea. His methods may change, but his love and care do not.

51:12-16 God's people feared Babylon but not God. They had reason to fear Babylon for the harm it wanted to do, but they should also have realized that God's power is much greater than Babylon's. Babylon was interested in making the people captives; God was interested in setting them free. The people had misplaced their fear and their love. Jerusalem should have feared God's power and loved his mercy.

enemies from morning till night? 14 Soon all you captives will be released! Imprisonment, starvation, and death will not be your fate! 15 For I am the LORD your God, who
stirs up the sea, causing its waves to roar. My name is the LORD Almighty. 16 And I have
put my words in your mouth and hidden you safely within my hand. I set all the stars in
space and established the earth. I am the one who says to Israel, 'You are mine!'"
17 Wake up, wake up, O Jerusalem! You have drunk enough from the cup of the LORD's
fury. You have drunk the cup of terror, tipping out its last drops. 18 Not one of your children
is left alive to help you or tell you what to do. 19 These two things have been your lot:
desolation and destruction, famine and war. And who is left to sympathize? Who is left to
comfort you? 20 For your children have fainted and lie in the streets, helpless as antelopes
caught in a net. The LORD has poured out his fury; God has rebuked them.
21 But now listen to this, you afflicted ones, who sit in a drunken stupor, though not
from drinking wine. 22 This is what the Sovereign LORD, your God and Defender, says:
"See, I am taking the terrible cup from your hands. You will drink no more of my fury.
It is gone at last! 23 But I will put that cup into the hands of those who tormented you. I
will give it to those who trampled you into the dust and walked on your backs."

Deliverance for Jerusalem

52 Wake up, wake up, O Zion! Clothe yourselves with strength. Put on your beautiful clothes, O holy city of Jerusalem, for unclean and godless people will no
longer enter your gates. 2 Rise from the dust, O Jerusalem. Remove the slave bands from
your neck, O captive daughter of Zion. 3 For this is what the LORD says: "When I sold
you into exile, I received no payment. Now I can redeem you without paying for you."
4 This is what the Sovereign LORD says: "Long ago my people went to live as resident
foreigners in Egypt. Now they have been oppressed without cause by Assyria. 5 And now,
what is this?" asks the LORD. "Why are my people enslaved again? Those who rule them
shout in exultation. My name is being blasphemed all day long. 6 But I will reveal my
name to my people, and they will come to know its power. Then at last they will
recognize that it is I who speaks to them."
7 How beautiful on the mountains are the feet of those who bring good news of peace
and salvation, the news that the God of Israel* reigns! 8 The watchmen shout and sing with
joy, for before their very eyes they see the LORD bringing his people home to Jerusalem.*
9 Let the ruins of Jerusalem break into joyful song, for the LORD has comforted his people.
He has redeemed Jerusalem. 10 The LORD will demonstrate his holy power before the eyes
of all the nations. The ends of the earth will see the salvation of our God.
11 Go now, leave your bonds and slavery. Put Babylon behind you, with everything it
represents, for it is unclean to you. You are the LORD's holy people. Purify yourselves, you
who carry home the vessels of the LORD. 12 You will not leave in a hurry, running for your
lives. For the LORD will go ahead of you, and the God of Israel will protect you from behind.

The LORD's Suffering Servant

13 See, my servant will prosper; he will be highly exalted. 14 Many were amazed when
they saw him*—beaten and bloodied, so disfigured one would scarcely know he was a
person. 15 And he will again startle* many nations. Kings will stand speechless in his
presence. For they will see what they had not previously been told about; they will
understand what they had not heard about.

51:14 Isa 49:10
51:15 Ps 107:25
51:16 Exod 33:22; Deut 18:18
51:17 Jer 25:15
51:18 Ps 142:4
51:20 Isa 66:15; Jer 14:16
51:21 Isa 29:9
51:22 Jer 50:34
51:23 Jer 25:15-17, 26, 28
52:1 Exod 28:2, 40; Neh 11:1; Isa 48:2; 61:10; Matt 4:5; Rev 21:2, 27
52:3 Ps 44:12; Isa 63:4
52:5 Ezek 36:20, 23; †Rom 2:24
52:7 Ps 93:1; †Rom 10:15
52:8 Isa 62:6
52:9 Ps 98:4; Isa 61:4
52:10 Ps 98:1-3; Luke 3:6
52:11 Isa 1:16; †2 Cor 6:17; 2 Tim 2:19
52:12 Exod 12:11, 33; 14:19-20; Isa 26:7
52:13 Phil 2:9
52:14 Ps 22:6-7
52:15 †Rom 15:21

52:7 Hebrew *of Zion.* **52:8** Hebrew *to Zion.* **52:14** As in Syriac version; Hebrew reads *you.* **52:15** Or *cleanse.*

51:17–52:10 Jerusalem was God's holy city, the city with God's Temple. But the people of Judah experienced ruin instead of prosperity, destruction instead of liberty. Because of their sins, the people suffered. But God promised to restore Jerusalem as a holy city where sinners cannot enter. God reigns. He is in control.

52:7 God says that the feet of those who bring good news are "beautiful." It is a wonderful privilege to be able to share God's Good News with others, his news of redemption, salvation, and peace. To whom do you need to give the Good News?

52:12 The people did not have to leave in fearful haste because Cyrus, God's anointed (45:1), decreed that the Jewish exiles could return safely to Jerusalem (Ezra 1:1-4). They had the king's approval, his guaranteed protection. More important, the Lord would go ahead to point the way and be behind to protect them.

52:13 The *servant,* as the term is used here, is the Messiah, our Lord Jesus. He would be highly exalted because of his sacrifice, described in chapter 53.

52:14, 15 This servant, Christ, would be "disfigured"; but through his suffering, he would cleanse the nations (Hebrews 10:14; 1 Peter 1:2).

53:1
†Rom 10:16
53:3
Luke 18:31-33
John 1:10-11
53:4
†Matt 8:17
1 Pet 2:24
53:5
Rom 4:25
1 Cor 15:3
Heb 5:8; 9:28
†1 Pet 2:24-25
53:7
Matt 27:12-14
Luke 23:9
53:8
†Acts 8:32-33
53:9
Matt 27:57-60
†1 Pet 2:22
Rev 14:5
53:10
John 1:29
53:11
John 10:14-18
Rom 5:18-19
53:12
Matt 26:38-39, 42
†Mark 15:27
†Luke 22:37
2 Cor 5:21
Phil 2:9-11
1 Pet 2:24

53 Who has believed our message? To whom will the LORD reveal his saving power?
2My servant grew up in the LORD's presence like a tender green shoot, sprouting
from a root in dry and sterile ground. There was nothing beautiful or majestic about his
appearance, nothing to attract us to him. 3He was despised and rejected—a man of
sorrows, acquainted with bitterest grief. We turned our backs on him and looked the other
way when he went by. He was despised, and we did not care.
4Yet it was our weaknesses he carried; it was our sorrows* that weighed him down.
And we thought his troubles were a punishment from God for his own sins! 5But he was
wounded and crushed for our sins. He was beaten that we might have peace. He was
whipped, and we were healed! 6All of us have strayed away like sheep. We have left
God's paths to follow our own. Yet the LORD laid on him the guilt and sins of us all.
7He was oppressed and treated harshly, yet he never said a word. He was led as a lamb
to the slaughter. And as a sheep is silent before the shearers, he did not open his mouth.
8From prison and trial they led him away to his death. But who among the people
realized that he was dying for their sins—that he was suffering their punishment? 9He
had done no wrong, and he never deceived anyone. But he was buried like a criminal;
he was put in a rich man's grave.
10But it was the LORD's good plan to crush him and fill him with grief. Yet when his
life is made an offering for sin, he will have a multitude of children, many heirs. He will
enjoy a long life, and the LORD's plan will prosper in his hands. 11When he sees all that
is accomplished by his anguish, he will be satisfied. And because of what he has
experienced, my righteous servant will make it possible for many to be counted righteous, for he will bear all their sins. 12I will give him the honors of one who is mighty
and great, because he exposed himself to death. He was counted among those who were
sinners. He bore the sins of many and interceded for sinners.

Future Glory for Jerusalem

54:1
Isa 62:4
†Gal 4:27
54:3
Gen 28:14
Isa 14:1-2

54 "Sing, O childless woman! Break forth into loud and joyful song, O Jerusalem,
even though you never gave birth to a child. For the woman who could bear no
children now has more than all the other women," says the LORD. 2"Enlarge your house;
build an addition; spread out your home! 3For you will soon be bursting at the seams.
Your descendants will take over other nations and live in their cities.

53:4 Or *Yet it was our sicknesses he carried; it was our diseases.*

53:1ff This chapter continues to speak of the Messiah, Jesus, who would suffer for the sins of all people. Such a prophecy is astounding! Who would believe that God would choose to save the world through a humble, suffering servant rather than a glorious king? The idea is contrary to human pride and worldly thinking. But God often works in ways we don't expect. The Messiah's strength is shown by humility, suffering, and mercy.

53:2 There was nothing beautiful or majestic in the physical appearance of this servant. Israel would miscalculate the servant's importance—they would consider him an ordinary man. But even though Jesus would not attract a large following based on his physical appearance, he would bring salvation and healing. Many people miscalculate the importance of Jesus' life and work, and they need faithful Christians to point out his extraordinary nature.

53:3 This man of sorrows was despised and rejected by those around him, and he is still despised and rejected by many today. Some reject Christ by standing against him. Others despise Christ and his great gift of forgiveness. Do you despise him, reject him, or accept him?

53:4, 5 How could an Old Testament person understand the idea of Christ dying for our sins—actually bearing the punishment that we deserved? The sacrifices suggested this idea, but it is one thing to kill a lamb, and something quite different to think of God's chosen servant as that Lamb. But God was pulling aside the curtain of time to let the people of Isaiah's day look ahead to the suffering of the future Messiah and the resulting forgiveness made available to all people.

53:6 Isaiah speaks of Israel straying from God and compares them to wandering sheep. Yet God would send the Messiah to bring them back into the fold. We have the hindsight to see and know the identity of the promised Messiah, who has come and died for our sins. But if we know all that Jesus did and still reject him, our sin is much greater than that of the ancient Israelites, who could not see what we have seen. Have you given your life to Jesus Christ, the "good shepherd" (John 10:11-16), or are you still like a wandering sheep?

53:7-12 In the Old Testament, people offered animals as sacrifices for their sins. Here, the sinless servant of the Lord offers himself for our sins. He is the Lamb (53:7) offered for the sins of all people (John 1:29; Revelation 5:6-14). The Messiah suffered for our sake, bearing our sins to make us acceptable to God. What can we say to such love? How will we respond to him?

53:11 This verse tells of the enormous family of believers who will become righteous, not by their own works, but by the Messiah's great work on the cross. They are justified because they have claimed Christ, the righteous servant, as their Savior and Lord (see Romans 10:9; 2 Corinthians 5:21). Their life of sin is stripped away, and they are clothed with Christ's goodness (Ephesians 4:22-24).

54:1 To be childless at that time was a woman's great shame, a disgrace. Families depended on children for survival, especially when the parents became elderly. Israel (Jerusalem) was unfruitful, like a childless woman, but God would permit her to have many children and change her mourning into singing.

4"Fear not; you will no longer live in shame. The shame of your youth and the sorrows
of widowhood will be remembered no more, 5for your Creator will be your husband.
The LORD Almighty is his name! He is your Redeemer, the Holy One of Israel, the God
of all the earth. 6For the LORD has called you back from your grief—as though you were
a young wife abandoned by her husband," says your God. 7"For a brief moment I
abandoned you, but with great compassion I will take you back. 8In a moment of anger
I turned my face away for a little while. But with everlasting love I will have compassion
on you," says the LORD, your Redeemer.
9"Just as I swore in the time of Noah that I would never again let a flood cover the
earth and destroy its life, so now I swear that I will never again pour out my anger on
you. 10For the mountains may depart and the hills disappear, but even then I will remain
loyal to you. My covenant of blessing will never be broken," says the LORD, who has
mercy on you.
11"O storm-battered city, troubled and desolate! I will rebuild you on a foundation of
sapphires and make the walls of your houses from precious jewels. 12I will make your
towers of sparkling rubies and your gates and walls of shining gems. 13I will teach all
your citizens, and their prosperity will be great. 14You will live under a government that
is just and fair. Your enemies will stay far away; you will live in peace. Terror will not
come near. 15If any nation comes to fight you, it will not be because I sent them to punish
you. Your enemies will always be defeated because I am on your side. 16I have created
the blacksmith who fans the coals beneath the forge and makes the weapons of destruction. And I have created the armies that destroy. 17But in that coming day, no weapon
turned against you will succeed. And everyone who tells lies in court will be brought to
justice. These benefits are enjoyed by the servants of the LORD; their vindication will
come from me. I, the LORD, have spoken!

Invitation to the LORD's Salvation

55 "Is anyone thirsty? Come and drink—even if you have no money! Come, take
your choice of wine or milk—it's all free! 2Why spend your money on food that
does not give you strength? Why pay for food that does you no good? Listen, and I will
tell you where to get food that is good for the soul!
3"Come to me with your ears wide open. Listen, for the life of your soul is at stake. I am
ready to make an everlasting covenant with you. I will give you all the mercies and unfailing
love that I promised to David. 4He displayed my power by being my witness and a leader
among the nations. 5You also will command the nations, and they will come running to
obey, because I, the LORD your God, the Holy One of Israel, have made you glorious."
6Seek the LORD while you can find him. Call on him now while he is near. 7Let the
people turn from their wicked deeds. Let them banish from their minds the very thought
of doing wrong! Let them turn to the LORD that he may have mercy on them. Yes, turn
to our God, for he will abundantly pardon.

54:5 Hos 2:19
54:6 Isa 62:4
54:7 Isa 11:12
54:8 Isa 49:10, 13; 60:10
54:9 Gen 9:9-11 Ezek 39:29
54:10 2 Sam 23:5 Pss 89:34; 102:25-26
54:11 Isa 28:16
54:13 Isa 66:12 Jer 31:34 †John 6:45
54:14 Isa 9:4, 7
54:15 Isa 41:11-16
54:17 Isa 29:8
55:1 Lam 5:4 Matt 10:8 John 4:14; 7:37 Rev 3:18; 21:6
55:2 Ps 22:26 Eccl 6:2
55:3 †Acts 13:34 Rom 10:5
55:5 Zech 8:22
55:6 Ps 32:6 2 Cor 6:1-2
55:7 Isa 1:16; 44:22

54:6-8 God said that he had abandoned Israel for a brief moment, so the nation was like a young wife rejected by her husband. But God still called Israel his own. The God we serve is holy, and he cannot tolerate sin. When his people blatantly sinned, God in his anger chose to punish them. Sin separates us from God and brings us pain and suffering. But if we confess our sin and repent, then God will forgive us. Have you ever been separated from a loved one and then experienced joy when that person returned? That is like the joy God experiences when you repent and return to him.

54:9-13 God made a covenant with Noah that he has never broken (Genesis 9:8-17). Likewise, God made a covenant of peace with the people of Israel that the time would come when he would stop pouring out his anger on them; he would teach their citizens and give them prosperity.

55:1-6 Food costs money, lasts only a short time, and meets only physical needs. But God offers us *free* nourishment that feeds our soul. How do we get it? We are to come (55:1), listen (55:2), seek, and call on God (55:6). God's salvation is freely offered, but to nourish our souls we must eagerly receive it. We will starve spiritually without this food as surely as we will starve physically without our daily bread.

55:3 God's covenant with David promised a permanent homeland for the Israelites, no threat from pagan nations, and no wars (2 Samuel 7:10, 11). But Israel did not fulfill its part of the covenant to obey God and stay away from idols. Even so, God was ready to renew his covenant again. He is a forgiving God!

55:6 Isaiah tells us to call on the Lord while he is near. God is not planning to move away from us, but we often move far from him or erect barriers of sin between us. Don't wait until you have drifted far away from God to seek him. Turning to him may be far more difficult later in life. Or God may come to judge the earth before you decide to turn to him. Seek God now, while you can, before it is too late.

8"My thoughts are completely different from yours," says the LORD. "And my ways
are far beyond anything you could imagine. 9For just as the heavens are higher than the
earth, so are my ways higher than your ways and my thoughts higher than your thoughts.
10"The rain and snow come down from the heavens and stay on the ground to water
the earth. They cause the grain to grow, producing seed for the farmer and bread for the
hungry. 11It is the same with my word. I send it out, and it always produces fruit. It will
accomplish all I want it to, and it will prosper everywhere I send it. 12You will live in joy
and peace. The mountains and hills will burst into song, and the trees of the field will
clap their hands! 13Where once there were thorns, cypress trees will grow. Where briers
grew, myrtles will sprout up. This miracle will bring great honor to the LORD's name; it
will be an everlasting sign of his power and love.

Blessings for All Nations

56 "Be just and fair to all," says the LORD. "Do what is right and good, for I am
coming soon to rescue you. 2Blessed are those who are careful to do this. Blessed
are those who honor my Sabbath days of rest by refusing to work. And blessed are those
who keep themselves from doing wrong.
3"And my blessings are for Gentiles, too, when they commit themselves to the LORD.
Do not let them think that I consider them second-class citizens. And my blessings are
also for the eunuchs. They are as much mine as anyone else. 4For I say this to the eunuchs
who keep my Sabbath days holy, who choose to do what pleases me and commit their
lives to me: 5I will give them—in my house, within my walls—a memorial and a name
far greater than the honor they would have received by having sons and daughters. For
the name I give them is an everlasting one. It will never disappear!
6"I will also bless the Gentiles who commit themselves to the LORD and serve him
and love his name, who worship him and do not desecrate the Sabbath day of rest, and
who have accepted his covenant. 7I will bring them also to my holy mountain of
Jerusalem and will fill them with joy in my house of prayer. I will accept their burnt
offerings and sacrifices, because my Temple will be called a house of prayer for all
nations. 8For the Sovereign LORD, who brings back the outcasts of Israel, says: I will
bring others, too, besides my people Israel."

Sinful Leaders Condemned

9Come, wild animals of the field! Come, wild animals of the forest! Come and devour my
people! 10For the leaders of my people—the LORD's watchmen, his shepherds—are blind
to every danger. They are like silent watchdogs that give no warning when danger comes.
They love to lie around, sleeping and dreaming. 11And they are as greedy as dogs, never
satisfied. They are stupid shepherds, all following their own path, all of them intent on
personal gain.
12"Come," they say. "We will get some wine and have a party. Let's all get drunk. Let
this go on and on, and tomorrow will be even better."

55:8 Isa 65:2
55:9 Ps 103:11
55:10 2 Cor 9:10
55:11 Isa 46:10
55:12 1 Chr 16:33; Jer 29:11
55:13 Jer 33:9
56:1 Ps 85:9; Isa 1:17
56:2 Exod 31:13-17; Ps 119:1-2; Ezek 20:12, 20
56:3 Acts 8:27, 37
56:5 Isa 2:2-3; 26:1; 62:2
56:6 Isa 60:10; 61:5
56:7 Isa 65:25; Mic 4:1-2; †Matt 21:13; †Mark 11:17; †Luke 19:46; Rom 12:1; Heb 13:15
56:8 John 10:16
56:9 Jer 12:9
56:10 Jer 14:13-14; Ezek 3:17
56:11 Jer 22:17; Mic 3:5, 11
56:12 Luke 12:19-20

55:8, 9 The people of Israel were foolish to act as if they knew what God was thinking and planning. His knowledge and wisdom are far greater than any human's. We are foolish to try to fit God into our mold—to make his plans and purposes conform to ours. Instead, we must strive to fit into *his* plans.

56:2 God commanded his people to rest and honor him on the Sabbath (Exodus 20:8-11). He wants us to serve him every day, but he wants us to make one day special when we rest and focus our thoughts on him. For the Israelites, this special day was the Sabbath (Saturday). Some Christians set Saturday aside as this special day, but many accept Sunday (the day of the week that Jesus rose from the dead) as the "Lord's Day," a day of rest and honor to God.

56:3 Isaiah clearly proclaims the radical message that God's blessings are for *all* people, even Gentiles and eunuchs, who were often excluded from worship and not even considered citizens in Israel. Whatever your race, social position, work, or financial situation, God's blessings are as much for you as for anyone else. No one must exclude in any way those God chooses to bless.

56:7 Jesus quoted from this verse when he threw the money changers out of the Temple (Mark 11:17). See the note on Mark 11:15-17.

56:9-11 The "watchmen" were the nation's leaders. The leaders of Israel were blind to every danger. Apathetic about their people's needs, they were more concerned about satisfying their own greed. Leadership's special privileges can cause leaders to either sacrifice for the good of their people or to sacrifice their people for their own greed. If you are in a leadership position, use it for the good of your people.

57 The righteous pass away; the godly often die before their time. And no one seems
to care or wonder why. No one seems to understand that God is protecting them
from the evil to come. 2For the godly who die will rest in peace.

Idolatrous Worship Condemned

3"But you—come here, you witches' children, you offspring of adulterers and prostitutes! 4Whom do you mock, making faces and sticking out your tongues? You children
of sinners and liars! 5You worship your idols with great passion beneath every green tree.
You slaughter your children as human sacrifices down in the valleys, under overhanging
rocks. 6Your gods are the smooth stones in the valleys. You worship them with drink
offerings and grain offerings. They, not I, are your inheritance. Does all this make me
happy? 7You have committed adultery on the mountaintops by worshiping idols there,
and so you have been unfaithful to me. 8Behind closed doors, you have set up your idols
and worship them instead of me. This is adultery, for you are loving these idols instead
of loving me. You have climbed right into bed with these detestable gods. 9You have
given olive oil and perfume to Molech* as your gift. You have traveled far, even into the
world of the dead,* to find new gods to love. 10You grew weary in your search, but you
never gave up. You strengthened yourself and went on. 11Why were you more afraid of
them than of me? How is it that you don't even remember me or think about me? Is it
because I have not corrected you that you have no fear of me?

12"Now I will expose your so-called good deeds that you consider so righteous. None
of them will benefit or save you. 13Let's see if your idols can do anything for you when
you cry to them for help. They are so helpless that a breath of wind can knock them
down! But whoever trusts in me will possess the land and inherit my holy mountain. 14I
will say, 'Rebuild the road! Clear away the rocks and stones so my people can return
from captivity.'"

God Forgives the Repentant

15The high and lofty one who inhabits eternity, the Holy One, says this: "I live in that high
and holy place with those whose spirits are contrite and humble. I refresh the humble and
give new courage to those with repentant hearts. 16For I will not fight against you forever;
I will not always show my anger. If I did, all people would pass away—all the souls I have
made. 17I was angry and punished these greedy people. I withdrew myself from them, but
they went right on sinning. 18I have seen what they do, but I will heal them anyway! I will
lead them and comfort those who mourn. 19Then words of praise will be on their lips. May
they have peace, both near and far, for I will heal them all," says the LORD. 20"But those
who still reject me are like the restless sea. It is never still but continually churns up mire
and dirt. 21There is no peace for the wicked," says my God.

True and False Worship

58 "Shout with the voice of a trumpet blast. Tell my people Israel* of their sins! 2Yet
they act so pious! They come to the Temple every day and seem delighted to hear
my laws. You would almost think this was a righteous nation that would never abandon
its God. They love to make a show of coming to me and asking me to take action on their

57:1 2 Kgs 22:19-20; Ps 12:1
57:2 Isa 26:7
57:3 Matt 16:4
57:5 Ps 106:37-38; Jer 2:20; 7:31
57:6 Jer 5:9, 29; 7:18; Hab 2:19
57:7 Ezek 16:16, 28
57:8 Ezek 23:18
57:9 Ezek 23:16, 40
57:10 Jer 2:25
57:11 Ps 50:21; Prov 29:25; Jer 2:32
57:12 Mic 3:1-4
57:13 Ps 37:3, 9; Jer 30:14
57:14 Isa 62:10
57:15 Deut 33:27; Ps 34:18
57:16 Mic 7:18
57:19 Acts 2:39; Eph 2:17; Heb 13:15
57:20 Job 18:5-14
57:21 Isa 48:22
58:2 Isa 29:13; Jer 7:9-10; Titus 1:16

57:9a Or *to the king.* **57:9b** Hebrew *into Sheol.* **58:1** Hebrew *Jacob.*

57:7, 8 Marriage is an exclusive relationship in which a man and a woman become one. Adultery breaks this beautiful bond of unity. When the people turned from God and gave their love to idols, God said they were committing adultery—breaking their exclusive commitment to God. How could people give their love to worthless wood and stone idols instead of to the God who made them and loved them so very much?

57:9 Molech was an Ammonite god whose worship included child sacrifice.

57:12 God says that he will expose their righteousness and good deeds for what they really were—mere pretentions of doing good. Isaiah warned these people that their righteousness and works would not save them any more than their weak, worthless idols. We cannot gain our salvation through good works because our best works are not good enough to outweigh our sins. Salvation is a gift from God, received only through faith in Christ, not good works (Ephesians 2:8, 9).

57:14-21 Verses 1-13 speak of pride and lust; verses 14-21 tell how God relates to those who are humble and repentant ("contrite"). The high and holy God came down to our level to save us because it is impossible for us to go up to his level to save ourselves (see 2 Chronicles 6:18; Psalm 51:1-7; Philippians 2).

58:1ff True worship was more than religious ritual, going to the Temple every day, fasting, and listening to Scripture readings. These people missed the point of a living, vital relationship with God. He doesn't want us to act pious when we have unforgiven sin in our heart and continue our sinful life-style. More important even than correct worship and doctrine is genuine compassion for the oppressed, the poor, and the helpless.

58:3 Zech 7:5-6 Luke 18:12
behalf. 3 'We have fasted before you!' they say. 'Why aren't you impressed? We have
done much penance, and you don't even notice it!'
"I will tell you why! It's because you are living for yourselves even while you are
58:4 1 Kgs 21:9-10
fasting. You keep right on oppressing your workers. 4 What good is fasting when you
keep on fighting and quarreling? This kind of fasting will never get you anywhere with
me. 5 You humble yourselves by going through the motions of penance, bowing your
heads like a blade of grass in the wind. You dress in sackcloth and cover yourselves with
ashes. Is this what you call fasting? Do you really think this will please the LORD?
58:6 Neh 5:10-12
6 "No, the kind of fasting I want calls you to free those who are wrongly imprisoned
and to stop oppressing those who work for you. Treat them fairly and give them what
58:7 Deut 22:1-4 Ezek 18:7, 16 Matt 25:35 Luke 3:11 Heb 13:2
they earn. 7 I want you to share your food with the hungry and to welcome poor
wanderers into your homes. Give clothes to those who need them, and do not hide from
relatives who need your help.
8 "If you do these things, your salvation will come like the dawn. Yes, your healing
58:8 Ps 85:13 Jer 30:17
will come quickly. Your godliness will lead you forward, and the glory of the LORD will
protect you from behind. 9 Then when you call, the LORD will answer. 'Yes, I am here,'
he will quickly reply.
"Stop oppressing the helpless and stop making false accusations and spreading vicious
58:10 Deut 15:7
rumors! 10 Feed the hungry and help those in trouble. Then your light will shine out from
58:11 Ps 107:9 Song 4:15 John 4:14; 7:37-38
the darkness, and the darkness around you will be as bright as day. 11 The LORD will guide
you continually, watering your life when you are dry and keeping you healthy, too. You
will be like a well-watered garden, like an ever-flowing spring. 12 Your children will
58:12 Ezek 36:10 Amos 9:11
rebuild the deserted ruins of your cities. Then you will be known as the people who
rebuild their walls and cities.
13 "Keep the Sabbath day holy. Don't pursue your own interests on that day, but enjoy
58:13 Ps 84:2, 10 Jer 17:21-27
the Sabbath and speak of it with delight as the LORD's holy day. Honor the LORD in
everything you do, and don't follow your own desires or talk idly. If you do this, 14 the
58:14 Deut 32:13
LORD will be your delight. I will give you great honor and give you your full share of
the inheritance I promised to Jacob, your ancestor. I, the LORD, have spoken!"

Warnings against Sin

59:1 Jer 32:17 Ezek 8:18
59 Listen! The LORD is not too weak to save you, and he is not becoming deaf. He
can hear you when you call. 2 But there is a problem—your sins have cut you off
59:2 Isa 1:15
from God. Because of your sin, he has turned away and will not listen anymore. 3 Your
59:3 Jer 2:30, 34 Hos 4:2
hands are the hands of murderers, and your fingers are filthy with sin. Your mouth is full
of lies, and your lips are tainted with corruption.
4 No one cares about being fair and honest. Their lawsuits are based on lies. They
59:4 Ps 7:14
spend their time plotting evil deeds and then doing them. 5 They spend their time and
59:5 Job 8:14
energy spinning evil plans that end up in deadly actions. 6 They cheat and shortchange
59:6 Jer 6:7
everyone. Nothing they do is productive; all their activity is filled with sin. Violence is
their trademark. 7 Their feet run to do evil, and they rush to commit murder. They think
59:7 Mark 7:21-22 †Rom 3:15-17
only about sinning. Wherever they go, misery and destruction follow them. 8 They do
not know what true peace is or what it means to be just and good. They continually do
wrong, and those who follow them cannot experience a moment's peace.

58:6-12 We cannot be saved without faith in Christ, but our faith lacks sincerity if it doesn't reach out to others. Fasting can be beneficial spiritually and physically, but at its best fasting helps only the person doing it. God says he wants our fasting to go beyond our own personal growth to acts of kindness, charity, justice, and generosity. This truly is pleasing to God.

58:13, 14 The day of rest should also be honored not only because Sabbath keeping is a commandment but also because it is best for us and it honors God. Keeping the Sabbath honors God, our Creator, who also rested on the seventh day (Genesis 2:3). It also unifies our family and sets priorities for them. Our day of rest refreshes us spiritually and physically—providing time when we can gather together for worship and reflect on God without the stress of our everyday activities.

59:1-14 Sin offends our holy God and separates us from him. Because God is holy, he cannot ignore, excuse, or tolerate sin as though it didn't matter. Sin cuts people off from him, forming a wall to isolate God from the people he loves. No wonder this long list of wretched sins makes God angry and forces him to look the other way. People who die with their life of sin unforgiven separate themselves eternally from God. God wants them to live with him forever, but he cannot take them into his holy presence unless their sin is removed. Have you confessed your sin to God, allowing him to remove it? The Lord can save you if you turn to him.

9 It is because of all this evil that deliverance is far from us. That is why God doesn't punish those who injure us. No wonder we are in darkness when we expected light. No wonder we are walking in the gloom. 10 No wonder we grope like blind people and stumble along. Even at brightest noontime, we fall down as though it were dark. No wonder we are like corpses when compared to vigorous young men! 11 We growl like hungry bears; we moan like mournful doves. We look for justice, but it is nowhere to be found. We look to be rescued, but it is far away from us. 12 For our sins are piled up before God and testify against us. Yes, we know what sinners we are. 13 We know that we have rebelled against the LORD. We have turned our backs on God. We know how unfair and oppressive we have been, carefully planning our deceitful lies. 14 Our courts oppose people who are righteous, and justice is nowhere to be found. Truth falls dead in the streets, and fairness has been outlawed. 15 Yes, truth is gone, and anyone who tries to live a godly life is soon attacked.

The LORD looked and was displeased to find that there was no justice. 16 He was amazed to see that no one intervened to help the oppressed. So he himself stepped in to save them with his mighty power and justice. 17 He put on righteousness as his body armor and placed the helmet of salvation on his head. He clothed himself with the robes of vengeance and godly fury. 18 He will repay his enemies for their evil deeds. His fury will fall on his foes in distant lands. 19 Then at last they will respect and glorify the name of the LORD throughout the world. For he will come like a flood tide driven by the breath of the LORD.

20 "The Redeemer will come to Jerusalem,*" says the LORD, "to buy back those in Israel* who have turned from their sins. 21 And this is my covenant with them," says the LORD. "My Spirit will not leave them, and neither will these words I have given you. They will be on your lips and on the lips of your children and your children's children forever. I, the LORD, have spoken!

59:9 Isa 5:30
59:10 Deut 28:29; Lam 3:6
59:11 Ezek 7:16
59:12 Ezra 9:6; Hos 5:5
59:13 Matt 10:33; Titus 1:16
59:14 Hab 1:4
59:15 Isa 1:21-23; 5:23
59:16 Ezek 22:30
59:17 Eph 6:14
59:19 Isa 30:28
59:20 Ezek 18:30-31; Acts 2:38-39; †Rom 11:26-27
59:21 Isa 44:3; Jer 31:31-34

3. The future kingdom

Future Glory for Jerusalem

60 "Arise, Jerusalem! Let your light shine for all the nations to see! For the glory of the LORD is shining upon you. 2 Darkness as black as night will cover all the nations of the earth, but the glory of the LORD will shine over you. 3 All nations will come to your light. Mighty kings will come to see your radiance.

4 "Look and see, for everyone is coming home! Your sons are coming from distant lands; your little daughters will be carried home. 5 Your eyes will shine, and your hearts will thrill with joy, for merchants from around the world will come to you. They will bring you the wealth of many lands. 6 Vast caravans of camels will converge on you, the camels of Midian and Ephah. From Sheba they will bring gold and incense for the worship of the LORD. 7 The flocks of Kedar will be given to you, and the rams of Nebaioth will be brought for my altars. In that day I will make my Temple glorious.

8 "And what do I see flying like clouds to Israel, like doves to their nests? 9 They are the ships of Tarshish, reserved to bring the people of Israel home. They will bring their

60:1 Eph 5:14
60:2 Col 1:13
60:3 Isa 2:3
60:5 Ps 34:5; Isa 61:6
60:6 Ps 72:10; Isa 42:10
60:9-10 Isa 49:22-23

59:20a Hebrew *to Zion.* **59:20b** Hebrew *in Jacob.*

59:15 Because of Israel's willful, persistent rebellion (chapters 56–59), the nation became unable to take action against its sins. Sin fills the vacuum left when God's truth no longer fills our life. Only God can defeat sin.

59:16, 17 God would, in fact, act to rescue the nation from enemy armies (Assyria and Babylon) and to punish wicked Israelites as well. He would also rescue his people from sin. Because redemption is an impossible task for any human, God himself, as the Messiah, would personally step in to help (Romans 11:26, 27). Whether we sin once or many times, out of rebellion or out of ignorance, our sin separates us from God and will continue to separate us until God forgives us and removes it.

59:21 When the Holy Spirit dwells within his people, they change. Their former desires no longer entice them; now their chief aim is to please God. We who are Christians today are the heirs of this prophecy; we are able to respond to God's will and distinguish between good and evil because the Holy Spirit dwells within us (John 14:26; Philippians 2:13; Hebrews 5:14).

60:1ff As we read these promises, we long for their fulfillment. But we must patiently wait for God's timing. He is in control of history, and he weaves together all our lives into his plan.

60:6, 7 The places mentioned belonged to obscure tribes in the Arabian desert hundreds of miles from Israel. All people would come to Jerusalem because God would be living there, and they would be attracted to his light. Don't be discouraged when you look around and see so few people turning to God; one day people throughout the earth will recognize him as the one true God.

wealth with them, and it will bring great honor to the LORD your God, the Holy One of
Israel, for he will fill you with splendor.
10“Foreigners will come to rebuild your cities. Kings and rulers will send you aid.
For though I have destroyed you in my anger, I will have mercy on you through my
grace. 11Your gates will stay open around the clock to receive the wealth of many
lands. The kings of the world will be led as captives in a victory procession. 12For the
nations that refuse to be your allies will be destroyed. 13The glory of Lebanon will be
yours—the forests of cypress, fir, and pine—to beautify my sanctuary. My Temple
will be glorious!
14“The children of your tormentors will come and bow before you. Those who
despised you will kiss your feet. They will call you the City of the LORD, and Zion of the
Holy One of Israel.
15“Though you were once despised and hated and rebuffed by all, you will be
beautiful forever. You will be a joy to all generations, for I will make you so.
16Powerful kings and mighty nations will bring the best of their goods to satisfy your
every need. You will know at last that I, the LORD, am your Savior and Redeemer, the
Mighty One of Israel.* 17I will exchange your bronze for gold, your iron for silver,
your wood for bronze, and your stones for iron. Peace and righteousness will be your
leaders! 18Violence will disappear from your land; the desolation and destruction of
war will end. Salvation will surround you like city walls, and praise will be on the lips
of all who enter there.
19“No longer will you need the sun or moon to give you light, for the LORD your
God will be your everlasting light, and he will be your glory. 20The sun will never
set; the moon will not go down. For the LORD will be your everlasting light. Your
days of mourning will come to an end. 21All your people will be righteous. They will
possess their land forever, for I will plant them there with my own hands in order to
bring myself glory. 22The smallest family will multiply into a large clan. The tiniest
group will become a mighty nation. I, the LORD, will bring it all to pass at the right
time.”

Good News for the Oppressed

61 The Spirit of the Sovereign LORD is upon me, because the LORD has appointed
me to bring good news to the poor. He has sent me to comfort the brokenhearted
and to announce that captives will be released and prisoners will be freed.* 2He has
sent me to tell those who mourn that the time of the LORD’s favor has come,* and with
it, the day of God’s anger against their enemies. 3To all who mourn in Israel,* he will
give beauty for ashes, joy instead of mourning, praise instead of despair. For the LORD
has planted them like strong and graceful oaks for his own glory.
4They will rebuild the ancient ruins, repairing cities long ago destroyed. They
will revive them, though they have been empty for many generations. 5Foreigners
will be your servants. They will feed your flocks and plow your fields and tend
your vineyards. 6You will be called priests of the LORD, ministers of our God. You
will be fed with the treasures of the nations and will boast in their riches. 7Instead
of shame and dishonor, you will inherit a double portion of prosperity and
everlasting joy.

60:11 Isa 26:2
60:12 Zech 14:17
60:13 Ps 132:7
60:14 Isa 1:26; 14:1-2; Rev 3:9
60:15 Isa 65:18; Jer 30:17
60:16 Isa 43:3, 11; 63:16
60:18 Isa 26:1
60:19 Isa 9:2; Zech 2:5; Rev 21:23; 22:5
60:20 Rev 21:4
60:21 Ps 37:22; Isa 45:24-25
60:22 Isa 51:2
61:1-2 Isa 49:8-9; †Luke 4:18-19
61:3 Ps 23:5; Jer 17:7-8
61:4 Ezek 36:33; Amos 9:14
61:5 Isa 14:2
61:6 Isa 66:21
61:7 Zech 9:12

60:16 Hebrew *of Jacob.* **61:1** Greek version reads *and the blind will see.* **61:2** Or *to proclaim the acceptable year of the LORD.* **61:3** Hebrew *in Zion.*

60:19, 20 See Revelation 21:23, 24 and 22:5, where this beautiful reality is also promised.

61:1, 2 Jesus quoted these words in Luke 4:18, 19. As he read to the people in the synagogue, he stopped in the middle of 61:2 after the words, “the time of the LORD’s favor has come.” Rolling up the scroll, he said, “This Scripture has come true today before your very eyes!” (Luke 4:21). The next phrase in 61:2, “and with it, the day of God’s anger against their enemies,” will come true when Jesus returns to earth again. We are now under God’s favor; his wrath is yet to come.

61:6 Under the old covenant, God ordained the priests of Israel to stand between him and his people. They brought God’s word to the people and the people’s needs and sins to God. Under the new covenant, all believers are priests of the Lord, reading God’s Word and seeking to understand it, confessing their sins directly to God, and ministering to others.

8“For I, the LORD, love justice. I hate robbery and wrongdoing. I will faithfully
reward my people for their suffering and make an everlasting covenant with them.
9Their descendants will be known and honored among the nations. Everyone will
realize that they are a people the LORD has blessed.”
10I am overwhelmed with joy in the LORD my God! For he has dressed me with the
clothing of salvation and draped me in a robe of righteousness. I am like a bridegroom
in his wedding suit or a bride with her jewels. 11The Sovereign LORD will show his
justice to the nations of the world. Everyone will praise him! His righteousness will be
like a garden in early spring, filled with young plants springing up everywhere.

Isaiah's Prayer for Jerusalem

62 Because I love Zion, because my heart yearns for Jerusalem, I cannot remain
silent. I will not stop praying for her until her righteousness shines like the dawn,
and her salvation blazes like a burning torch.
2The nations will see your righteousness. Kings will be blinded by your glory. And
the LORD will give you a new name. 3The LORD will hold you in his hands for all to
see—a splendid crown in the hands of God. 4Never again will you be called the
Godforsaken City* or the Desolate Land.* Your new name will be the City of God's
Delight* and the Bride of God,* for the LORD delights in you and will claim you as
his own. 5Your children will care for you with joy, O Jerusalem, just as a young man
cares for his bride. Then God will rejoice over you as a bridegroom rejoices over his
bride.
6O Jerusalem, I have posted watchmen on your walls; they will pray to the
LORD day and night for the fulfillment of his promises. Take no rest, all you who
pray. 7Give the LORD no rest until he makes Jerusalem the object of praise
throughout the earth. 8The LORD has sworn to Jerusalem by his own strength: “I
will never again hand you over to your enemies. Never again will foreign warriors
come and take away your grain and wine. 9You raised it, and you will keep it,
praising the LORD. Within the courtyards of the Temple, you yourselves will drink
the wine that you have pressed.”
10Go out! Prepare the highway for my people to return! Smooth out the road; pull
out the boulders; raise a flag for all the nations to see. 11The LORD has sent this
message to every land: “Tell the people of Israel,* ‘Look, your Savior is coming. See,
he brings his reward with him as he comes.’” 12They will be called the Holy People
and the People Redeemed by the LORD. And Jerusalem will be known as the Desirable
Place and the City No Longer Forsaken.

Judgment against the LORD's Enemies

63 Who is this who comes from Edom, from the city of Bozrah, with his clothing
stained red? Who is this in royal robes, marching in the greatness of his
strength?

61:8 Gen 17:7; Isa 5:16
61:9 Isa 44:3
61:10 Isa 51:3; 52:1
62:1 Isa 46:13
62:2 Isa 56:5
62:3 Zech 9:16; 1 Thes 2:19
62:4 Isa 54:6-7; Jer 32:41; Zeph 3:17-18
62:5 Isa 65:19
62:6 Jer 14:21; Ezek 33:7; Zeph 3:19-20
62:7 Luke 18:1-8
62:8 Lev 26:16; Deut 28:31, 33
62:9 Isa 65:13, 21-23
62:10 Isa 11:10
62:11 Isa 49:6; Zech 9:9; †Matt 21:5; Rev 22:12
62:12 Deut 7:6; 1 Pet 2:9
63:1 Jer 49:13; Amos 1:12; Zeph 3:17

62:4a Hebrew *Azubah,* which means “forsaken.” **62:4b** Hebrew *Shemamah,* which means “desolate.” **62:4c** Hebrew *Hephzibah,* which means “my delight is in her.” **62:4d** Hebrew *Beulah,* which means “married.” **62:11** Hebrew *Tell the daughter of Zion.*

61:8 We suffer for many reasons—our own mistakes, someone else's mistakes, injustice. When we suffer for our own mistakes, we get what we deserve. When we suffer because of others or because of injustice, God is angry. God in his mercy says that his people have suffered enough. God will reward those who suffer because of injustice. He will settle all accounts.

61:10 “Me” could refer to the Messiah, the person appointed by the Spirit of the Lord (61:1), or to Zion (62:1), which symbolizes God's people. The imagery of the bridegroom is often used in Scripture to depict the Messiah (see Matthew 9:15), while the imagery of the bride is used to depict God's people (see Revelation 19:6-8). We, too, can be clothed with the righteousness of Christ when we believe in him (2 Corinthians 5:21).

62:1-7 Many commentators believe Isaiah is speaking in verse 1. If so, Isaiah's zeal for his people and his desire to see the work of salvation completed caused him to pray without resting, hoping that Israel would be saved. We should have Isaiah's zeal to see God's will done. This is what we mean when we pray, “May your kingdom come soon. May your will be done here on earth, just as it is in heaven.” It is good to keep praying persistently for others.

62:12 The people of Jerusalem (Zion) will have new names: “the Holy People” and “the People Redeemed by the LORD.” Believers today also have new names—Christians. In 1 Peter 2:5, we are called “God's holy priests.”

63:1-4 Edom was a constant enemy of Israel despite its common ancestry in Isaac (Genesis 25:23). Edom rejoiced at any trouble Israel faced. The imagery in this passage is of a watchman on the wall of Jerusalem, seeing Edom approaching and

"It is I, the LORD, announcing your salvation! It is I, the LORD, who is mighty to
save!"
2 Why are your clothes so red, as if you have been treading out grapes?
3 "I have trodden the winepress alone; no one was there to help me. In my anger I have
trampled my enemies as if they were grapes. In my fury I have trampled my foes. It is
their blood that has stained my clothes. 4 For the time has come for me to avenge my
people, to ransom them from their oppressors. 5 I looked, but no one came to help my
people. I was amazed and appalled at what I saw. So I executed vengeance alone;
unaided, I passed down judgment. 6 I crushed the nations in my anger and made them
stagger and fall to the ground."

Praise for Deliverance

7 I will tell of the LORD's unfailing love. I will praise the LORD for all he has done. I will
rejoice in his great goodness to Israel, which he has granted according to his mercy and
love. 8 He said, "They are my very own people. Surely they will not be false again." And
he became their Savior. 9 In all their suffering he also suffered, and he personally rescued
them. In his love and mercy he redeemed them. He lifted them up and carried them
through all the years.
10 But they rebelled against him and grieved his Holy Spirit. That is why he became
their enemy and fought against them. 11 Then they remembered those days of old
when Moses led his people out of Egypt. They cried out, "Where is the one who
brought Israel through the sea, with Moses as their shepherd? Where is the one who
sent his Holy Spirit to be among his people? 12 Where is the one whose power divided
the sea before them, when Moses lifted up his hand, establishing his reputation
forever? 13 Where is the one who led them through the bottom of the sea? They were
like fine stallions racing through the desert, never stumbling. 14 As with cattle going
down into a peaceful valley, the Spirit of the LORD gave them rest. You led your
people, LORD, and gained a magnificent reputation."

Prayer for Mercy and Pardon

15 LORD, look down from heaven and see us from your holy, glorious home. Where is
the passion and the might you used to show on our behalf? Where are your mercy and
compassion now? 16 Surely you are still our Father! Even if Abraham and Jacob*

63:16 Hebrew *Israel.*

63:2 Rev 19:13, 15
63:3 Isa 22:5; Mic 7:10
63:4 Jer 51:6
63:5 Isa 52:10; 59:16
63:6 Isa 65:21
63:7 1 Kgs 8:66; Pss 25:6-7; 86:5; Eph 2:4
63:8 Exod 6:7
63:9 Exod 23:20-23; Judg 10:16
63:10 Ps 78:40; Acts 7:51; Eph 4:30
63:11 Num 11:17, 25, 29; Isa 51:9-10
63:12 Exod 6:6; 14:21-22
63:13 Jer 31:9
63:14 Josh 21:44
63:15 Pss 80:14; 123:1; Jer 31:20
63:16 Isa 41:8

THE SPIRIT IN ISAIAH

Reference	Main Teaching
11:2	The Spirit of the Lord brings wisdom, understanding, knowledge, and the fear of the Lord.
32:15	The Spirit of the Lord brings abundance.
34:16	The Spirit of the Lord carries out God's word.
40:13	The Spirit of the Lord is the Master Counselor.
42:1	The Messiah, God's Servant, will be given the Spirit.
44:3–5	Through the Spirit, God's true children will thrive.
48:16	The Spirit of the Lord sent Isaiah to prophesy.
61:1	God's servants (Isaiah and then Jesus) were appointed by the Spirit to proclaim the Good News.
63:10, 11	The Spirit of the Lord was grieved because of God's people.
63:14	The Spirit of the Lord gives rest.

fearing that the Edomite king in his red garment is leading an attack. But it turns out to be the Lord, in bloodstained clothes, who has trampled and destroyed Edom. Bozrah is a city in Edom. (For other prophecies against Edom, see Amos 1:11, 12; Obadiah 1:10, 11; Malachi 1:2-4.)

63:10 Grieving the Holy Spirit is willfully thwarting his leading by disobedience or rebellion. Isaiah mentions the work of the Holy Spirit more than any other Old Testament writer. See the note on Ephesians 4:28-32 for more on grieving the Holy Spirit.

63:15–64:7 On behalf of the faithful remnant, Isaiah asks God for two favors: to show mercy and compassion to them and to punish their enemies. Before making these requests, Isaiah recited the Lord's past favors, reminding him of his compassion in former days (63:7-14).

would disown us, LORD, you would still be our Father. You are our Redeemer from
ages past. 17 LORD, why have you allowed us to turn from your path? Why have you
given us stubborn hearts so we no longer fear you? Return and help us, for we are
your servants and your special possession. 18 How briefly your holy people possessed
the holy place, and now our enemies have destroyed it. 19 LORD, why do you treat us
as though we never belonged to you? Why do you act as though we had never been
known as your people?

64 Oh, that you would burst from the heavens and come down! How the mountains would quake in your presence! 2 As fire causes wood to burn and water to
boil, your coming would make the nations tremble. Then your enemies would learn
the reason for your fame! 3 When you came down long ago, you did awesome things
beyond our highest expectations. And oh, how the mountains quaked! 4 For since the
world began, no ear has heard, and no eye has seen a God like you, who works for
those who wait for him! 5 You welcome those who cheerfully do good, who follow
godly ways.
But we are not godly. We are constant sinners, so your anger is heavy on us. How can
people like us be saved? 6 We are all infected and impure with sin. When we proudly
display our righteous deeds, we find they are but filthy rags. Like autumn leaves, we
wither and fall. And our sins, like the wind, sweep us away. 7 Yet no one calls on your
name or pleads with you for mercy. Therefore, you have turned away from us and turned
us over to our sins.
8 And yet, LORD, you are our Father. We are the clay, and you are the potter. We are all
formed by your hand. 9 Oh, don't be so angry with us, LORD. Please don't remember our
sins forever. Look at us, we pray, and see that we are all your people.
10 Your holy cities are destroyed; even Jerusalem is a desolate wilderness. 11 The holy,
beautiful Temple where our ancestors praised you has been burned down, and all the
things of beauty are destroyed. 12 After all this, LORD, must you still refuse to help us?
Will you continue to be silent and punish us?

Judgment and Final Salvation

65 The LORD says, "People who never before inquired about me are now asking
about me. I am being found by people who were not looking for me. To them I
have said, 'I am here!'
2 "I opened my arms to my own people all day long, but they have rebelled. They
follow their own evil paths and thoughts. 3 All day long they insult me to my face by
worshiping idols in their sacred gardens. They burn incense on the rooftops of their
homes. 4 At night they go out among the graves and secret places to worship evil spirits.

63:17 Num 10:36; Isa 29:13-14
63:18 Ps 74:3-7
63:19 Lam 3:43-45
64:1 Exod 19:18; Judg 5:5; Nah 1:5
64:2 Ps 99:1
64:3 Pss 65:5; 66:5
64:4 Isa 40:31; †1 Cor 2:9
64:6 Ps 90:5-6; Isa 1:30; 48:1
64:7 Deut 31:18; Isa 1:15
64:8 Ps 100:3; Isa 45:9
64:9 Ps 79:13; Mic 7:18
64:11 Ps 74:5-7
64:12 Ps 83:1
65:1-2 †Rom 10:20-21
65:3 Job 2:5
65:4 Lev 11:7

64:1-6 God's appearance is so intense that it is like a consuming fire that burns everything in its path. If we are so impure, how can we be saved? Only by God's mercy. The Israelites had experienced God's presence at Mount Sinai (Exodus 19:16-19). When God met with Moses, there was a thunderstorm, smoke, and an earthquake. If God were to meet us today, his glory would overwhelm us, especially when we look at our "filthy rags" (64:6).

64:6 Sin makes us unclean so that we cannot approach God (6:5; Romans 3:23) any more than a beggar in filthy rags could dine at a king's table. Our best efforts are still infected with sin. Our only hope, therefore, is faith in Jesus Christ, who can cleanse us and bring us into God's presence (read Romans 3).

This passage can easily be misunderstood. It doesn't mean that God will reject us if we come to him in faith, nor that he despises our efforts to please him. It means that if we come to him demanding acceptance on the basis of our "good" conduct, God will point out that our righteousness is but filthy rags compared to his infinite righteousness. This message is primarily for the unrepentant person, not the true follower of God.

65:1 Israel considered itself to be the only people of God, but the time would come when other nations would seek him. Paul mentions Isaiah's statement in Romans 10:20 and points out that these other nations were the Gentiles. God's people today are those who accept Jesus as Savior and Lord, whether they are Jews or Gentiles. The gospel is for every person. Do not ignore or reject anyone when you share the gospel. You may be surprised at how many are sincerely searching for God.

65:3-5 God said these people directly disobeyed his laws when they worshiped and sacrificed to idols (Exodus 20:1-6), consulted the dead and evil spirits (Leviticus 19:31), and ate forbidden foods (Leviticus 11). But they were so perverse that they still thought they were more sacred than others. Jesus called such people hypocrites (Matthew 23:13-36).

65:5 Matt 9:11 Luke 8:9-12
65:6 Ps 50:3, 21 Isa 42:14
65:7 Jer 13:25 Ezek 20:27-28 Hos 2:13
65:9 Amos 9:11-15
65:10 Josh 7:24 Isa 33:9
65:11 Isa 1:4, 28
65:12 2 Chr 36:15-16 Prov 1:24
65:13 Isa 5:13
65:14 Matt 8:12 Luke 13:28
65:15 Jer 24:9
65:16 Isa 45:23
65:17 2 Cor 5:17 2 Pet 3:13
65:18 Ps 98:1-9 Isa 35:10
65:19 Jer 32:41 Rev 7:17
65:20 Eccl 8:12-13
65:21 Amos 9:14
65:23 Isa 61:9
65:24 Ps 91:15 Dan 10:12
65:25 Gen 3:14 Isa 11:6-7, 9

They also eat pork and other forbidden foods. 5 Yet they say to each other, 'Don't come
too close or you will defile me! I am holier than you!' They are a stench in my nostrils,
an acrid smell that never goes away.
6 "Look, my decree is written out in front of me: I will not stand silent; I will repay
them in full! Yes, I will repay them—7 both for their own sins and for those of their
ancestors," says the LORD. "For they also burned incense on the mountains and insulted
me on the hills. I will pay them back in full!
8 "But I will not destroy them all," says the LORD. "For just as good grapes are found
among a cluster of bad ones (and someone will say, 'Don't throw them all away—there
are some good grapes there!'), so I will not destroy all Israel. For I still have true servants
there. 9 I will preserve a remnant of the people of Israel* and of Judah to possess my land.
Those I choose will inherit it and serve me there. 10 For my people who have searched
for me, the plain of Sharon will again be filled with flocks, and the valley of Achor will
be a place to pasture herds.
11 "But because the rest of you have forsaken the LORD and his Temple and worship the
gods of Fate and Destiny, 12 I will 'destine' you to the sword. All of you will bow before the
executioner, for when I called, you did not answer. When I spoke, you did not listen. You
deliberately sinned—before my very eyes—and chose to do what you know I despise."
13 Therefore, this is what the Sovereign LORD says: "You will starve, but my
servants will eat. You will be thirsty, but they will drink. You will be sad and ashamed,
but they will rejoice. 14 You will cry in sorrow and despair, while my servants sing for
joy. 15 Your name will be a curse word among my people, for the Sovereign LORD will
destroy you and call his true servants by another name. 16 All who invoke a blessing
or take an oath will do so by the God of truth. For I will put aside my anger and forget
the evil of earlier days.
17 "Look! I am creating new heavens and a new earth—so wonderful that no one will
even think about the old ones anymore. 18 Be glad; rejoice forever in my creation! And
look! I will create Jerusalem as a place of happiness. Her people will be a source of joy.
19 I will rejoice in Jerusalem and delight in my people. And the sound of weeping and
crying will be heard no more.
20 "No longer will babies die when only a few days old. No longer will adults die
before they have lived a full life. No longer will people be considered old at one hundred!
Only sinners will die that young! 21 In those days, people will live in the houses they build
and eat the fruit of their own vineyards. 22 It will not be like the past, when invaders took
the houses and confiscated the vineyards. For my people will live as long as trees and
will have time to enjoy their hard-won gains. 23 They will not work in vain, and their
children will not be doomed to misfortune. For they are people blessed by the LORD, and
their children, too, will be blessed. 24 I will answer them before they even call to me.
While they are still talking to me about their needs, I will go ahead and answer their
prayers! 25 The wolf and lamb will feed together. The lion will eat straw like the ox.
Poisonous snakes will strike no more. In those days, no one will be hurt or destroyed on
my holy mountain. I, the LORD, have spoken!"

65:9 Hebrew *remnant of Jacob.*

65:6 God said he would pay back the people for their sins. Judgment is not our job but his because he alone is just. Who else knows our heart and mind? Who else knows what is a completely fair reward or punishment?

65:8, 9 God will always preserve a faithful remnant of his people. No matter how bad the world is, there are always a few who remain loyal to him. Jesus made this point in Matthew 13:36-43.

65:10 Sharon is a plain in the western part of Israel. The valley of Achor is in the east, near Jericho. The valley of Achor was also called the Valley of Trouble because Achan was executed there for hiding the devoted goods of battle (Joshua 7:10-26). Even in this valley there will be peace: The coming restoration will be complete.

65:17-25 In 65:17-19 we have a pictorial description of the new heavens and the new earth. They are eternal, and in them safety, peace, and plenty will be available to all (see also 66:22, 23; 2 Peter 3:13; Revelation 21:1). Verses 20-25 may refer to the reign of Christ on earth because sin and death have not yet been finally destroyed.

66 This is what the LORD says: "Heaven is my throne, and the earth is my footstool. Could you ever build me a temple as good as that? Could you build a dwelling place for me? 2My hands have made both heaven and earth, and they are mine. I, the LORD, have spoken!

"I will bless those who have humble and contrite hearts, who tremble at my word. 3But those who choose their own ways, delighting in their sins, are cursed. Their offerings will not be accepted. When such people sacrifice an ox, it is no more acceptable than a human sacrifice. When they sacrifice a lamb or bring an offering of grain, it is as bad as putting a dog or the blood of a pig on the altar! When they burn incense, it is as if they had blessed an idol. 4I will send great troubles against them—all the things they feared. For when I called, they did not answer. When I spoke, they did not listen. They deliberately sinned—before my very eyes—and chose to do what they know I despise."

5Hear this message from the LORD, and tremble at his words: "Your close relatives hate you and throw you out for being loyal to my name. 'Let the LORD be honored!' they scoff. 'Be joyful in him!' But they will be put to shame. 6What is all the commotion in the city? What is that terrible noise from the Temple? It is the voice of the LORD taking vengeance against his enemies.

7"Before the birth pains even begin, Jerusalem gives birth to a son. 8Who has ever seen or heard of anything as strange as this? Has a nation ever been born in a single day? Has a country ever come forth in a mere moment? But by the time Jerusalem's* birth pains begin, the baby will be born; the nation will come forth. 9Would I ever bring this nation to the point of birth and then not deliver it?" asks the LORD. "No! I would never keep this nation from being born," says your God.

10"Rejoice with Jerusalem! Be glad with her, all you who love her and mourn for her. 11Delight in Jerusalem! Drink deeply of her glory even as an infant drinks at its mother's generous breasts. 12Peace and prosperity will overflow Jerusalem like a river," says the LORD. "The wealth of the nations will flow to her. Her children will be nursed at her breasts, carried in her arms, and treated with love. 13I will comfort you there as a child is comforted by its mother."

14When you see these things, your heart will rejoice. Vigorous health will be yours! Everyone will see the good hand of the LORD on his people—and his anger against his enemies. 15See, the LORD is coming with fire, and his swift chariots of destruction roar like a whirlwind. He will bring punishment with the fury of his anger and the flaming fire of his hot rebuke. 16The LORD will punish the world by fire and by his sword, and many will be killed by the LORD.

17"Those who 'purify' themselves in a sacred garden, feasting on pork and rats and other forbidden meats, will come to a terrible end," says the LORD. 18"I can see what they are doing, and I know what they are thinking. So I will gather all nations and peoples together, and they will see my glory. 19I will perform a sign among them. And I will send those who survive to be messengers to the nations—to Tarshish, to the Libyans* and Lydians* (who are famous as archers), to Tubal and Greece,* and to all

66:1 Ps 11:4; Matt 5:34-35; John 4:20-21; †Acts 7:49-50
66:2 Ps 34:18; Matt 5:3-4; Luke 18:13-14
66:4 Prov 1:31-32; 10:24; Jer 7:13, 30
66:5 Ps 38:20; Matt 5:10-12; Luke 13:17; John 9:34
66:6 Joel 3:7
66:9 Isa 37:3
66:10 Ps 122:6; Rom 15:10
66:12 Isa 48:18; 60:5
66:13 2 Cor 1:4
66:14 Prov 3:8; Zech 10:7
66:16 Ezek 38:22
66:17 Lev 11:7
66:19 1 Chr 16:24; Isa 42:12

66:8 Hebrew *Zion's.* **66:19a** As in some Greek manuscripts, which read *Put* [Libya]; Hebrew reads *Pul.* **66:19b** Hebrew *Lud.* **66:19c** Hebrew *Javan.*

66:1 Even the beautiful Temple in Jerusalem was woefully inadequate for a God who is present everywhere. God cannot be confined to any human structure (see 2 Chronicles 6:18; Acts 7:49, 50). This chapter is a fitting climax to the book. God will lift up the humble, judge all people, destroy the wicked, bring all believers together, and establish the new heavens and the new earth. Let this hope encourage you each day.

66:2, 3 These key verses summarize Isaiah's message. He contrasted humble persons, who have a profound reverence for God's messages and their application to life, with those who choose their own ways. The sacrifices of the arrogant were only external compliance. In their hearts they were murderers, perverts, and idolaters. God shows mercy to the humble, but he curses the proud and self-sufficient (see Luke 1:51-53). Our society urges us to be assertive and to affirm ourselves. Don't let your freedom and right to choose lead you away from God's pathway to eternal life.

66:7-9 God will not leave his work of national restoration unfinished. In this image of birth, God shows that he will accomplish what he has promised. It is as unstoppable as the birth of a baby. When all the pain is over, the joy begins.

66:15-17 This is a vivid picture of the great judgment that will occur at Christ's second coming (2 Thessalonians 1:7-9).

66:19 God's people will go out as missionaries to all parts of the earth—to Tarshish (Spain), to the Libyans in northern Africa, to the Lydians in western Asia Minor, to northeastern Asia Minor (Tubal), and to Greece.

66:20 Isa 2:2; 43:5-6; 49:22; 52:11; 60:4
66:21 Isa 61:6; 1 Pet 2:5, 9
66:22 John 10:27-29; 2 Pet 3:13; Rev 21:1
66:23 Isa 27:13
66:24 Isa 1:31; Dan 12:2; †Mark 9:48

the lands beyond the sea that have not heard of my fame or seen my glory. There they
will declare my glory to the nations. 20 They will bring the remnant of your people
back from every nation. They will bring them to my holy mountain in Jerusalem as
an offering to the LORD. They will ride on horses, in chariots and wagons, and on
mules and camels," says the LORD. 21 "And I will appoint some of those who return
to be my priests and Levites. I, the LORD, have spoken!

22 "As surely as my new heavens and earth will remain, so will you always be my
people, with a name that will never disappear," says the LORD. 23 "All humanity will
come to worship me from week to week and from month to month. 24 And as they go out,
they will see the dead bodies of those who have rebelled against me. For the worms that
devour them will never die, and the fire that burns them will never go out. All who pass
by will view them with utter horror."

66:22-24 Isaiah brings his book to a close with great drama. For the faithless there is a sobering portrayal of judgment. For the faithful, there is a glorious picture of rich reward: "So will you always be my people, with a name that will never disappear." The contrast is so striking that it would seem that everyone would want to be God's follower. But we are often just as rebellious, foolish, and reluctant to change as the Israelites. We are just as negligent in feeding the hungry, working for justice, and obeying God's Word. Make sure you are among those who will be richly blessed.

JEREMIAH

Zephaniah becomes a prophet 640 B.C.

Jeremiah becomes a prophet 627

King Josiah killed in battle 609

Daniel taken captive 605

VITAL STATISTICS

PURPOSE:
To urge God's people to turn from their sins and back to God

AUTHOR:
Jeremiah

TO WHOM WRITTEN:
Judah (the southern kingdom) and its capital city, Jerusalem

DATE WRITTEN:
During Jeremiah's ministry, approximately 627–586 B.C.

SETTING:
Jeremiah ministered under Judah's last five kings—Josiah, Jehoahaz, Jehoiakim, Jehoiachin, and Zedekiah. The nation was sliding quickly toward destruction and was eventually conquered by Babylon in 586 B.C. (see 2 Kings 21—25). The prophet Zephaniah preceded Jeremiah, and Habakkuk was Jeremiah's contemporary.

KEY VERSE:
"Your own wickedness will punish you. You will see what an evil, bitter thing it is to forsake the LORD your God, having no fear of him. I, the Lord, the LORD Almighty, have spoken!" (2:19).

KEY PEOPLE:
Judah's kings (listed above), Baruch, Ebed-melech, King Nebuchadnezzar, the Recabites

KEY PLACES:
Anathoth, Jerusalem, Ramah, Egypt

SPECIAL FEATURES:
This book is a combination of history, poetry, and biography. Jeremiah often used symbolism to communicate his message.

WHAT is success? Most definitions include references to achieving goals and acquiring wealth, prestige, favor, and power. "Successful" people enjoy the good life—being financially and emotionally secure, being surrounded by admirers, and enjoying the fruits of their labors. They are leaders, opinion makers, and trendsetters. Their example is emulated; their accomplishments are noticed. They know who they are and where they are going, and they stride confidently to meet their goals.

By these standards, Jeremiah was a miserable failure. For 40 years he served as God's spokesman to Judah; but when Jeremiah spoke, nobody listened. Consistently and passionately he urged them to act, but nobody moved. And he certainly did not attain material success. He was poor and underwent severe deprivation to deliver his prophecies. He was thrown into prison (chapter 37) and into a cistern (chapter 38), and he was taken to Egypt against his will (chapter 43). He was rejected by his neighbors (11:19–21), his family (12:6), the false priests and prophets (20:1, 2; 28:1–17), friends (20:10), his audience (26:8), and the kings (36:23). Throughout his life, Jeremiah stood alone, declaring God's messages of doom, announcing the new covenant, and weeping over the fate of his beloved country. In the eyes of the world, Jeremiah was not a success.

But in God's eyes, Jeremiah was one of the most successful people in all of history. Success, as measured by God, involves obedience and faithfulness. Regardless of opposition and personal cost, Jeremiah courageously and faithfully proclaimed the word of God. He was obedient to his calling. Jeremiah's book begins with his call to be a prophet. The next 38 chapters are prophecies about Israel (the nation united) and Judah (the southern kingdom). Chapters 2—20 are general and undated, and chapters 21—39 are particular and dated. The basic theme of Jeremiah's message is simple: "Repent and turn to God, or he will punish." Because the people rejected this warning, Jeremiah then began predicting the destruction of Jerusalem. This terrible event is described in chapter 39. Chapters 40—45 describe events following Jerusalem's fall. The book concludes with prophecies concerning a variety of nations (chapters 46—52).

As you read Jeremiah, feel with him as he agonizes over the message he must deliver, pray with him for those who refuse to respond to the truth, and watch his example of faith and courage. Then commit yourself to being successful in God's eyes.

Ezekiel begins to prophesy in Babylonia 593

Judah falls; Jerusalem destroyed; Jeremiah's ministry ends 586

First exiles return to Judah 538

THE BLUEPRINT

A. GOD'S JUDGMENT ON JUDAH (1:1—45:5)
1. The call of Jeremiah
2. Jeremiah condemns Judah for its sins
3. Jeremiah prophesies destruction
4. Jeremiah accuses Judah's leaders
5. Restoration is promised
6. God's promised judgment arrives

Jeremiah confronts many people with their sins: kings, false prophets, those at the temples, and those at the gates. A lack of response made Jeremiah wonder if he was doing any good at all. He often felt discouraged and sometimes bitter. To bring such gloomy messages to these people was a hard task. We, too, have a responsibility to bring this news to a fallen world: Those who continue in their sinful ways are eternally doomed. Although we may feel discouraged at the lack of response, we must press on to tell others about the consequences of sin and the hope that God offers. Those who tell people only what they want to hear are being unfaithful to God's message.

B. GOD'S JUDGMENT ON THE NATIONS (46:1—52:34)
1. Prophecies about foreign nations
2. The fall of Jerusalem

Jeremiah lived to see many of his prophecies come true—most notably the fall of Jerusalem. The fulfillment of this and other prophecies against the foreign nations came as a result of sin. Those who refuse to confess their sin bring judgment upon themselves.

MEGATHEMES

THEME	EXPLANATION	IMPORTANCE
Sin	King Josiah's reformation failed because the people's repentance was shallow. They continued in their selfishness and worship of idols. All the leaders rejected God's law and will for the people. Jeremiah lists all their sins, predicts God's judgment, and begs for repentance.	Judah's deterioration and disaster came from a callous disregard and disobedience of God. When we ignore sin and refuse to listen to God's warning, we invite disaster. Don't settle for half measures in removing sin.
Punishment	Because of sin, Jerusalem was destroyed, the Temple was ruined, and the people were captured and carried off to Babylon. The people were responsible for their destruction and captivity because they refused to listen to God's message.	Unconfessed sin brings God's full punishment. It is useless to blame anyone else for our sin; we are accountable to God before anyone else. We must answer to him for how we live.
God Is Lord of All	God is the righteous Creator. He is accountable to no one but himself. He wisely and lovingly directs all creation to fulfill his plans, and he brings events to pass according to his timetable. He is Lord over all the world.	Because of God's majestic power and love, our only duty is to submit to his authority. By following his plans, not our own, we can have a loving relationship with him and serve him with our whole heart.
New Hearts	Jeremiah predicted that after the destruction of the nation, God would send a new shepherd, the Messiah. He would lead them into a new future, a new covenant, and a new day of hope. He would accomplish this by changing their sinful hearts into hearts of love for God.	God still transforms people by changing their hearts. His love can eliminate the problems created by sin. We can have assurance of a new heart by loving God, trusting Christ to save us, and repenting of our sin.
Faithful Service	Jeremiah served God faithfully for 40 years. During that time the people ignored, rejected, and persecuted him. Jeremiah's preaching was unsuccessful by human standards, yet he did not fail in his task. He remained faithful to God.	People's acceptance or rejection of us is not the measure of our success. God's approval alone should be our standard for service. We must bring God's message to others even when we are rejected. We must do God's work even if it means suffering for it.

A. GOD'S JUDGMENT ON JUDAH (1:1—45:5)

Jeremiah was called by God to be a prophet to Judah (the southern kingdom). He faithfully confronted the leaders and the people with their sin, prophesied both their 70-year captivity in Babylon and their eventual return from exile. After surviving the fall of Jerusalem, Jeremiah was forcefully taken to Egypt. Yet Jeremiah remained faithful in spite of Jerusalem's destruction. Years of obedience had made him strong and courageous. May we be able to stand through difficult times as did Jeremiah.

1. The call of Jeremiah

1 These are the words of Jeremiah son of Hilkiah, one of the priests from Anathoth, a
town in the land of Benjamin. 2 The LORD first gave messages to Jeremiah during
the thirteenth year of King Josiah's reign in Judah.* 3 He continued to give messages
throughout the reign of Josiah's son, King Jehoiakim, until the eleventh year of King
Zedekiah's reign in Judah. In August of that year,* the people of Jerusalem were taken
away as captives.

Jeremiah's Call and First Visions

4 The LORD gave me a message. He said, 5 "I knew you before I formed you in your
mother's womb. Before you were born I set you apart and appointed you as my
spokesman to the world."

6 "O Sovereign LORD," I said, "I can't speak for you! I'm too young!"

7 "Don't say that," the LORD replied, "for you must go wherever I send you and say
whatever I tell you. 8 And don't be afraid of the people, for I will be with you and take
care of you. I, the LORD, have spoken!"

9 Then the LORD touched my mouth and said, "See, I have put my words in your
mouth! 10 Today I appoint you to stand up against nations and kingdoms. You are to
uproot some and tear them down, to destroy and overthrow them. You are to build others
up and plant them."

11 Then the LORD said to me, "Look, Jeremiah! What do you see?"

And I replied, "I see a branch from an almond tree."

12 And the LORD said, "That's right, and it means that I am watching,* and I will surely
carry out my threats of punishment."

1:1 2 Chr 36:12, 21
1:2 1 Kgs 13:2; 2 Kgs 21:24
1:3 2 Kgs 23:34; Jer 25:1; 39:2
1:5 Ps 139:15-16; Isa 49:1, 5; Jer 25:15-26
1:6 Exod 4:10
1:7 Ezek 2:3-4
1:8 Jer 15:20; Ezek 2:6
1:9 Exod 4:11-16; Deut 18:18
1:10 Isa 44:26-28; Jer 24:6; 31:28; 2 Cor 10:4
1:11 Jer 24:3; Amos 7:8
1:12 Deut 32:35

1:2 The thirteenth year of Josiah's reign was 627 B.C. **1:3** Hebrew *In the fifth month,* of the Hebrew calendar. A number of events in Jeremiah can be cross-checked with dates in surviving Babylonian records and related accurately to our modern calendar. This month in the eleventh year of Zedekiah's reign occurred in August and September 586 B.C. Also see 52:12 and the note there. **1:12** The Hebrew word for "watching" sounds like the word for "almond tree."

1:1, 2 After King Solomon's death, the united kingdom of Israel had split into rival northern and southern kingdoms. The northern kingdom was called Israel; the southern, Judah. Jeremiah was from Anathoth, four miles north of Jerusalem in the southern kingdom. He lived and prophesied during the reigns of the last five kings of Judah. This was a chaotic time politically, morally, and spiritually. As Babylon, Egypt, and Assyria battled for world supremacy, Judah found itself caught in the middle of the triangle. Although Jeremiah prophesied for 40 years, he never saw his people heed his words and turn from their sins.

1:5 God knew you, as he knew Jeremiah, long before you were born or even conceived. He thought about you and planned for you. When you feel discouraged or inadequate, remember that God has always thought of you as valuable and that he has a purpose in mind for you.

1:5 Jeremiah was "appointed" by God as "spokesman to the world." God has a purpose for each Christian, but some people are appointed by God for specific kinds of work. Samson (Judges 13:3-5), David (1 Samuel 16:12, 13), John the Baptist (Luke 1:13-17), and Paul (Galatians 1:15, 16) were also called to do particular jobs for God. Whatever work you do should be done for the glory of God (Philippians 1:11). If God gives you a specific task, accept it cheerfully and do it with diligence. If God has not given you a specific call or assignment, then seek to fulfill the mission common to all believers—to love, obey, and serve God—until his guidance becomes more clear.

1:6-8 Often people struggle with new challenges because they lack self-confidence, feeling that they have inadequate ability, training, or experience. Jeremiah thought he was "too young" and inexperienced to be God's spokesman to the world. But God promised to be with him. We should not allow feelings of inadequacy to keep us from obeying God. He will *always* be with us. If God gives you a job to do, he will provide all you need to do it.

1:8 God promised to be with Jeremiah and take care of him, but not to keep trouble from coming. God did not insulate him from jailings, deportation, or insults. God does not keep us from encountering life's storms, but he will see us through them. In fact, God walks through these storms with us and rescues us.

1:10 God appointed Jeremiah to bring his word to "nations and kingdoms." Jeremiah's work was to warn not only the Jews but all the nations of the world about God's judgment for sin. Don't forget in reading the Old Testament that, while God was consistently working through the people of Judah and Israel, his plan was to communicate to every nation and person. We are included in Jeremiah's message of judgment and hope, and as believers we are to share God's desire to reach the whole world for him.

1:11-14 The vision of the branch of an almond tree revealed the beginning of God's judgment because the almond tree is among the first to blossom in the spring. God saw the sins of Judah and the nations, and he would carry out swift and certain judgment. The boiling pot tipping from the north and spilling over Judah pictured Babylon delivering God's scalding judgment against Jeremiah's people.

1:13 Ezek 11:3, 7 Zech 4:2
1:14 Isa 41:25 Jer 4:6; 10:22
1:15 Isa 22:7 Jer 9:11; 25:9
1:16 Isa 2:8; 37:19 Jer 7:9; 10:3-5; 19:4
1:17 Ezek 2:6; 3:16-18
1:19 Jer 1:8; 20:11

13 Then the LORD spoke to me again and asked, "What do you see now?"
And I replied, "I see a pot of boiling water, tipping from the north."
14 "Yes," the LORD said, "for terror from the north will boil out on the people of this
land. 15 Listen! I am calling the armies of the kingdoms of the north to come to Jerusalem.
They will set their thrones at the gates of the city. They will attack its walls and all the
other towns of Judah. 16 I will pronounce judgment on my people for all their evil—for
deserting me and worshiping other gods. Yes, they worship idols that they themselves
have made!
17 "Get up and get dressed. Go out, and tell them whatever I tell you to say. Do not be
afraid of them, or I will make you look foolish in front of them. 18 For see, today I have
made you immune to their attacks. You are strong like a fortified city that cannot be
captured, like an iron pillar or a bronze wall. None of the kings, officials, priests, or
people of Judah will be able to stand against you. 19 They will try, but they will fail. For
I am with you, and I will take care of you. I, the LORD, have spoken!"

2. Jeremiah condemns Judah for its sins

The LORD's Case against His People

2:2 Isa 58:1 Jer 11:6 Ezek 16:8
2:3 Exod 19:5-6 Deut 7:6; 14:2 Isa 41:11 Jer 30:16
2:5 2 Kgs 17:15 Jer 8:19 Mic 6:3
2:6 Deut 8:15; 32:10

2 The LORD gave me another message. He said, 2 "Go and shout in Jerusalem's streets:
'This is what the LORD says: I remember how eager you were to please me as a
young bride long ago, how you loved me and followed me even through the barren
wilderness. 3 In those days Israel was holy to the LORD, the first of my children.* All who
harmed my people were considered guilty, and disaster fell upon them. I, the LORD, have
spoken!'"
4 Listen to the word of the LORD, people of Jacob—all you families of Israel! 5 This is
what the LORD says: "What sin did your ancestors find in me that led them to stray so
far? They worshiped foolish idols, only to become foolish themselves. 6 They did not

2:3 Hebrew *the firstfruits of his harvest.*

JEREMIAH served as a prophet to Judah from 627 B.C. until the Exile in 586 B.C.

Climate of the times	Society was deteriorating economically, politically, spiritually. Wars and captivity dominated the world scene. God's word was deemed offensive.
Main message	Repentance from sin would postpone Judah's coming judgment at the hands of Babylon.
Importance of message	Repentance is one of the greatest needs in our immoral world. God's promises to the faithful shine brightly by bringing hope for tomorrow and strength for today.
Contemporary prophets	Habakkuk (612–588 B.C.), Zephaniah (640–621 B.C.)

1:14-19 The problems we face may not seem as ominous as Jeremiah's, but they are critical to us and may overwhelm us! God's promise to Jeremiah and to us is that nothing will defeat us completely; he will help us through the most agonizing problems. Face each day with the assurance that God will be with you and see you through.

1:16 The people of Judah sinned greatly by continuing to worship other gods. God had commanded them specifically against this (Exodus 20:3-6) because idolatry places trust in created things rather than the Creator. Although these people belonged to God, they chose to follow false gods. Many "gods" entice us to turn away from God. Material possessions, dreams for the future, approval of others, and vocational goals compete for our total commitment. Striving after these at the expense of our commitment to God puts our heart where Judah's was—and God severely punished Judah.

2:1–3:5 In this section, the marriage analogy sharply contrasts God's love for his people with their love for other gods and reveals Judah's faithlessness. Jeremiah condemned Judah (he sometimes called Judah "Jerusalem," the name of its capital city) for seeking security in worthless, changeable things rather than the unchangeable God. We may be tempted to seek security from possessions, people, or our own abilities, but these will fail us. There is no lasting security apart from the eternal God.

2:2 We appreciate a friend who remains true to his or her commitment, and we are disappointed with someone who fails to keep a promise. God was pleased when his people obeyed initially, but he became angry with them when they refused to keep their commitment. Temptations distract us from God. Think about your original commitment to obey God, and ask yourself if you are remaining truly devoted.

2:3 The firstfruits, or the first part, of the harvest were set aside for God (Deuteronomy 26:1-11). That's how Israel was dedicated to him in years gone by. Israel had been as eager to please God as if she were his young bride, a holy, devoted people. This contrasted greatly with the situation in Jeremiah's time.

2:4-8 The united nation of Israel included both the "people of Israel" and the "people of Jacob" (Judah). Jeremiah knew Israel's history well. The prophets recited history to the people for several reasons: (1) to remind them of God's faithfulness; (2) to make

ask, ‘Where is the LORD who brought us safely out of Egypt and led us through the barren wilderness—a land of deserts and pits, of drought and death, where no one lives or even travels?’

7“And when I brought you into a fruitful land to enjoy its bounty and goodness, you defiled my land and corrupted the inheritance I had promised you. 8The priests did not ask, ‘Where is the LORD?’ The judges ignored me, the rulers turned against me, and the prophets spoke in the name of Baal, wasting their time on nonsense. 9Therefore, I will bring my case against you and will keep on accusing you, even against your children’s children in the years to come. I, the LORD, have spoken!

10“Go west to the land of Cyprus*; go east to the land of Kedar. Think about what you see there. See if anyone has ever heard of anything as strange as this. 11Has any nation ever exchanged its gods for another god, even though its gods are nothing? Yet my people have exchanged their glorious God* for worthless idols! 12The heavens are shocked at such a thing and shrink back in horror and dismay, says the LORD. 13For my people have done two evil things: They have forsaken me—the fountain of living water. And they have dug for themselves cracked cisterns that can hold no water at all!

The Results of Israel’s Sin

14“Why has Israel become a nation of slaves? Why has she been carried away as plunder? 15Lions have roared against her. The land has been destroyed, and the cities are now in ruins. No one lives in them anymore. 16Egyptians, marching from their cities of Memphis* and Tahpanhes, have utterly destroyed Israel’s glory and power. 17And you have brought this on yourselves by rebelling against the LORD your God when he wanted to lead you and show you the way!

18“What have you gained by your alliances with Egypt and Assyria? What good to you are the waters of the Nile* and the Euphrates*? 19Your own wickedness will punish you. You will see what an evil, bitter thing it is to forsake the LORD your God, having no fear of him. I, the Lord, the LORD Almighty, have spoken! 20Long ago I broke your yoke and tore away the chains of your slavery, but still you would not obey me. On every hill and under every green tree, you have prostituted yourselves by bowing down to idols.

21“How could this happen? When I planted you, I chose a vine of the purest stock—the very best. How did you grow into this corrupt wild vine? 22No amount of soap or lye can make you clean. You are stained with guilt that cannot be washed away. I, the Sovereign LORD, have spoken!

2:7 Deut 8:7-9; 11:10-12 Jer 3:2; 16:18
2:8 Jer 10:21; 23:13 Hab 2:18 Mal 2:6-7
2:9 Ezek 20:35-36
2:10 Pss 106:20; 120:5 Isa 23:12; 37:19 Jer 49:28
2:13 Ps 36:9 Jer 17:13 John 4:14
2:16 Jer 44:1 Hos 9:6
2:17 Deut 32:10
2:18 Josh 13:3 Isa 30:2
2:19 Ps 36:1 Isa 3:9 Jer 3:8; 5:24 Hos 11:7 Amos 8:10
2:20 Lev 26:13 Deut 12:2 Isa 57:5 Jer 17:2; 32:6
2:21 Exod 15:17 Ps 80:8 Isa 5:2, 4
2:22 Jer 4:14

2:10 Hebrew *Kittim.* **2:11** Hebrew *their Glory.* **2:16** Hebrew *Noph.* **2:18a** Hebrew *of Shihor,* a branch of the Nile River. **2:18b** Hebrew *the river.*

---

sure the people wouldn’t forget (they didn’t have Bibles to read); (3) to emphasize God’s love for them; (4) to remind the people that there was a time when they *were* close to God. We should learn from history so we can build on the successes and avoid repeating the failures of others.

2:8 Baal was the chief male god of the Canaanite religion. “Images of Baal” (2:23) refers to the fact that Baal was worshiped in many centers in Canaanite practice. Baal was the god of fertility. Worship of Baal included animal sacrifice and sacred prostitution (male and female) in the high places. Jezebel, the wife of King Ahab, introduced Baal worship into the northern kingdom, and eventually it spread to Judah. The sexual orientation of this worship was a constant temptation to the Israelites, who were called to be holy.

2:10 God was saying that even pagan nations like Cyprus (in the west) and Kedar (the home of Arab tribes living in the desert east of Palestine) remained loyal to their national gods. But Israel had abandoned the one and only God for a completely worthless object of worship.

2:13 Who would set aside a fountain of living water for a cracked cistern, a pit that collected rainwater but could not hold it? God told the Israelites they were doing that very thing when they turned from him, the fountain of living water, to the worship of idols. Not only that, but the cisterns they chose were broken and empty. The people had built religious systems in which to store truth, but those systems were worthless. Why should we cling to the broken promises of unstable “cisterns” (money, power, religious systems, or whatever transitory thing we are putting in place of God) when God promises to constantly refresh us with living water (John 4:10)?

2:16, 17 Memphis was near modern Cairo’s present location in lower Egypt, and Tahpanhes was in northeastern Egypt. Jeremiah could be speaking of Pharaoh Shishak’s previous invasion of Judah in 926 B.C. (1 Kings 14:25), or he may have been predicting Pharaoh Neco’s invasion in 609 B.C. when King Josiah of Judah would be killed (2 Kings 23:29, 30). Jeremiah’s point is that the people brought this on themselves by rebelling against God.

2:22 The stain of sin is more than skin-deep. Israel had stains that could not be washed out, even with the strongest cleansers. Spiritual cleansing must reach deep into the heart—and this is a job that God alone can do. We cannot ignore the effects of sin and hope they will go away. Your sin has caused a deep stain that only God can remove if you are willing to let him cleanse you (Isaiah 1:18; Ezekiel 36:25).

Israel, an Unfaithful Wife

2:23 Prov 30:12; Jer 7:31; 9:14
2:25 Deut 32:16; Jer 14:10; 18:12
2:26 Jer 48:27
2:27 Isa 26:16; Jer 18:17

23 "You say, 'That's not true! We haven't worshiped the images of Baal!' But how can
you say that? Go and look in any valley in the land! Face the awful sins you have done.
You are like a restless female camel, desperate for a male! 24 You are like a wild donkey,
sniffing the wind at mating time. Who can restrain your lust? Those who desire you do
not even need to search, for you come running to them! 25 Why do you refuse to turn
from all this running after other gods? But you say, 'Don't waste your breath. I have
fallen in love with these foreign gods, and I can't stop loving them now!'
26 "Like a thief, Israel feels shame only when she gets caught. Kings, officials, priests,
and prophets—all are alike in this. 27 To an image carved from a piece of wood they say,
'You are my father.' To an idol chiseled out of stone they say, 'You are my mother.' They

JEREMIAH

Endurance is not a common quality. Many people lack the long-term commitment, caring, and willingness that are vital to sticking with a task against all odds. But Jeremiah was a prophet who endured.

Jeremiah's call by God teaches how intimately God knows us. He valued us before anyone else knew we would exist. He cared for us while we were in our mother's womb. He planned our life while our body was still being formed. He values us more highly than we value ourselves.

Jeremiah had to depend on God's love as he developed endurance. His audiences were usually antagonistic or apathetic to his messages. He was ignored; his life was often threatened. He saw both the excitement of a spiritual awakening and the sorrow of a national return to idolatry. With the exception of the good king Josiah, Jeremiah watched king after king ignore his warnings and lead the people away from God. He saw fellow prophets murdered. He himself was severely persecuted. Finally, he watched Judah's defeat at the hands of the Babylonians.

Jeremiah responded to all this with God's message and human tears. He felt firsthand God's love for his people and the people's rejection of that love. But even when he was angry with God and tempted to give up, Jeremiah knew he had to keep going. God had called him to endure. He expressed intense feelings but saw beyond the feelings to the God who was soon to execute justice but who afterward would show mercy.

It may be easy for us to identify with Jeremiah's frustrations and discouragement, but we need to realize that this prophet's life is also an encouragement to faithfulness.

Strengths and accomplishments
- Wrote two Old Testament books, Jeremiah and Lamentations
- Ministered during the reigns of the last five kings of Judah
- Was a catalyst for the great spiritual reformation under King Josiah
- Acted as God's faithful messenger in spite of many attempts on his life
- Was so deeply sorrowful for the fallen condition of Judah that he earned the title "Weeping Prophet"

Lessons from his life
- The majority opinion is not necessarily God's will
- Although punishment for sin is severe, there is hope in God's mercy
- God will not accept empty or insincere worship
- Serving God does not guarantee earthly security

Vital statistics
- Where: Anathoth
- Occupation: Prophet
- Relative: Father: Hilkiah
- Contemporaries: Josiah, Jehoahaz, Jehoiakim, Jehoiachin, Zedekiah, Baruch

Key verses
" 'O Sovereign LORD,' I said, 'I can't speak for you! I'm too young!' 'Don't say that,' the LORD replied, 'for you must go wherever I send you and say whatever I tell you. And don't be afraid of the people, for I will be with you and take care of you. I, the LORD, have spoken!' " (Jeremiah 1:6-8).

Jeremiah's story is told in the book of Jeremiah. He is also mentioned in Ezra 1:1; Daniel 9:2; Matthew 2:17; 16:14; 27:9. See also 2 Chronicles 34—35 for the story of the spiritual revival under Josiah.

2:23-27 The people are compared to animals who search for mates in mating season. Unrestrained, they rush for power, money, alliances with foreign powers, and other gods. The idols did not seek the people; the people sought the idols and ran wildly after them. Then they became so comfortable in their sin that they could not think of giving it up. Their only shame was in getting caught. If we desire something so much that we'll do anything to get it, it is a sign that we are addicted to it and out of tune with God.

turn their backs on me, but in times of trouble they cry out for me to save them! 28 Why
don't you call on these gods you have made? When danger comes, let them save you if
they can! For you have as many gods as there are cities and towns in Judah. 29 Why do
you accuse me of doing wrong? You are the ones who have rebelled, says the LORD. 30 I
have punished your children, but it did them no good. They still refuse to obey. You
yourselves have killed your prophets as a lion kills its prey.
31 "O my people, listen to the words of the LORD! Have I been like a desert to Israel?
Have I been to them a land of darkness? Why then do my people say, 'At last we are free
from God! We won't have anything to do with him anymore!' 32 Does a young woman
forget her jewelry? Does a bride hide her wedding dress? No! Yet for years on end my
people have forgotten me.
33 "How you plot and scheme to win your lovers. The most experienced prostitute
could learn from you! 34 Your clothing is stained with the blood of the innocent and the
poor. You killed them even though they didn't break into your houses! 35 And yet you
say, 'I haven't done anything wrong. Surely he isn't angry with me!' Now I will punish
you severely because you claim you have not sinned.
36 "First here, then there—you flit from one ally to another asking for help. But your
new friends in Egypt will let you down, just as Assyria did before. 37 In despair, you will
be led into exile with your hands on your heads, for the LORD has rejected the nations
you trust. You will not succeed despite their help.

3 "If a man divorces a woman and she marries someone else, he is not to take her back
again, for that would surely corrupt the land. But you have prostituted yourself with
many lovers, says the LORD. Yet I am still calling you to come back to me.
2 "Look all around you. Is there anywhere in the entire land where you have not been
defiled by your adulteries? You sit like a prostitute beside the road waiting for a client.
You sit alone like a nomad in the desert. You have polluted the land with your prostitution
and wickedness. 3 That is why even the spring rains have failed. For you are a prostitute
and are completely unashamed. 4 Yet you say to me, 'Father, you have been my guide
since the days of my youth. 5 Surely you won't be angry about such a little thing! Surely
you can forget it!' So you talk, and keep right on doing all the evil you can."

Judah Follows Israel's Example

6 During the reign of King Josiah, the LORD said to me, "Have you seen what fickle Israel
does? Like a wife who commits adultery, Israel has worshiped other gods on every hill and

2:28 Deut 32:37; 2 Kgs 17:30-31; Isa 45:20; Jer 11:12-13
2:29 Dan 9:11
2:30 Neh 9:26; Isa 1:5
2:31 Deut 32:15; Isa 45:19
2:32 Isa 17:10; Jer 3:21; Hos 8:14
2:34 2 Kgs 21:16; Jer 7:6; 19:4
2:35 Jer 25:31; 1 Jn 1:8, 10
2:36 2 Chr 28:16, 20-21; Hos 12:1; 1 Jn 1:8, 10
2:37 Jer 37:7-10
3:1 Deut 24:4; Jer 4:1; Ezek 16:26, 28-29; Zech 1:3
3:2 Deut 12:2; Jer 2:7, 20; Ezek 16:25
3:3 Lev 26:19; Jer 6:15; 14:3-6
3:4 Ps 71:17
3:6 Jer 17:2; Ezek 23:4-10

2:30 Being a prophet in Jeremiah's day was risky business. Prophets had to criticize the policies of evil kings, and this made them appear to be traitors. The kings hated the prophets for standing against their policies, and the people often hated the prophets for preaching against their idolatrous life-styles (see Acts 7:52).

2:31, 32 Forgetting can be dangerous, whether it is intentional or an oversight. Israel forgot God by focusing its affections on the allurements of the world. The more we focus on the pleasures of the world, the easier it becomes to forget God's care, his love, his dependability, his guidance, and most of all, God himself. What pleases you most? Have you been forgetting God lately?

2:36 God is not against alliances or working partnerships, but he is against people trusting others for the help that should come from him. This was the problem in Jeremiah's time. After the days of David and Solomon, Israel fell apart because the leaders turned to other nations and gods instead of the true God. They played power politics, thinking that their strong neighbors could protect them. But Judah would soon learn that its alliance with Egypt would be just as disappointing as its former alliance with Assyria (2 Kings 16:8, 9; Isaiah 7:13-25).

3:1 This law, found in Deuteronomy 24:1-4, says that a divorced woman who remarries can never be reunited with her first husband. Judah "divorced" God and "married" other gods. God had every right to permanently disown his wayward people, but in his mercy he was willing to take them back again.

3:2 "Like a nomad in the desert" means that Judah ran to idolatry as an Arab thief might hide and wait to plunder a passing caravan. It was a national preoccupation.

3:4, 5 In spite of their great sin, the people of Israel continued to talk like they were God's children. The only way they could do this was to minimize their sin. When we know we've done something wrong, we want to downplay the error and relieve some of the guilt we feel. As we minimize our sinfulness, we naturally shy away from making changes, and so we keep on sinning. But if we view every wrong attitude and action as a serious offense against God, we will begin to understand what living for God is all about. Is there any sin in your life that you've written off as too small to worry about? God says that we must confess and turn away from *every* sin.

3:6–6:30 The northern kingdom, Israel, had fallen to Assyria, and its people had been taken into captivity. The tragic lesson of their fall should have caused the southern kingdom, Judah, to return to God, but Judah paid no attention. Jeremiah urged Judah to return to God to avoid certain disaster. This message came between 627 and 621 B.C., during Josiah's reign. Although Josiah obeyed God's commands, his example apparently did not penetrate the hearts of the people. If the people refused to repent, God said he would destroy the nation because of the evils of Josiah's grandfather, King Manasseh (2 Kings 23:25-27).

under every green tree. 7 I thought that after she had done all this she would return to me.
But she did not come back. And though her faithless sister Judah saw this, 8 she paid no
attention. She saw that I had divorced faithless Israel and sent her away. But now Judah,
too, has left me and given herself to prostitution. 9 Israel treated it all so lightly—she thought
nothing of committing adultery by worshiping idols made of wood and stone. So now the
land has been greatly defiled. 10 But in spite of all this, her faithless sister Judah has never
sincerely returned to me. She has only pretended to be sorry," says the LORD.

Hope for Wayward Israel

11 Then the LORD said to me, "Even faithless Israel is less guilty than treacherous Judah!
12 Therefore, go and say these words to Israel,* 'This is what the LORD says: O Israel,
my faithless people, come home to me again, for I am merciful. I will not be angry with
you forever. 13 Only acknowledge your guilt. Admit that you rebelled against the LORD
your God and committed adultery against him by worshiping idols under every green
tree. Confess that you refused to follow me. I, the LORD, have spoken!'"

14 "Return home, you wayward children," says the LORD, "for I am your husband. I
will bring you again to the land of Israel*—one from here and two from there, from
wherever you are scattered. 15 And I will give you leaders after my own heart, who will
guide you with knowledge and understanding.

16 "And when your land is once more filled with people," says the LORD, "you will no
longer wish for 'the good old days' when you possessed the Ark of the LORD's covenant.
Those days will not be missed or even thought about, and there will be no need to rebuild
the Ark. 17 In that day Jerusalem will be known as The Throne of the LORD. All nations
will come there to honor the LORD. They will no longer stubbornly follow their own evil
desires. 18 In those days the people of Judah and Israel will return together from exile in
the north. They will return to the land I gave their ancestors as an inheritance forever.

3:7 Ezek 16:47
3:8 Isa 50:1; Ezek 16:46-47; 23:11
3:9 Isa 57:6; Jer 2:7, 27
3:10 Jer 12:2
3:12 Ps 86:15; Jer 31:20; 33:26
3:13 Deut 12:2; 30:1-3; Jer 14:20
3:14 Jer 50:4-5; Hos 2:19
3:15 Jer 23:4; Acts 20:28
3:16 Isa 65:17
3:17 Jer 12:15-16; 16:19; 17:12; Ezek 43:7
3:18 Isa 11:13; 60:9; Jer 16:14-15; 31:8; 50:4-5; Hos 1:11; Amos 9:15

3:12 Hebrew *toward the north.* **3:14** Hebrew *to Zion.*

THE KINGS OF JEREMIAH'S LIFETIME

King	*Story of his reign*	*Dates of his reign*	*Character of reign*	*Jeremiah's message to the king*
Josiah	2 Kings 22:1—23:30	640–609 B.C.	Mostly good	3:6–25
Jehoahaz	2 Kings 23:31–33	609 B.C.	Evil	22:11–17
Jehoiakim	2 Kings 23:34—24:7	609–598 B.C.	Evil	22:18–23; 25:1–38; 26:1–24; 27:1–11; 35:1–19; 36:1–32
Jehoiachin	2 Kings 24:8–17	598–597 B.C.	Evil	13:18–27; 22:24–30
Zedekiah	2 Kings 24:18—25:26	597–586 B.C.	Evil	21:1–14; 24:8–10; 27:12–22; 32:1–5; 34:1–22; 37:1–21; 38:1–28; 51:59–64

3:11-13 Israel was not even trying to look as if it were obeying God, but Judah maintained the appearance of faith without a true heart. Believing the right doctrines without heartfelt commitment is like offering sacrifices without true repentance. Judah's false repentance brought Jeremiah's words of condemnation. To live without faith is hopeless; to express sorrow without change is hypocritical. Being sorry for sin is not enough. Repentance demands a change of mind and heart that results in changed behavior.

3:12-18 The northern kingdom, Israel, was in captivity, being punished for its sins. The people of Judah undoubtedly looked down on these northern neighbors for their blatant heresy and degraded morals. Even so, Jeremiah promised the remnant of Israel God's blessings if they would turn to him. Judah, still secure in its own mind, should have turned to God after seeing the destruction of Israel. But the people of Judah refused, so Jeremiah startled them by telling about God's promise to Israel's remnant if they would repent.

3:15 God promised to give his people leaders who would follow him, filled with knowledge (wisdom) and understanding. God saw Israel's lack of direction, so he promised to provide the right kind of leadership. We look to and trust our leaders for guidance and direction. But if they do not follow God, they will lead us astray. Pray for God-honoring leaders in our nations, communities, and churches—those who will be good examples and bring us God's wisdom.

3:16, 17 In the days of David and Solomon's reign over a united Israel, the people had a beautiful Temple, where they worshiped God. The Temple housed the Ark of the Covenant, the symbol of God's presence with the people. The Ark held the tablets of the Ten Commandments (see Exodus 25:10-22). Those days with the Ark wouldn't be missed in the future Kingdom because God's presence by the Holy Spirit would be there personally among his people.

19“I thought to myself, ‘I would love to treat you as my own children!’ I wanted
nothing more than to give you this beautiful land—the finest inheritance in the world. I
looked forward to your calling me ‘Father,’ and I thought you would never turn away
from me again. 20But you have betrayed me, you people of Israel! You have been like a
faithless wife who leaves her husband,” says the LORD.

21Voices are heard high on the windswept mountains, the weeping and pleading of
Israel’s people. For they have forgotten the LORD their God and wandered far from his
ways.

22“My wayward children,” says the LORD, “come back to me, and I will heal your
wayward hearts.”

“Yes, we will come,” the people reply, “for you are the LORD our God. 23Our worship
of idols and our religious orgies on the hills and mountains are completely false. Only in
the LORD our God will Israel ever find salvation. 24From childhood we have watched as
everything our ancestors worked for—their flocks and herds, their sons and daughters—
was squandered on a delusion. 25Let us now lie down in shame and dishonor, for we and
our ancestors have always sinned against the LORD our God. We have never obeyed
him.”

4 “O Israel, come back to me,” says the LORD. “If you will throw away your detestable
idols and go astray no more, 2and if you will swear by my name alone, and begin to
live good, honest lives and uphold justice, then you will be a blessing to the nations of
the world, and all people will come and praise my name.”

Coming Judgment against Judah

3This is what the LORD says to the people of Judah and Jerusalem: “Plow up the hard
ground of your hearts! Do not waste your good seed among thorns. 4Cleanse your minds
and hearts before the LORD, or my anger will burn like an unquenchable fire because of
all your sins.

5“Shout to Jerusalem and to all Judah! Tell them to sound the alarm throughout the land:
‘Run for your lives! Flee to the fortified cities!’ 6Send a signal toward Jerusalem*: ‘Flee
now! Do not delay!’ For I am bringing terrible destruction upon you from the north.”

7A lion stalks from its den, a destroyer of nations. And it is headed for your land! Your
towns will lie in ruins, empty of people. 8So put on clothes of mourning and weep with
broken hearts, for the fierce anger of the LORD is still upon us.

9“In that day,” says the LORD, “the king and the officials will tremble in fear. The
priests and the prophets will be struck with horror.”

10Then I said, “O Sovereign LORD, the people have been deceived by what you said,
for you promised peace for Jerusalem. Yet the sword is even now poised to strike them
dead!”

11The time is coming when the LORD will say to the people of Jerusalem, “A burning
wind is blowing in from the desert. It is not a gentle breeze useful for winnowing grain.
12It is a roaring blast sent by me! Now I will pronounce your destruction!”

13Our enemy rushes down on us like a storm wind! His chariots are like whirlwinds;
his horses are swifter than eagles. How terrible it will be! Our destruction is sure!

4:6 Hebrew *Zion.*

3:19 Ps 16:6; Isa 63:16
3:20 Isa 48:8
3:21 Isa 15:2; Jer 2:32
3:22 Hos 6:1; 14:4
3:23 Pss 3:8; 121:1-2; Jer 17:14
3:25 Ezra 9:7; Jer 22:21
4:1 Joel 2:12
4:2 Gen 22:18; Deut 10:20; Gal 3:8
4:3 Hos 10:12; Matt 13:7, 22
4:4 Deut 10:16; Isa 30:27; Jer 9:25-26; 21:12; Mark 9:43, 48; Rom 2:28-29
4:5 Josh 10:20; Hos 8:1
4:7 Isa 1:7; 6:11; Jer 2:15; 5:6; 25:9, 38
4:8 Isa 5:25; 10:4; Jer 30:24
4:10 2 Thes 2:11; 14:13
4:11 Jer 51:1; Ezek 17:10; Hos 13:15
4:13 Deut 28:49; Isa 66:15; Lam 4:19

3:22-25 Jeremiah predicted a day when the nation would be reunited, true worship would be reinstated, and sin would be seen for what it is. Our world glorifies the thrill that comes from wealth, winning, and sexual pleasure, and it ignores the sin that is so often associated with these thrills. It is sad that so few see sin as it really is—a deception. Most people can’t see this until they are destroyed by the sin they pursue. The advantage of believing God’s Word is that we don’t have to learn by hard experience the destructive results of sin.

4:3 Jeremiah told the people to plow up the hardness of their hearts as a plow breaks up unplowed ground—soil that has not been tilled for a season. Good kings like Josiah had tried to turn the people back to God, but the people had continued to worship their idols in secret. Their hearts had become hardened to God’s will. Jeremiah said the people needed to remove the sin that hardened their hearts before the good seed of God’s commands could take root. Likewise we must remove our heart-hardening sin if we expect God’s Word to take root and grow in our life.

4:6, 7 The disaster from the north would come from Babylon when Nabopolassar and Nebuchadnezzar II would attack (see 2 Chronicles 36).

4:10 Jeremiah, deeply moved by God’s words, expressed his sorrow and confusion to God. Jeremiah was intercessor for the people. These people had false expectations because of the past promises of blessings, their blindness to their own sin, and the false prophets who kept telling them that all was well.

4:14 Isa 1:16; Jer 13:27; Jas 4:8
4:15 Jer 6:19
4:16 Jer 5:15; Ezek 21:22
4:17 2 Kgs 25:1; Jer 5:23
4:19 Isa 21:3; 22:4; Hab 3:16
4:20 Jer 10:20; Ezek 7:26
4:22 Jer 5:21; 10:8; 13:23; Rom 16:19
4:23 Isa 24:19
4:24 Isa 5:25; Ezek 38:20
4:25 Jer 9:10; 12:4; Zeph 1:3
4:28 Num 23:19; Isa 5:30; 50:3; Jer 23:20; 30:24; Hos 4:3; Joel 2:30-31
4:30 2 Kgs 9:30; Jer 22:20, 22; Ezek 23:9-10, 22
4:31 Isa 1:15; 42:14; Jer 13:21; Lam 1:17
5:1 Gen 18:26, 32; 2 Chr 16:9
5:2 Titus 1:16

14 O Jerusalem, cleanse your hearts that you may be saved. How long will you harbor
your evil thoughts? 15 From Dan and the hill country of Ephraim, your destruction has
been announced.
16 "Warn the surrounding nations and announce to Jerusalem: 'The enemy is coming
from a distant land, raising a battle cry against the towns of Judah. 17 They surround
Jerusalem like watchmen surrounding a field, for my people have rebelled against me,'"
says the LORD. 18 "Your own actions have brought this upon you. This punishment is a
bitter dose of your own medicine. It has pierced you to the heart!"

Jeremiah Weeps for His People

19 My heart, my heart—I writhe in pain! My heart pounds within me! I cannot be still.
For I have heard the blast of enemy trumpets and the roar of their battle cries. 20 Waves
of destruction roll over the land, until it lies in complete desolation. Suddenly, every tent
is destroyed; in a moment, every shelter is crushed. 21 How long must this go on? How
long must I be surrounded by war and death?
22 "My people are foolish and do not know me," says the LORD. "They are senseless
children who have no understanding. They are clever enough at doing wrong, but they
have no talent at all for doing right!"

Jeremiah's Vision of Coming Disaster

23 I looked at the earth, and it was empty and formless. I looked at the heavens, and there
was no light. 24 I looked at the mountains and hills, and they trembled and shook. 25 I
looked, and all the people were gone. All the birds of the sky had flown away. 26 I looked,
and the fertile fields had become a wilderness. The cities lay in ruins, crushed by the
LORD's fierce anger.
27 This is what the LORD says: "The whole land will be ruined, but I will not destroy
it completely. 28 The earth will mourn, the heavens will be draped in black, because of
my decree against my people. I have made up my mind and will not change it."
29 At the noise of marching armies, the people flee in terror from the cities. They hide
in the bushes and run for the mountains. All the cities have been abandoned—not a
person remains! 30 What are you doing, you who have been plundered? Why do you dress
up in your most beautiful clothing and jewelry? Why do you brighten your eyes with
mascara? It will do you no good! Your allies despise you and will kill you.
31 I hear a great cry, like that of a woman giving birth to her first child. It is the cry
of Jerusalem's people* gasping for breath, pleading for help, prostrate before their
murderers.

The Sins of Judah

5 "Run up and down every street in Jerusalem," says the LORD. "Look high and low;
search throughout the city! If you can find even one person who is just and honest,
I will not destroy the city. 2 Even when they are under oath, saying, 'As surely as the
LORD lives,' they all tell lies!"

4:31 Hebrew *the daughter of Zion.*

4:15 Disaster was announced first from Dan and then on to the hills of Ephraim because Dan was located at the northern border of Israel. Thus, the Danites would be the first to see the approaching armies as they invaded from the north. No one would be able to stop the armies because they would be coming as punishment for the people's sin.

4:19-31 Jeremiah was anguished by the sure devastation of the coming judgment. This judgment would continue until the people turned from their sin and listened to God. Although this prophecy refers to the future destruction by Babylon, it could also describe the judgment of all sinners at the end of the world.

4:22 Judah was clever at doing evil but did not know how to do what was right. Right living is more than simply avoiding sin. It requires decision and discipline. We must develop skills in right living because our behavior attracts attention to our God. We should pursue excellence in Christian living with as much effort as we pursue excellence at work.

4:27 God warned that destruction was certain, but he promised that the faithful remnant would be spared. God is committed to preserving those who are faithful to him.

5:1 Jerusalem was the capital city and center of worship for Judah. God was willing to spare the city if only one person who was just and honest could be found (he made a similar statement about Sodom; see Genesis 18:32). Think how significant your testimony may be in your city or community. You may represent the only witness for God to many people. Are you faithful to that opportunity?

3LORD, you are searching for honesty. You struck your people, but they paid no
attention. You crushed them, but they refused to turn from sin. They are determined, with
faces set like stone; they have refused to repent.
4Then I said, "But what can we expect from the poor and ignorant? They don't know
the ways of the LORD. They don't understand what God expects of them. 5I will go and
speak to their leaders. Surely they will know the LORD's ways and what God requires of
them." But the leaders, too, had utterly rejected their God. 6So now a lion from the forest
will attack them; a wolf from the desert will pounce on them. A leopard will lurk near
their towns, tearing apart any who dare to venture out. For their rebellion is great, and
their sins are many.
7"How can I pardon you? For even your children have turned from me. They have
sworn by gods that are not gods at all! I fed my people until they were fully satisfied.
But they thanked me by committing adultery and lining up at the city's brothels. 8They
are well-fed, lusty stallions, each neighing for his neighbor's wife. 9Should I not punish
them for this?" asks the LORD. "Should I not avenge myself against a nation such as this?
10"Go down the rows of the vineyards and destroy them, but leave a scattered few
alive. Strip the branches from the vine, for they do not belong to the LORD. 11The people
of Israel and Judah are full of treachery against me," says the LORD. 12"They have lied
about the LORD and have said, 'He won't bother us! No disasters will come upon us!
There will be no war or famine! 13God's prophets are windbags full of words with no
divine authority. Their predictions of disaster will fall on themselves!'"
14Therefore, this is what the LORD God Almighty says: "Because the people are
talking like this, I will give you messages that will burn them up as if they were kindling
wood. 15O Israel, I will bring a distant nation against you," says the LORD. "It is a mighty
nation, an ancient nation, a people whose language you do not know, whose speech you
cannot understand. 16Their weapons are deadly; their warriors are mighty. 17They will
eat your harvests and your children's bread, your flocks of sheep and your herds of cattle.
Yes, they will eat your grapes and figs. And they will destroy your fortified cities, which
you think are so safe.
18"Yet even in those days I will not blot you out completely," says the LORD. 19"And
when your people ask, 'Why is the LORD our God doing this to us?' you must reply, 'You
rejected him and gave yourselves to foreign gods in your own land. Now you will serve
foreigners in a land that is not your own.'

A Warning for God's People

20"Make this announcement to Israel* and to Judah: 21Listen, you foolish and senseless
people—who have eyes but do not see, who have ears but do not hear. 22Do you have
no respect for me? Why do you not tremble in my presence? I, the LORD, am the one who
defines the ocean's sandy shoreline, an everlasting boundary that the waters cannot
cross. The waves may toss and roar, but they can never pass the bounds I set.

5:3 Jer 7:26, 28; 8:5; 19:15; Ezek 3:8; Zeph 3:2
5:4 Isa 27:11; Jer 4:22; Hos 4:6
5:5 Jer 2:20; Mic 3:1
5:6 Jer 30:14-15; Hos 13:7; Hab 1:8
5:7 Deut 32:21; Josh 23:7; Jer 2:11; Zeph 1:5; Gal 4:8
5:8 Jer 13:27; 29:23; Ezek 22:11
5:10 Jer 4:27
5:12 2 Chr 36:16; Jer 43:1-4
5:13 Jer 14:13, 15
5:15 Deut 28:49; Isa 5:26; 28:11
5:17 Lev 26:16; Deut 28:31, 33; Jer 8:16; Hos 8:14
5:19 Deut 28:48; 29:24-26; 1 Kgs 9:8-9; Jer 16:10-13
5:21 Matt 13:14; †Mark 8:18
5:22 Deut 28:58; Job 38:8-11

5:20 Hebrew *to the house of Jacob.*

5:3 Nothing but truth is acceptable to God. When we pray, sing, speak, or serve, nothing closes the door of God's acceptance more than hypocrisy, lying, or pretense. God sees through us and refuses to listen. To be close to God, be honest with him.

5:4, 5 Even the leaders who knew God's laws and understood his words of judgment had rejected him. They were supposed to teach and guide the people, but instead they led them into sin. Jeremiah observed the poor and ignorant—those who were uninformed of God's ways—and realized they were not learning God's laws from their leaders. Thus, God's search in Jerusalem was complete. There were no true followers in any level of society.

5:7 God held these people responsible for the sins of their children because the children had followed their parents' example. The sin of leading others, especially our children, astray by our example is one for which God will hold us accountable.

5:15 Babylon was indeed an ancient nation. The old Babylonian Empire had lasted from about 1900 to 1550 B.C., and earlier kingdoms had been on her soil as early as 3000 B.C. Babylon in Jeremiah's day would shortly rebel against Assyrian domination, form its own army, conquer Assyria, and become the next dominant world power.

5:21 Have you ever spoken to someone, only to realize that the person didn't hear a word you were saying? Jeremiah told the people that their eyes and ears did them no good because they refused to see or hear God's message. The people of Judah and Israel were foolishly deaf when God promised blessings for obedience and destruction for disobedience. When God speaks through his Word or his messengers, we harm ourselves if we fail to listen. God's message will never change us unless we heed it.

5:22-24 What is your attitude when you come into God's presence? We should come with respect and trembling because God sets the boundaries of the roaring seas and sends the rain, assuring us of plentiful harvests. God had to strip away all the benefits that Judah and Israel had grown to respect more than him, with the hope that the people would turn back to God. Don't wait until God removes your cherished resources before committing yourself to him as you should.

23“But my people have stubborn and rebellious hearts. They have turned against me
and have chosen to practice idolatry. 24They do not say from the heart, ‘Let us live in
awe of the LORD our God, for he gives us rain each spring and fall, assuring us of
plentiful harvests.’ 25Your wickedness has deprived you of these wonderful blessings.
Your sin has robbed you of all these good things.
26“Among my people are wicked men who lie in wait for victims like a hunter hiding
in a blind. They are continually setting traps for other people. 27Like a cage filled with
birds, their homes are filled with evil plots. And the result? Now they are great and rich.
28They are well fed and well groomed, and there is no limit to their wicked deeds. They
refuse justice to orphans and deny the rights of the poor. 29Should I not punish them for
this?” asks the LORD. “Should I not avenge myself against a nation such as this?
30“A horrible and shocking thing has happened in this land—31the prophets give false
prophecies, and the priests rule with an iron hand. And worse yet, my people like it that
way! But what will you do when the end comes?

Jerusalem’s Last Warning

6 “Run for your lives, you people of Benjamin! Flee from Jerusalem! Sound the alarm
in Tekoa! Send up a signal at Beth-hakkerem! Warn everyone that a powerful army
is coming from the north to destroy this nation. 2O Jerusalem,* you are my beautiful and
delicate daughter—but I will destroy you! 3Enemy shepherds will surround you. They
will set up camp around the city and divide your pastures for their flocks. 4They shout,
‘Prepare for battle and attack at noon! But now the day is fading, and the evening
shadows are falling. 5So let us attack by night and destroy her palaces!’”
6This is what the LORD Almighty says: “Cut down the trees for battering rams. Build
ramps against the walls of Jerusalem. This is the city to be punished, for she is wicked
through and through. 7She spouts evil like a fountain! Her streets echo with the sounds
of violence and destruction. Her sickness and sores are ever before me. 8This is your last
warning, Jerusalem! If you do not listen, I will empty the land.”
9This is what the LORD Almighty says: “Disaster will fall upon you. Even the few who
remain in Israel will be gleaned again, as when a harvester checks each vine a second
time to pick the grapes that were missed.”

Israel’s Constant Rebellion

10To whom can I give warning? Who will listen when I speak? Their ears are closed, and
they cannot hear. They scorn the word of the LORD. They don’t want to listen at all. 11So
now I am filled with the LORD’s fury. Yes, I am weary of holding it in!
“I will pour out my fury over Jerusalem, even on children playing in the streets, on
gatherings of young men, and on husbands and wives and grandparents. 12Their homes
will be turned over to their enemies, and so will their fields and their wives. For I will
punish the people of this land,” says the LORD.
13“From the least to the greatest, they trick others to get what does not belong to them.
Yes, even my prophets and priests are like that! 14They offer superficial treatments for
my people’s mortal wound. They give assurances of peace when all is war. 15Are they
ashamed when they do these disgusting things? No, not at all—they don’t even blush!

5:24 Gen 8:22; Ps 147:8; Joel 2:23; Matt 5:45
5:26 Ps 10:9; Hab 1:15
5:28 Deut 32:15; Isa 1:23; Zech 7:10
5:30 Jer 23:14; Hos 6:10
5:31 Jer 14:14; Ezek 13:6; Mic 2:11
6:1 Neh 3:14; Jer 1:14; 4:6
6:2 Deut 28:56
6:3 2 Kgs 25:1; Jer 4:17; 12:10; Luke 19:43
6:5 Isa 32:14
6:6 Deut 20:19-20; Jer 22:17; 32:24
6:7 Jer 20:8; 30:12-13; Ezek 7:11, 23; Jas 3:10-12
6:9 Jer 8:3; 16:16; 49:9; Obad 1:5-6
6:10 Jer 7:26; 20:8; Acts 7:51
6:11 Job 32:18-19
6:12 Deut 28:30; Jer 8:10; 15:6
6:13 Isa 56:11; 57:17; Jer 22:17; Mic 3:5, 11
6:14 Jer 8:11-12; Ezek 13:10
6:15 Jer 3:3; 8:12

6:2 Hebrew *Zion.*

5:28, 29 People and nations who please God treat the fatherless (orphans) justly and care for the poor. Wicked men in Israel treated the defenseless unjustly, which displeased God greatly. Some defenseless people—orphans, the poor, the homeless, and the lonely—are within your reach. What action can you take to help at least one of them?

6:1 The Lord warned Jeremiah’s own tribe of Benjamin to flee, not to the security of the great walled city of Jerusalem because it would be under siege, but toward Tekoa, a town about 12 miles south of Jerusalem. The warning smoke signal was lit at Beth-hakkerem, halfway between Jerusalem and Bethlehem.

6:3 The shepherds were the leaders of Babylon’s armies, and their flocks were their troops.

6:9 The “few who remain in Israel” is not to be confused with the righteous remnant. This remnant refers to those left after the first wave of destruction. Like a grape gatherer, Babylon wouldn’t be satisfied until every person was taken. Babylonians invaded Judah three times until they destroyed the nation and its Temple completely (2 Kings 24–25).

6:10 The people became angry and closed their ears. They wanted no part of God’s commands because living for God did not appear very exciting. As in Jeremiah’s day, people today dislike God’s demand for disciplined living. As unsettling as people’s responses might be, we must continue to share God’s Word. Our responsibility is to present God’s Word; their responsibility is to accept it. We must not let what people want to hear determine what we say.

Therefore, they will lie among the slaughtered. They will be humbled beneath my
punishing anger," says the LORD.

Israel Rejects the LORD's Way

16 So now the LORD says, "Stop right where you are! Look for the old, godly way, and
walk in it. Travel its path, and you will find rest for your souls. But you reply, 'No, that's
not the road we want!' 17 I set watchmen over you who said, 'Listen for the sound of the
trumpet!' But you replied, 'No! We won't pay attention!'
18 "Therefore, listen to this, all you nations. Take note of my people's condition.
19 Listen, all the earth! I will bring disaster upon my people. It is the fruit of their own
sin because they refuse to listen to me. They have rejected all my instructions. 20 There
is no use now in offering me sweet incense from Sheba. Keep your expensive perfumes!
I cannot accept your burnt offerings. Your sacrifices have no sweet fragrance for me."
21 Therefore, this is what the LORD says: "I will put obstacles in my people's path.
Fathers and sons will both fall over them. Neighbors and friends will collapse together."

An Invasion from the North

22 This is what the LORD says: "See a great army marching from the north! A great nation
is rising against you from far-off lands. 23 They are fully armed for slaughter. They are
cruel and show no mercy. As they ride forward, the noise of their army is like a roaring
sea. They are marching in battle formation to destroy you, Jerusalem.*"
24 We have heard reports about the enemy, and we are weak with fright. Fear and pain
have gripped us, like that of a woman about to give birth. 25 Don't go out to the fields!
Don't travel the roads! The enemy is everywhere, and they are ready to kill. We are
terrorized at every turn! 26 Now my people, dress yourselves in sackcloth, and sit among
the ashes. Mourn and weep bitterly, as for the loss of an only son. For suddenly, the
destroying armies will be upon you!
27 "Jeremiah, I have made you a tester of metals, that you may determine the quality
of my people. 28 Are they not the worst of rebels, full of slander? They are as insolent as
bronze, as hard and cruel as iron. All of them lead others into corruption. 29 The bellows
blow fiercely. The refining fire grows hotter. But it will never purify and cleanse them
because there is no purity in them to refine. 30 I will label them 'Rejected Silver' because
I, the LORD, am discarding them."

Jeremiah Speaks at the Temple

7 The LORD gave another message to Jeremiah. He said, 2 "Go to the entrance of the
LORD's Temple, and give this message to the people: 'O Judah, listen to this
message from the LORD! Listen to it, all of you who worship here! 3 The LORD
Almighty, the God of Israel, says: Even now, if you quit your evil ways, I will let you

6:16 Jer 18:15; 31:21; Mal 4:4; †Matt 11:29
6:17 Isa 21:11; 58:1; Jer 25:4; Ezek 3:17
6:20 Pss 40:6; 50:7-9; Isa 1:11; 60:6; 66:3; Amos 5:21
6:21 Isa 8:14; 9:14-17; Jer 9:21-22; 13:16
6:22 Jer 1:15; 10:22; 50:41-43
6:23 Isa 5:30; Jer 4:29; 50:42
6:24 Isa 28:19; Jer 4:19-21
6:26 Jer 4:8; 25:34; Amos 8:10; Mic 1:10; Zech 12:10
6:27 Jer 1:18; 15:20
6:28 Ezek 22:18
6:30 Ps 119:119; Isa 1:22
7:2 Jer 17:19
7:3 Jer 4:1; 18:11; 26:13

6:23 Hebrew *daughter of Zion.*

6:14 "Ignore it and maybe it will go away!" Sound familiar? This was Israel's response to Jeremiah's warnings. They kept listening to predictions of peace because they did not like Jeremiah's condemnation of their sin. But denying the truth never changes it; what God says always happens. Sin is never removed by denying its existence. We must confess to God that we have sinned and ask him to forgive us.

6:16 The right path for living is ancient and has been marked out by God. But the people refused to take God's path, going their own way instead. We face the same decision today—going God's old but true way, or following a new path of our own choosing. Don't be misled. The only way to find peace and "rest for your souls" is to walk on God's path.

6:20 Sheba, located in southwest Arabia, was a center of trade in incense and spices used in pagan religious rituals.

6:29, 30 Metal is purified by fire. As it is heated, impurities are burned away and only the pure metal remains. As God tested the people of Judah, however, he could find no purity in their lives. They continued in their sinful ways. Do you see impurities in your life that should be burned away? Confess these to God and allow him to purify you as he sees fit. Take time right now to reflect on the areas of your life that he has already refined; then thank him for what he is doing.

7:1–10:25 As this section opens, God sends Jeremiah to the Temple gates to refute the false belief that God would not let harm come to the Temple or to those who lived near it. Jeremiah rebukes the people for their false and worthless religion, their idolatry, and the shameless behavior of the people and their leaders. Judah, he says, is ripe for judgment and exile. This happened during the reign of Jehoiakim, a puppet of Egypt. The nation, in shock over the death of Josiah, was going through a spiritual reversal that removed much of the good Josiah had done. The themes of this section are false religion, idolatry, and hypocrisy. Jeremiah was almost put to death for this sermon, but he was saved by the officials of Judah (see chapter 26).

7:2, 3 The people followed a worship ritual but maintained a sinful life-style. It was religion without personal commitment to God. Attending church, taking communion, teaching church school, singing in the choir—all are empty exercises unless we are truly doing them for God. It is good to do these activities, not because we ought to do them for the church, but because we want to do them for God.

stay in your own land. 4 But do not be fooled by those who repeatedly promise your
safety because the Temple of the LORD is here. 5 I will be merciful only if you stop
your wicked thoughts and deeds and are fair to others; 6 and if you stop exploiting
foreigners, orphans, and widows; and if you stop your murdering; and if you stop
worshiping idols as you now do to your own harm. 7 Then I will let you stay in this
land that I gave to your ancestors to keep forever.

8 " 'Do you think that because the Temple is here you will never suffer? Don't fool
yourselves! 9 Do you really think you can steal, murder, commit adultery, lie, and
worship Baal and all those other new gods of yours, 10 and then come here and stand
before me in my Temple and chant, "We are safe!"—only to go right back to all those
evils again? 11 Do you think this Temple, which honors my name, is a den of thieves? I
see all the evil going on there, says the LORD.

12 " 'Go to the place at Shiloh where I once put the Tabernacle to honor my name.
See what I did there because of all the wickedness of my people, the Israelites.
13 While you were doing these wicked things, says the LORD, I spoke to you about it
repeatedly, but you would not listen. I called out to you, but you refused to answer.
14 So just as I destroyed Shiloh, I will now destroy this Temple that was built to honor
my name, this Temple that you trust for help, this place that I gave to you and your
ancestors. 15 And I will send you into exile, just as I did your relatives, the people of
Israel.*'

Judah's Persistent Idolatry

16 "Pray no more for these people, Jeremiah. Do not weep or pray for them, and don't
beg me to help them, for I will not listen to you. 17 Do you not see what they are doing
throughout the towns of Judah and in the streets of Jerusalem? 18 No wonder I am so
angry! Watch how the children gather wood and the fathers build sacrificial fires. See
how the women knead dough and make cakes to offer to the Queen of Heaven. And they
give drink offerings to their other idol gods! 19 Am I the one they are hurting?" asks the
LORD. "Most of all, they hurt themselves, to their own shame."

20 So the Sovereign LORD says: "I will pour out my terrible fury on this place. Its
people, animals, trees, and crops will be consumed by the unquenchable fire of my
anger."

21 This is what the LORD Almighty, the God of Israel, says: "Away with your burnt
offerings and sacrifices! Eat them yourselves! 22 When I led your ancestors out of Egypt,
it was not burnt offerings and sacrifices I wanted from them. 23 This is what I told them:
'Obey me, and I will be your God, and you will be my people. Only do as I say, and all
will be well!'

24 "But my people would not listen to me. They kept on doing whatever they wanted,
following the stubborn desires of their evil hearts. They went backward instead of

7:4 Mic 3:11
7:5 Isa 1:19; Jer 21:12; 22:3
7:6 Exod 22:21-24; Deut 6:14-15; 8:19
7:7 Deut 4:40
7:9 Exod 20:3; Jer 11:13, 17; 19:4
7:10 Ezek 23:39
7:11 Matt 21:13; †Mark 11:17; †Luke 19:46
7:12 Josh 18:1, 10; Jer 26:6
7:14 1 Kgs 9:7; Jer 7:4, 12
7:15 2 Kgs 17:23
7:16 Jer 11:14; 15:1
7:18 Deut 32:16
7:19 Job 35:6; Jer 9:19
7:21 Hos 8:13; Amos 5:21
7:22 1 Sam 15:22; Ps 51:16; Hos 6:6
7:23 Exod 15:26; 19:5-6; Lev 26:12; Deut 6:3
7:24 Ps 81:11; Jer 11:8; Ezek 20:8, 13, 16, 21

7:15 Hebrew *of Ephraim*, referring to the northern kingdom of Israel.

7:9-11 There are several parallels between how the people of Judah viewed their Temple and how many today view their churches. (1) *They didn't make the Temple part of their daily living.* We may go to beautiful churches well-prepared for worship, but often we don't take the presence of God with us through the week. (2) *The image of the Temple became more important than the substance of faith.* Going to church and belonging to a group can become more important than a life changed for God. (3) *The people used their Temple as a sanctuary.* Many use religious affiliation as a hideout, thinking it will protect them from evil and problems.

7:11, 12 Jesus used these words from 7:11 in clearing the Temple (Mark 11:17; Luke 19:46). This passage applied to the evil in the Temple in Jesus' day as well as in Jeremiah's. God's Tabernacle had been at Shiloh, but Shiloh had been abandoned (Psalm 78:60; Jeremiah 26:6). If God did not preserve Shiloh because the Tabernacle was there, why would he preserve Jerusalem because of the Temple?

7:15 Israel, the northern kingdom, had been taken into captivity by Assyria in 722 B.C.

7:18 The Queen of Heaven was a name for Ishtar, the Mesopotamian goddess of love and fertility. After the fall of Jerusalem, the refugees from Judah who fled to Egypt continued to worship her (44:17). A papyrus dating from the 5th century B.C., found at Hermopolis in Egypt, mentions the Queen of Heaven among the gods honored by the Jewish community living there.

7:19 This verse answers the question, Who gets hurt when we turn away from God? We do! Separating ourselves from God is like keeping a green plant away from sunlight or water. God is our only source of spiritual strength. Cut yourself off from him, and you cut off life itself.

7:21-23 God had set up a system of sacrifices to encourage the people to joyfully obey him (see the book of Leviticus). He required the people to make these sacrifices, not because the sacrifices themselves pleased him, but because they caused the people to recognize their sin and refocus on living for God. They faithfully made the sacrifices but forgot the reason they were offering them, and thus they disobeyed God. Jeremiah reminded the people that unless they were prepared to obey God in all areas of life, acting out religious rituals was meaningless. (See the chart in Hosea 7.)

forward. [25]From the day your ancestors left Egypt until now, I have continued to send
my prophets—day in and day out. [26]But my people have not listened to me or even tried
to hear. They have been stubborn and sinful—even worse than their ancestors.

[27]"Tell them all this, but do not expect them to listen. Shout out your warnings, but
do not expect them to respond. [28]Say to them, 'This is the nation whose people will not
obey the LORD their God and who refuse to be taught. Truth has vanished from among
them; it is no longer heard on their lips. [29]O Jerusalem, shave your head in mourning,
and weep alone on the mountains. For the LORD has rejected and forsaken this generation
that has provoked his fury.'

The Valley of Slaughter

[30]"The people of Judah have sinned before my very eyes," says the LORD. "They have
set up their abominable idols right in my own Temple, defiling it. [31]They have built the
pagan shrines of Topheth in the valley of the son of Hinnom, where they sacrifice their
little sons and daughters in the fire. I have never commanded such a horrible deed; it
never even crossed my mind to command such a thing! [32]So beware, for the time is
coming," says the LORD, "when that place will no longer be called Topheth or the valley
of the son of Hinnom, but the Valley of Slaughter. They will bury so many bodies in
Topheth that there won't be room for all the graves. [33]The corpses of my people will be
food for the vultures and wild animals, and no one will be left to scare them away. [34]I
will put an end to the happy singing and laughter in the streets of Jerusalem. The joyful
voices of bridegrooms and brides will no longer be heard in the towns of Judah. The land
will lie in complete desolation.

8 "In that day," says the LORD, "the enemy will break open the graves of the kings and
officials of Judah, and the graves of the priests, prophets, and common people.
[2]They will dig out their bones and spread them out on the ground before the sun, moon,
and stars—the gods my people have loved, served, and worshiped. Their bones will not
be gathered up again or buried but will be scattered on the ground like dung. [3]And the
people of this evil nation who survive will wish to die rather than live where I will send
them. I, the LORD Almighty, have spoken!

Deception by False Prophets

[4]"Jeremiah, say to the people, 'This is what the LORD says: When people fall down, don't
they get up again? When they start down the wrong road and discover their mistake,
don't they turn back? [5]Then why do these people keep going along their self-destructive
path, refusing to turn back, even though I have warned them? [6]I listen to their conversations, and what do I hear? Is anyone sorry for sin? Does anyone say, "What a terrible
thing I have done"? No! All are running down the path of sin as swiftly as a horse rushing
into battle! [7]The stork knows the time of her migration, as do the turtledove, the swallow,
and the crane.* They all return at the proper time each year. But not my people! They do
not know what the LORD requires of them.

[8]" 'How can you say, "We are wise because we have the law of the LORD," when your
teachers have twisted it so badly? [9]These wise teachers will be shamed by exile for their

7:26 Jer 16:12; 17:23 Matt 23:32
7:27 Isa 65:12 Jer 26:2 Ezek 2:7
7:28 Jer 11:10
7:29 Isa 15:2; 22:12 Jer 6:30; 14:19; 16:6 Mic 1:16
7:30 2 Kgs 21:4 2 Chr 33:4-5, 7 Jer 32:34
7:31 2 Kgs 23:10 Jer 19:5
7:32 Jer 19:6-7
7:33 Deut 28:26 Jer 12:9
7:34 Isa 1:7; 24:7 Jer 4:27; 16:9 Ezek 26:13 Hos 2:11
8:1 Ezek 6:5
8:2 2 Kgs 23:5 Jer 22:19; 36:30 Zeph 1:5 Acts 7:42
8:3 Deut 30:1, 4
8:4 Prov 24:16 Mic 7:8
8:6 Job 39:21-25 Ps 14:2 Ezek 22:30 Mal 3:16
8:7 Prov 6:6-8 Song 2:12
8:8 Jer 4:22 Rom 1:22; 2:17
8:9 1 Cor 1:27

8:7 The identification of some of these birds is uncertain.

7:25 From the time of Moses to the end of the Old Testament period, God sent many prophets to Israel and Judah. No matter how bad the circumstances were, God always raised up a prophet to speak against their stubborn spiritual attitudes.

7:31, 32 The shrines of Topheth (meaning "fireplace") were set up in the valley of the son of Hinnom, where debris and rubbish from the city were thrown away. This altar was used to worship Molech—a god who required child sacrifice (2 Kings 23:10). Their valley of sacrifice would become their Valley of Slaughter by the Babylonians. At the place where the people had killed their children in sinful idol worship, they themselves would be slaughtered.

8:1, 2 The threat that the graves of Judah's people would be opened was horrible to a people who highly honored the dead and believed that it was the highest desecration to open graves. This would be an ironic punishment for idol worshipers—their bones would be laid out before the sun, moon, and stars—the gods they thought could save them.

8:4-6 When people fall down or realize that they are headed in the wrong direction, it only makes sense for them to get up or change directions. But as God watched the nation, he saw people living sinful lives by choice, deceiving themselves that there would be no consequences. They had lost perspective concerning God's will for their lives and were trying to minimize their sin. Are there some indicators that you have fallen down or are heading the wrong way? What are you doing to get back on the right path?

8:10 Deut 28:30 Isa 56:11
8:11 Jer 6:14; 14:13-14 Lam 2:14 Ezek 13:10
8:12 Deut 32:35 Isa 3:9; 9:14 Zeph 3:5
8:13 Matt 21:19
8:14 Deut 29:18 Ps 69:21 Jer 3:25; 4:5; 9:15; 14:20 Matt 27:34
8:16 Judg 5:22
8:17 Num 21:6 Deut 32:24 Ps 58:4-5
8:19 Deut 32:21 Ps 31:6
8:21 Joel 2:6 Nah 2:10
8:22 Gen 37:25 Jer 14:19; 30:13; 46:11
9:1 Jer 8:18; 13:17
9:2 Pss 55:6-7; 120:5-6
9:4 Gen 27:35 Prov 10:18
9:5 Mic 6:12
9:6 John 3:19-20
9:7 Isa 1:25 Jer 6:27 Mal 3:3

sin, for they have rejected the word of the LORD. Are they so wise after all? [10]I will give
their wives and their farms to others. From the least to the greatest, they trick others to
get what does not belong to them. Yes, even my prophets and priests are like that. [11]They
offer superficial treatments for my people's mortal wound. They give assurances of
peace when all is war. [12]Are they ashamed when they do these disgusting things? No,
not at all—they don't even blush! Therefore, they will lie among the slaughtered. They
will be humbled when they are punished, says the LORD. [13]I will take away their rich
harvests of figs and grapes. Their fruit trees will all die. All the good things I prepared
for them will soon be gone. I, the LORD, have spoken!'
[14]"Then the people will say, 'Why should we wait here to die? Come, let's go to the
fortified cities to die there. For the LORD our God has decreed our destruction and has
given us a cup of poison to drink because we sinned against the LORD. [15]We hoped for
peace, but no peace came. We hoped for a time of healing, but found only terror. [16]The
snorting of the enemies' warhorses can be heard all the way from the land of Dan in the
north! The whole land trembles at the approach of the terrible army, for it is coming to
devour the land and everything in it—cities and people alike.'
[17]"I will send these enemy troops among you like poisonous snakes you cannot
charm," says the LORD. "No matter what you do, they will bite you, and you will die."

Jeremiah Weeps for Sinful Judah

[18]My grief is beyond healing; my heart is broken. [19]Listen to the weeping of my people;
it can be heard all across the land.
"Has the LORD abandoned Jerusalem*?" the people ask. "Is her King no longer there?"
"Oh, why have they angered me with their carved idols and worthless gods?" asks the
LORD.
[20]"The harvest is finished, and the summer is gone," the people cry, "yet we are not
saved!"
[21]I weep for the hurt of my people. I am stunned and silent, mute with grief. [22]Is there
no medicine in Gilead? Is there no physician there? Why is there no healing for the
wounds of my people?

9 Oh, that my eyes were a fountain of tears; I would weep forever! I would sob day
and night for all my people who have been slaughtered. [2]Oh, that I could go away
and forget them and live in a shack in the desert, for they are all adulterous and
treacherous.

Judgment for Disobedience

[3]"My people bend their tongues like bows to shoot lies. They refuse to stand up for the
truth. And they only go from bad to worse! They care nothing for me," says the LORD.
[4]"Beware of your neighbor! Beware of your brother! They all take advantage of one
another and spread their slanderous lies. [5]They all fool and defraud each other; no one
tells the truth. With practiced tongues they tell lies; they wear themselves out with all
their sinning. [6]They pile lie upon lie and utterly refuse to come to me," says the LORD.
[7]Therefore, the LORD Almighty says, "See, I will melt them in a crucible and test them
like metal. What else can I do with them? [8]For their tongues aim lies like poisoned arrows.

8:19 Hebrew *Zion.*

8:16 Dan was the northernmost tribe in Israel.

8:18 Jeremiah was pleading with God to save his people.

8:20-22 These words vividly portray Jeremiah's emotion as he watched his people reject God. He responded with anguish to a world dying in sin. We watch that same world still dying in sin, still rejecting God. But how often is our heart broken for our lost friends and neighbors, our lost world? Only when we have Jeremiah's kind of passionate concern will we be moved to help. We must begin by asking God to break our heart for the world he loves.

8:22 Gilead was famous for its healing medicine. This is a rhetorical question. The obvious answer is, "Yes—God," but Israel was not applying the "medicine"; they were not obeying the Lord. Although the people's spiritual sickness was very deep, it could be healed. But the people refused the medicine. God could heal their self-inflicted wounds, but he would not force his healing on them.

9:1-6 Jeremiah felt conflicting emotions concerning his people. Lying, deceit, treachery, adultery, and idolatry had become common sins. He was angered by their sin, but he had compassion, too. He was set apart from them by his mission for God, but he was also one of them. Jesus had similar feelings when he stood before Jerusalem, the city that would reject him (Matthew 23:37).

They promise peace to their neighbors while planning to kill them. 9 Should I not punish
them for this?" asks the LORD. "Should I not avenge myself against a nation such as this?"
10 I will weep for the mountains and wail for the desert pastures. For they are desolate and
empty of life; the lowing of cattle is heard no more; the birds and wild animals all have fled.
11 "I will make Jerusalem into a heap of ruins," says the LORD. "It will be a place
haunted by jackals. The towns of Judah will be ghost towns, with no one living in them."
12 Who is wise enough to understand all this? Who has been instructed by the LORD
and can explain it to others? Why has the land been ruined so completely that no one
even dares to travel through it?
13 The LORD replies, "This has happened because my people have abandoned the
instructions I gave them; they have refused to obey my law. 14 Instead, they have
stubbornly followed their own desires and worshiped the images of Baal, as their
ancestors taught them. 15 So now, listen to what the LORD Almighty, the God of Israel,
says: Look! I will feed them with bitterness and give them poison to drink. 16 I will scatter
them around the world, and they will be strangers in distant lands. Their enemies will
chase them with the sword until I have destroyed them completely."

Weeping in Jerusalem

17 This is what the LORD Almighty says: "Think about what is going on! Call for the
mourners to come. 18 Quick! Begin your weeping! Let the tears flow from your eyes.
19 Hear the people of Jerusalem* crying in despair, 'We are ruined! Disaster has come
upon us! We must leave our land, because our homes have been torn down.'"
20 Listen, you women, to the words of the LORD; open your ears to what he has to say.
Teach your daughters to wail; teach one another how to lament. 21 For death has crept in
through our windows and has entered our mansions. It has killed off the flower of our
youth: Children no longer play in the streets, and young men no longer gather in the
squares. 22 And the LORD says, "Bodies will be scattered across the fields like dung, or
like bundles of grain after the harvest. No one will be left to bury them."
23 This is what the LORD says: "Let not the wise man gloat in his wisdom, or the mighty
man in his might, or the rich man in his riches. 24 Let them boast in this alone: that they
truly know me and understand that I am the LORD who is just and righteous, whose love
is unfailing, and that I delight in these things. I, the LORD, have spoken!
25 "A time is coming," says the LORD, "when I will punish all those who are circumcised in body but not in spirit—26 the Egyptians, Edomites, Ammonites, Moabites, the
people who live in distant places,* and yes, even the people of Judah. Like all these
pagan nations, the people of Israel also have uncircumcised hearts."

Idolatry Brings Destruction

10 Hear the word of the LORD, O Israel! 2 This is what the LORD says: "Do not act
like other nations who try to read their future in the stars. Do not be afraid of their
predictions, even though other nations are terrified by them. 3 Their ways are futile and
foolish. They cut down a tree and carve an idol. 4 They decorate it with gold and silver
and then fasten it securely with hammer and nails so it won't fall over. 5 There stands
their god like a helpless scarecrow in a garden! It cannot speak, and it needs to be carried
because it cannot walk. Do not be afraid of such gods, for they can neither harm you nor
do you any good."
6 LORD, there is no one like you! For you are great, and your name is full of power. 7 Who

9:19 Hebrew *Zion.* **9:26** Or *the people who clip the corners of their hair.*

9:10 Jer 4:24-25; 12:4 Ezek 14:15; 29:11; 33:28 Hos 4:3
9:12 Ps 107:43 Jer 23:10, 16 Hos 14:9
9:13 2 Chr 7:19-20 Ps 89:30 Jer 5:19; 22:9
9:14 Rom 1:21-24 1 Pet 1:18
9:15 Deut 29:18 Jer 8:14; 23:15
9:16 Lev 26:33 Deut 28:64 Ezek 5:2, 12
9:17 Amos 5:16
9:19 Deut 28:29 2 Chr 35:25
9:21 2 Chr 36:17 Jer 6:11; 18:21
9:23 1 Kgs 20:10-11 Ps 49:6-9 Eccl 9:11 Ezek 28:3-7
9:24 Exod 34:6-7 Pss 36:5, 7; 44:8 Isa 10:8-12; 61:8 Mic 7:18 †1 Cor 1:31 2 Cor 10:17 Gal 6:14
9:26 Lev 26:41 Ezek 44:7 Rom 2:28
10:2 Lev 18:3 Isa 47:12-14
10:5 Ps 115:5 1 Cor 12:12
10:6 Deut 33:26 Pss 48:1; 96:4 Isa 12:6 Jer 10:16
10:7 Ps 22:28 Dan 2:27-28 1 Cor 1:19-20

9:23, 24 People tend to admire three things about others: wisdom, power (might), and riches. But God puts a higher priority on knowing him personally and living a life that reflects his justice and righteousness. What do you want people to admire most about you?

9:25, 26 Circumcision went back to the time of Abraham. For the people of Israel, it was a symbol of their covenant relationship to God (Genesis 17:9-14). Circumcision was also practiced by pagan nations, but not as the sign of a covenant with God. By Jeremiah's time, the Israelites had forgotten the spiritual significance of circumcision even though they continued to do the physical ritual.

10:2, 3 Most people would like to know the future. Decisions would be easier, failures would be avoided, and successes would be assured. The people of Judah wanted to know the future, too, and they tried to discern it through reading the signs in the sky. God made the earth and the heavens, including stars that people consult and worship (10:12). No one will discover the future in man-made charts of God's stars. But God, who promises to guide you, knows your future and will be with you all the way. He will not reveal your future to you, but he will walk with you as the future unfolds. Don't trust the stars; trust the one who made the stars.

would not fear you, O King of nations? That title belongs to you alone! Among all the wise
people of the earth and in all the kingdoms of the world, there is no one like you.
8 The wisest of people who worship idols are stupid and foolish. The things they
worship are made of wood! 9 They bring beaten sheets of silver from Tarshish and gold
from Uphaz, and they give these materials to skillful craftsmen who make their idols.
Then they dress these gods in royal purple robes made by expert tailors. 10 But the LORD
is the only true God, the living God. He is the everlasting King! The whole earth trembles
at his anger. The nations hide before his wrath.
11 Say this to those who worship other gods: "Your so-called gods, who did not make
the heavens and earth, will vanish from the earth."*

12 But God made the earth by his power,
  and he preserves it by his wisdom.
He has stretched out the heavens
  by his understanding.
13 When he speaks, there is thunder in the heavens.
  He causes the clouds to rise over the earth.
He sends the lightning with the rain
  and releases the wind from his storehouses.
14 Compared to him, all people are foolish
  and have no knowledge at all!
They make idols, but the idols will disgrace their makers,
  for they are frauds.
  They have no life or power in them.
15 Idols are worthless; they are lies!
  The time is coming when they will all be destroyed.
16 But the God of Israel* is no idol!
  He is the Creator of everything that exists,
  including Israel, his own special possession.
The LORD Almighty is his name!

The Coming Destruction

17 "Pack your bag and prepare to leave; the siege is about to begin," 18 says the LORD.
"For suddenly, I will fling you from this land and pour great troubles upon you. At last
you will feel my anger."
19 My wound is desperate, and my grief is great. My sickness is incurable, but I must
bear it. 20 My home is gone, and no one is left to help me rebuild it. My children have
been taken away, and I will never see them again. 21 The shepherds of my people have
lost their senses. They no longer follow the LORD or ask what he wants of them.
Therefore, they fail completely, and their flocks are scattered. 22 Listen! Hear the
terrifying roar of great armies as they roll down from the north. The towns of Judah will
be destroyed and will become a haunt for jackals.

Jeremiah's Prayer

23 I know, LORD, that a person's life is not his own. No one is able to plan his own course.
24 So correct me, LORD, but please be gentle. Do not correct me in anger, for I would die.

10:8 Jer 4:22
10:9 Pss 72:10; 115:4; Isa 40:19; Dan 10:5
10:10 Pss 10:16; 29:10; 76:7; Isa 65:16; Jer 4:2; 50:46
10:11 Ps 96:5; Isa 2:18; Zeph 2:11
10:12 Job 9:8; 38:4-7; Pss 78:69; 148:4-5; Isa 40:22; 45:18; Jer 51:15
10:13 Job 36:27-29; Pss 29:3-9; 135:7
10:14 Jer 51:17
10:15 Isa 41:24; Jer 8:12; 14:22
10:16 Deut 32:9; Isa 45:7; Jer 10:12; 31:35; 32:18; 51:19
10:17 Ezek 12:3-12
10:18 1 Sam 25:29; Jer 14:17
10:19 Jer 4:31; Mic 7:9
10:20 Isa 51:18; Jer 4:20; 31:15; Lam 1:5; 2:4
10:21 Jer 23:2
10:23 Prov 20:24; Isa 26:7

10:11 The original text of this verse is in Aramaic. **10:16** Hebrew *the Portion of Jacob.*

10:8 Those who put their trust in a chunk of wood, even though it is carved well and looks beautiful, are foolish. The simplest person who worships God is wiser than the wisest person who worships a worthless substitute, because this person has discerned who God really is. In what or whom do you place your trust?

10:9 Tarshish was located at the westward limit of the ancient world, perhaps in what is now Spain (see Jonah 1:3). It was a source of silver, tin, lead, and iron for Tyre (Ezekiel 27:12). The location of Uphaz is unknown. Instead, it may be a metallurgical term for "refined gold." No matter how well made or how beautiful idols are, they can never have the power and life of the true and living God.

10:19-21 In this section, Jeremiah uses the picture of nomads wandering in the wilderness trying to pitch their tents. The shepherds of the nation are the evil leaders responsible for the distress. "Flocks" are the people of Judah. Instead of guiding the people to God, the leaders were leading them astray.

10:23, 24 God's ability to direct our life is far superior to our ability. Sometimes we are afraid of God's power andplans because we know his power would easily crush us if he used it against us. Don't be afraid to let God correct your plans. He will give you wisdom if you are willing.

25Pour out your wrath on the nations that refuse to recognize you—on nations that do
not call upon your name. For they have utterly devoured your people Israel,* making the
land a desolate wilderness.

3. Jeremiah prophesies destruction

Judah's Broken Covenant

11 The LORD gave another message to Jeremiah. He said, 2"Remind the people of
Judah and Jerusalem about the terms of their covenant with me. 3Say to them,
'This is what the LORD, the God of Israel, says: Cursed is anyone who does not obey the
terms of my covenant! 4For I said to your ancestors when I brought them out of slavery
in Egypt, "If you obey me and do whatever I command you, then you will be my people,
and I will be your God." 5I said this so I could keep my promise to your ancestors to give
you a land flowing with milk and honey—the land you live in today.'"

Then I replied, "So be it,* LORD!"

6Then the LORD said, "Broadcast this message in the streets of Jerusalem. Go from
town to town throughout the land and say, 'Remember the covenant your ancestors
made, and do everything they promised. 7For I solemnly warned your ancestors when I
brought them out of Egypt, repeating over and over again to this day: "Obey me!" 8But
your ancestors did not pay any attention; they would not even listen. Instead, they
stubbornly followed their own evil desires. And because they refused to obey, I brought
upon them all the curses described in our covenant.'"

9Again the LORD spoke to me and said, "I have discovered a conspiracy against me
among the people of Judah and Jerusalem. 10They have returned to the sins of their
forefathers. They have refused to listen to me and are worshiping idols. Israel and Judah
have both broken the covenant I made with their ancestors. 11Therefore, says the LORD,
I am going to bring calamity upon them, and they will not escape. Though they beg for
mercy, I will not listen to their cries. 12Then the people of Judah and Jerusalem will pray
to their idols and offer incense before them. But the idols will not save them when
disaster strikes! 13Look now, people of Judah, you have as many gods as there are cities
and towns. Your altars of shame—altars for burning incense to your god Baal—are along
every street in Jerusalem.

14"Pray no more for these people, Jeremiah. Do not weep or pray for them, for I will
not listen to them when they cry out to me in distress. 15What right do my beloved people
have to come to my Temple, where they have done so many immoral things? Can their
sacrifices avert their destruction? They actually rejoice in doing evil!

16"I, the LORD, once called them a thriving olive tree, beautiful to see and full of good
fruit. But now I have sent the fury of their enemies to burn them with fire, leaving them
charred and broken. 17I, the LORD Almighty, who planted this olive tree, have ordered it
destroyed. For the people of Israel and Judah have done evil, provoking my anger by
offering incense to Baal."

A Plot against Jeremiah

18Then the LORD told me about the plots my enemies were making against me. 19I had
been as unaware as a lamb on the way to its slaughter. I had no idea that they were

10:25 Ps 79:6; Jer 8:16; 50:7; Zeph 1:6; 3:8
11:3 Exod 19:5; Deut 27:26; Gal 3:10
11:4 Exod 24:3, 7; Deut 4:20; 1 Kgs 8:51; Jer 31:32; Zech 8:8
11:5 Exod 13:5; Deut 7:12; Jer 32:22
11:7 Exod 15:26; 2 Chr 36:15; Jer 7:25; 11:4
11:8 Lev 26:14-43; Ezek 20:8
11:9 Ezek 22:25
11:10 Deut 9:7; Judg 2:11-13; Jer 3:6-9; 13:10; Ezek 16:59
11:11 Jer 6:19; 25:35
11:12 Deut 32:37; Jer 44:17
11:13 Jer 2:28; 7:9-10
11:14 Ps 66:18; Jer 7:16; 14:11; Hos 5:6
11:15 Jer 13:27
11:16 Pss 52:8; 83:2; Isa 27:11; Jer 21:14
11:17 Jer 2:21; 32:29
11:18 1 Sam 23:11-12; 2 Kgs 6:9-10; Ezek 8:6

10:25 Hebrew *Jacob*. **11:5** Hebrew *Amen*.

11:1–13:27 This section concerns the broken covenant, and a rebuke for those who returned to idols after Josiah's reform. Jeremiah's rebuke prompted a threat against his life by his own countrymen. As Jeremiah suffered, he pondered the prosperity of the wicked. As he brought these words to a close, he used a rotten linen belt and filled wineskins as object lessons of God's coming judgment (see the note on 13:1-11).

11:14 At first glance this command is shocking: God tells Jeremiah not to pray and says he won't listen to the people if they pray. A time comes when God must dispense justice. Sin brings its own bitter reward. If the people were unrepentant and continued in their sin, neither their prayers nor Jeremiah's would prevent God's judgment. Their only hope was repentance—sorrow for sin, turning from it, and turning to God. How can we keep praying for God's help if we haven't committed our life to him? God's blessings come when we are committed to him, not when we selfishly hang on to our sinful ways.

11:18-23 To Jeremiah's surprise, the people of Anathoth, his hometown, were plotting to kill him. They wanted to silence Jeremiah's message for several reasons: (1) economic—his condemnation of idol worship would hurt the business of the idol makers; (2) religious—the message of doom and gloom made the people feel depressed and guilty; (3) political—he openly rebuked their hypocritical politics; and (4) personal—the people hated him for showing them that they were wrong. Jeremiah had two options: run and hide, or call on God. Jeremiah called, and God answered. Like Jeremiah, we can either run and hide when we face opposition because of our faithfulness to God, or we can call on God for help. Hiding compromises our message; calling on God lets him reinforce it.

planning to kill me! "Let's destroy this man and all his words," they said. "Let's kill him,
so his name will be forgotten forever."
20 O LORD Almighty, you are just, and you examine the deepest thoughts of hearts and
minds. Let me see your vengeance against them, for I have committed my cause to you.
21 The men of Anathoth wanted me dead. They said they would kill me if I did not stop
speaking in the LORD's name. 22 So this is what the LORD Almighty says about them: "I
will punish them! Their young men will die in battle, and their little boys and girls will
starve. 23 Not one of these plotters from Anathoth will survive, for I will bring disaster
upon them when their time of punishment comes."

Jeremiah Questions the LORD's Justice

12 LORD, you always give me justice when I bring a case before you. Now let me
bring you this complaint: Why are the wicked so prosperous? Why are evil people
so happy? 2 You have planted them, and they have taken root and prospered. Your name
is on their lips, but in their hearts they give you no credit at all. 3 But as for me, LORD,
you know my heart. You see me and test my thoughts. Drag these people away like
helpless sheep to be butchered! Set them aside to be slaughtered!
4 How long must this land weep? Even the grass in the fields has withered. The wild
animals and birds have disappeared because of the evil in the land. Yet the people say,
"The LORD won't do anything!"

The LORD's Reply to Jeremiah

5 Then the LORD replied to me, "If racing against mere men makes you tired, how will
you race against horses? If you stumble and fall on open ground, what will you do in the
thickets near the Jordan? 6 Even your own brothers, members of your own family, have
turned on you. They have plotted, raising a cry against you. Do not trust them, no matter
how pleasantly they speak.
7 "I have abandoned my people, my special possession. I have surrendered my dearest
ones to their enemies. 8 My chosen people have roared at me like a lion of the forest, so
I have treated them as though I hated them. 9 My chosen people have become as
disgusting to me as a vulture. And indeed, they are surrounded by vultures. Bring on the
wild beasts to pick their corpses clean!
10 "Many rulers have ravaged my vineyard, trampling down the vines and turning all
its beauty into a barren wilderness. 11 They have made it an empty wasteland; I hear its
mournful cry. The whole land is desolate, and no one even cares. 12 Destroying armies
plunder the land. The sword of the LORD kills people from one end of the nation to the
other. No one will escape! 13 My people have planted wheat but are harvesting thorns.
They have worked hard, but it has done them no good. They will harvest a crop of shame,
for the fierce anger of the LORD is upon them."

A Message for Israel's Neighbors

14 Now this is what the LORD says: "As for all the evil nations reaching out for the
inheritance I gave my people Israel, I will uproot them from their lands just as Judah will
be uprooted from hers. 15 But afterward I will return and have compassion on all of them.
I will bring them home to their own lands again, each nation to its own inheritance. 16 And
if these nations quickly learn the ways of my people, and if they learn to swear by my
name, saying, 'As surely as the LORD lives' (just as they taught my people to swear by
the name of Baal), then they will be given a place among my people. 17 But any nation
who refuses to obey me will be uprooted and destroyed. I, the LORD, have spoken!"

11:20 Ps 7:9; Jer 17:10; 20:12
11:21 Jer 1:1; 12:5-6; 20:10; 26:8; 38:4
11:22 Jer 18:21; 21:14
11:23 Jer 6:9; 23:12; Hos 9:7; Mic 7:4
12:1 Ezra 9:15; Job 13:3; Jer 5:27-28; 11:20; Hab 1:4
12:2 Isa 29:13; Ezek 17:5-10; 33:31; Titus 1:16
12:4 Jer 5:31; Hos 4:3; Joel 1:10-17
12:5 Jer 44:19; 50:44
12:7 Jer 7:29; 11:15; Hos 11:1-4
12:9 2 Kgs 24:2; Isa 56:9; Jer 7:33; 15:3; 34:20
12:10 Ps 80:8-16; Isa 5:1-7; Lam 1:10
12:12 Isa 34:6; Jer 47:6; Amos 9:4
12:13 Lev 26:16; Deut 28:38; Isa 55:2; Jer 4:26; 17:10; 25:37-38
12:14 Isa 11:11-16; Jer 2:3; 49:1; Zeph 2:8-10; Zech 2:8
12:16 Josh 23:7; Isa 49:6
12:17 Ps 2:8-12; Isa 60:12

12:1-6 Many people have asked, "Why are the wicked so prosperous?" (See, for example, Job 21:4-21 and Habakkuk 1:1-4.) Jeremiah knew that God's justice would ultimately come, but he was impatient because he wanted justice to come quickly. God didn't give a doctrinal answer; instead, he gave a challenge: If Jeremiah couldn't handle this, how would he handle the injustices ahead? It is natural for us to demand fair play and cry for justice against those who take advantage of others. But when we call for justice, we must realize that we ourselves would be in big trouble if God gave each of us what we truly deserve.

12:5, 6 Life was extremely difficult for Jeremiah despite his love for and obedience to God. When he called to God for relief, God's reply in effect was, "If you think this is bad, how are you going to cope when it gets really tough?" God's answers to prayer are not always nice or easy to handle. Any Christian who has experienced war, bereavement, or a serious illness knows this. We are to be committed to God even when the going gets tough and when our prayers for relief are not immediately answered.

Jeremiah's Linen Belt

13 This is what the LORD said to me: "Go and buy a linen belt and put it around your
waist, but do not wash it." 2 So I bought the belt as the LORD directed me and put
it around my waist. 3 Then the LORD gave me another message: 4 "Take the linen belt you
are wearing, and go to the Euphrates River.* Hide it there in a hole in the rocks." 5 So I
went and hid it at the Euphrates as the LORD had instructed me.
6 A long time afterward, the LORD said to me, "Go back to the Euphrates and get the linen
belt that I told you to hide there." 7 So I went to the Euphrates and dug it out of the hole
where I had hidden it. But now it was mildewed and falling apart. The belt was useless.
8 Then I received this message from the LORD: 9 "The LORD says: This illustrates how
I will rot away the pride of Judah and Jerusalem. 10 These wicked people refuse to listen
to me. They stubbornly follow their own desires and worship idols. Therefore, they will
become like this linen belt—good for nothing! 11 As a belt clings to a person's waist, so
I created Judah and Israel to cling to me," says the LORD. "They were to be my people,
my pride, my glory—an honor to my name. But they would not listen to me.
12 "So tell them, 'The LORD, the God of Israel, says: All your wineskins will be full of
wine.' And they will reply, 'Of course, you don't need to tell us how prosperous we will
be!' 13 Then tell them, 'No, this is what the LORD means: I will make everyone in this
land so confused that they will seem drunk—from the king sitting on David's throne and
from the priests and the prophets, right on down to the common people. 14 I will smash
them one against the other, even parents against children, says the LORD. I will not let
my pity or mercy or compassion keep me from destroying them.'"

A Warning against Pride

15 Listen! Do not be proud, for the LORD has spoken. 16 Give glory to the LORD your God
before it is too late. Acknowledge him before he brings darkness upon you, causing you
to stumble and fall on the dark mountains. For then, when you look for light, you will
find only terrible darkness. 17 And if you still refuse to listen, I will weep alone because
of your pride. My eyes will overflow with tears because the LORD's flock will be led
away into exile.
18 Say to the king and his mother, "Come down from your thrones and sit in the dust,
for your glorious crowns will soon be snatched from your heads." 19 The towns of the
Negev will close their gates, and no one will be able to open them. The people of Judah
will be taken away as captives. They will all be carried into exile.
20 See the armies marching down from the north! Where is your flock—your beautiful
flock—that he gave you to care for? 21 How will you feel when the LORD sets your
foreign allies over you as rulers? You will writhe in pain like a woman giving birth!
22 You may ask yourself, "Why is all this happening to me?" It is because of your many
sins! That is why you have been raped and destroyed by invading armies. 23 Can an
Ethiopian* change the color of his skin? Can a leopard take away its spots? Neither can
you start doing good, for you always do evil.

13:1 Jer 13:11
13:2 Isa 20:2
13:4 Jer 51:63
13:5 Exod 39:42-43; 40:16
13:9 Lev 26:19
13:10 Jer 13:15-17
13:11 Exod 19:5-6; Deut 32:10-11; Ps 81:11; Isa 43:21; Jer 7:24; 33:9
13:13 Pss 60:3; 75:8; Jer 25:27
13:14 Isa 27:11; Jer 6:21; 16:5; 19:9-11
13:15 Prov 16:5
13:16 Ps 96:8; Isa 5:30; 59:9; Amos 5:18
13:17 Jer 9:1; 23:1-2; Mal 2:2; Luke 19:41-42
13:18 2 Kgs 24:12, 15; 2 Chr 33:12, 19
13:20 Jer 1:15; 6:22; 13:17; 23:2
13:21 Isa 13:8; Jer 4:31; 38:22
13:22 Jer 2:17-19; 9:2-9
13:23 Prov 27:22; Jer 4:22

13:4 Hebrew *Perath;* also in 13:5, 6, 7. **13:23** Hebrew *a Cushite.*

13:1 A linen belt was one of the more intimate pieces of clothing, clinging close to the body. It was like underwear. Jeremiah's action showed how God would ruin Judah just as Jeremiah had ruined the linen belt.

13:1-11 Actions speak louder than words. Jeremiah often used vivid object lessons to arouse the people's curiosity and get his point across. This lesson of the linen belt illustrated Judah's destiny. Although the people had once been close to God, their pride had made them useless. Proud people may look important, but God says their pride makes them good for nothing, completely useless. Pride rots our hearts until we lose our usefulness to God.

13:15 While it is good to respect our country and our church, our loyalties always carry a hidden danger—arrogance. When is pride harmful? When it causes us to (1) look down on others; (2) be selfish with our resources; (3) force our solutions on others' problems; (4) think God is blessing us because of our own merits; (5) be content with our plans rather than seeking God's plans.

13:18 The king was Jehoiachin, and the queen mother was Nehushta. The king's father, Jehoiakim, had surrendered to Nebuchadnezzar but later rebelled. During Jehoiachin's reign, Nebuchadnezzar's armies besieged Jerusalem, and both Jehoiachin and Nehushta surrendered. Jehoiachin was sent to Babylon and imprisoned (2 Kings 24:1-15). Jeremiah's prophecy came true.

13:19 The Negev region is the dry wasteland stretching south from Beersheba. The towns in this area would be closed to any refugees fleeing the invading army.

13:23 Not even the threat of captivity could move the people to repent. The people had become so accustomed to doing evil that they had lost their ability to change. God never rejects those who sincerely turn to him. God was warning them to repent before it became impossible to change. We must never put off until tomorrow those changes God wants us to make. Our attitudes and patterns for living can become so set that we will lose all desire to change and will no longer fear the consequences.

24“I will scatter you, just as chaff is scattered by the winds blowing in from the desert.
25This is your allotment, that which is due you,” says the LORD. “I have measured it out
especially for you, because you have forgotten me and put your trust in false gods. 26I
myself will expose you to shame. 27I am keenly aware of your adultery and lust, and
your abominable idol worship out in the fields and on the hills. Your destruction is sure,
Jerusalem! How long will it be before you are pure?”

Judah's Terrible Drought

14 This message came to Jeremiah from the LORD, explaining why he was holding
back the rain: 2“Judah wilts; her businesses have ground to a halt. All the people
sit on the ground in mourning, and a great cry rises from Jerusalem. 3The nobles send
servants to get water, but all the wells are dry. The servants return with empty pitchers,
confused and desperate, covering their heads in grief. 4The ground is parched and
cracked for lack of rain. The farmers are afraid; they, too, cover their heads. 5The deer
abandons her newborn fawn because there is no grass. 6The wild donkeys stand on the
bare hills panting like thirsty jackals. They strain their eyes looking for grass to eat, but
there is none to be found.”

7The people say, “LORD, our wickedness has caught up with us. We have sinned
against you. So please, help us for the sake of your own reputation. 8O Hope of Israel,
our Savior in times of trouble! Why are you like a stranger to us? Why are you like
someone passing through the land, stopping only for the night? 9Are you also confused?
Are you helpless to save us? You are right here among us, LORD. We are known as your
people. Please don't abandon us now!”

10So the LORD replies to his people, “You love to wander far from me and do not
follow in my paths. Now I will no longer accept you as my people. I will remember all
your wickedness and will punish you for your sins.”

The LORD Forbids Jeremiah to Intercede

11Then the LORD said to me, “Do not pray for these people anymore. 12When they fast
in my presence, I will pay no attention. When they present their burnt offerings and grain
offerings to me, I will not accept them. In return, I will give them only war, famine, and
disease.”

13Then I said, “O Sovereign LORD, their prophets are telling them, ‘All is well—no
war or famine will come. The LORD will surely send you peace.’”

14Then the LORD said, “These prophets are telling lies in my name. I did not send them
or tell them to speak. I did not give them any messages. They prophesy of visions and
revelations they have never seen or heard. They speak foolishness made up in their own
lying hearts. 15Therefore, says the LORD, I will punish these lying prophets, for they have
spoken in my name even though I never sent them. They say that no war or famine will
come, but they themselves will die by war and famine! 16As for the people to whom they
prophesy—their bodies will be thrown out into the streets of Jerusalem, victims of
famine and war. There will be no one left to bury them. Husbands, wives, sons, and
daughters—all will be gone. For I will pour out their own wickedness on them.

17“Now, Jeremiah, say this to them: ‘Night and day my eyes overflow with tears. I
cannot stop weeping, for my virgin daughter—my precious people—has been run
through with a sword and lies mortally wounded on the ground. 18If I go out into the
fields, I see the bodies of people slaughtered by the enemy. If I walk the city streets, there
I see people who have died of starvation. The prophets and priests continue with their
work, but they do not know what they are doing.’”

13:24 Lev 26:33; Ezek 5:2, 12
13:26 Lam 1:8; Hos 2:10
13:27 Prov 1:22
14:2 Isa 3:26; Jer 11:11; Zech 7:13
14:3 2 Sam 15:30; 1 Kgs 18:5; 2 Kgs 18:31
14:6 Joel 11:18
14:7 Hos 5:5
14:8 Ps 9:9; Isa 43:3; 63:8; Jer 17:13
14:9 Num 11:23; Ps 46:5; Isa 50:2; 63:19; Jer 8:19; 15:16
14:10 Ps 119:101; Jer 2:25; 6:20; 44:21-23; Hos 8:13
14:11 Jer 7:16; 11:14
14:12 Isa 1:15; Jer 8:13
14:13 Jer 5:12; 6:14; 8:11; 23:17
14:14 Jer 5:31; 23:16, 25-26; 27:9-10
14:15 Ezek 14:10
14:16 Ps 79:2-3; Prov 1:31; Jer 7:33; 8:1-2; 13:22-25; 15:2-3
14:17 Jer 8:21; 9:1; Lam 2:13
14:18 Jer 6:25; Lam 1:20; Ezek 7:15

14:1–15:21 This section opens with God sending a drought on Judah and refusing to answer their prayers for rain. It continues with Jeremiah's description of judgment to come.

14:1ff Drought was a judgment with devastating consequences. As usual, when their backs were to the wall, the people cried out to God. But God rejected their plea because they did not repent; they merely wanted his rescue. Not even Jeremiah's prayers would help. Their only hope was to turn to God.

14:14 What made the people listen to the false prophets? These “prophets” said what the people wanted to hear. False teachers earn fame and money by telling people what they want to hear, but they lead people away from God. If we encourage false teachers, we are as guilty as they are.

A Prayer for Healing

19 LORD, have you completely rejected Judah? Do you really hate Jerusalem*? Why have
you wounded us past all hope of healing? We hoped for peace, but no peace came. We
hoped for a time of healing but found only terror.
20 LORD, we confess our wickedness and that of our ancestors, too. We all have sinned
against you. 21 For the sake of your own name, LORD, do not abandon us. Do not disgrace
yourself and the throne of your glory. Do not break your covenant with us. Please don't
forget us!
22 Can any of the foreign gods send us rain? Does it fall from the sky by itself? No, it
comes from you, the LORD our God! Only you can do such things. So we will wait for
you to help us.

Judah's Inevitable Doom

15 Then the LORD said to me, "Even if Moses and Samuel stood before me pleading
for these people, I wouldn't help them. Away with them! Get them out of my sight!
2 And if they say to you, 'But where can we go?' tell them, 'This is what the LORD says:
Those who are destined for death, to death; those who are destined for war, to war; those
who are destined for famine, to famine; those who are destined for captivity, to captivity.'
3 "I will send four kinds of destroyers against them," says the LORD. "I will send the
sword to kill, the dogs to drag away, the vultures to devour, and the wild animals to finish
up what is left. 4 Because of the wicked things Manasseh son of Hezekiah, king of Judah,
did in Jerusalem, I will make my people an object of horror to all the kingdoms of the
earth.
5 "Who will feel sorry for you, Jerusalem? Who will weep for you? Who will even
bother to ask how you are? 6 You have forsaken me and turned your back on me," says
the LORD. "Therefore, I will raise my clenched fists to destroy you. I am tired of always
giving you another chance. 7 I will winnow you like grain at the gates of your cities and
take away everything you hold dear. I will destroy my own people, because they refuse
to turn back to me from all their evil ways.
8 "There will be more widows than the grains of sand along the seashore. At noontime
I will bring a destroyer against the mothers of young men. I will cause anguish and terror
to come upon them suddenly. 9 The mother of seven grows faint and gasps for breath;
her sun has gone down while it is yet day. She sits childless now, disgraced and
humiliated. And those who are left, I will hand over to the enemy to be killed," says the
LORD.

Jeremiah's Complaint

10 Then I said, "What sadness is mine, my mother. Oh, that I had died at birth! I am hated
everywhere I go. I am neither a lender who has threatened to foreclose nor a borrower
who refuses to pay—yet they all curse me."
11 The LORD replied, "All will be well with you, Jeremiah. Your enemies will ask you
to plead on their behalf in times of trouble and distress. 12 Can a man break a bar of iron
from the north, or a bar of bronze? 13 Because of all my people's sins against me, I will
hand over their wealth and treasures as plunder to the enemy. 14 I will tell their enemies

14:19 Hebrew *Zion.*

14:19 Job 30:26; Jer 8:15; 30:13; 1 Thes 5:3
14:20 Ps 32:5
14:21 Jer 3:17; 14:7; 17:12
14:22 1 Kgs 17:1; Isa 41:29; Jer 5:24; 10:3; Lam 3:26
15:1 Exod 32:11-14; 1 Sam 7:9; Pss 99:6; 106:23; Jer 10:18; 52:3; Ezek 14:14, 20
15:2 Ezek 5:2, 12
15:3 Lev 26:16, 22, 25; Deut 28:26; Isa 18:6; Ezek 14:21
15:4 2 Kgs 23:26-27; 24:3-4; Jer 24:9; 29:18
15:5 Ps 69:20; Jer 13:14
15:6 Zeph 1:4
15:7 Jer 18:21; 51:2; Hos 9:12-16
15:8 Isa 3:25-26; 4:1; Jer 22:7
15:9 1 Sam 2:5; Isa 47:9; Amos 8:9
15:10 Deut 23:19; Job 3:3; Jer 1:18-19; 20:7-8, 14
15:11 Isa 41:10
15:13 Jer 17:3
15:14 Deut 28:64

14:19-22 Interceding for the people, Jeremiah asked God if Judah's repentance would bring his help. But God refused to come to their aid (15:1) because the people were insincere, wicked, and stubborn. They knew he wanted to bless them, and they knew what they needed to do to receive that blessing. They wanted God to do his part, but they did not want to do theirs. It's easy to express sorrow for wrong actions, especially when we want something, but we must be willing to stop doing what is wrong. God will forgive those who are truly repentant, but hypocrites will be severely punished.

15:1 Moses and Samuel were two of God's greatest prophets. Like Jeremiah, both interceded for the people before God (Exodus 32:11; Numbers 14:11-20; 1 Samuel 7:9; 12:17; Psalm 99:6). Intercession is often effective. In this case, however, the people were so wicked and stubborn that God knew they would not turn to him.

15:3, 4 The goal of these destroyers would be to destroy the living and devour the dead. Because of Manasseh's evil reign and the people's sin (2 Kings 21:1-16; 23:26; 24:3), the destruction would be complete. The people may have argued that they should not be held responsible for Manasseh's sins, but they were continuing what Manasseh began. If we follow corrupt leaders knowingly, we can't excuse ourselves by blaming their bad example.

to take them as captives to a foreign land. For my anger blazes forth like fire, and it will
consume them."
15 Then I said, "LORD, you know I am suffering for your sake. Punish my persecutors!
Don't let them kill me! Be merciful to me and give them what they deserve! 16 Your
words are what sustain me. They bring me great joy and are my heart's delight, for I bear
your name, O LORD God Almighty. 17 I never joined the people in their merry feasts. I
sat alone because your hand was on me. I burst with indignation at their sins. 18 Why then
does my suffering continue? Why is my wound so incurable? Your help seems as
uncertain as a seasonal brook. It is like a spring that has gone dry."
19 The LORD replied, "If you return to me, I will restore you so you can continue to
serve me. If you speak words that are worthy, you will be my spokesman. You are to
influence them; do not let them influence you! 20 They will fight against you like an
attacking army, but I will make you as secure as a fortified wall. They will not conquer
you, for I will protect and deliver you. I, the LORD, have spoken! 21 Yes, I will certainly
keep you safe from these wicked men. I will rescue you from their cruel hands."

Jeremiah Forbidden to Marry

16 The LORD gave me another message. He said, 2 "Do not marry or have children in
this place. 3 For this is what the LORD says about the children born here in this city
and about their mothers and fathers: 4 They will die from terrible diseases. No one will
mourn for them or bury them, and they will lie scattered on the ground like dung. They
will die from war and famine, and their bodies will be food for the vultures and wild
animals.

Judah's Coming Punishment

5 "Do not go to their funerals to mourn and show sympathy for them," says the LORD,
"for I have removed my protection and peace from them. I have taken away my unfailing
love and my mercy. 6 Both the great and the lowly will die in this land. No one will bury
them or mourn for them. Their friends will not cut themselves or shave their heads in
sadness. 7 No one will offer a meal to comfort those who mourn for the dead—not even
for the death of a mother or a father. No one will send a cup of wine to console them.
8 "And do not go to their feasts and parties. Do not eat and drink with them at all. 9 For
the LORD Almighty, the God of Israel, says: In your own lifetime, before your very eyes,
I will put an end to the happy singing and laughter in this land. The joyful voices of
bridegrooms and brides will no longer be heard.
10 "When you tell the people all these things, they will ask, 'Why has the LORD decreed
such terrible things against us? What have we done to deserve such treatment? What is
our sin against the LORD our God?' 11 Tell them that this is the LORD's reply: It is because
your ancestors were unfaithful to me. They worshiped other gods and served them. They
abandoned me. They did not keep my law. 12 And you are even worse than your
ancestors! You stubbornly follow your own evil desires and refuse to listen to me. 13 So
I will throw you out of this land and send you into a foreign land where you and your

15:16 Job 23:12; Ps 119:103; Jer 14:9
15:17 Ps 102:7; 2 Cor 6:17
15:18 Jer 30:15
15:19 Ezek 44:23
15:20 Ps 46:7; Isa 41:10; Jer 1:8, 18-19; Ezek 3:9
15:21 Ps 37:40; Isa 49:26; Jer 39:11-12
16:3 Jer 15:8
16:4 Pss 79:2; 83:10; Isa 18:6; Jer 15:2-3; 34:20
16:5 Isa 27:11; Ezek 24:16-23
16:6 Deut 14:1; Ezek 9:6
16:8 Eccl 7:2-4; Isa 22:12-14; Jer 15:17
16:9 Jer 7:34; 25:10; Hos 2:11
16:10 Deut 29:24-25; 1 Kgs 9:8-9
16:11 1 Pet 4:3
16:12 Mark 7:21
16:13 Deut 4:26-27; 28:36; Jer 5:19; 15:14

15:17-21 Jeremiah accused God of not helping him when he really needed it. Jeremiah had taken his eyes off God's purposes and was feeling sorry for himself. He was angry, hurt, and afraid. In response, God didn't get angry at Jeremiah; he answered by rearranging Jeremiah's priorities. As God's mouthpiece, he was to influence the people, not let them influence him. There are three important lessons in this passage: (1) In prayer we can reveal our deepest thoughts to God; (2) God expects us to trust him, no matter what; (3) we are here to influence others for God.

16:1–17:18 This section portrays the coming day of disaster. It begins by showing Jeremiah's loneliness. He is a social outcast because of his harsh messages and his celibate life-style. He must not marry, have children, or take part in funerals or festivals. The section concludes with another appeal to avoid judgment by turning to God. The people did not heed Jeremiah's words, however, and the first wave of destruction came almost immediately, in 605 B.C. (2 Kings 24:8-12). The second wave came in 597 B.C., and Judah was completely destroyed in 586 B.C.

16:5-7 In Jeremiah's culture, it was unthinkable not to show grief publicly. The absence of mourning showed the people how complete their devastation would be. So many people would die that it would be impossible to carry out customary mourning rituals for all of them.

16:8-13 Jeremiah was also told not to participate in parties or other joyful events to show how seriously God took the nation's sins. In both cases (no public grief or joy), Jeremiah's life was to be an attention getter and an illustration of God's truth. Sometimes we think that the only way to communicate is through speaking or teaching, but God can use a wide variety of means to bring his message. Use your creativity.

ancestors have never been. There you can worship idols all you like—and I will grant
you no favors!

Hope despite the Disaster

14“But the time is coming,” says the LORD, “when people who are taking an oath will no
longer say, ‘As surely as the LORD lives, who rescued the people of Israel from the land
of Egypt.’ 15Instead, they will say, ‘As surely as the LORD lives, who brought the people
of Israel back to their own land from the land of the north and from all the countries to
which he had exiled them.’ For I will bring them back to this land that I gave their
ancestors.

16“But now I am sending for many fishermen who will catch them,” says the LORD.
“I am sending for hunters who will search for them in the forests and caves. 17I am
watching them closely, and I see every sin. They cannot hope to hide from me. 18I will
punish them doubly for all their sins, because they have defiled my land with lifeless
images of their detestable gods and filled my inheritance with their evil deeds.”

Jeremiah's Prayer of Confidence

19LORD, you are my strength and fortress, my refuge in the day of trouble! Nations from
around the world will come to you and say, “Our ancestors were foolish, for they
worshiped worthless idols. 20Can people make their own god? The gods they make are
not real gods at all!”

21“So now I will show them my power and might,” says the LORD. “At last they will
know that I am the LORD.”

Judah's Sin and Punishment

17 The LORD says, “My people act as though their evil ways are laws to be obeyed,
inscribed with a diamond point on their stony hearts, or with an iron chisel on the
corners of their altars. 2Even their children go to worship at their sacred altars and
Asherah poles, beneath every green tree and on every high hill. 3So I will give all your
wealth and treasures—together with your pagan shrines—as plunder to your enemies,
for sin runs rampant in your land. 4The wonderful inheritance I have reserved for you
will slip out of your hands, and I will send you away as captives to a foreign land. For
you have kindled my anger into a roaring fire that will burn forever.”

Wisdom from the LORD

5This is what the LORD says: “Cursed are those who put their trust in mere humans and
turn their hearts away from the LORD. 6They are like stunted shrubs in the desert, with
no hope for the future. They will live in the barren wilderness, on the salty flats where
no one lives.

7“But blessed are those who trust in the LORD and have made the LORD their hope and

16:14 Deut 15:15; Isa 43:18-19
16:15 Isa 11:11-16
16:16 Isa 2:21; Amos 4:2; 9:1-3; Hab 1:14-15
16:17 Ps 90:8; Jer 23:24; 32:19; Luke 12:2; 1 Cor 4:5; Heb 4:13
16:18 Num 35:34; Jer 2:7; 3:9; Rev 18:6
16:19 Ps 18:1-2; Isa 25:4; Nah 1:7
16:21 Ps 83:18; Isa 43:3; Amos 5:8
17:1 Job 19:24; Prov 3:3; 7:3; 2 Cor 3:3
17:2 Exod 34:13; Isa 39:4-6
17:4 Deut 28:48; Isa 5:25; Jer 7:20; 12:7
17:5 2 Chr 32:8; Isa 30:1; 31:3; Ezek 29:6-7
17:7 Pss 34:8; 40:4; 84:12

16:14, 15 The book of Exodus records God's miraculous rescue of his people from Egyptian slavery (Exodus 1–15). The people's return from exile would be so momentous that it would overshadow even the exodus from Egypt. Even though his people had been so stubborn, God would once again show his great mercy.

16:17 Small children think that if they can't see you, then you can't see them. The people of Israel may have wished that hiding from God were as simple as closing their eyes. Although they closed their eyes to their sinful ways, their sins certainly weren't hidden from God. He who sees everything cannot be deceived. Do you have a sinful attitude or activity that you hope God won't notice? He knows about it. The first step of repentance is to acknowledge that God knows about your sins.

16:19 In this prayer, Jeremiah approached God with three descriptive names: strength, fortress, and refuge. Each name gives a slightly different glimpse of how Jeremiah experienced God's presence, and each is a picture of security and protection. Let God be your strength when you feel weak, your fortress when enemies come against you, and your refuge when you need to retreat from life's pressures.

17:1 God's people continued to sin even though they had the law, the prophets of God, and history replete with God's miracles. How could they do that? Why do we continue in sin even though we understand the eternal consequences? Jeremiah says the heart is deceitful (17:9), and “their evil ways are . . . inscribed with a diamond point on their stony hearts.” The Hebrews symbolized the various aspects of a person by locating them in certain physical organs. The heart was the organ of reason, intelligence, and will. So deep is our tendency to sin that only God's redemption can deliver us.

17:5-8 Two kinds of people are contrasted here: those who trust in human beings and those who trust in the Lord. The people of Judah were trusting in false gods and military alliances instead of God, and thus they were barren and unfruitful. In contrast, those who trust in the Lord flourish like trees planted along a riverbank (see Psalm 1). In times of trouble, those who trust in human beings will be impoverished and spiritually weak, so they will have no strength to draw on. But those who trust in the Lord will have abundant strength, not only for their own needs, but even for the needs of others. Are you satisfied with being unfruitful, or do you, like a well-watered tree, have strength for times of crisis and even some to share as you bear fruit for the Lord?

confidence. 8 They are like trees planted along a riverbank, with roots that reach deep
into the water. Such trees are not bothered by the heat or worried by long months of
drought. Their leaves stay green, and they go right on producing delicious fruit.
9 "The human heart is most deceitful and desperately wicked. Who really knows how
bad it is? 10 But I know! I, the LORD, search all hearts and examine secret motives. I give
all people their due rewards, according to what their actions deserve."

Jeremiah's Trust in the LORD

11 Like a bird that hatches eggs she has not laid, so are those who get their wealth by
unjust means. Sooner or later they will lose their riches and, at the end of their lives, will
become poor old fools.
12 But we worship at your throne—eternal, high, and glorious! 13 O LORD, the hope of
Israel, all who turn away from you will be disgraced and shamed. They will be buried in
a dry and dusty grave, for they have forsaken the LORD, the fountain of living water.
14 O LORD, you alone can heal me; you alone can save. My praises are for you alone!
15 People scoff at me and say, "What is this 'message from the LORD' you keep talking
about? Why don't your predictions come true?"
16 LORD, I have not abandoned my job as a shepherd for your people. I have not
urged you to send disaster. It is your message I have given them, not my own. 17 LORD,
do not desert me now! You alone are my hope in the day of disaster. 18 Bring shame
and terror on all who persecute me, but give me peace. Yes, bring double destruction
upon them!

Observing the Sabbath

19 Then the LORD said to me, "Go and stand in the gates of Jerusalem, first at the gate
where the king goes out, and then at each of the other gates. 20 Say to all the people,
'Listen to this message from the LORD, you kings of Judah and all you people of Judah
and everyone living in Jerusalem. 21 This is what the LORD says: Listen to my warning
and live! Stop carrying on your trade at Jerusalem's gates on the Sabbath day. 22 Do not
do your work on the Sabbath, but make it a holy day. I gave this command to your
ancestors, 23 but they did not listen or obey. They stubbornly refused to pay attention and
would not respond to discipline.
24 "'But if you obey me, says the LORD, and do not carry on your trade or work on
the Sabbath day, and if you keep it holy, 25 then this nation will continue forever. There
will always be a descendant of David sitting on the throne here in Jerusalem. Kings
and their officials will always ride among the people of Judah in chariots and on
horses, and this city will remain forever. 26 And from all around Jerusalem, from the
towns of Judah and Benjamin, from the western foothills* and the hill country and the
Negev, the people will come with their burnt offerings and sacrifices. They will bring
their grain offerings, incense, and thanksgiving offerings to the LORD's Temple.
27 "'But if you do not listen to me and refuse to keep the Sabbath holy, and if on the
Sabbath day you bring loads of merchandise through the gates of Jerusalem just as on
other days, then I will set fire to these gates. The fire will spread to the palaces, and no
one will be able to put out the roaring flames.'"

17:8 Pss 1:3; 92:12-14
17:9 Matt 13:15; Mark 2:17; 7:21-22; Rom 1:21; 7:11
17:10 Rom 8:27
17:12 Jer 14:21
17:13 Jer 14:8
17:14 Deut 10:21; Ps 54:1; Jer 33:6
17:15 Isa 5:19; Amos 5:18
17:16 Jer 12:3
17:17 Jer 16:19; Nah 1:7
17:18 Ps 35:4, 26; Jer 20:11
17:20 Jer 19:3-4
17:21 Num 15:32-36; Neh 13:15-21; Mark 4:24; John 5:9-12
17:22 Exod 20:8; 31:13; Ezek 20:12
17:23 Jer 7:26; 19:15
17:24 Exod 15:26; 20:8-11; Deut 11:13; Ezek 20:20
17:25 2 Sam 7:16; Ps 132:13-14; Jer 22:4; Luke 1:32; Heb 12:2
17:26 Ps 107:22; Jer 33:11
17:27 Jer 39:8; Ezek 20:47; Amos 2:5

17:26 Hebrew *the Shephelah.*

17:9, 10 God makes it clear why we sin—it's a matter of the heart. Our heart is inclined toward sin from the time we are born. It is easy to fall into the routine of forgetting and forsaking God. But we can still choose whether or not to continue in sin. We can yield to a specific temptation, or we can ask God to help us resist temptation when it comes.

17:11 There is a right way and a wrong way to do any task. Jeremiah says that the person who becomes rich by unjust means will end up foolish and poor. Whether at work, school, or play, we should strive to be honest in all our dealings. Getting a promotion, passing an exam, or gaining prestige by dishonest means will never bring God's blessing or lasting happiness.

17:19-27 The people were working on the Sabbath, their day of rest (Exodus 20:8-11). They considered making money more important than keeping God's law. If they would repent and put God first in their lives, God promised them honor among the nations. Over a century later, when Nehemiah led the exiles on their return to Jerusalem, one of his most important reforms was to reinstitute Sabbath observance (Nehemiah 13:15-22).

17:26 The Negev is the southern part of Judah.

The Potter and the Clay

18 The LORD gave another message to Jeremiah. He said, 2“Go down to the shop where
clay pots and jars are made. I will speak to you while you are there.” 3So I did as he
told me and found the potter working at his wheel. 4But the jar he was making did not turn
out as he had hoped, so the potter squashed the jar into a lump of clay and started again.
5Then the LORD gave me this message: 6“O Israel, can I not do to you as this potter
has done to his clay? As the clay is in the potter’s hand, so are you in my hand. 7If I
announce that a certain nation or kingdom is to be uprooted, torn down, and destroyed,
8but then that nation renounces its evil ways, I will not destroy it as I had planned. 9And
if I announce that I will build up and plant a certain nation or kingdom, making it strong
and great, 10but then that nation turns to evil and refuses to obey me, I will not bless that
nation as I had said I would.
11“Therefore, Jeremiah, go and warn all Judah and Jerusalem. Say to them, ‘This is
what the LORD says: I am planning disaster against you instead of good. So turn from
your evil ways, each of you, and do what is right.’”
12But they replied, “Don’t waste your breath. We will continue to live as we want to,
following our own evil desires.”
13Then the LORD said, “Has anyone ever heard of such a thing, even among the pagan
nations? My virgin Israel has done something too terrible to understand! 14Does the
snow ever melt high up in the mountains of Lebanon? Do the cold, flowing streams from
the crags of Mount Hermon ever run dry? 15These can be counted on, but not my people!
For they have deserted me and turned to worthless idols. They have stumbled off the
ancient highways of good, and they walk the muddy paths of sin. 16Therefore, their land
will become desolate, a monument to their stupidity. All who pass by will be astonished
and shake their heads in amazement at its utter desolation. 17I will scatter my people
before their enemies as the east wind scatters dust. And in all their trouble I will turn my
back on them and refuse to notice their distress.”

A Plot against Jeremiah

18Then the people said, “Come on, let’s find a way to stop Jeremiah. We have our own
priests and wise men and prophets. We don’t need him to teach the law and give us advice
and prophecies. Let’s spread rumors about him and ignore what he says.”
19LORD, help me! Listen to what they are planning to do to me! 20Should they repay
evil for good? They have set a trap to kill me, though I pleaded for them and tried to
protect them from your anger. 21So let their children starve! Let the sword pour out their
blood! Let their wives become widows without any children! Let their old men die in a
plague, and let their young men be killed in battle! 22Let screaming be heard from their
homes as warriors come suddenly upon them. For they have dug a pit for me, and they
have hidden traps along my path.
23LORD, you know all about their murderous plots against me. Don’t forgive their
crimes and blot out their sins. Let them die before you. Deal with them in your anger.

Jeremiah’s Shattered Jar

19 The LORD said to me, “Go and buy a clay jar. Then ask some of the leaders of the
people and of the priests to follow you. 2Go out into the valley of the son of Hinnom
by the entrance to the Potsherd Gate, and repeat to them the words that I give you. 3Say to

18:2 Jer 19:1-2; †Matt 27:9-10
18:6 Isa 45:9; 64:8; Matt 20:15; Rom 9:20-21
18:8 Jer 7:3-7; Ezek 18:21; Jon 3:10
18:9 Jer 31:28; Amos 9:11-15
18:10 1 Sam 2:30; Jer 7:24-28; Ezek 33:18
18:11 2 Kgs 17:13; Isa 1:16-19; Jer 4:6; 11:11; Acts 28:20
18:12 Deut 29:19; Jer 2:25; 16:12
18:13 Jer 2:10-11; 23:14; Hos 6:10
18:15 Isa 54:17; 62:10
18:16 Jer 25:9; 48:27; 50:13; Ezek 33:28-29
18:17 Jer 13:24
18:18 Ps 52:2; Mal 2:7
18:20 Pss 35:7; 57:6; 106:23
18:21 Ps 109:9-20; Jer 9:21; 11:22; 14:16
18:22 Ps 140:5; Jer 6:26
18:23 Jer 6:15, 21; 7:20; 17:4
19:2 Jer 7:31
19:3 1 Sam 3:11

18:1–19:15 The parables in these chapters, probably written during the early years of Jehoiakim’s reign, illustrate God’s sovereignty over the nation. God has power over the clay (Judah), and he continues to work with it to make it a useful vessel. But Judah must soon repent, or the clay will harden the wrong way. Then it will be worth nothing and will be broken and destroyed.

18:6 As the potter molded or shaped a clay pot on the potter’s wheel, defects often appeared. The potter had power over the clay, to permit the defects to remain or to reshape the pot. Likewise, God had power to reshape the nation to conform to his purposes. Our strategy should not be to become mindless and passive—one aspect of clay—but to be willing and receptive to God’s impact on us. As we yield to God, he begins reshaping us into valuable vessels.

18:12 Our society admires assertiveness, independence, and defiance of authority. In a relationship with God these qualities become stubbornness, self-importance, and refusal to listen or change. Left unchecked, stubbornness becomes a way of life hostile to God.

18:18 Jeremiah’s words and actions challenged the people’s social and moral behavior. He had openly spoken against the king, the officials, the priests and prophets, the teachers, and the wise (4:9; 8:8, 9). He wasn’t afraid to give unpopular criticism. The people could either obey him or silence him. They chose the latter. They did not think they needed Jeremiah; their false prophets told them what they wanted to hear. How do you respond to criticism? Listen carefully—God may be trying to tell you something.

19:4 Deut 28:20; 2 Kgs 21:6, 16; Isa 65:11; Jer 2:34; 7:6, 9; 11:13; 17:13; Dan 11:31
19:5 Lev 18:21; 2 Kgs 7:17; Ps 106:37-38; Jer 32:35
19:6 Jer 7:32
19:7 Ps 33:10-11; Isa 28:17-18; Jer 16:4
19:8 1 Kgs 9:8; 2 Chr 7:21; Jer 18:16
19:9 Deut 28:53, 55; Ezek 5:10; Lam 4:10
19:10 Jer 19:1
19:11 Ps 2:9; Isa 30:14; Jer 7:32; Rev 2:27
19:13 Deut 4:19; 2 Kgs 17:16; Jer 8:2; 7:18; 32:29; 52:13; Ezek 20:28; Zeph 1:5

them, 'Listen to this message from the LORD, you kings of Judah and citizens of Jerusalem!
This is what the LORD Almighty, the God of Israel, says: I will bring such a terrible disaster
on this place that the ears of those who hear about it will ring!
4 " 'For Israel has forsaken me and turned this valley into a place of wickedness.
The people burn incense to foreign gods—idols never before worshiped by this
generation, by their ancestors, or by the kings of Judah. And they have filled this place
with the blood of innocent children. 5 They have built pagan shrines to Baal, and there
they burn their sons as sacrifices to Baal. I have never commanded such a horrible
deed; it never even crossed my mind to command such a thing! 6 So beware, for the
time is coming, says the LORD, when this place will no longer be called Topheth or
the valley of the son of Hinnom, but the Valley of Slaughter. 7 For I will upset the battle
plans of Judah and Jerusalem and let invading armies slaughter them. The enemy will
leave the dead bodies as food for the vultures and wild animals. 8 I will wipe Jerusalem
from the face of the earth, making it a monument to their stupidity. All who pass by
will be appalled and will gasp at the destruction they see there. 9 I will see to it that
your enemies lay siege to the city until all the food is gone. Then those trapped inside
will have to eat their own sons and daughters and friends. They will be driven to utter
despair.'
10 "As these men watch, Jeremiah, smash the jar you brought with you. 11 Then say to
them, 'This is what the LORD Almighty says: As this jar lies shattered, so I will shatter
the people of Judah and Jerusalem beyond all hope of repair. They will bury the bodies
in Topheth until there is no more room. 12 This is what I will do to this place and its
people, says the LORD. I will cause this city to become defiled like Topheth. 13 Yes, all
the houses in Jerusalem, including the palace of Judah's kings, will become like
Topheth—all the houses where you burned incense on the rooftops to your star gods, and
where drink offerings were poured out to your idols.' "
14 Then Jeremiah returned from Topheth where he had delivered this message, and he

GOD'S OBJECT LESSONS IN JEREMIAH

Reference	Object Lesson	Significance
1:11, 12	Branch of an almond tree	God will carry out his threats of punishment.
1:13	Boiling pot, tipping southward	God will punish Judah.
13:1–11	A useless linen belt	Because the people refused to listen to God, they had become useless, good for nothing, like a useless linen belt.
18:1–17	Potter's clay	God could destroy his sinful people if he so desired. This is a warning to them to repent before he is forced to bring judgment.
19:1–12	Broken clay jars	God would smash Judah just as Jeremiah smashed the clay jars.
24:1–10	Two baskets of figs	Good figs represent God's remnant. Bad figs are the people left behind.
27:2–11	Yoke	Any nation who refused to submit to Babylon's yoke of control would be punished.
43:8–13	Large rocks	The rocks marked the place where Nebuchadnezzar would set his throne when God allowed him to conquer Egypt.
51:59–64	Scroll sunk in the river	Babylon would sink to rise no more.

19:6 The valley of the son of Hinnom was the garbage dump of Jerusalem and the place where children were sacrificed to the god Molech. It is also mentioned in 7:31, 32. Topheth was located in the valley and means "fireplace" and was probably where children were burned as sacrifices.

19:7-13 The horrible carnage that Jeremiah predicted happened twice: in 586 B.C. during the Babylonian invasion under Nebuchadnezzar and in A.D. 70 when Titus destroyed Jerusalem. During the Babylonian siege, food became so scarce that people became cannibals, even eating their own children. (See Leviticus 26:29 and Deuteronomy 28:53-57 for prophecies concerning this; and see 2 Kings 6:28, 29; Lamentations 2:20; 4:10 for accounts of actual occurrences.)

stopped in front of the Temple of the LORD. He said to the people there, 15“This is what the
LORD Almighty, the God of Israel, says: I will bring disaster upon this city and its
surrounding towns just as I promised, because you have stubbornly refused to listen to me.”

Jeremiah and Pashhur

20 Now Pashhur son of Immer, the priest in charge of the Temple of the LORD, heard
what Jeremiah was saying. 2So he arrested Jeremiah the prophet and had him
whipped and put in stocks at the Benjamin Gate of the LORD’s Temple.
3The next day, when Pashhur finally released him, Jeremiah said, “Pashhur, the LORD
has changed your name. From now on you are to be called ‘The Man Who Lives in
Terror.’* 4For this is what the LORD says: I will send terror upon you and all your friends,
and you will watch as they are slaughtered by the swords of the enemy. I will hand the
people of Judah over to the king of Babylon. He will take them captive to Babylon or
run them through with the sword. 5And I will let your enemies plunder Jerusalem. All
the famed treasures of the city—the precious jewels and gold and silver of your
kings—will be carried off to Babylon. 6As for you, Pashhur, you and all your household
will go as captives to Babylon. There you will die and be buried, you and all your friends
to whom you promised that everything would be all right.”

Jeremiah’s Complaint

7O LORD, you persuaded me, and I allowed myself to be persuaded. You are stronger
than I am, and you overpowered me. Now I am mocked by everyone in the city.
8Whenever I speak, the words come out in a violent outburst. “Violence and destruction!” I shout. So these messages from the LORD have made me a household joke. 9And
I can’t stop! If I say I’ll never mention the LORD or speak in his name, his word burns in
my heart like a fire. It’s like a fire in my bones! I am weary of holding it in!
10I have heard the many rumors about me. They call me “The Man Who Lives in
Terror.” And they say, “If you say anything, we will report it.” Even my old friends are
watching me, waiting for a fatal slip. “He will trap himself,” they say, “and then we will
get our revenge on him.”
11But the LORD stands beside me like a great warrior. Before him they will stumble.
They cannot defeat me. They will be shamed and thoroughly humiliated. Their dishonor
will never be forgotten. 12O LORD Almighty! You know those who are righteous, and
you examine the deepest thoughts of hearts and minds. Let me see your vengeance
against them, for I have committed my cause to you. 13Now I will sing out my thanks to
the LORD! Praise the LORD! For though I was poor and needy, he delivered me from my
oppressors.
14Yet I curse the day I was born! May the day of my birth not be blessed. 15I curse the
messenger who told my father, “Good news—you have a son!” 16Let him be destroyed
like the cities of old that the LORD overthrew without mercy. Terrify him all day long
with battle shouts, 17for he did not kill me at birth. Oh, that I had died in my mother’s
womb, that her body had been my grave! 18Why was I ever born? My entire life has been
filled with trouble, sorrow, and shame.

20:3 Hebrew *Magor-missabib,* which means “surrounded by terror”; also in 20:10.

19:15 Neh 9:17, 29; Ps 58:4; Jer 7:26; 17:23
20:1 1 Chr 24:14; Ezra 2:37-38
20:2 1 Kgs 22:27; 2 Chr 16:10; 24:21; Job 13:27; Zech 14:10
20:4 Jer 29:21; 39:6-7; Ezek 26:21
20:5 2 Kgs 20:17; 2 Chr 36:10; Jer 15:13; 17:3
20:6 Jer 14:14-15; Lam 2:14
20:7 Lam 3:14; Ezek 3:14; Mic 3:8
20:8 2 Chr 36:16; Jer 6:10
20:9 Job 32:18-20; Ps 39:3; Jer 4:19; Acts 4:20
20:10 1 Kgs 19:2; Neh 6:6-13; Pss 31:13; 41:9; Jer 18:18
20:12 Pss 7:9; 17:3; 59:10; 62:8; 139:23; Jer 11:20; 17:10
20:13 Pss 34:6; 69:33; Jer 15:21; 31:7
20:14 Job 3:3-6
20:15 Gen 21:6-7
20:17 Job 3:10-11, 16; 10:18-19
20:18 Job 3:20; 14:1; 1 Cor 4:9-13

20:1ff This event took place during the reign of Jehoiakim of Judah. Jeremiah preached at the valley of the son of Hinnom, the center of idolatry in the city. He also preached in the Temple, which should have been the center of true worship. Both places attracted many people; both were places of false worship.

20:1-3 Pashhur was the official in charge of maintaining order in the Temple (see 29:26 for a description of the responsibility). He was also a priest and had pretended to be a prophet. After hearing Jeremiah’s words, Pashhur had him whipped and put in the stocks (locked up) instead of taking his message to heart and acting on it. The truth sometimes stings, but our reaction to the truth shows what we are made of. We can deny the charges and destroy evidence of our misdeeds, or we can take the truth humbly to heart and let it change us. Pashhur may have thought he was a strong leader, but he was really a coward.

20:4-6 This prophecy of destruction came true in three waves of invasion by Babylon. The first wave happened within the year (605 B.C.). Pashhur was probably exiled to Babylon during the second wave in 597 B.C. when Jehoiachin was taken captive. The third invasion occurred in 586 B.C.

20:7-18 Jeremiah cried out in despair mixed with praise, unburdening his heart to God. He had faithfully proclaimed God’s word and had received nothing in return but persecution and sorrow. Yet when he withheld God’s word for a while, it became fire in his bones until he could hold it back no longer. When God’s living message of forgiveness and love becomes fire in your bones, you also will feel compelled to share it with others, regardless of the results.

4. Jeremiah accuses Judah's leaders

No Deliverance from Babylon

21:1 2 Kgs 25:18-21; 1 Chr 9:12; Jer 29:25, 29; 37:3
21:2 2 Kgs 25:1-2; Ps 44:1-4
21:4 Zech 14:2
21:5 Isa 5:25; 63:10; Jer 6:12
21:6 Jer 14:12; 32:24
21:7 2 Chr 36:17; Jer 13:14; Ezek 7:9; Hab 1:6-10
21:8 Deut 30:15, 19
21:10 2 Chr 36:19; Jer 32:28-29; 39:8; 44:11, 27; 52:13

21 The LORD spoke through Jeremiah when King Zedekiah sent Pashhur son of
Malkijah and Zephaniah son of Maaseiah, the priest, to speak with him. They
begged Jeremiah, 2"Please ask the LORD to help us. King Nebuchadnezzar* of Babylon
has begun his attack on Judah. Perhaps the LORD will be gracious and do a mighty
miracle as he has done in the past. Perhaps he will force Nebuchadnezzar to withdraw
his armies."
3Jeremiah replied, "Go back to King Zedekiah and tell him, 4'This is what the LORD,
the God of Israel, says: I will make your weapons useless against the king of Babylon
and the Babylonians* who are attacking you. Yes, I will bring your enemies right into
the heart of this city. 5I myself will fight against you with great power, for I am very
angry. You have made me furious! 6I will send a terrible plague upon this city, and both
people and animals will die. 7And then, says the LORD, even after King Zedekiah, his
officials, and everyone else in the city have survived war, famine, and disease, I will hand
them over to King Nebuchadnezzar of Babylon. He will slaughter them all without
mercy, pity, or compassion.'
8"Tell all the people, 'This is what the LORD says: Take your choice of life or death!
9Everyone who stays in Jerusalem will die from war, famine, or disease, but those who
go out and surrender to the Babylonians will live. 10For I have decided to bring disaster
and not good upon this city, says the LORD. It will be captured by the king of Babylon,
and he will reduce it to ashes.'

Judgment on Judah's Kings

21:12 Isa 1:17; Nah 1:6; Zech 7:9-10
21:13 2 Sam 5:6-7; Jer 49:4; Lam 4:12; Ezek 13:8; Obad 1:3-4
21:14 2 Chr 36:19

11"Say to the royal family of Judah, 'Listen to this message from the LORD! 12This is
what the LORD says to the dynasty of David: Give justice to the people you judge! Help
those who have been robbed; rescue them from their oppressors. Do what is right, or my
anger will burn like an unquenchable fire because of all your sins. 13I will fight against
this city of Jerusalem that boasts, "We are safe on our mountain! No one can touch us
here." 14And I myself will punish you for your sinfulness, says the LORD. I will light a
fire in your forests that will burn up everything around you.'"

A Message for Judah's Kings

22:2 Isa 9:7; Jer 17:25; 22:4, 20; Luke 1:32
22:3 Exod 22:21-24; Ps 72:4; Jer 7:6; 19:4; 21:12; 22:17

22 Then the LORD said to me, "Go over and speak directly to the king of Judah. Say
to him, 2'Listen to this message from the LORD, you king of Judah, sitting on
David's throne. Let your officials and your people listen, too. 3This is what the LORD
says: Be fair-minded and just. Do what is right! Help those who have been robbed; rescue
them from their oppressors. Quit your evil deeds! Do not mistreat foreigners, orphans,
and widows. Stop murdering the innocent! 4If you obey me, there will always be a

21:2 Hebrew *Nebuchadrezzar,* a variant name for Nebuchadnezzar; also in 21:7. **21:4** Or *Chaldeans;* also in 21:9.

21:1 Chapters 21–28 are Jeremiah's messages concerning Nebuchadnezzar's attacks on Jerusalem between 588 and 586 B.C. (see also 2 Kings 25). King Zedekiah decided to rebel against Nebuchadnezzar (2 Kings 24:20), and the nobles advised allying with Egypt. Jeremiah pronounced judgment on the kings (21:1–23:8) and false prophets (23:9-40) for leading the people astray.

21:1, 2 King Zedekiah probably was referring to God's deliverance of Jerusalem from Sennacherib, king of Assyria, in the days of Hezekiah (Isaiah 36–37). But Zedekiah's hopes were dashed. He was Judah's last ruler during the time of the Exile of 586 B.C.

21:1, 2 Pashhur came to the prophet for help. (This is not the same Pashhur as in 20:1.) God still had work for Jeremiah to do. In living out our faith, we may find that rejection, disappointment, or hard work has brought us to the point of despondency. But we are still needed. God has important work for us as well.

21:1-14 Jeremiah had foretold Jerusalem's destruction. The city's leaders had denied his word and mocked his pronouncements. In desperation, King Zedekiah turned to God for help, but without acknowledging God's warnings or admitting his sin. Too often we expect God to help us in our time of trouble even though we have ignored him in our time of prosperity. But God wants a lasting relationship. Are you trying to build a lasting friendship with God, or are you merely using him occasionally to escape trouble? What would you think of your family or friends if they thought of you only as a temporary resource?

21:13 Jerusalem was built on a plateau with valleys on three sides. Because of its strategic location, the inhabitants thought they were safe.

22:1ff Chapters 22–25 may not be in chronological order. In 21:8-10 God implied that it was too late for repentance. In 22:4, however, God said that there was still time to change. The events to which this chapter refer occurred before those of chapter 21.

22:3 God gave the king the basis for rebuilding the nation—turn from evil and do right. Doing what is right is more than simply believing all the right doctrines about God. It means living in obedience to God. Good deeds do not save us, but they display our faith (James 2:17-26).

descendant of David sitting on the throne here in Jerusalem. The king will ride through
the palace gates in chariots and on horses, with his parade of officials and subjects. 5 But
if you refuse to pay attention to this warning, I swear by my own name, says the LORD,
that this palace will become a pile of rubble.'"

A Message about the Palace

6 Now this is what the LORD says concerning the royal palace: "You are as beloved to
me as fruitful Gilead and the green forests of Lebanon. But I will destroy you and
leave you deserted, with no one living within your walls. 7 I will call for wreckers,
who will bring out their tools to dismantle you. They will tear out all your fine cedar
beams and throw them on the fire. 8 People from many nations will pass by the ruins
of this city and say to one another, 'Why did the LORD destroy such a great city?' 9 And
the answer will be, 'Because they violated their covenant with the LORD their God by
worshiping other gods.'"

A Message about Jehoahaz

10 Do not weep for the dead king or mourn his loss. Instead, weep for the captive king
being led away! For he will never return to see his native land again. 11 For this is what
the LORD says about Jehoahaz,* who succeeded his father, King Josiah, and was taken
away as a captive: "He will never return. 12 He will die in a distant land and never again
see his own country."

A Message about Jehoiakim

13 And the LORD says, "Destruction is certain for Jehoiakim,* who builds his palace with
forced labor.* By not paying wages, he builds injustice into its walls and oppression into its
doorframes and ceilings. 14 He says, 'I will build a magnificent palace with huge rooms and
many windows, paneled throughout with fragrant cedar and painted a lovely red.'

15 "But a beautiful palace does not make a great king! Why did your father, Josiah,
reign so long? Because he was just and right in all his dealings. That is why God blessed
him. 16 He made sure that justice and help were given to the poor and needy, and
everything went well for him. Isn't that what it means to know me?" asks the LORD.
17 "But you! You are full of selfish greed and dishonesty! You murder the innocent,
oppress the poor, and reign ruthlessly."

18 Therefore, this is the LORD's decree of punishment against King Jehoiakim, who
succeeded his father, Josiah, on the throne: "His family will not weep for him when he
dies. His subjects will not even care that he is dead. 19 He will be buried like a dead
donkey—dragged out of Jerusalem and dumped outside the gate! 20 Weep, for your allies
are all gone. Search for them in Lebanon. Shout for them at Bashan. Search for them in
the regions east of the river.* See, they are all destroyed. Not one is left to help you.

21 "When you were prosperous, I warned you, but you replied, 'Don't bother me.'
Since childhood you have been that way—you simply will not listen! 22 And now your
allies have all disappeared with a puff of wind. All your friends have been taken away
as captives. Surely at last you will see your wickedness and be ashamed. 23 It may be nice
to live in a beautiful palace lined with lumber from the cedars of Lebanon, but soon you
will cry and groan in anguish—anguish like that of a woman about to give birth.

22:5 Amos 6:8; Heb 6:13
22:6 Isa 6:11; Jer 7:34
22:8 Deut 29:24-26; 1 Kgs 9:8-9; 2 Chr 7:20, 22; Jer 16:10
22:9 2 Chr 34:25; Jer 11:3
22:10 Jer 16:7; 44:14
22:11 2 Kgs 23:30-34
22:12 2 Kgs 23:34
22:13 Jer 17:11; Hab 2:9; Jas 5:4
22:14 Isa 5:8-9; Hab 1:4
22:15 2 Kgs 23:25; Jer 21:12; 42:6
22:16 Ps 72:1-4, 12-13; Jer 9:24
22:17 Jer 6:13; 8:10; Luke 12:15-20
22:18 1 Kgs 13:30
22:19 Jer 36:30
22:20 Deut 32:49
22:21 Jer 3:24-25; 13:10; 19:15; 32:30
22:22 Jer 20:11; 30:14
22:23 Jer 4:31

22:11 Hebrew *Shallum,* another name for Jehoahaz. **22:13a** The brother and successor of the exiled Jehoahaz. **22:13b** Hebrew *by unrighteousness.* **22:20** Hebrew *in Abarim.*

22:10-12 Good King Josiah had died at the battle of Megiddo (2 Kings 23:29); his son Jehoahaz reigned for only three months in 609 B.C. before being taken away to Egypt by Pharaoh Neco. He would be the first ruler to die in exile. The people were told not to waste their tears on the death of Josiah but to cry for the king who was taken into exile and would never return.

22:15, 16 God passed judgment on King Jehoiakim. His father, Josiah, had been one of Judah's great kings, but Jehoiakim was evil. Josiah had been faithful to his responsibility to be a model of right living, but Jehoiakim had been unfaithful to his responsibility to imitate his father. God's judgment was on unfaithful Jehoiakim. He could not claim his father's blessings when he had not followed his father's God. We may inherit our parents' money, but we cannot inherit their faith. A godly heritage, a good education, or a beautiful home doesn't guarantee moral character. We must have our own relationship with God.

22:21 Jehoiakim had been hardheaded and hard-hearted since childhood. God warned him, but he refused to listen. His prosperity always took a higher priority than his relationship with God. If you ever find yourself so comfortable that you don't have time for God, stop and ask which is more important—the comforts of this life or a close relationship with God.

22:24 Hag 2:23
22:25 2 Kgs 24:15-16; Jer 34:20
22:28 Jer 15:1; Hos 8:8
22:29 Jer 6:19; Mic 1:2
22:30 Matt 1:12

A Message for Jehoiachin

24“And as surely as I live,” says the LORD, “I will abandon you, Jehoiachin* son of
Jehoiakim, king of Judah. Even if you were the signet ring on my right hand, I would
pull you off. 25I will hand you over to those who seek to kill you, of whom you are so
desperately afraid—to King Nebuchadnezzar* of Babylon and the mighty Babylonian*
army. 26I will expel you and your mother from this land, and you will die in a foreign
country. 27You will never again return to the land of your desire.

28“Why is this man Jehoiachin like a discarded, broken dish? Why are he and his
children to be exiled to distant lands? 29O earth, earth, earth! Listen to this message from
the LORD! 30This is what the LORD says: Let the record show that this man Jehoiachin
was childless, for none of his children will ever sit on the throne of David to rule in Judah.
His life will amount to nothing.”

23:1 Isa 56:9-12; Jer 10:21; 50:6; Ezek 13:3; 34:1-2; Zech 11:17
23:2 Exod 32:34; Jer 44:22
23:3 Isa 11:11-16; Jer 31:7-8; 32:37
23:4 Jer 3:15; 31:10; John 6:39; 10:28; 1 Pet 1:5
23:5 Isa 9:6-7; 11:1-5; 53:2; Jer 33:15-16; Zech 3:8; 6:12-13
23:6 Matt 1:21-23; Rom 3:21-22; 1 Cor 1:30
23:7 Isa 43:18-19; Jer 16:14-15

The Righteous Branch

23 “I will send disaster upon the leaders of my people—the shepherds of my
sheep—for they have destroyed and scattered the very ones they were expected
to care for,” says the LORD.

2This is what the LORD, the God of Israel, says to these shepherds: “Instead of leading
my flock to safety, you have deserted them and driven them to destruction. Now I will
pour out judgment on you for the evil you have done to them. 3But I will gather together
the remnant of my flock from wherever I have driven them. I will bring them back into
their own fold, and they will be fruitful and increase in number. 4Then I will appoint
responsible shepherds to care for them, and they will never be afraid again. Not a single
one of them will be lost or missing,” says the LORD.

5“For the time is coming,” says the LORD, “when I will place a righteous Branch on
King David’s throne. He will be a King who rules with wisdom. He will do what is just
and right throughout the land. 6And this is his name: ‘The LORD Is Our Righteousness.’*
In that day Judah will be saved, and Israel will live in safety.

7“In that day,” says the LORD, “when people are taking an oath, they will no longer
say, ‘As surely as the LORD lives, who rescued the people of Israel from the land of
Egypt.’ 8Instead, they will say, ‘As surely as the LORD lives, who brought the people of
Israel back to their own land from the land of the north and from all the countries to
which he had exiled them.’ Then they will live in their own land.”

23:9 Hab 3:16
23:10 Ps 107:34; Jer 5:7-8; 9:10; 12:4; Hos 4:2-3

Judgment on False Prophets

9My heart is broken because of the false prophets, and I tremble uncontrollably. I stagger
like a drunkard, like someone overcome by wine, because of the holy words the LORD
has spoken against them. 10For the land is full of adultery, and it lies under a curse. The
land itself is in mourning—its pastures are dried up. For the prophets do evil and abuse
their power.

22:24 Hebrew *Coniah,* a variant name for Jehoiachin; also in 22:28, 30. **22:25a** Hebrew *Nebuchadrezzar,* a variant name for Nebuchadnezzar. **22:25b** Or *Chaldean.* **23:6** Hebrew *Yahweh Tsidqenu.*

22:24, 25 A signet ring was extremely valuable because a king used it to authenticate important documents. Jehoiachin’s sins spoiled his usefulness to God. Even if he were God’s own signet ring, God would depose him because of his sins (see 24:1).

22:30 Zedekiah reigned after Jehoiachin but died before him (52:10, 11). Jehoiachin was the last king of David’s line to sit on the throne in Judah (1 Chronicles 3:15-20). He had seven sons, but not one served as king. Jehoiachin’s grandson Zerubbabel ruled after the return from exile (Ezra 2:2). He was only a governor, not a king.

23:1-4 Those responsible to lead Israel in God’s path were the very ones responsible for Israel’s present plight, and so God had decreed harsh judgment against them. Leaders are held responsible for those entrusted to their care. Whom has God placed in your care? Remember that you are accountable to God for those you influence and lead.

23:5, 6 Jeremiah contrasted the present corrupt leaders with the coming Messiah, the perfect King, who would come from David’s line to reign over Israel. The King is called a righteous Branch because he will sprout up from the stump of David’s fallen dynasty (Isaiah 11:1). This new growth will have God’s own characteristics. Like the Creator, the Branch will be righteous.

23:9-14 How did the nation become so corrupt? A major factor was false prophecy. The false prophets had a large, enthusiastic audience and were very popular because they made the people believe that all was well. By contrast, Jeremiah’s message from God was unpopular because it showed the people how bad they were.

There are four warning signs of false prophets—characteristics we need to watch for even today: (1) They may appear to speak God’s message, but they do not live according to God’s Word. (2) They water down God’s message in order to make it more palatable. (3) They encourage their listeners, often subtly, to disobey God. (4) They tend to be arrogant and self-serving, appealing to the desires of their audience instead of being true to God’s Word.

11“The priests are like the prophets, all ungodly, wicked men. I have seen their
despicable acts right here in my own Temple,” says the LORD. 12“Therefore, their paths
will be dark and slippery. They will be chased down dark and treacherous trails, where
they will fall. For I will bring disaster upon them when their time of punishment comes.
I, the LORD, have spoken!
13“I saw that the prophets of Samaria were terribly evil, for they prophesied by Baal
and led my people of Israel into sin. 14But now I see that the prophets of Jerusalem are
even worse! They commit adultery, and they love dishonesty. They encourage those who
are doing evil instead of turning them away from their sins. These prophets are as wicked
as the people of Sodom and Gomorrah once were.”
15Therefore, this is what the LORD Almighty says concerning the prophets: “I will feed
them with bitterness and give them poison to drink. For it is because of Jerusalem’s
prophets that wickedness fills this land. 16This is my warning to my people,” says the
LORD Almighty. “Do not listen to these prophets when they prophesy to you, filling you
with futile hopes. They are making up everything they say. They do not speak for the
LORD! 17They keep saying to these rebels who despise my word, ‘Don’t worry! The
LORD says you will have peace!’ And to those who stubbornly follow their own evil
desires, they say, ‘No harm will come your way!’
18“But can you name even one of these prophets who knows the LORD well enough
to hear what he is saying? Has even one of them cared enough to listen? 19Look! The
LORD’s anger bursts out like a storm, a whirlwind that swirls down on the heads of the
wicked. 20The anger of the LORD will not diminish until it has finished all his plans. In
the days to come, you will understand all this very clearly.
21“I have not sent these prophets, yet they claim to speak for me. I have given them
no message, yet they prophesy. 22If they had listened to me, they would have spoken my
words and turned my people from their evil ways. 23Am I a God who is only in one
place?” asks the LORD. “Do they think I cannot see what they are doing? 24Can anyone
hide from me? Am I not everywhere in all the heavens and earth?” asks the LORD.
25“I have heard these prophets say, ‘Listen to the dream I had from God last night.’
And then they proceed to tell lies in my name. 26How long will this go on? If they are
prophets, they are prophets of deceit, inventing everything they say. 27By telling these
false dreams, they are trying to get my people to forget me, just as their ancestors did by
worshiping the idols of Baal. 28Let these false prophets tell their dreams, but let my true
messengers faithfully proclaim my every word. There is a difference between chaff and
wheat! 29Does not my word burn like fire?” asks the LORD. “Is it not like a mighty
hammer that smashes rock to pieces?
30“Therefore,” says the LORD, “I stand against these prophets who get their messages
from each other—31these smooth-tongued prophets who say, ‘This prophecy is from the
LORD!’ 32Their imaginary dreams are flagrant lies that lead my people into sin. I did not
send or appoint them, and they have no message at all for my people,” says the LORD.

23:12 Isa 8:22; John 12:35
23:13 1 Kgs 18:18-21
23:14 Isa 1:9-10; Jer 5:30, 32; 29:23; Ezek 13:22-23; Matt 11:24
23:15 Deut 29:18; Jer 8:14; 9:15
23:16 Jer 14:14; Ezek 13:2-3, 6; Matt 7:15; 2 Cor 11:13-15; Gal 1:8-9; 1 Jn 4:1
23:17 Jer 5:12; 8:11; Amos 9:10; Mic 2:11; 3:11
23:18 Gen 49:11; Job 15:8; 33:11
23:19 Jer 30:23; Amos 1:14
23:20 Isa 55:11; Jer 30:24; Zech 1:5-6
23:22 Zech 1:4; 1 Thes 1:9-10
23:23 Ps 139:1-10
23:24 Job 22:13-14; Ps 139:7-12; Isa 29:15-16
23:25 Jer 8:6; 29:8
23:26 1 Tim 4:1-2
23:27 Deut 13:1-3; Judg 3:7; 8:33-34
23:28 1 Cor 3:12-13
23:29 2 Cor 10:4-5
23:30 Ezek 13:8

False Prophecies and False Prophets

33“Suppose one of the people or one of the prophets or priests asks you, ‘What prophecy
has the LORD burdened you with now?’ You must reply, ‘You are the burden!* The LORD

23:33 As in Greek version and Latin Vulgate; Hebrew reads *What burden?*

23:14 Sodom and Gomorrah were sinful cities destroyed by God (Genesis 19:23, 24). In the Bible they typify the ultimate in depraved, sinful behavior and rebellion against God.

23:20 "In the days to come, you will understand all this very clearly" means that the people would see the truth of this prophecy when Jerusalem fell.

23:28 True prophets and false prophets are as different as chaff and wheat. Chaff is useless for food and cannot compare to nourishing wheat. To share the gospel is a great responsibility because the way we present it and live it will encourage people either to accept it or reject it. Whether we speak from a pulpit, teach in a class, or share with friends, we must accurately communicate and live out God's Word. As you share God's Word with friends and neighbors, they will look for its effectiveness in your life. Unless it has changed you, why should they let it change them? If you preach it, make sure you live it!

23:33-40 People mocked Jeremiah by saying sarcastically, "What prophecy has the LORD burdened you with now?" It seemed that Jeremiah brought nothing but God's sad news of condemnation. But this sad news was the truth. If they had accepted it, they would have had to repent and turn to God. Because they did not want to do this, they rejected Jeremiah's message. Have you ever rejected a message or made fun of it because it would require you to change your ways? Before dismissing someone who brings sad news, look carefully at your motives.

23:34 Lam 2:14 Zech 13:3
23:35 Jer 33:3; 42:4
23:36 Jer 10:10 2 Pet 3:16

says he will abandon you!' [34]If any prophet, priest, or anyone else says, 'I have a
prophecy from the LORD,' I will punish that person along with his entire family. [35]You
should keep asking each other, 'What is the LORD's answer?' or 'What is the LORD
saying?' [36]But stop using this phrase, 'prophecy from the LORD.' For people are using it
to give authority to their own ideas, turning upside down the words of our God, the living
God, the LORD Almighty.

[37]"This is what you should say to the prophets: 'What is the LORD's answer?' or 'What
is the LORD saying?' [38]But suppose they respond, 'This is a prophecy from the LORD!'
Then you should say, 'This is what the LORD says: Because you have used this phrase,
"prophecy from the LORD," even though I warned you not to use it, [39]I will forget you
completely. I will expel you from my presence, along with this city that I gave to you
and your ancestors. [40]And I will make you an object of ridicule, and your name will be
infamous throughout the ages.'"

23:39 Jer 7:14-15 Ezek 8:18
23:40 Jer 20:11 Ezek 5:14-15

Good and Bad Figs

24:1 2 Kgs 24:10-16 2 Chr 36:10
24:2 Jer 29:17

24 After King Nebuchadnezzar* of Babylon exiled Jehoiachin* son of Jehoiakim,
king of Judah, to Babylon along with the princes of Judah and all the skilled
craftsmen, the LORD gave me this vision. I saw two baskets of figs placed in front of the
LORD's Temple in Jerusalem. [2]One basket was filled with fresh, ripe figs, while the other
was filled with figs that were spoiled and could not be eaten.

[3]Then the LORD said to me, "What do you see, Jeremiah?"

I replied, "Figs, some very good and some very bad."

[4]Then the LORD gave me this message: [5]"This is what the LORD, the God of Israel,
says: The good figs represent the exiles I sent from Judah to the land of the Babylonians.* [6]I have sent them into captivity for their own good. I will see that they are well
treated, and I will bring them back here again. I will build them up and not tear them
down. I will plant them and not uproot them. [7]I will give them hearts that will recognize
me as the LORD. They will be my people, and I will be their God, for they will return
to me wholeheartedly.

[8]"But the rotten figs," the LORD said, "represent King Zedekiah of Judah, his officials,
all the people left in Jerusalem, and those who live in Egypt. I will treat them like spoiled
figs, too rotten to eat. [9]I will make them an object of horror and evil to every nation on
earth. They will be disgraced and mocked, taunted and cursed, wherever I send them. [10]I
will send war, famine, and disease until they have vanished from the land of Israel, which
I gave to them and their ancestors."

24:5 Nah 1:7 Zech 13:9
24:6 Jer 29:10; 31:4; 32:37, 41; 33:7 Ezek 11:17
24:7 Jer 29:13; 31:33; 32:40 Zech 8:8 Heb 8:10
24:9 1 Kgs 9:7 Ps 44:13-14 Isa 65:15 Jer 15:4; 29:18; 34:17
24:10 Isa 51:19 Jer 21:9; 27:8 Ezek 5:12-17

Seventy Years of Captivity

25 This message for all the people of Judah came to Jeremiah from the LORD during
the fourth year of Jehoiakim's reign* over Judah. This was the year when King
Nebuchadnezzar* of Babylon began his reign.

24:1a Hebrew *Nebuchadrezzar,* a variant name for Nebuchadnezzar. **24:1b** Hebrew *Jeconiah,* a variant name for Jehoiachin. **24:5** Or *Chaldeans.* **25:1a** The fourth year of Jehoiakim's reign and the accession year of Nebuchadnezzar's reign was 605 B.C. **25:1b** Hebrew *Nebuchadrezzar,* a variant name for Nebuchadnezzar; also in 25:9.

24:1 In 597 B.C. Jehoiachin was taken to Babylon, and Zedekiah became king. Often royal officials were exiled to keep them from exerting power and starting a rebellion. Skilled craftsmen were taken because they were valuable for Babylon's building program. Jeremiah foretold this event in 22:24-28.

24:2-10 The fresh, ripe figs represented the exiles to Babylon, not because they themselves were good, but because their hearts would respond to God. He would preserve them and bring them back to the land. The spoiled figs represented those who remained in Judah or ran away to Egypt. Those people may have arrogantly believed they would be blessed if they remained in the land or escaped to Egypt, but the opposite was true because God would use the captivity to refine the exiles. We may assume we are blessed when life goes well and cursed when it does not. But trouble is a blessing when it makes us stronger, and prosperity is a curse if it entices us away from God. If you are facing trouble, ask God to help you grow stronger for him. If things are going your way, ask God to help you use your prosperity for him.

24:6 The exiles in Babylon were cared for by the Lord. Although they were moved to a foreign land, their captivity was not enslavement. The people could function in business and own homes. Some, like Daniel, even held high positions in the government (see Daniel 2:48).

25:1ff Jeremiah gave this message in 605 B.C., the year Nebuchadnezzar came to power. From verse 3 we learn that the beginning of Jeremiah's ministry was in 627 B.C. He predicted the 70 years of captivity a full 20 years before they began.

2Jeremiah the prophet said to the people in Judah and Jerusalem, 3“For the past
twenty-three years—from the thirteenth year of Josiah son of Amon,* king of Judah,
until now—the LORD has been giving me his messages. I have faithfully passed them on
to you, but you have not listened.
4“Again and again, the LORD has sent you his prophets, but you have not listened or
even tried to hear. 5Each time the message was this: ‘Turn from the evil road you are
traveling and from the evil things you are doing. Only then will I let you live in this land
that the LORD gave to you and your ancestors forever. 6Do not make me angry by
worshiping the idols you have made. Then I will not harm you.’
7“But you would not listen to me,” says the LORD. “You made me furious by
worshiping your idols, bringing on yourselves all the disasters you now suffer. 8And now
the LORD Almighty says: Because you have not listened to me, 9I will gather together all
the armies of the north under King Nebuchadnezzar of Babylon, whom I have appointed
as my deputy. I will bring them all against this land and its people and against the other
nations near you. I will completely destroy* you and make you an object of horror and
contempt and a ruin forever. 10I will take away your happy singing and laughter. The
joyful voices of bridegrooms and brides will no longer be heard. Your businesses will
fail, and all your homes will stand silent and dark. 11This entire land will become a
desolate wasteland. Israel and her neighboring lands will serve the king of Babylon for
seventy years.
12“Then, after the seventy years of captivity are over, I will punish the king of Babylon
and his people for their sins, says the LORD. I will make the country of the Babylonians*
an everlasting wasteland. 13I will bring upon them all the terrors I have promised in this
book—all the penalties announced by Jeremiah against the nations. 14Many nations and
great kings will enslave the Babylonians, just as they enslaved my people. I will punish
them in proportion to the suffering they cause my people.”

The Cup of the LORD's Anger

15Then the LORD, the God of Israel, said to me, “Take from my hand this cup filled to the
brim with my anger, and make all the nations to whom I send you drink from it. 16When
they drink from it, they will stagger, crazed by the warfare I will send against them.”
17So I took the cup of anger from the LORD and made all the nations drink from
it—every nation the LORD sent me to. 18I went to Jerusalem and the other towns of Judah,
and their kings and officials drank from the cup. From that day until this, they have been
a desolate ruin, an object of horror, contempt, and cursing. 19I went to Egypt and spoke
to Pharaoh, his officials, his princes, and his people. They, too, drank from that terrible
cup, 20along with all the foreigners living in that land. So did all the kings of the land of Uz
and the kings of the Philistine cities of Ashkelon, Gaza, Ekron, and what remains of Ashdod.
21Then I went to the nations of Edom, Moab, and Ammon, 22and the kings of Tyre and
Sidon, and the kings of the regions across the sea. 23I went to Dedan, Tema, and Buz,
and to the people who live in distant places.* 24I went to the kings of Arabia, the kings
of the nomadic tribes of the desert, 25and to the kings of Zimri, Elam, and Media. 26And
I went to the kings of the northern countries, far and near, one after the other—all the
kingdoms of the world. And finally, the king of Babylon* himself drank from the cup of
the LORD's anger.
27Then the LORD said to me, “Now tell them, ‘The LORD Almighty, the God of Israel,

25:2 Jer 1:2; 7:25-26; 11:7-8; 26:5; 36:2-3
25:3 2 Kgs 24:1-2; Jer 36:1; 46:2
25:5 Gen 17:8-10; Isa 55:6-7; Jer 4:1; 7:7; 35:15
25:6 Deut 6:14; 8:19; 2 Kgs 17:35
25:7 2 Kgs 17:17; 21:15; Jer 7:19; 32:30-33
25:8 Jer 18:16
25:10 Eccl 12:3-4; Isa 24:8-11; Jer 16:9; Ezek 26:13
25:11 Dan 9:2; Zech 7:5
25:12 Ezra 1:1; Isa 13:14; Jer 29:10, 50-51
25:13 Jer 36:4, 29, 32
25:14 Jer 27:7; 50:9
25:15 Jer 51:7
25:17 Jer 1:10
25:18 Isa 51:17
25:19 Jer 46:2-28
25:20 Job 1:1; Jer 47:1-7
25:21 Jer 48:1-47; 49:1-22
25:22 Jer 47:4; Zech 9:2-4
25:23 Jer 49:7-8
25:25 Jer 49:34
25:26 Jer 50:9; 51:41
25:27 Ezek 21:4-5; Hab 2:17

25:3 The thirteenth year of Josiah's reign was 627 B.C. **25:9** The Hebrew term used here refers to the complete consecration of things or people to the LORD, either by destroying them or by giving them as an offering. **25:12** Or *Chaldeans.* **25:23** Or *who clip the corners of their hair.* **25:26** Hebrew *of Sheshach,* a code name for Babylon.

25:2-6 Imagine preaching the same message for 23 years and continually being rejected! Jeremiah faced this; but because he had committed his life to God, he continued to proclaim the message “Turn from the evil road you are traveling and from the evil things you are doing.” Regardless of the people's response, Jeremiah did not give up. God never stops loving us, even when we reject him. We can thank God that he won't give up on us, and, like Jeremiah, we can commit ourselves to never forsaking him. No matter how people respond when you tell them about God, remain faithful to God's high call and continue to witness for him.

25:12 This event is further described in Daniel 5. The troops of Cyrus the Great entered Babylon in 539 B.C. and killed Belshazzar, the last Babylonian ruler.

25:15-38 Judah would not be the only nation to drink the cup of God's anger. Here Jeremiah listed other wicked nations that would experience God's wrath at the hands of Babylon. Finally, Babylon itself would be destroyed because of its sin.

says: Drink from this cup of my anger. Get drunk and vomit, and you will fall to rise no
more, for I am sending terrible wars against you.' 28And if they refuse to accept the cup,
tell them, 'The LORD Almighty says: You must drink from it. You cannot escape! 29I have
begun to punish Jerusalem, the city where my own name is honored. Now should I let
you go unpunished? No, you will not escape disaster. I will call for war against all the
nations of the earth. I, the LORD Almighty, have spoken!'
30"Now prophesy all these things, and say to them, 'The LORD will roar loudly against
his own land from his holy dwelling in heaven. He will shout against everyone on the
earth, like the harvesters do as they crush juice from the grapes. 31His cry of judgment
will reach the ends of the earth, for the LORD will bring his case against all the nations.
He will judge all the people of the earth, slaughtering the wicked with his sword. The
LORD has spoken!'"
32This is what the LORD Almighty says: "Look! Disaster will fall upon nation after
nation! A great whirlwind of fury is rising from the most distant corners of the earth!"
33In that day those the LORD has slaughtered will fill the earth from one end to the
other. No one will mourn for them or gather up their bodies to bury them. They will be
scattered like dung on the ground.
34Weep and moan, you evil shepherds! Roll in the dust, you leaders of the flock! The
time of your slaughter has arrived; you will fall and shatter like fragile pottery. 35You
will find no place to hide; there will be no way to escape.
36Listen to the frantic cries of the shepherds, to the leaders of the flock shouting in
despair, for the LORD is spoiling their pastures. 37Peaceful meadows will be turned into
a wasteland by the LORD's fierce anger. 38He has left his den like a lion seeking its prey,
and their land will be made desolate by the sword of the enemy and the LORD's fierce
anger.

Jeremiah's Escape from Death

26 This message came to Jeremiah from the LORD early in the reign of Jehoiakim son
of Josiah,* king of Judah. 2The LORD said, "Stand out in front of the Temple of
the LORD, and make an announcement to the people who have come there to worship
from all over Judah. Give them my entire message; include every word. 3Perhaps they
will listen and turn from their evil ways. Then I will be able to withhold the disaster I am
ready to pour out on them because of their sins.
4"Say to them, 'This is what the LORD says: If you will not listen to me and obey the
law I have given you, 5and if you will not listen to my servants, the prophets—for I sent
them again and again to warn you, but you would not listen to them—6then I will destroy
this Temple as I destroyed Shiloh, the place where the Tabernacle was located. And I will
make Jerusalem an object of cursing in every nation on earth.'"
7The priests, the prophets, and all the people listened to Jeremiah as he spoke in front
of the LORD's Temple. 8But when Jeremiah had finished his message, saying everything
the LORD had told him to say, the priests and prophets and all the people at the Temple
mobbed him. "Kill him!" they shouted. 9"What right do you have to prophesy in the
LORD's name that this Temple will be destroyed like Shiloh? What do you mean, saying

25:29 Prov 11:31; 1 Pet 4:17
25:30 Joel 2:11; 3:13; Amos 1:2
25:31 Isa 66:16; Hos 4:1
25:32 Isa 30:30; 34:2-3
25:33 Isa 5:25; Jer 16:4; Ezek 39:4, 7
25:34 Isa 34:7; Jer 50:27
25:35 Jer 11:11
25:37 Isa 27:11
25:38 Jer 4:7; 5:6; Hos 5:14; 13:7-8
26:2 Deut 4:2; Jer 7:2; 19:14; 42:4; Acts 20:20, 27
26:3 Isa 1:16-19; Jer 36:3-7
26:4 Lev 26:14; 1 Kgs 9:6; Isa 1:20; Jer 17:27; 22:5; 44:10, 23
26:5 Ezra 9:11; Jer 25:4
26:6 Ps 78:60-61; Jer 7:12, 14
26:7 Jer 5:31; 11:19; Mic 3:11

26:1 The first year of Jehoiakim's reign was 608 B.C.

26:1ff The events described in this chapter took place in 609–608 B.C., before the events described in chapter 25. Jehoiakim was a materialistic and self-centered king who persecuted and murdered innocent people (36:22-32; 2 Kings 23:36–24:6). Chapter 26 describes how and why Jeremiah was on trial for his life.

26:2 God reminded Jeremiah that he wanted his entire message given—"Include every word." Jeremiah may have been tempted to leave out the parts that would turn his audience against him, sound too harsh, or make him sound like a traitor. But by God's command, he was not to delete parts of God's message to suit himself, his audience, or the circumstances in which he found himself. Like Jeremiah, we must never ignore or exclude important parts of God's Word to please someone.

26:2-9 Shiloh was where the Tabernacle had been set up after the conquest of Canaan (Joshua 18:1). It was destroyed in 1050 B.C. by the Philistines. God said he would destroy the Temple as Shiloh had been destroyed. When Jeremiah said that Jerusalem, the city of God, would become an object of cursing and the Temple would be destroyed (26:6), the priests and false prophets were infuriated. The Temple was important to them because the people's reverence for it brought them power. By saying that the Temple would be destroyed, Jeremiah undermined their authority. Jesus also infuriated the religious leaders of his time by foretelling the destruction of Jerusalem and the Temple (Matthew 24:2).

26:11 Jeremiah was branded a traitor because he prophesied the destruction of the city and the Temple. But the "courageous" people advocated a foreign alliance to fight Babylon and retain their independence.

that Jerusalem will be destroyed?" And all the people threatened him as he stood in front
of the Temple.
10 When the officials of Judah heard what was happening, they rushed over from the
palace and sat down at the New Gate of the Temple to hold court. 11 The priests and
prophets presented their accusations to the officials and the people. "This man should
die!" they said. "You have heard with your own ears what a traitor he is, for he has
prophesied against this city."
12 Then Jeremiah spoke in his own defense. "The LORD sent me to prophesy against
this Temple and this city," he said. "The LORD gave me every word that I have spoken.
13 But if you stop your sinning and begin to obey the LORD your God, he will cancel this
disaster that he has announced against you. 14 As for me, I am helpless and in your
power—do with me as you think best. 15 But if you kill me, rest assured that you will be
killing an innocent man! The responsibility for such a deed will lie on you, on this city,
and on every person living in it. For it is absolutely true that the LORD sent me to speak
every word you have heard."
16 Then the officials and the people said to the priests and prophets, "This man does
not deserve the death sentence, for he has spoken to us in the name of the LORD our God."
17 Then some of the wise old men stood and spoke to the people there. 18 They said,
"Think back to the days when Micah of Moresheth prophesied during the reign of King
Hezekiah of Judah. He told the people of Judah, 'This is what the LORD Almighty says:
Mount Zion will be plowed like an open field; Jerusalem will be reduced to rubble! A
great forest will grow on the hilltop, where the Temple now stands.'* 19 But did King
Hezekiah and the people kill him for saying this? No, they turned from their sins and
worshiped the LORD. They begged him to have mercy on them. Then the LORD held back
the terrible disaster he had pronounced against them. If we kill Jeremiah, who knows
what will happen to us?"
20 (At this time, Uriah son of Shemaiah from Kiriath-jearim was also prophesying for
the LORD. And he predicted the same terrible disaster against the city and nation as
Jeremiah did. 21 When King Jehoiakim and the army officers and officials heard what he
was saying, the king sent someone to kill him. But Uriah heard about the plot and escaped
to Egypt. 22 Then King Jehoiakim sent Elnathan son of Acbor to Egypt along with several
other men to capture Uriah. 23 They took him prisoner and brought him back to King
Jehoiakim. The king then killed Uriah with a sword and had him buried in an unmarked
grave.)
24 Ahikam son of Shaphan also stood with Jeremiah and persuaded the court not to turn
him over to the mob to be killed.

Jeremiah Wears an Ox Yoke

27 This message came to Jeremiah from the LORD early in the reign of Zedekiah*
son of Josiah, king of Judah.
2 The LORD said to me, "Make a yoke, and fasten it on your neck with leather thongs.
3 Then send messages to the kings of Edom, Moab, Ammon, Tyre, and Sidon through
their ambassadors to King Zedekiah in Jerusalem. 4 Give them this message for their
masters: 'This is what the LORD Almighty, the God of Israel, says: 5 By my great power

26:10 Acts 21:31-32
26:11 Jer 18:23; 38:4; Matt 26:66; Acts 6:11-14
26:13 Jer 7:3, 5; 18:11
26:15 Num 35:33; Prov 6:16-17
26:16 Jer 36:19, 25; 38:7, 13; Acts 5:34-39; 23:9, 29; 25:25; 26:31
26:18 Mic 1:1; 3:12
26:19 2 Chr 29:6-11; 32:26; Isa 37:1, 15-20
26:20 Josh 9:17; 1 Sam 6:21
26:21 1 Kgs 19:2-4; 2 Chr 16:10; Jer 36:26; Matt 10:23, 28
26:22 Jer 36:12
26:23 Jer 2:30
26:24 2 Kgs 22:12-14; Jer 1:18-19; 39:14; 40:5-6
27:2 Jer 28:10, 13; 30:8
27:3 Jer 25:21-22
27:5 Deut 9:29; Pss 115:15-16; 146:5-6; Jer 10:12; 32:17; 51:15; Acts 17:26

26:18 Mic 3:12. **27:1** As in some Hebrew manuscripts and Syriac version (see also 27:3, 12); most Hebrew manuscripts read *Jehoiakim*.

26:17-19 The wise old men remembered the words of the prophet Micah (Micah 3:12), which were similar to the words Jeremiah spoke. When Micah called the people to repent, they turned from their wickedness. Although these people did not kill Jeremiah, they missed the main point—that the application of the story was for them. They spared Jeremiah, but they did not spare themselves by repenting of their sins. As you recall a great story of the Bible, ask how it can be applied to *your* life.

26:20-23 Uriah is an otherwise unknown prophet who was executed for faithfully proclaiming God's words. This shows us that God has had other prophets whose words are not included in the Bible.

27:1ff The year was 593 B.C., and Nebuchadnezzar had already invaded Judah once and had taken many captives. Jeremiah wore a yoke (a wooden frame used to fasten a team of animals to a plow) as a symbol of bondage. This was an object lesson, telling the people they must put themselves under Babylon's yoke or be destroyed.

27:5, 6 God punished the people of Judah in an unusual way, by appointing a foreign ruler to be his "servant." Nebuchadnezzar was not appointed to proclaim God's message, but to fulfill God's promise of judgment on sin. Because God is in control of all events, he uses whomever he wants. God may use unlikely people or circumstances to correct you. Be ready to accept God's guidance, even if it comes from unexpected sources.

I have made the earth and all its people and every animal. I can give these things of mine
to anyone I choose. 6Now I will give your countries to King Nebuchadnezzar of
Babylon, who is my servant. I have put everything, even the wild animals, under his
control. 7All the nations will serve him and his son and his grandson until his time is up.
But then many nations and great kings will conquer and rule over Babylon. 8So you must
submit to Babylon's king and serve him; put your neck under Babylon's yoke! I will
punish any nation that refuses to be his slave, says the LORD. I will send war, famine, and
disease upon that nation until Babylon has conquered it.
9"'Do not listen to your false prophets, fortune-tellers, interpreters of dreams, mediums, and sorcerers who say, "The king of Babylon will not conquer you." 10They are all
liars, and I will drive you from your land and send you far away to die. 11But the people
of any nation that submits to the king of Babylon will be allowed to stay in their own
country to farm the land as usual. I, the LORD, have spoken!'"
12Then I repeated this same message to King Zedekiah of Judah. "If you want to live,
submit to the king of Babylon and his people," I said. 13"Why do you insist on
dying—you and your people? Why should you choose war, famine, and disease, which
the LORD will bring against every nation that refuses to submit to Babylon's king? 14Do
not listen to the false prophets who keep telling you, 'The king of Babylon will not
conquer you.' They are liars. 15This is what the LORD says: I have not sent these
prophets! They are telling you lies in my name, so I will drive you from this land. You
will all die—you and all these prophets, too."
16Then I spoke to the priests and the people and said, "This is what the LORD says:
Do not listen to your prophets who claim that soon the gold utensils taken from my
Temple will be returned from Babylon. It is all a lie! 17Do not listen to them. Surrender
to the king of Babylon, and you will live. Why should this whole city be destroyed? 18If
they really are the LORD's prophets, let them pray to the LORD Almighty about the gold
utensils that are still left in the LORD's Temple and in the king's palace and in the palaces
of Jerusalem. Let them pray that these remaining articles will not be carried away with
you to Babylon!
19"For this is what the LORD Almighty says about the bronze pillars in front of the
Temple, the bronze Sea in the Temple courtyard, the bronze water carts, and all the other
ceremonial articles. 20King Nebuchadnezzar of Babylon left them here when he exiled
Jehoiachin* son of Jehoiakim, king of Judah, to Babylon, along with all the other
important people of Judah and Jerusalem. 21Yes, this is what the LORD Almighty, the God
of Israel, says about the precious things kept in the Temple and in the palace of Judah's
king: 22They will all be carried away to Babylon and will stay there until I send for them,
says the LORD. But someday I will bring them back to Jerusalem again."

Jeremiah Condemns Hananiah

28 One day in late summer* of that same year—the fourth year of the reign of Zedekiah,
king of Judah—Hananiah son of Azzur, a prophet from Gibeon, addressed me
publicly in the Temple while all the priests and people listened. He said, 2"The LORD
Almighty, the God of Israel, says: I will remove the yoke of the king of Babylon from your
necks. 3Within two years, I will bring back all the Temple treasures that King Nebuchadnezzar carried off to Babylon. 4And I will bring back Jehoiachin* son of Jehoiakim, king
of Judah, and all the other captives that were taken to Babylon. I will surely break the yoke
that the king of Babylon has put on your necks. I, the LORD, have spoken!"
5Jeremiah responded to Hananiah as they stood in front of all the priests and people

27:6 Jer 21:7; 22:25; 28:14; 43:10; Ezek 29:18-20
27:7 Isa 14:4-6; Jer 25:12; 44:30
27:8 Jer 24:10; 29:17; 42:15-16; Ezek 14:21; 17:19-21
27:9 Exod 22:18; Deut 18:10; Isa 8:19; Mal 3:5
27:10 Jer 23:25
27:11 Jer 21:9; 38:2; 40:9-12; 42:10-11
27:13 Jer 38:23; Ezek 18:31
27:14 2 Chr 11:13-15; Ezek 13:22
27:15 2 Chr 25:16; Jer 23:21, 25; 29:9
27:16 2 Kgs 24:13; 2 Chr 36:7, 10; Dan 1:2
27:18 1 Sam 7:8; 12:19, 23; 1 Kgs 18:24
27:19 1 Kgs 7:15; 2 Kgs 25:13, 17; Jer 52:17-23
27:20 2 Kgs 24:14-16
27:22 Ezra 5:13-15; 7:9; Jer 29:10; 32:5; 34:2-3
28:1 Jer 27:12
28:3 2 Chr 36:10; Jer 27:16; Dan 1:2
28:4 2 Kgs 25:27; Jer 22:10; 27:8

27:20 Hebrew *Jeconiah,* a variant name for Jehoiachin. **28:1** Hebrew *In the fifth month,* of the Hebrew calendar. This month in the fourth year of Zedekiah's reign occurred in August and September 593 B.C. Also see note on 1:3.
28:4 Hebrew *Jeconiah,* a variant name for Jehoiachin.

27:12-18 Zedekiah was in a tough spot. Jeremiah called on him to surrender to Nebuchadnezzar at a time when many of the other leaders wanted him to form an alliance and fight. It would be disgraceful for a king to surrender, and he would look like a coward. This was a great opportunity for the false prophets, who kept saying that the Babylonians would not defeat the great city of Jerusalem and that God would never allow the magnificent, holy Temple to be destroyed.

27:19-22 When Nebuchadnezzar invaded Judah, first in 605 and then in 597 B.C., he took away many important people living in Jerusalem—including Daniel and Ezekiel. Although these men were captives, they had a profound impact on the exiles and leaders in Babylon. Jeremiah predicted that more people, and even the precious objects in the Temple, would be taken. This happened in 586 B.C. during Babylon's third and last invasion.

at the Temple. 6 He said, "Amen! May your prophecies come true! I hope the LORD does
everything you say. I hope he does bring back from Babylon the treasures of this Temple
and all our loved ones. 7 But listen now to the solemn words I speak to you in the presence
of all these people. 8 The ancient prophets who preceded you and me spoke against many
nations, always warning of war, famine, and disease. 9 So a prophet who predicts peace
must carry the burden of proof. Only when his predictions come true can it be known
that he is really from the LORD."

10 Then Hananiah the prophet took the yoke off Jeremiah's neck and broke it. 11 And
Hananiah said again to the crowd that had gathered, "The LORD has promised that within
two years he will break the yoke of oppression from all the nations now subject to King
Nebuchadnezzar of Babylon." At that, Jeremiah left the Temple area.

12 Soon afterward the LORD gave this message to Jeremiah: 13 "Go and tell Hananiah,
'This is what the LORD says: You have broken a wooden yoke, but you have replaced it
with a yoke of iron. 14 The LORD Almighty, the God of Israel, says: I have put a yoke of
iron on the necks of all these nations, forcing them into slavery under King Nebuchadnezzar of Babylon. I have put everything, even the wild animals, under his control.'"

15 Then Jeremiah the prophet said to Hananiah, "Listen, Hananiah! The LORD has not
sent you, but the people believe your lies. 16 Therefore, the LORD says you must die. Your
life will end this very year because you have rebelled against the LORD."

17 Two months later,* Hananiah died.

A Letter to the Exiles

29 Jeremiah wrote a letter from Jerusalem to the elders, priests, prophets, and all the
people who had been exiled to Babylon by King Nebuchadnezzar. 2 This was after
King Jehoiachin,* the queen mother, the court officials, the leaders of Judah, and all the
craftsmen had been deported from Jerusalem. 3 He sent the letter with Elasah son of
Shaphan and Gemariah son of Hilkiah, when they went to Babylon as King Zedekiah's
ambassadors to Nebuchadnezzar. This is what Jeremiah's letter said:

> 4 The LORD Almighty, the God of Israel, sends this message to all the captives he
> has exiled to Babylon from Jerusalem: 5 "Build homes, and plan to stay. Plant gar-
> dens, and eat the food you produce. 6 Marry, and have children. Then find spouses
> for them, and have many grandchildren. Multiply! Do not dwindle away! 7 And
> work for the peace and prosperity of Babylon. Pray to the LORD for that city where
> you are held captive, for if Babylon has peace, so will you."
>
> 8 The LORD Almighty, the God of Israel, says, "Do not let the prophets and medi-
> ums who are there in Babylon trick you. Do not listen to their dreams 9 because they
> prophesy lies in my name. I have not sent them," says the LORD. 10 "The truth is
> that you will be in Babylon for seventy years. But then I will come and do for you
> all the good things I have promised, and I will bring you home again. 11 For I know

28:7 1 Kgs 22:28
28:8 1 Kgs 14:15; 17:1; 22:17
28:9 Deut 18:22
28:10 Jer 27:2
28:11 Jer 14:14-15; 27:10
28:12 Jer 1:2
28:13 Ps 107:16
28:14 Deut 28:48; Jer 25:11; 27:6, 8
28:15 Jer 29:31; Lam 2:14; Ezek 13:2-3, 22; 22:28
28:16 Gen 7:4; Deut 6:15; 13:5; 1 Kgs 13:34; Jer 20:6; 29:32
29:2 2 Kgs 24:12; Jer 22:24-28; 24:1
29:6 Jer 16:1-4
29:7 Ezra 6:10; Dan 4:27; 1 Tim 2:1-2
29:8 Jer 14:14; 23:21, 25, 27
29:9 Jer 27:15; 29:31
29:10 2 Chr 36:21-23; Jer 24:6-7; Dan 9:2; Zeph 2:7; Zech 7:5
29:11 Ps 40:5; Isa 40:9-11; Jer 23:5-6; 30:9-10, 18-22

28:17 Hebrew *In the seventh month of that same year.* See 28:1 and the note there. **29:2** Hebrew *Jeconiah,* a variant name for Jehoiachin.

28:8-17 Jeremiah spoke the truth, but it was unpopular; Hananiah spoke lies, but his deceitful words brought false hope and comfort to the people. God had already outlined the marks of a true prophet (Deuteronomy 13; 18:20-22): A true prophet's predictions always come true, and his words never contradict previous revelation. Jeremiah's predictions were already coming true, from Hananiah's death to the Babylonian invasions. But the people still preferred to listen to comforting lies rather than painful truth.

29:4-7 Jeremiah wrote to the captives in Babylon (29:4-23) instructing them to move ahead with their lives and to pray for the pagan nation that enslaved them. Life cannot grind to a halt during troubled times. In an unpleasant or distressing situation, we must adjust and keep moving. You may find it difficult to pray for those in authority if they are evil, but that is when your prayers are most needed (1 Timothy 2:1, 2). When you enter times of trouble or sudden change, pray diligently and move ahead, doing whatever you can rather than giving up because of fear and uncertainty.

29:10 Scholars differ on the exact dates of this 70-year period in Babylon. Some say it refers to the years 605–538 B.C., from the first deportation to Babylon to the arrival of the first exiles back in Jerusalem after Cyrus's freedom decree. Others point to the years 586–515 B.C., from the last deportation to Babylon and the destruction of the Temple until its rebuilding. A third possibility is that 70 years is an approximate number meaning a lifetime. All agree that God sent his people to Babylon for a long time, not the short captivity predicted by the false prophets.

29:11 We're all encouraged by a leader who stirs us to move ahead, someone who believes we can do the task he has given and who will be with us all the way. God is that kind of leader. He knows the future, and his plans for us are good and full of hope. As long as God, who knows the future, provides our agenda and goes with us as we fulfill his mission, we can have boundless hope. This does not mean that we will be spared pain, suffering, or hardship, but that God will see us through to a glorious conclusion.

the plans I have for you," says the LORD. "They are plans for good and not for
disaster, to give you a future and a hope. 12 In those days when you pray, I will
listen. 13 If you look for me in earnest, you will find me when you seek me. 14 I
will be found by you," says the LORD. "I will end your captivity and restore your
fortunes. I will gather you out of the nations where I sent you and bring you home
again to your own land."
15 You may claim that the LORD has raised up prophets for you in Babylon.
16 But this is what the LORD says about the king who sits on David's throne and all
those still living here in Jerusalem—your relatives who were not exiled to Babylon.
17 This is what the LORD Almighty says: "I will send war, famine, and disease upon
them and make them like rotting figs—too bad to eat. 18 Yes, I will pursue them
with war, famine, and disease, and I will scatter them around the world. In every
nation where I send them, I will make them an object of damnation, horror, contempt, and mockery. 19 For they refuse to listen to me, though I have spoken to them
repeatedly through my prophets. And you who are in exile have not listened either,"
says the LORD.
20 Therefore, listen to this message from the LORD, all you captives there in
Babylon. 21 This is what the LORD Almighty, the God of Israel, says about your
prophets—Ahab son of Kolaiah and Zedekiah son of Maaseiah—who are telling
you lies in my name: "I will turn them over to Nebuchadnezzar* for a public execution. 22 Their terrible fate will become proverbial, so that whenever the Judean
exiles want to curse someone they will say, 'May the LORD make you like Zedekiah
and Ahab, whom the king of Babylon burned alive!' 23 For these men have done
terrible things among my people. They have committed adultery with their neighbors' wives and have lied in my name. I am a witness to this," says the LORD.

A Message for Shemaiah

24 The LORD sent this message to Shemaiah the Nehelamite in Babylon: 25 "This is what
the LORD Almighty, the God of Israel, says: You wrote a letter on your own authority to
Zephaniah son of Maaseiah, the priest, and you sent copies to the other priests and people
in Jerusalem. You said to Zephaniah, 26 'The LORD has appointed you to replace Jehoiada
as the priest in charge of the house of the LORD. You are responsible to put anyone who
claims to be a prophet in the stocks and neck irons. 27 So why have you done nothing to
stop Jeremiah from Anathoth, who pretends to be a prophet among you? 28 Jeremiah sent
a letter here to Babylon, predicting that our captivity will be a long one. He said we
should build homes and plan to stay for many years. He said we should plant fruit trees,
because we will be here to eat the fruit for many years to come.'"
29 But when Zephaniah the priest received Shemaiah's letter, he took it to Jeremiah and
read it to him. 30 Then the LORD gave this message to Jeremiah: 31 "Send an open letter
to all the exiles in Babylon. Tell them, 'This is what the LORD says concerning Shemaiah
the Nehelamite: Since he has prophesied to you when I did not send him and has tricked
you into believing his lies, 32 I will punish him and his family. None of his descendants
will see the good things I will do for my people, for he has taught you to rebel against
me. I, the LORD, have spoken!'"

29:12 Ps 145:19; Jer 33:3
29:13 Deut 4:29; 1 Chr 22:19; 2 Chr 22:9; Jer 24:7
29:14 Deut 30:1-10; Isa 43:5-6; Jer 12:15; 16:14-15; 30:3
29:16 Jer 38:2-3
29:17 Jer 24:3
29:18 Isa 65:15; Jer 25:9; 42:18; Lam 2:15-16
29:19 Jer 6:19; 26:5
29:20 Jer 24:5; Ezek 11:9
29:21 Jer 14:14-15; Lam 2:14
29:22 Isa 65:15
29:23 2 Sam 13:12; Prov 5:21; Jer 5:8; 7:11
29:25 2 Kgs 25:18; Jer 21:1; 37:3
29:26 Deut 13:1-5; Jer 20:1-2; Hos 9:7; Zech 13:1-5; John 10:20; Acts 16:24; 26:24-25; 2 Cor 5:13
29:27 Jer 1:1
29:31 Jer 14:14-15; 28:15; Ezek 13:8, 16, 22-23
29:32 Deut 13:5; 1 Sam 2:30-34; Jer 22:30; 28:16; 36:31

29:21 Hebrew *Nebuchadrezzar,* a variant name for Nebuchadnezzar.

29:12-14 God did not forget his people, even though they were captives in Babylon. He planned to give them a new beginning with a new purpose—to turn them into new people. In times of dire circumstances, it may appear as though God has forgotten you. But God may be preparing you, as he did the people of Judah, for a new beginning with him at the center.

29:13 According to God's wise plan, his people were to have a future and a hope; consequently, they could call upon him in confidence. Although the exiles were in a difficult place and time, they need not despair because they had God's presence, the privilege of prayer, and God's grace. If we seek him wholeheartedly, he will be found. Neither a strange land, sorrow, persecution, nor physical problems can break our fellowship with God.

29:21 These false prophets, Ahab and Zedekiah, should not be confused with the kings who had the same names. Their family connections clearly identify them.

29:24-28 These verses describe the reaction of Shemaiah, a false prophet exiled in 597 B.C. who had protested about Jeremiah's letter. To discredit Jeremiah, Shemaiah accused him of false prophecy. Although Jeremiah's message was true and his words were from God, the people hated him because he told them to make the most of the Exile. Jeremiah's truth from God offered temporary correction and long-range benefit, while the false teachers' lies offered only temporary comfort and long-range punishment.

5. Restoration is promised

30 The LORD gave another message to Jeremiah. He said, 2“This is what the LORD, the God of Israel, says: Write down for the record everything I have said to you, Jeremiah. 3For the time is coming when I will restore the fortunes of my people of Israel and Judah. I will bring them home to this land that I gave to their ancestors, and they will possess it and live here again. I, the LORD, have spoken!”

4This is the message the LORD gave concerning Israel and Judah: 5“This is what the LORD says: I have heard the people crying; there is only fear and trembling. 6Now let me ask you a question: Do men give birth to babies? Then why do they stand there, ashen-faced, hands pressed against their sides like women about to give birth? 7In all history there has never been such a time of terror. It will be a time of trouble for my people Israel.* Yet in the end, they will be saved!

8“For in that day, says the LORD Almighty, I will break the yoke from their necks and snap their chains. Foreigners will no longer be their masters. 9For my people will serve the LORD their God and David their king, whom I will raise up for them.

10“So do not be afraid, Jacob, my servant; do not be dismayed, Israel, says the LORD. For I will bring you home again from distant lands, and your children will return from their exile. Israel will return and will have peace and quiet in their own land, and no one will make them afraid. 11For I am with you and will save you, says the LORD. I will completely destroy the nations where I have scattered you, but I will not destroy you. But I must discipline you; I cannot let you go unpunished.

12“This is what the LORD says: Yours is an incurable bruise, a terrible wound. 13There is no one to help you or bind up your injury. You are beyond the help of any medicine. 14All your allies have left you and do not care about you anymore. I have wounded you cruelly, as though I were your enemy. For your sins are many, and your guilt is great. 15Why do you protest your punishment—this wound that has no cure? I have had to punish you because your sins are many and your guilt is great.

16“But in that coming day, all who destroy you will be destroyed, and all your enemies will be sent into exile. Those who plunder you will be plundered, and those who attack you will be attacked. 17I will give you back your health and heal your wounds, says the LORD.

“Now you are called an outcast—‘Jerusalem* for whom nobody cares.’ 18But the LORD says this: When I bring you home again from your captivity and restore your fortunes, Jerusalem will be rebuilt on her ruins. The palace will be reconstructed as it was before. 19There will be joy and songs of thanksgiving, and I will multiply my people and make of them a great and honored nation. 20Their children will prosper as they did long ago. I will establish them as a nation before me, and I will punish anyone who hurts them. 21They will have their own ruler again, and he will not be a foreigner. I will invite him to approach me, says the LORD, for who would dare to come unless invited? 22You will be my people, and I will be your God.”

30:7 Hebrew *Jacob;* also in 30:10b. **30:17** Hebrew *Zion.*

30:2 Jer 25:13; 36:4, 28; Hab 2:2
30:3 Ezek 20:42; 36:24; Zeph 3:20
30:5 Isa 5:30; Jer 6:25; Amos 5:16-18
30:6 Jer 4:31; 6:24
30:7 Isa 2:12; Jer 2:27; 50:19; Lam 1:12; Dan 9:12; Joel 2:11
30:8 Isa 9:4; Ezek 34:27
30:9 Ezek 34:23-24; Hos 3:5; Luke 1:69; Acts 2:30; 13:23-24
30:10 Isa 35:9; 43:5; 44:2; Jer 23:3; 29:14; 46:27-28; Mic 4:4
30:13 Jer 14:19; 46:11
30:16 Isa 14:2; Jer 2:3; 10:25
30:17 Ps 107:20; Isa 56:8; Jer 8:22; 33:6, 24
30:18 1 Chr 29:1, 19; Pss 48:3; 122:7; Jer 31:38-40
30:19 Isa 12:1; 51:3; 55:5; 60:9; Jer 17:26; 33:11
30:21 Exod 3:5; Num 16:5
30:22 Exod 6:7; Jer 32:38; Hos 2:23; Zech 13:9

30:1ff Chapters 30 and 31 show that Jeremiah spoke of hope and consolation as well as trouble and gloom. The people would one day be restored to their land, and God would make a new covenant with them to replace the one they broke. Whereas once they sinned and disobeyed, eventually they would repent and obey.

30:8, 9 Like Isaiah, Jeremiah associated events of the near future and those of the distant future. Reading these prophecies is like looking at several mountain peaks in a range. From a distance they look as though they are next to each other, when actually they are miles apart. Jeremiah presents near and distant events as if they will all happen soon. He sees the Exile, but he sees also the future day when Christ will reign forever. The reference to David is not to King David, but to his famous descendant, the Messiah (Luke 1:69).

30:12, 13, 17 The medical language here conveys the idea that sin is terminal. Sinful people cannot be cured by being good or being religious. Beware of putting your confidence in useless cures while your sin spreads and causes you pain. God alone can cure the disease of sin, but you must be willing to let him do it.

30:15 Judah protested its punishment, even though the sin that caused the pain was scandalous. But punishment is an opportunity for growth because it makes us aware of sin's consequences. The people should have asked how they could profit from their mistakes. Remember this the next time you are corrected.

30:18 This prophecy that Jerusalem would be rebuilt was not completely fulfilled by the work of Ezra, Nehemiah, and Zerubbabel. The city was indeed rebuilt after the captivity, but the final restoration will occur when all believers are gathered in Christ's Kingdom. This restoration will include buildings (30:18), people (30:19), and rulers (30:21).

30:21 This verse refers to the restoration after the Babylonian captivity as well as to the final restoration under Christ.

30:23 Jer 23:19-20
30:24 Jer 4:8; 23:20

23 Look! The LORD's anger bursts out like a storm, a driving wind that swirls down on the heads of the wicked. 24 The fierce anger of the LORD will not diminish until it has finished all his plans. In the days to come, you will understand all this.

Hope for Restoration

31:1 Gen 17:7-8; Rom 11:26-28
31:3 Deut 4:37; 7:8; Ps 25:6
31:4 Isa 30:32; Jer 24:6; 33:7
31:5 Ps 107:37; Isa 65:21; Ezek 28:26
31:6 Isa 2:3; Mic 4:2
31:7 Pss 14:7; 28:9; Isa 37:31; 61:9
31:8 Deut 30:64; Isa 40:11; 43:6; 64:8; Ezek 34:16; Mic 4:6
31:10 Isa 40:11; 66:19
31:12 Isa 2:2; 35:10; 58:11; 60:20; 65:19; Hos 2:22; Joel 3:18; Mic 4:1; John 16:22
31:13 Ps 30:11; Isa 51:11; 61:3; Zech 8:4-5

31 "In that day," says the LORD, "I will be the God of all the families of Israel, and they will be my people. 2 I will care for the survivors as they travel through the wilderness. I will again come to give rest to the people of Israel."

3 Long ago the LORD said to Israel: "I have loved you, my people, with an everlasting love. With unfailing love I have drawn you to myself. 4 I will rebuild you, my virgin Israel. You will again be happy and dance merrily with tambourines. 5 Again you will plant your vineyards on the mountains of Samaria and eat from your own gardens there. 6 The day will come when watchmen will shout from the hill country of Ephraim, 'Come, let us go up to Jerusalem* to worship the LORD our God.'"

7 Now this is what the LORD says: "Sing with joy for Israel*! Shout for the greatest of nations! Shout out with praise and joy: 'Save your people, O LORD, the remnant of Israel!' 8 For I will bring them from the north and from the distant corners of the earth. I will not forget the blind and lame, the expectant mothers and women about to give birth. A great company will return! 9 Tears of joy will stream down their faces, and I will lead them home with great care. They will walk beside quiet streams and not stumble. For I am Israel's father, and Ephraim is my oldest child.

10 "Listen to this message from the LORD, you nations of the world; proclaim it in distant coastlands: The LORD, who scattered his people, will gather them together and watch over them as a shepherd does his flock. 11 For the LORD has redeemed Israel from those too strong for them. 12 They will come home and sing songs of joy on the heights of Jerusalem. They will be radiant because of the many gifts the LORD has given them—the good crops of wheat, wine, and oil, and the healthy flocks and herds. Their life will be like a watered garden, and all their sorrows will be gone. 13 The young women will dance for joy, and the men—old and young—will join in the celebration. I will turn their mourning into joy. I will comfort them and exchange their sorrow for rejoicing. 14 I will supply the priests with an abundance of offerings. I will satisfy my people with my bounty. I, the LORD, have spoken!"

Rachel's Sadness Turns to Joy

31:15 Ps 77:2; Jer 10:20; †Matt 2:17-18
31:16 Isa 25:8; 30:19; Jer 30:3; Ezek 11:17
31:18 Pss 80:3, 7, 19; 94:12; Jer 17:14; Hos 4:16
31:19 Ezek 36:31; Luke 18:13

15 This is what the LORD says: "A cry of anguish is heard in Ramah—mourning and weeping unrestrained. Rachel weeps for her children, refusing to be comforted—for her children are dead."

16 But now the LORD says, "Do not weep any longer, for I will reward you. Your children will come back to you from the distant land of the enemy. 17 There is hope for your future," says the LORD. "Your children will come again to their own land. 18 I have heard Israel* saying, 'You disciplined me severely, but I deserved it. I was like a calf that needed to be trained for the yoke and plow. Turn me again to you and restore me, for you alone are the LORD my God. 19 I turned away from God, but then I was sorry. I kicked myself for my stupidity! I was thoroughly ashamed of all I did in my younger days.'

31:6 Hebrew *Zion;* also in 31:12. **31:7** Hebrew *Jacob;* also in 31:11. **31:18** Hebrew *Ephraim,* referring to the northern kingdom of Israel; also in 31:20.

31:1 This promise is to all the families (tribes) of Israel, not only to the tribe of Judah. The restoration will include all people who trust God.

31:3 God reaches toward his people with kindness motivated by deep and everlasting love. He is eager to do the best for them if they will only let him. After many words of warning about sin, this reminder of God's magnificent love is a breath of fresh air. Rather than thinking of God with dread, look carefully and see him lovingly drawing us toward himself.

31:14 This means that many sacrifices will be made at the Temple so that the priests will have a feast with their portion. It is also a symbol of life and prosperity (Psalm 36:8; 63:5; Isaiah 55:2).

31:15 Rachel, Jacob's favorite wife, was the symbolic mother of the northern tribes, which were taken into captivity by the Assyrians. Rachel is pictured crying for the exiles at Ramah, a staging point of deportation. This verse is quoted in Matthew 2:18 to describe the sadness of the mothers of Bethlehem as the male children were killed. The weeping was great in both cases.

31:18-20 These words picture grief and mourning. Although Israel, the northern kingdom, had sunk into the most degrading sins, God still loved the people. A remnant would turn to God by repenting of their sins, and God would forgive. God still loves you despite anything you may have done. He will forgive you if you turn back to him.

20“Is not Israel still my son, my darling child?” asks the LORD. “I had to punish him, but I still love him. I long for him and surely will have mercy on him.

21“Set up road signs; put up guideposts. Mark well the path by which you came. Come back again, my virgin Israel; return to your cities here. 22How long will you wander, my wayward daughter? For the LORD will cause something new and different to happen—Israel will embrace her God.*”

23This is what the LORD Almighty, the God of Israel, says: “When I bring them back again, the people of Judah and its cities will again say, ‘The LORD bless you—O righteous home, O holy mountain!’ 24And city dwellers and farmers and shepherds alike will live together in peace and happiness. 25For I have given rest to the weary and joy to the sorrowing.”

26At this, I woke up and looked around. My sleep had been very sweet.

27“The time will come,” says the LORD, “when I will greatly increase the population and multiply the number of cattle here in Israel and Judah. 28In the past I uprooted and tore down this nation. I overthrew it, destroyed it, and brought disaster upon it. But in the future I will plant it and build it up,” says the LORD.

29“The people will no longer quote this proverb: ‘The parents eat sour grapes, but their children’s mouths pucker at the taste.’ 30All people will die for their own sins—those who eat the sour grapes will be the ones whose mouths will pucker.

31“The day will come,” says the LORD, “when I will make a new covenant with the people of Israel and Judah. 32This covenant will not be like the one I made with their ancestors when I took them by the hand and brought them out of the land of Egypt. They broke that covenant, though I loved them as a husband loves his wife,” says the LORD.

33“But this is the new covenant I will make with the people of Israel on that day,” says the LORD. “I will put my laws in their minds, and I will write them on their hearts. I will be their God, and they will be my people. 34And they will not need to teach their neighbors, nor will they need to teach their family, saying, ‘You should know the LORD.’ For everyone, from the least to the greatest, will already know me,” says the LORD. “And I will forgive their wickedness and will never again remember their sins.”

35It is the LORD who provides the sun to light the day and the moon and stars to light the night. It is he who stirs the sea into roaring waves. His name is the LORD Almighty, and this is what he says: 36“I am as likely to reject my people Israel as I am to do away with the laws of nature! 37Just as the heavens cannot be measured and the foundation of the earth cannot be explored, so I will not consider casting them away forever for their sins. I, the LORD, have spoken!

38“The time is coming,” says the LORD, “when all Jerusalem will be rebuilt for me, from the Tower of Hananel to the Corner Gate. 39A measuring line will be stretched out over the hill of Gareb and across to Goah. 40And the entire area—including the graveyard and ash dump in the valley, and all the fields out to the Kidron Valley on the east as far as the Horse Gate—will be holy to the LORD. The city will never again be captured or destroyed.”

31:22 Hebrew *a woman will court a suitor.*

31:20 Isa 55:7; Hos 11:8; 14:4
31:21 Isa 48:20; 52:11
31:23 Pss 48:1; 87:1; Isa 1:26
31:25 Ps 107:9; John 4:14
31:27 Ezek 36:9-11; Hos 2:23
31:28 Jer 1:10; Dan 9:14
31:29 Lam 5:7; Ezek 18:2
31:30 Deut 24:16; Ezek 18:4, 20
31:31-34 †Heb 8:8-12
31:31 Jer 32:40; Ezek 37:26; Luke 22:20; 1 Cor 11:25
31:32 Deut 1:31; 5:2-3
31:33 Heb 10:16
31:34 Isa 11:9; 43:25; Mic 7:18; Rom 11:27; 1 Thes 4:9; †Heb 10:17; 1 Jn 2:27
31:36 Ps 89:36-37; Isa 54:9-10; Jer 33:20-26; Amos 9:8-9
31:37 Isa 40:12; Jer 33:22, 24-26; Rom 11:2-5, 26-27
31:38 2 Chr 26:9; Neh 3:1; 12:39; Zech 14:10
31:40 2 Kgs 23:6; Neh 3:28; Joel 3:17; Zech 14:20

31:29, 30 The people tried to blame God’s judgment on the sins of their fathers. One person’s sin does indeed affect other people, but all people are still held personally accountable for the sin in their own life (Deuteronomy 24:16; Ezekiel 18:2). What excuses do you use for your sins?

31:33 God would write his law on their hearts rather than on tablets of stone, as he did the Ten Commandments. In 17:1 their sin was engraved on their hearts so that they wanted above all to disobey. This change seems to describe an experience very much like the new birth, with God taking the initiative. When we turn our life over to God, he, by his Holy Spirit, builds into us the desire to obey him.

31:33 The old covenant, broken by the people, would be replaced by a new covenant. The foundation of this new covenant is Christ (Hebrews 8:6). It is revolutionary, involving not only Israel and Judah but even the Gentiles. It offers a unique personal relationship with God himself, with his laws written on individuals’ hearts instead of on stone. Jeremiah looked forward to the day when Jesus would come to establish this covenant. But for us today, this covenant is here. We have the wonderful opportunity to make a fresh start and establish a permanent, personal relationship with God (see 29:11; 32:38-40).

31:35-37 God has the power to do away with the laws of nature or even to do away with his people. But he will do neither. This is not a prediction; it is a promise. This is God’s way of saying that he will not reject Israel any more than he will do away with nature’s laws.

31:38-40 These points mark the boundaries of restored Jerusalem in the days of Nehemiah. Gareb and Goah are unknown. The graveyard and ash dump are probably the valley of the son of Hinnom, where children were sacrified in pagan worship.

32:1 2 Kgs 25:1-2; Jer 39:1-2
32:2 Neh 3:25
32:3 Jer 21:4-7; 26:8-9; 34:2-3
32:4 2 Kgs 25:4-7; Jer 37:17; 39:4-7
32:5 Ezek 12:12-13; 17:9-10, 15
32:7 Lev 25:25; Ruth 4:3-4; †Matt 27:10
32:8 1 Sam 9:16-17; 10:3-7
32:9 Gen 23:16; 24:22; †Matt 27:9-10
32:10 Ruth 4:1, 9; Isa 8:1-2
32:11 Luke 2:27
32:15 Jer 30:18; 31:5, 12; Amos 9:14-15; Zech 3:10
32:17 Gen 18:14; 2 Kgs 19:15; Ps 102:25
32:18 Exod 34:6-7; Deut 7:9-10; 1 Kgs 16:1-3; Matt 23:32-36
32:19 Ps 62:12; Isa 28:29; Matt 16:27; John 5:29
32:21 Deut 4:34; 26:8; 1 Chr 17:21
32:22 Exod 13:5; Deut 1:8
32:23 Ezra 9:7; Dan 9:11-12

Jeremiah's Land Purchase

32 The following message came to Jeremiah from the LORD in the tenth year of the reign of Zedekiah,* king of Judah. This was also the eighteenth year of the reign of King Nebuchadnezzar.* [2]Jerusalem was under siege from the Babylonian army, and Jeremiah was imprisoned in the courtyard of the guard in the royal palace. [3]King Zedekiah had put him there because he continued to give this prophecy: "This is what the LORD says: I am about to hand this city over to the king of Babylon. [4]King Zedekiah will be captured by the Babylonians* and taken to the king of Babylon to be judged and sentenced. [5]I will take Zedekiah to Babylon and will deal with him there. If you fight against the Babylonians, you will never succeed."

[6]At that time the LORD sent me a message. He said, [7]"Your cousin Hanamel son of Shallum will come and say to you, 'Buy my field at Anathoth. By law you have the right to buy it before it is offered to anyone else.'"

[8]Then, just as the LORD had said he would, Hanamel came and visited me in the prison. He said, "Buy my field at Anathoth in the land of Benjamin. By law you have the right to buy it before it is offered to anyone else, so buy it for yourself." Then I knew for sure that the message I had heard was from the LORD.

[9]So I bought the field at Anathoth, paying Hanamel seventeen pieces* of silver for it. [10]I signed and sealed the deed of purchase before witnesses, weighed out the silver, and paid him. [11]Then I took the sealed deed and an unsealed copy of the deed, which contained the terms and conditions of the purchase, [12]and I handed them to Baruch son of Neriah and grandson of Mahseiah. I did all this in the presence of my cousin Hanamel, the witnesses who had signed the deed, and all the men of Judah who were there.

[13]Then I said to Baruch as they all listened, [14]"The LORD Almighty, the God of Israel, says: Take both this sealed deed and the unsealed copy, and put them into a pottery jar to preserve them for a long time. [15]For the LORD Almighty, the God of Israel, says: Someday people will again own property here in this land and will buy and sell houses and vineyards and fields."

Jeremiah's Prayer

[16]Then after I had given the papers to Baruch, I prayed to the LORD: [17]"O Sovereign LORD! You have made the heavens and earth by your great power. Nothing is too hard for you! [18]You are loving and kind to thousands, though children suffer for their parents' sins. You are the great and powerful God, the LORD Almighty. [19]You have all wisdom and do great and mighty miracles. You are very aware of the conduct of all people, and you reward them according to their deeds. [20]You performed miraculous signs and wonders in the land of Egypt—things still remembered to this day! And you have continued to do great miracles in Israel and all around the world. You have made your name very great, as it is today.

[21]"You brought Israel out of Egypt with mighty signs and wonders, with great power and overwhelming terror. [22]You gave the people of Israel this land that you had promised their ancestors long before—a land flowing with milk and honey. [23]Our ancestors came and conquered it and lived in it, but they refused to obey you or follow your law. They

32:1a The tenth year of Zedekiah's reign and the eighteenth year of Nebuchadnezzar's reign was 587 B.C. **32:1b** Hebrew *Nebuchadrezzar,* a variant name for Nebuchadnezzar; also in 32:28. **32:4** Or *Chaldeans;* also in 32:5, 24, 25, 28, 29, 43. **32:9** Hebrew *17 shekels,* about 7 ounces or 194 grams in weight.

32:1-12 God told Jeremiah to buy a field outside Jerusalem. The city had been under siege for a year, and Jeremiah bought land that the soldiers occupied—certainly a poor investment. In addition, Jeremiah was a prisoner in the palace. But Jeremiah was demonstrating his faith in God's promises to bring his people back and to rebuild Jerusalem.

32:6-17 Trust doesn't come easy. It wasn't easy for Jeremiah to publicly buy land already captured by the enemy. But he trusted God. It wasn't easy for David to believe that he would become king, even after he was anointed. But he trusted God (1 Samuel 16–31). It wasn't easy for Moses to believe that he and his people would escape Egypt, even after God spoke to him from a burning bush. But he trusted God (Exodus 3:1–4:20). It isn't easy for us to believe that God can fulfill his "impossible" promises either, but we must trust him. God, who worked in the lives of biblical heroes, will work in our life, too, if we will let him.

32:17-25 After Jeremiah bought the field, he began to wonder if such a move was wise. He sought relief in prayer from his nagging doubts. In this prayer, Jeremiah affirmed that God is the Creator of heaven and earth (32:17), the wise Judge, who is aware of our conduct (32:19), and our Redeemer, who has great power (32:21). God loves us and sees our situation. Whenever we doubt God's wisdom or wonder if it is practical to obey him, we can review what we already know about him. Such thoughts and prayers will quiet our doubts and calm our fears.

have hardly done one thing you told them to! That is why you have sent this terrible disaster upon them.

24“See how the siege ramps have been built against the city walls! Because of war, famine, and disease, the city has been handed over to the Babylonians, who will conquer it. Everything has happened just as you said it would. 25And yet, O Sovereign LORD, you have told me to buy the field—paying good money for it before these witnesses—even though the city will soon belong to the Babylonians.”

A Prediction of Jerusalem's Fall

26Then this message came to Jeremiah from the LORD: 27“I am the LORD, the God of all the peoples of the world. Is anything too hard for me? 28I will hand this city over to the Babylonians and to Nebuchadnezzar, king of Babylon, and he will capture it. 29The Babylonians outside the walls will come in and set fire to the city. They will burn down all these houses, where the people caused my fury to rise by offering incense to Baal on the rooftops and by pouring out drink offerings to other gods. 30Israel and Judah have done nothing but wrong since their earliest days. They have infuriated me with all their evil deeds,” says the LORD. 31“From the time this city was built until now, it has done nothing but anger me, so I am determined to get rid of it.

32“The sins of Israel and Judah—the sins of the people of Jerusalem, the kings, the officials, the priests, and the prophets—stir up my anger. 33My people have turned their backs on me and have refused to return. Day after day, year after year, I taught them right from wrong, but they would not listen or obey. 34They have set up their abominable idols right in my own Temple, defiling it. 35They have built pagan shrines to Baal in the valley of the son of Hinnom, and there they sacrifice their sons and daughters to Molech. I have never commanded such a horrible deed; it never even crossed my mind to command such a thing. What an incredible evil, causing Judah to sin so greatly!

A Promise of Restoration

36“Now I want to say something more about this city. You have been saying, ‘It will fall to the king of Babylon through war, famine, and disease.’ But this is what the LORD, the God of Israel, says: 37I will surely bring my people back again from all the countries where I will scatter them in my fury. I will bring them back to this very city and let them live in peace and safety. 38They will be my people, and I will be their God. 39And I will give them one heart and mind to worship me forever, for their own good and for the good of all their descendants.

40“And I will make an everlasting covenant with them, promising not to stop doing good for them. I will put a desire in their hearts to worship me, and they will never leave me. 41I will rejoice in doing good to them and will faithfully and wholeheartedly replant them in this land. 42Just as I have sent all these calamities upon them, so I will do all the good I have promised them. I, the LORD, have spoken!

43“Fields will again be bought and sold in this land about which you now say, ‘It has been ravaged by the Babylonians, a land where people and animals have all disappeared.’ 44Yes, fields will once again be bought and sold—deeds signed and sealed and witnessed—in the land of Benjamin and here in Jerusalem, in the towns of Judah and in the hill country, in the foothills of Judah* and in the Negev, too. For someday I will restore prosperity to them. I, the LORD, have spoken!”

32:44 Hebrew *the Shephelah.*

32:24 Josh 23:15-16 Ezek 14:21 Zech 1:6

32:27 Num 16:22; 27:16 Matt 19:26

32:28 Jer 19:7-12; 34:2-3

32:29 2 Chr 36:19

32:31 1 Kgs 11:7-8 2 Kgs 21:4-7, 15; 23:27; 24:3-4 Matt 23:37

32:32 Ezra 9:7 Isa 1:23 Jer 2:26; 44:17, 21

32:33 2 Chr 36:15-16 Jer 25:3; 26:5; 35:15

32:34 Jer 7:30 Ezek 8:5

32:35 Lev 18:21; 20:2-5 2 Chr 28:2-3; 33:6 Acts 7:43

32:37 Deut 30:3 Isa 11:11-16 Jer 23:6 Ezek 11:17; 34:25 Hos 1:11 Amos 9:14-15 Zech 14:11

32:38 †2 Cor 6:16

32:39 Deut 11:18-21 Ezek 37:25 John 17:21 Acts 4:32

32:40 Isa 55:3

32:41 Deut 30:9 Isa 65:19 Jer 31:28 Amos 9:15

32:42 Jer 31:28 Zech 8:14-15

32:43 Jer 32:15, 25 Ezek 37:11-14

32:35 These pagan shrines were where the most important and grotesque part of Molech worship took place. Children were offered in sacrifice to this pagan god.

32:36-42 God uses his power to accomplish *his* purposes through *his* people. God doesn't give you power to be all you want to be, but he gives you power to be all *he* wants you to be. The people of Israel had to learn that trusting God meant radically realigning their purposes and desires with his. God gave them “one heart” toward him (32:39). We must develop such singleness of heart and action to love God above anything else.

32:44 The hill country is in western Palestine. The Negev is the southern part of Judah.

33:2 Exod 3:15; 15:3
33:3 Ps 50:15; Isa 48:6; 55:6-7
33:4 Isa 32:13-14
33:5 Jer 21:10
33:6 Isa 66:12; Jer 17:14; Gal 5:22-23
33:7 Ps 85:1; Jer 30:18; 32:44; Amos 9:14-15
33:8 Ps 51:2; Jer 50:20; Heb 9:11-14
33:9 Ps 40:3; Isa 62:2, 4; Jer 16:19; 24:6; Hos 3:5
33:10 Isa 35:10
33:12 Ezek 34:12-14; Zeph 2:6-7
33:13 Lev 27:32; Jer 17:26; Luke 15:4
33:14 Hag 2:6-9
33:15 Ps 72:1-5; Isa 11:1-5
33:16 1 Cor 1:30; 2 Cor 5:21; Phil 3:9
33:17 1 Kgs 2:4; Ps 89:29-37
33:18 Deut 18:1; Ezek 44:15; Heb 13:15
33:20 2 Sam 23:5; 2 Chr 21:7; Ps 104:19-23; Isa 54:9
33:22 Gen 22:17

Promises of Peace and Prosperity

33 While Jeremiah was still confined in the courtyard of the guard, the LORD gave
him this second message: 2“The LORD, the Maker of the heavens and earth—the
LORD is his name—says this: 3Ask me and I will tell you some remarkable secrets about
what is going to happen here. 4For this is what the LORD, the God of Israel, says: Though
you have torn down the houses of this city and even the king’s palace to get materials to
strengthen the walls against the siege weapons of the enemy, 5the Babylonians* will still
enter. The men of this city are already as good as dead, for I have determined to destroy
them in my terrible anger. I have abandoned them because of all their wickedness.

6“Nevertheless, the time will come when I will heal Jerusalem’s damage and give her
prosperity and peace. 7I will restore the fortunes of Judah and Israel and rebuild their cities.
8I will cleanse away their sins against me, and I will forgive all their sins of rebellion. 9Then
this city will bring me joy, glory, and honor before all the nations of the earth! The people
of the world will see the good I do for my people and will tremble with awe!

10“This is what the LORD says: You say, ‘This land has been ravaged, and the people
and animals have all disappeared.’ Yet in the empty streets of Jerusalem and Judah’s other
towns, there will be heard once more 11the sounds of joy and laughter. The joyful voices
of bridegrooms and brides will be heard again, along with the joyous songs of people
bringing thanksgiving offerings to the LORD. They will sing,

‘Give thanks to the LORD Almighty, for the LORD is good.
His faithful love endures forever!’

For I will restore the prosperity of this land to what it was in the past, says the LORD.

12“This is what the LORD Almighty says: This land—though it is now desolate and
the people and animals have all disappeared—will once more see shepherds leading
sheep and lambs. 13Once again their flocks will prosper in the towns of the hill country,
the foothills of Judah,* the Negev, the land of Benjamin, the vicinity of Jerusalem, and
all the towns of Judah. I, the LORD, have spoken!

14“The day will come, says the LORD, when I will do for Israel and Judah all the good
I have promised them. 15At that time I will bring to the throne of David a righteous
descendant,* and he will do what is just and right throughout the land. 16In that day Judah
will be saved, and Jerusalem will live in safety. And their motto will be ‘The LORD is our
righteousness!’ 17For this is what the LORD says: David will forever have a descendant
sitting on the throne of Israel. 18And there will always be Levitical priests to offer burnt
offerings and grain offerings and sacrifices to me.”

19Then this message came to Jeremiah from the LORD: 20“If you can break my
covenant with the day and the night so that they do not come on their usual schedule,
21only then will my covenant with David, my servant, be broken. Only then will he no
longer have a descendant to reign on his throne. The same is true for my covenant with
the Levitical priests who minister before me. 22And as the stars cannot be counted and
the sand on the seashores cannot be measured, so I will multiply the descendants of
David, my servant, and the Levites who minister before me.”

23The LORD gave another message to Jeremiah. He said, 24“Have you heard what

33:5 Or *Chaldeans.* **33:13** Hebrew *the Shephelah.* **33:15** Hebrew *a righteous Branch.*

33:1ff God would restore Jerusalem, not because the people cried, but because it was part of his ultimate plan. The Babylonian disaster did not change God’s purposes for his people. Although Jerusalem would be destroyed, it would be restored (after the 70-year captivity and in the end times when the Messiah will rule). God’s justice is always tempered by his mercy.

33:3 God assured Jeremiah that he had only to ask God and God would answer (see also Psalm 145:18; Isaiah 58:9; Matthew 7:7). God is ready to answer our prayers, but we must ask for his assistance. Surely God could take care of our needs without our asking. But when we ask, we are acknowledging that he alone is God and that we cannot accomplish in our own strength all that is his domain to do. When we ask, we must humble ourselves, lay aside our willfulness and worry, and determine to obey him.

33:15, 16 These verses refer to both the first and second comings of Christ. At his first coming he would set up his reign in the hearts of believers; at his second coming he would execute justice and righteousness throughout the whole earth. Christ is the “righteous descendant” sprouting from David, the man after God’s own heart.

33:18 As Christ fulfills the role of King, he also fulfills the role of Priest, maintaining constant fellowship with God and mediating for the people. This verse does not mean that actual priests will perform sacrifices, for sacrifices will no longer be necessary (Hebrews 10:4, 11, 12). Now that Christ is our High Priest, all believers are priests of God, and we can come before him personally.

people are saying?—'The LORD chose Judah and Israel and then abandoned them!' They
are sneering and saying that Israel is not worthy to be counted as a nation. 25But this is the
LORD's reply: I would no more reject my people than I would change my laws of night
and day, of earth and sky. 26I will never abandon the descendants of Jacob or David, my
servant, or change the plan that David's descendants will rule the descendants of Abraham,
Isaac, and Jacob. Instead, I will restore them to their land and have mercy on them."

6. God's promised judgment arrives

A Warning for Zedekiah

34 King Nebuchadnezzar of Babylon came with all the armies from the kingdoms
he ruled, and he fought against Jerusalem and the towns of Judah. At that time
this message came to Jeremiah from the LORD: 2"Go to King Zedekiah of Judah, and tell
him, 'This is what the LORD, the God of Israel, says: I am about to hand this city over to
the king of Babylon, and he will burn it. 3You will not escape his grasp but will be taken
into captivity. You will stand before the king of Babylon to be judged and sentenced.
Then you will be exiled to Babylon.'

4"But listen to this promise from the LORD, O Zedekiah, king of Judah. This is what
the LORD says: 'You will not be killed in war 5but will die peacefully among your people.
They will burn incense in your memory, just as they did for your ancestors. They will
weep for you and say, "Alas, our king is dead!" This I have decreed, says the LORD.'"

6So Jeremiah the prophet delivered the message to King Zedekiah of Judah. 7At this
time the Babylonian army was besieging Jerusalem, Lachish, and Azekah—the only
cities of Judah with their walls still standing.

Freedom for Hebrew Slaves

8This message came to Jeremiah from the LORD after King Zedekiah made a covenant with
the people, proclaiming freedom for the slaves. 9He had ordered all the people to free their
Hebrew slaves—both men and women. No one was to keep a fellow Judean in bondage.
10The officials and all the people had obeyed the king's command, 11but later they changed
their minds. They took back the people they had freed, making them slaves again.

12So the LORD gave them this message through Jeremiah: 13"This is what the LORD,
the God of Israel, says: I made a covenant with your ancestors long ago when I rescued
them from their slavery in Egypt. 14I told them that every Hebrew slave must be freed
after serving six years. But this was never done. 15Recently you repented and did what
was right, following my command. You freed your slaves and made a solemn covenant
with me in my Temple. 16But now you have shrugged off your oath and defiled my name
by taking back the men and women you had freed, making them slaves once again.

17"Therefore, this is what the LORD says: Since you have not obeyed me by setting

33:24 Neh 4:2-4; Ps 44:13-14; Isa 11:13; Ezek 36:2
33:25 Ps 74:16-17
33:26 Hos 2:23
34:1 2 Kgs 25:1; Jer 1:15; Dan 2:37-38
34:2 2 Chr 36:11-12; Jer 37:1-4
34:3 2 Kgs 25:4-7; Jer 21:7
34:5 2 Chr 16:14; 21:19
34:7 Josh 10:3, 10; 2 Kgs 14:19; 2 Chr 11:5-10
34:8 Neh 5:1-13
34:11 Hos 6:4
34:13 Deut 5:2-3, 27; Jer 31:32
34:14 Exod 21:2; 1 Kgs 9:22; 2 Kgs 17:13-14
34:15 Neh 10:29
34:16 Exod 20:7; 1 Sam 15:11
34:17 Lev 26:34-35; Deut 28:25, 64; Matt 7:2

34:1ff This chapter describes the fulfillment of many of Jeremiah's predictions. In the book of Jeremiah, many prophecies were both given and quickly fulfilled.

34:8, 9 Babylon had laid siege to Jerusalem, and the city was about to fall. Zedekiah finally decided to listen to Jeremiah and try to appease God—so he freed the slaves. He thought he could win God's favor with a kind act, but what he needed was a change of heart. The people had been disobeying God's law from the beginning (Exodus 21:2-11; Leviticus 25:39-55; Deuteronomy 15:12-18). When the siege was temporarily lifted, the people became bold and returned to their sins (34:11-17; 37:5, 11).

34:15, 16 The people of Israel had a hard time keeping their promises to God. In the Temple, they would solemnly promise to obey God, but back in their homes and at work they wouldn't do it. God expressed his great displeasure. If you want to please God, make sure you keep your promises. God wants promises kept, not just piously made.

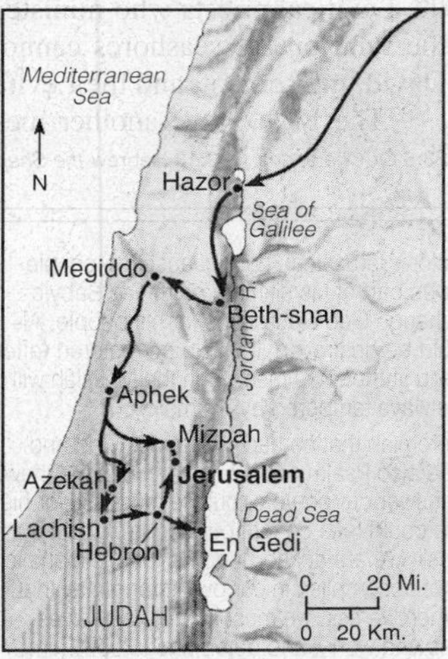

BABYLON ATTACKS JUDAH
Zedekiah incurred Babylon's wrath in allying with Egypt (37:5) and not surrendering as God told him through Jeremiah (38:17). Nebuchadnezzar attacked Judah for the third and final time, moving systematically until all its cities fell. Jerusalem withstood siege for several months but was burned, as Jeremiah predicted (chapter 39).

your countrymen free, I will set you free to be destroyed by war, famine, and disease.
You will be considered a disgrace by all the nations of the earth. 18 Because you have
refused the terms of our covenant, I will cut you apart just as you cut apart the calf when
you walked between its halves to solemnize your vows. 19 Yes, I will cut you apart,
whether you are officials of Judah or Jerusalem, court officials, priests, or common
people—for you have broken your oath. 20 I will give you to your enemies, and they will
kill you. Your bodies will be food for the vultures and wild animals. 21 I will hand over
King Zedekiah of Judah and his officials to the army of the king of Babylon. And though
Babylon's king has left this city for a while, 22 I will call the Babylonian armies back
again. They will fight against this city and will capture and burn it. I will see to it that all
the towns of Judah are destroyed and left completely empty."

The Faithful Recabites

35 This is the message the LORD gave Jeremiah when Jehoiakim son of Josiah was
king of Judah: 2 "Go to the settlement where the families of the Recabites live,
and invite them to the LORD's Temple. Take them into one of the inner rooms, and offer
them some wine."

3 So I went to see Jaazaniah son of Jeremiah and grandson of Habazziniah and all his
brothers and sons—representing all the Recabite families. 4 I took them to the Temple,
and we went into the room assigned to the sons of Hanan son of Igdaliah, a man of God.
This room was located next to the one used by the palace officials, directly above the
room of Maaseiah son of Shallum, the Temple gatekeeper.

5 I set cups and jugs of wine before them and invited them to have a drink, 6 but they
refused. "No," they said. "We don't drink wine, because Jehonadab* son of Recab, our
ancestor, gave us this command: 'You and your descendants must never drink wine. 7 And
do not build houses or plant crops or vineyards, but always live in tents. If you follow
these commands, you will live long, good lives in the land.' 8 So we have obeyed him in
all these things. We have never had a drink of wine since then, nor have our wives, our
sons, or our daughters. 9 We haven't built houses or owned vineyards or farms or planted
crops. 10 We have lived in tents and have fully obeyed all the commands of Jehonadab,
our ancestor. 11 But when King Nebuchadnezzar* of Babylon arrived in this country, we
were afraid of the Babylonian* and Aramean armies. So we decided to move to
Jerusalem. That is why we are here."

12 Then the LORD gave this message to Jeremiah: 13 "The LORD Almighty, the God of
Israel, says: Go and say to the people in Judah and Jerusalem, 'Come and learn a lesson
about how to obey me. 14 The Recabites do not drink wine because their ancestor
Jehonadab told them not to. But I have spoken to you again and again, and you refuse to
listen or obey. 15 I have sent you prophet after prophet to tell you to turn from your wicked
ways and to stop worshiping other gods, so that you might live in peace here in the land
I gave to you and your ancestors. But you would not listen to me or obey. 16 The families
of Recab have obeyed their ancestor completely, but you have refused to listen to me.'

34:18 Gen 15:10; Hos 6:7; Mic 7:1-5
34:20 1 Sam 17:46; Jer 19:7
34:21 2 Kgs 25:18-21; Ezek 17:16
34:22 Jer 44:22
35:1 2 Kgs 23:34-36; Dan 1:1
35:2 1 Kgs 6:5-6, 8; 1 Chr 2:55
35:4 1 Kgs 12:22; 1 Chr 9:18
35:5 Amos 2:12
35:6 Lev 10:9; 2 Kgs 10:15, 23; 1 Chr 2:55; Luke 1:15
35:7 Exod 20:12; 1 Chr 16:19; Heb 11:9
35:8 Prov 4:1-2, 10; 6:20; Col 3:20
35:9 Ps 37:16; 1 Tim 6:6
35:11 2 Kgs 24:1-2; Dan 1:1-2
35:13 Isa 28:9-12
35:14 2 Chr 36:15; Isa 30:9
35:15 Deut 6:14; Jer 29:19; Ezek 18:30-32; Acts 26:20
35:16 Mal 1:6

35:6 Hebrew *Jonadab,* a variant name for Jehonadab; also in 35:10, 14, 18, 19. See 2 Kgs 10:15. **35:11a** Hebrew *Nebuchadrezzar,* a variant name for Nebuchadnezzar. **35:11b** Or *Chaldean.*

34:18-20 Cutting a calf in two and walking between the halves was a customary way to ratify a contract (Genesis 15:9, 10). This action symbolized the judgment on anyone who broke the contract. God was saying, "You have broken the contract you made with me, so you know the judgment awaiting you!"

35:1ff The Recabites' code of conduct resembled that of the Nazirites, who took a special vow of dedication to God (Numbers 6). For 200 years they had obeyed their ancestor's vow to abstain from wine. While the rest of the nation was breaking its covenant with God, these people were steadfast in their commitment. God wanted the rest of his people to remain as committed to their covenant with him as the Recabites were to their vow. God had Jeremiah tempt the Recabites with wine to demonstrate their commitment and dedication. God knew they wouldn't break their vow.

35:6 Jehonadab son of Recab had joined Jehu in purging the northern kingdom of Baal worship (2 Kings 10:15-28).

35:13-17 There is a vivid contrast between the Recabites and the other Israelites. (1) The Recabites kept their vows to a fallible human leader; the people of Israel broke their covenant with their infallible divine Leader. (2) Jehonadab told his family one time not to drink, and they obeyed; God commanded Israel constantly to turn from sin, and they refused. (3) The Recabites obeyed laws that dealt with temporal issues; Israel refused to obey God's laws that dealt with eternal issues. (4) The Recabites had obeyed for hundreds of years; Israel had disobeyed for hundreds of years. (5) The Recabites would be rewarded; Israel would be punished. We often are willing to observe customs merely for the sake of tradition; how much more should we obey God's Word because it is eternal.

17"Therefore, the LORD God Almighty, the God of Israel, says: Because you refuse to
listen or answer when I call, I will send upon Judah and Jerusalem all the disasters I have
threatened."
18Then Jeremiah turned to the Recabites and said, "This is what the LORD Almighty,
the God of Israel, says: You have obeyed your ancestor Jehonadab in every respect,
following all his instructions. 19Because of this, Jehonadab son of Recab will always
have descendants who serve me. I, the LORD Almighty, the God of Israel, have spoken!"

Baruch Reads the LORD's Messages

36 During the fourth year that Jehoiakim son of Josiah was king in Judah,* the LORD
gave this message to Jeremiah: 2"Get a scroll, and write down all my messages
against Israel, Judah, and the other nations. Begin with the first message back in the days
of Josiah, and write down every message you have given, right up to the present time.
3Perhaps the people of Judah will repent if they see in writing all the terrible things I
have planned for them. Then I will be able to forgive their sins and wrongdoings."
4So Jeremiah sent for Baruch son of Neriah, and as Jeremiah dictated, Baruch wrote
down all the prophecies that the LORD had given him. 5Then Jeremiah said to Baruch,
"I am a prisoner here and unable to go to the Temple. 6So you go to the Temple on the
next day of fasting, and read the messages from the LORD that are on this scroll. On that
day people will be there from all over Judah. 7Perhaps even yet they will turn from their
evil ways and ask the LORD's forgiveness before it is too late. For the LORD's terrible
anger has been pronounced against them."
8Baruch did as Jeremiah told him and read these messages from the LORD to the
people at the Temple. 9This happened on the day of sacred fasting held in late autumn,*
during the fifth year of the reign of Jehoiakim son of Josiah. People from all over Judah
came to attend the services at the Temple on that day. 10Baruch read Jeremiah's words
to all the people from the Temple room of Gemariah son of Shaphan. This room was just
off the upper courtyard of the Temple, near the New Gate entrance.
11When Micaiah son of Gemariah and grandson of Shaphan heard the messages from
the LORD, 12he went down to the secretary's room in the palace where the administrative
officials were meeting. Elishama the secretary was there, along with Delaiah son of
Shemaiah, Elnathan son of Acbor, Gemariah son of Shaphan, Zedekiah son of Hananiah,
and all the others with official responsibilities. 13When Micaiah told them about the
messages Baruch was reading to the people, 14the officials sent Jehudi son of Nethaniah,
grandson of Shelemiah, and great-grandson of Cushi, to ask Baruch to come and read
the messages to them, too. So Baruch took the scroll and went to them. 15"Sit down and
read the scroll to us," the officials said, and Baruch did as they requested.
16By the time Baruch had finished reading, they were badly frightened. "We must tell
the king what we have heard," they said. 17"But first, tell us how you got these messages.
Did they come directly from Jeremiah?"
18So Baruch explained, "Jeremiah dictated them to me word by word, and I wrote
down his words with ink on this scroll."
19"You and Jeremiah should both hide," the officials told Baruch. "Don't tell anyone

35:17 Prov 1:24-25; Mic 3:12; Luke 13:34-35; Rom 10:21
35:18 Exod 20:12; Jer 15:19; Eph 6:1-3
35:19 Jer 15:19
36:1 Jer 25:1-3; 45:1
36:2 Jer 1:2-3, 5, 9-10; 25:9-29, 47-51; Zech 5:1-2
36:3 Isa 55:7; Jer 18:8, 11; 26:3; Mark 4:12; Acts 3:19
36:4 Jer 32:12; Ezek 2:9
36:5 Jer 32:2
36:6 Zech 8:19
36:7 1 Kgs 8:33; 2 Kgs 22:13; Jer 26:3
36:10 Jer 26:10
36:12 Jer 26:22
36:13 2 Kgs 22:9-10
36:16 Amos 7:10-11; Acts 24:25
36:18 Jer 36:4
36:19 1 Kgs 17:3; 18:4; Jer 26:20-24

36:1 The fourth year of Jehoiakim's reign was 605 B.C. **36:9** Hebrew *in the ninth month,* of the Hebrew calendar (also in 36:22). This month in the fifth year of Jehoiakim's reign occurred in November and December 604 B.C. Also see note on 1:3.

36:1ff This happened in the summer of 605 B.C., shortly after Nebuchadnezzar's victory over the Egyptian army at Carchemish, before the events recorded in chapters 34 and 35.

36:2-4 Most people in ancient times could neither read nor write, so those who could were highly esteemed. These men, called scribes or teachers, held positions of great importance and were very respected for their knowledge. Baruch was Jeremiah's scribe. Writing was often done on vellum or papyrus sheets that were sewn or glued together and stored in long rolls called scrolls. After the Exile, scribes became teachers of the law. In New Testament times, the scribes formed a powerful political party.

36:9 A time of fasting (when people abstained from eating food to show their humility and repentance) was often called during times of national emergency. Babylon was destroying city after city and closing in on Jerusalem. As the people came to the Temple, Baruch told them how to avert the coming tragedy, but they refused to listen.

36:10-32 God told Jeremiah to write his words on a scroll. Because he was not allowed to go to the Temple, Jeremiah asked his scribe, Baruch, to whom he had dictated the scroll to read it to the people gathered there. Baruch then read it to the officials, and finally Jehudi read it to the king himself. Although the king burned the scroll, he could not destroy the word of God. Today many people try to put God's Word aside or say that it contains errors and therefore cannot be trusted. People may reject God's Word, but they cannot destroy it. God's Word will stand forever (Psalm 119:89).

where you are!" [20]Then the officials left the scroll for safekeeping in the room of Elishama the secretary and went to tell the king.

King Jehoiakim Burns the Scroll

[21]The king sent Jehudi to get the scroll. Jehudi brought it from Elishama's room and read it to the king as all his officials stood by. [22]It was late autumn, and the king was in a winterized part of the palace, sitting in front of a fire to keep warm. [23]Whenever Jehudi finished reading three or four columns, the king took his knife and cut off that section of the scroll. He then threw it into the fire, section by section, until the whole scroll was burned up. [24]Neither the king nor his officials showed any signs of fear or repentance at what they heard. [25]Even when Elnathan, Delaiah, and Gemariah begged the king not to burn the scroll, he wouldn't listen.

[26]Then the king commanded his son Jerahmeel, Seraiah son of Azriel, and Shelemiah son of Abdeel to arrest Baruch and Jeremiah. But the LORD had hidden them.

Jeremiah Rewrites the Scroll

[27]After the king had burned Jeremiah's scroll, the LORD gave Jeremiah another message. He said, [28]"Get another scroll, and write everything again just as you did on the scroll King Jehoiakim burned. [29]Then say to the king, 'This is what the LORD says: You burned the scroll because it said the king of Babylon would destroy this land and everything in it. [30]Now this is what the LORD says about King Jehoiakim of Judah: He will have no heirs to sit on the throne of David. His dead body will be thrown out to lie unburied—exposed to hot days and frosty nights. [31]I will punish him and his family and his officials because of their sins. I will pour out on them and on all the people of Judah and Jerusalem all the disasters I have promised, for they would not listen to my warnings.'"

[32]Then Jeremiah took another scroll and dictated again to his secretary Baruch. He wrote everything that had been on the scroll King Jehoiakim had burned in the fire. Only this time, he added much more!

Zedekiah Calls for Jeremiah

37 Zedekiah son of Josiah succeeded Jehoiachin* son of Jehoiakim as the king of Judah. He was appointed by King Nebuchadnezzar* of Babylon. [2]But neither King Zedekiah nor his officials nor the people who were left in the land listened to what the LORD said through Jeremiah. [3]Nevertheless, King Zedekiah sent Jehucal son of Shelemiah and Zephaniah the priest, son of Maaseiah, to ask Jeremiah, "Please pray to the LORD our God for us." [4]Jeremiah had not yet been imprisoned, so he could come and go as he pleased.

[5]At this time the army of Pharaoh Hophra* of Egypt appeared at the southern border of Judah. When the Babylonian* army heard about it, they withdrew from their siege of Jerusalem. [6]Then the LORD gave this message to Jeremiah: [7]"This is what the LORD, the God of Israel, says: Tell the king of Judah, who sent you to ask me what is going to happen, that Pharaoh's army is about to return to Egypt, though he came here to help you. [8]Then the Babylonians* will come back and capture this city and burn it to the

36:21 2 Kgs 22:9-10; 2 Chr 34:18; Ezek 2:4-5
36:22 Amos 3:15
36:24 2 Kgs 19:1-2; Ps 36:1; Acts 5:34-39
36:26 1 Kgs 19:1-3, 10; Jer 15:20-21
36:28 Jer 28:13-14; Zech 1:5-6
36:29 Deut 29:19; Isa 30:10-11; 45:9; Jer 25:8-11; 26:9
36:30 2 Kgs 24:12-15; Jer 22:30
36:31 Deut 28:15-19; Prov 29:1; Jer 19:15
36:32 Exod 34:1
37:1 2 Kgs 24:17; 1 Chr 3:15-16; 2 Chr 36:9-10; Jer 22:24, 28; Ezek 17:12-21
37:2 2 Kgs 24:18-20; 2 Chr 36:12; Prov 29:12
37:3 Jer 2:26-27; 21:1-2; 52:24
37:5 Ezek 17:15-16
37:7 Isa 30:1-3; 31:1-3; Jer 21:1-2; Ezek 17:17

37:1a Hebrew *Coniah,* a variant name for Jehoiachin. **37:1b** Hebrew *Nebuchadrezzar,* a variant name for Nebuchadnezzar. **37:5a** Hebrew *army of Pharaoh;* see 44:30. **37:5b** Or *Chaldean;* also in 37:10, 11. **37:8** Or *Chaldeans;* also in 37:9, 13.

36:25 Only three leaders protested this evil act of burning the scroll containing God's word. This shows how complacent and insensitive to God the people had become.

36:30 Jehoiakim's son, Jehoiachin, was king for three months before he was taken into captivity, but this did not qualify as sitting "on the throne of David"—an expression that implied permanence. Jehoiakim did not secure a dynasty. Zedekiah, the next ruler, was Jehoiachin's uncle. Thus, the line of mortal human kings descended from David's son Solomon was finished, but in less than 600 years the eternal King would come through the descendants of Solomon's brother Nathan (see also the note on 22:30).

37:1ff King Jehoiakim died on the way to Babylon (2 Chronicles 36:6). His son Jehoiachin was appointed king but was taken captive to Babylon three months later. Nebuchadnezzar then appointed Zedekiah as his vassal in Judah.

37:2, 3 King Zedekiah and his officials did not want to listen to Jeremiah's words, but they wanted the blessings of his prayers. They wanted a superficial religion that wouldn't cost anything. God is not pleased with those who come to him seeking only what they can get rather than seeking to have a relationship with him. We would not accept that kind of relationship with someone else, and we shouldn't expect God to accept it from us.

37:5 When Nebuchadnezzar besieged Jerusalem in 589 B.C., Pharaoh Hophra marched against him at Zedekiah's invitation. Jerusalem looked to Egypt for help in spite of Jeremiah's warnings. But the Egyptians were no help, for as soon as the Babylonians turned on them, they retreated. Jeremiah's warnings had been correct.

ground. 9 The LORD says: Do not fool yourselves that the Babylonians are gone for good.
They aren't! 10 Even if you were to destroy the entire Babylonian army, leaving only a
handful of wounded survivors, they would still stagger from their tents and burn this city
to the ground!"

Jeremiah Is Imprisoned

11 When the Babylonian army left Jerusalem because of Pharaoh's approaching army,
12 Jeremiah started to leave the city on his way to the land of Benjamin, to see the property
he had bought. 13 But as he was walking through the Benjamin Gate, a sentry arrested
him and said, "You are defecting to the Babylonians!" The sentry making the arrest was
Irijah son of Shelemiah and grandson of Hananiah.

14 "That's not true!" Jeremiah protested. "I had no intention of doing any such thing."
But Irijah wouldn't listen, and he took Jeremiah before the officials. 15 They were furious
with Jeremiah and had him flogged and imprisoned in the house of Jonathan the
secretary. Jonathan's house had been converted into a prison. 16 Jeremiah was put into a
dungeon cell, where he remained for many days.

17 Later King Zedekiah secretly requested that Jeremiah come to the palace, where the
king asked him, "Do you have any messages from the LORD?"

"Yes, I do!" said Jeremiah. "You will be defeated by the king of Babylon."

18 Then Jeremiah asked the king, "What crime have I committed? What have I done
against you, your officials, or the people that I should be imprisoned like this? 19 Where
are your prophets now who told you the king of Babylon would not attack you? 20 Listen,
my lord the king, I beg you. Don't send me back to the dungeon in the house of Jonathan
the secretary, for I will die there."

21 So King Zedekiah commanded that Jeremiah not be returned to the dungeon.
Instead, he was imprisoned in the courtyard of the guard in the royal palace. The king
also commanded that Jeremiah be given a loaf of fresh bread every day as long as there
was any left in the city. So Jeremiah was put in the palace prison.

Jeremiah in a Cistern

38 Now Shephatiah son of Mattan, Gedaliah son of Pashhur, Jehucal* son of
Shelemiah, and Pashhur son of Malkijah heard what Jeremiah had been telling the
people. He was saying, 2 "This is what the LORD says: Everyone who stays in Jerusalem
will die from war, famine, or disease, but those who surrender to the Babylonians* will
live. 3 The LORD also says: The city of Jerusalem will surely be handed over to the army
of the king of Babylon, who will capture it."

4 So these officials went to the king and said, "Sir, this man must die! That kind of talk
will undermine the morale of the few fighting men we have left, as well as that of all the
people, too. This man is a traitor!"

5 So King Zedekiah agreed. "All right," he said. "Do as you like. I will do nothing to
stop you."

6 So the officials took Jeremiah from his cell and lowered him by ropes into an empty
cistern in the prison yard. It belonged to Malkijah, a member of the royal family. There was

38:1 Hebrew *Jucal,* a variant name for Jehucal; see 37:3. **38:2** Or *Chaldeans;* also in 38:18, 19, 23.

37:9 Jer 29:8
37:10 Isa 30:17; Joel 2:11
37:12 Jer 32:8
37:13 Jer 18:18; 20:10; Zech 14:10; Acts 24:5-9, 13
37:14 Ps 27:12; Jer 40:4-6; Matt 5:11-12
37:15 Jer 18:23; 38:6; Matt 21:35; Acts 5:18; Heb 11:36
37:17 Jer 21:7; 38:14-16; Ezek 12:12-13; 17:19-21
37:18 1 Sam 24:9; 26:18; John 10:32; Acts 25:8, 10-11
37:19 Deut 32:37-38
37:21 Job 5:20; Ps 33:18-19; Isa 33:16; Jer 52:6
38:1 Jer 21:8
38:2 Jer 21:9; 42:17
38:3 Jer 21:10; 32:3-5
38:4 1 Kgs 18:17-18; Jer 26:11; Amos 7:10; Acts 16:20-21
38:5 2 Sam 3:39
38:6 Pss 40:2; 69:1-2, 14; Jer 37:15-16; Zech 9:11; Acts 16:24

37:17 Zedekiah teetered between surrender and resistance. Too frightened and weak to exercise authority, he asked Jeremiah to come secretly to the palace, perhaps hoping for some better news from God. Zedekiah was desperate. He wanted to hear a word from the Lord, but he feared the political ramifications of being caught talking to Jeremiah.

38:4, 5 No wonder Judah was in turmoil: The king agreed with everybody. He listened to Jeremiah (37:21); then he agreed Jeremiah should be killed (38:5); and finally he rescued Jeremiah (38:10). Jeremiah was not popular; his words undermined the morale of the army and the people. Zedekiah couldn't decide between public opinion and God's will. What is most influential in your life—what others say and think or what God wants?

38:6 Officials put Jeremiah in a cistern to die. A cistern was a large hole in the ground lined with rocks to collect rainwater. The bottom would have been dark, damp, and, in this case, full of mud. Jeremiah could drown, die of exposure, or starve to death in the cistern.

38:6 Judah's leaders persecuted Jeremiah repeatedly for faithfully proclaiming God's messages. For 40 years of faithful ministry, he received no acclaim, no love, no popular following. He was beaten, jailed, threatened, and even forced to leave his homeland. Only the pagan Babylonians showed him any respect (39:11, 12). God does not guarantee that his servants will escape persecution, even when they are faithful. But God does promise that he will be with them and will give them strength to endure (2 Corinthians 1:3-7). As you minister to others, recognize that your service is for God and not just for human approval. God rewards our faithfulness, but not always during our lifetime.

no water in the cistern, but there was a thick layer of mud at the bottom, and Jeremiah sank down into it.

7 But Ebed-melech the Ethiopian,* an important palace official, heard that Jeremiah was in the cistern. At that time the king was holding court at the Benjamin Gate, 8 so Ebed-melech rushed from the palace to speak with him. 9 "My lord the king," he said, "these men have done a very evil thing in putting Jeremiah the prophet into the cistern. He will soon die of hunger, for almost all the bread in the city is gone."

10 So the king told Ebed-melech, "Take along thirty of my men, and pull Jeremiah out of the cistern before he dies."

11 So Ebed-melech took the men with him and went to a room in the palace beneath the treasury, where he found some old rags and discarded clothing. He carried these to the cistern and lowered them to Jeremiah on a rope. 12 Ebed-melech called down to Jeremiah, "Put these rags under your armpits to protect you from the ropes." Then when Jeremiah was ready, 13 they pulled him out. So Jeremiah was returned to the courtyard of the guard—the palace prison—where he remained.

Zedekiah Questions Jeremiah

14 One day King Zedekiah sent for Jeremiah to meet him at the third entrance of the LORD's Temple. "I want to ask you something," the king said. "And don't try to hide the truth."

15 Jeremiah said, "If I tell you the truth, you will kill me. And if I give you advice, you won't listen to me anyway."

16 So King Zedekiah secretly promised him, "As surely as the LORD our Creator lives, I will not kill you or hand you over to the men who want you dead."

17 Then Jeremiah said to Zedekiah, "The LORD God Almighty, the God of Israel, says: If you surrender to Babylon, you and your family will live, and the city will not be burned. 18 But if you refuse to surrender, you will not escape! This city will be handed over to the Babylonians, and they will burn it to the ground."

19 "But I am afraid to surrender," the king said, "for the Babylonians will hand me over to the Judeans who have defected to them. And who knows what they will do to me?"

20 Jeremiah replied, "You won't be handed over to them if you choose to obey the LORD. Your life will be spared, and all will go well for you. 21 But if you refuse to surrender, this is what the LORD has revealed to me: 22 All the women left in your palace will be brought out and given to the officers of the Babylonian army. Then the women will taunt you, saying, 'What fine friends you have! They have betrayed and misled you. When your feet sank in the mud, they left you to your fate!' 23 All your wives and children will be led out to the Babylonians, and you will not escape. You will be seized by the king of Babylon, and this city will be burned."

24 Then Zedekiah said to Jeremiah, "Don't tell anyone you told me this, or you will die! 25 My officials may hear that I spoke to you. Then they may say to you, 'Tell us what you and the king were talking about. If you don't tell us, we will kill you.' 26 If this happens, just tell them you begged me not to send you back to Jonathan's dungeon, for fear you would die there."

27 Sure enough, it wasn't long before the king's officials came to Jeremiah and asked him why the king had called for him. But Jeremiah followed the king's instructions, and they left without finding out the truth. No one had overheard the conversation between

38:9 Jer 37:21; 52:6
38:13 Jer 37:21; 39:14-15
38:14 1 Kgs 22:16; Jer 21:1-2; 37:17
38:15 Luke 22:67-68
38:16 Isa 42:5; Jer 37:17
38:17 2 Kgs 25:27-30; Ps 80:7, 14; Jer 21:8-10; 27:12, 17
38:18 2 Kgs 25:4-10; Jer 27:8; 37:8
38:19 Isa 51:12-13; 57:11; Jer 39:9; John 12:42
38:20 Isa 55:3; Jer 7:23; 11:4, 8; 26:13
38:22 Jer 6:12; 8:10; 43:6
38:23 2 Kgs 25:7; Jer 39:6; 41:10
38:26 Jer 37:15-16, 20
38:27 1 Sam 10:15-16; 16:2-5

38:7 Hebrew *the Cushite.*

38:7, 8 The Benjamin Gate was one of Jerusalem's city gates where legal matters were handled. A palace official, Ebed-melech, had access to the king. When Ebed-melech heard of Jeremiah's plight, he went immediately to deal with the injustice.

38:9-13 Ebed-melech feared God more than man. He alone among the palace officials stood up against the murder plot. His obedience could have cost him his life. Because he obeyed, however, he was spared when Jerusalem fell (39:15-18). You can either go along with the crowd or speak up for God. When someone is treated unkindly or unjustly, for example, reach out to that person with God's love. You may be the only one who does. And, when you are being treated unkindly yourself, be sure to thank God when he sends an "Ebed-melech" your way.

38:27 The officials wanted accurate information, but not God's truth. They wanted to use this information against God, his prophet, and the king. But Jeremiah told the officials only what the king ordered him to say. We must not withhold God's truth from others, but we should withhold information that will be used to bring evil to God's people.

Jeremiah and the king. [28]And Jeremiah remained a prisoner in the courtyard of the guard
until the day Jerusalem was captured.

The Fall of Jerusalem

39 It was in January* during the ninth year of King Zedekiah's reign that King
Nebuchadnezzar* and his army returned to besiege Jerusalem. [2]Two and a half
years later, on July 18,* the Babylonians broke through the wall, and the city fell. [3]All
the officers of the Babylonian army came in and sat in triumph at the Middle Gate:
Nergal-sharezer of Samgar, and Nebo-sarsekim,* a chief officer, and Nergal-sharezer,
the king's adviser, and many others.
[4]King Zedekiah and his royal guard saw the Babylonians in the city gate, so they fled
when the darkness of night arrived. They went out through a gate between the two walls
behind the king's garden and headed toward the Jordan Valley.* [5]But the Babylonians*
chased the king and caught him on the plains of Jericho. They took him to King
Nebuchadnezzar of Babylon, who was at Riblah in the land of Hamath. There the king
of Babylon pronounced judgment upon Zedekiah. [6]He made Zedekiah watch as they
killed his sons and all the nobles of Judah. [7]Then he gouged out Zedekiah's eyes, bound
him in chains, and sent him away to exile in Babylon.
[8]Meanwhile, the Babylonians burned Jerusalem, including the palace, and tore down
the walls of the city. [9]Then Nebuzaradan, the captain of the guard, sent to Babylon the
remnant of the population as well as those who had defected to him. [10]But Nebuzaradan
left a few of the poorest people in Judah, and he assigned them fields and vineyards to
care for.

Jeremiah Remains in Judah

[11]King Nebuchadnezzar had told Nebuzaradan to find Jeremiah. [12]"See that he isn't
hurt," he had said. "Look after him well, and give him anything he wants." [13]So
Nebuzaradan, the captain of the guard, and Nebushazban, a chief officer, and Nergal-
sharezer, the king's adviser, and the other officers of Babylon's king [14]sent messengers
to bring Jeremiah out of the prison. They put him under the care of Gedaliah son of
Ahikam and grandson of Shaphan, who was to take him back to his home. So Jeremiah
stayed in Judah among his own people.
[15]The LORD had given the following message to Jeremiah while he was still in prison:
[16]"Say to Ebed-melech the Ethiopian,* 'The LORD Almighty, the God of Israel, says: I
will do to this city everything I have threatened. I will send disaster, not prosperity. You
will see its destruction, [17]but I will rescue you from those you fear so much. [18]Because
you trusted me, I will preserve your life and keep you safe. I, the LORD, have spoken!'"

39:1a Hebrew *in the tenth month,* of the Hebrew calendar. A number of events in Jeremiah can be cross-checked with dates in surviving Babylonian records and related accurately to our modern calendar. This event occurred on January 15, 588 B.C.; see 52:4 and the note there. **39:1b** Hebrew *Nebuchadrezzar,* a variant name for Nebuchadnezzar; also in 39:11. **39:2** Hebrew *On the ninth day of the fourth month of the eleventh year of Zedekiah.* This event occurred on July 18, 586 B.C.; also see note on 39:1. **39:3** Or *Nergal-sharezer, Samgar-nebo, Sarsekim.* **39:4** Hebrew *the Arabah.* **39:5** Or *Chaldeans;* also in 39:8. **39:16** Hebrew *the Cushite.*

38:28 Jer 37:20-21; 39:13-14
39:1 2 Kgs 25:1-12
39:2 2 Kgs 25:4; Jer 52:7
39:4 2 Kgs 25:4; Isa 30:15-16; Jer 52:7; Amos 2:14
39:5 Jer 32:4-5; 52:8-9; Lam 4:20
39:6 Jer 24:8-10; 34:18-21; 52:10
39:7 2 Kgs 25:7; Jer 52:11; Ezek 12:13
39:8 2 Kgs 25:9-10; Neh 1:3
39:9 2 Kgs 25:11, 20; Jer 52:12-16, 26
39:10 2 Kgs 25:12
39:11 Job 5:15-16; Jer 1:8; 15:20-21
39:12 1 Pet 3:13
39:14 2 Kgs 22:12, 14; Jer 26:24; 40:1-6
39:16 Jer 21:10; Zech 1:6
39:17 Pss 41:1-2; 50:14-15
39:18 Ps 34:22; Jer 17:7-8; Rom 10:11

39:1ff Zedekiah, son of Josiah and last king of Judah, ruled 11 years, from 597 to 586 B.C. Zedekiah's two older brothers, Jehoahaz and Jehoiakim, and his nephew Jehoiachin ruled before him. When Jehoiachin was exiled to Babylon, Nebuchadnezzar made 21-year-old Mattaniah the king, changing his name to Zedekiah. Zedekiah rebelled against Nebuchadnezzar, who captured him, killed his sons in front of him, and then blinded him and took him back to Babylon, where he later died (see 2 Kings 24–25; 2 Chronicles 36; and Jeremiah 52).

39:5 Riblah was 200 miles north of Jerusalem. This was the Babylonian headquarters for ruling the region.

39:10 Babylon had a shrewd foreign policy toward conquered lands. They deported the rich and powerful, leaving only the very poor in charge, thus making them grateful to their conquerors. This policy assured that conquered populations would be too loyal and too weak to revolt.

39:11, 12 God had promised to rescue Jeremiah from his trouble (1:8). The superstitious Babylonians, who highly respected magicians and fortune-tellers, treated Jeremiah as a seer. Because he had been imprisoned by his own people, they assumed he was a traitor and on their side. They undoubtedly knew he had counseled cooperation with Babylon and predicted a Babylonian victory. So the Babylonians freed Jeremiah and protected him.

39:13, 14 What a difference there is between Jeremiah's fate and Zedekiah's! Jeremiah was freed; Zedekiah was imprisoned. Jeremiah was saved because of his faith; Zedekiah was destroyed because of his fear. Jeremiah was treated with respect; Zedekiah was treated with contempt. Jeremiah was concerned for the people; Zedekiah was concerned for himself.

39:17, 18 Ebed-melech had risked his life to save God's prophet Jeremiah (38:7-13). When Babylon conquered Jerusalem, God protected Ebed-melech from the Babylonians. God has special rewards for his faithful people, but not everyone will receive them in this life (see the note on 38:6).

40

The LORD gave a message to Jeremiah after Nebuzaradan, captain of the guard,
had released him at Ramah. He had found Jeremiah bound in chains among the
captives of Jerusalem and Judah who were being sent to exile in Babylon.
2 The captain of the guard called for Jeremiah and said, "The LORD your God has
brought this disaster on this land, 3 just as he said he would. For these people have sinned
against the LORD and disobeyed him. That is why it happened. 4 Now I am going to take
off your chains and let you go. If you want to come with me to Babylon, you are
welcome. I will see that you are well cared for. But if you don't want to come, you may
stay here. The whole land is before you—go wherever you like. 5 If you decide to stay,
then return to Gedaliah son of Ahikam and grandson of Shaphan. He has been appointed
governor of Judah by the king of Babylon. Stay there with the people he rules. But it's
up to you; go wherever you like."
Then Nebuzaradan gave Jeremiah some food and money and let him go. 6 So Jeremiah
returned to Gedaliah son of Ahikam at Mizpah and lived in Judah with the few who were
still left in the land.

Gedaliah Governs in Judah

7 The leaders of the Judean guerrilla bands in the countryside heard that the king of
Babylon had appointed Gedaliah son of Ahikam as governor over the poor people who
were left behind in Judah, and that he hadn't exiled everyone to Babylon. 8 So they came
to see Gedaliah at Mizpah. These are the names of the leaders who came: Ishmael son of
Nethaniah, Johanan and Jonathan, sons of Kareah, Seraiah son of Tanhumeth, the sons
of Ephai the Netophathite, Jaazaniah* son of the Maacathite, and all their men.
9 Gedaliah assured them that it would be safe for them to surrender to the Babylonians.* "Stay here, and serve the king of Babylon," he said, "and all will go well for you.
10 As for me, I will stay at Mizpah to represent you before the Babylonians who come to
meet with us. Settle in any town you wish, and live off the land. Harvest the grapes and
summer fruits and olives, and store them away."
11 When the Judeans in Moab, Ammon, Edom, and the other nearby countries heard
that the king of Babylon had left a few people in Judah and that Gedaliah was the
governor, 12 they began to return to Judah from the places to which they had fled. They
stopped at Mizpah to discuss their plans with Gedaliah and then went out into the Judean
countryside to gather a great harvest of grapes and other crops.

A Plot against Gedaliah

13 Soon after this, Johanan son of Kareah and the other guerrilla leaders came to
Gedaliah at Mizpah. 14 They said to him, "Did you know that Baalis, king of Ammon,
has sent Ishmael son of Nethaniah to assassinate you?" But Gedaliah refused to
believe them.
15 Later Johanan had a private conference with Gedaliah and volunteered to kill
Ishmael secretly. "Why should we let him come and murder you?" Johanan asked.
"What will happen then to the Judeans who have returned? Why should the few of us
who are still left be scattered and lost?"
16 But Gedaliah said to Johanan, "I forbid you to do any such thing, for you are lying
about Ishmael."

40:1 Jer 31:15; Eph 6:20
40:2 Deut 29:24-28; Jer 22:8-9; 50:7
40:3 Dan 9:11
40:4 Gen 20:15; Jer 39:11, 12
40:5 2 Kgs 25:23
40:6 Jer 39:14
40:7 2 Kgs 25:23-24; Jer 39:10; 52:16
40:8 Jer 41:1
40:9 2 Kgs 25:24; Jer 27:11
40:10 Jer 35:19; 39:10
40:11 1 Sam 11:1; Isa 11:14; 16:4-5
40:12 Jer 43:5
40:13 Jer 25:21; 41:10
40:15 1 Sam 26:8; 2 Sam 21:17; Jer 42:1-2
40:16 Matt 10:16

40:8 As in parallel text at 2 Kgs 25:23; Hebrew reads *Jezaniah,* a variant name for Jaazaniah. **40:9** Or *Chaldeans;* also in 40:10.

40–45 These six chapters cover events following Jerusalem's fall to Babylon.

40:2, 3 The Babylonian commander, who did not know God, acknowledged that God had given the Babylonians victory. It is strange for people to recognize that God exists and does miracles and yet not personally accept him. Knowing God is more than knowing about him. Be sure you know him personally.

40:4 Jeremiah was free to go anywhere. In Babylon he would have great comfort and power. In Judah he would continue to face hardship. In Babylon Jeremiah would have been favored by the Babylonians but hated by the Judean exiles. In Judah he would remain poor and unwanted, but the Judean remnant would know he was not a traitor. Jeremiah returned to Judah.

40:6 Mizpah was a few miles north of Jerusalem. Not thoroughly destroyed by the Babylonians, Mizpah served as a refuge after the destruction of Jerusalem.

40:13–41:3 Gedaliah, appointed governor of Judah, foolishly ignored the warnings of assassination. Ishmael, in the line of David, may have been angry that he had been passed over for leadership. This is similar to the chaotic political situation that Ezra and Nehemiah faced when they returned to rebuild the Temple and the city.

The Murder of Gedaliah

41 But in midautumn,* Ishmael son of Nethaniah and grandson of Elishama, who
was a member of the royal family, arrived in Mizpah accompanied by ten men.
Gedaliah invited them to dinner. While they were eating, 2 Ishmael and his ten men
suddenly drew their swords and killed Gedaliah, whom the king of Babylon had
appointed governor. 3 Then they went out and slaughtered all the Judean officials and
Babylonian* soldiers who were with Gedaliah at Mizpah.
4 The next day, before anyone had heard about Gedaliah's murder, 5 eighty men arrived
from Shechem, Shiloh, and Samaria. They had come to worship at the Temple of the
LORD. They had shaved off their beards, torn their clothes, and cut themselves, and had
brought along grain offerings and incense. 6 Ishmael left Mizpah to meet them, weeping
as he went. When he reached them, he said, "Oh, come and see what has happened to
Gedaliah!"
7 But as soon as they were all inside the town, Ishmael and his men killed all but ten
of them and threw their bodies into a cistern. 8 The other ten had talked Ishmael into
letting them go by promising to bring him their stores of wheat, barley, oil, and honey
that they had hidden away. 9 The cistern where Ishmael dumped the bodies of the men
he murdered was the large one made by King Asa when he fortified Mizpah to protect
himself against King Baasha of Israel. Ishmael son of Nethaniah filled it with corpses.
10 Ishmael made captives of the king's daughters and the other people who had been
left under Gedaliah's care in Mizpah by Nebuzaradan, captain of the guard. Taking them
with him, he started back toward the land of Ammon.
11 But when Johanan son of Kareah and the rest of the guerrilla leaders heard what
Ishmael had done, 12 they took all their men and set out to stop him. They caught up with
him at the pool near Gibeon. 13 The people Ishmael had captured shouted for joy when
they saw Johanan and his men. 14 And all the captives from Mizpah escaped and began
to help Johanan. 15 Meanwhile, Ishmael and eight of his men escaped from Johanan into
the land of Ammon.
16 Then Johanan son of Kareah and his officers led away all the people they had
rescued—warriors, women, children, and palace officials.* 17 They took them all to the
village of Geruth-kimham near Bethlehem, where they prepared to leave for Egypt.
18 They were afraid of what the Babylonians* would do when they heard that Ishmael
had killed Gedaliah, the governor appointed by the Babylonian king.

Warning to Stay in Judah

42 Then all the army officers, including Johanan son of Kareah and Jezaniah* son of
Hoshaiah, and all the people, from the least to the greatest, approached 2 Jeremiah
the prophet. They said, "Please pray to the LORD your God for us. As you know, we are
only a tiny remnant compared to what we were before. 3 Beg the LORD your God to show
us what to do and where to go."
4 "All right," Jeremiah replied. "I will pray to the LORD your God, and I will tell you
everything he says. I will hide nothing from you."
5 Then they said to Jeremiah, "May the LORD your God be a faithful witness against us
if we refuse to obey whatever he tells us to do! 6 Whether we like it or not, we will obey
the LORD our God to whom we send you with our plea. For if we obey him, everything
will turn out well for us."

41:1 2 Kgs 25:25; Jer 39:14; 40:5-8, 13-14
41:2 2 Sam 3:27; 20:8-10; Pss 41:9; 109:5; John 13:18
41:5 Deut 14:1; Josh 18:1; 1 Kgs 16:24; Ps 78:60; Jer 16:6
41:6 Jer 50:4
41:7 Isa 59:7; Ezek 22:27; 33:24
41:9 1 Sam 13:6; 1 Kgs 15:17-22; 2 Chr 16:1-6; Heb 11:37-38
41:10 Jer 40:11-12; 43:6
41:11 Jer 40:7-8, 13-16
41:12 2 Sam 2:13
41:15 Prov 28:17
41:16 Jer 42:8, 14; 43:4-7
41:17 2 Sam 19:37-38
41:18 Isa 57:11; Luke 12:4-5
42:1 Jer 40:8, 12-13
42:2 Deut 28:62; Isa 1:9; Acts 8:24
42:3 Ps 86:11; Prov 3:6; Mic 4:2
42:4 Ps 40:10; Jer 23:28
42:5 Mic 1:2
42:6 Exod 24:7; Deut 5:29

41:1 Hebrew *in the seventh month,* of the Hebrew calendar. This month occurred in October and November 586 B.C. Also see note on 39:1. **41:3** Or *Chaldean.* **41:16** Or *eunuchs.* **41:18** Or *Chaldeans.* **42:1** Greek version reads *Azariah;* compare 43:2.

41:4-9 The 80 men came from three cities of the northern kingdom to worship in Jerusalem. Ishmael probably killed them for the money and food they were carrying. Without a king, with no law and no loyalty to God, Judah was subjected to complete anarchy.

41:16, 17 Johanan and his group were already on their way to Egypt, headed south from Gibeon, stopping first at Geruth-kimham, near Bethlehem. Their visit to Jeremiah (42:1-6) was hypocritical, as Jeremiah later told them (42:20).

42:5, 6 Johanan and his associates spoke their own curse; Jeremiah merely elaborated on it. It was a tragic mistake to ask for God's guidance with no intention of following it. Be sure never to ask God for something that you know in your heart you really do not want. It is better not to pray than to pray hypocritically. God cannot be deceived.

42:9 2 Kgs 22:15
42:10 Jer 31:28; Hos 11:8; Joel 2:13; Jon 3:10; 4:2
42:11 Ps 46:7, 11; Isa 43:5; Jer 41:18; Rom 8:31
42:12 Ps 106:45-46; Prov 16:7
42:16 Jer 44:13, 27
42:17 Jer 44:13-14, 28
42:18 2 Chr 36:16-19; Jer 29:18-19; 39:1-9
42:19 Deut 17:16; Ezek 2:5
42:20 Ezek 14:3
42:21 Deut 11:26; Ezek 2:7
42:22 Jer 43:11; Hos 9:6

[7]Ten days later, the LORD gave his reply to Jeremiah. [8]So he called for Johanan son
of Kareah and the army officers, and for all the people, from the least to the greatest. [9]He
said to them, "You sent me to the LORD, the God of Israel, with your request, and this is
his reply: [10]'Stay here in this land. If you do, I will build you up and not tear you down;
I will plant you and not uproot you. For I am sorry for all the punishment I have had to
bring upon you. [11]Do not fear the king of Babylon anymore, says the LORD. For I am
with you and will save you and rescue you from his power. [12]I will be merciful to you
by making him kind, so he will let you stay here in your land.'
[13]"But if you refuse to obey the LORD your God and say, 'We will not stay here,' [14]and
if you insist on going to live in Egypt where you think you will be free from war, famine,
and alarms, [15]then this is what the LORD says to the remnant of Judah. The LORD Almighty,
the God of Israel, says: 'If you insist on going to Egypt, [16]the war and famine you fear
will follow close behind you, and you will die there. [17]That is the fate awaiting every one
of you who insists on going to live in Egypt. Yes, you will die from war, famine, and
disease. None of you will escape from the disaster I will bring upon you there.'
[18]"For the LORD Almighty, the God of Israel, says: 'Just as my anger and fury were
poured out on the people of Jerusalem, so they will be poured out on you when you enter
Egypt. You will become an object of damnation, horror, cursing, and mockery. And you
will never see your homeland again.'
[19]"Listen, you remnant of Judah. The LORD has told you: 'Do not go to Egypt!' Don't
forget this warning I have given you today. [20]For you were deceitful when you sent me
to pray to the LORD your God for you, saying, 'Just tell us what the LORD our God says,
and we will do it!' [21]And today I have told you exactly what he said, but you will not
obey the LORD your God any better now than you have in the past. [22]So you can be sure
that you will die from war, famine, and disease in Egypt, where you insist on going."

Jeremiah Taken to Egypt

43:2 2 Chr 36:13; Jer 5:12-13; 36:4, 10, 32; 38:4; 42:5
43:4 Jer 42:5-6, 10-12
43:5 Jer 40:11-12
43:6 Jer 40:7
43:8 Jer 44:1; 46:14; Ezek 30:18
43:10 Jer 25:8-9, 11; 27:6; 46:13
43:11 Isa 19:1-25; 44:13; Ezek 29:19-20
43:12 Jer 46:25; Ezek 30:13

43 When Jeremiah had finished giving this message from the LORD their God to all
the people, [2]Azariah son of Hoshaiah and Johanan son of Kareah and all the other
proud men said to Jeremiah, "You lie! The LORD our God hasn't forbidden us to go to
Egypt! [3]Baruch son of Neriah has convinced you to say this, so we will stay here and be
killed by the Babylonians* or be carried off into exile."
[4]So Johanan and all the army officers and all the people refused to obey the LORD's
command to stay in Judah. [5]Johanan and his officers took with them all the people who had
returned from the nearby countries to which they had fled. [6]In the crowd were men, women,
and children, the king's daughters, and all those whom Nebuzaradan, the captain of the
guard, had left with Gedaliah. Also included were the prophet Jeremiah and Baruch. [7]The
people refused to obey the LORD and went to Egypt, going as far as the city of Tahpanhes.
[8]Then at Tahpanhes, the LORD gave another message to Jeremiah. He said, [9]"While the
people of Judah are watching, bury large rocks between the pavement stones at the entrance
of Pharaoh's palace here in Tahpanhes. [10]Then say to the people of Judah, 'The LORD
Almighty, the God of Israel, says: I will surely bring my servant Nebuchadnezzar,* king of
Babylon, here to Egypt. I will set his throne on these stones that I have hidden. He will
spread his royal canopy over them. [11]And when he comes, he will destroy the land of Egypt.
He will bring death to those destined for death; he will bring captivity to those destined for
captivity; he will bring the sword against those destined for the sword. [12]He will set fire to

43:3 Or *Chaldeans.* **43:10** Hebrew *Nebuchadrezzar,* a variant name for Nebuchadnezzar.

43:1-3 Johanan and his tiny band had come to Jeremiah for God's approval of their plan, not for God's direction. This is a recurring problem for some of us—seeking God's approval of our desires rather than asking him for guidance. It is not good to make plans apart from God's guidance, and it is not good to pray unless we are willing to accept God's answer.

43:4-7 Afraid to obey the Lord, the people headed for Egypt, even forcing Jeremiah to go with them. (They thought that perhaps God would spare them if Jeremiah was with them.) Jeremiah had served as a prophet for 40 years. Many of his words had already come true, and he had turned down an offer to live comfortably in Babylon, returning instead to his beloved people. But the people still rejected Jeremiah's advice. The response of our audience is not necessarily a measure of our success. Jeremiah was doing all God asked, but he had been called to minister to a very stubborn group of people.

43:10-13 Nebuchadnezzar invaded Egypt in 568–567 B.C. Like Judah, Egypt rebelled against him and was quickly crushed. So much for the great empire on which Judah had constantly placed its hopes!

the temples of Egypt's gods, burning all their idols and carrying away the people as captives.
He will pick clean the land of Egypt as a shepherd picks fleas from his cloak. And he himself
will leave unharmed. 13He will break down the sacred pillars standing in the temple of the
sun* in Egypt, and he will burn down the temples of Egypt's gods.''

Judgment for Idolatry

44 This is the message Jeremiah received concerning the Judeans living in northern
Egypt in the cities of Migdol, Tahpanhes, and Memphis,* and throughout southern Egypt as well: 2"This is what the LORD Almighty, the God of Israel, says: You saw
what I did to Jerusalem and to all the towns of Judah. They now lie in ruins, and no one
lives in them. 3Because of all their wickedness, my anger rose high against them. They
burned incense and worshiped other gods—gods that neither they nor you nor any of
your ancestors have ever known.
4"Again and again I sent my servants, the prophets, to plead with them, 'Don't do
these horrible things that I hate so much.' 5But my people would not listen or turn back
from their wicked ways. They kept right on burning incense to these gods. 6And so my
fury boiled over and fell like fire on the towns of Judah and into the streets of Jerusalem,
and now they are a desolate ruin.
7"And now the LORD God Almighty, the God of Israel, asks you: Why are you
destroying yourselves? For not one of you will survive—not a man, woman, or child
among you who has come here from Judah, not even the babies in your arms. 8Why
arouse my anger by burning incense to the idols you have made here in Egypt? You will
only destroy yourselves and make yourselves an object of cursing and mockery for all
the nations of the earth. 9Have you forgotten the sins of your ancestors, the sins of the
kings and queens of Judah, and the sins you and your wives committed in Judah and
Jerusalem? 10To this very hour you have shown no remorse or reverence. No one has
chosen to follow my law and the decrees I gave to you and your ancestors before you.
11"Therefore, the LORD Almighty, the God of Israel, says: I have made up my mind
to destroy every one of you! 12I will take this remnant of Judah that insisted on coming
here to Egypt, and I will consume them. They will fall here in Egypt, killed by war and
famine. All will die, from the least to the greatest. They will be an object of damnation,
horror, cursing, and mockery. 13I will punish them in Egypt just as I punished them in
Jerusalem, by war, famine, and disease. 14Of those who fled to Egypt with dreams of
returning home to Judah, only a handful will escape."
15Then all the women present and all the men who knew that their wives had burned
incense to idols—a great crowd of all the Judeans living in Pathros, the southern region of

44:1 Isa 19:13; Jer 43:7; 46:14
44:2 Isa 6:11; Mic 3:12
44:3 Deut 13:6; 32:17; Jer 32:30-32
44:4 Jer 32:34-35; 35:15; Ezek 8:10; Zech 7:7
44:6 Isa 51:17-20; Jer 7:17, 34
44:7 Jer 9:21; Ezek 33:11
44:8 1 Kgs 9:7-8; 2 Kgs 17:15-17; 2 Chr 7:19-20; Jer 11:12, 17; 1 Cor 10:21-22
44:9 Jer 7:9-10, 17-18
44:10 Jer 6:15; 8:12
44:11 Lev 26:17; Amos 9:4
44:12 Isa 65:15; Jer 42:15-18, 22
44:13 Jer 24:10
44:14 Isa 10:20; Rom 9:27
44:15 Jer 5:1-5

43:13 Or *in Heliopolis*. **44:1** Hebrew *Noph*.

ESCAPE TO EGYPT
With Judah in turmoil after the murder of Gedaliah, the people turned to Jeremiah for guidance. Jeremiah had God's answer, "Stay in this land." But the leaders disobeyed and went to Egypt, taking Jeremiah with them. In Egypt, Jeremiah told them they were in grave danger.

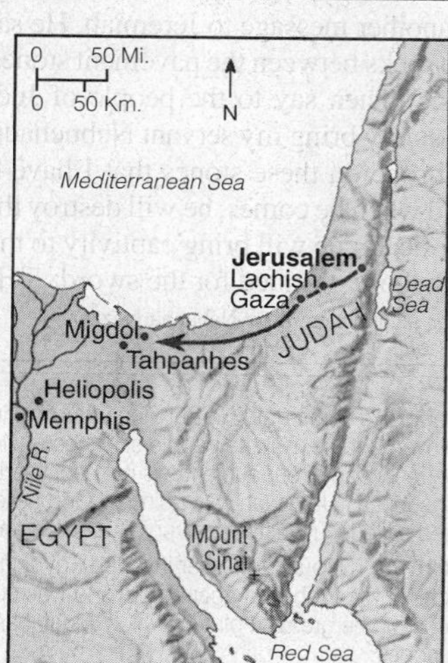

44:1ff This message, given in 580 B.C. while Jeremiah was in Egypt against his will, reminded the people that their idolatry had brought destruction on their land. Jeremiah told them that they would never return to Judah because the escape to Egypt had been against God's advice (42:9ff). But the people refused to learn any lessons from all the destruction their sins had caused.

44:9, 10 When we forget a lesson or refuse to learn it, we risk repeating our mistakes. The people of Judah struggled with this; to forget their former sins was to repeat them. To fail to learn from failure is to assure future failure. Your past is your school of experience. Let your past mistakes point you to God's way.

44:15-18 The farther we drift from God, the more confused our thinking becomes. Whatever spiritual life was left in the Israelites when they went to Egypt was lost as they sank into the depths of idolatry. (For more information on the "Queen of Heaven," see the note on 7:18.) The escape to Egypt had brought a change in their pagan worship habits, and they blamed their troubles on their neglect of their idols. But idol worship had started all their problems in the first place. The people refused to recognize the true source of their problems—departure from God's leading. When calamity forces you to examine your life, take a close look at God's instructions for you.

Egypt—answered Jeremiah, [16]"We will not listen to your messages from the LORD! [17]We
will do whatever we want. We will burn incense to the Queen of Heaven and sacrifice to
her just as much as we like—just as we and our ancestors did before us, and as our kings
and princes have always done in the towns of Judah and in the streets of Jerusalem. For in
those days we had plenty to eat, and we were well off and had no troubles! [18]But ever since
we quit burning incense to the Queen of Heaven and stopped worshiping her, we have been
in great trouble and have suffered the effects of war and famine."
[19]"And," the women added, "do you suppose that we were worshiping the Queen of
Heaven, pouring out drink offerings to her, and making cakes marked with her image,
without our husbands knowing it and helping us? Of course not!"
[20]Then Jeremiah said to all of them, men and women alike, who had given him that
answer, [21]"Do you think the LORD did not know that you and your ancestors, your kings
and officials, and all the people were burning incense to idols in the towns of Judah and
in the streets of Jerusalem? [22]It was because the LORD could no longer bear all the evil
things you were doing that he made your land an object of cursing—a desolate ruin
without a single inhabitant—as it is today. [23]The very reason all these terrible things have
happened to you is because you have burned incense to idols and sinned against the
LORD, refusing to obey him and follow his instructions, laws, and stipulations."
[24]Then Jeremiah said to them all, including the women, "Listen to this message from
the LORD, all you citizens of Judah who live in Egypt. [25]The LORD Almighty, the God
of Israel, says: You and your wives have said that you will never give up your devotion
and sacrifices to the Queen of Heaven, and you have proved it by your actions. Then go
ahead and carry out your promises and vows to her!
[26]"But listen to this message from the LORD, all you Judeans now living in Egypt: I
have sworn by my great name, says the LORD, that my name will no longer be spoken
by any of the Judeans in the land of Egypt. None of you may invoke my name or use this
oath: 'As surely as the Sovereign LORD lives!' [27]For I will watch over you to bring you
disaster and not good. You will suffer war and famine until all of you are dead.
[28]"Only a small number will escape death and return to Judah from Egypt. Then all
those who came to Egypt will find out whose words are true, mine or theirs! [29]And this
is the proof I give you, says the LORD, that all I have threatened will happen to you and
that I will punish you here: [30]I will turn Pharaoh Hophra, king of Egypt, over to his
enemies who want to kill him, just as I turned King Zedekiah of Judah over to King
Nebuchadnezzar* of Babylon. I, the LORD, have spoken!"

A Message for Baruch

45 The prophet Jeremiah gave a message to Baruch son of Neriah in the fourth year
of the reign of Jehoiakim son of Josiah,* after Baruch had written down everything Jeremiah had dictated to him. He said, [2]"This is what LORD, the God of Israel, says
to you, Baruch: [3]You have said, 'I am overwhelmed with trouble! Haven't I had enough
pain already? And now the LORD has added more! I am weary of my own sighing and
can find no rest.'
[4]"Baruch, this is what the LORD says: I will destroy this nation that I built. I will uproot
what I planted. [5]Are you seeking great things for yourself? Don't do it! But don't be
discouraged. I will bring great disaster upon all these people, but I will protect you
wherever you go. I, the LORD, have spoken!"

44:16 Jer 8:6; 13:10
44:17 Exod 16:3; 2 Kgs 17:16; Jer 7:18; Hos 2:5-9; Phil 3:19
44:18 Num 11:5-6; Mal 3:13-15
44:19 Num 30:6-7
44:21 Jer 11:13; 14:10; Ezek 8:10-11; 16:24; Hos 7:2
44:22 Isa 7:13; Jer 4:4; 25:11, 18, 38; 30:14
44:23 1 Kgs 9:9; Jer 7:13-15; 40:3; Dan 9:11-12
44:24 Jer 43:7
44:25 Ezek 20:39; Jas 1:13-15
44:26 Gen 22:16; Deut 32:40; Ps 50:16-17; Heb 6:13, 18
44:27 Jer 1:10
44:28 Isa 14:27; 46:9-10; Zech 1:5-6
44:29 Isa 40:8; Matt 24:15-16, 32
44:30 2 Kgs 25:4-7; Jer 46:25; Ezek 29:3
45:1 Jer 25:1; 36:4, 18, 32
45:3 Ps 6:6; 2 Cor 4:1, 16; Gal 6:9
45:4 Jer 18:7-10
45:5 Isa 66:16; Matt 6:25, 31-32; Rom 12:16

44:30 Hebrew *Nebuchadrezzar,* a variant name for Nebuchadnezzar. **45:1** The fourth year of Jehoiakim's reign was 605 B.C.

44:28 After Jeremiah's forced move to Egypt, there is no word in the Bible about the events in the rest of his life.

44:30 Pharaoh Hophra ruled Egypt from 588 to 569 B.C. and was killed by Ahmose, one of his generals, who was then crowned in his place.

45:1ff The event relating to this chapter is recorded in 36:1-8. The chapter was written in 605–604 B.C. Baruch was the scribe who recorded Jeremiah's words on a scroll.

45:5 Baruch had long been serving this unpopular prophet, writing his book of struggles and judgments, and now he was upset. God told Baruch to take his eyes off himself and whatever rewards he thought he deserved. If Baruch did this, God would protect him. It is easy to lose the joy of serving our God when we take our eyes off him. The more we look away from God's purposes toward our own sacrifices, the more frustrated we will become. As you serve God, beware of focusing on what you are giving up. When this happens, ask God's forgiveness; then look at him rather than at yourself.

B. GOD'S JUDGMENT ON THE NATIONS (46:1—52:34)

All of Jeremiah's prophecies against foreign nations have been grouped together. Many of the people in these nations assumed that they were free from judgment and punishment for their sin. Following these prophecies is a historical appendix recounting the fall of Jerusalem. Just as Jerusalem received its punishment, these nations were certain to receive theirs as well. Those today who think that judgment will never touch them are forewarned.

1. Prophecies about foreign nations

46 The following messages were given to Jeremiah the prophet from the LORD
concerning foreign nations.

Messages about Egypt

2 This message concerning Egypt was given in the fourth year of the reign of Jehoiakim
son of Josiah,* the king of Judah, on the occasion of the battle of Carchemish when
Pharaoh Neco, king of Egypt, and his army were defeated beside the Euphrates River by
King Nebuchadnezzar* of Babylon.
3 "Buckle on your armor and advance into battle! 4 Harness the horses, and prepare to
mount them. Put on your helmets, sharpen your spears, and prepare your armor. 5 But
look! The Egyptian army flees in terror. The bravest of its fighting men run without a
backward glance. They are terrorized at every turn, says the LORD. 6 The swiftest cannot
flee; the mightiest warriors cannot escape. By the Euphrates River to the north they
stumble and fall.
7 "Who is this, rising like the Nile River at floodtime, overflowing all the land? 8 It is
the Egyptian army, boasting that it will cover the earth like a flood, destroying every foe.
9 Then come, you horses and chariots and mighty warriors of Egypt! Come, all you allies
from Ethiopia, Libya, and Lydia* who are skilled with the shield and bow! 10 For this is
the day of the Lord, the LORD Almighty, a day of vengeance on his enemies. The sword
will devour until it is satisfied, yes, drunk with your blood! The Lord, the LORD
Almighty, will receive a sacrifice today in the north country beside the Euphrates River.
11 Go up to Gilead to get ointment, O virgin daughter of Egypt! But your many medicines
will bring you no healing. 12 The nations have heard of your shame. The earth is filled
with your cries of despair. Your mightiest warriors will stumble across each other and
fall together."
13 Then the LORD gave the prophet Jeremiah this message about King Nebuchadnezzar's plans to attack Egypt.
14 "Shout it out in Egypt! Publish it in the cities of Migdol, Memphis,* and Tahpanhes!
Mobilize for battle, for the sword of destruction will devour everyone around you.
15 Why have your warriors fled in terror? They cannot stand because the LORD has driven
them away. 16 They stumble and fall over each other and say among themselves, 'Come,
let's go back to our homeland where we were born. Let's get away from the sword of the
enemy!' 17 There they will say, 'Pharaoh, the king of Egypt, is a loudmouth who missed
his opportunity!'
18 "As surely as I live," says the King, whose name is the LORD Almighty, "one is
coming against Egypt who is as tall as Mount Tabor or Mount Carmel by the sea! 19 Pack
up! Get ready to leave for exile, you citizens of Egypt! The city of Memphis will be

46:1 Jer 1:10; Ezek 29-32
46:2 2 Kgs 23:29; 2 Chr 35:20
46:3 Joel 3:9
46:5 Isa 42:17; Jer 6:25; 49:29; Ezek 39:18
46:6 Isa 30:16; Dan 11:18
46:8 Isa 10:13; 37:24
46:9 Nah 2:4; 3:9
46:10 Isa 31:8; 34:6; Zeph 1:7
46:11 Jer 8:22; 30:13; Ezek 30:21-26; Nah 3:19
46:12 Jer 2:36; Nah 3:8-10
46:13 Isa 19:1; Jer 43:10-11
46:14 Jer 44:1; Nah 2:13
46:15 Pss 18:39; 68:1-2
46:16 Lev 26:36-37; Jer 51:9
46:17 Exod 15:9-10; 1 Kgs 20:10-11; Isa 19:11-16
46:18 1 Kgs 18:42; Ps 89:12; Jer 48:15
46:19 Isa 20:4; Ezek 30:13

46:2a The fourth year of Jehoiakim's reign was 605 B.C. **46:2b** Hebrew *Nebuchadrezzar,* a variant name for Nebuchadnezzar; also in 46:13, 26. **46:9** Hebrew *Cush, Put, and Lud.* **46:14** Hebrew *Noph;* also in 46:19.

46:1ff In this chapter, we gain several insights about God and his plan for this world. (1) Although God chose Israel for a special purpose, he loves all people and wants all to come to him. (2) God is holy and will not tolerate sin. (3) God's judgments are not based on prejudice and a desire for revenge but on fairness and justice. (4) God does not delight in judgment but in salvation. (5) God is impartial—he judges everyone by the same standard.

46:2 At the battle of Carchemish in 605 B.C., Babylon and Egypt, the two major world powers after Assyria's fall, clashed. The Babylonians entered Carchemish by surprise and defeated Egypt. This battle, which passed world leadership to Babylon, was Nebuchadnezzar's first victory, establishing him in his new position as king of the Babylonian Empire. With Egypt's power declining, it was both poor strategy and disobedience to God for Judah to form an alliance with Egypt.

46:9 The soldiers from Ethiopia and Libya were from eastern and northern Africa. The men of Lydia may have been from Greece.

46:17 In 589 B.C. when Nebuchadnezzar besieged Jerusalem, Pharaoh Hophra marched against him at Zedekiah's invitation. But when the Babylonians stood up to the Egyptians, Pharaoh Hophra and his troops retreated. Jeremiah had prophesied that Pharaoh Hophra would be killed by his enemies (44:30). This was fulfilled nearly 20 years later when his co-regent Ahmose led a revolt.

destroyed, without a single person living there. [20]Egypt is as sleek as a young cow, but
a gadfly from the north is on its way! [21]Egypt's famed mercenaries have become like
fattened calves. They turn and run, for it is a day of great disaster for Egypt, a time of
great punishment. [22]Silent as a serpent gliding away, Egypt flees. The invading army
marches in; they come against her with axes like woodsmen. [23]They will cut down her
people like trees," says the LORD, "for they are more numerous than grasshoppers.
[24]Egypt will be humiliated; she will be handed over to men from the north."

46:25 Isa 20:5-6; Jer 43:12-13; Ezek 30:13-16

[25]The LORD Almighty, the God of Israel, says: "I will punish Amon, the god of
Thebes,* and all the other gods of Egypt. I will punish its rulers and Pharaoh, too, and

46:26 Jer 44:30; Ezek 29:8-14; 32:11

all who trust in him. [26]I will hand them over to those who want them killed—to King
Nebuchadnezzar of Babylon and his army. But afterward the land will recover from the
ravages of war. I, the LORD, have spoken!

46:27 Isa 41:13-14; Jer 23:3-4; 30:10-11; 50:19

[27]"But do not be afraid, Jacob, my servant; do not be dismayed, Israel. For I will bring
you home again from distant lands, and your children will return from their exile. Israel*

46:28 Ps 46:7; Isa 43:2; Jer 10:24; Amos 9:8-9

will return and will have peace and quiet, and nothing will make them afraid. [28]Fear not,
Jacob, my servant," says the LORD, "for I am with you. I will destroy the nations to which
I have exiled you, but I will not destroy you. But I must discipline you; I cannot let you go
unpunished."

A Message about Philistia

47:1 Jer 25:17, 20; Amos 1:6; Zeph 2:4

47 This is the LORD's message to the prophet Jeremiah concerning the Philistines of
Gaza, before it was captured by the Egyptian army.

47:2 Isa 14:31

[2]This is what the LORD says: "A flood is coming from the north to overflow the land. It
will destroy the land and everything in it—cities and people alike. People will scream in
terror, and everyone in the land will weep. [3]Hear the clatter of hooves and the rumble of

47:4 Gen 10:13-14; Isa 14:31; 23:5; Amos 9:7

wheels as the chariots rush by. Terrified fathers run madly, without a backward glance at
their helpless children.

47:5 Jer 25:19-20; Amos 1:7-8; Zeph 2:4, 7; 9:5

[4]"The time has come for the Philistines to be destroyed, along with their allies from
Tyre and Sidon. Yes, the LORD is destroying the Philistines, those colonists from Crete.*
[5]The city of Gaza will be demolished; Ashkelon will lie in ruins. You remnant of the

47:6 Jer 12:12

Mediterranean plain,* how long will you lament and mourn?

47:7 Ezek 14:17; Mic 6:9

[6]"Now, O sword of the LORD, when will you be at rest again? Go back into your
sheath; rest and be still! [7]But how can it be still when the LORD has sent it on an errand?
For the city of Ashkelon and the people living along the sea must be destroyed."

A Message about Moab

48:1 Num 32:37-38; Jer 48:22-23; Ezek 25:9-10

48 This message was given concerning Moab.
This is what the LORD Almighty, the God of Israel, says: "Destruction is certain
for the city of Nebo; it will soon lie in ruins. The city of Kiriathaim will be humiliated and

48:2 Isa 15:4-5; 16:13-14

captured; the fortress will be humiliated and broken down. [2]No one will ever brag about
Moab again, for there is a plot against her life. In Heshbon plans have been completed to
destroy her. 'Come,' they say, 'we will cut her off from being a nation.' The city of
Madmen,* too, will be silenced; the sword will follow you there. [3]And then the roar of battle

48:5 Isa 15:5

will surge against Horonaim, [4]for all Moab is being destroyed. Her little ones will cry out.*
[5]Her refugees will climb the hills of Luhith, weeping bitterly, while cries of terror rise from

48:7 Num 21:29; Jer 9:23

Horonaim below. [6]Flee for your lives! Hide in the wilderness!* [7]Because you have trusted

46:25 Hebrew *No.* **46:27** Hebrew *Jacob.* **47:4** Hebrew *from Caphtor.* **47:5** Hebrew *the plain.* **48:2** *Madmen* sounds like the Hebrew word for "silence"; it should not be confused with the English word *madmen.* **48:4** Greek version reads *Her cries are heard as far away as Zoar.* **48:6** Or *Be like* [the town of] *Aroer in the wilderness.*

46:28 God punished his people in order to bring them back to himself, and he punishes us to correct and purify us. No one welcomes punishment, but we should all welcome its results: correction and purity.

47:1 Located on the coastal plain next to Judah, Philistia had always been a thorn in Israel's side. The two nations battled constantly. Other prophets who spoke against Philistia include Isaiah (14:28-32), Ezekiel (25:15-17), Amos (1:6-8), and Zephaniah (2:4-7).

48:1 The Moabites were descendants of Lot through an incestuous relationship with one of his daughters (Genesis 19:30-37). They led the Israelites into idolatry (Numbers 25:1-3) and joined the bands of raiders Nebuchadnezzar sent into Judah in 602 B.C. They were later conquered by Babylon and disappeared as a nation.

48:7 Chemosh was the main god of the nation of Moab (Numbers 21:29), and child sacrifice was an important part of his worship (2 Kings 3:26, 27).

in your wealth and skill, you will be taken captive. Your god Chemosh, with his priests and princes, will be exiled to distant lands!

8“All the towns will be destroyed, both on the plateaus and in the valleys, for the LORD has spoken. 9Oh, that Moab had wings so she could fly away, for her cities will be left empty, with no one living in them. 10Cursed be those who refuse to do the work the LORD has given them, who hold back their swords from shedding blood!

11“From her earliest history, Moab has lived in peace. She is like wine that has been allowed to settle. She has not been poured from flask to flask, and she is now fragrant and smooth. 12But the time is coming soon,” says the LORD, “when I will send troublemakers to pour her from her jar. They will pour her out, then shatter the jar! 13At last Moab will be ashamed of her idol Chemosh, as Israel was ashamed of her gold calf at Bethel.*

14“You used to boast, ‘We are heroes, mighty men of war.’ 15But now Moab and her towns will be destroyed. Her most promising youth are doomed to slaughter,” says the King, whose name is the LORD Almighty. 16“Calamity is coming fast to Moab; it threatens ominously.

17“You friends of Moab, weep for her and cry! See how the strong scepter is broken, how the beautiful staff is shattered! 18Come down from your glory and sit in the dust, you people of Dibon, for those who destroy Moab will shatter Dibon, too. They will tear down all your towers. 19The people of Aroer stand anxiously beside the road to watch. They shout to those who flee from Moab, ‘What has happened there?’

20“And the reply comes back, ‘Moab lies in ruins; weep and wail! Tell it by the banks of the Arnon River: Moab has been destroyed!’ 21All the cities of the plateau lie in ruins, too. Judgment has been poured out on them all—on Holon and Jahaz* and Mephaath, 22and on Dibon and Nebo and Beth-diblathaim, 23and on Kiriathaim and Beth-gamul and Beth-meon, 24and on Kerioth and Bozrah—all the cities of Moab, far and near.

25“The strength of Moab has ended. Her horns have been cut off, and her arms have been broken,” says the LORD. 26“Let her stagger and fall like a drunkard, for she has rebelled against the LORD. Moab will wallow in her own vomit, ridiculed by all. 27Did you not make Israel the object of your ridicule? Was she caught in the company of thieves that you should despise her as you do?

28“You people of Moab, flee from your cities and towns! Live in the caves like doves that nest in the clefts of the rocks. 29We have heard of the pride of Moab, for it is very great. We know of her loftiness, her arrogance, and her haughty heart. 30I know about her insolence,” says the LORD, “but her boasts are false; they accomplish nothing. 31Yes, I wail for Moab; my heart is broken for the men of Kir-hareseth.*

32“You people of Sibmah, rich in vineyards, I will weep for you even more than I did for Jazer. Your spreading vines once reached as far as the Dead Sea,* but the destroyer has stripped you bare! He has harvested your grapes and summer fruits. 33Joy and gladness are gone from fruitful Moab. The presses yield no wine. No one treads the grapes with shouts of joy. There is shouting, yes, but not of joy. 34Instead, their awful cries of terror can be heard from Heshbon clear across to Elealeh and Jahaz; from Zoar all the way to Horonaim and Eglath-shelishiyah. Even the waters of Nimrim are dried up now.

35“I will put an end to Moab,” says the LORD, “for they offer sacrifices at the pagan shrines and burn incense to their false gods. 36My heart moans like a flute for Moab and Kir-hareseth, for all their wealth has disappeared. 37They shave their heads and beards in mourning. They slash their hands and put on clothes made of sackcloth. 38Crying and sorrow will be in every Moabite home and on every street. For I have smashed Moab

48:8 Josh 13:10, 17, 21
48:9 Isa 16:2
48:10 1 Kgs 20:42
48:11 Zeph 1:12; Zech 1:15
48:13 1 Kgs 12:29; Isa 45:16; Hos 10:6
48:14 Ps 33:16-17; Isa 10:13-16
48:15 Jer 46:18; 50:27
48:16 Isa 13:22
48:17 Isa 14:5
48:18 Josh 13:9, 17; Isa 47:1
48:19 Josh 12:2
48:20 Num 21:13; Isa 16:7
48:21 Josh 13:18; Isa 15:4
48:23 Josh 13:19
48:24 Amos 2:2
48:25 Pss 10:15; 75:10; Zech 1:19-21
48:27 Lam 2:15-17; Zeph 2:8
48:28 Ps 55:6; Song 2:14; Isa 2:19
48:29 Ps 138:6; Isa 16:6; Zeph 2:8
48:31 Isa 15:5; 16:7, 11
48:32 Isa 16:8-9
48:33 Isa 16:10
48:34 Gen 13:10; Isa 15:4-6
48:36 Isa 16:11
48:37 Isa 15:2-3

48:13 Hebrew *ashamed when they trusted in Bethel.* **48:21** Hebrew *Jahzah,* a variant name for Jahaz. **48:31** Hebrew *Kir-heres,* a variant name for Kir-hareseth; also in 48:36. **48:32** Hebrew *the sea of Jazer.*

48:11, 12 When making wine, the grapes were crushed. After 40 days, the wine was poured off from the dregs in the bottom of the jar. If this was not done, the wine would be inferior. The prophet was saying that because of Moab's complacency and refusal to do God's work, Moab would be totally destroyed.

48:13 After Israel divided into northern and southern kingdoms, the northern kingdom set up gold calf idols in Bethel and Dan to keep people from going to worship in Jerusalem, capital of the southern kingdom (1 Kings 12:25-29).

48:29 Moab was condemned for its pride. God cannot tolerate pride because pride is taking personal credit for what God has done or looking down on others. God does not condemn our taking satisfaction in what we do (Ecclesiastes 3:22), but he stands against overestimates of our own importance. Romans 12:3 teaches us to have an honest estimate of ourselves.

48:31 Kir-hareseth was a stronghold city in Moab. God's compassion reaches to all creation, even to his enemies.

like an old, unwanted bottle. 39 How it is broken! Hear the wailing! See the shame of
48:40 Jer 49:22 Moab! She has become an object of ridicule, an example of ruin to all her neighbors.
40 "An eagle swoops down on the land of Moab," says the LORD. 41 "Her cities will
48:41 Jer 30:6; 49:22 fall; her strongholds will be seized. Even the mightiest warriors will be as frightened as
48:42 Ps 83:4 Jer 48:26 a woman about to give birth. 42 Moab will no longer be a nation, for she has boasted
against the LORD.
48:43 Isa 24:17 Lam 3:47 43 "Terror and traps and snares will be your lot, O Moab," says the LORD. 44 "Those
who flee in terror will fall into a trap, and those who escape the trap will step into a snare.
48:44 1 Kgs 19:17 Amos 5:19 I will see to it that you do not get away, for the time of your judgment has come," says
the LORD. 45 "The people flee as far as Heshbon but are unable to go on. For a fire comes
48:45 Num 21:28-29 Ps 135:10-11 from Heshbon, King Sihon's ancestral home, to devour the entire land with all its
rebellious people.
48:46 Num 21:29 46 "O Moab, your destruction is sure! The people of the god Chemosh are destroyed!
Your sons and daughters have been taken away as captives. 47 But in the latter days I will
48:47 Jer 12:17; 49:39 restore the fortunes of Moab," says the LORD.
This is the end of Jeremiah's prophecy concerning Moab.

A Message about Ammon

49:1 Ezek 25:2 Amos 1:13 **49** This message was given concerning the Ammonites.
This is what the LORD says: "What are you doing? Are there no descendants of
49:2 2 Sam 11:1 Isa 14:2 Ezek 21:28 Israel to inherit the land of Gad? Why are you, who worship Molech,* living in its towns?
2 I will punish you for this," says the LORD, "by destroying your city of Rabbah. It will
become a desolate heap, and the neighboring towns will be burned. Then Israel will come
49:3 Josh 7:2-5; 8:1-29 Jer 48:2, 7 and take back the land you took from her," says the LORD.
3 "Cry out, O Heshbon, for the town of Ai is destroyed. Weep, O people of Rabbah!
49:4 Ps 62:10-11 Ezek 28:4-5 1 Tim 6:17 Put on your clothes of mourning. Weep and wail, hiding in the hedges, for your god
Molech will be exiled along with his princes and priests. 4 You are proud of your fertile
valleys, but they will soon be ruined. You rebellious daughter, you trusted in your wealth
49:5 Jer 16:16 Lam 4:15 and thought no one could ever harm you. 5 But look! I will bring terror upon you," says
the Lord, the LORD Almighty. "Your neighbors will chase you from your land, and no
49:6 Jer 48:47; 49:39 one will help your exiles as they flee. 6 But afterward I will restore the fortunes of the
Ammonites," says the LORD.

Messages about Edom

49:7 Gen 36:11, 15 Isa 34:5-6 Amos 1:12 7 This message was given concerning Edom.
This is what the LORD Almighty says: "Where are all the wise men of Teman? Is there
49:8 Isa 21:13 Jer 25:23 no one left to give wise counsel? 8 Turn and flee! Hide in deep caves, you people of
Dedan! For when I bring disaster on Edom,* I will punish you, too! 9 Those who harvest
grapes always leave a few for the poor. If thieves came at night, even they would not take
49:9 Obad 1:5 everything. 10 But I will strip bare the land of Edom, and there will be no place left to
hide. Its children, its brothers, and its neighbors—all will be destroyed—and Edom itself
49:11 Ps 68:5 Zech 7:10 will be no more. 11 But I will preserve the orphans who remain among you. Your widows,
too, will be able to depend on me for help."
49:12 Jer 25:15, 28-29 1 Pet 4:17 12 And this is what the LORD says: "If the innocent must suffer, how much more must
49:13 Isa 34:6, 9-15 you! You will not go unpunished! You must drink this cup of judgment! 13 For I have sworn
by my own name," says the LORD, "that Bozrah will become an object of horror and a heap
of rubble; it will be mocked and cursed. All its towns and villages will be desolate forever."

49:1 Hebrew *Milcom,* a variant name for Molech; also in 49:3. **49:8** Hebrew *Esau;* also in 49:10.

49:1 The Ammonites were descendants of Lot through an incestuous relationship with one of his daughters (as were the Moabites; see Genesis 19:30-38). They were condemned for stealing land from God's people and for worshiping the idol Molech, to whom they made child sacrifices.

49:7 The Israelites descended from Jacob, and the Edomites descended from his twin brother, Esau; thus, both nations descended from their father, Isaac. There was constant conflict between these nations, and Edom rejoiced at the fall of Jerusalem (see the book of Obadiah). Teman, a town in the northern part of Edom, was known for its wisdom and was the hometown of Eliphaz, one of Job's friends (Job 2:11). But even the wisdom of Teman could not save Edom from God's wrath.

49:8 Dedan was a flourishing city that supported caravan travel. God told its inhabitants to flee to the caves or they would also be destroyed. Teman and Dedan were at opposite ends of the country, so this shows the completeness of God's destruction of Edom. Bozrah (49:13) is a town in northern Edom.

[14]I have heard a message from the LORD that an ambassador was sent to the nations
to say, "Form a coalition against Edom, and prepare for battle!"
[15]This is what the LORD says: "I will cut you down to size among the nations, Edom.
You will be despised by all. [16]You are proud that you inspire fear in others. And you are
proud because you live in a rock fortress and hide high in the mountains. But don't fool
yourselves! Though you live among the peaks with the eagles, I will bring you crashing
down," says the LORD.
[17]"Edom will be an object of horror. All who pass by will be appalled and will gasp
at the destruction they see there. [18]It will be like the destruction of Sodom and Gomorrah
and their neighboring towns," says the LORD. "No one will live there anymore. [19]I will
come like a lion from the thickets of the Jordan, leaping on the sheep in the pasture. I
will chase Edom from its land, and I will appoint the leader of my choice. For who is
like me, and who can challenge me? What ruler can oppose my will?"
[20]Listen to the LORD's plans for Edom and the people of Teman. Even the little
children will be dragged off, and their homes will be empty. [21]The earth will shake with
the noise of Edom's fall, and its cry of despair will be heard all the way to the Red Sea.*
[22]The enemy will come as swiftly as an eagle, and he will spread his wings against
Bozrah. Even the mightiest warriors will be as frightened as a woman about to give birth.

A Message about Damascus

[23]This message was given concerning Damascus.
This is what the LORD says: "The towns of Hamath and Arpad are struck with fear,
for they have heard the news of their destruction. Their hearts are troubled like a wild
sea in a raging storm. [24]Damascus has become feeble, and all her people turn to flee.
Fear, anguish, and pain have gripped her as they do a woman giving birth. [25]That famous
city, a city of joy, will be forsaken! [26]Her young men will fall in the streets and die. Her
warriors will all be killed," says the LORD Almighty. [27]"And I will start a fire at the edge
of Damascus that will burn up the palaces of Ben-hadad."

A Message about Kedar and Hazor

[28]This message was given concerning Kedar and the kingdoms of Hazor, which were
attacked by King Nebuchadnezzar* of Babylon.
This is what the LORD says: "Advance against Kedar! Blot out the warriors from the
East! [29]Their flocks and tents will be captured, and their household goods and camels
will be taken away. Everywhere shouts of panic will be heard: 'We are terrorized at every
turn!' [30]Flee for your lives," says the LORD. "Hide yourselves in deep caves, you people
of Hazor, for King Nebuchadnezzar of Babylon has plotted against you and is preparing
to destroy you.
[31]"Go up and attack those self-sufficient nomadic tribes," says the LORD. "They live
alone in the desert without walls or gates. [32]Their camels and cattle will all be yours. I
will scatter to the winds these people who live in distant places.* I will bring calamity
upon them from every direction," says the LORD. [33]"Hazor will be inhabited by jackals,
and it will be desolate forever. No one will live there anymore."

A Message about Elam

[34]This message concerning Elam came to the prophet Jeremiah from the LORD at the
beginning of the reign of King Zedekiah of Judah.

49:21 Hebrew *sea of reeds.* **49:28** Hebrew *Nebuchadrezzar,* a variant name for Nebuchadnezzar; also in 49:30.
49:32 Or *who clip the corners of their hair.*

49:14 Jer 50:14
49:15 Luke 1:51
49:16 Isa 14:13-15; Amos 9:2
49:17 Jer 51:37; Ezek 35:7
49:18 Gen 19:24-25; Deut 29:23; Amos 4:11
49:19 Isa 46:9; Jer 50:44
49:20 Isa 14:24, 27; Mal 1:4-5
49:21 Ezek 26:15, 18
49:22 Isa 13:8; Jer 48:40-41
49:23 Exod 15:15; Isa 10:9; 57:20; Jer 39:5; Amos 6:2; Nah 2:10
49:26 Jer 50:30
49:27 1 Kgs 15:18-20; Amos 1:3-5
49:28 Isa 21:16-17
49:29 Jer 46:5
49:30 Jer 25:8-9, 24; 27:6
49:31 Judg 18:7; Isa 47:8
49:32 Jer 9:25-26; 25:23; Ezek 12:14-15
49:33 Isa 13:20-22; Zeph 2:9, 13-15
49:34 Gen 10:22; 2 Kgs 24:17-18; Isa 11:11; Dan 8:2

49:16 Edom was located in a rock fortress that today is known as Petra, in southern Jordan. Edom thought it was invincible because of its location. Edom was destroyed because of its pride. Pride destroys nations as well as individuals. It deludes us into thinking that we can take care of ourselves without God's help. Even serving God and others can lead us into pride. Take inventory of your life and service for God; ask God to point out and remove any pride you may be harboring.

49:23-26 Damascus was the capital of Aram, north of Israel. This city was defeated by both Assyria and Babylon. Nebuchadnezzar attacked and defeated Damascus in 605 B.C. (Amos 1:4, 5). It is difficult to attribute the defeat of the army to a particular event, but God utterly destroyed Aram.

49:28 Kedar and Hazor were nomadic tribes east of Israel and south of Aram, in the desert. In 599 B.C. Nebuchadnezzar destroyed them.

49:34 Elam lay east of Babylon and was attacked by Nebuchadnezzar in 597 B.C. Later Elam became the nucleus of the Persian Empire (Daniel 8:2) and the residence of Darius.

49:35 Isa 22:6; Jer 51:56
49:36 Ezek 5:10; Rev 7:1
49:37 Jer 6:19; 30:24
49:39 Jer 48:47

35 This is what the LORD Almighty says: "I will destroy the archers of Elam—the best
of their marksmen. 36 I will bring enemies from all directions, and I will scatter the people
of Elam to the four winds. They will be exiled to countries around the world. 37 I myself
will go with Elam's enemies to shatter it. My fierce anger will bring great disaster upon
the people of Elam," says the LORD. "Their enemies will chase them with the sword until
I have destroyed them completely. 38 I will set my throne in Elam," says the LORD, "and
I will destroy its king and princes. 39 But in the latter days I will restore the fortunes of
Elam," says the LORD.

A Message about Babylon

50:1 Isa 13:1; Rev 14:8
50:2 Isa 46:1; Jer 51:31
50:3 Zeph 1:3

50 The LORD gave Jeremiah the prophet this message concerning Babylon and the
land of the Babylonians.*
2 This is what the LORD says: "Tell the whole world, and keep nothing back! Raise a
signal flag so everyone will know that Babylon will fall! Her images and idols will be
shattered. Her gods Bel and Marduk will be utterly disgraced. 3 For a nation will attack
her from the north and bring such destruction that no one will live in her again.
Everything will be gone; both people and animals will flee.

Hope for Israel and Judah

50:4 Ezra 3:12-13; Isa 11:12-13; Jer 31:9; Hos 1:11
50:5 Isa 55:3; Jer 6:16; 32:40
50:6 Isa 53:6; Jer 13:16; Ezek 34:15-16; Matt 9:36
50:7 Jer 17:13
50:8 Jer 51:6; Rev 18:4
50:10 Jer 51:24, 35

4 "Then the people of Israel and Judah will join together," says the LORD, "weeping and
seeking the LORD their God. 5 They will ask the way to Jerusalem* and will start back
home again. They will bind themselves to the LORD with an eternal covenant that will
never again be broken.
6 "My people have been lost sheep. Their shepherds have led them astray and turned
them loose in the mountains. They have lost their way and cannot remember how to get
back to the fold. 7 All who found them devoured them. Their enemies said, 'We are
allowed to attack them freely, for they have sinned against the LORD, their place of rest,
the hope of their ancestors.'
8 "But now, flee from Babylon! Leave the land of the Babylonians. Lead my people
home again. 9 For look, I am raising up an army of great nations from the north. I will
bring them against Babylon to attack her, and she will be captured. The enemies' arrows
will go straight to the mark; they will not miss! 10 Babylonia* will be plundered until the
attackers are glutted with plunder," says the LORD.

Babylon's Sure Fall

50:11 Jer 12:14; 46:20
50:12 Jer 22:6
50:13 Jer 18:16
50:14 Hab 2:8, 17
50:15 Ps 137:8
50:16 Jer 46:16

11 "You rejoice and are glad, you plunderers of my chosen people. You frisk about like
a calf in a meadow and neigh like a stallion. 12 But your homeland* will be overwhelmed with shame and disgrace. You will become the least of nations—a wilderness, a dry and desolate land. 13 Because of the LORD's anger, Babylon will become a
deserted wasteland. All who pass by will be horrified and will gasp at the destruction
they see there.
14 "Yes, prepare to attack Babylon, all you nations round about. Let your archers shoot
at her. Spare no arrows, for she has sinned against the LORD. 15 Shout against her from
every side. Look! She surrenders! Her walls have fallen. The LORD has taken vengeance,
so do not spare her. Do to her as she has done to others! 16 Lead from Babylon all those
who plant crops; send all the harvesters away. Let the captives escape the sword of the
enemy and rush back to their own lands.

50:1 Or *Chaldeans;* also in 50:8, 25, 35, 45. **50:5** Hebrew *Zion;* also in 50:28. **50:10** Or *Chaldea.* **50:12** Hebrew *your mother.*

49:38 The throne represents God's judgment and sovereignty. God would preside over Elam's destruction. He is the King over all kings, including Elam's.

50:1ff At the height of its power, the Babylonian Empire seemed immovable. But when Babylon had finished serving God's purpose of punishing Judah for her sins, it would be punished and crushed for its own. Babylon was destroyed in 539 B.C. by the Medo-Persians (Daniel 5:30, 31). Babylon is also used in Scripture as a symbol of all evil. This message can thus apply to the end times when God will wipe out all evil once and for all.

50:3 The nation from the north was Medo-Persia, an alliance of Media and Persia that would become the next world power. Cyrus took the city of Babylon by surprise and brought the nation to its knees in 539 B.C. (Daniel 5:30, 31). The complete destruction of the city was accomplished by later Persian kings.

Hope for God's People

17“The Israelites are like sheep that have been scattered by lions. First the king of Assyria
ate them up. Then King Nebuchadnezzar* of Babylon cracked their bones.” 18Therefore,
the LORD Almighty, the God of Israel, says: “Now I will punish the king of Babylon and
his land, just as I punished the king of Assyria. 19And I will bring Israel home again to
her own land, to feed in the fields of Carmel and Bashan, and to be satisfied once more
on the hill country of Ephraim and Gilead. 20In those days,” says the LORD, “no sin will
be found in Israel or in Judah, for I will forgive the remnant I preserve.

The LORD's Judgment on Babylon

21“Go up, my warriors, against the land of Merathaim and against the people of Pekod.
Yes, march against Babylon, the land of rebels, a land that I will judge! Pursue, kill, and
completely destroy* them, as I have commanded you,” says the LORD. 22“Let the battle
cry be heard in the land, a shout of great destruction. 23Babylon, the mightiest hammer
in all the earth, lies broken and shattered. Babylon is desolate among the nations!
24Listen, Babylon, for I have set a trap for you. You are caught, for you have fought
against the LORD.

25“The LORD has opened his armory and brought out weapons to vent his fury against
his enemies. The terror that falls upon the Babylonians will be the work of the Sovereign
LORD Almighty. 26Yes, come against her from distant lands. Break open her granaries.
Crush her walls and houses into heaps of rubble. Destroy her completely, and leave
nothing! 27Even destroy her cattle—it will be terrible for them, too! Slaughter them all!
For the time has come for Babylon to be devastated. 28Listen to the people who have
escaped from Babylon, as they declare in Jerusalem how the LORD our God has taken
vengeance against those who destroyed his Temple.

29“Send out a call for archers to come to Babylon. Surround the city so none can escape.
Do to her as she has done to others, for she has defied the LORD, the Holy One of Israel.
30Her young men will fall in the streets and die. Her warriors will all be killed,” says the
LORD.

31“See, I am your enemy, O proud people,” says the Lord, the LORD Almighty. “Your day
of reckoning has arrived. 32O land of pride, you will stumble and fall, and no one will raise
you up. For I will light a fire in the cities of Babylon that will burn everything around them.”

33And now the LORD Almighty says this: “The people of Israel and Judah have been
wronged. Their captors hold them and refuse to let them go. 34But the one who redeems
them is strong. His name is the LORD Almighty. He will defend them and give them rest
again in Israel. But the people of Babylon—there will be no rest for them!

35“The sword of destruction will strike the Babylonians,” says the LORD. “It will
strike the people of Babylon—her princes and wise men, too. 36And when it strikes her
wise counselors, they will become fools! When it strikes her mightiest warriors, panic
will seize them! 37When it strikes her horses and chariots, her allies from other lands will
become as weak as women. When it strikes her treasures, they all will be plundered. 38It
will even strike her water supply, causing it to dry up. And why? Because the whole land
is filled with idols, and the people are madly in love with them.

39“Soon this city of Babylon will be inhabited by ostriches and jackals. It will be a
home for the wild animals of the desert. Never again will people live there; it will lie
desolate forever. 40I will destroy it just as I* destroyed Sodom and Gomorrah and their
neighboring towns,” says the LORD. “No one will live there anymore.

50:17 2 Kgs 18:9-13; 24:1, 10-12
50:18 Isa 10:12; Nah 1:1; 3:7, 18-19
50:20 Jer 31:34; Mic 7:19
50:21 Ezek 23:23
50:22 Jer 4:19-21
50:23 Jer 51:20-24
50:24 Job 9:4; 40:2, 9; Jer 48:43
50:25 Isa 13:4-5
50:26 Isa 14:23
50:27 Ps 37:13; Ezek 7:7
50:28 Ps 149:6-9; Isa 48:20; Lam 1:10
50:29 Exod 10:3; Ps 137:8
50:30 Jer 18:21
50:31 Nah 2:13
50:32 Isa 10:12-15; Jer 21:14
50:33 Isa 14:17; 58:6
50:34 Isa 14:3-7; 43:14; Mic 7:9
50:35 Jer 47:6; Dan 5:1-2, 7-8
50:36 Isa 44:25
50:37 Ps 20:7-8; Jer 25:19-20; 48:41
50:39 Isa 13:20
50:40 Gen 19:24-25; Luke 17:28-30; 2 Pet 2:6; Jude 1:7

50:17 Hebrew *Nebuchadrezzar,* a variant name for Nebuchadnezzar. **50:21** The Hebrew term used here refers to the complete consecration of things or people to the LORD, either by destroying them or by giving them as an offering. **50:40** Hebrew *just as God.*

50:17-20 God would punish wicked Babylon as he punished Assyria for what it had done to Israel. Assyria was crushed by Babylon, which Assyria had once ruled. Babylon in turn would be crushed by Medo-Persia, formerly under its authority. These verses also look to the time when the Messiah will rule and Israel will be fully restored. No sin will then be found in Israel because God's people will seek him and be forgiven.

50:21 Merathaim was located in southern Babylonia; Pekod was in eastern Babylonia.

50:32 Pride was Babylon's characteristic sin. Pride comes from feeling self-sufficient or believing that we don't need God. Proud nations or persons, however, will eventually fail because they refuse to recognize God as the ultimate power. Getting rid of pride is not easy, but if we can admit that it often rules us and ask God to forgive us, he will help us overcome it. The best antidote to pride is to focus our attention on the greatness and goodness of God.

50:39 Babylon remains a wasteland to this day. See also Isaiah 13:19-22.

50:41 Isa 13:2-5 41 "Look! A great army is marching from the north! A great nation and many kings are
50:42 Isa 13:17-18 Hab 1:8 rising against you from far-off lands. 42 They are fully armed for slaughter. They are cruel
and show no mercy. As they ride forward, the noise of their army is like a roaring sea.
50:43 Jer 30:6 They are marching in battle formation to destroy you, Babylon. 43 The king of Babylon
has received reports about the enemy, and he is weak with fright. Fear and pain have
gripped him, like that of a woman about to give birth.
50:44 Num 16:5 Job 41:10 Isa 46:9 44 "I will come like a lion from the thickets of the Jordan, leaping on the sheep in the
pasture. I will chase Babylon from its land, and I will appoint the leader of my choice.
For who is like me, and who can challenge me? What ruler can oppose my will?"
45 Listen to the LORD's plans against Babylon and the land of the Babylonians. Even
50:46 Jer 10:10 Ezek 26:18 little children will be dragged off, and their homes will be empty. 46 The earth will shake
with the noise of Babylon's fall, and her cry of despair will be heard around the world.

51:1 Jer 4:11-12 **51** This is what the LORD says: "I will stir up a destroyer against Babylon and the
people of Babylonia.* 2 Foreigners will come and winnow her, blowing her away
51:2 Jer 15:7 Matt 3:12 as chaff. They will come from every side to rise against her in her day of trouble. 3 Don't
let the archers put on their armor or draw their bows. No one will be spared! Young and
51:3 Jer 46:4 old alike will be completely destroyed.* 4 They will fall dead in the land of the
Babylonians,* slashed to death in her streets. 5 For the LORD Almighty has not forsaken
51:5 Isa 54:7-8 Jer 33:24-26 Israel and Judah. He is still their God, even though their land was filled with sin against
the Holy One of Israel."
51:6 Num 16:26 Rev 18:4 6 Flee from Babylon! Save yourselves! Don't get trapped in her punishment! It is the
LORD's time for vengeance; he will fully repay her. 7 Babylon has been like a golden cup
51:7 Jer 25:15 Rev 14:8-10; 18:3 in the LORD's hands, a cup from which he made the whole earth drink and go mad. 8 But
now suddenly, Babylon, too, has fallen. Weep for her, and give her medicine. Perhaps
51:9 Jer 46:16 she can yet be healed. 9 We would have helped her if we could, but nothing can save her
now. Let her go; abandon her. Return now to your own land, for her judgment will be so
51:10 Isa 40:2 Mic 7:9 great it cannot be measured. 10 The LORD has vindicated us. Come, let us announce in
Jerusalem* everything the LORD our God has done.
51:11 Joel 3:9-10 11 Sharpen the arrows! Lift up the shields! For the LORD has stirred up the spirit of the
51:12 Jer 4:28 kings of the Medes to march against Babylon and destroy her. This is his vengeance
against those who desecrated his Temple. 12 Raise the battle flag against Babylon!
Reinforce the guard and station the watchmen. Prepare an ambush, for the LORD will
fulfill all his plans against Babylon.
51:13 Hab 2:9-11 13 You are a city rich with water, a great center of commerce, but your end has come.
51:14 Nah 3:15 The thread of your life is cut. 14 The LORD Almighty has taken this vow and has sworn
to it by his own name: "Your cities will be filled with enemies, like fields filled with
locusts, and they will lift their shouts of triumph over you."

A Hymn of Praise to the LORD

51:15 Ps 146:5-6 Jer 10:12-16 Rom 1:20 15 He made the earth by his power,
and he preserves it by his wisdom.
He has stretched out the heavens
by his understanding.
51:16 Job 37:2-5 Pss 18:13; 135:7 Jon 1:4 16 When he speaks, there is thunder in the heavens.
He causes the clouds to rise over the earth.
He sends the lightning with the rain
and releases the wind from his storehouses.

51:1 Hebrew *of Leb-kamai,* a code name for Babylonia. **51:3** The Hebrew term used here refers to the complete consecration of things or people to the LORD, either by destroying them or by giving them as an offering. **51:4** Or *Chaldeans;* also in 51:54. **51:10** Hebrew *Zion;* also in 51:24, 35a.

50:44-46 This invader was Cyrus, who attacked Babylon by surprise and overthrew it. The world was shocked that its greatest empire was overthrown so quickly. No earthly power, no matter how great, can last forever.

51:2 Winnowers worked to separate the wheat from the chaff. When they threw the mixture into the air, the wind blew away the worthless chaff while the wheat settled to the floor. Babylon would be blown away like chaff in the wind. (See also Matthew 3:12 where John the Baptist says Jesus will separate the wheat from the chaff.)

51:11 Cyrus, king of Persia, had allied himself with Babylon to defeat Nineveh (capital of the Assyrian Empire) in 612 B.C. Then the Medes joined Persia to defeat Babylon (539 B.C.).

17 Compared to him, all people are foolish
and have no knowledge at all!
They make idols, but the idols will disgrace their makers,
for they are frauds.
They have no life or power in them.
18 Idols are worthless; they are lies!
The time is coming when they will all be destroyed.
19 But the God of Israel* is no idol!
He is the Creator of everything that exists,
including his people, his own special possession.
The LORD Almighty is his name!

51:17 Isa 44:18-20 Hab 2:18-19
51:19 Jer 10:16

Babylon's Great Punishment

20"You* are my battle-ax and sword," says the LORD. "With you I will shatter nations
and destroy many kingdoms. 21 With you I will shatter armies, destroying the horse and
rider, the chariot and charioteer. 22 With you I will shatter men and women, old people
and children, young men and maidens. 23 With you I will shatter shepherds and flocks,
farmers and oxen, captains and rulers.
24"As you watch, I will repay Babylon and the people of Babylonia* for all the wrong
they have done to my people in Jerusalem," says the LORD.
25"Look, O mighty mountain, destroyer of the earth! I am your enemy," says the LORD.
"I will raise my fist against you, to roll you down from the heights. When I am finished,
you will be nothing but a heap of rubble. 26 You will be desolate forever. Even your stones
will never again be used for building. You will be completely wiped out," says the LORD.
27 Signal many nations to mobilize for war against Babylon. Sound the battle cry!
Bring out the armies of Ararat, Minni, and Ashkenaz. Appoint a leader, and bring a
multitude of horses! 28 Bring against her the armies of the kings of the Medes and their
generals, and the armies of all the countries they rule.
29 Babylon trembles and writhes in pain, for everything the LORD has planned against
her stands unchanged. Babylon will be left desolate without a single inhabitant. 30 Her
mightiest warriors no longer fight. They stay in their barracks. Their courage is gone.
They have become as fearful as women. The invaders have burned the houses and broken
down the city gates. 31 Messengers from every side come running to the king to tell him
all is lost! 32 All the escape routes are blocked. The fortifications are burning, and the
army is in panic.
33 For the LORD Almighty, the God of Israel, says: "Babylon is like wheat on a
threshing floor, about to be trampled. In just a little while her harvest will begin."
34"King Nebuchadnezzar* of Babylon has eaten and crushed us and emptied out our
strength. He has swallowed us like a great monster and filled his belly with our riches.
He has thrown us out of our own country. 35 May Babylon be repaid for all the violence
she did to us," say the people of Jerusalem. "May the people of Babylonia be paid in full
for all the blood they spilled," says Jerusalem.

51:20 Mic 4:12-13
51:21 Exod 15:1
51:22 Isa 13:15-16, 18
51:25 Rev 8:8
51:26 Isa 13:19-22
51:27 Gen 8:4; 10:3 2 Kgs 19:37 Isa 13:2-5
51:29 Jer 10:10 Amos 8:8
51:30 Ps 76:5 Isa 13:7-8; 45:1
51:33 Isa 21:10 Joel 3:13
51:34 Job 20:15 Ps 137:8 Isa 24:1-3
51:35 Ps 137:8

The LORD's Vengeance on Babylon

36 The LORD says to Jerusalem, "I will be your lawyer to plead your case, and I will
avenge you. I will dry up her river, her water supply, 37 and Babylon will become a heap
of rubble, haunted by jackals. It will be an object of horror and contempt, without a single
person living there.

51:36 Ps 140:12 Rom 12:19

51:19 Hebrew *the Portion of Jacob.* **51:20** Possibly Cyrus, who was used of God to conquer Babylon. Compare Isa 44:28; 45:1. **51:24** Or *Chaldea;* also in 51:35. **51:34** Hebrew *Nebuchadrezzar,* a variant name for Nebuchadnezzar.

51:17-19 It is foolish to trust in man-made images rather than in God. It is easy to think that the things we see and touch will bring us more security than God. But things rust, rot, and decay. God is eternal. Why put your trust in something that will disappear within a few years?

51:33 Grain was threshed on a threshing floor, where sheaves were brought from the field. The stalks of grain were distributed on the floor, a large level section of hard ground. There the grain was crushed to separate the kernels from the stalk; then the kernels were beaten with a wooden tool. Sometimes a wooden sledge was pulled over the grain by animals to break the kernels loose. Babylon would soon be "threshed" as God judged it for its sins.

51:36 This verse may refer to an event accomplished by Cyrus, who took Babylon by surprise by diverting the river that ran through the city far upstream and walking beneath the city's fortifications on the dry riverbed. More likely it is saying that Babylon will be deprived of life-giving water. Unlike Jerusalem, Babylon will not be restored.

51:39 Ps 76:5 Jer 25:27 38 "In their drunken feasts, the people of Babylon roar like lions. 39 And while they lie
inflamed with all their wine, I will prepare a different kind of feast for them. I will make
them drink until they fall asleep, never again to waken," says the LORD. 40 "I will bring
them like lambs to the slaughter, like rams and goats to be sacrificed.
51:42 Dan 9:26 41 "How Babylon* is fallen—great Babylon, praised throughout the earth! The world
can scarcely believe its eyes at her fall! 42 The sea has risen over Babylon; she is covered
51:43 Isa 13:20 by its waves. 43 Her cities now lie in ruins; she is a dry wilderness where no one lives or
51:44 Ezra 1:7 Isa 2:2 even passes by. 44 And I will punish Bel, the god of Babylon, and pull from his mouth
what he has taken. The nations will no longer come and worship him. The wall of
Babylon has fallen.

A Message for the Exiles

51:45 Gen 19:12-16 Isa 48:20 Acts 2:40 45 "Listen, my people, flee from Babylon. Save yourselves! Run from the LORD's fierce
anger. 46 But do not panic when you hear the first rumor of approaching forces. For
51:46 Isa 19:2 rumors will keep coming year by year. Then there will be a time of violence as the leaders
fight against each other. 47 For the time is surely coming when I will punish this great
51:47 Isa 21:9; 46:1-2 city and all her idols. Her whole land will be disgraced, and her dead will lie in the streets.
51:48 Isa 44:23 Rev 18:20 48 The heavens and earth will rejoice, for out of the north will come destroying armies
against Babylon," says the LORD. 49 "Just as Babylon killed the people of Israel and
others throughout the world, so must her people be killed. 50 Go, you who escaped the
sword! Do not stand and watch—flee while you can! Remember the LORD, even though
you are in a far-off land, and think about your home in Jerusalem."
51:51 Lam 1:10 51 "We are ashamed," the people say. "We are insulted and disgraced because the
LORD's Temple has been defiled by foreigners."
52 "Yes," says the LORD, "but the time is coming when Babylon's idols will be
destroyed. The groans of her wounded people will be heard throughout the land.
51:53 Job 20:6-7 53 Though Babylon reaches as high as the heavens, and though she increases her strength
immeasurably, I will send enemies to plunder her," says the LORD.

Babylon's Complete Destruction

54 Listen! Hear the cry of Babylon, the sound of great destruction from the land of the
51:55 Ps 69:2 Babylonians. 55 For the LORD is destroying Babylon. He will silence her. Waves of
51:56 Pss 76:3; 94:1-2 enemies pound against her; the noise of battle rings through the city. 56 Destroying armies
come against Babylon. Her mighty men are captured, and their weapons break in their
hands. For the LORD is a God who gives just punishment, and he is giving Babylon all
she deserves.
51:57 Ps 76:5-6 57 "I will make drunk her officials, wise men, rulers, captains, and warriors," says the
King, whose name is the LORD Almighty. "They will fall asleep and never wake up
again!"
51:58 Hab 2:13 58 This is what the LORD Almighty says: "The wide walls of Babylon will be leveled
to the ground, and her high gates will be burned. The builders from many lands have
worked in vain, for their work will be destroyed by fire!"

Jeremiah's Message Sent to Babylon

59 The prophet Jeremiah gave this message to Zedekiah's staff officer, Seraiah son of
Neriah and grandson of Mahseiah, when he went to Babylon with King Zedekiah of
Judah. This was during the fourth year of Zedekiah's reign.* 60 Jeremiah had recorded
51:62 Isa 13:19-22 Ezek 35:9 on a scroll all the terrible disasters that would soon come upon Babylon. 61 He said to
Seraiah, "When you get to Babylon, read aloud everything on this scroll. 62 Then say,

51:41 Hebrew *Sheshach,* a code name for Babylon. **51:59** The fourth year of Zedekiah's reign was 593 B.C.

51:44 Bel is one of the names of Marduk, the chief god of the city of Babylon.

51:51 The people were paralyzed with guilt over their past. The Babylonian armies had desecrated the Temple, and the people were ashamed to return to Jerusalem. But God told them to return to the city because he would destroy Babylon for its sins.

51:59 Jeremiah could not visit Babylon, so he sent the message with Seraiah, the officer who cared for the comforts of the army. Seraiah was probably Baruch's brother (32:12).

51:60-64 In this last of Jeremiah's messages, we find again the twin themes of God's sovereignty and his judgment. Babylon had been allowed to oppress the people of Israel, but Babylon itself would be judged. Although God brings good out of evil, he does not allow evil to remain unpunished. The wicked may succeed for a while, but resist the temptation to follow them or you may share in their judgment.

'LORD, you have said that you will destroy Babylon so that neither people nor animals
will remain here. She will lie empty and abandoned forever.' 63 Then, when you have **51:63**
finished reading the scroll, tie it to a stone, and throw it into the Euphrates River. 64 Then Rev 18:21
say, 'In this same way Babylon and her people will sink, never again to rise, because of **51:64** Nah 1:8-9
the disasters I will bring upon her.'"
This is the end of Jeremiah's messages.

2. The fall of Jerusalem

52 Zedekiah was twenty-one years old when he became king, and he reigned in **52:1** 2 Kgs 8:22;
Jerusalem eleven years. His mother's name was Hamutal, the daughter of Jere- 24:18-20
miah from Libnah. 2 But Zedekiah did what was evil in the LORD's sight, just as **52:2** Jer 36:30-31
Jehoiakim had done. 3 So the LORD, in his anger, finally banished the people of Jerusalem **52:3**
and Judah from his presence and sent them into exile. 2 Chr 36:13
Then Zedekiah rebelled against the king of Babylon. 4 So on January 15,* during the **52:4** 2 Kgs 25:1-7
ninth year of Zedekiah's reign, King Nebuchadnezzar* of Babylon led his entire army Jer 39:1
against Jerusalem. They surrounded the city and built siege ramps against its walls.
5 Jerusalem was kept under siege until the eleventh year of King Zedekiah's reign.
6 By July 18 of Zedekiah's eleventh year,* the famine in the city had become very **52:6** Jer 38:9
severe, with the last of the food entirely gone. 7 Then a section of the city wall was broken **52:7**
down, and all the soldiers made plans to escape from the city. But since the city was Jer 39:2, 4-7
surrounded by the Babylonians,* they waited for nightfall and fled through the gate
between the two walls behind the king's gardens. They made a dash across the fields, in
the direction of the Jordan Valley.*
8 But the Babylonians chased after them and caught King Zedekiah on the plains of **52:8** Jer 21:7; 38:23
Jericho, for by then his men had all abandoned him. 9 They brought him to the king of **52:9** 2 Kgs 25:6
Babylon at Riblah, in the land of Hamath, where sentence was passed against him. Jer 39:5
10 There at Riblah, the king of Babylon made Zedekiah watch as all his sons were killed; **52:10**
they also killed all the other leaders of Judah. 11 Then they gouged out Zedekiah's eyes, Jer 39:6
bound him in bronze chains, and led him away to Babylon. Zedekiah remained there in **52:11**
prison for the rest of his life. Ezek 12:13

The Temple Destroyed

12 On August 17 of that year,* which was the nineteenth year of Nebuchadnezzar's reign, **52:12** 2 Kgs 25:8-21
Nebuzaradan, captain of the guard, an official of the Babylonian king, arrived in
Jerusalem. 13 He burned down the Temple of the LORD, the royal palace, and all the **52:13**
houses of Jerusalem. He destroyed all the important buildings in the city. 14 Then the 2 Chr 36:19
captain of the guard supervised the entire Babylonian* army as they tore down the walls Ps 74:6-8 Jer 39:8
of Jerusalem. 15 Nebuzaradan, captain of the guard, then took as exiles some of the **52:14**
poorest of the people and those who remained in the city, along with the rest of the 2 Kgs 25:10
craftsmen and the troops who had declared their allegiance to the king of Babylon. 16 But
Nebuzaradan allowed some of the poorest people to stay behind in Judah to care for the
vineyards and fields.
17 The Babylonians broke up the bronze pillars, the bronze water carts, and the bronze **52:17**
Sea that were at the LORD's Temple, and they carried all the bronze away to Babylon. 1 Kgs 7:15-36
18 They also took all the pots, shovels, lamp snuffers, basins, dishes, and all the other **52:18**
bronze utensils used for making sacrifices at the Temple. 19 Nebuzaradan, captain of the 1 Kgs 7:45 **52:19**
guard, also took the small bowls, firepans, basins, pots, lampstands, dishes, bowls used 1 Kgs 7:50
for drink offerings, and all the other utensils made of pure gold or silver.

52:4a Hebrew *on the tenth day of the tenth month,* of the Hebrew calendar. A number of events in Jeremiah can be cross-checked with dates in surviving Babylonian records and related accurately to our modern calendar. This event occurred on January 15, 588 B.C. **52:4b** Hebrew *Nebuchadrezzar,* a variant name for Nebuchadnezzar; also in 52:12, 28, 29, 30. **52:6** Hebrew *By the ninth day of the fourth month* [of Zedekiah's eleventh year]. This event of the Hebrew lunar calendar occurred on July 18, 586 B.C.; also see note on 52:4a. **52:7a** Or *Chaldeans;* also in 50:8, 17. **52:7b** Hebrew *the Arabah.* **52:12** Hebrew *On the tenth day of the fifth month,* of the Hebrew calendar. This day was August 17, 586 B.C.; also see note on 52:4a. **52:14** Or *Chaldean.*

52:1ff This chapter provides more detail about the destruction of Jerusalem recorded in chapter 39 (similar material is found in 2 Kings 24:18–25:21). This appendix shows that Jeremiah's prophecies concerning the destruction of Jerusalem and the Babylonian captivity happened just as he predicted. For more information on Zedekiah, see the note on 39:1ff.

52:8, 9 Riblah was 200 miles north of Jerusalem. This was the Babylonian headquarters for ruling the region. Hamath was the district of Aram containing the nation's capital.

52:20 1 Kgs 7:47 20 The bronze from the two pillars, the water carts, and the Sea with the twelve bulls
beneath it was too great to be measured. These things had been made for the LORD's
52:22 Temple in the days of King Solomon. 21 Each of the pillars was 27 feet tall and 18 feet
1 Kgs 7:20, 42 in circumference.* They were hollow, with walls 3 inches thick.* 22 The bronze capital
on top of each pillar was 7½ feet* high and was decorated with a network of bronze
pomegranates all the way around. 23 There were ninety-six pomegranates on the sides,
52:24 and a total of one hundred on the network around the top.
2 Kgs 25:18 24 The captain of the guard took with him as prisoners Seraiah the chief priest, his
Ezra 7:1 assistant Zephaniah, and the three chief gatekeepers. 25 And of the people still hiding in
Esth 1:14 the city, he took an officer of the Judean army, seven of the king's personal advisers, the
army commander's chief secretary, who was in charge of recruitment, and sixty other
citizens. 26 Nebuzaradan the commander took them all to the king of Babylon at Riblah.
52:27 Jer 13:19 27 And there at Riblah in the land of Hamath, the king of Babylon had them all put to
Mic 4:10 death. So the people of Judah were sent into exile from their land.
52:28 2 Kgs 24:2-3, 12-16 28 The number of captives taken to Babylon in the seventh year of Nebuchadnezzar's
reign* was 3,023. 29 Then in Nebuchadnezzar's eighteenth year* he took 832 more. 30 In
his twenty-third year* he sent Nebuzaradan, his captain of the guard, who took 745
more—a total of 4,600 captives in all.

Hope for Israel's Royal Line

52:31 2 Kgs 25:27-30 31 In the thirty-seventh year of King Jehoiachin's exile in Babylon, Evil-merodach
Ps 3:3 ascended to the Babylonian throne. He was kind to Jehoiachin and released him from
52:33 prison on March 31 of that year.* 32 He spoke pleasantly to Jehoiachin and gave him
2 Sam 9:7, 13 preferential treatment over all the other exiled kings in Babylon. 33 He supplied Jehoiachin with new clothes to replace his prison garb and allowed him to dine at the king's
table for the rest of his life. 34 The Babylonian king also gave him a regular allowance to
cover his living expenses until the day of his death.

52:21a Hebrew *18 cubits* [8.1 meters] *tall and 12 cubits* [5.4 meters] *in circumference.* **52:21b** Hebrew *4 fingers thick* [8 centimeters]. **52:22** Hebrew *5 cubits* [2.3 meters]. **52:28** This exile in the seventh year of Nebuchadnezzar's reign occurred in 597 B.C. **52:29** This exile in the eighteenth year of Nebuchadnezzar's reign occurred in 586 B.C. **52:30** This exile in the twenty-third year of Nebuchadnezzar's reign occurred in 581 B.C. **52:31** Hebrew *on the twenty-fifth day of the twelfth month,* of the Hebrew calendar. This day was March 31, 561 B.C.; also see note on 52:4a.

52:31 Babylon's king showed kindness to Jehoiachin. In 561 B.C. Jehoiachin was released from prison and allowed to eat with the king. God continued to show kindness to the descendants of King David, even in exile.

52:34 In the world's eyes, Jeremiah looked totally unsuccessful. He had no money, family, or friends. He prophesied the destruction of the nation, the capital city, and the Temple, but the political and religious leaders would not accept or follow his advice. No group of people liked him or listened to him. Yet as we look back, we see that he successfully completed the work God gave him to do. Success must never be measured by popularity, fame, or fortune, for these are temporal measures. King Zedekiah, for example, lost everything by pursuing selfish goals. God measures our success with the yardsticks of obedience, faithfulness, and righteousness. If you are faithfully doing the work God has given you, you are successful in his eyes.

LAMENTATIONS

VITAL STATISTICS

PURPOSE:
To teach people that to disobey God is to invite disaster, and to show that God suffers when his people suffer

AUTHOR:
Jeremiah

DATE WRITTEN:
Soon after the fall of Jerusalem in 586 B.C.

SETTING:
Jerusalem had been destroyed by Babylon and her people killed, tortured, or taken captive.

KEY VERSE:
"I have cried until the tears no longer come. My heart is broken, my spirit poured out, as I see what has happened to my people. Little children and tiny babies are fainting and dying in the streets" (2:11).

KEY PEOPLE:
Jeremiah, the people of Jerusalem

KEY PLACE:
Jerusalem

SPECIAL FEATURES:
Three strands of Hebrew thought meet in Lamentations—prophecy, ritual, and wisdom. Lamentations is written in the rhythm and style of ancient Jewish funeral songs or chants. It contains five poems corresponding to the five chapters (see the second note on 3:1ff).

TEARS are defined simply as "drops of salty fluid flowing from the eyes." They can be caused by irritation or laughter but are usually associated with weeping, sorrow, and grief. When we cry, friends wonder what's wrong and try to console us. Babies cry for food; children cry at the loss of a pet; adults cry when confronted with trauma and death.

Jeremiah's grief ran deep. He is remembered as the "weeping prophet," and his tears flowed from a broken heart. As God's spokesman, he knew what lay ahead for Judah, his country, and for Jerusalem, the capital and "the city of God." God's judgment would fall and destruction would come. And so Jeremiah wept. His tears were not self-centered, mourning over personal suffering or loss. He wept because the people had rejected their God—the God who had made them, loved them, and sought repeatedly to bless them. Jeremiah's heart was broken because he knew that the selfishness and sinfulness of the people would bring them much suffering and an extended exile. Jeremiah's tears were tears of empathy and sympathy. His heart was broken with those things that break God's heart.

Jeremiah's two books focus on one event—the destruction of Jerusalem. The book of Jeremiah predicts it, and Lamentations looks back on it. Known as the book of tears, Lamentations is a dirge, a funeral song written for the fallen city of Jerusalem.

What makes a person cry says a lot about that person—whether he or she is self-centered or God-centered. The book of Lamentations allows us to see what made Jeremiah sorrowful. As one of God's choice servants, he stands alone in the depth of his emotions, broken by his care for the people, his love for the nation, and his devotion to God.

What causes your tears? Do you weep because your selfish pride has been wounded or because the people around you lead sinful lives and reject the God who loves them dearly? Do you weep because you have lost something of value or because people all around you will suffer for their sinfulness? Our world is filled with injustice, poverty, war, and rebellion against God, all of which should move us to tears and to action. Read Lamentations and learn what it means to grieve with God.

THE BLUEPRINT

1. Jeremiah mourns for Jerusalem (1:1–22)
2. God's anger at sin (2:1–22)
3. Hope in the midst of affliction (3:1–66)
4. God's anger is satisfied (4:1–22)
5. Jeremiah pleads for restoration (5:1–22)

Jeremiah grieves deeply because of the destruction of Jerusalem and the devastation of his nation. But in the middle of the book, in the depths of his grief, there shines a ray of hope. God's compassion is ever present. His faithfulness is great. Jeremiah realizes that it is only the Lord's mercy that has prevented total annihilation. This book shows us the serious consequences of sin and how we can still have hope in the midst of tragedy because God is able to turn it around for good. We see the timeless importance of prayer and confession of sin. We will all face tragedy in our life. But in the midst of our afflictions, there is hope in God.

MEGATHEMES

THEME	EXPLANATION	IMPORTANCE
Destruction of Jerusalem	Lamentations is a sad funeral song for the great capital city of the Jews. The Temple has been destroyed, the king is gone, and the people are in exile. God had warned that he would destroy them if they abandoned him. Now, afterward, the people realize their condition and confess their sin.	God's warnings are justified. He does what he says he will do. His punishment for sin is certain. Only by confessing and renouncing our sin can we turn to him for deliverance. How much better to do so before his warnings are fulfilled.
God's Mercy	God's compassion was at work even when the Israelites were experiencing the affliction of their Babylonian conquerors. Although the people had been unfaithful, God's faithfulness was great. He used this affliction to bring his people back to him.	God will always be faithful to his people. His merciful, refining work is evident even in affliction. At those times, we must pray for forgiveness and then turn to him for deliverance.
Sin's Consequences	God was angry at the prolonged rebellion by his people. Sin was the cause of their misery, and destruction was the result of their sin. The destruction of the nation shows the vanity of human glory and pride.	To continue in rebellion against God is to invite disaster. We must never trust our own leadership, resources, intelligence, or power more than God. If we do, we will experience consequences similar to Jerusalem's.
Hope	God's mercy in sparing some of the people offers hope for better days. One day, the people will be restored to a true and fervent relationship with God.	Only God can deliver us from sin. Without him there is no comfort or hope for the future. Because of Christ's death for us and his promise to return, we have a bright hope for tomorrow.

1. Jeremiah mourns for Jerusalem

1:1 Isa 22:2; Jer 31:7; 40:9
1:2 Job 19:13-14; Pss 6:6; 77:2-6; Jer 2:25; 22:20-22; Mic 7:5
1:3 Lev 26:39; Deut 28:64-67; 2 Kgs 25:4-5
1:4 Jer 9:11; 10:22; Lam 2:6-7; Joel 1:8-13

1 Jerusalem's streets, once bustling with people, are now silent. Like a widow broken
with grief, she sits alone in her mourning. Once the queen of nations, she is now a slave.
2 She sobs through the night; tears stream down her cheeks. Among all her lovers, there
is no one left to help her. All her friends have betrayed her; they are now her enemies.
3 Judah has been led away into captivity, afflicted and enslaved. She lives among
foreign nations and has no place of rest. Her enemies have chased her down, and she has
nowhere to turn.
4 The roads to Jerusalem* are in mourning, no longer filled with crowds on their way
to celebrate the Temple festivals. The city gates are silent, her priests groan, her young
women are crying—how bitterly Jerusalem weeps!

1:1 Each of the first four chapters of this book is an acrostic, laid out in the order of the Hebrew alphabet. The first word of each verse begins with a successive Hebrew letter. Chapters 1, 2, and 4 have one verse for each of the 22 Hebrew letters. Chapter 3 contains 22 stanzas of three verses each. Though chapter 5 is not an acrostic, it also has 22 verses. **1:4** Hebrew *Zion;* also in 1:17.

1:1 This is the prophet Jeremiah's song of sorrow for Jerusalem's destruction. The nation of Judah had been utterly defeated, the Temple destroyed, and captives taken away to Babylon. Jeremiah's tears were for the suffering and humiliation of the people, but those tears penetrated even deeper into his heart. He wept because God had rejected the people for their rebellious ways. Each year this book was read aloud to remind all the Jews that their great city fell because of their stubborn sinfulness.

1:2 The term *lovers* refers to nations such as Egypt, to whom Judah kept turning for help. As the Babylonians closed in on Jerusalem, the nation of Judah turned away from God and sought help and protection from other nations instead.

5 Her oppressors have become her masters, and her enemies prosper, for the LORD has punished Jerusalem for her many sins. Her children have been captured and taken away to distant lands.

6 All the beauty and majesty of Jerusalem* are gone. Her princes are like starving deer searching for pasture, too weak to run from the pursuing enemy.

7 And now in the midst of her sadness and wandering, Jerusalem remembers her ancient splendor. But then she fell to her enemy, and there was no one to help her. Her enemy struck her down and laughed as she fell.

8 Jerusalem has sinned greatly, so she has been tossed away like a filthy rag. All who once honored her now despise her, for they have seen her stripped naked and humiliated. All she can do is groan and hide her face.

9 She defiled herself with immorality with no thought of the punishment that would follow. Now she lies in the gutter with no one to lift her out. "LORD, see my deep misery," she cries. "The enemy has triumphed."

10 The enemy has plundered her completely, taking everything precious that she owns. She has seen foreigners violate her sacred Temple, the place the LORD had forbidden them to enter.

11 Her people groan as they search for bread. They have sold their treasures for food to stay alive. "O LORD, look," she mourns, "and see how I am despised.

12 "Is it nothing to you, all you who pass by? Look around and see if there is any suffering like mine, which the LORD brought on me in the day of his fierce anger.

13 "He has sent fire from heaven that burns in my bones. He has placed a trap in my path and turned me back. He has made me desolate, racked with sickness all day long.

14 "He wove my sins into ropes to hitch me to a yoke of captivity. The Lord sapped my strength and gave me to my enemies; I am helpless in their hands.

15 "The Lord has treated my mighty men with contempt. At his command a great army has come to crush my young warriors. The Lord has trampled his beloved city* as grapes are trampled in a winepress.

16 "For all these things I weep; tears flow down my cheeks. No one is here to comfort me; any who might encourage me are far away. My children have no future, for the enemy has conquered us."

17 Jerusalem pleads for help, but no one comforts her. Regarding his people,* the LORD has said, "Let their neighbors be their enemies! Let them be thrown away like a filthy rag!"

18 "And the LORD is right," she groans, "for I rebelled against him. Listen, people everywhere; look upon my anguish and despair, for my sons and daughters have been taken captive to distant lands.

19 "I begged my allies for help, but they betrayed me. My priests and leaders starved to death in the city, even as they searched for food to save their lives.

20 "LORD, see my anguish! My heart is broken and my soul despairs, for I have rebelled against you. In the streets the sword kills, and at home there is only death.

21 "Others heard my groans, but no one turned to comfort me. When my enemies heard of my troubles, they were happy to see what you had done. Oh, bring the day you promised, when you will destroy them as you have destroyed me.

1:5 Ps 90:7-8; Ezek 8:17-18; 9:9-10
1:6 Jer 13:18
1:7 Jer 37:7; Lam 4:17
1:8 Isa 59:2-13
1:9 Ps 74:23; Eccl 4:1; Isa 3:8; Jer 13:17-18; Ezek 24:13
1:10 Ps 74:4-8; Isa 64:10-11; Jer 51:51
1:11 1 Sam 30:12; Jer 15:19
1:12 Isa 13:13; Jer 4:8; 18:16; 48:27
1:13 Job 19:6; 30:30; Ps 22:14; Jer 44:6; Hab 3:16
1:14 Prov 5:22; Isa 47:6; Jer 28:13-14; 32:3; Ezek 25:4, 7
1:15 Isa 41:2; Jer 13:24; 37:10
1:16 Ps 69:20; Eccl 4:1; Lam 1:2
1:17 2 Kgs 24:2-4; Isa 1:15; Jer 4:31
1:18 Deut 28:32, 41; 1 Sam 12:14-15; Ps 119:75; Jer 12:1
1:19 Job 19:13-19; Jer 14:15; Lam 1:2; 2:20
1:20 Isa 16:11; Jer 4:19
1:21 Ps 35:15; Isa 14:5-6; 47:6; Jer 30:16

1:6 Hebrew *the daughter of Zion.* **1:15** Hebrew *the virgin daughter of Judah.* **1:17** Hebrew *Jacob.*

1:9 The warning was loud and clear: If Judah played with fire, its people would get burned. Jerusalem foolishly took a chance and lost, refusing to believe that immoral living brings God's punishment. The ultimate consequence of sin is punishment (Romans 6:23). We can choose to ignore God's warnings, but as surely as judgment came upon Jerusalem, so it will come upon those who defy God. Are you listening to God's Word? Are you obeying it? Obedience is a sure sign of your love for God.

1:14 At first, sin seems to offer freedom. But the liberty to do anything we want gradually becomes a desire to do everything. Then we become captive to sin, bound by its "yoke." Freedom from sin's captivity comes only from God. He gives us freedom, not to do anything we want, but to do what he knows is best for us. Strange as it may seem, true freedom comes in obeying God—following his guidance so that we can receive his best.

1:16 God is the comforter, but because of the people's sins, he had to turn away from them and become their judge.

1:19 Jerusalem's allies could not come to help because, like Jerusalem, they failed to seek God. Though these allies appeared strong, they were actually weak because God was not with them. Dependable assistance can come only from an ally whose power is from God. When you seek wise counsel, go to Christians who get their wisdom from the all-knowing God.

22 "Look at all their evil deeds, LORD. Punish them, as you have punished me for all my sins. My groans are many, and my heart is faint."

2. God's anger at sin

2 The Lord in his anger has cast a dark shadow over Jerusalem.* The fairest of Israel's cities lies in the dust, thrown down from the heights of heaven. In his day of awesome fury, the Lord has shown no mercy even to his Temple.*

2 Without mercy the Lord has destroyed every home in Israel.* In his anger he has broken down the fortress walls of Jerusalem.* He has brought to dust the kingdom and all its rulers.

3 All the strength of Israel vanishes beneath his fury. The Lord has withdrawn his protection as the enemy attacks. He consumes the whole land of Israel like a raging fire.

4 He bends his bow against his people as though he were their enemy. His strength is used against them to kill their finest youth. His fury is poured out like fire on beautiful Jerusalem.*

5 Yes, the Lord has vanquished Israel like an enemy. He has destroyed her forts and palaces. He has brought unending sorrow and tears to Jerusalem.

6 He has broken down his Temple as though it were merely a garden shelter. The LORD has blotted out all memory of the holy festivals and Sabbath days. Kings and priests fall together before his anger.

7 The Lord has rejected his own altar; he despises his own sanctuary. He has given Jerusalem's palaces to her enemies. They shout in the LORD's Temple as though it were a day of celebration.

8 The LORD was determined to destroy the walls of Jerusalem. He made careful plans for their destruction, then he went ahead and did it. Therefore, the ramparts and walls have fallen down before him.

9 Jerusalem's gates have sunk into the ground. All their locks and bars are destroyed, for he has smashed them. Her kings and princes have been exiled to distant lands; the law is no more. Her prophets receive no more visions from the LORD.

10 The leaders of Jerusalem sit on the ground in silence, clothed in sackcloth. They throw dust on their heads in sorrow and despair. The young women of Jerusalem hang their heads in shame.

11 I have cried until the tears no longer come. My heart is broken, my spirit poured out, as I see what has happened to my people. Little children and tiny babies are fainting and dying in the streets.

12 "Mama, we want food," they cry, and then collapse in their mothers' arms. Their lives ebb away like the life of a warrior wounded in battle.

2:1a Hebrew *the daughter of Zion;* also in 2:8, 10, 18. **2:1b** Hebrew *footstool.* **2:2a** Hebrew *Jacob;* also in 2:3. **2:2b** Hebrew *the daughter of Judah;* also in 2:5. **2:4** Hebrew *on the tent of the daughter of Zion.*

1:22 Neh 4:4-5; Ps 137:7-8
2:1 Pss 99:5; 132:7; Isa 64:11; Ezek 28:14-16
2:2 Pss 21:9; 89:39-40; Lam 3:43
2:3 Ps 75:5, 10; Isa 42:25; Jer 21:14
2:4 Job 6:4; 16:13; Jer 7:20; Lam 3:12-13
2:5 Jer 52:13; Lam 2:2
2:6 Lam 1:4; Zeph 3:18
2:7 Ps 74:3-8; Isa 64:11; Ezek 7:20-22
2:8 2 Kgs 21:13; Isa 34:11; Amos 7:7-9
2:9 Neh 1:3; Jer 14:14; 23:16
2:10 Job 2:13; Isa 3:26; Amos 8:3; Jon 3:6-8
2:11 Job 16:13; Jer 4:19; Lam 2:19
2:12 Job 30:16; Ps 42:4

1:22 Babylon, although sinful, was God's instrument for punishing Judah and its capital, Jerusalem. The people of Jerusalem were pleading for God to punish sinful Babylon as he had punished them ("punish them, as you have punished me"). God would do this, for he had already passed judgment on Babylon (see Jeremiah 50:1-27).

2:6 King Solomon's Temple in Jerusalem represented God's presence with the people (1 Kings 8:1-11). The Temple was the central place of worship. Its destruction symbolized God's rejection of his people—that he no longer lived among them.

2:7 Our place of worship is not as important to God as our pattern of worship. A church building may be beautiful, but if its people don't sincerely follow God, the church will decay from within. The people of Judah, despite their beautiful Temple, had rejected in their daily lives what they proclaimed in their worship rituals. Thus, their worship had turned into a mocking lie. When you worship, are you saying words you don't really mean? Do you pray for help you don't really believe will come? Do you express love for God you don't really have? Earnestly seek God and catch a fresh vision of his love and care. Then worship him wholeheartedly.

2:9 Four powerful symbols and sources of security were lost: the protection of the *gates,* the leadership of the *kings and princes,* the guidance of the *law,* and the vision of the *prophets.* With those four factors present, the people were lulled into a false sense of security and felt comfortable with their sins. But after each was removed, the people were confronted with the choice of repenting and returning to God or continuing on this path of suffering. Don't substitute symbols, even good ones, for the reality of a living, personal relationship with God himself.

2:11 Jeremiah's tears were sincere and full of compassion. Sorrow does not mean that we lack faith or strength. There is nothing wrong with crying—Jesus himself felt sorrow and even wept (John 11:35). How do we react to the tearing down of our society and to moral degradation? This may not be as obvious as an invading enemy army, but the destruction is just as certain. We, too, should be deeply moved when we see the moral decay that surrounds us.

13In all the world has there ever been such sorrow? O daughter of Jerusalem, to what
can I compare your anguish? O virgin daughter of Zion, how can I comfort you? For
your wound is as deep as the sea. Who can heal you?
14Your "prophets" have said so many foolish things, false to the core. They did not try
to hold you back from exile by pointing out your sins. Instead, they painted false pictures,
filling you with false hope.
15All who pass by jeer at you. They scoff and insult Jerusalem,* saying, "Is this the
city called 'Most Beautiful in All the World' and 'Joy of All the Earth'?"
16All your enemies deride you. They scoff and grind their teeth and say, "We have
destroyed her at last! Long have we awaited this day, and it is finally here!"
17But it is the LORD who did it just as he warned. He has fulfilled the promises of
disaster he made long ago. He has destroyed Jerusalem without mercy and caused her
enemies to rejoice over her and boast of their power.
18Cry aloud* before the Lord, O walls of Jerusalem! Let your tears flow like a river.
Give yourselves no rest from weeping day or night.
19Rise during the night and cry out. Pour out your hearts like water to the Lord. Lift
up your hands to him in prayer. Plead for your children as they faint with hunger in the
streets.
20"O LORD, think about this!" Jerusalem cries. "You are doing this to your own
people! Should mothers eat their little children, those they once bounced on their knees?
Should priests and prophets die within the Lord's Temple?
21"See them lying in the streets—young and old, boys and girls, killed by the swords
of the enemy. You have killed them in your anger, slaughtering them without mercy.
22"You have invited terrors from all around as though you were calling them to a day
of feasting. In the day of the LORD's anger, no one has escaped or survived. The enemy
has killed all the children I bore and raised."

3. Hope in the midst of affliction

3 I am the one who has seen the afflictions that come from the rod of the LORD's anger.
2He has brought me into deep darkness, shutting out all light. 3He has turned against
me. Day and night his hand is heavy upon me.
4He has made my skin and flesh grow old. He has broken my bones. 5He has attacked
me and surrounded me with anguish and distress. 6He has buried me in a dark place, like
a person long dead.
7He has walled me in, and I cannot escape. He has bound me in heavy chains. 8And
though I cry and shout, he shuts out my prayers. 9He has blocked my path with a high
stone wall. He has twisted the road before me with many detours.
10He hid like a bear or a lion, waiting to attack me. 11He dragged me off the path and

2:13 Lam 1:12
2:14 Ezek 22:25, 28; 23:36; Mic 3:8
2:15 Job 27:23; Pss 48:2; 50:2; Jer 18:16
2:16 Pss 22:13; 56:2; Lam 3:46; Obad 1:12-15
2:17 Deut 28:43-44; Ps 89:42; Lam 1:5
2:18 Lam 2:8; Hos 7:14; Hab 2:11
2:19 1 Sam 1:15; Isa 51:20
2:20 Exod 32:11; Deut 9:26; Jer 23:11-12; Lam 4:13, 16
2:21 2 Chr 36:17; Jer 6:11; Zech 11:6
2:22 Isa 24:17-18; Jer 16:2-4
3:2 Jer 4:23
3:3 Isa 5:25
3:4 Jer 50:17
3:5 Jer 23:15
3:7 Jer 40:4
3:9 Isa 63:17
3:11 Hos 6:1

2:15 Hebrew *the daughter of Jerusalem.* **2:18** Hebrew *Their heart cried.*

2:14 False prophets were everywhere in Jeremiah's day. They gave false and misleading messages. While Jeremiah warned the people of coming destruction and lengthy captivity, the false prophets said that all was well so the people need not fear. All of Jeremiah's words came true because he was a true prophet of God (Jeremiah 14:14-16).

2:19 Chapter 1 describes Jerusalem's desolation and calls for God's revenge on his enemies. Chapter 2 includes a call for God's people to pour out their hearts in the Lord's presence. The people must turn from their sins; they must sincerely mourn over their wrongs against God (3:40-42). The people had much to cry about. Because of their stubborn rebellion against God, they had brought great suffering to all, especially to the innocent. Was this suffering God's fault? No, it was the fault of the wayward people. Sinful people brought destruction on themselves, but tragically, sin's consequences affected everyone—good and evil alike.

2:19 The people's suffering and sin should have brought them to the Lord, weeping for forgiveness. Only when sin breaks our hearts can God come to our rescue. Just feeling sorry about experiencing sin's consequences does not bring forgiveness. But if we cry out to God, he will forgive us.

2:21, 22 This horrible scene could have been avoided. Jeremiah had warned the people for years that this day of destruction would come, and it broke his heart to see it fulfilled. We are always shocked when we hear of tragedy striking the innocent. But often innocent bystanders are victims of judgment on a nation. Sin has a way of causing great sorrow and devastation to many.

3:1ff In Jeremiah's darkest moment, his hope was strengthened with this assurance: God had been faithful and would continue to be faithful. Jeremiah saw both God's judgment and God's steadfast love. In the time of judgment, Jeremiah could still cling to God's love, just as in times of prosperity he had warned of God's judgment.

3:1ff In the original Hebrew, the first four chapters in Lamentations are acrostic poems. Each verse in each chapter begins with a successive letter of the Hebrew alphabet. Chapter 3 has 66 verses rather than 22 because it is a triple acrostic: The first three verses begin with the equivalent of *A,* the next three with *B,* and so on. This was a typical form of Hebrew poetry. Other examples of acrostics are Psalms 37, 119, and 145, and Proverbs 31:10-31.

tore me with his claws, leaving me helpless and desolate. [12]He bent his bow and aimed it squarely at me.

[13]He shot his arrows deep into my heart. [14]My own people laugh at me. All day long they sing their mocking songs. [15]He has filled me with bitterness. He has given me a cup of deep sorrow to drink.

[16]He has made me grind my teeth on gravel. He has rolled me in the dust. [17]Peace has been stripped away, and I have forgotten what prosperity is. [18]I cry out, "My splendor is gone! Everything I had hoped for from the LORD is lost!"

[19]The thought of my suffering and homelessness is bitter beyond words.* [20]I will never forget this awful time, as I grieve over my loss. [21]Yet I still dare to hope when I remember this:

[22]The unfailing love of the LORD never ends! By his mercies we have been kept from complete destruction. [23]Great is his faithfulness; his mercies begin afresh each day. [24]I say to myself, "The LORD is my inheritance; therefore, I will hope in him!"

[25]The LORD is wonderfully good to those who wait for him and seek him. [26]So it is good to wait quietly for salvation from the LORD. [27]And it is good for the young to submit to the yoke of his discipline.

[28]Let them sit alone in silence beneath the LORD's demands. [29]Let them lie face down in the dust; then at last there is hope for them. [30]Let them turn the other cheek to those who strike them. Let them accept the insults of their enemies.

[31]For the Lord does not abandon anyone forever. [32]Though he brings grief, he also shows compassion according to the greatness of his unfailing love. [33]For he does not enjoy hurting people or causing them sorrow.

[34]But the leaders of his people trampled prisoners underfoot. [35]They deprived people of their God-given rights in defiance of the Most High. [36]They perverted justice in the courts. Do they think the Lord didn't see it?

[37]Can anything happen without the Lord's permission? [38]Is it not the Most High who helps one and harms another? [39]Then why should we, mere humans, complain when we are punished for our sins?

[40]Instead, let us test and examine our ways. Let us turn again in repentance to the LORD. [41]Let us lift our hearts and hands to God in heaven and say, [42]"We have sinned and rebelled, and you have not forgiven us.

[43]"You have engulfed us with your anger, chased us down, and slaughtered us without mercy. [44]You have hidden yourself in a cloud so our prayers cannot reach you. [45]You have discarded us as refuse and garbage among the nations.

[46]"All our enemies have spoken out against us. [47]We are filled with fear, for we are trapped, desolate, and ruined." [48]Streams of tears flow from my eyes because of the destruction of my people!

3:19 Hebrew *is wormwood and gall.*

3:14 Lam 3:63
3:15 Jer 9:15
3:16 Prov 20:17
3:17 Isa 59:11; Jer 12:12
3:18 Job 17:15; Ezek 37:11
3:19 Lam 3:5, 15
3:22 Jer 3:12; Mal 3:6
3:25 Isa 25:9; 26:9
3:28 Jer 15:17
3:29 Job 16:15; 40:4
3:30 Isa 50:6; Matt 5:39
3:31 Isa 54:7-10
3:32 Hos 11:8
3:35 Prov 17:15
3:36 Jer 22:3; Hab 1:13
3:38 Job 2:10; Jer 32:42
3:39 Mic 7:9; Heb 12:5-6
3:40 2 Cor 13:5
3:42 Neh 9:26; Jer 14:20
3:45 1 Cor 4:13
3:46 Lam 2:16
3:47 Jer 48:43-44

3:21-23 Jeremiah saw one ray of hope in all the sin and sorrow surrounding him: "The unfailing love of the LORD never ends. . . . Great is his faithfulness; his mercies begin afresh each day." God willingly responds with help when we ask. Perhaps there is some sin in your life that you thought God would not forgive. God's steadfast love and mercy are greater than any sin, and he promises forgiveness.

3:23 Jeremiah knew from personal experience about God's faithfulness. God had promised that punishment would follow disobedience, and it did. But God also had promised future restoration and blessing, and Jeremiah knew that God would keep that promise also. Trusting in God's faithfulness day by day makes us confident in his great promises for the future.

3:27-33 To "submit to the yoke" means to willingly come under God's discipline and learn what he wants to teach. This involves several important factors: (1) silent reflection on what God wants, (2) repentant humility, (3) self-control in the face of adversity, and (4) confident patience, depending on the divine Teacher to bring about loving lessons in our life. God has several long-term and short-term lessons for you right now. Are you doing your homework?

3:30 This call to "turn the other cheek" reminds us that sometimes God calls us to suffer criticism and abuse for his purposes. Jesus taught his followers to turn the other cheek (Matthew 5:39), and he exemplified this at the highest level just before his crucifixion (Matthew 27:27-31; Luke 22:64; John 18:22; 19:3). This, however, should never be used to justify anyone's continued suffering of spousal or any other kind of abuse.

3:39-42 Parents discipline children to produce right behavior. God disciplined Judah to produce right living and genuine worship. We must not complain about discipline but learn from it, trusting God and being willing to change. We must allow God's correction to bring about the kind of behavior in our life that pleases him.

49 My tears flow down endlessly. They will not stop 50 until the LORD looks down from
heaven and sees. 51 My heart is breaking over the fate of all the women of Jerusalem.
52 My enemies, whom I have never harmed, chased me like a bird. 53 They threw me
into a pit and dropped stones on me. 54 The water flowed above my head, and I cried out,
"This is the end!"
55 But I called on your name, LORD, from deep within the well, 56 and you heard me!
You listened to my pleading; you heard my weeping! 57 Yes, you came at my despairing
cry and told me, "Do not fear."
58 Lord, you are my lawyer! Plead my case! For you have redeemed my life. 59 You
have seen the wrong they have done to me, LORD. Be my judge, and prove me right.
60 You have seen the plots my enemies have laid against me.
61 LORD, you have heard the vile names they call me. You know all about the plans
they have made—62 the plots my enemies whisper and mutter against me all day long.
63 Look at them! In all their activities, they constantly mock me with their songs.
64 Pay them back, LORD, for all the evil they have done. 65 Give them hard and stubborn
hearts, and then let your curse fall upon them! 66 Chase them down in your anger,
destroying them from beneath the LORD's heavens.

4. God's anger is satisfied

4 How the gold has lost its luster! Even the finest gold has become dull. The sacred
gemstones lie scattered in the streets!
2 See how the precious children of Jerusalem,* worth their weight in gold, are now
treated like pots of clay.
3 Even the jackals feed their young, but not my people Israel. They ignore their
children's cries, like the ostriches of the desert.
4 The parched tongues of their little ones stick with thirst to the roofs of their mouths.
The children cry for bread, but no one has any to give them.
5 The people who once ate only the richest foods now beg in the streets for anything
they can get. Those who once lived in palaces now search the garbage pits for food.
6 The guilt* of my people is greater than that of Sodom, where utter disaster struck in
a moment with no one to help them.
7 Our princes were once glowing with health; they were as clean as snow and as elegant
as jewels.
8 But now their faces are blacker than soot. No one even recognizes them. Their skin
sticks to their bones; it is as dry and hard as wood.
9 Those killed by the sword are far better off than those who die of hunger, wasting
away for want of food.
10 Tenderhearted women have cooked their own children and eaten them in order to
survive the siege.
11 But now the anger of the LORD is satisfied. His fiercest anger has now been poured
out. He started a fire in Jerusalem* that burned the city to its foundations.
12 Not a king in all the earth—no one in all the world—would have believed an enemy
could march through the gates of Jerusalem.

4:2 Hebrew *sons of Zion.* **4:6** Or *punishment.* **4:11** Hebrew *in Zion.*

3:52 1 Sam 26:20
3:53 Jer 37:16
3:54 Jon 2:3-5
3:56 Job 34:28
3:57 Isa 41:10-14
3:58 Jer 50:34; 51:36
3:61 Lam 5:1
3:62 Ezek 36:3
3:63 Lam 3:14
3:64 Jer 51:24
3:65 Deut 2:30
4:1 2 Kgs 25:9-10
4:2 Isa 30:14; Jer 19:1, 11
4:3 Job 39:14-16; Lam 2:12
4:4 Jer 14:3
4:5 Jer 6:2; Amos 6:3-7
4:6 Gen 19:25; Jer 20:16; Ezek 16:48
4:7 Ps 51:7
4:8 Ps 102:5; Lam 5:10
4:9 Lev 26:39
4:10 Deut 28:53-55; 2 Kgs 6:26-30; Lam 2:20
4:11 Deut 32:22
4:12 Jer 21:13

3:52-57 At one point in his ministry, Jeremiah was thrown into an empty cistern, and he was left to die in the mire at the bottom (Jeremiah 38:6-13). But God rescued him. Jeremiah used this experience as a picture of the nation sinking into sin. If they turned to God, he would rescue them.

4:1ff This chapter contrasts the situation before the siege of Jerusalem with the situation after the siege. The sights and sounds of prosperity were gone because of the people's sin. This chapter warns us not to assume that when life is going well, it will always stay that way. We must be careful not to glory in our prosperity and fall into spiritual bankruptcy.

4:1-10 When a city was under siege, the city wall—built for protection—sealed the people inside. They could not get out to the fields to get food and water because the enemy was camped around the city. As food in the city ran out, the people watched their enemies harvest and eat the food in the fields. The siege was a test of wills to see which army could outlast the other. Jerusalem was under siege for two years. Life became so harsh that people even ate their own children, and dead bodies were left to rot in the streets. All hope was gone.

4:6 Sodom, destroyed by burning sulfur from heaven because of its wickedness (Genesis 18:20–19:29), became a symbol of God's ultimate judgment. Yet the sin of Jerusalem was even greater than the sin of Sodom!

4:13 Jer 2:30; 26:8-9; Ezek 22:26
4:14 Deut 28:28-29; Isa 29:10; 56:10; 59:9-10
4:15 Lev 13:45-46; Jer 45:5
4:16 Isa 9:14-16; Jer 52:24-27
4:17 Jer 37:7; Ezek 29:16
4:18 Jer 5:31; 16:16; Amos 8:2
4:19 Deut 28:49; Isa 5:26-28; Jer 4:13
4:20 Jer 39:5; Ezek 12:12-13
4:21 Isa 34:7; Amos 1:11
4:22 Isa 40:2; Jer 49:10

13 Yet it happened because of the sins of her prophets and priests, who defiled the city
by shedding innocent blood.
14 They wandered blindly through the streets, so defiled by blood that no one dared to
touch them.
15 "Get away!" the people shouted at them. "You are defiled! Don't touch us!" So they
fled to distant lands and wandered there among foreign nations, but none would let them
stay.
16 The LORD himself has scattered them, and he no longer helps them. The priests and
leaders are no longer honored and respected.
17 We looked in vain for our allies to come and save us, but we were looking to nations
that could offer no help at all.
18 We couldn't go into the streets without danger to our lives. Our end was near; our
days were numbered. We were doomed!
19 Our enemies were swifter than the eagles. If we fled to the mountains, they found
us. If we hid in the wilderness, they were waiting for us there.
20 Our king, the LORD's anointed, the very life of our nation, was caught in their snares.
We had foolishly boasted that under his protection we could hold our own against any
nation on earth!
21 Are you rejoicing in the land of Uz, O people of Edom? But you, too, must drink
from the cup of the LORD's anger. You, too, will be stripped naked in your drunkenness.
22 O Jerusalem,* your punishment will end; you will soon return from exile. But
Edom, your punishment is just beginning; soon your many sins will be revealed.

5. Jeremiah pleads for restoration

5:2 Isa 1:7; Hos 8:7-8; Zeph 1:13
5:7 Jer 14:20; 16:12
5:8 Neh 5:15; Zech 11:6
5:9 Jer 40:9-12
5:11 Isa 13:16; Zech 14:2
5:12 Isa 47:6
5:14 Isa 24:8; Jer 7:34

5 LORD, remember everything that has happened to us. See all the sorrows we bear!
2 Our inheritance has been turned over to strangers, our homes to foreigners. 3 We
are orphaned and fatherless. Our mothers are widowed. 4 We have to pay for water to
drink, and even firewood is expensive. 5 Those who pursue us are at our heels; we are
exhausted but are given no rest. 6 We submitted to Egypt and Assyria to get enough food
to survive. 7 It was our ancestors who sinned, but they died before the hand of judgment
fell. We have suffered the punishment they deserved!
8 Slaves have now become our masters; there is no one left to rescue us. 9 We must hunt
for food in the wilderness at the risk of our lives. 10 Because of the famine, our skin has
been blackened as though baked in an oven. 11 Our enemies rape the women and young
girls in Jerusalem* and throughout the towns of Judah. 12 Our princes are being hanged
by their thumbs, and the old men are treated with contempt. 13 The young men are led
away to work at millstones, and the children stagger under heavy loads of wood. 14 The
old men no longer sit in the city gates; the young men no longer dance and sing.

4:22 Hebrew *daughter of Zion.* **5:11** Hebrew *Zion.*

4:13-15 To be defiled or unclean meant to be unfit to enter the Temple or to worship before God. The priests and prophets should have been the most careful to maintain ceremonial purity so that they could continue to perform their duties before God. But many priests and prophets did evil and were defiled. As the nation's leaders, their example led the people into sin and caused the ultimate downfall of the nation and its capital city, Jerusalem.

4:17 Judah asked Egypt to help it fight the Babylonian army. Egypt gave Judah false hope by starting to help, but then it retreated (Jeremiah 37:5-7). Jeremiah warned Judah not to ally itself with Egypt. He told the leaders to rely on God, but they refused to listen.

4:20 King Zedekiah, although called "the LORD's anointed," had little spiritual depth and leadership power. Instead of putting his faith in God and listening to God's true prophet, Jeremiah, he listened to the false prophets. To make matters worse, the people chose to follow and trust in their king (2 Chronicles 36:11-16). They chose the path of complacency, wanting to feel secure rather than to follow the directives God was giving his people through Jeremiah. But the source of their confidence—King Zedekiah—was captured.

4:21, 22 Edom was Judah's archenemy, even though they had a common ancestor, Isaac (see Genesis 25:19-26; 36:1). Edom had actively aided Babylon in the siege of Jerusalem. As a reward, Nebuchadnezzar gave the outlying lands of Judah to Edom. Jeremiah said that Edom would be judged for her treachery against her brothers. (See also Jeremiah 49:7-22; Ezekiel 25:12-14; Amos 9:12; Obadiah 1:1-21.)

5:1ff At a time of grief, the true believer should turn to God in prayer. Here Jeremiah prayed for mercy for his people. At the end of his prayer, he wondered if God had "utterly rejected" his people because of his great anger toward them. But God would not stay angry with them forever. "You cannot stay angry with your people forever because you delight in showing mercy" (Micah 7:18).

5:14 During peace and prosperity, the leaders and elders of the city would sit at the city gate and talk over politics, theology, and philosophy, and conduct business.

15 The joy of our hearts has ended; our dancing has turned to mourning. 16 The garlands have* fallen from our heads. Disaster has fallen upon us because we have sinned. 17 Our hearts are sick and weary, and our eyes grow dim with tears. 18 For Jerusalem* is empty and desolate, a place haunted by jackals.

19 But LORD, you remain the same forever! Your throne continues from generation to generation. 20 Why do you continue to forget us? Why have you forsaken us for so long? 21 Restore us, O LORD, and bring us back to you again! Give us back the joys we once had! 22 Or have you utterly rejected us? Are you angry with us still?

5:16 Or *The crown has.* **5:18** Hebrew *Mount Zion.*

5:15
Jer 25:10
Amos 8:10

5:17
Job 17:7
Isa 1:5

5:19
Pss 45:6; 102:12

5:21
Ps 80:3
Isa 60:20-22
Jer 31:18

5:22 A high calling flouted by low living results in deep suffering. Lamentations gives us a portrait of the bitter suffering the people of Jerusalem experienced when sin caught up with them and God turned his back on them. Every material goal they had lived for collapsed. But although God turned away from them because of their sin, he did not abandon them—that was their great hope. Despite their sinful past, God would restore them if they returned to him. Hope is found only in the Lord. Thus, our grief should turn us toward him, not away from him.

EZEKIEL

Jeremiah becomes a prophet to Judah 627 B.C.	Daniel taken captive to Babylon 605	Ezekiel taken captive to Babylon 597	Ezekiel becomes a prophet to exiles 593	Judah falls; Jerusalem destroyed 586	Ezekiel's ministry ends 571	Babylon overthrown by Cyrus 539	First exiles return to Judah 538

A COMPUTER can be programmed to respond at your command. And by conditioning a dog with rewards and punishments, you can teach it to obey. But as every parent knows, children are not so easily taught. People have wills and must choose to submit, to follow the instructions of those who have authority over them. Surely discipline is part of the process—boys and girls should know that they will reap the consequences of disobedience.

God's children must learn to obey their heavenly Father. Created in his image, they have a choice, and God allows them to choose.

Ezekiel was a man who chose to obey God. Although he was a priest (1:3), he served as a Jewish "street preacher" in Babylon for 22 years, telling everyone about God's judgment and salvation, and calling them to repent and obey. And Ezekiel *lived* what he preached. During his ministry God told him to illustrate his messages with dramatic object lessons. Some of these acts included (1) lying on his side for 390 days during which he could eat only one eight-ounce meal a day cooked over manure, (2) shaving his head and beard, and (3) showing no sorrow when his wife died. He obeyed and faithfully proclaimed God's word.

God may not ask you to do anything quite so dramatic or difficult; but if he did, would you do it?

The book of Ezekiel chronicles the prophet's life and ministry. Beginning with his call as a prophet and commissioning as a "watchman for Israel" (chapters 1—3), Ezekiel immediately began to preach and demonstrate God's truth, as he predicted the approaching siege and destruction of Jerusalem (chapters 4—24). This devastation would be God's judgment for the people's idolatry. Ezekiel challenged them to turn from their wicked ways. In the next section, he spoke to the surrounding nations, prophesying that God would judge them for their sins as well (chapters 25—32). The book concludes with a message of hope, as Ezekiel proclaimed the faithfulness of God and foretold the future blessings for God's people (chapters 33—48).

As you read this exciting record, observe how Ezekiel fearlessly preach the word of God to the exiled Jews in the streets of Babylon, and hear the timeless truth of God's love and power. Think about each person's responsibility to trust God and about the inevitability of God's judgment against idolatry, rebellion, and indifference. Then commit yourself to obey God, whatever, wherever, and whenever he asks.

VITAL STATISTICS

PURPOSE:
To announce God's judgment on Israel and other nations and to foretell the eventual salvation of God's people

AUTHOR:
Ezekiel son of Buzi, a Zadokite priest

TO WHOM WRITTEN:
The Jews in captivity in Babylonia and God's people everywhere

DATE WRITTEN:
Approximately 571 B.C.

SETTING:
Ezekiel was a younger contemporary of Jeremiah. While Jeremiah ministered to the people still in Judah, Ezekiel prophesied to those already exiled in Babylonia after the defeat of Jehoiachin. He was taken there in 597 B.C.

KEY VERSES:
"For I will gather you up from all the nations and bring you home again to your land. Then I will sprinkle clean water on you, and you will be clean. Your filth will be washed away, and you will no longer worship idols. And I will give you a new heart with new and right desires, and I will put a new spirit in you. I will take out your stony heart of sin and give you a new, obedient heart. (36:24–26).

KEY PEOPLE:
Ezekiel, Israel's leaders, Ezekiel's wife, Nebuchadnezzar, "the prince"

KEY PLACES:
Jerusalem, Babylon, and Egypt

THE BLUEPRINT

A. MESSAGES OF DOOM (1:1—24:27)
1. Ezekiel's call and commission
2. Visions of sin and judgment
3. Punishment is certain

While Jeremiah was prophesying in Jerusalem that the city would soon fall to the Babylonians, Ezekiel was giving the same message to the captives who were already in Babylon. Like those in Jerusalem, the captives stubbornly believed that Jerusalem would not fall and that they would soon return to their land. Ezekiel warned them that punishment was certain because of their sins and that God was purifying his people. God will always punish sin, whether we believe it or not.

B. MESSAGES AGAINST FOREIGN NATIONS (25:1—32:32)

Ezekiel condemns the sinful actions of seven nations. The people in these nations were saying that God was obviously too weak to defend his people and the city of Jerusalem. But God was allowing his people to be defeated in order to punish them for their sins. These pagan nations, however, would face a similar fate, and then they would know that God is all-powerful. Those who dare to mock God today will also face a terrible fate.

C. MESSAGES OF HOPE (33:1—48:35)
1. Restoring the people of God
2. Restoring the worship of God

After the fall of Jerusalem, Ezekiel delivered messages of future restoration and hope for the people. God is holy, but Jerusalem and the Temple had become defiled. The nation had to be cleansed through 70 years of captivity. Ezekiel gives a vivid picture of the unchangeable holiness of God. We, too, must gain a vision of the glory of God, a fresh sense of his greatness, as we face the struggles of daily life.

MEGATHEMES

THEME	EXPLANATION	IMPORTANCE
God's Holiness	Ezekiel saw a vision that revealed God's absolute moral perfection. God was spiritually and morally superior to members of Israel's corrupt and compromising society. Ezekiel wrote to let the people know that God in his holiness was also present in Babylon, not just in Jerusalem.	Because God is morally perfect, he can help us live above our tendency to compromise with this world. When we focus on his greatness, he gives us the power to overcome sin and to reflect his holiness.
Sin	Israel had sinned, and God's punishment came. The fall of Jerusalem and the Babylonian exile were used by God to correct the rebels and draw them back from their sinful way of life. Ezekiel warned them that not only was the nation responsible for sin but each individual was also accountable to God.	We cannot excuse ourselves from our responsibilities before God. We are accountable to God for our choices. Rather than neglect him, we must recognize sin for what it is—rebellion against God—and choose to follow him instead.
Restoration	Ezekiel consoles the people by telling them that the day will come when God will restore those who turn from sin. God will be their King and shepherd. He will give his people a new heart to worship him, and he will establish a new government and a new Temple.	The certainty of future restoration encourages believers in times of trial. But we must be faithful to God because we love him, not merely for what he can do for us. Is our faith in *him* or merely in our future benefits?
Leaders	Ezekiel condemned the shepherds (unfaithful priests and leaders), who led the people astray. By contrast, he served as a caring shepherd and a faithful watchman to warn the people about their sin. One day God's perfect shepherd, the Messiah, will lead his people.	Jesus is our perfect leader. If we truly want him to lead us, our devotion must be more than talk. If we are given the responsibility of leading others, we must take care of them even if it means sacrificing personal pleasure, happiness, time, or money. We are responsible for those we lead.
Worship	An angel gave Ezekiel a vision of the Temple in great detail. God's holy presence had departed from Israel and the Temple because of sin. The building of a future Temple portrays the return of God's glory and presence. God will cleanse his people and restore true worship.	All of God's promises will be fulfilled under the rule of the Messiah. The faithful followers will be restored to perfect fellowship with God and with one another. To be prepared for this time, we must focus on God. We do this through regular worship. Through worship we learn about God's holiness and the changes we must make in how we live.

A. MESSAGES OF DOOM (1:1—24:27)

Ezekiel prophesied to the exiles in Babylon. He had to dispel the false hope that Israel's captivity would be short, explain the reasons for the severe judgments on their nation, and bring a message of future hope. Although the people did not respond positively, they heard the messages and knew the truth. God's people were not left without explanation and direction, and neither are we.

1. Ezekiel's call and commission

A Vision of Living Beings

1:1 Ezek 3:23; 40:2; Dan 8:1-2; Rev 4:1; 19:11
1:2 2 Kgs 24:12
1:4 Isa 21:1; Jer 23:19
1:5 Rev 4:6-8
1:6 Ezek 10:14, 21
1:7 Dan 10:6; Rev 1:15; 2:18

1 On July 31* of my thirtieth year,* while I was with the Judean exiles beside the
Kebar River in Babylon, the heavens were opened to me, and I saw visions of God.
2 This happened during the fifth year of King Jehoiachin's captivity. 3 The LORD gave a
message to me, Ezekiel son of Buzi, a priest, there beside the Kebar River in the land of
the Babylonians,* and I felt the hand of the LORD take hold of me.
4 As I looked, I saw a great storm coming toward me from the north, driving before it
a huge cloud that flashed with lightning and shone with brilliant light. The fire inside the
cloud glowed like gleaming amber. 5 From the center of the cloud came four living beings
that looked human, 6 except that each had four faces and two pairs of wings. 7 Their legs
were straight like human legs, but their feet were split like calves' feet and shone like

1:1a Hebrew *On the fifth day of the fourth month,* of the Hebrew calendar. A number of dates in Ezekiel can be cross-checked with dates in surviving Babylonian records and related accurately to our modern calendar. This event occurred on July 31, 593 B.C. **1:1b** Or *in the thirtieth year.* **1:3** Or *Chaldeans.*

EZEKIEL served as a prophet to the exiles in Babylon from 593–571 B.C.

Climate of the times	Ezekiel and his people are taken to Babylon as captives. The Jews become foreigners in a strange land ruled by an authoritarian government.
Main message	Because of the people's sins, God allowed the nation of Judah to be destroyed. But there was still hope—God promised to restore the land to those who remained faithful to him.
Importance of message	God never forgets those who faithfully seek to obey him. They have a glorious future ahead.
Contemporary prophets	Daniel (605–536 B.C.), Habakkuk (612–588 B.C.), Jeremiah (627–586 B.C.)

1:1 Ezekiel, born and raised in the land of Judah, was preparing to become a priest in God's Temple when the Babylonians attacked in 597 B.C. and carried him away along with 10,000 other captives (2 Kings 24:10-14). The nation was on the brink of complete destruction. Five years later, when Ezekiel was 30 (the normal age for becoming a priest), God called him to be a prophet. During the first six years when Ezekiel ministered in Babylonia (1:3), Jeremiah was preaching to the Jews still in Judah, and Daniel was serving in Nebuchadnezzar's court. The Kebar River connected to the Euphrates in Babylonia and was the location of a Jewish settlement of exiles.

1:1 Why did the Jewish exiles in Babylonia need a prophet? God wanted Ezekiel to (1) help the exiles understand why they had been taken captive, (2) dispel the false hope that the captivity was going to be short, (3) bring a new message of hope, and (4) call the people to a new awareness of their dependence upon God.

1:1 God communicated to Ezekiel in visions. A vision is a miraculous revelation of God's truth. These visions seem strange to us because they are *apocalyptic.* This means that Ezekiel saw symbolic pictures that vividly conveyed an idea. Daniel and John were other Bible writers who used apocalyptic imagery. The people in exile had lost their perspective of God's purpose and presence, and Ezekiel came to them with a vision from God to show God's awesome glory and holiness and to warn the exiles of sin's consequences before it was too late.

1:1ff Ezekiel's latest dated message from God (29:17) was given in 571 B.C. He was taken captive during the second Babylonian invasion of Judah in 597 B.C. The Babylonians invaded Judah a third and final time in 586 B.C., completely destroying Jerusalem, burning the Temple, and deporting the rest of the people (see 2 Kings 25). Ezekiel dates all his messages from the year he was taken captive (597). His first prophecy to the exiles occurred four years after he arrived in the land of Babylon (593 B.C.).

1:3 The name *Ezekiel* means "God is strong" or "God strengthens." In a very real sense, this sums up the basic message of the book: that in spite of the captivity, God's sovereign strength prevails, and he will judge his enemies and restore his true people.

1:4ff In this first vision, God called Ezekiel to be a prophet (see 2:5). Nothing in Ezekiel's previous experience had prepared him for such a display of God's glorious presence and power. The huge cloud flashed with lightning and was surrounded by a brilliant light. From the fire in the cloud came four living beings. They showed Ezekiel that Jerusalem's coming destruction was God's punishment of Judah for its sins. (These living beings are also seen in Revelation 4:6, 7.)

When Ezekiel received this vision, he was far away from the Temple in Jerusalem, the physical symbol of God's presence. Through this vision, he learned that God is present everywhere and that God's activities in heaven are shaping the events on earth.

1:5-12 Each of the four living beings had four faces, symbolizing God's perfect nature. Some believe that the lion represented strength; the ox, diligent service; the human, intelligence; and the eagle, divinity. Others see these as the most majestic of God's creatures and say that they therefore represent God's whole creation. The early church fathers saw a connection between these beings and the four Gospels: the lion with Matthew, presenting Christ as the Lion of Judah; the ox with Mark, portraying Christ as the Servant; the human with Luke, portraying Christ as the perfect human; the eagle with John, portraying Christ as the Son of God, exalted and divine. The vision of John in Revelation 4 parallels Ezekiel's vision.

burnished bronze. 8Beneath each of their wings I could see human hands. 9The wings
of each living being touched the wings of the two beings beside it. The living beings were
able to fly in any direction without turning around. 10Each had a human face in the front,
the face of a lion on the right side, the face of an ox on the left side, and the face of an
eagle at the back. 11Each had two pairs of outstretched wings—one pair stretched out to
touch the wings of the living beings on either side of it, and the other pair covered its
body. 12They went in whatever direction the spirit chose, and they moved straight
forward in all directions without having to turn around.
13The living beings looked like bright coals of fire or brilliant torches, and it looked
as though lightning was flashing back and forth among them. 14And the living beings
darted to and fro like flashes of lightning.
15As I looked at these beings, I saw four wheels on the ground beneath them, one wheel
belonging to each. 16The wheels sparkled as if made of chrysolite. All four wheels looked
the same; each wheel had a second wheel turning crosswise within it. 17The beings could
move forward in any of the four directions they faced, without turning as they moved.
18The rims of the four wheels were awesomely tall, and they were covered with eyes all
around the edges. 19When the four living beings moved, the wheels moved with them.
When they flew upward, the wheels went up, too. 20The spirit of the four living beings
was in the wheels. So wherever the spirit went, the wheels and the living beings went, too.
21When the living beings moved, the wheels moved. When the living beings stopped, the
wheels stopped. When the living beings flew into the air, the wheels rose up. For the spirit
of the living beings was in the wheels.
22There was a surface spread out above them like the sky. It sparkled like crystal.
23Beneath this surface the wings of each living being stretched out to touch the others'
wings, and each had two wings covering its body. 24As they flew their wings roared like
waves crashing against the shore, or like the voice of the Almighty,* or like the shouting
of a mighty army. When they stopped, they let down their wings. 25As they stood with
their wings lowered, a voice spoke from beyond the crystal surface above them.
26Above the surface over their heads was what looked like a throne made of blue
sapphire. And high above this throne was a figure whose appearance was like that of a
man. 27From his waist up, he looked like gleaming amber, flickering like a fire. And from
his waist down, he looked like a burning flame, shining with splendor. 28All around him
was a glowing halo, like a rainbow shining through the clouds. This was the way the glory
of the LORD appeared to me. When I saw it, I fell face down in the dust, and I heard
someone's voice speaking to me.

1:24 Hebrew *Shaddai.*

1:8 Ezek 10:8, 21
1:9 Ezek 10:22
1:10 Ezek 10:14; Rev 4:7
1:11 Isa 6:2; Ezek 10:16, 19
1:12 Ezek 1:9, 20
1:13 Ps 104:4; Rev 4:5
1:14 Matt 24:27
1:16 Ezek 10:9-13
1:17 Ezek 1:12
1:18 Ezek 10:9-13; Rev 4:6, 8
1:19 Ezek 10:16-17, 19
1:21 Ezek 10:17
1:22 Ezek 10:1
1:24 2 Kgs 7:6; Ezek 10:5; 43:2; Dan 10:6; Rev 1:15; 19:6
1:26 Exod 24:10; Isa 6:1; 54:11; Ezek 10:1; 24:10; 43:6; Rev 1:13
1:27 Ezek 3:23
1:28 Rev 1:17; 4:3; 10:1

EXILE IN BABYLON Ezekiel worked for God right where he was—among the exiles in various colonies near the Kebar River in Babylonia. Jerusalem and its Temple lay over 500 miles away, but Ezekiel helped the people understand that, although they were far from home, they did not need to be far from God.

1:16-18 Ezekiel described two wheels at right angles to each other, one on a north-south and the other on an east-west axis. Able to move anywhere, these wheels show that God is present everywhere and is able to see all things (1:18). God is not restricted to Jerusalem but rules all of life and history. Though the exiles had experienced great change, God was still in control.

1:26 This figure "like that of a man" revealed God's holiness and prepared Ezekiel for what God was about to tell him. The figure represented God himself on the throne. In a similar way, Christ revealed God in human form and prepared us for his message of salvation. Christ came into history in a real, human body.

1:27, 28 The glory of the Lord appeared like fire and a glowing halo or rainbow to Ezekiel. Ezekiel fell face down, overwhelmed by the contrast between God's holiness and his own sinfulness and insignificance. Eventually every person will fall before God, either out of reverence and awe for his mercy or out of fear of his judgment. Based on the way you are living today, how will you respond to God's holiness?

1:27, 28 The four living beings and the four wheels are powerful pictures of judgment, yet the rainbow over the throne symbolizes God's never-ending faithfulness to his people. Just as God sent a rainbow to Noah to symbolize his promise never again to destroy the earth by a flood (Genesis 9:8-17), so this rainbow symbolizes God's promise to preserve those who remain faithful to him. The purpose of God's judgment is to correct us and, ultimately, to allow perfect peace and righteousness to reign on the earth forever.

2:2 Dan 8:18
2:3 1 Sam 8:7-8; Jer 3:25; Dan 9:5-13
2:4 Isa 48:4; Jer 5:3
2:5 Matt 10:12-15; Luke 10:10-11; John 15:22
2:6 Isa 51:12; Jer 1:8; Mic 7:4
2:8 Jer 15:16; Rev 10:9
2:9 Jer 36:2; Rev 5:1-5; 10:8-11

Ezekiel's Call and Commission

2 “Stand up, son of man,” said the voice. “I want to speak with you.” 2The Spirit came
into me as he spoke and set me on my feet. I listened carefully to his words. 3“Son of
man,” he said, “I am sending you to the nation of Israel, a nation that is rebelling against
me. Their ancestors have rebelled against me from the beginning, and they are still in revolt
to this very day. 4They are a hard-hearted and stubborn people. But I am sending you to say
to them, ‘This is what the Sovereign LORD says!’ 5And whether they listen or not—for
remember, they are rebels—at least they will know they have had a prophet among them.
6“Son of man, do not fear them. Don't be afraid even though their threats are sharp as
thorns and barbed like briers, and they sting like scorpions. Do not be dismayed by their
dark scowls. For remember, they are rebels! 7You must give them my messages whether
they listen or not. But they won't listen, for they are completely rebellious! 8Son of man,
listen to what I say to you. Do not join them in being a rebel. Open your mouth, and eat
what I give you.”
9Then I looked and saw a hand reaching out to me, and it held a scroll. 10He unrolled
it, and I saw that both sides were covered with funeral songs, other words of sorrow, and
pronouncements of doom.

3:2 Jer 25:17
3:3 Jer 6:11; 15:16; Rev 10:9-10
3:5 Jon 1:2; 3:2-4; Acts 26:17-18
3:7 John 15:20
3:8 Jer 1:18
3:10 Job 22:22

3 The voice said to me, “Son of man, eat what I am giving you—eat this scroll! Then
go and give its message to the people of Israel.” 2So I opened my mouth, and he fed
me the scroll. 3“Eat it all,” he said. And when I ate it, it tasted as sweet as honey.
4Then he said, “Son of man, go to the people of Israel with my messages. 5I am not
sending you to some foreign people whose language you cannot understand. 6No, I am
not sending you to people with strange and difficult speech. If I did, they would listen!
7I am sending you to the people of Israel, but they won't listen to you any more than they
listen to me! For the whole lot of them are hard-hearted and stubborn. 8But look, I have
made you as hard and stubborn as they are. 9I have made you as hard as rock! So don't
be afraid of them or fear their angry looks, even though they are such rebels.”
10Then he added, “Son of man, let all my words sink deep into your own heart first.
Listen to them carefully for yourself. 11Then go to your people in exile and say to them,
‘This is what the Sovereign LORD says!’ Do this whether they listen to you or not.”

2:1 The immortal God addressed Ezekiel by calling him “son of man,” emphasizing the distance between them. It is amazing that God chooses to work his divine will on earth through finite, imperfect beings. We are made from the dust of the ground, yet God chooses to place within us his life and breath and to ask us to serve him.

2:2 We can only imagine what it was like for Ezekiel to experience this vision. Certainly there was much he did not understand, but Ezekiel knew that each part had significance because it came from God. When God saw Ezekiel's open and obedient attitude, he filled him with his Spirit and gave him power for the job ahead. God doesn't expect us to understand everything about him, but to be willing and obedient servants, faithful to what we know is true and right.

2:3-5 The world of business defines success in terms of giving customers what they want. Ezekiel, however, was called to give God's message to the people, whether they would listen or not. The measure of Ezekiel's success would not be how well the people responded, but how well he obeyed God and thus fulfilled God's purpose for him. Isaiah and Jeremiah also prophesied with little positive response (see Isaiah 6:9-12; Jeremiah 1:17-19). God's truth does not depend on how people respond. God will not judge us for how well others respond to our faith but for how faithful we have been. God always gives us the strength to accomplish what he asks us to do.

2:4, 5 God called the people “hard-hearted and stubborn” because they refused to admit their sin. Rebelliousness was the nation's primary characteristic at this time. Even when God pointed out their wrongdoing, the people ignored the truth. Is God pointing at some sin in your life? Don't be stubborn—confess your sin and begin to live for God. By obeying him now you will be ready for God's final review of your life (Matthew 25:31-46).

2:6-8 God gave Ezekiel the difficult responsibility of presenting his message to ungrateful and abusive people. Sometimes we must be an example to or share our faith with unkind people. The Lord told Ezekiel not to be afraid, but to speak his words, whether or not the people would listen. He also wants us to tell the Good News, whether it's convenient or not (2 Timothy 4:2).

2:6-10 Three times God told Ezekiel not to be afraid or dismayed. When God's Spirit is within us, we can lay aside our fears of rejection or ridicule. God's strength is powerful enough to help us live for him even under the heaviest criticism.

2:9, 10 Ancient books were usually scrolls, one page (up to 30 feet long) rolled up simultaneously from both ends. Normally, scrolls had writing on only one side. But in this case, the warnings overflowed to the scroll's other side, showing the full measure of judgment about to descend on Judah.

3:1-3 In his vision, Ezekiel ate God's message and found this spiritual food not only good for him but also sweet as honey (see Revelation 10:8-10 for a similar use of this image). If you “digest” God's Word, you will find that not only does it make you stronger in your faith, but its wisdom also sweetens your life. You need to feed yourself spiritually just as you do physically. This means doing more than simply giving God's Word a casual glance. You must make digesting God's Word a regular part of your life.

3:10, 11 Ezekiel needed to take God's words to heart before preaching them to others. God's message must sink deep into your heart and show in your actions before you can effectively help others understand and apply the gospel.

12 Then the Spirit lifted me up, and I heard a loud rumbling sound behind me. (May the glory of the LORD be praised in his place!)* 13 It was the sound of the wings of the living beings as they brushed against each other and the rumbling of their wheels beneath them.

14 The Spirit lifted me up and took me away. I went in bitterness and turmoil, but the LORD's hold on me was strong. 15 Then I came to the colony of Judean exiles in Tel-abib, beside the Kebar River. I sat there among them for seven days, overwhelmed.

A Watchman for Israel

16 At the end of the seven days, the LORD gave me a message. He said, 17 "Son of man, I have appointed you as a watchman for Israel. Whenever you receive a message from me, pass it on to the people immediately. 18 If I warn the wicked, saying, 'You are under the penalty of death,' but you fail to deliver the warning, they will die in their sins. And I will hold you responsible, demanding your blood for theirs. 19 If you warn them and they keep on sinning and refuse to repent, they will die in their sins. But you will have saved your life because you did what you were told to do. 20 If good people turn bad and don't listen to my warning, they will die. If you did not warn them of the consequences, then they will die in their sins. Their previous good deeds won't help them, and I will hold you responsible, demanding your blood for theirs. 21 But if you warn them and they repent, they will live, and you will have saved your own life, too."

22 Then the LORD took hold of me, and he said to me, "Go out into the valley, and I will talk to you there." 23 So I got up and went, and there I saw the glory of the LORD, just as I had seen it in my first vision by the Kebar River. And I fell face down in the dust.

24 Then the Spirit came into me and set me on my feet. He talked to me and said, "Go, shut yourself up in your house. 25 There you will be bound with ropes so you cannot go out among the people. 26 And I will make your tongue stick to the roof of your mouth so you won't be able to pray for them, for they are rebellious. 27 But whenever I give you a message, I will loosen your tongue and let you speak. Then you will say to them, 'This is what the Sovereign LORD says!' Some of them will listen, but some will ignore you, for they are rebels.

3:12 Ezek 8:3; Acts 2:2; 8:39
3:13 2 Sam 5:24; Ezek 1:15, 24; 10:5, 16-17
3:14 Ezek 8:1
3:17 Isa 52:8; 58:1; 62:6; Jer 6:17; Ezek 33:7-9
3:18 Ezek 33:6, 8
3:19 2 Kgs 17:13-14; Ezek 33:3, 9; Acts 18:6
3:20 Jer 6:21; Ezek 18:24; 33:18; Zeph 1:6
3:21 Acts 20:31
3:22 Acts 9:6
3:23 Ezek 1:1, 28; Acts 7:55
3:24 Ezek 2:2
3:25 Ezek 4:8
3:26 Luke 1:20, 22
3:27 Ezek 33:22

3:12 A likely reading for this verse is *Then the Spirit lifted me up, and as the glory of the LORD rose from its place, I heard behind me a loud rumbling sound.*

3:14, 15 Ezekiel was bitter and angry, not at God, but at the sins and attitudes of the people. Ezekiel's extraordinary vision had ended, and he had to begin the tedious job of prophesying among his people, who cared little about God's messages. Before the Exile, the people had heard Jeremiah, but they would not listen. Here Ezekiel had to give a similar message, and he expected to be rejected as well. But Ezekiel had the vision of the four living beings and the wheels to back up his message. He had nothing to fear because God was with him. Despite knowing the probable outcome, Ezekiel obeyed God.

As we grow, we will have times of great joy when we feel close to God and times when sins, struggles, or everyday tasks overwhelm us. Like Ezekiel, we should obey God even when we don't feel like it. Don't let feelings hinder your obedience.

3:15 Ezekiel sat quietly among the people for seven days. This was the customary period of mourning for the dead (Genesis 50:10; 1 Samuel 31:13; Job 2:13). Ezekiel was mourning for those who were spiritually dead. Tel-abib was the location of one of the settlements of Jews who were exiled from Jerusalem.

3:17, 18 A watchman's job was to stand on the city wall and warn the people of approaching danger. Ezekiel's role was to be a spiritual watchman, warning the people of the judgment to come. Some think that "I will hold you responsible, demanding your blood for theirs" means that just as a watchman on the wall would pay with his life if he failed to warn the city of approaching enemies, Ezekiel would pay with his life if he refused to warn the people of coming judgment. Others believe this phrase simply means that God would hold Ezekiel accountable.

3:18-21 In these verses, God is not talking about loss of salvation but rather about physical death. If the people back in Judah continued in their sins, they and their land and cities would be destroyed by Nebuchadnezzar's armies. If, on the other hand, the people would turn to God, God would spare them. God would hold Ezekiel responsible for his fellow Jews if he failed to warn them of the consequences of their sins. All people are individually responsible to God, but believers have a special responsibility to warn unbelievers of the consequences of rejecting God. If we fail to do this, God will hold us responsible for what happens to them. This should motivate us to begin sharing our faith with others—in word and deed—and to avoid becoming callous or unconcerned in our attitude.

3:23 Ezekiel recognized his helplessness before God and fell face down in his presence. Sometimes our prosperity, popularity, or physical strength blinds us to our spiritual helplessness. But nothing we do on our own can accomplish much for God. Only when God is in control of our wills can we accomplish great tasks for him. The first step to being God's person is to admit that you need his help; then you can begin to see what God can really do in your life.

3:24-27 Ezekiel was allowed to speak only when God had a message for the people. Thus, the people knew that whatever Ezekiel said was God's message. They did not have to wonder whether Ezekiel was speaking by God's authority or his own.

2. Visions of sin and judgment

A Sign of the Coming Siege

4:1 Isa 20:2 Jer 13:1; 19:1
4:3 Isa 8:18; 20:3 Jer 39:1-2
4:4 Lev 10:17 Num 18:1

4 "And now, son of man, take a large brick and set it down in front of you. Then draw
a map of the city of Jerusalem on it. 2Build siege ramps against the city walls.
Surround it with enemy camps and battering rams. 3Then take an iron griddle and place
it between you and the city. Turn toward it and demonstrate how the enemy will attack
Jerusalem. This will be a warning to the people of Israel.
4"Now lie on your left side and place the sins of Israel on yourself. You are to bear

Although Ezekiel's visions and prophecies were clear and vivid, very little is known about the prophet's personal life. He was among the thousands of young men deported from Judah to Babylon when King Jehoiachin surrendered. Until those tragic days, Ezekiel was being trained for the priesthood. But during the exile in Babylon, God called Ezekiel to be his prophet during one of Israel's darkest times.

Ezekiel experienced the same kind of shocking encounter with God that Isaiah had reported 150 years earlier. Like Isaiah, Ezekiel was never the same after his personal encounter with God. Although God's messages through both these prophets had many points in common, the conditions under which they lived were very different. Isaiah warned of the coming storm; Ezekiel spoke in the midst of the storm of national defeat that devastated his people. He announced that even Jerusalem would not escape destruction. In addition, during this time Ezekiel had to endure the pain of his wife's death.

God's description of Ezekiel as a watchman on the walls of the city captures the personal nature of his ministry. A watchman's job was dangerous. If he failed at his post, he and the entire city might be destroyed. His own safety depended on the quality of his work. The importance of each person's accountability before God was a central part of Ezekiel's message. He taught the exiles that God expected personal obedience and worship from each of them.

As in Ezekiel's day, it is easy for us today to forget that God has a personal interest in each one of us. We may feel insignificant or out of control when we look at world events. But knowing that God is ultimately in control, that he cares, and that he is willing to be known by us can bring a new sense of purpose to our lives. How do you measure your worth? Are you valuable because of your achievements and potential or because God, your Creator and Designer, declares you valuable?

Strengths and accomplishments
- Was a priest by training, a prophet by God's call
- Received vivid visions and delivered powerful messages
- Served as God's messenger during Israel's captivity in Babylon
- Became a tough and courageous man so he could reach a hard and stubborn people (Ezekiel 3:8)

Lessons from his life
- Even the repeated failures of his people will not prevent God's plan for the world from being fulfilled
- Each person's response to God determines his or her eternal destiny
- God has people through whom he can work even in seemingly hopeless situations

Vital statistics
- Where: Babylon
- Occupation: Prophet to the captives in Babylon
- Relatives: Father: Buzi. Wife: Unknown
- Contemporaries: Jehoiachin, Jeremiah, Jehoiakim, Nebuchadnezzar

Key verses
"Then he added, 'Son of man, let all my words sink deep into your own heart first. Listen to them carefully for yourself. Then go to your people in exile and say to them, "This is what the Sovereign LORD says!" Do this whether they listen to you or not' " (Ezekiel 3:10, 11).

Ezekiel's story is told in the book of Ezekiel and 2 Kings 24:10-17.

4:1ff Ezekiel acted out the coming siege and fall of Jerusalem before it actually happened. God gave Ezekiel specific instructions about what to do and say and how to do and say it. Each detail had a specific meaning. Often we ignore or disregard the smaller details of God's Word, thinking God probably doesn't care. Like Ezekiel, we should want to obey God completely, even in the details.

4:4-17 Ezekiel's unusual actions symbolically portrayed the fate of Jerusalem. He lay on his left side for 390 days to show that Israel would be punished for 390 years; then he lay on his right side for 40 days to show that Judah would be punished for 40 years. Ezekiel was not allowed to move, symbolizing the fact that the people of Jerusalem would be imprisoned within the walls of the city. We know that Ezekiel did not have to lie on his side all day because these verses tell of other tasks God asked him to do during this time. The small amount of food he was allowed to eat represented the normal ration provided to those living in a city under siege by enemy armies. The food that was to be cooked over human dung was a symbol of Judah's spiritual uncleanness.

Certainly many people saw these spectacles and, in the process, heard Ezekiel's occasional speeches (3:27). How many of us would be willing to so dramatically portray the sins of our nation? We need to pray for greater boldness in our witness.

their sins for the number of days you lie there on your side. 5 You will bear Israel's sins
for 390 days—one day for each year of their sin. 6 After that, turn over and lie on your
right side for 40 days—one day for each year of Judah's sin.
7 "Meanwhile, continue your demonstration of the siege of Jerusalem. Lie there with
your arm bared and prophesy her destruction. 8 I will tie you up with ropes so you won't
be able to turn from side to side until the days of your siege have been completed.
9 "Now go and get some wheat, barley, beans, lentils, millet, and spelt, and mix them
together in a storage jar. Use this food to make bread for yourself during the 390 days
you will be lying on your side. 10 Ration this out to yourself, eight ounces* of food for
each day, and eat it at set times. 11 Then measure out a jar* of water for each day, and
drink it at set times. 12 Each day prepare your bread as you would barley cakes. While all
the people are watching, bake it over a fire using dried human dung as fuel and then eat
the bread. 13 For this is what the LORD says: Israel will eat defiled bread in the Gentile
lands, where I will banish them!"
14 Then I said, "O Sovereign LORD, must I be defiled by using human dung? For I have
never been defiled before. From the time I was a child until now I have never eaten any
animal that died of sickness or that I found dead. And I have never eaten any of the
animals that our laws forbid."
15 "All right," the LORD said. "You may bake your bread with cow dung instead of
human dung." 16 Then he told me, "Son of man, I will cause food to be very scarce in
Jerusalem. It will be weighed out with great care and eaten fearfully. The water will be
portioned out drop by drop, and the people will drink it with dismay. 17 Food and water
will be so scarce that the people will look at one another in terror, and they will waste
away under their punishment.

A Sign of the Coming Judgment

5 "Son of man, take a sharp sword and use it as a razor to shave your head and beard.
Use a scale to weigh the hair into three equal parts. 2 Place a third of it at the center
of your map of Jerusalem. After acting out the siege, burn it there. Scatter another third
across your map and slash at it with a sword. Scatter the last third to the wind, for I will
scatter my people with the sword. 3 Keep just a bit of the hair and tie it up in your robe.
4 Then take a few of these hairs out and throw them into the fire, burning them up. A fire
will then spread from this remnant and destroy all of Israel.
5 "This is what the Sovereign LORD says: This is an illustration of what will happen to
Jerusalem. I placed her at the center of the nations, 6 but she has rebelled against my
regulations and has been even more wicked than the surrounding nations. She has
refused to obey the laws I gave her to follow. 7 So this is what the Sovereign LORD says:
Since you have refused to obey my laws and regulations and have behaved even worse
than your neighbors, 8 I myself, the Sovereign LORD, am now your enemy. I will punish
you publicly while all the nations watch. 9 Because of your detestable idols, I will punish
you more severely than I have punished anyone before or ever will again. 10 Parents will
eat their own children, and children will eat their parents. And I will punish you by
scattering the few who survive to the far reaches of the earth.

4:10 Hebrew *20 shekels* [228 grams]. **4:11** Hebrew *1/6 of a hin,* about 1.3 pints or 0.6 liters.

4:5 Num 14:34
4:6 Dan 9:24-26; Rev 11:2-3
4:7 Ezek 21:2
4:8 Ezek 3:25
4:9 Exod 9:32; Isa 28:25
4:10 Ezek 45:12
4:12 Isa 36:12
4:13 Dan 1:8; Hos 9:3
4:14 Lev 17:15; 22:8; Deut 14:3-5; Isa 65:4; 66:17; Ezek 9:8; 20:49; Acts 10:14
4:16 Lev 26:26; Isa 3:1; Lam 5:4; Ezek 5:16; 12:18-19
4:17 Lev 26:39; Ezek 24:23; 33:10
5:1 Lev 21:5; Isa 7:20; Dan 5:27
5:2 Lev 26:33; Jer 39:1-2
5:3 Jer 39:10
5:4 Jer 41:12
5:5 Jer 6:6; Lam 1:1
5:8 Jer 24:9; Zech 14:2
5:9 Dan 9:12; Matt 24:21
5:10 Lev 26:29; Jer 19:9; Amos 9:9; Zech 2:6; 7:14

4:12-14 Ezekiel asked God not to make him use human dung for fuel because it violated the laws for purity (Leviticus 21–22; Deuteronomy 23:12-14). As a priest, Ezekiel would have been careful to keep all these laws. To use human dung for fuel would paint a dramatic picture of ruin. If nothing was left in the city that could be burned, it would be impossible to continue to follow God's laws for sacrifices.

5:1-10 Shaving one's head and beard signified mourning, humiliation, and repentance. God told Ezekiel to shave his head and beard and then to divide the hair into three parts, symbolizing what was going to happen to the people in Jerusalem (see 5:12). Along with verbal prophecies, God asked Ezekiel to use dramatic visual images to command the people's attention and to burn an indelible impression on their minds. Just as God gave Ezekiel creative ways to communicate his message to the exiles, we can creatively communicate the Good News about God to a lost generation.

5:3, 4 The few strands of hair Ezekiel put in his robe symbolized the small remnant of faithful people whom God would preserve. But even some from this remnant would be judged and destroyed because their faith was not genuine. Where will you stand in the coming judgment? Matthew 7:22, 23 warns that many who believe they will be saved won't be. Make sure your commitment to the Lord is genuine.

5:7 The people's wickedness was so great that they couldn't even be compared favorably with the pagan nations around them, not to mention how they would appear with respect to God's laws.

11“As surely as I live, says the Sovereign LORD, I will cut you off completely. I will
show you no pity at all because you have defiled my Temple with idols and vile practices.
12A third of your people will die in the city from famine and disease. A third of them will
be slaughtered by the enemy outside the city walls. And I will scatter a third to the winds
and chase them with my sword. 13Then at last my anger will be spent, and I will be
satisfied. And when my fury against them has subsided, all Israel will know that I, the
LORD, have spoken to them in my jealous anger.
14“So I will turn you into a ruin, a mockery in the eyes of the surrounding nations and
to everyone who travels by. 15You will become an object of mockery and taunting and
horror. You will be a warning to all the nations around you. They will see what happens
when the LORD turns against a nation in furious rebuke. I, the LORD, have spoken!
16“I will shower you with the deadly arrows of famine to destroy you. The famine will
become more and more severe until every crumb of food is gone. 17And along with the
famine, wild animals will attack you, robbing you of your children. Disease and war will
stalk your land, and I will bring the sword of the enemy against you. I, the LORD, have
spoken!”

5:11 Jer 7:9-11; Ezek 8:5-6, 16, 18
5:12 Jer 15:2; 44:27; Ezek 6:11-12; 12:14; Amos 9:9; Zech 2:6
5:13 Isa 1:24; 59:17; Lam 4:11; Ezek 36:6; 38:19
5:14 Pss 74:3-10; 79:1-4; Ezek 22:4
5:15 Isa 66:15-16; Jer 22:8-9; Ezek 25:17; 1 Cor 10:11
5:16 Deut 32:23-24

Judgment against Israel's Mountains

6 Again a message came to me from the LORD: 2“Son of man, look over toward the
mountains of Israel and prophesy against them. 3Give the mountains of Israel this
message from the Sovereign LORD. This is what the Sovereign LORD says to the
mountains and hills and to the ravines and valleys: I am about to bring war upon you,
and I will destroy your pagan shrines. 4All your altars will be demolished, and your
incense altars will be smashed. I will kill your people in front of your idols. 5I will lay
your corpses in front of your idols and scatter your bones around your altars. 6Wherever
you live there will be desolation. I will destroy your pagan shrines, your altars, your
idols, your incense altars, and all the other religious objects you have made. 7Then when
the place is littered with corpses, you will know that I am the LORD.

6:2 Ezek 36:1
6:3 Ezek 36:4
6:4 Lev 26:30; 2 Chr 14:5; Isa 27:9; Ezek 6:6
6:6 Zech 13:2

EZEKIEL'S ACTS OF OBEDIENCE

Reference	Act
2:1	Stood and received God's message
3:24–27	Shut himself inside his house
3:27	Faithfully proclaimed God's message
4:1ff	Drew the city of Jerusalem on a large brick (clay tablet)
4:4, 5	Lay on his left side for 390 days
4:6	Lay on his right side for 40 days
4:9–17	Followed specific cooking instructions
5:1–4	Shaved his head and beard
12:3–7	Left home to demonstrate exile
13:1ff	Spoke against false prophets
19:1ff	Sang a funeral song concerning the leaders
21:2	Prophesied against Israel and the Temple
21:19–23	Marked out two routes for Babylon's king
24:16, 17	Did not mourn his wife's death

5:11 It was a serious sin to defile the Temple, God's sanctuary, by worshiping idols and practicing evil within its very walls. In the New Testament, we learn that God now makes his home *within* those who are his. Our body is God's temple (see 1 Corinthians 6:19). We defile God's temple today by allowing gossiping, bitterness, love of money, lying, or any other wrong actions or attitudes to be a part of our life. By asking the Holy Spirit's help, we can keep from defiling his temple, our body.

5:13 Have you ever seen someone try to discipline a child by saying, “If you do that one more time . . .”? If the parent doesn't follow through, the child learns not to listen. Empty threats backfire. God was going to punish the Israelites for their blatant sins, and he wanted them to know that he would do what he said. The people learned the hard way that God always follows through on his word. Too many people ignore God's warnings, treating them as empty threats. Don't make the mistake of thinking God doesn't really mean what he says.

6:1ff This is the beginning of a two-part message. Remember that Ezekiel could speak only when giving messages from God. The message in chapter 6 is that Judah's idolatry will surely call down God's judgment. The message in chapter 7 describes the nature of that judgment—utter destruction of the nation. Nevertheless God in his mercy saved a remnant. Ezekiel prophesies against the mountains of Israel because mountains were sites of the pagan shrines used to worship idols.

8 “But I will let a few of my people escape destruction, and they will be scattered among the nations of the world. 9 Then when they are exiled among the nations, they will remember me. They will recognize how grieved I am by their unfaithful hearts and lustful eyes that long for other gods. Then at last they will hate themselves for all their wickedness. 10 They will know that I alone am the LORD and that I was serious when I predicted that all this would happen to them.

11 “This is what the Sovereign LORD says: Clap your hands in horror, and stamp your feet. Cry out, ‘Alas!’ because of all the evil that the people of Israel have done. Now they are going to die from war and famine and disease. 12 Disease will strike down those who are far away in exile. War will destroy those who are nearby. And anyone who survives will be killed by famine. So at last I will spend my fury on them. 13 When their dead lie scattered among their idols and altars, on every hill and mountain and under every green tree and great oak where they offered incense to their gods, then they will know that I alone am the LORD. 14 I will crush them and make their cities desolate from the wilderness in the south to Riblah* in the north. Then they will know that I am the LORD.”

The Coming of the End

7 Then this message came to me from the LORD: 2 “Son of man, this is what the Sovereign LORD says to Israel: The end is here! Wherever you look—east, west, north, or south—your land is finished. 3 No hope remains, for I will unleash my anger against you. I will call you to account for all your disgusting behavior. 4 I will turn my eyes away and show no pity, repaying you in full for all your evil. Then you will know that I am the LORD!

5 “This is what the Sovereign LORD says: With one blow after another I will bring total disaster! 6 The end has come! It has finally arrived! Your final doom is waiting! 7 O people of Israel, the day of your destruction is dawning. The time has come; the day of trouble is near. It will ring with shouts of anguish, not shouts of joy. 8 Soon I will pour out my fury to complete your punishment for all your disgusting behavior. 9 I will neither spare nor pity you. I will repay you for all your detestable practices. Then you will know that it is I, the LORD, who is striking the blow.

10 “The day of judgment is here; your destruction awaits! The people’s wickedness and pride have reached a climax. 11 Their violence will fall back on them as punishment for their wickedness. None of these proud and wicked people will survive. All their wealth will be swept away. 12 Yes, the time has come; the day is here! There is no reason for buyers to rejoice over the bargains they find or for sellers to grieve over their losses, for all of them will fall under my terrible anger. 13 And if any merchants should survive, they will never return to their business. For what God has said applies to everyone—it will not be changed! Not one person whose life is twisted by sin will recover.

6:14 As in some Hebrew manuscripts; most Hebrew manuscripts read *Diblah*.

6:8
Isa 6:13
Jer 44:14, 28

6:9
Deut 30:2
Job 42:6
Ps 78:40
Isa 7:13; 43:24
Hos 11:8

6:12
Lam 4:11-12
Dan 9:7

6:13
1 Kgs 14:23
2 Kgs 16:4
Isa 57:5-7
Hos 4:13

6:14
Isa 5:25
Ezek 14:13

7:2
Ezek 11:13
Amos 8:2, 10

7:4
Ezek 6:7; 11:21; 22:31
Hos 9:7

7:5
2 Kgs 21:12-13
Nah 1:9

7:7
Isa 22:5
Ezek 12:23-25, 28

7:8
Isa 42:25
Ezek 9:8; 14:19; 33:20; 36:19
Nah 1:6

7:10
Ps 89:32
Isa 10:5

7:12
Isa 5:13-14
Ezek 6:11-12
1 Cor 7:29-31
Jas 5:8-9

7:13
Lev 25:24-28, 31

6:8-10 A ray of light appears in this prophecy of darkness—God would spare a remnant of people, but only after they had learned some hard lessons. God sometimes has to break a person in order to bring him or her to true repentance. The people needed to change their attitudes, but they wouldn’t until God broke their hearts with humiliation, pain, suffering, and defeat. Does your heart long for God enough to change those areas displeasing him? Or will God have to break your heart?

6:11 Prophets often used this threefold description of judgment upon Jerusalem—war, famine, and disease—as a way of saying that the destruction would be complete. War meant death in battle; famine came when enemies besieged a city; disease was always a danger during famine. Don’t make the mistake of underestimating the extent of God’s judgment. If you ignore the biblical warnings and turn away from God, God’s punishment awaits you.

6:14 The phrase “then they will know that I am the LORD” (or a variation of this phrase) occurs 65 times in the book of Ezekiel. The purpose of all God’s punishment was not to take revenge but to impress upon the people the truth that the Lord is the only true and living God. People in Ezekiel’s day were worshiping man-made idols and calling them gods. Today money, sex, and power have become idols for many. Punishment will come upon all who put other things ahead of God. It is easy to forget that the Lord alone is God, the supreme authority and the only source of eternal love and life. Remember that God may use the difficulties of your life to teach you that he alone is God.

7:10, 11 In chapter 7, Ezekiel predicts the complete destruction of Judah. The wicked and proud will finally get what they deserve. If it seems as though God ignores the evil and proud people of our day, be assured that a day of judgment will come, just as it came for the people of Judah. God is waiting patiently for sinners to repent (see 2 Peter 3:9), but when his judgment comes, “none of these proud and wicked people will survive.” What you decide about God now will determine your fate then.

7:12, 13 The nation of Judah trusted in its prosperity and possessions instead of in God. So God planned to destroy the basis of its prosperity. Whenever we begin to trust in jobs, the economy, a political system, or military might for our security, we put God in the backseat.

The Desolation of Israel

14"The trumpets call Israel's army to mobilize, but no one listens, for my fury is against
them all. 15Any who leave the city walls will be killed by enemy swords. Those who stay
inside will die of famine and disease. 16The few who survive and escape to the mountains
will moan like doves, weeping for their sins. 17Everyone's hands will be feeble; their
knees will be as weak as water. 18They will dress themselves in sackcloth; horror and
shame will cover them. They will shave their heads in sorrow and remorse.

19"They will throw away their money, tossing it out like worthless trash. It won't buy
their deliverance in that day of the LORD's anger. It will neither satisfy nor feed them, for
their love of money made them stumble into sin. 20They were proud of their gold jewelry
and used it to make vile and detestable idols. That is why I will make all their wealth
disgusting to them. 21I will give it as plunder to foreigners from the most wicked of
nations, and they will defile it. 22I will hide my eyes as these robbers invade my treasured
land and corrupt it.

23"Prepare chains for my people, for the land is bloodied by terrible crimes. Jerusalem
is filled with violence. 24I will bring the most ruthless of nations to occupy their homes.
I will break down their proud fortresses and defile their sanctuaries. 25Terror and
trembling will overcome my people. They will look for peace but will not find it.
26Calamity will follow calamity; rumor will follow rumor. They will look in vain for a
vision from the prophets. They will receive no teaching from the priests and no counsel
from the leaders. 27The king and the prince will stand helpless, weeping in despair, and
the people's hands will tremble with fear. I will bring against them the evil they have
done to others, and they will receive the punishment they so richly deserve. Then they
will know that I am the LORD!"

Idolatry in the Temple

8 Then on September 17,* during the sixth year of King Jehoiachin's captivity, while
the leaders of Judah were in my home, the Sovereign LORD took hold of me. 2I saw
a figure that appeared to be a man. From the waist down he looked like a burning flame.
From the waist up he looked like gleaming amber. 3He put out what seemed to be a hand
and took me by the hair. Then the Spirit lifted me up into the sky and transported me in
a vision of God to Jerusalem. I was taken to the north gate of the inner courtyard of the
Temple, where there is a large idol that has made the LORD very angry. 4Suddenly, the
glory of the God of Israel was there, just as I had seen it before in the valley.

5Then the LORD said to me, "Son of man, look toward the north." So I looked, and
there to the north, beside the entrance to the gate of the altar, stood the idol that had made
the LORD so angry.

8:1 Hebrew *on the fifth day of the sixth month,* of the Hebrew calendar. This event occurred on September 17, 592 B.C.; also see note on 1:1.

7:14 Jer 4:5
7:15 Jer 14:18
7:16 Isa 38:14; 59:11; Nah 2:7
7:17 Isa 13:7; Heb 12:12
7:18 Isa 15:3; Amos 8:10
7:19 Prov 11:4; Isa 2:20; 30:22; Zeph 1:8
7:20 Jer 7:20
7:21 2 Kgs 24:13
7:22 Jer 18:17
7:23 Jer 27:4; Hos 4:2
7:24 2 Chr 7:20
7:26 Jer 4:20; 18:18; Mic 3:6
8:2 Ezek 1:4, 27-28
8:3 Ezek 3:12; 11:1; Dan 5:5
8:4 Ezek 1:27-28
8:5 Ps 78:58; Jer 3:2; 7:30; 32:34; Ezek 8:3; Zech 5:5

7:19 God's people had allowed their love of money to lead them into sin. And for this, God would destroy them. Money has a strange power to lead people into sin. Paul said that "the love of money is at the root of all kinds of evil" (1 Timothy 6:10). It is ironic that we use money—a gift of God—to buy things that separate us from him. It is tragic that we spend so much money seeking to satisfy ourselves and so little time seeking God, the true source of satisfaction.

7:20 God gave the people silver and gold, but they used that silver and gold to make idols. The resources God gives us should be used to do his work and carry out his will, but too often we use them to satisfy our own desires. When we abuse God's gifts or use resources selfishly, we miss the real purpose God had in mind. This is as shortsighted as idolatry.

7:24 The people of Jerusalem took great pride in their buildings. The Temple itself was a source of pride (see 24:20, 21). This pride would be crushed when the evil and godless Babylonians destroyed Jerusalem's fortresses and sanctuaries. If you are going through a humiliating experience, God may be using that experience to weed out pride in your life.

8:1ff This prophecy's date corresponds to 592 B.C. The message of chapters 8–11 is directed specifically toward Jerusalem and its leaders. Chapter 8 records Ezekiel being taken in a vision from Babylon to the Temple in Jerusalem to see the great wickedness being practiced there. The people and their religious leaders were thoroughly corrupt. While Ezekiel's first vision (chapters 1–3) showed that judgment was from God, this vision showed that their sin was the reason for judgment.

8:2 This person could have been an angel or a manifestation of God himself. In Ezekiel's previous vision, a man with a similar appearance was pictured as God on his throne (1:26-28).

8:3-5 This "idol that has made the LORD very angry" could be an image of Asherah, the Canaanite goddess of fertility, whose character encouraged sexual immorality and self-gratification. King Manasseh had placed such an idol in the Temple (2 Kings 21:7). King Josiah had burned the Asherah pole (2 Kings 23:6), but there were certainly many other idols around.

6"Son of man," he said, "do you see what they are doing? Do you see the great sins
the people of Israel are doing to drive me from my Temple? But come, and you will see
even greater sins than these!" 7Then he brought me to the door of the Temple courtyard,
where I could see an opening in the wall. 8He said to me, "Now, son of man, dig into the
wall." So I dug into the wall and uncovered a door to a hidden room.
9"Go in," he said, "and see the unspeakable wickedness going on in there!" 10So I
went in and saw the walls engraved with all kinds of snakes, lizards, and hideous
creatures. I also saw the various idols worshiped by the people of Israel. 11Seventy
leaders of Israel were standing there with Jaazaniah son of Shaphan in the middle. Each
of them held an incense burner, so there was a thick cloud of incense above their heads.
12Then the LORD said to me, "Son of man, have you seen what the leaders of Israel are
doing with their idols in dark rooms? They are saying, 'The LORD doesn't see us; he has
deserted our land!'" 13Then he added, "Come, and I will show you greater sins than these!"
14He brought me to the north gate of the LORD's Temple, and some women were sitting
there, weeping for the god Tammuz. 15"Have you seen this?" he asked. "But I will show
you even greater sins than these!"
16Then he brought me into the inner courtyard of the LORD's Temple. At the entrance,
between the foyer and the bronze altar, about twenty-five men were standing with their
backs to the LORD's Temple. They were facing eastward, worshiping the sun!
17"Have you seen this, son of man?" he asked. "Is it nothing to the people of Judah that
they commit these terrible sins, leading the whole nation into violence, thumbing their
noses at me, and rousing my fury against them? 18Therefore, I will deal with them in fury.
I will neither pity nor spare them. And though they scream for mercy, I will not listen."

The Slaughter of Idolaters

9 Then the LORD thundered, "Bring on the men appointed to punish the city! Tell them
to bring their weapons with them!" 2Six men soon appeared from the upper gate that
faces north, each carrying a battle club in his hand. One of them was dressed in linen and
carried a writer's case strapped to his side. They all went into the Temple courtyard and
stood beside the bronze altar.
3Then the glory of the God of Israel rose up from between the cherubim, where it had
rested, and moved to the entrance of the Temple. And the LORD called to the man dressed
in linen who was carrying the writer's case. 4He said to him, "Walk through the streets
of Jerusalem and put a mark on the foreheads of all those who weep and sigh because of
the sins they see around them."

8:6 2 Kgs 23:4-5; Ezek 5:11; 8:9, 17
8:8 Isa 29:15
8:10 Exod 20:4
8:11 Num 11:16, 25; 16:17, 35; Jer 19:1; Luke 10:1
8:14 Ezek 44:4; 46:9
8:16 Deut 4:19; 17:3; 2 Chr 29:6; Job 31:26-28; Jer 2:27; 44:17
8:17 Jer 7:18-19; Amos 3:10; Mic 2:2
8:18 Isa 1:15; Jer 11:11; Mic 3:4; Zech 7:13
9:2 Ezek 10:2
9:3 Ezek 10:4; 11:22-23
9:4 Exod 12:7, 13; Ps 119:53, 136; Jer 13:17; 2 Cor 1:22; 2 Tim 2:19; Rev 7:2-3

8:6ff In scene after scene, God revealed to Ezekiel the extent to which the people had embraced idolatry and wickedness. God's Spirit works within us in a similar way, revealing sin that lurks in our life. How comfortable would you feel if God held an open house in your life today?

8:14 Tammuz was the Babylonian god of spring. He was the husband or lover of the goddess Ishtar. The followers of this cult believed that the green vegetation shriveled and died in the hot summer because Tammuz had died and descended into the underworld. Thus, the worshipers wept and mourned his death. In the springtime, when the new vegetation appeared, they rejoiced, believing that Tammuz had come back to life. God was showing Ezekiel that many people were no longer worshiping the *true* God of life and vegetation. We must also be careful not to spend so much time thinking about the benefits of creation that we lose sight of the Creator.

9:1ff This chapter presents a picture of coming judgment. After Ezekiel had seen how corrupt Jerusalem had become, God called one man to spare the small minority that had been faithful. Then he called six men to slaughter the wicked people in the city. This judgment was ordered by God himself (9:5-7).

9:2 The writer's case was a common object in Ezekiel's day. It included a long narrow board with a groove to hold the reed brush that was used to write on parchment, papyrus, or dried clay. The board had hollowed out areas for holding cakes of black and red ink that had to be moistened before use.

9:3 What is God's glory? It is the manifestation of God's character—his ultimate power, transcendence, and moral perfection. God is completely above humans and their limitations. Yet God reveals himself to us so that we can worship and follow him.

9:3 Cherubim (*cherub* is singular) are an order of powerful angelic beings created to glorify God. They are associated with God's absolute holiness and moral perfection. God placed cherubim at the entrance of Eden to keep Adam and Eve out after they sinned (Genesis 3:24). Representations of cherubim were used to decorate the Tabernacle and Temple. The lid of the Ark of the Covenant, called the atonement cover, was adorned with two gold cherubim (Exodus 37:6-9). It was a symbol of the very presence of God. The cherubim seen by Ezekiel left the Temple along with the glory of God (chapter 10). Ezekiel then recognized them as the living beings he had seen in his first vision (see chapter 1).

9:4, 5 God told the man with the writer's case to put a mark on those who were faithful to God. Their faithfulness was determined by their sorrow over their nation's sin. Those with the mark were spared when the six men began to destroy the wicked people. During the Exodus, the Israelites put a mark of blood on their doorframes to save them from death. In the final days, God will mark the foreheads of those destined for salvation (Revelation 7:3), and Satan will mark his followers (Revelation 13:16, 17), who, like him, are destined for destruction. When God punishes sin, he won't forget his promise to preserve his people.

9:6 2 Chr 36:17 Ezek 5:11; 8:11-12 Rev 9:4
9:7 Ezek 7:20-22
9:8 1 Chr 21:16 Ezek 11:13 Amos 7:2-6
9:9 2 Kgs 21:16 Pss 10:11; 94:7 Isa 29:15 Ezek 7:23; 8:12; 22:2-3, 29 Mic 3:1-3; 7:3
9:10 Isa 65:6 Ezek 7:4; 8:18; 11:21; 24:14 Hos 9:7
10:1 Exod 24:10 Ezek 1:22, 26 Rev 4:2-3
10:2 Ps 18:10-13 Isa 6:6 Ezek 1:15-21; 10:13 Rev 8:5
10:3 Ezek 8:3, 16
10:4 Exod 40:34-35 Isa 6:1-4 Ezek 1:27-28; 9:3; 11:22-23
10:5 Job 40:9 Ezek 1:24 Rev 10:3
10:9 Ezek 1:16-17
10:11 Ezek 1:17
10:12 Ezek 1:18 Rev 4:6, 8
10:14 1 Kgs 7:27-30, 36 Ezek 1:6, 10; 10:21 Rev 4:7

[5]Then I heard the LORD say to the other men, "Follow him through the city and kill
everyone whose forehead is not marked. Show no mercy; have no pity! [6]Kill them
all—old and young, girls and women and little children. But do not touch anyone with
the mark. Begin your task right here at the Temple." So they began by killing the seventy
leaders. [7]"Defile the Temple!" the LORD commanded. "Fill its courtyards with the bodies
of those you kill! Go!" So they went throughout the city and did as they were told.

[8]While they were carrying out their orders, I was all alone. I fell face down in the dust
and cried out, "O Sovereign LORD! Will your fury against Jerusalem wipe out everyone
left in Israel?"

[9]Then he said to me, "The sins of the people of Israel and Judah are very great. The
entire land is full of murder; the city is filled with injustice. They are saying, 'The LORD
doesn't see it! The LORD has forsaken the land!' [10]So I will not spare them or have any
pity on them. I will fully repay them for all they have done."

[11]Then the man in linen clothing, who carried the writer's case, reported back and
said, "I have finished the work you gave me to do."

The LORD's Glory Leaves the Temple

10 As I looked, I saw what appeared to be a throne of blue sapphire above the crystal
surface over the heads of the cherubim. [2]Then the LORD spoke to the man in linen
clothing and said, "Go in between the whirling wheels beneath the cherubim, and take a
handful of glowing coals and scatter them over the city." He did this as I watched. [3]The
cherubim were standing at the south end of the Temple when the man went in, and the
cloud of glory filled the inner courtyard. [4]Then the glory of the LORD rose up from above
the cherubim and went over to the door of the Temple. The Temple was filled with this
cloud of glory, and the Temple courtyard glowed brightly with the glory of the LORD.
[5]The moving wings of the cherubim sounded like the voice of God Almighty and could
be heard clearly in the outer courtyard.

[6]The LORD said to the man in linen clothing, "Go between the cherubim and take some
burning coals from between the wheels." So the man went in and stood beside one of the
wheels. [7]Then one of the cherubim reached out his hand and took some live coals from
the fire burning among them. He put the coals into the hands of the man in linen clothing,
and the man took them and went out. [8](All the cherubim had what looked like human
hands hidden beneath their wings.)

[9]Each of the four cherubim had a wheel beside him, and the wheels sparkled like
chrysolite. [10]All four wheels looked the same; each wheel had a second wheel turning
crosswise within it. [11]The cherubim could move forward in any of the four directions
they faced, without turning as they moved. They went straight in the direction in which
their heads were turned, never turning aside. [12]Both the cherubim and the wheels were
covered with eyes. The cherubim had eyes all over their bodies, including their hands,
their backs, and their wings. [13]I heard someone refer to the wheels as "the whirling
wheels." [14]Each of the four cherubim had four faces—the first was the face of an ox,*

10:14 Hebrew *the face of a cherub;* compare 1:10.

9:6 The spiritual leaders of Israel blatantly promoted their idolatrous beliefs, and the people abandoned God and followed them. Spiritual leaders are especially accountable to God because they are entrusted with the task of teaching the truth (see James 3:1). When they pervert the truth, they can lead countless people away from God and even cause a nation to fall. It is not surprising, then, that when God began to judge the nation, he started at the Temple and worked outward (see 1 Peter 4:17). How sad it is that in the Temple, the one place where they should have been teaching God's truth, they were teaching lies.

9:9, 10 The people said that the Lord had forsaken the land and wouldn't see their sin. People have many convenient explanations to make it easier to sin: "It doesn't matter," "Everybody's doing it," or "Nobody will ever know." Do you find yourself making excuses for sin? Rationalizing sin makes it easier to commit, but rationalization does not convince God or cancel the punishment.

10:1ff Chapters 8–11 depict God's glory departing from the Temple. In 8:3, 4, his glory was over the north gate. It then moved to the entrance (9:3), then the south end of the Temple (10:3, 4), the east gate (10:18, 19; 11:1), and finally the mountain east of the Temple (11:23), probably the Mount of Olives. Because of the nation's sins, God's glory had departed.

10:2 God's perfect holiness demands judgment for sin. The cherubim are mighty angels. The glowing coals scattered over the city represent the purging of sin. For Jerusalem, this meant the destruction of all the people who blatantly sinned and refused to repent. Shortly after this prophecy, the Babylonians destroyed Jerusalem by fire (2 Kings 25:9; 2 Chronicles 36:19).

the second was a human face, the third was the face of a lion, and the fourth was the face
of an eagle.
15 Then the cherubim rose upward. These were the same living beings I had seen
beside the Kebar River. 16 When the cherubim moved, the wheels moved with them.
When they rose into the air, the wheels stayed beside them, going with them as they flew.
17 When the cherubim stood still, the wheels also stopped, for the spirit of the living
beings was in the wheels.
18 Then the glory of the LORD moved from the door of the Temple and hovered above
the cherubim. 19 And as I watched, the cherubim flew with their wheels to the east gate
of the LORD's Temple. And the glory of the God of Israel hovered above them.
20 These were the same living beings I had seen beneath the God of Israel when I was
by the Kebar River. I knew they were cherubim, 21 for each had four faces and four wings
and what looked like human hands under their wings. 22 Their faces, too, were just like
the faces of the beings I had seen at the Kebar, and they traveled straight ahead, just as
the others had.

Judgment on Israel's Leaders

11 Then the Spirit lifted me and brought me over to the east gateway of the LORD's
Temple, where I saw twenty-five prominent men of the city. Among them were
Jaazaniah son of Azzur and Pelatiah son of Benaiah, who were leaders among the
people.
2 Then the Spirit said to me, "Son of man, these are the men who are responsible for
the wicked counsel being given in this city. 3 They say to the people, 'Is it not a good
time to build houses? Our city is like an iron pot. Inside it we will be like meat—safe
from all harm.*' 4 Therefore, son of man, prophesy against them loudly and clearly."
5 Then the Spirit of the LORD came upon me, and he told me to say, "This is what the
LORD says to the people of Israel: Is that what you are saying? Yes, I know it is, for I
know every thought that comes into your minds. 6 You have murdered endlessly and
filled your streets with the dead.
7 "Therefore, this is what the Sovereign LORD says: This city is an iron pot, but the
victims of your injustice are the pieces of meat. And you are not safe, for I will soon drag
you from the city. 8 I will expose you to the war you so greatly fear, says the Sovereign
LORD. 9 I will drive you out of Jerusalem and hand you over to foreigners who will carry
out my judgments against you. 10 You will be slaughtered all the way to the borders of
Israel, and then you will know that I am the LORD. 11 No, this city will not be an iron pot
for you, and you will not be the meat, safe inside. I will judge you even to the borders of
Israel, 12 and you will know that I am the LORD. For you have refused to obey me; instead,
you have copied the sins of the nations around you."
13 While I was still speaking, Pelatiah son of Benaiah suddenly died. Then I fell face
down in the dust and cried out, "O Sovereign LORD, are you going to kill everyone in
Israel?"

11:3 Hebrew *This city is the pot, and we are the meat.*

10:15 Ezek 1:3-6, 19-21
10:17 Ezek 1:12
10:18 Ps 18:10
10:19 Ezek 1:22
10:20 Ezek 1:5, 26; 10:15
10:21 Ezek 1:6, 8; 10:14; 41:18-20
10:22 Ezek 1:10, 12
11:1 Ezek 8:3; 43:5
11:2 Isa 30:1 Mic 2:1
11:3 Jer 1:13 Ezek 24:3, 6 2 Pet 3:4
11:4 Ezek 3:4, 17
11:5 Jer 11:20; 17:10
11:6 Isa 1:15 Ezek 7:23; 22:2-6, 9, 12, 27 Matt 23:35
11:7 2 Kgs 25:18-22 Jer 52:24-27
11:9 Deut 28:36, 49-50 Ps 106:41
11:10 Num 34:8-9 Josh 13:5
11:12 Ezek 8:10, 14, 16; 18:8-9
11:13 Ezek 9:8

10:18 God's glory departed from the Temple and was never completely present again until Christ himself visited it in New Testament times. God's holiness required that he leave the Temple because the people had so defiled it. God had to completely destroy what people had perverted in order for true worship to be revived. We must commit ourselves, our families, our churches, and our nation to follow God faithfully so that we never have to experience God's abandoning us.

11:1-4 God had abandoned his altar and Temple (chapters 9–11); here his judgment was complete as his glory stopped above the mountain east of the city (11:23). The city gate was where merchants and politicians conducted business, so the 25 men may have represented the nation's rulers. Because of their leadership positions, they were responsible for leading the people astray. They had wrongly said that they were secure from another attack by the Babylonians. "Our city is like an iron pot. Inside it we will be like meat" means they believed that they were the elite, the influential, the ones who would be protected from all harm. However, without God our situation is always precarious.

11:5 God knew everything about the Israelites, even their thoughts. He also knows everything about us, even the sins we try to hide. Instead of worrying about people noticing how we look or what we do, we should care about what God thinks, for he sees everything. Trying to hide our thoughts and actions from God is futile. "Secret" sins are never secret from God. The only effective way to deal with our sins is to confess them and ask God to help us overcome them.

11:12 From the time they entered the Promised Land, the Israelites were warned not to copy the customs and religious practices of other nations. Disobeying this command and following pagan customs instead of God's laws always got them into trouble. Today, believers are still tempted to conform to the ways of the world. But we must get our standards of right and wrong from God, not from the popular trends of society.

11:15 Ezek 33:24
11:16 Jer 29:7, 11
11:17 Isa 11:11-16; Jer 24:5
11:18 Ezek 5:11; 37:23
11:19 Jer 24:7; 32:39; Ezek 36:26; Zech 7:12; 2 Cor 3:3
11:20 Ezek 36:27
11:21 Jer 16:18

Hope for Exiled Israel

14 Then this message came to me from the LORD: 15 "Son of man, the people still left in
Jerusalem are talking about their relatives in exile, saying, 'They are far away from the
LORD, so now he has given their land to us!' 16 Therefore, give the exiles this message
from the Sovereign LORD: Although I have scattered you in the countries of the world, I
will be a sanctuary to you during your time in exile. 17 I, the Sovereign LORD, will gather
you back from the nations where you are scattered, and I will give you the land of Israel
once again.

18 "When the people return to their homeland, they will remove every trace of their
detestable idol worship. 19 And I will give them singleness of heart and put a new spirit
within them. I will take away their hearts of stone and give them tender hearts* instead,
20 so they will obey my laws and regulations. Then they will truly be my people, and I
will be their God. 21 But as for those who long for idols, I will repay them fully for their
sins, says the Sovereign LORD."

11:22 Ezek 10:19
11:23 Ezek 8:4; Zech 14:4
11:24 Ezek 8:3; 37:1

The LORD's Glory Leaves Jerusalem

22 Then the cherubim lifted their wings and rose into the air with their wheels beside
them, and the glory of the God of Israel hovered above them. 23 Then the glory of the
LORD went up from the city and stopped above the mountain to the east.

24 Afterward the Spirit of God carried me back again to Babylonia,* to the Judeans in
exile there. And so ended the vision of my visit to Jerusalem. 25 And I told the exiles
everything the LORD had shown me.

3. Punishment is certain

Signs of the Coming Exile

12:2 Isa 6:9-10; Jer 5:21; Ezek 2:6-8; Matt 13:13-14; John 9:39-41
12:3 Jer 26:3; 36:3, 7; Luke 20:13; 2 Tim 2:25
12:4 2 Kgs 25:4; Jer 39:4; 52:7
12:6 Ezek 4:3; 24:24

12 Again a message came to me from the LORD: 2 "Son of man, you live among rebels
who could see the truth if they wanted to, but they don't want to. They could hear
me if they would listen, but they won't listen because they are rebellious. 3 So now put on a
demonstration to show them what it will be like to go off into exile. Pack whatever you can
carry on your back and leave your home to go on a journey. Make your preparations in broad
daylight so the people can see you, for perhaps they will even yet consider what this means,
even though they are such rebels. 4 Bring your baggage outside during the day so they can
watch you. Then as they are watching, leave your house in the evening, just as captives do
when they begin a long march to distant lands. 5 Dig a hole through the wall while they are
watching and carry your possessions out through it. 6 As they watch, lift your pack to your

11:19 Hebrew *hearts of flesh.* **11:24** Or *Chaldea.*

11:14ff God promised the exiles in Babylonia that he would continue to be with them even though they were not in Jerusalem. This was a major concern to the Jews because they believed that God was present primarily in the Temple. But God assured them that he would continue to be their God regardless of where they were. In the midst of Ezekiel's burning message of judgment stands a cool oasis—God's promise to restore the faithful few to their homeland. God's arms are now open to receive those who will repent of their sins.

11:15-21 God's messages through Ezekiel are full of irony. Here God says that the Jews in captivity are the faithful ones, and those in Jerusalem are the sinful and wicked ones. This was the opposite of the people's perception. Appearances can be deceiving. God will evaluate your life by your faith and obedience, not by your apparent earthly success. Furthermore, we should not judge others by outward appearances.

11:16 God was a sanctuary for the righteous remnant. Idolatrous people, even though they worshiped in the Jerusalem Temple (11:15), would find no true sanctuary; but the faithful exiles, even though they were far from home, would be protected by God. Likewise, our external circumstances do not truly indicate our standing with God. Those who appear safe and secure may be far from him, while those going through difficult times may be safely under God's protection. We can depend on God to keep us safe if we pledge ourselves to his care.

11:18, 19 "Singleness of heart" indicates a unanimous singleness of purpose. No longer will God's people seek many gods; they will be content with God. The hard, deaf, immovable heart of stone will be radically transplanted with a tender, receptive, and responsive heart of flesh (see Jeremiah 32:39; Ezekiel 18:31; 36:26). This new life can only be the work of the Holy Spirit. It is God's work, but we must recognize and turn from our sin. When we do, God will give us new motives, new guidelines, and new purpose. Have you received your new heart?

11:23 God's glory left Jerusalem and stopped above a mountain on the east side of the city—almost certainly the Mount of Olives. Ezekiel 43:1-4 implies that God will return the same way he left, when he comes back to earth to set up his perfect Kingdom.

12:1ff Ezekiel played the role of a captive being led away to exile, portraying what was about to happen to King Zedekiah and the people remaining in Jerusalem. The exiles knew exactly what Ezekiel was doing because only six years earlier they had made similar preparations as they left Jerusalem for Babylonia. This was to show the people that they should not trust the king or the capital city to save them from the Babylonian army—only God could do that. And the exiles who hoped for an early return from exile would be disappointed. Ezekiel's graphic demonstration was proven correct to the last detail. But when he warned them, many refused to listen.

shoulders and walk away into the night. Cover your face and don't look around. All of these
actions will be a sign for the people of Israel."
7So I did as I was told. In broad daylight I brought my pack outside, filled with the things
I might carry into exile. Then in the evening while the people looked on, I dug through the
wall with my hands and went out into the darkness with my pack on my shoulder.
8The next morning this message came to me from the LORD: 9"Son of man, these rebels,
the people of Israel, have asked you what all this means. 10Say to them, 'This is what the
Sovereign LORD says: These actions contain a message for Zedekiah in Jerusalem* and for
all the people of Israel.' 11Then explain that your actions are a demonstration of what will
soon happen to them, for they will be driven from their homes and sent away into exile.
12"Even Zedekiah will leave Jerusalem at night through a hole in the wall, taking only
what he can carry with him. He will cover his face, and his eyes will never see his homeland
again. 13Then I will spread out my net and capture him in my snare. I will bring him to
Babylon, the land of the Babylonians,* though he will never see it, and he will die there. 14I
will scatter his servants and guards to the four winds and send the sword after them. 15And
when I scatter them among the nations, they will know that I am the LORD. 16But I will spare
a few of them from death by war, famine, or disease, so they can confess to their captors
about how wicked they have been. Then they will know that I am the LORD!"
17Then this message came to me from the LORD: 18"Son of man, tremble as you eat
your food. Drink your water with fear, as if it were your last. 19Give the people this
message from the Sovereign LORD concerning those living in Israel and Jerusalem: They
will eat their food with trembling and sip their tiny portions of water in utter despair,
because their land will be stripped bare on account of their violence. 20The cities will be
destroyed and the farmland deserted. Then you will know that I am the LORD."

A New Proverb for Israel

21Again a message came to me from the LORD: 22"Son of man, what is that proverb they
quote in Israel: 'Time passes, making a liar of every prophet'? 23Give the people this
message from the Sovereign LORD: I will put an end to this proverb, and you will soon
stop quoting it. Now give them this new proverb to replace the old one: 'The time has
come for every prophecy to be fulfilled!'
24"Then you will see what becomes of all the false visions and misleading predictions
about peace in Israel. 25For I am the LORD! What I threaten always happens. There will
be no more delays, you rebels of Israel! I will fulfill my threat of destruction in your own
lifetime, says the Sovereign LORD."
26Then this message came to me from the LORD: 27"Son of man, the people of Israel
are saying, 'His visions won't come true for a long, long time.' 28Therefore, give them
this message from the Sovereign LORD: No more delay! I will now do everything I have
threatened! I, the Sovereign LORD, have spoken!"

Judgment against False Prophets

13 Then this message came to me from the LORD: 2"Son of man, speak against the false
prophets of Israel who are inventing their own prophecies. Tell them to listen to the
word of the LORD. 3This is what the Sovereign LORD says: Destruction is certain for the
false prophets who are following their own imaginations and have seen nothing at all!
4"O people of Israel, these prophets of yours are like jackals digging around in the ruins.

12:7 Ezek 24:18
12:9 Ezek 2:5-8; 17:12; 24:19
12:10 2 Kgs 9:25; Isa 13:1; Mal 1:1
12:11 Jer 15:2, 28-30
12:12 2 Kgs 25:4; Jer 39:4; 52:7
12:13 Isa 24:17; Jer 39:7; 52:11; Hos 7:12
12:16 Jer 22:8-9
12:19 Isa 6:11; Zech 7:14
12:20 Isa 7:23-24; Jer 25:9; Dan 9:17
12:22 Jer 5:12; Amos 6:3; 2 Pet 3:3-4
12:23 Joel 2:11; Zeph 1:14
12:24 Jer 14:13-16; Zech 13:2-4
12:25 Num 14:28-34; Hab 1:5
12:27 Dan 10:14
13:2 Isa 9:15; 56:9-12; Jer 37:19
13:3 Jer 23:28-32; Lam 2:14

12:10 Hebrew *the prince in Jerusalem;* also in 12:12. **12:13** Or *Chaldeans.*

12:10-12 Zedekiah, Judah's last king (597–586 B.C.), was reigning in Jerusalem when Ezekiel gave these messages from God. Ezekiel showed the people what would happen to Zedekiah. Jerusalem would be attacked again, and Zedekiah would join the exiles already in Babylon. Zedekiah would be unable to see because Nebuchadnezzar would have his eyes gouged out (2 Kings 25:3-7; Jeremiah 52:10, 11).

12:21-28 These two short messages were warnings that God's words would come true—*soon!* Less than six years later, Jerusalem would be destroyed. Yet the people were skeptical. Unbelief and false security led them to believe it would never happen. The apostle Peter dealt with this problem in the church (2 Peter 3:9). It is dangerous to say Christ will never return or to regard his coming as so far in the future as to be irrelevant today. All that God says is sure to happen. Don't dare assume that you have plenty of time to get right with God.

13:1ff This warning was directed against false prophets, whose messages were not from God but were lies intended to win popularity by saying whatever made the people happy. False prophets did not care about the truth as Ezekiel did. They lulled people into a false sense of security, making Ezekiel's job even more difficult. Beware of people who bend the truth in their quest for popularity and power.

5They have done nothing to strengthen the breaks in the walls around the nation. They have not helped it to stand firm in battle on the day of the LORD. 6Instead, they have lied and said, 'My message is from the LORD,' even though the LORD never sent them. And yet they expect him to fulfill their prophecies! 7Can your visions be anything but false if you claim, 'This message is from the LORD,' when I have not even spoken to you?

8"Therefore, this is what the Sovereign LORD says: Because what you say is false and your visions are a lie, I will stand against you, says the Sovereign LORD. 9I will raise my fist against all the lying prophets, and they will be banished from the community of Israel. I will blot their names from Israel's record books, and they will never again see their own land. Then you will know that I am the Sovereign LORD!

10"These evil prophets deceive my people by saying, 'All is peaceful!' when there is no peace at all! It's as if the people have built a flimsy wall, and these prophets are trying to hold it together by covering it with whitewash! 11Tell these whitewashers that their wall will soon fall down. A heavy rainstorm will undermine it; great hailstones and mighty winds will knock it down. 12And when the wall falls, the people will cry out, 'Where is the whitewash you applied?'

13"Therefore, this is what the Sovereign LORD says: I will sweep away your whitewashed wall with a storm of indignation, with a great flood of anger, and with hailstones of fury. 14I will break down your wall right to the foundation, and when it falls, it will crush you. Then you will know that I am the LORD! 15At last my anger against the wall and those who covered it with whitewash will be satisfied. Then I will say to you: 'The wall and those who whitewashed it are both gone. 16They were lying prophets who claimed peace would come to Jerusalem when there was no peace. I, the Sovereign LORD, have spoken!'

Judgment against False Women Prophets

17"Now, son of man, also speak out against the women who prophesy from their own imaginations. 18This is what the Sovereign LORD says: Destruction is certain for you women who are ensnaring the souls of my people, both young and old alike. You tie magic charms on their wrists and furnish them with magic veils. Do you think you can trap others without bringing destruction on yourselves? 19You turn my people away from me for a few handfuls of barley or a piece of bread. By lying to my people who love to listen to lies, you kill those who should not die, and you promise life to those who should not live.

20"And so the Sovereign LORD says: I am against all your magic charms, which you use to ensnare my people like birds. I will tear them from your arms, setting my people free like birds set free from a cage. 21I will tear off the magic veils and save my people from your grasp. They will no longer be your victims. Then you will know that I am the LORD. 22You have discouraged the righteous with your lies, when I didn't want them to suffer grief. And you have encouraged the wicked by promising them life, even though they continue in their sins. 23But you will no longer talk of seeing visions that you never saw, nor will you practice your magic. For I will rescue my people from your grasp. Then you will know that I am the LORD."

The Idolatry of Israel's Leaders

14 Then some of the leaders of Israel visited me, and while they were there, 2this message came to me from the LORD: 3"Son of man, these leaders have set up idols in their hearts. They have embraced things that lead them into sin. Why should I let them ask me anything? 4Give them this message from the Sovereign LORD: I, the LORD, will

13:5 Ps 106:23; Isa 58:12
13:6 Jer 28:15; 29:8
13:8 Nah 2:13
13:9 Ezra 2:59-63; Ps 69:28; Jer 20:3-6; Dan 12:1
13:10 Jer 8:11; 50:6
13:13 Exod 9:24-25; Ps 18:12-13; Rev 11:19; 16:21
13:14 Mic 1:6
13:16 Isa 57:21
13:17 Judg 4:4; 2 Kgs 22:14; Luke 2:36; Acts 21:9; Rev 2:20
13:18 2 Pet 2:14
13:19 Prov 28:21; Jer 23:14, 17; Mic 3:5
13:21 Pss 91:3; 124:7
13:22 Amos 5:12; 2 Pet 2:18-19
13:23 Mic 3:6; Zech 13:3
14:1 2 Kgs 6:32
14:4 1 Kgs 21:20-24; 2 Kgs 1:16

13:10-12 These false prophets covered their lies (a "flimsy wall") with "whitewash"—a pleasing front. Such superficiality can't hold up under God's scrutiny.

13:17 In the Bible, the gift of prophecy was given to women as well as men. Miriam (Exodus 15:20), Deborah (Judges 4:4), and Huldah (2 Kings 22:14) were prophets. But the women mentioned here are more like the witch of 1 Samuel 28:7, and they are condemned for discouraging the righteous (13:22).

13:18 These magic charms and veils were used in witchcraft practices as good luck charms, but they ensnared the people in idolatry.

14:3 God condemned the elders for setting up idols in their hearts and then daring to come to God's prophet for advice. On the outside, they appeared to worship God, making regular visits to the Temple to offer sacrifices. But they were not sincere. It is easy for us to criticize the Israelites for worshiping idols when they so clearly needed God instead. But we have idols in our hearts when we pursue reputation, acceptance, wealth, or sensual pleasure with the intensity and commitment that should be reserved for serving God.

14:3-5 For Hebrew writers, important functions of life were assigned to different physical organs. The heart was considered the core of a person's intellect and spirit. Because all people have someone or something as the object of their heart's

punish the people of Israel who set up idols in their hearts so they fall into sin and then come to a prophet asking for help. 5 I will do this to capture the minds and hearts of all my people who have turned from me to worship their detestable idols.

6 "Therefore, give the people of Israel this message from the Sovereign LORD: Repent and turn away from your idols, and stop all your loathsome practices. 7 I, the LORD, will punish all those, both Israelites and foreigners, who reject me and set up idols in their hearts so they fall into sin, and who then come to a prophet asking for my advice. 8 I will turn against such people and make a terrible example of them, destroying them. Then you will know that I am the LORD. 9 And if a prophet is deceived and gives a message anyway, it is because I, the LORD, have deceived that prophet. I will stand against such prophets and cut them off from the community of Israel. 10 False prophets and hypocrites—evil people who claim to want my advice—will all be punished for their sins. 11 In this way, the people of Israel will learn not to stray from me, polluting themselves with sin. They will be my people, and I will be their God, says the Sovereign LORD."

The Certainty of the LORD's Judgment

12 Then this message came to me from the LORD: 13 "Son of man, suppose the people of a country were to sin against me, and I lifted my fist to crush them, cutting off their food supply and sending a famine to destroy both people and animals alike. 14 Even if Noah, Daniel, and Job were there, their righteousness would save no one but themselves, declares the Sovereign LORD.

15 "Or suppose I were to send an invasion of dangerous wild animals to devastate the land and kill the people. 16 Even if these three men were there, the Sovereign LORD swears that it would do no good—it wouldn't save the people from destruction. Those three alone would be saved, but the land would be devastated.

17 "Or suppose I were to bring war against the land, and I told enemy armies to come and destroy everything. 18 Even if these three men were in the land, the Sovereign LORD swears that they could not save the people. They alone would be saved.

19 "Or suppose I were to pour out my fury by sending an epidemic of disease into the land, and the plague killed people and animals alike. 20 Even if Noah, Daniel, and Job were living there, the Sovereign LORD swears that they could not save the people. They alone would be saved by their righteousness.

21 "Now this is what the Sovereign LORD says: How terrible it will be when all four of these fearsome punishments fall upon Jerusalem—war, famine, beasts, and plague—destroying all her people and animals. 22 Yet there will be survivors, and they will come here to join you as exiles in Babylon. You will see with your own eyes how wicked they are, and then you will feel better about what I have done to Jerusalem. 23 When you meet them and see their behavior, you will agree that these things are not being done to Israel without cause, says the Sovereign LORD."

Jerusalem—a Useless Vine

15 Then this message came to me from the LORD: 2 "Son of man, how does a grapevine compare to a tree? Is a vine's wood as useful as the wood of a tree? 3 Can its wood be used for making things, like pegs to hang up pots and pans? 4 No, it can only

14:5 Jer 2:11; Hos 10:2; Zech 7:12
14:6 1 Sam 7:3; Neh 1:9; Isa 30:22; 55:6-7
14:7 Exod 12:48; 20:10
14:8 Isa 65:15
14:9 Jer 6:14-15
14:11 Ezek 11:20; 44:10, 15
14:13 Ezek 15:8; 20:27
14:14 Gen 6:8; Job 1:1, 5; Dan 10:11; Heb 11:7
14:16 Gen 19:29
14:17 Ezek 5:12; 21:3-4; 25:13; Zeph 1:3
14:19 Jer 14:12; Ezek 5:12
14:21 Amos 4:6-10; Rev 6:4-8
14:22 Ezek 36:20
14:23 Jer 22:8-9
15:2 John 15:1-6
15:4 Heb 6:8

devotion, they have the potential for idolatry within them. God wants to recapture the hearts of his people. We must never let anything captivate our allegiance or imagination in such a way that it replaces or weakens our devotion to God.

14:6-11 The people of Judah, although eager to accept the messages of false prophets, considered the presence of a few God-fearing men in the nation an insurance policy against disaster. In a pinch, they could always ask God's prophets for advice. We must remember that the relationship our pastor, family, or friends have with God will not protect us from the consequences of our own sins. Each person is responsible for his or her own relationship with God. Is your faith personal and real, or are you resting in what others have done?

14:14 Noah, Daniel, and Job were great men in Israel's history, renowned for their relationship with God and for their wisdom (see Genesis 6:8, 9; Daniel 2:47, 48; Job 1:1). Daniel had been taken into captivity during Babylon's first invasion of Judah in 605 B.C., eight years before Ezekiel was taken captive. At the time of Ezekiel's message, Daniel occupied a high government position in Babylon. But even these great men of God could not have saved the people of Judah because God had already passed judgment on the nation's pervasive evil.

15:1ff The messages given to Ezekiel in chapters 15–17 provided further evidence that God was going to destroy Jerusalem. The first message was about a vine, useless at first and even more useless after being burned. The people of Jerusalem were useless to God because of their idol worship, and so they would be destroyed and their cities burned. Isaiah also compared the nation of Israel to a vineyard (see Isaiah 5:1-7). Have you become apathetic and unfruitful to God? How can you begin fulfilling his plan for you?

be used for fuel, and even as fuel, it burns too quickly. 5Vine branches are useless both
before and after being put into the fire!
6"And this is what the Sovereign LORD says: The people of Jerusalem are like
grapevines growing among the trees of the forest. Since they are useless, I have set them
aside to be burned! 7And I will see to it that if they escape from one fire, they will fall
into another. When this happens, you will know that I am the LORD. 8And I will make
the land desolate because my people have been unfaithful to me, says the Sovereign
LORD."

Jerusalem—an Unfaithful Wife

16 Then another message came to me from the LORD: 2"Son of man, confront
Jerusalem with her loathsome sins. 3Give her this message from the Sovereign
LORD: You are nothing but a Canaanite! Your father was an Amorite and your mother a
Hittite! 4When you were born, no one cared about you. Your umbilical cord was left
uncut, and you were never washed, rubbed with salt, and dressed in warm clothing. 5No
one had the slightest interest in you; no one pitied you or cared for you. On the day you
were born, you were dumped in a field and left to die, unwanted.
6"But I came by and saw you there, helplessly kicking about in your own blood. As
you lay there, I said, 'Live!' 7And I helped you to thrive like a plant in the field. You grew
up and became a beautiful jewel. Your breasts became full, and your hair grew, though
you were still naked. 8And when I passed by and saw you again, you were old enough
to be married. So I wrapped my cloak around you to cover your nakedness and declared
my marriage vows. I made a covenant with you, says the Sovereign LORD, and you
became mine.
9"Then I bathed you and washed off your blood, and I rubbed fragrant oils into your
skin. 10I gave you expensive clothing of linen and silk, beautifully embroidered, and
sandals made of fine leather. 11I gave you lovely jewelry, bracelets, and beautiful
necklaces, 12a ring for your nose and earrings for your ears, and a lovely crown for your
head. 13And so you were made beautiful with gold and silver. Your clothes were made
of fine linen and were beautifully embroidered. You ate the finest foods—fine flour,
honey, and olive oil—and became more beautiful than ever. You looked like a queen, and
so you were! 14Your fame soon spread throughout the world on account of your beauty,
because the splendor I bestowed on you perfected your beauty, says the Sovereign LORD.
15"But you thought you could get along without me, so you trusted instead in your
fame and beauty. You gave yourself as a prostitute to every man who came along. Your
beauty was theirs for the asking! 16You used the lovely things I gave you to make shrines
for idols, where you carried out your acts of prostitution. Unbelievable! How could such
a thing ever happen? 17You took the very jewels and gold and silver ornaments I had
given you and made statues of men and worshiped them, which is adultery against me.
18You used the beautifully embroidered clothes I gave you to cover your idols. Then you
used my oil and incense to worship them. 19Imagine it! You set before them as a lovely
sacrifice the fine flour and oil and honey I had given you, says the Sovereign LORD.
20"Then you took your sons and daughters—the children you had borne to me—and
sacrificed them to your gods. Was it not enough that you should be a prostitute? 21Must

15:7 Lev 26:17; 1 Kgs 19:17; Isa 24:18; Amos 5:19; 9:1-4
16:2 Isa 58:1; Hos 8:1
16:4 Hos 2:3
16:5 Deut 32:10
16:7 Exod 1:7
16:8 Gen 22:16-18; Exod 19:5; 24:7-8; Ruth 3:9; Jer 2:2; Hos 2:18-20
16:11 Gen 24:22, 47; Isa 3:18-19
16:12 Jer 13:18
16:13 Deut 32:13-14; Ps 45:13-14
16:14 1 Kgs 10:1, 24; Ps 50:2; Lam 2:15
16:15 Isa 57:8; Jer 2:20; Ezek 27:3
16:19 Hos 2:8
16:20 Exod 13:2, 12; Ps 106:37-38; Jer 7:31
16:21 2 Kgs 17:17; Jer 19:5

16:1ff This message reminded Jerusalem of its former despised status among the Canaanite nations. Using the imagery of a young baby growing to mature womanhood, God reminded Jerusalem that he raised her from a lowly state to great glory as his bride. However, she betrayed God's trust and prostituted herself by seeking alliances with pagan nations and adopting their customs. If we push God aside for anything, even education, family, career, or pleasure, we are abandoning him in the same way.

16:3 *Canaan* was the name of the territory taken over by the children of Israel. The Bible often uses this name to refer to all the corrupt pagan nations of the region. The Amorites and Hittites, two Canaanite peoples, were known for their wickedness. But here God implies that his people are no better than the Canaanites.

16:15 God cared for and loved Judah, only to have it turn away to other nations and their false gods. The nation had grown to maturity and become famous, but the people forgot who had given them their life (16:22). This is a picture of spiritual adultery (called apostasy—turning from the one true God). As you become wise and more mature, don't turn away from the one who truly loves you.

16:20, 21 Child sacrifice had been practiced by the Canaanites long before Israel invaded their land. But it was strictly forbidden by God (Leviticus 20:1-3). By Ezekiel's time, however, the people were openly sacrificing their own children (2 Kings 16:3; 21:6). Jeremiah confirmed that this was a common practice (Jeremiah 7:31; 32:35). Because of such vile acts among the people and priesthood, the Temple became unfit for God to inhabit. When God left the Temple, he was no longer Judah's guide and protector.

you also slaughter my children by sacrificing them to idols? 22 In all your years of adultery and loathsome sin, you have not once thought of the days long ago when you lay naked in a field, kicking about in your own blood.

23 "Your destruction is certain, says the Sovereign LORD. In addition to all your other wickedness, 24 you built a pagan shrine and put altars to idols in every town square. 25 On every street corner you defiled your beauty, offering your body to every passerby in an endless stream of prostitution. 26 Then you added lustful Egypt to your lovers, fanning the flames of my anger with your increasing promiscuity. 27 That is why I struck you with my fist and reduced your boundaries. I handed you over to your enemies, the Philistines, and even they were shocked by your lewd conduct! 28 You have prostituted yourselves with the Assyrians, too. It seems you can never find enough new lovers! And after your prostitution there, you still were not satisfied. 29 You added to your lovers by embracing that great merchant land of Babylonia*—but you still weren't satisfied!

30 "What a sick heart you have, says the Sovereign LORD, to do such things as these, acting like a shameless prostitute. 31 You build your pagan shrines on every street corner and your altars to idols in every square. You have been worse than a prostitute, so eager for sin that you have not even demanded payment for your love! 32 Yes, you are an adulterous wife who takes in strangers instead of her own husband. 33 Prostitutes charge for their services—but not you! You give gifts to your lovers, bribing them to come to you. 34 So you are the opposite of other prostitutes. No one pays you; instead, you pay them!

Judgment on Jerusalem's Prostitution

35 "Therefore, you prostitute, listen to this message from the LORD! 36 This is what the Sovereign LORD says: Because you have exposed yourself in prostitution to all your lovers, and because you have worshiped detestable idols, and because you have slaughtered your children as sacrifices to your gods, 37 this is what I am going to do. I will gather together all your allies—these lovers of yours with whom you have sinned, both those you loved and those you hated—and I will strip you naked in front of them so they can stare at you. 38 I will punish you for your murder and adultery. I will cover you with blood in my jealous fury. 39 Then I will give you to your lovers—these many nations—and they will destroy you. They will knock down your pagan shrines and the altars to your idols. They will strip you and take your beautiful jewels, leaving you completely naked and ashamed. 40 They will band together in a mob to stone you and run you through with swords. 41 They will burn your homes and punish you in front of many women. I will see to it that you stop your prostitution and end your payments to your many lovers.

42 "Then at last my fury against you will be spent, and my jealous anger will subside. I will be calm and will not be angry with you anymore. 43 But first, because you have not remembered your youth but have angered me by doing all these evil things, I will fully repay you for all of your sins, says the Sovereign LORD. For to all your disgusting sins, you have added these lewd acts. 44 Everyone who makes up proverbs will say of you, 'Like mother, like daughter.' 45 For your mother loathed her husband and her children, and so do you. And you are exactly like your sisters, for they despised their husbands and their children. Truly your mother must have been a Hittite and your father an Amorite.

46 "Your older sister was Samaria, who lived with her daughters in the north. Your younger sister was Sodom, who lived with her daughters in the south. 47 But you have not merely sinned as they did—no, that was nothing to you. In a very short time you far surpassed them! 48 As surely as I live, says the Sovereign LORD, Sodom and her daughters

16:24 Ps 78:58; Isa 57:5-7
16:25 Prov 9:14
16:26 Jer 7:18-19
16:27 Isa 9:12
16:28 2 Kgs 16:7-18; 2 Chr 28:16-23
16:30 Prov 9:13; Isa 3:9; Rev 17:1-6
16:31 Isa 52:3
16:33 Hos 8:9-10; Joel 3:3; Luke 15:30
16:36 Jer 19:5; Ezek 20:31; 23:37
16:37 Isa 47:3; Nah 3:5-6
16:38 Ps 79:3, 5; Jer 18:21; Zeph 1:17; Rev 16:6
16:41 2 Kgs 25:9
16:42 2 Sam 24:25; Isa 40:1-2; 54:9-10
16:43 Ps 78:42; Isa 63:10
16:45 Isa 1:4; Zech 11:8
16:46 Gen 13:11-13; Jer 3:8-11
16:47 1 Kgs 16:31; 2 Kgs 21:9; Ezek 5:6-7
16:48 Matt 11:23-24

16:29 Or *Chaldea.*

16:27 The conduct of the Jews was so lewd that even those who worshiped other gods, including their great enemy the Philistines, would have been ashamed to behave that way. The Jews outdid them in doing evil.

16:44-52 The city of Sodom, a symbol of total corruption, was completely destroyed by God for its wickedness (Genesis 19:24, 25). Samaria, the capital of what had been the northern kingdom (Israel), was despised and rejected by the Jews in Judah. To be called a sister of Samaria and Sodom was bad enough, but to be called more wicked than they were meant that Judah's sins were an unspeakable abomination and that its doom was inevitable. The reason it was considered worse was not necessarily that Judah's sins were worse but that Judah knew better. In that light, we who live in an age when God's message is made clear to us through the Bible are worse than Judah if we continue in sin (see Matthew 11:20-24).

16:49 Gen 13:10; Ps 138:6; Isa 22:13; Luke 12:16-20
16:50 Gen 19:24-25
16:51 Jer 3:8-11; Matt 12:41-42
16:53 Isa 19:24-25
16:54 Jer 2:26
16:57 2 Kgs 16:5-7; 2 Chr 28:5-6, 18-23; Hos 2:10; 7:1
16:58 Ezek 23:49
16:59 Isa 24:5
16:60 Jer 32:40
16:62 Jer 24:7
16:63 Ps 39:9; Dan 9:7-8; Rom 3:19

were never as wicked as you and your daughters. 49 Sodom's sins were pride, laziness,
and gluttony, while the poor and needy suffered outside her door. 50 She was proud and
did loathsome things, so I wiped her out, as you have seen.

51 "Even Samaria did not commit half your sins. You have done far more loathsome
things than your sisters ever did. They seem righteous compared to you! 52 You should
be deeply ashamed because your sins are so terrible. In comparison, you make your
sisters seem innocent!

53 "But someday I will restore the fortunes of Sodom and Samaria, and I will restore
you, too. 54 Then you will be truly ashamed of everything you have done, for your sins
make them feel good in comparison. 55 Yes, your sisters, Sodom and Samaria, and all
their people will be restored, and at that time you also will be restored. 56 In your proud
days you held Sodom in contempt. 57 But now your greater wickedness has been exposed
to all the world, and you are the one who is scorned—by Edom* and all her neighbors
and by Philistia. 58 This is your punishment for all your disgusting sins, says the LORD.

59 "Now this is what the Sovereign LORD says: I will give you what you deserve, for
you have taken your solemn vows lightly by breaking your covenant. 60 Yet I will keep
the covenant I made with you when you were young, and I will establish an everlasting
covenant with you. 61 Then you will remember with shame all the evil you have done. I
will make your sisters, Samaria and Sodom, to be your daughters, even though they are
not part of our covenant. 62 And I will reaffirm my covenant with you, and you will know
that I am the LORD. 63 You will remember your sins and cover your mouth in silence and
shame when I forgive you of all that you have done, says the Sovereign LORD."

A Story of Two Eagles

17:2 Ezek 20:49; 24:3
17:3 Jer 22:23; 48:40; Dan 4:22
17:5 Deut 8:7-9; Isa 44:4
17:7 Ezek 31:4
17:10 Ezek 19:12-14; Hos 13:15

17 Then this message came to me from the LORD: 2 "Son of man, tell this story to the
people of Israel. 3 Give them this message from the Sovereign LORD: A great eagle
with broad wings full of many-colored feathers came to Lebanon. He took hold of the
highest branch of a cedar tree 4 and plucked off its topmost shoot. Then he carried it away
to a city filled with merchants, where he planted it.

5 "Then he planted one of its seedlings in fertile ground beside a broad river, where it
would grow as quickly as a willow tree. 6 It took root there and grew into a low, spreading
vine. Its branches turned up toward the eagle, and its roots grew down beneath it. It soon
produced strong branches and luxuriant leaves. 7 But then another great eagle with broad
wings and full plumage came along. So the vine sent its roots and branches out toward him
for water. 8 The vine did this even though it was already planted in good soil and had plenty
of water so it could grow into a splendid vine and produce rich leaves and luscious fruit.

9 "So now the Sovereign LORD asks: Should I let this vine grow and prosper? No! I
will pull it out, roots and all! I will cut off its fruit and let its leaves wither and die. I will
pull it out easily enough—it won't take a strong arm or a large army to do it. 10 Then
when the vine is transplanted, will it thrive? No, it will wither away completely when the
east wind blows against it. It will die in the same good soil where it had grown so well."

16:57 Many ancient manuscripts read *Aram.*

16:49 It is easy to judge and condemn Sodom, especially for its terrible sexual sins. Ezekiel reminded Judah, however, that Sodom was destroyed because of its pride, laziness, gluttony, and unconcern for the poor and needy. It is easy to be selective in what we consider gross sin. If we do not commit such horrible sins as adultery, homosexuality, stealing, and murder, we may think we are living good enough lives. But what about sins like pride, laziness, gluttony, and indifference to the needy? These sins may not be as shocking to you as the others, but they are also forbidden by God.

16:59-63 Although the people had broken their promises and did not deserve anything but punishment, God would not break his promises. If the people turned back to him, he would again forgive them and renew his covenant. This covenant was put into effect when Jesus paid for everyone's sins by his death on the cross (Hebrews 10:8-10). No one is beyond the reach of God's forgiveness. Although we don't deserve anything but punishment for our sins, God's arms are still outstretched. He will not break his promise to give us salvation and forgiveness if we repent and turn to him.

17:1ff The first eagle in this chapter represents King Nebuchadnezzar of Babylon (see 17:12), who appointed or "planted" Zedekiah as king in Jerusalem. Zedekiah rebelled against this arrangement and tried to ally with Egypt, the second eagle, to battle against Babylon. This took place while Ezekiel, miles away in Babylon, was describing these events. Jeremiah, a prophet in Judah, was also warning Zedekiah not to form this alliance (Jeremiah 2:36, 37). Although many miles apart, the prophets had the same message because both spoke for God. God still directs his chosen spokespeople to speak his truth all around the world.

17:10 This east wind was the hot, dry wind blowing off the desert, a wind that could wither a flourishing crop. The hot wind of Nebuchadnezzar's armies was about to overcome the nation of Judah.

The Riddle Explained

11 Then this message came to me from the LORD: 12 "Say to these rebels of Israel: Don't
you understand the meaning of this riddle of the eagles? I will tell you, says the
Sovereign LORD. The king of Babylon came to Jerusalem, took away her king and
princes, and brought them to Babylon. 13 He made a treaty with a member of the royal
family and made him take an oath of loyalty. He also exiled Israel's most influential
leaders, 14 so Israel would not become strong again and revolt. Only by keeping her treaty
with Babylon could Israel maintain her national identity.

15 "Nevertheless, this man of Israel's royal family rebelled against Babylon, sending
ambassadors to Egypt to request a great army and many horses. Can Israel break her
sworn treaties like that and get away with it? 16 No! For as surely as I live, says the
Sovereign LORD, the king of Israel will die in Babylon, the land of the king who put him
in power and whose treaty he despised and broke. 17 Pharaoh and all his mighty army
will fail to help Israel when the king of Babylon lays siege to Jerusalem again and
destroys the lives of many. 18 For the king of Israel broke his treaty after swearing to
obey; therefore, he will not escape.

19 "So this is what the Sovereign LORD says: As surely as I live, I will punish him for
breaking my covenant and despising the solemn oath he made in my name. 20 I will throw
my net over him and capture him in my snare. I will bring him to Babylon and deal with
him there for this treason against me. 21 And all the best warriors of Israel will be killed
in battle, and those remaining in the city will be scattered to the four winds. Then you
will know that I, the LORD, have spoken these words.

22 "And the Sovereign LORD says: I will take a tender shoot from the top of a tall cedar,
and I will plant it on the top of Israel's highest mountain. 23 It will become a noble cedar,
sending forth its branches and producing seed. Birds of every sort will nest in it, finding
shelter beneath its branches. 24 And all the trees will know that it is I, the LORD, who cuts
down the tall tree and helps the short tree to grow tall. It is I who makes the green tree
wither and gives new life to the dead tree. I, the LORD, have spoken! I will do what I have
said."

The Justice of a Righteous God

18 Then another message came to me from the LORD: 2 "Why do you quote this proverb
in the land of Israel: 'The parents have eaten sour grapes, but their children's mouths
pucker at the taste'? 3 As surely as I live, says the Sovereign LORD, you will not say this
proverb anymore in Israel. 4 For all people are mine to judge—both parents and children
alike. And this is my rule: The person who sins will be the one who dies.

5 "Suppose a certain man is just and does what is lawful and right, 6 and he has not
feasted in the mountains before Israel's idols or worshiped them. And suppose he does
not commit adultery or have intercourse with a woman during her menstrual period.
7 Suppose he is a merciful creditor, not keeping the items given in pledge by poor debtors,
and does not rob the poor but instead gives food to the hungry and provides clothes for
people in need. 8 And suppose he grants loans without interest, stays away from injustice,
is honest and fair when judging others, 9 and faithfully obeys my laws and regulations.
Anyone who does these things is just and will surely live, says the Sovereign LORD.

17:13 2 Kgs 24:15-17; 2 Chr 36:13
17:14 Jer 27:12-17; 38:17
17:15 2 Kgs 24:20; 2 Chr 36:13
17:16 Jer 52:11
17:17 Isa 36:6; Jer 37:7
17:18 1 Chr 29:24
17:20 Ezek 12:13; 20:36; 32:3
17:21 2 Kgs 25:5, 11; Amos 9:1-10
17:22 Pss 72:16; 80:15; Ezek 20:40; Zech 3:8; 4:12-14
17:24 Ps 96:12; Isa 55:12; Amos 9:11
18:2 Jer 31:29
18:4 Num 16:22; 27:16; Isa 42:5; 57:16
18:6 Deut 4:19
18:7 Lev 19:13; Matt 25:35-40
18:8 Exod 22:25; Lev 25:36; Deut 23:19; Zech 8:16
18:9 Hab 2:4; Rom 1:17

17:22, 23 Ezekiel's prophecy of judgment ends in hope. When the people put their hope in foreign alliances, they were disappointed. Only God could give them true hope. God said he would plant a tender shoot, the Messiah, whose Kingdom would grow and become a shelter for all who come to him (see Isaiah 11:1-5). This prophecy was fulfilled at the coming of Jesus Christ.

18:1ff The people of Judah believed they were being punished for the sins of their ancestors, not their own. They thought this way because this was the teaching of the Ten Commandments (Exodus 20:5). Ezekiel taught that the destruction of Jerusalem was due to the spiritual decay in previous generations. But this belief in the corporate life of Israel led to fatalism and irresponsibility. So Ezekiel gave God's new policy because the people had misconstrued the old one. God judges each person individually. Although we often suffer from the effects of sins committed by those who came before us, God does not punish us for someone else's sins, and we can't use their mistakes as an excuse for our sins. Each person is accountable to God for his or her actions.

In addition, some people of Judah used the corporate umbrella of God's blessing as an excuse for disobeying God. They thought that because of their righteous ancestors (18:5-9), they would live. God told them that they would not; they were the evil children of righteous parents and, as such, would die (18:10-13). If, however, anyone returned to God, he or she would live (18:14-18).

18:8 The law of Moses had rules about charging interest (Exodus 22:25; Leviticus 25:36; Deuteronomy 23:19, 20) to prevent God's people from taking advantage of the poor among them.

10 "But suppose that man has a son who grows up to be a robber or murderer and
refuses to do what is right. 11 And suppose that son does all the evil things his father
would never do—worships idols on the mountains, commits adultery, 12 oppresses the
poor and helpless, steals from debtors by refusing to let them redeem what they have
given in pledge, worships idols and takes part in loathsome practices, 13 and lends
money at interest. Should such a sinful person live? No! He must die and must take
full blame.
14 "But suppose that sinful son, in turn, has a son who sees his father's wickedness
but decides against that kind of life. 15 Suppose this son refuses to worship idols on
the mountains, does not commit adultery, 16 and does not exploit the poor, but instead
is fair to debtors and does not rob them. And suppose this son feeds the hungry,
provides clothes for the needy, 17 helps the poor, does not lend money at interest, and
obeys all my regulations and laws. Such a person will not die because of his father's
sins; he will surely live. 18 But the father will die for the many sins he committed—for
being cruel and robbing close relatives, doing what was clearly wrong among his
people.
19 "'What?' you ask. 'Doesn't the child pay for the parent's sins?' No! For if the
child does what is right and keeps my laws, that child will surely live. 20 The one who
sins is the one who dies. The child will not be punished for the parent's sins, and the
parent will not be punished for the child's sins. Righteous people will be rewarded for
their own goodness, and wicked people will be punished for their own wickedness.
21 But if wicked people turn away from all their sins and begin to obey my laws and
do what is just and right, they will surely live and not die. 22 All their past sins will be
forgotten, and they will live because of the righteous things they have done.
23 "Do you think, asks the Sovereign LORD, that I like to see wicked people die? Of
course not! I only want them to turn from their wicked ways and live. 24 However, if
righteous people turn to sinful ways and start acting like other sinners, should they be
allowed to live? No, of course not! All their previous goodness will be forgotten, and
they will die for their sins.
25 "Yet you say, 'The Lord isn't being just!' Listen to me, O people of Israel. Am I
the one who is unjust, or is it you? 26 When righteous people turn from being good
and start doing sinful things, they will die for it. Yes, they will die because of their
sinful deeds. 27 And if wicked people turn away from their wickedness, obey the law,
and do what is just and right, they will save their lives. 28 They will live, because after
thinking it over, they decided to turn from their sins. Such people will not die. 29 And
yet the people of Israel keep saying, 'The Lord is unjust!' O people of Israel, it is you
who are unjust, not I.
30 "Therefore, I will judge each of you, O people of Israel, according to your actions,
says the Sovereign LORD. Turn from your sins! Don't let them destroy you! 31 Put all your
rebellion behind you, and get for yourselves a new heart and a new spirit. For why should
you die, O people of Israel? 32 I don't want you to die, says the Sovereign LORD. Turn
back and live!

18:12 2 Kgs 21:11; Isa 59:6-7; Amos 4:1
18:13 Ezek 33:4-5
18:14 2 Chr 29:6-10; 34:21
18:16 Job 31:16; Ps 41:1
18:19 Exod 20:5; Zech 1:3-6
18:20 Deut 24:16; Matt 16:27; Rom 2:6-9
18:21 Ezek 33:12, 19
18:22 Ps 18:20-24; Ezek 33:16; Mic 7:19
18:23 Ps 147:11; Ezek 33:11; 2 Pet 3:9
18:24 1 Sam 15:11; Prov 21:16; Ezek 33:18; Gal 3:3-4
18:25 Gen 18:25; Deut 32:4; Ezek 33:17, 20; Zeph 3:5; Mal 3:13-15
18:30 Ezek 14:6; 33:11; Hos 12:6
18:31 Ps 51:10; Isa 1:16-17; 55:17; Acts 3:19

18:12 Returning what one took in pledge referred to the lender letting the debtor use the cloak each night that he had placed as security on his loan. Without the cloak, the debtor would be cold at night. (See Exodus 22:26 and Deuteronomy 24:10-13 for the giving of this law.)

18:23 God is a God of love, but he is also a God of perfect justice. His perfect love causes him to be merciful to those who recognize their sin and turn back to him, but he cannot wink at those who willfully sin. Wicked people die both physically and spiritually. God takes no joy in their deaths; he would prefer that they turn to him and have eternal life. Likewise, we should not rejoice in the misfortunes of nonbelievers. Instead, we should do all in our power to bring them to faith.

18:25 A typical childish response to punishment is to say, "That isn't fair!" In reality, God is fair, but *we* have broken the rules. It is not God who must live up to our ideas of fairness; instead, we must live up to his. Don't spend your time looking for the loopholes in God's law. Instead, live up to God's standards.

18:30-32 Ezekiel's solution to the problem of inherited guilt is for each person to have a changed life. This is God's work in us and not something we can do for ourselves. The Holy Spirit does it (Psalm 51:10-12). If we renounce our life's direction of sin and rebellion and turn to God, he will give us a new direction, a new love, and a new power to change. You can begin by faith, trusting in God's power to change your heart and mind. Then determine to live each day with him in control (Ephesians 4:22-24).

A Funeral Song for Israel's Kings

19 "Sing this funeral song for the princes of Israel: 19:1 2 Kgs 25:5-7

2 'What is your mother?
A lioness among lions!
She lay down among the young lions
and reared her cubs.
3 She raised one of her cubs 19:3 2 Kgs 23:31-34
to become a strong young lion.
He learned to catch and devour prey,
and he became a man-eater.
4 Then the nations heard about him, 19:4 2 Chr 36:4
and he was trapped in their pit.
They led him away in chains
to the land of Egypt.
5 'When the mother lion saw
that all her hopes for him were gone,
she took another of her cubs
and taught him to be a strong lion.
6 He prowled among the other lions 19:6 2 Kgs 24:9
and became a leader among them.
He learned to catch and devour prey,
and he, too, became a man-eater.
7 He demolished fortresses in nearby nations*
and destroyed their towns and cities.
Their farms were desolated,
and their crops were destroyed.
Everyone in the land trembled in fear
when they heard him roar.
8 Then the armies of the nations attacked him,
surrounding him from every direction.
They spread out their nets for him
and captured him in their pit.
9 With hooks, they dragged him into a cage 19:9 2 Kgs 24:15 2 Chr 36:6
and brought him before the king of Babylon.
They held him in captivity,
so his voice could never again be heard
on the mountains of Israel.
10 'Your mother was like a vine 19:10 Ps 80:8-11
planted by the water's edge.
It had lush, green foliage
because of the abundant water.
11 Its branches became very strong,
strong enough to be a ruler's scepter.
It soon became very tall,
towering above all the others.
It stood out because of its height
and because of its many lush branches.

19:7 As in Greek version; Hebrew reads *He consorted with widows.*

19:1ff Ezekiel used illustrations to communicate many of his messages. With the picture of the lioness and her cubs, he raised the curiosity of his listeners. The lioness symbolized the nation of Judah, and the two cubs were two of its kings. The first cub was King Jehoahaz, who was taken captive to Egypt in 609 B.C. by Pharaoh Neco (2 Kings 23:31-33). The second cub was either King Jehoiachin, who had already been taken into captivity in Babylon (2 Kings 24:8ff), or King Zedekiah, who soon would be (2 Kings 25:7). This illustration showed that for Judah, there was no hope for a quick return from exile and no escape from the approaching Babylonian armies.

19:11, 12 Not even the political and military might of Judah's kings could save the nation. Like branches of a vine, they would be cut off and uprooted by "the desert wind"—the powerful Babylonian army.

12 But the vine was uprooted in fury
and thrown down to the ground.
The desert wind dried up its fruit
and tore off its branches.
Its stem was destroyed by fire.
13 Now the vine is growing in the wilderness,
where the ground is hard and dry.
14 A fire has come from its branches
and devoured its fruit.
None of the remaining limbs
is strong enough to be a ruler's scepter.'

This is a funeral song, and it is now time for the funeral."

The Rebellion of Israel

20 On August 14,* during the seventh year of King Jehoiachin's captivity, some of
the leaders of Israel came to request a message from the LORD. They sat down in
front of me to wait for his reply. 2 Then this message came to me from the LORD: 3 "Son
of man, give the leaders of Israel this message from the Sovereign LORD: How dare you
come to ask for my help? As surely as I live, I will tell you nothing. This is the word of
the Sovereign LORD!

4 "Son of man, bring judgment against them and condemn them. Make them realize
how loathsome the actions of their ancestors really were. 5 Give them this message from
the Sovereign LORD: When I chose Israel and revealed myself to her in Egypt, I swore
that I, the LORD, would be her God. 6 I promised that I would bring her and her
descendants out of Egypt to a land I had discovered and explored for them—a good land,
a land flowing with milk and honey, the best of all lands anywhere. 7 Then I said to them,
'Each of you, get rid of your idols. Do not defile yourselves with the Egyptian gods, for
I am the LORD your God.'

8 "But they rebelled against me and would not listen. They did not get rid of their idols
or forsake the gods of Egypt. Then I threatened to pour out my fury on them to satisfy
my anger while they were still in Egypt. 9 But I didn't do it, for I acted to protect the honor
of my name. That way the surrounding nations wouldn't be able to laugh at Israel's God,
who had promised to deliver his people. 10 So I brought my people out of Egypt and led
them into the wilderness. 11 There I gave them my laws so they could live by keeping
them. Yes, all those who keep them will live! 12 And I gave them my Sabbath days of rest
as a sign between them and me. It was to remind them that I, the LORD, had set them
apart to be holy, making them my special people.

13 "But the people of Israel rebelled against me, and they refused to obey my laws there
in the wilderness. They wouldn't obey my instructions even though obedience would
have given them life. And they also violated my Sabbath days. So I threatened to pour
out my fury on them, and I made plans to utterly consume them in the desert. 14 But again
I held back in order to protect the honor of my name. That way the nations who saw me
lead my people out of Egypt wouldn't be able to claim I destroyed them because I
couldn't take care of them. 15 But I swore to them in the wilderness that I would not bring
them into the land I had given them, a land flowing with milk and honey, the most
beautiful place on earth. 16 I told them this because they had rejected my laws, ignored

19:12 Jer 31:28; Ezek 17:10; 28:17; Hos 13:15; John 15:6
19:13 2 Kgs 24:12-16; Hos 2:3
20:1 Ezek 8:1, 11-12
20:3 Ezek 14:3
20:4 Ezek 16:2; 22:2
20:5 Exod 6:2-3, 7; Deut 7:6; 14:2; Ezek 6:2-9; 33:3
20:6 Ps 48:2; Jer 33:24
20:7 Exod 20:2; Deut 29:16-18
20:8 Isa 63:10
20:9 Exod 32:11-14; Num 14:13
20:11 Exod 20:1-23; Lev 18:5
20:12 Exod 31:13, 17; Ezek 20:20
20:13 Num 14:11, 22; Isa 56:6
20:15 Ps 95:11
20:16 Ezek 11:21; 14:3-7

20:1 Hebrew *In the fifth month, on the tenth day,* of the Hebrew calendar. This event occurred on August 14, 591 B.C.; also see note on 1:1.

20:1ff Here Ezekiel gives a panoramic view of Israel's history of rebellion. The emphasis is on God's attempts to bring the nation back to himself and on God's mercy for his constantly rebellious and disobedient people. Ezekiel gives the message that the people alone are responsible for the troubles and judgments they have experienced. Those who persist in rebellion God will purge out (20:38), while he will bring the faithful into the land of Israel. The reason: that "you will know that I am the LORD" (20:42).

20:12, 13 The Sabbath, instituted by God at creation, was entrusted to Israel as a sign that God had created and redeemed them (Exodus 20:8-11; Deuteronomy 5:12-15). This day of rest was a gift from a loving God, not a difficult obligation. But the people repeatedly violated the Sabbath and ignored God (see also 20:20, 21). It was meant to be a reminder that they were God's special people. Today many Christians celebrate the Lord's Day, Sunday, as their Sabbath. Whatever the day, we must be careful to fulfill God's purpose for the Sabbath. He wants us to rest, to refocus, and to remember him.

my will for them, and violated my Sabbath days. Their hearts were given to their idols.
17 Nevertheless, I pitied them and held back from destroying them in the wilderness.
18 "Then I warned their children and told them not to follow in their parents' footsteps,
defiling themselves with their idols. 19 'I am the LORD your God,' I told them. 'Follow
my laws, pay attention to my instructions, 20 and keep my Sabbath days holy, for they are
a sign to remind you that I am the LORD your God.'
21 "But their children, too, rebelled against me. They refused to keep my laws and
follow my instructions, even though obeying them would have given them life. And they
also violated my Sabbath days. So again I threatened to pour out my fury on them in the
wilderness. 22 Nevertheless, I withdrew my judgment against them to protect the honor
of my name among the nations who had seen my power in bringing them out of Egypt.
23 But I took a solemn oath against them while they were in the wilderness. I vowed I
would scatter them among all the nations 24 because they did not obey my laws. They
scorned my instructions by violating my Sabbath days and longing for the idols of their
ancestors. 25 I gave them over to worthless customs and laws that would not lead to life.
26 I let them pollute themselves with the very gifts I had given them, and I allowed them
to give their firstborn children as offerings to their gods—so I might devastate them and
show them that I alone am the LORD.

Judgment and Restoration

27 "Therefore, son of man, give the people of Israel this message from the Sovereign
LORD: Your ancestors continued to blaspheme and betray me, 28 for when I brought them
into the land I had promised them, they offered sacrifices and incense on every high hill
and under every green tree they saw! They roused my fury as they offered up sacrifices
to their gods. They brought their perfumes and incense and poured out their drink
offerings to them! 29 I said to them, 'What is this high place where you are going?' (This
idol shrine has been called Bamah—'high place'—ever since.)
30 "Therefore, give the people of Israel this message from the Sovereign LORD: Do
you plan to pollute yourselves just as your ancestors did? Do you intend to keep
prostituting yourselves by worshiping detestable idols? 31 For when you offer gifts to
them and give your little children to be burned as sacrifices,* you continue to pollute
yourselves to this day. Should I listen to you or help you, O people of Israel? As surely
as I live, says the Sovereign LORD, I will not give you a message even though you have
come to me requesting one.
32 "You say, 'We want to be like the nations all around us, who serve idols of wood
and stone.' But what you have in mind will never happen. 33 As surely as I live, says
the Sovereign LORD, I will rule you with an iron fist in great anger and with awesome
power. 34 With might and fury I will bring you out from the lands where you are
scattered. 35 I will bring you into the wilderness of the nations, and there I will judge
you face to face. 36 I will judge you there just as I did your ancestors in the wilderness
after bringing them out of Egypt, says the Sovereign LORD. 37 I will count you
carefully and hold you to the terms of the covenant. 38 I will purge you of all those
who rebel and sin against me. I will bring them out of the countries where they are in
exile, but they will never enter the land of Israel. And when that happens, you will
know that I am the LORD.

20:17 Jer 4:27; 5:18
20:18 Deut 4:3-4
20:19 Exod 6:7; 20:2 Deut 5:32
20:21 Num 25:1-3
20:22 Isa 48:9-11
20:23 Deut 28:64-68 Jer 15:4
20:24 Ezek 6:9
20:25 Ps 81:12 Rom 1:21-25, 28 2 Thes 2:9-11
20:26 Ezek 6:7; 20:30 Rom 11:8
20:30 Judg 2:19
20:31 Ps 106:37-39 Jer 7:31 Ezek 16:20
20:32 Jer 2:25; 44:17 Ezek 16:20
20:34 Jer 42:18; 44:6 Lam 2:4 †2 Cor 6:17
20:36 Deut 32:10 1 Cor 10:5-10
20:38 Ps 95:11 Ezek 34:17-22 Amos 9:9-10 Heb 4:3

20:31 Or *and make your little children pass through the fire.*

20:23, 24 At the very beginning of Israel's history, God clearly warned the people about the consequences of disobedience (Deuteronomy 28:15ff). When the people disobeyed, God let them experience those devastating consequences to remind them of the seriousness of their sins. If you choose to live for yourself, apart from God, you may experience similar destructive consequences. However, even through such consequences, God may be drawing you to himself. Let your misfortunes bring you to your senses and to the merciful God before it is too late.

20:25 These "worthless" laws do not refer to any aspect of the Mosaic law—Ezekiel reinforces that law (20:11, 13, 21). Evidently the Jews had taken Exodus 13:12 and 22:29, the dedication of firstborn animals and children, as a justification for child sacrifice to the Canaanite god Molech. God was giving them over to this delusion to get them to acknowledge him, to jar their consciences, and to revitalize their faith (20:26).

20:35–38 When the Israelites disobeyed God by refusing to enter the Promised Land the first time, God chose to purify his people by forcing them to wander in the wilderness until that entire generation died (Numbers 14:26-35). Here he promised to purge the nation of its rebellious people again as they crossed the vast wilderness from their captivity in Babylon. Only those who faithfully followed God would be able to return to their land. The purpose of this wilderness judgment would be to purge out all those who worshiped idols and to restore all those faithful to God.

20:39 Isa 1:12-15 Jer 44:25-26 Ezek 23:38-39
20:40 Isa 56:7; 60:7 Ezek 43:12, 27
20:41 Isa 27:12-13
20:43 Zech 12:10-14
20:46 Jer 13:19
20:47 Isa 9:18
20:48 Jer 7:20; 17:27
20:49 Matt 13:12-13 John 16:25
21:2 Ezek 20:46
21:3 Isa 57:1 Jer 21:13 Ezek 5:8 Nah 2:13; 3:5
21:4 Jer 12:12 Ezek 7:2; 20:47
21:5 1 Sam 3:12 Nah 1:9
21:7 Isa 13:7 Ezek 7:26
21:9 Deut 32:41
21:10 Isa 34:5-6

39“As for you, O people of Israel, this is what the Sovereign LORD says: If you insist,
go right ahead and worship your idols, but then don’t turn around and bring gifts to me.
Such desecration of my holy name must stop! 40For on my holy mountain, says the
Sovereign LORD, the people of Israel will someday worship me, and I will accept them.
There I will require that you bring me all your offerings and choice gifts and sacrifices.
41When I bring you home from exile, you will be as pleasing to me as an offering of
perfumed incense. And I will display my holiness in you as all the nations watch. 42Then
when I have brought you home to the land I promised your ancestors, you will know that
I am the LORD. 43You will look back at all your sins and hate yourselves because of the
evil you have done. 44You will know that I am the LORD, O people of Israel, when I have
honored my name by treating you mercifully in spite of your wickedness, says the
Sovereign LORD.”

Judgment against the Negev

45Then this message came to me from the LORD: 46“Son of man, look toward the south*
and speak out against it; prophesy against the fields of the Negev. 47Give the southern
wilderness this message from the Sovereign LORD: Hear the word of the LORD! I will set
you on fire, O forest, and every tree will be burned—green and dry trees alike. The
terrible flames will not be quenched; they will scorch everything from south to north.
48And all the world will see that I, the LORD, have set this fire. It will not be put out.”
49Then I said, “O Sovereign LORD, they are saying of me, ‘He only talks in riddles!’”

The LORD’s Sword of Judgment

21 Then this message came to me from the LORD: 2“Son of man, look toward
Jerusalem and prophesy against Israel and her sanctuaries. 3Give her this message
from the LORD: I am your enemy, O Israel, and I am about to unsheath my sword to
destroy your people—the righteous and the wicked alike. 4Yes, I will not spare even the
righteous! I will make a clean sweep throughout the land from south to north. 5All the
world will know that I am the LORD. My sword is in my hand, and it will not return to
its sheath until its work is finished.
6“Son of man, groan before the people! Groan before them with bitter anguish and a
broken heart. 7When they ask you why, tell them, ‘I groan because of the terrifying news
I have heard. When it comes true, the boldest heart will melt with fear; all strength will
disappear. Every spirit will faint; strong knees will tremble and become as weak as water.
And the Sovereign LORD says: It is coming! It’s on its way!’”
8Then the LORD said to me, 9“Son of man, give the people this message from the
LORD: A sword is being sharpened and polished. 10It is being prepared for terrible
slaughter; it will flash like lightning! Now will you laugh? Those far stronger than you
have fallen beneath its power!* 11Yes, the sword is now being sharpened and polished;
it is being prepared for the executioner!

20:46 Hebrew *Teman.* **21:10** The meaning of the Hebrew is uncertain.

20:39 The Israelites were worshiping idols and giving gifts to God at the same time! They did not believe in their God as the one true God; instead, they worshiped him along with the other gods of the land. Perhaps they enjoyed the immoral pleasures of idol worship; or perhaps they didn’t want to miss out on the benefits the idols might give them. Often people believe in God and give him gifts of church attendance or service, while still holding on to their idols of money, power, or pleasure. They don’t want to miss out on any possible benefits. But God wants all of our life and all of our devotion; devotion to anything else is idol worship. Beware of trying to please God while also pursuing the pleasures of sin. You must choose one or the other.

20:45-47 “Toward the south” refers to Jerusalem and Judah. “The southern wilderness” is the region of the Negev, which is compared to a forest about to be destroyed by fire.

20:49 Ezekiel was exasperated and discouraged. Many Israelites were complaining that he spoke only in riddles, so they refused to listen. No matter how important our work or how significant our ministry, we will have moments of discouragement. Apparently God did not answer Ezekiel’s plea; instead, he gave Ezekiel another message to proclaim. What has been discouraging you? Have you felt like giving up? Instead, continue doing what God has told you to do. He promises to reward the faithful (Mark 13:13). God’s cure for discouragement may be another assignment. In serving others, we may find the renewal we need.

21:1ff The short message in 20:45-48 introduces the first of three messages about the judgments that would come upon Jerusalem: (1) the sword of the Lord (21:1-7); (2) the sharpened sword (21:8-17); (3) the sword of Nebuchadnezzar (21:18-22). The city would be destroyed because it was defiled. According to Jewish law, defiled objects were to be passed through fire in order to purify them (see Numbers 31:22, 23; Psalm 66:10-12; Proverbs 17:3). God’s judgment is designed to purify; destruction is often a necessary part of that process.

12“Son of man, cry out and wail; pound your thighs in anguish, for that sword will
slaughter my people and their leaders—everyone will die! 13It will put them all to the
test! So now the Sovereign LORD asks: What chance do they have?*
14“Son of man, prophesy to them and clap your hands vigorously. Then take the sword
and brandish it twice, even three times, to symbolize the great massacre they will face!
15Let their hearts melt with terror, for the sword glitters at every gate. It flashes like
lightning; it is polished for slaughter! 16O sword, slash to the right, and slash to the left,
wherever you will, wherever you want. 17I, too, will clap my hands, and I will satisfy
my fury. I, the LORD, have spoken!”

A Signpost for Babylon’s King

18Then this message came to me from the LORD: 19“Son of man, make a map and trace
two routes on it for the sword of Babylon’s king to follow. Put a signpost on the road that
comes out of Babylon where the road forks into two—20one road going to Ammon and
its capital, Rabbah, and the other to Judah and fortified Jerusalem. 21The king of Babylon
now stands at the fork, uncertain whether to attack Jerusalem or Rabbah. He will call his
magicians to use divination. They will cast lots by shaking arrows from the quiver. They
will inspect the livers of their animal sacrifices. 22Then they will decide to turn toward
Jerusalem! With battering rams they will go against the gates, shouting for the kill. They
will put up siege towers and build ramps against the walls to reach the top. 23The people
of Jerusalem will think it is a mistake, because of their treaty with the Babylonians. But
the king of Babylon will remind the people of their rebellion. Then he will attack and
capture them.
24“Therefore, this is what the Sovereign LORD says: Again and again your guilt cries
out against you, for you are not ashamed of your sin. You don’t even try to hide it!
Wherever you go, whatever you do, all your actions are filled with sin. So now the time
of your punishment has come!
25“O you corrupt and wicked prince of Israel, your final day of reckoning is here!
26Take off your jeweled crown, says the Sovereign LORD. The old order changes—now
the lowly are exalted, and the mighty are brought low. 27Destruction! Destruction! I will
surely destroy the kingdom. And it will not be restored until the one appears who has the
right to judge it. Then I will hand it over to him.

A Message for the Ammonites

28“And now, son of man, prophesy concerning the Ammonites and their mockery.
Give them this message from the Sovereign LORD: My sword is drawn for your
slaughter; it is sharpened to destroy, flashing like lightning! 29Your magicians and
false prophets have given false visions and told lies about the sword. And now it will
fall with even greater force on the wicked for whom the day of final reckoning has
come. 30Should I return my sword to its sheath before I deal with you? No, I will
destroy you in your own country, the land of your birth. 31I will pour out my fury on
you and blow on you with the fire of my anger. I will hand you over to cruel men who
are skilled in destruction. 32You are fuel for the fire, and your blood will be spilled in
your own land. You will be utterly wiped out, your memory lost to history. I, the LORD,
have spoken!”

21:13 The meaning of the Hebrew is uncertain.

21:12 Joel 1:13
21:14 Lev 26:21, 24
21:15 Josh 2:11; 2 Sam 17:10; Jer 17:27
21:17 Ezek 5:13
21:19 Deut 3:11; Amos 1:14
21:20 Jer 49:2; Ezek 25:5; Amos 1:14
21:21 Num 23:23; Judg 17:5; Prov 16:33
21:22 Ezek 4:2; 26:9
21:23 Num 5:15; Ezek 17:16-18; 29:16
21:25 Ps 37:13; Ezek 7:2-7
21:26 Ps 75:7; Jer 13:18; Ezek 16:12; 17:24
21:27 Ps 2:6; Jer 23:5-6; Ezek 34:24; 37:24; Hag 2:21-22
21:28 Isa 31:8; Jer 12:12; Zeph 2:8-10
21:29 Jer 27:9
21:30 Jer 47:6-7
21:31 Ps 18:15; Nah 1:6; Hab 1:6, 10
21:32 Ezek 25:10; Mal 4:1

21:12 Pounding the thighs was a gesture of grief.

21:18-23 Ammon evidently rebelled against Babylon about the same time as King Zedekiah of Judah. In 589 B.C. the nations of Judah and Ammon were among those who conspired against Babylon (Jeremiah 27:3). Ezekiel gave this message to the exiles who had heard the news and were again filled with hope of returning to their homeland. Ezekiel said that Babylon's king would march his armies into the region to stop the rebellion. Traveling from the north, he would stop at a fork in the road, one way leading to Rabbah, the capital of Ammon, and the other leading to Jerusalem, the capital of Judah. He had to decide which city to destroy. Just as Ezekiel predicted, King Nebuchadnezzar went to Jerusalem and besieged it.

21:21 Nebuchadnezzar had two ways to get advice on the future. One was shaking arrows, much like drawing straws, to see which course of action was right; the second was having priests inspect the liver of a sacrificed animal to see if its shape and size would indicate a decision.

21:28 The Ammonites and Israelites were usually fighting with each other. God told the Israelites not to ally with foreign nations, but Judah and Ammon united against Babylon in 589 B.C. (Jeremiah 27:3). God first judged Judah when Nebuchadnezzar first went to Jerusalem (21:22); but Ammon would also be judged, not for allying with Judah, but for watching Jerusalem's destruction with insulting delight.

The Sins of Jerusalem

22 Now this message came to me from the LORD: 2“Son of man, are you ready to
judge Jerusalem? Are you ready to judge this city of murderers? Denounce her
terrible deeds in public, 3and give her this message from the Sovereign LORD: O city of
murderers, doomed and damned—city of idols, filthy and foul—4you are guilty of both
murder and idolatry. Your day of destruction has come! You have reached the end of your
years. I will make you an object of mockery throughout the world. 5O infamous city,
filled with confusion, you will be mocked by people both far and near.
6“Every leader in Israel who lives within your walls is bent on murder. 7Fathers and
mothers are contemptuously ignored. Resident foreigners are forced to pay for protection. Orphans and widows are wronged and oppressed. 8Inside your walls you despise
my holy things and violate my Sabbath days of rest. 9People accuse others falsely and
send them to their death. You are filled with idol worshipers and people who take part in
lewd activities. 10Men sleep with their fathers’ wives and have intercourse with women
who are menstruating. 11Within your walls live men who commit adultery with their
neighbors’ wives, who defile their daughters-in-law or who rape their own sisters.
12There are hired murderers, loan racketeers, and extortioners everywhere! They never
even think of me and my commands, says the Sovereign LORD.
13“But now I clap my hands in indignation over your dishonest gain and bloodshed.
14How strong and courageous will you be in my day of reckoning? I, the LORD, have
spoken! I will do what I have said. 15I will scatter you among the nations and purge you
of your wickedness. 16And when you have been dishonored among the nations, you will
know that I am the LORD.”

The LORD’s Refining Furnace

17Then this message came to me from the LORD: 18“Son of man, the people of Israel are
the worthless slag that remains after silver is smelted. They are the dross that is left
over—a useless mixture of copper, tin, iron, and lead. 19So give them this message from
the Sovereign LORD: Because you are all worthless slag, I will bring you to my crucible
in Jerusalem. 20I will melt you down in the heat of my fury, just as copper, tin, iron, and
lead are melted down in a furnace. 21I will gather you together and blow the fire of my
anger upon you, 22and you will melt like silver in fierce heat. Then you will know that
I, the LORD, have poured out my fury on you.”

The Sins of Israel’s Leaders

23Again a message came to me from the LORD: 24“Son of man, give the people of Israel
this message: In the day of my indignation, you will become like an uncleared wilderness
or a desert without rain. 25Your princes* plot conspiracies just as lions stalk their prey.
They devour innocent people, seizing treasures and extorting wealth. They increase the
number of widows in the land. 26Your priests have violated my laws and defiled my holy
things. To them there is no difference between what is holy and what is not. And they do
not teach my people the difference between what is ceremonially clean and unclean.
They disregard my Sabbath days so that my holy name is greatly dishonored among
them. 27Your leaders are like wolves, who tear apart their victims. They actually destroy

22:3 Zeph 3:3
22:4 2 Kgs 21:16
22:6 Isa 1:23
22:7 Exod 22:22; 23:9 Prov 22:22-23
22:9 Hos 4:2, 10, 14
22:10 Lev 18:8, 19
22:11 Lev 18:15 2 Sam 13:14
22:12 Lev 19:13; 25:36 Deut 27:25 Mic 7:2-3
22:13 Prov 28:8 Isa 33:15 Amos 2:6-8
22:15 Deut 4:27 Zech 7:14
22:16 Ezek 6:4-7
22:18 Ps 119:119 Prov 17:3 Isa 1:22; 48:10 Jer 6:28
22:22 Ezek 20:8, 33 Hos 5:10
22:24 Isa 9:13 Jer 2:30 Ezek 24:13 Zeph 3:2
22:25 Jer 2:34; 15:8 Hos 6:9
22:26 Lev 10:10 1 Sam 2:12-17 Ezek 44:23 Hag 2:11-14

22:25 As in Greek version; Hebrew reads *prophets.*

22:1ff Chapter 22 explains why Jerusalem’s judgment would come (22:2-16), how it would come (22:17-22), and who would be affected by it (22:23-31).

22:6-13 The leaders, whom God chose, were responsible for the moral climate of the nation. The same is true today (see James 3:1). Unfortunately, many of the sins mentioned here have been committed in recent years by Christian leaders. We are living in a time of unprecedented attacks by Satan. We must uphold our leaders in prayer, and leaders must seek accountability in order to help them maintain their moral and spiritual integrity.

22:17-22 Precious metals are refined with intense heat to remove the impurities. When heated, the dross (impurities) rises to the top of the molten metal and is skimmed off and thrown away. The purpose of the invasion of Jerusalem was to refine the people, but the refining process showed that the people, like worthless dross, had nothing good in them.

22:26 The priests were supposed to keep God’s worship pure and teach the people right living. But the worship of God had become commonplace to them; they ignored the Sabbath, and they refused to teach the people. They no longer carried out their God-given duties (Leviticus 10:10, 11; Ezekiel 44:23). When doing God’s work becomes no more important than any mundane task, we are no longer giving God the reverence he deserves. Instead of bringing God down to our sinful human level, we should live in ways that reflect his holiness.

people's lives for profit! 28 And your prophets announce false visions and speak false
messages. They say, 'My message is from the Sovereign LORD,' when the LORD hasn't
spoken a single word to them. They repair cracked walls with whitewash! 29 Even
common people oppress the poor, rob the needy, and deprive foreigners of justice.
30 "I looked for someone who might rebuild the wall of righteousness that guards the
land. I searched for someone to stand in the gap in the wall so I wouldn't have to destroy
the land, but I found no one. 31 So now I will pour out my fury on them, consuming them
in the fire of my anger. I will heap on them the full penalty for all their sins, says the
Sovereign LORD."

The Adultery of Two Sisters

23 This message came to me from the LORD: 2 "Son of man, once there were two
sisters who were daughters of the same mother. 3 They became prostitutes in
Egypt. Even as young girls, they allowed themselves to be fondled and caressed. 4 The
older girl was named Oholah, and her sister was Oholibah. I married them, and they bore
me sons and daughters. I am speaking of Samaria and Jerusalem, for Oholah is Samaria
and Oholibah is Jerusalem.
5 "Then Oholah lusted after other lovers instead of me, and she gave her love to the
Assyrians, her neighbors. 6 They were all attractive young men, captains and commanders
dressed in handsome blue, dashing about on their horses. 7 And so she prostituted herself
with the most desirable men of Assyria, worshiping their idols and defiling herself. 8 For
when she left Egypt, she did not leave her spirit of prostitution behind. She was still as
lewd as in her youth, when the Egyptians satisfied their lusts with her and robbed her of
her virginity. 9 And so I handed her over to her Assyrian lovers, whom she desired so much.
10 They stripped her and killed her and took away her children as their slaves. Her name
was known to every woman in the land as a sinner who had received what she deserved.
11 "Yet even though Oholibah saw what had happened to Oholah, her sister, she
followed right in her footsteps. And she was even more depraved, abandoning herself to
her lust and prostitution. 12 She fawned over her Assyrian neighbors, those handsome
young men on fine horses, those captains and commanders in handsome uniforms—all of
them desirable. 13 I saw the way she was going, defiling herself just like her older sister.
14 "Then she carried her prostitution even further. She fell in love with pictures that
were painted on a wall—pictures of Babylonian* military officers, outfitted in striking
red uniforms. 15 Handsome belts encircled their waists, and flowing turbans crowned
their heads. They were dressed like chariot officers from the land of Babylonia.* 16 When
she saw these paintings, she longed to give herself to them, so she sent messengers to
Babylonia to invite them to come to her. 17 So they came and committed adultery with

22:28 Jer 23:25-32; Ezek 13:6
22:29 Exod 23:9; Isa 5:7; Amos 3:10; Jas 5:4
22:30 Ps 106:23; Jer 5:1; Ezek 13:5
23:2 Jer 3:7-10; Ezek 16:46
23:5 Ezek 16:28; Hos 8:9-10
23:6 Ezek 23:12, 23
23:7 Hos 5:3; 6:10
23:8 Exod 32:4; 1 Kgs 12:28; 2 Kgs 17:16
23:9-10 Ezek 16:37
23:11 Jer 3:8-11
23:12 2 Kgs 16:7
23:14 Ezek 8:10; 16:29
23:16 Matt 5:28
23:17 2 Kgs 24:17

23:14 Or *Chaldean.* **23:15** Or *Chaldea;* also in 23:16.

22:30 The wall spoken of here is not made of stones but of faithful people united in their efforts to resist evil. This wall was in disrepair because there was no one who could lead the people back to God. The feeble attempts to repair the gap—through religious rituals or messages based on opinion rather than God's will—were as worthless as whitewash, only covering over the real problems. What the people really needed was total spiritual reconstruction! When we give the appearance of loving God without living his way, we are covering up sins that could eventually damage us deeply. Don't use religion as a whitewash; repair your life by applying the principles of God's Word. Then you can join with others to stand "in the gap" and make a difference for God in the world.

23:1ff Ezekiel continued his discussion of the reasons for God's judgment by telling a further allegory. He compared the northern and southern kingdoms to two sisters who became prostitutes. The proud citizens of Jerusalem had long scorned their sister city of Samaria, thinking that they were superior. But God called both of these cities prostitutes—a shock to the people of Jerusalem, who thought that they were so righteous. Just as the imagery of this message was shocking and distasteful to the people, so our sins are repugnant to God.

23:4-6 Oholah (meaning "her tent"), the northern kingdom of Israel, was lured away from God by the dashing Assyrians. The people of Israel coveted their youth, strength, power, wealth, and pleasure—the same qualities people think will bring happiness today.

23:11ff Oholibah (meaning "my tent is in her") was shown to be worse, because she did not learn from the judgment upon her sister but continued in her lust for the Assyrians and Babylonians. Therefore, her judgment was equally certain. Just as Oholibah was privileged and should have known better, so we are privileged because we know about Christ. We need to be doubly sure that we follow him.

23:12 "She fawned over her Assyrian neighbors" probably means Judah excessively tried to please Assyria and may refer to Ahaz's paying protection money to Tiglath-pileser III (2 Kings 16:7, 8).

23:16 An invitation to Babylonia was given by Hezekiah to the envoys from Babylon (2 Kings 20:12ff; Isaiah 39).

23:17 At first, Judah made an alliance with Babylonia, but then changed its mind. During the reigns of Jehoiakim and Zedekiah, Judah looked to Egypt for help. Judah's unfaithfulness (its alliances with godless nations) cost it the only real protection it ever had—God.

her, defiling her in the bed of love. But later, she became disgusted with them and broke off their relationship.

[18]"So I became disgusted with Oholibah, just as I was with her sister, because she flaunted herself before them and gave herself to satisfy their lusts. [19]But that didn't bother her. She turned to even greater prostitution, remembering her youth when she was a prostitute in Egypt. [20]She lusted after lovers whose attentions were gross and bestial. [21]And so, Oholibah, you celebrated your former days as a young girl in Egypt, when you first allowed yourself to be fondled and caressed.

The LORD's Judgment of Oholibah

[22]"Therefore, Oholibah, this is what the Sovereign LORD says: I will send your lovers against you—those very nations from which you turned away in disgust. [23]For the Babylonians will come with all the Chaldeans from Pekod and Shoa and Koa. And all the Assyrians will come with them—handsome young captains, commanders, chariot officers, and other high-ranking officers, riding their horses. [24]They will all come against you from the north with chariots, wagons, and a great army fully prepared for attack. They will take up positions on every side, surrounding you with men armed for battle. And I will hand you over to them so they can do with you as they please. [25]I will turn my jealous anger against you, and they will deal furiously with you. They will cut off your nose and ears, and any survivors will then be slaughtered by the sword. Your children will be taken away as captives, and everything that is left will be burned. [26]They will strip you of your beautiful clothes and jewels. [27]In this way, I will put a stop to the lewdness and prostitution you brought from Egypt. You will never again cast longing eyes on those things or fondly remember your time in Egypt.

[28]"For this is what the Sovereign LORD says: I will surely hand you over to your enemies, to those you loathe. [29]They will deal with you in hatred and rob you of all you own, leaving you naked and bare. The shame of your prostitution will be exposed to all the world. [30]You brought all this on yourself by prostituting yourself to other nations, defiling yourself with all their idols. [31]Because you have followed in your sister's footsteps, I will punish you with the same terrors that destroyed her.

[32]"Yes, this is what the Sovereign LORD says: You will drink from the same cup of terror as your sister—a cup that is large and deep. And all the world will mock and scorn you in your desolation. [33]You will reel like a drunkard beneath the awful blows of sorrow and distress, just as your sister Samaria did. [34]In deep anguish you will drain that cup of terror to the very bottom. Then you will smash it to pieces and beat your breast in anguish. For I, the Sovereign LORD, have spoken! [35]And because you have forgotten me and turned your back on me, says the Sovereign LORD, you must bear the consequences of all your lewdness and prostitution."

The LORD's Judgment on Both Sisters

[36]The LORD said to me, "Son of man, you must accuse Oholah and Oholibah of all their awful deeds. [37]They have committed both adultery and murder—adultery by worshiping idols and murder by burning their children as sacrifices on their altars. [38]Then after doing these terrible things, they defiled my Temple and violated my Sabbath day! [39]On the very day that they murdered their children in front of their idols, they boldly came into my Temple to worship! They came in and defiled my house!

[40]"You sisters sent messengers to distant lands to get men. Then when they arrived, you bathed yourselves, painted your eyelids, and put on your finest jewels for them. [41]You sat with them on a beautifully embroidered couch and put my incense and my oil on a table that was spread before you. [42]From your room came the sound of many men carousing. They were lustful men and drunkards from the wilderness, who put bracelets on your wrists and beautiful crowns on your heads. [43]Then I said, 'If they really want to sleep with worn-out, old prostitutes like these, let them!' [44]And that is what they did.

23:20 Ezek 17:15
23:21 Jer 3:9
23:23 Gen 25:18; 2 Kgs 20:14-17; 24:2; Job 1:17; Jer 50:21; Ezek 21:19
23:24 Jer 39:5-6
23:25 Ezek 8:17-18; 23:47; Zeph 1:18
23:26 Ezek 16:39
23:27 Ezek 16:41
23:28 Jer 21:7-10; Ezek 16:37
23:29 Deut 28:48
23:30 Ezek 6:9
23:31 2 Kgs 21:13
23:32 Ps 60:3; Ezek 5:14-15
23:33 Jer 25:15
23:34 Ps 75:8; Isa 51:17
23:35 1 Kgs 14:9; Neh 9:26; Hos 13:6
23:36 Isa 58:1; Jer 1:10
23:38 2 Kgs 21:4, 7; Jer 17:27
23:39 Jer 7:9-11
23:40 2 Kgs 9:30
23:41 Jer 44:17
23:42 Gen 24:30; Jer 51:7; Ezek 16:11-12, 49; Amos 6:3-6

23:22-26 This predicts the last attack on Jerusalem that would destroy the city and bring to Babylonia the third wave of captives in 586 B.C. (2 Kings 25; Jeremiah 52). The first attack came in 605 B.C., the second in 597 B.C. Pekod, Shoa, and Koa were Babylonian allies.

23:39 The Israelites went so far as to sacrifice their own children to idols and then to sacrifice to the Lord the same day. This made a mockery of worship. We cannot praise God and willfully sin at the same time. That would be like going to bed with a neighbor and then celebrating one's wedding anniversary.

They slept with Oholah and Oholibah, these shameless prostitutes, with all the zest of
lustful young men. 45 But righteous people will judge these sister cities for what they
really are—adulteresses and murderers. They will sentence them to all the punishment
they deserve.
46 "Now this is what the Sovereign LORD says: Bring an army against them and hand
them over to be terrorized and plundered. 47 For their enemies will stone them and kill
them with swords. They will butcher their sons and daughters and burn their homes. 48 In
this way, I will put an end to lewdness and idolatry in the land, and my judgment will be
a warning to others not to follow their wicked example. 49 You will be fully repaid for all
your prostitution—your worship of idols. Yes, you will suffer the full penalty! Then you
will know that I am the Sovereign LORD."

The Sign of the Cooking Pot

24 On January 15,* during the ninth year of King Jehoiachin's captivity, this message
came to me from the LORD: 2 "Son of man, write down today's date, because on
this very day the king of Babylon is beginning his attack against Jerusalem. 3 Then show
these rebels an illustration; give them a message from the Sovereign LORD. Put a pot of
water on the fire to boil. 4 Fill it with choice meat—the rump and the shoulder and all the
most tender cuts. 5 Use only the best sheep from the flock and heap fuel on the fire
beneath the pot. Bring the pot to a boil, and cook the bones along with the meat.
6 "Now this is what the Sovereign LORD says: Destruction is certain for Jerusalem, the
city of murderers! She is a pot filled with corruption. So take the meat out chunk by chunk
in whatever order it comes, 7 for her wickedness is evident to all. She murders boldly,
leaving blood on the rocks for all to see. She doesn't even try to cover it! 8 So I will splash
her blood on a rock as an open expression of my anger and vengeance against her.
9 "This is what the Sovereign LORD says: Destruction is certain for Jerusalem, the city
of murderers! I myself will pile up the fuel beneath her. 10 Yes, heap on the wood! Let
the fire roar to make the pot boil. Cook the meat well with many spices. Then empty the
pot and burn the bones. 11 Now set the empty pot on the coals to scorch away the filth
and corruption. 12 But it's hopeless; the corruption remains. So throw it into the fire! 13 It
is the filth and corruption of your lewdness and idolatry. And now, because I tried to
cleanse you but you refused, you will remain filthy until my fury against you has been
satisfied. 14 I, the LORD, have spoken! The time has come and I won't hold back; I will
not change my mind. You will be judged on the basis of all your wicked actions, says the
Sovereign LORD."

The Death of Ezekiel's Wife

15 Then this message came to me from the LORD: 16 "Son of man, I am going to take away
your dearest treasure. Suddenly she will die. Yet you must not show any sorrow. Do not
weep; let there be no tears. 17 You may sigh but only quietly. Let there be no wailing at
her grave. Do not uncover your head or take off your sandals. Do not perform the rituals
of mourning or accept any food brought to you by consoling friends."

23:45 Ezek 16:38
23:46 Jer 15:4; 24:9; 29:18 Ezek 16:38
23:47 Jer 29:8
23:49 Isa 59:18 Ezek 9:10
24:2 2 Kgs 25:1 Jer 39:1; 52:4
24:3 Jer 1:13-14
24:4 Mic 3:2-3
24:5 Jer 52:10, 24-27
24:6 2 Kgs 24:3-4 Nah 3:1
24:7 Lev 17:13 Deut 12:16
24:8 Isa 26:21
24:9 Hab 2:12
24:11 Mal 4:1
24:13 Ezek 8:18
24:14 Ps 33:9 Isa 55:11
24:16 Job 23:2 Song 7:10 Jer 13:17; 16:5; 22:10
24:17 Lev 21:10-12 2 Sam 15:30 Jer 16:7

24:1 Hebrew *On the tenth day of the tenth month,* of the Hebrew calendar. This event occurred on January 15, 588 B.C.; also see note on 1:1.

24:1-14 Ezekiel gave this illustration in 588 B.C., about three years after the first of the previous messages (see 20:1, 2). The people in Judah thought they were the choice meat because they hadn't been taken into captivity in 597 when the Babylonians last invaded the land. Ezekiel used this illustration before (chapter 11) to show that, although the people thought they were safe and secure inside the cooking pot, this pot would actually be the place of their destruction. This message was given to the exiles in Babylonia the very day that the Babylonians attacked Jerusalem (24:2), beginning a siege that lasted over two years and resulted in the city's destruction. When God's punishment comes, it is relentless.

24:6-13 The city of Jerusalem was like a pot so encrusted with sin that it would not come clean. God wanted to cleanse the lives of those who lived in Jerusalem, and he wants to cleanse our lives today. Sometimes he tries to purify us through difficulties and troublesome circumstances. When you face tough times, allow the sin to be burned from your life. Look at your problems as opportunities for your faith to grow. When these times come, unnecessary priorities and diversions are purged away. We can reexamine our lives so that we will do what really counts.

24:15-18 God told Ezekiel that his wife would die and that he should not grieve for her. Ezekiel obeyed God fully, even as Hosea did when he was told to marry a prostitute (Hosea 1:2, 3). In both cases, these unusual events were intended as symbolic acts to illustrate God's relationship with his people. Obeying God can carry a high price, but not obeying God will cost you more—eternal life. We should be wholehearted in our obedience to God as Ezekiel was. We can begin by doing all that God commands us to do, even when we don't feel like it. Are you willing to serve God as completely as Ezekiel did?

18 So I proclaimed this to the people the next morning, and in the evening my wife
died. The next morning I did everything I had been told to do. 19 Then the people asked,
"What does all this mean? What are you trying to tell us?"

24:21 Ps 27:4 Jer 16:11 Ezek 23:47

20 So I said to them, "A message came to me from the LORD, 21 and I was told to give
this message to the people of Israel. This is what the Sovereign LORD says: I will
desecrate my Temple, the source of your security and pride. Your sons and daughters in
Judea will be slaughtered by the sword. 22 Then you will do as Ezekiel has done. You will

24:23 Job 27:15 Ps 78:64

not mourn in public or console yourselves by eating the food brought to you by
sympathetic friends. 23 Your heads must remain covered, and your sandals must not be
taken off. You will not mourn or weep, but you will waste away because of your sins.

24:24 Ezek 4:3 Luke 11:29-30

You will mourn privately for all the evil you have done. 24 Ezekiel is an example for you
to follow; you will do as he has done. And when that time comes, you will know that I
am the LORD."

24:25 Pss 48:2; 122:1-9 Jer 7:4; 11:22

25 Then the LORD said to me, "Son of man, on the day I take away their stronghold—

24:26 1 Sam 4:12 Job 1:15-19 Ezek 33:21-22

their joy and glory, their heart's desire, their dearest treasure—I will also take away their
sons and daughters. 26 And on that day a refugee from Jerusalem will come to you in
Babylon and tell you what has happened. 27 And when he arrives, your voice will

24:27 Ezek 3:26; 33:22

suddenly return so you can talk to him, and you will be a symbol for these people. Then
they will know that I am the LORD."

B. MESSAGES AGAINST FOREIGN NATIONS (25:1—32:32)

These messages were given concerning seven nations which surrounded Judah. The Ammonites were judged because of their joy over the desecration of the Temple, the Moabites because they scorned Judah as special people, the Edomites because of their special hatred of the Jews, and the Philistines because of their vengeance. All these nations would soon realize that God is supreme. Nations today are also under limits imposed by God.

A Message for Ammon

25:2 Amos 1:13 Zeph 2:9

25 Then this message came to me from the LORD: 2 "Son of man, look toward the
land of Ammon and prophesy against its people. 3 Give the Ammonites this

25:4 Deut 28:33, 51 Judg 6:3, 33 Isa 1:7

message from the Sovereign LORD: Hear the word of the Sovereign LORD! Because you
scoffed when my Temple was desecrated, mocked Israel in her desolation, and laughed
at Judah as she went away into exile, 4 I will allow nomads from the eastern deserts to

25:5 2 Sam 12:26 Jer 49:2 Zeph 2:14-15

overrun your country. They will set up their camps among you and pitch their tents on
your land. They will harvest all your fruit and steal your livestock. 5 And I will turn the
city of Rabbah into a pasture for camels, and all the land of the Ammonites into an

25:6 Job 27:23 Zeph 2:8, 10

enclosure for sheep. Then you will know that I am the LORD.
6 "And the Sovereign LORD says: Because you clapped and stamped and cheered with

24:20-24 Ezekiel was not allowed to mourn for his dead wife in order to show his fellow exiles that they were not to mourn publicly over Jerusalem when it was destroyed. Any personal sorrow felt would soon be eclipsed by national sorrow over the horror of the city's total destruction. The individuals would waste away because of their sins, which caused the city's destruction.

24:27 For some time Ezekiel had not been allowed to speak except when God gave him a message to deliver to the people (3:25-27). This restriction would soon end when Jerusalem was destroyed and all Ezekiel's prophecies about Judah and Jerusalem had come true (33:21, 22).

25:1ff Chapters 25–32 are God's word concerning the seven nations surrounding Judah. The judgments in these chapters are not simply the vengeful statements of Jews against their enemies; they are God's judgments on nations that failed to acknowledge the one true God and fulfill the good purposes God intended for them. The Ammonites were judged because of their joy over the desecration of the Temple (25:1-7), the Moabites because they found pleasure in Judah's wickedness (25:8-11), the Edomites because of their racial hatred for the Jews (25:12-14), and the Philistines because they sought revenge against Judah for defeating them in battle (25:15-17).

25:5 Rabbah was the capital city of the Ammonites.

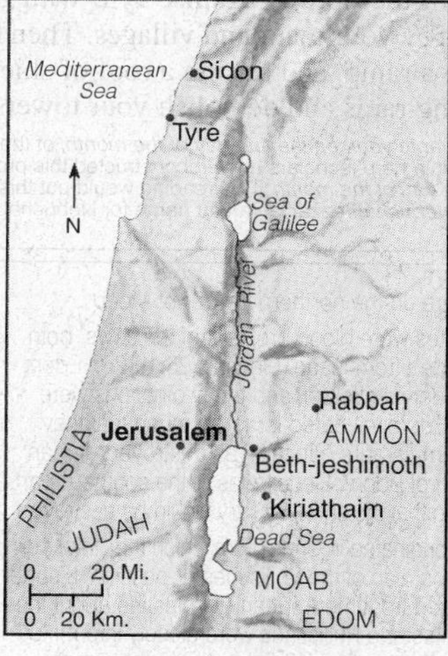

JUDAH'S ENEMIES
Ammon, Moab, Edom, and Philistia, although once united with Judah against Babylon, had abandoned Judah and rejoiced to see its ruin. But these nations were as sinful as Judah and would also feel the sting of God's judgment.

glee at the destruction of my people, 7I will lift up my fist against you. I will give you as plunder to many nations. I will cut you off from being a nation and destroy you completely. Then you will know that I am the LORD.

25:7 Amos 1:14-15

A Message for Moab

8"And the Sovereign LORD says: Because the people of Moab have said that Judah is just like all the other nations, 9I will open up their eastern flank and wipe out their glorious frontier cities—Beth-jeshimoth, Baal-meon, and Kiriathaim. 10And I will hand Moab over to nomads from the eastern deserts, just as I handed over Ammon. Yes, the Ammonites will no longer be counted among the nations. 11And in the same way, I will bring my judgment down on the Moabites. Then they will know that I am the LORD.

25:8 Isa 15:1; Jer 48:1; Amos 2:1
25:9 Num 32:37-38; Josh 13:17-20; 1 Chr 5:8; Jer 48:23

A Message for Edom

12"And the Sovereign LORD says: The people of Edom have sinned greatly by avenging themselves against the people of Judah. 13Therefore, says the Sovereign LORD, I will raise my fist of judgment against Edom. I will wipe out their people, cattle, and flocks with the sword. I will make a wasteland of everything from Teman to Dedan. 14By the hand of my people of Israel, I will accomplish this. They will carry out my furious vengeance, and Edom will know it is from me. I, the Sovereign LORD, have spoken!

25:13 Gen 36:34; Jer 49:7; Mal 1:3-4
25:14 Ezek 34:11; Nah 1:2-4; Heb 10:30-31

A Message for Philistia

15"And the Sovereign LORD says: The people of Philistia have acted against Judah out of revenge and long-standing contempt. 16Therefore, says the Sovereign LORD, I will raise my fist of judgment against the land of the Philistines. I will wipe out the Kerethites and utterly destroy the people who live by the sea. 17I will execute terrible vengeance against them to rebuke them for what they have done. And when I have inflicted my revenge, then they will know that I am the LORD."

25:15 Isa 14:29-31; Joel 3:4; Amos 1:6-8; Zeph 2:4-7; Zech 9:5-8
25:16 1 Sam 30:14

A Message for Tyre

26 On February 3, during the twelfth year of King Jehoiachin's captivity,* this message came to me from the LORD: 2"Son of man, Tyre has rejoiced over the fall of Jerusalem, saying, 'Ha! She who controlled the rich trade routes to the east has been broken, and I am the heir! Because she has been destroyed, I will become wealthy!'

3"Therefore, this is what the Sovereign LORD says: I am your enemy, O Tyre, and I will bring many nations against you, like the waves of the sea crashing against your shoreline. 4They will destroy the walls of Tyre and tear down its towers. I will scrape away its soil and make it a bare rock! 5The island of Tyre will become uninhabited. It will be a place for fishermen to spread their nets, for I have spoken, says the Sovereign LORD. Tyre will become the prey of many nations, 6and its mainland villages will be destroyed by the sword. Then they will know that I am the LORD.

7"For the Sovereign LORD says: I will bring King Nebuchadnezzar* of Babylon—the king of kings from the north—against Tyre with his cavalry, chariots, and great army. 8First he will destroy your mainland villages. Then he will attack you by building a siege wall, constructing a ramp, and raising a roof of shields against you. 9He will pound your walls with battering rams and demolish your towers with sledgehammers. 10The hooves

26:2 2 Sam 5:11; Isa 23:1; Jer 25:22
26:3 Jer 50:42; 51:42
26:4 Isa 23:11; Amos 1:10
26:7 Dan 2:37, 47; Nah 2:3-4
26:8 Jer 6:6; 32:24; 52:4
26:10 Jer 39:3

26:1 Hebrew *In the eleventh year, on the first day of the month,* of the Hebrew calendar year. Since an element is missing in the date formula here, scholars have reconstructed this probable reading: *In the eleventh [month of the twelfth] year, on the first day of the month.* This reading would put this message on February 3, 585 B.C.; also see note on 1:1. **26:7** Hebrew *Nebuchadrezzar,* a variant name for Nebuchadnezzar.

25:9 These towns were on the northern border of Moab.

25:13, 14 The Edomites were blood brothers of the Jews, both nations having descended from Isaac (Genesis 25:19-26). Edom shared its northern border with Israel, and the two nations were always in conflict. The Edomites hated Israel so much that they rejoiced when Jerusalem, Israel's capital, was destroyed. Teman was in the northern part of Edom; Dedan was in the southern part. Thus, Ezekiel was saying that the entire country would be destroyed.

25:16 The Kerethites originated in Crete, from which they take their name. They were either a clan of the Philistines or possibly a separate people who migrated from the Aegean to Palestine about the same time. The Kerethites and Philistines were closely intermixed once they were in Palestine and are often mentioned together.

26:1ff This message came to Ezekiel in 586 B.C. Chapters 26 and 27 are a prophecy against Tyre, the capital of Phoenicia, just north of Israel. Part of the city was on the coastline, and part was on a beautiful island. Tyre rejoiced when Jerusalem fell, because Tyre and Judah always competed for the lucrative trade that came through their lands from Egypt in the south and Mesopotamia to the north. Tyre dominated the sea trading routes, while Judah dominated the land caravan routes. After Judah was defeated, Tyre thought it had all the trade routes to itself. But this gloating didn't last long. In 586 B.C., Nebuchadnezzar attacked the city. It took him 15 years to capture Tyre (586-571) because the city's back side lay on the sea so fresh supplies could be shipped in daily.

of his cavalry will choke the city with dust, and your walls will shake as the horses gallop through your broken gates, pulling chariots behind them. 11 His horsemen will trample every street in the city. They will butcher your people, and your famous pillars will topple.

12 "They will plunder all your riches and merchandise and break down your walls. They will destroy your lovely homes and dump your stones and timbers and even your dust into the sea. 13 I will stop the music of your songs. No more will the sound of harps be heard among your people. 14 I will make your island a bare rock, a place for fishermen to spread their nets. You will never be rebuilt, for I, the LORD, have spoken! This is the word of the Sovereign LORD.

The Effect of Tyre's Destruction

15 "This is what the Sovereign LORD says to Tyre: The whole coastline will tremble at the sound of your fall, as the screams of the wounded echo in the continuing slaughter. 16 All the seaport rulers will step down from their thrones and take off their royal robes and beautiful clothing. They will sit on the ground trembling with horror at what they have seen. 17 Then they will wail for you, singing this funeral song:

'O famous island city,
  once ruler of the sea,
  how you have been destroyed!
Your people, with their naval power,
  once spread fear around the world.
18 Now the coastlands tremble at your fall.
  The islands are dismayed as you pass away.'

19 "For the Sovereign LORD says: I will make Tyre an uninhabited ruin. You will sink beneath the terrible waves of enemy attack. Great seas will swallow you. 20 I will send you to the pit to lie there with those who descended there long ago. Your city will lie in ruins, buried beneath the earth, like those in the pit who have entered the world of the dead. Never again will you be given a position of respect here in the land of the living. 21 I will bring you to a terrible end, and you will be no more. You will be looked for, but you will never be found. I, the Sovereign LORD, have spoken!"

The End of Tyre's Glory

27 Then this message came to me from the LORD: 2 "Son of man, sing a funeral song for Tyre, 3 that mighty gateway to the sea, the trading center of the world. Give Tyre this message from the Sovereign LORD: You claimed, O Tyre, to be perfect in beauty. 4 You extended your boundaries into the sea. Your builders made you glorious! 5 You were like a great ship built of the finest cypress from Senir.* They took a cedar from Lebanon to make a mast for you. 6 They carved oars for you from the oaks of Bashan. They made your deck of pine wood, brought from the southern coasts of Cyprus.* Then they inlaid it with ivory. 7 Your sails were made of Egypt's finest linen, and they flew as a banner above you. You stood beneath blue and purple awnings made bright with dyes from the coasts of Elishah.

8 "Your oarsmen came from Sidon and Arvad; your helmsmen were skilled men from Tyre itself. 9 Wise old craftsmen from Gebal did all the caulking. Ships came with goods from every land to barter for your trade. 10 Men from distant Persia, Lydia, and Libya*

27:5 Or *Hermon.* **27:6** Hebrew *Kittim.* **27:10** Hebrew *Paras, Lud, and Put.*

26:11 Isa 5:28; 26:5
26:12 2 Chr 32:27; Isa 23:8, 18
26:13 Isa 24:8-9; Amos 6:5
26:14 Deut 13:16; Isa 14:27
26:15 Jer 49:21
26:16 Ps 35:26; Jon 3:6
26:17 Isa 14:12; Jer 48:39; 50:23
26:18 Isa 23:5-7, 10-15
26:19 Isa 8:7-8
26:20 Ps 88:6; Jon 2:2, 6; Zech 2:8
26:21 Ezek 27:36
27:2 Jer 7:20; 9:10
27:5 Deut 3:9; Song 4:8
27:6 Num 21:33; Jer 22:20; Zech 11:2
27:7 Exod 25:4; Prov 7:16; Jer 10:9
27:8 Gen 10:18; 1 Kgs 9:27; 1 Chr 1:16
27:9 1 Kgs 5:18

26:14 After a 15-year siege, Nebuchadnezzar could not conquer the part of Tyre located on the island; thus, certain aspects of the description in 26:12, 14 exceed the actual damage done to Tyre by Nebuchadnezzar. But the prophecy predicted what would happen to the island settlement later during the conquests of Alexander the Great. Alexander threw the rubble of the mainland city into the sea until it made a bridge to the island. Then he marched across the bridge and destroyed the island (332 B.C.). Today the island city is still a pile of rubble, a testimony to God's judgment.

27:1ff Chapter 27 is a funeral lament over Tyre's fall. It compares the city to a ship (27:1-9), mentions many of its trading partners (27:10-25), and then describes how the ship sank (27:26-36). Jesus spoke of Tyre in Matthew 11:22 as a city worthy of God's judgment.

27:3, 4 The beauty of Tyre was the source of its pride, and Tyre's pride guaranteed its judgment. Conceit or pride in our own accomplishments should be a danger signal to us (see James 4:13-17). God is not against our taking pleasure or finding satisfaction in what we do; he is against arrogance and inflated self-esteem that looks down on others. We must acknowledge God as the basis and source of our life.

served in your great army. They hung their shields and helmets on your walls, giving you
great honor. 11 Men from Arvad and from Helech stood on your walls as sentinels. Your
towers were manned by men from Gammad. Their shields hung on your walls, perfecting
your splendor.
12 "Tarshish was your agent, trading your wares in exchange for silver, iron, tin, and
lead. 13 Merchants from Greece,* Tubal, and Meshech brought slaves and bronze dishes.
14 From Togarmah came riding horses, chariot horses, and mules. All these things were
exchanged for your manufactured goods. 15 Merchants came to you from Dedan.*
Numerous coastlands were your captive markets; they brought payment in ivory tusks
and ebony wood.
16 "Aram* sent merchants to buy your wares. They traded turquoise, purple dyes,
embroidery, fine linen, and jewelry of coral and rubies. 17 Judah and Israel traded for your
wares, offering wheat from Minnith, early figs,* honey, oil, and balm. 18 Damascus
traded for your rich variety of goods, bringing wine from Helbon and white wool from
Zahar. 19 Greeks from Uzal* came to trade for your merchandise. Wrought iron, cassia,
and calamus were bartered for your wares. 20 Dedan traded their expensive saddle
blankets with you.
21 "The Arabians and the princes of Kedar brought lambs and rams and goats in
trade for your goods. 22 The merchants of Sheba and Raamah came with all kinds of
spices, jewels, and gold in exchange for your wares. 23 Haran, Canneh, Eden, Sheba,
Asshur, and Kilmad came with their merchandise, too. 24 They brought choice fabrics
to trade—blue cloth, embroidery, and many-colored carpets bound with cords and
made secure. 25 The ships of Tarshish were your ocean caravans. Your island ware-
house was filled to the brim!

The Destruction of Tyre

26 "But look! Your oarsmen are rowing your ship of state into a hurricane! Your mighty
vessel flounders in the heavy eastern gale. You are shipwrecked in the heart of the sea!
27 Everything is lost—your riches and wares, your sailors and helmsmen, your ship
builders, merchants, and warriors. On that day of vast ruin, everyone on board sinks into
the depths of the sea.
28 "Your cities by the sea tremble as your helmsmen cry out in terror. 29 All the
oarsmen abandon their ships; the sailors and helmsmen come to stand on the shore.
30 They weep bitterly as they throw dust on their heads and roll in ashes. 31 They shave
their heads in grief because of you and dress themselves in sackcloth. They weep for
you with bitter anguish and deep mourning. 32 As they wail and mourn, they sing this
sad funeral song:

'Was there ever such a city as Tyre,
now silent at the bottom of the sea?
33 The merchandise you traded
satisfied the needs of many nations.
Kings at the ends of the earth
were enriched by your trade.
34 Now you are a wrecked ship,
broken at the bottom of the sea.
All your merchandise and your crew
have passed away with you.
35 All who live along the coastlands
are appalled at your terrible fate.
Their kings are filled with horror
and look on with twisted faces.
36 The merchants of the nations
shake their heads at the sight of you,*
for you have come to a horrible end
and will be no more.'"

27:13 Gen 10:2-3; Isa 66:19; Ezek 38:2; Joel 3:3; Rev 18:13
27:14 Gen 10:13
27:15 Rev 18:12
27:16 Ezek 16:13, 18
27:17 Judg 11:33
27:18 Gen 14:15; Ezek 47:16-18
27:21 Isa 21:13; 60:7
27:22 Gen 10:7; 43:11; 1 Kgs 10:2; Isa 60:6; Ezek 38:13
27:23 2 Kgs 19:12; Isa 37:12; Amos 1:5; 6:2
27:26 Ps 48:7
27:29 Rev 18:17-19
27:30 1 Sam 4:12; 2 Sam 1:2; Jon 3:6; Rev 18:19
27:31 Isa 16:9; 22:12; Ezek 7:18; 29:18
27:32 Rev 18:18
27:34 Zech 9:3-4
27:36 Ps 37:10, 36; Jer 49:17; Zeph 2:15

27:13 Hebrew *Javan*. **27:15** Greek version reads *Rhodes*. **27:16** Some manuscripts read *Edom*. **27:17** The meaning of the Hebrew is uncertain. **27:19** Hebrew *Vedan and Javan from Uzal*. The meaning of the Hebrew is uncertain. **27:36** Hebrew *hiss at you*.

28:2 Ps 82:6-7; 2 Thes 2:4
28:3 Dan 1:20
28:4 Zech 9:2-4
28:5 Job 31:24-25; Ps 52:7; Hos 12:7-8; 13:6
28:6 Exod 9:17
28:7 Dan 7:7; Hab 1:6-8
28:8 Ezek 27:26-27, 34
28:10 1 Sam 17:26, 36; Ezek 31:18
28:12 Ezek 27:2
28:13 Gen 2:8; Exod 28:17-20; 39:10-21; Isa 51:3; 54:11-12
28:14 Exod 25:17-20; Ezek 20:40; Rev 18:16
28:15 Isa 14:12
28:16 Ezek 8:17; Hab 2:8, 17
28:17 Isa 19:11
28:18 Amos 1:9-10; Mal 4:3
28:19 Jer 51:64
28:21 Gen 10:15-19; Isa 23:2-4, 12
28:23 Jer 51:52; Ezek 38:22

A Message for Tyre's King

28 Then this message came to me from the LORD: 2 "Son of man, give the prince of
Tyre this message from the Sovereign LORD: In your great pride you claim, 'I am
a god! I sit on a divine throne in the heart of the sea.' But you are only a man and not a
god, though you boast that you are like a god. 3 You regard yourself as wiser than Daniel
and think no secret is hidden from you. 4 With your wisdom and understanding you have
amassed great wealth—gold and silver for your treasuries. 5 Yes, your wisdom has made
you very rich, and your riches have made you very proud.
6 "Therefore, this is what the Sovereign LORD says: Because you think you are as
wise as a god, 7 I will bring against you an enemy army, the terror of the nations. They
will suddenly draw their swords against your marvelous wisdom and defile your
splendor! 8 They will bring you down to the pit, and you will die there on your island
home in the heart of the sea, pierced with many wounds. 9 Will you then boast, 'I am
a god!' to those who kill you? To them you will be no god but merely a man! 10 You
will die like an outcast at the hands of foreigners. I, the Sovereign LORD, have
spoken!"
11 Then this further message came to me from the LORD: 12 "Son of man, weep for the
king of Tyre. Give him this message from the Sovereign LORD: You were the perfection
of wisdom and beauty. 13 You were in Eden, the garden of God. Your clothing was
adorned with every precious stone*—red carnelian, chrysolite, white moonstone, beryl,
onyx, jasper, sapphire, turquoise, and emerald—all beautifully crafted for you and set in
the finest gold. They were given to you on the day you were created. 14 I ordained and
anointed you as the mighty angelic guardian.* You had access to the holy mountain of
God and walked among the stones of fire.
15 "You were blameless in all you did from the day you were created until the day evil
was found in you. 16 Your great wealth filled you with violence, and you sinned. So I
banished you from the mountain of God. I expelled you, O mighty guardian, from your
place among the stones of fire. 17 Your heart was filled with pride because of all your
beauty. You corrupted your wisdom for the sake of your splendor. So I threw you to the
earth and exposed you to the curious gaze of kings. 18 You defiled your sanctuaries with
your many sins and your dishonest trade. So I brought fire from within you, and it
consumed you. I let it burn you to ashes on the ground in the sight of all who were
watching. 19 All who knew you are appalled at your fate. You have come to a terrible end,
and you are no more."

A Message for Sidon

20 Then another message came to me from the LORD: 21 "Son of man, look toward the
city of Sidon and prophesy against it. 22 Give the people of Sidon this message from
the Sovereign LORD: I am your enemy, O Sidon, and I will reveal my glory by what
happens to you. When I bring judgment against you and reveal my holiness among
you, everyone watching will know that I am the LORD. 23 I will send a plague against
you, and blood will be spilled in your streets. The attack will come from every

28:13 The identification of some of these gemstones is uncertain. **28:14** Hebrew *guardian cherub;* also in 28:16.

28:1ff Previously Ezekiel had prophesied against the city of Tyre (chapters 26–27). Here he focused his prophecy on Tyre's leader. The chief sin of Tyre's king was pride—believing himself to be a god. But Ezekiel also may have made a broader spiritual application, speaking about the spiritual king of Tyre, Satan, whom the people were really following (see the note on 28:12-19).

28:2, 3 Daniel, an important official in Nebuchadnezzar's kingdom (14:14), was already renowned for his wisdom. Daniel proclaimed that all his wisdom came from God (Daniel 2:20-23). By contrast, the king of Tyre thought that he himself *was* a god. As truly wise people get closer to God, they recognize their need to depend on him for guidance.

28:6-10 The enemy army that attacked Tyre was the Babylonian army under Nebuchadnezzar. This attack occurred in 573/572 B.C.

28:12-19 Some of the phrases in this passage describing the human king of Tyre may describe Satan. Great care must be taken to interpret these verses with discernment. It is clear that at times Ezekiel describes this king in terms that could not apply to a mere man. This king had been in the Garden of Eden (28:13), had been "ordained and anointed . . . as the mighty angelic guardian" (28:14), and had access to the holy mountain of God (28:14), but was banished from there (28:16, 17). Ezekiel, therefore, may have been condemning not only the king of Tyre but Satan, who had motivated the king to sin.

28:20, 21 Sidon was another famous seaport, located about 25 miles north of Tyre. God charged this city with contempt for his people. Sidon's economy was bound to Tyre's, so when Tyre fell to Nebuchadnezzar, Sidon was doomed to follow.

direction, and your people will lie slaughtered within your walls. Then everyone will
know that I am the LORD. 24 No longer will Israel's scornful neighbors prick and tear
at her like thorns and briers. For then they will know that I am the Sovereign LORD.

Restoration for Israel

25 "This is what the Sovereign LORD says: The people of Israel will again live in their
own land, the land I gave my servant Jacob. For I will gather them from the distant lands
where I have scattered them. I will reveal to the nations of the world my holiness among
my people. 26 They will live safely in Israel and build their homes and plant their
vineyards. And when I punish the neighboring nations that treated them with contempt,
they will know that I am the LORD their God."

A Message for Egypt

29 On January 7,* during the tenth year of King Jehoiachin's captivity, this
message came to me from the LORD: 2 "Son of man, turn toward Egypt and
prophesy against Pharaoh the king and all the people of Egypt. 3 Give them this
message from the Sovereign LORD: I am your enemy, O Pharaoh, king of Egypt—you
great monster, lurking in the streams of the Nile. For you have said, 'The Nile River
is mine; I made it for myself!' 4 I will put hooks in your jaws and drag you out on the
land with fish sticking to your scales. 5 I will leave you and all your fish stranded in
the desert to die. You will lie unburied on the open ground, for I have given you as
food to the wild animals and birds.

6 "All the people of Egypt will discover that I am the LORD, for you collapsed like
a reed when Israel looked to you for help. 7 Israel leaned on you, but like a cracked
staff, you splintered and stabbed her in the armpit. When she put her weight on you,
you gave way, and her back was thrown out of joint. 8 So now the Sovereign LORD
says: I will bring an army against you, O Egypt, and destroy both people and animals.
9 The land of Egypt will become a desolate wasteland, and the Egyptians will know
that I am the LORD.

"Because you said, 'The Nile River is mine; I made it,' 10 I am now the enemy of
both you and your river. I will utterly destroy the land of Egypt, from Migdol to
Aswan, as far south as the border of Ethiopia.* 11 For forty years not a soul will pass
that way, neither people nor animals. It will be completely uninhabited. 12 I will make
Egypt desolate, and it will be surrounded by other desolate nations. Its cities will be
empty and desolate for forty years, surrounded by other desolate cities. I will scatter
the Egyptians to distant lands.

28:24 Num 33:35; Josh 23:13; Isa 55:13
28:25 Ps 106:47; Isa 11:12-13; Jer 23:8
28:26 Jer 32:15, 43-44; Amos 9:13-14
29:2 Isa 19:1-17; Jer 46:2-25
29:3 Isa 27:1
29:4 2 Kgs 19:28; Isa 37:29; Ezek 38:4
29:5 Jer 7:33; 34:20
29:6 Isa 36:6
29:7 Jer 37:5-11; Ezek 17:15-17
29:9 Prov 18:12; 29:23
29:11 Jer 43:11-12
29:12 Jer 25:15-19; 27:6-11

29:1 Hebrew *On the twelfth day of the tenth month,* of the Hebrew calendar. A number of dates in Ezekiel can be cross-checked with dates in surviving Babylonian records and related accurately to our modern calendar. This event occurred on January 7, 587 B.C. **29:10** Hebrew *Cush.*

28:24-26 This promise that God's people will live in complete safety has yet to be fulfilled. While many were allowed to return from exile under Zerubbabel, Ezra, and Nehemiah, and although the political nation is restored today, the inhabitants do not yet live in complete safety (28:26). Therefore, this promise will have its ultimate fulfillment when Christ sets up his eternal Kingdom. Then all people who have been faithful to God will dwell together in harmony and complete safety.

29:1ff There are seven prophecies in chapters 29–32, all dealing with judgment on Egypt. This is probably the first prophecy that was given by Ezekiel in 587 B.C. Hezekiah, Jehoiakim, and Zedekiah (kings of Judah) had all sought help from Egypt despite God's warnings.

There are three key reasons for this prophecy: (1) Egypt was an ancient enemy of the Jews, having once enslaved them for more than 400 years; (2) Egypt worshiped many gods; (3) Egypt's wealth and power made it seem like a good ally. Egypt offered to help Judah only because of the benefits it hoped to receive from such an alliance. When the Egyptians didn't get what they hoped for, they bailed out of their agreement without regard to any promises they had made.

29:2ff Egypt had great artistic treasures, a flourishing civilization, and world-renowned military power. Unfortunately, it was also evil, egotistical, idolatrous, and it treated slaves cruelly. For those sins God condemned Egypt. At the battle of Carchemish in 605 B.C., Babylon crushed Egypt along with Assyria, its rivals for the position of world ruler.

29:9, 10 The Nile was Egypt's pride and joy, a life-giving river cutting through the middle of the desert. Rather than thanking God, however, Egypt declared, "The Nile River is mine; I made it." We do the same when we say, "This house is mine; I built it," or "I have brought myself to the place where I am today," or "I have built this church, business, or reputation from the ground up." These statements reveal our pride. Sometimes we take for granted what God has given us, thinking we have made it ourselves. Of course, we have put forth a lot of hard effort, but God supplied the resources, gave us the abilities, and provided us with the opportunities to make it happen. Instead of proclaiming our own greatness, as the Egyptians did, we should proclaim God's greatness and give him the credit. (Migdol is in the north of Egypt, and Aswan in the south. Thus, this meant all of Egypt.)

29:13 Isa 19:22; Jer 46:26
29:14 Isa 11:11; Jer 44:1
29:15 Dan 11:42-43
29:16 Isa 30:1-3; 64:9; Hos 5:13; 8:13; 9:9

13“But the Sovereign LORD also says: At the end of the forty years I will bring the
Egyptians home again from the nations to which they have been scattered. 14I will restore
the prosperity of Egypt and bring its people back to the land of Pathros in southern Egypt
from which they came. But Egypt will remain an unimportant, minor kingdom. 15It will
be the lowliest of all the nations, never again great enough to rise above its neighbors.
16“Then Israel will no longer be tempted to trust in Egypt for help. Egypt’s shattered
condition will remind Israel of how sinful she was to trust Egypt in earlier days. Then
Israel will know that I alone am the Sovereign LORD.”

Nebuchadnezzar to Conquer Egypt

29:17 Ezek 24:1; 30:20
29:18 Jer 25:9; 27:6; Ezek 26:7-12
29:19 Jer 43:10-13; Ezek 30:10-12
29:20 Isa 10:6-7; 45:1-3
29:21 1 Sam 2:10; Ps 92:10; 132:17; Amos 3:7-8; Luke 21:15

17On April 26,* during the twenty-seventh year of King Jehoiachin’s captivity, this
message came to me from the LORD: 18“Son of man, the army of King Nebuchadnezzar*
of Babylon fought so hard against Tyre that the warriors’ heads were rubbed bare and
their shoulders were raw and blistered. Yet Nebuchadnezzar and his army won no
plunder to compensate them for all their work. 19Therefore, this is what the Sovereign
LORD says: I will give the land of Egypt to Nebuchadnezzar, king of Babylon. He will
carry off their wealth, plundering everything they have to pay his army. 20Yes, I have
given him the land of Egypt as a reward for his work, says the Sovereign LORD, because
he was working for me when he destroyed Tyre.
21“And the day will come when I will cause the ancient glory of Israel to revive, and
then at last your words will be respected. Then they will know that I am the LORD.”

A Sad Day for Egypt

30:2 Isa 13:6; 65:14; Joel 1:5, 11, 13, 15
30:5 Jer 25:20, 24
30:6 Isa 20:3-6
30:8 Ps 58:11; Amos 1:4, 7, 10-14
30:9 Isa 18:1-2; Ezek 32:9-10; 38:11
30:12 Ezek 29:3, 9

30 This is another message that came to me from the LORD: 2“Son of man, prophesy
and give this message from the Sovereign LORD: Weep, 3for the terrible day is
almost here—the day of the LORD! It is a day of clouds and gloom, a day of despair for
the nations! 4A sword will come against Egypt, and those who are slaughtered will cover
the ground. Their wealth will be carried away and their foundations destroyed. The land
of Ethiopia* will be ravished. 5Ethiopia, Libya,* Lydia,* and Arabia, with all their other
allies, will be destroyed in that war.
6“For this is what the LORD says: All of Egypt’s allies will fall, and the pride of their
power will end. From Migdol to Aswan they will be slaughtered by the sword, says the
Sovereign LORD. 7Egypt will be desolate, surrounded by desolate nations, and its cities
will be in ruins, surrounded by other ruined cities. 8And the people of Egypt will know
that I am the LORD when I have set Egypt on fire and destroyed all their allies. 9At that
time I will send swift messengers in ships to terrify the complacent Ethiopians. Great
panic will come upon them on that day of Egypt’s certain destruction.
10“For this is what the Sovereign LORD says: Through King Nebuchadnezzar* of
Babylon, I will destroy the hordes of Egypt. 11He and his armies—ruthless among the
nations—have been sent to demolish the land. They will make war against Egypt until
slaughtered Egyptians cover the ground. 12I will dry up the Nile River and hand the land
over to wicked men. I will destroy the land of Egypt and everything in it, using foreigners
to do it. I, the LORD, have spoken!

29:17 Hebrew *On the first day of the first month,* of the Hebrew calendar. This event occurred on April 26, 571 B.C.; also see note on 29:1. **29:18** Hebrew *Nebuchadrezzar,* a variant name for Nebuchadnezzar; also in 29:19. **30:4** Hebrew *Cush;* also in 30:5, 9. **30:5a** Hebrew *Put . . . Kub.* Both *Put* and *Kub* are associated with Libya. **30:5b** Hebrew *Lud.* **30:10** Hebrew *Nebuchadrezzar,* a variant name for Nebuchadnezzar.

29:13-16 This 40-year period of desolation in Egypt is hard to pinpoint. Nebuchadnezzar attacked Egypt around 572 B.C. and carried many people off to Babylon, while others fled for safety to surrounding nations. Approximately 33 years later, Cyrus, king of the Persian Empire, conquered Babylon and allowed the nations that Babylon had conquered to return to their homelands. Adding a possible seven-year regrouping and travel period, this could then make up that 40-year time period. Since that time, Egypt has never returned to its previous dominance as a world power.

29:17, 18 This prophecy was given in 571 B.C. and is actually the latest prophecy in Ezekiel. Nebuchadnezzar had finally conquered Tyre after a long and costly 15-year siege (586–571 B.C.). He had not counted on such an expense, so he went south and conquered Egypt to make up for all he had lost in taking Tyre. Ezekiel placed this prophecy here to describe *who* would bring this punishment to Egypt. God was using Nebuchadnezzar, an evil man, as an instrument of his judgment on Tyre, Judah, and Egypt—evil nations themselves. When Babylon didn’t recognize God’s favor, he judged it, too.

30:1-19 This is a lament for Egypt and its allies. Because of the Egyptians’ pride and idolatry, they would be brought down.

30:12 Egypt’s pharaohs claimed that they had made the Nile—the river on which the entire nation depended. If God dried up the Nile, the nation would be doomed.

13 “This is what the Sovereign LORD says: I will smash the idols of Egypt and the
images at Memphis.* There will be no rulers left in Egypt; anarchy will prevail
throughout the land! 14 I will destroy Pathros, Zoan, and Thebes,* and they will lie in
ruins, burned up by my anger. 15 I will pour out my fury on Pelusium,* the strongest
fortress of Egypt, and I will stamp out the people of Thebes. 16 Yes, I will set fire to all
Egypt! Pelusium will be racked with pain; Thebes will be torn apart; Memphis will live
in constant terror. 17 The young men of Heliopolis and Bubastis* will die in battle, and
the women* will be taken away as slaves. 18 When I come to break the proud strength of
Egypt, it will be a dark day for Tahpanhes, too. A dark cloud will cover Tahpanhes, and
its daughters will be led away as captives. 19 And so I will greatly punish Egypt, and they
will know that I am the LORD.”

The Broken Arms of Pharaoh

20 On April 29,* during the eleventh year of King Jehoiachin’s captivity, this message
came to me from the LORD: 21 “Son of man, I have broken the arm of Pharaoh, the king
of Egypt. His arm has not been put in a cast so that it may heal. Neither has it been bound
up with a splint to make it strong enough to hold a sword. 22 Therefore, this is what the
Sovereign LORD says: I am the enemy of Pharaoh, the king of Egypt! I will break both
of his arms—the good arm along with the broken one—and I will make his sword clatter
to the ground. 23 I will scatter the Egyptians to many lands throughout the world. 24 I will
strengthen the arms of Babylon’s king and put my sword in his hand. But I will break
the arms of Pharaoh, king of Egypt, and he will lie there mortally wounded, groaning in
pain. 25 I will strengthen the arms of the king of Babylon, while the arms of Pharaoh fall
useless to his sides. And when I put my sword in the hand of Babylon’s king and he
brings it against the land of Egypt, Egypt will know that I am the LORD. 26 I will scatter
the Egyptians among the nations. Then they will know that I am the LORD.”

Egypt Compared to Fallen Assyria

31 On June 21,* during the eleventh year of King Jehoiachin’s captivity, this message came to me from the LORD: 2 “Son of man, give this message to Pharaoh,
king of Egypt, and all his people: To whom would you compare your greatness? 3 You
are as Assyria was—a great and mighty nation. Assyria, too, was once like a cedar of
Lebanon, full of thick branches that cast deep forest shade with its top high among the
clouds. 4 Deep springs watered it and helped it to grow tall and luxuriant. The water was
so abundant that there was enough for all the trees nearby. 5 This great tree towered above
all the other trees around it. It prospered and grew long thick branches because of all the
water at its roots. 6 The birds nested in its branches, and in its shade all the wild animals
gave birth to their young. All the great nations of the world lived in its shadow. 7 It was
strong and beautiful, for its roots went deep into abundant water. 8 This tree became taller
than any of the other cedars in the garden of God. No cypress had branches equal to it;
no plane tree had boughs to compare. No tree in the garden of God came close to it in

30:13 Isa 2:18; Jer 44:1; 46:14
30:14 Ps 78:12, 43; Isa 19:11, 13
30:17 Gen 41:45
30:18 Lev 26:13; Jer 43:8-13
30:19 Ps 9:16; Ezek 5:8, 15
30:20 Ezek 26:1
30:21 Pss 10:15; 37:17; Jer 30:13; 46:11
30:22 2 Kgs 24:7; Jer 37:7; 46:1-12, 21-25
30:24 Isa 45:1, 5; Zeph 2:12; Zech 10:12
30:25 Josh 8:18; 1 Chr 21:16; Isa 5:25
31:2 Nah 3:8-9
31:4 Ezek 17:5, 8; Rev 17:1, 15
31:5 Ps 1:3
31:6 Ezek 17:23; Dan 4:12, 21; Matt 13:32
31:8 Gen 2:8-9; 13:10; Ps 80:10; Isa 51:3

30:13 Hebrew *Noph;* also in 30:16. **30:14** Hebrew *No;* also in 30:15, 16. **30:15** Hebrew *Sin;* also in 30:16. **30:17a** Hebrew *of Awen and Pi-beseth.* **30:17b** Or *her cities.* **30:20** Hebrew *On the seventh day of the first month,* of the Hebrew calendar. This event occurred on April 29, 587 B.C.; also see note on 29:1. **31:1** Hebrew *On the first day of the third month,* of the Hebrew calendar. This event occurred on June 21, 587 B.C.; also see note on 29:1.

30:13-19 The list of cities to be destroyed shows the breadth of the destruction; the drying up of the Nile (30:12) shows how deep the devastation would reach. Egypt would be completely incapacitated. This was a clear message to Judah not to trust Egypt for help against the Babylonians.

30:20, 21 This message came in 587 B.C. while Jerusalem was under attack from Babylon. Judah had rebelled against Babylon and made an alliance with Egypt in spite of God’s warnings (Jeremiah 2:36, 37). Pharaoh Hophra made a half-hearted attempt to help Jerusalem, but when Nebuchadnezzar’s army turned on him, he fled back to Egypt (Jeremiah 37:5-7). This defeat is what Ezekiel meant when he said that God had broken the arm of Pharaoh.

30:21-26 This prophecy was given to Ezekiel in 587 B.C. God destroyed Egypt’s military superiority and gave it to Babylon. God allows nations to rise to power to accomplish a particular purpose, often beyond our immediate understanding. When you read about armies and wars, don’t despair. Remember that God is sovereign and in charge of everything, even military might. Besides praying for your military and government leaders, pray that God’s greater purposes would be carried out and that his will would be done “on earth, just as it is in heaven” (see Matthew 6:10).

31:1ff This message was given in 587 B.C. Ezekiel compared Egypt to Assyria, calling Assyria a great cedar tree. The Egyptians were to look at the fall of the mighty nation of Assyria (whose demise they had seen) as an example of what would happen to them. Just like Assyria, Egypt took pride in its strength and beauty; this would be its downfall. She would crash like a mighty tree and be sent to the place of the dead. There is no permanence apart from God, even for a great society with magnificent culture and military power.

beauty. 9 Because of the magnificence I gave this tree, it was the envy of all the other
trees of Eden, the garden of God.
10 "Therefore, this is what the Sovereign LORD says: Because it became proud and
arrogant, and because it set itself so high above the others, reaching to the clouds, 11 I
handed it over to a mighty nation that destroyed it as its wickedness deserved. I myself
discarded it. 12 A foreign army—the terror of the nations—cut it down and left it fallen
on the ground. Its branches were scattered across the mountains and valleys and ravines
of the land. All those who lived beneath its shadow went away and left it lying there.
13 The birds roosted on its fallen trunk, and the wild animals lay among its branches.
14 Let no other nation proudly exult in its own prosperity, though it be higher than the
clouds, for all are doomed. They will land in the pit along with all the proud people of
the world.
15 "This is what the Sovereign LORD says: When Assyria went down into the grave,*
I made the deep places mourn, and I restrained the mighty waters. I clothed Lebanon in
black and caused the trees of the field to wilt. 16 I made the nations shake with fear at the
sound of its fall, for I sent it down to the grave with all the others like it. And all the other
proud trees of Eden, the most beautiful and the best of Lebanon, the ones whose roots
went deep into the water, were relieved to find it there with them in the pit. 17 Its allies,
too, were all destroyed and had passed away. They had gone down to the grave—all those
nations that had lived in its shade.
18 "O Egypt, to which of the trees of Eden will you compare your strength and glory?
You, too, will be brought down to the pit with all these other nations. You will lie there
among the outcasts who have died by the sword. This will be the fate of Pharaoh and all
his teeming hordes. I, the Sovereign LORD, have spoken!"

A Warning for Pharaoh

32 On March 3,* during the twelfth year of King Jehoiachin's captivity, this message
came to me from the LORD: 2 "Son of man, mourn for Pharaoh, king of Egypt, and
give him this message: You think of yourself as a strong young lion among the nations,
but you are really just a sea monster, heaving around in your own rivers, stirring up mud
with your feet.
3 "Therefore, this is what the Sovereign LORD says: I will send many people to catch
you in my net and haul you out of the water. 4 I will leave you stranded on the land to die.
All the birds of the heavens will land on you, and the wild animals of the whole earth
will gorge themselves on you. 5 I will cover the hills with your flesh and fill the valleys
with your bones. 6 I will drench the earth with your gushing blood all the way to the
mountains, filling the ravines to the brim. 7 When I blot you out, I will veil the heavens
and darken the stars. I will cover the sun with a cloud, and the moon will not give you
its light. 8 Yes, I will bring darkness everywhere across your land. Even the brightest stars
will become dark above you. I, the Sovereign LORD, have spoken!
9 "And when I bring your shattered remains to distant nations that you have never seen,
I will disturb many hearts. 10 Yes, I will bring terror to many lands, and their kings will
be terrified because of all I do to you. They will shudder in fear for their lives as I
brandish my sword before them on the day of your fall.
11 "For this is what the Sovereign LORD says: The sword of the king of Babylon will
come against you. 12 I will destroy you with the swords of mighty warriors—the terror

31:10 2 Chr 32:25; Isa 14:13-14; Dan 5:20
31:11 Deut 18:12; Dan 5:18-19; Nah 3:18
31:12 Dan 4:14; Hab 1:6; Matt 3:17-18
31:13 Isa 18:6; Rev 19:17-18
31:14 Num 16:30-33; Ps 63:9; Jon 2:2, 6; Eph 4:9
31:15 Nah 2:8-10
31:16 Isa 14:8; Hag 2:7
31:17 Ps 9:17; Dan 4:11-12
31:18 Ps 52:7; Jer 9:25-26; Matt 13:19
32:2 Jer 46:7-8; Nah 2:11-13
32:3 Ezek 12:13
32:4 Jer 8:2
32:6 Exod 7:17; Isa 34:3, 7; Rev 14:20
32:7 Prov 13:9; Amos 8:9
32:8 Gen 1:14
32:9 Exod 15:14-16; Rev 18:10-15
32:10 Ezek 26:16; 27:35
32:11 Jer 46:26
32:12 Ezek 28:7

31:15 Hebrew *to Sheol;* also in 31:16, 17. 32:1 Hebrew *On the first day of the twelfth month,* of the Hebrew calendar. This event occurred on March 3, 585 B.C.; also see note on 29:1.

31:9 "All the other trees of Eden" may refer to all the other nations of the world, which were jealous of Assyria's power and grandeur.

31:11 The "mighty nation" may refer to Babylon (see Daniel 2:37, 38).

32:1ff This prophecy was given in 585 B.C., two months after the news of Jerusalem's fall had reached the exiles in Babylon. Ezekiel prophesied numerous judgments upon many wicked nations. These judgments served a positive purpose: They showed that evil forces are continually being overcome and that one day God will overthrow all evil, making the world the perfect place he intended. They also serve as warnings that God alone is sovereign. Even the mightiest rulers, like Pharaoh, will fall before God. All are accountable to him.

32:2 Although Pharaoh thought of himself as a strong lion, in God's eyes he was nothing but a crocodile ("sea monster") muddying the water. God's judgment would reduce Pharaoh to his true size. Anyone who defies God will face his judgment.

of the nations. They will shatter the pride of Egypt, and all its hordes will be destroyed.
13 I will destroy all your flocks and herds that graze beside the streams. Never again will
people or animals disturb those waters with their feet. 14 Then I will let the waters of
Egypt become calm again, and they will flow as smoothly as olive oil, says the Sovereign
LORD. 15 And when I destroy Egypt and wipe out everything you have and strike down
all your people, then you will know that I am the LORD. 16 Yes, this is the funeral song
they will sing for Egypt. Let all the nations mourn for Egypt and its hordes. I, the
Sovereign LORD, have spoken!"

Egypt Falls into the Pit

17 On March 17,* during the twelfth year, another message came to me from the LORD:
18 "Son of man, weep for the hordes of Egypt and for the other mighty nations. For I
will send them down to the world below in company with those who descend to the
pit. 19 Say to them, 'O Egypt, are you lovelier than the other nations? No! So go down
to the pit and lie there among the outcasts.' 20 The Egyptians will fall with the many
who have died by the sword, for the sword is drawn against them. Egypt will be
dragged away to its judgment. 21 Down in the grave* mighty leaders will mockingly
welcome Egypt and its allies, saying, 'They have come down; they lie among the
outcasts, all victims of the sword.'

22 "Assyria lies there surrounded by the graves of all its people, those who were
slaughtered by the sword. 23 Their graves are in the depths of the pit, and they are
surrounded by their allies. These mighty men who once struck terror in the hearts of
people everywhere are now dead at the hands of their enemies.

24 "Elam lies there buried with its hordes who descended as outcasts to the world
below. They terrorized the nations while they lived, but now they lie in the pit and share
the humiliation of those who have gone to the world of the dead. 25 They have a resting
place among the slaughtered, surrounded by the graves of all their people. Yes, they
terrorized the nations while they lived, but now they lie in shame in the pit, all of them
outcasts, slaughtered by the sword.

26 "Meshech and Tubal are there, surrounded by the graves of all their hordes. They
once struck terror into the hearts of all people. But now they are outcasts, all victims
of the sword. 27 They are not buried in honor like the fallen heroes of the outcasts, who
went down to the grave* with their weapons—their shields covering their bodies,*
and their swords beneath their heads. They brought terror to everyone while they were
still alive.

28 "You too, Egypt, will lie crushed and broken among the outcasts, all victims of the
sword.

29 "Edom is there with its kings and princes. Mighty as they were, they also lie among
those killed by the sword, with the outcasts who have gone down to the pit. 30 All the
princes of the north and the Sidonians are there, all victims of the sword. Once a terror,

32:15 Exod 7:5; 14:4, 18; Ps 83:17-18
32:16 2 Sam 3:33-34; 2 Chr 35:25; Jer 9:17
32:18 Jer 1:10; Hos 6:5
32:19 Jer 9:25-26
32:20 Ps 28:3
32:21 Isa 14:9-12; Luke 16:23-24
32:23 Isa 14:15
32:24 Gen 10:22; Job 28:13; Ps 52:5; Jer 49:32-39
32:25 Ps 139:8
32:26 Gen 10:2; Isa 66:19
32:27 Prov 14:32
32:29 Isa 34:5-15; Jer 49:7-22; Ezek 25:13
32:30 Jer 1:15; 25:26; Ezek 28:21-23; 38:15

32:17 Hebrew *On the fifteenth day of the month,* presumably in the twelfth month of the Hebrew calendar (see 32:1). This would put this message at the end of King Jehoiachin's twelfth year of captivity, on March 17, 585 B.C.; also see note on 29:1. Greek version reads *On the fifteenth day of the first month,* which would put this message on April 27, 586 B.C., at the beginning of Jehoiachin's twelfth year. **32:21** Hebrew *in Sheol.* **32:27a** Hebrew *to Sheol.* **32:27b** The meaning of the Hebrew phrase here is uncertain.

32:18 The Hebrews believed in an afterlife for all people, good and bad. Ezekiel predicted that Egypt would share the same fate as that of the evil nations already sent to the "pit." The words here are more poetic than doctrinal (see Job 24:19; Psalm 16:10; Isaiah 38:10, and the note on Matthew 25:46). The Egyptians had a preoccupation with the afterlife and built pyramids to ensure the pharaohs' comfort in the next life. God alone controls our future and life after death.

32:21-32 In these verses, Ezekiel conducts a guided tour of the grave, the region of the afterlife. In the grave, all of God's enemies are condemned in judgment; many of them experience the fate they so quickly imposed on others. Though Babylon is not mentioned, Ezekiel's readers would have concluded that if all the other nations would be judged for their rebellion against God, Babylon would be judged as well. These words would comfort the captives.

32:24-26 Elam was a nation of fierce warriors from the region east of Assyria. They were conquered by Nebuchadnezzar (Jeremiah 49:34-39) and eventually rebuilt themselves and became part of Persia. Meshech and Tubal were territories located in the eastern region of Asia Minor, now eastern and central Turkey. In chapters 38 and 39 they are described as allies of Gog, the chief prince of a confederacy. They are included with the evil nations that will be judged for fighting against God's people.

32:30 The princes of the north were probably the princes of the Phoenician city-states.

they now lie there in shame. They lie there as outcasts with all the other dead who have
descended to the pit.
31“When Pharaoh arrives, he will be relieved to find that he is not alone in having his
entire army killed, says the Sovereign LORD. 32For I have caused my terror to fall upon
all the living. And Pharaoh and his hordes will lie there among the outcasts who have
died by the sword. I, the Sovereign LORD, have spoken!”

32:31 Ezek 31:16

C. MESSAGES OF HOPE (33:1—48:35)

This section begins a new direction in Ezekiel's prophecies. Ezekiel is reminded that he is the nation's watchman. Before Jerusalem's fall, he told the people of their punishment and dispersion. Now he is to proclaim the hope of restoration, but even this message does not improve the people's response. They listen to him with curiosity and then live as they please. Today we have the good news of forgiveness, but how easy it is to ignore the message and continue to live sinful lives.

1. Restoring the people of God

Ezekiel as Israel's Watchman

33 Once again a message came to me from the LORD: 2“Son of man, give your people
this message: When I bring an army against a country, the people of that land
choose a watchman. 3When the watchman sees the enemy coming, he blows the alarm
to warn the people. 4Then if those who hear the alarm refuse to take action—well, it is
their own fault if they die. 5They heard the warning but wouldn't listen, so the
responsibility is theirs. If they had listened to the warning, they could have saved their
lives. 6But if the watchman sees the enemy coming and doesn't sound the alarm to warn
the people, he is responsible for their deaths. They will die in their sins, but I will hold
the watchman accountable.
7“Now, son of man, I am making you a watchman for the people of Israel. Therefore,
listen to what I say and warn them for me. 8If I announce that some wicked people are
sure to die and you fail to warn them about changing their ways, then they will die in
their sins, but I will hold you responsible for their deaths. 9But if you warn them to repent
and they don't repent, they will die in their sins, but you will not be held responsible.

33:2 2 Sam 18:24-25, 2 Kgs 9:17
33:3 Neh 4:18-20, Hos 8:1, Joel 2:1
33:4 Jer 6:17, Zech 1:4
33:5 Exod 9:19-21, 25, Heb 11:7
33:6 Isa 56:10
33:7 Isa 62:6-7, Jer 26:2

The Watchman's Message

10“Son of man, give the people of Israel this message: You are saying, ‘Our sins are
heavy upon us; we are wasting away! How can we survive?’ 11As surely as I live, says
the Sovereign LORD, I take no pleasure in the death of wicked people. I only want them
to turn from their wicked ways so they can live. Turn! Turn from your wickedness,
O people of Israel! Why should you die?
12“Son of man, give your people this message: The good works of righteous people
will not save them if they turn to sin, nor will the sins of evil people destroy them if they
repent and turn from their sins. 13When I tell righteous people that they will live, but then
they sin, expecting their past righteousness to save them, then none of their good deeds

33:10 Lev 26:39, Isa 49:14
33:11 Hos 11:8, Acts 3:19, 1 Tim 2:4, 2 Pet 3:9
33:12 2 Chr 7:14
33:13 Heb 10:38, 2 Pet 2:20-21

32:32 After reading Ezekiel's prophecies against all these foreign nations, we may wonder if he was blindly loyal to his own nation. But Ezekiel spoke only when God gave him a message (3:27). Besides, God's prophets pronounced judgment on God's sinful people just as much as on God's enemies. But if Babylon was God's enemy, why isn't it mentioned in Ezekiel's judgments? Perhaps because (1) God wanted to foster a spirit of cooperation between the exiles and Babylon in order to preserve his people; (2) God was still using Babylon to refine his own people; (3) God wanted to use Daniel, a powerful official in Babylon, to draw the Babylonians to him.

33:1ff This chapter sets forth a new direction for Ezekiel's prophecies. Up to this point, Ezekiel has pronounced judgment upon Judah (chapters 1–24) and the surrounding evil nations (chapters 25–32) for their sins. After Jerusalem fell, he turned from messages of doom and judgment to messages of comfort, hope, and future restoration for God's people (chapters 33–48). God previously appointed Ezekiel to be a watchman, warning the nation of coming judgment (see 3:17-21). Here God appointed him to be a watchman again, but this time he was to preach a message of hope. There are still sections full of warnings (33:23–34:10; 36:1-7), but these are part of the larger picture of hope. God will remember to bless those who are faithful to him. We must pay attention to both aspects of Ezekiel's message: warning and promise. Those who persist in rebelling against God should take warning. Those faithful to God should find encouragement and hope.

33:10-12 The exiles were discouraged by their past sins. This is an important turning point in this book—elsewhere in Ezekiel the people had refused to face their sins. Here, they felt heavy guilt for rebelling against God for so many years. Therefore, God assured them of forgiveness if they repented. God wants *everyone* to turn to him. He looks at what we are and will become, not what we have been. God gives you the opportunity to turn to him if you will. Sincerely follow God, and ask him to forgive you when you fail.

will be remembered. I will destroy them for their sins. 14And suppose I tell some wicked
people that they will surely die, but then they turn from their sins and do what is just and
right. 15For instance, they might give back a borrower's pledge, return what they have
stolen, and obey my life-giving laws, no longer doing what is evil. If they do this, then
they will surely live and not die. 16None of their past sins will be brought up again, for
they have done what is just and right, and they will surely live.
17"Your people are saying, 'The Lord is not just,' but it is they who are not just. 18For
again I say, when righteous people turn to evil, they will die. 19But if wicked people turn
from their wickedness and do what is just and right, they will live. 20O people of Israel,
you are saying, 'The Lord is not just.' But I will judge each of you according to your
deeds."

Explanation of Jerusalem's Fall

21On January 8,* during the twelfth year of our captivity, a man who had escaped from
Jerusalem came to me and said, "The city has fallen!" 22The previous evening the LORD
had taken hold of me and opened my mouth, so I would be able to speak when this man
arrived the next morning.
23Then this message came to me from the LORD: 24"Son of man, the scattered
remnants of Judah living among the ruined cities keep saying, 'Abraham was only one
man, and yet he gained possession of the entire land! We are many; surely the land should
be given to us as a possession.' 25Now give these people this message from the Sovereign
LORD: You eat meat with blood in it, you worship idols, and you murder the innocent.
Do you really think the land should be yours? 26Murderers! Idolaters! Adulterers!
Should the land belong to you?
27"Give them this message from the Sovereign LORD: As surely as I live, those living
in the ruins will die by the sword. Those living in the open fields will be eaten by wild
animals. Those hiding in the forts and caves will die of disease. 28I will destroy the land
and demolish her pride. Her arrogant power will come to an end. The mountains of Israel
will be so ruined that no one will even travel through them. 29When I have ruined the
land because of their disgusting sins, then they will know that I am the LORD.
30"Son of man, your people are whispering behind your back. They talk about you in
their houses and whisper about you at the doors, saying, 'Come on, let's have some fun!
Let's go hear the prophet tell us what the LORD is saying!' 31So they come pretending to
be sincere and sit before you listening. But they have no intention of doing what I tell
them. They express love with their mouths, but their hearts seek only after money. 32You
are very entertaining to them, like someone who sings love songs with a beautiful voice
or plays fine music on an instrument. They hear what you say, but they don't do it! 33But
when all these terrible things happen to them—as they certainly will—then they will
know a prophet has been among them."

33:21 Hebrew *On the fifth day of the tenth month,* of the Hebrew calendar. This event occurred on January 8, 585 B.C.; also see note on 29:1.

33:14 Isa 55:7; Ezek 18:27; Hos 14:1, 4; Mic 6:8
33:15 Lev 6:4-5; Num 5:6-8; Luke 19:8
33:16 Isa 1:18; 43:25; Ezek 18:22
33:17 Ezek 18:24-29
33:21 Jer 39:1-2; Ezek 24:1-2, 26
33:22 Luke 1:64
33:24 Isa 51:1-2; Jer 39:10; Acts 7:5; Rom 4:12
33:25 Lev 17:10-14; Deut 12:16, 23; Jer 7:9-10
33:26 Mic 2:1-2; Zeph 3:3
33:27 Isa 2:19; Jer 15:2-4
33:28 Jer 44:22; Ezek 6:14; 36:34
33:29 Isa 29:13; 58:2; Ezek 23:33, 35
33:30 Ezek 14:3
33:31 Isa 29:13; Matt 13:22; Luke 12:15; 1 Jn 3:18
33:32 Mark 6:20
33:33 Ezek 2:5; 33:29

33:13 Past good deeds will not save a person who decides to turn to a life of sin. Some people think that if they do enough good deeds, they can hold on to the sins they don't want to give up. But it's useless to try to be good in some areas so you can be deliberately bad in others. God wants wholehearted love and obedience.

33:15 While good deeds will not save us, our salvation must lead to righteous actions (see Ephesians 2:10; James 2:14-17). This includes restitution for past sins (as exemplified in the story of Zacchaeus, see Luke 19:1-10). God expects us to make restitution, whenever necessary, for the wrongs we have committed.

33:21, 22 Near the beginning of his ministry, Ezekiel was unable to speak except to give specific messages from God (3:26, 27). After Ezekiel's prophecies came true and the false prophets were exposed, Ezekiel was again able to talk freely. No longer needing to prove himself, he was free to offer God's message of restoration and hope.

33:30-32 The people refused to act upon Ezekiel's message. When people mock your witness for Christ or ignore your advice, don't give up. You cannot make someone accept the message of salvation. Your part is to be faithful in delivering it.

33:31 In your heart, do you really love God? These people gave the appearance of following God, but they loved their money more. Many today also give the outward impression of being religious while remaining inwardly greedy. Jesus warned that we cannot love God and money at the same time (Matthew 6:24). It's easy to say, "I surrender all" when we don't have much. It's when we start accumulating wealth that it becomes difficult to avoid loving it.

33:32 The people were coming to listen to Ezekiel in order to be entertained. They listened to the message from the Lord but had no intention of putting it into practice. Many people regard church as entertainment. They enjoy the music, the people, and the activities, but they don't take the messages to heart. They are apathetic toward serving the Lord. Have you reduced church services to the level of entertainment, or does your worship truly have an impact on your life? Listen to God's words and then obey—apply his words and put them into practice in your life.

The Shepherds of Israel

34 Then this message came to me from the LORD: 2“Son of man, prophesy against
the shepherds, the leaders of Israel. Give them this message from the Sovereign
LORD: Destruction is certain for you shepherds who feed yourselves instead of your
flocks. Shouldn’t shepherds feed their sheep? 3You drink the milk, wear the wool, and
butcher the best animals, but you let your flocks starve. 4You have not taken care of the
weak. You have not tended the sick or bound up the broken bones. You have not gone
looking for those who have wandered away and are lost. Instead, you have ruled them
with force and cruelty. 5So my sheep have been scattered without a shepherd. They are
easy prey for any wild animal. 6They have wandered through the mountains and hills,
across the face of the earth, yet no one has gone to search for them.
7“Therefore, you shepherds, hear the word of the LORD: 8As surely as I live, says
the Sovereign LORD, you abandoned my flock and left them to be attacked by every
wild animal. Though you were my shepherds, you didn’t search for my sheep when
they were lost. You took care of yourselves and left the sheep to starve. 9Therefore, you
shepherds, hear the word of the LORD. 10This is what the Sovereign LORD says: I now
consider these shepherds my enemies, and I will hold them responsible for what has
happened to my flock. I will take away their right to feed the flock, along with their
right to feed themselves. I will rescue my flock from their mouths; the sheep will no
longer be their prey.

34:2 Jer 10:21; 23:1; Mic 3:1-3; John 10:11; 21:15-17
34:3 Isa 56:11; Zech 11:5, 16; 22:27
34:4 Zech 11:15-16; Matt 9:36; 18:12-13; 1 Pet 5:3
34:5 Jer 10:21; 23:2
34:6 Ps 142:4; 1 Pet 2:25
34:8 Acts 20:29

The Good Shepherd

11“For this is what the Sovereign LORD says: I myself will search and find my sheep.
12I will be like a shepherd looking for his scattered flock. I will find my sheep and
rescue them from all the places to which they were scattered on that dark and cloudy
day. 13I will bring them back home to their own land of Israel from among the peoples
and nations. I will feed them on the mountains of Israel and by the rivers in all the
places where people live. 14Yes, I will give them good pastureland on the high hills
of Israel. There they will lie down in pleasant places and feed in lush mountain
pastures. 15I myself will tend my sheep and cause them to lie down in peace, says the
Sovereign LORD. 16I will search for my lost ones who strayed away, and I will bring
them safely home again. I will bind up the injured and strengthen the weak. But I will
destroy those who are fat and powerful. I will feed them, yes—feed them justice!

34:11 Matt 13:11-12; John 10:16
34:12 Jer 23:3; 31:10; Joel 2:2; Luke 19:10
34:13 Isa 30:25; Ezek 36:29-30
34:14 Ps 23:2; John 10:9
34:16 Isa 10:16; 49:26

BAD SHEPHERDS VERSUS GOOD SHEPHERDS

Bad Shepherds	*Good Shepherds*
Take care of themselves	Take care of their flock
Worry about their own health	Strengthen the weak and sick, search for the lost
Rule harshly and brutally	Rule lovingly and gently
Abandon and scatter the sheep	Gather and protect the sheep
Keep the best for themselves	Give their best to the sheep

34:1ff Ezekiel called the exiles “Israel,” referring to all Jews in captivity from both the northern and southern kingdoms. Ezekiel criticized Israel’s leaders for taking care of themselves rather than taking care of their people. He outlined their sins (34:1-6) and pronounced judgment upon them (34:7-10). Then he promised that a good shepherd (the Messiah) would come who would take care of the people as the other leaders were supposed to do (34:11-31). This beautiful message portrays the fate of the present shepherds, the work of the new shepherd, and the future of the sheep.

34:4-6 God would judge the religious leaders because they were selfishly caught up in their own concerns and were neglecting their service to others. Spiritual leaders must be careful not to pursue self-development at the expense of broken, lost people. When we give too much attention to our own needs and ideas, we may push God aside and abandon those who depend on us.

34:9, 10 Those shepherds who failed their flock would be removed from office and held responsible for what happened to the people they were supposed to lead. Christian leaders must heed this warning and care for their flock, or total failure and judgment will be the result (see 1 Corinthians 9:24-27). True leadership focuses on helping others, not just on getting ahead.

34:11-16 God promises to take over as shepherd of his scattered flock. When our leaders fail us, we must not despair but remember that God is in control and that he promises to return and care for his flock. Thus, we know that we can turn to God for help. He is still in control and can transform any tragic situation into good for his Kingdom (see Genesis 50:20; Romans 8:28).

17 "And as for you, my flock, my people, this is what the Sovereign LORD says: I will
judge between one sheep and another, separating the sheep from the goats. 18 Is it not
enough for you to keep the best of the pastures for yourselves? Must you also trample
down the rest? Is it not enough for you to take the best water for yourselves? Must you
also muddy the rest with your feet? 19 All that is left for my flock to eat is what you have
trampled down. All they have to drink is water that you have fouled.
20 "Therefore, this is what the Sovereign LORD says: I will surely judge between the
fat sheep and the scrawny sheep. 21 For you fat sheep push and butt and crowd my sick
and hungry flock until they are scattered to distant lands. 22 So I will rescue my flock,
and they will no longer be abused and destroyed. And I will judge between one sheep
and another. 23 And I will set one shepherd over them, even my servant David. He will
feed them and be a shepherd to them. 24 And I, the LORD, will be their God, and my
servant David will be a prince among my people. I, the LORD, have spoken!

The LORD's Covenant of Peace

25 "I will make a covenant of peace with them and drive away the dangerous animals
from the land. Then my people will be able to camp safely in the wildest places and sleep
in the woods without fear. 26 I will cause my people and their homes around my holy hill
to be a blessing. And I will send showers, showers of blessings, which will come just
when they are needed. 27 The orchards and fields of my people will yield bumper crops,
and everyone will live in safety. When I have broken their chains of slavery and rescued
them from those who enslaved them, then they will know that I am the LORD. 28 They
will no longer be prey for other nations, and wild animals will no longer attack them.
They will live in safety, and no one will make them afraid.
29 "And I will give them a land famous for its crops, so my people will never again go
hungry or be shamed by the scorn of foreign nations. 30 In this way, they will know that
I, the LORD their God, am with them. And they will know that they, the people of Israel,
are my people, says the Sovereign LORD. 31 You are my flock, the sheep of my pasture.
You are my people, and I am your God, says the Sovereign LORD."

A Message for Edom

35 Again a message came to me from the LORD: 2 "Son of man, turn toward Mount
Seir, and prophesy against its people. 3 Give them this message from the Sovereign LORD: I am your enemy, O Mount Seir, and I will raise my fist against you to destroy
you completely. 4 I will demolish your cities and make you desolate, and then you will
know that I am the LORD. 5 Your continual hatred for the people of Israel led you to
butcher them when they were helpless, when I had already punished them for all their
sins. 6 As surely as I live, says the Sovereign LORD, since you show no distaste for blood,
I will give you a bloodbath of your own. Your turn has come! 7 I will make Mount Seir
utterly desolate, killing off all who try to escape and any who return. 8 I will fill your
mountains with the dead. Your hills, your valleys, and your streams will be filled with
people slaughtered by the sword. 9 I will make you desolate forever. Your cities will never
be rebuilt. Then you will know that I am the LORD.
10 "For you said, 'The lands of Israel and Judah will be ours. We will take possession
of them. What do we care that the LORD is there!' 11 Therefore, as surely as I live, says

34:17 Zech 10:3; Matt 25:32
34:18 Num 16:9, 13; 2 Sam 7:19
34:21 Deut 33:17; Luke 13:14-16
34:22 Jer 23:2-3; Zech 11:7-9
34:23 Isa 40:11; Jer 23:4-6; 30:9; John 10:11
34:24 Jer 30:9
34:25 Isa 11:6-9; Jer 33:16; Hos 2:18
34:26 Gen 12:2; Deut 28:12; Isa 32:15; 44:3
34:27 Lev 26:13; Isa 52:2-3
34:28 Jer 30:10
34:29 Isa 60:21
34:31 Mic 7:14; John 10:11
35:2 Gen 36:6-8
35:3 Jer 49:13, 17-18
35:4 Mal 1:2-4
35:7 Ezek 25:13
35:8 Isa 34:5-6
35:9 Jer 49:13
35:10 Ps 48:1-3
35:11 Pss 9:16; 137:7; Amos 1:11

34:18-20 A bad shepherd is not only selfish but destructive. A minister who muddies the waters for others by causing unnecessary fears, teaching false ideas, and acting sinfully is a detriment to his flock's spiritual nourishment.

34:23-25 In contrast to the present evil shepherds (leaders) of God's people (34:1-6), God will send a perfect shepherd, the Messiah ("my servant David"), who will take care of every need his people have and set up a Kingdom of perfect peace and justice (see Psalm 23; Jeremiah 23:5, 6; John 10:11; Hebrews 13:20, 21; Revelation 21). *Peace* here means more than the absence of conflict. It is contentment, fulfillment, and security.

35:1ff Ezekiel gave another prophecy against Edom (also called Seir); his first prophecy against Edom is found in 25:12-14. In this prophecy, Ezekiel is probably using Edom to represent *all* the nations opposed to God's people. Chapter 36 says that Israel will be restored, while this chapter says that Edom (God's enemies) will be made "desolate."

35:2 Edom offered to help destroy Jerusalem and rejoiced when the city fell. Edom's long-standing hostility against God's people resulted in God's judgment.

35:6-8 Ezekiel prophesied not only against the people of Edom but also against their mountains and land. Their home territory was Mount Seir. Mountains, symbols of strength and power, represented the pride of these people, who thought they could get away with evil. Their desire for revenge turned against them. Edom received the punishment it was so hasty to give out. God has a way of allowing our treatment of others to boomerang on us. So be careful in your judgment of others (Matthew 7:1, 2).

the Sovereign LORD, I will pay back your angry deeds with mine. I will punish you for
all your acts of anger, envy, and hatred. And I will bring honor to my name by what I do
to you. 12 Then you will know that I, the LORD, have heard every contemptuous word
you spoke against the mountains of Israel. For you said, 'They have been destroyed; they
have been given to us as food to eat!' 13 In saying that, you boasted proudly against me,
and I have heard it all!

14 "This is what the Sovereign LORD says: The whole world will rejoice when I make
you desolate. 15 You rejoiced at the desolation of Israel's inheritance. Now I will rejoice
at yours! You will be wiped out, you people of Mount Seir and all who live in Edom!
Then you will know that I am the LORD!

Restoration for Israel

36 "Son of man, prophesy to Israel's mountains. Give them this message: O mountains
of Israel, hear the word of the LORD! 2 This is what the Sovereign LORD says: Your
enemies have taunted you, saying, 'Aha! Now the ancient heights belong to us!' 3 Therefore,
son of man, give the mountains of Israel this message from the Sovereign LORD: Your
enemies have attacked you from all directions, and now you are possessed by many nations.
You are the object of much mocking and slander. 4 Therefore, O mountains of Israel, hear
the word of the Sovereign LORD. He speaks to the hills and mountains, ravines and valleys,
and to ruined wastes and long-deserted cities that have been destroyed and mocked by
foreign nations everywhere. 5 This is what the Sovereign LORD says: My jealous anger is
on fire against these nations, especially Edom, because they have shown utter contempt for
me by gleefully taking my land for themselves as plunder.

6 "Therefore, prophesy to the hills and mountains, the ravines and valleys of Israel.
Give them this message from the Sovereign LORD: I am full of fury because you have
suffered shame before the surrounding nations. 7 Therefore, says the Sovereign LORD, I
have raised my hand and sworn an oath that those nations will soon have their turn at
suffering shame. 8 But the mountains of Israel will produce heavy crops of fruit to
prepare for my people's return—and they will be coming home again soon! 9 See, I am
concerned for you, and I will come to help you. Your ground will be tilled and your crops
planted. 10 I will greatly increase the population of Israel, and the ruined cities will be
rebuilt and filled with people. 11 Not only the people, but your flocks and herds will also
greatly multiply. O mountains of Israel, I will bring people to live on you once again. I
will make you even more prosperous than you were before. Then you will know that I
am the LORD. 12 I will cause my people to walk on you once again, and you will be their
inheritance. You will never again devour their children.

13 "This is what the Sovereign LORD says: Now the other nations taunt you, saying,
'Israel is a land that devours her own people!' 14 But you will never again devour your
people or bereave your nation, says the Sovereign LORD. 15 I will not allow those foreign
nations to sneer at you, and you will no longer be shamed by them or cause your nation
to fall, says the Sovereign LORD."

16 Then this further message came to me from the LORD: 17 "Son of man, when the people
of Israel were living in their own land, they defiled it by their evil deeds. To me their conduct

35:12 Jer 50:7; Ezek 36:2
35:13 Isa 10:13-14; Ezek 36:3; Dan 11:36
35:14 Isa 44:23; 49:13; Jer 51:48
35:15 Isa 34:5-6; Lam 4:21; Obad 1:12, 15
36:2 Deut 32:13; Isa 58:14; Ezek 35:10; Hab 3:19
36:3 Jer 2:15; 51:34; Ezek 35:13
36:4 Deut 11:11; Ps 79:4; Jer 48:27
36:5 Isa 66:15-16; Jer 50:11; Ezek 35:15; Mic 7:8
36:6 Ezek 34:29
36:8 Isa 27:6; Ezek 17:22-23; 34:26-29
36:9 Lev 26:9; Ezek 28:26; 34:14
36:10 Isa 27:6; 49:17-22; Jer 31:27-28; Ezek 37:21-22
36:11 Jer 30:18; Ezek 16:55
36:12 Ezek 34:13-14; 47:14
36:13 Num 13:32
36:15 Isa 54:4; Jer 18:15
36:17 Jer 2:7

OLD AND NEW COVENANTS

Old Covenant	*New Covenant*
Placed upon stone	Placed upon people's hearts
Based on the law	Based on desire to love and serve God
Must be taught	Known by all
Legal relationship with God	Personal relationship with God

36:1ff In this prophecy, Ezekiel said that Israel would be restored as a nation and would return to its own land. The mountains were symbolic of Israel's strength (see the note on 35:6-8). To the exiles in Babylon, this seemed impossible. This message again emphasized God's sovereignty and trustworthiness. He would first judge the nations used to punish Israel (36:1-7) and then restore his people (36:8-15).

36:2 "The ancient heights" refers to the Promised Land—the land of Israel. Israel's enemies challenged not only their boundaries but also God's promises to Israel.

was as filthy as a bloody rag. 18 They polluted the land with murder and by worshiping idols,
so I poured out my fury on them. 19 I scattered them to many lands to punish them for the
evil way they had lived. 20 But when they were scattered among the nations, they brought
dishonor to my holy name. For the nations said, 'These are the people of the LORD, and he
couldn't keep them safe in his own land!' 21 Then I was concerned for my holy name, which
had been dishonored by my people throughout the world.

22 "Therefore, give the people of Israel this message from the Sovereign LORD: I am
bringing you back again but not because you deserve it. I am doing it to protect my holy
name, which you dishonored while you were scattered among the nations. 23 I will show
how holy my great name is—the name you dishonored among the nations. And when I
reveal my holiness through you before their very eyes, says the Sovereign LORD, then
the nations will know that I am the LORD. 24 For I will gather you up from all the nations
and bring you home again to your land.

25 "Then I will sprinkle clean water on you, and you will be clean. Your filth will be
washed away, and you will no longer worship idols. 26 And I will give you a new heart
with new and right desires, and I will put a new spirit in you. I will take out your stony
heart of sin and give you a new, obedient heart.* 27 And I will put my Spirit in you so you
will obey my laws and do whatever I command.

28 "And you will live in Israel, the land I gave your ancestors long ago. You will be my
people, and I will be your God. 29 I will cleanse you of your filthy behavior. I will give
you good crops, and I will abolish famine in the land. 30 I will give you great harvests
from your fruit trees and fields, and never again will the surrounding nations be able to
scoff at your land for its famines. 31 Then you will remember your past sins and hate
yourselves for all the evil things you did. 32 But remember, says the Sovereign LORD, I
am not doing this because you deserve it. O my people of Israel, you should be utterly
ashamed of all you have done!

33 "This is what the Sovereign LORD says: When I cleanse you from your sins, I will
bring people to live in your cities, and the ruins will be rebuilt. 34 The fields that used
to lie empty and desolate—a shock to all who passed by—will again be farmed. 35 And
when I bring you back, people will say, 'This godforsaken land is now like Eden's
garden! The ruined cities now have strong walls, and they are filled with people!'
36 Then the nations all around—all those still left—will know that I, the LORD, rebuilt
the ruins and planted lush crops in the wilderness. For I, the LORD, have promised
this, and I will do it.

37 "This is what the Sovereign LORD says: I am ready to hear Israel's prayers for these
blessings, and I am ready to grant them their requests. 38 I will multiply them like the
sacred flocks that fill Jerusalem's streets at the time of her festivals. The ruined cities will
be crowded with people once more, and everyone will know that I am the LORD."

36:26 Hebrew *a heart of flesh.*

36:18 2 Chr 34:21, 25; Lam 2:4; 4:11; Ezek 22:18-20
36:19 Deut 28:64; Ezek 22:15; Amos 9:9; Rom 2:6
36:20 Isa 52:5; Jer 33:24; †Rom 2:24
36:21 Ps 74:18; Isa 48:9
36:22 Deut 9:5-7; Ps 106:8
36:23 Ps 126:2; Ezek 20:41; 39:7
36:24 Isa 43:5-6
36:25 Isa 52:15; Zech 13:1; John 3:5; Titus 3:5-6; Heb 10:22
36:26 Ps 51:10; 2 Cor 5:17
36:27 Isa 59:21; Ezek 37:14
36:28 Jer 30:22
36:29 Ezek 34:27-29; Hos 2:21-23
36:30 Lev 26:4
36:32 Deut 9:5
36:33 Isa 58:12; Zech 8:7-8
36:35 Isa 51:3
36:36 Hos 14:4-7
36:38 1 Kgs 8:63; 2 Chr 35:7-9

36:21-23 Why did God want to protect his holy name—his reputation—among the nations of the world? God was concerned about the salvation of not only his people but also the whole world. To allow his people to remain in sin and be permanently destroyed by their enemies would lead other nations to conclude that their pagan gods were more powerful than Israel's God (Isaiah 48:11). Thus, to protect his holy name, God would return a remnant of his people to their land. God will not share his glory with false gods—he alone is the one true God. The people had the responsibility to represent God to the rest of the world. Believers today have that same responsibility. How do you represent God to your world?

36:25-27 God promised to restore Israel not only physically but spiritually. To accomplish this, God would give them a new heart for following him and put his Spirit within them (see 11:19, 20; Psalm 51:7-11) to transform them and empower them to do his will. Again the new covenant was promised (16:61-63; 34:23-25), ultimately to be fulfilled in Christ. No matter how impure your life is right now, God offers you a fresh start. You can have your sins washed away, receive a new heart for God, and have his Spirit within you—if you accept God's promise. Why try to patch up your old life when you can have a new one?

36:31, 32 God said his people should be ashamed of their sins. The people had become so callous that they had lost all sensitivity to sin. First they had to "remember" their sins, be ashamed of them, and finally repent of them (see James 4:8, 9). As we examine our life, we may find that we, too, have lost our sensitivity to certain sins. But as we measure ourselves against God's standards of right living, we will be ashamed. To regain sensitivity we must recognize our sin for what it is, be sorry for displeasing God, and ask his forgiveness. The Holy Spirit will guide us, making us responsive and receptive to God's truth (John 14:26; 16:8, 13).

36:37, 38 God said that he was ready to answer Israel's prayers. We cannot expect God to answer our prayers, however, until we have received a new heart from him (36:26). Is your heart right with God?

A Valley of Dry Bones

37 The LORD took hold of me, and I was carried away by the Spirit of the LORD to a
valley filled with bones. 2He led me around among the old, dry bones that covered
the valley floor. They were scattered everywhere across the ground. 3Then he asked me,
"Son of man, can these bones become living people again?"
"O Sovereign LORD," I replied, "you alone know the answer to that."
4Then he said to me, "Speak to these bones and say, 'Dry bones, listen to the word of the
LORD! 5This is what the Sovereign LORD says: Look! I am going to breathe into you and
make you live again! 6I will put flesh and muscles on you and cover you with skin. I will
put breath into you, and you will come to life. Then you will know that I am the LORD.'"
7So I spoke these words, just as he told me. Suddenly as I spoke, there was a rattling
noise all across the valley. The bones of each body came together and attached themselves as they had been before. 8Then as I watched, muscles and flesh formed over the
bones. Then skin formed to cover their bodies, but they still had no breath in them.
9Then he said to me, "Speak to the winds and say: 'This is what the Sovereign LORD
says: Come, O breath, from the four winds! Breathe into these dead bodies so that they
may live again.'"
10So I spoke as he commanded me, and the wind entered the bodies, and they began
to breathe. They all came to life and stood up on their feet—a great army of them.
11Then he said to me, "Son of man, these bones represent the people of Israel. They are
saying, 'We have become old, dry bones—all hope is gone.' 12Now give them this message
from the Sovereign LORD: O my people, I will open your graves of exile and cause you to
rise again. Then I will bring you back to the land of Israel. 13When this happens, O my
people, you will know that I am the LORD. 14I will put my Spirit in you, and you will live
and return home to your own land. Then you will know that I am the LORD. You will see
that I have done everything just as I promised. I, the LORD, have spoken!"

Reunion of Israel and Judah

15Again a message came to me from the LORD: 16"Son of man, take a stick and carve on
it these words: 'This stick represents Judah and its allied tribes.' Then take another stick
and carve these words on it: 'This stick represents the northern tribes of Israel.'* 17Now
hold them together in your hand as one stick. 18When your people ask you what your
actions mean, 19say to them, 'This is what the Sovereign LORD says: I will take the
northern tribes and join them to Judah. I will make them one stick in my hand.' 20Then
hold out the sticks you have inscribed, so the people can see them. 21And give them this
message from the Sovereign LORD: I will gather the people of Israel from among the
nations. I will bring them home to their own land from the places where they have been
scattered. 22I will unify them into one nation in the land. One king will rule them all; no
longer will they be divided into two nations. 23They will stop polluting themselves with
their detestable idols and other sins, for I will save them from their sinful backsliding. I
will cleanse them. Then they will truly be my people, and I will be their God.
24"My servant David will be their king, and they will have only one shepherd. They
will obey my regulations and keep my laws. 25They will live in the land of Israel where

37:1 Jer 7:32–8:2; Acts 8:39
37:3 Deut 32:29; 1 Sam 2:6; Isa 26:19
37:4 Isa 42:18
37:5 Ps 104:29-30; John 20:22; Eph 2:5; Rev 11:11
37:6 Joel 2:27; 3:17
37:7 Jer 13:5-7
37:9 Ps 104:30; Hos 13:14
37:10 Jer 30:19; Rev 11:11
37:11 Ps 141:7; Isa 49:14
37:12 Deut 32:39; Isa 26:19; Hos 13:14; Amos 9:14-15
37:14 Joel 2:28-29
37:16 1 Kgs 12:16-20; 2 Chr 10:17-19
37:17 Isa 11:13; 50:4; Hos 1:11
37:21 Isa 43:5-6; Ezek 39:27
37:22 Isa 11:13; Jer 50:4; Ezek 34:13-14; Hos 1:11
37:23 Ezek 11:18
37:24 Jer 30:21; Hos 3:5
37:25 Isa 11:1

37:16 Hebrew *Ephraim's stick, representing Joseph and all the house of Israel.*

37:1ff This vision illustrates the promise of chapter 36—new life and a nation restored, both physically and spiritually. The dry bones are a picture of the Jews in captivity—scattered and dead. The two sticks (37:15-17) represent the reunion of the entire nation of Israel that had divided into northern and southern kingdoms after Solomon. The scattered exiles of both Israel and Judah would be released from the "graves" of captivity and one day regathered in their homeland, with the Messiah as their leader. This vision has yet to be fulfilled. Ezekiel felt he was speaking to the dead as he preached to the exiles because they rarely responded to his message. But these bones responded! And just as God brought life to the dead bones, he would bring life again to his spiritually dead people.

37:4, 5 The dry bones represented the people's spiritually dead condition. Your church may seem like a heap of dry bones to you, spiritually dead with no hope of vitality. But just as God promised to restore his nation, he can restore any church, no matter how dry or dead it may be. Rather than give up, pray for renewal, for God can restore it to life. The hope and prayer of every church should be that God will put his Spirit into it (37:14). In fact, God is at work calling his people back to himself, bringing new life into dead churches.

37:16 The first stick was for Judah, being the leading tribe in the southern kingdom. The other was for Joseph, because he was the father of Ephraim, the leading tribe in the northern kingdom.

37:24, 25 The Messiah was often called David because he is David's descendant. David was a good king, but the Messiah would be the perfect King (Revelation 17:14; 19:16).

their ancestors lived, the land I gave my servant Jacob. They and their children and their
grandchildren after them will live there forever, generation after generation. And my
servant David will be their prince forever. 26 And I will make a covenant of peace with
them, an everlasting covenant. I will give them their land and multiply them, and I will
put my Temple among them forever. 27 I will make my home among them. I will be their
God, and they will be my people. 28 And since my Temple will remain among them forever,
the nations will know that I, the LORD, have set Israel apart for myself to be holy."

A Message for Gog

38 This is another message that came to me from the LORD: 2 "Son of man, prophesy
against Gog of the land of Magog, the prince who rules over the nations of
Meshech and Tubal. 3 Give him this message from the Sovereign LORD: Gog, I am your
enemy! 4 I will turn you around and put hooks into your jaws to lead you out to your
destruction. I will mobilize your troops and cavalry and make you a vast and mighty
horde, all fully armed. 5 Persia, Ethiopia, and Libya* will join you, too, with all their
weapons. 6 Gomer and all its hordes will also join you, along with the armies of
Beth-togarmah from the distant north and many others.
7 "Get ready; be prepared! Keep all the armies around you mobilized, and take
command of them. 8 A long time from now you will be called into action. In the distant
future you will swoop down on the land of Israel, which will be lying in peace after her
recovery from war and after the return of her people from many lands. 9 You and all your
allies—a vast and awesome horde—will roll down on them like a storm and cover the
land like a cloud.
10 "This is what the Sovereign LORD says: At that time evil thoughts will come to your
mind, and you will devise a wicked scheme. 11 You will say, 'Israel is an unprotected land
filled with unwalled villages! I will march against her and destroy these people who live
in such confidence! 12 I will go to those once-desolate cities that are again filled with
people who have returned from exile in many nations. I will capture vast amounts of
plunder and take many slaves, for the people are rich with cattle now, and they think the
whole world revolves around them!' 13 But Sheba and Dedan and the merchants of
Tarshish will ask, 'Who are you to rob them of silver and gold? Who are you to drive
away their cattle and seize their goods and make them poor?'
14 "Therefore, son of man, prophesy against Gog. Give him this message from the
Sovereign LORD: When my people are living in peace in their land, then you will rouse
yourself.* 15 You will come from your homeland in the distant north with your vast
cavalry and your mighty army, 16 and you will cover the land like a cloud. This will
happen in the distant future. I will bring you against my land as everyone watches, and
my holiness will be displayed by what happens to you. Then all the nations will know
that I am the LORD.
17 "This is what the Sovereign LORD says: You are the one I was talking about long ago,
when I announced through Israel's prophets that in future days I would bring you against
my people. 18 But when Gog invades the land of Israel, says the Sovereign LORD, my fury
will rise! 19 For in my jealousy and blazing anger, I promise a mighty shaking in the land of
Israel on that day. 20 All living things—all the fish, birds, animals, and people—will quake

37:26 Jer 30:19; Heb 13:20
37:27 Lev 26:11; †2 Cor 6:16
37:28 Exod 31:13; Zeph 3:15
38:2 Ezek 39:1, 9; Rev 20:8-9
38:4 Isa 43:17; Ezek 39:2; Dan 11:40
38:5 Gen 10:6-7; Ezek 27:10; 30:4-5
38:6 Gen 10:2-3; Ezek 27:14
38:8 Isa 11:11; Ezek 34:13
38:9 Isa 5:28; Jer 4:13; Joel 2:2
38:10 Ps 36:4; Mic 2:1
38:11 Isa 37:24-25; Zech 2:4-5
38:12 Isa 10:6; Ezek 29:19
38:13 Isa 10:5-7
38:14 Jer 23:5-6; Zech 2:5, 8
38:16 Ezek 36:23
38:17 Isa 5:26-30; 34:1-6
38:18 Ps 18:7-8
38:19 Ezek 36:5-6; Joel 3:16; Hag 2:6-7; Heb 12:26-29
38:20 Jer 4:24; Nah 1:5-6; Zech 14:4-5

38:5 Hebrew *Paras, Cush, and Put.* **38:14** As in Greek version; Hebrew reads *then you will know.*

37:26, 27 God's promise here goes beyond the physical and geographical restoration of Israel. He promises to breathe new spiritual life into his people so that their hearts and attitudes will be right with him and united with one another. This same process is described throughout God's Word as the cleansing and renewing of our hearts by God's Spirit (Titus 3:4-6).

38:1ff In chapter 37, Ezekiel revealed how Israel (God's people) would be restored to their land from many parts of the world. Once Israel became strong, a confederacy of nations from the north would attack, led by Gog (see also Revelation 20:8). Their purpose would be to destroy God's people. Gog's allies would come from the mountainous area southeast of the Black Sea and southwest of the Caspian Sea (central Turkey), as well as from the area that is present-day Iran, Ethiopia, Libya, and possibly Russia. Gog could be a person (he sometimes is identified with Gyges, king of Lydia in 660 B.C.), or Gog could also be a symbol of all the evil in the world. Whether symbolic or literal, Gog represents the aggregate military might of all the forces opposed to God.

Many say that the battle Ezekiel described will occur at the end of human history, but there are many differences between the events described here and those in Revelation 20. Regardless of when this battle will occur, the message is clear: God will deliver his people—no enemy can stand before his mighty power.

38:13 Sheba and Dedan, great trading centers in Arabia, would in effect say to Gog, "Who are you to usurp our position as the world's trade leaders?" Sheba and Dedan would then join this confederacy. Tarshish was the leading trade center in the west; many believe it was in Spain.

in terror at my presence. Mountains will be thrown down; cliffs will crumble; walls will fall to the earth. 21I will summon the sword against you throughout Israel, says the Sovereign LORD. Your men will turn against each other in mortal combat. 22I will punish you and your hordes with disease and bloodshed; I will send torrential rain, hailstones, fire, and burning sulfur! 23Thus will I show my greatness and holiness, and I will make myself known to all the nations of the world. Then they will know that I am the LORD!

The Slaughter of Gog's Armies

39 "Son of man, prophesy against Gog. Give him this message from the Sovereign LORD: I am your enemy, O Gog, ruler of the nations of Meshech and Tubal. 2I will turn you and drive you toward the mountains of Israel, bringing you from the distant north. 3I will knock your weapons from your hands and leave you helpless. 4You and all your vast hordes will die on the mountains. I will give you as food to the vultures and wild animals. 5You will fall in the open fields, for I have spoken, says the Sovereign LORD. 6And I will rain down fire on Magog and on all your allies who live safely on the coasts. Then they will know that I am the LORD.

7"Thus, I will make known my holy name among my people of Israel. I will not let it be desecrated anymore. And the nations, too, will know that I am the LORD, the Holy One of Israel. 8That day of judgment will come, says the Sovereign LORD. Everything will happen just as I have declared it.

9"Then the people in the towns of Israel will go out and pick up your small and large shields, bows and arrows, javelins and spears, and they will use them for fuel. There will be enough to last them seven years! 10They will need nothing else for their fires. They won't need to cut wood from the fields or forests, for these weapons will give them all they need. They will take plunder from those who planned to plunder them, says the Sovereign LORD.

11"And I will make a vast graveyard for Gog and his hordes in the Valley of the Travelers, east of the Dead Sea.* The path of those who travel there will be blocked by this burial ground, and they will change the name of the place to the Valley of Gog's Hordes. 12It will take seven months for the people of Israel to cleanse the land by burying the bodies. 13Everyone in Israel will help, for it will be a glorious victory for Israel when I demonstrate my glory on that day, says the Sovereign LORD. 14At the end of the seven months, special crews will be appointed to search the land for any skeletons and to bury them, so the land will be made clean again. 15Whenever some bones are found, a marker will be set up beside them so the burial crews will see them and take them to be buried in the Valley of Gog's Hordes. 16(There will be a town there named Hamonah—which means 'horde.') And so the land will finally be cleansed.

17"And now, son of man, call all the birds and wild animals, says the Sovereign LORD. Say to them: Gather together for my great sacrificial feast. Come from far and near to the mountains of Israel, and there eat the flesh and drink the blood! 18Eat the flesh of mighty men and drink the blood of princes as though they were rams, lambs, goats, and fat young bulls of Bashan! 19Gorge yourselves with flesh until you are glutted; drink blood until you are drunk. This is the sacrificial feast I have prepared for you. 20Feast at my banquet table—feast on horses, riders, and valiant warriors, says the Sovereign LORD.

21"Thus, I will demonstrate my glory among the nations. Everyone will see the punishment I have inflicted on them and the power I have demonstrated. 22And from that

39:11 Hebrew *the sea.*

38:21 Judg 7:22; 2 Chr 20:23; Hag 2:22
38:22 Ps 11:6; Zech 14:12-15; Rev 16:21
39:1 Ezek 38:2-4
39:2 Ezek 38:15
39:3 Pss 46:9; 76:3; Jer 21:4-5; Ezek 30:21-24; Hos 1:5
39:4 Isa 14:24-25; Ezek 29:5; 32:4-5
39:6 Jer 25:22; Ezek 30:8, 16; 38:22; Amos 1:4-7; Nah 1:6
39:7 Exod 20:7; Ezek 20:39
39:9 Ps 46:9
39:10 Isa 14:2; Mic 5:8; Hab 2:8
39:13 Jer 33:9; Ezek 28:22; Zeph 3:19-20
39:17 Isa 34:6-7; Jer 46:10; Zeph 1:7; Rev 19:17-18
39:18 Deut 32:14; Ps 22:12; Jer 51:40; Amos 4:1
39:20 Ps 75:5-6; Ezek 38:4; Hag 2:22; Rev 19:18
39:21 Exod 9:16; Ezek 38:16, 23

38:21 God will directly intervene in the defense of Israel, unleashing severe natural disasters on the invaders from the north. In the end, the stricken pagan nations will turn on themselves in confusion and panic. All those who set themselves against God will be destroyed.

39:1ff The story of the battle continues. The defeat of the evil forces will be final and complete; they will be destroyed by divine intervention. Because of this victory, God's name will be known throughout the world. His glory will be evident, and the nations will understand that he alone is in charge of human history. God will clearly show his love for his people by restoring them to their homeland.

39:12-16 Two themes are intertwined: God's total victory over his enemies, and the need to cleanse the land to make it holy. After the final battle, special crews will be appointed to give proper burial to the bodies of the dead enemies in order for the land to be cleansed. The land would have been defiled by unburied corpses. Those who would come in contact with the corpses out in the open would become ceremonially unclean (according to Numbers 19:14-16). There will be so many bodies that all kinds of birds will be called in order to help dispose of them (39:17-20). The message for us is an exciting one: With God on our side, we are assured of ultimate victory over his foes because God will fight on our behalf (see also Zephaniah 3:14-17; Romans 8:38, 39).

time on the people of Israel will know that I am the LORD their God. 23 The nations will
then know why Israel was sent away to exile—it was punishment for sin, for they acted
in treachery against their God. Therefore, I turned my back on them and let their enemies
destroy them. 24 I turned my face away and punished them in proportion to the vileness
of their sins.

Restoration for God's People

25 "So now the Sovereign LORD says: I will end the captivity of my people*; I will
have mercy on Israel, for I am jealous for my holy reputation! 26 They will accept
responsibility for their past shame and treachery against me after they come home to
live in peace and safety in their own land. And then no one will bother them or make
them afraid. 27 When I bring them home from the lands of their enemies, my holiness
will be displayed to the nations. 28 Then my people will know that I am the LORD their
God—responsible for sending them away to exile and responsible for bringing them
home. I will leave none of my people behind. 29 And I will never again turn my back
on them, for I will pour out my Spirit upon them, says the Sovereign LORD."

2. Restoring the worship of God

The New Temple Area

40 On April 28,* during the twenty-fifth year of our captivity—fourteen years after
the fall of Jerusalem—the LORD took hold of me. 2 In a vision of God he took me
to the land of Israel and set me down on a very high mountain. From there I could see
what appeared to be a city across from me toward the south. 3 As he brought me nearer,
I saw a man whose face shone like bronze standing beside a gateway entrance. He was
holding in his hand a measuring tape and a measuring rod.

4 He said to me, "Son of man, watch and listen. Pay close attention to everything I
show you. You have been brought here so I can show you many things. Then you will
return to the people of Israel and tell them everything you have seen."

39:25 Hebrew *of Jacob.* **40:1** Hebrew *At the beginning of the year, on the tenth day of the month,* of the Hebrew calendar. A number of dates in Ezekiel can be cross-checked with dates in surviving Babylonian records and related accurately to our modern calendar. This event occurred on April 28, 573 B.C.

39:23 Isa 59:2; Ezek 29:29; 36:18-19
39:24 2 Kgs 17:7; Jer 2:17, 19; 4:18; Ezek 36:19
39:25 Jer 33:7; Ezek 34:13; 36:10; Hos 1:11
39:26 Ezek 34:25-28; Mic 4:4
39:27 Ezek 28:25-26
39:29 Isa 32:15; Ezek 36:27; 37:14; Joel 2:28-29; Acts 2:17
40:1 2 Kgs 25:1-7; Jer 39:1-9
40:2 Ps 48:2; Ezek 17:23; 20:40; Mic 4:1; Rev 21:10
40:3 Dan 10:5-6; Zech 2:1-2; Rev 11:1; 21:15
40:4 Jer 26:2; Ezek 43:10; 44:5; Acts 20:27

39:29 Both in this prophecy and in Joel 2:28, 29, God promises to pour out his Spirit on his people. The early church believed this began to be fulfilled at Pentecost, when God's Holy Spirit came to live in all believers (Acts 2:1-18).

40:1ff The building of the Temple envisioned a time of complete restoration to the exiles, a time when God would return to his people. The Temple was built from 520 to 515 B.C. (see Ezra 5, 6) but fell short of Ezekiel's plan (Haggai 2:3; Zechariah 4:10). This vision of the Temple has been interpreted in four main ways: (1) This is the Temple Zerubbabel should have built from 520 to 515 B.C. and is the actual blueprint Ezekiel intended. But due to disobedience (43:2-10), it was never followed. (2) This is a literal Temple to be rebuilt during the millennial reign of Christ. (3) This Temple is symbolic of the true worship of God by the Christian church right now. (4) This Temple is symbolic of the future and eternal reign of God when his presence and blessing fill the earth.

Whether the Temple is literal or symbolic, it seems clear that this is a vision of God's final perfect Kingdom. This gave hope to the people of Ezekiel's time who had just seen their nation and its Temple destroyed with no hope of rebuilding it in the near future. The details given in this vision gave the people even more hope that what Ezekiel saw had come from God and would surely happen in the future.

40:1ff One argument against the view that Ezekiel's Temple is a literal building of the future is that sacrifices are mentioned (40:38-43). If the sacrifices were to be reinstituted in the last days, then Christ's final sacrifice would not have been final. The New Testament makes it clear that Christ died once and for all (Romans 6:10; Hebrews 9:12; 10:10, 18). Our sins have been removed; no further sacrifice is needed.

In Ezekiel's day, however, the only kind of worship the people knew was the kind that involved sacrifices and ceremonies as described in Exodus through Deuteronomy. Ezekiel had to explain the new order of worship in terms the people would understand. The next nine chapters tell how the Temple is the focal point of everything, showing that the ideal relationship with God is when all of life centers on him.

40:1ff Ezekiel explained God's dwelling place in words and images the people could understand. God wanted them to see the great splendor he had planned for those who lived faithfully. This kind of Temple was never built, but it was a vision intended to typify God's perfect plan for his people—the centrality of worship, the presence of the Lord, the blessings flowing from it, and the orderliness of worship and worship duties. Don't let the details obscure the point of this vision: One day all those who have been faithful to God will enjoy eternal life with him. Let the majesty of this vision lift you and teach you about the God you worship and serve.

40:1–43:27 This vision came to Ezekiel in 573 B.C. Chapters 40–43 give the Temple's measurements and then describe how it would be filled with God's glory. Because Ezekiel was a priest, he would have been familiar with the furnishings and ceremonies of Solomon's Temple. As in Revelation 11:1, 2, the command to "measure" defines the areas God has marked out for special use. As you read all these details, remember that God is sovereign over all our worship and over the timetable for restoring the faithful to himself.

40:3, 4 Who was this man? He was obviously not a human being, so he may have been the angel in 9:1-11 or one like him. Some say he may have been Christ himself because he speaks as God had been speaking to Ezekiel, calling him "son of man."

The East Gateway

40:5 Ezek 42:20

5 I could see a wall completely surrounding the Temple area. The man took a measuring
rod that was 10½ feet* long and measured the wall, and the wall was 10½ feet thick and
10½ feet high.

40:6 Ezek 8:16; 11:1; 43:1

40:7 1 Kgs 6:5-10; 2 Chr 31:11; Jer 35:4; Ezek 29:33, 36

6 Then he went over to the gateway that goes through the eastern wall. He climbed the
steps and measured the threshold of the gateway; it was 10½ feet deep.* 7 There were
guard alcoves on each side built into the gateway passage. Each of these alcoves was
10½ feet square, with a distance between them of 8¾ feet along the passage wall. The
gateway's inner threshold, which led to the foyer at the inner end of the gateway passage,
was 10½ feet deep. 8 He also measured the foyer of the gateway* 9 and found it to be
14 feet deep, with supporting columns 3½ feet thick. This foyer was at the inner end of
the gateway structure, facing toward the Temple.

10 There were three guard alcoves on each side of the gateway passage. Each had the
same measurements, and the dividing walls separating them were also identical. 11 The
man measured the gateway entrance, which was 17½ feet wide at the opening and 22¾
feet wide in the gateway passage. 12 In front of each of the guard alcoves was a 21-inch
curb. The alcoves themselves were 10½ feet square.

40:14 Exod 27:9; 1 Chr 28:6; Ps 100:4; Isa 62:9; Ezek 42:1

40:16 1 Kgs 6:4; Ezek 41:26; 1 Cor 13:12

13 Then he measured the entire width of the gateway, measuring the distance between
the back walls of facing guard alcoves; this distance was 43¾ feet. 14 He measured the
dividing walls all along the inside of the gateway up to the gateway's foyer; this distance
was 105 feet.* 15 The full length of the gateway passage was 87½ feet from one end to
the other. 16 There were recessed windows that narrowed inward through the walls of the
guard alcoves and their dividing walls. There were also windows in the foyer structure.
The surfaces of the dividing walls were decorated with carved palm trees.

The Outer Courtyard

40:17 1 Chr 9:26; 2 Chr 31:11; Ezek 46:21; Rev 11:2

17 Then the man brought me through the gateway into the outer courtyard of the Temple.
A stone pavement ran along the walls of the courtyard, and thirty rooms were built
against the walls, opening onto the pavement. 18 This pavement flanked the gates and
extended out from the walls into the courtyard the same distance as the gateway entrance.
This was the lower pavement. 19 Then the man measured across the Temple's outer
courtyard between the outer and inner gateways; the distance was 175 feet.

The North Gateway

20 There was a gateway on the north just like the one on the east, and the man measured
it. 21 Here, too, there were three guard alcoves on each side, with dividing walls and a
foyer. All the measurements matched those of the east gateway. The gateway passage
was 87½ feet long and 43¾ feet wide between the back walls of facing guard alcoves.

40:22 1 Kgs 6:29-35; 7:36; 2 Chr 3:5; Rev 7:9

40:23 Exod 27:9-18; 38:9-12

22 The windows, the foyer, and the palm tree decorations were identical to those in the
east gateway. There were seven steps leading up to the gateway entrance, and the foyer
was at the inner end of the gateway passage. 23 Here on the north side, just as on the east,
there was another gateway leading to the Temple's inner courtyard directly opposite this
outer gateway. The distance between the two gateways was 175 feet.

The South Gateway

40:24 Ezek 46:9

24 Then the man took me around to the south gateway and measured its various parts, and
he found they were exactly the same as in the others. 25 It had windows along the walls
as the others did, and there was a foyer where the gateway passage opened into the outer
courtyard. And like the others, the gateway passage was 87½ feet long and 43¾ feet wide
between the back walls of facing guard alcoves. 26 This gateway also had a stairway of
seven steps leading up to it, and there were palm tree decorations along the dividing

40:5 Hebrew *6 long cubits* [3.2 meters], *each being a cubit* [18 inches or 45 centimeters] *and a handbreadth* [3 inches or 8 centimeters] *in length.* In this chapter, the distance measures are calculated using the Hebrew long cubit, which equals 21 inches or 53 centimeters. **40:6** Greek version; Hebrew reads *one rod* [10.5 feet or 3.2 meters] *deep, and one threshold, one rod deep.* **40:8** Many Hebrew manuscripts add *which faced inward toward the Temple; it was one rod* [10.5 feet or 3.2 meters] *deep.* 9 *Then he measured the foyer of the gateway, . . .* **40:14** The meaning of the Hebrew in this verse is uncertain.

40:38, 39 The washing of the sacrifices was done according to the standards of preparation established in Leviticus 1:6-9. This washing was part of the process of presenting an acceptable sacrifice to God.

walls. 27And here again, directly opposite the outer gateway, was another gateway that
led into the inner courtyard. The distance between the two gateways was 175 feet.

Gateways to the Inner Courtyard

28Then the man took me to the south gateway leading into the inner courtyard. He
measured it and found that it had the same measurements as the other gateways. 29Its
guard alcoves, dividing walls, and foyer were the same size as those in the others. It also
had windows along its walls and in the foyer structure. And like the others, the gateway
passage was 87½ feet long and 43¾ feet wide. 30(The foyers of the gateways leading into
the inner courtyard were 8¾ feet deep and 43¾ feet wide.) 31The foyer of the south
gateway faced into the outer courtyard. It had palm tree decorations on its columns, and
there were eight steps leading to its entrance.

32Then he took me to the east gateway leading to the inner courtyard. He measured it
and found that it had the same measurements as the other gateways. 33Its guard alcoves,
dividing walls, and foyer were the same size as those of the others, and there were
windows along the walls and in the foyer structure. The gateway passage measured
87½ feet long and 43¾ feet wide. 34Its foyer faced into the outer courtyard. It had palm
tree decorations on its columns, and there were eight steps leading to its entrance.

35Then he took me around to the north gateway leading to the inner courtyard. He
measured it and found that it had the same measurements as the other gateways. 36The
guard alcoves, dividing walls, and foyer of this gateway had the same measurements as
in the others and the same window arrangements. The gateway passage measured 87½
feet long and 43¾ feet wide. 37Its foyer faced into the outer courtyard, and it had palm
tree decorations on the columns. There were eight steps leading to its entrance.

40:35 Ezek 44:4; 47:2

Rooms for Preparing Sacrifices

38A door led from the foyer of the inner gateway on the north side into a side room where
the meat for sacrifices was washed before being taken to the altar. 39On each side of this
foyer were two tables, where the sacrificial animals were slaughtered for the burnt offerings,
sin offerings, and guilt offerings. 40Outside the foyer, on each side of the stairs going up to
the north entrance, there were two more tables. 41So there were eight tables in all, four inside
and four outside, where the sacrifices were cut up and prepared. 42There were also four
tables of hewn stone for preparation of the burnt offerings, each 31½ inches square and
21 inches high. On these tables were placed the butchering knives and other implements
and the sacrificial animals. 43There were hooks, each three inches* long, fastened to the
foyer walls and set on the tables where the sacrificial meat was to be laid.

40:38 1 Kgs 6:8; 1 Chr 28:12; 2 Chr 4:6; Neh 13:5, 9; Ezek 41:10; 42:13
40:39 Lev 1:2-17; 4:2-3; 5:6; 6:6; 7:1-2; Ezek 46:2
40:42 Exod 20:25

Rooms for the Priests

44Inside the inner courtyard there were two one-room buildings for the singers, one
beside the north gateway, facing south, and the other beside the south* gateway, facing
north. 45And the man said to me, "The building beside the north inner gate is for the
priests who supervise the Temple maintenance. 46The building beside the south inner
gate is for the priests in charge of the altar—the descendants of Zadok—for they alone
of all the Levites may approach the LORD to minister to him."

40:44 1 Chr 6:31-32; 16:41-43; 25:1-7
40:45 Lev 8:35; 1 Chr 9:23
40:46 1 Kgs 2:35

The Inner Courtyard and Temple

47Then the man measured the inner courtyard and found it to be 175 feet square. The
altar stood there in the courtyard in front of the Temple. 48Then he brought me to the
foyer of the Temple. He measured its supporting columns and found them to be 8¾ feet
square. The entrance was 24½ feet wide with walls 5¼ feet thick. 49The depth of the foyer
was 35 feet and the width was 19¼ feet. There were ten steps leading up to it, with a
column on each side.

40:48 1 Kgs 6:3
40:49 Jer 52:17-23; Rev 3:12

41 After that, the man brought me into the Holy Place, the large main room of the
Temple, and he measured the columns that framed its doorway. They were 10½
feet* square. 2The entrance was 17½ feet wide, and the walls on each side were 8¾ feet
wide. The Holy Place itself was 70 feet long and 35 feet wide.

3Then he went into the inner room at the end of the Holy Place. He measured the columns

41:1 Ezek 40:2-3, 17
41:2 1 Kgs 6:2, 17; 2 Chr 3:3

40:43 Hebrew *a handbreadth* [8 centimeters]. **40:44** As in Greek version; Hebrew reads *east.* **41:1** Hebrew *6 cubits* [3.2 meters]. In this chapter, the distance measures are calculated using the Hebrew long cubit, which equals 21 inches or 53 centimeters.

at the entrance and found them to be 3½ feet thick. The entrance was 10½ feet wide, and the
walls on each side of the entrance extended 12¼ feet to the corners of the inner room. 4 The
inner room was 35 feet square. "This," he told me, "is the Most Holy Place."
5 Then he measured the wall of the Temple and found that it was 10½ feet thick. There
was a row of rooms along the outside wall; each room was 7 feet wide. 6 These rooms
were built in three levels, one above the other, with thirty rooms on each level. The
supports for these rooms rested on ledges in the Temple wall, but the supports did not
extend into the wall. 7 Each level was wider than the one below it, corresponding to the
narrowing of the Temple wall as it rose higher. A stairway led up from the bottom level
through the middle level to the top level.
8 I noticed that the Temple was built on a terrace, which provided a foundation for the side
rooms. This terrace was 10½ feet high. 9 The outer wall of the Temple's side rooms was
8¾ feet thick. This left an open area between these side rooms 10 and the row of rooms along
the outer wall of the inner courtyard. This open area measured 35 feet in width, and it went
all the way around the Temple. 11 Two doors opened from the side rooms into the terrace
yard, which was 8¾ feet wide. One door faced north and the other south.
12 A large building stood on the west, facing the Temple courtyard. It was 122½ feet
wide and 157½ feet long, and its walls were 8¾ feet thick. 13 Then the man measured the
Temple, and he found it to be 175 feet long. The courtyard around the building, including
its walls, was an additional 175 feet in length. 14 The inner courtyard to the east of the
Temple was also 175 feet wide. 15 The building to the west, including its two walls, was
also 175 feet wide.
The Holy Place, the Most Holy Place, and the foyer of the Temple were all paneled
with wood, 16 as were the frames of the recessed windows. The inner walls of the Temple
were paneled with wood above and below the windows. 17 The space above the door
leading into the Most Holy Place was also paneled. 18 All the walls were decorated with
carvings of cherubim, each with two faces, and there was a palm tree carving between
each of the cherubim. 19 One face—that of a man—looked toward the palm tree on one
side. The other face—that of a young lion—looked toward the palm tree on the other
side. The figures were carved all along the inside of the Temple, 20 from the floor to the
top of the walls, including the outer wall of the Holy Place.
21 There were square columns at the entrance to the Holy Place, and the ones at the
entrance of the Most Holy Place were similar. 22 There was an altar made of wood, 3½
feet square and 5¼ feet high. Its corners, base, and sides were all made of wood. "This,"
the man told me, "is the table that stands in the LORD's presence."
23 Both the Holy Place and the Most Holy Place had double doorways, 24 each with
two swinging doors. 25 The doors leading into the Holy Place were decorated with carved
cherubim and palm trees just as on the walls. And there was a wooden canopy over the
front of the Temple's foyer. 26 On both sides of the foyer there were recessed windows
decorated with carved palm trees.

Rooms for the Priests

42 Then the man led me out of the Temple courtyard by way of the north gateway.
We entered the outer courtyard and came to a group of rooms against the north
wall of the inner courtyard. 2 This group of structures, whose entrance opened toward
the north, was 175 feet long and 87½ feet wide.* 3 One block of rooms overlooked the

41:4 Exod 26:33-34; 1 Kgs 6:20; 2 Chr 3:8; Heb 9:3-8
41:5 1 Kgs 6:5
41:6 1 Kgs 6:6, 10
41:7 1 Kgs 6:8
41:8 Ezek 40:5
41:10 Ezek 40:17
41:12 Ezek 42:1; Rev 21:27; 22:14-15
41:13 Ezek 40:47
41:15 Ezek 42:1, 10, 13
41:16 1 Kgs 6:4, 15
41:18 1 Kgs 6:29; 7:36; 2 Chr 3:5; Ezek 10:18
41:19 Ezek 1:10; 10:14
41:21 1 Kgs 6:33
41:22 Exod 30:1-3, 8; Ezek 44:16; Mal 1:7, 12; Rev 8:3
41:23 1 Kgs 6:31-35
41:24 1 Kgs 6:34
41:26 Ezek 40:7-12
42:1 Ezek 40:2-3, 17; 41:9, 12-15
42:2 Ezek 41:13

41:4 God's holiness is a central theme throughout both the Old and New Testaments. The Most Holy Place was the innermost room in the Temple (Exodus 26:33, 34). This was where the Ark of the Covenant was kept and where God's glory was said to dwell. This room was entered only once a year by the high priest, who performed a ceremony to atone for the nation's sins.

41:18 Cherubim are mighty angels.

41:22 The dimensions given would fit either the table of the Bread of the Presence (Exodus 25:30) or the altar of incense (Exodus 30:1-3).

42:14 Approaching our holy God must not be taken lightly. The holy garments the priests were required to wear may symbolize the importance of having a holy heart when approaching God. The priests had to wear these special clothes in order to minister in the inner rooms of the Temple. Because the garments were holy, the priests had to change their clothes before going back out to the public.

42:16-20 The perfect symmetry of Ezekiel's Temple may represent the order and harmony in God's future Kingdom.

43:1ff This is the culmination of chapters 40–42 because God's glory returns to the Temple. It reverses the negative tone of the book and serves as a fitting end for all the passages dealing with the blessings reserved for the restored remnant. All true believers should long for that moment when God's name will finally be glorified and he will live among his people forever.

35-foot width of the inner courtyard. Another block of rooms looked out onto the **42:3** Ezek 40:17; 41:10
pavement of the outer courtyard. The two blocks were built three levels high and stood
across from each other. 4 Between the two blocks of rooms ran a walkway 17½ feet **42:4** Ezek 46:19
wide. It extended the entire 175 feet of the complex, and all the doors faced toward
the north. 5 Each of the two upper levels of rooms was narrower than the one beneath
it because the upper levels had to allow space for walkways in front of them. 6 Since **42:6** Ezek 41:6
there were three levels and they did not have supporting columns as in the courtyards,
each of the upper levels was set back from the level beneath it. 7 There was an outer **42:7** Ezek 41:13-14
wall that separated the rooms from the outer courtyard; it was 87½ feet long. 8 This
wall added length to the outer block of rooms, which extended for only 87½ feet,
while the inner block—the rooms toward the Temple—extended for 175 feet. 9 There **42:9** Ezek 44:5; 46:19
was an entrance from the outer courtyard to these rooms from the east.

10 On the south* side of the Temple there were two blocks of rooms just south of
the inner courtyard between the Temple and the outer courtyard. These rooms were
arranged just like the rooms on the north. 11 There was a walkway between the two
blocks of rooms just like the complex on the north side of the Temple. This complex
of rooms was the same length and width as the other one, and it had the same entrances
and doors. The dimensions of each were identical. 12 So there was an entrance in the
wall facing the doors of the inner block of rooms, and another on the east at the end
of the interior walkway.

13 Then the man told me, "These rooms that overlook the Temple from the north **42:13**
and south are holy. It is there that the priests who offer sacrifices to the LORD will eat Lev 6:25, 29; 7:6; 10:13-17
the most holy offerings. And they will use these rooms to store the grain offerings, sin Num 18:9-10
offerings, and guilt offerings because these rooms are holy. 14 When the priests leave **42:14**
the Holy Place, they must not go directly to the outer courtyard. They must first take Exod 29:4-9
off the clothes they wore while ministering because these clothes are holy. They must Isa 61:10 Zech 3:4-5
put on other clothes before entering the parts of the building complex open to the
public."

15 When the man had finished taking these measurements, he led me out through the **42:15**
east gateway to measure the entire Temple area. 16 He measured the east side; it was 875 Ezek 43:1
feet long. 17 He also measured the north side and got the same measurement. 18 The south **42:16**
side was the same length, 19 and so was the west side. 20 So the area was 875 feet on each Ezek 40:3, 5
side with a wall all around it to separate the holy places from the common.

The LORD's Glory Returns

43 After this, the man brought me back around to the east gateway. 2 Suddenly, the **43:1**
glory of the God of Israel appeared from the east. The sound of his coming was Ezek 10:19; 40:6; 44:1; 46:1
like the roar of rushing waters, and the whole landscape shone with his glory. 3 This **43:2**
vision was just like the others I had seen, first by the Kebar River and then when he came Isa 6:3
to destroy Jerusalem. And I fell down before him with my face in the dust. 4 And the glory Ezek 10:4, 18-19
of the LORD came into the Temple through the east gateway. Rev 1:15; 18:1

5 Then the Spirit took me up and brought me into the inner courtyard, and the glory **43:3** Jer 1:10
of the LORD filled the Temple. 6 And I heard someone speaking to me from within the Ezek 3:23
Temple. (The man who had been measuring was still standing beside me.) 7 And the **43:4**
LORD said to me, "Son of man, this is the place of my throne and the place where I Ezek 44:2
will rest my feet. I will remain here forever, living among the people of Israel. They **43:5** 1 Kgs 8:10-11
and their kings will not defile my holy name any longer by their adulterous worship 2 Cor 12:2-4
of other gods or by raising monuments in honor of their dead kings.* 8 They put their **43:7** Lev 26:30 Ps 47:8 Jer 16:18

42:2 Hebrew *100 cubits* [53 meters] *long and 50 cubits* [26.5 meters] *wide.* In this chapter, the distance measures are calculated using the Hebrew long cubit, which equals 21 inches or 53 centimeters. **42:10** As in Greek version; Hebrew reads *east.* **43:7** Or *by raising pillars on their high places.*

43:2 In 11:23, God's glory stopped over the Mount of Olives, to the east of Jerusalem, before leaving the city. This prophecy states that his glory would also return from the east.

43:2-4 It was completely devastating for Ezekiel when God's glory departed (11:23) from his Temple, but he was overwhelmed with awe and joy beyond expression when he saw God's glory return.

43:3 The Kebar River connected with the Euphrates River and was the location of a Jewish settlement of exiles in Babylonia.

idol altars right next to mine with only a wall between them and me. They defiled my
holy name by such wickedness, so I consumed them in my anger. 9 Now let them put
away their idols and the sacred pillars erected to honor their kings, and I will live
among them forever.
10 "Son of man, describe to the people of Israel the Temple I have shown you. Tell
them its appearance and its plan so they will be ashamed of all their sins. 11 And if they
are ashamed of what they have done, describe to them all the specifications of its
construction—including its entrances and doors—and everything else about it. Write
down all these specifications and directions as they watch so they will be sure to
remember them. 12 And this is the basic law of the Temple: absolute holiness! The entire
top of the hill where the Temple is built is holy. Yes, this is the primary law of the
Temple.

The Altar

13 "These are the measurements of the altar*: There is a gutter all around the altar
21 inches wide and 21 inches deep, with a curb 9 inches* wide around its edge. And
this is the height of the altar: 14 From the gutter the altar rises 3½ feet to a ledge that
surrounds the altar; this lower ledge is 21 inches wide. From the lower ledge the altar
rises 7 feet to the upper ledge; this upper ledge is also 21 inches wide. 15 The top of
the altar, the hearth, rises still 7 feet higher, with a horn rising up from each of the four
corners. 16 The top of the altar is square, measuring 21 feet by 21 feet. 17 The upper
ledge also forms a square, measuring 24½ feet on each side, with a 21-inch gutter and
a 10½-inch curb all around the edge. There are steps going up the east side of the
altar."
18 Then he said to me, "Son of man, this is what the Sovereign LORD says: These will
be the regulations for the burning of offerings and the sprinkling of blood when the altar
is built. 19 At that time, the Levitical priests of the family of Zadok, who minister before
me, are to be given a young bull for a sin offering, says the Sovereign LORD. 20 You will
take some of its blood and smear it on the four horns of the altar, the four corners of the
upper ledge, and the curb that runs around that ledge. This will cleanse and make
atonement for the altar. 21 Then take the young bull for the sin offering and burn it at the
appointed place outside the Temple area.
22 "On the second day, sacrifice as a sin offering a young male goat that has no physical
defects. Then cleanse and make atonement for the altar again, just as you did with the
young bull. 23 When you have finished the cleansing ceremony, offer another young bull
that has no defects and a perfect ram from the flock. 24 You are to present them to the LORD,
and the priests are to sprinkle salt on them and offer them as a burnt offering to the LORD.
25 "Every day for seven days a male goat, a young bull, and a ram from the flock will
be sacrificed as a sin offering. None of these animals may have physical defects of any
kind. 26 Do this each day for seven days to cleanse and make atonement for the altar, thus
setting it apart for holy use. 27 On the eighth day, and on each day afterward, the priests
will sacrifice on the altar the burnt offerings and peace offerings of the people. Then I
will accept you, says the Sovereign LORD."

43:9 Ezek 18:30, 31
43:10 Ezek 40:4
43:11 Ezek 11:20; 12:3; 36:27; 44:5
43:12 Ezek 40:2
43:13 Exod 27:1-8; 2 Chr 4:1
43:15 Exod 27:2; Lev 9:9; 1 Kgs 1:49-50; Ps 118:27
43:16 Exod 27:1
43:17 Exod 20:26; Ezek 40:6
43:18 Exod 40:29; Lev 1:5, 11; Ezek 2:1; Heb 9:21-22
43:19 1 Kgs 2:35; Ezek 40:46; 44:15; Heb 7:27
43:20 Lev 8:15; 9:9
43:21 Exod 29:14; Lev 4:11-12; Heb 13:11
43:23 Exod 29:1
43:24 Lev 2:13; Num 18:19; Mark 9:49-50; Col 4:6
43:25 Exod 29:35-37; Lev 8:33, 35
43:27 Lev 3:1; 9:1; 17:5; Ezek 20:40

43:13a Hebrew *measurements of the altar in long cubits, each being a cubit* [18 inches or 45 centimeters] *and a handbreadth* [3 inches or 8 centimeters] *in length.* In this chapter, the distance measures are calculated using the Hebrew long cubit, which equals 21 inches or 53 centimeters. **43:13b** Hebrew *1 span* [23 centimeters].

43:9-11 God's departure from the city had been a signal for the destruction of the city and the Temple. Now for God to return, his conditions had to be met: Idolatry had to be removed. Some commentators feel these verses indicate that Ezekiel was commanding the people of his day to build this Temple according to the designs and regulations that the angelic architect had given. But the people never repented and the conditions were not met, so the fulfillment was postponed.

43:12 The basic law of God's Temple was holiness. In all he does, God is holy, perfect, and blameless. There is no trace of evil or sin in him. Just as God is holy, so we are to be holy (Leviticus 19:2; 1 Peter 1:15, 16). People are holy when they are devoted to God and separated from sin. It is important to understand the concept of holiness in order that we may progress in our Christian growth.

43:18-27 This vision was simultaneously flashing back to Mount Sinai and forward to Mount Calvary. When the people returned from exile, they would seek forgiveness through the sacrificial system instituted in Moses' day. Today, Christ's death has made the forgiveness of our sins possible, making us acceptable to God (Hebrews 9:9-15). God stands ready to forgive those who come to him in faith.

The Prince, Levites, and Priests

44 Then the man brought me back to the east gateway in the outer wall, but it was
closed. 2And the LORD said to me, "This gate must remain closed; it will never again
be opened. No man will ever pass through it, for the LORD, the God of Israel, entered here.
Thus, it must always remain shut. 3Only the prince himself may sit inside this gateway to
feast in the LORD's presence. But he may come and go only through the gateway's foyer."
4Then the man brought me through the north gateway to the front of the Temple. I
looked and saw that the glory of the LORD filled the Temple of the LORD, and I fell to the
ground with my face in the dust.
5And the LORD said to me, "Son of man, take careful notice; use your eyes and ears.
Listen to everything I tell you about the regulations concerning the LORD's Temple. Take
careful note of who may be admitted to the Temple and who is to be excluded from it.
6And give these rebels, the people of Israel, this message from the Sovereign LORD:
O people of Israel, enough of your disgusting sins! 7You have brought uncircumcised
foreigners into my sanctuary—people who have no heart for God. In this way, you
profaned my Temple even as you offered me my food, the fat and blood of sacrifices.
Thus, in addition to all your other disgusting sins, you have broken my covenant. 8You
have not kept the laws I gave you concerning these sacred rituals, for you have hired
foreigners to take charge of my sanctuary.
9"So this is what the Sovereign LORD says: No foreigners, including those who live
among the people of Israel, will enter my sanctuary if they have not been circumcised
and do not love the LORD. 10And the men of the tribe of Levi who abandoned me when
Israel strayed away from me to worship idols must bear the consequences of their
unfaithfulness. 11They may still be Temple guards and gatemen, and they may still
slaughter the animals brought for burnt offerings and be present to help the people. 12But
they encouraged my people to worship other gods, causing Israel to fall into deep sin.
So I have raised my hand and taken an oath that they must bear the consequences for
their sins, says the Sovereign LORD. 13They may not approach me to minister as priests.
They may not touch any of my holy things or the holy offerings, for they must bear the
shame of all the sins they have committed. 14They are to serve as the Temple caretakers
and are relegated to doing maintenance work and helping the people in a general way.
15"However, the Levitical priests of the family of Zadok continued to minister
faithfully in the Temple when Israel abandoned me for idols. These men will serve as my
ministers. They will stand in my presence and offer the fat and blood of the sacrifices,
says the Sovereign LORD. 16They are the ones who will enter my sanctuary and approach
my table to serve me. They are the ones who will fulfill all my requirements. 17When
they enter the gateway to the inner courtyard, they must wear only linen clothing. They
must wear no wool while on duty in the inner courtyard or in the Temple itself. 18They
must wear linen turbans and linen undergarments. They must not wear anything that
would cause them to perspire. 19When they return to the outer courtyard where the
people are, they must take off the clothes they wear while ministering to me. They must
leave them in the sacred rooms and put on other clothes so they do not harm the people
by transmitting holiness to them through this clothing.
20"They must neither let their hair grow too long nor shave it off completely. Instead,

44:2 Ezek 43:4
44:3 Gen 31:54; Exod 24:9-11; Zech 6:12-13
44:4 Ezek 1:28; 3:23
44:5 Deut 12:32; 32:46; Ezek 40:4; 43:10-11
44:6 Ezek 2:5-7; 3:9; 1 Pet 4:3
44:7 Gen 17:14; Exod 12:43-49; Lev 22:25; 26:41; Jer 4:4; 9:26
44:8 Num 18:7
44:9 Joel 3:17; Zech 14:21
44:10 Num 18:23; 2 Kgs 23:8-9; Ezek 22:26
44:11 Num 3:5-37; 4:1-33; 16:8-9; 18:2, 6; 1 Chr 26:1; 2 Chr 29:34
44:12 2 Kgs 16:10-16; Ezek 14:3-4; Hos 4:6; 5:1
44:13 Num 18:3; 2 Kgs 23:9
44:14 Num 18:4, 6; 1 Chr 23:28, 32
44:15 Num 18:7; Jer 33:18-22; Ezek 48:11
44:16 Mal 1:17, 21
44:17 Exod 39:27-29
44:18 Exod 28:40, 42
44:19 Lev 16:23-24
44:20 Lev 21:5; Num 6:5

44:2 Why was this east gate to remain closed? Several reasons have been suggested: (1) This was the gate through which God entered the Temple, and no one else could walk where God had (43:4); (2) the closed gate indicated that God would never again leave the Temple (10:19; 11:23); (3) it would prevent people from worshiping the sun as it rises in the east from within the Temple grounds (8:16).

44:3 Although Christ is called a prince (37:25), this prince is probably not Christ because he offers a sacrifice to God (46:4) and he can enter only by the "gateway's foyer." He is a princely ruler of the city, but he is distinguished from other princes because he will be just and fair (see 45:9). Some, however, have understood this prince to be a prophetic image that anticipates the coming of Christ, who would offer himself as a sacrifice to God.

44:9 Unbelievers would not be allowed to enter the Temple. Ezekiel's vision was for a restored, purified worship in which only those who prepared themselves physically and spiritually could participate. In 47:22, 23, we find that people from other nations are allowed to join in worship by accepting the standards of faith and practice declared in the law (see Leviticus 24:22; Numbers 15:29).

44:15 Zadok's descendants are mentioned because many of the priests in Zadok's line had remained faithful to God, while others had become corrupt. Zadok supported God's choice of Solomon to succeed David and was therefore appointed high priest during his reign (1 Kings 1:32-35; 2:27, 35). Zadok's descendants were considered the true priestly line throughout the time between the Old and New Testaments.

44:20-31 These laws were originally given to God's people in the wilderness. They are recorded in the books of Exodus and Leviticus. They reveal the importance of approaching God respectfully, and they give guidelines for the priests to live above

they must trim it regularly. 21 The priests must never drink wine before entering the inner
courtyard. 22 They may choose their wives only from among the virgins of Israel or the
widows of the priests. They may not marry other widows or divorced women. 23 They
will teach my people the difference between what is holy and what is common, what is
ceremonially clean and unclean.
24 "They will serve as judges to resolve any disagreements among my people. Their
decisions must be based on my regulations. And the priests themselves must obey my
instructions and laws at all the sacred festivals, and they will see to it that the Sabbath is
set apart as a holy day. 25 A priest must never defile himself by being in the presence of
a dead person unless it is his father, mother, child, brother, or unmarried sister. In such
cases it is permitted. 26 But such a priest can only return to his Temple duties after being
ritually cleansed and then waiting for seven days. 27 The first day he returns to work and
enters the inner courtyard and the sanctuary, he must offer a sin offering for himself, says
the Sovereign LORD.
28 "As to property, the priests will not have any, for I alone am their inheritance.
29 Their food will come from the gifts and sacrifices brought to the Temple by the
people—the grain offerings, the sin offerings, and the guilt offerings. Whatever anyone
sets apart* for the LORD will belong to the priests. 30 The first of the ripe fruits and all
the gifts brought to the LORD will go to the priests. The first samples of each grain harvest
and the first of your flour must also be given to the priests so the LORD will bless your
homes. 31 The priests may never eat meat from any bird or animal that dies a natural death
or that dies after being attacked by another animal.

Division of the Land

45 "When you divide the land among the tribes of Israel, you must set aside a section
of it for the LORD as his holy portion. This piece of land will be 8⅓ miles long and
6⅔ miles wide.* The entire area will be holy ground. 2 A section of this land, measuring
875 feet by 875 feet, will be set aside for the Temple. An additional strip of land 87½ feet
wide is to be left empty all around it. 3 Within the larger sacred area, measure out a portion
of land 8⅓ miles long and 3⅓ miles wide. Within it the sanctuary of the Most Holy Place
will be located. 4 This area will be a holy land, set aside for the priests who minister to
the LORD in the sanctuary. They will use it for their homes, and my Temple will be located
within it. 5 The strip of sacred land next to it, also 8⅓ miles long and 3⅓ miles wide, will
be a living area for the Levites who work at the Temple. It will be their possession and
a place for their towns.*
6 "Adjacent to the larger sacred area will be a section of land 8⅓ miles long and 1⅔
miles wide. This will be set aside to be a city where anyone in Israel can come and live.
7 "Two special sections of land will be set apart for the prince. One section will share
a border with the east side of the sacred lands and city, and the second section will share
a border on the west side. Then the far eastern and western borders of the prince's lands
will line up with the eastern and western boundaries of the tribal areas. 8 These sections
of land will be the prince's allotment.

Rules for the Prince

"My princes will no longer oppress and rob my people; they will assign the rest of the
land to the people, giving an allotment to each tribe. 9 For this is what the Sovereign LORD
says: Enough, you princes of Israel! Stop all your violence and oppression and do what
is just and right. Quit robbing and cheating my people out of their land! Stop expelling

44:21 Lev 10:8-9
44:22 Lev 21:7, 13-15
44:23 Lev 10:10; Deut 33:10
44:24 Deut 17:8-9; 21:5; 2 Chr 19:8-10
44:25 Lev 21:1-3
44:26 Num 19:13-19
44:27 Num 6:9-11
44:28 Num 18:20; Deut 10:9; Josh 13:33
44:29 Lev 27:21, 28; Num 18:9, 14-15; Josh 13:14
44:30 Num 15:20; 18:12; 2 Chr 31:4-6, 10
44:31 Lev 22:8; Deut 14:21
45:1 Josh 13:7; 14:2; Ps 16:5-6; Ezek 47:21; 48:8-9
45:2 Ezek 42:16-20
45:3 Ezek 48:10
45:4 Num 16:5; Ezek 40:45; 44:13-14; 48:10-11
45:5 Ezek 48:12-14
45:6 Ezek 48:15-16
45:7 Ezek 46:16-18; 48:21-22
45:8 Josh 11:23; Isa 11:3-5; Jer 23:5-6; Ezek 22:27; 46:18
45:9 Jer 6:7; 22:3; Nah 5:1-5; Zech 8:16

44:29 The Hebrew term used here refers to the complete consecration of things or people to the LORD, either by destroying them or by giving them as an offering. **45:1** Reflecting the Greek reading *25,000 cubits* [13.3 kilometers] *long and 20,000 cubits* [10.6 kilometers] *wide;* Hebrew reads *25,000 cubits long and 10,000 cubits wide.* Compare 45:3, 5; 48:9. In this chapter, the distance measures are calculated using the Hebrew long cubit, which equals 21 inches or 53 centimeters. **45:5** As in Greek version; Hebrew reads *They will have as their possession 20 rooms.*

reproach so they could carry out their responsibility to teach the people "the difference between what is holy and what is common, what is ceremonially clean and unclean" (44:23).

45:1-7 The land allotted to the Temple was in the center of the nation. God is central to life. He must be our first priority.

45:8-12 Greed and extortion were two of the major social sins of the nation during this time (see Amos 5:10-13). In the new economy there would be plenty of land for the "princes" (45:7, 8) and no longer any basis for greed. Therefore, God commanded the princes and the people to do what was just and right, especially in their business dealings. Consider the ways that you measure goods, money, or services. If you are paid for an hour of work, be sure you work for a full hour. If you sell a bushel of apples, make sure it is a full bushel. God is completely trustworthy, and his followers should be, too.

them from their homes! 10 You must use only honest weights and scales, honest dry
volume measures, and honest liquid volume measures.* 11 The homer* will be your
standard unit for measuring volume. The ephah and the bath* will each measure
one-tenth of a homer. 12 The standard unit for weight will be the silver shekel.* One
shekel consists of twenty gerahs, and sixty shekels are equal to one mina.*

Special Offerings and Celebrations

13 "This is the tax you must give to the prince: one bushel of wheat or barley for every
sixty* you harvest, 14 one percent of your olive oil,* 15 and one sheep for every two
hundred in your flocks in Israel. These will be the grain offerings, burnt offerings, and
peace offerings that will make atonement for the people who bring them, says the
Sovereign LORD. 16 All the people of Israel must join the prince in bringing their
offerings. 17 The prince will be required to provide offerings that are given at the religious
festivals, the new moon celebrations, the Sabbath days, and all other similar occasions.
He will provide the sin offerings, burnt offerings, grain offerings, drink offerings, and
peace offerings to make reconciliation for the people of Israel.

18 "This is what the Sovereign LORD says: In early spring, on the first day of each new
year,* sacrifice a young bull with no physical defects to purify the Temple. 19 The priest
will take some of the blood of this sin offering and put it on the doorposts of the Temple,
the four corners of the upper ledge on the altar, and the gateposts at the entrance to the
inner courtyard. 20 Do this also on the seventh day of the new year for anyone who has
sinned through error or ignorance. In that way, you will make atonement for the Temple.

21 "On the fourteenth day of the new year, you must celebrate the Passover. This
festival will last for seven days. Only bread without yeast may be eaten during that time.
22 On the day of Passover the prince will provide a young bull as a sin offering for himself
and the people of Israel. 23 On each of the seven days of the feast he will prepare a burnt
offering to the LORD. This daily offering will consist of seven young bulls and seven
rams without any defects. A male goat will also be given each day for a sin offering.
24 The prince will provide a half bushel of flour as a grain offering and a gallon of olive
oil* with each young bull and ram.

25 "During the seven days of the Festival of Shelters, which occurs every year in early
autumn,* the prince will provide these same sacrifices for the sin offering, the burnt
offering, and the grain offering, along with the required olive oil.

46 "This is what the Sovereign LORD says: The east gateway of the inner wall will
be closed during the six workdays each week, but it will be open on Sabbath days
and the days of new moon celebrations. 2 The prince will enter the foyer of the gateway
from the outside. Then he will stand by the gatepost while the priest offers his burnt
offering and peace offering. He will worship inside the gateway passage and then go
back out the way he came. The gateway will not be closed until evening. 3 The common
people will worship the LORD in front of this gateway on Sabbath days and the days of
new moon celebrations.

4 "Each Sabbath day the prince will present to the LORD a burnt offering of six lambs
and one ram, all with no physical defects. 5 He will present a grain offering of a half

45:10 Lev 19:35-36; Deut 25:13-15; Prov 11:1; 16:11; Mic 6:10-11
45:12 Exod 30:13
45:15 Lev 1:4; 6:30
45:17 Lev 23:1-44; 1 Kgs 8:62-64; 2 Chr 31:3; Ezek 46:4-12
45:18 Exod 12:2; Lev 16:16, 20; 22:20; Heb 9:14
45:19 Lev 16:18-20
45:20 Lev 4:27; Ps 19:12
45:21 Exod 12:18; Lev 23:5-8; Num 9:2-3; 28:16-17
45:22 Lev 4:14
45:23 Lev 23:8; Num 28:16-25; Job 42:8
45:24 Num 28:12-15
45:25 Lev 23:33-36; Num 29:12-38
46:1 Exod 20:9-10; Isa 66:23; Ezek 44:1-2
46:2 Ezek 44:3
46:3 Luke 1:10
46:4 Ezek 45:17
46:5 Ezek 45:24

45:10 Hebrew *use honest scales, an honest ephah, and an honest bath.* **45:11a** The *homer* measures about 40 gallons or 182 liters. **45:11b** The *ephah* is a dry measure; the *bath* is a liquid measure. **45:12a** The shekel weighs about 0.4 ounces or 11 grams. **45:12b** Elsewhere the mina is equated to 50 shekels. **45:13** Hebrew *1/6 of an ephah from each homer of wheat . . . and of barley.* **45:14** Hebrew *the portion of oil, measured by the bath, is 1/10 of a bath from each cor, which consists of 10 baths or 1 homer, for 10 baths are equivalent to a homer.* **45:18** Hebrew *On the first day of the first month,* of the Hebrew calendar. This day of the Hebrew lunar calendar occurs in late March or early April. **45:24** Hebrew *an ephah* [18 liters] *of flour . . . a hin* [3.8 liters] *of olive oil.* **45:25** Hebrew *the festival which begins on the fifteenth day of the seventh month* (see Lev 23:33). This day of the Hebrew lunar calendar occurs in late September or October.

45:17 The conditions and regulations for these offerings are described in detail in Leviticus 1–7.

45:21 The Passover was an annual seven-day festival instituted by God so that his people would remember when he brought them out of slavery in Egypt. On that first Passover night, the destroyer passed over the homes marked by lamb's blood; he struck only the unmarked homes (see Exodus 11–12).

45:25 This annual festival was celebrated in October. It commemorates God's protection of his people as they traveled through the wilderness from Egypt to the Promised Land (see Leviticus 23:33-43; Deuteronomy 16:13-17).

46:1-15 Ezekiel continued to describe various aspects of daily worship. While allowing for diversity in worship, God prescribed order and continuity. This continuity gave a healthy rhythm to the spiritual life of his people.

bushel of flour to go with the ram and whatever amount of flour he chooses to go with each lamb. He is to offer one gallon of olive oil* for each half bushel of flour. 6At the new moon celebrations, he will bring one young bull, six lambs, and one ram, all with no physical defects. 7With the young bull he must bring a half bushel of flour for a grain offering. With the ram he must bring another half bushel of flour. And with each lamb he is to bring whatever amount of flour that he decides to give. With each half bushel of flour he must offer one gallon of olive oil.

8"The prince must enter the gateway through the foyer, and he must leave the same way he came. 9But when the people come in through the north gateway to worship the LORD during the religious festivals, they must leave by the south gateway. And those who entered through the south gateway must leave by the north gateway. They must never leave by the same gateway they came in; they must always use the opposite gateway. 10The prince will enter and leave with the people on these occasions.

11"So at the special feasts and sacred festivals, the grain offering will be a half bushel of flour with each young bull, another half bushel of flour with each ram, and as much flour as the prince chooses to give with each lamb. One gallon of oil is to be given with each half bushel of flour. 12Whenever the prince offers a voluntary burnt offering or peace offering to the LORD, the east gateway to the inner courtyard will be opened for him to enter, and he will offer his sacrifices just as he does on Sabbath days. Then he will turn and leave the way he entered, and the gateway will be shut behind him.

13"Each morning a year-old lamb with no physical defects must be sacrificed as a burnt offering to the LORD. 14With the lamb, a grain offering must also be given to the LORD—about two and a half quarts of flour with a third of a gallon of olive oil* to moisten the flour. This will be a permanent law for you. 15The lamb, the grain offering, and the olive oil must be given as a daily sacrifice every morning without fail.

16"This is what the Sovereign LORD says: If the prince gives a gift of land to one of his sons, it will belong to him and his descendants forever. 17But if he gives a gift of land to one of his servants, the servant may keep it only until the Year of Jubilee, which comes every fiftieth year.* At that time the servant will be set free, and the land will return to the prince. Only the gifts given to the prince's sons will be permanent. 18And the prince may never take anyone's property by force. If he gives property to his sons, it must be from his own land, for I do not want any of my people unjustly evicted from their property."

The Temple Kitchens

19Then the man brought me through the entrance beside the gateway and led me to the sacred rooms assigned to the priests, which faced toward the north. He showed me a place at the extreme west end of these rooms. 20He explained, "This is where the priests will cook the meat from the guilt offerings and sin offerings and bake the flour from the grain offerings into bread. They will do it here to avoid carrying the sacrifices through the outer courtyard and harming the people by transmitting holiness to them."

21Then he brought me back to the outer courtyard and led me to each of its four corners. In each corner I saw an enclosure. 22Each of these enclosures was 70 feet long and 52½ feet wide,* surrounded by walls. 23Along the inside of these walls was a ledge of stone with fireplaces under the ledge all the way around. 24The man said to me, "These are the kitchens to be used by the Temple assistants to boil the sacrifices offered by the people."

The River of Healing

47 Then the man brought me back to the entrance of the Temple. There I saw a stream flowing eastward from beneath the Temple threshold. This stream then passed to the right of the altar on its south side. 2The man brought me outside the wall through the north gateway and led me around to the eastern entrance. There I could see the stream flowing out through the south side of the east gateway. 3Measuring as he went, he led

46:7 Deut 16:17
46:8 Ezek 44:1-3
46:9 Exod 23:14-17; Deut 16:16; Ps 84:7
46:10 2 Chr 6:3; 7:4; Ps 42:4
46:11 Ezek 45:17
46:12 Lev 23:38; 2 Chr 29:31; Ezek 44:3; 45:17
46:13 Exod 29:38; Num 28:3-4; Isa 50:4
46:14 Exod 29:42; Num 28:5-6
46:15 Exod 29:42; Num 28:6
46:16 2 Chr 21:3
46:17 Lev 25:10
46:18 Ezek 45:8; Mic 2:1-2
46:20 Lev 2:4-7; 2 Chr 35:13
47:1 Ps 46:4; Joel 2:13; Zech 13:1; Rev 22:1, 17
47:2 Ezek 44:1-4
47:3 Ezek 40:3

46:5 Hebrew *an ephah* [18 liters] *of flour . . . a hin* [3.8 liters] *of olive oil;* also in 46:7, 11. **46:14** Hebrew *1/6 of an ephah* [2.9 liters] *of flour with 1/3 of a hin* [1.3 liters] *of olive oil.* **46:17** Hebrew *until the Year of Release;* see Lev 25:8-17. **46:22** Hebrew *40 cubits* [21.2 meters] *long and 30 cubits* [15.9 meters] *wide.* The distances are calculated using the Hebrew long cubit, which equals 21 inches or 53 centimeters.

47:1-12 This river is similar to the river mentioned in Revelation 22:1, 2. Both are associated with the river in the Garden of Eden (see Genesis 2:10). The river symbolizes life from God and the blessings that flow from his throne. It is a gentle, safe, deep river, expanding as it flows.

me along the stream for 1,750 feet* and told me to go across. At that point the water was
up to my ankles. [4]He measured off another 1,750 feet and told me to go across again.
This time the water was up to my knees. After another 1,750 feet, it was up to my waist.
[5]Then he measured another 1,750 feet, and the river was too deep to cross without
swimming.
[6]He told me to keep in mind what I had seen; then he led me back along the
riverbank. [7]Suddenly, to my surprise, many trees were now growing on both sides of
the river! [8]Then he said to me, "This river flows east through the desert into the Jordan
Valley,* where it enters the Dead Sea.* The waters of this stream will heal the salty
waters of the Dead Sea and make them fresh and pure. [9]Everything that touches the
water of this river will live. Fish will abound in the Dead Sea, for its waters will be
healed. Wherever this water flows, everything will live. [10]Fishermen will stand along
the shores of the Dead Sea, fishing all the way from En-gedi to En-eglaim. The shores
will be covered with nets drying in the sun. Fish of every kind will fill the Dead Sea,
just as they fill the Mediterranean*! [11]But the marshes and swamps will not be purified;
they will be sources of salt. [12]All kinds of fruit trees will grow along both sides of the
river. The leaves of these trees will never turn brown and fall, and there will always be
fruit on their branches. There will be a new crop every month, without fail! For they
are watered by the river flowing from the Temple. The fruit will be for food and the
leaves for healing."

Boundaries for the Land

[13]This is what the Sovereign LORD says: "Follow these instructions for dividing the land
for the twelve tribes of Israel: The tribe of Joseph will be given two shares of land.*
[14]Otherwise each tribe will receive an equal share. I swore that I would give this land to
your ancestors, and it will now come to you as your inheritance.

[15]"The northern border will run from the Mediterranean toward Hethlon, then on
through Lebo-hamath to Zedad; [16]then it will run to Berothah and Sibraim, which
are on the border between Damascus and Hamath, and finally to Hazer-hatticon, on
the border of Hauran. [17]So the northern border will run from the Mediterranean to
Hazar-enan, on the border between Hamath to the north and Damascus to the south.
[18]"The eastern border starts at a point between Hauran and Damascus and runs southward along the Jordan River between Israel and Gilead, past the Dead Sea* and as
far south as Tamar.* This will be the eastern border.
[19]"The southern border will go west from Tamar to the waters of Meribah at Kadesh*
and then follow the course of the brook of Egypt to the Mediterranean. This will be
the southern border.
[20]"On the west side the Mediterranean itself will be your border from the southern
border to the point where the northern border begins, opposite Lebo-hamath.

[21]"Divide the land within these boundaries among the tribes of Israel. [22]Distribute the
land as an inheritance for yourselves and for the foreigners who have joined you and are
raising their families among you. They will be just like native-born Israelites to you, and
they will receive an inheritance among the tribes. [23]All these immigrants are to be given
land within the territory of the tribe with whom they now live. I, the Sovereign LORD,
have spoken!

47:5 Isa 11:9; Hab 2:14
47:6 Ezek 40:4; 44:5
47:7 Isa 60:21; 61:3; Rev 22:2
47:8 Deut 3:17; Isa 35:6-7; 41:17-19; 44:3
47:9 Isa 12:3; John 4:14; 7:37-38; Rev 21:6
47:10 Num 34:6; 2 Chr 20:2; Ps 104:25; Ezek 26:5; 48:28; Matt 13:47; Luke 5:5-9
47:12 Gen 2:9; Ps 1:3; Jer 17:8; Rev 22:2
47:13 Gen 48:5; Num 34:1-13; 1 Chr 5:1; Ezek 48:4-5
47:14 Gen 12:7; Deut 1:8; Ezek 20:5-6
47:15 Num 34:7-9; Ezek 48:1
47:16 Num 13:21; 1 Kgs 8:65
47:17 Num 34:9; Ezek 48:1
47:18 Gen 13:10-11; Num 34:10-12
47:19 Num 34:3-5; Deut 32:51; Isa 27:12
47:20 Num 34:6
47:22 Isa 14:1; 56:6-7; Acts 11:18; Rom 10:12; Eph 2:12-14; Col 3:11

47:3 Hebrew *1,000 cubits* [530 meters]; also in 47:4, 5. The distances are calculated using the Hebrew long cubit, which equals 21 inches or 53 centimeters. **47:8a** Hebrew *the Arabah.* **47:8b** Hebrew *the sea;* also in 47:10. **47:10** Hebrew *the great sea;* also in 47:15, 17, 19, 20. **47:13** A share of land for each of Joseph's two oldest sons, Ephraim and Manasseh. **47:18a** Hebrew *the eastern sea.* **47:18b** As in Greek version; Hebrew reads *you will measure.* **47:19** Hebrew *waters of Meribath-kadesh.*

47:8, 9 The Jordan Valley is the geological depression in which the Dead Sea lies. The Dead Sea is a body of water so salty that nothing can live in it. The river will freshen the Dead Sea's water so it can support life. This is another picture of the life-giving nature of the water that flows from God's Temple. God's power can transform us no matter how lifeless or corrupt we may be. Even when we feel messed up and beyond hope, his power can heal us.

47:10 En-gedi and En-eglaim were on the western shore of the Dead Sea.

47:22, 23 In the restoration there will be room for foreigners. The regulations of Leviticus 24:22 and Numbers 15:29 provided for this. Isaiah also taught it (Isaiah 56:3-8). The children of foreigners will even inherit property like Israelites. Anyone who accepts the standards and is willing to obey may enjoy the blessings of God's rule.

48:1 Exod 1:1; Josh 19:40-48
48:2 Gen 30:12-13; Josh 19:24-31
48:3 Gen 30:7-8; Josh 19:32-39
48:4 Gen 30:22-24; 41:51; 48:5, 14-20; Josh 13:29-31; 17:1-11
48:5 Josh 16:5-10; 17:8-10, 14-18; 19:9
48:6 Josh 13:15-21
48:7 Josh 15:1-63
48:8 Ezek 45:1-6; Rev 21:3, 22
48:10 Ezek 44:28; 45:4
48:11 Ezek 44:10-15
48:14 Lev 25:32-34
48:15 Ezek 42:20; 45:6
48:16 Rev 21:16
48:21 Ezek 34:24; 45:7
48:23 Gen 35:16-19; Josh 18:21-28
48:24 Gen 29:33; 49:5-7; Josh 19:1-9
48:25 Gen 30:14-18; Josh 19:17-23
48:26 Gen 30:19-20; Josh 19:10-16
48:27 Gen 30:10-11; Josh 13:24-28; Ezek 47:19-20
48:28 Num 34:6
48:29 Ezek 47:13-23
48:31 Rev 21:12-13

Division of the Land

48 "Here is the list of the tribes of Israel and the territory each is to receive. The
territory of Dan is in the extreme north. Its boundary line follows the Hethlon
road to Lebo-hamath and then runs on to Hazar-enan on the border of Damascus, with
Hamath to the north. Dan's territory extends all the way across the land of Israel from
east to west. 2 Asher's territory lies south of Dan's and also extends from east to west.
3 Naphtali's land lies south of Asher's, also extending from east to west. 4 Then comes
Manasseh south of Naphtali, and its territory also extends from east to west. 5 South
of Manasseh is Ephraim, 6 and then Reuben, 7 and then Judah, all of whose boundaries
extend from east to west.

8 "South of Judah is the land set aside for a special purpose. It will be 8⅓ miles wide
and will extend as far east and west as the tribal territories, with the Temple at the
center.

9 "The area set aside for the LORD's Temple will be 8⅓ miles long and 6⅔ miles
wide.* 10 For the priests there will be a strip of land measuring 8⅓ miles long by 3⅓
miles wide, with the LORD's Temple at the center. 11 This area is set aside for the
ordained priests, the descendants of Zadok who obeyed me and did not go astray when
the people of Israel and the rest of the Levites did. 12 It will be their special portion when
the land is distributed, the most sacred land of all. Next to the priests' territory will lie
the land where the other Levites will live. 13 The land allotted to the Levites will be the
same size and shape as that belonging to the priests—8⅓ miles long and 3⅓ miles wide.
Together these portions of land will measure 8⅓ miles long by 6⅔ miles wide.* 14 None
of this special land will ever be sold or traded or used by others, for it belongs to the
LORD; it is set apart as holy.

15 "An additional strip of land 8⅓ miles long by 1⅔ miles wide, south of the sacred Temple
area, will be allotted for public use—homes, pasturelands, and common lands, with a city
at the center. 16 The city will measure 1½ miles* on each side. 17 Open lands will surround
the city for 150 yards* in every direction. 18 Outside the city there will be a farming area that
stretches 3⅓ miles to the east and 3⅓ miles to the west along the border of the sacred area.
This farmland will produce food for the people working in the city. 19 Those who come from
the various tribes to work in the city may farm it. 20 This entire area—including the sacred
lands and the city—is a square that measures 8⅓ miles on each side.

21 "The areas that remain, to the east and to the west of the sacred lands and the city,
will belong to the prince. Each of these areas will be 8⅓ miles wide, extending in
opposite directions to the eastern and western borders of Israel. 22 So the prince's land
will include everything between the territories allotted to Judah and Benjamin, except
for the areas set aside for the sacred lands and the city.

23 "These are the territories allotted to the rest of the tribes. Benjamin's territory lies
just south of the prince's lands, and it extends across the entire land of Israel from east
to west. 24 South of Benjamin's territory lies that of Simeon, also extending across the
land from east to west. 25 Next is the territory of Issachar with the same eastern and
western boundaries. 26 Then comes the territory of Zebulun, which also extends across
the land from east to west. 27 The territory of Gad is just south of Zebulun with the same
borders to the east and west. 28 The southern border of Gad runs from Tamar to the waters
of Meribah at Kadesh* and then follows the brook of Egypt to the Mediterranean.*
29 These are the allotments that will be set aside for each tribe's inheritance, says the
Sovereign LORD.

The Gates of the City

30 "These will be the exits to the city: On the north wall, which is 1½ miles long, 31 there
will be three gates, each one named after a tribe of Israel. The first will be named for

48:9 Reflecting the Greek reading in 45:1: *25,000 cubits* [13.3 kilometers] *long and 20,000 cubits* [10.6 kilometers] *wide;* Hebrew reads *25,000 cubits long and 10,000 cubits wide.* Compare 45:1-5; 48:10-13. In this chapter, the distance measures are calculated using the Hebrew long cubit, which equals 21 inches or 53 centimeters. **48:13** See note on 48:9. **48:16** Hebrew *4,500 cubits* [2.4 kilometers]; also in 48:30, 32, 33, 34. **48:17** Hebrew *250 cubits* [133 meters]. **48:28a** Hebrew *waters of Meribath-kadesh.* **48:28b** Hebrew *the great sea.*

48:1ff The land would be divided into 13 parallel portions (one for each tribe plus a sacred district) that would stretch from the Jordan River or Dead Sea to the Mediterranean Sea. The division of the land shows that in God's Kingdom there is a place for all who believe in and obey the one true God (see John 14:1-6).

Reuben, the second for Judah, and the third for Levi. 32On the east wall, also 1½ miles
long, the gates will be named for Joseph, Benjamin, and Dan. 33The south wall, also
1½ miles long, will have gates named for Simeon, Issachar, and Zebulun. 34And on the
west wall, also 1½ miles long, the gates will be named for Gad, Asher, and Naphtali.
35"The distance around the entire city will be six miles.* And from that day the name
of the city will be 'The LORD Is There.'*"

48:35 Isa 12:6; 24:23 Jer 3:17; 23:6; 33:16 Joel 3:21 Zech 2:10 Rev 21:3; 22:3

48:35a Hebrew *18,000 cubits* [9.6 kilometers]. **48:35b** Hebrew *Yahweh Shammah.*

48:35 The book of Ezekiel begins by describing the holiness of God that Israel had despised and ignored. As a result, God's presence departed from the Temple, the city, and the people. The book ends with a detailed vision of the new Temple, the new city, and the new people—all demonstrating God's holiness. The pressures of everyday life may cause us to focus on the here and now and thus forget God. That is why, worship is so important; it takes our eyes off our current worries, gives us a glimpse of God's holiness, and allows us to look toward his future Kingdom. God's presence makes everything glorious, and worship brings us into his presence.

DANIEL

Daniel taken captive to Babylon 605 B.C.	Ezekiel becomes a prophet to exiles 593	Judah falls; Jerusalem is destroyed; Jeremiah's ministry ends 586	Daniel's first vision 553	Babylon overthrown; Daniel thrown to lions 539	First exiles return to Judah 538	Daniel's ministry ends 535

AN EARTHQUAKE shakes the foundation of our security; a tornado blows away a lifetime of treasures; an assassin's bullet changes national history; a drunk driver claims an innocent victim; a divorce shatters a home. International and personal tragedies make our world seem a fearful place, overflowing with evil and seemingly out of control. And the litany of bombings, coups, murders, and natural disasters could cause us to think that God is absent or impotent. "Where is God?" we cry, engulfed by sorrow and despair.

Twenty-five centuries ago, Daniel could have despaired. He and thousands of his countrymen had been deported to a foreign land after Judah was conquered. Daniel found himself facing an egocentric despot and surrounded by idolaters. Instead of giving in or giving up, this courageous young man held fast to his faith in his God. Daniel knew that despite the circumstances, God was sovereign and was working out his plan for nations and individuals. The book of Daniel centers around this profound truth—the sovereignty of God.

After a brief account of Nebuchadnezzar's siege and defeat of Jerusalem, the scene quickly shifts to Daniel and his three friends, Hananiah, Mishael, and Azariah (Shadrach, Meshach, and Abednego). These men held prominent positions within the Babylonian government. Daniel, in particular, held such a position because of his ability to interpret the king's dreams that tell of God's unfolding plan (chapters 2 and 4). Sandwiched between the dreams is the fascinating account of Daniel's three friends and the furnace (chapter 3). Because they refused to bow down to an image of gold, they were condemned to a fiery death. But God intervened and spared their lives.

Belshazzar ruled Babylon after Nebuchadnezzar, and chapter 5 tells of his encounter with God's message written on a wall. Daniel, who was summoned to interpret the message, predicted Babylon's fall to the Medes and Persians. This prediction came true that very night, and Darius the Mede conquered the Babylonian kingdom.

Daniel became one of Darius's most trusted advisers. His privileged position angered other administrators, who plotted his death by convincing the king to outlaw prayer. In spite of the law, Daniel continued to pray to his sovereign Lord. As a result, he was condemned to die in a den of hungry lions. Again, God intervened and saved him, shutting the mouths of the lions (chapter 6).

The book concludes with a series of visions that Daniel had during the reigns of Belshazzar (chapters 7—8), Darius (chapter 9), and Cyrus (chapters 10—12). These dreams dramatically outline God's future plans, beginning with Babylon and continuing to the end of the age. They give a preview of God's redemption and have been called the key to all biblical prophecy.

God is sovereign. He was in control in Babylon, and he has been moving in history, controlling the destinies of people ever since. And he is here now! Despite news reports or personal stress, we can be confident that God is in control. As you read Daniel, watch God work and find your security in his sovereignty.

VITAL STATISTICS

PURPOSE:
To give a historical account of the faithful Jews who lived in captivity and to show how God is in control of heaven and earth, directing the forces of nature, the destiny of nations, and the care of his people

AUTHOR:
Daniel

TO WHOM WRITTEN:
The other captives in Babylon and God's people everywhere

DATE WRITTEN:
Approximately 535 B.C., recording events that occurred from about 605–535 B.C.

SETTING:
Daniel had been taken captive and deported to Babylon by Nebuchadnezzar in 605 B.C. There he served in the government for about 70 years during the reigns of Nebuchadnezzar, Belshazzar, Darius, and Cyrus.

KEY VERSE:
"He [God] reveals deep and mysterious things and knows what lies hidden in darkness, though he himself is surrounded by light" (2:22).

KEY PEOPLE:
Daniel, Nebuchadnezzar, Shadrach, Meshach, Abednego, Belshazzar, Darius

KEY PLACES:
Nebuchadnezzar's palace, the blazing furnace, Belshazzar's feast, the den of lions

SPECIAL FEATURES:
Daniel's apocalyptic visions (chapters 7—12) give a glimpse of God's plan for the ages, including a direct prediction of the Messiah.

THE BLUEPRINT

A. DANIEL'S LIFE (1:1—6:28)	Daniel and his three friends chose not to eat the king's food. They did not bow down to the king's image, even under penalty of death. Daniel continued to pray even though he knew he might be noticed and sentenced to death. These men are inspiring examples for us of how to live a godly life in a sinful world. When we face trials, we can expect God to also be with us through them. May God grant us similar courage to remain faithful under pressure.
B. DANIEL'S VISIONS (7:1—12:13)	These visions gave the captives added confidence that God is in control of history. They were to wait patiently in faith and not worship the gods of Babylon or accept that society's way of life. God still rules over human activities. Evil will be overcome, so we should wait patiently and not give in to the temptations and pressures of the sinful way of life around us.

MEGATHEMES

THEME	EXPLANATION	IMPORTANCE
God Is in Control	God is all-knowing, and he is in charge of world events. God overrules and removes rebellious leaders who defy him. God will overcome evil; no one is exempt. But he will deliver the faithful who follow him.	Although nations vie for world control now, one day Christ's Kingdom will replace and surpass the kingdoms of this world. Our faith is sure because our future is secure in Christ. We must have courage and put our faith in God, who controls everything.
Purpose in Life	Daniel and his three friends are examples of dedication and commitment. They determined to serve God regardless of the consequences. They did not give in to pressures from an ungodly society because they had a clear purpose in life.	It is wise to make trusting and obeying God alone our true purpose in life. This will give us direction and peace in spite of the circumstances or consequences. We should disobey anyone who asks us to disobey God. Our first allegiance must be to God.
Perseverance	Daniel served for 70 years in a foreign land that was hostile to God, yet he did not compromise his faith in God. He was truthful, persistent in prayer, and disinterested in power for personal glory.	In order to fulfill your life's purpose, you need staying power. Don't let your Christian distinctness become blurred. Be relentless in your prayers, maintain your integrity, and be content to serve God wherever he puts you.
God's Faithfulness	God was faithful in Daniel's life. He delivered him from prison, from a den of lions, and from enemies who hated him. God cares for his people and deals patiently with them.	We can trust God to be with us through any trial. Because he has been faithful to us, we should remain faithful to him.

A. DANIEL'S LIFE (1:1—6:28)

While Ezekiel was ministering to the captives in Babylon, Daniel was drafted as a counselor to King Nebuchadnezzar. With God's help, Daniel interpreted two of the king's dreams, Daniel's three friends were rescued from certain death in the blazing furnace, and Daniel was rescued from a lions' den. Daniel's life is a picture of the triumph of faith. May God grant us this type of faith so that we may also live courageously each day.

Daniel in Nebuchadnezzar's Court

1 During the third year of King Jehoiakim's reign in Judah,* King Nebuchadnezzar
of Babylon came to Jerusalem and besieged it with his armies. [2]The Lord gave him
victory over King Jehoiakim of Judah. When Nebuchadnezzar returned to Babylon, he
took with him some of the sacred objects from the Temple of God and placed them in
the treasure-house of his god in the land of Babylonia.*

1:1 2 Kgs 24:1; 2 Chr 36:6
1:2 Isa 11:11; Jer 27:19-20; Zech 5:5-11

1:1 The third year of Jehoiakim's reign, according to the Hebrew system of reckoning, was 605 B.C. **1:2** Hebrew *the land of Shinar.*

1:1, 2 Born during the middle of Josiah's reign (2 Kings 22–23), Daniel grew up during the king's reforms. During this time, Daniel probably heard Jeremiah, a prophet he quoted in 9:2. In 609 B.C. Josiah was killed in a battle against Egypt, and within four years, the southern kingdom of Judah had returned to its evil ways.

In 605 B.C. Nebuchadnezzar became king of Babylon. In September of that year, he swept into Palestine and surrounded Jerusalem, making Judah his vassal state. To demonstrate his dominance, Nebuchadnezzar took many of Jerusalem's wisest men and most beautiful women to Babylon as captives. Daniel was among this group.

1:3 Isa 39:7 3 Then the king ordered Ashpenaz, who was in charge of the palace officials, to bring
to the palace some of the young men of Judah's royal family and other noble families,
who had been brought to Babylon as captives. 4 "Select only strong, healthy, and
good-looking young men," he said. "Make sure they are well versed in every branch of
learning, are gifted with knowledge and good sense, and have the poise needed to serve
1:5 in the royal palace. Teach these young men the language and literature of the Babyloni-
Dan 1:8, 19 ans.*" 5 The king assigned them a daily ration of the best food and wine from his own
kitchens. They were to be trained for a three-year period, and then some of them would
be made his advisers in the royal court.

1:6 6 Daniel, Hananiah, Mishael, and Azariah were four of the young men chosen, all from
Ezek 14:14, 20; 28:3; Matt 24:15 the tribe of Judah. 7 The chief official renamed them with these Babylonian names:

1:7 Dan 2:49; 3:12-30; 4:8; 5:12

Daniel was called Belteshazzar.
Hananiah was called Shadrach.
Mishael was called Meshach.
Azariah was called Abednego.

1:8 Lev 11:47 8 But Daniel made up his mind not to defile himself by eating the food and wine given
Deut 32:38; Ezek 4:13-14; Hos 9:3 to them by the king. He asked the chief official for permission to eat other things instead.

1:4 Or *of the Chaldeans.*

DANIEL served as a prophet to the exiles in Babylon from 605–536 B.C.

Climate of the times	The people of Judah were captives in a strange land, feeling hopeless.
Main message	God is sovereign over all of human history, past, present, and future.
Importance of message	We should spend less time wondering when future events will happen and more time learning how we should live now.
Contemporary prophets	Jeremiah (627–586 B.C.), Habakkuk (612–588 B.C.), Ezekiel (593–571 B.C.)

1:1, 2 Nebuchadnezzar, the supreme leader of Babylon, was feared throughout the world. When he invaded a country, defeat was certain. After a victory, the Babylonians usually took the most talented and useful people back to Babylon and left only the poor behind to take whatever land they wanted and to live peacefully there (2 Kings 24:14). This system fostered great loyalty from conquered lands and ensured a steady supply of wise and talented people for civil service.

1:2 At certain times God allows his work to suffer. In this instance, the Babylonians raided the Temple of God and took the worship articles to the temple of a god in Babylon. This god may have been Bel, also called Marduk, the chief god of the Babylonians. Those who loved the Lord must have felt disheartened and discouraged. We feel greatly disappointed when our churches suffer physical damage, split, close down for financial reasons, or are rocked by scandals. We do not know why God allows his church to experience these calamities. But like the people who witnessed the plundering of the Temple by the Babylonians, we must trust that God is in control and that he is watching over all who trust in him.

1:4 The common language of Babylon was Aramaic, while the language of scholarship included the ancient and complicated Babylonian language. The academic program would have included mathematics, astronomy, history, science, and magic. These young men demonstrated not only aptitude but also discipline. This character trait, combined with integrity, served them well in their new culture.

1:7 Nebuchadnezzar changed the names of Daniel and his friends because he wanted to make them Babylonian—in their own eyes and in the eyes of the Babylonian people. New names would help them to be assimilated into the culture. Daniel means "God is my judge" in Hebrew; his name was changed to Belteshazzar, meaning "Bel, protect his life!" (Bel, also called Marduk, was the chief Babylonian god.) Hananiah means "the LORD shows grace"; his new name, Shadrach, probably means "under the command of Aku" (the moon god). Mishael means "who is like God?"; his new name, Meshach, probably means "who is like Aku?" Azariah means "the LORD helps"; his new name, Abednego, means "servant of Nego/Nebo" (or Nabu, the god of learning and writing). This was how the king attempted to change the religious loyalty of these young men from Judah's God to Babylon's gods.

1:8 Daniel resolved not to eat this food, either because it was forbidden by Jewish law, such as pork (see Leviticus 11), or because accepting the king's food and drink was the first step toward depending on his gifts and favors. Although Daniel was in a culture that did not honor God, he still obeyed God's laws.

1:8 Daniel "made up his mind" to be devoted to principle and to be committed to a course of action. When Daniel made up his mind not to defile himself, he was being true to a lifelong determination to do what was right and not to give in to the pressures around him. We, too, are often assaulted by pressures to compromise our standards and live more like the world around us. Merely wanting or preferring God's will and way is not enough to stand against the onslaught of temptation. Like Daniel, we must resolve to obey God.

1:8 It is easier to resist temptation if you have thought through your convictions before the temptation arises. Daniel and his friends made their decision to be faithful to the laws of God before they were faced with the king's delicacies, so they did not hesitate to stick with their convictions. We will get into trouble if we have not previously decided where to draw the line. Before such situations arise, decide on your commitments and what you will do. Then when temptation comes, you will be ready to say no.

9 Now God had given the chief official great respect for Daniel. 10 But he was alarmed
by Daniel's suggestion. "My lord the king has ordered that you eat this food and wine,"
he said. "If you become pale and thin compared to the other youths your age, I am afraid
the king will have me beheaded for neglecting my duties."
11 Daniel talked it over with the attendant who had been appointed by the chief official
to look after Daniel, Hananiah, Mishael, and Azariah. 12 "Test us for ten days on a diet
of vegetables and water," Daniel said. 13 "At the end of the ten days, see how we look
compared to the other young men who are eating the king's rich food. Then you can
decide whether or not to let us continue eating our diet." 14 So the attendant agreed to
Daniel's suggestion and tested them for ten days.
15 At the end of the ten days, Daniel and his three friends looked healthier and better
nourished than the young men who had been eating the food assigned by the king. 16 So
after that, the attendant fed them only vegetables instead of the rich foods and wines.
17 God gave these four young men an unusual aptitude for learning the literature and
science of the time. And God gave Daniel special ability in understanding the meanings
of visions and dreams.
18 When the three-year training period ordered by the king was completed, the chief
official brought all the young men to King Nebuchadnezzar. 19 The king talked with each
of them, and none of them impressed him as much as Daniel, Hananiah, Mishael, and
Azariah. So they were appointed to his regular staff of advisers. 20 In all matters requiring
wisdom and balanced judgment, the king found the advice of these young men to be ten
times better than that of all the magicians and enchanters in his entire kingdom.
21 Daniel remained there until the first year of King Cyrus's reign.*

1:21 The first year of Cyrus's reign was 538 B.C.

1:9 Ps 106:46; Prov 16:7
1:12 Dan 1:16
1:15 Exod 23:25; Prov 10:22
1:16 Dan 1:12
1:17 1 Kgs 3:12, 28; Job 32:8; Dan 1:20; 2:19; 7:1; 8:1
1:19 Gen 41:46; Jer 15:1; Dan 1:5
1:20 Num 14:22; Isa 19:3; Dan 1:17; 2:2, 27-28; 4:18; 5:7
1:21 Dan 6:28; 10:1

TAKEN TO BABYLON Daniel, as a captive of Babylonian soldiers, faced a long and difficult march to a new land. The 500-mile trek, under harsh conditions, certainly tested his faith in God.

1:9 God moved with an unseen hand to change the heart of this Babylonian official. The strong moral conviction of these four young men made an impact. God promises to be with his people in times of trial and temptation (Psalm 106:46; Isaiah 43:2-5; 1 Corinthians 10:13). His active intervention often comes just when we take a stand for him. Stand for God and trust him to protect you in ways you may not be able to see.

1:10 Anything short of complete obedience meant execution for the officials who served Nebuchadnezzar. Even in such a small matter as this, the official feared for his life.

1:12 The Babylonians were trying to change their *thinking* by giving them a Babylonian education, their *loyalty* by changing their names, and their *life-style* by changing their diet. Without compromising, Daniel found a way to live by God's standards in a culture that did not honor God. Wisely choosing to negotiate rather than to rebel, Daniel suggested an experimental 10-day diet of vegetables and water instead of the royal foods and wine the king offered. Without compromising, Daniel quickly thought of a practical, creative solution that saved his life and the lives of his companions. As God's people, we may adjust to our culture as long as we do not compromise God's laws.

1:17 Daniel and his friends learned all they could about their new culture so they could do their work with excellence. But while they learned, they maintained steadfast allegiance to God, and God gave them skill and wisdom. Culture need not be God's enemy. If it does not violate his commands, it can aid in accomplishing his purpose. We who follow God are free to be competent leaders in our culture, but we are required to pledge our allegiance to God first.

1:20 Nebuchadnezzar put Daniel and his friends on his staff of advisers. This staff included many "magicians and enchanters." These were astrologers who claimed to be able to tell the future through occult practices. They were masters at communicating their message so that it sounded authoritative—as though it came directly from their gods. In addition to knowledge, Daniel and his three friends had wisdom and understanding, given to them by God. Thus, the king was far more pleased with them than with his magicians and enchanters. As we serve others, we must not merely pretend to have God's wisdom. Our wisdom will be genuine when we are rightly related to God.

1:20 How did the captives survive in a foreign culture? They learned about the culture, achieved excellence in their work, served the people, prayed for God's help, and maintained their integrity. We may feel like foreigners whenever we experience change. Alien cultures come in many forms: a new job, a new school, a new neighborhood. We can use the same principles to help us adapt to our new surroundings without abandoning God.

1:21 Daniel was one of the first captives taken to Babylon, and he lived to see the first exiles return to Jerusalem in 538 B.C. Throughout this time Daniel honored God, and God honored him. While serving as an adviser to the kings of Babylon, Daniel was God's spokesman to the Babylonian Empire. Babylon was a wicked nation, but it would have been much worse without Daniel's influence.

2:1-11 Dreams were considered to be messages from the

2:1 Gen 40:5-8; 41:1, 8 Esth 6:1 Job 33:15-17 Dan 6:18
2:3 Dan 4:5
2:4 Ezra 4:7 Isa 36:11 Dan 3:9; 5:10
2:5 Ezra 6:11 Dan 2:12; 3:29
2:6 Dan 2:48; 5:7, 16, 29
2:9 Esth 4:11 Isa 41:23
2:10 Dan 2:27
2:11 Gen 41:39 Exod 29:45 Isa 57:15 Dan 5:11

Nebuchadnezzar's Dream

2 One night during the second year of his reign,* Nebuchadnezzar had a dream that
disturbed him so much that he couldn't sleep. 2He called in his magicians, enchanters, sorcerers, and astrologers,* and he demanded that they tell him what he had
dreamed. As they stood before the king, 3he said, "I have had a dream that troubles me.
Tell me what I dreamed, for I must know what it means."
4Then the astrologers answered the king in Aramaic,* "Long live the king! Tell us the
dream, and we will tell you what it means."
5But the king said to the astrologers, "I am serious about this. If you don't tell me what
my dream was and what it means, you will be torn limb from limb, and your houses will
be demolished into heaps of rubble! 6But if you tell me what I dreamed and what the
dream means, I will give you many wonderful gifts and honors. Just tell me the dream
and what it means!"
7They said again, "Please, Your Majesty. Tell us the dream, and we will tell you what
it means."
8The king replied, "I can see through your trick! You are trying to stall for time
because you know I am serious about what I said. 9If you don't tell me the dream, you
will be condemned. You have conspired to tell me lies in hopes that something will
change. But tell me the dream, and then I will know that you can tell me what it means."
10The astrologers replied to the king, "There isn't a man alive who can tell Your
Majesty his dream! And no king, however great and powerful, has ever asked such a
thing of any magician, enchanter, or astrologer! 11This is an impossible thing the king

2:1 The second year of Nebuchadnezzar's reign was 603 B.C. **2:2** Or *Chaldeans;* also in 2:4, 5, 10. **2:4** The original text from this point through chapter 7 is in Aramaic.

THE FULFILLMENT OF DANIEL'S INTERPRETATION

The large statue in Nebuchadnezzar's dream (2:24–45) represented the four kingdoms that would dominate as world powers. We recognize these as the Babylonian Empire, the Medo-Persian Empire, the Grecian Empire, and the Roman Empire. All of these will be crushed and brought to an end by the Kingdom of God, which will continue forever.

Part	*Material*	*Empire*	*Period of Domination*
Head	Gold	Babylonian	606 B.C.–539 B.C.
Chest and Arms	Silver	Medo-Persian	539 B.C.–331 B.C.
Belly and Thighs	Bronze	Grecian	331 B.C.–146 B.C.
Legs and Feet	Iron and Clay	Roman	146 B.C.–A.D. 476

gods, and the astrologers were expected to interpret them. Usually the astrologers could give some sort of interpretation as long as they knew what the dream was about. This time, however, Nebuchadnezzar demanded to be told the dream also. God sent a series of dreams to Nebuchadnezzar with prophetic messages that could be revealed and understood only by a servant of God. People from other time periods who received dreams from God include Jacob (Genesis 28:10-15), Joseph (Genesis 37:5-11), Pharaoh's cup-bearer and his baker (Genesis 40), Pharaoh (Genesis 41), Solomon (1 Kings 3:5-15), and Joseph (Matthew 1:20-24).

2:10, 11 The astrologers told the king that "there isn't a man alive" who could know the dreams of another person. What the king asked was humanly impossible. But Daniel could tell what the king had dreamed, and he could also give the interpretation because God was working through him. In daily life, we face many apparently impossible situations that would be hopeless if we had to handle them with our limited strength. But God specializes in working through us to achieve the impossible.

2:10, 11 The astrologers were unable to persuade the king with any amount of logic or rational argument. The king asked for something impossible and didn't want anyone to change his mind. When power goes to a leader's head, whether at work, at home, or in the church, that leader may sometimes demand the impossible from subordinates. At times, he may motivate workers to achieve more than they thought they could. At other times, they may ignore his rantings and ravings. Just as Daniel dealt wisely in the situation, we can ask God to give us wisdom to know how to deal with unreasonable bosses.

2:11 The astrologers admitted that their gods did not "live among people." Of course their gods didn't—they didn't even exist! This exposed the limitations of the astrologers. They could invent interpretations of dreams but could not tell Nebuchadnezzar *what* he had dreamed. Although his request was unreasonable, Nebuchadnezzar was infuriated by their reply. It was not unusual in these times for astrologers to be in conflict with the king. They sometimes used their craft to gain political power.

requires. No one except the gods can tell you your dream, and they do not live among
people."
12 The king was furious when he heard this, and he sent out orders to execute all the
wise men of Babylon. 13 And because of the king's decree, men were sent to find and kill
Daniel and his friends. 14 When Arioch, the commander of the king's guard, came to kill
them, Daniel handled the situation with wisdom and discretion. 15 He asked Arioch,
"Why has the king issued such a harsh decree?" So Arioch told him all that had
happened. 16 Daniel went at once to see the king and requested more time so he could tell
the king what the dream meant.
17 Then Daniel went home and told his friends Hananiah, Mishael, and Azariah what
had happened. 18 He urged them to ask the God of heaven to show them his mercy by
telling them the secret, so they would not be executed along with the other wise men of
Babylon. 19 That night the secret was revealed to Daniel in a vision. Then Daniel praised
the God of heaven, 20 saying,

"Praise the name of God forever and ever,
for he alone has all wisdom and power.
21 He determines the course of world events;
he removes kings and sets others on the throne.
He gives wisdom to the wise
and knowledge to the scholars.
22 He reveals deep and mysterious things
and knows what lies hidden in darkness,
though he himself is surrounded by light.
23 I thank and praise you, God of my ancestors,
for you have given me wisdom and strength.
You have told me what we asked of you
and revealed to us what the king demanded."

Daniel Interprets the Dream

24 Then Daniel went in to see Arioch, who had been ordered to execute the wise men of
Babylon. Daniel said to him, "Don't kill the wise men. Take me to the king, and I will
tell him the meaning of his dream."
25 Then Arioch quickly took Daniel to the king and said, "I have found one of the
captives from Judah who will tell Your Majesty the meaning of your dream!"
26 The king said to Daniel (also known as Belteshazzar), "Is this true? Can you tell me
what my dream was and what it means?"

2:12 Ps 76:10; Dan 2:5; 3:13
2:13 Dan 1:19-20
2:14 Dan 2:24
2:18 Gen 18:28; Esth 4:15; Isa 37:4; Jer 33:3; Ezek 36:27; Dan 2:23
2:19 Num 12:6; 2 Kgs 6:8-12; Job 33:15-16; Dan 7:2, 7
2:20 1 Chr 29:11-12; Job 12:13; Pss 103:1-2; 113:2; Dan 2:21-23
2:21 1 Kgs 3:9-10; 4:29; Job 12:18-19; Ps 75:6-7; Dan 7:25; Jas 1:5
2:22 Job 12:22; 26:6; Ps 139:12; Isa 45:7; Jer 23:24; Dan 2:19, 28; Jas 1:17; 1 Jn 1:5
2:23 Gen 31:42; Dan 2:21
2:24 Dan 2:12-13; Acts 27:24
2:25 Gen 41:14; Dan 1:6; 5:13; 6:13

2:11 By answering that the gods "do not live among people," the astrologers betrayed their concept of the gods. Theirs was a hollow religion, a religion of convenience. They believed in the gods, but that belief made no difference in their conduct. Today, many people profess to believe in God, but it is also a hollow belief. In essence, they are practical atheists because they don't listen to him or do what he says. Do you believe in God? He *does* live among people, and he wants to change your life.

2:16-18 Daniel was at a crisis point. Imagine going to see the powerful, temperamental king who had just angrily ordered your death! Daniel did not shrink back in fear, however, but confidently believed God would tell him all the king wanted to know. When the king gave Daniel time to find the answer, Daniel found his three friends and they prayed. When you find yourself in a tight spot, share your needs with trusted friends who also believe in God's power. Prayer is more effective than panic. Panic confirms your hopelessness; prayer confirms your hope in God. Daniel's trust in God saved not only himself but also his three friends and all the other wise men of Babylon.

2:19-23 After Daniel asked God to reveal Nebuchadnezzar's dream to him, he saw a vision of the dream. Daniel's prayer was answered. Before rushing to Arioch with the news, Daniel took time to give God credit for all wisdom and power, thanking God for answering his request. How do you feel when your prayers are answered? Excited, surprised, relieved? There are times when we seek God in prayer and, after having been answered, dash off in our excitement, forgetting to give God credit for the answer. Match your persistence in prayer with gratitude when your requests are answered.

2:21 If you know that you still have much to learn in life, and if you have ever wished that you knew more about how to deal with people, then look to God for wisdom. While educational institutions provide diplomas at great expense, God gives wisdom freely to all who ask. (See James 1:5 for more on asking God for wisdom.)

2:21 When we see evil leaders who live long and good leaders who die young, we may wonder if God is still in control. Daniel saw evil rulers with almost limitless power, but he knew that God "removes kings and sets others on the throne" and that he controls everything that happens. God governs the world according to his purposes. You may be dismayed when you see evil people prosper, but God is in control. Let this knowledge give you confidence and peace no matter what happens.

2:24 Daniel did not use his success to promote his own self-interest. He thought of others. When striving to succeed or survive, remember the needs of others.

2:27 Dan 2:2, 10-11; 5:7-8
2:28 Gen 40:8; 41:16 Dan 2:22, 45
2:30 Gen 41:16 Ps 139:2 Isa 43:3 Dan 1:17
2:31 Hab 1:7
2:34 Dan 8:25 Zech 4:6

27 Daniel replied, "There are no wise men, enchanters, magicians, or fortune-tellers
who can tell the king such things. 28 But there is a God in heaven who reveals secrets,
and he has shown King Nebuchadnezzar what will happen in the future. Now I will tell
you your dream and the visions you saw as you lay on your bed.
29 "While Your Majesty was sleeping, you dreamed about coming events. The revealer
of mysteries has shown you what is going to happen. 30 And it is not because I am wiser
than any living person that I know the secret of your dream, but because God wanted
you to understand what you were thinking about.
31 "Your Majesty, in your vision you saw in front of you a huge and powerful statue
of a man, shining brilliantly, frightening and awesome. 32 The head of the statue was
made of fine gold, its chest and arms were of silver, its belly and thighs were of bronze,
33 its legs were of iron, and its feet were a combination of iron and clay. 34 But as you

DANIEL

Daniel's early life demonstrates that there is more to being young than making mistakes. No characteristic wins the hearts of adults more quickly than wisdom in the words and actions of a young person. Daniel and his friends had been taken from their homes in Judah and exiled. Their futures were in doubt, but they all had personal traits that qualified them for jobs as servants in the king's palace. They took advantage of the opportunity without letting the opportunity take advantage of them.

Our first hint of Daniel's greatness comes in his quiet refusal to give up his convictions. He had applied God's will to his own life, and he resisted changing the good habits he had formed. Both his physical and spiritual diets were an important part of his relationship with God. He ate carefully and lived prayerfully. One of the benefits of being in training for royal service was eating food from the king's table. Daniel tactfully chose a simpler menu and proved it was a healthy choice. As with Daniel, mealtimes are obvious and regular tests of our efforts to control our appetites.

While Daniel limited his food intake, he indulged in prayer. He was able to communicate with God because he made it a habit. He put into practice his convictions, even when that meant being thrown into a den of hungry lions. His life proved he made the right choice.

Do you hold so strongly to your faith in God that whatever happens you will do what God says? Such conviction keeps you a step ahead of temptation; such conviction gives you wisdom and stability in changing circumstances. Prayerfully live out your convictions in everyday life and trust God for the results.

Strengths and accomplishments
- Although young when deported, remained true to his faith
- Served as an adviser to two Babylonian kings and two Medo-Persian kings
- Was a man of prayer and a statesman with the gift of prophecy
- Survived the lions' den

Lessons from his life
- Quiet convictions often earn long-term respect
- Don't wait until you are in a tough situation to learn about prayer
- God can use people wherever they are

Vital statistics
- Where: Judah and the courts of both Babylon and Persia
- Occupation: A captive from Israel who became an adviser of kings
- Contemporaries: Hananiah, Mishael, Azariah, Nebuchadnezzar, Belshazzar, Darius, Cyrus

Key verse
"This man Daniel, whom the king named Belteshazzar, has a sharp mind and is filled with divine knowledge and understanding. He can interpret dreams, explain riddles, and solve difficult problems. Call for Daniel, and he will tell you what the writing means" (Daniel 5:12).

Daniel's story is told in the book of Daniel. He is also mentioned in Matthew 24:15.

2:27-30 Before Daniel told the king anything else, he gave credit to God, explaining that he did not know the dream through his own wisdom but only because God revealed it. How easily we take credit for what God does through us! This robs God of the honor that he alone deserves. Instead, we should be like Daniel and point people to God so that we give him the glory.

2:31ff The head of gold on the statue in the dream represented Nebuchadnezzar, ruler of the Babylonian Empire. The silver chest and two arms represented the Medo-Persian Empire, which conquered Babylon in 539 B.C. The belly and thighs of bronze were Greece and Macedonia under Alexander the Great, who conquered the Medo-Persian Empire (334–330 B.C.). The legs of iron represented Rome, which conquered the Greeks in 63 B.C. The feet of clay and iron represented the breakup of the Roman Empire, when the territory Rome ruled divided into a mixture of strong and weak nations. The type of metal in each part depicted the strength of the political power it represented. The rock cut out of the mountain depicted God's Kingdom, which would be ruled eternally by the Messiah, the King of kings. The dream revealed Daniel's God as the power behind all earthly kingdoms.

watched, a rock was cut from a mountain by supernatural means.* It struck the feet of iron and clay, smashing them to bits. 35 The whole statue collapsed into a heap of iron, clay, bronze, silver, and gold. The pieces were crushed as small as chaff on a threshing floor, and the wind blew them all away without a trace. But the rock that knocked the statue down became a great mountain that covered the whole earth.

36 "That was the dream; now I will tell Your Majesty what it means. 37 Your Majesty, you are a king over many kings. The God of heaven has given you sovereignty, power, strength, and honor. 38 He has made you the ruler over all the inhabited world and has put even the animals and birds under your control. You are the head of gold.

39 "But after your kingdom comes to an end, another great kingdom, inferior to yours, will rise to take your place. After that kingdom has fallen, yet a third great kingdom, represented by the bronze belly and thighs, will rise to rule the world. 40 Following that kingdom, there will be a fourth great kingdom, as strong as iron. That kingdom will smash and crush all previous empires, just as iron smashes and crushes everything it strikes. 41 The feet and toes you saw that were a combination of iron and clay show that this kingdom will be divided. 42 Some parts of it will be as strong as iron, and others as weak as clay. 43 This mixture of iron and clay also shows that these kingdoms will try to strengthen themselves by forming alliances with each other through intermarriage. But this will not succeed, just as iron and clay do not mix.

44 "During the reigns of those kings, the God of heaven will set up a kingdom that will never be destroyed; no one will ever conquer it. It will shatter all these kingdoms into nothingness, but it will stand forever. 45 That is the meaning of the rock cut from the mountain by supernatural means, crushing to dust the statue of iron, bronze, clay, silver, and gold.

"The great God has shown Your Majesty what will happen in the future. The dream is true, and its meaning is certain."

Nebuchadnezzar Rewards Daniel

46 Then King Nebuchadnezzar bowed to the ground before Daniel and worshiped him, and he commanded his people to offer sacrifices and burn sweet incense before him. 47 The king said to Daniel, "Truly, your God is the God of gods, the Lord over kings, a revealer of mysteries, for you have been able to reveal this secret."

48 Then the king appointed Daniel to a high position and gave him many valuable gifts. He made Daniel ruler over the whole province of Babylon, as well as chief over all his wise men. 49 At Daniel's request, the king appointed Shadrach, Meshach, and Abednego to be in charge of all the affairs of the province of Babylon, while Daniel remained in the king's court.

Nebuchadnezzar's Gold Statue

3 King Nebuchadnezzar made a gold statue ninety feet tall and nine feet wide* and set it up on the plain of Dura in the province of Babylon. 2 Then he sent messages to the princes, prefects, governors, advisers, counselors, judges, magistrates, and all the pro-

2:35 Pss 1:4; 37:10; Isa 17:13; Hos 13:3
2:37 Isa 10:8; 47:5; Jer 27:6-7; Ezek 26:7; Hos 8:10
2:38 Ps 50:10
2:40 Dan 7:7, 23
2:44 Pss 2:9; 145:13; Isa 9:6-7; 60:12; Ezek 37:25; Mic 4:7
2:45 Gen 41:28, 32; Deut 10:17; 2 Sam 7:22; Dan 2:29; Rev 22:6
2:46 Lev 26:31; Acts 10:25; 14:13; Rev 19:10; 22:8
2:47 Deut 10:17; Amos 3:7
2:48 Gen 41:39-43
2:49 Esth 2:19, 21; Amos 5:15
3:1 Isa 46:6; Jer 16:20; Dan 2:31; Hab 2:19

2:34 Aramaic *not by human hands;* also in 2:45. **3:1** Aramaic *60 cubits* [27 meters] *tall and 6 cubits* [2.7 meters] *wide.*

2:44 God's Kingdom will never be destroyed. If you are upset by threats of war and the prosperity of evil leaders, remember that God, not world leaders, decides the outcome of history. Under God's protection, God's Kingdom is indestructible. Those who trust in God are members of his Kingdom and are secure in him.

2:47 Nebuchadnezzar honored Daniel and Daniel's God. If Daniel had taken the credit himself, the king would have honored only Daniel. Because Daniel gave God the credit, the king honored both of them. Part of our mission in this world is to show unbelievers what God is like. We can do that by acts of love and compassion; and if we give God credit for our actions, they will want to know more about him. Give thanks to God for what he is doing in and through you.

2:49 After being named ruler over the whole province of Babylon and placed in charge of the wise men, Daniel requested that his companions, Shadrach, Meshach, and Abednego, be appointed as his assistants. Daniel knew that he could not handle such an enormous responsibility without capable assistants, so he chose the best men he knew—his three Hebrew companions. A competent leader never does all the work alone; he or she knows how to delegate and supervise. Moses, Israel's greatest leader, shared the burden of administration with dozens of assistants. (This story is in Exodus 18:13-27.)

3:1 In Babylon's religious culture, statues were frequently worshiped. Nebuchadnezzar hoped to use this huge image (90 feet high by 9 feet wide) as a strategy to unite the nation and solidify his power by centralizing worship. This gold image may have been inspired by his dream. Instead of having only a head of gold, however, it was gold from head to toe. Nebuchadnezzar wanted his kingdom to last forever. When he made the statue, Nebuchadnezzar showed that his devotion to Daniel's God was short-lived. He neither feared nor obeyed the God who was behind the dream.

3:2 Dan 3:3, 27; 6:1-7
3:4 Isa 40:9; 58:1; Dan 3:7; 4:1; 6:25; Rev 18:2
3:5 Dan 3:7, 10
3:6 Jer 29:22; Dan 3:11, 15, 21; 6:7; Matt 13:42; Rev 9:2; 14:11
3:8 Ezra 4:12-16; Esth 3:8-9
3:10 Dan 6:12

vincial officials to come to the dedication of the statue he had set up. 3When all these
officials* had arrived and were standing before the image King Nebuchadnezzar had set
up, 4a herald shouted out, "People of all races and nations and languages, listen to the
king's command! 5When you hear the sound of the horn, flute, zither, lyre, harp, pipes,
and other instruments,* bow to the ground to worship King Nebuchadnezzar's gold
statue. 6Anyone who refuses to obey will immediately be thrown into a blazing furnace."
7So at the sound of the musical instruments,* all the people, whatever their race or
nation or language, bowed to the ground and worshiped the statue that King Nebuchadnezzar had set up.
8But some of the astrologers* went to the king and informed on the Jews. 9They
said to King Nebuchadnezzar, "Long live the king! 10You issued a decree requiring

3:3 Aramaic *the princes, prefects, governors, advisers, counselors, judges, magistrates, and all the provincial officials.* **3:5** The identification of some of these musical instruments is uncertain. **3:7** Aramaic *the horn, flute, zither, lyre, harp, and other instruments of the musical ensemble.* **3:8** Aramaic *Chaldeans.*

Shadrach/Meshach/Abednego

Friendships make life enjoyable and difficult times bearable. Friendships are tested and strengthened by hardships. Such was the relationship between three young Jewish men deported to Babylon along with Daniel. Shadrach, Meshach, and Abednego help us think about the real meaning of friendship. As much as these friends meant to each other, they never allowed their friendship to usurp God's place in their lives—not even in the face of death.

Together they silently defied King Nebuchadnezzar's order to fall down and worship the image of gold. They shared a courageous act, while others, eager to get rid of them, told the king that the three Jews were being disloyal. While this was not true, Nebuchadnezzar could not spare them without losing face.

This was the moment of truth. Death was about to end their friendship. A small compromise would have allowed them to live and go on enjoying each other, serving God, and serving their people while in this foreign land. But they were wise enough to see that compromise would have poisoned the very conviction that bound them so closely—each had a higher allegiance to God. So they did not hesitate to place their lives in the hands of God. The rest was victory!

When we leave God out of our most important relationships, we tend to expect those relationships to meet needs in us that only God can meet. Friends are helpful, but they cannot meet our deepest spiritual needs. Leaving God out of our relationships indicates how unimportant he really is in our own life. Our relationship with God should be important enough to touch our other relationships—especially our closest friendships.

Strengths and accomplishment
- Stood with Daniel against eating food from the king's table
- Shared a friendship that stood the tests of hardship, success, wealth, and possible death
- Unwilling to compromise their convictions even in the face of death
- Survived the blazing furnace

Lessons from their lives
- There is great strength in real friendship
- It is important to stand with others with whom we share convictions
- God can be trusted even when we can't predict the outcome

Vital statistics
- Where: Babylon
- Occupations: King's servants and advisers
- Contemporaries: Daniel, Nebuchadnezzar

Key verses
"Shadrach, Meshach, and Abednego replied, 'O Nebuchadnezzar, we do not need to defend ourselves before you. If we are thrown into the blazing furnace, the God whom we serve is able to save us. He will rescue us from your power, Your Majesty. But even if he doesn't, Your Majesty can be sure that we will never serve your gods or worship the gold statue you have set up'" (Daniel 3:16–18).

The story of Shadrach (Hananiah), Meshach (Mishael), and Abednego (Azariah) is told in the book of Daniel.

3:6 This blazing furnace was not a small oven for cooking dinner or heating a house; it was a huge industrial furnace that could have been used for baking bricks or smelting metals. The temperatures were hot enough to assure that no one could survive. The roaring flames could be seen leaping from its top opening, and a fiery blast killed the soldiers who went up to the large opening (3:22).

all the people to bow down and worship the gold statue when they hear the sound of
the musical instruments.* 11That decree also states that those who refuse to obey must
be thrown into a blazing furnace. 12But there are some Jews—Shadrach, Meshach,
and Abednego—whom you have put in charge of the province of Babylon. They have
defied Your Majesty by refusing to serve your gods or to worship the gold statue you
have set up."

13Then Nebuchadnezzar flew into a rage and ordered Shadrach, Meshach, and
Abednego to be brought before him. When they were brought in, 14Nebuchadnezzar
said to them, "Is it true, Shadrach, Meshach, and Abednego, that you refuse to serve
my gods or to worship the gold statue I have set up? 15I will give you one more
chance. If you bow down and worship the statue I have made when you hear the sound
of the musical instruments, all will be well. But if you refuse, you will be thrown
immediately into the blazing furnace. What god will be able to rescue you from my
power then?"

16Shadrach, Meshach, and Abednego replied, "O Nebuchadnezzar, we do not need to
defend ourselves before you. 17If we are thrown into the blazing furnace, the God whom
we serve is able to save us. He will rescue us from your power, Your Majesty. 18But even
if he doesn't, Your Majesty can be sure that we will never serve your gods or worship
the gold statue you have set up."

The Blazing Furnace

19Nebuchadnezzar was so furious with Shadrach, Meshach, and Abednego that his face
became distorted with rage. He commanded that the furnace be heated seven times hotter
than usual. 20Then he ordered some of the strongest men of his army to bind Shadrach,
Meshach, and Abednego and throw them into the blazing furnace. 21So they tied them
up and threw them into the furnace, fully clothed. 22And because the king, in his anger,
had demanded such a hot fire in the furnace, the flames leaped out and killed the soldiers
as they threw the three men in! 23So Shadrach, Meshach, and Abednego, securely tied,
fell down into the roaring flames.

24But suddenly, as he was watching, Nebuchadnezzar jumped up in amazement and
exclaimed to his advisers, "Didn't we tie up three men and throw them into the furnace?"

"Yes," they said, "we did indeed, Your Majesty."

3:13 Dan 2:12; 3:19
3:14 Isa 46:1; Dan 3:1; 4:8
3:15 Exod 5:2; Isa 36:18-20; Jer 50:2; Dan 2:47
3:16 Dan 1:7; 3:12
3:17 1 Sam 17:37; Ps 27:1-2; Isa 26:3-4; Jer 1:8
3:18 Josh 24:15; 1 Kgs 19:14; Dan 3:28
3:19 Lev 26:18-28
3:22 Dan 2:15

3:10 Aramaic *the horn, flute, zither, lyre, harp, pipes, and other instruments of the musical ensemble;* also in 3:15.

3:12 We don't know if other Jews refused to fall down and worship the image, but these three were singled out as public examples. Why didn't the three men just bow to the image and tell God that they didn't mean it? They had determined never to worship another god, and they courageously took their stand. As a result, they were condemned and led away to be executed. The men did not know whether they would be delivered from the fire; all they knew was that they would not fall down and worship an idol. Are you ready to take a stand for God no matter what? When you stand for God, you will stand out. It may be painful, and it may not always have a happy ending. Be prepared to say, "If he rescues me, or if he doesn't, I will serve only God."

3:13 Nebuchadnezzar had lost control. How could anyone dare to disobey his commands? As the supreme ruler of Babylon, he expected absolute obedience. But his pride had caused him to go beyond his own authority. His demands were unjust and his reactions extreme. If you find yourself angered when people don't follow your directions, ask yourself, Why am I reacting this way? Your ego may be overly involved with your authority.

3:15 The three men were given one more chance. Here are eight excuses they could have used to bow to the image and save their lives: (1) We will fall down but not actually *worship* the idol. (2) We won't become idol worshipers but will worship it this one time, and then ask God for forgiveness. (3) The king has absolute power, and we must obey him. God will understand. (4) The king appointed us—we owe this to him. (5) This is a foreign land, so God will excuse us for following the customs of the land. (6) Our ancestors set up idols in God's Temple! This isn't half as bad! (7) We're not hurting anybody. (8) If we get ourselves killed and some pagans take our high positions, they won't help our people in exile!

Although all these excuses sound sensible at first, they are dangerous rationalizations. To fall down and worship the image would violate God's command in Exodus 20:3, "Do not worship any other gods besides me." It would also erase their testimony for God forever. Never again could they talk about the power of their God above all other gods. What excuses do you use for not standing up for him?

3:16-18 Shadrach, Meshach, and Abednego were pressured to deny God, but they chose to be faithful to him no matter what happened! They trusted God to deliver them, but they were determined to be faithful regardless of the consequences. If God always rescued those who were true to him, Christians would not need faith. Their religion would be a great insurance policy, and there would be lines of selfish people ready to sign up. We should be faithful to serve God whether he intervenes on our behalf or not. Our eternal reward is worth any suffering we may have to endure first.

3:25 Isa 43:2; Jer 1:8, 19
3:26 Deut 4:20; 1 Kgs 8:51
3:27 Isa 43:2; Dan 3:2; Heb 11:34

25 "Look!" Nebuchadnezzar shouted. "I see four men, unbound, walking around in the
fire. They aren't even hurt by the flames! And the fourth looks like a divine being*!"
26 Then Nebuchadnezzar came as close as he could to the door of the flaming furnace
and shouted: "Shadrach, Meshach, and Abednego, servants of the Most High God, come
out! Come here!" So Shadrach, Meshach, and Abednego stepped out of the fire. 27 Then
the princes, prefects, governors, and advisers crowded around them and saw that the fire

3:25 Aramaic *like a son of the gods.*

NEBUCHADNEZZAR

Nebuchadnezzar was one world leader who decided he could get more cooperation from the people he conquered by letting them keep their gods. Their lands he took, their riches he robbed, their lives he controlled, but their idols he allowed them to worship, sometimes even worshiping them himself. Nebuchadnezzar's plan worked well, with one glaring exception. When he conquered the little nation of Judah, he met a God who demanded *exclusive* worship—not just his share among many gods. In a sense, Nebuchadnezzar had always been able to rule the gods. This new God was different; this God dared to claim that he had made Nebuchadnezzar all that he was. One of the great conquerors in history was himself conquered by his Creator.

The Bible allows us to note the ways in which God worked on Nebuchadnezzar. God allowed him victories, but he was accomplishing God's purposes. God allowed him to deport the best young Jewish leaders as his palace servants, while placing close to him a young man named Daniel, who would change the king's life. God allowed Nebuchadnezzar to attempt to kill three of his servants to teach the king that he did not really have power over life and death. God warned him of the dangers in his pride and then allowed Nebuchadnezzar to live through seven years of insanity before restoring him to the throne. God showed the king who was really in control!

These lessons are clear to us today because of our place in history. When our attention shifts to our own life, we find ourselves unable to see how God is working. But we do have the advantage of God's Word as our guide for today's challenges. We are commanded to obey God; we are also commanded to trust him. Trusting him covers those times when we are not sure about the outcome. God has entrusted us with this day; have we trusted him with our life?

Strengths and accomplishments
- Greatest of the Babylonian kings
- Known as a builder of cities
- Described in the Bible as one of the foreign rulers God used for his purposes

Weaknesses and mistakes
- Thought of himself as a god and was persuaded to build an image of gold that all were to worship
- Became extremely proud, which led to a bout of insanity
- Tended to forget the demonstrations of God's power he had witnessed

Lessons from his life
- History records the actions of God's willing servants and those who were his unwitting tools
- A leader's greatness is affected by the quality of his advisers
- Uncontrolled pride is self-destructive

Vital statistics
- Where: Babylon
- Occupation: King
- Relatives: Father: Nabopolassar. Son: Evil-merodach. Grandson: Belshazzar
- Contemporaries: Jeremiah, Ezekiel, Daniel, Jehoiakim, Jehoiachin

Key verse
"Now I, Nebuchadnezzar, praise and glorify and honor the King of heaven. All his acts are just and true, and he is able to humble those who are proud" (Daniel 4:37).

Nebuchadnezzar's story is told in 2 Kings 24—25; 2 Chronicles 36; Jeremiah 21—52; Daniel 1—4.

3:25 It was obvious to those watching that this fourth person was supernatural. We cannot be certain who the fourth man was. It could have been an angel or a preincarnate appearance of Christ. In either case, God sent a heavenly visitor to accompany these faithful men during their time of great trial.

3:25-30 God's deliverance of Shadrach, Meshach, and Abednego was a great victory of faith for the Jews in captivity. They were protected from harm, they were comforted in trial, God was glorified, and they were rewarded. Let us determine to be true to God no matter how difficult the pressure or punishment. God's protection transcends anything we could imagine.

3:27 These young men had been completely untouched by the fire and heat. Only the rope that bound them had been burned. No human can bind us if God wants us to be free. The power available to us is the same that delivered Shadrach, Meshach, and Abednego and raised Christ from the dead (Ephesians 1:18-20). Trust God in every situation. There are eternal reasons for temporary trials; so be thankful that your destiny is in God's hands, not in human hands.

had not touched them. Not a hair on their heads was singed, and their clothing was not
scorched. They didn't even smell of smoke!
28 Then Nebuchadnezzar said, "Praise to the God of Shadrach, Meshach, and Abednego! He sent his angel to rescue his servants who trusted in him. They defied the king's
command and were willing to die rather than serve or worship any god except their own
God. 29 Therefore, I make this decree: If any people, whatever their race or nation or
language, speak a word against the God of Shadrach, Meshach, and Abednego, they will
be torn limb from limb, and their houses will be crushed into heaps of rubble. There is
no other god who can rescue like this!" 30 Then the king promoted Shadrach, Meshach,
and Abednego to even higher positions in the province of Babylon.

Nebuchadnezzar's Dream about a Tree

4 King Nebuchadnezzar sent this message to the people of every race and nation and
language throughout the world:

"Peace and prosperity to you!

2 "I want you all to know about the miraculous signs and wonders the Most High
God has performed for me.

3 How great are his signs,
how powerful his wonders!
His kingdom will last forever,
his rule through all generations.

4 "I, Nebuchadnezzar, was living in my palace in comfort and prosperity. 5 But
one night I had a dream that greatly frightened me; I saw visions that terrified me as
I lay in my bed. 6 So I issued an order calling in all the wise men of Babylon, so they
could tell me what my dream meant. 7 When all the magicians, enchanters, astrologers,* and fortune-tellers came in, I told them the dream, but they could not tell me
what it meant. 8 At last Daniel came in before me, and I told him the dream. (He
was named Belteshazzar after my god, and the spirit of the holy gods is in him.)
9 "I said to him, 'O Belteshazzar, master magician, I know that the spirit of the
holy gods is in you and that no mystery is too great for you to solve. Now tell me
what my dream means.
10 "'While I was lying in my bed, this is what I dreamed. I saw a large tree in the
middle of the earth. 11 The tree grew very tall and strong, reaching high into the
heavens for all the world to see. 12 It had fresh green leaves, and it was loaded with
fruit for all to eat. Wild animals lived in its shade, and birds nested in its branches.
All the world was fed from this tree.
13 "'Then as I lay there dreaming, I saw a messenger,* a holy one, coming down
from heaven. 14 The messenger shouted, "Cut down the tree; lop off its branches!
Shake off its leaves, and scatter its fruit! Chase the animals from its shade and the
birds from its branches. 15 But leave the stump and the roots in the ground, bound
with a band of iron and bronze and surrounded by tender grass. Now let him be
drenched with the dew of heaven, and let him live like an animal among the plants
of the fields. 16 For seven periods of time, let him have the mind of an animal

3:28 Ps 34:7-8; Isa 37:36; Dan 3:25; 6:22; Acts 5:19; 12:7
3:29 Ezra 6:11; Dan 3:12, 15
3:30 Dan 2:49; 3:12
4:1 Dan 6:25
4:3 Deut 4:34; Ps 77:19; Isa 25:1; Dan 2:44; 4:34; 6:26
4:4 Ps 30:6; Isa 47:7-8
4:5 Dan 4:10, 13
4:6 Gen 41:8; Dan 2:2
4:7 Isa 44:25; Jer 27:9-10; Dan 2:7
4:8 Dan 1:7; 4:9, 18
4:9 Gen 41:38; Ezek 28:3; Dan 1:20; 2:4-5, 47-48; 4:8; 5:11
4:10 Ezek 31:3-4
4:12 Jer 27:6-7; Ezek 31:7; Matt 13:32; Luke 13:19
4:13 Deut 33:2; Ps 89:7; Dan 8:13
4:14 Jer 51:5-6; Ezek 31:10-14; Matt 3:10; 7:19; Rev 10:3; 18:2
4:15 Job 14:7-9
4:16 Dan 7:25

4:7 Or *Chaldeans.* **4:13** Aramaic *a watcher;* also in 4:23.

3:28, 29 Nebuchadnezzar was not making a commitment here to serve the Hebrews' God alone. Instead, he was acknowledging that God is powerful, and he commanded his people not to speak against God. Nebuchadnezzar didn't tell the people to throw away all the other gods but to add this one to the list.

3:30 Where was Daniel in this story? The Bible doesn't say, but there are several possibilities: (1) He may have been on official business in another part of the kingdom. (2) He may have been present, but because he was a ruler, the officials didn't accuse him of not falling down and worshiping the image. (3) He may have been in the capital city handling the administration while Nebuchadnezzar was away. (4) He may have been considered exempt from bowing down to the image because of his reputation for interpreting dreams through his God. Whether Daniel was there or not, we can be sure that he would not have worshiped the image.

4:2, 3 Although Nebuchadnezzar praised Daniel's God, he still did not believe in him completely or submit to him alone (4:8). Many people attend church and use Christian language, but they really don't honor God with their lives. Profession doesn't always mean possession. Does your life match your profession of faith?

instead of a human. 17For this has been decreed by the messengers*; it is commanded by the holy ones. The purpose of this decree is that the whole world may
understand that the Most High rules over the kingdoms of the world and gives them
to anyone he chooses—even to the lowliest of humans."
18"'O Belteshazzar, that was the dream that I, King Nebuchadnezzar, had. Now
tell me what it means, for no one else can help me. All the wisest men of my kingdom have failed me. But you can tell me because the spirit of the holy gods is in
you.'"

Daniel Explains the Dream

19Upon hearing this, Daniel (also known as Belteshazzar) was overcome for a time,
aghast at the meaning of the dream. Finally, the king said to him, "Belteshazzar,
don't be alarmed by the dream and what it means."
Belteshazzar replied, "Oh, how I wish the events foreshadowed in this dream
would happen to your enemies, my lord, and not to you! 20You saw a tree growing
very tall and strong, reaching high into the heavens for all the world to see. 21It had
fresh green leaves, and it was loaded with fruit for all to eat. Wild animals lived in
its shade, and birds nested in its branches. 22That tree, Your Majesty, is you. For
you have grown strong and great; your greatness reaches up to heaven, and your
rule to the ends of the earth.
23"Then you saw a messenger, a holy one, coming down from heaven and saying, 'Cut down the tree and destroy it. But leave the stump and the roots in the
ground, bound with a band of iron and bronze and surrounded by tender grass. Let
him be drenched with the dew of heaven. Let him eat grass with the animals of the
field for seven periods of time.'
24"This is what the dream means, Your Majesty, and what the Most High has
declared will happen to you. 25You will be driven from human society, and you will
live in the fields with the wild animals. You will eat grass like a cow, and you will
be drenched with the dew of heaven. Seven periods of time will pass while you live
this way, until you learn that the Most High rules over the kingdoms of the world
and gives them to anyone he chooses. 26But the stump and the roots were left in the
ground. This means that you will receive your kingdom back again when you have
learned that heaven rules.
27"O King Nebuchadnezzar, please listen to me. Stop sinning and do what is
right. Break from your wicked past by being merciful to the poor. Perhaps then you
will continue to prosper."

The Dream's Fulfillment

28But all these things did happen to King Nebuchadnezzar. 29Twelve months later,
he was taking a walk on the flat roof of the royal palace in Babylon. 30As he looked

4:17 1 Sam 2:8; Ps 9:16; Dan 4:25; 11:21
4:18 Gen 41:8; 1 Kgs 14:2-3; Dan 4:7; 5:8
4:19 1 Sam 3:17; 2 Sam 18:32; Dan 7:15, 28; 8:27
4:22 2 Sam 12:7; Jer 27:6-7; Dan 2:37-38
4:24 Job 40:11-12; Ps 107:40
4:25 Ps 75:7; Jer 27:5; Dan 4:17, 33; 5:21
4:26 Dan 4:31
4:27 Gen 41:33-37; 1 Kgs 21:29; Ps 41:1-3; Prov 28:13; Isa 55:6-7; Ezek 18:21-22; Jon 3:9
4:28 Zech 1:6
4:29 2 Pet 3:9

4:17 Aramaic *the watchers.*

4:17 One of the most difficult lessons to learn is that God is sovereign. He is above all of those who are above us. He limits the power and authority of all the government, business, and religious leaders in the world. Those who live in freedom and with a relatively high degree of autonomy find this difficult to understand. While we may feel as though we are free to do what we please, God is sovereign over all of our plans and desires.

4:19 When Daniel understood Nebuchadnezzar's dream, he was stunned, and he wondered how to break the news. He told the king he wished what the dream foreshadowed would happen to the king's enemies and not to Nebuchadnezzar. How could Daniel be so deeply grieved at the fate of Nebuchadnezzar—the king who was responsible for the destruction of Daniel's home and nation? Daniel had forgiven Nebuchadnezzar, and so God was able to use Daniel. Very often when we have been wronged by someone, we find it difficult to forget the past. We may even be glad when that person suffers. Forgiveness means putting the past behind us. Can you love someone who has hurt you? Can you serve someone who mistreated you? Ask God to help you forgive, forget, and love. God may use you in an extraordinary way in that person's life!

4:23ff Although much of the world thought that Nebuchadnezzar was a mighty (even divine) king, God demonstrated that Nebuchadnezzar was an ordinary man. The king would go insane and become like an animal for a set period of time ("seven periods of time"). God humiliated Nebuchadnezzar to show that almighty God, not Nebuchadnezzar, was Lord of the nations. No matter how powerful a person may become, self-centered pride will push God from his or her life. Pride may be one of the most dangerous temptations you will face. Don't let your accomplishments cause you to forget God.

4:27-33 Daniel pleaded with Nebuchadnezzar to change his ways, and God gave Nebuchadnezzar 12 months to do it. Unfortunately, there was no repentance in the heart of this proud king, and so the dream was fulfilled.

out across the city, he said, "Just look at this great city of Babylon! I, by my own
mighty power, have built this beautiful city as my royal residence and as an expression of my royal splendor."
31 While he was still speaking these words, a voice called down from heaven,
"O King Nebuchadnezzar, this message is for you! You are no longer ruler of this
kingdom. 32 You will be driven from human society. You will live in the fields with
the wild animals, and you will eat grass like a cow. Seven periods of time will pass
while you live this way, until you learn that the Most High rules over the kingdoms
of the world and gives them to anyone he chooses."
33 That very same hour the prophecy was fulfilled, and Nebuchadnezzar was driven
from human society. He ate grass like a cow, and he was drenched with the dew of
heaven. He lived this way until his hair was as long as eagles' feathers and his nails
were like birds' claws.

Nebuchadnezzar Praises God

34 "After this time had passed, I, Nebuchadnezzar, looked up to heaven. My sanity
returned, and I praised and worshiped the Most High and honored the one who
lives forever.

His rule is everlasting,
and his kingdom is eternal.
35 All the people of the earth
are nothing compared to him.
He has the power to do as he pleases
among the angels of heaven
and with those who live on earth.
No one can stop him or challenge him,
saying, 'What do you mean by doing these things?'

36 "When my sanity returned to me, so did my honor and glory and kingdom. My
advisers and officers sought me out, and I was reestablished as head of my kingdom, with even greater honor than before.
37 "Now I, Nebuchadnezzar, praise and glorify and honor the King of heaven. All
his acts are just and true, and he is able to humble those who are proud."

The Writing on the Wall

5 A number of years later, King Belshazzar gave a great feast for a thousand of his nobles
and drank wine with them. 2 While Belshazzar was drinking, he gave orders to bring in
the gold and silver cups that his predecessor,* Nebuchadnezzar, had taken from the Temple
in Jerusalem, so that he and his nobles, his wives, and his concubines might drink from
them. 3 So they brought these gold cups taken from the Temple of God in Jerusalem, and
the king and his nobles, his wives, and his concubines drank from them. 4 They drank toasts
from them to honor their idols made of gold, silver, bronze, iron, wood, and stone.
5 At that very moment they saw the fingers of a human hand writing on the plaster wall

4:30 Hab 2:4
4:33 Dan 4:25; 5:21
4:34 Ps 102:24 Jer 10:10 Dan 4:2; 5:18, 21 Rev 4:10; 10:6
4:35 Job 42:2 Ps 135:6 Isa 40:17; 43:13; 45:9 Dan 6:27 Rom 9:20
4:36 2 Chr 33:12-13 Prov 22:4 Dan 2:31
4:37 Exod 18:11 Ps 33:4-5 Matt 23:12
5:1 Esth 1:3 Isa 22:12-14
5:2 2 Kgs 24:13 Ezra 1:7-11 Dan 1:2
5:4 Rev 9:20

5:2 Aramaic *father;* also in 5:11, 13, 18.

4:34 Ancient kings tried to avoid mentioning their weaknesses or defeats in their monuments and official records. From Nebuchadnezzar's records, however, we can infer that for a time during his 43-year reign he did not rule. The Bible, however, explains Nebuchadnezzar's pride and punishment.

4:36 Nebuchadnezzar's pilgrimage with God is one of the themes of this book. In 2:47, he acknowledged that God revealed mysteries to Daniel. In 3:28, 29 he praised the God who rescued the three Hebrews. Despite Nebuchadnezzar's recognition that God exists and works great miracles, in 4:30 we see that he still did not acknowledge God as his Lord. We may recognize that God exists and does wonderful miracles, but so do many unbelievers! To be a child of God, you must invite him to be Lord of your life.

5:1 Sixty-six years have elapsed since chapter 1, which tells of Nebuchadnezzar's strike against Jerusalem in 605 B.C. Nebuchadnezzar died in 562 B.C. after a reign of 43 years. His son, Evil-merodach, ruled from 562 to 560 B.C.; his brother-in-law Neriglissar reigned four years from 560 to 556 B.C. After a two-month reign by Labashi-marduk in 556 B.C., the Babylonian Empire continued from 556 to 539 B.C. under the command of Nabonidus. Belshazzar was the son of Nabonidus. He co-reigned with his father from 553 to 539 B.C.

5:1 Archaeologists have recently discovered Belshazzar's name on several documents. He ruled with his father, Nabonidus, staying home to administer the affairs of the kingdom while his father tried to reopen trade routes taken over by Cyrus and the Persians. Belshazzar was in charge of the city of Babylon when it was captured.

5:6 Ps 69:23 Ezek 7:17; 21:7 Dan 7:28 Nah 2:10
5:7 Gen 41:42-44 Isa 44:25; 47:13 Ezek 16:11 Dan 5:11, 16, 29; 6:2-3
5:9 Job 18:11-14 Ps 18:14 Isa 21:2-4 Jer 6:24 Dan 5:6
5:10 Dan 3:9; 6:6
5:11 Gen 41:11-15 Dan 2:47; 4:8-9; 5:14
5:12 Dan 4:18
5:13 Dan 1:1; 2:25
5:15 Isa 47:12 Dan 5:8
5:16 Gen 40:8
5:17 2 Kgs 5:16
5:18 Jer 25:5-7 Dan 2:37; 4:2, 17; 5:21
5:19 Prov 16:14 Dan 2:12; 3:6; 11:3
5:20 Exod 9:17 Isa 14:13-15 Jer 13:18 Dan 4:30 Luke 18:14
5:21 Exod 9:14-16 Ps 83:17-18 Ezek 17:24

of the king's palace, near the lampstand. The king himself saw the hand as it wrote, [6]and his face turned pale with fear. Such terror gripped him that his knees knocked together and his legs gave way beneath him.

[7]The king shouted for the enchanters, astrologers,* and fortune-tellers to be brought before him. He said to these wise men of Babylon, "Whoever can read this writing and tell me what it means will be dressed in purple robes of royal honor and will wear a gold chain around his neck. He will become the third highest ruler in the kingdom!" [8]But when all the king's wise men came in, none of them could read the writing or tell him what it meant. [9]So the king grew even more alarmed, and his face turned ashen white. His nobles, too, were shaken.

[10]But when the queen mother heard what was happening, she hurried to the banquet hall. She said to Belshazzar, "Long live the king! Don't be so pale and afraid about this. [11]There is a man in your kingdom who has within him the spirit of the holy gods. During Nebuchadnezzar's reign, this man was found to have insight, understanding, and wisdom as though he himself were a god. Your predecessor, King Nebuchadnezzar, made him chief over all the magicians, enchanters, astrologers, and fortune-tellers of Babylon. [12]This man Daniel, whom the king named Belteshazzar, has a sharp mind and is filled with divine knowledge and understanding. He can interpret dreams, explain riddles, and solve difficult problems. Call for Daniel, and he will tell you what the writing means."

Daniel Explains the Writing

[13]So Daniel was brought in before the king. The king asked him, "Are you Daniel, who was exiled from Judah by my predecessor, King Nebuchadnezzar? [14]I have heard that you have the spirit of the gods within you and that you are filled with insight, understanding, and wisdom. [15]My wise men and enchanters have tried to read this writing on the wall, but they cannot. [16]I am told that you can give interpretations and solve difficult problems. If you can read these words and tell me their meaning, you will be clothed in purple robes of royal honor, and you will wear a gold chain around your neck. You will become the third highest ruler in the kingdom."

[17]Daniel answered the king, "Keep your gifts or give them to someone else, but I will tell you what the writing means. [18]Your Majesty, the Most High God gave sovereignty, majesty, glory, and honor to your predecessor, Nebuchadnezzar. [19]He made him so great that people of all races and nations and languages trembled before him in fear. He killed those he wanted to kill and spared those he wanted to spare. He honored those he wanted to honor and disgraced those he wanted to disgrace. [20]But when his heart and mind were hardened with pride, he was brought down from his royal throne and stripped of his glory. [21]He was driven from human society. He was given the mind of an animal, and he lived among the wild donkeys. He ate grass like a cow, and he was drenched with the dew of heaven, until he learned that the Most High God rules the kingdoms of the world and appoints anyone he desires to rule over them.

5:7 Or *Chaldeans;* also in 5:11.

5:7 Belshazzar served as co-regent with his father, Nabonidus. Thus, Nabonidus was the first ruler and his son Belshazzar, the second. The person who could read the writing would be given third place, which was the highest position and honor that Belshazzar could offer.

5:8 Although the writing on the wall contained only three words in Aramaic, a language understood by Babylonians (see 2:4), the people could not determine its prophetic significance. God gave Daniel alone the ability to interpret the message of doom to Babylon. The wise men of the kingdom were ignorant of God's wisdom, no matter how great the reward. Daniel did not rush into the banquet hall with the others. His loyalty was to God, not money.

5:10 This queen mother was either Nabonidus's wife or the wife of one of his predecessors, possibly even of Nebuchadnezzar. She was not Belshazzar's wife, because his wives were with him in the banquet hall.

5:17 The king offered Daniel beautiful gifts and great power if he would explain the writing, but Daniel turned him down. Daniel was not motivated by material rewards. His entire life had been characterized by doing right. Daniel was not showing disrespect in refusing the gifts, but he was growing older himself and knew the gifts would do him little good. Daniel wanted to show that he was giving an unbiased interpretation to the king. Doing right should be our first priority, not gaining power or rewards. Do you love God enough to do what is right, even if it means giving up personal rewards?

5:21-23 Belshazzar knew Babylonian history, and so he knew how God had humbled Nebuchadnezzar. Nevertheless Belshazzar's feast was open defiance to God's authority as he took the sacred cups from God's Temple and drank from them. No one who understands that God is the Creator of the universe should be foolish enough to challenge him.

22“You are his successor,* O Belshazzar, and you knew all this, yet you have not
humbled yourself. 23For you have defied the Lord of heaven and have had these cups
from his Temple brought before you. You and your nobles and your wives and concubines have been drinking wine from them while praising gods of silver, gold, bronze,
iron, wood, and stone—gods that neither see nor hear nor know anything at all. But you
have not honored the God who gives you the breath of life and controls your destiny!
24So God has sent this hand to write a message.
25“This is the message that was written: MENE, MENE, TEKEL, PARSIN. 26This is what
these words mean:

Mene means ‘numbered’—God has numbered the days of your reign and has brought it to an end.
27 *Tekel* means ‘weighed’—you have been weighed on the balances and have failed the test.
28 *Parsin** means ‘divided’—your kingdom has been divided and given to the Medes and Persians.”

29Then at Belshazzar’s command, Daniel was dressed in purple robes, a gold chain
was hung around his neck, and he was proclaimed the third highest ruler in the kingdom.
30That very night Belshazzar, the Babylonian* king, was killed.* 31And Darius the
Mede took over the kingdom at the age of sixty-two.

Daniel in the Lions’ Den

6 Darius the Mede decided to divide the kingdom into 120 provinces, and he appointed
a prince to rule over each province. 2The king also chose Daniel and two others as
administrators to supervise the princes and to watch out for the king’s interests. 3Daniel soon
proved himself more capable than all the other administrators and princes. Because of his
great ability, the king made plans to place him over the entire empire. 4Then the other
administrators and princes began searching for some fault in the way Daniel was handling
his affairs, but they couldn’t find anything to criticize. He was faithful and honest and
always responsible. 5So they concluded, “Our only chance of finding grounds for accusing
Daniel will be in connection with the requirements of his religion.”

5:22 Aramaic *son.* 5:28 Aramaic *Peres,* the singular of *Parsin.* 5:30a Or *Chaldean.* 5:30b The Persians and Medes conquered Babylon in October 539 B.C.

5:22 Exod 10:3; 2 Chr 33:23; 36:12
5:23 2 Kgs 14:10; Job 3:14; 12:10; Jer 10:23; 50:29; Dan 5:3-4; Hab 2:18-19
5:26 Isa 13:6, 17; Jer 50:41-43
5:27 Job 31:6; Ps 62:9
5:28 Isa 21:2; 45:1-2; Dan 5:31; 6:28
5:30 Isa 21:4-9; Jer 51:11, 31, 39, 57
5:31 Dan 6:1; 9:1
6:1 Esth 1:1
6:2 Ezra 4:22; Esth 7:4
6:3 Gen 41:40; Dan 5:12
6:4 Gen 43:18; Luke 23:14-15; Phil 2:15
6:5 Acts 24:13-16

5:22 Often kings would kill the bearer of bad news. But Daniel was not afraid to tell the truth to the king even though it was not what he wanted to hear. We should be just as courageous in telling the truth under pressure.

5:23, 24 Belshazzar used the cups from the Temple for his party, and God condemned him for this act. We must not use for sinful purposes what has been dedicated to God. Today this would include church buildings, financial donations, and anything else that has been set apart for serving God. Be careful how you use what is God’s.

5:27 The writing on the wall was a message for all those who defy God. Although Belshazzar had power and wealth, his kingdom was totally corrupt, and he could not withstand the judgment of God. God’s time of judgment comes for all people. If you have forgotten God and slipped into a sinful way of life, turn away from your sin now before he removes any opportunities to repent. Ask God to forgive you, and begin to live by his standards of justice.

5:28 The Medes and Persians joined forces to overthrow Babylon. This event was predicted in the second phase of Nebuchadnezzar’s dream in chapter 2—the silver chest and arms.

5:31 Darius and his soldiers entered Babylon by diverting the river that ran through the city, then walking in on the dry riverbed.

5:31 This Darius is not to be confused with Darius I, mentioned in Ezra, Haggai, and Zechariah, or Darius II (the Persian), mentioned in Nehemiah. Darius the Mede is named only in the book of Daniel. Other records name no king between Belshazzar and Cyrus. Thus, Darius may have been (1) appointed by Cyrus to rule over Babylon as a province of Persia, (2) another name for Cyrus himself or for his son, Cambyses, or (3) a descendant of Xerxes I.

6:1-3 At this time, Daniel was over 80 years old and one of Darius’s top three administrators. Daniel was working with those who did not believe in his God, but he worked more efficiently and capably than all the rest. Thus, he attracted the attention of the pagan king and earned a place of respect. One of the best ways to influence non-Christian employers is to work diligently and responsibly. How well do you represent God to your employer?

6:3, 4 Daniel made enemies at work by doing a good job. Perhaps you have had a similar experience. When you begin to excel, you will find that co-workers may look for ways to hold you back and tear you down. How should you deal with those who would cheer at your downfall and even try to hasten it? Conduct your life above reproach. Then you will have nothing to hide, and your enemies will have a difficult time finding legitimate charges against you. Of course, this will not always save you from attacks, and, like Daniel, you will have to rely on God for protection.

6:4, 5 The jealous administrators and princes couldn’t find anything about Daniel’s life to criticize, so they attacked his religion. If you face jealous critics because of your faith, be glad they’re criticizing that part of your life—perhaps they had to focus on your religion as a last resort! Respond by continuing to believe and live as you should. Then remember that God is in control, fighting this battle for you.

6:6 Neh 2:3
6:7 Pss 59:3; 62:4; 64:2-6; Matt 12:14
6:8 Esth 1:19; 3:12; Isa 10:1; Matt 24:35
6:9 Pss 118:9; 146:3
6:10 1 Kgs 8:48-49; Pss 34:1; 95:6; 1 Thes 5:17-18
6:11 Ps 37:32-33; Dan 6:6
6:12 Esth 1:19; Acts 16:19-21
6:13 Esth 3:8; Acts 5:29
6:14 Mark 6:26
6:15 Esth 8:8; Ps 94:20-21
6:16 Job 5:19; Ps 37:39-40; Jer 38:5

6 So the administrators and princes went to the king and said, "Long live King Darius!
7 We administrators, prefects, princes, advisers, and other officials have unanimously
agreed that Your Majesty should make a law that will be strictly enforced. Give orders
that for the next thirty days anyone who prays to anyone, divine or human—except to
Your Majesty—will be thrown to the lions. 8 And let Your Majesty issue and sign this law
so it cannot be changed, a law of the Medes and Persians, which cannot be revoked." 9 So
King Darius signed the law.
10 But when Daniel learned that the law had been signed, he went home and knelt down
as usual in his upstairs room, with its windows open toward Jerusalem. He prayed three
times a day, just as he had always done, giving thanks to his God. 11 The officials went
together to Daniel's house and found him praying and asking for God's help. 12 So they
went back to the king and reminded him about his law. "Did you not sign a law that for
the next thirty days anyone who prays to anyone, divine or human—except to Your
Majesty—will be thrown to the lions?"
"Yes," the king replied, "that decision stands; it is a law of the Medes and Persians,
which cannot be revoked."
13 Then they told the king, "That man Daniel, one of the captives from Judah, is paying
no attention to you or your law. He still prays to his God three times a day."
14 Hearing this, the king was very angry with himself for signing the law, and he tried
to find a way to save Daniel. He spent the rest of the day looking for a way to get Daniel
out of this predicament. 15 In the evening the men went together to the king and said,
"Your Majesty knows that according to the law of the Medes and the Persians, no law
that the king signs can be changed."
16 So at last the king gave orders for Daniel to be arrested and thrown into the den of

KINGS DANIEL SERVED

Name	*Empire*	*Story told in*	*Memorable event*
Nebuchadnezzar	Babylonia	chapters 1—4	Shadrach, Meshach, and Abednego thrown into blazing furnace; Nebuchadnezzar became insane for 7 years
Belshazzar	Babylonia	chapters 5, 7, 8	Daniel read the writing on the wall, which signaled the end of the Babylonian Empire
Darius	Medo-Persia	chapters 6, 9	Daniel thrown into a lions' den
Cyrus	Medo-Persia	chapters 10—12	The exiles return to their homeland in Judah and their capital city, Jerusalem

6:8, 9 In Babylon, the king's word *was* the law. In the Medo-Persian Empire, however, when a law was made, even the king couldn't change it. Darius was an effective government administrator, but he had a fatal flaw—pride. By appealing to his vanity, the men talked Darius into signing a law effectively making himself a god for 30 days. This law could not be broken—not even by an important official like Daniel. Another example of the irrevocable nature of the laws of the Medes and Persians appears in Esther 8:8.

6:10 Daniel stood alone. Although he knew about the law against praying to anyone except the king, he continued to pray three times a day as he always had. Daniel had a disciplined prayer life. Our prayers are usually interrupted, not by threats, but simply by the pressure of our schedules. Don't let threats or pressures cut into your prayer time. Pray regularly, no matter what, for prayer is your lifeline to God.

6:10 Daniel made no attempt to hide his daily prayer routine from his enemies in government, even though he knew he would be disobeying the new law. Hiding his daily prayers would have been futile because surely the conspirators would have caught him at something else during the month. Also, hiding would have demonstrated that he was afraid of the other government officials. Daniel continued to pray because he could not look to the king for the guidance and strength that he needed during this difficult time. Only God could provide what he really needed.

6:16 Lions roamed the countryside and forests in Mesopotamia, and the people feared them and greatly respected their power. Some kings hunted lions for sport. The Persians captured lions, keeping them in large parks where they were fed and attended. Lions were also used for executing people. But God has ways of delivering his people (6:22) that none of us can imagine. It is always premature to give up and give in to the pressure of unbelievers, because God has power they know nothing about. God can even shut the lions' mouths.

6:16 Even unbelievers witnessed to Daniel's consistency. By his continual service, Daniel had demonstrated his faithful devotion to God. What can unbelievers determine about your life?

lions. The king said to him, "May your God, whom you worship continually, rescue
you." 17A stone was brought and placed over the mouth of the den. The king sealed the
stone with his own royal seal and the seals of his nobles, so that no one could rescue
Daniel from the lions. 18Then the king returned to his palace and spent the night fasting.
He refused his usual entertainment and couldn't sleep at all that night.

19Very early the next morning, the king hurried out to the lions' den. 20When he got
there, he called out in anguish, "Daniel, servant of the living God! Was your God, whom
you worship continually, able to rescue you from the lions?"

21Daniel answered, "Long live the king! 22My God sent his angel to shut the lions'
mouths so that they would not hurt me, for I have been found innocent in his sight. And
I have not wronged you, Your Majesty."

23The king was overjoyed and ordered that Daniel be lifted from the den. Not a scratch
was found on him because he had trusted in his God. 24Then the king gave orders to
arrest the men who had maliciously accused Daniel. He had them thrown into the lions'
den, along with their wives and children. The lions leaped on them and tore them apart
before they even hit the floor of the den.

25Then King Darius sent this message to the people of every race and nation and
language throughout the world:

"Peace and prosperity to you!

26"I decree that everyone throughout my kingdom should tremble with fear before
the God of Daniel.

For he is the living God,
and he will endure forever.
His kingdom will never be destroyed,
and his rule will never end.
27 He rescues and saves his people;
he performs miraculous signs and wonders
in the heavens and on earth.
He has rescued Daniel
from the power of the lions."

28So Daniel prospered during the reign of Darius and the reign of Cyrus the Persian.*

6:17 Lam 3:53; Matt 27:66
6:18 2 Sam 12:16-17; Esth 6:1; Rev 18:22
6:20 Jer 32:17; Dan 3:17; Hos 12:6
6:22 Ps 91:11-13; Acts 12:11; 2 Tim 4:17; Heb 11:33
6:23 Ps 118:8; Isa 26:3; Dan 3:17, 28
6:24 Deut 19:18-19; 2 Kgs 14:6
6:25 Ezra 1:1-2; Esth 3:12; 8:9; Hos 1:10; 1 Pet 1:2
6:26 Ps 93:1-2
6:27 Dan 4:3

B. DANIEL'S VISIONS (7:1—12:13)

Daniel had many dreams and visions he did not understand. He dreamed of four beasts, which represented four kingdoms of the world, and of a ram and goat, which depicted two of those kingdoms in greater detail. Daniel's visions reveal that the Messiah will be the ruler of a spiritual Kingdom that will overpower and overshadow all other earthly kingdoms. These visions help us see that we should interpret all of history in light of God's eternal Kingdom.

Daniel's Vision of Four Beasts

7 Earlier, during the first year of King Belshazzar's reign in Babylon, Daniel had a dream
and saw visions as he lay in his bed. He wrote the dream down, and this is what he saw.
2In my vision that night, I, Daniel, saw a great storm churning the surface of a great

7:1 Job 33:14-16; Jer 36:4; Joel 2:28
7:2 Rev 7:1

6:28 Or *of Darius, that is, the reign of Cyrus the Persian.*

6:21-23 The man or woman who trusts in God and obeys his will is untouchable until God takes him or her. To trust God is to have immeasurable peace. God, who delivered Daniel, will deliver you. Do you trust him with your life?

6:24 In accordance with Persian custom, this cruel punishment was transferred to those who had conspired against the king by provoking him into an unjust action (see also Esther 7:9, 10). The king's great anger resulted in the execution of the evil officials and their families. Evil deeds often backfire on those who plan cruelty.

6:25-27 Nebuchadnezzar had come to believe that Israel's God was real because of the faithfulness of Daniel and his friends. Here Darius was also convinced of God's power because Daniel was faithful and God rescued him. Although Daniel was captive in a strange land, his devotion to God was a testimony to powerful rulers. If you find yourself in new surroundings, take the opportunity to testify about God's power in your life. Be faithful to God so he can use you to make an impact on others.

7:1 Chronologically, this chapter takes place before chapter 5. At this time, Belshazzar had just been given a position of authority (553 B.C.), and Daniel was probably in his late sixties. The first six chapters of Daniel present history; the last six chapters are visions relating mainly to the future.

7:1ff Daniel had a vision of four huge beasts, each representing a world empire. This was similar to Nebuchadnezzar's

7:3 Rev 13:1 sea, with strong winds blowing from every direction. 3 Then four huge beasts came up
out of the water, each different from the others.
4 The first beast was like a lion with eagles' wings. As I watched, its wings were pulled
off, and it was left standing with its two hind feet on the ground, like a human being. And
a human mind was given to it.
5 Then I saw a second beast, and it looked like a bear. It was rearing up on one side,
and it had three ribs in its mouth between its teeth. And I heard a voice saying to it, "Get
up! Devour many people!"
6 Then the third of these strange beasts appeared, and it looked like a leopard. It had
four wings like birds' wings on its back, and it had four heads. Great authority was given
to this beast.
7:7 Rev 12:3; 13:1 7 Then in my vision that night, I saw a fourth beast, terrifying, dreadful, and very
strong. It devoured and crushed its victims with huge iron teeth and trampled what
was left beneath its feet. It was different from any of the other beasts, and it had ten
7:9 Ezek 1:13; 10:2, 6 horns. 8 As I was looking at the horns, suddenly another small horn appeared among
Mark 9:3 them. Three of the first horns were wrenched out, roots and all, to make room for it.
Rev 1:14 This little horn had eyes like human eyes and a mouth that was boasting arrogantly.
7:10 Pss 50:3; 97:3 9 I watched as thrones were put in place and the Ancient One* sat down to judge. His
Isa 30:27 Dan 7:22, 26; 12:1 clothing was as white as snow, his hair like whitest wool. He sat on a fiery throne with
Rev 5:11; 20:11-15 wheels of blazing fire, 10 and a river of fire flowed from his presence. Millions of angels
ministered to him, and a hundred million stood to attend him. Then the court began its
session, and the books were opened.
7:11 Rev 19:20; 20:10 11 I continued to watch because I could hear the little horn's boastful speech. I kept
7:13 †Matt 26:64 watching until the fourth beast was killed and its body was destroyed by fire. 12 As for
†Mark 13:26 the other three beasts, their authority was taken from them, but they were allowed to live
†Luke 21:27 Rev 1:13; 14:14 for a while longer.*
13 As my vision continued that night, I saw someone who looked like a man* coming
7:14 Pss 2:6-8; 72:17; 102:22 with the clouds of heaven. He approached the Ancient One and was led into his presence.
Dan 7:27 14 He was given authority, honor, and royal power over all the nations of the world, so
Eph 1:20-22 Heb 12:28 that people of every race and nation and language would obey him. His rule is eternal—it
Rev 1:6 will never end. His kingdom will never be destroyed.

The Vision Is Explained

7:16 Dan 8:13-16; 15 I, Daniel, was troubled by all I had seen, and my visions terrified me. 16 So I
10:5-6, 11-12 Zech 1:8-11 approached one of those standing beside the throne and asked him what it all meant. He
Rev 5:5; 7:13-14

7:9 Aramaic *an Ancient of Days;* also in 7:13, 22. **7:12** Aramaic *for a season and a time.* **7:13** Or *a Son of Man;* Aramaic reads *a son of man.*

dream in chapter 2. Nebuchadnezzar's dream covered the political aspects of the empires; Daniel's dream depicted their moral characteristics. These nations, which would reign over Israel, were evil and cruel; but Daniel also saw God's everlasting, indestructible Kingdom arrive and conquer them all.

7:4-8 The lion with eagles' wings represents Babylon with its swift conquests (statues of winged lions have been recovered from Babylon's ruins). The bear that ravaged the lion is Medo-Persia. The three ribs in its mouth represent the conquests of three major enemies. The leopard is Greece. Its wings show the swiftness of Alexander the Great's campaign as he conquered much of the civilized world in four years (334–330 B.C.). The leopard's four heads are the four divisions of the Greek Empire after Alexander's death.

The fourth beast points to both Rome and the end times. Many Bible scholars believe that the horns correspond to 10 kings who will reign shortly before God sets up his everlasting Kingdom. These 10 kings had still not come to power at the time of John's vision recorded in the book of Revelation (Revelation 17:12). The little horn is a future human ruler or the Antichrist (see also 2 Thessalonians 2:3, 4). God is illustrating the final end of all worldly kingdoms in contrast to his eternal Kingdom.

7:9 Here the prophecy shifts to the end times. This judgment scene is similar to one that was seen by the apostle John (Revelation 1:14, 15). The Ancient One is almighty God, who assigns power to kingdoms and who will himself judge those kingdoms in the end.

7:10 Daniel saw God judging millions of people as they stood before him. We all must stand before almighty God and give an account of our lives. If your life were judged by God today, what would he say about it? How would he measure it against his will for you? We should live each day with the full awareness that we must appear before God to give account for how we used our life. How will your life measure up?

7:11, 12 The slaying of the beast represents the fall of Rome. While this beast was destroyed, the other beasts were allowed to live for a period of time. The kingdoms (or their cultures) continued to be recognizable in some form; history did not end when God intervened with his judgment.

7:13, 14 This one "who looked like a man" is the Messiah. Jesus used this verse to refer to himself (Matthew 26:64; Luke 21:27; John 1:51). The clouds of heaven portray the Son of Man as divine; throughout the Bible, clouds represent his majesty and awesome presence. God's glory appeared in a cloud in Exodus 16:10 and 19:9 at the giving of the law at Sinai.

explained it to me like this: 17“These four huge beasts represent four kingdoms that will
arise from the earth. 18But in the end, the holy people of the Most High will be given the
kingdom, and they will rule forever and ever.”
19Then I wanted to know the true meaning of the fourth beast, the one so different
from the others and so terrifying. It devoured and crushed its victims with iron teeth and
bronze claws, and it trampled what was left beneath its feet. 20I also asked about the ten
horns on the fourth beast’s head and the little horn that came up afterward and destroyed
three of the other horns. This was the horn that seemed greater than the others and had
human eyes and a mouth that was boasting arrogantly. 21As I watched, this horn was
waging war against the holy people and was defeating them, 22until the Ancient One
came and judged in favor of the holy people of the Most High. Then the time arrived for
the holy people to take over the kingdom.
23Then he said to me, “This fourth beast is the fourth world power that will rule the
earth. It will be different from all the others. It will devour the whole world, trampling
everything in its path. 24Its ten horns are ten kings that will rule that empire. Then another
king will arise, different from the other ten, who will subdue three of them. 25He will
defy the Most High and wear down the holy people of the Most High. He will try to
change their sacred festivals and laws, and they will be placed under his control for a
time, times, and half a time.
26“But then the court will pass judgment, and all his power will be taken away and
completely destroyed. 27Then the sovereignty, power, and greatness of all the kingdoms
under heaven will be given to the holy people of the Most High. They will rule forever,
and all rulers will serve and obey them.”
28That was the end of the vision. I, Daniel, was terrified by my thoughts and my face
was pale with fear, but I kept these things to myself.

Daniel’s Vision of a Ram and Goat

8 During the third year of King Belshazzar’s reign, I, Daniel, saw another vision,
following the one that had already appeared to me. 2This time I was at the fortress
of Susa, in the province of Elam, standing beside the Ulai River.*
3As I looked up, I saw in front of me a ram with two long horns standing beside the
river.* One of the horns was longer than the other, even though it had begun to grow later
than the shorter one. 4The ram butted everything out of its way to the west, to the north,
and to the south, and no one could stand against it or help its victims. It did as it pleased
and became very great.
5While I was watching, suddenly a male goat appeared from the west, crossing the
land so swiftly that it didn’t even touch the ground. This goat, which had one very large
horn between its eyes, 6headed toward the two-horned ram that I had seen standing

7:18 Isa 60:12-14; Dan 7:22, 25, 27; Rev 2:26-27; 20:4
7:21 Rev 13:7
7:22 Dan 7:10; 1 Cor 6:2-3
7:24 Rev 17:12
7:25 Dan 4:2; 11:36; 12:7, 14; Rev 12:14; 13:6-7; 18:24
7:26 Rev 17:14; 19:2
7:27 Pss 2:6-12; 22:27; 86:9; 145:13; Isa 60:12; Dan 2:44; 4:34; 7:14, 18, 22; Luke 1:33; Rev 11:1, 5; 20:4
8:2 Gen 10:22; 14:1; Esth 1:2; Isa 11:11; Jer 25:25; Dan 7:2, 15
8:3 Dan 8:20
8:4 Deut 33:17; 1 Kgs 22:11; Ezek 34:21
8:5 Dan 8:8, 21; 11:3

8:2 Or *the Ulai Gate;* also in 8:16. **8:3** Or *the gate;* also in 8:6.

7:18 The “holy people of the Most High” are the true Israel, the people ruled by the Messiah. Jesus Christ gave the Kingdom to the new Israel, his church, made up of all faithful believers. His coming ushered in the Kingdom of God, and all believers are its citizens (see also 7:22, 27). Although God may allow persecution to continue for a while, the destiny of his followers is to possess the Kingdom and be with him forever.

7:24 The 10 horns, or 10 kings, are also mentioned in Revelation 17:12. There were also 10 toes in Nebuchadnezzar’s vision (2:41, 42). While all do not agree concerning the identity of these 10 kings, we are reminded in Revelation 17:12-14 that these kings will make war against Christ, but, as the King of kings, he will conquer them. The other king mentioned here in verse 24 is the future man of lawlessness of 2 Thessalonians 2:3, 4.

7:25 While the exact meaning of this “time, times, and half a time” is debated, we do know that God told Daniel that persecution would continue only a relatively short time. God has promised to give his Kingdom to his holy people.

8:1 As with chapter 7, this chapter precedes chapter 5 chronologically; the dream probably occurred in 551 B.C. when Daniel was about 70 years old. Chapters 7 and 8 correspond to the first and third years of Belshazzar and belong chronologically between chapters 4 and 5. Chapter 9 took place at approximately the same time as chapter 6. It gives us more details about the Medo-Persian and Greek Empires, the two world powers that ruled after Babylonia.

8:2 Susa was one of the capitals of the Babylonian Empire. Located in what is now Iran, Susa was a well-developed city. It was the winter capital of the Persian Empire and a mighty fortress (citadel). In his vision, Daniel saw himself in this important location. The earliest known code of law, the Code of Hammurabi, was found there. Susa rivaled Babylon itself in cultural sophistication.

8:3 The two horns were the kings of Media and Persia (8:20). The longer horn represented the growing dominance of Persia in the Medo-Persian Empire.

8:5-7 The goat represented Greece, and its large horn, Alexander the Great (8:21). This is an amazing prediction because Greece was not yet considered a world power when this prophecy was given. Alexander the Great conquered the world with great speed and military strategy, indicated by the goat’s rapid movement. The shattering of both horns symbolized Alexander breaking both parts of the Medo-Persian Empire.

beside the river. 7 The goat charged furiously at the ram and struck it, breaking off both
its horns. Now the ram was helpless, and the goat knocked it down and trampled it. There
was no one who could rescue the ram from the goat's power.
8 The goat became very powerful. But at the height of its power, its large horn was
broken off. In the large horn's place grew four prominent horns pointing in the four
directions of the earth. 9 From one of the prominent horns came a small horn whose
power grew very great. It extended toward the south and the east and toward the
glorious land of Israel. 10 His power reached to the heavens where it attacked the
heavenly armies, throwing some of the heavenly beings and stars to the ground and
trampling them. 11 He even challenged the Commander of heaven's armies by canceling the daily sacrifices offered to him and by destroying his Temple. 12 But the army
of heaven was restrained from destroying him for this sin. As a result, sacrilege was
committed against the Temple ceremonies, and truth was overthrown. The horn
succeeded in everything it did.*
13 Then I heard two of the holy ones talking to each other. One of them said, "How
long will the events of this vision last? How long will the rebellion that causes
desecration stop the daily sacrifices? How long will the Temple and heaven's armies be
trampled on?"
14 The other replied, "It will take twenty-three hundred evenings and mornings; then
the Temple will be restored."

Gabriel Explains the Vision

15 As I, Daniel, was trying to understand the meaning of this vision, someone who
looked like a man suddenly stood in front of me. 16 And I heard a human voice calling
out from the Ulai River, "Gabriel, tell this man the meaning of his vision."
17 As Gabriel approached the place where I was standing, I became so terrified that I
fell to the ground. "Son of man," he said, "you must understand that the events you have
seen in your vision relate to the time of the end."
18 While he was speaking, I fainted and lay there with my face to the ground. But
Gabriel roused me with a touch and helped me to my feet. 19 Then he said, "I am here
to tell you what will happen later in the time of wrath. What you have seen pertains
to the very end of time. 20 The two-horned ram represents the kings of Media and
Persia. 21 The shaggy male goat represents the king of Greece,* and the large horn
between its eyes represents the first king of the Greek Empire. 22 The four prominent
horns that replaced the one large horn show that the Greek Empire will break into four
sections with four kings, none of them as great as the first.
23 "At the end of their rule, when their sin is at its height, a fierce king, a master of
intrigue, will rise to power. 24 He will become very strong, but not by his own power.
He will cause a shocking amount of destruction and succeed in everything he does.

8:8 2 Chr 26:16; Dan 5:20; 7:2; 8:22; Rev 7:1
8:9 Dan 8:23; 11:16, 41
8:10 Jer 48:26, 42; Ezek 46:14; Dan 7:7; 8:7; 11:31; Rev 12:4
8:11 Ezek 46:14; Dan 11:31, 36-37; 12:11
8:12 Isa 59:14
8:13 Pss 74:10; 79:5; Dan 4:13, 23; 12:6, 8; Luke 10:22; 21:24; Heb 10:29; Rev 6:10; 11:2
8:14 Dan 7:25; 12:7, 11; Rev 11:2-3; 12:14; 13:5
8:15 Dan 7:13; 10:16, 18
8:16 Dan 9:21; Luke 1:19, 26
8:17 Ezek 1:28; 6:2; 44:4; Dan 2:46; 8:19; 11:35, 40; Rev 1:17
8:18 Ezek 2:2; Dan 10:9-10, 16, 18; Luke 9:32
8:19 Dan 8:15-17
8:24 Dan 8:11-13; 11:36; 12:7; Rev 13:3-9; 16:6; 17:12-17

8:11-12 The meaning of the Hebrew for these verses is uncertain. **8:21** Hebrew *of Javan.*

8:8 Alexander the Great died in his thirties at the height of his power. His kingdom was split into four parts under four generals: Ptolemy I of Egypt and Palestine; Seleucus of Babylonia and Syria; Lysimachus of Asia Minor; and Antipater of Macedonia and Greece.

8:9 Israel ("the glorious land") was attacked by Antiochus IV Epiphanes (the small horn) in the second century B.C. He was the eighth ruler of the Seleucid Empire (Babylonia and Syria). He overthrew the high priest, looted the Temple, and replaced worship of God with a Greek form of worship. A further fulfillment of this prophecy of a powerful horn will occur in the future with the coming of the Antichrist (see 8:17, 19, 23; 11:36; 2 Thessalonians 2:4).

8:11 The "Commander of heaven's armies" here refers to a heavenly authority, perhaps an angel or even God himself (see also Joshua 5:13-15).

8:14 The phrase "evenings and mornings" means evening and morning sacrifices, and refers to the time from the desecration of the altar in the Temple by Antiochus IV Epiphanes to the restoration of Temple worship under Judas Maccabeus in 165 B.C.

8:16 Gabriel is an angel, the heavenly messenger God used to explain Daniel's visions (9:21). He also announced the birth of John the Baptist (Luke 1:11) and the Messiah (Luke 1:26).

8:17 The "time of the end," in this case, refers to the whole period from the end of the Exile until the second coming of Christ. Many of the events that would happen under Antiochus IV Epiphanes will be repeated on a broader scale just before Christ's second coming. During these times, God deals with Israel in a radically different way, with divine discipline coming through Gentile nations. This period is sometimes referred to as the "age of the Gentiles" (Luke 21:24).

8:23 This fierce king describes both Antiochus IV Epiphanes and the Antichrist at the end of human history.

He will destroy powerful leaders and devastate the holy people. 25 He will be a master
of deception, defeating many by catching them off guard. Without warning he will
destroy them. He will even take on the Prince of princes in battle, but he will be
broken, though not by human power.
26 "This vision about the twenty-three hundred evenings and mornings* is true. But
none of these things will happen for a long time, so do not tell anyone about them yet."
27 Then I, Daniel, was overcome and lay sick for several days. Afterward I got up and
performed my duties for the king, but I was greatly troubled by the vision and could not
understand it.

Daniel's Prayer for His People

9 It was the first year of the reign of Darius the Mede, the son of Ahasuerus, who became
king of the Babylonians.* 2 During the first year of his reign, I, Daniel, was studying
the writings of the prophets. I learned from the word of the LORD, as recorded by Jeremiah
the prophet, that Jerusalem must lie desolate for seventy years.* 3 So I turned to the Lord
God and pleaded with him in prayer and fasting. I wore rough sackcloth and sprinkled
myself with ashes.
4 I prayed to the LORD my God and confessed: "O Lord, you are a great and awesome
God! You always fulfill your promises of unfailing love to those who love you and keep
your commands. 5 But we have sinned and done wrong. We have rebelled against you
and scorned your commands and regulations. 6 We have refused to listen to your servants
the prophets, who spoke your messages to our kings and princes and ancestors and to all
the people of the land.
7 "Lord, you are in the right; but our faces are covered with shame, just as you see
us now. This is true of us all, including the people of Judah and Jerusalem and all
Israel, scattered near and far, wherever you have driven us because of our disloyalty
to you. 8 O LORD, we and our kings, princes, and ancestors are covered with shame
because we have sinned against you. 9 But the Lord our God is merciful and forgiving,
even though we have rebelled against him. 10 We have not obeyed the LORD our God,
for we have not followed the laws he gave us through his servants the prophets. 11 All
Israel has disobeyed your law and turned away, refusing to listen to your voice.

8:25 Job 34:20; Dan 2:34, 45
8:27 Dan 7:28; 8:17; Hab 3:16
9:1 Dan 5:31; 11:1
9:2 2 Chr 36:21; Ezra 1:1; Jer 25:11; 29:10; Zech 7:5
9:4 Deut 7:9, 21; Neh 9:32
9:5 Isa 53:6; Lam 1:18, 20
9:6 2 Chr 36:16; Jer 44:4-5, 21
9:7 Ezra 9:6-7; Jer 2:26-27; 3:25; 23:6; 33:16
9:9 Neh 9:17; Pss 106:43; 130:4
9:10 2 Kgs 17:13-15; 18:12
9:11 Isa 1:2-4; Jer 8:5-10

8:26 Hebrew *about the evenings and mornings;* compare 8:14. **9:1** Or *the Chaldeans.* **9:2** See Jer 25:11-12; 29:10.

8:25 This Prince of princes is God himself. No human power could defeat the king whom Daniel saw in his vision, but God would bring him down. Antiochus IV Epiphanes reportedly went insane and died in Persia in 164 B.C. God's power and justice will prevail, so we should never give up our faith or lose hope, no matter how powerful God's enemies may seem.

9:1 The vision in chapter 9 was given to Daniel during the same time period of chapter 6. This Darius is the person mentioned in chapter 6. The Ahasuerus (or Xerxes) mentioned here is not Esther's husband. The events described in the book of Esther happened about 50 years later.

9:2, 3 Daniel pleaded with God to bring about the promised return of his people to their land. The prophet Jeremiah had written that God would not allow the captives to return to their land for 70 years (Jeremiah 25:11, 12; 29:10). Daniel knew of this prophecy and realized that this 70-year period was coming to an end.

9:3ff In Daniel's prayer for the nation he confessed his own sin, using the pronoun *we* throughout. In times of adversity, it's easy to blame others and excuse our own actions. If any Israelite was righteous, it was Daniel; and yet he confessed his sinfulness and need for God's forgiveness. Instead of looking for others to blame, first examine yourself and confess your own sins to God.

9:3-19 Daniel knew how to pray. As he prayed, he fasted, confessed his sins, and pleaded that God would reveal his will. He prayed with complete surrender to God and with complete openness to what God was saying to him. When you pray, do you speak openly to God? Examine your attitude. Talk to God with openness, vulnerability, and honesty, and be ready for God's reply.

9:4-6 The captives from Judah had rebelled against God. Their sins had led to their captivity. But God is merciful even to rebels if they confess their sins and return to him. Don't let your past disobedience keep you from returning to God. He is waiting for you and wants you to return to him.

9:6 God had sent many prophets to speak to his people through the years, but their messages had been ignored. The truth was too painful to hear. God still speaks clearly and accurately through the Bible, and he also speaks through preachers, teachers, and concerned friends. Sometimes the truth hurts, and we would rather hear words that soothe, even if they are false. If you are unwilling to accept God's message, maybe you are trying to avoid making a painful change. Don't settle for a soothing lie that will bring harsh judgment. Accepting the truth even if it is painful can only help you.

9:11-13 Daniel mentioned the curses outlined in Deuteronomy 28. God had given the people of Israel a choice: Obey me and receive blessings, or disobey me and face curses. The affliction was meant to turn the people to God. When we face difficult circumstances, we should ask ourselves if God has reason to send judgment. If we think so, we must seek his forgiveness. Then we can ask him to help us through our troubles.

9:12 Isa 44:26 Jer 44:2-6 Ezek 5:9 Zech 1:6
9:13 Lev 26:14-45 Deut 28:15-68 Isa 9:13 Jer 2:30; 5:3
9:14 Jer 31:28; 44:27
9:15 Deut 5:15 Neh 9:10 Jer 32:20
9:16 Ps 87:1-3 Ezek 5:14 Joel 3:17 Zech 8:3
9:17 Num 6:24-26 Ps 80:3, 7, 19 Lam 5:18
9:18 Ps 80:14 Isa 37:17 Jer 7:12; 36:7
9:19 Pss 44:23; 74:10-11
9:20 Ps 145:18 Isa 6:5; 58:9
9:21 Exod 29:39 1 Kgs 18:36 Ezra 9:4
9:22 Zech 1:9, 14
9:23 Matt 24:15
9:24 Lev 25:8 Num 14:34 2 Chr 29:24 Isa 51:6, 8; 53:10 Rom 3:21; 5:10
9:25 Isa 9:6 John 1:41; 4:25

"So now the solemn curses and judgments written in the law of Moses, the servant
of God, have been poured out against us because of our sin. 12 You have done exactly
what you warned you would do against us and our rulers. Never in all history has there
been a disaster like the one that happened in Jerusalem. 13 Every curse written against
us in the law of Moses has come true. All the troubles he predicted have taken place.
But we have refused to seek mercy from the LORD our God by turning from our sins
and recognizing his truth. 14 The LORD has brought against us the disaster he prepared,
for we did not obey him, and the LORD our God is just in everything he does.
15 "O Lord our God, you brought lasting honor to your name by rescuing your
people from Egypt in a great display of power. But we have sinned and are full of
wickedness. 16 In view of all your faithful mercies, Lord, please turn your furious
anger away from your city of Jerusalem, your holy mountain. All the neighboring
nations mock Jerusalem and your people because of our sins and the sins of our
ancestors.
17 "O our God, hear your servant's prayer! Listen as I plead. For your own sake, Lord,
smile again on your desolate sanctuary.
18 "O my God, listen to me and hear my request. Open your eyes and see our wretched-
ness. See how your city lies in ruins—for everyone knows that it is yours. We do not ask
because we deserve help, but because you are so merciful.
19 "O Lord, hear. O Lord, forgive. O Lord, listen and act! For your own sake, O my
God, do not delay, for your people and your city bear your name."

Gabriel's Message about the Exile

20 I went on praying and confessing my sin and the sins of my people, pleading with the
LORD my God for Jerusalem, his holy mountain. 21 As I was praying, Gabriel, whom I
had seen in the earlier vision, came swiftly to me at the time of the evening sacrifice.
22 He explained to me, "Daniel, I have come here to give you insight and understanding.
23 The moment you began praying, a command was given. I am here to tell you what it
was, for God loves you very much. Now listen, so you can understand the meaning of
your vision.
24 "A period of seventy sets of seven* has been decreed for your people and your
holy city to put down rebellion, to bring an end to sin, to atone for guilt, to bring in
everlasting righteousness, to confirm the prophetic vision, and to anoint the Most
Holy Place.* 25 Now listen and understand! Seven sets of seven plus sixty-two sets of
seven* will pass from the time the command is given to rebuild Jerusalem until the
Anointed One* comes. Jerusalem will be rebuilt with streets and strong defenses,*
despite the perilous times.

9:24a Hebrew *70 sevens.* **9:24b** Or *the Most Holy One.* **9:25a** Hebrew *Seven sevens plus 62 sevens.* **9:25b** Or *an anointed one.* **9:25c** Or *and a moat,* or *and trenches.*

9:14 Daniel spoke about how God continually tried to bring Israel back to himself. Yet even after disaster struck them, they refused to obey him. God still uses circumstances, other people, and, most important, his Word to bring his people back to him. What would it take for God to get your attention?

9:17-19 It would be a mistake to read the Bible as dry history and miss the deep personal feelings. In this section, Daniel was crying out to the Lord. He had a deep concern for his nation and his people. So often our prayers are without passion and true compassion for others. Are you willing to pray by pouring out your deep feelings to God?

9:18 Daniel begged for mercy, not for help, because he knew that his people deserved God's wrath and punishment. God sends his help, not because we deserve it, but because he wants to show great mercy. If God would refuse to help us because of our sin, how could we complain? But when he sends mercy instead of the punishment we deserve, how can we withhold our praise and thanksgiving?

9:23 Just as God answered Daniel's prayer, so we can have confidence that God hears and answers our prayers.

9:24, 25 Each day of these 70 weeks ("seventy sets of seven") may represent one year. The Bible often uses round numbers to make a point, not to give an exact count. For example, Jesus said we are to forgive others "seventy times seven" (Matthew 18:22). He did not mean a literal 77 times only, but that we should be abundantly forgiving. Similarly, some scholars see this figure of 70 weeks as a figurative time period. Others, however, interpret this time period as a literal 70 weeks or 490 years, observing that Christ's death came at the end of the 69 weeks (i.e., 483 years later). One interpretation places the 70th week as the seven years of the great tribulation, still in the future. Consequently the number would symbolize both the first and second comings of Christ.

9:25 These "strong defenses" show that Jerusalem will be rebuilt as a complete, fully functioning city.

26 "After this period of sixty-two sets of seven,* the Anointed One will be killed,
appearing to have accomplished nothing, and a ruler will arise whose armies will
destroy the city and the Temple. The end will come with a flood, and war and its
miseries are decreed from that time to the very end. 27 He will make a treaty with the
people for a period of one set of seven,* but after half this time, he will put an end to
the sacrifices and offerings. Then as a climax to all his terrible deeds,* he will set up
a sacrilegious object that causes desecration,* until the end that has been decreed is
poured out on this defiler."

Daniel's Vision of a Messenger

10 In the third year of the reign of King Cyrus of Persia, Daniel (also known as
Belteshazzar) had another vision. It concerned events certain to happen in the
future—times of war and great hardship—and Daniel understood what the vision
meant.
2 When this vision came to me, I, Daniel, had been in mourning for three weeks.
3 All that time I had eaten no rich food or meat, had drunk no wine, and had used no
fragrant oils. 4 On April 23,* as I was standing beside the great Tigris River, 5 I looked
up and saw a man dressed in linen clothing, with a belt of pure gold around his waist.
6 His body looked like a dazzling gem. From his face came flashes like lightning, and
his eyes were like flaming torches. His arms and feet shone like polished bronze, and
his voice was like the roaring of a vast multitude of people.
7 I, Daniel, am the only one who saw this vision. The men with me saw nothing, but
they were suddenly terrified and ran away to hide. 8 So I was left there all alone to
watch this amazing vision. My strength left me, my face grew deathly pale, and I felt
very weak. 9 When I heard him speak, I fainted and lay there with my face to the
ground.
10 Just then a hand touched me and lifted me, still trembling, to my hands and knees.
11 And the man said to me, "O Daniel, greatly loved of God, listen carefully to what I
have to say to you. Stand up, for I have been sent to you." When he said this to me, I
stood up, still trembling with fear.
12 Then he said, "Don't be afraid, Daniel. Since the first day you began to pray for
understanding and to humble yourself before your God, your request has been heard in
heaven. I have come in answer to your prayer. 13 But for twenty-one days the spirit
prince* of the kingdom of Persia blocked my way. Then Michael, one of the archangels,*
came to help me, and I left him there with the spirit prince of the kingdom of Persia.*
14 Now I am here to explain what will happen to your people in the future, for this vision
concerns a time yet to come."

9:26 Isa 53:8; Matt 24:2; Mark 9:12; 13:2; Luke 19:43-44; 24:26
9:27 Isa 10:23; 28:22; †Matt 24:15; †Mark 13:14; †Luke 21:20
10:1 Dan 1:17, 21; 2:21; 6:28
10:2 Ezra 9:4-5; Neh 1:4
10:4 Ezek 1:3; Dan 8:2
10:5 Jer 10:9; Ezek 9:2; Dan 12:6-7; Rev 1:13; 15:6
10:6 Rev 1:14; 2:18
10:7 2 Kgs 6:17; Ezek 12:18; Acts 9:7
10:8 Gen 32:34; Dan 7:28; 8:27; Hab 3:16
10:9 Gen 15:12; Dan 8:18
10:10 Jer 1:9
10:11 Job 4:14-15; Ezek 2:1; Dan 8:16-17
10:12 Dan 9:20-23; 10:2-3, 19
10:13 Dan 10:21; 12:1; Jude 1:9; Rev 12:7
10:14 Dan 2:28; 8:26; 12:4, 9

9:26 Hebrew *After 62 sevens.* **9:27a** Hebrew *for one seven.* **9:27b** Hebrew *on the wing of abominations;* the meaning of the Hebrew is uncertain. **9:27c** Hebrew *an abomination of desolation.* **10:4** Hebrew *On the twenty-fourth day of the first month.* This date in the book of Daniel can be cross-checked with dates in surviving Persian records and can be related accurately to our modern calendar. This day of the Hebrew lunar calendar occurred on April 23, 536 B.C. **10:13a** Hebrew *the prince;* also in 10:13c, 20. **10:13b** Hebrew *the chief princes.* **10:13c** As in one Greek version; Hebrew reads *and I was left there with the kings of Persia.* The meaning of the Hebrew is uncertain.

9:26 The Messiah, the Anointed One, will be rejected and killed by his own people. His perfect eternal Kingdom will come later.

9:26, 27 There has been much discussion on the numbers, times, and events in these verses, and there are three basic views: (1) The prophecy was fulfilled in the past at the desecration of the Temple by Antiochus IV Epiphanes from 168 to 167 B.C. (see 11:31); (2) it was fulfilled in the past at the destruction of the Temple by the Roman general Titus in A.D. 70 when one million Jews were killed; or (3) it is still to be fulfilled in the future under the Antichrist (see Matthew 24:15).

10:1ff This is Daniel's final vision (536 B.C.). In it, he was given further insight into the great spiritual battle between God's people and those who want to destroy them. There is also more detailed information on the future, specifically the struggles between the Ptolemies (kings of the south) and the Seleucids (kings of the north).

10:1ff Prior to this vision, Cyrus allowed the Jews to return to Jerusalem, but Daniel stayed in Babylon. Why didn't Daniel return to Jerusalem? He may have been too old to make the long, hazardous journey (he was over 80); his government duties could have prevented him; or God may have told him to stay behind to complete the work he was called to do.

10:3 Daniel refrained from eating choice foods and using oils because these were signs of feasting and rejoicing.

10:5, 6 The man seen by Daniel was a heavenly being. Some commentators believe that this was an appearance of Christ (see Revelation 1:13-15), while others think it was an angel (because he required Michael's help—10:13). In either case, Daniel caught a glimpse of the battle between good and evil supernatural powers.

10:15 Ezek 24:27; Luke 1:20
10:16 Jer 1:9; Dan 7:15; 8:15
10:17 Exod 24:10-11; Isa 6:1-5
10:18 Isa 35:3-4
10:19 Josh 1:6-9; Judg 6:23; Isa 35:4; 43:1; Dan 10:12
10:20 Dan 8:21; 11:2
10:21 Dan 12:1, 4

15 While he was speaking to me, I looked down at the ground, unable to say a word.
16 Then the one who looked like a man* touched my lips, and I opened my mouth and
began to speak. I said to the one standing in front of me, "I am terrified by the vision
I have seen, my lord, and I am very weak. 17 How can someone like me, your servant,
talk to you, my lord? My strength is gone, and I can hardly breathe."
18 Then the one who looked like a man touched me again, and I felt my strength
returning. 19 "Don't be afraid," he said, "for you are deeply loved by God. Be at peace;
take heart and be strong!"
As he spoke these words, I suddenly felt stronger and said to him, "Now you may
speak, my lord, for you have strengthened me."
20 He replied, "Do you know why I have come? Soon I must return to fight against the
spirit prince of the kingdom of Persia, and then against the spirit prince of the kingdom
of Greece.* 21 But before I do that, I will tell you what is written in the Book of Truth.
(There is no one to help me against these spirit princes except Michael, your spirit
prince.* 1 I have been standing beside Michael* as his support and defense since the first
year of the reign of Darius the Mede.)

Kings of the South and North

11:1 Dan 5:31; 9:1
11:2 Dan 8:21, 26; 10:1, 20-21
11:3 Dan 5:19; 8:4-5, 21; 11:16, 36
11:4 Jer 49:36; Ezek 37:9; Dan 7:2; 8:8; Zech 2:6; Rev 7:1
11:5 Dan 11:9, 11, 14, 25, 40

11 2 "Now then, I will reveal the truth to you. Three more Persian kings will reign, to
be succeeded by a fourth, far richer than the others. Using his wealth for political
advantage, he will stir up everyone to war against the kingdom of Greece.*
3 "Then a mighty king will rise to power who will rule a vast kingdom and accomplish
everything he sets out to do. 4 But at the height of his power, his kingdom will be broken
apart and divided into four parts. It will not be ruled by the king's descendants, nor will
the kingdom hold the authority it once had. For his empire will be uprooted and given to
others.
5 "The king of the south will increase in power, but one of this king's own officials
will become more powerful than he and will rule his kingdom with great strength.

10:16 As in most manuscripts of the Masoretic Text; one manuscript of the Masoretic Text and one Greek version read *Then something that looked like a human hand.* **10:20** Hebrew *of Javan.* **10:21** Hebrew *against these except Michael, your prince.* **11:1** Hebrew *him.* **11:2** Hebrew *of Javan.*

10:10-18 Daniel was frightened by this vision, but the messenger reassured him. Daniel lost his speech, but the messenger's touch restored it. Daniel felt weak and helpless, but the messenger's words strengthened him. God can bring us healing when we are hurt, peace when we are troubled, and strength when we are weak. Trust God to minister to you as he did to Daniel.

10:12, 13 Although God sent a messenger to Daniel, a powerful spiritual being ("the spirit prince of the kingdom of Persia") detained the messenger for three weeks. Daniel faithfully continued praying and fasting, and God's messenger eventually arrived, assisted by Michael, the archangel. Answers to our prayers may be hindered by unseen obstacles. Don't expect God's answers to come too easily or too quickly. Prayer may be challenged by evil forces, so pray fervently and pray earnestly. Then expect God to answer at the right time.

10:20, 21 The heavenly warfare was to be directed against Persia and then Greece. Each of these nations was to have power over God's people. Both Persia and Greece were represented by evil "spirit princes," or demons. But God is in control of the past, present, and future, and he has all events recorded in his "Book of Truth."

11:2 The angelic messenger was revealing Israel's future (see 10:20, 21). Only God can reveal future events so clearly. God's work not only deals with the sweeping panorama of history but also focuses on the intricate details of people's lives. And his plans—whether for nations or individuals—are unshakable.

11:2 The fourth Persian king may have been Xerxes I (also called Ahasuerus, 486–465 B.C.), who launched an all-out effort against Greece in 480 (Esther 1:1).

11:2ff Babylon was defeated by Medo-Persia. Medo-Persia was defeated by Greece under Alexander the Great, who conquered most of the Mediterranean and Middle Eastern lands. After Alexander's death, the empire was divided into four parts. The Ptolemies gained control of the southern section of Palestine, and the Seleucids took the northern part. Verses 2-20 show the conflict between the Ptolemies and Seleucids over control of Palestine in 300–200 B.C. Verses 21-35 describe the persecution of Israel under Antiochus IV Epiphanes. In verses 36-45 the prophecy shifts to the end times. Antiochus IV fades from view, and the Antichrist of the last days becomes the center of attention.

11:3 This mighty king of Greece was Alexander the Great, who conquered Medo-Persia and built a huge empire in only four years.

11:4, 5 Eventually Alexander the Great's empire was divided into four nations. These four weaker nations were comprised of the following regions: (1) Egypt, (2) Babylonia and Syria, (3) Asia Minor, and (4) Macedonia and Greece. The king of Egypt ("the king of the south") was Ptolemy I or perhaps a reference to the Ptolemaic dynasty in general.

6“Some years later, an alliance will be formed between the king of the north and the king of the south. The daughter of the king of the south will be given in marriage to the king of the north to secure the alliance, but she will lose her influence over him, and so will her father. She will be given up along with her supporters. 7But when one of her relatives* becomes king of the south, he will raise an army and enter the fortress of the king of the north and defeat him. 8When he returns again to Egypt, he will carry back their idols with him, along with priceless gold and silver dishes. For some years afterward he will leave the king of the north alone.

9“Later the king of the north will invade the realm of the king of the south but will soon return to his own land. 10However, the sons of the king of the north will assemble a mighty army that will advance like a flood and carry the battle as far as the enemy's fortress. 11Then the king of the south, in great anger, will rally against the vast forces assembled by the king of the north and will defeat them. 12After the enemy army is swept away, the king of the south will be filled with pride and will have many thousands of his enemies killed. But his success will be short lived.

13“A few years later, the king of the north will return with a fully equipped army far greater than the one he lost. 14At that time there will be a general uprising against the king of the south. Lawless ones among your own people will join them in order to fulfill the vision, but they will not succeed. 15Then the king of the north will come and lay siege to a fortified city and capture it. The best troops of the south will not be able to stand in the face of the onslaught.

16“The king of the north will march onward unopposed; none will be able to stop him. He will pause in the glorious land of Israel, intent on destroying it. 17He will make plans to come with the might of his entire kingdom and will form an alliance with the king of the south. He will give him a daughter in marriage in order to overthrow the kingdom from within, but his plan will fail.

18“After this, he will turn his attention to the coastal cities and conquer many. But a commander from another land will put an end to his insolence and will cause him to retreat in shame. 19He will take refuge in his own fortresses but will stumble and fall, and he will be seen no more.

20“His successor will be remembered as the king who sent a tax collector to maintain the royal splendor, but after a very brief reign, he will die, though neither in battle nor open conflict.

21“The next to come to power will be a despicable man who is not directly in line for royal succession. But he will slip in when least expected and take over the kingdom by flattery and intrigue. 22Before him great armies will be swept away, including a covenant prince. 23By making deceitful promises, he will make various alliances. With a mere handful of followers, he will become strong. 24Without warning he will enter the richest areas of the land and do something that none of his predecessors ever did—distribute among his followers the plunder and wealth of the rich. He will plot the overthrow of strongholds, but this will last for only a short while.

25“Then he will stir up his courage and raise a great army against the king of the

11:6 Dan 11:7, 13, 15, 40
11:7 Dan 11:19, 38-39
11:8 Isa 37:19; 46:1-2 Jer 43:12-13
11:10 Isa 8:8 Jer 46:7-8; 51:42 Dan 11:26, 40
11:13 Dan 4:16; 12:7
11:15 Jer 6:6 Ezek 4:2; 17:17
11:16 Josh 1:5 Dan 5:19; 8:9; 11:3, 36, 41
11:17 2 Kgs 12:17 Ezek 4:3, 7
11:18 Gen 10:5 Isa 66:19 Hos 12:14 Zeph 2:11
11:19 Pss 27:2; 37:36 Jer 46:6 Ezek 26:21
11:20 Isa 60:17
11:24 Num 13:20 Neh 9:25 Ezek 34:14

11:7 Hebrew *a branch from her roots.*

11:6, 7 These prophecies seem to have been fulfilled many years later in the Seleucid wars between Egypt and Syria. In 252 B.C., Ptolemy II of Egypt ("the south") gave his daughter Berenice in marriage to Antiochus II of Syria ("the north") to finalize a peace treaty between their two lands. But Berenice was murdered in Antioch by Antiochus II's former wife, Laodice. Berenice's brother, Ptolemy III, ascended the Egyptian throne and declared war against the Seleucids to avenge his sister's murder.

11:9-11 The king of Syria ("the north") was Seleucus II, and the king of Egypt ("the south") was Ptolemy IV.

11:13 This king of the north may have been Antiochus III (the Great). He defeated many Egyptian cities (11:15) and established himself in Israel ("the glorious Land," 11:16). He was later defeated by the Romans at Magnesia (11:18).

11:17 The invader, Antiochus III, tried to bring peace between Egypt and Syria by having his daughter marry Ptolemy V Epiphanes of Egypt, but the plan failed.

11:20 The successor to Antiochus III was Seleucus IV. He sent Heliodorus to collect money from the Temple treasury in Jerusalem.

11:21 Seleucus IV was succeeded by his brother, Antiochus IV Epiphanes, who found favor with the Romans.

11:22 The "great armies" refer to the way all opposition against Antiochus IV will be broken. The covenant prince may be the high priest Onias III, who was assassinated by Menelaus in 170 B.C.

11:27 Pss 52:1; 64:6 Jer 9:3-5 Dan 11:35, 40 Hab 2:3 Acts 17:31

11:30 Gen 10:4 Num 24:24 Jer 2:10

11:31 Dan 8:11-13; 9:27; 12:11 Matt 24:15 Mark 13:14

11:32 Dan 11:21, 34 Mic 5:7-9 Zech 9:13-16; 10:3-6

11:33 Matt 24:9 John 16:2 Heb 11:36-38

11:34 Dan 11:21, 32 Matt 7:15 Rom 16:18

11:35 Deut 8:16 Prov 17:3 Dan 12:10 Zech 13:9 John 15:2

11:36 Deut 10:17 Ps 136:2 Isa 10:25; 14:13; 26:20 Dan 2:47; 5:20; 7:8, 11; 8:11; 9:27; 11:3 2 Thes 2:4 Rev 13:5-6

south. The king of the south will go to battle with a mighty army, but to no avail, for
plots against him will succeed. 26 Those of his own household will bring his downfall.
His army will be swept away, and many will be killed. 27 Seeking nothing but each
other's harm, these kings will plot against each other at the conference table, attempting to deceive each other. But it will make no difference, for an end will still come at
the appointed time.
28 "The king of the north will then return home with great riches. On the way he will
set himself against the people of the holy covenant, doing much damage before continuing his journey.
29 "Then at the appointed time he will once again invade the south, but this time the
result will be different. 30 For warships from western coastlands* will scare him off, and
he will withdraw and return home. But he will vent his anger against the people of the
holy covenant and reward those who forsake the covenant. 31 His army will take over the
Temple fortress, polluting the sanctuary, putting a stop to the daily sacrifices, and setting
up the sacrilegious object that causes desecration.* 32 He will flatter those who have
violated the covenant and win them over to his side. But the people who know their God
will be strong and will resist him.
33 "Those who are wise will give instruction to many. But for a time many of these
teachers will die by fire and sword, or they will be jailed and robbed. 34 While all these
persecutions are going on, a little help will arrive, though many who join them will not
be sincere. 35 And some who are wise will fall victim to persecution. In this way, they
will be refined and cleansed and made pure until the time of the end, for the appointed
time is still to come.
36 "The king will do as he pleases, exalting himself and claiming to be greater than
every god there is, even blaspheming the God of gods. He will succeed—until the time
of wrath is completed. For what has been determined will surely take place. 37 He will
have no regard for the gods of his ancestors, or for the god beloved of women, or for
any other god, for he will boast that he is greater than them all. 38 Instead of these, he
will worship the god of fortresses—a god his ancestors never knew—and lavish on
him gold, silver, precious stones, and costly gifts. 39 Claiming this foreign god's help,
he will attack the strongest fortresses. He will honor those who submit to him,

11:30 Hebrew *from Kittim.* **11:31** Hebrew *the abomination of desolation.*

11:27 These two treacherous kings were probably Antiochus IV of Syria and Ptolemy VI of Egypt. Treachery and deceit are a power broker's way to position himself over someone else. When two power brokers try to gain the upper hand, it is a mutually weakening and self-destructive process. It is also futile because God ultimately holds all power in his hands.

11:29-31 Antiochus IV would again invade "the south," but enemy ships would cause him to retreat. On his way back, he plundered Jerusalem, desecrated the Temple, and stopped the Jews' daily sacrifices. The Temple was desecrated when he sacrificed pigs on an altar erected in honor of Zeus. According to Jewish law, pigs were unclean and were not to be touched or eaten. To sacrifice a pig in the Temple was the worst kind of insult an enemy could level against the Jews. This happened from 168 to 167 B.C.

11:32 This reference to those who have violated the covenant may include Menelaus, the high priest, who was won over by Antiochus and who conspired with him against the Jews who were loyal to God. The "people who know their God" may refer to the Maccabees and their sympathizers, but a further fulfillment may lie in the future.

11:33, 34 Those who are wise will teach many, but they will also face great persecution. Difficult times show up our weaknesses and our inability to cope. We want answers, leadership, and clear direction. During these times, God's Word begins to interest even those who would never look at it otherwise. We should look for opportunities to share God's Word in hard times. We must also be prepared to face persecution and rejection as we teach and preach.

11:35 God's messenger described a time of trial when even wise believers would fall victim to persecution. If we persevere in our faith, any such experience will only refine us and make us stronger. Are you facing trials? Recognize them as opportunities to strengthen your faith. If you remain steadfast in these experiences, you will be stronger in your faith and closer to God.

11:36-39 These verses could refer to Antiochus IV Epiphanes, Titus (the Roman general), or the Antichrist. Some of these events may have been fulfilled in the past, and some have yet to be fulfilled.

11:37 The "god beloved of women" may refer to Tammuz, a Babylonian fertility god. Tammuz is also mentioned in Ezekiel 8:14. In other words, this person won't recognize any deity or religions at all, not even pagan ones. Instead, he will proclaim himself to be divine and the ultimate power.

11:38 The "god of fortresses" is believed by some to be Jupiter or Zeus. The implication is that this king will make *war* his god. More than all his predecessors, he will wage war and glorify its horrors.

appointing them to positions of authority and dividing the land among them as their
reward.*
40 “Then at the time of the end, the king of the south will attack him, and the king
of the north will storm out against him with chariots, cavalry, and a vast navy. He will
invade various lands and sweep through them like a flood. 41 He will enter the glorious
land of Israel, and many nations will fall, but Moab, Edom, and the best part of
Ammon will escape. 42 He will conquer many countries, and Egypt will not escape.
43 He will gain control over the gold, silver, and treasures of Egypt, and the Libyans
and Ethiopians* will be his servants.
44 “But then news from the east and the north will alarm him, and he will set out in
great anger to destroy many as he goes. 45 He will halt between the glorious holy
mountain and the sea and will pitch his royal tents there, but while he is there, his time
will suddenly run out, and there will be no one to help him.

The Time of the End

12 “At that time Michael, the archangel* who stands guard over your nation, will
arise. Then there will be a time of anguish greater than any since nations first
came into existence. But at that time every one of your people whose name is written
in the book will be rescued. 2 Many of those whose bodies lie dead and buried will
rise up, some to everlasting life and some to shame and everlasting contempt.
3 Those who are wise will shine as bright as the sky, and those who turn many to
righteousness will shine like stars forever. 4 But you, Daniel, keep this prophecy a
secret; seal up the book until the time of the end. Many will rush here and there, and
knowledge will increase.”
5 Then I, Daniel, looked and saw two others standing on opposite banks of the river.
6 One of them asked the man dressed in linen, who was now standing above the river,
“How long will it be until these shocking events happen?”
7 The man dressed in linen, who was standing above the river, raised both his hands
toward heaven and took this solemn oath by the one who lives forever: “It will go on for
a time, times, and half a time. When the shattering of the holy people has finally come
to an end, all these things will have happened.”
8 I heard what he said, but I did not understand what he meant. So I asked, “How will
all this finally end, my lord?”
9 But he said, “Go now, Daniel, for what I have said is for the time of the end. 10 Many
will be purified, cleansed, and refined by these trials. But the wicked will continue in

11:39 Or *at a price.* **11:43** Hebrew *Cushites.* **12:1** Hebrew *the great prince.*

11:40 Isa 5:28; Jer 4:13; Dan 11:27, 35; 12:4, 9
11:41 Jer 48:47; 49:6
11:43 2 Chr 12:3; Ezek 30:4-5; Nah 3:9
11:45 Isa 65:25; 66:20; Dan 9:16, 20
12:1 Jer 30:7; Ezek 5:9; Matt 24:21; Mark 13:19; Rev 16:18
12:2 Isa 26:19; Ezek 37:12-14; Matt 25:46; John 5:28-29
12:3 Isa 53:11; John 5:35
12:4 Isa 8:16; 11:9; Rev 22:10
12:6 Ezek 9:2; Zech 1:12-13; Matt 24:3; Mark 13:4
12:7 Ezek 20:5; Luke 21:24; Rev 10:5-7; 12:14
12:10 Isa 32:6-7; Rev 22:11

11:40 The Antichrist of the last days becomes the center of attention from this point through the rest of the book of Daniel.

11:45 “The glorious holy mountain” is Mount Zion or the city of Jerusalem.

12:1 Great suffering is in store for God’s people throughout the years ahead. This way of describing the future is also used by Jeremiah (Jeremiah 30:7) and Jesus (Matthew 24:21ff). Yet the great suffering is tempered by a great promise of hope for true believers.

12:2 This is a clear reference to the resurrection of both the righteous and the wicked, although the eternal destiny of each will be quite different. Up to this point in time, teaching about the resurrection was not common, although every Israelite believed that one day he or she would be included in the restoration of the new Kingdom. This reference to a bodily resurrection of both the saved and the lost was a sharp departure from common belief. (See also Job 19:25, 26; Psalm 16:10; and Isaiah 26:19 for other Old Testament references to the resurrection.)

12:3 Many people try to be stars in the world of entertainment, only to find their stardom temporary. God tells us how we can be eternal “stars”—by being wise and leading many to God’s righteousness. If we share our Lord with others, we can be true stars—radiantly beautiful in God’s sight!

12:4 Closing and sealing up the book meant that it was to be kept safe and preserved. This was to be done so that believers of all times could look back on God’s work in history and find hope. Daniel did not understand the exact meaning of the times and events in his vision. We can see events as they unfold, for we are in the end times. The whole book will not be understood until the climax of earth’s history.

12:7 “Time, times, and half a time” may add up to 3½ years and may be taken as either literal or figurative.

12:7 “The holy people” seem to be shattered again and again throughout history. God’s recurring purpose in this is to break the pride and self-sufficiency of his rebellious people and to bring them to accept him as their Lord.

12:10 Trials and persecutions make very little sense to us when we experience them. But they can purify us if we are willing to learn from them. After you come through a difficult time, seek to learn from it so that it can help you in the future. See Romans 5:3-5 for more on God’s purpose in our sufferings.

12:11 Dan 9:27; 11:31 Matt 24:15 Mark 13:14

12:12 Isa 30:18 Dan 8:14 Rev 11:2; 12:6; 13:5

12:13 Ps 16:5 Rev 14:13

their wickedness, and none of them will understand. Only those who are wise will know
what it means.
11 "From the time the daily sacrifice is taken away and the sacrilegious object that
causes desecration* is set up to be worshiped, there will be 1,290 days. 12 And blessed
are those who wait and remain until the end of the 1,335 days!
13 "As for you, go your way until the end. You will rest, and then at the end of the days,
you will rise again to receive the inheritance set aside for you."

12:11 Hebrew *the abomination of desolation.*

12:11 "The sacrilegious object that causes desecration" set up in the Temple refers to the altar of Zeus, where Antiochus IV Epiphanes sacrificed a pig. Some think it will have another fulfillment in the Antichrist and one of his horrible acts of evil (Matthew 24:15). However, this and the predictions at the early part of the chapter may refer specifically to Antiochus IV Epiphanes, and the rest of the prophecy may refer to the end times.

12:11, 12 Either these are further calculations relating to the persecution of the Jews under Antiochus IV Epiphanes, or they refer to the end times. The abolishing of the daily sacrifices means the removal of worship of the true God, as well as oppression of believers. There is much speculation about these numbers in verses 11 and 12. The point is that this time of persecution has an end; God is in control of it, and he will be victorious over evil.

12:13 The promise of resurrection was reaffirmed to Daniel. He would one day see the fulfillment of his words, but he was not to spend the rest of his life wondering what his visions might mean. Instead, he was to rest in the comfort of God's sovereignty and look forward to the time when he would rise to receive and share eternal life with God. God does not reveal everything to us in this life. We must be content with the partial picture until he wants us to see more. He will tell us all we need to know.

12:13 Daniel stands tall in the gallery of God's remarkable servants. Born of royal heritage, yet taken into captivity when only a teenager, Daniel determined to remain faithful to God in the land of his captivity. Even at great personal cost, Daniel spent his entire lifetime advising his captors with unusual wisdom. God chose him as his servant to record some of the events of the captivity and some significant events concerning the future. As an old man, having been faithful to God throughout his years, Daniel was assured by God that he would rise from the dead and receive his portion in God's eternal Kingdom. Faithfulness to God has a rich reward, not necessarily in this life, but most certainly in the life to come.

HOSEA

Jeroboam II becomes king of Israel 793 B.C.

Amos becomes a prophet 760

VITAL STATISTICS

PURPOSE:
To illustrate God's love for his sinful people

AUTHOR:
Hosea son of Beeri ("Hosea" means "salvation")

TO WHOM WRITTEN:
Israel (the northern kingdom) and God's people everywhere

DATE WRITTEN:
Approximately 715 B.C., recording events from about 753–715 B.C.

SETTING:
Hosea began his ministry during the end of the prosperous but morally declining reign of Jeroboam II of Israel (the upper classes were doing well, but they were oppressing the poor). He prophesied until shortly after the fall of Samaria in 722 B.C.

KEY VERSE:
"Then the LORD said to me, 'Go and get your wife again. Bring her back to you and love her, even though she loves adultery. For the LORD still loves Israel even though the people have turned to other gods, offering them choice gifts'" (3:1).

KEY PEOPLE:
Hosea, Gomer, their children

KEY PLACES:
The northern kingdom (Israel), Samaria, Ephraim

SPECIAL FEATURES:
Hosea employs many images from daily life: God is depicted as husband, father, lion, leopard, bear, dew, rain, moth, and others; Israel is pictured as wife, sick person, vine, grapes, early fruit, olive tree, woman in childbirth, oven, morning mist, chaff, and smoke, to name a few.

GROOMSMEN stand at attention as the music swells and the bride begins her long walk down the aisle, arm in arm with her father. The smiling, but nervous, husband-to-be follows every step, his eyes brimming with love. Then happy tears are shed, vows stated, and families merged. A wedding is a joyous celebration of love. It is the holy mystery of two becoming one, of beginning life together, and of commitment. Marriage is ordained by God and illustrates his relationship with his people. Thus, there is perhaps no greater tragedy than the violation of those sacred vows.

God told Hosea to find a wife and revealed to him ahead of time that she would be unfaithful to him. Although she would bear many children, some of these offspring would be fathered by others. In obedience to God, Hosea married Gomer. His relationship with her, her adultery, and their children became living, prophetic examples to Israel.

The book of Hosea is a love story—real, tragic, and true. Transcending the tale of young man and wife, it tells of God's love for his people and the response of his "bride." A covenant had been made, and God had been faithful. His love was steadfast, and his commitment unbroken. But Israel, like Gomer, was adulterous and unfaithful, spurning God's love and turning instead to false gods. Then after warning of judgment, God reaffirmed his love and offered reconciliation. His love and mercy were overflowing, but justice would be served.

The book begins with God's marriage instructions to Hosea. After Hosea's marriage, children were born, and each given a name signifying a divine message (chapter 1). Then, as predicted, Gomer left Hosea to pursue her lusts (chapter 2). But Hosea (whose name means "salvation") found her, redeemed her, and brought her home again, fully reconciled (chapter 3). Images of God's love, judgment, grace, and mercy were woven into their relationship. Next, God outlined his case against the people of Israel: Their sins would ultimately cause their destruction (chapters 4; 6; 7; 12) and would rouse his anger, resulting in punishment (chapters 5; 8—10; 12—13). But even in the midst of Israel's immorality, God was merciful and offered hope, expressing his infinite love for his people (chapter 11) and the fact that their repentance would bring about blessing (chapter 14).

The book of Hosea dramatically portrays our God's constant and persistent love. As you read this book, watch the prophet submit himself willingly to his Lord's direction; grieve with him over the unfaithfulness of his wife and his people; and hear the clear warning of judgment. Then reaffirm your commitment to being God's person, faithful in your love and true to your vows.

Hosea becomes a prophet; King Zechariah of Israel is killed 753	*King Shallum of Israel is killed 752*	*Tiglath-pileser III invades Israel 743*	*Micah becomes a prophet to Judah 742*	*Isaiah becomes a prophet to Judah 740*	*Israel (northern kingdom) falls 722*	*Hosea's ministry ends 715*

THE BLUEPRINT

A. HOSEA'S WAYWARD WIFE (1:1—3:5)	Hosea was commanded by God to marry a woman who would be unfaithful to him and would cause him many heartaches. Just as Gomer lost interest in Hosea and ran after other lovers, we, too, can easily lose appreciation for our special relationship with God and pursue dreams and goals that do not include him. When we compromise our Christian life-styles and adopt the ways of the world, we are being unfaithful.
B. GOD'S WAYWARD PEOPLE (4:1—14:9) 1. Israel's sinfulness 2. Israel's punishment 3. God's love for Israel	God wanted the people in the northern kingdom to turn from their sin and return to worshiping him alone, but they persisted in their wickedness. Throughout the book, Israel is described as ignorant of God, with no desire to please him. Israel did not understand God at all, just as Gomer did not understand Hosea. Like a loving husband or patient father, God wants people to know him and to turn to him daily.

MEGATHEMES

THEME	EXPLANATION	IMPORTANCE
The Nation's Sin	Just as Hosea's wife, Gomer, was unfaithful to him, so the nation of Israel had been unfaithful to God. Israel's idolatry was like adultery. They sought illicit relationships with Assyria and Egypt in pursuit of military might, and they mixed Baal worship with the worship of God.	Like Gomer, we can chase after other loves—love of power, pleasure, money, or recognition. The temptations in this world can be very seductive. Are we loyal to God, remaining completely faithful, or have other loves taken his rightful place?
God's Judgment	Hosea solemnly warned Judah against following Israel's example. Because Judah broke the covenant, turned away from God, and forgot her Maker, she experienced a devastating invasion and exile. Sin has terrible consequences.	Disaster surely follows ingratitude toward God and rebellion. The Lord is our only true refuge. If we harden our heart against him, there is no safety or security anywhere else. We cannot escape God's judgment.
God's Love	Just as Hosea went after his unfaithful wife to bring her back, so the Lord pursues us with his love. His love is tender, loyal, unchanging, and undying. No matter what, God still loves us.	Have you forgotten God and become disloyal to him? Don't let prosperity diminish your love for him or let success blind you to your need for his love.
Restoration	Although God will discipline his people for sin, he encourages and restores those who have repented. True repentance opens the way to a new beginning. God forgives and restores.	There is still hope for those who turn back to God. No loyalty, achievement, or honor can be compared to loving him. Turn to the Lord while the offer is still good. No matter how far you have strayed, God is willing to forgive you.

A. HOSEA'S WAYWARD WIFE (1:1—3:5)

Hosea highlights the parallels between his relationship with Gomer and God's relationship with the nation of Israel. Although the people made a covenant with the one true God, they went after false gods. In the same way, Hosea married Gomer, knowing ahead of time that she would leave him. Hosea tenderly dealt with his wife in spite of her sin. And God was merciful toward the people of Israel despite their sins. God has not changed; he is still merciful and forgiving.

1 The LORD gave these messages to Hosea son of Beeri during the years when Uzziah, **1:1**
Jotham, Ahaz, and Hezekiah were kings of Judah, and Jeroboam son of Jehoash* 2 Chr 26:1-23; 27:1-9; 28:1-27; 29:1-32
was king of Israel. Mic 1:1

Hosea's Wife and Children

2When the LORD first began speaking to Israel through Hosea, he said to him, "Go and **1:2**
marry a prostitute,* so some of her children will be born to you from other men. This Jer 3:1
will illustrate the way my people have been untrue to me, openly committing adultery Hos 2:5; 3:1
against the LORD by worshiping other gods."
3So Hosea married Gomer, the daughter of Diblaim, and she became pregnant and
gave Hosea a son. 4And the LORD said, "Name the child Jezreel, for I am about to punish **1:4**
King Jehu's dynasty to avenge the murders he committed at Jezreel. 5In fact, I will put 2 Kgs 10:1-28
an end to Israel's independence by breaking its military power in the Jezreel Valley."
6Soon Gomer became pregnant again and gave birth to a daughter. And the LORD said
to Hosea, "Name your daughter Lo-ruhamah—'Not loved'—for I will no longer show **1:7**
love to the people of Israel or forgive them. 7But I, the LORD their God, will show love Ps 44:3-7
to the people of Judah. I will personally free them from their enemies without any help Isa 30:18
from weapons or armies."
8After Gomer had weaned Lo-ruhamah, she again became pregnant and gave birth to **1:9**
a second son. 9And the LORD said, "Name him Lo-ammi—'Not my people'—for Israel †1 Pet 2:10

1:1 Hebrew *Joash,* a variant name for Jehoash. **1:2** Or *a promiscuous woman.*

1:1 Hosea was a prophet to the northern kingdom of Israel. He served from 753 to 715 B.C. Under the reign of Jeroboam II, the northern kingdom had prospered materially but had decayed spiritually. The people were greedy and had adopted the moral behavior and idolatrous religion of the surrounding Canaanites.

Hosea's role was to show how the people of the northern kingdom had been unfaithful to God, their "husband" and provider, and had married themselves to Baal and the gods of Canaan. He warned that unless they repented of their sin and turned back to God, they were headed for destruction. Hosea spoke of God's characteristics—his powerful love and justice—and how their practical experience of these should affect their lives and make them return to God. Unfortunately, the people had broken their covenant with God, and they would receive the punishments God had promised (Deuteronomy 27–28).

1:2, 3 Did God really order his prophet to marry a woman who was a prostitute? Some who find it difficult to believe God could make such a request view this story as an illustration, not a historical event. Many, however, think the story is historical and give one of these explanations: (1) According to God's law, a priest could not marry a prostitute or a divorced woman (Leviticus 21:7). However, Hosea was not a priest. (2) It is possible that Gomer was not a prostitute when Hosea married her and that God was letting Hosea know that Gomer would later turn to adultery and prostitution. In any case, Hosea knew ahead of time that his wife would be unfaithful and that their married life would become a living object lesson to the adulterous northern kingdom. Hosea's marriage to an unfaithful woman would illustrate God's relationship to the unfaithful nation of Israel.

1:2, 3 It is difficult to imagine Hosea's feelings when God told him to marry a woman who would be unfaithful to him. He may not have wanted to do it, but he obeyed. God often required extraordinary obedience from his prophets who were facing extraordinary times. God may ask you to do something difficult and extraordinary, too. If he does, how will you respond? Will you obey him, trusting that he who knows everything has a special purpose for his request? Will you be able to accept the fact that the pain involved in obedience may benefit those you serve and not you personally?

1:4, 5 Elijah had predicted that the family of Israel's King Ahab would be destroyed because of their wickedness (1 Kings 21:20-22), but Jehu went too far in carrying out God's command (2 Kings 10:1-11). Therefore, Jehu's dynasty would also be punished—in the Jezreel Valley, the very place where he carried out the massacre of Ahab's family. God's promise to put an end to Israel as an independent kingdom came true 25 years later when the Assyrians conquered the northern kingdom and carried the people into captivity.

1:6, 8 In 1:3, we read that Gomer "gave *Hosea* a son." In 1:6 and 1:8, we learn that Gomer gave birth to two more children, but there is no indication that Hosea was their natural father; some translations imply that he was not. The key to this part of the story is found in the names God chose for the children, showing his reaction to Israel's unfaithfulness. God's reaction to unfaithfulness is no different today. He wants our complete devotion.

1:7 God said he would personally rescue the people of Judah from their enemies with no help from their weapons or armies. Although God asks us to do our part, we should remember that he is not limited to human effort. God often chooses to work through people, but only because it is good for *them.* He can accomplish all his purposes without any help from us if he so chooses. You are very important to God, but on your own you have neither the ability to fulfill nor the power to disrupt God's plans.

1:9 Here God was in essence dissolving the covenant (Jeremiah 7:23). The name of the third child conveys the finality of God's judgment. God's warnings recorded in Deuteronomy 28:15-68 were beginning to come true: Israel was abandoning God, and in turn, he was leaving them alone and without his blessings.

1:10
Gen 22:17; 32:12
Isa 63:16; 64:8
Jer 33:22
†Romans 9:26

1:11
Isa 11:12
Jer 3:5-6; 30:21
Ezek 37:21-24
Hos 3:5

is not my people, and I am not their God. [10]Yet the time will come when Israel will
prosper and become a great nation. In that day its people will be like the sands of the
seashore—too many to count! Then, at the place where they were told, 'You are not my
people,' it will be said, 'You are children of the living God.' [11]Then the people of Judah
and Israel will unite under one leader, and they will return from exile together. What a
day that will be—the day of Jezreel*—when God will again plant his people in his land.
[1]In that day you will call your brothers Ammi—'My people.' And you will call your
sisters Ruhamah—'The ones I love.'

Charges against an Unfaithful Wife

2:2
Isa 50:1
Hos 4:5

2:3
Isa 20:2-3; 32:13-14
Jer 14:3
Ezek 16:7, 22, 29
Amos 8:11-13

2:5
Jer 2:25; 3:1-2
Ezek 23:16-17

2:7
2 Chr 28:20-22
Jer 2:2; 3:1
Ezek 23:4

2 [2]"But now, call Israel* to account, for she is no longer my wife, and I am no longer
her husband. Tell her to take off her garish makeup and suggestive clothing and to
stop playing the prostitute. [3]If she doesn't, I will strip her as naked as she was on the day
she was born. I will leave her to die of thirst, as in a desert or a dry and barren wilderness.
[4]And I will not love her children as I would my own because they are not my children!
They were conceived in adultery. [5]For their mother is a shameless prostitute and became
pregnant in a shameful way. She said, 'I'll run after other lovers and sell myself to them
for food and drink, for clothing of wool and linen, and for olive oil.'
[6]"But I will fence her in with thornbushes. I will block the road to make her lose her
way. [7]When she runs after her lovers, she won't be able to catch up with them. She will

1:11 *Jezreel* means "God plants." **2:2** Hebrew *call your mother.*

HOSEA served as a prophet to Israel (the northern kingdom) from 753–715 B.C.

Climate of the times	Israel's last six kings were especially wicked; they promoted heavy taxes, oppression of the poor, idol worship, and total disregard for God. Israel was subjected to Assyria and was forced to pay tribute, which depleted its few remaining resources.
Main message	The people of Israel had sinned against God, as an adulterous woman sins against her husband. Judgment was sure to come for living in total disregard for God and fellow humans. Israel fell to Assyria in 722 B.C.
Importance of message	When we sin, we sever our relationship with God, breaking our commitment to him. While all must answer to God for their sins, those who seek God's forgiveness are spared eternal judgment.
Contemporary prophets	Jonah (793–753 B.C.), Amos (760–750 B.C.), Micah (742–687 B.C.), Isaiah (740–681 B.C.)

1:10 The Old Testament prophetic books sometimes use the word *Israel* to refer to the people of the united kingdom (north and south) and sometimes just to the northern kingdom. In talking about past events, Hosea usually thought of Israel as the northern kingdom with its capital in Samaria. But when Hosea spoke about future events relating to God's promises of restoration, it is difficult to understand his words as applying only to the northern kingdom because the exiled northerners would become hopelessly intermingled with their conquerors. Thus, most scholars see the promises of return as either: (1) conditional—the Israelites chose not to return to God, and therefore they were not entitled to the blessings included in the promises of restoration, or (2) unconditional—God's promises of restoration have been fulfilled in Jesus Christ, and therefore the church (the new Israel) receives his blessings (Romans 9:25, 26; 1 Peter 2:10).

1:10, 11 Although Israel was unfaithful, God's commitment remained unchanged. This promise of a future reuniting confirmed the covenant made with Moses (Deuteronomy 30:1-10) and foreshadowed the prophecies of Jeremiah (Jeremiah 29:11-14; 31:31-40) and Ezekiel (Ezekiel 11:16-21). It was a prediction of the day when all the people of God will be united under Christ. Today all believers everywhere are God's chosen people, "a kingdom of priests, God's holy nation" (see 1 Peter 2:9).

1:11 Just as the other children's names carried significance, so did *Jezreel.* In verse 4, the name depicts divine judgment; here it represents the scattering. The name means "God scatters." Here it represents the scattering a farmer does when he plants seeds. This was a sign of a new day and a new relationship between God and Israel.

2:2ff Israel's punishment and restoration are the themes of this chapter. As in a court case, the prostitute is brought to trial and found guilty. But after her punishment, she is joyfully and tenderly restored to God.

2:5-7 The Israelites were thanking false gods (specifically Baal, the god whom they believed controlled weather and thus farming) for their food, shelter, and clothing, instead of the true God, who gave those blessings. Therefore, God would fence Israel in "with thornbushes" and "block the road" by making the rewards of idol worship so disappointing that the people would be persuaded to turn back to God. Despite Israel's unfaithfulness, God was still faithful and merciful. He would continue to hold his arms out to his people, even to the point of placing obstacles in their wayward path to turn them back to him.

2:7 Just as Gomer would return to her husband if she thought she would be better off with him, so people often return to God when they find life's struggle too difficult to handle. Returning to God out of desperation is better than rebelling against him, but it is better yet to turn to God out of gratitude for his care.

search for them but not find them. Then she will think, 'I might as well return to my
husband because I was better off with him than I am now.' 8She doesn't realize that it
was I who gave her everything she has—the grain, the wine, the olive oil. Even the gold
and silver she used in worshiping the god Baal were gifts from me!
9"But now I will take back the wine and ripened grain I generously provided each
harvest season. I will take away the linen and wool clothing I gave her to cover her
nakedness. 10I will strip her naked in public, while all her lovers look on. No one will be
able to rescue her from my hands. 11I will put an end to her annual festivals, her new
moon celebrations, and her Sabbath days—all her appointed festivals. 12I will destroy
her vineyards and orchards, things she claims her lovers gave her. I will let them grow
into tangled thickets, where only wild animals will eat the fruit. 13I will punish her for
all the times she deserted me, when she burned incense to her images of Baal, put on her
earrings and jewels, and went out looking for her lovers," says the LORD.

The LORD's Love for Unfaithful Israel

14"But then I will win her back once again. I will lead her out into the desert and speak
tenderly to her there. 15I will return her vineyards to her and transform the Valley of
Trouble* into a gateway of hope. She will give herself to me there, as she did long ago
when she was young, when I freed her from her captivity in Egypt.
16"In that coming day," says the LORD, "you will call me 'my husband' instead of 'my
master.'* 17O Israel, I will cause you to forget your images of Baal; even their names
will no longer be spoken. 18At that time I will make a covenant with all the wild animals
and the birds and the animals that scurry along the ground so that they will not harm you.
I will remove all weapons of war from the land, all swords and bows, so you can live
unafraid in peace and safety. 19I will make you my wife forever, showing you righteousness and justice, unfailing love and compassion. 20I will be faithful to you and make you
mine, and you will finally know me as LORD.
21"In that day," says the LORD, "I will answer the pleading of the sky for clouds, which
will pour down water on the earth in answer to its cries for rain. 22Then the earth will
answer the thirsty cries of the grain, the grapes, and the olive trees for moisture. And the
whole grand chorus will sing together, 'Jezreel'—'God plants!'
23"At that time I will plant a crop of Israelites and raise them for myself! I will show

2:8 Ezek 16:18; Hos 8:4
2:10 Ezek 16:37; Hos 8:7; 9:2
2:11 Isa 1:13-14; Jer 7:34; 16:9
2:12 Jer 5:17; 8:13
2:13 Jer 7:9; Ezek 23:40-42; Hos 4:13; 11:2
2:14 Ezek 20:33-38
2:15 Josh 7:26; Jer 2:1-3; Ezek 16:8, 22
2:16 Isa 54:5
2:18 Lev 26:5-6; Job 5:23; Isa 2:4; Ezek 34:25; 39:1-10
2:20 Jer 31:34; Hos 6:6; 13:4
2:21 Isa 55:10; Zech 8:12
2:22 Jer 31:27; Joel 2:19
2:23 †Rom 9:25; †1 Pet 2:10

2:15 Hebrew *valley of Achor.* **2:16** Hebrew *'my baal.'*

2:8 Material possessions are success symbols in most societies. Israel was a wealthy nation at this time, and Gomer may have accumulated silver and gold. But Gomer didn't realize that Hosea had given her all she owned, just as Israel did not recognize God as the giver of blessings. Both Gomer and Israel used their possessions irresponsibly as they ran after other lovers and other gods. How do you use your possessions? Use what God has given you to honor him.

2:12 The Israelites were so immersed in idolatry that they actually believed pagan gods gave them their vineyards and orchards. They had forgotten that the entire land was a gift from God (Deuteronomy 32:49). Today many people give credit to everything and everyone but God for their prosperity—luck, hard work, quick thinking, the right contacts. When *you* succeed, who gets the credit?

2:13 Baal was the most important of the Canaanite gods, and his name came to be used to describe all the local deities worshiped throughout the land occupied by Israel. Unfortunately, the Israelites did not get rid of the idols and pagan worship centers as they had been commanded. Instead, they tolerated and frequently joined Baal worshipers, often through the influence of corrupt kings. One Israelite king especially noted for his Baal worship was Ahab. The prophet Elijah, in a dramatic showdown with Ahab's hired prophets, proved God's power far superior to Baal's (1 Kings 18).

2:14, 15 God was promising (1) to bring the people to the desert, a place free from distractions, so he could clearly communicate with them, and (2) to change what had been a time of difficulty into a day of hope. The Valley of Trouble is the site where Achan had sinned by keeping forbidden war plunder (see Joshua 7). He had brought great disaster to Joshua's troops when they were attempting to conquer the land. God uses even our negative experiences to create opportunities to turn back to him. As you face problems and trials, remember that God speaks to you in the "desert" and not just in times of prosperity.

2:16 Not until Judah's exile would the entire nation begin to come to its senses, give up its idols, and turn back to God; and not until that day when God rules through Jesus the Messiah will the relationship between God and his people be restored. In that day, God will no longer be like a master to them; he will be like a husband (Isaiah 54:4-8). The relationship will be deep and personal, the kind of relationship we can know, though imperfectly, in marriage.

2:19, 20 The time will come when unfaithfulness will be impossible. God will bind us to himself in his perfect righteousness, justice, love, compassion, and faithfulness. God was promising a fresh new beginning, not just a temporary rewriting of a tired old agreement (see Jeremiah 31:31-34).

2:19, 20 God's wedding gift to his people, both in Hosea's day and in our own, is his compassion. Through no merit of our own, God forgives us and makes us right with him. There is no way for us by our own efforts to reach God's high standards, but he graciously accepts us, forgives us, and draws us into a relationship with himself. In that relationship we have personal and intimate communion with him.

love to those I called ‘Not loved.’* And to those I called ‘Not my people,’* I will say,
‘Now you are my people.’ Then they will reply, ‘You are our God!’”

Hosea’s Wife Is Redeemed

3:1 **3** Then the LORD said to me, “Go and get your wife again. Bring her back to you and
2 Sam 6:19 1 Chr 16:3 love her, even though she loves adultery. For the LORD still loves Israel even though
Song 2:5 the people have turned to other gods, offering them choice gifts.*”
3:2 2So I bought her back for fifteen pieces of silver* and about five bushels of barley and
Ruth 4:10 a measure of wine.* 3Then I said to her, “You must live in my house for many days and
stop your prostitution. During this time, you will not have sexual intercourse with
anyone, not even with me.*”
3:4 4This illustrates that Israel will be a long time without a king or prince, and without
Judg 17:5 sacrifices, temple, priests, or even idols! 5But afterward the people will return to the
3:5 Jer 50:4-5 LORD their God and to David’s descendant, their king.* They will come trembling in awe
Ezek 34:24 to the LORD, and they will receive his good gifts in the last days.

B. GOD’S WAYWARD PEOPLE (4:1—14:9)

The rest of the book deals with Israel’s sin and her impending judgment. Hosea points out the moral and spiritual decay of the nation. He describes the punishment awaiting the people and pleads with them to return to God. Although judgment and condemnation of sin are prevalent in the book, a strand of love and restoration runs throughout. Even in the midst of judgment, God is merciful and will restore those who repent and turn to him.

2:23a Hebrew *Lo-ruhamah;* see 1:6. **2:23b** Hebrew *Lo-ammi;* see 1:9. **3:1** Hebrew *raisin cakes.* **3:2a** Hebrew *15 shekels of silver,* about 6 ounces or 171 grams in weight. **3:2b** As in Greek version, which reads *a homer* [182 liters] *of barley and a measure of wine;* Hebrew reads *a homer of barley and a lethech* [2.5 bushels or 91 liters] *of barley.* **3:3** Or *and I will live with you.* **3:5** Hebrew *to David their king.*

SPIRITUAL UNFAITHFULNESS

Spiritual adultery and physical adultery are alike in many ways, and both are dangerous. God was disappointed with his people, because they had committed spiritual adultery against him, as Gomer had committed physical adultery against Hosea.

Parallels	*The Danger*
Both spiritual and physical adultery are against God’s law.	When we break God’s law in full awareness of what we’re doing, our hearts become hardened to the sin, and our relationship with God is broken.
Both spiritual and physical adultery begin with disappointment and dissatisfaction—either real or imagined—with an already existing relationship.	The feeling that God disappoints can lead you away from him. Feelings of disappointment and dissatisfaction are normal and, when endured, will pass.
Both spiritual and physical adultery begin with diverting affection from one object of devotion to another.	The diverting of our affection is the first step in the blinding process that leads into sin.
Both spiritual and physical adultery involve a process of deterioration; it is not usually an impulsive decision.	The process is dangerous because you don’t always realize it is happening until it is too late.
Both spiritual and physical adultery involve the creation of a fantasy about what a new object of love can do for you.	Such fantasy creates unrealistic expectations of what a new relationship can do and only leads to disappointment in all existing and future relationships.

3:1 This short chapter pictures the nation’s exile and return. Israel would experience a time of purification in a foreign land, but God would still love the people and would be willing to accept them back. God commanded Hosea to show the same forgiving spirit to Gomer. Although Hosea had good reason to divorce Gomer, he was told to buy her back and love her.

3:2 Apparently Gomer was on her own for a while. Needing to support herself, she must have either sold herself into slavery or become the mistress of another man. In either case, Hosea had to pay to get her back—although the required amount was pitifully small. Gomer was no longer worth much to anyone except Hosea, but he loved her just as God loved Israel. No matter how low we sink, God is willing to buy us back—to redeem us—and to lift us up again.

3:3 After this, Gomer is no longer mentioned by Hosea. This is explained in 3:4. Gomer’s isolation showed how God would deal with the northern kingdom (5:6, 15). It is dangerous to rebel against God. If he were ever to withdraw his love and mercy, we would be without hope.

3:4 God would separate the Israelites from their treasured idolatrous practices. The sacrifices and temple mentioned were those used for idol worship. The priests served the idols; the idols were household gods, which were strictly forbidden for God’s people.

3:4, 5 The northern kingdom had rebelled against David’s dynasty and had taken Jeroboam as their king (1 Kings 12–13). Their rebellion was both political and religious. At that time, they reverted back to the worship of gold idols. “David’s descendant, their king” refers to the time of Messiah’s rule when all people will bow before him in humility and submission. Those who won’t accept Christ’s blessings now will face his power and judgment later. How much better it is to love and follow Christ now than face his angry judgment later.

1. Israel's sinfulness

The LORD's Case against Israel

4 Hear the word of the LORD, O people of Israel! The LORD has filed a lawsuit against
you, saying: "There is no faithfulness, no kindness, no knowledge of God in your
land. 2 You curse and lie and kill and steal and commit adultery. There is violence
everywhere, with one murder after another. 3 That is why your land is not producing. It
is filled with sadness, and all living things are becoming sick and dying. Even the
animals, birds, and fish have begun to disappear.

4 "Don't point your finger at someone else and try to pass the blame! Look, you priests,
my complaint is with you!* 5 As a sentence for your crimes, you will stumble in broad
daylight, just as you might at night, and so will your false prophets. And I will destroy
your mother, Israel. 6 My people are being destroyed because they don't know me. It is
all your fault, you priests, for you yourselves refuse to know me. Now I refuse to
recognize you as my priests. Since you have forgotten the laws of your God, I will forget
to bless your children. 7 The more priests there are, the more they sin against me. They
have exchanged* the glory of God for the disgrace of idols.

8 "The priests get fed when the people sin and bring their sin offerings to them. So the
priests are glad when the people sin! 9 'Like priests, like people'—since the priests are
wicked, the people are wicked, too. So now I will punish both priests and people for all
their wicked deeds. 10 They will eat and still be hungry. Though they do a big business
as prostitutes, they will have no children, for they have deserted the LORD to worship
other gods.

11 "Alcohol and prostitution have robbed my people of their brains. 12 They are asking
a piece of wood to tell them what to do! They think a stick can tell them the future! Longing
after idols has made them foolish. They have played the prostitute, serving other gods and
deserting their God. 13 They offer sacrifices to idols on the tops of mountains. They go up
into the hills to burn incense in the pleasant shade of oaks, poplars, and other trees.

4:1 Isa 59:4 Jer 7:28 Hos 12:2 Mic 6:2
4:2 Hos 6:8-9; 7:1-4; 10:4
4:3 Isa 24:4; 33:9 Zeph 1:3
4:4 Deut 17:12 Ezek 3:26 Amos 5:10, 13
4:5 Ezek 14:3, 7 Hos 5:5
4:6 Hos 4:14 Zech 11:8-9, 15-17 Mal 2:7-8
4:7 Hos 2:16; 10:1; 13:6 Hab 2:16
4:9 Isa 24:2 Jer 5:31
4:11 Isa 5:12; 28:7
4:12 Jer 2:27
4:13 Jer 2:20; 3:6 Ezek 6:13 Hos 2:13; 11:2

4:4 Hebrew *Your people are like those with a complaint against the priests.* **4:7** As in Syriac version and an ancient Hebrew tradition; Masoretic Text reads *I will exchange.*

4:1ff In this chapter, God brings a charge of disobedience against Israel. The religious leaders had failed to turn the people to God, and ritual prostitution had replaced right worship. The nation had declined spiritually and morally, breaking the laws that God had given them. The people found it easy to condemn Hosea's wife for her adultery. They were not so quick to see that *they* had been unfaithful to God.

4:1-3 God explained the reasons for Israel's suffering. Their lawless behavior had brought the twin judgments of increased violence and ecological crisis. There is not always a direct cause-and-effect relationship between our actions and the problems we face. Nevertheless, when we are facing difficulties, we should seriously ask, Have I done anything sinful or irresponsible that has caused my suffering? If we discover that we are at fault, even partially, we must change our ways before God will help us.

4:2 This verse may allude to the assassinations of kings during Hosea's lifetime. Shallum killed Zechariah (the king, not the prophet) and took the throne. Then Menahem killed Shallum and destroyed an entire city because it refused to accept him as king (2 Kings 15:8-16). God pointed out that even murder was being taken casually in Israel.

4:4-9 Hosea leveled his charges against the religious leaders. Who were these religious leaders? When Jeroboam I rebelled against Solomon's son Rehoboam and set up a rival kingdom in the north, he also set up his own religious system (see 1 Kings 12:25-33). In violation of God's law, he made two gold calves and told the people to worship them. He also appointed his own priests, who were not descendants of Aaron. At first the residents of the northern kingdom continued to worship God, even though they were doing it in the wrong way; but very soon they also began to worship Canaanite gods. Before long they had substituted Baal for God and no longer worshiped God at all. It is not surprising that Jeroboam's false priests were unable to preserve the true worship of God.

4:6-9 God accused the religious leaders of keeping the people from knowing him. They were supposed to be spiritual leaders, but they had become leaders in wrongdoing. The people may have said to one another, "It must be OK if the priests do it." Spiritual leadership is a heavy responsibility. Whether you teach a church school class, hold a church office, or lead a Bible study, don't take your leadership responsibilities lightly. Be a leader who leads others to God.

4:8 The priests relished the people's sins. Every time a person brought a sin offering, the priest received a portion of it. The more the people sinned, the more the priests received. Because they couldn't eat all of the offerings themselves, they sold some and gave some to their relatives. The priests profited from the continuation of sin; it gave them power and position in the community. So instead of trying to lead the people out of sin, they encouraged sin to increase their profits.

4:10-12 The chief Canaanite gods, Baal and Asherah, represented the power of fertility and sexual reproduction. Not surprisingly, their worship included rituals with vile sexual practices. Male worshipers had sex with female temple prostitutes or female priests, and young women wishing to bear children had sex with male priests. But God said their efforts to increase fertility would not succeed.

4:12 The "stick," or divining rod, was a way of attempting to tell the future. By divorcing themselves from God's authoritative religion centered in Jerusalem, inhabitants of the northern kingdom had effectively cut themselves off from God's word and from his way of forgiveness. The drive to be free from all restrictions can move us completely out of God's will.

"That is why your daughters turn to prostitution, and your daughters-in-law commit adultery. [14]Why should I punish them? For you men are doing the same thing, sinning with whores and shrine prostitutes. O foolish people! You will be destroyed, for you refuse to understand.

[15]"Though Israel is a prostitute, may Judah avoid such guilt. O Judah, do not join with those who worship me insincerely at Gilgal and at Beth-aven.* Their worship is mere pretense as they take oaths in the LORD's name. [16]Israel is as stubborn as a heifer, so the LORD will put her out to pasture. She will stand alone and unprotected, like a helpless lamb in an open field. [17]Leave her alone because she is married to idolatry. [18]The men of Israel finish up their drinking bouts and off they go to find some prostitutes. Their love for shame is greater than their love for honor.* [19]So a mighty wind will sweep them away. They will die in shame because they offer sacrifices to idols.

The Failure of Israel's Leaders

5 "Hear this, you priests and all of Israel's leaders! Listen, all you men of the royal family! These words of judgment are for you: You are doomed! For you have led the people into a snare by worshiping the idols at Mizpah and Tabor. [2]You have dug a deep pit to trap them at Acacia.* But never forget—I will settle with all of you for what you have done. [3]I know what you are like, O Israel! You have left me as a prostitute leaves her husband; you are utterly defiled. [4]Your deeds won't let you return to your God. You are a prostitute through and through, and you cannot know the LORD.

[5]"The arrogance of Israel* testifies against her; she will stumble under her load of guilt. Judah, too, will fall with her. [6]Then at last, they will come with their flocks and herds to offer sacrifices to the LORD. But it will be too late! They will not find him, because he has withdrawn from them, and they are now alone. [7]For they have betrayed the honor of the LORD, bearing children that aren't his. Now their false religion will devour them, along with their wealth.

[8]"Blow the ram's horn in Gibeah! Sound the alarm in Ramah! Raise the battle cry in Beth-aven*! Lead on into battle, O warriors of Benjamin! [9]One thing is certain, Israel*: When your day of punishment comes, you will become a heap of rubble.

[10]"The leaders of Judah have become as bad as thieves.* So I will pour my anger down on them like a waterfall. [11]The people of Israel will be crushed and broken by my judgment because they are determined to worship idols. [12]I will destroy Israel as a moth consumes wool. I will sap Judah's strength as dry rot weakens wood.

[13]"When Israel and Judah saw how sick they were, Israel turned to Assyria, to the great king there, but he could neither help nor cure them. [14]I will tear at Israel and Judah

4:14 Deut 23:17
4:16 Pss 23:2-3; 78:8 Isa 5:17; 7:25
4:17 Ps 81:12
4:19 Hos 12:1; 13:15
5:3 Amos 5:12
5:4 Hos 4:6, 14
5:5 2 Kgs 17:19-20 Ezek 23:31-35
5:6 Isa 1:15 Ezek 8:6 Mic 6:6-7
5:7 Hos 2:4
5:9 Isa 28:1-4; 37:3 Hos 9:11-17
5:10 Deut 27:17 Pss 32:6; 93:3-4 Ezek 7:8
5:12 Ps 39:11 Isa 51:8
5:13 Jer 30:12
5:14 Pss 7:2; 50:22 Hos 13:7

4:15 *Beth-aven* means "house of wickedness"; it is being used as another name for Bethel, which means "house of God." **4:18** As in Greek version; the meaning of the Hebrew is uncertain. **5:2** Hebrew *at Shittim.* The meaning of the Hebrew for this sentence is uncertain. **5:5** Hebrew *Israel and Ephraim* **5:8** *Beth-aven* means "house of wickedness"; it is being used as another name for Bethel, which means "house of God." **5:9** Hebrew *Ephraim,* referring to the northern kingdom of Israel; also in 5:11, 12, 13, 14. **5:10** Hebrew *have become as those who move a boundary marker.*

4:15 God sent a warning to the southern kingdom of Judah that its priests should not become like those in Israel. (The southern kingdom was called Judah after its most powerful tribe.) Israel's priests who remained in the north had forgotten their spiritual heritage and had sold out to Baal. They were promoting idol worship and ritual prostitution. Israel would not escape punishment, but Judah could if it refused to follow Israel's example.

4:19 The mighty wind that would sweep Israel away refers to the Assyrian invasion that would destroy the nation about 20 years later.

5:1, 2 Mizpah and Tabor may have been sites prominent in the false worship of Baal. The leaders likely even encouraged the people to sin at these places. With both their civil and religious leaders hopelessly corrupt, the people of Israel did not have much of a chance. They looked to their leaders for guidance, and they should have found it. Today we can often choose our own leaders, but we still need to be aware of whether they are taking us toward or away from God. God held the people responsible for what they did. Similarly, God holds us responsible for our actions and choices.

5:4 Persistent sin hardens a person's heart, making it difficult to repent. Deliberately choosing to disobey God can sear the conscience; each sin makes the next one easier to commit. Don't allow sin to groove a hard path deep within you. Steer as far away from sinful practices as possible.

5:8 Gibeah and Ramah were Israelite cities near Jerusalem. Hosea prophesied that these cities would sound the alarm of the coming judgment.

5:13 During the reigns of Menahem and Hoshea, Israel turned to Assyria for help (2 Kings 15:19, 20; 17:3, 4). But even the great world powers of that time could not help Israel, for God himself had determined to judge the nation. If we neglect God's call to repentance, how can we escape? (See Hebrews 2:3.)

as a lion rips apart its prey. I will carry them off, and there will be no one left to rescue
them. 15 Then I will return to my place until they admit their guilt and look to me for help.
For as soon as trouble comes, they will search for me."

2. Israel's punishment

A Call to Repentance

6 "Come, let us return to the LORD! He has torn us in pieces; now he will heal us. He
has injured us; now he will bandage our wounds. 2 In just a short time, he will restore
us so we can live in his presence. 3 Oh, that we might know the LORD! Let us press on to
know him! Then he will respond to us as surely as the arrival of dawn or the coming of
rains in early spring."
4 "O Israel* and Judah, what should I do with you?" asks the LORD. "For your love
vanishes like the morning mist and disappears like dew in the sunlight. 5 I sent my
prophets to cut you to pieces. I have slaughtered you with my words, threatening you
with death. My judgment will strike you as surely as day follows night. 6 I want you to
be merciful; I don't want your sacrifices. I want you to know God; that's more important
than burnt offerings.
7 "But like Adam, you broke my covenant and rebelled against me. 8 Gilead is a city
of sinners, tracked with footprints of blood. 9 Its citizens are bands of robbers, lying in
ambush for their victims. Gangs of priests murder travelers along the road to Shechem
and practice every kind of sin. 10 Yes, I have seen a horrible thing in Israel: My people
have defiled themselves by chasing after other gods!
11 "O Judah, a harvest of punishment is also waiting for you, though I wanted so much
to restore the fortunes of my people!

Israel's Love for Wickedness

7 "I wanted to heal Israel, but its sins were far too great. Samaria is filled with liars,
thieves, and bandits! 2 Its people don't realize I am watching them. Their sinful deeds
are all around them; I see them all! 3 The people make the king glad with their
wickedness. The princes laugh about the people's many lies. 4 They are all adulterers,
always aflame with lust. They are like an oven that is kept hot even while the baker is
still kneading the dough.

6:4 Hebrew *Ephraim,* referring to the northern kingdom of Israel.

5:15 Isa 64:7-9; Jer 2:27
6:1 Isa 30:26; Jer 50:4; Hos 14:4; Zeph 2:1-3
6:2 1 Cor 15:4
6:3 Ps 19:6; Isa 2:3; 5:6; Joel 2:2-3; Mic 4:2; 5:2
6:4 Ps 78:34-37; Hos 13:3
6:5 Heb 4:12
6:6 Matt 9:13; 12:7
6:9 Jer 7:9; Ezek 22:9
6:11 Jer 51:33; Joel 3:13
7:1 Ezek 24:13
7:2 Jer 2:19; Hos 8:13
7:3 Mic 7:3
7:4 Jer 9:2; 23:10

6:1-3 This is presumption, not genuine repentance. The people did not understand the depth of their sins. They did not turn from idols, repent of their sins, or pledge to make changes. They thought that God's wrath would last only a few days; little did they know that their nation would soon be taken into exile. Israel was interested in God only for the material benefits he provided; they did not value the eternal benefits that come from worshiping him. Before judging Israel, however, consider your attitude. What do you hope to gain from your religion? Do you "repent" easily, without seriously considering what changes need to take place in your life?

6:4 God answered his people, pointing out that their profession of loyalty, like mist and dew, evaporated easily and had no substance. Many find it easy and comfortable to maintain the appearance of being committed without deep and sincere loyalty. If you profess loyalty to God, back it up with your actions.

6:6 Religious rituals can help people understand God and nourish their relationship with him. That is why God instituted circumcision and the sacrificial system in the Old Testament and baptism and the Lord's Supper in the New Testament. But a religious ritual is helpful only if it is carried out with an attitude of love for and obedience to God. If a person's heart is far from God, ritual will become empty mockery. God didn't want the Israelites' rituals; he wanted their hearts. Why do you worship? What is the motive behind your "sacrifices" and "offerings"?

6:7 One of Hosea's key themes is that Israel had broken the covenant God had made with them at Mount Sinai (Exodus 19–20). God wanted to make Israel a blessing and a light to all the nations (Genesis 12:2, 3; Isaiah 49:6); and if God's chosen people obeyed him and proclaimed him to the world, he would give them special blessings. If they broke the covenant, however, they would suffer severe penalties, as they should have known (see Deuteronomy 28:15-68). Sadly, the people broke the agreement and proved themselves unfaithful to God. How about you? Have you also broken faith with God? What about your forgotten promises to serve him?

6:8, 9 Gilead was once a sacred place, but here it was corrupt. Shechem was once a city of refuge designated by Joshua (Joshua 20:1, 2, 7, 8); Gilead was a region that included Ramoth, also a city of refuge. At this time these areas were associated with murder and crime, with bands of evil priests lying in wait to murder travelers passing through the territory.

6:11 So that the people of Judah would not become proud as they saw the northern kingdom's destruction, Hosea interjected a solemn warning about God's "harvest." God's Temple was in Judah (Jerusalem), and the people thought that what happened in Israel could never happen to them. But when they had become utterly corrupt, they, too, were led off into captivity (see 2 Kings 25).

7:1, 2 God sees and knows everything. We, like Israel, often forget this. Thoughts like "No one will ever know," or "No one is watching" may tempt us to try to get away with sin. If you are facing difficult temptations, you will be less likely to give in if you remind yourself that God is watching. When faced with the opportunity to sin, remember that God sees everything.

7:5 Isa 28:1 5"On royal holidays, the princes get drunk. The king makes a fool of himself and
7:6 Ps 21:9 drinks with those who are making fun of him. 6Their hearts blaze like a furnace with
intrigue. Their plot smolders through the night, and in the morning it flames forth like
7:7 Isa 64:7 a raging fire. 7They kill their kings one after another, and no one cries out to me for
help.

8"My people of Israel* mingle with godless foreigners, picking up their evil ways.
7:9 Isa 1:7 Now they have become as worthless as a half-baked cake! 9Worshiping foreign gods
has sapped their strength, but they don't even know it. Israel is like an old man with
7:10 Hos 5:5 graying hair, unaware of how weak and old he has become. 10His arrogance testifies
against him, yet he doesn't return to the LORD his God or even try to find him.

7:11 Hos 12:1 11"The people of Israel have become like silly, witless doves, first calling to Egypt,
7:12 Ezek 12:13 then flying to Assyria. 12But as they fly about, I will throw my net over them and bring
them down like a bird from the sky. I will punish them for all their evil ways.*

7:13 Matt 23:37 13"How terrible it will be for my people who have deserted me! Let them die, for
they have rebelled against me. I wanted to redeem them, but they have only spoken
7:14 Amos 2:8 lies about me. 14They do not cry out to me with sincere hearts. Instead, they sit on
their couches and wail. They cut themselves, begging foreign gods for crops and
prosperity.

7:15 Nah 1:9 15"I trained them and made them strong, yet now they plot evil against me. 16They
7:16 Ps 78:57; Ezek 23:32; Hos 9:3, 6 look everywhere except to heaven, to the Most High. They are like a crooked bow that
always misses its target. Their leaders will be killed by their enemies because of their
insolence toward me. Then the people of Egypt will laugh at them.

7:8 Hebrew *Ephraim,* referring to the northern kingdom of Israel; also in 7:11. **7:12** Hebrew *I will punish them because of what was reported against them in the assembly.*

OBEDIENCE VERSUS SACRIFICES

God says many times that he doesn't want our gifts and sacrifices when we give them out of ritual or hypocrisy. God wants us first to love and obey him.

1 Samuel 15:22, 23	Obedience is far better than sacrifice.
Psalm 40:6–8	God doesn't want burnt offerings; he wants our lifelong service.
Psalm 51:16–19	God isn't interested in penance; he wants a broken and repentant heart.
Jeremiah 7:21–23	It isn't sacrifices God wants; he desires our obedience and promises that he will be our God and we will be his people.
Hosea 6:6	God doesn't want sacrifices; he wants our loving loyalty. He doesn't want offerings; he wants us to acknowledge him.
Amos 5:21–24	God hates pretense and hypocrisy; he wants to see justice roll on like a river.
Micah 6:6–8	God is not satisfied with offerings; he wants us to do what is right, love mercy, and walk humbly with him.
Matthew 9:13	God doesn't want sacrifices; he wants us to be merciful.

7:6 "Their hearts blaze like a furnace" refers to the lust for power and intrigue that was burning in these leaders' hearts. Three Israelite kings were assassinated during Hosea's lifetime—Zechariah, Shallum, and Pekahiah (2 Kings 15:8-26). The kings' foreign relations and domestic lives were ruined because they ignored God and his word.

7:8 The people of Israel had intermarried with foreign people and had picked up their evil ways. When we spend a lot of time with unbelievers, either professionally or socially, we can easily pick up their attitudes and begin to imitate their actions. Beware of the influence they may have on you. Instead of drifting into bad habits, see if you can have a positive influence and point these people to God.

7:10 Arrogance (pride) keeps a person from turning to God because arrogance claims no need of help from anyone, human or divine. Pride intensifies all our other sins because we cannot repent of any of them without first giving up our pride.

7:11 Israel's King Menahem had paid Assyria to support him in power (2 Kings 15:19, 20); King Hoshea turned against Assyria and went to Egypt for help (2 Kings 17:4). Israel's kings went back and forth, allying themselves with different nations when they should have allied themselves with God.

7:16 A crooked bow is unreliable. Its arrows miss the target, and its owner would be quite vulnerable in battle. Life without God is as unreliable as a crooked bow. Without God's direction, our thoughts are filled with lust, cheating, selfishness, and deceit. As long as we are warped by sin, we will never reach our true potential.

7:16 People look everywhere except to God for happiness and fulfillment, pursuing possessions, recreation, and relationships. In reality, only God can truly satisfy the deep longings of the soul. Look first to heaven, to the Most High God. He will meet your *spiritual* needs, not all your materialistic wants.

Israel Harvests the Whirlwind

8 "Sound the alarm! The enemy descends like an eagle on the people of the LORD, 8:1
for they have broken my covenant and revolted against my law. 2 Now Israel Hab 1:8
pleads with me, 'Help us, for you are our God!' 3 But it is too late! The people of Israel
have rejected what is good, and now their enemies will chase after them. 4 The people
have appointed kings and princes, but not with my consent. By making idols for 8:4 Hos 2:8; 13:10
themselves from their silver and gold, they have brought about their own destruction.
5 "O Samaria, I reject this calf—this idol you have made. My fury burns against
you. How long will you be incapable of innocence? 6 This calf you worship was 8:5 Jer 13:27
crafted by your own hands! It is not God! Therefore, it must be smashed to bits. 8:6 Hos 13:2
7 "They have planted the wind and will harvest the whirlwind. The stalks of wheat
wither, producing no grain. And if there is any grain, foreigners will eat it. 8 The 8:7 Isa 66:15
people of Israel have been swallowed up; they lie among the nations like an old pot Nah 1:3
that no one wants. 9 Like a wild donkey looking for a mate, they have gone up to 8:8 Jer 51:34
Assyria. The people of Israel* have sold themselves to many lovers. 10 But though 8:9 Jer 2:24
they have sold themselves to many lands, I will now gather them together. Then they Ezek 16:33
will writhe under the burden of the great king!
11 "Israel has built many altars to take away sin, but these very altars became places 8:10 Jer 42:2
for sinning! 12 Even though I gave them all my laws, they act as if those laws don't Ezek 16:37
apply to them. 13 The people of Israel love their rituals of sacrifice, but to me their Hos 10:10
sacrifices are all meaningless! I will call my people to account for their sins, and I will 8:13 Hos 7:2
punish them. They will go back down to Egypt. 1 Cor 4:5
14 "Israel has built great palaces, and Judah has fortified its cities. But they have both 8:14 Jer 17:27
forgotten their Maker. Therefore, I will send down fire on their palaces and burn their Hos 2:13; 4:6; 13:6
fortresses."

8:9 Hebrew *Ephraim,* referring to the northern kingdom of Israel; also in 8:11.

8:1-4 "The enemy descends like an eagle on the people of the LORD" refers to Assyria coming to attack Israel and take the people into captivity (2 Kings 15:28, 29). The people would call to God, but it would be too late because they had stubbornly refused to give up their idols. We, like Israel, often call on God to ease our pain without wanting him to change our behavior. And we, like Israel, may repent after it is too late to avoid the painful consequences of sin.

8:5 Samaria was the capital of the northern kingdom, and sometimes it stands for the whole kingdom of Israel. Jeroboam I had set up worship of calf idols at Bethel and Dan and had encouraged the people to worship them (1 Kings 12:25-33). Thus, the people were worshiping the image of a created animal rather than the Creator.

8:7 Crop yield is the result of good seed planted in good soil and given the proper proportions of sunlight, moisture, and fertilizer. A single seed can produce multiple fruit in good conditions. Israel, however, had sown its spiritual seed to the wind—it had invested itself in activities without substance. Like the wind that comes and goes, its idolatry and foreign alliances offered no protection. In seeking self-preservation apart from God, it had brought about its own destruction. Like a forceful whirlwind, God's judgment would come upon Israel by means of the Assyrians. When we seek security in anything except God, we expose ourselves to great danger. Without God there is no lasting security.

8:11 The altars that were supposed to remove sin were actually increasing sin through their misuse in worshiping Baal.

8:12 Though the laws were written for *them,* the people of Israel acted as if those laws didn't apply to them. It is easy to listen to a sermon and think of all the people we know who should be listening, or to read the Bible and think of those who should do what the passage teaches. The Israelites did this constantly, applying God's laws to others but not to themselves to avoid making needed changes. As you think of others who need to apply what you are hearing or reading, check to see if the same application could fit you. Apply the lessons to your own life first because often our own faults are the very first ones we see in others.

8:13 The people's sacrifices had become mere ritual, and God refused to accept them. We have rituals, too: attending church, observing a regular quiet time, celebrating Christian holidays, praying before meals. Rituals give us security in a changing world. Because they are repeated often, they can drive God's lessons deep within us. But rituals can be abused. Beware if you find yourself observing a religious ritual for any of the following reasons: (1) to gain community approval, (2) to avoid the risks of doing something different, (3) to make thought unnecessary, (4) to substitute for personal relationships, (5) to make up for bad behavior, (6) to earn God's favor. We should not reject the rituals of our worship, but we must be careful to think about why we do them. Focus on God, and perform every act with sincere devotion.

8:13 In Egypt, the Israelites had been slaves (Exodus 1:11). The people would not literally return to Egypt, but they would return to slavery—this time scattered throughout the Assyrian Empire.

8:14 Israel had placed its confidence in military strength, strong defenses, and economic stability, just as nations do today. But because of the people's inner moral decay, their apparent sources of strength were inadequate. There is a tendency in many nations toward removing all traces of God from daily life. But if a nation forgets its Maker, its strengths may prove worthless when put to the test.

Hosea Announces Israel's Punishment

9:1 **9** O people of Israel, do not rejoice as others do. For you have been unfaithful to your
Isa 17:11; 22:12-13 God, hiring yourselves out like prostitutes, offering sacrifices to other gods on every
9:2 Hos 2:9 threshing floor. 2 So now your harvests will be too small to feed you. The grapes you gather
9:3 will not quench your thirst. 3 You may no longer stay here in this land of the LORD. You will
Ezek 4:13 be carried off to Egypt and Assyria, where you will live on food that is ceremonially unclean.
9:4 4 There, far from home, you will not be allowed to pour out wine as a sacrifice to the
Exod 29:40; Hag 2:14 LORD. None of the sacrifices you offer there will please him. Such sacrifices will be
unclean, just as food touched by a person in mourning is unclean. All who present such
sacrifices will be defiled. They may eat this food to feed themselves, but they may not
offer it to the LORD.
9:5 Hos 2:11 5 What then will you do on festival days? What will you do on days of feasting in the
Joel 1:13 LORD's presence? 6 Even if you escape destruction from Assyria, you will be conquered
9:6 Isa 5:6; 7:23 by Egypt. Memphis* will bury you. Briers will take over your treasures of silver;
Hos 10:8 brambles will fill your homes.
9:7 Isa 10:3 7 The time of Israel's punishment has come; the day of payment is almost here. Soon
Jer 10:15; 29:26 Israel will know this all too well. "The prophets are crazy!" the people shout. "The
Lam 2:14; Ezek 7:2-7; 13:3, 10 inspired men are mad!" So they taunt, for the nation is burdened with sin and shows only
hatred for those who love God.
8 The prophet is a watchman for my God over Israel,* yet traps are laid in front of him
9:9 Isa 31:6 wherever he goes. He faces hostility even in the house of God. 9 The things my people
Hos 7:2; 8:13 do are as depraved as what they did in Gibeah long ago. God will not forget. He will
surely punish them for their sins.
9:10 Num 25:1-9 10 The LORD says, "O Israel, when I first found you, it was like finding fresh grapes
Jer 24:2 in the desert! When I saw your ancestors, it was like seeing the first ripe figs of the
Mic 7:1 season! But then they deserted me for Baal-peor, giving themselves to that shameful
9:11 Hos 4:7 idol. Soon they became as vile as the god they worshiped. 11 The glory of Israel will fly
away like a bird, for your children will die at birth or perish in the womb or never even
9:12 Hos 7:13 be conceived. 12 Even if your children do survive to grow up, I will take them from you.
It will be a terrible day when I turn away and leave you alone. 13 I have watched Israel
become as beautiful and pleasant as Tyre. But now Israel will bring out her children to
be slaughtered."
14 O LORD, what should I request for your people? I will ask for wombs that don't give
birth and breasts that give no milk.

9:6 Memphis was the capital of northern Egypt. **9:8** Hebrew *Ephraim,* referring to the northern kingdom of Israel; also in 9:11, 13, 16.

9:1 A threshing floor was a flat area, often built on a hilltop, where harvesters beat the wheat and separated it from the chaff. Often men would stay overnight at the threshing floor to protect their grain, so prostitutes would visit there. Because of the location of threshing floors in the hilltops, they began to be used as places to sacrifice to false gods.

9:6 Israel's leaders vacillated between alliances with Egypt and alliances with Assyria. Hosea was saying that both were wrong. Breaking an alliance with untrustworthy Assyria and fleeing for help to the equally untrustworthy Egypt would not forestall Israel's destruction. Its only hope was to return to God.

9:7 By the time Israel began to experience the consequences of its sins, it was no longer listening to God's messengers. Refusing to hear the truth from prophets who spoke out so clearly about its sins, the nation did not hear God's warnings about what was soon to happen. We all listen and read selectively, focusing on what seems to support our present life-style and ignoring a radical reordering of our priorities. In doing this, we are likely to miss the warning signs. Listen to people who think your approach is all wrong. Read articles that present viewpoints you would be unlikely to take. Ask yourself, Is God speaking to me through these speakers and writers? Is there something I need to change?

9:9 A couple had stopped to stay overnight in Gibeah when some wicked men gathered around the house and demanded that the man come out so they could have sex with him. Instead, the traveler gave them his concubine. They raped and abused her all night and then left her dead on the doorstep (Judges 19:14-30). That horrible act revealed the depths to which the people had sunk. Gibeah was destroyed for its evil (Judges 20:8-48), but Hosea said that the whole nation was now as evil as that city. Just as the city didn't escape punishment, neither would the nation.

9:10 Baal-peor was the god of Peor, a mountain in Moab. In Numbers 22, Balaam, a prophet, was hired by King Balak of Moab to curse the Israelites as they were coming through his land. The Moabites enticed the Israelites into sexual sin and Baal worship. Before long, the Israelites became as corrupt as the gods they worshiped. People soon begin to copy the characteristics and life-styles of those around them. What do you worship? Are you becoming more like God, or are you becoming more like the world?

9:14 Hosea prayed this prayer when he foresaw the destruction that Israel's sins would bring (2 Kings 17:7-23). This vision of Israel's terrible fate moved him to pray that women would not get pregnant and that children would die as infants so they would not have to experience the tremendous suffering and pain that lay ahead.

15The LORD says, "All their wickedness began at Gilgal; there I began to hate them. I
will drive them from my land because of their evil actions. I will love them no more
because all their leaders are rebels. 16The people of Israel are stricken. Their roots are
dried up; they will bear no more fruit. And if they give birth, I will slaughter their beloved
children."
17My God will reject the people of Israel because they will not listen or obey. They
will be wanderers, homeless among the nations.

The LORD's Judgment against Israel

10 How prosperous Israel is—a luxuriant vine loaded with fruit! But the more wealth
the people got, the more they poured it on the altars of their foreign gods. The
richer the harvests they brought in, the more beautiful the statues and idols they built.
2The hearts of the people are fickle; they are guilty and must be punished. The LORD will
break down their foreign altars and smash their many idols.
3Then they will say, "We have no king because we didn't fear the LORD. But what's
the difference? What could a king do for us anyway?" 4They spout empty words and
make promises they don't intend to keep. So perverted justice springs up among them
like poisonous weeds in a farmer's field.
5The people of Samaria tremble for their calf idol at Beth-aven.* The people mourn
over it, and the priests wail for it, because its glory will be stripped away. 6This idol they
love so much will be carted away with them when they go as captives to Assyria, a gift
to the great king there. Israel will be laughed at and shamed because its people have
trusted in this idol. 7Samaria will be cut off, and its king will disappear like a chip of
wood on an ocean wave. 8And the pagan shrines of Aven,* the place of Israel's sin, will
crumble. Thorns and thistles will grow up around them. They will beg the mountains to
bury them and the hills to fall on them.
9The LORD says, "O Israel, ever since that awful night in Gibeah, there has been only sin
and more sin! You have made no progress whatsoever. Was it not right that the wicked men
of Gibeah were attacked? 10Now I will attack you, too, for your rebellion and disobedience.
I will call out the armies of the nations to punish you for your multiplied sins.
11"Israel* is like a trained heifer accustomed to treading out the grain—an easy job
that she loves. Now I will put a heavy yoke on her tender neck. I will drive her in front
of the plow. Israel* and Judah must now break up the hard ground; their days of ease are
gone. 12I said, 'Plant the good seeds of righteousness, and you will harvest a crop of my
love. Plow up the hard ground of your hearts, for now is the time to seek the LORD, that
he may come and shower righteousness upon you.'

10:5 *Beth-aven* means "house of wickedness"; it is being used as another name for Bethel, which means "house of God." **10:8** *Aven* is a reference to Beth-aven; see 10:5 and the note there. **10:11a** Hebrew *Ephraim,* referring to the northern kingdom of Israel. **10:11b** Hebrew *Jacob.*

9:15 Isa 1:23 Hos 7:2; 12:2 Amos 4:4; 5:5
9:16 Ezek 24:21
10:1 1 Kgs 14:23 Isa 5:1-7 Ezek 15:1-5 Hos 8:11; 12:11
10:2 1 Kgs 18:21 Hos 10:8 Mic 5:13 Zeph 1:5
10:3 Ps 12:4
10:4 Hos 4:2
10:5 Hos 8:5
10:6 Hos 10:5
10:8 Hos 5:8; 9:6; 10:5 †Luke 23:30 Rev 6:16
10:10 Ezek 5:13
10:11 Jer 28:14
10:12 Prov 11:18 Isa 45:8

9:15 At Gilgal, both the political and the religious failure of the nation began. Here idols and kings were substituted for God. Saul, the united nation's first king, was crowned at Gilgal (1 Samuel 11:15), but by Hosea's time, Baal worship flourished there (4:15; 12:11).

10:1 Israel prospered under Jeroboam II, gaining military and economic strength. But the more prosperous the nation became, the more love it lavished on idols. It seems as though the more God gives, the more we spend. We want bigger houses, better cars, and finer clothes. But the finest things the world offers line the pathway to destruction. As you prosper, consider where your money is going. Is it being used for God's purposes, or are you consuming it all on yourself?

10:4 God was angry with the people of Israel for their insincere promises. Because the people did not keep their word, there were many lawsuits. People break their promises, but God always keeps his. Are you remaining true to your promises, both to other people and to God? If not, ask God for forgiveness and help to get back on track. Then be careful about the promises you make. Never make a promise unless you are sure you can keep it.

10:5 *Beth-aven* means "house of wickedness," and it refers to Bethel ("house of God"), where false worship took place. If the Israelites' idols were really gods, they should have been able to protect them. How ironic that the people were fearing for their gods' safety! For more information on this calf idol, see the notes on 3:4, 5 and 8:5.

10:9, 10 For information on "that awful night in Gibeah," see the note on 9:9 or read Judges 19 and 20. Gibeah stands for cruelty and sensuality, as in Judges, and for rebellion as in Saul's day (Gibeah was Saul's hometown; see 1 Samuel 10:5; 11:4).

10:12 Hosea repeatedly uses illustrations about fields and crops. Here he envisions a plowed field. It is no longer stony and hard; it has been carefully prepared, and it is ready for planting. Is your life ready for God to work in it? You can break up the unplowed ground of your heart by acknowledging your sins and receiving God's forgiveness and guidance.

10:13 Ps 33:16; Gal 6:7-8
10:14 2 Kgs 17:3

13“But you have cultivated wickedness and raised a thriving crop of sins. You have
eaten the fruit of lies—trusting in your military might, believing that great armies could
make your nation safe! 14Now the terrors of war will rise among your people. All your
fortifications will fall, just as they did when Shalman destroyed Beth-arbel. Even
mothers and children were dashed to death there. 15You will share that fate, Bethel,
because of your great wickedness. When the day of judgment dawns, the king of Israel
will be completely destroyed.

3. God’s love for Israel

11:1 Exod 4:22; Hos 2:15; 12:9, 13; 13:4; Matt 2:15
11:3 Deut 1:31; Jer 30:17
11:4 Exod 16:32; Ps 78:25; Jer 31:2-3
11:6 Hos 13:16
11:7 Jer 8:5
11:8 Gen 14:8; Deut 29:23; Hos 6:4; 7:1
11:9 Deut 13:17; Isa 5:24; 12:6; 41:14; Jer 26:3

11 “When Israel was a child, I loved him as a son, and I called my son out of Egypt.
2But the more I* called to him, the more he rebelled, offering sacrifices to the
images of Baal and burning incense to idols. 3It was I who taught Israel* how to walk,
leading him along by the hand. But he doesn’t know or even care that it was I who took
care of him. 4I led Israel along with my ropes of kindness and love. I lifted the yoke from
his neck, and I myself stooped to feed him.

5“But since my people refuse to return to me, they will go back to Egypt and will be
forced to serve Assyria. 6War will swirl through their cities; their enemies will crash
through their gates and destroy them, trapping them in their own evil plans. 7For my
people are determined to desert me. They call me the Most High, but they don’t truly
honor me.

8“Oh, how can I give you up, Israel? How can I let you go? How can I destroy you
like Admah and Zeboiim? My heart is torn within me, and my compassion overflows.
9No, I will not punish you as much as my burning anger tells me to. I will not completely
destroy Israel, for I am God and not a mere mortal. I am the Holy One living among you,
and I will not come to destroy.

11:2 As in Greek version; Hebrew reads *they.* **11:3** Hebrew *Ephraim,* referring to the northern kingdom of Israel; also in 11:8, 9, 12.

10:13 The Israelites were taken in by the lie that military power could keep them safe. Believers today sometimes fall for lies. Those who lead others astray often follow these rules: Make it big; keep it simple; repeat it often. Believers can avoid falling for lies by asking: (1) Am I believing this because there is personal gain in it for me? (2) Am I discounting important facts? (3) Does this conflict with a direct command of Scripture? (4) Are there any biblical parallels to the situation I’m facing that would help me know what to believe?

10:14 Some say Shalman was Shalmaneser, king of Assyria; others say Shalman was Salmanu, a Moabite king mentioned in the inscriptions of Tiglath-pileser. Shalman had invaded Gilead around 740 B.C. and destroyed the city of Beth-arbel, killing many people, including women and children. This kind of cruelty was not uncommon in ancient warfare. Hosea was saying such would be Israel’s fate.

10:15 Because Israel had put its confidence in military might rather than in God, it would be destroyed by military power. Israel’s king, who had led the people into idol worship, would be the first to fall. Divine judgment is *sometimes* swift, but it is *always* sure.

11:1ff In the final four chapters, Hosea shifts to the theme of God’s intense love for Israel. God had always loved Israel as a parent loves a stubborn child, and that is why he would not release Israel from the consequences of its behavior. The Israelites were sinful, and they would be punished like a rebellious son brought by his parents before the elders (Deuteronomy 21:18-21). All through Israel’s sad history, God repeatedly offered to restore the nation if it would only turn to him. By stubbornly refusing God’s invitation, the northern kingdom had sealed its doom. It would be destroyed, never to rise again. Even so, Israel as a nation was not finished. A remnant of faithful Israelites would return to Jerusalem, where one day the Messiah would come, offering pardon and reconciliation to all who would faithfully follow him.

11:3 God had consistently provided for his people, but they refused to see what he had done, and they showed no interest in thanking him. Ungratefulness is a common human fault. For example, when was the last time you thanked your parents for caring for you? your pastor for the service he gives your church? your child’s teacher for the care taken with each day’s activities? your heavenly Father for his guidance? Many of the benefits and privileges we enjoy are the result of loving actions done long ago. Look for hidden acts of nurturing, and thank those who make the world better through their love. But begin by thanking God for all his blessings.

11:4 God’s discipline requires times of leading and times of feeding. Sometimes the rope is taut; sometimes it is slack. God’s discipline is always loving, and its object is always the well-being of the beloved. When you are called to discipline others—children, students, employees, or church members—do not be rigid. Vary your approach according to the goals you are seeking to accomplish. In each case, ask yourself, Does this person need guidance, or does he or she need to be nurtured?

11:5 The northern kingdom survived for only two centuries after its break with Jerusalem. Its spiritual and political leaders did not help the people learn the way to God, so as a nation they would never repent. Hosea prophesied its downfall, which happened when Shalmaneser of Assyria conquered Israel in 722 B.C. Judah also would go into captivity, but a remnant would return to its homeland.

11:8 Admah and Zeboiim were cities of the plain that perished with Sodom and Gomorrah (Genesis 14:8; Deuteronomy 29:23).

11:9 “I am God and not a mere mortal.” It is easy for us to define God in terms of our own expectations and behavior. In so doing, we make him just slightly larger than ourselves. In reality, God is infinitely greater than we are. We should seek to become like him rather than attempt to remake him in our image.

10“For someday the people will follow the LORD. I will roar like a lion, and my people
will return trembling from the west. 11Like a flock of birds, they will come from Egypt.
Flying like doves, they will return from Assyria. And I will bring them home again,” says
the LORD.

Charges against Israel and Judah

12Israel surrounds me with lies and deceit, but Judah still walks with God and is faithful
to the Holy One.*

12 The people of Israel* feed on the wind; they chase after the east wind all day long.
They multiply lies and violence; they make alliances with Assyria and cut deals
with the Egyptians.

2Now the LORD is bringing a lawsuit against Judah. He is about to punish Jacob* for
all his deceitful ways. 3Before Jacob was born, he struggled with his brother; when he
became a man, he even fought with God. 4Yes, he wrestled with the angel and won. He
wept and pleaded for a blessing from him. There at Bethel he met God face to face, and
God spoke to him*—5the LORD God Almighty, the LORD is his name! 6So now, come
back to your God! Act on the principles of love and justice, and always live in confident
dependence on your God.

7But no, the people are like crafty merchants selling from dishonest scales—they love
to cheat. 8Israel boasts, “I am rich, and I’ve gotten it all by myself! No one can say I got
it by cheating! My record is spotless!”

9“I am the LORD your God, who rescued you from your slavery in Egypt. And I will
make you live in tents again, as you do each year when you celebrate the Festival of
Shelters.* 10I sent my prophets to warn you with many visions and parables.”

11But Gilead is filled with sinners who worship idols. And in Gilgal, too, they
sacrifice bulls; their altars are lined up like the heaps of stone along the edges of a
plowed field. 12Jacob fled to the land of Aram and earned a wife by tending sheep.

11:10 Isa 31:4; 66:2, 5; Joel 3:16
11:11 Isa 11:11; 60:8
12:1 Gen 41:6; Jer 22:22; Ezek 17:10
12:2 Hos 4:1; Mic 6:2
12:3 Gen 25:26
12:4 Gen 28:13-15; 32:24-30; 35:10-15
12:5 Exod 3:15
12:6 Mic 7:7
12:7 Prov 11:1; Amos 8:5; Mic 6:11
12:8 Hos 13:6; Rev 3:17
12:10 2 Kgs 17:13; Ezek 17:2; 20:49
12:12 Gen 28:5; 29:20

11:12 Or *and Judah is unruly against God, the faithful Holy One.* **12:1** Hebrew *Ephraim,* referring to the northern kingdom of Israel; also in 12:8, 14. **12:2** *Jacob* means “he grasps at the heel”; this can also figuratively mean “he deceives.” **12:4** As in Greek and Syriac versions; Hebrew reads *to us.* **12:9** Hebrew *as in the days of your appointed feast.*

11:12 Unlike Israel, Judah had some fairly good kings—Asa, Jehoshaphat, Joash, Amaziah, Azariah (Uzziah), Jotham, and especially Hezekiah and Josiah. Under some of these kings, God’s law was dusted off and taught to the people. The priests continued to serve in God’s appointed Temple in Jerusalem, and the festivals were celebrated at least some of the time. Unfortunately, the political or religious leaders were unable to completely wipe out idol worship and pagan rites (although Hezekiah and Josiah came close), which continued to fester until they eventually erupted and infected the whole country. Still, the influence of the good kings enabled Judah to survive more than 150 years longer than Israel, and that memory of their positive influence fortified a small group—a remnant—of faithful people who would one day return and restore their land and Temple.

12:2-5 Jacob, whose name was later changed to Israel, was the common ancestor of all 12 tribes of Israel (both northern and southern kingdoms). Like the nations that descended from him, Jacob practiced deceit. Unlike Israel and Judah, however, he constantly searched for God. Jacob wrestled with the angel in order to be blessed, but his descendants thought their blessings came from their own successes. Jacob purged his house of idols (Genesis 35:2), but his descendants could not quit their idol worship.

12:6 The two principles that Hosea called his nation to live by, love and justice, are at the very foundation of God’s character. They are essential to his followers, but they are not easy to keep in balance. Some people are loving to the point that they excuse wrongdoing. Others are just to the extent that they forget love. Love without justice leaves people in their sins, because it is not aiming at a higher standard. Justice without love drives people away from God because it has no heart. To specialize in one at the expense of the other is to distort our witness. Today’s church, just like Hosea’s nation, must live by both principles.

12:7, 8 In Israel, dishonesty had become an accepted means of attaining wealth. Israelites who were financially successful could not imagine that God would consider them sinful. They thought that their wealth was a sign of God’s approval, and they didn’t bother to consider how they had gotten it. But God said that Israel’s riches would not make up for its sin. Remember that God’s measure of success is different from ours. He calls us to faithfulness, not to affluence. Character is more important to him than our purses.

12:8 Rich people and nations often claim that their material success is due to their own hard work, initiative, and intelligence. Because they have bought whatever they wanted, they don’t feel the need for God. They believe that their riches are their own and that they have the right to use them any way they please. If you find yourself feeling proud of your accomplishments, remember that all your opportunities, abilities, and resources come from God and that you hold them in sacred trust for him.

12:9 Once a year the Israelites spent a week living in tents during the Festival of Shelters, which commemorated God’s protection as they wandered in the wilderness for 40 years (see Deuteronomy 1:19–2:1). Here, because of their sin, God would cause them to live in tents again—this time not as part of a festival but in actual bondage.

12:12 Hosea was using this reference to Jacob to say, “Don’t forget your humble beginnings. What you have is not a result of your own efforts, but it is yours because God has been gracious to you.”

13 Then the LORD led Jacob's descendants, the Israelites, out of Egypt by a prophet,
who guided and protected them. 14 But the people of Israel have bitterly provoked the
LORD, so their Lord will now sentence them to death in payment for their sins.

The LORD's Anger against Israel

13 In the past when the tribe of Ephraim spoke, the people shook with fear because
the other Israelite tribes looked up to them. But the people of Ephraim sinned by
worshiping Baal and thus sealed their destruction. 2 Now they keep on sinning by making
silver idols to worship—images shaped skillfully with human hands. "Sacrifice to
these," they cry, "and kiss the calf idols!" 3 Therefore, they will disappear like the
morning mist, like dew in the morning sun, like chaff blown by the wind, like smoke
from a chimney.

4 "I am the LORD your God, who rescued you from your slavery in Egypt. You have
no God but me, for there is no other savior. 5 I took care of you in the wilderness, in that
dry and thirsty land. 6 But when you had eaten and were satisfied, then you became proud
and forgot me. 7 So now I will attack you like a lion, or like a leopard that lurks along the
road. 8 I will rip you to pieces like a bear whose cubs have been taken away. I will tear
you apart and devour you like a hungry lion.

9 "You are about to be destroyed, O Israel, though I am your helper. 10 Where now is*
your king? Why don't you call on him for help? Where are all the leaders of the land?
You asked for them, now let them save you! 11 In my anger I gave you kings, and in my
fury I took them away.

12 "The sins of Ephraim have been collected and stored away for punishment. 13 The
people have been offered new birth, but they are like a child who resists being born.
How stubborn they are! How foolish! 14 Should I ransom them from the grave? Should
I redeem them from death? O death, bring forth your terrors! O grave, bring forth
your plagues! For I will not relent! 15 Ephraim was the most fruitful of all his brothers,
but the east wind—a blast from the LORD—will arise in the desert. It will blow hard
against the people of Ephraim, drying up their land. All their flowing springs and
wells will disappear. Every precious thing they have will be plundered and carried
away. 16 The people of Samaria must bear the consequences of their guilt because
they rebelled against their God. They will be killed by an invading army, their
little ones dashed to death against the ground, their pregnant women ripped open by
swords."

13:10 As in Greek and Syriac versions and Latin Vulgate; Hebrew reads *I will be.*

12:13 Exod 14:19-22
12:14 2 Kgs 17:7-18
13:1 Judg 8:1; 12:1; Hos 2:8-17
13:2 Isa 44:17-20; 46:6; Jer 10:2-5
13:3 Ps 68:2; Isa 17:13; Dan 2:35; Hos 6:4
13:4 Exod 20:3; Isa 43:11; 45:21-22
13:5 Deut 2:7; 8:15; 32:10
13:6 Hos 2:13; 4:6; 8:14
13:8 Ps 50:22
13:10 2 Kgs 17:4; Hos 8:4
13:11 1 Sam 8:7; 1 Kgs 14:7-10
13:12 Deut 32:34-35; Rom 2:5
13:13 Mic 4:9-10
13:14 Isa 25:8; Ezek 37:12-13; †1 Cor 15:55; Phil 3:21
13:15 Jer 51:36; Hos 10:1
13:16 2 Kgs 15:16

CYCLES OF JUDGMENT/ SALVATION IN HOSEA

Judgment . . . . 1:2-9; 2:2-13; 4:1—5:14; 6:4—11:7; 11:12—13:16
Salvation . . . . . 1:10—2:1; 2:14—3:5; 5:15—6:3; 11:8-11; 14:1-9

God promises to judge, but he also promises mercy. Here you can see the cycles of judgment and salvation in Hosea. Prophecies of judgment are consistently followed by prophecies of forgiveness.

12:13 The prophet who brought Israel out of Egypt was Moses (Exodus 13:17-19).

13:1 Israel, represented here by the northern tribe of Ephraim, had been great, but by Hosea's time the people had rebelled against God and had lost their authority among the nations. Greatness in the past is no guarantee of greatness in the future. It is good to remember what God has done for you and through you, but it is equally important to keep your relationship with him vital and up to date. Commit yourself to God moment by moment.

13:4-6 When abundant possessions made Israel feel self-sufficient, it turned its back on God and forgot him. Self-sufficiency is as destructive today as it was in Hosea's time. Do you see your constant need of God's presence and help? Learn to rely on God, both in good times and bad. If you are traveling along a smooth and easy path right now, beware of forgetting who gave you your good fortune. Don't depend on your gifts; depend on the Giver. See Deuteronomy 6:10-12 and 8:7-20 for God's warning.

13:11 God had warned the people of Israel that kings would cause more problems than they would solve, and he reluctantly gave them Saul as their first king (1 Samuel 8:4-22). The second king, David, was a good king, and Solomon, David's son, had his strengths. But after the nation divided in two, the northern kingdom never had another good ruler. Evil kings led the nations deeper into idolatry and unwise political alliances. Eventually the evil kings destroyed the nation; with Hoshea, the northern kingdom's kings were cut off (2 Kings 17:1-6).

13:12 Ephraim's (Israel's) sins were recorded for later punishment. All our sins are known and will be revealed at the day of judgment (2 Corinthians 5:10; Revelation 20:11-15).

13:14 The apostle Paul used this passage to teach the resurrection of our bodies from death (1 Corinthians 15:55). For those who have trusted in Christ for deliverance from sin, death holds no threat of annihilation.

Healing for the Repentant

14 Return, O Israel, to the LORD your God, for your sins have brought you down.
2 Bring your petitions, and return to the LORD. Say to him, "Forgive all our sins
and graciously receive us, so that we may offer you the sacrifice of praise. 3 Assyria
cannot save us, nor can our strength in battle. Never again will we call the idols we have
made 'our gods.' No, in you alone do the orphans find mercy."
4 The LORD says, "Then I will heal you of your idolatry and faithlessness, and my love
will know no bounds, for my anger will be gone forever! 5 I will be to Israel like a
refreshing dew from heaven. It will blossom like the lily; it will send roots deep into the
soil like the cedars in Lebanon. 6 Its branches will spread out like those of beautiful olive
trees, as fragrant as the cedar forests of Lebanon. 7 My people will return again to the
safety of their land. They will flourish like grain and blossom like grapevines. They will
be as fragrant as the wines of Lebanon.
8 "O Israel,* stay away from idols! I am the one who looks after you and cares for you.
I am like a tree that is always green, giving my fruit to you all through the year."
9 Let those who are wise understand these things. Let those who are discerning listen
carefully. The paths of the LORD are true and right, and righteous people live by walking
in them. But sinners stumble and fall along the way.

14:2 Mic 7:18-19; Heb 13:15
14:3 Pss 10:14; 68:5; Mic 5:10
14:4 Isa 57:18; Zeph 3:17
14:5 Song 2:1; Matt 6:28
14:6 Ps 52:8; Jer 11:16
14:7 Ps 91:1-4; Ezek 17:23
14:8 Isa 41:19
14:9 Ps 107:43; Isa 1:28; 26:7; Jer 9:12

14:8 Hebrew *Ephraim,* referring to the northern kingdom of Israel.

14:1ff Verses 1-3 are Hosea's call to repent. Verses 4-8 are God's promise of restoration. God had to punish Israel for its gross and repeated violations of his law, but he would do so with a heavy heart. What God really wanted to do was restore the nation and make it prosper.

14:1, 2 The people could return to God by asking him to forgive their sins. The same is true for us: We can pray Hosea's prayer and know our sins are forgiven because Christ died for them on the cross (John 3:16).

Forgiveness begins when we see the destructiveness of sin and the futility of life without God. Then we must admit we cannot save ourselves; our only hope is in God's mercy. When we seek forgiveness, we must recognize that we do not deserve it and therefore cannot demand it. Our appeal must be for God's love and mercy, not for his justice. Although we cannot demand forgiveness, we can be confident that we have received it because God is gracious and loving and wants to restore us to himself, just as he wanted to restore Israel.

14:2 "The sacrifice of praise" refers to thank offerings to God. God desired real, heartfelt repentance, not merely annual sacrifices.

14:3-8 When our will is weak, when our thinking is confused, and when our conscience is burdened with a load of guilt, we must remember that God cares for us continually; his compassion never fails. When friends and family desert us, when co-workers don't understand us, and when we are tired of being good, God's compassion never fails. When we can't see the way or seem to hear God's voice, and when we lack courage to go on, God's compassion never fails. When our shortcomings and our awareness of our sins overcome us, God's compassion never fails.

14:9 Hosea closes with an appeal to listen, learn, and benefit from God's word. To those receiving the Lord's message through Hosea, this meant the difference between life and death. For you, the reader of the book of Hosea, the choice is similar: You can either listen to the book's message and follow God's ways or refuse to walk along the Lord's path. But people who insist on following their own direction without God's guidance are in "complete darkness" and "have no idea what they are stumbling over" (Proverbs 4:19). If you are lost, you can find the way by turning from your sin and following God.

14:9 God's concern for *justice* that requires faithfulness and for *love* that offers forgiveness can be seen in his dealings with Hosea. We can err by forgetting God's love, feeling that our sins are hopeless; but we can also err by forgetting his wrath against our sins, thinking he will continue to accept us no matter how we act. *Forgiveness* is a key word: When God forgives us, he judges the sin but shows mercy to the sinner. We should never be afraid to come to God for a clean slate and a renewed life.

JOEL

King Ahab dies in battle 853 B.C.	Elisha becomes a prophet 848	Jehu becomes king of Israel; Athaliah seizes Judah's throne 841	Joel becomes a prophet? Joash becomes king of Judah 835	Jehoahaz becomes king of Israel 814	Jehoash becomes king of Israel 798	Joel's ministry ends 796?

A SINGLE bomb devastates a city, and the world is ushered into the nuclear age. A split atom—power and force such as we had never seen.

At a launch site, rockets roar and a payload is thrust into space. Discoveries dreamed of for centuries are ours as we begin to explore the edge of the universe.

Volcanos, earthquakes, tidal waves, hurricanes, and tornados unleash uncontrollable and unstoppable force. And we can only avoid them and then pick up the pieces.

Power, strength, might—we stand in awe at the natural and man-made display. But these forces cannot touch the power of omnipotent God. Creator of galaxies, atoms, and natural laws, the Sovereign Lord rules all there is and ever will be. How silly to live without him; how foolish to run and hide from him; how ridiculous to disobey him. But we do. Since Eden, we have sought independence from his control, as though we were gods and could control our destiny. And he has allowed our rebellion. But soon *the day of the Lord* will come.

It is about this day that the prophet Joel speaks, and it is the theme of his book. On this day God will judge all unrighteousness and disobedience—all accounts will be settled and the crooked made straight.

We know very little about Joel—only that he was a prophet and the son of Pethuel. He may have lived in Jerusalem because his audience was Judah, the southern kingdom. Whoever he was, Joel speaks forthrightly and forcefully in this short and powerful book. His message is one of foreboding and warning, but it is also filled with hope. Joel states that our Creator, the omnipotent Judge, is also merciful, and he wants to bless all those who trust him.

Joel begins by describing a terrible plague of locusts that covers the land and devours the crops. The devastation wrought by these creatures is but a foretaste of the coming judgment of God, the "day of the LORD." Joel, therefore, urges the people to turn from their sin and turn back to God. Woven into this message of judgment and the need for repentance is an affirmation of God's kindness and the blessings he promises for all who follow him. In fact, "anyone who calls on the name of the LORD will be saved" (2:32).

As you read Joel, catch his vision of the power and might of God and of God's ultimate judgment of sin. Choose to follow, obey, and worship God alone as your sovereign Lord.

VITAL STATISTICS

PURPOSE:
To warn Judah of God's impending judgment because of its sins and to urge the people to turn back to God

AUTHOR:
Joel son of Pethuel

TO WHOM WRITTEN:
The people of Judah, the southern kingdom, and God's people everywhere

DATE WRITTEN:
Probably during the time Joel may have prophesied, from approximately 835–796 B.C.

SETTING:
The people of Judah had become prosperous and complacent. Taking God for granted, they had turned to self-centeredness, idolatry, and sin. Joel warned them that this kind of life-style would inevitably bring down God's judgment.

KEY VERSES:
"That is why the LORD says, 'Turn to me now, while there is time! Give me your hearts. Come with fasting, weeping, and mourning. Don't tear your clothing in your grief; instead, tear your hearts.' Return to the LORD your God, for he is gracious and merciful. He is not easily angered. He is filled with kindness and is eager not to punish you" (2:12, 13).

KEY PEOPLE:
Joel, the people of Judah

KEY PLACE:
Jerusalem

THE BLUEPRINT

1. The day of the locusts (1:1—2:27) 2. The day of the LORD (2:28—3:21)	The locust plague was only a foretaste of the judgment to come in the day of the Lord. This is a timeless call to repentance with the promise of blessing. Just as the people faced the tragedy of their crops being destroyed, we, too, will face tragic judgment if we live in sin. But God's grace is available to us both now and in that coming day.

MEGATHEMES

THEME	EXPLANATION	IMPORTANCE
Punishment	Like a destroying army of locusts, God's punishment for sin is overwhelming, dreadful, and unavoidable. When it comes, there will be no food, no water, no protection, and no escape. The day for settling accounts with God for how we have lived is fast approaching.	God is the one with whom we all must reckon—not nature, the economy, or a foreign invader. We can't ignore or offend God forever. We must pay attention to his message now, or we will face his anger later.
Forgiveness	God stood ready to forgive and restore all those who would come to him and turn away from sin. God wanted to shower his people with his love and restore them to a proper relationship with him.	Forgiveness comes by turning from sin and turning toward God. It is not too late to receive God's forgiveness. God's greatest desire is for you to come to him.
Promise of the Holy Spirit	Joel predicts the time when God will pour out his Holy Spirit on all people. It will be the beginning of new and fresh worship of God by those who believe in him, as well as the beginning of judgment on all who reject him.	God is in control. Justice and restoration are in his hands. The Holy Spirit confirms God's love for us just as he did for the first Christians (Acts 2). We must be faithful to God and place our life under the guidance and power of his Holy Spirit.

1. The day of the locusts

1 The LORD gave this message to Joel son of Pethuel.

Mourning over the Locust Plague

2 Hear this, you leaders of the people! Everyone listen! In all your history, has anything
like this ever happened before? 3 Tell your children about it in the years to come. Pass
the awful story down from generation to generation. 4 After the cutting locusts finished
eating the crops, the swarming locusts took what was left! After them came the hopping
locusts, and then the stripping locusts,* too!
5 Wake up, you drunkards, and weep! All the grapes are ruined, and all your new wine
is gone! 6 A vast army of locusts* has invaded my land. It is a terrible army, too numerous
to count! Its teeth are as sharp as the teeth of lions! 7 They have destroyed my grapevines
and fig trees, stripping their bark and leaving the branches white and bare.

1:2 Jer 30:7; Joel 2:2, 16
1:3 Exod 10:2
1:4 Deut 28:38-39; Isa 33:4; Nah 3:15-16
1:6 Rev 9:8
1:7 Isa 5:6; Amos 4:9

1:4 The precise identification of the four kinds of locusts mentioned here is uncertain. **1:6** Hebrew *A nation.*

1:1 Joel was a prophet to the nation of Judah, also known as the southern kingdom. The book does not mention when Joel lived, but many believe that he prophesied during the reign of King Joash (835–796 B.C.). But the date of Joel's book is not nearly so important as its timeless message: Sin brings God's judgment; yet with God's justice there is also great mercy.

1:3 God urged parents to pass their history down to their children, telling over and over the important lessons they learned. One of the greatest gifts you can give young people is your life's story to help them repeat your successes and avoid your mistakes.

1:4 A locust plague can be as devastating as an invading army. Locusts gather in swarms too great to number (1:6) and fly several feet above the ground, seeming to darken the sun as they pass by (2:2). When they land, they devour almost every piece of vegetation (1:7-12), covering and entering everything in their path (2:9).

1:4 Joel's detailed description has caused many to believe that he was referring to an actual locust plague that had come or was about to come upon the land. Another view is that the locusts symbolize an invading enemy army. In either case, the locusts represent devastation, and Joel's point was that God would punish the people because of their sin. Joel calls this judgment the "day of the LORD" (see the note on 1:15).

1:5 The people's physical and moral senses were dulled, making them oblivious to sin. Joel called them to awaken from their complacency and admit their sins before it was too late. Otherwise everything would be destroyed, even the grapes that caused their drunkenness. Our times of peace and prosperity can lull us to sleep. We must never let material abundance hinder our spiritual readiness.

1:9 Hos 9:4
1:10 Isa 24:4, 7
1:11 Amos 5:16
1:12 Song 2:3; Hab 3:17-18; Hag 2:19
1:13 1 Kgs 21:27; Jer 4:8
1:14 Jon 3:8
1:15 Isa 13:9; Jer 30:7; Ezek 7:2-13
1:16 Isa 3:7; Amos 4:6-7
1:17 Isa 17:10-11
1:19 Pss 50:15; 91:15; Mic 7:7
1:20 1 Kgs 17:7; 18:5; Ps 104:21

8 Weep with sorrow, as a virgin weeps when her fiancé has died. 9 There is no grain or
wine to offer at the Temple of the LORD. The priests are mourning because there are no
offerings. Listen to the weeping of these ministers of the LORD! 10 The fields are ruined
and empty of crops. The grain, the wine, and the olive oil are gone.

11 Despair, all you farmers! Wail, all you vine growers! Weep, because the wheat and
barley—yes, all the field crops—are ruined. 12 The grapevines and the fig trees have all
withered. The pomegranate trees, palm trees, and apple trees—yes, all the fruit trees—
have dried up. All joy has dried up with them.

13 Dress yourselves in sackcloth, you priests! Wail, you who serve before the altar!
Come, spend the night in sackcloth, you ministers of my God! There is no grain or wine
to offer at the Temple of your God. 14 Announce a time of fasting; call the people together
for a solemn meeting. Bring the leaders and all the people into the Temple of the LORD
your God, and cry out to him there. 15 The day of the LORD is on the way, the day when
destruction comes from the Almighty. How terrible that day will be!

16 We watch as our food disappears before our very eyes. There are no joyful
celebrations in the house of our God. 17 The seeds die in the parched ground, and the
grain crops fail. The barns and granaries stand empty and abandoned. 18 How the animals
moan with hunger! The cattle wander about confused because there is no pasture for
them. The sheep bleat in misery.

19 LORD, help us! The fire has consumed the pastures and burned up all the trees.
20 Even the wild animals cry out to you because they have no water to drink. The streams
have dried up, and fire has consumed the pastures.

Locusts Invade like an Army

2:1 Zeph 1:16
2:2 Dan 9:12

2 Blow the trumpet in Jerusalem*! Sound the alarm on my holy mountain! Let
everyone tremble in fear because the day of the LORD is upon us. 2 It is a day of
darkness and gloom, a day of thick clouds and deep blackness. Suddenly, like dawn

2:1 Hebrew *Zion;* also in 2:15, 23.

JOEL served as a prophet to Judah, possibly from 835–796 B.C.

Climate of the times	Wicked Queen Athaliah seized power in a bloody coup but was overthrown after a few years. Joash was crowned king, but he was only seven years old and in great need of spiritual guidance. Joash followed God in his early years but then turned away from him.
Main message	A plague of locusts had come to discipline the nation. Joel called the people to turn back to God before an even greater judgment occurred.
Importance of message	God judges all people for their sins, but he is merciful to those who turn to him and offers them eternal salvation.
Contemporary prophets	Elisha (848–797 B.C.), Jonah (793–753 B.C.)

1:9 Because of the devastation, there was no fine flour or wine for the grain or drink offerings (see Leviticus 1 and 2 for a detailed explanation of these offerings).

1:13 Sackcloth is the clothing put on by mourners at a funeral. Used here, it would be a sign of repentance.

1:14 A fast was a period of time when no food was eaten and people approached God with humility, sorrow for sin, and urgent prayer. In the Old Testament, people often would fast during times of calamity in order to focus their attention on God and to demonstrate their change of heart and their true devotion (see, for example, Judges 20:26; 1 Kings 21:27; Ezra 8:21; Jonah 3:5). This solemn meeting was a public religious gathering, called so that everyone could repent and pray to God for mercy.

1:15 The "day of the LORD" is a common phrase in the Old Testament and in the book of Joel (see 2:1, 11, 31; 3:14). It always refers to some extraordinary happening, whether a present event (like a locust plague), an event in the near future (like the destruction of Jerusalem or the defeat of enemy nations), or the final period of history when God will defeat all the forces of evil.

Even when the day of the Lord refers to a present event, it also foreshadows the *final* day of the Lord. This final event of history has two aspects to it: (1) the last judgment on all evil and sin and (2) the final reward for faithful believers. Righteousness and truth will prevail, but not before much suffering (Zechariah 14:1-3). If you trust the Lord, looking toward this final day should give you hope, because then all who are faithful will be united forever with God.

1:15-19 Without God, destruction is sure. Those who have not personally accepted God's love and forgiveness will stand before him with no appeal. Be sure to avail yourself of God's love and mercy while you have the opportunity (2:32).

2:1ff Joel was still describing the devastating effects of the locust plague (see 2:25). The alarm showed that the crisis was at hand. However, Joel implied that the locust plague would be only the forerunner of an even greater crisis if the people didn't turn from their sins.

spreading across the mountains, a mighty army appears! How great and powerful they
are! The likes of them have not been seen before and never will be seen again.
[3]Fire burns in front of them and follows them in every direction! Ahead of them the
land lies as fair as the Garden of Eden in all its beauty. Behind them is nothing but
desolation; not one thing escapes. [4]They look like tiny horses, and they run as fast.
[5]Look at them as they leap along the mountaintops! Listen to the noise they make—like
the rumbling of chariots, like the roar of a fire sweeping across a field, or like a mighty
army moving into battle.
[6]Fear grips all the people; every face grows pale with fright. [7]The attackers march
like warriors and scale city walls like trained soldiers. Straight forward they march,
never breaking rank. [8]They never jostle each other; each moves in exactly the right
place. They lunge through the gaps, and no weapon can stop them. [9]They swarm over
the city and run along its walls. They enter all the houses, climbing like thieves
through the windows.
[10]The earth quakes as they advance, and the heavens tremble. The sun and moon grow
dark, and the stars no longer shine. [11]The LORD leads them with a shout! This is his
mighty army, and they follow his orders. The day of the LORD is an awesome, terrible
thing. Who can endure it?

A Call to Repentance

[12]That is why the LORD says, "Turn to me now, while there is time! Give me your hearts.
Come with fasting, weeping, and mourning. [13]Don't tear your clothing in your grief;
instead, tear your hearts." Return to the LORD your God, for he is gracious and merciful.
He is not easily angered. He is filled with kindness and is eager not to punish you. [14]Who
knows? Perhaps even yet he will give you a reprieve, sending you a blessing instead of
this terrible curse. Perhaps he will give you so much that you will be able to offer grain
and wine to the LORD your God as before!
[15]Blow the trumpet in Jerusalem! Announce a time of fasting; call the people together
for a solemn meeting. [16]Bring everyone—the elders, the children, and even the babies.
Call the bridegroom from his quarters and the bride from her private room. [17]The priests,
who minister in the LORD's presence, will stand between the people and the altar,
weeping. Let them pray, "Spare your people, LORD! They belong to you, so don't let
them become an object of mockery. Don't let their name become a proverb of unbelieving foreigners who say, 'Where is the God of Israel? He must be helpless!'"

The LORD's Promise of Restoration

[18]Then the LORD will pity his people and be indignant for the honor of his land! [19]He
will reply, "Look! I am sending you grain and wine and olive oil, enough to satisfy your
needs. You will no longer be an object of mockery among the surrounding nations. [20]I
will remove these armies from the north and send them far away. I will drive them back
into the parched wastelands, where they will die. Those in the rear will go into the Dead
Sea; those at the front will go into the Mediterranean.* The stench of their rotting bodies
will rise over the land."

2:20 Hebrew *the eastern sea; . . . the western sea.*

2:3 Gen 2:8; Ps 105:34-35; Isa 51:3
2:4 Rev 9:7
2:5 Isa 5:24; 30:30; Rev 9:9
2:6 Isa 13:8; Jer 30:6
2:7 Isa 5:26-29
2:9 Exod 10:6; Jer 9:21; John 10:1
2:10 Isa 13:10; Nah 1:5; Matt 24:29; 27:51; †Mark 13:24-25
2:12 Deut 4:29-30
2:13 Exod 34:6; Amos 7:2-6
2:14 Hag 2:19
2:15 Num 10:3; Joel 2:1
2:16 Ps 19:5
2:17 Pss 44:13; 79:10; Isa 37:20; Ezek 8:16
2:18 Isa 60:10; Zech 1:14
2:19 Ezek 34:29; 36:15; Hos 2:21-22
2:20 Deut 11:24; Jer 1:14-15; Zech 14:8

2:3 The Garden of Eden was Adam and Eve's first home (Genesis 2:8). Known for its beauty, it is used here to describe the beauty of the land prior to the devastation.

2:12, 13 God told the people to turn to him while there was still time. Destruction would soon be upon them. Time is also running out for us. Because we don't know when our life will end, we should trust and obey God now while we can. Don't let anything hinder you from turning to him.

2:13 Deep remorse was often shown by tearing one's clothes. But God didn't want an outward display of penitence without true inward repentance (1 Samuel 16:7; Matthew 23:1-36). Be sure your attitude toward God is correct, not just your outward actions.

2:18 Joel reached a turning point in his message, moving from prophesying about an outpouring of God's judgment to prophesying about an outpouring of God's forgiveness and blessing. But this would come only if the people began to live as God wanted them to, giving up their sins. Where there is repentance, there is hope. This section of the book inspires that hope. Without it, Joel's prophecy could bring only despair. This promise of forgiveness should have encouraged the people to repent.

2:20 Joel foresaw the invasion from the north by the armies of Assyria and Babylon, typified by the locusts.

2:22 Ps 65:12-13
2:23 Ps 149:2; Hos 6:3; Zech 10:1
2:26 Ps 67:5-7; Isa 45:17
2:27 Lev 26:11-12; Isa 45:5-6, 18; Joel 3:17, 21

Surely the LORD has done great things! 21 Don't be afraid, my people! Be glad now
and rejoice because the LORD has done great things. 22 Don't be afraid, you animals of
the field! The pastures will soon be green. The trees will again be filled with luscious
fruit; fig trees and grapevines will flourish once more. 23 Rejoice, you people of Jerusalem! Rejoice in the LORD your God! For the rains he sends are an expression of his grace.
Once more the autumn rains will come, as well as the rains of spring. 24 The threshing
floors will again be piled high with grain, and the presses will overflow with wine and
olive oil.

25 The LORD says, "I will give you back what you lost to the stripping locusts, the
cutting locusts, the swarming locusts, and the hopping locusts.* It was I who sent this
great destroying army against you. 26 Once again you will have all the food you want,
and you will praise the LORD your God, who does these miracles for you. Never again
will my people be disgraced like this. 27 Then you will know that I am here among my
people of Israel and that I alone am the LORD your God. My people will never again be
disgraced like this.

2. The day of the Lord

The LORD's Promise of His Spirit

2:28-32 †Acts 2:17-21
2:29 1 Cor 12:13; Gal 3:28
2:30-31 Joel 2:1, 10; 3:15; †Matt 24:29; †Mark 13:24-25
2:32 Isa 4:2; †Rom 10:13

28 "Then after I have poured out my rains again, I will pour out my Spirit upon all people.
Your sons and daughters will prophesy. Your old men will dream dreams. Your young
men will see visions. 29 In those days, I will pour out my Spirit even on servants, men
and women alike.

30 "I will cause wonders in the heavens and on the earth—blood and fire and pillars
of smoke. 31 The sun will be turned into darkness, and the moon will turn bloodred
before that great and terrible day of the LORD arrives. 32 And anyone who calls on the
name of the LORD will be saved. There will be people on Mount Zion in Jerusalem
who escape, just as the LORD has said. These will be among the survivors whom the
LORD has called.

2:25 The precise identification of the four kinds of locusts mentioned here is uncertain.

2:21 Joel contrasts the fear of God's judgment (2:1) with the joy of God's intervention (2:21). On the day of the Lord, sin will bring judgment, and only God's forgiveness will bring rejoicing. Unless you repent, your sin will result in punishment. Let God intervene in your life. Then you will be able to rejoice in that day because you will have nothing to fear. Before, there were fasting, plagues, and funeral dirges; then, there will be feasting, harvesting, and songs of praise. When God rules, his restoration will be complete. In the meantime, we must remember that God does not promise that all his followers will be prosperous now. When God pardons, he restores our relationship with him, but this does not guarantee individual wealth. Instead, God promises to meet the deepest needs of those who love him by loving us, forgiving us, giving us purpose in life, and giving us a caring Christian community.

2:26, 27 If the Jews would never again experience a disaster like this locust plague ("never again will my people be disgraced like this"), how do we explain the captivity in Babylon, the Jews' slavery under the Greeks and Romans, and their persecution under Hitler? It is important not to take these verses out of context. This is still part of the "blessings" section of Joel's prophecy. Only if the people truly repented would they avoid a disaster like the one Joel had described. God's blessings are promised only to those who sincerely and consistently follow him. God does promise that after the final day of judgment, his people will never again experience this kind of disaster (Zechariah 14:9-11; Revelation 21).

2:28-32 Peter quoted this passage (see Acts 2:16-21); the outpouring of the Spirit predicted by Joel occurred on Pentecost. While in the past God's Spirit seemed available to kings, prophets, and judges, Joel envisioned a time when the Spirit would be available to every believer. Ezekiel also spoke of an outpouring of the Spirit (Ezekiel 39:28, 29). God's Spirit is available today to anyone who calls on the Lord for salvation (2:32).

2:30 These "wonders" would give a hint or a picture of a coming event.

2:31, 32 The "day of the LORD" is used here as God's appointed time to judge the nations (see the note on 1:15). Judgment and mercy go hand in hand. Joel had said that if the people repented, the Lord would save them from judgment (2:12-14). In this day of judgment and catastrophe, therefore, some will be saved. God's intention is not to destroy but to heal and to save. However, we must accept his salvation or we will certainly perish with the unrepentant.

Judgment against Enemy Nations

3 “At that time, when I restore the prosperity of Judah and Jerusalem,” says the
LORD, 2“I will gather the armies of the world into the valley of Jehoshaphat.*
There I will judge them for harming my people, for scattering my inheritance among
the nations, and for dividing up my land. 3They cast lots to decide which of my people
would be their slaves. They traded young boys for prostitutes and little girls for
enough wine to get drunk.
4“What do you have against me, Tyre and Sidon and you cities of Philistia? Are
you trying to take revenge on me? If you are, then watch out! I will strike swiftly and
pay you back for everything you have done. 5You have taken my silver and gold and
all my precious treasures, and you have carried them off to your pagan temples. 6You
have sold the people of Judah and Jerusalem to the Greeks,* who took them far from
their homeland. 7But I will bring them back again from all these places to which you
sold them, and I will pay you back for all you have done. 8I will sell your sons and
daughters to the people of Judah, and they will sell them to the peoples of Arabia,* a
nation far away. I, the LORD, have spoken!”
9Say to the nations far and wide: “Get ready for war! Call out your best warriors! Let
all your fighting men advance for the attack! 10Beat your plowshares into swords and
your pruning hooks into spears. Train even your weaklings to be warriors. 11Come
quickly, all you nations everywhere! Gather together in the valley.”
And now, O LORD, call out your warriors!
12“Let the nations be called to arms. Let them march to the valley of Jehoshaphat.
There I, the LORD, will sit to pronounce judgment on them all. 13Now let the sickle
do its work, for the harvest is ripe. Come, tread the winepress because it is full. The
storage vats are overflowing with the wickedness of these people.”
14Thousands upon thousands are waiting in the valley of decision. It is there that
the day of the LORD will soon arrive. 15The sun and moon will grow dark, and the
stars will no longer shine. 16The LORD’s voice will roar from Zion and thunder from
Jerusalem, and the earth and heavens will begin to shake. But to his people of Israel,
the LORD will be a welcoming refuge and a strong fortress.

Blessings for God’s People

17“Then you will know that I, the LORD your God, live in Zion, my holy mountain.
Jerusalem will be holy forever, and foreign armies will never conquer her again.

3:2 Isa 66:16, 18 Ezek 36:1-5 Joel 3:12, 14
3:3 Obad 1:11 Nah 3:10
3:4 Ezek 25:15-17
3:5 2 Kgs 12:18 2 Chr 21:16-17
3:7 Isa 43:5-6 Jer 23:8
3:9 Isa 34:1 Jer 46:3; 51:27 Zech 14:2-3
3:10 Isa 2:4 Mic 4:3
3:12 Ps 76:8-9 Isa 3:13 Joel 3:2, 14
3:13 Hos 6:11 Matt 13:39 Mark 4:29 Rev 14:15-19
3:14 Isa 34:2-8 Joel 2:1; 3:2, 12
3:15 Joel 1:10, 31
3:16 Hos 11:10 Amos 1:2
3:17 Isa 11:9 Ezek 20:40

3:2 *Jehoshaphat* means “the LORD judges.” **3:6** Hebrew *to the peoples of Javan.* **3:8** Hebrew *to the Sabeans.*

3:1, 2 The phrase “at that time” refers to the time when those who call on the Lord will be saved (2:32). God will not only bless believers with everything they need; he will also bless them by destroying all evil and ending the pain and suffering on earth. This prophecy had three fulfillments: immediate, ongoing, and final. Its immediate interpretation could apply to King Jehoshaphat’s recent battle against several enemy nations, including Moab and Ammon (2 Chronicles 20). Its ongoing fulfillment could be the partial restoration of the people to their land after the exile to Babylon. The final fulfillment will come in the great battle that precedes the Messiah’s reign over the earth (Revelation 20:7-9).

3:2 The geographic location of the valley of Jehoshaphat is not known, and some suggest it is being used as a symbol for the place where the Lord is to judge. Some think it may be a future valley created by the splitting of the Mount of Olives when the Messiah returns (Zechariah 14:4). The most important fact for us is that the name means “the LORD judges.”

3:4 Tyre and Sidon were major cities in Phoenicia to the northwest of Israel; Philistia was the nation southwest of Judah. Phoenicia and Philistia were small countries that rejoiced at the fall of Judah and Israel because they would benefit from the increased trade. God would judge them for their wrong attitude.

3:6 Jews were sold to Greeks, a pagan and unclean people. Some think this verse and 3:1 indicate that Joel lived after the captivity in Babylon (586 B.C.), when the Greek culture began to flourish. But archaeological studies have shown that the Greeks were trading with Phoenicia as early as 800 B.C. Also 3:4 mentions Tyre, Sidon, and Philistia. These places were contemporary with Judah before their captivity.

3:8 The “peoples of Arabia” are also referred to as Sabeans, who came from Sheba, a nation in southwestern Arabia. One of Sheba’s queens had visited Solomon over a century earlier (1 Kings 10:1-13). The Sabeans controlled the eastern trade routes.

3:14 Joel described multitudes waiting in the “valley of decision” (the valley of judgment of verses 2 and 12). Billions of people have lived on earth, and every one of them—dead, living, and yet to be born—will face judgment. Look around you. See your friends—those with whom you work and live. Have they received God’s forgiveness? Have they been warned about sin’s consequences? If we understand the severity of God’s final judgment, we will want to take God’s offer of hope to those we know.

3:17 The last word will be God’s; his ultimate sovereignty will be revealed in the end. We cannot predict when that end will come, but we can have confidence in his control over the world’s events. The world’s history, as well as our own pilgrimage, is in God’s hands. We can be secure in his love and trust him to guide our decisions.

3:18 Exod 3:8 Amos 9:13
3:19 Amos 1:11 Obad 1:10
3:20 Ezek 37:25 Amos 9:15
3:21 Isa 4:4 Ezek 36:25, 29

18 In that day the mountains will drip with sweet wine, and the hills will flow with
milk. Water will fill the dry streambeds of Judah, and a fountain will burst forth from
the LORD's Temple, watering the arid valley of acacias.* 19 Egypt will become a
wasteland and Edom a wilderness, because they attacked Judah and killed her
innocent people.

20 "But Judah will remain forever, and Jerusalem will endure through all future
generations. 21 I will pardon my people's crimes, which I have not yet pardoned; and I,
the LORD, will make my home in Jerusalem* with my people."

3:18 Hebrew *valley of Shittim.* **3:21** Hebrew *Zion.*

3:18 The picture of this restored land is one of perfect beauty, similar to the Garden of Eden. The life-giving fountain flowing from the Lord's Temple illustrates the blessings that come from God. Those who trust in him will be forever fruitful. (See also Ezekiel 47:1-12; Revelation 22:1, 2.)

3:19 Egypt and Edom were two of Israel's most persistent enemies. They represent all the nations hostile to God's people. God's promise that they would be destroyed is also a promise that all evil in the world will one day be destroyed.

3:20, 21 The word *Judah* is used here to refer to all God's people—anyone who has called on the name of the Lord. There is full assurance of victory and peace for those who trust in God (2:32).

3:21 Joel began with a prophecy about the destruction of the land and ended with a prophecy about its restoration. He began by stressing the need for repentance and ended with the promise of forgiveness that repentance brings. Joel was trying to convince the people to wake up (1:5), get rid of their complacency, and realize the danger of living apart from God. His message to us is that there is still time; anyone who calls on God's name can be saved (2:12-14, 32). Those who turn to God will enjoy the blessings mentioned in Joel's prophecy; those who refuse will face destruction.

AMOS

Jeroboam II becomes king of Israel 793 B.C.

VITAL STATISTICS

PURPOSE:
To pronounce God's judgment upon Israel, the northern kingdom, for its complacency, idolatry, and oppression of the poor

AUTHOR:
Amos

TO WHOM WRITTEN:
Israel, the northern kingdom, and God's people everywhere

DATE WRITTEN:
Probably during the reigns of Jeroboam II of Israel and Uzziah (Azariah) of Judah (approximately 760–750 B.C.)

SETTING:
The wealthy people of Israel were enjoying peace and prosperity. They were quite complacent and were oppressing the poor, even selling them into slavery. Soon, however, Israel would be conquered by Assyria, and the rich would themselves become slaves.

KEY VERSE:
"Instead, I want to see a mighty flood of justice, a river of righteous living that will never run dry" (5:24).

KEY PEOPLE:
Amos, Amaziah, Jeroboam II

KEY PLACES:
Bethel, Samaria

SPECIAL FEATURES:
Amos uses striking metaphors from his shepherding and farming experience—a loaded wagon (2:13), a roaring lion (3:8), a mutilated sheep (3:12), fat cows (4:1), and a basket of ripe fruit (8:1, 2).

WHEN we hear, "He's a man of God," the images that most often come to mind are some famous evangelist, a "Reverend," a missionary, or the campus minister—professionals, Christian workers, those who preach and teach the Word as a vocation.

Surely Amos was a man of God, a person whose life was devoted to serving the Lord and whose life-style reflected this devotion—but he was a layperson. Herding sheep and tending sycamore-fig trees in the Judean countryside, Amos was not the son of a prophet; he was not the son of a priest. As a humble shepherd, he could have stayed in Tekoa, doing his job, providing for his family, and worshiping his God. But God gave Amos a vision of the future (1:1) and told him to take his message to Israel, the northern kingdom (7:15). Amos obeyed and thus proved he was a man of God.

Amos's message has had an impact on God's people throughout the centuries, and it needs to be heard today by individuals and nations. Although they were divided from their southern brothers and sisters in Judah, the northern Israelites were still God's people. But they were living beneath a pious veneer of religion, worshiping idols and oppressing the poor. Amos, a fiery, fearless, and honest shepherd from the south, confronted them with their sin and warned them of the impending judgment.

The book of Amos opens with this humble shepherd watching his sheep. God then gave him a vision of what was about to happen to the nation of Israel. God condemned all the nations who had sinned against him and harmed his people. Beginning with Aram, he moved quickly through Philistia, Tyre, Edom, Ammon, and Moab. All were condemned, and we can almost hear the Israelites shouting, "Amen!" And then, even Judah, Amos's homeland, was included in God's scathing denunciation (2:4, 5). How Amos's listeners must have enjoyed hearing those words! Suddenly, however, Amos turned to the people of Israel and pronounced God's judgment on *them.* The next four chapters enumerate and describe their sins. It is no wonder that Amaziah the priest intervened and tried to stop the preaching (7:10–13). Fearlessly, Amos continued to relate the visions of future judgment that God gave to him (chapters 8—9). After all the chapters on judgment, the book concludes with a message of hope. Eventually God will restore his people and make them great again (9:8–15).

As you read Amos's book, put yourself in the place of those Israelites and listen to God's message. Have you grown complacent? Have other concerns taken God's place in your life? Do you ignore those in need or oppress the poor? Picture yourself as Amos, faithfully doing what God calls you to do. You, too, can be God's person. Listen for his clear call and do what he says, wherever it leads.

Amos becomes a prophet to Israel 760	Hosea becomes a prophet to Israel 753	King Shallum of Israel is assassinated 752	Amos's ministry ends 750	Isaiah becomes a prophet to Judah 740

THE BLUEPRINT

1. Announcement of judgment (1:1—2:16)
2. Reasons for judgment (3:1—6:14)
3. Visions of judgment (7:1—9:15)

Amos speaks with brutal frankness in denouncing sin. He collided with the false religious leaders of his day and was not intimidated by priest or king. He continued to speak his message boldly. God requires truth and goodness, justice and righteousness, from all people and nations today as well. Many of the conditions in Israel during Amos's time are evident in today's society. We need Amos's courage to ignore danger and stand against sin.

MEGATHEMES

THEME	EXPLANATION	IMPORTANCE
Everyone Answers to God	Amos pronounced judgment from God on all the surrounding nations. Then he included Judah and Israel. God is in supreme control of all the nations. Everyone is accountable to him.	All people will have to account for their sin. When those who reject God seem to get ahead, don't envy their prosperity or feel sorry for yourself. Remember that we all must answer to God for how we live.
Complacency	Everyone was optimistic, business was booming, and people were happy (except for the poor and oppressed). With all the comfort and luxury came self-sufficiency and a false sense of security. But prosperity brought corruption and destruction.	A complacent present leads to a disastrous future. Don't congratulate yourself for the blessings and benefits you now enjoy. They are from God. If you are more satisfied with yourself than with God, remember that everything is meaningless without him. A self-sufficient attitude may be your downfall.
Oppressing the Poor	The wealthy and powerful people of Samaria, the capital of Israel, had become prosperous, greedy, and unjust. Illegal and immoral slavery came as the result of over-taxation and land-grabbing. There was also cruelty and indifference towards the poor. God is weary of greed and will not tolerate injustice.	God made all people; therefore, to ignore the poor is to ignore those whom God loves and whom Christ came to save. We must go beyond feeling bad for the poor and oppressed. We must act compassionately to stop injustice and to help care for those in need.
Superficial Religion	Although many people had abandoned real faith in God, they still pretended to be religious. They were carrying on superficial religious exercises instead of having spiritual integrity and practicing heartfelt obedience toward God.	Merely participating in ceremony or ritual falls short of true religion. God wants simple trust in him, not showy external actions. Don't settle for impressing others with external rituals when God wants heartfelt obedience and commitment.

1. Announcement of judgment

1 This message was given to Amos, a shepherd from the town of Tekoa in Judah. He received this message in visions two years before the earthquake, when Uzziah was king of Judah and Jeroboam II, the son of Jehoash,* was king of Israel.

1:1
2 Sam 14:2
2 Kgs 14:23-29
Zech 14:5

1:1 Hebrew *Joash*, a variant name for Jehoash.

1:1 Amos was a shepherd and fig grower from the southern kingdom (Judah), but he prophesied to the northern kingdom (Israel). Israel was politically at the height of its power with a prosperous economy, but the nation was spiritually corrupt. Idols were worshiped throughout the land and especially at Bethel, which was supposed to be the nation's religious center. Like Hosea, Amos was sent by God to denounce this social and religious corruption. About 30 or 40 years after Amos prophesied, Assyria destroyed the capital city, Samaria, and conquered Israel (722 B.C.). Uzziah reigned in Judah from 792–740; Jeroboam II reigned in Israel from 793–753.

1:1 Tekoa, Amos's hometown, was located in the rugged sheep country of Judah, about 10 miles south of Jerusalem. Long before Amos was born, a woman of Tekoa had helped reconcile David and his rebellious son, Absalom (2 Samuel 14:1-23).

1:1 Amos raised sheep—not a particularly "spiritual" job; yet he became a channel of God's message to others. Your job may

2 This is his report of what he saw and heard: "The LORD's voice roars from his Temple
on Mount Zion; he thunders from Jerusalem! Suddenly, the lush pastures of the shepherds dry up. All the grass on Mount Carmel withers and dies."

God's Judgment on Israel's Neighbors

3 This is what the LORD says: "The people of Damascus have sinned again and again,
and I will not forget it. I will not let them go unpunished any longer! They beat down my
people in Gilead as grain is threshed with threshing sledges of iron. 4 So I will send down
fire on King Hazael's palace, and the fortresses of King Ben-hadad will be destroyed. 5 I
will break down the gates of Damascus and slaughter its people all the way to the valley
of Aven.* I will destroy the ruler in Beth-eden, and the people of Aram will return to Kir
as slaves. I, the LORD, have spoken!"

6 This is what the LORD says: "The people of Gaza have sinned again and again, and
I will not forget it. I will not let them go unpunished any longer! They sent my people
into exile, selling them as slaves in Edom. 7 So I will send down fire on the walls of Gaza,
and all its fortresses will be destroyed. 8 I will slaughter the people of Ashdod and destroy
the king of Ashkelon. Then I will turn to attack Ekron, and the few Philistines still left
will be killed. I, the Sovereign LORD, have spoken!"

9 This is what the LORD says: "The people of Tyre have sinned again and again, and I
will not forget it. I will not let them go unpunished any longer! They broke their treaty
of brotherhood with Israel, selling whole villages as slaves to Edom. 10 So I will send
down fire on the walls of Tyre, and all its fortresses will be destroyed."

11 This is what the LORD says: "The people of Edom have sinned again and again, and
I will not forget it. I will not let them go unpunished any longer! They chased down their
relatives, the Israelites, with swords. They showed them no mercy and were unrelenting
in their anger. 12 So I will send down fire on Teman, and the fortresses of Bozrah will be
destroyed."

13 This is what the LORD says: "The people of Ammon have sinned again and again,
and I will not forget it. I will not let them go unpunished any longer! When they attacked
Gilead to extend their borders, they committed cruel crimes, ripping open pregnant

1:2 Isa 42:13; Jer 12:4; 14:2; Amos 9:3
1:3 Isa 8:4
1:4 1 Kgs 20:1; 2 Kgs 6:24
1:5 Jer 51:30; Lam 2:9
1:6 1 Sam 6:17; Jer 47:1, 5; Ezek 35:5
1:8 Isa 14:29-31; Jer 47:1-7; Ezek 25:16; Zeph 2:4-7; Zech 9:6
1:9 1 Kgs 5:1; 9:11-14; Isa 23:1-18
1:11 Num 20:14-21; Isa 34:5-6; 57:16; 63:1-3; Jer 49:7-22; Ezek 25:12-14; Mic 7:18
1:12 Jer 49:7, 20
1:13 2 Kgs 15:16; Jer 49:1-6; Ezek 25:2-7; Hos 13:16

1:5 *Aven* means "wickedness."

not cause you to feel spiritual or successful, but it is vital work if you are in the place God wants you to be. God can work through you to do extraordinary things, no matter how ordinary your occupation.

1:1 The prophet Zechariah and other historical records from this period mention an earthquake that occurred at this time (Zechariah 14:5).

1:2 In the Bible, God is often pictured as a shepherd and his people as sheep. As a shepherd, God leads and protects his flock. But here God is depicted as a ferocious lion ready to devour those who are evil or unfaithful (see also Hosea 11:10).

1:2 *Carmel* means "fertile field." It was a very fertile area. A drought capable of drying up this area would have to be quite severe.

1:3 Damascus was the capital of Aram. In the past, Aram had been one of Israel's most formidable enemies. After the defeat of Aram by Assyria in 732 B.C. (2 Kings 16:9), Damascus was no longer a real threat.

1:3–2:6 Amos pronounced God's judgment on nation after nation around Israel's borders—even Judah. Perhaps the people of Israel cheered when they heard the rebukes leveled against those nations. But then Amos proclaimed God's judgment on the people of Israel. They could not excuse their own sin just because the sins of their neighbors seemed worse. God is no respecter of persons. He judges all people fairly and impartially.

1:3–2:6 The accusation "The people . . . have sinned again and again, and I will not forget it" echoes through these verses as God evaluates nation after nation. Each nation had persistently refused to follow God's commands. A sinful practice can become a way of life. Ignoring or denying the problem will not help us. We must begin the process of correction by confessing our sins to God and asking him to forgive us. Otherwise we have no hope but to continue our pattern of sin.

1:4 King Hazael was king of Aram. Ben-hadad was Hazael's son (2 Kings 13:24).

1:5 The Arameans had been slaves in Kir, but here they were free (9:7). Decreeing that the Arameans should go back to Kir was like saying the Israelites should go back to Egypt as slaves (Exodus 1).

1:7, 8 Gaza, Ashdod, Ashkelon, and Ekron were four of the five major cities of Philistia, an enemy who often threatened Israel. The fifth city, Gath, had probably already been destroyed. Therefore, Amos was saying that the entire nation of Philistia would be destroyed for its sins.

1:9 Tyre was one of two major cities in Phoenicia. Several treaties had been made with this city, which supplied the cedar used to build David's palace and God's Temple (2 Samuel 5:11; 1 Kings 5).

1:11, 12 Both Edom and Israel had descended from Isaac: Edom from Isaac's son Esau, and Israel from Esau's twin brother, Jacob (Genesis 25:19-28; 27). But these two nations, like the two brothers, were always fighting. Edom had rejoiced at Israel's misfortunes. As a result, God promised to destroy Edom completely, from Teman in the south to Bozrah in the north.

1:13-15 The Ammonites had descended from an incestuous relationship between Lot and his younger daughter (Genesis 19:30-38). The Ammonites were hostile to Israel; and although Israel began to worship their idols, the Ammonites still attacked

1:14 Isa 9:5 Jer 49:2 Ezek 21:22
1:15 Jer 49:3

women with their swords. 14So I will send down fire on the walls of Rabbah, and all its
fortresses will be destroyed. There will be wild shouts during the battle, swirling like a
whirlwind in a mighty storm. 15And their king* and his princes will go into exile
together. I, the LORD, have spoken!"

2:1 Isa 15:1-9; 16:1-14 Jer 48:1-7 Zech 2:8-9
2:2 Jer 48:24, 41, 45
2:3 Isa 40:23

2 This is what the LORD says: "The people of Moab have sinned again and again, and
I will not forget it. I will not let them go unpunished any longer! They desecrated
the tomb of Edom's king and burned his bones to ashes. 2So I will send down fire on the
land of Moab, and all the fortresses in Kerioth will be destroyed. The people will fall in
the noise of battle, as the warriors shout and the trumpets blare. 3And I will destroy their
king and slaughter all their princes. I, the LORD, have spoken!"

God's Judgment on Judah and Israel

2:4 Judg 2:17-20 2 Kgs 17:19
2:5 Jer 17:27 Hos 8:14
2:6 2 Kgs 18:12 Joel 3:3, 6
2:7 Hos 4:14 Amos 5:12; 8:4
2:8 Exod 22:26 Amos 4:1; 6:6

4This is what the LORD says: "The people of Judah have sinned again and again, and I
will not forget it. I will not let them go unpunished any longer! They have rejected the
laws of the LORD, refusing to obey him. They have been led astray by the same lies that
deceived their ancestors. 5So I will send down fire on Judah, and all the fortresses of
Jerusalem will be destroyed."
6This is what the LORD says: "The people of Israel have sinned again and again, and
I will not forget it. I will not let them go unpunished any longer! They have perverted
justice by selling honest people for silver and poor people for a pair of sandals. 7They
trample helpless people in the dust and deny justice to those who are oppressed. Both
father and son sleep with the same woman, corrupting my holy name. 8At their religious

1:15 Hebrew *malcam*, possibly referring to their god Molech.

AMOS served as a prophet to Israel (the northern kingdom) from 760–750 B.C.

Climate of the times .... Israel was enjoying peace and economic prosperity. But this blessing had caused her to become a selfish, materialistic society. Those who were well-off ignored the needs of those less fortunate. The people were self-centered and indifferent toward God.

Main message .... Amos spoke against those who exploited or ignored the needy.

Importance of message ..... Believing in God is more than a matter of individual faith. God calls all believers to work against injustices in society and to aid those less fortunate.

Contemporary prophets ..... Jonah (793–753 B.C.), Hosea (753–715 B.C.)

(Judges 10:6-8). After Saul had been anointed Israel's king, his first victory in battle was against the Ammonites (1 Samuel 11). Rabbah was Ammon's capital city. Amos's prophecy of Ammon's destruction was fulfilled through the Assyrian invasion.

2:1-3 The Moabites had descended from an incestuous relationship between Lot and his older daughter (Genesis 19:30-37). Balak, king of Moab, had tried to hire the prophet Balaam to curse the Israelites so they could be defeated (Numbers 22–24). Balaam spoke the Lord's word of blessing instead, but some of the Moabites had succeeded in getting Israel to worship Baal (Numbers 25:1-3). The Moabites were known for their atrocities (2 Kings 3:26, 27). An archaeological artifact, the Moabite Stone, reveals that Moab was always ready to profit from the downfall of others.

2:4-6 After Solomon died, the kingdom divided, and the tribes of Judah and Benjamin became the southern kingdom (Judah) under Solomon's son Rehoboam. The other 10 tribes became the northern kingdom (Israel) and followed Jeroboam, who had rebelled against Rehoboam.

God had punished other nations harshly for their evil actions and atrocities. But God also promised to judge both Israel and Judah because they ignored the revealed law of God. The other nations were ignorant, but Judah and Israel, God's people, knew what God wanted. Still they ignored him and joined pagan nations in worshiping idols. If we know God's Word and refuse to obey it, like Israel, our guilt is greater than those who are ignorant of it.

2:4-6 Amos must have won over his audience as he proclaimed God's judgment against the evil nations surrounding Israel. But then he even spoke against his own nation, Judah, before focusing on God's indictment of Israel.

2:6ff God condemned Israel for five specific sins: (1) selling the poor as slaves (see Deuteronomy 15:7-11; Amos 8:6), (2) exploiting the poor (see Exodus 23:6; Deuteronomy 16:19), (3) engaging in perverse sexual sins (see Leviticus 20:11, 12), (4) taking illegal collateral for loans (see Exodus 22:26, 27; Deuteronomy 24:6, 12, 13), and (5) worshiping false gods (see Exodus 20:3-5).

2:6, 7 Amos was speaking to the upper class. There was no middle class in the country—only the very rich and the very poor. The rich observed religious rituals. They gave extra tithes, went to places of worship, and offered sacrifices. But they were greedy and unjust, and they took advantage of the helpless. Be sure that you do not neglect the needs of the poor while you faithfully attend church and fulfill your religious obligations. God expects us to live out our faith—this means responding to those in need.

festivals, they lounge around in clothing stolen from their debtors. In the house of their
god, they present offerings of wine purchased with stolen money.
9"Yet think of all I did for my people! I destroyed the Amorites before my people
arrived in the land. The Amorites were as tall as cedar trees and strong as oaks, but I
destroyed their fruit and dug out their roots. 10It was I who rescued you from Egypt and
led you through the desert for forty years so you could possess the land of the Amorites.
11I chose some of your sons to be prophets and others to be Nazirites. Can you deny this,
my people of Israel?" asks the LORD. 12"But you caused the Nazirites to sin by making
them drink your wine, and you said to my prophets, 'Shut up!'
13"So I will make you groan as a wagon groans when it is loaded down with grain.
14Your fastest runners will not get away. The strongest among you will become weak.
Even the mightiest warriors will be unable to save themselves. 15The archers will fail to
stand their ground. The swiftest soldiers won't be fast enough to escape. Even warriors
on horses won't be able to outrun the danger. 16On that day, the most courageous of your
fighting men will drop their weapons and run for their lives. I, the LORD, have spoken!"

2:9 Ezek 17:9; Mal 4:1
2:10 Exod 3:8; 12:51; Deut 2:7; 8:2-4
2:11 Num 6:2-3; Jer 7:25
2:12 Isa 30:10; Jer 11:21; Amos 7:13, 16
2:14 Ps 33:16; Isa 30:16-17; Jer 9:23
2:15 Isa 31:3; Jer 51:56; Ezek 39:3

2. Reasons for judgment

3 Listen to this message that the LORD has spoken against you, O people of Israel and
Judah—the entire family I rescued from Egypt: 2"From among all the families on
the earth, I chose you alone. That is why I must punish you for all your sins."

Witnesses against Guilty Israel

3Can two people walk together without agreeing on the direction? 4Does a lion ever roar
in a thicket without first finding a victim? Does a young lion growl in its den without
first catching its prey? 5Does a bird ever get caught in a trap that has no bait? Does a trap
ever spring shut when there's nothing there to catch? 6When the war trumpet blares,
shouldn't the people be alarmed? When disaster comes to a city, isn't it because the LORD
planned it?
7"But always, first of all, I warn you through my servants the prophets. I, the
Sovereign LORD, have now done this."
8The lion has roared—tremble in fear! The Sovereign LORD has spoken—I dare not
refuse to proclaim his message!
9Announce this to the leaders of Philistia* and Egypt: "Take your seats now on the
hills around Samaria, and witness the scandalous spectacle of all Israel's crimes."

3:9 Hebrew *Ashdod.*

3:2 Exod 19:5-6; Deut 7:6; Rom 2:9
3:3 Gen 5:22; 6:9; Lev 26:23-24
3:4 Ps 104:21; Hos 11:10
3:6 Isa 14:24-27; Jer 6:1; Hos 5:8
3:7 Gen 18:17; Dan 9:22-27; John 15:15
3:8 Jer 20:9; Acts 4:20

2:9-11 The prophets were constantly challenging people to remember what God had done! When we read a list like this one, we are amazed at Israel's forgetfulness. But what would the prophets say about us? God's past faithfulness should have reminded the Israelites to obey him; likewise, what he has done for us should remind us to live for him.

2:11 The Nazirites took a vow of service to God. The vow included abstaining from wine and never cutting their hair. But instead of being respected for their disciplined and temperate lives, they were being urged to break their vows. If the Nazirites were corrupted, there would remain little influence for good among the Israelites.

2:16 "That day" refers to the time when Assyria would attack Israel, destroy Samaria, and take the people captive (722 B.C.). This military defeat came only a few decades after this pronouncement.

2:16 Television and movies are filled with images of people who seem to have no fear. Many today have modeled their lives after these images—they want to be tough. But God is not impressed with bravado. He says that even the toughest people will run in fear when God's judgment comes. Do you know people who think they can make it through life without God? Don't be swayed by their self-assured rhetoric. Recognize that God fears no one, and one day all people will fear him.

3:2 God chose Israel to be the people through whom all other nations of the world could know him. He made this promise to Abraham, father of the Israelites (Genesis 12:1-3). Israel didn't have to do anything to be chosen; God had given them this special privilege because he wanted to, not because they deserved special treatment (Deuteronomy 9:4-6). Pride in their privileged position, however, ruined Israel's sensitivity to the will of God and to the plight of others.

3:3-6 With a series of seven rhetorical questions, Amos shows how two events can be linked together. Once one event takes place, the second will surely follow. Amos was showing that God's revelation to him was the sure sign that judgment would follow.

3:6 This verse means that God himself would be sending disaster to Israel.

3:7 Even in anger, God is merciful: He always warned his people through prophets before punishing them so they could not rationalize or complain when judgment came. Warnings about sin and judgment apply to people today just as they did to Israel. Because we have been warned about our sin, we have no excuse when punishment comes. Do not take lightly the warnings in God's Word about judgment. His warnings are a way of showing mercy to you.

3:9 Amos pictured Philistia and Egypt summoned to witness Israel's great sins. Even Israel's most wicked and idolatrous neighbors would see God judge Israel.

3:10 Ps 14:4; Jer 4:22; Hab 2:8-11; Zeph 1:9; Zech 5:3-4
3:12 1 Sam 17:34-37; Ps 132:3
3:13 Ezek 2:7
3:14 Amos 4:4; 5:5-6
3:15 Judg 3:20; 1 Kgs 22:39; Jer 36:22

10“My people have forgotten what it means to do right,” says the LORD. “Their fortresses are filled with wealth taken by theft and violence. 11Therefore,” says the Sovereign LORD, “an enemy is coming! He will surround them and shatter their defenses. Then he will plunder all their fortresses.”

12This is what the LORD says: “A shepherd who tries to rescue a sheep from a lion's mouth will recover only two legs and a piece of ear. So it will be when the Israelites in Samaria are rescued with only a broken chair and a tattered pillow. 13Now listen to this, and announce it throughout all Israel,*” says the Lord, the LORD God Almighty. 14“On the very day I punish Israel for its sins, I will destroy the pagan altars at Bethel. The horns of the altar will be cut off and fall to the ground. 15And I will destroy the beautiful homes of the wealthy—their winter mansions and their summer houses, too—all their palaces filled with ivory. I, the LORD, have spoken!”

Israel's Failure to Learn

4:1 Ps 22:12; Ezek 39:18
4:2 Isa 37:29; Jer 16:16; Ezek 29:4; 38:4
4:5 Lev 7:13; 22:18-21; Hos 9:1, 10
4:6 Isa 3:1; Jer 14:18; Hag 2:17
4:7 1 Kgs 8:35-36; Zech 14:17
4:8 1 Kgs 18:5; Jer 14:3-4; Ezek 4:16; Mic 6:14; Hag 1:6
4:9 Deut 28:22, 42; Joel 2:25
4:10 Exod 9:3-6; Lev 26:25; Isa 9:13; Jer 11:22; 18:21

4 Listen to me, you “fat cows” of Samaria, you women who oppress the poor and crush the needy and who are always asking your husbands for another drink! 2The Sovereign LORD has sworn this by his holiness: “The time will come when you will be led away with hooks in your noses. Every last one of you will be dragged away like a fish on a hook! 3You will leave by going straight through the breaks in the wall; you will be thrown from your fortresses.* I, the LORD, have spoken!

4“Go ahead and offer your sacrifices to the idols at Bethel and Gilgal. Keep on disobeying—your sins are mounting up! Offer sacrifices each morning and bring your tithes every three days! 5Present your bread made with yeast as an offering of thanksgiving. Then give your extra voluntary offerings so you can brag about it everywhere! This is the kind of thing you Israelites love to do,” says the Sovereign LORD.

6“I brought hunger to every city and famine to every town. But still you wouldn't return to me,” says the LORD.

7“I kept the rain from falling when you needed it the most, ruining all your crops. I sent rain on one town but withheld it from another. Rain fell on one field, while another field withered away. 8People staggered from one town to another for a drink of water, but there was never enough. But still you wouldn't return to me,” says the LORD.

9“I struck your farms and vineyards with blight and mildew. Locusts devoured all your fig and olive trees. But still you wouldn't return to me,” says the LORD.

10“I sent plagues against you like the plagues I sent against Egypt long ago. I killed your young men in war and slaughtered all your horses. The stench of death filled the air! But still you wouldn't return to me,” says the LORD.

3:13 Hebrew *the house of Jacob.* **4:3** Hebrew *thrown out toward Harmon,* possibly a reference to Mount Hermon.

3:10 The people of Israel no longer knew how to do what was right. The more they sinned, the harder it was to remember what God wanted. The same is true for us. The longer we wait to deal with sin, the greater the hold it has on us. Finally, we forget what it means to do right. Are you on the verge of forgetting?

3:11, 12 The enemy mentioned here was Assyria, which conquered Israel and did just as Amos predicted. The people were scattered to foreign lands, and foreigners were placed in the land to keep the peace. Israel's leaders had robbed their defenseless countrymen, and here they would be rendered defenseless by the Assyrians. Amos added that even if the Israelites tried to repent, it would be too late. The destruction would be so complete that nothing of value would be left.

3:14 God's judgment against Israel's altars shows that he was rejecting Israel's entire religious system because it was so polluted. The horns of the altar stood for protection (1 Kings 1:49-53), and the false altars would soon be gone. Then the people would have no sanctuary or protection (see 4:4) when judgment came.

4:1 Israel's wealthy women were called “fat cows”—pampered, sleek, and well fed (see Psalm 22:12). These women selfishly pushed their husbands to oppress the helpless in order to support their lavish life-styles. Be careful not to desire material possessions so much that you are willing to oppress others and displease God to get them.

4:4 Amos sarcastically invited the people to sin in Bethel and Gilgal, where they worshiped idols instead of God. Bethel was where God had renewed his covenant to Abraham with Jacob (Genesis 28:10-22). At this time, Bethel was the religious center of the northern kingdom, and Jeroboam had placed an idol there to discourage the people from traveling to Jerusalem in the southern kingdom to worship (1 Kings 12:26-29). Gilgal was Israel's first campground after entering the Promised Land (Joshua 4:19). Here Joshua had renewed the covenant and the rite of circumcision, and the people had celebrated the Passover (Joshua 5:2-11). Saul was crowned Israel's first king in Gilgal (1 Samuel 11:15).

4:6-13 No matter how God warned the people—through famine, drought, blight, locusts, plagues, or war—they still ignored him. Because the Israelites didn't get the message, they would have to meet God face to face in judgment. No longer would they ignore God; they would have to face the one they had rejected, the one they had refused to obey when he commanded them to care for the poor. One day each of us will meet God face to face to give account for what we have done or refused to do. Are you prepared to meet him?

11 “I destroyed some of your cities, as I destroyed* Sodom and Gomorrah. Those of
you who survived were like half-burned sticks snatched from a fire. But still you
wouldn’t return to me,” says the LORD.
12 “Therefore, I will bring upon you all these further disasters I have announced.
Prepare to meet your God as he comes in judgment, you people of Israel!”
13 For the LORD is the one who shaped the mountains, stirs up the winds, and reveals
his every thought. He turns the light of dawn into darkness and treads the mountains
under his feet. The LORD God Almighty is his name!

A Call to Repentance

5 Listen, you people of Israel! Listen to this funeral song I am singing:

2 “The virgin Israel has fallen,
never to rise again!
She lies forsaken on the ground,
with none to raise her up.”

3 The Sovereign LORD says: “When one of your cities sends a thousand men to battle,
only a hundred will return. When a town sends a hundred, only ten will come back alive.”
4 Now this is what the LORD says to the family of Israel: “Come back to me and live!
5 Don’t go to worship the idols of Bethel, Gilgal, or Beersheba. For the people of Gilgal
will be dragged off into exile, and the people of Bethel will come to nothing.”
6 Come back to the LORD and live! If you don’t, he will roar through Israel* like a fire,
devouring you completely. Your gods in Bethel certainly won’t be able to quench the
flames! 7 You wicked people! You twist justice, making it a bitter pill for the poor and
oppressed. Righteousness and fair play are meaningless fictions to you.
8 It is the LORD who created the stars, the Pleiades and Orion. It is he who turns
darkness into morning and day into night. It is he who draws up water from the oceans
and pours it down as rain on the land. The LORD is his name! 9 With blinding speed and
power he destroys the strong, crushing all their defenses.
10 How you hate honest judges! How you despise people who tell the truth! 11 You
trample the poor and steal what little they have through taxes and unfair rent.
Therefore, you will never live in the beautiful stone houses you are building. You will
never drink wine from the lush vineyards you are planting. 12 For I know the vast
number of your sins and rebellions. You oppress good people by taking bribes and
deprive the poor of justice in the courts. 13 So those who are wise will keep quiet, for
it is an evil time.
14 Do what is good and run from evil—that you may live! Then the LORD God

4:11 Gen 19:24-25; Jer 23:14
4:12 Ezek 13:5
4:13 Job 38:4-11; Pss 135:7; 139:2; Dan 2:28, 30; Amos 5:8; 8:9
5:1 Jer 9:10; Ezek 19:1, 14
5:2 Isa 51:18; Jer 14:17; 50:32; Amos 8:14
5:4 Deut 4:29; 32:46-47
5:6 Deut 4:24
5:7 Amos 2:3; 5:12; 6:12
5:8 Job 9:9; 12:22; 37:13; 38:31-34; Amos 9:6
5:9 Amos 2:14; Mic 5:11
5:10 Jer 17:16-17; Amos 5:15
5:11 Isa 59:15; Mic 6:15
5:12 Isa 1:23; Amos 2:6
5:14 Mic 3:11

4:11 Hebrew *as when God destroyed.* **5:6** Hebrew *the house of Joseph.*

5:1 Amos shocked his listeners by singing a funeral song for them as though they had already been destroyed. The Israelites believed that their wealth and religious ritual made them secure, but Amos lamented their sure destruction.

5:6 There is one sure remedy for a world that is sick and dying in sin: “Come back to the LORD and live.” Sin seeks to destroy, but hope is found in seeking God. In times of difficulty, seek God. In personal discomfort and struggle, seek God. When others are struggling, encourage them to seek God, too.

5:7 The courts should have been places of justice where the poor and oppressed could find relief. Instead, they had become places of greed and injustice.

5:8 Pleiades and Orion are star constellations. For thousands of years, navigators have staked lives and fortunes on the reliability of the stars. The constancy and orderliness of the heavens challenge us to look beyond them to their Creator.

5:10-12 A society is in trouble when those who try to do right are hated for their commitment to justice. Any society that exploits the poor and defenseless or hates the truth is bent on destroying itself.

5:12 Why does God put so much emphasis on the way we treat the poor and needy? Because how we treat the poor reflects our true character. We know we can expect nothing in return. Do we, like Christ, give without thought of gain? We should treat the poor as we would like God to treat us.

5:12 Here are eight common excuses for not helping the poor and needy: (1) They don’t deserve help. They got themselves into poverty; let them get themselves out. (2) God’s call to help the poor applies to another time. (3) We don’t know any people like this. (4) I have my own needs. (5) Any money I give will be wasted, stolen, or spent. The poor will never see it. (6) I may become a victim myself. (7) I don’t know where to start, and I don’t have time. (8) My little bit won’t make any difference.

Instead of making lame excuses, ask what can be done to help. Does your church have programs to help the needy? Could you volunteer to work with a community group that fights poverty? As one individual, you may not be able to accomplish much, but join with similarly motivated people and watch mountains begin to move.

5:15 Ps 97:10 Joel 2:14 Rom 12:9
5:16 Amos 8:3, 10 Joel 1:8, 11
5:17 Isa 16:10

Almighty will truly be your helper, just as you have claimed he is. 15 Hate evil and love
what is good; remodel your courts into true halls of justice. Perhaps even yet the LORD
God Almighty will have mercy on his people who remain.*
16 Therefore, this is what the Lord, the LORD God Almighty, says: "There will be
crying in all the public squares and in every street. Call for the farmers to weep with you,
and summon professional mourners to wail and lament. 17 There will be wailing in every
vineyard, for I will pass through and destroy them all. I, the LORD, have spoken!"

Warning of Coming Judgment

5:18 Isa 5:30 Jer 30:7 Joel 1:15; 2:1, 4, 31
5:19 Job 20:24
5:20 Isa 13:10
5:21 Lev 26:31 Isa 1:11-16 Jer 14:12 Hos 5:6
5:22 Isa 66:3
5:24 Jer 22:3 Mic 6:8

18 How terrible it will be for you who say, "If only the day of the LORD were here! For
then the LORD would rescue us from all our enemies." But you have no idea what you
are wishing for. That day will not bring light and prosperity, but darkness and disaster.
19 In that day you will be like a man who runs from a lion—only to meet a bear. After
escaping the bear, he leans his hand against a wall in his house—and is bitten by a snake.
20 Yes, the day of the LORD will be a dark and hopeless day, without a ray of joy or hope.
21 "I hate all your show and pretense—the hypocrisy of your religious festivals and
solemn assemblies. 22 I will not accept your burnt offerings and grain offerings. I won't
even notice all your choice peace offerings. 23 Away with your hymns of praise! They are
only noise to my ears. I will not listen to your music, no matter how lovely it is. 24 Instead,
I want to see a mighty flood of justice, a river of righteous living that will never run dry.
25 "Was it to me you were bringing sacrifices and offerings during the forty years in
the wilderness, Israel? 26 No, your real interest was in your pagan gods—Sakkuth your
king god and Kaiwan your star god—the images you yourselves made.* 27 So I will send
you into exile, to a land east of Damascus," says the LORD, whose name is God Almighty.

6:1 Exod 19:5 Isa 32:9-11
6:2 Gen 10:10 1 Sam 17:23 2 Kgs 18:34 2 Chr 26:6 Isa 10:9
6:4 Ezek 34:2-3

6 How terrible it will be for you who lounge in luxury and think you are secure in
Jerusalem* and Samaria! You are famous and popular in Israel, you to whom the
people go for help. 2 Go over to Calneh and see what happened there. Then go to the great
city of Hamath and on down to the Philistine city of Gath. You are no better than they
were, and look at how they were destroyed. 3 You push away every thought of coming
disaster, but your actions only bring the day of judgment closer.
4 How terrible it will be for you who sprawl on ivory beds surrounded with luxury,

5:15 Hebrew *on the remnant of Joseph.* **5:26** Greek version reads *You took up the shrine of Molech, and the star of your god Rephan, and the images you made for yourselves.* **6:1** Hebrew *Zion.*

5:15 If Israel were to sweep away the corrupt system of false accusations, bribery, and corruption, and were to insist that only just decisions be given, this would show their change of heart. We dare not read this passage lightly or write it off simply as encouragement to be good. It is a command to reform our own legal and social system.

5:16 Failure to honor the dead was considered horrible in Israel, so loud weeping was common at funerals. Paid mourners, usually women, cried and mourned loudly with dirges and eulogies. Amos said there would be so many funerals that there would be a shortage of professional mourners, so farmers would be called from the fields to help (see also Jeremiah 9:17-20).

5:18 Here "the day of the LORD" means the imminent destruction by the Assyrian army as well as the future day of God's judgment. For the faithful, "the day of the LORD" will be glorious, but for the unfaithful it will be a day of darkness and doom. (See Joel 1:15 for more discussion of the day of the Lord.)

5:18-24 These people were calling for the day of the Lord, thinking it would bring an end to their troubles. But God said, "You have no idea what you are wishing for." This "day of the LORD" would bring justice, and justice would bring the punishment the people deserved for their sins.

5:21-23 God hates worship by people who go through the motions only for show. If we are living sinful lives and using religious rituals and traditions to make ourselves look good, God will despise our worship and not accept what we offer. He wants sincere hearts, not praise from hypocrites. When you worship at church, are you more concerned about your image or your attitude toward God?

5:26 In days past, Israel had turned to worshiping stars and planets, preferring nature over nature's God (2 Kings 23:4, 5). Pagan religion allowed them to indulge in sexual immorality and to become wealthy through any means possible. Because they refused to worship and obey the one true God, they would cause their own destruction.

5:27 Israel's captivity was indeed beyond Damascus—the people were taken to Assyria. God's punishment was more than defeat; it was complete exile from their homeland.

6:1-6 Amos leveled his attack at those living in complacency and luxury in both Israel and Judah. Great wealth and comfortable life-styles may make people think they are secure, but God is not pleased if we isolate ourselves from others' needs. God wants us to care for others as he cares for us. His Kingdom has no place for selfishness or indifference. We must learn to put the needs of others before our wants. Using our wealth to help others is one way to guard against pride and complacency.

6:2 Great cities to the east, north, and west had been destroyed because of their pride. What happened to them would happen to Israel because Israel's sin was just as great as theirs.

6:4 Ivory was an imported luxury, rare and extremely expensive. Even a small amount of ivory symbolized wealth. Something as extravagant as a bed inlaid with ivory shows the gross waste of resources that should have been used to help the poor.

eating the meat of tender lambs and choice calves. 5 You sing idle songs to the sound of **6:5**
the harp, and you fancy yourselves to be great musicians, as King David was. 6 You drink 1 Chr 15:16; 23:5
wine by the bowlful, and you perfume yourselves with exotic fragrances, caring nothing Isa 5:12
at all that your nation* is going to ruin. 7 Therefore, you will be the first to be led away
as captives. Suddenly, all your revelry will end.
8 The Sovereign LORD has sworn by his own name, and this is what he, the LORD God **6:8**
Almighty, says: "I despise the pride and false glory of Israel,* and I hate their beautiful Lev 26:30
homes. I will give this city and everything in it to their enemies."
9 If there are ten men left in one house, they will all die. 10 And when a close **6:9**
relative—one who is responsible for burning the dead—goes into the house to carry Amos 5:3
away a dead body, he will ask the last survivor, "Is there anyone else with you?" And the **6:10**
person will answer, "No!" Then he will say, "Hush! Don't even whisper the name of the 1 Sam 31:12
LORD. He might hear you!" Amos 5:13; 8:3
11 When the LORD gives the command, homes both great and small will be smashed **6:11**
to pieces. 12 Can horses gallop over rocks? Can oxen be used to plow rocks? Stupid Amos 3:15
even to ask—but that's how stupid you are when you turn justice into poison and make **6:12**
bitter the sweet fruit of righteousness. 13 And just as stupid is this bragging about your Hos 10:4
conquest of Lo-debar.* You boast, "Didn't we take Karnaim* by our own strength and Amos 5:7, 11-12
power?"
14 "O people of Israel, I am about to bring an enemy nation against you," says the **6:14**
LORD God Almighty. "It will oppress you bitterly throughout your land—from Lebo-ha- Num 34:7-8
math in the north to the Arabah Valley in the south." 2 Kgs 8:65; 14:25
Jer 5:15

3. Visions of judgment

A Vision of Locusts

7 The Sovereign LORD showed me a vision. I saw him preparing to send a vast swarm **7:1**
of locusts over the land. This was after the king's share had been harvested from the Exod 10:12-16
fields and as the main crop was coming up. 2 In my vision the locusts ate everything in Nah 3:15-17
sight that was green. Then I said, "O Sovereign LORD, please forgive your people! **7:2**
Unless you relent, Israel* will not survive, for we are only a small nation." Exod 10:15
3 So the LORD relented and did not fulfill the vision. "I won't do it," he said. Isa 37:4
Jer 14:7; 42:2
Ezek 9:8; 11:13

A Vision of Fire

4 Then the Sovereign LORD showed me another vision. I saw him preparing to punish his **7:4**
people with a great fire. The fire had burned up the depths of the sea and was devouring Isa 66:15-16
the entire land. 5 Then I said, "O Sovereign LORD, please don't do it. Unless you relent, Amos 2:5
Israel will not survive, for we are only a small nation." **7:6**
6 Then the LORD turned from this plan, too. "I won't do that either," said the Sovereign Amos 7:3
LORD.

A Vision of a Plumb Line

7 Then he showed me another vision. I saw the Lord standing beside a wall that had been
built using a plumb line. He was checking it with a plumb line to see if it was straight. **7:8**
8 And the LORD said to me, "Amos, what do you see?" Isa 28:17; 34:11
I answered, "A plumb line." Amos 8:2

6:6 Hebrew *Joseph.* **6:8** Hebrew *Jacob.* **6:13a** *Lo-debar* means "nothing." **6:13b** *Karnaim* means "horns," a term that symbolizes strength. **7:2** Hebrew *Jacob;* also in 7:5.

6:8-11 The people had built luxurious homes to flaunt their achievements. While it is not wrong to live in comfortable houses, we must not let them become sources of inflated pride and self-glorification. God gave our homes to us, and they are to be used for service, not just for show.

6:10 Amos gives us a picture of God's fearful judgment: The people hesitated to speak God's name, even during a time of grief, for fear that they would attract his attention and be judged also.

6:13, 14 Karnaim was a city northeast of Israel, an insignificant border town compared to the nation they were about to face, Assyria. Lebo-hamath was to the north, and the Arabah Valley to the south. The entire nation would be destroyed by Assyria (2 Kings 17).

7:1ff The following series of visions conveyed God's message to the people, using images that were familiar to them—locusts, fire, and a plumb line.

7:1-6 Twice Amos was shown a vision of Israel's impending punishment, and his immediate response was to pray that God would spare Israel. Prayer is a powerful privilege. Amos's prayers should remind us to pray for our nation.

7:7-9 A plumb line is a device used to ensure the straightness of a wall. A wall that is not straight will eventually collapse. God wants people to be right with him; he wants the sin that makes us crooked removed immediately. God's Word is the plumb line that helps us be aware of our sin. How do you measure up to God's plumb line?

And the Lord replied, "I will test my people with this plumb line. I will no longer
7:9 2 Kgs 15:8-10 ignore all their sins. 9 The pagan shrines of your ancestors* and the temples of Israel will
be destroyed, and I will bring the dynasty of King Jeroboam to a sudden end."

Amos and Amaziah

7:10 1 Kgs 12:31-32 2 Kgs 14:23-24 10 But when Amaziah, the priest of Bethel, heard what Amos was saying, he rushed a
message to King Jeroboam: "Amos is hatching a plot against you right here on your very
doorstep! What he is saying is intolerable. It will lead to rebellion all across the land.
11 He is saying, 'Jeroboam will soon be killed and the people of Israel will be sent away
7:12 1 Sam 9:9 into exile.'"

12 Then Amaziah sent orders to Amos: "Get out of here, you seer! Go on back to the
7:13 1 Kgs 12:29, 32; 13:1 Amos 2:12 Acts 4:17-18 land of Judah and do your preaching there! 13 Don't bother us here in Bethel with your
prophecies, especially not here where the royal sanctuary is!"

14 But Amos replied, "I'm not one of your professional prophets. I certainly never
7:14 1 Kgs 20:35 2 Kgs 2:3-7; 4:38 trained to be one. I'm just a shepherd, and I take care of fig trees. 15 But the LORD called
me away from my flock and told me, 'Go and prophesy to my people in Israel.'

7:15 Jer 1:7 Ezek 2:3-4 16 "Now then, listen to this message from the LORD! You say, 'Don't prophesy against
Israel. Stop preaching against my people.*' 17 But this is what the LORD says: Because
7:16 Amos 7:13 Mic 2:6 you have refused to listen, your wife will become a prostitute in this city, and your sons
and daughters will be killed. Your land will be divided up, and you yourself will die in a
7:17 Jer 14:16; 20:6 Hos 4:13-14 foreign land. And the people of Israel will certainly become captives in exile, far from
their homeland."

A Vision of Ripe Fruit

8 Then the Sovereign LORD showed me another vision. In it I saw a basket filled with
8:2 Jer 24:1-3 Amos 7:8 ripe fruit. 2 "What do you see, Amos?" he asked.

I replied, "A basket full of ripe fruit."

Then the LORD said, "This fruit represents my people of Israel—ripe for punishment!
8:3 Hos 10:5-6 Amos 5:23 I will not delay their punishment again. 3 In that day the riotous sounds of singing in the
Temple will turn to wailing. Dead bodies will be scattered everywhere. They will be
carried out of the city in silence. I, the Sovereign LORD, have spoken!"

7:9 Hebrew *of Isaac.* **7:16** Hebrew *against the house of Isaac.*

AMOS'S VISIONS

Vision/Reference	*Significance*
Swarm of locusts 7:1–3	God was preparing punishment, which he delayed only because of Amos's intervention.
Fire 7:4–6	God was preparing to devour the land, but Amos intervened on behalf of the people.
Wall and plumb line 7:7–9	God would see if the people were crooked, and if they were, he would punish them.
Basket of ripe fruit 8:1ff	The people were ripe for punishment; though once beautiful, they were now rotten.
God standing by the altar 9:1ff	Punishment was executed.

Amos had a series of visions concerning God's judgment on Israel. God was planning to judge Israel by sending a swarm of locusts or by sending fire. In spite of Amos's intercession on Israel's behalf, God would still carry out his judgment because Israel persisted in her disobedience.

7:10 Prophets like Amos were often seen as traitors and conspirators because they spoke out against the king and his advisers, questioning their authority and exposing their sin. The kings often saw the prophets as enemies rather than as God's spokesmen who were really trying to help them and the nation.

7:10ff Amaziah was the chief priest in Bethel, representing Israel's official religion. He was not concerned about hearing God's message; he was only worried about his own position. Maintaining his position was more important than listening to the truth. Don't let your desire for prestige, authority, or money keep you tied to a job or position you should leave. Don't let anything come between you and obeying God.

7:14, 15 Without any special preparation, education, or upbringing, Amos obeyed God's call to "go and prophesy to my people in Israel." Obedience is the test of a faithful servant of God. Are you obeying God's call to you?

4Listen to this, you who rob the poor and trample the needy! 5You can't wait for the
Sabbath day to be over and the religious festivals to end so you can get back to cheating
the helpless. You measure out your grain in false measures and weigh it out on dishonest
scales. 6And you mix the wheat you sell with chaff swept from the floor! Then you
enslave poor people for a debt of one piece of silver or a pair of sandals.
7Now the LORD has sworn this oath by his own name, the Pride of Israel*: "I will
never forget the wicked things you have done! 8The earth will tremble for your deeds,
and everyone will mourn. The land will rise up like the Nile River at floodtime, toss
about, and sink again. 9At that time," says the Sovereign LORD, "I will make the sun go
down at noon and darken the earth while it is still day. 10I will turn your celebrations into
times of mourning, and your songs of joy will be turned to weeping. You will wear
funeral clothes and shave your heads as signs of sorrow, as if your only son had died.
How very bitter that day will be!
11"The time is surely coming," says the Sovereign LORD, "when I will send a famine
on the land—not a famine of bread or water but of hearing the words of the LORD. 12People
will stagger everywhere from sea to sea, searching for the word of the LORD, running here
and going there, but they will not find it. 13Beautiful girls and fine young men will grow
faint and weary, thirsting for the LORD's word. 14And those who worship and swear by the
idols of Samaria, Dan, and Beersheba will fall down, never to rise again."

A Vision of God at the Altar

9 Then I saw a vision of the Lord standing beside the altar. He said, "Strike the tops
of the Temple columns so hard that the foundation will shake. Smash the columns
so the roof will crash down on the people below. Then those who survive will be
slaughtered in battle. No one will escape!
2"Even if they dig down to the place of the dead,* I will reach down and pull them
up. Even if they climb up into the heavens, I will bring them down. 3Even if they hide
at the very top of Mount Carmel, I will search them out and capture them. Even if they
hide at the bottom of the ocean, I will send the great sea serpent after them to bite and
destroy them. 4Even if they are driven into exile, I will command the sword to kill them
there. I am determined to bring disaster upon them and not to help them."
5The Lord, the LORD Almighty, touches the land and it melts, and all its people mourn.
The ground rises like the Nile River at floodtime, and then it sinks again. 6The upper stories
of the LORD's home are in the heavens, while its foundation is on the earth. He draws up
water from the oceans and pours it down as rain on the land. The LORD is his name!
7"Do you Israelites think you are more important to me than the Ethiopians*?" asks
the LORD. "I brought you out of Egypt, but have I not done as much for other nations,
too? I brought the Philistines from Crete* and led the Arameans out of Kir.

8:5 Neh 13:15-21 Hos 12:7
8:7 Deut 33:26-29 Hos 7:2; 8:13
8:8 Pss 18:7; 114:3-7 Jer 46:8
8:9 Mic 3:6 Matt 27:45 Mark 15:33 Luke 23:44-45
8:10 Isa 15:2-3 Ezek 7:18 Amos 5:23; 6:4-7
8:12 Ezek 20:3, 31
8:13 Isa 41:17 Lam 1:18; 2:21 Hos 2:3
8:14 1 Kgs 12:28-29
9:1 Zeph 2:14
9:2 Ps 139:7-10
9:3 Job 34:22 Ps 139:9-11 Isa 27:1 Jer 16:16
9:4 Lev 26:33 Jer 44:11
9:5 Ps 46:2, 6 Isa 64:1
9:6 Ps 104:3, 6, 13
9:7 2 Chr 14:9, 12 Isa 20:4; 43:3

8:7 Hebrew *the pride of Jacob.* **9:2** Hebrew *to Sheol.* **9:7a** Hebrew *the Cushites.* **9:7b** Hebrew *Caphtor.*

8:5, 6 These merchants were keeping the religious festivals, but not in spirit. They couldn't wait for the holy days and Sabbaths to be over so they could go back to making money. Their real interest was in enriching themselves, even if that meant cheating (shortchanging the quantity while boosting the price, or even selling chaff as wheat). Do you take a day to rest and worship God at least once a week, or is making money more important to you than anything else? When you give time to God, is your heart in your worship? Or is your religion only a front for unethical practices?

8:11-13 The people had no appetite for God's word when prophets like Amos brought it. Because of their apathy, God said he would take away even the opportunity to hear his word. We have God's Word, the Bible. But many still look everywhere for answers to life's problems *except* in Scripture. You can help them by directing them to the Bible, showing them the parts that speak to their special needs and questions. God's Word is available to us. Let us help people know it before a time comes when they cannot find it.

9:1 Judgment would begin at the altar, the center of the nation's life, the place where the people expected protection and blessing. This judgment would cover all 12 tribes. Commentators disagree concerning this altar. Some think it was the altar at Bethel; more likely it was the altar in the Temple in Jerusalem. God would destroy their base of security in order to bring them to himself. But in 9:11 he promises to restore his renewed people and their broken world.

9:2-4 The "place of the dead" was the grave. The grave and Mount Carmel were symbols of inaccessibility. No one can escape God's judgment. This was good news for the faithful but bad news for the unfaithful. Whether we go to the mountaintops or the bottom of the sea, God will find us and judge us for our deeds. Amos pictured the judgment of the wicked as a sea serpent, relentlessly pursuing the condemned. For God's faithful followers, however, the judgment brings a new earth of peace and prosperity. Does God's judgment sound like good news or bad news to you?

9:7 Ethiopia, south of Egypt, was a remote and exotic land to the Israelites. Crete was where the Philistines lived as they migrated to Palestine. God would judge Israel no differently than he judges foreign nations. He is not the God of Israel only; he is God of the universe, and he controls all nations.

9:8 Jer 5:10 | 8 "I, the Sovereign LORD, am watching this sinful nation of Israel, and I will uproot it
Joel 2:32 | and scatter its people across the earth. Yet I have promised that I will never completely
Amos 7:17 | destroy the family of Israel,*" says the LORD. 9 "For I have commanded that Israel be
9:9 Isa 30:28 | persecuted by the other nations as grain is sifted in a sieve, yet not one true kernel will
be lost. 10 But all the sinners will die by the sword—all those who say, 'Nothing bad will
happen to us.'

A Promise of Restoration

9:11 Isa 16:5; 63:11 | 11 "In that day I will restore the fallen kingdom of David. It is now like a house in ruins,
but I will rebuild its walls and restore its former glory. 12 And Israel will possess what is
left of Edom and all the nations I have called to be mine. I, the LORD, have spoken, and
I will do these things.

9:13 Lev 26:5 | 13 "The time will come," says the LORD, "when the grain and grapes will grow faster
Joel 3:18, 20 | than they can be harvested. Then the terraced vineyards on the hills of Israel will drip
9:14 Isa 61:4 | with sweet wine! 14 I will bring my exiled people of Israel back from distant lands, and
Jer 30:18; 31:28 | they will rebuild their ruined cities and live in them again. They will plant vineyards
9:15 Ezek 34:28 | and gardens; they will eat their crops and drink their wine. 15 I will firmly plant them
there in the land I have given them," says the LORD your God. "Then they will never
be uprooted again."

9:8 Hebrew *the house of Jacob.*

9:8 Amos assured the Israelites that God would "never completely destroy" Israel—in other words, the punishment would not be permanent or total. God wants to redeem, not punish. But when punishment is necessary, he doesn't withhold it. Like a loving father, God disciplines those he loves in order to correct them. If God disciplines you, accept it as a sign of his love.

9:8, 9 Although Assyria would destroy Israel and take the people into exile, some would be preserved. This exile had been predicted hundreds of years earlier (Deuteronomy 28:63-68). Although the nation would be purified through this invasion and captivity, not one true believer would be eternally lost. Our system of justice is not perfect, but God's is. Sinners will not get away, and the faithful will not be forgotten. True believers will not be lost.

9:11, 12 In the punishment, the house of David was reduced to a "house in ruins." God's covenant with David stated that one of David's descendants would always sit on his throne (2 Samuel 7:12-16). The exile made this promise seem impossible. But "in that day" God would raise up and restore the kingdom to its promised glory. This was a promise to both Israel and Judah, not to be fulfilled by an earthly, political ruler, but by the Messiah, who would renew the spiritual Kingdom and rule forever.

James quoted these verses (Acts 15:16, 17), finding the promise fulfilled in Christ's resurrection and in the presence of both Jews and Gentiles in the church. "Possess what is left of Edom" envisions the messianic Kingdom, which will be universal and include Gentiles. When God brings in the Gentiles, he is restoring the ruins. After the Gentiles are called together, God will renew and restore the fortunes of the new Israel. All the land that was once under David's rule will again be part of God's nation.

9:13 This verse describes a time of such an abundance of crops that the people won't be able to harvest them all.

9:13-15 The Jews of Amos's day had lost sight of God's care and love for them. The rich were carefree and comfortable, refusing to help others in need. They observed their religious rituals in hopes of appeasing God, but they did not truly love him. Amos announced God's warnings of destruction for their evil ways.

We must not assume that going to church and being good are enough. God expects our belief in him to affect all areas of our conduct and to extend to all people and circumstances. We should let Amos's words inspire us to live faithfully according to God's desires.

OBADIAH

VITAL STATISTICS

PURPOSE:
To show that God judges those who have harmed his people

AUTHOR:
Obadiah. Very little is known about this man, whose name means "servant (or worshiper) of the LORD"

TO WHOM WRITTEN:
The Edomites, the Jews in Judah, and God's people everywhere

DATE WRITTEN:
Possibly during the reign of Jehoram in Judah, 853–841 B.C., or possibly during Jeremiah's ministry, 627–586 B.C.

SETTING:
Historically, Edom had constantly harassed the Jews. Prior to the time this book was written, they had participated in attacks against Judah. Given the dates above, this prophecy came after the division of Israel into the northern and southern kingdoms and before the conquering of Judah by Nebuchadnezzar in 586 B.C.

KEY VERSE:
"The day is near when I, the LORD, will judge the godless nations! As you have done to Israel, so it will be done to you. All your evil deeds will fall back on your own heads" (1:15).

KEY PEOPLE:
The Edomites

KEY PLACES:
Edom, Jerusalem

SPECIAL FEATURES:
The book of Obadiah uses vigorous poetic language and is written in the form of a dirge of doom.

WRINKLED face, tiny hands with fingernail chips, folds of new skin, and miniature eyes, nose, and mouth—she's a newborn. After months of formation, she burst forth into the world and into her family. "She has her mother's eyes." "I can sure tell who her parents are." "Now that's your nose." Relatives and friends gaze into the little face and see her mom and dad. Mother and Father rejoice in their daughter, a miracle, a new member of the family. As loving parents, they will feed, protect, nurture, guide, and discipline her. This is their duty and joy.

God, too, has children—men and women whom he has chosen as his very own. There have always been individuals marked as his, but with Abraham he promised to build a nation. Israel was to be God's country, and her people, the Jews, his very own sons and daughters. Down through the centuries, God meted out discipline and punishment, but always with love and mercy. God, the eternal Father, protected and cared for his children.

Obadiah, the shortest book in the Old Testament, is a dramatic example of God's response to anyone who would harm his children. Edom was a mountainous nation, occupying the region southeast of the Dead Sea including Petra, the spectacular city discovered by archaeologists a few decades ago. As descendants of Esau (Genesis 25:19—27:45), the Edomites were blood relatives of Israel, and like their father, they were rugged, fierce, and proud warriors with a seemingly invincible mountain home. Of all people, they should have rushed to the aid of their northern brothers. Instead, however, they gloated over Israel's problems, captured and delivered fugitives to the enemy, and even looted Israel's countryside.

Obadiah gave God's message to the Edomites. Because of their indifference to and defiance of God, their cowardice and pride, and their treachery toward their brothers in Judah, they stood condemned and would be destroyed. The book begins with the announcement that disaster was coming to Edom (1:1–9). Despite their "impregnable" cliffs and mountains, they would not be able to escape God's judgment. Obadiah then gave the reasons for their destruction (1: 10–14)—their blatant arrogance toward God and their persecution of God's children. This concise prophecy ends with a description of the "day of the LORD," when judgment will fall on all who have harmed God's people (1:15–21).

Today, God's holy nation is his church—all who have trusted Christ for their salvation and have given their lives to him. These men and women are God's born-again and adopted children. As you read Obadiah, catch a glimpse of what it means to be God's child, under his love and protection. See how the heavenly Father responds to all who would attack those whom he loves.

THE BLUEPRINT

1. Edom's destruction (1:1–16)
2. Israel's restoration (1:17–21)

The book of Obadiah shows the outcome of the ancient feud between Edom and Israel. Edom was proud of its high position, but God would bring her down. Those who are high and powerful today should not be overconfident in themselves, whether they are a nation, a corporation, a church, or a family. Just as Edom was destroyed for its pride, so will anyone be who lives in defiance of God.

MEGATHEMES

THEME	EXPLANATION	IMPORTANCE
Justice	Obadiah predicted that God would destroy Edom as punishment for standing by when Babylon invaded Judah. Because of their treachery, Edom's land would be given to Judah in the day when God rights the wrongs against his people.	God will judge and fiercely punish all who harm his people. We can be confident in God's final victory. He is our champion, and we can trust him to bring about true justice.
Pride	Because of their seemingly invincible rock fortress, the Edomites were proud and self-confident. But God humbled them and their nation disappeared from the face of the earth.	All those who defy God will meet their doom as Edom did. Any nation who trusts in its power, wealth, technology, or wisdom more than in God will be brought low. All who are proud will one day be shocked to discover that no one is exempt from God's justice.

1. Edom's destruction

1:1 Isa 34:5-15; 63:1-6 Jer 49:7-22

This is the vision that the Sovereign LORD revealed to Obadiah concerning the land of
Edom.

Edom's Judgment Announced

We have heard a message from the LORD that an ambassador was sent to the nations to
say, "Get ready, everyone! Let's assemble our armies and attack Edom!"

1:2 Num 24:15-19

[2]The LORD says, "I will cut you down to size among the nations, Edom; you will be

1:3 Isa 16:6 Jer 49:15-16

small and despised. [3]You are proud because you live in a rock fortress and make your
home high in the mountains. 'Who can ever reach us way up here?' you ask boastfully.

1:1 Obadiah was a prophet from Judah who told of God's judgment against the nation of Edom. There are two commonly accepted dates for this prophecy: (1) between 853 and 841 B.C., when King Jehoram and Jerusalem were attacked by a Philistine/Arab coalition (2 Chronicles 21:16ff); and (2) 586 B.C., when Jerusalem was completely destroyed by the Babylonians (2 Kings 25; 2 Chronicles 36). Edom had rejoiced over the misfortunes of both Israel and Judah, and yet the Edomites and Jews descended from two brothers—Esau and Jacob (Genesis 25:19-26). But just as these two brothers were constantly fighting, so were Israel and Edom. God pronounced judgment on Edom for its callous and malicious actions toward his people.

1:3 Edom was Judah's southern neighbor, sharing a common boundary. But neighbors are not always friends, and Edom liked nothing about Judah. Edom's capital at this time was Sela (perhaps the later city of Petra), a city considered impregnable because it was cut into rock cliffs and set in a canyon that could be entered only through a narrow gap. What Edom perceived as its strengths would be its downfall: (1) safety in their city (1:3, 4)—God would send them plummeting from the heights; (2) pride in their self-sufficiency (1:4)—God would humble them; (3) wealth (1:5, 6)—thieves would steal all they had; (4) allies (1:7)—God would cause them to turn against Edom; (5) wisdom (1:8, 9)—the wise would be destroyed.

1:3 The Edomites felt secure, and they were proud of their self-sufficiency. But they were fooling themselves because there is no lasting security apart from God. Is your security in objects or people? Ask yourself how much lasting security they really offer. Possessions and people can disappear in a moment, but God does not change. Only he can supply true security.

Don't fool yourselves! 4 Though you soar as high as eagles and build your nest among
the stars, I will bring you crashing down. I, the LORD, have spoken!
5 "If thieves came at night and robbed you, they would not take everything. Those who
harvest grapes always leave a few for the poor. But your enemies will wipe you out
completely! 6 Every nook and cranny of Edom* will be searched and looted. Every
treasure will be found and taken.
7 "All your allies will turn against you. They will help to chase you from your land.
They will promise you peace, while plotting your destruction. Your trusted friends will
set traps for you, and you won't even know about it. 8 At that time not a single wise person
will be left in the whole land of Edom!" says the LORD. "For on the mountains of Edom
I will destroy everyone who has wisdom and understanding. 9 The mightiest warriors of
Teman will be terrified, and everyone on the mountains of Edom will be cut down in the
slaughter.

Reasons for Edom's Punishment

10 "And why? Because of the violence you did to your close relatives in Israel.* Now you
will be destroyed completely and filled with shame forever. 11 For you deserted your
relatives in Israel during their time of greatest need. You stood aloof, refusing to lift a
finger to help when foreign invaders carried off their wealth and cast lots to divide up
Jerusalem. You acted as though you were one of Israel's enemies.
12 "You shouldn't have done this! You shouldn't have gloated when they exiled your
relatives to distant lands. You shouldn't have rejoiced because they were suffering such
misfortune. You shouldn't have crowed over them as they suffered these disasters. 13 You

1:4 Job 39:26-30; Isa 14:12-15
1:5-6 Jer 49:9-10
1:7 Isa 19:11-14; Jer 30:14
1:8 Job 5:12-14; Isa 19:3, 13-14; 29:14
1:9 Jer 49:20-22; Amos 1:12-13
1:10 Ezek 25:12-14
1:11 Ps 137:7; Joel 3:3; Nah 3:10
1:12 Ezek 35:15; Mic 4:11
1:13 Ezek 35:5

6 Hebrew *Esau;* also in 8b, 9, 18, 19, 21. **10** Hebrew *your brother Jacob.*

HISTORY OF THE CONFLICT BETWEEN ISRAEL AND EDOM

The nation of Israel descended from Jacob; the nation of Edom descended from Esau.	Genesis 25:23
Jacob and Esau struggled in their mother's womb.	Genesis 25:19–26
Esau sold his birthright and blessing to Jacob.	Genesis 25:29–34
Edom refused to let the Israelites pass through its land.	Numbers 20:14–22
Israel's kings had constant conflict with Edom.	
• Saul	1 Samuel 14:47
• David	2 Samuel 8:13, 14
• Solomon	1 Kings 11:14–22
• Jehoram	2 Kings 8:20–22; 2 Chronicles 21:8ff
• Ahaz	2 Chronicles 28:16
Edom urged Babylon to destroy Jerusalem.	Psalm 137:7

1:4 The Edomites were proud of their city carved right into the rock. Today Sela, or Petra, is considered one of the marvels of the ancient world, but only as a tourist attraction. The Bible warns that pride is the surest route to self-destruction (Proverbs 16:18). Just as Petra and Edom fell, so will proud people fall. A humble person is more secure than a proud person because humility gives a more accurate perspective of oneself and the world.

1:4-9 God did not pronounce these harsh judgments against Edom out of vengeance but in order to bring about justice. God is morally perfect and demands complete justice and fairness. The Edomites were simply getting what they deserved. Because they murdered, they would be murdered. Because they robbed, they would be robbed. Because they took advantage of others, they would be used. Don't talk yourself into sin, thinking that "nobody will know" or "I won't get caught." God knows all our sins, and he will be just.

1:8 Edom was noted for its wise men. There is a difference, however, between human wisdom and God's wisdom. The Edomites may have been wise in the ways of the world, but they were foolish because they ignored and even mocked God.

1:9 Eliphaz, one of Job's three friends (Job 2:11), was from Teman, about five miles east of Petra. Teman was named after Esau's grandson (Genesis 36:11).

1:10, 11 The Israelites had descended from Jacob, and the Edomites, from his brother, Esau (Genesis 25:19-26). Instead of helping Israel and Judah when they were in need, Edom allowed them to be destroyed and even plundered what was left behind. Edom, therefore, acted like a stranger, and it would be punished. Anyone who does not help God's people is God's enemy. If you have withheld your help from someone in a time of need, this is sin (James 4:17). Sin includes not only what we do, but also what we refuse to do. Don't ignore or refuse to help those in need.

1:12 The Edomites were glad to see Judah in trouble. Their hatred made them want the nation destroyed. For their wrong attitudes and actions, God wiped out the Edomites. How often do you find yourself rejoicing at the misfortunes of others? Because God alone is the judge, we must never be happy about others' misfortunes, even if we think they deserve them (see Proverbs 24:17).

shouldn't have plundered the land of Israel when they were suffering such calamity. You
shouldn't have gloated over the destruction of your relatives, looting their homes and
making yourselves rich at their expense. 14 You shouldn't have stood at the crossroads,
killing those who tried to escape. You shouldn't have captured the survivors, handing
them over to their enemies in that terrible time of trouble.

Edom Destroyed, Israel Restored

1:15 Jer 50:29 15 "The day is near when I, the LORD, will judge the godless nations! As you have done
Ezek 30:3 Joel 1:15 to Israel, so it will be done to you. All your evil deeds will fall back on your own heads.
Hab 2:8 16 Just as you swallowed up my people on my holy mountain, so you and the surrounding
1:16 nations will swallow the punishment I pour out on you. Yes, you nations will drink and
Jer 25:15; 49:12 stagger and disappear from history, as though you had never even existed.

2. Israel's restoration

1:17 Isa 14:1-3 17 "But Jerusalem* will become a refuge for those who escape; it will be a holy place.
Amos 9:11-15 And the people of Israel* will come back to reclaim their inheritance. 18 At that time
1:18 Zech 12:6 Israel will be a raging fire, and Edom, a field of dry stubble. The fire will roar across the
field, devouring everything and leaving no survivors in Edom. I, the LORD, have spoken!
1:19 Jer 31:5; 32:44 19 "Then my people living in the Negev will occupy the mountains of Edom. Those
living in the foothills of Judah* will possess the Philistine plains and take over the fields
of Ephraim and Samaria. And the people of Benjamin will occupy the land of Gilead.
1:20 1 Kgs 17:9 20 The exiles of Israel will return to their land and occupy the Phoenician coast as far
north as Zarephath. The captives from Jerusalem exiled in the north* will return to their
1:21 Ps 22:28 homeland and resettle the villages of the Negev. 21 Deliverers will go up to* Mount Zion
Zech 14:9 in Jerusalem to rule over the mountains of Edom. And the LORD himself will be king!"
Rev 11:15; 19:6

17a Hebrew *Mount Zion.* **17b** Hebrew *house of Jacob;* also in 18. **19** Hebrew *the Shephelah.* **20** Hebrew *in Sepharad.* **21** Or *from.*

OBADIAH served as a prophet to Judah possibly around 853 B.C.

Climate of the times . . . . Edom was a constant thorn in Judah's side. The Edomites often participated in attacks initiated by other enemies.

Main message . . . . God will judge Edom for its evil actions toward God's people.

Importance of message . . . . Just as Edom was destroyed and disappeared as a nation, so God will destroy proud and wicked people.

Contemporary prophets . . . Elijah (875–848 B.C.), Micaiah (865–853 B.C.), Jehu (855–840? B.C.)

1:12-14 Of all Israel and Judah's neighbors, the Edomites were the only ones not promised any mercy from God. This was because they looted Jerusalem and rejoiced at the misfortunes of Israel and Judah. They betrayed their blood brothers in times of crisis and aided their brothers' enemies. (See also Psalm 137:7; Jeremiah 49:7-22; Ezekiel 25:12-14; Amos 1:11, 12.)

1:15 Why will God's judgment fall on all the nations? Edom was not the only nation to rejoice at Judah's fall. All nations and individuals will be judged for the way they have treated God's people. Some nations today treat God's people favorably, while others are hostile toward them. God will judge all people according to the way they treat others, especially believers (Revelation 20:12, 13). Jesus talked about this in Matthew 25:31-46.

1:17-21 The Edomites were routed by Judas Maccabeus in 164 B.C. The nation no longer existed by the first century A.D. At the time of Obadiah's prophecy, Edom may have seemed more likely to survive than Judah. Yet Edom has vanished, and Judah still exists. This demonstrates the absolute certainty of God's word and of the punishment awaiting all who have mistreated God's people.

1:19 The Negev was the southern part of Judah, a dry, hot region. The foothills were in the western part of Judah.

1:20 The boundaries of the kingdom would be extended to include Phoenicia as far north as Zarephath, located between Tyre and Sidon on the Mediterranean coast.

1:21 Obadiah brought God's message of judgment on Edom. God was displeased with both their inward and their outward rebellion. People today are much the same as people in Obadiah's time, filled with arrogance, envy, and dishonesty. We may wonder how much longer evil will continue. Regardless of sin's effects, however, God is in control. Don't despair or give up hope. Know that when all is said and done, the Lord is still sovereign, and the confidence you place in him will not be in vain.

1:21 Edom is an example to all the nations that are hostile to God. Nothing can break God's promise to protect his people from complete destruction. In the book of Obadiah we see four aspects of God's message of judgment: (1) Evil will certainly be punished; (2) those faithful to God have hope for a new future; (3) God is sovereign in human history; (4) God's ultimate purpose is to establish his eternal Kingdom. The Edomites had been cruel to God's people. They were arrogant and proud, and they took advantage of others' misfortunes. Any nation that mistreats people who obey God will be punished, regardless of how invincible they appear. Similarly we, as individuals, cannot allow ourselves to feel so comfortable with our wealth or security that we fail to help God's people. This is sin. And because God is just, sin will be punished.

JONAH

Jeroboam II becomes king; Jonah becomes a prophet 793 B.C.	Uzziah (Azariah) becomes king of Judah 792	Jonah preaches to Nineveh 785?	Shalmaneser IV becomes king of Assyria 783	Ashur-dan III becomes king of Assyria 772

VITAL STATISTICS

PURPOSE:
To show the extent of God's grace—the message of salvation is for *all* people

AUTHOR:
Jonah son of Amittai

TO WHOM WRITTEN:
Israel and God's people everywhere

DATE WRITTEN: Approximately 785–760 B.C.

SETTING:
Jonah preceded Amos and ministered under Jeroboam II, Israel's most powerful king (793–753 B.C.; see 2 Kings 14:23–25). Assyria was Israel's great enemy; it conquered Israel in 722 B.C. Nineveh's repentance must have been short-lived, for it was destroyed in 612 B.C.

KEY VERSE:
"But Nineveh has more than 120,000 people living in spiritual darkness, not to mention all the animals. Shouldn't I feel sorry for such a great city?" (4:11).

KEY PEOPLE:
Jonah, the ship's captain and crew

KEY PLACES:
Joppa, Nineveh

SPECIAL FEATURES:
This book is different from the other prophetic books because it tells the story of the prophet and does not center on his prophecies. In fact, only one verse summarizes his message to the people of Nineveh (3:4). Jonah is a historical narrative. It is also mentioned by Jesus as a picture of his death and resurrection (Matthew 12:38–42).

SIN runs rampant in society—daily headlines and overflowing prisons bear dramatic witness to that fact. With child abuse, pornography, serial killings, terrorism, anarchy, and ruthless dictatorships, the world seems to be filled to overflowing with violence, hatred, and corruption. Reading and hearing about these tragedies—and perhaps even experiencing them—we begin to understand the necessity of God's judgment. We may even find ourselves wishing for vengeance by any means upon the violent perpetrators. Surely they are beyond redemption! But suppose that in the midst of such thoughts, God told you to take the gospel to the worst of the offenders—how would you respond?

Jonah was given such a task. Assyria—a great but evil empire—was Israel's most dreaded enemy. The Assyrians flaunted their power before God and the world through numerous acts of heartless cruelty. So when Jonah heard God tell him to go to Assyria and call the people to repentance, he ran in the opposite direction.

The book of Jonah tells the story of this prophet's flight and how God stopped him and turned him around. But it is much more than a story of a man and a great fish. Jonah's story is a profound illustration of God's mercy and grace. No one deserved God's favor less than the people of Nineveh, Assyria's capital. Jonah knew this. But he knew that God would forgive and bless them if they would turn from their sin and worship him. Jonah also knew the power of God's message, that even through his own weak preaching, they would respond and be spared God's judgment. But Jonah hated the Assyrians, and he wanted vengeance, not mercy. So he ran. Eventually, Jonah obeyed and preached in the streets of Nineveh, and the people repented and were delivered from judgment. Then Jonah sulked and complained to God, "I knew that you were a gracious and compassionate God, slow to get angry and filled with unfailing love. I knew how easily you could cancel your plans for destroying these people" (4:2). In the end, God confronted Jonah about his self-centered values and lack of compassion, saying, "But Nineveh has more than 120,000 people living in spiritual darkness, not to mention all the animals. Shouldn't I feel sorry for such a great city?" (4:11).

As you read Jonah, see the full picture of God's love and compassion and realize that no one is beyond redemption. The gospel is for all who will repent and believe. Begin to pray for those who seem to be farthest from the kingdom, and look for ways to tell them about God. Learn from the story of this reluctant prophet and determine to obey God, doing whatever he asks and going wherever he leads.

Amos becomes a prophet 760	*Ashur-nirari V becomes king of Assyria 754*	*Jonah's ministry ends 753*	*Israel falls to Assyria 722*

THE BLUEPRINT

1. Jonah forsakes his mission (1:1—2:10)
2. Jonah fulfills his mission (3:1—4:11)

Jonah was a reluctant prophet given a mission he found distasteful. He chose to run away from God rather than obey him. Like Jonah, we may have to do things in life that we don't want to do. Sometimes we find ourselves wanting to turn and run. But it is better to obey God than to defy him or run away. Often, in spite of our defiance, God in his mercy will give us another chance to serve him when we return to him.

MEGATHEMES

THEME	EXPLANATION	IMPORTANCE
God's Sovereignty	Although the prophet Jonah tried to run away from God, God was in control. By controlling the stormy seas and a great fish, God displayed his absolute, yet loving guidance.	Rather than running from God, trust him with your past, present, and future. Saying no to God quickly leads to disaster. Saying yes brings new understanding of God and his purpose in the world.
God's Message to All the World	God had given Jonah a purpose—to preach to the great Assyrian city of Nineveh. Jonah hated Nineveh, and so he responded with anger and indifference. Jonah had yet to learn that God loves all people. Through Jonah, God reminded Israel of its missionary purpose.	We must not limit our focus to our own people. God wants his people to proclaim his love in words and actions to the whole world. He wants us to be his missionaries wherever we are, wherever he sends us.
Repentance	When the reluctant preacher went to Nineveh, there was a great response. The people repented and turned to God. This was a powerful rebuke to the people of Israel, who thought they were better but refused to respond to God's message. God will forgive all those who turn from their sin.	God doesn't honor sham or pretense. He wants the sincere devotion of each person. It is not enough to share the privileges of Christianity; we must ask God to forgive us and to remove our sin. Refusing to repent shows that we still love our sin.
God's Compassion	God's message of love and forgiveness was not for the Jews alone. God loves all the people of the world. The Assyrians didn't deserve it, but God spared them when they repented. In his mercy, God did not reject Jonah for aborting his mission. God has great love, patience, and forgiveness.	God loves each of us, even when we fail him. But he also loves other people, including those not of our group, background, race, or denomination. When we accept his love, we must also learn to accept all those whom he loves. We will find it much easier to love others when we truly love God.

1. Jonah forsakes his mission

Jonah Runs from the LORD

1:1 2 Kgs 14:25

1:3 Acts 9:36

1 The LORD gave this message to Jonah son of Amittai: 2"Get up and go to the great
city of Nineveh! Announce my judgment against it because I have seen how wicked
its people are."
3But Jonah got up and went in the opposite direction in order to get away from the

1:1, 2 Jonah is mentioned in 2 Kings 14:25. He prophesied during the reign of Jeroboam II, the king of Israel from 793 to 753 B.C. He may have been a member of the company of prophets mentioned in connection with Elisha's ministry (2 Kings 2:3).

God told Jonah to preach to Nineveh, the most important city in Assyria, the rising world power of Jonah's day. Within 50 years, Nineveh would become the capital of the vast Assyrian Empire. Jonah doesn't say much about Nineveh's wickedness, but the prophet Nahum gives us more insight. Nahum says that Nineveh was guilty of (1) evil plots against God (Nahum 1:9); (2) exploitation of the helpless (Nahum 2:12); (3) cruelty in war (Nahum 2:12, 13); and (4) idolatry, prostitution, and witchcraft (Nahum 3:4). God told Jonah to go to Nineveh, about 500 miles northeast of Israel, to warn of judgment and to declare that the people could receive mercy and forgiveness if they repented.

LORD. He went down to the seacoast, to the port of Joppa, where he found a ship leaving
for Tarshish. He bought a ticket and went on board, hoping that by going away to the
west he could escape from the LORD.

4But as the ship was sailing along, suddenly the LORD flung a powerful wind over
the sea, causing a violent storm that threatened to send them to the bottom. 5Fearing
for their lives, the desperate sailors shouted to their gods for help and threw the cargo
overboard to lighten the ship. And all this time Jonah was sound asleep down in the
hold. 6So the captain went down after him. "How can you sleep at a time like this?"
he shouted. "Get up and pray to your god! Maybe he will have mercy on us and spare
our lives."

7Then the crew cast lots to see which of them had offended the gods and caused the
terrible storm. When they did this, Jonah lost the toss. 8"What have you done to bring
this awful storm down on us?" they demanded. "Who are you? What is your line of
work? What country are you from? What is your nationality?"

9And Jonah answered, "I am a Hebrew, and I worship the LORD, the God of heaven,
who made the sea and the land." 10Then he told them that he was running away from the
LORD.

The sailors were terrified when they heard this. "Oh, why did you do it?" they
groaned. 11And since the storm was getting worse all the time, they asked him, "What
should we do to you to stop this storm?"

12"Throw me into the sea," Jonah said, "and it will become calm again. For I know
that this terrible storm is all my fault."

1:5 1 Kgs 18:26; Acts 27:18-19, 38
1:6 Ps 107:28; Jon 3:8-9
1:7 Josh 7:14; 1 Sam 14:41
1:8 Gen 47:3; Josh 7:18-19; 1 Sam 14:42
1:9 Gen 1:9; Ezra 1:2; 5:11; Neh 1:4; 9:6
1:12 John 11:50

1:3 Nineveh was a powerful and wicked city. Jonah had grown up hating the Assyrians and fearing their atrocities. His hatred was so strong that he didn't want them to receive God's mercy. Jonah was actually afraid the people would repent (4:2, 3). Jonah's attitude is representative of Israel's reluctance to share God's love and mercy with others, even though this was their God-given mission (Genesis 12:3). They, like Jonah, did not want non-Jews (Gentiles) to obtain God's favor.

1:3 Jonah knew that God had a specific job for him, but he didn't want to do it. Tarshish could be one of any number of Phoenicia's western ports. Nineveh was toward the east. Jonah decided to go as far west as he could. When God gives us directions through his Word, sometimes we run in fear or in stubbornness, claiming that God is asking too much. It may have been fear or anger at the wideness of God's mercy that made Jonah run. But running got him into worse trouble. In the end, Jonah understood that it is best to do what God asks in the first place. But by then he had paid a costly price for running. It is far better to obey from the start.

1:4 Before settling in the Promised Land, the Israelites had been nomads, wandering from place to place, seeking good pastureland for their flocks. Although they were not a seafaring people, their location along the Mediterranean Sea and near the neighboring maritime powers of Phoenicia and Philistia allowed much contact with ships and sailors. The ship Jonah sailed on was probably a large trading vessel with a deck.

1:4 Jonah's disobedience to God endangered the lives of the ship's crew. We have a great responsibility to obey God's Word because our sin and disobedience can hurt others around us.

1:4, 5 While the storm raged, Jonah was sound asleep below deck. Even as he ran from God, Jonah's actions apparently didn't bother his conscience. But the absence of guilt isn't always a barometer of whether we are doing right. Because we can deny reality, we cannot measure obedience by our feelings. Instead, we must compare what we do with God's standards for living.

1:7 The crew cast lots to find the guilty person, relying on their superstition to give them the answer. Their system worked, but only because God intervened to let Jonah know that he couldn't run away.

1:9-12 You cannot seek God's love and run from him at the same time. Jonah soon realized that no matter where he went, he couldn't get away from God. But before Jonah could return to God, he first had to stop going in the opposite direction. What has God told you to do? If you want more of God's love and power, you must be willing to carry out the responsibilities he gives you. You cannot say that you truly believe in God if you don't do what he says (1 John 2:3-6).

1:12 Jonah knew that he had disobeyed and that the storm was his fault, but he didn't say anything until the crew cast lots and he lost the toss (1:7). Then Jonah was willing to give his life to save the sailors, although he had refused to do the same for the people of Nineveh. Jonah's hatred for the Assyrians had affected his perspective.

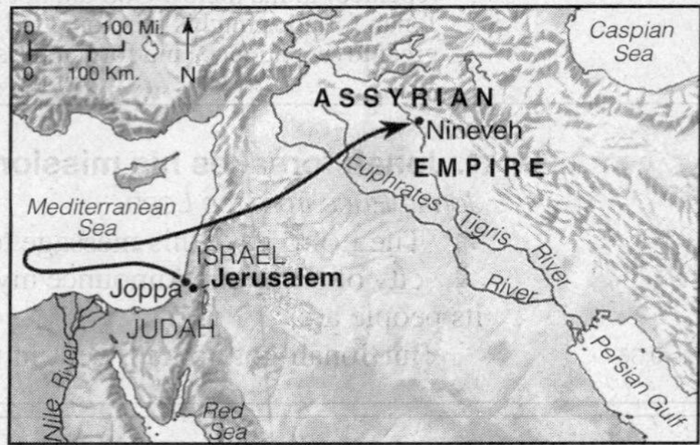

JONAH'S ROUNDABOUT JOURNEY God told Jonah to go to Nineveh, the capital of the Assyrian Empire. Many of Jonah's countrymen had experienced the atrocities of these fierce people. The last place Jonah wanted to go was on a missionary trip to Nineveh! So he went in the opposite direction. He boarded a ship in Joppa that was headed for Tarshish. But Jonah could not run from God.

13 Instead, the sailors tried even harder to row the boat ashore. But the stormy sea was
too violent for them, and they couldn't make it. 14 Then they cried out to the LORD,
Jonah's God. "O LORD," they pleaded, "don't make us die for this man's sin. And don't
hold us responsible for his death, because it isn't our fault. O LORD, you have sent this
storm upon him for your own good reasons."

1:15 Ps 89:9; Mark 4:41
15 Then the sailors picked Jonah up and threw him into the raging sea, and the storm
stopped at once! 16 The sailors were awestruck by the LORD's great power, and they
1:16 Ps 66:13-14
offered him a sacrifice and vowed to serve him.

1:17 Matt 12:40; 16:4
17 Now the LORD had arranged for a great fish to swallow Jonah. And Jonah was inside
the fish for three days and three nights.

Jonah's Prayer

2:2 Pss 18:4-6; 22:24
2 Then Jonah prayed to the LORD his God from inside the fish. 2 He said, "I cried out
to the LORD in my great trouble, and he answered me. I called to you from the world
2:3 Ps 42:7
of the dead,* and LORD, you heard me! 3 You threw me into the ocean depths, and I sank
2:4 1 Kgs 8:38; Pss 5:7; 31:22
down to the heart of the sea. I was buried beneath your wild and stormy waves. 4 Then I
said, 'O LORD, you have driven me from your presence. How will I ever again see your
2:5 Ps 69:1; Lam 3:54
holy Temple?'

5 "I sank beneath the waves, and death was very near. The waters closed in around me,
2:6 Pss 16:10; 30:3; Isa 38:17; 40:12
and seaweed wrapped itself around my head. 6 I sank down to the very roots of the
mountains. I was locked out of life and imprisoned in the land of the dead. But you,
O LORD my God, have snatched me from the yawning jaws of death!

2:7 2 Chr 30:27; Pss 18:6; 77:10-11; 142:3
7 "When I had lost all hope, I turned my thoughts once more to the LORD. And my
earnest prayer went out to you in your holy Temple. 8 Those who worship false gods turn

2:2 Hebrew *from Sheol.*

JONAH served as a prophet to Israel and Assyria from 793–753 B.C.

Climate of the times . . . . Nineveh was the most important city in Assyria and would soon become the capital of the huge Assyrian Empire. But Nineveh was also a very wicked city.

Main message . . . . Jonah, who hated the powerful and wicked Assyrians, was called by God to warn the Assyrians that they would receive judgment if they did not repent.

Importance of message . . . . . Jonah didn't want to go to Nineveh, so he tried to run from God. But God has ways of teaching us to obey and follow him. When Jonah preached, the city repented and God withheld his judgment. Even the most wicked will be saved if they truly repent of their sins and turn to God.

Contemporary prophets . . . . . Joel (853–796? B.C.), Amos (760–750 B.C.)

1:13 By trying to save Jonah's life, the pagan sailors showed more compassion than Jonah, because Jonah did not want to warn the Ninevites of the coming judgment of God. Believers should be ashamed when unbelievers show more concern and compassion than they do. God wants us to be concerned for all of his people, lost and saved.

1:14-16 Jonah had disobeyed God. While he was running away, he stopped and submitted to God. Then the ship's crew began to worship God because they saw that the storm had stopped. God is able to use even our mistakes to help others come to know him. It may be painful, but admitting our sins can be a powerful example to those who don't know God. Ironically, the pagan sailors did what the entire nation of Israel would not do—prayed to God and vowed to serve him.

1:17 Many have tried to dismiss this miraculous event as fiction, but the Bible does not describe it as a dream or a legend. We should not explain away this miracle as if we could pick and choose which of the miracles in the Bible we believe and which ones we don't. That kind of attitude would allow us to question any part of the Bible and cause us to lose our trust in the Bible as God's true and reliable Word. Jonah's experience was used by Christ himself as an illustration of his death and resurrection (Matthew 12:39, 40).

2:1ff This is a prayer of thanksgiving, not a prayer for deliverance. Jonah was simply thankful that he had not drowned. He was delivered in a most spectacular way and was overwhelmed that he had escaped certain death. Even from inside the fish, Jonah's prayer was heard by God. We can pray anywhere and at any time, and God will hear us. Your sin is never too great, your predicament never too difficult, for God.

2:1-7 Jonah said, "When I had lost all hope, I turned my thoughts once more to the LORD" (2:7). Often we act the same way. When life is going well, we tend to take God for granted; but when we lose hope, we cry out to him. This kind of relationship with God can result only in an inconsistent, up-and-down spiritual life. A consistent, daily commitment to God promotes a solid relationship with him. Look to God during both the good and bad times, and you will have a stronger spiritual life.

2:2 Jonah pictured his predicament inside the fish as though he had been buried alive.

2:8 Those who worship worthless idols (false gods) forfeit God's grace and abandon any hope for mercy from the Lord. Any object of our devotion that replaces God is a lying vanity. We deceive ourselves with something that is ultimately empty and foolish. Make sure that nothing takes God's rightful place in your life.

their backs on all God's mercies. 9But I will offer sacrifices to you with songs of praise,
and I will fulfill all my vows. For my salvation comes from the LORD alone."
10Then the LORD ordered the fish to spit up Jonah on the beach, and it did.

2:9 Pss 3:8; 50:14; 68:20 Hos 14:2

2. Jonah fulfills his mission

Jonah Goes to Nineveh

3 Then the LORD spoke to Jonah a second time: 2"Get up and go to the great city of
Nineveh, and deliver the message of judgment I have given you."
3This time Jonah obeyed the LORD's command and went to Nineveh, a city so large
that it took three days to see it all. 4On the day Jonah entered the city, he shouted to the
crowds: "Forty days from now Nineveh will be destroyed!" 5The people of Nineveh
believed God's message, and from the greatest to the least, they decided to go without
food and wear sackcloth to show their sorrow.
6When the king of Nineveh heard what Jonah was saying, he stepped down from his
throne and took off his royal robes. He dressed himself in sackcloth and sat on a heap of
ashes. 7Then the king and his nobles sent this decree throughout the city: "No one, not
even the animals, may eat or drink anything at all. 8Everyone is required to wear
sackcloth and pray earnestly to God. Everyone must turn from their evil ways and stop
all their violence. 9Who can tell? Perhaps even yet God will have pity on us and hold
back his fierce anger from destroying us."
10When God saw that they had put a stop to their evil ways, he had mercy on them
and didn't carry out the destruction he had threatened.

3:2 Jer 1:17 Ezek 2:7
3:3 Jon 1:2; 4:11
3:4 Matt 12:41 Luke 11:32
3:7 2 Chr 20:3
3:8 Ps 130:1-2 Jon 1:6, 14
3:9 Joel 2:14
3:10 Jer 18:8 Amos 7:3, 6

Jonah's Anger at the LORD's Mercy

4 This change of plans upset Jonah, and he became very angry. 2So he complained to
the LORD about it: "Didn't I say before I left home that you would do this, LORD?
That is why I ran away to Tarshish! I knew that you were a gracious and compassionate

4:2 Exod 34:6 Ps 86:5 Jer 20:7 Joel 2:13

2:9 Obviously Jonah was not in a position to bargain with God. Instead, he simply thanked God for saving his life. Our troubles should cause us to cling tightly to God, not attempt to bargain our way out of the pain. We can thank and praise God for what he has already done for us, and for his love and mercy.

2:9 It took a miracle of deliverance to get Jonah to do as God had commanded. As a prophet, Jonah was obligated to obey God's word, but he had tried to escape his responsibilities. At this time, he pledged to keep his vows. Jonah's story began with a tragedy, but a greater tragedy would have happened if God had allowed him to keep running. When you know God wants you to do something, don't run. God may not stop you as he did Jonah.

3:1, 2 Jonah had run away from God but was given a second chance to participate in God's work. You may feel as though you are disqualified from serving God because of past mistakes. But serving God is not an earned position. No one qualifies for God's service, but God still asks us to carry out his work. You may yet have another chance.

3:1, 2 Jonah was to preach only what God told him—a message of doom to one of the most powerful cities in the world. This was not the most desirable assignment, but those who bring God's word to others should not let social pressures or fear of people dictate their words. They are called to preach God's message and his truth, no matter how unpopular it may be.

3:3 Nineveh was a huge city. The Hebrew text makes no distinction between the city proper (the walls of which were only about eight miles in circumference, accommodating a population of about 175,000 persons) and the administrative district of Nineveh that was about 30 to 60 miles across.

3:4-9 God's word is for everyone. Despite the wickedness of the Ninevite people, they were open to God's message and repented immediately. If we simply proclaim God's message of salvation, we may be surprised at how many people will listen.

3:10 The pagan people of Nineveh believed Jonah's message and repented. What a miraculous effect God's words had on those evil people! Their repentance stood in stark contrast to Israel's stubbornness. The people of Israel had heard many messages from the prophets, but they had refused to repent. The people of Nineveh only needed to hear God's message once. Jesus said that at the judgment, the people of Nineveh will stand up to condemn the Israelites for their failure to repent (Matthew 12:39-41). It is not our hearing God's Word that pleases him, but our responding obediently to it.

3:10 God responded in mercy by canceling his threatened destruction. God had said that any nation on which he had pronounced judgment would be saved if it repented (Jeremiah 18:7, 8). God forgave Nineveh, just as he had forgiven Jonah. The purpose of God's judgment is correction, not revenge. He is always ready to show compassion to anyone willing to seek him.

4:1 Why did Jonah become angry when God spared Nineveh? The Jews did not want to share God's message with Gentile nations in Jonah's day, just as they resisted that role in Paul's day (1 Thessalonians 2:14-16). They had forgotten their original purpose as a nation—to be a blessing to the rest of the world by sharing God's message with other nations (Genesis 22:18). Jonah thought that God should not freely give his salvation to a wicked pagan nation. Yet this is exactly what God does for all who come to him today in faith.

4:1, 2 Jonah revealed the reason for his reluctance to go to Nineveh (1:3). He didn't want the Ninevites forgiven; he wanted them destroyed. Jonah did not understand that the God of Israel was also the God of the whole world. Are you surprised when some unlikely person turns to God? Is it possible that your view is as narrow as Jonah's? We must not forget that, in reality, *we* do not deserve to be forgiven by God.

God, slow to get angry and filled with unfailing love. I knew how easily you could cancel
4:3 1 Kgs 19:4 — your plans for destroying these people. 3 Just kill me now, LORD! I'd rather be dead than
Job 6:8-9 — alive because nothing I predicted is going to happen."
4 The LORD replied, "Is it right for you to be angry about this?"
5 Then Jonah went out to the east side of the city and made a shelter to sit under as he
waited to see if anything would happen to the city. 6 And the LORD God arranged for a
leafy plant to grow there, and soon it spread its broad leaves over Jonah's head, shading
him from the sun. This eased some of his discomfort, and Jonah was very grateful for
4:7 — the plant.
Joel 1:12 — 7 But God also prepared a worm! The next morning at dawn the worm ate through the
4:8 — stem of the plant, so that it soon died and withered away. 8 And as the sun grew hot, God
Isa 49:10 Ezek 19:12 — sent a scorching east wind to blow on Jonah. The sun beat down on his head until he
Hos 13:15 — grew faint and wished to die. "Death is certainly better than this!" he exclaimed.
9 Then God said to Jonah, "Is it right for you to be angry because the plant died?"
"Yes," Jonah retorted, "even angry enough to die!"
10 Then the LORD said, "You feel sorry about the plant, though you did nothing to put
4:11 — it there. And a plant is only, at best, short lived. 11 But Nineveh has more than 120,000
Jon 1:2; 3:2; 3:10 — people living in spiritual darkness,* not to mention all the animals. Shouldn't I feel sorry
for such a great city?"

4:11 Hebrew *people who don't know their right hands from their left.*

MIRACLES IN THE BOOK OF JONAH		
	God sent a violent storm	1:4
	God provided a great fish to swallow Jonah	1:17
	God ordered the fish to spit up Jonah	2:10
	God made a leafy plant to shade Jonah	4:6
	God provided a worm to eat the plant	4:7
	God provided a scorching wind to blow on Jonah	4:8

4:3 Jonah had run from the job of delivering God's message of destruction to Nineveh (1:2, 3); then he wanted to die because the destruction wouldn't happen. How quickly Jonah had forgotten God's mercy for him when he was inside the fish (2:9, 10). Jonah was happy when God saved him, but he was angry when Nineveh was saved. But Jonah was learning a valuable lesson about God's mercy and forgiveness. God's forgiveness was not only for Jonah or for Israel alone; it extends to all who repent and believe.

4:3 Jonah may have been more concerned about his own reputation than God's. He knew that if the people repented, none of his warnings to Nineveh would come true. This would embarrass him, although it would give glory to God. Are you more interested in getting glory for God or for yourself?

4:5-11 God ministered tenderly to Jonah just as he had done to Nineveh and to Israel—and just as he does to us. God could have destroyed Jonah for his defiant anger, but instead he gently taught him a lesson. If we will obey God, he will lead us. His harsh judgment is reserved for those who persist in rebellion.

4:9 Jonah was angry at the withering of the plant, but not over what could have happened to Nineveh. Most of us have cried at the death of a pet or when an object with sentimental value is broken, but have we cried over the fact that a friend does not know God? How easy it is to be more sensitive to our own interests than to the spiritual needs of people around us.

4:10, 11 Sometimes people wish that judgment and destruction would come upon sinful people whose wickedness seems to demand immediate punishment. But God is more merciful than we can imagine. God feels compassion for the sinners we want judged, and he devises plans to bring them to himself. What is your attitude toward those who are especially wicked? Do you want them destroyed? Or do you wish that they could experience God's mercy and forgiveness?

4:11 God spared the sailors when they pleaded for mercy. God saved Jonah when he prayed from inside the fish. God saved the people of Nineveh when they responded to Jonah's preaching. God answers the prayers of those who call upon him. God will always work his will, and he desires that all come to him, trust in him, and be saved. We can be saved if we heed God's warnings to us through his Word. If we respond in obedience, God will be gracious, and we will receive his mercy, not his punishment.

MICAH

Hosea becomes a prophet 753 B.C.	Jotham becomes king of Judah 750	Tiglath-pileser III invades Israel 743	Micah becomes a prophet; Pekahiah becomes king 742	Isaiah becomes a prophet 740	Ahaz becomes king of Judah 735

VITAL STATISTICS

PURPOSE:
To warn God's people that judgment is coming and to offer pardon to all who repent

AUTHOR:
Micah, a native of Moresheth, near Gath, about 20 miles southwest of Jerusalem

TO WHOM WRITTEN:
The people of Israel (the northern kingdom) and of Judah (the southern kingdom)

DATE WRITTEN:
Possibly during the reigns of Jotham, Ahaz, and Hezekiah (742–687 B.C.)

SETTING:
The political situation is described in 2 Kings 15—20 and 2 Chronicles 26—30. Micah was a contemporary of Isaiah and Hosea.

KEY VERSE:
"No, O people, the LORD has already told you what is good, and this is what he requires: to do what is right, to love mercy, and to walk humbly with your God" (6:8).

KEY PEOPLE:
The people of Samaria and Jerusalem

KEY PLACES:
Samaria, Jerusalem, Bethlehem

SPECIAL FEATURES:
This is a beautiful example of classical Hebrew poetry. There are three parts, each beginning with "Attention!" or "Listen" (1:2; 3:1; 6:1) and closing with a promise.

"I HATE YOU!" she screams and runs from the room. Words from a child thrown as emotional darts. Perhaps she learned the phrase from Mom and Dad, or maybe it just burst forth from that inner well of "sinful nature." Whatever the case, hate and love have become society's bywords, almost tired clichés, tossed carelessly at objects, situations, and even people.

The casual use of such words as *love* and *hate* has emptied them of their meaning. We no longer understand statements that describe a loving God who hates sin. So we picture God as gentle and kind—a cosmic "pushover"; and our concept of what he hates is tempered by our misconceptions and wishful thinking.

The words of the prophets stand in stark contrast to such misconceptions. God's hatred is real—burning, consuming, and destroying. He hates sin, and he stands as the righteous Judge, ready to mete out just punishment to all who defy his rule. God's love is also real. So real that he sent his Son, the Messiah, to save and accept judgment in the sinner's place. Love and hate are together—both unending, irresistible, and unfathomable.

In seven short chapters, Micah presents this true picture of God—the almighty Lord who hates sin and loves the sinner. Much of the book is devoted to describing God's judgment on Israel (the northern kingdom), on Judah (the southern kingdom), and on all the earth. This judgment will come "because of the sins and rebellion of Israel and Judah" (1:5). And the prophet lists their despicable sins, including fraud (2:2), theft (2:8), greed (2:9), debauchery (2:11), oppression (3:3), hypocrisy (3:4), heresy (3:5), injustice (3:9), extortion and lying (6:12), murder (7:2), and other offenses. God's judgment will come.

In the midst of this overwhelming prediction of destruction, Micah gives hope and consolation because he also describes God's love. The truth is that judgment comes only after countless opportunities to repent, to turn back to true worship and obedience—"to do what is right, to love mercy, and to walk humbly with your God" (6:8). But even in the midst of judgment, God promises to deliver the small minority who have continued to follow him. He states, "Your king will lead you; the LORD himself will guide you." (2:13). The king, of course, is Jesus; and we read in 5:2 that he will be born as a baby in Bethlehem, an obscure Judean village.

As you read Micah, catch a glimpse of God's anger in action as he judges and punishes sin. See God's love in action as he offers eternal life to all who repent and believe. And then determine to join the faithful remnant of God's people, who live according to his will.

Israel (the northern kingdom) falls 722	*Hosea's ministry ends; Hezekiah becomes king of Judah 715*	*Sennacherib surrounds Jerusalem 701*	*Micah's ministry ends 687*

THE BLUEPRINT

1. The trial of the capitals (1:1—2:13)
2. The trial of the leaders (3:1—5:15)
3. The trial of the people (6:1—7:20)

Micah emphasized the need for justice and peace. Like a lawyer, he set forth God's case against Israel and Judah, their leaders, and their people. Throughout the book are prophecies about Jesus, the Messiah, who will gather the people into one nation. He will be their king and ruler, acting mercifully toward them. Micah makes it clear that God hates unkindness, idolatry, injustice, and empty ritual—and he still hates these today. But God is very willing to pardon the sins of any who repent.

MEGATHEMES

THEME	EXPLANATION	IMPORTANCE
Perverting Faith	God will judge the false prophets, dishonest leaders, and selfish priests in Israel and Judah. While they publicly carried out religious ceremonies, they were privately seeking to gain money and influence. To mix selfish motives with an empty display of religion is to pervert faith.	Don't try to mix your own selfish desires with true faith in God. One day God will reveal how foolish it is to substitute anything for loyalty to him. Coming up with your own private blend of religion will pervert your faith.
Oppression	Micah predicted ruin for all nations and leaders who were oppressive toward others. The upper classes oppressed and exploited the poor. Yet no one was speaking against them or doing anything to stop them. God will not put up with such injustice.	We dare not ask God to help us while we ignore those who are needy and oppressed, or while we silently condone the actions of those who oppress them.
The Messiah—King of Peace	God promised to provide a new king to bring strength and peace to his people. Hundreds of years before Christ's birth, God promised that the eternal King would be born in Bethlehem. It was God's great plan to restore his people through the Messiah.	Christ our king leads us just as God promised. But until his final judgment, his leadership is only visible among those who welcome his authority. We can have God's peace now by giving up our sins and welcoming him as king.
Pleasing God	Micah preached that God's greatest desire was not the offering of sacrifices at the Temple. God delights in faith that produces justice, love for others, and obedience to him.	True faith in God generates kindness, compassion, justice, and humility. We can please God by seeking these attributes in our work, our family, our church, and our neighborhood.

1. The trial of the capitals

1:1 1 Chr 3:12-13 Jer 26:18

1 The LORD gave these messages to Micah of Moresheth during the years when
Jotham, Ahaz, and Hezekiah were kings of Judah. The messages concerned both
Samaria and Jerusalem, and they came to Micah in the form of visions.

Grief over Samaria and Jerusalem

1:2 Ps 50:7 Jer 6:19

2 Attention! Let all the people of the world listen! The Sovereign LORD has made
accusations against you; the Lord speaks from his holy Temple.

1:1 Micah and Isaiah lived at the same time, about 750–680 B.C., and undoubtedly knew of each other. Micah directed his message mainly to Judah, the southern kingdom, but he also had some words for Israel, the northern kingdom. Judah was enjoying great prosperity at this time. Of the three kings mentioned, Jotham (750–732) and Hezekiah (715–686) had tried to follow God (2 Kings 15:32-38; 18–20), but Ahaz (735–715) was one of the most evil kings ever to reign in Judah (2 Kings 16). Moresheth was a Judean village near Gath, on the border with Philistia.

3Look! The LORD is coming! He leaves his throne in heaven and comes to earth,
walking on the high places. 4They melt beneath his feet and flow into the valleys like
wax in a fire, like water pouring down a hill.
5And why is this happening? Because of the sins and rebellion of Israel and Judah.*
Who is to blame for Israel's rebellion? Samaria, its capital city! Where is the center of
idolatry in Judah? In Jerusalem, its capital!
6"So I, the LORD, will make the city of Samaria a heap of rubble. Her streets will be
plowed up for planting vineyards. I will roll the stones of her walls down into the valley
below, exposing all her foundations. 7All her carved images will be smashed to pieces.
All her sacred treasures will be burned up. These things were bought with the money
earned by her prostitution, and they will now be carried away to pay prostitutes
elsewhere."
8Because of all this, I will mourn and lament. I will walk around naked and barefoot
in sorrow and shame. I will howl like a jackal and wail like an ostrich. 9For my
people's wound is far too deep to heal. It has reached into Judah, even to the gates of
Jerusalem.
10Don't tell our enemies in the city of Gath*; don't weep at all.* You people in
Beth-leaphrah,* roll in the dust to show your anguish and despair. 11You people of
Shaphir,* go as captives into exile—naked and ashamed. The people of Zaanan* dare
not come outside their walls. The people of Beth-ezel* mourn because the very foundations of their city have been swept away. 12The people of Maroth* anxiously wait for
relief, but only bitterness awaits them as the LORD's judgment reaches even to the gates
of Jerusalem.
13Quick! Use your swiftest chariots and flee, you people of Lachish.* You were the
first city in Judah to follow Israel in the sin of idol worship, and so you led Jerusalem*
into sin. 14Send a farewell gift to Moresheth-gath; there is no hope of saving it. The town
of Aczib* has deceived the kings of Israel, for it promised help it could not give. 15You
people of Mareshah,* I will bring a conqueror to capture your town. And the leaders* of
Israel will go to Adullam.
16Weep, you people of Judah! Shave your heads in sorrow, for the children you love
will be snatched away, and you will never see them again. Make yourselves as bald as
an eagle, for your little ones will be exiled to distant lands.

1:3 Isa 26:21; Amos 4:13
1:4 Ps 97:5; Isa 64:1-2; Nah 1:5
1:5 2 Chr 34:3-4; Amos 8:14
1:6 Jer 31:5; Lam 4:1; Ezek 13:14
1:7 Deut 9:21; 23:18; 2 Chr 34:7; Isa 23:17
1:8 Isa 13:21-22; 20:2-4
1:9 Jer 30:11-15; Mic 1:12
1:11 Ezek 23:29
1:12 Job 30:26; Isa 59:9-11; Jer 8:15; 14:19
1:13 Josh 10:3
1:14 Josh 15:18, 44; 2 Kgs 16:8
1:15 Josh 12:15; 15:35, 44
1:16 2 Kgs 17:6; Isa 22:12

1:5 Hebrew *and Jacob.* **1:10a** *Gath* sounds like the Hebrew term for "tell." **1:10b** Greek version reads *weep not in Acco.* **1:10c** *Beth-leaphrah* means "house of dust." **1:11a** *Shaphir* means "pleasant." **1:11b** *Zaanan* sounds like the Hebrew term for "come out." **1:11c** *Beth-ezel* means "adjoining house." **1:12** *Maroth* sounds like the Hebrew term for "bitter." **1:13a** *Lachish* sounds like the Hebrew term for "team of horses." **1:13b** Hebrew *the daughter of Zion.* **1:14** *Aczib* means "deception." **1:15a** *Mareshah* sounds like the Hebrew term for "conqueror." **1:15b** Hebrew *the glory.*

1:3 "High places" could simply mean "mountaintops" or may refer to the altars dedicated to various idols, usually placed in such elevated areas (see also 1:5).

1:3-7 Jerusalem was the capital city of Judah (the southern kingdom); Samaria was the capital city of Israel (the northern kingdom). The destruction of Samaria was literally fulfilled during Micah's lifetime, in 722 B.C. (2 Kings 17:1-18), just as he had predicted.

1:5 There are two sins identified in Micah's message: the perversion of worship (1:7; 3:5-7, 11; 5:12, 13) and injustice toward others (2:1, 2, 8, 9; 3:2, 3, 9-11; 7:2-6). Rampant in the capital cities, these sins infiltrated and infected the entire country.

1:9 Samaria's sins were incurable, and God's judgment on the city had already begun. This sin was not like a gash in the skin but more like a stab wound in a vital organ, causing an injury that would soon prove fatal (Samaria was, in fact, destroyed early in Micah's ministry). Tragically, Samaria's sin had influenced Jerusalem, and judgment would come to its very gates. This probably refers to Sennacherib's siege in 701 B.C. (see 2 Kings 18–19).

1:10-16 Micah declared God's judgment on city after city because of the people's sins. There is a clever wordplay in the Hebrew of 1:10-13 (see the textual notes). Micah bitterly denounced each town by using puns. *Shaphir* sounds like the Hebrew word for "pleasant"; *Zaanan* sounds like the verb meaning "come out"; and *Maroth* sounds like a word for "bitter." Read 1:11-12 aloud, substituting the meaning for each city's name, and you will realize the effect of Micah's word choice. Not all these cities can be identified now, but Lachish was on the border with Philistia and took the brunt of the Assyrian invasion.

1:13 The people of Lachish had influenced many to follow their evil example. They "led Jerusalem into sin." We often do the same when we sin. Regardless of whether you consider yourself a leader, your daily actions and words are observed by others who may choose to follow your example, whether you know it or not.

1:14 Moresheth-gath was Micah's hometown (1:1).

1:15 The terrain surrounding Adullam had numerous caves. Micah was warning that when the enemy approached, Judah's proud princes would be forced to flee and hide in these caves.

1:16 Micah pictured the devastating sorrow of parents seeing their children taken away to be slaves in a distant land. This happened frequently in both Israel and Judah, most horribly when each nation was completely conquered—Israel in 722 B.C. and Judah in 586 B.C.

Judgment against Wealthy Oppressors

2:1 Prov 3:27; Isa 32:7; Hos 7:6-7
2:2 Isa 5:8

2 How terrible it will be for you who lie awake at night, thinking up evil plans. You rise at dawn and hurry to carry out any of the wicked schemes you have power to accomplish. [2]When you want a certain piece of land, you find a way to seize it. When you want someone's house, you take it by fraud and violence. No one's family or inheritance is safe with you around!

2:3 Isa 2:11-12; Jer 18:11

[3]But this is what the LORD says: "I will reward your evil with evil; you won't be able to escape! After I am through with you, none of you will ever again walk proudly in the streets."

2:4 Jer 6:12; 8:10; Hab 2:6

[4]In that day your enemies will make fun of you by singing this song of despair about your experience:

"We are finished,
  completely ruined!
God has confiscated our land,
  taking it from us.
He has given our fields
  to those who betrayed us.*"

2:5 Deut 32:8; Josh 18:4, 10

[5]Others will set your boundaries then, and the LORD's people will have no say in how the land is divided.

True and False Prophets

2:6 Isa 30:10; Amos 2:12

[6]"Don't say such things," the people say. "Don't prophesy like that. Such disasters will never come our way!"

2:7 Jer 15:16
2:8 Jer 12:8; Mic 3:2-3; 7:2-3
2:9 Jer 10:20
2:10 Lev 18:24-28; Deut 12:9

[7]Should you talk that way, O family of Israel*? Will the LORD have patience with such behavior? If you would do what is right, you would find my words to be good. [8]Yet to this very hour my people rise against me! You steal the shirts right off the backs of those who trusted you, making them as ragged as men who have just come home from battle. [9]You have evicted women from their homes and stripped their children of all their God-given rights. [10]Up! Begone! This is no longer your land and home, for you have filled it with sin and ruined it completely.

2:4 Or *to those who took us captive.* **2:7** Hebrew *house of Jacob.*

MICAH served as a prophet to Judah from 742–687 B.C.

Climate of the times	King Ahaz set up pagan idols in the Temple and finally nailed the Temple doors shut. Four different nations harassed Judah. When Hezekiah became king, the nation began a slow road to recovery and economic strength. Hezekiah probably heeded much of Micah's advice.
Main message	Prediction of the fall of both the northern kingdom of Israel and the southern kingdom of Judah. This was God's discipline upon the people, actually showing how much he cared for them. Hezekiah's good reign helped postpone Judah's punishment.
Importance of message	Choosing to live a life apart from God is making a commitment to sin. Sin leads to judgment and death. God alone shows us the way to eternal peace. His discipline often keeps us on the right path.
Contemporary prophets	Hosea (753–715 B.C.), Isaiah (740–681 B.C.)

2:1, 2 Micah spoke out against those who planned evil deeds at night and rose at dawn to do them. A person's thoughts and plans reflect his or her character. What do you think about as you lie down to sleep? Do your desires involve greed or stepping on others to achieve your goals? Evil thoughts lead to evil deeds.

2:5 Those who have been oppressing others will find the tables turned. They will end up not having any share in the decisions to divide the land because they won't have any surviving relatives.

2:6, 7 If these messages seem harsh, remember that God did not want to take revenge on Israel; he wanted to get them back on the right path. The people had rejected what was true and right, and they needed stern discipline. Children may think discipline is harsh, but it helps keep them going in the right direction. If we only want God's comforting messages, we may miss what he has for us. Listen whenever God speaks, even when the message is hard to take.

[11]Suppose a prophet full of lies were to say to you, "I'll preach to you the joys of wine
and drink!" That's just the kind of prophet you would like!

2:11 Jer 5:31 Mic 3:5, 11

Hope for Restoration

[12]"Someday, O Israel, I will gather the few of you who are left. I will bring you together
again like sheep in a fold, like a flock in its pasture. Yes, your land will again be filled
with noisy crowds! [13]Your leader will break out and lead you out of exile. He will bring
you through the gates of your cities of captivity, back to your own land. Your king will
lead you; the LORD himself will guide you."

2:12 Isa 11:11 Mic 4:7; 5:7; 7:18

2. The trial of the leaders

Judgment against Israel's Leaders

3 Listen, you leaders of Israel! You are supposed to know right from wrong, [2]but you
are the very ones who hate good and love evil. You skin my people alive and tear
the flesh off their bones. [3]You eat my people's flesh, cut away their skin, and break their
bones. You chop them up like meat for the cooking pot. [4]Then you beg the LORD for help
in times of trouble! Do you really expect him to listen? After all the evil you have done,
he won't even look at you!

[5]This is what the LORD says to you false prophets: "You are leading my people astray!
You promise peace for those who give you food, but you declare war on anyone who
refuses to pay you. [6]Now the night will close around you, cutting off all your visions.
Darkness will cover you, making it impossible for you to predict the future. The sun will
set for you prophets, and your day will come to an end. [7]Then you seers will cover your
faces in shame, and you diviners will be disgraced. And you will admit that your
messages were not from God."

[8]But as for me, I am filled with power and the Spirit of the LORD. I am filled with
justice and might, fearlessly pointing out Israel's sin and rebellion. [9]Listen to me, you
leaders of Israel! You hate justice and twist all that is right. [10]You are building Jerusalem
on a foundation of murder and corruption. [11]You rulers govern for the bribes you can
get; you priests teach God's laws only for a price; you prophets won't prophesy unless
you are paid. Yet all of you claim you are depending on the LORD. "No harm can come
to us," you say, "for the LORD is here among us."

3:1 Jer 5:5
3:2 Ezek 22:27
3:3 Ezek 11:7 Zeph 3:3
3:4 Deut 31:17 Prov 1:28 Isa 1:15; 59:2
3:5 Jer 6:14; 14:14-15
3:6 Isa 8:20-22; 29:10 Amos 8:9-10
3:7 Isa 44:25 Zech 13:4
3:8 Isa 58:1; 61:1-2
3:10 Jer 22:13-17 Ezek 22:25-28 Hab 2:9-12
3:11 Isa 48:2 Hos 4:18

2:11 The people liked the false prophets who told them only what they wanted to hear. Micah spoke against prophets who encouraged the people to feel comfortable in their sin. Preachers are popular when they don't ask too much of us and when they tell us our greed or lust might even be good for us. But a true teacher of God speaks the truth, regardless of what the listeners want to hear.

2:12, 13 Micah's prophecy telescopes two great events—Judah's return from captivity in Babylon, and the great gathering of all believers when the Messiah returns. God gave his prophets visions of various future events, but not necessarily the ability to discern when these events would happen. For example, they could not see the long period of time between the Babylonian captivity and the coming of the Messiah, but they could clearly see that the Messiah was coming. The purpose of this prophecy was not to predict exactly *how* this would occur but *that* it would. This gave the people hope and helped them turn from sin.

3:1ff Micah denounced the sins of the leaders, including priests and prophets—those responsible for teaching the people right from wrong. The leaders, who should have known the law and taught it to the people, had set the law aside and had become the worst of sinners. They were taking advantage of the very people they were supposed to serve. All sin is bad, but the sin that leads others astray is the worst of all.

3:2-4 The leaders had no compassion or respect for those they were supposed to serve. They were treating the people miserably in order to satisfy their own desires, and then they had the gall to ask for God's help when they found themselves in trouble. We, like the leaders, should not treat God like a light switch to be turned on only as needed. Instead, we should always rely on him.

3:5-7 Micah remained true to his calling and proclaimed God's words. In contrast, the false prophets' messages were geared to the favors they received. Not all those who claim to have messages from God really do. Micah prophesied that one day the false prophets would be shamed by their actions.

3:8 Micah attributed the power of his ministry to the Spirit of the Lord. Our power comes from the same source. Jesus told his followers they would receive power to witness about him when the Holy Spirit came on them (Acts 1:8). You can't witness effectively by relying on your own strength, because fear will keep you from speaking out for God. Only by relying on the power of the Holy Spirit can you live and witness for him.

3:11 Micah warned the rulers, priests, and prophets of his day to avoid bribes. Pastors today accept bribes when they allow those who are big contributors to control the church. If fear of losing money or members influences pastors to remain silent when they should speak up for what is right, their churches are in danger. We should remember that Judah was finally destroyed because of the behavior of its religious leaders. A similar warning must be directed at those who have money—*never* use your resources to influence or manipulate God's ministers—that is bribery.

12 So because of you, Mount Zion will be plowed like an open field; Jerusalem will be
reduced to rubble! A great forest will grow on the hilltop, where the Temple now stands.

The LORD's Future Reign

4 In the last days, the Temple of the LORD in Jerusalem will become the most important
place on earth. People from all over the world will go there to worship. 2 Many
nations will come and say, "Come, let us go up to the mountain of the LORD, to the
Temple of the God of Israel.* There he will teach us his ways, so that we may obey him."
For in those days the LORD's teaching and his word will go out from Jerusalem.
3 The LORD will settle international disputes. All the nations will beat their swords into
plowshares and their spears into pruning hooks. All wars will stop, and military training will
come to an end. 4 Everyone will live quietly in their own homes in peace and prosperity, for
there will be nothing to fear. The LORD Almighty has promised this! 5 Even though the
nations around us worship idols, we will follow the LORD our God forever and ever.

Israel's Return from Exile

6 "In that coming day," says the LORD, "I will gather together my people who are lame,
who have been exiles, filled with grief. 7 They are weak and far from home, but I will
make them strong again, a mighty nation. Then I, the LORD, will rule from Jerusalem*
as their king forever."
8 As for you, O Jerusalem, the citadel of God's people, your royal might and power will
come back to you again. The kingship will be restored to my precious Jerusalem. 9 But why
are you now screaming in terror? Have you no king to lead you? He is dead! Have you no
wise people to counsel you? All are gone! Pain has gripped you like it does a woman in
labor. 10 Writhe and groan in terrible pain, you people of Jerusalem,* for you must leave this
city to live in the open fields. You will soon be sent into exile in distant Babylon. But the
LORD will rescue you there; he will redeem you from the grip of your enemies.
11 True, many nations have gathered together against you, calling for your blood, eager
to gloat over your destruction. 12 But they do not know the LORD's thoughts or under-

4:2 Hebrew *of Jacob.* **4:7** Hebrew *Mount Zion.* **4:10** Hebrew *O daughter of Zion.*

3:12 Jer 9:11; 26:18
4:1 Pss 22:27; 86:9; Jer 3:17
4:2 Ps 25:8-12; Isa 2:3; 4:3; 42:1-4; Jer 31:6; Zech 14:8-9
4:3 Isa 11:3-5
4:4 Lev 26:6; Isa 1:20; 40:5
4:5 2 Kgs 17:29, 34
4:6 Zeph 3:19
4:7 Isa 9:6-7; 24:23
4:8 Ps 48:12; Isa 1:26; Zech 9:10
4:9 Jer 8:19
4:10 2 Kgs 20:18; Isa 48:20; Hos 2:14; Mic 7:8-12
4:11 Isa 5:25-30
4:12 Ps 147:19-20; Isa 55:8

MICAH'S CHARGES OF INJUSTICE
Micah charged the people with injustice of many kinds.

Charge	Reference
Plotting evil	2:1
Fraud, coveting, violence	2:2
Stealing, dishonesty	2:8
Evicting widows from their homes	2:9
Hating good, loving evil	3:1, 2
Despising justice, distorting what is right	3:9
Murder	3:10
Taking bribes	3:11

3:12 Jerusalem would be destroyed just as Samaria was (1:6). This happened in 586 B.C. when Nebuchadnezzar and the Babylonian army attacked the city (2 Kings 25). Although Micah blamed the corrupt leaders, the people were not without fault. They allowed the corruption to continue without turning to God or calling for justice.

4:1ff The phrase "in the last days" describes the days when God will reign over his perfect Kingdom (see 4:1-8). The "mountain of the LORD" is Mount Zion. This will be an era of peace and blessing, a time when war will be forever ended. We cannot pinpoint its date, but God has promised that it *will* arrive (see also Isaiah 2:2; Jeremiah 16:15; Joel 3:1ff; Zechariah 14:9-11; Malachi 3:17, 18; Revelation 19–22).

Verses 9-13 predicted the Babylonian captivity in 586 B.C., even before Babylon became a powerful empire. Just as God promises a time of peace and prosperity, he also promises judgment and punishment for all who refuse to follow him. Both results are certain.

4:9-13 Micah predicted the end of the kings. This was a drastic statement to the people of Judah, who thought that their kingdom would last forever. Micah also said that Babylon would destroy the land of Judah and carry away its king, but that after a while God would help his people return to their land. This all happened just as Micah prophesied, and these events are recorded in 2 Chronicles 36:9-23 and Ezra 1–2.

4:12 When God reveals the future, his purpose goes beyond satisfying our curiosity. He wants us to change our present behavior because of what we know about the future. Forever begins now; and a glimpse of God's plan for his followers should motivate us to serve him, no matter what the rest of the world may do.

stand his plan. These nations don't know that he is gathering them together to be beaten
and trampled like bundles of grain on a threshing floor.
13 "Rise up and destroy the nations, O Jerusalem!"* says the LORD. "For I will give
you iron horns and bronze hooves, so you can trample many nations to pieces. Then you
will give all the wealth they acquired as offerings to me, the Lord of all the earth."

A Ruler from Bethlehem

5 Mobilize! Marshal your troops! The enemy is laying siege to Jerusalem. With a rod
they will strike the leader of Israel in the face.
2 But you, O Bethlehem Ephrathah, are only a small village in Judah. Yet a ruler of
Israel will come from you, one whose origins are from the distant past. 3 The people
of Israel will be abandoned to their enemies until the time when the woman in labor
gives birth to her son. Then at last his fellow countrymen will return from exile to
their own land. 4 And he will stand to lead his flock with the LORD's strength, in the
majesty of the name of the LORD his God. Then his people will live there undisturbed,
for he will be highly honored all around the world. 5 And he will be the source of our
peace.
When the Assyrians invade our land and break through our defenses, we will appoint
seven rulers to watch over us, eight princes to lead us. 6 They will rule Assyria with drawn
swords and enter the gates of the land of Nimrod. They* will rescue us from the
Assyrians when they pour over the borders to invade our land.

The Remnant Purified

7 Then the few left in Israel* will go out among the nations. They will be like dew sent
by the LORD or like rain falling on the grass, which no one can hold back. 8 The remnant
of Israel will go out among the nations and be as strong as a lion. And the other nations
will be like helpless sheep, with no one to rescue them. 9 The people of Israel will stand
up to their foes, and all their enemies will be wiped out.
10 "At that same time," says the LORD, "I will destroy all your weapons—your
horses and chariots. 11 I will tear down your walls and demolish the defenses of your
cities. 12 I will put an end to all witchcraft; there will be no more fortune-tellers to
consult. 13 I will destroy all your idols and sacred pillars, so you will never again
worship the work of your own hands. 14 I will abolish your pagan shrines with their
Asherah poles and destroy the cities where your idol temples stand. 15 I will pour out
my vengeance on all the nations that refuse to obey me."

4:13 Isa 41:15-16; 60:9
5:1 Jer 5:7; Lam 3:30
5:2 Jer 30:21; Zech 9:9; †Matt 2:6; John 1:1-2; 7:42
5:3 Isa 10:20-22; Hos 11:8
5:4 Isa 52:10
5:5 Isa 8:7-8; 9:6
5:6 Gen 10:8-11; Isa 37:36-37; Nah 2:11-13
5:7 Deut 32:2
5:8 Gen 49:9; Zech 10:5
5:10 Hos 14:3; Zech 9:10
5:11 Isa 2:12-17; Hos 10:14
5:12 Deut 18:10-12
5:14 Exod 34:13
5:15 Isa 1:24; 65:12

4:13 Hebrew *"Rise up and thresh, O daughter of Zion."* **5:6** Hebrew *He.* **5:7** Hebrew *Jacob;* also in 5:8.

5:1 This leader was probably King Zedekiah, who was reigning in Jerusalem when Nebuchadnezzar conquered the city (2 Kings 25:1, 2). Zedekiah was the last of the kings in David's line to sit on the throne in Jerusalem. Micah said that the next king in David's line would be the Messiah, who would establish a Kingdom that would never end.

5:1ff Jerusalem's leaders were obsessed with wealth and position, but Micah prophesied that mighty Jerusalem, with all its wealth and power, would be besieged and destroyed. Its king could not save it. In contrast, Bethlehem, a tiny town, would be the birthplace of the only ruler who could save his people. This deliverer, the Messiah, would be born as a baby in Bethlehem (Luke 2:4-7) and eventually would reign as the eternal King (Revelation 19–22).

5:2 Ephrathah was the district in which Bethlehem was located.

5:2 This ruler is Jesus, the Messiah. Micah accurately predicted Christ's birthplace hundreds of years before Jesus was born. The promised eternal King in David's line, who would come to live as a man, had been alive forever—"whose origins are from the distant past." Although eternal, Christ entered human history as the man, Jesus of Nazareth.

5:5 This chapter provides one of the clearest Old Testament prophecies of Christ's coming. The key descriptive phrase is "he will be the source of our peace." In one of Christ's final talks he said, "I am leaving you with a gift—peace of mind and heart. And the peace I give isn't like the peace the world gives. So don't be troubled or afraid" (John 14:27). Because of Christ's first coming, we have the opportunity to experience peace with God with no more fear of judgment and no more conflict and guilt. Christ's peace gives us assurance even though wars continue. At Christ's second coming, all wars and weapons will be destroyed (4:3-5).

5:5 Micah's prophecy of seven rulers and eight princes is a figurative way of saying that the Messiah will raise up many good leaders when he returns to reign. This contrasts with Micah's words in chapter 3 about Judah's corrupt leaders. "The Assyrians" symbolically refer to all nations in every age that oppose God's people. These good leaders will help Christ defeat all evil in the world.

5:6 The land of Nimrod is another name for Assyria, which, in this case, is a symbol of all the evil nations in the world.

5:10 When God rules in his eternal Kingdom, our strength and deliverance will not be found in military might but in God's almighty power. God will destroy all the weapons that people use for security. There will be no need for armies because God will rule in the heart of every person. Instead of being overwhelmed by fear of invasion or nuclear attack, we should have confidence in God.

5:12-14 Idols, sacred pillars, and Asherah poles were all part of pagan worship.

3. The trial of the people

The LORD's Case against Israel

6:2 Hos 4:1; 12:2 **6** Listen to what the LORD is saying: "Stand up and state your case against me. Let the
mountains and hills be called to witness your complaints.
6:3 Jer 2:5, 31 [2]"And now, O mountains, listen to the LORD's complaint! He has a case against his
people Israel! He will prosecute them to the full extent of the law. [3]O my people, what
6:4 Exod 20:1-2 Ps 77:20 have I done to make you turn from me? Tell me why your patience is exhausted! Answer
me! [4]For I brought you out of Egypt and redeemed you from your slavery. I sent Moses,
6:5 Num 22:5-6; 25:1 Josh 5:9-10 Aaron, and Miriam to help you.
[5]"Don't you remember, my people, how King Balak of Moab tried to have you cursed
and how Balaam son of Beor blessed you instead? And remember your journey from
6:6 Pss 40:6-8; 51:16-17 Acacia* to Gilgal, when I, the LORD, did everything I could to teach you about my
faithfulness."
6:7 Lev 18:21; 20:1-5 Ps 50:9 Isa 40:16 [6]What can we bring to the LORD to make up for what we've done? Should we bow
before God with offerings of yearling calves? [7]Should we offer him thousands of rams
and tens of thousands of rivers of olive oil? Would that please the LORD? Should we
6:8 Deut 10:12-13 Isa 57:15 sacrifice our firstborn children to pay for the sins of our souls? Would that make him glad?
[8]No, O people, the LORD has already told you what is good, and this is what he
requires: to do what is right, to love mercy, and to walk humbly with your God.

Israel's Guilt and Punishment

6:10 Jer 5:26-27 Amos 3:10; 8:5 [9]Listen! Fear the LORD if you are wise! His voice is calling out to everyone in Jerusalem:
"The armies of destruction are coming; the LORD is sending them.* [10]Will there be no
end of your getting rich by cheating? The homes of the wicked are filled with treasures
6:12 Isa 3:8 gained by dishonestly measuring out grain in short measures.* [11]And how can I tolerate
all your merchants who use dishonest scales and weights? [12]The rich among you have
become wealthy through extortion and violence. Your citizens are so used to lying that
6:13 Isa 1:7; 6:11 their tongues can no longer tell the truth.
6:14 Lev 26:26 Isa 9:20; 30:6 [13]"Therefore, I will wound you! I will bring you to ruin for all your sins. [14]You will
eat but never have enough. Your hunger pangs and emptiness will still remain. And
6:15 Deut 28:38-40 Jer 12:13 Amos 5:11 Zeph 1:13 though you try to save your money, it will come to nothing in the end. You will save a
little, but I will give it to those who conquer you. [15]You will plant crops but not harvest
them. You will press your olives but not get enough oil to anoint yourselves. You will
6:16 1 Kgs 16:25, 29-33 Jer 7:24; 18:15-16; 25:9 trample the grapes but get no juice to make your wine.
[16]"The only laws you keep are those of evil King Omri; the only example you
follow is that of wicked King Ahab! Therefore, I will make an example of you,

6:5 Hebrew *Shittim.* **6:9** Hebrew *"Listen to the rod. Who appointed it?"* **6:10** Hebrew *by using the short ephah;* the ephah was a unit for measuring grain.

6:1ff Here Micah pictures a courtroom. God, the Judge, tells his people what he requires of them and recites all the ways they have wronged both him and others. Chapters 4 and 5 are full of hope; chapters 6 and 7 proclaim judgment and appeal to the people to repent.

6:1, 2 God called to the mountains to confirm the people's guilt. The mountains would serve as excellent witnesses, for it was in the high places that the people had built pagan altars and had sacrificed to false gods (1 Kings 14:23; Jeremiah 17:2, 3; Ezekiel 20:28).

6:3 The people would never be able to answer this question because God had done nothing wrong. In fact, God had been exceedingly patient with them, had always lovingly guided them, and had given them every opportunity to return to him. If God asked you, "What have I done to you?" how would you reply?

6:5 The story of Balak and Balaam is found in Numbers 22–24. Acacia was the Israelites' campsite east of the Jordan River just before they entered the Promised Land (Joshua 2:1). There the people received many of God's instructions about how to live. Gilgal, their first campsite after crossing the Jordan (Joshua 4:19), was where the people renewed their covenant with God (Joshua 5:3-9). These two places represent God's loving care for his people: his willingness both to protect them and to warn them about potential troubles. In Micah's day, the people had forgotten this covenant and its benefits and had turned away from God.

6:5 God continued to be kind to his forgetful people, but their short memory and lack of thankfulness condemned them. When people refuse to see how fortunate they are and begin to take God's gifts for granted, they become self-centered. Regularly remember God's goodness and thank him. Remembering God's past protection will help you see his present provision.

6:8 People have tried all kinds of ways to please God (6:6, 7), but God has made his wishes clear: He wants his people to do what is right, love mercy, and walk humbly with him. In your efforts to please God, examine these areas on a regular basis. Are you fair in your dealings with people? Do you show mercy to those who wrong you? Are you learning humility?

6:16 Omri reigned over Israel and led the people into idol worship (1 Kings 16:21-26). Ahab, his son, was Israel's most wicked king (1 Kings 16:29-33). If the people were following the commands and practices of these kings, they were in bad shape. Such pervasive evil was ripe for punishment.

bringing you to complete ruin. You will be treated with contempt, mocked by all who
see you."

Misery Turned to Hope

7 What misery is mine! I feel like the fruit picker after the harvest who can find
nothing to eat. Not a cluster of grapes or a single fig can be found to satisfy my
hunger. 2The godly people have all disappeared; not one fair-minded person is left on
the earth. They are all murderers, even setting traps for their own brothers. 3They go
about their evil deeds with both hands. How skilled they are at using them! Officials and
judges alike demand bribes. The people with money and influence pay them off, and
together they scheme to twist justice. 4Even the best of them is like a brier; the straightest
is more crooked than a hedge of thorns. But your judgment day is coming swiftly now.
Your time of punishment is here.

5Don't trust anyone—not your best friend or even your wife! 6For the son despises
his father. The daughter defies her mother. The daughter-in-law defies her mother-in-law.
Your enemies will be right in your own household.

7As for me, I look to the LORD for his help. I wait confidently for God to save me, and
my God will certainly hear me. 8Do not gloat over me, my enemies! For though I fall, I
will rise again. Though I sit in darkness, the LORD himself will be my light. 9I will be
patient as the LORD punishes me, for I have sinned against him. But after that, he will
take up my case and punish my enemies for all the evil they have done to me. The LORD
will bring me out of my darkness into the light, and I will see his righteousness. 10Then
my enemies will see that the LORD is on my side. They will be ashamed that they taunted
me, saying, "Where is the LORD—that God of yours?" With my own eyes I will see them
trampled down like mud in the streets.

11In that day, Israel, your cities will be rebuilt, and your borders will be extended.
12People from many lands will come and honor you—from Assyria all the way to the
towns of Egypt, and from Egypt all the way to the Euphrates River,* and from many
distant seas and mountains. 13But the land* will become empty and desolate because of
the wickedness of those who live there.

The LORD's Compassion on Israel

14O LORD, come and rule your people; lead your flock in green pastures. Help them to
live in peace and prosperity. Let them enjoy the fertile pastures of Bashan and Gilead as
they did long ago.

15"Yes," says the LORD, "I will do mighty miracles for you, like those I did when I
rescued you from slavery in Egypt."

16All the nations of the world will stand amazed at what the LORD will do for
you. They will be embarrassed that their power is so insignificant. They will stand
in silent awe, deaf to everything around them. 17They will come to realize what

7:1 Hos 9:10
7:2 Isa 57:1; 59:7 Jer 5:26 Hos 5:1
7:3 Prov 4:16-17
7:4 Isa 10:3; 22:5 Ezek 2:6; 28:24 Nah 1:10
7:5 Jer 9:4-5
7:6 †Matt 10:35-36 †Luke 12:53
7:7 Pss 4:3; 130:5
7:8 Prov 24:15-16 Isa 9:2 Amos 9:11
7:9 Ps 37:6 Jer 50:34
7:10 Isa 51:23 Zech 10:5
7:11 Amos 9:11
7:12 Isa 11:16; 19:23-25
7:13 Isa 3:10-11
7:14 Lev 27:32 Amos 9:11
7:15 Exod 3:20
7:16 Mic 3:7
7:17 Gen 3:14 Pss 9:20; 72:9

7:12 Hebrew *the river.* **7:13** Or *earth.*

7:1ff This chapter begins in gloom (7:1-6) and ends in hope (7:8-20). Micah watched as society rotted around him. Rulers demanded gifts; judges accepted bribes; corruption was universal. But God promised to lead the people out of the darkness of sin and into his light. Then the people would praise him for his faithfulness. God alone is perfectly faithful.

7:1-4 Micah could not find a fair-minded person anywhere in the land. Even today, fair-mindedness (uprightness, honesty, integrity) is difficult to find. Society rationalizes sin, and even believers sometimes compromise Christian principles in order to do what they want. It is easy to convince ourselves that we deserve a few breaks, especially when "everyone else" is doing it. But the standards for honesty come from God, not society. We are honest because God is truth, and we are to be like him.

7:5, 6 Sin had affected the government leaders and society in general. Deceit and dishonesty had even ruined the family, the core of society. As a result, the only way left to purify the people was God's judgment. This would draw the nation back to God and restore them from the inside out.

7:7-10 Micah showed great faith in God both personally (7:7) and on Israel's behalf (7:8-10) as he proclaimed that (1) he would wait upon God because God hears and saves when help is needed, (2) God would bring his people through when times were tough, (3) Israel must be patient in punishment because God would bring them out of the darkness, and (4) their enemies would be punished. We, too, can have a relationship with God that can allow us to have confidence like Micah's. It doesn't take unusual talent; it simply takes faith in God and a willingness to act on that faith.

7:14 Bashan and Gilead were fertile areas east of the Jordan, previously the territory of Reuben, Gad, and the half-tribe of Manasseh.

7:18
Exod 34:9
Num 14:18-19
Jer 4:2; 32:41

7:19
Isa 43:25
Jer 50:20

7:20
Gen 24:27; 32:10
Deut 7:8, 12
Luke 1:72

lowly creatures they really are. Like snakes crawling from their holes, they will come
out to meet the LORD our God. They will fear him greatly, trembling in terror at his
presence.
18 Where is another God like you, who pardons the sins of the survivors among his
people? You cannot stay angry with your people forever, because you delight in showing
mercy. 19 Once again you will have compassion on us. You will trample our sins under
your feet and throw them into the depths of the ocean! 20 You will show us your
faithfulness and unfailing love as you promised with an oath to our ancestors Abraham
and Jacob long ago.

7:18 God delights to show mercy! He does not forgive grudgingly but is glad when we repent, and he offers forgiveness to all who come back to him. Today you can confess your sins and receive his loving forgiveness. Don't be too proud to accept God's free offer.

7:20 In an age when religion was making little difference in people's lives, Micah said that God expected his people to do what is right, show mercy, and walk humbly with him (6:8). He requires the same of Christians today. In a world that is unjust, we must act justly and do what is right. In a world of tough breaks, we must be merciful. In a world of pride and self-sufficiency, we must walk humbly with God. Only when we live according to God's way will we begin to affect our homes, our society, and our world.

NAHUM

Manasseh becomes king of Judah 697 B.C.

Ashurbanipal becomes king of Assyria 669

The fall of Thebes; Nahum becomes a prophet 663

VITAL STATISTICS

PURPOSE:
To pronounce God's judgment on Assyria and to comfort Judah with this truth

AUTHOR:
Nahum

TO WHOM WRITTEN:
The people of Nineveh and Judah

DATE WRITTEN:
Sometime during Nahum's prophetic ministry (probably between 663 and 612 B.C.)

SETTING:
This particular prophecy took place after the fall of Thebes in 663 B.C. (see 3:8–10).

KEY VERSES:
"The LORD is good. When trouble comes, he is a strong refuge. And he knows everyone who trusts in him. But he sweeps away his enemies in an overwhelming flood. He pursues his foes into the darkness of night. Why are you scheming against the LORD? He will destroy you with one blow; he won't need to strike twice!" (1:7–9).

KEY PLACE:
Nineveh

THE SHRILL whistle pierces the air, and all the action on the court abruptly stops. Pointing to the offending player, the referee shouts, "Foul!"

Rules, fouls, and penalties are part of any game and are regulated and enforced vigorously by referees, umpires, judges, and other officials. Every participant knows that boundaries must be set and behavior monitored, or the game will degenerate into chaos.

There are laws in the world as well—boundaries and rules for living established by God. But men and women regularly flaunt these regulations, hiding their infractions or overpowering others and declaring that might makes right. God calls this sin—willful disobedience, rebellion against his control, or apathy. And at times it seems as though the violators succeed—no whistles blow, no fouls are called, and individual dictators rule. The truth is, however, that ultimately justice will be served in the world. God will settle all accounts.

Assyria was the most powerful nation on earth. Proud in their self-sufficiency and military might, they plundered, oppressed, and slaughtered their victims. One hundred years earlier, Jonah had preached in the streets of the great city Nineveh; the people had heard God's message and had turned from their evil. But generations later, evil was again reigning, and the prophet Nahum pronounced judgment on this wicked nation. Nineveh is called a "city of murder" (3:1), a city of cruelty (3:19), and the Assyrians are judged for their arrogance (1:11), idolatry (1:14), murder, lies, treachery, and social injustice (3:1–19). Nahum predicted that this proud and powerful nation would be utterly destroyed because of its sins. The end came within 50 years.

In this judgment of Assyria and its capital city, Nineveh, God is judging a sinful world. And the message is clear: Disobedience, rebellion, and injustice will not prevail but will be punished severely by a righteous and holy God, who rules over all the earth.

As you read Nahum, sense God's wrath as he avenges sin and brings about justice. Then decide to live under his guidance and within his rules, commands, and guidelines for life.

THE BLUEPRINT

1. Nineveh's judge (1:1–15)
2. Nineveh's judgment (2:1—3:19)

Nineveh, the capital of the Assyrian Empire, is the subject of Nahum's prophecy. The news of its coming destruction was a relief for Judah, who was subject to Assyrian domination. No longer would Judah be forced to pay tribute as insurance against invasions. Judah was comforted to know that God was still in control. Nineveh is an example to all rulers and nations of the world today. God is sovereign over even those who are seemingly invincible. We can be confident that God's power and justice will one day conquer all evil.

Josiah becomes king of Judah; Zephaniah becomes a prophet 640	Jeremiah becomes a prophet 627	Nineveh falls 612	Assyria completely conquered 609	Babylonians win battle of Carchemish 605	Judah falls to Babylon 586

MEGATHEMES

THEME	EXPLANATION	IMPORTANCE
God Judges	God would judge the city of Nineveh for its idolatry, arrogance, and oppression. Although Assyria was the leading military power in the world, God would completely destroy this "invincible" nation. God allows no person or power to usurp or scoff at his authority.	Anyone who remains arrogant and resists God's authority will face his anger. No ruler or nation will get away with rejecting him. No individual will be able to hide from his judgment. Yet those who keep trusting God will be kept safe forever.
God Rules	God rules over all the earth, even over those who don't acknowledge him. God is all-powerful, and no one can thwart his plans. God will overcome any who attempt to defy him. Human power is futile against God.	If you are impressed by or afraid of any weapons, armies, or powerful people, remember that God alone can truly rescue you from fear or oppression. We must place our confidence in God because he alone rules all of history, all the earth, and our life.

1. Nineveh's judge

1:2 Exod 20:5 Deut 4:24; 32:35
1:3 Exod 34:5-7 Pss 50:3; 104:3
1:4 Isa 33:9 Matt 8:26
1:5 Exod 19:19 2 Sam 22:8-9
1:6 1 Kgs 19:11

1 This message concerning Nineveh came as a vision to Nahum, who lived in Elkosh.

The LORD's Anger against Nineveh

2The LORD is a jealous God, filled with vengeance and wrath. He takes revenge on all
who oppose him and furiously destroys his enemies! 3The LORD is slow to get angry, but
his power is great, and he never lets the guilty go unpunished. He displays his power in
the whirlwind and the storm. The billowing clouds are the dust beneath his feet. 4At his
command the oceans and rivers dry up, the lush pastures of Bashan and Carmel fade, and
the green forests of Lebanon wilt. 5In his presence the mountains quake, and the hills
melt away; the earth trembles, and its people are destroyed. 6Who can stand before his
fierce anger? Who can survive his burning fury? His rage blazes forth like fire, and the
mountains crumble to dust in his presence.

1:1 Nahum, like Jonah, was a prophet to Nineveh, the capital of the Assyrian Empire, and he prophesied between 663 and 612 B.C. Jonah had seen Nineveh repent a century earlier (see the book of Jonah), but the city had fallen back into wickedness. Assyria, the world power controlling the Fertile Crescent, seemed unstoppable. Its ruthless and savage warriors had already conquered Israel, the northern kingdom, and were causing great suffering in Judah. So Nahum proclaimed God's anger against Assyria's evil. Within a few decades, the mighty Assyrian Empire would be toppled by Babylon.

1:1 Elkosh was a village thought by some to be in southwest Judah.

1:2 God alone has the right to be jealous and to carry out vengeance. *Jealousy* and *vengeance* may be surprising terms to associate with God. When humans are jealous and take vengeance, they are usually acting in a spirit of selfishness. But it is appropriate for God to insist on our complete allegiance, and it is just for him to punish unrepentant evildoers. His jealousy and vengeance are unmixed with selfishness. Their purpose is to remove sin and restore peace to the world (Deuteronomy 4:24; 5:9).

1:3 God is slow to get angry, but when he is ready to punish, even the earth trembles. Often people avoid God because they see evildoers in the world and hypocrites in the church. They don't realize that because God is slow to anger, he gives his true followers time to share his love and truth with evildoers. But judgment *will* come; God will not allow sin to go unchecked forever. When people wonder why God doesn't punish evil immediately, help them remember that if he did, none of us would be here. We can all be thankful that God gives people time to turn to him.

1:4 Bashan and Carmel were very fertile areas.

1:6 No person on earth can safely defy God, the Almighty, the Creator of all the universe. God, who controls the sun, the galaxies, and the vast stretches beyond, also controls the rise and fall of nations. How could a small temporal kingdom like Assyria, no matter how powerful, challenge God's awesome power? If only Assyria could have looked ahead to see the desolate mound of rubble that it would become—and yet God would still be alive and well! Don't defy God; he will be here forever with greater power than that of all armies and nations combined.

1:6-8 To people who refuse to believe, God's punishment is like an angry fire. To those who love him, his mercy is a refuge, supplying all their needs without diminishing his supply. But to God's enemies he is an overwhelming flood that will sweep them away. The relationship we have with God is up to us. What kind of relationship will you choose?

[7]The LORD is good. When trouble comes, he is a strong refuge. And he knows
everyone who trusts in him. [8]But he sweeps away his enemies in an overwhelming flood.
He pursues his foes into the darkness of night.
[9]Why are you scheming against the LORD? He will destroy you with one blow; he
won't need to strike twice! [10]His enemies, tangled up like thorns, staggering like drunks,
will be burned like dry straw in a field. [11]Who is this king of yours who dares to plot evil
against the LORD?
[12]This is what the LORD says: "Even though the Assyrians have many allies, they will
be destroyed and disappear. O my people, I have already punished you once, and I will
not do it again. [13]Now I will break your chains and release you from Assyrian oppression."
[14]And this is what the LORD says concerning the Assyrians in Nineveh: "You will have
no more children to carry on your name. I will destroy all the idols in the temples of your
gods. I am preparing a grave for you because you are despicable and don't deserve to live!"
[15]Look! A messenger is coming over the mountains with good news! He is bringing
a message of peace. Celebrate your festivals, O people of Judah, and fulfill all your
vows, for your enemies from Nineveh will never invade your land again. They have been
completely destroyed!

1:7 1 Chr 16:34; Pss 25:8; 100:5
1:8 Isa 8:7
1:9 Pss 2:1-4; 21:11
1:10 Isa 9:18; Mal 4:1
1:13 Isa 9:4; Jer 2:20
1:14 Nah 3:4-6
1:15 Isa 29:7-8; 40:9; 52:7; †Rom 10:15

2. Nineveh's judgment

The Fall of Nineveh

2 Nineveh, you are already surrounded by enemy armies! Sound the alarm! Man the
ramparts! Muster your defenses, and keep a sharp watch for the enemy attack to
begin! [2]For the land of Israel lies empty and broken after your attacks, but the LORD will
restore its honor and power again.
[3]Shields flash red in the sunlight! The attack begins! See their scarlet uniforms! Watch
as their glittering chariots move into position, with a forest of spears waving above them.
[4]The chariots race recklessly along the streets and through the squares, swift as lightning,
flickering like torches. [5]The king shouts to his officers; they stumble in their haste,
rushing to the walls to set up their defenses. [6]But too late! The river gates are open! The
enemy has entered! The palace is about to collapse!
[7]Nineveh's exile has been decreed, and all the servant girls mourn its capture. Listen
to them moan like doves; watch them beat their breasts in sorrow. [8]Nineveh is like a
leaking water reservoir! The people are slipping away. "Stop, stop!" someone shouts, but
the people just keep on running.
[9]Loot the silver! Plunder the gold! There seems no end to Nineveh's many treasures—
its vast, uncounted wealth. [10]Soon the city is an empty shambles, stripped of its wealth.
Hearts melt in horror, and knees shake. The people stand aghast, their faces pale and
trembling.
[11]Where now is that great Nineveh, lion of the nations, full of fight and boldness,
where the old and feeble and the young and tender lived with nothing to fear? [12]O Nineveh, you were once a mighty lion! You crushed your enemies to feed your cubs and your
mate. You filled your city and your homes with captives and plunder.

2:1 Jer 51:20
2:2 Isa 60:15; Ezek 37:21-23
2:3 Ezek 23:14-15
2:4 Jer 4:3; Nah 3:2
2:5 Jer 46:12
2:7 Isa 32:12; 59:11
2:8 Jer 46:5
2:10 Josh 2:11
2:11 Isa 5:29

1:11 The one "who dares to plot evil against the LORD" could have been (1) Ashurbanipal (669–627 B.C.), king of Assyria during much of Nahum's life and the one who brought Assyria to the zenith of its power; (2) Sennacherib (705–681), who openly defied God (2 Kings 18:13-35), epitomizing rebellion against God; (3) no one king in particular, but the entire evil monarchy. The point is that Nineveh would be destroyed for rebelling against God.

1:12-15 The good news for Judah, whom Assyria afflicted, was that its conquerors and tormentors would be destroyed and would never rise to torment it again. Nineveh was so completely wiped out that its ruins were not identified until 1845.

2:1ff This chapter predicts the events of 612 B.C., when the combined armies of the Babylonians and the Medes sacked the seemingly impregnable Nineveh.

2:2 Assyria had plundered and crushed the northern kingdom (Israel) and had deported its people in 722 B.C. (2 Kings 17:3-6; 18:9-11). Assyria had also attacked the southern kingdom and had forced it to pay tribute.

2:6 This reference to the opening of river gates could refer either to the enemy flowing into Nineveh like a flood (1:8) or to an actual flood of water. Some scholars suggest that dam gates, which were found in archaeological excavations, were closed to dam up the river. When an enormous amount of water had been accumulated, the gates were opened, allowing the water to flood Nineveh.

2:12–3:1 The major source of wealth for the Assyrian economy was the plunder taken from other nations. The Assyrians had taken the food of innocent people to maintain their luxurious standard of living, depriving others to supply their excesses. Depriving innocent people to support the luxury of a few is a sin that angers God. As Christians we must stand firm against this common but evil practice.

2:13 Ps 46:9 13"I am your enemy!" says the LORD Almighty. "Your chariots will soon go up in
smoke. The finest of your youth will be killed in battle. Never again will you bring back
plunder from conquered nations. Never again will the voices of your proud messengers
be heard."

3:1 *The LORD's Judgment against Nineveh*

Ezek 24:6-9 **3** How terrible it will be for Nineveh, the city of murder and lies! She is crammed with
3:2 Nah 2:3-4 wealth to be plundered. 2Listen! Hear the crack of the whips as the chariots rush
3:3 forward against her. Wheels rumble, horses' hooves pound, and chariots clatter as they
Isa 34:13 bump wildly through the streets. 3See the flashing swords and glittering spears in the
upraised arms of the cavalry! The dead are lying in the streets—dead bodies, heaps of
3:4 Isa 23:17; 47:9 bodies, everywhere. People stumble over them, scramble to their feet, and fall again. 4All
Rev 17:1-6; 18:2-3 this because Nineveh, the beautiful and faithless city, mistress of deadly charms, enticed
the nations with her beauty. She taught them all to worship her false gods, enchanting
3:5 people everywhere.
Isa 47:3 5"No wonder I am your enemy!" declares the LORD Almighty. "And now I will lift
3:6 Job 9:31 your skirts so all the earth will see your nakedness and shame. 6I will cover you with
Isa 14:16 filth and show the world how vile you really are. 7All who see you will shrink back in
3:7 Isa 51:19 horror and say, 'Nineveh lies in utter ruin.' Yet no one anywhere will regret your
Jer 15:5 destruction."
3:8 Isa 19:6-8 8Are you any better than Thebes,* surrounded by rivers, protected by water on all
Jer 46:25 sides? 9Ethiopia* and the land of Egypt were the source of her strength, which seemed
Ezek 30:14-16 without limit. The nations of Put and Libya also helped and supported her. 10Yet Thebes
3:9 Isa 20:5-6 fell, and her people were led away as captives. Her babies were dashed to death against
Jer 46:9 the stones of the streets. Soldiers cast lots to see who would get the Egyptian officers as
3:10 2 Kgs 8:12 servants. All their leaders were bound in chains.
Ps 137:9 11And you, Nineveh, will also stagger like a drunkard. You will hide for fear of the
Hos 13:16 attacking enemy. 12All your fortresses will fall. They will be devoured like the ripe figs
3:11 Isa 49:26 that fall into the mouths of those who shake the trees. 13Your troops will be as weak and
Jer 25:15-27 helpless as women. The gates of your land will be opened wide to the enemy and set on
3:13 Isa 19:16 fire and burned.
Jer 50:37; 51:30 **3:8** Hebrew *No-amon;* also in 3:10. **3:9** Hebrew *Cush.*

NAHUM served as a prophet to Judah from 663–612 B.C.

Climate of the times	Manasseh, one of Judah's most wicked kings, ruled the land. He openly defied God and persecuted God's people. Assyria, the world power at that time, made Judah one of its vassal states. The people of Judah wanted to be like the Assyrians, who seemed to have all the power and possessions they wanted.
Main message	The mighty empire of Assyria that oppressed God's people would soon tumble.
Importance of message	Those who do evil and oppress others will one day meet a bitter end.
Contemporary prophets	Zephaniah (640–621 B.C.)

2:13 God had given the people of Nineveh a chance to repent, which they did after hearing Jonah (see the book of Jonah). But they had returned to their sin, and its consequences were destroying them. There is a point for people, cities, and nations after which there is no turning back; Assyria had passed that point. We must warn others to repent while there is still time.

3:4 Nineveh had used its beauty, prestige, and power to seduce other nations. Like a harlot, she had enticed them into false friendships. Then when the other nations relaxed, thinking Assyria was a friend, Assyria destroyed and plundered them. Beautiful and impressive on the outside, Nineveh was vicious and deceitful on the inside. Beneath beautiful facades sometimes lie seduction and death. Don't let an attractive institution, company, movement, or person seduce you into lowering your standards or compromising your moral principles.

3:8-10 Thebes was a city in Egypt, the previous world power, which stood in the path of Assyria's expansion in the south. The Assyrians conquered Thebes 51 years before this prophecy was given. To Judah, surrounded to the north and south by Assyria, the situation appeared hopeless. But God said that the same atrocities done in Thebes would happen in Nineveh.

3:8-10 No power on earth can protect us from God's judgment or be a suitable substitute for his power in our life. Thebes and Assyria put their trust in alliances and military power, but history would show that these were inadequate. Don't insist on learning through personal experience; instead, learn the lessons history has already taught. Put your trust in God above all else.

14 Get ready for the siege! Store up water! Strengthen the defenses! Make bricks to
repair the walls! Go into the pits to trample clay, and pack it into molds! 15 But in the
middle of your preparations, the fire will devour you; the sword will cut you down. The
enemy will consume you like locusts, devouring everything they see. There will be no
escape, even if you multiply like grasshoppers. 16 Merchants, as numerous as the stars,
have filled your city with vast wealth. But like a swarm of locusts, they strip the land and
then fly away. 17 Your princes and officials are also like locusts, crowding together in the
hedges to survive the cold. But like locusts that fly away when the sun comes up to warm
the earth, all of them will fly away and disappear.

18 O Assyrian king, your princes lie dead in the dust. Your people are scattered across
the mountains. There is no longer a shepherd to gather them together. 19 There is no
healing for your wound; your injury is fatal. All who hear of your destruction will clap
their hands for joy. Where can anyone be found who has not suffered from your cruelty?

3:14 2 Chr 32:3-4, 11; Nah 2:1
3:15 Isa 66:15-16; Joel 1:4
3:17 Jer 51:27
3:18 1 Kgs 22:17; Ps 76:5-6; Isa 56:10; Jer 50:18
3:19 Jer 30:13; Lam 2:15; Mic 1:9

3:19 All the nations hated to be ruled by the merciless Assyrians, but the nations wanted to be like Assyria—powerful, wealthy, prestigious—and they courted Assyria's friendship. In the same way, we don't like the idea of being ruled harshly, so we do what we can to stay on good terms with a powerful leader. And deep down, we would like to have that kind of power. The thought of being on top can be captivating. But power is seductive, so we should not scheme to get it or hold on to it. Those who lust after power will be powerfully destroyed, as was the mighty Assyrian Empire.

HABAKKUK

Jeremiah becomes a prophet 627 B.C.	Habakkuk becomes a prophet 612	King Josiah dies in battle 609	Daniel taken captive to Babylon 605	Ezekiel a captive in Babylon; Zedekiah becomes king 597	Habakkuk's ministry ends 588	Fall of Judah; Jerusalem destroyed 586

FROM innocent childhood queries to complex university discussions, life is filled with questions. Asking how and why and when, we probe beneath the surface to find satisfying answers. But not all questions have answers wrapped and neatly tied. These unanswered interrogations create more questions and nagging, spirit-destroying doubt. Some choose to live with their doubts, ignoring them and moving on with life. Others become cynical and hardened. But there are those who reject those options and continue to ask, looking for answers.

Habakkuk was a man who sought answers. Troubled by what he observed, he asked difficult questions. These questions were not merely intellectual exercises or bitter complaints. Habakkuk saw a dying world, and it broke his heart. Why is there evil in the world? Why do the wicked seem to be winning? He boldly and confidently took his complaints directly to God. And God answered with an avalanche of proof and prediction.

The prophet's questions and God's answers are recorded in this book. As we turn the pages, we are immediately confronted with his urgent cries, "How long, O LORD, must I call for help? But you do not listen! 'Violence!' I cry, but you do not come to save" (1:2). In fact, most of the first chapter is devoted to his questions. As chapter two begins, Habakkuk declares that he will wait to hear God's answers to his complaints. Then God begins to speak, telling the prophet to write his answer plainly so that all will see and understand. It may seem, God says, as though the wicked triumph, but eventually they will be judged, and righteousness will prevail. Judgment may not come quickly, but it *will* come. God's answers fill chapter two. Then Habakkuk concludes his book with a prayer of triumph. With questions answered and a new understanding of God's power and love, Habakkuk rejoices in who God is and in what he will do. "Yet I will rejoice in the LORD! I will be joyful in the God of my salvation. The Sovereign LORD is my strength! He will make me as surefooted as a deer and bring me safely over the mountains" (3:18, 19).

Listen to the profound questions that Habakkuk boldly brings to God, and realize that you can also bring your complaints and inquiries to him. Listen to God's answers and rejoice that he is at work in the world and in your life.

VITAL STATISTICS

PURPOSE:
To show that God is still in control of the world despite the apparent triumph of evil

AUTHOR:
Habakkuk

TO WHOM WRITTEN:
Judah (the southern kingdom), and God's people everywhere

DATE WRITTEN:
Between 612 and 588 B.C.

SETTING:
Babylon was becoming the dominant world power, and Judah would soon feel Babylon's destructive force.

KEY VERSE:
"I have heard all about you, LORD, and I am filled with awe by the amazing things you have done. In this time of our deep need, begin again to help us, as you did in years gone by. Show us your power to save us. And in your anger, remember your mercy" (3:2).

KEY PEOPLE:
Habakkuk, the Babylonians

KEY PLACE:
Judah

THE BLUEPRINT

1. Habakkuk's complaints (1:1—2:20)
2. Habakkuk's prayer (3:1–19)

When Habakkuk was troubled, he brought his concerns directly to God. After receiving God's answers, he responded with a prayer of faith. Habakkuk's example is one that should encourage us as we struggle to move from doubt to faith. We don't have to be afraid to ask questions of God. The problem is not with God and his ways but with our limited understanding of him.

MEGATHEMES

THEME	EXPLANATION	IMPORTANCE
Struggle and Doubt	Habakkuk asked God why the wicked in Judah were not being punished for their sin. He couldn't understand why a just God would allow such evil to exist. God promised to use the Babylonians to punish Judah. When Habakkuk cried out for answers in his time of struggle, God answered him with words of hope.	God wants us to come to him with our struggles and doubts. But his answers may not be what we expect. God sustains us by revealing himself to us. Trusting him leads to quiet hope, not bitter resignation.
God's Sovereignty	Habakkuk asked God why he would use the wicked Babylonians to punish his people. God said that he would also punish the Babylonians after they had fulfilled his purpose.	God is still in control of this world in spite of the apparent triumph of evil. God doesn't overlook sin. One day he will rule the whole earth with perfect justice.
Hope	God is the Creator; he is all-powerful. He has a plan, and he will carry it out. He will punish sin. He is our strength and our place of safety. We can have confidence that he will love us and guard our relationship with him forever.	Hope means going beyond our unpleasant daily experiences to the joy of knowing God. We live by trusting in him, not by the benefits, happiness, or success we may experience in this life. Our hope comes from God.

1. Habakkuk's complaints

1 This is the message that the prophet Habakkuk received from the LORD in a vision. 1:1 Isa 13:1 Nah 1:1

Habakkuk's Complaint

2 How long, O LORD, must I call for help? But you do not listen! "Violence!" I cry, but 1:2 Pss 13:1-4; 22:1-2
you do not come to save. 3 Must I forever see this sin and misery all around me? Jer 14:9
Wherever I look, I see destruction and violence. I am surrounded by people who love to 1:3
argue and fight. 4 The law has become paralyzed and useless, and there is no justice given Jer 20:8
in the courts. The wicked far outnumber the righteous, and justice is perverted with 1:4 Pss 22:12; 119:126
bribes and trickery. Isa 5:20

The LORD's Reply

5 The LORD replied, "Look at the nations and be amazed! Watch and be astounded at what 1:5 Isa 29:9
I will do! For I am doing something in your own day, something you wouldn't believe †Acts 13:41
even if someone told you about it. 6 I am raising up the Babylonians* to be a new power 1:6
on the world scene. They are a cruel and violent nation who will march across the world Deut 28:49 2 Kgs 24:2
and conquer it. 7 They are notorious for their cruelty. They do as they like, and no one 1:7
can stop them. 8 Their horses are swifter than leopards. They are a fierce people, more Jer 39:5-9
fierce than wolves at dusk. Their horsemen race forward from distant places. Like eagles 1:8 Jer 4:13
they swoop down to pounce on their prey.

1:6 Or *Chaldeans.*

1:1 Habakkuk lived in Judah during the reign of Jehoiakim (2 Kings 23:36–24:5). He prophesied between the fall of Nineveh (the capital of Assyria) in 612 B.C. and the Babylonian invasion of Judah in 588 B.C. With Assyria in disarray, Babylon was becoming the dominant world power. This book records the prophet's dialogue with God concerning the questions Why does God often seem indifferent in the face of evil? and Why do evil people seem to go unpunished? While other prophetic books brought God's word to people, this brought people's questions to God. A "vision" is a message from God.

1:2-4 Saddened by the violence and corruption he saw around him, Habakkuk poured out his heart to God. Today injustice is still rampant, but don't let your concern cause you to doubt God or rebel against him. Instead, consider the message that God gave Habakkuk and recognize God's long-range plans and purposes. Realize that God is doing right, even when you do not understand why he works as he does.

1:5 God responded to Habakkuk's questions and concerns by stating that he would do amazing acts that would astound Habakkuk. When circumstances around us become almost unbearable, we wonder if God has forgotten us. But remember, he is in control. God has a plan and will judge evildoers in his time. If we are truly humble, we will be willing to accept God's answers and await his timing.

1:5ff God told the inhabitants of Jerusalem that they would be utterly amazed at what he was about to do. The people would, in fact, see a series of unbelievable events: (1) Their own independent and prosperous kingdom, Judah, would suddenly become a vassal nation; (2) Egypt, a world power for centuries, would be crushed almost overnight; (3) Nineveh, the capital of the Assyrian Empire, would be so completely ransacked that people would forget where it had been; and (4) the Babylonians would rise to power. Though these words were indeed amazing, the people saw them fulfilled during their lifetime.

1:6 The Babylonians, who lived northwest of the Persian Gulf, made a rapid rise to power around 630 B.C. They began to assert themselves against the Assyrian Empire and by 605 B.C. had conquered Assyria and Egypt to become the strongest world power. But they were as wicked as the Assyrians, for they loved to collect prisoners (1:9), were proud of their warfare tactics (1:10), and trusted in their military strength (1:11).

9 “On they come, all of them bent on violence. Their hordes advance like a wind from
the desert, sweeping captives ahead of them like sand. 10 They scoff at kings and princes
and scorn all their defenses. They simply pile ramps of earth against their walls and
capture them! 11 They sweep past like the wind and are gone. But they are deeply guilty,
for their own strength is their god.”

Habakkuk's Second Complaint

12 O LORD my God, my Holy One, you who are eternal—is your plan in all of this to
wipe us out? Surely not! O LORD our Rock, you have decreed the rise of these
Babylonians to punish and correct us for our terrible sins. 13 You are perfectly just in
this. But will you, who cannot allow sin in any form, stand idly by while they swallow
us up? Should you be silent while the wicked destroy people who are more righteous
than they?

14 Are we but fish to be caught and killed? Are we but creeping things that have no
leader to defend them from their enemies? 15 Must we be strung up on their hooks and
dragged out in their nets while they rejoice? 16 Then they will worship their nets and
burn incense in front of them. “These nets are the gods who have made us rich!” they
will claim.

17 Will you let them get away with this forever? Will they succeed forever in their
heartless conquests?

2 I will climb up into my watchtower now and wait to see what the LORD will say to
me and how he will answer my complaint.

The LORD's Second Reply

2 Then the LORD said to me, “Write my answer in large, clear letters on a tablet, so that
a runner can read it and tell everyone else. 3 But these things I plan won't happen right

1:10 2 Kgs 25:6-7; 2 Chr 36:6; Jer 32:24; 33:4-5; Ezek 26:7-11
1:11 Jer 4:11-12
1:12 Deut 32:4, 30-31; Isa 10:6
1:13 Ps 50:21; 1 Pet 1:15-16
1:15 Jer 16:16
1:16 Jer 44:17-18
1:17 Isa 14:6; 19:8
2:2 Deut 27:8; Isa 8:1; Rev 1:19
2:3 Dan 8:17-19; 9:24-27; 10:1, 14; †Heb 10:37

HABAKKUK served as a prophet to Judah from 612–588 B.C.

Climate of the times	Judah's last four kings were wicked men who rejected God and oppressed their own people. Babylon invaded Judah twice before finally destroying it in 586 B.C.. It was a time of fear, oppression, persecution, lawlessness, and immorality.
Main message	Habakkuk couldn't understand why God seemed to do nothing about the wickedness in society. Then he realized that faith in God alone would supply the answers to his questions.
Importance of message	Instead of questioning the ways of God, we should realize that he is totally just, and we should have faith that he is in control and that one day evil will be utterly destroyed.
Contemporary prophets	Jeremiah (627–586 B.C.), Daniel (605–536 B.C.), Ezekiel (593–571 B.C.)

1:10 Armies were able to take walled cities by building earthen ramps—heaping mounds of earth against the walls.

1:11 Babylon was proud of its military might, strategies, armies, and weapons. With no regard for humanity, the armies brought home riches, plunder, prisoners, and tribute from the nations they conquered. Such is the essence of idolatry—asking the gods we make to help us get all we want. The essence of Christianity is asking the God *who made us* to help us give all we can in service to him. The goal of idolatry is self-glory; the aim of Christianity is God's glory.

1:13 Judah's forthcoming punishment would be at the hands of the Babylonians. Habakkuk was appalled that God would use a nation even more wicked than Judah to punish it. But the Babylonians did not know they were being used by God to help Judah return to him, and Babylon's pride in its victories would be its downfall. Evil is self-destructive, and it is never beyond God's control. God may use whatever unusual instrument he chooses to correct or punish us. When we deserve punishment or correction, how can we complain about the kind of “rod” God uses on us?

2:1 The watchman and watchtower, often used by the prophets to show an attitude of expectation (Isaiah 21:8, 11; Jeremiah 6:17; Ezekiel 3:17), are pictures of Habakkuk's attitude of patient waiting and watching for God's response. Stone watchtowers were built on city walls or ramparts so that watchmen could see people (enemies or messengers) approaching their city while still at a distance. Watchtowers were also erected in vineyards to help guard the ripening grapes (Isaiah 5:2). Habakkuk wanted to be in the best position to receive God's message.

2:2ff This chapter records God's answers to Habakkuk's questions: (1) How long would evil prevail (1:2, 3)? (2) Why was Babylon chosen to punish Judah (1:13)? God said that the judgment, though slow to come, was certain. Although God used Babylon against Judah, he knew Babylon's sins and would punish it in due time.

2:3 Evil and injustice seem to have the upper hand in the world. Like Habakkuk, Christians often feel angry and discouraged as they see what goes on. Habakkuk complained vigorously to God about the situation. God's answer to Habakkuk is the same answer he would give us, “If it seems slow, wait patiently, for it will surely take place.” It isn't easy to be patient, but it helps to remember that God hates sin even more than we do. Punishment of sin will certainly come. As God told Habakkuk, “Wait patiently.” We must trust God even when we don't understand why events occur as they do.

away. Slowly, steadily, surely, the time approaches when the vision will be fulfilled. If it
seems slow, wait patiently, for it will surely take place. It will not be delayed.
4"Look at the proud! They trust in themselves, and their lives are crooked;* but the
righteous will live by their faith.* 5Wealth* is treacherous, and the arrogant are never at
rest. They range far and wide, with their mouths opened as wide as death,* but they are
never satisfied. In their greed they have gathered up many nations and peoples. 6But the
time is coming when all their captives will taunt them, saying, 'You thieves! At last
justice has caught up with you! Now you will get what you deserve for your oppression
and extortion!' 7Suddenly, your debtors will rise up in anger. They will turn on you and
take all you have, while you stand trembling and helpless. 8You have plundered many
nations; now they will plunder you. You murderers! You have filled the countryside with
violence and all the cities, too.
9"How terrible it will be for you who get rich by unjust means! You believe your
wealth will buy security, putting your families beyond the reach of danger. 10But by the
murders you committed, you have shamed your name and forfeited your lives. 11The
very stones in the walls of your houses cry out against you, and the beams in the ceilings
echo the complaint.
12"How terrible it will be for you who build cities with money gained by murder and
corruption! 13Has not the LORD Almighty promised that the wealth of nations will turn
to ashes? They work so hard, but all in vain! 14For the time will come when all the earth
will be filled, as the waters fill the sea, with an awareness of the glory of the LORD.
15"How terrible it will be for you who make your neighbors drunk! You force your
cup on them so that you can gloat over their nakedness and shame. 16But soon it will be
your turn! Come, drink and be exposed! Drink from the cup of the LORD's judgment, and
all your glory will be turned to shame. 17You cut down the forests of Lebanon. Now you
will be cut down! You terrified the wild animals you caught in your traps. Now terror
will strike you because of your murder and violence in cities everywhere!
18"What have you gained by worshiping all your man-made idols? How foolish to
trust in something made by your own hands! What fools you are to believe such lies!
19How terrible it will be for you who beg lifeless wooden idols to save you. You ask
speechless stone images to tell you what to do. Can an idol speak for God? They may be
overlaid with gold and silver, but they are lifeless inside. 20But the LORD is in his holy
Temple. Let all the earth be silent before him."

2. Habakkuk's prayer

3 This prayer was sung by the prophet Habakkuk:*
2I have heard all about you, LORD, and I am filled with awe by the amazing
things you have done. In this time of our deep need, begin again to help us, as you did
in years gone by. Show us your power to save us. And in your anger, remember your
mercy.

2:4 Pss 10:4; 49:17-20; Prov 3:6; 16:3; †Rom 1:17; †Gal 3:11; †Heb 10:38
2:6 Isa 14:4-5, 10; Jer 50:13, 34-35; Hab 2:9, 12, 15, 19
2:7 Prov 29:1
2:8 Isa 33:1; Zech 2:8-9
2:9 Jer 22:13
2:11 Josh 24:27; Luke 19:40
2:12 Mic 3:10; Hab 2:9, 15, 19
2:13 Isa 50:11
2:14 Pss 22:27; 86:9; Isa 11:9; Zech 14:9
2:15 Hos 7:5
2:16 Jer 25:15-16
2:17 Jer 51:35
2:18 Isa 42:17; Jer 2:27-28; 50:2
2:19 1 Kgs 18:26-29; Jer 10:4-5
2:20 Zeph 1:7; Zech 2:13
3:2 Pss 78:38-39; 85:6; Isa 54:8; Jer 10:7

2:4a Greek version reads *I will have no pleasure in anyone who turns away.* **2:4b** Or *the just will live by their faithfulness.* **2:5a** As in Dead Sea Scroll 1QpHab; other Hebrew manuscripts read *Wine.* **2:5b** Hebrew *as Sheol.*
3:1 Hebrew adds *according to shigionoth,* probably indicating the musical setting for the prayer.

2:4 The wicked Babylonians trusted in themselves and would fall; but the righteous live by their faith and trust in God. This verse has inspired countless Christians. Paul quotes it in Romans 1:17 and Galatians 3:11. The writer of Hebrews quotes it in 10:38, just before the famous chapter on faith. And it is helpful to all Christians who must live through difficult times without seeing signs of hope. Christians must trust that God is directing all things according to his purposes.

2:9-13 Babylon's riches had come from the misfortunes of others, but these riches would only be fuel for the fire. The victims and their cities would cry out against Babylon. Money is not evil, but God condemns the love of riches and the evil means of acquiring them (1 Timothy 6:10). Be careful not to hunger for wealth so much that you lose your appetite for God. Do not allow money to take the place of family, friends, or God.

2:18 Idolatry may seem like a sin that modern people do not commit. But idolatry is not just bowing down to idols; it is trusting in what one has made and, therefore, in one's own power as creator and sustainer. If we say we worship God but put our trust in bank accounts, homes, businesses, and organizations, then we are idolaters. Do you trust God more than you trust what your hands have made?

2:20 Idols have no life, no personhood, no power; they are empty chunks of wood or stone. Temples built to idols are equally empty; no one lives there. But the Lord *is* in his Temple. He is real, alive, and powerful. He is truly and fully God. Idolaters command their idols to save them, but we who worship the living God come to him in silent awe and reverence. We acknowledge that God is in control and knows what he is doing. Idols remain silent because they cannot answer. The living God, by contrast, speaks through his Word. Approach God reverently and wait silently to hear what he has to say.

3 I see God, the Holy One, moving across the deserts from Edom* and Mount Paran.*
His brilliant splendor fills the heavens, and the earth is filled with his praise! What a
wonderful God he is! 4 Rays of brilliant light flash from his hands. He rejoices in his
awesome power.* 5 Pestilence marches before him; plague follows close behind. 6 When
he stops, the earth shakes. When he looks, the nations tremble. He shatters the everlasting
mountains and levels the eternal hills. But his power is not diminished in the least! 7 I see
the peoples of Cushan and Midian trembling in terror.

8 Was it in anger, LORD, that you struck the rivers and parted the sea? Were you
displeased with them? No, you were sending your chariots of salvation! 9 You were
commanding your weapons of power! You split open the earth with flowing rivers!
10 The mountains watched and trembled. Onward swept the raging waters. The mighty
deep cried out, lifting its hands to the LORD. 11 The lofty sun and moon began to fade,
obscured by brilliance from your arrows and the flashing of your glittering spear.

12 You marched across the land in awesome anger and trampled the nations in your
fury. 13 You went out to rescue your chosen people, to save your anointed ones. You
crushed the heads of the wicked and laid bare their bones from head to toe. 14 With their
own weapons, you destroyed those who rushed out like a whirlwind, thinking Israel
would be easy prey. 15 You trampled the sea with your horses, and the mighty waters piled
high.

16 I trembled inside when I heard all this; my lips quivered with fear. My legs gave way
beneath me,* and I shook in terror. I will wait quietly for the coming day when disaster
will strike the people who invade us. 17 Even though the fig trees have no blossoms, and
there are no grapes on the vine; even though the olive crop fails, and the fields lie empty
and barren; even though the flocks die in the fields, and the cattle barns are empty, 18 yet
I will rejoice in the LORD! I will be joyful in the God of my salvation. 19 The Sovereign
LORD is my strength! He will make me as surefooted as a deer* and bring me safely over
the mountains.

(For the choir director: This prayer is to be accompanied by stringed instruments.)

3:3 Deut 5:24; Pss 48:10; 113:4; 148:13
3:4 Job 26:14; Pss 18:12; 104:1
3:5 Exod 12:29-30; Deut 32:24-25
3:7 Exod 15:14
3:8 Exod 7:19-20
3:10 Ps 93:3
3:11 Josh 10:12-14
3:12 Isa 41:15
3:13 Ps 110:6
3:14 Judg 7:22; Dan 11:40
3:15 Hab 3:8
3:17 Jer 5:17; Joel 1:10-12; Amos 4:9
3:18 Ps 97:12; Isa 12:2; Luke 1:47; Phil 4:4
3:19 Pss 18:13; 46:1-5

3:3a Hebrew *Teman.* **3:3b** Hebrew adds *selah;* also in 3:9, 13. The meaning of this Hebrew term is uncertain; it is probably a musical or literary term. **3:4** Or *He veils his awesome power.* **3:16** Hebrew *Decay entered my bones.* **3:19** Or *will give me the speed of a deer.*

3:1ff Habakkuk praised God for answering his questions. Evil will not triumph forever; God is in control, and he can be completely trusted to vindicate those who are faithful to him. We must patiently wait for him to act (3:16).

3:2 Habakkuk knew that God was going to discipline the people of Judah and that it wasn't going to be a pleasant experience. But Habakkuk accepted God's will, asking for help and mercy. Habakkuk did not ask to escape the discipline, but he accepted the truth that Judah needed to learn a lesson. God still disciplines in love to bring his children back to him (Hebrews 12:5, 6). Accept God's discipline gladly, and ask him to help you change.

3:17-19 Crop failure and the death of animals would devastate Judah. But Habakkuk affirmed that even in the times of starvation and loss, he would still rejoice in the Lord. Habakkuk's feelings were not controlled by the events around him but by faith in God's ability to give him strength. When nothing makes sense, and when troubles seem more than you can bear, remember that God gives strength. Take your eyes off your difficulties and look to God.

3:19 God will give his followers strength and confidence in difficult times. They will run surefooted as deer across rough and dangerous terrain. At the proper time, God will bring about his justice and completely rid the world of evil. In the meantime, God's people need to live in the strength of his Spirit, confident in his ultimate victory over evil.

3:19 The note to the choir director was to be used when this passage was sung as a psalm in Temple worship.

3:19 Habakkuk had asked God why evil people prosper while the righteous suffer. God's answer: They don't, not in the long run. Habakkuk saw his own limitations in contrast to God's unlimited power and control of all the world's events. God is alive and in control of the world and its events. We cannot see all that God is doing, and we cannot see all that God will do. But we can be assured that he is God and will do what is right. Knowing this can give us confidence and hope in a confusing world.

ZEPHANIAH

Zephaniah becomes a prophet; Josiah becomes king of Judah 640 B.C.

Jeremiah becomes a prophet 627

Book of the Law found in the Temple 622

Zephaniah's ministry ends 621

Habakkuk becomes a prophet 612

VITAL STATISTICS

PURPOSE:
To shake the people of Judah out of their complacency and urge them to return to God

AUTHOR:
Zephaniah

TO WHOM WRITTEN:
Judah and all nations

DATE WRITTEN:
Probably near the end of Zephaniah's ministry (640–621 B.C.), when King Josiah's great reforms began

SETTING:
King Josiah of Judah was attempting to reverse the evil trends set by the two previous kings of Judah—Manasseh and Amon. Josiah was able to extend his influence because there wasn't a strong superpower dominating the world at that time (Assyria was declining rapidly). Zephaniah's prophecy may have been the motivating factor in Josiah's reform. Zephaniah was a contemporary of Jeremiah.

KEY VERSE:
"Beg the LORD to save you—all you who are humble, all you who uphold justice. Walk humbly and do what is right. Perhaps even yet the LORD will protect you from his anger on that day of destruction" (2:3).

KEY PLACE:
Jerusalem

OVERWHELMING grief, prolonged distress, incessant abuse, continual persecution, and imminent punishment breed hopelessness and despair. "If only," we cry, as we search our mind for a way out and look to the skies for rescue. With just a glimmer of hope, we would take courage and carry on, enduring until the end.

Hope is the silver shaft of sun breaking through the storm-darkened sky, words of comfort in the intensive care unit, a letter from across the sea, the first spring bird perched on a snow-covered twig, and the finish line in sight. It is a rainbow, a song, a loving touch. Hope is knowing God and resting in his love.

As God's prophet, Zephaniah was bound to speak the truth. This he did clearly, thundering certain judgment and horrible punishment for all who would defy the Lord. God's awful wrath would sweep away everything in the land and destroy it. "'I will sweep away both people and animals alike. Even the birds of the air and the fish in the sea will die. I will reduce the wicked to heaps of rubble, along with the rest of humanity,' says the LORD" (1:3). No living thing in the land would escape. And that terrible day was coming soon: "That terrible day of the LORD is near. Swiftly it comes—a day when strong men will cry bitterly. It is a day when the LORD'S anger will be poured out. It is a day of terrible distress and anguish, a day of ruin and desolation, a day of darkness and gloom, of clouds, [and] blackness" (1:14, 15). We can sense the oppression and depression his listeners must have felt. They were judged guilty, and they were doomed.

But in the midst of this terrible pronouncement, there is hope. The first chapter of Zephaniah's prophecy is filled with terror. In chapter two, however, a whispered promise appears. "Beg the LORD to save you—all you who are humble, all you who uphold justice. Walk humbly and do what is right. Perhaps even yet the LORD will protect you from his anger" (2:3). And a few verses later we read of "the few survivors of the tribe of Judah" (2:7) who will be restored.

Finally in chapter three, the quiet refrain grows to a crescendo as God's salvation and deliverance for those who are faithful to him is declared. "Sing, O daughter of Zion; shout aloud, O Israel! Be glad and rejoice with all your heart, O daughter of Jerusalem! For the LORD will remove his hand of judgment and will disperse the armies of your enemy. And the LORD himself, the King of Israel, will live among you! At last your troubles will be over, and you will fear disaster no more" (3:14, 15). This is true hope, grounded in the knowledge of God's justice and in his love for his people.

As you read Zephaniah, listen carefully to the words of judgment. God does not take sin lightly, and it will be punished. But be encouraged by the words of hope—our God reigns, and he will rescue his own. Decide to be part of that faithful remnant of souls who humbly worship and obey the living Lord.

Josiah dies in battle 609	First captives taken to Babylon 605	Babylon's second attack on Judah 597	Judah (the southern kingdom) falls 586

THE BLUEPRINT

1. The day of judgment (1:1—3:8)
2. The day of hope (3:9–20)

Zephaniah warned the people of Judah that if they refused to repent, the entire nation, including the beloved city of Jerusalem, would be lost. The people knew that God would eventually bless them, but Zephaniah made it clear that there would be judgment first, then blessing. This judgment would not be merely punishment for sin, but it would also be a means of purifying the people. Though we live in a fallen world surrounded by evil, we can hope in the perfect Kingdom of God to come, and we can allow any punishment that touches us now to purify us from sin.

MEGATHEMES

THEME	EXPLANATION	IMPORTANCE
Day of Judgment	Destruction was coming because Judah had forsaken the Lord. The people worshiped Baal, Molech, and the starry hosts. Even the priests mixed pagan practices with faith in God. God's punishment for sin was on the way.	To escape God's judgment we must listen to him, accept his correction, trust him, and seek his guidance. If we accept him as our Lord, we can escape his condemnation.
Indifference to God	Although there had been occasional attempts at renewal, Judah had no sorrow for its sins. The people were prosperous, and they no longer cared about God. God's demands for righteous living seemed irrelevant to the people, whose security and wealth made them complacent.	Don't let material comfort be a barrier to your commitment to God. Prosperity can lead to an attitude of proud self-sufficiency. We need to admit that money won't save us and that we cannot save ourselves. Only God can save us.
Day of Cheer	The day of judgment will also be a day of cheer. God will judge all those who mistreat his people. He will purify his people, purging away all sin and evil. God will restore his people and give them hope.	When people are purged of sin, there is great relief and hope. No matter how difficult our experience now, we can look forward to the day of celebration when God will completely restore us. It will truly be a day to rejoice!

1. The day of judgment

1:1 2 Kgs 22:1–23:28; 2 Chr 34:1–35:26
1:2 Isa 6:11
1:3 Isa 6:11-12; Jer 4:25; 9:10

1 The LORD gave these messages to Zephaniah when Josiah son of Amon was king of
Judah. Zephaniah was the son of Cushi, son of Gedaliah, son of Amariah, son of
Hezekiah.

Coming Judgment against Judah

2"I will sweep away everything in all your land," says the LORD. 3"I will sweep away
both people and animals alike. Even the birds of the air and the fish in the sea will

1:1 Zephaniah prophesied in the days of Josiah king of Judah (640–609 B.C.). Josiah followed God, and during his reign the Book of the Law was discovered in the Temple. After reading it, Josiah began a great religious revival in Judah (2 Kings 22:1–23:25). Zephaniah helped fan the revival by warning the people that judgment would come if they did not turn from their sins. Although this great revival turned the nation back to God, it did not fully eliminate idolatry and lasted only a short time. Just four years after Josiah's death, Nebuchadnezzar swept into Palestine and took the first wave of Israelite captives into exile.

1:2ff The people of Judah were clearly warned by the highest authority of all—God. They refused to listen, either because they doubted God's prophet and thus did not believe that the message was from God, or because they doubted God himself and thus did not believe that he would do what he said. If we refuse to listen to God's Word, the Bible, we are as shortsighted as the people of Judah, and like them, we will be punished.

die. I will reduce the wicked to heaps of rubble,* along with the rest of humanity,”
says the LORD. 4“I will crush Judah and Jerusalem with my fist and destroy every
last trace of their Baal worship. I will put an end to all the idolatrous priests, so
that even the memory of them will disappear. 5For they go up to their roofs and bow
to the sun, moon, and stars. They claim to follow the LORD, but then they worship
Molech,* too. So now I will destroy them! 6And I will destroy those who used to
worship me but now no longer do. They no longer ask for the LORD’s guidance or seek
my blessings.”

7Stand in silence in the presence of the Sovereign LORD, for the awesome day of the
LORD’s judgment has come. The LORD has prepared his people for a great slaughter and
has chosen their executioners.* 8“On that day of judgment,” says the LORD, “I will
punish the leaders and princes of Judah and all those following pagan customs. 9Yes, I
will punish those who participate in pagan worship ceremonies, and those who steal and
kill to fill their masters’ homes with loot.

10“On that day,” says the LORD, “a cry of alarm will come from the Fish Gate and echo
throughout the newer Mishneh section* of the city. And a great crashing sound will come
from the surrounding hills. 11Wail in sorrow, all you who live in the market area, for all
who buy and sell there will die.

12“I will search with lanterns in Jerusalem’s darkest corners to find and punish
those who sit contented in their sins, indifferent to the LORD, thinking he will do
nothing at all to them. 13They are the very ones whose property will be plundered by
the enemy, whose homes will be ransacked. They will never have a chance to live in
the new homes they have built. They will never drink wine from the vineyards they
have planted.

14“That terrible day of the LORD is near. Swiftly it comes—a day when strong men
will cry bitterly. 15It is a day when the LORD’s anger will be poured out. It is a day of
terrible distress and anguish, a day of ruin and desolation, a day of darkness and gloom,

1:4 2 Kgs 23:4-7
1:5 1 Kgs 11:33
1:6 Isa 1:4; 9:13
1:7 Isa 34:6; Hab 2:20; Zech 2:13
1:8 Isa 24:21-23
1:9 Amos 3:10
1:10 2 Chr 33:14; Neh 3:3; 12:39
1:12 Jer 16:16-17; Amos 6:1
1:13 Deut 28:30; Amos 5:11
1:14 Ezek 7:16-18
1:15 Isa 22:5; Joel 2:2

1:3 The meaning of the Hebrew is uncertain. **1:5** Hebrew *Malcam,* another name for Molech; or it could possibly mean *their king.* **1:7** Hebrew *has prepared a sacrifice and sanctified his guests.* **1:10** Or *the Second Quarter,* a newer section of Jerusalem.

1:4 When the Israelites arrived in the Promised Land, God had commanded that they completely rid the land of its pagan inhabitants, who worshiped idols. But the Israelites failed to do so, and gradually they began to worship the Canaanites’ gods. The Canaanites believed in many gods that represented many aspects of life, and the chief god was Baal, symbolizing strength and fertility. God was extremely angry when his people turned from him to Baal.

1:4-6 Idols have been worshiped down through history. More than just a stone statue, an idol can be anything reverenced more than God. Thus, idol worship is prevalent even today: People trust in themselves, money, or power and not in God. But ultimately all idols will prove worthless, and the true God will prevail. Seek God first (Matthew 6:33), and have no other gods before him (Exodus 20:3).

1:5 The people had become polytheistic, worshiping the Lord *and* all the other gods of the land. They added the “best” of pagan worship to the worship of God. But God commands that he alone be worshiped (Exodus 20:1-5); thus, the people committed a horrible sin. One of these other gods was Molech, the national god of the Ammonites. The worship of Molech included child sacrifice, an abominable sin. From the time of Moses, the Israelites had been warned about worshiping this false god (Leviticus 18:21; 20:5), but they refused to take heed. Because of their sins, God would destroy them.

1:7 A day of judgment and great slaughter occurred during the lifetime of these people when Babylon invaded the land. The prophet saw these prophecies as future events, but he could not see when or in what order these events would take place. Many think that these prophecies have a double fulfillment—one for the near future (soon after the prophecy was made) and another for the distant future (possibly during the end times). Some scholars believe that these prophecies of judgment refer to events entirely in the future.

1:8, 9 Following pagan customs involved not only imitating foreign ways but also worshiping foreign gods. Leaders who should have been good examples to the people were adopting foreign practices and thus showing their contempt for the Lord by ignoring his commands against adopting the pagan culture.

1:12 God would search the city with lanterns and punish those who deserved punishment. Because they did not search their own hearts, and because they were content with the moral chaos around them and indifferent to God, God would use the Babylonians to judge them. Within 20 years, the Babylonians would enter Jerusalem, drag people out of hiding, and take them captive or kill them. No one would escape God’s judgment; there would be no place to hide.

1:12-14 Some people think of God as an indulgent heavenly grandfather, nice to have around but not a real force in shaping modern life. They don’t believe in his power or his coming judgment. But God is holy, and therefore he will actively judge and justly punish everyone who is content to live in sin, indifferent to him, or unconcerned about justice. When people are indifferent to God, they tend to think that he is indifferent to them and their sin. They will be surprised to find that the “terrible day of the LORD is near.”

1:14-18 The day of the Lord was near; the Babylonians would soon come and destroy Jerusalem. The day of the Lord is also near for us. God promises a final judgment, a day of worldwide destruction (Revelation 20:12-15). The Babylonian conquest occurred just as surely and horribly as Zephaniah had predicted. And God’s final day of judgment is also sure—but so is his ability to save. To be spared from judgment, recognize that you have sinned, that your sin will

1:16 Isa 2:12-15; Jer 4:19
1:17 Deut 28:28-29; Pss 79:3; 83:10; Isa 59:10; Jer 8:2; 9:22
1:18 Zeph 3:8

of clouds, blackness, 16 trumpet calls, and battle cries. Down go the walled cities and
strongest battlements!
17 "Because you have sinned against the LORD, I will make you as helpless as a blind
man searching for a path. Your blood will be poured out into the dust, and your bodies
will lie there rotting on the ground."
18 Your silver and gold will be of no use to you on that day of the LORD's anger. For
the whole land will be devoured by the fire of his jealousy. He will make a terrifying end
of all the people on earth.*

A Call to Repentance

2:1 2 Chr 20:4; Jer 3:3; 6:15; Joel 1:14
2:2 Zeph 1:18
2:3 Ps 57:1; Amos 5:6, 14-15

2 Gather together and pray, you shameless nation. 2 Gather while there is still time,
before judgment begins and your opportunity is blown away like chaff. Act now,
before the fierce fury of the LORD falls and the terrible day of the LORD's anger begins.
3 Beg the LORD to save you—all you who are humble, all you who uphold justice. Walk
humbly and do what is right. Perhaps even yet the LORD will protect you from his anger
on that day of destruction.

Judgment against Philistia

2:4 Amos 1:6-8; Zech 9:5
2:5 Isa 14:29, 31; Amos 3:1
2:7 Isa 32:14; Zeph 3:20

4 Gaza, Ashkelon, Ashdod, Ekron—these Philistine cities, too, will be rooted out and left
in desolation. 5 And how terrible it will be for you Philistines* who live along the coast
and in the land of Canaan, for this judgment is against you, too! The LORD will destroy
you until not one of you is left. 6 The coastal area will become a pasture, a place of
shepherd camps and enclosures for sheep.
7 The few survivors of the tribe of Judah will pasture there. They will lie down to rest
in the abandoned houses in Ashkelon. For the LORD their God will visit his people in
kindness and restore their prosperity again.

1:18 Or *the people living in the land.* **2:5** Hebrew *Kerethites.*

ZEPHANIAH served as a prophet to Judah from 640–621 B.C.

Climate of the times	Josiah was the last good king in Judah. His bold attempts to reform the nation and turn it back to God were probably influenced by Zephaniah.
Main message	A day will come when God, as judge, will severely punish all nations. But after judgment, he will show mercy to all who have been faithful to him.
Importance of message	We will all be judged for our disobedience to God; but if we remain faithful to him, he will show us mercy.
Contemporary prophet	Jeremiah (627–586 B.C.)

---

bring judgment, that you cannot save yourself, and that God alone can save you.

1:18 Money is not evil in itself, but it is useless to save us. In this life, money can warp our perspective, giving us feelings of security and power. Just as the Israelites' wealth could not save them from the Babylonian invasion, so at the final judgment, our riches will be worthless. Only Christ's redemptive work on our behalf matters for eternity. Christ alone will ransom us if we believe in him. Don't trust money; trust Christ.

2:1-3 There was still time for the people to avert God's judgment. They simply had to turn from their sins, humble themselves, and obey God. The Old Testament prophets announced news of destruction, but they also offered the only means of escape and protection—turning from sin and walking with God (see also Micah 6:8).

2:4 The four cities mentioned here are in Philistia, the nation southwest of Judah on the coast of the Mediterranean Sea. Age-old enemies of Israel from the days of Joshua, the Philistines were known for their cruelty. God judged these cities for their idolatry and their constant taunting of Israel. These four cities were four of the five capitals. The fifth (Gath) had probably already been destroyed.

2:7 All the prophets, even while prophesying doom and destruction, speak of "the few survivors"—a small group of God's people who remain faithful to him and whom God will restore to the land. Although God said he would destroy Judah, he also promised to save some, thus keeping his original covenant to preserve Abraham's descendants (Genesis 17:4-8). Because God is holy, he cannot allow sin to continue. But God is also faithful to his promises. He cannot stay angry forever with Israel or with you, if you are his child, because he loves his children and always seeks their good.

Judgment against Moab and Ammon

8 “I have heard the taunts of the people of Moab and Ammon, mocking my people and invading their borders. 9 Now, as surely as I live,” says the LORD Almighty, the God of Israel, “Moab and Ammon will be destroyed as completely as Sodom and Gomorrah. Their land will become a place of stinging nettles, salt pits, and eternal desolation. Those of my people who are left will plunder them and take their land.”

10 They will receive the wages of their pride, for they have scoffed at the people of the LORD Almighty. 11 The LORD will terrify them as he destroys all the gods in the land. Then people from nations around the world will worship the LORD, each in their own land.

Judgment against Ethiopia and Assyria

12 “You Ethiopians* will also be slaughtered by my sword,” says the LORD.

13 And the LORD will strike the lands of the north with his fist. He will destroy Assyria and make its great capital, Nineveh, a desolate wasteland, parched like a desert. 14 The city that once was so proud will become a pasture for sheep and cattle. All sorts of wild animals will settle there. Owls of many kinds will live among the ruins of its palaces, hooting from the gaping windows. Rubble will block all the doorways, and the cedar paneling will lie open to the wind and weather.

15 This is the fate of that boisterous city, once so secure. “In all the world there is no city as great as I,” it boasted. But now, look how it has become an utter ruin, a place where animals live! Everyone passing that way will laugh in derision or shake a defiant fist.

Jerusalem's Rebellion and Redemption

3 How terrible it will be for rebellious, polluted Jerusalem, the city of violence and crime. 2 It proudly refuses to listen even to the voice of the LORD. No one can tell it anything; it refuses all correction. It does not trust in the LORD or draw near to its God.

2:8 Ezek 25:3, 8
2:9 Isa 11:14; 15:1-9
2:10 Isa 16:6-10; Jer 48:28-31; Zeph 2:8
2:11 Joel 2:11; Zeph 1:4; 3:4
2:12 Isa 20:3-4
2:13 Nah 3:7
2:14 Isa 34:11
2:15 1 Kgs 9:7-8; Isa 22:2-7; 32:14; 47:8
3:1 Jer 6:6
3:2 Ps 78:22; Jer 5:3

2:12 Hebrew *Cushites.*

2:8 The Moabites and Ammonites lived to the east of Judah, and they often ridiculed and attacked Judah. These nations worshiped Chemosh and Molech (1 Kings 11:7). Moab's king once sacrificed his son on the city wall to stop an invasion (2 Kings 3:26, 27). God would judge these nations for their wickedness and for their treatment of his people.

2:8-11 Judah had been taunted and mocked by the neighboring nations, Moab and Ammon, but God reminded them that he had “heard the taunts” (2:8), and that the taunters would be punished for their pride (2:10). At times the whole world seems to mock God and those who have faith in him. When you are ridiculed, remember that God hears and will answer. Eventually, in God's timing, justice will be carried out.

2:9 The nations of Moab and Ammon trace their roots to Lot's incest with his daughters after escaping the destruction of evil Sodom and Gomorrah (Genesis 19). Ironically, Moab and Ammon would be the same kind of perpetual wasteland that God had made those evil cities. Sodom and Gomorrah were so completely destroyed that their exact location is still unknown.

2:12 Ethiopia, at the southern end of the Red Sea, controlled Egypt at this time. No one can escape deserved judgment. The Ethiopians were also “slaughtered by my sword” when the Babylonians invaded Egypt in 605 B.C. (See Isaiah 18 and Ezekiel 30:9 for other prophecies concerning Ethiopia, also called Cush.)

2:13 Zephaniah mentioned the large nation to the south and then moved to the nation that invaded from the north, Assyria. Though declining, Assyria was still the strongest military power of the day, dominating the world for three centuries and destroying any nation in its path. Nineveh, the large capital city, was considered impregnable. However, just as Zephaniah predicted, Nineveh was wiped out in 612 B.C. by the Babylonians, who would become the next world power.

2:13-15 To predict the destruction of Nineveh 10 years before it happened would be equivalent to predicting the destruction of Tokyo, Moscow, or New York. Nineveh was the ancient Near Eastern center for culture, technology, and beauty. It had great libraries, buildings, and a vast irrigation system that created lush gardens in the city. The city wall was 60 miles long, 100 feet high, and over 30 feet wide and was fortified with 1,500 towers. Yet the entire city was destroyed so completely that its very existence was questioned until it was discovered, with great difficulty, by 19th-century archaeologists. Nineveh had indeed become as desolate and dry as the desert.

3:1ff After predicting the destruction of the surrounding nations, Zephaniah returned to the problem at hand—sin in Jerusalem. The city of God, and God's people themselves, had become “polluted”—as sinful as their pagan neighbors. The people pretended to worship and serve God, but in their hearts they had rejected him and continued to be complacent about their sins. They no longer cared about the consequences of turning away from God.

3:2 Do you know people who refuse to listen when someone disagrees with their opinions? Their root problem is pride—inflated self-esteem. God's people had become so proud that they would not even listen to God's voice. Do you find it difficult to listen to the spiritual counsel of others or God's words from the Bible? Don't let pride make you unable or unwilling to let God work in your life. You will be more willing to listen when you consider how weak and sinful you really are compared to God.

3:3 Ezek 22:6-12
3:4 Ezek 22:26; Mal 2:7-9
3:5 Jer 3:3
3:6 Zeph 2:5
3:7 Hos 9:9
3:8 Ps 27:14; Ezek 38:14-23; Zeph 1:18
3:9 Ps 22:27
3:10 Ps 68:31; Isa 60:7
3:11 Isa 11:9
3:12 Nah 1:7
3:13 Hos 2:18; Mic 4:7; Zech 8:3; Rev 14:5
3:15 Isa 33:22; Ezek 37:26-28
3:16 Isa 35:3-4; Heb 12:12-13

3 Its leaders are like roaring lions hunting for their victims—out for everything they can get. Its judges are like ravenous wolves at evening time, who by dawn have left no trace of their prey. 4 Its prophets are arrogant liars seeking their own gain. Its priests defile the Temple by disobeying God's laws. 5 But the LORD is still there in the city, and he does no wrong. Day by day his justice is more evident, but no one takes notice—the wicked know no shame.

6 "I have wiped out many nations, devastating their fortress walls and towers. Their cities are now deserted; their streets are in silent ruin. There are no survivors to even tell what happened. 7 I thought, 'Surely they will have reverence for me now! Surely they will listen to my warnings, so I won't need to strike again.' But no; however much I punish them, they continue their evil practices from dawn till dusk and dusk till dawn." 8 So now the LORD says: "Be patient; the time is coming soon when I will stand up and accuse these evil nations. For it is my decision to gather together the kingdoms of the earth and pour out my fiercest anger and fury on them. All the earth will be devoured by the fire of my jealousy.

2. The day of hope

9 "On that day I will purify the lips of all people, so that everyone will be able to worship the LORD together. 10 My scattered people who live beyond the rivers of Ethiopia* will come to present their offerings. 11 And then you will no longer need to be ashamed of yourselves, for you will no longer be rebels against me. I will remove all the proud and arrogant people from among you. There will be no pride on my holy mountain. 12 Those who are left will be the lowly and the humble, for it is they who trust in the name of the LORD. 13 The people of Israel who survive will do no wrong to each other, never telling lies or deceiving one another. They will live peaceful lives, lying down to sleep in safety; there will be no one to make them afraid."

14 Sing, O daughter of Zion; shout aloud, O Israel! Be glad and rejoice with all your heart, O daughter of Jerusalem! 15 For the LORD will remove his hand of judgment and will disperse the armies of your enemy. And the LORD himself, the King of Israel, will live among you! At last your troubles will be over, and you will fear disaster no more.

16 On that day the announcement to Jerusalem will be, "Cheer up, Zion! Don't be

3:10 Hebrew *Cush.*

3:3, 4 Leading God's people is a privilege and a responsibility. Through Zephaniah, God rebuked many different leaders in Jerusalem—judges, prophets, and priests— because of their callous disobedience, irresponsibility, and sin. If you are a leader in the church, consider yourself in a privileged position, but be careful. God holds you responsible for the purity of your actions, the quality of your example, and the truth of your words.

3:5 Jerusalem's citizens, of all people, had no excuse for their sins. Jerusalem, where the Temple was located, was the religious center of the nation. But even though the people didn't follow God, God was still there in the city, present in the midst of corruption, persecution, and unbelief. No matter how spiritually desolate the world seems, God is here, and he is at work. Ask yourself, What is he doing now, and how can I be part of his work?

3:7 We may wonder how the Israelites could have had such clear warnings and still not turn to God. The problem was that they had allowed sin to so harden them that they no longer cared to follow God. They refused to heed God's warnings, and they refused to repent. The more God punished them, the more they sinned. If you are living in disobedience to God now, your heart may grow hard, and you may lose all desire for God.

3:8 In the last days, God will judge all people according to what they have done (Revelation 20:12). Justice will prevail; evildoers will be punished; and the obedient will be blessed. Don't try to avenge yourself. Be patient, and God's justice will come.

3:9 God will purify lips and unify language so that all his people from all nations will be able to worship him together. In the new earth, all believers will be able to understand each other; the confusion of languages at the tower of Babel will be reversed (Genesis 11). God will purify our hearts, so that the words coming from our lips will be pure as well.

3:10 The "scattered people" refers to Jews dispersed beyond the rivers of Ethiopia. It symbolizes that all Jews, no matter how far they have been scattered, will return to worship God.

3:11, 12 God will remove the proud people and leave the lowly and humble. God is opposed to the proud and arrogant of every generation. But those who are lowly (meek) and humble, both physically and spiritually, will be rewarded because they trust in God. Self-reliance and arrogance have no place among God's people or in his Kingdom.

3:14-18 The Lord himself will remove his hand of judgment, disperse Israel's enemies, and come to live among his people. He will give them gladness. Zephaniah points out that gladness results when we allow God to be with us. We do that by faithfully following him and obeying his commands. Then God rejoices over us with singing. If you want to be happy, draw close to the source of happiness by obeying God.

afraid! 17For the LORD your God has arrived to live among you. He is a mighty savior.
He will rejoice over you with great gladness. With his love, he will calm all your fears.
He will exult over you by singing a happy song."
18"I will gather you who mourn for the appointed festivals; you will be disgraced no
more.* 19And I will deal severely with all who have oppressed you. I will save the weak
and helpless ones; I will bring together those who were chased away. I will give glory
and renown to my former exiles, who have been mocked and shamed. 20On that day I
will gather you together and bring you home again. I will give you a good name, a name
of distinction among all the nations of the earth. They will praise you as I restore your
fortunes before their very eyes. I, the LORD, have spoken!"

3:17 Isa 62:5; 63:1
3:19 Isa 60:14; Ezek 34:16
3:20 Isa 56:5; 66:22; Ezek 37:12; Zeph 2:7

3:18 The meaning of the Hebrew for this verse is uncertain.

3:20 "Before their very eyes" does not necessarily mean that this promise would be fulfilled during Zephaniah's generation. Rather, it means that the restoration will be an obvious work of the Lord.

3:20 The message of doom in the beginning of the book becomes a message of hope by the end. There will be a new day when God will bless his people. If the leaders in the church today were to hear a message from a prophet of God, the message would probably resemble the book of Zephaniah. Under Josiah's religious reforms, the people did return to God *outwardly,* but their hearts were far from him. Zephaniah encouraged the nation to gather together and pray for salvation. We must also ask ourselves: Is our reform merely an outward show, or is it changing our hearts and lives? We need to gather together and pray, to walk humbly with God, to do what is right, and to hear the message of hope regarding the new world to come.

HAGGAI

Babylon overthrown by Cyrus 539 B.C.	Cyrus's decree allowing the exiles to return 538	Temple construction begins 536	Temple work halted 530	Haggai, Zechariah become prophets; Temple work resumed 520	Temple completed 515

PRESSURES, demands, expectations, and tasks push in from all sides and assault our schedules. Do this! Be there! Finish that! Call them! It seems as though everyone wants something from us—family, friends, employer, school, church, clubs. Soon there is little left to give, as we run out of energy and time. We find ourselves rushing through life, attending to the necessary, the immediate, and the urgent. The important is all too often left in the dust. Our problem is not the volume of demands or lack of scheduling skills, but values—what is *truly* important to us.

Our values and priorities are reflected in how we use our resources—time, money, strength, and talent. Often our actions belie our words. We say God is number one, but then we relegate him to a lesser number on our "to do" lists.

Twenty-five centuries ago, a voice was heard, calling men and women to the right priorities. Haggai knew what was important and what had to be done, and he challenged God's people to respond.

In 586 B.C., the armies of Babylon had destroyed the Temple in Jerusalem—God's house, the symbol of his presence. In 538 B.C. King Cyrus decreed that Jews could return to their beloved city and rebuild the Temple. So they traveled to Jerusalem and began the work. But then they forgot their purpose and lost their priorities, as opposition and apathy brought the work to a standstill (Ezra 4:4, 5). Then Haggai spoke, calling them back to God's values. "Why are you living in luxurious houses while my house lies in ruins?" (1:4). The people were more concerned with their own needs than with doing God's will, and, as a result, they suffered. Then Haggai called them to action: "This is what the LORD Almighty says: Consider how things are going for you! Now go up into the hills, bring down timber, and rebuild my house. Then I will take pleasure in it and be honored, says the LORD" (1:7, 8). And God's message through his servant Haggai became the catalyst for finishing the work.

Although Haggai is a small book, it is filled with challenge and promise, reminding us of God's claim on our life and our priorities. As you read Haggai, imagine him walking the streets and alleys of Jerusalem, urging the people to get back to doing God's work. And listen to Haggai speaking to you, urging you to reorder your priorities in accordance with God's will. What has God told you to do? Put all else aside and obey him.

VITAL STATISTICS

PURPOSE:
To call the people to complete the rebuilding of the Temple

AUTHOR:
Haggai

TO WHOM WRITTEN:
The people living in Jerusalem and those who had returned from exile

DATE WRITTEN:
520 B.C.

SETTING:
The Temple in Jerusalem had been destroyed in 586 B.C. Cyrus allowed the Jews to return to their homeland and rebuild their temple in 538 B.C. They began the work but were unable to complete it. Through the ministry of Haggai and Zechariah, the Temple was completed (520–515 B.C.).

KEY VERSE:
"Why are you living in luxurious houses while my house lies in ruins?" (1:4).

KEY PEOPLE:
Haggai, Zerubbabel, Jeshua

KEY PLACE:
Jerusalem

SPECIAL FEATURES:
Haggai was the first of the postexilic prophets. The other two were Zechariah and Malachi. The literary style of this book is simple and direct.

THE BLUEPRINT

1. The call to rebuild the Temple (1:1–15)
2. Encouragement to complete the Temple (2:1–23)

When the exiles first returned from Babylon, they set about rebuilding the Temple right away. Although they began with the right attitudes, they slipped back into wrong behavior, and the work came to a standstill. In this regard, we need to be on guard to keep our priorities straight. Remain active in your service to God and continue to put first things first.

MEGATHEMES

THEME	EXPLANATION	IMPORTANCE
Right Priorities	God had given the Jews the assignment to finish the Temple in Jerusalem when they returned from captivity. After 15 years, they still had not completed it. They were more concerned about building their own homes than finishing God's work. Haggai told them to get their priorities straight.	It is easy to make other priorities more important than doing God's work. But God wants us to follow through and build up his Kingdom. Don't stop and don't make excuses. Set your heart on what is right and do it. Get your priorities straight.
God's Encouragement	Haggai encouraged the people as they worked. He assured them of the divine presence of the Holy Spirit and of final victory, and instilled in them the hope that the Messiah would reign.	If God gives you a task, don't be afraid to get started. His resources are infinite. God will help you complete it by giving you encouragement from others along the way.

1. The call to rebuild the Temple

1 On August 29* of the second year of King Darius's reign, the LORD gave a message
through the prophet Haggai to Zerubbabel son of Shealtiel, governor of Judah, and
to Jeshua* son of Jehozadak, the high priest. 2 "This is what the LORD Almighty says:
The people are saying, 'The time has not yet come to rebuild the LORD's house—the
Temple.'"
3 So the LORD sent this message through the prophet Haggai: 4 "Why are you living
in luxurious houses while my house lies in ruins? 5 This is what the LORD Almighty
says: Consider how things are going for you! 6 You have planted much but harvested
little. You have food to eat, but not enough to fill you up. You have wine to drink, but
not enough to satisfy your thirst. You have clothing to wear, but not enough to keep
you warm. Your wages disappear as though you were putting them in pockets filled
with holes!
7 "This is what the LORD Almighty says: Consider how things are going for you! 8 Now
go up into the hills, bring down timber, and rebuild my house. Then I will take pleasure
in it and be honored, says the LORD. 9 You hoped for rich harvests, but they were poor.
And when you brought your harvest home, I blew it away. Why? Because my house lies
in ruins, says the LORD Almighty, while you are all busy building your own fine houses.
10 That is why the heavens have withheld the dew and the earth has withheld its crops.

1:1 Ezra 2:2; 3:8; 5:1-2; 6:6-14 Zech 6:11
1:4 Hag 1:9
1:6 Hag 1:9; 2:16
1:8 Ezra 3:7-13 Ps 132:13-14 Hag 2:7, 9
1:9 Isa 40:7 Hag 1:4
1:10 Deut 28:24 1 Kgs 8:35-36; 17:1 Joel 1:18-20

1:1a Hebrew *On the first day of the sixth month,* of the Hebrew calendar. A number of dates in Haggai can be cross-checked with dates in surviving Persian records and related accurately to our modern calendar. This event occurred on August 29, 520 B.C. **1:1b** Hebrew *Joshua,* a variant name for Jeshua; also in 1:12, 14.

1:1 Zerubbabel, governor of Judah, and Jeshua, the high priest, were key leaders in rebuilding the Temple. They had already reestablished the altar, but work on the Temple had slowed. Haggai gave a message to these outstanding leaders and to the exiles who had returned from Babylon, encouraging them to complete the rebuilding of the Temple in Jerusalem.

1:1ff The Jews who had returned from Babylon in 538 B.C. to rebuild the Temple in Jerusalem were not able to finish their work because they were hindered by their enemies. After opposition put a halt to progress, no further work had been done on the Temple for over 15 years. In August 520 B.C., Haggai delivered a message to encourage the people to rebuild the Temple. Haggai was probably born in captivity in Babylon and returned to Jerusalem with Zerubbabel in 538 B.C. (Ezra 1–2). Haggai and Zechariah, two prophets who encouraged the Temple rebuilding, are mentioned in Ezra 5:1.

1:2-15 Haggai encouraged the people to finish rebuilding the Temple. Opposition from hostile neighbors had caused them to feel discouraged and to neglect the Temple and thus neglect God. But Haggai's message turned them around and motivated them to pick up their tools and continue the work they had begun.

1:3-6 God asked his people how they could live in luxury when his house was lying in ruins. The Temple was the focal point of Judah's relationship with God, but it was still demolished. Instead of rebuilding the Temple, the people put their energies into beautifying their own homes. However, the harder the people worked for themselves, the less they had, because they ignored their spiritual lives. The same happens to us. If we put God first, he will provide for our deepest needs. If we put him in any other place, all our efforts will be futile. Caring only for your physical needs while ignoring your relationship with God will lead to ruin.

1:6 Because the people had not given God first place in their lives, their work was not fruitful or productive, and their material possessions did not satisfy. While they concentrated on building and beautifying their own homes, God's blessing was withheld because they no longer put him first. Moses had predicted that this would be the result if the people neglected God (Deuteronomy 28:38-45).

1:9 Judah's problem was confused priorities. Like Judah, our priorities involving occupation, family, and God's work are often confused. Jobs, homes, vacations, and leisure activities may rank higher on our list of importance than God. What is most important to you? Where is God on your list of priorities?

1:11 Deut 28:22-24 11 I have called for a drought on your fields and hills—a drought to wither the grain and
grapes and olives and all your other crops, a drought to starve both you and your cattle
and to ruin everything you have worked so hard to get."

Obedience to God's Call

1:12 Ps 112:1 12 Then Zerubbabel son of Shealtiel, Jeshua son of Jehozadak, the high priest, and the
Isa 50:10 whole remnant of God's people obeyed the message from the LORD their God. It had
Hag 1:1 been delivered by the prophet Haggai, whom the LORD their God had sent, and the people
1:13 Mal 2:7; 3:1 worshiped the LORD in earnest. 13 Then Haggai, the LORD's messenger, gave the people
1:14-15 this message from the LORD: "I am with you, says the LORD!" 14 So the LORD sparked
Ezra 5:2 the enthusiasm of Zerubbabel son of Shealtiel, governor of Judah, Jeshua son of
Neh 4:6 Hag 1:1 Jehozadak, the high priest, and the whole remnant of God's people. They came and began
their work on the house of the LORD Almighty, their God. 15 This was on September 21*
of the second year of King Darius's reign.

2. Encouragement to complete the Temple

The New Temple's Splendor

2 Then on October 17* of that same year, the LORD sent another message through the
prophet Haggai. 2 "Say this to Zerubbabel son of Shealtiel, governor of Judah, and
to Jeshua* son of Jehozadak, the high priest, and to the remnant of God's people there
2:3 Ezra 3:12 in the land: 3 Is there anyone who can remember this house—the Temple—as it was
before? In comparison, how does it look to you now? It must seem like nothing at all!
2:4 Deut 31:23 4 But now take courage, Zerubbabel, says the LORD. Take courage, Jeshua son of
Acts 7:9 Eph 6:10-12 Jehozadak, the high priest. Take courage, all you people still left in the land, says the
2:5 Exod 29:45-46 LORD. Take courage and work, for I am with you, says the LORD Almighty. 5 My Spirit
Neh 9:10 remains among you, just as I promised when you came out of Egypt. So do not be afraid.
Isa 63:11, 14

1:15 Hebrew *on the twenty-fourth day of the sixth month,* of the Hebrew calendar. This event occurred on September 21, 520 B.C.; also see note on 1:1a. **2:1** Hebrew *on the twenty-first day of the seventh month,* of the Hebrew calendar. This event occurred on October 17, 520 B.C.; also see note on 1:1a. **2:2** Hebrew *Joshua,* a variant name for Jeshua; also in 2:4.

HAGGAI served as a prophet to Judah about 520 B.C., after the return from exile.

Climate of the times	The people of Judah had been exiled to Babylon in 586 B.C., and Jerusalem and the Temple had been destroyed. Under Cyrus, king of Persia, the Jews were allowed to return to Judah and rebuild their Temple.
Main message	The people returned to Jerusalem to begin rebuilding the Temple, but they hadn't finished. Haggai's message encouraged the people to finish rebuilding God's Temple.
Importance of message	The Temple lay half-finished while the people lived in beautiful homes. Haggai warned them against putting their possessions and jobs ahead of God. We must put God first in our lives.
Contemporary prophet	Zechariah (520–480 B.C.)

1:11 Grain, grapes for wine, and olives for oil were Israel's major crops. The people depended on these for security while neglecting the worship of God. As a result, God would send a drought to destroy their livelihood and call them back to himself.

1:14, 15 The people began rebuilding the Temple just 23 days after Haggai's first message. Rarely did a prophet's message produce such a quick response. How often we hear a sermon and respond, "That was an excellent point—I ought to do that," only to leave church and forget to act. These people put their words into action. When you hear a good sermon or lesson, ask what you should *do* about it, and then make plans to put it into practice.

2:1-9 This is Haggai's second message. It was given during the Festival of Shelters in October 520 B.C. The older people could remember the incredible beauty of Solomon's Temple, destroyed 66 years earlier. Many were discouraged because the rebuilt Temple was inferior to Solomon's. But Haggai encouraged them with God's message that the glory of this Temple would surpass that of its predecessor. The most important part of the Temple is God's presence. Some 500 years later, Jesus Christ would walk in the Temple courts.

2:4 "Take courage and work, for I am with you." Judah's people had returned to worshiping God, and God had promised to bless their efforts. But it was time for them to *work.* We must be people of prayer, Bible study, and worship, but eventually we must get out and *do* the work God has prepared for us. He wants to change the world through us, his ambassadors. God has given you a job to do in the church, at your place of employment, and at home. The time has come to take courage and get going because God is with you!

2:5 The Israelites had been led from captivity in Egypt to their Promised Land. They were God's chosen people, guided and cared for by his Holy Spirit. Although God had punished them for their sins, he kept his promise and never left them (Exodus 29:45, 46). No matter what difficulties we face or how frustrating our work may be, God's Spirit is with us.

6“For this is what the LORD Almighty says: In just a little while I will again shake
the heavens and the earth. I will shake the oceans and the dry land, too. 7I will shake
all the nations, and the treasures of all the nations will come to this Temple. I will fill
this place with glory, says the LORD Almighty. 8The silver is mine, and the gold is
mine, says the LORD Almighty. 9The future glory of this Temple will be greater than
its past glory, says the LORD Almighty. And in this place I will bring peace. I, the LORD
Almighty, have spoken!”

2:6 Ezek 38:19 †Heb 12:26
2:7 1 Kgs 8:11 Isa 60:4-9

Blessings Promised for Obedience

10On December 18* of the second year of King Darius’s reign, the LORD sent this
message to the prophet Haggai: 11“This is what the LORD Almighty says! Ask the priests
this question about the law: 12If one of you is carrying a holy sacrifice in his robes and
happens to brush against some bread or stew, wine or oil, or any other kind of food, will
it also become holy?”
The priests replied, “No.”
13Then Haggai asked, “But if someone becomes ceremonially unclean by touching a
dead person and then brushes against any of the things mentioned, will it be defiled?”
And the priests answered, “Yes.”
14Then Haggai said, “That is how it is with this people and this nation, says the LORD.
Everything they do and everything they offer is defiled. 15So think about this from now
on—consider how things were going for you before you began to lay the foundation of
the LORD’s Temple. 16When you hoped for a twenty-bushel crop, you harvested only ten.
When you expected to draw fifty gallons from the winepress, you found only twenty. 17I
sent blight and mildew and hail to destroy all the produce of your labor. Yet, even so, you
refused to return to me, says the LORD.
18“On this eighteenth day of December—the day when the foundation of the LORD’s
Temple was laid—carefully consider this: 19I am giving you a promise now while the
seed is still in the barn, before you have harvested your grain and before the grapevine,
the fig tree, the pomegranate, and the olive tree have produced their crops. From this day
onward I will bless you.”

2:10 Hag 1:15
2:12 Exod 29:37 Ezek 44:19 Matt 23:19
2:13 Num 19:11-12, 22
2:14 Prov 15:8 Isa 1:11-15
2:15 Ezra 3:10; 4:24 Hag 1:5
2:16 Hag 1:9
2:18 Hag 2:10

2:10 Hebrew *On the twenty-fourth day of the ninth month,* of the Hebrew calendar (also in 2:18). This event occurred on December 18, 520 B.C.; also see note on 1:1a.

2:6-9 The focus shifts from the local Temple being rebuilt in Jerusalem to the worldwide reign of the Messiah on earth. The words “in just a little while” are not limited to the immediate historical context; they refer to God’s control of history—he can act anytime he chooses. God will act *in his time* (see also Hebrews 12:26, 27).

2:7 When God promised to shake all the nations with his judgment, he was speaking of both his present judgment on evil nations and future judgment during the last days.

2:8, 9 God wanted the Temple to be rebuilt, and he had the gold and silver to do it, but he needed willing hands. God has chosen to do his work through people. He provides the resources, but willing hands must do the work. Are your hands available for God’s work in the world?

2:10-19 The point of this message (delivered in December 520 B.C.) is that holiness will not rub off on others, but contamination will. As the people began to obey God, God promised to encourage and prosper them. But they needed to understand that activities in the Temple would not clean up their sin; only repentance and obedience could do that. If we insist on harboring wrong attitudes and sins or on maintaining close relationships with sinful people, we will be defiled. Holy living will come only when we are empowered by God’s Holy Spirit.

2:14 When a child eats spaghetti sauce, very soon his or her face, hands, and clothes become red. Sin and selfish attitudes produce the same result—they stain everything they touch. Even good deeds done for God can be tainted by sinful attitudes. The only remedy is God’s cleansing.

2:16 For many years, the grain had only given 50 percent of the expected yield, and wine had done even worse.

2:18, 19 The people relaid the Temple foundation, and immediately God blessed them. He did not wait for the project to be completed. God often sends his encouragement and approval with our first few obedient steps. He is eager to bless us!

Promises for Zerubbabel

2:21 Hag 2:6 Heb 12:26
2:22 Mic 5:10

20 The LORD sent this second message to Haggai on December 18*: 21 "Tell Zerubbabel,
the governor of Judah, that I am about to shake the heavens and the earth. 22 I will
overthrow royal thrones, destroying the power of foreign kingdoms. I will overturn their
chariots and charioteers. The horses will fall, and their riders will kill each other. 23 But
when this happens, says the LORD Almighty, I will honor you, Zerubbabel son of
Shealtiel, my servant. I will treat you like a signet ring on my finger, says the LORD, for
I have specially chosen you. I, the LORD Almighty, have spoken!"

2:20 Hebrew *on the twenty-fourth day of the month; see note on 2:10.*

2:20-23 Haggai's final message acknowledged that he was merely the messenger who brings the word of the Lord. It is addressed to Zerubbabel, the governor of Judah.

2:23 A signet ring was used to guarantee the authority and authenticity of a letter. It served as a signature when pressed in soft wax on a written document. God was reaffirming and guaranteeing his promise of a Messiah through David's line (Matthew 1:12).

2:23 God closed his message to Zerubbabel with this tremendous affirmation: "I have specially chosen you." Such a proclamation applies to us as well: Each of us has been chosen by God (Ephesians 1:4). This truth should make us see how much God loves us and motivate us to work for him. When you feel down, remind yourself: God has chosen me!

2:23 Haggai's message to the people sought to get their priorities straight, help them quit worrying, and motivate them to rebuild the Temple. Like them, we often place a higher priority on our personal comfort than on God's work and true worship. But God is pleased and promises strength and guidance when we give him first place in our life.

ZECHARIAH

Daniel taken to Babylon 605 B.C.

Ezekiel taken to Babylon 597

Jerusalem falls 586

Babylon overthrown by Cyrus 539

Cyrus's decree allowing the exiles to return 538

VITAL STATISTICS

PURPOSE:
To give hope to God's people by revealing God's future deliverance through the Messiah

AUTHOR:
Zechariah

TO WHOM WRITTEN:
The Jews in Jerusalem who had returned from their captivity in Babylon and to God's people everywhere

DATE WRITTEN:
Chapters 1—8 were written approximately 520–518 B.C. Chapters 9—14 were written around 480 B.C.

SETTING:
The exiles had returned from Babylon to rebuild the Temple, but the work had been thwarted and stalled. Haggai and Zechariah confronted the people with their task and encouraged them to complete it.

KEY VERSES:
"Rejoice greatly, O people of Zion! Shout in triumph, O people of Jerusalem! Look, your king is coming to you. He is righteous and victorious, yet he is humble, riding on a donkey—even on a donkey's colt. . . . Your king will bring peace to the nations. His realm will stretch from sea to sea and from the Euphrates River to the ends of the earth" (9:9, 10).

KEY PEOPLE:
Zerubbabel, Jeshua

KEY PLACE:
Jerusalem

SPECIAL FEATURES:
This book is the most apocalyptic and messianic of all the minor prophets.

THE FUTURE—that vast uncharted sea of the unknown, holding joy or terror, comfort or pain, love or loneliness. Some people fear the days to come, wondering what evils lurk in the shadows; others consult seers and future-telling charlatans, trying desperately to discover its secrets. But tomorrow's story is known only to God and to those special messengers called prophets, to whom God has revealed a chapter or two.

A prophet's primary task was to proclaim the word of the Lord, pointing out sin, explaining its consequences, and calling men and women to repentance and obedience. Elijah, Elisha, Isaiah, Jeremiah, Ezekiel, Hosea, and Amos stand with scores of others who faithfully delivered God's message despite rejection, ridicule, and persecution. And at times they were given prophetic visions foretelling coming events.

Nestled near the end of the Old Testament, among what are known as "minor prophets," is the book of Zechariah. As one of three post-exilic prophets, along with Haggai and Malachi, Zechariah ministered to the small remnant of Jews who had returned to Judah to rebuild the Temple and their nation. Like Haggai, he encouraged the people to finish rebuilding the Temple, but his message went far beyond those physical walls and contemporary issues. With spectacular apocalyptic imagery and graphic detail, Zechariah told of the Messiah, the one whom God would send to rescue his people and to reign over all the earth. Zechariah is one of our most important prophetic books, giving detailed messianic references that were clearly fulfilled in the life of Jesus Christ. The rebuilding of the Temple, he says, was just the first act in the drama of the end and the ushering in of the messianic age. Zechariah proclaimed a stirring message of hope to these ex-captives and exiles—their King was coming!

Jesus is Messiah, the promised "great deliverer" of Israel. Unlike Zechariah's listeners, we can look back at Christ's ministry and mission. As you study Zechariah's prophecy, you will see details of Christ's life that were written 500 years before their fulfillment. Read and stand in awe of our God, who keeps his promises. But there is also a future message that has not yet been fulfilled—the return of Christ at the end of the age. As you read Zechariah, think through the implications of this promised event. *Your King is coming,* and he will reign forever and ever.

God knows and controls the future. We may never see more than a moment ahead, but we can be secure if we trust in him. Read Zechariah and strengthen your faith in God—he alone is your hope and security.

Temple construction begins 536	Temple work halted 530	Haggai, Zechariah become prophets; Temple work resumed 520	Temple completed 515	Ezra comes to Jerusalem 458	Nehemiah comes to Jerusalem 445

THE BLUEPRINT

A. MESSAGES WHILE REBUILDING THE TEMPLE (1:1—8:23)
1. Zechariah's night visions
2. Zechariah's words of encouragement

Zechariah encouraged the people to put away the sin in their lives and to continue rebuilding the Temple. His visions described the judgment of Israel's enemies, the blessings to Jerusalem, and the need for God's people to remain pure—avoiding hypocrisy, superficiality, and sin. Zechariah's visions provided hope for the people. We also need to carefully follow the instruction to remain pure until Christ returns.

B. MESSAGES AFTER COMPLETING THE TEMPLE (9:1—14:21)

Besides encouragement and hope, Zechariah's messages were also a warning that God's messianic Kingdom would not begin as soon as the Temple was complete. Israel's enemies would be judged and the King would come, but God's people would themselves face many difficult circumstances before experiencing the blessing of the messianic Kingdom. We, too, may face much sorrow, disappointment, and distress before coming into Christ's eternal Kingdom.

MEGATHEMES

THEME	EXPLANATION	IMPORTANCE
God's Jealousy	God was angry at his people for ignoring his prophets through the years, and he was concerned that they not follow the careless and false leaders who exploited them. Disobedience was the root of their problems and the cause of their misery. God was jealous for their devotion to him.	God is jealous for our devotion. To avoid Israel's ruin, don't walk in their steps. Don't reject God, follow false teachers, or lead others astray. Turn to God, faithfully obey his commands, and make sure you are leading others correctly.
Rebuild the Temple	The Jews were discouraged. They were free from exile, yet the Temple was not completed. Zechariah encouraged them to rebuild it. God would both protect his workmen and empower them by his Holy Spirit to carry out his work.	More than the rebuilding of the Temple was at stake—the people were staging the first act in God's wonderful drama of the end times. Those of us who love God must complete his work. To do so we must have the Holy Spirit's help. God will empower us with his Spirit.
The King Is Coming	The Messiah will come both to rescue people from sin and to reign as king. He will establish his Kingdom, conquer all his enemies, and rule over all the earth. Everything will one day be under his loving and powerful control.	The Messiah came as a servant to die for us. He will return as a victorious king. At that time, he will usher in peace throughout the world. Submit to his leadership now to be ready for the King's triumphant return.
God's Protection	There was opposition to God's plan in Zechariah's day, and he prophesied future times of trouble. But God's Word endures. God remembers the agreements he makes with his people. He cares for his people and will deliver them from all the world powers that oppress them.	Although evil is still present, God's infinite love and personal care have been demonstrated through the centuries. God keeps his promises. Although our bodies may be destroyed, we need never fear our ultimate destiny if we love and obey him.

A. MESSAGES WHILE REBUILDING THE TEMPLE (1:1—8:23)

Zechariah begins by describing eight visions that came to him at night. Then he gives a collection of messages about the crowning of Jeshua, answers to questions of feasting and fasting, and encouragment to continue rebuilding the Temple. We, too, can be inspired to continue following God in faithfulness throughout our life.

1. Zechariah's night visions

A Call to Return to the LORD

1 In midautumn* of the second year of King Darius's reign, the LORD gave this **1:1** Ezra 4:24; 5:1
message to the prophet Zechariah son of Berekiah and grandson of Iddo. Neh 12:4, 16
2"I, the LORD, was very angry with your ancestors. 3Therefore, say to the people, **1:2**
'This is what the LORD Almighty says: Return to me, and I will return to you, says the 2 Chr 36:16 **1:3**
LORD Almighty.' 4Do not be like your ancestors who would not listen when the earlier Isa 31:6
prophets said to them, 'This is what the LORD Almighty says: Turn from your evil ways Mal 3:7 **1:4**
and stop all your evil practices.' 2 Chr 24:19;
5"Your ancestors and their prophets are now long dead. 6But all the things I said 29:6-10; 36:15
through my servants the prophets happened to your ancestors, just as I said they would. Jer 6:17; 11:6-8 **1:6**
As a result, they repented and said, 'We have received what we deserved from the LORD Jer 12:16-17
Almighty. He has done what he said he would do.'" Lam 2:17

A Man among the Myrtle Trees

7Then on February 15* of the second year of King Darius's reign, the LORD sent
another message to the prophet Zechariah son of Berekiah and grandson of Iddo. **1:8** Neh 8:15
Zechariah said: Isa 41:19; 55:13
8In a vision during the night, I saw a man sitting on a red horse that was standing Zech 6:2-3 Rev 6:4
among some myrtle trees in a small valley. Behind him were red, brown, and white **1:9**
horses, each with its own rider. 9I asked the angel who was talking with me, "My lord, Zech 2:3
what are all those horses for?"
"I will show you," the angel replied.
10So the man standing among the myrtle trees explained, "They are the ones the LORD **1:11**
has sent out to patrol the earth." Isa 14:7
11Then the other riders reported to the angel of the LORD, who was standing among **1:12**
the myrtle trees, "We have patrolled the earth, and the whole earth is at peace." Pss 69:5; 74:10 Isa 64:9-12
12Upon hearing this, the angel of the LORD prayed this prayer: "O LORD Almighty, for Jer 25:11-12
seventy years now you have been angry with Jerusalem and the towns of Judah. How Dan 9:2

1:1 Hebrew *In the eighth month.* A number of dates in Zechariah can be cross-checked with dates in surviving Persian records and related accurately to our modern calendar. This month of the Hebrew lunar calendar occurred in October and November 520 B.C. **1:7** Hebrew *on the twenty-fourth day of the eleventh month, the month of Shebat,* of the Hebrew calendar. This event occurred on February 15, 519 B.C.; also see note on 1:1.

1:1 Born in Babylon during the Exile, Zechariah was a fairly young man when he returned to Jerusalem in 538 B.C. King Cyrus of Persia had defeated Babylon in 539 and had decreed that captives in exile could return to their homelands. Zechariah and Haggai were among the first to leave. Zechariah, a prophet and a priest, began ministering at the same time as the prophet Haggai (520–518 B.C.). His first prophecy was delivered two months after Haggai's first prophecy.

Like Haggai, Zechariah encouraged the people to continue rebuilding the Temple, whose reconstruction had been halted for nearly 15 years. Zechariah combated the people's spiritual apathy, despair over pressures from their enemies, and discouragement about the smaller scale of the new Temple foundation. Neglect of our spiritual priorities can be just as devastating today to fulfilling God's purpose.

1:2-6 The familiar phrase "Like father, like son" implies that children turn out like their parents. But here, God warned Israel *not* to be like their forefathers, who disobeyed him and reaped the consequences—his punishment. We are responsible before God for our actions. We can't use our heredity or environment as excuses for our sins. We are free to choose, and individually we must return to God and follow him.

1:5, 6 The words God had spoken through his prophets a century earlier, before the captivity, also applied to Zechariah's generation, and they are still relevant for us. Because God's Word endures, we must read, study, and apply what is preserved for us in Scripture. Learn the lessons of God's Word so you will not have to repeat the mistakes of others.

1:7-17 The man among the myrtle trees was the angel of the Lord (1:11). The horses and their colors were symbols of God's involvement in world governments. The full meaning of the colors is unknown, although the red horse is often associated with war and the white horse with final victory.

1:11 The angel of the Lord saw that all the nations were secure and at peace, while Israel was still oppressed and despised. But God was planning a change. He had released his people, and he would allow them to return and rebuild his Temple.

1:12 Seventy years was the time that God had decreed for Israel to remain in captivity (Jeremiah 25:11; 29:10). This time was over, and the angel asked God to act swiftly to complete the promised return of his people to Jerusalem.

1:13 Isa 40:1-2; Zech 4:1
long will it be until you again show mercy to them?" 13 And the LORD spoke kind and
comforting words to the angel who talked with me.

1:14 Zech 1:17; 8:2
14 Then the angel said to me, "Shout this message for all to hear: 'This is what the
LORD Almighty says: My love for Jerusalem and Mount Zion is passionate and strong.

1:15 Ps 123:4; Amos 1:11
15 But I am very angry with the other nations that enjoy peace and security. I was
only a little angry with my people, but the nations punished them far beyond my
intentions.

1:16 Ezra 6:14-15; Isa 54:8-10; Zech 2:10
16 "'Therefore, this is what the LORD says: I have returned to show mercy to Jerusalem.
My Temple will be rebuilt, says the LORD Almighty, and plans will be made for the

1:17 Isa 44:26; 51:3
reconstruction of Jerusalem.*' 17 Say this also: 'This is what the LORD Almighty says:
The towns of Israel will again overflow with prosperity, and the LORD will again comfort
Zion and choose Jerusalem as his own.'"

1:19 1 Kgs 22:11

Four Horns and Four Blacksmiths

18 Then I looked up and saw four animal horns. 19 "What are these?" I asked the angel
who was talking with me.

1:20 Isa 44:12; 54:16
He replied, "These horns represent the world powers that scattered Judah, Israel, and
Jerusalem."

1:21 Ps 75:10; Zech 1:18-19
20 Then the LORD showed me four blacksmiths. 21 "What are these men coming to do?"
I asked.

The angel replied, "The blacksmiths have come to terrify the four horns that scattered
and humbled Judah. They will throw them down and destroy them."

Future Prosperity of Jerusalem

2:1 Ezek 40:3-5
2 When I looked around me again, I saw a man with a measuring line in his hand.
2 "Where are you going?" I asked.

2:2 Jer 31:39; Rev 21:15-17
He replied, "I am going to measure Jerusalem, to see how wide and how long it is."
3 Then the angel who was with me went to meet a second angel who was coming

2:4 Jer 1:6; Ezek 38:11; 1 Tim 4:12
toward him. 4 The other angel said, "Hurry, and say to that young man, 'Jerusalem
will someday be so full of people that it won't have room enough for everyone! Many
will live outside the city walls, with all their livestock—and yet they will be safe. 5 For

2:5 Zech 2:10-11
I, myself, will be a wall of fire around Jerusalem, says the LORD. And I will be the
glory inside the city!'"

1:16 Hebrew *and the measuring line will be stretched out over Jerusalem.*

ZECHARIAH served as a prophet to Judah about 520 B.C., after the return from exile.

Climate of the times . . . . The exiles had returned from captivity to rebuild their Temple. But work on the Temple had stalled, and the people were ignoring their service to God.

Main message . . . . Zechariah, like Haggai, encouraged the people to finish rebuilding the Temple. His visions gave the people hope. He told the people of a future king who would one day establish an eternal kingdom.

Importance of message . . . . . Even in times of discouragement and despair, God is working out his plan. God protects and guides us; we must trust and follow him.

Contemporary prophet . . . . . . Haggai (approximately 520 B.C.)

1:13 God's people had lived under his judgment for 70 years during their captivity in Babylon. But here God spoke words of comfort and assurance. God promises that when we return to him, he will heal us (Hosea 6:1). If you feel wounded and crushed by the events of your life, turn to God so he can heal and comfort you.

1:15 Although the pagan nations afflicted God's people beyond his intentions, God was not powerless to stop them. God used these nations to punish his sinful people. When the nations went beyond his plans by trying to destroy Israel as a nation, he intervened.

1:18-21 The horns were the four world powers that oppressed Israel—Egypt, Assyria, Babylon, and Medo-Persia. The four blacksmiths (1:20) were the nations used to overthrow Israel's enemies. God raised them up to judge the oppressors of his people.

2:1 The man with the measuring line symbolizes the hope of a rebuilt Jerusalem and a restored people. The man would be measuring to mark out the boundaries for a foundation (see 1:16; and Jeremiah 31:38-40).

The Exiles Are Called Home

6 The LORD says, "Come away! Flee from the north, for I have scattered you to the four
winds. 7 Come away! Escape to Jerusalem,* you who are exiled in Babylon!"
8 "After a period of glory, the LORD Almighty sent me against the nations who
oppressed you. For he said, 'Anyone who harms you harms my most precious possession.* 9 I will raise my fist to crush them, and their own slaves will plunder them.' Then
you will know that the LORD Almighty has sent me."
10 The LORD says, "Shout and rejoice, O Jerusalem,* for I am coming to live among
you. 11 Many nations will join themselves to the LORD on that day, and they, too, will be
my people. I will live among you, and you will know that the LORD Almighty sent me to
you. 12 The land of Judah will be the LORD's inheritance in the holy land, and he will once
again choose Jerusalem to be his own city. 13 Be silent before the LORD, all humanity, for
he is springing into action from his holy dwelling."

Cleansing for the High Priest

3 Then the angel showed me Jeshua* the high priest standing before the angel of the
LORD. Satan* was there at the angel's right hand, accusing Jeshua of many things.
2 And the LORD said to Satan, "I, the LORD, reject your accusations, Satan. Yes, the LORD,
who has chosen Jerusalem, rebukes you. This man is like a burning stick that has been
snatched from a fire."
3 Jeshua's clothing was filthy as he stood there before the angel. 4 So the angel said to
the others standing there, "Take off his filthy clothes." And turning to Jeshua he said,
"See, I have taken away your sins, and now I am giving you these fine new clothes."
5 Then I said, "Please, could he also have a clean turban on his head?" So they put a
clean priestly turban on his head and dressed him in new clothes while the angel of the
LORD stood by.
6 Then the angel of the LORD spoke very solemnly to Jeshua and said, 7 "This is what
the LORD Almighty says: If you follow my ways and obey my requirements, then you
will be given authority over my Temple and its courtyards. I will let you walk in and out

2:6 Isa 48:20; Jer 3:18; 31:10
2:8 Deut 32:10; Isa 60:7-14
2:11 Mic 4:2
2:12 Deut 32:9; Zech 1:17
2:13 Ps 78:65; Hab 2:20; Zeph 1:7
3:1 Ezra 5:2; Job 1:6-12; Ps 109:6; Hag 1:1; Zech 6:11
3:2 2 Chr 6:6; Amos 4:11; Zech 2:12; Jude 1:23
3:3 Ezra 9:15
3:4 Isa 43:25; 61:10; Zech 3:9
3:7 Deut 17:9; 1 Kgs 3:14; Isa 62:9

2:7 Hebrew *to Zion.* **2:8** Hebrew *harms the apple of my eye.* **2:10** Hebrew *O daughter of Zion.* **3:1a** Hebrew *Joshua,* a variant name for Jeshua; also in 3:3, 4, 6, 8, 9. **3:1b** Or *The Accuser;* Hebrew reads *The Adversary;* also in 3:2.

2:6, 7 Many of the captive Israelites did not return to Jerusalem because they had become accustomed to the security and wealth they had in Babylon. But Zechariah instructed them to leave Babylon quickly. This was an urgent request because Babylon would be destroyed and its decadent culture would cause God's people to forget their spiritual priorities. A vast majority of the Israelites rejected these warnings and remained in Babylon.

2:8 Believers are precious to God (Psalm 116:15); they are his very own children (Psalm 103:13). Treating any believer unkindly is the same as treating God that way. As Jesus told his disciples, when we help others we are helping him; when we neglect or abuse them, we are neglecting or abusing him (Matthew 25:34-46). Be careful, therefore, how you treat fellow believers—that is the way you are treating God.

2:9-12 *Me* (2:9) may refer to the Messiah, who, in the end, will judge all who have oppressed God's people. God promises to live among his people, and he says that many nations will come to know him (John 1:14; Revelation 21:3).

2:11, 12 God did not forget his words to Abraham, "All the families of the earth will be blessed through you" (Genesis 12:3). Abraham, the father of the nation of Israel, was promised that his descendants would bless the whole world. Since the coming of Jesus, the Messiah, this promise is being fulfilled—people from all nations are coming to God through him.

3:1 Jeshua was Israel's high priest when the remnant returned to Jerusalem and began rebuilding the walls (Haggai 1:1, 12; 2:4).

3:1-3 Satan accused Jeshua, who here represents the nation of Israel. The accusations were accurate—Jeshua stood in "filthy" clothes (sins). Yet God revealed his mercy, stating that he chose to save his people in spite of their sin. Satan is always accusing people of their sins before God (Job 1:6). But he greatly misunderstands the breadth of God's mercy and forgiveness toward those who believe in him. Satan the Accuser will ultimately be destroyed (Revelation 12:10), while everyone who is a believer will be saved (John 3:16). To be prepared, we can ask God to remove our clothing of sin and dress us with his goodness.

3:2 God punished Judah through the fire of great trials, but he rescued the nation before it was completely destroyed, like "a burning stick that has been snatched from a fire."

3:2-4 Zechariah's vision graphically portrays how we receive God's mercy. We do nothing ourselves. God removes our filthy clothes (sins), then provides us with fine, new clothes (the righteousness and holiness of God—2 Corinthians 5:21; Ephesians 4:24; Revelation 19:8). All we need to do is repent and ask God to forgive us. When Satan tries to make you feel dirty and unworthy, remember that the clean clothes of Christ's righteousness make you worthy to draw near to God.

3:5-7 The Greek name for Jeshua is Jesus, meaning "the LORD saves." He is seen here as a symbol of Jesus, the Messiah.

3:7-10 There was no priesthood during the Exile, so it had to be reinstated upon the return to the land. In this vision, Jeshua is installed as high priest. One of the high priest's duties was to offer a sacrifice on the Day of Atonement to make amends for all the sins of the people. The priest was the mediator between God and the nation. Thus, he represented the coming Messiah (Isaiah 11:1), who would change the entire order of God's dealing with people's sin (Hebrews 10:8-14 explains this in detail). Jesus, the Messiah, was the High Priest who offered, once for all, the sacrifice of himself to take away our sins. In the new order, every Christian is a priest, offering a holy, cleansed life to God (1 Peter 2:9; Revelation 5:10).

3:8
Isa 4:2; 8:18; 11:1; 53:2
Jer 33:15
Ezek 12:11
Zech 6:12

of my presence along with these others standing here. 8Listen to me, O Jeshua the high
priest, and all you other priests. You are symbols of the good things to come. Soon I am
going to bring my servant, the Branch. 9Now look at the jewel I have set before Jeshua,
a single stone with seven facets.* I will engrave an inscription on it, says the LORD

3:9 Hebrew *7 eyes.*

ZECHARIAH'S VISIONS

Vision	*Reference*	*Significance*
Zechariah sees messengers reporting to God that the surrounding nations that have oppressed Judah are living in careless and sinful ease.	1:7–17	Israel was asking, "Why isn't God punishing the wicked?" Wicked nations may prosper, but not forever. God will bring upon them the judgment they deserve.
Zechariah sees four horns, representing the four world powers that oppressed and scattered the people of Judah and Israel. Then he sees four blacksmiths who will throw down the horns.	1:18–21	God will do what he promised. After the evil nations have carried out his will in punishing his people, God will destroy those nations for their sin.
Zechariah sees a man measuring the city of Jerusalem. The city will one day be full of people, and God himself will be a wall around the city.	2:1–13	The city will be restored in God's future Kingdom. God will keep his promise to protect his people.
Zechariah sees Jeshua the high priest standing before God. Jeshua's filthy clothes are exchanged for fine new clothes; Satan's accusations against him are rejected by God.	3:1–10	The story of Jeshua the high priest pictures how the filthy clothes of sin are replaced with the pure linen of God's righteousness. Christ has taken our clothes of sin and replaced them with God's righteousness. (See Ephesians 4:24; 1 John 1:9.)
Zechariah sees a lampstand that is continually kept burning by an unlimited reservoir of oil. This picture reminds the people that it is only through God's Spirit that they will succeed, not by their own might and resources.	4:1–14	The Spirit of God is given without measure. Human effort does not make a difference. The work of God is not accomplished in human strength.
Zechariah sees a flying scroll, which represents God's curse.	5:1–4	By God's word and Spirit, every person will be judged. The individual's sin is the focus here, not the sins of the nation. Each person is responsible for his or her deeds; no one has an excuse. God's curse is a symbol of destruction; all sin will be judged and removed.
Zechariah sees a vision of a woman in a basket. She represents the wickedness of the nations. The angel packed the woman back into the basket and sent her back to Babylon.	5:5–11	Sins of the individual were judged in the last vision (5:1–4); now sin is being removed from society. Sin has to be eradicated in order to clean up the nation and the individual.
Zechariah sees a vision of four horses and chariots. The horses represent God's judgment on the world—one is sent north, the direction from which most of Judah's enemies came. The other horses are patrolling the world, ready to execute judgment at God's command.	6:1–8	Judgment will come upon those who oppress God's people—it will come in God's time and at his command.

3:8, 9 The "Branch" refers to the Messiah. The meaning of the stone with seven facets is unclear. It could mean (1) the Branch himself as the foundation stone of the Temple, (2) the rock struck by Moses that produced water for the Israelites (Numbers 20:7-11), or (3) the renewed spiritual priesthood of the church (1 Peter 2:5). These verses were fulfilled hundreds of years later by Jesus Christ. God said, "I will remove the sins of this land in a single day," and this was fulfilled in Christ who "died for our sins

Almighty, and I will remove the sins of this land in a single day. 10And on that day, says
the LORD Almighty, each of you will invite your neighbor into your home to share your
peace and prosperity."

A Lampstand and Two Olive Trees

4 Then the angel who had been talking with me returned and woke me, as though I
had been asleep. 2"What do you see now?" he asked.
I answered, "I see a solid gold lampstand with a bowl of oil on top of it. Around the
bowl are seven lamps, each one having seven spouts with wicks. 3And I see two olive
trees, one on each side of the bowl."
4Then I asked the angel, "What are these, my lord? What do they mean?"
5"Don't you know?" the angel asked.
"No, my lord," I replied.
6Then he said to me, "This is what the LORD says to Zerubbabel: It is not by force nor
by strength, but by my Spirit, says the LORD Almighty. 7Nothing, not even a mighty
mountain, will stand in Zerubbabel's way; it will flatten out before him! Then Zerubbabel will set the final stone of the Temple in place, and the people will shout: 'May God
bless it! May God bless it!'"
8Then another message came to me from the LORD: 9"Zerubbabel is the one who laid
the foundation of this Temple, and he will complete it. Then you will know that the LORD
Almighty has sent me. 10Do not despise these small beginnings, for the LORD rejoices to
see the work begin, to see the plumb line in Zerubbabel's hand. For these seven lamps
represent the eyes of the LORD that search all around the world."
11Then I asked the angel, "What are these two olive trees on each side of the
lampstand, 12and what are the two olive branches that pour out golden oil through two
gold tubes?"
13"Don't you know?" he asked.
"No, my lord," I replied.
14Then he said to me, "They represent the two anointed ones who assist the Lord of
all the earth."

A Flying Scroll

5 I looked up again and saw a scroll flying through the air.
2"What do you see?" the angel asked.
"I see a flying scroll," I replied. "It appears to be about thirty feet long and fifteen feet
wide.*"

3:10 1 Kgs 4:25; Isa 36:16; Mic 4:4
4:1 Zech 1:9
4:2 Exod 25:31, 37; Rev 4:5
4:3 Zech 4:11-12, 14; Rev 11:4
4:5 Zech 1:9
4:6 Isa 11:2-4; Hos 1:7; Hag 2:4-5; Eph 6:17
4:7 Ezra 3:11-13; Jer 51:25
4:9 Ezra 3:8-10; 5:16; Zech 6:12-15
4:10 Amos 7:2, 7-8; Hag 2:3; Zech 1:10; 3:9; Rev 8:2
4:14 Exod 29:7; Isa 61:1-3; Dan 9:24-26; Mic 4:13; Zech 3:1-7
5:1 Jer 36:1-6; Ezek 2:9-10

5:2 Hebrew *20 cubits* [9 meters] *long and 10 cubits* [4.5 meters] *wide.*

---

once for all time . . . that he might bring us safely home to God" (1 Peter 3:18). You cannot remove your sins by your own effort. You must allow God to remove them through Christ.

3:10 God promises that each person will have his or her own place of security during Christ's reign (see also Micah 4:4).

4:1-3 The gold lampstand with a bowl and seven lamps on it represents a steady supply of oil, signifying that God's power would be reflected in the light. Oil was obtained from crushed olives and used in bowls with wicks to produce light. The two olive trees stood for the priestly and royal offices.

4:6 Zerubbabel was given the responsibility of rebuilding the Temple in Jerusalem (Ezra 3:2, 8; Haggai 1:1; 2:23). While the prophets Haggai and Zechariah gave the moral and spiritual encouragement to resume work on the Temple, Zerubbabel saw that the task was carried out. As the work was being completed, the prophets encouraged Zerubbabel and told him of a time when spiritual apathy and foreign oppression would forever be abolished.

4:6 Many people believe that to survive in this world a person must be tough, strong, unbending, and harsh. But God says, "Not by force nor by strength, but by my Spirit." The key words are "by my Spirit." It is *only* through God's Spirit that anything of lasting value is accomplished. The returned exiles were indeed weak—harassed by their enemies, tired, discouraged, and poor. But actually they had God on their side! As you live for God, determine not to trust in your own strength or abilities. Instead, depend on God and work in the power of his Spirit! (See also Hosea 1:7.)

4:9 The Temple was completed in 515 B.C. (Ezra 6:14, 15).

4:10 Many of the older Jews were disheartened when they realized this new Temple would not match the size and splendor of the previous Temple built during King Solomon's reign. But bigger and more beautiful is not always better. What you do for God may seem small and insignificant at the time, but God rejoices in what is right, not necessarily in what is big. Be faithful in the small opportunities. Begin where you are and do what you can, and leave the results to God.

4:14 The two anointed ones may be Jeshua and Zerubbabel, dedicated for this special task. Also note that in Revelation 11:3, two witnesses arise to prophesy to the nations during the time of tribulation. These witnesses will be killed but will rise again.

5:1-9 The judgment of the flying scroll was leveled against those who violated God's law, specifically by stealing and lying (5:1-4). The woman in a basket personified wickedness, and so this vision showed that wickedness would be not only severely punished (the vision of the flying scroll) but also banished (the vision of the woman in a basket, 5:6-9).

5:3 Exod 20:15; Jer 26:6; Mal 3:8-9
5:4 Lev 14:34-45; Jer 2:26; Hab 2:9-11; Mal 3:5

3Then he said to me, "This scroll contains the curse that is going out over the entire
land. One side says that those who steal will be banished from the land; the other side
says that those who swear falsely will be banished from the land. 4And this is what the
LORD Almighty says: I am sending this curse into the house of every thief and into the
house of everyone who swears falsely by my name. And my curse will remain in that
house until it is completely destroyed—even its timbers and stones."

5:5 Zech 1:9
5:6 Lev 19:36; Amos 8:5

A Woman in a Basket

5Then the angel who was talking with me came forward and said, "Look up! Something
is appearing in the sky."
6"What is it?" I asked.
He replied, "It is a basket for measuring grain,* and it is filled with the sins* of
everyone throughout the land."

5:8 Hos 12:7; Mic 6:11
5:9 Lev 11:13-19; Ps 104:17; Jer 8:7

7When the heavy lead cover was lifted off the basket, there was a woman sitting inside
it. 8The angel said, "The woman's name is Wickedness," and he pushed her back into
the basket and closed the heavy lid again.
9Then I looked up and saw two women flying toward us, with wings gliding on the
wind. Their wings were like those of a stork, and they picked up the basket and flew with
it into the sky.

5:11 Gen 10:10; Isa 11:11; Dan 1:2

10"Where are they taking the basket?" I asked the angel.
11He replied, "To the land of Babylonia,* where they will build a temple for the
basket. And when the temple is ready, they will set the basket there on its pedestal."

6:1 Zech 1:18; 6:5
6:2 Rev 6:4-5
6:3 Rev 6:2
6:5 Ezek 37:9; Dan 7:2; 11:4; Matt 24:31; Rev 7:1
6:6 Ezek 1:4; Dan 11:5-6, 9, 40
6:8 Ezek 5:13

Four Chariots

6 Then I looked up again and saw four chariots coming from between two bronze
mountains. 2The first chariot was pulled by red horses, the second by black horses,
3the third by white horses, and the fourth by dappled-gray horses. 4"And what are these,
my lord?" I asked the angel who was talking with me.
5He replied, "These are the four spirits* of heaven who stand before the Lord of all
the earth. They are going out to do his work. 6The chariot with black horses is going
north, the chariot with white horses is going west,* and the chariot with dappled-gray
horses is going south."
7The powerful horses were eager to be off, to patrol back and forth across the earth.
And the LORD said, "Go and patrol the earth!" So they left at once on their patrol.
8Then the LORD summoned me and said, "Those who went north have vented the
anger of my Spirit* there."

2. Zechariah's words of encouragement

6:9 Zech 1:1; 7:1; 8:1
6:10 Ezra 7:14-16; 8:26-30

The Crowning of Jeshua

9Then I received another message from the LORD: 10"Heldai, Tobijah, and Jedaiah will
bring gifts of silver and gold from the Jews exiled in Babylon. As soon as they arrive,
meet them at the home of Josiah son of Zephaniah. 11Accept their gifts and make a

5:6a Hebrew *an ephah,* about half a bushel or 18 liters; also in 5:7, 8, 9, 10, 11. **5:6b** As in Greek version; Hebrew reads *the appearance.* **5:11** Hebrew *the land of Shinar.* **6:5** Or *the four winds.* **6:6** Hebrew *is going after them.* **6:8** Hebrew *have given my Spirit rest.*

5:9-11 The woman in a basket was carried away "to the land of Babylonia," which had become a symbol for the center of world idolatry and wickedness. This woman was a picture to Zechariah that wickedness and sin would be taken away from Israel and one day sin would be removed from the entire earth. When Christ died, he removed sin's power and penalty. When we trust Christ to forgive us, he removes the penalty of sin and gives us the power to overcome sin in our life. When Christ returns, he will remove all sin from the earth, allowing people to live in eternal safety and security.

6:1-8 The four chariots were similar to the four horsemen in the first vision. These chariots represent the four angels of God's judgment on the earth.

6:6, 8 The black horses that went north executed God's judgment in the north country. God is angry with sin and with the wicked (Psalm 7:11), and his anger is expressed in judgment. As much as we like to concentrate on God's love and mercy, anger and judgment are also part of his righteous character. If you have unconfessed or habitual sin in your life, confess it and turn away from it. Confession releases God's mercy, but refusing to repent invites his judgment.

6:9-15 This vision is about the Messiah, the King-Priest. In the days of the kings and after the Exile, Judah's government was to be ruled by two distinct persons—the king, ruling the nation's political life, and the high priest, ruling its religious life. Kings and priests had often been corrupt. God was telling Zechariah that someone worthy of the crown would come to rule as both king ("rule as king from his throne") and priest ("as priest from his throne"). This was an unlikely combination for that day.

crown* from the silver and gold. Then put the crown on the head of Jeshua* son of
Jehozadak, the high priest. 12 Tell him that the LORD Almighty says: Here is the man
called the Branch. He will branch out where he is and build the Temple of the LORD. 13 He
will build the LORD's Temple, and he will receive royal honor and will rule as king from
his throne. He will also serve as priest from his throne,* and there will be perfect
harmony between the two.
14 "The crown will be a memorial in the Temple of the LORD to honor those who gave
it—Heldai,* Tobijah, Jedaiah, and Josiah* son of Zephaniah."
15 Many will come from distant lands to rebuild the Temple of the LORD. And when
this happens, you will know my messages have been from the LORD Almighty. All this
will happen if you carefully obey the commands of the LORD your God.

A Call to Justice and Mercy

7 On December 7* of the fourth year of King Darius's reign, another message came
to Zechariah from the LORD. 2 The people of Bethel had sent Sharezer and Regemmelech,* along with their men, to seek the LORD's favor. 3 They were to ask this question
of the prophets and of the priests at the Temple of the LORD Almighty: "Should we
continue to mourn and fast each summer on the anniversary of the Temple's destruction,*
as we have done for so many years?"
4 The LORD Almighty sent me this message: 5 "Say to all your people and your priests,
'During those seventy years of exile, when you fasted and mourned in the summer and
at the festival in early autumn,* was it really for me that you were fasting? 6 And even
now in your holy festivals, you don't think about me but only of pleasing yourselves.
7 Isn't this the same message the LORD proclaimed through the prophets years ago when
Jerusalem and the towns of Judah were bustling with people, and the Negev and the
foothills of Judah* were populated areas?'"
8 Then this message came to Zechariah from the LORD: 9 "This is what the LORD
Almighty says: Judge fairly and honestly, and show mercy and kindness to one another.
10 Do not oppress widows, orphans, foreigners, and poor people. And do not make evil
plans to harm each other.
11 "Your ancestors would not listen to this message. They turned stubbornly away and
put their fingers in their ears to keep from hearing. 12 They made their hearts as hard as
stone, so they could not hear the law or the messages that the LORD Almighty had sent
them by his Spirit through the earlier prophets. That is why the LORD Almighty was so
angry with them.
13 "Since they refused to listen when I called to them, I would not listen when they

6:12 Isa 4:2-3; 11:1; Jer 23:5-6; Zech 3:8; 4:6-9
6:13 Ps 110:4; Isa 9:6; 11:10
6:15 Isa 56:6-8; 60:10; Zech 3:7
7:2 Jer 26:19; Zech 8:21
7:3 Ezra 3:10-12
7:5 Isa 58:5; Zech 1:12; Matt 5:16-18; 6:2, 5, 16; 23:5
7:7 Jer 17:26; 22:21; Zech 1:4
7:9 Mic 6:8; Zech 8:16
7:10 Exod 22:22; Deut 24:14-18; Prov 22:22-23; Zech 8:17
7:11 Ps 58:4-5; Jer 8:5; Acts 7:57
7:12 Neh 9:30; Jer 17:1; Ezek 3:9; Dan 9:11-12
7:13 Prov 1:24-28; Isa 1:15; Jer 11:10-14

6:11a As in Greek and Syriac versions; Hebrew reads *crowns.* **6:11b** Hebrew *Joshua,* a variant name for Jeshua. **6:13** Or *There will be a priest by his throne.* **6:14a** As in Syriac version (compare 6:10); Hebrew reads *Helem.* **6:14b** As in Syriac version (compare 6:10); Hebrew reads *Hen.* **7:1** Hebrew *On the fourth day of the ninth month, the month of Kislev,* of the Hebrew calendar. This event occurred on December 7, 518 B.C.; also see note on 1:1. **7:2** Or *Bethel-sharezer had sent Regemmelech.* **7:3** Hebrew *mourn and fast in the fifth month.* This month of the Hebrew lunar calendar usually occurs in July and August. **7:5** Hebrew *fasted and mourned in the fifth and seventh months.* The fifth month of the Hebrew lunar calendar usually occurs in July and August. The seventh month usually occurs in September and October; both the Day of Atonement and the Festival of Shelters were celebrated in the seventh month. **7:7** Hebrew *the Shephelah.*

6:15 Some of God's promises are conditional—we must obey him to receive them. The rebuilding of the Temple required careful obedience. God would protect the people as long as they obeyed. Casual or occasional obedience, the result of a half-hearted or divided commitment, would not lead to blessing. Many of God's blessings come to us as a result of diligent obedience. Inconsistent obedience can't produce consistent blessing.

7:1ff The fourth year of King Darius's reign was 518 B.C. For the previous 70 years, the people had been holding a fast in August to remember the destruction of Jerusalem. Because Jerusalem was being rebuilt, they came to the Temple to ask if they had to continue this annual fast. God did not answer their question directly. Instead, he told them that their acts of justice and mercy were more important than their fasting. What he wanted from his people was true justice in their dealings and mercy and compassion for the weak.

7:5-7 The Israelites had lost their sincere desire for a loving relationship with God. Zechariah told them that they had been fasting without a proper attitude of repentance or worship. They fasted and mourned during their exile with no thought of God or their sins that had caused it in the first place. When you go to church, pray, or have fellowship with other believers, are you doing these things from habit or for what you can get out of them? God says that an attitude of worship without a sincere desire to know and love him will lead to ruin.

7:7 The Negev was the southern part of Judah.

7:11, 12 Zechariah explained to the people that their ancestors brought God's great wrath on themselves by hardening their hearts. Any sin seems more natural the second time—as we become hardened, each repetition is easier. Ignoring or refusing God's warning hardens you each time you do wrong. Read God's Word and apply it to your life. Sensitivity and submission to God's Word can soften your heart and allow you to live as you should.

7:14 Deut 28:64; Jer 12:10; 23:19; 44:6
8:3 Zech 2:10
8:4 Isa 65:20-22
8:5 Jer 30:19-20
8:6 Ps 118:23; Jer 32:17, 27
8:7 Ps 107:2-3; Isa 11:11; 43:5; Amos 9:14-15
8:8 Ezek 37:28; Zech 2:11; 10:10
8:9 Ezra 5:1; 6:14; Hag 2:4
8:10 Isa 19:2; Amos 3:6; 9:4; Hag 1:6-11; 2:16-19
8:11 Isa 12:1
8:12 Gen 27:28
8:13 Ps 72:17; Jer 29:18; Dan 9:11; Zech 14:11
8:14 Jer 4:28; 29:11-14; Ezek 24:14
8:15 Jer 29:11
8:16 †Eph 4:25
8:17 Zech 5:3-4; 7:10; Mal 3:5

called to me, says the LORD Almighty. 14I scattered them as with a whirlwind among the distant nations, where they lived as strangers. Their land became so desolate that no one even traveled through it. The land that had been so pleasant became a desert."

Promised Blessings for Jerusalem

8 Then another message came to me from the LORD Almighty: 2"This is what the LORD Almighty says: My love for Mount Zion is passionate and strong; I am consumed with passion for Jerusalem! 3And now the LORD says: I am returning to Mount Zion, and I will live in Jerusalem. Then Jerusalem will be called the Faithful City; the mountain of the LORD Almighty will be called the Holy Mountain. 4This is what the LORD Almighty says: Once again old men and women will walk Jerusalem's streets with a cane and sit together in the city squares. 5And the streets of the city will be filled with boys and girls at play.

6"This is what the LORD Almighty says: All this may seem impossible to you now, a small and discouraged remnant of God's people. But do you think this is impossible for me, the LORD Almighty? 7This is what the LORD Almighty says: You can be sure that I will rescue my people from the east and from the west. 8I will bring them home again to live safely in Jerusalem. They will be my people, and I will be faithful and just toward them as their God.

9"This is what the LORD Almighty says: Take heart and finish the task! You have heard what the prophets have been saying about building the Temple of the LORD Almighty ever since the foundation was laid. 10Before the work on the Temple began, there were no jobs and no wages for either people or animals. No traveler was safe from the enemy, for there were enemies on all sides. I had turned everyone against each other. 11But now I will not treat the remnant of my people as I treated them before, says the LORD Almighty. 12For I am planting seeds of peace and prosperity among you. The grapevines will be heavy with fruit. The earth will produce its crops, and the sky will release the dew. Once more I will make the remnant in Judah and Israel the heirs of these blessings. 13Among the nations, Judah and Israel had become symbols of what it means to be cursed. But no longer! Now I will rescue you and make you both a symbol and a source of blessing! So don't be afraid or discouraged, but instead get on with rebuilding the Temple!

14"For this is what the LORD Almighty says: I did not change my mind when your ancestors angered me and I promised to punish them, says the LORD Almighty. 15Neither will I change my decision to bless Jerusalem and the people of Judah. So don't be afraid. 16But this is what you must do: Tell the truth to each other. Render verdicts in your courts that are just and that lead to peace. 17Do not make evil plots to harm each other. And stop this habit of swearing to things that are false. I hate all these things, says the LORD."

8:3 One day Christ will reign in his Kingdom on earth. There all his people will live with him. This truth should encourage us to look forward to the Messiah's reign.

8:4, 5 In troubled times, the very old and very young are the first to suffer and die. But both groups are plentiful in this vision, filling the streets with their normal everyday activities. This is a sign of the complete peace and prosperity of God's new earth.

8:6 The remnant was the small group of exiles who had returned from Babylon to rebuild Jerusalem and the Temple. Struggling to survive in the land, they became discouraged over the opposition they often faced from hostile neighbors. It was hard to believe that one day God himself would reign from this city and that their land would enjoy great peace and prosperity. Our God is all-powerful; he can do anything! When confronting seemingly impossible tasks or situations, remember that "with God everything is possible" (Matthew 19:26).

8:8 The covenant relationship will be renewed, and the whole community will be filled with the presence of God. This promise of forgiveness and restoration extends to all God's people wherever they may be found. (For other references to this promise, see Exodus 6:6, 7; 19:5, 6; 29:45; Leviticus 26:12; Deuteronomy 7:6; Jeremiah 31:1, 33.)

8:9 God had to give the Temple workers a little push to get them moving. They had heard the prophets' words of encouragement; at this time they needed to stop just listening and get to work. We need to listen to what God says, but after he has made our course of action plain, we need to "take heart" and do what he wants.

8:13-15 For more than 15 years, God and his prophets had been urging the people to finish building the Temple. Here again, God encouraged them with visions of the future. We may be tempted to slow down for many reasons: People aren't responding; we feel physically or emotionally drained; the workers are uncooperative; the work is distasteful, too difficult, or not worth the effort. God's promises about the future should encourage us *now.* He knows what the results of our labors will be, and thus he can give us a perspective that will help us continue in our work for him.

8:14-17 God promised to give his people rich rewards, reassuring them that despite the punishments they had endured, he would not change his mind to bless them. But he also said they had a job to do: "This is what you must do." God will be faithful, but we also have responsibilities: to tell the truth, exercise justice, and live peacefully. If you expect God to do his part, be sure to do yours.

[18]Here is another message that came to me from the LORD Almighty. [19]"This is
what the LORD Almighty says: The traditional fasts and times of mourning you have
kept in early summer, midsummer, autumn, and winter* are now ended. They will
become festivals of joy and celebration for the people of Judah. So love truth and
peace.
[20]"This is what the LORD Almighty says: People from nations and cities around the
world will travel to Jerusalem. [21]The people of one city will say to the people in
another, 'Let us go to Jerusalem to ask the LORD to bless us and to seek the LORD
Almighty. We are planning to go ourselves.' [22]People from many nations, even
powerful nations, will come to Jerusalem to seek the LORD Almighty and to ask the
LORD to bless them.
[23]"This is what the LORD Almighty says: In those days ten people from nations and
languages around the world will clutch at the hem of one Jew's robe. And they will say,
'Please let us walk with you, for we have heard that God is with you.'"

8:19 Isa 12:1; Jer 39:2; Zech 7:3-5; 8:16; Luke 1:74-75
8:20 Zech 2:11; 14:16
8:22 Isa 49:6, 22-23; 60:3-12
8:23 Isa 45:14; 60:14

B. MESSAGES AFTER COMPLETING THE TEMPLE (9:1—14:21)

After the Temple was completed, Zechariah gave several prophecies about Israel's future, which describe the first and second comings of Jesus Christ. This book contains more about the person, work, and glory of Christ than the other minor prophets combined. Israel's King would come, but he would be rejected by his people. They would later repent and be restored to God. The King who is coming is our king. May we be found faithful and pure in his sight when we meet him face to face.

Judgment against Israel's Enemies

9 This is the message* from the LORD against the land of Aram* and the city of
Damascus, for the eyes of all humanity, including the people of Israel, are on the
LORD. [2]Doom is certain for Hamath, near Damascus, and for the cities of Tyre and Sidon,
too, though they are so clever. [3]Tyre has built a strong fortress and has piled up so much
silver and gold that it is as common as dust in the streets! [4]But now the Lord will strip
away Tyre's possessions and hurl its fortifications into the Mediterranean Sea.* Tyre will
be set on fire and burned to the ground.
[5]The city of Ashkelon will see Tyre fall and will be filled with fear. Gaza will shake
with terror, and so will Ekron, for their hopes will be dashed. Gaza will be conquered
and its king killed, and Ashkelon will be completely deserted. [6]Foreigners will occupy
the city of Ashdod. Thus, I will destroy the pride of the Philistines. [7]They will no longer
eat meat with blood in it or feed on other forbidden foods. All the surviving Philistines
will worship our God and be adopted as a new clan in Judah.* And the Philistines of
Ekron will join my people, just as the Jebusites once did. [8]I will guard my Temple and
protect it from invading armies. I am closely watching their movements. No foreign
oppressor will ever again overrun my people's land.

9:1 Amos 1:3-5
9:2 Jer 49:23; Ezek 12:21-26; 28:3-5
9:3 Josh 19:29; Ezek 27:33
9:4 Isa 23:1-7; Ezek 28:16, 18
9:8 Isa 52:1; 54:14

8:19 Hebrew *in the fourth, fifth, seventh, and tenth months.* The fourth month of the Hebrew lunar calendar usually occurs in June and July. The fifth month usually occurs in July and August. The seventh month usually occurs in September and October. The tenth month usually occurs in December and January. **9:1a** Hebrew *An Oracle: The message.* **9:1b** Hebrew *land of Hadrach.* **9:4** Hebrew *the sea.* **9:7** Hebrew *and will become a leader in Judah.*

8:19-22 There will come a time when fasting for sins will be replaced by feasting and joy. People from all nations will "seek the LORD Almighty." This was also promised in 2:11.

8:23 In the past, Jerusalem had often borne the brunt of cruel jokes from other nations (8:13). The city was not respected; its citizens had sinned so much that God let them be kicked around by their enemies. But eventually, says Zechariah, Jerusalem will be a holy place—highly respected throughout the world because its people will have a change of heart toward God. People from other nations will see how God has rewarded his people for their faithfulness and want to be included in their great blessings.

9:1-17 The last six chapters of the book are two messages delivered late in Zechariah's life. These messages point to the Messiah and his second coming. Some of these prophecies were fulfilled before the Messiah came, perhaps by Alexander the Great; others were fulfilled during the Messiah's time on earth; and others will be fulfilled when he returns. Those who oppressed Jerusalem—Aram, Philistia, Phoenicia—would be crushed. Zion's promised King would come—first as a servant on a donkey's colt, later as a powerful ruler and judge.

9:5-7 Zechariah mentions four key cities in Philistia: Ashkelon, Gaza, and Ekron would be destroyed, and Ashdod would be overtaken by foreigners. This would happen because of their great evil and idolatry. But those left in the land would be adopted into Israel as a new clan, as the Jebusites were. (When David conquered Jerusalem, he did not wipe out the Jebusites, but absorbed them into Judah.)

9:8 Several centuries after Zechariah's day, Antiochus IV Epiphanes would invade Israel; and in A.D. 70, Titus, a Roman general, would completely destroy the Temple. This promise, therefore, may have been conditional upon the people's obedience. The day will come, however, when God's people will never again have to worry about invading enemies (Joel 3:17).

9:9
Ps 97:6-8
Isa 9:6-7; 57:15
Jer 23:5-6
Zeph 3:5
Zech 2:10
†Matt 21:5
†John 12:15

9:10
Ps 72:17
Isa 57:18-19
Mic 4:2-10; 5:4

9:11
Exod 24:8
Heb 10:29

9:12
Isa 61:7
Joel 3:16

9:13
Ps 45:3
Jer 51:20
Joel 3:6-8

9:14
Ps 18:14
Isa 27:13; 31:5

9:15
Zech 12:6

9:16
Isa 62:3

Zion's Coming King

9 Rejoice greatly, O people* of Zion! Shout in triumph, O people of Jerusalem! Look, your king is coming to you. He is righteous and victorious, yet he is humble, riding on a donkey—even on a donkey's colt. 10 I will remove the battle chariots from Israel* and the warhorses from Jerusalem, and I will destroy all the weapons used in battle. Your king will bring peace to the nations. His realm will stretch from sea to sea and from the Euphrates River* to the ends of the earth.*

11 Because of the covenant I made with you, sealed with blood, I will free your prisoners from death in a waterless dungeon. 12 Come back to the place of safety, all you prisoners, for there is yet hope! I promise this very day that I will repay you two mercies for each of your woes! 13 Judah is my bow, and Israel is my arrow! Jerusalem* is my sword, and like a warrior, I will brandish it against the Greeks.*

14 The LORD will appear above his people; his arrows will fly like lightning! The Sovereign LORD will sound the trumpet; he will go out against his enemies like a whirlwind from the southern desert. 15 The LORD Almighty will protect his people, and they will subdue their enemies with sling stones. They will shout in battle as though drunk with wine, shedding the blood of their enemies. They will be filled with blood like a bowl, drenched with blood like the corners of the altar.

16 When that day arrives, the LORD their God will rescue his people, just as a shepherd rescues his sheep. They will sparkle in his land like jewels in a crown. 17 How wonderful and beautiful they will be! The young men and women will thrive on the abundance of grain and new wine.

10:1
Jer 10:13
Hos 6:3
Joel 2:23-24

10:2
Ezek 34:5, 8
Mic 3:6-11
†Matt 9:36
†Mark 6:34

10:3
Ezek 34:2, 7, 12

10:4
Zech 9:10

10:5
2 Sam 22:43

The LORD Will Restore His People

10 Ask the LORD for rain in the spring, and he will give it. It is the LORD who makes storm clouds that drop showers of rain so that every field becomes a lush pasture. 2 Household gods give false advice, fortune-tellers predict only lies, and interpreters of dreams pronounce comfortless falsehoods. So my people are wandering like lost sheep, without a shepherd to protect and guide them.

3 "My anger burns against your shepherds, and I will punish these leaders.* For the LORD Almighty has arrived to look after his flock of Judah; he will make them strong and glorious, like a proud warhorse in battle. 4 From Judah will come the cornerstone, the tent peg, the battle bow, and all the rulers. 5 They will be like mighty warriors in battle, trampling their enemies in the mud under their feet. Since the LORD is with them as they fight, they will overthrow even the horsemen of the enemy.

9:9 Hebrew *daughter.* **9:10a** Hebrew *from Ephraim;* also in 9:13. **9:10b** Hebrew *the river.* **9:10c** Or *the end of the land.* **9:13a** Hebrew *Zion.* **9:13b** Hebrew *the sons of Javan.* **10:3** Or *these male goats.*

9:9 The triumphal entry of Jesus riding into Jerusalem (Matthew 21:1-11) was predicted here more than 500 years before it happened. Just as this prophecy was fulfilled when Jesus came to earth, so the prophecies of his second coming are just as certain to come true. We are to be ready for his return, for he is coming!

9:10 "Israel" refers to the northern kingdom. When we view two distant mountains, they appear to be close together, perhaps even to touch each other. But as we approach them, we can see that they are, in fact, far apart, even separated by a huge valley. This is the situation with many Old Testament prophecies. Verse 9 was clearly fulfilled in Christ's first coming, but verse 10 can now be seen to refer to his second coming. At that time all nations will be subject to Christ, and his rule will extend over the whole earth. In Philippians 2:9-11, we are told that at that time every knee will bow to Christ and every tongue will confess him as Lord.

9:11 Covenants in Old Testament times were sealed or confirmed with blood, much as we would sign our name to a contract. The old covenant was sealed by the blood of sacrifices, pointing ahead to the blood Christ would shed at Calvary, his "signature" that confirmed God's new covenant with his people. Because God had made a covenant with these people, he delivered them from the "waterless dungeon," the cisternlike prison of exile.

9:14-17 After Solomon's reign, the kingdom was divided into the northern kingdom (called Israel or Ephraim) and the southern kingdom (called Judah, with Jerusalem as the capital). This prophecy says that all Israel, north and south, will someday be reunited. The first part of this chapter tells how God will help his people avoid war; here God explains that he will come to help his people when war is inevitable. Verses 14-16 explain how the Jews will win over the Greeks, but it is also a figurative picture of the ultimate future victory over evil by God's people.

10:2 We often create idols of money, power, fame, or success, and then we expect them to give us happiness and security. But these idols can't supply what we need any more than a stone image can make it rain. How foolish it is to trust in idols. Instead, trust God's promises for your future.

10:4 Zechariah's prophecy, more than 500 years before Christ's first coming, called Christ the "cornerstone" (see also Isaiah 28:16), the "tent peg" (Isaiah 22:23), the "battle bow," and a ruler who was a man of action (see also Genesis 49:10; Micah 5:2). This Messiah would be strong, stable, victorious, and trustworthy—in all ways, the answer to Israel's problems. Only in the Messiah will all the promises to God's people be fulfilled.

6“I will strengthen Judah and save Israel*; I will reestablish them because I love
them. It will be as though I had never rejected them, for I am the LORD their God, who
will hear their cries. 7The people of Israel* will become like mighty warriors, and
their hearts will be happy as if by wine. Their children, too, will see it all and be glad;
their hearts will rejoice in the LORD. 8When I whistle to them, they will come
running, for I have redeemed them. From the few that are left, their population
will grow again to its former size. 9Though I have scattered them like seeds among
the nations, still they will remember me in distant lands. With their children, they will
survive and come home again to Israel. 10I will bring them back from Egypt and
Assyria and resettle them in Gilead and Lebanon. There won't be enough room for
them all! 11They will pass safely through the sea of distress,* for the waves of the sea
will be held back. And the waters of the Nile will become dry. The pride of Assyria
will be crushed, and the rule of Egypt will end. 12I will make my people strong in my
power, and they will go wherever they wish by my authority. I, the LORD, have
spoken!”

10:6 Isa 54:8
10:7 Isa 54:13
10:8 Isa 5:26; 7:18-19 Jer 33:22 Ezek 36:11
10:9 1 Kgs 8:47-48 Ezek 6:9
10:10 Isa 11:11-16; 49:19-21
10:11 Isa 19:5-7 Ezek 30:13 Zeph 2:13
10:12 Mic 4:5

11 Open your doors, Lebanon, so that fire may sweep through your cedar forests.
2Weep, you cypress trees, for all the ruined cedars; the tallest and most beautiful
of them are fallen. Weep, you oaks of Bashan, as you watch the thickest forests being
felled. 3Listen to the wailing of the shepherds, for their wealth is gone. Hear the young
lions roaring, for their thickets in the Jordan Valley have been destroyed.

11:1 Jer 22:6-7 Ezek 31:3
11:3 Jer 2:15; 25:34-36; 50:44

The Good and Evil Shepherds

4This is what the LORD my God says: “Go and care for a flock that is intended for
slaughter. 5The buyers will slaughter their sheep without remorse. The sellers will say,
‘Praise the LORD, I am now rich!’ Even the shepherds have no compassion for them.
6And likewise, I will no longer have pity on the inhabitants of the land,” says the LORD.
“I will let them fall into each other's clutches, as well as into the clutches of their king.
They will turn the land into a wilderness, and I will not protect them.”
7So I cared for the flock intended for slaughter—the flock that was oppressed. Then
I took two shepherd's staffs and named one Favor and the other Union. 8I got rid of their
three evil shepherds in a single month. But I became impatient with these sheep—this
nation—and they hated me, too. 9So I told them, “I won't be your shepherd any longer.
If you die, you die. If you are killed, you are killed. And those who remain will devour
each other!”
10Then I took my staff called Favor and snapped it in two, showing that I had revoked
the covenant I had made with all the nations. 11That was the end of my covenant with
them. Those who bought and sold sheep were watching me, and they knew that the LORD

11:5 Jer 50:7 Ezek 34:2-6 Hos 12:8 1 Tim 6:9
11:6 Isa 9:19-21 Jer 13:14 Zech 8:10; 14:13
11:7 Pss 27:4; 90:17; 133:1 Ezek 37:16-23
11:8 Hos 5:7
11:9 Ps 69:22-28 Jer 15:2-3
11:10 Jer 14:21

10:6 Hebrew *save the house of Joseph.* **10:7** Hebrew *of Ephraim.* **10:11** Or *the sea of Egypt,* referring to the Red Sea.

10:6 Judah refers to the southern kingdom, and Israel refers to the northern kingdom. One day God will unite all his people. This verse tells about God's reuniting of the Jews (see also Jeremiah 31:10). This was a startling idea. The people of the northern kingdom of Israel were so completely absorbed into other cultures after their captivity in 722 B.C. that a regathering could only be accomplished by God.

10:6, 12 God promises to strengthen his people. When we stay closely connected to God, his Spirit will enable us to do his will, despite the obstacles. When we stray away from God, we will be cut off from our power source.

10:10 This pictured return from Egypt and Assyria was a symbolic way of saying that the people would be returned from all the countries where they had been dispersed. Egypt and Assyria evoked memories of slavery and separation.

10:11 The “sea of distress” refers to the Red Sea, through which the Israelites were miraculously delivered from Egypt. As the Israelites returned once again from Egypt and other lands, they would be protected by God's miraculous power.

11:4-17 In this message, God told Zechariah to act out the roles of two different kinds of shepherds. The first type of shepherd demonstrated how God would reject his people (the sheep) because they rejected him (11:4-14). The second type of shepherd demonstrated how God would let his people fall into the clutches of evil shepherds (11:15-17). (See Ezekiel 34 for a detailed portrayal of the evil shepherds of Israel.)

11:4 God told Zechariah to take a job as shepherd of a flock of sheep being fattened for slaughter. The Messiah would shepherd God's people during a time of spiritual and political confusion. The flock represented the people feeding on their own greed and evil desires until they were ripe for God's judgment.

11:7 Zechariah took two shepherd's staffs and named them “Favor” and “Union.” He broke the first one (“Favor”) to show that God's gracious covenant with his people was broken. He broke the second one (“Union”) to show that “the bond of unity between Judah and Israel was broken” (11:14).

11:8 The identity of the three evil shepherds is not known. But God knew they were unfit to shepherd his people, and so he removed them.

11:12-13 †Matt 27:9-10; Acts 1:18-19
11:14 Zech 11:6
11:15 Zech 11:17
11:16 Jer 23:2, 22; Ezek 34:2-6
11:17 Zech 10:2; 11:15

was speaking to them through my actions. 12And I said to them, "If you like, give me
my wages, whatever I am worth; but only if you want to." So they counted out for my
wages thirty pieces* of silver.
13And the LORD said to me, "Throw it to the potters*"—this magnificent sum at which
they valued me! So I took the thirty coins and threw them to the potters in the Temple of
the LORD. 14Then I broke my other staff, Union, to show that the bond of unity between
Judah and Israel was broken.
15Then the LORD said to me, "Go again and play the part of a worthless shepherd.
16This will illustrate how I will give this nation a shepherd who will not care for the sheep
that are threatened by death, nor look after the young, nor heal the injured, nor feed the
healthy. Instead, this shepherd will eat the meat of the fattest sheep and tear off their
hooves. 17Doom is certain for this worthless shepherd who abandons the flock! The
sword will cut his arm and pierce his right eye! His arm will become useless, and his
right eye completely blind!"

Future Deliverance for Jerusalem

12:1 Job 26:7; Pss 102:23, 26; Isa 57:16; Jer 51:15; Heb 1:10-12; 12:9
12:2 Ps 75:8; Isa 51:17, 22-23
12:3 Dan 2:34-35, 44-45; Matt 21:44
12:6 Isa 10:16-18; Obad 1:18
12:7 Amos 9:11
12:8 Exod 14:19; Lev 26:8; Pss 8:6; 82:6; Mic 7:8; Zech 9:14-15

12 This* message concerning the fate of Israel came from the LORD: "This message
is from the LORD, who stretched out the heavens, laid the foundations of the earth,
and formed the spirit within humans. 2I will make Jerusalem and Judah like an intoxicating drink to all the nearby nations that send their armies to besiege Jerusalem. 3On
that day I will make Jerusalem a heavy stone, a burden for the world. None of the nations
who try to lift it will escape unscathed.
4"On that day, says the LORD, I will cause every horse to panic and every rider to lose
his nerve. I will watch over the people of Judah, but I will blind the horses of her enemies.
5And the clans of Judah will say to themselves, 'The people of Jerusalem have found
strength in the LORD Almighty, their God.'
6"On that day I will make the clans of Judah like a brazier that sets a woodpile ablaze
or like a burning torch among sheaves of grain. They will burn up all the neighboring
nations right and left, while the people living in Jerusalem remain secure. 7The LORD
will give victory to the rest of Judah first, before Jerusalem, so that the people of
Jerusalem and the royal line of David will not have greater honor than the rest of Judah.
8On that day the LORD will defend the people of Jerusalem; the weakest among them
will be as mighty as King David! And the royal descendants will be like God, like the
angel of the LORD who goes before them! 9For my plan is to destroy all the nations that
come against Jerusalem.

11:12 Hebrew *30 shekels,* about 12 ounces or 342 grams in weight. **11:13** Syriac version reads *into the treasury;* also in 11:13b. **12:1** Hebrew *An Oracle: This.*

11:12 To pay this shepherd 30 pieces of silver was an insult—this was the price paid to an owner for a slave gored by an ox (Exodus 21:32). This is also the amount Judas received for betraying Jesus (Matthew 27:3-10). The priceless Messiah was sold for the price of a slave.

11:13 Potters were in the lowest social class. "This magnificent sum" (a sarcastic comment) was so little that it could be thrown to the potters. It is significant that the 30 pieces of silver paid to Judas for betraying Jesus were returned to the Temple and used to buy a potter's field (Matthew 27:3-10).

11:14 Because the people had rejected the Messiah, God would reject them—symbolized by Zechariah breaking the staff called "Union." Not long after Zechariah's time, the Jews began to divide into numerous factions: Pharisees, Sadducees, Essenes, Herodians, and Zealots. The discord among these groups was a key factor leading to the destruction of Jerusalem in A.D. 70.

11:15-17 Israel would not only reject the true shepherd; it would accept instead a worthless shepherd. This shepherd would serve his own concerns rather than the concerns of his flock and would destroy rather than defend them. Condemnation is his rightful fate because he trusted his arm (military might) and his right eye (intellect). God would destroy both areas.

11:17 It is a great tragedy for God's people when their leaders fail to care for them adequately. God holds leaders particularly accountable for the condition of his people. The New Testament tells church leaders, "Not many of you should become teachers in the church, for we who teach will be judged by God with greater strictness" (James 3:1). If God puts you in a position of leadership, remember that it is also a place of great responsibility.

12:1-14 This chapter pictures the final siege against the people of Jerusalem.

12:3, 4 This speaks of a great future battle against Jerusalem. Some say it is Armageddon, the last great battle on earth. Those who oppose God's people will not prevail forever. Eventually, evil, pain, and oppression will be abolished once and for all.

12:7 As water flows downhill, so a city's influence usually flows to its surrounding countryside. But this time, the countryside of Judah would have priority over Jerusalem so that the people of Jerusalem would not become proud. Don't think that you must witness to only "important" people—professional athletes, movie stars, and prominent businesspeople. Christ came to seek and save the lost (Luke 19:10), even the "down-and-out" lost. We must be careful to avoid spiritual pride, or we, like Jerusalem, may be the last to know what God is doing.

10 “Then I will pour out a spirit of grace and prayer on the family of David and on all
the people of Jerusalem. They will look on me whom they have pierced and mourn for
him as for an only son. They will grieve bitterly for him as for a firstborn son who has
died. 11 The sorrow and mourning in Jerusalem on that day will be like the grievous
mourning of Hadad-rimmon in the valley of Megiddo.
12 “All Israel will weep in profound sorrow, each family by itself, with the husbands
and wives in separate groups. The family of David will mourn, along with the family of
Nathan, 13 the family of Levi, and the family of Shimei. 14 Each of the surviving families
from Judah will mourn separately, husbands and wives apart.

A Fountain of Cleansing

13 “On that day a fountain will be opened for the dynasty of David and for the people
of Jerusalem, a fountain to cleanse them from all their sins and defilement.
2 “And on that day, says the LORD Almighty, I will get rid of every trace of idol worship
throughout the land, so that even the names of the idols will be forgotten. I will remove
from the land all false prophets and the unclean spirits that inspire them. 3 If anyone
begins prophesying again, his own father and mother will tell him, ‘You must die, for
you have prophesied lies in the name of the LORD.’ Then his own father and mother will
stab him.
4 “No one will be boasting then of a prophetic gift! No one will wear prophet’s clothes
to try to fool the people. 5 ‘No,’ he will say. ‘I’m not a prophet; I’m a farmer. The soil has
been my means of livelihood from my earliest youth.’ 6 And if someone asks, ‘Then what
are those scars on your chest*?’ he will say, ‘I was wounded at the home of friends!’

The Scattering of the Sheep

7 “Awake, O sword, against my shepherd, the man who is my partner, says the LORD
Almighty. Strike down the shepherd, and the sheep will be scattered, and I will turn
against the lambs. 8 Two-thirds of the people in the land will be cut off and die, says the
LORD. But a third will be left in the land. 9 I will bring that group through the fire and
make them pure, just as gold and silver are refined and purified by fire. They will call on
my name, and I will answer them. I will say, ‘These are my people,’ and they will say,
‘The LORD is our God.’ ”

12:10 Joel 2:28-29; John 19:34-37; Rev 1:7
12:11 Matt 24:30
13:1 Num 19:9-22
13:2 Exod 23:13; 1 Kgs 22:22
13:3 Deut 13:6-11; Jer 23:25
13:4 2 Kgs 1:8; Isa 20:2; Jer 6:15; 8:9; Matt 3:4
13:5 Amos 7:14
13:6 2 Kgs 9:24
13:7 Isa 40:11; 53:4-5; †Matt 26:31; †Mark 14:27
13:8 Zech 11:6-9
13:9 Isa 48:10; Hos 2:23; Zech 12:10

13:6 Or *scars between your hands.*

12:10 The Holy Spirit was poured out at Pentecost, 50 days after Christ’s resurrection (see Acts 2). Zechariah calls the Spirit “a spirit of grace and prayer.” It is this Spirit who convicts us of sin, reveals to us God’s righteousness and judgment, and helps us as we pray. “And the Holy Spirit helps us in our distress. For we don’t even know what we should pray for, nor how we should pray. But the Holy Spirit prays for us with groanings that cannot be expressed in words” (Romans 8:26). Ask God to fill you with his Spirit.

12:10-14 Eventually *all* people will realize that Jesus, the man who was pierced and killed, is indeed the Messiah. There will be an awakening, with sorrow for sin and genuine revival. The crucified Messiah will be clearly revealed (Philippians 2:10; Revelation 5:13).

12:11 Hadad-rimmon could refer to the place near the plain of Megiddo, where King Josiah was killed. Josiah’s death was greatly mourned by his people (see 2 Chronicles 35:22-25).

12:12-14 These verses are saying that all Israel will mourn—king, prophet, priest, and people. Each family will go into private mourning, husbands and wives by themselves, to face their sorrow.

13:1ff There will be a never-ending supply of God’s mercy, forgiveness, and cleansing power. This picture of a fountain is similar to the never-ending stream flowing out from the Temple (Ezekiel 47:1). The fountain is used in Scripture to symbolize God’s forgiveness. In John 4, Jesus tells of his “living water” that satisfies completely. Are you spiritually thirsty? Do you need to experience God’s forgiveness? Drink from the fountain—ask Jesus to forgive you and give you his salvation.

13:2-6 This chapter pictures the final days of the earth as we know it. For God’s new era to begin, there must be a cleansing—all evil must be abolished. Therefore, idols will be banished, and false prophets will be ashamed of themselves and no longer try to deceive God’s people.

13:7 Just before his arrest, Jesus quoted from this verse, referring to himself and his disciples (Matthew 26:31, 32). He knew beforehand that his disciples would scatter when he was arrested. The Roman “sword” was the military power that put Christ to death.

13:8, 9 This “third” was a remnant, a small part of the whole. Throughout the history of Israel, whenever the whole nation seemed to turn against God, God said that a righteous remnant still trusted and followed him. These believers were refined like silver and gold through the fire of their difficult circumstances. Determine to be part of God’s remnant, that small part of the whole that is obedient to him. Obey God no matter what the rest of the world does. This may mean trials and troubles at times; but as fire purifies gold and silver, you will be purified and made more like Christ.

The LORD Will Rule the Earth

14:1 Mal 4:1
14:4 Ezek 11:23; 47:1-10; Mic 1:3-4; Zech 4:7
14:5 Isa 29:6; Matt 16:27; 25:31; Jude 1:14
14:6 Acts 2:16, 19
14:7 Rev 21:23-25; 22:5
14:8 Ezek 47:1-12; John 7:37-38; Rev 22:1-2
14:9 Deut 6:4; Ps 47:7; Zech 9:9
14:10 2 Kgs 14:13
14:11 Ps 48:8; Rev 22:3
14:14 Zech 12:2
14:16 Isa 60:6-9; 66:18-21
14:17 Jer 14:4

14 Watch, for the day of the LORD is coming when your possessions will be plundered
right in front of you! 2On that day I will gather all the nations to fight against
Jerusalem. The city will be taken, the houses plundered, and the women raped. Half the
population will be taken away into captivity, and half will be left among the ruins of the
city.
3Then the LORD will go out to fight against those nations, as he has fought in times
past. 4On that day his feet will stand on the Mount of Olives, which faces Jerusalem on
the east. And the Mount of Olives will split apart, making a wide valley running from
east to west, for half the mountain will move toward the north and half toward the south.
5You will flee through this valley, for it will reach across to Azal.* Yes, you will flee as
you did from the earthquake in the days of King Uzziah of Judah. Then the LORD my
God will come, and all his holy ones with him.*
6On that day the sources of light will no longer shine,* 7yet there will be continuous
day! Only the LORD knows how this could happen! There will be no normal day and
night, for at evening time it will still be light. 8On that day life-giving waters will flow
out from Jerusalem, half toward the Dead Sea and half toward the Mediterranean,*
flowing continuously both in summer and in winter.
9And the LORD will be king over all the earth. On that day there will be one LORD—his
name alone will be worshiped. 10All the land from Geba, north of Judah, to Rimmon,
south of Jerusalem, will become one vast plain. But Jerusalem will be raised up in its
original place and will be inhabited all the way from the Benjamin Gate over to the site
of the old gate, then to the Corner Gate, and from the Tower of Hananel to the king's
winepresses. 11And Jerusalem will be filled, safe at last, never again to be cursed and
destroyed.
12And the LORD will send a plague on all the nations that fought against Jerusalem.
Their people will become like walking corpses, their flesh rotting away. Their eyes will
shrivel in their sockets, and their tongues will decay in their mouths. 13On that day they
will be terrified, stricken by the LORD with great panic. They will fight against each other
in hand-to-hand combat; 14Judah, too, will be fighting at Jerusalem. The wealth of all
the neighboring nations will be captured—great quantities of gold and silver and fine
clothing. 15This same plague will strike the horses, mules, camels, donkeys, and all the
other animals in the enemy camps.
16In the end, the enemies of Jerusalem who survive the plague will go up to Jerusalem
each year to worship the King, the LORD Almighty, and to celebrate the Festival of
Shelters. 17And any nation anywhere in the world that refuses to come to Jerusalem to
worship the King, the LORD Almighty, will have no rain. 18And if the people of Egypt
refuse to attend the festival, the LORD will punish them with the same plague that he
sends on the other nations who refuse to go. 19Egypt and the other nations will all be
punished if they don't go to celebrate the festival.

14:5a The meaning of the Hebrew is uncertain. **14:5b** As in Greek version; Hebrew reads *with you.* **14:6** Hebrew *there will be no light, no cold or frost.* The meaning of the Hebrew is uncertain. **14:8** Hebrew *half toward the eastern sea and half toward the western sea.*

14:1 Many times in the Bible we are encouraged to watch for the day of the Lord. What if you knew exactly when this would happen? Would you live differently? Christ could return at any moment. Be ready for him by studying the Scriptures carefully and by making sure that you live as he intends—in obedience and spiritual readiness.

14:1-21 This chapter portrays the eventual triumph of the Messiah over all the earth and his reign over God's people. But the chronological order of these future events is not clear. They show that God has various ways of dealing with his people. Now we are to watch as the events unfold and God provides an escape for his people.

14:4 On the Mount of Olives, Jesus spoke with his disciples about the end times (Matthew 24). Near this mountain, an angel promised that Jesus would return in the same manner as he had left (Acts 1:11; see also Ezekiel 11:23).

14:5 Only God's people will escape God's punishment (Matthew 24:16-20). In this time of confusion, God will clearly know who his people are. (See the note on Amos 1:1 concerning the earthquake in King Uzziah's day.)

14:10 Jerusalem is honored as the city of God and the focal point of all the world's worship. Jerusalem's elevation is a dramatic way of showing God's supremacy.

14:16 This Festival of Shelters is the only festival still appropriate during the Messiah's reign. The Passover was fulfilled in Christ's death; the Day of Atonement, in acceptance of Christ's salvation; the Festival of Firstfruits, in his resurrection; and Pentecost, with the arrival of the Holy Spirit. But the Festival of Shelters, a festival of thanksgiving, celebrates the harvest of human souls for the Lord. Jesus may have alluded to it in John 4:35.

20 On that day even the harness bells of the horses will be inscribed with these words:
SET APART AS HOLY TO THE LORD. And the cooking pots in the Temple of the LORD will
be as sacred as the basins used beside the altar. 21 In fact, every cooking pot in Jerusalem
and Judah will be set apart as holy to the LORD Almighty. All who come to worship will
be free to use any of these pots to boil their sacrifices. And on that day there will no longer
be traders* in the Temple of the LORD Almighty.

14:20 Exod 39:30 Ezek 46:20 Rev 20:6

14:21 Neh 8:10 Rom 14:6-7 1 Cor 10:31

14:21 Hebrew *Canaanites.*

14:20, 21 In the future, even such common objects as horses' bells and cooking pots will be holy. This vision of a restored, holy Jerusalem stands in contrast to its broken walls and unpleasant living conditions. One day God would fulfill the people's dreams for Jerusalem beyond what they could imagine. God wants to do much more for us than we can imagine (Ephesians 3:20). As we walk with him, we will discover this day by day.

14:21 Zechariah was speaking to a people who were enduring hardships: They were being harassed by neighbors; they were discouraged over their small numbers and seemingly inadequate Temple; and their worship was apathetic. But God said, "My love for Jerusalem and Mount Zion is passionate and strong" (1:14). He promised to restore their land, their city, and their Temple. Like other prophets, Zechariah blended prophecies of the present, near future, and final days into one sweeping panorama. Through his message we learn that our hope is found in God and his Messiah, who are in complete control of the world.

MALACHI

First exiles return to Jerusalem 538 B.C.	Temple reconstruction begins 536	Haggai, Zechariah become prophets 520	Temple completed 515	Ezra comes to Jerusalem 458	Nehemiah comes to Jerusalem 445	Malachi becomes a prophet 430

A VASE shatters, brushed by a careless elbow; a toy breaks, handled roughly by young fingers; and fabric rips, pulled by strong and angry hands. Spills and rips take time to clean up, effort to repair, and money to replace, but far more costly are shattered relationships. Unfaithfulness, untruths, hateful words, and forsaken vows tear delicate personal bonds and inflict wounds not easily healed. Most tragic, however, is a broken relationship with God.

God loves perfectly and completely. And his love is a love of action—giving, guiding, and guarding. He is altogether faithful, true to his promises to his chosen people. But consistently they spurn their loving God, breaking the covenant, following other gods, and living for themselves. So their relationship with him is shattered.

But the breach is not irreparable; all hope is not lost. God can heal and mend and reweave the fabric. Forgiveness is available. And that is grace.

This is the message of Malachi, God's prophet in Jerusalem. His words reminded the Jews, God's chosen nation, of their willful disobedience, beginning with the priests (1:1—2:9) and then including every person (2:10—3:15). They had shown contempt for God's name (1:6), offered defiled sacrifices (1:7–14), led others into sin (2:7–9), broken God's laws (2:11–16), called evil "good" (2:17), kept God's tithes and offerings for themselves (3:8–9), and become arrogant (3:13–15). The relationship was broken, and judgment and punishment would be theirs. In the midst of this wickedness, however, there were a faithful few—the remnant—who loved and honored God. God would shower his blessings upon these men and women (3:16–18).

Malachi paints a stunning picture of Israel's unfaithfulness that clearly shows the people to be worthy of punishment, but woven throughout this message is hope—the possibility of forgiveness. This is beautifully expressed in 4:2—"But for you who fear my name, the Sun of Righteousness will rise with healing in his wings. And you will go free, leaping with joy like calves let out to pasture."

Malachi concludes with a promise of the coming of "the prophet Elijah," who will offer God's forgiveness to all people through repentance and faith (4:5, 6).

The book of Malachi forms a bridge between the Old Testament and the New Testament. As you read Malachi, see yourself as the recipient of this word of God to his people. Evaluate the depth of your commitment, the sincerity of your worship, and the direction of your life. Then allow God to restore your relationship with him through his love and forgiveness.

VITAL STATISTICS

PURPOSE:
To confront the people with their sins and to restore their relationship with God

AUTHOR:
Malachi

TO WHOM WRITTEN:
The Jews in Jerusalem and God's people everywhere

DATE WRITTEN:
Approximately 430 B.C.

SETTING:
Malachi, Haggai, and Zechariah were postexilic prophets to Judah (the southern kingdom). Haggai and Zechariah rebuked the people for their failure to rebuild the Temple. Malachi confronted them with their neglect of the Temple and their false and profane worship.

KEY VERSES:
"The day of judgment is coming, burning like a furnace. . . . But for you who fear my name, the Sun of Righteousness will rise with healing in his wings. And you will go free, leaping with joy like calves let out to pasture" (4:1, 2).

KEY PEOPLE:
Malachi, the priests

KEY PLACES:
Jerusalem, the Temple

SPECIAL FEATURES:
Malachi's literary style employs a dramatic use of questions asked by God and his people (for example, see 3:7, 8).

THE BLUEPRINT

1. The sinful priests (1:1—2:9)
2. The sinful people (2:10—3:15)
3. The faithful few (3:16—4:6)

Malachi rebuked the people and the priests for neglecting the worship of God and failing to live according to his will. The priests were corrupt; how could they lead the people? They had become stumbling blocks instead of spiritual leaders. The men were divorcing their wives and marrying pagan women; how could they have godly children? Their relationship to God had become inconsequential. If our relationship with God is unimportant, we need to take stock of ourselves by setting aside our sinful habits, putting the Lord first, and giving God our best each day.

MEGATHEMES

THEME	EXPLANATION	IMPORTANCE
God's Love	God loves his people even when they ignore or disobey him. He has great blessings to bestow on those who are faithful to him. His love never ends.	Because God loves us so much, he hates hypocrisy and careless living. This kind of living denies him the relationship he wants to have with us. What we give and how we live reflects the sincerity of our love for God.
The Sin of the Priests	Malachi singled out the priests for condemnation. They knew what God required, yet their sacrifices were unworthy and their service was insincere; they were lazy, arrogant, and insensitive. They had a casual attitude toward the worship of God and observance of God's standards.	If religious leaders go wrong, how will the people be led? We are all leaders in some capacity. Don't neglect your responsibilities or be ruled by what is convenient. Neglect and insensitivity are acts of disobedience. God wants leaders who are faithful and sincere.
The Sin of the People	The people had not learned the lesson of the Exile, nor had they listened to the prophets. Men were callously divorcing their faithful wives to marry younger pagan women. This was against God's law because it disobeyed his commands about marriage and threatened the religious training of the children. But pride had hardened the hearts of the people.	God deserves our very best honor, respect, and faithfulness. But sin hardens our heart to our true condition. Pride is unwarranted self-esteem; it is setting your own judgment above God's and looking down on others. Don't let pride keep you from giving God your devotion, money, marriage, and family.
The Lord's Coming	God's love for his faithful people is demonstrated by the Messiah's coming. The Messiah will lead the people to the realization of all their fondest hopes. The day of the Lord's coming will be a day of comfort and healing for a faithful few, and a day of judgment for those who reject him.	At Christ's first coming, he refined and purified all those who believed in him. Upon his return, he will expose and condemn those who are proud, insensitive, or unprepared. Yet God is able to heal and forgive. Forgiveness is available to all who come to him.

1. The sinful priests

1 This is the message* that the LORD gave to Israel through the prophet Malachi.*

The LORD's Love for Israel

2"I have loved you deeply," says the LORD. 1:2-3 †Rom 9:13
But you retort, "Really? How have you loved us?"
And the LORD replies, "I showed my love for you by loving your ancestor Jacob. Yet
Esau was Jacob's brother, 3and I rejected Esau and devastated his hill country. I turned
Esau's inheritance into a desert for jackals."
4And Esau's descendants in Edom may say, "We have been shattered, but we will 1:4 Isa 9:10
rebuild the ruins."
But this is what the LORD Almighty says: "They may try to rebuild, but I will demolish
them again! Their country will be known as 'The Land of Wickedness,' and their people
will be called 'The People with Whom the LORD Is Forever Angry.' 5When you see the 1:5 Pss 35:27; 48:1
destruction for yourselves, you will say, 'Truly, the LORD's great power reaches far
beyond our borders!'"

1:1a Hebrew *An Oracle: The message.* **1:1b** *Malachi* means "my messenger."

1:1 Malachi, the last Old Testament prophet, preached after Haggai, Zechariah, and Nehemiah—about 430 B.C. The Temple had been rebuilt for almost a century, and the people were losing their enthusiasm for worship. Apathy and disillusionment had set in because the exciting messianic prophecies of Isaiah, Jeremiah, and Micah had not been fulfilled. Many of the sins that had brought the downfall of Jerusalem in 586 B.C. were still being practiced in Judah. Malachi confronted the hypocrites with their sins by portraying a graphic dialogue between a righteous God and his hardened people.

1:2 God's first message through Malachi was "I have loved you deeply." Although this message applied specifically to Israel, it is a message of hope for all people in all times. Unfortunately, many people are cynical about God's love, using political and economic progress as a measure of success. Because the government was corrupt and the economy poor, the Israelites assumed that God didn't love them. They were wrong. God loves all people because he made them; however, his *eternal* rewards go only to those who are faithful to him.

1:2-5 The phrase "I rejected Esau" does not refer to Esau's eternal destiny. It simply means that God chose Jacob, not his brother Esau, to be the one through whom the nation of Israel and the Messiah would come (see Romans 9:10-13). God allowed Esau to father a nation, but this nation, Edom, later became one of Israel's chief enemies. The story of Jacob and Esau is found in Genesis 25:19-26. Because God chose Jacob and his descendants as the nation through whom the world would be blessed, God cared for them in a special way. Ironically, they rejected God after he chose them.

Unworthy Sacrifices

1:6 6 The LORD Almighty says to the priests: "A son honors his father, and a servant respects
Exod 20:12 Deut 31:12 his master. I am your father and master, but where are the honor and respect I deserve?
Isa 1:2 You have despised my name!
"But you ask, 'How have we ever despised your name?'
1:7 7 "You have despised my name by offering defiled sacrifices on my altar.
Lev 21:6-8 "Then you ask, 'How have we defiled the sacrifices*?'
"You defile them by saying the altar of the LORD deserves no respect. 8 When you give
1:8 Lev 1:3 blind animals as sacrifices, isn't that wrong? And isn't it wrong to offer animals that are
Deut 15:21 crippled and diseased? Try giving gifts like that to your governor, and see how pleased
he is!" says the LORD Almighty.
1:9 9 "Go ahead, beg God to be merciful to you! But when you bring that kind of offering,
Lev 23:33-44 Ps 51:17 why should he show you any favor at all?" asks the LORD Almighty.
1:10 Isa 1:13 10 "I wish that someone among you would shut the Temple doors so that these worthless
Jer 14:12 sacrifices could not be offered! I am not at all pleased with you," says the LORD Almighty,
1:11 Ps 113:3 "and I will not accept your offerings. 11 But my name is honored by people of other nations
Isa 60:6-7 from morning till night. All around the world they offer sweet incense and pure offerings in
honor of my name. For my name is great among the nations," says the LORD Almighty.
12 "But you dishonor my name with your actions. By bringing contemptible food, you are
1:13 Isa 43:22-24 saying it's all right to defile the Lord's table. 13 You say, 'It's too hard to serve the LORD,'

1:7 As in Greek version; Hebrew reads *defiled you.*

MALACHI served as a prophet to Judah about 430 B.C. He was the last of the Old Testament prophets.

Climate of the times . . . . The city of Jerusalem and the Temple had been rebuilt for almost a century, but the people had become complacent in their worship of God.

Main message . . . . The people's relationship with God was broken because of their sin, and they would soon be punished. But the few who repented would receive God's blessing, highlighted in his promise to send a Messiah.

Importance of message . . . . . Hypocrisy, neglecting God, and careless living have devastating consequences. Serving and worshiping God must be the primary focus of our life, both now and in eternity.

Contemporary prophets . . . . . None

1:6ff God charged the priests with failing to honor him (to the point of despising his name) and failing to be good spiritual examples to the people. The Temple had been rebuilt in 515 B.C., and worship was being conducted there, but the priests did not worship God properly. They were not following his laws for the sacrifices. Ezra the priest had sparked a great revival around 458 B.C. However, by Malachi's time, the nation's leaders had once again fallen away from God, and the people right along with them. The worship of God was no longer from heartfelt adoration; instead, it was simply a burdensome job for the priests.

1:6-8 God's law required that only perfect animals be offered to God (see, for example, Leviticus 1:3). But these priests were allowing the people to offer blind, crippled, and diseased animals to God. God accused them of dishonoring him by offering imperfect sacrifices, and he was greatly displeased. The New Testament says that our lives should be living sacrifices to God (Romans 12:1). If we give God only our leftover time, money, and energy, we repeat the same sin as these worshipers, who didn't want to bring anything valuable to God. What we give God reflects our true attitude toward him.

1:7, 8 The people sacrificed to God wrongly through (1) expedience—being as cheap as possible, (2) neglect—not caring how they offered the sacrifice, and (3) outright disobedience—sacrificing their own way and not as God had commanded. Their methods of giving showed their real attitudes toward God. How about your attitude? Do expedience, neglect, or disobedience characterize your giving?

1:10 As intermediaries between God and the people, priests were responsible for reflecting God's attitudes and character. By accepting imperfect sacrifices, they were leading the people to believe that God accepted those sacrifices as well. But God says, "I am not at all pleased with you." As Christians, we are often in the same position as these priests because we reflect God to our friends and family. What image of God's character and attitudes do they see in you? If you casually accept sin, you are like these priests in Malachi's day, and God is not pleased with you.

1:11 A theme that can be heard throughout the Old Testament is affirmed in this book: "My name is great among the nations." God had a chosen people, the Jews, through whom he planned to save and bless the entire world. Today God still wants to save and bless the world through all who believe in him—Jews and Gentiles. Christians are now his chosen people, and our offering to the Lord is our life. Are you available to God to be used in making his name great to the nations? This mission begins in our home and in our neighborhood, but it doesn't stop there. We must work and pray so that God's name will be honored everywhere.

1:13 Worship was "too hard" according to these priests. Some people think that following God is supposed to make life more comfortable. They are looking for a God of convenience. The truth is that it takes commitment and hard work to live by God's high standards. We may have to face poverty or suffering. But if serving God is more important to us than anything else, what we give up is nothing compared to what we gain—eternal life with God.

and you turn up your noses at his commands," says the LORD Almighty. "Think of it!
Animals that are stolen and mutilated, crippled and sick—presented as offerings! Should I
accept from you such offerings as these?" asks the LORD. 14"Cursed is the cheat who
promises to give a fine ram from his flock but then sacrifices a defective one to the Lord.
For I am a great king," says the LORD Almighty, "and my name is feared among the nations!

1:14 Exod 12:5; Lev 22:18-21; Ps 72:8-11

A Warning for the Priests

2 "Listen, you priests; this command is for you! 2Listen to me and take it to heart.
Honor my name," says the LORD Almighty, "or I will bring a terrible curse against
you. I will curse even the blessings you receive. Indeed, I have already cursed them,
because you have not taken my warning seriously. 3I will rebuke your descendants and
splatter your faces with the dung of your festival sacrifices, and I will add you to the dung
heap. 4Then at last you will know it was I who sent you this warning so that my covenant
with the Levites may continue," says the LORD Almighty.
5"The purpose of my covenant with the Levites was to bring life and peace, and this is
what I gave them. This called for reverence from them, and they greatly revered me and
stood in awe of my name. 6They passed on to the people all the truth they received from
me. They did not lie or cheat; they walked with me, living good and righteous lives, and
they turned many from lives of sin. 7The priests' lips should guard knowledge, and people
should go to them for instruction, for the priests are the messengers of the LORD Almighty.
8But not you! You have left God's paths. Your 'guidance' has caused many to stumble into
sin. You have corrupted the covenant I made with the Levites," says the LORD Almighty.
9"So I have made you despised and humiliated in the eyes of all the people. For you have
not obeyed me but have shown partiality in your interpretation of the law."

2:1 Num 6:23-27
2:4 Num 3:12
2:5 Num 25:12
2:6 Deut 33:10
2:7 Lev 10:11; Num 27:21; Deut 17:8-11
2:8 Neh 13:29; Isa 9:16; Jer 18:15; Ezek 44:10
2:9 Deut 1:17; 1 Sam 2:30

2. The sinful people

A Call to Faithfulness

10Are we not all children of the same Father? Are we not all created by the same God?
Then why are we faithless to each other, violating the covenant of our ancestors? 11In
Judah, in Israel, and in Jerusalem there is treachery, for the men of Judah have defiled
the LORD's beloved sanctuary by marrying women who worship idols. 12May the LORD
cut off from the nation of Israel* every last man who has done this and yet brings an
offering to the LORD Almighty.

2:10 Exod 19:5; Josh 24:3; Jer 31:9
2:11 Ezra 9:1-2; Jer 3:7-9

2:12 Hebrew *from the tents of Jacob.*

2:1, 2 God warned the priests that if they did not honor his name, he would punish them. Like these priests, we, too, are called to honor God's name—to worship him. This means acknowledging God for who he is—the almighty Creator of the universe, who alone is perfect and who reaches down to sinful people with perfect love. According to this definition, are you honoring God's name?

2:1, 2 The priests didn't take seriously God's priority, even though he had reminded them through his word many times. How do you find out what is most important to God? Begin by loving him with all your heart, soul, and strength (Deuteronomy 6:5). This means listening to what God says in his Word and then setting your heart, mind, and will on doing what he says. When we love God, his Word becomes a shining light that guides our daily activities. The priests in Malachi's day had stopped loving God, and thus they did not know nor care what he wanted.

2:4-6 Levi "walked with [God]," and "turned many from lives of sin" (2:6). Levi was the ancestor of the tribe of Levites, the tribe set apart for service to God (Numbers 1:47-54). The Levites became God's ministers, first in the Tabernacle, then in the Temple. In these verses, God was addressing the priests who were from this tribe, admonishing them for corrupting the laws he gave their ancestor Levi and not following his example.

2:7, 8 Malachi was angry at the priests because, although they were to be God's messengers, they did not know God's will. And this lack of knowledge caused them to lead God's people astray. Their ignorance was willful and inexcusable. Pastors and leaders of God's people *must* know God's Word—what it says, what it means, and how it applies to daily life. How much time do you spend in God's Word?

2:9 The priests had allowed influential and favored people to break the law. The priests were so dependent on these people for support that they could not afford to confront them when they did wrong. In your church, are certain people allowed to do wrong without criticism? There should be no double standard based on wealth or position. Let your standards be those presented in God's Word. Playing favorites is contemptible in God's sight (see James 2:1-9).

2:10-16 The people were being unfaithful. Though not openly saying they rejected God, they were living as if he did not exist. Men were marrying pagan women who worshiped idols. Divorce was common, occurring for no reason other than a desire for change. People acted as if they could do anything without being punished. And they wondered why God refused to accept their offerings and bless them (2:13)! We cannot successfully separate our dealings with God from the rest of our life. He must be Lord of all.

2:11, 12 After the Temple had been rebuilt and the walls completed, the people were excited to see past prophecies coming true. But as time passed, the prophecies about the destruction of God's enemies and a coming Messiah were not immediately fulfilled. The people became discouraged, and they grew complacent about obeying all of God's laws. This complacency gradually led to blatant sin, such as marriage to those who worshiped idols. Ezra and Nehemiah also had confronted this problem years earlier (Ezra 9–10; Nehemiah 13:23-31).

13Here is another thing you do. You cover the LORD's altar with tears, weeping and
groaning because he pays no attention to your offerings, and he doesn't accept them with
2:14 Prov 5:18
pleasure. 14You cry out, "Why has the LORD abandoned us?" I'll tell you why! Because the
LORD witnessed the vows you and your wife made to each other on your wedding day when
you were young. But you have been disloyal to her, though she remained your faithful
2:15 Gen 2:24 Matt 19:4-6 1 Cor 7:10, 14
companion, the wife of your marriage vows. 15Didn't the LORD make you one with your
wife? In body and spirit you are his.* And what does he want? Godly children from your
union. So guard yourself; remain loyal to the wife of your youth. 16"For I hate divorce!"
2:16 Matt 5:31; 19:6-8 Mark 10:4-5
says the LORD, the God of Israel. "It is as cruel as putting on a victim's bloodstained coat,"
says the LORD Almighty. "So guard yourself; always remain loyal to your wife."
2:17 Isa 5:20; 43:22, 24 Zeph 1:12
17You have wearied the LORD with your words.
"Wearied him?" you ask. "How have we wearied him?"
You have wearied him by suggesting that the LORD favors evildoers since he does not
punish them. You have wearied him by asking, "Where is the God of justice?"

The Coming Day of Judgment

3:1 †Matt 11:10 †Mark 1:2 †Luke 7:27
3 "Look! I am sending my messenger, and he will prepare the way before me. Then the
Lord you are seeking will suddenly come to his Temple. The messenger of the
3:2 Ezek 22:14 Matt 3:10-12 Rev 6:17
covenant, whom you look for so eagerly, is surely coming," says the LORD Almighty. 2"But
who will be able to endure it when he comes? Who will be able to stand and face him when
he appears? For he will be like a blazing fire that refines metal or like a strong soap that
3:3 Dan 12:10
whitens clothes. 3He will sit and judge like a refiner of silver, watching closely as the dross
is burned away. He will purify the Levites, refining them like gold or silver, so that they may
3:4 2 Chr 7:3 Ps 51:19
once again offer acceptable sacrifices to the LORD. 4Then once more the LORD will accept
the offerings brought to him by the people of Judah and Jerusalem, as he did in former times.
3:5 Exod 22:22 Jer 7:9 Jas 5:4
5At that time I will put you on trial. I will be a ready witness against all sorcerers and
adulterers and liars. I will speak against those who cheat employees of their wages, who
oppress widows and orphans, or who deprive the foreigners living among you of justice,
for these people do not fear me," says the LORD Almighty.

A Call to Repentance

6"I am the LORD, and I do not change. That is why you descendants of Jacob are not
3:7 Zech 1:3
already completely destroyed. 7Ever since the days of your ancestors, you have scorned
my laws and failed to obey them. Now return to me, and I will return to you," says the
LORD Almighty.

2:15 Or *Did not one God make us and preserve our life and breath?* or *Did not one God make her, both flesh and spirit?* The meaning of the Hebrew is uncertain.

2:14 The people were complaining about their adverse circumstances when they had only themselves to blame. People often try to avoid guilt feelings by shifting the blame. But this doesn't solve the problem. When you face problems, look first at yourself. If you changed your attitude or behavior, would the problem be solved?

2:14, 15 Divorce in these times was practiced exclusively by men. They were disloyal to their wives and ignored the wedding vows they had made before God, thus corrupting his purpose for them to rear godly children who love the Lord. Not only were men unfaithful to their wives, but they also were ignoring the fact that this bonding relationship was an illustration of their union with God.

2:15, 16 "Guard yourself; always remain loyal to your wife" means to have the same commitment to marriage that God has to his promises for his people. Our passion should be reserved exclusively for our spouse.

2:17–3:6 God was tired of the way the people had cynically twisted his truths. He would punish those who insisted that because God was silent, he approved of their actions or at least would never punish them. God would also punish those who professed a counterfeit faith while acting sinfully (see 3:5).

3:1 There are two messengers in this verse. The first is usually understood to be John the Baptist (Matthew 11:10; Luke 7:27). The second messenger is Jesus, the Messiah, for whom both Malachi and John the Baptist prepared the way.

3:2, 3 In the process of refining metals, the raw metal is heated with fire until it melts. The impurities separate from it and rise to the surface. They are skimmed off, leaving the pure metal. Without this heating and melting, there could be no purifying. As the impurities are skimmed off the top, the reflection of the worker appears in the clear, pure surface. As we are purified by God, his reflection in our life will become more and more clear to those around us. God says that the Levites (Israel's leaders) should be especially open to his purification process in their lives. The strong soap was alkali used to whiten cloth, also used here as a symbol of the purifying process.

3:7 God's patience seems endless! Throughout history, his people have disobeyed, even scorned, his laws, but he has always been willing to accept them back. Here, however, the people have the nerve to imply that they never disobeyed ("How can we return when we have never gone away?")! Many people have turned their backs on forgiveness and restoration because they have refused to admit their sin. Don't follow their example. God is ready to return to us if we are willing to return to him.

"But you ask, 'How can we return when we have never gone away?'
8"Should people cheat God? Yet you have cheated me!
"But you ask, 'What do you mean? When did we ever cheat you?'
"You have cheated me of the tithes and offerings due to me. 9You are under a curse,
for your whole nation has been cheating me. 10Bring all the tithes into the storehouse so
there will be enough food in my Temple. If you do," says the LORD Almighty, "I will
open the windows of heaven for you. I will pour out a blessing so great you won't have
enough room to take it in! Try it! Let me prove it to you! 11Your crops will be abundant,
for I will guard them from insects and disease.* Your grapes will not shrivel before they
are ripe," says the LORD Almighty. 12"Then all nations will call you blessed, for your
land will be such a delight," says the LORD Almighty.
13"You have said terrible things about me," says the LORD.
"But you say, 'What do you mean? How have we spoken against you?'
14"You have said, 'What's the use of serving God? What have we gained by obeying
his commands or by trying to show the LORD Almighty that we are sorry for our sins?
15From now on we will say, "Blessed are the arrogant." For those who do evil get rich,
and those who dare God to punish them go free of harm.'"

3. The faithful few

The LORD's Promise of Mercy

16Then those who feared the LORD spoke with each other, and the LORD listened to what
they said. In his presence, a scroll of remembrance was written to record the names of
those who feared him and loved to think about him. 17"They will be my people," says
the LORD Almighty. "On the day when I act, they will be my own special treasure. I will
spare them as a father spares an obedient and dutiful child. 18Then you will again see the
difference between the righteous and the wicked, between those who serve God and
those who do not."

The Coming Day of Judgment

4 The LORD Almighty says, "The day of judgment is coming, burning like a furnace.
The arrogant and the wicked will be burned up like straw on that day. They will be
consumed like a tree—roots and all.
2"But for you who fear my name, the Sun of Righteousness will rise with healing in
his wings.* And you will go free, leaping with joy like calves let out to pasture. 3On the

3:8 Neh 13:11
3:12 Deut 28:3-12; Isa 61:9; 62:4
3:14-15 Ps 73:13
3:16 Ps 56:8
3:17 Neh 13:22; 1 Pet 2:9
3:18 Ps 58:11
4:1 Isa 5:24; Mal 3:2
4:2 Isa 30:26; 35:6
4:3 Ezek 28:18; Mic 7:10

3:11 Hebrew *from the devourer.* **4:2** Or *the sun of righteousness will rise with healing in its wings.*

3:8-12 Malachi urged the people to stop holding back their tithes, to stop cheating God. The tithing system began during the time of Moses (Leviticus 27:30-34; Deuteronomy 14:22). The Levites received some of the tithe because they could not possess land of their own (Numbers 18:20, 21). During Malachi's day, the people were not giving tithes, so the Levites went to work to earn a living, thereby neglecting their God-given responsibilities to care for the Temple and for the service of worship. Everything we have is from God; so when we refuse to return to him a part of what he has given, we rob him. Do you selfishly want to keep 100 percent of what God gives, or are you willing to return at least 10 percent to help advance God's Kingdom?

3:8-12 The people of Malachi's day ignored God's command to give a tithe of their income to his Temple. They may have feared losing what they had worked so hard to get, but in this they misjudged God. "If you give, you will receive," he says (Luke 6:38). When we give, we must remember that the blessings God promises are not always material and may not be experienced completely here on earth, but we will certainly receive them in our future life with him.

3:10 The "storehouse" was a place in the Temple for storing grain and other food given as tithes. The priests lived off these gifts. We also need to give from the plenty that God has given us in order to support those who serve God by ministering to the spiritual needs of others.

3:13-15 These verses describe the people's arrogant attitude toward God. When we ask, "What's the use of serving God?" we are really asking, "What good does it do for *me?"* Our focus is selfish. Our real question should be, "What good does it do for God?" We must serve God just because he is God and deserves to be served.

3:16 God will remember those who remain faithful to him, and who love, fear, honor, and respect him.

3:17 God's special treasure are those faithful to him. This fulfills the promise he made in the covenant to his people (Exodus 19:5). According to 1 Peter 2:9, believers are God's very own possession. Have you committed your life to God for safekeeping?

4:2 In the day of the Lord, God's wrath toward the wicked will burn like a furnace (4:1). But he will be like the healing warmth of the sun to those who love and obey him. John the Baptist prophesied that with the coming of Jesus, the dawn was about to break with light for those in sin's darkness (Luke 1:76-79). In Isaiah 60:20 and Revelation 21:23, 24, we learn that no light will be needed in God's holy city, because God himself will be the light.

4:2ff These last verses of the Old Testament are filled with hope. Regardless of how life looks now, God controls the future, and everything will be made right. We who have loved and served God look forward to a joyful celebration. This hope for the future becomes ours when we trust God with our lives.

day when I act, you will tread upon the wicked as if they were dust under your feet," says
the LORD Almighty.
4"Remember to obey the instructions of my servant Moses, all the laws and regulations that I gave him on Mount Sinai* for all Israel.
5"Look, I am sending you the prophet Elijah before the great and dreadful day of the
LORD arrives. 6His preaching will turn the hearts of parents* to their children, and the
hearts of children to their parents. Otherwise I will come and strike the land with a
curse."

4:4 Exod 20:3
4:5 Matt 11:14; Mark 9:11-13; Luke 1:17; John 1:21
4:6 Isa 11:4; Luke 1:17; Rev 19:15

4:4 Hebrew *Horeb,* another name for Sinai. **4:6** Hebrew *fathers;* also in 4:6b.

4:4 These laws, given to Moses at Mount Sinai, were the foundation of the nation's civil, moral, and ceremonial life (Exodus 20; Deuteronomy 4:5, 6). We still must obey these moral laws because they apply to all generations.

4:5, 6 Elijah was one of the greatest prophets who ever lived (his story is recorded in 1 Kings 17–2 Kings 2). With Malachi's death, the voice of God's prophets would be silent for 400 years. Then a prophet would come, like Elijah, to herald the Messiah's coming (Matthew 17:10-13; Luke 1:17). This prophet was John the Baptist. John prepared people's hearts for Jesus by urging people to repent of their sins. Christ's coming would bring not only unity and peace but also judgment on those who refused to turn from their sins.

4:6 Malachi gives us practical guidelines about commitment to God: God deserves the best we have to offer (1:7-10). We must be willing to change our wrong ways of living (2:1, 2). We should make our family a lifelong priority (2:13-16). We should be sensitive to God's refining process in our life (3:3). We should tithe our income (3:8-12). There is no room for pride (3:13-15).

Malachi closes his messages by pointing to that great final day of judgment. For those who are committed to God, judgment day will be a day of joy because it will usher in eternity in God's presence. Those who have ignored God will be "straw," to be burned up (4:1). To help the people prepare for that day of judgment, God would send a prophet like Elijah (John the Baptist), who would prepare the way for Jesus, the Messiah. The New Testament begins with this prophet calling the people to turn from their sins to God. Such a commitment to God demands great sacrifice on our part, but we can be sure it will be worth it all in the end.

THE NEW TESTAMENT

MATTHEW

Herod the Great begins to rule 37 B.C.	Jesus is born 6/5 B.C.	Escape to Egypt 5/4 B.C.	Herod the Great dies 4 B.C.	Return to Nazareth 4/3 B.C.	Judea becomes a Roman province A.D. 6	Jesus visits Temple as a boy 6/7

VITAL STATISTICS

PURPOSE:
To prove that Jesus is the Messiah, the eternal King

AUTHOR:
Matthew (Levi)

TO WHOM WRITTEN:
Matthew wrote especially to the Jews

DATE WRITTEN:
Approximately A.D. 60–65

SETTING:
Matthew was a Jewish tax collector who became one of Jesus' disciples. This Gospel forms the connecting link between the Old and New Testaments because of its emphasis on the fulfillment of prophecy.

KEY VERSE:
"Don't misunderstand why I have come. I did not come to abolish the law of Moses or the writings of the prophets. No, I came to fulfill them" (5:17).

KEY PEOPLE:
Jesus, Mary, Joseph, John the Baptist, the disciples, the religious leaders, Caiaphas, Pilate, Mary Magdalene

KEY PLACES:
Bethlehem, Jerusalem, Capernaum, Galilee, Judea

SPECIAL FEATURES:
Matthew is filled with messianic language ("Son of David" is used throughout) and Old Testament references (53 quotes and 76 other references). This Gospel was not written as a chronological account; its purpose was to present the clear evidence that Jesus is the Messiah, the Savior.

AS the motorcade slowly winds through the city, thousands pack the sidewalks hoping to catch a glimpse. Marching bands with great fanfare announce the arrival, and protective agents scan the crowd and run alongside the limousine. Pomp, ceremony, protocol—modern symbols of position and evidences of importance—herald the arrival of a head of state. Whether they are leaders by birth or election, we honor and respect them.

The Jews waited for a leader who had been promised centuries before by prophets. They believed that this leader—the Messiah ("anointed one")—would rescue them from their Roman oppressors and establish a new kingdom. As their king, he would rule the world with justice. However, many Jews overlooked prophecies that also spoke of this king as a suffering servant who would be rejected and killed. It is no wonder, then, that few recognized Jesus as the Messiah. How could this humble carpenter's son from Nazareth be their king? But Jesus was and is the King of all the earth!

Matthew (Levi) was one of Jesus' 12 disciples. Once he was a despised tax collector, but his life was changed by this man from Galilee. Matthew wrote this Gospel to his fellow Jews to prove that Jesus is the Messiah and to explain God's Kingdom.

Matthew begins his account by giving Jesus' genealogy. He then tells of Jesus' birth and early years, including the family's escape to Egypt from the murderous Herod and their return to Nazareth. Following Jesus' baptism by John (3:16, 17) and his defeat of Satan in the wilderness, Jesus begins his public ministry by calling his first disciples and giving the Sermon on the Mount (chapters 5—7). Matthew shows Christ's authority by reporting his miracles of healing the sick and the demon-possessed, and even raising the dead.

Despite opposition from the Pharisees and others in the religious establishment (chapters 12—15), Jesus continued to teach concerning the Kingdom of Heaven (chapters 16—20). During this time, Jesus spoke with his disciples about his imminent death and resurrection (16:21) and revealed his true identity to Peter, James, and John (17:1–5). Near the end of his ministry, Jesus entered Jerusalem in a triumphant procession (21:1–11). But soon opposition mounted, and Jesus knew that his death was near. So he taught his disciples about the future—what they could expect before his return (chapter 24) and how to live until then (chapter 25).

In Matthew's finale (chapters 26—28), he focuses on Jesus' final days on earth—the Last Supper, his prayer in Gethsemane, the betrayal by Judas, the flight of the disciples, Peter's denial, the trials before Caiaphas and Pilate, Jesus' final words on the cross, and his burial in a borrowed tomb. But the story does not end there, for the Messiah rose from the dead—conquering death and then telling his followers to continue his work by making disciples in all nations.

As you read this Gospel, listen to Matthew's clear message: Jesus is the Christ, the King of kings and Lord of lords. Celebrate his victory over evil and death, and make Jesus the Lord of your life.

Tiberius Caesar becomes emperor	*Pontius Pilate appointed governor*	*Jesus begins his ministry*	*Jesus chooses twelve disciples*	*Jesus feeds 5,000*	*Jesus is crucified, rises again, and ascends*
14	*26*	*26/27*	*28*	*29*	*30*

THE BLUEPRINT

A. BIRTH AND PREPARATION OF JESUS, THE KING (1:1—4:11)

The people of Israel were waiting for the Messiah, their king. Matthew begins his book by showing how Jesus Christ was a descendant of David. But Matthew goes on to show that God did not send Jesus to be an earthly king but a heavenly King. His Kingdom would be much greater than David's because it would never end. Even at Jesus' birth, many recognized him as a King. Herod, the ruler, as well as Satan, was afraid of Jesus' kingship and tried to stop him, but others worshiped him and brought royal gifts. We must be willing to recognize Jesus for who he really is and worship him as King of our life.

B. MESSAGE AND MINISTRY OF JESUS, THE KING (4:12—25:46)

1. Jesus begins his ministry
2. Jesus gives the Sermon on the Mount
3. Jesus performs many miracles
4. Jesus teaches about the Kingdom
5. Jesus encounters differing reactions to his ministry
6. Jesus faces conflict with the religious leaders
7. Jesus teaches on the Mount of Olives

Jesus gave the Sermon on the Mount, directions for living in his Kingdom. He also told many parables about the difference between his Kingdom and the kingdoms of earth. Forgiveness, peace, and putting others first are some of the characteristics that make one great in the Kingdom of God. And to be great in God's Kingdom, we must live by God's standards right now. Jesus came to show us how to live as faithful subjects in his Kingdom.

C. DEATH AND RESURRECTION OF JESUS, THE KING (26:1—28:20)

Jesus was formally presented to the nation of Israel but was rejected. How strange for the King to be accused, arrested, and crucified. But Jesus demonstrated his power, even over death, through his resurrection and gained access for us into his Kingdom. With all this evidence that Jesus is God's Son, we, too, should accept him as our Lord.

MEGATHEMES

THEME	EXPLANATION	IMPORTANCE
Jesus Christ, the King	Jesus is revealed as the King of kings. His miraculous birth, his life and teaching, his miracles, and his triumph over death show his true identity.	Jesus cannot be equated with any person or power. He is the supreme ruler of time and eternity, heaven and earth, humans and angels. We should give him his rightful place as King of our life.
The Messiah	Jesus was the Messiah, the one for whom the Jews had waited to deliver them from Roman oppression. Yet, tragically, they didn't recognize him when he came because his kingship was not what they expected. The true purpose of God's anointed deliverer was to die for all people to free them from sin's oppression.	Because Jesus was sent by God, we can trust him with our life. It is worth everything we have to acknowledge him and give ourselves to him, because he came to be our Messiah, our Savior.
Kingdom of God	Jesus came to earth to begin his Kingdom. His full Kingdom will be realized at his return and will be made up of anyone who has faithfully followed him.	The way to enter God's Kingdom is by faith—believing in Christ to save us from sin and change our life. We must do the work of his Kingdom now to be prepared for his return.

Teachings	Jesus taught the people through sermons, illustrations, and parables. Through his teachings, he showed the true ingredients of faith and how to guard against a fruitless and hypocritical life.	Jesus' teachings show us how to prepare for life in his eternal Kingdom by living properly right now. He lived what he taught, and we, too, must practice what we preach.
Resurrection	When Jesus rose from the dead, he rose in power as the true King. In his victory over death, he established his credentials as King and his power and authority over evil.	The Resurrection shows Jesus' all-powerful life for us—not even death could stop his plan of offering eternal life. Those who believe in Jesus can hope for a resurrection like his. Our role is to tell his story to all the earth so that everyone may share in his victory.

KEY PLACES IN MATTHEW

Jesus' earthly story begins in the town of Bethlehem in the Roman province of Judea (2:1). A threat to kill the infant king led Joseph to take his family to Egypt (2:14). When they returned, God led them to settle in Nazareth in Galilee (2:22, 23). At about age 30, Jesus was baptized in the Jordan River and was tempted by Satan in the Judean wilderness (3:13; 4:1). Jesus set up his base of operations in Capernaum (4:12, 13) and from there ministered throughout Israel, telling parables, teaching about the Kingdom, and healing the sick. He traveled to Gadara and healed two demon-possessed men (8:28ff); fed over 5,000 people with five loaves and two fish on the shores of Galilee near Bethsaida (14:15ff); healed the sick in Gennesaret (14:34ff); ministered to the Gentiles in Tyre and Sidon (15:21ff); visited Caesarea Philippi, where Peter declared him to be the Messiah (16:13ff); and taught in Perea, across the Jordan (19:1). As he set out on his last visit to Jerusalem, he told the disciples what would happen to him there (20:17ff). He spent some time in Jericho (20:29) and then stayed in Bethany at night as he went back and forth to Jerusalem during his last week (21:17ff). In Jerusalem he would be crucified, but he would rise again.

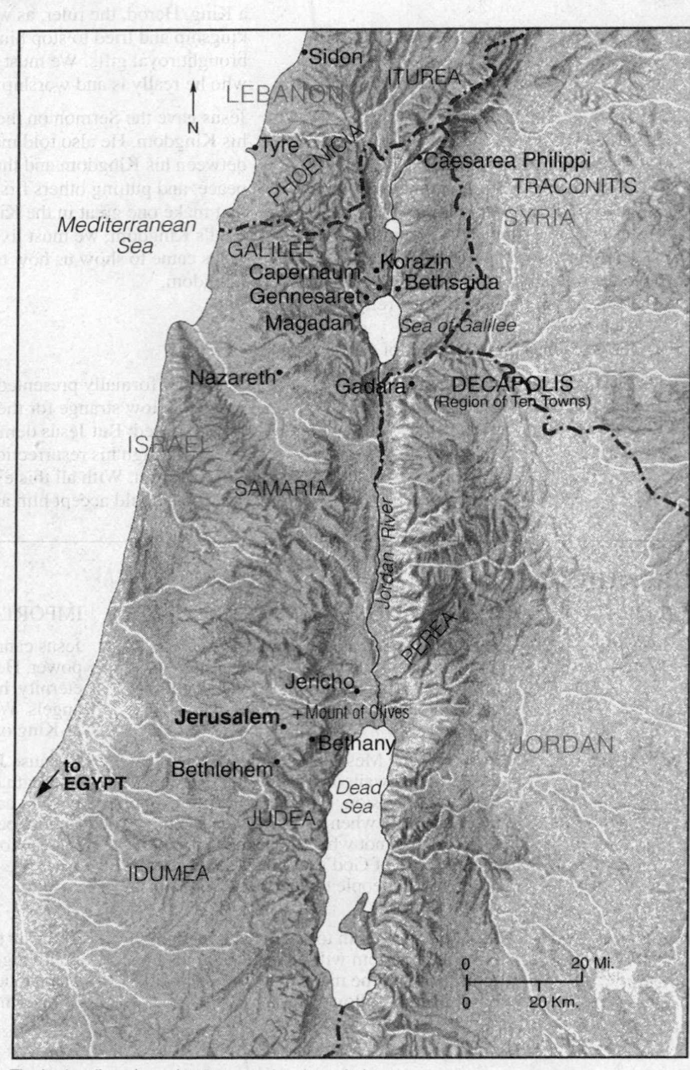

The broken lines (—·—) indicate modern boundaries.

A. BIRTH AND PREPARATION OF JESUS, THE KING (1:1—4:11)

Matthew opens his Gospel with a genealogy to prove that Jesus is a descendant of both King David and Abraham, just as the Old Testament had predicted. Jesus' birth didn't go unnoticed, for both shepherds and astrologers came to worship him. The Jewish people were waiting for the Messiah to appear. However, after he was born, the Jews didn't recognize him because they were looking for a different kind of king.

The Record of Jesus' Ancestors (**3**/Luke 3:23-38)

1 This is a record of the ancestors of Jesus the Messiah, a descendant of King David and of Abraham:

2 Abraham was the father of Isaac.
Isaac was the father of Jacob.
Jacob was the father of Judah and his brothers.
3 Judah was the father of Perez and Zerah (their mother was Tamar).
Perez was the father of Hezron.
Hezron was the father of Ram.*
4 Ram was the father of Amminadab.
Amminadab was the father of Nahshon.
Nahshon was the father of Salmon.
5 Salmon was the father of Boaz (his mother was Rahab).
Boaz was the father of Obed (his mother was Ruth).
Obed was the father of Jesse.
6 Jesse was the father of King David.
David was the father of Solomon (his mother was Bathsheba, the widow of Uriah).
7 Solomon was the father of Rehoboam.
Rehoboam was the father of Abijah.
Abijah was the father of Asaph.*
8 Asaph was the father of Jehoshaphat.
Jehoshaphat was the father of Jehoram.*
Jehoram was the father* of Uzziah.
9 Uzziah was the father of Jotham.
Jotham was the father of Ahaz.
Ahaz was the father of Hezekiah.
10 Hezekiah was the father of Manasseh.
Manasseh was the father of Amos.*
Amos was the father of Josiah.
11 Josiah was the father of Jehoiachin* and his brothers (born at the time of the exile to Babylon).

1:1 Gen 22:18; 2 Sam 7:12-14; 1 Chr 17:11; Pss 89:3-4; 132:11; Isa 9:6; 11:1; Matt 22:42; John 7:42; Rom 1:3; Gal 3:16; Rev 22:16
1:2 Gen 21:3, 12; 25:26; 29:35; 1 Chr 1:34
1:3 Gen 38:29-30; Ruth 4:12, 18-19; 1 Chr 2:4-5, 9
1:4-5 Ruth 4:13, 17-20; 1 Chr 2:10-12, 15; Heb 11:31
1:6 Ruth 4:17, 22; 2 Sam 12:24; 1 Chr 2:13-15
1:7-10 1 Chr 3:10-14
1:11 2 Kgs 24:14-16; 1 Chr 3:15-16; Jer 27:20; Dan 1:1-2

1:3 Greek *Aram;* also in 1:4. See 1 Chr 2:9-10. **1:7** *Asaph* is the same person as Asa; also in 1:8. See 1 Chr 3:10. **1:8a** Greek *Joram.* See 1 Kgs 22:50 and note at 1 Chr 3:11. **1:8b** Or *ancestor;* also in 1:11. **1:10** *Amos* is the same person as Amon. See 1 Chr 3:14. **1:11** Greek *Jeconiah;* also in 1:12. See 2 Kgs 24:6 and note at 1 Chr 3:16.

1:1 Presenting this genealogy was one of the most interesting ways that Matthew could begin a book for a Jewish audience. Because a person's family line proved his or her standing as one of God's chosen people, Matthew began by showing that Jesus was a descendant of Abraham, the father of all Jews, and a direct descendant of David, fulfilling Old Testament prophecies about the Messiah's line. The facts of this ancestry were carefully preserved. This is the first of many proofs recorded by Matthew to show that Jesus is the true Messiah.

1:1ff More than 400 years had passed since the last Old Testament prophecies, and faithful Jews all over the world were still waiting for the Messiah (Luke 3:15). Matthew wrote this book to Jews to present Jesus as King and Messiah, the promised descendant of David who would reign forever (Isaiah 11:1-5). The Gospel of Matthew links the Old and New Testaments and contains many references that show how Jesus fulfilled Old Testament prophecy.

1:1ff Jesus entered human history when the land of Palestine was controlled by Rome and considered an insignificant outpost of the vast and mighty Roman Empire. The presence of Roman soldiers in Israel gave the Jews military peace, but at the price of oppression, slavery, injustice, and immorality. Into this kind of world came the promised Messiah.

1:1-17 In the first 17 verses we meet 46 people whose lifetimes span 2,000 years. All were ancestors of Jesus, but they varied considerably in personality, spirituality, and experience. Some were heroes of faith—like Abraham, Isaac, Ruth, and David. Some had shady reputations—like Rahab and Tamar. Many were very ordinary—like Hezron, Ram, Nahshon, and Akim. And others were evil—like Manasseh and Abijah. God's work in history is not limited by human failures or sins, and he works through ordinary people. Just as God used all kinds of people to bring his Son into the world, he uses all kinds today to accomplish his will. And God wants to use you.

1:11 The Exile occurred in 586 B.C. when Nebuchadnezzar, king of Babylon, conquered Judah, destroyed Jerusalem, and took thousands of captives to Babylon.

12 After the Babylonian exile:
Jehoiachin was the father of Shealtiel.
Shealtiel was the father of Zerubbabel.
13 Zerubbabel was the father of Abiud.
Abiud was the father of Eliakim.
Eliakim was the father of Azor.
14 Azor was the father of Zadok.
Zadok was the father of Akim.
Akim was the father of Eliud.
15 Eliud was the father of Eleazar.
Eleazar was the father of Matthan.
Matthan was the father of Jacob.
16 Jacob was the father of Joseph, the husband of Mary.
Mary was the mother of Jesus, who is called the Messiah.

1:12 1 Chr 3:17, 19 Ezra 3:2

1:16 Matt 27:17, 22 Luke 2:11

17All those listed above include fourteen generations from Abraham to King David, and fourteen from David's time to the Babylonian exile, and fourteen from the Babylonian exile to the Messiah.

An Angel Appears to Joseph (**8**)

18Now this is how Jesus the Messiah was born. His mother, Mary, was engaged to be
married to Joseph. But while she was still a virgin, she became pregnant by the Holy
Spirit. 19Joseph, her fiancé, being a just man, decided to break the engagement quietly,
so as not to disgrace her publicly.
20As he considered this, he fell asleep, and an angel of the Lord appeared to him in a
dream. "Joseph, son of David," the angel said, "do not be afraid to go ahead with your
marriage to Mary. For the child within her has been conceived by the Holy Spirit. 21And

1:18 Luke 1:27, 35 Gal 4:4

1:19 Deut 24:1

1:20 Luke 1:35

1:16 Because Mary was a virgin when she became pregnant, Matthew lists Joseph only as the husband of Mary, not the father of Jesus. Matthew's genealogy gives Jesus' legal (or royal) lineage through Joseph. Mary's ancestral line is recorded in Luke 3:23-38. Both Mary and Joseph were direct descendants of David.

Matthew traced the genealogy back to Abraham, while Luke traced it back to Adam. Matthew wrote to the Jews, so Jesus was shown as a descendant of their father, Abraham. Luke wrote to the Gentiles, so he emphasized Jesus as the Savior of all people.

1:17 Matthew breaks Israel's history into three sets of 14 generations, but there were probably more generations than those listed here. Genealogies often compressed history, meaning that not every generation of ancestors was specifically listed. Thus, the phrase *the father of* can also be translated "the ancestor of."

1:18 There were three steps in a Jewish marriage. First, the two families agreed to the union. Second, a public announcement was made. At this point, the couple was "engaged." This was similar to engagement today except that their relationship could be broken only through death or divorce (even though sexual relations were not yet permitted). Third, the couple was married and began living together. Because Mary and Joseph were engaged, Mary's apparent unfaithfulness carried a severe social stigma. According to Jewish civil law, Joseph had a right to divorce her, and the Jewish authorities could have had her stoned to death (Deuteronomy 22:23, 24).

1:18 Why is the Virgin Birth important to the Christian faith? Jesus Christ, God's Son, had to be free from the sinful nature passed on to all other human beings by Adam. Because Jesus was born of a woman, he was a human being; but as the Son of God, Jesus was born without any trace of human sin. Jesus is both fully human and fully divine.

Because Jesus lived as a man, we know that he fully understands our experiences and struggles (Hebrews 4:15, 16). Because he is God, he has the power and authority to deliver us from sin (Colossians 2:13-15). We can tell Jesus all our thoughts, feelings, and needs. He has been where we are now, and he has the ability to help.

1:18-25 Joseph was faced with a difficult choice after discovering that Mary was pregnant. Although he knew that taking Mary as his wife could be humiliating, Joseph chose to obey the angel's command to marry her. His action revealed four admirable qualities: (1) righteousness (1:19), (2) discretion and sensitivity (1:19), (3) responsiveness to God (1:24), and (4) self-discipline (1:25).

1:19 Perhaps Joseph thought he had only two options: divorce Mary quietly or have her stoned. But God gave a third option—marry her (1:20-23). In view of the circumstances, this had not occurred to Joseph. But God often shows us that there are more options available than we think. Although Joseph seemed to be doing the right thing by breaking the engagement, only God's guidance helped him make the best decision. When our decisions affect the lives of others, we must always seek God's wisdom.

1:20 The conception and birth of Jesus Christ are supernatural events beyond human logic or reasoning. Because of this, God sent angels to help certain people understand the significance of what was happening (see 2:13, 19; Luke 1:11, 26; 2:9).

Angels are spiritual beings created by God who help carry out his work on earth. They bring God's messages to people (Luke 1:26), protect God's people (Daniel 6:22), offer encouragement (Genesis 16:7ff), give guidance (Exodus 14:19), carry out punishment (2 Samuel 24:16), patrol the earth (Zechariah 1:9-14), and fight the forces of evil (2 Kings 6:16-18; Revelation 20:1, 2). There are both good and bad angels (Revelation 12:7), but because bad angels are allied with the Devil, or Satan, they have considerably less power and authority than good angels. Eventually the main role of angels will be to offer continuous praise to God (Revelation 7:11, 12).

1:20-23 The angel declared to Joseph that Mary's child was conceived by the Holy Spirit and would be a son. This reveals an important truth about Jesus—he is both God and human. The infinite, unlimited God took on the limitations of humanity so he could live and die for the salvation of all who would believe in him.

1:21 Luke 1:31; 2:11, 21 Acts 5:31; 13:23 Heb 7:25

1:23 †Isa 7:14; 8:8, 10 John 1:14 1 Tim 3:16

she will have a son, and you are to name him Jesus,* for he will save his people from
their sins." 22All of this happened to fulfill the Lord's message through his prophet:

23 "Look! The virgin will conceive a child!
She will give birth to a son,
and he will be called Immanuel*
(meaning, God is with us)."

1:21 *Jesus* means "The LORD saves." **1:23** Isa 7:14; 8:8, 10.

JOSEPH

The strength of what we believe is measured by how much we are willing to suffer for those beliefs. Joseph was a man with strong beliefs. He was prepared to do what was right, despite the pain he knew it would cause. But Joseph had another trait: He not only tried to do what was right, he also tried to do it in the right way.

When Mary told Joseph about her pregnancy, Joseph knew the child was not his. His respect for Mary's character and the explanation she gave him, as well as her attitude toward the expected child, must have made it hard to think his bride had done something wrong. Still, someone else was the child's father—and it was mind-boggling to accept that the "someone else" was God.

Joseph decided he had to break the engagement, but he was determined to do it in a way that would not cause public shame to Mary. He intended to act with justice and love.

At this point, God sent a messenger to Joseph to confirm Mary's story and open another way of obedience for Joseph—to take Mary as his wife. Joseph obeyed God, married Mary, and honored her virginity until the baby was born.

We do not know how long Joseph lived his role as Jesus' earthly father—he is last mentioned when Jesus was 12 years old. But Joseph trained his son in the trade of carpentry, made sure he had good spiritual training in Nazareth, and took the whole family on the yearly trip to Jerusalem for the Passover, which Jesus continued to observe during his adult years.

Joseph knew Jesus was someone special from the moment he heard the angel's words. His strong belief in that fact and his willingness to follow God's leading empowered him to be Jesus' chosen earthly father.

Strengths and accomplishments
- A man of integrity
- A descendant of King David
- Jesus' legal and earthly father
- A person sensitive to God's guidance and willing to do God's will no matter what the consequence

Lessons from his life
- God honors integrity
- Social position is of little importance when God chooses to use us
- Being obedient to the guidance we have from God leads to more guidance from him
- Feelings are not accurate measures of the rightness or wrongness of an action

Vital statistics
- Where: Nazareth, Bethlehem
- Occupation: Carpenter
- Relatives: Wife: Mary. Children: Jesus, James, Joses, Judas, Simon, and daughters
- Contemporaries: Herod the Great, John the Baptist, Simeon, Anna

Key verses
"Joseph, her fiancé, being a just man, decided to break the engagement quietly, so as not to disgrace her publicly. As he considered this, he fell asleep, and an angel of the Lord appeared to him in a dream. 'Joseph, son of David,' the angel said, 'do not be afraid to go ahead with your marriage to Mary. For the child within her has been conceived by the Holy Spirit' " (Matthew 1:19, 20).

Joseph's story is told in Matthew 1:16—2:23; Luke 1:26—2:52.

1:21 *Jesus* means "the Lord saves." Jesus came to earth to save us because we can't save ourselves from sin and its consequences. No matter how good we are, we can't eliminate the sinful nature present in all of us. Only Jesus can do that. Jesus didn't come to help people save themselves; he came to be their Savior from the power and penalty of sin. Thank Christ for his death on the cross for your sin, and then ask him to take control of your life. Your new life begins at that moment.

1:23 Jesus was to be called *Immanuel* ("God is with us"), as predicted by Isaiah the prophet (Isaiah 7:14). Jesus was God in the flesh; thus, God was literally among us, "with us." Through the Holy Spirit, Christ is present today in the life of every believer. Perhaps not even Isaiah understood how far-reaching the meaning of *Immanuel* would be.

24 When Joseph woke up, he did what the angel of the Lord commanded. He brought
Mary home to be his wife, 25 but she remained a virgin until her son was born. And **1:25** Luke 1:31
Joseph named him Jesus.

Visitors Arrive from Eastern Lands (**12**)

2 Jesus was born in the town of Bethlehem in Judea, during the reign of King Herod. **2:1** Luke 1:5; 2:4-7
About that time some wise men* from eastern lands arrived in Jerusalem, asking,
2 "Where is the newborn king of the Jews? We have seen his star as it arose,* and we **2:2** Num 24:17
have come to worship him." Jer 23:5

3 Herod was deeply disturbed by their question, as was all of Jerusalem. 4 He called a Matt 2:9; 27:11 Rev 22:16
meeting of the leading priests and teachers of religious law. "Where did the prophets say
the Messiah would be born?" he asked them.

2:1 Or *royal astrologers;* Greek reads *magi;* also in 2:7, 16. **2:2** Or *in the east.*

1:24 Joseph changed his plans quickly after learning that Mary had not been unfaithful to him (1:19). He obeyed God and proceeded with the marriage plans. Although others may have disapproved of his decision, Joseph went ahead with what he knew was right. Sometimes we avoid doing what is right because of what others might think. Like Joseph, we must choose to obey God rather than seek the approval of others.

2:1 Bethlehem is a small town five miles south of Jerusalem. It sits on a high ridge over 2,000 feet above sea level. It is mentioned in more detail in the Gospel of Luke. Luke also explains why Joseph and Mary were in Bethlehem when Jesus was born, rather than in Nazareth, their hometown.

2:1 The land of Israel was divided into four political districts and several lesser territories. Judea was to the south, Samaria in the middle, Galilee to the north, and Idumea to the southwest. Bethlehem of Judea (also called Judah, 2:6) had been prophesied as the Messiah's birthplace (Micah 5:2). Jerusalem was also in Judea and was the seat of government for Herod the Great, king over all four political districts. After Herod's death, the districts were divided among three separate rulers (see the note on 2:19-22). Although he was a ruthless, evil man who murdered many in his own family, Herod the Great supervised the renovation of the Temple, making it much larger and more beautiful. This made him popular with many Jews. Jesus would visit Jerusalem many times because the great Jewish festivals were held there.

2:1, 2 Not much is known about these astrologers (traditionally called wise men). We don't know where they came from or how many there were. Tradition says they were men of high position from Parthia, near the site of ancient Babylon. How did they know that the star represented the Messiah? (1) They could have been Jews who remained in Babylon after the Exile and knew the Old Testament predictions of the Messiah's coming. (2) They may have been eastern astrologers who studied ancient manuscripts from around the world. Because of the Jewish exile centuries earlier, they would have had copies of the Old Testament in their land. (3) They may have had a special message from God directing them to the Messiah. Some scholars say these astrologers were each from a different land, representing the entire world bowing before Jesus. These men from faraway lands recognized Jesus as the Messiah when most of God's chosen people in Israel did not. Matthew pictures Jesus as the King over the whole world, not just Judea.

2:1, 2 The astrologers traveled thousands of miles to see the king of the Jews. When they finally found him, they responded with joy, worship, and gifts. This is so different from the approach people often take today. We expect God to come looking for us, to explain himself, prove who he is, and give *us* gifts. But those who are wise still seek and worship Jesus today, not for what they can get, but for who he is.

2:2 The astrologers said they saw Jesus' star. Balaam referred to a coming "star . . . from Jacob" (Numbers 24:17). Some say this star may have been a conjunction of Jupiter, Saturn, and Mars in 6 B.C., and others offer other explanations. But couldn't God, who created the heavens, have created a special star to signal the arrival of his Son? Whatever the nature of the star, these astrologers traveled thousands of miles searching for a king, and they found him.

2:3 Herod the Great was quite disturbed when the astrologers asked about a newborn king of the Jews because (1) Herod was not the rightful heir to the throne of David; therefore, many Jews hated him as a usurper. If Jesus really was an heir, trouble would arise. (2) Herod was ruthless, and because of his many enemies, he was suspicious that someone would try to overthrow him. (3) Herod didn't want the Jews, a religious people, to unite around a religious figure. (4) If these astrologers were of Jewish descent and from Parthia (the most powerful region next to Rome), they would have welcomed a Jewish king who could swing the balance of power away from Rome. The land of Israel, far from Rome, would have been easy prey for a nation trying to gain more control.

2:4 The leading priests and teachers of religious law were aware of Micah 5:2 and other prophecies about the Messiah. The astrologers' news troubled Herod because he knew that the Jewish people expected the Messiah to come soon (Luke 3:15). Most Jews expected the Messiah to be a great military and political deliverer, like Alexander the Great. Herod's counselors would have told Herod this. No wonder this ruthless man took no chances and ordered all the baby boys in Bethlehem killed (2:16)!

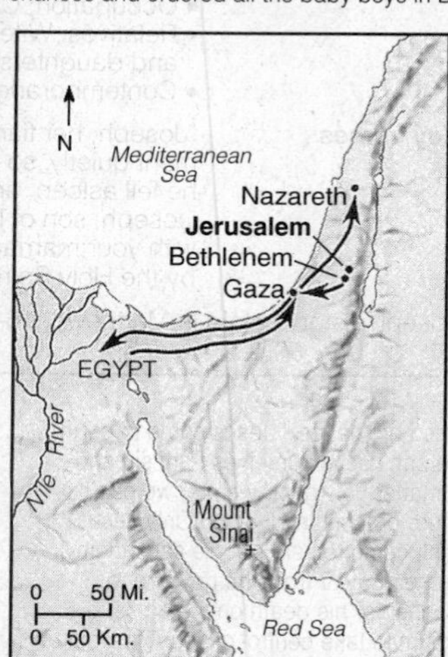

THE FLIGHT TO EGYPT
Herod planned to kill the baby Jesus, whom he perceived to be a future threat to his position. Warned of this treachery in a dream, Joseph took his family to Egypt until Herod's death, which occurred a year or two later. They then planned to return to Judea, but God led them instead to Nazareth in Galilee.

2:5 John 7:42 — 5“In Bethlehem,” they said, “for this is what the prophet wrote:

2:6 †Mic 5:2 — 6 ‘O Bethlehem of Judah,
you are not just a lowly village in Judah,
for a ruler will come from you
who will be the shepherd for my people Israel.’*”

7Then Herod sent a private message to the wise men, asking them to come see him.
At this meeting he learned the exact time when they first saw the star. 8Then he told them,
“Go to Bethlehem and search carefully for the child. And when you find him, come back
and tell me so that I can go and worship him, too!”

2:9 Matt 2:2 — 9After this interview the wise men went their way. Once again the star appeared to
them, guiding them to Bethlehem. It went ahead of them and stopped over the place
2:11 Ps 72:10; Isa 60:6 — where the child was. 10When they saw the star, they were filled with joy! 11They entered
the house where the child and his mother, Mary, were, and they fell down before him and
2:12 Matt 2:22 — worshiped him. Then they opened their treasure chests and gave him gifts of gold,
frankincense, and myrrh. 12But when it was time to leave, they went home another way,
because God had warned them in a dream not to return to Herod.

The Escape to Egypt (**13**)

2:13 Matt 1:20; 2:19 — 13After the wise men were gone, an angel of the Lord appeared to Joseph in a dream.
“Get up and flee to Egypt with the child and his mother,” the angel said. “Stay there until

2:6 Mic 5:2; 2 Sam 5:2.

GOSPEL ACCOUNTS FOUND ONLY IN MATTHEW

Passage	Subject
1:20–24	Joseph’s dream*
2:1–12	The visit of the astrologers
2:13–15	Escape to Egypt*
2:16–18	Slaughter of the children*
27:3–10	The death of Judas*
27:19	The dream of Pilate’s wife
27:52	The other resurrections
28:11–15	The bribery of the guards
28:19, 20	The baptism emphasis in the great commission*

Matthew records nine special events that are not mentioned in any of the other Gospels. In each case, the most apparent reason for Matthew’s choice has to do with his purpose in communicating the gospel to Jewish people. Five cases are fulfillments of Old Testament prophecies (marked with asterisks above). The other four would have been of particular interest to the Jews of Matthew’s day.

2:5, 6 Matthew often quoted Old Testament prophets. This prophecy, paraphrasing Micah 5:2, had been delivered seven centuries earlier.

2:6 Most religious leaders believed in a literal fulfillment of all Old Testament prophecy; therefore, they believed the Messiah would be born in Bethlehem. Ironically, when Jesus was born, these same religious leaders became his greatest enemies. When the Messiah for whom they had been waiting finally came, they didn’t recognize him.

2:8 Herod did not want to worship Christ—he was lying. This was a trick to get the astrologers to return to him and reveal the whereabouts of the newborn king. Herod’s plan was to kill Jesus.

2:11 Jesus was probably one or two years old when the astrologers found him. By this time, Mary and Joseph were married, living in a house, and intending to stay in Bethlehem for a while. For more on Joseph and Mary’s stay there, see the note on Luke 2:39.

2:11 The astrologers gave these expensive gifts because they were worthy presents for a future king. Bible students have seen in the gifts symbols of Christ’s identity and what he would accomplish. Gold was a gift for a king; frankincense was a gift for deity; and myrrh was a spice used to anoint a body for burial. These gifts may have provided the financial resources for the trip to Egypt and back.

2:11 The astrologers brought gifts and worshiped Jesus for who he was. This is the essence of true worship—honoring Christ for who he is and being willing to give him what is valuable to you. Worship God because he is the perfect, just, and almighty Creator of the universe, worthy of the best you have to give.

2:12 After finding Jesus and worshiping him, the astrologers were warned by God not to return through Jerusalem as they had intended. Finding Jesus may mean that your life must take a different direction, one that is responsive and obedient to God’s Word. Are you willing to be led a different way?

2:13 This was the second dream or vision that Joseph received from God. Joseph’s first dream revealed that Mary’s child would be the Messiah (1:20, 21). His second dream told him how to protect the child’s life. Although Joseph was not Jesus’ natural father, he was Jesus’ legal father and was responsible for his safety and well-being. Divine guidance comes only to prepared hearts. Joseph remained receptive to God’s guidance.

I tell you to return, because Herod is going to try to kill the child." 14 That night Joseph
left for Egypt with the child and Mary, his mother, 15 and they stayed there until Herod's
death. This fulfilled what the Lord had spoken through the prophet: "I called my Son out
of Egypt."*

16 Herod was furious when he learned that the wise men had outwitted him. He sent
soldiers to kill all the boys in and around Bethlehem who were two years old and under,
because the wise men had told him the star first appeared to them about two years
earlier.* 17 Herod's brutal action fulfilled the prophecy of Jeremiah:

18 "A cry of anguish is heard in Ramah—
weeping and mourning unrestrained.
Rachel weeps for her children,
refusing to be comforted—for they are dead."*

The Return to Nazareth (**14**)

19 When Herod died, an angel of the Lord appeared in a dream to Joseph in Egypt and
told him, 20 "Get up and take the child and his mother back to the land of Israel,
because those who were trying to kill the child are dead." 21 So Joseph returned
immediately to Israel with Jesus and his mother. 22 But when he learned that the new
ruler was Herod's son Archelaus, he was afraid. Then, in another dream, he was
warned to go to Galilee. 23 So they went and lived in a town called Nazareth. This
fulfilled what was spoken by the prophets concerning the Messiah: "He will be called
a Nazarene."

John the Baptist Prepares the Way for Jesus (**16**/Mark 1:1-8; Luke 3:1-17)

3 In those days John the Baptist began preaching in the Judean wilderness. His
message was, 2 "Turn from your sins and turn to God, because the Kingdom of
Heaven is near.*" 3 Isaiah had spoken of John when he said,

2:15 †Hos 11:1
2:18 †Jer 31:15
2:19 Matt 1:20; 2:12
2:20 Exod 4:19
2:22 Matt 2:12
2:23 Isa 11:1; 53:2; Luke 2:39; John 1:45-46; Acts 4:10; 24:5
3:2 Matt 4:17; 10:7; Mark 1:15

2:15 Hos 11:1. **2:16** Or *according to the time he calculated from the wise men.* **2:18** Jer 31:15. **3:2** Or *has come* or *is coming soon.*

2:14, 15 Going to Egypt was not unusual because there were colonies of Jews in several major Egyptian cities. These colonies had developed during the time of the great captivity (see Jeremiah 43–44). There is an interesting parallel between this flight to Egypt and Israel's history. As an infant nation, Israel went to Egypt, just as Jesus did as a child. God led Israel out (Hosea 11:1); God brought Jesus back. Both events show God working to save his people.

2:16 Herod, the king of the Jews, killed all the boys under two years of age in an obsessive attempt to kill Jesus, the newborn king. He stained his hands with blood, but he did not harm Jesus. Herod was king by a human appointment; Jesus was King by a divine appointment. No one can thwart God's plans.

2:16 Herod was afraid that this newborn king would one day take his throne. He completely misunderstood the reason for Christ's coming. Jesus didn't want Herod's throne; he wanted to be king of Herod's life. Jesus wanted to give Herod eternal life, not take away his present life. Today people are often afraid that Christ wants to take things away when, in reality, he wants to give them real freedom, peace, and joy. Don't fear Christ—give him the throne of your life.

2:17, 18 Rachel was the wife of Jacob, one of the great men of God in the Old Testament. From Jacob's 12 sons had come the 12 tribes of Israel. Rachel was buried near Bethlehem (Genesis 35:19). For more about the significance of this verse, see the note on Jeremiah 31:15, from which this verse was quoted.

2:19-22 Herod the Great died in 4 B.C. of an incurable disease. Rome trusted him but didn't trust his sons. Herod knew that Rome wouldn't give his successor as much power, so he divided his kingdom into three parts, one for each son. Archelaus received Judea, Samaria, and Idumea; Herod Antipas received Galilee and Perea; Herod Philip II received Traconitis. Archelaus, a violent man, began his reign by slaughtering 3,000 influential people. Nine years later, he was banished. God didn't want Joseph's family to go into the region of this evil ruler.

2:23 Nazareth sat in the hilly area of southern Galilee near the crossroads of great caravan trade routes. The town itself was rather small. The Roman garrison in charge of Galilee was housed there. The people of Nazareth had constant contact with people from all over the world, so world news reached them quickly. The people of Nazareth had an attitude of independence that many of the Jews despised. This may have been why Nathanael commented "Nazareth! . . . Can anything good come from there?" (John 1:46).

2:23 The Old Testament does not record this specific statement, "He will be called a Nazarene." Many scholars believe, however, that Matthew is referring to Isaiah 11:1, where the Hebrew word for "branch" is similar to the word for "Nazarene." Or he may be referring to a prophecy unrecorded in the Bible. In any case, Matthew paints the picture of Jesus as the true Messiah announced by God through the prophets; and he makes the point that Jesus, the Messiah, had unexpectedly humble beginnings, just as the Old Testament had predicted (see Micah 5:2).

3:1, 2 Almost 30 years had passed since the events of chapter 2. Here John the Baptist burst onto the scene. His theme was "Turn from your sins!" The people needed to repent—make a 180-degree turn—from the kind of self-centeredness that leads to wrong actions, such as lying, cheating, stealing, gossiping, taking revenge, abusing, and indulging in sexual immorality. A person who turns from sin stops rebelling and begins following God's way of living prescribed in his Word. The first step in turning to God is to admit your sin, as John urged. Then God will receive you and help you live the way he wants. Remember that only God can get rid of sin. He doesn't expect us to clean up our life *before* we come to him.

3:1, 2 John the Baptist's Profile is found in John 1.

3:3 †Isa 40:3 Mal 3:1 Luke 1:76

"He is a voice shouting in the wilderness:
'Prepare a pathway for the Lord's coming!
Make a straight road for him!' "*

3:4 Lev 11:22 2 Kgs 1:8

[4]John's clothes were woven from camel hair, and he wore a leather belt; his food was

3:3 Isa 40:3.

HEROD

The Bible records history. It has proven itself an accurate and reliable record of people, events, and places. Independent historical accounts verify the Bible's descriptions and details of many famous lives. One of these was the father of the Herodian family, Herod the Great.

Herod is remembered as a builder of cities and the lavish rebuilder of the Temple in Jerusalem. But he also destroyed people. He showed little greatness in either his personal actions or his character. He was ruthless in ruling his territory. His suspicions and jealousy led to the murder of several of his children and the death of his wife Mariamne.

Herod's title, king of the Jews, was granted by Rome but never accepted by the Jewish people. He was not part of the Davidic family line, and he was only partly Jewish. Although Israel benefited from Herod's lavish efforts to repair the Temple in Jerusalem, he won little admiration because he also rebuilt various pagan temples. Herod's costly attempt to gain the loyalty of the people failed because it was superficial. His only loyalty was to himself.

Because his royal title was not genuine, Herod was constantly worried about losing his position. His actions when hearing from the astrologers about their search for the new king are consistent with all that we know about Herod. He planned to locate and kill the child before he could become a threat. The murder of innocent children that followed is a tragic lesson in what can happen when actions are motivated by selfishness. Herod's suspicions did not spare even his own family. His life was self-destructive.

Strengths and accomplishments
- Was given the title king of the Jews by the Romans
- Held on to his power for more than 30 years
- Was an effective, though ruthless, ruler
- Sponsored a great variety of large building projects

Weaknesses and mistakes
- Tended to treat those around him with fear, suspicion, and jealousy
- Had several of his own children and at least one wife killed
- Ordered the killing of the infants in Bethlehem
- Although claiming to be a God-worshiper, he was still involved in many forms of pagan religion

Lessons from his life
- Great power brings neither peace nor security
- No one can prevent God's plans from being carried out
- Superficial loyalty does not impress people or God

Vital statistics
- Occupation: King of Judea from 37 to 4 B.C.
- Relatives: Father: Antipater. Sons: Archelaus, Antipater, Antipas, Philip, and others. Wives: Doris, Mariamne, and others
- Contemporaries: Zechariah, Elizabeth, Mary, Joseph, Mark Antony, Augustus

Key verse
"Herod was furious when he learned that the astrologers had outwitted him. He sent soldiers to kill all the boys in and around Bethlehem who were two years old and under" (Matthew 2:16).

Herod the Great is mentioned in Matthew 2:1–22 and Luke 1:5.

3:2 The Kingdom of Heaven began when God himself entered human history as a man. Today Jesus Christ reigns in the hearts of believers, but the Kingdom of Heaven will not be fully realized until all evil in the world is judged and removed. Christ came to earth first as a suffering servant; he will come again as king and judge to rule victoriously over all the earth.

3:3 The prophecy quoted is Isaiah 40:3. Isaiah was one of the greatest prophets of the Old Testament and one of the most quoted in the New. Like Isaiah, John was a prophet who urged the people to confess their sins and live for God. Both prophets taught that the message of repentance is good news to those who listen and seek the healing forgiveness of God's love but terrible news to those who refuse to listen and thus cut off their only hope.

3:3 John the Baptist *prepared* the way for Jesus. People who do not know Jesus need to get ready to meet him. We can prepare them by explaining their need for forgiveness, demonstrating Christ's teachings by our conduct, and telling them how Christ can give their lives meaning. We can "make a straight road for him" by correcting misconceptions that might be hindering people from coming to Christ. Someone you know may be open to a relationship with Christ. What can you do to prepare the way for this person?

3:4 John was markedly different from other religious leaders of his day. While many were greedy, selfish, and preoccupied with winning the praise of the people, John was concerned only with the praise of God. Having separated himself from the evil and hypocrisy of his day, John lived differently from other people to show that his message was new. John not only preached God's law, he *lived* it. Do you practice what you preach? Could people discover what you believe by observing the way you live?

3:4-6 John must have presented a strange image! Many people came to hear this preacher, who wore odd clothes and ate unusual food. Some probably came simply out of curiosity and ended up turning from their sins as they listened to his powerful message.

locusts and wild honey. [5]People from Jerusalem and from every section of Judea and
from all over the Jordan Valley went out to the wilderness to hear him preach. [6]And
when they confessed their sins, he baptized them in the Jordan River.
[7]But when he saw many Pharisees and Sadducees coming to be baptized, he denounced them. "You brood of snakes!" he exclaimed. "Who warned you to flee God's
coming judgment? [8]Prove by the way you live that you have really turned from your sins
and turned to God. [9]Don't just say, 'We're safe—we're the descendants of Abraham.'
That proves nothing. God can change these stones here into children of Abraham. [10]Even
now the ax of God's judgment is poised, ready to sever your roots. Yes, every tree that
does not produce good fruit will be chopped down and thrown into the fire.
[11]"I baptize with* water those who turn from their sins and turn to God. But
someone is coming soon who is far greater than I am—so much greater that I am not
even worthy to be his slave.* He will baptize you with the Holy Spirit and with fire.*

3:7 Matt 12:34; 23:33 Luke 3:7; 21:23 John 8:44 Rom 1:8; 5:9 Eph 5:6 Col 3:6

3:9 John 8:33, 37, 39 Acts 13:26 Rom 4:12

3:10 Matt 7:19 Luke 13:7 John 15:6

3:11 John 1:26-33 Acts 1:5; 2:3-4; 13:24; 19:4

3:11a Or *in.* **3:11b** Greek *to carry his sandals.* **3:11c** Or *in the Holy Spirit and in fire.*

People may be curious about your Christian life-style and values. You can use their simple curiosity as an opener to share how Christ makes a difference in you.

3:5 Why did John attract so many people? He was the first true prophet in 400 years. He blasted both Herod and the religious leaders, daring acts that fascinated the common people. But John also had strong words for his audience: They, too, were sinners and needed to turn from their sins. His message was powerful and true. The people were expecting a prophet like Elijah (Malachi 4:5; Luke 1:17), and John seemed to be the one!

3:6 When you wash dirty hands, the results are immediately visible. But turning from sins (repentance) happens inside with a cleansing that isn't seen right away. So John used a symbolic action that people could see: baptism. The Jews used baptism to initiate converts, so John's audience was familiar with the rite. Here, baptism was used as a sign of repentance and forgiveness. Turning from sins implies a change in behavior, turning from sin toward God. Have you turned from sin in your life? Can others see the difference it makes in you? A changed life with new and different behavior makes your repentance real and visible.

3:6 The Jordan River is about 70 miles long, its main section stretching between the Sea of Galilee and the Dead Sea. Jerusalem lies about 20 miles west of the Jordan. This river was Israel's eastern border, and many significant events in the nation's history took place there. It was by the Jordan River that the Israelites renewed their covenant with God before entering the Promised Land (Joshua 1–2). Here John the Baptist calls them to renew their covenant with God again, this time through baptism.

3:7 The Jewish religious leaders were divided into several groups. Two of the most prominent groups were the Pharisees and the Sadducees. The Pharisees separated themselves from anything non-Jewish and carefully followed both the Old Testament laws and the oral traditions handed down through the centuries. The Sadducees believed the Pentateuch alone (Genesis—Deuteronomy) to be God's Word. They were descended mainly from priestly nobility, while the Pharisees came from all classes of people. The two groups disliked each other greatly, and both opposed Jesus. John the Baptist criticized the Pharisees for being legalistic and hypocritical, following the letter of the law while ignoring its true intent. He criticized the Sadducees for using religion to advance their political position. For more information on these two groups, see the chart in Mark 2.

3:8 John the Baptist called people to more than words or ritual; he told them to change their behavior. "Prove by the way you live that you have really turned from your sins" means that God looks beyond our words and religious activities to see if our conduct backs up what we say, and he judges our words by the actions that accompany them. Do your actions match your words?

3:9, 10 Just as a fruit tree is expected to bear fruit, God's people should produce a crop of good deeds. God has no use for people who call themselves Christians but who live otherwise. Like many people in John's day who were God's people in name only, we are of no value if we are Christians in name only. If others can't see our faith in the way we treat them, we may not be God's people at all.

3:10 God's message hasn't changed since the Old Testament: People will be judged for their unproductive lives. God calls us to be *active* in our obedience. John compared people who claim they believe God but don't live for God to unproductive trees that will be cut down. To be productive for God, we must obey his teachings, resist temptation, actively serve and help others, and share our faith. How productive are you for God?

3:11 John baptized people as a sign that they had asked God to forgive their sins and had decided to live as he wanted them to live. Baptism was an *outward* sign of commitment. To be effective, it had to be accompanied by an *inward* change of attitude leading to a changed life—the work of the Holy Spirit. John said that Jesus would baptize with the Holy Spirit and fire. This looked ahead to Pentecost (Acts 2), when the Holy Spirit would be sent by Jesus in the form of tongues of fire, empowering his followers to preach the Good News. John's statement also symbolizes the work of the Holy Spirit in bringing God's judgment on those who refuse to turn from their sins. Everyone will one day be baptized—either now by God's Holy Spirit or later by the fire of his judgment.

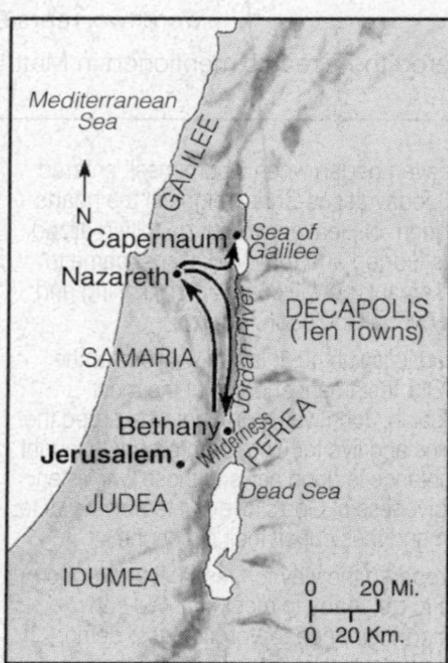

JESUS BEGINS HIS MINISTRY
From his childhood home, Nazareth, Jesus set out to begin his earthly ministry. He was baptized by John the Baptist in the Jordan River, tempted by Satan in the wilderness, and then returned to Galilee. Between the temptation and his move to Capernaum (4:12, 13), he ministered in Judea, Samaria, and Galilee (see John 1—4).

3:12 Matt 13:30

12 He is ready to separate the chaff from the grain with his winnowing fork. Then he
will clean up the threshing area, storing the grain in his barn but burning the chaff
with never-ending fire."

The Baptism of Jesus (**17**/Mark 1:9-11; Luke 3:21-22)

3:13-17 Mark 1:9-11; Luke 3:21-22; John 1:31-34
3:16 Isa 11:2
3:17 Gen 22:2; Ps 2:7; Isa 42:1; Matt 12:18; 17:5; Mark 9:7; Luke 9:35

13 Then Jesus went from Galilee to the Jordan River to be baptized by John. 14 But John
didn't want to baptize him. "I am the one who needs to be baptized by you," he said, "so
why are you coming to me?"
15 But Jesus said, "It must be done, because we must do everything that is right.*" So
then John baptized him.
16 After his baptism, as Jesus came up out of the water, the heavens were opened and
he saw the Spirit of God descending like a dove and settling on him. 17 And a voice from
heaven said, "This is my beloved Son, and I am fully pleased with him."

3:15 Or *we must fulfill all righteousness.*

THE PHARISEES AND SADDUCEES

The Pharisees and Sadducees were the two major religious groups in Israel at the time of Christ. The Pharisees were more religiously minded, while the Sadducees were more politically minded. Although the groups disliked and distrusted each other, they became allies in their common hatred for Jesus.

Name	*Positive Characteristics*	*Negative Characteristics*
PHARISEES	• Were committed to obeying all of God's commands • Were admired by the common people for their apparent piety • Believed in a bodily resurrection and eternal life • Believed in angels and demons	• Behaved as though their own religious rules were just as important as God's rules for living • Their piety was often hypocritical, and their efforts often forced others to try to live up to standards they themselves could not live up to • Believed that salvation came from perfect obedience to the law and was not based on forgiveness of sins • Became so obsessed with obeying their legal interpretations in every detail that they completely ignored God's message of mercy and grace • Were more concerned with appearing to be good than obeying God
SADDUCEES	• Believed strongly in the Mosaic law and in Levitical purity • Were more practically minded than the Pharisees	• Relied on logic while placing little importance on faith • Did not believe all the Old Testament was God's Word • Did not believe in a bodily resurrection or eternal life • Did not believe in angels or demons • Were often willing to compromise their values with the Romans and others in order to maintain their status and influential positions

3:12 A winnowing fork is a pitchfork used to toss wheat in the air to separate grain from chaff. The grain is the part of the plant that is useful; chaff is the worthless outer shell. Because it is useless, chaff is burned; grain, however, is gathered. "Winnowing" is often used as a picture of God's judgment. Unrepentant people will be judged and discarded because they are worthless in doing God's work; those who repent and believe will be saved and used by God.

3:13-15 John had been explaining that Jesus' baptism would be much greater than his, when suddenly Jesus came to him and asked to be baptized! John felt unqualified. He wanted Jesus to baptize him. Why did Jesus ask to be baptized? It was not for repentance for sin because Jesus never sinned. "We must do everything that is right" refers to accomplishing God's mission. Jesus saw his baptism as advancing God's work. Jesus was baptized because (1) he was confessing sin on behalf of the nation, as Nehemiah, Ezra, Moses, and Daniel had done; (2) he was showing support for what John was doing; (3) he was inaugurating his public ministry; (4) he was identifying with the penitent people of God, not with the critical Pharisees who were only watching. Jesus, the perfect man, didn't need baptism for sin, but he accepted baptism in obedient service to the Father, and God showed his approval.

3:15 Put yourself in John's shoes. Your work is going well, people are taking notice, everything is growing. But you know that the purpose of your work is to prepare the people for Jesus (John 1:35-37). Then Jesus arrives, and his coming tests your integrity. Will you be able to turn your followers over to him? John passed the test by publicly baptizing Jesus. Soon he would say, "He must become greater and greater, and I must become less and less" (John 3:30). Can we, like John, put our egos and profitable work aside in order to point others to Jesus? Are we willing to lose some of our status so that everyone will benefit?

3:16, 17 The doctrine of the Trinity means that God is three persons and yet one in essence. In this passage, all three persons of the Trinity are present and active. God the Father speaks; God the Son is baptized; God the Holy Spirit descends on Jesus. God is one, yet in three persons at the same time. This is one of God's incomprehensible mysteries. Other Bible references that speak of the Father, Son, and Holy Spirit are Matthew 28:19; John 15:26; 1 Corinthians 12:4-13; 2 Corinthians 13:14; Ephesians 2:18; 1 Thessalonians 1:2-5; and 1 Peter 1:2.

Satan Tempts Jesus in the Wilderness (**18**/Mark 1:12-13; Luke 4:1-13)

4 Then Jesus was led out into the wilderness by the Holy Spirit to be tempted there by — **4:1** Gen 3:1-7; 1 Thes 3:5
the Devil. 2For forty days and forty nights he ate nothing and became very hungry.
3Then the Devil* came and said to him, "If you are the Son of God, change these stones — **4:2** Exod 34:28; 1 Kgs 19:8
into loaves of bread."
4But Jesus told him, "No! The Scriptures say, — **4:4** †Deut 8:3

'People need more than bread for their life;
they must feed on every word of God.'*"

5Then the Devil took him to Jerusalem, to the highest point of the Temple, 6and said, — **4:6** †Ps 91:11-12
"If you are the Son of God, jump off! For the Scriptures say,

'He orders his angels to protect you.
And they will hold you with their hands
to keep you from striking your foot on a stone.'*"

4:3 Greek *the tempter.* **4:4** Deut 8:3. **4:6** Ps 91:11-12.

4:1 This time of testing showed that Jesus really was the Son of God, able to overcome the Devil and his temptations. A person has not shown true obedience if he or she has never had an opportunity to disobey. We read in Deuteronomy 8:2 that God led Israel into the wilderness to humble and test them. God wanted to see whether or not his people would really obey him. We, too, will be tested. Because we know that testing will come, we should be alert and ready for it. Remember, your convictions are only strong if they hold up under pressure!

4:1 The Devil, also called Satan, tempted Eve in the Garden of Eden, and here he tempted Jesus in the wilderness. Satan is a fallen angel. He is *real,* not symbolic, and is constantly fighting against those who follow and obey God. Satan's temptations are real, and he is always trying to get us to live his way or our way rather than God's way. Jesus will one day reign over all creation, but Satan tried to force his hand and get him to declare his kingship prematurely. If Jesus had given in, his mission on earth—to die for our sins and give us the opportunity to have eternal life—would have been lost. When temptations seem especially strong, or when you think you can rationalize giving in, consider whether Satan may be trying to block God's purposes for your life or for someone else's life.

4:1ff This temptation by the Devil shows us that Jesus was human, and it gave Jesus the opportunity to reaffirm God's plan for his ministry. It also gives us an example to follow when we are tempted. Jesus' temptation was an important demonstration of his sinlessness. He would face temptation and not give in.

4:1ff Jesus was tempted by the Devil, but he never sinned! Although we may feel dirty after being tempted, we should remember that temptation itself is not sin. We sin when we give in and disobey God. Remembering this will help us turn away from the temptation.

4:1ff Jesus wasn't tempted inside the Temple or at his baptism but in the wilderness, where he was tired, alone, and hungry, and thus most vulnerable. The Devil often tempts us when we are vulnerable—when we are under physical or emotional stress (for example, lonely, tired, weighing big decisions, or faced with uncertainty). But he also likes to tempt us through our strengths, where we are most susceptible to pride (see the note on Luke 4:3ff). We must guard at all times against his attacks.

4:1-10 The Devil's temptations focused on three crucial areas: (1) physical needs and desires, (2) possessions and power, and (3) pride (see 1 John 2:15, 16 for a similar list). But Jesus did not give in. Hebrews 4:15 says that Jesus "faced all of the same temptations we do, yet he did not sin." He knows firsthand what we are experiencing, and he is willing and able to help us in our struggles. When you are tempted, turn to him for strength.

4:3, 4 Jesus was hungry and weak after fasting for 40 days, but he chose not to use his divine power to satisfy his natural desire for food. Food, hunger, and eating are good, but the timing was wrong. Jesus was in the wilderness to fast, not to eat. And because Jesus had given up the unlimited, independent use of his divine power in order to experience humanity fully, he wouldn't use his power to change the stones to bread. We also may be tempted to satisfy a perfectly normal desire in a wrong way or at the wrong time. If we indulge in sex before marriage or if we steal to get food, we are trying to satisfy God-given desires in wrong ways. Remember, many of your desires are normal and good, but God wants you to satisfy them in the right way and at the right time.

4:3, 4 Jesus was able to resist all of the Devil's temptations because he not only knew Scripture, but he also obeyed it. Ephesians 6:17 says that God's Word is a sword to use in spiritual combat. Knowing Bible verses is an important step in helping us resist the Devil's attacks, but we must also obey the Bible. Note that Satan had memorized Scripture, but he failed to obey it. Knowing and obeying the Bible helps us follow God's desires rather than the Devil's.

4:5 The Temple was the religious center of the Jewish nation and the place where the people expected the Messiah to arrive (Malachi 3:1). Herod the Great had renovated the Temple in hopes of gaining the Jews' confidence. The Temple was the tallest building in the area, and this "highest point" was probably the corner wall that jutted out of the hillside, overlooking the valley below. From this spot, Jesus could see all of Jerusalem behind him and the country for miles in front of him.

4:5-7 God is not our magician in the sky ready to perform on request. In response to Satan's temptations, Jesus said not to put God to a test (Deuteronomy 6:16). You may want to ask God to do something to prove his existence or his love for you. Jesus once taught through a parable that people who don't believe what is written in the Bible won't believe even if someone were to come back from the dead to warn them (Luke 16:31)! God wants us to live by faith, not by magic. Don't try to manipulate God by asking for signs.

4:6 The Devil used Scripture to try to convince Jesus to sin! Sometimes friends or associates will present attractive and convincing reasons why you should try something you know is wrong. They may even find Bible verses that *seem* to support their viewpoint. Study the Bible carefully, especially the broader contexts of specific verses, so that you understand God's principles for living and what he wants for your life. Only if you really understand what the *whole* Bible says will you be able to recognize errors of interpretation when people take verses out of context and twist them to say what they want them to say.

4:7 †Deut 6:16

[7]Jesus responded, "The Scriptures also say, 'Do not test the Lord your God.'*"
[8]Next the Devil took him to the peak of a very high mountain and showed him the
nations of the world and all their glory. [9]"I will give it all to you," he said, "if you will
only kneel down and worship me."

4:10 †Deut 6:13

[10]"Get out of here, Satan," Jesus told him. "For the Scriptures say,

4:11 Luke 22:43 Heb 1:14 Jas 4:7

'You must worship the Lord your God;
serve only him.'*"

[11]Then the Devil went away, and angels came and cared for Jesus.

B. MESSAGE AND MINISTRY OF JESUS, THE KING (4:12—25:46)

Matthew features Jesus' sermons. The record of Jesus' actions is interspersed with great passages of his teaching. This section of Matthew is topical rather than chronological. Matthew records for us the Sermon on the Mount, the parables of the Kingdom, Jesus' teachings on forgiveness, and parables about the end of the age.

4:7 Deut 6:16. **4:10** Deut 6:13.

THE TEMPTATIONS

Temptation	*Real needs used as basis for temptation*	*Possible doubts that made the temptations real*	*Potential weaknesses Satan sought to exploit*	*Jesus' answer*
Make bread	Physical need: Hunger	Would God provide food?	Hunger, impatience, need to "prove his sonship"	Deuteronomy 8:3 "Depend on God" Focus: God's purpose
Dare God to rescue you (based on misapplied Scripture, Psalm 91:11, 12)	Emotional need: Security	Would God protect?	Pride, insecurity, need to test God	Deuteronomy 6:16 "Don't test God" Focus: God's plan
Worship me! (Satan)	Psychological need: significance, power, achievement	Would God rule?	Desire for quick power, easy solutions, need to prove equality with God	Deuteronomy 6:13 "No compromise with evil" Focus: God's person

As if going through a final test of preparation, Jesus was tempted by Satan in the wilderness. Three specific parts of the Temptation are listed by Matthew. They are familiar because we face the same kinds of temptations. As the chart shows, temptation is often the combination of a real need and a possible doubt that creates an inappropriate desire. Jesus demonstrates both the importance and effectiveness of knowing and applying Scripture to combat temptation.

4:8, 9 Did the Devil have the power to give Jesus the nations of the world? Didn't God, the Creator of the world, have control over these nations? The Devil may have been lying about his implied power, or he may have based his offer on his temporary control and free rein over the earth because of humanity's sinfulness. The temptation before Jesus was to take the world as a political ruler right then, without carrying out his plan to save the world from sin. Satan was trying to distort Jesus' perspective by making him focus on worldly power and not on God's plans.

4:8-10 The Devil offered the whole world to Jesus if Jesus would only kneel down and worship him. Today the Devil offers us the world by trying to entice us with materialism and power. We can resist temptations the same way Jesus did. If you find yourself craving something that the world offers, quote Jesus' words to the Devil: "You must worship the Lord your God; serve only him."

4:11 Angels, like these who waited on Jesus, have a significant role as God's messengers. These spiritual beings were involved in Jesus' life on earth by (1) announcing Jesus' birth to Mary, (2) reassuring Joseph, (3) naming Jesus, (4) announcing Jesus' birth to the shepherds, (5) protecting Jesus by sending his family to Egypt, and (6) ministering to Jesus in Gethsemane. For more on angels, see the note on 1:20.

1. Jesus begins his ministry

Jesus Preaches in Galilee (**30**/Mark 1:14-15; Luke 4:14-15; John 4:43-45)

[12]When Jesus heard that John had been arrested, he left Judea and returned to Galilee.
[13]But instead of going to Nazareth, he went to Capernaum, beside the Sea of Galilee, in
the region of Zebulun and Naphtali. [14]This fulfilled Isaiah's prophecy:

15 "In the land of Zebulun and of Naphtali,
beside the sea, beyond the Jordan River—
in Galilee where so many Gentiles live—
16 the people who sat in darkness
have seen a great light.
And for those who lived in the land where death casts its shadow,
a light has shined."*

4:15-16 †Isa 9:1-2; 42:6-7 Luke 2:32

[17]From then on, Jesus began to preach, "Turn from your sins and turn to God, because
the Kingdom of Heaven is near.*"

4:17 Matt 3:2; 10:7

Four Fishermen Follow Jesus (**33**/Mark 1:16-20)

[18]One day as Jesus was walking along the shore beside the Sea of Galilee, he saw two
brothers—Simon, also called Peter, and Andrew—fishing with a net, for they were
commercial fishermen. [19]Jesus called out to them, "Come, be my disciples, and I will
show you how to fish for people!" [20]And they left their nets at once and went with him.
[21]A little farther up the shore he saw two other brothers, James and John, sitting in a
boat with their father, Zebedee, mending their nets. And he called them to come, too.
[22]They immediately followed him, leaving the boat and their father behind.

4:19 Matt 16:17-18 John 1:42

4:20 Mark 10:28 Luke 18:28

Jesus Preaches throughout Galilee (**36**/Mark 1:35-39; Luke 4:42-44)

[23]Jesus traveled throughout Galilee teaching in the synagogues, preaching everywhere the Good News about the Kingdom. And he healed people who had every kind

4:23 Matt 9:35 Mark 1:39 Luke 4:15

4:15-16 Isa 9:1-2. **4:17** Or *has come* or *is coming soon.*

4:12, 13 Jesus moved from Nazareth, his hometown, to Capernaum, about 20 miles farther north. Capernaum became Jesus' home base during his ministry in Galilee. Jesus probably moved (1) to get away from intense opposition in Nazareth, (2) to have an impact on the greatest number of people (Capernaum was a busy city, and Jesus' message could reach more people and spread more quickly), and (3) to utilize extra resources and support for his ministry.

Jesus' move fulfilled the prophecy of Isaiah 9:1, 2, which states that the Messiah would be a light to the land of Zebulun and Naphtali, the region of Galilee where Capernaum was located. Zebulun and Naphtali were two of the original 12 tribes of Israel.

4:14-16 By quoting from the book of Isaiah, Matthew continues to tie Jesus' ministry to the Old Testament. This was helpful for his Jewish readers, who were familiar with these Scriptures. In addition, it shows the unity of God's purposes as he works with his people throughout all ages.

4:17 The "Kingdom of Heaven" has the same meaning as the "Kingdom of God" in Mark and Luke. Matthew uses this phrase because the Jews, out of their intense reverence and respect, did not pronounce God's name. The Kingdom of Heaven is still near because it has arrived in our heart. See the note on 3:2 for more on the Kingdom of Heaven.

4:17 Jesus started his ministry with the same message people had heard John the Baptist say: "Turn from your sins." The message is the same today as when Jesus and John gave it. Becoming a follower of Christ means turning away from our self-centeredness and "self" control and turning our life over to Christ's direction and control.

4:18 The Sea of Galilee is really a large lake. About 30 fishing towns surrounded it during Jesus' day, and Capernaum was the largest.

4:18-20 Jesus told Peter and Andrew to leave their fishing business and begin fishing "for people," helping others find God. Jesus was calling them away from their productive trade to be productive spiritually. We all need to fish for souls. If we practice Christ's teachings and share the Good News with others, we will be able to draw those around us to Christ like a fisherman who pulls fish into his boat with nets.

4:19, 20 These men already knew Jesus. He had talked to Peter and Andrew previously (John 1:35-42) and had been preaching in the area. When Jesus called them, they knew what kind of man he was and were willing to follow him. They were not in a hypnotic trance when they followed but had been thoroughly convinced that following him would change their lives forever.

4:21, 22 James and his brother, John, along with Peter and Andrew, were the first disciples that Jesus called to work with him. Jesus' call motivated these men to get up and leave their jobs—immediately. They didn't make excuses about why it wasn't a good time. They left at once and followed. Jesus calls each of us to follow him. When Jesus asks us to serve him, we must be like the disciples and do it at once.

4:23 Jesus was teaching, preaching, and healing. These were the three main aspects of his ministry. *Teaching* shows Jesus' concern for understanding; *preaching* shows his concern for commitment; and *healing* shows his concern for wholeness. His miracles of healing authenticated his teaching and preaching, proving that he truly was from God.

4:23 Jesus soon developed a powerful preaching ministry and often spoke in the synagogues. Most towns that had 10 or more Jewish families had a synagogue. The building served as a religious gathering place on the Sabbath and as a school during the week. The leader of the synagogue was not a preacher as much as an administrator. His job was to find and invite rabbis to teach and preach. It was customary to invite visiting rabbis like Jesus to speak.

of sickness and disease. [24]News about him spread far beyond the borders of Galilee so that the sick were soon coming to be healed from as far away as Syria. And whatever their illness and pain, or if they were possessed by demons, or were epileptics, or were paralyzed—he healed them all. [25]Large crowds followed him wherever he went—people from Galilee, the Ten Towns,* Jerusalem, from all over Judea, and from east of the Jordan River.

2. Jesus gives the Sermon on the Mount

Jesus Gives the Beatitudes (**49**/Luke 6:17-26)

5:1 Luke 6:12 John 6:3

5 One day as the crowds were gathering, Jesus went up the mountainside with his disciples and sat down to teach them.

4:25 Greek *Decapolis.*

KEY LESSONS FROM THE SERMON ON THE MOUNT

Beatitude	Old Testament anticipation	Clashing worldly values	God's reward	How to develop this attitude
Realize need for God (5:3)	Isaiah 57:15	Pride and personal independence	Kingdom of Heaven	James 4:7–10
Mourn (5:4)	Isaiah 61:1, 2	Happiness at any cost	Comfort (2 Corinthians 1:4)	Psalm 51 James 4:7–10
Gentle and lowly (5:5)	Psalm 37:5–11	Power	Receive the earth	Matthew 11:27–30
Hunger and thirst for justice (5:6)	Isaiah 11:4, 5; 42:1–4	Pursuing personal needs	See it happen	John 16:5–11 Philippians 3:7–11
Merciful (5:7)	Psalm 41:1	Strength without feeling	Be shown mercy	Ephesians 5:1, 2
Pure in heart (5:8)	Psalm 24:3, 4; 51:10	Deception is acceptable	See God	1 John 3:1–3
Work for peace (5:9)	Isaiah 57:18, 19; 60:17	Personal peace is pursued without concern for the world's chaos	Be called children of God	Romans 12:9–21 Hebrews 12:10, 11
Persecuted (5:10)	Isaiah 52:13; 53:12	Weak commitments	Inherit the Kingdom of Heaven	2 Timothy 3:12

In his longest recorded sermon, Jesus began by describing the traits he was looking for in his followers. He called those who lived out those traits blessed because God had something special in store for them. Each beatitude is an almost direct contradiction of society's typical way of life. In the last beatitude, Jesus even points out that a serious effort to develop these traits is bound to create opposition. The best example of each trait is found in Jesus himself. If our goal is to become like him, the Beatitudes will challenge the way we live each day.

4:23, 24 Jesus preached the gospel—the Good News—to everyone who wanted to hear it. The Good News is that the Kingdom of Heaven has come, that God is with us, and that he cares for us. Christ can heal us, not just of physical sickness, but of spiritual sickness as well. There's no sin or problem too great or too small for him to handle. Jesus' words were good news because they offered freedom, hope, peace of heart, and eternal life with God.

4:25 The "Ten Towns" was a league of 10 Gentile cities east of the Sea of Galilee, joined together for better trade and mutual defense. The word about Jesus was out, and Jews and Gentiles were coming long distances to hear him.

5:1ff Matthew 5–7 is called the Sermon on the Mount because Jesus gave it on a hillside near Capernaum. This "sermon" probably covered several days of preaching. In it, Jesus proclaimed his attitude toward the law. Position, authority, and money are not important in his Kingdom—what matters is faithful obedience from the heart. The Sermon on the Mount challenged the proud and legalistic religious leaders of the day. It called them back to the messages of the Old Testament prophets, who, like Jesus, taught that heartfelt obedience is more important than legalistic observance.

5:1, 2 Enormous crowds were following Jesus—he was the talk of the town, and everyone wanted to see him. The disciples, who were the closest associates of this popular man, were certainly tempted to feel important, proud, and possessive. Being with Jesus gave them not only prestige but also opportunity for receiving money and power.

The crowds were gathering once again. But before speaking to them, Jesus pulled his disciples aside and warned them about the temptations they would face as his associates. Don't expect fame and fortune, Jesus was saying, but mourning, hunger, and persecution. Nevertheless, Jesus assured his disciples that they would be rewarded—but perhaps not in this life. There may be times when following Jesus will bring us great popularity. If we don't live by Jesus' words in this sermon, we will find ourselves using God's message only to promote our personal interests.

2 This is what he taught them:

3 "God blesses those who realize their need for him,*
for the Kingdom of Heaven is given to them.
4 God blesses those who mourn,
for they will be comforted.
5 God blesses those who are gentle and lowly,
for the whole earth will belong to them.
6 God blesses those who are hungry and thirsty for justice,
for they will receive it in full.
7 God blesses those who are merciful,
for they will be shown mercy.
8 God blesses those whose hearts are pure,
for they will see God.
9 God blesses those who work for peace,
for they will be called the children of God.
10 God blesses those who are persecuted because they live for God,
for the Kingdom of Heaven is theirs.

11 "God blesses you when you are mocked and persecuted and lied about because you
are my followers. 12 Be happy about it! Be very glad! For a great reward awaits you in
heaven. And remember, the ancient prophets were persecuted, too.

Jeus Teaches about Salt and Light (**50**)

13 "You are the salt of the earth. But what good is salt if it has lost its flavor? Can you
make it useful again? It will be thrown out and trampled underfoot as worthless.
14 You are the light of the world—like a city on a mountain, glowing in the night for
all to see. 15 Don't hide your light under a basket! Instead, put it on a stand and let it
shine for all. 16 In the same way, let your good deeds shine out for all to see, so that
everyone will praise your heavenly Father.

5:3-12 Luke 6:20-23
5:3 Isa 57:15; Matt 25:34
5:4 Isa 61:2-3
5:5 Ps 37:11
5:6 Isa 55:1-2
5:7 Matt 18:33; Jas 2:13
5:8 Ps 24:3-4
5:9 Heb 12:14; Jas 3:18
5:10 2 Tim 2:12; 1 Pet 3:14
5:11 Matt 10:22; 1 Pet 4:14
5:12 Acts 7:52; Heb 11:32-38; Jas 5:10
5:13 Mark 9:50; Luke 14:34-35
5:15 Mark 4:21; Luke 8:16; 11:33
5:16 Eph 5:8-9; 1 Pet 2:12

5:3 Greek *the poor in spirit.*

5:3-5 Jesus began his sermon with words that seem to contradict each other. But God's way of living usually contradicts the world's. If you want to live for God, you must be ready to say and do what seems strange to the world. You must be willing to give when others take, to love when others hate, to help when others abuse. By giving up your own rights in order to serve others, you will one day receive everything God has in store for you.

5:3-12 There are at least four ways to understand the Beatitudes: (1) They are a code of ethics for the disciples and a standard of conduct for all believers. (2) They contrast Kingdom values (what is eternal) with worldly values (what is temporary). (3) They contrast the superficial "faith" of the Pharisees with the real faith that Christ demands. (4) They show how the Old Testament expectations will be fulfilled in the new Kingdom. These Beatitudes are not multiple choice—pick what you like and leave the rest. They must be taken as a whole. They describe what we should be like as Christ's followers.

5:3-12 Each Beatitude tells how to be *blessed* by God. *Blessed* means more than happiness. It implies the fortunate or enviable state of those who are in God's Kingdom. The Beatitudes don't promise laughter, pleasure, or earthly prosperity. Being "blessed" by God means the experience of hope and joy, independent of outward circumstances. To find hope and joy, the deepest form of happiness, follow Jesus no matter what the cost.

5:3-12 With Jesus' announcement that the Kingdom was near (4:17), people were naturally asking, "How do I qualify to be in God's Kingdom?" Jesus said that God's Kingdom is organized differently from worldly kingdoms. In the Kingdom of Heaven, wealth and power and authority are unimportant. Kingdom people seek different blessings and benefits, and they have different attitudes. Are your attitudes a carbon copy of the world's selfishness, pride, and lust for power, or do they reflect the humility and self-sacrifice of Jesus, your king?

5:11, 12 Jesus said to rejoice when we're persecuted for our faith. Persecution can be good because (1) it takes our eyes off earthly rewards, (2) it strips away superficial belief, (3) it strengthens the faith of those who endure, and (4) our attitude through it serves as an example to others who follow. We can be comforted knowing that God's greatest prophets were persecuted (Elijah, Jeremiah, Daniel). The fact that we are being persecuted proves that we have been faithful; faithless people would be unnoticed. In the future God will reward the faithful by receiving them into his eternal Kingdom, where there is no more persecution.

5:13 If a seasoning has no flavor, it has no value. If Christians make no effort to affect the world around them, they are of little value to God. If we are too much like the world, we are worthless. Christians should not blend in with everyone else. Instead, we should affect others positively, just as seasoning brings out the best flavor in food.

5:14-16 Can you hide a city that is sitting on top of a mountain? Its light at night can be seen for miles. If we live for Christ, we will glow like lights, showing others what Christ is like. We hide our light by (1) being quiet when we should speak, (2) going along with the crowd, (3) denying the light, (4) letting sin dim our light, (5) not explaining our light to others, or (6) ignoring the needs of others. Be a beacon of truth—don't shut your light off from the rest of the world.

Jesus Teaches about the Law (**51**)

5:17 Rom 3:31 [17]"Don't misunderstand why I have come. I did not come to abolish the law of Moses
or the writings of the prophets. No, I came to fulfill them. [18]I assure you, until heaven
5:18 Luke 16:17; 21:33 and earth disappear, even the smallest detail of God's law will remain until its purpose
5:19 Jas 2:10 is achieved. [19]So if you break the smallest commandment and teach others to do the
same, you will be the least in the Kingdom of Heaven. But anyone who obeys God's
laws and teaches them will be great in the Kingdom of Heaven.
5:20 Matt 6:1 [20]"But I warn you—unless you obey God better than the teachers of religious law and
the Pharisees do, you can't enter the Kingdom of Heaven at all!

SIX WAYS TO THINK LIKE CHRIST

Reference	*Example*	*It's not enough to*	*We must also*
5:21, 22	Murder	Avoid killing	Avoid anger and hatred
5:23–26	Offerings	Offer regular gifts	Have right relationships with God and others
5:27–30	Adultery	Avoid adultery	Keep our hearts from lusting and be faithful
5:31, 32	Divorce	Be legally married	Live out marriage commitments
5:33–37	Vows	Keep a vow	Avoid casual and irresponsible commitments to God
5:38–47	Revenge	Seek justice for ourselves	Show mercy and love to others

We, more often than not, avoid the extreme sins but regularly commit the types of sins with which Jesus was most concerned. In these six examples, our real struggle with sin is exposed. Jesus pointed out what kind of lives would be required of his followers. Are you living as Jesus taught?

5:17 God's moral and ceremonial laws were given to help people love God with all their hearts and minds. Throughout Israel's history, however, these laws had often been misquoted and misapplied. By Jesus' time, religious leaders had turned the laws into a confusing mass of rules. When Jesus talked about a new way to understand God's law, he was actually trying to bring people back to its *original* purpose. Jesus did not speak against the law itself but against the abuses and excesses to which it had been subjected (see John 1:17).

5:17-20 If Jesus did not come to abolish the law, does that mean all the Old Testament laws still apply to us today? In the Old Testament, there were three categories of law: ceremonial, civil, and moral.

(1) The *ceremonial law* related specifically to Israel's worship (see Leviticus 1:2, 3, for example). Its primary purpose was to point forward to Jesus Christ; these laws, therefore, were no longer necessary after Jesus' death and resurrection. While we are no longer bound by ceremonial law, the principles behind them—to worship and love a holy God—still apply. Jesus was often accused by the Pharisees of violating ceremonial law.

(2) The *civil law* applied to daily living in Israel (see Deuteronomy 24:10, 11, for example). Because modern society and culture are so radically different from that time and setting, all of these guidelines cannot be followed specifically. But the principles behind the commands are timeless and should guide our conduct. Jesus demonstrated these principles by example.

(3) The *moral law* (such as the Ten Commandments) is the direct command of God, and it requires strict obedience (see Exodus 20:13, for example). The moral law reveals the nature and will of God, and it still applies today. Jesus obeyed the moral law completely.

5:19 Some of those in the crowd were experts at telling others what to do, but they missed the central point of God's laws themselves. Jesus made it clear, however, that obeying God's laws is more important than explaining them. It's much easier to study God's laws and tell others to obey them than to put them into practice. How are you doing at obeying God *yourself?*

5:20 The Pharisees were exacting and scrupulous in their attempts to follow their laws. So how could Jesus reasonably call us to greater obedience than theirs? The Pharisees' weakness was that they were content to obey the laws outwardly without allowing God to change their hearts (or attitudes). Jesus was saying, therefore, that the *quality* of our goodness should be greater than that of the Pharisees. They looked pious, but they were far from the Kingdom of Heaven. God judges our heart as well as our deeds, for it is in the heart that our real allegiance lies. Be just as concerned about your attitudes that people don't see as about your actions that are seen by all.

5:20 Jesus was saying that his listeners needed a different kind of obedience altogether (out of love for God), not just a more intense version of the Pharisees' obedience (which was mere legal compliance). Our obedience must (1) come from what God does in us, not what we can do by ourselves, (2) be God-centered, not self-centered, (3) be based on reverence for God, not approval from people, and (4) go beyond keeping the law to living by the principles behind the law.

Jesus Teaches about Anger (**52**)

21"You have heard that the law of Moses says, 'Do not murder. If you commit murder,
you are subject to judgment.'* 22 But I say, if you are angry with someone,* you are
subject to judgment! If you say to your friend, 'You idiot,'* you are in danger of being
brought before the court. And if you curse someone,* you are in danger of the fires
of hell.
23"So if you are standing before the altar in the Temple, offering a sacrifice to God,
and you suddenly remember that someone has something against you, 24 leave your
sacrifice there beside the altar. Go and be reconciled to that person. Then come and
offer your sacrifice to God. 25 Come to terms quickly with your enemy before it is too
late and you are dragged into court, handed over to an officer, and thrown in jail. 26 I
assure you that you won't be free again until you have paid the last penny.

Jesus Teaches about Lust (**53**)

27"You have heard that the law of Moses says, 'Do not commit adultery.'* 28 But I
say, anyone who even looks at a woman with lust in his eye has already committed
adultery with her in his heart. 29 So if your eye—even if it is your good eye*—
causes you to lust, gouge it out and throw it away. It is better for you to lose one part
of your body than for your whole body to be thrown into hell. 30 And if your
hand—even if it is your stronger hand*—causes you to sin, cut it off and throw it
away. It is better for you to lose one part of your body than for your whole body to be
thrown into hell.

5:21 †Exod 20:13 †Deut 5:17 Matt 19:18 Mark 10:19 Luke 18:20 Rom 13:9 Jas 2:11
5:22 Eph 4:26 Jas 1:19-20 1 Jn 3:15
5:25-26 Matt 18:34-35 Luke 12:58-59
5:27 †Exod 20:14 †Deut 5:18 Matt 19:18 Mark 10:19 Luke 18:20 Rom 13:9 Jas 2:11
5:29-30 Matt 18:8-9 Mark 9:43-47

5:21 Exod 20:13; Deut 5:17. **5:22a** Some manuscripts add *without cause.* **5:22b** Literally *'Raca,'* an Aramaic term of contempt. **5:22c** Greek *if you say, 'You fool.'* **5:27** Exod 20:14; Deut 5:18. **5:29** Greek *your right eye.* **5:30** Greek *your right hand.*

5:21, 22 When Jesus said, "But I say," he was not doing away with the law or adding his own beliefs. Rather, he was giving a fuller understanding of why God made that law in the first place. For example, Moses said, "Do not murder" (Exodus 20:13); Jesus taught that we should not even become angry enough to murder, for then we have already committed murder in our heart. The Pharisees read this law and, not having literally murdered anyone, felt that they had obeyed it. Yet they were angry enough with Jesus that they would soon plot his death, though they would not do the dirty work themselves. We miss the intent of God's Word when we read his rules for living without trying to understand why he made them. When do you keep God's rules but close your eyes to his intent?

5:21, 22 Killing is a terrible sin, but *anger* is a great sin, too, because it also violates God's command to love. Anger in this case refers to a seething, brooding bitterness against someone. It is a dangerous emotion that always threatens to leap out of control, leading to violence, emotional hurt, increased mental stress, and spiritual damage. Anger keeps us from developing a spirit pleasing to God. Have you ever been proud that you didn't strike out and say what was really on your mind? Self-control is good, but Christ wants us to practice thought-control as well. Jesus said that we will be held accountable even for our attitudes.

5:23, 24 Broken relationships can hinder our relationship with God. If we have a problem or grievance with a friend, we should resolve the problem as soon as possible. We are hypocrites if we claim to love God while we hate others. Our attitudes toward others reflect our relationship with God (1 John 4:20).

5:25, 26 In Jesus' day, someone who couldn't pay a debt was thrown into prison until the debt was paid. Unless someone came to pay the debt for the prisoner, he or she would probably die there. It is practical advice to resolve our differences with our enemies before their anger causes more trouble (Proverbs 25:8-10). You may not get into a disagreement that takes you to court, but even small conflicts mend more easily if you try to make peace right away. In a broader sense, these verses advise us to get things right with our brothers and sisters before we have to stand before God.

5:27, 28 The Old Testament law said that it is wrong for a person to have sex with someone other than his or her spouse (Exodus 20:14). But Jesus said that the *desire* to have sex with someone other than your spouse is mental adultery and thus sin. Jesus emphasized that if the *act* is wrong, then so is the *intention.* To be faithful to your spouse with your body but not your mind is to break the trust so vital to a strong marriage. Jesus is condemning not natural interest in the opposite sex or even healthy sexual desire but the deliberate and repeated filling of one's mind with fantasies that would be evil if acted out.

5:27, 28 Some think that if lustful thoughts are sin, why shouldn't a person go ahead and do the lustful actions, too? Acting out sinful desires is harmful in several ways: (1) It causes people to excuse sin rather than to stop sinning; (2) it destroys marriages; (3) it is deliberate rebellion against God's Word; (4) it always hurts someone else in addition to the sinner. Sinful actions are more dangerous than sinful desires, and that is why desires should not be acted out. Nevertheless, sinful desires are just as damaging to obedience. Left unchecked, wrong desires will result in wrong actions and turn people away from God.

5:29, 30 When Jesus said to get rid of your hand or your eye, he was speaking figuratively. He didn't mean literally to gouge out your eye, because even a blind person can lust. But if that were the only choice, it would be better to go into heaven with one eye or hand than to go to hell with two. We sometimes tolerate sins in our life that, left unchecked, could eventually destroy us. It is better to experience the pain of removal (getting rid of a bad habit or something we treasure, for instance) than to allow the sin to bring judgment and condemnation. Examine your life for anything that causes you to sin, and take every necessary action to remove it.

5:31 †Deut 24:1 Matt 19:7 Mark 10:4
5:32 1 Cor 7:10-11

Jesus Teaches about Divorce (**54**)
31 “You have heard that the law of Moses says, ‘A man can divorce his wife by merely
giving her a letter of divorce.’* 32 But I say that a man who divorces his wife, unless she
has been unfaithful, causes her to commit adultery. And anyone who marries a divorced
woman commits adultery.

5:33 Lev 19:12 Num 30:2 Deut 23:21
5:34 Isa 66:1 Jas 5:12
5:35 Isa 66:1
5:37 Jas 5:12

Jesus Teaches about Vows (**55**)
33 “Again, you have heard that the law of Moses says, ‘Do not break your vows; you must
carry out the vows you have made to the Lord.’* 34 But I say, don’t make any vows! If you
say, ‘By heaven!’ it is a sacred vow because heaven is God’s throne. 35 And if you say, ‘By
the earth!’ it is a sacred vow because the earth is his footstool. And don’t swear, ‘By
Jerusalem!’ for Jerusalem is the city of the great King. 36 Don’t even swear, ‘By my head!’
for you can’t turn one hair white or black. 37 Just say a simple, ‘Yes, I will,’ or ‘No, I won’t.’
Your word is enough. To strengthen your promise with a vow shows that something is
wrong.*

5:38 †Exod 21:24 †Lev 24:20 †Deut 19:21

Jesus Teaches about Revenge (**56**)
38 “You have heard that the law of Moses says, ‘If an eye is injured, injure the eye of
the person who did it. If a tooth gets knocked out, knock out the tooth of the person

5:31 Deut 24:1. **5:33** Num 30:2. **5:37** Or *Anything beyond this is from the evil one.*

JESUS AND THE OLD TESTAMENT LAW

Reference	*Examples of Old Testament mercy in justice:*
Leviticus 19:18	“Never seek revenge or bear a grudge against anyone. But love your neighbor as yourself, for I am the LORD.”
Proverbs 24:28, 29	“Do not testify spitefully against innocent neighbors; don’t lie about them. And don’t say, ‘Now I can pay them back for all their meanness to me! I’ll get even!’ ”
Proverbs 25:21, 22	“If your enemies are hungry, give them food to eat. If they are thirsty, give them water to drink. You will heap burning coals on their head, and the LORD will reward you.”
Lamentations 3:30, 31	“Let them turn the other cheek to those who strike them. Let them accept the awful insults of their enemies. For the Lord does not abandon anyone forever.”

What seems to be a case of Jesus contradicting the laws of the Old Testament deserves a careful look. It is too easy to overlook how much mercy was written into the Old Testament laws. Above are several examples. What God designed as a system of justice with mercy had been distorted over the years into a license for revenge. It was this misapplication of the law that Jesus attacked.

5:31, 32 Divorce is as hurtful and destructive today as in Jesus’ day. God intends marriage to be a lifetime commitment (Genesis 2:24). When entering into marriage, people should never consider divorce an option for solving problems or a way out of a relationship that seems dead. In these verses, Jesus is also attacking those who purposefully abuse the marriage contract, using divorce to satisfy their lustful desire to marry someone else. Are your actions today helping your marriage grow stronger, or are you tearing it apart?

5:32 Jesus said that divorce is not permissible except for unfaithfulness. This does not mean that divorce should automatically occur when a spouse commits adultery. The word translated “unfaithful” implies a sexually immoral life-style, not a confessed and repented act of adultery. Those who discover that their partner has been unfaithful should first make every effort to forgive, reconcile, and restore their relationship. We are always to look for reasons to restore the marriage relationship rather than for excuses to leave it.

5:33ff Here, Jesus was emphasizing the importance of telling the truth. People were breaking vows and using sacred language casually and carelessly. Keeping vows and promises is important; it builds trust and makes committed human relationships possible. The Bible condemns making vows or taking oaths casually, giving your word while knowing that you won’t keep it, or swearing falsely in God’s name (Exodus 20:7; Leviticus 19:12; Numbers 30:1, 2; Deuteronomy 19:16-20). Vows are needed in certain situations only because we live in a sinful society that breeds distrust.

5:33-37 Vows were common, but Jesus told his followers not to use them—their word alone should be enough (see James 5:12). Are you known as a person of your word? Truthfulness seems so rare that we feel we must end our statements with “I promise.” If we tell the truth all the time, we will have less pressure to back up our words with an oath or promise.

5:38 God’s purpose behind this law was an expression of mercy. The law was given to judges and said, in effect, “Make the punishment fit the crime.” It was not a guide for personal revenge (Exodus 21:23-25; Leviticus 24:19, 20; Deuteronomy 19:21). These laws were given to *limit* vengeance and help the court administer punishment that was neither too strict nor too lenient. Some people, however, were using this phrase to justify their vendettas against others. People still try to excuse their acts of revenge by saying, “I was just doing to him what he did to me.”

5:38-42 When we are wronged, often our first reaction is to get even. Instead, Jesus said we should do *good* to those who wrong us! Our desire should not be to keep score but to love and forgive. This is not natural—it is supernatural. Only God can give us the strength to love as he does. Instead of planning vengeance, pray for those who hurt you.

who did it.'* 39But I say, don't resist an evil person! If you are slapped on the right
cheek, turn the other, too. 40If you are ordered to court and your shirt is taken from
you, give your coat, too. 41If a soldier demands that you carry his gear for a mile,*
carry it two miles. 42Give to those who ask, and don't turn away from those who want
to borrow.

5:39 1 Cor 6:7; 1 Pet 3:9
5:40 1 Cor 6:7
5:42 Deut 15:8

Jesus Teaches about Loving Enemies (**57**/Luke 6:27-36)

43"You have heard that the law of Moses says, 'Love your neighbor'* and hate your
enemy. 44But I say, love your enemies!* Pray for those who persecute you! 45In that
way, you will be acting as true children of your Father in heaven. For he gives his
sunlight to both the evil and the good, and he sends rain on the just and on the unjust,
too. 46If you love only those who love you, what good is that? Even corrupt tax
collectors do that much. 47If you are kind only to your friends, how are you different
from anyone else? Even pagans do that. 48But you are to be perfect, even as your
Father in heaven is perfect.

5:43 †Lev 19:18; Matt 19:19; 22:39; Mark 12:31; Luke 10:27; Rom 13:9
5:44 Exod 23:4-5; Luke 23:34
5:48 Luke 6:36; 1 Pet 1:16

Jesus Teaches about Giving to the Needy (**58**)

6 "Take care! Don't do your good deeds publicly, to be admired, because then you will
lose the reward from your Father in heaven. 2When you give a gift to someone in
need, don't shout about it as the hypocrites do—blowing trumpets in the synagogues and
streets to call attention to their acts of charity! I assure you, they have received all the
reward they will ever get. 3But when you give to someone, don't tell your left hand what
your right hand is doing. 4Give your gifts in secret, and your Father, who knows all
secrets, will reward you.

6:1-2 Matt 23:5
6:4 Matt 6:6, 18

Jesus Teaches about Prayer (**59**)

5"And now about prayer. When you pray, don't be like the hypocrites who love to pray
publicly on street corners and in the synagogues where everyone can see them. I assure

6:5 Matt 6:16; 23:5; Mark 11:25; Luke 18:10-14

5:38 Greek *'An eye for an eye and a tooth for a tooth.'* Exod 21:24; Lev 24:20; Deut 19:21. **5:41** Greek *milion* [4,854 feet or 1,478 meters]. **5:43** Lev 19:18. **5:44** Some manuscripts add *Bless those who curse you, do good to those who hate you.*

5:39-44 To many Jews of Jesus' day, these statements were offensive. Any Messiah who would turn the other cheek was not the military leader they wanted to lead a revolt against Rome. Since they were under Roman oppression, they wanted retaliation against their enemies, whom they hated. But Jesus suggested a new, radical response to injustice: Instead of demanding rights, give them up freely! According to Jesus, it is more important to *give* justice and mercy than to receive it.

5:43, 44 By telling us not to retaliate, Jesus keeps us from taking the law into our own hands. By loving and praying for our enemies, we can overcome evil with good.

The Pharisees interpreted Leviticus 19:18 as teaching that they should love only those who love in return, and Psalm 139:19-22 and 140:9-11 as meaning that they should hate their enemies. But Jesus says we are to love our enemies. If you love your enemies and treat them well, you will truly show that Jesus is Lord of your life. This is possible only for those who give themselves fully to God, because only he can deliver people from natural selfishness. We must trust the Holy Spirit to help us *show* love to those for whom we may not *feel* love.

5:48 How can we be perfect? (1) *In character:* In this life we cannot be flawless, but we can aspire to be as much like Christ as possible. (2) *In holiness:* Like the Pharisees, we are to separate ourselves from the world's sinful values. But unlike the Pharisees, we are to be devoted to God's desires rather than our own and carry his love and mercy into the world. (3) *In maturity:* We can't achieve Christlike character and holy living all at once, but we must grow toward maturity and wholeness. Just as we expect different behavior from a baby, a child, a teenager, and an adult, so God expects different behavior from us, depending on our stage of spiritual development. (4) *In love:* We can seek to love others as completely as God loves us.

We can be perfect if our behavior is appropriate for our maturity level—perfect, yet with much room to grow. Our tendency to sin must never deter us from striving to be more like Christ. Christ calls all of his disciples to excel, to rise above mediocrity, and to mature in every area, becoming like him. Those who strive to become perfect will one day be perfect, even as Christ is perfect (1 John 3:2, 3).

6:2 The term *hypocrites,* as used here, describes people who do good acts for appearances only—not out of compassion or other good motives. Their actions may be good, but their motives are hollow. These empty acts are their only reward, but God will reward those who are sincere in their faith.

6:3 When Jesus says not to let your left hand know what your right hand is doing, he is teaching that our motives for giving to God and to others must be pure. It is easy to give with mixed motives, to do something for someone if it will benefit us in return. But believers should avoid all scheming and give for the pleasure of giving and as a response to God's love. Why do *you* give?

6:3, 4 It's easier to do what's right when we gain recognition and praise. To be sure our motives are not selfish, we should do our good deeds quietly or in secret, with no thought of reward. Jesus says we should check our motives in three areas: generosity (6:4), prayer (6:6), and fasting (6:18). Those acts should not be self-centered but God-centered, done not to make us look good but to make God look good. The reward God promises is not material, and it is never given to those who seek it. Doing something only for ourselves is not a loving sacrifice. With your next good deed, ask, Would I still do this if no one would ever know I did it?

6:5, 6 Some people, especially the religious leaders, wanted to be seen as "holy," and public prayer was one way to get attention. Jesus saw through their self-righteous acts, however, and taught that the essence of prayer is not public style but private

6:6 2 Kgs 4:33; Isa 26:20
6:7 Eccl 5:1-2
6:8 Matt 6:32; Luke 12:30
6:9-13 Luke 11:2-4
6:9 1 Pet 1:17
6:10 Matt 26:39, 42; Luke 22:42
6:11 Prov 30:8; John 6:32
6:13 Luke 22:40, 46; John 17:15
6:14 Mark 11:25; Eph 4:32; Col 3:13
6:15 Matt 18:35

you, that is all the reward they will ever get. 6 But when you pray, go away by yourself,
shut the door behind you, and pray to your Father secretly. Then your Father, who knows
all secrets, will reward you.
7 "When you pray, don't babble on and on as people of other religions do. They think
their prayers are answered only by repeating their words again and again. 8 Don't be like
them, because your Father knows exactly what you need even before you ask him! 9 Pray
like this:

Our Father in heaven,
may your name be honored.
10 May your kingdom come soon.
May your will be done here on earth,
just as it is in heaven.
11 Give us our food for today.*
12 and forgive us our sins,
just as we have forgiven those who have sinned against us.
13 And don't let us yield to temptation,
but deliver us from the evil one.*

14 "If you forgive those who sin against you, your heavenly Father will forgive you.
15 But if you refuse to forgive others, your Father will not forgive your sins.

Jesus Teaches about Fasting (**60**)

6:16 Isa 58:5; Matt 6:5; 23:5
6:18 Matt 6:4, 6

16 "And when you fast, don't make it obvious, as the hypocrites do, who try to look pale
and disheveled so people will admire them for their fasting. I assure you, that is the only
reward they will ever get. 17 But when you fast, comb your hair and wash your face.
18 Then no one will suspect you are fasting, except your Father, who knows what you do
in secret. And your Father, who knows all secrets, will reward you.

6:11 Or *for tomorrow.* **6:13** Or *from evil.* Some manuscripts add *For yours is the kingdom and the power and the glory forever. Amen.*

---

communication with God. There is a place for public prayer, but to pray only where others will notice you indicates that your real audience is not God.

6:7, 8 Repeating the same words over and over like a magic incantation is no way to ensure that God will hear your prayer. It's not wrong to come to God many times with the same requests—Jesus encourages *persistent* prayer. But he condemns the shallow repetition of words that are not offered with a sincere heart. We can never pray too much if our prayers are honest and sincere. Before you start to pray, make sure you mean what you say.

6:9 This is often called the Lord's Prayer because Jesus gave it to the disciples. It can be a pattern for our prayers. We should praise God, pray for his work in the world, pray for our daily needs, and pray for help in our daily struggles.

6:9 The phrase "Our Father in heaven" indicates that God is not only majestic and holy but also personal and loving. The first line of this model prayer is a statement of praise and a commitment to hallow, or honor, God's holy name. We can honor God's name by being careful to use it respectfully. If we use God's name lightly, we aren't remembering God's holiness.

6:10 The phrase "May your kingdom come soon" is a reference to God's spiritual reign, not Israel's freedom from Rome. God's Kingdom was announced in the covenant with Abraham (8:11; Luke 13:28), is present in Christ's reign in believers' hearts (Luke 17:21), and will be complete when all evil is destroyed and God establishes the new heaven and earth (Revelation 21:1).

6:10 When we pray "May your will be done," we are not resigning ourselves to fate but praying that God's perfect purpose will be accomplished in this world as well as in the next.

6:11 When we pray "Give us our food for today," we are acknowledging that God is our sustainer and provider. It is a misconception to think that we provide for our needs ourselves. We must trust God *daily* to provide what he knows we need.

6:13 God sometimes allows us to be tested by temptation. As disciples, we should pray to be delivered from these trying times and for deliverance from Satan ("the evil one") and his deceit. All Christians struggle with temptation. Sometimes it is so subtle that we don't even realize what is happening to us. God has promised that he won't allow us to be tempted beyond what we can bear (1 Corinthians 10:13). Ask God to help you recognize temptation and to give you strength to overcome it and choose God's way instead. For more on temptation, see the notes on 4:1.

6:14, 15 Jesus gives a startling warning about forgiveness: If we refuse to forgive others, God will also refuse to forgive us. Why? Because when we don't forgive others, we are denying our common ground as sinners in need of God's forgiveness. God's forgiveness of sin is not the direct result of our forgiving others, but it is based on our realizing what forgiveness means (see Ephesians 4:32). It is easy to ask God for forgiveness but difficult to grant it to others. Whenever we ask God to forgive us for sin, we should ask, Have I forgiven the people who have wronged me?

6:16 Fasting—going without food in order to spend time in prayer—is noble *and* difficult. It gives us time to pray, teaches self-discipline, reminds us that we can live with a lot less, and helps us appreciate God's gifts. Jesus was not condemning fasting, but hypocrisy—fasting in order to gain public approval. Fasting was mandatory for the Jewish people once a year on the Day of Atonement (Leviticus 23:32). The Pharisees voluntarily fasted twice a week to impress the people with their "holiness." Jesus commended acts of self-sacrifice done quietly and sincerely. He wanted people to adopt spiritual disciplines for the right reasons, not from a selfish desire for praise.

6:17 In these words, Jesus was telling people to go about their normal daily routine when they fasted, instead of making a show of it.

Jesus Teaches about Money (**61**)

19 "Don't store up treasures here on earth, where they can be eaten by moths and get rusty,
and where thieves break in and steal. 20 Store your treasures in heaven, where they will
never become moth-eaten or rusty and where they will be safe from thieves. 21 Wherever
your treasure is, there your heart and thoughts will also be.
22 "Your eye is a lamp for your body. A pure eye lets sunshine into your soul. 23 But an
evil eye shuts out the light and plunges you into darkness. If the light you think you have
is really darkness, how deep that darkness will be!
24 "No one can serve two masters. For you will hate one and love the other, or be
devoted to one and despise the other. You cannot serve both God and money.

Jesus Teaches about Worry (**62**)

25 "So I tell you, don't worry about everyday life—whether you have enough food, drink,
and clothes. Doesn't life consist of more than food and clothing? 26 Look at the birds.
They don't need to plant or harvest or put food in barns because your heavenly Father
feeds them. And you are far more valuable to him than they are. 27 Can all your worries
add a single moment to your life? Of course not.
28 "And why worry about your clothes? Look at the lilies and how they grow.
They don't work or make their clothing, 29 yet Solomon in all his glory was not
dressed as beautifully as they are. 30 And if God cares so wonderfully for flowers
that are here today and gone tomorrow, won't he more surely care for you? You
have so little faith!
31 "So don't worry about having enough food or drink or clothing. 32 Why be like the
pagans who are so deeply concerned about these things? Your heavenly Father already
knows all your needs, 33 and he will give you all you need from day to day if you live for
him and make the Kingdom of God your primary concern.
34 "So don't worry about tomorrow, for tomorrow will bring its own worries. Today's
trouble is enough for today.

6:19 Prov 23:4; Jas 5:2-3
6:20 Matt 19:21; Mark 10:21; Luke 18:22; 1 Tim 6:19
6:23 Matt 20:15; Mark 7:22
6:25 Phil 4:6; 1 Tim 6:6, 8; 1 Pet 5:7
6:26 Job 38:41
6:29 1 Kgs 10:4-7
6:30 Matt 8:26; 14:31; 16:8
6:32 Matt 6:8; Luke 12:30
6:33 Ps 37:4, 25; Mark 10:29, 30
6:34 Exod 16:4

6:20 Storing treasures in heaven is not limited to tithing but is accomplished by all acts of obedience to God. There is a sense in which giving our money to God's work is like investing in heaven. But we should seek to please God not only in our giving but also in fulfilling God's purposes in all we do.

6:22, 23 Spiritual vision is our capacity to see clearly what God wants us to do and to see the world from his point of view. But this spiritual insight can be easily clouded. Self-serving desires, interests, and goals block that vision. Serving God is the best way to restore it. A "pure" eye is one that is fixed on God.

6:24 Jesus says we can have only one master. We live in a materialistic society where many people serve money. They spend all their lives collecting and storing it, only to die and leave it behind. Their desire for money and what it can buy far outweighs their commitment to God and spiritual matters. Whatever you store up, you will spend much of your time and energy thinking about. Don't fall into the materialistic trap, because "the love of money is at the root of all kinds of evil" (1 Timothy 6:10). Can you honestly say that God, and not money, is your master? One test is to ask yourself which one occupies more of your thoughts, time, and efforts.

6:24 Jesus contrasted heavenly values with earthly values when he explained that our first loyalty should be to those things that do not fade, cannot be stolen or used up, and never wear out. We should not be fascinated with our possessions, lest *they* possess *us*. This means we may have to do some cutting back if our possessions are becoming too important to us. Jesus is calling for a decision that allows us to live contentedly with whatever we have because we have chosen what is eternal and lasting.

6:25 Because of the ill effects of worry, Jesus tells us not to worry about those needs that God promises to supply. Worry may (1) damage your health, (2) disrupt your productivity, (3) negatively affect the way you treat others, and (4) reduce your ability to trust in God. How many ill effects of worry are you experiencing? Here is the difference between worry and genuine concern—worry immobilizes, but concern moves you to action.

6:33 To "make the Kingdom of God your primary concern" means to put God first in your life, to fill your thoughts with his desires, to take his character for your pattern, and to serve and obey him in everything. What is really important to you? People, objects, goals, and other desires all compete for priority. Any of these can quickly bump God out of first place if you don't actively choose to give him first place in *every* area of your life.

6:34 Planning for tomorrow is time well spent; worrying about tomorrow is time wasted. Sometimes it's difficult to tell the difference. Careful planning is thinking ahead about goals, steps, and schedules, and trusting in God's guidance. When done well, planning can help alleviate worry. Worriers, by contrast, are consumed by fear and find it difficult to trust God. They let their plans interfere with their relationship with God. Don't let worries about tomorrow affect your relationship with God today.

Jesus Teaches about Judging Others (**63**/Luke 6:37-42)

7:1-2 Luke 6:37-42; Rom 2:1-3; 14:4; 1 Cor 4:5; 5:12; Jas 4:11-12
7:3-5 Luke 6:37-38, 41-42

7 "Stop judging others, and you will not be judged. 2 For others will treat you as you treat
them.* Whatever measure you use in judging others, it will be used to measure how
you are judged. 3 And why worry about a speck in your friend's eye when you have a log
in your own? 4 How can you think of saying, 'Friend, let me help you get rid of that speck
in your eye,' when you can't see past the log in your own eye? 5 Hypocrite! First get rid of
the log from your own eye; then perhaps you will see well enough to deal with the speck in
your friend's eye.

6 "Don't give what is holy to unholy people.* Don't give pearls to swine! They will
trample the pearls, then turn and attack you.

Jesus Teaches about Asking, Looking, Knocking (**64**)

7:7-11 Luke 11:9-13
7:7 Matt 21:22; Mark 11:24; Luke 11:9-13; John 14:13-14; 15:7; 16:23-24; Jas 1:5-6; 1 Jn 3:21-22; 5:14-15
7:12 Luke 6:31; Rom 13:8-10; Gal 5:14

7 "Keep on asking, and you will be given what you ask for. Keep on looking, and you will
find. Keep on knocking, and the door will be opened. 8 For everyone who asks, receives.
Everyone who seeks, finds. And the door is opened to everyone who knocks. 9 You
parents—if your children ask for a loaf of bread, do you give them a stone instead? 10 Or if
they ask for a fish, do you give them a snake? Of course not! 11 If you sinful people know
how to give good gifts to your children, how much more will your heavenly Father give
good gifts to those who ask him.

12 "Do for others what you would like them to do for you. This is a summary of all that
is taught in the law and the prophets.

7:2 Or *For God will treat you as you treat others;* Greek reads *For with the judgment you judge you will be judged.*
7:6 Greek *Don't give the sacred to dogs.*

SEVEN REASONS NOT TO WORRY

6:25	The same God who created life in you can be trusted with the details of your life.
6:26	Worrying about the future hampers your efforts for today.
6:27	Worrying is more harmful than helpful.
6:28–30	God does not ignore those who depend on him.
6:31, 32	Worrying shows a lack of faith in and understanding of God.
6:33	Worrying keeps us from real challenges God wants us to pursue.
6:34	Living one day at a time keeps us from being consumed with worry.

7:1, 2 Jesus tells us to examine our own motives and conduct instead of judging others. The traits that bother us in others are often the habits we have ourselves. Our bad habits and behavior patterns are the very ones that we most want to change in others. Do you find it easy to magnify others' faults while excusing your own? If you are ready to criticize someone, check to see if you deserve the same criticism. Judge yourself first, and then lovingly forgive and help your neighbor.

7:1-5 Jesus' statement, "Stop judging," is against the kind of hypocritical, judgmental attitude that tears others down in order to build oneself up. It is not a blanket statement to overlook wrong behavior of others but a call to be *discerning* rather than negative. Jesus said to expose false prophets (7:15-23), and Paul taught that we should exercise church discipline (1 Corinthians 5:1, 2) and trust God to be the final Judge (1 Corinthians 4:3-5).

7:6 Swine were unclean animals according to God's law (Deuteronomy 14:8). Anyone who touched an unclean animal became "ceremonially unclean" and could not go to the Temple to worship until the uncleanness was removed. Jesus says that we should not entrust holy teachings to unholy or unclean people. It is futile to try to teach holy concepts to people who don't want to listen and will only tear apart what we say. We should not stop giving God's Word to unbelievers, but we should be wise and discerning in our witnessing, so that we will not be wasting our time.

7:7, 8 Jesus tells us to persist in pursuing God. People often give up after a few halfhearted efforts and conclude that God cannot be found. But knowing God takes faith, focus, and follow-through, and Jesus assures us that we will be rewarded. Don't give up in your efforts to seek God. Continue to ask him for more knowledge, patience, wisdom, love, and understanding. He will give them to you.

7:9, 10 The children in Jesus' example asked their father for bread and fish—good and necessary items. If the children had asked for a poisonous snake, would the wise father have granted the request? Sometimes God knows we are praying for "snakes" and does not give us what we ask for, even though we persist in our prayers. As we learn to know God better as a loving Father, we learn to ask for what is good for us, and then he grants it.

7:11 Christ is showing us the heart of God the Father. God is not selfish, begrudging, or stingy, and we don't have to beg or grovel as we come with our requests. He is a loving Father, who understands, cares, and comforts. If humans can be kind, imagine how kind God, the Creator of kindness, can be.

7:11 Jesus used the expression "you sinful people" to contrast sinful and fallible human beings with the holy and perfect God.

7:12 This is commonly known as the Golden Rule. In many religions it is stated negatively: "Don't do to others what you don't want done to you." By stating it positively, Jesus made it more significant. It is not very hard to refrain from harming others; it is much more difficult to take the initiative in doing something good for them. The Golden Rule, as Jesus formulated it, is the foundation of active goodness and mercy—the kind of love God shows to us every day. Think of a good and merciful action you can do today.

Jesus Teaches about the Way to Heaven (**65**)
13“You can enter God’s Kingdom only through the narrow gate. The highway to hell* is
broad, and its gate is wide for the many who choose the easy way. 14But the gateway to
life is small, and the road is narrow, and only a few ever find it.

Jesus Teaches about Fruit in People’s Lives (**66**/Luke 6:43-45)
15“Beware of false prophets who come disguised as harmless sheep, but are really
wolves that will tear you apart. 16You can detect them by the way they act, just as you
can identify a tree by its fruit. You don’t pick grapes from thornbushes, or figs from
thistles. 17A healthy tree produces good fruit, and an unhealthy tree produces bad
fruit. 18A good tree can’t produce bad fruit, and a bad tree can’t produce good
fruit. 19So every tree that does not produce good fruit is chopped down and
thrown into the fire. 20Yes, the way to identify a tree or a person is by the kind of
fruit that is produced.

Jesus Teaches about Building on a Solid Foundation (**67**/Luke 6:46-49)
21“Not all people who sound religious are really godly. They may refer to me as
‘Lord,’ but they still won’t enter the Kingdom of Heaven. The decisive issue is
whether they obey my Father in heaven. 22On judgment day many will tell me, ‘Lord,
Lord, we prophesied in your name and cast out demons in your name and performed
many miracles in your name.’ 23But I will reply, ‘I never knew you. Go away; the
things you did were unauthorized.*’

24“Anyone who listens to my teaching and obeys me is wise, like a person who builds
a house on solid rock. 25Though the rain comes in torrents and the floodwaters rise and
the winds beat against that house, it won’t collapse, because it is built on rock. 26But
anyone who hears my teaching and ignores it is foolish, like a person who builds a house
on sand. 27When the rains and floods come and the winds beat against that house, it will
fall with a mighty crash.”

28After Jesus finished speaking, the crowds were amazed at his teaching, 29for he
taught as one who had real authority—quite unlike the teachers of religious law.

7:14 John 14:6; Acts 14:22
7:15 Jer 23:16; Matt 24:11, 24; Luke 6:26; Acts 20:29; Rom 16:17; 2 Pet 2:1; 1 Jn 4:1
7:16-20 Matt 12:33
7:21 Luke 6:46; Jas 1:22
7:22 Acts 19:13-15
7:23 Matt 25:12, 41; Luke 13:25-27
7:24 2 Tim 2:19; Jas 1:22
7:26 Jas 1:23
7:27 Ezek 13:10-12
7:28 Matt 13:54; Mark 1:22; 6:2; Luke 4:32; John 7:46

7:13 Greek *The way that leads to destruction.* **7:23** Or *unlawful.*

7:13, 14 The gate that leads to eternal life (John 10:7-9) is called “narrow.” This does not mean that it is difficult to become a Christian but that there is only *one* way to eternal life with God and that only a few decide to walk that road. Believing in Jesus is the only way to heaven, because he alone died for our sins and made us right before God. Living his way may not be popular, but it is true and right. Thank God there is one way!

7:15 False prophets were common in Old Testament times. They prophesied only what the king and the people wanted to hear, claiming it was God’s message. False teachers are just as common today. Jesus says to beware of those whose words sound religious but who are motivated by money, fame, or power. You can tell who they are because in their teaching they minimize Christ and glorify themselves.

7:20 We should evaluate teachers’ words by examining their lives. Just as trees are consistent in the kind of fruit they produce, good teachers consistently exhibit good behavior and high moral character as they seek to live out the truths of Scripture. This does not mean we should have witch-hunts, throwing out Sunday school teachers, pastors, and others who are less than perfect. Every one of us is subject to sin, and we must show the same mercy to others that we expect for ourselves. When Jesus talks about bad trees, he means teachers who deliberately teach false doctrine. We must examine the teachers’ motives, the direction they are taking, and the results they are seeking.

7:21 Some self-professed athletes can “talk” a great game, but that tells you nothing about their athletic skills. And not everyone who talks about heaven belongs to God’s Kingdom. Jesus is more concerned about our *walk* than our *talk*. He wants us to *do* right, not just *say* the right words. Your house (which represents your life, 7:24) will withstand the storms of life only if you do what is right instead of just talking about it. What you do cannot be separated from what you believe.

7:21-23 Jesus exposed those people who sounded religious but had no personal relationship with him. On “judgment day” only our relationship with Christ—our acceptance of him as Savior and our obedience to him—will matter. Many people think that if they are “good” people and say religious things, they will be rewarded with eternal life. In reality, faith in Christ is what will count at the judgment.

7:22 “Judgment day” is the final day of reckoning when God will settle all accounts, judging sin and rewarding faith.

7:24 To build “on solid rock” means to be a hearing, responding disciple, not a phony, superficial one. Practicing obedience becomes the solid foundation to weather the storms of life. See James 1:22-27 for more on putting into practice what we hear.

7:26 Like a house of cards, the fool’s life crumbles. Most people do not deliberately seek to build on a false or inferior foundation; instead, they just don’t think about their life’s purpose. Many people are headed for destruction, not out of stubbornness but out of thoughtlessness. Part of our responsibility as believers is to help others stop and think about where their lives are headed and to point out the consequences of ignoring Christ’s message.

7:29 The teachers of religious law (religious scholars) often cited traditions and quoted authorities to support their arguments and interpretations. But Jesus spoke with a new authority—his own. He didn’t need to quote anyone because he was the original Word (John 1:1).

3. Jesus performs many miracles

Jesus Heals a Man with Leprosy (**38**/Mark 1:40-45; Luke 5:12-16)

8 Large crowds followed Jesus as he came down the mountainside. [2]Suddenly, a man
with leprosy approached Jesus. He knelt before him, worshiping. "Lord," the man
said, "if you want to, you can make me well again."
[3]Jesus touched him. "I want to," he said. "Be healed!" And instantly the leprosy
8:4 Lev 14:1-32 Luke 17:4 disappeared. [4]Then Jesus said to him, "Go right over to the priest and let him examine
you. Don't talk to anyone along the way. Take along the offering required in the law of
Moses for those who have been healed of leprosy, so everyone will have proof of your
healing."

A Roman Officer Demonstrates Faith (**68**/Luke 7:1-10)

8:5-7 John 4:43-54 [5]When Jesus arrived in Capernaum, a Roman officer came and pleaded with him,
[6]"Lord, my young servant lies in bed, paralyzed and racked with pain."
[7]Jesus said, "I will come and heal him."
8:8 Ps 107:20 [8]Then the officer said, "Lord, I am not worthy to have you come into my home. Just
say the word from where you are, and my servant will be healed! [9]I know, because I am
under the authority of my superior officers and I have authority over my soldiers. I only
need to say, 'Go,' and they go, or 'Come,' and they come. And if I say to my slaves, 'Do
8:10-12 Ps 107:3 Matt 13:41-42; 21:43 Acts 10:45; 11:18; 14:27 Eph 3:6 this or that,' they do it."
[10]When Jesus heard this, he was amazed. Turning to the crowd, he said, "I tell you the
truth, I haven't seen faith like this in all the land of Israel! [11]And I tell you this, that many
Gentiles will come from all over the world and sit down with Abraham, Isaac, and Jacob
at the feast in the Kingdom of Heaven. [12]But many Israelites—those for whom the

8:2, 3 Leprosy, like AIDS today, was a terrifying disease because there was no known cure. In Jesus' day, the Greek word for "leprosy" was used for a variety of similar diseases, and some forms were contagious. If a person contracted the contagious type, a priest declared him a leper and banished him from his home and city. The leper was sent to live in a community with other lepers until he either got better or died. Yet when the leper begged Jesus to heal him, Jesus reached out and touched him, even though his skin was covered with the dread disease.

Sin is also an incurable disease—and we all have it. Only Christ's healing touch can miraculously take away our sins and restore us to real living. But first, just like the leper, we must realize our inability to cure ourselves and ask for Christ's saving help.

8:4 The law required a healed leper to be examined by the priest (Leviticus 14). Jesus wanted this man to give his story firsthand to the priest to prove that his leprosy was completely gone so that he could be restored to his community.

8:5, 6 The Roman officer could have let many obstacles stand between him and Jesus—pride, doubt, money, language, distance, time, self-sufficiency, power, race. But he didn't. If he did not let these barriers block his approach to Jesus, we don't need to either. What keeps you from Christ?

8:8-12 This Roman officer (also called a centurion) was a career military officer in the Roman army with control over 100 soldiers. Roman soldiers, of all people, were hated by the Jews for their oppression, control, and ridicule. Yet this man's genuine faith amazed Jesus! This hated Gentile's faith put to shame the pompous piety of many of the Jewish religious leaders.

8:10-12 Jesus told the crowd that many religious Jews who should be in the Kingdom would be excluded because of their lack of faith. Entrenched in their religious traditions, they could not accept Christ and his new message. We must be careful not to become so set in our religious habits that we expect God to work only in specified ways. Don't limit God by your mind-set and lack of faith.

8:11, 12 Faithful people of God from "all over the world" will be gathered to feast with the Messiah (Isaiah 25:6; 55). The Jews should have known that when the Messiah came, his blessings would be for Gentiles too (see Isaiah 66:12, 19). But this message came as a shock because they were too wrapped up in their own affairs and destiny. In claiming God's promises, we must not apply them so personally that we forget to see what God wants to do to reach *all* the people he loves.

8:11, 12 Matthew emphasizes this universal theme—Jesus' message is for everyone. The Old Testament prophets knew this (see Isaiah 56:3, 6-8; 66:12, 19; Malachi 1:11), but many New Testament Jewish leaders chose to ignore it. Each individual has to choose to accept or reject the Good News, and no one can become part of God's Kingdom on the basis of heritage or connections. Having Christian parents is a wonderful blessing, but it won't guarantee you eternal life. *You* must believe in and follow Christ.

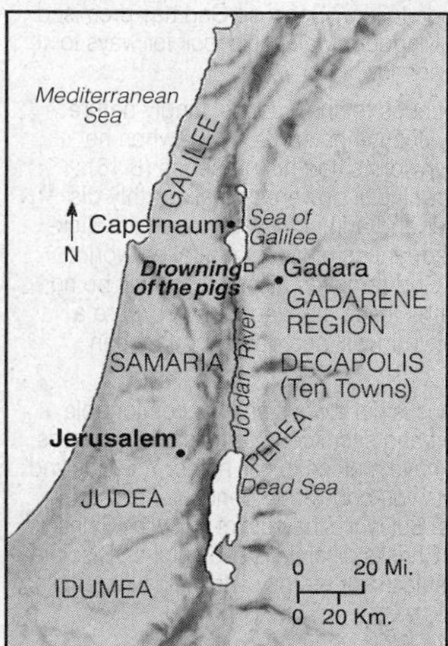

JESUS' MIRACULOUS POWER DISPLAYED
Jesus finished the sermon he had given on a hillside near Galilee and returned to Capernaum. As he and his disciples crossed the Sea of Galilee, Jesus calmed a fierce storm. Then, in the Gentile Gadarene region, Jesus commanded demons to come out of two men.

Kingdom was prepared—will be cast into outer darkness, where there will be weeping
and gnashing of teeth."
13 Then Jesus said to the Roman officer, "Go on home. What you have believed has **8:13** Matt 9:29; 15:28 John 4:50-51
happened." And the young servant was healed that same hour.

Jesus Heals Peter's Mother-in-Law and Many Others (**35**/Mark 1:29-34; Luke 4:38-41)

14 When Jesus arrived at Peter's house, Peter's mother-in-law was in bed with a high
fever. 15 But when Jesus touched her hand, the fever left her. Then she got up and
prepared a meal for him.
16 That evening many demon-possessed people were brought to Jesus. All the spirits
fled when he commanded them to leave; and he healed all the sick. 17 This fulfilled the **8:17** †Isa 53:4
word of the Lord through Isaiah, who said, "He took our sicknesses and removed our
diseases."*

Jesus Teaches about the Cost of Following Him (**122**/Luke 9:51-62)

18 When Jesus noticed how large the crowd was growing, he instructed his disciples to
cross to the other side of the lake.
19 Then one of the teachers of religious law said to him, "Teacher, I will follow you
no matter where you go!"
20 But Jesus said, "Foxes have dens to live in, and birds have nests, but I, the Son of **8:22** Matt 9:9 Mark 2:14 Luke 9:59 John 1:43; 21:19
Man, have no home of my own, not even a place to lay my head."
21 Another of his disciples said, "Lord, first let me return home and bury my father."
22 But Jesus told him, "Follow me now! Let those who are spiritually dead care for
their own dead."*

Jesus Calms the Storm (**87**/Mark 4:35-41; Luke 8:22-25)

23 Then Jesus got into the boat and started across the lake with his disciples. 24 Suddenly,
a terrible storm came up, with waves breaking into the boat. But Jesus was sleeping.
25 The disciples went to him and woke him up, shouting, "Lord, save us! We're going to
drown!"

8:17 Isa 53:4. **8:22** Greek *Let the dead bury their own dead.*

8:14 Peter was one of Jesus' 12 disciples. His Profile is found in chapter 27.

8:14, 15 Peter's mother-in-law gives us a beautiful example to follow. Her response to Jesus' touch was to wait on Jesus and his disciples—immediately. Has God ever helped you through a dangerous or difficult situation? If so, you should ask, How can I express my gratitude to him? Because God has promised us all the rewards of his Kingdom, we should look for ways to serve him and his followers now.

8:16, 17 Matthew continues to show Jesus' kingly nature. Through a single touch, Jesus healed (8:3, 15); when he spoke a single word, evil spirits fled his presence (8:16). Jesus has authority over all evil powers and all earthly disease. He also has power and authority to conquer sin. Sickness and evil are consequences of living in a fallen world. But in the future, when God removes all sin, there will be no more sickness and death. Jesus' healing miracles were a taste of what the whole world will one day experience in God's Kingdom.

8:19, 20 Following Jesus is not always easy or comfortable. Often it means great cost and sacrifice, with no earthly rewards or security. Jesus didn't have a place to call home. You may find that following Christ costs you popularity, friendships, leisure time, or treasured habits. But while the cost of following Christ is high, the value of being Christ's disciple is even higher. Discipleship is an investment that lasts for eternity and yields incredible rewards.

8:21, 22 It is possible that this disciple was not asking permission to go to his father's funeral but rather to put off following Jesus until his elderly father died. Perhaps he was the firstborn son and wanted to be sure to claim his inheritance. Perhaps he didn't want to face his father's wrath if he left the family business to follow an itinerant preacher. Whether his concern was financial security, family approval, or something else, he did not want to commit himself to Jesus just yet. Jesus, however, would not accept his excuse.

8:21, 22 Jesus was always direct with those who wanted to follow him. He made sure they counted the cost and set aside any conditions they might have for following him. As God's Son, Jesus did not hesitate to demand complete loyalty. Even family loyalty was not to take priority over the demands of obedience. His direct challenge forces us to ask ourselves about our own priorities in following him. The decision to follow Jesus should not be put off, even though other loyalties compete for our attention. Nothing should be placed above a total commitment to iving for him.

8:23 This would have been a fishing boat because many of Jesus' disciples were fishermen. Josephus, an ancient historian, wrote that there were usually more than 300 fishing boats on the Sea of Galilee at one time. This boat was large enough to hold Jesus and his 12 disciples and was powered both by oars and sails. During a storm, however, the sails were taken down to keep them from ripping and to make the boat easier to control.

8:24 The Sea of Galilee is an unusual body of water. It is relatively small (13 miles long, 7 miles wide), but it is 150 feet deep, and the shoreline is 680 feet below sea level. Sudden storms can appear over the surrounding mountains with little warning, stirring the water into violent 20-foot waves. The disciples had not foolishly set out in a storm. They had been caught without warning, and their danger was great.

8:26 Pss 89:10; 107:25-32 Matt 6:30

[26]And Jesus answered, "Why are you afraid? You have so little faith!" Then he stood
up and rebuked the wind and waves, and suddenly all was calm. [27]The disciples just sat
there in awe. "Who is this?" they asked themselves. "Even the wind and waves obey
him!"

Jesus Sends Demons into a Herd of Pigs (**88**/Mark 5:1-20; Luke 8:26-39)

[28]When Jesus arrived on the other side of the lake in the land of the Gadarenes,* two
men who were possessed by demons met him. They lived in a cemetery and were so
8:29 Mark 1:24 Luke 4:34 2 Pet 2:4
dangerous that no one could go through that area. [29]They began screaming at him, "Why
are you bothering us, Son of God? You have no right to torture us before God's appointed
time!" [30]A large herd of pigs was feeding in the distance, [31]so the demons begged, "If
you cast us out, send us into that herd of pigs."

[32]"All right, go!" Jesus commanded them. So the demons came out of the men and
entered the pigs, and the whole herd plunged down the steep hillside into the lake and
drowned in the water. [33]The herdsmen fled to the nearby city, telling everyone what
8:34 Acts 16:39
happened to the demon-possessed men. [34]The entire town came out to meet Jesus, but
they begged him to go away and leave them alone.

Jesus Heals a Paralyzed Man (**39**/Mark 2:1-12; Luke 5:17-26)

9 Jesus climbed into a boat and went back across the lake to his own town. [2]Some
people brought to him a paralyzed man on a mat. Seeing their faith, Jesus said to the
paralyzed man, "Take heart, son! Your sins are forgiven."

8:28 Some manuscripts read *Gerasenes;* other manuscripts read *Gergesenes.* See Mark 5:1; Luke 8:26.

8:25 Although the disciples had witnessed many miracles, they panicked in this storm. As experienced sailors, they knew its danger; what they did not know was that Christ could control the forces of nature. We often encounter storms in our life, where we feel God can't or won't work. When we truly understand who God is, however, we will realize that he controls both the storms of nature and the storms of the troubled heart. Jesus' power that calmed this storm can also help us deal with the problems we face. Jesus is willing to help if we only ask him. We should never discount his power even in terrible trials.

8:28 The land of the Gadarenes is located southeast of the Sea of Galilee, near the town of Gadara, one of the most important cities of the region (see map). Gadara was a member of the Ten Towns (see the note on Mark 5:20), towns with independent governments that were largely inhabited by Gentiles. This explains the herd of pigs (8:30), for the Jews did not raise pigs because pigs were considered unclean and thus unfit to eat.

8:28 Demon-possessed people are under the control of one or more demons. Demons are fallen angels who joined Satan in his rebellion against God and are now evil spirits under Satan's control. They help Satan tempt people to sin and have great destructive powers. But whenever they are confronted by Jesus, they lose their power. These demons recognized Jesus as God's Son (8:29), but they didn't think they had to obey him. Just believing is not enough (see James 2:19 for a discussion of belief and demons). Faith is more than belief. By faith, you accept what Jesus has done for you, receive him as the only one who can save you from sin, and live out your faith by obeying his commands.

8:28 Matthew says there were two demon-possessed men, while Mark and Luke refer only to one. Apparently Mark and Luke mention only the man who did the talking.

8:28 According to Jewish ceremonial laws, the men Jesus encountered were unclean in three ways: They were Gentiles (non-Jews), they were demon possessed, and they lived in a cemetery. Jesus helped them anyway. We should not turn our backs on people who are "unclean" or repulsive to us or who violate our moral standards and religious beliefs. Instead, we must realize that every human individual is a unique creation of God, needing to be touched by his love.

8:29 The Bible tells us that at the end of the world the Devil and his angels will be thrown into the lake of fire that burns with sulfur (Revelation 20:10). When the demons asked if Jesus had come to torment them "before God's appointed time," they showed they knew their ultimate fate.

8:32 When the demons entered the pigs, they drove the animals into the sea. The demons' action proves their destructive intent—if they could not destroy the men, they would destroy the pigs. Jesus' action, by contrast, shows the value he places on each human life.

8:34 Why did the people ask Jesus to leave? Unlike their own pagan gods, Jesus could not be contained, controlled, or appeased. They feared Jesus' supernatural power, a power that they had never before witnessed. And they were upset about losing a herd of pigs more than they were glad about the deliverance of the demon-possessed men. Are you more concerned about property and programs than people? Human beings are created in God's image and have eternal value. How foolish and yet how easy it is to value possessions, investments, and even animals above human life. Would you rather have Jesus leave you than finish his work in you?

9:1 "His own town" was Capernaum, a good choice for Jesus' base of operations. It was a wealthy city due to fishing and trade. Situated on the Sea of Galilee in a densely populated area, Capernaum housed the Roman garrison that kept peace in the region. The city was a cultural melting pot, greatly influenced by Greek and Roman manners, dress, architecture, and politics.

9:2 Among the first words Jesus said to the paralyzed man were "Your sins are forgiven." Then he healed the man. We must be careful not to concentrate more on God's power to heal physical sickness than on his power to forgive spiritual sickness in the form of sin. Jesus saw that even more than physical health, this man needed spiritual health. Spiritual health comes only from Jesus' healing touch.

9:2 Both the man's body and his spirit were paralyzed—he could not walk, and he did not know Jesus. But the man's spiritual state was Jesus' first concern. If God does not heal us or someone we love, we need to remember that physical healing is not Christ's only concern. We will all be completely healed in Christ's coming Kingdom; but first we have to come to know Jesus.

3“Blasphemy! This man talks like he is God!” some of the teachers of religious law
said among themselves.
4Jesus knew what they were thinking, so he asked them, “Why are you thinking such
evil thoughts? 5Is it easier to say, ‘Your sins are forgiven’ or ‘Get up and walk’? 6I will
prove that I, the Son of Man, have the authority on earth to forgive sins.” Then Jesus
turned to the paralyzed man and said, “Stand up, take your mat, and go on home, because
you are healed!”
7And the man jumped up and went home! 8Fear swept through the crowd as they saw
this happen right before their eyes. They praised God for sending a man with such great
authority.

Jesus Eats with Sinners at Matthew's House (**40**/Mark 2:13-17; Luke 5:27-32)

9As Jesus was going down the road, he saw Matthew sitting at his tax-collection booth.
“Come, be my disciple,” Jesus said to him. So Matthew got up and followed him.
10That night Matthew invited Jesus and his disciples to be his dinner guests, along
with his fellow tax collectors and many other notorious sinners. 11The Pharisees were
indignant. “Why does your teacher eat with such scum*?” they asked his disciples.
12When he heard this, Jesus replied, “Healthy people don't need a doctor—sick
people do.” 13Then he added, “Now go and learn the meaning of this Scripture: ‘I want
you to be merciful; I don't want your sacrifices.’* For I have come to call sinners, not
those who think they are already good enough.”

Religious Leaders Ask Jesus about Fasting (**41**/Mark 2:18-22; Luke 5:33-39)

14One day the disciples of John the Baptist came to Jesus and asked him, “Why do we
and the Pharisees fast, but your disciples don't fast?”
15Jesus responded, “Should the wedding guests mourn while celebrating with the
groom? Someday he will be taken from them, and then they will fast. 16And who would
patch an old garment with unshrunk cloth? For the patch shrinks and pulls away from

9:3 Matt 26:65; John 10:33
9:4 Matt 12:25; Luke 6:8; 9:47; 11:17
9:6-8 Matt 15:31; Luke 7:16; Acts 9:33-35
9:11 Matt 11:19; Luke 5:30; 15:1-2; 19:7
9:13 †Hos 6:6; Mic 6:6-8; Matt 12:7; Luke 19:10; 1 Tim 1:15
9:15 John 3:29

9:11 Greek *with tax collectors and sinners.* **9:13** Hos 6:6.

9:3 Blaspheming is claiming to be God and applying his characteristics to yourself. The religious leaders rightly saw that Jesus was claiming to be God. What they did not understand was that he *is* God and thus has the authority to heal and to forgive sins.

9:5, 6 It's easy to tell someone his sins are forgiven; it's a lot more difficult to reverse a case of paralysis! Jesus backed up his words by healing the man's legs. Jesus' action showed that his words were true; he had the power to forgive as well as to heal. Talk is cheap, but our words lack meaning if our actions do not back them up. We can say we love God or others, but if we are not taking practical steps to demonstrate that love, our words are empty and meaningless. How well do your actions back up what you say?

9:9 Matthew was a Jew who was appointed by the Romans to be the area's tax collector. He collected taxes from the citizens as well as from merchants passing through town. Tax collectors were expected to take a commission on the taxes they collected, but most of them overcharged and kept the profits. Thus, tax collectors were hated by the Jews because of their reputation for cheating and because of their support of Rome.

9:9 When Jesus called Matthew to be one of his disciples, Matthew got up and followed, leaving a lucrative career. When God calls you to follow or obey him, do you do it with as much abandon as Matthew? Sometimes the decision to follow Christ requires difficult or painful choices. Like Matthew, we must decide to leave behind those things that would keep us from following Christ.

9:10-13 When he visited Matthew, Jesus hurt his own reputation. Matthew was cheating the people, but Jesus found and changed him. We should not be afraid to reach out to people who are living in sin—God's message can change anyone.

9:11, 12 The Pharisees constantly tried to trap Jesus, and they thought his association with these “lowlifes” was the perfect opportunity. They were more concerned with their own appearance of holiness than with helping people, with criticism than encouragement, with outward respectability than practical help. But God is concerned for all people, including the sinful and hurting ones. The Christian life is not a popularity contest! Following Jesus' example, we should share the Good News with the poor, immoral, lonely, and outcast, not just the rich, moral, popular, and powerful.

9:13 Those who are sure that they are good enough can't be saved because the first step in following Jesus is acknowledging our need and admitting that we don't have all the answers. For more on “I want you to be merciful; I don't want your sacrifices,” see the chart in Hosea 7.

9:14 John's disciples fasted (went without food) as a sign of mourning for sin and preparation for the Messiah's coming. Jesus' disciples did not need to fast because he is the Messiah and was with them! Jesus did not condemn fasting—he himself fasted (4:2). He emphasized that fasting must be done for the right reasons.

9:14 John the Baptist's message was harsh, and it focused on law. When people look at God's law and compare themselves to it, they realize how far they fall short and how badly they need to repent. Jesus' message focused on life, the result of turning from sin and turning to him. John's disciples had the right start, but they needed to take the next step and trust in Jesus. Where is your focus—on law or on Christ?

9:15 The arrival of the Kingdom of Heaven was like a wedding feast with Jesus as the groom. His disciples, therefore, were filled with joy. It would not be right to mourn or fast when the groom was present.

the old cloth, leaving an even bigger hole than before. 17 And no one puts new wine into old wineskins. The old skins would burst from the pressure, spilling the wine and ruining the skins. New wine must be stored in new wineskins. That way both the wine and the wineskins are preserved."

Jesus Heals a Bleeding Woman and Restores a Girl to Life (**89**/Mark 5:21-43; Luke 8:40-56)

18 As Jesus was saying this, the leader of a synagogue came and knelt down before him. "My daughter has just died," he said, "but you can bring her back to life again if you just come and lay your hand upon her."

MATTHEW

More than any other disciple, Matthew had a clear idea of how much it would cost to follow Jesus, yet he did not hesitate a moment. When he left his tax-collecting booth, he guaranteed himself unemployment. For several of the other disciples, there was always fishing to return to, but for Matthew, there was no turning back.

Two changes happened to Matthew when he decided to follow Jesus. First, Jesus gave him a new life. He not only belonged to a new group; he belonged to the Son of God. He was not just accepting a different way of life; he was now an accepted person. For a despised tax collector, that change must have been wonderful! Second, Jesus gave Matthew a new purpose for his skills. When he followed Jesus, the only tool from his past job that he carried with him was his pen. From the beginning, God had made him a record keeper. Jesus' call eventually allowed him to put his skills to their finest work. Matthew was a keen observer, and he undoubtedly recorded what he saw going on around him. The Gospel that bears his name came as a result.

Matthew's experience points out that each of us, from the beginning, is one of God's works in progress. Much of what God has for us he gives long before we are able to consciously respond to him. He trusts us with skills and abilities ahead of schedule. He has made each of us capable of being his servant. When we trust him with what he has given us, we begin a life of real adventure. Matthew couldn't have known that God would use the very skills he had sharpened as a tax collector to record the greatest story ever lived. And God has no less meaningful a purpose for each one of us. Have you recognized Jesus saying to you, "Follow me"? What has been your response?

Strengths and accomplishments
- Was one of Jesus' 12 disciples
- Responded immediately to Jesus' call
- Invited many friends to his home to meet Jesus
- Compiled the Gospel of Matthew
- Clarified for his Jewish audience Jesus' fulfillment of Old Testament prophecies

Lessons from his life
- Jesus consistently accepted people from every level of society
- Matthew was given a new life, and his God-given skills of record keeping and attention to detail were given new purpose
- Having been accepted by Jesus, Matthew immediately tried to bring others into contact with Jesus

Vital statistics
- Where: Capernaum
- Occupations: Tax collector, disciple of Jesus
- Relative: Father: Alphaeus
- Contemporaries: Jesus, Pilate, Herod, other disciples

Key verse
"As Jesus was going down the road, he saw Matthew sitting at his tax-collection booth. 'Come, be my disciple,' Jesus said to him. So Matthew got up and followed him" (Matthew 9:9).

Matthew's story is told in the Gospels. He is also mentioned in Acts 1:13.

9:17 In Bible times wine was not kept in glass bottles but in goatskins sewn around the edges to form watertight bags. New wine expanded as it fermented, stretching its wineskin. After the wine had aged, the stretched skin would burst if more new wine was poured into it. New wine, therefore, was always put into new wineskins.

9:17 Jesus did not come to patch up the old religious system of Judaism with its rules and traditions. If he had, his message would have damaged it. His purpose was to bring in something new, though it had been prophesied for centuries. This new message, the Good News, said that Jesus Christ, God's Son, came to earth to offer all people forgiveness of sins and reconciliation with God. The Good News did not fit into the old rigid legalistic system of religion. It needed a fresh start. The message will always remain "new" because it must be accepted and applied in every generation. When we follow Christ, we must be prepared for new ways to live, new ways to look at people, and new ways to serve.

9:18 Mark and Luke say this man's name was Jairus (Mark 5:22; Luke 8:41). As leader of the synagogue, Jairus was responsible for administration—looking after the building, supervising worship, running the school on weekdays, and finding rabbis to teach on the Sabbath. For more information on synagogues, read the first note on Mark 1:21.

19 As Jesus and the disciples were going to the official's home, 20 a woman who had
had a hemorrhage for twelve years came up behind him. She touched the fringe of his
robe, 21 for she thought, "If I can just touch his robe, I will be healed."
22 Jesus turned around and said to her, "Daughter, be encouraged! Your faith has made
you well." And the woman was healed at that moment.
23 When Jesus arrived at the official's home, he noticed the noisy crowds and heard
the funeral music. 24 He said, "Go away, for the girl isn't dead; she's only asleep." But
the crowd laughed at him. 25 When the crowd was finally outside, Jesus went in and took
the girl by the hand, and she stood up! 26 The report of this miracle swept through the
entire countryside.

Jesus Heals the Blind and Mute **(90)**

27 After Jesus left the girl's home, two blind men followed along behind him, shouting,
"Son of David, have mercy on us!"
28 They went right into the house where he was staying, and Jesus asked them, "Do
you believe I can make you see?"
"Yes, Lord," they told him, "we do."
29 Then he touched their eyes and said, "Because of your faith, it will happen." 30 And
suddenly they could see! Jesus sternly warned them, "Don't tell anyone about this."
31 But instead, they spread his fame all over the region.
32 When they left, some people brought to him a man who couldn't speak because he
was possessed by a demon. 33 So Jesus cast out the demon, and instantly the man could
talk. The crowds marveled. "Nothing like this has ever happened in Israel!" they
exclaimed.
34 But the Pharisees said, "He can cast out demons because he is empowered by the
prince of demons."

9:22 Matt 9:29; Mark 10:52; Luke 7:50; 17:19; Acts 3:16
9:23 2 Chr 35:25; Jer 9:17-18
9:24 John 11:11-13
9:27 Matt 20:29-31; Mark 10:47
9:30 Mark 7:36
9:31 Mark 7:36
9:32-33 Matt 12:22; Mark 7:32, 35; 9:17, 25; Luke 11:14
9:34 Matt 12:24; Mark 3:22; Luke 11:15

9:20-22 This woman had suffered for 12 years with a hemorrhage (perhaps a menstrual disorder). In our times of desperation, we don't have to worry about the correct way to reach out to God. Like this woman, we can simply reach out in faith. He will respond.

9:22 God changed a situation that had been a problem for years. Like the leper and the demon-possessed men (see the note on 8:2, 3 and the second note on 8:28), this woman was considered unclean. For 12 years, she, too, had been one of the "untouchables" and had not been able to lead a normal life. But Jesus changed that and restored her. Sometimes we are tempted to give up on people or situations that have not changed for many years. God can change what seems unchangeable, giving new purpose and hope.

9:23-26 The synagogue leader didn't come to Jesus until his daughter was dead—it was too late for anyone else to help. But Jesus simply went to the girl and raised her! In our lives, Christ can make a difference when it seems too late for anyone else to help. He can bring healing to broken relationships, release from addicting habits, and forgiveness and healing to emotional scars. If your situation looks hopeless, remember that Christ can do the impossible.

9:27 "Son of David" was a popular way of addressing Jesus as the Messiah because it was known that the Messiah would be a descendant of David (Isaiah 9:7). This is the first time the title is used in Matthew. Jesus' ability to give sight to the blind was prophesied in Isaiah 29:18; 35:5; 42:7.

9:27-30 Jesus didn't respond immediately to the blind men's pleas. He waited to see if they had faith. Not everyone who says he wants help really believes God can help him. Jesus may have waited and questioned these men to emphasize and increase their faith. When you think that God is too slow in answering your prayers, consider that he might be testing you as he did the blind men. Do you believe that God can help you? Do you *really* want his help?

9:28 These blind men were persistent. They went right into the house where Jesus was staying. They knew Jesus could heal them, and they would let nothing stop them from finding him. That's real faith in action. If you believe Jesus is the answer to your every need, don't let anything or anyone stop you from reaching out to him.

9:30 Jesus told the people to keep quiet about his healings because he did not want to be known only as a miracle worker. He healed because he had compassion on people, but he also wanted to bring *spiritual* healing to a sin-sick world.

9:32 While Jesus was on earth, demonic forces seemed especially active. Although we cannot always be sure why or how demon possession occurs, it causes both physical and mental problems. In this case, the demon made the man unable to talk. For more on demons and demon possession, read the notes on 8:28 and Mark 1:23.

9:34 In chapter 9, the Pharisees accuse Jesus of four different sins: blasphemy, befriending outcasts, impiety, and serving Satan. Matthew shows how Jesus was maligned by those who should have received him most gladly. Why did the Pharisees do this? (1) Jesus bypassed their religious authority. (2) He weakened their control over the people. (3) He challenged their cherished beliefs. (4) He exposed their insincere motives.

9:34 While the Pharisees questioned, debated, and dissected Jesus, people were being healed and lives changed right in front of them. Their skepticism was based not on insufficient evidence but on jealousy of Jesus' popularity.

Jesus Urges the Disciples to Pray for Workers (**92**)
9:35 Matt 4:23 — 35 Jesus traveled through all the cities and villages of that area, teaching in the
synagogues and announcing the Good News about the Kingdom. And wherever he
9:36 †Num 27:17 †2 Chr 18:16 †Zech 10:2 Mark 6:34 — went, he healed people of every sort of disease and illness. 36 He felt great pity for the
crowds that came, because their problems were so great and they didn't know where
to go for help. They were like sheep without a shepherd. 37 He said to his disciples,
9:37-38 Luke 10:2 John 4:35 — "The harvest is so great, but the workers are so few. 38 So pray to the Lord who is in
charge of the harvest; ask him to send out more workers for his fields."

Jesus Sends Out the Twelve Disciples (**93**/Mark 6:7-13; Luke 9:1-6)

10 Jesus called his twelve disciples to him and gave them authority to cast out evil
10:2-4 John 1:40-49 Acts 1:13 — spirits and to heal every kind of disease and illness. 2 Here are the names of the
twelve apostles:

first Simon (also called Peter),
then Andrew (Peter's brother),
James (son of Zebedee),
John (James's brother),
3 Philip,
Bartholomew,
Thomas,
Matthew (the tax collector),
James (son of Alphaeus),
Thaddeus,

COUNTING THE COST OF FOLLOWING CHRIST

Jesus helped his disciples prepare for the rejection many of them would experience by being Christians. Being God's person will usually create reactions from others who are resisting him.

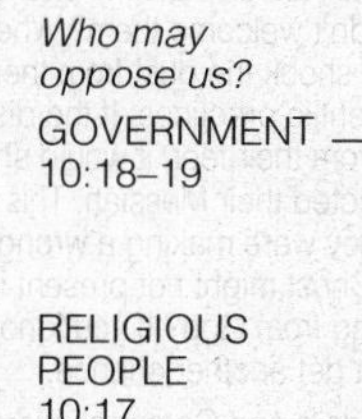

Who may oppose us?	*Natural response*	*Possible pressures*		*Needed truth*
GOVERNMENT 10:18–19		Threats 10:26	→	The truth will be revealed (10:26)
		Physical harm 10:28	→	Our soul cannot be harmed (10:28)
RELIGIOUS PEOPLE 10:17	Fear and worry	Public ridicule 10:22	→	God himself will acknowledge us if we acknowledge him (10:32)
FAMILY 10:21		Rejection by loved ones 10:34–37	→	God's love can sustain us (10:31)

9:35 The Good News about the Kingdom was that the promised and long-awaited Messiah had finally come. His healing miracles were a sign that his teaching was true.

9:35-38 Jesus needs workers who know how to deal with people's problems. We can comfort others and show them the way to live because we have been helped with our problems by God and his laborers (2 Corinthians 1:3-7).

9:36 Ezekiel also compared Israel to sheep without a shepherd (Ezekiel 34:5, 6). Jesus came to be the Shepherd, the one who could show people how to avoid life's pitfalls (see John 10:14).

9:37, 38 Jesus looked at the crowds following him and referred to them as a field ripe for harvest. Many people are ready to give their lives to Christ if someone would show them how. Jesus commands us to pray that people will respond to this need for workers. Often, when we pray for something, God answers our prayers by using *us*. Be prepared for God to use you to show another person the way to him.

10:1 Jesus *called* his 12 disciples. He didn't draft them, force them, or ask them to volunteer; he chose them to serve him in a special way. Christ calls us today. He doesn't twist our arms and make us do something we don't want to do. We can choose to join him or remain behind. When Christ calls you to follow him, how do you respond?

10:2-4 The list of Jesus' 12 disciples doesn't give us many details—probably because there weren't many impressive details to tell. Jesus called people from all walks of life—fishermen, political activists, tax collectors. He called common people and uncommon leaders; rich and poor; educated and uneducated. Today, many people think only certain people are fit to follow Christ, but this was not the attitude of the Master himself. God can use anyone, no matter how insignificant he or she appears. When you feel small and useless, remember that God uses ordinary people to do his extraordinary work.

10:3 Bartholomew is probably another name for Nathanael, whom we meet in John 1:45-51. Thaddeus is also known as Judas son of James. The disciples are also listed in Mark 3:16-19; Luke 6:14-16; and Acts 1:13.

4 Simon (the Zealot*),
Judas Iscariot (who later betrayed him).

5 Jesus sent the twelve disciples out with these instructions: "Don't go to the Gentiles
or the Samaritans, 6 but only to the people of Israel—God's lost sheep. 7 Go and announce
to them that the Kingdom of Heaven is near.* 8 Heal the sick, raise the dead, cure those
with leprosy, and cast out demons. Give as freely as you have received!
9 "Don't take any money with you. 10 Don't carry a traveler's bag with an extra coat
and sandals or even a walking stick. Don't hesitate to accept hospitality, because those
who work deserve to be fed.* 11 Whenever you enter a city or village, search for a worthy
man and stay in his home until you leave for the next town. 12 When you are invited into
someone's home, give it your blessing. 13 If it turns out to be a worthy home, let your
blessing stand; if it is not, take back the blessing. 14 If a village doesn't welcome you or
listen to you, shake off the dust of that place from your feet as you leave. 15 I assure you,
the wicked cities of Sodom and Gomorrah will be better off on the judgment day than
that place will be.

Jesus Prepares the Disciples for Persecution (**94**)

16 "Look, I am sending you out as sheep among wolves. Be as wary as snakes and
harmless as doves. 17 But beware! For you will be handed over to the courts and beaten
in the synagogues. 18 And you must stand trial before governors and kings because you
are my followers. This will be your opportunity to tell them about me—yes, to witness
to the world. 19 When you are arrested, don't worry about what to say in your defense,

10:4 Matt 26:25; 27:3; Mark 14:44
10:5 2 Kgs 17:24; John 4:9
10:6 Jer 50:6; Matt 15:24
10:7 Matt 3:2; 4:17
10:9-10 1 Cor 9:14; 1 Tim 5:18
10:15 Gen 18:20–19:29; Matt 11:23-24; 2 Pet 2:6; Jude 1:7
10:16 Luke 10:3; Acts 20:29
10:17 Acts 5:40; 22:19; 26:11
10:19-20 Luke 12:11-12; Acts 4:8

10:4 Greek *the Cananean.* **10:7** Or *has come* or *is coming soon.* **10:10** Or *the worker is worthy of support.*

10:4 Simon the zealot may have been a member of the Zealots, a radical political party working for the violent overthrow of Roman rule in Israel.

10:5, 6 Why didn't Jesus send the disciples to the Gentiles or the Samaritans? A Gentile is anyone who is not a Jew. The Samaritans were a race that resulted from intermarriage between Jews and Gentiles after the Old Testament captivities (see 2 Kings 17:24). Jesus asked his disciples to go only to the Jews because he came *first* to the Jews (Romans 1:16). God chose them to tell the rest of the world about him. Jewish disciples and apostles preached the Good News of the risen Christ all around the Roman Empire, and soon Gentiles were pouring into the church. The Bible clearly teaches that God's message of salvation is for *all* people, regardless of race, sex, or national origin (Genesis 12:3; Isaiah 25:6; 56:3-7; Malachi 1:11; Acts 10:34, 35; Romans 3:29, 30; Galatians 3:28).

10:7 The Jews were waiting for the Messiah to usher in his Kingdom. They hoped for a political and military kingdom that would free them from Roman rule and bring back the days of glory under David and Solomon. But Jesus was talking about a spiritual Kingdom. The Good News today is that the Kingdom is still *near.* Jesus, the Messiah, has already begun his Kingdom on earth in the hearts of his followers. One day the Kingdom will be fully realized. Then evil will be destroyed and all people will live in peace with one another.

10:8 Jesus gave the disciples a principle to guide their actions as they ministered to others: "Give as freely as you have received." Because God has showered us with his blessings, we should give generously to others of our time, love, and possessions.

10:10 Jesus said that those who minister are to be cared for. The disciples could expect food and shelter in return for the spiritual service they provided. Who ministers to you? Make sure you take care of the pastors, missionaries, and teachers who serve God by serving you (see 1 Corinthians 9:9, 10; 1 Timothy 5:17).

10:10 Mark's account (6:8) says to take a walking stick, and Matthew and Luke (9:3) say not to. Jesus may have meant that they were not to take an *extra* pair of sandals, walking stick, and bag. In any case, the principle was that they were to go out ready for duty and travel, unencumbered by excess material goods.

10:14 Why did Jesus tell his disciples to shake the dust off their feet if a city or home didn't welcome them? When leaving Gentile cities, pious Jews often shook the dust from their feet to show their separation from Gentile practices. If the disciples shook the dust of a *Jewish* town from their feet, it would show their separation from Jews who rejected their Messiah. This gesture was to show the people that they were making a wrong choice—that the opportunity to choose Christ might not present itself again. Are you receptive to teaching from God? If you ignore the Spirit's prompting, you may not get another chance.

10:15 The cities of Sodom and Gomorrah were destroyed by fire from heaven because of their wickedness (Genesis 19:24, 25). Those who reject the Good News when they hear it will be worse off than the wicked people of these destroyed cities, who never heard the Good News at all.

10:16 The opposition of the Pharisees would be like ravaging wolves. The disciples' only hope would be to look to their Shepherd for protection. We may face similar hostility. Like the disciples, we are not to be sheeplike in our attitude but sensible and prudent. We are not to be gullible pawns, but neither are we to be deceitful connivers. We must find a balance between wisdom and vulnerability to accomplish God's work.

10:17, 18 Later the disciples experienced these hardships (Acts 5:40; 12:1-3), not only from without (governments, courts), but also from within (friends, family; 10:21). Living for God often brings on persecution, but with it comes the opportunity to tell the Good News of salvation. In times of persecution, we can be confident because Jesus has "overcome the world" (John 16:33). And those who endure to the end will be saved (Matthew 10:22).

10:19, 20 Jesus told the disciples that when arrested for preaching the Good News, they should not worry about what to say in their defense—God's Spirit would speak through them. This promise was fulfilled in Acts 4:8-14 and elsewhere. Some mistakenly think this means we don't have to prepare to present the Good News because God will take care of everything. Scripture teaches, however, that we are to make carefully prepared, thoughtful statements (Colossians 4:6). Jesus is telling us not to stop preparing but to stop worrying.

because you will be given the right words at the right time. 20 For it won't be you doing
the talking—it will be the Spirit of your Father speaking through you.
21 "Brother will betray brother to death, fathers will betray their own children, and
children will rise against their parents and cause them to be killed. 22 And everyone will
hate you because of your allegiance to me. But those who endure to the end will be saved.
23 When you are persecuted in one town, flee to the next. I assure you that I, the Son of
Man, will return before you have reached all the towns of Israel.
24 "A student is not greater than the teacher. A servant is not greater than the master.
25 The student shares the teacher's fate. The servant shares the master's fate. And since
I, the master of the household, have been called the prince of demons,* how much more
will it happen to you, the members of the household! 26 But don't be afraid of those who
threaten you. For the time is coming when everything will be revealed; all that is secret
will be made public. 27 What I tell you now in the darkness, shout abroad when daybreak
comes. What I whisper in your ears, shout from the housetops for all to hear!
28 "Don't be afraid of those who want to kill you. They can only kill your body; they
cannot touch your soul. Fear only God, who can destroy both soul and body in hell. 29 Not
even a sparrow, worth only half a penny, can fall to the ground without your Father
knowing it. 30 And the very hairs on your head are all numbered. 31 So don't be afraid;
you are more valuable to him than a whole flock of sparrows.
32 "If anyone acknowledges me publicly here on earth, I will openly acknowledge that
person before my Father in heaven. 33 But if anyone denies me here on earth, I will deny
that person before my Father in heaven.
34 "Don't imagine that I came to bring peace to the earth! No, I came to bring a
sword. 35 I have come to set a man against his father, and a daughter against her
mother, and a daughter-in-law against her mother-in-law. 36 Your enemies will be right
in your own household! 37 If you love your father or mother more than you love me,
you are not worthy of being mine; or if you love your son or daughter more than me,
you are not worthy of being mine. 38 If you refuse to take up your cross and follow
me, you are not worthy of being mine. 39 If you cling to your life, you will lose it; but
if you give it up for me, you will find it.
40 "Anyone who welcomes you is welcoming me, and anyone who welcomes me is

10:21 Mic 7:6
10:22 John 15:21
10:24 John 13:16; 15:20
10:26 Mark 4:22
10:28 Isa 8:12-13; Heb 10:31
10:29 Luke 12:6
10:30 1 Sam 14:45; 2 Sam 14:11; Luke 21:18; Acts 27:34
10:31 Matt 6:26; 12:12
10:32 Rom 10:9; Rev 3:5
10:33 Mark 8:38; Luke 9:26; 2 Tim 2:12
10:35-36 †Mic 7:6
10:37 Luke 14:26
10:38 Matt 16:24; Mark 8:34; Luke 9:23; 14:27
10:39 Matt 16:25; Mark 8:35; Luke 9:24; 17:33; John 12:25
10:40 John 12:44; 13:20

10:25 Greek *Beelzeboul.*

10:22 Enduring to the end is not a way to be saved but the evidence that a person is really committed to Jesus. Persistence is not a means to earn salvation; it is the by-product of a truly devoted life.

10:23 Christ warned the disciples against premature martyrdom. They were to leave before the persecution got too great. We have plenty of work to do and many people to reach. Our work won't be finished until Christ returns. And only after he returns will the whole world realize his true identity (see 24:14; Romans 14:9-12).

10:25 The prince of demons was Satan, also known as Beelzebub and the lord of flies. The Pharisees accused Jesus of using Satan's power to drive out demons (see 12:24). Good is sometimes labeled evil. If Jesus, who is perfect, was called evil, his followers should expect that similar accusations will be directed at them. But those who endure will be vindicated (10:22).

10:29-31 Jesus said that God is aware of everything that happens even to sparrows, and you are far more valuable to him than they are. You are so valuable that God sent his only Son to die for you (John 3:16). Because God places such value on you, you need never fear personal threats or difficult trials. These can't shake God's love or dislodge his Spirit from within you.

But this doesn't mean that God will take away all your troubles (see 10:16). The real test of value is how well something holds up under the wear, tear, and stress of everyday life. Those who stand up for Christ in spite of their troubles truly have lasting value and will receive great rewards (see 5:11, 12).

10:34 Jesus did not come to bring the kind of peace that glosses over deep differences just for the sake of superficial harmony. Conflict and disagreement will arise between those who choose to follow Christ and those who don't. Yet we can look forward to the day when all conflict will be resolved. For other verses on Jesus as peacemaker, see Isaiah 9:6; Matthew 5:9; John 14:27.

10:34-39 Christian commitment may separate friends and loved ones. In saying this, Jesus was not encouraging disobedience to parents or conflict at home. Rather, he was showing that his presence demands a decision. Because some will follow Christ and some won't, conflict will inevitably arise. As we take up our cross and follow him, our different values, morals, and goals will set us apart from others. Don't neglect your family, but remember that your commitment to God is even more important than it is. God should be your first priority.

10:37 Christ calls us to a higher mission than to find comfort and tranquility in this life. Love of family is a law of God, but even this love can be self-serving and used as an excuse not to serve God or do his work.

10:38 To take up our cross and follow Jesus means to be willing to publicly identify with him, to experience certain opposition, and to be willing to face even suffering and death for his sake.

10:39 This verse is a positive and negative statement of the same truth: Clinging to this life may cause us to forfeit the best from Christ in this world *and* in the next. The more we love this life's rewards (leisure, power, popularity, financial security), the more we will discover how empty they really are. The best way to enjoy life, therefore, is to loosen our greedy grasp on earthly rewards so that we can be free to follow Christ. In doing so, we will inherit eternal life and begin at once to experience the benefits of following Christ.

welcoming the Father who sent me. 41 If you welcome a prophet as one who speaks for
God,* you will receive the same reward a prophet gets. And if you welcome good and
godly people because of their godliness, you will be given a reward like theirs. 42 And
if you give even a cup of cold water to one of the least of my followers, you will surely
be rewarded."

4. Jesus teaches about the Kingdom

Jesus Eases John's Doubt (**70**/Luke 7:18-35)

11 When Jesus had finished giving these instructions to his twelve disciples, he went
off teaching and preaching in towns throughout the country.
2 John the Baptist, who was now in prison, heard about all the things the Messiah was
doing. So he sent his disciples to ask Jesus, 3 "Are you really the Messiah we've been
waiting for, or should we keep looking for someone else?"
4 Jesus told them, "Go back to John and tell him about what you have heard and seen—
5 the blind see, the lame walk, the lepers are cured, the deaf hear, the dead are raised to
life, and the Good News is being preached to the poor. 6 And tell him: 'God blesses those
who are not offended by me.*' "
7 When John's disciples had gone, Jesus began talking about him to the crowds. "Who
is this man in the wilderness that you went out to see? Did you find him weak as a reed,
moved by every breath of wind? 8 Or were you expecting to see a man dressed in
expensive clothes? Those who dress like that live in palaces, not out in the wilderness.
9 Were you looking for a prophet? Yes, and he is more than a prophet. 10 John is the man
to whom the Scriptures refer when they say,

'Look, I am sending my messenger before you,
and he will prepare your way before you.'*

11 "I assure you, of all who have ever lived, none is greater than John the Baptist. Yet even
the most insignificant person in the Kingdom of Heaven is greater than he is! 12 And
from the time John the Baptist began preaching and baptizing until now, the Kingdom
of Heaven has been forcefully advancing, and violent people attack it.* 13 For
before John came, all the teachings of the Scriptures looked forward to this present
time. 14 And if you are willing to accept what I say, he is Elijah, the one the prophets
said would come.* 15 Anyone who is willing to hear should listen and understand!
16 "How shall I describe this generation? These people are like a group of children
playing a game in the public square. They complain to their friends, 17 'We played
wedding songs, and you weren't happy, so we played funeral songs, but you weren't

10:41 1 Kgs 17:9-24; 2 Kgs 4:8-37
11:3 Ps 118:26; Mal 3:1
11:5 Isa 35:4-6; 42:7, 18; 61:1; Luke 4:18-19
11:6 Matt 13:57; 26:31
11:7 Matt 3:5
11:9 Matt 14:5; 21:26; Luke 1:76
11:10 Exod 23:20; †Mal 3:1; Mark 1:2; Luke 7:27
11:12-13 Luke 16:16
11:14 Mal 4:5; Matt 17:10-13; Mark 9:11-13; Luke 1:17; John 1:21
11:15 Matt 13:9, 43; Mark 4:9, 23; Luke 8:8; 14:35; Rev 2:7

10:41 Greek *welcome a prophet in the name of a prophet.* **11:6** Or *who don't fall away because of me.* **11:10** Mal 3:1. **11:12** Or *until now, eager multitudes have been pressing into the Kingdom of Heaven.* **11:14** See Mal 4:5.

10:42 How much we love God can be measured by how well we treat others. Jesus' example of giving a cup of cold water to a thirsty child is a good model of unselfish service. A child usually can't or won't return a favor. God notices every good deed we do or don't do as if he were the one receiving it. Is there something unselfish you can do for someone else today? Although no one else may see you, God will notice.

11:2, 3 John had been put in prison by Herod. Herod had married his own sister-in-law, and John publicly rebuked Herod's flagrant sin (14:3-5). John's Profile is found in John 1. Herod's Profile is found in Mark 6.

11:4-6 As John sat in prison, he began to have some doubts about whether Jesus really was the Messiah. If John's purpose was to prepare people for the coming Messiah (3:3), and if Jesus really was that Messiah, then why was John in prison when he could have been preaching to the crowds, preparing their hearts?

Jesus answered John's doubts by pointing to Jesus' acts of healing the blind, lame, and deaf, curing the lepers, raising the dead, and preaching the Good News to the poor. With so much evidence, Jesus' identity was obvious. If you sometimes doubt your salvation, the forgiveness of your sins, or God's work in your life, look at the evidence in Scripture and the changes in your life. When you doubt, don't turn away from Christ; turn *to* him.

11:11 No person ever fulfilled his God-given purpose better than John. Yet in God's coming Kingdom all members will have a greater spiritual heritage than John because they will have seen and known Christ and his finished work on the cross.

11:12 There are three common views about the meaning of this verse: (1) Jesus may have been referring to a vast movement toward God, the momentum that began with John's preaching. (2) He may have been reflecting the Jewish activists' expectation that God's Kingdom would come through a violent overthrow of Rome. (3) Or he may have meant that entering God's Kingdom takes courage, unwavering faith, determination, and endurance because of the growing opposition leveled at Jesus' followers.

11:14 John was not a resurrected Elijah, but he took on Elijah's prophetic role—boldly confronting sin and pointing people to God (Malachi 3:1). See Elijah's Profile in 1 Kings 18.

11:16-19 Jesus condemned the attitude of his generation. No matter what he said or did, they took the opposite view. They were cynical and skeptical because he challenged their comfortable, secure, and self-centered lives. Too often we justify our inconsistencies because listening to God may require us to change the way we live.

11:18 Matt 3:4; Luke 1:15 sad.' 18 For John the Baptist didn't drink wine and he often fasted, and you say, 'He's
demon possessed.' 19 And I, the Son of Man, feast and drink, and you say, 'He's a
11:19 Matt 9:11, 14 glutton and a drunkard, and a friend of the worst sort of sinners!' But wisdom is shown
to be right by what results from it."

Jesus Promises Rest for the Soul (**71**)

20 Then Jesus began to denounce the cities where he had done most of his miracles,
11:21-22 Isa 23:1-8; Ezek 26–28; Joel 3:4-8; Amos 1:9-10; Zech 9:2-4; Matt 10:15 because they hadn't turned from their sins and turned to God. 21 "What horrors
await you, Korazin and Bethsaida! For if the miracles I did in you had been done
in wicked Tyre and Sidon, their people would have sat in deep repentance long
ago, clothed in sackcloth and throwing ashes on their heads to show their remorse.
11:23 †Isa 14:13, 15 22 I assure you, Tyre and Sidon will be better off on the judgment day than you!
23 And you people of Capernaum, will you be exalted to heaven? No, you will be
brought down to the place of the dead.* For if the miracles I did for you had been
done in Sodom, it would still be here today. 24 I assure you, Sodom will be better
off on the judgment day than you."

11:25-27 Eph 1:17-18 25 Then Jesus prayed this prayer: "O Father, Lord of heaven and earth, thank you for
hiding the truth from those who think themselves so wise and clever, and for revealing
it to the childlike. 26 Yes, Father, it pleased you to do it this way!

11:27 Matt 28:18; John 3:35; 10:15; 17:2, 25-26 27 "My Father has given me authority over everything. No one really knows the Son
except the Father, and no one really knows the Father except the Son and those to whom
the Son chooses to reveal him."

28 Then Jesus said, "Come to me, all of you who are weary and carry heavy burdens,
11:29 †Jer 6:16 and I will give you rest. 29 Take my yoke upon you. Let me teach you, because I am
11:30 1 Jn 5:3 humble and gentle, and you will find rest for your souls. 30 For my yoke fits perfectly,
and the burden I give you is light."

The Disciples Pick Wheat on the Sabbath (**45**/Mark 2:23-28; Luke 6:1-5)

12:2 Exod 20:10; Deut 5:14; Luke 13:14; 14:3; John 5:10; 7:23; 9:16 **12** At about that time Jesus was walking through some grainfields on the Sabbath.
His disciples were hungry, so they began breaking off heads of wheat and eating
the grain. 2 Some Pharisees saw them do it and protested, "Your disciples shouldn't be
doing that! It's against the law to work by harvesting grain on the Sabbath."
12:3 1 Sam 21:1-6 3 But Jesus said to them, "Haven't you ever read in the Scriptures what King David

11:23 Greek *to Hades.*

11:21-24 Tyre, Sidon, and Sodom were ancient cities with a long-standing reputation for wickedness (Genesis 18–19; Ezekiel 27–28). Each was destroyed by God for its evil. The people of Bethsaida, Korazin, and Capernaum saw Jesus first-hand, and yet they stubbornly refused to repent of their sins and believe in him. Jesus said that if some of the wickedest cities in the world had seen him, they would have repented. Because Bethsaida, Korazin, and Capernaum saw Jesus and didn't believe, they would suffer even greater punishment than would the wicked cities that didn't see Jesus. Similarly, nations and cities with churches on every corner and Bibles in every home will have no excuse on judgment day if they do not repent and believe.

11:25 Jesus mentioned two kinds of people in his prayer: the "wise and clever"—arrogant in their own knowledge—and the "childlike"—humbly open to receive the truth of God's Word. Are you wise in your own eyes, or do you seek the truth in childlike faith, realizing that only God holds all the answers?

11:27 In the Old Testament, *know* means more than knowledge. It implies an intimate relationship. The communion between God the Father and God the Son is the core of their relationship. For anyone else to know God, God must reveal himself to that person, by the Son's choice. How fortunate we are that Jesus has clearly revealed God to us, as well as his truth and how we can know him.

11:28-30 A yoke is a heavy wooden harness that fits over the shoulders of an ox or oxen. It is attached to a piece of equipment the oxen are to pull. A person may be carrying heavy burdens of (1) sin, (2) excessive demands of religious leaders (23:4; Acts 15:10), (3) oppression and persecution, or (4) weariness in the search for God.

Jesus frees people from all these burdens. The rest that Jesus promises is love, healing, and peace with God, not the end of all labor. A relationship with God changes meaningless, wearisome toil into spiritual productivity and purpose.

12:1, 2 The Pharisees had established 39 categories of actions forbidden on the Sabbath, based on interpretations of God's law and on Jewish custom. Harvesting was one of those forbidden actions. By picking wheat and rubbing it in their hands, the disciples were technically harvesting, according to the Pharisees. Jesus and the disciples were picking grain because they were hungry, not because they wanted to harvest the grain for a profit. They were not working on the Sabbath. The Pharisees, however, could not (and did not want to) see beyond their law's technicalities. They had no room for compassion, and they were determined to accuse Jesus of wrongdoing.

did when he and his companions were hungry? 4He went into the house of God, and they 12:4 Lev 24:5-9
ate the special bread reserved for the priests alone. That was breaking the law, too. 5And
haven't you ever read in the law of Moses that the priests on duty in the Temple may 12:5 Num 28:9-10
work on the Sabbath? 6I tell you, there is one here who is even greater than the Temple! 12:6
7But you would not have condemned those who aren't guilty if you knew the meaning Matt 12:41-42 Luke 11:31-32
of this Scripture: 'I want you to be merciful; I don't want your sacrifices.'* 8For I, the 12:7
Son of Man, am master even of the Sabbath." Mic 6:6-8

Jesus Heals a Man's Hand on the Sabbath (**46**/Mark 3:1-6; Luke 6:6-11)

9Then he went over to the synagogue, 10where he noticed a man with a deformed hand. 12:10 Luke 13:14; 14:3
The Pharisees asked Jesus, "Is it legal to work by healing on the Sabbath day?" (They John 9:16
were, of course, hoping he would say yes, so they could bring charges against him.)
11And he answered, "If you had one sheep, and it fell into a well on the Sabbath, 12:11 Luke 14:5
wouldn't you get to work and pull it out? Of course you would. 12And how much more 12:12
valuable is a person than a sheep! Yes, it is right to do good on the Sabbath." 13Then he Matt 6:26; 10:31
said to the man, "Reach out your hand." The man reached out his hand, and it became
normal, just like the other one. 14Then the Pharisees called a meeting and discussed plans
for killing Jesus.

Large Crowds Follow Jesus (**47**/Mark 3:7-12)

15But Jesus knew what they were planning. He left that area, and many people followed
him. He healed all the sick among them, 16but he warned them not to say who he was. 12:16 Matt 8:4
17This fulfilled the prophecy of Isaiah concerning him:

12:7 Hos 6:6.

12:4 This story is recorded in 1 Samuel 21:1-6. The Bread of the Presence was replaced every week, and the old loaves were eaten by the priests. The loaves given to David were the old loaves that had just been replaced with fresh ones. Although the priests were the only ones allowed to eat this bread, God did not punish David because his need for food was more important than the priestly regulations. Jesus was saying, "If you condemn me, you must also condemn David," something the religious leaders could never do without causing a great uproar among the people. Jesus was not condoning disobedience to God's laws. Instead, he was emphasizing discernment and compassion in enforcing the laws.

12:5 The Ten Commandments require that the Sabbath be kept holy (Exodus 20:8-11). The Pharisees had interpreted that to require a long list of actions that could not be done on the Sabbath, forcing the people to "rest." That was the *letter* of the law. But because the *purpose* of the Sabbath is to rest and to worship God, the priests were allowed to work by performing sacrifices and conducting worship services. This "Sabbath work" was serving and worshiping God. Jesus always emphasized the intent of the law, the meaning behind the letter. The Pharisees had lost the spirit of the law and were rigidly demanding that the letter (and their interpretation of it) be obeyed.

12:6 The Pharisees were so concerned about religious rituals that they missed the whole purpose of the Temple—to bring people to God. And because Jesus Christ is even greater than the Temple, how much better can he bring people to God. God is far more important than the created instruments of worship. If we become more concerned with the means of worship than with the one we worship, we will miss God even as we think we are worshiping him.

12:7 Jesus repeated to the Pharisees words the Jewish people had heard time and again throughout their history (1 Samuel 15:22, 23; Psalm 40:6-8; Isaiah 1:11-17; Jeremiah 7:21-23; Hosea 6:6). Our heart attitude toward God comes first. Only then can we properly obey and observe religious regulations and rituals.

12:8 When Jesus said he was master of the Sabbath, he claimed to be greater than the law and above the law. To the Pharisees, this was heresy. They did not realize that Jesus, the divine Son of God, had created the Sabbath. The Creator is always greater than his creation; thus, Jesus had the authority to overrule their traditions and regulations.

12:9 For more information on synagogues, read the first note on Mark 1:21 and 5:22.

12:10 As they pointed to the man with the deformed hand, the Pharisees tried to trick Jesus by asking him if it was legal to heal on the Sabbath. Their Sabbath rules said that people could be helped on the Sabbath only if their lives were in danger. Jesus healed on the Sabbath several times, and none of those healings were in response to emergencies. If Jesus had waited until another day, he would have been submitting to the Pharisees' authority, showing that their petty rules were equal to God's law. If he healed the man on the Sabbath, the Pharisees could claim that because Jesus broke their rules, his power was not from God. But Jesus made it clear how ridiculous and petty their rules were. God is a God of people, not rules. The best time to reach out to someone is when he or she needs help.

12:10-12 The Pharisees placed their laws above human need. They were so concerned about Jesus' breaking one of their rules that they did not care about the man's deformed hand. What is your attitude toward others? If your convictions don't allow you to help certain people, your convictions may not be in tune with God's Word. Don't allow dogma to blind you to human need.

12:14 The Pharisees plotted Jesus' death because they were outraged. Jesus had overruled their authority (Luke 6:11) and had exposed their evil attitudes in front of the entire crowd in the synagogue. Jesus had showed that the Pharisees were more loyal to their religious system than to God.

12:15 Up to this point, Jesus had been aggressively confronting the Pharisees' hypocrisy. Here he decided to withdraw from the synagogue before a major confrontation developed because it was not yet time for him to die. Jesus had many lessons still to teach his disciples and the people.

12:16 Jesus did not want those he healed to tell others about his miracles because he didn't want the people coming to him for the wrong reasons. That would hinder his teaching ministry and arouse false hopes about an earthly kingdom. But the news of Jesus' miracles spread, and many came to see for themselves (see Mark 3:7, 8).

12:18-21 †Isa 42:1-4 [18] "Look at my Servant,
whom I have chosen.
He is my Beloved,
and I am very pleased with him.
I will put my Spirit upon him,
and he will proclaim justice to the nations.
[19] He will not fight or shout;
he will not raise his voice in public.
[20] He will not crush those who are weak,
or quench the smallest hope,
until he brings full justice with his final victory.
[21] And his name will be the hope
of all the world."*

Religious Leaders Accuse Jesus of Getting His Power from Satan (**74**/Mark 3:20-30)

12:22-23 [22] Then a demon-possessed man, who was both blind and unable to talk, was brought to
Matt 9:32-33 Jesus. He healed the man so that he could both speak and see. [23] The crowd was amazed.
12:24 "Could it be that Jesus is the Son of David, the Messiah?" they wondered out loud.
Matt 9:34 [24] But when the Pharisees heard about the miracle, they said, "No wonder he can cast
12:25 out demons. He gets his power from Satan,* the prince of demons."
Matt 9:4 [25] Jesus knew their thoughts and replied, "Any kingdom at war with itself is doomed.
A city or home divided against itself is doomed. [26] And if Satan is casting out Satan, he
12:27 Matt 9:34 is fighting against himself. His own kingdom will not survive. [27] And if I am empowered
Acts 19:13 by the prince of demons,* what about your own followers? They cast out demons, too,
12:28 Acts 10:38 so they will judge you for what you have said. [28] But if I am casting out demons by the
Spirit of God, then the Kingdom of God has arrived among you. [29] Let me illustrate this.
You can't enter a strong man's house and rob him without first tying him up. Only then
12:30 Mark 9:40 can his house be robbed!* [30] Anyone who isn't helping me opposes me, and anyone who
Luke 9:50 isn't working with me is actually working against me.
12:31-32 Mark 3:28-30 [31] "Every sin or blasphemy can be forgiven—except blasphemy against the Holy
Luke 12:10 Spirit, which can never be forgiven. [32] Anyone who blasphemes against me, the Son of
Man, can be forgiven, but blasphemy against the Holy Spirit will never be forgiven,
12:33 either in this world or in the world to come.
Matt 7:16-20 Luke 6:43-45 [33] "A tree is identified by its fruit. Make a tree good, and its fruit will be good. Make

12:18-21 Isa 42:1-4. **12:24** Greek *Beelzeboul.* **12:27** Greek *by Beelzeboul.* **12:29** Or *One cannot rob Satan's kingdom without first tying him up. Only then can his demons be cast out.*

12:17-21 The people expected the Messiah to be a king. This quotation from Isaiah's prophecy (Isaiah 42:1-4) showed that the Messiah was indeed a king, but it illustrated what *kind* of king—a quiet, gentle ruler who brings justice to the nations. Like the crowd in Jesus' day, we may want Christ to rule as a king and bring great and visible victories in our life. But often Christ's work is quiet, and it happens according to *his* perfect timing, not ours.

12:24 The Pharisees had already accused Jesus of being empowered by the prince of demons (9:34). They were trying to discredit him by using an emotional argument. Refusing to believe that Jesus came from God, they said he was in league with Satan. Jesus easily exposed the foolishness of their argument.

12:25 In the Incarnation, Jesus gave up the complete and unlimited use of his supernatural abilities. But he still had profound insight into human nature. His discernment stopped the religious leaders' attempts to trick him. The resurrected Christ knows all our thoughts. This can be comforting because he knows what we really mean when we speak to him. It can be threatening because we cannot hide from him, and he knows our selfish motives.

12:29 At Jesus' birth, Satan's power and control were disrupted. In the wilderness Jesus overcame Satan's temptations, and at the Resurrection he defeated Satan's ultimate weapon—death. Eventually Satan will be constrained forever (Revelation 20:10), and evil will no longer pervade the earth. Jesus has complete power and authority over Satan and all his forces.

12:30 It is impossible to be neutral about Christ. Anyone who is not actively following him has chosen to reject him. Any person who tries to remain neutral in the struggle of good against evil is choosing to be separated from God, who alone is good. To refuse to follow Christ is to choose to be on Satan's team.

12:31, 32 The Pharisees had blasphemed against the Spirit by attributing the power by which Christ did miracles to Satan (12:24) instead of the Holy Spirit. The unpardonable sin is the deliberate refusal to acknowledge God's power in Christ. It indicates a deliberate and irreversible hardness of heart. Sometimes believers worry that they have accidently committed this unforgivable sin. But only those who have turned their backs on God and rejected all faith have any need to worry. Jesus said they can't be forgiven—not because their sin is worse than any other but because they will never ask for forgiveness. Whoever rejects the prompting of the Holy Spirit removes himself or herself from the only force that can lead him or her to repentance and restoration to God.

a tree bad, and its fruit will be bad. 34You brood of snakes! How could evil men like you
speak what is good and right? For whatever is in your heart determines what you say.
35A good person produces good words from a good heart, and an evil person produces
evil words from an evil heart. 36And I tell you this, that you must give an account on
judgment day of every idle word you speak. 37The words you say now reflect your fate
then; either you will be justified by them or you will be condemned."

Religious Leaders Ask Jesus for a Miraculous Sign (**75**)

38One day some teachers of religious law and Pharisees came to Jesus and said,
"Teacher, we want you to show us a miraculous sign to prove that you are from God."
39But Jesus replied, "Only an evil, faithless generation would ask for a miraculous sign;
but the only sign I will give them is the sign of the prophet Jonah. 40For as Jonah was in
the belly of the great fish for three days and three nights, so I, the Son of Man, will be in
the heart of the earth for three days and three nights. 41The people of Nineveh will rise up
against this generation on judgment day and condemn it, because they repented at the
preaching of Jonah. And now someone greater than Jonah is here—and you refuse to
repent. 42The queen of Sheba* will also rise up against this generation on judgment day
and condemn it, because she came from a distant land to hear the wisdom of Solomon.
And now someone greater than Solomon is here—and you refuse to listen to him.
43"When an evil spirit leaves a person, it goes into the desert, seeking rest but finding
none. 44Then it says, 'I will return to the person I came from.' So it returns and finds its
former home empty, swept, and clean. 45Then the spirit finds seven other spirits more
evil than itself, and they all enter the person and live there. And so that person is worse
off than before. That will be the experience of this evil generation."

Jesus Describes His True Family (**76**/Mark 3:31-35; Luke 8:19-21)

46As Jesus was speaking to the crowd, his mother and brothers were outside, wanting to
talk with him. 47Someone told Jesus, "Your mother and your brothers are outside, and
they want to speak to you."
48Jesus asked, "Who is my mother? Who are my brothers?" 49Then he pointed to his
disciples and said, "These are my mother and brothers. 50Anyone who does the will of
my Father in heaven is my brother and sister and mother!"

12:42 Greek *The queen of the south.*

12:34 Matt 3:7; 23:33
12:38 Matt 16:1; Mark 8:11-12; Luke 11:16; John 2:18; 6:30; 1 Cor 1:22
12:38-42 Matt 16:4
12:40 Jon 1:17
12:41 Jon 1:2; 3:5
12:42 1 Kgs 10:1-10; 2 Chr 9:1-12; Matt 12:6
12:45 2 Pet 2:20
12:46 Mark 6:3; John 2:12; 7:3-5; Acts 1:14
12:50 John 15:14

12:34-36 Jesus reminds us that what we say reveals what is in our heart. What kinds of words come from your mouth? That is an indication of what is in your heart. You can't solve your heart problem, however, just by cleaning up your speech. You must allow the Holy Spirit to fill you with new attitudes and motives; then your speech will be cleansed at its source.

12:38-40 The Pharisees were asking for another miraculous sign, but they were not sincerely seeking to know Jesus. Jesus knew they had already seen enough miraculous proof to convince them that he was the Messiah if they would just open their hearts. But they had already decided not to believe in him, and more miracles would not change that.

Many people have said, "If I could just see a real miracle, then I could really believe in God." But Jesus' response to the Pharisees applies to us. We have plenty of evidence—Jesus' birth, death, resurrection, and ascension, and centuries of his work in believers around the world. Instead of looking for additional evidence or miracles, accept what God has already given and move forward. He may use your life as evidence to reach another person.

12:39-41 Jonah was a prophet sent to the Assyrian city of Nineveh (see the book of Jonah). Because Assyria was such a cruel and warlike nation, Jonah tried to run from his assignment and ended up spending three days in the belly of a huge fish. When Jonah got out, he grudgingly went to Nineveh, preached God's message, and saw the city repent. By contrast, when Jesus came to his people, they refused to repent. Here Jesus is clearly saying that his resurrection will prove he is the Messiah. Three days after his death, Jesus will come back to life, just as Jonah was given a new chance at life after three days in the fish.

12:41, 42 In Jonah's day, Nineveh was the capital of the Assyrian Empire, and it was as evil as it was powerful (Jonah 1:2). But the entire city repented at Jonah's preaching. The queen of Sheba traveled far to see Solomon, king of Israel, and learn about his great wisdom (1 Kings 10:1-10; also see the note on Luke 11:31, 32 for more on the queen of Sheba). These Gentiles recognized the truth about God when it was presented to them, unlike these religious leaders, who ignored the truth even though it stared them in the face. How have you responded to the evidence and truth that you have?

12:43-45 Jesus was describing the attitude of the nation of Israel and the religious leaders in particular. Just cleaning up one's life without filling it with God leaves plenty of room for Satan to enter. The book of Ezra records how the people rid themselves of idolatry but failed to replace it with love for God and obedience to him. Ridding our life of sin is the first step. We must also take the second step: filling our life with God's Word and the Holy Spirit. Unfilled and complacent people are easy targets for Satan.

12:46-50 Jesus was not denying his responsibility to his earthly family. On the contrary, he criticized the religious leaders for not following the Old Testament command to honor their parents (15:1-9). He provided for his mother's security as he hung on the cross (John 19:25-27). His mother and brothers were present in the upper room at Pentecost (Acts 1:14). Instead, Jesus was pointing out that spiritual relationships are as binding as physical ones, and he was paving the way for a new community of believers (the universal church), our spiritual family.

Jesus Tells the Parable of the Four Soils (**77**/Mark 4:1-9; Luke 8:4-8)

13 Later that same day, Jesus left the house and went down to the shore, 2where an
immense crowd soon gathered. He got into a boat, where he sat and taught as the
people listened on the shore. 3He told many stories such as this one:
"A farmer went out to plant some seed. 4As he scattered it across his field, some
seeds fell on a footpath, and the birds came and ate them. 5Other seeds fell on shallow
soil with underlying rock. The plants sprang up quickly, 6but they soon wilted beneath
the hot sun and died because the roots had no nourishment in the shallow soil. 7Other
seeds fell among thorns that shot up and choked out the tender blades. 8But some seeds
fell on fertile soil and produced a crop that was thirty, sixty, and even a hundred times
13:9 Matt 11:15; 13:43
as much as had been planted. 9Anyone who is willing to hear should listen and
understand!"

Jesus Explains the Parable of the Four Soils (**78**/Mark 4:10-25; Luke 8:9-18)

10His disciples came and asked him, "Why do you always tell stories when you talk to
the people?"

13:11 Matt 11:25; 16:17; 1 Cor 2:10, 14; Col 1:27; 1 Jn 2:20, 27
11Then he explained to them, "You have been permitted to understand the secrets of
the Kingdom of Heaven, but others have not. 12To those who are open to my teaching,
more understanding will be given, and they will have an abundance of knowledge. But
13:12 Matt 25:29; Mark 4:25; Luke 19:26
to those who are not listening, even what they have will be taken away from them. 13That
is why I tell these stories, because people see what I do, but they don't really see. They
hear what I say, but they don't really hear, and they don't understand. 14This fulfills the
13:13 Jer 5:21
prophecy of Isaiah, which says:

13:14-15 †Isa 6:9-10

'You will hear my words,
  but you will not understand;
you will see what I do,
  but you will not perceive its meaning.
15For the hearts of these people are hardened,
  and their ears cannot hear,
  and they have closed their eyes—
so their eyes cannot see,
  and their ears cannot hear,
  and their hearts cannot understand,
and they cannot turn to me
  and let me heal them.'*

13:17 John 8:56; Heb 11:13; 1 Pet 1:10-12
16"But blessed are your eyes, because they see; and your ears, because they hear. 17I
assure you, many prophets and godly people have longed to see and hear what you have
seen and heard, but they could not.
18"Now here is the explanation of the story I told about the farmer sowing grain: 19The
seed that fell on the hard path represents those who hear the Good News about the Kingdom

13:14-15 Isa 6:9-10.

13:2, 3 Jesus used many stories, or parables (13:34), when speaking to the crowds. These stories compare something familiar to something unfamiliar, helping us understand spiritual truth by using everyday objects and relationships. Jesus' parables compel listeners to discover truth, while at the same time concealing the truth from those too lazy or too stubborn to see it. To those who are honestly searching, the truth becomes clear. We must be careful not to read too much into parables, forcing them to say what they don't mean. All parables have one meaning unless otherwise specified by Jesus.

13:8 This parable should encourage spiritual "farmers"—those who teach, preach, and seek to lead others to the Lord. The farmer sowed good seed, but not all the seed sprouted; even the plants that grew had varying yields. Don't be discouraged if you do not always see results as you faithfully teach the Word. Belief cannot be forced to follow a mathematical formula (i.e., a 4:1 ratio of seeds planted to seeds sprouted). Rather, it is a miracle of God's Holy Spirit using your words to produce faith in Christ.

13:9 Human ears hear many sounds, but there is a deeper kind of listening that results in spiritual understanding. If you honestly seek God's will, you have spiritual hearing, and these stories will give you new perspectives.

13:10 When speaking in parables, Jesus was not hiding truth from sincere seekers, because those who were receptive to spiritual truth understood the illustrations. To others they were only stories without meaning. This allowed Jesus to give spiritual food to those who hungered for it while preventing his enemies from trapping him sooner than they might otherwise have done.

13:12 This phrase means that we are responsible to use well what we have. When people reject Jesus, their hardness of heart drives away or renders useless even the little understanding they had.

and don't understand it. Then the evil one comes and snatches the seed away from their
hearts. 20The rocky soil represents those who hear the message and receive it with joy. 21But
like young plants in such soil, their roots don't go very deep. At first they get along fine, but
they wilt as soon as they have problems or are persecuted because they believe the word.
22The thorny ground represents those who hear and accept the Good News, but all too
quickly the message is crowded out by the cares of this life and the lure of wealth, so no
crop is produced. 23The good soil represents the hearts of those who truly accept God's
message and produce a huge harvest—thirty, sixty, or even a hundred times as much as had
been planted."

13:22 Matt 19:23; Luke 12:16-21; 1 Tim 6:9-10, 17

Jesus Tells the Parable of the Weeds (**80**)

24Here is another story Jesus told: "The Kingdom of Heaven is like a farmer who planted
good seed in his field. 25But that night as everyone slept, his enemy came and planted
weeds among the wheat. 26When the crop began to grow and produce grain, the weeds
also grew. 27The farmer's servants came and told him, 'Sir, the field where you planted
that good seed is full of weeds!'

28"'An enemy has done it!' the farmer exclaimed.

"'Shall we pull out the weeds?' they asked.

29"He replied, 'No, you'll hurt the wheat if you do. 30Let both grow together until the
harvest. Then I will tell the harvesters to sort out the weeds and burn them and to put the
wheat in the barn.'"

13:24 Mark 4:26-29
13:30 Matt 3:12

Jesus Tells the Parable of the Mustard Seed (**81**/Mark 4:30-34)

31Here is another illustration Jesus used: "The Kingdom of Heaven is like a mustard seed
planted in a field. 32It is the smallest of all seeds, but it becomes the largest of garden
plants and grows into a tree where birds can come and find shelter in its branches."

13:32 Ps 104:12; Ezek 17:23; 31:6

Jesus Tells the Parable of the Yeast (**82**)

33Jesus also used this illustration: "The Kingdom of Heaven is like yeast used by a
woman making bread. Even though she used a large amount* of flour, the yeast
permeated every part of the dough."

34Jesus always used stories and illustrations like these when speaking to the crowds.
In fact, he never spoke to them without using such parables. 35This fulfilled the prophecy
that said,

"I will speak to you in parables.
I will explain mysteries hidden since the creation of the world."*

13:33 1 Cor 5:6; Gal 5:9
13:34 John 16:25
13:35 †Ps 78:2

Jesus Explains the Parable of the Weeds (**83**)

36Then, leaving the crowds outside, Jesus went into the house. His disciples said, "Please
explain the story of the weeds in the field."

13:36 Matt 15:15

13:33 Greek *3 measures.* **13:35** Ps 78:2.

13:22 How easy it is to agree with Christ with no intention of obeying. It is easy to denounce worries of this life and the deceitfulness of wealth and still do nothing to change our ways. In light of eternal life with God, are your present worries justified? If you had everything you could want but forfeited eternal life with God, would those things be so desirable?

13:23 The four types of soil represent different responses to God's message. People respond differently because they are in different states of readiness. Some are hardened, others are shallow, others are contaminated by distracting worries, and some are receptive. How has God's Word taken root in your life? What kind of soil are you?

13:24ff Jesus gives the meaning of this parable in verses 36-43. All the parables in this chapter teach us about God and his Kingdom. They explain what the Kingdom is really like as opposed to our expectations of it. The Kingdom of Heaven is not a geographic location but a spiritual realm where God rules and where we share in his eternal life. We join that Kingdom when we trust in Christ as Savior.

13:30 The young weeds and the young blades of wheat look the same and can't be distinguished until they are grown and ready for harvest. Weeds (unbelievers) and wheat (believers) must live side by side in this world. God allows unbelievers to remain for a while, just as a farmer allows weeds to remain in his field so the surrounding wheat isn't uprooted with them. At the harvest, however, the weeds will be uprooted and thrown away. God's harvest (judgment) of all people is coming. We are to make ourselves ready by making sure that our faith is sincere.

13:31, 32 The mustard seed was the smallest seed a farmer used. Jesus used this parable to show that the Kingdom has small beginnings but will grow and produce great results.

13:33 In other Bible passages, yeast is used as a symbol of evil or uncleanness. Here it is a positive symbol of growth. Although yeast looks like a minor ingredient, it permeates the whole loaf. Although the Kingdom began small and was nearly invisible, it would soon grow and have a great impact on the world.

13:38 John 8:44; 1 Jn 3:10
13:39 Joel 3:13; Rev 14:15

37“All right,” he said. “I, the Son of Man, am the farmer who plants the good seed. 38The
field is the world, and the good seed represents the people of the Kingdom. The weeds are
the people who belong to the evil one. 39The enemy who planted the weeds among the
wheat is the Devil. The harvest is the end of the world, and the harvesters are the angels.
40“Just as the weeds are separated out and burned, so it will be at the end of the world.

13:41 Matt 24:31; Mark 13:27
13:42 Matt 8:12; 13:50; 22:13; 24:51; 25:30; Luke 13:28

41I, the Son of Man, will send my angels, and they will remove from my Kingdom
everything that causes sin and all who do evil, 42and they will throw them into the
furnace and burn them. There will be weeping and gnashing of teeth. 43Then the godly
will shine like the sun in their Father’s Kingdom. Anyone who is willing to hear should
listen and understand!

Jesus Tells the Parable of the Hidden Treasure (**84**)

13:44 Phil 3:7-8

44“The Kingdom of Heaven is like a treasure that a man discovered hidden in a field. In
his excitement, he hid it again and sold everything he owned to get enough money to buy
the field—and to get the treasure, too!

Jesus Tells the Parable of the Pearl Merchant (**85**)

45“Again, the Kingdom of Heaven is like a pearl merchant on the lookout for choice pearls.
46When he discovered a pearl of great value, he sold everything he owned and bought it!

Jesus Tells the Parable of the Fishing Net (**86**)

13:47 Matt 22:10

47“Again, the Kingdom of Heaven is like a fishing net that is thrown into the water and
gathers fish of every kind. 48When the net is full, they drag it up onto the shore, sit down,
sort the good fish into crates, and throw the bad ones away. 49That is the way it will be
at the end of the world. The angels will come and separate the wicked people from the

13:50 Matt 8:12; 13:42; 22:13; 24:51; 25:30; Luke 13:28

godly, 50throwing the wicked into the fire. There will be weeping and gnashing of teeth.
51Do you understand?”
“Yes,” they said, “we do.”
52Then he added, “Every teacher of religious law who has become a disciple in the

---

13:40-43 At the end of the world, angels will separate the evil from the good. There are true and false believers in churches today, but we should be cautious in our judgments because only Christ is qualified to make the final separation. If you start judging, you may damage some of the good “plants.” It’s more important to judge our own response to God than to analyze others’ responses.

13:42 Jesus often uses these terms to refer to the coming judgment. The weeping indicates sorrow or remorse, and gnashing of teeth shows extreme anxiety or pain. Those who say they don’t care what happens to them after they die don’t realize what they are saying. They will be punished for living in selfishness and indifference to God.

13:43 Those who will shine like the sun in God’s Kingdom stand in contrast to those who receive his judgment. A similiar illustration is used in Daniel 12:3.

13:44-46 The Kingdom of Heaven is more valuable than anything else we can have, and a person must be willing to give up everything to obtain it. The man who discovered the treasure in the field stumbled upon it by accident but knew its value when he found it. The merchant was earnestly searching for the pearl of great value, and when he found it, he sold everything he had to purchase it.

13:47-49 The parable of the fishing net has the same meaning as the parable of the wheat and weeds. We are to obey God and tell others about his grace and goodness, but we cannot dictate who is part of the Kingdom of Heaven and who is not. This sorting will be done at the last judgment by those infinitely more qualified than we.

13:52 Anyone who understands God’s real purpose in the law as revealed in the Old Testament has a real treasure. The Old Testament points the way to Jesus, the Messiah. Jesus always upheld its authority and relevance. But there is a double benefit for those who understand Jesus’ teaching about the Kingdom of Heaven. This was a new treasure that Jesus was revealing. Both the old and new teaching give practical guidelines for faith and for living in the world. The teachers of religious law, however, were trapped in the old and blind to the new. They were looking for a future kingdom *preceded* by judgment. Jesus, however, taught that the Kingdom was *now,* and the judgment was future. The religious leaders were looking for a physical and temporal kingdom (via military rebellion and physical rule), but they were blind to the spiritual significance of the Kingdom that Christ brought.

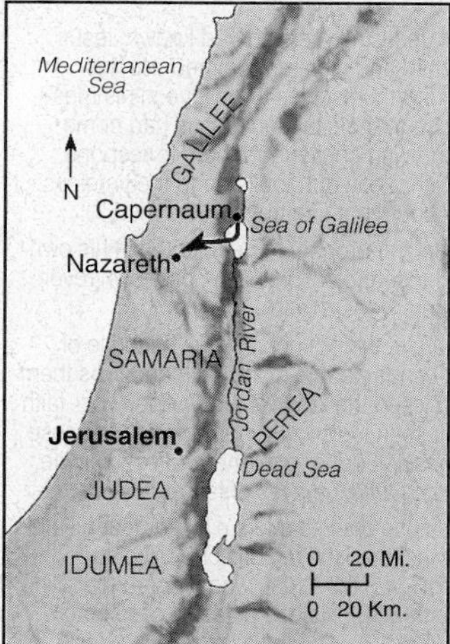

NAZARETH REJECTS JESUS
Chronologically, this return to Nazareth occurred after Jesus was in the Gadarene region and healed the demon-possessed men (8:28–34), then recrossed the sea to Capernaum. From there he traveled to Nazareth, where he had grown up, only to discover that the people refused to believe he was the Christ.

Kingdom of Heaven is like a person who brings out of the storehouse the new teachings
as well as the old."

5. Jesus encounters differing reactions to his ministry

The People of Nazareth Refuse to Believe (**91**/Mark 6:1-6)

53When Jesus had finished telling these stories, he left that part of the country. 54He 13:53 Matt 7:28
returned to Nazareth, his hometown. When he taught there in the synagogue, everyone
was astonished and said, "Where does he get his wisdom and his miracles? 55He's just 13:54 John 7:15
a carpenter's son, and we know Mary, his mother, and his brothers—James, Joseph, 13:55 Matt 12:46
Simon, and Judas. 56All his sisters live right here among us. What makes him so great?" Luke 3:23
57And they were deeply offended and refused to believe in him. John 6:42

Then Jesus told them, "A prophet is honored everywhere except in his own hometown 13:57 Luke 4:24
and among his own family." 58And so he did only a few miracles there because of their John 4:44
unbelief.

Herod Kills John the Baptist (**95**/Mark 6:14-29; Luke 9:7-9)

14 When Herod Antipas* heard about Jesus, 2he said to his advisers, "This must be
John the Baptist come back to life again! That is why he can do such miracles." 14:3 Luke 3:19-20
3For Herod had arrested and imprisoned John as a favor to his wife Herodias (the former 14:4
wife of Herod's brother Philip). 4John kept telling Herod, "It is illegal for you to marry Lev 18:16; 20:21
her." 5Herod would have executed John, but he was afraid of a riot, because all the people 14:5 Matt 11:9; 21:26
believed John was a prophet.

6But at a birthday party for Herod, Herodias's daughter performed a dance that
greatly pleased him, 7so he promised with an oath to give her anything she wanted. 8At
her mother's urging, the girl asked, "I want the head of John the Baptist on a tray!"
9The king was sorry, but because of his oath and because he didn't want to back down
in front of his guests, he issued the necessary orders. 10So John was beheaded in the 14:10 Matt 17:12
prison, 11and his head was brought on a tray and given to the girl, who took it to her 14:12
mother. 12John's disciples came for his body and buried it. Then they told Jesus what Acts 8:2
had happened.

Jesus Feeds Five Thousand (**96**/Mark 6:30-44; Luke 9:10-17; John 6:1-15)

13As soon as Jesus heard the news, he went off by himself in a boat to a remote area to be
alone. But the crowds heard where he was headed and followed by land from many villages.
14A vast crowd was there as he stepped from the boat, and he had compassion on them and 14:14 Matt 9:36
healed their sick. Mark 1:41 Heb 2:17-18; 4:15;

15That evening the disciples came to him and said, "This is a desolate place, and it is getting 5:1-3
late. Send the crowds away so they can go to the villages and buy food for themselves."

14:1 Greek *Herod the tetrarch.* He was a son of King Herod and was ruler over one of the four districts in Palestine.

13:55 The residents of Jesus' hometown had known Jesus since he was a young child and were acquainted with his family; they could not bring themselves to believe in his message. They were too close to the situation. Jesus had come to them as a prophet, one who challenged them to respond to unpopular spiritual truth. They did not listen to the timeless message because they could not see beyond the man.

13:57 Jesus was not the first prophet to be rejected in his own country. Jeremiah experienced rejection in his hometown, even by members of his own family (Jeremiah 12:5, 6).

13:58 Jesus did few miracles in his hometown "because of their unbelief." Unbelief blinds people to the truth and robs them of hope. These people missed the Messiah. How does your faith measure up? If you can't see God's work, perhaps it is because of your unbelief. Believe, ask God for a mighty work in your life, and expect him to act. Look with the eyes of faith.

14:1 Herod Antipas was one of three rulers over the four districts of Palestine. His territory included the regions of Galilee and Perea. He was the son of Herod the Great, who ordered the killing of the babies in Bethlehem (2:16). He heard Jesus' case before Jesus' crucifixion (Luke 23:6-12). His Profile is found in Mark 6.

14:2 For more information on John the Baptist, see his Profile in John 1.

14:3 Philip, Herod's half brother, was another of Palestine's three rulers. His territories were Iturea and Traconitis, northeast of the Sea of Galilee (Luke 3:1). Philip's wife, Herodias, left Philip to live with Herod Antipas. John the Baptist condemned the two for living immorally (see Mark 6:17, 18).

14:9 Herod did not want to kill John the Baptist, but he gave the order so that he wouldn't be embarrassed in front of his guests. How easy it is to give in to the crowd and to let ourselves be pressured into doing wrong. Don't get in a situation where it will be too embarrassing to do what is right. Determine to do what is right, no matter how embarrassing or painful it may be.

14:13, 14 Jesus sought solitude after the news of John's death. Sometimes we may need to deal with our grief alone. Jesus did not dwell on his grief but returned to the ministry he came to do.

14:14 Jesus performed some miracles as signs of his identity. He used other miracles to teach important truths. But here we read that he healed people because he "had compassion on them." Jesus was, and is, a loving, caring, and feeling person. When you are suffering, remember that Jesus hurts with you. He has compassion on you.

14:16-20 2 Kgs 4:42-44

16 But Jesus replied, "That isn't necessary—you feed them."
17 "Impossible!" they exclaimed. "We have only five loaves of bread and two fish!"

14:19-22 Matt 15:35-39 Mark 8:6-10

18 "Bring them here," he said. 19 Then he told the people to sit down on the grass.
And he took the five loaves and two fish, looked up toward heaven, and asked God's
blessing on the food. Breaking the loaves into pieces, he gave some of the bread
and fish to each disciple, and the disciples gave them to the people. 20 They all ate
as much as they wanted, and they picked up twelve baskets of leftovers. 21 About
five thousand men had eaten from those five loaves, in addition to all the women and
children!

Jesus Walks on Water (**97**/Mark 6:45-52; John 6:16-21)

22 Immediately after this, Jesus made his disciples get back into the boat and cross to the

14:23 Luke 9:28

other side of the lake while he sent the people home. 23 Afterward he went up into the
hills by himself to pray. Night fell while he was there alone. 24 Meanwhile, the disciples
were in trouble far away from land, for a strong wind had risen, and they were fighting
heavy waves.

14:26 Luke 24:37

25 About three o'clock in the morning* Jesus came to them, walking on the water.
26 When the disciples saw him, they screamed in terror, thinking he was a ghost. 27 But
Jesus spoke to them at once. "It's all right," he said. "I am here! Don't be afraid."
28 Then Peter called to him, "Lord, if it's really you, tell me to come to you by walking
on water."
29 "All right, come," Jesus said.
So Peter went over the side of the boat and walked on the water toward Jesus. 30 But

14:31 Matt 6:30

when he looked around at the high waves, he was terrified and began to sink. "Save me,
Lord!" he shouted.

14:33 Ps 2:7 Matt 16:16; 26:63; 27:54 Mark 1:1 Luke 22:70 John 1:49; 6:69 Rom 1:4

31 Instantly Jesus reached out his hand and grabbed him. "You don't have much faith,"
Jesus said. "Why did you doubt me?" 32 And when they climbed back into the boat, the
wind stopped.
33 Then the disciples worshiped him. "You really are the Son of God!" they exclaimed.

14:25 Greek *In the fourth watch of the night.*

14:19-21 Jesus multiplied five loaves and two fish to feed over 5,000 people. What he was originally given seemed insufficient, but in his hands it became more than enough. We often feel that our contribution to Jesus is meager, but he can use and multiply whatever we give him, whether it is talent, time, or treasure. It is when we give them to Jesus that our resources are multiplied.

14:21 The text states that there were 5,000 men present, *besides* women and children. Therefore, the total number of people Jesus fed could have been 10,000 to 15,000. The number of men is listed separately because in the Jewish culture of the day, men and women usually ate separately when in public. The children ate with the women.

14:23 Seeking solitude was an important priority for Jesus (see also 14:13). He made room in his busy schedule to be alone with the Father. Spending time with God in prayer nurtures a vital relationship with him and equips us to meet life's challenges and struggles. Develop the discipline of spending time alone with God. It will help you grow spiritually and become more and more like Christ.

14:28 Peter was not putting Jesus to the test, something we are told not to do (4:7). Instead, he was the only one in the boat to react in faith. His impulsive request led him to experience a rather unusual demonstration of God's power. Peter started to sink because he took his eyes off Jesus and focused on the high waves around him. His faith wavered when he realized what he was doing. We probably will not walk on water, but we may walk through tough situations. If we focus on the waves of difficult circumstances around us without faith in Jesus to help, we, too, may despair and sink. To maintain your faith when situations are difficult, focus on Jesus' power rather than on your inadequacies.

14:30, 31 Although we start out with good intentions, sometimes our faith falters. This doesn't necessarily mean we have failed. When Peter's faith faltered, he reached out to Christ, the only one who could help. He was afraid, but he still looked to Christ. When you are apprehensive about the troubles around you and doubt Christ's presence or ability to help, remember that he is always with you and is the *only* one who can really help.

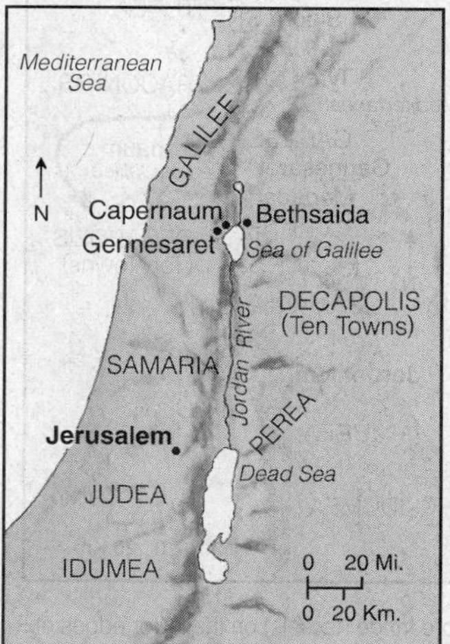

JESUS WALKS ON THE SEA
The miraculous feeding of the 5,000 occurred on the shores of the Sea of Galilee near Bethsaida. Jesus then sent his disciples across the lake. Several hours later they encountered a storm, and Jesus came to them—walking on the water. The boat then landed at Gennesaret.

Jesus Heals All Who Touch Him (**98**/Mark 6:53-56)

34 After they had crossed the lake, they landed at Gennesaret. 35 The news of their arrival
spread quickly throughout the whole surrounding area, and soon people were bringing **14:36**
all their sick to be healed. 36 The sick begged him to let them touch even the fringe of his Matt 9:20-21
robe, and all who touched it were healed.

Jesus Teaches about Inner Purity (**102**/Mark 7:1-23)

15 Some Pharisees and teachers of religious law now arrived from Jerusalem to
interview Jesus. 2 "Why do your disciples disobey our age-old traditions?" they **15:2**
demanded. "They ignore our tradition of ceremonial hand washing before they eat." Luke 11:38
3 Jesus replied, "And why do you, by your traditions, violate the direct commandments **15:4**
of God? 4 For instance, God says, 'Honor your father and mother,' and 'Anyone who †Exod 20:12; 21:17 †Lev 20:9
speaks evil of father or mother must be put to death.'* 5 But you say, 'You don't need to †Deut 5:16 Matt 19:19
honor your parents by caring for their needs if you give the money to God instead.' 6 And Mark 10:19 Luke 18:20
so, by your own tradition, you nullify the direct commandment of God. 7 You hypocrites! Eph 6:2
Isaiah was prophesying about you when he said,

8 'These people honor me with their lips, **15:8-9** †Isa 29:13
but their hearts are far away.
9 Their worship is a farce, **15:9** Col 2:20-22
for they replace God's commands with their own man-made teachings.'*"

10 Then Jesus called to the crowds and said, "Listen to what I say and try to understand. **15:11**
11 You are not defiled by what you eat; you are defiled by what you say and do.*" Matt 12:34 Acts 10:14-15

15:4 Exod 20:12; 21:17; Lev 20:9; Deut 5:16. **15:8-9** Isa 29:13. **15:11** Or *what comes out of the mouth defiles a person.*

14:34 Gennesaret was located on the west side of the Sea of Galilee in a fertile, well-watered area.

14:35, 36 The people recognized Jesus as a great healer, but how many understood who he truly was? They came to Jesus for physical healing, but did they come for spiritual healing? They came to prolong their lives on earth, not to seek eternal life. People may follow Jesus to learn valuable lessons from his life or in hopes of finding relief from pain. But we miss Jesus' whole message if we seek him only to heal our bodies but not our souls, if we look to him for help only in this life, rather than for his eternal plan for us. Only when we understand the real Jesus Christ can we appreciate how he can truly change our life.

MINISTRY IN PHOENICIA
After preaching again in Capernaum, Jesus left Galilee for Phoenicia, where he preached in Tyre and Sidon. On his return, he traveled through the region of the Decapolis (Ten Towns), fed the 4,000 beside the sea, then crossed to Magadan.

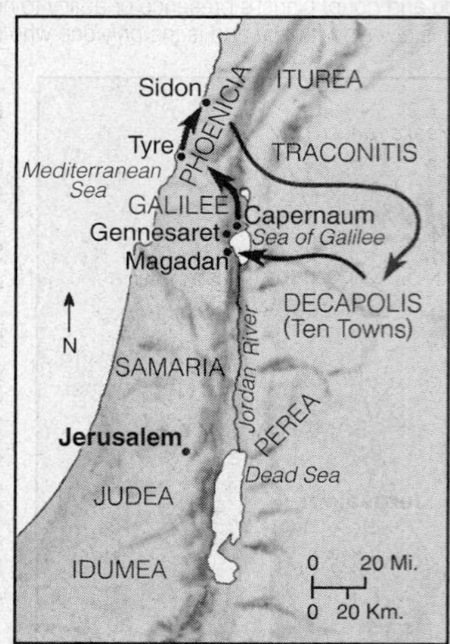

14:36 Jewish men wore fringe (tassels) on the lower edges of their robes according to God's command (Deuteronomy 22:12). By Jesus' day, this fringe was seen as a sign of holiness (23:5). It was natural that people seeking healing should reach out and touch these. But as one sick woman learned, healing came from faith and not from Jesus' robe (9:19-22).

15:1, 2 The Pharisees and teachers of religious law came from Jerusalem, the center of Jewish authority, to scrutinize Jesus' activities. Over the centuries since the Jews' return from Babylonian captivity, hundreds of religious traditions had been added to God's laws. The Pharisees and teachers of religious law considered them all equally important. Many traditions are not bad in themselves. Certain religious traditions can add richness and meaning to life. But we must not assume that because our traditions have been practiced for years, they should be elevated to a sacred standing. God's principles never change, and his law doesn't need additions. Traditions should help us understand God's laws better, not become laws themselves.

15:5, 6 This was the practice of *Corban* (literally, "offering"; see Mark 7:11). Anyone who made a Corban vow was required to dedicate money to God's Temple that otherwise would have gone to support his parents. Corban had become a religiously acceptable way to neglect parents, circumventing the child's responsibility to them. Although the action—giving money to God—seemed worthy and no doubt conferred prestige on the giver, many people who took the Corban vow were disregarding God's command to care for needy parents. These religious leaders were ignoring God's clear command to honor their parents.

15:8, 9 The prophet Isaiah also criticized hypocrites (Isaiah 29:13), and Jesus applied Isaiah's words to these religious leaders. When we claim to honor God while our heart is far from him, our worship means nothing. It is not enough to act religious. Our actions and our attitudes must be sincere. If they are not, Isaiah's words also describe us.

15:9 The Pharisees knew a lot about God, but they didn't know God. It is not enough to study about religion or even to study the Bible. We must respond to God himself.

15:11 Jesus was referring to the Jewish regulations concerning food and drink. This verse could be paraphrased: "You aren't made unclean by eating nonkosher food! It is what you *say* and *think* that makes you unclean!" This statement offended the Pharisees, who were very concerned about what people ate and drank.

15:13 Isa 60:21; 61:3 John 15:2 1 Cor 3:9
15:14 Matt 23:16, 24 Luke 6:39 Rom 2:19
15:18 Matt 12:34 Jas 3:6
15:19 Rom 1:29-31 1 Cor 5:10-11; 6:9-10 Gal 5:19-21

12 Then the disciples came to him and asked, "Do you realize you offended the
Pharisees by what you just said?"
13 Jesus replied, "Every plant not planted by my heavenly Father will be rooted up,
14 so ignore them. They are blind guides leading the blind, and if one blind person guides
another, they will both fall into a ditch."
15 Then Peter asked Jesus, "Explain what you meant when you said people aren't
defiled by what they eat."
16 "Don't you understand?" Jesus asked him. 17 "Anything you eat passes through the
stomach and then goes out of the body. 18 But evil words come from an evil heart and defile
the person who says them. 19 For from the heart come evil thoughts, murder, adultery, all
other sexual immorality, theft, lying, and slander. 20 These are what defile you. Eating with
unwashed hands could never defile you and make you unacceptable to God!"

Jesus Sends a Demon Out of a Girl (**103**/Mark 7:24-30)

21 Jesus then left Galilee and went north to the region of Tyre and Sidon. 22 A Gentile*
woman who lived there came to him, pleading, "Have mercy on me, O Lord, Son of
David! For my daughter has a demon in her, and it is severely tormenting her."
23 But Jesus gave her no reply—not even a word. Then his disciples urged him to send
her away. "Tell her to leave," they said. "She is bothering us with all her begging."

15:24 Matt 10:6 Rom 15:8
15:25 Matt 8:2
15:28 Matt 8:10

24 Then he said to the woman, "I was sent only to help the people of Israel—God's lost
sheep—not the Gentiles."
25 But she came and worshiped him and pleaded again, "Lord, help me!"
26 "It isn't right to take food from the children and throw it to the dogs," he said.
27 "Yes, Lord," she replied, "but even dogs are permitted to eat crumbs that fall beneath
their master's table."
28 "Woman," Jesus said to her, "your faith is great. Your request is granted." And her
daughter was instantly healed.

Jesus Heals Many People (**104**/Mark 7:31-37)

15:30 Isa 35:5-6 Matt 4:23; 11:5 Luke 7:22

29 Jesus returned to the Sea of Galilee and climbed a hill and sat down. 30 A vast crowd
brought him the lame, blind, crippled, mute, and many others with physical difficulties,

15:22 Greek *Canaanite.*

15:13, 14 Jesus told his disciples to leave the Pharisees alone because the Pharisees were blind to God's truth. Anyone who listened to their teaching would risk spiritual blindness as well. Not all religious leaders clearly see God's truth. Make sure that those you listen to and learn from are those with good spiritual eyesight—they teach and follow the principles of Scripture.

15:15 Later Peter would be faced with the issue of clean and unclean food (see the notes on 15:11 and Acts 10:12). Then he would learn that nothing should be a barrier to proclaiming the Good News to the Gentiles (non-Jews).

15:16-20 We work hard to keep our outward appearance attractive, but what is deep down in our heart (where others can't see) is more important to God. What are you like inside? When people become Christians, God makes them different on the inside. He will continue the process of change inside them if they only ask. God wants us to have healthy thoughts and motives, not just healthy bodies.

15:22 This woman is called "a Gentile, born in Syrian Phoenicia" in Mark's Gospel (7:26), indicating that she was from the territory northwest of Galilee, where the cities of Tyre and Sidon were located. Matthew calls her a Gentile, indicating her separation from the Jews. Matthew's Jewish audience would have immediately understood the significance of Jesus helping this woman.

15:23 The disciples asked Jesus to get rid of the woman because she was bothering them with her persistent begging. They showed no compassion for her or sensitivity to her needs. It is possible to become so occupied with spiritual matters that we become oblivious to the needs around us. This may be true especially if we are prejudiced against needy people or if they cause us inconvenience. Instead of being annoyed, be aware of the opportunities that surround you, and make an effort to look for ways to minister to others.

15:24 Jesus' words do not contradict the truth that God's message is for all people (Psalm 22:27; Isaiah 56:7; Matthew 28:19; Romans 15:9-12). After all, when Jesus said these words, he was in Gentile territory on a mission to Gentile people. He ministered to Gentiles on many other occasions also. Jesus was simply telling the woman that Jews were to have the first opportunity to accept him as the Messiah because God wanted them to present the message of salvation to the rest of the world (see Genesis 12:3). Jesus was not rejecting the Gentile woman. He may have wanted to test her faith, or he may have wanted to use the situation as another opportunity to teach that faith is available to all people.

15:26-28 *Dog* was a term the Jews commonly applied to Gentiles because the Jews considered these pagan people no more likely than dogs to receive God's blessing. Jesus was not degrading the woman by using this term; he was reflecting the Jews' attitude so as to contrast it with his own. The woman did not argue. Instead, using Jesus' choice of words, she agreed to be considered a dog as long as she could receive God's blessing for her daughter. Ironically, many Jews would lose God's blessing and salvation because they rejected Jesus, and many Gentiles would find salvation because they recognized and accepted him.

15:29-31 A vast crowd was brought to Jesus to be healed, and he healed them all. Jesus is still able to heal people who are suffering physically, emotionally, and spiritually, and we can be the ones who bring suffering people to him. Whom do you know that needs Christ's healing touch? You can bring them to Jesus through prayer or through explaining to them the reason for the hope that you have (1 Peter 3:15). Then let Christ do the healing.

and they laid them before Jesus. And he healed them all. 31 The crowd was amazed!
Those who hadn't been able to speak were talking, the crippled were made well, the lame
were walking around, and those who had been blind could see again! And they praised
the God of Israel.

Jesus Feeds Four Thousand (**105**/Mark 8:1-10)

32 Then Jesus called his disciples to him and said, "I feel sorry for these people. They **15:32** Matt 9:36
have been here with me for three days, and they have nothing left to eat. I don't want to
send them away hungry, or they will faint along the road."

33 The disciples replied, "And where would we get enough food out here in the **15:33** Mark 6:37; John 6:5
wilderness for all of them to eat?"

34 Jesus asked, "How many loaves of bread do you have?"

They replied, "Seven, and a few small fish." 35 So Jesus told all the people to sit **15:34-37** Matt 14:17-20; Mark 6:38-43; Luke 9:13-17; John 6:9-13
down on the ground. 36 Then he took the seven loaves and the fish, thanked God for
them, broke them into pieces, and gave them to the disciples, who distributed the food
to the crowd.

37 They all ate until they were full, and when the scraps were picked up, there were **15:37** Matt 16:10
seven large baskets of food left over! 38 There were four thousand men who were fed that **15:38** Matt 14:21; Mark 6:44
day, in addition to all the women and children. 39 Then Jesus sent the people home, and
he got into a boat and crossed over to the region of Magadan.

Leaders Demand a Miraculous Sign (**106**/Mark 8:11-13)

16 One day the Pharisees and Sadducees came to test Jesus' claims by asking him to **16:1** Matt 12:38; Luke 11:16; John 6:30
show them a miraculous sign from heaven.

2 He replied, "You know the saying, 'Red sky at night means fair weather tomorrow, **16:2-3** Luke 12:54-56
3 red sky in the morning means foul weather all day.' You are good at reading the weather
signs in the sky, but you can't read the obvious signs of the times!* 4 Only an evil, **16:4** Matt 12:39; Luke 11:29
faithless generation would ask for a miraculous sign, but the only sign I will give them
is the sign of the prophet Jonah." Then Jesus left them and went away.

Jesus Warns against Wrong Teaching (**107**/Mark 8:14-21)

5 Later, after they crossed to the other side of the lake, the disciples discovered they had
forgotten to bring any food. 6 "Watch out!" Jesus warned them. "Beware of the yeast of **16:6** Luke 12:1
the Pharisees and Sadducees."

7 They decided he was saying this because they hadn't brought any bread. 8 Jesus knew
what they were thinking, so he said, "You have so little faith! Why are you worried about

16:2-3 Several manuscripts do not include any of the words in 16:2-3 after *He replied.*

15:32ff This feeding of 4,000 is a separate event from the feeding of the 5,000 (14:13-21), confirmed by Mark 8:19, 20. This was the beginning of Jesus' expanded ministry to the Gentiles.

15:33 Jesus had already fed more than 5,000 people with five loaves and two fish. Here, in a similar situation, the disciples were again perplexed. How easily we throw up our hands in despair when faced with difficult situations. Like the disciples, we often forget that if God has cared for us in the past, he will do the same now. When facing a difficult situation, remember that God cares for you and trust him to work faithfully again.

15:39 Magadan was located on the west shore of the Sea of Galilee. Also known as Dalmanutha (Mark 8:10), this was Mary Magdalene's hometown.

16:1 The Pharisees and Sadducees were Jewish religious leaders of two different parties, and their views were diametrically opposed on many issues. The Pharisees carefully followed their religious rules and traditions, believing that this was the way to God. They also believed in the authority of all Scripture and in the resurrection of the dead. The Sadducees accepted only the books of Moses as Scripture and did not believe in life after death. In Jesus, however, these two groups had a common enemy, and they joined forces to try to kill him. For more information on the Pharisees and Sadducees, see the charts in chapter 3 and Mark 2.

16:1 The Pharisees and Sadducees demanded a sign "from heaven." They tried to explain away Jesus' other miracles as sleight of hand, coincidence, or use of evil power, but they believed that only God could do a sign in the sky. This, they were sure, would be a feat beyond Jesus' power. Although Jesus could have easily impressed them, he refused. He knew that even a miracle in the sky would not convince them he was the Messiah because they had already decided not to believe in him.

16:4 By using the sign of Jonah, who was inside a great fish for three days, Jesus was predicting his death and resurrection (see also 12:38-42).

16:4 Many people, like these Jewish leaders, say they want to see a miracle so that they can believe. But Jesus knew that miracles never convince the skeptical. Jesus had been healing, raising people from the dead, and feeding thousands, and still people wanted him to prove himself. Do you doubt Christ because you haven't *seen* a miracle? Do you expect God to prove himself to you personally before you believe? Jesus says, "Blessed are those who haven't seen me and believe anyway" (John 20:29). We have miracles recorded in the Old and New Testaments, 2,000 years of church history, and the witness of thousands. With all this evidence, those who won't believe are either too proud or too stubborn. If you simply step forward in faith and believe, then you will begin to see the miracles that God can do in your life!

16:9 Matt 14:17-21 Mark 6:34-44 Luke 9:11-17 John 6:1-13
16:10 Matt 15:32-38 Mark 8:1-9
16:11 Luke 12:1

having no food? 9Won't you ever understand? Don't you remember the five thousand I
fed with five loaves, and the baskets of food that were left over? 10Don't you remember
the four thousand I fed with seven loaves, with baskets of food left over? 11How could
you even think I was talking about food? So again I say, 'Beware of the yeast of the
Pharisees and Sadducees.'"
12Then at last they understood that he wasn't speaking about yeast or bread but about
the false teaching of the Pharisees and Sadducees.

Peter Says Jesus Is the Messiah (**109**/Mark 8:27-30; Luke 9:18-20)

16:14 Mark 6:14-15
16:16 Matt 1:16; 14:33; 26:23 Mark 14:61 John 1:34, 49; 6:69; 11:27; 20:31
16:18 John 1:42 1 Cor 3:11 Eph 2:20-22; 4:15-16 1 Pet 2:4-5
16:19 Isa 22:22 Matt 18:18 John 20:23 Rev 1:18; 3:7

13When Jesus came to the region of Caesarea Philippi, he asked his disciples, "Who do
people say that the Son of Man is?"
14"Well," they replied, "some say John the Baptist, some say Elijah, and others say
Jeremiah or one of the other prophets."
15Then he asked them, "Who do you say I am?"
16Simon Peter answered, "You are the Messiah, the Son of the living God."
17Jesus replied, "You are blessed, Simon son of John,* because my Father in heaven
has revealed this to you. You did not learn this from any human being. 18Now I say to you
that you are Peter,* and upon this rock I will build my church, and all the powers of hell*
will not conquer it. 19And I will give you the keys of the Kingdom of Heaven. Whatever
you lock on earth will be locked in heaven, and whatever you open on earth will be opened
in heaven." 20Then he sternly warned them not to tell anyone that he was the Messiah.

16:17 Greek *Simon son of Jonah;* see John 1:42; 21:15-17. **16:18a** *Peter* means "stone" or "rock." **16:18b** Greek *and the gates of Hades.*

16:12 Yeast is put into bread to make it rise, and it takes only a little to affect a whole batch of dough. Jesus used yeast as an example of how a small amount of evil can affect a large group of people. The wrong teachings of the Pharisees and Sadducees were leading many people astray. Beware of the tendency to say, "How can this little wrong possibly affect anyone?"

16:13 Caesarea Philippi was located several miles north of the Sea of Galilee, in the territory ruled by Philip. The influence of Greek and Roman culture was everywhere, and pagan temples and idols abounded. When Philip became ruler, he rebuilt and renamed the city after the emperor (Caesar) and himself. The city was originally called Caesarea, the same name as the capital city of Philip's brother Herod's territory.

16:13-17 The disciples answered Jesus' question with the common view—that Jesus was one of the great prophets come back to life. This belief may have stemmed from Deuteronomy 18:18, where God said he would raise up a prophet from among the people. (John the Baptist's Profile is in John 1; Elijah's Profile is in 1 Kings 18; and Jeremiah's Profile is in Jeremiah 2.) Peter, however, confessed Jesus as divine and as the promised and long-awaited Messiah. If Jesus were to ask you this question, how would you answer? Is he your Lord and Messiah?

16:18 The rock on which Jesus would build his church has been identified as (1) Jesus himself (his work of salvation by dying for us on the cross); (2) Peter (the first great leader in the church at Jerusalem); (3) the confession of faith that Peter gave and that all subsequent true believers would give. It seems most likely that the rock refers to Peter as the leader of the church (for his function, not necessarily his character). Just as Peter had revealed the true identity of Christ, so Jesus revealed Peter's identity and role.

Later, Peter reminds Christians that they are the church built on the foundation of the apostles and prophets, with Jesus Christ as the cornerstone (1 Peter 2:4-6). All believers are joined into this church by faith in Jesus Christ as Savior, the same faith that Peter expressed here (see also Ephesians 2:20, 21). Jesus praised Peter for his confession of faith. It is faith like Peter's that is the foundation of Christ's Kingdom.

16:19 The meaning of this verse has been a subject of debate for centuries. Some say the keys represent the authority to carry out church discipline, legislation, and administration (18:15-18); while others say the keys give the authority to announce the forgiveness of sins (John 20:23). Still others say the keys may be the opportunity to bring people to the Kingdom of Heaven by presenting them with the message of salvation found in God's Word (Acts 15:7-9). The religious leaders thought they held the keys of the Kingdom, and they tried to shut some people out. We cannot decide to open or close the Kingdom of Heaven for others, but God uses us to help others find the way inside. To all who believe in Christ and obey his words, the Kingdom doors are swung wide open.

16:20 Jesus warned the disciples not to publicize Peter's confession because they did not yet fully understand the kind of Messiah he had come to be—not a military commander but a suffering servant. They needed to come to a full understanding of Jesus and their mission as disciples before they could proclaim it to others in a way that would not cause a rebellion. They would have a difficult time understanding what Jesus came to do until his earthly mission was complete.

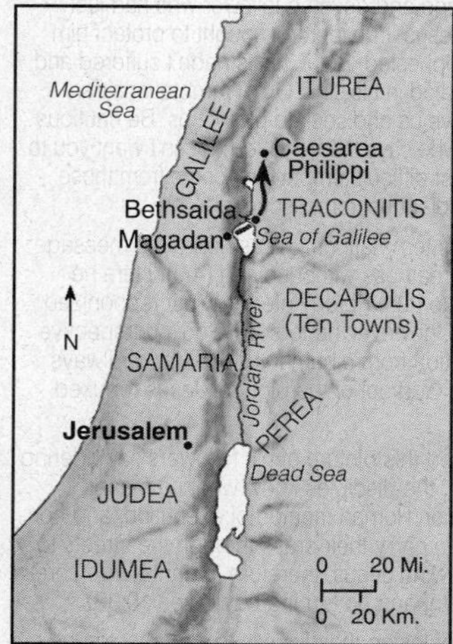

JOURNEY TO CAESAREA PHILIPPI
Jesus left Magadan, crossed the lake, and landed in Bethsaida. There he healed a man who had been born blind. From there, he and his disciples went to Caesarea Philippi, where Peter confessed Jesus as the Messiah and Son of God.

Jesus Predicts His Death the First Time (**110**/Mark 8:31—9:1; Luke 9:21-27)
21 From then on Jesus began to tell his disciples plainly that he had to go to Jerusalem, **16:21** John 2:19 1 Cor 15:3-4
and he told them what would happen to him there. He would suffer at the hands of the
leaders and the leading priests and the teachers of religious law. He would be killed, and
he would be raised on the third day.
22 But Peter took him aside and corrected him. "Heaven forbid, Lord," he said. "This
will never happen to you!" **16:23** Matt 4:10
23 Jesus turned to Peter and said, "Get away from me, Satan! You are a dangerous trap **16:24** Matt 10:38 Luke 14:27
to me. You are seeing things merely from a human point of view, and not from God's."
24 Then Jesus said to the disciples, "If any of you wants to be my follower, you must **16:25** Matt 10:39 Luke 17:33 John 12:25
put aside your selfish ambition, shoulder your cross, and follow me.
25 If you try to keep
your life for yourself, you will lose it. But if you give up your life for me, you will find
true life.
26 And how do you benefit if you gain the whole world but lose your own soul* **16:26** Ps 49:7-9 Matt 4:8-9
in the process? Is anything worth more than your soul?
27 For I, the Son of Man, will
come in the glory of my Father with his angels and will judge all people according to **16:27** Prov 24:12 Matt 25:31 Rev 22:12
their deeds.
28 And I assure you that some of you standing here right now will not die
before you see me, the Son of Man, coming in my Kingdom."

Jesus Is Transfigured on the Mountain (**111**/Mark 9:2-13; Luke 9:28-36)

17 Six days later Jesus took Peter and the two brothers, James and John, and led them
up a high mountain.
2 As the men watched, Jesus' appearance changed so that his **17:2** 2 Pet 1:16-18
face shone like the sun, and his clothing became dazzling white.
3 Suddenly, Moses and
Elijah appeared and began talking with Jesus.
4 Peter blurted out, "Lord, this is wonder-
ful! If you want me to, I'll make three shrines,* one for you, one for Moses, and one for
Elijah."

16:26 Or *your life.* **17:4** Or *shelters;* Greek reads *tabernacles.*

16:21 The phrase "From then on" marks a turning point. In 4:17 it signaled Jesus' announcement of the Kingdom of Heaven. Here it points to his new emphasis on his death and resurrection. The disciples still didn't grasp Jesus' true purpose because of their preconceived notions about what the Messiah should be. This is the first of three times that Jesus predicted his death (see 17:22, 23; 20:18 for others).

16:21-28 This passage corresponds to Daniel's prophecies: The Messiah would be cut off (Daniel 9:26); there would be a period of trouble (Daniel 9:27); and the king would come in glory (Daniel 7:13, 14). The disciples would endure the same suffering as their King and, like him, would be rewarded in the end.

16:22 Peter, Jesus' friend and devoted follower who had just eloquently proclaimed Jesus' true identity, sought to protect him from the suffering he prophesied. But if Jesus hadn't suffered and died, Peter would have died in his sins. Great temptations can come from those who love us and seek to protect us. Be cautious of advice from a friend who says, "Surely God doesn't want you to face this." Often our most difficult temptations come from those who are only trying to protect us from discomfort.

16:23 In his wilderness temptations, Jesus heard the message that he could achieve greatness without dying (4:9). Here he heard the same message from Peter. Peter had just recognized Jesus as Messiah; here, however, he forsook God's perspective and evaluated the situation from a human one. Satan is always trying to get us to leave God out of the picture. Jesus rebuked Peter for this attitude.

16:24 When Jesus used this picture of his followers shouldering their cross to follow him, the disciples knew what he meant. Crucifixion was a common Roman method of execution, and condemned criminals had to carry their cross through the streets to the execution site. Following Jesus, therefore, meant a true commitment, the risk of death, and no turning back (see 10:39).

16:25 The possibility of losing their lives was very real for the disciples as well as for Jesus. Real discipleship implies real commitment—pledging our whole existence to his service. If we try to save our physical life from death, pain, or discomfort, we may risk losing eternal life. If we protect ourselves from the pain God calls us to suffer, we begin to die spiritually and emotionally. Our lives turn inward, and we lose our intended purpose. When we give our life in service to Christ, however, we discover the real purpose of living.

16:26 When we don't know Christ, we make choices as though there were no afterlife. In reality, this life is just the introduction to eternity. How we live this brief span determines our eternal state. What we accumulate on earth has no value in gaining eternal life. Even the highest social or civic honors cannot earn us entrance into heaven. Evaluate your life-style from an eternal perspective, and you will find your values and decisions changing.

16:27 Jesus Christ has been given the authority to judge all the earth (Romans 14:9-11; Philippians 2:9-11). Although his judgment is already working in our lives, there is a future, final judgment when Christ returns (25:31-46) and everyone's life will be reviewed and evaluated. This will not be confined to unbelievers; Christians, too, will face a judgment. Their eternal destiny is secure, but Jesus will look at how they handled gifts, opportunities, and responsibilities in order to determine their heavenly rewards. At the time of judgment, God will deliver the righteous and condemn the wicked. We should not judge others' salvation; that is God's work.

16:28 Because all the disciples died *before* Christ's return, many believe that Jesus' words were fulfilled at the Transfiguration when Peter, James, and John saw his glory (17:1-3). Others say this statement refers to Pentecost (Acts 2) and the beginning of Christ's church. In either case, certain disciples were eyewitnesses to the power and glory of Christ's Kingdom.

17:1ff The Transfiguration was a vision, a brief glimpse of the true glory of the King (16:27, 28). This was a special revelation of Jesus' divinity to three of the disciples, and it was God's divine affirmation of everything Jesus had done and was about to do.

17:3-5 Moses and Elijah were the two greatest prophets in the Old Testament. Moses represents the law, or the old covenant. He wrote the Pentateuch, and he predicted the coming of a great

17:5
Ps 2:7
Matt 3:17; 12:18
Mark 1:11
Luke 3:22
2 Pet 1:17

5 But even as he said it, a bright cloud came over them, and a voice from the cloud said, "This is my beloved Son, and I am fully pleased with him. Listen to him." 6 The disciples were terrified and fell face down on the ground.

7 Jesus came over and touched them. "Get up," he said, "don't be afraid." 8 And when they looked, they saw only Jesus with them. 9 As they descended the mountain, Jesus commanded them, "Don't tell anyone what you have seen until I, the Son of Man, have been raised from the dead."

17:10-11
Mal 4:5-6
Luke 1:16-17

17:12
Matt 11:14

10 His disciples asked, "Why do the teachers of religious law insist that Elijah must return before the Messiah comes*?"

11 Jesus replied, "Elijah is indeed coming first to set everything in order. 12 But I tell you, he has already come, but he wasn't recognized, and he was badly mistreated. And soon the Son of Man will also suffer at their hands." 13 Then the disciples realized he had been speaking of John the Baptist.

Jesus Heals a Demon-Possessed Boy (**112**/Mark 9:14-29; Luke 9:37-43)

14 When they arrived at the foot of the mountain, a huge crowd was waiting for them. A man came and knelt before Jesus and said, 15 "Lord, have mercy on my son, because he has seizures and suffers terribly. He often falls into the fire or into the water. 16 So I brought him to your disciples, but they couldn't heal him."

17:17
Deut 32:5, 20

17:18
Matt 8:13; 9:22; 15:28

17 Jesus replied, "You stubborn, faithless people! How long must I be with you until you believe? How long must I put up with you? Bring the boy to me." 18 Then Jesus rebuked the demon in the boy, and it left him. From that moment the boy was well.

19 Afterward the disciples asked Jesus privately, "Why couldn't we cast out that demon?"

17:20
Matt 21:21
Mark 11:23
Luke 17:6
1 Cor 13:2

20 "You didn't have enough faith," Jesus told them. "I assure you, even if you had faith as small as a mustard seed you could say to this mountain, 'Move from here to there,' and it would move. Nothing would be impossible."*

17:10 Greek *that Elijah must come first.* **17:20** Some manuscripts add verse 21, *But this kind of demon won't leave unless you have prayed and fasted.*

---

prophet (Deuteronomy 18:15-19). Elijah represents the prophets who foretold the coming of the Messiah (Malachi 4:5, 6). Moses' and Elijah's presence with Jesus confirmed Jesus' messianic mission: to fulfill God's law and the words of God's prophets. Just as God's voice in the cloud over Mount Sinai gave authority to his law (Exodus 19:9), God's voice at the Transfiguration gave authority to Jesus' words.

17:4 Peter wanted to build three shrines for these three great men to show how the Festival of Shelters was fulfilled in the coming of God's Kingdom. Peter had the right idea about Christ, but his timing was wrong. Peter wanted to act, but this was a time for worship and adoration. He wanted to memorialize the moment, but he was supposed to learn and move on.

17:5 Jesus is more than just a great leader, a good example, a good influence, or a great prophet. He is the Son of God. When you understand this profound truth, the only adequate response is worship. When you have a correct understanding of Christ, you will obey him.

17:9 Jesus told Peter, James, and John not to tell anyone what they had seen until after his resurrection because Jesus knew that they didn't fully understand it and could not explain what they didn't understand. Their question (17:10ff) revealed their misunderstandings. They knew that Jesus was the Messiah, but they had much more to learn about the significance of his death and resurrection.

17:10-12 Based on Malachi 4:5, 6, the teachers of the Old Testament law believed that Elijah must appear before the Messiah would appear. Jesus referred to John the Baptist, not to the Old Testament prophet Elijah. John the Baptist took on Elijah's prophetic role, boldly confronting sin and pointing people to God. Malachi had prophesied that a prophet like Elijah would come (Malachi 4:5).

17:17 The disciples had been given the authority to do the healing, but they had not yet learned how to appropriate the power of God. Jesus' frustration is with the unbelieving and unresponsive generation. His disciples were merely a reflection of that attitude in this instance. Jesus' purpose was not to criticize the disciples but to encourage them to greater faith.

17:17-20 The disciples were unable to cast out this demon, and they asked Jesus why. He said their faith was too small. It is the power of God, plus our faith, that moves mountains. The mustard seed was the smallest particle imaginable. Jesus said that even faith as small or undeveloped as a mustard seed would have been sufficient. Perhaps the disciples had tried to cast out the demon with their own ability rather than God's. There is great power in even a little faith when we trust in God's power to act. If we feel weak or powerless as Christians, we should examine our faith, making sure we are trusting God's power, not our own ability to produce results.

17:20 Jesus wasn't condemning the disciples for substandard faith; he was trying to show how important faith would be in their future ministry. If you are facing a problem that seems as big and immovable as a mountain, turn your eyes from the mountain and look to Christ for more faith. Only then will you be able to overcome the obstacles that may stand in your way.

Jesus Predicts His Death the Second Time (**113**/Mark 9:30-32; Luke 9:44-45)
22 One day after they had returned to Galilee, Jesus told them, "The Son of Man is going
to be betrayed. 23 He will be killed, but three days later he will be raised from the dead."
And the disciples' hearts were filled with grief.

Peter Finds the Coin in the Fish's Mouth (**114**)
24 On their arrival in Capernaum, the tax collectors for the Temple tax came to Peter and
asked him, "Doesn't your teacher pay the Temple tax?"

25 "Of course he does," Peter replied. Then he went into the house to talk to Jesus
about it.

But before he had a chance to speak, Jesus asked him, "What do you think, Peter*?
Do kings tax their own people or the foreigners they have conquered?"

26 "They tax the foreigners," Peter replied.

"Well, then," Jesus said, "the citizens are free! 27 However, we don't want to offend
them, so go down to the lake and throw in a line. Open the mouth of the first fish you
catch, and you will find a coin. Take the coin and pay the tax for both of us."

The Disciples Argue about Who Would Be the Greatest (**115**/Mark 9:33-37; Luke 9:46-48)

18 About that time the disciples came to Jesus and asked, "Which of us is greatest in
the Kingdom of Heaven?"

2 Jesus called a small child over to him and put the child among them. 3 Then he said,
"I assure you, unless you turn from your sins and become as little children, you will
never get into the Kingdom of Heaven. 4 Therefore, anyone who becomes as humble as
this little child is the greatest in the Kingdom of Heaven. 5 And anyone who welcomes a
little child like this on my behalf is welcoming me. 6 But if anyone causes one of these
little ones who trusts in me to lose faith, it would be better for that person to be thrown
into the sea with a large millstone tied around the neck.

17:24 Exod 30:13
17:25 Matt 22:17-22; Rom 13:7
18:3 Matt 19:14; Mark 10:15; Luke 18:17; 1 Pet 2:2
18:4 Matt 20:26-27; Mark 10:43-44; Luke 22:26
18:5 Matt 10:40; Luke 10:16; John 13:20
18:6-9 1 Cor 8:12-13

17:25 Greek *Simon*.

17:22, 23 Once again Jesus predicted his death (see also 16:21); but more important, he told of his resurrection. Unfortunately, the disciples heard only the first part of Jesus' words and became discouraged. They couldn't understand why Jesus wanted to go back to Jerusalem, where he would walk right into trouble.

The disciples didn't fully comprehend the purpose of Jesus' death and resurrection until Pentecost (Acts 2). We shouldn't get upset at ourselves for being unable to understand everything about Jesus. After all, the disciples spent three years with him, saw his miracles, heard his words, and still had difficulty understanding. Despite their questions and doubts, however, they believed. We should do no less.

17:22, 23 The disciples didn't understand why Jesus kept talking about his death because they expected him to set up a political kingdom. The thought of his death dashed their hopes. They didn't know that Jesus' death and resurrection would make his Kingdom possible.

17:24 All Jewish males had to pay a Temple tax to support Temple upkeep (Exodus 30:11-16). Tax collectors set up booths to collect these taxes. Only Matthew records this incident— perhaps because he had been a tax collector himself.

17:24-27 As usual, Peter answered a question without really knowing the answer, putting Jesus and the disciples in an awkward position. Jesus used this situation, however, to emphasize his kingly role. Just as kings pay no taxes and collect none from their family, Jesus, the King, owed no taxes. But Jesus supplied the tax payment for both himself and Peter rather than offend those who didn't understand his kingship. Although Jesus supplied the tax money, Peter had to go and get it. Ultimately all that we have comes to us from God's supply, but he may want us to be active in the process.

17:24-27 As God's people, we are foreigners on earth because our loyalty is always to our real King—Jesus. Still we have to cooperate with the authorities and be responsible citizens. An ambassador to another country keeps the local laws in order to represent well the one who sent him. We are Christ's ambassadors (2 Corinthians 5:20). Are you being a good foreign ambassador for him to this world?

18:1 From Mark's Gospel we learn that Jesus precipitated this conversation by asking the disciples what they had been discussing among themselves earlier (Mark 9:33, 34).

18:1-4 Jesus used a child to help his self-centered disciples get the point. We are not to be *childish* (like the disciples, arguing over petty issues) but *childlike,* with humble and sincere hearts. Are you being childlike or childish?

18:3, 4 The disciples had become so preoccupied with the organization of Jesus' earthly kingdom that they had lost sight of its divine purpose. Instead of seeking a place of service, they sought positions of advantage. It is easy to lose our eternal perspective and compete for promotions or status in the church. It is difficult to identify with "children"—weak and dependent people with no status or influence.

18:6 Children are trusting by nature. Because they trust adults, they are easily led to faith in Christ. God holds parents and other adults accountable for how they influence these little ones. Jesus warned that anyone who turns little children away from faith in him will receive severe punishment.

Jesus Warns against Temptation (**117**/Mark 9:42-50)

18:8-9 Matt 5:29-30

7"How terrible it will be for anyone who causes others to sin. Temptation to do wrong
is inevitable, but how terrible it will be for the person who does the tempting. 8So if
your hand or foot causes you to sin, cut it off and throw it away. It is better to enter
heaven* crippled or lame than to be thrown into the unquenchable fire with both of
your hands and feet. 9And if your eye causes you to sin, gouge it out and throw it
away. It is better to enter heaven half blind than to have two eyes and be thrown into
hell.

Jesus Warns against Looking Down on Others (**118**)

18:10 Acts 12:15; Heb 1:14

10"Beware that you don't despise a single one of these little ones. For I tell you that in
heaven their angels are always in the presence of my heavenly Father.*
12"If a shepherd has one hundred sheep, and one wanders away and is lost, what will
he do? Won't he leave the ninety-nine others and go out into the hills to search for the
lost one? 13And if he finds it, he will surely rejoice over it more than over the ninety-nine
that didn't wander away! 14In the same way, it is not my heavenly Father's will that even
one of these little ones should perish.

Jesus Teaches How to Treat a Believer Who Sins (**119**)

18:15 Lev 19:17; Gal 6:1; Jas 5:19-20
18:16 †Deut 19:15; 2 Cor 13:1; 1 Tim 5:19
18:17 1 Cor 6:1-6

15"If another believer sins against you, go privately and point out the fault. If the other
person listens and confesses it, you have won that person back. 16But if you are unsuccessful, take one or two others with you and go back again, so that everything you say may be
confirmed by two or three witnesses. 17If that person still refuses to listen, take your case
to the church. If the church decides you are right, but the other person won't accept it, treat

18:8 Greek *enter life;* also in 18:9. **18:10** Some manuscripts add verse 11, *And I, the Son of Man, have come to save the lost.*

JESUS AND FORGIVENESS

Jesus forgave	*Reference*
the paralyzed man lowered on a mat through the roof.	Matthew 9:2–8
the woman caught in adultery.	John 8:3–11
the woman who anointed his feet with perfume.	Luke 7:47–50
Peter, for denying he knew Jesus.	John 18:15–18, 25–27; 21:15–19
the criminal on the cross.	Luke 23:39–43
the people who crucified him.	Luke 23:34

Jesus not only taught frequently about forgiveness, he also demonstrated his own willingness to forgive. Here are several examples that should be an encouragement to recognize his willingness to forgive us also.

18:7ff Jesus warned the disciples about two ways to cause others to sin: tempting them (18:7-9) and neglecting or demeaning them (18:10-14). As leaders, we are to help young people or new believers avoid anything or anyone that could cause them to stumble in their faith and lead them to sin. We must never take lightly the spiritual education and protection of those young in age or in the faith.

18:8, 9 We must remove stumbling blocks that cause us to sin. This does not mean to cut off a part of the body. For the church it means that any person, program, or teaching that threatens the spiritual growth of the body must be removed. For the individual, any relationship, practice, or activity that leads to sin should be stopped. Jesus says it would be better to go to heaven with one hand than to hell with both. Sin, of course, affects more than our hands; it affects our mind and heart.

18:14 Just as a shepherd is concerned enough about one lost sheep to go search the hills for it, so God is concerned about every human being he has created (he "does not want anyone to perish," 2 Peter 3:9). If you come in contact with children in your neighborhood who need Christ, steer them toward him by your example, your words, and your acts of kindness.

18:15-17 These are Jesus' guidelines for dealing with those who sin against us. They were meant for (1) Christians, not unbelievers, (2) sins committed against *you* and not others, and (3) conflict resolution in the context of the church, not the community at large. Jesus' words are not a license for a frontal attack on every person who hurts or slights us. They are not a license to start a destructive gossip campaign or to call for a church trial. They are designed to reconcile those who disagree so that all Christians can live in harmony.

When someone wrongs us, we often do the opposite of what Jesus recommends. We turn away in hatred or resentment, seek revenge, or engage in gossip. By contrast, we should go to that person *first,* as difficult as that may be. Then we should forgive that person as often as he or she needs it (18:21, 22). This will create a much better chance of restoring the relationship.

that person as a pagan or a corrupt tax collector. [18]I tell you this: Whatever you prohibit on earth is prohibited in heaven, and whatever you allow on earth is allowed in heaven.

[19]"I also tell you this: If two of you agree down here on earth concerning anything you ask, my Father in heaven will do it for you. [20]For where two or three gather together because they are mine,* I am there among them."

Jesus Tells the Parable of the Unforgiving Debtor (**120**)

[21]Then Peter came to him and asked, "Lord, how often should I forgive someone who sins against me? Seven times?"

[22]"No!" Jesus replied, "seventy times seven!*

[23]"For this reason, the Kingdom of Heaven can be compared to a king who decided to bring his accounts up to date with servants who had borrowed money from him. [24]In the process, one of his debtors was brought in who owed him millions of dollars.* [25]He couldn't pay, so the king ordered that he, his wife, his children, and everything he had be sold to pay the debt. [26]But the man fell down before the king and begged him, 'Oh, sir, be patient with me, and I will pay it all.' [27]Then the king was filled with pity for him, and he released him and forgave his debt.

[28]"But when the man left the king, he went to a fellow servant who owed him a few thousand dollars.* He grabbed him by the throat and demanded instant payment. [29]His fellow servant fell down before him and begged for a little more time. 'Be patient and I will pay it,' he pleaded. [30]But his creditor wouldn't wait. He had the man arrested and jailed until the debt could be paid in full.

[31]"When some of the other servants saw this, they were very upset. They went to the king and told him what had happened. [32]Then the king called in the man he had forgiven and said, 'You evil servant! I forgave you that tremendous debt because you pleaded with me. [33]Shouldn't you have mercy on your fellow servant, just as I had mercy on you?' [34]Then the angry king sent the man to prison until he had paid every penny.

[35]"That's what my heavenly Father will do to you if you refuse to forgive your brothers and sisters in your heart."

6. Jesus faces conflict with the religious leaders

Jesus Teaches about Marriage and Divorce (**173**/Mark 10:1-12)

19 After Jesus had finished saying these things, he left Galilee and went southward to the region of Judea and into the area east of the Jordan River. [2]Vast crowds followed him there, and he healed their sick.

18:18 Matt 16:19; John 20:23
18:19 Matt 7:7; 21:22; Mark 11:24; John 15:7; 16:23; 1 Jn 3:22; 5:14-15
18:20 Matt 28:20; John 14:23
18:21-22 Luke 17:3-4
18:23 Matt 25:19
18:25 Exod 21:2; Lev 25:39; 2 Kgs 4:1; Neh 5:5
18:27 Luke 7:42
18:34 Matt 5:25-26; Luke 12:58-59
18:35 Matt 6:15; Mark 11:25; Eph 4:32; Col 3:13
19:1 Matt 7:28
19:2 Matt 4:23

18:20 Greek *gather together in my name.* **18:22** Or *77 times.* **18:24** Greek *10,000 talents.* **18:28** Greek *100 denarii.* A denarius was the equivalent of a full day's wage.

18:18 This *prohibiting* and *allowing* refers to the decisions of the church in conflicts. Among believers, there is no court of appeals beyond the church. Ideally, the church's decisions should be God-guided and based on discernment of his Word. Believers have the responsibility, therefore, to bring their problems to the church, and the church has the responsibility to use God's guidance in seeking to resolve conflicts. Handling problems God's way will have an impact now and for eternity.

18:19, 20 Jesus looked ahead to a new day when he would be present with his followers not in body, but through his Holy Spirit. In the body of believers (the church), the sincere agreement of two people in prayer is more powerful than the superficial agreement of thousands, because Christ's Holy Spirit is with them. Two or more believers, *filled with the Holy Spirit,* will pray according to God's will, not their own; thus, their requests will be granted.

18:22 The rabbis taught that people should forgive those who offend them—but only three times. Peter, trying to be especially generous, asked Jesus if seven (the "perfect" number) was enough times to forgive someone. But Jesus answered, "Seventy times seven," meaning that we shouldn't even keep track of how many times we forgive someone. We should always forgive those who are truly repentant, no matter how many times they ask.

18:30 In Bible times, serious consequences awaited those who could not pay their debts. A person lending money could seize the borrower who couldn't pay and force him or his family to work until the debt was paid. The debtor could also be thrown into prison, or his family could be sold into slavery to help pay off the debt. It was hoped that the debtor, while in prison, would sell off his landholdings or that relatives would pay the debt. If not, the debtor could remain in prison for life.

18:35 Because God has forgiven all our sins, we should not withhold forgiveness from others. As we realize how completely Christ has forgiven us, it should produce an attitude of forgiveness toward others. When we don't forgive others, we are setting ourselves above Christ's law of love.

19:3 Matt 5:31 — 3 Some Pharisees came and tried to trap him with this question: "Should a man be
allowed to divorce his wife for any reason?"
19:4 †Gen 1:27; 5:2 — 4 "Haven't you read the Scriptures?" Jesus replied. "They record that from the
beginning 'God made them male and female.'* 5 And he said, 'This explains why a man
19:5 †Gen 2:24; 1 Cor 6:16; Eph 5:31 — leaves his father and mother and is joined to his wife, and the two are united into one.'*
6 Since they are no longer two but one, let no one separate them, for God has joined them
together."
19:7 †Deut 24:1; Matt 5:31 — 7 "Then why did Moses say a man could merely write an official letter of divorce and
send her away?"* they asked.
8 Jesus replied, "Moses permitted divorce as a concession to your hard-hearted
19:9 Matt 5:32; Luke 16:18; 1 Cor 7:10-11 — wickedness, but it was not what God had originally intended. 9 And I tell you this, a man
who divorces his wife and marries another commits adultery—unless his wife has been
unfaithful.*"
10 Jesus' disciples then said to him, "Then it is better not to marry!"
19:11 1 Cor 7:7-9, 17 — 11 "Not everyone can accept this statement," Jesus said. "Only those whom God helps.
19:12 1 Cor 7:32, 34 — 12 Some are born as eunuchs, some have been made that way by others, and some choose
not to marry for the sake of the Kingdom of Heaven. Let anyone who can, accept this
statement."

Jesus Blesses the Children (**174**/Mark 10:13-16; Luke 18:15-17)

13 Some children were brought to Jesus so he could lay his hands on them and pray for
19:14 Matt 18:2-3 — them. The disciples told them not to bother him. 14 But Jesus said, "Let the children come
to me. Don't stop them! For the Kingdom of Heaven belongs to such as these." 15 And
he put his hands on their heads and blessed them before he left.

19:4 Gen 1:27; 5:2. **19:5** Gen 2:24. **19:7** Deut 24:1. **19:9** Some manuscripts add *And the man who marries a divorced woman commits adultery.*

19:3-12 John was put in prison and killed, at least in part for his public opinions on marriage and divorce, so the Pharisees hoped to trap Jesus, too. They were trying to trick Jesus by having him choose sides in a theological controversy. Two schools of thought represented two opposing views of divorce. One group supported divorce for almost any reason. The other believed that divorce could be allowed only for marital unfaithfulness. This conflict hinged on how each group interpreted Deuteronomy 24:1-4. In his answer, however, Jesus focused on marriage rather than divorce. He pointed out that God intended marriage to be permanent and gave four reasons for the importance of marriage (19:4-6).

19:7, 8 This law is found in Deuteronomy 24:1-4. In Moses' day, as well as in Jesus' day, the practice of marriage fell far short of God's intention. The same is true today. Jesus said that Moses gave this law only because of the people's hard hearts—permanent marriage was God's intention. But because sinful human nature made divorce inevitable, Moses instituted some laws to help its victims. These were civil laws designed especially to protect the women who, in that culture, were quite vulnerable when living alone. Because of Moses' law, a man could no longer just throw his wife out—he had to write a formal letter of dismissal. This was a radical step toward civil rights, for it made men think twice about divorce. God designed marriage to be indissoluble. Instead of looking for reasons to leave each other, husbands and wives should concentrate on how to stay together (19:3-9).

19:10-12 Although divorce was relatively easy in Old Testament times (19:7), it is not what God originally intended. Couples should decide against divorce from the start and build their marriage on mutual commitment. There are also many good reasons for not marrying, one being to have more time to work for God's Kingdom. Don't assume that God wants everyone to marry. For many it may be better if they don't. Be sure that you prayerfully seek God's will before you plunge into the lifelong commitment of marriage.

19:12 A "eunuch" is an emasculated male—a man with no testicles.

19:12 Some have physical limitations that prevent their marrying, while others choose not to marry because, in their particular situation, they can serve God better as single people. Jesus was not teaching us to avoid marriage because it is inconvenient or takes away our freedom. That would be selfishness. A good reason to remain single is to use the time and freedom to serve God. Paul elaborates on this in 1 Corinthians 7.

19:13-15 The disciples must have forgotten what Jesus had said about children (18:4-6). Jesus wanted little children to come to him because he loves them and because they have a guileless trust in God. He didn't mean that heaven is only for children but that all people need childlike faith in God. The receptiveness of little children was a great contrast to the stubbornness of the religious leaders, who let their education and sophistication stand in the way of the simple faith needed to believe in Jesus.

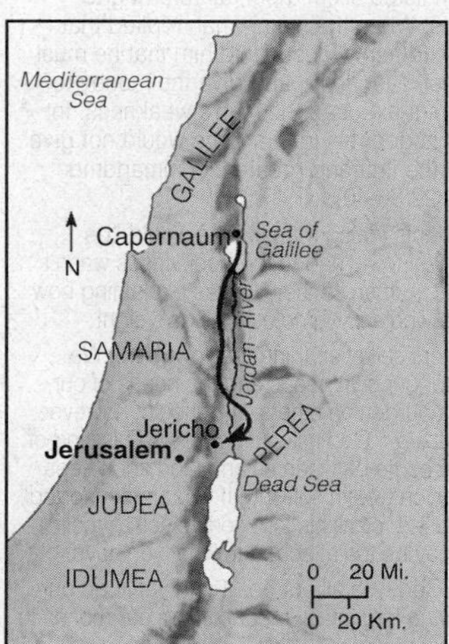

JESUS TRAVELS TOWARD JERUSALEM
Jesus left Galilee for the last time—heading toward Jerusalem and death. He again crossed the Jordan, spending some time in Perea before going on to Jericho.

Jesus Speaks to the Rich Young Man (**175**/Mark 10:17-31; Luke 18:18-30)

16 Someone came to Jesus with this question: "Teacher,* what good things must I do to
have eternal life?"
17 "Why ask me about what is good?" Jesus replied. "Only God is good. But to answer
your question, you can receive eternal life if you keep the commandments."
18 "Which ones?" the man asked.
And Jesus replied: "'Do not murder. Do not commit adultery. Do not steal. Do not
testify falsely. 19 Honor your father and mother. Love your neighbor as yourself.'*"
20 "I've obeyed all these commandments," the young man replied. "What else must I do?"
21 Jesus told him, "If you want to be perfect, go and sell all you have and give the
money to the poor, and you will have treasure in heaven. Then come, follow me." 22 But
when the young man heard this, he went sadly away because he had many possessions.
23 Then Jesus said to his disciples, "I tell you the truth, it is very hard for a rich person
to get into the Kingdom of Heaven. 24 I say it again—it is easier for a camel to go through
the eye of a needle than for a rich person to enter the Kingdom of God!"
25 The disciples were astounded. "Then who in the world can be saved?" they asked.
26 Jesus looked at them intently and said, "Humanly speaking, it is impossible. But
with God everything is possible."
27 Then Peter said to him, "We've given up everything to follow you. What will we
get out of it?"
28 And Jesus replied, "I assure you that when I, the Son of Man, sit upon my glorious
throne in the Kingdom,* you who have been my followers will also sit on twelve thrones,
judging the twelve tribes of Israel. 29 And everyone who has given up houses or brothers
or sisters or father or mother or children or property, for my sake, will receive a hundred
times as much in return and will have eternal life. 30 But many who seem to be important
now will be the least important then, and those who are considered least here will be the
greatest then.*

19:16 Matt 19:29; Luke 10:25
19:17 Lev 18:5; Luke 10:28
19:18 †Exod 20:12-16; †Deut 5:16-21
19:19 †Lev 19:18; Matt 5:43; 22:39; Luke 10:27; Rom 13:9
19:21 Acts 2:45; 4:34-37
19:23 Matt 13:22; 1 Tim 6:9-10
19:26 Gen 18:14; Job 42:2; Jer 32:17; Zech 8:6
19:27 Matt 4:19
19:28 Luke 22:28-30; Rev 3:21
19:30 Matt 20:16; Mark 10:31; Luke 13:30

19:16 Some manuscripts read *Good Teacher.* **19:18-19** Exod 20:12-16; Lev 19:18; Deut 5:16-20. **19:28** Greek *in the regeneration.* **19:30** Greek *But many who are first will be last; and the last, first.*

19:16 To this man seeking assurance of eternal life, Jesus pointed out that salvation does not come from good deeds unaccompanied by love for God. The man needed a whole new starting point. Instead of adding another commandment to keep or good deed to perform, the young man needed to submit humbly to the lordship of Christ.

19:17ff In response to the young man's question about how to have eternal life, Jesus told him to keep God's Ten Commandments. Jesus then listed six of them, all referring to relationships with others. When the young man replied that he had kept the commandments, Jesus told him that he must do something more—sell everything and give the money to the poor. Jesus' statement exposed the man's weakness. In reality, his wealth was his god, his idol, and he would not give it up. Thus, he violated the first and greatest commandment (Exodus 20:3; Matthew 22:36-40).

19:21 When Jesus told this young man that he would "be perfect" if he gave everything he had to the poor, Jesus wasn't speaking in the temporal, human sense. He was explaining how to be justified and made whole or complete in God's sight.

19:21 Should all believers sell everything they own? No. We are responsible to care for our own needs and the needs of our families so as not to be a burden on others. We should, however, be willing to give up anything if God asks us to do so. This kind of attitude allows nothing to come between us and God and keeps us from using our God-given wealth selfishly. If you are comforted by the fact that Christ did not tell all his followers to sell all their possessions, then you may be too attached to what you have.

19:22 We cannot love God with all our heart and yet keep our money to ourselves. Loving him totally means using our money in ways that please him.

19:24 Because it is impossible for a camel to go through the eye of a needle, it appears impossible for a rich person to get into the Kingdom of Heaven. Jesus explained, however, that "with God everything is possible" (19:26). Even rich people can enter the Kingdom if God brings them in. Faith in Christ, not in self or riches, is what counts. On what are you counting for salvation?

19:25, 26 The disciples were astounded. They thought that if anyone could be saved, it would be the rich, whom their culture considered especially blessed by God.

19:27 In the Bible, God gives rewards to his people according to his justice. In the Old Testament, obedience often brought reward in this life (Deuteronomy 28), but obedience and immediate reward are not always linked. If they were, good people would always be rich, and suffering would always be a sign of sin. As believers, our reward is God's presence and power through his indwelling Holy Spirit. Later, in eternity, we will be rewarded for our faith and service. If material rewards in this life came to us for every faithful deed, we would be tempted to boast about our achievements and act out of wrong motivations.

19:29 Jesus assured the disciples that anyone who gives up something valuable for his sake will be repaid many times over in this life, although not necessarily in the same form. For example, a person may be rejected by his or her family for accepting Christ, but he or she will gain the larger family of believers.

19:30 Jesus turned the world's values upside down. Consider the most powerful or well-known people in our world—how many got where they are by being humble, self-effacing, and gentle? Not many! But in the life to come, the last will be first. Don't forfeit eternal rewards for temporary benefits. Be willing to make sacrifices now for greater rewards later. Be willing to accept human disapproval, while knowing that you have God's approval.

Jesus Tells the Parable of the Vineyard Workers (**176**)

20:1 Matt 21:28, 33

20 "For the Kingdom of Heaven is like the owner of an estate who went out early
one morning to hire workers for his vineyard. 2He agreed to pay the normal daily
wage* and sent them out to work.
3"At nine o'clock in the morning he was passing through the marketplace and saw
some people standing around doing nothing. 4So he hired them, telling them he would
pay them whatever was right at the end of the day. 5At noon and again around three
o'clock he did the same thing. 6At five o'clock that evening he was in town again and
saw some more people standing around. He asked them, 'Why haven't you been working
today?'
7"They replied, 'Because no one hired us.'
"The owner of the estate told them, 'Then go on out and join the others in my
vineyard.'

20:8 Lev 19:13 Deut 24:15

8"That evening he told the foreman to call the workers in and pay them, beginning
with the last workers first. 9When those hired at five o'clock were paid, each received a
full day's wage. 10When those hired earlier came to get their pay, they assumed they
would receive more. But they, too, were paid a day's wage. 11When they received their
pay, they protested, 12'Those people worked only one hour, and yet you've paid them
just as much as you paid us who worked all day in the scorching heat.'
13"He answered one of them, 'Friend, I haven't been unfair! Didn't you agree to work

20:15 Deut 15:9 Matt 6:23 Mark 7:22

all day for the usual wage? 14Take it and go. I wanted to pay this last worker the same
as you. 15Is it against the law for me to do what I want with my money? Should you be
angry because I am kind?'

20:16 Matt 19:30 Mark 10:31 Luke 13:30

16"And so it is, that many who are first now will be last then; and those who are last
now will be first then."

Jesus Predicts His Death the Third Time (**177**/Mark 10:32-34; Luke 18:31-34)

17As Jesus was on the way to Jerusalem, he took the twelve disciples aside privately and
told them what was going to happen to him. 18"When we get to Jerusalem," he said, "the

20:18-19 Matt 16:21; 17:22-23 Luke 9:22 Acts 2:23

Son of Man will be betrayed to the leading priests and the teachers of religious law. They
will sentence him to die. 19Then they will hand him over to the Romans to be mocked,
whipped, and crucified. But on the third day he will be raised from the dead."

Jesus Teaches about Serving Others (**178**/Mark 10:35-45)

20:21 Matt 19:28

20Then the mother of James and John, the sons of Zebedee, came to Jesus with her sons.
She knelt respectfully to ask a favor. 21"What is your request?" he asked.

20:2 Greek *a denarius,* the payment for a full day's labor; also in 20:9, 10, 13.

20:1ff Jesus further clarified the membership rules of the Kingdom of Heaven: Entrance is by God's grace alone. In this parable, God is the owner of the estate, and believers are the workers. This parable speaks especially to those who feel superior because of heritage or position, to those who feel superior because they have spent so much time with Christ, and to new believers as reassurance of God's grace.

20:15 This parable is not about rewards but about salvation. It is a strong teaching about *grace,* God's generosity. We shouldn't begrudge those who turn to God in the last moments of life, because, in reality, *no one* deserves eternal life.

Many people we don't expect to see in the Kingdom will be there. The criminal who repented as he was dying (Luke 23:40-43) will be there along with people who have believed and served God for many years. Do you resent God's gracious acceptance of the despised, the outcast, and the sinners who have turned to him for forgiveness? Have you ever been jealous of what God has given to another person? Instead, focus on God's gracious benefits to you, and be thankful for what you have.

20:17-19 Jesus predicted his death and resurrection for the third time (see 16:21 and 17:22, 23 for the first two times). But the disciples still didn't understand what he meant. They continued to argue greedily over their positions in Christ's Kingdom (20:20-28).

20:20 The mother of James and John came to Jesus and "knelt respectfully to ask a favor." She gave Jesus worship, but her real motive was to get something from him. Too often this happens in our churches and in our life. We play religious games, expecting God to give us something in return. True worship, however, adores and praises Christ for who he is and for what he has done.

20:20 The mother of James and John asked Jesus to give her sons special positions in his Kingdom. Parents naturally want to see their children promoted and honored, but this desire is dangerous if it causes them to stand in the way of God's specific will for their children. God may have different work in mind for them—perhaps not as glamorous but just as important. Thus, parents' desires for their children's advancement must be held in check as they pray that God's will be done in their children's lives.

20:20 According to 27:56, the mother of James and John was at the cross when Jesus was crucified. Some have suggested that she was the sister of Mary, the mother of Jesus. A close family relationship could have prompted her to make this request for her sons.

She replied, "In your Kingdom, will you let my two sons sit in places of honor next
to you, one at your right and the other at your left?"
22 But Jesus told them, "You don't know what you are asking! Are you able to drink
from the bitter cup of sorrow I am about to drink?"
"Oh yes," they replied, "we are able!"
23 "You will indeed drink from it," he told them. "But I have no right to say who will sit on
the thrones next to mine. My Father has prepared those places for the ones he has chosen."
24 When the ten other disciples heard what James and John had asked, they were
indignant. 25 But Jesus called them together and said, "You know that in this world kings
are tyrants, and officials lord it over the people beneath them. 26 But among you it should
be quite different. Whoever wants to be a leader among you must be your servant, 27 and
whoever wants to be first must become your slave. 28 For even I, the Son of Man, came
here not to be served but to serve others, and to give my life as a ransom for many."

20:22 Matt 26:39, 42 Mark 14:36 Luke 22:42 John 18:11
20:23 Acts 12:2 Rev 1:9
20:26 Matt 23:11 Mark 9:35 Luke 9:48
20:28 Isa 53:10 Phil 2:7 1 Tim 2:6 1 Pet 1:18-19

Jesus Heals Two Blind Beggars (**179**/Mark 10:46-52; Luke 18:35-43)

29 As Jesus and the disciples left the city of Jericho, a huge crowd followed behind. 30 Two
blind men were sitting beside the road. When they heard that Jesus was coming that way,
they began shouting, "Lord, Son of David, have mercy on us!" 31 The crowd told them
to be quiet, but they only shouted louder, "Lord, Son of David, have mercy on us!"
32 Jesus stopped in the road and called, "What do you want me to do for you?"
33 "Lord," they said, "we want to see!" 34 Jesus felt sorry for them and touched their
eyes. Instantly they could see! Then they followed him.

Jesus Rides into Jerusalem on a Donkey
(**183**/Mark 11:1-11; Luke 19:28-44; John 12:12-19)

21 As Jesus and the disciples approached Jerusalem, they came to the town of Bethphage on the Mount of Olives. Jesus sent two of them on ahead. 2 "Go into the village
over there," he said, "and you will see a donkey tied there, with its colt beside it. Untie them

---

20:22 James, John, and their mother failed to grasp Jesus' previous teachings on rewards (19:16-30) and eternal life (20:1-16). They failed to understand the suffering they must face before living in the glory of God's Kingdom. The "cup" was the suffering and crucifixion that Christ faced. Both James and John would also face great suffering. James would be put to death for his faith, and John would be exiled.

20:23 Jesus was showing that he was under the authority of the Father, who alone makes the decisions about leadership in heaven. Such rewards are not granted as favors. They are for those who have maintained their commitment to Jesus in spite of severe trials.

PREPARATION FOR THE TRIUMPHAL ENTRY
On their way from Jericho, Jesus and the disciples neared Bethphage, on the slope of the Mount of Olives, just outside Jerusalem. Two disciples went into the village, as Jesus told them, to bring back a donkey and its colt. Jesus rode into Jerusalem on the colt, an unmistakable sign of his kingship.

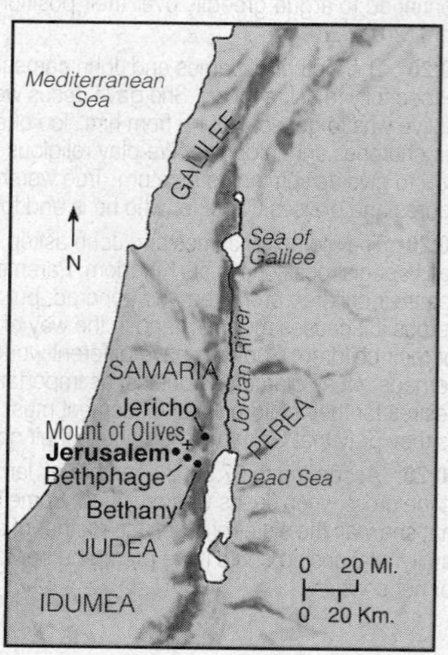

20:24 The other disciples were upset with James and John for trying to grab the top positions. *All* the disciples wanted to be the greatest (18:1), but Jesus taught them that the greatest person in God's Kingdom is the servant of all. Authority is given, not for self-importance, ambition, or respect, but for useful service to God and his creation.

20:27 Jesus described leadership from a new perspective. Instead of using people, we are to serve them. Jesus' mission was to serve others and to give his life away. A real leader has a servant's heart. Servant leaders appreciate others' worth and realize that they're not above any job. If you see something that needs to be done, don't wait to be asked. Take the initiative and do it like a faithful servant.

20:28 A "ransom" was the price paid to release a slave from bondage. Jesus often told his disciples that he must die, but here he told them why—to redeem all people from the bondage of sin and death. The disciples thought that as long as Jesus was alive, he could save them. But Jesus revealed that only his death would save them and the world.

20:29-34 Matthew records that there were two blind men, while Mark and Luke mention only one. This is probably the same event, but Mark and Luke singled out the more vocal of the two men.

20:30 The blind men called Jesus "Son of David" because the Jews knew that the Messiah would be a descendant of David (see Isaiah 9:6, 7; 11:1; Jeremiah 23:5, 6). These blind beggars could *see* that Jesus was the long-awaited Messiah, while the religious leaders who witnessed Jesus' miracles were blind to his identity, refusing to open their eyes to the truth. Seeing with your eyes doesn't guarantee seeing with your heart.

20:32, 33 Although Jesus was concerned about the coming events in Jerusalem, he demonstrated what he had just told the disciples about service (20:28) by stopping to care for the blind men.

21:2-5 Matthew mentions a donkey and a colt, while the other Gospels mention only the colt. This was the same event, but

and bring them here. 3 If anyone asks what you are doing, just say, 'The Lord needs them,'
and he will immediately send them." 4 This was done to fulfill the prophecy,

21:5 †Isa 62:11 †Zech 9:9

5 "Tell the people of Israel,*
'Look, your King is coming to you.
He is humble, riding on a donkey—
even on a donkey's colt.'"*

6 The two disciples did as Jesus said. 7 They brought the animals to him and threw their
garments over the colt, and he sat on it.*

21:9 †Pss 118:25-26; 148:1 Matt 22:39 Luke 13:35

8 Most of the crowd spread their coats on the road ahead of Jesus, and others cut
branches from the trees and spread them on the road. 9 He was in the center of the
procession, and the crowds all around him were shouting,

"Praise God* for the Son of David!
Bless the one who comes in the name of the Lord!
Praise God in highest heaven!"*

21:11 Luke 7:16, 39 John 1:21, 25; 6:14; 7:40; 9:17

10 The entire city of Jerusalem was stirred as he entered. "Who is this?" they asked.
11 And the crowds replied, "It's Jesus, the prophet from Nazareth in Galilee."

Jesus Clears the Temple Again (**184**/Mark 11:12-19; Luke 19:45-48)

21:13 †Isa 56:7 †Jer 7:11

21:14 Isa 35:5-6

21:15 Matt 21:9

21:16 †Ps 8:3

21:17 Mark 11:1 John 11:1, 18; 12:1

12 Jesus entered the Temple and began to drive out the merchants and their customers. He
knocked over the tables of the money changers and the stalls of those selling doves. 13 He
said, "The Scriptures declare, 'My Temple will be called a place of prayer,' but you have
turned it into a den of thieves!"*
14 The blind and the lame came to him, and he healed them there in the Temple. 15 The
leading priests and the teachers of religious law saw these wonderful miracles and heard
even the little children in the Temple shouting, "Praise God for the Son of David." But
they were indignant 16 and asked Jesus, "Do you hear what these children are saying?"
"Yes," Jesus replied. "Haven't you ever read the Scriptures? For they say, 'You have
taught children and infants to give you praise.'*" 17 Then he returned to Bethany, where
he stayed overnight.

Jesus Says the Disciples Can Pray for Anything (**188**/Mark 11:20-26)

18 In the morning, as Jesus was returning to Jerusalem, he was hungry, 19 and he noticed
a fig tree beside the road. He went over to see if there were any figs on it, but there were
only leaves. Then he said to it, "May you never bear fruit again!" And immediately the
fig tree withered up.

21:5a Greek *Tell the daughter of Zion.* Isa 62:11. **21:5b** Zech 9:9. **21:7** Greek *over them, and he sat on them.* **21:9a** Greek *Hosanna,* an exclamation of praise that literally means "save now"; also in 21:9b, 15. **21:9b** Pss 118:25-26; 148:1. **21:13** Isa 56:7; Jer 7:11. **21:16** Ps 8:2.

Matthew focuses on the prophecy in Zechariah 9:9, where a donkey and a colt are mentioned. He shows how Jesus' actions fulfilled the prophet's words, thus giving another indication that Jesus was indeed the Messiah. When Jesus entered Jerusalem on a donkey's colt, he affirmed his messianic royalty as well as his humility.

21:8 This verse is one of the few places where the Gospels record that Jesus' glory is recognized on earth. Jesus boldly declared himself King, and the crowd gladly joined him. But these same people would bow to political pressure and desert him in just a few days. Today we celebrate this event on Palm Sunday. That day should remind us to guard against superficial acclaim for Christ.

21:12 This is the second time Jesus cleared the Temple (see John 2:13-17). Merchants and money changers set up their booths in the Court of the Gentiles in the Temple, crowding out the Gentiles who had come from all over the civilized world to worship God. The merchants sold sacrificial animals at high prices, taking advantage of those who had come long distances. The money changers exchanged all international currency for the special Temple coins—the only money the merchants would accept. They often deceived foreigners who didn't know the exchange rates. Their commercialism in God's house frustrated people's attempts at worship. This, of course, greatly angered Jesus. Any practice that interferes with worshiping God should be stopped.

21:19 Why did Jesus curse the fig tree? This was not a thoughtless, angry act but an acted-out parable. Jesus was showing his anger at religion without substance. Just as the fig tree looked good from a distance but was fruitless on close examination, so the Temple looked impressive at first glance, but its sacrifices and other activities were hollow because they were not done to worship God sincerely (see 21:43). If you only appear to have faith without putting it to work in your life, you are like the fig tree that withered and died because it bore no fruit. Genuine faith means bearing fruit for God's Kingdom. For more information about the fig tree, see the note on Mark 11:13-26.

20 The disciples were amazed when they saw this and asked, “How did the fig tree
wither so quickly?”
21 Then Jesus told them, “I assure you, if you have faith and don’t doubt, you can do
things like this and much more. You can even say to this mountain, ‘May God lift you
up and throw you into the sea,’ and it will happen. 22 If you believe, you will receive
whatever you ask for in prayer.”

21:21 Matt 17:20; Luke 17:6; 1 Cor 13:2; Jas 1:6
21:22 Matt 7:7-11; John 14:13-14

Religious Leaders Challenge Jesus’ Authority (**189**/Mark 11:27-33; Luke 20:1-8)

23 When Jesus returned to the Temple and began teaching, the leading priests and other
leaders came up to him. They demanded, “By whose authority did you drive out the
merchants from the Temple?* Who gave you such authority?”
24 “I’ll tell you who gave me the authority to do these things if you answer one
question,” Jesus replied. 25 “Did John’s baptism come from heaven or was it merely
human?”
They talked it over among themselves. “If we say it was from heaven, he will ask why
we didn’t believe him. 26 But if we say it was merely human, we’ll be mobbed, because
the people think he was a prophet.” 27 So they finally replied, “We don’t know.”
And Jesus responded, “Then I won’t answer your question either.

21:23 Acts 4:7
21:26 Matt 11:9

Jesus Tells the Parable of the Two Sons (**190**)

28 “But what do you think about this? A man with two sons told the older boy, ‘Son, go
out and work in the vineyard today.’ 29 The son answered, ‘No, I won’t go,’ but later he
changed his mind and went anyway. 30 Then the father told the other son, ‘You go,’ and
he said, ‘Yes, sir, I will.’ But he didn’t go. 31 Which of the two was obeying his father?”
They replied, “The first, of course.”
Then Jesus explained his meaning: “I assure you, corrupt tax collectors and prostitutes
will get into the Kingdom of God before you do. 32 For John the Baptist came and showed
you the way to life, and you didn’t believe him, while tax collectors and prostitutes did.
And even when you saw this happening, you refused to turn from your sins and believe
him.

21:28 Luke 15:11
21:32 Matt 3:1-12; Luke 3:12-13; 7:29-30

Jesus Tells the Parable of the Evil Farmers (**191**/Mark 12:1-12; Luke 20:9-19)

33 “Now listen to this story. A certain landowner planted a vineyard, built a wall around
it, dug a pit for pressing out the grape juice, and built a lookout tower. Then he leased
the vineyard to tenant farmers and moved to another country. 34 At the time of the grape
harvest he sent his servants to collect his share of the crop. 35 But the farmers grabbed

21:33 Isa 5:1-2
21:35 Matt 23:34, 37

21:23 Or *By whose authority do you do these things?*

21:21 Many have wondered about Jesus’ statement that if we have faith and don’t doubt, we can move mountains. Jesus, of course, was not suggesting that his followers use prayer as “magic” and perform capricious “mountain moving” acts. Instead, he was making a strong point about the disciples’ (and our) lack of faith. What kinds of mountains do you face? Have you talked to God about them? How strong is your faith?

21:22 This verse is not a guarantee that we can get *anything* we want simply by asking Jesus and believing. God does not grant requests that would hurt us or others or that would violate his own nature or will. Jesus’ statement is not a blank check. To be fulfilled, our requests must be in harmony with the principles of God’s Kingdom. The stronger our belief, the more likely our prayers will be in line with God’s will, and then God will be happy to grant them.

21:23-25 In Jesus’ world, as in ours, people looked for the outward sign of authority—education, title, position, connections. But Jesus’ authority came from who he was, not from any outward and superficial trappings. If we are followers of Christ, God has given us authority. We can confidently speak and act on his behalf because he has authorized us. Are you exercising your authority?

21:23-27 The Pharisees demanded to know where Jesus got his authority. If Jesus said his authority came from God, they would accuse him of blasphemy. If he said that he was acting on his own authority, the crowds would be convinced that the Pharisees had the greater authority. But Jesus answered them with a seemingly unrelated question that exposed their real motives. They didn’t really want an answer to their question; they only wanted to trap him. Jesus showed that the Pharisees wanted the truth only if it supported their own views and causes.

21:25 For more information on John the Baptist, see Matthew 3 and his Profile in John 1.

21:30 The son who said he would obey and then didn’t represented the people of Israel in Jesus’ day. They said they wanted to do God’s will, but they constantly disobeyed. They were phony, just going through the motions. It is dangerous to pretend to obey God when our heart is far from him because God knows our true intentions. Our actions must match our words.

21:33ff The main elements in this parable are (1) the landowner—God, (2) the vineyard—Israel, (3) the tenant farmers—the Jewish religious leaders, (4) the landowner’s servants—the prophets and priests who remained faithful to God and preached to Israel, (5) the son—Jesus (21:38), and (6) the other tenants—the Gentiles. Jesus was exposing the religious leaders’ murderous plot (21:45).

his servants, beat one, killed one, and stoned another. 36 So the landowner sent a larger
group of his servants to collect for him, but the results were the same.
37 "Finally, the owner sent his son, thinking, 'Surely they will respect my son.'
38 "But when the farmers saw his son coming, they said to one another, 'Here comes
the heir to this estate. Come on, let's kill him and get the estate for ourselves!' 39 So they
grabbed him, took him out of the vineyard, and murdered him.
40 "When the owner of the vineyard returns," Jesus asked, "what do you think he will
do to those farmers?"

21:41 Matt 8:11-12; Luke 21:24; Acts 13:46

41 The religious leaders replied, "He will put the wicked men to a horrible death and
lease the vineyard to others who will give him his share of the crop after each harvest."

21:42 †Ps 118:22-23; Isa 28:16; Acts 4:11; Eph 2:20; 1 Pet 2:6-7

42 Then Jesus asked them, "Didn't you ever read this in the Scriptures?

'The stone rejected by the builders
  has now become the cornerstone.
This is the Lord's doing,
  and it is marvelous to see.'*

21:44 Isa 8:14-15; Dan 2:34-35, 44-45

43 What I mean is that the Kingdom of God will be taken away from you and given to
a nation that will produce the proper fruit. 44 Anyone who stumbles over that stone will
be broken to pieces, and it will crush anyone on whom it falls.*"

21:46 Matt 21:26

45 When the leading priests and Pharisees heard Jesus, they realized he was pointing
at them—that they were the farmers in his story. 46 They wanted to arrest him, but they
were afraid to try because the crowds considered Jesus to be a prophet.

Jesus Tells the Parable of the Wedding Dinner (192)

22 Jesus told them several other stories to illustrate the Kingdom. He said, 2 "The
Kingdom of Heaven can be illustrated by the story of a king who prepared a great

22:3 Matt 21:34

wedding feast for his son. 3 Many guests were invited, and when the banquet was ready,
he sent his servants to notify everyone that it was time to come. But they all refused! 4 So

22:4 Matt 21:36

he sent other servants to tell them, 'The feast has been prepared, and choice meats have
been cooked. Everything is ready. Hurry!' 5 But the guests he had invited ignored them

22:6 Matt 21:35

and went about their business, one to his farm, another to his store. 6 Others seized his
messengers and treated them shamefully, even killing some of them.

22:7 Luke 19:27

7 "Then the king became furious. He sent out his army to destroy the murderers and
burn their city. 8 And he said to his servants, 'The wedding feast is ready, and the guests

22:8 Acts 13:46

I invited aren't worthy of the honor. 9 Now go out to the street corners and invite everyone
you see.'

22:10 Matt 13:47-48

10 "So the servants brought in everyone they could find, good and bad alike, and the
banquet hall was filled with guests. 11 But when the king came in to meet the guests, he

22:12 Matt 20:13; 26:50

noticed a man who wasn't wearing the proper clothes for a wedding. 12 'Friend,' he asked,

21:42 Ps 118:22-23. **21:44** This verse is omitted in some early manuscripts.

21:37 In trying to reach us with his love, God finally sent his own Son. Jesus' perfect life, his words of truth, and his sacrifice of love are meant to cause us to listen to him and to follow him as Lord. If we ignore God's gracious gift of his Son, we reject God himself.

21:42 Jesus refers to himself as "the stone rejected by the builders." Although Jesus was rejected by many of his people, he will become the cornerstone of his new building, the church (see Acts 4:11; 1 Peter 2:7).

21:44 Jesus used this metaphor to show that one stone can affect people in different ways, depending on how they relate to it (see Isaiah 8:14, 15; 28:16; Daniel 2:34, 44, 45). Ideally they will build on it; many, however, will trip over it. And at the Last Judgment God's enemies will be crushed by it. In the end, Christ, the "building block," will become the "crushing stone." He offers mercy and forgiveness *now* and promises judgment later. We should choose him now!

22:1-14 In this culture, two invitations were expected when banquets were given. The first asked the guests to attend; the second announced that all was ready. In this story the king invited his guests three times, and each time they rejected his invitation. God wants us to join him at his banquet, which will last for eternity. That's why he sends us invitations again and again. Have you accepted his invitation?

22:11, 12 It was customary for wedding guests to be given wedding clothes to wear to the banquet. It was unthinkable to refuse to wear these clothes. That would insult the host, who could only assume that the guest was arrogant and thought he didn't need these clothes, or that he did not want to take part in the wedding celebration. The wedding clothes picture the righteousness needed to enter God's Kingdom—the total acceptance in God's eyes that Christ gives every believer. Christ has provided these clothes of righteousness for everyone, but each person must choose to put them on in order to enter the King's banquet (eternal life). There is an open invitation, but we must be ready. For more on the imagery of clothes of righteousness and salvation, see Psalm 132:16; Isaiah 61:10; Zechariah 3:3-5; Revelation 3:4, 5; 19:7, 8.

'how is it that you are here without wedding clothes?' And the man had no reply. [13]Then **22:13** Matt 8:12; 25:30
the king said to his aides, 'Bind him hand and foot and throw him out into the outer darkness, **22:14** 2 Pet 1:10
where there is weeping and gnashing of teeth.' [14]For many are called, but few are chosen." Rev 17:14

Religious Leaders Question Jesus about Paying Taxes
(**193**/Mark 12:13-17; Luke 20:20-26)

[15]Then the Pharisees met together to think of a way to trap Jesus into saying something
for which they could accuse him. [16]They decided to send some of their disciples, along
with the supporters of Herod, to ask him this question: "Teacher, we know how honest
you are. You teach about the way of God regardless of the consequences. You are
impartial and don't play favorites. [17]Now tell us what you think about this: Is it right to **22:17** Matt 17:25
pay taxes to the Roman government or not?"

[18]But Jesus knew their evil motives. "You hypocrites!" he said. "Whom are you
trying to fool with your trick questions? [19]Here, show me the Roman coin used for
the tax." When they handed him the coin,* [20]he asked, "Whose picture and title are
stamped on it?"

[21]"Caesar's," they replied. **22:21** Rom 13:7

"Well, then," he said, "give to Caesar what belongs to him. But everything that
belongs to God must be given to God." [22]His reply amazed them, and they went away.

Religious Leaders Question Jesus about the Resurrection
(**194**/Mark 12:18-27; Luke 20:27-40)

[23]That same day some Sadducees stepped forward—a group of Jews who say there is **22:23** Acts 23:8
no resurrection after death. They posed this question: [24]"Teacher, Moses said, 'If a man 1 Cor 15:12
dies without children, his brother should marry the widow and have a child who will be **22:24**
the brother's heir.'* [25]Well, there were seven brothers. The oldest married and then died †Deut 25:5-6
without children, so the second brother married the widow. [26]This brother also died
without children, and the wife was married to the next brother, and so on until she had
been the wife of each of them. [27]And then she also died. [28]So tell us, whose wife will she
be in the resurrection? For she was the wife of all seven of them!"

[29]Jesus replied, "Your problem is that you don't know the Scriptures, and you don't **22:29**
know the power of God. [30]For when the dead rise, they won't be married. They will be John 20:9

22:19 Greek *a denarius.* **22:24** Deut 25:5-6.

22:15-17 The Pharisees, a religious group, opposed the Roman occupation of Palestine. The supporters of Herod, a political party, supported Herod Antipas and the policies instituted by Rome. Normally these two groups were bitter enemies, but here they united against Jesus. Thinking they had a foolproof plan to corner him, together their representatives asked Jesus about paying Roman taxes. If Jesus agreed that it was right to pay taxes to Caesar, the Pharisees would say he was opposed to God, the only King they recognized. If Jesus said the taxes should not be paid, the supporters of Herod would hand him over to Herod on the charge of rebellion. In this case the Pharisees were not motivated by love for God's laws, and Herod's supporters were not motivated by love for Roman justice. Jesus' answer exposed their evil motives and embarrassed them both.

22:17 The Jews were required to pay taxes to support the Roman government. They hated this taxation because the money went directly into Caesar's treasury, where some of it went to support the pagan temples and decadent life-style of the Roman aristocracy. Caesar's image on the coins was a constant reminder of Israel's subjection to Rome.

22:19 The coin, a denarius, was the usual day's wage for a laborer.

22:21 Jesus avoided this trap by showing that we have dual citizenship (1 Peter 2:17). Our citizenship in the nation requires that we pay money for the services and benefits we receive. Our citizenship in the Kingdom of Heaven requires that we pledge to God our obedience and commitment.

22:23ff After the Pharisees and supporters of Herod had failed to trap Jesus, the Sadducees smugly stepped in to try. They did not believe in the resurrection because the Pentateuch (Genesis—Deuteronomy) has no direct teaching on it. The Pharisees had never been able to come up with a convincing argument from the Pentateuch for the resurrection, and the Sadducees thought they had trapped Jesus for sure. But Jesus was about to show them otherwise (see 22:31, 32 for Jesus' answer).

22:24 For more information on Moses, see his Profile in Exodus 14.

22:24 The law said that when a woman's husband died without having a son, the man's brother had a responsibility to marry and care for the widow (Deuteronomy 25:5, 6). This law protected women who were left alone, because in that culture they usually had no other means to support themselves.

22:29, 30 The Sadducees asked Jesus what marriage would be like in heaven. Jesus said it was more important to understand God's power than know what heaven will be like. In every generation and culture, ideas of eternal life tend to be based on images and experiences of present life. Jesus answered that these faulty ideas are caused by ignorance of God's Word. We must not make up our own ideas about eternity and heaven by thinking of it and God in human terms. We should concentrate more on our relationship with God than about what heaven will look like. Eventually we will find out, and it will be far beyond our greatest expectations.

22:32 †Exod 3:6, 15-16; Acts 7:32
22:33 Matt 7:28; 13:54; Mark 11:18

like the angels in heaven. [31]But now, as to whether there will be a resurrection of the
dead—haven't you ever read about this in the Scriptures? Long after Abraham, Isaac,
and Jacob had died, God said,* [32]'I am the God of Abraham, the God of Isaac, and the
God of Jacob.'* So he is the God of the living, not the dead."
[33]When the crowds heard him, they were impressed with his teaching.

Religious Leaders Question Jesus about the Greatest Commandment
(**195**/Mark 12:28-34)

22:35 Luke 10:25
22:37 †Deut 6:5
22:39 †Lev 19:18; Matt 5:43; 19:19; Mark 12:31; Luke 10:27; Rom 13:9
22:40 Matt 7:12; Luke 10:25-28; Rom 13:10

[34]But when the Pharisees heard that he had silenced the Sadducees with his reply, they
thought up a fresh question of their own to ask him. [35]One of them, an expert in religious
law, tried to trap him with this question: [36]"Teacher, which is the most important
commandment in the law of Moses?"
[37]Jesus replied, "'You must love the Lord your God with all your heart, all your soul,
and all your mind.'* [38]This is the first and greatest commandment. [39]A second is equally
important: 'Love your neighbor as yourself.'* [40]All the other commandments and all the
demands of the prophets are based on these two commandments."

Religious Leaders Cannot Answer Jesus' Question (**196**/Mark 12:35-37; Luke 20:41-44)

22:43 2 Sam 23:2; Acts 2:30; 2 Pet 1:20-21
22:44 †Ps 110:1; Acts 2:34-35; Heb 1:13
22:46 Mark 12:34; Luke 20:40

[41]Then, surrounded by the Pharisees, Jesus asked them a question: [42]"What do you think
about the Messiah? Whose son is he?"
They replied, "He is the son of David."
[43]Jesus responded, "Then why does David, speaking under the inspiration of the Holy
Spirit, call him Lord? For David said,

[44]'The LORD said to my Lord,
Sit in honor at my right hand
until I humble your enemies beneath your feet.'*

[45]Since David called him Lord, how can he be his son at the same time?"
[46]No one could answer him. And after that, no one dared to ask him any more questions.

Jesus Warns against the Religious Leaders (**197**/Mark 12:38-40; Luke 20:45-47)

23:2 Ezra 7:6, 25; Neh 8:1-4
23:4 Luke 11:46; Acts 15:20; Gal 6:13

23 Then Jesus said to the crowds and to his disciples, [2]"The teachers of religious law
and the Pharisees are the official interpreters of the Scriptures. [3]So practice and
obey whatever they say to you, but don't follow their example. For they don't practice
what they teach. [4]They crush you with impossible religious demands and never lift a
finger to help ease the burden.

22:31 Greek *in the Scriptures? God said.* **22:32** Exod 3:6. **22:37** Deut 6:5. **22:39** Lev 19:18. **22:44** Ps 110:1.

22:31, 32 Because the Sadducees accepted only the Pentateuch as God's divine Word, Jesus answered them from the book of Exodus (3:6). God would not have said, "I am the God of your ancestors—the God of Abraham, the God of Isaac, and the God of Jacob" if God thought of Abraham, Isaac, and Jacob as dead. From God's perspective, they are alive. Jesus' use of the present tense pointed to the resurrection and the eternal life that all believers enjoy in him.

22:34 We might think the Pharisees would have been glad to see the Sadducees silenced. The question that the Sadducees had always used to trap them was finally answered by Jesus. But the Pharisees were too proud to be impressed. Jesus' answer gave them a theological victory over the Sadducees, but they were more interested in defeating Jesus than in learning the truth.

22:35-40 The Pharisees, who had classified over 600 laws, often tried to distinguish the more important from the less important. So one of them, an "expert in religious law," asked Jesus to identify the most important law. Jesus quoted from Deuteronomy 6:5 and Leviticus 19:18. By fulfilling these two commands, a person keeps all the others. They summarize the Ten Commandments and the other Old Testament moral laws.

22:37-40 Jesus said that if we truly love God and our neighbor, we will naturally keep the commandments. This is looking at God's law positively. Rather than worrying about all we should *not* do, we should concentrate on all we *can* do to show our love for God and others.

22:41-45 The Pharisees, Sadducees, and supporters of Herod had asked their questions. Then Jesus turned the tables and asked them a penetrating question—who they thought the Messiah was. The Pharisees knew that the Messiah would be a descendant of David, but they did not understand that he would be God himself. Jesus quoted from Psalm 110:1 to show that the Messiah would be greater than David. (Hebrews 1:13 uses the same text as proof of Christ's deity.) The most important question we will ever answer is what we believe about Christ. Other theological questions are irrelevant until we believe that Jesus is who he said he is.

23:2, 3 The Pharisees' traditions and their interpretations and applications of the laws had become as important to them as God's law itself. Their laws were not all bad—some were beneficial. Problems arose when the religious leaders (1) held that man-made rules were equal to God's laws, (2) told the people to obey these rules but did not do so themselves, or (3) obeyed the rules, not to honor God, but to make themselves look good. Usually Jesus did not condemn what the Pharisees taught but what they *were*—hypocrites.

5“Everything they do is for show. On their arms they wear extra wide prayer boxes
with Scripture verses inside,* and they wear extra long tassels on their robes. 6And how
they love to sit at the head table at banquets and in the most prominent seats in the
synagogue! 7They enjoy the attention they get on the streets, and they enjoy being called
‘Rabbi.’* 8Don’t ever let anyone call you ‘Rabbi,’ for you have only one teacher, and all
of you are on the same level as brothers and sisters. 9And don’t address anyone here on
earth as ‘Father,’ for only God in heaven is your spiritual Father. 10And don’t let anyone
call you ‘Master,’ for there is only one master, the Messiah. 11The greatest among you
must be a servant. 12But those who exalt themselves will be humbled, and those who
humble themselves will be exalted.

Jesus Condemns the Religious Leaders (198)

13“How terrible it will be for you teachers of religious law and you Pharisees. Hypocrites! For you won’t let others enter the Kingdom of Heaven, and you won’t go in
yourselves.* 15Yes, how terrible it will be for you teachers of religious law and you
Pharisees. For you cross land and sea to make one convert, and then you turn him into
twice the son of hell as you yourselves are.

16“Blind guides! How terrible it will be for you! For you say that it means nothing to
swear ‘by God’s Temple’—you can break that oath. But then you say that it is binding
to swear ‘by the gold in the Temple.’ 17Blind fools! Which is greater, the gold, or the
Temple that makes the gold sacred? 18And you say that to take an oath ‘by the altar’ can
be broken, but to swear ‘by the gifts on the altar’ is binding! 19How blind! For which is
greater, the gift on the altar, or the altar that makes the gift sacred? 20When you swear
‘by the altar,’ you are swearing by it and by everything on it. 21And when you swear ‘by
the Temple,’ you are swearing by it and by God, who lives in it. 22And when you swear
‘by heaven,’ you are swearing by the throne of God and by God, who sits on the throne.

23“How terrible it will be for you teachers of religious law and you Pharisees.
Hypocrites! For you are careful to tithe even the tiniest part of your income,* but you
ignore the important things of the law—justice, mercy, and faith. You should tithe, yes,
but you should not leave undone the more important things. 24Blind guides! You strain
your water so you won’t accidentally swallow a gnat; then you swallow a camel!

23:5 Exod 13:9; Num 15:37-40; Deut 6:8
23:11 Matt 20:26-27; Mark 9:35; 10:43-45; Luke 9:48; 22:26
23:12 Job 22:29; Prov 29:23; Ezek 21:26; Luke 14:11; 18:14
23:13 Luke 11:52
23:15 Acts 13:43
23:16 Isa 9:16; Matt 5:33-35; 15:14; Rom 2:19
23:19 Exod 29:37
23:21 1 Kgs 8:13; Ps 26:8
23:22 Ps 11:4; Isa 66:1; Matt 5:34; Acts 7:49
23:23 Lev 27:30; Hos 6:6; Mic 6:8; Zech 7:9; Luke 11:42
23:24 Matt 23:16

23:5 Greek *They enlarge their phylacteries.* **23:7** *Rabbi,* from Aramaic, means “master” or “teacher.” **23:13** Some manuscripts add verse 14, *How terrible it will be for you teachers of religious law and you Pharisees. Hypocrites! You shamelessly cheat widows out of their property, and then, to cover up the kind of people you really are, you make long prayers in public. Because of this, your punishment will be the greater.* **23:23** Greek *to tithe the mint, the dill, and the cumin.*

23:5 These “prayer boxes” were leather boxes containing Scripture verses. Very religious people wore these boxes on their foreheads and arms in order to obey Deuteronomy 6:8 and Exodus 13:9, 16. But the prayer boxes had been made extra wide and had become more important for the status they gave than for the truth they contained.

23:5-7 Jesus again exposed the hypocritical attitudes of the religious leaders. They knew the Scriptures but did not live by them. They didn’t care about *being* holy—just *looking* holy in order to receive people’s admiration and praise. Today, like the Pharisees, many people say they know the Bible but do not let it change their lives. They say they follow Jesus, but they don’t live by his standards of love. We must make sure that our actions match our beliefs.

23:5-7 People desire positions of leadership not only in business but also in the church. It is dangerous when love for position grows stronger than loyalty to God. This is what happened to the Pharisees and teachers of religious law. Jesus is not against all leadership—we need Christian leaders—but against leadership that serves itself rather than others.

23:11, 12 Jesus challenged society’s norms. To him, greatness comes from serving—giving of yourself to help God and others. Service keeps us aware of others’ needs, and it stops us from focusing only on ourselves. Jesus came as a servant. What kind of greatness do you seek?

23:13, 14 Being a religious leader in Jerusalem was very different from being a pastor in a secular society today. Israel’s history, culture, and daily life centered around its relationship with God. The religious leaders were the best known, most powerful, and most respected of all leaders. Jesus made these stinging accusations because the leaders’ hunger for more power, money, and status had made them lose sight of God, and their blindness was spreading to the whole nation.

23:15 The Pharisees’ converts were attracted to Pharisaism, not to God. By getting caught up in the details of their additional laws and regulations, they completely missed God, to whom the laws pointed. A religion of deeds puts pressure on people to surpass others in what they know and do. Thus, a hypocritical teacher was likely to have students who were even more hypocritical. We must make sure we are not creating Pharisees by emphasizing outward obedience at the expense of inner renewal.

23:23, 24 It’s possible to obey the details of the laws but still be disobedient in our general behavior. For example, we could be very precise and faithful about giving 10 percent of our money to God but refuse to give one minute of our time in helping others. Tithing is important, but giving a tithe does not exempt us from fulfilling God’s other directives.

23:24 The Pharisees strained their water so they wouldn’t accidentally swallow a gnat—an unclean insect according to the law. Meticulous about the details of ceremonial cleanliness, they nevertheless had lost their perspective on inner purity. They were ceremonially clean on the outside but had corrupt hearts.

23:25 Mark 7:4

25“How terrible it will be for you teachers of religious law and you Pharisees.
Hypocrites! You are so careful to clean the outside of the cup and the dish, but inside you
are filthy—full of greed and self-indulgence! 26Blind Pharisees! First wash the inside of
the cup, and then the outside will become clean, too.

23:27 Luke 11:44; Acts 23:3

23:28 Luke 16:15

27“How terrible it will be for you teachers of religious law and you Pharisees.
Hypocrites! You are like whitewashed tombs—beautiful on the outside but filled on the
inside with dead people’s bones and all sorts of impurity. 28You try to look like upright
people outwardly, but inside your hearts are filled with hypocrisy and lawlessness.

23:31 Acts 7:52

23:32 1 Thes 2:16

29“How terrible it will be for you teachers of religious law and you Pharisees.
Hypocrites! For you build tombs for the prophets your ancestors killed and decorate the
graves of the godly people your ancestors destroyed. 30Then you say, ‘We never would
have joined them in killing the prophets.’

23:33 Matt 3:7; 12:34; Luke 3:7

23:34 Matt 10:23; Acts 7:52; 22:19; 2 Cor 11:23-25; 1 Thes 2:15

23:35 Gen 4:8; 2 Chr 24:20-21; Zech 1:1; Heb 11:4

31“In saying that, you are accusing yourselves of being the descendants of those who
murdered the prophets. 32Go ahead. Finish what they started. 33Snakes! Sons of vipers!
How will you escape the judgment of hell? 34I will send you prophets and wise men and
teachers of religious law. You will kill some by crucifixion and whip others in your
synagogues, chasing them from city to city. 35As a result, you will become guilty of
murdering all the godly people from righteous Abel to Zechariah son of Barachiah,
whom you murdered in the Temple between the altar and the sanctuary. 36I assure you,
all the accumulated judgment of the centuries will break upon the heads of this very
generation.

Jesus Grieves over Jerusalem Again (**199**)

37“O Jerusalem, Jerusalem, the city that kills the prophets and stones God’s messengers!
How often I have wanted to gather your children together as a hen protects her chicks

THE SEVEN WOES

23:14	Not letting others enter the Kingdom of Heaven and not entering yourselves
23:15	Converting people away from God to be like yourselves
23:16–22	Blindly leading God’s people to follow man-made traditions instead of God’s Word
23:23, 24	Involving yourself in every last detail and ignoring what is really important: justice, mercy, and faith
23:25, 26	Keeping up appearances while your private world is corrupt
23:27, 28	Acting spiritual to cover up sin
23:29–36	Pretending to have learned from past history, but your present behavior shows you have learned nothing

Jesus mentioned seven ways to guarantee God’s anger, often called the “seven woes.” These seven statements about the religious leaders must have been spoken with a mixed tone of judgment and sorrow. They were strong and unforgettable. They are still applicable anytime we become so involved in perfecting the practice of religion that we forget that God is also concerned with mercy, real love, and forgiveness.

23:25-28 Jesus condemned the Pharisees and religious leaders for outwardly appearing upright and holy but inwardly remaining full of corruption and greed. Living our Christianity merely as a show for others is like washing only the outside of a cup. When we are clean on the inside, our cleanliness on the outside won’t be a sham.

23:34-36 These prophets, wise men, and teachers were probably leaders in the early church who were persecuted, scourged, and killed, as Jesus predicted. The people of Jesus’ generation said they would not act as their fathers did in killing the prophets whom God had sent to them (23:30), but they were about to kill the Messiah himself and his faithful followers. Thus, they would become guilty of all the righteous blood shed through the centuries.

23:35 Jesus was giving a brief history of Old Testament martyrdom. Abel was the first martyr (Genesis 4); Zechariah was the last mentioned in the Hebrew Bible, which ended with 2 Chronicles. Zechariah is a classic example of a man of God who was killed by those who claimed to be God’s people (see 2 Chronicles 24:20, 21).

23:37 Jesus wanted to gather his people together as a hen protects her chicks under her wings, but they wouldn’t let him. Jesus also wants to protect us if we will just come to him. Many times we hurt and don’t know where to turn. We reject Christ’s help because we don’t think he can give us what we need. But who knows our needs better than our Creator? Those who turn to Jesus will find that he helps and comforts as no one else can.

23:37 Jerusalem was the capital city of God’s chosen people, the ancestral home of David, Israel’s greatest king, and the location of the Temple, the earthly dwelling place of God. It was intended to be the center of worship of the true God and a symbol of justice to all people. But Jerusalem had become blind to God and insensitive to human need. Here we see the depth of Jesus’ feelings for lost people and for his beloved city, which would soon be destroyed.

beneath her wings, but you wouldn't let me. 38 And now look, your house is left to you,
empty and desolate. 39 For I tell you this, you will never see me again until you say, 'Bless
the one who comes in the name of the Lord!'*"

7. Jesus teaches on the Mount of Olives

Jesus Tells about the Future (**201**/Mark 13:1-23; Luke 21:5-24)

24 As Jesus was leaving the Temple grounds, his disciples pointed out to him the various
Temple buildings. 2 But he told them, "Do you see all these buildings? I assure you,
they will be so completely demolished that not one stone will be left on top of another!"
3 Later, Jesus sat on the slopes of the Mount of Olives. His disciples came to him
privately and asked, "When will all this take place? And will there be any sign ahead of
time to signal your return and the end of the world*?"
4 Jesus told them, "Don't let anyone mislead you. 5 For many will come in my name,
saying, 'I am the Messiah.' They will lead many astray. 6 And wars will break out near
and far, but don't panic. Yes, these things must come, but the end won't follow
immediately. 7 The nations and kingdoms will proclaim war against each other, and there
will be famines and earthquakes in many parts of the world. 8 But all this will be only the
beginning of the horrors to come.
9 "Then you will be arrested, persecuted, and killed. You will be hated all over the
world because of your allegiance to me. 10 And many will turn away from me and betray
and hate each other. 11 And many false prophets will appear and will lead many people
astray. 12 Sin will be rampant everywhere, and the love of many will grow cold. 13 But
those who endure to the end will be saved. 14 And the Good News about the Kingdom
will be preached throughout the whole world, so that all nations will hear it; and then,
finally, the end will come.

23:39 †Ps 118:26; Matt 21:9; Mark 11:10; Luke 19:38
24:2 Luke 19:44
24:3 Matt 13:39; 28:20; Luke 17:30
24:4 Mark 13:5
24:5 Matt 24:11, 23-24; John 5:43; 1 Jn 2:18
24:6 Dan 2:28-29
24:7 Isa 19:2
24:9-14 Matt 10:17-22
24:9 John 16:2
24:11 Matt 24:5, 24
24:14 Matt 28:19; Rev 3:10; 16:14

23:39 Ps 118:26. **24:3** Or *the age.*

24:1, 2 Although no one knows exactly what this Temple looked like, it must have been beautiful. Herod had helped the Jews remodel and beautify it, no doubt to stay on friendly terms with his subjects. Next to the inner Temple, where the sacred objects were kept and the sacrifices offered, there was a large area called the Court of the Gentiles (where the money changers and merchants had their booths). Outside these courts were long porches. Solomon's porch was 1,562 feet long; the royal portico was decorated with 160 columns stretching along its 921-foot length. Gazing at this glorious and massive structure, the disciples found Jesus' words about its destruction difficult to believe. But the Temple was indeed destroyed only 40 years later when the Romans sacked Jerusalem in A.D. 70.

24:3ff Jesus was sitting on the Mount of Olives, the very place where the prophet Zechariah had predicted that the Messiah would stand when he came to establish his Kingdom (Zechariah 14:4). It was a fitting place for the disciples to ask Jesus when he would come in power and what they could expect then. Jesus' reply emphasized the events that would take place before the end of the age. He pointed out that his disciples should be less concerned with knowing the exact date and more concerned with being prepared—living God's way consistently so that no matter when Jesus came, they would be ready.

24:4 The disciples asked Jesus for the sign of his coming and of the end of the age. Jesus' first response was "Don't let anyone mislead you." The fact is that whenever we look for signs, we become very susceptible to being deceived. There are many "false prophets" (24:11, 24) around with counterfeit signs of spiritual power and authority. The only sure way to keep from being deceived is to focus on Christ and his words. Don't look for special signs, and don't spend time looking at other people. Look at Christ.

24:9-13 You may not be facing intense persecution now, but Christians in other parts of the world are. As you hear about Christians suffering for their faith, remember that they are your brothers and sisters in Christ. Pray for them. Ask God what you can do to help them in their troubles. When one part of the body suffers, the *whole* body suffers. But when all the parts join together to ease the suffering, the whole body benefits (1 Corinthians 12:26).

24:11 The Old Testament frequently mentions false prophets (see 2 Kings 3:13; Isaiah 44:25; Jeremiah 23:16; Ezekiel 13:2, 3; Micah 3:5; Zechariah 13:2). False prophets claimed to receive messages from God, but they preached a "health and wealth" message. They said what the people wanted to hear, even when the nation was not following God as it should. There were false prophets in Jesus' day, and we have them today. They are the popular leaders who tell people what they want to hear, such as "God wants you to be rich," "Do whatever your desires tell you," or "There is no such thing as sin or hell." Jesus said false teachers would come, and he warned his disciples, as he warns us, not to listen to their dangerous words.

24:12 With false teaching and loose morals comes a particularly destructive disease—the loss of true love for God and others. Sin cools your love for God and others by turning your focus on yourself. You cannot truly love if you think only of yourself.

24:13 Jesus predicted that his followers would be severely persecuted by those who hated what he stood for. In the midst of terrible persecutions, however, they could have hope, knowing that salvation was theirs. Times of trial serve to sift true Christians from unbelievers or fair-weather Christians. When you are pressured to give up and turn your back on Christ, don't do it. Remember the benefits of standing firm, and continue to live for Christ.

24:14 Jesus said that before he returns, the Good News about the Kingdom (the message of salvation) would be preached throughout the world. This was the disciples' mission—and it is ours today. Jesus talked about the end times and final judgment to show his followers the urgency of spreading the Good News of salvation to everyone.

24:15 Dan 9:27; 11:31; 12:11
24:17 Luke 17:31
24:21 Dan 12:1; Joel 2:2; Rev 3:10; 7:14
24:23-24 Luke 17:21-23; 2 Thes 2:9-10; 1 Jn 4:1-3; Rev 13:13-14
24:26-27 Luke 17:23-24
24:28 Luke 17:37; Rev 19:17
24:29 Isa 13:10; 34:4; Ezek 32:7; Joel 2:10, 31; 3:15; Rev 6:12-13
24:30 †Dan 7:13; Zech 12:10-14; Rev 1:7
24:31 1 Cor 15:52; 1 Thes 4:16; Rev 8:2; 11:15
24:33 Jas 5:9
24:34 Matt 16:28
24:35 Matt 5:18; Luke 16:17

15“The time will come when you will see what Daniel the prophet spoke about: the
sacrilegious object that causes desecration* standing in the holy place”—reader, pay
attention! 16“Then those in Judea must flee to the hills. 17A person outside the house*
must not go inside to pack. 18A person in the field must not return even to get a coat.
19How terrible it will be for pregnant women and for mothers nursing their babies in
those days. 20And pray that your flight will not be in winter or on the Sabbath. 21For that
will be a time of greater horror than anything the world has ever seen or will ever see
again. 22In fact, unless that time of calamity is shortened, the entire human race will be
destroyed. But it will be shortened for the sake of God’s chosen ones.
23“Then if anyone tells you, ‘Look, here is the Messiah,’ or ‘There he is,’ don’t pay
any attention. 24For false messiahs and false prophets will rise up and perform great
miraculous signs and wonders so as to deceive, if possible, even God’s chosen ones.
25See, I have warned you.

Jesus Tells about His Return (**202**/Mark 13:24-31; Luke 21:25-33)

26“So if someone tells you, ‘Look, the Messiah is out in the desert,’ don’t bother to go
and look. Or, ‘Look, he is hiding here,’ don’t believe it! 27For as the lightning lights up
the entire sky, so it will be when the Son of Man comes. 28Just as the gathering of vultures
shows there is a carcass nearby, so these signs indicate that the end is near.*
29“Immediately after those horrible days end,

the sun will be darkened,
the moon will not give light,
the stars will fall from the sky,
and the powers of heaven will be shaken.*

30And then at last, the sign of the coming of the Son of Man will appear in the heavens,
and there will be deep mourning among all the nations of the earth. And they will see
the Son of Man arrive on the clouds of heaven with power and great glory.* 31And he
will send forth his angels with the sound of a mighty trumpet blast, and they will gather
together his chosen ones from the farthest ends of the earth and heaven.
32“Now learn a lesson from the fig tree. When its buds become tender and its leaves
begin to sprout, you know without being told that summer is near. 33Just so, when you
see the events I’ve described beginning to happen, you can know his return is very near,
right at the door. 34I assure you, this generation* will not pass from the scene before all
these things take place. 35Heaven and earth will disappear, but my words will remain
forever.

24:15 Greek *the abomination of desolation.* See Dan 9:27; 11:31; 12:11. **24:17** Greek *on the roof.* **24:28** Greek *Wherever the carcass is, the vultures gather.* **24:29** See Isa 13:10; 34:4; Joel 2:10. **24:30** See Dan 7:13. **24:34** Or *this age,* or *this nation.*

24:15, 16 What was “the sacrilegious object that causes desecration” mentioned by both Daniel and Jesus? Rather than one specific object, event, or person, it could be seen as any deliberate attempt to mock and deny the reality of God’s presence. Daniel’s prediction came true in 168 B.C. when Antiochus Epiphanes sacrificed a pig to Zeus on the sacred Temple altar (Daniel 9:27; 11:30, 31). Jesus’ words were remembered in A.D. 70 when Titus placed an idol on the site of the burned Temple after destroying Jerusalem. In the end times the Antichrist will set up an image of himself and order everyone to worship it (2 Thessalonians 2:4; Revelation 13:14, 15). These are all abominations to God.

24:21, 22 Jesus, talking about the end times, telescoped near future and far future events, as did the Old Testament prophets. Many of these persecutions have already occurred; more are yet to come. But God is in control of even the length of persecutions. He will not forget his people. This is all we need to know about the future to motivate us to live rightly now.

24:23, 24 Jesus’ warnings about false teachers still hold true. Upon close examination it becomes clear that many nice-sounding messages don’t agree with God’s message in the Bible. Only a solid foundation in God’s Word can equip us to perceive the errors and distortions in false teaching.

24:24-28 In times of persecution even strong believers will find it difficult to be loyal. To keep from being deceived by false messiahs, we must understand that Jesus’ return will be unmistakable (Mark 13:26); no one will doubt that it is he. If you have to be told that the Messiah has come, then he hasn’t (24:27). Christ’s coming will be obvious to everyone.

24:30 The nations of the earth will mourn because unbelievers will suddenly realize they have chosen the wrong side. Everything they have scoffed about will be happening, and it will be too late for them.

Jesus Tells about Remaining Watchful (**203**/Mark 13:32-37; Luke 21:34-38)

36“However, no one knows the day or the hour when these things will happen, not even
the angels in heaven or the Son himself.* Only the Father knows.
37“When the Son of Man returns, it will be like it was in Noah’s day. 38In those days
before the Flood, the people were enjoying banquets and parties and weddings right up
to the time Noah entered his boat. 39People didn’t realize what was going to happen until
the Flood came and swept them all away. That is the way it will be when the Son of Man
comes.
40“Two men will be working together in the field; one will be taken, the other left.
41Two women will be grinding flour at the mill; one will be taken, the other left. 42So be
prepared, because you don’t know what day your Lord is coming.
43“Know this: A homeowner who knew exactly when a burglar was coming would
stay alert and not permit the house to be broken into. 44You also must be ready all the
time. For the Son of Man will come when least expected.
45“Who is a faithful, sensible servant, to whom the master can give the responsibility
of managing his household and feeding his family? 46If the master returns and finds that
the servant has done a good job, there will be a reward. 47I assure you, the master will
put that servant in charge of all he owns. 48But if the servant is evil and thinks, ‘My
master won’t be back for a while,’ 49and begins oppressing the other servants, partying,
and getting drunk— 50well, the master will return unannounced and unexpected. 51He
will tear the servant apart and banish him with the hypocrites. In that place there will be
weeping and gnashing of teeth.

Jesus Tells the Parable of the Ten Bridesmaids (**204**)

25 “The Kingdom of Heaven can be illustrated by the story of ten bridesmaids* who
took their lamps and went to meet the bridegroom. 2Five of them were foolish,
and five were wise. 3The five who were foolish took no oil for their lamps, 4but the other
five were wise enough to take along extra oil. 5When the bridegroom was delayed, they
all lay down and slept. 6At midnight they were roused by the shout, ‘Look, the
bridegroom is coming! Come out and welcome him!’
7“All the bridesmaids got up and prepared their lamps. 8Then the five foolish ones
asked the others, ‘Please give us some of your oil because our lamps are going out.’ 9But

24:36 Acts 1:7; 1 Thes 5:1-2
24:37-39 Gen 6:9–7:24
24:40-41 Luke 17:34-35
24:42 Matt 25:13; Luke 12:40; 1 Thes 5:6; Rev 3:3; 16:15
24:51 Matt 8:12; 25:30
25:1 Luke 12:35-38
25:5 1 Thes 5:6
25:8 Luke 12:35-40

24:36 Some manuscripts omit the phrase *or the Son himself.* **25:1** Or *virgins;* also in 25:7, 11.

24:36 It is good that we don’t know exactly when Christ will return. If we knew the precise date, we might be tempted to be lazy in our work for Christ. Worse yet, we might plan to keep sinning and then turn to God right at the end. Heaven is not our only goal; we have work to do here. And we must keep on doing it until death or until we see the unmistakable return of our Savior.

24:40-42 Christ’s second coming will be swift and sudden. There will be no opportunity for last-minute repentance or bargaining. The choice we have already made will determine our eternal destiny.

24:44 Jesus’ purpose in telling about his return is not to stimulate predictions and calculations about the date but to warn us to be prepared. Will you be ready? The only safe choice is to obey him *today* (24:46).

24:45-47 Jesus asks us to spend the time of waiting taking care of his people and doing his work here on earth, both within the church and outside it. This is the best way to prepare for Christ’s return.

24:50 Knowing that Christ’s return will be sudden and unexpected should motivate us to be prepared. We are to live responsibly—not using his tarrying as an excuse to not do God’s work of building his Kingdom or to pursue pleasure, nor developing a false security based on someone’s calculations of events.

24:51 “Weeping and gnashing of teeth” is a phrase used to describe despair. God’s coming judgment is as certain as Jesus’ return to earth.

25:1ff Jesus told the following parables to clarify further what it means to be ready for his return and how to live until he comes. In the story of the 10 bridesmaids (25:1-13), we are taught that every person is responsible for his or her own spiritual condition. The story of the three servants (25:14-30) shows the necessity of using well what God has entrusted to us. The parable of the sheep and goats (25:31-46) stresses the importance of serving others in need. No parable by itself *completely* describes our preparation. Instead, each paints one part of the whole picture.

25:1ff This parable is about a wedding. On the wedding day the bridegroom went to the bride’s house for the ceremony; then the bride and groom, along with a great procession, returned to the groom’s house, where a feast took place, often lasting a full week.

These ten bridesmaids were waiting to join the procession, and they hoped to take part in the marriage feast. But when the groom didn’t come at the expected time, five of them were out of lamp oil. By the time they had purchased extra oil, it was too late to join the feast.

When Jesus returns to take his people to heaven, we must be ready. Spiritual preparation cannot be bought or borrowed at the last minute. Our relationship with God must be our own.

the others replied, ‘We don’t have enough for all of us. Go to a shop and buy some for
yourselves.’

25:10 Luke 13:24-25; Rev 19:9

10“But while they were gone to buy oil, the bridegroom came, and those who were
ready went in with him to the marriage feast, and the door was locked. 11Later, when the
other five bridesmaids returned, they stood outside, calling, ‘Sir, open the door for us!’
12But he called back, ‘I don’t know you!’

25:13 Matt 24:42, 44; Mark 13:35; Luke 12:40

13“So stay awake and be prepared, because you do not know the day or hour of my
return.

Jesus Tells the Parable of the Loaned Money (**205**)

14“Again, the Kingdom of Heaven can be illustrated by the story of a man going on a
trip. He called together his servants and gave them money to invest for him while he was

25:15 Matt 18:24-25; Rom 12:3, 6

gone. 15He gave five bags of gold* to one, two bags of gold to another, and one bag of
gold to the last—dividing it in proportion to their abilities—and then left on his trip.
16The servant who received the five bags of gold began immediately to invest the money
and soon doubled it. 17The servant with two bags of gold also went right to work and
doubled the money. 18But the servant who received the one bag of gold dug a hole in the
ground and hid the master’s money for safekeeping.

25:19 Matt 18:23

19“After a long time their master returned from his trip and called them to give an
account of how they had used his money. 20The servant to whom he had entrusted the
five bags of gold said, ‘Sir, you gave me five bags of gold to invest, and I have doubled

25:21 Matt 24:45-46; Luke 16:10

the amount.’ 21The master was full of praise. ‘Well done, my good and faithful servant.
You have been faithful in handling this small amount, so now I will give you many more
responsibilities. Let’s celebrate together!’
22“Next came the servant who had received the two bags of gold, with the report, ‘Sir,
you gave me two bags of gold to invest, and I have doubled the amount.’ 23The master said,
‘Well done, my good and faithful servant. You have been faithful in handling this small
amount, so now I will give you many more responsibilities. Let’s celebrate together!’
24“Then the servant with the one bag of gold came and said, ‘Sir, I know you are a
hard man, harvesting crops you didn’t plant and gathering crops you didn’t cultivate. 25I
was afraid I would lose your money, so I hid it in the earth and here it is.’
26“But the master replied, ‘You wicked and lazy servant! You think I’m a hard man,
do you, harvesting crops I didn’t plant and gathering crops I didn’t cultivate? 27Well, you
should at least have put my money into the bank so I could have some interest. 28Take
the money from this servant and give it to the one with the ten bags of gold. 29To those

25:29 Matt 13:12; Mark 4:25; Luke 8:18

who use well what they are given, even more will be given, and they will have an
abundance. But from those who are unfaithful,* even what little they have will be taken

25:30 Matt 8:12; Luke 13:28

away. 30Now throw this useless servant into outer darkness, where there will be weeping
and gnashing of teeth.’

25:15 Greek *talents;* also throughout the story. A talent is equal to 75 pounds or 34 kilograms. **25:29** Or *who have nothing.*

25:15 The master divided the money among his servants according to their abilities. No one received more or less than he could handle. If he failed in his assignment, his excuse could not be that he was overwhelmed. Failure would indicate only laziness or hatred toward the master. The bags of gold represent any kind of resource we are given. God gives us time, gifts, and other resources according to our abilities, and he expects us to invest them wisely until he returns. We are responsible to use well what God has given us. The issue is not how much we have but how well we use what we have.

25:21 Jesus is coming back—we know this is true. Does this mean we must quit our jobs in order to serve God? No, it means we are to use our time, talents, and treasures diligently in order to serve God completely in whatever we do. For a few people, this may mean changing professions. For most of us, it means doing our daily work out of love for God.

25:24-30 This last man was thinking only of himself. He hoped to play it safe and protect himself from his hard master, but he was judged for his self-centeredness. We must not make excuses to avoid doing what God calls us to do. If God truly is our Master, we must obey willingly. Our time, abilities, and money aren’t ours in the first place—we are caretakers, not owners. When we ignore, squander, or abuse what we are given, we are rebellious and deserve to be punished.

25:29, 30 This parable describes the consequences of two attitudes toward Christ’s return. The person who diligently prepares for it by investing his or her time and talents to serve God will be rewarded. The person who has no heart for the work of the Kingdom will be punished. God rewards faithfulness. Those who bear no fruit for God’s Kingdom cannot expect to be treated the same as those who are faithful.

Jesus Tells about the Final Judgment (**206**)

31"But when the Son of Man comes in his glory, and all the angels with him, then he will
sit upon his glorious throne. 32All the nations will be gathered in his presence, and he will
separate them as a shepherd separates the sheep from the goats. 33He will place the sheep
at his right hand and the goats at his left. 34Then the King will say to those on the right,
'Come, you who are blessed by my Father, inherit the Kingdom prepared for you from the
foundation of the world. 35For I was hungry, and you fed me. I was thirsty, and you gave
me a drink. I was a stranger, and you invited me into your home. 36I was naked, and you
gave me clothing. I was sick, and you cared for me. I was in prison, and you visited me.'
37"Then these righteous ones will reply, 'Lord, when did we ever see you hungry and
feed you? Or thirsty and give you something to drink? 38Or a stranger and show you
hospitality? Or naked and give you clothing? 39When did we ever see you sick or in
prison, and visit you?' 40And the King will tell them, 'I assure you, when you did it to
one of the least of these my brothers and sisters, you were doing it to me!'
41"Then the King will turn to those on the left and say, 'Away with you, you cursed
ones, into the eternal fire prepared for the Devil and his demons! 42For I was hungry, and
you didn't feed me. I was thirsty, and you didn't give me anything to drink. 43I was a
stranger, and you didn't invite me into your home. I was naked, and you gave me no
clothing. I was sick and in prison, and you didn't visit me.'
44"Then they will reply, 'Lord, when did we ever see you hungry or thirsty or a
stranger or naked or sick or in prison, and not help you?' 45And he will answer, 'I assure
you, when you refused to help the least of these my brothers and sisters, you were
refusing to help me.' 46And they will go away into eternal punishment, but the righteous
will go into eternal life."

25:31 Dan 7:13; Zech 14:5; Rev 20:11
25:32 Ezek 34:17, 20; Rev 20:12
25:33 Luke 12:32
25:34 Luke 22:30; 1 Cor 15:50; Gal 5:21
25:35-36 Isa 58:7; Heb 13:3; Jas 2:15-16
25:40 Prov 19:17; Matt 10:40, 42
25:41 Matt 7:23; Mark 9:48; 2 Pet 2:4; Rev 20:10
25:45 Prov 14:31; 17:5
25:46 Dan 12:2; John 3:15, 36; 5:29; Acts 13:46-48; Rom 2:7-8; Gal 6:8

C. DEATH AND RESURRECTION OF JESUS, THE KING (26:1—28:20)

After facing much opposition for his teaching, Jesus is betrayed by Judas, denied by the disciples, crucified, and he dies. Three days later he rises from the dead and appears to the disciples, confirming that he is indeed King over life and death. The long-awaited King has brought in his Kingdom, but it is different than expected, for he reigns in our heart until the day he comes again to establish a new and perfect world.

Religious Leaders Plot to Kill Jesus (**207**/Mark 14:1-2; Luke 22:1-2)

26 When Jesus had finished saying these things, he said to his disciples, 2"As you
know, the Passover celebration begins in two days, and I, the Son of Man, will be
betrayed and crucified."

26:2 Exod 12:1-27

25:31-46 God will separate his obedient followers from pretenders and unbelievers. The real evidence of our belief is the way we act. To treat all persons we encounter as if they were Jesus is no easy task. What we do for others demonstrates what we really think about Jesus' words to us: Feed the hungry, give the homeless a place to stay, look after the sick. How well do your actions separate you from pretenders and unbelievers?

25:32 Jesus used sheep and goats to picture the division between believers and unbelievers. Sheep and goats often grazed together but were separated when it came time to shear the sheep. Ezekiel 34:17-24 also refers to the separation of sheep and goats.

25:34-40 This parable describes acts of mercy we all can do every day. These acts do not depend on wealth, ability, or intelligence; they are simple acts freely given and freely received. We have no excuse to neglect those who have deep needs, and we cannot hand over this responsibility to the church or government. Jesus demands our personal involvement in caring for others' needs (Isaiah 58:7).

25:40 There has been much discussion about the identity of the "brothers and sisters." Some have said they are the Jews; others say they are all Christians; still others say they are suffering people everywhere. Such a debate is much like the lawyer's earlier question to Jesus, "Who is my neighbor?" (Luke 10:29). The point of this parable is not the *who,* but the *what*—the importance of serving where service is needed. The focus of this parable is that we should love every person and serve anyone we can. Such love for others glorifies God by reflecting our love for him.

25:46 Eternal punishment takes place in hell (the lake of fire, or Gehenna), the place of punishment after death for all those who refuse to repent. In the Hebrew, three words were used in connection with eternal punishment.

(1) *Sheol,* or "the grave," was used in the Hebrew Old Testament to mean the place of the dead, generally thought to be under the earth. (In the Hebrew, this word occurs in Job 24:19; Psalm 16:10; Isaiah 38:10.)

(2) *Hades* is the Greek word for the underworld, the realm of the dead. It is the word used in the New Testament for Sheol. (In the Greek, this word occurs in Matthew 16:18; Revelation 1:18; 20:13, 14.)

(3) *Gehenna,* or hell, was named after the valley of the son of Hinnom near Jerusalem, where children were sacrificed by fire to the pagan gods (see 2 Kings 23:10; 2 Chronicles 28:3). This is the place of eternal fire (Matthew 5:22; 10:28; Mark 9:43; Luke 12:5; James 3:6; Revelation 19:20) prepared for the Devil, his angels, and all those who do not believe in God (25:46; Revelation 20:9, 10). This is the final and eternal state of the wicked after the resurrection and the Last Judgment.

When Jesus warns against unbelief, he is trying to save us from agonizing punishment.

26:3
Ps 2:2
John 11:47-53
Acts 4:6

3 At that same time the leading priests and other leaders were meeting at the residence
of Caiaphas, the high priest, 4 to discuss how to capture Jesus secretly and put him to
death. 5 "But not during the Passover," they agreed, "or there will be a riot."

A Woman Anoints Jesus with Perfume (**182**/Mark 14:3-9; John 12:1-11)

6 Meanwhile, Jesus was in Bethany at the home of Simon, a man who had leprosy.
7 During supper, a woman came in with a beautiful jar* of expensive perfume and
poured it over his head. 8 The disciples were indignant when they saw this. "What a
waste of money," they said. 9 "She could have sold it for a fortune and given the
money to the poor."

26:7 Greek *an alabaster jar.*

MARY
LAZARUS'S SISTER

Hospitality is an art. Making sure a guest is welcomed, warmed, and well fed requires creativity, organization, and teamwork. Their ability to accomplish these goals makes Mary and her sister, Martha, one of the best hospitality teams in the Bible. Their frequent guest was Jesus Christ.

For Mary, hospitality meant giving more attention to the guest himself than to the needs he might have. She would rather talk than cook. She was more interested in her guest's words than in the cleanliness of her home or the timeliness of her meals. She let her older sister, Martha, take care of those details. Mary's approach to events shows her to be mainly a "responder." She did little preparation—her role was participation. Unlike her sister, who had to learn to stop and listen, Mary needed to learn that action is often appropriate and necessary.

We first meet Mary during a visit Jesus paid to her home. She simply sat at his feet and listened. When Martha became irritated at her sister's lack of help, Jesus stated that Mary's choice to enjoy his company was the most appropriate response at the time. Our last glimpse of Mary shows her to have become a woman of thoughtful and worshipful action. Again she was at Jesus' feet, washing them with perfume and wiping them with her hair. She seemed to understand, better even than the disciples, why Jesus was going to die. Jesus said her act of worship would be told everywhere, along with the gospel, as an example of costly service.

What kind of hospitality does Jesus receive from your life? Are you so busy planning and running your life that you neglect precious time with him? Or do you respond to him by listening to his Word, then finding ways to worship him with your life? It is that kind of hospitality he longs for from each of us.

Strengths and accomplishments
- Perhaps the only person who understood and accepted Jesus' coming death, taking time to anoint his body while he was still living
- Learned when to listen and when to act

Lessons from her life
- The busyness of serving God can become a barrier to knowing him personally
- Small acts of obedience and service have widespread effects

Vital statistics
- Where: Bethany
- Relatives: Sister: Martha. Brother: Lazarus

Key verses
"She has poured this perfume on me to prepare my body for burial. I assure you, wherever the Good News is preached throughout the world, this woman's deed will be talked about in her memory" (Matthew 26:12, 13).

Mary's story is told in Matthew 26:6–13; Mark 14:3–9; Luke 10:38–42; John 11:17–45; 12:1–11.

26:3 Caiaphas was the ruling high priest during Jesus' ministry. He was the son-in-law of Annas, the previous high priest. The Roman government had taken over the process of appointing all political and religious leaders. Caiaphas served for 18 years, longer than most high priests, suggesting that he was gifted at cooperating with the Romans. He was the first to recommend Jesus' death in order to "save" the nation (John 11:49, 50).

26:3-5 This was a deliberate plot to kill Jesus. Without this plot, there would have been no groundswell of popular opinion against him. In fact, because of Jesus' popularity, the religious leaders were afraid to arrest him during the Passover. They did not want their actions to incite a riot.

26:6-13 Matthew and Mark put this event just before the Last Supper, while John has it just before the Triumphal Entry. Of the three, John places this event in the most likely chronological order. We must remember that the main purpose of the Gospel writers was to give an accurate record of Jesus' message, not to present an exact chronological account of his life. Matthew and Mark may have chosen to place this event here to contrast the complete devotion of Mary with the betrayal of Judas, the next event they record in their Gospels.

26:7 This woman was Mary, the sister of Martha and Lazarus, who lived in Bethany (John 12:1-3). Alabaster jars were carved from a translucent gypsum. These jars were used to hold perfumed oil.

26:8 All the disciples were indignant, but John's Gospel singles out Judas Iscariot as especially so (John 12:4).

10 But Jesus replied, "Why berate her for doing such a good thing to me? 11 You will always — 26:11 Deut 15:11
have the poor among you, but I will not be here with you much longer. 12 She has poured
this perfume on me to prepare my body for burial. 13 I assure you, wherever the Good
News is preached throughout the world, this woman's deed will be talked about in her
memory."

Judas Agrees to Betray Jesus (**208**/Mark 14:10-11; Luke 22:3-6)
14 Then Judas Iscariot, one of the twelve disciples, went to the leading priests 15 and asked, — 26:14-16 John 11:57
"How much will you pay me to betray Jesus to you?" And they gave him thirty pieces of — 26:15 Exod 21:32; Zech 11:12
silver. 16 From that time on, Judas began looking for the right time and place to betray Jesus.

Disciples Prepare for the Passover (**209**/Mark 14:12-16; Luke 22:7-13)
17 On the first day of the Festival of Unleavened Bread, the disciples came to Jesus and — 26:17 Exod 12:18-20; Deut 16:5-8
asked, "Where do you want us to prepare the Passover supper?"
18 "As you go into the city," he told them, "you will see a certain man. Tell him, 'The
Teacher says, My time has come, and I will eat the Passover meal with my disciples at your
house.'" 19 So the disciples did as Jesus told them and prepared the Passover supper there.

Jesus and the Disciples Share the Last Supper
(**211**/Mark 14:17-25; Luke 22:14-30; John 13:21-30)
20 When it was evening, Jesus sat down at the table with the twelve disciples. 21 While
they were eating, he said, "The truth is, one of you will betray me."
22 Greatly distressed, one by one they began to ask him, "I'm not the one, am I, Lord?"
23 He replied, "One of you who is eating with me now* will betray me. 24 For I, the — 26:23 Ps 41:9
Son of Man, must die, as the Scriptures declared long ago. But how terrible it will be for — 26:24 Ps 22:7-8, 16-18; Isa 53:8-9; Luke 24:25-27, 46; 1 Pet 1:10-11
my betrayer. Far better for him if he had never been born!"
25 Judas, the one who would betray him, also asked, "Teacher, I'm not the one, am I?"
And Jesus told him, "You have said it yourself."
26 As they were eating, Jesus took a loaf of bread and asked God's blessing on it.

26:23 Or *The one who has dipped his hand in the bowl with me.*

26:11 Here Jesus brought back to mind Deuteronomy 15:11: "There will always be some among you who are poor." This statement does not justify ignoring the needs of the poor. Scripture continually exhorts us to care for the needy. The passage in Deuteronomy continues: "That is why I am commanding you to share your resources freely with the poor and with other Israelites in need." Rather, by saying this, Jesus highlighted the special sacrifice Mary made for him.

VISIT IN BETHANY
Chronologically, the events of Matthew 26:6–13 precede the events of 21:1ff. In 20:29, Jesus left Jericho, heading toward Jerusalem. Then he arrived in Bethany, where a woman anointed him. From there he went toward Bethphage, where two of his disciples got the colt that he would ride into Jerusalem.

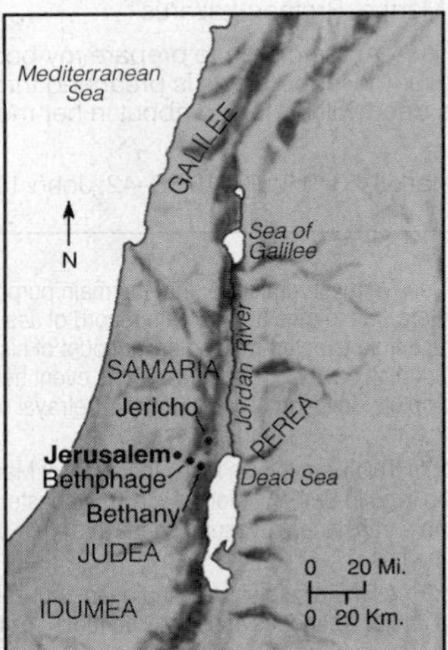

26:14, 15 Why would Judas want to betray Jesus? Judas, like the other disciples, expected Jesus to start a political rebellion and overthrow Rome. As treasurer, Judas certainly assumed (as did the other disciples—see Mark 10:35-37) that he would be given an important position in Jesus' new government. But when Jesus praised Mary for pouring out perfume worth a year's salary, Judas may have realized that Jesus' Kingdom was not physical or political but spiritual. Judas's greedy desire for money and status could not be realized if he followed Jesus, so he betrayed Jesus in exchange for money and favor from the religious leaders.

26:15 Matthew alone records the exact amount of money Judas accepted to betray Jesus—30 silver coins, the price of a slave (Exodus 21:32). The religious leaders had planned to wait until after the Passover to take Jesus, but with Judas's unexpected offer, they accelerated their plans.

26:17 The Passover took place on one night and at one meal, but the Festival of Unleavened Bread, which was celebrated with it, continued for a week. The people removed all yeast from their homes in commemoration of their ancestors' exodus from Egypt, when they did not have time to let the bread dough rise. Thousands of people poured into Jerusalem from all over the Roman Empire for this festival. For more information on how the Passover was celebrated, see the notes on Mark 14:1 and in Exodus 12.

26:23 In Jesus' time, some food was eaten from a common bowl into which everyone dipped their hand.

26:26 Each name we use for this sacrament brings out a different dimension to it. It is the *Lord's Supper* because it commemorates the Passover meal Jesus ate with his disciples; it is the *Eucharist* (thanksgiving) because in it we thank God for Christ's work for us; it is *Communion* because through it we commune with God and with other believers. As we eat the bread and drink the wine, we should be quietly reflective as we recall Jesus' death and his promise to come again, grateful for God's wonderful gift to us, and joyful as we meet with Christ and the body of believers.

26:28 Exod 24:8 Jer 31:31 Zech 9:11 Heb 9:20
Then he broke it in pieces and gave it to the disciples, saying, "Take it and eat it, for
this is my body." 27And he took a cup of wine and gave thanks to God for it. He gave
it to them and said, "Each of you drink from it, 28for this is my blood, which seals the
26:29 Acts 10:41
covenant* between God and his people. It is poured out to forgive the sins of many.
29Mark my words—I will not drink wine again until the day I drink it new with you
26:30 Pss 113–118
in my Father's Kingdom." 30Then they sang a hymn and went out to the Mount of
Olives.

Jesus Again Predicts Peter's Denial (**222**/Mark 14:26-31)

26:31 †Zech 13:7 John 16:32
31"Tonight all of you will desert me," Jesus told them. "For the Scriptures say,

'God* will strike the Shepherd,
and the sheep of the flock will be scattered.'*

26:32 Matt 28:7
32But after I have been raised from the dead, I will go ahead of you to Galilee and meet
you there."

26:34 Matt 26:69-75 Mark 14:66-72 Luke 22:56-62 John 18:25-27
33Peter declared, "Even if everyone else deserts you, I never will."
34"Peter," Jesus replied, "the truth is, this very night, before the rooster crows, you
will deny me three times."
26:35 John 13:37
35"No!" Peter insisted. "Not even if I have to die with you! I will never deny you!"
And all the other disciples vowed the same.

Jesus Agonizes in the Garden (**223**/Mark 14:32-42; Luke 22:39-46)

26:36 John 18:1
36Then Jesus brought them to an olive grove called Gethsemane, and he said, "Sit here while
I go on ahead to pray." 37He took Peter and Zebedee's two sons, James and John, and he
26:38 †Pss 42:6, 12; 43:5 John 12:27
began to be filled with anguish and deep distress. 38He told them, "My soul is crushed with
grief to the point of death. Stay here and watch with me."

26:28 Some manuscripts read *the new covenant.* **26:31a** Greek *I.* **26:31b** Zech 13:7.

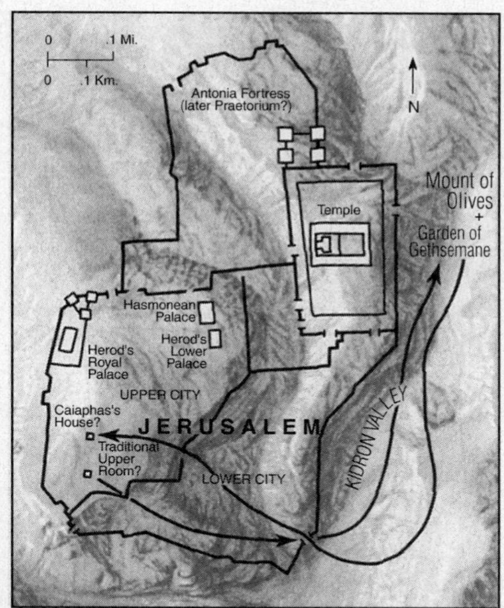

THE PASSOVER MEAL AND GETHSEMANE Jesus, who would soon be the final Passover Lamb, ate the traditional Passover meal with his disciples in the upper room of a house in Jerusalem. During the meal they partook of the bread and wine, which would be the elements of future Communion celebrations, and then went out to the Garden of Gethsemane on the Mount of Olives.

26:28 How does Jesus' blood relate to the new covenant? People under the old covenant (those who lived before Jesus) could approach God only through a priest and an animal sacrifice. Now all people can come directly to God through faith because Jesus' death has made us acceptable in God's eyes (Romans 3:21-24).

The old covenant was a shadow of the new (Jeremiah 31:31; Hebrews 8:1ff), pointing forward to the day when Jesus himself would be the final and ultimate sacrifice for sin. Rather than an unblemished lamb slain on the altar, the perfect Lamb of God was slain on the cross, a sinless sacrifice, so that our sins could be forgiven once and for all. All those who believe in Christ receive that forgiveness.

26:29 Again Jesus assured his disciples of victory over death and of their future with him. The next few hours would bring apparent defeat, but soon they would experience the power of the Holy Spirit and witness the great spread of the Good News. And one day they would all be together again in God's new Kingdom.

26:30 It is possible that the hymn the disciples sang was from Psalms 115–118, the traditional psalms sung as part of the Passover meal.

26:35 All the disciples declared that they would die before denying Jesus. A few hours later, however, they all scattered. Talk is cheap. It is easy to say we are devoted to Christ, but our claims are meaningful only when they are tested in the crucible of persecution. How strong is your faith? Is it strong enough to stand up under intense trial?

26:37, 38 Jesus was in great anguish over his approaching physical pain, separation from the Father, and death for the sins of the world. The divine course was set, but he, in his human nature, still struggled (Hebrews 5:7-9). Because of the anguish Jesus experienced, he can relate to our suffering. Jesus' strength to obey came from his relationship with God the Father, who is also the source of our strength (John 17:11, 15, 16, 21, 26).

[39]He went on a little farther and fell face down on the ground, praying, "My Father!
If it is possible, let this cup of suffering be taken away from me. Yet I want your will, not
mine." [40]Then he returned to the disciples and found them asleep. He said to Peter,
"Couldn't you stay awake and watch with me even one hour? [41]Keep alert and pray.
Otherwise temptation will overpower you. For though the spirit is willing enough, the
body is weak!"
[42]Again he left them and prayed, "My Father! If this cup cannot be taken away until
I drink it, your will be done." [43]He returned to them again and found them sleeping, for
they just couldn't keep their eyes open.
[44]So he went back to pray a third time, saying the same things again. [45]Then he came
to the disciples and said, "Still sleeping? Still resting?* Look, the time has come. I, the
Son of Man, am betrayed into the hands of sinners. [46]Up, let's be going. See, my betrayer
is here!"

Jesus Is Betrayed and Arrested (**224**/Mark 14:43-52; Luke 22:47-53; John 18:1-11)

[47]And even as he said this, Judas, one of the twelve disciples, arrived with a mob that
was armed with swords and clubs. They had been sent out by the leading priests and
other leaders of the people. [48]Judas had given them a prearranged signal: "You will
know which one to arrest when I go over and give him the kiss of greeting." [49]So
Judas came straight to Jesus. "Greetings, Teacher!" he exclaimed and gave him the
kiss.
[50]Jesus said, "My friend, go ahead and do what you have come for." Then the others
grabbed Jesus and arrested him. [51]One of the men with Jesus pulled out a sword and
slashed off an ear of the high priest's servant.
[52]"Put away your sword," Jesus told him. "Those who use the sword will be killed by
the sword. [53]Don't you realize that I could ask my Father for thousands* of angels to

26:39 Matt 20:22; John 5:30; 6:38; Heb 5:7-8
26:41 Matt 6:13
26:45 John 12:23-27; 13:1; 17:1
26:52 Gen 9:6; Rev 13:10
26:53 2 Kgs 6:16-17; Ps 91:11; Dan 7:10

26:45 Or *Sleep on, take your rest.*

26:39 Jesus was not rebelling against his Father's will when he asked that the cup of suffering and separation be taken away. In fact, he reaffirmed his desire to do God's will by saying, "Yet I want your will, not mine." His prayer reveals to us his terrible suffering. His agony was worse than death because he paid for *all* sin by being separated from God. The sinless Son of God took our sins upon himself to save us from suffering and separation.

26:39 In times of suffering people sometimes wish they knew the future, or they wish they could understand the reason for their anguish. Jesus knew what lay ahead of him, and he knew the reason. Even so, his struggle was intense—more wrenching than any struggle we will ever have to face. What does it take to be able to say, "I want your will"? It takes firm trust in God's plans; it takes prayer and obedience each step of the way.

26:40, 41 Jesus used Peter's drowsiness to warn him about the kinds of temptation he would soon face. The way to overcome temptation is to keep alert and pray. Keeping alert means being aware of the possibilities of temptation, sensitive to the subtleties, and spiritually equipped to fight it. Because temptation strikes where we are most vulnerable, we can't resist it alone. Prayer is essential because God's strength can shore up our defenses and defeat Satan's power.

26:48 Judas had told the crowd to arrest the man he kissed. This was not an arrest by Roman soldiers under Roman law but an arrest by the religious leaders. Judas pointed Jesus out, not because Jesus was hard to recognize, but because Judas had agreed to be the formal accuser in case a trial was called. Judas was able to lead the group to one of Jesus' retreats, where no onlookers would interfere with the arrest.

26:51-53 The man who cut off the servant's ear was Peter (John 18:10). Peter was trying to prevent what he saw as *defeat.* He didn't realize that Jesus had to die in order to gain *victory.* But Jesus demonstrated perfect commitment to his Father's will. His Kingdom would not be advanced with swords but with faith and obedience.

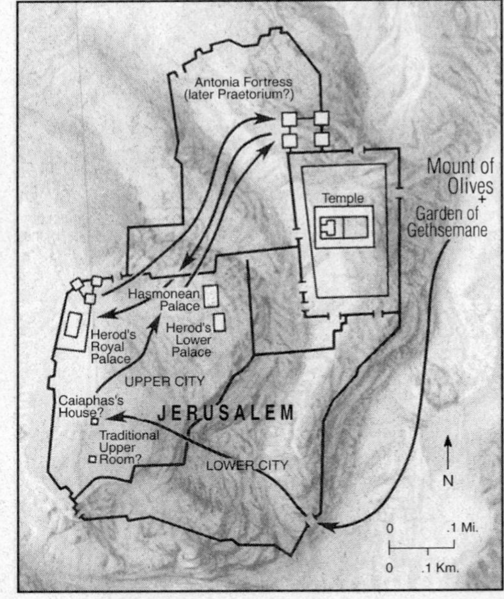

JESUS' TRIAL After Judas singled Jesus out for arrest, the mob took Jesus first to Caiaphas, the high priest. This trial, a mockery of justice, ended at daybreak with their decision to kill him; but the Jews needed Rome's permission for the death sentence. Jesus was taken to Pilate (who was probably in the Praetorium), then to Herod (Luke 23:5–12), and back to Pilate, who sentenced him to die.

26:54 Ps 22:7-8, 16-18; Isa 53:8-9; Luke 24:25-27, 46; 1 Pet 1:10-11
26:56 Isa 53:7; Zech 13:7; Matt 26:31
26:58 Mark 14:66; Luke 22:55; John 18:15
26:60 Deut 19:15; Ps 27:12
26:61 Matt 27:40; John 2:19; Acts 6:14
26:63 Lev 5:1; Matt 16:16-18
26:64 Ps 110:1; †Dan 7:13; Matt 24:30; Rev 1:7
26:65-66 Lev 24:16; John 19:7

protect us, and he would send them instantly? 54 But if I did, how would the Scriptures
be fulfilled that describe what must happen now?"
55 Then Jesus said to the crowd, "Am I some dangerous criminal, that you have come
armed with swords and clubs to arrest me? Why didn't you arrest me in the Temple? I was
there teaching every day. 56 But this is all happening to fulfill the words of the prophets as
recorded in the Scriptures." At that point, all the disciples deserted him and fled.

Caiaphas Questions Jesus (**226**/Mark 14:53-65)

57 Then the people who had arrested Jesus led him to the home of Caiaphas, the high
priest, where the teachers of religious law and other leaders had gathered. 58 Meanwhile, Peter was following far behind and eventually came to the courtyard of the high
priest's house. He went in, sat with the guards, and waited to see what was going to
happen to Jesus.
59 Inside, the leading priests and the entire high council* were trying to find witnesses
who would lie about Jesus, so they could put him to death. 60 But even though they found
many who agreed to give false witness, there was no testimony they could use. Finally,
two men were found 61 who declared, "This man said, 'I am able to destroy the Temple
of God and rebuild it in three days.'"
62 Then the high priest stood up and said to Jesus, "Well, aren't you going to answer
these charges? What do you have to say for yourself?" 63 But Jesus remained silent. Then
the high priest said to him, "I demand in the name of the living God that you tell us
whether you are the Messiah, the Son of God."
64 Jesus replied, "Yes, it is as you say. And in the future you will see me, the Son of
Man, sitting at God's right hand in the place of power and coming back on the clouds of
heaven."*
65 Then the high priest tore his clothing to show his horror, shouting, "Blasphemy!
Why do we need other witnesses? You have all heard his blasphemy. 66 What is your
verdict?"

26:53 Greek *12 legions.* **26:59** Greek *the Sanhedrin.* **26:64** See Ps 110:1; Dan 7:13.

BETRAYED!

Delilah betrayed Samson to the Philistines.	Judges 16:16–21
Absalom betrayed David, his father.	2 Samuel 15:10–17
Jehu betrayed Joram and killed him.	2 Kings 9:14–27
Officials betrayed Joash and killed him.	2 Kings 12:20, 21
Judas betrayed Jesus.	Matthew 26:46–56

Scripture records a number of occasions on which a person or group was betrayed. The tragedies caused by these violations of trust are a strong lesson about the importance of keeping our commitments.

26:55 Although the religious leaders could have arrested Jesus at any time, they came at night because they were afraid of the crowds that followed him each day (see 26:5).

26:56 A few hours earlier, this band of men had said they would rather die than desert their Lord (see the note on 26:35).

26:57 Earlier in the evening, Jesus had been questioned by Annas (the former high priest and the father-in-law of Caiaphas). Annas then sent Jesus to Caiaphas's home to be questioned (John 18:12-24). Because of their haste to complete the trial and see Jesus die before the Sabbath, less than 24 hours away, the religious leaders met in Caiaphas's home at night instead of waiting for daylight and meeting in the Temple.

26:59 The high council was the most powerful religious and political body of the Jewish people. Although the Romans controlled Israel's government, they gave the people power to handle religious disputes and some civil disputes, so the high council made many of the local decisions affecting daily life. But a death sentence had to be approved by the Romans (John 18:31).

26:60, 61 The high council tried to find witnesses who would distort some of Jesus' teachings. Finally, they found two witnesses who distorted Jesus' words about the Temple (see John 2:19). They claimed that Jesus had said he could destroy the Temple—a blasphemous boast. Actually Jesus had said, "Destroy this temple, and in three days I will raise it up." Jesus, of course, was talking about his body, not the building. Ironically, the religious leaders were about to destroy Jesus' body just as he had said, and three days later he would rise from the dead.

26:64 Jesus declared his royalty in no uncertain terms. In saying he was the Son of Man, Jesus was claiming to be the Messiah, as his listeners well knew. He knew this declaration would be his undoing, but he did not panic. He was calm, courageous, and determined.

26:65, 66 The high priest accused Jesus of blasphemy—calling himself God. To the Jews, this was a great crime, punishable by death (Leviticus 24:16). The religious leaders refused even to consider that Jesus' words might be true. They had decided to kill Jesus, and in so doing, they sealed their own fate as well as his. Like the members of the high council, you must decide whether Jesus' words are blasphemy or truth. Your decision has eternal implications.

"Guilty!" they shouted. "He must die!"
67 Then they spit in Jesus' face and hit him with their fists. And some slapped him,
68 saying, "Prophesy to us, you Messiah! Who hit you that time?"

26:67 Isa 50:6; 53:5

Peter Denies Knowing Jesus (**227**/Mark 14:66-72; Luke 22:54-65; John 18:25-27)

69 Meanwhile, as Peter was sitting outside in the courtyard, a servant girl came over and said to him, "You were one of those with Jesus the Galilean."
70 But Peter denied it in front of everyone. "I don't know what you are talking about," he said.
71 Later, out by the gate, another servant girl noticed him and said to those standing around, "This man was with Jesus of Nazareth."
72 Again Peter denied it, this time with an oath. "I don't even know the man," he said.
73 A little later some other bystanders came over to him and said, "You must be one of them; we can tell by your Galilean accent."
74 Peter said, "I swear by God, I don't know the man." And immediately the rooster
crowed. 75 Suddenly, Jesus' words flashed through Peter's mind: "Before the rooster crows, you will deny me three times." And he went away, crying bitterly.

26:75 Matt 26:34 Mark 14:30 Luke 22:34 John 13:38

The Council of Religious Leaders Condemns Jesus (**228**/Mark 15:1; Luke 22:66-71)

27 Very early in the morning, the leading priests and other leaders met again to discuss how to persuade the Roman government to sentence Jesus to death. 2 Then
they bound him and took him to Pilate, the Roman governor.

27:1-2 Mark 15:1 Luke 23:1-2 John 18:28

Judas Hangs Himself (**229**)

3 When Judas, who had betrayed him, realized that Jesus had been condemned to die, he was filled with remorse. So he took the thirty pieces of silver back to the leading priests and other leaders. 4 "I have sinned," he declared, "for I have betrayed an innocent man."
"What do we care?" they retorted. "That's your problem." 5 Then Judas threw the money
onto the floor of the Temple and went out and hanged himself. 6 The leading priests picked

27:3 Matt 26:14-15

27:5-10 Acts 1:18-19

26:69ff There were three stages to Peter's denial. First, he acted confused and tried to divert attention from himself by changing the subject. Second, using an oath he denied that he knew Jesus. Third, he swore that he did not know Jesus. Believers who deny Christ often begin doing so subtly by pretending not to know him. When opportunities to discuss religious issues come up, they walk away or pretend they don't know the answers. With only a little more pressure, they can be induced to deny flatly their relationship with Christ. If you find yourself subtly diverting conversation so you don't have to talk about Christ, watch out. You may be on the road to denying him.

26:72-74 That Peter denied that he knew Jesus, using an oath and swearing, does not mean he used foul language. This was the kind of swearing that a person does in a court of law. Peter was swearing that he did not know Jesus and was invoking a curse on himself if his words were untrue. In effect he was saying, "May God strike me dead if I am lying."

27:1, 2 The religious leaders had to persuade the Roman government to sentence Jesus to death because they did not have the authority to do it themselves. The Romans had taken away the religious leaders' authority to inflict capital punishment. Politically, it looked better for the religious leaders anyway if someone else was responsible for killing Jesus. They wanted the death to appear Roman sponsored so the crowds couldn't blame them. The Jewish leaders had arrested Jesus on theological grounds—blasphemy; but because this charge would be thrown out of a Roman court, they had to come up with a political reason for Jesus' death. Their strategy was to show Jesus as a rebel who claimed to be a king and thus a threat to Caesar.

27:2 Pilate was the Roman governor for the regions of Samaria and Judea from A.D. 26 to 36. Jerusalem was located in Judea. Pilate took special pleasure in demonstrating his authority over the Jews; for example, he impounded money from the Temple treasuries to build an aqueduct. Pilate was not popular, but the religious leaders had no other way to get rid of Jesus than to go to him. Ironically, when Jesus, a Jew, came before him for trial, Pilate found him innocent. He could not find a single fault in Jesus, nor could he contrive one.

27:3, 4 Jesus' formal accuser (see 26:48 note) wanted to drop his charges, but the religious leaders refused to halt the trial. When he betrayed Jesus, perhaps Judas was trying to force Jesus' hand to get him to lead a revolt against Rome. This did not work, of course. Whatever his reason, Judas changed his mind, but it was too late. Many of the plans we set into motion cannot be reversed. It is best to think of the potential consequences before we launch into an action we may later regret.

27:4 The priests' job was to teach people about God and act as intercessors for them, helping administer the sacrifices to cover their sins. Judas returned to the priests, exclaiming that he had sinned. Rather than helping him find forgiveness, however, the priests said, "That's your problem." Not only had they rejected the Messiah, they had rejected their role as priests.

27:5 According to Matthew, Judas hanged himself. Acts 1:18, however, says that he fell and burst open. The best explanation is that the limb from which he was hanging broke, and the resulting fall split open his body.

27:6 These chief priests felt no guilt in giving Judas money to betray an innocent man, but when Judas returned the money, the priests couldn't accept it because it was wrong to accept payment for murder! Their hatred for Jesus had caused them to lose all sense of justice.

up the money. "We can't put it in the Temple treasury," they said, "since it's against the law
to accept money paid for murder." 7After some discussion they finally decided to buy the
potter's field, and they made it into a cemetery for foreigners. 8That is why the field is still
called the Field of Blood. 9This fulfilled the prophecy of Jeremiah that says,

27:9-10 †Jer 32:6-9 †Zech 11:12-13

"They took* the thirty pieces of silver—
the price at which he was valued by the people of Israel—
10 and purchased the potter's field,
as the Lord directed.*"

Jesus Stands Trial before Pilate (**230**/Mark 15:2-5; Luke 23:1-5; John 18:28-38)

11Now Jesus was standing before Pilate, the Roman governor. "Are you the King of the
Jews?" the governor asked him.
Jesus replied, "Yes, it is as you say."
12But when the leading priests and other leaders made their accusations against him,
Jesus remained silent. 13"Don't you hear their many charges against you?" Pilate
demanded. 14But Jesus said nothing, much to the governor's great surprise.

27:12 Isa 53:7 Matt 26:63 John 19:9 1 Pet 2:22

27:14 Mark 14:61

27:9 Or *I took.* **27:9-10** Greek *as the Lord directed me.* Zech 11:12-13; Jer 32:6-9.

PETER

Jesus' first words to Simon Peter were "Come, be my disciple" (Mark 1:17). His last words to him were "You follow me" (John 21:22). Every step of the way between those two challenges, Peter never failed to follow—even though he often stumbled.

When Jesus entered Peter's life, this plain fisherman became a new person with new goals and new priorities. He did not become a perfect person, however, and he never stopped being Simon Peter. We may wonder what Jesus saw in Simon that made him greet this potential disciple with a new name: Peter—the "rock." Impulsive Peter certainly didn't act like a rock much of the time. But when Jesus chose his followers, he wasn't looking for models; he was looking for real people. He chose people who could be changed by his love, and then he sent them out to communicate that his acceptance was available to anyone—even to those who often fail.

We may wonder what Jesus sees in us when he calls us to follow him. But we know Jesus accepted Peter, and, in spite of his failures, Peter went on to do great things for God. Are you willing to keep following Jesus, even when you fail?

Strengths and accomplishments
- Became the recognized leader among Jesus' disciples—one of the inner group of three
- Was the first great voice of the gospel during and after Pentecost
- Probably knew Mark and gave him information for the Gospel of Mark
- Wrote 1 and 2 Peter

Weaknesses and mistakes
- Often spoke without thinking; was brash and impulsive
- During Jesus' trial, denied three times that he even knew Jesus
- Later found it hard to treat Gentile Christians as equals

Lessons from his life
- Enthusiasm has to be backed up by faith and understanding, or it fails
- God's faithfulness can compensate for our greatest unfaithfulness
- It is better to be a follower who sometimes fails than one who fails to follow

Vital statistics
- Occupations: Fisherman, disciple
- Relatives: Father: John. Brother: Andrew
- Contemporaries: Jesus, Pilate, Herod

Key verse "Now I say to you that you are Peter, and upon this rock I will build my church, and all the powers of hell will not conquer it" (Matthew 16:18).

Peter's story is told in the Gospels and the book of Acts. He is mentioned in Galatians 1:18 and 2:7-14; and he wrote the books of 1 and 2 Peter.

27:9, 10 This prophecy is found specifically in Zechariah 11:12, 13 but may also have been taken from Jeremiah 18:1-4; 19:1-11; or 32:6-15. In Old Testament times, Jeremiah was considered the collector of some of the prophets' writings, so perhaps his name is cited rather than Zechariah.

27:12 Standing before Pilate, the religious leaders accused Jesus of a different crime than the ones for which they had arrested him. They arrested him for blasphemy (claiming to be God), but that charge would mean nothing to the Romans. So the religious leaders had to accuse Jesus of crimes that would have concerned the Roman government, such as encouraging the people not to pay taxes, claiming to be a king, and causing riots. These accusations were not true, but the religious leaders were determined to kill Jesus, and they broke several commandments in order to do so.

Pilate Hands Jesus Over to Be Crucified
(**232**/Mark 15:6-15; Luke 23:13-25; John 18:39—19:16)
15 Now it was the governor's custom to release one prisoner to the crowd each year
during the Passover celebration—anyone they wanted. 16 This year there was a notorious
criminal in prison, a man named Barabbas.* 17 As the crowds gathered before Pilate's
house that morning, he asked them, "Which one do you want me to release to you—Barabbas, or Jesus who is called the Messiah?" 18 (He knew very well that the Jewish leaders
had arrested Jesus out of envy.)
19 Just then, as Pilate was sitting on the judgment seat, his wife sent him this message: **27:19** Job 33:14-16
"Leave that innocent man alone, because I had a terrible nightmare about him last night."
20 Meanwhile, the leading priests and other leaders persuaded the crowds to ask for **27:20** Acts 3:14
Barabbas to be released and for Jesus to be put to death. 21 So when the governor asked
again, "Which of these two do you want me to release to you?" the crowd shouted back
their reply: "Barabbas!"
22 "But if I release Barabbas," Pilate asked them, "what should I do with Jesus who is **27:22** Matt 1:16
called the Messiah?"
And they all shouted, "Crucify him!"
23 "Why?" Pilate demanded. "What crime has he committed?"
But the crowd only roared the louder, "Crucify him!"
24 Pilate saw that he wasn't getting anywhere and that a riot was developing. So he sent **27:24** Deut 21:5-9 Ps 26:6

27:16 Some manuscripts read *Jesus Barabbas;* also in 27:17.

27:14 Jesus' silence fulfilled the words of the prophet (Isaiah 53:7). Pilate was amazed that Jesus didn't try to defend himself. He recognized the obvious plot against Jesus and wanted to let him go, but Pilate was already under pressure from Rome to keep peace in his territory. The last thing he needed was a rebellion over this quiet and seemingly insignificant man.

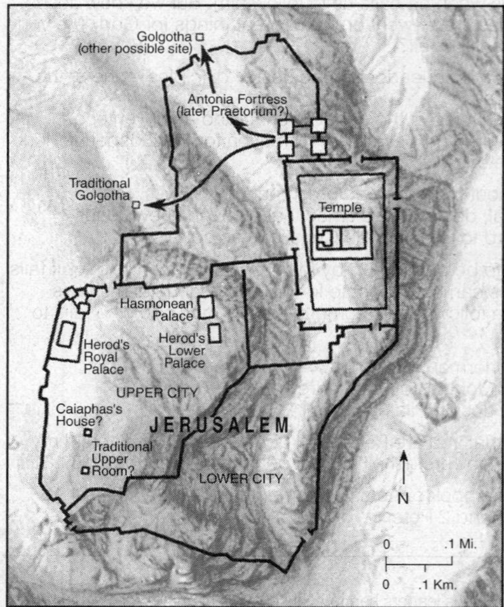

THE WAY OF THE CROSS The Roman soldiers took Jesus into the Praetorium and mocked him, dressing him in a scarlet robe and a crown of thorns. They then led him to the crucifixion site outside the city. He was so weakened by his beatings that he could not carry his cross, and a man from Cyrene was forced to carry it to Golgotha.

27:15, 16 Barabbas had taken part in a rebellion against the Roman government (Mark 15:7). Although an enemy to Rome, he may have been a hero to the Jews. Ironically, Barabbas was guilty of the crime for which Jesus was accused. *Barabbas* means "son of the father," which was actually Jesus' position with God.

27:19 For a leader who was supposed to administer justice, Pilate proved to be more concerned about political expediency than about doing what was right. He had several opportunities to make the right decision. His conscience told him Jesus was innocent; Roman law said an innocent man should not be put to death; and his wife had a nightmare. Pilate had no good excuse to condemn Jesus, but he was afraid of the crowd.

27:21 Crowds are fickle. They loved Jesus on Sunday because they thought he was going to inaugurate his Kingdom. Then they hated him on Friday when his power appeared broken. In the face of the mass uprising against Jesus, his friends were afraid to speak up.

27:21 Faced with a clear choice, the people chose Barabbas, a revolutionary and murderer, over the Son of God. Faced with the same choice today, people are still choosing "Barabbas." They would rather have the tangible force of human power than the salvation offered by the Son of God.

27:24 At first Pilate hesitated to give the religious leaders permission to crucify Jesus. He thought they were simply jealous of a teacher who was more popular with the people than they were. But when the Jews threatened to report Pilate to Caesar (John 19:12), Pilate became afraid. Historical records indicate that the Jews had already threatened to lodge a formal complaint against Pilate for his stubborn flouting of their traditions—and such a complaint would most likely have led to his recall by Rome. His job was in jeopardy. The Roman government could not afford to put large numbers of troops in all the regions under their control, so one of Pilate's main duties was to do whatever was necessary to maintain peace.

27:24 In making no decision, Pilate made the decision to let the crowds crucify Jesus. Although he washed his hands, the guilt remained. Washing your hands of a tough situation doesn't cancel your guilt. It merely gives you a false sense of peace. Don't make excuses—take responsibility for the decisions you make.

for a bowl of water and washed his hands before the crowd, saying, "I am innocent of
the blood of this man. The responsibility is yours!"
27:25 Acts 5:28 — 25 And all the people yelled back, "We will take responsibility for his death—we and
our children!"*
27:26 Isa 53:5 — 26 So Pilate released Barabbas to them. He ordered Jesus flogged with a lead-tipped
John 19:1 — whip, then turned him over to the Roman soldiers to crucify him.

Roman Soldiers Mock Jesus (**233**/Mark 15:16-20)

27 Some of the governor's soldiers took Jesus into their headquarters and called out the
27:29 Ps 22:8 — entire battalion. 28 They stripped him and put a scarlet robe on him. 29 They made a crown
Isa 53:3 — of long, sharp thorns and put it on his head, and they placed a stick in his right hand as
John 19:2-3 — a scepter. Then they knelt before him in mockery, yelling, "Hail! King of the Jews!"
27:30 Isa 50:6 — 30 And they spit on him and grabbed the stick and beat him on the head with it. 31 When
27:31 Isa 53:7 — they were finally tired of mocking him, they took off the robe and put his own clothes
on him again. Then they led him away to be crucified.

Jesus Is Led Away to Be Crucified (**234**/Mark 15:21-24; Luke 23:26-31; John 19:17)
Jesus Is Placed on the Cross (**235**/Mark 15:25-32; Luke 23:32-43; John 19:18-27)

32 As they were on the way, they came across a man named Simon, who was from
27:34 — Cyrene,* and they forced him to carry Jesus' cross. 33 Then they went out to a place called
Ps 69:21 — Golgotha (which means Skull Hill). 34 The soldiers gave him wine mixed with bitter gall,
27:35 †Ps 22:18 — but when he had tasted it, he refused to drink it.
35 After they had nailed him to the cross, the soldiers gambled for his clothes by
throwing dice.* 36 Then they sat around and kept guard as he hung there. 37 A signboard
was fastened to the cross above Jesus' head, announcing the charge against him. It read:
27:38 Isa 53:12 — "This is Jesus, the King of the Jews."
27:39 — 38 Two criminals were crucified with him, their crosses on either side of his. 39 And the
Pss 22:7; 109:25 Lam 2:15 — people passing by shouted abuse, shaking their heads in mockery. 40 "So! You can
27:40 Matt 26:61 — destroy the Temple and build it again in three days, can you? Well then, if you are the
John 2:19-20 — Son of God, save yourself and come down from the cross!"

27:25 Greek *"His blood be on us and on our children."* **27:32** *Cyrene* was a city in northern Africa. **27:35** Greek *by casting lots.* A few late manuscripts add *This fulfilled the word of the prophet: "They divided my clothes among themselves and cast lots for my robe."* See Ps 22:18.

THE SEVEN LAST WORDS OF JESUS ON THE CROSS

Statement	Reference
"Father, forgive these people because they don't know what they are doing."	Luke 23:34
"I assure you, today you will be with me in paradise."	Luke 23:43
Speaking to John and Mary, "Woman, he is your son. . . . She is your mother."	John 19:26, 27
"My God, my God, why have you forsaken me?"	Matthew 27:46; Mark 15:34
"I am thirsty."	John 19:28
"It is finished."	John 19:30
"Father, I entrust my spirit into your hands!"	Luke 23:46

The statements that Jesus made from the cross have been treasured by all who have followed him as Lord. They demonstrate both his humanity and his divinity. They also capture the last moments of all that Jesus went through to gain our forgiveness.

27:27 A battalion was a division of the Roman legion, containing about 200 men.

27:29 People often make fun of Christians for their faith, but believers can take courage from the fact that Jesus himself was mocked more than most people. Taunting may hurt our feelings, but we should never let it change our faith (see 5:11, 12).

27:32 Condemned prisoners had to carry their own crosses to the execution site. Jesus, weakened from the beatings he had received, was physically unable to carry his cross any farther. Thus, a bystander, Simon, was forced to do so. Simon was from Cyrene, in northern Africa, and was probably one of the thousands of Jews visiting Jerusalem for the Passover.

27:33 Some scholars say Golgotha ("Skull Hill") derives its name from its appearance. Golgotha may have been a regular place of execution in a prominent public place outside the city. Executions held there would serve as a deterrent to criminals.

27:34 Wine mixed with gall was offered to Jesus to help reduce his pain, but Jesus refused to drink it. Gall is generally understood to be a narcotic that was used to deaden pain. Jesus would suffer fully conscious and with a clear mind.

27:35 The soldiers customarily took the clothing of those they crucified. These soldiers threw dice and divided Jesus' clothing among themselves, fulfilling the prophecy made by David. Much of Psalm 22 parallels Jesus' crucifixion.

41 The leading priests, the teachers of religious law, and the other leaders also
mocked Jesus. 42 "He saved others," they scoffed, "but he can't save himself! So he
is the king of Israel, is he? Let him come down from the cross, and we will believe in
him! 43 He trusted God—let God show his approval by delivering him! For he said, 'I
am the Son of God.'" 44 And the criminals who were crucified with him also shouted
the same insults at him.

Jesus Dies on the Cross (**236**/Mark 15:33-41; Luke 23:44-49; John 19:28-37)

45 At noon, darkness fell across the whole land until three o'clock. 46 At about three **27:45**
o'clock, Jesus called out with a loud voice, "*Eli, Eli, lema sabachthani?*" which means, Amos 8:9
"My God, my God, why have you forsaken me?"* **27:46** †Ps 22:1
47 Some of the bystanders misunderstood and thought he was calling for the prophet
Elijah. 48 One of them ran and filled a sponge with sour wine, holding it up to him on a **27:48**
stick so he could drink. 49 But the rest said, "Leave him alone. Let's see whether Elijah Ps 69:21 John 19:29-30
will come and save him."*
50 Then Jesus shouted out again, and he gave up his spirit. 51 At that moment the curtain **27:51**
in the Temple was torn in two, from top to bottom. The earth shook, rocks split apart, Exod 26:31-33 Heb 10:19-20
52 and tombs opened. The bodies of many godly men and women who had died were **27:52**
raised from the dead 53 after Jesus' resurrection. They left the cemetery, went into the Ezek 37:12
holy city of Jerusalem, and appeared to many people.*
54 The Roman officer and the other soldiers at the crucifixion were terrified by the
earthquake and all that had happened. They said, "Truly, this was the Son of God!"
55 And many women who had come from Galilee with Jesus to care for him were **27:55-56**
watching from a distance. 56 Among them were Mary Magdalene, Mary (the mother of Luke 8:2-3
James and Joseph), and Zebedee's wife, the mother of James and John.

Jesus Is Laid in the Tomb (**237**/Mark 15:42-47; Luke 23:50-56; John 19:38-42)

57 As evening approached, Joseph, a rich man from Arimathea who was one of Jesus'
followers, 58 went to Pilate and asked for Jesus' body. And Pilate issued an order to **27:60**
release it to him. 59 Joseph took the body and wrapped it in a long linen cloth. 60 He placed Matt 28:2 Mark 16:3-4
it in his own new tomb, which had been carved out of the rock. Then he rolled a great Luke 24:2 John 20:1

27:46 Ps 22:1. **27:49** Some manuscripts add *And another took a spear and pierced his side, and out came water and blood.* **27:51-53** Or *The earth shook, rocks split apart, tombs opened, and the bodies of many godly men and women who had died were raised from the dead. After Jesus' resurrection, they left the cemetery, went into the holy city of Jerusalem, and appeared to many people.*

27:40 This accusation was used against Jesus in his trial by the high council (26:61). It is ironic that Jesus was in the very process of fulfilling his own prophecy. Because Jesus is the Son of God, who always obeys the will of the Father, he did not come down from the cross.

27:44 Later one of these criminals repented. Jesus promised that the repentant criminal would join him in paradise (Luke 23:39-43).

27:45 We do not know how this darkness occurred, but it is clear that God caused it. Nature testified to the gravity of Jesus' death, while Jesus' friends and enemies alike fell silent in the encircling gloom. The darkness on that Friday afternoon was both physical and spiritual.

27:46 Jesus was not questioning God; he was quoting the first line of Psalm 22—a deep expression of the anguish he felt when he took on the sins of the world, which caused him to be separated from his Father. *This* was what Jesus dreaded as he prayed to God in the garden to take the cup from him (26:39). The physical agony was horrible, but even worse was the period of spiritual separation from God. Jesus suffered this double death so that we would never have to experience eternal separation from God.

27:47 The bystanders misinterpreted Jesus' words and thought he was calling for Elijah. Because Elijah ascended into heaven without dying (2 Kings 2:11), they thought he would return again to rescue them from great trouble (Malachi 4:5). At their annual Passover meal, each family set an extra place for Elijah in expectation of his return.

27:51 The Temple had three main parts: the courts, the Holy Place (where only the priests could enter), and the Most Holy Place (where only the high priest could enter, and only once a year, to atone for the sins of the nation—Leviticus 16:1-35). The curtain separating the Holy Place from the Most Holy Place was torn in two at Christ's death, symbolizing that the barrier between God and humanity was removed. Now all people are free to approach God because of Christ's sacrifice for our sins (see Hebrews 9:1-14; 10:19-22).

27:52, 53 Christ's death was accompanied by at least four miraculous events: darkness, the tearing in two of the curtain in the Temple, an earthquake, and dead people rising from their tombs. Jesus' death, therefore, could not have gone unnoticed. Everyone knew something significant had happened.

27:57, 58 Joseph of Arimathea was a secret disciple of Jesus. He was a religious leader, an honored member of the high council (Mark 15:43). In the past, Joseph had been afraid to speak against the religious leaders who opposed Jesus; now he was bold, courageously asking to take Jesus' body from the cross and to bury it. The disciples who publicly followed Jesus had fled, but this Jewish leader, who followed Jesus in secret, came forward and did what was right.

27:60 The tomb where Jesus was laid was probably a manmade cave cut out of one of the many limestone hills in the area. These caves were often large enough to walk into.

stone across the entrance as he left. 61 Both Mary Magdalene and the other Mary were
sitting nearby watching.

Guards are Posted at the Tomb (**238**)

62 The next day—on the first day of the Passover ceremonies*—the leading priests and
Pharisees went to see Pilate. 63 They told him, "Sir, we remember what that deceiver once
said while he was still alive: 'After three days I will be raised from the dead.' 64 So we
request that you seal the tomb until the third day. This will prevent his disciples from
coming and stealing his body and then telling everyone he came back to life! If that
happens, we'll be worse off than we were at first."

65 Pilate replied, "Take guards and secure it the best you can." 66 So they sealed the
tomb and posted guards to protect it.

Jesus Rises from the Dead (**239**/Mark 16:1-8; Luke 24:1-12; John 20:1-10)

28 Early on Sunday morning,* as the new day was dawning, Mary Magdalene and
the other Mary went out to see the tomb. 2 Suddenly there was a great earthquake,
because an angel of the Lord came down from heaven and rolled aside the stone and sat
on it. 3 His face shone like lightning, and his clothing was as white as snow. 4 The guards
shook with fear when they saw him, and they fell into a dead faint.

5 Then the angel spoke to the women. "Don't be afraid!" he said. "I know you are
looking for Jesus, who was crucified. 6 He isn't here! He has been raised from the dead,

27:63 Matt 12:40; 16:21; 17:23; 20:19; Mark 8:31; 9:31; 10:34; Luke 9:22; 18:33
27:64 Matt 28:13
27:66 Dan 6:17
28:3 Dan 7:9; 10:5-6
28:6 Matt 12:40; 16:21; 17:23; 20:19; Mark 8:31; 9:31; 10:34; Luke 9:22; 18:33; 24:7

27:62 Or *On the next day, which is after the Preparation.* **28:1** Greek *After the Sabbath, on the first day of the week.*

HOW JESUS' TRIAL WAS ILLEGAL

1. Even before the trial began, it had been determined that Jesus must die (John 11:50; Mark 14:1). There was no "innocent until proven guilty" approach.
2. False witnesses were sought to testify against Jesus (Matthew 26:59). Usually the religious leaders went through an elaborate system of screening witnesses to ensure justice.
3. No defense for Jesus was sought or allowed (Luke 22:67–71).
4. The trial was conducted at night (Mark 14:53–65; 15:1), which was illegal according to the religious leaders' own laws.
5. The high priest put Jesus under oath, but then incriminated him for what he said (Matthew 26:63–66).
6. Cases involving such serious charges were to be tried only in the high council's regular meeting place, not in the high priest's palace (Mark 14:53–65).

The religious leaders were not interested in giving Jesus a fair trial. In their minds, Jesus had to die. This blind obsession led them to pervert the justice they were appointed to protect. Above are many examples of the actions taken by the religious leaders that were illegal according to their own laws.

27:64 The religious leaders took Jesus' resurrection claims more seriously than the disciples did. The disciples didn't remember Jesus' teaching about his resurrection (20:17-19); but the religious leaders did. Because of his claims, they were almost as afraid of Jesus after his death as when he was alive. They tried to take every precaution that his body would remain in the tomb.

27:66 The Pharisees were so afraid of Jesus' predictions about his resurrection that they made sure the tomb was thoroughly sealed and guarded. Because the tomb was hewn out of rock in the side of a hill, there was only one entrance. The tomb was sealed by stringing a cord across the stone that was rolled over the entrance. The cord was sealed at each end with clay. But the religious leaders took a further precaution, asking that guards be placed at the tomb's entrance. With such precautions, the only way the tomb could be empty would be for Jesus to rise from the dead. The Pharisees failed to understand that no rock, seal, guard, or army could prevent the Son of God from rising again.

28:1 The other Mary was not Jesus' mother. She could have been the wife of Clopas (John 19:25). Or, she may have been Jesus' aunt, the mother of James and John (Matthew 27:56).

28:2 The stone was not rolled back so Jesus could get out, but so others could get in and see that Jesus had indeed risen from the dead, just as he had promised.

28:5-7 The angel who announced the good news of the Resurrection to the women gave them four messages: (1) *Don't be afraid.* The reality of the Resurrection brings joy, not fear. When you are afraid, remember the empty tomb. (2) *He isn't here.* Jesus is not dead and is not to be looked for among the dead. He is alive, with his people. (3) *Come, see.* The women could check the evidence themselves. The tomb was empty then, and it is empty today. The Resurrection is a historical fact. (4) *Go quickly and tell.* They were to spread the joy of the Resurrection. We, too, are to spread the great news about Jesus' resurrection.

28:6 Jesus' resurrection is the key to the Christian faith. Why? (1) Just as he promised, Jesus rose from the dead. We can be confident, therefore, that he will accomplish all he has promised. (2) Jesus' bodily resurrection shows us that the living Christ is ruler of God's eternal Kingdom, not a false prophet or impostor. (3) We can be certain of our resurrection because he was resurrected. Death is not the end—there is future life. (4) The power that brought Jesus back to life is available to us to bring our spiritually dead selves back to life. (5) The Resurrection is the basis for the church's witness to the world. Jesus is more than just a human leader; he is the Son of God.

just as he said would happen. Come, see where his body was lying. 7 And now, go quickly 28:7 Matt 26:32
and tell his disciples he has been raised from the dead, and he is going ahead of you to Mark 14:28; 16:7
Galilee. You will see him there. Remember, I have told you."

Jesus Appears to the Women (**241**)

8 The women ran quickly from the tomb. They were very frightened but also filled with
great joy, and they rushed to find the disciples to give them the angel's message. 9 And
as they went, Jesus met them. "Greetings!" he said. And they ran to him, held his feet, 28:10 John 20:17
and worshiped him. 10 Then Jesus said to them, "Don't be afraid! Go tell my brothers to Rom 8:29
leave for Galilee, and they will see me there." Heb 2:11-13, 17

Religious Leaders Bribe the Guards (**242**)

11 As the women were on their way into the city, some of the men who had been guarding
the tomb went to the leading priests and told them what had happened. 12 A meeting of 28:13
all the religious leaders was called, and they decided to bribe the soldiers. 13 They told Matt 27:64
the soldiers, "You must say, 'Jesus' disciples came during the night while we were
sleeping, and they stole his body.' 14 If the governor hears about it, we'll stand up for you
and everything will be all right." 15 So the guards accepted the bribe and said what they
were told to say. Their story spread widely among the Jews, and they still tell it today.

Jesus Gives the Great Commission (**248**/Mark 16:15-18)

16 Then the eleven disciples left for Galilee, going to the mountain where Jesus had told 28:18
them to go. 17 When they saw him, they worshiped him—but some of them still doubted! John 3:35; 13:3; 17:2
18 Jesus came and told his disciples, "I have been given complete authority in heaven Eph 1:20-22
and on earth. 19 Therefore, go and make disciples of all the nations, baptizing them in the Phil 2:9-10
name of the Father and the Son and the Holy Spirit. 20 Teach these new disciples to obey 28:19 Luke 24:47
all the commands I have given you. And be sure of this: I am with you always, even to Acts 1:8; 2:38
the end of the age."

28:10 By "brothers," Jesus probably meant his disciples. This showed that he had forgiven them, even after they had denied and deserted him. Their relationship would now be even stronger than before.

28:10 Jesus told the women to pass a message on to the disciples—that he would meet them in Galilee, as he had previously told them (Mark 14:28). But the disciples, afraid of the religious leaders, stayed hidden behind locked doors in Jerusalem (John 20:19). So Jesus met them first there (Luke 24:36) and then later in Galilee (John 21).

28:11-15 Jesus' resurrection was already causing a great stir in Jerusalem. A group of women was moving quickly through the streets, looking for the disciples to tell them the amazing news that Jesus was alive. At the same time, a group of religious leaders was plotting how to cover up the Resurrection.

Today there is still a great stir over the Resurrection, and there are still only two choices: to believe that Jesus rose from the dead, or to be closed to the truth—denying it, ignoring it, or trying to explain it away.

28:18 God gave Jesus authority over heaven and earth. On the basis of that authority, Jesus told his disciples to make more disciples as they preached, baptized, and taught. With this same authority, Jesus still commands us to tell others the Good News and make them disciples for the Kingdom.

28:18-20 When someone is dying or leaving us, his or her last words are very important. Jesus left the disciples with these last words of instruction: They were under his authority; they were to make more disciples; they were to baptize and teach these new disciples to obey Christ; Christ would be with them always. Whereas in previous missions Jesus had sent his disciples only to the Jews (10:5, 6), their mission from now on would be worldwide. Jesus is Lord of the earth, and he died for the sins of people from all nations.

We are to go—whether it is next door or to another country—and make disciples. It is not an option but a command to all who call Jesus "Lord." We are not all evangelists in the formal sense, but we have all received gifts that we can use to help fulfill the great commission. As we obey, we have comfort in the knowledge that Jesus is always with us.

28:19 Jesus' words affirm the reality of the Trinity. Some people accuse theologians of making up the concept of the Trinity and reading it into Scripture. As we see here, the concept comes directly from Jesus himself. He did not say baptize them in the *names,* but in the *name* of the Father, Son, and Holy Spirit. The word *Trinity* does not occur in Scripture, but it well describes the three-in-one nature of the Father, Son, and Holy Spirit.

28:19 The disciples were to baptize people because baptism unites believers with Jesus Christ in their death to sin and their resurrection to new life. Baptism symbolizes submission to Christ, a willingness to live God's way, and identification with God's covenant people.

28:20 How is Jesus "with us"? Jesus was with the disciples physically until he ascended into heaven and then spiritually through the Holy Spirit (Acts 1:4). The Holy Spirit would be Jesus' presence that would never leave them (John 14:26). Jesus continues to be with us today through his Spirit.

28:20 The Old Testament prophecies and genealogies in the book of Matthew present Jesus' credentials for being King of the world—not a military or political leader, as the disciples had originally hoped, but a spiritual King who can overcome all evil and rule in the heart of every person. If we refuse to serve the King faithfully, we are disloyal subjects, fit only to be banished from the Kingdom. We must make Jesus King of our life and worship him as our Savior, King, and Lord.

KEY PLACES IN MARK

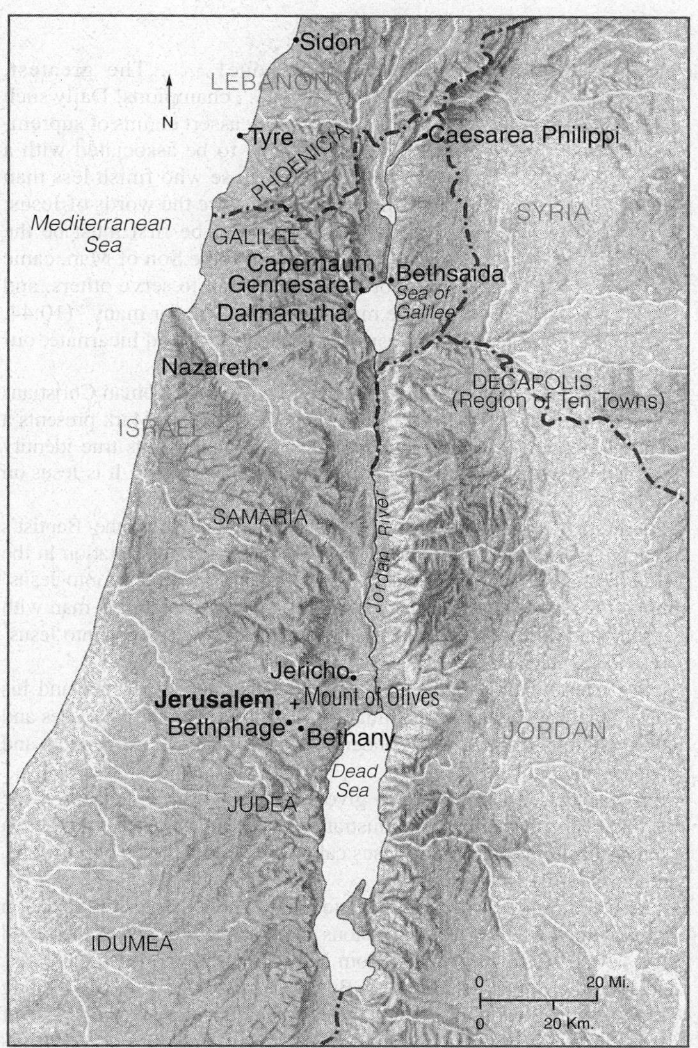

The broken lines (–··–··–) indicate modern boundaries.

Of the four Gospels, Mark's narrative is the most chronological—that is, most of the stories are positioned in the order they actually occurred. Though the shortest of the four, the Gospel of Mark contains the most events; it is action-packed. Most of this action centers in Galilee, where Jesus began his ministry. Capernaum served as his base of operation (1:21; 2:1; 9:33), from which he would go out to cities like Bethsaida, where he healed a blind man (8:22ff); Gennesaret, where he performed many healings (6:53ff); Tyre and Sidon (to the far north), where he healed many, drove out demons, and met the woman from Syrian Phoenicia (3:8; 7:24ff); and Caesarea Philippi, where Peter declared him to be the Messiah (8:27ff). After his ministry in Galilee and the surrounding regions, Jesus headed for Jerusalem (10:1). Before going there, Jesus told his disciples three times that he would be crucified there and then come back to life (8:31; 9:31; 10:33, 34).

MARK

Herod the Great begins to rule 37 B.C.	Jesus is born 6/5 B.C.	Escape to Egypt 5/4 B.C.	Herod the Great dies 4 B.C.	Return to Nazareth 4/3 B.C.	Jesus visits Temple as a boy A.D. 6/7

VITAL STATISTICS

PURPOSE:
To present the person, work, and teachings of Jesus

AUTHOR:
John Mark. He was not one of the 12 disciples, but he accompanied Paul on his first missionary journey (Acts 13:13).

TO WHOM WRITTEN:
The Christians in Rome, where he wrote the Gospel

DATE WRITTEN:
Between A.D. 55 and 65

SETTING:
The Roman Empire under Tiberius Caesar. The empire, with its common language and excellent transportation and communication systems, was ripe to hear Jesus' message, which spread quickly from nation to nation.

KEY VERSE:
"For even I, the Son of Man, came here not to be served but to serve others, and to give my life as a ransom for many" (10:45).

KEY PEOPLE:
Jesus, the 12 disciples, Pilate, the Jewish religious leaders

KEY PLACES:
Capernaum, Nazareth, Caesarea Philippi, Jericho, Bethany, Mount of Olives, Jerusalem, Golgotha

SPECIAL FEATURES:
Mark was probably the first Gospel written. The other Gospels quote all but 31 verses of Mark. Mark records more miracles than does any other Gospel.

WE'RE number one! . . . The greatest, strongest, prettiest . . . champions! Daily such proclamations boldly assert claims of supremacy. Everyone wants to be associated with a winner. Losers are those who finish less than first. In direct contrast are the words of Jesus: "And whoever wants to be first must be the slave of all. For even I, the Son of Man, came here not to be served but to serve others, and to give my life as a ransom for many" (10:44, 45). Jesus *is* the greatest—God incarnate, our Messiah—but he entered history as a servant.

This is the message of Mark. Written to encourage Roman Christians and to prove beyond a doubt that Jesus is the Messiah, Mark presents a rapid succession of vivid pictures of Jesus in action—his true identity revealed by what he does, not necessarily by what he says. It is Jesus on the move.

Omitting the birth of Jesus, Mark begins with John the Baptist's preaching. Then, moving quickly past Jesus' baptism, temptation in the wilderness, and call of the disciples, Mark takes us directly into Jesus' public ministry. We see Jesus confronting a demon, healing a man with leprosy, and forgiving and healing the paralyzed man lowered into Jesus' presence by friends.

Next, Jesus calls Matthew (Levi) and has dinner with him and his questionable associates. This initiates the conflict with the Pharisees and other religious leaders, who condemn Jesus for eating with sinners and breaking the Sabbath.

In chapter 4, Mark pauses to give a sample of Jesus' teaching—the parable of the farmer and the illustration of the mustard seed—and then plunges back into the action. Jesus calms the waves, drives out demons, and heals Jairus's daughter.

After returning to Nazareth for a few days and experiencing rejection in his hometown, Jesus commissions the disciples to spread the Good News everywhere. Opposition from Herod and the Pharisees increases, and John the Baptist is beheaded. But Jesus continues to move, feeding 5,000, reaching out to the woman from Syrian Phoenicia, healing the deaf man, and feeding 4,000.

Finally, it is time to reveal his true identity to the disciples. Do they really know who Jesus is? Peter proclaims him Messiah but then promptly shows that he does not understand Jesus' mission. After the Transfiguration, Jesus continues to teach and heal, confronting the Pharisees about divorce and the rich young man about eternal life. Blind Bartimaeus is healed.

Events move rapidly toward a climax. The Last Supper, the betrayal, the Crucifixion, and the Resurrection are dramatically portrayed, along with more examples of Jesus' teachings. Mark shows us Jesus—moving, serving, sacrificing, and saving! As you read Mark, be ready for action, be open for God's move in your life, and be challenged to move into your world to serve.

Tiberius Caesar becomes emperor 14	*John's ministry begins 26*	*Jesus begins his ministry 26/27*	*Jesus chooses twelve disciples 28*	*Jesus feeds 5,000 29*	*Jesus is crucified, rises again, and ascends 30*

THE BLUEPRINT

A. BIRTH AND PREPARATION OF JESUS, THE SERVANT (1:1–13)

Jesus did not arrive unannounced or unexpected. The Old Testament prophets had clearly predicted the coming of a great one, sent by God himself, who would offer salvation and eternal peace to Israel and the entire world. Then came John the Baptist, who announced that the long-awaited Messiah had finally come and would soon be among the people. In God's work in the world today, Jesus does not come unannounced or unexpected. Yet many still reject him. We have the witness of the Bible, but some choose to ignore it, just as many ignored John the Baptist in his day.

B. MESSAGE AND MINISTRY OF JESUS, THE SERVANT (1:14—13:37)
1. Jesus' ministry in Galilee
2. Jesus' ministry beyond Galilee
3. Jesus' ministry in Jerusalem

Jesus had all the power of almighty God: He raised the dead, gave sight to the blind, restored deformed bodies, and quieted stormy seas. But with all this power, Jesus came to mankind as a servant. We can use his life as a pattern for how to live today. As Jesus served God and others, so should we.

C. DEATH AND RESURRECTION OF JESUS, THE SERVANT (14:1—16:20)

Jesus came as a servant, so many did not recognize or acknowledge him as the Messiah. We must be careful that we also don't reject God or his will because he doesn't quite fit our image of what God should be.

MEGATHEMES

THEME	EXPLANATION	IMPORTANCE
Jesus Christ	Jesus Christ alone is the Son of God. In Mark, Jesus demonstrates his divinity by overcoming disease, demons, and death. Although he had the power to be king of the earth, Jesus chose to obey the Father and die for us.	When Jesus rose from the dead, he proved that he was God, that he could forgive sin, and that he has the power to change our lives. By trusting in him for forgiveness, we can begin a new life with him as our guide.
Servant	As the Messiah, Jesus fulfilled the prophecies of the Old Testament by coming to earth. He did not come as a conquering king; he came as a servant. He helped people by telling them about God and healing them. Even more, by giving his life as a sacrifice for sin, he performed the ultimate act of service.	Because of Jesus' example, we should be willing to serve God and others. Real greatness in Christ's kingdom is shown by service and sacrifice. Ambition or love of power or position should not be our motive; instead, we should do God's work because we love him.
Miracles	Mark records more of Jesus' miracles than sermons. Jesus is clearly a man of power and action, not just words. Jesus did miracles to convince the people who he was and to confirm to the disciples his true identity—God.	The more convinced we become that Jesus is God, the more we will see his power and his love. His mighty works show us he is able to save anyone regardless of his or her past. His miracles of forgiveness bring healing, wholeness, and changed lives to those who trust him.

Spreading the Gospel	Jesus directed his public ministry to the Jews first. When the Jewish leaders opposed him, Jesus also went to the non-Jewish world, healing and preaching. Roman soldiers, Syrians, and other Gentiles heard the Good News. Many believed and followed him. Jesus' final message to his disciples challenged them to go into all the world and preach the gospel of salvation.	Jesus crossed national, racial, and economic barriers to spread his Good News. Jesus' message of faith and forgiveness is for the whole world—not just our church, neighborhood, or nation. We must reach out beyond our own people and needs to fulfill the worldwide vision of Jesus Christ so that people everywhere may hear this great message and be saved from sin and death.

A. BIRTH AND PREPARATION OF JESUS, THE SERVANT (1:1-13)

Mark, the shortest of the four Gospels, opens with Jesus' baptism and temptation. Moving right into action, Mark quickly prepares us for Christ's ministry. The Gospel of Mark is concise, straightforward, and chronological.

John the Baptist Prepares the Way for Jesus (**16**/Matthew 3:1-12; Luke 3:1-18)

1 Here begins the Good News about Jesus the Messiah, the Son of God.*
[2]In the book of the prophet Isaiah, God said,

"Look, I am sending my messenger before you,
and he will prepare your way.*
3 He is a voice shouting in the wilderness:
'Prepare a pathway for the Lord's coming!
Make a straight road for him!'*"

1:1 Ps 2:7; Matt 1:1; John 1:34; 1 Jn 4:15
1:2-3 †Isa 40:3; †Mal 3:1; John 1:23

1:1 Some manuscripts do not include *the Son of God.* **1:2** Mal 3:1. **1:3** Isa 40:3.

1:1 When you experience the excitement of a big event, you naturally want to tell someone. Telling the story can bring back that original thrill as you relive the experience. Reading Mark's first words, you can sense his excitement. Picture yourself in the crowd as Jesus heals and teaches. Imagine yourself as one of the disciples. Respond to his words of love and encouragement. And remember that Jesus came for us who live today as well as for those who lived 2,000 years ago.

JESUS BEGINS HIS MINISTRY When Jesus came from his home in Nazareth to begin his ministry, he first took two steps in preparation—baptism by John in the Jordan River and temptation by Satan in the rough Judean wilderness. After the temptations, Jesus returned to Galilee and later set up his home base in Capernaum.

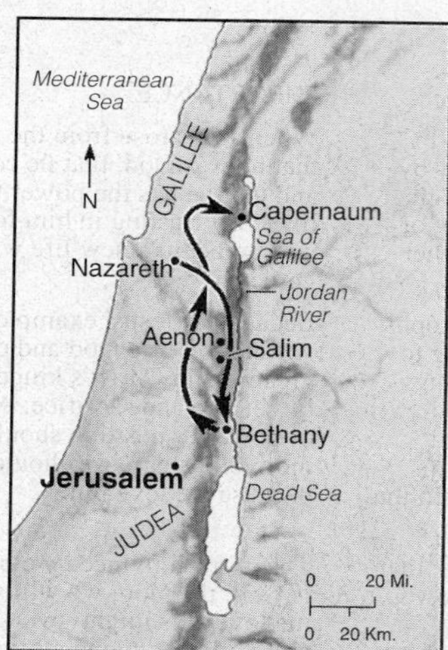

1:1 Mark was not one of the 12 disciples of Jesus, but he probably knew Jesus personally. Mark wrote his Gospel in the form of a fast-paced story, like a popular novel. The book portrays Jesus as a man who backed up his words with action that constantly proved who he is—the Son of God. Because Mark wrote his Gospel for Christians in Rome, where many gods were worshiped, he wanted his readers to know that Jesus is *the one true* Son of God.

1:2 Jesus came at a time in history when the entire civilized world was relatively peaceful under Roman rule, travel was easy, and there was a common language. The news about Jesus' life, death, and resurrection could spread quickly throughout the vast Roman Empire.

In Israel, common men and women were ready for Jesus, too. There had been no God-sent prophets for 400 years, since the days of Malachi (who wrote the last book of the Old Testament). There was growing anticipation that a great prophet, or the Messiah mentioned in the Old Testament, would soon come (see Luke 3:15).

1:2, 3 Isaiah was one of the greatest prophets of the Old Testament. The second half of the book of Isaiah is devoted to the promise of salvation. Isaiah wrote about the coming of the Messiah, Jesus Christ, and the man who would announce his coming, John the Baptist. John's call to "make a straight road for him" meant that people should give up their selfish way of living, renounce their sins, seek God's forgiveness, and establish a relationship with the almighty God by believing and obeying his words as found in Scripture (Isaiah 1:18-20; 57:15).

1:2, 3 Mark 1:2, 3 is a composite quotation, taken first from Malachi 3:1 and then from Isaiah 40:3.

1:2, 3 Hundreds of years earlier, the prophet Isaiah had predicted that John the Baptist and Jesus would come. How did he know? God promised Isaiah that a Redeemer would come to Israel and that a messenger calling in the wilderness would prepare the way for him. Isaiah's words comforted many people as they looked forward to the Messiah, and knowing that God keeps his promises can comfort you, too. As you read the book of Mark, realize that it is more than just a story; it is part of God's Word. In it God is revealing to you his plans for human history.

1:4 Acts 13:24; 19:4
1:6 Lev 11:22; 2 Kgs 1:8; Zech 13:4
1:7 Acts 13:25
1:8 Joel 2:28; Acts 2:4; 10:45; 11:16

4 This messenger was John the Baptist. He lived in the wilderness and was preaching
that people should be baptized to show that they had turned from their sins and turned
to God to be forgiven.* 5 People from Jerusalem and from all over Judea traveled out
into the wilderness to see and hear John. And when they confessed their sins, he
baptized them in the Jordan River. 6 His clothes were woven from camel hair, and he
wore a leather belt; his food was locusts and wild honey. 7 He announced: "Someone is
coming soon who is far greater than I am—so much greater that I am not even worthy
to be his slave.* 8 I baptize you with* water, but he will baptize you with the Holy
Spirit!"

The Baptism of Jesus (**17**/Matthew 3:13-17; Luke 3:21-22)

1:11 Gen 22:2; Ps 2:7; Isa 42:1; Matt 12:18; 17:5; Mark 9:7; Luke 9:35; 2 Pet 1:17

9 One day Jesus came from Nazareth in Galilee, and he was baptized by John in the
Jordan River. 10 And when Jesus came up out of the water, he saw the heavens split
open and the Holy Spirit descending like a dove on him. 11 And a voice came from
heaven saying, "You are my beloved Son, and I am fully pleased with you."

1:4 Greek *preaching a baptism of repentance for the forgiveness of sins.* **1:7** Greek *to stoop down and untie his sandals.* **1:8** Or *in.*

1:4 Why does the Gospel of Mark begin with the story of John the Baptist and not mention the story of Jesus' birth? Important Roman officials of this day were always preceded by an announcer or herald. When the herald arrived in town, the people knew that someone of prominence would soon arrive. Because Mark's audience was primarily Roman Christians, he began his book with John the Baptist, whose mission it was to announce the coming of Jesus, the most important man who ever lived. Roman Christians would have been less interested in Jesus' birth than in this messenger who prepared the way.

1:4 John chose to live in the wilderness (1) to get away from distractions so he could hear God's instructions; (2) to capture the undivided attention of the people; (3) to symbolize a sharp break with the hypocrisy of the religious leaders who preferred their luxurious homes and positions of authority over doing God's work; (4) to fulfill Old Testament prophecies that said John would be the voice of someone shouting, "Make a highway for the LORD through the wilderness. Make a straight, smooth road through the desert for our God" (Isaiah 40:3).

1:4 In John's ministry, baptism was a visible sign that a person had decided to change his or her life, giving up a sinful and selfish way of living and turning to God. John took a known custom and gave it new meaning. The Jews often baptized non-Jews who had converted to Judaism. But to baptize a Jew as a sign of repentance was a radical departure from Jewish custom. The early church took baptism a step further, associating it with Jesus' death and resurrection (see, for example, Romans 6:3, 4; 1 Peter 3:21).

1:5 The purpose of John's preaching was to prepare people to accept Jesus as God's Son. When John challenged the people to confess sin individually, he signaled the start of a new way to relate to God.

Is change needed in your life before you can hear and understand Jesus' message? You have to admit that you need forgiveness before you can accept it. To prepare to receive Christ, repent. Denounce the world's dead-end attractions, sinful temptations, and harmful attitudes.

1:6 John's clothes were not the latest style of his day. He dressed much like the prophet Elijah (2 Kings 1:8) in order to distinguish himself from the religious leaders, whose flowing robes reflected their great pride in their position (12:38). John's striking appearance reinforced his striking message.

1:7, 8 Although John was the first genuine prophet in 400 years, Jesus the Messiah would be infinitely greater than he. John was pointing out how insignificant he was compared to the one who was coming. John was not even worthy of being his slave. What John began, Jesus finished. What John prepared, Jesus fulfilled.

1:8 John said Jesus would baptize them with the Holy Spirit, sending the Holy Spirit to live within each believer. John's baptism with water prepared a person to receive Christ's message. This baptism demonstrated repentance, humility, and willingness to turn from sin. This was the *beginning* of the spiritual process.

When Jesus baptizes with the Holy Spirit, however, the entire person is transformed by the Spirit's power. Jesus offers to us both forgiveness of sin and the power to live for him.

1:9 If John's baptism was for repentance from sin, why was Jesus baptized? While even the greatest prophets (Isaiah, Jeremiah, Ezekiel) had to confess their sinfulness and need for repentance, Jesus didn't need to admit sin—he was sinless. Although Jesus didn't need forgiveness, he was baptized for the following reasons: (1) to begin his mission to bring the message of salvation to all people; (2) to show support for John's ministry; (3) to identify with our humanness and sin; (4) to give us an example to follow. We know that John's baptism was different from Christian baptism in the church because Paul had John's followers baptized again (see Acts 19:2-5).

1:9 Jesus grew up in Nazareth, where he had lived since he was a young boy (Matthew 2:22, 23). Nazareth was a small town in Galilee, located about halfway between the Sea of Galilee and the Mediterranean Sea. The city was despised and avoided by many Jews because it had a reputation for independence. Nazareth was a crossroads for trade routes and had contact with other cultures. (See also John 1:46.)

1:10, 11 The Spirit descended like a dove on Jesus, and the voice from heaven proclaimed the Father's approval of Jesus as his divine Son. The fact that Jesus is God's divine Son informs everything that we read about Jesus in the Gospels. Here we see all three members of the Trinity together—God the Father, God the Son, and God the Holy Spirit.

Satan Tempts Jesus in the Wilderness (**18**/Matthew 4:1-11; Luke 4:1-13)
12 Immediately the Holy Spirit compelled Jesus to go into the wilderness. 13 He was there
for forty days, being tempted by Satan. He was out among the wild animals, and angels
took care of him.

B. MESSAGE AND MINISTRY OF JESUS, THE SERVANT (1:14—13:37)

Mark tells us dramatic, action-packed stories. He gives us the most vivid account of Christ's activities. He features facts and actions, rather than teachings. The way Jesus lived his life is the perfect example of how we should live our lives today.

1. Jesus' ministry in Galilee

Jesus Preaches in Galilee (**30**/Matthew 4:12-17; Luke 4:14-15; John 4:43-45)
14 Later on, after John was arrested by Herod Antipas, Jesus went to Galilee to preach **1:14** Mark 6:17-18
God's Good News. 15 "At last the time has come!" he announced. "The Kingdom of God **1:15** Gal 4:4
is near! Turn from your sins and believe this Good News!" Eph 1:10

Four Fishermen Follow Jesus (**33**/Matthew 4:18-22)
16 One day as Jesus was walking along the shores of the Sea of Galilee, he saw Simon*
and his brother, Andrew, fishing with a net, for they were commercial fishermen. 17 Jesus
called out to them, "Come, be my disciples, and I will show you how to fish for people!"
18 And they left their nets at once and went with him.
19 A little farther up the shore Jesus saw Zebedee's sons, James and John, in a boat **1:19** Matt 10:2
mending their nets. 20 He called them, too, and immediately they left their father, Mark 3:17; 10:35
Zebedee, in the boat with the hired men and went with him. Luke 5:10

Jesus Teaches with Authority (**34**/Luke 4:31-37)
21 Jesus and his companions went to the town of Capernaum, and every Sabbath day
he went into the synagogue and taught the people. 22 They were amazed at his **1:22**
teaching, for he taught as one who had real authority—quite unlike the teachers of Matt 7:28-29
religious law.

1:16 *Simon* is called *Peter* in 3:16 and thereafter.

1:12, 13 Jesus left the crowds and went into the wilderness, where he was tempted by Satan. Temptation is bad for us only when we give in. We should not hate or resent times of inner testing, because through them God can strengthen our character and teach us valuable lessons. When you face Satan and must deal with his temptations and the turmoil he brings, remember Jesus. He used God's Word against Satan and won. You can do the same.

1:12, 13 Satan is an angel who rebelled against God. He is real, not symbolic, and is constantly working against God and those who obey him. Satan tempted Eve in the garden and persuaded her to sin; he tempted Jesus in the wilderness and did not persuade him to fall. To be tempted is not a sin. Tempting others or giving in to temptation *is* sin. For a more detailed account of Jesus' temptation, read Matthew 4:1-11.

1:12, 13 To identify fully with human beings, Jesus had to endure Satan's temptations. Although Jesus is God, he is also man. And as fully human, he was not exempt from Satan's attacks. Because Jesus faced temptations and overcame them, he can assist us in two important ways: (1) as an example of how to face temptation without sinning, and (2) as a helper who knows just what we need because he went through the same experience. (See Hebrews 4:15 for more on Jesus and temptation.)

1:14, 15 What is God's Good News? These first words spoken by Jesus in Mark gave the core of his teaching: that the long-awaited Messiah had come to break the power of sin and begin God's personal reign on earth. Most of the people who heard this message were oppressed, poor, and without hope. Jesus' words were good news because they offered freedom, justice, and hope.

1:16 Fishing was a major industry around the Sea of Galilee. Fishing with nets was the most common method. Capernaum, the largest of the more than 30 fishing towns around the lake at that time, became Jesus' new home (Matthew 4:12, 13).

1:16-20 We often assume that Jesus' disciples were great men of faith from the first time they met Jesus. But they had to grow in their faith just as all believers do (14:48-50, 66-72; John 14:1-9; 20:26-29). This is apparently not the only time Jesus called Peter (Simon), James, and John to follow him (see Luke 5:1-11 and John 1:35-42 for two other times). Although it took time for Jesus' call and his message to get through, the disciples *followed.* In the same way, we may question and falter, but we must never stop following Jesus.

1:21 Because the Temple in Jerusalem was too far for many Jews to travel to regularly for worship, many towns had synagogues serving both as places of worship and as schools. Beginning in the days of Ezra, about 450 B.C., a group of 10 Jewish families could start a synagogue. There, during the week, Jewish boys were taught the Old Testament law and Jewish religion. Girls could not attend. Each Saturday, the Sabbath, the Jewish men would gather to listen to a rabbi teach from the Scriptures. Because there was no permanent rabbi or teacher, it was customary for the synagogue leader to ask visiting teachers to speak. This is why Jesus often spoke in the synagogues in the towns he visited.

1:21 Jesus had recently moved to Capernaum from Nazareth (Matthew 4:12, 13). Capernaum was a thriving town with great wealth as well as great sin and decadence. Because it was the headquarters for many Roman troops, pagan influences from all over the Roman Empire were pervasive. This was an ideal place for Jesus to challenge both Jews and non-Jews with the Good News of God's Kingdom.

1:24 23 A man possessed by an evil spirit was in the synagogue, 24 and he began shouting,
Matt 8:29 "Why are you bothering us, Jesus of Nazareth? Have you come to destroy us? I know
John 6:69 who you are—the Holy One sent from God!"
1:26 25 Jesus cut him short. "Be silent! Come out of the man." 26 At that, the evil spirit
Mark 9:20 screamed and threw the man into a convulsion, but then he left him.
27 Amazement gripped the audience, and they began to discuss what had happened.
1:28 "What sort of new teaching is this?" they asked excitedly. "It has such authority! Even
Mark 9:26 evil spirits obey his orders!" 28 The news of what he had done spread quickly through
that entire area of Galilee.

Jesus Heals Peter's Mother-in-Law and Many Others (**35**/Matthew 8:14-17; Luke 4:38-41)

29 After Jesus and his disciples left the synagogue, they went over to Simon and Andrew's
home, and James and John were with them. 30 Simon's mother-in-law was sick in bed
with a high fever. They told Jesus about her right away. 31 He went to her bedside, and
as he took her by the hand and helped her to sit up, the fever suddenly left, and she got
up and prepared a meal for them.
32 That evening at sunset, many sick and demon-possessed people were brought to
1:34 Jesus. 33 And a huge crowd of people from all over Capernaum gathered outside the
Mark 3:12 door to watch. 34 So Jesus healed great numbers of sick people who had many different
kinds of diseases, and he ordered many demons to come out of their victims. But
because they knew who he was, he refused to allow the demons to speak.

Jesus Preaches throughout Galilee (**36**/Matthew 4:23-25; Luke 4:42-44)

35 The next morning Jesus awoke long before daybreak and went out alone into the
wilderness to pray. 36 Later Simon and the others went out to find him. 37 They said,
1:38 "Everyone is asking for you."
Isa 61:1 38 But he replied, "We must go on to other towns as well, and I will preach to them,
1:39 Matt 4:23; 9:35 too, because that is why I came." 39 So he traveled throughout the region of Galilee,
preaching in the synagogues and expelling demons from many people.

1:22 The Jewish teachers often quoted from well-known rabbis to give their words more authority. But Jesus didn't have that need. Because Jesus is God, he knew exactly what the Scriptures said and meant. He was the ultimate authority.

1:23 Evil spirits, or demons, are ruled by Satan. They work to tempt people to sin. They were not created by Satan—because God is the Creator of all. Rather they are fallen angels who joined Satan in his rebellion. Though not all disease comes from Satan, demons can cause a person to become mute, deaf, blind, or insane. But in every case where demons confronted Jesus, they lost their power. Thus, God limits what evil spirits can do; they can do nothing without his permission. During Jesus' life on earth, demons were allowed to be very active to demonstrate once and for all Christ's power and authority over them.

1:23ff Many psychologists dismiss all accounts of demon possession as a primitive way to describe mental illness. Although throughout history mental illness has often been wrongly diagnosed as demon possession, clearly a hostile outside force controlled the man described here. Mark emphasized Jesus' conflict with evil powers to show his superiority over them, so he recorded many stories about Jesus driving out evil spirits. Jesus didn't have to conduct an elaborate exorcism ritual. His word was enough to send out the demons.

1:23, 24 The evil spirit knew at once that Jesus was the Holy One sent from God. By including this event in his Gospel, Mark was establishing Jesus' credentials, showing that even the spiritual underworld recognized Jesus as the Messiah.

1:29-31 Each Gospel writer had a slightly different perspective as he wrote; thus, the comparable stories in the Gospels often highlight different details. In Matthew, Jesus touched the woman's hand. In Mark, he helped her up. In Luke, he spoke to the fever, and it left her. The accounts do not conflict. Each writer chose to emphasize different details of the story in order to emphasize a certain characteristic of Jesus.

1:32, 33 The people came to Jesus in the evening after sunset. This was the Sabbath (1:21), their day of rest, lasting from sunset Friday to sunset Saturday. The Jewish leaders had proclaimed that it was against the law to be healed on the Sabbath (Matthew 12:10; Luke 13:14). The people didn't want to break this law or the Jewish law that prohibited traveling on the Sabbath, so they waited until sunset. After the sun went down, the crowds were free to find Jesus so he could heal them.

1:34 Why didn't Jesus want the demons to reveal who he was? (1) By commanding the demons to remain silent, Jesus proved his authority and power over them. (2) Jesus wanted the people to believe he was the Messiah because of what he said and did, not because of the demons' words. (3) Jesus wanted to reveal his identity as the Messiah according to his timetable, not according to Satan's timetable. Satan wanted the people to follow Jesus around for what they could get out of him, not because he was the Son of God who could truly set them free from sin's guilt and power.

1:35 Jesus took time to pray. Finding time to pray is not easy, but prayer is the vital link between us and God. Like Jesus, we must break away from others to talk with God, even if we have to get up very early in the morning to do it!

1:39 The Romans divided the land of Israel into three separate regions: Galilee, Samaria, and Judea. Galilee was the northernmost region, an area about 60 miles long and 30 miles wide. Jesus did much of his ministry in this area, an ideal place for him to teach because there were over 250 towns concentrated there, with many synagogues.

Jesus Heals a Man with Leprosy (**38**/Matthew 8:1-4; Luke 5:12-16)

40 A man with leprosy came and knelt in front of Jesus, begging to be healed. "If you
want to, you can make me well again," he said.
41 Moved with pity,* Jesus touched him. "I want to," he said. "Be healed!" 42 Instantly
the leprosy disappeared—the man was healed. 43 Then Jesus sent him on his way and
told him sternly, 44 "Go right over to the priest and let him examine you. Don't talk to — 1:44 Lev 14:1-32
anyone along the way. Take along the offering required in the law of Moses for those
who have been healed of leprosy, so everyone will have proof of your healing."
45 But as the man went on his way, he spread the news, telling everyone what had
happened to him. As a result, such crowds soon surrounded Jesus that he couldn't enter
a town anywhere publicly. He had to stay out in the secluded places, and people from
everywhere came to him there.

Jesus Heals a Paralyzed Man (**39**/Matthew 9:1-8; Luke 5:17-26)

2 Several days later Jesus returned to Capernaum, and the news of his arrival spread
quickly through the town. 2 Soon the house where he was staying was so packed with — 2:2 Eph 2:17
visitors that there wasn't room for one more person, not even outside the door. And he — Heb 2:3
preached the word to them. 3 Four men arrived carrying a paralyzed man on a mat. 4 They
couldn't get to Jesus through the crowd, so they dug through the clay roof above his head.
Then they lowered the sick man on his mat, right down in front of Jesus. 5 Seeing their — 2:5 Luke 7:48
faith, Jesus said to the paralyzed man, "My son, your sins are forgiven."
6 But some of the teachers of religious law who were sitting there said to themselves, — 2:7 Ps 130:3-4
7 "What? This is blasphemy! Who but God can forgive sins!" — Isa 43:25
8 Jesus knew what they were discussing among themselves, so he said to them, "Why — 2:8 Matt 16:8
do you think this is blasphemy? 9 Is it easier to say to the paralyzed man, 'Your sins are
forgiven' or 'Get up, pick up your mat, and walk'? 10 I will prove that I, the Son of Man,
have the authority on earth to forgive sins." Then Jesus turned to the paralyzed man and
said, 11 "Stand up, take your mat, and go on home, because you are healed!"
12 The man jumped up, took the mat, and pushed his way through the stunned — 2:12 Matt 9:33
onlookers. Then they all praised God. "We've never seen anything like this before!" they
exclaimed.

1:41 Some manuscripts read *Moved with anger.*

1:40, 41 In keeping with the law in Leviticus 13 and 14, Jewish leaders declared people with leprosy unclean. This meant that lepers were unfit to participate in any religious or social activity. Because the law said that contact with any unclean person made a person unclean, too, some people even threw rocks at lepers to keep them at a safe distance. Even the mention of the name of this disabling disease terrified people. But Jesus touched this man who had leprosy.

The real value of a person is inside, not outside. Although a person's body may be diseased or deformed, the person inside is no less valuable to God. No person is too disgusting for God's touch. In a sense, we are all people with leprosy because we have all been deformed by the ugliness of sin. By sending his Son, Jesus, God has touched us, giving us the opportunity to be healed. When you feel repulsed by someone, stop and remember how God feels about that person—and about you.

1:43, 44 Although leprosy was incurable, many different types of skin diseases were classified together as "leprosy." According to the Old Testament laws about leprosy (Leviticus 13–14), when a leper was cured, he or she had to go to a priest to be examined. Then the leper was to give a thank offering at the Temple. Jesus adhered to these laws by sending the man to the priest, demonstrating Jesus' complete regard for God's law. Sending a healed leper to a priest was also a way to verify Jesus' great miracle to the community.

2:3 The paralyzed man's need moved his friends to action, and they brought him to Jesus. When you recognize someone's need, do you act? Many people have physical and spiritual needs you can meet, either by yourself or with others who are also concerned. Human need moved these four men; let it also move you to compassionate action.

2:4 Houses in Bible times were built of stone. They had flat roofs made of mud mixed with straw. Outside stairways led to the roofs. These friends may have carried the paralyzed man up the outside stairs to the roof. They then could easily have taken apart the mud and straw mixture to make a hole through which to lower their friend to Jesus.

2:5-7 Before saying to the paralyzed man, "Get up," Jesus said, "Your sins are forgiven." To the Jewish leaders this statement was blasphemous, claiming to do something only God could do. According to the law, the punishment for this sin was death (Leviticus 24:15, 16).

The religious leaders understood correctly that Jesus was claiming divine prerogatives, but their judgment of him was wrong. Jesus was not blaspheming because his claim was true. Jesus is God, and he proved his claim by healing the paralyzed man (2:9-12).

2:10 This is the first time in Mark that Jesus is referred to as the "Son of Man." The title *Son of Man* emphasizes that Jesus is fully human, while *Son of God* (see, for example, John 20:31) emphasizes that he is fully God. As God's Son, Jesus has the authority to forgive sin. As a man, he can identify with our deepest needs and sufferings and help us overcome sin (see the note on 8:29-31).

Jesus Eats with Sinners at Matthew's House (**40**/Matthew 9:9-13; Luke 5:27-32)

[13]Then Jesus went out to the lakeshore again and taught the crowds that gathered around
2:14 John 1:43 him. [14]As he walked along, he saw Levi son of Alphaeus sitting at his tax-collection
booth. "Come, be my disciple," Jesus said to him. So Levi got up and followed him.
[15]That night Levi invited Jesus and his disciples to be his dinner guests, along with
his fellow tax collectors and many other notorious sinners. (There were many people of
this kind among the crowds that followed Jesus.) [16]But when some of the teachers of

PROMINENT JEWISH RELIGIOUS AND POLITICAL GROUPS

Name and Selected References	*Description*	*Agreement with Jesus*	*Disagreement with Jesus*
PHARISEES Matthew 5:20 Matthew 23:1–36 Luke 6:2 Luke 7:36–47	Strict group of religious Jews who advocated obedience to the most minute portions of the Jewish law and traditions. Very influential in the synagogues.	Respect for the law, belief in the resurrection of the dead, committed to obeying God's will.	Rejected Jesus' claim to be Messiah because he did not follow all their traditions and associated with notoriously wicked people.
SADDUCEES Matthew 3:7 Matthew 16:11, 12 Mark 12:18	Wealthy, upper class, Jewish priestly party. Rejected the authority of the Bible beyond the five books of Moses. Profited from business in the Temple. They, along with the Pharisees, were one of the two major parties of the Jewish high council.	Showed great respect for the five books of Moses, as well as the sanctity of the Temple.	Denied the resurrection of the dead. Thought the Temple could also be used as a place to transact business.
TEACHERS OF RELIGIOUS LAW Matthew 7:29 Mark 2:6 Mark 2:16	Professional interpreters of the law—who especially emphasized the traditions. Many teachers of religious law were Pharisees.	Respect for the law. Committed to obeying God.	Denied Jesus' authority to reinterpret the law. Rejected Jesus as Messiah because he did not obey all of their traditions.
SUPPORTERS OF HEROD Matthew 22:16 Mark 3:6 Mark 12:13	A Jewish political party of King Herod's supporters.	Unknown. In the Gospels they tried to trap Jesus with questions and plotted to kill him.	Afraid of Jesus causing political instability. They saw Jesus as a threat to their political future at a time when they were trying to regain from Rome some of their lost political power.
ZEALOTS Luke 6:15 Acts 1:14	A fiercely dedicated group of Jewish patriots determined to end Roman rule in Israel.	Concerned about the future of Israel. Believed in the Messiah but did not recognize Jesus as the one sent by God.	Believed that the Messiah must be a political leader who would deliver Israel from Roman occupation.
ESSENES none	Jewish monastic group practicing ritual purity and personal holiness.	Emphasized justice, honesty, commitment.	Believed ceremonial rituals made them righteous.

2:14 Levi is another name for Matthew, the disciple who wrote the Gospel of Matthew. See Matthew's Profile in Matthew 9 for more information.

2:14 Capernaum (2:1) was a key military center for Roman troops as well as a thriving business community. Several major highways intersected in Capernaum, with merchants passing through from as far away as Egypt to the south and Mesopotamia to the north.

Levi (Matthew), a Jew, was appointed by the Romans to be the area's tax collector. He collected taxes from citizens as well as from merchants passing through town. Tax collectors were expected to take a commission on the taxes they collected. Most of them overcharged and vastly enriched themselves. Tax collectors were despised by the Jews because of their reputation for cheating and their support of Rome. The Jews must also have hated to think that some of the money collected went to support pagan religions and temples.

2:14, 15 The day that Levi met Jesus, Levi held a meeting at his house to introduce others to Jesus. Levi didn't waste any time starting to witness! Some people feel that new believers should wait for maturity or training before they begin to tell others about Christ. But, like Levi, new believers can share their faith right away with whatever knowledge, skill, or experience they already have.

2:16, 17 The self-righteous Pharisees were indignant that Jesus would eat a meal with such sinners. But Jesus gladly associated with sinners because he loved them and because he knew that they needed to hear what he had to say. Jesus spent time with whoever needed or wanted to hear his message—poor, rich, bad, good. We, too, must befriend those who need Christ, even if they do not seem to be ideal companions. Are there people you have been neglecting because of their reputation? They may be the ones who most need to see and hear the message of Christ's love in and from you.

religious law who were Pharisees* saw him eating with people like that, they said to his
disciples, "Why does he eat with such scum*?"
17 When Jesus heard this, he told them, "Healthy people don't need a doctor—sick 2:17 Luke 19:10
people do. I have come to call sinners, not those who think they are already good enough." 1 Tim 1:15

Religious Leaders Ask Jesus about Fasting (**41**/Matthew 9:14-17; Luke 5:33-39)

18 John's disciples and the Pharisees sometimes fasted. One day some people came to Jesus
and asked, "Why do John's disciples and the Pharisees fast, but your disciples don't fast?"
19 Jesus replied, "Do wedding guests fast while celebrating with the groom? Of course 2:19
not. They can't fast while they are with the groom. 20 But someday he will be taken away John 3:29
from them, and then they will fast. 21 And who would patch an old garment with Rev 19:7
unshrunk cloth? For the new patch shrinks and pulls away from the old cloth, leaving an 2:20 Luke 17:22
even bigger hole than before. 22 And no one puts new wine into old wineskins. The wine 2:22 Gal 3:1-3
would burst the wineskins, spilling the wine and ruining the skins. New wine needs new
wineskins."

The Disciples Pick Wheat on the Sabbath (**45**/Matthew 12:1-8; Luke 6:1-5)

23 One Sabbath day as Jesus was walking through some grainfields, his disciples began 2:23
breaking off heads of wheat. 24 But the Pharisees said to Jesus, "They shouldn't be doing Deut 23:25
that! It's against the law to work by harvesting grain on the Sabbath."
25 But Jesus replied, "Haven't you ever read in the Scriptures what King David did 2:25-26 1 Sam 21:1-7
when he and his companions were hungry? 26 He went into the house of God (during the
days when Abiathar was high priest), ate the special bread reserved for the priests alone, 2:27
and then gave some to his companions. That was breaking the law, too." 27 Then he said Exod 23:12 Deut 5:14
to them, "The Sabbath was made to benefit people, and not people to benefit the Sabbath. John 7:21-24
28 And I, the Son of Man, am master even of the Sabbath!"

2:16a Greek *the scribes of the Pharisees.* **2:16b** Greek *with tax collectors and sinners.*

2:18ff John had two goals: to lead people to repent of their sin, and to prepare them for Christ's coming. John's message was sobering, so he and his followers fasted. Fasting is both an outward sign of humility and regret for sin, and an inner discipline that clears the mind and keeps the spirit alert. Fasting empties the body of food; repentance empties the life of sin. Jesus' disciples did not need to fast to prepare for his coming because he was with them. Jesus did not condemn fasting, however. He himself fasted for 40 days (Matthew 4:2). Nevertheless, Jesus emphasized fasting with the right motives. The Pharisees fasted twice a week to show others how holy they were. Jesus explained that if people fast only to impress others, they will be twisting the purpose of fasting.

2:19 Jesus compared himself to a groom. In the Bible, the image of a bride is often used for God's people, and the image of a groom for the God who loves them (Isaiah 62:5; Matthew 25:1-13; Revelation 21:2).

2:22 A wineskin was a goatskin sewed together at the edges to form a watertight bag. New wine, expanding as it aged, stretched the wineskin. New wine, therefore, could not be put into a wineskin that had already been stretched, or the taut skin would burst.

The Pharisees had become rigid like old wineskins. They could not accept faith in Jesus that would not be contained or limited by man-made ideas or rules. Your heart, like a wineskin, can become rigid and prevent you from accepting the new life that Christ offers. Keep your heart pliable and open to accepting the life-changing truths of Christ.

2:23 Jesus and his disciples were not stealing when they picked the grain. Leviticus 19:9, 10 and Deuteronomy 23:25 say that farmers were to leave the edges of their fields unharvested so that some of their crops could be picked by travelers and by the poor. Just as walking on a sidewalk is not trespassing on private property, picking heads of grain at the edge of a field was not stealing.

2:24 God's law said that crops should not be harvested on the Sabbath (Exodus 34:21). This law prevented farmers from becoming greedy and ignoring God on the Sabbath. It also protected laborers from being overworked.

The Pharisees interpreted the action of Jesus and his disciples—picking the grain and eating it as they walked through the fields—as harvesting; and so they judged Jesus a lawbreaker. But Jesus and the disciples clearly were not harvesting the grain for personal gain; they were simply looking for something to eat. The Pharisees were so focused on the words of the rule that they missed its intent.

2:24 Many of the Pharisees were so caught up in their man-made laws and traditions that they lost sight of what was good and right. Jesus implied in Mark 3:4 that the Sabbath is a day to do good. God provided the Sabbath as a day of rest and worship, but he didn't mean that concern for rest should keep us from lifting a finger to help others. Don't allow your Sabbath to become a time of selfish indulgence.

2:25-28 Jesus used the example of David to point out how ridiculous the Pharisees' accusations were (this incident occurred in 1 Samuel 21:1-6). God created the Sabbath for our benefit, not his own. God derives no benefit from having us rest on the Sabbath, but we are restored both physically and spiritually when we take time to rest and to focus on God. For the Pharisees, Sabbath laws had become more important than Sabbath rest. Both David and Jesus understood that the intent of God's law is to promote love for God and others. When we apply a law to other people, we should make sure that we understand its purpose and intent so we don't make harmful or inappropriate judgments.

2:26 The "special bread reserved for the priests" was the bread set before God in the Tabernacle. Every Sabbath, 12 baked loaves of bread were placed on the table in the Holy Place. Then the priests ate the old ones. See Exodus 25:30 and Leviticus 24:5-9 for more about the Bread of the Presence.

Jesus Heals a Man's Hand on the Sabbath (**46**/Matthew 12:9-14; Luke 6:6-11)

3 Jesus went into the synagogue again and noticed a man with a deformed hand.
2 Since it was the Sabbath, Jesus' enemies watched him closely. Would he heal the
man's hand on the Sabbath? If he did, they planned to condemn him. 3 Jesus said to the
man, "Come and stand in front of everyone." 4 Then he turned to his critics and asked,
"Is it legal to do good deeds on the Sabbath, or is it a day for doing harm? Is this a day
3:5 Mark 6:52; 8:17 to save life or to destroy it?" But they wouldn't answer him. 5 He looked around at them
angrily, because he was deeply disturbed by their hard hearts. Then he said to the man,
"Reach out your hand." The man reached out his hand, and it became normal again! 6 At
3:6 Matt 22:15-16; Mark 12:13 once the Pharisees went away and met with the supporters of Herod to discuss plans for
killing Jesus.

Large Crowds Follow Jesus (**47**/Matthew 12:15-21)

3:7-8 Matt 4:25 7 Jesus and his disciples went out to the lake, followed by a huge crowd from all over
Galilee, Judea, 8 Jerusalem, Idumea, from east of the Jordan River, and even from as far
away as Tyre and Sidon. The news about his miracles had spread far and wide, and vast
numbers of people came to see him for themselves.
3:10 Mark 4:1 9 Jesus instructed his disciples to bring around a boat and to have it ready in case he was
crowded off the beach. 10 There had been many healings that day. As a result, many sick
3:11-12 Mark 1:24-25, 34; Luke 4:41; Acts 16:16-17 people were crowding around him, trying to touch him. 11 And whenever those possessed
by evil spirits caught sight of him, they would fall down in front of him shrieking, "You
are the Son of God!" 12 But Jesus strictly warned them not to say who he was.

Jesus Chooses the Twelve Disciples (**48**/Luke 6:12-16)

3:14 Mark 6:30 13 Afterward Jesus went up on a mountain and called the ones he wanted to go with him.
And they came to him. 14 Then he selected twelve of them to be his regular companions,

---

3:2 Already the Pharisees had turned against Jesus. They were jealous of his popularity, his miracles, and the authority in his teaching and actions. They valued their status in the community and their opportunity for personal gain so much that they lost sight of their goal as religious leaders—to point people toward God. Of all people, the Pharisees should have recognized the Messiah, but they refused to acknowledge him because they were not willing to give up their treasured position and power. When Jesus exposed their attitudes, he became their enemy instead of their Messiah, and they began looking for ways to turn the people against him.

3:5 Jesus was angry about the Pharisees' uncaring attitudes. Anger itself is not wrong. It depends on what makes us angry and what we do with our anger. Too often we express our anger in selfish and harmful ways. By contrast, Jesus expressed his anger by correcting a problem—healing the man's hand. Use your anger to find constructive solutions rather than to tear people down.

3:6 The Pharisees were a Jewish religious group that zealously followed the Old Testament laws as well as their own religious traditions. They were highly respected in the community, but they hated Jesus because he challenged their proud attitudes and dishonorable motives.

The supporters of Herod were a Jewish political party that hoped to restore Herod the Great's line to the throne. Jesus was a threat to them as well because he challenged their political ambitions. The Pharisees and supporters of Herod, normally enemies, joined forces against Jesus because he exposed them for what they were.

3:6 The Pharisees accused Jesus of breaking their law that said medical attention could be given to no one on the Sabbath except in matters of life and death. Ironically, the Pharisees themselves were breaking God's law by plotting murder.

3:7, 8 While Jesus was drawing fire from the religious leaders, he was gaining great popularity among the people. Some were curious, some sought healing, some wanted evidence to use against him, and others wanted to know if Jesus truly was the Messiah. Most of them could only dimly guess at the real meaning of what was happening among them. Today crowds still follow Jesus, and they come for the same variety of reasons. What is your primary reason for following Jesus?

3:11 The evil spirits knew that Jesus was the Son of God, but they refused to turn from their evil purposes. Knowing about Jesus, or even believing that he is God's Son, does not guarantee salvation. You must also want to follow and obey him (see also James 2:17).

3:12 Jesus warned the evil spirits not to reveal his identity because he did not want them to reinforce a popular misconception. The huge crowds were looking for a political and military leader who would free them from Rome's control, and they thought that the Messiah predicted by the Old Testament prophets would be this kind of man. Jesus wanted to teach the people about the kind of Messiah he really was—one who was far different from their expectations. Christ's Kingdom is spiritual. It begins with the overthrow of sin in people's hearts, not with the overthrow of governments.

3:14 From the hundreds of people who followed him from place to place, Jesus chose 12 to be his *apostles. Apostle* means "messenger or authorized representative." He did not choose these 12 to be his associates and companions because of their faith; their faith often faltered. He didn't choose them because of their talent and ability; no one stood out with unusual ability. The disciples represented a wide range of backgrounds and life experiences, but apparently they had no more leadership potential than those who were not chosen. The one characteristic they all shared was their willingness to obey Jesus. After Jesus' ascension, they were filled with the Holy Spirit and empowered to carry out special roles in the growth of the early church. We should not disqualify ourselves from service to Christ because we do not have the expected credentials. Being a good disciple is simply a matter of following Jesus with a willing heart.

3:14, 15 Why did Jesus choose 12 men? The number 12 corresponds to the 12 tribes of Israel (Matthew 19:28), showing the continuity between the old religious system and the new one based on Jesus' message. Many people followed Jesus, but these 12 received the most intense training. We see the impact of these men throughout the rest of the New Testament.

THE TWELVE

Name	Occupation	Outstanding Characteristics	Major Events in His Life
SIMON PETER (son of John)	Fisherman	Impulsive; later—bold in preaching about Jesus	One of three in core group of disciples; recognized Jesus as the Messiah; denied Christ and repented; preached Pentecost sermon; a leader of the Jerusalem church; baptized Gentiles; wrote 1 and 2 Peter.
JAMES (son of Zebedee), he and his brother, John, were called the "Sons of Thunder"	Fisherman	Ambitious, short-tempered, judgmental, deeply committed to Jesus	Also in core group; he and his brother, John, asked Jesus for places of honor in his Kingdom; wanted to call fire down to destroy a Samaritan village; first disciple to be martyred.
JOHN (son of Zebedee), James's brother, and "the disciple whom Jesus loved"	Fisherman	Ambitious, judgmental, later—very loving	Third disciple in core group; asked Jesus for a place of honor in his Kingdom; wanted to call down fire on a Samaritan village; a leader of the Jerusalem church; wrote the Gospel of John and 1, 2, 3 John and Revelation.
ANDREW (Peter's brother)	Fisherman	Eager to bring others to Jesus	Accepted John the Baptist's testimony about Jesus; told Peter about Jesus; he and Philip told Jesus that Greeks wanted to see him.
PHILIP	Fisherman	Questioning attitude	Told Nathanael about Jesus; wondered how Jesus could feed the 5,000; asked Jesus to show his followers God the Father; he and Andrew told Jesus that Greeks wanted to see him.
BARTHOLOMEW (Nathanael)	Unknown	Honest and straightforward	Initially rejected Jesus because Jesus was from Nazareth but acknowledged him as the "Son of God" and "King of Israel" when they met.
MATTHEW (Levi)	Tax collector	Despised outcast because of his dishonest career	Abandoned his corrupt (and financially profitable) way of life to follow Jesus; invited Jesus to a party with his notorious friends; wrote the Gospel of Matthew.
THOMAS (the Twin)	Unknown	Courage and doubt	Suggested the disciples go with Jesus to Bethany—even if it meant death; asked Jesus about where he was going; refused to believe Jesus was risen until he could see Jesus alive and touch his wounds.
JAMES (son of Alphaeus)	Unknown	Unknown	Became one of Jesus' disciples.
THADDAEUS (Judas son of James)	Unknown	Unknown	Asked Jesus why he would reveal himself to his followers and not to the world.
SIMON THE ZEALOT	Unknown	Fierce patriotism	Became a disciple of Jesus.
JUDAS ISCARIOT	Unknown	Treacherous and greedy	Became one of Jesus' disciples; betrayed Jesus; killed himself.

Jesus' faithful disciples were ordinary men who became extraordinary because of Jesus Christ. Despite their confusion and lack of understanding during his lifetime, they became powerful witnesses to his resurrection. Their lives were transformed by God's power. The story of Jesus' disciples does not end with the Gospels. It continues in the book of Acts and many of the letters.

DISCIPLES

What Jesus Said about Him	A Key Lesson from His Life	Selected References
Named him Peter, "rock"; called him "Satan" when he urged Jesus to reject the cross; said he would fish for people; he received revelation from God; he would deny Jesus; he would later be crucified for his faith.	Christians falter at times, but when they return to Jesus, he forgives them and strengthens their faith	Matthew 4:18–20 Mark 8:29–33 Luke 22:31–34 John 21:15–19 Acts 2:14–41 Acts 10:1—11:18
Called James and John "Sons of Thunder"; said he would fish for people; would drink the cup Jesus drank.	Christians must be willing to die for Jesus.	Mark 3:17 Mark 10:35–40 Luke 9:52–56 Acts 12:1, 2
Called James and John "Sons of Thunder"; said he would fish for people; would drink the cup Jesus drank; would take care of Jesus' mother after Jesus' death.	The transforming power of the love of Christ is available to all.	Mark 1:19 Mark 10:35–40 Luke 9:52–56 John 19:26, 27 John 21:20–24
Said he would fish for people.	Christians are to tell other people about Jesus.	Matthew 4:18–20 John 1:35–42; 6:8, 9 John 12:20–22
Asked if Philip realized that to know and see him was to know and see the Father.	God uses our questions to teach us.	Matthew 10:3 John 1:43–46; 6:2–7 John 12:20–22 John 14:8–11
Called him "a true son of Israel" and "an honest man."	Jesus respects honesty in people—even if they challenge him because of it.	Mark 3:18 John 1:45–51 John 21:1–13
Called him to be a disciple.	Christianity is not for people who think they're already good; it is for people who know they've failed and want help.	Matthew 9:9–13 Mark 2:15–17 Luke 5:27–32
Said Thomas believed because he actually saw Jesus after the Resurrection.	Even when Christians experience serious doubts, Jesus reaches out to them to restore their faith.	Matthew 10:3 John 14:5; 20:24–29 John 21:1–13
Unknown	Unknown	Matthew 10:3 Mark 3:18 Luke 6:15
Unknown	Christians follow Jesus because they believe in him; they do not always understand the details of God's plan.	Matthew 10:3 Mark 3:18 John 14:22
Unknown	If we are willing to give up our plans for the future, we can participate in Jesus' plans.	Matthew 10:4 Mark 3:18 Luke 6:15
Called him "a devil"; said Judas would betray Jesus.	It is not enough to be familiar with Jesus' teachings. Jesus' true followers love and obey him.	Matthew 26:20–25 Luke 22:47, 48 John 12:4–8

calling them apostles.* He sent them out to preach, 15 and he gave them authority to cast 3:16
out demons. 16 These are the names of the twelve he chose: Matt 16:17-18 John 1:42

Simon (he renamed him Peter),
17 James and John (the sons of Zebedee, but Jesus nicknamed them "Sons of Thunder"*), 3:17 Luke 9:54
18 Andrew,
Philip,
Bartholomew,
Matthew,
Thomas,
James (son of Alphaeus),
Thaddaeus,
Simon (the Zealot*),
19 Judas Iscariot (who later betrayed him).

Religious Leaders Accuse Jesus of Getting His Power from Satan (**74**/Matthew 12:22-37)
20 When Jesus returned to the house where he was staying, the crowds began to gather
again, and soon he and his disciples couldn't even find time to eat. 21 When his family
heard what was happening, they tried to take him home with them. "He's out of his
mind," they said.
22 But the teachers of religious law who had arrived from Jerusalem said, "He's possessed 3:22
by Satan,* the prince of demons. That's where he gets the power to cast out demons." John 7:20; 8:48, 52; 10:20
23 Jesus called them over and said to them by way of illustration, "How can Satan cast
out Satan? 24 A kingdom at war with itself will collapse. 25 A home divided against itself
is doomed. 26 And if Satan is fighting against himself, how can he stand? He would never
survive. 27 Let me illustrate this. You can't enter a strong man's house and rob him 3:27 Isa 49:24-25
without first tying him up. Only then can his house be robbed!*
28 "I assure you that any sin can be forgiven, including blasphemy; 29 but anyone who 3:28-30 Luke 12:10
blasphemes against the Holy Spirit will never be forgiven. It is an eternal sin." 30 He told 1 Jn 5:16
them this because they were saying he had an evil spirit.

Jesus Describes His True Family (**76**/Matthew 12:46-50; Luke 8:19-21)
31 Jesus' mother and brothers arrived at the house where he was teaching. They stood 3:31 Mark 6:3
outside and sent word for him to come out and talk with them. 32 There was a crowd John 7:3-5
around Jesus, and someone said, "Your mother and your brothers and sisters* are
outside, asking for you."

3:14 Some manuscripts do not include *calling them apostles.* **3:17** Greek *whom he named Boanerges, which means Sons of Thunder.* **3:18** Greek *the Cananean.* **3:22** Greek *Beelzeboul.* **3:27** Or *One cannot rob Satan's kingdom without first tying him up. Only then can his demons be cast out.* **3:32** Some manuscripts do not include *and sisters.*

3:18 Zealots were Jewish nationalists who opposed the Roman occupation of Palestine.

3:21 With the crowds pressing in on him, Jesus didn't even take time to eat. Because of this, his friends and family came to take charge of him (3:31, 32), thinking he had gone "over the edge" as a religious fanatic. They were concerned for him, but they missed the point of his ministry. Even those who were closest to Jesus were slow to understand who he was and what he had come to do.

3:22-27 The teachers of religious law could not deny the reality of Jesus' miracles and supernatural power. They refused to believe that his power was from God, however, because then they would have had to accept him as the Messiah. Their pride would not let them do that. So in an attempt to destroy Jesus' popularity among the people, the teachers of religious law accused him of having power from Satan. Jesus' reply showed that their argument didn't make sense.

3:27 Although God permits Satan to work in our world, God is still in control. Because he is God, Jesus has power over Satan and is able to drive out demons, thus ending their terrible work in people's lives. One day Satan will be bound forever (Revelation 20:10).

3:28, 29 Christians sometimes wonder if they have committed this sin of blasphemy against the Holy Spirit. Christians need not worry because this sin is attributing to the Devil the work of the Holy Spirit. It reveals a heart attitude of unbelief and unrepentance. Deliberate, ongoing rejection of the work of the Holy Spirit is blasphemy because it is rejecting God himself. The religious leaders accused Jesus of blasphemy, but ironically they were the guilty ones when they looked Jesus in the face and accused him of being possessed by Satan.

3:31-35 Jesus' mother was Mary (Luke 1:30, 31), and his brothers were probably the other children Mary and Joseph had after Jesus (see also 6:3). Some Christians believe the ancient tradition that Jesus was Mary's only child. If this is true, the "brothers" were possibly cousins (cousins were often called brothers in those days). Some have offered yet another suggestion: When Joseph married Mary, he was a widower, and these were his children by his first marriage. Most likely, these were Jesus' half brothers (see Mark 6:3, 4).

Jesus' family did not yet fully understand his ministry, as can be seen in verse 21. Jesus explained that in our spiritual family, the relationships are ultimately more important and longer lasting than those formed in our physical families.

3:34 John 20:17 Rom 8:29 Heb 2:11

33 Jesus replied, "Who is my mother? Who are my brothers?" 34 Then he looked at those around him and said, "These are my mother and brothers. 35 Anyone who does God's will is my brother and sister and mother."

Jesus Tells the Parable of the Four Soils (**77**/Matthew 13:1-9; Luke 8:4-8)

4:2 Mark 4:33-34

4 Once again Jesus began teaching by the lakeshore. There was such a large crowd along the shore that he got into a boat and sat down and spoke from there. 2 He began to teach the people by telling many stories such as this one:

3 "Listen! A farmer went out to plant some seed. 4 As he scattered it across his field, some seed fell on a footpath, and the birds came and ate it. 5 Other seed fell on shallow soil with underlying rock. The plant sprang up quickly, 6 but it soon wilted beneath the hot sun and died because the roots had no nourishment in the shallow soil. 7 Other seed fell among thorns that shot up and choked out the tender blades so that it produced no grain. 8 Still other seed fell on fertile soil and produced a crop that was thirty, sixty, and even a hundred times as much as had been planted." Then he said, 9 "Anyone who is willing to hear should listen and understand!"

4:9 Matt 11:15 Mark 4:23

Jesus Explains the Parable of the Four Soils (**78**/Matthew 13:10-23; Luke 8:9-18)

10 Later, when Jesus was alone with the twelve disciples and with the others who were gathered around, they asked him, "What do your stories mean?"

4:12 †Isa 6:9-10 John 12:39-40 Acts 28:26-27

11 He replied, "You are permitted to understand the secret about the Kingdom of God. But I am using these stories to conceal everything about it from outsiders, 12 so that the Scriptures might be fulfilled:

'They see what I do,
  but they don't perceive its meaning.
They hear my words,
  but they don't understand.
So they will not turn from their sins
  and be forgiven.'*

4:14 Eph 3:8 Jas 1:18 1 Pet 1:23-25

4:15 2 Cor 4:4 1 Pet 5:8

13 "But if you can't understand this story, how will you understand all the others I am going to tell? 14 The farmer I talked about is the one who brings God's message to others. 15 The seed that fell on the hard path represents those who hear the message, but then Satan comes at once and takes it away from them. 16 The rocky soil represents those who hear the message and receive it with joy. 17 But like young plants in such

4:12 Isa 6:9-10.

3:33-35 God's family is accepting and doesn't exclude anyone. Although Jesus cared for his mother and brothers, he also cared for all those who loved him. Jesus did not show partiality; he allowed everyone the privilege of obeying God and becoming part of his family. In our increasingly computerized, impersonal world, warm relationships among members of God's family take on major importance. The church can give the loving, personalized care that many people find nowhere else.

4:2 Jesus taught the people by telling stories called parables, using familiar scenes to explain spiritual truths. This method of teaching compels the listener to think. It conceals the truth from those who are too stubborn or prejudiced to hear what is being taught. Most parables have one main point, so we must be careful not to go beyond what Jesus intended to teach.

4:3 Seed was planted by hand. As the farmer walked across the field, he threw handfuls of seed onto the ground from a large bag slung across his shoulders. The plants did not grow in neat rows as they do with today's machine planting. No matter how skillful, no farmer could keep some of his seed from falling on the footpath, from being scattered among rocks and thorns, or from being carried off by the wind. So the farmer would throw the seed liberally, and enough would fall on good ground to ensure the harvest.

4:9 We hear with our ears, but there is a deeper kind of listening with the mind and heart that is necessary in order to gain spiritual understanding from Jesus' words. Some people in the crowd were looking for evidence to use against Jesus; others truly wanted to learn and grow. Jesus' words were for the honest seekers.

4:11, 12 Some people do not understand God's truth because they are not ready for it. God reveals truth to people who will act on it and make it visible in their lives. When you talk with people about God, be aware that they will not understand if they are not yet ready. Be patient, taking every chance to tell them more about God and praying that the Holy Spirit will open their minds and hearts to receive the truth and act on it.

4:14-20 The four soils represent four different ways people respond to God's message. Usually we think that Jesus was talking about four different kinds of people. But he may also have been talking about (1) different times or phases in a person's life or (2) how we willingly apply God's message to some areas of our life but resist applying it to others. For example, you may be open to God about your future but closed concerning how you spend your money. You may respond like good soil to God's demand for worship but respond like rocky soil to his demand to give to people in need. Strive to be like good soil in every area of your life at all times.

soil, their roots don't go very deep. At first they get along fine, but they wilt as soon
as they have problems or are persecuted because they believe the word. 18 The thorny
ground represents those who hear and accept the Good News, 19 but all too quickly **4:19** 1 Tim 6:9-10, 17
the message is crowded out by the cares of this life, the lure of wealth, and the desire 1 Jn 2:15-17
for nice things, so no crop is produced. 20 But the good soil represents those who hear
and accept God's message and produce a huge harvest—thirty, sixty, or even a
hundred times as much as had been planted."

21 Then Jesus asked them, "Would anyone light a lamp and then put it under a basket **4:21-25** Matt 5:15
or under a bed to shut out the light? Of course not! A lamp is placed on a stand, where **4:22**
its light will shine. Matt 10:26 Luke 12:2

22 "Everything that is now hidden or secret will eventually be brought to light. **4:23**
23 Anyone who is willing to hear should listen and understand! 24 And be sure to pay Matt 11:15; 13:43
attention to what you hear. The more you do this, the more you will understand—and
even more, besides. 25 To those who are open to my teaching, more understanding will **4:25** Matt 13:12; 25:29
be given. But to those who are not listening, even what they have will be taken away Luke 19:26
from them."

Jesus Tells the Parable of the Growing Seed (**79**)

26 Jesus also said, "Here is another illustration of what the Kingdom of God is like: A **4:26-27** 1 Cor 3:6-7
farmer planted seeds in a field, 27 and then he went on with his other activities. As the
days went by, the seeds sprouted and grew without the farmer's help, 28 because the earth **4:28-29** Matt 9:37-38
produces crops on its own. First a leaf blade pushes through, then the heads of wheat are Rev 14:15
formed, and finally the grain ripens. 29 And as soon as the grain is ready, the farmer
comes and harvests it with a sickle."

Jesus Tells the Parable of the Mustard Seed (**81**/Matthew 13:31-32)

30 Jesus asked, "How can I describe the Kingdom of God? What story should I use to
illustrate it? 31 It is like a tiny mustard seed. Though this is one of the smallest of seeds,
32 it grows to become one of the largest of plants, with long branches where birds can **4:32** Ezek 17:23; 31:6
come and find shelter." Dan 4:12, 21

33 He used many such stories and illustrations to teach the people as much as **4:33** Matt 13:34-35
they were able to understand. 34 In fact, in his public teaching he taught only with par- **4:34**
ables, but afterward when he was alone with his disciples, he explained the meaning John 16:25
to them.

Jesus Calms the Storm (**87**/Matthew 8:23-27; Luke 8:22-25)

35 As evening came, Jesus said to his disciples, "Let's cross to the other side of the lake."
36 He was already in the boat, so they started out, leaving the crowds behind (although
other boats followed). 37 But soon a fierce storm arose. High waves began to break into
the boat until it was nearly full of water.

4:19 Cares of this life, the lure of wealth, and the desire for nice things plagued first-century disciples as they do us today. How easy it is for our daily routines to become overcrowded. A life packed with materialistic pursuits deafens us to God's Word. Stay free so you can hear God when he speaks.

4:21 If a lamp doesn't help people see, it is useless. Does your life show other people how to find God and how to live for him? If not, ask what "baskets" have extinguished your light. Complacency, resentment, stubbornness of heart, or disobedience could keep God's light from shining through you to others.

4:24, 25 The light of Jesus' truth is revealed to us, not hidden. But we may not be able to see or to use all of that truth right now. Only as we put God's teachings into practice will we understand and see more of the truth. The truth is clear, but our ability to understand is imperfect. As we obey, we will sharpen our vision and increase our understanding (see James 1:22-25).

4:25 This verse simply means that we are responsible to use well what we have. How much we have is not nearly as important as what we do with it.

4:26-29 This parable about the Kingdom of God, recorded only by Mark, reveals that spiritual growth is a continual, gradual process that is finally consummated in a harvest of spiritual maturity. We can understand the process of spiritual growth by comparing it to the slow but certain growth of a plant.

4:30-32 Jesus used this parable to explain that although Christianity had very small beginnings, it would grow into a worldwide community of believers. When you feel alone in your stand for Christ, realize that God is building a worldwide Kingdom. He has faithful followers in every part of the world, and your faith, no matter how small, can join with that of others to accomplish great things.

4:33, 34 Jesus adapted his methods to his audience's ability and desire to understand. He didn't speak in parables to confuse people but to challenge sincere seekers to discover the meaning of his words. Much of Jesus' teaching was against hypocrisy and impure motives—characteristics of the religious leaders. Had Jesus spoken against the leaders directly, his public ministry would have been hampered. Those who listened carefully to Jesus knew what he was talking about.

[38]Jesus was sleeping at the back of the boat with his head on a cushion. Frantically
4:39 Pss 65:8; 89:10; 107:25-32 they woke him up, shouting, "Teacher, don't you even care that we are going to drown?"
[39]When he woke up, he rebuked the wind and said to the water, "Quiet down!"
Suddenly the wind stopped, and there was a great calm. [40]And he asked them, "Why are
you so afraid? Do you still not have faith in me?"
4:41 Ps 33:8-9 [41]And they were filled with awe and said among themselves, "Who is this man, that
even the wind and waves obey him?"

Jesus Sends Demons into a Herd of Pigs (**88**/Matthew 8:28-34; Luke 8:26-39)

5 So they arrived at the other side of the lake, in the land of the Gerasenes.* [2]Just as
Jesus was climbing from the boat, a man possessed by an evil spirit ran out from a
cemetery to meet him. [3]This man lived among the tombs and could not be restrained,
even with a chain. [4]Whenever he was put into chains and shackles—as he often was—he

5:1 Some manuscripts read *Gadarenes;* others read *Gergesenes.* See Matt 8:28; Luke 8:26.

THE TOUCH OF JESUS

What kind of people did Jesus associate with? Whom did he consider important enough to touch? Here we see many of the people Jesus came to know. Some reached out to him; he reached out to them all. Regardless of how great or unknown, rich or poor, young or old, sinner or saint—Jesus cares equally for all. No person is beyond the loving touch of Jesus.

Jesus talked with . . .	*Reference*
A despised tax collector	Matthew 9:9
An insane hermit	Mark 5:1–15
The Roman governor	Mark 15:1–15
A young boy	Mark 9:17–27
A prominent religious leader	John 3:1–21
A homemaker	Luke 10:38–42
An expert in religious law	Matthew 22:35
A criminal	Luke 23:40–43
A synagogue leader	Mark 5:22
Fishermen	Matthew 4:18–20
A king	Luke 23:7–11
A poor widow	Luke 7:11–17; 21:1–4
A Roman captain	Luke 7:1–10
A group of children	Mark 10:13–16
A prophet	Matthew 3
An adulterous woman	John 8:1–11
The Jewish high council	Luke 22:66–71
A sick woman	Mark 5:25–34
A rich man	Mark 10:17–23
A blind beggar	Mark 10:46
Jewish political leaders	Mark 12:13
A group of women	Luke 8:2, 3
The high priest	Matthew 26:62–68
An outcast with leprosy	Luke 17:11–19
A government official	John 4:46–53
A young girl	Mark 5:41, 42
A traitor	John 13:1–3, 27
A helpless and paralyzed man	Mark 2:1–12
An angry mob of soldiers and guards	John 18:3–9
A woman from a foreign land	Mark 7:25–30
A doubting follower	John 20:24–29
An enemy who hated him	Acts 9:1–9
A Samaritan woman	John 4:1–26

4:35, 37 The "lake" is the Sea of Galilee, a body of water 680 feet below sea level and surrounded by hills. Winds blowing across the land intensify close to the sea, often causing violent and unexpected storms. The disciples were seasoned fishermen, who had spent their lives fishing on this huge lake, but during this squall they panicked.

4:38-40 The disciples panicked because the storm threatened to destroy them all, and Jesus seemed unaware and unconcerned. Theirs was a physical storm, but storms come in other forms. Think about the storms in your life—the situations that cause you great anxiety. Whatever your difficulty, you have two options: You can worry and assume that Jesus no longer cares, or you can resist fear, putting your trust in him. When you feel like panicking, confess your need for God and then trust him to care for you.

4:41 The disciples lived with Jesus, but they underestimated him. They did not see that his power applied to their very own situation. Jesus has been with his people for 20 centuries, and yet we, like the disciples, underestimate his power to handle crises in our lives. The disciples did not yet know enough about Jesus. We cannot make the same excuse.

5:1, 2 Although we cannot be sure why demon possession occurs, we know that evil spirits can use the human body to distort and destroy people's relationship with God and likeness to him. Even today, demons are dangerous, powerful, and destructive. While it is important to recognize their evil activity so that we can stay away from demons, we should avoid any curiosity about or involvement with demonic forces or the occult (Deuteronomy 18:10-12). If we resist the Devil and his influences, he will flee from us (James 4:7).

snapped the chains from his wrists and smashed the shackles. No one was strong enough
to control him. 5All day long and throughout the night, he would wander among the
tombs and in the hills, screaming and hitting himself with stones.

6When Jesus was still some distance away, the man saw him. He ran to meet Jesus and
fell down before him. 7He gave a terrible scream, shrieking, "Why are you bothering
me, Jesus, Son of the Most High God? For God's sake, don't torture me!" 8For Jesus had
already said to the spirit, "Come out of the man, you evil spirit."

9Then Jesus asked, "What is your name?"

And the spirit replied, "Legion, because there are many of us here inside this man."
10Then the spirits begged him again and again not to send them to some distant place.
11There happened to be a large herd of pigs feeding on the hillside nearby. 12"Send us
into those pigs," the evil spirits begged. 13Jesus gave them permission. So the evil spirits
came out of the man and entered the pigs, and the entire herd of two thousand pigs
plunged down the steep hillside into the lake, where they drowned.

14The herdsmen fled to the nearby city and the surrounding countryside, spreading
the news as they ran. Everyone rushed out to see for themselves. 15A crowd soon
gathered around Jesus, but they were frightened when they saw the man who had been
demon possessed, for he was sitting there fully clothed and perfectly sane. 16Those who
had seen what happened to the man and to the pigs told everyone about it, 17and the
crowd began pleading with Jesus to go away and leave them alone.

18When Jesus got back into the boat, the man who had been demon possessed begged
to go, too. 19But Jesus said, "No, go home to your friends, and tell them what wonderful
things the Lord has done for you and how merciful he has been." 20So the man started
off to visit the Ten Towns* of that region and began to tell everyone about the great things
Jesus had done for him; and everyone was amazed at what he told them.

5:7-8 Acts 16:17; Heb 7:1
5:15 Matt 4:24
5:18 Ps 116:12
5:20 Ps 116:16; Isa 63:7; 1 Tim 1:13-14

5:20 Greek *Decapolis.*

5:9 The evil spirit said its name was Legion. A legion was the largest unit of the Roman army, consisting of 3,000 to 6,000 soldiers. Obviously this man was possessed by many demons.

HEALING A DEMON-POSSESSED MAN
From Capernaum, Jesus and his disciples crossed the Sea of Galilee. A storm blew up unexpectedly, but Jesus calmed it. Landing in the region of the Gerasenes, Jesus sent demons out of a man and into a herd of pigs that plunged over the steep bank into the lake.

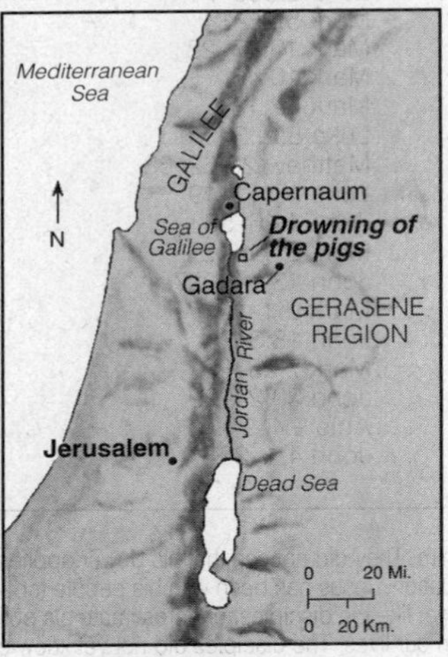

5:10 Mark often highlights the supernatural struggle between Jesus and Satan. The demons' goal was to control the humans they inhabited; Jesus' goal was to give people freedom from sin and Satan's control. The demons knew they had no power over Jesus; so when they saw Jesus, they begged not to be sent to some distant place ("the Bottomless Pit" in Luke 8:31). Jesus granted their request to enter into the herd of pigs (5:13) but ended their destructive work in people. Perhaps Jesus let the demons destroy the pigs to demonstrate his own superiority over a very powerful yet destructive force. He could have sent them to hell, but he did not, because the time for judgment had not yet come. In the end, the Devil and all his angels will be sent into eternal fire (Matthew 25:41).

5:11 According to Old Testament law (Leviticus 11:7), pigs were "unclean" animals. This meant that they could not be eaten or even touched by a Jew. This incident took place southeast of the Sea of Galilee in the region of the Gerasenes, a Gentile region, which explains how a herd of pigs could be involved.

5:17 After such a wonderful miracle of saving a man's life, why did the people want Jesus to leave? They were undoubtedly afraid of his supernatural power. They may have also feared that Jesus would continue destroying their pigs. They would rather give up Jesus than lose their source of income and security.

5:19 Jesus told this man to tell his friends about the miraculous healing. Most of the time, Jesus urged those he healed to keep quiet. Why the difference? Here are possible answers: (1) The demon-possessed man had been alone and unable to speak. Telling others what Jesus did for him would prove that he was healed. (2) This was mainly a Gentile and pagan area, so Jesus was not expecting great crowds to follow him or religious leaders to hinder him. (3) By sending the man away with this Good News, Jesus was expanding his ministry to people who were not Jews.

5:19, 20 This man had been demon possessed but became a living example of Jesus' power. He wanted to go with Jesus, but Jesus told him to go home and share his story with his friends. If you have experienced Jesus' power in your life, are you, like this man, enthusiastically sharing the good news with those around you? Just as we would tell others about a doctor who cured a physical disease, we should tell about Christ who cures our sin.

5:20 These Ten Towns were located southeast of the Sea of Galilee. Ten cities, each with its own independent government, formed an alliance for protection and for increased trade opportunities. These cities had been settled several centuries earlier by Greek traders and immigrants. Although Jews also lived in the area, they were not in the majority. Many people from the Ten Towns followed Jesus (Matthew 4:25).

Jesus Heals a Bleeding Woman and Restores a Girl to Life
(**89**/Matthew 9:18-26; Luke 8:40-56)

21 When Jesus went back across to the other side of the lake, a large crowd gathered around
him on the shore. 22 A leader of the local synagogue, whose name was Jairus, came and fell
down before him, 23 pleading with him to heal his little daughter. "She is about to die," he
said in desperation. "Please come and place your hands on her; heal her so she can live."
24 Jesus went with him, and the crowd thronged behind. 25 And there was a woman in
the crowd who had had a hemorrhage for twelve years. 26 She had suffered a great deal
from many doctors through the years and had spent everything she had to pay them, but
she had gotten no better. In fact, she was worse. 27 She had heard about Jesus, so she came
up behind him through the crowd and touched the fringe of his robe. 28 For she thought
to herself, "If I can just touch his clothing, I will be healed." 29 Immediately the bleeding
stopped, and she could feel that she had been healed!
30 Jesus realized at once that healing power had gone out from him, so he turned
around in the crowd and asked, "Who touched my clothes?"
31 His disciples said to him, "All this crowd is pressing around you. How can you ask,
'Who touched me?' "
32 But he kept on looking around to see who had done it. 33 Then the frightened woman,
trembling at the realization of what had happened to her, came and fell at his feet and
told him what she had done. 34 And he said to her, "Daughter, your faith has made you
well. Go in peace. You have been healed."
35 While he was still speaking to her, messengers arrived from Jairus's home with the
message, "Your daughter is dead. There's no use troubling the Teacher now."
36 But Jesus ignored their comments and said to Jairus, "Don't be afraid. Just trust me."
37 Then Jesus stopped the crowd and wouldn't let anyone go with him except Peter and
James and John. 38 When they came to the home of the synagogue leader, Jesus saw the
commotion and the weeping and wailing. 39 He went inside and spoke to the people. "Why
all this weeping and commotion?" he asked. "The child isn't dead; she is only asleep."
40 The crowd laughed at him, but he told them all to go outside. Then he took the girl's
father and mother and his three disciples into the room where the girl was lying.
41 Holding her hand, he said to her, "Get up, little girl!"* 42 And the girl, who was twelve
years old, immediately stood up and walked around! Her parents were absolutely over-

5:23 Matt 8:3; Mark 6:5; 7:32; 8:23, 25; Luke 4:40; 13:13; Acts 9:12, 17; 28:8
5:25 Lev 15:25-30
5:27 Mark 3:10; Acts 19:11-12
5:30 Luke 6:19
5:34 Mark 10:52; Luke 7:50; 17:19; 18:42; Acts 14:9
5:36 John 11:25-40
5:39 John 11:11
5:40 Acts 9:40
5:41-42 Luke 7:14

5:41 Greek text uses Aramaic *"Talitha cumi"* and then translates it as "Get up, little girl."

5:22 Jesus recrossed the Sea of Galilee, probably landing at Capernaum. Jairus was the elected leader of the local synagogue. He was responsible for supervising worship, running the weekly school, and caring for the building. Many synagogue leaders had close ties to the Pharisees. It is likely, therefore, that some synagogue rulers had been pressured not to support Jesus. For Jairus to bow before Jesus was a significant and perhaps daring act of respect and worship.

5:25-34 This woman had a seemingly incurable condition causing her to bleed constantly. This may have been a menstrual or uterine disorder that would have made her ritually unclean (Leviticus 15:25-27) and would have excluded her from most social contact. She desperately wanted Jesus to heal her, but she knew that her bleeding would cause Jesus to be unclean under Jewish law if she touched him. Still, the woman reached out by faith and was healed. Sometimes we feel that our problems will keep us from God. But he is always ready to help. We should never allow our fear to keep us from approaching him.

5:32-34 Jesus was not angry with this woman for touching him. He knew she had touched him, but he stopped and asked who did it in order to teach her something about faith. Although the woman was healed when she touched him, Jesus said her faith caused the cure. Genuine faith involves action. Faith that isn't put into action is not faith at all.

5:35, 36 Jairus's crisis made him feel confused, afraid, and without hope. Jesus' words to Jairus in the midst of crisis speak to us as well: "Don't be afraid. Just trust me." In Jesus' mind, there was both hope and promise. The next time you feel hopeless and afraid, look at your problem from Jesus' point of view. He is the source of all hope and promise.

5:38 Loud weeping and wailing were customary at a person's death. Lack of them was the ultimate disgrace and disrespect. There were some people, usually women, who made mourning a profession and were paid by the dead person's family to weep over the body. On the day of death, the body was carried through the streets, followed by mourners, family members, and friends.

5:39, 40 The mourners began to laugh at Jesus when he said, "The child isn't dead; she is only asleep." The girl was dead, but Jesus used the image of sleep to indicate that her condition was temporary and that she would be restored.

Jesus tolerated the crowd's abuse in order to teach an important lesson about maintaining hope and trust in him. Today, most of the world laughs at Christ's claims, which seem ridiculous to them. When you are belittled for expressing faith in Jesus and hope for eternal life, remember that unbelievers don't see from God's perspective. For a clear statement about life after death, see 1 Thessalonians 4:13, 14.

5:41, 42 Jesus not only demonstrated great power, he also showed tremendous compassion. Jesus' power over nature, evil spirits, and death was motivated by compassion—for a demon-possessed man who lived among tombs, for a diseased woman, and for the family of a dead girl. The rabbis of the day considered such people unclean. Polite society avoided them. But Jesus reached out and helped anyone in need.

whelmed. 43 Jesus commanded them not to tell anyone what had happened, and he told 5:43 Matt 8:4
them to give her something to eat. Mark 1:44; 7:36

The People of Nazareth Refuse to Believe (**91**/Matthew 13:53-58)

6 Jesus left that part of the country and returned with his disciples to Nazareth, his
hometown. 2 The next Sabbath he began teaching in the synagogue, and many who 6:2
heard him were astonished. They asked, "Where did he get all his wisdom and the power John 7:15
to perform such miracles? 3 He's just the carpenter, the son of Mary and brother of James, 6:3
Joseph,* Judas, and Simon. And his sisters live right here among us." They were deeply John 6:42
offended and refused to believe in him.
4 Then Jesus told them, "A prophet is honored everywhere except in his own home- 6:4
town and among his relatives and his own family." 5 And because of their unbelief, he John 4:44 6:5
couldn't do any mighty miracles among them except to place his hands on a few sick Matt 9:18
people and heal them. 6 And he was amazed at their unbelief.

Jesus Sends Out the Twelve Disciples (**93**/Matthew 10:1-15; Luke 9:1-6)

Then Jesus went out from village to village, teaching. 7 And he called his twelve disciples 6:7
together and sent them out two by two, with authority to cast out evil spirits. 8 He told Luke 10:1
them to take nothing with them except a walking stick—no food, no traveler's bag, no 6:8-9 Matt 10:9-10
money. 9 He told them to wear sandals but not to take even an extra coat. 10 "When you Luke 9:3; 10:4
enter each village, be a guest in only one home," he said. 11 "And if a village won't 6:10 Luke 10:7
welcome you or listen to you, shake off its dust from your feet as you leave. It is a sign 6:11
that you have abandoned that village to its fate." Luke 10:11

6:3 Greek *Joses;* see Matt 13:55. Acts 13:51

5:43 Jesus told the girl's parents not to spread the news of the miracle. He wanted the facts to speak for themselves, and the time was not yet right for a major confrontation with the religious leaders. Jesus still had much to accomplish, and he didn't want people following him just to see his miracles.

6:2, 3 Jesus was teaching effectively and wisely, but the people of his hometown saw him as only a carpenter. "Where did he get all his wisdom and power to perform such miracles?" they asked. They were offended that others could be impressed by Jesus and follow him. They rejected his authority because he was one of their peers. They thought they knew him, but their preconceived notions about who he was made it impossible for them to accept his message. Don't let prejudice blind you to truth. As you learn more about Jesus, try to see him for who he really is.

PREACHING IN GALILEE
After returning to his hometown, Nazareth, from Capernaum, Jesus preached in the villages of Galilee and sent his disciples out to preach as well. After meeting back in Capernaum, they left by boat to rest, only to be met by the crowds who followed the boat along the shore.

6:4 Jesus said that a prophet (in other words, a worker for God) is never honored in his hometown. But that doesn't make his work any less important. A person doesn't need to be respected or honored to be useful to God. If friends, neighbors, or family don't respect your Christian work, don't let their rejection keep you from serving God.

6:5 Jesus could have done greater miracles in Nazareth, but he chose not to because of the people's pride and unbelief. The miracles he did had little effect on the people because they did not accept his message or believe that he was from God. Therefore, Jesus looked elsewhere, seeking those who would respond to his miracles and message.

6:7 The disciples were sent out in pairs. Individually they could have reached more areas of the country, but this was not Christ's plan. One advantage in going out by twos was that they could strengthen and encourage each other, especially when they faced rejection. Our strength ultimately comes from God, but he meets many of our needs through our teamwork with others. As you serve Christ, don't try to go it alone.

6:8, 9 Mark records that the disciples were instructed to take nothing with them *except* walking sticks, while Matthew and Luke record that Jesus told them *not* to take walking sticks. One explanation is that Matthew and Luke were referring to a club used for protection, whereas Mark was talking about a shepherd's crook. In any case, the point in all three accounts is the same—the disciples were to leave at once, without extensive preparation, trusting in God's care rather than in their own resources.

6:11 Pious Jews shook the dust from their feet after passing through Gentile cities or territory to show their separation from Gentile influences and practices. When the disciples shook the dust from their feet after leaving a *Jewish* town, it was a vivid sign that they wished to remain separate from people who had rejected Jesus and his message. Jesus made it clear that all who heard the gospel were responsible for what they did with it. The disciples were not to blame if the message was rejected, as long as they had faithfully and carefully presented it. We are not responsible when others reject Christ's message of salvation, but we do have the responsibility to share the Good News clearly and faithfully.

6:13 Luke 10:34 Jas 5:14 12 So the disciples went out, telling all they met to turn from their sins. 13 And they cast
out many demons and healed many sick people, anointing them with olive oil.

Herod Kills John the Baptist (**95**/Matthew 14:1-12; Luke 9:7-9)

14 Herod Antipas, the king, soon heard about Jesus, because people everywhere were
talking about him. Some were saying,* "This must be John the Baptist come back to life
6:15 Matt 16:14 again. That is why he can do such miracles." 15 Others thought Jesus was the ancient
prophet Elijah. Still others thought he was a prophet like the other great prophets of the
past. 16 When Herod heard about Jesus, he said, "John, the man I beheaded, has come

6:14 Some manuscripts read *He was saying.*

HEROD ANTIPAS

Most people dislike having their sins pointed out, especially in public. The shame of being exposed is often stronger than the guilt brought on by the wrongdoing. Herod Antipas was a man experiencing both guilt and shame.

Herod's ruthless ambition was public knowledge, as was his illegal marriage to his brother's wife, Herodias. One man made Herod's sin a public issue. That man was John the Baptist. John had been preaching in the wilderness, and thousands flocked to hear him. Apparently it was no secret that John had rebuked Herod for his adulterous marriage. Herodias was particularly anxious to have John silenced. As a solution, Herod imprisoned John.

Herod liked John. John was probably one of the few people he met who spoke only the truth to him. But the truth about his sin was a bitter pill to swallow, and Herod wavered at the point of conflict: He couldn't afford to have John constantly reminding the people of their leader's sinfulness, but he was afraid to have John killed. He put off the choice. Eventually Herodias forced his hand, and John was executed. Of course, this only served to increase Herod's guilt.

Upon hearing about Jesus, Herod immediately identified him with John. He couldn't decide what to do about Jesus. He didn't want to repeat the mistake he had made with John, so he tried to threaten Jesus just before his final journey to Jerusalem. When the two met briefly during Jesus' trial, Jesus would not speak to Herod. Herod had proved himself a poor listener to John, and Jesus had nothing to add to John's words. Herod responded with spite and mocking. Having rejected the messenger, he found it easy to reject the Messiah.

For each person, God chooses the best possible ways to reveal himself. He uses his Word, various circumstances, our mind, or other people to get our attention. He is persuasive and persistent but never forces himself on us. To miss or resist God's message, as did Herod, is a tragedy. How aware are you of God's attempts to enter your life? Have you welcomed him?

Strengths and accomplishments
- Built the city of Tiberias and oversaw other architectural projects
- Ruled the region of Galilee for the Romans

Weaknesses and mistakes
- Consumed with his quest for power
- Put off decisions or made wrong ones under pressure
- Divorced his wife to marry the wife of his half brother, Philip
- Imprisoned John the Baptist and later ordered his execution
- Had a minor part in the execution of Jesus

Lessons from his life
- A life motivated by ambition is usually characterized by self-destruction
- Opportunities to do good usually come to us in the form of choices to be made

Vital statistics
- Where: Jerusalem
- Occupation: Roman ruler of the region of Galilee and Perea
- Relatives: Father: Herod the Great. Mother: Malthace. First wife: daughter of Aretas IV. Second wife: Herodias
- Contemporaries: John the Baptist, Jesus, Pilate

Key verse "Herod was disturbed whenever he talked with John, but even so, he liked to listen to him" (Mark 6:20).

Herod Antipas's story is told in the Gospels. He is also mentioned in Acts 4:27; 13:1.

6:14, 15 Herod, along with many others, wondered who Jesus really was. Unable to accept Jesus' claim to be God's Son, many people made up their own explanations for his power and authority. Herod thought that Jesus was John the Baptist come back to life, while those who were familiar with the Old Testament thought he was Elijah (Malachi 4:5). Still others believed that Jesus was a teaching prophet in the tradition of Moses, Isaiah, or Jeremiah. Today people still have to make up their minds about Jesus. Some think that if they can name what he is—prophet, teacher, good man—they can weaken the power of his claim on their lives. But what they *think* does not change who Jesus *is.*

back from the dead." 17 For Herod had sent soldiers to arrest and imprison John as a favor 6:17-18 Lev 18:15-16; 20:21
to Herodias. She had been his brother Philip's wife, but Herod had married her. 18 John Luke 3:19-20
kept telling Herod, "It is illegal for you to marry your brother's wife." 19 Herodias was
enraged and wanted John killed in revenge, but without Herod's approval she was
powerless. 20 And Herod respected John, knowing that he was a good and holy man, so
he kept him under his protection. Herod was disturbed whenever he talked with John,
but even so, he liked to listen to him.
21 Herodias's chance finally came. It was Herod's birthday, and he gave a party for his
palace aides, army officers, and the leading citizens of Galilee. 22 Then his daughter, also
named Herodias,* came in and performed a dance that greatly pleased them all. "Ask me
for anything you like," the king said to the girl, "and I will give it to you." 23 Then he 6:23
promised, "I will give you whatever you ask, up to half of my kingdom!" Esth 5:3-6; 7:2
24 She went out and asked her mother, "What should I ask for?"
Her mother told her, "Ask for John the Baptist's head!"
25 So the girl hurried back to the king and told him, "I want the head of John the
Baptist, right now, on a tray!"
26 Then the king was very sorry, but he was embarrassed to break his oath in front of
his guests. 27 So he sent an executioner to the prison to cut off John's head and bring it
to him. The soldier beheaded John in the prison, 28 brought his head on a tray, and gave
it to the girl, who took it to her mother. 29 When John's disciples heard what had
happened, they came for his body and buried it in a tomb.

Jesus Feeds Five Thousand (**96**/Matthew 14:13-21; Luke 9:10-17; John 6:1-15)

30 The apostles returned to Jesus from their ministry tour and told him all they had done 6:30 Luke 9:10; 10:17
and what they had taught. 31 Then Jesus said, "Let's get away from the crowds for a while 6:31
and rest." There were so many people coming and going that Jesus and his apostles didn't Mark 3:20
even have time to eat. 32 They left by boat for a quieter spot. 33 But many people saw them
leaving, and people from many towns ran ahead along the shore and met them as they 6:34
landed. 34 A vast crowd was there as he stepped from the boat, and he had compassion †Num 27:17 †1 Kgs 22:17
on them because they were like sheep without a shepherd. So he taught them many †2 Chr 18:16 †Zech 10:2
things. Matt 9:36

6:22 Some manuscripts read *the daughter of Herodias herself.*

JESUS WALKS ON THE WATER
After feeding the people who had followed to hear him at Bethsaida, Jesus sent the people home, sent his disciples by boat toward Bethsaida, and went to pray. The disciples encountered a storm, and Jesus walked to them on the water. They landed at Gennesaret.

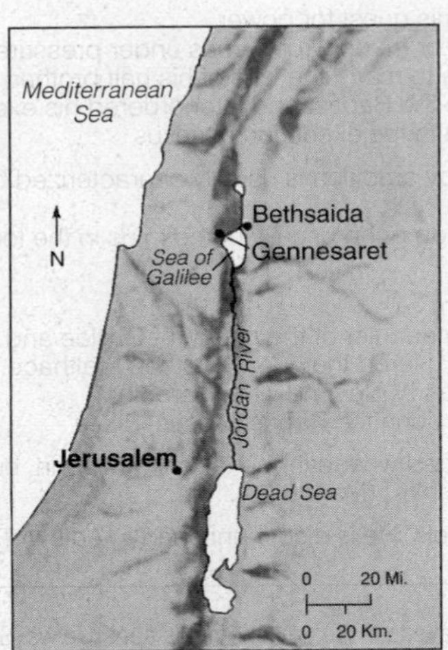

6:17-19 Palestine was divided into four territories, each with a different ruler. Herod Antipas, called Herod in the Gospels, was ruler over Galilee; his brother Philip ruled over Traconitis and Idumea. Philip's wife was Herodias, but she left him to marry Herod Antipas. When John confronted the two for committing adultery, Herodias formulated a plot to kill him. Instead of trying to get rid of her sin, Herodias tried to get rid of the one who brought it to public attention. This is exactly what the religious leaders were trying to do to Jesus.

6:20 Herod arrested John the Baptist under pressure from his wife and advisers. Though Herod respected John's integrity, in the end Herod had John killed because of pressure from his peers and family. What you do under pressure often shows what you are really like.

6:22, 23 As a ruler under Roman authority, Herod had no kingdom to give. The offer of half his kingdom was Herod's way to say that he would give Herodias's daughter almost anything she wanted. When Herodias asked for John's head, Herod would have been greatly embarrassed in front of his guests if he had denied her request. Words are powerful. Because they can lead to great sin, we should use them with great care.

6:30 Mark uses the word *apostles* here and in 3:14. *Apostle* means "one sent" as messenger, authorized agent, or missionary. The word became an official title for Jesus' 12 disciples after his death and resurrection (Acts 1:25, 26; Ephesians 2:20).

6:31 When the disciples had returned from their mission, Jesus took them away to rest. Doing God's work is very important, but Jesus recognized that to do it effectively we need periodic rest and renewal. Jesus and his disciples, however, did not always find it easy to get the rest they needed!

6:34 This crowd was as pitiful as a flock of sheep without a shepherd. Sheep are easily scattered; without a shepherd they are in grave danger. Jesus was the Shepherd who could teach them what they needed to know and keep them from straying from God. See Psalm 23; Isaiah 40:11; Ezekiel 34:5ff; and John 10:11-16 for descriptions of the good shepherd.

35 Late in the afternoon his disciples came to him and said, "This is a desolate place,
and it is getting late. 36 Send the crowds away so they can go to the nearby farms and
villages and buy themselves some food."

6:37 2 Kgs 4:42-44; Matt 15:33; Mark 8:4

37 But Jesus said, "You feed them."
"With what?" they asked. "It would take a small fortune* to buy food for all this crowd!"

6:38 Matt 15:34; Mark 8:5

38 "How much food do you have?" he asked. "Go and find out."
They came back and reported, "We have five loaves of bread and two fish." 39 Then
Jesus told the crowd to sit down in groups on the green grass. 40 So they sat in groups of
fifty or a hundred.

6:41 Matt 14:19

41 Jesus took the five loaves and two fish, looked up toward heaven, and asked God's
blessing on the food. Breaking the loaves into pieces, he kept giving the bread and fish
to the disciples to give to the people. 42 They all ate as much as they wanted, 43 and they
picked up twelve baskets of leftover bread and fish. 44 Five thousand men had eaten from
those five loaves!

Jesus Walks on Water (**97**/Matthew 14:22-33; John 6:16-21)

45 Immediately after this, Jesus made his disciples get back into the boat and head out across
the lake to Bethsaida, while he sent the people home. 46 Afterward he went up into the hills
by himself to pray.
47 During the night, the disciples were in their boat out in the middle of the lake, and
Jesus was alone on land. 48 He saw that they were in serious trouble, rowing hard and
struggling against the wind and waves. About three o'clock in the morning* he came to
them, walking on the water. He started to go past them, 49 but when they saw him walking
on the water, they screamed in terror, thinking he was a ghost. 50 They were all terrified

6:52 Mark 8:17-21

when they saw him. But Jesus spoke to them at once. "It's all right," he said. "I am here!
Don't be afraid." 51 Then he climbed into the boat, and the wind stopped. They were
astonished at what they saw. 52 They still didn't understand the significance of the
miracle of the multiplied loaves, for their hearts were hard and they did not believe.

6:37 Greek *200 denarii.* A denarius was the equivalent of a full day's wage. **6:48** Greek *About the fourth watch of the night.*

REAL LEADERSHIP
Mark gives us some of the best insights into Jesus' character.

Herod as a leader	*Jesus as a leader*
Selfish	Compassionate
Murderer	Healer
Immoral	Just and good
Political opportunist	Servant
King over small territory	King over all creation

6:37 In this chapter different people have examined Jesus' life and ministry: his neighbors and family, Herod the king, and the disciples. Yet none of these appreciated Jesus for who he was. The disciples were still pondering, still confused, still unbelieving. They did not realize that Jesus could provide for them. They were so preoccupied with the immensity of the task that they could not see what was possible with God. Do you let what seems impossible about Christianity keep you from believing?

6:37-42 When Jesus asked the disciples to provide food for over 5,000 people, they were amazed and said it would take a small fortune to feed such a crowd. How do you react when you are given an impossible task? A situation that seems impossible with human resources is simply an opportunity for God. The disciples did everything they could by gathering the available food and organizing the people into groups. Then, in answer to prayer, God did the impossible. When facing a seemingly impossible task, do what you can and ask God to do the rest. He may see fit to make the impossible happen.

6:49 The disciples were surprised to see Jesus walking beside them on the water. But they should have realized that Jesus would help them when they were in trouble. Though they had lost sight of Jesus, he had not lost sight of them. His concern for them overcame their lack of faith. The next time you are in "deep water," remember that Christ knows your struggle and cares for you.

6:49, 50 The disciples were afraid, but Jesus' presence calmed their fears. We all experience fear. Do we try to deal with it ourselves, or do we let Jesus deal with it? In times of fear and uncertainty, it is calming to know that Christ is always with us (Matthew 28:20). To recognize Christ's presence is the antidote for fear.

6:52 The disciples didn't want to believe, perhaps because (1) they couldn't accept the fact that this human named Jesus was really the Son of God; (2) they dared not believe that the Messiah would choose them as his followers—it was too good to be true; (3) they still did not understand the real purpose for Jesus' coming to earth. Their disbelief took the form of misunderstanding.

Even after watching Jesus miraculously feed 5,000 people, they still could not take the final step of faith and believe that he was God's Son. If they had, they would not have been amazed that Jesus could walk on water. The disciples did not transfer the truth they already knew about Jesus to their own lives. We read that Jesus walked on the water, and yet we often marvel that he is able to work in our life. We must not only believe that these miracles really occurred; we must also transfer the truth to our own life situations.

Jesus Heals All Who Touch Him (**98**/Matthew 14:34-36)
53 When they arrived at Gennesaret on the other side of the lake, they anchored the boat
54 and climbed out. The people standing there recognized him at once, 55 and they ran
throughout the whole area and began carrying sick people to him on mats. 56 Wherever **6:56** Matt 9:20
he went—in villages and cities and out on the farms—they laid the sick in the market Mark 5:27
plazas and streets. The sick begged him to let them at least touch the fringe of his robe, Luke 8:44
and all who touched it were healed.

Jesus Teaches about Inner Purity (**102**/Matthew 15:1-20)
7 One day some Pharisees and teachers of religious law arrived from Jerusalem to
confront Jesus. 2 They noticed that some of Jesus' disciples failed to follow the usual **7:2** Luke 11:38
Jewish ritual of hand washing before eating. 3 (The Jews, especially the Pharisees, do not Acts 10:14, 28
eat until they have poured water over their cupped hands,* as required by their ancient **7:3**
traditions. 4 Similarly, they eat nothing bought from the market unless they have im- Gal 1:14 Col 2:8
mersed their hands in water. This is but one of many traditions they have clung to—such **7:4** Matt 23:25
as their ceremony of washing cups, pitchers, and kettles.*) 5 So the Pharisees and Luke 11:39
teachers of religious law asked him, "Why don't your disciples follow our age-old
customs? For they eat without first performing the hand-washing ceremony." **7:6-7**
6 Jesus replied, "You hypocrites! Isaiah was prophesying about you when he said, †Isa 29:13 Col 2:22

7 'These people honor me with their lips,
but their hearts are far away.
Their worship is a farce,
for they replace God's commands with their own man-made teachings.'* **7:9** Isa 24:4-5

8 For you ignore God's specific laws and substitute your own traditions." **7:10** †Exod 20:12; 21:17
9 Then he said, "You reject God's laws in order to hold on to your own traditions. 10 For †Lev 20:9 †Deut 5:16 1 Tim 5:8

7:3 Greek *washed with the fist.* **7:4** Some Greek manuscripts add *and dining couches.* **7:7** Isa 29:13.

6:53 Gennesaret was a small fertile plain located on the west side of the Sea of Galilee. Capernaum, Jesus' home, sat at the northern edge of this plain.

7:1ff The religious leaders sent some investigators from their headquarters in Jerusalem to check up on Jesus. The delegation didn't like what they found, however, because Jesus scolded them for keeping the law and the traditions in order to look holy instead of to honor God. The prophet Isaiah accused the religious leaders of his day of doing the same thing (Isaiah 29:13). Jesus used Isaiah's words to accuse these men.

MINISTRY IN PHOENICIA
Jesus' ministry was to all people—first to Jews but also to Gentiles. Jesus took his disciples from Galilee to Tyre and Sidon, large cities in Phoenicia, where he healed a Gentile woman's daughter.

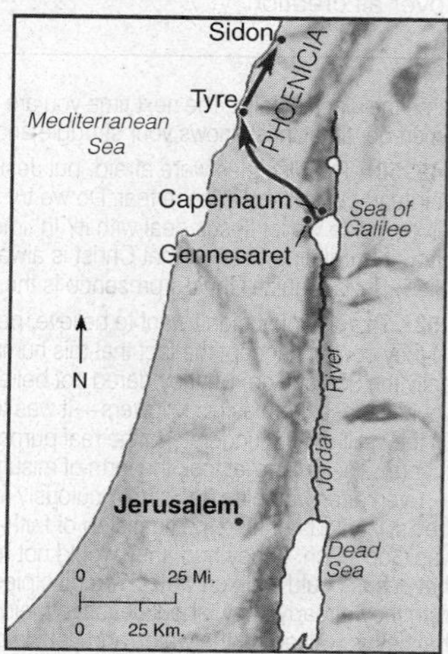

7:3, 4 Mark explained these Jewish rituals because he was writing to a non-Jewish audience. Before each meal, devout Jews performed a short ceremony, washing their hands and arms in a specific way. The disciples did not have dirty hands, but they were simply not carrying out this traditional cleansing. The Pharisees thought this ceremony cleansed them from any contact they might have had with anything considered unclean. Jesus said they were wrong in thinking they were acceptable to God just because they were clean on the outside.

7:6, 7 Hypocrisy is pretending to be something you are not and have no intention of being. Jesus called the Pharisees hypocrites because they worshiped God for the wrong reasons. Their worship was not motivated by love but by a desire to attain profit, to appear holy, and to increase their status. We become hypocrites when we (1) pay more attention to reputation than to character, (2) carefully follow certain religious practices while allowing our hearts to remain distant from God, and (3) emphasize our virtues but others' sins.

7:8, 9 The Pharisees added hundreds of their own petty rules and regulations to God's holy laws, and then they tried to force people to follow these rules. These men claimed to know God's will in every detail of life. There are still religious leaders today who add rules and regulations to God's Word, causing much confusion among believers. It is idolatry to claim that your interpretation of God's Word is as important as God's Word itself. It is especially dangerous to set up unbiblical standards for *others* to follow. Instead, look to Christ for guidance about your own behavior, and let him lead others in the details of their lives.

7:10, 11 The Pharisees used God as an excuse to avoid helping their families. They thought it was more important to put money in the Temple treasury than to help their needy parents, although God's law specifically says to honor fathers and mothers (Exodus 20:12) and to care for those in need (Leviticus 25:35-43). (For vowing to give money to God, see the note on Matthew 15:5, 6.) We should give money and time to God, but we must never use God as an excuse to neglect our responsibilities. Helping those in need is one of the most important ways to honor God.

instance, Moses gave you this law from God: 'Honor your father and mother,' and
'Anyone who speaks evil of father or mother must be put to death.'* 11 But you say it is
all right for people to say to their parents, 'Sorry, I can't help you. For I have vowed to
give to God what I could have given to you.'* 12 You let them disregard their needy
parents. 13 As such, you break the law of God in order to protect your own tradition. And
this is only one example. There are many, many others."

14 Then Jesus called to the crowd to come and hear. "All of you listen," he said, "and try to
understand. 15 You are not defiled by what you eat; you are defiled by what you say and do!*"
17 Then Jesus went into a house to get away from the crowds, and his disciples asked
him what he meant by the statement he had made. 18 "Don't you understand either?" he
asked. "Can't you see that what you eat won't defile you? 19 Food doesn't come in
contact with your heart, but only passes through the stomach and then comes out again."
(By saying this, he showed that every kind of food is acceptable.)
20 And then he added, "It is the thought-life that defiles you. 21 For from within, out of
a person's heart, come evil thoughts, sexual immorality, theft, murder, 22 adultery, greed,
wickedness, deceit, eagerness for lustful pleasure, envy, slander, pride, and foolishness.
23 All these vile things come from within; they are what defile you and make you
unacceptable to God."

7:15 1 Cor 8:8; 1 Tim 4:4
7:17 Mark 9:28
7:19 Acts 10:15; 11:9; Rom 14:1-12; Col 2:16; 1 Tim 4:3-5
7:21-22 Rom 1:29-31; Gal 5:19-21; Titus 1:15

2. Jesus' ministry beyond Galilee

Jesus Sends a Demon Out of a Girl (**103**/Matthew 15:21-28)

24 Then Jesus left Galilee and went north to the region of Tyre.* He tried to keep it secret
that he was there, but he couldn't. As usual, the news of his arrival spread fast. 25 Right
away a woman came to him whose little girl was possessed by an evil spirit. She had
heard about Jesus, and now she came and fell at his feet. 26 She begged him to release
her child from the demon's control.
Since she was a Gentile, born in Syrian Phoenicia, 27 Jesus told her, "First I should

7:10 Exod 20:12; 21:17; Lev 20:9; Deut 5:16. **7:11** Greek *'What I could have given to you is Corban' (that is, a gift).* **7:15** Some manuscripts add verse 16, *Anyone who is willing to hear should listen and understand.* **7:24** Some Greek manuscripts add *and Sidon.*

GOSPEL ACCOUNTS FOUND ONLY IN MARK

Section	Topic	Significance
4:26–29	Story of the growing seed	We must share the Good News of Jesus with other people, but only God makes it grow in their lives.
7:31–37	Jesus heals a deaf man who could hardly talk	Jesus cares about our physical as well as spiritual needs.
8:22–26	Jesus heals the blind man at Bethsaida	Jesus is considerate because he makes sure this man's sight is fully restored.

7:18, 19 Do we worry more about what is in our diet than what is in our heart and mind? As they interpreted the dietary laws (Leviticus 11), the Jews believed they could be clean before God because of what they refused to eat. But Jesus pointed out that sin actually begins in the attitudes and intentions of the inner person. Jesus did not degrade the law, but he paved the way for the change made clear in Acts 10:9-29 when God removed the cultural restrictions regarding food. We are not pure because of outward acts—we become pure on the inside as Christ renews our mind and transforms us into his image.

7:20-23 An evil action begins with a single thought. Allowing our mind to dwell on lust, envy, hatred, or revenge will lead to sin. Don't defile yourself by focusing on evil. Instead, follow Paul's advice in Philippians 4:8 and think about what is true, honorable, right, pure, lovely, and admirable.

7:24 Jesus traveled about 30 miles to Tyre. Tyre and the nearby city of Sidon were port cities on the Mediterranean Sea north of Israel. Both cities had flourishing trade and were very wealthy. They were proud, historic Canaanite cities.

In David's day, Tyre was on friendly terms with Israel (2 Samuel 5:11), but soon afterward the city became known for its wickedness. Its king even claimed to be God (Ezekiel 28:1ff). Tyre rejoiced when Jerusalem was destroyed in 586 B.C., because without Israel's competition, Tyre's trade and profits would increase. It was into this evil and materialistic culture that Jesus brought his message. It is interesting that Jesus stressed the importance of inner purity just before visiting Tyre.

7:26 This woman is called a Gentile, born in Syrian Phoenicia. Mark's designation refers to her political background. His Roman audience would easily identify her by the part of the empire that was her home.

7:27, 28 "Dog" refers to little dogs or house pets, not outdoor scavengers. Jesus was saying that his first priority was to provide food for the children (teach his disciples), not to allow pets to interrupt the family meal.

The woman did not try to argue. Using Jesus' choice of imagery, she pointed out that she was willing to be considered an interruption as long as she could receive God's healing for her daughter. Ironically, many Jews would lose God's spiritual healing because they rejected Jesus, while many Gentiles, whom the Jews rejected, would find salvation because they recognized Jesus.

help my own family, the Jews.* It isn't right to take food from the children and throw
it to the dogs."
28 She replied, "That's true, Lord, but even the dogs under the table are given some
crumbs from the children's plates."
29 "Good answer!" he said. "And because you have answered so well, I have healed
your daughter." 30 And when she arrived home, her little girl was lying quietly in bed,
and the demon was gone.

Jesus Heals Many People (**104**/Matthew 15:29-31)

31 Jesus left Tyre and went to Sidon, then back to the Sea of Galilee and the region of the
Ten Towns.* 32 A deaf man with a speech impediment was brought to him, and the people
begged Jesus to lay his hands on the man to heal him. 33 Jesus led him to a private place **7:33**
away from the crowd. He put his fingers into the man's ears. Then, spitting onto his own Mark 8:23
fingers, he touched the man's tongue with the spittle. 34 And looking up to heaven, he John 9:6
sighed and commanded, "Be opened!"* 35 Instantly the man could hear perfectly and **7:34** Matt 14:19
speak plainly! Mark 6:41 John 11:41; 17:1
36 Jesus told the crowd not to tell anyone, but the more he told them not to, the more **7:36**
they spread the news, 37 for they were completely amazed. Again and again they said, Matt 8:4
"Everything he does is wonderful. He even heals those who are deaf and mute." **7:37** Isa 35:5-6

Jesus Feeds Four Thousand (**105**/Matthew 15:32-39)

8 About this time another great crowd had gathered, and the people ran out of food **8:1-10**
again. Jesus called his disciples and told them, 2 "I feel sorry for these people. They Mark 6:32-44
have been here with me for three days, and they have nothing left to eat. 3 And if I send **8:2**
them home without feeding them, they will faint along the road. For some of them have Matt 9:36
come a long distance."
4 "How are we supposed to find enough food for them here in the wilderness?" his **8:4** Num 11:21-22
disciples asked. 2 Kgs 4:42-43
5 "How many loaves of bread do you have?" he asked.
"Seven," they replied. 6 So Jesus told all the people to sit down on the ground. Then
he took the seven loaves, thanked God for them, broke them into pieces, and gave them
to his disciples, who distributed the bread to the crowd. 7 A few small fish were found, **8:7** Matt 14:19
too, so Jesus also blessed these and told the disciples to pass them out.
8 They ate until they were full, and when the scraps were picked up, there were seven

7:27 Greek *Let the children eat first.* **7:31** Greek *Decapolis.* **7:34** Greek text uses Aramaic *"Ephphatha"* and then translates it as "Be opened."

CONTINUED MINISTRY
After taking a roundabout way back to Galilee through Decapolis (the Ten Towns), Jesus returned to Dalmanutha where Jewish leaders questioned his authority. From there he went to Bethsaida and on to Caesarea Philippi. Here he talked with his disciples about his authority and coming events.

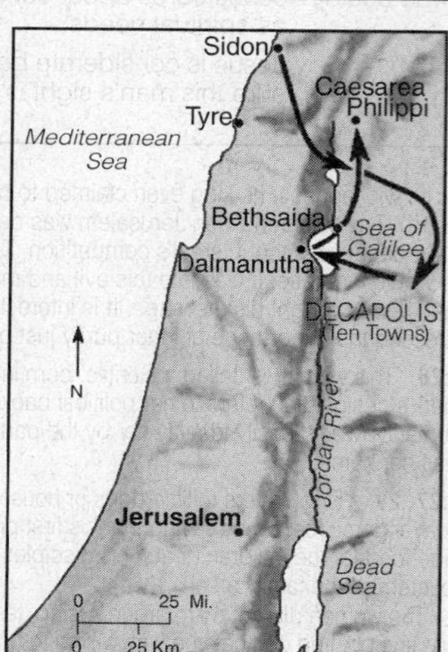

7:29 This miracle shows that Jesus' power over demons is so great that he doesn't need to be present physically in order to free someone. His power transcends any distance.

7:36 Jesus asked the people not to talk about this healing, because he didn't want to be seen simply as a miracle worker. He didn't want the people to miss his real message. We must not be so concerned about what Jesus can do for us that we forget to listen to his message.

8:1ff This is a different miracle from the feeding of the 5,000 described in chapter 6. At that time, those fed were mostly Jews. This time Jesus was ministering to a non-Jewish crowd in the Gentile region of the Ten Towns. Jesus' actions and message were beginning to have an impact on large numbers of Gentiles. That Jesus would compassionately minister to non-Jews was very reassuring to Mark's primarily Roman audience.

8:1-3 Do you ever feel that God is so busy with important concerns that he can't possibly be aware of your needs? Just as Jesus was concerned about these people's need for food, he is concerned about our daily needs. At another time Jesus said, "So don't worry about having enough food or drink or clothing. . . . Your heavenly Father already knows all your needs" (Matthew 6:31, 32). Do you have concerns that you think would not interest God? There is nothing too large for him to handle and no need too small to escape his interest.

large baskets of food left over! 9 There were about four thousand people in the crowd that
8:10 Matt 15:39 day, and he sent them home after they had eaten. 10 Immediately after this, he got into a
boat with his disciples and crossed over to the region of Dalmanutha.

Leaders Demand a Miraculous Sign (**106**/Matthew 16:1-4)

8:11-21 Luke 11:16, 29 John 6:30 11 When the Pharisees heard that Jesus had arrived, they came to argue with him. Testing
him to see if he was from God, they demanded, "Give us a miraculous sign from heaven
to prove yourself."
12 When he heard this, he sighed deeply and said, "Why do you people keep demanding a miraculous sign? I assure you, I will not give this generation any such sign." 13 So
he got back into the boat and left them, and he crossed to the other side of the lake.

Jesus Warns against Wrong Teaching (**107**/Matthew 16:5-12)

14 But the disciples discovered they had forgotten to bring any food, so there was only
8:15 Luke 12:1 one loaf of bread with them in the boat. 15 As they were crossing the lake, Jesus warned
them, "Beware of the yeast of the Pharisees and of Herod."
8:17 Isa 6:9-10 Mark 6:52 16 They decided he was saying this because they hadn't brought any bread. 17 Jesus
knew what they were thinking, so he said, "Why are you so worried about having no
8:18 †Jer 5:21 Ezek 12:2 Matt 13:13 food? Won't you ever learn or understand? Are your hearts too hard to take it in? 18 'You
have eyes—can't you see? You have ears—can't you hear?'* Don't you remember
anything at all? 19 What about the five thousand men I fed with five loaves of bread? How
8:19 Mark 6:41-44 Luke 9:17 John 6:13 many baskets of leftovers did you pick up afterward?"
"Twelve," they said.
8:20 Matt 15:37 20 "And when I fed the four thousand with seven loaves, how many large baskets of
leftovers did you pick up?"
"Seven," they said.
21 "Don't you understand even yet?" he asked them.

Jesus Restores Sight to a Blind Man (**108**)

22 When they arrived at Bethsaida, some people brought a blind man to Jesus, and they
8:23 Mark 7:33 John 9:6 begged him to touch and heal the man. 23 Jesus took the blind man by the hand and led
him out of the village. Then, spitting on the man's eyes, he laid his hands on him and
asked, "Can you see anything now?"
24 The man looked around. "Yes," he said, "I see people, but I can't see them very
clearly. They look like trees walking around."
25 Then Jesus placed his hands over the man's eyes again. As the man stared intently,
8:26 Matt 8:4 his sight was completely restored, and he could see everything clearly. 26 Jesus sent him
home, saying, "Don't go back into the village on your way home."

8:18 Jer 5:21.

8:11 The Pharisees had tried to explain away Jesus' previous miracles by claiming they were done by luck, coincidence, or evil power. Here they demanded a sign from heaven—something only God could do. Jesus refused their demand because he knew that even this kind of miracle would not convince them. They had already decided not to believe. Hearts can become so hard that even the most convincing facts and demonstrations will not change them.

8:15 Mark mentions the yeast of the Pharisees and of Herod, while Matthew talks about the yeast of the Pharisees and Sadducees. Mark's audience, mostly non-Jews, would have known about Herod but not necessarily about the Jewish religious sect of the Sadducees. Thus, Mark quoted the part of Jesus' statement that his readers would understand. This reference to Herod may mean the supporters of Herod, a group of Jews who supported the king. Many supporters of Herod were also Sadducees.

8:15ff Yeast in this passage symbolizes evil. Just as only a small amount of yeast is needed to make a batch of bread rise, so the hard-heartedness of the religious and political leaders could permeate and contaminate the entire society and make it rise up against Jesus.

8:17, 18 How could the disciples experience so many of Jesus' miracles and yet be so slow to comprehend who he was? They had already seen Jesus feed over 5,000 people with five loaves and two fish (6:35-44), yet here they doubted whether he could feed another large group.

Sometimes we are also slow to catch on. Although Christ has brought us through trials and temptations in the past, we don't believe that he will do so in the future. Is your heart too closed to take in all that God can do for you? Don't be like the disciples. Remember what Christ has done, and have faith that he will do it again.

8:25 Why did Jesus touch the man a second time before he could see? This miracle was not too difficult for Jesus, but he chose to do it in stages, possibly to show the disciples that some healing would be gradual rather than instantaneous or to demonstrate that spiritual truth is not always perceived clearly at first. Before Jesus left, however, the man was healed completely.

Peter Says Jesus Is the Messiah (**109**/Matthew 16:13-20; Luke 9:18-20)
27 Jesus and his disciples left Galilee and went up to the villages of Caesarea Philippi. As
they were walking along, he asked them, "Who do people say I am?"
28 "Well," they replied, "some say John the Baptist, some say Elijah, and others say
you are one of the other prophets."
29 Then Jesus asked, "Who do you say I am?"
Peter replied, "You are the Messiah." 30 But Jesus warned them not to tell anyone about
him.

Jesus Predicts His Death the First Time (**110**/Matthew 16:21-28; Luke 9:21-27)
31 Then Jesus began to tell them that he, the Son of Man, would suffer many terrible
things and be rejected by the leaders, the leading priests, and the teachers of religious
law. He would be killed, and three days later he would rise again. 32 As he talked about
this openly with his disciples, Peter took him aside and told him he shouldn't say things
like that.*
33 Jesus turned and looked at his disciples and then said to Peter very sternly, "Get
away from me, Satan! You are seeing things merely from a human point of view, not
from God's."
34 Then he called his disciples and the crowds to come over and listen. "If any of you
wants to be my follower," he told them, "you must put aside your selfish ambition, shoulder
your cross, and follow me. 35 If you try to keep your life for yourself, you will lose it. But if
you give up your life for my sake and for the sake of the Good News, you will find true life.

8:32 Or *and began to correct him.*

8:27-30 John 6:67-71
8:28 Matt 14:2
8:29 Matt 16:20; Luke 9:21; John 6:69; 11:27
8:34 Matt 10:38; Luke 14:27
8:35 Matt 10:39; Luke 17:33; John 12:25

8:27 Caesarea Philippi was an especially pagan city known for its worship of Greek gods and its temples devoted to the ancient god Pan. The ruler Philip, referred to in Mark 6:17, changed the city's name from Caesarea to Caesarea Philippi so that it would not be confused with the coastal city of Caesarea (Acts 8:40), the capital of the territory ruled by his brother Herod Antipas. This pagan city where many gods were recognized was a fitting place for Jesus to ask the disciples to recognize him as the Son of God.

8:28 For the story of John the Baptist, see Mark 1:1-11 and 6:14-29. For the story of Elijah, see 1 Kings 17–20 and 2 Kings 1–2.

8:29 Jesus asked the disciples who other people thought he was; then he asked them the same question. It is not enough to know what others say about Jesus: You must know, understand, and accept for yourself that he is the Messiah. You must move from curiosity to commitment, from admiration to adoration.

8:29-31 The name for Jesus, *Son of Man,* is Jesus' most common title for himself. It comes from Daniel 7:13, where the Son of Man is a heavenly figure who, in the end times, has authority and power. The name refers to Jesus as the Messiah, the representative man, the human agent of God who is vindicated by God. In this passage, *Son of Man* is linked closely with Peter's confession of Jesus as the Christ and confirms its messianic significance.

From this point on, Jesus spoke plainly and directly to his disciples about his death and resurrection. He began to prepare them for what was going to happen to him by telling them three times that he would soon die (8:31; 9:31; 10:33, 34).

8:30 Why did Jesus warn his own disciples not to tell anyone the truth about him? Jesus knew they needed more instruction about the work he would accomplish through his death and resurrection. Without more teaching, the disciples would have only half the picture. When they confessed Jesus as the Christ, they still didn't know all that it meant.

8:32, 33 In this moment, Peter was not considering God's purposes but only his own natural human desires and feelings. Peter wanted Christ to be king, but not the suffering servant prophesied in Isaiah 53. He was ready to receive the glory of following the Messiah but not the persecution.

The Christian life is not a paved road to wealth and ease. It often involves hard work, persecution, deprivation, and deep suffering. Peter saw only part of the picture. Don't repeat his mistake. Instead, focus on the good that God can bring out of apparent evil and the Resurrection that follows the Crucifixion.

8:33 Peter was often the spokesman for all the disciples. In singling him out, Jesus may have been addressing all of them indirectly. Unknowingly, the disciples were trying to prevent Jesus from going to the cross and thus fulfilling his mission on earth. Satan also tempted Jesus to avoid the way of the cross (Matthew 4). Whereas Satan's motives were evil, the disciples were motivated by love and admiration for Jesus. Nevertheless, the disciples' job was not to guide and protect Jesus but to follow him. Only after Jesus' death and resurrection would they fully understand why he had to die.

8:34 The Romans, Mark's original audience, knew what shouldering the cross meant. Death on a cross was a form of execution used by Rome for dangerous criminals. A prisoner carried his own cross to the place of execution, signifying submission to Rome's power.

Jesus used the image of carrying a cross to illustrate the ultimate submission required of his followers. He is not against pleasure, nor was he saying that we should seek pain needlessly. Jesus was talking about the heroic effort needed to follow him moment by moment, to do his will even when the work is difficult and the future looks bleak.

8:35 We should be willing to lose our life for the sake of the Good News, not because our life is useless but because nothing—not even life itself—can compare to what we gain with Christ. Jesus wants us to *choose* to follow him rather than to lead a life of sin and self-satisfaction. He wants us to stop trying to control our own destiny and to let him direct us. This makes good sense because, as the Creator, Christ knows better than we do what real life is about. He asks for submission, not self-hatred; he asks us only to lose our self-centered determination to be in charge.

36 And how do you benefit if you gain the whole world but lose your own soul* in the
8:38 Matt 10:33 Luke 12:9
process? 37 Is anything worth more than your soul? 38 If a person is ashamed of me and my
message in these adulterous and sinful days, I, the Son of Man, will be ashamed of that
person when I return in the glory of my Father with the holy angels."

9 Jesus went on to say, "I assure you that some of you standing here right now will
not die before you see the Kingdom of God arrive in great power!"

Jesus Is Transfigured on the Mountain (**111**/Matthew 17:1-13; Luke 9:28-36)

9:2-10 2 Pet 1:17-18
2 Six days later Jesus took Peter, James, and John to the top of a mountain. No one else
9:3 Dan 7:9 Matt 28:3
was there. As the men watched, Jesus' appearance changed, 3 and his clothing became
dazzling white, far whiter than any earthly process could ever make it. 4 Then Elijah and
Moses appeared and began talking with Jesus.
5 "Teacher, this is wonderful!" Peter exclaimed. "We will make three shrines*—one
for you, one for Moses, and one for Elijah." 6 He didn't really know what to say, for they
were all terribly afraid.
9:7 Exod 40:34 Deut 18:15 Heb 1:2; 2:3; 12:25
7 Then a cloud came over them, and a voice from the cloud said, "This is my beloved
Son. Listen to him." 8 Suddenly they looked around, and Moses and Elijah were gone,
and only Jesus was with them. 9 As they descended the mountainside, he told them not
to tell anyone what they had seen until he, the Son of Man, had risen from the dead. 10 So
they kept it to themselves, but they often asked each other what he meant by "rising from
the dead."
11 Now they began asking him, "Why do the teachers of religious law insist that Elijah
must return before the Messiah comes?"
12 Jesus responded, "Elijah is indeed coming first to set everything in order. Why then

8:36 Or *your life;* also in 8:37. **9:5** Or *shelters;* Greek reads *tabernacles.*

8:36, 37 Many people spend all their energy seeking pleasure. Jesus said, however, that worldliness, which is centered on possessions, position, or power, is ultimately worthless. Whatever you have on earth is only temporary; it cannot be exchanged for your soul. If you work hard at getting what you want, you might eventually have a "pleasurable" life, but in the end you will find it hollow and empty. Are you willing to make the pursuit of God more important than the selfish pursuits? Follow Jesus, and you will know what it means to live abundantly now and to have eternal life as well.

8:38 Jesus constantly turns the world's perspective upside down with talk of first and last, saving and losing. Here he gives us a choice. We can reject Jesus now and be rejected by him at his second coming, or we can accept him now and be accepted by him then. Rejecting Christ may help us escape shame for the time being, but it will guarantee an eternity of shame later.

9:1 What did Jesus mean when he said that some of the disciples would see the Kingdom of God arrive in power? There are several possibilities. He could have been foretelling his transfiguration, resurrection and ascension, the coming of the Holy Spirit at Pentecost, or his second coming. The Transfiguration is a strong possibility because Mark immediately tells that story. In the Transfiguration (9:2-8), Peter, James, and John saw Jesus glorified as the Son of God (2 Peter 1:16).

9:2 We don't know why Jesus singled out Peter, James, and John for this special revelation of his glory and purity. Perhaps they were the ones most ready to understand and accept this great truth. These three disciples were the inner circle of the group of 12. They were among the first to hear Jesus' call (1:16-19). They headed the Gospel lists of disciples (3:16). And they were present at certain healings where others were excluded (Luke 8:51).

9:2 Jesus took the disciples to either Mount Hermon or Mount Tabor. A mountain was often associated with closeness to God and readiness to receive his words. God had appeared to both Moses (Exodus 24:12-18) and Elijah (1 Kings 19:8-18) on mountains.

9:3ff The Transfiguration revealed Christ's divine nature. God's voice exalted Jesus above Moses and Elijah as the long-awaited Messiah with full divine authority. Moses represented the law, and Elijah, the prophets. Their appearance showed Jesus as the fulfillment of both the Old Testament law and the prophetic promises.

Jesus was not a reincarnation of Elijah or Moses. He was not merely one of the prophets. As God's only Son, he far surpasses them in authority and power. Many voices try to tell us how to live and how to know God personally. Some of these are helpful, many are not. We must first listen to the Bible, and then evaluate all other authorities in light of God's revelation.

9:9, 10 Jesus told Peter, James, and John not to speak about what they had seen because they would not fully understand it until Jesus had risen from the dead. Then they would realize that only through dying could Jesus show his power over death and his authority to be King of all. The disciples would not be powerful witnesses for God until they had grasped this truth.

It was natural for the disciples to be confused about Jesus' death and resurrection because they could not see into the future. We, on the other hand, have God's revealed Word, the Bible, to give us the full meaning of Jesus' death and resurrection. We have no excuse for our unbelief.

9:11-13 When Jesus said that Elijah had already come, he was speaking of John the Baptist (Matthew 17:11-13), who had fulfilled the role prophesied for Elijah.

9:12, 13 It was difficult for the disciples to grasp the idea that their Messiah would have to suffer. The Jews who studied the Old Testament prophecies expected the Messiah to be a great king like David, who would overthrow the enemy, Rome. Their vision was limited to their own time and experience.

They could not understand that the values of God's eternal Kingdom were different from the values of the world. They wanted relief from their present problems. But deliverance from sin is far more important than deliverance from physical suffering or political oppression. Our understanding and appreciation of Jesus must go beyond what he can do for us here and now.

is it written in the Scriptures that the Son of Man must suffer and be treated with utter
contempt? 13But I tell you, Elijah has already come, and he was badly mistreated, just
as the Scriptures predicted."

Jesus Heals a Demon-Possessed Boy (**112**/Matthew 17:14-21; Luke 9:37-43)

14At the foot of the mountain they found a great crowd surrounding the other disciples,
as some teachers of religious law were arguing with them. 15The crowd watched Jesus
in awe as he came toward them, and then they ran to greet him. 16"What is all this arguing
about?" he asked.

17One of the men in the crowd spoke up and said, "Teacher, I brought my son for you
to heal him. He can't speak because he is possessed by an evil spirit that won't let him
talk. 18And whenever this evil spirit seizes him, it throws him violently to the ground and
makes him foam at the mouth and grind his teeth and become rigid.* So I asked your
disciples to cast out the evil spirit, but they couldn't do it."

19Jesus said to them, "You faithless people! How long must I be with you until you
believe? How long must I put up with you? Bring the boy to me." 20So they brought the
boy. But when the evil spirit saw Jesus, it threw the child into a violent convulsion, and
he fell to the ground, writhing and foaming at the mouth. 21"How long has this been
happening?" Jesus asked the boy's father.

He replied, "Since he was very small. 22The evil spirit often makes him fall into the
fire or into water, trying to kill him. Have mercy on us and help us. Do something if you
can."

23"What do you mean, 'If I can'?" Jesus asked. "Anything is possible if a person
believes."

24The father instantly replied, "I do believe, but help me not to doubt!"

25When Jesus saw that the crowd of onlookers was growing, he rebuked the evil spirit.
"Spirit of deafness and muteness," he said, "I command you to come out of this child
and never enter him again!" 26Then the spirit screamed and threw the boy into another
violent convulsion and left him. The boy lay there motionless, and he appeared to be
dead. A murmur ran through the crowd, "He's dead." 27But Jesus took him by the hand
and helped him to his feet, and he stood up.

28Afterward, when Jesus was alone in the house with his disciples, they asked him,
"Why couldn't we cast out that evil spirit?"

29Jesus replied, "This kind can be cast out only by prayer.*"

Jesus Predicts His Death the Second Time (**113**/Matthew 17:22-23; Luke 9:44-45)

30Leaving that region, they traveled through Galilee. Jesus tried to avoid all publicity
31in order to spend more time with his disciples and teach them. He said to them, "The
Son of Man is going to be betrayed. He will be killed, but three days later he will rise

9:13 Ps 22:6-7; Isa 50:6; 53:3; Matt 11:14
9:20 Mark 1:26
9:23 Matt 21:21; Mark 11:23-24; Luke 17:6; John 11:40; Acts 14:9
9:24 Luke 17:5
9:25 Acts 10:38
9:26 Mark 1:26
9:27 Matt 8:15
9:31 Matt 16:21; Mark 8:31; Luke 9:22

9:18 Or *become weak.* **9:29** Some manuscripts add *and fasting.*

9:18 Why couldn't the disciples cast out the evil spirit? In 6:13 we read that they cast out demons while on their mission to the villages. Perhaps they had special authority only for that trip, or perhaps their faith was faltering. Mark tells this story to show that the battle with Satan is a difficult, ongoing struggle. Victory over sin and temptation comes through faith in Jesus Christ, not through our own efforts.

9:23 Jesus' words do not mean that we can automatically obtain anything we want if we just think positively. Jesus meant that anything is *possible* if we believe, because nothing is too difficult for God. We cannot have everything we pray for as if by magic, but with faith, we can have everything we need to serve him.

9:24 The attitude of trust and confidence that the Bible calls *belief* or *faith* (Hebrews 11:1, 6) is not something we can obtain without help. Faith is a gift from God (Ephesians 2:8, 9). No matter how much faith we have, we never reach the point of being self-sufficient. Faith is not stored away like money in the bank. Growing in faith is a constant process of daily renewing our trust in Jesus.

9:29 The disciples would often face difficult situations that could be resolved only through prayer. Prayer is the key that unlocks faith in our life. Effective prayer needs both an attitude—complete dependence—and an action—asking. Prayer demonstrates our reliance on God as we humbly invite him to fill us with faith and power. There is no substitute for prayer, especially in circumstances that seem impossible.

9:30, 31 At times, Jesus limited his public ministry in order to train his disciples in depth. He knew the importance of equipping them to carry on when he returned to heaven. It takes time to learn. Spiritual growth isn't instant, regardless of the quality of experience or teaching. If even the disciples needed to lay aside their work periodically in order to learn from the Master, how much more do we need to alternate working and learning.

9:30, 31 Leaving Caesarea Philippi, Jesus began his last tour through the region of Galilee.

from the dead." 32But they didn't understand what he was saying, and they were afraid
to ask him what he meant.

The Disciples Argue about Who Would Be the Greatest
(**115**/Matthew 18:1-6; Luke 9:46-48)

33After they arrived at Capernaum, Jesus and his disciples settled in the house where they
9:34 Luke 22:24 would be staying. Jesus asked them, "What were you discussing out on the road?" 34But
they didn't answer, because they had been arguing about which of them was the greatest.
9:35 Matt 20:27 35He sat down and called the twelve disciples over to him. Then he said, "Anyone who
wants to be the first must take last place and be the servant of everyone else."
9:37 Matt 10:40; Luke 10:16; John 13:20 36Then he put a little child among them. Taking the child in his arms, he said to them,
37"Anyone who welcomes a little child like this on my behalf welcomes me, and anyone
who welcomes me welcomes my Father who sent me."

The Disciples Forbid Another to Use Jesus' Name (**116**/Luke 9:49-50)

9:38-41 Num 11:26-29 38John said to Jesus, "Teacher, we saw a man using your name to cast out demons, but
9:39 1 Cor 12:3 we told him to stop because he isn't one of our group."
39"Don't stop him!" Jesus said. "No one who performs miracles in my name will soon
9:40 Matt 12:30; Luke 11:23 be able to speak evil of me. 40Anyone who is not against us is for us. 41If anyone gives
you even a cup of water because you belong to the Messiah, I assure you, that person
9:41 Matt 10:42 will be rewarded.

Jesus Warns against Temptation (**117**/Matthew 18:7-9)

42"But if anyone causes one of these little ones who trusts in me to lose faith, it would
be better for that person to be thrown into the sea with a large millstone tied around the
9:43 Matt 5:30; 18:8 neck. 43If your hand causes you to sin, cut it off. It is better to enter heaven* with only
one hand than to go into the unquenchable fires of hell with two hands.* 45If your foot

9:43a Greek *enter life;* also in 9:45. **9:43b** Some manuscripts add verse 44 (which is identical with 9:48).

9:32 Why were the disciples afraid to ask Jesus about his prediction of his death? Perhaps it was because the last time they reacted to Jesus' sobering words they were scolded (8:32, 33). In their minds, Jesus seemed morbidly preoccupied with death. Actually it was the disciples who were wrongly preoccupied—constantly thinking about the Kingdom they hoped Jesus would bring and their positions in it. If Jesus died, the Kingdom as they imagined it could not come. Consequently they preferred not to ask him about his predictions.

9:34 The disciples, caught up in their constant struggle for personal success, were embarrassed to answer Jesus' question. It is always painful to compare our motives with Christ's. It is not wrong for believers to be industrious or ambitious. But when ambition pushes obedience and service to one side, it becomes sin. Pride or insecurity can cause us to overvalue position and prestige. In God's Kingdom, such motives are destructive. The only safe ambition is directed toward Christ's Kingdom, not our own advancement.

9:36, 37 Jesus taught the disciples to welcome children. This was a new approach in a society where children were usually treated as second-class citizens. It is important not only to treat children well but also to teach them about Jesus. Children's ministries should never be regarded as less important than those for adults.

9:38 The disciples were jealous of a man who healed in Jesus' name because they were more concerned about their own group's position than in helping to free those troubled by demons. We do the same today when we refuse to associate with Christians from other denominations because (1) other people or groups are not affiliated with our denomination, (2) their projects do not involve the kind of people with whom we feel most comfortable, (3) others don't do things the way we are used to doing things, or (4) our efforts won't receive enough recognition. Correct theology is important but should never be an excuse to avoid helping people in need.

9:40 Jesus was not saying that being indifferent or neutral toward him is as good as being committed. As he explained in Matthew 12:30, "Anyone who isn't helping me opposes me, and anyone who isn't working with me is actually working against me." In both cases, Jesus was pointing out that neutrality toward him is not possible. Nevertheless his followers will not all resemble each other or belong to the same groups. People who are on Jesus' side have the same goal of building up the Kingdom of God, and they should not let their differences interfere with this goal. Those who share a common faith in Christ should cooperate. People don't have to be just like us to be following Jesus with us.

9:41, 42 Luke 9:48 states, "Whoever is the least among you is the greatest." In Jesus' eyes, whoever welcomes a child welcomes Jesus; giving a cup of cold water to a person in need is the same as giving an offering to God. By contrast, harming others or failing to care for them is a sin, even if they are unimportant people in the world's eyes. It is possible for thoughtless, selfish people to gain a measure of worldly greatness, but lasting greatness is measured by God's standards. What do you use as your measure—personal achievement or unselfish service?

9:42 This caution against harming little ones in the faith applies both to what we do individually as teachers and examples and to what we allow to fester in our Christian fellowship. Our thoughts and actions must be motivated by love (1 Corinthians 13), and we must be careful about judging others (Matthew 7:1-5; Romans 14:1–15:4). However, we also have a responsibility to confront flagrant sin within the church (1 Corinthians 5:12, 13).

9:43ff Jesus used startling language to stress the importance of cutting sin out of our life. Painful self-discipline is required of his true followers. Giving up a relationship, job, or habit that is against God's will may seem just as painful as cutting off a hand. Our high goal, however, is worth any sacrifice; Christ is worth any possible loss. Nothing should stand in the way of faith. We must be ruthless in removing sin from our life now in order to avoid being suffering for eternity. Make your choices from an eternal perspective.

causes you to sin, cut it off. It is better to enter heaven with only one foot than to be
thrown into hell with two feet.* 47And if your eye causes you to sin, gouge it out. It is **9:47** Matt 5:29
better to enter the Kingdom of God half blind than to have two eyes and be thrown into **9:49** Lev 2:13
hell, 48'where the worm never dies and the fire never goes out.'*
49"For everyone will be purified with fire.* 50Salt is good for seasoning. But if it loses **9:50** Matt 5:13; Luke 14:34; Rom 12:18; Col 4:6
its flavor, how do you make it salty again? You must have the qualities of salt among
yourselves and live in peace with each other."

Jesus Teaches about Marriage and Divorce (**173**/Matthew 19:1-12)

10 Then Jesus left Capernaum and went southward to the region of Judea and into
the area east of the Jordan River. As always there were the crowds, and as usual
he taught them.
2Some Pharisees came and tried to trap him with this question: "Should a man be
allowed to divorce his wife?"
3"What did Moses say about divorce?" Jesus asked them.
4"Well, he permitted it," they replied. "He said a man merely has to write his wife an
official letter of divorce and send her away."* **10:4** †Deut 24:1-3
5But Jesus responded, "He wrote those instructions only as a concession to your
hard-hearted wickedness. 6But God's plan was seen from the beginning of creation, for **10:6** †Gen 1:27; 5:2
'He made them male and female.'* 7'This explains why a man leaves his father and
mother and is joined to his wife,* 8and the two are united into one.'* Since they are no **10:7-8** †Gen 2:24; 1 Cor 6:16; Eph 5:31
longer two but one, 9let no one separate them, for God has joined them together."
10Later, when he was alone with his disciples in the house, they brought up the **10:11** Matt 5:32; Luke 16:18; 1 Cor 7:10-11
subject again. 11He told them, "Whoever divorces his wife and marries someone else

9:45 Some manuscripts add verse 46 (which is identical with 9:48). **9:48** Isa 66:24. **9:49** Greek *salted with fire.* Some manuscripts add *and every sacrifice will be salted with salt.* **10:4** Deut 24:1. **10:6** Gen 1:27; 5:2. **10:7** Some manuscripts do not include *and is joined to his wife.* **10:7-8** Gen 2:24.

9:48, 49 With these strange words, Jesus pictured the serious and eternal consequences of sin. To the Jews, worms and fire represented both internal and external pain. Nothing could be worse.

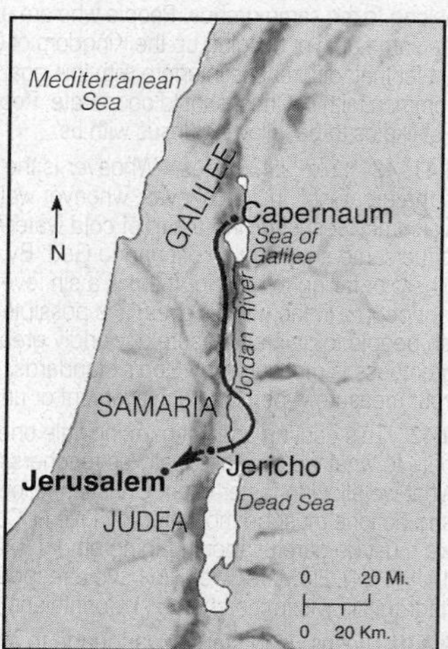

FINAL TRIP TO JUDEA
Jesus quietly left Capernaum, heading toward the borders of Judea before crossing the Jordan River. He preached there before going to Jericho. This trip from Galilee was his last; he would not return before his death.

9:50 Jesus used salt to illustrate three qualities that should be found in his people: (1) *We should remember God's faithfulness,* just as salt when used with a sacrifice recalled God's covenant with his people (Leviticus 2:13). (2) *We should make a difference in the "flavor" of the world we live in,* just as salt changes meat's flavor (see Matthew 5:13). (3) *We should counteract the moral decay in society,* just as salt preserves food from decay. When we lose this desire to "salt" the earth with the love and message of God, we become useless to him.

10:2 The Pharisees were trying to trap Jesus with their question. If he supported divorce, he would be upholding the Pharisees' procedures, and they doubted that he would do that. If Jesus spoke against divorce, however, some members of the crowd would dislike his position; some may have even used the law to their advantage to divorce their wives. More important, he might incur the wrath of Herod, who had already killed John the Baptist for speaking out against divorce and adultery (6:17-28). This is what the Pharisees wanted.

The Pharisees saw divorce as a legal issue rather than a spiritual one. Jesus used this test as an opportunity to review God's intended purpose for marriage and to expose the Pharisees' selfish motives. They were not thinking about what God intended for marriage but had settled for marriages of convenience. In addition, they were quoting Moses unfairly and out of context. Jesus showed these legal experts how superficial their knowledge really was.

10:5-9 God allowed divorce as a concession to people's sinfulness. Divorce was not approved, but it was instituted to protect the injured party in a bad situation. Unfortunately, the Pharisees used Deuteronomy 24:1 as a proof text for divorce. Jesus explained that this was not God's intent; instead, God wants married people to consider their marriage permanent. Don't enter marriage with the option of getting out. Your marriage is more likely to be happy if from the outset you are committed to permanence. Don't be hardhearted like these Pharisees, but be hardheaded in your determination, with God's help, to stay together.

10:6-9 Women were often treated as property. Marriage and divorce were regarded as transactions similar to buying and selling land. But Jesus condemned this attitude, clarifying God's original intention—that marriage bring oneness (Genesis 2:24). Jesus held up God's ideal for marriage and told his followers to live by that ideal.

commits adultery against her. 12 And if a woman divorces her husband and remarries,
she commits adultery."

Jesus Blesses the Children (**174**/Matthew 19:13-15; Luke 18:15-17)

13 One day some parents brought their children to Jesus so he could touch them and bless
them, but the disciples told them not to bother him. 14 But when Jesus saw what was
happening, he was very displeased with his disciples. He said to them, "Let the children
10:15 Matt 18:3 come to me. Don't stop them! For the Kingdom of God belongs to such as these. 15 I
assure you, anyone who doesn't have their kind of faith will never get into the Kingdom
10:16 Mark 9:36 of God." 16 Then he took the children into his arms and placed his hands on their heads
and blessed them.

Jesus Speaks to the Rich Young Man (**175**/Matthew 19:16-30; Luke 18:18-30)

17 As he was starting out on a trip, a man came running up to Jesus, knelt down, and asked,
"Good Teacher, what should I do to get eternal life?"
10:19 †Exod 20:12-16 †Deut 5:16-20 Rom 13:9 18 "Why do you call me good?" Jesus asked. "Only God is truly good. 19 But as for
your question, you know the commandments: 'Do not murder. Do not commit adultery.
Do not steal. Do not testify falsely. Do not cheat. Honor your father and mother.'*"
20 "Teacher," the man replied, "I've obeyed all these commandments since I was a
10:21 Matt 6:19-20 Luke 12:33 Acts 2:44-45 child."
21 Jesus felt genuine love for this man as he looked at him. "You lack only one thing,"
he told him. "Go and sell all you have and give the money to the poor, and you will have
treasure in heaven. Then come, follow me." 22 At this, the man's face fell, and he went
sadly away because he had many possessions.
23 Jesus looked around and said to his disciples, "How hard it is for rich people to get
10:24 Matt 7:13-14 John 3:5 into the Kingdom of God!" 24 This amazed them. But Jesus said again, "Dear children,
it is very hard* to get into the Kingdom of God. 25 It is easier for a camel to go through
the eye of a needle than for a rich person to enter the Kingdom of God!"

10:19 Exod 20:12-16; Deut 5:16-20. **10:24** Some manuscripts add *for those who trust in riches.*

10:13-16 Jesus was often criticized for spending too much time with the wrong people—children, tax collectors, and sinners (Matthew 9:11; Luke 15:1, 2; 19:7). Some, including the disciples, thought Jesus should be spending more time with important leaders and the devout, because this was the way to improve his position and avoid criticism. But Jesus didn't need to improve his position. He was God, and he wanted to speak to those who needed him most.

10:14 To feel secure, all children need is a loving look and gentle touch from someone who cares. They believe us because they trust us. Jesus said that people should trust in him with this kind of childlike faith. We do not have to understand all the mysteries of the universe; it should be enough to know that God loves us and provides forgiveness for our sin. This doesn't mean that we should be childish or immature, but we should trust God with a child's simplicity and receptivity.

10:17-23 This man wanted to be sure he would get eternal life, so he asked what he could *do*. He said he'd never once broken any of the laws Jesus mentioned (10:19), and perhaps he had even kept the Pharisees' loophole-filled version of them. But Jesus lovingly broke through the man's pride with a challenge that brought out his true motives: "Go and sell all you have and give the money to the poor." This challenge exposed the barrier that could keep this man out of the Kingdom: his love of money. Money represented his pride of accomplishment and self-effort. Ironically, his attitude made him unable to keep the first commandment: to let nothing be more important than God (Exodus 20:3). He could not meet the one requirement Jesus gave—to turn his whole heart and life over to God. The man came to Jesus wondering what he could do; he left seeing what he was unable to do. What barriers are keeping you from turning your life over to Christ?

10:18 When Jesus asked this question, he was saying, "Do you really know the one to whom you are talking?" Because only God is truly good, the man was calling Jesus "God," whether or not he realized it.

10:21 What does your money mean to you? Although Jesus wanted this man to sell everything and give his money to the poor, this does not mean that all believers should sell all their possessions. Most of his followers did not sell everything, although they used their possessions to serve others. Instead, this incident shows us that we must not let our possessions or money keep us from following Jesus. We must remove all barriers to serving him fully. If Jesus asked, could you give up your house? your car? your level of income? your position on the ladder of promotion? Your reaction may show your attitude toward money—whether it is your servant or your master.

10:21 Jesus showed genuine love for this man, even though he knew that the man might not follow him. Love is able to give tough advice; it doesn't hedge on the truth. Christ loved us enough to die for us, and he also loves us enough to talk straight to us. If his love were superficial, he would give us only his approval; but because his love is complete, he gives us life-changing challenges.

10:23 Jesus said it was very difficult for the rich to enter the Kingdom of God because the rich, having their basic physical needs met, often become self-reliant. When they feel empty, they buy something new to try to fill the void that only God can fill. Their abundance and self-sufficiency become their deficiency. The person who has everything on earth can still lack what is most important—eternal life.

26 The disciples were astounded. "Then who in the world can be saved?" they asked.
27 Jesus looked at them intently and said, "Humanly speaking, it is impossible. But not with God. Everything is possible with God."
28 Then Peter began to mention all that he and the other disciples had left behind. "We've given up everything to follow you," he said.
29 And Jesus replied, "I assure you that everyone who has given up house or brothers or sisters or mother or father or children or property, for my sake and for the Good News,
30 will receive now in return, a hundred times over, houses, brothers, sisters, mothers, children, and property—with persecutions. And in the world to come they will have eternal life. 31 But many who seem to be important now will be the least important then, and those who are considered least here will be the greatest then.*"

10:27 Gen 18:14 Job 42:2 Mark 14:36
10:28 Mark 1:18
10:30 2 Tim 3:12
10:31 Matt 20:16 Luke 13:30

Jesus Predicts His Death the Third Time (**177**/Matthew 20:17-19; Luke 18:31-34)

32 They were now on the way to Jerusalem, and Jesus was walking ahead of them. The disciples were filled with dread and the people following behind were overwhelmed with fear. Taking the twelve disciples aside, Jesus once more began to describe everything that was about to happen to him in Jerusalem. 33 "When we get to Jerusalem," he told them, "the Son of Man will be betrayed to the leading priests and the teachers of religious law. They will sentence him to die and hand him over to the Romans. 34 They will mock him, spit on him, beat him with their whips, and kill him, but after three days he will rise again."

10:33 Matt 16:21; 17:22-23 Mark 8:31; 9:31 Luke 24:7
10:34 Isa 50:6

Jesus Teaches about Serving Others (**178**/Matthew 20:20-28)

35 Then James and John, the sons of Zebedee, came over and spoke to him. "Teacher," they said, "we want you to do us a favor."
36 "What is it?" he asked.
37 "In your glorious Kingdom, we want to sit in places of honor next to you," they said, "one at your right and the other at your left."
38 But Jesus answered, "You don't know what you are asking! Are you able to drink from the bitter cup of sorrow I am about to drink? Are you able to be baptized with the baptism of suffering I must be baptized with?"

10:38 Luke 12:50 John 18:11

10:31 Greek *But many who are first will be last; and the last, first.*

10:26 The disciples were amazed. Was not wealth a blessing from God, a reward for being good? This misconception is still common today. Although many believers enjoy material prosperity, many others live in poverty. Wealth is not a sign of faith or of partiality on God's part.

10:29, 30 Jesus assured the disciples that anyone who gives up something valuable for his sake will be repaid a hundred times over in this life, although not necessarily in the same way. For example, someone may be rejected by his family for accepting Christ, but he or she will gain the larger family of believers. Along with these rewards, however, we experience persecution because the world hates God. Jesus emphasized persecution to make sure that we do not selfishly follow him only for the rewards.

10:31 Jesus explained that in the world to come, the values of this world will be reversed. Those who seek status and importance here will have none in heaven. Those who are humble here will be great in heaven. The corrupt condition of our society encourages confusion in values. We are bombarded by messages that tell us how to be important and how to feel good, and Jesus' teaching about service to others seems alien. But those who have humbly served others are most qualified to be great in heaven.

10:32 Because Jesus had just spoken to them about facing persecution, the disciples were filled with dread as they thought about what awaited them in Jerusalem.

10:33, 34 Jesus' death and resurrection should have come as no surprise to the disciples. Here he clearly explained to them what would happen to him. Unfortunately, they didn't really hear what he was saying. Jesus said he was the Messiah, but they thought the Messiah would be a conquering king. He spoke to them of resurrection, but they heard only his words about death. Because Jesus often spoke in parables, the disciples may have thought that his words on death and resurrection were another parable they weren't astute enough to understand. Jesus' predictions of his death and resurrection show that these events were God's plan from the beginning and not accidents.

10:35 Mark records that John and James went to Jesus with their request; in Matthew, their mother also made the request. There is no contradiction in the accounts—mother and sons were in agreement in requesting honored places in Christ's Kingdom.

10:37 The disciples, like most Jews of that day, had the wrong idea of the Messiah's Kingdom as predicted by the Old Testament prophets. They thought Jesus would establish an earthly kingdom that would free Israel from Rome's oppression, and James and John wanted honored places in it. But Jesus' Kingdom is not of this world; it is not centered in palaces and thrones but in the hearts and lives of his followers. The disciples did not understand this until after Jesus' resurrection.

10:38, 39 James and John said they were willing to face any trial for Christ. Both did suffer: James died as a martyr (Acts 12:2), and John was forced to live in exile (Revelation 1:9). It is easy to say we will endure anything for Christ, and yet most of us complain about the most minor problems. We may say that we are willing to suffer for Christ, but are we willing to suffer the minor irritations that sometimes come with serving others?

10:38-40 Jesus didn't ridicule James and John for asking, but he denied their request. We can feel free to ask God for anything, but our request may be denied. God wants to give us what is best for us, not merely what we want. He denies some requests for our own good.

10:39 Acts 12:2; Rev 1:9
10:42 Luke 22:25-27; 1 Pet 5:3
10:43-44 Matt 23:11; Mark 9:35; Luke 22:26
10:45 Matt 20:28; John 13:14; Phil 2:7; 1 Tim 2:5-6; Titus 2:14

39 “Oh yes,” they said, “we are able!”
And Jesus said, “You will indeed drink from my cup and be baptized with my baptism,
40 but I have no right to say who will sit on the thrones next to mine. God has prepared
those places for the ones he has chosen.”
41 When the ten other disciples discovered what James and John had asked, they
were indignant. 42 So Jesus called them together and said, “You know that in this
world kings are tyrants, and officials lord it over the people beneath them. 43 But
among you it should be quite different. Whoever wants to be a leader among you must
be your servant, 44 and whoever wants to be first must be the slave of all. 45 For even
I, the Son of Man, came here not to be served but to serve others, and to give my life
as a ransom for many.”

Jesus Heals a Blind Beggar (**179**/Matthew 20:29-34; Luke 18:35-43)

10:47 Isa 11:1; Jer 23:5-6; Matt 9:27; 15:22

46 And so they reached Jericho. Later, as Jesus and his disciples left town, a great
crowd was following. A blind beggar named Bartimaeus (son of Timaeus) was sitting
beside the road as Jesus was going by. 47 When Bartimaeus heard that Jesus from
Nazareth was nearby, he began to shout out, “Jesus, Son of David, have mercy on
me!”
48 “Be quiet!” some of the people yelled at him.
But he only shouted louder, “Son of David, have mercy on me!”
49 When Jesus heard him, he stopped and said, “Tell him to come here.”
So they called the blind man. “Cheer up,” they said. “Come on, he’s calling you!”
50 Bartimaeus threw aside his coat, jumped up, and came to Jesus.
51 “What do you want me to do for you?” Jesus asked.
“Teacher,” the blind man said, “I want to see!”
52 And Jesus said to him, “Go your way. Your faith has healed you.” And instantly the
blind man could see! Then he followed Jesus down the road.*

10:52 Matt 9:22; Mark 5:34; Luke 7:50; 8:48; 17:19

10:52 Or *on the way.*

10:42-45 James and John wanted the highest positions in Jesus’ Kingdom. But Jesus told them that true greatness comes in serving others. Peter, one of the disciples who had heard this message, expands the thought in 1 Peter 5:1-4.

Businesses, organizations, and institutions measure greatness by personal achievement. In Christ’s Kingdom, however, service is the way to get ahead. The desire to be on top will hinder, not help. Rather than seeking to have your needs met, look for ways that you can minister to the needs of others.

10:45 This verse reveals not only the motive for Jesus’ ministry but also the basis for our salvation. A ransom was the price paid to release a slave. Jesus paid a ransom for us because we could not pay it ourselves. His death released all of us from our slavery to sin. The disciples thought Jesus’ life and power would save them from Rome; Jesus said his *death* would save them from sin, an even greater slavery than Rome’s. More about the ransom Jesus paid for us is found in 1 Peter 1:18, 19.

10:46 Jericho was a popular resort city rebuilt by Herod the Great in the Judean desert, not far from the Jordan River crossing. Jesus was on his way to Jerusalem (10:32), and, after crossing over from Perea, he would naturally enter Jericho.

10:46 Beggars were a common sight in most towns. Because most occupations of that day required physical labor, anyone with a crippling disease or disability was at a severe disadvantage and was usually forced to beg, even though God’s laws commanded care for such needy people (Leviticus 25:35-38). Blindness was considered a curse from God for sin (John 9:2), but Jesus refuted this idea when he reached out to heal the blind.

10:47 “Son of David” was a popular way of addressing Jesus as the Messiah, because it was known that the Messiah would be a descendant of King David (Isaiah 9:7). The fact that Bartimaeus called Jesus the Son of David shows that he recognized Jesus as the Messiah. His faith in Jesus as the Messiah brought about his healing.

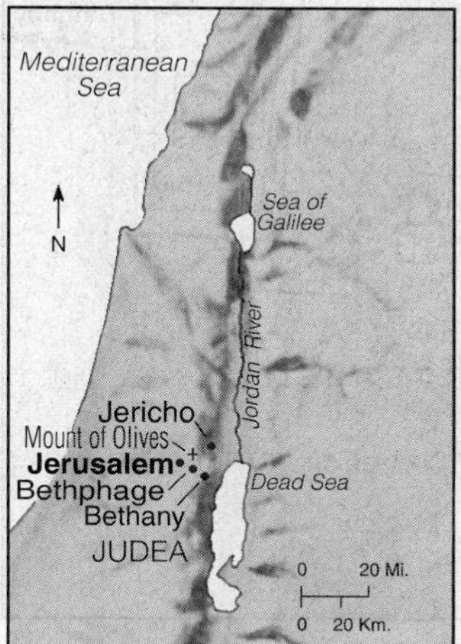

JESUS NEARS JERUSALEM Leaving Jericho, Jesus headed toward acclaim, then crucifixion, in Jerusalem. During his last week, he stayed outside the city in Bethany, a village on the eastern slope of the Mount of Olives, entering Jerusalem to teach, eat the Passover, and finally be crucified.

3. Jesus' ministry in Jerusalem

Jesus Rides into Jerusalem on a Donkey
(**183**/Matthew 21:1-11; Luke 19:28-44; John 12:12-19)

11 As Jesus and his disciples approached Jerusalem, they came to the towns of
Bethphage and Bethany, on the Mount of Olives. Jesus sent two of them on ahead.
2"Go into that village over there," he told them, "and as soon as you enter it, you will **11:2** 1 Sam 6:7
see a colt tied there that has never been ridden. Untie it and bring it here. 3If anyone asks Zech 9:9
what you are doing, just say, 'The Lord needs it and will return it soon.'"
4The two disciples left and found the colt standing in the street, tied outside a house.
5As they were untying it, some bystanders demanded, "What are you doing, untying that
colt?" 6They said what Jesus had told them to say, and they were permitted to take it.
7Then they brought the colt to Jesus and threw their garments over it, and he sat on it.
8Many in the crowd spread their coats on the road ahead of Jesus, and others cut leafy
branches in the fields and spread them along the way. 9He was in the center of the **11:9-10** †Pss 118:25-26;
procession, and the crowds all around him were shouting, 148:1

"Praise God!*
Bless the one who comes in the name of the Lord!
10 Bless the coming kingdom of our ancestor David!
Praise God in highest heaven!"*

11So Jesus came to Jerusalem and went into the Temple. He looked around carefully **11:11** Matt 21:10, 17
at everything, and then he left because it was late in the afternoon. Then he went out to
Bethany with the twelve disciples.

Jesus Clears the Temple Again (**184**/Matthew 21:12-17; Luke 19:45-48)
12The next morning as they were leaving Bethany, Jesus felt hungry. 13He noticed a

11:9 Greek *Hosanna,* an exclamation of praise that literally means "save now"; also in 11:10. **11:9-10** Pss 118:25-26; 148:1.

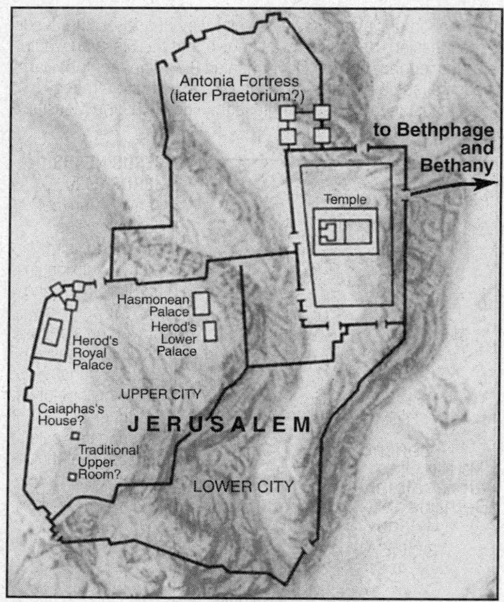

CLEARING THE TEMPLE On Monday morning of his last week, Jesus left Bethany, entered Jerusalem, and cleared the Temple of money changers and merchants.

11:1, 2 This was Sunday of the week that Jesus would be crucified, and the great Passover festival was about to begin. Jews came to Jerusalem from all over the Roman world during this week-long celebration to remember the great exodus from Egypt (see Exodus 12:37-51). Many in the crowds had heard of or seen Jesus and were hoping he would come to the Temple (John 11:55-57).

Jesus did come, not as a warring king on a horse or in a chariot, but as a gentle and peaceable King on a donkey's colt, just as Zechariah 9:9 had predicted. Jesus knew that those who would hear him teach at the Temple would return to their homes throughout the world and announce the coming of the Messiah.

11:9, 10 The people exclaimed "Praise God!" because they recognized that Jesus was fulfilling the prophecy in Zechariah 9:9 (see also Psalm 24:7-10; 118:26). They spoke of David's kingdom because of God's words to David in 2 Samuel 7:12-14. The crowd correctly saw Jesus as the fulfillment of these prophecies, but they did not understand where Jesus' kingship would lead him. This same crowd cried out, "Crucify him!" when Jesus stood on trial only a few days later.

11:11-21 In this passage, two unusual incidents are related: the cursing of the fig tree and the clearing of the Temple. The cursing of the fig tree was an acted-out parable related to the clearing of the Temple. The Temple was supposed to be a place of worship, but true worship had disappeared. The fig tree showed promise of fruit, but it produced none. Jesus was showing his anger at religious life without substance. If you claim to have faith without putting it to work in your life, you are like the barren fig tree. Genuine faith has great potential; ask God to help you bear fruit for his Kingdom.

11:13-26 Fig trees, a popular source of inexpensive food in Israel, require three years from the time they are planted until they can bear fruit. Each tree yields a great amount of fruit twice a year, in late spring and in early autumn. This incident occurred early in the spring when the leaves were beginning to bud. The figs normally grow as the leaves fill out, but this tree, though full of leaves, had none. The tree looked promising but offered no fruit. Jesus' harsh words to the fig tree could be applied to the nation of Israel. Fruitful in appearance only, Israel was spiritually barren.

fig tree a little way off that was in full leaf, so he went over to see if he could find any
figs on it. But there were only leaves because it was too early in the season for fruit.
[14]Then Jesus said to the tree, "May no one ever eat your fruit again!" And the
disciples heard him say it.

[15]When they arrived back in Jerusalem, Jesus entered the Temple and began to drive
out the merchants and their customers. He knocked over the tables of the money
changers and the stalls of those selling doves, [16]and he stopped everyone from bringing
11:17 †Isa 56:7 †Jer 7:11 in merchandise. [17]He taught them, "The Scriptures declare, 'My Temple will be called
a place of prayer for all nations,' but you have turned it into a den of thieves."*

11:18 Matt 21:46 Mark 12:12 Luke 20:19 [18]When the leading priests and teachers of religious law heard what Jesus had done,
they began planning how to kill him. But they were afraid of him because the people
were so enthusiastic about Jesus' teaching. [19]That evening Jesus and the disciples* left
the city.

Jesus Says the Disciples Can Pray for Anything (**188**/Matthew 21:18-22)

[20]The next morning as they passed by the fig tree he had cursed, the disciples noticed it
was withered from the roots. [21]Peter remembered what Jesus had said to the tree on the
previous day and exclaimed, "Look, Teacher! The fig tree you cursed has withered!"

11:22 Matt 17:20 Luke 17:6 [22]Then Jesus said to the disciples, "Have faith in God. [23]I assure you that you can say
to this mountain, 'May God lift you up and throw you into the sea,' and your command

11:17 Isa 56:7; Jer 7:11. **11:19** Greek *they;* some manuscripts read *he.*

KEY CHARACTERISTICS OF CHRIST IN THE GOSPELS

Characteristic	*Reference*
Jesus is the Son of God.	Matthew 16:15, 16; Mark 1:1; Luke 22:70, 71; John 8:24
Jesus is God who became human.	John 1:1, 2, 14; 20:28
Jesus is the Christ, the Messiah.	Matthew 26:63, 64; Mark 14:61, 62; Luke 9:20; John 4:25, 26
Jesus came to help sinners.	Matthew 9:13; Luke 5:32
Jesus has power to forgive sins.	Mark 2:9–12; Luke 24:47
Jesus has authority over death.	Matthew 28:5, 6; Mark 5:22–24, 35–42; Luke 24:5, 6; John 11:1–44
Jesus has power to give eternal life.	John 10:28; 17:2
Jesus healed the sick.	Matthew 8:5–13; Mark 1:32–34; Luke 5:12–15; John 9:1–7
Jesus taught with authority.	Matthew 7:29; Mark 1:21, 22
Jesus was compassionate.	Matthew 9:36; Mark 1:41; 8:2
Jesus experienced sorrow.	Matthew 26:38; John 11:35
Jesus never disobeyed God.	Matthew 3:15; John 8:46

11:15-17 Jesus became angry, but he did not sin. There is a place for righteous indignation. Christians are right to be upset about sin and injustice and should take a stand against them. Unfortunately, believers are often passive about these important issues and instead get angry over personal insults and petty irritations. Make sure your anger is directed toward the right issues.

11:15-17 Money changers and merchants did big business during Passover. Those who came from foreign countries had to have their money changed into Temple currency because this was the only money accepted for the Temple tax and for the purchase of sacrificial animals. Often the inflated exchange rate enriched the money changers, and the exorbitant prices of animals made the merchants wealthy. Their stalls were set up in the Temple's court of the Gentiles, frustrating the intentions of non-Jews, who had come to worship God (Isaiah 56:6, 7). Jesus became angry because God's house of worship had become a place of extortion and a barrier to Gentiles who wanted to worship.

11:22, 23 The kind of prayer that moves mountains is prayer for the fruitfulness of God's Kingdom. It would seem impossible to move a mountain into the sea, so Jesus used that illustration to show that God can do the impossible. God will answer your prayers but not as a result of your positive mental attitude. Other conditions must be met: (1) You must be a believer; (2) you must not hold a grudge against another person; (3) you must not pray with selfish motives; (4) your request must be for the good of God's Kingdom. To pray effectively, you need faith in God, not faith in the object of your request. If you focus only on your request, you will be left with nothing if your request is refused.

will be obeyed. All that's required is that you really believe and do not doubt in your
heart. 24 Listen to me! You can pray for anything, and if you believe, you will have it. 11:24 Matt 7:7
25 But when you are praying, first forgive anyone you are holding a grudge against, so 11:25 Matt 5:23; 6:14
that your Father in heaven will forgive your sins, too.*"

Religious Leaders Challenge Jesus' Authority (**189**/Matthew 21:23-27; Luke 20:1-8)

27 By this time they had arrived in Jerusalem again. As Jesus was walking through the
Temple area, the leading priests, the teachers of religious law, and the other leaders came
up to him. They demanded, 28 "By whose authority did you drive out the merchants from
the Temple?* Who gave you such authority?"

29 "I'll tell who gave me authority to do these things if you answer one question," Jesus
replied. 30 "Did John's baptism come from heaven or was it merely human? Answer me!"

31 They talked it over among themselves. "If we say it was from heaven, he will ask
why we didn't believe him. 32 But do we dare say it was merely human?" For they were 11:32 Matt 14:5; 21:46
afraid that the people would start a riot, since everyone thought that John was a prophet.
33 So they finally replied, "We don't know."

And Jesus responded, "Then I won't answer your question either."

Jesus Tells the Parable of the Evil Farmers (**191**/Matthew 21:33-46; Luke 20:9-19)

12 Then Jesus began telling them stories: "A man planted a vineyard, built a wall 12:1 Isa 5:1-2
around it, dug a pit for pressing out the grape juice, and built a lookout tower. Then
he leased the vineyard to tenant farmers and moved to another country. 2 At grape-picking time he sent one of his servants to collect his share of the crop. 3 But the farmers
grabbed the servant, beat him up, and sent him back empty-handed.

4 "The owner then sent another servant, but they beat him over the head and treated
him shamefully. 5 The next servant he sent was killed. Others who were sent were either 12:5 2 Chr 24:21; 36:15-16 Neh 9:26 Matt 23:34-37 Acts 7:52 1 Thes 2:15
beaten or killed, 6 until there was only one left—his son whom he loved dearly. The
owner finally sent him, thinking, 'Surely they will respect my son.'

7 "But the farmers said to one another, 'Here comes the heir to this estate. Let's kill
him and get the estate for ourselves!' 8 So they grabbed him and murdered him and threw 12:6 Rom 8:3 Gal 4:4
his body out of the vineyard.

9 "What do you suppose the owner of the vineyard will do?" Jesus asked. "I'll tell 12:8 Heb 13:12
you—he will come and kill them all and lease the vineyard to others. 10 Didn't you ever 12:10-11 †Ps 118:22-23 Acts 4:11 Rom 9:33 Eph 2:20 1 Pet 2:5-7
read this in the Scriptures?

'The stone rejected by the builders
has now become the cornerstone.
11 This is the Lord's doing,
and it is marvelous to see.'*"

11:25 Some manuscripts add verse 26, *But if you do not forgive, neither will your Father who is in heaven forgive your sins.* **11:28** Or *By whose authority do you do these things?* **12:10-11** Ps 118:22-23.

11:24 Jesus, our example, prayed, "Everything is possible for you. . . . Yet I want your will, not mine" (14:36). Our prayers are often motivated by our own interests and desires. We like to hear that we can have anything. But Jesus prayed with *God's* interests in mind. When we pray, we can express our desires, but we should want his will above ours. Check yourself to see if your prayers focus on your interests or God's.

11:27ff The religious leaders asked Jesus who gave him the authority to chase away the merchants and money changers. Their question was a trap. If Jesus said his authority was from God, they would accuse him of blasphemy; if he said his authority was his own, they would dismiss him as a fanatic. To expose their real motives, Jesus countered their question with a question about John the Baptist. The leaders' silence proved that they were not interested in the truth. They simply wanted to get rid of Jesus because he was undermining their authority.

11:30 For more information, see John the Baptist's Profile in John 1.

12:1 Jesus' stories, also called parables, were illustrations that used something familiar to help us understand something new. This method of teaching compels listeners to discover truth for themselves. The message gets through only to those who are willing to listen and learn.

12:1 Israel, pictured as a vineyard, was the nation that God had cultivated to bring salvation to the world. The religious leaders not only frustrated their nation's purpose but also killed those who were trying to fulfill it. They were so jealous and possessive that they ignored the welfare of the very people they were supposed to be bringing to God.

12:1ff In this parable, the man who planted the vineyard is God; the vineyard is the nation Israel; the tenant farmers are Israel's religious leaders; the servants are the prophets and priests who remained faithful to God; the son is Jesus; and the others are the Gentiles. By telling this story, Jesus exposed the religious leaders' plot to kill him and warned that their sins would be punished.

12:10, 11 Jesus referred to himself as the stone rejected by the builders. Although he would be rejected by most of the Jewish leaders, he would become the cornerstone of a new "building," the church (Acts 4:11, 12). The cornerstone was used as a base to make sure the other stones of the building were straight and level. Likewise, Jesus' life and teaching would be the church's foundation.

12:12
Mark 11:18

[12]The Jewish leaders wanted to arrest him for using this illustration because they
realized he was pointing at them—they were the wicked farmers in his story. But they
were afraid to touch him because of the crowds. So they left him and went away.

Religious Leaders Question Jesus about Paying Taxes
(**193**/Matthew 22:15-22; Luke 20:20-26)

[13]The leaders sent some Pharisees and supporters of Herod to try to trap Jesus into saying
something for which he could be arrested. [14]"Teacher," these men said, "we know how
honest you are. You are impartial and don't play favorites. You sincerely teach the ways
of God. Now tell us—is it right to pay taxes to the Roman government or not? [15]Should
we pay them, or should we not?"
Jesus saw through their hypocrisy and said, "Whom are you trying to fool with your
trick questions? Show me a Roman coin,* and I'll tell you." [16]When they handed it to
him, he asked, "Whose picture and title are stamped on it?"
"Caesar's," they replied.

12:15 Greek *a denarius.*

WHAT JESUS SAID ABOUT LOVE

In Mark 12:28 a teacher of religious law asked Jesus which of all the commandments was the most important to follow. Jesus mentioned two commandments, one from Deuteronomy 6:5, the other from Leviticus 19:18. Both had to do with love. Why is love so important? Jesus said that all of the commandments were given for two simple reasons: to help us love God and love others as we should.

What else did Jesus say about love?	*Reference*
God loves us.	John 3:16
We are to love God.	Matthew 22:37
Because God loves us, he cares for us.	Matthew 6:25–34
God wants everyone to know how much he loves them.	John 17:23
God loves even those who hate him; we are to do the same.	Matthew 5:43–47; Luke 6:35
God seeks out even those most alienated from him.	Luke 15
God must be your first love.	Matthew 6:24; 10:37
You love God when you obey him.	John 14:21; 15:10
God loves Jesus, his Son.	John 5:20; 10:17
Jesus loves God.	John 14:31
Those who refuse Jesus don't have God's love.	John 5:41–44
Jesus loves us just as God loves Jesus.	John 15:9
Jesus proved his love for us by dying on the cross so that we could live eternally with him.	John 3:14, 15; 15:13, 14
The love between God and Jesus is the perfect example of how we are to love others.	John 17:21–26
We are to love one another (John 13:34, 35) and demonstrate that love.	Matthew 5:40–42; 10:42
We are *not* to love the praise of people (John 12:43), selfish recognition (Matthew 23:6), earthly belongings (Luke 6: 19–31), or anything more than God.	Luke 16:13
Jesus' love extends to each individual.	Mark 10:21; John 10:11–15
Jesus wants us to love him through the good and through the difficult times.	Matthew 26:31–35
Jesus wants our love to be genuine.	John 21:15–17

12:13 The Pharisees were primarily a religious group concerned for ritual purity; the supporters of Herod were a Jewish political group that approved of Herod's compromises with Rome. Normally the two groups had nothing to do with each other.

The Pharisees did not like Jesus because he exposed their hypocrisy. The supporters of Herod also saw Jesus as a threat. Supporters of the dynasty of Herod the Great, they had lost political control when, as a result of reported unrest, Rome deposed Archelaus (Herod's son with authority over Judea), and replaced him with a Roman governor. The supporters of Herod feared that Jesus would cause still more instability in Judea and that Rome might react by never allowing the Roman leaders to step down and be replaced by a descendant of Herod.

12:14 Anyone who avoided paying taxes faced harsh penalties. The Jews hated to pay taxes to Rome because the money supported their oppressors and symbolized their subjection. Much of the tax money also went to maintain the pagan temples and luxurious life-styles of Rome's upper class. The Pharisees and supporters of Herod hoped to trap Jesus with this tax question. Either a yes or a no could lead him into trouble. A yes would mean he supported Rome, which would turn the people against him. A no would bring accusations of treason and rebellion against Rome and could lead to civil penalties.

12:15 This coin represented the usual day's wage for a laborer.

[17]"Well, then," Jesus said, "give to Caesar what belongs to him. But everything that
belongs to God must be given to God." This reply completely amazed them. 12:17 Rom 13:7

Religious Leaders Question Jesus about the Resurrection
(**194**/Matthew 22:23-33; Luke 20:27-40)

[18]Then the Sadducees stepped forward—a group of Jews who say there is no resurrec- 12:18-27
tion after death. They posed this question: [19]"Teacher, Moses gave us a law that if a man Acts 23:8
dies, leaving a wife without children, his brother should marry the widow and have a 1 Cor 15:12
child who will be the brother's heir.* [20]Well, there were seven brothers. The oldest of 12:19 †Gen 38:8
them married and then died without children. [21]So the second brother married the †Deut 25:5
widow, but soon he too died and left no children. Then the next brother married her and
died without children. [22]This continued until all the brothers had married her and died,
and still there were no children. Last of all, the woman died, too. [23]So tell us, whose wife
will she be in the resurrection? For all seven were married to her."

[24]Jesus replied, "Your problem is that you don't know the Scriptures, and you don't 12:25
know the power of God. [25]For when the dead rise, they won't be married. They will be 1 Cor 15:42, 49, 52
like the angels in heaven. [26]But now, as to whether the dead will be raised—haven't you 12:26
ever read about this in the writings of Moses, in the story of the burning bush? Long after †Exod 3:6
Abraham, Isaac, and Jacob had died, God said to Moses,* 'I am the God of Abraham, 12:27
the God of Isaac, and the God of Jacob.'* [27]So he is the God of the living, not the dead. Matt 22:32 Luke 20:38
You have made a serious error."

Religious Leaders Question Jesus about the Greatest Commandment (**195**/Matthew 22:34-40)

[28]One of the teachers of religious law was standing there listening to the discussion. He
realized that Jesus had answered well, so he asked, "Of all the commandments, which is
the most important?" 12:29-30

[29]Jesus replied, "The most important commandment is this: 'Hear, O Israel! The Lord †Deut 6:4-5 †Josh 22:5 Luke 10:27
our God is the one and only Lord. [30]And you must love the Lord your God with all your 12:31
heart, all your soul, all your mind, and all your strength.'* [31]The second is equally impor- †Lev 19:18
tant: 'Love your neighbor as yourself.'* No other commandment is greater than these." Rom 13:9 Gal 5:14 Jas 2:8

12:19 Deut 25:5-6. **12:26a** Greek *in the story of the bush? God said to him.* **12:26b** Exod 3:6. **12:29-30** Deut 6:4-5. **12:31** Lev 19:18.

12:17 The Pharisees and supporters of Herod thought they had the perfect question to trap Jesus. But Jesus answered wisely, once again exposing their self-interest and wrong motives. Jesus said that the coin bearing the emperor's image should be given to the emperor. Our life, which bears God's image, belongs to God. Are you giving God all that is rightfully his? Give your life to God—you bear his image.

12:18-23 After the Pharisees and supporters of Herod failed to trap Jesus with their tax question, the Sadducees stepped in with a question they were sure would stump him. This was a question that they had successfully used against the Pharisees, who could not come up with an answer. The Sadducees did not believe in life after death because the Pentateuch (Genesis—Deuteronomy) had no direct teaching about it, and the writings of Moses were the only Scriptures they followed. But Jesus was about to point out that Moses' books support the idea of eternal life (12:26).

12:19 According to Old Testament law, when a man died without a son, his brother had to marry the widow and produce children to care for her and allow the family line to continue. The first son of this marriage was considered the heir of the dead man (Deuteronomy 25:5, 6).

12:24 What life will be like after the resurrection is far beyond our ability to understand or imagine (Isaiah 64:4; 1 Corinthians 2:9). We need not be afraid of eternal life because of the unknowns, however. Instead of wondering what God's coming Kingdom will be like, we should concentrate on our relationship with Christ right now because in the new Kingdom, we will be with him. If we learn to love and trust Christ *now,* we will not be afraid of what he has in store for us then.

12:25-27 Jesus' statement does not mean that people won't recognize their partners in the coming Kingdom. It simply means that God's new order will not be an extension of this life and that the same physical and natural rules won't apply. Jesus' comment in verse 25 was not intended to be the final word on marriage in heaven. Instead, this response was Jesus' refusal to answer the Sadducees' riddle and fall into their trap. Sidestepping their question about the much-married woman, he gave a definitive answer to their question about the resurrection.

12:26 The Sadducees' real question was not about marriage but about the doctrine of resurrection. Because the Sadducees believed only in the Pentateuch (Genesis—Deuteronomy), Jesus quoted from Exodus 3:6 to prove that there is life after death. The Pharisees had overlooked this verse in their debates with the Sadducees. God spoke of Abraham, Isaac, and Jacob years after their deaths as if they *still lived.* God's covenant with all people exists beyond death.

12:28 By Jesus' time, the Jews had accumulated hundreds of laws—613 by one historian's count. Some religious leaders tried to distinguish between major and minor laws, and some taught that all laws were equally binding and that it was dangerous to make any distinctions. This teacher's question could have provoked controversy among these groups, but Jesus' answer summarized all of God's laws.

12:29-31 God's laws are not burdensome. They can be reduced to two simple principles: Love God and love others. These commands are from the Old Testament (Deuteronomy 6:5; Leviticus 19:18). When you love God completely and care for others as you care for yourself, then you have fulfilled the intent of the Ten Commandments and the other Old Testament laws. According to Jesus, these two commandments summarize all God's laws. Let them rule your thoughts, decisions, and actions. When you are uncertain about what to do, ask yourself which course of action best demonstrates love for God and love for others.

12:32 †Deut 4:35, 39; 6:4; 1 Cor 8:4-6 [32]The teacher of religious law replied, "Well said, Teacher. You have spoken the truth
by saying that there is only one God and no other. [33]And I know it is important to love
12:33 †Lev 19:18; Mic 6:6-8 him with all my heart and all my understanding and all my strength, and to love my
neighbors as myself. This is more important than to offer all of the burnt offerings and
sacrifices required in the law."
12:34 Matt 22:46; Luke 20:40 [34]Realizing this man's understanding, Jesus said to him, "You are not far from the
Kingdom of God." And after that, no one dared to ask him any more questions.

Religious Leaders Cannot Answer Jesus' Question
(**196**/Matthew 22:41-46; Luke 20:41-44)

[35]Later, as Jesus was teaching the people in the Temple, he asked, "Why do the teachers
12:36 2 Sam 23:2; †Ps 110:1 of religious law claim that the Messiah will be the son of David? [36]For David himself,
speaking under the inspiration of the Holy Spirit, said,

'The LORD said to my Lord,
Sit in honor at my right hand
until I humble your enemies beneath your feet.'*

12:37 Rom 1:3; 9:5; Rev 22:16 [37]Since David himself called him Lord, how can he be his son at the same time?" And
the crowd listened to him with great interest.

Jesus Warns against the Religious Leaders (**197**/Matthew 23:1-12; Luke 20:45-47)

[38]Here are some of the other things he taught them at this time: "Beware of these teachers
of religious law! For they love to parade in flowing robes and to have everyone bow to
12:39 Luke 11:43 them as they walk in the marketplaces. [39]And how they love the seats of honor in the
synagogues and at banquets. [40]But they shamelessly cheat widows out of their property,
and then, to cover up the kind of people they really are, they make long prayers in public.
Because of this, their punishment will be the greater."

A Poor Widow Gives All She Has (**200**/Luke 21:1-4)

12:41 2 Kgs 12:9; John 8:20 [41]Jesus went over to the collection box in the Temple and sat and watched as the crowds
dropped in their money. Many rich people put in large amounts. [42]Then a poor widow
12:43-44 2 Cor 8:12 came and dropped in two pennies.* [43]He called his disciples to him and said, "I assure
you, this poor widow has given more than all the others have given. [44]For they gave a
tiny part of their surplus, but she, poor as she is, has given everything she has."

12:36 Ps 110:1. **12:42** Greek *2 lepta, which is a kodrantes.*

12:32-34 This man had grasped the intent of God's law as it is so often stressed in the Old Testament—that true obedience comes from the heart. Because all the Old Testament commands lead to Christ, his next step was faith in Jesus himself. This, however, was the most difficult step to take.

12:35-37 Jesus quoted Psalm 110:1 to show that David considered the Messiah to be his Lord, not just his son. The religious leaders did not understand that the Messiah would be far more than a human descendant of David; he would be God himself in human form.

12:38-40 Jesus again exposed the religious leaders' impure motives. The teachers of religious law received no pay, so they depended on the hospitality extended by devout Jews. Some of them used this custom to exploit people, cheating the poor out of everything they had and taking advantage of the rich. Through their pious actions they hoped to gain status, recognition, and respect.

12:38-40 Jesus warned against trying to make a good impression. These teachers of religious law were religious hypocrites who had no love for God. True followers of Christ are not distinguished by showy spirituality. Reading the Bible, praying in public, or following church rituals can be phony if the motive for doing them is to be noticed or honored. Let your actions be consistent with your beliefs. Live for Christ, even when no one is looking.

12:40 The punishment for these teachers of religious law would be especially severe because as teachers they were responsible for shaping the faith of the people. But they saddled people with petty rules, while they lived greedily and deceitfully. Their behavior oppressed and misled the very people they were supposed to lead.

12:41 There were several boxes in the Temple where money could be placed. Some were for collecting the Temple tax from Jewish males; the others were for freewill offerings. These particular collection boxes were probably in the Court of the Women.

12:41-44 In the Lord's eyes, this poor widow gave more than all the others put together, although her gift was by far the smallest. The value of a gift is not determined by its amount but by the spirit in which it is given. A gift given grudgingly or for recognition loses its value. When you give, remember that gifts of any size are pleasing to God when they are given out of gratitude and a spirit of generosity.

Jesus Tells about the Future (**201**/Matthew 24:1-25; Luke 21:5-24)

13 As Jesus was leaving the Temple that day, one of his disciples said, "Teacher, look
at these tremendous buildings! Look at the massive stones in the walls!"
2 Jesus replied, "These magnificent buildings will be so completely demolished that
not one stone will be left on top of another."
3 Later, Jesus sat on the slopes of the Mount of Olives across the valley from the
Temple. Peter, James, John, and Andrew came to him privately and asked him, 4 "When
will all this take place? And will there be any sign ahead of time to show us when all this
will be fulfilled?"
5 Jesus replied, "Don't let anyone mislead you, 6 because many will come in my
name, claiming to be the Messiah.* They will lead many astray. 7 And wars will break
out near and far, but don't panic. Yes, these things must come, but the end won't
follow immediately. 8 Nations and kingdoms will proclaim war against each other, and
there will be earthquakes in many parts of the world, and famines. But all this will be
only the beginning of the horrors to come. 9 But when these things begin to happen,
watch out! You will be handed over to the courts and beaten in the synagogues. You
will be accused before governors and kings of being my followers. This will be your
opportunity to tell them about me.* 10 And the Good News must first be preached to
every nation. 11 But when you are arrested and stand trial, don't worry about what to
say in your defense. Just say what God tells you to. Then it is not you who will be
speaking, but the Holy Spirit.
12 "Brother will betray brother to death, fathers will betray their own children, and
children will rise against their parents and cause them to be killed. 13 And everyone
will hate you because of your allegiance to me. But those who endure to the end will
be saved.

13:2 Luke 19:44
13:5 2 Thes 2:3, 10-12; 1 Tim 4:1; 2 Tim 3:13; 1 Jn 4:6
13:6 John 5:43
13:8 2 Chr 15:6; Isa 19:2
13:10 Rom 10:18
13:11 Matt 10:19-20; Luke 12:11-12
13:12 Mic 7:6
13:13 Matt 10:22; John 15:18-21

13:6 Greek *name, saying, 'I am.'* **13:9** Or *This will be your testimony against them.*

13:1, 2 About 15 years before Jesus was born (20 B.C.), Herod the Great began to remodel and rebuild the Temple, which had stood for nearly 500 years since the days of Ezra (Ezra 6:14, 15). Herod made the Temple one of the most beautiful buildings in Jerusalem, not to honor God, but to appease the Jews whom he ruled. The magnificent building project was not completely finished until A.D. 64. Jesus' prophecy that not one stone would be left on another was fulfilled in A.D. 70, when the Romans completely destroyed the Temple and the entire city of Jerusalem.

13:3ff The disciples wanted to know when the Temple would be destroyed. Jesus gave them a prophetic picture of that time, including events leading up to it. He also talked about future events connected with his return to earth to judge all people. Jesus predicted both near and distant events without putting them in chronological order. Some of the disciples lived to see the destruction of Jerusalem in A.D. 70. This event would assure them that everything else Jesus predicted would also happen.

Jesus warned his followers about the future so that they could learn how to live in the present. Many predictions Jesus made in this passage have not yet been fulfilled. He did not make them so that we would guess when they might be fulfilled but to help us to be spiritually alert and prepared at all times as we wait for his return.

13:3, 4 The Mount of Olives rises above Jerusalem to the east. From its slopes a person can look down into the city and see the Temple. Zechariah 14:1-4 predicts that the Messiah will stand on this very mountain when he returns to set up his eternal Kingdom.

13:5-7 What are the signs of the end times? There have been people in every generation since Christ's resurrection claiming to know exactly when Jesus would return. No one has been right yet, however, because Christ will return on God's timetable, not ours. Jesus predicted that before his return, many believers would be misled by false teachers claiming to have revelations from God.

According to Scripture, one clear sign of Christ's return will be his unmistakable appearance in the clouds, which will be seen by all people (13:26; Revelation 1:7). In other words, you do not have to wonder whether a certain person is the Messiah or whether these are the "end times." When Jesus returns, *you will know* beyond a doubt, because it will be evident to all true believers. Beware of groups who claim special knowledge of Christ's return because no one knows when that time will be (13:32). Be cautious about saying, "This is it!" but be bold in your total commitment to have your heart and life ready for Christ's return.

13:9, 10 As the early church began to grow, most of the disciples experienced the kind of persecution Jesus was talking about. Since the time of Christ, Christians have been persecuted in their own lands and on foreign mission fields. Though you may be safe from persecution now, your vision of God's Kingdom must not be limited by what happens only to you. A glance at a newspaper will reveal that many Christians in other parts of the world daily face hardships and persecution. Persecutions are an opportunity for Christians to witness for Christ to those opposed to him. God's desire is that the Good News be proclaimed to everyone in spite of persecution.

13:11 Jesus did not imply that studying the Bible and gaining knowledge is useless or wrong. Before and after his resurrection Jesus himself taught his disciples what to say and how to say it. But Jesus was teaching the kind of attitude we should have when we must take a stand for the Good News. We don't have to be fearful or defensive about our faith because the Holy Spirit will be present to give us the right words to say.

13:13 To believe in Jesus and "endure to the end" will take perseverance because our faith will be challenged and opposed. Severe trials will sift true Christians from fair-weather believers. Enduring to the end does not earn salvation for us but marks us as already saved. The assurance of our salvation will keep us strong in times of persecution.

13:14 †Dan 9:27; 11:31; 12:11; Matt 24:15; 2 Thes 2:3
13:17 Luke 23:29
13:19 Dan 9:26; 12:1; Joel 2:2; Rev 7:14
13:21 Luke 17:23
13:22 Deut 13:1-3; 2 Thes 2:9-10; Rev 13:13

14 “The time will come when you will see the sacrilegious object that causes desecration* standing where it should not be”—reader, pay attention! “Then those in Judea must
flee to the hills. 15 A person outside the house* must not go back into the house to pack.
16 A person in the field must not return even to get a coat. 17 How terrible it will be for
pregnant women and for mothers nursing their babies in those days. 18 And pray that your
flight will not be in winter. 19 For those will be days of greater horror than at any time
since God created the world. And it will never happen again. 20 In fact, unless the Lord
shortens that time of calamity, the entire human race will be destroyed. But for the sake
of his chosen ones he has shortened those days.
21 “And then if anyone tells you, ‘Look, here is the Messiah,’ or, ‘There he is,’ don’t
pay any attention. 22 For false messiahs and false prophets will rise up and perform
miraculous signs and wonders so as to deceive, if possible, even God’s chosen ones.
23 Watch out! I have warned you!

Jesus Tells about His Return (**202**/Matthew 24:26-35; Luke 21:25-33)

13:24-25 †Isa 13:10; 34:4; Ezek 32:7-8; †Joel 2:10, 31; 3:15; Rev 6:12-14; 8:12

24 “At that time, after those horrible days end,
the sun will be darkened,
the moon will not give light,
25 the stars will fall from the sky,
and the powers of heaven will be shaken.*

13:26 †Dan 7:13; Matt 16:27; Rev 1:7
13:27 Deut 30:4; Zech 2:6

26 Then everyone will see the Son of Man arrive on the clouds with great power and
glory.* 27 And he will send forth his angels to gather together his chosen ones from all
over the world—from the farthest ends of the earth and heaven.
28 “Now, learn a lesson from the fig tree. When its buds become tender and its leaves
begin to sprout, you know without being told that summer is near. 29 Just so, when you

13:14 Greek *the abomination of desolation.* See Dan 9:27; 11:31; 12:11. **13:15** Greek *on the roof.* **13:24-25** See Isa 13:10; 34:4; Joel 2:10. **13:26** See Dan 7:13.

JESUS' PROPHECIES IN THE OLIVET DISCOURSE	*Type of Prophecy*	*Old Testament References*	*Other New Testament References*
	The Last Days Mark 13:1–23 Matthew 24:1–28 Luke 21:5–24	Daniel 9:26, 27 Daniel 11:31 Joel 2:2	John 15:21 Revelation 11:2 1 Timothy 4:1, 2
	The Second Coming of Christ Mark 13:24–27 Luke 21:25–28 Matthew 24:29–31	Isaiah 13:6–10 Ezekiel 32:7 Daniel 7:13, 14	Revelation 6:12 Mark 14:62 1 Thessalonians 4:16

In Mark 13, often called the Olivet discourse, Jesus talked a lot about two things: the end times and his second coming. Jesus was not trying to encourage his disciples to speculate about exactly when he would return by sharing these prophecies with them. Instead, he urges all his followers to be watchful and prepared for his coming. If we serve Jesus faithfully now, we will be ready when he returns.

13:14 The “sacrilegious object that causes desecration” refers to the desecration of the Temple by God’s enemies. This happened repeatedly in Israel’s history: in 597 B.C. when Nebuchadnezzar looted the Temple and took Judean captives to Babylon (2 Chronicles 36); in 168 B.C. when Antiochus Epiphanes sacrificed a pig to Zeus on the sacred Temple altar (Daniel 9:27; 11:30, 31); in A.D. 70 when the Roman general Titus placed an idol on the site of the burned-out Temple after the destruction of Jerusalem. Just a few years after Jesus gave this warning, in A.D. 38, the emperor Caligula made plans to put his own statue in the Temple, but he died before this could be carried out.

13:20 The “chosen ones” are God’s chosen people, those who are saved. See Romans 8:29, 30 and Ephesians 1:4, 5 for more on God’s choice.

13:22, 23 Is it possible for Christians to be deceived? Yes. So convincing will be the arguments and proofs from deceivers in the end times that it will be difficult *not* to fall away from Christ. If we are prepared, Jesus says, we can remain faithful. But if we are not prepared, we will turn away. To penetrate the disguises of false teachers we can ask: (1) Have their predictions come true, or do they have to revise them to fit what’s already happened? (2) Does any teaching utilize a small section of the Bible to the neglect of the whole? (3) Does the teaching contradict what the Bible says about God? (4) Are the practices meant to glorify the teacher or Christ? (5) Do the teachings promote hostility toward other Christians?

see the events I've described beginning to happen, you can be sure that his return is very
near, right at the door. 30 I assure you, this generation* will not pass from the scene until
all these events have taken place. 31 Heaven and earth will disappear, but my words will
remain forever.

13:31 Matt 5:18; Luke 16:17

Jesus Tells about Remaining Watchful (**203**/Matthew 24:36-51; Luke 21:34-38)

32 "However, no one knows the day or hour when these things will happen, not even the
angels in heaven or the Son himself. Only the Father knows. 33 And since you don't know
when they will happen, stay alert and keep watch.*

34 "The coming of the Son of Man can be compared with that of a man who left home
to go on a trip. He gave each of his employees instructions about the work they were to
do, and he told the gatekeeper to watch for his return. 35 So keep a sharp lookout! For
you do not know when the homeowner will return—at evening, midnight, early dawn,
or late daybreak. 36 Don't let him find you sleeping when he arrives without warning.
37 What I say to you I say to everyone: Watch for his return!"

13:32 Acts 1:7
13:33-37 Matt 25:13-14; Luke 12:35-40; Rom 13:11; Eph 6:17-18; Col 4:2; 1 Thes 5:6

C. DEATH AND RESURRECTION OF JESUS, THE SERVANT (14:1—16:20)

Mark tells us about Jesus' ultimate deed of servanthood—dying for us on the cross. Jesus died for our sin so we wouldn't have to. Now we can have eternal fellowship with God instead of eternal suffering and death. When first written in Rome, this Gospel was encouraging to Roman Christians during times of persecution. Christ's victory through suffering can encourage us during difficult times, too.

Religious Leaders Plot to Kill Jesus (**207**/Matthew 26:1-5; Luke 22:1-2)

14 It was now two days before the Passover celebration and the Festival of Unleavened Bread. The leading priests and the teachers of religious law were still looking
for an opportunity to capture Jesus secretly and put him to death. 2 "But not during the
Passover," they agreed, "or there will be a riot."

14:1-2 John 11:55-57

A Woman Anoints Jesus with Perfume (**182**/Matthew 26:6-13; John 12:1-11)

3 Meanwhile, Jesus was in Bethany at the home of Simon, a man who had leprosy.
During supper, a woman came in with a beautiful jar of expensive perfume.* She

14:3 Luke 7:37-38

13:30 Or *this age*, or *this nation.* **13:33** Some manuscripts add *and pray.* **14:3** Greek *an alabaster jar of expensive ointment, pure nard.*

13:31 In Jesus' day the world seemed concrete, dependable, and permanent. These days many people fear its destruction by nuclear war. Jesus tells us, however, that even if the earth passes away, the truth of his words will never be changed or abolished. God and his Word provide the only stability in our unstable world. How shortsighted people are who spend all their time and energy learning about this temporary world and accumulating its possessions, while neglecting the Bible and its eternal truths!

13:32 When Jesus said that even he did not know the time of the end, he was affirming his humanity. Of course God the Father knows the time, and Jesus and the Father are one. But when Jesus became a man, he voluntarily gave up the unlimited use of his divine attributes.

The emphasis of this verse is not on Jesus' lack of knowledge, but rather on the fact that no one knows. It is God the Father's secret to be revealed when he wills. No one can predict by Scripture or science the exact day of Jesus' return. Jesus is teaching that preparation, not calculation, is needed.

13:33, 34 Months of planning go into a wedding, the birth of a baby, a career change, a speaking engagement, the purchase of a home. Do you place the same importance on preparing for Christ's return, the most important event in your life? Its results will last for eternity. You dare not postpone your preparations because you do not know when his return will occur. The way to prepare is to study God's Word and live by its instructions each day. Only then will you be ready.

13:35-37 The entire thirteenth chapter of Mark tells us how to live while we wait for Christ's return: (1) We are not to be misled by confusing claims or speculative interpretations of what will happen (13:5, 6). (2) We should not be afraid to tell people about Christ, despite what they might say or do to us (13:9-11). (3) We must stand firm by faith and not be surprised by persecution (13:13). (4) We must be morally alert, obedient to the commands for living found in God's Word. This chapter was not given to promote discussions on prophetic timetables but to stimulate right living for God in a world where he is largely ignored.

14:1 The Passover commemorated the night the Israelites were freed from Egypt (Exodus 12), when God "passed over" homes marked by the blood of a lamb while killing firstborn sons in unmarked homes. The day of Passover was followed by a seven-day festival called the Festival of Unleavened Bread. This, too, recalled the Israelites' quick escape from Egypt when they didn't have time to let their bread rise, so they baked it without yeast. This holiday found people gathering for a special meal that included lamb, wine, bitter herbs, and unleavened bread. Eventually the whole week came to be called Passover.

14:1 The Jewish leaders plotted secretly to kill Jesus—his murder was carefully planned. The murder plot was not being planned because popular opinion had turned against Jesus. In fact, the leaders were afraid of Jesus' popularity.

14:3 Bethany is located on the eastern slope of the Mount of Olives (Jerusalem is on the western side). This town was the home of Jesus' friends Lazarus, Mary, and Martha, who were also present at this dinner (John 11:2). The woman who anointed Jesus' feet was Mary, Lazarus and Martha's sister (John 12:1-3).

JUDAS ISCARIOT

It is easy to overlook the fact that Jesus chose Judas to be his disciple. We may also forget that while Judas betrayed Jesus, *all* the disciples abandoned him. With the other disciples, Judas shared a persistent misunderstanding of Jesus' mission. They all expected Jesus to make the right political moves. When he kept talking about dying, they all felt varying degrees of anger, fear, and disappointment. They didn't understand why they had been chosen if Jesus' mission was doomed to fail.

We do not know the exact motivation behind Judas's betrayal. What is clear is that Judas allowed his desires to place him in a position where Satan could manipulate him. Judas accepted payment to set Jesus up for the religious leaders. He identified Jesus for the guards in the dimly lit Garden of Gethsemane. It is possible that he was trying to force Jesus' hand: Would Jesus now rebel against Rome and set up a new political government?

Whatever his plan, though, at some point Judas realized he didn't like the way things were turning out. He tried to undo the evil he had done by returning the money to the priests, but it was too late. The wheels of God's sovereign plan had been set into motion. How sad that Judas ended his life in despair without ever experiencing the gift of reconciliation God could give even to him through Jesus Christ.

Human feelings toward Judas have always been mixed. Some have fervently hated him for his betrayal. Others have pitied him for not realizing what he was doing. A few have tried to make him a hero for his part in ending Jesus' earthly mission. Some have questioned God's fairness in allowing one man to bear such guilt. While there are many feelings about Judas, there are some facts to consider as well. He, by his own choice, betrayed God's Son into the hands of soldiers (Luke 22:48). He was a thief (John 12:6). Jesus knew that Judas's life of evil would not change (John 6:70). Judas's betrayal of Jesus was part of God's sovereign plan (Psalm 41:9; Zechariah 11:12, 13; Matthew 20:18; 26:20–25; Acts 1:16, 20).

In betraying Jesus, Judas made the greatest mistake in history. But the fact that Jesus knew Judas would betray him doesn't mean that Judas was a puppet of God's will. Judas made the choice. God knew what that choice would be and confirmed it. Judas didn't lose his relationship with Jesus; rather, he never found Jesus in the first place. He is called "the one headed for destruction" (John 17:12) because he was never saved.

Judas does us a favor if he makes us think a second time about our commitment to God and the presence of God's Spirit within us. Are we true disciples and followers, or uncommitted pretenders? We can choose despair and death, or we can choose repentance, forgiveness, hope, and eternal life. Judas's betrayal sent Jesus to the cross to guarantee that second choice, our only chance. Will we accept Jesus' free gift, or, like Judas, betray him?

Strengths and accomplishments
- He was chosen as one of the 12 disciples; the only non-Galilean
- He was in charge of the disciples' funds
- He was able to recognize the evil in his betrayal of Jesus

Weaknesses and mistakes
- He was greedy (John 12:6)
- He betrayed Jesus
- He committed suicide instead of seeking forgiveness

Lessons from his life
- Evil plans and motives leave us open to being used by Satan for even greater evil
- The consequences of evil are so devastating that even small lies and little wrongdoings have serious results
- God's plan and his purposes are worked out even in the worst possible events

Vital statistics
- Where: Possibly from the town of Kerioth
- Occupation: Disciple of Jesus
- Relative: Father: Simon
- Contemporaries: Jesus, Pilate, Herod, the other 11 disciples

Key verses
"Then Satan entered into Judas Iscariot, who was one of the twelve disciples, and he went over to the leading priests and captains of the Temple guard to discuss the best way to betray Jesus to them" (Luke 22:3, 4).

Judas's story is told in the Gospels. He is also mentioned in Acts 1:18, 19.

14:3-9 Matthew and Mark placed this event just before the Last Supper, while John placed it a week earlier, just before the Triumphal Entry. It must be remembered that the main purpose of the Gospel writers was not to present an exact chronological account of Christ's life but to give an accurate record of his message. Matthew and Mark may have chosen to place this event here to contrast the complete devotion of Mary with the betrayal of Judas, the next event in both Gospels.

broke the seal and poured the perfume over his head. 4 Some of those at the table were
indignant. "Why was this expensive perfume wasted?" they asked. 5 "She could have
sold it for a small fortune* and given the money to the poor!" And they scolded her
harshly.
6 But Jesus replied, "Leave her alone. Why berate her for doing such a good thing to
me? 7 You will always have the poor among you, and you can help them whenever you 14:7 Deut 15:11
want to. But I will not be here with you much longer. 8 She has done what she could and 14:8
has anointed my body for burial ahead of time. 9 I assure you, wherever the Good News John 19:40
is preached throughout the world, this woman's deed will be talked about in her
memory."

Judas Agrees to Betray Jesus (**208**/Matthew 26:14-16; Luke 22:3-6)

10 Then Judas Iscariot, one of the twelve disciples, went to the leading priests to arrange
to betray Jesus to them. 11 The leading priests were delighted when they heard why he
had come, and they promised him a reward. So he began looking for the right time and
place to betray Jesus.

Disciples Prepare for the Passover (**209**/Matthew 26:17-19; Luke 22:7-13)

12 On the first day of the Festival of Unleavened Bread (the day the Passover lambs were 14:12 Exod 12:14-21
sacrificed), Jesus' disciples asked him, "Where do you want us to go to prepare the Pass- Deut 16:1-4
over supper?" 1 Cor 5:7-8
13 So Jesus sent two of them into Jerusalem to make the arrangements. "As you go into
the city," he told them, "a man carrying a pitcher of water will meet you. Follow him.
14 At the house he enters, say to the owner, 'The Teacher asks, Where is the guest room 14:14
where I can eat the Passover meal with my disciples?' 15 He will take you upstairs to a Exod 12:8
large room that is already set up. That is the place; go ahead and prepare our supper Lev 23:5
there." 16 So the two disciples went on ahead into the city and found everything just as
Jesus had said, and they prepared the Passover supper there.

14:5 Greek *300 denarii.* A denarius was the equivalent of a full day's wage.

14:4, 5 Where Mark says "some of those at the table," John specifically mentions Judas (John 12:4, 5). Judas's indignation over Mary's act of worship was based not on concern for the poor but on greed. Because Judas was the treasurer of Jesus' ministry and had embezzled funds (John 12:6), he no doubt wanted the perfume sold so that he could benefit from the proceeds.

14:6, 7 Jesus was not saying that we should neglect the poor, nor was he justifying indifference to them. (For Jesus' teaching about the poor, see Matthew 6:2-4; Luke 6:20, 21; 14:13, 21; 18:22.) Jesus was praising Mary for her unselfish act of worship. The essence of worshiping Christ is to regard him with utmost love, respect, and devotion and to be willing to sacrifice to him what is most precious.

14:10 Why would Judas want to betray Jesus? Very likely, Judas expected Jesus to start a political rebellion and overthrow Rome. As treasurer, Judas certainly assumed (as did the other disciples—see 10:35-37) that he would be given an important position in Jesus' new government. But when Jesus praised Mary for pouring out the perfume, thought to be worth a day's salary, Judas finally began to realize that Jesus' Kingdom was not physical or political but spiritual. Judas's greedy desire for money and status could not be fulfilled if he followed Jesus, so he betrayed him in exchange for money and favor from the religious leaders.

14:13 The two men Jesus sent were Peter and John (Luke 22:8).

14:14, 15 Many homes had large upstairs rooms, sometimes with stairways both inside and outside the house. The preparations for the Passover would have included setting the table and buying and preparing the Passover lamb, unleavened bread, sauces, and other ceremonial food and drink.

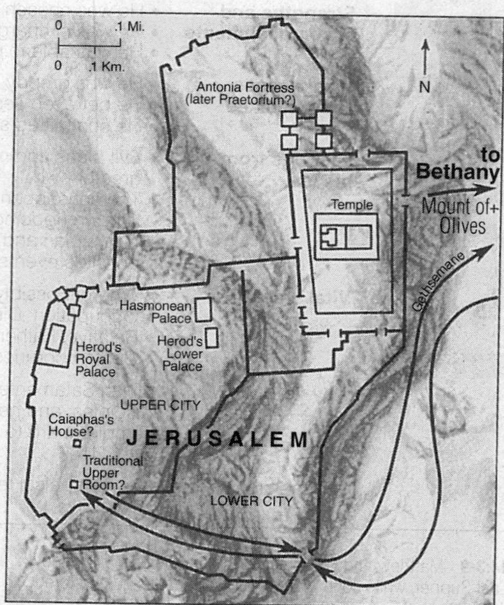

UPPER ROOM AND GETHSEMANE Jesus and the disciples ate the traditional Passover meal in an upper room in the city and then went to the Mount of Olives into a garden called Gethsemane. In the cool of the evening, Jesus prayed for strength to face the trial and suffering ahead.

Jesus and the Disciples Share the Last Supper
(**211**/Matthew 26:20-30; Luke 22:14-30; John 13:21-30)
14:18 †Ps 41:9 17 In the evening Jesus arrived with the twelve disciples. 18 As they were sitting around
the table eating, Jesus said, "The truth is, one of you will betray me, one of you who is
here eating with me."
19 Greatly distressed, one by one they began to ask him, "I'm not the one, am I?"
14:21 Ps 22:1-21 Isa 53:3-8 20 He replied, "It is one of you twelve, one who is eating with me now.* 21 For I, the
Son of Man, must die, as the Scriptures declared long ago. But how terrible it will be for
my betrayer. Far better for him if he had never been born!"
14:22-25 1 Cor 11:23-25 22 As they were eating, Jesus took a loaf of bread and asked God's blessing on it. Then
he broke it in pieces and gave it to the disciples, saying, "Take it, for this is my body."
14:23 1 Cor 10:16 23 And he took a cup of wine and gave thanks to God for it. He gave it to them, and
they all drank from it. 24 And he said to them, "This is my blood, poured out for many,
sealing the covenant* between God and his people. 25 I solemnly declare that I will not
drink wine again until that day when I drink it new in the Kingdom of God." 26 Then they
sang a hymn and went out to the Mount of Olives.

Jesus Again Predicts Peter's Denial (**222**/Matthew 26:31-35)
14:27 †Zech 13:7 27 "All of you will desert me," Jesus told them. "For the Scriptures say,

'God* will strike the Shepherd,
and the sheep will be scattered.'*

14:28 Mark 16:7 28 But after I am raised from the dead, I will go ahead of you to Galilee and meet you
there."
29 Peter said to him, "Even if everyone else deserts you, I never will."
30 "Peter," Jesus replied, "the truth is, this very night, before the rooster crows twice,
you will deny me three times."
31 "No!" Peter insisted. "Not even if I have to die with you! I will never deny you!"
And all the others vowed the same.

Jesus Agonizes in the Garden (**223**/Matthew 26:36-46; Luke 22:39-46)
14:33 Matt 17:1 Mark 9:2 Luke 9:28 32 And they came to an olive grove called Gethsemane, and Jesus said, "Sit here while I
go and pray." 33 He took Peter, James, and John with him, and he began to be filled with
14:34 †Pss 42:6, 12; 43:5 John 12:27 horror and deep distress. 34 He told them, "My soul is crushed with grief to the point of
death. Stay here and watch with me."

14:20 Or *one who is dipping bread into the bowl with me.* **14:24** Some manuscripts read *the new covenant.* **14:27a** Greek *I.* **14:27b** Zech 13:7.

14:19 Judas, the very man who would betray Jesus, was at the table with the others. Judas had already determined to betray Jesus, but in cold-blooded hypocrisy he shared the fellowship of this meal. It is easy to become enraged or shocked by what Judas did; yet professing commitment to Christ and then denying him with one's life is also betraying him. It is denying Christ's love to disobey him; it is denying his truth to distrust him; it is denying his deity to reject his authority. Do your words and actions match? If not, consider a change of mind and heart that will protect you from making a terrible mistake.

14:20 It was often the practice to eat from a common bowl. Meat or bread was dipped into a bowl filled with sauce often made from fruit.

14:22-25 Mark records the origin of the Lord's Supper, also called Communion or Eucharist (thanksgiving), which is still celebrated in worship services today. Jesus and his disciples ate a meal, sang psalms, read Scripture, and prayed. Then Jesus took two traditional parts of the Passover meal, the passing of bread and the drinking of wine, and gave them new meaning as representations of his body and blood. He used the bread and wine to explain the significance of what he was about to do on the cross. For more on the significance of the Last Supper, see 1 Corinthians 11:23-29.

14:24 Jesus' death for us on the cross seals a new covenant between God and us. The old covenant involved forgiveness of sins through the blood of an animal sacrifice (Exodus 24:6-8). But instead of a spotless lamb on the altar, Jesus offered himself, the spotless Lamb of God, as a sacrifice that would forgive sin once and for all. Jesus was the final sacrifice for sins, and his blood sealed the new agreement between God and us. Now all of us can come to God through Jesus, in full confidence that God will hear us and save us from our sins.

14:26 The hymn they sang was most likely taken from Psalms 115–118, traditionally sung at the Passover meal.

14:27 It's easy to think that Satan temporarily gained the upper hand in Jesus' death. But we see later that God was in control, even in the death of his Son. Satan gained no victory—everything occurred exactly as God had planned.

14:27-31 This was the second time in the same evening that Jesus predicted the disciples' denial and desertion, which probably explains their strong reaction (14:31). For Jesus' earlier prediction, see Luke 22:31-34 and John 13:36-38.

35 He went on a little farther and fell face down on the ground. He prayed that, if it
were possible, the awful hour awaiting him might pass him by. 36 "Abba,* Father," he
said, "everything is possible for you. Please take this cup of suffering away from me. Yet
I want your will, not mine."
37 Then he returned and found the disciples asleep. "Simon!" he said to Peter. "Are
you asleep? Couldn't you stay awake and watch with me even one hour? 38 Keep alert
and pray. Otherwise temptation will overpower you. For though the spirit is willing
enough, the body is weak."
39 Then Jesus left them again and prayed, repeating his pleadings. 40 Again he returned
to them and found them sleeping, for they just couldn't keep their eyes open. And they
didn't know what to say.
41 When he returned to them the third time, he said, "Still sleeping? Still resting?*
Enough! The time has come. I, the Son of Man, am betrayed into the hands of sinners.
42 Up, let's be going. See, my betrayer is here!"

Jesus Is Betrayed and Arrested (**224**/Matthew 26:47-56; Luke 22:47-53; John 18:1-11)

43 And immediately, as he said this, Judas, one of the twelve disciples, arrived with a mob
that was armed with swords and clubs. They had been sent out by the leading priests, the
teachers of religious law, and the other leaders. 44 Judas had given them a prearranged
signal: "You will know which one to arrest when I go over and give him the kiss of
greeting. Then you can take him away under guard."
45 As soon as they arrived, Judas walked up to Jesus. "Teacher!" he exclaimed, and
gave him the kiss. 46 Then the others grabbed Jesus and arrested him. 47 But someone
pulled out a sword and slashed off an ear of the high priest's servant.
48 Jesus asked them, "Am I some dangerous criminal, that you come armed with swords
and clubs to arrest me? 49 Why didn't you arrest me in the Temple? I was there teaching
every day. But these things are happening to fulfill what the Scriptures say about me."
50 Meanwhile, all his disciples deserted him and ran away. 51 There was a young man

14:36 Matt 20:22; John 5:30; 6:38; 18:11; Rom 8:15; Gal 4:6
14:38 Rom 7:22-23
14:47 John 18:10
14:49 Isa 53:7-9; Luke 24:44
14:50 Ps 88:8; John 16:32

14:36 *Abba* is an Aramaic term for "father." **14:41** Or *Sleep on, take your rest.*

14:35, 36 Was Jesus trying to get out of his task? Jesus expressed his true feelings, but he did not deny or rebel against God's will. He reaffirmed his desire to do what God wanted. Jesus' prayer highlights the terrible suffering he had to endure—an agony so much more magnified because he had to take on the sins of the whole world. This "cup" was the agony of alienation from God, his Father, at the cross (Hebrews 5:7-9). The sinless Son of God took on our sins and was separated for a while from God so that we could be eternally saved.

14:36 While praying, Jesus was aware of what doing the Father's will would cost him. He understood the suffering he was about to encounter, and he did not want to have to endure the horrible experience. But Jesus prayed, "Yet I want your will, not mine." Anything worth having costs something. What does your commitment to God cost you? We must be willing to pay whatever the price to gain what is priceless—eternal life.

14:38 In times of great stress, we are vulnerable to temptation, even if we have a willing spirit. Jesus gave us an example of what to do to resist: (1) Pray to God (14:35); (2) seek support of friends and loved ones (14:33, 37, 40, 41); (3) focus on the purpose God has given us (14:36).

14:43-45 Judas was given a contingent of police and soldiers (John 18:3) in order to seize Jesus and bring him before the religious court for trial. The religious leaders had issued a warrant for Jesus' arrest, and Judas was acting as Jesus' official accuser.

14:47 According to John 18:10, the person who pulled out a sword was Peter. Luke 22:51 records that Jesus immediately healed the man's ear and prevented any further bloodshed.

14:50 Just hours earlier, these disciples had vowed never to desert Jesus (14:31).

14:51, 52 Tradition says that this young man may have been John Mark, the writer of this Gospel. The incident is not mentioned in any of the other accounts.

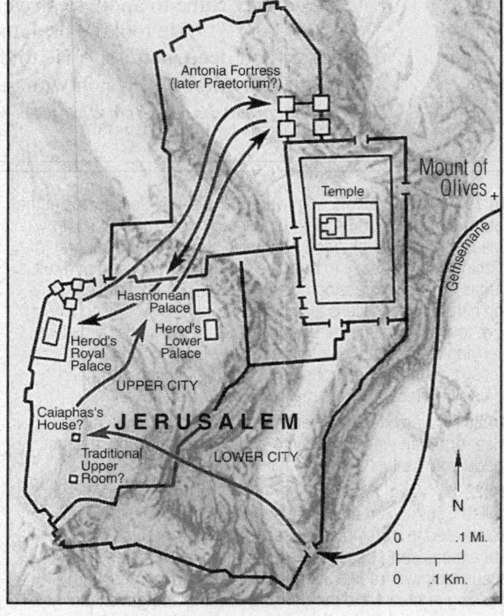

JESUS' TRIAL From Gethsemane, Jesus' trial began at the home of Caiaphas, the high priest. Jesus was then taken to Pilate, the Roman governor. Luke records that Pilate sent him to Herod, who was in Jerusalem—presumably in one of his two palaces (Luke 23:5-12). Herod sent him back to Pilate, who handed Jesus over to be crucified.

following along behind, clothed only in a linen nightshirt. When the mob tried to grab
him, 52 they tore off his clothes, but he escaped and ran away naked.

Caiaphas Questions Jesus (**226**/Matthew 26:57-68)

14:54 Matt 26:3 John 18:18

53 Jesus was led to the high priest's home where the leading priests, other leaders, and
teachers of religious law had gathered. 54 Meanwhile, Peter followed far behind and then

MAJOR EVENTS OF PASSION WEEK

Sunday through Wednesday Jesus spent each night in Bethany, just two miles east of Jerusalem on the opposite slope of the Mount of Olives. He probably stayed at the home of Mary, Martha, and Lazarus. Jesus spent Thursday night praying in the Garden of Gethsemane. Friday and Saturday nights Jesus' body lay in the garden tomb.

Day	*Event*	*References*
Sunday	Triumphal Entry into Jerusalem	Matthew 21:1–11 Mark 11:1–10 Luke 19:29–40 John 12:12–19
Monday	Jesus clears the Temple	Matthew 21:12, 13 Mark 11:15–17 Luke 19:45, 46
Tuesday	Jesus' authority challenged in the Temple	Matthew 21:23–27 Mark 11:27–33 Luke 20:1–8
	Jesus teaches in stories and confronts the Jewish leaders	Matthew 21:28—23:36 Mark 12:1–40 Luke 20:9–47
	Greeks ask to see Jesus	John 12:20–26
	The Olivet discourse	Matthew 24 Mark 13 Luke 21:5–38
	Judas agrees to betray Jesus	Matthew 26:14–16 Mark 14:10, 11 Luke 22:3–6
Wednesday	The Bible does not say what Jesus did on this day; he probably remained in Bethany with his disciples	
Thursday	The Last Supper	Matthew 26:26–29 Mark 14:22–25 Luke 22:14–20
	Jesus speaks to the disciples in the upper room	John 13—17
	Jesus struggles in Gethsemane	Matthew 26:36–46 Mark 14:32–42 Luke 22:39–46 John 18:1
	Jesus is betrayed and arrested	Matthew 26:47–56 Mark 14:43–52 Luke 22:47–53 John 18:2–12
Friday	Jesus is tried by Jewish and Roman authorities and is denied by Peter	Matthew 26:57—27:2, 11–31 Mark 14:53—15:20 Luke 22:54—23:25 John 18:13—19:16
	Jesus is crucified	Matthew 27:31–56 Mark 15:20–41 Luke 23:26–49 John 19:17–30
Sunday	The Resurrection	Matthew 28:1–10 Mark 16:1–11 Luke 24:1–12 John 20:1–18

14:53ff This trial by the high council had two phases. A small group met at night (John 18:12-24), and then the full high council met at daybreak (Luke 22:66-71). They tried Jesus for religious offenses, such as calling himself the Son of God, which, according to law, was blasphemy. The trial was fixed: These religious leaders had already decided to kill Jesus (Luke 22:2).

slipped inside the gates of the high priest's courtyard. For a while he sat with the guards,
warming himself by the fire.
55 Inside, the leading priests and the entire high council* were trying to find witnesses who would testify against Jesus, so they could put him to death. But their efforts
were in vain. 56 Many false witnesses spoke against him, but they contradicted each
other. 57 Finally, some men stood up to testify against him with this lie: 58 "We heard
him say, 'I will destroy this Temple made with human hands, and in three days I will
build another, made without human hands.'" 59 But even then they didn't get their
stories straight!
60 Then the high priest stood up before the others and asked Jesus, "Well, aren't you
going to answer these charges? What do you have to say for yourself?" 61 Jesus made no
reply. Then the high priest asked him, "Are you the Messiah, the Son of the blessed God?"
62 Jesus said, "I am, and you will see me, the Son of Man, sitting at God's right hand
in the place of power and coming back on the clouds of heaven."*
63 Then the high priest tore his clothing to show his horror and said, "Why do we need
other witnesses? 64 You have all heard his blasphemy. What is your verdict?" And they
all condemned him to death.
65 Then some of them began to spit at him, and they blindfolded him and hit his face
with their fists. "Who hit you that time, you prophet?" they jeered. And even the guards
were hitting him as they led him away.

Peter Denies Knowing Jesus (**227**/Matthew 26:69-75; Luke 22:54-65; John 18:25-27)

66 Meanwhile, Peter was below in the courtyard. One of the servant girls who worked for
the high priest 67 noticed Peter warming himself at the fire. She looked at him closely and
then said, "You were one of those with Jesus, the Nazarene."
68 Peter denied it. "I don't know what you're talking about," he said, and he went out
into the entryway. Just then, a rooster crowed.*
69 The servant girl saw him standing there and began telling the others, "That man is
definitely one of them!" 70 Peter denied it again.
A little later some other bystanders began saying to Peter, "You must be one of them
because you are from Galilee."
71 Peter said, "I swear by God, I don't know this man you're talking about." 72 And
immediately the rooster crowed the second time. Suddenly, Jesus' words flashed through
Peter's mind: "Before the rooster crows twice, you will deny me three times." And he
broke down and cried.

14:56 Ps 35:11; Prov 6:16-19; 19:5
14:58 Mark 15:29; John 2:19
14:61 Isa 53:7; 1 Pet 2:23
14:62 †Ps 110:1; †Dan 7:13; Matt 16:27; 24:30; Mark 8:38; 13:26; Acts 1:11; 1 Thes 4:16; 2 Thes 1:7; Rev 1:7; 22:20
14:63 Lev 10:6; 21:10; Num 14:6
14:64 Lev 24:16; John 19:7
14:65 Isa 50:6; 53:5
14:70 Acts 2:7
14:72 Mark 14:30

14:55 Greek *the Sanhedrin.* **14:62** See Ps 110:1; Dan 7:13. **14:68** Some manuscripts do not include *Just then, a rooster crowed.*

14:55 The Romans controlled Israel, but the Jews were given some authority over religious and minor civil disputes. The Jewish ruling body, the high council, was made up of 71 of Israel's religious leaders. It was assumed that these men would be just. Instead, they showed great injustice in the trial of Jesus, even to the point of making up lies to use against him (14:57).

14:58 The statement that the false witnesses finally agreed to use as an accusation twisted Jesus' actual words. Jesus did not say, "I will destroy this Temple made with human hands;" he said, "Destroy this temple, and in three days I will raise it up" (John 2:19). Jesus was not talking about Herod's Temple but about his own body.

14:60-64 To the first question, Jesus made no reply because it was based on confusing and erroneous evidence. Not answering was wiser than trying to clarify the fabricated accusations. But if Jesus had refused to answer the second question, it could have been taken as a denial of his mission. Instead, his answer predicted a powerful role reversal. Sitting at God's right hand in the place of power, he would come to judge his accusers, and they would have to answer *his* questions (Psalm 110:1; Revelation 20:11-13).

14:63, 64 Of all people, the high priest and members of the high council should have recognized the Messiah because they knew the Scriptures thoroughly. Their job was to point people to God, but they were more concerned about preserving their reputation and holding on to their authority. They valued human security more than eternal security.

14:66, 67 Caiaphas's house, where Jesus was tried (14:53), was part of a huge palace with several courtyards. John was apparently acquainted with the high priest, and he was let into the courtyard along with Peter (John 18:15, 16).

14:71 Peter was making the strongest denial he could think of by denying with an oath that he knew Jesus. He was saying, in effect, "May God strike me dead if I'm lying."

14:71 It is easy to get angry at the high council and the Roman governor for their injustice in condemning Jesus, but Peter and the rest of the disciples also contributed to Jesus' pain by deserting him (14:50). While most of us may not be like the Jewish and Roman leaders, we are like the disciples because all of us have been guilty of denying Christ as Lord in vital areas of our lives. We may pride ourselves that we have not committed certain sins, but we are all guilty of sin. Don't try to excuse yourself by pointing at others whose sins seem worse than yours.

15:1 Why did the Jewish leaders send Jesus to Pilate, the Roman governor? The Romans had taken away the Jews' right to inflict capital punishment; so in order for Jesus to be condemned to death, he had to be sentenced by a Roman leader. The Jewish leaders wanted Jesus executed on a cross, a

The Council of Religious Leaders Condemns Jesus (**228**/Matthew 27:1-2; Luke 22:66-71)

15:1 Matt 27:1 Luke 23:1 John 18:28

15 Very early in the morning the leading priests, other leaders, and teachers of religious
law—the entire high council*—met to discuss their next step. They bound Jesus and
took him to Pilate, the Roman governor.

Jesus Stands Trial before Pilate
(**230**/Matthew 27:11-14; Luke 23:1-5; John 18:28-37)

2 Pilate asked Jesus, "Are you the King of the Jews?"
Jesus replied, "Yes, it is as you say."

15:5 Isa 53:7 Mark 14:60-61 Luke 23:9

3 Then the leading priests accused him of many crimes, 4 and Pilate asked him, "Aren't
you going to say something? What about all these charges against you?" 5 But Jesus said
nothing, much to Pilate's surprise.

15:1 Greek *the Sanhedrin;* also in 15:43.

PILATE

In Jesus' day, any death sentence had to be approved by the Roman official in charge of the administrative district. Pontius Pilate was governor of the province of Judea, where Jerusalem was located. When the Jewish leaders had Jesus in their power and wanted to kill him, they had to obtain Pilate's permission. So it happened that early one morning Pilate found a crowd at his door demanding a man's death.

Pilate's relationship with the Jews had always been stormy. His Roman toughness and fairness had been weakened by cynicism, compromises, and mistakes. On several occasions his actions had deeply offended the religious leaders. The resulting riots and chaos must have made Pilate wonder what he had gotten himself into. He was trying to control people who treated their Roman conquerors without respect. Jesus' trial was another episode in Pilate's ongoing problems.

For Pilate, there was never a doubt about Jesus' innocence. Three separate times he declared Jesus not guilty. He couldn't understand why these people wanted to kill Jesus, but his fear of the Jews' political pressure made him decide to allow Jesus' crucifixion. Because of the people's threat to inform the emperor that Pilate hadn't eliminated a rebel against Rome, Pilate went against what he knew was right. In desperation, he chose to do wrong.

We share a common humanity with Pilate. At times we know what is right but choose what is wrong. He had his moment in history, and now we have ours. What have we done with our opportunities and responsibilities? What judgment have we passed on Jesus?

Strength and accomplishment
- Roman governor of Judea

Weaknesses and mistakes
- He failed in his attempt to rule a people who were defeated militarily but never dominated by Rome
- His constant political struggles made him a cynical and uncaring compromiser, susceptible to pressure
- Although he realized Jesus was innocent, he bowed to the public demand for his execution

Lessons from his life
- Great evil can happen when truth is at the mercy of political pressures
- Resisting the truth leaves a person without purpose or direction

Vital statistics
- Where: Judea
- Occupation: Roman governor of Judea
- Relative: Wife: unnamed
- Contemporaries: Jesus, Caiaphas, Herod

Key verses
" 'What is truth?' Pilate asked. Then he went out again to the people and told them, 'He is not guilty of any crime. But you have a custom of asking me to release someone from prison each year at Passover. So if you want me to, I'll release the King of the Jews' " (John 18:38, 39).

Pilate's story is told in the Gospels. He is also mentioned in Acts 3:13; 4:27; 13:28; 1 Timothy 6:13.

method of death that they believed brought a curse from God (see Deuteronomy 21:23). They hoped to persuade the people that Jesus was cursed, not blessed, by God.

15:3, 4 The Jewish leaders had to fabricate new accusations against Jesus when they brought him before Pilate. The charge of blasphemy would mean nothing to the Roman governor, so they accused Jesus of three other crimes: (1) encouraging the people to not pay their taxes to Rome, (2) claiming he was a king—"the King of the Jews," and (3) causing riots all over the countryside. Tax evasion, treason, and terrorism—all these would be cause for Pilate's concern (see also Luke 23:2).

15:5 Why didn't Jesus answer Pilate's questions? It would have been futile to answer, and the time had come to give his life to save the world. Jesus had no reason to try to prolong the trial or save himself. His was the ultimate example of self-assurance and peace, which no ordinary criminal could imitate. Nothing would stop him from completing the work he had come to earth to do (Isaiah 53:7).

Pilate Hands Jesus Over to Be Crucified
(**232**/Matthew 27:15-26; Luke 23:13-25; John 18:38—19:16)
6 Now it was the governor's custom to release one prisoner each year at Passover
time—anyone the people requested. 7 One of the prisoners at that time was Barabbas,
convicted along with others for murder during an insurrection. 8 The mob began to crowd
in toward Pilate, asking him to release a prisoner as usual. 9 "Should I give you the King
of the Jews?" Pilate asked. 10 (For he realized by now that the leading priests had arrested
Jesus out of envy.) 11 But at this point the leading priests stirred up the mob to demand **15:11** Acts 3:14
the release of Barabbas instead of Jesus. 12 "But if I release Barabbas," Pilate asked them,
"what should I do with this man you call the King of the Jews?"
13 They shouted back, "Crucify him!"
14 "Why?" Pilate demanded. "What crime has he committed?"
But the crowd only roared the louder, "Crucify him!"
15 So Pilate, anxious to please the crowd, released Barabbas to them. He ordered Jesus **15:15** Isa 53:6
flogged with a lead-tipped whip, then turned him over to the Roman soldiers to crucify him.

Roman Soldiers Mock Jesus (**233**/Matthew 27:27-31)
16 The soldiers took him into their headquarters* and called out the entire battalion.
17 They dressed him in a purple robe and made a crown of long, sharp thorns and put it

15:16 Greek *the courtyard, which is the praetorium.*

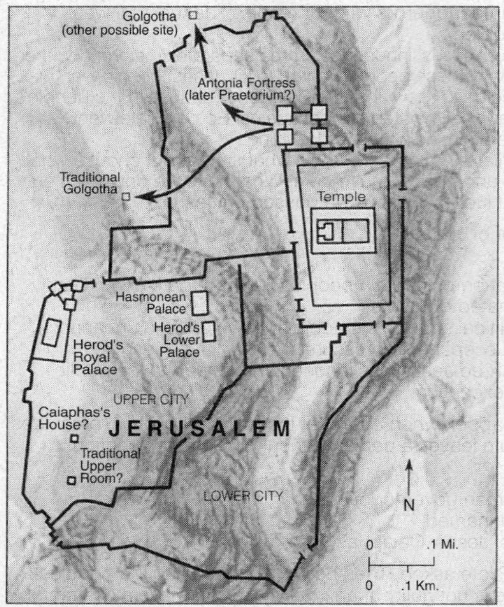

JESUS' ROUTE TO GOLGOTHA After being sentenced by Pilate, Jesus was taken from the Praetorium to Golgotha, a place outside the city, for crucifixion.

15:7 Barabbas was arrested for his part in a rebellion against the Roman government, and, although he had committed a murder, he may have been a hero among the Jews. The fiercely independent Jews hated to be ruled by pagan Romans. They hated paying taxes to support the despised government and its gods. Most of the Roman authorities who had to settle Jewish disputes hated the Jews in return. The time was ripe for rebellion.

15:8 This mob was most likely a group of people loyal to the Jewish leaders. But where were the disciples and the crowds who days earlier had shouted, "Praise God in highest heaven" (11:10)? Jesus' sympathizers were afraid of the Jewish leaders, so they went into hiding. Another possibility is that the multitude included many people who were in the Palm Sunday parade but who turned against Jesus when they saw that he was not going to be an earthly conqueror and their deliverer from Rome.

15:10 The Jews hated Pilate, but they went to him for the favor of condemning Jesus to crucifixion. Pilate could see that this was a frame-up. Why else would these people, who hated him and the Roman Empire he represented, ask him to convict one of their fellow Jews of treason and give him the death penalty?

15:13 Crucifixion was the Roman penalty for rebellion. Only slaves or those who were not Roman citizens could be crucified. If Jesus died by crucifixion, he would die the death of a rebel and slave, not of the king he claimed to be. This is just what the Jewish religious leaders wanted and the reason they whipped the mob into a frenzy. In addition, crucifixion would put the responsibility for killing Jesus on the Romans, and thus the crowds could not blame the religious leaders.

15:14, 15 Who was guilty of Jesus' death? In reality, everyone was at fault. The disciples deserted him in terror. Peter denied that he ever knew Jesus. Judas betrayed him. The crowds who had followed him stood by and did nothing. Pilate tried to blame the crowds. The religious leaders actively promoted Jesus' death. The Roman soldiers tortured him. If you had been there, watching these trials, what would your response have been?

15:15 The region of Judea where Pilate ruled as governor was little more than a hot and dusty outpost of the Roman Empire. Because Judea was so far from Rome, Pilate was given just a small army. His primary job was to keep the peace. We know from historical records that Pilate had already been warned about other uprisings in his region. Although he may have seen no guilt in Jesus and no reason to condemn him to death, Pilate wavered when the Jews in the crowd threatened to report him to Caesar (John 19:12). Such a report, accompanied by a riot, could cost him his position and hopes for advancement.

15:15 Although Jesus was innocent according to Roman law, Pilate caved in to political pressure. He abandoned what he knew was right. Trying to second-guess the Jewish leaders, Pilate gave a decision that would please everyone while keeping himself safe. When we ignore God's clear statements of right and wrong and make decisions based on the preferences of our audience, we fall into compromise and lawlessness. God promises to honor those who do right, not those who make everyone happy.

on his head. 18 Then they saluted, yelling, "Hail! King of the Jews!" 19 And they beat him
on the head with a stick, spit on him, and dropped to their knees in mock worship.
20 When they were finally tired of mocking him, they took off the purple robe and put his
own clothes on him again. Then they led him away to be crucified.

Jesus Is Led Away to Be Crucified (**234**/Matthew 27:32-34; Luke 23:26-31; John 19:17)
21 A man named Simon, who was from Cyrene,* was coming in from the country just then,
and they forced him to carry Jesus' cross. (Simon is the father of Alexander and Rufus.)
15:23 Ps 69:21 22 And they brought Jesus to a place called Golgotha (which means Skull Hill). 23 They
offered him wine drugged with myrrh, but he refused it. 24 Then they nailed him to the cross.
15:24 †Ps 22:18 They gambled for his clothes, throwing dice* to decide who would get them.

Jesus Is Placed on the Cross (**235**/Matthew 27:35-44; Luke 23:32-43; John 19:18-27)
15:25 John 19:14 25 It was nine o'clock in the morning when the crucifixion took place. 26 A signboard was
fastened to the cross above Jesus' head, announcing the charge against him. It read: "The
King of the Jews." 27 Two criminals were crucified with him, their crosses on either side
15:29 Pss 22:7; 109:2 Mark 14:58 John 2:19 of his.* 29 And the people passing by shouted abuse, shaking their heads in mockery.
"Ha! Look at you now!" they yelled at him. "You can destroy the Temple and rebuild it
in three days, can you? 30 Well then, save yourself and come down from the cross!"
31 The leading priests and teachers of religious law also mocked Jesus. "He saved
15:32 Zeph 3:15 others," they scoffed, "but he can't save himself! 32 Let this Messiah, this king of Israel,

15:21 *Cyrene* was a city in northern Africa. **15:24** Greek *casting lots.* See Ps 22:18. **15:27** Some manuscripts add verse 28, *And the Scripture was fulfilled that said, "He was counted among those who were rebels."* See Isa 53:12.

WHY DID JESUS HAVE TO DIE?		
	The Problem	We have all done things that are wrong, and we have failed to obey God's laws. Because of this, we have been separated from God our Creator. Separation from God is death; but, by ourselves, we can do nothing to become united with God.
	Why Jesus Could Help	Jesus was not only a man; he was God's unique Son. Because Jesus never disobeyed God and never sinned, only he can bridge the gap between the sinless God and sinful people.
	The Solution	Jesus freely offered his life for us, dying on the cross in our place, taking all our wrongdoing upon himself, and saving us from the consequences of sin—including God's judgment and death.
	The Results	Jesus took our past, present, and future sins upon himself so that we could have new life. Because all our wrongdoing is forgiven, we are reconciled to God. Furthermore, Jesus' resurrection from the dead is the proof that his substitutionary sacrifice on the cross was acceptable to God, and his resurrection has become the source of new life for those who believe that Jesus is the Son of God. All who believe in him may have this new life and live it in union with him.

15:19 The soldiers mocked Jesus by pretending to worship him.

15:21 Colonies of Jews existed outside Judea. Simon had made a Passover pilgrimage to Jerusalem all the way from Cyrene in North Africa. His sons, Alexander and Rufus, are mentioned here probably because they became well known later in the early church (Romans 16:13).

15:24 Throwing dice was a way of making a decision by chance. The soldiers gambled to decide who would receive Jesus' clothing. Roman soldiers had the right to take for themselves the clothing of those crucified. This act fulfilled the prophecy of Psalm 22:18.

15:25 Crucifixion was a feared and shameful form of execution. The victim was forced to carry his cross along the longest possible route to the crucifixion site as a warning to bystanders. There were several shapes for crosses and several different methods of crucifixion. Jesus was nailed to the cross; condemned men were sometimes tied to their crosses with ropes. In either case, death came by suffocation as the person lost strength and the weight of the body made breathing more and more difficult.

15:26 A sign stating the condemned man's crime was often placed on a cross as a warning. Because Jesus was never found guilty, the only accusation placed on his sign was the "crime" of being King of the Jews.

15:27 Luke records that one of these criminals repented before his death, and Jesus promised that criminal that he would be with him in paradise (Luke 23:39-43).

15:31 Jesus could have saved himself, but he endured this suffering because of his love for us. He could have chosen not to take the pain and humiliation and killed those who mocked him. But he suffered through it all because he loved even his enemies. We had a significant part in the drama that afternoon because our sins were on the cross, too. Jesus died on that cross for us, and the penalty for our sins was paid by his death. The only adequate response we can make is to confess our sins and gratefully accept the fact that Jesus paid for them so we wouldn't have to. Don't insult God with indifference toward the greatest act of genuine love in history.

15:32 When James and John had asked Jesus for the places of honor next to him in his Kingdom, Jesus had told them that they didn't know what they were asking (10:35-39). Here, as Jesus was preparing to inaugurate his Kingdom through his death, the places on his right and on his left were taken by dying men—criminals. As Jesus explained to his two power-hungry disciples, a person

come down from the cross so we can see it and believe him!" Even the two criminals
who were being crucified with Jesus ridiculed him.

Jesus Dies on the Cross (**236**/Matthew 27:45-56; Luke 23:44-49; John 19:28-37)
33 At noon, darkness fell across the whole land until three o'clock. 34 Then, at that time **15:34** †Ps 22:1
Jesus called out with a loud voice, "*Eloi, Eloi, lema sabachthani?*" which means, "My
God, my God, why have you forsaken me?"*
35 Some of the bystanders misunderstood and thought he was calling for the prophet Elijah.
36 One of them ran and filled a sponge with sour wine, holding it up to him on a stick so he **15:36** Ps 69:21
could drink. "Leave him alone. Let's see whether Elijah will come and take him down!" he said.
37 Then Jesus uttered another loud cry and breathed his last. 38 And the curtain in the **15:38** Exod 26:31-33
Temple was torn in two, from top to bottom. 39 When the Roman officer who stood facing Heb 10:19-20
him saw how he had died, he exclaimed, "Truly, this was the Son of God!"
40 Some women were there, watching from a distance, including Mary Magdalene, **15:40-41** Luke 8:2-3
Mary (the mother of James the younger and of Joseph*), and Salome. 41 They had been
followers of Jesus and had cared for him while he was in Galilee. Then they and many
other women had come with him to Jerusalem.

Jesus Is Laid in the Tomb (**237**/Matthew 27:57-61; Luke 23:50-56; John 19:38-42)
42 This all happened on Friday, the day of preparation,* the day before the Sabbath. As
evening approached, 43 an honored member of the high council, Joseph from Arimathea **15:43** Luke 2:25, 38
(who was waiting for the Kingdom of God to come), gathered his courage and went to Pilate
to ask for Jesus' body. 44 Pilate couldn't believe that Jesus was already dead, so he called for
the Roman military officer in charge and asked him. 45 The officer confirmed the fact, and
Pilate told Joseph he could have the body. 46 Joseph bought a long sheet of linen cloth, and **15:46** Acts 13:29
taking Jesus' body down from the cross, he wrapped it in the cloth and laid it in a tomb that
had been carved out of the rock. Then he rolled a stone in front of the entrance. 47 Mary
Magdalene and Mary the mother of Joseph saw where Jesus' body was laid.

15:34 Ps 22:1. **15:40** Greek *Joses;* also in 15:47. See Matt 27:56. **15:42** Greek *on the day of preparation.*

---

who wants to be close to Jesus must be prepared to suffer and die as he himself was doing. The way to the Kingdom is the way of the cross. If we want the glory of the Kingdom, we must be willing to be united with the crucified Christ.

15:34 Jesus did not ask this question in surprise or despair. He was quoting the first line of Psalm 22. The whole psalm is a prophecy expressing the deep agony of the Messiah's death for the world's sin. Jesus knew that he would be temporarily separated from God the moment he took upon himself the sins of the world. This separation was what he had dreaded as he prayed in Gethsemane. The physical agony was horrible, but the spiritual alienation from God was the ultimate torture.

15:37 Jesus' loud cry may have been his last words, "It is finished" (John 19:30).

15:38 A heavy curtain hung in front of the Temple room called the Most Holy Place, a place reserved by God for himself. Symbolically, the curtain separated the holy God from sinful people. The room was entered only once a year, on the Day of Atonement, by the high priest as he made a sacrifice to gain forgiveness for the sins of all the people. When Jesus died, the curtain was torn in two, showing that his death for our sins had opened up the way for us to approach our holy God. And it was torn from top to bottom, showing that *God* had opened the way. Read Hebrews 9 for a more complete explanation.

15:42ff The Sabbath began at sundown on Friday and ended at sundown on Saturday. Jesus died just a few hours before sundown on Friday. It was against Jewish law to do physical work or to travel on the Sabbath. It was also against Jewish law to let a dead body remain exposed overnight (Deuteronomy 21:23). Joseph came to bury Jesus' body before the Sabbath began. If Jesus had died on the Sabbath when Joseph was unavailable, his body would have been taken down by the Romans. Had the Romans taken Jesus' body, no Jews could have confirmed his death, and opponents could have disputed his resurrection.

15:42, 43 After Jesus died on the cross, Joseph of Arimathea asked for his body and then sealed it in a new tomb. Although an honored member of the high council, Joseph was a secret disciple of Jesus. Not all the Jewish leaders hated Jesus. Joseph risked his reputation to give a proper burial to his Lord. It is frightening to risk one's reputation even for what is right. If your Christian witness endangers your reputation, remember Joseph. Today he is remembered with admiration in the Christian church. How many other members of the Jewish high council can you name?

15:44 Pilate was surprised that Jesus had died so quickly, so he asked an officer to verify the report. Today, in an effort to deny the Resurrection, there are those who say that Jesus didn't really die. His death, however, was confirmed by the officer, Pilate, Joseph of Arimathea, the religious leaders, and the women who witnessed his burial. Jesus suffered actual physical death on the cross.

15:46 This tomb was probably a man-made cave hewn from a hill. It was large enough to walk into. Joseph wrapped Jesus' body, placed it in the tomb, and rolled a heavy stone across the entrance. The religious leaders also watched where Jesus was buried. They stationed guards by the tomb and sealed the stone to make sure that no one would steal Jesus' body and claim he had risen from the dead (Matthew 27:62-66).

15:47 These women could do very little. They couldn't speak before the high council in Jesus' defense; they couldn't appeal to Pilate; they couldn't stand against the crowds; they couldn't overpower the Roman guards. But they did what they could. They stayed at the cross when the disciples had fled; they followed Jesus' body to its tomb; and they prepared spices for his body. Because these women used the opportunities they had, they were the first to witness the Resurrection. God blessed their devotion and diligence. As believers, we should take advantage of the opportunities we have and do what we *can* for Christ, instead of worrying about what we *cannot* do.

16:1 Luke 23:56; John 19:39-40
16:3 Mark 15:46
16:5 John 20:12; Acts 1:10; 10:30
16:6 Acts 2:23-32; Rom 1:3-4; 1 Cor 15:4-12, 20; Rev 1:18
16:7 Matt 26:32; Mark 14:28; John 21:1

Jesus Rises from the Dead (**239**/Matthew 28:1-7; Luke 24:1-12; John 20:1-10)

16 The next evening, when the Sabbath ended, Mary Magdalene and Salome and Mary
the mother of James went out and purchased burial spices to put on Jesus' body. 2 Very
early on Sunday morning,* just at sunrise, they came to the tomb. 3 On the way they were
discussing who would roll the stone away from the entrance to the tomb. 4 But when they
arrived, they looked up and saw that the stone—a very large one—had already been rolled
aside. 5 So they entered the tomb, and there on the right sat a young man clothed in a white
robe. The women were startled, 6 but the angel said, "Do not be so surprised. You are looking
for Jesus, the Nazarene, who was crucified. He isn't here! He has been raised from the dead!
Look, this is where they laid his body. 7 Now go and give this message to his disciples,
including Peter: Jesus is going ahead of you to Galilee. You will see him there, just as he
told you before he died!" 8 The women fled from the tomb, trembling and bewildered,
saying nothing to anyone because they were too frightened to talk.*

16:2 Greek *on the first day of the week;* also in 16:9. **16:8** The most reliable early manuscripts conclude the Gospel of Mark at verse 8. Other manuscripts include various endings to the Gospel. Two of the more noteworthy endings are printed here.

EVIDENCE THAT JESUS ACTUALLY DIED AND AROSE

This evidence demonstrates Jesus' uniqueness in history and proves that he is God's Son. No one else was able to predict his own resurrection and then accomplish it.

Proposed Explanations for Empty Tomb	*Evidence against These Explanations*	*References*
Jesus was only unconscious and later revived.	A Roman soldier told Pilate that Jesus was dead.	Mark 15:44, 45
	The Roman soldiers did not break Jesus' legs because he had already died, and one of them pierced Jesus' side with a spear.	John 19:32–34
	Joseph of Arimathea and Nicodemus wrapped Jesus' body and placed it in the tomb.	John 19:38–40
The women made a mistake and went to the wrong tomb.	Mary Magdalene and Mary the mother of Joseph saw Jesus placed in the tomb.	Matthew 27:59–61 Mark 15:47 Luke 23:55
Unknown thieves stole Jesus' body.	On Sunday morning Peter and John also went to the same tomb.	John 20:3–9
The disciples stole Jesus' body.	The tomb was sealed and guarded by Roman soldiers.	Matthew 27:65, 66
	The disciples were ready to die for their faith. Stealing Jesus' body would have been admitting that their faith was meaningless.	Acts 12:2
The religious leaders stole Jesus' body to produce it later.	If the religious leaders had taken Jesus' body, they would have produced it to stop the rumors of his resurrection.	None

16:1, 2 The women purchased the spices on Saturday evening after the Sabbath had ended so they could go to the tomb early the next morning and anoint Jesus' body as a sign of love, devotion, and respect. Bringing spices to the tomb was like bringing flowers to a grave today.

16:4 The angel did not roll away the stone so Jesus could get out but so others could get in and see for themselves that Jesus had indeed risen from the dead, just as he said.

16:5 Mark says that one angel met the women at the tomb, while Luke mentions two angels. These accounts are not contradictory. Each Gospel writer chose to highlight different details as he explained the same story, just as eyewitnesses to a news story each may highlight a different aspect of that event. Mark probably emphasized only the angel who spoke. The unique emphasis of each Gospel shows that the four accounts were written independently. This should give us confidence that all four are true and reliable.

16:6 The Resurrection is vitally important for many reasons: (1) Jesus kept his promise to rise from the dead, so we can believe he will keep all his other promises. (2) The Resurrection ensures that the ruler of God's eternal Kingdom will be the living Christ, not just an idea, hope, or dream. (3) Christ's resurrection gives us the assurance that we also will be resurrected. (4) The power of God that brought Christ's body back from the dead is available to us to bring our morally and spiritually dead selves back to life so that we can change and grow (1 Corinthians 15:12-19). (5) The Resurrection provides the substance of the church's witness to the world. We do not merely tell lessons from the life of a good teacher; we proclaim the reality of the resurrection of Jesus Christ.

16:7 The angel made special mention of Peter to show that, in spite of Peter's denials, Jesus had not disowned or deserted him. Jesus had great responsibilities for Peter to fulfill in the church that was not yet in existence.

16:7 The angel told the disciples to meet Jesus in Galilee "as he told you" (see 14:28). This is where Jesus had called most of them and had said they would "fish for people" (Matthew 4:19), and it would be where this mission would be restated (John 21). But the disciples, filled with fear, remained behind locked doors in Jerusalem (John 20:19). Jesus met them first in Jerusalem (Luke 24:36) and later in Galilee (John 21). Then he returned to Jerusalem, where he ascended into heaven from the Mount of Olives (Acts 1:12).

[Shorter Ending of Mark]

Then they reported all these instructions briefly to Peter and his companions. Afterward Jesus himself sent them out from east to west with the sacred and unfailing message of salvation that gives eternal life. Amen.

[Longer Ending of Mark]

Jesus Appears to Mary Magdalene (**240**/John 20:11-18)

9It was early on Sunday morning when Jesus rose from the dead, and the first person who
saw him was Mary Magdalene, the woman from whom he had cast out seven demons. 10She
went and found the disciples, who were grieving and weeping. 11But when she told them
that Jesus was alive and she had seen him, they didn't believe her.

16:9-11 Matt 28:9-10 John 20:11-18

Jesus Appears to Two Believers Traveling on the Road (**243**/Luke 24:13-34)

12Afterward he appeared to two who were walking from Jerusalem into the country, but
they didn't recognize him at first because he had changed his appearance. 13When they
realized who he was, they rushed back to tell the others, but no one believed them.

16:12-13 Luke 24:13-35

Jesus Appears to Thomas (**245**/John 20:24-31)

14Still later he appeared to the eleven disciples as they were eating together. He rebuked
them for their unbelief—their stubborn refusal to believe those who had seen him after
he had risen.

16:14-18 Matt 28:16-20 Luke 24:36-49 John 20:19-23 Acts 1:6-8

Jesus Gives the Great Commission (**248**/Matthew 28:16-20)

15And then he told them, "Go into all the world and preach the Good News to everyone,
everywhere. 16Anyone who believes and is baptized will be saved. But anyone who
refuses to believe will be condemned. 17These signs will accompany those who believe:
They will cast out demons in my name, and they will speak new languages.* 18They will
be able to handle snakes with safety, and if they drink anything poisonous, it won't hurt
them. They will be able to place their hands on the sick and heal them."

16:16 Acts 2:38; 16:31, 33

16:17 Acts 2:4, 11; 8:7; 10:46; 16:18; 19:6

16:18 Luke 10:19 Acts 28:3-6

Jesus Ascends into Heaven (**250**/Luke 24:50-53)

19When the Lord Jesus had finished talking with them, he was taken up into heaven and
sat down in the place of honor at God's right hand. 20And the disciples went everywhere
and preached, and the Lord worked with them, confirming what they said by many
miraculous signs.

16:19-20 Luke 24:50-53 Acts 1:9-11

16:19 Rom 8:34 Col 3:1 Heb 1:3

16:17 Or *new tongues.* Some manuscripts omit *new.*

16:13 When the two finally realized who Jesus was, they rushed back to Jerusalem. It's not enough to read about Christ as a personality or to study his teachings. You must also believe he is God, trust him to save you, and accept him as Lord of your life. This is the difference between knowing Jesus and knowing about him. Only when you know Christ will you be motivated to share with others what he has done for you.

16:15 Jesus told his disciples to go into all the world, telling everyone that he had paid the penalty for sin and that those who believe in him can be forgiven and live eternally with God. Christians today in all parts of the world are telling this Good News to people who haven't heard about Christ. The driving power that carries missionaries around the world and sets Christ's church in motion is the faith that comes from the Resurrection. Do you ever feel as though you don't have the skill or determination to be a witness for Christ? You must personally realize that Jesus rose from the dead and lives for you today. As you grow in your relationship with Christ, he will give you both the opportunities and the inner strength to tell his message.

16:16 It is not the water of baptism that saves but God's grace accepted through faith in Christ. Because of Jesus' response to the criminal on the cross who died with him, we know it is possible to be saved without being baptized (Luke 23:43). Baptism alone, without faith, does not guarantee that a person will go to heaven. Those who refuse to accept Jesus as their Savior will be condemned, regardless of whether or not they have been baptized.

16:18 There are times when God intervenes miraculously to protect his followers. Occasionally he gives them special powers. Paul handled a snake safely (Acts 28:5), and the disciples healed the sick (Matthew 10:1; Acts 3:7, 8). This does not mean, however, that we should test God by putting ourselves in dangerous situations.

16:19 When Jesus ascended into heaven, his physical presence left the disciples (Acts 1:9). Jesus' sitting at God's right hand signifies the completion of his work, his authority as God, and his coronation as King.

16:20 Mark's Gospel emphasizes Christ's power as well as his servanthood. Jesus' life and teaching turned the world upside down and continue to do so. The world sees power as a way to gain control over others. But Jesus, with all authority and power in heaven and earth, chose to serve others. He held children in his arms, healed the sick, washed the disciples' feet, and died for the sins of the world. Jesus' followers today receive this same power to serve. As believers, we are called to be servants of Christ. As Christ served, so we are to serve.

KEY PLACES IN LUKE

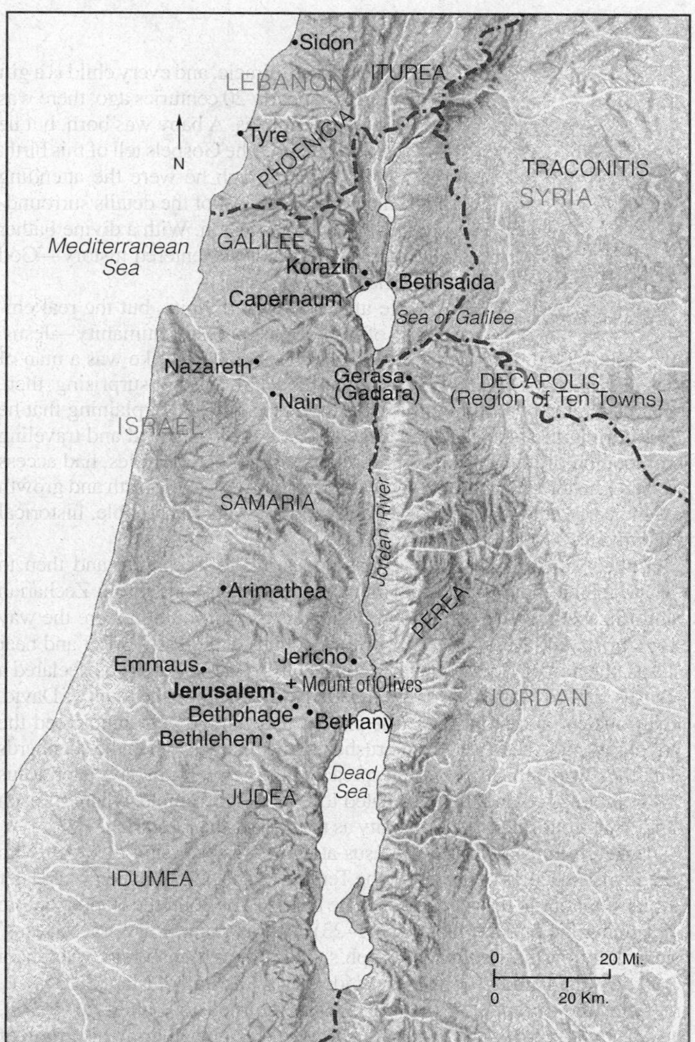

The broken lines (—·—·) indicate modern boundaries.

Luke begins his account in the Temple in Jerusalem, giving us the background for the birth of John the Baptist, then moves on to the town of Nazareth and the story of Mary, chosen to be Jesus' mother (1:26ff). As a result of Caesar's call for a census, Mary and Joseph had to travel to Bethlehem, where Jesus was born in fulfillment of prophecy (2:1ff). Jesus grew up in Nazareth and began his earthly ministry by being baptized by John (3:21, 22) and tempted by Satan (4:1ff). Much of his ministry focused on Galilee: He set up his "home" in Capernaum (4:31ff), and from there he taught throughout the region (8:1ff). Later he visited Gerasa (also called Gadara), where he healed a demon-possessed man (8:36ff). He fed more than 5,000 people with one lunch on the shores of the Sea of Galilee near Bethsaida (9:10ff). Jesus always traveled to Jerusalem for the major festivals, and he enjoyed visiting friends in nearby Bethany (10:38ff). He healed 10 men with leprosy on the border between Galilee and Samaria (17:11) and helped a dishonest tax collector in Jericho turn his life around (19:1ff). The little villages of Bethphage and Bethany on the Mount of Olives were Jesus' resting places during his last days on earth. He was crucified outside Jerusalem's walls, but he would rise again. Two of Jesus' followers walking on the road leading to Emmaus were among the first to see the resurrected Christ (24:13ff).

LUKE

Herod the Great begins to rule 37 B.C.	Jesus is born 6/5 B.C.	Escape to Egypt 5/4 B.C.	Herod the Great dies 4 B.C.	Return to Nazareth 4/3 B.C.	Jesus visits Temple as a boy A.D. 6/7

VITAL STATISTICS

PURPOSE:
To present an accurate account of the life of Christ and to present Christ as the perfect human and Savior

AUTHOR:
Luke—a doctor (Colossians 4:14), a Greek, and Gentile Christian. He is the only known Gentile author in the New Testament. Luke was a close friend and companion of Paul. He also wrote Acts, and the two books go together.

TO WHOM WRITTEN:
Theophilus ("one who loves God"), Gentiles, and people everywhere

DATE WRITTEN:
About A.D. 60

SETTING:
Luke wrote from Rome or possibly from Caesarea.

KEY VERSES:
"Jesus responded, 'Salvation has come to this home today, for this man has shown himself to be a son of Abraham. And I, the Son of Man, have come to seek and save those like him who are lost'" (19:9, 10).

KEY PEOPLE:
Jesus, Elizabeth, Zechariah, John the Baptist, Mary, the disciples, Herod the Great, Pilate, Mary Magdalene

KEY PLACES:
Bethlehem, Galilee, Judea, Jerusalem

SPECIAL FEATURES:
This is the most comprehensive Gospel. The general vocabulary and diction show that the author was educated. He makes frequent references to illnesses and diagnoses. Luke stresses Jesus' relationships with people; emphasizes prayer, miracles, and angels; records inspired hymns of praise; and gives a prominent place to women. Most of 9:51—18:35 is not found in any other Gospel.

EVERY birth is a miracle, and every child is a gift from God. But nearly 20 centuries ago, there was the miracle of miracles. A baby was born, but he was the Son of God. The Gospels tell of this birth, but Dr. Luke, as though he were the attending physician, provides most of the details surrounding this awesome occasion. With a divine Father and human mother, Jesus entered history—God in the flesh.

Luke affirms Jesus' divinity, but the real emphasis of his book is on Jesus' humanity—Jesus, the Son of God, is also the Son of Man. As a doctor, Luke was a man of science, and as a Greek, he was a man of detail. It is not surprising, then, that he begins by outlining his extensive research and explaining that he is reporting the facts (1:1–4). Luke also was a close friend and traveling companion of Paul, so he could interview the other disciples, had access to other historical accounts, and was an eyewitness to the birth and growth of the early church. His Gospel and book of Acts are reliable, historical documents.

Luke's story begins with angels appearing to Zechariah and then to Mary, telling them of the upcoming births of their sons. From Zechariah and Elizabeth would come John the Baptist, who would prepare the way for Christ. And Mary would conceive a child by the Holy Spirit and bear Jesus, the Son of God. Soon after John's birth, Caesar Augustus declared a census, and so Mary and Joseph traveled to Bethlehem, the town of David, their ancient ancestor. There the child was born. Angels announced the joyous event to shepherds, who rushed to the manger. When the shepherds left, they were praising God and spreading the news. Eight days later, Jesus was circumcised and then dedicated to God in the Temple, where Simeon and Anna confirmed Jesus' identity as the Savior, their Messiah.

Luke gives us a glimpse of Jesus at age 12—discussing theology with the Jewish teachers of the law at the Temple (2:41–52). Eighteen years later Jesus went out in the wilderness to be baptized by John the Baptist before beginning his public ministry (3:1–23). At this point, Luke traces Jesus' genealogy on his stepfather Joseph's side, through David and Abraham back to Adam, underscoring Jesus' identity as the Son of Man (3:23–38).

After the Temptation (4:1–13), Jesus returned to Galilee to preach, teach, and heal (4:14ff). During this time, he began gathering his group of 12 disciples (5:1–11, 27–29). Later Jesus commissioned the disciples and sent them out to proclaim the Kingdom of God. When they returned, Jesus revealed to them his mission, his true identity, and what it means to be his disciple (9:18–62). His mission would take him to Jerusalem (9:51–53), where he would be rejected, tried, and crucified.

While Jesus carried his own cross to Golgotha, some women in Jerusalem wept for him, but Jesus told them to weep for themselves and for their children (23:28). Luke's Gospel does not end in sadness, however. It concludes with the thrilling account of Jesus' resurrection from the dead, his appearances to the disciples, and his promise to send the Holy Spirit (24:1–53). Read Luke's beautifully written and accurate account of the life of Jesus, Son of Man and Son of God. Then praise God for sending the Savior—our risen and triumphant Lord—for all people.

Tiberius Caesar becomes emperor 14	John's ministry begins 26	Jesus begins his ministry 26/27	Jesus chooses twelve disciples 28	Jesus feeds 5,000 29	Jesus is crucified, rises again, and ascends 30

THE BLUEPRINT

A. BIRTH AND PREPARATION OF JESUS, THE SAVIOR (1:1—4:13)

From an infant who could do nothing on his own, Jesus grew to become completely able to fulfill his mission on earth. He was fully human, developing in all ways like us. Yet he remained fully God. He took no shortcuts and was not isolated from the pressures and temptations of life. There are no shortcuts for us either as we prepare for a life of service to God.

B. MESSAGE AND MINISTRY OF JESUS, THE SAVIOR (4:14—21:38)

1. Jesus' ministry in Galilee
2. Jesus' ministry on the way to Jerusalem
3. Jesus' ministry in Jerusalem

Jesus taught great crowds of people, especially through parables, which are stories that illustrate great truths. But only those with ears to hear will understand. We should pray that God's Spirit would help us understand the implications of these truths for our life so we can become more and more like Jesus.

C. DEATH AND RESURRECTION OF JESUS, THE SAVIOR (22:1—24:53)

The Savior of the world was arrested and executed. But death could not destroy him, and Jesus came back to life and ascended to heaven. In Luke's careful, historical account, we receive the facts about Jesus' resurrection. We must not only believe that these facts are true, but we must also trust Christ as our Savior. It is shortsighted to neglect the facts, but how sad it is to accept the facts and neglect the forgiveness that Jesus offers to each of us.

MEGATHEMES

THEME	EXPLANATION	IMPORTANCE
Jesus Christ, the Savior	Luke describes how God's Son entered human history. Jesus lived as the perfect example of a human. After a perfect ministry, he provided a perfect sacrifice for our sin so we could be saved.	Jesus is our perfect leader and Savior. He offers forgiveness to all who will accept him as Lord of their lives and believe that what he says is true.
History	Luke was a medical doctor and historian. He put great emphasis on dates and details, connecting Jesus to events and people in history.	Luke gives details so we can believe in the reliability of the history of Jesus' life. Even more important, we can believe with certainty that Jesus is God.
People	Jesus was deeply interested in people and relationships. He showed warm concern for his followers and friends—men, women, and children.	Jesus' love for people is good news for everyone. His message is for all people in every nation. Each one of us has an opportunity to respond to him in faith.
Compassion	As a perfect human, Jesus showed tender sympathy to the poor, the despised, the hurt, and the sinful. No one was rejected or ignored by him.	Jesus is more than a good teacher—he cares for you. Because of his deep love for you, he can satisfy your needs.
Holy Spirit	The Holy Spirit was present at Jesus' birth, baptism, ministry, and resurrection. As a perfect example for us, Jesus lived in dependence on the Holy Spirit.	The Holy Spirit was sent by God as confirmation of Jesus' authority. The Holy Spirit is given to enable people to live for Christ. By faith we can have the indwelling Holy Spirit's presence and power to witness and to serve.

A. BIRTH AND PREPARATION OF JESUS, THE SAVIOR (1:1—4:13)

Luke gives us the most detailed account of Jesus' birth. In describing Jesus' birth, childhood, and development, Luke lifts up the humanity of Jesus. Our Savior was the ideal human. Fully prepared, the ideal human was now ready to live the perfect life.

Luke's Purpose in Writing (**1**)

1 Most honorable Theophilus:
Many people have written accounts about the events that took place* among us. **1:1-2**
[2]They used as their source material the reports circulating among us from the early John 15:27
disciples and other eyewitnesses of what God has done in fulfillment of his promises. Acts 1:21-22 Heb 2:3
[3]Having carefully investigated all of these accounts from the beginning, I have decided 2 Pet 1:16
to write a careful summary for you, [4]to reassure you of the truth of all you were taught. 1 Jn 1:1-4 **1:3**

An Angel Promises the Birth of John to Zechariah (**4**) Acts 1:1

[5]It all begins with a Jewish priest, Zechariah, who lived when Herod was king of Judea.
Zechariah was a member of the priestly order of Abijah. His wife, Elizabeth, was also **1:5** 1 Chr 24:10
from the priestly line of Aaron. [6]Zechariah and Elizabeth were righteous in God's eyes, 2 Chr 31:2
careful to obey all of the Lord's commandments and regulations. [7]They had no children Matt 2:1
because Elizabeth was barren, and now they were both very old.
[8]One day Zechariah was serving God in the Temple, for his order was on duty that
week. [9]As was the custom of the priests, he was chosen by lot to enter the sanctuary and **1:8**
burn incense in the Lord's presence. [10]While the incense was being burned, a great 1 Chr 24:19 2 Chr 8:14
crowd stood outside, praying. **1:9**
[11]Zechariah was in the sanctuary when an angel of the Lord appeared, standing to the Exod 30:7
right of the incense altar. [12]Zechariah was overwhelmed with fear. [13]But the angel said,

1:1 Or *have been fulfilled.*

1:1, 2 Luke tells Jesus' story from Luke's unique perspective of a Gentile, a physician, and the first historian of the early church. Though not an eyewitness of Jesus' ministry, Luke nevertheless is concerned that eyewitness accounts be preserved accurately and that the foundations of Christian belief be transmitted intact to the next generation. In Luke's Gospel are many of Jesus' parables. In addition, more than any other Gospel, it gives specific instances of Jesus' concern for women.

1:1-4 There was a lot of interest in Jesus, and many people had written firsthand accounts about him. Luke may have used these accounts and all other available resources as material for an accurate and complete account of Jesus' life, teachings, and ministry. Because truth was important to Luke, he relied heavily on eyewitness accounts. Christianity doesn't say, "Close your eyes and believe," but rather, "Check it out for yourself." The Bible encourages you to investigate its claims thoroughly (John 1:46; 21:24; Acts 17:11, 12), because your conclusion about Jesus is a life-and-death matter.

1:1-4 *Theophilus* means "one who loves God." The book of Acts, also written by Luke, is likewise addressed to Theophilus. This preface may be a general dedication to all Christian readers. Theophilus may have been Luke's patron, who helped to finance the book's writing. More likely, Theophilus was a Roman acquaintance of Luke's with a strong interest in the new Christian religion.

1:3, 4 As a medical doctor, Luke knew the importance of being thorough. He used his skills in observation and analysis to thoroughly investigate the stories about Jesus. His diagnosis: The Good News of Jesus Christ is true! You can read Luke's account of Jesus' life with confidence that it was written by a clear thinker and a thoughtful researcher. Because the Good News is founded on historical truth, our spiritual growth must involve careful, disciplined, and thorough investigation of God's Word so that we can understand how God has acted in history. If this kind of study is not part of your life, find a pastor, teacher, or even a book to help you get started and to guide you in this important part of Christian growth.

1:5 This was Herod the Great, confirmed by the Roman Senate as king of the Jews. Only half-Jewish himself and eager to please his Roman superiors, Herod expanded and beautified the Jerusalem Temple—but he placed a Roman eagle over the entrance. When he helped the Jews, it was for political purposes and not because he cared about their God. Herod the Great later ordered a massacre of infants in a futile attempt to kill the infant Jesus, whom some were calling the new "king of the Jews" (Matthew 2:16-18).

1:5 A Jewish priest was a minister of God who worked at the Temple managing its upkeep, teaching the people the Scriptures, and directing the worship services. At this time there were about 20,000 priests throughout the country—far too many to minister in the Temple at one time. Therefore the priests were divided into 24 separate groups of about 1,000 each, according to David's directions (1 Chronicles 24:3-19).

Zechariah was a member of the Abijah division, on duty this particular week. Each morning a priest was to enter the Holy Place in the Temple and burn incense. Lots were cast to decide who would enter the sanctuary, and one day the lot fell to Zechariah. But it was not by chance that Zechariah was on duty and that he was chosen that day to enter the Holy Place—perhaps a once-in-a-lifetime opportunity. God was guiding the events of history to prepare the way for Jesus to come to earth.

1:6 Zechariah and Elizabeth didn't merely go through the motions in following God's laws; they backed up their outward compliance with inward obedience. Unlike the religious leaders whom Jesus called hypocrites, Zechariah and Elizabeth did not stop with the letter of the law. Their obedience was from the heart, and that is why they are called "righteous in God's eyes."

1:9 Incense was burned in the Temple twice daily. When the people saw the smoke from the burning incense, they prayed. The smoke drifting heavenward symbolized their prayers ascending to God's throne.

1:11, 12 Angels are spirit beings who live in God's presence and do his will. Only two angels are mentioned by name in Scripture—Michael and Gabriel—but there are many who act as God's messengers. Here, Gabriel (1:19) delivered a special message to Zechariah. This was not a dream or a vision. The angel appeared in visible form and spoke audible words to the priest.

1:15
Num 6:3
Judg 13:4
Jer 1:5
Matt 11:11
1:16
Mal 4:5-6
1:17
Matt 17:11-13

"Don't be afraid, Zechariah! For God has heard your prayer, and your wife, Elizabeth,
will bear you a son! And you are to name him John. [14]You will have great joy and
gladness, and many will rejoice with you at his birth, [15]for he will be great in the eyes
of the Lord. He must never touch wine or hard liquor, and he will be filled with the Holy
Spirit, even before his birth.* [16]And he will persuade many Israelites to turn to the Lord
their God. [17]He will be a man with the spirit and power of Elijah, the prophet of old. He
will precede the coming of the Lord, preparing the people for his arrival. He will turn the

1:15 Or *even from birth.*

ZECHARIAH

Zechariah, a Jewish priest, was told before anyone else that God was setting in motion his own visit to earth. Zechariah and his wife, Elizabeth, were known for their personal holiness. They were well suited to doing a special work for God. But they shared the pain of not having children, and in Jewish culture this was considered not having God's blessing. Zechariah and Elizabeth were old, and they had stopped even asking for children.

One day while on duty at the Temple in Jerusalem, Zechariah received an unexpected blessing. He was chosen to be the priest who would enter the Holy Place to offer incense to God for the people. Suddenly, much to his surprise and terror, he found himself face to face with an angel. The angel's message was too good to be true! But the news of the coming Savior was eclipsed by doubts about his own ability to father the child the angel promised him. His age spoke more loudly than God's promise. As a result, God prevented Zechariah from speaking until the promise became a reality.

The record of the prayer in Luke 1 is our last glimpse of Zechariah. Like so many of God's most faithful servants, he passed quietly from the scene once his part was done. He becomes our hero for those times when we doubt God and yet are willing to obey. We gain hope from Zechariah's story that God can do great things through anyone who is available to him.

Strengths and accomplishments
- Known as a righteous man
- Was a priest of God
- One of the few people to be directly addressed by an angel
- Fathered John the Baptist

Weakness and mistake
- Momentarily doubted the angel's promise of a son because of his own old age

Lessons from his life
- Physical limitations do not limit God
- God accomplishes his will, sometimes in unexpected ways

Vital statistics
- Occupation: Priest
- Relatives: Wife: Elizabeth. Son: John the Baptist

Key verses: "Zechariah and Elizabeth were righteous in God's eyes, careful to obey all of the Lord's commandments and regulations. They had no children because Elizabeth was barren, and now they were both very old" (Luke 1:6, 7).

Zechariah's story is told in Luke 1.

1:13 While burning incense on the altar, Zechariah was also praying, perhaps for a son or for the coming of the Messiah. In either case, his prayer was answered. He would soon have a son, who would prepare the way for the Messiah. God answers prayer in his own way and in his own time. He worked in an "impossible" situation—Zechariah's wife was barren—to bring about the fulfillment of all the prophecies concerning the Messiah. If we want to have our prayers answered, we must be open to what God can do in impossible situations. And we must wait for God to work in his way, in his time.

1:13 *John* means "the LORD is gracious," and *Jesus* means "the LORD saves." Both names were prescribed by God, not chosen by human parents. Throughout the Gospels, God acts graciously and saves his people. He will not withhold salvation from anyone who sincerely comes to him.

1:15 John was set apart for special service to God. He may have been forbidden to drink wine as part of the Nazirite vow, an ancient vow of consecration to God (see Numbers 6:1-8). Samson (Judges 13) was under the Nazirite vow, and Samuel may have been also (1 Samuel 1:11).

1:15 This is Luke's first mention of the Holy Spirit, the Third Person of the Trinity; Luke refers to the Holy Spirit more than any other Gospel writer. Because Luke also wrote the book of Acts, we know he was thoroughly informed about the work of the Holy Spirit. Luke recognized and emphasized the Holy Spirit's work in directing the beginnings of Christianity and in guiding the early church. The presence of the Spirit was God's gift given to the entire church at Pentecost. Prior to that, God's Spirit was given to the faithful for special tasks. We need the Holy Spirit's help to do God's work effectively.

1:17 John's role was to be almost identical to that of an Old Testament prophet: to encourage people to turn away from sin and back to God. John is often compared to the great prophet Elijah, who was known for standing up to evil rulers (Malachi 4:5; Matthew 11:14; 17:10-13). See Elijah's Profile in 1 Kings 18.

1:17 In preparing people for the Messiah's arrival, John would seek to take stony hearts and exchange them for hearts that were soft, pliable, trusting, and open to change. (See Ezekiel 11:19, 20 and 36:25-29 for more on "heart transplants.") Are you as open to God as you should be? Or do you need a change of heart?

hearts of the fathers to their children, and he will change disobedient minds to accept
godly wisdom."*
18Zechariah said to the angel, "How can I know this will happen? I'm an old man now, **1:18** Gen 18:11
and my wife is also well along in years."
19Then the angel said, "I am Gabriel! I stand in the very presence of God. It was he **1:19** Dan 8:16;
who sent me to bring you this good news! 20And now, since you didn't believe what I 9:21
said, you won't be able to speak until the child is born. For my words will certainly come **1:20** Ezek 3:26
true at the proper time."
21Meanwhile, the people were waiting for Zechariah to come out, wondering why he
was taking so long. 22When he finally did come out, he couldn't speak to them. Then
they realized from his gestures that he must have seen a vision in the Temple sanctuary.
23He stayed at the Temple until his term of service was over, and then he returned
home. 24Soon afterward his wife, Elizabeth, became pregnant and went into seclusion
for five months. 25"How kind the Lord is!" she exclaimed. "He has taken away my **1:25** Gen 30:23
disgrace of having no children!" Isa 4:1

An Angel Promises the Birth of Jesus to Mary **(5)**

26In the sixth month of Elizabeth's pregnancy, God sent the angel Gabriel to Nazareth, **1:26** Matt 2:23
a village in Galilee, 27to a virgin named Mary. She was engaged to be married to a man
named Joseph, a descendant of King David. 28Gabriel appeared to her and said, **1:27** Matt 1:16, 18
"Greetings, favored woman! The Lord is with you!*" Luke 2:5
29Confused and disturbed, Mary tried to think what the angel could mean. 30"Don't be
frightened, Mary," the angel told her, "for God has decided to bless you! 31You will become **1:31** Isa 7:14
Matt 1:21-23

1:17 See Mal 4:5-6. **1:28** Some manuscripts add *Blessed are you among women.*

1:18 When told he would have a son, Zechariah doubted the angel's word. From Zechariah's human perspective, his doubts were understandable—but with God, anything is possible. Although Zechariah and Elizabeth were past the age of child-bearing, God gave them a child. It is easy to doubt or misunderstand what God wants to do in our life. Even God's people sometimes make the mistake of trusting their intellect or experience rather than God. When you are tempted to think that one of God's promises is impossible, remember his work throughout history. God's power is not confined by narrow perspective or bound by human limitations. Trust him completely.

1:20 Zechariah thought it incredible that he and his wife, in their old age, could conceive a child. But what God promises, he delivers. And God delivers *on time!* You can have complete confidence that God will keep his promises. Their fulfillment may not be the next day, but they will be "at the proper time." If you are waiting for God to answer some request or to fill some need, remain patient. No matter how impossible God's promises may seem, what he has said in his Word will come true at the right time.

1:21 The people were waiting outside for Zechariah to come out and pronounce the customary blessing upon them as found in Numbers 6:24-26.

1:25 Zechariah and Elizabeth were both godly people, and yet they were suffering. Some Jews at that time did not believe in a bodily resurrection, so their hope of immortality was in their children. In addition, children cared for their parents in their old age and added to the family's financial security and social status. Children were considered a blessing, and childlessness was seen as a curse. Zechariah and Elizabeth had been childless for many years, and at this time they were too old to expect any change in their situation. They felt humiliated and hopeless. But God was waiting for the right time to encourage them and take away their disgrace.

1:26 Gabriel appeared not only to Zechariah and to Mary but also to the prophet Daniel more than 500 years earlier (Daniel 8:15-17; 9:21). Each time Gabriel appeared, he brought important messages from God.

1:26 Nazareth, Joseph and Mary's hometown, was a long way from Jerusalem, the center of Jewish life and worship. Located on a major trade route, Nazareth was frequently visited by Gentile merchants and Roman soldiers. It was known for its independent and aloof attitude. Jesus was born in Bethlehem but grew up in Nazareth. Nevertheless the people of Nazareth would reject him as the Messiah (4:22-30).

1:27, 28 Mary was young, poor, female—all characteristics that, to the people of her day, would make her seem unusable by God for any major task. But God chose Mary for one of the most important acts of obedience he has ever demanded of anyone. You may feel that your ability, experience, or education makes you an unlikely candidate for God's service. Don't limit God's choices. He can use you if you trust him.

1:30, 31 God's favor does not automatically bring instant success or fame. His blessing on Mary, the honor of being the mother of the Messiah, would lead to much pain: her peers would ridicule her; her fiancé would come close to leaving her; her son would be rejected and murdered. But through her son would come the world's only hope, and this is why Mary has been praised by countless generations. Her submission was part of God's plan to bring about our salvation. If sorrow weighs you down and dims your hope, think of Mary and wait patiently for God to finish working out his plan.

1:31-33 *Jesus,* a Greek form of the Hebrew name *Joshua,* was a common name meaning "the LORD saves." Just as Joshua had led Israel into the Promised Land (see Joshua 1:1, 2), so Jesus would lead his people into eternal life. The symbolism of his name was not lost on the people of his day, who took names seriously and saw them as a source of power. In Jesus' name, people were healed, demons were banished, and sins were forgiven.

1:32 Isa 9:6-7; 16:5 Jer 23:5 Phil 2:10 1 Tim 6:15
1:33 Ps 89:3-4 Isa 9:7 Jer 33:17 Dan 2:44; 7:14, 27 Heb 1:8
1:35 Matt 1:20 Mark 1:1 John 1:34; 20:31 Rom 1:4
1:41 Gen 25:22 Luke 1:15

pregnant and have a son, and you are to name him Jesus. 32 He will be very great and will
be called the Son of the Most High. And the Lord God will give him the throne of his
ancestor David. 33 And he will reign over Israel* forever; his Kingdom will never end!"
34 Mary asked the angel, "But how can I have a baby? I am a virgin."
35 The angel replied, "The Holy Spirit will come upon you, and the power of the Most
High will overshadow you. So the baby born to you will be holy, and he will be called
the Son of God. 36 What's more, your relative Elizabeth has become pregnant in her old
age! People used to say she was barren, but she's already in her sixth month. 37 For
nothing is impossible with God."
38 Mary responded, "I am the Lord's servant, and I am willing to accept whatever he
wants. May everything you have said come true." And then the angel left.

Mary Visits Elizabeth (**6**)

39 A few days later Mary hurried to the hill country of Judea, to the town 40 where
Zechariah lived. She entered the house and greeted Elizabeth. 41 At the sound of
Mary's greeting, Elizabeth's child leaped within her, and Elizabeth was filled with the
Holy Spirit.

1:33 Greek *over the house of Jacob.*

GOD'S UNUSUAL METHODS

One of the best ways to understand God's willingness to communicate to people is to note the various methods, some of them quite unexpected, that he has used to give his message. Following is a sample of his methods and the people he contacted.

Person/Group	*Method*	*Reference*
Jacob, Zechariah, Mary, shepherds	Angels	Genesis 32:22–32; Luke 1:13, 30; 2:10
Jacob, Joseph, a baker, a cup-bearer, Pharaoh, Isaiah, Joseph, the astrologers	Dreams	Genesis 28:10–22; 37:5–10; 40:5; 41:7, 8; Isaiah 1:1; Matthew 1:20; 2:12, 13
Belshazzar	Writing on the wall	Daniel 5:5–9
Balaam	Talking donkey	Numbers 22:21–35
People of Israel	Pillars of cloud and fire	Exodus 13:21, 22
Jonah	Being swallowed by a fish	Jonah 2
Abraham, Moses, Jesus at his baptism, Paul	Verbally	Genesis 12:1–4; Exodus 7:8; Matthew 3:13–17; Acts 18:9
Moses	Fire	Exodus 3:2
Us	God's Son	Hebrews 1:1, 2

1:32, 33 Centuries earlier, God had promised David that David's kingdom would last forever (2 Samuel 7:16). This promise was fulfilled in the coming of Jesus, a direct descendant of David, whose reign will continue throughout eternity.

1:34 The birth of Jesus to a virgin is a miracle that many people find hard to believe. These three facts can aid our faith: (1) Luke was a medical doctor, and he knew perfectly well how babies are made. It would have been just as hard for him to believe in a virgin birth as it is for us, and yet he reports it as fact. (2) Luke was a painstaking researcher who based his Gospel on eyewitness accounts. Tradition holds that he talked with Mary about the events he recorded in the first two chapters. This is Mary's story, not a fictional invention. (3) Christians and Jews, who worship God as the Creator of the universe, should have no doubts that God has the power to create a child in a virgin's womb.

1:35 Jesus was born without the sin that entered the world through Adam. He was born holy, just as Adam was created sinless. In contrast to Adam, who disobeyed God, Jesus obeyed God and was thus able to face sin's consequences in our place and make us acceptable to God (Romans 5:14-19).

1:38 A young unmarried girl who became pregnant risked disaster. Unless the father of the child agreed to marry her, she would probably remain unmarried for life. If her own father rejected her, she could be forced into begging or prostitution in order to earn her living. And Mary, with her story about becoming pregnant by the Holy Spirit, risked being considered crazy as well. Still Mary said, despite the possible risks, "May everything you have said come true." When Mary said that, she didn't know about the tremendous opportunity she would have. She only knew that God was asking her to serve him, and she willingly obeyed. Don't wait to see the bottom line before offering your life to God. Offer yourself willingly, even when the outcome seems disastrous.

1:38 God's announcement of the birth of a special child was met with various responses throughout Scripture. Sarah, Abraham's wife, laughed (Genesis 18:9-15). Zechariah doubted (Luke 1:18). By contrast, Mary graciously submitted. She believed the angel's words and agreed to bear the child, even under humanly impossible circumstances. God is able to do the impossible. Our response to his demands should not be laughter or doubt but willing acceptance.

[42]Elizabeth gave a glad cry and exclaimed to Mary, "You are blessed by God above
all other women, and your child is blessed. [43]What an honor this is, that the mother of
my Lord should visit me! [44]When you came in and greeted me, my baby jumped for joy
the instant I heard your voice! [45]You are blessed, because you believed that the Lord
would do what he said."

[46]Mary responded,

"Oh, how I praise the Lord.
47 How I rejoice in God my Savior!
48 For he took notice of his lowly servant girl,
and now generation after generation
will call me blessed.
49 For he, the Mighty One, is holy,
and he has done great things for me.
50 His mercy goes on from generation to generation,
to all who fear him.
51 His mighty arm does tremendous things!
How he scatters the proud and haughty ones!
52 He has taken princes from their thrones
and exalted the lowly.
53 He has satisfied the hungry with good things
and sent the rich away with empty hands.
54 And how he has helped his servant Israel!
He has not forgotten his promise to be merciful.
55 For he promised our ancestors—Abraham and his children—
to be merciful to them forever."

[56]Mary stayed with Elizabeth about three months and then went back to her own
home.

John the Baptist Is Born (**7**)

[57]Now it was time for Elizabeth's baby to be born, and it was a boy. [58]The word spread
quickly to her neighbors and relatives that the Lord had been very kind to her, and
everyone rejoiced with her.
[59]When the baby was eight days old, all the relatives and friends came for the

1:42 Judg 5:24
1:43 Luke 2:11
1:46-55 1 Sam 2:1-10 Ps 34:2-3
1:47 1 Tim 1:1; 2:3 Titus 1:3; 2:10; 3:4
1:48 1 Sam 1:11
1:49 Ps 111:9
1:50 Ps 103:13, 17
1:51 2 Sam 22:28 Ps 89:10
1:52 Job 5:12; 12:19
1:53 1 Sam 2:5 Ps 107:9
1:54 Ps 98:3 Isa 41:8
1:55 Gen 17:7; 22:17
1:59 Gen 17:12 Lev 12:3 Luke 2:21 Phil 3:5

1:41-43 Apparently the Holy Spirit told Elizabeth that Mary's child was the Messiah because Elizabeth called her young relative "the mother of my Lord" as she greeted her. As Mary rushed off to visit her relative, she must have been wondering if the events of the last few days were real. Elizabeth's greeting must have strengthened her faith. Mary's pregnancy may have seemed impossible, but her wise relative believed in the Lord's faithfulness and rejoiced in Mary's blessed condition.

1:42, 43 Even though she herself was pregnant with a long-awaited son, Elizabeth could have envied Mary, whose son would be even greater than her own. Instead, she was filled with joy that the mother of her Lord would visit her. Have you ever envied people whom God has apparently singled out for special blessing? A cure for jealousy is to rejoice with those people, realizing that God uses his people in ways best suited to his purpose.

1:46-55 This song is often called the *Magnificat*, the first word in the Latin translation of this passage. Mary's song has often been used as the basis for choral music and hymns. Like Hannah, the mother of Samuel (1 Samuel 2:1-10), Mary glorified God in song for what he was going to do for the world through her. Notice that in both songs, God is pictured as a champion of the poor, the oppressed, and the despised.

1:48 When Mary said, "And now generation after generation will call me blessed," was she being proud? No, she was recognizing and accepting the gift God had given her. If Mary had denied her incredible position, she would have been throwing God's blessing back at him. Pride is refusing to accept God's gifts or taking credit for what God has done; humility is accepting the gifts and using them to praise and serve God. Don't deny, belittle, or ignore your gifts. Thank God for them and use them to his glory.

1:54, 55 God kept his promise to Abraham to be merciful to God's people forever (Genesis 22:16-18). Christ's birth fulfilled the promise, and Mary understood this. She was not surprised when her special son eventually announced that he was the Messiah. She had known Jesus' mission from before his birth. Some of God's promises to Israel are found in 2 Samuel 22:50, 51; Psalms 89:2-4; 103:17, 18; Micah 7:18-20.

1:56 Because travel was not easy, long visits were customary. Mary must have been a great help to Elizabeth, who was experiencing the discomforts of a first pregnancy in old age.

1:59 The circumcision ceremony was an important event to the family of a Jewish baby boy. God commanded circumcision when he was beginning to form his holy nation (Genesis 17:4-14), and he reaffirmed it through Moses (Leviticus 12:1-3). This ceremony was a time of joy when friends and family members celebrated the baby's becoming part of God's covenant nation.

1:59 Family lines and family names were important to the Jews. The people naturally assumed the child would receive Zechariah's name or at least a family name. Thus, they were surprised that both Elizabeth and Zechariah wanted to name the boy John. This was the name the angel had given them (see 1:13).

circumcision ceremony. They wanted to name him Zechariah, after his father. 60 But
Elizabeth said, "No! His name is John!"
61 "What?" they exclaimed. "There is no one in all your family by that name." 62 So
they asked the baby's father, communicating to him by making gestures. 63 He motioned
for a writing tablet, and to everyone's surprise he wrote, "His name is John!" 64 Instantly
Zechariah could speak again, and he began praising God.
65 Wonder fell upon the whole neighborhood, and the news of what had happened
spread throughout the Judean hills. 66 Everyone who heard about it reflected on these
events and asked, "I wonder what this child will turn out to be? For the hand of the Lord
is surely upon him in a special way."
67 Then his father, Zechariah, was filled with the Holy Spirit and gave this prophecy:

68 "Praise the Lord, the God of Israel,
because he has visited his people and redeemed them.
69 He has sent us a mighty Savior
from the royal line of his servant David,
70 just as he promised
through his holy prophets long ago.
71 Now we will be saved from our enemies
and from all who hate us.
72 He has been merciful to our ancestors
by remembering his sacred covenant with them,
73 the covenant he gave to our ancestor Abraham.
74 We have been rescued from our enemies,
so we can serve God without fear,
75 in holiness and righteousness forever.

76 "And you, my little son,
will be called the prophet of the Most High,
because you will prepare the way for the Lord.

1:66 Luke 2:19; Acts 11:21
1:67 Joel 2:28
1:68 Pss 41:13; 72:18; 106:48; 111:9
1:69 1 Sam 2:1-10; Pss 18:2; 132:17; Ezek 29:21
1:70 Jer 23:5; Acts 3:21; Rom 1:2-4
1:71 Ps 106:10
1:72-73 Pss 105:8-9; 106:45-46
1:73-74 Gen 22:16-18
1:75 Eph 4:24
1:76 Isa 40:3; Mal 3:1

DOUBTERS IN THE BIBLE

Doubter	*Doubtful Moment*	*Reference*
Abraham	When told he would be a father in old age	Genesis 17:17
Sarah	When she heard she would be a mother in old age	Genesis 18:12
Moses	When told to return to Egypt to lead the people	Exodus 3:10–15
Israelites	Whenever they faced difficulties in the wilderness	Exodus 16:1–3
Gideon	When told he would be a judge and leader	Judges 6:14–23
Zechariah	When told he would be a father in old age	Luke 1:18
Thomas	When told Jesus had risen from the dead	John 20:24, 25

Many of the people God used to accomplish great things started out as real doubters. With all of them, God showed great patience. Honest doubt was not a bad starting point as long as they didn't stay there. How great a part does doubt have in your willingness to trust God?

1:62 Zechariah's relatives talked to him by gestures, because he was apparently deaf as well as speechless and had not heard what his wife had said.

1:67-79 Zechariah praised God with his first words after months of silence. In a song that is often called the *Benedictus* after the first words in the Latin translation of this passage, Zechariah prophesied the coming of a Savior who would redeem his people, and he predicted that his son, John, would prepare the Messiah's way. All the Old Testament prophecies were coming true—no wonder Zechariah praised God! The Messiah would come in Zechariah's lifetime, and his son had been chosen to pave the way.

1:71 The Jews were eagerly awaiting the Messiah, but they thought he would come to save them from the powerful Roman Empire. They were ready for a military Savior, but not for a peaceful Messiah who would conquer sin.

1:72, 73 This was God's promise to Abraham to bless all peoples through him (see Genesis 12:3). It would be fulfilled through the Messiah, Abraham's descendant.

1:76 Zechariah had just recalled hundreds of years of God's sovereign work in history, beginning with Abraham and going on into eternity. Then, in tender contrast, he personalized the story. His son had been chosen for a key role in the drama of the ages. Although God has unlimited power, he chooses to work through frail humans who begin as helpless babies. Don't minimize what God can do through those who are faithful to him.

[77] You will tell his people how to find salvation
through forgiveness of their sins.
[78] Because of God's tender mercy,
the light from heaven is about to break upon us,
[79] to give light to those who sit in darkness and in the shadow of death,
and to guide us to the path of peace."

[80] John grew up and became strong in spirit. Then he lived out in the wilderness until
he began his public ministry to Israel.

1:77 Jer 31:34
1:78 Mal 4:2
1:79 Isa 9:2; 58:8; 60:1-2; Matt 4:16
1:80 Luke 2:40, 52

Jesus Is Born in Bethlehem (**9**)

2 At that time the Roman emperor, Augustus, decreed that a census should be taken
throughout the Roman Empire. [2] (This was the first census taken when Quirinius was
governor of Syria.) [3] All returned to their own towns to register for this census. [4] And
because Joseph was a descendant of King David, he had to go to Bethlehem in Judea,
David's ancient home. He traveled there from the village of Nazareth in Galilee. [5] He
took with him Mary, his fiancée, who was obviously pregnant by this time.

[6] And while they were there, the time came for her baby to be born. [7] She gave birth to
her first child, a son. She wrapped him snugly in strips of cloth and laid him in a manger,
because there was no room for them in the village inn.

2:1-7 Matt 1:18-25
2:5 Luke 1:27
2:6 Matt 1:25; Gal 4:4

THE JOURNEY TO BETHLEHEM
Caesar's decree for a census of the entire Roman Empire made it necessary for Joseph and Mary to leave their hometown, Nazareth, and journey the 70 miles to the Judean village of Bethlehem.

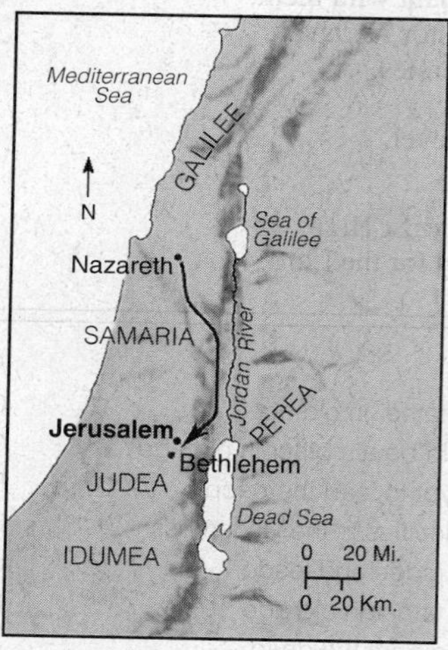

1:80 Why did John live out in the wilderness? Prophets used the isolation of the uninhabited wilderness to enhance their spiritual growth and to focus their message on God. By being in the wilderness, John remained separate from the economic and political powers so that he could aim his message against them. He also remained separate from the hypocritical religious leaders of his day. His message was different from theirs, and his life proved it.

2:1 Luke is the only Gospel writer who related the events he recorded to world history. His account was addressed to a predominantly Greek audience that would have been interested in and familiar with the political situation. Palestine was under the rule of the Roman Empire; Emperor Caesar Augustus, the first Roman emperor, was in charge. The Roman rulers, considered to be like gods, stood in contrast to the tiny baby in a manger who was truly God in the flesh.

2:1 A Roman census (registration) was taken to aid military conscription or tax collection. The Jews didn't have to serve in the Roman army, but they could not avoid paying taxes. Augustus's decree went out in God's perfect timing and according to God's perfect plan to bring his Son into the world.

2:3-6 The government forced Joseph to make a long trip just to pay his taxes. His fiancée, who had to go with him, was going to have a baby any moment. But when they arrived in Bethlehem, they couldn't even find a place to stay. When we do God's will, we are not guaranteed a comfortable life. But we are promised that everything, even our discomfort, has meaning in God's plan.

2:4 God controls all history. By the decree of Emperor Augustus, Jesus was born in the very town prophesied for his birth (Micah 5:2), even though his parents did not live there.

2:4 Joseph and Mary were both descendants of David. The Old Testament is filled with prophecies that the Messiah would be born in David's royal line (see, for example, Isaiah 11:1; Jeremiah 33:15; Ezekiel 37:24; Hosea 3:5).

2:7 Strips of cloth were used to keep a baby warm and give him a sense of security. These cloths were believed to protect his internal organs. The custom of wrapping infants this way is still practiced in many Mideastern countries.

2:7 This mention of the manger is the basis for the traditional belief that Jesus was born in a stable. Stables were often caves with feeding troughs (mangers) carved into the rock walls. Despite popular Christmas card pictures, the surroundings were dark and dirty. This was not the atmosphere the Jews expected as the birthplace of the Messiah-King. They thought their promised Messiah would be born in royal surroundings. We should not limit God by our expectations. He is at work wherever he is needed in our sin-darkened and dirty world.

2:7 Although our first picture of Jesus is as a baby in a manger, it must not be our last. The Christ child in the manger has been the subject of a beautiful Christmas scene, but we cannot leave him there. This tiny, helpless baby lived an amazing life, died for us, ascended to heaven, and will come back to this earth as King of kings. Christ will rule the world and judge all people according to their decisions about him. Do you still picture Jesus as a baby in a manger—or is he your Lord? Make sure you don't underestimate Jesus. Let him grow up in your life.

Shepherds Visit Jesus (**10**)

[8]That night some shepherds were in the fields outside the village, guarding their flocks of
2:9 Acts 5:19 sheep. [9]Suddenly, an angel of the Lord appeared among them, and the radiance of the Lord's
glory surrounded them. They were terribly frightened, [10]but the angel reassured them.
"Don't be afraid!" he said. "I bring you good news of great joy for everyone! [11]The
2:11 John 4:42; 11:21; 20:31 Savior—yes, the Messiah, the Lord—has been born tonight in Bethlehem, the city of
David! [12]And this is how you will recognize him: You will find a baby lying in a manger,
wrapped snugly in strips of cloth!"
2:13 Ps 103:20 Rev 5:11 [13]Suddenly, the angel was joined by a vast host of others—the armies of heaven—
praising God:

2:14 Isa 57:19 Luke 19:38 [14] "Glory to God in the highest heaven,
and peace on earth to all whom God favors.*"

[15]When the angels had returned to heaven, the shepherds said to each other, "Come
on, let's go to Bethlehem! Let's see this wonderful thing that has happened, which the
Lord has told us about."
[16]They ran to the village and found Mary and Joseph. And there was the baby, lying
2:17 Luke 2:10-12 in the manger. [17]Then the shepherds told everyone what had happened and what the
2:19 Luke 2:51 angel had said to them about this child. [18]All who heard the shepherds' story were
astonished, [19]but Mary quietly treasured these things in her heart and thought about

2:14 Or *and peace on earth for all those pleasing God.* Some manuscripts read *and peace on earth, goodwill among people.*

TO FEAR OR NOT TO FEAR

Person	*Reference*
Abraham	Genesis 15:1
Moses	Numbers 21:34 Deuteronomy 3:2
Joshua	Joshua 8:1
Jeremiah	Lamentations 3:57
Daniel	Daniel 10:12, 19
Zechariah	Luke 1:13
Mary	Luke 1:30
Shepherds	Luke 2:10
Peter	Luke 5:10
Paul	Acts 27:23, 24
John	Revelation 1:17, 18

People in the Bible who were confronted by God or his angels all had one consistent response—fear. To each of them, God's response was always the same—don't be afraid. As soon as they sensed that God accepted them and wanted to communicate with them, their fear subsided. He had given them freedom to be his friends. Has he given you the same freedom?

2:8 God continued to reveal his Son, but not to those we might expect. Luke records that Jesus' birth was announced to shepherds in the fields. These may have been the shepherds who supplied the lambs for the Temple sacrifices that were performed for the forgiveness of sin. Here the angels invited these shepherds to greet the Lamb of God (John 1:36), who would take away the sins of the whole world forever.

2:8-15 What a birth announcement! The shepherds were terrified, but their fear turned to joy as the angels announced the Messiah's birth. First the shepherds ran to see the baby; then they spread the word. Jesus is *your* Messiah, *your* Savior. Do you look forward to meeting him in prayer and in his Word each day? Have you discovered a Lord so wonderful that you can't help sharing your joy with your friends?

2:9, 10 The greatest event in history had just happened! The Messiah had been born! For ages the Jews had waited for this, and when it finally occurred, the announcement came to humble shepherds. The Good News about Jesus is that he comes to all, including the plain and the ordinary. He comes to anyone with a heart humble enough to accept him. Whoever you are, whatever you do, you can have Jesus in your life. Don't think you need extraordinary qualifications—he accepts you as you are.

2:11-14 Some of the Jews were waiting for a savior to deliver them from Roman rule; others hoped the Christ (Messiah) would deliver them from physical ailments. But Jesus, while healing their illnesses and establishing a spiritual Kingdom, delivered them from sin. His work is more far-reaching than anyone could imagine. Christ paid the price for sin and opened the way to peace with God. He offers us more than temporary political or physical changes—he offers us new hearts that will last for eternity.

2:14 The story of Jesus' birth resounds with music that has inspired composers for 2,000 years. The angels' song, often called the *Gloria* after its first word in the Latin translation, is the basis for many modern choral works, traditional Christmas carols, and ancient liturgical chants.

them often. 20 The shepherds went back to their fields and flocks, glorifying and
praising God for what the angels had told them, and because they had seen the child,
just as the angel had said.

Mary and Joseph Bring Jesus to the Temple (**11**)

21 Eight days later, when the baby was circumcised, he was named Jesus, the name given
him by the angel even before he was conceived.

22 Then it was time for the purification offering, as required by the law of Moses after
the birth of a child; so his parents took him to Jerusalem to present him to the Lord. 23 The
law of the Lord says, "If a woman's first child is a boy, he must be dedicated to the
Lord."* 24 So they offered a sacrifice according to what was required in the law of the
Lord—"either a pair of turtledoves or two young pigeons."*

25 Now there was a man named Simeon who lived in Jerusalem. He was a righteous
man and very devout. He was filled with the Holy Spirit, and he eagerly expected the
Messiah to come and rescue Israel. 26 The Holy Spirit had revealed to him that he
would not die until he had seen the Lord's Messiah. 27 That day the Spirit led him to
the Temple. So when Mary and Joseph came to present the baby Jesus to the Lord as
the law required, 28 Simeon was there. He took the child in his arms and praised God,
saying,

29 "Lord, now I can die in peace!
As you promised me,
30 I have seen the Savior
31 you have given to all people.
32 He is a light to reveal God to the nations,
and he is the glory of your people Israel!"

33 Joseph and Mary were amazed at what was being said about Jesus. 34 Then
Simeon blessed them, and he said to Mary, "This child will be rejected by many in
Israel, and it will be their undoing. But he will be the greatest joy to many others.
35 Thus, the deepest thoughts of many hearts will be revealed. And a sword will pierce
your very soul."

36 Anna, a prophet, was also there in the Temple. She was the daughter of Phanuel, of
the tribe of Asher, and was very old. She was a widow, for her husband had died when

2:21 Gen 17:12; Lev 12:3; Matt 1:21
2:22 Lev 12:2-6
2:23 †Exod 13:2, 12, 15
2:24 †Lev 5:11; 12:8
2:25 †Isa 40:1; 49:13
2:26 Ps 89:48; John 8:51; Heb 11:5
2:30-31 Isa 40:5; 52:10; Acts 4:12
2:32 Isa 42:6-7; 46:13; 49:6
2:34 Isa 8:14; 1 Cor 1:23; 1 Pet 2:7-8

2:23 Exod 13:2. **2:24** Lev 12:8.

2:21-24 Jewish families went through several ceremonies soon after a baby's birth: (1) *Circumcision.* Every boy was circumcised and named on the eighth day after birth (Leviticus 12:3; Luke 1:59, 60). Circumcision symbolized the Jews' separation from Gentiles and their unique relationship with God (see the notes on 1:59). (2) *Redemption of the firstborn.* A firstborn son was presented to God one month after birth (Exodus 13:2, 11-16; Numbers 18:15, 16). The ceremony included buying back—"redeeming"—the child from God through an offering. Thus, the parents acknowledged that the child belonged to God, who alone has the power to give life. (3) *Purification of the mother.* For 40 days after the birth of a son and 80 days after the birth of a daughter, the mother was ceremonially unclean and could not enter the Temple. At the end of her time of separation, the parents were to bring a lamb for a burnt offering and a dove or pigeon for a sin offering. The priest would sacrifice these animals and declare her to be clean. If a lamb was too expensive, the parents could bring a second dove or pigeon instead. This is what Mary and Joseph did.

Jesus was God's Son, but his family carried out these ceremonies according to God's law. Jesus was not born above the law; instead, he fulfilled it perfectly.

2:28-32 When Mary and Joseph brought Jesus to the Temple to be dedicated to God, they met an old man who told them what their child would become. Simeon's song is often called the *Nunc Dimittis,* because these are the first words of its Latin translation. Simeon could die in peace because he had seen the Messiah.

2:32 The Jews were well acquainted with the Old Testament prophecies that spoke of the Messiah's blessings to their nation. They did not always give equal attention to the prophecies saying that he would bring salvation to the entire world, not just the Jews (see, for example, Isaiah 49:6). Many thought that Christ had come to save only his own people. Luke made sure his Greek audience understood that Christ had come to save *all* who believe, Gentiles as well as Jews.

2:33 Joseph and Mary were amazed for three reasons: Simeon said that Jesus was a gift from God; Simeon recognized Jesus as the Messiah; and Simeon said Jesus would be a light to the entire world. This was at least the second time that Mary had been greeted with a prophecy about her son; the first time was when Elizabeth welcomed her as the mother of her Lord (1:42-45).

2:34, 35 Simeon prophesied that Jesus would have a paradoxical effect on Israel. Some would fall because of him (see Isaiah 8:14, 15), while others would rise (see Malachi 4:2). With Jesus, there would be no neutral ground: People would either joyfully accept him or totally reject him. As Jesus' mother, Mary would be grieved by the widespread rejection he would face. This is the first note of sorrow in Luke's Gospel.

2:36 Although Simeon and Anna were very old, they had never lost their hope that they would see the Messiah. Led by the Holy Spirit, they were among the first to bear witness to Jesus. In the Jewish culture, elders were respected, so because of Simeon's and Anna's age, their prophecies carried extra weight. Our society, however, values youthfulness over wisdom, and contributions by the elderly are often ignored. As Christians, we should reverse

they had been married only seven years. 37 She was now eighty-four years old. She never
left the Temple but stayed there day and night, worshiping God with fasting and prayer.
38 She came along just as Simeon was talking with Mary and Joseph, and she began
praising God. She talked about Jesus to everyone who had been waiting for the promised
King to come and deliver Jerusalem.
39 When Jesus' parents had fulfilled all the requirements of the law of the Lord, they
returned home to Nazareth in Galilee. 40 There the child grew up healthy and strong.
He was filled with wisdom beyond his years, and God placed his special favor upon
him.

2:37 1 Tim 5:5
2:38 Isa 52:9; Luke 1:68; 24:21
2:39 Matt 2:23
2:40 Luke 1:80

ELIZABETH

In societies like Israel, in which a woman's value was largely measured by her ability to bear children, to be without children often led to personal hardship and public shame. For Elizabeth, a childless old age was a painful and lonely time but during which she remained faithful to God.

Both Elizabeth and Zechariah came from priestly families. For two weeks each year, Zechariah had to go to the Temple in Jerusalem to attend to his priestly duties. After one of those trips, Zechariah returned home excited but speechless. He had to write down his good news, because he couldn't give it any other way. And what a wonderful surprise he had for his wife: Their faded dream would become an exciting reality! Soon Elizabeth became pregnant, and she knew her child was a long-hoped-for gift from God.

News traveled fast among the family. Seventy miles to the north, in Nazareth, Elizabeth's relative Mary also unexpectedly became pregnant. Within days after the angel's message that she would bear the Messiah, Mary went to visit Elizabeth. They were instantly bound together by the unique gifts God had given them. Elizabeth knew that Mary's son would be even greater than her own, for John would be the messenger for Mary's son.

When her baby was born, Elizabeth insisted on his God-given name: John. Zechariah's written agreement freed his tongue, and everyone in town wondered what would become of this obviously special child.

Elizabeth whispered her praise as she cared for God's gift. Knowing about Mary must have made her marvel at God's timing. Things had worked out even better than she could have planned. We, too, need to remember that God is in control of every situation. When did you last pause to recognize God's timing in the events of your life?

Strengths and accomplishments
- Known as a deeply spiritual woman
- Showed no doubts about God's ability to fulfill his promise
- Mother of John the Baptist
- The first woman besides Mary to hear of the coming Savior

Lessons from her life
- God does not forget those who have been faithful to him
- God's timetable and methods do not have to conform to what we expect

Vital statistics
- Occupation: Homemaker
- Relatives: Husband: Zechariah. Son: John the Baptist. Relative: Mary
- Contemporaries: Joseph, Herod the Great

Key verses
"What an honor this is, that the mother of my Lord should visit me! When you came in and greeted me, my baby jumped for joy the instant I heard your voice! You are blessed, because you believed that the Lord would do what he said" (Luke 1:43–45).

Elizabeth's story is told in Luke 1:5–80.

---

those values wherever we can. Encourage older people to share their wisdom and experience. Listen carefully when they speak. Offer them your friendship, and help them find ways to continue to serve God.

2:36, 37 Anna was called a prophet, indicating that she was unusually close to God. Prophets did not necessarily predict the future. Their main role was to speak for God, proclaiming his truth.

2:39 Did Mary and Joseph return immediately to Nazareth, or did they remain in Bethlehem for a time (as implied in Matthew 2)? Apparently there is a gap of several years between verses 38 and 39—ample time for them to find a place to live in Bethlehem, flee to Egypt to escape Herod's wrath, and return to Nazareth when it was safe to do so.

2:40 Jesus was filled with wisdom, which is not surprising since he stayed in close contact with his heavenly Father. James 1:5 says God gives wisdom generously to all who ask. Like Jesus, we can grow in wisdom by walking with God.

Jesus Speaks with the Religious Teachers (**15**)
41 Every year Jesus' parents went to Jerusalem for the Passover festival. 42 When Jesus **2:41** Exod 12:24-27
was twelve years old, they attended the festival as usual. 43 After the celebration was over, Deut 16:1-8
they started home to Nazareth, but Jesus stayed behind in Jerusalem. His parents didn't
miss him at first, 44 because they assumed he was with friends among the other travelers.
But when he didn't show up that evening, they started to look for him among their **2:47**
relatives and friends. 45 When they couldn't find him, they went back to Jerusalem to Matt 7:28 John 7:15
search for him there. 46 Three days later they finally discovered him. He was in the **2:48**
Temple, sitting among the religious teachers, discussing deep questions with them. Matt 12:26 Luke 3:23; 4:22
47 And all who heard him were amazed at his understanding and his answers. **2:49**
48 His parents didn't know what to think. "Son!" his mother said to him. "Why have John 2:16
you done this to us? Your father and I have been frantic, searching for you everywhere." **2:50**
49 "But why did you need to search?" he asked. "You should have known that I would Mark 9:32
be in my Father's house."* 50 But they didn't understand what he meant. **2:51** Luke 2:19
51 Then he returned to Nazareth with them and was obedient to them; and his mother **2:52**
stored all these things in her heart. 52 So Jesus grew both in height and in wisdom, and 1 Sam 2:26 Prov 3:4
he was loved by God and by all who knew him. Luke 1:80

John the Baptist Prepares the Way for Jesus (**16**/Matthew 3:1-12; Mark 1:1-8)
3 It was now the fifteenth year of the reign of Tiberius, the Roman emperor. Pilate was
governor over Judea; Herod Antipas was ruler* over Galilee; his brother Philip was **3:2**
ruler* over Iturea and Traconitis; Lysanias was ruler over Abilene. 2 Annas and Caiaphas Luke 1:80

2:49 Or *"Didn't you realize that I should be involved with my Father's affairs?"* **3:1a** Greek *Herod was tetrarch.* Herod Antipas was a son of King Herod. **3:1b** Greek *tetrarch;* also in 3:19.

2:41, 42 According to God's law, every male was required to go to Jerusalem three times a year for the great festivals (Deuteronomy 16:16). In the spring, the Passover was celebrated, followed immediately by the weeklong Festival of Unleavened Bread. Passover commemorated the night of the Jews' escape from Egypt when God had killed the Egyptian firstborn but had passed over Israelite homes (see Exodus 12:21-36). Passover was the most important of the three annual festivals.

2:43-45 At age 12, Jesus was considered almost an adult, and so he didn't spend a lot of time with his parents during the festival. Those who attended these festivals often traveled in caravans for protection from robbers along the Palestine roads. It was customary for the women and children to travel at the front of the caravan, with the men bringing up the rear. A 12-year-old boy conceivably could have been in either group, and both Mary and Joseph assumed Jesus was with the other one. But when the caravan left Jerusalem, Jesus stayed behind, absorbed in his discussion with the religious leaders.

2:46, 47 The Temple courts were famous throughout Judea as a place of learning. The apostle Paul studied in Jerusalem, perhaps in the Temple courts, under Gamaliel, one of its foremost teachers (Acts 22:3). At the time of the Passover, the greatest rabbis of the land would assemble to teach and to discuss great truths among themselves. The coming Messiah would no doubt have been a popular discussion topic, for everyone was expecting him soon. Jesus would have been eager to listen and to ask probing questions. It was not his youth but the depth of his wisdom that astounded these teachers.

2:48 Mary had to let go of her child and let him become a man, God's Son, the Messiah. Fearful that she hadn't been careful enough with this God-given child, she searched frantically for him. But she was looking for a boy, not the young man who was in the Temple astounding the religious leaders with his questions. It is hard to let go of people or projects we have nurtured. It is both sweet and painful to see our children growing into adults, our students into teachers, our subordinates into managers, our inspirations into institutions. But when the time comes we must step back and let go—in spite of the hurt. Then our protégés can exercise their wings, take flight, and soar to the heights God intended for them.

2:49, 50 This is the first mention of Jesus' awareness that he was God's Son. But even though he knew his real Father, he did not reject his earthly parents. He went back to Nazareth with them and lived under their authority for another 18 years. God's people do not despise human relationships or family responsibilities. If the Son of God obeyed his human parents, how much more should we honor our family members! Don't use commitment to God's work to justify neglecting your family.

2:50 Jesus' parents didn't understand what he meant about his Father's house. They didn't realize he was making a distinction between his earthly father and his heavenly Father. Jesus knew that he had a unique relationship with God. Although Mary and Joseph knew he was God's Son, they didn't understand what his mission would involve. Besides, they had to raise him, along with his brothers and sisters (Matthew 13:55, 56), as a normal child. They knew he was unique, but they did not know what was going on in his mind.

2:52 The Bible does not record any events of the next 18 years of Jesus' life, but Jesus undoubtedly was learning and maturing. As the oldest in a large family, he assisted Joseph in his carpentry work. Joseph may have died during this time, leaving Jesus to provide for the family. The normal routines of daily life gave Jesus a solid understanding of the Judean people.

2:52 The second chapter of Luke shows us that although Jesus was unique, he had a normal childhood and adolescence. In terms of development, he went through the same progression we do. He grew physically and mentally, he related to other people, and he was loved by God. A full human life is not unbalanced. It was important to Jesus—and it should be important to all believers—to develop fully and harmoniously in each of these key areas: physical, mental, social, and spiritual.

3:1 Tiberius, the Roman emperor, ruled from A.D. 14 to 37. Pilate was the Roman governor responsible for the province of Judea; Herod Antipas and Philip were half brothers and sons of the cruel Herod the Great, who had been dead more than 20 years. Antipas, Philip, Pilate, and Lysanias apparently had equal powers in governing their separate territories. All were subject to Rome and responsible for keeping peace in their respective lands.

3:2 Under Jewish law there was only one high priest. He was

3:3 Acts 13:24; 19:4

3:4-6 †Isa 40:3-5

were the high priests. At this time a message from God came to John son of Zechariah, who
was living out in the wilderness. [3]Then John went from place to place on both sides of the
Jordan River, preaching that people should be baptized to show that they had turned from
their sins and turned to God to be forgiven.* [4]Isaiah had spoken of John when he said,

3:3 Greek *preaching a baptism of repentance for the forgiveness of sins.*

Motherhood is a painful privilege. Young Mary of Nazareth had the unique privilege of being mother to the very Son of God. Yet the pains and pleasures of her motherhood can be understood by mothers everywhere. Mary was the only human present at Jesus' birth who also witnessed his death. She saw him arrive as her baby son, and she watched him die as her Savior.

Until Gabriel's unexpected visit, Mary's life was quite satisfactory. She had recently become engaged to a carpenter, Joseph, and was anticipating married life. But her life was about to change forever.

Angels don't usually make appointments before visiting. Feeling as if she were being congratulated for winning the grand prize in a contest she had never entered, Mary found the angel's greeting puzzling and his presence frightening. What she heard next was the news almost every woman in Israel hoped to hear—that her child would be the Messiah, God's promised Savior. Mary did not doubt the message but rather asked how pregnancy would be possible. Gabriel told her the baby would be God's Son. Her answer was the one God waits in vain to hear from so many other people: "I am the Lord's servant. . . . May everything you have said come true" (Luke 1:38). Later her song of joy shows us how well she knew God, for her thoughts were filled with his words from the Old Testament.

Within a few weeks of his birth, Jesus was taken to the Temple to be dedicated to God. There Joseph and Mary were met by two devout people, Simeon and Anna, who recognized the child as the Messiah and praised God. Simeon directed some words to Mary that must have come to her mind many times in the years that followed: "A sword will pierce your very soul" (Luke 2:35). A big part of her painful privilege of motherhood would be to see her son rejected and crucified by the people he came to save.

We can imagine that even if she had known all she would suffer as Jesus' mother, Mary would still have given the same response. Are you, like Mary, available to be used by God?

Strengths and accomplishments
- The mother of Jesus, the Messiah
- The one human who was with Jesus from birth to death
- Willing to be available to God
- Knew and applied Old Testament Scriptures

Lessons from her life
- God's best servants are often ordinary people who make themselves available to him
- God's plans involve extraordinary events in ordinary people's lives
- A person's character is revealed by his or her response to the unexpected

Vital statistics
- Where: Nazareth, Bethlehem
- Occupation: Homemaker
- Relatives: Husband: Joseph. Relatives: Zechariah and Elizabeth. Children: Jesus, James, Joseph, Judas, Simon, and daughters

Key verse
"Mary responded, 'I am the Lord's servant, and I am willing to accept whatever he wants. May everything you have said come true.' And then the angel left" (Luke 1:38).

Mary's story is told throughout the Gospels. She is also mentioned in Acts 1:14.

appointed from Aaron's line, and he held his position for life. By this time, however, the religious system had been corrupted, and the Roman government was appointing its own religious leaders to maintain greater control over the Jews. Apparently the Roman authorities had deposed the Jewish-appointed Annas and had replaced him with Annas's son-in-law, Caiaphas. Nevertheless Annas retained his title (see Acts 4:6) and probably also much of the power it carried. Because the Jews believed the high priest's position to be for life, they would have continued to call Annas their high priest.

3:2 This is John the Baptist, whose birth story is told in chapter 1. See his Profile in John 1.

3:2 Pilate, Herod, and Caiaphas were the most powerful leaders in Palestine, but they were upstaged by a wilderness prophet from rural Judea. God chose to speak through the loner John the Baptist, who has gone down in history as greater than any of the rulers of his day. How often we judge people by our culture's standards—power, wealth, beauty—and miss the truly great people through whom God works! Greatness is measured not by what you have but by your faith in God. Like John, give yourself entirely to God so God's power can work through you.

3:3 To turn from sins means turning *away* from sins and turning *toward* God. To truly turn from our sins, we must do both. We can't just say we believe and then live any way we choose (see 3:7, 8), and neither can we simply live a morally correct life without a personal relationship with God, because that cannot bring forgiveness from sin. Determine to rid your life of any sins God points out, and put your trust in him alone to guide you.

"He is a voice shouting in the wilderness:
'Prepare a pathway for the Lord's coming!
Make a straight road for him!
5 Fill in the valleys,
and level the mountains and hills!
Straighten the curves,
and smooth out the rough places!
6 And then all people will see
the salvation sent from God.'"*

3:6 Luke 2:30-31 Acts 28:28 Titus 2:11

7 Here is a sample of John's preaching to the crowds that came for baptism: "You brood
of snakes! Who warned you to flee God's coming judgment? 8 Prove by the way you live
that you have really turned from your sins and turned to God. Don't just say, 'We're
safe—we're the descendants of Abraham.' That proves nothing. God can change these
stones here into children of Abraham. 9 Even now the ax of God's judgment is poised,
ready to sever your roots. Yes, every tree that does not produce good fruit will be chopped
down and thrown into the fire."

3:7 Matt 12:34; 23:33
3:8 John 8:33, 37, 39 Acts 3:25
3:9 Matt 7:19 John 15:6

10 The crowd asked, "What should we do?"

11 John replied, "If you have two coats, give one to the poor. If you have food, share
it with those who are hungry."

3:11 Jas 2:15 1 Jn 3:17

12 Even corrupt tax collectors came to be baptized and asked, "Teacher, what should
we do?"

3:12 Luke 7:29

13 "Show your honesty," he replied. "Make sure you collect no more taxes than the
Roman government requires you to."

3:13 Luke 19:8

14 "What should we do?" asked some soldiers.
John replied, "Don't extort money, and don't accuse people of things you know they
didn't do. And be content with your pay."

3:14 Exod 23:1 Lev 19:11

3:4-6 Isa 40:3-5.

3:4, 5 In John's day, before a king took a trip, messengers would tell those he was planning to visit to prepare the roads for him. Similarly John told his listeners to make their lives ready so the Lord could come to them. To prepare for Jesus' coming to us, we must focus on him, read his Word, and respond obediently to his directions.

3:6 This book was written to a non-Jewish audience. Luke quoted from Isaiah to show that salvation is for all people, not just the Jews (Isaiah 40:3-5; 52:10). John the Baptist called all people to prepare to meet Jesus. That includes you, no matter what your religious affiliation or position. Don't let feelings of being an outsider cause you to hold back. No one who wants to follow Jesus is an outsider in God's Kingdom.

3:7 What motivates your faith—fear of the future, or a desire to be a better person in a better world? Some people wanted to be baptized by John so they could escape eternal punishment, but they didn't turn to God for salvation. John had harsh words for such people. He knew that God values reformation above ritual. Is your faith motivated by a desire for a new, changed life, or is it only like a vaccination or insurance policy against possible disaster?

3:8 Many of John's hearers were shocked when he said that being Abraham's descendants was not enough for God. The religious leaders relied more on family lines than on faith for their standing with God. For them, religion was inherited. But a personal relationship with God is not handed down from parents to children. Everyone has to make a personal decision of whether or not to trust Christ. Don't rely on someone else's faith for your salvation. Put your faith in Jesus, and live it every day.

3:8, 9 Confession of sins and a changed life are inseparable. Faith without deeds is dead (James 2:14-26). Jesus' harshest words were to the respectable religious leaders, who lacked the desire for real change. They wanted to be known as religious authorities, but they didn't want to change their hearts and minds. Thus, their lives were unproductive. Turning from sin must be tied to action, or it isn't real. Following Jesus means more than saying the right words; it means acting on what he says.

3:11-14 John's message demanded at least three specific responses: (1) Share what you have with those who need it, (2) whatever your job is, do it well and with fairness, and (3) be content with your earnings. John had not been commissioned to bring comforting messages to those who lived sinful lives; he was calling the people to right living. What changes can you make in sharing what you have, doing your work honestly and well, and being content?

3:12 Tax collectors were notorious for their dishonesty. Romans gathered funds for their government by farming out the collection privilege. Tax collectors earned their own living by adding a sizable sum—whatever they could get away with—to the total and keeping this money for themselves. Unless the people revolted and risked Roman retaliation, they had to pay whatever was demanded. Obviously they hated the tax collectors, who were generally dishonest, greedy, and ready to betray their own countrymen for cold cash. Yet, said John, God would accept even these men; God desires to pour out mercy on those who confess their sins and then to give them strength to live changed lives.

3:12-14 John's message took root in unexpected places—among the poor, the dishonest, and even the hated occupation army. These people were painfully aware of their needs. Too often we confuse respectability with right living. They are not the same. Respectability can even hinder right living if it keeps us from seeing our need for God. If you had to choose, would you protect your character or your reputation?

3:14 These soldiers were the Roman troops sent to keep peace in this distant province. Many of them oppressed the poor and used their power to take advantage of all the people. John called them to turn from their sins and change their ways.

3:16 Mark 1:4; John 1:26, 33; Acts 1:5; 2:3; 11:16; 13:25; 19:4
3:17 Matt 13:30

15 Everyone was expecting the Messiah to come soon, and they were eager to know
whether John might be the Messiah. 16 John answered their questions by saying, "I
baptize with* water; but someone is coming soon who is greater than I am—so much
greater that I am not even worthy to be his slave.* He will baptize you with the Holy
Spirit and with fire.* 17 He is ready to separate the chaff from the grain with his
winnowing fork. Then he will clean up the threshing area, storing the grain in his barn
but burning the chaff with never-ending fire." 18 John used many such warnings as he
announced the Good News to the people.

Herod Puts John in Prison (**26**)

3:19-20 Matt 14:3; Mark 6:17

19 John also publicly criticized Herod Antipas, ruler of Galilee, for marrying Herodias,
his brother's wife, and for many other wrongs he had done. 20 So Herod put John in
prison, adding this sin to his many others.

The Baptism of Jesus (**17**/Matthew 3:13-17; Mark 1:9-11)

3:22 Gen 22:2; Ps 2:7; Isa 42:1; Matt 12:18; 17:5; Mark 9:7; Luke 9:35; 2 Pet 1:17

21 One day when the crowds were being baptized, Jesus himself was baptized. As he was
praying, the heavens opened, 22 and the Holy Spirit descended on him in the form of a
dove. And a voice from heaven said, "You are my beloved Son, and I am fully pleased
with you.*"

3:16a Or *in.* **3:16b** Greek *to untie his sandals.* **3:16c** Or *in the Holy Spirit and in fire.* **3:22** Some manuscripts read *and today I have become your Father.*

3:15 There had not been a prophet in Israel for more than 400 years. It was widely believed that when the Messiah came, prophecy would reappear (Joel 2:28, 29; Malachi 3:1; 4:5). When John burst onto the scene, the people were excited. He was obviously a great prophet, and they were sure that the eagerly awaited age of the Messiah had come. Some, in fact, thought John himself was the Messiah. John spoke like the prophets of old, saying that the people must turn from their sin to God to avoid punishment and to experience his mercy and approval. This is a message for all times and places, but John spoke it with particular urgency; he was preparing the people for the coming Messiah.

3:16 John's baptism with water symbolized the washing away of sins. His baptism followed his message of repentance and reformation. Jesus' baptism with fire equips one with power to do God's will. The baptism with the Holy Spirit was first given at Pentecost (Acts 2) when the Holy Spirit came upon believers in the form of tongues of fire, empowering them to proclaim Jesus' resurrection in many languages. The baptism with fire also symbolizes the work of the Holy Spirit in bringing God's judgment on those who refuse to repent.

3:17 John warned of impending judgment by comparing those who refuse to live for God to chaff, the useless outer husk of the grain. By contrast, he compared those who repent and reform their lives to the nourishing grain itself. The winnowing fork was a pitchfork used to toss wheat so that the kernels would separate from the husks. Those who refuse to be used by God will be discarded because they have no value in furthering God's work. Those who repent and believe, however, hold great value in God's eyes because they are beginning a new life of productive service for him.

3:19, 20 In these two verses Luke flashes forward to continue his explanation about John the Baptist. See the Harmony of the Gospels for the chronological order of events.

3:19, 20 This is Herod Antipas (see Mark 6 for his Profile). Herodias was Herod's niece and also his brother's wife. She treacherously plotted John the Baptist's death (Matthew 14:1-12). The Herods were a murderous and deceitful family. Rebuking a tyrannical Roman official who could imprison and execute him was extremely dangerous, yet that is what John did. Herod seemingly had the last word, but the story is not finished. At the Last Judgment, Herod, not John, will be the one in danger.

3:21 Luke emphasizes Jesus' human nature. Jesus was born to humble parents, a birth unannounced except to shepherds and foreigners. This baptism recorded here was the first public declaration of Jesus' ministry. Instead of going to Jerusalem and identifying with the established religious leaders, Jesus went to a river and identified himself with those who were repenting of sin. When Jesus, at age 12, visited the Temple, he understood his mission (2:49). Eighteen years later, at his baptism, he began carrying it out. And as Jesus prayed, God spoke and confirmed his decision to act. God was breaking into human history through Jesus the Christ.

3:21, 22 If baptism was a sign of repentance from sin, why did Jesus ask to be baptized? Several explanations are often given: (1) Jesus' baptism was one step in fulfilling his earthly mission of identifying with our humanity and sin; (2) by endorsing the rite of baptism, Jesus was giving us an example to follow; (3) Jesus was announcing the beginning of his public ministry; (4) Jesus was being baptized for the sins of the nation. The Holy Spirit's appearance in the form of a dove showed that God's plan for salvation was centered in Jesus. He was the perfect human who didn't need baptism for repentance, but he was baptized anyway on our behalf.

3:21, 22 This is one of several places in Scripture where all the members of the Trinity are mentioned—Father, Son, and Holy Spirit. In the traditional words of the church, the one God exists in three persons but one substance, coeternal and coequal. No amount of explanation can adequately portray the power and intricacy of this unique relationship. There are no perfect analogies in nature because there is no other relationship like the Trinity.

The Record of Jesus' Ancestors (**3**/Matthew 1:1-17)

23 Jesus was about thirty years old when he began his public ministry.

Jesus was known as the son of Joseph.
Joseph was the son of Heli.
24 Heli was the son of Matthat.
Matthat was the son of Levi.
Levi was the son of Melki.
Melki was the son of Jannai.
Jannai was the son of Joseph.
25 Joseph was the son of Mattathias.
Mattathias was the son of Amos.
Amos was the son of Nahum.
Nahum was the son of Esli.
Esli was the son of Naggai.
26 Naggai was the son of Maath.
Maath was the son of Mattathias.
Mattathias was the son of Semein.
Semein was the son of Josech.
Josech was the son of Joda.
27 Joda was the son of Joanan.
Joanan was the son of Rhesa.
Rhesa was the son of Zerubbabel.
Zerubbabel was the son of Shealtiel.
Shealtiel was the son of Neri.
28 Neri was the son of Melki.
Melki was the son of Addi.
Addi was the son of Cosam.
Cosam was the son of Elmadam.
Elmadam was the son of Er.
29 Er was the son of Joshua.
Joshua was the son of Eliezer.
Eliezer was the son of Jorim.
Jorim was the son of Matthat.
Matthat was the son of Levi.
30 Levi was the son of Simeon.
Simeon was the son of Judah.
Judah was the son of Joseph.
Joseph was the son of Jonam.
Jonam was the son of Eliakim.
31 Eliakim was the son of Melea.
Melea was the son of Menna.
Menna was the son of Mattatha.
Mattatha was the son of Nathan.
Nathan was the son of David.
32 David was the son of Jesse.
Jesse was the son of Obed.

3:23
Luke 4:22
John 6:42

3:27
1 Chr 3:17
Ezra 3:2

3:31-33
Ruth 4:18-22
1 Sam 16:1, 13
2 Sam 5:14
1 Chr 2:9-12; 3:5

3:23 Imagine the Savior of the world working in a small-town carpenter's shop until he was 30 years old! It seems incredible that Jesus would have been content to remain in Nazareth all that time, but he patiently trusted his Father's timing for his life and ministry. Thirty was the prescribed age for priests to begin their ministry (Numbers 4:3). Joseph was 30 years old when he began serving the king of Egypt (Genesis 41:46), and David was 30 years old when he began to reign over Judah (2 Samuel 5:4). Age 30, then, was a good time to begin an important task in the Jewish culture. Like Jesus, we need to resist the temptation to jump ahead before receiving the Spirit's direction. Are you waiting and wondering what your next step should be? Don't jump ahead—trust God's timing.

3:23 Heli may have been Joseph's father-in-law. If that were the case, this would be Mary's genealogy that Luke may have received personally from her. It is fitting that Luke would show Mary's genealogy because of the prominence he gives women in his Gospel.

3:23-38 Matthew's genealogy goes back to Abraham and shows that Jesus was related to all Jews (Matthew 1). Luke's genealogy goes back to Adam, showing that Jesus is related to all human beings. This is consistent with Luke's picture of Jesus as the Savior of the whole world.

Obed was the son of Boaz.
Boaz was the son of Salmon.*
Salmon was the son of Nahshon.
33 Nahshon was the son of Amminadab.
Amminadab was the son of Admin.
Admin was the son of Arni.*
Arni was the son of Hezron.
Hezron was the son of Perez.
Perez was the son of Judah.
34 Judah was the son of Jacob.
Jacob was the son of Isaac.
Isaac was the son of Abraham.
Abraham was the son of Terah.
Terah was the son of Nahor.
35 Nahor was the son of Serug.
Serug was the son of Reu.
Reu was the son of Peleg.
Peleg was the son of Eber.
Eber was the son of Shelah.
36 Shelah was the son of Cainan.
Cainan was the son of Arphaxad.
Arphaxad was the son of Shem.
Shem was the son of Noah.
Noah was the son of Lamech.
37 Lamech was the son of Methuselah.
Methuselah was the son of Enoch.
Enoch was the son of Jared.
Jared was the son of Mahalalel.
Mahalalel was the son of Kenan.
38 Kenan was the son of Enosh.*
Enosh was the son of Seth.
Seth was the son of Adam.
Adam was the son of God.

3:34-36 Gen 11:10-26; 1 Chr 1:24-27
3:36-38 Gen 4:25–5:32; 1 Chr 1:1-4
3:38 Gen 1:26-27, 2:7; 5:1-2

Satan Tempts Jesus in the Wilderness (**18**/Matthew 4:1-11; Mark 1:12-13)

4 Then Jesus, full of the Holy Spirit, left the Jordan River. He was led by the Spirit to
go out into the wilderness, [2]where the Devil tempted him for forty days. He ate
nothing all that time and was very hungry.

4:1 Isa 11:2; 61:1
4:2 Exod 34:28; 1 Kgs 19:8; Heb 4:15

3:32 Greek *Sala;* see Ruth 4:22. **3:33** *Arni* is the same person as Ram; see 1 Chr 2:9-10. **3:38** Greek *Enos;* see Gen 5:6.

4:1 Sometimes we feel that if the Holy Spirit leads us, it will always be "beside peaceful streams" (Psalm 23:2). But that is not necessarily true. He led Jesus into the wilderness for a long and difficult time of testing, and he may also lead us into difficult situations. When facing trials, first make sure you haven't brought them on yourself through sin or unwise choices. If you find no sin to confess or unwise behavior to change, then ask God to strengthen you for your test. Finally, be careful to follow faithfully wherever the Holy Spirit leads.

4:1 Temptation will often come after a high point in our spiritual life or ministry (see 1 Kings 18–19 for Elijah's story of great victory followed by despair). Remember that Satan chooses the times for his attacks. We need to be on our guard in times of victory just as much as in times of discouragement. See the third note on Matthew 4:1ff for a comment on how Satan tempts us when we're vulnerable.

4:1, 2 The Devil, who tempted Adam and Eve in the garden, also tempted Jesus in the wilderness. Satan is a real being, a created but rebellious fallen angel, and not a symbol or an idea. He constantly fights against God and those who follow and obey God. Jesus was a prime target for the Devil's temptations. Satan succeeded with Adam and Eve, and he hoped to succeed with Jesus, too.

4:1-13 Knowing and obeying God's Word is an effective weapon against temptation, the only *offensive* weapon provided in the Christian's "armor" (Ephesians 6:17). Jesus used Scripture to counter Satan's attacks, and you can, too. But to use it effectively, you must have faith in God's promises, because Satan also knows Scripture and is adept at twisting it to suit his purposes. Obeying the Scriptures is more important than simply having a verse to quote, so read them daily and apply them to your life. Then your "sword" will always be sharp.

4:2 Why was it necessary for Jesus to be tempted? First, temptation is part of the human experience. For Jesus to be fully human, for him to understand us completely, he had to face temptation (see Hebrews 4:15). Second, Jesus had to undo Adam's work. Adam, though created perfect, gave in to temptation and passed sin on to the whole human race. Jesus, by contrast, resisted Satan. His victory offers salvation to all of Adam's descendants (see Romans 5:12-19).

3 Then the Devil said to him, "If you are the Son of God, change this stone into a loaf
of bread."
4 But Jesus told him, "No! The Scriptures say, 'People need more than bread for their
life.'*"
5 Then the Devil took him up and revealed to him all the kingdoms of the world in a
moment of time. 6 The Devil told him, "I will give you the glory of these kingdoms and
authority over them—because they are mine to give to anyone I please. 7 I will give it all
to you if you will bow down and worship me."
8 Jesus replied, "The Scriptures say,

'You must worship the Lord your God;
serve only him.'*"

9 Then the Devil took him to Jerusalem, to the highest point of the Temple, and said,
"If you are the Son of God, jump off! 10 For the Scriptures say,

'He orders his angels to protect and guard you.
11 And they will hold you with their hands
to keep you from striking your foot on a stone.'*"

12 Jesus responded, "The Scriptures also say, 'Do not test the Lord your God.'*"
13 When the Devil had finished tempting Jesus, he left him until the next opportunity
came.

4:4 †Deut 8:3
4:6 Matt 28:18; John 12:31; 14:30; 1 Jn 5:19; Rev 13:2
4:8 †Deut 6:13; 10:20
4:10-11 †Ps 91:11-12
4:12 †Deut 6:16
4:13 Heb 4:15

4:4 Deut 8:3. **4:8** Deut 6:13. **4:10-11** Ps 91:11-12. **4:12** Deut 6:16.

JESUS' TEMPTATION AND RETURN TO GALILEE
Jesus was tempted by Satan in the rough Judean wilderness before returning to his boyhood home, Nazareth. John's Gospel tells of Jesus' journeys in Galilee, Samaria, and Judea (see John 1—4) before he moved to Capernaum to set up his base of operations (see Matthew 4:12, 13).

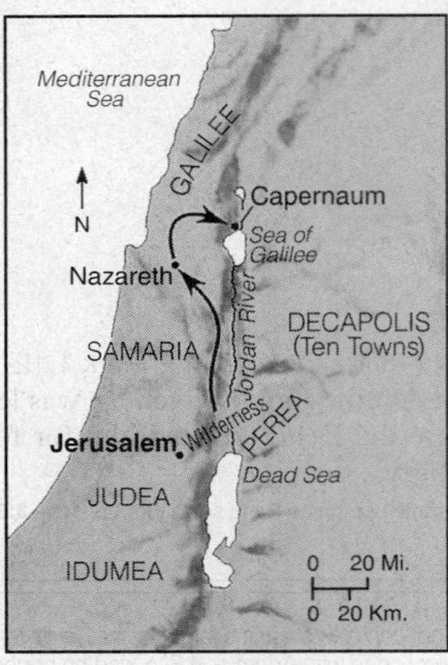

4:3 Satan may tempt us to doubt Christ's true identity. He knows that once we begin to question whether or not Jesus is God, it's far easier to get us to do what he wants. Times of questioning can help us sort out our beliefs and strengthen our faith, but those times can also be dangerous. If you are dealing with doubt, be aware that you are especially vulnerable to temptation. Even as you search for answers, protect yourself by meditating on the unshakable truths of God's Word.

4:3 Sometimes what we are tempted to do isn't wrong in itself. Turning a stone into bread wasn't necessarily bad. The sin was not in the act but in the reason behind it. The Devil was trying to get Jesus to take a shortcut, to solve Jesus' immediate problem at the expense of his long-range goals, to seek comfort at the sacrifice of his discipline. Satan often works that way—persuading us to take action, even right action, for the wrong reason or at the wrong time. The fact that something is not wrong in itself does not mean that it is good for you at a given time. Many people sin by attempting to fulfill legitimate desires outside of God's will or ahead of his timetable. First ask Is the Holy Spirit leading me to do this? Or is Satan trying to get me off the track?

4:3ff Often we are tempted not through our weaknesses, but through our strengths. The Devil tempted Jesus where he was strong. Jesus had power over stones, the kingdoms of the world, and even angels, and Satan wanted him to use that power without regard for his mission. When we give in to the Devil and wrongly use our strengths, we become proud and self-reliant. Trusting in our own powers, we feel little need of God. To avoid this trap, we must realize that all our strengths are God's gifts to us, and we must dedicate those strengths to his service.

4:6, 7 The Devil arrogantly hoped to succeed in his rebellion against God by diverting Jesus from his mission and winning his worship. "This world is mine, not God's," he was saying, "and if you hope to do anything worthwhile here, you'd better recognize that fact." Jesus didn't argue with Satan about who owns the world, but Jesus refused to validate Satan's claim by worshiping him. Jesus knew that he would redeem the world through giving up his life on the cross, not through making an alliance with a corrupt angel.

4:9-11 Here the Devil misinterpreted Scripture. The intention of Psalm 91 is to show God's protection of his people, not to incite them to use God's power for sensational or foolish displays.

4:13 Christ's defeat of the Devil in the wilderness was decisive but not final. Throughout his ministry, Jesus would confront Satan in many forms. Too often we see temptation as once and for all. In reality, we need to be constantly on guard against the Devil's ongoing attacks. Where are you most susceptible to temptation right now? How are you preparing to withstand it?

B. MESSAGE AND MINISTRY OF JESUS, THE SAVIOR (4:14—21:38)

Luke accurately records the actions and teachings of Christ, helping us understand the way of salvation. There is much unique material in Luke, especially the parables of Jesus. Jesus came to teach us how to live and how to find salvation. How carefully, then, we should study the words and life of our Savior.

1. Jesus' ministry in Galilee

Jesus Preaches in Galilee (**30**/Matthew 4:12-17; Mark 1:14-15; John 4:43-45)

14 Then Jesus returned to Galilee, filled with the Holy Spirit's power. Soon he became
well known throughout the surrounding country. 15 He taught in their synagogues and
was praised by everyone.

Jesus Is Rejected at Nazareth (**32**)

16 When he came to the village of Nazareth, his boyhood home, he went as usual to the
synagogue on the Sabbath and stood up to read the Scriptures. 17 The scroll containing
the messages of Isaiah the prophet was handed to him, and he unrolled the scroll to the
place where it says:

4:18-19 †Isa 61:1-2

18 "The Spirit of the Lord is upon me,
for he has appointed me to preach Good News to the poor.
He has sent me to proclaim
that captives will be released,
that the blind will see,
that the downtrodden will be freed from their oppressors,
19 and that the time of the Lord's favor has come.*"

4:19 Lev 25:8-10; 2 Cor 6:2

20 He rolled up the scroll, handed it back to the attendant, and sat down. Everyone in
the synagogue stared at him intently. 21 Then he said, "This Scripture has come true today
before your very eyes!"
22 All who were there spoke well of him and were amazed by the gracious words that
fell from his lips. "How can this be?" they asked. "Isn't this Joseph's son?"
23 Then he said, "Probably you will quote me that proverb, 'Physician, heal yourself'—meaning, 'Why don't you do miracles here in your hometown like those you did
in Capernaum?' 24 But the truth is, no prophet is accepted in his own hometown.
25 "Certainly there were many widows in Israel who needed help in Elijah's time,
when there was no rain for three and a half years and hunger stalked the land. 26 Yet Elijah
was not sent to any of them. He was sent instead to a widow of Zarephath—a foreigner
in the land of Sidon. 27 Or think of the prophet Elisha, who healed Naaman, a Syrian,
rather than the many lepers in Israel who needed help."
28 When they heard this, the people in the synagogue were furious. 29 Jumping up,

4:22 Luke 2:47; John 6:42; 7:15
4:23 Matt 4:13; 11:23; Mark 1:21-28; 2:1-12
4:24 Matt 13:57; Mark 6:4; John 4:44
4:25-26 1 Kgs 17:1-9; 18:1; Jas 5:17
4:27 2 Kgs 5:1-14
4:29 Num 15:35; Acts 7:58; Heb 13:12

4:18-19 Or *and to proclaim the acceptable year of the Lord.* Isa 61:1-2.

4:16 Synagogues were very important in Jewish religious life. During the Exile when the Jews no longer had their Temple, synagogues were established as places of worship on the Sabbath and as schools for young boys during the week. Synagogues continued to exist even after the Temple was rebuilt. A synagogue could be set up in any town where there were at least 10 Jewish families. It was administered by one leader and an assistant. At the synagogue, the leader often would invite a visiting rabbi to read from the Scriptures and to teach.

4:16 Jesus went to the synagogue "as usual." Even though he was the perfect Son of God and his local synagogue undoubtedly left much to be desired, Jesus attended services every week. His example makes our excuses for not attending church sound weak and self-serving. Make regular worship a part of your life.

4:17-21 Jesus was quoting from Isaiah 61:1, 2. Isaiah pictures the deliverance of Israel from exile in Babylon as a Year of Jubilee when all debts are cancelled, all slaves are freed, and all property is returned to original owners (Leviticus 25). But the release from Babylonian exile had not brought the fulfillment the people had expected; they were still a conquered and oppressed people. So Isaiah must have been referring to a future messianic age. Jesus boldly announced, "This Scripture has come true today before your very eyes!" Jesus was proclaiming himself as the one who would bring this Good News to pass but in a way that the people would not yet be able to grasp.

4:24 Even Jesus himself was not accepted as a prophet in his hometown. Many people have a similar attitude—an expert is anyone who carries a briefcase and comes from more than 200 miles away. Don't be surprised when your Christian life and faith are not easily understood or accepted by those who know you well.

4:28 Jesus' remarks angered the people of Nazareth because he was saying that God sometimes chose to reach Gentiles rather than Jews. Jesus implied that his hearers were as unbelieving as the citizens of the northern kingdom of Israel in the days of Elijah and Elisha, a time notorious for its great wickedness.

they mobbed him and took him to the edge of the hill on which the city was built. They **4:30**
intended to push him over the cliff, 30 but he slipped away through the crowd and left John 8:59
them.

Jesus Teaches with Great Authority (**34**/Mark 1:21-28)

31 Then Jesus went to Capernaum, a town in Galilee, and taught there in the synagogue **4:31**
every Sabbath day. 32 There, too, the people were amazed at the things he said, because Matt 4:13-16 John 2:12
he spoke with authority. **4:32**
33 Once when he was in the synagogue, a man possessed by a demon began shouting Matt 7:28-29 John 7:46
at Jesus, 34 "Go away! Why are you bothering us, Jesus of Nazareth? Have you come to **4:34**
destroy us? I know who you are—the Holy One sent from God." Luke 4:41 John 6:69
35 Jesus cut him short. "Be silent!" he told the demon. "Come out of the man!" The **4:35**
demon threw the man to the floor as the crowd watched; then it left him without hurting Luke 4:39-41
him further.
36 Amazed, the people exclaimed, "What authority and power this man's words
possess! Even evil spirits obey him and flee at his command!" 37 The story of what he
had done spread like wildfire throughout the whole region.

Jesus Heals Peter's Mother-in-Law and Many Others (**35**/Matthew 8:14-17; Mark 1:29-34)

38 After leaving the synagogue that day, Jesus went to Simon's home, where he found
Simon's mother-in-law very sick with a high fever. "Please heal her," everyone begged.
39 Standing at her bedside, he spoke to the fever, rebuking it, and immediately her
temperature returned to normal. She got up at once and prepared a meal for them.
40 As the sun went down that evening, people throughout the village brought sick **4:40-41**
family members to Jesus. No matter what their diseases were, the touch of his hand Matt 8:16-17 Mark 1:32-34
healed every one. 41 Some were possessed by demons; and the demons came out at his **4:41**
command, shouting, "You are the Son of God." But because they knew he was the Mark 3:11
Messiah, he stopped them and told them to be silent.

Jesus Preaches throughout Galilee (**36**/Matthew 4:23-25; Mark 1:35-39)

42 Early the next morning Jesus went out into the wilderness. The crowds searched every- **4:42-44**
where for him, and when they finally found him, they begged him not to leave them. 43 But Matt 4:23

4:31 Jesus had recently moved to Capernaum from Nazareth (Matthew 4:13). Capernaum was a thriving city with great wealth as well as great decadence. Because it was the headquarters for many Roman troops, word about Jesus could spread all over the Roman Empire.

4:31 Why was Jesus allowed to teach in the synagogues? Jesus was taking advantage of the policy of allowing visitors to teach. Itinerant rabbis were always welcome to speak to those gathered each Sabbath in the synagogues. The apostle Paul also took advantage of this practice (see Acts 13:5; 14:1).

4:33 A man possessed by a demon was in the synagogue where Jesus was teaching. This man made his way into the place of worship and verbally abused Jesus. It is naive to think that we will be sheltered from evil in the church. Satan is happy to invade our presence wherever and whenever he can. But Jesus' authority is much greater than Satan's; and where Jesus is present, demons cannot stay for long.

4:34-36 The people were amazed at Jesus' authority to drive out demons—evil spirits ruled by Satan and sent to harass people and tempt them to sin. Demons are fallen angels who have joined Satan in rebellion against God. Demons can cause a person to become mute, deaf, blind, or insane. Jesus faced many demons during his time on earth, and he always exerted authority over them. Not only did the evil spirit leave this man; Luke records that the man was not even injured.

4:36 Evil permeates our world, and it is no wonder that people are often fearful. But Jesus' power is far greater than Satan's. The first step toward conquering fear of evil is to recognize Jesus' authority and power. He has overcome all evil, including Satan himself.

4:39 Jesus healed Simon's (Peter's) mother-in-law so completely that not only did the fever leave but her strength was restored, and immediately she got up and took care of others' needs. What a beautiful attitude of service she showed! God gives us health so that we may serve others.

4:40 The people came to Jesus when the sun was setting because this was the Sabbath (4:31), their day of rest. Sabbath lasted from sunset on Friday to sunset on Saturday. The people didn't want to break the law that prohibited travel on the Sabbath, so they waited until the Sabbath hours were over before coming to Jesus. Then, as Luke the physician notes, they came with all kinds of diseases, and Jesus healed each one.

4:41 Why didn't Jesus want the demons to reveal who he was? (1) Jesus commanded them to remain silent to show his authority over them. (2) Jesus wanted his listeners to believe he was the Messiah because of his words, not because of the demons' words. (3) Jesus was going to reveal his identity according to God's timetable, and he would not be pushed by Satan's evil plans. The demons called Jesus "Son of God" or "the Holy One sent from God" (4:34) because they knew he was the Christ. But Jesus was going to show himself to be the suffering servant before he became the great King. To reveal his identity as King too soon would stir up the crowds with the wrong expectations of what he had come to do.

4:42 Jesus had to get up very early just to get some time alone. If Jesus needed solitude for prayer and refreshment, how much more is this true for us? Don't become so busy that life turns into a flurry of activity leaving no room for quiet fellowship alone with God. No matter how much you have to do, you should always have time for prayer.

4:43 Luke 8:1 he replied, "I must preach the Good News of the Kingdom of God in other places, too,
4:44 Matt 4:23 Mark 1:39 because that is why I was sent." 44So he continued to travel around, preaching in synagogues throughout Judea.*

Jesus Provides a Miraculous Catch of Fish (**37**)

5 One day as Jesus was preaching on the shore of the Sea of Galilee,* great crowds
pressed in on him to listen to the word of God. 2He noticed two empty boats at the
water's edge, for the fishermen had left them and were washing their nets. 3Stepping into
one of the boats, Jesus asked Simon,* its owner, to push it out into the water. So he sat
in the boat and taught the crowds from there.

5:4 John 21:6 4When he had finished speaking, he said to Simon, "Now go out where it is deeper
and let down your nets, and you will catch many fish."
5:5 John 21:3 5"Master," Simon replied, "we worked hard all last night and didn't catch a thing. But
5:6 John 21:11 if you say so, we'll try again." 6And this time their nets were so full they began to tear!
7A shout for help brought their partners in the other boat, and soon both boats were filled
with fish and on the verge of sinking.
5:8 Gen 18:27 Job 42:5-6 8When Simon Peter realized what had happened, he fell to his knees before Jesus and
said, "Oh, Lord, please leave me—I'm too much of a sinner to be around you." 9For he
was awestruck by the size of their catch, as were the others with him. 10His partners,
James and John, the sons of Zebedee, were also amazed.
Jesus replied to Simon, "Don't be afraid! From now on you'll be fishing for people!"
5:11 Matt 19:27 11And as soon as they landed, they left everything and followed Jesus.

Jesus Heals a Man with Leprosy (**38**/Matthew 8:1-4; Mark 1:40-45)

12In one of the villages, Jesus met a man with an advanced case of leprosy. When the
man saw Jesus, he fell to the ground, face down in the dust, begging to be healed. "Lord,"
he said, "if you want to, you can make me well again."
13Jesus reached out and touched the man. "I want to," he said. "Be healed!" And
5:14 Lev 14:2-32 instantly the leprosy disappeared. 14Then Jesus instructed him not to tell anyone what
had happened. He said, "Go right to the priest and let him examine you. Take along the

4:44 Some manuscripts read *Galilee*. **5:1** Greek *Lake Gennesaret*, another name for the Sea of Galilee. **5:3** *Simon* is called *Peter* in 6:14 and thereafter.

4:43 The Kingdom of God was Good News! It was Good News to the Jews because they had been awaiting the coming of the promised Messiah ever since the Babylonian captivity. It is Good News for us also because it means freedom from slavery to sin and selfishness. The Kingdom of God is here and now because the Holy Spirit lives in the hearts of believers. Yet it is also in the future because Jesus will return to reign over a perfect Kingdom, where sin and evil no longer exist.

5:2 Fishermen on the Sea of Galilee used nets, often bell-shaped nets with lead weights around the edges. A net would be thrown flat onto the water, and the lead weights would cause it to sink around the fish. Then the fishermen would pull on a cord, drawing the net around the fish. Nets had to be kept in good condition, so they were washed to remove weeds and then mended.

5:8 Simon Peter was awestruck at this miracle, and his first response was to feel his own insignificance in comparison to this man's greatness. Peter knew that Jesus had healed the sick and driven out demons, but he was amazed that Jesus cared about his day-to-day routine and understood his needs. God is interested not only in saving us but also in helping us in our daily activities.

5:11 There are two requirements for coming to God. Like Peter, we must recognize our own sinfulness. Then, like these fishermen, we must realize that we can't save ourselves and that we need help. If we know that Jesus is the only one who can help us, we will be ready to leave everything and follow him.

5:11 This was the disciples' second call. After the first call (Matthew 4:18-22; Mark 1:16-20), Peter, Andrew, James, and John had gone back to fishing. They continued to watch Jesus, however, as he established his authority in the synagogue, healed the sick, and drove out demons. Here he also established his authority in their lives—he met them on their level and helped them in their work. From this point on, they left their nets and remained with Jesus. For us, following Jesus means more than just acknowledging him as Savior. We must leave our past behind and commit our future to him.

5:12 Leprosy was a feared disease because there was no known cure for it, and some forms of it were highly contagious. Leprosy had a similar emotional impact and terror associated with it as AIDS does today. (Sometimes called Hansen's disease, leprosy still exists today in a less contagious form that can be treated.) The priests monitored the disease, banishing lepers who were in a contagious stage to prevent the spread of infection and readmitting lepers whose disease was in remission. Because leprosy destroys the nerve endings, lepers often would unknowingly damage their fingers, toes, and noses. This man with leprosy had an advanced case, so he undoubtedly had lost much bodily tissue. Still, he believed that Jesus could heal him of every trace of the disease.

5:13 Lepers were considered untouchable because people feared contracting their disease. Yet Jesus reached out and touched the leper to heal him. We may consider certain people who are diseased or disabled to be untouchable or repulsive. We must not be afraid to reach out and touch them with God's love. Whom do you know who needs God's touch of love?

offering required in the law of Moses for those who have been healed of leprosy, so everyone will have proof of your healing." 15 Yet despite Jesus' instructions, the report of his power spread even faster, and vast crowds came to hear him preach and to be healed of their diseases. 16 But Jesus often withdrew to the wilderness for prayer.

Jesus Heals a Paralyzed Man (**39**/Matthew 9:1-8; Mark 2:1-12)

17 One day while Jesus was teaching, some Pharisees and teachers of religious law were sitting nearby. (It seemed that these men showed up from every village in all Galilee and Judea, as well as from Jerusalem.) And the Lord's healing power was strongly with Jesus. 18 Some men came carrying a paralyzed man on a sleeping mat. They tried to push through the crowd to Jesus, 19 but they couldn't reach him. So they went up to the roof, took off some tiles, and lowered the sick man down into the crowd, still on his mat, right in front of Jesus. 20 Seeing their faith, Jesus said to the man, "Son, your sins are forgiven."

21 "Who does this man think he is?" the Pharisees and teachers of religious law said to each other. "This is blasphemy! Who but God can forgive sins?"

22 Jesus knew what they were thinking, so he asked them, "Why do you think this is blasphemy? 23 Is it easier to say, 'Your sins are forgiven' or 'Get up and walk'? 24 I will prove that I, the Son of Man, have the authority on earth to forgive sins." Then Jesus turned to the paralyzed man and said, "Stand up, take your mat, and go on home, because you are healed!"

25 And immediately, as everyone watched, the man jumped to his feet, picked up his mat, and went home praising God. 26 Everyone was gripped with great wonder and awe. And they praised God, saying over and over again, "We have seen amazing things today."

Jesus Eats with Sinners at Matthew's House (**40**/Matthew 9:9-13; Mark 2:13-17)

27 Later, as Jesus left the town, he saw a tax collector named Levi sitting at his tax-collection booth. "Come, be my disciple!" Jesus said to him. 28 So Levi got up, left everything, and followed him.

29 Soon Levi held a banquet in his home with Jesus as the guest of honor. Many of Levi's fellow tax collectors and other guests were there. 30 But the Pharisees and their teachers of religious law complained bitterly to Jesus' disciples, "Why do you eat and drink with such scum*?"

5:15 Matt 9:26
5:20 Luke 7:48
5:21 Isa 43:25; 55:7 Luke 7:49
5:22 Luke 6:8; 9:47
5:24-25 John 5:8-9
5:29-30 Luke 15:1-2

5:30 Greek *with tax collectors and sinners.*

5:16 People were flocking to hear Jesus preach and to have their diseases healed, but Jesus made sure he often withdrew to quiet, solitary places to pray. Many things clamor for our attention, and we often run ourselves ragged attending to them. Like Jesus, however, we should take time to withdraw to a quiet and deserted place to pray. Strength comes from God, and we can only be strengthened by spending time with him.

5:17 The religious leaders spent much time defining and discussing the huge body of religious tradition that had been accumulating for more than 400 years since the Jews' return from exile. They were so concerned with these man-made traditions, in fact, that they often lost sight of Scripture. Here these leaders felt threatened because Jesus challenged their sincerity and because the people were flocking to him.

5:18, 19 In Bible times, houses were built of stone and had flat roofs made of mud mixed with straw. Outside stairways led to the roof. These men carried their friend up the stairs to the roof, where they took apart as much as was necessary to lower him in front of Jesus.

5:18-20 It wasn't the paralyzed man's faith that impressed Jesus but the faith of his friends. Jesus responded to their faith and healed the man. For better or worse, our faith affects others. We cannot make another person a Christian, but we can do much through our words, actions, and love to give him or her a chance to respond. Look for opportunities to bring your friends to the living Christ.

5:21 When Jesus told the paralyzed man his sins were forgiven, the Jewish leaders accused Jesus of blasphemy—claiming to be God or to do what only God can do. In Jewish law, blasphemy was punishable by death (Leviticus 24:16). In labeling Jesus' claim to forgive sins blasphemous, the religious leaders showed they did not understand that Jesus *is* God, and he has God's power to heal both the body and the soul. Forgiveness of sins was a sign that the messianic age had come (Isaiah 40:2; Joel 2:32; Micah 7:18, 19; Zechariah 13:1).

5:27 For more about Levi (who was also named Matthew), the disciple and author of the Good News of Matthew, see his Profile in Matthew 9.

5:28, 29 Levi left a lucrative, though probably dishonest, tax-collecting business to follow Jesus. Then he responded as Jesus would want all his followers to do. He held a reception for his fellow tax collectors and other notorious "sinners" so they could meet Jesus, too. Levi, who left behind a material fortune in order to gain a spiritual fortune, was proud to be associated with Jesus.

5:30-32 The Pharisees wrapped their sin in respectability. They made themselves appear good by publicly doing good deeds and pointing at the sins of others. Jesus chose to spend time not with these proud, self-righteous religious leaders, but with people who sensed their own sin and knew that they were not good enough for God. In order to come to God, we must repent; and in order to renounce our sin, we must first acknowledge it.

31 Jesus answered them, "Healthy people don't need a doctor—sick people do.
32 I have come to call sinners to turn from their sins, not to spend my time with those
who think they are already good enough."

Religious Leaders Ask Jesus about Fasting (**41**/Matthew 9:14-17; Mark 2:18-22)

33 The religious leaders complained that Jesus' disciples were feasting instead of fasting.
"John the Baptist's disciples always fast and pray," they declared, "and so do the
disciples of the Pharisees. Why are yours always feasting?"
5:34 John 3:29 — 34 Jesus asked, "Do wedding guests fast while celebrating with the groom? 35 Someday
5:35 Luke 9:22; 17:22 — he will be taken away from them, and then they will fast."
36 Then Jesus gave them this illustration: "No one tears a piece of cloth from a new
garment and uses it to patch an old garment. For then the new garment would be torn,
and the patch wouldn't even match the old garment. 37 And no one puts new wine into
old wineskins. The new wine would burst the old skins, spilling the wine and ruining the
skins. 38 New wine must be put into new wineskins. 39 But no one who drinks the old
wine seems to want the fresh and the new. 'The old is better,' they say."

The Disciples Pick Wheat on the Sabbath (**45**/Matthew 12:1-8; Mark 2:23-28)

6:1 Deut 23:25 — **6** One Sabbath day as Jesus was walking through some grainfields, his disciples broke
off heads of wheat, rubbed off the husks in their hands, and ate the grains. 2 But some
6:2 John 5:10 — Pharisees said, "You shouldn't be doing that! It's against the law to work by harvesting
6:3-4 1 Sam 21:6 — grain on the Sabbath."
3 Jesus replied, "Haven't you ever read in the Scriptures what King David did when
6:4 Lev 24:5-9 — he and his companions were hungry? 4 He went into the house of God, ate the special
bread reserved for the priests alone, and then gave some to his friends. That was
breaking the law, too." 5 And Jesus added, "I, the Son of Man, am master even of the
Sabbath."

Jesus Heals a Man's Hand on the Sabbath (**46**/Matthew 12:9-14; Mark 3:1-6)

6 On another Sabbath day, a man with a deformed right hand was in the synagogue
6:7 Luke 14:1 — while Jesus was teaching. 7 The teachers of religious law and the Pharisees watched
closely to see whether Jesus would heal the man on the Sabbath, because they were
6:8 Luke 5:22; 9:47 — eager to find some legal charge to bring against him. 8 But Jesus knew their thoughts.
He said to the man with the deformed hand, "Come and stand here where everyone

---

5:35 Jesus knew his death was coming. After that time, fasting would be in order. Although he was fully human, Jesus knew he was God and why he had come—to die for the sins of the world.

5:36-39 "Wineskins" were goatskins sewn together at the edges to form watertight bags. Because new wine expands as it ages, it had to be put in new, pliable wineskins. A used skin, having become more rigid, would burst and spill the wine. Like old wineskins, the Pharisees were too rigid to accept Jesus, who could not be contained in their traditions or rules. Christianity required new approaches, new traditions, new structures. Our church programs and ministries should not be so structured that they have no room for a fresh touch of the Spirit, a new method, or a new idea. We, too, must be careful that our heart does not become so rigid that it prevents us from accepting new ways of thinking that Christ brings. We need to keep our heart pliable so we can accept Jesus' life-changing message.

6:1, 2 In Jewish legal tradition, there were 39 categories of activities forbidden on the Sabbath, and harvesting was one of them. The teachers of religious law even went so far as to describe different methods of harvesting. One method was to rub the heads of grain between the hands, as the disciples were doing here. God's law said farmers were to leave the edges of their fields unplowed so travelers and the poor could eat from this bounty (Deuteronomy 23:25), so the disciples were not guilty of stealing grain. Neither were they breaking the Sabbath by doing their daily work on it. In fact, though they may have been violating the Pharisees' rules, they were not breaking any divine law.

6:2 The Pharisees thought their religious system had all the answers. They could not accept Jesus because he did not fit into their system. We could miss Christ for the same reason. Beware of thinking that you or your church has all the answers. No religious system is big enough to contain Christ completely or to fulfill perfectly all his desires for the world.

6:3-5 Each week 12 consecrated loaves of bread, representing the 12 tribes of Israel, were placed on a table in the Temple. This bread was called the Bread of the Presence. After its use in the Temple, it was to be eaten only by priests. Jesus, accused of Sabbath breaking, referred to a well-known story about David (1 Samuel 21:1-6). On one occasion, when fleeing from Saul, David and his men ate this special bread. Their need was more important than ceremonial regulations. Jesus was appealing to the same principle: Human need is more important than human regulations and rules. By comparing himself and his disciples with David and his men, Jesus was saying, "If you condemn me, you must also condemn David."

6:5 When Jesus said that he was "master even of the Sabbath," he meant that he had the authority to overrule the Pharisees' traditions and regulations because he had created the Sabbath. The Creator is always greater than the creation.

6:6, 7 According to the tradition of the religious leaders, no healing could be done on the Sabbath. Healing, they argued, was practicing medicine, and a person could not practice his or her profession on the Sabbath. It was more important for the religious leaders to protect their laws than to free a person from painful suffering.

can see." So the man came forward. 9 Then Jesus said to his critics, "I have a question
for you. Is it legal to do good deeds on the Sabbath, or is it a day for doing harm? Is
this a day to save life or to destroy it?" 10 He looked around at them one by one and
then said to the man, "Reach out your hand." The man reached out his hand, and it
became normal again! 11 At this, the enemies of Jesus were wild with rage and began
to discuss what to do with him.

Jesus Chooses the Twelve Disciples (**48**/Mark 3:13-19)

12 One day soon afterward Jesus went to a mountain to pray, and he prayed to God all
night. 13 At daybreak he called together all of his disciples and chose twelve of them to **6:13** John 6:70
be apostles. Here are their names:

14 Simon (he also called him Peter), **6:14-15** Acts 1:13
Andrew (Peter's brother),
James,
John,
Philip,
Bartholomew,
15 Matthew,
Thomas,
James (son of Alphaeus),
Simon (the Zealot),
16 Judas (son of James),
Judas Iscariot (who later betrayed him).

Jesus Gives the Beatitudes (**49**/Matthew 5:1-12)

17 When they came down the slopes of the mountain, the disciples stood with Jesus on a
large, level area, surrounded by many of his followers and by the crowds. There were
people from all over Judea and from Jerusalem and from as far north as the seacoasts of **6:19**
Tyre and Sidon. 18 They had come to hear him and to be healed, and Jesus cast out many Matt 9:20
evil spirits. 19 Everyone was trying to touch him, because healing power went out from Mark 5:30
him, and they were all cured.
20 Then Jesus turned to his disciples and said, **6:20-23** Matt 5:1-12

"God blesses you who are poor,
for the Kingdom of God is given to you.

6:11 Jesus' enemies were furious. Not only had he read their minds; he also flouted their laws and exposed the hatred in their hearts. It is ironic that it was their hatred, combined with their zeal for the law, that drove them to plot murder—an act that was clearly against the law.

6:12 The Gospel writers note that before every important event in Jesus' life, he took time to go off by himself and pray. This time Jesus was preparing to choose his inner circle, the 12 apostles. Make sure that all your important decisions are grounded in prayer.

6:13 Jesus had many *disciples* (learners), but he chose only 12 *apostles* (messengers). The apostles were his inner circle, to whom he gave special training and whom he sent out with his own authority. These were the men who started the Christian church. In the Gospels these 12 men are usually called the disciples, but in the book of Acts they are called apostles.

6:13-16 Jesus selected "ordinary" men with a mixture of backgrounds and personalities to be his disciples. Today, God calls "ordinary" people together to build his church, teach salvation's message, and serve others out of love. Alone we may feel unqualified to serve Christ effectively, but together we make up a group strong enough to serve God in any way. Ask for patience to accept the diversity of people in your church, and build on the variety of strengths represented in your group.

6:14-16 The disciples are not always listed by the same names. For example, Simon is sometimes called Peter or Cephas. Matthew is also known as Levi. Bartholomew is thought to be the same person as Nathanael (John 1:45). Judas the son of James is also called Thaddaeus.

6:19 Once word of Jesus' healing power spread, crowds gathered just to touch him. For many, he had become a magician or a symbol of good fortune. Instead of desiring God's pardon and love, they only wanted physical healing or a chance to see spectacular events. Some people still see God as a cosmic magician and consider prayer as a way to get God to do his tricks. But God is not a magician—he is the Master. Prayer is not a way for us to control God; it is a way for us to put ourselves under his control.

6:20ff This may be Luke's account of the sermon that Matthew records in Matthew 5–7, or it may be that Jesus gave similar sermons on several different occasions. Some believe that this was not one sermon, but a composite based on Jesus' customary teachings.

6:20-23 These verses are called the *Beatitudes,* from the Latin word meaning "blessing." They describe what it means to be Christ's follower; they are standards of conduct; they contrast Kingdom values with worldly values, showing what Christ's followers can expect from the world and what God will give them; they contrast fake piety with true humility; and finally, they show how Old Testament expectations are fulfilled in God's Kingdom.

6:21 Isa 55:1; 61:3 Rev 7:16-17

21 God blesses you who are hungry now,
for you will be satisfied.
God blesses you who weep now,
for the time will come when you will laugh with joy.

6:22 John 15:19; 16:2 1 Pet 4:14

22 God blesses you who are hated and excluded and mocked and cursed
because you are identified with me, the Son of Man.

6:23 2 Chr 36:16 Acts 5:41; 7:52 Jas 1:2

23 "When that happens, rejoice! Yes, leap for joy! For a great reward awaits you in
heaven. And remember, the ancient prophets were also treated that way by your
ancestors.

24 "What sorrows await you who are rich,
for you have your only happiness now.

6:24 Jas 5:1

6:25 Isa 5:22; 65:13

25 What sorrows await you who are satisfied and prosperous now,
for a time of awful hunger is before you.
What sorrows await you who laugh carelessly,
for your laughing will turn to mourning and sorrow.

6:26 Jas 4:4

26 What sorrows await you who are praised by the crowds,
for their ancestors also praised false prophets.

Jesus Teaches about Loving Enemies (**57**/Matthew 5:43-48)

6:27 Prov 25:21 Rom 12:20

6:28 Rom 12:14

6:30 Deut 15:7-8, 10

6:31 Matt 7:12

6:33-35 Lev 25:35-36

27 "But if you are willing to listen, I say, love your enemies. Do good to those who hate
you. 28 Pray for the happiness of those who curse you. Pray for those who hurt you. 29 If
someone slaps you on one cheek, turn the other cheek. If someone demands your coat,
offer your shirt also. 30 Give what you have to anyone who asks you for it; and when
things are taken away from you, don't try to get them back. 31 Do for others as you would
like them to do for you.
32 "Do you think you deserve credit merely for loving those who love you? Even
the sinners do that! 33 And if you do good only to those who do good to you, is that
so wonderful? Even sinners do that much! 34 And if you lend money only to those who
can repay you, what good is that? Even sinners will lend to their own kind for a full
return.
35 "Love your enemies! Do good to them! Lend to them! And don't be concerned
that they might not repay. Then your reward from heaven will be very great, and you
will truly be acting as children of the Most High, for he is kind to the unthankful and

6:36 Matt 5:48

to those who are wicked. 36 You must be compassionate, just as your Father is
compassionate.

6:21 Some believe that the hunger about which Jesus spoke is a hunger for righteousness (Matthew 5:6). Others say this is physical hunger. In any case, in a nation where riches were seen as a sign of God's favor, Jesus startled his hearers by pronouncing blessings on the hungry. In doing so, however, he was in line with an ancient tradition. The Old Testament is filled with texts proclaiming God's concern for the poor and needy. See, for example, 1 Samuel 2:5; Psalm 146:7; Isaiah 58:6, 7; and Jesus' own mother's prayer in Luke 1:53.

6:24 If you are trying to find fulfillment only through riches, wealth may be the only reward you will ever get—and it does not last. We should not seek comfort now at the expense of eternal life.

6:26 There were many false prophets in Old Testament times. They were praised by kings and crowds because their predictions—prosperity and victory in war—were exactly what the people wanted to hear. But popularity is no guarantee of truth, and human flattery does not bring God's approval. Sadness lies ahead for those who chase after the crowd's praise rather than God's truth.

6:27 The Jews despised the Romans because they oppressed God's people, but Jesus told the people to love these enemies. Such words turned many away from Christ. But Jesus wasn't talking about having affection for enemies; he was talking about an act of the will. You can't "fall into" this kind of love—it takes conscious effort. Loving our enemies means acting in their best interests. We can pray for them, and we can think of ways to help them. Jesus loved the whole world, even though the world was in rebellion against God. Jesus asks us to follow his example by loving our enemies. Grant your enemies the same respect and rights as you desire for yourself.

6:35 Love means action. One way to put love to work is to take the initiative in meeting specific needs. This is easy to do with people who love us, people whom we trust; but love means doing this even to those who dislike us or hurt us. The money we give others should be a gift, not a high-interest loan that will put a burden on them. Give as though you are giving to God.

Jesus Teaches about Judging Others (**63**/Matthew 7:1-6)
37“Stop judging others, and you will not be judged. Stop criticizing others, or it will all
come back on you. If you forgive others, you will be forgiven. 38If you give, you will **6:38** Ps 79:12
receive. Your gift will return to you in full measure, pressed down, shaken together to Mark 4:24
make room for more, and running over. Whatever measure you use in giving—large or
small—it will be used to measure what is given back to you.”
39Then Jesus gave the following illustration: “What good is it for one blind person **6:39** Matt 15:14
to lead another? The first one will fall into a ditch and pull the other down also. 40A **6:40**
student is not greater than the teacher. But the student who works hard will become like Matt 10:24-25 John 13:16; 15:20
the teacher.
41“And why worry about a speck in your friend’s eye when you have a log in your
own? 42How can you think of saying, ‘Friend, let me help you get rid of that speck in
your eye,’ when you can’t see past the log in your own eye? Hypocrite! First get rid of
the log from your own eye; then perhaps you will see well enough to deal with the speck
in your friend’s eye!

Jesus Teaches about Fruit in People’s Lives (**66**/Matthew 7:15-20)
43“A good tree can’t produce bad fruit, and a bad tree can’t produce good fruit. 44A tree is **6:44** Matt 12:33
identified by the kind of fruit it produces. Figs never grow on thornbushes or grapes on
bramble bushes. 45A good person produces good deeds from a good heart, and an evil
person produces evil deeds from an evil heart. Whatever is in your heart determines what
you say.

Jesus Teaches about Building on a Solid Foundation (**67**/Matthew 7:21-29)
46“So why do you call me ‘Lord,’ when you won’t obey me? 47I will show you what it’s **6:46** Mal 1:6
like when someone comes to me, listens to my teaching, and then obeys me. 48It is like a Matt 7:21
person who builds a house on a strong foundation laid upon the underlying rock. When the
floodwaters rise and break against the house, it stands firm because it is well built. 49But
anyone who listens and doesn’t obey is like a person who builds a house without a
foundation. When the floods sweep down against that house, it will crumble into a heap of
ruins.”

A Roman Officer Demonstrates Faith (**68**/Matthew 8:5-13)
7 When Jesus had finished saying all this, he went back to Capernaum. 2Now the **7:1** Matt 7:28
highly valued slave of a Roman officer was sick and near death. 3When the officer **7:2**
heard about Jesus, he sent some respected Jewish leaders to ask him to come and heal John 4:47

6:37, 38 A forgiving spirit demonstrates that a person has received God’s forgiveness. Jesus uses the picture of measuring grain in a basket to ensure the full amount. If we are critical rather than compassionate, we will also receive criticism. If we treat others generously, graciously, and compassionately, however, these qualities will come back to us in full measure. We are to love others, not judge them.

6:39, 40 Make sure you’re following the right teachers and leaders, because you will go no farther than they do. Look for leaders who will show you more about faith and whose guidance you can trust.

6:41 Jesus doesn’t mean we should ignore wrongdoing, but we should not be so worried about others’ sins that we overlook our own. We often rationalize our sins by pointing out the same mistakes in others. What kinds of specks in others’ eyes are the easiest for you to criticize? Remember your own “logs” when you feel like criticizing, and you may find that you have less to say.

6:42 We should not be so afraid of the label *hypocrite* that we stand still in our Christian life, hiding our faith and making no attempts to grow. A person who tries to do right but often fails is not a hypocrite. Neither are those who fulfill their duty even when they don’t feel like doing it. It is often necessary and good to set aside our desires in order to do what needs doing. It is not hypocrisy to be weak in faith. A hypocrite is a person who puts on religious behavior in order to gain attention, approval, or admiration from others.

6:45 Jesus reminds us that our speech and actions reveal the true underlying beliefs, attitudes, and motivations. The good impressions we try to make cannot last if our heart is deceptive. What is in your heart will come out in your speech and behavior.

6:46-49 Obeying God is like building a house on a strong, solid foundation that stands firm when storms come. When life is calm, our foundations don’t seem to matter. But when crises come, our foundations are tested. Be sure your life is built on the solid foundation of knowing and trusting Jesus Christ.

6:49 Why would people build a house without a foundation? Perhaps to save time and avoid the hard work of preparing a stone foundation. Possibly because the waterfront scenery is more attractive or because beach houses have higher social status than cliff houses. Perhaps because they want to join their friends who have already settled in sandy areas. Maybe because they haven’t heard about the violent storms coming, or because they have discounted the reports, or for some reason they think disaster can’t happen to them. Whatever their reason, those with no foundation are shortsighted, and they will be sorry. When you find yourself listening but not obeying, what are your reasons?

7:2 This Roman officer was a captain in charge of 100 men. This man came to Jesus, not as a last resort or magic charm, but because he believed Jesus was sent from God. Apparently the officer recognized that the Jews were God’s special people. It is recorded that he loved the Jews and built a synagogue. Thus, in his time of need, it was natural for him to turn to Jesus.

7:5 his slave. 4So they earnestly begged Jesus to come with them and help the man. "If
Acts 10:2 anyone deserves your help, it is he," they said, 5"for he loves the Jews and even built a
synagogue for us."

6So Jesus went with them. But just before they arrived at the house, the officer sent
7:7 some friends to say, "Lord, don't trouble yourself by coming to my home, for I am not
Ps 107:20 worthy of such an honor. 7I am not even worthy to come and meet you. Just say the word
from where you are, and my servant will be healed. 8I know because I am under the
authority of my superior officers, and I have authority over my soldiers. I only need to
say, 'Go,' and they go, or 'Come,' and they come. And if I say to my slaves, 'Do this or
that,' they do it."

9When Jesus heard this, he was amazed. Turning to the crowd, he said, "I tell you, I
haven't seen faith like this in all the land of Israel!" 10And when the officer's friends
returned to his house, they found the slave completely healed.

Jesus Raises a Widow's Son from the Dead (**69**)

7:11-16 11Soon afterward Jesus went with his disciples to the village of Nain, with a great crowd
1 Kgs 17:17-24; 2 Kgs 4:32-37 following him. 12A funeral procession was coming out as he approached the village gate.
7:13 The boy who had died was the only son of a widow, and many mourners from the village
Luke 8:52 were with her. 13When the Lord saw her, his heart overflowed with compassion. "Don't
7:14 Luke 8:54 cry!" he said. 14Then he walked over to the coffin and touched it, and the bearers
John 11:43; Acts 9:40 stopped. "Young man," he said, "get up." 15Then the dead boy sat up and began to talk
7:16 to those around him! And Jesus gave him back to his mother.
Luke 1:65-68; 19:44 16Great fear swept the crowd, and they praised God, saying, "A mighty prophet has
risen among us," and "We have seen the hand of God at work today." 17The report of
what Jesus had done that day spread all over Judea and even out across its borders.

7:3 Why did the officer send Jewish leaders to Jesus instead of going himself? Since he was well aware of the Jewish hatred for Roman soldiers, he may not have wanted to interrupt a Jewish gathering. As an army officer, he daily delegated work and sent groups on missions, so this was how he chose to get his message to Jesus.

7:3 Matthew 8:5 says the Roman officer visited Jesus himself, while Luke 7:3 says he sent Jewish leaders to present his request to Jesus. In dealing with the messengers, Jesus was dealing with the officer. For his Jewish audience, Matthew emphasized the man's faith. For his Gentile audience, Luke highlighted the good relationship between the Jewish leaders and the Roman officer.

7:9 The Roman officer didn't come to Jesus, and he didn't expect Jesus to come to him. Just as this officer did not need to be present to have his orders carried out, so Jesus didn't need to be present to heal. The officer's faith was especially amazing, because he was a Gentile who had not been brought up to know a loving God.

7:11-15 The widow's situation was serious. She had lost her husband, and here her only son was dead—her last means of support. The crowd of mourners would go home, and she would be left penniless and alone. The widow was probably past the age of childbearing and would not marry again. Unless a relative came to her aid, her future was bleak. She would be an easy prey for swindlers, and she would likely be reduced to begging for food. In fact, as Luke repeatedly emphasizes, this woman was just the kind of person Jesus had come to help—and help her he did. Jesus has the power to bring hope out of any tragedy.

7:11-17 This story illustrates salvation. The whole world was dead in sin (Ephesians 2:1), just as the widow's son was dead. Being dead, we could do nothing to help ourselves—we couldn't even ask for help. But God had compassion on us, and he sent Jesus to raise us to life with him (Ephesians 2:4-7). The dead man did not earn his second chance at life, and we cannot earn our new life in Christ. But we can accept God's gift of life, praise God for it, and use our life to do his will.

7:12 Honoring the dead was important in Jewish tradition. A funeral procession, with relatives of the dead person following the body that was wrapped and carried on a kind of stretcher, would make its way through town, and bystanders would be expected to join the procession. In addition, hired mourners would cry aloud and draw attention to the procession. The family's mourning would continue for 30 days.

7:16 The people thought of Jesus as a prophet because, like the Old Testament prophets, he boldly proclaimed God's message and sometimes raised the dead. Both Elijah and Elisha raised children from the dead (1 Kings 17:17-24; 2 Kings 4:18-37). The people were correct in thinking that Jesus was a prophet, but he was much more—he is God himself.

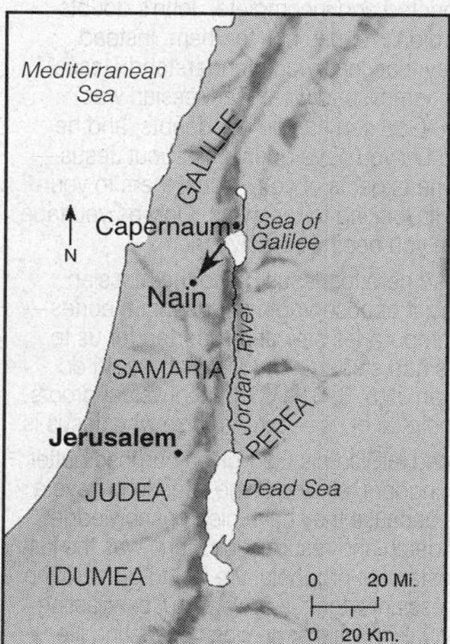

JESUS RAISES A WIDOW'S SON
Jesus traveled to Nain and met a funeral procession leaving the village. A widow's only son had died, leaving her virtually helpless, but Jesus brought the young man back to life. This miracle, recorded only in Luke, reveals Jesus' compassion for people's needs.

Jesus Eases John's Doubt (**70**/Matthew 11:1-19)

18 The disciples of John the Baptist told John about everything Jesus was doing. So John
called for two of his disciples, 19 and he sent them to the Lord to ask him, "Are you the
Messiah we've been expecting, or should we keep looking for someone else?"
20 John's two disciples found Jesus and said to him, "John the Baptist sent us to ask, 'Are
you the Messiah we've been expecting, or should we keep looking for someone else?'"
21 At that very time, he cured many people of their various diseases, and he cast out
evil spirits and restored sight to the blind. 22 Then he told John's disciples, "Go back to
John and tell him what you have seen and heard—the blind see, the lame walk, the lepers
are cured, the deaf hear, the dead are raised to life, and the Good News is being preached
to the poor. 23 And tell him, 'God blesses those who are not offended by me.*'"
24 After they left, Jesus talked to the crowd about John. "Who is this man in the
wilderness that you went out to see? Did you find him weak as a reed, moved by every
breath of wind? 25 Or were you expecting to see a man dressed in expensive clothes? No,
people who wear beautiful clothes and live in luxury are found in palaces, not in the
wilderness. 26 Were you looking for a prophet? Yes, and he is more than a prophet. 27 John
is the man to whom the Scriptures refer when they say,

> 'Look, I am sending my messenger before you,
> and he will prepare your way before you.'*

28 I tell you, of all who have ever lived, none is greater than John. Yet even the most
insignificant person in the Kingdom of God is greater than he is!"
29 When they heard this, all the people, including the unjust tax collectors, agreed that
God's plan was right,* for they had been baptized by John. 30 But the Pharisees and
experts in religious law had rejected God's plan for them, for they had refused John's
baptism.
31 "How shall I describe this generation?" Jesus asked. "With what will I compare
them? 32 They are like a group of children playing a game in the public square. They
complain to their friends, 'We played wedding songs, and you weren't happy, so we
played funeral songs, but you weren't sad.' 33 For John the Baptist didn't drink wine and
he often fasted, and you say, 'He's demon possessed.' 34 And I, the Son of Man, feast and
drink, and you say, 'He's a glutton and a drunkard, and a friend of the worst sort of
sinners!' 35 But wisdom is shown to be right by the lives of those who follow it.*"

7:19 Mal 3:1-3
7:22 †Isa 29:18-19; 35:5-6; 42:18; 61:1 Luke 4:18
7:26 Luke 1:76
7:27 †Exod 23:20 †Mal 3:1
7:28 Luke 1:15
7:29-30 Matt 21:32 Luke 3:7, 12
7:33 Luke 1:15
7:35 1 Cor 1:24

7:23 Or *who don't fall away because of me.* **7:27** Mal 3:1. **7:29** Or *praised God.* **7:35** Or *But wisdom is justified by all her children.*

7:18-23 John was confused because the reports he received about Jesus were unexpected and incomplete. John's doubts were natural, and Jesus didn't rebuke him for them. Instead, Jesus responded in a way that John would understand: Jesus explained that he had accomplished what the Messiah was supposed to accomplish. God can handle our doubts, and he welcomes our questions. Do you have questions about Jesus—about who he is or what he expects of you? Admit them to yourself and to God, and begin looking for answers. Only as you face your doubts honestly can you begin to resolve them.

7:20-22 The proofs listed here for Jesus being the Messiah are significant. They consist of observable deeds, not theories—actions that Jesus' contemporaries saw and reported for us to read today. The prophets had said that the Messiah would do these very acts (see Isaiah 35:5, 6; 61:1). These physical proofs helped John—and will help all of us—to recognize who Jesus is.

7:28 Of all people, no one fulfilled his God-given purpose better than John. Yet in God's Kingdom, all who come after John have a greater spiritual heritage because they have clearer knowledge of the purpose of Jesus' death and resurrection. John was the last to function like the Old Testament prophets, the last to prepare the people for the coming messianic age. Jesus was not contrasting the man John with individual Christians; he was contrasting life before Christ with life in the fullness of Christ's Kingdom.

7:29, 30 The tax collectors (who embodied evil in most people's minds) and common people heard John's message and repented. In contrast, the Pharisees and experts in the law—religious leaders—rejected his words. Wanting to live their own way, they justified their own point of view and refused to listen to other ideas. Rather than trying to force your plans on God, try to discover his plan for you.

7:31-35 The religious leaders hated anyone who spoke the truth and exposed their own hypocrisy, and they did not bother to be consistent in their faultfinding. They criticized John the Baptist because he fasted and drank no wine; they criticized Jesus because he ate heartily and drank wine with tax collectors and "sinners." Their real objection to both men, of course, had nothing to do with dietary habits. What the Pharisees and experts in the law couldn't stand was being exposed for their hypocrisy.

7:33, 34 The Pharisees weren't troubled by their inconsistency toward John the Baptist and Jesus. They were good at justifying their "wisdom." Most of us can find compelling reasons to do or believe whatever suits our purposes. If we do not examine our ideas in the light of God's truth, however, we may be just as obviously self-serving as the Pharisees.

7:35 Those who "followed" wisdom were the followers of Jesus and John. These followers lived changed lives. Their righteous living demonstrated the wisdom that Jesus and John taught.

A Sinful Woman Anoints Jesus' Feet (**72**)

7:36-50 Matt 26:6-13 Mark 14:3-9 John 12:1-8
36 One of the Pharisees asked Jesus to come to his home for a meal, so Jesus accepted the
invitation and sat down to eat. 37 A certain immoral woman heard he was there and
brought a beautiful jar* filled with expensive perfume. 38 Then she knelt behind him at
7:37 Luke 8:2
his feet, weeping. Her tears fell on his feet, and she wiped them off with her hair. Then
she kept kissing his feet and putting perfume on them.
7:39 Matt 21:11
39 When the Pharisee who was the host saw what was happening and who the woman
was, he said to himself, "This proves that Jesus is no prophet. If God had really sent him,
he would know what kind of woman is touching him. She's a sinner!"
40 Then Jesus spoke up and answered his thoughts. "Simon," he said to the Pharisee,
"I have something to say to you."
"All right, Teacher," Simon replied, "go ahead."
41 Then Jesus told him this story: "A man loaned money to two people—five hundred
7:42 Matt 18:27 Col 2:13
pieces of silver* to one and fifty pieces to the other. 42 But neither of them could repay
him, so he kindly forgave them both, canceling their debts. Who do you suppose loved
him more after that?"
43 Simon answered, "I suppose the one for whom he canceled the larger debt."
7:44 Gen 18:4 1 Tim 5:10
"That's right," Jesus said. 44 Then he turned to the woman and said to Simon, "Look
at this woman kneeling here. When I entered your home, you didn't offer me water to
wash the dust from my feet, but she has washed them with her tears and wiped them with
7:45 Rom 16:16 1 Cor 16:20 2 Cor 13:12 1 Thes 5:26 1 Pet 5:14
her hair. 45 You didn't give me a kiss of greeting, but she has kissed my feet again and
again from the time I first came in. 46 You neglected the courtesy of olive oil to anoint
my head, but she has anointed my feet with rare perfume. 47 I tell you, her sins—and they
are many—have been forgiven, so she has shown me much love. But a person who is
7:46 2 Sam 12:20 Ps 23:5
forgiven little shows only little love." 48 Then Jesus said to the woman, "Your sins are
forgiven."
7:48-49 Luke 5:20-21
49 The men at the table said among themselves, "Who does this man think he is, going
around forgiving sins?"
7:50 Matt 9:22
50 And Jesus said to the woman, "Your faith has saved you; go in peace."

Women Accompany Jesus and the Disciples (**73**)

8:1 Matt 4:23
8 Not long afterward Jesus began a tour of the nearby cities and villages to announce
the Good News concerning the Kingdom of God. He took his twelve disciples with
8:2 Matt 27:55-56 Mark 15:40-41 Luke 23:49
him, 2 along with some women he had healed and from whom he had cast out evil spirits.
Among them were Mary Magdalene, from whom he had cast out seven demons;

7:37 Greek *an alabaster jar.* **7:41** Greek *500 denarii.* A denarius was the equivalent of a full day's wage.

7:36 A similar incident occurred later in Jesus' ministry (see Matthew 26:6-13; Mark 14:3-9; John 12:1-11).

7:38 Although the woman was not an invited guest, she entered the house anyway and knelt behind Jesus at his feet. In Jesus' day, it was customary to recline while eating. Dinner guests would lie on couches with their heads near the table, propping themselves up on one elbow and stretching their feet out behind them. The woman could easily anoint Jesus' feet without approaching the table.

7:44ff Again Luke contrasts the Pharisees with sinners—and again the sinners come out ahead. Simon had committed several social errors in neglecting to wash Jesus' feet (a courtesy extended to guests because sandaled feet got very dirty), anoint his head with oil, and offer him the kiss of greeting. Did Simon perhaps feel that he was too good to treat Jesus as an equal? The sinful woman, by contrast, lavished tears, expensive perfume, and kisses on her Savior. In this story it is the grateful immoral woman, and not the stingy religious leader, whose sins were forgiven. Although it is God's grace through faith that saves us, and not acts of love or generosity, this woman's act demonstrated her true faith, and Jesus honored her faith.

7:47 Overflowing love is the natural response to forgiveness and the appropriate consequence of faith. But only those who realize the depth of their sin can appreciate the complete forgiveness God offers them. Jesus has rescued all of his followers, whether they were once extremely wicked or conventionally good, from eternal death. Do you appreciate the wideness of God's mercy? Are you grateful for his forgiveness?

7:49, 50 The Pharisees believed that only God could forgive sins, so they wondered why this man Jesus was saying that the woman's sins were forgiven. They did not grasp the fact that Jesus was indeed God.

8:2, 3 Jesus lifted women up from the agony of degradation and servitude to the joy of fellowship and service. In Jewish culture, women were not supposed to learn from rabbis. By allowing these women to travel with him, Jesus was showing that all people are equal under God. These women supported Jesus' ministry with their own money. They owed a great debt to him because he had driven demons out of some and had healed others.

8:2, 3 Here we catch a glimpse of a few of the people behind the scenes in Jesus' ministry. The ministry of those in the foreground is often supported by those whose work is less visible but just as essential. Offer your resources to God, whether or not you will be on center stage.

3Joanna, the wife of Chuza, Herod's business manager; Susanna; and many others who **8:3** Matt 14:1
were contributing from their own resources to support Jesus and his disciples.

Jesus Tells the Parable of the Four Soils (**77**/Matthew 13:1-9; Mark 4:1-9)

4One day Jesus told this story to a large crowd that had gathered from many towns to
hear him: 5"A farmer went out to plant some seed. As he scattered it across his field,
some seed fell on a footpath, where it was stepped on, and the birds came and ate it.
6Other seed fell on shallow soil with underlying rock. This seed began to grow, but
soon it withered and died for lack of moisture. 7Other seed fell among thorns that shot
up and choked out the tender blades. 8Still other seed fell on fertile soil. This seed
grew and produced a crop one hundred times as much as had been planted." When he
had said this, he called out, "Anyone who is willing to hear should listen and
understand!"

Jesus Explains the Parable of the Four Soils (**78**/Matthew 13:10-23; Mark 4:10-25)

9His disciples asked him what the story meant. 10He replied, "You have been permitted **8:10** †Isa 6:9-10
to understand the secrets of the Kingdom of God. But I am using these stories to conceal
everything about it from outsiders, so that the Scriptures might be fulfilled:

'They see what I do,
 but they don't really see;
they hear what I say,
 but they don't understand.'*

11"This is the meaning of the story: The seed is God's message. 12The seed that fell **8:11** 1 Pet 1:23
on the hard path represents those who hear the message, but then the Devil comes and
steals it away and prevents them from believing and being saved. 13The rocky soil **8:12** 1 Cor 1:21
represents those who hear the message with joy. But like young plants in such soil, their
roots don't go very deep. They believe for a while, but they wilt when the hot winds of
testing blow. 14The thorny ground represents those who hear and accept the message, **8:14** Matt 19:23
but all too quickly the message is crowded out by the cares and riches and pleasures of 1 Tim 6:9, 10
this life. And so they never grow into maturity. 15But the good soil represents honest, 2 Tim 4:10
good-hearted people who hear God's message, cling to it, and steadily produce a huge
harvest.

16"No one would light a lamp and then cover it up or put it under a bed. No, lamps are **8:16** Matt 5:15
mounted in the open, where they can be seen by those entering the house. 17For Luke 11:33
everything that is hidden or secret will eventually be brought to light and made plain to **8:17** Matt 10:26

8:10 Isa 6:9.

8:4 Jesus often communicated spiritual truth through short stories (often called parables). These parables describe a familiar object or situation and give it a startling new twist. By linking the known with the hidden and forcing listeners to think, parables can point to spiritual truths. A parable compels listeners to discover the truth for themselves, and it conceals the truth from those too lazy or dull to understand it. In reading Jesus' parables, we must be careful not to read too much into them. Most have only one point and one meaning.

8:5 Why would a farmer allow precious seed to land on the footpath, on rocks, or among thorns? This is not an irresponsible farmer scattering seeds at random. He is using the acceptable method of seeding a large field—tossing it by handfuls as he walks through the field. His goal is to get as much seed as possible to take root in good soil, but there is inevitable waste as some falls or is blown into less productive areas. That some of the seed produced no crop was not the fault of the faithful farmer or of the seed. The yield depended on the condition of the soil where the seed fell. It is our responsibility to spread the seed (God's message), but we should not give up when some of our efforts fail. Remember, not every seed falls on good soil.

8:10 Why didn't the crowds understand Jesus' words? Perhaps they were looking for a military leader or a political Messiah and could not fit his gentle teaching style into their preconceived idea. Perhaps they were afraid of pressure from religious leaders and did not want to look too deeply into Jesus' words. God told Isaiah that people would hear without understanding and see without perceiving (Isaiah 6:9), and that kind of reaction confronted Jesus. The story of the sower was an accurate picture of the people's reaction to the rest of his stories.

8:11-15 "Path" people, like many of the religious leaders, refused to believe God's message. "Rock" people, like many in the crowds who followed Jesus, believed his message but never got around to doing anything about it. "Thorn patch" people, overcome by worries and the lure of materialism, left no room in their lives for God. "Good soil" people, in contrast to all the other groups, followed Jesus no matter what the cost. Which type of soil are you?

8:16, 17 When the light of the truth about Jesus illuminates us, it is our duty to shine that light to help others. Our witness for Christ should be public, not hidden. We should not keep the benefits for ourselves alone but pass them on to others. In order to be helpful, we need to be well placed. Seek opportunities to be there when unbelievers need help.

8:18 Matt 25:29 Luke 19:26
all. [18]So be sure to pay attention to what you hear. To those who are open to my teaching,
more understanding will be given. But to those who are not listening, even what they
think they have will be taken away from them."

Jesus Describes His True Family (**76**/Matthew 12:46-50; Mark 3:31-35)

[19]Once when Jesus' mother and brothers came to see him, they couldn't get to him
because of the crowds. [20]Someone told Jesus, "Your mother and your brothers are
outside, and they want to see you."

[21]Jesus replied, "My mother and my brothers are all those who hear the message of
God and obey it."

Jesus Calms the Storm (**87**/Matthew 8:23-27; Mark 4:35-41)

[22]One day Jesus said to his disciples, "Let's cross over to the other side of the lake." So
they got into a boat and started out. [23]On the way across, Jesus lay down for a nap, and
while he was sleeping the wind began to rise. A fierce storm developed that threatened
to swamp them, and they were in real danger.

[24]The disciples woke him up, shouting, "Master, Master, we're going to drown!"

So Jesus rebuked the wind and the raging waves. The storm stopped and all was calm!
[25]Then he asked them, "Where is your faith?"

And they were filled with awe and amazement. They said to one another, "Who is this
man, that even the winds and waves obey him?"

JESUS AND WOMEN

Jesus talks to a Samaritan woman at the well	John 4:1–26
Jesus raises a widow's son from the dead	Luke 7:11–17
A sinful woman anoints Jesus' feet	Luke 7:36–50
The adulterous woman	John 8:1–11
The group of women travels with Jesus	Luke 8:1–3
Jesus visits Mary and Martha	Luke 10:38–42
Jesus heals a crippled woman	Luke 13:10–17
Jesus heals the daughter of a Gentile woman	Mark 7:24–30
Weeping women follow Jesus on his way to the cross	Luke 23:27–31
Jesus' mother and other women gather at the cross	John 19:25–27
Jesus appears to Mary Magdalene	Mark 16:9–11
Jesus appears to other women after his resurrection	Matthew 28:8–10

As a non-Jew recording the words and works of Jesus' life, Luke demonstrates a special sensitivity to other "outsiders" with whom Jesus came into contact. For instance, Luke records five events involving women that are not mentioned in the other Gospels. In first-century Jewish culture, women were usually treated as second-class citizens with few of the rights men had. But Jesus crossed those barriers, and Luke showed the special care Jesus had for women. Jesus treated all people with equal respect. The above passages tell of his encounters with women.

8:18 Applying God's Word helps us grow. This is a principle of growth in physical, mental, and spiritual life. For example, a muscle, when exercised, will grow stronger, but an unused muscle will grow weak and flabby. If you are not growing stronger, you are growing weaker; it is impossible for you to stand still. How are you using what God has taught you?

8:21 Jesus' true family is comprised of those who hear *and* obey his words. Hearing without obeying is not enough. As Jesus loved his mother (see John 19:25-27), so he loves us. Christ offers us an intimate family relationship with him.

8:23 The Sea of Galilee (actually a large lake) is even today the scene of fierce storms, sometimes with waves as high as 20 feet. Jesus' disciples were not frightened without cause. Even though several of them were expert fishermen and knew how to handle a boat, their peril was real.

8:25 When caught in the storms of life, it is easy to think that God has lost control and that we're at the mercy of the winds of fate. In reality, God is sovereign. He controls the history of the world as well as our personal destiny. Just as Jesus calmed the waves, he can calm whatever storms you may face.

Jesus Sends Demons into a Herd of Pigs (**88**/Matthew 8:28-34; Mark 5:1-20)
26 So they arrived in the land of the Gerasenes,* across the lake from Galilee. 27 As Jesus
was climbing out of the boat, a man who was possessed by demons came out to meet
him. Homeless and naked, he had lived in a cemetery for a long time. 28 As soon as he — **8:28**
saw Jesus, he shrieked and fell to the ground before him, screaming, "Why are you — Matt 8:29; Mark 1:23-24
bothering me, Jesus, Son of the Most High God? Please, I beg you, don't torture me!"
29 For Jesus had already commanded the evil spirit to come out of him. This spirit had
often taken control of the man. Even when he was shackled with chains, he simply broke
them and rushed out into the wilderness, completely under the demon's power.
30 "What is your name?" Jesus asked.
"Legion," he replied—for the man was filled with many demons. 31 The demons kept — **8:31**
begging Jesus not to send them into the Bottomless Pit. 32 A large herd of pigs was feeding — Rev 9:1-2, 11; 20:3
on the hillside nearby, and the demons pleaded with him to let them enter into the pigs. Jesus
gave them permission. 33 So the demons came out of the man and entered the pigs, and the
whole herd plunged down the steep hillside into the lake, where they drowned.
34 When the herdsmen saw it, they fled to the nearby city and the surrounding
countryside, spreading the news as they ran. 35 A crowd soon gathered around Jesus, for
they wanted to see for themselves what had happened. And they saw the man who had
been possessed by demons sitting quietly at Jesus' feet, clothed and sane. And the whole
crowd was afraid. 36 Then those who had seen what happened told the others how the
demon-possessed man had been healed. 37 And all the people in that region begged Jesus — **8:37**
to go away and leave them alone, for a great wave of fear swept over them. — Acts 16:39
So Jesus returned to the boat and left, crossing back to the other side of the lake. 38 The
man who had been demon possessed begged to go, too, but Jesus said, 39 "No, go back

8:26 Some manuscripts read *Gadarenes;* other manuscripts read *Gergesenes.* See Matt 8:28; Mark 5:1.

HEALING A DEMON-POSSESSED MAN
As he traveled through Galilee, Jesus told many parables and met many people, as recorded in Matthew and Mark. Later, from Capernaum, Jesus and the disciples set out in a boat, only to encounter a fierce storm. Jesus calmed the storm and, when they landed, exorcised a "legion" of demons.

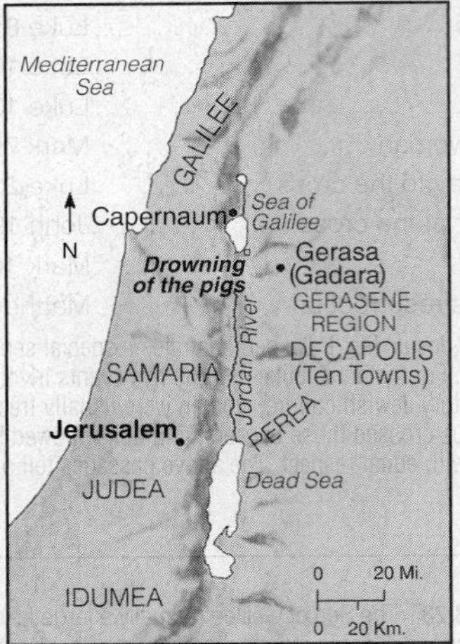

8:26 The land of the Gerasenes was a Gentile region southeast of the Sea of Galilee, home of the Ten Towns. These were Greek cities that belonged to no country and were self-governing. Although Jews would not have raised pigs because the Jewish religion labeled them unclean, the Gentiles had no such aversion.

8:27, 28 These demons recognized Jesus and his authority immediately. They knew who Jesus was and what his great power could do to them. Demons, Satan's messengers, are powerful and destructive. Still active today, they attempt to distort and destroy people's relationship with God. Demons and demon possession are real. It is vital that believers recognize the power of Satan and his demons, but we shouldn't let curiosity lead us to get involved with demonic forces (Deuteronomy 18:10-12). Demons are powerless against those who trust in Jesus. If we resist the Devil, he will leave us alone (James 4:7).

8:29-31 The demons begged Jesus to spare them from the Bottomless Pit, which is also mentioned in Revelation 9:1 and 20:1-3 as the place of confinement for Satan and his messengers. The demons, of course, knew all about this place of confinement, and they didn't want to go there.

8:30 The demon's name was Legion. A legion was the largest unit in the Roman army, having between 3,000 and 6,000 soldiers. The man was possessed by not one but many demons.

8:33 Why didn't Jesus just destroy these demons—or send them to the Bottomless Pit? Because the time for such work had not yet come. He healed many people of the destructive effects of demon possession, but he did not yet destroy demons. The same question could be asked today—why doesn't Jesus stop all the evil in the world? His time for that has not yet come. But it will come. The book of Revelation portrays the future victory of Jesus over Satan, his demons, and all evil.

8:33-37 The demons destroyed the pigs, which hurt the finances of those tending the pigs, but can pigs and money compare with a human life? A man had been freed from the Devil's power, but the people thought only about their livestock. People have always tended to value financial gain above needy people. Throughout history, most wars have been fought to protect economic interests. Much injustice and oppression, both at home and abroad, is the direct result of some individual's or company's urge to get rich. People are continually being sacrificed to the god of money. Don't think more highly of "pigs" than of people. Think carefully about how your decisions will affect other human beings, and be willing to choose a simpler life-style if it will keep other people from being harmed.

8:38, 39 Often Jesus asked those he healed to be quiet about the healing, but he urged this man to return to his family and tell them what God had done for him. Why? (1) Jesus knew the man would be an effective witness to those who knew his previous condition and could attest to the miraculous healing. (2) Jesus wanted to expand his ministry by introducing his message into this Gentile area. (3) Jesus knew that the Gentiles, since they were not expecting a Messiah, would not divert his ministry by trying to crown him king. When God touches your life, don't be afraid to share the wonderful events with your family and friends.

to your family and tell them all the wonderful things God has done for you." So he went
all through the city telling about the great thing Jesus had done for him.

Jesus Heals a Bleeding Woman and Restores a Girl to Life
(**89**/Matthew 9:18-26; Mark 5:21-43)

40On the other side of the lake the crowds received Jesus with open arms because they
had been waiting for him. 41And now a man named Jairus, a leader of the local
synagogue, came and fell down at Jesus' feet, begging him to come home with him. 42His
only child was dying, a little girl twelve years old.

8:43 Lev 15:25-30

As Jesus went with him, he was surrounded by the crowds. 43And there was a woman
in the crowd who had had a hemorrhage for twelve years. She had spent everything she
had on doctors* and still could find no cure. 44She came up behind Jesus and touched
the fringe of his robe. Immediately, the bleeding stopped.
45"Who touched me?" Jesus asked.
Everyone denied it, and Peter said, "Master, this whole crowd is pressing up against
you."

8:46 Luke 5:17; 6:19

46But Jesus told him, "No, someone deliberately touched me, for I felt healing power
go out from me." 47When the woman realized that Jesus knew, she began to tremble and
fell to her knees before him. The whole crowd heard her explain why she had touched

8:48 Matt 9:22 Mark 5:34 Luke 7:50; 17:19; 18:42

him and that she had been immediately healed. 48"Daughter," he said to her, "your faith
has made you well. Go in peace."
49While he was still speaking to her, a messenger arrived from Jairus's home with the
message, "Your little girl is dead. There's no use troubling the Teacher now."
50But when Jesus heard what had happened, he said to Jairus, "Don't be afraid. Just
trust me, and she will be all right."
51When they arrived at the house, Jesus wouldn't let anyone go in with him except Peter,

8:52 Luke 7:13

James, John, and the little girl's father and mother. 52The house was filled with people
weeping and wailing, but he said, "Stop the weeping! She isn't dead; she is only asleep."
53But the crowd laughed at him because they all knew she had died. 54Then Jesus took

8:54 Luke 7:14

her by the hand and said in a loud voice, "Get up, my child!" 55And at that moment her
life returned, and she immediately stood up! Then Jesus told them to give her something
to eat. 56Her parents were overwhelmed, but Jesus insisted that they not tell anyone what

8:56 Matt 8:4 Mark 7:36 Luke 5:14

had happened.

8:43 Some manuscripts omit *She had spent everything she had on doctors.*

8:41 The synagogue was the local center of worship. The synagogue leader was responsible for administration, building maintenance, and worship supervision. It would have been quite unusual for a respected synagogue leader to fall at the feet of an itinerant preacher and beg him to heal his daughter. Jesus honored this man's humble faith (8:50, 54-56).

8:43-48 Many people surrounded Jesus as he made his way toward Jairus's house. It was virtually impossible to get through the multitude, but one woman fought her way desperately through the crowd in order to touch Jesus. As soon as she did so, she was healed. What a difference there is between the crowds that are curious about Jesus and the few who reach out and touch him! Today, many people are familiar with who Jesus is, but nothing in their lives is changed by knowing he is God's Son. It is only faith in Christ that releases God's healing power. Are you just curious about God, or do you reach out to him in faith, knowing that his mercy will bring healing to your body, soul, and spirit?

8:45 It isn't that Jesus didn't know who had touched him; it's that he wanted the woman to step forward and identify herself. Jesus wanted to teach her that his cloak did not have magical properties; it was her faith in him that had healed her. He may also have wanted to teach the crowds a lesson. According to Jewish law, a man who touched a menstruating woman became ceremonially unclean (Leviticus 15:19-28). This was true whether her bleeding was normal or, as in this woman's case, the result of an abnormal condition. To protect themselves from such defilement, Jewish men carefully avoided touching, speaking to, or even looking at women. By contrast, Jesus proclaimed to hundreds of people that this "unclean" woman had touched him—and then he healed her. In Jesus' mind, this suffering woman was not to be overlooked. As God's creation, she deserved attention and respect.

8:56 Jesus told the parents not to talk about their daughter's healing because he knew the facts would speak for themselves. Besides, Jesus was concerned for his ministry. He did not want to be known as just a miracle worker; he wanted people to listen to his words that could heal their broken spiritual lives.

Jesus Sends Out the Twelve Apostles (**93**/Matthew 10:1-15; Mark 6:7-13)

9 One day Jesus called together his twelve apostles and gave them power and authority
to cast out demons and to heal all diseases. 2 Then he sent them out to tell everyone
about the coming of the Kingdom of God and to heal the sick. 3 "Don't even take along **9:3**
a walking stick," he instructed them, "nor a traveler's bag, nor food, nor money. Not even Luke 10:4; 22:35
an extra coat. 4 When you enter each village, be a guest in only one home. 5 If the people **9:4** Luke 10:5-7
of the village won't receive your message when you enter it, shake off its dust from your **9:5**
feet as you leave. It is a sign that you have abandoned that village to its fate." Luke 10:10-11 Acts 13:51
6 So they began their circuit of the villages, preaching the Good News and healing the
sick.

Herod Kills John the Baptist (**95**/Matthew 14:1-12; Mark 6:14-29)

7 When reports of Jesus' miracles reached Herod Antipas,* he was worried and puzzled
because some were saying, "This is John the Baptist come back to life again." 8 Others **9:8**
were saying, "It is Elijah or some other ancient prophet risen from the dead." Matt 11:14
9 "I beheaded John," Herod said, "so who is this man about whom I hear such strange **9:9** Luke 23:8
stories?" And he tried to see him.

Jesus Feeds Five Thousand (**96**/Matthew 14:13-21; Mark 6:30-44; John 6:1-15)

10 When the apostles returned, they told Jesus everything they had done. Then he slipped
quietly away with them toward the town of Bethsaida. 11 But the crowds found out where
he was going, and they followed him. And he welcomed them, teaching them about the
Kingdom of God and curing those who were ill. 12 Late in the afternoon the twelve

9:7 Greek *Herod the tetrarch.* He was a son of King Herod and was ruler over one of the four districts in Palestine.

9:1-10 Note Jesus' methods of leadership. He empowered his disciples (9:1), gave them specific instructions so they knew what to do (9:3, 4), told them how to deal with tough times (9:5), and held them accountable (9:10). As you lead others, study the Master Leader's pattern. Which of these elements do you need to incorporate into your leadership?

9:2 Jesus announced his Kingdom by both preaching and healing. If he had limited himself to preaching, people might have seen his Kingdom as spiritual only. On the other hand, if he had healed without preaching, people might not have realized the spiritual importance of his mission. Most of his listeners expected a Messiah who would bring wealth and power to their nation; they preferred material benefits to spiritual discernment. The truth about Jesus is that he is both God and man, both spiritual and physical; and the salvation that he offers is both for the soul and the body. Any group or teaching that emphasizes soul at the expense of body, or body at the expense of soul, is in danger of distorting Jesus' Good News.

9:3, 4 Why were the disciples instructed to depend on others while they went from town to town preaching the Good News? Their purpose was to blanket Judea with Jesus' message, and by traveling light they could move quickly. Their dependence on others had other good effects as well: (1) It clearly showed that the Messiah had not come to offer wealth to his followers; (2) it forced the disciples to rely on God's power and not on their own provision; (3) it involved the villagers and made them more eager to hear the message. This was an excellent approach for the disciples' short-term mission; it was not intended, however, to be a permanent way of life for them.

9:4 The disciples were told to stay in only one home in each town because they were not to offend their hosts by moving to a home that was more comfortable or socially prominent. To remain in one home was not a burden for the homeowner, because the disciples' stay in each community was short.

9:5 Shaking the dust of unaccepting towns from their feet had deep cultural implications. Pious Jews would do this after passing through Gentile cities to show their separation from Gentile practices. If the disciples shook the dust of a *Jewish* town from their feet, it would show their separation from Jews who rejected their Messiah. This action also showed that the disciples were not responsible for how the people responded to their message. Neither are we responsible if we have carefully and truthfully presented Christ but our message is rejected. Like the disciples, we must move on to others whom God desires to reach.

9:7 For more information on Herod Antipas, see his Profile in Mark 6.

9:7, 8 It was so difficult for the people to accept Jesus as the Son of God that they tried to come up with other solutions—most of which sound quite unbelievable to us. Many thought that he must be someone who had come back to life, perhaps John the Baptist or another prophet. Some suggested that he was Elijah, the great prophet who did not die but was taken to heaven in a chariot of fire (2 Kings 2:1-11). Very few found the correct answer, as Peter did (9:20). For many people today, it is still not easy to accept Jesus as the fully human yet fully divine Son of God. People are still trying to find alternate explanations—a great prophet, a radical political leader, a self-deceived rabble-rouser. None of these explanations can account for Jesus' miracles or especially his glorious resurrection—so these realities, too, have to be explained away. In the end, the attempts to explain away Jesus are far more difficult to believe than the truth.

9:9 For the story of why Herod had John beheaded, see Mark 6:14-29.

9:10, 11 Jesus had tried to slip quietly away from the crowds, but they found out where he was going and followed him. Instead of showing impatience at this interruption, Jesus welcomed the people and ministered to their needs. How do you see people who interrupt your schedule—as nuisances or as the reason for your life and ministry?

9:11 The Kingdom of God was a focal point of Jesus' teaching. He explained that it was not just a future Kingdom; it was among them, embodied in him, the Messiah. Even though the Kingdom will not be complete until Jesus comes again in glory, we do not have to wait to taste it. The Kingdom of God begins in the hearts of those who believe in Jesus (17:21). It is as present with us today as it was with the Judeans almost 2,000 years ago.

disciples came to him and said, "Send the crowds away to the nearby villages and farms,
so they can find food and lodging for the night. There is nothing to eat here in this
deserted place."
[13]But Jesus said, "You feed them."
"Impossible!" they protested. "We have only five loaves of bread and two fish. Or are
you expecting us to go and buy enough food for this whole crowd?" [14]For there were
about five thousand men there.
"Just tell them to sit down on the ground in groups of about fifty each," Jesus replied.
[15]So the people all sat down. [16]Jesus took the five loaves and two fish, looked up toward
heaven, and asked God's blessing on the food. Breaking the loaves into pieces, he kept
9:17 2 Kgs 4:44 giving the bread and fish to the disciples to give to the people. [17]They all ate as much as
they wanted, and they picked up twelve baskets of leftovers!

Jesus singled out three of his 12 disciples for special training. James, his brother John, and Peter made up this inner circle. Each eventually played a key role in the early church. Peter became a great speaker, John became a major writer, and James was the first of the 12 disciples to die for his faith.

The fact that his name is always mentioned before John's indicates that James was the older brother. Zebedee, their father, owned a fishing business in which they worked alongside Peter and Andrew. When Peter, Andrew, and John left Galilee to see John the Baptist, James stayed back with the boats and fishing nets. Later, when Jesus called them, James was as eager as his partners to follow.

James enjoyed being in the inner circle of Jesus' disciples, but he misunderstood Jesus' purpose. He and his brother even tried to secure their role in Jesus' Kingdom by asking Jesus to promise them each a special position. Like the other disciples, James had a limited view of what Jesus was doing on earth, picturing only an earthly kingdom that would overthrow Rome and restore Israel's former glory. But above all, James wanted to be with Jesus. He had found the right leader, even though he was still on the wrong timetable. It took Jesus' death and resurrection to correct his view.

James was the first of the 12 disciples to die for the gospel. He was willing to die because he knew Jesus had conquered death, the doorway to eternal life. Our expectations about life will be limited if this life is all we can see. Jesus promised eternal life to those willing to trust him. If we believe this promise, he will give us the courage to stand for him even during dangerous times.

Strengths and accomplishments
- One of the 12 disciples
- One of a special inner circle of three with Peter and John
- First of the 12 disciples to be killed for his faith

Weaknesses and mistakes:
- Two outbursts from James indicate struggles with temper (Luke 9:54) and selfishness (Mark 10:37). Both times, he and his brother, John, spoke as one

Lesson from his life:
- Loss of life is not too heavy a price to pay for following Jesus

Vital statistics:
- Where: Galilee
- Occupations: Fisherman, disciple
- Relatives: Father: Zebedee. Mother: Salome. Brother: John
- Contemporaries: Jesus, Pilate, Herod Agrippa

Key verses: "Then James and John, the sons of Zebedee, came over and spoke to him. 'Teacher,' they said, 'we want you to do us a favor.' 'What is it?' he asked. 'In your glorious Kingdom, we want to sit in places of honor next to you,' they said, 'one at your right and the other at your left'." (Mark 10:35–37).

James's story is told in the Gospels. He is also mentioned in Acts 1:13 and 12:2.

9:13, 14 When the disciples expressed concern about where the crowd of thousands would eat, Jesus offered a surprising solution: "You feed them." The disciples protested, focusing their attention on what they didn't have (food and money). Do you think God would ask you to do something that you and he together couldn't handle? Don't let your lack of resources blind you to God's power.

9:16, 17 Why did Jesus bother to feed these people? He could just as easily have sent them on their way. But Jesus does not ignore needs. He is concerned with every aspect of our life—the physical as well as the spiritual. As we work to bring wholeness to people's lives, we must never ignore the fact that all of us have both physical and spiritual needs. It is impossible to minister effectively to one type of need without considering the other.

Peter Says Jesus Is the Messiah (**109**/Matthew 16:13-20; Mark 8:27-30)

18 One day as Jesus was alone, praying, he came over to his disciples and asked them,
"Who do people say I am?"
19 "Well," they replied, "some say John the Baptist, some say Elijah, and others say
you are one of the other ancient prophets risen from the dead."
20 Then he asked them, "Who do you say I am?"
Peter replied, "You are the Messiah sent from God!"

9:19 Luke 9:7-8
9:20 John 6:68-69

Jesus Predicts His Death the First Time (**110**/Matthew 16:21-28; Mark 8:31—9:1)

21 Jesus warned them not to tell anyone about this. 22 "For I, the Son of Man, must suffer
many terrible things," he said. "I will be rejected by the leaders, the leading priests, and the
teachers of religious law. I will be killed, but three days later I will be raised from the dead."
23 Then he said to the crowd, "If any of you wants to be my follower, you must put
aside your selfish ambition, shoulder your cross daily, and follow me. 24 If you try to keep
your life for yourself, you will lose it. But if you give up your life for me, you will find
true life. 25 And how do you benefit if you gain the whole world but lose or forfeit your
own soul in the process? 26 If a person is ashamed of me and my message, I, the Son of
Man, will be ashamed of that person when I return in my glory and in the glory of the
Father and the holy angels. 27 And I assure you that some of you standing here right now
will not die before you see the Kingdom of God."

9:23 Matt 10:38; Luke 14:27
9:24 Matt 10:39; Luke 17:33; John 12:25
9:26 Matt 10:33; Luke 12:9; 2 Tim 2:12

Jesus Is Transfigured on the Mountain (**111**/Matthew 17:1-13; Mark 9:2-13)

28 About eight days later Jesus took Peter, James, and John to a mountain to pray. 29 And
as he was praying, the appearance of his face changed, and his clothing became dazzling
white. 30 Then two men, Moses and Elijah, appeared and began talking with Jesus.
31 They were glorious to see. And they were speaking of how he was about to fulfill God's
plan by dying in Jerusalem.

9:31-32 2 Pet 1:15-16

9:18-20 The Christian faith goes beyond knowing what others believe. It requires us to hold beliefs for ourselves. When Jesus asks, "Who do you say I am?" he wants us to take a stand. Who do *you* say Jesus is?

9:21 Jesus told his disciples not to tell anyone that he was the Christ, because at this point they didn't fully understand the significance of that confession—nor would anyone else. Everyone still expected the Messiah to come as a conquering king. But even though Jesus was the Messiah, he still had to suffer, be rejected by the leaders, be killed, and rise from the dead. When the disciples saw all this happen to Jesus, they would understand what the Messiah had come to do. Only then would they be equipped to share the Good News around the world.

9:22 This was the turning point in Jesus' instruction to his disciples. From then on he began teaching clearly and specifically what they could expect, so that they would not be surprised when it happened. He explained that he would not *now* be the conquering Messiah because he first had to suffer, die, and rise again. But one day he would return in great glory to set up his eternal Kingdom.

9:23 Christians follow their Lord by imitating his life and obeying his commands. To shoulder one's cross meant to carry one's own cross to the place of crucifixion. Many Galileans had been killed that way by the Romans. Applied to the disciples, it meant to identify completely with Christ's message, even if it meant death. We must deny our selfish desires to use our time and money our own way and to choose our own direction in life without regard to Christ. Following Christ in this life may be costly, but in the long run, it is well worth the pain and effort.

9:23-26 People are willing to pay a high price for something they value. Is it any surprise that Jesus would demand this much commitment from his followers? There are at least three conditions that must be met by people who want to follow Jesus. We must be willing to deny self, to shoulder our cross, and to follow him. Anything less is superficial lip service.

9:24, 25 If this present life is most important to you, you will do everything you can to protect it. You will not want to do anything that might endanger your safety, health, or comfort. By contrast, if following Jesus is most important, you may find yourself in unsafe, unhealthy, and uncomfortable places. You may risk death, but you will not fear it because you know that Jesus will raise you to eternal life. Nothing material can compensate for the loss of eternal life. Jesus' disciples are not to use their lives on earth for their own pleasure; they should spend their lives serving God and others.

9:26 Luke's Greek audience would have found it difficult to understand a God who could die, just as Jesus' Jewish audience would have been perplexed by a Messiah who would let himself be captured. Both would be ashamed of Jesus if they did not look past his death to his glorious resurrection and second coming. Then they would see Jesus, not as a loser, but as the Lord of the universe, who through his death brought salvation to all people.

9:27 When Jesus said some would not die without seeing the Kingdom, he was referring (1) to Peter, James, and John, who would witness the Transfiguration eight days later, or, in a broader sense, (2) to all who would witness the Resurrection and Ascension, or (3) to all who would take part in the spread of the church after Pentecost. Jesus' listeners were not going to have to wait for another, future Messiah. The Kingdom was among them, and it would soon come in power.

9:29, 30 Jesus took Peter, James, and John to the top of a mountain to show them who he really was—not just a great prophet, but God's own Son. Moses, representing the Law, and Elijah, representing the Prophets, appeared with Jesus. Then God's voice singled out Jesus as the long-awaited Messiah, who possessed divine authority. Jesus would fulfill both the Law and the Prophets (Matthew 5:17).

32 Peter and the others were very drowsy and had fallen asleep. Now they woke up and
saw Jesus' glory and the two men standing with him. 33 As Moses and Elijah were starting
to leave, Peter, not even knowing what he was saying, blurted out, "Master, this is
wonderful! We will make three shrines*—one for you, one for Moses, and one for
Elijah." 34 But even as he was saying this, a cloud came over them; and terror gripped
9:35 Deut 18:15 Ps 2:7 Isa 42:1 Matt 3:17 2 Pet 1:17
them as it covered them.
35 Then a voice from the cloud said, "This is my Son, my Chosen One.* Listen to him."
36 When the voice died away, Jesus was there alone. They didn't tell anyone what they
had seen until long after this happened.

Jesus Heals a Demon-Possessed Boy (**112**/Matthew 17:14-21; Mark 9:14-29)

9:38 Luke 7:12
37 The next day, after they had come down the mountain, a huge crowd met Jesus. 38 A
man in the crowd called out to him, "Teacher, look at my boy, who is my only son. 39 An
evil spirit keeps seizing him, making him scream. It throws him into convulsions so that
he foams at the mouth. It is always hitting and injuring him. It hardly ever leaves him
alone. 40 I begged your disciples to cast the spirit out, but they couldn't do it."
41 "You stubborn, faithless people," Jesus said, "how long must I be with you and put
up with you? Bring him here." 42 As the boy came forward, the demon knocked him to
the ground and threw him into a violent convulsion. But Jesus rebuked the evil spirit and
9:43b-45 2 Pet 1:16
healed the boy. Then he gave him back to his father. 43 Awe gripped the people as they
saw this display of God's power.

Jesus Predicts His Death the Second Time (**113**/Matthew 17:22-23; Mark 9:30-32)

9:44 Luke 18:32
While everyone was marveling over all the wonderful things he was doing, Jesus said to
his disciples, 44 "Listen to me and remember what I say. The Son of Man is going to be
9:45 Mark 9:32 Luke 18:34
betrayed." 45 But they didn't know what he meant. Its significance was hidden from
them, so they could not understand it, and they were afraid to ask him about it.

The Disciples Argue about Who Would Be the Greatest
(**115**/Matthew 18:1-6; Mark 9:33-37)

46 Then there was an argument among them as to which of them would be the greatest.
9:47 Matt 9:4
47 But Jesus knew their thoughts, so he brought a little child to his side. 48 Then he said

9:33 Or *shelters;* Greek reads *tabernacles.* **9:35** Some manuscripts read *This is my beloved Son.*

9:33 When Peter suggested making three shrines, he may have been thinking of the Festival of Shelters, where shelters were set up to commemorate the Exodus, God's deliverance from slavery in Egypt. Peter wanted to keep Moses and Elijah with them. But this was not what God wanted. Peter's desire to build shrines for Jesus, Moses, and Elijah may also show his understanding that real faith is built on three cornerstones: the Law, the Prophets, and Jesus. But Peter grew in his understanding, and eventually he would write of Jesus as the "chosen cornerstone" of the church (1 Peter 2:6).

9:33 Peter, James, and John experienced a wonderful moment on the mountain, and they didn't want to leave. Sometimes we too have such an inspiring experience that we want to stay where we are—away from the reality and problems of our daily life. Knowing that struggles await us in the valley encourages us to linger on the mountaintop. Yet staying on top of a mountain prohibits our ministering to others. Instead of becoming spiritual giants, we would soon become dwarfed by our self-centeredness. We need times of retreat and renewal, but only so we can return to minister to the world. Our faith must make sense off the mountain as well as on it.

9:35 As God's Son, Jesus has God's power and authority; thus, his words should be our final authority. If a person's teaching is true, it will agree with Jesus' teachings. Test everything you hear against Jesus' words, and you will not be led astray. Don't be hasty to seek advice and guidance from merely human sources and thereby neglect Christ's message.

9:35 God clearly identified Jesus as his Son before saying that Peter and the others were to listen to Jesus and not to their own ideas and desires. The ability to follow Jesus comes from confidence about who he is. If we believe he is God's Son, then we surely will want to do what he says.

9:37-39 As the disciples came down from the mountain with Jesus, they passed from a reassuring experience of God's presence to a frightening experience of evil. The beauty they had just seen must have made the ugliness seem even uglier. As our spiritual vision improves and allows us to see and understand God better, we will also be able to see and understand evil better. We would be overcome by its horror if we did not have Jesus with us to take us through it safely.

9:40 Why couldn't the disciples cast out the evil spirit? For a possible answer, see the note on Mark 9:18.

9:45, 46 The disciples didn't understand Jesus' words about his death. They still thought of Jesus as only an earthly king, and they were concerned about their places in the Kingdom he would set up. So they ignored Jesus' words about his death and began arguing about who would be the greatest.

9:48 Our care for others is a measure of our greatness. How much concern do you show for others? This is a vital question that can accurately measure your greatness in God's eyes. How have you expressed your care for others lately, especially the helpless, the needy, the poor—those who can't return your love and concern? Your honest answer to that question will give you a good idea of your real greatness.

to them, "Anyone who welcomes a little child like this on my behalf welcomes me, and **9:48** Matt 10:40
anyone who welcomes me welcomes my Father who sent me. Whoever is the least Luke 10:16
among you is the greatest."

The Disciples Forbid Another to Use Jesus' Name (**116**/Mark 9:38-41)

49 John said to Jesus, "Master, we saw someone using your name to cast out demons. We
tried to stop him because he isn't in our group." **9:50** Matt 12:30
50 But Jesus said, "Don't stop him! Anyone who is not against you is for you." Luke 11:23

2. Jesus' ministry on the way to Jerusalem

Jesus Teaches about the Cost of Following Him (**122**/Matthew 8:18-22)

51 As the time drew near for his return to heaven, Jesus resolutely set out for Jerusalem. **9:51** Mark 16:19
52 He sent messengers ahead to a Samaritan village to prepare for his arrival. 53 But Luke 13:22; 17:11;
they were turned away. The people of the village refused to have anything to do with 18:31; 19:28
Jesus because he had resolved to go to Jerusalem. 54 When James and John heard **9:54**
about it, they said to Jesus, "Lord, should we order down fire from heaven to burn 2 Kgs 1:10, 12
them up*?" 55 But Jesus turned and rebuked them.* 56 So they went on to another
village.
57 As they were walking along someone said to Jesus, "I will follow you no matter
where you go."
58 But Jesus replied, "Foxes have dens to live in, and birds have nests, but I, the Son
of Man, have no home of my own, not even a place to lay my head."
59 He said to another person, "Come, be my disciple."
The man agreed, but he said, "Lord, first let me return home and bury my father."
60 Jesus replied, "Let those who are spiritually dead care for their own dead.* Your **9:60** Matt 3:2
duty is to go and preach the coming of the Kingdom of God."
61 Another said, "Yes, Lord, I will follow you, but first let me say good-bye to my **9:61**
family." 1 Kgs 19:20
62 But Jesus told him, "Anyone who puts a hand to the plow and then looks back is **9:62**
not fit for the Kingdom of God." Phil 3:13

9:54 Some manuscripts add *as Elijah did.* **9:55** Some manuscripts add *And he said, "You don't realize what your hearts are like.* 56*For the Son of Man has not come to destroy men's lives, but to save them."* **9:60** Greek *Let the dead bury their own dead.*

9:49, 50 The disciples were jealous. Nine of them together were unable to cast out a single evil spirit (9:40), but when they saw a man who was not one of their group casting out demons, they told him to stop. Our pride is hurt when someone else succeeds where we have failed, but Jesus says there is no room for such jealousy in the spiritual warfare of his Kingdom. Share Jesus' open-arms attitude toward Christian workers outside your group.

9:51 Although Jesus knew he would face persecution and death in Jerusalem, he was determined to go there. That kind of resolve should characterize our life too. When God gives us a course of action, we must move steadily toward our destination, no matter what potential hazards await us there.

9:53 After Assyria invaded Israel, the northern kingdom, and resettled it with its own people (2 Kings 17:24-41), the mixed race that developed became known as the Samaritans. "Purebred" Jews hated these "half-breeds," and the Samaritans in turn hated the Jews. So many tensions arose between the two peoples that Jewish travelers between Galilee and southern Judea often walked around rather than through Samaritan territory, even though this lengthened their trip considerably. Jesus held no such prejudices, and he sent messengers ahead to get things ready in a Samaritan village. But the village refused to welcome these Jewish travelers.

9:54 When James and John were rejected by the Samaritan village, they didn't want to stop at shaking the dust from their feet (9:5). They wanted to retaliate by calling down fire from heaven on the people, as Elijah did on the servants of a wicked king of Israel (2 Kings 1). When others reject or scorn us, we, too, may feel like retaliating. We must remember that judgment belongs to God, and we must not expect him to use his power to carry out our personal vendettas.

9:59 Luke does not tell us whether the father is already dead or whether he's terminally ill. It seems likely that if the father were dead, the son would have been fulfilling the burial duties. Jesus was saying that true discipleship requires instant action. Jesus did not teach people to forsake responsibilities to family, but he often gave commands to people in light of their real motives. Perhaps this man wanted to delay following Christ and used his father as an excuse. There is a cost to following Jesus, and each of us must be ready to serve, even when it requires sacrifice.

9:62 What does Jesus want from us? Total dedication, not halfhearted commitment. We can't pick and choose among Jesus' ideas and follow him selectively; we have to accept the cross along with the crown, judgment as well as mercy. We must count the cost and be willing to abandon everything else that has given us security. With our focus on Jesus, we should allow nothing to distract us from the manner of living that he calls good and true.

Jesus Sends Out Seventy-Two Messengers (130)

10:1 Mark 6:7 — **10** The Lord now chose seventy-two* other disciples and sent them on ahead in pairs
to all the towns and villages he planned to visit. 2 These were his instructions to them:
10:2 Matt 9:37-38; John 4:35 — "The harvest is so great, but the workers are so few. Pray to the Lord who is in charge of
the harvest, and ask him to send out more workers for his fields. 3 Go now, and remember
10:3 Matt 10:16 — that I am sending you out as lambs among wolves. 4 Don't take along any money, or a
10:4 2 Kgs 4:29; Luke 9:3 — traveler's bag, or even an extra pair of sandals. And don't stop to greet anyone on the road.
5 "Whenever you enter a home, give it your blessing. 6 If those who live there are
10:7 1 Cor 9:6-14; 1 Tim 5:18 — worthy, the blessing will stand; if they are not, the blessing will return to you. 7 When
you enter a town, don't move around from home to home. Stay in one place, eating and
drinking what they provide you. Don't hesitate to accept hospitality, because those who
work deserve their pay.
10:9 Matt 3:2 — 8 "If a town welcomes you, eat whatever is set before you 9 and heal the sick. As you
heal them, say, 'The Kingdom of God is near you now.' 10 But if a town refuses to
welcome you, go out into its streets and say, 11 'We wipe the dust of your town from our
feet as a public announcement of your doom. And don't forget the Kingdom of God is
10:12 Gen 19:24-25; Matt 10:15 — near!' 12 The truth is, even wicked Sodom will be better off than such a town on the
judgment day.

10:1 Some manuscripts read *70;* also in 10:17.

A COLLECTION OF ATTITUDES

To the expert in religious law	the wounded man was a subject to discuss.
To the bandits	the wounded man was someone to use and exploit.
To the religious men	the wounded man was a problem to be avoided.
To the innkeeper	the wounded man was a customer to serve for a fee.
To the Samaritan	the wounded man was a human being worth being cared for and loved.
To Jesus	all of them and all of us were worth dying for.

Confronting the needs of others brings out various attitudes in us. Jesus used the story of the good but despised Samaritan to make clear what attitude was acceptable to him. If we are honest, we often will find ourselves in the place of the expert in religious law, needing to learn again who our neighbor is. Note these different attitudes toward the wounded man.

10:1, 2 Far more than 12 people had been following Jesus. Here Jesus designated a group of 72 to prepare a number of towns for Jesus' later visit. These disciples were not unique in their qualifications. They were not better educated, more capable, or of higher status than other followers of Jesus. What prepared them for this mission was that they had been equipped with Jesus' power and their vision to reach all the people. It is important to dedicate our skills to God's Kingdom, but we must also be equipped with his power and have a clear vision of what he wants us to do.

10:2 Jesus was sending 36 teams of two to reach the multitudes. These teams were not to try to do the job without help; rather, they were to ask God for more workers. Some people, as soon as they understand the Good News, want to go to work immediately contacting unsaved people. This story suggests a different approach: Begin by mobilizing people to pray. And before praying for unsaved people, pray that other concerned disciples will join you in reaching out to them.

10:2 In Christian service, there is no unemployment. God has work enough for everyone. Don't just sit back and watch others work—look for ways to help with the harvest.

10:3 Jesus said he was sending his disciples out "as lambs among wolves." They would have to be careful because they would surely meet with opposition. We, too, are sent into the world like lambs among wolves. Be alert, and remember to face your enemies, not with aggression but with love and gentleness. A dangerous mission requires sincere commitment.

10:7 Jesus' direction to stay in one house avoided certain problems. Shifting from house to house could offend the families who first took them in. Some families might begin to compete for the disciples' presence, and some might think they weren't good enough to hear their message. If the disciples appeared not to appreciate the hospitality offered them, the town might not accept Jesus when he followed them there. In addition, by staying in one place, the disciples did not have to worry continually about getting good accommodations. They could settle down and do their appointed task.

10:7 Jesus told his disciples to accept hospitality graciously because their work entitled them to it. Ministers of the Good News deserve to be supported, and it is our responsibility to make sure they have what they need. There are several ways to encourage those who serve God in his church: (1) See that they have an adequate salary; (2) see that they are supported emotionally—plan special times to express appreciation for something they have done; (3) lift their spirits with special surprises from time to time. Our ministers deserve to know we are giving to them cheerfully and generously.

10:8, 9 Jesus gave two rules for the disciples to follow as they traveled. They were to eat what was set before them—that is, they were to accept hospitality without being picky—and they were to heal the sick. Because of the healings, people would be willing to listen to the Good News.

10:12 Sodom was an evil city that God destroyed because of its great sinfulness (Genesis 19). The city's name is often used to symbolize wickedness and immorality. Sodom will suffer on judgment day, but cities who saw the Messiah and rejected him will suffer even more.

13“What horrors await you, Korazin and Bethsaida! For if the miracles I did in you
had been done in wicked Tyre and Sidon, their people would have sat in deep repentance
long ago, clothed in sackcloth and throwing ashes on their heads to show their remorse.
14 Yes, Tyre and Sidon will be better off on the judgment day than you. 15 And you people
of Capernaum, will you be exalted to heaven? No, you will be brought down to the place
of the dead.*”

16 Then he said to the disciples, “Anyone who accepts your message is also accepting
me. And anyone who rejects you is rejecting me. And anyone who rejects me is rejecting
God who sent me.”

The Seventy-Two Messengers Return (**131**)

17 When the seventy-two disciples returned, they joyfully reported to him, “Lord, even
the demons obey us when we use your name!”

18“Yes,” he told them, “I saw Satan falling from heaven as a flash of lightning! 19 And
I have given you authority over all the power of the enemy, and you can walk among
snakes and scorpions and crush them. Nothing will injure you. 20 But don’t rejoice just
because evil spirits obey you; rejoice because your names are registered as citizens of
heaven.”

21 Then Jesus was filled with the joy of the Holy Spirit and said, “O Father, Lord of
heaven and earth, thank you for hiding the truth from those who think themselves so
wise and clever, and for revealing it to the childlike. Yes, Father, it pleased you to do it
this way.

22“My Father has given me authority over everything. No one really knows the Son
except the Father, and no one really knows the Father except the Son and those to whom
the Son chooses to reveal him.”

23 Then when they were alone, he turned to the disciples and said, “How privileged
you are to see what you have seen. 24 I tell you, many prophets and kings have longed to
see and hear what you have seen and heard, but they could not.”

10:15 Greek *to Hades.*

10:14 Isa 23; Ezek 26–28
10:15 †Isa 14:13, 15
10:16 Matt 10:40; John 5:23; 1 Thes 4:8
10:18 John 12:31; Rev 12:8-9
10:19 Acts 28:3-5
10:20 Exod 32:32; Isa 4:3; Phil 4:3; Rev 3:5
10:22 Matt 28:18; John 1:18; 3:35
10:24 1 Pet 1:10-14

10:13 Korazin was a city near the Sea of Galilee, probably about two miles north of Capernaum. Tyre and Sidon were cities destroyed by God as punishment for their wickedness (see Ezekiel 26–28).

10:15 Capernaum was Jesus’ base for his Galilean ministry. The city was located at an important crossroads used by traders and the Roman army, so a message proclaimed in Capernaum was likely to go far. But many people of Capernaum did not understand Jesus’ miracles or believe his teaching, and the city was included among those who would be judged for rejecting him.

10:17-20 The disciples had seen tremendous results as they ministered in Jesus’ name and with his authority. They were elated by the victories they had witnessed, and Jesus shared their enthusiasm. He helped them get their priorities right, however, by reminding them of their most important victory—that their names were registered in heaven. This honor was more important than any of their accomplishments. As we see God’s wonders at work in and through us, we should not lose sight of the greatest wonder of all—our heavenly citizenship.

10:18, 19 Jesus may have been looking ahead to his victory over Satan at the cross. John 12:31, 32 indicates that Satan would be judged and driven out at the time of Jesus’ death. On the other hand, Jesus may have been warning his disciples against pride. Perhaps he was referring to Isaiah 14:12-17, which begins, “How you are fallen from heaven, O shining star, son of the morning!” Some interpreters identify this verse with Satan and explain that Satan’s pride led to all the evil we see on earth today. To Jesus’ disciples, who were thrilled with their power over evil spirits (“snakes and scorpions”), he may have been giving this stern warning: “Yours is the kind of pride that led to Satan’s downfall. Be careful!”

10:21 Jesus thanked God that spiritual truth was for everyone and not just for the elite. Many of life’s rewards seem to go to the intelligent, the rich, the good looking, or the powerful, but the Kingdom of God is equally available to all, regardless of position or abilities. We come to Jesus, not through strength or brains, but through childlike trust. Jesus is not opposed to engaging in scholarly pursuits; he is opposed to spiritual pride (being wise in one’s own eyes). Join Jesus in thanking God that we all have equal access to him. Trust in God’s grace, not in your personal qualifications, for your citizenship in the Kingdom.

10:22 Christ’s mission was to reveal God the Father to people. His words brought difficult ideas down to earth. He explained God’s love through stories, teachings, and, most of all, his life. By examining Jesus’ actions, principles, and attitudes, we can understand God more clearly.

10:23, 24 The disciples had a fantastic opportunity—they were eyewitnesses of Christ, the Son of God. But for many months they took Jesus for granted, not really listening to him or obeying him. We also have a privileged position: the legacy of 2,000 years of church history, the availability of the Bible in hundreds of languages and translations, and access to many excellent pastors and speakers. Yet often we take these for granted. Remember, with privilege comes responsibility. Because we are privileged to know so much about Christ, we must be careful to follow him.

10:24 Old Testament men of God, such as David and the prophet Isaiah, made many God-inspired predictions that Jesus fulfilled. As Peter later wrote, these prophets wondered what their words meant and when they would be fulfilled (1 Peter 1:10-13). In Jesus’ words, they “longed to see and hear what you have seen and heard”—the coming of God’s Kingdom.

Jesus Tells the Parable of the Good Samaritan (**132**)
25 One day an expert in religious law stood up to test Jesus by asking him this question: "Teacher, what must I do to receive eternal life?"
26 Jesus replied, "What does the law of Moses say? How do you read it?"
27 The man answered, "'You must love the Lord your God with all your heart, all your soul, all your strength, and all your mind.' And, 'Love your neighbor as yourself.'"*

10:27 †Deut 6:5 †Lev 19:18

10:27 Deut 6:5; Lev 19:18.

MARTHA

Many older brothers and sisters have an irritating tendency to take charge, a habit developed while growing up. We can easily see this pattern in Martha, the older sister of Mary and Lazarus. She was used to being in control.

The fact that Martha, Mary, and Lazarus are remembered for their hospitality takes on added significance when we note that hospitality was a social requirement in their culture. It was considered shameful to turn anyone away from your door. Apparently Martha's family met this requirement very well.

Martha worried about details. She wished to please, to serve, to do the right thing—but she often succeeded in making everyone around her uncomfortable. Perhaps as the oldest she feared shame if her home did not measure up to expectations. She tried to do everything she could to make sure that wouldn't happen. As a result, she found it hard to relax and enjoy her guests and even harder to accept Mary's lack of cooperation in all the preparations. Martha's frustration was so intense that she finally asked Jesus to settle the matter. He gently corrected her attitude and showed her that her priorities, though good, were not the best. The personal attention she gave her guests should be more important than the comforts she tried to provide for them.

Later, following her brother Lazarus's death, Martha could hardly help being herself. When she heard Jesus was finally coming, she rushed out to meet him and expressed her inner conflict of disappointment and hope. Jesus pointed out that her hope was too limited. He was not only Lord over death; he was the resurrection and the life! Moments later, Martha again spoke without thinking, pointing out that four-day-old corpses are well on their way to decomposition. Her awareness of details sometimes kept her from seeing the whole picture, but Jesus was consistently patient with her.

In our last picture of Martha, she is once again serving a meal to Jesus and his disciples. She has not stopped serving. But the Bible records her silence this time. She has begun to learn what her younger sister already knew—that worship begins with silence and listening.

Strengths and accomplishments
- Known as a hospitable homemaker
- Believed in Jesus with growing faith
- Had a strong desire to do everything exactly right

Weaknesses and mistakes
- Expected others to agree with her priorities
- Was overly concerned with details
- Tended to feel sorry for herself when her efforts were not recognized
- Limited Jesus' power to this life

Lessons from her life
- Getting caught up in details can make us forget the main reasons for our actions
- There is a proper time to listen to Jesus and a proper time to work for him

Vital statistics
- Where: Bethany
- Relatives: Sister: Mary. Brother: Lazarus

Key verse
"But Martha was worrying over the big dinner she was preparing. She came to Jesus and said, 'Lord, doesn't it seem unfair to you that my sister just sits here while I do all the work? Tell her to come and help me' " (Luke 10:40).

Martha's story is told in Luke 10:38–42 and John 11:17–45.

10:27 This expert in religious law was quoting Deuteronomy 6:5 and Leviticus 19:18. He correctly understood that the law demanded total devotion to God and love for one's neighbor. Jesus talked more about these laws elsewhere (see Matthew 19:16-22 and Mark 10:17-22).

10:27-37 The legal expert viewed the wounded man as a topic for discussion; the bandits, as an object to exploit; the priest, as a problem to avoid; and the Temple assistant, as an object of curiosity. Only the Samaritan treated him as a person to love.

10:27-37 From the illustration we learn three principles about loving our neighbor: (1) Lack of love is often easy to justify, even though it is never right; (2) our neighbor is anyone of any race, creed, or social background who is in need; and (3) love means acting to meet the person's need. Wherever you live, there are needy people close by. There is no good reason for refusing to help.

28 "Right!" Jesus told him. "Do this and you will live!" 10:28 Lev 18:5 Rom 10:5
29 The man wanted to justify his actions, so he asked Jesus, "And who is my
neighbor?" 10:29 Luke 16:15
30 Jesus replied with an illustration: "A Jewish man was traveling on a trip from
Jerusalem to Jericho, and he was attacked by bandits. They stripped him of his clothes
and money, beat him up, and left him half dead beside the road.
31 "By chance a Jewish priest came along; but when he saw the man lying there, he
crossed to the other side of the road and passed him by. 32 A Temple assistant* walked 10:31 Lev 21:1-3
over and looked at him lying there, but he also passed by on the other side.
33 "Then a despised Samaritan came along, and when he saw the man, he felt deep
pity. 34 Kneeling beside him, the Samaritan soothed his wounds with medicine and
bandaged them. Then he put the man on his own donkey and took him to an inn, where
he took care of him. 35 The next day he handed the innkeeper two pieces of silver* and
told him to take care of the man. 'If his bill runs higher than that,' he said, 'I'll pay
the difference the next time I am here.'
36 "Now which of these three would you say was a neighbor to the man who was
attacked by bandits?" Jesus asked.
37 The man replied, "The one who showed him mercy."
Then Jesus said, "Yes, now go and do the same."

Jesus Visits Martha and Mary (**133**)

38 As Jesus and the disciples continued on their way to Jerusalem, they came to a 10:38 John 11:1; 12:2-3
village where a woman named Martha welcomed them into her home. 39 Her sister,
Mary, sat at the Lord's feet, listening to what he taught. 40 But Martha was worrying
over the big dinner she was preparing. She came to Jesus and said, "Lord, doesn't it
seem unfair to you that my sister just sits here while I do all the work? Tell her to come
and help me." 10:41 Matt 6:25-34 Luke 12:11, 22
41 But the Lord said to her, "My dear Martha, you are so upset over all these details!
42 There is really only one thing worth being concerned about. Mary has discovered 10:42 Ps 27:4 Phil 3:13-14
it—and I won't take it away from her."

10:32 Greek *A Levite.* **10:35** Greek *2 denarii.* A denarius was the equivalent of a full day's wage.

10:33 There was deep hatred between Jews and Samaritans. The Jews saw themselves as pure descendants of Abraham, while the Samaritans were a mixed race produced when Jews from the northern kingdom intermarried with other peoples after Israel's exile. To this legal expert, the person least likely to act correctly would be the Samaritan. In fact, he could not bear to say *Samaritan* in answer to Jesus' question. This expert's attitude betrayed his lack of the very thing that he had earlier said the law commanded—love.

10:38-42 Mary and Martha both loved Jesus. On this occasion they were both serving him. But Martha thought Mary's style of serving was inferior to hers. She didn't realize that in her desire to serve, she was actually neglecting her guest. Are you so busy doing things *for* Jesus that you're not spending any time *with* him? Don't let your service become self-serving.

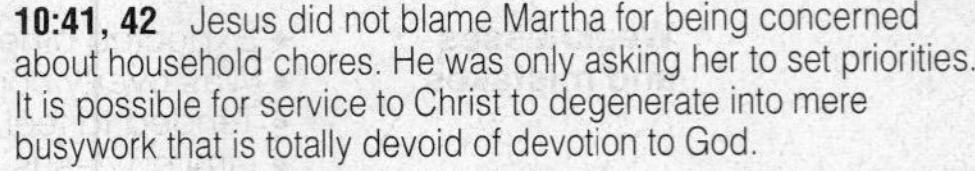

10:41, 42 Jesus did not blame Martha for being concerned about household chores. He was only asking her to set priorities. It is possible for service to Christ to degenerate into mere busywork that is totally devoid of devotion to God.

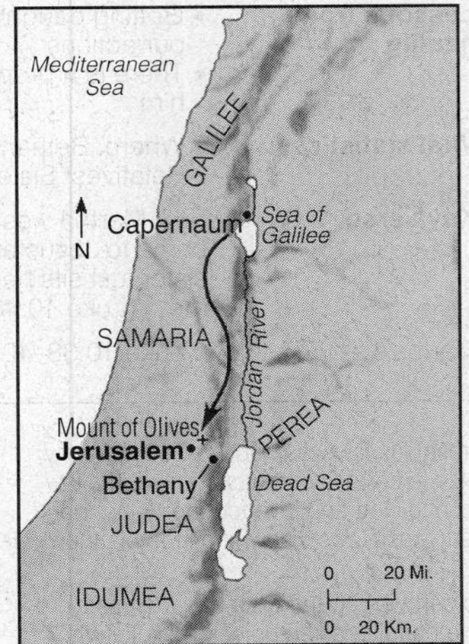

JESUS VISITS MARY AND MARTHA
After teaching throughout Galilee, Jesus returned to Jerusalem for the Festival of Shelters (John 7:2ff). He spoke in Jerusalem and then visited his friends Mary and Martha in Bethany, a tiny village on the eastern slope of the Mount of Olives.

Jesus Teaches His Disciples about Prayer (**134**)

11:1 Luke 3:21 **11** Once when Jesus had been out praying, one of his disciples came to him as he
finished and said, "Lord, teach us to pray, just as John taught his disciples."
11:2-4 Matt 6:9-13 2 He said, "This is how you should pray:

"Father, may your name be honored.
May your Kingdom come soon.
3 Give us our food day by day.
11:4 Matt 18:35 Mark 11:25 4 And forgive us our sins—
just as we forgive those who have sinned against us.
And don't let us yield to temptation.*"

5 Then, teaching them more about prayer, he used this illustration: "Suppose you went
to a friend's house at midnight, wanting to borrow three loaves of bread. You would say
to him, 6 'A friend of mine has just arrived for a visit, and I have nothing for him to eat.'
11:7 Matt 26:10 Luke 18:5 Gal 6:17 7 He would call out from his bedroom, 'Don't bother me. The door is locked for the night,
and we are all in bed. I can't help you this time.' 8 But I tell you this—though he won't
do it as a friend, if you keep knocking long enough, he will get up and give you what
11:8 Luke 18:1-6 you want so his reputation won't be damaged.*
9 "And so I tell you, keep on asking, and you will be given what you ask for. Keep on
looking, and you will find. Keep on knocking, and the door will be opened. 10 For
everyone who asks, receives. Everyone who seeks, finds. And the door is opened to
everyone who knocks.
11 "You fathers—if your children ask* for a fish, do you give them a snake instead?
11:13 Jas 1:17 12 Or if they ask for an egg, do you give them a scorpion? Of course not! 13 If you sinful
people know how to give good gifts to your children, how much more will your heavenly
Father give the Holy Spirit to those who ask him."

Jesus Answers Hostile Accusations (**135**)

11:15 Matt 9:34 14 One day Jesus cast a demon out of a man who couldn't speak, and the man's voice
returned to him. The crowd was amazed, 15 but some said, "No wonder he can cast out

11:2-4 Some manuscripts add additional portions of the Lord's Prayer as it reads in Matt 6:9-13. **11:8** Greek *in order to avoid shame,* or *because of [your] persistence.* **11:11** Some manuscripts add *for bread, do you give them a stone? Or if they ask.*

11:1-4 Notice the order in this prayer. First, Jesus praised God; then he made his requests. Praising God first puts us in the right frame of mind to tell him about our needs. Too often our prayers are more like shopping lists than conversations.

11:2-13 These verses focus on three aspects of prayer: its content (11:2-4), our persistence (11:5-10), and God's faithfulness (11:11-13).

11:3 God's provision is daily, not all at once. We cannot store it up and then cut off communication with God. And we dare not be self-satisfied. If you are running low on strength, ask yourself, How long have I been away from the Source?

11:4 When Jesus taught his disciples to pray, he made forgiveness the cornerstone of their relationship with God. God has forgiven our sins; we must now forgive those who have wronged us. To remain unforgiving shows we have not understood that we ourselves deeply need to be forgiven. Think of some people who have wronged you. Have you forgiven them? How will God deal with you if he treats you as you treat others?

11:8 Persistence, or boldness, in prayer overcomes our insensitivity, not God's. To practice persistence does more to change our heart and mind than his, and it helps us understand and express the intensity of our need. Persistence in prayer helps us recognize God's work.

11:13 Even though good fathers make mistakes, they treat their children well. How much better our perfect heavenly Father treats his children! The most important gift he could ever give us is the Holy Spirit (Acts 2:1-4), whom he promised to give all believers after his death, resurrection, and return to heaven (John 15:26).

11:14-23 A similar and possibly separate event is reported in Matthew 12:22-45 and Mark 3:20-30. The event described by Luke happened in Judea, while the other took place in Galilee. According to Luke, Jesus spoke to the crowds; in Matthew and Mark, he accused the Pharisees.

11:15-20 There are two common interpretations of these verses: (1) Some of the Pharisees' followers drove out demons. If this was so, the Pharisees' accusations were becoming more desperate. To accuse Jesus of being empowered by Satan, the prince of demons, because Jesus was driving out demons was also to say that the Pharisees' own followers were doing Satan's work. Jesus turned the religious leaders' accusation against them. (2) Another possibility is that the Pharisees' followers were *not* driving out demons; and even if they tried, they did not succeed. Jesus first dismissed their claim as absurd (Why would the Devil drive out his own demons?). Then he engaged in a little irony ("What about your own followers?"). Finally, he concluded that his work of driving out demons proved that the Kingdom of God had arrived.

Satan, who had controlled the kingdom of this world for thousands of years, was now being controlled and overpowered by Jesus and the Kingdom of Heaven. Jesus' Kingdom began to come into power at Jesus' birth and grew as he resisted the wilderness temptations. It established itself through his teachings and healings, blossomed in victory at his resurrection and at Pentecost, and will become permanent and universal at his second coming. Although these two interpretations may differ, they arrive at the same conclusion: The Kingdom of God arrived with the coming of Jesus Christ.

demons. He gets his power from Satan,* the prince of demons!" 16 Trying to test Jesus,
others asked for a miraculous sign from heaven to see if he was from God.
17 He knew their thoughts, so he said, "Any kingdom at war with itself is doomed. A
divided home is also doomed. 18 You say I am empowered by the prince of demons.* But
if Satan is fighting against himself by empowering me to cast out his demons, how can
his kingdom survive? 19 And if I am empowered by the prince of demons, what about
your own followers? They cast out demons, too, so they will judge you for what you
have said. 20 But if I am casting out demons by the power of God, then the Kingdom of
God has arrived among you. 21 For when Satan,* who is completely armed, guards his
palace, it is safe—22 until someone who is stronger attacks and overpowers him, strips
him of his weapons, and carries off his belongings.
23 "Anyone who isn't helping me opposes me, and anyone who isn't working with me
is actually working against me.
24 "When an evil spirit leaves a person, it goes into the desert, searching for rest. But
when it finds none, it says, 'I will return to the person I came from.' 25 So it returns and
finds that its former home is all swept and clean. 26 Then the spirit finds seven other
spirits more evil than itself, and they all enter the person and live there. And so that
person is worse off than before."
27 As he was speaking, a woman in the crowd called out, "God bless your mother—the
womb from which you came, and the breasts that nursed you!"
28 He replied, "But even more blessed are all who hear the word of God and put it into
practice."

Jesus Warns against Unbelief (**136**)

29 As the crowd pressed in on Jesus, he said, "These are evil times, and this evil
generation keeps asking me to show them a miraculous sign. But the only sign I will give
them is the sign of the prophet Jonah. 30 What happened to him was a sign to the people
of Nineveh that God had sent him. What happens to me will be a sign that God has sent
me, the Son of Man, to these people.
31 "The queen of Sheba* will rise up against this generation on judgment day and
condemn it, because she came from a distant land to hear the wisdom of Solomon. And

11:16 Matt 12:38; 16:1
11:17 Matt 9:4
11:20 Exod 8:19
11:22 Isa 49:24; 53:12
11:24-26 Matt 12:43-45
11:27 Luke 1:28, 42, 48
11:28 Luke 6:47; 8:21
11:29-32 Matt 12:38-42; 1 Cor 1:22
11:30 Jon 1:17; 2:10
11:31 1 Kgs 10:1-10; 2 Chr 9:1-12

11:15 Greek *Beelzeboul.* **11:18** Greek *by Beelzeboul;* also in 11:19. **11:21** Greek *the strong one.* **11:31** Greek *the queen of the south.*

11:21, 22 Jesus may have been referring to Isaiah 49:24-26. Regardless of how great Satan's power is, Jesus is stronger still. He will overpower Satan and dispose of him for eternity (see Revelation 20:2, 10).

11:23 How does this verse relate to 9:50: "Anyone who is not against you is for you"? In the earlier passage, Jesus was talking about a person who was driving out demons in Jesus' name. Those who fight evil, he was saying, are on the same side as the one driving out demons in Jesus' name. Here, by contrast, he was talking about the conflict between God and the Devil. In this battle, if a person is not on God's side, he or she is on Satan's. There is no neutral ground. Because God has already won the battle, why be on the losing side? If you aren't actively for Christ, you are against him.

11:24-26 Jesus was illustrating an unfortunate human tendency: Our desire to reform often does not last long. In Israel's history, almost as soon as a good king would pull down idols, a bad king would set them up again. It is not enough to be emptied of evil; we must then be filled with the power of the Holy Spirit to accomplish God's new purpose in our life (see also Matthew 12:43-45; Galatians 5:22).

11:27, 28 Jesus was speaking to people who put extremely high value on family ties. Their genealogies were important guarantees that they were part of God's chosen people. A man's value came from his ancestors, and a woman's value came from the sons she bore. Jesus' response to the woman meant that a person's obedience to God is more important than his or her place on the family tree. Consistent obedience is more important than the honor of bearing a respected son.

11:29, 30 What was the sign of the prophet Jonah? God had asked Jonah to preach repentance to the Gentiles (non-Jews). Jesus was affirming Jonah's message. Salvation is not only for Jews but for all people. Matthew 12:40 adds another explanation: Jesus would die and rise after three days, just as the prophet Jonah was rescued after three days in the belly of the great fish.

11:29-32 The cruel, warlike men of Nineveh, capital of Assyria, repented when Jonah preached to them—and Jonah did not even care about them. The pagan queen of Sheba praised the God of Israel when she heard Solomon's wisdom, and Solomon was full of faults. By contrast, Jesus, the perfect Son of God, had come to people that he loved dearly—but they rejected him. Thus, God's chosen people made themselves more liable to judgment than either a notoriously wicked nation or a powerful pagan queen. Compare 10:12-15, where Jesus says the evil cities of Sodom, Tyre, and Sidon will be judged less harshly than the cities in Judea and Galilee that rejected Jesus' message.

11:31, 32 The people of Nineveh and the queen of Sheba had turned to God with far less evidence than Jesus was giving his listeners—and far less than we have today. We have eyewitness reports of the risen Jesus, the continuing power of the Holy Spirit unleashed at Pentecost, easy access to the Bible, and knowledge of 2,000 years of Christ's acts through his church. With the knowledge and insight available to us, our response to Christ ought to be even more complete and wholehearted.

11:32 Jon 3:5, 8, 10 now someone greater than Solomon is here—and you refuse to listen to him. [32]The
people of Nineveh, too, will rise up against this generation on judgment day and
condemn it, because they repented at the preaching of Jonah. And now someone greater
than Jonah is here—and you refuse to repent.

Jesus Teaches about the Light Within (**137**)

11:33 Matt 5:15 Luke 8:16 [33]"No one lights a lamp and then hides it or puts it under a basket. Instead, it is put on a
lampstand to give light to all who enter the room. [34]Your eye is a lamp for your body. A
11:34-36 Matt 6:22-23 pure eye lets sunshine into your soul. But an evil eye shuts out the light and plunges you
into darkness. [35]Make sure that the light you think you have is not really darkness. [36]If
you are filled with light, with no dark corners, then your whole life will be radiant, as
though a floodlight is shining on you."

Jesus Criticizes the Religious Leaders (**138**)

[37]As Jesus was speaking, one of the Pharisees invited him home for a meal. So he went
11:38 Mark 7:3-4 in and took his place at the table. [38]His host was amazed to see that he sat down to eat
11:39 Matt 23:25 Mark 7:20-23 without first performing the ceremonial washing required by Jewish custom. [39]Then the
Lord said to him, "You Pharisees are so careful to clean the outside of the cup and the
dish, but inside you are still filthy—full of greed and wickedness! [40]Fools! Didn't God
11:41 Luke 12:33 make the inside as well as the outside? [41]So give to the needy what you greedily possess,
and you will be clean all over.
11:42 Lev 27:30 Matt 23:23 [42]"But how terrible it will be for you Pharisees! For you are careful to tithe even
the tiniest part of your income,* but you completely forget about justice and the love
of God. You should tithe, yes, but you should not leave undone the more important
things.
11:43 Matt 23:6-7 Mark 12:38-39 [43]"How terrible it will be for you Pharisees! For how you love the seats of honor in
the synagogues and the respectful greetings from everyone as you walk through the
11:44 Matt 23:27-28 markets! [44]Yes, how terrible it will be for you. For you are like hidden graves in a field.
People walk over them without knowing the corruption they are stepping on."
[45]"Teacher," said an expert in religious law, "you have insulted us, too, in what you
11:46 Matt 23:4 just said."
[46]"Yes," said Jesus, "how terrible it will be for you experts in religious law! For you
crush people beneath impossible religious demands, and you never lift a finger to help
11:47 Matt 23:29-32 ease the burden. [47]How terrible it will be for you! For you build tombs for the very

11:42 Greek *to tithe the mint and the rue and every herb.*

11:33-36 The lamp is Christ; the eye represents spiritual understanding and insight. Evil desires make the eye less sensitive and blot out the light of Christ's presence. If you have a hard time seeing God at work in the world and in your life, check your vision. Are any sinful desires blinding you to Christ?

11:37-39 This ceremonial washing was done not for health reasons but as a symbol of washing away any contamination from touching anything unclean. Not only did the Pharisees make a public show of their washing, but they also commanded everyone else to follow a practice originally intended only for the priests.

11:41 The Pharisees loved to think of themselves as "clean," but their stinginess toward God and the poor proved that they were not as clean as they thought. How do you use the resources God has entrusted to you? Are you generous in meeting the needs around you? Your generosity reveals much about the purity of your heart.

11:42 It is easy to rationalize not helping others because we have already given to the church, but a person who follows Jesus should share with needy neighbors. While tithing is important to the life of the church, our compassion must not stop there. Where we can help, we should help.

11:42-52 Jesus criticized the Pharisees and the experts in religious law harshly because they (1) washed their outsides but not their insides, (2) remembered to give a tenth of even their garden herbs but neglected justice, (3) loved praise and attention, (4) loaded people down with burdensome religious demands, (5) would not accept the truth about Jesus, and (6) prevented others from believing the truth. They went wrong by focusing on outward appearances and ignoring the inner condition of their hearts. We do the same when our service comes from a desire to be seen rather than from a pure heart that is full of love for others. People may sometimes be fooled, but God isn't. Don't be a Christian on the outside only. Bring your inner life under God's control, and your outer life will naturally reflect him.

11:44 The Old Testament laws said a person who touched a grave was unclean (Numbers 19:16). Jesus accused the Pharisees of making others unclean by their spiritual rottenness. Like unmarked graves hidden in a field, the Pharisees corrupted everyone who came in contact with them.

11:46 These "demands" were the details the Pharisees had added to God's law. To the commandment, "Remember to observe the Sabbath day by keeping it holy" (Exodus 20:8), for example, they had added instructions regarding how far a person could walk on the Sabbath, which kinds of knots could be tied, and how much weight could be carried. Healing a person was considered unlawful work on the Sabbath, although rescuing a trapped animal was permitted (14:5). No wonder Jesus condemned their additions to the law.

prophets your ancestors killed long ago. 48 Murderers! You agree with your ancestors that
what they did was right. You would have done the same yourselves. 49 This is what God
in his wisdom said about you:* 'I will send prophets and apostles to them, and they will
kill some and persecute the others.'
50 "And you of this generation will be held responsible for the murder of all God's
prophets from the creation of the world—51 from the murder of Abel to the murder of
Zechariah, who was killed between the altar and the sanctuary. Yes, it will surely be
charged against you.
52 "How terrible it will be for you experts in religious law! For you hide the key to
knowledge from the people. You don't enter the Kingdom yourselves, and you prevent
others from entering."
53 As Jesus finished speaking, the Pharisees and teachers of religious law were furious.
From that time on they grilled him with many hostile questions, 54 trying to trap him into
saying something they could use against him.

Jesus Speaks against Hypocrisy **(139)**

12 Meanwhile, the crowds grew until thousands were milling about and crushing
each other. Jesus turned first to his disciples and warned them, "Beware of the
yeast of the Pharisees—beware of their hypocrisy. 2 The time is coming when everything
will be revealed; all that is secret will be made public. 3 Whatever you have said in the
dark will be heard in the light, and what you have whispered behind closed doors will
be shouted from the housetops for all to hear!
4 "Dear friends, don't be afraid of those who want to kill you. They can only kill the
body; they cannot do any more to you. 5 But I'll tell you whom to fear. Fear God, who
has the power to kill people and then throw them into hell.
6 "What is the price of five sparrows? A couple of pennies? Yet God does not forget a
single one of them. 7 And the very hairs on your head are all numbered. So don't be
afraid; you are more valuable to him than a whole flock of sparrows.
8 "And I assure you of this: If anyone acknowledges me publicly here on earth, I,
the Son of Man, will openly acknowledge that person in the presence of God's angels.
9 But if anyone denies me here on earth, I will deny that person before God's angels.

11:48 Acts 7:51-53; 8:1
11:49-51 Matt 23:34-36; 1 Cor 1:24, 30
11:51 Gen 4:8; 2 Chr 24:20-21
11:52 Matt 23:13
11:54 Luke 20:20
12:1 Matt 16:6, 11, 12
12:2 Mark 4:22
12:4 John 15:14-15
12:5 Heb 10:31
12:8 Luke 15:10; Rev 3:5
12:9 Mark 8:38; Luke 9:26; 2 Tim 2:12

11:49 Greek *Therefore, the wisdom of God said.*

11:49 God's prophets have been persecuted and murdered throughout history. But this generation was rejecting more than a human prophet—they were rejecting God himself. This quotation is not from the Old Testament. Jesus, the greatest prophet of all, was directly giving them God's message.

11:51 Abel's death is recorded in Genesis 4:8. For more about him, see his Profile in Genesis 5. Zechariah's death is recorded in 2 Chronicles 24:20-22 (the last book in the Hebrew canon). Why would all these sins come upon this particular generation? Because they were rejecting the Messiah himself, the one to whom all their history and prophecy were pointing.

11:52 How did the legal experts hide the "key to knowledge"? Through their erroneous interpretations of Scripture and their added man-made rules, they made God's truth hard to understand and practice. On top of that, these men were bad examples, arguing their way out of the demanding rules they placed on others. Caught up in a religion of their own making, they could no longer lead the people to God. They had closed the door of God's love to the people and had thrown away the key.

11:53, 54 The teachers of religious law and the Pharisees hoped to arrest Jesus for blasphemy, heresy, and lawbreaking. They were enraged by Jesus' words about them, but they couldn't arrest him for merely speaking words. They had to find a legal way to get rid of Jesus.

12:1, 2 As Jesus watched the huge crowds waiting to hear him, he warned his disciples against hypocrisy—trying to appear holy when one's heart is far from God. The Pharisees could not keep their attitudes hidden forever. Their selfishness would act like yeast, and soon they would expose themselves for what they really were—power-hungry impostors, not devoted religious leaders. It is easy to be angry at the blatant hypocrisy of the Pharisees, but each of us must resist the temptation to settle for the appearance of respectability when our hearts are far from God.

12:4, 5 Fear of opposition or ridicule can weaken our witness for Christ. Often we cling to peace and comfort, even at the cost of our walk with God. Jesus reminds us here that we should fear God, who controls eternal, not merely temporal, consequences. Don't allow fear of a person or group to keep you from standing up for Christ.

12:7 Our true value is God's estimate of our worth, not our peers'. Other people evaluate and categorize us according to how we perform, what we achieve, and how we look. But God cares for us, as he does for all of his creatures, because we belong to him. So we can face life without fear.

12:8, 9 We deny Jesus when we (1) hope no one will find out we are Christians, (2) decide *not* to speak up for what is right, (3) are silent about our relationship with God, (4) blend into society, and (5) accept our culture's non-Christian values. By contrast, we acknowledge him when we (1) live a moral, upright, Christ-honoring life, (2) look for opportunities to share our faith with others, (3) help others in need, (4) take a stand for justice, (5) love others, (6) acknowledge our loyalty to Christ, and (7) use our life and resources to carry out his desires rather than our own.

12:10 Matt 12:31-32 Mark 3:28-29 1 Jn 5:16

10 Yet those who speak against the Son of Man may be forgiven, but anyone who
speaks blasphemies against the Holy Spirit will never be forgiven.

12:11-12 Matt 10:19-20 Mark 13:11 Luke 21:12-15

11 "And when you are brought to trial in the synagogues and before rulers and
authorities, don't worry about what to say in your defense, 12 for the Holy Spirit will
teach you what needs to be said even as you are standing there."

Jesus Tells the Parable of the Rich Fool (**140**)

13 Then someone called from the crowd, "Teacher, please tell my brother to divide our
father's estate with me."

12:14 Exod 2:14 Acts 7:27, 35

14 Jesus replied, "Friend, who made me a judge over you to decide such things as
that?" 15 Then he said, "Beware! Don't be greedy for what you don't have. Real life is
not measured by how much we own."

12:15 Job 20:20; 31:24 Ps 62:10 1 Tim 6:9-10

16 And he gave an illustration: "A rich man had a fertile farm that produced fine crops.
17 In fact, his barns were full to overflowing. 18 So he said, 'I know! I'll tear down my

12:19 Prov 27:1 1 Cor 15:32 Jas 5:1-5

barns and build bigger ones. Then I'll have room enough to store everything. 19 And I'll
sit back and say to myself, My friend, you have enough stored away for years to come.
Now take it easy! Eat, drink, and be merry!'

12:20 Job 27:8 Ps 39:6-7

20 "But God said to him, 'You fool! You will die this very night. Then who will get it
all?'

21 "Yes, a person is a fool to store up earthly wealth but not have a rich relationship
with God."

Jesus Warns about Worry (**141**)

22 Then turning to his disciples, Jesus said, "So I tell you, don't worry about everyday
life—whether you have enough food to eat or clothes to wear. 23 For life consists of

12:24 Job 38:41 Ps 147:9

far more than food and clothing. 24 Look at the ravens. They don't need to plant or
harvest or put food in barns because God feeds them. And you are far more valuable
to him than any birds! 25 Can all your worries add a single moment to your life? Of
course not! 26 And if worry can't do little things like that, what's the use of worrying
over bigger things?

12:10 Jesus said that blasphemy against the Holy Spirit is unforgivable. This has worried many sincere Christians, but it does not need to. The unforgivable sin is attributing to Satan the work that the Holy Spirit accomplishes (see the notes on Matthew 12:31, 32; Mark 3:28, 29). Thus, it is the deliberate and ongoing rejection of the Holy Spirit's work and even of God himself. A person who has committed this sin is far from God and totally unaware of any sin at all. If you fear you have committed this sin, be assured that your very concern shows that you have not sinned in this way.

12:11, 12 The disciples knew they could never get the upper hand in a religious dispute with the well-educated Jewish leaders. Nevertheless, they would not be left unprepared. Jesus promised that the Holy Spirit would give them the appropriate words in their time of need. The disciples' testimony might not make them look impressive, but it would still point out God's work in the world through Jesus' life. We need to pray for opportunities to witness for Christ, and then trust him to help us with our words. This promise of the Spirit's help, however, does not compensate for lack of preparation. Remember that these disciples had three years of teaching and practical application. We need to study God's Word. Then God will bring his truths to mind when we most need them, helping us present them in the most effective way.

12:13ff Problems like this were often brought to rabbis for them to settle. Jesus' response, though not directed to the topic, is not a change of subject. Rather, Jesus is pointing to a higher issue—a correct attitude toward the accumulation of wealth. Life is more than material goods; far more important is our relationship with God. Jesus put his finger on this questioner's heart. When we bring problems to God in prayer, he often responds in the same way, showing us how we need to change and grow in our attitude toward the problem. This answer is often not the one we were looking for, but it is more effective in helping us trace God's hand in our life.

12:15 Jesus says that the good life has nothing to do with being wealthy, so be on guard against greed (desire for what we don't have). This is the exact opposite of what society usually says. Advertisers spend millions of dollars to entice us to think that if we buy more and more of their products, we will be happier, more fulfilled, more comfortable. How do you respond to the constant pressure to buy? Learn to tune out expensive enticements and concentrate instead on the truly fulfilled life—living in a relationship with God and doing his work.

12:16-21 The rich man in Jesus' story died before he could begin to use what was stored in his big barns. Planning for retirement—preparing for life *before* death—is wise, but neglecting life *after* death is disastrous. If you accumulate wealth only to enrich yourself, with no concern for helping others, you will enter eternity empty-handed.

12:18-20 Why do you save money? Are you saving for retirement? to buy more expensive cars or toys? to be secure? Jesus challenges us to think beyond earthbound goals and to use what we have been given for God's Kingdom. Faith, service, and obedience are the way to become rich toward God.

12:22-34 Jesus commands us not to worry. But how can we avoid it? Only faith can free us from the anxiety caused by greed and covetousness. It is good to work and plan responsibly; it is bad to dwell on all the ways our planning could go wrong. Worry is pointless because it can't fill any of our needs; worry is foolish because the Creator of the universe loves us and knows what we need. He promises to meet all our real needs but not necessarily all our desires.

27 "Look at the lilies and how they grow. They don't work or make their clothing, yet **12:27** 1 Kgs 10:1-10
Solomon in all his glory was not dressed as beautifully as they are. 28 And if God cares
so wonderfully for flowers that are here today and gone tomorrow, won't he more surely
care for you? You have so little faith! 29 And don't worry about food—what to eat and
drink. Don't worry whether God will provide it for you. 30 These things dominate the **12:30** Matt 6:8
thoughts of most people, but your Father already knows your needs. 31 He will give you
all you need from day to day if you make the Kingdom of God your primary concern.
32 "So don't be afraid, little flock. For it gives your Father great happiness to give you **12:32** Luke 22:29
the Kingdom.
33 "Sell what you have and give to those in need. This will store up treasure for you in **12:33** Matt 19:21
heaven! And the purses of heaven have no holes in them. Your treasure will be safe—no Acts 2:45
thief can steal it and no moth can destroy it. 34 Wherever your treasure is, there your heart
and thoughts will also be.

Jesus Warns about Preparing for His Coming (**142**)

35 "Be dressed for service and well prepared, 36 as though you were waiting for your **12:35-36** Matt 25:1-13
master to return from the wedding feast. Then you will be ready to open the door and let Mark 13:33-37
him in the moment he arrives and knocks. 37 There will be special favor for those who **12:35** †Exod 12:11
are ready and waiting for his return. I tell you, he himself will seat them, put on an apron,
and serve them as they sit and eat! 38 He may come in the middle of the night or just **12:37** Luke 17:7-8
before dawn.* But whenever he comes, there will be special favor for his servants who John 13:4
are ready!
39 "Know this: A homeowner who knew exactly when a burglar was coming would **12:39** 1 Thes 5:2
not permit the house to be broken into. 40 You must be ready all the time, for the Son of Rev 16:15
Man will come when least expected." **12:40** Mark 13:33
41 Peter asked, "Lord, is this illustration just for us or for everyone?"
42 And the Lord replied, "I'm talking to any faithful, sensible servant to whom the **12:42** Luke 7:13
master gives the responsibility of managing his household and feeding his family. 43 If
the master returns and finds that the servant has done a good job, there will be a reward.
44 I assure you, the master will put that servant in charge of all he owns. 45 But if the
servant thinks, 'My master won't be back for a while,' and begins oppressing the other
servants, partying, and getting drunk—46 well, the master will return unannounced and
unexpected. He will tear the servant apart and banish him with the unfaithful. 47 The **12:47** Deut 25:2
servant will be severely punished, for though he knew his duty, he refused to do it. Jas 4:17

12:38 Greek *in the second or third watch.*

12:31 Making the Kingdom of God your primary concern means making Jesus the Lord and King of your life. He must control every area—your work, play, plans, relationships. Is the Kingdom only one of your many concerns, or is it central to all you do? Are you holding back any areas of your life from God's control? As Lord and Creator, he wants to help provide what you need as well as guide how you use what he provides.

12:33 Money seen as an end in itself quickly traps us and cuts us off from both God and the needy. The key to using money wisely is to see how much we can use for God's purposes, not how much we can accumulate for ourselves. Does God's love touch your wallet? Does your money free you to help others? If so, you are storing up lasting treasures in heaven. If your financial goals and possessions hinder you from giving generously, loving others, or serving God, sell what you must to bring your life into perspective.

12:34 If you concentrate your money in your business, your thoughts will center on making the business profitable. If you direct it toward other people, you will become concerned with their welfare. Where do you put your time, money, and energy? What do you think about most? How should you change the way you use your resources in order to reflect Kingdom values more accurately?

12:35-40 Jesus repeatedly said that he would leave this world but would return at some future time (see Matthew 24–25; John 14:1-3). He also said that a Kingdom is being prepared for his followers. Many Greeks envisioned this as a heavenly, idealized, spiritual Kingdom. Jews—like Isaiah and John, the writer of Revelation—saw it as a restored earthly Kingdom.

12:40 Christ's return at an unexpected time is not a trap, a trick by which God hopes to catch us off guard. In fact, God is delaying his return so more people will have the opportunity to follow him (see 2 Peter 3:9). Before Christ's return, we have time to live out our beliefs and to reflect Jesus' love as we relate to others.

People who are ready for their Lord's return are (1) not hypocritical but sincere (12:1), (2) not fearful but ready to witness (12:4-9), (3) not worried but trusting (12:25, 26), (4) not greedy but generous (12:34), (5) not lazy but diligent (12:37). May your life be more like Christ's so that when he comes, you will be ready to greet him joyfully.

12:42-44 Jesus promises a reward for those who have been faithful to the Master. While we sometimes experience immediate and material rewards for our obedience to God, this is not always the case. If so, we would be tempted to boast about our achievements and only do good for what we get. Jesus said that if we look for rewards now, we will lose them later (see Mark 8:36). Our heavenly rewards will be the most accurate reflection of what we have done on earth, and they will be far greater than we can imagine.

12:48 Lev 5:17 Num 15:27-30

48“But people who are not aware that they are doing wrong will be punished only
lightly. Much is required from those to whom much is given, and much more is required
from those to whom much more is given.

Jesus Warns about Coming Division (**143**)

49“I have come to bring fire to the earth, and I wish that my task were already completed!

12:50 Mark 10:38-39

50There is a terrible baptism ahead of me, and I am under a heavy burden until it is
accomplished. 51Do you think I have come to bring peace to the earth? No, I have come
to bring strife and division! 52From now on families will be split apart, three in favor of

12:53 †Mic 7:6

me, and two against—or the other way around. 53There will be a division between father
and son, mother and daughter, mother-in-law and daughter-in-law.”

Jesus Warns about the Future Crisis (**144**)

12:54-56 Matt 16:2-3

54**Then Jesus turned to the crowd and said,** “When you see clouds beginning to form
in the west, you say, ‘Here comes a shower.’ And you are right. 55When the south wind
blows, you say, ‘Today will be a scorcher.’ And it is. 56You hypocrites! You know how
to interpret the appearance of the earth and the sky, but you can’t interpret these
present times.

12:58-59 Matt 5:25-26

57“Why can’t you decide for yourselves what is right? 58If you are on the way to court
and you meet your accuser, try to settle the matter before it reaches the judge, or you may
be sentenced and handed over to an officer and thrown in jail. 59And if that happens, you
won’t be free again until you have paid the last penny.”

Jesus Calls the People to Repent (**145**)

13:2 John 9:2-3

13 **About this time Jesus was informed that Pilate had murdered some people from
Galilee as they were sacrificing at the Temple in Jerusalem.** 2“Do you think those

13:3 Ps 7:12

Galileans were worse sinners than other people from Galilee?” **he asked.** “Is that why

13:4 John 9:7, 11

they suffered? 3Not at all! And you will also perish unless you turn from your evil ways
and turn to God. 4And what about the eighteen men who died when the Tower of Siloam

13:6 Matt 21:19 Mark 11:12-14

fell on them? Were they the worst sinners in Jerusalem? 5No, and I tell you again that
unless you repent, you will also perish.”

13:7 Hab 3:17 Matt 3:10

6**Then Jesus used this illustration:** “A man planted a fig tree in his garden and came
again and again to see if there was any fruit on it, but he was always disappointed. 7Finally,

---

12:48 Jesus has told us how to live until he comes: We must watch for him, work diligently, and obey his commands. Such attitudes are especially necessary for leaders. Watchful and faithful leaders will be given increased opportunities and responsibilities. The more resources, talents, and understanding we have, the more we are required to use them effectively. God will not hold us responsible for gifts he has not given us, but all of us have been given enough gifts and duties to keep us busy until Jesus comes.

12:50 The “baptism” to which Jesus referred was his coming crucifixion. Jesus was dreading the physical pain, of course, but even worse would be the spiritual pain of complete separation from God that would accompany his death for the sins of the world.

12:51-53 In these strange and unsettling words, Jesus revealed that his coming often results in conflict. Because he demands a response, families may be split apart when some choose to follow him and others refuse to do so. There is no middle ground with Jesus. He demands loyalty and commitment, sometimes to the point of severing other relationships. Are you willing to risk your family’s disapproval in order to gain eternal life?

12:54-57 For most of recorded history, the world’s principal occupation was farming. The farmer depended directly on the weather for his livelihood. He needed just the right amounts of sun and rain—not too much, not too little—to make his living, and he grew skilled at interpreting natural signs. Jesus was announcing an earthshaking event that would be much more important than the year’s crops—the coming of God’s Kingdom. Just as dark clouds forewarn of a rainstorm, there were signs that the Kingdom would soon arrive. But Jesus’ hearers, though skilled at interpreting weather signs, were intentionally ignoring the signs of the times.

13:1-5 Pilate may have killed the Galileans because he thought they were rebelling against Rome; those killed by the Tower of Siloam may have been working for the Romans on an aqueduct there. The Pharisees, who were opposed to using force to deal with Rome, would have said that the Galileans deserved to die for rebelling. The Zealots, a group of anti-Roman terrorists, would have said the aqueduct workers deserved to die for cooperating. Jesus said that neither the Galileans nor the workers should be blamed for their calamity. And instead of blaming others, everyone should look to his or her own day of judgment.

13:5 Whether a person is killed in a tragic accident or miraculously survives is not a measure of righteousness. Everyone has to die; that’s part of being human. But we will not stay dead. Jesus promises that those who believe in him will not perish but have eternal life (John 3:16).

13:6-9 In the Old Testament, a fruitful tree was often used as a symbol of godly living (see, for example, Psalm 1:3 and Jeremiah 17:7, 8). Jesus pointed out what would happen to the other kind of tree—the kind that took valuable time and space and still produced nothing for the patient gardener. By this illustration Jesus warned his listeners that God would not tolerate forever their lack of productivity. (Luke 3:9 records John the Baptist’s version of the same message.) Have you been enjoying God’s special treatment without giving anything in return? If so, respond to the Gardener’s patient care, and begin to bear the fruit God has created you to produce.

he said to his gardener, 'I've waited three years, and there hasn't been a single fig! Cut it
down. It's taking up space we can use for something else.'
8"The gardener answered, 'Give it one more chance. Leave it another year, and I'll (13:8 2 Pet 3:9, 15)
give it special attention and plenty of fertilizer. 9If we get figs next year, fine. If not, you
can cut it down.'"

Jesus Heals the Crippled Woman **(146)**

10One Sabbath day as Jesus was teaching in a synagogue, 11he saw a woman who had (13:10 Matt 4:23)
been crippled by an evil spirit. She had been bent double for eighteen years and was
unable to stand up straight. 12When Jesus saw her, he called her over and said, "Woman,
you are healed of your sickness!" 13Then he touched her, and instantly she could stand (13:13 Mark 5:23)
straight. How she praised and thanked God!
14But the leader in charge of the synagogue was indignant that Jesus had healed her (13:14 Exod 20:9-10; Deut 5:13-14; Matt 12:10; Mark 3:2; Luke 6:7; John 5:16)
on the Sabbath day. "There are six days of the week for working," he said to the crowd.
"Come on those days to be healed, not on the Sabbath."
15But the Lord replied, "You hypocrite! You work on the Sabbath day! Don't you untie
your ox or your donkey from their stalls on the Sabbath and lead them out for water?
16Wasn't it necessary for me, even on the Sabbath day, to free this dear woman* from (13:15 Luke 14:5)
the bondage in which Satan has held her for eighteen years?" 17This shamed his enemies. (13:16 Luke 19:9)
And all the people rejoiced at the wonderful things he did.

Jesus Teaches about the Kingdom of God **(147)**

18Then Jesus said, "What is the Kingdom of God like? How can I illustrate it? 19It is like
a tiny mustard seed planted in a garden; it grows and becomes a tree, and the birds come
and find shelter among its branches."
20He also asked, "What else is the Kingdom of God like? 21It is like yeast used by a
woman making bread. Even though she used a large amount* of flour, the yeast
permeated every part of the dough."

Jesus Teaches about Entering the Kingdom **(153)**

22Jesus went through the towns and villages, teaching as he went, always pressing on (13:24 Mark 10:25; 1 Tim 6:12)
toward Jerusalem. 23Someone asked him, "Lord, will only a few be saved?"
He replied, 24"The door to heaven is narrow. Work hard to get in, because many will (13:25 Matt 25:10-11)
try to enter, 25but when the head of the house has locked the door, it will be too late. Then
you will stand outside knocking and pleading, 'Lord, open the door for us!' But he will

13:16 Greek *this woman, a daughter of Abraham.* **13:21** Greek *3 measures.*

13:10-17 Why was healing considered work? The religious leaders saw healing as part of a doctor's profession, and practicing one's profession on the Sabbath was prohibited. The synagogue leader could not see beyond the law to Jesus' compassion in healing this crippled woman. Jesus shamed him and the other leaders by pointing out their hypocrisy. They would untie their animals and care for them, but they refused to rejoice when a human being was freed from Satan's bondage.

13:15, 16 The Pharisees hid behind their own set of laws to avoid love's obligations. We, too, can use the letter of the law to rationalize away our obligation to care for others (for example, by tithing regularly and then refusing to help a needy neighbor). But people's needs are more important than rules and regulations. Take time to help others, even if doing so might compromise your public image.

13:16 In our fallen world, disease and disability are common. Their causes are many and often multiple—inadequate nutrition, contact with a source of infection, lowered defenses, and even direct attack by Satan. Whatever the immediate cause of our illness, we can trace its original source to Satan, the author of all the evil in our world. The Good News is that Jesus is more powerful than the Devil or any disease. He often brings physical healing in this life; and when he returns, he will put an end to all disease and disability.

13:18-21 The general expectation among Jesus' hearers was that the Messiah would come as a great king and leader, freeing the nation from Rome and restoring Israel's former glory. But Jesus said his Kingdom was beginning quietly. Like the tiny mustard seed that grows into an enormous tree, or the spoonful of yeast that makes the bread dough double in size, the Kingdom of God would eventually push outward until the whole world was changed.

13:22 This is the second time Luke reminds us that Jesus was intentionally going to Jerusalem (the other time is in 9:51). Jesus knew he was on his way to die, but he continued preaching to large crowds. The prospect of death did not deter Jesus from his mission.

13:24, 25 Finding salvation requires more concentrated effort than most people are willing to put forth. Obviously we cannot save ourselves—there is no way we can work ourselves into God's favor. We "work hard to get in" through the narrow door by earnestly desiring to know Jesus and diligently striving to follow him whatever the cost. We dare not put off making this decision because the door will not stay open forever.

13:27 †Ps 6:8; Matt 25:12
13:29 Ps 107:3; Isa 43:5; 49:12; 59:19; Rev 14:15; 21:13; 22:16
13:30 Matt 19:30; 20:16; Mark 10:31

reply, 'I do not know you.' 26You will say, 'But we ate and drank with you, and you
taught in our streets.' 27And he will reply, 'I tell you, I don't know you. Go away, all you
who do evil.'

28"And there will be great weeping and gnashing of teeth, for you will see Abraham,
Isaac, Jacob, and all the prophets within the Kingdom of God, but you will be thrown
out. 29Then people will come from all over the world to take their places in the Kingdom
of God. 30And note this: Some who are despised now will be greatly honored then; and
some who are greatly honored now will be despised then.*"

Jesus Grieves over Jerusalem (**154**)

31A few minutes later some Pharisees said to him, "Get out of here if you want to live,
because Herod Antipas wants to kill you!"

13:33 Matt 16:21
13:34-35 Luke 19:41-44
13:35 †Ps 118:26; Jer 12:7; 22:5; Luke 19:38

32Jesus replied, "Go tell that fox that I will keep on casting out demons and doing
miracles of healing today and tomorrow; and the third day I will accomplish my purpose.
33Yes, today, tomorrow, and the next day I must proceed on my way. For it wouldn't do
for a prophet of God to be killed except in Jerusalem!

34"O Jerusalem, Jerusalem, the city that kills the prophets and stones God's messengers! How often I have wanted to gather your children together as a hen protects her
chicks beneath her wings, but you wouldn't let me. 35And now look, your house is left
to you empty. And you will never see me again until you say, 'Bless the one who comes
in the name of the Lord!'*"

13:30 Greek *Some are last who will be first, and some are first who will be last.* **13:35** Ps 118:26.

SEVEN SABBATH MIRACLES

Jesus sends a demon out of a man	Mark 1:21–28
Jesus heals Peter's mother-in-law	Mark 1:29–31
Jesus heals a lame man by the pool of Bethesda	John 5:1–18
Jesus heals a man with a deformed hand	Mark 3:1–6
Jesus restores a crippled woman	Luke 13:10–17
Jesus heals a man with dropsy	Luke 14:1–6
Jesus heals a man born blind	John 9:1–16

Over the centuries, the Jewish religious leaders had added rule after rule to God's law. For example, God's law said the Sabbath is a day of rest (Exodus 20:10, 11). But the religious leaders added to that law, creating one that said, "You cannot heal on the Sabbath" because that is "work." Seven times Jesus healed people on the Sabbath. In doing this, he was challenging these religious leaders to look beyond their rules to their true purpose—to honor God by helping those in need. Would God have been pleased if Jesus had ignored these people?

13:26, 27 We may not necessarily see the people we expect to find in the Kingdom of God. Some perfectly respectable religious leaders claiming allegiance to Jesus will not be there because secretly they were morally corrupt.

13:27 The people were eager to know who would be in God's Kingdom. Jesus explained that, although many people know something about God, only a few have acknowledged their sins and accepted his forgiveness. Just listening to Jesus' words or admiring his miracles is not enough. We must turn from sin and trust in God to save us.

13:29 God's Kingdom will include people from every part of the world. Israel's rejection of Jesus as Messiah would not stop God's plan. True Israel includes all people who believe in God. This was an important fact for Luke to stress as he was directing his Good News to a Gentile audience (see also Romans 4:16-25; Galatians 3:6-9).

13:30 There will be many surprises in God's Kingdom. Some who are despised now will be greatly honored then; some influential people here will be left outside the gates. Many "great" people on this earth (in God's eyes) are virtually ignored by the rest of the world. What matters to God is not a person's earthly popularity, status, wealth, heritage, or power but his or her commitment to Christ. How do your values match those of the Bible? Put God in first place, and you will join people from all over the world who will take their places at the feast in the Kingdom of Heaven.

13:31-33 The Pharisees weren't interested in protecting Jesus from danger. They were trying to trap him themselves. The Pharisees urged Jesus to leave because they wanted to stop him from going to Jerusalem, not because they feared Herod. But Jesus' life, work, and death were not to be determined by Herod or the Pharisees. His life was planned and directed by God himself, and his mission would unfold in God's time and according to God's plan.

13:33, 34 Why was Jesus focusing on Jerusalem? Jerusalem, the city of God, symbolized the entire nation. It was Israel's largest city, the nation's spiritual and political capital, and Jews from around the world visited it frequently. But Jerusalem had a history of rejecting God's prophets (1 Kings 19:10; 2 Chronicles 24:19; Jeremiah 2:30; 26:20-23), and it would reject the Messiah, just as it had rejected his forerunners.

Jesus Heals a Man with Swollen Limbs **(155)**

14 One Sabbath day Jesus was in the home of a leader of the Pharisees. The people 14:1
were watching him closely, 2because there was a man there whose arms and Luke 7:36; 11:37
legs were swollen.* 3Jesus asked the Pharisees and experts in religious law, "Well, is 14:3
it permitted in the law to heal people on the Sabbath day, or not?" 4When they refused Luke 6:9
to answer, Jesus touched the sick man and healed him and sent him away. 5Then he 14:5
turned to them and asked, "Which of you doesn't work on the Sabbath? If your son* Matt 12:11
or your cow falls into a pit, don't you proceed at once to get him out?" 6Again they
had no answer.

Jesus Teaches about Seeking Honor **(156)**

7When Jesus noticed that all who had come to the dinner were trying to sit near the head 14:7
of the table, he gave them this advice: 8"If you are invited to a wedding feast, don't Matt 23:6
always head for the best seat. What if someone more respected than you has also been 14:8-11
invited? 9The host will say, 'Let this person sit here instead.' Then you will be embar- Prov 25:6-7
rassed and will have to take whatever seat is left at the foot of the table!

10"Do this instead—sit at the foot of the table. Then when your host sees you, he will
come and say, 'Friend, we have a better place than this for you!' Then you will be
honored in front of all the other guests. 11For the proud will be humbled, but the humble 14:11
will be honored." Matt 23:12 Luke 18:14

12Then he turned to his host. "When you put on a luncheon or a dinner," he said,
"don't invite your friends, brothers, relatives, and rich neighbors. For they will repay you
by inviting you back. 13Instead, invite the poor, the crippled, the lame, and the blind. 14:14
14Then at the resurrection of the godly, God will reward you for inviting those who could Acts 24:15
not repay you."

Jesus Tells the Parable of the Great Festival **(157)**

15Hearing this, a man sitting at the table with Jesus exclaimed, "What a privilege it
would be to have a share in the Kingdom of God!"

16Jesus replied with this illustration: "A man prepared a great feast and sent out many
invitations. 17When all was ready, he sent his servant around to notify the guests that it

14:2 Traditionally translated *who had dropsy.* **14:5** Some manuscripts read *donkey.*

14:1-6 Earlier Jesus had been invited to a Pharisee's home for discussion (7:36). This time a prominent Pharisee invited Jesus to his home specifically to trap him into saying or doing something for which he could be arrested. It may be surprising to see Jesus on the Pharisees' turf after he had denounced them so many times. But he was not afraid to face them, even though he knew that their purpose was to trick him into breaking their laws.

14:7-11 Jesus advised people not to rush for the best places at a feast. People today are just as eager to raise their social status, whether by being with the right people, dressing for success, or driving the right car. Whom do you try to impress? Rather than aiming for prestige, look for a place where you can serve. If God wants you to serve on a wider scale, he will invite you to take a higher place.

14:7-14 Jesus taught two lessons here. First, he spoke to the guests, telling them not to seek places of honor. Service is more important in God's Kingdom than status. Second, he told the host not to be exclusive about whom he invited. God opens his Kingdom to everyone.

14:11 How can we humble ourselves? Some people try to give the appearance of humility in order to manipulate others. Others think that humility means putting themselves down. Truly humble people compare themselves only with Christ, realize their sinfulness, and understand their limitations. On the other hand, they also recognize their gifts and strengths and are willing to use them as Christ directs. Humility is not self-degradation; it is realistic self-assessment and commitment to serve.

14:15-24 The man sitting at the table with Jesus saw the glory of God's Kingdom, but he did not yet understand how to get in. In Jesus' story, many people turned down the invitation to the feast because the timing was inconvenient. We, too, may resist or delay responding to God's invitation, and our excuses may sound reasonable—work duties, family responsibilities, financial needs, or whatever they may be. Nevertheless, God's invitation is the most important event in our life, no matter how inconveniently it may be timed. Are you making excuses to avoid responding to God's call? Jesus reminds us that the time will come when God will pull his invitation and offer it to others—then it will be too late to get into the feast.

14:16ff It was customary to send two invitations to a party: the first to announce the event, the second to tell the guests that everything was ready. The guests in Jesus' story insulted the host by making excuses when he issued the second invitation. In Israel's history, God's first invitation came from Moses and the prophets; the second came from his Son. The religious leaders accepted the first invitation. They believed that God had called them to be his people, but they insulted God by refusing to accept his Son. Thus, as the master in the story sent his servant into the streets to invite the needy to his feast, so God sent his Son to a whole world of needy people to tell them that God's Kingdom had arrived and was ready for them.

14:16ff In this chapter we read Jesus' words against seeking status and in favor of hard work and even suffering. Let us not lose sight of the end result of all our humility and self-sacrifice—a joyous banquet with our Lord! God never asks us to suffer for the sake of suffering. He never asks us to give up something good unless he plans to replace it with something even better. Jesus is not calling us to join him in a labor camp but in a feast—the wedding feast of the Lamb (Revelation 19:6-9), when God and his beloved church will be joined forever.

was time for them to come. [18]But they all began making excuses. One said he had just
bought a field and wanted to inspect it, so he asked to be excused. [19]Another said he had

14:20 Deut 24:5; 1 Cor 7:33

just bought five pair of oxen and wanted to try them out. [20]Another had just been
married, so he said he couldn't come.
[21]"The servant returned and told his master what they had said. His master was angry
and said, 'Go quickly into the streets and alleys of the city and invite the poor, the
crippled, the lame, and the blind.' [22]After the servant had done this, he reported, 'There
is still room for more.' [23]So his master said, 'Go out into the country lanes and behind

14:24 Matt 21:43; Acts 13:46

the hedges and urge anyone you find to come, so that the house will be full. [24]For none
of those I invited first will get even the smallest taste of what I had prepared for them.'"

Jesus Teaches about the Cost of Being a Disciple (**158**)

14:26 Deut 33:9; Matt 16:24; Mark 8:34; Luke 9:23; 18:29; John 12:25

[25]Great crowds were following Jesus. He turned around and said to them, [26]"If you want
to be my follower you must love me more than* your own father and mother, wife and
children, brothers and sisters—yes, more than your own life. Otherwise, you cannot be
my disciple. [27]And you cannot be my disciple if you do not carry your own cross and

14:27 Matt 10:38; 16:24; Mark 8:34; Luke 9:23

follow me.
[28]"But don't begin until you count the cost. For who would begin construction of a
building without first getting estimates and then checking to see if there is enough money
to pay the bills? [29]Otherwise, you might complete only the foundation before running
out of funds. And then how everyone would laugh at you! [30]They would say, 'There's
the person who started that building and ran out of money before it was finished!'
[31]"Or what king would ever dream of going to war without first sitting down with his
counselors and discussing whether his army of ten thousand is strong enough to defeat

14:33 Phil 3:7-8

the twenty thousand soldiers who are marching against him? [32]If he is not able, then
while the enemy is still far away, he will send a delegation to discuss terms of peace.

14:34 Matt 5:13; Mark 9:50

[33]So no one can become my disciple without giving up everything for me.
[34]"Salt is good for seasoning. But if it loses its flavor, how do you make it salty again?

14:35 Matt 11:15

[35]Flavorless salt is good neither for the soil nor for fertilizer. It is thrown away. Anyone
who is willing to hear should listen and understand!"

Jesus Tells the Parable of the Lost Sheep (**159**)

15:1 Matt 9:11; Luke 5:29; Gal 2:12

15 Tax collectors and other notorious sinners often came to listen to Jesus teach.
[2]This made the Pharisees and teachers of religious law complain that he was
associating with such despicable people—even eating with them!

14:26 Greek *you must hate.*

14:27 Jesus' audience was well aware of what it meant to carry one's own cross. When the Romans led a criminal to his execution site, he was forced to carry the cross on which he would die. This showed his submission to Rome and warned observers that they had better submit, too. Jesus spoke this teaching to get the crowds to think through their enthusiasm for him. He encouraged those who were superficial either to go deeper or to turn back. Following Christ means total submission to him—perhaps even to the point of death.

14:28-30 When a builder doesn't count the cost or estimates it inaccurately, his building may be left half completed. Will your Christian life be abandoned after a little while because you did not count the cost of commitment to Jesus? What are those costs? Christians may face loss of social status or wealth. They may have to give up control of their money, their time, or their career. They may be hated, separated from their family, and even put to death. Following Christ does not mean a trouble-free life. We must carefully count the cost of becoming Christ's disciples so that we will firmly hold to our faith and won't be tempted later to turn back later.

14:34 Salt can lose its flavor. When it gets wet and then dries, nothing is left but a tasteless residue. Many Christians blend into the world and avoid the cost of standing up for Christ. But Jesus says if Christians lose their distinctive saltiness, they become worthless. Just as salt flavors and preserves food, we are to preserve the good in the world and bring new flavor to life. This requires careful planning, willing sacrifice, and unswerving commitment to Christ's Kingdom. But if a Christian fails to be "salty," he or she fails to represent Christ in the world. How salty are you?

15:2 Why were the Pharisees and teachers of religious law bothered that Jesus associated with these people? The religious leaders were always careful to stay "clean" according to Old Testament law. In fact, they went well beyond the law in their avoidance of certain people and situations and in their ritual washings. By contrast, Jesus took their concept of "cleanness" lightly. He risked defilement by touching those who had leprosy and by neglecting to wash in the Pharisees' prescribed manner, and he showed complete disregard for their sanctions against associating with certain classes of people. He came to offer salvation to sinners and to show that God loves them. Jesus didn't worry about the accusations. Instead, he continued going to those who needed him, regardless of the effect these rejected people might have on his reputation. What keeps you away from people who need Christ?

3So Jesus used this illustration: 4"If you had one hundred sheep, and one of them
strayed away and was lost in the wilderness, wouldn't you leave the ninety-nine others
to go and search for the lost one until you found it? 5And then you would joyfully carry
it home on your shoulders. 6When you arrived, you would call together your friends and
neighbors to rejoice with you because your lost sheep was found. 7In the same way,
heaven will be happier over one lost sinner who returns to God than over ninety-nine
others who are righteous and haven't strayed away!

Jesus Tells the Parable of the Lost Coin **(160)**

8"Or suppose a woman has ten valuable silver coins* and loses one. Won't she light a
lamp and look in every corner of the house and sweep every nook and cranny until she
finds it? 9And when she finds it, she will call in her friends and neighbors to rejoice with
her because she has found her lost coin. 10In the same way, there is joy in the presence
of God's angels when even one sinner repents."

Jesus Tells the Parable of the Lost Son **(161)**

11To illustrate the point further, Jesus told them this story: "A man had two sons. 12The **15:12**
younger son told his father, 'I want my share of your estate now, instead of waiting until Deut 21:17
you die.' So his father agreed to divide his wealth between his sons.

13"A few days later this younger son packed all his belongings and took a trip to a
distant land, and there he wasted all his money on wild living. 14About the time his
money ran out, a great famine swept over the land, and he began to starve. 15He
persuaded a local farmer to hire him to feed his pigs. 16The boy became so hungry that
even the pods he was feeding the pigs looked good to him. But no one gave him anything.

17"When he finally came to his senses, he said to himself, 'At home even the hired
men have food enough to spare, and here I am, dying of hunger! 18I will go home to my **15:18** Ps 51:4
father and say, "Father, I have sinned against both heaven and you, 19and I am no longer
worthy of being called your son. Please take me on as a hired man."'

20"So he returned home to his father. And while he was still a long distance away, his **15:20**
father saw him coming. Filled with love and compassion, he ran to his son, embraced Gen 45:14-15; 46:29

15:8 Greek *10 drachmas.* A drachma was the equivalent of a full day's wage.

15:3-6 It may seem foolish for the shepherd to leave 99 sheep to go search for just one. But the shepherd knew that the 99 would be safe in the sheepfold, whereas the lost sheep was in danger. Because each sheep was of high value, the shepherd knew that it was worthwhile to search diligently for the lost one. God's love for each individual is so great that he seeks out each one and rejoices when he or she is "found." Jesus associated with sinners because he wanted to bring the lost sheep—people considered beyond hope—the Good News of God's Kingdom. Before you were a believer, God sought you; and his love is still seeking those who are yet lost.

15:4, 5 We may be able to understand a God who would forgive sinners who come to him for mercy. But a God who tenderly searches for sinners and then joyfully forgives them must possess an extraordinary love! This is the kind of love that prompted Jesus to come to earth to search for lost people and save them. This is the kind of extraordinary love that God has for you. If you feel far from God, don't despair. He is seaching for you.

15:8-10 Palestinian women received 10 silver coins as a wedding gift. Besides their monetary value, these coins held sentimental value like that of a wedding ring, and to lose one would be extremely distressing. Just as a woman would rejoice at finding her lost coin or ring, so the angels rejoice over a repentant sinner. Each individual is precious to God. He grieves over every loss and rejoices whenever one of his children is found and brought into the Kingdom. Perhaps we would have more joy in our churches if we shared Jesus' love and concern for the lost.

15:12 The younger son's share of the estate would have been one-third, with the older son receiving two-thirds (Deuteronomy 21:17). In most cases he would have received this at his father's death, although fathers sometimes chose to divide up their inheritance early and retire from managing their estates. What is unusual here is that the younger one initiated the division of the estate. This showed arrogant disregard for his father's authority as head of the family.

15:15, 16 According to Moses' law, pigs were unclean animals (Leviticus 11:2-8; Deuteronomy 14:8). This meant that pigs could not be eaten or used for sacrifices. To protect themselves from defilement, Jews would not even touch pigs. For a Jew to stoop to feeding pigs was a great humiliation, and for this young man to eat food that the pigs had touched was to be degraded beyond belief. The younger son had truly sunk to the depths.

15:17 The younger son, like many who are rebellious and immature, wanted to be free to live as he pleased, and he had to hit bottom before he came to his senses. It often takes great sorrow and tragedy to cause people to look to the only one who can help them—Jesus. Are you trying to live life your own way, selfishly pushing aside any responsibility or commitment that gets in your way? Stop and look before you hit bottom. You will save yourself and your family much grief.

15:20 In the two preceding stories, the seeker actively looked for the coin and the sheep, which could not return by themselves. In this story, the father watched and waited. He was dealing with a human being with a will of his own, but he was ready to greet his son if he returned. In the same way, God's love is constant and patient and welcoming. He will search for us and give us opportunities to respond, but he will not force us to come to him. Like the father in this story, God waits patiently for us to come to our senses.

him, and kissed him. 21His son said to him, 'Father, I have sinned against both heaven
15:22 Gen 41:42 Zech 3:4 Rev 6:11 — and you, and I am no longer worthy of being called your son.*'
22"But his father said to the servants, 'Quick! Bring the finest robe in the house and
put it on him. Get a ring for his finger, and sandals for his feet. 23And kill the calf we
15:24 Eph 2:1, 5; 5:14 — have been fattening in the pen. We must celebrate with a feast, 24for this son of mine was
dead and has now returned to life. He was lost, but now he is found.' So the party began.
25"Meanwhile, the older son was in the fields working. When he returned home, he
heard music and dancing in the house, 26and he asked one of the servants what was going
on. 27'Your brother is back,' he was told, 'and your father has killed the calf we were
fattening and has prepared a great feast. We are celebrating because of his safe return.'
28"The older brother was angry and wouldn't go in. His father came out and begged
him, 29but he replied, 'All these years I've worked hard for you and never once refused
to do a single thing you told me to. And in all that time you never gave me even one
young goat for a feast with my friends. 30Yet when this son of yours comes back after
15:31 Prov 29:3 John 17:10, 24 — squandering your money on prostitutes, you celebrate by killing the finest calf we have.'
31"His father said to him, 'Look, dear son, you and I are very close, and everything I
have is yours. 32We had to celebrate this happy day. For your brother was dead and has
come back to life! He was lost, but now he is found!'"

Jesus Tells the Parable of the Shrewd Manager **(162)**

16:1 Luke 15:13, 30 — **16** Jesus told this story to his disciples: "A rich man hired a manager to handle his
affairs, but soon a rumor went around that the manager was thoroughly dishonest.
2So his employer called him in and said, 'What's this I hear about your stealing from
me? Get your report in order, because you are going to be dismissed.'
3"The manager thought to himself, 'Now what? I'm through here, and I don't have
the strength to go out and dig ditches, and I'm too proud to beg. 4I know just the thing!
And then I'll have plenty of friends to take care of me when I leave!'
5"So he invited each person who owed money to his employer to come and discuss
the situation. He asked the first one, 'How much do you owe him?' 6The man replied, 'I
owe him eight hundred gallons of olive oil.' So the manager told him, 'Tear up that bill
and write another one for four hundred gallons.*'
7"'And how much do you owe my employer?' he asked the next man. 'A thousand
bushels of wheat,' was the reply. 'Here,' the manager said, 'take your bill and replace it
with one for only eight hundred bushels.*'
16:8 John 12:36 Eph 5:8 1 Thes 5:5 — 8"The rich man had to admire the dishonest rascal for being so shrewd. And it is true
that the citizens of this world are more shrewd than the godly are. 9I tell you, use your

15:21 Some manuscripts add *Please take me on as a hired man.* **16:6** Greek *100 baths . . . 50 [baths].* **16:7** Greek *100 korous . . . 80 [korous].*

15:24 The sheep was lost because it may have foolishly wandered away (15:4); the coin was lost through no fault of its own (15:8); and the son left out of selfishness (15:12). God's great love reaches out and finds sinners no matter why or how they got lost.

15:25-31 It was hard for the older brother to accept his younger brother when he returned, and it is just as difficult to accept "younger brothers and sisters" today. People who repent after leading notoriously sinful lives are often held in suspicion; churches are sometimes unwilling to admit them to membership. Instead, we should rejoice like the angels in heaven when an unbeliever repents and turns to God. Like the father, accept repentant sinners wholeheartedly and give them the support and encouragement that they need to grow in Christ.

15:30 In the story of the lost son, the father's response is contrasted with the older brother's. The father forgave because he was filled with love. The son refused to forgive because he was bitter about the injustice of it all. His resentment rendered him just as lost to the father's love as his younger brother had been. Don't let anything keep you from forgiving others. If you are refusing to forgive people, you are missing a wonderful opportunity to experience joy and share it with others. Make your joy grow: Forgive somebody who has hurt you.

15:32 In Jesus' story, the older brother represented the Pharisees, who were angry and resentful that sinners were being welcomed into God's Kingdom. "After all," the Pharisees must have thought, "we have sacrificed and done *so much* for God." How easy it is to resent God's gracious forgiveness of others whom we consider to be far worse sinners than ourselves. But if our self-righteousness gets in the way of rejoicing when others come to Jesus, we are no better than the Pharisees.

16:1-8 Our use of money is a good test of the lordship of Christ. (1) Let us use our resources wisely because they belong to God, and not to us. (2) Money can be used for good or evil; let us use ours for good. (3) Money has a lot of power, so we must use it carefully and thoughtfully. (4) We must use our material goods in a way that will foster faith and obedience (see 12:33, 34).

16:9 We are to make wise use of the financial opportunities we have, not to earn heaven but to help people find Christ. If we use our money to help those in need or to help others find Christ, our earthly investment will bring eternal benefit. When we obey God's will, the unselfish use of possessions will follow.

worldly resources to benefit others and make friends. In this way, your generosity stores
up a reward for you in heaven.*
10 “Unless you are faithful in small matters, you won’t be faithful in large ones. If you
cheat even a little, you won’t be honest with greater responsibilities. 11 And if you are
untrustworthy about worldly wealth, who will trust you with the true riches of heaven?
12 And if you are not faithful with other people’s money, why should you be trusted with
money of your own?
13 “No one can serve two masters. For you will hate one and love the other, or be
devoted to one and despise the other. You cannot serve both God and money.”
14 The Pharisees, who dearly loved their money, naturally scoffed at all this. 15 Then
he said to them, “You like to look good in public, but God knows your evil hearts. What
this world honors is an abomination in the sight of God.
16 “Until John the Baptist began to preach, the laws of Moses and the messages of the
prophets were your guides. But now the Good News of the Kingdom of God is preached,
and eager multitudes are forcing their way in. 17 But that doesn’t mean that the law has lost
its force in even the smallest point. It is stronger and more permanent than heaven and earth.
18 “Anyone who divorces his wife and marries someone else commits adultery, and
anyone who marries a divorced woman commits adultery.”

Jesus Tells about the Rich Man and the Beggar **(163)**

19 Jesus said, “There was a certain rich man who was splendidly clothed and who lived
each day in luxury. 20 At his door lay a diseased beggar named Lazarus. 21 As Lazarus lay
there longing for scraps from the rich man’s table, the dogs would come and lick his open
sores. 22 Finally, the beggar died and was carried by the angels to be with Abraham.* The
rich man also died and was buried, 23 and his soul went to the place of the dead.* There,
in torment, he saw Lazarus in the far distance with Abraham.
24 “The rich man shouted, ‘Father Abraham, have some pity! Send Lazarus over here
to dip the tip of his finger in water and cool my tongue, because I am in anguish in these
flames.’

16:10-12 Matt 25:20-30; Luke 19:17-26
16:13 Matt 6:24
16:14 Luke 23:35; 1 Tim 3:3
16:15 Prov 24:12; Matt 23:28; Luke 8:9-14
16:16 Matt 11:12-13
16:17 Matt 5:18
16:18 Matt 5:32; 19:9; Mark 10:11-12; 1 Cor 7:10-11
16:22 Matt 8:11; John 1:18
16:24 Luke 3:8

16:9 Or *Then when you run out at the end of this life, your friends will welcome you into eternal homes.* **16:22** Greek *into Abraham’s bosom.* **16:23** Greek *to Hades.*

16:10, 11 Our integrity is often put on the line in money matters. God calls us to be honest even in small details we could easily ignore. Heaven’s riches are far more valuable than earthly wealth. But if we are not trustworthy with our money here (no matter how much or little we have), we will be unfit to handle the vast riches of God’s Kingdom. See that you maintain your integrity in all matters, whether big or small.

16:13 Money has the power to take God’s place in your life. It can become your master. How can you tell if you are a slave to money? (1) Do you think and worry about it frequently? (2) Do you give up doing what you should do or would like to do in order to make more money? (3) Do you spend a great deal of your time caring for your possessions? (4) Is it hard for you to give money away? (5) Are you in debt?

Money is a hard master and a deceptive one. Wealth promises power and control, but often it cannot deliver. Great fortunes can be made—and lost—overnight, and no amount of money can provide health, happiness, or eternal life. How much better it is to let God be your master. His servants have peace of mind and security, both now and forever.

16:14 Because the Pharisees loved money, they took exception to Jesus’ teaching. We live in an age that measures people’s worth by how much money they make. Do we scoff at Jesus’ warnings against serving money? Do we try to explain them away? Do we apply them to someone else—the Pharisees, for example? Unless we take Jesus’ statements seriously, we may be acting like Pharisees ourselves.

16:15 The Pharisees acted piously to get praise from others, but God knew what was in their hearts. They considered their wealth to be a sign of God’s approval. God detested their wealth because it caused them to abandon true spirituality. Though prosperity may earn people’s praise, it must never substitute for devotion and service to God.

16:16, 17 John the Baptist’s ministry was the dividing line between the Old and New Testaments (John 1:15-18). With the arrival of Jesus came the realization of all the prophets’ hopes. Jesus emphasized that his Kingdom fulfilled the law (the Old Testament); it did not cancel it (Matthew 5:17). His was not a new system but the culmination of the old. The same God who worked through Moses was working through Jesus.

16:18 Most religious leaders of Jesus’ day permitted a man to divorce his wife for nearly any reason. Jesus’ teaching about divorce went beyond Moses’ (Deuteronomy 24:1-4). Stricter than any of the then-current schools of thought, Jesus’ teachings shocked his hearers (see Matthew 19:10) just as they shake today’s readers. Jesus says in no uncertain terms that marriage is a lifetime commitment. To leave your spouse for another person may be legal, but it is adultery in God’s eyes. As you think about marriage, remember that God intends it to be a permanent commitment.

16:19-31 The Pharisees considered wealth to be a proof of a person’s righteousness. Jesus startled them with this story in which a diseased beggar is rewarded and a rich man is punished. The rich man did not go to hell because of his wealth but because he was selfish, refusing to feed Lazarus, take him in, or care for him. The rich man was hard-hearted in spite of his great blessings. The amount of money we have is not as important as the way we use it. What is your attitude toward your money and possessions? Do you hoard them selfishly, or do you use them to help others?

16:20 This Lazarus should not be confused with the Lazarus whom Jesus raised from the dead in John 11.

16:25 Luke 6:24 25“But Abraham said to him, ‘Son, remember that during your lifetime you had
everything you wanted, and Lazarus had nothing. So now he is here being comforted,
and you are in anguish. 26And besides, there is a great chasm separating us. Anyone who
wanted to cross over to you from here is stopped at its edge, and no one there can cross
over to us.’
16:28 Acts 18:5 27“Then the rich man said, ‘Please, Father Abraham, send him to my father’s home.
28For I have five brothers, and I want him to warn them about this place of torment so
they won’t have to come here when they die.’
16:29 Luke 24:27, 44; John 1:45; 5:45-47; Acts 15:21 29“But Abraham said, ‘Moses and the prophets have warned them. Your brothers can
read their writings anytime they want to.’
30“The rich man replied, ‘No, Father Abraham! But if someone is sent to them from
the dead, then they will turn from their sins.’
16:31 Matt 6:24; John 11:44-48 31“But Abraham said, ‘If they won’t listen to Moses and the prophets, they won’t
listen even if someone rises from the dead.’”

Jesus Tells about Forgiveness and Faith (**164**)

17:1-3 Matt 18:7; Mark 9:42 **17** One day Jesus said to his disciples, “There will always be temptations to sin,
but how terrible it will be for the person who does the tempting. 2It would be
better to be thrown into the sea with a large millstone tied around the neck than to face
17:3 Matt 18:15 the punishment in store for harming one of these little ones. 3I am warning you! If
another believer sins, rebuke him; then if he repents, forgive him. 4Even if he wrongs
you seven times a day and each time turns again and asks forgiveness, forgive him.”
17:5 Mark 9:24 5One day the apostles said to the Lord, “We need more faith; tell us how to get it.”
17:6 Matt 17:20; 21:21 6“Even if you had faith as small as a mustard seed,” the Lord answered, “you could
say to this mulberry tree, ‘May God uproot you and throw you into the sea,’ and it would
obey you!
7“When a servant comes in from plowing or taking care of sheep, he doesn’t just
sit down and eat. 8He must first prepare his master’s meal and serve him his supper
before eating his own. 9And the servant is not even thanked, because he is merely
doing what he is supposed to do. 10In the same way, when you obey me you should
17:10 1 Cor 9:16 say, ‘We are not worthy of praise. We are servants who have simply done our duty.’”

16:29-31 The rich man thought that his five brothers would surely believe a messenger who had been raised from the dead. But Jesus said that if they did not believe Moses and the prophets, who spoke constantly of caring for the poor, not even a resurrection would convince them. Notice the irony in Jesus' statement; on his way to Jerusalem to die, he was fully aware that even when he had risen from the dead, most of the religious leaders would not accept him. They were set in their ways, and neither Scripture nor God's Son himself would shake them loose.

17:1-3 Jesus may have been directing this warning at the religious leaders who taught their converts their own hypocritical ways (see Matthew 23:15). They were perpetuating an evil system. A person who teaches others has a solemn responsibility (James 3:1). Like physicians, a teacher should keep this ancient oath in mind: "First, do no harm."

17:3, 4 To rebuke does not mean to point out every sin we see; it means to bring sin to a person's attention with the purpose of restoring him or her to God and to fellow humans. When you feel you must rebuke another Christian for a sin, check your attitudes before you speak. Do you love that person? Are you willing to forgive? Unless rebuke is tied to forgiveness, it will not help the sinning person.

17:5, 6 The disciples' request was genuine; they wanted the faith necessary for such radical forgiveness. But Jesus didn't directly answer their question because the amount of faith is not as important as its genuineness. What is faith? It is complete trust and loyalty to God that results in a willingness to do his will. Faith is not something we use to put on a show for others. It is complete and humble obedience to God's will, readiness to do whatever he calls us to do. The amount of faith isn't as important as the right kind of faith—faith in our all-powerful God.

17:6 A mustard seed is small, but it is alive and growing. Almost invisible at first, it will begin to spread, first under the ground and then visibly. Like a tiny seed, a small amount of genuine faith in God will take root and grow. Although each change will be gradual and imperceptible, soon this faith will have produced major results that will uproot and destroy competing loyalties. We don't need more faith; a tiny seed of faith is enough if it is alive and growing.

17:7-10 If we have obeyed God, we have only done our duty, and we should regard it as a privilege. Do you sometimes feel that you deserve extra credit for serving God? Remember, obedience is not something extra we do; it is our duty. Jesus is not suggesting that our service is meaningless or useless, nor is he advocating doing away with rewards. He is attacking unwarranted self-esteem and spiritual pride.

Jesus Heals Ten Men with Leprosy **(169)**

11 As Jesus continued on toward Jerusalem, he reached the border between Galilee and **17:11** Luke 9:51-52; 13:22
Samaria. 12 As he entered a village there, ten lepers stood at a distance, 13 crying out, **17:12** Lev 13:46
"Jesus, Master, have mercy on us!"
14 He looked at them and said, "Go show yourselves to the priests." And as they went, **17:14** Lev 14:2-3 Luke 5:14
their leprosy disappeared.
15 One of them, when he saw that he was healed, came back to Jesus, shouting, "Praise
God, I'm healed!" 16 He fell face down on the ground at Jesus' feet, thanking him for **17:16** Matt 10:5
what he had done. This man was a Samaritan.
17 Jesus asked, "Didn't I heal ten men? Where are the other nine? 18 Does only this
foreigner return to give glory to God?" 19 And Jesus said to the man, "Stand up and go. **17:19** Matt 9:22 Luke 7:50; 18:42
Your faith has made you well."

Jesus Teaches about the Coming of the Kingdom of God **(170)**

20 One day the Pharisees asked Jesus, "When will the Kingdom of God come?" **17:20** John 3:3; 18:36
Jesus replied, "The Kingdom of God isn't ushered in with visible signs.* 21 You
won't be able to say, 'Here it is!' or 'It's over there!' For the Kingdom of God is among
you.*"
22 Later he talked again about this with his disciples. "The time is coming when you
will long to share in the days of the Son of Man, but you won't be able to," he said. **17:23** Mark 13:21 Luke 17:21; 21:8
23 "Reports will reach you that the Son of Man has returned and that he is in this place
or that. Don't believe such reports or go out to look for him. 24 For when the Son of Man **17:24** 1 Tim 6:15
returns, you will know it beyond all doubt. It will be as evident as the lightning that
flashes across the sky. 25 But first the Son of Man must suffer terribly* and be rejected **17:25** Matt 16:21 Mark 8:31 Luke 9:22
by this generation.

17:20 Or *by your speculations.* **17:21** Or *within you.* **17:25** Or *suffer many things.*

17:11-14 People who had leprosy were required to try to stay away from other people and to announce their presence if they had to come near. Sometimes leprosy went into remission. If a leper thought his leprosy had gone away, he was supposed to present himself to a priest, who could declare him clean (Leviticus 14). Jesus sent the 10 lepers to the priest *before* they were healed—and they went! They responded in faith, and Jesus healed them on the way. Is your trust in God so strong that you act on what he says even before you see evidence that it will work?

17:16 Jesus healed all 10 lepers, but only one returned to thank him. It is possible to receive God's great gifts with an ungrateful spirit—9 of the 10 men did so. Only the thankful man, however, learned that his faith had played a role in his healing; and only grateful Christians grow in understanding God's grace. God does not demand that we thank him, but he is pleased when we do so. And he uses our responsiveness to teach us more about himself.

17:16 Not only was this man a leper, he was also a Samaritan—a race despised by the Jews as idolatrous half-breeds (see the note on 10:33). Once again Luke is pointing out that God's grace is for everybody.

17:20, 21 The Pharisees asked when God's Kingdom would come, not knowing that it had already arrived. The Kingdom of God is not like an earthly kingdom with geographical boundaries. Instead, it begins with the work of God's Spirit in people's lives and in relationships. We must resist looking to institutions or programs for evidence of the progress of God's Kingdom. Instead, we should look for what God is doing in people's hearts.

17:23, 24 Many will claim to be the Messiah, and many will claim that the Son of Man has returned—and people will believe them. Jesus warns us never to take such reports seriously, no matter how convincing they may sound. When Jesus returns, his power and presence will be evident to everyone. No one will need to spread the message because all will see for themselves.

17:23-36 Life will be going on as usual on the day Christ returns. There will be no warning. Most people will be going about their everyday tasks, indifferent to the demands of God. They will be as surprised by Christ's return as the people in Noah's day were by the Flood (Genesis 6–8) or the people in Lot's day by the destruction of Sodom (Genesis 19). We don't know the time of Christ's return, but we do know that he is coming. He may come today, tomorrow, or centuries in the future. Whenever he comes, we must be morally and spiritually ready. Live as if Jesus were returning today.

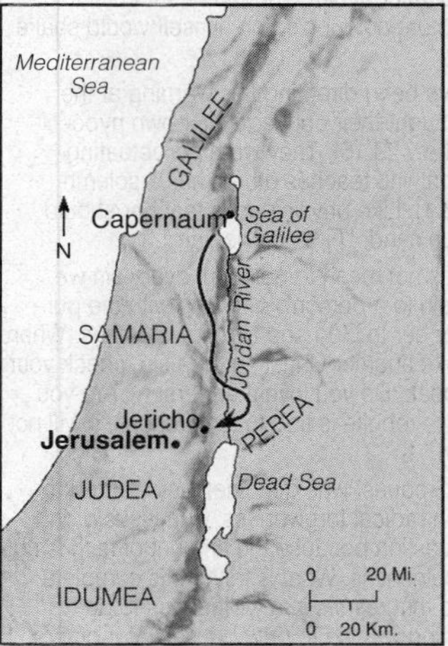

LAST TRIP FROM GALILEE
Jesus left Galilee for the last time—he would not return before his death. He passed through Samaria, met and healed 10 men who had leprosy, and continued to Jerusalem. He spent some time east of the Jordan (Mark 10:1) before going to Jericho (Luke 19:1).

17:26-27 Matt 24:37-39 26“When the Son of Man returns, the world will be like the people were in Noah’s day.
27In those days before the flood, the people enjoyed banquets and parties and weddings
right up to the time Noah entered his boat and the flood came to destroy them all.
17:28 Gen 19:1-28 28“And the world will be as it was in the days of Lot. People went about their daily
business—eating and drinking, buying and selling, farming and building—29until the
morning Lot left Sodom. Then fire and burning sulfur rained down from heaven and
17:30 2 Thes 1:7 destroyed them all. 30Yes, it will be ‘business as usual’ right up to the hour when the Son
17:31 Matt 24:17-18 Mark 13:15-16 of Man returns.* 31On that day a person outside the house* must not go into the house
to pack. A person in the field must not return to town. 32Remember what happened to
Lot’s wife! 33Whoever clings to this life will lose it, and whoever loses this life will save
17:33 Matt 10:39; 16:25 Mark 8:35 Luke 9:24 John 12:25 it. 34That night two people will be asleep in one bed; one will be taken away, and the
other will be left. 35Two women will be grinding flour together at the mill; one will be
taken, the other left.*”
17:35 Matt 24:41 37“Lord, where will this happen?” the disciples asked.
17:37 Matt 24:28 Jesus replied, “Just as the gathering of vultures shows there is a carcass nearby, so
these signs indicate that the end is near.”*

Jesus Tells the Parable of the Persistent Widow (171)

18:1 Rom 12:12 Col 4:2 1 Thes 5:17 **18** One day Jesus told his disciples a story to illustrate their need for constant prayer
and to show them that they must never give up. 2“There was a judge in a certain
city,” he said, “who was a godless man with great contempt for everyone. 3A widow of
that city came to him repeatedly, appealing for justice against someone who had harmed
her. 4The judge ignored her for a while, but eventually she wore him out. ‘I fear neither
18:5 Luke 11:7-8 God nor man,’ he said to himself, 5‘but this woman is driving me crazy. I’m going to see
that she gets justice, because she is wearing me out with her constant requests!’”
18:7 Rev 6:10 6Then the Lord said, “Learn a lesson from this evil judge. 7Even he rendered a just
decision in the end, so don’t you think God will surely give justice to his chosen people
18:8 1 Tim 4:1 who plead with him day and night? Will he keep putting them off? 8I tell you, he will
grant justice to them quickly! But when I, the Son of Man, return, how many will I find
who have faith?”

Jesus Tells the Parable of Two Men Who Prayed (172)

9Then Jesus told this story to some who had great self-confidence and scorned everyone
else: 10“Two men went to the Temple to pray. One was a Pharisee, and the other was a
18:11 Matt 6:5 dishonest tax collector. 11The proud Pharisee stood by himself and prayed this prayer: ‘I
thank you, God, that I am not a sinner like everyone else, especially like that tax collector

17:30 Or *on the day the Son of Man is revealed.* **17:31** Greek *on the roof.* **17:35** Some manuscripts add verse 36, *Two men will be working in the field; one will be taken, the other left.* **17:37** Greek *Wherever the carcass is, the vultures gather.*

17:26-35 Jesus warned against false security. We are to abandon the values and attachments of this world in order to be ready for Christ’s return. His return will happen suddenly, and when he comes, there will be no second chances. Some will be taken to be with him; the rest will be left behind.

17:37 To answer the disciples’ question, Jesus quoted a familiar proverb. One vulture circling overhead does not mean much, but a gathering of vultures means that a dead body is nearby. Likewise, one sign of the end may not be significant, but when many signs occur, the Second Coming is near.

18:1 To persist in prayer and not give up does not mean endless repetition or painfully long prayer sessions. Constant prayer means keeping our requests continually before God as we live for him day by day, believing he will answer. When we live by faith, we are not to give up. God may delay answering, but his delays always have good reasons. As we persist in prayer, we grow in character, faith, and hope.

18:3 Widows and orphans were among the most vulnerable of all God’s people, and both Old Testament prophets and New Testament apostles insisted that these needy people be properly cared for. See, for example, Exodus 22:22-24; Isaiah 1:17; 1 Timothy 5:3; James 1:27.

18:6, 7 If godless judges respond to constant pressure, how much more will a great and loving God respond to us. If we know he loves us, we can believe he will hear our cries for help.

18:10 The people who lived near Jerusalem often went to the Temple to pray. The Temple was the center of their worship.

18:11-14 The Pharisee did not go to the Temple to pray to God but to announce to all within earshot how good he was. The tax collector went recognizing his sin and begging for mercy. Self-righteousness is dangerous. It leads to pride, causes a person to despise others, and prevents him or her from learning anything from God. The tax collector’s prayer should be our prayer because we all need God’s mercy every day. Don’t let pride in your achievements cut you off from God.

over there! For I never cheat, I don't sin, I don't commit adultery, 12 I fast twice a week, **18:12** Matt 23:23
and I give you a tenth of my income.'
13 "But the tax collector stood at a distance and dared not even lift his eyes to heaven
as he prayed. Instead, he beat his chest in sorrow, saying, 'O God, be merciful to me, for
I am a sinner.' 14 I tell you, this sinner, not the Pharisee, returned home justified before **18:14** Matt 23:12
God. For the proud will be humbled, but the humble will be honored." Luke 14:11

Jesus Blesses the Children (**174**/Matthew 19:13-15; Mark 10:13-16)

15 One day some parents brought their little children to Jesus so he could touch them and
bless them, but the disciples told them not to bother him. 16 Then Jesus called for the
children and said to the disciples, "Let the children come to me. Don't stop them! For
the Kingdom of God belongs to such as these. 17 I assure you, anyone who doesn't have **18:17** Matt 18:3
their kind of faith will never get into the Kingdom of God."

Jesus Speaks to the Rich Young Man (**175**/Matthew 19:16-30; Mark 10:17-31)

18 Once a religious leader asked Jesus this question: "Good teacher, what should I do to
get eternal life?"
19 "Why do you call me good?" Jesus asked him. "Only God is truly good. 20 But as **18:20** †Exod 20:13-16
for your question, you know the commandments: 'Do not commit adultery. Do not †Deut 5:17-20
murder. Do not steal. Do not testify falsely. Honor your father and mother.'*"
21 The man replied, "I've obeyed all these commandments since I was a child."
22 "There is still one thing you lack," Jesus said. "Sell all you have and give the money **18:22** Matt 6:20
to the poor, and you will have treasure in heaven. Then come, follow me." 23 But when
the man heard this, he became sad because he was very rich.
24 Jesus watched him go and then said to his disciples, "How hard it is for rich people
to get into the Kingdom of God! 25 It is easier for a camel to go through the eye of a needle
than for a rich person to enter the Kingdom of God!"
26 Those who heard this said, "Then who in the world can be saved?"
27 He replied, "What is impossible from a human perspective is possible with God."
28 Peter said, "We have left our homes and followed you." **18:28** Matt 4:19
29 "Yes," Jesus replied, "and I assure you, everyone who has given up house or wife
or brothers or parents or children, for the sake of the Kingdom of God, 30 will be repaid
many times over in this life, as well as receiving eternal life in the world to come."

18:20 Exod 20:12-16; Deut 5:16-20.

18:15-17 It was customary for a mother to bring her children to a rabbi for a blessing, and that is why these mothers gathered around Jesus. The disciples, however, thought the children were unworthy of the Master's time—less important than whatever else he was doing. But Jesus welcomed them, because little children have the kind of faith and trust needed to enter God's Kingdom. It is important that we introduce our children to Jesus and that we ourselves approach him with childlike attitudes of acceptance, faith, and trust.

18:18ff This leader sought reassurance, some way of knowing for sure that he had eternal life. He wanted Jesus to measure and grade his qualifications, or to give him some task he could do to assure his own immortality. So Jesus gave him a task—the one thing the rich man knew he could not do. "Then who in the world can be saved?" the bystanders asked. "No one can, by his or her own achievements," Jesus' answer implied. "What is impossible from a human perspective is possible with God." Salvation cannot be earned—it is God's gift (see Ephesians 2:8-10).

18:18, 19 Jesus' question to the leader who came and called him "Good teacher" was, in essence, "Do you know who I am?" Undoubtedly the man did not catch the implications of Jesus' reply—that the man was right in calling him good because Jesus truly is God.

18:22, 23 This man's wealth made his life comfortable and gave him power and prestige. When Jesus told him to sell everything he owned, Jesus was touching the very basis of his security and identity. The man did not understand that he would be even more secure if he followed Jesus than he was with all his wealth. Jesus does not ask believers to sell everything they have, although this may be his will for some. He does ask us all, however, to get rid of anything that has become more important in our life than God. If your possessions take first place in your life, it would be better for you to get rid of them.

18:24-27 Because money represents power, authority, and success, often it is difficult for wealthy people to realize their need and their powerlessness to save themselves. The rich in talent or intelligence suffer the same difficulty. Unless God reaches down into their lives, they will not come to him. Jesus surprised some of his hearers by offering salvation to the poor; he may surprise some people today by offering it to the rich. It is difficult for a self-sufficient person to realize his or her need and come to Jesus, but "what is impossible from a human perspective is possible with God."

18:26-30 Peter and the other disciples had paid a high price—leaving their homes and jobs—to follow Jesus. But Jesus reminded Peter that following him has its benefits as well as its sacrifices. Any believer who has had to give up something to follow Christ will be paid back in this life as well as in the next. For example, if you must give up a secure job, you will find that God offers a secure relationship with himself now and forever. If you must give up your family's approval, you will gain the love of the family of God. The disciples had begun to pay the price of following Jesus, and he said they would be rewarded. Don't dwell on what you have given up; think about what you have gained and give thanks for it. You can never outgive God.

Jesus Predicts His Death the Third Time (**177**/Matthew 20:17-19; Mark 10:32-34)

18:31 Ps 22; Isa 53; Luke 9:51; 24:25-27, 44
18:32 Matt 16:21; Luke 9:22, 44

31 Gathering the twelve disciples around him, Jesus told them, "As you know, we are
going to Jerusalem. And when we get there, all the predictions of the ancient prophets
concerning the Son of Man will come true. 32 He will be handed over to the Romans to
be mocked, treated shamefully, and spit upon. 33 They will whip him and kill him, but on
the third day he will rise again."
34 But they didn't understand a thing he said. Its significance was hidden from them,
and they failed to grasp what he was talking about.

Jesus Heals a Blind Beggar (**179**/Matthew 20:29-34; Mark 10:46-52)

18:38 Matt 9:27
18:41 Mark 10:36
18:42 Matt 9:22; Luke 7:50; 17:19
18:43 Luke 19:37

35 As they approached Jericho, a blind beggar was sitting beside the road. 36 When he
heard the noise of a crowd going past, he asked what was happening. 37 They told him
that Jesus of Nazareth was going by. 38 So he began shouting, "Jesus, Son of David, have
mercy on me!" 39 The crowds ahead of Jesus tried to hush the man, but he only shouted
louder, "Son of David, have mercy on me!"
40 When Jesus heard him, he stopped and ordered that the man be brought to him.
41 Then Jesus asked the man, "What do you want me to do for you?"
"Lord," he pleaded, "I want to see!"
42 And Jesus said, "All right, you can see! Your faith has healed you." 43 Instantly
the man could see, and he followed Jesus, praising God. And all who saw it praised
God, too.

Jesus Brings Salvation to Zacchaeus's Home (**180**)

19:1 Luke 18:35
19:4 1 Kgs 10:27; 1 Chr 27:28
19:7 Matt 9:11; Luke 5:30; 15:2
19:8 Exod 22:1; Num 5:7; Luke 3:12-13

19 Jesus entered Jericho and made his way through the town. 2 There was a man there
named Zacchaeus. He was one of the most influential Jews in the Roman
tax-collecting business, and he had become very rich. 3 He tried to get a look at Jesus,
but he was too short to see over the crowds. 4 So he ran ahead and climbed a sycamore
tree beside the road, so he could watch from there.
5 When Jesus came by, he looked up at Zacchaeus and called him by name. "Zacchaeus!" he said. "Quick, come down! For I must be a guest in your home today."
6 Zacchaeus quickly climbed down and took Jesus to his house in great excitement and
joy. 7 But the crowds were displeased. "He has gone to be the guest of a notorious sinner,"
they grumbled.
8 Meanwhile, Zacchaeus stood there and said to the Lord, "I will give half my wealth
to the poor, Lord, and if I have overcharged people on their taxes, I will give them back
four times as much!"

18:31-34 Some predictions about what would happen to Jesus are found in Psalm 41:9 (betrayal); Psalm 22:16-18 and Isaiah 53:4-7 (crucifixion); Psalm 16:10 (resurrection). The disciples didn't understand Jesus, apparently because they focused on what he said about his death and ignored what he said about his resurrection. Even though Jesus spoke plainly, they would not grasp the significance of his words until they saw the risen Christ face to face.

18:35 Beggars often waited along the roads near cities, because that was where they were able to contact the most people. Usually disabled in some way, beggars were unable to earn a living. Medical help was not available for their problems, and people tended to ignore their obligation to care for the needy (Leviticus 25:35-38). Thus, beggars had little hope of escaping their degrading way of life. But this blind beggar took hope in the Messiah. He shamelessly cried out for Jesus' attention, and Jesus said that his faith allowed him to see. No matter how desperate your situation may seem, if you call out to Jesus in faith, he will help you.

18:38 The blind man called Jesus "Son of David," a title for the Messiah (Isaiah 11:1-3). This means that he understood Jesus to be the long-awaited Messiah. It is interesting to note that a poor and blind beggar could *see* that Jesus was the Messiah, while the religious leaders who saw his miracles were blinded to his identity and refused to recognize him as the Messiah.

19:1-10 To finance their great world empire, the Romans levied heavy taxes on all nations under their control. The Jews opposed these taxes because they supported a secular government and its pagan gods, but they were still forced to pay. Tax collectors were among the most unpopular people in Israel. Jews by birth, they chose to work for Rome and were considered traitors. Besides, it was common knowledge that tax collectors were making themselves rich by gouging their fellow Jews. No wonder the people muttered when Jesus went home with the tax collector Zacchaeus. But despite the fact that Zacchaeus was both a cheater and a turncoat, Jesus loved him; and in response, this tax collector was converted. In every society, certain groups of people are considered "untouchable" because of their political views, their immoral behavior, or their life-style. We should not give in to social pressure to avoid these people. Jesus loves them, and they need to hear his Good News.

19:8 Judging from the crowd's reaction to him, Zacchaeus must have been a very crooked tax collector. But after he met Jesus, he realized that his life needed straightening out. By giving to the poor and making restitution—with generous interest—to those he had cheated, Zacchaeus demonstrated inner change by outward action. It is not enough to follow Jesus in your head or heart alone. You must show your faith by changed behavior. Has your faith resulted in action? What changes do you need to make?

[9]Jesus responded, "Salvation has come to this home today, for this man has shown **19:9** Matt 9:13
himself to be a son of Abraham. [10]And I, the Son of Man, have come to seek and save Acts 16:31-34
those like him who are lost." 1 Tim 1:15

Jesus Tells the Parable of the King's Ten Servants (**181**)

[11]The crowd was listening to everything Jesus said. And because he was nearing **19:11-27** Matt 25:14-30
Jerusalem, he told a story to correct the impression that the Kingdom of God would begin
right away. [12]He said, "A nobleman was called away to a distant empire to be crowned **19:11** Acts 1:6
king and then return. [13]Before he left, he called together ten servants and gave them ten **19:12** Mark 13:34
pounds of silver* to invest for him while he was gone. [14]But his people hated him and
sent a delegation after him to say they did not want him to be their king.
[15]"When he returned, the king called in the servants to whom he had given the money.
He wanted to find out what they had done with the money and what their profits were.
[16]The first servant reported a tremendous gain—ten times as much as the original
amount! [17]'Well done!' the king exclaimed. 'You are a trustworthy servant. You have **19:17** Luke 16:10
been faithful with the little I entrusted to you, so you will be governor of ten cities as
your reward.'
[18]"The next servant also reported a good gain—five times the original amount.
[19]'Well done!' the king said. 'You can be governor over five cities.'
[20]"But the third servant brought back only the original amount of money and said, 'I
hid it and kept it safe. [21]I was afraid because you are a hard man to deal with, taking what
isn't yours and harvesting crops you didn't plant.'
[22]"'You wicked servant!' the king roared. 'Hard, am I? If you knew so much about **19:22** Job 15:6
me and how tough I am, [23]why didn't you deposit the money in the bank so I could at Matt 12:37
least get some interest on it?' [24]Then turning to the others standing nearby, the king
ordered, 'Take the money from this servant, and give it to the one who earned the most.'
[25]"'But, master,' they said, 'that servant has enough already!'
[26]"'Yes,' the king replied, 'but to those who use well what they are given, even more **19:26** Matt 13:12
will be given. But from those who are unfaithful,* even what little they have will be taken Mark 4:25
away. [27]And now about these enemies of mine who didn't want me to be their king— Luke 8:18
bring them in and execute them right here in my presence.'" **19:27** Luke 19:14

19:13 Greek *10 minas;* 1 mina was worth about 3 months' wages. **19:26** Or *who have nothing.*

19:9, 10 When Jesus said Zacchaeus was a son of Abraham and yet was lost, he must have shocked his hearers in at least two ways: (1) They would not have liked to acknowledge that this unpopular tax collector was a fellow son of Abraham, and (2) they would not have wished to admit that sons of Abraham could be lost. But a person is not saved because of a good heritage or condemned by a bad one; faith is more important than genealogy. Jesus came to save all the lost no matter what their background or previous way of life. Through faith, the lost can be forgiven and made new.

19:11ff The people still hoped for a political leader who would set up an earthly kingdom and get rid of Roman domination. Jesus' story showed that his Kingdom would not take this form right away. First, he would go away for a while, and his followers would need to be faithful and productive during his absence. Upon his return, Jesus would inaugurate a Kingdom more powerful and just than anything they could expect.

19:11ff This story showed Jesus' followers what they were to do during the time between Jesus' departure and his second coming. Because we live in that time period, it applies directly to us. We have been given excellent resources to build and expand God's Kingdom. Jesus expects us to use these talents so that they multiply and the Kingdom grows. He asks each of us to account for what we do with his gifts. While awaiting the coming of the Kingdom of God in glory, we must do Christ's work.

19:20-27 Why was the king so hard on this man who had not increased the money? He punished the man because (1) he didn't share his master's interest in the Kingdom, (2) he didn't trust his master's intentions, (3) his only concern was for himself, and (4) he did nothing to use the money. Like the king in this story, God has given you gifts to use for the benefit of his Kingdom. Do you want the Kingdom to grow? Do you trust God to govern it fairly? Are you as concerned for others' welfare as you are for your own? Are you willing to use faithfully what he has entrusted to you?

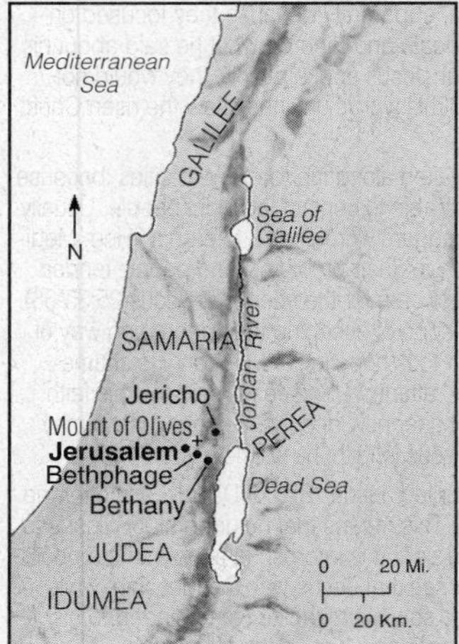

LAST WEEK IN JERUSALEM
As they approached Jerusalem from Jericho (19:1), Jesus and the disciples came to the villages of Bethany and Bethphage, nestled on the eastern slope of the Mount of Olives, only a few miles outside Jerusalem. Jesus stayed in Bethany during the nights of that last week, entering Jerusalem during the day.

3. Jesus' ministry in Jerusalem

Jesus Rides into Jerusalem on a Donkey

(**183**/Matthew 21:1-11; Mark 11:1-11; John 12:12-19)

28 After telling this story, Jesus went on toward Jerusalem, walking ahead of his disciples.
29 As they came to the towns of Bethphage and Bethany, on the Mount of Olives, he sent
two disciples ahead. 30 "Go into that village over there," he told them, "and as you enter
it, you will see a colt tied there that has never been ridden. Untie it and bring it here. 31 If
anyone asks what you are doing, just say, 'The Lord needs it.'"

32 So they went and found the colt, just as Jesus had said. 33 And sure enough, as they
were untying it, the owners asked them, "Why are you untying our colt?"

34 And the disciples simply replied, "The Lord needs it." 35 So they brought the colt to
Jesus and threw their garments over it for him to ride on.

19:36 2 Kgs 9:13
36 Then the crowds spread out their coats on the road ahead of Jesus. 37 As they reached
the place where the road started down from the Mount of Olives, all of his followers
began to shout and sing as they walked along, praising God for all the wonderful miracles
they had seen.

19:38 †Pss 118:25-26; 148:1; Luke 2:14; 13:35
38 "Bless the King who comes in the name of the Lord!
Peace in heaven
and glory in highest heaven!"*

39 But some of the Pharisees among the crowd said, "Teacher, rebuke your followers
for saying things like that!"

19:40 Hab 2:11
40 He replied, "If they kept quiet, the stones along the road would burst into cheers!"

19:38 Pss 118:26; 148:1.

GOSPEL ACCOUNTS FOUND ONLY IN LUKE

1:5–80	Special events leading up to birth of John the Baptist and Jesus
2:1–52	Events from Jesus' childhood
3:19, 20	Herod puts John in prison
4:16–30	Jesus is rejected at Nazareth
5:1–11	Jesus provides a miraculous catch of fish
7:11–17	Jesus raises a widow's son from the dead
7:36–50	A sinful woman anoints Jesus' feet
8:1–3	Women travel with Jesus
10:1—18:14	Events, miracles, and teachings during the months prior to Christ's death
19:1–27	Jesus meets Zacchaeus and later tells the parable of the king's 10 servants
23:6–12	Jesus' trial before Herod
24:44–49	Some of Jesus' last words before his ascension

19:30-35 By this time Jesus was extremely well known. Everyone coming to Jerusalem for the Passover festival had heard of him, and, for a time, the popular mood was favorable toward him. "The Lord needs it" was all the disciples had to say, and the colt's owners gladly turned their animal over to them.

19:35-38 Christians celebrate this event on Palm Sunday. The people lined the road, praising God, waving palm branches, and throwing their cloaks in front of the colt as it passed before them. "Long live the King" was the meaning behind their joyful shouts, because they knew that Jesus was intentionally fulfilling the prophecy in Zechariah 9:9: "Look, your king is coming to you. He is righteous and victorious, yet he is humble, riding on a donkey—even on a donkey's colt." To announce that he was indeed the Messiah, Jesus chose a *time* when all Israel would be gathered at Jerusalem, a *place* where huge crowds could see him, and a *way* of proclaiming his mission that was unmistakable. The people went wild. They were sure their liberation was at hand.

19:38 The people who were praising God for giving them a king had the wrong idea about Jesus. They expected him to be a national leader who would restore their nation to its former glory, and thus they were deaf to the words of their prophets and blind to Jesus' real mission. When it became apparent that Jesus was not going to fulfill their hopes, many people turned against him.

19:39, 40 The Pharisees thought the crowd's words were sacrilegious and blasphemous. They didn't want someone challenging their power and authority, and they didn't want a revolt that would bring the Roman army down on them. So they asked Jesus to keep his people quiet. But Jesus said that if the people were quiet, the stones would burst into cheers. Why? Not because Jesus was setting up a powerful political kingdom but because he was establishing God's eternal Kingdom, a reason for the greatest celebration of all.

[41]But as they came closer to Jerusalem and Jesus saw the city ahead, he began to cry.
[42]"I wish that even today you would find the way of peace. But now it is too late, and
peace is hidden from you. [43]Before long your enemies will build ramparts against your
walls and encircle you and close in on you. [44]They will crush you to the ground, and
your children with you. Your enemies will not leave a single stone in place, because you
have rejected the opportunity God offered you."

19:43 Isa 29:3 Jer 6:6 Ezek 4:2 Luke 21:20

19:44 Ps 137:9 Luke 21:6

Jesus Clears the Temple Again (**184**/Matthew 21:12-17; Mark 11:12-19)

[45]Then Jesus entered the Temple and began to drive out the merchants from their stalls.
[46]He told them, "The Scriptures declare, 'My Temple will be a place of prayer,' but you
have turned it into a den of thieves."*

[47]After that, he taught daily in the Temple, but the leading priests, the teachers of
religious law, and the other leaders of the people began planning how to kill him. [48]But
they could think of nothing, because all the people hung on every word he said.

19:46 †Isa 56:7 †Jer 7:11

19:47 Matt 26:55 Luke 21:37; 22:53 John 18:20

Religious Leaders Challenge Jesus' Authority
(**189**/Matthew 21:23-27; Mark 11:27-33)

20 One day as Jesus was teaching and preaching the Good News in the Temple, the
leading priests and teachers of religious law and other leaders came up to him.
[2]They demanded, "By whose authority did you drive out the merchants from the
Temple?* Who gave you such authority?"

[3]"Let me ask you a question first," he replied. [4]"Did John's baptism come from
heaven, or was it merely human?"

[5]They talked it over among themselves. "If we say it was from heaven, he will ask
why we didn't believe him. [6]But if we say it was merely human, the people will stone
us, because they are convinced he was a prophet." [7]Finally they replied, "We don't
know."

[8]And Jesus responded, "Then I won't answer your question either."

20:2 John 2:18 Acts 4:7; 7:27

20:4 Mark 1:4

20:6 Luke 7:29

Jesus Tells the Parable of the Evil Farmers (**191**/Matthew 21:33-46; Mark 12:1-12)

[9]Now Jesus turned to the people again and told them this story: "A man planted a
vineyard, leased it out to tenant farmers, and moved to another country to live for several
years. [10]At grape-picking time, he sent one of his servants to collect his share of the crop.
But the farmers attacked the servant, beat him up, and sent him back empty-handed. [11]So
the owner sent another servant, but the same thing happened; he was beaten up and
treated shamefully, and he went away empty-handed. [12]A third man was sent and the
same thing happened. He, too, was wounded and chased away.

[13]"'What will I do?' the owner asked himself. 'I know! I'll send my cherished son.
Surely they will respect him.'

20:9-19 Isa 5:1-7

20:10-12 2 Chr 36:15-16

19:46 Isa 56:7; Jer 7:11. **20:2** Or *By whose authority do you do these things?*

19:41-44 The Jewish leaders had rejected their King (19:47). They had gone too far. They had refused God's offer of salvation in Jesus Christ when they were visited by God himself, and soon their nation would suffer. God did not turn away from the Jewish people who obeyed him, however, and he continues to offer salvation to the people he loves, both Jews and Gentiles. Eternal life is within your reach; accept it while the opportunity is still offered.

19:43, 44 About 40 years after Jesus said these words, they came true. In A.D. 66, the Jews revolted against Roman control. Three years later Titus, son of the emperor Vespasian, was sent to crush the rebellion. Roman soldiers attacked Jerusalem and broke through the northern wall but still couldn't take the city. Finally, they laid siege to it, and in A.D. 70 they were able to enter the severely weakened city and burn it. Six hundred thousand Jews were killed during Titus's onslaught.

19:47 Who were the "other leaders of the people"? This group probably included wealthy leaders in politics, commerce, and law. They had several reasons for wanting to get rid of Jesus. He had damaged business in the Temple by driving the merchants out. In addition, he was preaching against injustice, and his teachings often favored the poor over the rich. Furthermore, his great popularity was in danger of attracting Rome's attention, and the leaders of Israel wanted as little as possible to do with Rome.

20:1-8 This group of leaders wanted to get rid of Jesus, so they tried to trap him with their question. If Jesus would answer that his authority came from God—if he stated openly that he was the Messiah and the Son of God—they would accuse him of blasphemy and bring him to trial. Jesus did not let himself be caught. Instead, he turned the question on them. Thus, he exposed their motives and avoided their trap.

20:9-16 The characters in this story are easily identified. Even the religious leaders understood it. The owner of the vineyard is God; the vineyard is Israel; the tenant farmers are the religious leaders; the servants are the prophets and priests God sent to Israel; the son is the Messiah, Jesus; and the others are the Gentiles. Jesus' parable indirectly answered the religious leaders' question about his authority; it also showed them that he knew about their plan to kill him.

20:14 Heb 1:2

[14]“But when the farmers saw his son, they said to each other, ‘Here comes the heir to
this estate. Let’s kill him and get the estate for ourselves!’ [15]So they dragged him out of
the vineyard and murdered him.
“What do you suppose the owner of the vineyard will do to those farmers?” Jesus
asked. [16]“I’ll tell you—he will come and kill them all and lease the vineyard to others.”
“But God forbid that such a thing should ever happen,” his listeners protested.

20:17 †Ps 118:22; Acts 4:11

[17]Jesus looked at them and said, “Then what do the Scriptures mean?

‘The stone rejected by the builders
has now become the cornerstone.’*

20:18 Isa 8:14-15; Dan 2:34, 35

[18]All who stumble over that stone will be broken to pieces, and it will crush anyone on
whom it falls.”
[19]When the teachers of religious law and the leading priests heard this story, they wanted
to arrest Jesus immediately because they realized he was pointing at them—that they were
the farmers in the story. But they were afraid there would be a riot if they arrested him.

Religious Leaders Question Jesus about Paying Taxes
(**193**/Matthew 22:15-22; Mark 12:13-17)

[20]Watching for their opportunity, the leaders sent secret agents pretending to be honest
men. They tried to get Jesus to say something that could be reported to the Roman
governor so he would arrest Jesus. [21]They said, “Teacher, we know that you speak and
teach what is right and are not influenced by what others think. You sincerely teach the
ways of God. [22]Now tell us—is it right to pay taxes to the Roman government or not?”
[23]He saw through their trickery and said, [24]“Show me a Roman coin.* Whose picture
and title are stamped on it?”
“Caesar’s,” they replied.

20:25 Luke 23:2; Rom 13:6-7

[25]“Well then,” he said, “give to Caesar what belongs to him. But everything that
belongs to God must be given to God.” [26]So they failed to trap him in the presence of
the people. Instead, they were amazed by his answer, and they were silenced.

Religious Leaders Question Jesus about the Resurrection
(**194**/Matthew 22:23-33; Mark 12:18-27)

20:27 Acts 23:8

20:28 †Deut 25:5

[27]Then some Sadducees stepped forward—a group of Jews who say there is no resurrection after death. [28]They posed this question: “Teacher, Moses gave us a law that if a
man dies, leaving a wife but no children, his brother should marry the widow and have
a child who will be the brother’s heir.* [29]Well, there were seven brothers. The oldest
married and then died without children. [30]His brother married the widow, but he also
died. Still no children. [31]And so it went, one after the other, until each of the seven had
married her and died, leaving no children. [32]Finally, the woman died, too. [33]So tell us,
whose wife will she be in the resurrection? For all seven were married to her!”

20:17 Ps 118:22. **20:24** Greek *a denarius.* **20:28** Deut 25:5-6.

20:17-19 Quoting Psalm 118:22, Jesus showed the unbelieving leaders that even their rejection of the Messiah had been prophesied in Scripture. Ignoring the cornerstone was dangerous. A person could be tripped or crushed (judged and punished). Jesus’ comments were veiled, but the religious leaders had no trouble interpreting them. They immediately wanted to arrest him.

20:20-26 Jesus turned his enemies’ attempt to trap him into a powerful lesson: As God’s followers, we have legitimate obligations to both God and the government. But it is important to keep our priorities straight. When the two authorities conflict, our duty to God always must come before our duty to the government.

20:21 These spies, pretending to be honest men, flattered Jesus before asking him their trick question, hoping to catch him off guard. But Jesus knew what they were trying to do and stayed out of their trap. Beware of flattery. With God’s help, you can detect it and avoid the trap that often follows.

20:22 This was a loaded question. The Jews were enraged at having to pay taxes to Rome, thus supporting the pagan government and its gods. They hated the system that allowed tax collectors to charge exorbitant rates and keep the extra for themselves. If Jesus said they should pay taxes, they would call him a traitor to their nation and their religion. But if he said they should not, they could report him to Rome as a rebel. Jesus’ questioners thought they had him this time, but he outwitted them again.

20:24 This Roman coin was a denarius, the usual pay for one day’s work.

20:27-38 The Sadducees, a group of conservative religious leaders, honored only the Pentateuch—Genesis through Deuteronomy—as Scripture. They also did not believe in a resurrection of the dead because they could find no mention of it in those books. The Sadducees decided to try their hand at tricking Jesus, so they brought him a question that had always stumped the Pharisees. After addressing their question about marriage, Jesus answered their *real* question about the resurrection. Basing his answer on the writings of Moses—an authority they respected—he upheld belief in the resurrection.

[34]Jesus replied, "Marriage is for people here on earth. [35]But that is not the way it will be
in the age to come. For those worthy of being raised from the dead won't be married then.
[36]And they will never die again. In these respects they are like angels. They are children of
God raised up to new life. [37]But now, as to whether the dead will be raised—even Moses
proved this when he wrote about the burning bush. Long after Abraham, Isaac, and Jacob
had died, he referred to the Lord* as 'the God of Abraham, the God of Isaac, and the God
of Jacob.'* [38]So he is the God of the living, not the dead. They are all alive to him."
[39]"Well said, Teacher!" remarked some of the teachers of religious law who were
standing there. [40]And that ended their questions; no one dared to ask any more.

20:36 John 1:12; Gal 4:5-7; 1 Jn 3:1-2
20:37 †Exod 3:6

Religious Leaders Cannot Answer Jesus' Question
(**196**/Matthew 22:41-46; Mark 12:35-37)

[41]Then Jesus presented them with a question. "Why is it," he asked, "that the Messiah
is said to be the son of David? [42]For David himself wrote in the book of Psalms:

'The LORD said to my Lord,
Sit in honor at my right hand
[43] until I humble your enemies,
making them a footstool under your feet.'*

[44]Since David called him Lord, how can he be his son at the same time?"

20:42-43 †Ps 110:1

Jesus Warns against the Religious Leaders (**197**/Matthew 23:1-12; Mark 12:38-40)

[45]Then, with the crowds listening, he turned to his disciples and said, [46]"Beware of these
teachers of religious law! For they love to parade in flowing robes and to have everyone
bow to them as they walk in the marketplaces. And how they love the seats of honor in
the synagogues and at banquets. [47]But they shamelessly cheat widows out of their
property, and then, to cover up the kind of people they really are, they make long prayers
in public. Because of this, their punishment will be the greater."

A Poor Widow Gives All She Has (**200**/Mark 12:41-44)

21 While Jesus was in the Temple, he watched the rich people putting their gifts
into the collection box. [2]Then a poor widow came by and dropped in two
pennies.* [3]"I assure you," he said, "this poor widow has given more than all the rest

20:37a Greek *when he wrote about the bush. He referred to the Lord.* **20:37b** Exod 3:6. **20:42-43** Ps 110:1.
21:2 Greek *2 lepta.*

20:34, 35 Jesus' statement does not mean that people will not recognize their partners in heaven. It simply means that we must not think of heaven as an extension of life as we now know it. Our relationships in this life are limited by time, death, and sin. We don't know everything about our resurrection life, but Jesus affirms that relationships will be different from what we are used to here and now.

20:37, 38 The Sadducees came to Jesus with a trick question. Not believing in the resurrection, they wanted Jesus to say something they could refute. Even so, Jesus did not ignore or belittle their question. He answered it, and then he went beyond it to the real issue. People may ask you tough religious questions, such as "How can a loving God allow people to starve?" "If God knows what I'm going to do, do I have any free choice?" If they do, follow Jesus' example. First, answer them to the best of your ability; then look for the real issue: hurt over a personal tragedy, for example, or difficulty in making a decision. Often the spoken question is only a test, not of your ability to answer hard questions, but of your willingness to listen and care.

20:41-44 The Pharisees and Sadducees had asked their questions. Then Jesus turned the tables and asked them a question that went right to the heart of the matter—what they thought about the Messiah's identity. The Pharisees knew that the Messiah would be a descendant of David, but they did not understand that he would be more than a human descendant—he would be God in the flesh. Jesus quoted from Psalm 110:1 to show that David knew that the Messiah would be both human and divine. The Pharisees expected only a human ruler to restore Israel's greatness as in the days of David and Solomon.

The central issue of life is what we believe about Jesus. Other spiritual questions are irrelevant unless we first decide to believe that Jesus is who he said he is. The Pharisees and Sadducees could not do this. They remained confused over Jesus' identity.

20:45-47 The teachers of religious law loved the benefits associated with their position, and they sometimes cheated the poor in order to get even more benefits. Every job has its rewards, but gaining rewards should never become more important than doing the job faithfully. God will punish people who use their position of responsibility to cheat others. Use whatever resources you have been given to help others and not just yourself.

20:47 How strange to think that the teachers of religious law would receive the worst punishment. But behind their appearance of holiness and respectability, they were arrogant, crafty, selfish, and uncaring. Jesus exposed their evil hearts. He showed that despite their pious words, they were neglecting God's laws and doing as they pleased. Religious deeds do not cancel sin. Jesus said that God's most severe judgment awaited these teachers because they should have been living examples of mercy and justice.

21:1, 2 Jesus was in the area of the Temple called the Court of Women. In this area were seven boxes in which worshipers could deposit their Temple tax and six boxes for freewill offerings, like the one this woman gave. This widow was not only poor but had few resources for making money. Her small gift was a sacrifice, but she gave it willingly.

of them. 4 For they have given a tiny part of their surplus, but she, poor as she is, has
given everything she has."

Jesus Tells about the Future (**201**/Matthew 24:1-25; Mark 13:1-23)

5 Some of his disciples began talking about the beautiful stonework of the Temple and
21:6 Luke 19:44 the memorial decorations on the walls. But Jesus said, 6 "The time is coming when all
these things will be so completely demolished that not one stone will be left on top of
another."

7 "Teacher," they asked, "when will all this take place? And will there be any sign
ahead of time?"

21:8 Luke 17:23 8 He replied, "Don't let anyone mislead you. For many will come in my name,
claiming to be the Messiah* and saying, 'The time has come!' But don't believe them.
9 And when you hear of wars and insurrections, don't panic. Yes, these things must come,
21:10 2 Chr 15:6 Isa 19:2 but the end won't follow immediately." 10 Then he added, "Nations and kingdoms will
proclaim war against each other. 11 There will be great earthquakes, and there will be
famines and epidemics in many lands, and there will be terrifying things and great
21:12 Acts 12:4 miraculous signs in the heavens.

12 "But before all this occurs, there will be a time of great persecution. You will be
21:13 Phil 1:12 dragged into synagogues and prisons, and you will be accused before kings and
governors of being my followers. 13 This will be your opportunity to tell them about
21:14 Luke 12:11-12 me. 14 So don't worry about how to answer the charges against you, 15 for I will give
21:15 Acts 6:10 you the right words and such wisdom that none of your opponents will be able to reply!

21:8 Greek *name, saying, 'I am.'*

21:1-4 In contrast to the way most of us handle our money, this widow gave all she had to live on. When we consider ourselves generous in giving a small percentage of our income to the Lord, we resemble those who gave "a tiny part of their surplus." Here, Jesus admired her generous and sacrificial giving. As believers, we should consider increasing our giving—whether money, time, or talents—to a point beyond mere convenience.

21:5, 6 The Temple the disciples were admiring was not Solomon's Temple—that had been destroyed by the Babylonians early in the sixth century B.C. This Temple had been built by Ezra after the return from exile later in the sixth century B.C. It was desecrated by the Seleucids in the second century B.C., reconsecrated by the Maccabees soon afterward, and enormously expanded by Herod the Great over a 46-year period. It was a beautiful, imposing structure with a significant history, but Jesus said that it would be completely destroyed. This happened in A.D. 70 when the Roman army burned Jerusalem.

21:7ff Jesus did not leave his disciples unprepared for the difficult years ahead. He warned them about false messiahs, natural disasters, and persecutions; but he assured them that he would be with them to protect them and make his Kingdom known through them. In the end, Jesus promised that he would return in power and glory to save them. Jesus' warnings and promises to his disciples also apply to us as we look forward to his return.

21:12, 13 These persecutions soon began. Luke recorded many of them in the book of Acts. Paul wrote from prison that he suffered gladly because it helped him know Christ better and do Christ's work for the church (Philippians 3:10; Colossians 1:24). The early church thrived despite intense persecution. In fact, late in the second century the church father Tertullian wrote, "The blood of Christians is seed," because opposition helped spread Christianity.

21:14-19 Jesus warned that in the coming persecutions his followers would be betrayed by their family members and friends. Christians of every age have had to face this possibility. It is reassuring to know that even when we feel completely abandoned, the Holy Spirit will stay with us. He will comfort us, protect us, and give us the words we need. This assurance can give us the courage and hope to stand firm for Christ no matter how difficult the situation.

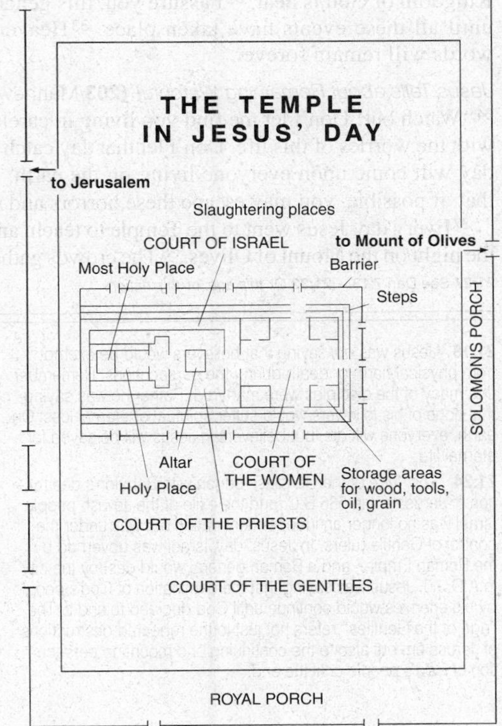

16 Even those closest to you—your parents, brothers, relatives, and friends—will betray
you. And some of you will be killed. 17 And everyone will hate you because of your
allegiance to me. 18 But not a hair of your head will perish! 19 By standing firm, you will **21:18** Matt 10:30
win your souls.

20 "And when you see Jerusalem surrounded by armies, then you will know that the
time of its destruction has arrived. 21 Then those in Judea must flee to the hills. Let those **21:22** Deut 32:35 Dan 9:24-27 Hos 9:7
in Jerusalem escape, and those outside the city should not enter it for shelter. 22 For those
will be days of God's vengeance, and the prophetic words of the Scriptures will be
fulfilled. 23 How terrible it will be for pregnant women and for mothers nursing their **21:23** 1 Cor 7:26, 28
babies. For there will be great distress in the land and wrath upon this people. 24 They **21:24** Isa 5:5; 63:18 Dan 8:13 2 Pet 3:10, 12 Rev 11:2
will be brutally killed by the sword or sent away as captives to all the nations of the
world. And Jerusalem will be conquered and trampled down by the Gentiles until the age
of the Gentiles comes to an end.

Jesus Tells about His Return (**202**/Matthew 24:26-35; Mark 13:24-31)

25 "And there will be strange events in the skies—signs in the sun, moon, and stars. And
down here on earth the nations will be in turmoil, perplexed by the roaring seas and
strange tides. 26 The courage of many people will falter because of the fearful fate they **21:26** †Isa 34:4
see coming upon the earth, because the stability of the very heavens will be broken up.
27 Then everyone will see the Son of Man arrive on the clouds with power and great **21:27** †Dan 7:13 Matt 26:64 Rev 1:7; 14:14
glory.* 28 So when all these things begin to happen, stand straight and look up, for your
salvation is near!"

29 Then he gave them this illustration: "Notice the fig tree, or any other tree.
30 When the leaves come out, you know without being told that summer is near. 31 Just
so, when you see the events I've described taking place, you can be sure that the
Kingdom of God is near. 32 I assure you, this generation* will not pass from the scene **21:33** Isa 40:6-8 Matt 5:18
until all these events have taken place. 33 Heaven and earth will disappear, but my
words will remain forever.

Jesus Tells about Remaining Watchful (**203**/Matthew 24:36-51; Mark 13:32-37)

34 "Watch out! Don't let me find you living in careless ease and drunkenness, and filled **21:34** Matt 24:48-50 Rom 13:13 1 Thes 5:3
with the worries of this life. Don't let that day catch you unaware, 35 as in a trap. For that
day will come upon everyone living on the earth. 36 Keep a constant watch. And pray **21:36** Mark 13:33
that, if possible, you may escape these horrors and stand before the Son of Man."

37 Every day Jesus went to the Temple to teach, and each evening he returned to spend **21:37** Luke 19:47; 22:39 John 8:1-2
the night on the Mount of Olives. 38 The crowds gathered early each morning to hear him.

21:27 See Dan 7:13. **21:32** Or *this age*, or *this nation.*

21:18 Jesus was *not* saying that believers would be exempt from physical harm or death during the persecutions. Remember that many of the disciples were martyred. Rather he was saying that none of his followers would suffer spiritual or eternal loss. On earth, everyone will die, but believers in Jesus will be saved for eternal life.

21:24 The "age of the Gentiles" began with Babylon's destruction of Jerusalem in 586 B.C. and the exile of the Jewish people. Israel was no longer an independent nation but was under the control of Gentile rulers. In Jesus' day, Israel was governed by the Roman Empire, and a Roman general would destroy the city in A.D. 70. Jesus was saying that the domination of God's people by his enemies would continue until God decided to end it. The "age of the Gentiles" refers not just to the repeated destructions of Jerusalem but also to the continuing and mounting persecution of God's people until the end.

21:28 The picture of the coming persecutions and natural disasters is gloomy, but ultimately it is a cause not for worry but for great joy. As believers see these events happening, they will know that the return of their Messiah is near, and they can look forward to his reign of justice and peace. Rather than being terrified by what is happening in our world, we should confidently await Christ's return to bring justice and restoration to his people.

21:34-36 Jesus told the disciples to keep a constant watch for his return. Although nearly 2,000 years have passed since he spoke these words, their truth remains: Christ is coming again, and we need to watch and be spiritually fit. This means working faithfully at the tasks God has given us. Don't let your mind and spirit be dulled by careless living, drinking, or the foolish pursuit of pleasure. Don't let the cares of this life weigh you down. Be ready to move at God's command.

21:36 Only days after telling the disciples to pray that they might escape persecution, Jesus himself asked God to spare him the agonies of the cross, if that was God's will (22:41, 42). It is abnormal to *want* to suffer, but as Jesus' followers, we must be willing to suffer if by doing so we can help build God's Kingdom. We have two wonderful promises to help us as we suffer: God will always be with us (Matthew 28:20), and he will one day rescue us and give us eternal life (Revelation 21:1-4).

C. DEATH AND RESURRECTION OF JESUS, THE SAVIOR (22:1—24:53)

The perfect man was a high ideal in Greek culture. Written with Greeks in mind, Luke's Gospel shows how Jesus was the perfect man given as the perfect sacrifice for the sin of all people. Christ is the ideal human—the perfect model for us to follow. We must stand in awe of his character, which met humanity's highest ideals as well as God's demand for an atonement for sin. He is, at one and the same time, our model and our Savior.

Religious Leaders Plot to Kill Jesus (**207**/Matthew 26:1-5; Mark 14:1-2)

22 The Festival of Unleavened Bread, which begins with the Passover celebration,
was drawing near. 2 The leading priests and teachers of religious law were actively
plotting Jesus' murder. But they wanted to kill him without starting a riot, a possibility
they greatly feared.

Judas Agrees to Betray Jesus (**208**/Matthew 26:14-16; Mark 14:10-11)

22:3 John 13:2, 27; Acts 1:17 — 3 Then Satan entered into Judas Iscariot, who was one of the twelve disciples, 4 and he
went over to the leading priests and captains of the Temple guard to discuss the best way
22:5 Zech 11:12; 1 Tim 6:10 — to betray Jesus to them. 5 They were delighted that he was ready to help them, and they
promised him a reward. 6 So he began looking for an opportunity to betray Jesus so they
could arrest him quietly when the crowds weren't around.

Disciples Prepare for the Passover (**209**/Matthew 26:17-19; Mark 14:12-16)

7 Now the Festival of Unleavened Bread arrived, when the Passover lambs were sacri-
22:8 Exod 12:8-11 — ficed. 8 Jesus sent Peter and John ahead and said, "Go and prepare the Passover meal, so
we can eat it together."

9 "Where do you want us to go?" they asked him.
22:10 1 Sam 10:2-7 — 10 He replied, "As soon as you enter Jerusalem, a man carrying a pitcher of water will
meet you. Follow him. At the house he enters, 11 say to the owner, 'The Teacher asks,
Where is the guest room where I can eat the Passover meal with my disciples?' 12 He will
take you upstairs to a large room that is already set up. That is the place. Go ahead and
prepare our supper there." 13 They went off to the city and found everything just as Jesus
had said, and they prepared the Passover supper there.

Jesus and the Disciples Share the Last Supper
(**211**/Matthew 26:20-30; Mark 14:17-26; John 13:21-30)

22:15-20 1 Cor 11:23-26 — 14 Then at the proper time Jesus and the twelve apostles sat down together at the table.
15 Jesus said, "I have looked forward to this hour with deep longing, anxious to eat this
22:16 Luke 14:15 — Passover meal with you before my suffering begins. 16 For I tell you now that I won't eat
it again until it comes to fulfillment in the Kingdom of God."

22:1 All Jewish males over the age of 12 were required to go to Jerusalem for the Passover festival, which was followed by a seven-day celebration called the Festival of Unleavened Bread. For these festivals, Jews from all over the Roman Empire converged on Jerusalem to celebrate one of the most important events in their history. To learn more about the Passover and the Festival of Unleavened Bread, see the first note on Mark 14:1.

22:3 Satan's part in the betrayal of Jesus does not remove any of the responsibility from Judas. Disillusioned because Jesus was talking about dying rather than about setting up his Kingdom, Judas may have been trying to force Jesus' hand and make him use his power to prove he was the Messiah. Or perhaps Judas, not understanding Jesus' mission, no longer believed that Jesus was God's chosen one. (For more information on Judas, see his Profile in Mark 14.) Whatever Judas thought, Satan assumed that Jesus' death would end his mission and thwart God's plan. Like Judas, he did not know that Jesus' death and resurrection were the most important parts of God's plan all along.

22:7, 8 The Passover meal included the sacrifice of a lamb because of the association with the Jews' exodus from Egypt. When the Jews were getting ready to leave, God told them to kill a lamb and paint its blood on the doorframes of their houses. They then were to prepare the meat for food. Peter and John had to buy and prepare the lamb as well as the unleavened bread, herbs, wine, and other ceremonial food.

22:10 Ordinarily women, not men, went to the well and brought home the water. So this man would have stood out in the crowd.

22:14-18 The Passover commemorated Israel's escape from Egypt when the blood of a lamb painted on their doorframes saved their firstborn sons from death. This event foreshadowed Jesus' work on the cross. As the spotless Lamb of God, his blood would be spilled in order to save his people from the penalty of death brought by sin.

17 Then he took a cup of wine, and when he had given thanks for it, he said, "Take this
and share it among yourselves. 18 For I will not drink wine again until the Kingdom of
God has come."

19 Then he took a loaf of bread; and when he had thanked God for it, he broke it in **22:19**
pieces and gave it to the disciples, saying, "This is my body, given for you. Do this in Luke 24:30
remembrance of me." 20 After supper he took another cup of wine and said, "This wine Acts 27:35 **22:20**
is the token of God's new covenant to save you—an agreement sealed with the blood I Exod 24:8 Jer 31:31-34
will pour out for you.* Heb 9:15-18

21 "But here at this table, sitting among us as a friend, is the man who will betray me. **22:21**
22 For I, the Son of Man, must die since it is part of God's plan. But how terrible it will Ps 41:9
be for my betrayer!" 23 Then the disciples began to ask each other which of them would John 13:21 **22:22**
ever do such a thing. Acts 2:23; 4:28

24 And they began to argue among themselves as to who would be the greatest in the
coming Kingdom. 25 Jesus told them, "In this world the kings and great men order their
people around, and yet they are called 'friends of the people.' 26 But among you, those **22:26**
who are the greatest should take the lowest rank, and the leader should be like a servant. Matt 23:11 Mark 9:35
27 Normally the master sits at the table and is served by his servants. But not here! For I 1 Pet 5:5 **22:27**
am your servant. 28 You have remained true to me in my time of trial. 29 And just as my John 13:4-16
Father has granted me a Kingdom, I now grant you the right 30 to eat and drink at my
table in that Kingdom. And you will sit on thrones, judging the twelve tribes of Israel.

Jesus Predicts Peter's Denial (**212**/John 13:31-38)

31 "Simon, Simon, Satan has asked to have all of you, to sift you like wheat. 32 But I have **22:31** Job 1:6-12
pleaded in prayer for you, Simon, that your faith should not fail. So when you have Amos 9:9
repented and turned to me again, strengthen and build up your brothers." **22:32** John 17:9, 15; 21:15

22:19-20 Some manuscripts omit 22:19b-20, *given for you . . . I will pour out for you.*

22:17, 20 Luke mentions two cups of wine, while Matthew and Mark mention only one. In the traditional Passover meal, the wine is served four times. Christ spoke the words about his body and his blood when he offered the fourth and last cup.

22:17-20 Christians differ in their interpretation of the meaning of the commemoration of the Lord's Supper. There are three main views: (1) The bread and wine actually become Christ's body and blood; (2) the bread and wine remain unchanged, yet Christ is spiritually present by faith in and through them; (3) the bread and wine, which remain unchanged, are lasting memorials of Christ's sacrifice. No matter which view they favor, all Christians agree that the Lord's Supper commemorates Christ's death on the cross for our sins and points to the coming of his Kingdom in glory. When we partake of it, we show our deep gratitude for Christ's work on our behalf, and our faith is strengthened.

22:19 Jesus asked the disciples to eat the broken bread "in remembrance of me." He wanted them to remember his sacrifice, the basis for forgiveness of sins, and also his friendship, which they could continue to enjoy through the work of the Holy Spirit. Although the exact meaning of Communion has been strongly debated throughout church history, Christians still take bread and wine in remembrance of their Lord and Savior, Jesus Christ. Do not neglect participating in the Lord's Supper. Let it remind you of what Christ did for you.

22:20 In Old Testament times, God agreed to forgive people's sins if they brought animals for the priests to sacrifice. When this sacrificial system was inaugurated, the agreement between God and his people was sealed with the blood of animals (Exodus 24:8). But animal blood did not in itself remove sin (only God can forgive sin), and animal sacrifices had to be repeated day after day and year after year. Jesus instituted a "new covenant" or agreement between God and his people. Under this new covenant, Jesus would die in the place of sinners. Unlike the blood of animals, his blood (because he is God) would remove the sins of all who put their faith in him. Jesus' sacrifice would never have to be repeated; it would be good for all eternity (Hebrews 9:23-28). The prophets looked forward to this new covenant that would fulfill the old sacrificial agreement (Jeremiah 31:31-34), and John the Baptist called Jesus "the Lamb of God who takes away the sin of the world" (John 1:29).

22:21 From the accounts of Mark and John, we know that the betrayer was Judas Iscariot. Although the other disciples were confused by Jesus' words, Judas knew what he meant.

22:24 The most important event in human history was about to take place, and the disciples were still arguing about their prestige in the Kingdom! Looking back, we see that this was no time to worry about status. But the disciples, wrapped up in their own concerns, did not perceive what Jesus had been trying to tell them about his approaching death and resurrection. What are your major concerns today? Twenty years from now, as you look back, will these worries look petty and inappropriate? Get your eyes off yourself and get ready for Christ's coming into human history for the second time.

22:24-27 The world's system of leadership is very different from leadership in God's Kingdom. Worldly leaders are often selfish and arrogant as they claw their way to the top. (Some kings in the ancient world gave themselves the title "Benefactor," friend of the people). But among Christians, the leader is to be the one who *serves* best. There are different styles of leadership—some lead through public speaking, some through administering, some through relationships—but every Christian leader needs a servant's heart. Ask the people you lead how you can serve them better.

22:31, 32 Satan wanted to crush Simon Peter and the other disciples like grains of wheat. He hoped to find only chaff and blow it away. But Jesus assured Peter that his faith, although it would falter, would not be destroyed. It would be renewed, and Peter would become a powerful leader.

22:33 John 11:16 33 Peter said, "Lord, I am ready to go to prison with you, and even to die with you."
34 But Jesus said, "Peter, let me tell you something. The rooster will not crow
tomorrow morning until you have denied three times that you even know me."
22:35 Matt 10:9-10 Luke 9:3 35 Then Jesus asked them, "When I sent you out to preach the Good News and you did
not have money, a traveler's bag, or extra clothing, did you lack anything?"
"No," they replied.
36 "But now," he said, "take your money and a traveler's bag. And if you don't have a
22:37 †Isa 53:12 Mark 15:28 sword, sell your clothes and buy one! 37 For the time has come for this prophecy about
me to be fulfilled: 'He was counted among those who were rebels.'* Yes, everything
written about me by the prophets will come true."
38 "Lord," they replied, "we have two swords among us."
"That's enough," he said.

Jesus Agonizes in the Garden (**223**/Matthew 26:36-46; Mark 14:32-42)

39 Then, accompanied by the disciples, Jesus left the upstairs room and went as usual to
22:40 Matt 6:13 the Mount of Olives. 40 There he told them, "Pray that you will not be overcome by
temptation."
41 He walked away, about a stone's throw, and knelt down and prayed, 42 "Father, if
you are willing, please take this cup of suffering away from me. Yet I want your will, not
mine." 43 Then an angel from heaven appeared and strengthened him. 44 He prayed more
fervently, and he was in such agony of spirit that his sweat fell to the ground like great
drops of blood.* 45 At last he stood up again and returned to the disciples, only to find
them asleep, exhausted from grief. 46 "Why are you sleeping?" he asked. "Get up and
pray. Otherwise temptation will overpower you."

Jesus Is Betrayed and Arrested (**224**/Matthew 26:47-56; Mark 14:43-52; John 18:1-11)

47 But even as he said this, a mob approached, led by Judas, one of his twelve disciples.
Judas walked over to Jesus and greeted him with a kiss. 48 But Jesus said, "Judas, how
can you betray me, the Son of Man, with a kiss?"
49 When the other disciples saw what was about to happen, they exclaimed, "Lord,
should we fight? We brought the swords!" 50 And one of them slashed at the high priest's
servant and cut off his right ear.
51 But Jesus said, "Don't resist anymore." And he touched the place where the man's
ear had been and healed him. 52 Then Jesus spoke to the leading priests and captains of

22:37 Isa 53:12. **22:43-44** These verses are not included in many ancient manuscripts.

22:33, 34 Jesus told the disciples that one of them would betray him and that calamity awaited the traitor (22:22). Jesus then told Peter that he would deny that he knew Jesus, but later Peter would repent and receive a commission to feed Jesus' lambs (John 21:15). Betraying and denying—one is just about as bad as the other. But the two men had entirely different fates because one repented.

22:35-38 Here Jesus reversed his earlier advice regarding how to travel (9:3). The disciples were to bring bags, money, and swords. They would be facing hatred and persecution and would need to be prepared. When Jesus said, "That's enough," he may have meant it was not time to think of using swords. In either case, mention of a sword vividly communicated the trials they were soon to face.

22:39 The Mount of Olives was located just to the east of Jerusalem. Jesus went up the southwestern slope to an olive grove called Gethsemane, which means "oil press."

22:40 Jesus asked the disciples to pray that they would not fall into temptation because he knew that he would soon be leaving them. Jesus also knew that they would need extra strength to face the temptations ahead—temptations to run away or to deny their relationship with him. They were about to see Jesus die. Would they still think he was the Messiah? The disciples' strongest temptation would undoubtedly be to think they had been deceived.

22:41, 42 Was Jesus trying to get out of his mission? It is never wrong to express our true feelings to God. Jesus exposed his dread of the coming trials, but he also reaffirmed his commitment to do what God wanted. The cup he spoke of meant the terrible agony he knew he would endure—not only the horror of the crucifixion but, even worse, the total separation from God that he would have to experience in order to die for the world's sins.

22:44 Only Luke tells us that Jesus' sweat resembled drops of blood. Jesus was in extreme agony, but he did not give up or give in. He went ahead with the mission for which he had come.

22:46 These disciples were asleep. How tragic it is that many Christians act as if they are sound asleep when it comes to devotion to Christ and service for him. Don't be found insensitive to or unprepared for Christ's work.

22:47 A kiss was and still is the traditional greeting among men in certain parts of the world. In this case, it was also the agreed-upon signal to point out Jesus (Matthew 26:48). It is ironic that a gesture of greeting would be the means of betrayal. It was a hollow gesture because of Judas's treachery. Have any of your religious practices become empty gestures? We still betray Christ when our acts of service or giving are insincere or carried out merely for show.

22:50 We learn from the Gospel of John that the man who cut off the servant's ear was Peter (John 18:10).

the Temple guard and the other leaders who headed the mob. "Am I some dangerous
criminal," he asked, "that you have come armed with swords and clubs to arrest me?
53 Why didn't you arrest me in the Temple? I was there every day. But this is your
moment, the time when the power of darkness reigns."

22:53 Luke 19:47 John 7:30

Peter Denies Knowing Jesus (**227**/Matthew 26:69-75; Mark 14:66-72; John 18:25-27)

54 So they arrested him and led him to the high priest's residence, and Peter was following
far behind. 55 The guards lit a fire in the courtyard and sat around it, and Peter joined
them there. 56 A servant girl noticed him in the firelight and began staring at him. Finally
she said, "This man was one of Jesus' followers!"
57 Peter denied it. "Woman," he said, "I don't even know the man!"
58 After a while someone else looked at him and said, "You must be one of them!"
"No, man, I'm not!" Peter replied.
59 About an hour later someone else insisted, "This must be one of Jesus' disciples
because he is a Galilean, too."
60 But Peter said, "Man, I don't know what you are talking about." And as soon as he
said these words, the rooster crowed. 61 At that moment the Lord turned and looked at
Peter. Then Peter remembered that the Lord had said, "Before the rooster crows
tomorrow morning, you will deny me three times." 62 And Peter left the courtyard, crying
bitterly.
63 Now the guards in charge of Jesus began mocking and beating him. 64 They
blindfolded him; then they hit him and asked, "Who hit you that time, you prophet?"
65 And they threw all sorts of terrible insults at him.

22:61 Luke 7:13

The Council of Religious Leaders Condemns Jesus (**228**/Matthew 27:1-2; Mark 15:1)

66 At daybreak all the leaders of the people assembled, including the leading priests and
the teachers of religious law. Jesus was led before this high council,* 67 and they said,
"Tell us if you are the Messiah."

22:66 Greek *before their Sanhedrin.*

22:53 The religious leaders had not arrested Jesus in the Temple for fear of a riot. Instead, they came secretly at night, under the influence of the power of darkness, Satan himself. Although it looked as if Satan was getting the upper hand, everything was proceeding according to God's plan. It was time for Jesus to die.

22:54 Jesus was immediately taken to the high priest's residence, even though this was the middle of the night. The Jewish leaders were in a hurry—they wanted to complete the execution before the Sabbath and get on with the Passover celebration. This residence was a palace with outer walls enclosing a courtyard, where servants and soldiers warmed themselves around a fire.

22:55 Peter's experiences in the next few hours would change his life. He would change from a halfhearted follower to a repentant disciple, and finally to the kind of person Christ could use to build his church. For more information on Peter, see his Profile in Matthew 27.

22:62 Peter wept bitterly, not only because he realized that he had denied his Lord, the Messiah, but also because he had turned away from a very dear friend, a person who had loved and taught him for three years. Peter had said that he would *never* deny Christ, despite Jesus' prediction (Mark 14:29-31; Luke 22:33, 34). But when frightened, he went against all he had boldly promised. Unable to stand up for his Lord for even 12 hours, he had failed as a disciple and as a friend. We need to be aware of our own breaking points and not become overconfident or self-sufficient. If we fail him, we must remember that Christ can use those who recognize their failure. From this humiliating experience Peter learned much that would help him later when he assumed leadership of the young church.

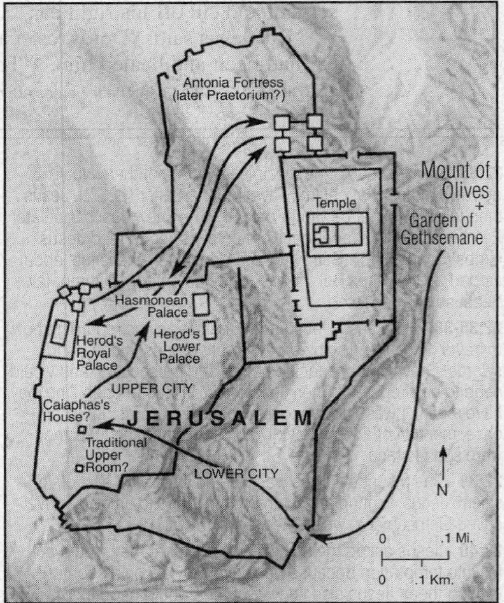

JESUS' TRIAL Taken from Gethsemane, Jesus first appeared before the Jewish high council, which had convened at daybreak at Caiaphas's house. From there he went to Pilate, the Roman governor; then to Herod, tetrarch of Galilee, who was visiting in Jerusalem; and back to Pilate, who, in desperation, sentenced Jesus to die.

But he replied, "If I tell you, you won't believe me. 68 And if I ask you a question, you
22:69 Ps 110:1 Dan 7:13 Acts 7:56 won't answer. 69 But the time is soon coming when I, the Son of Man, will be sitting at
God's right hand in the place of power."*
70 They all shouted, "Then you claim you are the Son of God?"
22:70 Matt 4:3 And he replied, "You are right in saying that I am."
71 "What need do we have for other witnesses?" they shouted. "We ourselves heard
him say it."

Jesus Stands Trial before Pilate (**230**/Matthew 27:11-14; Mark 15:2-5; John 18:28-37)

23 Then the entire council took Jesus over to Pilate, the Roman governor. 2 They
23:2 John 19:12 began at once to state their case: "This man has been leading our people to ruin
by telling them not to pay their taxes to the Roman government and by claiming he is
the Messiah, a king."
3 So Pilate asked him, "Are you the King of the Jews?"
Jesus replied, "Yes, it is as you say."
23:4 1 Tim 6:13 4 Pilate turned to the leading priests and to the crowd and said, "I find nothing wrong
with this man!"
5 Then they became desperate. "But he is causing riots everywhere he goes, all over
Judea, from Galilee to Jerusalem!"

22:69 See Ps 110:1.

JESUS' TRIAL
Jesus' trial was actually a series of hearings, carefully controlled to accomplish the death of Jesus. The verdict was predecided, but certain "legal" procedures were necessary. A lot of effort went into condemning and crucifying an innocent man. Jesus went through an unfair trial in our place so that we would not have to face a fair trial and receive the well-deserved punishment for our sins.

Event	*Probable Reasons*	*References*
Trial before Annas (powerful ex–high priest)	Although no longer the high priest, he may have still wielded much power	John 18:13–23
Trial before Caiaphas (the ruling high priest)	To gather evidence for the full high council hearing to follow	Matthew 26:57–68 Mark 14:53–65 Luke 22:54, 63–65 John 18:24
Trial before the high council (Sanhedrin)	Formal religious trial and condemnation to death	Matthew 27:1 Mark 15:1 Luke 22:66–71
Trial before Pilate (highest Roman authority)	All death sentences needed Roman approval	Matthew 27:2, 11–14 Mark 15:1–5 Luke 23:1–6 John 18:28–38
Trial before Herod (ruler of Galilee)	A courteous and guilt-sharing act by Pilate because Jesus was from Galilee, Herod's district	Luke 23:7–12
Trial before Pilate	Pilate's last effort to avoid condemning an obviously innocent man	Matthew 27:15–26 Mark 15:6–15 Luke 23:13–25 John 18:39—19:16

22:70 Jesus in effect agreed that he was the Son of God when he simply turned the high priest's question around by saying, "You are right in saying that I am." And Jesus identified himself with God by using a familiar title for God found in the Old Testament: "I am" (Exodus 3:14). The high priest recognized Jesus' claim and could accuse him of blasphemy. For any other human this claim would have been blasphemy, but in this case it was true. Blasphemy, the sin of claiming to be God or of attacking God's authority and majesty in any way, was punishable by death. The Jewish leaders had the evidence they wanted.

23:1 Pilate was the Roman governor of Judea, where Jerusalem was located. He seemed to take special pleasure in harassing the Jews. For example, Pilate had taken money from the Temple treasury and had used it to build an aqueduct. And he had insulted the Jewish religion by bringing imperial images into the city. As Pilate well knew, such acts could backfire. If the people were to lodge a formal complaint against his administration, Rome might remove him from his post. Pilate was already beginning to feel insecure in his position when the Jewish leaders brought Jesus to trial. Would he continue to badger the Jews and risk his political future, or would he give in to their demands and condemn a man who, he was quite sure, was innocent? That was the question facing Pilate that springtime Friday morning nearly 2,000 years ago. For more about Pilate, see his Profile in Mark 15.

Jesus Stands Trial before Herod (**231**)
6“Oh, is he a Galilean?” Pilate asked. 7When they answered that he was, Pilate sent him
to Herod Antipas, because Galilee was under Herod’s jurisdiction, and Herod happened
to be in Jerusalem at the time.
8Herod was delighted at the opportunity to see Jesus, because he had heard about him **23:8**
and had been hoping for a long time to see him perform a miracle. 9He asked Jesus Luke 9:9
question after question, but Jesus refused to answer. 10Meanwhile, the leading priests **23:9** John 19:9
and the teachers of religious law stood there shouting their accusations. 11Now Herod
and his soldiers began mocking and ridiculing Jesus. Then they put a royal robe on him
and sent him back to Pilate. 12Herod and Pilate, who had been enemies before, became **23:12** Acts 4:27
friends that day.

Pilate Hands Jesus Over to Be Crucified
(**232**/Matthew 27:15-26; Mark 15:6-15; John 18:39—19:16)
13Then Pilate called together the leading priests and other religious leaders, along with
the people, 14and he announced his verdict. “You brought this man to me, accusing him
of leading a revolt. I have examined him thoroughly on this point in your presence and
find him innocent. 15Herod came to the same conclusion and sent him back to us.
Nothing this man has done calls for the death penalty. 16So I will have him flogged, but **23:16** John 19:1
then I will release him.”* Acts 16:37
18Then a mighty roar rose from the crowd, and with one voice they shouted, “Kill him, **23:18**
and release Barabbas to us!” 19(Barabbas was in prison for murder and for taking part in Acts 3:13-14
an insurrection in Jerusalem against the government.) 20Pilate argued with them, because
he wanted to release Jesus. 21But they shouted, “Crucify him! Crucify him!”

23:16 Some manuscripts add verse 17, *For it was necessary for him to release one [prisoner] for them during the feast.*

23:7 Herod Antipas was in Jerusalem that weekend for the Passover celebration. (This was the Herod who killed John the Baptist.) Pilate hoped to pass Jesus off on Herod because he knew that Jesus had lived and worked in Galilee. But Herod was not much help. He was curious about Jesus and enjoyed making fun of him. But when Herod sent Jesus back to Pilate, it was with the verdict of “not guilty.” For more about Herod Antipas, see his Profile in Mark 6.

23:12 Herod was the part-Jewish ruler of Galilee and Perea. Pilate was the Roman governor of Judea and Samaria. Those four provinces, together with several others, had been united under Herod the Great. But when Herod died in 4 B.C., the kingdom was divided among his sons. Archelaus, the son who had received Judea and Samaria, was removed from office within 10 years, and his provinces were then ruled by a succession of Roman governors, of whom Pilate was the fifth.

Herod Antipas had two advantages over Pilate: He came from a hereditary, part-Jewish monarchy, and he had held his position much longer. But Pilate had two advantages over Herod: He was a Roman citizen and an envoy of the emperor, and his position was created to replace that of Herod’s ineffective half brother. It is not surprising that the two men were uneasy around each other. Jesus’ trial, however, brought them together. Because Pilate had recognized Herod’s authority over Galilee, Herod stopped feeling threatened by the Roman politician. And because neither man knew what to do in this predicament, their common problem united them.

23:13-25 Pilate wanted to release Jesus, but the crowd loudly demanded his death; so Pilate sentenced Jesus to die. No doubt Pilate did not want to risk losing his position, which may already have been shaky, by allowing a riot to occur in his province. As a career politician, he knew the importance of compromise, and he saw Jesus more as a political threat than as a human being with rights and dignity.

When the stakes are high, it is difficult to stand up for what is right, and it is easy to see our opponents as problems to be solved rather than as people to be respected. Had Pilate been a man of real courage, he would have released Jesus no matter what the consequences. But the crowd roared, and Pilate buckled. We are like Pilate when we know what is right but decide not to do it. When you have a difficult decision to make, don’t discount the effects of peer pressure. Realize beforehand that the right decision could have unpleasant consequences: social rejection, career derailment, public ridicule. Then think of Pilate and resolve to stand up for what is right no matter what other people pressure you to do.

23:15 Jesus was tried six times, by both Jewish and Roman authorities, but he was never convicted of a crime deserving death. Even when condemned to execution, he had been convicted of no felony. Today, no one can find fault in Jesus. But just like Pilate, Herod, and the religious leaders, many still refuse to acknowledge him as Lord.

23:18, 19 Barabbas had been part of a rebellion against the Roman government (Mark 15:7). As a political insurgent, he was no doubt a hero among some of the Jews. How ironic it is that Barabbas, who was released, was guilty of the very crime Jesus was accused of (23:14).

23:18, 19 Who was Barabbas? Jewish men had names that identified them with their fathers. Simon Peter, for example, is called Simon son of John (Matthew 16:17). Barabbas is never identified by his given name, and this name is not much help either—*bar-abbas* means “son of *Abba*” (or “son of daddy”). He could have been anybody’s son—and that’s just the point. Barabbas, son of an unnamed father, committed a crime. Because Jesus died in his place, this man was set free. We, too, are sinners and criminals who have broken God’s holy law. Like Barabbas, we deserve to die. But Jesus has died in our place, for our sins, and we have been set free. We don’t have to be “very important people” to accept our freedom in Christ. In fact, thanks to Jesus, God adopts us all as his own sons and daughters and gives us the right to call him our dear Father (see Galatians 4:4-6).

[22]For the third time he demanded, "Why? What crime has he committed? I have found
no reason to sentence him to death. I will therefore flog him and let him go."
[23]But the crowd shouted louder and louder for Jesus' death, and their voices prevailed.
[24]So Pilate sentenced Jesus to die as they demanded. [25]As they had requested, he
released Barabbas, the man in prison for insurrection and murder. But he delivered Jesus
over to them to do as they wished.

Jesus Is Led Away to Be Crucified
(**234**/Matthew 27:32-34; Mark 15:21-24; John 19:17)

[26]As they led Jesus away, Simon of Cyrene,* who was coming in from the country
just then, was forced to follow Jesus and carry his cross. [27]Great crowds trailed along
behind, including many grief-stricken women. [28]But Jesus turned and said to them,
"Daughters of Jerusalem, don't weep for me, but weep for yourselves and for your
children. [29]For the days are coming when they will say, 'Fortunate indeed are the
women who are childless, the wombs that have not borne a child and the breasts that
have never nursed.' [30]People will beg the mountains to fall on them and the hills to
bury them. [31]For if these things are done when the tree is green, what will happen
when it is dry?*"

23:29 Luke 21:23
23:30 Isa 2:19; †Hos 10:8; Rev 6:16

Jesus Is Placed on the Cross (**235**/Matthew 27:35-44; Mark 15:25-32; John 19:18-27)

[32]Two others, both criminals, were led out to be executed with him. [33]Finally, they came
to a place called The Skull.* All three were crucified there—Jesus on the center cross,
and the two criminals on either side.

23:32 Isa 53:12; Matt 27:38; Mark 15:27; John 19:18

23:26 *Cyrene* was a city in northern Africa. **23:31** Or *If these things are done to me, the living tree, what will happen to you, the dry tree?* **23:33** Sometimes rendered *Calvary,* which comes from the Latin word for "skull."

23:22 When Pilate said he would have Jesus flogged, he was referring to a punishment that could have killed Jesus. The usual procedure was to bare the upper half of the victim's body and tie his hands to a pillar before whipping him with a three-pronged whip. The number of lashes was determined by the severity of the crime; up to 40 were permitted under Jewish law. After being flogged, Jesus also endured other agonies as recorded in Matthew and Mark. He was slapped, struck with fists, and mocked. A crown of thorns was placed on his head, and he was beaten with a stick and stripped before being hung on the cross.

23:23, 24 Pilate did not want to give Jesus the death sentence. He thought the Jewish leaders were simply jealous men who wanted to get rid of a rival. When they threatened to report Pilate to Caesar (John 19:12), however, Pilate became frightened. Historical records indicate that Pilate had already been warned by Roman authorities about tensions in this region. The last thing he needed was a riot in Jerusalem at Passover time, when the city was crowded with Jews from all over the empire. So Pilate turned Jesus over to the mob to do with as they pleased.

23:27-29 Luke alone mentions the tears of the Jewish women while Jesus was being led through the streets to his execution. Jesus told them not to weep for him but for themselves. He knew that in only about 40 years, Jerusalem and the Temple would be destroyed by the Romans.

23:31 This proverb is difficult to interpret. Some feel it means: If the innocent Jesus (green tree) suffered at the hands of the Romans, what would happen to the guilty Jews (dry tree)?

23:32, 33 The place called The Skull, or Golgotha, was probably a hill outside Jerusalem along a main road. The Romans executed people publicly as examples to the people.

23:32, 33 When James and John asked Jesus for the places of honor next to him in his Kingdom, he told them they didn't know what they were asking (Mark 10:35-39). Here, as Jesus was preparing to inaugurate his Kingdom through his death, the places on his right and on his left were taken by dying men—criminals. As Jesus explained to his two position-conscious disciples, a person who wants to be close to Jesus must be prepared to suffer and die. The way to the Kingdom is the way of the cross.

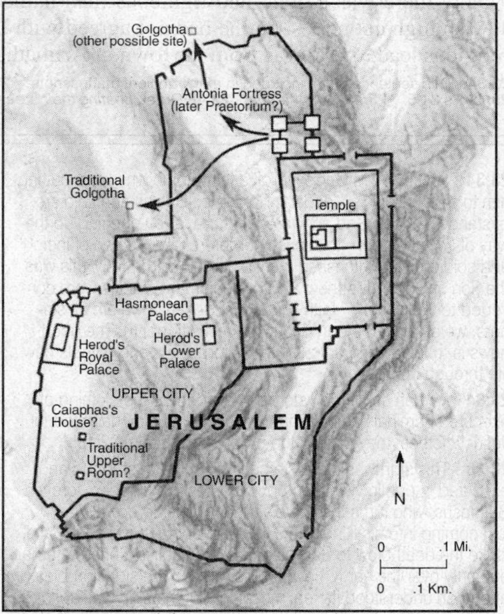

JESUS LED AWAY TO DIE As Jesus was led away through the streets of Jerusalem, he could no longer carry his cross, and Simon of Cyrene was given the burden. Jesus was crucified, along with common criminals, on a hill outside Jerusalem.

34 Jesus said, "Father, forgive these people, because they don't know what they are
doing."* And the soldiers gambled for his clothes by throwing dice.*
35 The crowd watched, and the leaders laughed and scoffed. "He saved others," they
said, "let him save himself if he is really God's Chosen One, the Messiah." 36 The soldiers
mocked him, too, by offering him a drink of sour wine. 37 They called out to him, "If you
are the King of the Jews, save yourself!" 38 A signboard was nailed to the cross above
him with these words: "This is the King of the Jews."
39 One of the criminals hanging beside him scoffed, "So you're the Messiah, are you?
Prove it by saving yourself—and us, too, while you're at it!"
40 But the other criminal protested, "Don't you fear God even when you are dying?
41 We deserve to die for our evil deeds, but this man hasn't done anything wrong." 42 Then
he said, "Jesus, remember me when you come into your Kingdom."
43 And Jesus replied, "I assure you, today you will be with me in paradise."

23:34 †Ps 22:18
23:35 Ps 22:17
23:36 Pss 22:7; 69:21 Matt 27:48
23:43 2 Cor 12:3-4 Rev 2:7

Jesus Dies on the Cross (**236**/Matthew 27:45-56; Mark 15:33-41; John 19:28-37)

44 By this time it was noon, and darkness fell across the whole land until three o'clock.
45 The light from the sun was gone. And suddenly, the thick veil hanging in the Temple
was torn apart. 46 Then Jesus shouted, "Father, I entrust my spirit into your hands!"* And
with those words he breathed his last.
47 When the captain of the Roman soldiers handling the executions saw what had
happened, he praised God and said, "Surely this man was innocent.*" 48 And when the
crowd that came to see the crucifixion saw all that had happened, they went home in deep
sorrow.* 49 But Jesus' friends, including the women who had followed him from Galilee,
stood at a distance watching.

23:45 Exod 26:31-33 Heb 9:3, 8; 10:19-20
23:46 †Ps 31:5
23:48 Luke 18:13
23:49 Ps 38:11

Jesus Is Laid in the Tomb (**237**/Matthew 27:57-61; Mark 15:42-47; John 19:38-42)

50 Now there was a good and righteous man named Joseph. He was a member of the
Jewish high council, 51 but he had not agreed with the decision and actions of the other
religious leaders. He was from the town of Arimathea in Judea, and he had been waiting

23:34a This sentence is not included in many ancient manuscripts. **23:34b** Greek *by casting lots.* See Ps 22:18. **23:46** Ps 31:5. **23:47** Or *righteous.* **23:48** Greek *beating their breasts.*

23:34 Jesus asked God to forgive the people who were putting him to death—Jewish leaders, Roman politicians and soldiers, bystanders—and God answered that prayer by opening up the way of salvation even to Jesus' murderers. The Roman officer and soldiers who witnessed the Crucifixion said, "Truly, this was the Son of God!" (Matthew 27:54). Soon many priests were converted to the Christian faith (Acts 6:7). Because we are all sinners, we all played a part in putting Jesus to death. The good news is that God is gracious. He will forgive us and give us new life through his Son.

23:34 Roman soldiers customarily divided up the clothing of executed criminals among themselves. When they gambled for Jesus' clothes, they fulfilled the prophecy in Psalm 22:18.

23:38 This sign was meant to be ironic. A king, stripped and executed in public view, had obviously lost his kingdom forever. But Jesus, who turns the world's wisdom upside down, was just coming into his Kingdom. His death and resurrection would strike the deathblow to Satan's rule and establish Christ's eternal authority over the earth. Few people reading the sign that bleak afternoon understood its real meaning, but the sign was absolutely true. All was not lost. Jesus is King of the Jews—and of the Gentiles and the whole universe.

23:39-43 As this man was about to die, he turned to Christ for forgiveness, and Christ accepted him. This shows that our deeds don't save us—our faith in Christ does. It is never too late to turn to God. Even in his misery, Jesus had mercy on this criminal who decided to believe in him. Our life will be much more useful and fulfilling if we turn to God early, but even those who repent at the very last moment will be with God in paradise.

23:42, 43 The dying criminal had more faith than the rest of Jesus' followers put together. Although the disciples continued to love Jesus, their hopes for the Kingdom were shattered. Most of them had gone into hiding. As one of his followers sadly said two days later, "We had thought he was the Messiah who had come to rescue Israel" (24:21). By contrast, the criminal looked at the man who was dying next to him and said, "Jesus, remember me when you come into your Kingdom." By all appearances, the Kingdom was finished. How awe-inspiring is the faith of this man who alone saw beyond the present shame to the coming glory!

23:44 Darkness covered the entire land for about three hours in the middle of the day. All nature seemed to mourn over the stark tragedy of the death of God's Son.

23:45 This significant event symbolized Christ's work on the cross. The Temple had three parts: the courts for all the people; the Holy Place, where only priests could enter; and the Most Holy Place, where the high priest alone could enter once a year to atone for the sins of the people. It was in the Most Holy Place that the Ark of the Covenant, and God's presence with it, rested. The curtain that was torn was the one that closed off the Most Holy Place from view. At Christ's death, the barrier between God and humanity was split in two. Now all people can approach God directly through Christ (Hebrews 9:1-14; 10:19-22).

23:50-52 Joseph of Arimathea was a wealthy and honored member of the Jewish high council. He was also a secret disciple of Jesus (John 19:38). The disciples who had publicly followed Jesus fled, but Joseph boldly took a stand that could have cost him dearly. He cared enough about Jesus to ask for his body so he could give it a proper burial.

23:53 The tomb was likely a man-made cave cut out of one of the many limestone hills in the area around Jerusalem. Such a tomb was large enough to walk into. After burial, a large stone would have been rolled across the entrance (John 20:1).

23:53 Luke 19:30
23:55 Luke 8:2; 23:49
23:56 Exod 12:16; 20:10 Lev 23:8

for the Kingdom of God to come. 52 He went to Pilate and asked for Jesus' body. 53 Then
he took the body down from the cross and wrapped it in a long linen cloth and laid it in
a new tomb that had been carved out of rock. 54 This was done late on Friday afternoon,
the day of preparation* for the Sabbath.
55 As his body was taken away, the women from Galilee followed and saw the tomb
where they placed his body. 56 Then they went home and prepared spices and ointments
to embalm him. But by the time they were finished it was the Sabbath, so they rested all
that day as required by the law.

Jesus Rises from the Dead (**239**/Matthew 28:1-7; Mark 16:1-8; John 20:1-10)

24:1 John 20:19 Acts 20:17 1 Cor 16:2
24:3 Mark 16:19 Acts 1:21; 4:33
24:4 Acts 1:10
24:6 Matt 16:21 Luke 9:22
24:8 John 2:22
24:10 Matt 27:56 Luke 8:1-3
24:11 Mark 16:11

24 But very early on Sunday morning* the women came to the tomb, taking the
spices they had prepared. 2 They found that the stone covering the entrance had
been rolled aside. 3 So they went in, but they couldn't find the body of the Lord Jesus.
4 They were puzzled, trying to think what could have happened to it. Suddenly, two
men appeared to them, clothed in dazzling robes. 5 The women were terrified and
bowed low before them. Then the men asked, "Why are you looking in a tomb for
someone who is alive? 6 He isn't here! He has risen from the dead! Don't you
remember what he told you back in Galilee, 7 that the Son of Man must be betrayed
into the hands of sinful men and be crucified, and that he would rise again the third
day?"
8 Then they remembered that he had said this. 9 So they rushed back to tell his eleven
disciples—and everyone else—what had happened. 10 The women who went to the tomb
were Mary Magdalene, Joanna, Mary the mother of James, and several others. They told
the apostles what had happened, 11 but the story sounded like nonsense, so they didn't

23:54 Greek *on the day of preparation.* **24:1** Greek *But on the first day of the week, very early in the morning.*

23:55 The Galilean women followed Joseph to the tomb, so they knew exactly where to find Jesus' body when they returned after the Sabbath with their spices and perfumes. These women could not do "great" things for Jesus—they were not permitted to stand up before the Jewish high council or the Roman governor and testify on his behalf—but they did what they could. They stayed at the cross when most of the disciples had fled, and they got ready to anoint their Lord's body. Because of their devotion, they were the first to know about the Resurrection. As believers, we may feel we can't do much for Jesus. But we are called to take advantage of the opportunities given us, doing what we *can* do and not worrying about what we cannot do.

24:1 The women brought spices to the tomb as we would bring flowers—as a sign of love and respect. The women went home and kept the Sabbath as the law required, from sundown Friday to sundown Saturday, before gathering up their spices and perfumes and returning to the tomb.

24:1-9 The two angels (appearing as "two men . . . clothed in dazzling robes") asked the women why they were looking in a tomb for someone who was alive. Often we run into people who are looking for God among the dead. They study the Bible as a mere historical document and go to church as if going to a memorial service. But Jesus is not among the dead—he lives! He reigns in the hearts of Christians, and he is the head of his church. Do you look for Jesus among the living? Do you expect him to be active in the world and in the church? Look for signs of his power—they are all around you.

24:4 We learn from Matthew and John that these two men in dazzling robes were angels. When angels appeared to people, they looked like humans.

24:6, 7 The angels reminded the women that Jesus had accurately predicted all that had happened to him (9:22, 44; 18:31-33).

24:6, 7 The resurrection of Jesus from the dead is the central fact of Christian history. On it, the church is built; without it, there would be no Christian church today. Jesus' resurrection is unique. Other religions have strong ethical systems, concepts about paradise and the afterlife, and various holy scriptures. Only Christianity has a God who became human, literally died for his people, and was raised again in power and glory to rule his church forever.

Why is the Resurrection so important? (1) Because Christ was raised from the dead, we know that the Kingdom of Heaven has broken into earth's history. Our world is now headed for redemption, not disaster. God's mighty power is at work destroying sin, creating new lives, and preparing us for Jesus' second coming. (2) Because of the Resurrection, we know that death has been conquered and we, too, will be raised from the dead to live forever with Christ. (3) The Resurrection gives authority to the church's witness in the world. Look at the early evangelistic sermons in the book of Acts: The apostles' most important message was the proclamation that Jesus Christ had been raised from the dead! (4) The Resurrection gives meaning to the church's sacrament of the Lord's Supper. Like Jesus' followers on the Emmaus Road, we break bread with our risen Lord, who comes in power to save us. (5) The Resurrection helps us find meaning even in great tragedy. No matter what happens to us as we walk with the Lord, the Resurrection gives us hope for the future. (6) The Resurrection assures us that Christ is alive and ruling his Kingdom. He is not a legend; he is alive and real. (7) God's power that brought Jesus back from the dead is available to us so that we can live for him in an evil world.

Christians can look very different from one another, and they can hold widely varying beliefs about politics, life-style, and even theology. But one central belief unites and inspires all true Christians: Jesus Christ rose from the dead! (For more on the importance of the Resurrection, see 1 Corinthians 15:3-7, 12-58.)

24:11, 12 People who hear about the Resurrection for the first time may need time before they can comprehend this amazing story. Like the disciples, they may pass through four stages of belief: (1) At first, they may think it is a fairy tale, impossible to believe. (2) Like Peter, they may check out the facts but still be puzzled about what happened. (3) Only when they encounter Jesus personally will they be able to accept the fact of the Resurrection. (4) Then, as they commit themselves to Jesus and devote their lives to serving him, they will begin fully to understand the reality of his presence with them.

believe it. 12 However, Peter ran to the tomb to look. Stooping, he peered in and saw the **24:12** John 20:3-7
empty linen wrappings; then he went home again, wondering what had happened.*

Jesus Appears to Two Believers Traveling on the Road (**243**/Mark 16:12-13)

13 That same day two of Jesus' followers were walking to the village of Emmaus, seven
miles* out of Jerusalem. 14 As they walked along they were talking about everything that
had happened. 15 Suddenly, Jesus himself came along and joined them and began **24:15** Matt 18:20
walking beside them. 16 But they didn't know who he was, because God kept them from **24:16** John 20:14; 21:4
recognizing him.

17 "You seem to be in a deep discussion about something," he said. "What are you so
concerned about?"

They stopped short, sadness written across their faces. 18 Then one of them, Cleopas, **24:18** John 19:25
replied, "You must be the only person in Jerusalem who hasn't heard about all the things
that have happened there the last few days."

19 "What things?" Jesus asked.

"The things that happened to Jesus, the man from Nazareth," they said. "He was a
prophet who did wonderful miracles. He was a mighty teacher, highly regarded by both
God and all the people. 20 But our leading priests and other religious leaders arrested him **24:20** Luke 23:13
and handed him over to be condemned to death, and they crucified him. 21 We had
thought he was the Messiah who had come to rescue Israel. That all happened three days **24:21** Luke 1:68; Acts 1:6
ago. 22 Then some women from our group of his followers were at his tomb early this
morning, and they came back with an amazing report. 23 They said his body was missing, **24:22-23** Matt 28:1-8; Mark 16:1-8
and they had seen angels who told them Jesus is alive! 24 Some of our men ran out to see,
and sure enough, Jesus' body was gone, just as the women had said."

25 Then Jesus said to them, "You are such foolish people! You find it so hard to believe

24:12 Some manuscripts do not include this verse. **24:13** Greek *60 stadia* [11.1 kilometers].

24:12 From John 20:3, 4, we learn that another disciple ran to the tomb with Peter. That other disciple was almost certainly John, the author of the fourth Gospel.

24:13ff The two followers returning to Emmaus at first missed the significance of history's greatest event because they were too focused on their disappointments and problems. In fact, they didn't recognize Jesus when he was walking beside them. To compound the problem, they were walking in the wrong direction—away from the fellowship of believers in Jerusalem. We are likely to miss Jesus and withdraw from the strength found in other believers when we become preoccupied with our dashed hopes and frustrated plans. Only when we are looking for Jesus in our midst will we experience the power and help he can bring.

24:18 The news about Jesus' crucifixion had spread throughout Jerusalem. Because this was Passover week, Jewish pilgrims visiting the city from all over the Roman Empire now knew about his death. This was not a small, insignificant event, affecting only the disciples—the whole nation was interested.

24:21 These followers from Emmaus were counting on Jesus to redeem Israel, that is, to rescue the nation from its enemies. Most Jews believed that the Old Testament prophecies pointed to a military and political Messiah; they didn't realize that the Messiah had come to redeem people from slavery to sin. When Jesus died, therefore, they lost all hope. They didn't understand that Jesus' death offered the greatest hope possible.

24:24 These followers knew that the tomb was empty but didn't understand that Jesus had risen, and they were filled with sadness. Despite the women's witness, which was verified by some of the disciples, and despite the biblical prophecies of this very event, they still didn't believe. Today the Resurrection still catches people by surprise. In spite of 2,000 years of evidence and witness, many people refuse to believe. What more will it take? For these disciples it took the living Jesus in their midst. For many people today, it takes the presence of alive Christians.

24:25 Why did Jesus call these disciples foolish? Even though they well knew the biblical prophecies, they failed to understand that Christ's suffering was his path to glory. They could not understand why God did not intervene to save Jesus from the cross. They were so caught up in the world's admiration of political power and military might that they were blind to God's Kingdom values—that the last will be first, and that life grows out of death. The world has not changed its values. The suffering servant is no more popular today than he was 2,000 years ago. But we have not only the witness of the Old Testament prophets; we also have the witness of the New Testament apostles and the history of the Christian church testifying to Jesus' victory over death. Will we confront the values of our culture and put our faith in Jesus? Or will we foolishly continue to ignore this Good News?

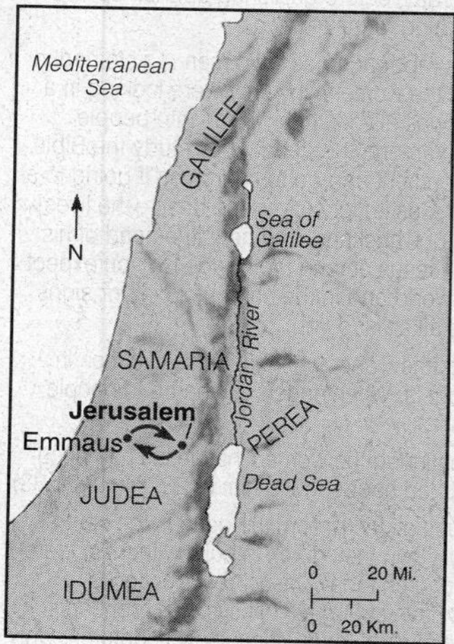

ON THE ROAD TO EMMAUS
After Jesus' death, two of his followers were walking from Jerusalem back toward Emmaus when a stranger joined them. During dinner in Emmaus, Jesus revealed himself to them and then disappeared. They immediately returned to Jerusalem to tell the disciples the good news that Jesus was alive!

24:26
Matt 26:24
Luke 24:7, 44
John 12:23-24;
13:31-32
Acts 17:3
Heb 2:10; 5:5

all that the prophets wrote in the Scriptures. 26 Wasn't it clearly predicted by the prophets
that the Messiah would have to suffer all these things before entering his time of glory?"
27 Then Jesus quoted passages from the writings of Moses and all the prophets, explaining what all the Scriptures said about himself.
28 By this time they were nearing Emmaus and the end of their journey. Jesus would
have gone on, 29 but they begged him to stay the night with them, since it was getting
late. So he went home with them. 30 As they sat down to eat, he took a small loaf of bread,
asked God's blessing on it, broke it, then gave it to them. 31 Suddenly, their eyes were
opened, and they recognized him. And at that moment he disappeared!
32 They said to each other, "Didn't our hearts feel strangely warm as he talked with us
on the road and explained the Scriptures to us?" 33 And within the hour they were on their
way back to Jerusalem, where the eleven disciples and the other followers of Jesus were
gathered. When they arrived, they were greeted with the report, 34 "The Lord has really
risen! He appeared to Peter*!"

24:34
1 Cor 15:5

Jesus Appears to His Disciples (**244**/John 20:19-23)

35 Then the two from Emmaus told their story of how Jesus had appeared to them as they
were walking along the road and how they had recognized him as he was breaking the
bread. 36 And just as they were telling about it, Jesus himself was suddenly standing there
among them. He said, "Peace be with you."* 37 But the whole group was terribly
frightened, thinking they were seeing a ghost! 38 "Why are you frightened?" he asked.
"Why do you doubt who I am? 39 Look at my hands. Look at my feet. You can see that
it's really me. Touch me and make sure that I am not a ghost, because ghosts don't have
bodies, as you see that I do!" 40 As he spoke, he held out his hands for them to see, and
he showed them his feet.*
41 Still they stood there doubting, filled with joy and wonder. Then he asked them, "Do
you have anything here to eat?" 42 They gave him a piece of broiled fish, 43 and he ate it
as they watched.

Jesus Appears to the Disciples in Jerusalem (**249**)

24:44
Luke 24:27

44 Then he said, "When I was with you before, I told you that everything written about
me by Moses and the prophets and in the Psalms must all come true." 45 Then he opened
their minds to understand these many Scriptures. 46 And he said, "Yes, it was written long

24:34 Greek *Simon.* **24:36** Some manuscripts do not include *He said, "Peace be with you."* **24:40** Some manuscripts do not include this verse.

24:25-27 After the two followers had explained their sadness and confusion, Jesus responded by going to Scripture and applying it to his ministry. When we are puzzled by questions or problems, we, too, can go to Scripture and find authoritative help. If we, like these two, do not understand what the Bible means, we can turn to other believers who know the Bible and have the wisdom to apply it to our situation.

24:27 Beginning with the promised offspring in Genesis (Genesis 3:15) and going through the suffering servant in Isaiah (Isaiah 53), the pierced one in Zechariah (Zechariah 12:10), and the messenger of the covenant in Malachi (Malachi 3:1), Jesus reintroduced these disciples to the Old Testament. Christ is the thread woven through all the Scriptures, the central theme that binds them together. Following are several key passages Jesus may have mentioned on this walk to Emmaus: Genesis 3; 12; Psalms 22; 69; 110; Isaiah 53; Jeremiah 31; Zechariah 9; 13; Malachi 3.

24:33, 34 Paul also mentions that Jesus appeared to Peter alone (1 Corinthians 15:5). This appearance is not further described in the Gospels. Jesus showed individual concern for Peter because Peter felt completely unworthy after denying his Lord. But Peter repented, and Jesus approached him and forgave him. Soon God would use Peter in building Christ's church (see the first half of the book of Acts).

24:36-43 Jesus' body wasn't just a figment of the imagination or the appearance of a ghost—the disciples touched him, and he ate food. On the other hand, his body wasn't merely a restored human body like Lazarus's (John 11)—he was able to appear and disappear. Jesus' resurrected body was immortal. This is the kind of body we will be given at the resurrection of the dead (see 1 Corinthians 15:42-50).

24:44 Many days may have elapsed between verses 43 and 44 because Jesus and his followers traveled to Galilee and back before he returned to heaven (Matthew 28:16; John 21). In his second book, Acts, Luke makes it clear that Jesus spent 40 days with his disciples between his resurrection and ascension.

24:44-46 "The writings by Moses, the prophets, and in the Psalms" refers to the entire Old Testament. In other words, the entire Old Testament points to the Messiah. For example, his role as prophet was foretold in Deuteronomy 18:15-20; his sufferings were prophesied in Psalm 22 and Isaiah 53; his resurrection was predicted in Psalm 16:9-11 and Isaiah 53:10, 11.

24:45 Jesus opened these people's minds to understand the Scriptures. The Holy Spirit still does this in our life today when we study the Bible. Have you ever wondered how to understand a difficult Bible passage? Besides reading surrounding passages, asking other people, and consulting reference works, pray that the Holy Spirit will open your mind to understand, giving you the needed insight to put God's Word into action in your life.

ago that the Messiah must suffer and die and rise again from the dead on the third day.
47 With my authority, take this message of repentance to all the nations, beginning in
Jerusalem: 'There is forgiveness of sins for all who turn to me.' 48 You are witnesses of
all these things.
49 "And now I will send the Holy Spirit, just as my Father promised. But stay here in
the city until the Holy Spirit comes and fills you with power from heaven."

24:47 Acts 2:38; 10:43; 13:38; 26:18
24:48 John 15:27
24:49 Acts 2:1-4

Jesus Ascends into Heaven (**250**/Mark 16:19-20)

50 Then Jesus led them to Bethany, and lifting his hands to heaven, he blessed them.
51 While he was blessing them, he left them and was taken up to heaven.* 52 They
worshiped him and* then returned to Jerusalem filled with great joy. 53 And they spent
all of their time in the Temple, praising God.

24:50-53 Mark 16:19; Acts 1:4-14
24:53 Acts 2:46; 3:1; 5:42

24:51 Some manuscripts do not include *and was taken up to heaven.* **24:52** Some manuscripts do not include *worshiped him and.*

24:47 Luke wrote to the Greek-speaking world. He wanted them to know that Christ's message of God's love and forgiveness should go to all the world. We must never ignore the worldwide scope of Christ's Good News. God wants all the world to hear the Good News of salvation.

24:50-53 As the disciples stood and watched, Jesus began rising into the air, and soon he disappeared into heaven. Seeing Jesus leave must have been frightening, but the disciples knew that Jesus would keep his promise to send the Holy Spirit to be with them. This same Jesus, who lived with the disciples, who died and was buried, and who rose from the dead, loves us and promises to be with us always. We can get to know him better by studying the Scriptures, praying, and allowing the Holy Spirit to make us more like Jesus.

24:51 Jesus' physical presence left the disciples when he returned to heaven (Acts 1:9), but the Holy Spirit soon came to comfort them and empower them to spread the Good News of salvation (Acts 2:1-4). Today Jesus' work of salvation is complete, and he is sitting at God's right hand, where he has authority over heaven and earth.

24:53 Luke's Gospel portrays Jesus as a perfect life lived according to God's plan. As a child, he was obedient to his parents and amazed the religious leaders in the Temple. As an adult, he served God and others through preaching and healing, and finally, as a condemned man, he suffered without complaint. This portrayal of Jesus was well suited to Luke's Greek audience, who placed high value on being an example and improving oneself, and who often discussed the meaning of perfection. The Greeks, however, had a difficult time understanding the spiritual importance of the physical world. To them, the spiritual was always more important than the physical. To help them understand the God-man, who united the spiritual and the physical, Luke emphasized that Jesus was not a phantom but a real human being who healed people and fed them because he was concerned with their physical health as well as the state of their souls.

As believers living according to God's plan, we, too, should obey our Lord in every detail as we seek to bring wholeness to people's bodies and souls. If others want to know how to live a perfect life, we can point them to Jesus.

OLD TESTAMENT PASSAGES QUOTED BY CHRIST

New Testament	*Old Testament*	*Occasion*
Matthew 4:4	Deuteronomy 8:3	Temptation
Matthew 4:7	Deuteronomy 6:16	
Matthew 4:10	Deuteronomy 6:13	
Matthew 5:21	Exodus 20:13	Sermon on the Mount
Matthew 5:27	Exodus 20:14	
Luke 4:18, 19	Isaiah 61:1, 2	Hometown Sermon
Matthew 9:13	Hosea 6:6	Confrontations with the Jewish Rulers
Mark 10:7, 8	Genesis 2:24	
Mark 12:29, 30	Deuteronomy 6:4, 5	
Matthew 15:7-9	Isaiah 29:13	
John 8:17	Deuteronomy 17:6	
Luke 7:27	Malachi 3:1	Tribute to John
Matthew 21:16	Psalm 8:2	Triumphal Entry
Luke 19:46	Isaiah 56:7	Temple Cleansing
Matthew 21:42, 44	Psalm 118:22, 23	Parable about Israel
Mark 12:36	Psalm 110:1	Temple Question Session
John 15:25	Psalm 35:19; 69:4	Last Passover
Matthew 27:46	Psalm 22:1	On the Cross
Luke 23:46	Psalm 31:5	

JOHN

Herod the Great begins to rule 37 B.C.	*Jesus is born 6/5 B.C.*	*Escape to Egypt 5/4 B.C.*	*Herod the Great dies 4 B.C.*	*Return to Nazareth 4/3 B.C.*	*Judea becomes a Roman province A.D. 6*

VITAL STATISTICS

PURPOSE:
To prove conclusively that Jesus is the Son of God and that all who believe in him will have eternal life

AUTHOR:
John the apostle, son of Zebedee, brother of James, called a "Son of Thunder"

TO WHOM WRITTEN:
New Christians and searching non-Christians

DATE WRITTEN:
Probably A.D. 85–90

SETTING:
Written after the destruction of Jerusalem in A.D. 70 and before John's exile to the island of Patmos

KEY VERSES:
"Jesus' disciples saw him do many other miraculous signs besides the ones recorded in this book. But these are written so that you may believe that Jesus is the Messiah, the Son of God, and that by believing in him you will have life" (20:30, 31).

KEY PEOPLE:
Jesus, John the Baptist, the disciples, Mary, Martha, Lazarus, Jesus' mother, Pilate, Mary Magdalene

KEY PLACES:
Judean countryside, Samaria, Galilee, Bethany, Jerusalem

SPECIAL FEATURES:
Of the eight miracles recorded, six are unique (among the Gospels) to John, as is the "Upper Room Discourse" (chapters 14—17). Over 90 percent of John is unique to his Gospel— John does not contain a genealogy or any record of Jesus' birth, childhood, temptation, transfiguration, appointment of the disciples, nor any account of Jesus' parables, ascension, or great commission.

HE SPOKE, and galaxies whirled into place, stars burned the heavens, and planets began orbiting their suns—words of awesome, unlimited, unleashed power. He spoke again, and the waters and lands were filled with plants and creatures, running, swimming, growing, and multiplying—words of animating, breathing, pulsing life. Again he spoke, and man and woman were formed, thinking, speaking, and loving—words of personal and creative glory. Eternal, infinite, unlimited—he was, is, and always will be the Maker and Lord of all that exists.

And then he came in the flesh to a speck in the universe called planet Earth. The mighty Creator became a part of the creation, limited by time and space and susceptible to aging, sickness, and death. But love propelled him, and so he came to rescue and save those who were lost and to give them the gift of eternity. He is the Word; he is Jesus, the Messiah.

It is this truth that the apostle John brings to us in this book. John's Gospel is not a life of Christ; it is a powerful argument for the incarnation, a conclusive demonstration that Jesus was, and is, the very heaven-sent Son of God and the only source of eternal life.

John discloses Jesus' identity with his very first words, "In the beginning the Word already existed. He was with God, and he was God. He was in the beginning with God" (1:1, 2); and the rest of the book continues the theme. John, the eyewitness, chose eight of Jesus' miracles (or miraculous signs, as he calls them) to reveal his divine/human nature and his life-giving mission. These signs are (1) turning water to wine (2:1–11), (2) healing the official's son (4:46–54), (3) healing the lame man at the Pool of Bethesda (5:1–9), (4) feeding the 5,000 with just a few loaves and fish (6:1–14), (5) walking on the water (6:15–21), (6) restoring sight to the blind man (9:1–41), (7) raising Lazarus from the dead (11:1–44), and, after the Resurrection, (8) giving the disciples an overwhelming catch of fish (21:1–14).

In every chapter Jesus' deity is revealed. And Jesus' true identity is underscored through the titles he is given—the Word, the only Son, Lamb of God, Son of God, true bread, life, resurrection, vine. And the formula is "I am." When Jesus uses this phrase, he affirms his preexistence and eternal deity. Jesus says, *I am* the bread of life (6:35); *I am* the light of the world (8:12; 9:5); *I am* the gate (10:7); *I am* the good shepherd (10:11, 14); *I am* the resurrection and the life (11:25); *I am* the way, the truth, and the life (14:6); and *I am* the true vine (15:1).

The greatest sign, of course, is the Resurrection, and John provides a stirring eyewitness account of finding the empty tomb. Then he records various post-Resurrection appearances by Jesus.

John, the devoted follower of Christ, has given us a personal and powerful look at Jesus Christ, the eternal Son of God. As you read his story, commit yourself to believe in and follow him.

Tiberius Caesar becomes emperor 14	Pontius Pilate appointed governor 26	Jesus begins his ministry 26/27	Jesus and Nicodemus 27	Jesus chooses twelve disciples 28	Jesus feeds 5,000 29	Jesus is crucified, rises again, and ascends 30

THE BLUEPRINT

A. BIRTH AND PREPARATION OF JESUS, THE SON OF GOD (1:1—2:12)

John makes it clear that Jesus is not just a man; he is the eternal Son of God. He is the light of the world because he offers this gift of eternal life to all people. How blind and foolish to call Jesus nothing more than an unusually good man or moral teacher. Yet we sometimes act as if this were true when we casually toss around his words and go about living our own way. If Jesus is the eternal Son of God, we should pay attention to his divine identity and life-giving message.

B. MESSAGE AND MINISTRY OF JESUS, THE SON OF GOD (2:13—12:50)
1. Jesus encounters belief and unbelief from the people
2. Jesus encounters conflict with the religious leaders
3. Jesus encounters crucial events in Jerusalem

Jesus meets with individuals, preaches to great crowds, trains his disciples, and debates with the religious leaders. The message that he is the Son of God receives a mixed reaction. Some worship him, some are puzzled, some shrink back, and some move to silence him. We see the same varied reactions today. Times have changed, but people's hearts remain hard. May we see ourselves in these encounters Jesus had with people, and may our response be to worship and follow him.

C. DEATH AND RESURRECTION OF JESUS, THE SON OF GOD (13:1—21:25)
1. Jesus teaches his disciples
2. Jesus completes his mission

Jesus carefully instructed the disciples how to continue to believe even after his death, yet they could not take it in. After he died and the first reports came back that Jesus was alive, the disciples could not believe it. Thomas is especially remembered as one who refused to believe even when he heard the eyewitness accounts from other disciples. May we not be like Thomas, demanding a physical face-to-face encounter, but may we accept the eyewitness testimony of the disciples that John has recorded in this Gospel.

MEGATHEMES

THEME	EXPLANATION	IMPORTANCE
Jesus Christ, Son of God	John shows us that Jesus is unique as God's special Son, yet he is fully God. Because he is fully God, Jesus is able to reveal God to us clearly and accurately.	Because Jesus is God's Son, we can perfectly trust what he says. By trusting him, we can gain an open mind to understand God's message and fulfill his purpose in our lives.
Eternal Life	Because Jesus is God, he lives forever. Before the world began, he lived with God, and he will reign forever with him. In John we see Jesus revealed in power and magnificence even before his resurrection.	Jesus offers eternal life to us. We are invited to begin living in a personal, eternal relationship with him now. Although we must grow old and die, by trusting him we can have a new life that lasts forever.
Belief	John records eight specific signs, or miracles, that show the nature of Jesus' power and love. We see his power over everything created, and we see his love of all people. These signs encourage us to believe in him.	Believing is active, living, and continuous trust in Jesus as God. When we believe in his life, his words, his death, and his resurrection, we are cleansed from sin and receive power to follow him. But we must respond to him by believing.
Holy Spirit	Jesus taught his disciples that the Holy Spirit would come after he ascended from earth. The Holy Spirit would then indwell, guide, counsel, and comfort those who follow Jesus. Through the Holy Spirit, Christ's presence and power are multiplied in all who believe.	Through God's Holy Spirit, we are drawn to him in faith. We must know the Holy Spirit to understand all Jesus taught. We can experience Jesus' love and guidance as we allow the Holy Spirit to do his work in us.

Resurrection	On the third day after he died, Jesus rose from the dead. This was verified by his disciples and many eyewitnesses. This reality changed the disciples from frightened deserters to dynamic leaders in the new church. This fact is the foundation of the Christian faith.	We can be changed as the disciples were and have confidence that our bodies will one day be raised to live with Christ forever. The same power that raised Christ to life can give us the ability to follow Christ each day.

KEY PLACES IN JOHN

John's story begins as John the Baptist ministers near Bethany east of the Jordan (1:28ff). Jesus also begins his ministry, talking to some of the men who would later become his 12 disciples. Jesus' ministry in Galilee began with a visit to a wedding in Cana (2:1ff). Then he went to Capernaum, which became his new home (2:12). He journeyed to Jerusalem for the special festivals (2:13) and there met with Nicodemus, a religious leader (3:1ff). When Jesus left Judea, he traveled through Samaria and ministered to the Samaritans (4:1ff). Jesus did miracles in Galilee (4:46ff) and in Judea and Jerusalem (5:1ff). We follow him as he fed 5,000 near Bethsaida beside the Sea of Galilee (Sea of Tiberias) (6:1ff), walked on the water to his frightened disciples (6:16ff), preached through Galilee (7:1), returned to Jerusalem (7:2ff), preached beyond the Jordan in Perea (10:40), raised Lazarus from the dead in Bethany (11:1ff), and finally entered Jerusalem for the last time to celebrate the Passover with his disciples and give them key teachings about what was to come and how they should act. His last hours before his crucifixion were spent in the city (13:1ff), in a grove of olive trees (the Garden of Gethsemane) (18:1ff), and finally in various buildings in Jerusalem during his trial (18:12ff). He would be crucified, but he would rise again as he had promised.

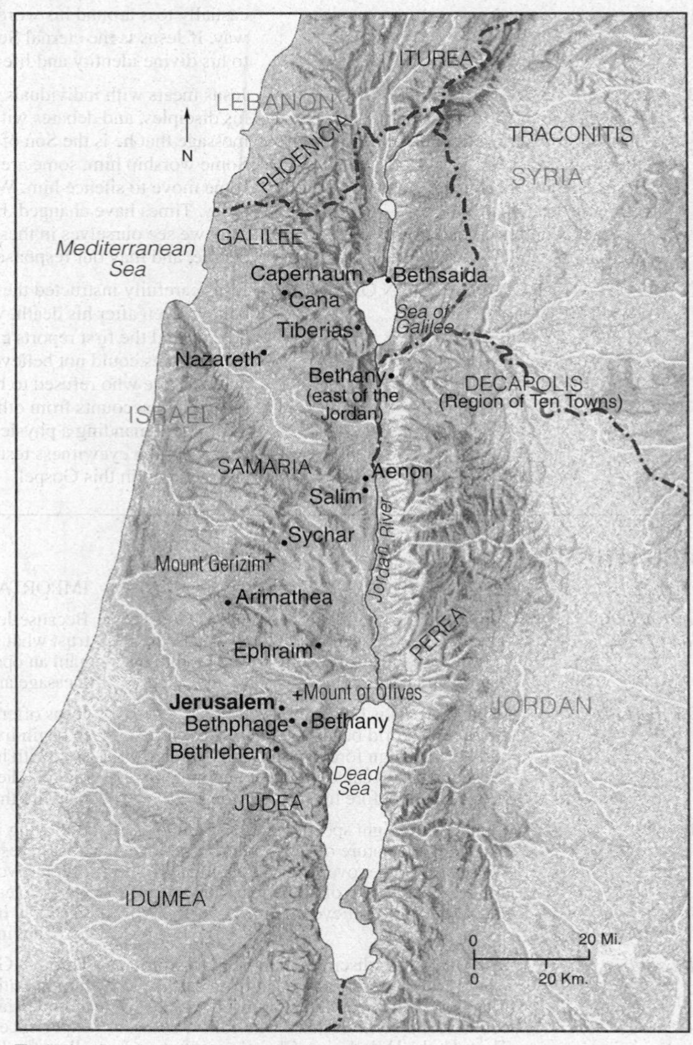

The broken lines (—·—) indicate modern boundaries.

A. BIRTH AND PREPARATION OF JESUS, THE SON OF GOD (1:1—2:12)

In this Gospel, John provides clear evidence that Jesus is the Son of God and that by believing in him we may have eternal life. John also provides unique material about Jesus' birth. He did not come into being when he was born, because he is eternal.

God Became a Human (**2**)

1:1 Gen 1:1 Phil 2:6 1 Jn 5:21
1:3 1 Cor 8:6 Col 1:16-17 Heb 1:2
1:4 John 3:15-16, 36; 6:35, 48; 8:12; 1 Jn 5:12, 20
1:9 1 Jn 2:8

1 In the beginning the Word already existed. He was with God, and he was God.
[2]He was in the beginning with God. [3]He created everything there is. Nothing
exists that he didn't make. [4]Life itself was in him, and this life gives light to
everyone. [5]The light shines through the darkness, and the darkness can never
extinguish it.
[6]God sent John the Baptist [7]to tell everyone about the light so that everyone might
believe because of his testimony. [8]John himself was not the light; he was only a witness
to the light. [9]The one who is the true light, who gives light to everyone, was going to come
into the world.
[10]But although the world was made through him, the world didn't recognize him when
he came. [11]Even in his own land and among his own people, he was not accepted. [12]But

---

1:1 What Jesus taught and what he did are tied inseparably to who he is. John shows Jesus as fully human and fully God. Although Jesus took upon himself full humanity and lived as a man, he never ceased to be the eternal God who has always existed, the Creator and Sustainer of all things, and the source of eternal life. This is the truth about Jesus, and the foundation of all truth. If we cannot or do not believe this basic truth, we will not have enough faith to trust our eternal destiny to him. That is why John wrote this Gospel—to build faith and confidence in Jesus Christ so that we may believe that he truly was and is the Son of God (20:30, 31).

1:1 John wrote to believers everywhere, both Jews and non-Jews (Gentiles). As one of Jesus' 12 disciples, John was an eyewitness so his story is accurate. His book is not a biography (like the book of Luke); it is a thematic presentation of Jesus' life. Many in John's original audience had a Greek background. Greek culture encouraged worship of many mythological gods, whose supernatural characteristics were as important to Greeks as genealogies were to Jews. John shows that Jesus is not only different from but superior to these gods of mythology.

1:1ff What does John mean by "the Word"? *The Word* was a term used by theologians and philosophers, both Jews and Greeks, in many different ways. In Hebrew Scripture, *the Word* was an agent of creation (Psalm 33:6), the source of God's message to his people through the prophets (Hosea 4:1), and God's law, his standard of holiness (Psalm 119:11). In Greek philosophy, *the Word* was the principle of reason that governed the world, or the thought still in the mind, while in Hebrew thought, *the Word* was another expression for God. John's description shows clearly that he is speaking of Jesus (see especially 1:14)—a human being he knew and loved, but at the same time the Creator of the universe, the ultimate revelation of God, the living picture of God's holiness, the one who "holds all creation together" (Colossians 1:17). To Jewish readers, to say this man Jesus "was God" was blasphemous. To Greek readers, "the Word became human" (1:14) was unthinkable. To John, this new understanding of the Word was the Good News of Jesus Christ.

1:3 When God created, he made something from nothing. Because we are created beings, we have no basis for pride. Remember that you exist only because God made you, and you have special gifts only because God gave them to you. With God you are something valuable and unique; apart from God you are nothing, and if you try to live without him, you will be abandoning the purpose for which you were made.

1:3-5 Do you ever feel that your life is too complex for God to understand? Remember, God created the entire universe, and nothing is too difficult for him. God created you; he is alive today, and his love is bigger than any problem you may face.

1:4, 5 "The darkness can never extinguish it" means the darkness of evil never has and never will overcome God's light. Jesus Christ is the Creator of life, and his life brings light to humankind. In his light, we see ourselves as we really are (sinners in need of a Savior). When we follow Jesus, the true Light, we can avoid walking blindly and falling into sin. He lights the path ahead of us so we can see how to live. He removes the darkness of sin from our lives. Have you allowed the light of Christ to shine into your life? Let Christ guide your life, and you'll never need to stumble in darkness.

1:6-8 For more information on John the Baptist, see his Profile in this chapter.

1:8 We, like John the Baptist, are not the source of God's light; we merely reflect that light. Jesus Christ is the true Light; he helps us see our way to God and shows us how to walk along that way. But Christ has chosen to reflect his light through his followers to an unbelieving world, perhaps because unbelievers are not able to bear the full blazing glory of his light firsthand. The word *witness* indicates our role as reflectors of Christ's light. We are never to present ourselves as the light to others, but are always to point them to Christ, the Light.

1:10, 11 Although Christ created the world, the people he created didn't recognize him (1:10). Even the people chosen by God to prepare the rest of the world for the Messiah rejected him (1:11), although the entire Old Testament pointed to his coming.

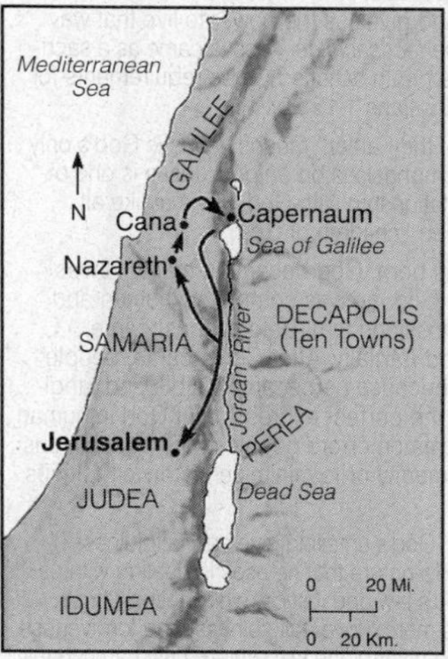

JESUS' FIRST TRAVELS After his baptism by John in the Jordan River and the temptation by Satan in the wilderness (see the map in Mark 1), Jesus returned to Galilee. He visited Nazareth, Cana, and Capernaum, and then returned to Jerusalem for the Passover.

to all who believed him and accepted him, he gave the right to become children of God.
13 They are reborn! This is not a physical birth resulting from human passion or
plan—this rebirth comes from God.
14 So the Word became human and lived here on earth among us. He was full of
unfailing love and faithfulness.* And we have seen his glory, the glory of the only Son
of the Father.
15 John pointed him out to the people. He shouted to the crowds, "This is the one I
was talking about when I said, 'Someone is coming who is far greater than I am, for
he existed long before I did.'"
16 We have all benefited from the rich blessings he brought to us—one gracious
blessing after another.* 17 For the law was given through Moses; God's unfailing
love and faithfulness came through Jesus Christ. 18 No one has ever seen God. But
his only Son, who is himself God,* is near to the Father's heart; he has told us
about him.

John the Baptist Declares His Mission (**19**)

19 This was the testimony of John when the Jewish leaders sent priests and Temple
assistants* from Jerusalem to ask John whether he claimed to be the Messiah. 20 He flatly
denied it. "I am not the Messiah," he said.
21 "Well then, who are you?" they asked. "Are you Elijah?"
"No," he replied.
"Are you the Prophet?"*
"No."
22 "Then who are you? Tell us, so we can give an answer to those who sent us. What
do you have to say about yourself?"

1:12 Rom 8:15-16, 29; 1 Jn 3:1, 23
1:14 Rom 1:3; 8:3; Gal 4:4; Phil 2:6-8; Col 2:9; 1 Tim 3:16; Heb 2:14; 1 Jn 1:1; 4:2-3
1:16 Col 2:9-10
1:17 Exod 31:18; 34:28; John 7:19
1:18 Exod 33:20; 2 Cor 4:4, 6; Col 1:15
1:19-28 Matt 3:1-12; Mark 1:2-8; Luke 3:1-16
1:20 Luke 3:15; John 3:28
1:21 Deut 18:15; Mal 4:5; Matt 11:14

1:14 Greek *grace and truth;* also in 1:17. **1:16** Greek *grace upon grace.* **1:18** Some manuscripts read *his one and only Son.* **1:19** Greek *and Levites.* **1:21** See Deut 18:15, 18; Mal 4:5-6.

1:12, 13 All who welcome Jesus Christ as Lord of their lives are reborn spiritually, receiving new life from God. Through faith in Christ, this new birth changes us from the inside out—rearranging our attitudes, desires, and motives. Being born makes you physically alive and places you in your parents' family (1:13). Being born of God makes you spiritually alive and puts you in God's family (1:12). Have you asked Christ to make you a new person? This fresh start in life is available to all who believe in Christ.

1:14 "The Word became human." By doing so, Christ became (1) *the perfect teacher*—in Jesus' life we see how God thinks and therefore how we should think (Philippians 2:5-11); (2) *the perfect example*—as a model of what we are to become, he shows us how to live and gives us the power to live that way (1 Peter 2:21); (3) *the perfect sacrifice*—Jesus came as a sacrifice for all sins, and his death satisfied God's requirements for the removal of sin (Colossians 1:15-23).

1:14 "The only Son of the Father" means Jesus is God's only and unique Son. The emphasis is on *unique.* Jesus is one of a kind and enjoys a relationship with God. He is unlike all believers, who are called "children of God."

1:14 When Jesus was born, God became a man. He was not part man and part God; he was completely human and completely divine (Colossians 2:9). Before Christ came, people could know God partially. After Christ came, people could know God fully because he became visible and tangible in Christ. Christ is the perfect expression of God in human form. The two most common errors people make about Jesus are to minimize his humanity or to minimize his divinity. Jesus is both God and man.

1:17 Law and grace ("God's unfailing love and faithfulness") are both aspects of God's nature that he uses in dealing with us. Moses emphasized God's law and justice, while Jesus Christ came to highlight God's mercy, love, faithfulness, and forgiveness. Moses could only be the giver of the law, while Christ came to fulfill the law (Matthew 5:17). The nature and will of God were revealed in the law; now the nature and will of God are revealed in Jesus Christ. Rather than coming through cold stone tablets, God's revelation now comes through a person's life. As we get to know Christ better, our understanding of God will increase.

1:18 God communicated through various people in the Old Testament, usually prophets who were told to give specific messages. But no one ever *saw* God. Jesus is both God and the Father's unique Son. In Christ, God revealed his nature and essence in a way that could be seen and touched. In Christ, God became a man who lived on earth.

1:19 The priests and Temple assistants (also called Levites) were respected religious leaders in Jerusalem. Priests served in the Temple, and Temple assistants helped them. The Pharisees (1:24) were a group that both John the Baptist and Jesus often denounced. Many of them outwardly obeyed God's laws to look pious, while inwardly their hearts were filled with pride and greed. The Pharisees believed that their own oral traditions were just as important as God's inspired Word. For more information on the Pharisees, see the charts in Matthew 3 and Mark 2.

These leaders came to see John the Baptist for several reasons: (1) Their duty as guardians of the faith caused them to want to investigate any new preaching (Deuteronomy 13:1-5; 18:20-22). (2) They wanted to find out if John had the credentials of a prophet. (3) John had quite a following, and it was growing. They were probably jealous and wanted to see why this man was so popular.

1:21-23 In the religious leaders' minds, there were four options regarding John the Baptist's identity: He was (1) the Prophet foretold by Moses (Deuteronomy 18:15), (2) Elijah (Malachi 4:5), (3) the Messiah, or (4) a false prophet. John denied being the first three personages. Instead, he called himself, in the words of the Old Testament prophet Isaiah, "The voice of someone shouting, "Make a highway for the LORD through the wilderness. Make a straight, smooth road through the desert for our God"' (Isaiah

1:23
†Isa 40:3

[23]John replied in the words of Isaiah:

"I am a voice shouting in the wilderness,
'Prepare a straight pathway for the Lord's coming!'"*

1:26
Mal 3:1
Matt 3:11
Mark 1:8
Luke 3:16

1:27
Mark 1:7
John 1:15
Acts 13:25

[24]Then those who were sent by the Pharisees [25]asked him, "If you aren't the Messiah
or Elijah or the Prophet, what right do you have to baptize?"
[26]John told them, "I baptize with* water, but right here in the crowd is someone you
do not know, [27]who will soon begin his ministry. I am not even worthy to be his slave.*"

1:23 Isa 40:3. **1:26** Or *in;* also in 1:31, 33. **1:27** Greek *to untie his sandals.*

JOHN THE BAPTIST

There's no getting around it—John the Baptist was unique. He wore odd clothes and ate strange food and preached an unusual message to the Judeans who went out to the wastelands to see him.

But John did not aim at uniqueness for its own sake. Instead, he aimed at obedience. He knew he had a specific role to play in the world—announcing the coming of the Savior—and he put all his energies into this task. Luke tells us that John was in the wilderness when God's word of direction came to him. John was ready and waiting. The angel who had announced John's birth to Zechariah had made it clear this child was to be a Nazirite—one set apart for God's service. John remained faithful to that calling.

This wild-looking man had no power or position in the Jewish political system, but he spoke with almost irresistible authority. People were moved by his words because he spoke the truth, challenging them to turn from their sins and baptizing them as a symbol of their repentance. They responded by the hundreds. But even as people crowded to him, he pointed beyond himself, never forgetting that his main role was to announce the coming of the Savior.

The words of truth that moved many to repentance goaded others to resistance and resentment. John even challenged Herod to admit his sin. Herodias, the woman Herod had married illegally, decided to get rid of this wilderness preacher. Although she was able to have him killed, she was not able to stop his message. The one John had announced was already on the move. John had accomplished his mission.

God has given each of us a purpose for living, and we can trust him to guide us. John did not have the complete Bible as we know it today, but he focused his life on the truth he knew from the available Old Testament Scriptures. Likewise, we can discover in God's Word the truths he wants us to know. And as these truths work in us, others will be drawn to him. God can use you in a way he can use no one else. Let him know your willingness to follow him today.

Strengths and accomplishments
- The God-appointed messenger to announce the arrival of Jesus
- A preacher whose theme was repentance
- A fearless confronter
- Known for his remarkable life-style
- Uncompromising

Lessons from his life
- God does not guarantee an easy or safe life to those who serve him
- Doing what God desires is the greatest possible life investment
- Standing for the truth is more important than life itself

Vital statistics
- Where: Judea
- Occupation: Prophet
- Relatives: Father: Zechariah. Mother: Elizabeth. Distant relative: Jesus
- Contemporaries: Herod, Herodias

Key verse
"I assure you, of all who have ever lived, none is greater than John the Baptist. Yet even the most insignificant person in the Kingdom of Heaven is greater than he is!" (Matthew 11:11).

John's story is told in all four Gospels. His coming was predicted in Isaiah 40:3 and Malachi 4:5; and he is mentioned in Acts 1:5, 22; 10:37; 11:16; 13:24, 25; 18:25; 19:3, 4.

40:3). The leaders kept pressing John to say who he was because people were expecting the Messiah to come (Luke 3:15). But John emphasized only *why* he had come—to prepare the way for the Messiah. The Pharisees missed the point. They wanted to know who John was, but John wanted them to know who Jesus was.

1:25, 26 John was baptizing Jews. The Essenes (a strict, monastic sect of Judaism) practiced baptism for purification, but normally only non-Jews (Gentiles) were baptized when they converted to Judaism. When the Pharisees questioned John's authority to baptize, they were asking who gave John the right to treat God's chosen people like Gentiles. John said, "I baptize with water"—he was merely helping the people perform a symbolic act of repentance. But soon one would come who would truly *forgive* sins, something only the Son of God—the Messiah—could do.

1:27 John the Baptist said he was not even worthy to be Christ's slave. But according to Luke 7:28, Jesus said that John was the greatest of all prophets. If such a great person felt inadequate even to be Christ's slave, how much more should we lay aside our pride to serve Christ! When we truly understand who Christ is, our pride and self-importance melt away.

28 This incident took place at Bethany, a village east of the Jordan River, where John was
baptizing.

John the Baptist Proclaims Jesus as the Messiah (**20**)

29 The next day John saw Jesus coming toward him and said, "Look! There is the
Lamb of God who takes away the sin of the world! 30 He is the one I was talking about
when I said, 'Soon a man is coming who is far greater than I am, for he existed long
before I did.' 31 I didn't know he was the one, but I have been baptizing with water in
order to point him out to Israel."

32 Then John said, "I saw the Holy Spirit descending like a dove from heaven and
resting upon him. 33 I didn't know he was the one, but when God sent me to baptize
with water, he told me, 'When you see the Holy Spirit descending and resting upon
someone, he is the one you are looking for. He is the one who baptizes with the Holy
Spirit.' 34 I saw this happen to Jesus, so I testify that he is the Son of God.*"

The First Disciples Follow Jesus (**21**)

35 The following day, John was again standing with two of his disciples. 36 As Jesus
walked by, John looked at him and then declared, "Look! There is the Lamb of God!"
37 Then John's two disciples turned and followed Jesus.

38 Jesus looked around and saw them following. "What do you want?" he asked them.
They replied, "Rabbi" (which means Teacher), "where are you staying?"

39 "Come and see," he said. It was about four o'clock in the afternoon when they
went with him to the place, and they stayed there the rest of the day.

40 Andrew, Simon Peter's brother, was one of these men who had heard what John
said and then followed Jesus. 41 The first thing Andrew did was to find his brother,
Simon, and tell him, "We have found the Messiah" (which means the Christ).

1:28 John 3:26; 10:40
1:29 Isa 53:7; 1 Cor 5:7; 1 Pet 1:19
1:32 Matt 3:16; Mark 1:10; Luke 3:22
1:33 Luke 3:16; Acts 1:5
1:34 John 1:49; 10:36
1:40 Matt 4:18-22; Mark 1:16; Luke 5:2-11
1:41 Ps 2:2; John 4:25

1:34 Some manuscripts read *the chosen One of God.*

1:29 Every morning and evening, a lamb was sacrificed in the Temple for the sins of the people (Exodus 29:38-42). Isaiah 53:7 prophesied that the Messiah, God's servant, would be led to the slaughter like a lamb. To pay the penalty for sin, a life had to be given—and God chose to provide the sacrifice himself. The sins of the world were removed when Jesus died as the perfect sacrifice. This is the way our sins are forgiven (1 Corinthians 5:7). The "sin of the world" means everyone's sin, the sin of each individual. Jesus paid the price of *your* sin by his death. You can receive forgiveness by confessing your sin to him and asking for his forgiveness.

1:30 Although John the Baptist was a well-known preacher who attracted large crowds, he was content for Jesus to take the higher place. This is true humility, the basis for greatness in preaching, teaching, or any other work we do for Christ. When you are content to do what God wants you to do and let Jesus Christ be honored for it, God will do great things through you.

1:31-34 At Jesus' baptism, John the Baptist had declared Jesus to be the Messiah. At that time God had given John a sign to show him that Jesus truly had been sent from God (1:33). John and Jesus were related (see Luke 1:36), so John probably knew who he was. But it wasn't until Jesus' baptism that John understood that Jesus was the Messiah. Jesus' baptism is described in Matthew 3:13-17; Mark 1:9-11; and Luke 3:21, 22.

1:33 John the Baptist's baptism with water was preparatory, because it was for repentance and symbolized the washing away of sins. Jesus, by contrast, would baptize with the Holy Spirit. He would send the Holy Spirit upon all believers, empowering them to live and to teach the message of salvation. This outpouring of the Spirit came after Jesus had risen from the dead and ascended into heaven (see 20:22; Acts 2).

1:34 John the Baptist's job was to point people to Jesus, their long-awaited Messiah. Today people are looking for someone to give them security in an insecure world. Our job is to point them to Christ and to show that he is the one whom they seek.

1:35ff These new disciples used several names for Jesus: Lamb of God (1:36), Rabbi (1:38), Messiah (1:41), Son of God (1:49), and King of Israel (1:49). As they got to know Jesus, their appreciation for him grew. The more time we spend getting to know Christ, the more we will understand and appreciate who he is. We may be drawn to him for his teaching, but we will come to know him as the Son of God. Although these disciples made this verbal shift in a few days, they would not fully understand Jesus until three years later (Acts 2). What they so easily professed had to be worked out in experience. We may find that words of faith come easily, but deep appreciation for Christ comes with living by faith.

1:37 One of the two disciples was Andrew (1:40). The other was probably John, the writer of this book. Why did these disciples leave John the Baptist? Because that's what John wanted them to do—he was pointing the way to Jesus, the one John had prepared them to follow. These were Jesus' first disciples, along with Simon Peter (1:42) and Nathanael (1:45).

1:38 When the two disciples began to follow Jesus, he asked them, "What do you want?" Following Christ is not enough; we must follow him for the right reasons. To follow Christ for our own purposes would be asking Christ to follow us—to align with us to support and advance our cause, not his. We must examine our motives for following him. Are we seeking his glory or ours?

1:40-42 Andrew accepted John the Baptist's testimony about Jesus and immediately went to tell his brother, Simon, about him. There was no question in Andrew's mind that Jesus was the Messiah. Not only did he tell his brother, but he was also eager to introduce others to Jesus (see 6:8, 9; 12:22).

1:42 Matt 16:18; 1 Cor 15:5; 1 Pet 2:5
1:43 John 6:5-6; 12:20-22
1:45 Gen 3:15; Num 21:8-9; 24:17; Deut 18:15, 18; Isa 7:14; 11:1-10; 52:10, 13; 53:1-12; Jer 23:5-6; 30:9; Ezek 34:23-24; 37:24-25; Hos 11:1; Mic 5:2; Zech 3:8-9; 6:12-13; 9:9; Mal 3:1; 4:2, 5
1:49 2 Sam 7:14; Ps 2:2; John 1:34; 20:31
1:51 Gen 28:12
2:1 John 1:35, 43
2:4 John 7:30; 8:20

42 Then Andrew brought Simon to meet Jesus. Looking intently at Simon, Jesus said, "You are Simon, the son of John—but you will be called Cephas" (which means Peter*).

43 The next day Jesus decided to go to Galilee. He found Philip and said to him, "Come, be my disciple." 44 Philip was from Bethsaida, Andrew and Peter's hometown.

45 Philip went off to look for Nathanael and told him, "We have found the very person Moses and the prophets wrote about! His name is Jesus, the son of Joseph from Nazareth."

46 "Nazareth!" exclaimed Nathanael. "Can anything good come from there?"

"Just come and see for yourself," Philip said.

47 As they approached, Jesus said, "Here comes an honest man—a true son of Israel."

48 "How do you know about me?" Nathanael asked.

And Jesus replied, "I could see you under the fig tree before Philip found you."

49 Nathanael replied, "Teacher, you are the Son of God—the King of Israel!"

50 Jesus asked him, "Do you believe all this just because I told you I had seen you under the fig tree? You will see greater things than this." 51 Then he said, "The truth is, you will all see heaven open and the angels of God going up and down upon the Son of Man."*

Jesus Turns Water into Wine (22)

2 The next day* Jesus' mother was a guest at a wedding celebration in the village of Cana in Galilee. 2 Jesus and his disciples were also invited to the celebration. 3 The wine supply ran out during the festivities, so Jesus' mother spoke to him about the problem. "They have no more wine," she told him.

4 "How does that concern you and me?" Jesus asked. "My time has not yet come."

5 But his mother told the servants, "Do whatever he tells you."

1:42 The names *Cephas* and *Peter* both mean "rock." **1:51** See Gen 28:10-17, the account of Jacob's ladder. **2:1** Greek *On the third day;* see 1:35, 43.

1:42 Jesus saw not only who Simon was, but who he would become. That is why he gave him a new name—*Cephas* in Aramaic, *Peter* in Greek (the name means "a rock"). Peter is not presented as rock-solid throughout the Gospels, but he became a solid rock in the days of the early church, as we learn in the book of Acts. By giving Simon a new name, Jesus introduced a change in character. For more on Simon Peter, see his Profile in Matthew 27.

1:46 Nazareth was despised by the Jews because a Roman army garrison was located there. Some have speculated that an aloof attitude or a poor reputation in morals and religion on the part of the people of Nazareth led to Nathanael's harsh comment. Nathanael's hometown was Cana, about four miles from Nazareth.

1:46 When Nathanael heard that the Messiah was from Nazareth, he was surprised. Philip responded, "Come and see for yourself." Fortunately for Nathanael, he went to meet Jesus and became a disciple. If he had stuck to his prejudice without investigating further, he would have missed the Messiah! Don't let people's stereotypes about Christ cause them to miss his power and love. Invite them to come and see who Jesus really is.

1:47-49 Jesus knew about Nathanael before the two ever met. Jesus also knows what we are really like. An honest person will feel comfortable with the thought that Jesus knows him or her through and through. A dishonest person will feel uncomfortable. You can't pretend to be something you're not. God knows the real you and wants *you* to follow him.

1:51 This is a reference to Jacob's dream recorded in Genesis 28:12. As the unique God-man, Jesus would be the ladder between heaven and earth. Jesus is not saying that this would be a physical experience (that they would see the ladder with their eyes) like the Transfiguration, but that they would have spiritual insight into Jesus' true nature and purpose for coming.

2:1, 2 Jesus was on a mission to save the world, the greatest mission in the history of humankind. Yet he took time to attend a wedding and take part in its festivities. We may be tempted to think we should not take time out from our "important" work for social occasions. But maybe these social occasions are part of our mission. Jesus valued these wedding festivities because they involved people, and Jesus came to be with people. Our mission can often be accomplished in joyous times of celebration with others. Bring balance to your life by bringing Jesus into times of pleasure as well as times of work.

2:1-3 Weddings in Jesus' day were week-long festivals. Banquets would be prepared for many guests, and the week would be spent celebrating the new life of the married couple. Often the whole town was invited, and everybody would come—it was considered an insult to refuse an invitation to a wedding. To accommodate many people, careful planning was needed. To run out of wine was more than embarrassing; it broke the strong unwritten laws of hospitality. Jesus was about to respond to a heartfelt need.

2:4 Mary was probably not asking Jesus to do a miracle; she was simply hoping that her son would help solve this major problem and find some wine. Tradition says that Joseph, Mary's husband, was dead, so she probably was used to asking for her son's help in certain situations. Jesus' answer to Mary is difficult to understand, but maybe that is the point. Although Mary did not understand what Jesus was going to do, she trusted him to do what was right. Those who believe in Jesus but run into situations they cannot understand must continue to trust that he will work in the best way.

2:5 Mary submitted to Jesus' way of doing things. She recognized that Jesus was more than her human son—he was the Son of God. When we bring our problems to Christ, we may think we know how he should take care of them. But he may have a completely different plan. Like Mary, we should submit and allow him to deal with the problem as he sees best.

6 Six stone waterpots were standing there; they were used for Jewish ceremonial 2:6 Mark 7:3-4
purposes and held twenty to thirty gallons* each. 7 Jesus told the servants, "Fill the jars John 3:25
with water." When the jars had been filled to the brim, 8 he said, "Dip some out and take
it to the master of ceremonies." So they followed his instructions.
9 When the master of ceremonies tasted the water that was now wine, not knowing 2:9 John 4:46
where it had come from (though, of course, the servants knew), he called the bridegroom over. 10 "Usually a host serves the best wine first," he said. "Then, when
everyone is full and doesn't care, he brings out the less expensive wines. But you have
kept the best until now!"
11 This miraculous sign at Cana in Galilee was Jesus' first display of his glory. And his 2:11 John 2:23; 3:2; 4:54; 6:14; 11:47;
disciples believed in him. 12:37
12 After the wedding he went to Capernaum for a few days with his mother, his 2:12
brothers, and his disciples. Matt 12:46-50

B. MESSAGE AND MINISTRY OF JESUS, THE SON OF GOD (2:13—12:50)

John stresses the deity of Christ. He gives us eight miracles that serve as signs that Jesus is the Messiah. In this section he records Jesus describing himself as the bread of life, the water of life, the light of the world, the door, and the good shepherd. John provides teachings of Jesus found nowhere else. This is the most theological of the four Gospels.

1. Jesus encounters belief and unbelief from the people

Jesus Clears the Temple (**23**)

13 It was time for the annual Passover celebration, and Jesus went to Jerusalem. 14 In the 2:13-22 Matt 21:12-17
Temple area he saw merchants selling cattle, sheep, and doves for sacrifices; and he saw Mark 11:15-19
money changers behind their counters. 15 Jesus made a whip from some ropes and chased Luke 19:45-48

2:6 Greek *2 or 3 measures* [75 to 113 liters].

2:6 The six stone waterpots were normally used for ceremonial washing. When full, the pots would hold 20 to 30 gallons. According to the Jews' ceremonial law, people became symbolically unclean by touching objects of everyday life. Before eating, the Jews would pour water over their hands to cleanse themselves of any bad influences associated with what they had touched.

2:10 People look everywhere but to God for excitement and meaning. For some reason, they expect God to be dull and lifeless. Just as the wine Jesus made was the best, so life in him is better than life on our own. Why wait until everything else runs out before trying God? Why save the best until last?

2:11 When the disciples saw Jesus' miracle, they believed. The miracle showed his power over nature and revealed the way he would go about his ministry—helping others, speaking with authority, and being in personal touch with people.

2:11 Miracles are not merely superhuman events, but events that demonstrate God's power. Almost every miracle Jesus did was a renewal of fallen creation—restoring sight, making the lame walk, even restoring life to the dead. Believe in Christ not because he is a superman but because he is the God who continues his creation, even in those of us who are poor, weak, crippled, orphaned, blind, deaf, or with some other desperate need for re-creation.

2:12 Capernaum became Jesus' home base during his ministry in Galilee. Located on a major trade route, it was an important city in the region, with a Roman garrison and a customs station. At Capernaum, Matthew was called to be a disciple (Matthew 9:9). The city was also the home of several other disciples (Matthew 4:13-19) and a high-ranking government official (4:46). It had at least one major synagogue. Although Jesus made this city his base of operations in Galilee, he condemned it for the people's unbelief (Matthew 11:23; Luke 10:15).

2:13 The Passover celebration took place yearly at the Temple in Jerusalem. Every Jewish male was expected to make a pilgrimage to Jerusalem during this time (Deuteronomy 16:16). This was a week-long festival—the Passover was one day, and the Festival of Unleavened Bread lasted the rest of the week. The entire week commemorated the freeing of the Jews from slavery in Egypt (Exodus 12:1-13).

2:13 Jerusalem was both the religious and the political seat of Palestine, and the place where the Messiah was expected to arrive. The Temple was located there, and many Jewish families from all over the world would travel to Jerusalem during the key festivals. The Temple was on an imposing site, a hill overlooking the city. Solomon had built the first Temple on this same site almost 1,000 years earlier (959 B.C.), but his Temple had been destroyed by the Babylonians (2 Kings 25). The Temple was rebuilt in 515 B.C., and Herod the Great had enlarged and remodeled it.

2:14 The Temple area was always crowded during Passover with thousands of out-of-town visitors. The religious leaders crowded it even further by allowing money changers and merchants to set up booths in the Court of the Gentiles. They rationalized this practice as a convenience for the worshipers and as a way to make money for Temple upkeep. But the religious leaders did not seem to care that the Court of the Gentiles was so full of merchants that foreigners found it difficult to worship. And worship was the main purpose for visiting the Temple. No wonder Jesus was angry!

2:14 The Temple tax had to be paid in local currency, so foreigners had to have their money changed. But the money changers often would charge exorbitant exchange rates. The people also were required to make sacrifices for sins. Because of the long journey, many could not bring their own animals. Some who brought animals would have them rejected for imperfections. So animal merchants would do a flourishing business in the Temple courtyard. The price of sacrificial animals was much higher in the Temple area than elsewhere. Jesus was angry at the dishonest, greedy practices of the money changers and merchants, and he particularly disliked their presence on the Temple grounds. They were making a mockery of God's house of worship.

2:14ff John records this first clearing, or cleansing, of the Temple. A second clearing occurred at the end of Jesus' ministry, about three years later, and that event is recorded in Matthew 21:12-17; Mark 11:12-19; Luke 19:45-48.

them all out of the Temple. He drove out the sheep and oxen, scattered the money
2:16 Luke 2:49 changers' coins over the floor, and turned over their tables. 16 Then, going over to the
people who sold doves, he told them, "Get these things out of here. Don't turn my
Father's house into a marketplace!"
2:17 †Ps 69:9 17 Then his disciples remembered this prophecy from the Scriptures: "Passion for
God's house burns within me."*
18 "What right do you have to do these things?" the Jewish leaders demanded. "If you
2:19 Matt 26:61; 27:40 Mark 14:58 Acts 6:14 have this authority from God, show us a miraculous sign to prove it."
19 "All right," Jesus replied. "Destroy this temple, and in three days I will raise it up."

2:17 Or *"Concern for God's house will be my undoing."* Ps 69:9.

NICODEMUS

God specializes in finding and changing people we consider out of reach. It took a while for Nicodemus to come out of the dark, but God was patient with this "undercover" believer.

Afraid of being discovered, Nicodemus made an appointment to see Jesus at night. Daylight conversations between Pharisees and Jesus tended to be antagonistic, but Nicodemus really wanted to learn. He probably got a lot more than he expected—a challenge to a new life! We know very little about Nicodemus, but we know that he left that evening's encounter a changed man. He came away with a whole new understanding of both God and himself.

Nicodemus next appears as part of the Jewish high council (7:50). As the group discussed ways to eliminate Jesus, Nicodemus raised the question of justice. Although his objection was overruled, he had spoken up. He had begun to change.

Our last picture of Nicodemus shows him joining Joseph of Arimathea in asking for Jesus' body in order to provide for its burial (19:39). Realizing what he was risking, Nicodemus was making a bold move. He was continuing to grow.

God looks for steady growth, not instant perfection. How well does your present level of spiritual growth match up with how long you have known Jesus?

Strengths and accomplishments
- One of the few religious leaders who believed in Jesus
- A member of the powerful Jewish high council
- A Pharisee who was attracted by Jesus' character and miracles
- Joined with Joseph of Arimathea in burying Jesus

Weakness and mistake
- Limited by his fear of being publicly exposed as Jesus' follower

Lessons from his life
- Unless we are born again, we can never be part of the Kingdom of God
- God is able to change those we might consider unreachable
- God is patient, but persistent
- If we are available, God can use us

Vital statistics
- Where: Jerusalem
- Occupation: Religious leader
- Contemporaries: Jesus, Annas, Caiaphas, Pilate, Joseph of Arimathea

Key verse
" 'What do you mean?' exclaimed Nicodemus. 'How can an old man go back into his mother's womb and be born again?' " (John 3:4).

Nicodemus's story is told in John 3:1–21; 7:50–52; and 19:39, 40.

2:14-16 God's Temple was being misused by people who had turned it into a marketplace. They had forgotten, or didn't care, that God's house is a place of worship, not a place for making a profit. Our attitude toward the church is wrong if we see it as a place for personal contacts or business advantage. Make sure you attend church to worship God.

2:15, 16 Jesus was obviously angry at the merchants who exploited those who had come to God's house to worship. There is a difference between uncontrolled rage and righteous indignation—yet both are called anger. We must be very careful how we use the powerful emotion of anger. It is right to be angry about injustice and sin; it is wrong to be angry over trivial personal offenses.

2:15, 16 Jesus made a whip and chased out the money changers. Does his example permit us to use violence against wrongdoers? Certain authority is granted to some, but not to all. For example, the authority to use weapons and restrain people is granted to police officers, but not to the general public. The authority to imprison people is granted to judges, but not to individual citizens. Jesus had God's authority, something we cannot have. While we want to live like Christ, we should never try to claim his authority where it has not been given to us.

2:17 Jesus took the evil acts in the Temple as an insult against God, and thus, he did not deal with them halfheartedly. He was consumed with righteous anger against such flagrant disrespect for God.

2:19, 20 The Jews understood Jesus to mean the Temple out of which he had just driven the merchants and money changers. This was the Temple Zerubbabel had built over 500 years earlier, but Herod the Great had begun remodeling it, making it much larger and far more beautiful. It had been 46 years since this remodeling had started (20 B.C.), and it still wasn't completely finished. They understood Jesus' words to mean that this imposing building could be torn down and rebuilt in three days, and they were startled.

[20]“What!” they exclaimed. “It took forty-six years to build this Temple, and you can
do it in three days?” [21]But by “this temple,” Jesus meant his body. [22]After he was raised
from the dead, the disciples remembered that he had said this. And they believed both
Jesus and the Scriptures.
[23]Because of the miraculous signs he did in Jerusalem at the Passover celebration,
many people were convinced that he was indeed the Messiah. [24]But Jesus didn’t trust
them, because he knew what people were really like. [25]No one needed to tell him about
human nature.

Nicodemus Visits Jesus at Night (**24**)

3 After dark one evening, a Jewish religious leader named Nicodemus, a Pharisee,
[2]came to speak with Jesus. “Teacher,” he said, “we all know that God has sent you
to teach us. Your miraculous signs are proof enough that God is with you.”
[3]Jesus replied, “I assure you, unless you are born again,* you can never see the
Kingdom of God.”
[4]“What do you mean?” exclaimed Nicodemus. “How can an old man go back into his
mother’s womb and be born again?”
[5]Jesus replied, “The truth is, no one can enter the Kingdom of God without being born
of water and the Spirit.* [6]Humans can reproduce only human life, but the Holy Spirit
gives new life from heaven. [7]So don’t be surprised at my statement that you* must be

2:21 John 10:38; 14:2, 10; 17:21; 1 Cor 3:16; 6:19

2:22 Luke 24:6-8; John 12:16; 14:26

2:23 John 7:31; 11:47-48

3:1-2 John 7:50; 19:39

3:2 Matt 22:16; Acts 2:22; 10:38

3:3 John 1:13

3:5 Ezek 36:26-27; Titus 3:5; 2 Pet 1:11

3:6 John 1:13; Rom 8:15-16; 1 Cor 15:50; Gal 4:6

3:3 Or *born from above;* also in 3:7. **3:5** Or *spirit.* The Greek word for *Spirit* can also be translated *wind;* see 3:8.
3:7 The Greek word for *you* is plural; also in 3:12.

2:21, 22 Jesus was not talking about the Temple made of stones, but about his body. His listeners didn’t realize it, but Jesus was greater than the Temple (Matthew 12:6). His words would take on meaning for his disciples after his resurrection. That Christ so perfectly fulfilled this prediction became the strongest proof for his claims to be God.

2:23-25 The Son of God knows all about human nature. Jesus was well aware of the truth of Jeremiah 17:9, which states, “The human heart is most deceitful and desperately wicked. Who really knows how bad it is?” Jesus was discerning, and he knew that the faith of some followers was superficial. Some of the same people claiming to believe in Jesus at this time would later yell “Crucify him!” It’s easy to believe when it is exciting and everyone else believes the same way. But keep your faith firm even when it isn’t popular to follow Christ.

3:1 Nicodemus was a Pharisee and a member of the ruling council (called the high council, or the Sanhedrin). The Pharisees were a group of religious leaders whom Jesus and John the Baptist often criticized for being hypocrites (see the note on Matthew 3:7 for more on the Pharisees). Most Pharisees were intensely jealous of Jesus because he undermined their authority and challenged their views. But Nicodemus was searching, and he believed that Jesus had some answers. A learned teacher himself, he came to Jesus to be taught. No matter how intelligent and well educated you are, you must come to Jesus with an open mind and heart so he can teach you the truth about God.

3:1ff Nicodemus came to Jesus personally, although he could have sent one of his assistants. He wanted to examine Jesus for himself to separate fact from rumor. Perhaps Nicodemus was afraid of what his peers, the Pharisees, would say about his visit, so he came after dark. Later, when he understood that Jesus was truly the Messiah, he spoke up boldly in his defense (7:50, 51). Like Nicodemus, we must examine Jesus for ourselves—others cannot do it for us. Then, if we believe he is who he says, we will want to speak up for him.

3:3 What did Nicodemus know about the Kingdom? From the Bible he knew it would be ruled by God, it would be restored on earth, and it would incorporate God’s people. Jesus revealed to this devout Pharisee that the Kingdom would come to the whole world (3:16), not just the Jews, and that Nicodemus wouldn’t be a part of it unless he was personally born again (3:5). This was a revolutionary concept: The Kingdom is personal, not national or ethnic, and its entrance requirements are repentance and spiritual rebirth. Jesus later taught that God’s Kingdom has *already begun* in the hearts of believers (Luke 17:21). It will be fully realized when Jesus returns again to judge the world and abolish evil forever (Revelation 21–22).

3:5, 6 “Of water and the Spirit” could refer to (1) the contrast between physical birth (water) and spiritual birth (Spirit), or (2) being regenerated by the Spirit and signifying that rebirth by Christian baptism. The water may also represent the cleansing action of God’s Holy Spirit (Titus 3:5). Nicodemus undoubtedly would have been familiar with God’s promise in Ezekiel 36:25, 26. Jesus was explaining the importance of a spiritual rebirth, saying that people don’t enter the Kingdom by living a better life, but by being spiritually reborn.

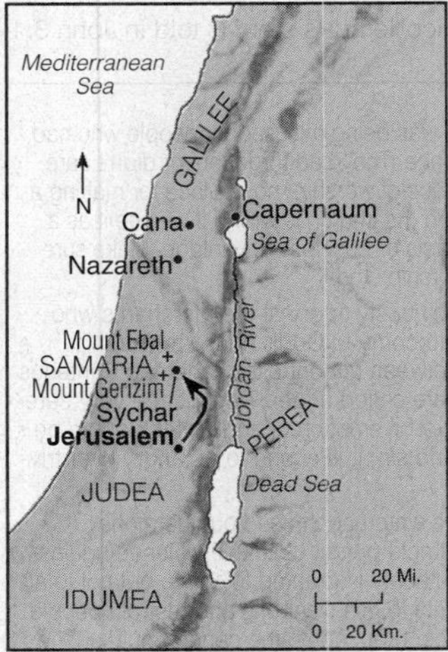

THE VISIT IN SAMARIA
Jesus went to Jerusalem for the Passover, cleared the Temple, and talked with Nicodemus, a religious leader, about eternal life. He then left Jerusalem and traveled in Judea. On his way to Galilee, he visited Sychar and other villages in Samaria. Unlike most Jews of the day, he did not try to avoid the region of Samaria.

3:8 Eccl 11:5
3:13 John 6:38, 42; Eph 4:8-10
3:14 Num 21:8-9; John 8:28; 12:34
3:15 John 20:31; 1 Jn 5:11, 12
3:16 Rom 5:8; 8:32; 1 Jn 4:9-10; 5:13
3:17 John 12:47
3:18 John 5:24
3:19 John 1:5, 9; 8:12; 9:5; 12:46
3:20 Eph 5:11-13
3:21 1 Jn 1:6

born again. 8 Just as you can hear the wind but can't tell where it comes from or where
it is going, so you can't explain how people are born of the Spirit."
9 "What do you mean?" Nicodemus asked.
10 Jesus replied, "You are a respected Jewish teacher, and yet you don't understand
these things? 11 I assure you, I am telling you what we know and have seen, and yet you
won't believe us. 12 But if you don't even believe me when I tell you about things that
happen here on earth, how can you possibly believe if I tell you what is going on in
heaven? 13 For only I, the Son of Man,* have come to earth and will return to heaven
again. 14 And as Moses lifted up the bronze snake on a pole in the wilderness, so I, the
Son of Man, must be lifted up on a pole,* 15 so that everyone who believes in me will
have eternal life.
16 "For God so loved the world that he gave his only Son, so that everyone who
believes in him will not perish but have eternal life. 17 God did not send his Son into the
world to condemn it, but to save it.
18 "There is no judgment awaiting those who trust him. But those who do not trust him
have already been judged for not believing in the only Son of God. 19 Their judgment is
based on this fact: The light from heaven came into the world, but they loved the
darkness more than the light, for their actions were evil. 20 They hate the light because
they want to sin in the darkness. They stay away from the light for fear their sins will be
exposed and they will be punished. 21 But those who do what is right come to the light
gladly, so everyone can see that they are doing what God wants."

3:13 Some manuscripts add *who lives in heaven.* **3:14** Greek *must be lifted up.*

3:6 Who is the Holy Spirit? God is three persons in one—the Father, the Son, and the Holy Spirit. God became a man in Jesus so that Jesus could die for our sins. Jesus rose from the dead to offer salvation to all people through spiritual renewal and rebirth. When Jesus ascended into heaven, his physical presence left the earth, but he promised to send the Holy Spirit so that his spiritual presence would still be among humankind (see Luke 24:49). The Holy Spirit first became available to all believers at Pentecost (Acts 2). Whereas in Old Testament days the Holy Spirit empowered specific individuals for specific purposes, now all believers have the power of the Holy Spirit available to them. For more on the Holy Spirit, read 14:16-28; Romans 8:9; 1 Corinthians 12:13; and 2 Corinthians 1:22.

3:8 Jesus explained that we cannot control the work of the Holy Spirit. He works in ways we cannot predict or understand. Just as you did not control your physical birth, so you cannot control your spiritual birth. It is a gift from God through the Holy Spirit (Romans 8:16; 1 Corinthians 2:10-12; 1 Thessalonians 1:5, 6).

3:10, 11 This Jewish teacher of the Bible knew the Old Testament thoroughly, but he didn't understand what it said about the Messiah. Knowledge is not salvation. You should know the Bible, but even more important, you should understand the God whom the Bible reveals and the salvation that God offers.

3:14, 15 When the Israelites were wandering in the wilderness, God sent a plague of snakes to punish the people for their rebellious attitudes. Those doomed to die from snakebite could be healed by obeying God's command to look up at the elevated bronze snake and by believing that God would heal them if they did (see Numbers 21:8, 9). Similarly, our salvation happens when we look up to Jesus, believing he will save us. God has provided this way for us to be healed of sin's deadly bite.

3:16 The message of the Good News comes to a focus in this verse. God's love is not static or self-centered; it reaches out and draws others in. Here God sets the pattern of true love, the basis for all love relationships—when you love someone dearly, you are willing to give freely to the point of self-sacrifice. God paid dearly with the life of his Son, the highest price he could pay. Jesus accepted our punishment, paid the price for our sins, and then offered us the new life that he had bought for us. When we share the Good News with others, our love must be like Jesus'—willingly giving up our own comfort and security so that others might join us in receiving God's love.

3:16 Some people are repulsed by the idea of eternal life because their lives are miserable. But eternal life is not an extension of a person's miserable, mortal life; eternal life is God's life embodied in Christ given to all believers now as a guarantee that they will live forever. In eternal life there is no death, sickness, enemy, evil, or sin. When we don't know Christ, we make choices as though this life is all we have. In reality, this life is just the introduction to eternity. Receive this new life by faith and begin to evaluate all that happens from an eternal perspective.

3:16 To "believe" is more than intellectual agreement that Jesus is God. It means to put our trust and confidence in him that he alone can save us. It is to put Christ in charge of our present plans and eternal destiny. Believing is both trusting his words as reliable, and relying on him for the power to change. If you have never trusted Christ, let this promise of everlasting life be yours—and believe.

3:18 People often try to protect themselves from their fears by putting their faith in something they do or have: good deeds, skill or intelligence, money or possessions. But only God can save us from the one thing that we really need to fear—eternal condemnation. We believe in God by recognizing the insufficiency of our own efforts to find salvation and by asking him to do his work in us. When Jesus talks about unbelievers, he means those who reject or ignore him completely, not those who have momentary doubts.

3:19-21 Many people don't want their lives exposed to God's light because they are afraid of what will be revealed. They don't want to be changed. Don't be surprised when these same people are threatened by your desire to obey God and do what is right, because they are afraid that the light in you may expose some of the darkness in their lives. Rather than giving in to discouragement, keep praying that they will come to see how much better it is to live in light than in darkness.

John the Baptist Tells More about Jesus **(25)**

[22]Afterward Jesus and his disciples left Jerusalem, but they stayed in Judea for a while **3:22** John 3:26; 4:1-2
and baptized there.
[23]At this time John the Baptist was baptizing at Aenon, near Salim, because there
was plenty of water there and people kept coming to him for baptism. [24]This was **3:24** Matt 4:12
before John was put into prison. [25]At that time a certain Jew began an argument with
John's disciples over ceremonial cleansing. [26]John's disciples came to him and said, **3:26** John 1:7, 34
"Teacher, the man you met on the other side of the Jordan River, the one you said was
the Messiah, is also baptizing people. And everybody is going over there instead of
coming here to us."
[27]John replied, "God in heaven appoints each person's work. [28]You yourselves **3:27** 1 Cor 4:7
know how plainly I told you that I am not the Messiah. I am here to prepare the Heb 5:4
way for him—that is all. [29]The bride will go where the bridegroom is. A bride- **3:28** Mal 3:1
groom's friend rejoices with him. I am the bridegroom's friend, and I am filled **3:29**
with joy at his success. [30]He must become greater and greater, and I must become Matt 9:15
less and less. Rev 21:9
[31]"He has come from above and is greater than anyone else. I am of the earth, and **3:31** 1 Jn 4:5
my understanding is limited to the things of earth, but he has come from heaven.* **3:33**
[32]He tells what he has seen and heard, but how few believe what he tells them! 1 Jn 5:10
[33]Those who believe him discover that God is true. [34]For he is sent by God. He speaks **3:34** Luke 4:18
God's words, for God's Spirit is upon him without measure or limit. [35]The Father **3:35**
loves his Son, and he has given him authority over everything. [36]And all who believe John 5:20; 15:9
in God's Son have eternal life. Those who don't obey the Son will never experience **3:36** John 3:16
eternal life, but the wrath of God remains upon them." 1 Jn 5:12-13

Jesus Talks to a Woman at the Well **(27)**

4 Jesus* learned that the Pharisees had heard, "Jesus is baptizing and making more **4:1** John 3:22, 26
disciples than John" [2](though Jesus himself didn't baptize them—his disciples did).
[3]So he left Judea to return to Galilee.

3:31 Some manuscripts omit *but he has come from heaven.* **4:1** Some manuscripts read *The Lord.*

3:25ff Some people look for points of disagreement so they can sow seeds of discord, discontent, and doubt. John the Baptist ended this theological argument by focusing on his devotion to Christ. It is divisive to try to force others to believe our way. Instead, let's witness about what Christ has done for us. How can anyone argue with us about that?

3:26 John the Baptist's disciples were disturbed because people were following Jesus instead of John. It is easy to grow jealous of the popularity of another person's ministry. But we must remember that our true mission is to influence people to follow Christ, not us.

3:27 Why did John the Baptist continue to baptize after Jesus came onto the scene? Why didn't he become a disciple, too? John explained that because God had given him his work, he had to continue it until God called him to do something else. John's main purpose was to point people to Christ. Even with Jesus beginning his own ministry, John could still turn people to Jesus.

3:30 John's willingness to decrease in importance shows unusual humility. Pastors and other Christian leaders can be tempted to focus more on the success of their ministries than on Christ. Beware of those who put more emphasis on their own achievements than on God's Kingdom.

3:31-35 Jesus' testimony was trustworthy because he had come from heaven and was speaking of what he had seen there. His words were the very words of God. Your whole spiritual life depends on your answer to one question: Who is Jesus Christ? If you accept Jesus as only a prophet or teacher, you have to reject his teaching, for he claimed to be God's Son, even God himself. The heartbeat of John's Gospel is the dynamic truth that Jesus Christ is God's Son, the Messiah, the Savior, who existed from the beginning and will continue to live forever. This same Jesus has invited us to accept him and live with him eternally. When we understand who Jesus is, we are compelled to believe what he said.

3:34 God's Spirit was upon Jesus without measure or limit. Thus, Jesus was the highest revelation of God to humanity (Hebrews 1:2).

3:36 Jesus says that those who believe in him *have* (not *will have*) eternal life. To receive eternal life is to join in God's life, which by nature is eternal. Thus, eternal life begins at the moment of spiritual rebirth.

3:36 John, the author of this Gospel, has been demonstrating that Jesus is the true Son of God. Jesus sets before us the greatest choice in life. We are responsible to decide today whom we will obey (Joshua 24:15), and God wants us to choose him and life (Deuteronomy 30:15-20). The wrath of God is God's final judgment and rejection of the sinner. To put off the choice is to choose not to follow Christ. Indecision is a fatal decision.

4:1-3 Already opposition was rising against Jesus, especially from the Pharisees. They resented Jesus' popularity as well as his message, which challenged much of their teachings. Because Jesus was just beginning his ministry, it wasn't yet time to confront these leaders openly; so he left Jerusalem and traveled north toward Galilee.

4:4 Matt 10:5 Luke 9:52
4:5-6 Gen 33:19; 48:22 Josh 24:32
4:7 Gen 24:17 1 Kgs 17:10
4:9 Ezra 4:1-3; 9–10 Matt 10:5 Luke 9:52-53 John 8:48 Acts 10:48
4:10 Isa 12:3; 44:3 Jer 2:13; 17:13 John 7:37-39 1 Cor 12:13 Rev 7:17; 21:6; 22:17
4:14 John 6:35; 7:38

4 He had to go through Samaria on the way. 5 Eventually he came to the Samaritan
village of Sychar, near the parcel of ground that Jacob gave to his son Joseph. 6 Jacob's
well was there; and Jesus, tired from the long walk, sat wearily beside the well about
noontime. 7 Soon a Samaritan woman came to draw water, and Jesus said to her, "Please
give me a drink." 8 He was alone at the time because his disciples had gone into the
village to buy some food.

9 The woman was surprised, for Jews refuse to have anything to do with Samaritans.
She said to Jesus, "You are a Jew, and I am a Samaritan woman. Why are you asking me
for a drink?"

10 Jesus replied, "If you only knew the gift God has for you and who I am, you would
ask me, and I would give you living water."

11 "But sir, you don't have a rope or a bucket," she said, "and this is a very deep well.
Where would you get this living water? 12 And besides, are you greater than our ancestor
Jacob who gave us this well? How can you offer better water than he and his sons and
his cattle enjoyed?"

13 Jesus replied, "People soon become thirsty again after drinking this water. 14 But the
water I give them takes away thirst altogether. It becomes a perpetual spring within them,
giving them eternal life."

4:4 After the northern kingdom, with its capital at Samaria, fell to the Assyrians, many Jews were deported to Assyria, and foreigners were brought in to settle the land and help keep the peace (2 Kings 17:24). The intermarriage between those foreigners and the remaining Jews resulted in a mixed race, impure in the opinion of Jews who lived in the southern kingdom. Thus, the pure Jews hated this mixed race, called Samaritans, because they felt that their fellow Jews who had intermarried had betrayed their people and nation. The Samaritans had set up an alternate center for worship on Mount Gerizim (4:20) to parallel the Temple at Jerusalem, but it had been destroyed 150 years earlier. The Jews did everything they could to avoid traveling through Samaria. But Jesus had no reason to live by such cultural restrictions. The route through Samaria was shorter, and that was the route he took.

4:5-7 Jacob's well was on the property originally owned by Jacob (Genesis 33:18, 19). It was not a spring-fed well, but a well into which water seeped from rain and dew, collecting at the bottom. Wells were almost always located outside the city along the main road. Twice each day, morning and evening, women came to draw water. This woman came at noon, however, probably to avoid meeting people who knew her reputation. Jesus gave this woman an extraordinary message about fresh and pure water that would quench her spiritual thirst forever.

4:7-9 This woman (1) was a Samaritan, a member of the hated mixed race, (2) was known to be living in sin, and (3) was in a public place. No respectable Jewish man would talk to a woman under such circumstances. But Jesus did. The Good News is for every person, no matter what his or her race, social position, or past sins. We must be prepared to share this Good News at any time and in any place. Jesus crossed all barriers to share the Good News, and we who follow him must do no less.

4:10 What did Jesus mean by "living water"? In the Old Testament, many verses speak of thirsting after God as one thirsts for water (Psalm 42:1; Isaiah 55:1; Jeremiah 2:13; Zechariah 13:1). God is called the fountain of life (Psalm 36:9) and the fountain of living water (Jeremiah 17:13). In saying he would bring living water that could forever quench a person's thirst for God, Jesus was claiming to be the Messiah. Only the Messiah could give this gift that satisfies the soul's desire.

4:13-15 Many spiritual functions parallel physical functions. As our bodies hunger and thirst, so do our souls. But our souls need *spiritual* food and water. The woman confused the two kinds of water, perhaps because no one had ever talked with her about her spiritual hunger and thirst before. We would not think of depriving our bodies of food and water when they hunger or thirst. Why then should we deprive our souls? The living Word, Jesus Christ, and the written Word, the Bible, can satisfy our hungry and thirsty souls.

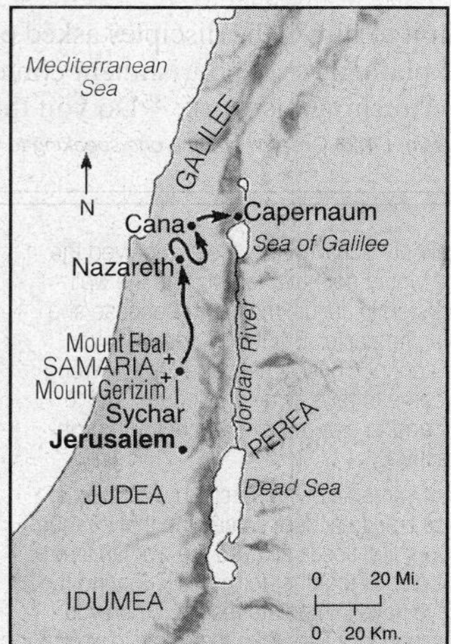

JESUS RETURNS TO GALILEE
Jesus stayed in Sychar for two days, then went on to Galilee. He visited Nazareth and various towns in Galilee before arriving in Cana. From there he spoke the word of healing, and a government official's son in Capernaum was healed. The Gospel of Matthew tells us Jesus then settled in Capernaum (Matthew 4:12, 13).

15"Please, sir," the woman said, "give me some of that water! Then I'll never be thirsty
again, and I won't have to come here to haul water."
16"Go and get your husband," Jesus told her.
17"I don't have a husband," the woman replied.
Jesus said, "You're right! You don't have a husband—18for you have had five
husbands, and you aren't even married to the man you're living with now."
19"Sir," the woman said, "you must be a prophet. 20So tell me, why is it that you Jews
insist that Jerusalem is the only place of worship, while we Samaritans claim it is here at
Mount Gerizim,* where our ancestors worshiped?"
21Jesus replied, "Believe me, the time is coming when it will no longer matter
whether you worship the Father here or in Jerusalem. 22You Samaritans know so little
about the one you worship, while we Jews know all about him, for salvation comes
through the Jews. 23But the time is coming and is already here when true worshipers
will worship the Father in spirit and in truth. The Father is looking for anyone who will
worship him that way. 24For God is Spirit, so those who worship him must worship in
spirit and in truth."
25The woman said, "I know the Messiah will come—the one who is called Christ.
When he comes, he will explain everything to us."
26Then Jesus told her, "I am the Messiah!"*

Jesus Tells about the Spiritual Harvest (**28**)

27Just then his disciples arrived. They were astonished to find him talking to a woman,
but none of them asked him why he was doing it or what they had been discussing. 28The
woman left her water jar beside the well and went back to the village and told everyone,
29"Come and meet a man who told me everything I ever did! Can this be the Messiah?"
30So the people came streaming from the village to see him.
31Meanwhile, the disciples were urging Jesus to eat. 32"No," he said, "I have food you
don't know about."
33"Who brought it to him?" the disciples asked each other.
34Then Jesus explained: "My nourishment comes from doing the will of God, who
sent me, and from finishing his work. 35Do you think the work of harvesting will not

4:15 John 6:34
4:19 Matt 21:46; John 7:40; 9:17
4:20 Deut 11:29; 12:5-14; Josh 8:33
4:21 Mal 1:11; 1 Tim 2:8
4:22 2 Kgs 17:28-41; Isa 2:3; Rom 3:1-2; 9:4-5
4:23-24 2 Cor 3:17-18; Phil 3:3
4:25 Deut 18:15
4:26 Mark 14:61-62; John 9:37
4:29 Matt 9:37; John 7:26
4:34 John 5:30, 36; 6:38; 17:4
4:35 Matt 9:37; Luke 10:2

4:20 Greek *on this mountain.* **4:26** Greek *"I am, the one speaking to you."*

4:15 The woman mistakenly believed that if she received the water Jesus offered, she would not have to return to the well each day. She was interested in Jesus' message because she thought it could make her life easier. But if that were always the case, people would accept Christ's message for the wrong reasons. Christ did not come to take away challenges, but to change us on the inside and to empower us to deal with problems from God's perspective.

4:15 The woman did not immediately understand what Jesus was talking about. It takes time to accept something that changes the very foundations of your life. Jesus allowed the woman time to ask questions and put pieces together for herself. Sharing the Good News will not always have immediate results. When you ask people to let Jesus change their lives, give them time to weigh the matter.

4:16-20 When this woman discovered that Jesus knew all about her private life, she quickly changed the subject. Often people become uncomfortable when the conversation is too close to home, and they try to talk about something else. As we witness, we should gently guide the conversation back to Christ. His presence exposes sin and makes people squirm, but only Christ can forgive sins and give new life.

4:20-24 The woman brought up a popular theological issue—the correct place to worship. But her question was a smoke screen to keep Jesus away from her deepest need. Jesus directed the conversation to a much more important point: The *location* of worship is not nearly as important as the *attitude* of the worshipers.

4:21-24 "God is Spirit" means he is not a physical being limited to one place. He is present everywhere, and he can be worshiped anywhere, at any time. It is not where we worship that counts, but how we worship. Is your worship genuine and true? Do you have the Holy Spirit's help? How does the Holy Spirit help us worship? The Holy Spirit prays for us (Romans 8:26), teaches us the words of Christ (14:26), and tells us we are loved (Romans 5:5).

4:22 When Jesus said, "Salvation comes through the Jews," he meant that only through the Jewish Messiah would the whole world find salvation. God had promised that through the Jewish race the whole earth would be blessed (Genesis 12:3). The Old Testament prophets had called the Jews to be a light to the other nations of the world, bringing them to a knowledge of God; and they had predicted the Messiah's coming. The woman at the well may have known of these passages and was expecting the Messiah, but she didn't realize that she was talking to him!

4:34 The "food" about which Jesus was speaking was his spiritual nourishment. It includes more than Bible study, prayer, and attending church. Spiritual nourishment also comes from doing God's will and helping to bring his work of salvation to completion. We are nourished not only by what we take in, but also by what we give out for God. In 17:4, Jesus refers to completing God's work on earth.

4:35 Sometimes Christians excuse themselves from witnessing by saying that their family or friends aren't ready to believe. Jesus, however, makes it clear that around us a continual harvest waits to

begin until the summer ends four months from now? Look around you! Vast fields are
ripening all around us and are ready now for the harvest. 36 The harvesters are paid
good wages, and the fruit they harvest is people brought to eternal life. What joy
4:37 Job 31:8 Mic 6:15 awaits both the planter and the harvester alike! 37 You know the saying, 'One person
plants and someone else harvests.' And it's true. 38 I sent you to harvest where you
didn't plant; others had already done the work, and you will gather the harvest."

Many Samaritans Believe in Jesus (**29**)

39 Many Samaritans from the village believed in Jesus because the woman had said, "He
told me everything I ever did!" 40 When they came out to see him, they begged him to
stay at their village. So he stayed for two days, 41 long enough for many of them to hear
4:42 Luke 2:11 1 Jn 4:14 his message and believe. 42 Then they said to the woman, "Now we believe because we
have heard him ourselves, not just because of what you told us. He is indeed the Savior
of the world."

Jesus Preaches in Galilee (**30**/Matthew 4:12-17; Mark 1:14-15; Luke 4:14-15)

4:44 Matt 13:57 Luke 4:24 43 At the end of the two days' stay, Jesus went on into Galilee. 44 He had previously
said, "A prophet is honored everywhere except in his own country." 45 The Galileans
welcomed him, for they had been in Jerusalem at the Passover celebration and had
seen all his miraculous signs.

Jesus Heals a Government Official's Son (**31**)

4:46 John 2:1-11 46 In the course of his journey through Galilee, he arrived at the town of Cana, where he
had turned the water into wine. There was a government official in the city of Capernaum
whose son was very sick. 47 When he heard that Jesus had come from Judea and was
traveling in Galilee, he went over to Cana. He found Jesus and begged him to come to
Capernaum with him to heal his son, who was about to die.

4:48 1 Cor 1:22 48 Jesus asked, "Must I do miraculous signs and wonders before you people will
believe in me?"

49 The official pleaded, "Lord, please come now before my little boy dies."

4:50 Matt 8:13 Mark 7:29 50 Then Jesus told him, "Go back home. Your son will live!" And the man believed
Jesus' word and started home.

51 While he was on his way, some of his servants met him with the news that his son
was alive and well. 52 He asked them when the boy had begun to feel better, and they
4:53 Acts 11:14; 16:14-15 replied, "Yesterday afternoon at one o'clock his fever suddenly disappeared!" 53 Then
the father realized it was the same time that Jesus had told him, "Your son will live."

---

be reaped. Don't let Jesus find you making excuses. Look around. You will find people ready to hear God's Word.

4:36-38 The wages Jesus offers are the joy of working for him and seeing the harvest of believers. These wages come to planter and harvester alike because both find joy in seeing new believers come into Christ's Kingdom. The phrase "others had already done the work" (4:38) may refer to the Old Testament prophets and to John the Baptist, who paved the way for the Good News.

4:39 The Samaritan woman immediately shared her experience with others. Despite her reputation, many took her invitation and came out to meet Jesus. Perhaps there are sins in our past of which we're ashamed. But Christ changes us. As people see these changes, they become curious. Use these opportunities to introduce them to Christ.

4:46-49 This government official was probably an officer in Herod's service. He had walked 20 miles to see Jesus and addressed him as "Lord," putting himself under Jesus even though he had legal authority over Jesus.

4:48 This miracle was more than a favor to one official; it was a sign to all the people. John's Gospel was written to all humankind to urge faith in Christ. Here a government official had faith that Jesus could do what he claimed. The official believed; *then* he saw a miraculous sign.

4:50 This government official not only believed Jesus could heal; he also obeyed Jesus by returning home, thus demonstrating his faith. It isn't enough for us to say we believe that Jesus can take care of our problems. We need to act as if he can. When you pray about a need or problem, live as though you believe Jesus can do what he says.

4:51 Jesus' miracles were not mere illusions, the product of wishful thinking. Although the official's son was 20 miles away, he was healed when Jesus spoke the word. Distance was no problem because Christ has mastery over space. We can never put so much space between ourselves and Christ that he can no longer help us.

4:53 Notice how the official's faith grew. First, he believed enough to ask Jesus to help his son. Second, he believed Jesus' assurance that his son would live, and he acted on it. Third, he and his whole house believed in Jesus. Faith is a gift that grows as we use it.

And the officer and his entire household believed in Jesus. 54This was Jesus' second 4:54
miraculous sign in Galilee after coming from Judea. John 2:11

Jesus Heals a Lame Man by a Pool **(42)**

5 Afterward Jesus returned to Jerusalem for one of the Jewish holy days. 2Inside the 5:1
city, near the Sheep Gate, was the pool of Bethesda,* with five covered porches. Lev 23:1-2
3Crowds of sick people—blind, lame, or paralyzed—lay on the porches.* 5One of the Deut 16:1 John 2:13
men lying there had been sick for thirty-eight years. 6When Jesus saw him and knew 5:2
how long he had been ill, he asked him, "Would you like to get well?" Neh 3:1; 12:39
7"I can't, sir," the sick man said, "for I have no one to help me into the pool when the
water is stirred up. While I am trying to get there, someone always gets in ahead of me."
8Jesus told him, "Stand up, pick up your sleeping mat, and walk!" 5:8
9Instantly, the man was healed! He rolled up the mat and began walking! But this miracle Matt 9:6 Mark 2:11
happened on the Sabbath day. 10So the Jewish leaders objected. They said to the man who Luke 5:24
was cured, "You can't work on the Sabbath! It's illegal to carry that sleeping mat!" 5:10
11He replied, "The man who healed me said to me, 'Pick up your sleeping mat and Neh 13:15-20 Jer 17:21
walk.'" Matt 12:2
12"Who said such a thing as that?" they demanded.
13The man didn't know, for Jesus had disappeared into the crowd. 14But afterward 5:14
Jesus found him in the Temple and told him, "Now you are well; so stop sinning, or John 8:11
something even worse may happen to you." 15Then the man went to find the Jewish
leaders and told them it was Jesus who had healed him.

Jesus Claims to Be the Son of God **(43)**

16So the Jewish leaders began harassing Jesus for breaking the Sabbath rules. 17But 5:18 Phil 2:6
Jesus replied, "My Father never stops working, so why should I?" 18So the Jewish Titus 2:13 2 Pet 1:1 1 Jn 5:21

5:2 Some manuscripts read *Beth-zatha;* other manuscripts read *Bethsaida.* **5:3** Some manuscripts add *waiting for a certain movement of the water,* [4]*for an angel of the Lord came from time to time and stirred up the water. And the first person to step down into it afterward was healed.*

JESUS TEACHES IN JERUSALEM
Between chapters 4 and 5 of John, Jesus ministered throughout Galilee, especially in Capernaum. He had been calling certain men to follow him, but it wasn't until after this trip to Jerusalem (5:1) that he chose his 12 disciples from among them.

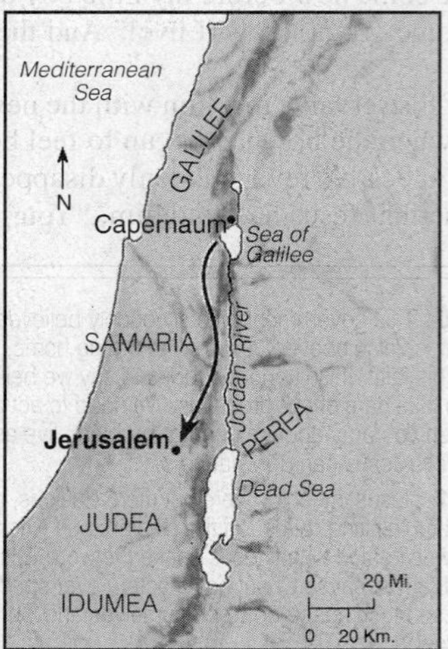

5:1 Three festivals (or "holy days") required all Jewish males to come to Jerusalem: (1) the Festival of Passover and Unleavened Bread, (2) the Festival of Pentecost (also called the Festival of Harvest or the Festival of Weeks), and (3) the Festival of Shelters.

5:6 After 38 years, this man's problem had become a way of life. No one had ever helped him. He had no hope of ever being healed and no desire to help himself. The man's situation looked hopeless. But no matter how trapped you feel in your infirmities, God can minister to your deepest needs. Don't let a problem or hardship cause you to lose hope. God may have special work for you to do in spite of your condition, or even because of it. Many have ministered effectively to hurting people because they have triumphed over their own hurts.

5:10 According to the Pharisees, carrying a mat on the Sabbath was work and was therefore unlawful. It did not break an Old Testament law, but it broke the Pharisees' *interpretation* of God's command to "remember to observe the Sabbath day by keeping it holy" (Exodus 20:8). This was just one of hundreds of rules they had added to the Old Testament law.

5:10 A man who hadn't walked for 38 years had been healed, but the Pharisees were more concerned about their petty rules than the life and health of a human being. It is easy to get so caught up in our man-made structures and rules that we forget the people involved. Are your guidelines for living God-made or man-made? Are they helping people, or have they become needless stumbling blocks?

5:14 This man had been lame, or paralyzed, and suddenly he could walk. This was a great miracle. But he needed an even greater miracle—to have his sins forgiven. The man was delighted to be physically healed, but he had to turn from his sins and seek God's forgiveness to be spiritually healed. God's forgiveness is the greatest gift you will ever receive. Don't neglect his gracious offer.

5:16 The Jewish leaders saw both a mighty miracle of healing and a broken rule. They threw the miracle aside as they focused their attention on the broken rule, because the rule was more important to them than the miracle. God is prepared to work in our lives, but we can shut out his miracles by limiting our views about how he works.

5:17 If God stopped every kind of work on the Sabbath, nature would fall into chaos, and sin would overrun the world. Genesis 2:2 says that God rested on the seventh day, but this can't mean that he stopped doing good. Jesus wanted to teach that when the opportunity to do good presents itself, it should not be ignored, even on the Sabbath.

leaders tried all the more to kill him. In addition to disobeying the Sabbath rules, he had
5:19 John 8:28; 12:49; 14:10 — spoken of God as his Father, thereby making himself equal with God.
[19]Jesus replied, "I assure you, the Son can do nothing by himself. He does only what
5:21 John 11:25 — he sees the Father doing. Whatever the Father does, the Son also does. [20]For the Father
loves the Son and tells him everything he is doing, and the Son will do far greater things
5:22 John 3:17; 5:27 — than healing this man. You will be astonished at what he does. [21]He will even raise from
5:23 1 Jn 2:23 — the dead anyone he wants to, just as the Father does. [22]And the Father leaves all judgment
to his Son, [23]so that everyone will honor the Son, just as they honor the Father. But if
5:24 John 3:15; 20:30-31; 1 Jn 3:14; 5:13 — you refuse to honor the Son, then you are certainly not honoring the Father who sent him.
[24]"I assure you, those who listen to my message and believe in God who sent me have
5:25 John 4:21; 6:63, 68 — eternal life. They will never be condemned for their sins, but they have already passed
5:26 John 1:4; 6:57; 1 Jn 5:11-12 — from death into life.
[25]"And I assure you that the time is coming, in fact it is here, when the dead will
hear my voice—the voice of the Son of God. And those who listen will live. [26]The

THE CLAIMS OF CHRIST

Those who read the life of Christ are faced with one unavoidable question—was Jesus God? Part of any reasonable conclusion has to include the fact that he did claim to be God. We have no other choice but to agree or disagree with his claim. Eternal life is at stake in the choice.

Jesus claimed to be:	*Matthew*	*Mark*	*Luke*	*John*
the fulfillment of Old Testament prophecies	5:17; 14:33; 16:16, 17; 26:31, 53–56; 27:43	14:21, 61, 62	4:16–21; 7:18–23; 18:31; 22:37; 24:44	2:22; 5:45–47; 6:45; 7:40; 10:34–36; 13:18; 15:25; 20:9
the Son of Man	8:20; 12:8; 16:27; 19:28; 20:18, 19; 24:27, 44; 25:31; 26:2, 45, 64	8:31, 38; 9:9; 10:45; 14:41	6:22; 7:33, 34; 12:8; 17:22; 18:8, 31; 19:10; 21:36	1:51; 3:13, 14; 6:27, 53; 12:23, 34
the Son of God	11:27; 14:33; 16:16, 17; 27:43	3:11, 12; 14:61, 62	8:28; 10:22	1:18; 3:35, 36; 5:18–26; 6:40; 10:36; 11:4; 17:1; 19:7
the Messiah/ the Christ	23:9, 10; 26:63, 64	8:29, 30	4:41; 23:1, 2; 24:25–27	4:25, 26; 10:24, 25; 11:27
Teacher/Master	26:18			13:13, 14
one with authority to forgive		2:1–12	7:48, 49	
Lord		5:19		13:13, 14; 20:28, 29
Savior			19:10	3:17; 10:9

5:17ff Jesus was identifying himself with God, his Father. There could be no doubt as to his claim to be God. Jesus does not leave us the option to believe in God while ignoring God's Son (5:23). The Pharisees also called God their Father, but they realized Jesus was claiming a unique relationship with him. In response to Jesus' claim, the Pharisees had two choices: to believe him, or to accuse him of blasphemy. They chose the second.

5:19-23 Because of his unity with God, Jesus lived as God wanted him to live. Because of our identification with Jesus, we must honor him and live as he wants us to live. The questions "What would Jesus do?" and "What would Jesus have me do?" may help us make the right choices.

5:24 "Eternal life"—living forever with God—begins when you accept Jesus Christ as Savior. At that moment, new life begins in you (2 Corinthians 5:17). It is a completed transaction. You still will face physical death, but when Christ returns again, your body will be resurrected to live forever (1 Corinthians 15).

5:25 In saying that the dead will hear his voice, Jesus was talking about the spiritually dead who hear, understand, and accept him. Those who accept Jesus, the Word, will have eternal life. Jesus was also talking about the physically dead. He raised several dead people while he was on earth, and at his second coming, "all the Christians who have died" will rise to meet him (1 Thessalonians 4:16).

5:26 God is the source and Creator of life, for there is no life apart from God, here or hereafter. The life in us is a gift from him (see Deuteronomy 30:20; Psalm 36:9). Because Jesus is eternally existent with God, the Creator, he, too, is "the life" (14:6) through whom we may live eternally (see 1 John 5:11).

Father has life in himself, and he has granted his Son to have life in himself. 27 And
he has given him authority to judge all mankind because he is the Son of Man. 28 Don't
be so surprised! Indeed, the time is coming when all the dead in their graves will hear
the voice of God's Son, 29 and they will rise again. Those who have done good will
rise to eternal life, and those who have continued in evil will rise to judgment. 30 But
I do nothing without consulting the Father. I judge as I am told. And my judgment is
absolutely just, because it is according to the will of God who sent me; it is not merely
my own.

Jesus Supports His Claim (**44**)

31 "If I were to testify on my own behalf, my testimony would not be valid. 32 But
someone else is also testifying about me, and I can assure you that everything he says
about me is true. 33 In fact, you sent messengers to listen to John the Baptist, and he
preached the truth. 34 But the best testimony about me is not from a man, though I have
reminded you about John's testimony so you might be saved. 35 John shone brightly
for a while, and you benefited and rejoiced. 36 But I have a greater witness than
John—my teachings and my miracles. They have been assigned to me by the Father,
and they testify that the Father has sent me. 37 And the Father himself has also testified
about me. You have never heard his voice or seen him face to face, 38 and you do not
have his message in your hearts, because you do not believe me—the one he sent to
you.

39 "You search the Scriptures because you believe they give you eternal life. But the
Scriptures point to me! 40 Yet you refuse to come to me so that I can give you this
eternal life.

41 "Your approval or disapproval means nothing to me, 42 because I know you don't
have God's love within you. 43 For I have come to you representing my Father, and you
refuse to welcome me, even though you readily accept others who represent only
themselves. 44 No wonder you can't believe! For you gladly honor each other, but you
don't care about the honor that comes from God alone.

45 "Yet it is not I who will accuse you of this before the Father. Moses will accuse you!
Yes, Moses, on whom you set your hopes. 46 But if you had believed Moses, you would
have believed me because he wrote about me. 47 And since you don't believe what he
wrote, how will you believe what I say?"

Jesus Feeds Five Thousand (**96**/Matthew 14:13-21; Mark 6:30-44; Luke 9:10-17)

6 After this, Jesus crossed over the Sea of Galilee, also known as the Sea of Tiberias.
2 And a huge crowd kept following him wherever he went, because they saw his
miracles as he healed the sick. 3 Then Jesus went up into the hills and sat down with his

5:27 John 9:39; Acts 10:42; 17:31
5:29 Dan 12:2; Matt 25:46; Acts 24:15
5:30 John 5:19; 6:38
5:31 John 8:13-14
5:32 John 8:18
5:36 John 10:25, 38; 14:11; 15:24; 1 Jn 5:9
5:37 Deut 4:12; John 1:18; 8:18; 1 Tim 1:17
5:38 1 Jn 2:14
5:39 Luke 24:27, 44; Acts 13:27; Rom 2:17-20
5:41 John 12:43
5:45 John 9:28; Rom 2:17
5:46 Gen 3:15; Deut 18:15, 18; Luke 24:27, 44; Acts 26:22, 23
5:47 Luke 16:31

5:27 The Old Testament mentioned three signs of the coming Messiah. In this chapter, John shows that Jesus has fulfilled all three signs. Authority to judge is given to him as the Son of Man (cf. 5:27 with Daniel 7:13, 14). The lame and sick are healed (cf. 5:20, 21 with Isaiah 35:6; Jeremiah 31:8, 9). The dead are raised to life (cf. 5:21, 28 with Deuteronomy 32:39; 1 Samuel 2:6; 2 Kings 5:7).

5:29 Those who have rebelled against Christ will be resurrected, too, but they will hear God's judgment against them and will be sentenced to eternity apart from him. There are those who wish to live well on earth, ignore God, and then see death as final rest. Jesus does not allow unbelieving people to see death as the end of it all. There is a judgment to face.

5:31ff Jesus claimed to be equal with God (5:18), to give eternal life (5:24), to be the source of life (5:26), and to judge sin (5:27). These statements make it clear that Jesus was claiming to be divine—an almost unbelievable claim, but one that was supported by another witness, John the Baptist.

5:39, 40 The religious leaders knew what the Bible said but failed to apply its words to their lives. They knew the teachings of the Scriptures but failed to see the Messiah to whom the Scriptures pointed. They knew the rules but missed the Savior. Entrenched in their own religious system, they refused to let the Son of God change their lives. Don't become so involved in "religion" that you miss Christ.

5:41 Whose praise do you seek? The religious leaders enjoyed great prestige in Israel, but their stamp of approval meant nothing to Jesus. He was concerned about God's approval. This is a good principle for us. If even the highest officials in the world approve of our actions and God does not, we should be concerned. But if God approves, even though others don't, we should be content.

5:45 The Pharisees prided themselves on being the true followers of their ancestor Moses. They were trying to follow every one of his laws to the letter, and they even added some of their own. Jesus' warning that Moses would accuse them stung them to fury. Moses wrote about Jesus (Genesis 3:15; Numbers 21:9; 24:17; Deuteronomy 18:15), yet the religious leaders refused to believe Jesus when he came.

6:4 John 11:55
6:5 John 1:43
6:8 John 1:40
6:9 2 Kgs 4:43 John 21:9, 13
6:14 Deut 18:15, 18 Acts 3:22; 7:37
6:19 Job 9:8

disciples around him. 4(It was nearly time for the annual Passover celebration.) 5Jesus
soon saw a great crowd of people climbing the hill, looking for him. Turning to Philip,
he asked, "Philip, where can we buy bread to feed all these people?" 6He was testing
Philip, for he already knew what he was going to do.

7Philip replied, "It would take a small fortune* to feed them!"

8Then Andrew, Simon Peter's brother, spoke up. 9"There's a young boy here with five
barley loaves and two fish. But what good is that with this huge crowd?"

10"Tell everyone to sit down," Jesus ordered. So all of them—the men alone
numbered five thousand—sat down on the grassy slopes. 11Then Jesus took the
loaves, gave thanks to God, and passed them out to the people. Afterward he did the
same with the fish. And they all ate until they were full. 12"Now gather the leftovers,"
Jesus told his disciples, "so that nothing is wasted." 13There were only five barley
loaves to start with, but twelve baskets were filled with the pieces of bread the people
did not eat!

14When the people saw this miraculous sign, they exclaimed, "Surely, he is the
Prophet* we have been expecting!" 15Jesus saw that they were ready to take him by force
and make him king, so he went higher into the hills alone.

Jesus Walks on Water (**97**/Matthew 14:22-33; Mark 6:45-52)

16That evening his disciples went down to the shore to wait for him. 17But as darkness
fell and Jesus still hadn't come back, they got into the boat and headed out across the
lake toward Capernaum. 18Soon a gale swept down upon them as they rowed, and the
sea grew very rough. 19They were three or four miles* out when suddenly they saw Jesus

6:7 Greek *200 denarii.* A denarius was the equivalent of a full day's wage. **6:14** See Deut 18:15, 18. **6:19** Greek *25 or 30 stadia* [4.6 or 5.5 kilometers].

6:5 If anyone knew where to get food, it would have been Philip because he was from Bethsaida, a town about nine miles away (1:44). Jesus was testing Philip to strengthen his faith. By asking for a human solution (knowing that there was none), Jesus highlighted the powerful and miraculous act that he was about to perform.

6:5-7 When Jesus asked Philip where they could buy a great amount of bread, Philip started assessing the probable cost. Jesus wanted to teach him that financial resources are not the most important ones. We can limit what God does in us by assuming what is and is not possible. Is there some impossible task that you believe God wants you to do? Don't let your estimate of what can't be done keep you from taking on the task. God can do the miraculous; trust him to provide the resources.

6:8, 9 The disciples are contrasted with the youngster who brought what he had. They certainly had more resources than the boy, but they knew they didn't have enough, so they didn't give anything at all. The boy gave what little he had, and it made all the difference. If we offer nothing to God, he will have nothing to use. But he can take what little we have and turn it into something great.

6:8, 9 In performing his miracles, Jesus usually preferred to work through people. Here he took what a young child offered and used it to accomplish one of the most spectacular miracles recorded in the Gospels. Age is no barrier to Christ. Never think you are too young or old to be of service to him.

6:13 There is a lesson in the leftovers. God gives in abundance. He takes whatever we can offer him in time, ability, or resources and multiplies its effectiveness beyond our wildest expectations. If you take the first step in making yourself available to God, he will show you how greatly you can be used to advance the work of his Kingdom.

6:14 "The Prophet" is the one prophesied by Moses (Deuteronomy 18:15).

6:18 The Sea of Galilee is 650 feet below sea level, 150 feet deep, and surrounded by hills. These physical features make it subject to sudden windstorms that would cause extremely high waves. Such storms were expected on this lake, but they were nevertheless frightening. When Jesus came to the disciples during a storm, walking on the water (three and a half miles from shore), he told them not to be afraid. We often face spiritual and emotional storms and feel tossed about like a small boat on a big lake. In spite of terrifying circumstances, if we trust our lives to Christ for his safekeeping, he will give us peace in any storm.

6:18, 19 The disciples, terrified, probably thought they were seeing a ghost (Mark 6:49). But if they had thought about all they had already seen Jesus do, they could have accepted this miracle. They were frightened—they didn't expect Jesus to come, and they weren't prepared for his help. Faith is a mind-set that *expects* God to act. When we act on this expectation, we can overcome our fears.

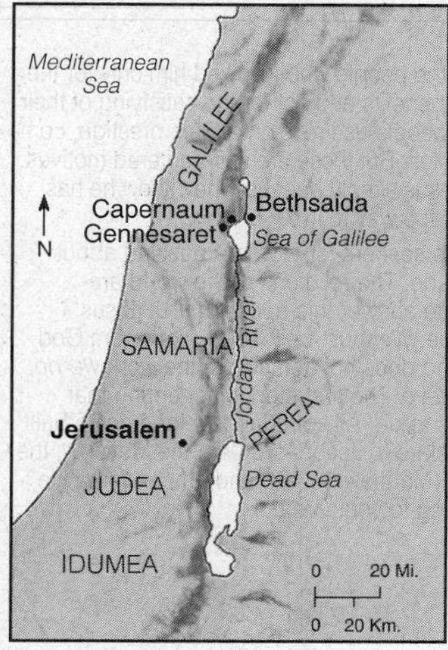

JESUS WALKS ON THE WATER
Jesus fed the 5,000 on a hill near the Sea of Galilee at Bethsaida. The disciples set out across the sea toward Capernaum. But they encountered a storm—and Jesus came walking to them on the water! The boat landed at Gennesaret (Mark 6:53); from there they went back to Capernaum.

walking on the water toward the boat. They were terrified, 20 but he called out to them,
"I am here! Don't be afraid." 21 Then they were eager to let him in, and immediately the
boat arrived at their destination!

Jesus Is the True Bread from Heaven (**99**)

22 The next morning, back across the lake, crowds began gathering on the shore, waiting
to see Jesus. For they knew that he and his disciples had come over together and that the
disciples had gone off in their boat, leaving him behind. 23 Several boats from Tiberias
landed near the place where the Lord had blessed the bread and the people had eaten.
24 When the crowd saw that Jesus wasn't there, nor his disciples, they got into the boats
and went across to Capernaum to look for him. 25 When they arrived and found him, they
asked, "Teacher, how did you get here?"

26 Jesus replied, "The truth is, you want to be with me because I fed you, not because
you saw the miraculous sign. 27 But you shouldn't be so concerned about perishable
things like food. Spend your energy seeking the eternal life that I, the Son of Man, can
give you. For God the Father has sent me for that very purpose."

28 They replied, "What does God want us to do?"

29 Jesus told them, "This is what God wants you to do: Believe in the one he has
sent."

30 They replied, "You must show us a miraculous sign if you want us to believe in
you. What will you do for us? 31 After all, our ancestors ate manna while they
journeyed through the wilderness! As the Scriptures say, 'Moses gave them bread
from heaven to eat.'*"

32 Jesus said, "I assure you, Moses didn't give them bread from heaven. My Father
did. And now he offers you the true bread from heaven. 33 The true bread of God is the
one who comes down from heaven and gives life to the world."

34 "Sir," they said, "give us that bread every day of our lives."

35 Jesus replied, "I am the bread of life. No one who comes to me will ever be
hungry again. Those who believe in me will never thirst. 36 But you haven't believed
in me even though you have seen me. 37 However, those the Father has given me will
come to me, and I will never reject them. 38 For I have come down from heaven to do
the will of God who sent me, not to do what I want. 39 And this is the will of God, that
I should not lose even one of all those he has given me, but that I should raise them
to eternal life at the last day. 40 For it is my Father's will that all who see his Son and
believe in him should have eternal life—that I should raise them at the last day."

6:20 Matt 14:27
6:23 John 6:11
6:27 Matt 3:17; 17:5; Mark 1:11; 9:7; Luke 3:22; John 1:33; 4:14; 6:50-51, 54, 58; Acts 2:22; Rom 6:23
6:29 1 Jn 3:23
6:31 Exod 16:15; Num 11:7-9; Neh 9:15; †Pss 78:24; 105:40
6:33 John 6:41, 50
6:35 John 4:14; 6:48; 7:37-38
6:37 John 10:28-29; 17:2, 24
6:38 John 4:34; 5:30
6:39 John 10:28-29; 17:12; 18:9
6:40 John 12:45

6:31 Exod 16:4; Ps 78:24.

6:26 Jesus criticized the people who followed him only for the physical and temporal benefits and not for the satisfying of their spiritual hunger. Many people use religion to gain prestige, comfort, or even political votes. But those are self-centered motives. True believers follow Jesus simply because they know he has the truth and his way is the way to live.

6:28, 29 Many sincere seekers for God are puzzled about what he wants them to do. The religions of the world are humankind's attempts to answer this question. But Jesus' reply is brief and simple: We must believe on him whom God has sent. Satisfying God does not come from the work we *do*, but from whom we *believe*. The first step is accepting that Jesus is who he claims to be. All spiritual development is built on this affirmation. Declare to Jesus, "You are the Messiah, the Son of the living God" (Matthew 16:16), and embark on a life of belief that is satisfying to your Creator.

6:35 People eat bread to satisfy physical hunger and to sustain physical life. We can satisfy spiritual hunger and sustain spiritual life only by a right relationship with Jesus Christ. No wonder he called himself the bread of life. But bread must be eaten to sustain life, and Christ must be invited into our daily walk to sustain spiritual life.

6:37, 38 Jesus did not work independently of God the Father, but in union with him. This should give us even more assurance of being welcomed into God's presence and being protected by him. Jesus' purpose was to do the will of God, not to satisfy Jesus' human desires. When we follow Jesus, we should have the same purpose.

6:39 Jesus said he would not lose even one person whom the Father had given him. Thus, anyone who makes a sincere commitment to believe in Jesus Christ as Savior is secure in God's promise of eternal life. Christ will not let his people be overcome by Satan and lose their salvation (see also 17:12; Philippians 1:6).

6:40 Those who put their faith in Christ will be resurrected from physical death to eternal life with God when Christ comes again (see 1 Corinthians 15:52; 1 Thessalonians 4:16).

6:41 John 6:33, 35, 51
6:42 Luke 4:22; John 7:27-28
6:44 Jer 31:3; John 6:65; 12:32
6:45 †Isa 54:13; Jer 31:33-34; 1 Thes 4:9; Heb 8:10, 11
6:46 John 1:18; 5:37
6:47 John 3:15, 16, 36
6:48 John 6:35, 41, 51, 58
6:51 John 10:10-11; Heb 10:10
6:54 John 6:39-40, 44
6:56 John 14:20; 15:4-7; 17:21-23; 1 Jn 2:24; 3:24
6:57 John 5:26
6:58 John 6:31
6:62 Acts 1:9-11; Eph 4:8
6:63 Rom 8:2; 1 Cor 15:45; 1 Pet 3:18

The People Disagree That Jesus Is from Heaven (**100**)

41 Then the people* began to murmur in disagreement because he had said, "I am the
bread from heaven." 42 They said, "This is Jesus, the son of Joseph. We know his father
and mother. How can he say, 'I came down from heaven'?"
43 But Jesus replied, "Don't complain about what I said. 44 For people can't come to
me unless the Father who sent me draws them to me, and at the last day I will raise them
from the dead. 45 As it is written in the Scriptures, 'They will all be taught by God.'*
Everyone who hears and learns from the Father comes to me. 46 (Not that anyone has
ever seen the Father; only I, who was sent from God, have seen him.)
47 "I assure you, anyone who believes in me already has eternal life. 48 Yes, I am the
bread of life! 49 Your ancestors ate manna in the wilderness, but they all died. 50 However,
the bread from heaven gives eternal life to everyone who eats it. 51 I am the living bread
that came down out of heaven. Anyone who eats this bread will live forever; this bread
is my flesh, offered so the world may live."
52 Then the people began arguing with each other about what he meant. "How can this
man give us his flesh to eat?" they asked.
53 So Jesus said again, "I assure you, unless you eat the flesh of the Son of Man and
drink his blood, you cannot have eternal life within you. 54 But those who eat my flesh
and drink my blood have eternal life, and I will raise them at the last day. 55 For my flesh
is the true food, and my blood is the true drink. 56 All who eat my flesh and drink my
blood remain in me, and I in them. 57 I live by the power of the living Father who sent
me; in the same way, those who partake of me will live because of me. 58 I am the true
bread from heaven. Anyone who eats this bread will live forever and not die as your
ancestors did, even though they ate the manna."
59 He said these things while he was teaching in the synagogue in Capernaum.

Many Disciples Desert Jesus (**101**)

60 Even his disciples said, "This is very hard to understand. How can anyone accept it?"
61 Jesus knew within himself that his disciples were complaining, so he said to them,
"Does this offend you? 62 Then what will you think if you see me, the Son of Man, return
to heaven again? 63 It is the Spirit who gives eternal life. Human effort accomplishes

6:41 Greek *Jewish people;* also in 6:52. **6:45** Isa 54:13.

6:41 The religious leaders grumbled because they could not accept Jesus' claim of divinity. They saw him only as a carpenter from Nazareth. They refused to believe that Jesus was God's divine Son, and they could not tolerate his message. Many people reject Christ because they say they cannot believe he is the Son of God. In reality, the demands that Christ makes for their loyalty and obedience are what they can't accept. So to protect themselves from the message, they reject the messenger.

6:44 God, not people, plays the most active role in salvation. When someone chooses to believe in Jesus Christ as Savior, he or she does so only in response to the urging of God's Holy Spirit. God does the urging; then we decide whether or not to believe. Thus, no one can believe in Jesus without God's help.

6:45 Jesus was alluding to an Old Testament view of the messianic Kingdom in which all people are taught directly by God (Isaiah 54:13; Jeremiah 31:31-34). He was stressing the importance of not merely hearing, but learning. We are taught by God through the Bible, our experiences, the thoughts the Holy Spirit brings, and relationships with other Christians. Are you open to God's teaching?

6:47 As used here, *believes* means "continues to believe." We do not believe merely once; we keep on believing in and trusting Jesus.

6:47ff The religious leaders frequently asked Jesus to prove to them why he was better than the prophets they already had. Jesus here referred to the manna that Moses had given their ancestors in the wilderness (see Exodus 16). This bread was physical and temporal. The people ate it, and it sustained them for a day. But they had to get more bread every day, and this bread could not keep them from dying. Jesus, who is much greater than Moses, offers himself as the spiritual bread from heaven that satisfies completely and leads to eternal life.

6:51 How can Jesus give us his flesh as bread to eat? To eat living bread means to accept Christ into our lives and become united with him. We are united with Christ in two ways: (1) by believing in his death (the sacrifice of his flesh) and resurrection and (2) by devoting ourselves to living as he requires, depending on his teaching for guidance and trusting in the Holy Spirit for power.

6:56 This was a shocking message—to eat flesh and drink blood sounded cannibalistic. The idea of drinking any blood, let alone human blood, was repugnant to the religious leaders because the law forbade it (Leviticus 17:10, 11). Jesus was not talking about literal blood, of course. He was saying that his life had to become their own, but they could not accept this concept. The apostle Paul later used the body and blood imagery in talking about Communion (see 1 Corinthians 11:23-26).

6:63, 65 The Holy Spirit gives spiritual life; without the work of the Holy Spirit, we cannot even see our need for new life (14:17). All spiritual renewal begins and ends with God. He reveals truth to us, lives within us, and then enables us to respond to that truth.

nothing. And the very words I have spoken to you are spirit and life. 64 But some of you
don't believe me." (For Jesus knew from the beginning who didn't believe, and he knew
who would betray him.) 65 Then he said, "That is what I meant when I said that people
can't come to me unless the Father brings them to me."
66 At this point many of his disciples turned away and deserted him. 67 Then Jesus
turned to the Twelve and asked, "Are you going to leave, too?"
68 Simon Peter replied, "Lord, to whom would we go? You alone have the words that
give eternal life. 69 We believe them, and we know you are the Holy One of God."
70 Then Jesus said, "I chose the twelve of you, but one is a devil." 71 He was speaking
of Judas, son of Simon Iscariot, one of the Twelve, who would betray him.

6:64 John 13:11
6:65 John 6:44
6:68 John 6:63
6:69 Matt 16:16; Mark 1:24; 8:29; Luke 9:20; 1 Jn 2:20

2. Jesus encounters conflict with the religious leaders

Jesus' Brothers Ridicule Him (**121**)

7 After this, Jesus stayed in Galilee, going from village to village. He wanted to stay
out of Judea where the Jewish leaders were plotting his death. 2 But soon it was time
for the Festival of Shelters, 3 and Jesus' brothers urged him to go to Judea for the
celebration. "Go where your followers can see your miracles!" they scoffed. 4 "You can't
become a public figure if you hide like this! If you can do such wonderful things, prove
it to the world!" 5 For even his brothers didn't believe in him.
6 Jesus replied, "Now is not the right time for me to go. But you can go anytime, and
it will make no difference. 7 The world can't hate you, but it does hate me because I
accuse it of sin and evil. 8 You go on. I am not yet* ready to go to this festival, because
my time has not yet come." 9 So Jesus remained in Galilee.

Jesus Teaches Openly at the Temple (**123**)

10 But after his brothers had left for the festival, Jesus also went, though secretly,
staying out of public view. 11 The Jewish leaders tried to find him at the festival and

7:1 John 5:18; 7:19; 8:37, 40
7:2 Lev 23:34; Deut 16:16
7:3 Matt 12:46
7:6 John 2:4; 7:30; 8:20
7:7 John 15:18
7:11 John 11:56

7:8 Some manuscripts omit *yet*.

6:66 Why did Jesus' words cause many of his followers to desert him? (1) They may have realized that he wasn't going to be the conquering Messiah-King they expected. (2) He refused to give in to their self-centered requests. (3) He emphasized faith, not deeds. (4) His teachings were difficult to understand, and some of his words were offensive. As we grow in our faith, we may be tempted to turn away because Jesus' lessons are difficult. Will your response be to give up, ignore certain teachings, or reject Christ? Instead, ask God to show you what the teachings mean and how they apply to your life. Then have the courage to act on God's truth.

6:67 There is no middle ground with Jesus. When he asked the disciples if they would also leave, he was showing that they could either accept or reject him. Jesus was not trying to repel people with his teachings. He was simply telling the truth. The more the people heard Jesus' real message, the more they divided into two camps—the honest seekers who wanted to understand more, and those who rejected Jesus because they didn't like what they had heard.

6:67, 68 After many of Jesus' followers had deserted him, he asked the 12 disciples if they were also going to leave. Peter replied, "To whom would we go?" In his straightforward way, Peter answered for all of us—there is no other way. Though there are many philosophies and self-styled authorities, Jesus alone has the words of eternal life. People look everywhere for eternal life and miss Christ, the only source. Stay with him, especially when you are confused or feel alone.

6:70 In response to Jesus' message, some people left; others stayed and truly believed; and some, like Judas, stayed but tried to use Jesus for personal gain. Many people today turn away from Christ. Others pretend to follow, going to church for status, approval of family and friends, or business contacts. But there are only two real responses to Jesus—you either accept him or reject him. How have you responded to Christ?

6:71 For more information on Judas, see his Profile in Mark 14.

7:2 The Festival of Shelters is described in Leviticus 23:33ff. This event occurred in October, about six months after the Passover celebration mentioned in John 6:2-5. The festival commemorated the days when the Israelites wandered in the wilderness and lived in shelters (Leviticus 23:43).

7:3-5 Jesus' brothers had a difficult time believing in him. Some of these brothers would eventually become leaders in the church (James, for example), but for several years they were embarrassed by Jesus. After Jesus died and rose again, they finally believed. We today have every reason to believe because we have the full record of Jesus' miracles, death, and resurrection. We also have the evidence of what the Good News has done in people's lives through the centuries. Don't miss this opportunity to believe in God's Son.

7:7 Because the world hated Jesus, we who follow him can expect that many people will hate us as well. If circumstances are going too well, ask if you are following Christ as you should. We can be grateful when life goes well, but we must make sure it is not at the cost of following Jesus halfheartedly or not at all.

7:10 Jesus came with the greatest gift ever offered, so why did he often act secretly? The religious leaders hated him, and many would refuse his gift of salvation, no matter what he said or did. The more Jesus taught and worked publicly, the more these leaders would cause trouble for him and his followers. So it was necessary for Jesus to teach and work as quietly as possible. Many people today have the privilege of teaching, preaching, and worshiping publicly with little persecution. These believers should be grateful and make the most of their opportunities to proclaim the Good News.

kept asking if anyone had seen him. 12 There was a lot of discussion about him among
the crowds. Some said, "He's a wonderful man," while others said, "He's nothing but
a fraud, deceiving the people." 13 But no one had the courage to speak favorably about
him in public, for they were afraid of getting in trouble with the Jewish leaders.
14 Then, midway through the festival, Jesus went up to the Temple and began to
teach. 15 The Jewish leaders were surprised when they heard him. "How does he know
so much when he hasn't studied everything we've studied?" they asked.
16 So Jesus told them, "I'm not teaching my own ideas, but those of God who sent me.
17 Anyone who wants to do the will of God will know whether my teaching is from God
or is merely my own. 18 Those who present their own ideas are looking for praise for
themselves, but those who seek to honor the one who sent them are good and genuine.
19 None of you obeys the law of Moses! In fact, you are trying to kill me."
20 The crowd replied, "You're demon possessed! Who's trying to kill you?"
21 Jesus replied, "I worked on the Sabbath by healing a man, and you were offended.
22 But you work on the Sabbath, too, when you obey Moses' law of circumcision.
(Actually, this tradition of circumcision is older than the law of Moses; it goes back to
Abraham.) 23 For if the correct time for circumcising your son falls on the Sabbath, you
go ahead and do it, so as not to break the law of Moses. So why should I be condemned
for making a man completely well on the Sabbath? 24 Think this through and you will
see that I am right."
25 Some of the people who lived there in Jerusalem said among themselves, "Isn't
this the man they are trying to kill? 26 But here he is, speaking in public, and they say
nothing to him. Can it be that our leaders know that he really is the Messiah? 27 But
how could he be? For we know where this man comes from. When the Messiah comes,
he will simply appear; no one will know where he comes from."
28 While Jesus was teaching in the Temple, he called out, "Yes, you know me, and
you know where I come from. But I represent one you don't know, and he is true.
29 I know him because I have come from him, and he sent me to you." 30 Then the
leaders tried to arrest him; but no one laid a hand on him, because his time had not
yet come.
31 Many among the crowds at the Temple believed in him. "After all," they said,
"would you expect the Messiah to do more miraculous signs than this man has done?"

7:12 John 7:40-43
7:13 John 9:22-23
7:15 Matt 13:54; Luke 2:47; Acts 4:13
7:16 John 8:28; 12:49; 14:10
7:18 John 5:41, 44; 8:50, 54
7:19 John 1:17; 7:1, 25; 8:37-40
7:20 John 8:48, 52; 10:20
7:21-22 Gen 17:10-13; Lev 12:3
7:23 John 5:8-10, 16; Acts 7:8
7:24 Isa 11:3-4; John 8:15
7:27 John 9:29
7:28-29 John 8:26, 55; 17:25
7:30 John 8:20
7:31 John 2:23; 8:30; 10:42; 11:45; 12:11, 42

7:13 The religious leaders had a great deal of power over the common people. Apparently these leaders couldn't do much to Jesus at this time, but they threatened anyone who might publicly support him, most likely with excommunication. Excommunication from the synagogue was one of the reprisals for believing in Jesus (9:22). To a Jew, this was a severe punishment.

7:13 Everyone was talking about Jesus! But when it came time to speak up for him in public, no one said a word. All were afraid. Fear can stifle our witness. Although many people talk about Christ in church, when it comes to making a public statement about their faith, they are often embarrassed. Jesus says that he will acknowledge us before God if we acknowledge him before others (Matthew 10:32). Be courageous! Speak up for Christ!

7:16-18 Those who attempt to know God's will and do it will know intuitively that Jesus was telling the truth about himself. Have you ever listened to religious speakers and wondered if they were telling the truth? Test them: (1) Their words should agree with, not contradict, the Bible; (2) their words should point to God and his will, not to themselves.

7:19 The Pharisees spent their days trying to achieve holiness by keeping the meticulous rules that they had added to God's laws. Jesus' accusation that they didn't keep Moses' laws stung them deeply. In spite of their pompous pride in themselves and their rules, they did not even fulfill a legalistic religion, for they were living far below what the law of Moses required. Murder was certainly against the law. Jesus' followers should do *more* than the moral law requires, not by adding to its requirements, but by going beyond and beneath the mere dos and don'ts of the law to the spirit of the law.

7:20 Most of the people were probably not aware of the plot to kill Jesus (5:18). There was a small group looking for the right opportunity to kill him, but most were still trying to decide what they believed about him.

7:21-23 According to Moses' law, circumcision was to be performed eight days after a baby's birth (Genesis 17:9-14; Leviticus 12:3). This rite was carried out on all Jewish males to demonstrate their identity as part of God's covenant people. If the eighth day after birth was a Sabbath, the circumcision would still be performed (even though it was considered work). While the religious leaders allowed certain exceptions to Sabbath laws, they allowed none to Jesus, who was simply showing mercy to those who needed healing.

7:26 This chapter shows the many reactions people had toward Jesus. They called him a wonderful man (7:12), a fraud (7:12), a demon-possessed man (7:20), the Messiah (7:26), and the Prophet, whose coming had been predicted by Moses (7:40). We must make up our own minds about who Jesus is, knowing that whatever we decide will have eternal consequences.

7:27 There was a popular tradition that the Messiah would simply appear. But those who believed this tradition were ignoring the Scriptures that clearly predicted the Messiah's birthplace (Micah 5:2).

Religious Leaders Attempt to Arrest Jesus (**124**)
32 When the Pharisees heard that the crowds were murmuring such things, they and the
leading priests sent Temple guards to arrest Jesus. 33 But Jesus told them, "I will be here
a little longer. Then I will return to the one who sent me. 34 You will search for me but
not find me. And you won't be able to come where I am."
35 The Jewish leaders were puzzled by this statement. "Where is he planning to
go?" they asked. "Maybe he is thinking of leaving the country and going to the Jews
in other lands, or maybe even to the Gentiles! 36 What does he mean when he says,
'You will search for me but not find me,' and 'You won't be able to come where I
am'?"
37 On the last day, the climax of the festival, Jesus stood and shouted to the crowds,
"If you are thirsty, come to me! 38 If you believe in me, come and drink! For the
Scriptures declare that rivers of living water will flow out from within."* 39 (When he
said "living water," he was speaking of the Spirit, who would be given to everyone
believing in him. But the Spirit had not yet been given, because Jesus had not yet
entered into his glory.)
40 When the crowds heard him say this, some of them declared, "This man surely is
the Prophet."* 41 Others said, "He is the Messiah." Still others said, "But he can't be!
Will the Messiah come from Galilee? 42 For the Scriptures clearly state that the Messiah
will be born of the royal line of David, in Bethlehem, the village where King David was
born."* 43 So the crowd was divided in their opinion about him. 44 And some wanted him
arrested, but no one touched him.
45 The Temple guards who had been sent to arrest him returned to the leading priests
and Pharisees. "Why didn't you bring him in?" they demanded.
46 "We have never heard anyone talk like this!" the guards responded.
47 "Have you been led astray, too?" the Pharisees mocked. 48 "Is there a single one of
us rulers or Pharisees who believes in him? 49 These ignorant crowds do, but what do
they know about it? A curse on them anyway!"
50 Nicodemus, the leader who had met with Jesus earlier, then spoke up. 51 "Is it legal
to convict a man before he is given a hearing?" he asked.

7:33 John 13:33; 16:5
7:34 John 8:21; 13:33
7:37 Isa 55:1; John 4:10, 14; 6:35; Rev 22:17
7:38 Prov 18:4; Isa 58:11; Ezek 47:1-10; Joel 3:18
7:39 John 14:17-18; 16:7; 20:22; Rom 8:9; 1 Cor 15:45; 2 Cor 3:17
7:40 Deut 18:15; John 6:14
7:41 John 1:46
7:42 2 Sam 7:12; Mic 5:2; Matt 1:1; 2:5-10; Luke 2:4
7:44 John 7:30
7:46 Matt 7:28
7:48 John 12:42
7:50 John 3:1-2; 19:39
7:51 Deut 1:16

7:37-38 Or *"Let anyone who is thirsty come to me and drink. 38 For the Scriptures declare that rivers of living water will flow from the heart of those who believe in me."* **7:40** See Deut 18:15, 18. **7:42** See Mic 5:2.

7:38 Jesus' words, "come and drink," alluded to the theme of many Bible passages that talk about the Messiah's life-giving blessings (Isaiah 12:2, 3; 44:3, 4; 58:11). In promising to give the Holy Spirit to all who believed, Jesus was claiming to be the Messiah, for that was something only the Messiah could do.

7:38 Jesus used the term *living water* in 4:10 to indicate eternal life. Here he uses the term to refer to the Holy Spirit. The two go together: Wherever the Holy Spirit is accepted, he brings eternal life. Jesus teaches more about the Holy Spirit in chapters 14–16. The Holy Spirit empowered Jesus' followers at Pentecost (Acts 2) and has since been available to all who believe in Jesus as Savior.

7:40-44 The crowd was asking questions about Jesus. Some believed, others were hostile, and others disqualified Jesus as the Messiah because he was from Nazareth, not Bethlehem (Micah 5:2). But he *was* born in Bethlehem (Luke 2:1-7), although he grew up in Nazareth. If they had looked more carefully, they would not have jumped to the wrong conclusions. When you search for God's truth, make sure you look carefully and thoughtfully at the Bible with an open heart and mind. Don't jump to conclusions before knowing more of what the Bible says.

7:44-46 Although the Romans ruled Palestine, they gave the Jewish religious leaders authority over minor civil and religious affairs. The religious leaders supervised their own Temple guards and gave the officers power to arrest anyone causing a disturbance or breaking any of their ceremonial laws. Because these leaders had developed hundreds of trivial laws, it was almost impossible for anyone, even the leaders themselves, not to break, neglect, or ignore at least a few of them some of the time. But these Temple guards couldn't find one reason to arrest Jesus. And as they listened to Jesus to try to find evidence, they couldn't help hearing the wonderful words he said.

7:46-49 The Jewish leaders saw themselves as an elite group that alone had the truth, and they resisted the truth about Christ because it wasn't *theirs* to begin with. It is easy to think that we have the truth and that those who disagree with us do not have any truth at all. But God's truth is available to everyone. Don't copy the Pharisees' self-centered and narrow attitude.

7:50-52 This passage offers additional insight into Nicodemus, the Pharisee who visited Jesus at night (chapter 3). Apparently Nicodemus had become a secret believer. Since most of the Pharisees hated Jesus and wanted to kill him, Nicodemus risked his reputation and high position when he spoke up for Jesus. His statement was bold, and the Pharisees immediately became suspicious. After Jesus' death, Nicodemus brought spices for his body (19:39). That is the last time he is mentioned in Scripture.

7:51 Nicodemus confronted the Pharisees with their failure to keep their own laws. The Pharisees were losing ground—the Temple guards came back impressed by Jesus (7:46), and one of the Pharisees' own, Nicodemus, was defending him. With their hypocritical motives being exposed and their prestige slowly eroding, they began to move to protect themselves. Pride would interfere with their ability to reason, and soon they would become obsessed with getting rid of Jesus just to save face. What was good and right no longer mattered.

7:52 Isa 9:1-2 Matt 4:14-16 John 1:46

52They replied, "Are you from Galilee, too? Search the Scriptures and see for
yourself—no prophet ever comes from Galilee!"

[The most ancient Greek manuscripts do not include John 7:53–8:11.]

Jesus Forgives an Adulterous Woman (**125**)

53Then the meeting broke up and everybody went home.

8:2 Matt 26:55

8 Jesus returned to the Mount of Olives, 2but early the next morning he was back again
at the Temple. A crowd soon gathered, and he sat down and taught them. 3As he was
speaking, the teachers of religious law and Pharisees brought a woman they had caught
in the act of adultery. They put her in front of the crowd.

4"Teacher," they said to Jesus, "this woman was caught in the very act of adultery.
5The law of Moses says to stone her. What do you say?"

8:5 Lev 20:10 Deut 22:22-24 Job 31:11
8:6 Matt 22:15
8:7 Deut 17:7

6They were trying to trap him into saying something they could use against him, but
Jesus stooped down and wrote in the dust with his finger. 7They kept demanding an
answer, so he stood up again and said, "All right, stone her. But let those who have never
sinned throw the first stones!" 8Then he stooped down again and wrote in the dust.

9When the accusers heard this, they slipped away one by one, beginning with the
oldest, until only Jesus was left in the middle of the crowd with the woman. 10Then Jesus
stood up again and said to her, "Where are your accusers? Didn't even one of them
condemn you?"

11"No, Lord," she said.

8:11 John 5:14

And Jesus said, "Neither do I. Go and sin no more."

8:12 Isa 9:1-2 John 1:4-5, 9; 3:19; 9:5; 12:35-36, 46 2 Cor 4:6

Jesus Is the Light of the World (**126**)

12Jesus said to the people, "I am the light of the world. If you follow me, you won't be
stumbling through the darkness, because you will have the light that leads to life."

13The Pharisees replied, "You are making false claims about yourself!"

8:3-6 The Jewish leaders had already disregarded the law by arresting the woman without the man. The law required that both parties to adultery be stoned (Leviticus 20:10; Deuteronomy 22:22). The leaders were using the woman as a trap so they could trick Jesus. If Jesus said the woman should not be stoned, they would accuse him of violating Moses' law. If he urged them to execute her, they would report him to the Romans, who did not permit the Jews to carry out their own executions (18:31).

8:7 This is a significant statement about judging others. Because Jesus upheld the legal penalty for adultery, stoning, he could not be accused of being against the law. But by saying that only a sinless person could throw the first stone, he highlighted the importance of compassion and forgiveness. When others are caught in sin, are you quick to pass judgment? To do so is to act as though you have never sinned. It is God's role to judge, not ours. Our role is to show forgiveness and compassion.

8:8 It is uncertain whether Jesus was merely ignoring the accusers by writing on the ground, listing their sins, or writing out the Ten Commandments.

8:9 When Jesus said that only someone who had not sinned should throw the first stone, the leaders slipped quietly away, from oldest to youngest. Evidently the older men were more aware of their sins than the younger. Age and experience often temper youthful self-righteousness. But whatever your age, take an honest look at your life. Recognize your sinful nature, and look for ways to help others rather than hurt them.

8:11 Jesus didn't condemn the woman accused of adultery, but neither did he ignore or condone her sin. He told her to leave her life of sin. Jesus stands ready to forgive any sin in your life, but confession and repentance mean a change of heart. With God's help we can accept Christ's forgiveness and stop our wrongdoing.

8:12 To understand what Jesus meant by "the light of the world," see the note on 1:4, 5.

8:12 Jesus was speaking in the part of the Temple where the offerings were put (8:20), where candles burned to symbolize the pillar of fire that led the people of Israel through the wilderness (Exodus 13:21, 22). In this context, Jesus called himself the light of the world. The pillar of fire represented God's presence, protection, and guidance. Jesus brings God's presence, protection, and guidance. Is he the light of *your* world?

8:12 What does it mean to follow Christ? As a soldier follows his captain, so we should follow Christ, our commander. As a slave follows his master, so we should follow Christ, our Lord. As we follow the advice of a trusted counselor, so we should follow Jesus' commands to us in Scripture. As we follow the laws of our nation, so we should follow the laws of the Kingdom of Heaven.

8:13, 14 The Pharisees thought Jesus was either a lunatic or a liar. Jesus provided them with a third alternative: He was telling the truth. Because most of the Pharisees refused to consider the third alternative, they never recognized him as Messiah and Lord. If you are seeking to know who Jesus is, do not close any door before looking through it honestly. Only with an open mind will you know the truth that he is Messiah and Lord.

8:13-18 The Pharisees argued that Jesus' claim was legally invalid because he had no other witnesses. Jesus responded that his confirming witness was God himself. Jesus and the Father made two witnesses, the number required by the law (Deuteronomy 19:15).

[14]Jesus told them, "These claims are valid even though I make them about myself.
For I know where I came from and where I am going, but you don't know this about me.
[15]You judge me with all your human limitations,* but I am not judging anyone. [16]And
if I did, my judgment would be correct in every respect because I am not alone—I have
with me the Father who sent me. [17]Your own law says that if two people agree about
something, their witness is accepted as fact.* [18]I am one witness, and my Father who
sent me is the other."
[19]"Where is your father?" they asked.
Jesus answered, "Since you don't know who I am, you don't know who my Father is.
If you knew me, then you would know my Father, too." [20]Jesus made these statements
while he was teaching in the section of the Temple known as the Treasury. But he was
not arrested, because his time had not yet come.

Jesus Warns of Coming Judgment (**127**)

[21]Later Jesus said to them again, "I am going away. You will search for me and die in
your sin. You cannot come where I am going."
[22]The Jewish leaders asked, "Is he planning to commit suicide? What does he mean,
'You cannot come where I am going'?"
[23]Then he said to them, "You are from below; I am from above. You are of this world;
I am not. [24]That is why I said that you will die in your sins; for unless you believe that I
am who I say I am, you will die in your sins."
[25]"Tell us who you are," they demanded.
Jesus replied, "I am the one I have always claimed to be.* [26]I have much to say about
you and much to condemn, but I won't. For I say only what I have heard from the one
who sent me, and he is true." [27]But they still didn't understand that he was talking to
them about his Father.
[28]So Jesus said, "When you have lifted up the Son of Man on the cross, then you will
realize that I am he and that I do nothing on my own, but I speak what the Father taught
me. [29]And the one who sent me is with me—he has not deserted me. For I always do
those things that are pleasing to him." [30]Then many who heard him say these things
believed in him.

Jesus Speaks about God's True Children (**128**)

[31]Jesus said to the people* who believed in him, "You are truly my disciples if you keep
obeying my teachings. [32]And you will know the truth, and the truth will set you free."
[33]"But we are descendants of Abraham," they said. "We have never been slaves to
anyone on earth. What do you mean, 'set free'?"
[34]Jesus replied, "I assure you that everyone who sins is a slave of sin. [35]A slave is not
a permanent member of the family, but a son is part of the family forever. [36]So if the Son
sets you free, you will indeed be free. [37]Yes, I realize that you are descendants of
Abraham. And yet some of you are trying to kill me because my message does not find
a place in your hearts. [38]I am telling you what I saw when I was with my Father. But you
are following the advice of your father."
[39]"Our father is Abraham," they declared.

8:14 John 7:28; 9:29
8:16 John 5:30
8:17-18 Deut 17:6; 19:15; John 5:37; 1 Jn 5:7-9
8:19 John 14:7, 9
8:20 Mark 12:41; John 7:30
8:21 John 7:34, 36; 13:33
8:22 John 7:35
8:23 John 3:31; 17:14
8:24 Exod 3:14-15; John 4:26; 8:28, 58; 13:19
8:26 John 3:32-34; 12:49
8:28 John 3:14; 5:19; 8:24; 12:32
8:29 John 4:34; 6:38; 8:16; 14:10; 16:32
8:30 John 7:31
8:31 John 15:7; 2 Jn 1:9
8:32 Rom 8:2; 2 Cor 3:17; Gal 5:1, 13
8:33 Matt 3:9; Luke 3:8
8:34 Rom 6:16, 20; 2 Pet 2:19
8:35 Gen 21:10; Gal 4:30

8:15 Or *judge me by human standards.* **8:17** See Deut 19:15. **8:25** Or *"Why do I speak to you at all?"* **8:31** Greek *Jewish people;* also in 8:48, 52, 57.

8:20 The Temple Treasury was located in the Court of Women. In this area, 13 collection boxes were set up to receive money offerings. Seven of the boxes were for the Temple tax; the other 6 were for freewill offerings. On another occasion, a widow placed her money in one of these boxes, and Jesus taught a profound lesson from her action (Luke 21:1-4).

8:24 People will die in their sins if they reject Christ, because they are rejecting the only way to be rescued from sin. Sadly, many are so taken up with the values of this world that they are blind to the priceless gift Christ offers. Where are you looking? Don't focus on this world's values and miss what is most valuable—eternal life with God.

8:32 Jesus himself is the truth that sets us free (8:36). He is the source of truth, the perfect standard of what is right. He frees us from the consequences of sin, from self-deception, and from deception by Satan. He shows us clearly the way to eternal life with God. Thus, Jesus does not give us freedom to do what we want, but freedom to follow God. As we seek to serve God, Jesus' perfect truth frees us to be all that God meant us to be.

8:34, 35 Sin has a way of enslaving us, controlling us, dominating us, and dictating our actions. Jesus can free you from this slavery that keeps you from becoming the person God created you to be. If sin is restraining, mastering, or enslaving you, Jesus can break its power over your life.

8:39 Matt 3:9; John 8:33; Gal 3:7, 14, 29
8:41 Deut 32:6; Isa 63:16; 64:8; Mal 1:6
8:42 1 Jn 5:1
8:44 Gen 3:4; 4:9; 1 Jn 3:8
8:45 John 18:37
8:47 1 Jn 4:6
8:50 John 5:41
8:51 John 5:24; 11:25, 26
8:53 John 4:12
8:54 John 16:14; 17:5
8:55 John 7:28-29; 15:10
8:56 Gen 18:18; 22:17-18; Matt 13:17; Heb 11:13
8:58 Exod 3:14; Isa 43:10, 13; John 1:1; 8:24, 28

"No," Jesus replied, "for if you were children of Abraham, you would follow his
good example.* 40 I told you the truth I heard from God, but you are trying to kill me.
Abraham wouldn't do a thing like that. 41 No, you are obeying your real father when
you act that way."

They replied, "We were not born out of wedlock! Our true Father is God himself."

42 Jesus told them, "If God were your Father, you would love me, because I have come
to you from God. I am not here on my own, but he sent me. 43 Why can't you understand
what I am saying? It is because you are unable to do so! 44 For you are the children of
your father the Devil, and you love to do the evil things he does. He was a murderer from
the beginning and has always hated the truth. There is no truth in him. When he lies, it
is consistent with his character; for he is a liar and the father of lies. 45 So when I tell the
truth, you just naturally don't believe me! 46 Which of you can truthfully accuse me of
sin? And since I am telling you the truth, why don't you believe me? 47 Anyone whose
Father is God listens gladly to the words of God. Since you don't, it proves you aren't
God's children."

Jesus States He Is Eternal (**129**)

48 The people retorted, "You Samaritan devil! Didn't we say all along that you were
possessed by a demon?"

49 "No," Jesus said, "I have no demon in me. For I honor my Father—and you
dishonor me. 50 And though I have no wish to glorify myself, God wants to glorify me.
Let him be the judge. 51 I assure you, anyone who obeys my teaching will never die!"

52 The people said, "Now we know you are possessed by a demon. Even Abraham and
the prophets died, but you say that those who obey your teaching will never die! 53 Are
you greater than our father Abraham, who died? Are you greater than the prophets, who
died? Who do you think you are?"

54 Jesus answered, "If I am merely boasting about myself, it doesn't count. But it is
my Father who says these glorious things about me. You say, 'He is our God,' 55 but you
do not even know him. I know him. If I said otherwise, I would be as great a liar as you!
But it is true—I know him and obey him. 56 Your ancestor Abraham rejoiced as he looked
forward to my coming. He saw it and was glad."

57 The people said, "You aren't even fifty years old. How can you say you have seen
Abraham?*"

58 Jesus answered, "The truth is, I existed before Abraham was even born!"*

8:39 Some manuscripts read *if you are children of Abraham, follow his example.* **8:57** Some manuscripts read *How can you say Abraham has seen you?* **8:58** Or *"Truly, truly, before Abraham was, I am."*

8:41 Jesus made a distinction between hereditary children and *true* children. The religious leaders were hereditary children of Abraham (founder of the Jewish nation) and therefore claimed to be children of God. But their actions showed them to be true children of Satan, for they lived under Satan's guidance. True children of Abraham (faithful followers of God) would not act as they did. Your church membership and family connections will not make you a true child of God. Your true father is the one you imitate and obey.

8:43 The religious leaders were unable to understand because they refused to listen. Satan used their stubbornness, pride, and prejudices to keep them from believing in Jesus.

8:44, 45 The attitudes and actions of these leaders clearly identified them as followers of Satan. They may not have been conscious of this, but their hatred of truth, their lies, and their murderous intentions indicated how much control the Devil had over them. They were his tools in carrying out his plans; they spoke the very same language of lies. Satan still uses people to obstruct God's work (Genesis 4:8; Romans 5:12; 1 John 3:12).

8:46 No one could accuse Jesus of a single sin. People who hated him and wanted him dead scrutinized his behavior but could find nothing wrong. Jesus proved he was God in the flesh by his sinless life. He is the only perfect example for us to follow.

8:46, 47 In a number of places Jesus intentionally challenged his listeners to test him. He welcomed those who wanted to question his claims and character as long as they were willing to follow through on what they discovered. Jesus' challenge clarifies the two most frequent reasons that people miss when encountering him: (1) They never accept his challenge to test him, or (2) they test him but are not willing to believe what they discover. Have you made either of those mistakes?

8:51 When Jesus says those who obey won't die, he is talking about spiritual death, not physical death. Even physical death, however, will eventually be overcome. Those who follow Christ will be raised to live eternally with him.

8:56 God told Abraham, the father of the Jewish nation, that through him all nations would be blessed (Genesis 12:1-7; 15:1-21). Abraham had been able to see this through the eyes of faith. Jesus, a descendant of Abraham, blessed all people through his death, resurrection, and offer of salvation.

8:58 This is one of the most powerful statements uttered by Jesus. When he said that he existed before Abraham was born, he undeniably proclaimed his divinity. Not only did Jesus say that he existed before Abraham; he also applied God's holy name (*I AM*—Exodus 3:14) to himself (see NLT text note). This claim demands a response. It cannot be ignored. The Jewish leaders tried to stone Jesus for blasphemy because he claimed equality with God. But Jesus *is* God. How have you responded to Jesus, the Son of God?

59At that point they picked up stones to kill him. But Jesus hid himself from them and
left the Temple.

Jesus Heals the Man Who Was Born Blind (**148**)

9 As Jesus was walking along, he saw a man who had been blind from birth.
2"Teacher," his disciples asked him, "why was this man born blind? Was it a result
of his own sins or those of his parents?"
3"It was not because of his sins or his parents' sins," Jesus answered. "He was born
blind so the power of God could be seen in him. 4All of us must quickly carry out the
tasks assigned us by the one who sent me, because there is little time left before the night
falls and all work comes to an end. 5But while I am still here in the world, I am the light
of the world."
6Then he spit on the ground, made mud with the saliva, and smoothed the mud over
the blind man's eyes. 7He told him, "Go and wash in the pool of Siloam" (Siloam means
Sent). So the man went and washed, and came back seeing!
8His neighbors and others who knew him as a blind beggar asked each other, "Is this
the same man—that beggar?" 9Some said he was, and others said, "No, but he surely
looks like him!"
And the beggar kept saying, "I am the same man!"
10They asked, "Who healed you? What happened?"
11He told them, "The man they call Jesus made mud and smoothed it over my eyes
and told me, 'Go to the pool of Siloam and wash off the mud.' I went and washed, and
now I can see!"
12"Where is he now?" they asked.
"I don't know," he replied.

Religious Leaders Question the Blind Man (**149**)

13Then they took the man to the Pharisees. 14Now as it happened, Jesus had healed the
man on a Sabbath. 15The Pharisees asked the man all about it. So he told them, "He
smoothed the mud over my eyes, and when it was washed away, I could see!"
16Some of the Pharisees said, "This man Jesus is not from God, for he is working on
the Sabbath." Others said, "But how could an ordinary sinner do such miraculous signs?"
So there was a deep division of opinion among them.
17Then the Pharisees once again questioned the man who had been blind and demanded, "This man who opened your eyes—who do you say he is?"
The man replied, "I think he must be a prophet."
18The Jewish leaders wouldn't believe he had been blind, so they called in his parents.
19They asked them, "Is this your son? Was he born blind? If so, how can he see?"

9:2 Exod 20:5; Ezek 18:20; Luke 13:2; John 9:34
9:3 John 11:4
9:4 John 5:17; 11:9; 12:35
9:5 Isa 49:6; John 1:4-5, 9; 8:12; 12:46
9:6 Mark 8:23
9:7 2 Kgs 5:10; Isa 35:5
9::8 Acts 3:10
9:14 Luke 13:14; John 5:9
9:16 John 3:2; 7:43
9:17 Matt 21:11

8:59 In accordance with the law given in Leviticus 24:16, the religious leaders were ready to stone Jesus for claiming to be God. They well understood what Jesus was claiming, and because they didn't believe he was God, they charged him with blasphemy. It is ironic that *they* were really the blasphemers, cursing and attacking the very God they claimed to serve!

9:1ff In chapter 9, we see four different reactions to Jesus. The neighbors revealed surprise and skepticism; the Pharisees showed disbelief and prejudice; the parents believed but kept quiet for fear of excommunication; and the healed man showed consistent, growing faith.

9:2, 3 A common belief in Jewish culture was that calamity or suffering was the result of some great sin. But Christ used this man's suffering to teach about faith and to glorify God. We live in a fallen world where good behavior is not always rewarded and bad behavior not always punished. Therefore, innocent people sometimes suffer. If God took suffering away whenever we asked, we would follow him for comfort and convenience, not out of love and devotion. Regardless of the reasons for our suffering, Jesus has the power to help us deal with it. When you suffer from a disease, tragedy, or disability, try not to ask, Why did this happen to me? or What did I do wrong? Instead, ask God to give you strength for the trial and a clearer perspective on what is happening.

9:7 The pool of Siloam was built by Hezekiah. His workers constructed an underground tunnel from a spring outside the city walls to carry water into the city. Thus, the people could always get water without fear of being attacked. This was especially important during times of siege (see 2 Kings 20:20; 2 Chronicles 32:30).

9:13-17 While the Pharisees conducted investigations and debated about Jesus, people were being healed and lives were being changed. The Pharisees' skepticism was based not on insufficient evidence, but on jealousy of Jesus' popularity and his influence on the people.

9:14-16 The Jewish Sabbath, Saturday, was the weekly holy day of rest. The Pharisees had made a long list of specific dos and don'ts regarding the Sabbath. Kneading the clay and healing the man were considered work and therefore were forbidden. Jesus may have purposely made the clay in order to emphasize his teaching about the Sabbath—that it is right to care for others' needs even if it involves working on a day of rest.

20 His parents replied, "We know this is our son and that he was born blind, 21 but
we don't know how he can see or who healed him. He is old enough to speak for
himself. Ask him." 22 They said this because they were afraid of the Jewish leaders,
who had announced that anyone saying Jesus was the Messiah would be expelled
from the synagogue. 23 That's why they said, "He is old enough to speak for himself.
Ask him."
24 So for the second time they called in the man who had been blind and told him,
"Give glory to God by telling the truth,* because we know Jesus is a sinner."
25 "I don't know whether he is a sinner," the man replied. "But I know this: I was blind,
and now I can see!"
26 "But what did he do?" they asked. "How did he heal you?"
27 "Look!" the man exclaimed. "I told you once. Didn't you listen? Why do you want
to hear it again? Do you want to become his disciples, too?"
28 Then they cursed him and said, "You are his disciple, but we are disciples of Moses.
29 We know God spoke to Moses, but as for this man, we don't know anything about
him."
30 "Why, that's very strange!" the man replied. "He healed my eyes, and yet you don't
know anything about him! 31 Well, God doesn't listen to sinners, but he is ready to hear
those who worship him and do his will. 32 Never since the world began has anyone been
able to open the eyes of someone born blind. 33 If this man were not from God, he
couldn't do it."
34 "You were born in sin!" they answered. "Are you trying to teach us?" And they
threw him out of the synagogue.

Jesus Teaches about Spiritual Blindness (**150**)

35 When Jesus heard what had happened, he found the man and said, "Do you believe in
the Son of Man*?"
36 The man answered, "Who is he, sir, because I would like to."
37 "You have seen him," Jesus said, "and he is speaking to you!"
38 "Yes, Lord," the man said, "I believe!" And he worshiped Jesus.
39 Then Jesus told him, "I have come to judge the world. I have come to give sight to
the blind and to show those who think they see that they are blind."
40 The Pharisees who were standing there heard him and asked, "Are you saying we
are blind?"
41 "If you were blind, you wouldn't be guilty," Jesus replied. "But you remain guilty
because you claim you can see.

9:22 Luke 6:22; John 7:13; 12:42; 16:2; 19:38; Acts 5:13
9:24 Josh 7:19
9:28 John 5:45
9:29 John 8:14
9:31 Job 27:8-9; Pss 34:15; 66:18; 145:19; Prov 15:29; Isa 1:15; Jer 11:11; 14:12; Mic 3:4; Zech 7:13
9:33 John 3:2
9:34 John 9:2
9:37 John 4:26
9:39 Luke 4:18
9:40 Rom 2:19
9:41 John 15:22

9:24 Or *Give glory to God, not to Jesus;* Greek reads *Give glory to God.* **9:35** Some manuscripts read *the Son of God.*

9:25 By now the man who had been blind had heard the same questions over and over. He did not know how or why he was healed, but he knew that his life had been miraculously changed, and he was not afraid to tell the truth. You don't need to know all the answers in order to share Christ with others. It is important to tell them how he has changed your life. Then trust that God will use your words to help others believe in him, too.

9:28, 34 The man's new faith was severely tested by some of the authorities. He was cursed and evicted from the synagogue. Persecution may come when you follow Jesus. You may lose friends; you may even lose your life. But no one can ever take away the eternal life that Jesus gives you.

9:38 The longer this man experienced his new life through Christ, the more confident he became in the one who had healed him. He gained not only physical sight but also spiritual sight as he recognized Jesus first as a prophet (9:17), then as his Lord. When you turn to Christ, you begin to see him differently. The longer you walk with him, the better you will understand who he is. Peter tells us to "grow in the special favor and knowledge of our Lord and Savior Jesus Christ" (2 Peter 3:18). If you want to know more about Jesus, keep walking with him.

9:40, 41 The Pharisees were shocked that Jesus thought they were spiritually blind. Jesus countered by saying that it was only blindness (stubbornness and stupidity) that could excuse their behavior. To those who remained open and recognized how sin had truly blinded them from knowing the truth, he gave spiritual understanding and insight. But he rejected those who had become complacent, self-satisfied, and blind.

Jesus Is the Good Shepherd (**151**)

10 "I assure you, anyone who sneaks over the wall of a sheepfold, rather than going
through the gate, must surely be a thief and a robber! 2 For a shepherd enters
through the gate. 3 The gatekeeper opens the gate for him, and the sheep hear his voice
and come to him. He calls his own sheep by name and leads them out. 4 After he has
gathered his own flock, he walks ahead of them, and they follow him because they
recognize his voice. 5 They won't follow a stranger; they will run from him because they
don't recognize his voice."

6 Those who heard Jesus use this illustration didn't understand what he meant, 7 so he
explained it to them. "I assure you, I am the gate for the sheep," he said. 8 "All others
who came before me were thieves and robbers. But the true sheep did not listen to them.
9 Yes, I am the gate. Those who come in through me will be saved. Wherever they go,
they will find green pastures. 10 The thief's purpose is to steal and kill and destroy. My
purpose is to give life in all its fullness.

11 "I am the good shepherd. The good shepherd lays down his life for the sheep. 12 A hired
hand will run when he sees a wolf coming. He will leave the sheep because they aren't his
and he isn't their shepherd. And so the wolf attacks them and scatters the flock. 13 The hired
hand runs away because he is merely hired and has no real concern for the sheep.

14 "I am the good shepherd; I know my own sheep, and they know me, 15 just as my
Father knows me and I know the Father. And I lay down my life for the sheep. 16 I have
other sheep, too, that are not in this sheepfold. I must bring them also, and they will listen
to my voice; and there will be one flock with one shepherd.

17 "The Father loves me because I lay down my life that I may have it back again. 18 No
one can take my life from me. I lay down my life voluntarily. For I have the right to lay
it down when I want to and also the power to take it again. For my Father has given me
this command."

19 When he said these things, the people* were again divided in their opinions about
him. 20 Some of them said, "He has a demon, or he's crazy. Why listen to a man like that?"

10:19 Greek *Jewish people.*

10:2 Acts 20:28
10:4 Ps 80:2; John 10:27
10:6 John 16:25
10:7 John 14:6
10:8 Jer 23:1-2; Ezek 34:2-3
10:9 Ps 118:20; John 14:6
10:10 John 5:40; Acts 20:29; 2 Pet 2:1
10:11 Isa 40:11; Ezek 34:11-16, 23; Heb 13:20; 1 Pet 2:25; 1 Jn 3:16; Rev 7:17
10:14 2 Tim 2:19
10:15 Matt 11:27
10:16 Isa 56:8; Ezek 37:24; John 11:52; Eph 2:14-18
10:17-18 Phil 2:8-9; Heb 5:8; 7:16

10:1 At night, sheep were often gathered into a sheepfold to protect them from thieves, weather, or wild animals. The sheepfolds were caves, sheds, or open areas surrounded by walls made of stones or branches. The shepherd often slept in the fold to protect the sheep. Just as a shepherd cares for his sheep, Jesus, the good shepherd, cares for his flock (those who follow him). The prophet Ezekiel, in predicting the coming of the Messiah, called him a shepherd (Ezekiel 34:23).

MINISTRY EAST OF THE JORDAN
Jesus had been in Jerusalem for the Festival of Shelters (7:2); then he preached in various towns, probably in Judea, before returning to Jerusalem for Hanukkah. He again angered the religious leaders, who tried to arrest him, but he left the city and went to the region east of the Jordan to preach.

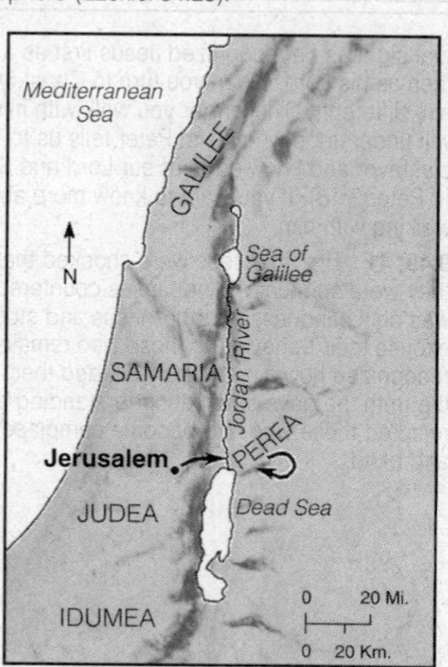

10:7 In the sheepfold, the shepherd functioned as a gate, letting the sheep in and protecting them. Jesus is the gate to God's salvation for us. He offers access to safety and security. Christ is our protector. Some people resent that Jesus is the gate, the only way of access to God. But Jesus is God's Son—why should we seek any other way or want to customize a different approach to God? (See also the notes on 14:6.)

10:10 In contrast to the thief who takes life, Jesus gives life. The life he gives right now is abundantly rich and full. It is eternal, yet it begins immediately. Life in Christ is lived on a higher plane because of his overflowing forgiveness, love, and guidance. Have you taken Christ's offer of life?

10:11, 12 A hired hand tends the sheep for money, while the shepherd does it out of love. The shepherd owns the sheep and is committed to them. Jesus is not merely doing a job; he is committed to love us and even lay down his life for us. False teachers and false prophets do not have this commitment.

10:16 The "other sheep" were non-Jews. Jesus came to save Gentiles as well as Jews. This is an insight into his worldwide mission—to die for the sins of the world. People tend to want to restrict God's blessings to their own group, but Jesus refuses to be limited by the fences we build.

10:17, 18 Jesus' death and resurrection, as part of God's plan for the salvation of the world, were under God's full control. No one could kill Jesus without his consent.

10:19, 20 If Jesus had been merely a man, his claims to be God would have proven him insane. But his miracles proved his words true—he really was God. The Jewish leaders could not see beyond their own prejudices, and they looked at Jesus only from a human perspective—Jesus confined in a human box. But Jesus was not limited by their restricted vision.

21 Others said, "This doesn't sound like a man possessed by a demon! Can a demon open
the eyes of the blind?"

Religious Leaders Surround Jesus at the Temple (**152**)

22 It was now winter, and Jesus was in Jerusalem at the time of Hanukkah.* 23 He was at
the Temple, walking through the section known as Solomon's Colonnade. 24 The Jewish
leaders surrounded him and asked, "How long are you going to keep us in suspense? If
you are the Messiah, tell us plainly."
25 Jesus replied, "I have already told you, and you don't believe me. The proof is what
I do in the name of my Father. 26 But you don't believe me because you are not part of
my flock. 27 My sheep recognize my voice; I know them, and they follow me. 28 I give
them eternal life, and they will never perish. No one will snatch them away from me,
29 for my Father has given them to me, and he is more powerful than anyone else. So no
one can take them from me. 30 The Father and I are one."
31 Once again the Jewish leaders picked up stones to kill him. 32 Jesus said, "At my
Father's direction I have done many things to help the people. For which one of these
good deeds are you killing me?"

10:23 Acts 3:11; 5:12
10:24 Luke 22:67
10:25 John 5:36; 10:38; 14:11
10:26 John 8:47
10:28 John 6:37, 39; 17:12
10:29 John 14:28 17:2, 6, 24
10:30 John 1:1; 10:38; 14:8-11; 17:21-24

10:22 Or *the Festival of Dedication.*

THE NAMES OF JESUS
In different settings, Jesus gave himself names that pointed to special roles he was ready to fulfill for people. Some of these refer back to the Old Testament promises of the Messiah. Others were ways to help people understand him.

Reference	*Name*	*Significance*
6:27	Son of Man	Jesus' favorite reference to himself. It emphasized his humanity—but the way he used it, it was a claim to divinity.
6:35	Bread of life	Refers to his life-giving role—that he is the only source of eternal life.
8:12	Light of the world	Light is a symbol of spiritual truth. Jesus is the universal answer for people's need of spiritual truth.
10:7	Gate for the sheep	Jesus is the only way into God's Kingdom.
10:11	Good shepherd	Jesus appropriated the prophetic images of the Messiah pictured in the Old Testament. This is a claim to divinity, focusing on Jesus' love and guidance.
11:25	The resurrection and the life	Not only is Jesus the source of life; he is the power over death.
14:6	The way, the truth, and the life	Jesus is the method, the message, and the meaning for all people. With this title, he summarized his purpose in coming to earth.
15:1	The true vine	This title has an important second part, "you are the branches." As in so many of his other names, Jesus reminds us that just as branches gain life from the vine and cannot live apart from it, so we are completely dependent on Christ for spiritual life.

10:22, 23 Hanukkah commemorated the cleansing of the Temple under Judas Maccabeus in 164 B.C. after Antiochus Epiphanes had defiled it by sacrificing a pig on the altar of burnt offering. The festival was celebrated toward the end of December.

10:23 Solomon's Colonnade was a roofed walkway supported by large stone columns, just inside the walls of the Temple courtyard.

10:24 Many people asking for proof do so for the wrong reasons. Most of these questioners didn't want to follow Jesus in the way that he wanted to lead them. They hoped that Jesus would declare himself Messiah for perverted reasons. They, along with the disciples and everyone else in the Jewish nation, would have been delighted to have him drive out the Romans. Many of them didn't think he was going to do that, however. These doubters hoped he would identify himself so they could accuse him of telling lies (as the Pharisees did in 8:13).

10:28, 29 Just as a shepherd protects his sheep, Jesus protects his people from eternal harm. While believers can expect to suffer on earth, Satan cannot harm their souls or take away their eternal life with God. There are many reasons to be afraid here on earth because this is the Devil's domain (1 Peter 5:8). But if you choose to follow Jesus, he will give you everlasting safety.

10:30 This is the clearest statement of Jesus' divinity he ever made. Jesus and his Father are not the same person, but they are one in essence and nature. Thus, Jesus is not merely a good teacher—he is God. His claim to be God was unmistakable. The religious leaders wanted to kill him because their laws said that anyone claiming to be God should die. Nothing could persuade them that Jesus' claim was true.

10:31 The Jewish leaders attempted to carry out the directive found in Leviticus 24:16 regarding those who blaspheme (claim to be God). They intended to stone Jesus.

33 They replied, "Not for any good work, but for blasphemy, because you, a mere man,
have made yourself God."
34 Jesus replied, "It is written in your own law that God said to certain leaders of the
people, 'I say, you are gods!'* 35 And you know that the Scriptures cannot be altered. So
if those people, who received God's message, were called 'gods,' 36 why do you call it
blasphemy when the Holy One who was sent into the world by the Father says, 'I am the
Son of God'? 37 Don't believe me unless I carry out my Father's work. 38 But if I do his
work, believe in what I have done, even if you don't believe me. Then you will realize
that the Father is in me, and I am in the Father."
39 Once again they tried to arrest him, but he got away and left them. 40 He went beyond
the Jordan River to stay near the place where John was first baptizing. 41 And many
followed him. "John didn't do miracles," they remarked to one another, "but all his
predictions about this man have come true." 42 And many believed in him there.

10:33 Lev 24:16; Matt 26:63-66; John 1:1, 18; 5:18; 20:28; Rom 9:5; Phil 2:6; Titus 2:13; 2 Pet 1:1; 1 Jn 5:20
10:34 †Ps 82:6
10:36 John 5:17-20
10:42 John 2:23; 7:31; 8:30; 11:45; 12:11, 42

3. Jesus encounters crucial events in Jerusalem

Lazarus Becomes Ill and Dies **(165)**

11 A man named Lazarus was sick. He lived in Bethany with his sisters, Mary and
Martha. 2 This is the Mary who poured the expensive perfume on the Lord's feet
and wiped them with her hair.* Her brother, Lazarus, was sick. 3 So the two sisters sent
a message to Jesus telling him, "Lord, the one you love is very sick."
4 But when Jesus heard about it he said, "Lazarus's sickness will not end in death. No,
it is for the glory of God. I, the Son of God, will receive glory from this." 5 Although
Jesus loved Martha, Mary, and Lazarus, 6 he stayed where he was for the next two days
and did not go to them. 7 Finally after two days, he said to his disciples, "Let's go to Judea
again."
8 But his disciples objected. "Teacher," they said, "only a few days ago the Jewish
leaders in Judea were trying to kill you. Are you going there again?"
9 Jesus replied, "There are twelve hours of daylight every day. As long as it is light,
people can walk safely. They can see because they have the light of this world. 10 Only
at night is there danger of stumbling because there is no light." 11 Then he said, "Our
friend Lazarus has fallen asleep, but now I will go and wake him up."

10:34 Ps 82:6. **11:2** This incident is recorded in chapter 12.

11:1 Matt 21:17; Luke 10:38
11:2 John 12:3
11:4 John 9:3
11:8 John 8:59; 10:31
11:9 John 9:4
11:10 John 12:35
11:11 Dan 12:2; Matt 9:24; 27:52; Mark 5:39; Luke 8:52; Acts 7:60; 1 Cor 11:30

10:34-36 Jesus referred to Psalm 82:6, where the Israelite rulers and judges are called "gods" (see also Exodus 4:16; 7:1). If God called the Israelite leaders gods because they were agents of God's revelation and will, how could it be blasphemy for Jesus to call himself the Son of God? Jesus was rebuking the religious leaders, because he is the Son of God in a unique, unparalleled relationship of oneness with the Father.

10:35 "The Scriptures cannot be altered" is a clear statement of the truth of the Bible. If we accept Christ as Lord, we also must accept his testimony to the Bible as God's Word.

11:1 The village of Bethany was located about two miles east of Jerusalem on the road to Jericho. It was near enough to Jerusalem for Jesus and the disciples to be in danger, but far enough away so as not to attract attention prematurely.

11:3 As their brother grew very sick, Mary and Martha turned to Jesus for help. They believed in his ability to help because they had seen his miracles. We, too, know of Jesus' miracles, both from Scripture and through changed lives we have seen. When we need extraordinary help, Jesus offers extraordinary resources. We should not hesitate to ask him for assistance.

11:4 Any trial a believer faces can ultimately bring glory to God because God can bring good out of any bad situation (Genesis 50:20; Romans 8:28). When trouble comes, do you grumble, complain, and blame God, or do you see your problems as opportunities to honor him?

11:5-7 Jesus loved this family and often stayed with them. He knew their pain but did not respond immediately. His delay had a specific purpose. God's timing, especially his delays, may make us think he is not answering or is not answering the way we want. But he will meet all our needs according to his perfect schedule and purpose (Philippians 4:19). Patiently await his timing.

11:9, 10 "Daylight" symbolizes the knowledge of God's will, and "night," the absence of this knowledge. When we move ahead in darkness, we will be likely to stumble.

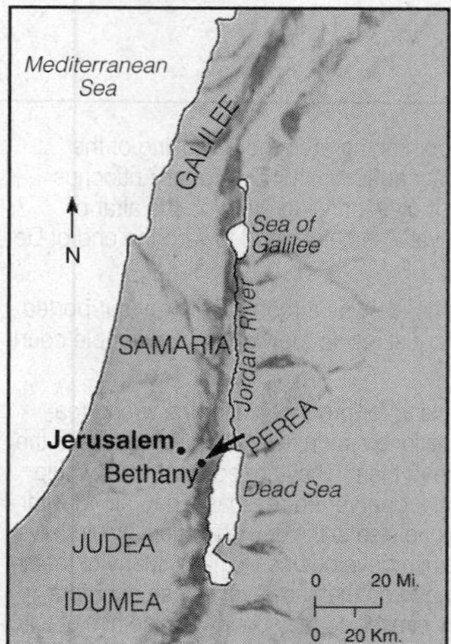

JESUS RAISES LAZARUS
Jesus had been preaching in the villages beyond the Jordan, probably in Perea, when he received the news of Lazarus's sickness. Jesus did not leave immediately, but waited two days before returning to Judea. He knew Lazarus would be dead when he arrived in Bethany, but he was going to do a great miracle.

12 The disciples said, "Lord, if he is sleeping, that means he is getting better!" 13 They
thought Jesus meant Lazarus was having a good night's rest, but Jesus meant Lazarus
had died.

14 Then he told them plainly, "Lazarus is dead. 15 And for your sake, I am glad I wasn't
there, because this will give you another opportunity to believe in me. Come, let's go see
him."

16 Thomas, nicknamed the Twin,* said to his fellow disciples, "Let's go, too—and die
with Jesus."

Jesus Comforts Mary and Martha (**166**)

17 When Jesus arrived at Bethany, he was told that Lazarus had already been in his grave
for four days. 18 Bethany was only a few miles* down the road from Jerusalem, 19 and
many of the people* had come to pay their respects and console Martha and Mary on
their loss. 20 When Martha got word that Jesus was coming, she went to meet him. But
Mary stayed at home. 21 Martha said to Jesus, "Lord, if you had been here, my brother
would not have died. 22 But even now I know that God will give you whatever you ask."

23 Jesus told her, "Your brother will rise again."

24 "Yes," Martha said, "when everyone else rises, on resurrection day."

25 Jesus told her, "I am the resurrection and the life.* Those who believe in me, even
though they die like everyone else, will live again. 26 They are given eternal life for
believing in me and will never perish. Do you believe this, Martha?"

11:16 Matt 10:3; John 14:5; 20:24-28; 21:2; Acts 1:3
11:20 Luke 10:38-42
11:22 John 16:30
11:23-24 Dan 12:2; John 5:28-29; Acts 24:15; Phil 3:21; 1 Thes 4:14
11:25 John 1:4; 3:36; 5:21; 6:39-40; 14:6; Col 1:18; 3:4; 1 Jn 1:1-2; 5:10-11; Rev 1:17-18
11:26 John 8:51

11:16 Greek *the one who was called Didymus.* **11:18** Greek *was about 15 stadia* [about 2.8 kilometers]. **11:19** Greek *Jewish people;* also 11:31, 33, 36, 45, 54. **11:25** Some manuscripts do not include *and the life.*

GREAT EXPECTATIONS
Wherever he went, Jesus exceeded people's expectations.

What was expected	*What Jesus did*	*Reference*
A man looked for healing.	Jesus also forgave his sins.	Mark 2:1–12
The disciples were expecting an ordinary day of fishing.	They found the Savior.	Luke 5:1–11
A widow was resigned to bury her dead son.	Jesus restored her son to life.	Luke 7:11–17
The religious leaders wanted a miracle.	Jesus offered them the Creator of miracles.	Matthew 12:38–45
A woman who wanted to be healed touched Jesus.	Jesus helped her see it was her faith that had healed her.	Mark 5:25–34
The disciples thought the crowd should be sent home because there was no food.	Jesus used a small meal to feed thousands, and there were leftovers!	John 6:1–15
The crowds looked for a political leader to set up a new kingdom to overthrow Rome's control.	Jesus offered them an eternal, spiritual kingdom to overthrow sin's control.	A theme throughout the Gospels
The disciples wanted to eat the Passover meal with Jesus, their Master.	Jesus washed their feet, showing that he was also their servant.	John 13:1–20
The religious leaders wanted Jesus killed and got their wish.	But Jesus rose from the dead!	John 11:53; 19:30; 20:1–29

11:14, 15 If Jesus had been with Lazarus during the final moments of Lazarus's sickness, he might have healed him rather than let him die. But Lazarus died so that Jesus' power over death could be shown to his disciples and others. The raising of Lazarus was an essential display of his power, and the resurrection from the dead is a crucial belief of the Christian faith. Jesus not only raised himself from the dead (10:18), but he has the power to raise others.

11:16 We often remember Thomas as "the doubter," because he doubted Jesus' resurrection. But here he demonstrated love and courage. The disciples knew the dangers of going with Jesus to Jerusalem, and they tried to talk him out of it. Thomas merely expressed what all of them felt. When their objections failed, they were willing to go and even die with Jesus. They may not have understood why Jesus would be killed, but they were loyal. There are unknown dangers in doing God's work. It is wise to consider the high cost of being Jesus' disciple.

11:25, 26 Jesus has power over life and death as well as power to forgive sins. This is because he is the Creator of life (see 14:6). He who *is* life can surely restore life. Whoever believes in Christ has a spiritual life that death cannot conquer or diminish in any way. When we realize his power and how wonderful his offer to us really is, how can we not commit our lives to him? To those of us who believe, what wonderful assurance and certainty we have: "I will live again, and you will, too" (14:19).

27 "Yes, Lord," she told him. "I have always believed you are the Messiah, the Son of God, the one who has come into the world from God." 28 Then she left him and returned to Mary. She called Mary aside from the mourners and told her, "The Teacher is here and wants to see you." 29 So Mary immediately went to him.

30 Now Jesus had stayed outside the village, at the place where Martha met him. 31 When the people who were at the house trying to console Mary saw her leave so hastily, they assumed she was going to Lazarus's grave to weep. So they followed her there. 32 When Mary arrived and saw Jesus, she fell down at his feet and said, "Lord, if you had been here, my brother would not have died."

33 When Jesus saw her weeping and saw the other people wailing with her, he was moved with indignation and was deeply troubled. 34 "Where have you put him?" he asked them.

They told him, "Lord, come and see." 35 Then Jesus wept. 36 The people who were standing nearby said, "See how much he loved him." 37 But some said, "This man healed a blind man. Why couldn't he keep Lazarus from dying?"

Jesus Raises Lazarus from the Dead (**167**)

38 And again Jesus was deeply troubled. Then they came to the grave. It was a cave with a stone rolled across its entrance. 39 "Roll the stone aside," Jesus told them.

But Martha, the dead man's sister, said, "Lord, by now the smell will be terrible because he has been dead for four days."

40 Jesus responded, "Didn't I tell you that you will see God's glory if you believe?" 41 So they rolled the stone aside. Then Jesus looked up to heaven and said, "Father, thank you for hearing me. 42 You always hear me, but I said it out loud for the sake of all these people standing here, so they will believe you sent me." 43 Then Jesus shouted, "Lazarus, come out!" 44 And Lazarus came out, bound in graveclothes, his face wrapped in a headcloth. Jesus told them, "Unwrap him and let him go!"

Religious Leaders Plot to Kill Jesus (**168**)

45 Many of the people who were with Mary believed in Jesus when they saw this happen. 46 But some went to the Pharisees and told them what Jesus had done. 47 Then the leading priests and Pharisees called the high council* together to discuss the situation. "What are we going to do?" they asked each other. "This man certainly performs many

11:27 Matt 16:16 John 6:14
11:35 Luke 19:41
11:37 John 9:6-7
11:39 John 11:17
11:41 Matt 11:25
11:42 John 12:30
11:43 Luke 7:14
11:47 Matt 26:3-5

11:47 Greek *the Sanhedrin.*

11:27 Martha is best known for being too busy to sit down and talk with Jesus (Luke 10:38-42). But here we see her as a woman of deep faith. Her statement of faith is exactly the response that Jesus wants from us.

TIME WITH THE DISCIPLES
Lazarus's return to life became the last straw for the religious leaders, who were bent on killing Jesus. So Jesus stopped his public ministry and took his disciples away from Jerusalem to Ephraim. From there they returned to Galilee for a while (see the map in Luke 17).

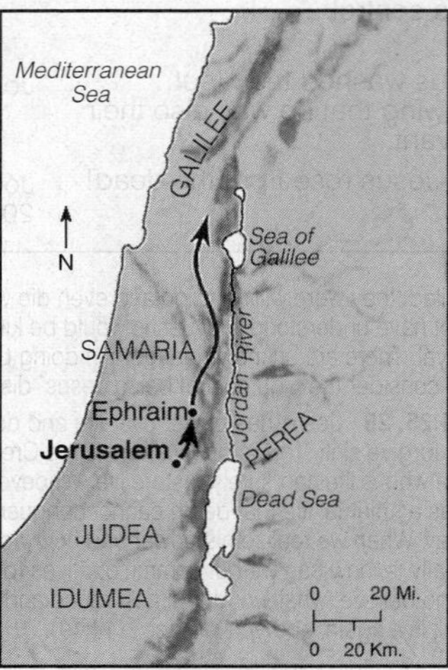

11:33-38 John stresses that we have a God who cares. This portrait contrasts with the Greek concept of God that was popular in that day—a God with no emotions and no messy involvement with humans. Here we see many of Jesus' emotions—compassion, indignation, sorrow, even frustration. He often expressed deep emotion, and we must never be afraid to reveal our true feelings to him. He understands them, for he experienced them. Be honest, and don't try to hide anything from your Savior. He cares.

11:35 When Jesus saw the weeping and wailing, he too wept openly. Perhaps he empathized with their grief, or perhaps he was troubled at their unbelief. In either case, Jesus showed that he cares enough for us to weep with us in our sorrow.

11:38 Tombs at this time were usually caves carved in the limestone rock of a hillside. A tomb was often large enough for people to walk inside. Several bodies would be placed in one tomb. After burial, a large stone was rolled across the entrance to the tomb.

11:44 Jesus raised others from the dead, including Jairus's daughter (Matthew 9:18-26; Mark 5:42, 43; Luke 8:40-56) and a widow's son (Luke 7:11-15).

11:45-53 Even when confronted point-blank with the power of Jesus' deity, some refused to believe. These eyewitnesses not only rejected Jesus; they plotted his murder. They were so hardened that they preferred to reject God's Son rather than admit that they were wrong. Beware of pride. If we allow it to grow, it can lead us into enormous sin.

miraculous signs. 48 If we leave him alone, the whole nation will follow him, and then
the Roman army will come and destroy both our Temple and our nation.”
11:49 Matt 26:3
49 And one of them, Caiaphas, who was high priest that year, said, “How can you be
11:50 John 18:13-14
so stupid? 50 Why should the whole nation be destroyed? Let this one man die for the
people.”
11:51 Exod 28:30 Num 27:21
51 This prophecy that Jesus should die for the entire nation came from Caiaphas in his
position as high priest. He didn’t think of it himself; he was inspired to say it. 52 It was a
11:52 Isa 49:6 John 10:16 1 Jn 2:2
prediction that Jesus’ death would be not for Israel only, but for the gathering together
of all the children of God scattered around the world.
11:53 Matt 26:4
53 So from that time on the Jewish leaders began to plot Jesus’ death. 54 As a result,
Jesus stopped his public ministry among the people and left Jerusalem. He went to a
place near the wilderness, to the village of Ephraim, and stayed there with his disciples.
11:55 Exod 12:13 2 Chr 30:17-19 Matt 26:1-2 Mark 14:1
55 It was now almost time for the celebration of Passover, and many people from the
country arrived in Jerusalem several days early so they could go through the cleansing
ceremony before the Passover began. 56 They wanted to see Jesus, and as they talked in
the Temple, they asked each other, “What do you think? Will he come for the Passover?”
57 Meanwhile, the leading priests and Pharisees had publicly announced that anyone
seeing Jesus must report him immediately so they could arrest him.

A Woman Anoints Jesus with Perfume (**182**/Matthew 26:6-13; Mark 14:3-9)

12:1 John 11:1
12 Six days before the Passover ceremonies began, Jesus arrived in Bethany, the home
of Lazarus—the man he had raised from the dead. 2 A dinner was prepared in Jesus’
12:2 Luke 10:38-42
honor. Martha served, and Lazarus sat at the table with him. 3 Then Mary took a twelve-
12:3 Luke 7:37-38
ounce jar* of expensive perfume made from essence of nard, and she anointed Jesus’ feet
with it and wiped his feet with her hair. And the house was filled with fragrance.
12:4 John 6:71
4 But Judas Iscariot, one of his disciples—the one who would betray him—said,
5 “That perfume was worth a small fortune.* It should have been sold and the money
12:6 John 13:29
given to the poor.” 6 Not that he cared for the poor—he was a thief who was in charge of
the disciples’ funds, and he often took some for his own use.
12:7 John 19:40
7 Jesus replied, “Leave her alone. She did it in preparation for my burial. 8 You will
12:8 Deut 15:11
always have the poor among you, but I will not be here with you much longer.”
9 When all the people* heard of Jesus’ arrival, they flocked to see him and also to see
12:10 Luke 16:31
Lazarus, the man Jesus had raised from the dead. 10 Then the leading priests decided to
kill Lazarus, too, 11 for it was because of him that many of the people had deserted them
and believed in Jesus.

12:3 Greek *took 1 litra* [327 grams]. **12:5** Greek *300 denarii.* A denarius was equivalent to a full day’s wage.
12:9 Greek *Jewish people;* also in 12:11.

11:48 The Jewish leaders knew that if they didn’t stop Jesus, the Romans would discipline them. Rome gave partial freedom to the Jews as long as they were quiet and obedient. Jesus’ miracles often caused a disturbance. The leaders feared that Rome’s displeasure would bring additional hardship to their nation.

11:51 John regarded Caiaphas’s statement as a prophecy. As high priest, Caiaphas was used by God to explain Jesus’ death even though Caiaphas didn’t realize what he was doing.

12:3 Essence of nard was a fragrant ointment imported from the mountains of India. Thus, it was very expensive. The amount Mary used was worth a year’s wages.

12:4-6 Judas often dipped into the disciples’ money bag for his own use. Quite likely, Jesus knew what Judas was doing (2:24, 25; 6:64), but never did or said anything about it. Similarly, when we choose the way of sin, God may not immediately do anything to stop us, but this does not mean he approves of our actions. What we deserve will come.

12:5, 6 Judas used a pious phrase to hide his true motives. But Jesus knew what was in his heart. Judas’s life had become a lie, and the Devil was entering into him (13:27). Satan is the father of lies, and a lying character opens the door to his influence. Jesus’ knowledge of us should make us want to keep our actions consistent with our words. Because we have nothing to fear with him, we should have nothing to hide.

12:7, 8 This act and Jesus’ response to it do not teach us to ignore the poor so we can spend money extravagantly for Christ. This was a unique act for a specific occasion—an anointing that anticipated Jesus’ burial and a public declaration of faith in him as Messiah. Jesus’ words should have taught Judas a valuable lesson about the worth of money. Unfortunately, Judas did not take heed; soon he would sell his Master’s life for 30 pieces of silver.

12:10, 11 The leading priests’ blindness and hardness of heart caused them to sink ever deeper into sin. They rejected the Messiah and planned to kill him, and then plotted to murder Lazarus as well. One sin leads to another. From the Jewish leaders’ point of view, they could accuse Jesus of blasphemy because he claimed equality with God. But Lazarus had done nothing of the kind. They wanted Lazarus dead simply because he was a living witness to Jesus’ power. This is a warning to us to avoid sin. Sin leads to more sin, a downward spiral that can be stopped only by repentance and the power of the Holy Spirit to change our behavior.

Jesus Rides into Jerusalem on a Young Donkey
(**183**/Matthew 21:1-11; Mark 11:1-11; Luke 19:28-44)

12 The next day, the news that Jesus was on the way to Jerusalem swept through the city. A huge crowd of Passover visitors 13 took palm branches and went down the road to meet him. They shouted,

"Praise God!*
Bless the one who comes in the name of the Lord!
Hail to the King of Israel!"*

14 Jesus found a young donkey and sat on it, fulfilling the prophecy that said:

15 "Don't be afraid, people of Israel.*
Look, your King is coming,
sitting on a donkey's colt."*

16 His disciples didn't realize at the time that this was a fulfillment of prophecy. But after Jesus entered into his glory, they remembered that these Scriptures had come true before their eyes.

17 Those in the crowd who had seen Jesus call Lazarus back to life were telling others all about it. 18 That was the main reason so many went out to meet him—because they had heard about this mighty miracle. 19 Then the Pharisees said to each other, "We've lost. Look, the whole world has gone after him!"

Jesus Explains Why He Must Die (**185**)

20 Some Greeks who had come to Jerusalem to attend the Passover 21 paid a visit to Philip, who was from Bethsaida in Galilee. They said, "Sir, we want to meet Jesus." 22 Philip told Andrew about it, and they went together to ask Jesus.

23 Jesus replied, "The time has come for the Son of Man to enter into his glory. 24 The truth is, a kernel of wheat must be planted in the soil. Unless it dies it will be alone—a single seed. But its death will produce many new kernels—a plentiful harvest of new lives. 25 Those who love their life in this world will lose it. Those who despise their life in this world will keep it for eternal life. 26 All those who want to be my disciples must

12:13 Lev 23:40 †Ps 118:25-26 Zeph 3:15
12:15 Isa 35:4 †Zech 9:9
12:16 John 2:22; 7:39
12:17 John 11:43-44
12:18 John 12:11; 19:37
12:21 John 1:43-44
12:23 John 13:32; 17:1
12:24 1 Cor 15:36
12:25 Matt 10:39 Luke 9:24; 17:33
12:26 John 14:3; 17:24

12:13a Greek *Hosanna,* an exclamation of praise that literally means "save now." **12:13b** Ps 118:25-26; Zeph 3:15. **12:15a** Greek *daughter of Zion.* **12:15b** Zech 9:9.

12:13 Jesus began his last week on earth by riding into Jerusalem on a donkey under a canopy of palm branches, with crowds hailing him as their king. To announce that he was indeed the Messiah, Jesus chose a *time* when all Israel would be gathered at Jerusalem, a *place* where huge crowds could see him, and a *way* of proclaiming his mission that was unmistakable. On Palm Sunday we celebrate Jesus' Triumphal Entry into Jerusalem.

12:13 The people who were praising God for giving them a king had the wrong idea about Jesus. They were sure he would be a national leader who would restore their nation to its former glory, and thus, they were deaf to the words of their prophets and blind to Jesus' real mission. When it became apparent that Jesus was not going to fulfill their hopes, many people turned against him.

12:16 After Jesus' resurrection, the disciples understood for the first time many of the prophecies that they had missed along the way. Jesus' words and actions took on new meaning and made more sense. In retrospect, the disciples saw how Jesus had led them into a deeper and better understanding of his truth. Stop now and think about the events in your life leading up to where you are now. How has God led you to this point? As you grow older, you will look back and see God's involvement more clearly than you do now.

12:18 The people flocked to Jesus because they had heard about his great miracle in raising Lazarus from the dead. Their adoration was short-lived and their commitment shallow, for in a few days they would do nothing to stop his crucifixion. Devotion based only on curiosity or popularity fades quickly.

12:20, 21 These Greeks probably were converts to the Jewish faith. They may have gone to Philip because, though he was a Jew, he had a Greek name.

12:23-25 This is a beautiful picture of the necessary sacrifice of Jesus. Unless a kernel of wheat is planted in the soil, it will not become a blade of wheat producing many more seeds. Jesus had to die to pay the penalty for our sin, but also to show his power over death. His resurrection proves he has eternal life. Because Jesus is God, Jesus can give this same eternal life to all who believe in him.

12:25 We must be so committed to living for Christ that we "despise" our lives by comparison. This does not mean that we long to die or that we are careless or destructive with the life God has given, but that we are willing to die if doing so will glorify Christ. We must disown the tyrannical rule of our own self-centeredness. By laying aside our striving for advantage, security, and pleasure, we can serve God lovingly and freely. Releasing control of our lives and transferring control to Christ bring eternal life and genuine joy.

12:26 Many believed that Jesus came for the Jews only. But when Jesus said, "All those who want to be my disciples must come and follow me," he was talking to these Greeks as well. No matter who the sincere seekers are, Jesus welcomes them. His message is for everyone. Don't allow social or racial differences to become barriers to the Good News. Take the Good News to all people.

come and follow me, because my servants must be where I am. And if they follow me,
the Father will honor them. [27]Now my soul is deeply troubled. Should I pray, 'Father,
save me from what lies ahead'? But that is the very reason why I came! [28]Father, bring
glory to your name."
Then a voice spoke from heaven, saying, "I have already brought it glory, and I will
do it again." [29]When the crowd heard the voice, some thought it was thunder, while
others declared an angel had spoken to him.
[30]Then Jesus told them, "The voice was for your benefit, not mine. [31]The time of
judgment for the world has come, when the prince of this world* will be cast out.

12:27 Ps 6:3; Matt 26:38; Mark 14:34
12:28 Matt 3:17; 17:5; Mark 1:11; 9:7; Luke 3:22; 9:35; 2 Pet 1:17-18
12:31 John 14:30; 16:11; Eph 2:2

12:31 *The prince of this world* is a name for Satan.

CAIAPHAS

Caiaphas was the leader of the religious group called the Sadducees. Educated and wealthy, they were politically influential in the nation. As the elite group, they were on fairly good terms with Rome. They hated Jesus because he endangered their secure life-styles and taught a message they could not accept. A kingdom in which leaders *served* had no appeal to them.

Caiaphas's usual policy was to remove any threats to his power by whatever means necessary. For Caiaphas, whether Jesus should die was not in question; the only point to be settled was *when* his death should take place. Not only did Jesus have to be captured and tried; the Jewish high council also needed Roman approval before they could carry out the death sentence. Caiaphas's plans were unexpectedly helped by Judas's offer to betray Christ.

Caiaphas did not realize that his schemes were actually part of a wonderful plan God was carrying out. Caiaphas's willingness to sacrifice another man to preserve his own security was decidedly selfish. By contrast, Jesus' willingness to die for us was a clear example of loving self-sacrifice. Caiaphas thought he had won the battle as Jesus hung on the cross, but he did not count on the Resurrection!

Caiaphas's mind was closed. He couldn't accept the Resurrection even when the evidence was overwhelming, and he attempted to silence those whose lives had been forever changed by the risen Christ (Matthew 28:12, 13). Caiaphas represents those people who will not believe because they think it will cost them too much to accept Jesus as Lord. They choose the fleeting power, prestige, and pleasures of this life instead of the eternal life God offers those who receive his Son. What is your choice?

Strength and accomplishment
- High priest for 18 years

Weaknesses and mistakes
- One of those most directly responsible for Jesus' death
- Used his office as a means to power and personal security
- Planned Jesus' capture, carried out his illegal trial, pressured Pilate to approve the Crucifixion, attempted to prevent the Resurrection, and later tried to cover up the fact of the Resurrection
- Kept up religious appearances while compromising with Rome
- Involved in the later persecution of Christians

Lessons from his life
- God uses even the twisted motives and actions of his enemies to bring about his will
- When we cover selfish motives with spiritual objectives and words, God still sees our intentions

Vital statistics
- Where: Jerusalem
- Occupation: High priest
- Relative: Father-in-law: Annas
- Contemporaries: Jesus, Pilate, Herod Antipas

Key verses
"And one of them, Caiaphas, who was high priest that year, said, 'How can you be so stupid? Why should the whole nation be destroyed? Let this one man die for the people' " (John 11:49, 50).

12:27 Jesus knew his crucifixion lay ahead, and because he was human, he dreaded it. He knew he would have to take the sins of the world on himself, and he knew this would separate him from his Father. He wanted to be delivered from this horrible death, but he knew that God sent him into the world to die for our sins, in our place. Jesus said no to his human desires in order to obey his Father and glorify him. Although we will never have to face such a difficult and awesome task, we are still called to obedience. Whatever the Father asks, we should do his will and bring glory to his name.

12:31 The prince of this world is Satan, an angel who rebelled against God. Satan is real, not symbolic, and is constantly working against God and those who obey him. Satan tempted Eve in the garden and persuaded her to sin; he tempted Jesus in the wilderness and did not persuade him to fall (Matthew 4:1-11). Satan has great power, but people can be delivered from his reign of spiritual darkness because of Christ's victory on the cross. Satan is powerful, but Jesus is much more powerful. Jesus' resurrection shattered Satan's deathly power (Colossians 1:13, 14). To overcome Satan we need faithful allegiance to God's Word, determination to stay away from sin, and the support of other believers.

32 And when I am lifted up on the cross,* I will draw everyone to myself." 33 He said
this to indicate how he was going to die.
34 "Die?" asked the crowd. "We understood from Scripture that the Messiah would
live forever. Why are you saying the Son of Man will die? Who is this Son of Man you
are talking about?"
35 Jesus replied, "My light will shine out for you just a little while longer. Walk in it
while you can, so you will not stumble when the darkness falls. If you walk in the
darkness, you cannot see where you are going. 36 Believe in the light while there is still
time; then you will become children of the light." After saying these things, Jesus went
away and was hidden from them.

12:32 John 3:14; 6:44
12:34 Pss 89:4, 36; 110:4; Isa 9:7; Ezek 37:25; Dan 7:14
12:35 John 8:12; 9:4; 12:46
12:36 Luke 16:8; John 8:59; Eph 5:8; 1 Thes 5:5

Most of the People Do Not Believe in Jesus (**186**)

37 But despite all the miraculous signs he had done, most of the people did not believe in
him. 38 This is exactly what Isaiah the prophet had predicted:

"Lord, who has believed our message?
 To whom will the Lord reveal his saving power?"*

39 But the people couldn't believe, for as Isaiah also said,

40 "The Lord has blinded their eyes
 and hardened their hearts—
so their eyes cannot see,
 and their hearts cannot understand,
and they cannot turn to me
 and let me heal them."*

41 Isaiah was referring to Jesus when he made this prediction, because he was given a
vision of the Messiah's glory. 42 Many people, including some of the Jewish leaders,
believed in him. But they wouldn't admit it to anyone because of their fear that the
Pharisees would expel them from the synagogue. 43 For they loved human praise more
than the praise of God.

12:38 †Isa 53:1; Rom 10:16
12:40 †Isa 6:10; Matt 13:14
12:41 Isa 6:1
12:42 John 7:13, 48; 9:22-23; 12:11
12:43 John 5:44

Jesus Summarizes His Message (**187**)

44 Jesus shouted to the crowds, "If you trust me, you are really trusting God who sent me.
45 For when you see me, you are seeing the one who sent me. 46 I have come as a light to

12:46 John 1:4; 3:19; 8:12; 9:5

12:32 Greek *lifted up from the earth.* **12:38** Isa 53:1. **12:40** Isa 6:10.

12:32-34 The crowd could not believe what Jesus was saying about the Messiah. They were waving palm branches for a victorious Messiah who would set up a political, earthly kingdom that would never end. From their reading of certain Scriptures, they thought the Messiah would never die (Psalms 89:35, 36; 110:4; Isaiah 9:7). Other passages, however, showed that he would die (Isaiah 53:5-9). Jesus' words did not mesh with their concept of the Messiah. First he had to suffer and die—then he would one day set up his eternal Kingdom. What kind of Messiah, or Savior, are you seeking? Beware of trying to force Jesus into your own mold—he won't fit.

12:35, 36 Jesus said he would be with them in person for only a short time, and they should take advantage of his presence while they had it. Like a light shining in a dark place, he would point out the way they should walk. If they walked in his light, they would become "children of the light," revealing the truth and pointing people to God. As Christians, we are to be Christ's light bearers, letting his light shine through us. How brightly is your light shining? Can others see Christ in your actions?

12:37, 38 Jesus had performed many miracles, but most people still didn't believe in him. Likewise, many today won't believe despite all God does. Don't be discouraged if your witness for Christ doesn't turn as many to him as you'd like. Your job is to continue as a faithful witness. You are responsible to reach out to others, but they are responsible for their own decisions.

12:39-41 People in Jesus' time, like those in the time of Isaiah, would not believe despite the evidence (12:37). As a result, God hardened their hearts. Does that mean God intentionally prevented these people from believing in him? No, he simply confirmed their own choices. After a lifetime of resisting God, they had become so set in their ways that they wouldn't even try to understand Jesus' message. For such people, it is virtually impossible to come to God—their hearts have been permanently hardened. Other instances of hardened hearts because of constant stubbornness are recorded in Exodus 9:12, Romans 1:24-28, and 2 Thessalonians 2:8-12.

12:42, 43 Along with those who refused to believe, many believed but refused to admit it. This is just as bad, and Jesus had strong words for such people (see Matthew 10:32, 33). People who will not take a stand for Jesus are afraid of rejection or ridicule. Many Jewish leaders wouldn't admit to faith in Jesus because they feared excommunication from the synagogue (which was their livelihood) and loss of their prestigious place in the community. But the praise of others is fickle and short-lived. We should be much more concerned about God's eternal acceptance than about the temporary approval of other people.

12:45 We often wonder what God is like. How can we know the Creator when he doesn't make himself visible? Jesus said plainly that those who see him see God, because he *is* God. If you want to know what God is like, study the person and words of Jesus Christ.

shine in this dark world, so that all who put their trust in me will no longer remain in the
12:47 John 3:17; 8:15 darkness. 47If anyone hears me and doesn't obey me, I am not his judge—for I have come
to save the world and not to judge it. 48But all who reject me and my message will be judged
at the day of judgment by the truth I have spoken. 49I don't speak on my own authority. The
Father who sent me gave me his own instructions as to what I should say. 50And I know his
instructions lead to eternal life; so I say whatever the Father tells me to say!"

C. DEATH AND RESURRECTION OF JESUS, THE SON OF GOD (13:1—21:25)

John begins his Gospel with eternity and ends with Jesus coming to earth again. He features Jesus teaching his disciples privately just before his arrest and death. We see, clearly, the deep love Jesus has for the believer and the peace that comes from faith. Knowing the love Jesus has for believers, we, too, should believe and allow Jesus to forgive our sins. Only then will we experience peace in a world filled with turmoil.

1. Jesus teaches his disciples

Jesus Washes the Disciples' Feet (**210**)

13:1 John 16:28; 17:1 **13** Before the Passover celebration, Jesus knew that his hour had come to leave this
world and return to his Father. He now showed the disciples the full extent of his
13:2 Luke 22:3 John 6:70-71 love.* 2It was time for supper, and the Devil had already enticed Judas, son of Simon
Iscariot, to carry out his plan to betray Jesus. 3Jesus knew that the Father had given him
13:4 Luke 12:37; 22:27 authority over everything and that he had come from God and would return to God. 4So
he got up from the table, took off his robe, wrapped a towel around his waist, 5and poured
13:5 Luke 7:44 John 12:3 water into a basin. Then he began to wash the disciples' feet and to wipe them with the
towel he had around him.
6When he came to Simon Peter, Peter said to him, "Lord, why are you going to wash
my feet?"
7Jesus replied, "You don't understand now why I am doing it; someday you will."
13:8 Ezek 36:25 1 Cor 6:11 Eph 5:26 Titus 3:5 8"No," Peter protested, "you will never wash my feet!"
Jesus replied, "But if I don't wash you, you won't belong to me."
9Simon Peter exclaimed, "Then wash my hands and head as well, Lord, not just my
feet!"
13:10 John 15:3 10Jesus replied, "A person who has bathed all over does not need to wash, except for
the feet,* to be entirely clean. And you are clean, but that isn't true of everyone here."

13:1 Or *He loved his disciples to the very end.* **13:10** Some manuscripts do not include *except for the feet.*

12:48 The purpose of Jesus' first mission on earth was not to judge people, but to show them the way to find salvation and eternal life. When he comes again, one of his main purposes will be to judge people for how they lived on earth. Christ's words that we would *not* accept and obey will condemn us. On the day of judgment, those who accepted Jesus and lived his way will be raised to eternal life (1 Corinthians 15:51-57; 1 Thessalonians 4:15-18; Revelation 21:1-7), and those who rejected Jesus and lived any way they pleased will face eternal punishment (Revelation 20:11-15). Decide now which side you'll be on, for the consequences of your decision last forever.

13:1 Jesus knew he would be betrayed by one of his disciples, denied by another, and deserted by all of them for a time. Still he "now showed the disciples the full extent of his love." God knows us completely, as Jesus knew his disciples (2:24, 25; 6:64). He knows the sins we have committed and the ones we will yet commit. Still, he loves us. How do you respond to that kind of love?

13:1ff Chapters 13–17 tell us what Jesus said to his disciples on the night before his death. These words were all spoken in one evening when, with only the disciples as his audience, he gave final instructions to prepare them for his death and resurrection, events that would change their lives forever.

13:1-3 For more information on Judas Iscariot, see his Profile in Mark 14.

13:1-17 Jesus was the model servant, and he showed his servant attitude to his disciples. Washing guests' feet was a job for a household servant to carry out when guests arrived. But Jesus wrapped a towel around his waist, as the lowliest slave would do, and washed and dried his disciples' feet. If even he, God in the flesh, is willing to serve, we his followers must also be servants, willing to serve in any way that glorifies God. Are you willing to follow Christ's example of serving? Whom can you serve today? There is a special blessing for those who not only agree that humble service is Christ's way, but who also follow through and do it (13:17).

13:6, 7 Imagine being Peter and watching Jesus wash the others' feet, all the while moving closer to you. Seeing his Master behave like a slave must have confused Peter. He still did not understand Jesus' teaching that to be a leader, a person must be a servant. This is not a comfortable passage for leaders who find it hard to serve those beneath them. How do you treat those who work under you (whether children, employees, or volunteers)?

[11]For Jesus knew who would betray him. That is what he meant when he said, "Not all of you are clean."

[12]After washing their feet, he put on his robe again and sat down and asked, "Do you understand what I was doing? [13]You call me 'Teacher' and 'Lord,' and you are right, because it is true. [14]And since I, the Lord and Teacher, have washed your feet, you ought to wash each other's feet. [15]I have given you an example to follow. Do as I have done to you. [16]How true it is that a servant is not greater than the master. Nor are messengers more important than the one who sends them. [17]You know these things—now do them! That is the path of blessing.

[18]"I am not saying these things to all of you; I know so well each one of you I chose. The Scriptures declare, 'The one who shares my food has turned against me,'* and this will soon come true. [19]I tell you this now, so that when it happens you will believe I am the Messiah. [20]Truly, anyone who welcomes my messenger is welcoming me, and anyone who welcomes me is welcoming the Father who sent me."

Jesus and the Disciples Share the Last Supper
(**211**/Matthew 26:20-30; Mark 14:17-26; Luke 22:14-30)

[21]Now Jesus was in great anguish of spirit, and he exclaimed, "The truth is, one of you will betray me!"

[22]The disciples looked at each other, wondering whom he could mean. [23]One of Jesus' disciples, the one Jesus loved, was sitting next to Jesus at the table.* [24]Simon Peter motioned to him to ask who would do this terrible thing. [25]Leaning toward Jesus, he asked, "Lord, who is it?"

[26]Jesus said, "It is the one to whom I give the bread dipped in the sauce." And when he had dipped it, he gave it to Judas, son of Simon Iscariot. [27]As soon as Judas had eaten the bread, Satan entered into him. Then Jesus told him, "Hurry. Do it now." [28]None of the others at the table knew what Jesus meant. [29]Since Judas was their treasurer, some thought Jesus was telling him to go and pay for the food or to give some money to the poor. [30]So Judas left at once, going out into the night.

Jesus Predicts Peter's Denial (**212**/Luke 22:31-38)

[31]As soon as Judas left the room, Jesus said, "The time has come for me, the Son of Man, to enter into my glory, and God will receive glory because of all that happens to me. [32]And God will bring* me into my glory very soon. [33]Dear children, how brief are these moments before I must go away and leave you! Then, though you search for me, you cannot come to me—just as I told the Jewish leaders. [34]So now I am giving you a new commandment: Love each other. Just as I have loved you, you should love each other. [35]Your love for one another will prove to the world that you are my disciples."

13:11 John 6:64, 70-71; 13:2
13:13 1 Cor 12:3
13:14 Luke 22:27; 1 Tim 5:10; 1 Pet 5:5
13:15 Phil 2:5-7; 1 Pet 5:3-5; 1 Jn 2:6; 3:16
13:17 Jas 1:25
13:18 †Ps 41:9
13:20 Matt 10:40; Luke 10:16
13:23 John 19:26
13:25 John 21:20
13:27 Luke 22:3; John 13:2
13:29 John 12:6
13:30 Luke 22:53
13:34 Lev 19:18; Eph 5:2; 1 Thes 4:9; 1 Pet 1:22; 1 Jn 2:8; 3:23; 4:10-11
13:35 1 Jn 3:14; 4:20

13:18 Ps 41:9. **13:23** Greek *was reclining on Jesus' bosom.* The "disciple whom Jesus loved" was probably John. **13:32** Some manuscripts read *And if God is glorified in him [the Son of Man], God will bring.*

13:12ff Jesus did not wash his disciples' feet just to get them to be nice to each other. His far greater goal was to extend his mission on earth after he was gone. These men were to move into the world serving God, serving each other, and serving all people to whom they took the message of salvation.

13:22 Judas was not the obvious betrayer. After all, he was the one the disciples trusted to keep the money (12:6; 13:29).

13:26 The honored guest at a meal was often singled out like this.

13:27 Satan's part in the betrayal of Jesus does not remove any of the responsibility from Judas. Disillusioned because Jesus was talking about dying rather than setting up his Kingdom, Judas may have been trying to force Jesus' hand and make him use his power to prove he was the Messiah. Or perhaps Judas, not understanding Jesus' mission, no longer believed Jesus was God's chosen one. Whatever Judas thought, Satan assumed that Jesus' death would end his mission and thwart God's plan. Like Judas, Satan did not know that Jesus' death was the most important part of God's plan all along.

13:27-38 John describes these few moments in clear detail. We can see that Jesus knew exactly what was going to happen. He knew about Judas and about Peter, but he did not change the situation, nor did he stop loving them. In the same way, Jesus knows exactly what you will do to hurt him. Yet he still loves you unconditionally and will forgive you whenever you ask him. Judas couldn't understand this, and his life ended tragically. Peter understood, and despite his shortcomings, his life ended triumphantly because he never let go of his faith in the one who loved him.

13:34 To love others was not a new commandment (see Leviticus 19:18), but to love others as much as Christ loved others was revolutionary. Now we are to love others based on Jesus' sacrificial love for us. Such love will not only bring unbelievers to Christ; it will also keep believers strong and united in a world hostile to God. Jesus was a living example of God's love, as we are to be living examples of Jesus' love.

13:34, 35 Jesus says that our Christlike love will show we are his disciples. Do people see petty bickering, jealousy, and division in your church? Or do they know you are Jesus' followers by your love for one another?

13:35 Love is more than simply warm feelings; it is an attitude that reveals itself in action. How can we love others as Jesus loves

13:36-38 Matt 26:33-35 Mark 14:29-31 Luke 22:33-34

13:36 John 21:18 2 Pet 1:14

14:2 Ps 90:1 John 2:16, 19-21

36 Simon Peter said, "Lord, where are you going?"
And Jesus replied, "You can't go with me now, but you will follow me later."
37 "But why can't I come now, Lord?" he asked. "I am ready to die for you."
38 Jesus answered, "Die for me? No, before the rooster crows tomorrow morning, you
will deny three times that you even know me.

Jesus Is the Way to the Father (**213**)

14 "Don't be troubled. You trust God, now trust in me. 2 There are many rooms in
my Father's home, and I am going to prepare a place for you. If this were not
so, I would tell you plainly. 3 When everything is ready, I will come and get you, so

---

JOHN

Being loved is the most powerful motivation in the world! Our ability to love is often shaped by our experience of love. We usually love others as we have been loved.

Some of the greatest statements about God's loving nature were written by a man who experienced God's love in a unique way. John, Jesus' disciple, expressed his relationship to the Son of God by calling himself "the disciple Jesus loved" (21:20). Although Jesus' love is clearly communicated in all the Gospels, in John's Gospel it is a central theme. Because his own experience of Jesus' love was so strong and personal, John was sensitive to those words and actions of Jesus that illustrated how the one who *is* love loved others.

Jesus knew John fully and loved him fully. He gave John and his brother James the nickname "Sons of Thunder," perhaps from an occasion when the brothers asked Jesus for permission to "order down fire from heaven" (Luke 9:54) on a village that had refused to welcome Jesus and the disciples. In John's Gospel and letters, we see the great God of love, while the thunder of God's justice bursts from the pages of Revelation.

Jesus confronts each of us as he confronted John. We cannot know the depth of Jesus' love unless we are willing to face the fact that he knows us completely. Otherwise we are fooled into believing he must love the people we pretend to be, not the sinners we actually are. John and all the disciples convince us that God is able and willing to accept us as we are. Being aware of God's love is a great motivator for change. His love is not given in exchange for our efforts; his love frees us to really live. Have you accepted that love?

Strengths and accomplishments
- Before following Jesus, was one of John the Baptist's disciples
- One of the 12 disciples and, with Peter and James, one of the inner three, closest to Jesus
- Wrote five New Testament books: the Gospel of John; 1, 2, and 3 John; and Revelation

Weaknesses and mistakes
- Along with James, shared a tendency to outbursts of selfishness and anger
- Asked for a special position in Jesus' Kingdom

Lessons from his life
- Those who realize how much they are loved are able to love much
- When God changes a life, he does not take away personality characteristics, but puts them to effective use in his service

Vital statistics
- Occupations: Fisherman, disciple
- Relatives: Father: Zebedee. Mother: Salome. Brother: James
- Contemporaries: Jesus, Pilate, Herod

Key verses
"Dear friends, I am not writing a new commandment, for it is an old one you have always had, right from the beginning. This commandment—to love one another—is the same message you heard before. Yet it is also new. This commandment is true in Christ and is true among you, because the darkness is disappearing and the true light is already shining" (1 John 2:7, 8).

John's story is told throughout the Gospels, Acts, and Revelation.

---

us? By helping when it's not convenient, by giving when it hurts, by devoting energy to others' welfare rather than our own, by absorbing hurts from others without complaining or fighting back. This kind of loving is hard to do. That is why people notice when you do it and know you are empowered by a supernatural source. The Bible has another beautiful description of love in 1 Corinthians 13.

13:37, 38 Peter proudly told Jesus that he was ready to die for him. But Jesus corrected him. He knew Peter would deny that he knew Jesus that very night to protect himself (18:15-18, 25-27). In our enthusiasm, it is easy to make promises, but God knows the extent of our commitment. Paul tells us not to think of ourselves more highly than we ought (Romans 12:3). Instead of bragging, demonstrate your commitment step by step as you grow in your knowledge of God's Word and in your faith.

14:1-3 Jesus' words show that the way to eternal life, though unseen, is secure—as secure as your trust in Jesus. He has already prepared the way to eternal life. The only issue that may still be unsettled is your willingness to believe.

14:2, 3 There are few verses in Scripture that describe eternal life, but these few verses are rich with promises. Here Jesus says, "I am going to prepare a place for you," and "I will come and get you." We can look forward to eternal life because Jesus has promised it to all who believe in him. Although the details of eternity are unknown, we need not fear because Jesus is preparing for us and will spend eternity with us.

that you will always be with me where I am. 4And you know where I am going and
how to get there."
5"No, we don't know, Lord," Thomas said. "We haven't any idea where you are going,
so how can we know the way?"
6Jesus told him, "I am the way, the truth, and the life. No one can come to the Father
except through me. 7If you had known who I am, then you would have known who my
Father is.* From now on you know him and have seen him!"
8Philip said, "Lord, show us the Father and we will be satisfied."
9Jesus replied, "Philip, don't you even yet know who I am, even after all the time I
have been with you? Anyone who has seen me has seen the Father! So why are you
asking to see him? 10Don't you believe that I am in the Father and the Father is in me?
The words I say are not my own, but my Father who lives in me does his work through
me. 11Just believe that I am in the Father and the Father is in me. Or at least believe
because of what you have seen me do.
12"The truth is, anyone who believes in me will do the same works I have done, and
even greater works, because I am going to be with the Father. 13You can ask for anything
in my name, and I will do it, because the work of the Son brings glory to the Father.
14Yes, ask anything in my name, and I will do it!

Jesus Promises the Holy Spirit **(214)**

15"If you love me, obey my commandments. 16And I will ask the Father, and he will
give you another Counselor,* who will never leave you. 17He is the Holy Spirit, who
leads into all truth. The world at large cannot receive him, because it isn't looking for
him and doesn't recognize him. But you do, because he lives with you now and later will
be in you. 18No, I will not abandon you as orphans—I will come to you. 19In just a little

14:6 John 1:4, 14, 16; 8:32; 10:10; 11:25 Rom 5:2 Eph 2:18 Heb 10:20 1 Jn 5:20

14:7 John 6:46; 8:19 1 Jn 2:13

14:9 John 1:14, 18; 12:45 2 Cor 4:4 Col 1:15 Heb 1:3

14:10 John 5:19; 10:38; 17:11, 21-24

14:16 John 14:26; 15:26

14:17 Rom 8:15-16 1 Jn 3:24

14:18 Rom 8:9-11 2 Cor 3:17-18

14:7 Some manuscripts read *If you really have known me, you will know who my Father is.* **14:16** Or *Comforter,* or *Encourager,* or *Advocate.* Greek *Paraclete;* also in 14:26.

14:5, 6 This is one of the most basic and important passages in Scripture. How can we know the way to God? Only through Jesus. Jesus is the way because he is both God and man. By uniting our lives with his, we are united with God. Trust Jesus to take you to the Father, and all the benefits of being God's child will be yours.

14:6 Jesus says he is the *only* way to God the Father. Some people may argue that this way is too narrow. In reality, it is wide enough for the whole world, if the world chooses to accept it. Instead of worrying about how limited it sounds to have only one way, we should be saying, "Thank you, God, for providing a sure way to get to you!"

14:6 As the *way,* Jesus is our path to the Father. As the *truth,* he is the reality of all God's promises. As the *life,* he joins his divine life to ours, both now and eternally.

14:9 Jesus is the visible, tangible image of the invisible God. He is the complete revelation of what God is like. Jesus explained to Philip, who wanted to see the Father, that to know Jesus is to know God. The search for God, for truth and reality, ends in Christ. (See also Colossians 1:15; Hebrews 1:1-4.)

14:12, 13 Jesus is not saying that his disciples would do greater works—after all, raising the dead is about as amazing as you can get. Rather, the disciples, working in the power of the Holy Spirit, would carry the Good News of God's Kingdom out of Palestine and into the whole world.

14:14 When Jesus says we can ask for anything, we must remember that our asking must be in his name—that is, according to God's character and will. God will not grant requests contrary to his nature or his will, and we cannot use his name as a magic formula to fulfill our selfish desires. If we are sincerely following God and seeking to do his will, then our requests will be in line with what he wants, and he will grant them. (See also 15:16; 16:23.)

14:15, 16 Jesus was soon going to leave the disciples, but he would remain with them. How could this be? The Counselor—the Spirit of God himself—would come after Jesus was gone to care for and guide the disciples. The regenerating power of the Spirit came on the disciples just before Jesus' ascension (20:22), and the Spirit was poured out on all the believers at Pentecost (Acts 2), shortly after Jesus ascended to heaven. The Holy Spirit is the very presence of God within us and all believers, helping us live as God wants and building Christ's church on earth. By faith we can appropriate the Spirit's power each day.

14:16 The word translated "Counselor" combines the ideas of comfort and counsel (see NLT text note). The Holy Spirit is a powerful person on our side, working for and with us.

14:17ff The following chapters teach these truths about the Holy Spirit: He will never leave us (14:16); the world at large cannot receive him (14:17); he lives with us and in us (14:17); he teaches us (14:26); he reminds us of Jesus' words (14:26; 15:26); he convinces us of sin, shows us God's righteousness, and announces God's judgment on evil (16:8); he guides into truth and gives insight into future events (16:13); he brings glory to Christ (16:14). The Holy Spirit has been active among people from the beginning of time, but after Pentecost (Acts 2) he came to live in all believers. Many people are unaware of the Holy Spirit's activities, but to those who hear Christ's words and understand the Spirit's power, the Spirit gives a whole new way to look at life.

14:18 When Jesus said, "I will come to you," he meant it. Although Jesus ascended to heaven, he sent the Holy Spirit to live in believers, and to have the Holy Spirit is to have Jesus himself.

14:19-21 Sometimes people wish they knew the future so they could prepare for it. God has chosen not to give us this knowledge. He alone knows what will happen, but he tells us all we need to know to *prepare* for the future. When we live by his standards, he will not leave us; he will come to us, he will be in us, and he will show himself to us. God knows what will happen, and because he will be with us through it all, we need not fear. We don't have to know the future to have faith in God; we have to have faith in God to be secure about the future.

14:20 John 10:38; 15:4-5; 16:16, 23; 17:21-24
14:21 John 15:10; 16:27; 1 Jn 2:5; 2 Jn 1:6
14:22 Luke 6:16; Acts 10:41
14:23 Ps 91:1; John 15:10; Eph 3:17; 1 Jn 4:16; 5:3; Rev 3:20; 21:3
14:24 John 7:16; 14:10
14:26 John 1:33; 15:26; 16:7; 20:22; 1 Jn 2:20, 27
14:27 John 16:33; 20:19; Phil 4:7; Col 3:15
14:29 John 13:19
14:30 John 12:31
14:31 John 10:18; 12:49
15:3 John 17:17; Eph 5:26

while the world will not see me again, but you will. For I will live again, and you will,
too. [20]When I am raised to life again, you will know that I am in my Father, and you are
in me, and I am in you. [21]Those who obey my commandments are the ones who love
me. And because they love me, my Father will love them, and I will love them. And I
will reveal myself to each one of them."

[22]Judas (not Judas Iscariot, but the other disciple with that name) said to him, "Lord,
why are you going to reveal yourself only to us and not to the world at large?"

[23]Jesus replied, "All those who love me will do what I say. My Father will love them,
and we will come to them and live with them. [24]Anyone who doesn't love me will not
do what I say. And remember, my words are not my own. This message is from the Father
who sent me. [25]I am telling you these things now while I am still with you. [26]But when
the Father sends the Counselor as my representative—and by the Counselor I mean the
Holy Spirit—he will teach you everything and will remind you of everything I myself
have told you.

[27]"I am leaving you with a gift—peace of mind and heart. And the peace I give isn't
like the peace the world gives. So don't be troubled or afraid. [28]Remember what I told
you: I am going away, but I will come back to you again. If you really love me, you will
be very happy for me, because now I can go to the Father, who is greater than I am. [29]I
have told you these things before they happen so that you will believe when they do
happen.

[30]"I don't have much more time to talk to you, because the prince of this world
approaches. He has no power over me, [31]but I will do what the Father requires of me, so
that the world will know that I love the Father. Come, let's be going.

Jesus Teaches about the Vine and the Branches (215)

15 "I am the true vine, and my Father is the gardener. [2]He cuts off every branch that
doesn't produce fruit, and he prunes the branches that do bear fruit so they will
produce even more. [3]You have already been pruned for greater fruitfulness by the

---

14:21 Jesus said that his followers show their love for him by obeying him. Love is more than lovely words; it is commitment and conduct. If you love Christ, then prove it by obeying what he says in his Word.

14:22, 23 Because the disciples were still expecting Jesus to establish an earthly kingdom and overthrow Rome, they found it hard to understand why he did not tell the world at large that he was the Messiah. Not everyone, however, could understand Jesus' message. Ever since Pentecost, the Good News of the Kingdom has been proclaimed in the whole world, and yet not everyone is receptive to it. Jesus saves the deepest revelations of himself for those who love and obey him.

14:26 Jesus promised the disciples that the Holy Spirit would help them remember what he had been teaching them. This promise ensures the validity of the New Testament. The disciples were eyewitnesses of Jesus' life and teachings, and the Holy Spirit helped them remember without taking away their individual perspectives. We can be confident that the Gospels are accurate records of what Jesus taught and did (see 1 Corinthians 2:10-14). The Holy Spirit can help us in the same way. As we study the Bible, we can trust him to plant truth in our mind, convince us of God's will, and remind us when we stray from it.

14:27 The end result of the Holy Spirit's work in our lives is deep and lasting peace. Unlike worldly peace, which is usually defined as the absence of conflict, this peace is confident assurance in any circumstance; with Christ's peace, we have no need to fear the present or the future. If your life is full of stress, allow the Holy Spirit to fill you with Christ's peace (see Philippians 4:6, 7 for more on experiencing God's peace).

14:27-29 Sin, fear, uncertainty, doubt, and numerous other forces are at war within us. The peace of God moves into our hearts and lives to restrain these hostile forces and offer comfort in place of conflict. Jesus says he will give us that peace if we are willing to accept it from him.

14:28 As God the Son, Jesus willingly submits to God the Father. On earth, Jesus also submitted to many of the physical limitations of his humanity (Philippians 2:6).

14:30, 31 Although Satan, the prince of this world, was unable to overpower Jesus (Matthew 4), he still had the arrogance to try. Satan's power exists only because God allows him to act. But because Jesus is sinless, Satan has no power over him. If we obey Jesus and align ourselves closely with God's purposes, Satan can have no power over us.

14:31 "Come, let's be going" suggests that chapters 15–17 may have been spoken en route to the Garden of Gethsemane. Another view is that Jesus was asking the disciples to get ready to leave the upper room, but they did not actually do so until 18:1.

15:1 The grapevine is a prolific plant; a single vine bears many grapes. In the Old Testament, grapes symbolized Israel's fruitfulness in doing God's work on the earth (Psalm 80:8; Isaiah 5:1-7; Ezekiel 19:10-14). In the Passover meal, the fruit of the vine symbolized God's goodness to his people.

15:1ff Christ is the vine, and God is the gardener who cares for the branches to make them fruitful. The branches are all those who claim to be followers of Christ. The fruitful branches are true believers who by their living union with Christ produce much fruit. But those who become unproductive—those who turn back from following Christ after making a superficial commitment—will be separated from the vine. Unproductive followers are as good as dead and will be cut off and tossed aside.

15:2, 3 Jesus makes a distinction between two kinds of pruning: (1) cutting off and (2) cutting back branches. Fruitful branches are cut back to promote growth. In other words, God must sometimes discipline us to strengthen our character and faith. But branches that don't bear fruit are cut off at the trunk not only because they are worthless but also because they often infect the rest of the tree. People who don't bear fruit for God or who try to block the efforts of God's followers will be cut off from his life-giving power.

message I have given you. 4 Remain in me, and I will remain in you. For a branch cannot
produce fruit if it is severed from the vine, and you cannot be fruitful apart from me.
5 "Yes, I am the vine; you are the branches. Those who remain in me, and I in them,
will produce much fruit. For apart from me you can do nothing. 6 Anyone who parts from
me is thrown away like a useless branch and withers. Such branches are gathered into a
pile to be burned. 7 But if you stay joined to me and my words remain in you, you may
ask any request you like, and it will be granted! 8 My true disciples produce much fruit.
This brings great glory to my Father.
9 "I have loved you even as the Father has loved me. Remain in my love. 10 When
you obey me, you remain in my love, just as I obey my Father and remain in his love.
11 I have told you this so that you will be filled with my joy. Yes, your joy will overflow!
12 I command you to love each other in the same way that I love you. 13 And here is how
to measure it—the greatest love is shown when people lay down their lives for their
friends. 14 You are my friends if you obey me. 15 I no longer call you servants, because
a master doesn't confide in his servants. Now you are my friends, since I have told you
everything the Father told me. 16 You didn't choose me. I chose you. I appointed you
to go and produce fruit that will last, so that the Father will give you whatever you ask
for, using my name. 17 I command you to love each other.

Jesus Warns about the World's Hatred (**216**)

18 "When the world hates you, remember it hated me before it hated you. 19 The world
would love you if you belonged to it, but you don't. I chose you to come out of the world,
and so it hates you. 20 Do you remember what I told you? 'A servant is not greater than
the master.' Since they persecuted me, naturally they will persecute you. And if they had
listened to me, they would listen to you! 21 The people of the world will hate you because
you belong to me, for they don't know God who sent me. 22 They would not be guilty if
I had not come and spoken to them. But now they have no excuse for their sin. 23 Anyone
who hates me hates my Father, too. 24 If I hadn't done such miraculous signs among them
that no one else could do, they would not be counted guilty. But as it is, they saw all that
I did and yet hated both of us—me and my Father. 25 This has fulfilled what the Scriptures
said: 'They hated me without cause.'*

15:25 Pss 35:19; 69:4.

15:4 John 6:56
15:6 Matt 3:10; 7:19; 13:42
15:8 Matt 5:16
15:9 John 3:35
15:10 John 14:15
15:11 John 17:13; 1 Jn 1:4
15:12 John 13:34
15:13 John 10:11; Rom 5:6-8
15:16 Rom 1:13; Phil 1:22
15:18 John 7:7; 1 Jn 3:13
15:19 John 17:14; 1 Jn 4:5
15:21 Matt 5:11; 1 Pet 4:14
15:22 John 9:41
15:24 John 5:36; 9:41
15:25 †Pss 35:19; 69:4

15:5 "Fruit" is not limited to soul winning. In this chapter, answered prayer, joy, and love are mentioned as fruit (15:7, 11, 12). Galatians 5:22-24 and 2 Peter 1:5-8 describe additional fruit: qualities of Christian character.

15:5, 6 Remaining in Christ means (1) believing that he is God's Son (1 John 4:15), (2) receiving him as Savior and Lord (John 1:12), (3) doing what God says (1 John 3:24), (4) continuing to believe the Good News (1 John 2:24), and (5) relating in love to the community of believers, Christ's body (John 15:12).

15:5-8 Many people try to be good, honest people who do what is right. But Jesus says that the only way to live a truly good life is to stay close to him, like a branch attached to the vine. Apart from Christ our efforts are unfruitful. Are you receiving the nourishment and life offered by Christ, the vine? If not, you are missing a special gift he has for you.

15:8 When a vine produces "much fruit," God is glorified, for daily he sent the sunshine and rain to make the crops grow, and constantly he nurtured each tiny plant and prepared it to blossom. What a moment of glory for the Lord of the harvest when the harvest is brought into the barns, mature and ready for use! He made it all happen! This farming analogy shows how God is glorified when people come into a right relationship with him and begin to "produce much fruit" in their lives.

15:11 When things are going well, we feel elated. When hardships come, we sink into depression. But true joy transcends the rolling waves of circumstance. Joy comes from a consistent relationship with Jesus Christ. When our lives are intertwined with his, he will help us walk through adversity without sinking into debilitating lows and manage prosperity without moving into deceptive highs. The joy of living with Jesus Christ daily will keep us levelheaded, no matter how high or low our circumstances.

15:12, 13 We are to love each other as Jesus loved us, and he loved us enough to give his life for us. We may not have to die for someone, but there are other ways to practice sacrificial love: listening, helping, encouraging, giving. Think of someone in particular who needs this kind of love today. Give all the love you can, and then try to give a little more.

15:15 Because Jesus Christ is Lord and Master, he should call us servants; instead, he calls us friends. How comforting and reassuring to be chosen as Christ's friends. Because he is Lord and Master, we owe him our unqualified obedience, but most of all, Jesus asks us to obey him because we love him.

15:16 Jesus made the first choice—to love and to die for us, to invite us to live with him forever. We make the next choice—to accept or reject his offer. Without *his* choice, we would have no choice to make.

15:17 Christians will get plenty of hatred from the world; from each other we need love and support. Do you allow small problems to get in the way of loving other believers? Jesus commands that you love them, and he will give you the strength to do it.

15:26 John 14:17; 1 Jn 5:7

26 "But I will send you the Counselor*—the Spirit of truth. He will come to you from
the Father and will tell you all about me. 27 And you must also tell others about me
because you have been with me from the beginning.

16:2 John 9:22
16:3 John 15:21
16:4 John 13:19

16 "I have told you these things so that you won't fall away. 2 For you will be expelled
from the synagogues, and the time is coming when those who kill you will think
they are doing God a service. 3 This is because they have never known the Father or me.
4 Yes, I'm telling you these things now, so that when they happen, you will remember I
warned you. I didn't tell you earlier because I was going to be with you for a while longer.

Jesus Teaches about the Holy Spirit (217)

16:5 John 7:33; 13:36
16:7 John 14:26; 15:26
16:9 John 15:22
16:10 Acts 3:14; 7:52; Rom 1:17; 1 Pet 3:18
16:11 John 12:31
16:13 John 14:17, 26
16:15 John 17:10

5 "But now I am going away to the one who sent me, and none of you has asked me
where I am going. 6 Instead, you are very sad. 7 But it is actually best for you that I go
away, because if I don't, the Counselor* won't come. If I do go away, he will come
because I will send him to you. 8 And when he comes, he will convince the world of
its sin, and of God's righteousness, and of the coming judgment. 9 The world's sin is
unbelief in me. 10 Righteousness is available because I go to the Father, and you will
see me no more. 11 Judgment will come because the prince of this world has already
been judged.

12 "Oh, there is so much more I want to tell you, but you can't bear it now. 13 When the
Spirit of truth comes, he will guide you into all truth. He will not be presenting his own
ideas; he will be telling you what he has heard. He will tell you about the future. 14 He
will bring me glory by revealing to you whatever he receives from me. 15 All that the
Father has is mine; this is what I mean when I say that the Spirit will reveal to you
whatever he receives from me.

Jesus Teaches about Using His Name in Prayer (218)

16:16 John 14:18-24

16 "In just a little while I will be gone, and you won't see me anymore. Then, just a little
while after that, you will see me again."

17 The disciples asked each other, "What does he mean when he says, 'You won't see
me, and then you will see me'? And what does he mean when he says, 'I am going to the
Father'? 18 And what does he mean by 'a little while'? We don't understand."

15:26 Or *Comforter,* or *Encourager,* or *Advocate.* Greek *Paraclete.* **16:7** Or *Comforter,* or *Encourager,* or *Advocate.* Greek *Paraclete.*

15:26 Once again Jesus offers hope. The Holy Spirit gives strength to endure the unreasonable hatred and evil in our world and the hostility many have toward Christ. This is especially comforting for those facing persecution.

15:26 Jesus uses two names for the Holy Spirit—"Counselor" and "Spirit of truth." The word *Counselor* conveys the helping, encouraging, and strengthening work of the Spirit. *Spirit of truth* points to the teaching, illuminating, and reminding work of the Spirit. The Holy Spirit ministers to both the head and the heart, and both dimensions are important.

16:1-16 In his last moments with his disciples, Jesus (1) warned them about further persecution, (2) told them where, when, and why he was going, and (3) assured them that they would not be left alone, but that the Spirit would come. Jesus knew what lay ahead, and he did not want the disciples' faith shaken or destroyed. God wants you to know you are not alone. You have the Holy Spirit to comfort you, teach you truth, and help you.

16:2 Saul (who later became Paul), under the authority of the high priest, went through the land hunting down and persecuting Christians, convinced that he was doing the right thing (Acts 9:1, 2; 26:9-11).

16:5 Although the disciples had asked Jesus about his death (13:36; 14:5), they had never wondered about its meaning. They were mostly concerned about themselves. If Jesus went away, what would become of them?

16:7 Unless Jesus did what he came to do, there would be no Good News. If he did not die, he could not remove our sins; he could not rise again and defeat death. If he did not go back to the Father, the Holy Spirit would not come. Christ's presence on earth was limited to one place at a time. His leaving meant he could be present to the whole world through the Holy Spirit.

16:8-11 Three important tasks of the Holy Spirit are (1) convincing the world of its sin and calling it to repentance, (2) revealing the standard of God's righteousness to anyone who believes, because Christ would no longer be physically present on earth, and (3) demonstrating Christ's judgment over Satan.

16:9 According to Jesus, not believing in him is *sin.*

16:10, 11 Christ's death on the cross made a personal relationship with God available to us. When we confess our sin, God declares us righteous and delivers us from judgment for our sins.

16:13 The truth into which the Holy Spirit guides us is the truth about Christ. The Spirit also helps us through patient practice to discern right from wrong.

16:13 Jesus said the Holy Spirit would tell them "about the future"—the nature of their mission, the opposition they would face, and the final outcome of their efforts. They didn't fully understand these promises until the Holy Spirit came after Jesus' death and resurrection. Then the Holy Spirit revealed truths to the disciples that they wrote down in the books that now form the New Testament.

16:16 Jesus was referring to his death, now only a few hours away, and his resurrection three days later.

19 Jesus realized they wanted to ask him, so he said, "Are you asking yourselves what I
meant? I said in just a little while I will be gone, and you won't see me anymore. Then, just
a little while after that, you will see me again. 20 Truly, you will weep and mourn over what
is going to happen to me, but the world will rejoice. You will grieve, but your grief will
suddenly turn to wonderful joy when you see me again. 21 It will be like a woman
experiencing the pains of labor. When her child is born, her anguish gives place to joy
because she has brought a new person into the world. 22 You have sorrow now, but I will see
you again; then you will rejoice, and no one can rob you of that joy. 23 At that time you won't
need to ask me for anything. The truth is, you can go directly to the Father and ask him, and
he will grant your request because you use my name. 24 You haven't done this before. Ask,
using my name, and you will receive, and you will have abundant joy.

25 "I have spoken of these matters in parables, but the time will come when this will
not be necessary, and I will tell you plainly all about the Father. 26 Then you will ask
in my name. I'm not saying I will ask the Father on your behalf, 27 for the Father
himself loves you dearly because you love me and believe that I came from God.
28 Yes, I came from the Father into the world, and I will leave the world and return to
the Father."

29 Then his disciples said, "At last you are speaking plainly and not in parables. 30 Now
we understand that you know everything and don't need anyone to tell you anything.*
From this we believe that you came from God."

31 Jesus asked, "Do you finally believe? 32 But the time is coming—in fact, it is already
here—when you will be scattered, each one going his own way, leaving me alone. Yet I
am not alone because the Father is with me. 33 I have told you all this so that you may
have peace in me. Here on earth you will have many trials and sorrows. But take heart,
because I have overcome the world."

Jesus Prays for Himself (**219**)

17 When Jesus had finished saying all these things, he looked up to heaven and said,
"Father, the time has come. Glorify your Son so he can give glory back to you.
2 For you have given him authority over everyone in all the earth. He gives eternal life
to each one you have given him. 3 And this is the way to have eternal life—to know you,
the only true God, and Jesus Christ, the one you sent to earth. 4 I brought glory to you
here on earth by doing everything you told me to do. 5 And now, Father, bring me into
the glory we shared before the world began.

16:30 Or *don't need that anyone should ask you anything.*

16:20 Mark 16:10; Luke 23:27; John 20:20
16:21 Isa 13:8; 21:3; 26:17; Acts 13:33; Col 1:18
16:22 Isa 66:14; John 20:20
16:23 John 14:20; 16:26
16:24 John 15:11
16:25 Ps 78:2; John 10:6
16:27 John 8:42; 14:21; 17:8
16:28 John 13:3
16:32 Zech 13:7; Matt 26:31; John 8:29
16:33 John 14:27; Rom 5:1; 8:37; 1 Jn 5:4
17:1 John 13:31
17:2 Matt 28:18; John 6:37, 39
17:3 Phil 3:8; 1 Jn 5:20
17:5 John 1:1-2; 17:24; Phil 2:6

16:20 What a contrast between the disciples and the world! The world rejoiced as the disciples wept, but the disciples would see Jesus again (in three days) and rejoice. The world's values are often the opposite of God's values. This can cause Christians to feel like misfits. But even if life is difficult now, one day we will rejoice. Keep your eye on the future and on God's promises!

16:23-27 Jesus is talking about a new relationship between the believer and God. Previously, people approached God through priests. After Jesus' resurrection, any believer could approach God directly. A new day has dawned and now all believers are priests, talking with God personally and directly (see Hebrews 10:19-23). We approach God, not because of our own merit, but because Jesus, our great High Priest, has made us acceptable to God.

16:30 The disciples believed Jesus' words because they were convinced that he knew everything. But their belief was only a first step toward the great faith they would receive when the Holy Spirit came to live in them.

16:31-33 As Christians, we should expect continuing tension with an unbelieving world that is "out of sync" with Christ, his Good News, and his people. At the same time, we can expect our relationship with Christ to produce peace and comfort because we are "in sync" with him.

16:32 The disciples scattered after Jesus was arrested (see Mark 14:50).

16:33 Jesus summed up all he had told them this night, tying together themes from 14:27-29; 16:1-4; and 16:9-11. With these words he told his disciples to take courage. In spite of the inevitable struggles they would face, they would not be alone. Jesus does not abandon us to our struggles either. If we remember that the ultimate victory has already been won, we can claim the peace of Christ in the most troublesome times.

17:1ff This entire chapter is Jesus' prayer. From it, we learn that the world is a tremendous battleground where the forces under Satan's power and those under God's authority are at war. Satan and his forces are motivated by bitter hatred for Christ and his forces. Jesus prayed for his disciples, including those of us who follow him today. He prayed that God would keep his chosen believers safe from Satan's power, setting them apart and making them pure and holy, uniting them through his truth.

17:3 How do we get eternal life? Jesus tells us clearly here—by knowing God the Father himself through his Son, Jesus Christ. Eternal life requires entering into a personal relationship with God in Jesus Christ. When we admit our sin and turn away from it, Christ's love lives in us by the Holy Spirit.

17:5 Before Jesus came to earth, he was one with God. At this point, when his mission on earth was almost finished, Jesus was asking his Father to restore him to his original place of honor and authority. Jesus' resurrection and ascension—and Stephen's dying exclamation (Acts 7:56)—attest that Jesus did return to his exalted position at the right hand of God.

Jesus Prays for His Disciples (**220**)

17:6 John 17:26 6 “I have told these men about you. They were in the world, but then you gave them to
me. Actually, they were always yours, and you gave them to me; and they have kept your
17:8 John 13:3; 16:30 word. 7 Now they know that everything I have is a gift from you, 8 for I have passed on
17:9 1 Jn 5:19 to them the words you gave me; and they accepted them and know that I came from you,
and they believe you sent me.
17:10 John 16:15 9 “My prayer is not for the world, but for those you have given me, because they
belong to you. 10 And all of them, since they are mine, belong to you; and you have given
17:11 John 10:30; 17:21 Gal 3:28 them back to me, so they are my glory! 11 Now I am departing the world; I am leaving
them behind and coming to you. Holy Father, keep them and care for them—all those
17:12 John 6:39 you have given me—so that they will be united just as we are. 12 During my time here, I
have kept them safe.* I guarded them so that not one was lost, except the one headed for
destruction, as the Scriptures foretold.
17:13 John 7:33; 15:11 13 “And now I am coming to you. I have told them many things while I was with them
17:14 John 15:18-19 so they would be filled with my joy. 14 I have given them your word. And the world hates
17:15 1 Jn 5:18 them because they do not belong to the world, just as I do not. 15 I’m not asking you to
take them out of the world, but to keep them safe from the evil one. 16 They are not part
17:17 John 15:3 of this world any more than I am. 17 Make them pure and holy by teaching them your
17:18 John 20:21 words of truth. 18 As you sent me into the world, I am sending them into the world. 19 And
17:19 Heb 2:11 I give myself entirely to you so they also might be entirely yours.

Jesus Prays for Future Believers (**221**)

17:20 John 17:9 20 “I am praying not only for these disciples but also for all who will ever believe in me
17:21 John 10:38 Gal 3:28 because of their testimony. 21 My prayer for all of them is that they will be one, just as
you and I are one, Father—that just as you are in me and I am in you, so they will be in
us, and the world will believe you sent me.
17:22 John 17:11 22 “I have given them the glory you gave me, so that they may be one, as we are—23 I
17:23 John 16:27; 17:5 in them and you in me, all being perfected into one. Then the world will know that you
17:24 John 1:14; 12:26 sent me and will understand that you love them as much as you love me. 24 Father, I want
these whom you’ve given me to be with me, so they can see my glory. You gave me the
glory because you loved me even before the world began!

17:12 Greek *I have kept in your name those whom you have given me.*

17:10 What did Jesus mean when he said “they are my glory”? God’s glory is the revelation of his character and presence. The lives of Jesus’ disciples reveal his character, and he is present to the world through them. Does your life reveal Jesus’ character and presence?

17:11 Jesus was asking that the disciples be united in harmony and love as the Father, Son, and Holy Spirit are united—the strongest of all unions. (See the notes on 17:21-23.)

17:12 Judas was the “one headed for destruction,” who was lost because he betrayed Jesus and never sought forgiveness (see Psalm 41:9).

17:13 Joy is a common theme in Christ’s teachings—he wants us to be joyful (see 15:11; 16:24). The key to immeasurable joy is living in intimate contact with Christ, the source of all joy. When we do, we will experience God’s special care and protection and see the victory God brings even when defeat seems certain.

17:14 The world hates Christians because Christians’ values differ from the world’s. Because Christ’s followers don’t cooperate with the world by joining in their sin, they are living accusations against the world’s immorality. The world follows Satan’s agenda, and Satan is the avowed enemy of Jesus and his people.

17:17 A follower of Christ becomes pure and holy through believing and obeying the Word of God (Hebrews 4:12). He or she has already accepted forgiveness through Christ’s sacrificial death (Hebrews 7:26, 27). But daily application of God’s Word has a purifying effect on our minds and hearts. Scripture points out sin, motivates us to confess, renews our relationship with Christ, and guides us back to the right path.

17:18 Jesus didn’t ask God to take believers *out* of the world but instead to use them *in* the world. Because Jesus sends us into the world, we should not try to escape from the world, nor should we avoid all relationships with non-Christians. We are called to be salt and light (Matthew 5:13-16), and we are to do the work that God sent us to do.

17:20 Jesus prayed for all who would follow him, including you and others you know. He prayed for unity (17:11), protection from the evil one (17:15), and holiness (17:17). Knowing that Jesus prayed for us should give us confidence as we work for his Kingdom.

17:21-23 Jesus’ great desire for his disciples was that they would become one. He wanted them unified as a powerful witness to the reality of God’s love. Are you helping to unify the body of Christ, the church? You can pray for other Christians, avoid gossip, build others up, work together in humility, give your time and money, exalt Christ, and refuse to get sidetracked arguing over divisive matters.

17:21-23 Jesus prayed for unity among believers based on the believers’ unity with him and the Father. Christians can know unity among themselves if they are living in union with God. For example, each branch living in union with the vine is united with all other branches doing the same.

25 “O righteous Father, the world doesn’t know you, but I do; and these disciples know 17:25
you sent me. 26 And I have revealed you to them and will keep on revealing you. I will Matt 11:27
do this so that your love for me may be in them and I in them.” 17:26 John 15:9

2. Jesus completes his mission

Jesus Is Betrayed and Arrested

(**224**/Matthew 26:47-56; Mark 14:43-52; Luke 22:47-53)

18 After saying these things, Jesus crossed the Kidron Valley with his disciples and 18:1
entered a grove of olive trees. 2 Judas, the betrayer, knew this place, because 2 Sam 15:23 Matt 26:36
Jesus had gone there many times with his disciples. 3 The leading priests and Pharisees Mark 14:32
had given Judas a battalion of Roman soldiers and Temple guards to accompany him. 18:3 John 7:32, 45
Now with blazing torches, lanterns, and weapons, they arrived at the olive grove.
4 Jesus fully realized all that was going to happen to him. Stepping forward to meet 18:4
them, he asked, “Whom are you looking for?” John 6:64
5 “Jesus of Nazareth,” they replied.
“I am he,”* Jesus said. Judas was standing there with them when Jesus identified
himself. 6 And as he said, “I am he,” they all fell backward to the ground! 7 Once more
he asked them, “Whom are you searching for?”
And again they replied, “Jesus of Nazareth.”
8 “I told you that I am he,” Jesus said. “And since I am the one you want, let these
others go.” 9 He did this to fulfill his own statement: “I have not lost a single one of those 18:9 John 6:39; 17:12
you gave me.”* 18:10
10 Then Simon Peter drew a sword and slashed off the right ear of Malchus, the high Luke 22:36, 38
priest’s servant. 11 But Jesus said to Peter, “Put your sword back into its sheath. Shall I 18:11 Matt 20:22; 26:39
not drink from the cup the Father has given me?” Mark 10:38; 14:36 Luke 22:42

18:5 Greek *I am;* also in 18:6, 8. **18:9** See John 6:39 and 17:12.

18:3 The Jewish religious leaders were given authority by the Romans to make arrests for minor infractions. The Roman soldiers may not have participated in the arrest but accompanied the Temple guards to make sure matters didn’t get out of control.

18:4, 5 John does not record Judas’s kiss of greeting (Matthew 26:49; Mark 14:45; Luke 22:47, 48), but Judas’s kiss marked a turning point for the disciples. With Jesus’ arrest, each one’s life would be radically different. For the first time, Judas openly betrayed Jesus before the other disciples. For the first time, Jesus’ loyal disciples ran away from him (Matthew 26:56). The band of disciples would undergo severe testing before they were transformed from hesitant followers to dynamic leaders.

18:5, 6 The men may have been startled by the boldness of Jesus’ question or by the words “I am he,” a declaration of his divinity (Exodus 3:14). Or perhaps they were overcome by his obvious power and authority.

18:10, 11 Trying to protect Jesus, Peter pulled a sword and wounded the high priest’s servant. But Jesus told Peter to put away his sword and allow God’s plan to unfold. At times it is tempting to take matters into our own hands, to force the issue. Most often such moves lead to sin. Instead, we must trust God to work out his plan. Think of it—if Peter had had his way, Jesus would not have gone to the cross, and God’s plan of redemption would have been thwarted.

18:11 “The cup” refers to the suffering, isolation, and death that Jesus would have to endure in order to atone for the sins of the world.

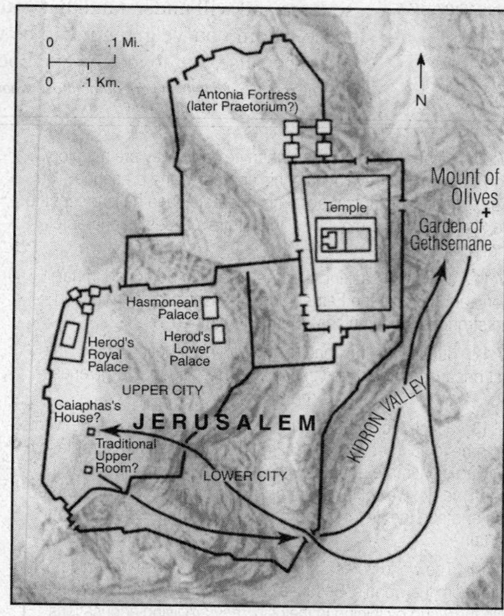

BETRAYAL IN THE GARDEN After eating the Passover meal in the upper room, Jesus and his disciples went to Gethsemane, where Judas led the Temple guard to arrest Jesus. Jesus was then taken to Caiaphas’s house for his first of many trials.

Annas Questions Jesus (**225**)

18:12-14 Matt 26:57-58 Mark 14:53-54 Luke 22:54
18:13 Luke 3:2 John 18:24

[12]So the soldiers, their commanding officer, and the Temple guards arrested Jesus and tied him up. [13]First they took him to Annas, the father-in-law of Caiaphas, the high priest that year. [14]Caiaphas was the one who had told the other Jewish leaders, "Better that one should die for all."

THE SIX STAGES OF JESUS' TRIAL
Although Jesus' trial lasted less than 18 hours, he was taken to six different hearings.

BEFORE JEWISH AUTHORITIES	Preliminary Hearing before Annas (John 18:12–24)	Because the office of high priest was for life, Annas was still the "official" high priest in the eyes of the Jews, even though the Romans had appointed another. Thus, Annas still carried much weight in the high council.
	Hearing before Caiaphas (Matthew 26:57–68)	Like the hearing before Annas, this hearing was conducted at night in secrecy. It was full of illegalities that made a mockery of justice (see the chart in Matthew 28).
	Trial before the High Council (Matthew 27:1, 2)	Just after daybreak, 70 members of the high council met to rubber-stamp their approval of the previous hearings to make them appear legal. The purpose of this trial was not to determine justice, but to justify their own preconceptions of Jesus' guilt.
BEFORE ROMAN AUTHORITIES	First Hearing before Pilate (Luke 23:1–5)	The religious leaders had condemned Jesus to death on religious grounds, but only the Roman government could grant the death penalty. Thus, they took Jesus to Pilate, the Roman governor, and accused him of treason and rebellion, crimes for which the Roman government gave the death penalty. Pilate saw at once that Jesus was innocent, but he was afraid about the uproar being caused by the religious leaders.
	Hearing before Herod (Luke 23:6–12)	Because Jesus' home was in the region of Galilee, Pilate sent Jesus to Herod Antipas, the ruler of Galilee, who was in Jerusalem for the Passover celebration. Herod was eager to see Jesus do a miracle, but when Jesus remained silent, Herod wanted nothing to do with him and sent him back to Pilate.
	Last Hearing before Pilate (Luke 23:13–25)	Pilate didn't like the religious leaders. He wasn't interested in condemning Jesus because he knew Jesus was innocent. However, he knew that another uprising in his district might cost him his job. First he tried to compromise with the religious leaders by having Jesus beaten, an illegal action in itself. But finally he gave in and handed Jesus over to be executed. Pilate's self-interest was stronger than his sense of justice.

18:12, 13 Jesus was immediately taken to the high priest's residence, even though this was the middle of the night. The religious leaders were in a hurry—they wanted to complete the execution before the Sabbath and get on with the Passover celebration. This residence was a palace whose outer walls enclosed a courtyard, where servants and soldiers could warm themselves around a fire.

18:13 Both Annas and Caiaphas had been high priests. Annas was Israel's high priest from A.D. 6 to 15, when he was deposed by Roman rulers. Caiaphas, Annas's son-in-law, was appointed high priest from A.D. 18 to 36/37. According to Jewish law, the office of high priest was held for life. Many Jews, therefore, still considered Annas the high priest and still called him by that title. But although Annas retained much authority among the Jews, Caiaphas made the final decisions.

Both Caiaphas and Annas cared more about their political ambitions than about their responsibility to lead the people to God. Though religious leaders, they had become evil. As the nation's spiritual leaders, they should have been sensitive to God's revelation. They should have known that Jesus was the Messiah about whom the Scriptures spoke, and they should have pointed the people to him. But when deceitful men and women pursue evil, they want to eliminate all opposition. Instead of honestly evaluating Jesus' claims based on their knowledge of Scripture, these religious leaders sought to further their own selfish ambitions and were even willing to kill God's Son, if that's what it took, to do it.

15 Simon Peter followed along behind, as did another of the disciples. That other
disciple was acquainted with the high priest, so he was allowed to enter the courtyard
with Jesus. 16 Peter stood outside the gate. Then the other disciple spoke to the woman **18:16-18** Matt 26:69-70
watching at the gate, and she let Peter in. 17 The woman asked Peter, "Aren't you one of Mark 14:66-68
Jesus' disciples?" Luke 22:55-57

"No," he said, "I am not."

18 The guards and the household servants were standing around a charcoal fire they **18:18**
had made because it was cold. And Peter stood there with them, warming himself. Mark 14:54, 67

19 Inside, the high priest began asking Jesus about his followers and what he had been **18:19-24**
teaching them. 20 Jesus replied, "What I teach is widely known, because I have preached Matt 26:59-68 Mark 14:55-65
regularly in the synagogues and the Temple. I have been heard by people* everywhere, Luke 22:63-71
and I teach nothing in private that I have not said in public. 21 Why are you asking me **18:20** Matt 26:55
this question? Ask those who heard me. They know what I said." John 7:26

22 One of the Temple guards standing there struck Jesus on the face. "Is that the way **18:22** John 19:3
to answer the high priest?" he demanded.

23 Jesus replied, "If I said anything wrong, you must give evidence for it. Should you **18:23** Matt 5:39
hit a man for telling the truth?" Acts 23:2-5

24 Then Annas bound Jesus and sent him to Caiaphas, the high priest. **18:24** Matt 26:3

Peter Denies Knowing Jesus

(**227**/Matthew 26:69-75; Mark 14:66-72; Luke 22:54-65)

25 Meanwhile, as Simon Peter was standing by the fire, they asked him again, "Aren't
you one of his disciples?"

"I am not," he said.

26 But one of the household servants of the high priest, a relative of the man whose ear

18:20 Greek *Jewish people;* also in 18:38.

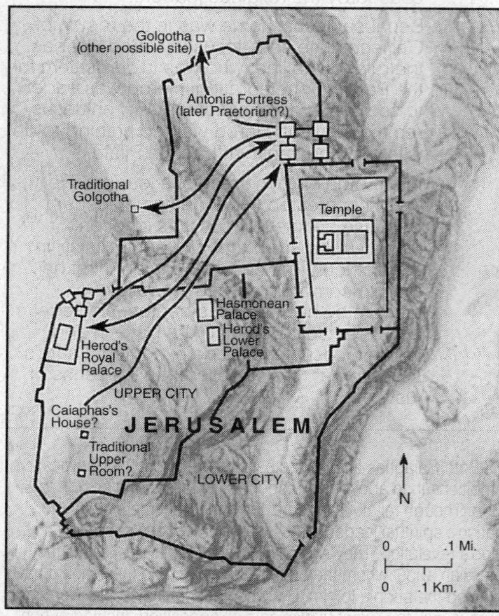

JESUS' TRIAL AND CRUCIFIXION Jesus was taken from trial before the Jewish high council to trial before the Roman governor, Pilate, in Pilate's palace. Pilate sent him to Herod (Luke 23:5–12), but Herod just returned Jesus to Pilate. Responding to threats from the mob, Pilate finally turned Jesus over to be crucified.

18:15, 16 The other disciple is probably John, the author of this Gospel. He knew the high priest and identified himself to the woman at the door. Because of his connections, John got himself and Peter into the courtyard. But Peter refused to identify himself as Jesus' follower. Peter's experiences in the next few hours would change his life. For more information about Peter, see his Profile in Matthew 27.

18:19ff During the night, Jesus had a pretrial hearing before Annas before he was taken to Caiaphas and the entire high council (Mark 14:53-65). The religious leaders knew they had no grounds for charging Jesus, so they tried to build evidence against him by using false witnesses (Mark 14:55-59).

18:22-27 We can easily get angry at the high council for their injustice in condemning Jesus, but we must remember that Peter and the rest of the disciples also contributed to Jesus' pain by deserting and denying him (Matthew 26:56, 75). While most of us are not like the religious leaders, we are all like the disciples, for all of us have been guilty of denying that Christ is Lord in vital areas of our lives or of keeping secret our identity as believers in times of pressure. Don't excuse yourself by pointing at others whose sins seem worse than yours. Instead, come to Jesus for forgiveness and healing.

18:25 The other three Gospels say that Peter's three denials happened near a fire in the courtyard outside Caiaphas's palace. John places the first denial outside Annas's home and the other two denials outside Caiaphas's home. This was very likely the same courtyard. The high priest's residence was large, and Annas and Caiaphas undoubtedly lived near each other.

18:25-27 Imagine standing outside while Jesus, your Lord and Master, is questioned. Imagine watching this man, whom you have come to believe is the long-awaited Messiah, being abused and beaten. Naturally Peter was confused and afraid. It is a serious sin to deny Christ, but Jesus forgave Peter (21:15-17). No sin is too great for Jesus to forgive if you are

18:27 Peter had cut off, asked, “Didn’t I see you out there in the olive grove with Jesus?”
John 13:38 27 Again Peter denied it. And immediately a rooster crowed.

Jesus Stands Trial before Pilate (**230**/Matthew 27:11-14; Mark 15:2-5; Luke 23:1-5)

28 Jesus’ trial before Caiaphas ended in the early hours of the morning. Then he was
taken to the headquarters of the Roman governor. His accusers didn’t go in themselves
because it would defile them, and they wouldn’t be allowed to celebrate the Passover
feast. 29 So Pilate, the governor, went out to them and asked, “What is your charge
against this man?”
30 “We wouldn’t have handed him over to you if he weren’t a criminal!” they
retorted.
31 “Then take him away and judge him by your own laws,” Pilate told them.
“Only the Romans are permitted to execute someone,” the Jewish leaders replied.
18:32 Matt 20:19 32 This fulfilled Jesus’ prediction about the way he would die.*
John 12:32 33 Then Pilate went back inside and called for Jesus to be brought to him. “Are you the
18:33 King of the Jews?” he asked him.
Luke 23:3 John 19:9 34 Jesus replied, “Is this your own question, or did others tell you about me?”
35 “Am I a Jew?” Pilate asked. “Your own people and their leading priests brought you
here. Why? What have you done?”
18:36 36 Then Jesus answered, “I am not an earthly king. If I were, my followers would have
Matt 26:53 Luke 17:21 fought when I was arrested by the Jewish leaders. But my Kingdom is not of this world.”
John 6:15 37 Pilate replied, “You are a king then?”
18:37 “You say that I am a king, and you are right,” Jesus said. “I was born for that purpose.
John 8:47 1 Jn 4:6 And I came to bring truth to the world. All who love the truth recognize that what I say is
true.”

Pilate Hands Jesus Over to Be Crucified
(**232**/Matthew 27:15-26; Mark 15:6-15; Luke 23:13-25)

38 “What is truth?” Pilate asked. Then he went out again to the people and told them,
“He is not guilty of any crime. 39 But you have a custom of asking me to release

18:32 See John 12:32-33.

truly repentant. He will forgive even your worst sin if you turn from it and ask his pardon.

18:27 This fulfilled Jesus’ words to Peter after he promised he would never deny him (Mark 14:31; John 13:38).

18:28 By Jewish law, entering the house of a Gentile would cause a Jewish person to be ceremonially defiled. As a result, he could not take part in worship at the Temple or celebrate the festivals until he was restored to a state of “cleanness.” Afraid of being defiled, these men stayed outside the house where they had taken Jesus for trial. They kept the ceremonial requirements of their religion while harboring murder and treachery in their hearts.

18:29 This Roman governor, Pilate, was in charge of Judea (the region where Jerusalem was located) from A.D. 26 to 36. Pilate was unpopular with the Jews because he had raided the Temple treasuries for money to build an aqueduct. He did not like the Jews, but when Jesus, the King of the Jews, stood before him, Pilate found him innocent.

18:30 Pilate knew what was going on; he knew that the religious leaders hated Jesus, and he did not want to act as their executioner. They could not sentence him to death themselves—permission had to come from a Roman leader. But Pilate initially refused to sentence Jesus without sufficient evidence. Jesus’ life became a pawn in a political power struggle.

18:31ff Pilate made four attempts to deal with Jesus: (1) He tried to put the responsibility on someone else (18:31); (2) he tried to find a way of escape so he could release Jesus (18:39); (3) he tried to compromise by having Jesus flogged rather than handing him over to die (19:1-3); and (4) he tried a direct appeal to the sympathy of the accusers (19:15). Everyone has to decide what to do with Jesus. Pilate tried to let everyone else decide for him—and in the end, he lost.

18:32 This prediction is recorded in Matthew 20:19 and John 12:32, 35. Crucifixion was a common method of execution for criminals who were not Roman citizens.

18:34 If Pilate was asking this question in his role as the Roman governor, he would have been inquiring whether Jesus was setting up a rebel government. But the Jews were using the word *king* to mean their religious ruler, the Messiah. Israel was a captive nation, under the authority of the Roman Empire. A rival king might have threatened Rome; a Messiah could have been a purely religious leader.

18:36, 37 Pilate asked Jesus a straightforward question, and Jesus answered clearly. Jesus is a King, but one whose Kingdom is not of this world. There seems to have been no question in Pilate’s mind that Jesus spoke the truth and was innocent of any crime. It also seems apparent that while recognizing the truth, Pilate chose to reject it. It is a tragedy when we fail to recognize the truth. It is a greater tragedy when we recognize the truth but fail to heed it.

18:38 Pilate was cynical; he thought that all truth was relative. To many government officials, truth was whatever the majority of people agreed with or whatever helped advance their own personal power and political goals. When there is no basis for truth, there is no basis for moral right and wrong. Justice becomes whatever works or whatever helps those in power. In Jesus and his Word we have a standard for truth and for our moral behavior.

someone from prison each year at Passover. So if you want me to, I'll release the King
of the Jews."
40 But they shouted back, "No! Not this man, but Barabbas!" (Barabbas was a criminal.)

19 Then Pilate had Jesus flogged with a lead-tipped whip. 2 The soldiers made a **19:1**
crown of long, sharp thorns and put it on his head, and they put a royal purple robe Isa 50:6; 53:5
on him. 3 "Hail! King of the Jews!" they mocked, and they hit him with their fists. **19:3**
4 Pilate went outside again and said to the people, "I am going to bring him out to you John 18:22
now, but understand clearly that I find him not guilty." 5 Then Jesus came out wearing **19:4** Luke 23:4
the crown of thorns and the purple robe. And Pilate said, "Here is the man!" John 18:38
6 When they saw him, the leading priests and Temple guards began shouting, "Crucify! **19:6**
Crucify!" John 18:31
"You crucify him," Pilate said. "I find him not guilty."
7 The Jewish leaders replied, "By our laws he ought to die because he called himself **19:7**
the Son of God." Lev 24:16
8 When Pilate heard this, he was more frightened than ever. 9 He took Jesus back into Matt 26:63-66
the headquarters again and asked him, "Where are you from?" But Jesus gave no answer.
10 "You won't talk to me?" Pilate demanded. "Don't you realize that I have the power to
release you or to crucify you?"
11 Then Jesus said, "You would have no power over me at all unless it were given to **19:11**
you from above. So the one who brought me to you has the greater sin." Rom 13:1
12 Then Pilate tried to release him, but the Jewish leaders told him, "If you release this **19:12** Luke 23:2
man, you are not a friend of Caesar. Anyone who declares himself a king is a rebel against Acts 17:7
Caesar."
13 When they said this, Pilate brought Jesus out to them again. Then Pilate sat down **19:13**
on the judgment seat on the platform that is called the Stone Pavement (in Hebrew, Matt 27:19
Gabbatha). 14 It was now about noon of the day of preparation for the Passover. And
Pilate said to the people,* "Here is your king!"

19:14 Greek *Jewish people;* also in 19:20.

18:40 Barabbas was a rebel against Rome, and although he had committed murder, he was probably a hero among the Jews. The Jews hated being governed by Rome and paying taxes to the despised government. Barabbas, who had led a rebellion and failed, was released instead of Jesus, the only one who could truly help Israel. For more on Barabbas, see the note on Luke 23:18, 19.

19:1ff To grasp the full picture of Jesus' crucifixion, read John's perspective along with the other three accounts in Matthew 27, Mark 15, and Luke 23. Each writer adds meaningful details, but each has the same message—Jesus died on the cross, in fulfillment of Old Testament prophecy, so that we could be saved from our sins and be given eternal life.

19:1-3 Flogging could have killed Jesus. The usual procedure was to bare the upper half of the victim's body and tie his hands to a pillar before whipping him with a three-pronged whip, with pieces of lead in the prongs. The number of lashes was determined by the severity of the crime; up to 40 were permitted under Jewish law (Deuteronomy 25:3). After being flogged, Jesus also endured other agonies recorded here and in the other Gospels.

19:2-5 The soldiers went beyond their orders to whip Jesus—they also mocked his claim to royalty by placing a crown on his head and a royal robe on his shoulders.

19:7 The truth finally came out—the religious leaders had not brought Jesus to Pilate because he was causing rebellion against Rome, but because they thought he had broken their religious laws. Blasphemy, one of the most serious crimes in Jewish law, deserved the death penalty. Accusing Jesus of blasphemy would give credibility to their case in the eyes of Jews; accusing Jesus of treason would give credibility to their case in the eyes of the Romans. They didn't care which accusation Pilate listened to, as long as he would cooperate with them in killing Jesus.

19:10 Throughout the trial we see that Jesus was in control, not Pilate or the religious leaders. Pilate vacillated, the Jewish leaders reacted out of hatred and anger, but Jesus remained composed. He knew the truth, he knew God's plan, and he knew the reason for his trial. Despite the pressure and persecution, Jesus remained unmoved. It was really Pilate and the religious leaders who were on trial, not Jesus. When you are questioned or ridiculed because of your faith, remember that while you may be on trial before your accusers, they are on trial before God.

19:11 When Jesus said the man who delivered him to Pilate was guiltier than Pilate, he was not excusing Pilate for reacting to the political pressure placed on him. Pilate was responsible for his decision about Jesus. Caiaphas and the other religious leaders were guilty of a greater sin because they premeditated Jesus' murder.

19:12, 13 These words pressured Pilate into allowing Jesus to be crucified. As Roman governor of the area, Pilate was expected to keep the peace. Because Rome could not afford to keep large numbers of troops in the outlying regions, they maintained control by crushing rebellions immediately with brute force. Pilate was afraid that reports to Caesar of insurrection in his region would cost Pilate his job and perhaps even his life. When we face a tough decision, we can take the easy way out, or we can stand for what is right regardless of the cost. If we know the good we ought to do and don't do it, we sin (James 4:17).

19:13 The Stone Pavement was part of the Tower of Antonia bordering the northwest corner of the Temple complex.

15“Away with him,” they yelled. “Away with him—crucify him!”
“What? Crucify your king?” Pilate asked.
“We have no king but Caesar,” the leading priests shouted back.
16Then Pilate gave Jesus to them to be crucified.

Jesus Is Led Away to Be Crucified
(**234**/Matthew 27:32-37; Mark 15:21-24; Luke 23:26-31)
So they took Jesus and led him away. 17Carrying the cross by himself, Jesus went to the
place called Skull Hill (in Hebrew, *Golgotha*).

Jesus Is Placed on the Cross (**235**/Matthew 27:35-44; Mark 15:25-32; Luke 23:32-43)
18There they crucified him. There were two others crucified with him, one on either side,
with Jesus between them. 19And Pilate posted a sign over him that read, “Jesus of Nazareth,
the King of the Jews.” 20The place where Jesus was crucified was near the city; and the sign
was written in Hebrew, Latin, and Greek, so that many people could read it.
21Then the leading priests said to Pilate, “Change it from ‘The King of the Jews’ to
‘He said, I am King of the Jews.’”
22Pilate replied, “What I have written, I have written. It stays exactly as it is.”
23When the soldiers had crucified Jesus, they divided his clothes among the four of
them. They also took his robe, but it was seamless, woven in one piece from the top. 24So
19:24 †Ps 22:18 they said, “Let’s not tear it but throw dice* to see who gets it.” This fulfilled the Scripture
19:25 Matt 27:55-56; Mark 15:40-41; Luke 8:2; 23:49 that says, “They divided my clothes among themselves and threw dice for my robe.”*
25So that is what they did.
Standing near the cross were Jesus’ mother, and his mother’s sister, Mary (the wife of
19:26 John 2:4; 13:23; 20:2; 21:7, 20 Clopas), and Mary Magdalene. 26When Jesus saw his mother standing there beside the
disciple he loved, he said to her, “Woman, he is your son.” 27And he said to this disciple,
“She is your mother.” And from then on this disciple took her into his home.

Jesus Dies on the Cross (**236**/Matthew 27:45-56; Mark 15:33-41; Luke 23:44-49)
19:28 †Pss 22:15; 69:21 28Jesus knew that everything was now finished, and to fulfill the Scriptures he said, “I
am thirsty.”* 29A jar of sour wine was sitting there, so they soaked a sponge in it, put it

19:24a Greek *cast lots.* **19:24b** Ps 22:18. **19:28** See Pss 22:15; 69:21.

19:15 The Jewish leaders were so desperate to get rid of Jesus that, despite their intense hatred for Rome, they shouted, “We have no king but Caesar.” How ironic that they feigned allegiance to Rome while rejecting their own Messiah! Their own words condemned them, for God was to be their only true King, and they had abandoned every trace of loyalty to him. The priests had truly lost their reason for existence—instead of turning people to God, they claimed allegiance to Rome in order to kill their Messiah.

19:17 This place called Skull Hill was probably a hill outside Jerusalem along a main road. Many executions took place here so the Romans could use them as an example to the people.

19:18 Crucifixion was a Roman form of execution. The condemned man was forced to carry his cross along a main road to the execution site, as a warning to the people. Types of crosses and methods of crucifixion varied. Jesus was nailed to his cross; some people were tied with ropes. Death came by suffocation because the weight of the body made breathing difficult as the victim lost strength. Crucifixion was a hideously slow and painful death.

19:19 This sign was meant to be ironic. A king, stripped nearly naked and executed in public view, had obviously lost his kingdom forever. But Jesus, who turns the world’s wisdom upside down, was just coming into his Kingdom. His death and resurrection would strike the deathblow to Satan’s rule and would establish Jesus’ eternal authority over the earth. Few people reading the sign that bleak afternoon understood its real meaning, but the sign was absolutely true. All was not lost. Jesus was King of the Jews—and of the Gentiles, and of the whole universe.

19:20 The sign was written in three languages: Hebrew for the native Jews, Latin for the Roman occupation forces, and Greek for foreigners and Jews visiting from other lands.

19:23, 24 Roman soldiers in charge of crucifixions customarily took for themselves the clothes of the condemned men. They divided Jesus’ clothing, throwing dice to determine who would get his seamless garment, the most valuable piece of clothing. This fulfilled the prophecy in Psalm 22:18.

19:25-27 Even while dying on the cross, Jesus was concerned about his family. He instructed John to care for Mary, Jesus’ mother. Our families are precious gifts from God, and we should value and care for them under all circumstances. Neither Christian work nor key responsibilities in any job or position excuse us from caring for our families. What can you do today to show your love to your family?

19:27 Jesus asked his close friend John, the writer of this Gospel, to care for Jesus’ mother, Mary, whose husband, Joseph, must have been dead by this time. Why didn’t Jesus assign this task to his brothers? As the oldest son, Jesus entrusted his mother to a person who stayed with him at the cross—and that was John.

19:29 This sour wine was a cheap wine that the Roman soldiers drank while waiting for those crucified to die.

on a hyssop branch, and held it up to his lips. 30 When Jesus had tasted it, he said, "It is
finished!" Then he bowed his head and gave up his spirit.
31 The Jewish leaders didn't want the victims hanging there the next day, which was the
Sabbath (and a very special Sabbath at that, because it was the Passover), so they asked
Pilate to hasten their deaths by ordering that their legs be broken. Then their bodies could
be taken down. 32 So the soldiers came and broke the legs of the two men crucified with
Jesus. 33 But when they came to Jesus, they saw that he was dead already, so they didn't
break his legs. 34 One of the soldiers, however, pierced his side with a spear, and blood and
water flowed out. 35 This report is from an eyewitness giving an accurate account; it is
presented so that you also can believe. 36 These things happened in fulfillment of the
Scriptures that say, "Not one of his bones will be broken,"* 37 and "They will look on him
whom they pierced."*

Jesus Is Laid in the Tomb (**237**/Matthew 27:57-61; Mark 15:42-47; Luke 23:50-56)

38 Afterward Joseph of Arimathea, who had been a secret disciple of Jesus (because he
feared the Jewish leaders), asked Pilate for permission to take Jesus' body down. When
Pilate gave him permission, he came and took the body away. 39 Nicodemus, the man
who had come to Jesus at night, also came, bringing about seventy-five pounds* of
embalming ointment made from myrrh and aloes. 40 Together they wrapped Jesus' body
in a long linen cloth with the spices, as is the Jewish custom of burial. 41 The place of
crucifixion was near a garden, where there was a new tomb, never used before. 42 And
so, because it was the day of preparation before the Passover and since the tomb was
close at hand, they laid Jesus there.

19:30 Job 19:26-27
19:31 Deut 21:22-23
19:35 John 20:30-31; 21:24; 1 Jn 1:1
19:36 †Exod 12:46; Num 9:12; †Ps 34:20
19:37 †Zech 12:10; Rev 1:7
19:39 John 3:1-2; 7:50
19:40 Luke 24:12; John 20:5-7

19:36 Exod 12:46; Num 9:12; Ps 34:20. **19:37** Zech 12:10. **19:39** Greek *100 litras* [32.7 kilograms].

19:30 Until this time, a complicated system of sacrifices had atoned for sins. Sin separates people from God, and only through the sacrifice of an animal, a substitute, could people be forgiven and become clean before God. But people sin continually, so frequent sacrifices were required. Jesus, however, became the final and ultimate sacrifice for sin. The word *finished* is the same as "paid in full." Jesus came to *finish* God's work of salvation (4:34; 17:4), to pay the full penalty for our sins. With his death, the complex sacrificial system ended because Jesus took all sin upon himself. Now we can freely approach God because of what Jesus did for us. Those who believe in Jesus' death and resurrection can live eternally with God and escape the penalty that comes from sin.

19:31 It was against God's law to leave the body of a dead person exposed overnight (Deuteronomy 21:23), and it was also against the law to work after sundown on Friday, when the Sabbath began. This is why the religious leaders urgently wanted to get Jesus' body off the cross and buried by sundown.

19:31-35 These Romans were experienced soldiers. They knew from many previous crucifixions whether a man was dead or alive. There was no question that Jesus was dead when they checked him, so they decided not to break his legs as they had done to the other victims. Piercing his side and seeing the sudden flow of blood and water (indicating that the sac surrounding the heart and the heart itself had been pierced) was further proof of his death. Some people say Jesus didn't really die, that he only passed out—and that's how he came back to life. But we have the witness of an impartial party, the Roman soldiers, that Jesus died on the cross (see Mark 15:44, 45).

19:32 The Roman soldiers would break victims' legs to hasten the death process. When a person hung on a cross, death came by suffocation, but the victim could push against the cross with his legs to hold up his body and keep breathing. With broken legs, he would suffocate almost immediately.

19:34, 35 The graphic details of Jesus' death are especially important in John's record because he was an eyewitness.

19:36, 37 Jesus died as the lambs for the Passover meal were being slain. Not a bone was to be broken in these sacrificial lambs (Exodus 12:46; Numbers 9:12). Jesus, the Lamb of God, was the perfect sacrifice for the sins of the world (1 Corinthians 5:7).

19:38, 39 Four people were changed in the process of Jesus' death. The criminal, dying on the cross beside Jesus, asked Jesus to include him in his Kingdom (Luke 23:39-43). The Roman officer proclaimed that Jesus was surely the Son of God (Mark 15:39). Joseph and Nicodemus, members of the Jewish high council and secret followers of Jesus (7:50-52), came out of hiding. These men were changed more by Jesus' death than by his life. They realized who Jesus was, and that realization brought out their belief, proclamation, and action. When confronted with Jesus and his death, we should be changed—to believe, proclaim, and act.

19:38-42 Joseph of Arimathea and Nicodemus were secret followers of Jesus. They were afraid to make this allegiance known because of their positions in the Jewish community. Joseph was a leader and honored member of the Jewish high council. Nicodemus, also a member of the high council, had come to Jesus by night (3:1) and later tried to defend him before the other religious leaders (7:50-52). Yet they risked their reputations to provide for Jesus' burial. Are you a secret believer? Do you hide your faith from your friends and fellow workers? This is an appropriate time to step out of hiding and let others know whom you follow.

19:42 This tomb was probably a cave carved out of the stone hillside. It was large enough for a person to walk into, so Joseph and Nicodemus carried Jesus' body into it. A large stone was rolled in front of the entrance.

19:42 As they buried Jesus, Nicodemus and Joseph had to hurry to avoid working on the Sabbath, which began Friday evening at sundown.

Jesus Rises from the Dead (**239**/Matthew 28:1-7; Mark 16:1-8; Luke 24:1-12)

20 Early Sunday morning,* while it was still dark, Mary Magdalene came to the
tomb and found that the stone had been rolled away from the entrance. 2 She
ran and found Simon Peter and the other disciple, the one whom Jesus loved. She said,
"They have taken the Lord's body out of the tomb, and I don't know where they have
put him!"
3 Peter and the other disciple ran to the tomb to see. 4 The other disciple outran Peter
and got there first. 5 He stooped and looked in and saw the linen cloth lying there, but
he didn't go in. 6 Then Simon Peter arrived and went inside. He also noticed the linen
wrappings lying there, 7 while the cloth that had covered Jesus' head was folded up
and lying to the side. 8 Then the other disciple also went in, and he saw and believed—

20:2 John 13:23
20:3 Luke 24:12
20:5 John 19:40
20:7 John 11:44

20:1 Greek *On the first day of the week.*

MARY MAGDALENE

The absence of women among the 12 disciples has bothered a few people. But it is clear that there were many women among Jesus' followers. It is also clear that Jesus did not treat women as others in his culture did; he treated them with dignity, as people with worth.

Mary of Magdala was an early follower of Jesus who certainly deserves to be called a disciple. An energetic, impulsive, caring woman, she not only traveled with Jesus, but also contributed to the needs of the group. She was present at the Crucifixion and was on her way to anoint Jesus' body on Sunday morning when she discovered the empty tomb. Mary was the first to see Jesus after his resurrection.

Mary Magdalene is a heartwarming example of thankful living. Her life was miraculously freed by Jesus when he drove seven demons out of her. In every glimpse we have of her, she was acting out her appreciation for the freedom Christ had given her. That freedom allowed her to stand under Christ's cross when all the disciples except John were hiding in fear. After Jesus' death, she intended to give his body every respect. Like the rest of Jesus' followers, she never expected his bodily resurrection— but she was overjoyed to discover it.

Mary's faith was not complicated, but it was direct and genuine. She was more eager to believe and obey than to understand everything. Jesus honored her childlike faith by appearing to her first and by entrusting her with the first message of his resurrection.

Strengths and accomplishments
- Contributed to the needs of Jesus and his disciples
- One of the few faithful followers present at Jesus' death on the cross
- First to see the risen Christ

Weakness and mistake
- Jesus had to drive seven demons out of her

Lessons from her life
- Those who are obedient grow in understanding
- Women are vital to Jesus' ministry
- Jesus relates to women as he created them—as equal reflectors of God's image

Vital statistics
- Where: Magdala, Jerusalem
- Occupation: We are not told, but she seems to have been wealthy
- Contemporaries: Jesus, the 12 disciples, Mary, Martha, Lazarus, Jesus' mother Mary

Key verse
"It was early on Sunday morning when Jesus rose from the dead, and the first person who saw him was Mary Magdalene, the woman from whom he had cast out seven demons" (Mark 16:9).

Mary Magdalene's story is told in Matthew 27—28; Mark 15—16; Luke 23—24; and John 19—20. She is also mentioned in Luke 8:2.

20:1 Other women came to the tomb along with Mary Magdalene. The other Gospel accounts give their names. For more information on Mary Magdalene, see her Profile in chapter 20.

20:1 The stone was not rolled away from the entrance to the tomb so Jesus could get out. He could have left easily without moving the stone. It was rolled away so others could get *in* and see that Jesus was gone.

20:1ff People who hear about the Resurrection for the first time may need time before they can comprehend this amazing story. Like Mary and the disciples, they may pass through four stages of belief. (1) At first, they may think the story is a fabrication, impossible to believe (20:2). (2) Like Peter, they may check out the facts and still be puzzled about what happened (20:6). (3) Only when they encounter Jesus personally are they able to accept the fact of the Resurrection (20:16). (4) Then, as they commit themselves to the risen Lord and devote their lives to serving him, they begin to understand fully the reality of his presence with them (20:28).

20:7 The linen wrappings were left as if Jesus had passed right through them. The cloth that covered Jesus' head was still rolled up in the shape of a head, and it was at about the right distance from the wrappings that had enveloped Jesus' body. A grave robber couldn't possibly have made off with Jesus' body and left the linens as if they were still shaped around it.

9 for until then they hadn't realized that the Scriptures said he would rise from the
dead. 10 Then they went home.

20:9 John 2:22

Jesus Appears to Mary Magdalene (**240**/Mark 16:9-11)

11 Mary was standing outside the tomb crying, and as she wept, she stooped and looked
in. 12 She saw two white-robed angels sitting at the head and foot of the place where the
body of Jesus had been lying. 13 "Why are you crying?" the angels asked her.
"Because they have taken away my Lord," she replied, "and I don't know where they
have put him."
14 She glanced over her shoulder and saw someone standing behind her. It was Jesus,
but she didn't recognize him. 15 "Why are you crying?" Jesus asked her. "Who are you
looking for?"
She thought he was the gardener. "Sir," she said, "if you have taken him away, tell me
where you have put him, and I will go and get him."
16 "Mary!" Jesus said.
She turned toward him and exclaimed, "Teacher!"*
17 "Don't cling to me," Jesus said, "for I haven't yet ascended to the Father. But go
find my brothers and tell them that I am ascending to my Father and your Father, my God
and your God."
18 Mary Magdalene found the disciples and told them, "I have seen the Lord!" Then
she gave them his message.

20:11-18 Mark 16:9-11
20:12 Mark 16:5; Luke 24:4
20:14 Mark 16:9; Luke 24:16; John 21:4
20:17 Matt 28:10; John 16:28; Rom 8:29; Col 1:18; Heb 2:11

Jesus Appears to His Disciples (**244**/Luke 24:36-43)

19 That evening, on the first day of the week, the disciples were meeting behind locked doors
because they were afraid of the Jewish leaders. Suddenly, Jesus was standing there among
them! "Peace be with you," he said. 20 As he spoke, he held out his hands for them to see,
and he showed them his side. They were filled with joy when they saw their Lord! 21 He
spoke to them again and said, "Peace be with you. As the Father has sent me, so I send you."
22 Then he breathed on them and said to them, "Receive the Holy Spirit. 23 If you forgive
anyone's sins, they are forgiven. If you refuse to forgive them, they are unforgiven."

20:19-23 Matt 28:16-20; Luke 24:36-49
20:20 John 16:20-22
20:21 Matt 28:19; John 17:18
20:22 John 7:37-39; 14:16-18, 26

20:16 Greek *and said in Hebrew, "Rabboni," which means "Teacher."*

20:9 As further proof that the disciples did not fabricate this story, we find that Peter and John were surprised that Jesus was not in the tomb. When John saw the linen wrappings looking like an empty cocoon from which Jesus had emerged, he believed that Jesus had risen. It wasn't until after they had seen the empty tomb that they remembered what the Scriptures and Jesus had said—he would die, but he would also rise again!

20:9 Jesus' resurrection is the key to the Christian faith. Why? (1) Just as he said, Jesus rose from the dead. We can be confident, therefore, that he will accomplish all he has promised. (2) Jesus' bodily resurrection shows us that the living Christ, not a false prophet or imposter, is ruler of God's eternal Kingdom. (3) We can be certain of our own resurrection because Jesus was resurrected. Death is not the end—there is future life. (4) The divine power that brought Jesus back to life is now available to us to bring our spiritually dead selves back to life. (5) The Resurrection is the basis for the church's witness to the world.

20:17 Mary did not want to lose Jesus again. She had not yet understood the Resurrection. Perhaps she thought this was his promised second coming (14:3). But Jesus did not want to be detained at the tomb. If he did not ascend to heaven, the Holy Spirit could not come. Both he and Mary had important work to do.

20:18 Mary didn't recognize Jesus at first. Her grief had blinded her; she couldn't see him because she didn't expect to see him. Then he spoke her name, and immediately she recognized him. Imagine the love that flooded her heart when she heard her Savior saying her name. Jesus is near you, and he is calling your name. Can you, like Mary, regard him as your Lord?

20:18 Mary did not meet the risen Christ until she had discovered the empty tomb. She responded with joy and obedience by going to tell the disciples. We cannot meet Christ until we discover that he is indeed alive, that his tomb is empty. Are you filled with joy by this good news, and do you share it with others?

20:21 Jesus again identified himself with his Father. He told the disciples by whose authority he did his work. Then he passed the job to his disciples of spreading the Good News of salvation around the world. Whatever God has asked you to do, remember: (1) Your authority comes from God, and (2) Jesus has demonstrated by words and actions how to accomplish the job he has given you. As the Father sent Jesus, Jesus sends his followers . . . and you.

20:22 This may have been a special filling of the Holy Spirit for the disciples, a foretaste of what all believers would experience from the time of Pentecost (Acts 2) and forever after. To do God's work, we need the guidance and power of the Holy Spirit. We must avoid trying to do his work in our own strength.

20:22 There is life in the breath of God. Man was created but did not come alive until God breathed into him the breath of life (Genesis 2:7). God's first breath made man different from all other forms of creation. Now, through the breath of Jesus, God imparted eternal, spiritual life. With this inbreathing came the power to do God's will on earth.

Jesus Appears to Thomas (**245**/Mark 16:14)

20:24 John 11:16

[24]One of the disciples, Thomas (nicknamed the Twin*), was not with the others when
Jesus came. [25]They told him, "We have seen the Lord!" But he replied, "I won't believe
it unless I see the nail wounds in his hands, put my fingers into them, and place my hand
into the wound in his side."

20:24 Greek *the one who was called Didymus.*

THOMAS

Thomas, so often remembered as "Doubting Thomas," deserves to be respected for his faith. He was a doubter, but his doubts had a purpose—he wanted to know the truth. Thomas did not idolize his doubts; he gladly believed when given reasons to do so. He expressed his doubts fully and had them answered completely. Doubting was only his way of responding, not his way of life.

Although our glimpses of Thomas are brief, his character comes through with consistency. He struggled to be faithful to what he knew, despite what he felt. At one point, when it was plain to everyone that Jesus' life was in danger, only Thomas put into words what most were feeling, "Let's go, too—and die with Jesus" (John 11:16). He didn't hesitate to follow Jesus.

We don't know why Thomas was absent the first time Jesus appeared to the disciples after the Resurrection, but he was reluctant to believe their witness to Christ's resurrection. Not even 10 friends could change his mind!

We can doubt without having to live a doubting way of life. Doubt encourages rethinking. Its purpose is more to sharpen the mind than to change it. Doubt can be used to pose the question, get an answer, and push for a decision. But doubt was never meant to be a permanent condition. Doubt is one foot lifted, poised to step forward or backward. There is no motion until the foot comes down.

When you experience doubt, take encouragement from Thomas. He didn't stay in his doubt but allowed Jesus to bring him to belief. Take encouragement also from the fact that countless other followers of Christ have struggled with doubts. The answers God gave them may help you, too. Don't settle into doubts, but move on from them to decision and belief. Find another believer with whom you can share your doubts. Silent doubts rarely find answers.

Strengths and accomplishments
- One of Jesus' 12 disciples
- Intense both in doubt and belief
- Was a loyal and honest man

Weaknesses and mistakes
- Along with the others, abandoned Jesus at his arrest
- Refused to believe the others' claims to have seen Christ and demanded proof
- Struggled with a pessimistic outlook

Lessons from his life
- Jesus does not reject doubts that are honest and directed toward belief
- Better to doubt out loud than to disbelieve in silence

Vital statistics
- Where: Galilee, Judea, Samaria
- Occupation: Disciple of Jesus
- Contemporaries: Jesus, other disciples, Herod, Pilate

Key verses
"Then he said to Thomas, 'Put your finger here and see my hands. Put your hand into the wound in my side. Don't be faithless any longer. Believe!' 'My Lord and my God!' Thomas exclaimed" (John 20:27, 28).

Thomas's story is told in the Gospels. He is also mentioned in Acts 1:13.

20:23 Jesus was giving the disciples their Spirit-powered and Spirit-guided mission—to preach the Good News about Jesus so people's sins might be forgiven. The disciples did not have the power to forgive sins (only God can forgive sins), but Jesus gave them the privilege of telling new believers that their sins *have been* forgiven because they have accepted Jesus' message (see the note on Matthew 16:19). All believers have this same privilege. We can announce forgiveness of sins with certainty when we ourselves have found repentance and faith.

20:24-29 Have you ever wished you could actually see Jesus, touch him, and hear his words? Are there times you want to sit down with him and get his advice? Thomas wanted Jesus' physical presence. But God's plan is wiser. He has not limited himself to one physical body; he wants to be present with you at all times. Even now he is with you in the form of the Holy Spirit. You can talk to him, and you can find his words to you in the pages of the Bible. He can be as real to you as he was to Thomas.

20:25-28 Jesus wasn't hard on Thomas for his doubts. Despite his skepticism, Thomas was still loyal to the believers and to Jesus himself. Some people need to doubt before they believe. If doubt leads to questions, questions lead to answers, and the answers are accepted, then doubt has done good work. It is when doubt becomes stubbornness and stubbornness becomes a life-style that doubt harms faith. When you doubt, don't stop there. Let your doubt deepen your faith as you continue to search for the answer.

26 Eight days later the disciples were together again, and this time Thomas was with
them. The doors were locked; but suddenly, as before, Jesus was standing among
them. He said, "Peace be with you." 27 Then he said to Thomas, "Put your finger here
and see my hands. Put your hand into the wound in my side. Don't be faithless any
longer. Believe!"
28 "My Lord and my God!" Thomas exclaimed.
29 Then Jesus told him, "You believe because you have seen me. Blessed are those who
haven't seen me and believe anyway."
30 Jesus' disciples saw him do many other miraculous signs besides the ones recorded
in this book. 31 But these are written so that you may believe* that Jesus is the Messiah,
the Son of God, and that by believing in him you will have life.

Jesus Appears to Seven Disciples (**246**)

21 Later Jesus appeared again to the disciples beside the Sea of Galilee.* This is
how it happened. 2 Several of the disciples were there—Simon Peter, Thomas
(nicknamed the Twin*), Nathanael from Cana in Galilee, the sons of Zebedee, and
two other disciples.
3 Simon Peter said, "I'm going fishing."
"We'll come, too," they all said. So they went out in the boat, but they caught nothing
all night.
4 At dawn the disciples saw Jesus standing on the beach, but they couldn't see who he
was. 5 He called out, "Friends, have you caught any fish?"
"No," they replied.
6 Then he said, "Throw out your net on the right-hand side of the boat, and you'll get
plenty of fish!" So they did, and they couldn't draw in the net because there were so many
fish in it.
7 Then the disciple whom Jesus loved said to Peter, "It is the Lord!" When Simon
Peter heard that it was the Lord, he put on his tunic (for he had stripped for work),
jumped into the water, and swam ashore. 8 The others stayed with the boat and pulled
the loaded net to the shore, for they were only out about three hundred feet.* 9 When
they got there, they saw that a charcoal fire was burning and fish were frying over it,
and there was bread.
10 "Bring some of the fish you've just caught," Jesus said. 11 So Simon Peter went
aboard and dragged the net to the shore. There were 153 large fish, and yet the net hadn't
torn.
12 "Now come and have some breakfast!" Jesus said. And no one dared ask him if he
really was the Lord because they were sure of it. 13 Then Jesus served them the bread and
the fish. 14 This was the third time Jesus had appeared to his disciples since he had been
raised from the dead.

20:28 John 1:1, 18; 10:30; 14:9; Phil 2:6; Col 2:9; Titus 2:13; 2 Pet 1:1; 1 Jn 5:20
20:29 1 Pet 1:8
20:30 John 21:25
20:31 John 3:15; 19:35; 1 Jn 5:13
21:2 John 1:45-51; 11:16; 20:24
21:3 Luke 5:5
21:4 Luke 24:16; John 20:14
21:6 Luke 5:4-7
21:7 John 13:23
21:9 John 18:18
21:14 John 20:19, 26

20:31 Some manuscripts read *may continue to believe.* **21:1** Greek *Sea of Tiberias,* another name for the Sea of Galilee. **21:2** Greek *the one who was called Didymus.* **21:8** Greek *200 cubits* [90 meters].

20:27 Jesus' resurrected body was unique. It was not the same kind of flesh and blood Lazarus had when he came back to life. Jesus' body was no longer subject to the same laws of nature as before his death. He could appear in a locked room; yet he was not a ghost or apparition because he could be touched and could eat. Jesus' resurrection was *literal* and *physical*—he was not a disembodied spirit.

20:29 Some people think they would believe in Jesus if they could see a definite sign or miracle. But Jesus says we are blessed if we can believe without seeing. We have all the proof we need in the words of the Bible and the testimony of believers. A physical appearance would not make Jesus any more real to us than he is now.

20:30, 31 To understand the life and mission of Jesus more fully, all we need to do is study the Gospels. John tells us that his Gospel records only a few of the many events in Jesus' life on earth. But the Good News includes everything we need to know to believe that Jesus is the Messiah, the Son of God, through whom we receive eternal life.

21:1ff This chapter tells how Jesus commissioned Peter. Perhaps Peter needed special encouragement after his denial—he may have felt completely worthless. Verses 1-14 set the scene for Jesus' conversation with Peter.

21:7 Only John ("the disciple whom Jesus loved") recognized Jesus in the dim morning light, undoubtedly because Jesus had performed a similar miracle earlier (Luke 5:1-11).

Jesus Challenges Peter (**247**)

21:15 Matt 26:33
15 After breakfast Jesus said to Simon Peter, "Simon son of John, do you love me more
than these?"
"Yes, Lord," Peter replied, "you know I love you."
"Then feed my lambs," Jesus told him.
21:16 Acts 20:28 Heb 13:20-21 1 Pet 5:2-3
16 Jesus repeated the question: "Simon son of John, do you love me?"
"Yes, Lord," Peter said, "you know I love you."
"Then take care of my sheep," Jesus said.
21:17 John 13:38; 16:30
17 Once more he asked him, "Simon son of John, do you love me?"
Peter was grieved that Jesus asked the question a third time. He said, "Lord, you know
everything. You know I love you."
Jesus said, "Then feed my sheep. 18 The truth is, when you were young, you were able
to do as you liked and go wherever you wanted to. But when you are old, you will stretch
out your hands, and others will direct you and take you where you don't want to go."
21:19 John 13:36 2 Pet 1:14
19 Jesus said this to let him know what kind of death he would die to glorify God. Then
Jesus told him, "Follow me."
21:20 John 13:23, 25
20 Peter turned around and saw the disciple Jesus loved following them—the one who
had leaned over to Jesus during supper and asked, "Lord, who among us will betray
you?" 21 Peter asked Jesus, "What about him, Lord?"

JESUS' APPEARANCES AFTER HIS RESURRECTION

Appearance	Reference
Mary Magdalene	Mark 16:9–11; John 20:11–18
The other women at the tomb	Matthew 28:8–10
Peter in Jerusalem	Luke 24:34; 1 Corinthians 15:5
The two travelers on the road	Mark 16:12, 13
Ten disciples behind closed doors	Mark 16:14; Luke 24:36–43; John 20:19–25
All the disciples, with Thomas (excluding Judas Iscariot)	John 20:26–31; 1 Corinthians 15:5
Seven disciples while fishing	John 21:1–14
Eleven disciples on the mountain	Matthew 28:16–20
A crowd of 500	1 Corinthians 15:6
Jesus' brother James	1 Corinthians 15:7
Those who watched Jesus ascend into heaven	Luke 24:44–49; Acts 1:3–8

The truth of Christianity rests heavily on the Resurrection. If Jesus rose from the grave, who saw him? How trustworthy were the witnesses? Those who claimed to have seen the risen Jesus went on to turn the world upside down. Most of them also died for being followers of Christ. People rarely die for halfhearted belief. These are the people who saw Jesus risen from the grave.

21:15-17 In this beach scene, Jesus led Peter through an experience that would remove the cloud of his denial. Peter had denied Jesus three times. Three times Jesus asked Peter if he loved him. When Peter answered yes, Jesus told him to feed his sheep. It is one thing to say you love Jesus, but the real test is willingness to serve him. Peter had repented, and here Jesus was asking him to commit his life. Peter's life changed when he finally realized who Jesus was. His occupation changed from fisherman to evangelist; his identity changed from impetuous to "rock"; and his relationship to Jesus changed—he was forgiven, and he finally understood the significance of Jesus' words about his death and resurrection.

21:15-17 Jesus asked Peter three times if he loved him. The first time Jesus said, "Do you love (Greek *agape:* volitional, self-sacrificial love) me more than these?" The second time, Jesus focused on Peter alone and still used the word translated into Greek, *agape.* The third time, Jesus used the word translated into Greek, *phileo* (signifying affection, affinity, or brotherly love) and asked, in effect, "Are you even my friend?" Each time Peter responded with the word translated into Greek as *phileo.* Jesus doesn't settle for quick, superficial answers. He has a way of getting to the heart of the matter. Peter had to face his true feelings and motives when Jesus confronted him. How would you respond if Jesus asked you, "Do you love me?" Do you really love Jesus? Are you even his friend?

21:18, 19 This was a prediction of Peter's death by crucifixion. Tradition indicates that Peter was crucified for his faith—upside down because he did not feel worthy of dying as his Lord did. Despite what Peter's future held, Jesus told him to follow him. We may be uncertain and fearful about our future. But if we know God is in control, we can confidently follow Christ.

21:21, 22 Peter asked Jesus how John would die. Jesus replied that Peter should not concern himself with that. We tend to compare our lives to others, whether to rationalize our own level of devotion to Christ or to question God's justice. Jesus responds to us as he did to Peter: "What is that to you? You follow me."

[22]Jesus replied, "If I want him to remain alive until I return, what is that to you? You
follow me." [23]So the rumor spread among the community of believers* that that disciple
wouldn't die. But that isn't what Jesus said at all. He only said, "If I want him to remain
alive until I return, what is that to you?"
[24]This is that disciple who saw these events and recorded them here. And we all know
that his account of these things is accurate.
[25]And I suppose that if all the other things Jesus did were written down, the whole
world could not contain the books.

21:22 Matt 16:27

21:24 John 15:27; 19:35; 1 Jn 1:1-3; 3 Jn 1:12

21:25 John 20:30

21:23 Greek *the brothers.*

21:23 Early church history reports that after John spent several years as an exile on the island of Patmos, he returned to Ephesus where he died as an old man, near the end of the first century.

21:25 John's stated purpose for writing his Gospel was to show that Jesus was the Son of God (20:31). He clearly and systematically presented the evidence for Jesus' claims. When evidence is presented in the courtroom, those who hear it must make a choice. Those who read the Gospel of John must also make a choice—is Jesus the Son of God, or isn't he? You are the jury. The evidence has been clearly presented. You must decide. Read John's Gospel and believe!

250 EVENTS IN THE LIFE OF CHRIST/ A HARMONY OF THE GOSPELS

All four books in the Bible that tell the story of Jesus Christ—Matthew, Mark, Luke, and John—stand alone, emphasizing a unique aspect of Jesus' life. But when these are blended into one complete account, or harmonized, we gain new insights about the life of Christ.

This harmony combines the four Gospels into a single chronological account of Christ's life on earth. It includes every chapter and verse of each Gospel, leaving nothing out.

The harmony is divided into 250 events. The title of each event is identical to the title found in the corresponding Gospel. Parallel passages found in more than one Gospel have identical titles, helping you to identify them quickly.

Each of the 250 events in the harmony is numbered. The number of the event corresponds to the number next to the title in the Bible text. When reading one of the Gospel accounts, you will notice, at times, that some numbers are missing or out of sequence. The easiest way to locate these events is to refer to the harmony.

In addition, if you are looking for a particular event in the life of Christ, the harmony can help you locate it more rapidly than paging through all four Gospels. Each of the 250 events has a distinctive title keyed to the main emphasis of the passage to help you locate and remember the events.

This harmony will help you to better visualize the travels of Jesus, study the four Gospels comparatively, and appreciate the unity of their message.

I. BIRTH AND PREPARATION OF JESUS CHRIST

	Matthew	*Mark*	*Luke*	*John*
1 Luke's purpose in writing			1:1–4	
2 God became a human				1:1–18
3 The record of Jesus' ancestors	1:1–17		3:23–38	
4 An angel promises the birth of John to Zechariah			1:5–25	
5 An angel promises the birth of Jesus to Mary			1:26–38	
6 Mary visits Elizabeth			1:39–56	
7 John the Baptist is born			1:57–80	
8 An angel appears to Joseph	1:18–25			
9 Jesus is born in Bethlehem			2:1–7	
10 Shepherds visit Jesus			2:8–20	
11 Mary and Joseph bring Jesus to the Temple			2:21–40	
12 Visitors arrive from eastern lands	2:1–12			
13 The escape to Egypt	2:13–18			
14 The return to Nazareth	2:19–23			
15 Jesus speaks with the religious teachers			2:41–52	
16 John the Baptist prepares the way for Jesus	3:1–12	1:1–8	3:1–18	
17 The baptism of Jesus	3:13–17	1:9–11	3:21, 22	

		Matthew	Mark	Luke	John
18	Satan tempts Jesus in the wilderness	4:1–11	1:12, 13	4:1–13	
19	John the Baptist declares his mission				1:19–28
20	John the Baptist proclaims Jesus as the Messiah				1:29–34
21	The first disciples follow Jesus				1:35–51
22	Jesus turns water into wine				2:1–12

II. MESSAGE AND MINISTRY OF JESUS CHRIST

		Matthew	Mark	Luke	John
23	Jesus clears the Temple				2:13–25
24	Nicodemus visits Jesus at night				3:1–21
25	John the Baptist tells more about Jesus				3:22–36
26	Herod puts John in prison			3:19, 20	
27	Jesus talks to a woman at the well				4:1–26
28	Jesus tells about the spiritual harvest				4:27–38
29	Many Samaritans believe in Jesus				4:39–42
30	Jesus preaches in Galilee	4:12–17	1:14, 15	4:14, 15	4:43–45
31	Jesus heals a government official's son				4:46–54
32	Jesus is rejected at Nazareth			4:16–30	
33	Four fishermen follow Jesus	4:18–22	1:16–20		
34	Jesus teaches with great authority		1:21–28	4:31–37	
35	Jesus heals Peter's mother-in-law and many others	8:14–17	1:29–34	4:38–41	
36	Jesus preaches throughout Galilee	4:23–25	1:35–39	4:42–44	
37	Jesus provides a miraculous catch of fish			5:1–11	
38	Jesus heals a man with leprosy	8:1–4	1:40–45	5:12–16	
39	Jesus heals a paralyzed man	9:1–8	2:1–12	5:17–26	
40	Jesus eats with sinners at Matthew's house	9:9–13	2:13–17	5:27–32	
41	Religious leaders ask Jesus about fasting	9:14–17	2:18–22	5:33–39	
42	Jesus heals a lame man by a pool				5:1–15
43	Jesus claims to be the Son of God				5:16–30
44	Jesus supports his claim				5:31–47
45	The disciples pick wheat on the Sabbath	12:1–8	2:23–28	6:1–5	
46	Jesus heals a man's hand on the Sabbath	12:9–14	3:1–6	6:6–11	
47	Large crowds follow Jesus	12:15–21	3:7–12		
48	Jesus chooses the twelve disciples		3:13–19	6:12–16	
49	Jesus gives the Beatitudes	5:1–12		6:17–26	
50	Jesus teaches about salt and light	5:13–16			
51	Jesus teaches about the law	5:17–20			
52	Jesus teaches about anger	5:21–26			
53	Jesus teaches about lust	5:27–30			
54	Jesus teaches about divorce	5:31, 32			
55	Jesus teaches about vows	5:33–37			
56	Jesus teaches about revenge	5:38–42			
57	Jesus teaches about loving enemies	5:43–48		6:27–36	
58	Jesus teaches about giving to the needy	6:1–4			
59	Jesus teaches about prayer	6:5–15			
60	Jesus teaches about fasting	6:16–18			
61	Jesus teaches about money	6:19–24			
62	Jesus teaches about worry	6:25–34			
63	Jesus teaches about judging others	7:1–6		6:37–42	
64	Jesus teaches about asking, looking, knocking	7:7–12			
65	Jesus teaches about the way to heaven	7:13, 14			
66	Jesus teaches about fruit in people's lives	7:15–20		6:43–45	
67	Jesus teaches about building on a solid foundation	7:21–29		6:46–49	
68	A Roman officer demonstrates faith	8:5–13		7:1–10	
69	Jesus raises a widow's son from the dead			7:11–17	
70	Jesus eases John's doubt	11:1–19		7:18–35	
71	Jesus promises rest for the soul	11:20–30			
72	A sinful woman anoints Jesus' feet			7:36–50	
73	Women accompany Jesus and the disciples			8:1–3	

	Matthew	Mark	Luke	John
74 Religious leaders accuse Jesus of getting his power from Satan	12:22–37	3:20–30		
75 Religious leaders ask Jesus for a miracle	12:38–45			
76 Jesus describes his true family	12:46–50	3:31–35	8:19–21	
77 Jesus tells the parable of the four soils	13:1–9	4:1–9	8:4–8	
78 Jesus explains the parable of the four soils	13:10–23	4:10–25	8:9–18	
79 Jesus tells the parable of the growing seed		4:26–29		
80 Jesus tells the parable of the weeds	13:24–30			
81 Jesus tells the parable of the mustard seed	13:31, 32	4:30–34		
82 Jesus tells the parable of the yeast	13:33–35			
83 Jesus explains the parable of the weeds	13:36–43			
84 Jesus tells the parable of hidden treasure	13:44			
85 Jesus tells the parable of the pearl merchant	13:45, 46			
86 Jesus tells the parable of the fishing net	13:47–52			
87 Jesus calms the storm	8:23–27	4:35–41	8:22–25	
88 Jesus sends demons into a herd of pigs	8:28–34	5:1–20	8:26–39	
89 Jesus heals a bleeding woman and restores a girl to life	9:18–26	5:21–43	8:40–56	
90 Jesus heals the blind and mute	9:27–34			
91 The people of Nazareth refuse to believe	13:53–58	6:1–6		
92 Jesus urges the disciples to pray for workers	9:35–38			
93 Jesus sends out the twelve disciples	10:1–15	6:7–13	9:1–6	
94 Jesus prepares the disciples for persecution	10:16–42			
95 Herod kills John the Baptist	14:1–12	6:14–29	9:7–9	
96 Jesus feeds five thousand	14:13–21	6:30–44	9:10–17	6:1–15
97 Jesus walks on water	14:22–33	6:45–52		6:16–21
98 Jesus heals all who touch him	14:34–36	6:53–56		
99 Jesus is the true bread from heaven				6:22–40
100 The people disagree that Jesus is from heaven				6:41–59
101 Many disciples desert Jesus				6:60–71
102 Jesus teaches about inner purity	15:1–20	7:1–23		
103 Jesus sends a demon out of a girl	15:21–28	7:24–30		
104 Jesus heals many people	15:29–31	7:31–37		
105 Jesus feeds four thousand	15:32–39	8:1–10		
106 Leaders demand a miraculous sign	16:1–4	8:11–13		
107 Jesus warns against wrong teaching	16:5–12	8:14–21		
108 Jesus restores sight to a blind man		8:22–26		
109 Peter says Jesus is the Messiah	16:13–20	8:27–30	9:18–20	
110 Jesus predicts his death the first time	16:21–28	8:31—9:1	9:21–27	
111 Jesus is transfigured on the mountain	17:1–13	9:2–13	9:28–36	
112 Jesus heals a demon-possessed boy	17:14–21	9:14–29	9:37–43	
113 Jesus predicts his death the second time	17:22, 23	9:30–32	9:44, 45	
114 Peter finds the coin in the fish's mouth	17:24–27			
115 The disciples argue about who would be the greatest	18:1–6	9:33–37	9:46–48	
116 The disciples forbid another to use Jesus' name		9:38–41	9:49, 50	
117 Jesus warns against temptation	18:7–9	9:42–50		
118 Jesus warns against looking down on others	18:10–14			
119 Jesus teaches how to treat a believer who sins	18:15–20			
120 Jesus tells the parable of the unforgiving debtor	18:21–35			
121 Jesus' brothers ridicule him				7:1–9
122 Jesus teaches about the cost of following him	8:18–22		9:51–62	
123 Jesus teaches openly at the Temple				7:10–31
124 Religious leaders attempt to arrest Jesus				7:32–52
125 Jesus forgives an adulterous woman				7:53—8:11
126 Jesus is the light of the world				8:12–20
127 Jesus warns of coming judgment				8:21–30
128 Jesus speaks about God's true children				8:31–47
129 Jesus states he is eternal				8:48–59
130 Jesus sends out seventy-two messengers			10:1–16	
131 The seventy-two messengers return			10:17–24	
132 Jesus tells the parable of the Good Samaritan			10:25–37	
133 Jesus visits Mary and Martha			10:38–42	
134 Jesus teaches his disciples about prayer			11:1–13	

		Matthew	Mark	Luke	John
135	Jesus answers hostile accusations			11:14–28	
136	Jesus warns against unbelief			11:29–32	
137	Jesus teaches about the light within			11:33–36	
138	Jesus criticizes the religious leaders			11:37–54	
139	Jesus speaks against hypocrisy			12:1–12	
140	Jesus tells the parable of the rich fool			12:13–21	
141	Jesus warns about worry			12:22–34	
142	Jesus warns about preparing for his coming			12:35–48	
143	Jesus warns about coming division			12:49–53	
144	Jesus warns about the future crisis			12:54–59	
145	Jesus calls the people to repent			13:1–9	
146	Jesus heals the crippled woman			13:10–17	
147	Jesus teaches about the Kingdom of God			13:18–21	
148	Jesus heals the man who was born blind				9:1–12
149	Religious leaders question the blind man				9:13–34
150	Jesus teaches about spiritual blindness				9:35–41
151	Jesus is the good shepherd				10:1–21
152	Religious leaders surround Jesus at the Temple				10:22–42
153	Jesus teaches about entering the Kingdom			13:22–30	
154	Jesus grieves over Jerusalem			13:31–35	
155	Jesus heals a man with swollen limbs			14:1–6	
156	Jesus teaches about seeking honor			14:7–14	
157	Jesus tells the parable of the great festival			14:15–24	
158	Jesus teaches about the cost of being a disciple			14:25–35	
159	Jesus tells the parable of the lost sheep			15:1–7	
160	Jesus tells the parable of the lost coin			15:8–10	
161	Jesus tells the parable of the lost son			15:11–32	
162	Jesus tells the parable of the shrewd manager			16:1–18	
163	Jesus tells about the rich man and the beggar			16:19–31	
164	Jesus tells about forgiveness and faith			17:1–10	
165	Lazarus becomes ill and dies				11:1–16
166	Jesus comforts Mary and Martha				11:17–37
167	Jesus raises Lazarus from the dead				11:38–44
168	Religious leaders plot to kill Jesus				11:45–57
169	Jesus heals ten men with leprosy			17:11–19	
170	Jesus teaches about the coming of the Kingdom of God			17:20–37	
171	Jesus tells the parable of the persistent widow			18:1–8	
172	Jesus tells the parable of two men who prayed			18:9–14	
173	Jesus teaches about marriage and divorce	19:1–12	10:1–12		
174	Jesus blesses the children	19:13–15	10:13–16	18:15–17	
175	Jesus speaks to the rich young man	19:16–30	10:17–31	18:18–30	
176	Jesus tells the parable of the vineyard workers	20:1–16			
177	Jesus predicts his death the third time	20:17–19	10:32–34	18:31–34	
178	Jesus teaches about serving others	20:20–28	10:35–45		
179	Jesus heals a blind beggar	20:29–34	10:46–52	18:35–43	
180	Jesus brings salvation to Zacchaeus's home			19:1–10	
181	Jesus tells the parable of the king's ten servants			19:11–27	
182	A woman anoints Jesus with perfume	26:6–13	14:3–9		12:1–11
183	Jesus rides into Jerusalem on a young donkey	21:1–11	11:1–11	19:28–44	12:12–19
184	Jesus clears the Temple again	21:12–17	11:12–19	19:45–48	
185	Jesus explains why he must die				12:20–36
186	Most of the people do not believe in Jesus				12:37–43
187	Jesus summarizes his message				12:44–50
188	Jesus says the disciples can pray for anything	21:18–22	11:20–26		
189	Religious leaders challenge Jesus' authority	21:23–27	11:27–33	20:1–8	
190	Jesus tells the parable of the two sons	21:28–32			
191	Jesus tells the parable of the evil farmers	21:33–46	12:1–12	20:9–19	
192	Jesus tells the parable of the wedding dinner	22:1–14			
193	Religious leaders question Jesus about paying taxes	22:15–22	12:13–17	20:20–26	
194	Religious leaders question Jesus about the Resurrection	22:23–33	12:18–27	20:27–40	
195	Religious leaders question Jesus about the greatest commandment	22:34–40	12:28–34		

		Matthew	Mark	Luke	John
196	Religious leaders cannot answer Jesus' question	22:41–46	12:35–37	20:41–44	
197	Jesus warns against the religious leaders	23:1–12	12:38–40	20:45–47	
198	Jesus condemns the religious leaders	23:13–36			
199	Jesus grieves over Jerusalem again	23:37–39			
200	A poor widow gives all she has		12:41–44	21:1–4	
201	Jesus tells about the future	24:1–25	13:1–23	21:5–24	
202	Jesus tells about his return	24:26–35	13:24–31	21:25–33	
203	Jesus tells about remaining watchful	24:36–51	13:32–37	21:34–38	
204	Jesus tells the parable of the ten bridesmaids	25:1–13			
205	Jesus tells the parable of the loaned money	25:14–30			
206	Jesus tells about the final judgment	25:31–46			

III. DEATH AND RESURRECTION OF JESUS CHRIST

		Matthew	Mark	Luke	John
207	Religious leaders plot to kill Jesus	26:1–5	14:1, 2	22:1, 2	
208	Judas agrees to betray Jesus	26:14–16	14:10, 11	22:3–6	
209	Disciples prepare for the Passover	26:17–19	14:12–16	22:7–13	
210	Jesus washes the disciples' feet				13:1–20
211	Jesus and the disciples share the Last Supper	26:20–30	14:17–26	22:14–30	13:21–30
212	Jesus predicts Peter's denial			22:31–38	13:31–38
213	Jesus is the way to the Father				14:1–14
214	Jesus promises the Holy Spirit				14:15–31
215	Jesus teaches about the vine and the branches				15:1–17
216	Jesus warns about the world's hatred				15:18—16:4
217	Jesus teaches about the Holy Spirit				16:5–15
218	Jesus teaches about using his name in prayer				16:16–33
219	Jesus prays for himself				17:1–5
220	Jesus prays for his disciples				17:6–19
221	Jesus prays for future believers				17:20–26
222	Jesus again predicts Peter's denial	26:31–35	14:27–31		
223	Jesus agonizes in the garden	26:36–46	14:32–42	22:39–46	
224	Jesus is betrayed and arrested	26:47–56	14:43–52	22:47–53	18:1–11
225	Annas questions Jesus				18:12–24
226	Caiaphas questions Jesus	26:57–68	14:53–65		
227	Peter denies knowing Jesus	26:69–75	14:66–72	22:54–65	18:25–27
228	The council of religious leaders condemns Jesus	27:1, 2	15:1	22:66–71	
229	Judas hangs himself	27:3–10			
230	Jesus' trial before Pilate	27:11–14	15:2–5	23:1–5	18:28–37
231	Jesus stands trial before Herod			23:6–12	
232	Pilate hands Jesus over to be crucified	27:15–26	15:6–15	23:13–25	18:38—19:16
233	Roman soldiers mock Jesus	27:27–31	15:16–20		
234	Jesus is led away to be crucified	27:32–34	15:21–24	23:26–31	19:17
235	Jesus is placed on the cross	27:35–44	15:25–32	23:32–43	19:18–27
236	Jesus dies on the cross	27:45–56	15:33–41	23:44–49	19:28–37
237	Jesus is laid in the tomb	27:57–61	15:42–47	23:50–56	19:38–42
238	Guards are posted at the tomb	27:62–66			
239	Jesus rises from the dead	28:1–7	16:1–8	24:1–12	20:1–10
240	Jesus appears to Mary Magdalene		16:9–11		20:11–18
241	Jesus appears to the women	28:8–10			
242	Religious leaders bribe the guards	28:11–15			
243	Jesus appears to two believers traveling on the road		16:12, 13	24:13–34	
244	Jesus appears to his disciples			24:35–43	20:19–23
245	Jesus appears to Thomas		16:14		20:24–31
246	Jesus appears to seven disciples				21:1–14
247	Jesus challenges Peter				21:15–25
248	Jesus gives the great commission	28:16–20	16:15–18		
249	Jesus appears to the disciples in Jerusalem			24:44–49	
250	Jesus ascends into heaven		16:19, 20	24:50–53	

THE PARABLES OF JESUS

I. Teaching Parables
- A. About the Kingdom of God
  1. The Soils (Matthew 13:3–8; Mark 4:4–8; Luke 8:5–8)
  2. The Weeds (Matthew 13:24–30)
  3. The Mustard Seed (Matthew 13:31, 32; Mark 4:30–32; Luke 13:18, 19)
  4. The Yeast (Matthew 13:33; Luke 13:20, 21)
  5. The Treasure (Matthew 13:44)
  6. The Pearl (Matthew 13:45, 46)
  7. The Fishing Net (Matthew 13:47–50)
  8. The Growing Wheat (Mark 4:26–29)
- B. About Service and Obedience
  1. The Workers in the Harvest (Matthew 20:1–16)
  2. The Loaned Money (Matthew 25:14–30)
  3. The Nobleman's Servants (Luke 19:11–27)
  4. The Servant's Role (Luke 17:7–10)
- C. About Prayer
  1. The Friend at Midnight (Luke 11:5–8)
  2. The Unjust Judge (Luke 18:1–8)
- D. About Neighbors
  1. The Good Samaritan (Luke 10:30–37)
- E. About Humility
  1. The Wedding Feast (Luke 14:7–11)
  2. The Proud Pharisee and the Corrupt Tax Collector (Luke 18:9–14)
- F. About Wealth
  1. The Rich Fool (Luke 12:16–21)
  2. The Great Festival (Luke 14:16–24)
  3. The Shrewd Manager (Luke 16:1–9)

II. Gospel Parables
- A. About God's Love
  1. The Lost Sheep (Matthew 18:12–14; Luke 15:3–7)
  2. The Lost Coin (Luke 15:8–10)
  3. The Lost Son (Luke 15:11–32)
- B. About Thankfulness
  1. The Forgiven Debts (Luke 7:41–43)

III. Parables of Judgment and the Future
- A. About Christ's Return
  1. The Ten Bridesmaids (Matthew 25:1–13)
  2. The Wise and Faithful Servants (Matthew 24:45–51; Luke 12:42–48)
  3. The Traveling Owner of the House (Mark 13:34–37)
- B. About God's Values
  1. The Two Sons (Matthew 21:28–32)
  2. The Evil Farmers (Matthew 21:33, 34; Mark 12:1–9; Luke 20:9–16)
  3. The Unproductive Fig Tree (Luke 13:6–9)
  4. The Wedding Feast (Matthew 22:1–14)
  5. The Unforgiving Servant (Matthew 18:23–35)

JESUS' MIRACLES

John and the other Gospel writers were able to record only a fraction of the people who were touched and healed by Jesus. But enough of Jesus' words and works have been saved so that we also might be able to know him and be his disciples in this day. There follows a listing of the miracles that are included in the Gospels. They were supernatural events that pointed people to God, and they were acts of love by one who is love.

	Matthew	*Mark*	*Luke*	*John*
Five thousand people are fed	14:15–21	6:35–44	9:12–17	6:5–14
Calming the storm	8:23–27	4:35–41	8:22–25	
Demons sent into the pigs	8:28–34	5:1–20	8:26–39	
Jairus's daughter raised	9:18–26	5:22–24, 35–43	8:41, 42, 49–56	
A sick woman is healed	9:20–22	5:25–34	8:43–48	
Jesus heals a paralytic	9:1–8	2:1–12	5:17–26	
A leper is healed at Gennesaret	8:1–4	1:40–45	5:12–15	
Peter's mother-in-law healed	8:14–17	1:29–31	4:38, 39	
A deformed hand is restored	12:9–13	3:1–5	6:6–11	
A boy with an evil spirit is healed	17:14–21	9:14–29	9:37–42	
Jesus walks on the water	14:22–33	6:45–52		6:17–21
Blind Bartimaeus receives sight	20:29–34	10:46–52	18:35–43	
A girl is freed from a demon	15:21–28	7:24–30		
Four thousand are fed	15:32–38	8:1–9		
Cursing the fig tree	21:18–22	11:12–14, 20–24		
A centurion's servant is healed	8:5–13		7:1–10	
An evil spirit is sent out of a man		1:23–27	4:33–36	
A mute demoniac is healed	12:22		11:14	
Two blind men find sight	9:27–31			
Jesus heals the mute man	9:32, 33			
A coin in a fish's mouth	17:24–27			
A deaf and mute man is healed		7:31–37		
A blind man sees at Bethsaida		8:22–26		
The first miraculous catch of fish			5:1–11	
A widow's son is raised			7:11–16	
A crippled woman is healed			13:10–17	
Jesus heals a sick man			14:1–6	
Ten lepers are healed			17:11–19	
Jesus restores a man's ear			22:49–51	
Jesus turns water into wine				2:1–11
An official's son is healed at Cana				4:46–54
A lame man is healed				5:1–16
Jesus heals a man born blind				9:1–7
Lazarus is raised from the dead				11:1–45
The second miraculous catch of fish				21:1–14

COMPARISON OF THE FOUR GOSPELS

All four Gospels present the life and teachings of Jesus. Each book, however, focuses on a unique facet of Jesus and his character. To understand more about the specific characteristics of Jesus, read any one of the four Gospels.

	Matthew	*Mark*	*Luke*	*John*
Jesus is . . .	The promised King	The Servant of God	The Son of Man	The Son of God
The original readers were . . .	Jews	Gentiles, Romans	Greeks	Christians throughout the world
Significant themes . . .	Jesus is the Messiah because he fulfilled Old Testament prophecy	Jesus backed up his words with action	Jesus was God but also fully human	Belief in Jesus is required for salvation
Character of the writer . . .	Teacher	Storyteller	Historian	Theologian
Greatest emphasis is on . . .	Jesus' sermons and words	Jesus' miracles and actions	Jesus' humanity	The principles of Jesus' teaching

	Old Testament Prophecies	New Testament Fulfillment
1. Messiah was to be born in Bethlehem	Micah 5:2	Matthew 2:1–6 Luke 2:1–20
2. Messiah was to be born of a virgin	Isaiah 7:14	Matthew 1:18–25 Luke 1:26–38
3. Messiah was to be a prophet like Moses	Deuteronomy 18:15, 18, 19	John 7:40
4. Messiah was to enter Jerusalem in triumph	Zechariah 9:9	Matthew 21:1–9 John 12:12–16
5. Messiah was to be rejected by his own people	Isaiah 53:1, 3 Psalm 118:22	Matthew 26:3, 4 John 12:37–43 Acts 4:1–12
6. Messiah was to be betrayed by one of his followers	Psalm 41:9	Matthew 26:14–16, 47–50 Luke 22:19–23
7. Messiah was to be tried and condemned	Isaiah 53:8	Matthew 27:1, 2 Luke 2:1–25
8. Messiah was to be silent before his accusers	Isaiah 53:7	Matthew 27:12–14 Mark 15:3–4 Luke 23:8–10
9. Messiah was to be struck and spat on by his enemies	Isaiah 50:6	Matthew 26:67; 27:30 Mark 14:65
10. Messiah was to be mocked and insulted	Psalm 22:7, 8	Matthew 27:39–44 Luke 23:11, 35
11. Messiah was to die by crucifixion	Psalm 22:14, 16, 17	Matthew 27:31 Mark 15:20, 25
12. Messiah was to suffer with criminals and pray for his enemies	Isaiah 53:12	Matthew 27:38 Mark 15:27, 28 Luke 23:32–34
13. Messiah was to be given vinegar	Psalm 69:21	Matthew 27:34 John 19:28–30
14. Others were to cast lots for Messiah's garments	Psalm 22:18	Matthew 27:35 John 19:23, 24
15. Messiah's bones were not to be broken	Exodus 12:46	John 19:31–36
16. Messiah was to die as a sacrifice for sin	Isaiah 53:5, 6, 8, 10, 11, 12	John 1:29; 11:49–52 Acts 10:43; 13:38, 39
17. Messiah was to be raised from the dead	Psalm 16:10	Matthew 28:1–10 Acts 2:22–32
18. Messiah is now at God's right hand	Psalm 110:1	Mark 16:19 Luke 24:50, 51

MESSIANIC PROPHECIES AND FULFILLMENTS
For the Gospel writers, one of the main reasons for believing in Jesus was the way his life fulfilled the Old Testament prophecies about the Messiah. Following is a list of some of the main prophecies.

KEY PLACES IN ACTS

Modern names and boundaries are shown in gray.

The apostle Paul, whose missionary journeys fill much of this book, traveled tremendous distances as he tirelessly spread the gospel across much of the Roman Empire. His combined trips, by land and sea, equal more than 13,000 air miles.

1 Judea Jesus ascended to heaven from the Mount of Olives, outside Jerusalem, and his followers returned to the city to await the infilling of the Holy Spirit, which occurred at Pentecost. Peter gave a powerful sermon that was heard by Jews from across the empire. The Jerusalem church grew, but Stephen was martyred for his faith by Jewish leaders who did not believe in Jesus (1:1—7:60).

2 Samaria After Stephen's death, persecution of Christians intensified, but it caused the believers to leave Jerusalem and spread the gospel to other cities in the empire. Philip took the gospel into Samaria, and even to a man from Ethiopia (8:1–40).

3 Syria Paul (Saul) began his story as a persecutor of Christians, only to be met by Jesus himself on the road to Damascus. He became a believer, but his new faith caused opposition, so he returned to Tarsus, his home, for safety. Barnabas sought out Paul in Tarsus and brought him to the church in Antioch of Syria, where they worked together. Meanwhile, Peter had received a vision that led him to Caesarea, where he presented the gospel to a Gentile family, who became believers (9:1—12:25).

4 Cyprus and Galatia Paul and Barnabas were dedicated by the church in Antioch of Syria for God's work of spreading the gospel to other cities. They set off on their first missionary journey through Cyprus and Galatia (13:1—14:28).

5 Jerusalem Controversy between Jewish Christians and Gentile Christians over the matter of keeping the law led to a special council, with delegates from the churches in Antioch and Jerusalem meeting in Jerusalem. Together, they resolved the conflict and the news was taken back to Antioch (15:1–35).

6 Macedonia Barnabas traveled to Cyprus while Paul took a second missionary journey. He revisited the churches in Galatia and headed toward Ephesus, but the Holy Spirit said no. So he turned north toward Bithynia and Pontus but again was told not to go. He then received the "Macedonian call," and followed the Spirit's direction into the cities of Macedonia (15:36—17:14).

7 Achaia Paul traveled from Macedonia to Athens and Corinth in Achaia, then traveled by ship to Ephesus before returning to Caesarea, Jerusalem, and finally back to Antioch (17:15—18:22).

8 Ephesus Paul's third missionary journey took him back through Cilicia and Galatia, this time straight to Ephesus in Asia. He visited other cities in Asia before going back to Macedonia and Achaia. He returned to Jerusalem by ship, despite his knowledge that arrest awaited him there (18:23—23:30).

9 Caesarea Paul was arrested in Jerusalem and taken to Antipatris, then on to Caesarea under Roman guard. Paul always took advantage of any opportunity to share the gospel, and he did so before many Gentile leaders. Because Paul appealed to Caesar, he began the long journey to Rome (23:31—26:32).

10 Rome After storms, layovers in Crete, and shipwreck on the island of Malta, Paul arrived in Sicily and finally in Italy, where he traveled by land, under guard, to his long-awaited destination: Rome, the capital of the empire (27:1—28:31).

ACTS

Jesus crucified; Pentecost; church begun A.D. 30	Stephen martyred; Paul's conversion 35	Paul returns to Tarsus 38	Barnabas goes to find Paul 43	James martyred; Peter in prison 44	Paul's first missionary journey 46–48	Jerusalem council 50	Paul's second missionary journey 50–52

VITAL STATISTICS

PURPOSE:
To give an accurate account of the birth and growth of the Christian church

AUTHOR:
Luke (a Gentile physician)

TO WHOM WRITTEN:
Theophilus and all lovers of God

DATE WRITTEN:
Between A.D. 63 and 70

SETTING:
Acts is the connecting link between Christ's life and the life of the church, between the Gospels and the Letters

KEY VERSE:
"But when the Holy Spirit has come upon you, you will receive power and will tell people about me everywhere—in Jerusalem, throughout Judea, in Samaria, and to the ends of the earth" (1:8).

KEY PEOPLE:
Peter, John, James, Stephen, Philip, Paul, Barnabas, Cornelius, James (Jesus' brother), Timothy, Lydia, Silas, Titus, Apollos, Agabus, Ananias, Felix, Festus, Agrippa, Luke

KEY PLACES:
Jerusalem, Samaria, Lydda, Joppa, Antioch, Cyprus, Pisidian Antioch, Iconium, Lystra, Derbe, Philippi, Thessalonica, Berea, Athens, Corinth, Ephesus, Caesarea, Malta, Rome

SPECIAL FEATURES:
Acts is a sequel to the Gospel of Luke. Because Acts ends so abruptly, Luke may have planned to write a third book, continuing the story.

WITH a flick of a match, friction occurs and a spark leaps from match to tinder. A small flame burns the edges and grows, fueled by wood and air. Heat builds, and soon the kindling is licked by reddish orange tongues. Higher and wider it spreads, consuming the wood. The flame has become a fire.

Nearly 2,000 years ago, a match was struck in Palestine. At first, just a few in that corner of the world were touched and warmed; but the fire spread beyond Jerusalem and Judea out to the world and to all people. Acts provides an eyewitness account of the flame and fire—the birth and spread of the church. Beginning in Jerusalem with a small group of disciples, the message traveled across the Roman Empire. Empowered by the Holy Spirit, this courageous band preached, taught, healed, and demonstrated love in synagogues, schools, homes, marketplaces, and courtrooms, and on streets, hills, ships, and desert roads—wherever God sent them, lives and history were changed.

Written by Luke as a sequel to his Gospel, Acts is an accurate historical record of the early church. But Acts is also a theological book, with lessons and living examples of the work of the Holy Spirit, church relationships and organization, the implications of grace, and the law of love. And Acts is an apologetic work, building a strong case for the validity of Christ's claims and promises.

The book of Acts begins with the outpouring of the promised Holy Spirit and the commencement of the proclamation of the gospel of Jesus Christ. This Spirit-inspired evangelism began in Jerusalem and eventually spread to Rome, covering most of the Roman Empire. The gospel first went to the Jews, but they, as a nation, rejected it. A remnant of Jews, of course, gladly received the Good News. But the continual rejection of the gospel by the vast majority of the Jews led to the ever-increasing proclamation of the gospel to the Gentiles. This was according to Jesus' plan: The gospel was to go from Jerusalem, to Judea, to Samaria, and to the ends of the earth (1:8). This, in fact, is the pattern that the Acts narrative follows. The glorious proclamation began in Jerusalem (chapters 1—7), went to Judea and Samaria (chapters 8 and following), and to the countries beyond Judea (11:19; 13:4 and on to the end of Acts). The second half of Acts is focused primarily on Paul's missionary journeys to many countries north of the Mediterranean Sea. He, with his companions, took the gospel first to the Jews and then to the Gentiles. Some of the Jews believed, and many of the Gentiles received the Good News with joy. New churches were started, and new believers began to grow in the Christian life.

As you read Acts, put yourself in the place of the disciples: Identify with them as they are filled with the Holy Spirit, and experience the thrill of seeing thousands respond to the gospel message. Sense their commitment as they give every ounce of talent and treasure to Christ. And as you read, watch the Spirit-led boldness of these first-century believers, who through suffering and in the face of death take every opportunity to tell of their crucified and risen Lord. Then decide to be a twentieth-century version of those men and women of God.

Paul's third missionary journey 53–57	*Nero becomes emperor 54*	*Paul imprisoned in Caesarea 57–59*	*Paul's journey to Rome 59*	*Paul released from prison 62*	*Paul martyred 67?*	*Rome destroys Jerusalem 70*

THE BLUEPRINT

A. PETER'S MINISTRY (1:1—12:25)
1. Establishment of the church
2. Expansion of the church

After the resurrection of Jesus Christ, Peter preached boldly and performed many miracles. Peter's actions demonstrate vividly the source and effects of Christian power. Because of the Holy Spirit, God's people were empowered so they could accomplish their tasks. The Holy Spirit is still available to empower believers today. We should turn to the Holy Spirit to give us the strength, courage, and insight to accomplish our work for God.

B. PAUL'S MINISTRY (13:1—28:31)
1. First missionary journey
2. The council at Jerusalem
3. Second missionary journey
4. Third missionary journey
5. Paul on trial

Paul's missionary adventures show us the progress of Christianity. The gospel could not be confined to one corner of the world. This was a faith that offered hope to all humanity. We, too, should venture forth and share in this heroic task to witness for Christ in all the world.

MEGATHEMES

THEME	EXPLANATION	IMPORTANCE
Church Beginnings	Acts is the history of how Christianity was founded and organized and solved its problems. The community of believers began by faith in the risen Christ and in the power of the Holy Spirit, who enabled them to witness, to love, and to serve.	New churches are continually being founded. By faith in Jesus Christ and through the power of the Holy Spirit, the church can be a vibrant agent for change. As we face new problems, Acts gives important remedies for solving them.
Holy Spirit	The church did not start or grow by its own power or enthusiasm. The disciples were empowered by God's Holy Spirit. He was the promised Counselor and Guide sent when Jesus went to heaven.	The Holy Spirit's work demonstrated that Christianity was supernatural. Thus, the church became more Holy Spirit conscious than problem conscious. By faith, any believer can claim the Holy Spirit's power to do Christ's work.
Church Growth	Acts presents the history of a dynamic, growing community of believers from Jerusalem to Syria, Africa, Asia, and Europe. In the first century, Christianity spread from believing Jews to non-Jews in 39 cities and 30 countries, islands, or provinces.	When the Holy Spirit works, there is movement, excitement, and growth. He gives us the motivation, energy, and ability to get the gospel to the whole world. How are you fitting into God's plan for spreading Christianity? What is your place in this movement?
Witnessing	Peter, John, Philip, Paul, Barnabas, and thousands more witnessed to their new faith in Christ. By personal testimony, preaching, or defense before authorities, they told the story with boldness and courage to groups of all sizes.	We are God's people, chosen to be part of his plan to reach the world. In love and by faith, we can have the Holy Spirit's help as we witness or preach. Witnessing is also beneficial to us because it strengthens our faith as we confront those who challenge it.
Opposition	Through imprisonment, beatings, plots, and riots, Christians were persecuted by both Jews and Gentiles. But the opposition became a catalyst for the spread of Christianity. Growth during times of oppression showed that Christianity was not the work of humans, but of God.	God can work through any opposition. When persecution from hostile unbelievers comes, realize that it has come because you have been a faithful witness and you have looked for the opportunity to present the Good News about Christ. Seize the opportunities that opposition brings.

A. PETER'S MINISTRY (1:1—12:25)

The book of Acts begins where the Gospels leave off, reporting the actions of the apostles and the work of the Holy Spirit. Beginning in Jerusalem, the church is established and grows rapidly, then faces intense persecution, which drives the believers out into the surrounding areas. Through this dispersion, Samaritans and Gentiles hear the Good News and believe.

1. Establishment of the church

The Promise of the Holy Spirit

1 Dear Theophilus:
In my first book* I told you about everything Jesus began to do and teach 2 until
the day he ascended to heaven after giving his chosen apostles further instructions from
the Holy Spirit. 3 During the forty days after his crucifixion, he appeared to the apostles
from time to time and proved to them in many ways that he was actually alive. On these
occasions he talked to them about the Kingdom of God.
4 In one of these meetings as he was eating a meal with them, he told them, "Do not
leave Jerusalem until the Father sends you what he promised. Remember, I have told you
about this before. 5 John baptized with* water, but in just a few days you will be baptized
with the Holy Spirit."

1:1 Luke 1:3
1:3 Luke 24:33-36; John 20:19, 26; 21:1, 14
1:4 Mark 16:19; Luke 24:49; John 14:16-17, 26; Acts 2:33
1:5 Luke 3:16

The Ascension of Jesus

6 When the apostles were with Jesus, they kept asking him, "Lord, are you going to free
Israel now and restore our kingdom?"

1:6 Luke 24:1

1:1 The reference is to the book of Luke. **1:5** Or *in;* also in 1:5b.

1:1 The book of Acts continues the story Luke began in his Gospel, covering the 30 years after Jesus was taken up into heaven. During that short time the church was established, and the Good News of salvation was taken throughout the world, even to the capital of the Roman Empire. Those preaching the Good News, though ordinary people with human frailties and limitations, were empowered by the Holy Spirit to take it all over the world. Throughout the book of Acts we learn about the nature of the church and how we today are also to go about turning our world upside down (17:6).

1:1ff Verses 1-11 are the bridge between the events recorded in the Gospels and the events marking the beginning of the church. Jesus spent 40 days teaching his disciples, and they were drastically changed. Before, they had argued with each other, deserted their Lord, and one (Peter) even lied about knowing Jesus. Here, in a series of meetings with the living, resurrected Christ, the disciples had many questions answered. They became convinced of the Resurrection, learned about the Kingdom of God, and learned about their power source—the Holy Spirit. By reading the Bible, we can sit with the resurrected Christ in his school of discipleship. By believing in him, we can receive his power through the Holy Spirit to be new people. By joining with other Christians, we can take part in doing his work on earth.

1:1-3 Luke says that the disciples were eyewitnesses to all that had happened to Jesus Christ—his life before his crucifixion, and the 40 days after his resurrection as he taught them more about the Kingdom of God. Today there are still people who doubt Jesus' resurrection. But Jesus appeared to the disciples on many occasions after his resurrection, proving that he was alive. Look at the change the Resurrection made in the disciples' lives. At Jesus' death, they scattered—they were disillusioned, and they feared for their lives. After seeing the resurrected Christ, they were fearless and risked everything to spread the Good News about him around the world. They faced imprisonment, beatings, rejection, and martyrdom, yet they never compromised their mission. These men would not have risked their lives for something they knew was a fraud. They knew Jesus was raised from the dead, and the early church was fired with their enthusiasm to tell others. It is important to know this so we can have confidence in their testimony. Twenty centuries later we can still be confident that our faith is based on fact.

1:3 Jesus explained that with his coming, the Kingdom of God was inaugurated. When he returned to heaven, God's Kingdom would remain in the hearts of all believers through the presence of the Holy Spirit. But the Kingdom of God will not be fully realized until Jesus Christ comes again to judge all people and remove all evil from the world. Until that time believers are to work to spread God's Kingdom across the world. The book of Acts records how this work was begun. What the early church started, we must continue.

1:4, 5 The *Trinity* is a description of the unique relationship of God the Father, the Son, and the Holy Spirit. If Jesus had stayed on earth, his physical presence would have limited the spread of the Good News, because physically he could be in only one place at a time. After Christ was taken up into heaven, he would be spiritually present everywhere through the Holy Spirit. The Holy Spirit was sent so that God would be with and within his followers after Christ returned to heaven. The Spirit would comfort them, guide them to know his truth, remind them of Jesus' words, give them the right words to say, and fill them with power (see John 14–16).

1:5 At Pentecost (2:1-4) the Holy Spirit was made available to all who believed in Jesus. We receive the Holy Spirit (are baptized with him) when we receive Jesus Christ as our Savior. The baptism of the Holy Spirit must be understood in the light of his total work in Christians.

(1) The Spirit marks the beginning of the Christian experience. We cannot be Christians without his Spirit (Romans 8:9); we cannot be joined to Christ without his Spirit (1 Corinthians 6:17); we cannot be adopted as his children without his Spirit (Romans 8:14-17; Galatians 4:6, 7); we cannot be in the body of Christ except by baptism in the Spirit (1 Corinthians 12:13).

(2) The Spirit is the power of our new lives. He begins a lifelong process of change as we become more like Christ (Galatians 3:3; Philippians 1:6). When we receive Christ by faith, we begin an immediate personal relationship with God. The Holy Spirit works in us to help us become like Christ.

(3) The Spirit unites the Christian community in Christ (Ephesians 2:19-22). The Holy Spirit can be experienced by all, and he works through all (1 Corinthians 12:11; Ephesians 4:4).

1:6 During the years of Jesus' ministry on earth, the disciples continually wondered about his Kingdom. When would it come? What would their role be? In the traditional view, the Messiah would be an earthly conqueror who would free Israel from Rome.

1:7 Matt 24:36; 1 Thes 5:1-2
1:8 Luke 24:48; John 15:27; Acts 2:1-4
1:9 Mark 16:19
1:11 Acts 2:7; Rev 1:7

7 “The Father sets those dates,” he replied, “and they are not for you to know. 8 But
when the Holy Spirit has come upon you, you will receive power and will tell people
about me everywhere—in Jerusalem, throughout Judea, in Samaria, and to the ends of
the earth.”
9 It was not long after he said this that he was taken up into the sky while they were
watching, and he disappeared into a cloud. 10 As they were straining their eyes to see him,
two white-robed men suddenly stood there among them. 11 They said, “Men of Galilee,
why are you standing here staring at the sky? Jesus has been taken away from you into
heaven. And someday, just as you saw him go, he will return!”

Matthias Replaces Judas

1:12 Luke 24:50, 52
1:13 Matt 10:2-4; Mark 3:16-19; Luke 6:14-16

12 The apostles were at the Mount of Olives when this happened, so they walked the half
mile* back to Jerusalem. 13 Then they went to the upstairs room of the house where they
were staying. Here is the list of those who were present:

Peter,
John,
James,
Andrew,
Philip,
Thomas,
Bartholomew,
Matthew,
James (son of Alphaeus),
Simon (the Zealot),
and Judas (son of James).

1:12 Greek *a Sabbath day's journey.*

But the Kingdom Jesus spoke about was first of all a *spiritual* Kingdom established in the hearts and lives of believers (Luke 17:21). God's presence and power dwell in believers in the person of the Holy Spirit.

1:6, 7 Like other Jews, the disciples chafed under their Roman rulers. They wanted Jesus to free Israel from Roman power and then become their king. Jesus replied that God the Father sets the timetable for all events—worldwide, national, and personal. If you want changes in your life that God hasn't yet made, don't become impatient. Instead, trust God's timetable.

1:8 Power from the Holy Spirit is not limited to strength beyond the ordinary. That power also involves courage, boldness, confidence, insight, ability, and authority. The disciples would need all these gifts to fulfill their mission. If you believe in Jesus Christ as your Savior, you can experience the power of the Holy Spirit in your life.

1:8 Jesus promised the disciples that they would receive power to witness after they received the Holy Spirit. Notice the progression: (1) They would receive the Holy Spirit, (2) he would give them power, and (3) they would witness with extraordinary results. Often we try to reverse the order and witness by our own power and authority. Witnessing is not showing what we can do for God. It is showing and telling what God has done for us.

1:8 Jesus had instructed his disciples to witness to people of all nations about him (Matthew 28:19, 20). But they were told to wait first for the Holy Spirit (Luke 24:49). God has important work for you to do for him, but you must do it by the power of the Holy Spirit. We often like to get on with the job, even if it means running ahead of God. But waiting is sometimes part of God's plan. Are you waiting and listening for God's complete instructions, or are you running ahead of his plans? We need God's timing and power to be truly effective.

1:8 This verse describes a series of ever-widening circles. The Good News was to spread, geographically, from Jerusalem, into Judea and Samaria, and finally to the whole world. It would begin with the devout Jews in Jerusalem and Samaria, spread to the mixed race in Samaria, and finally be offered to the Gentiles in the uttermost parts of the earth. God's Good News has not reached its final destination if someone in your family, your workplace, your school, or your community hasn't heard about Jesus Christ. Make sure that you are contributing in some way to the ever-widening circle of God's loving message.

1:9 It was important for the disciples to see Jesus taken up into heaven. Then they knew without a doubt that he was God and that his home was in heaven.

1:9-11 After 40 days with his disciples (1:3), Jesus returned to heaven. The two white-robed men were angels who proclaimed to the disciples that one day Jesus would return in the same way he went—bodily and visibly. History is not haphazard or cyclical; it is moving toward a specific point—the return of Jesus to judge and rule over the earth. We should be ready for his sudden return (1 Thessalonians 5:2), not by standing around "staring at the sky," but by working hard to share the Good News so that others will be able to share in God's great blessings.

1:12, 13 After Christ was taken up into heaven, the disciples immediately returned to Jerusalem and had a prayer meeting. Jesus had said they would be baptized with the Holy Spirit in a few days, so they waited and prayed. When you face a difficult task, an important decision, or a baffling dilemma, don't rush into the work and just hope it comes out the way it should. Instead, your first step should be to pray for the Holy Spirit's power and guidance.

1:13 A "zealot" could mean anyone zealous for the Jewish law. The zealots may have been a radical political party working for the violent overthrow of Roman rule in Israel.

14 They all met together continually for prayer, along with Mary the mother of Jesus,
several other women, and the brothers of Jesus.
15 During this time, on a day when about 120 believers were present, Peter stood up
and addressed them as follows:
16 "Brothers, it was necessary for the Scriptures to be fulfilled concerning Judas, who
guided the Temple police to arrest Jesus. This was predicted long ago by the Holy Spirit,
speaking through King David. 17 Judas was one of us, chosen to share in the ministry
with us."
18 (Judas bought a field with the money he received for his treachery, and falling there,
he burst open, spilling out his intestines. 19 The news of his death spread rapidly among
all the people of Jerusalem, and they gave the place the Aramaic name *Akeldama,* which
means "Field of Blood.")
20 Peter continued, "This was predicted in the book of Psalms, where it says, 'Let his
home become desolate, with no one living in it.' And again, 'Let his position be given to
someone else.'*
21 "So now we must choose someone else to take Judas's place. It must be someone
who has been with us all the time that we were with the Lord Jesus—22 from the time he
was baptized by John until the day he was taken from us into heaven. Whoever is chosen
will join us as a witness of Jesus' resurrection."
23 So they nominated two men: Joseph called Barsabbas (also known as Justus) and
Matthias. 24 Then they all prayed for the right man to be chosen. "O Lord," they said,
"you know every heart. Show us which of these men you have chosen 25 as an apostle to
replace Judas the traitor in this ministry, for he has deserted us and gone where he
belongs." 26 Then they cast lots, and in this way Matthias was chosen and became an
apostle with the other eleven.

The Holy Spirit Comes

2 On the day of Pentecost, seven weeks after Jesus' resurrection,* the believers were
meeting together in one place. 2 Suddenly, there was a sound from heaven like the
roaring of a mighty windstorm in the skies above them, and it filled the house where they
were meeting. 3 Then, what looked like flames or tongues of fire appeared and settled on

1:14 Acts 2:42
1:16 Ps 41:9
1:17 John 6:70-71; Acts 1:24-25
1:18 Matt 27:3-8
1:20 †Pss 69:25; 109:8
1:21-22 Mark 1:1-4
1:24 Acts 6:6
1:26 Prov 16:33
2:1 Lev 23:15-21; Deut 16:9-11; Acts 1:14; 20:16
2:2 Acts 4:31

1:20 Pss 69:25; 109:8. **2:1** Greek *When the day of Pentecost arrived.* This annual celebration came 50 days after the Passover ceremonies. See Lev 23:16.

1:14 At this time, Jesus' brothers were with the disciples. During Jesus' lifetime, they did not believe he was the Messiah (John 7:5), but his resurrection must have convinced them. Jesus' special appearance to James, one of his brothers, may have been an especially significant event in their conversion (see 1 Corinthians 15:7).

1:15-26 This was the first church business meeting. The small group of 11 had already grown to more than 120. The main order of business was to appoint a new disciple, or apostle, as the 11 were now called. While the apostles waited, they were doing what they could—praying, seeking God's guidance, and getting organized. Waiting for God to work does not mean sitting around doing nothing. We must do what we can, while we can, as long as we don't run ahead of God.

1:16, 17 How could someone who had been with Jesus daily betray him? Judas received the same calling and teaching as everyone else. But he chose to reject Christ's warning as well as his offers of mercy. Judas hardened his heart and joined in the plot with Jesus' enemies to put him to death. Judas remained unrepentant to the end, and he finally committed suicide. Although Jesus predicted this would happen, it was Judas's choice. Those privileged to be *close* to the truth are not necessarily *committed* to the truth. See Judas's Profile in Mark 14 for more information on his life.

1:18 Matthew says that Judas hanged himself (Matthew 27:5); Acts says that he fell. The traditional explanation is that when Judas hanged himself, the rope or branch broke, Judas fell, and his body burst open.

1:21, 22 There were many who consistently followed Jesus throughout his ministry on earth. The 12 disciples were his inner circle, but others shared the disciples' deep love for and commitment to Jesus.

1:21-25 The apostles had to choose a replacement for Judas Iscariot. They outlined specific criteria for making the choice. When the "finalists" had been chosen, the apostles prayed, asking God to guide the selection process. This gives us a good example of how to proceed when we are making important decisions. Set up criteria consistent with the Bible, examine the alternatives, and pray for wisdom and guidance to reach a wise decision.

1:26 The disciples became *apostles. Disciple* means "follower or learner," and *apostle* means "messenger or missionary." These men now had the special assignment of spreading the Good News of Jesus' death and resurrection.

2:1 Held 50 days after Passover, Pentecost was also called the Festival of Harvest. It was one of three major annual festivals (Deuteronomy 16:16), a festival of thanksgiving for the harvested crops. Jesus was crucified at Passover time, and he ascended 40 days after his resurrection. The Holy Spirit came 50 days after the Resurrection, 10 days after the Ascension. Jews of many nations gathered in Jerusalem for this festival. Thus, Peter's speech (2:14ff) was given to an international audience, and it resulted in a worldwide harvest of new believers—the first converts to Christianity.

A JOURNEY THROUGH THE BOOK OF ACTS

Beginning with a brief summary of Jesus' last days on earth with his disciples, his ascension, and the selection of a replacement for Judas Iscariot, Luke moves quickly to his subject—the spread of the gospel and the growth of the church. Pentecost, highlighted by the filling of the Holy Spirit (2:1–13) and Peter's powerful sermon (2:14–42), was the beginning. Then the **Jerusalem** church grew daily through the bold witness of Peter and John and the love of the believers (2:43—4:37). The infant church was not without problems, however, with external opposition (resulting in imprisonment, beatings, and death) and internal deceit and complaining. Greek-speaking Jewish believers were appointed to help with the administration of the church to free the apostles to preach. Stephen and Philip were among the first deacons, and Stephen became the church's first martyr (5:1—8:3).

Instead of stopping Christianity, opposition and persecution served as catalysts for its spread because the believers took the message with them wherever they fled (8:4). Soon there were converts throughout **Samaria** and even in **Ethiopia** (8:5–40).

At this point, Luke introduces us to a bright young Jew, zealous for the law and intent on ridding Judaism of the Jesus heresy. But on the way to **Damascus** to capture believers, Saul was converted when he was confronted in person by the risen Christ (9:1–9). Through the ministry of Ananias and the sponsorship of Barnabas, Saul (Paul) was welcomed into the fellowship and then sent to **Tarsus** for safety (9:10–30).

Meanwhile, the church continued to thrive throughout **Judea, Galilee,** and **Samaria.** Luke recounts Peter's preaching and how Peter healed Aeneas in Lydda and Dorcas in **Joppa** (9:31–43). While in Joppa, Peter learned through a vision that he could take the gospel to the "unclean" Gentiles. Peter understood, and he faithfully shared the truth with Cornelius, whose entire household became believers (chapter 10). This was startling news to the Jerusalem church; but when Peter told his story, they praised God for his plan for *all* people to hear the Good News (11:1–18). This pushed the church into even wider circles as the message was preached to Greeks in **Antioch,** where Barnabas went to encourage the believers. Then he went on to **Tarsus** to find Saul (11:20–26).

To please the Jewish leaders, Herod joined in the persecution of the Jerusalem church, killing James (John's brother) and imprisoning Peter. But God freed Peter, and Peter walked from prison to a prayer meeting on his behalf at John Mark's house (chapter 12).

Here Luke shifts the focus to Paul's ministry. Commissioned by the Antioch church for a missionary tour (13:1–3), Paul and Barnabas took the gospel to **Cyprus** and south **Galatia** with great success (13:4—14:28). But the Jewish-Gentile controversy still smoldered, and with so many Gentiles responding to Christ, the controversy threatened to divide the church. So a council met in Jerusalem to rule on the relationship of Gentile Christians to the Old Testament laws. After hearing both sides, James (Jesus' brother and the leader of the Jerusalem church) resolved the issue and sent messengers to the churches with the decision (15:1–31).

After the council, Paul and Silas preached in Antioch. Then they left for **Syria** and **Cilicia** as Barnabas and Mark sailed for **Cyprus** (15:35–41). On this second missionary journey, Paul and Silas traveled throughout **Macedonia** and **Achaia,** establishing churches in **Philippi, Thessalonica, Berea, Corinth,** and **Ephesus** before returning to Antioch (16:1—18:22). Luke also tells of the ministry of Apollos (18:24–28).

On Paul's third missionary trip, he traveled through **Galatia, Phrygia, Macedonia,** and **Achaia,** encouraging and teaching the believers (19:1—21:9). During this time, he felt compelled to go to Jerusalem; and although he was warned by Agabus and others of impending imprisonment (21:10–12), he continued his journey in that direction.

While in Jerusalem, Paul was accosted in the Temple by an angry mob and taken into protective custody by the Roman commander (21:17—22:29). Now we see Paul as a prisoner and on trial before the Jewish high council (23:1–9), Governor Felix (23:23—24:27), and Festus and Agrippa (25:1—26:32). In each case, Paul gave a strong and clear witness for his Lord.

Because Paul appealed to Caesar, however, he was sent to **Rome** for the final hearing of his case. But on the way, the ship was destroyed in a storm, and the sailors and prisoners had to swim ashore. Even in this circumstance Paul shared his faith (27:1—28:10). Eventually the journey continued and Paul arrived in Rome, where he was held under house arrest while awaiting trial (28:11–31).

Luke ends Acts abruptly with the encouraging word that Paul had freedom in his captivity as he talked to visitors and guards, "proclaiming the Kingdom of God with all boldness and teaching about the Lord Jesus Christ. And no one tried to stop him" (28:31).

each of them. 4And everyone present was filled with the Holy Spirit and began speaking
in other languages,* as the Holy Spirit gave them this ability.
5Godly Jews from many nations were living in Jerusalem at that time. 6When they
heard this sound, they came running to see what it was all about, and they were
bewildered to hear their own languages being spoken by the believers.
7They were beside themselves with wonder. "How can this be?" they exclaimed.
"These people are all from Galilee, 8and yet we hear them speaking the languages of the
lands where we were born! 9Here we are—Parthians, Medes, Elamites, people from
Mesopotamia, Judea, Cappadocia, Pontus, the province of Asia, 10Phrygia, Pamphylia,
Egypt, and the areas of Libya toward Cyrene, visitors from Rome (both Jews and
converts to Judaism), 11Cretans, and Arabians. And we all hear these people speaking in
our own languages about the wonderful things God has done!" 12They stood there
amazed and perplexed. "What can this mean?" they asked each other. 13But others in the
crowd were mocking. "They're drunk, that's all!" they said.

2:4 Mark 16:17; Acts 4:31; 10:44-46; 19:6; 1 Cor 12:10; 13:1
2:7 Acts 1:11
2:9 Acts 16:6; 19:10; 1 Pet 1:1
2:10 Matt 27:32; Acts 13:13; 16:6
2:13 1 Cor 14:23; Eph 5:18

Peter Preaches to a Crowd

14Then Peter stepped forward with the eleven other apostles and shouted to the crowd,
"Listen carefully, all of you, fellow Jews and residents of Jerusalem! Make no mistake
about this. 15Some of you are saying these people are drunk. It isn't true! It's much too
early for that. People don't get drunk by nine o'clock in the morning. 16No, what you
see this morning was predicted centuries ago by the prophet Joel:

17 'In the last days, God said,
I will pour out my Spirit upon all people.

2:17-21 †Joel 2:28-32

2:4 Or *in other tongues.*

2:3, 4 This was a fulfillment of John the Baptist's words about the Holy Spirit's baptizing with fire (Luke 3:16) and of the prophet Joel's words about the outpouring of the Holy Spirit (Joel 2:28, 29).

Why tongues of fire? Tongues symbolize speech and the communication of the Good News. Fire symbolizes God's purifying presence, which burns away the undesirable elements of our life and sets our heart aflame to ignite the lives of others. On Mount Sinai, God confirmed the validity of the Old Testament law with fire from heaven (Exodus 19:16-18). At Pentecost, God confirmed the validity of the Holy Spirit's ministry by sending fire. At Mount Sinai, fire came down on one place; at Pentecost, fire came down on many believers, symbolizing that God's presence is available to all who believe in him.

2:3, 4 God made his presence known to this group of believers in a spectacular way—violent wind, fire, and his Holy Spirit. Would you like God to reveal himself to you in such recognizable ways? He may do so, but be wary of forcing your expectations on God. In 1 Kings 19:10-13, Elijah also needed a message from God. There was a great wind, then an earthquake, and finally a fire. But God's message came in a "gentle whisper." God may use dramatic methods to work in your life—or he may speak in gentle whispers. Wait patiently and always listen.

2:4-11 These people literally spoke in other languages as the Spirit game them ability—a miraculous attention-getter for the international crowd gathered in town for the festival. All the nationalities represented recognized their own languages being spoken. But more than miraculous speaking drew people's attention; they saw the presence and power of the Holy Spirit. The apostles continued to minister in the power of the Holy Spirit wherever they went.

2:7, 8 Christianity is not limited to any race or group of people. Christ offers salvation to all people without regard to nationality. Visitors in Jerusalem were surprised to hear the apostles and other believers speaking in languages other than their own, the languages of other nationalities, but they need not have been. God works all kinds of miracles to spread the Good News, using many languages as he calls all kinds of people to become his followers. No matter what your race, color, nationality, or language, God speaks to you. Are you listening?

2:9-11 Why are all these places mentioned? This is a list of many lands from which Jews came to the festivals in Jerusalem. These Jews were not originally from Palestine because their ancestors had been dispersed to other parts of the world through captivities and persecutions. Very likely, some of the Jews who responded to Peter's message returned to their homelands with God's Good News of salvation. Thus, God prepared the way for the spread of the Good News. As you read Acts, you will see how the way was often prepared for Paul and other messengers by people who became believers at Pentecost. The church at Rome, for example, was probably begun by such Jewish believers.

2:14 Peter had been an unstable leader during Jesus' ministry, letting his bravado be his downfall, even denying that he knew Jesus (John 18:15-18, 25-27). But Christ had forgiven and restored him (John 21). This was a new Peter, humble but bold. His confidence came from the Holy Spirit, who made him a powerful and dynamic speaker. Have you ever felt as if you've made such bad mistakes that God could never forgive and use you? No matter what sins you have committed, God promises to forgive you and make you useful for his Kingdom. Allow him to forgive you and use you effectively to serve him.

2:14ff Peter tells the people why they should listen to the testimony of the believers: because the Old Testament prophecies concerning Jesus had been entirely fulfilled in him (2:14-21), because Jesus is the Messiah (2:25-36), and because the risen Christ could change their lives (2:37-40).

2:15 Peter answered accusations that they were all drunk (2:13) by saying it was much too early in the day for that.

2:16-21 Not everything mentioned in Joel 2:28, 29 was happening that particular morning. The "last days" include all the days between Christ's first and second comings and is another way of saying "from now on." "That great and glorious day of the Lord" (2:20) denotes the whole Christian age. Even Moses yearned for the Lord to put his Spirit upon everyone (Numbers 11:29). At Pentecost the Holy Spirit was released throughout the entire world—to men, women, slaves, Jews, Gentiles. Now *everyone* can receive the Spirit. This was a revolutionary thought for first- century Jews.

Your sons and daughters will prophesy,
your young men will see visions,
and your old men will dream dreams.

2:18 Num 11:29 1 Cor 12:10

18 In those days I will pour out my Spirit
upon all my servants, men and women alike,
and they will prophesy.
19 And I will cause wonders in the heavens above
and signs on the earth below—
blood and fire and clouds of smoke.

2:20 Matt 24:29

20 The sun will be turned into darkness,
and the moon will turn bloodred,
before that great and glorious day of the Lord arrives.

2:21 Acts 9:14 Rom 10:13

21 And anyone who calls on the name of the Lord
will be saved.'*

2:22 John 3:2
2:23 1 Pet 1:20
2:24 Acts 3:15
2:25-28 †Ps 16:8-11 Acts 13:30-35

22"People of Israel, listen! God publicly endorsed Jesus of Nazareth by doing wonderful
miracles, wonders, and signs through him, as you well know. 23But you followed God's
prearranged plan. With the help of lawless Gentiles, you nailed him to the cross and
murdered him. 24However, God released him from the horrors of death and raised him back
to life again, for death could not keep him in its grip. 25King David said this about him:

'I know the Lord is always with me.
I will not be shaken, for he is right beside me.
26 No wonder my heart is filled with joy,
and my mouth shouts his praises!
My body rests in hope.
27 For you will not leave my soul among the dead*
or allow your Holy One to rot in the grave.
28 You have shown me the way of life,
and you will give me wonderful joy in your presence.'*

2:29 1 Kgs 2:10 Acts 13:36
2:30 †2 Sam 7:12-14 †Pss 89:4; 132:11
2:31 †Ps 16:10
2:33 John 14:26 Acts 1:4, 8 Eph 4:8 Phil 2:9
2:34-35 †Ps 110:1

29"Dear brothers, think about this! David wasn't referring to himself when he spoke
these words I have quoted, for he died and was buried, and his tomb is still here among
us. 30But he was a prophet, and he knew God had promised with an oath that one of
David's own descendants would sit on David's throne as the Messiah. 31David was
looking into the future and predicting the Messiah's resurrection. He was saying that the
Messiah would not be left among the dead and that his body would not rot in the grave.
32"This prophecy was speaking of Jesus, whom God raised from the dead, and we all
are witnesses of this. 33Now he sits on the throne of highest honor in heaven, at God's
right hand. And the Father, as he had promised, gave him the Holy Spirit to pour out upon
us, just as you see and hear today. 34For David himself never ascended into heaven, yet
he said,

'The LORD said to my Lord,
Sit in honor at my right hand
35 until I humble your enemies,
making them a footstool under your feet.'*

2:17-21 Joel 2:28-32. **2:27** Greek *in Hades;* also in 2:31. **2:25-28** Ps 16:8-11. **2:34-35** Ps 110:1.

2:23 Everything that happened to Jesus was under God's control. His plans were never disrupted by the Roman government or the Jewish officials. This was especially comforting to those facing oppression during the time of the early Christian church.

2:24 Peter began with a public proclamation of the Resurrection at a time when it could be verified by many witnesses. This was a powerful statement, because many of the people listening to Peter's words had been in Jerusalem 50 days earlier at Passover and may have seen or heard about the Crucifixion and Resurrection of this "great teacher." Jesus' resurrection was the ultimate sign that what he said about himself was true. Without the Resurrection, we would have no reason to believe in Jesus (1 Corinthians 15:14).

2:25-32 Peter quoted from Psalm 16:8-11—a psalm written by David. He explained that David was not writing about himself, because David died and was buried (2:29). Instead, he wrote as a prophet (2:30) who spoke of the Messiah who would be resurrected. The emphasis here is that Jesus' body was *not* left to rot in the grave but was, in fact, resurrected and glorified.

36 So let it be clearly known by everyone in Israel that God has made this Jesus whom
you crucified to be both Lord and Messiah!"
37 Peter's words convicted them deeply, and they said to him and to the other apostles,
"Brothers, what should we do?"
38 Peter replied, "Each of you must turn from your sins and turn to God, and be
baptized in the name of Jesus Christ for the forgiveness of your sins. Then you will
receive the gift of the Holy Spirit. 39 This promise is to you and to your children, and
even to the Gentiles*—all who have been called by the Lord our God." 40 Then Peter
continued preaching for a long time, strongly urging all his listeners, "Save yourselves
from this generation that has gone astray!"
41 Those who believed what Peter said were baptized and added to the church—about
three thousand in all. 42 They joined with the other believers and devoted themselves to
the apostles' teaching and fellowship, sharing in the Lord's Supper and in prayer.

The Believers Meet Together

43 A deep sense of awe came over them all, and the apostles performed many miraculous
signs and wonders. 44 And all the believers met together constantly and shared everything
they had. 45 They sold their possessions and shared the proceeds with those in need.
46 They worshiped together at the Temple each day, met in homes for the Lord's Supper,
and shared their meals with great joy and generosity—47 all the while praising God and
enjoying the goodwill of all the people. And each day the Lord added to their group those
who were being saved.

Peter Heals a Crippled Beggar

3 Peter and John went to the Temple one afternoon to take part in the three o'clock
prayer service. 2 As they approached the Temple, a man lame from birth was being
carried in. Each day he was put beside the Temple gate, the one called the Beautiful Gate,

2:39 Greek *to those far away.*

2:36 Acts 5:30-31
2:37 Acts 16:30
2:38 Mark 16:16; Acts 3:19; 8:12; 22:16
2:39 Isa 44:3; 57:19; Joel 2:32; Eph 2:13
2:40 Deut 32:5; Phil 2:15
2:42 Acts 20:7
2:44-45 Acts 4:32-37
2:47 Acts 4:4; 6:7; Rom 14:18
3:1 Acts 10:3, 9, 30
3:2 Acts 14:8

2:37 After Peter's powerful, Spirit-filled message, the people were deeply moved and asked, "What should we do?" This is the basic question we must ask. It is not enough to be sorry for our sins. We must repent, ask God to forgive us, and then live like forgiven people. Has God spoken to you through his Word or through the words of another believer? Like Peter's audience, ask God what you should do, and then obey.

2:38, 39 If you want to follow Christ, you must "turn from your sins and turn to God, and be baptized." To turn from sin means to repent, changing the direction of your life from selfishness and rebellion against God's laws. At the same time, you must *turn to* Christ, depending on him for forgiveness, mercy, guidance, and purpose. We cannot save ourselves—only God can save us. Baptism identifies us with Christ and with the community of believers. It is a condition of discipleship and a sign of faith.

2:40-43 About 3,000 people became new believers when Peter preached the Good News about Christ. These new Christians were united with the other believers, taught by the apostles, and included in the prayer meetings and fellowship. New believers in Christ need to be in groups, where they can learn God's Word, pray, and mature in the faith. If you have just begun a relationship with Christ, seek out other believers for fellowship, prayer, and teaching. This is the way to grow.

2:42 "Sharing in the Lord's Supper" refers to Communion services that were celebrated in remembrance of Jesus and were patterned after the Last Supper that Jesus had with his disciples before his death (Matthew 26:26-29).

2:44 Recognizing the other believers as brothers and sisters in the family of God, the Christians in Jerusalem shared all they had so that all could benefit from God's gifts. It is tempting—especially if we have material wealth—to cut ourselves off from one another, concerning ourselves with only our interests and enjoying only our own little piece of the world. But as part of God's spiritual family, it is our responsibility to help one another in every way possible. God's family works best when its members work together.

2:46 A common misconception about the first Christians (who were Jews) was that they rejected the Jewish religion. But these believers saw Jesus' message and resurrection as the fulfillment of everything they knew and believed from the Old Testament. The Jewish believers at first did not separate themselves from the rest of the Jewish community. They still went to the Temple and synagogues for worship and instruction in the Scriptures. But their belief in Jesus created great friction with Jews who didn't believe that Jesus was the Messiah. Thus, believing Jews were forced to meet in private homes for Communion, prayer, and teaching about Christ. By the end of the first century, many of these Jewish believers were excommunicated from their synagogues.

2:47 A healthy Christian community attracts people to Christ. The Jerusalem church's zeal for worship and brotherly love was contagious. A healthy, loving church will grow in numbers. What are you doing to make your church the kind of place that will attract others to Christ?

3:1 The Jews observed three times of prayer—morning (9:00 A.M.), afternoon (3:00 P.M.), and evening (sunset). At these times devout Jews and Gentiles who believed in God often went to the Temple to pray. Peter and John were going to the Temple for the afternoon prayer service.

3:2 The Beautiful Gate was an entrance to the Temple, not to the city. It was one of the favored entrances, and many people passed through it on their way to worship. The lame man was begging where he would be seen by the most people.

3:2 Giving money to beggars was considered praiseworthy in the Jewish religion. So the beggar wisely placed himself where pious people might see him on their way to worship at the Temple.

so he could beg from the people going into the Temple. 3When he saw Peter and John
about to enter, he asked them for some money.
4Peter and John looked at him intently, and Peter said, "Look at us!" 5The lame man
looked at them eagerly, expecting a gift. 6But Peter said, "I don't have any money for you.
But I'll give you what I have. In the name of Jesus Christ of Nazareth, get up and walk!"
7Then Peter took the lame man by the right hand and helped him up. And as he did,
the man's feet and anklebones were healed and strengthened. 8He jumped up, stood on
his feet, and began to walk! Then, walking, leaping, and praising God, he went into the
Temple with them.
9All the people saw him walking and heard him praising God. 10When they realized
he was the lame beggar they had seen so often at the Beautiful Gate, they were absolutely
astounded! 11They all rushed out to Solomon's Colonnade, where he was holding tightly
to Peter and John. Everyone stood there in awe of the wonderful thing that had happened.

Peter Preaches in the Temple

12Peter saw his opportunity and addressed the crowd. "People of Israel," he said, "what
is so astounding about this? And why look at us as though we had made this man walk
by our own power and godliness? 13For it is the God of Abraham, the God of Isaac, the
God of Jacob, the God of all our ancestors who has brought glory to his servant Jesus by
doing this. This is the same Jesus whom you handed over and rejected before Pilate,
despite Pilate's decision to release him. 14You rejected this holy, righteous one and
instead demanded the release of a murderer. 15You killed the author of life, but God
raised him to life. And we are witnesses of this fact!
16"The name of Jesus has healed this man—and you know how lame he was before.
Faith in Jesus' name has caused this healing before your very eyes.
17"Friends,* I realize that what you did to Jesus was done in ignorance; and the same
can be said of your leaders. 18But God was fulfilling what all the prophets had declared
about the Messiah beforehand—that he must suffer all these things. 19Now turn from

3:4 Acts 13:9; 14:9
3:6 Acts 4:10
3:8 John 5:14
3:9 Acts 4:16, 21
3:10 John 9:8
3:11 John 10:23; Acts 5:12
3:13 †Exod 3:6, 15; Matt 22:32; Acts 5:30; 7:32
3:15 Acts 2:24; 5:30
3:17 Luke 23:34; Acts 13:27; 1 Tim 1:13
3:18 Pss 22; 41:9; 69:4, 21; Isa 50:6; 53:4-11; Zech 12:10; 13:7; Luke 24:27, 44, 46
3:19 Acts 2:38; 26:20

3:17 Greek *Brothers.*

3:5, 6 The lame man asked for money, but Peter gave him something much better—the use of his legs. We often ask God to solve a small problem, but he wants to give us a whole new life and help for *all* our problems. When we ask God for help, he may say, "I've got something even better for you." You may ask God for what you want, but don't be surprised when he gives you what you really *need.*

3:6 "In the name of Jesus Christ" means "by the authority of Jesus Christ." The apostles were doing this healing through the Holy Spirit's power, not their own.

3:7-10 In his excitement, the formerly lame man began to jump and walk around. He also praised God! And then others were also awed by God's power. Don't forget to thank people who help you, but also remember to praise God for his care and protection.

3:11 Solomon's Colonnade was a covered porch or entrance with columns.

3:11ff Peter had an audience, and he capitalized on the opportunity to share Jesus Christ. He clearly presented his message by telling (1) who Jesus is, (2) how the Jews had rejected him, (3) why their rejection was fatal, and (4) what they needed to do to change the situation. Peter told the crowd that they still had a choice; God still offered them the opportunity to believe and receive Jesus as their Messiah and as their Lord. Displays of God's mercy and grace, such as the healing of this lame man, often create teachable moments. Pray to have courage like Peter to see these opportunities and to use them to speak up for Christ.

3:13-15 Pilate had decided to release Jesus, but the people had clamored to have Barabbas, a murderer, released instead (see John 19:1-16). When Peter said, "You killed the author of life," he meant it literally. Jesus' trial and death had occurred right there in Jerusalem only weeks earlier. It wasn't an event of the distant past—most of these people had heard about it, and some may very well have taken part in condemning Jesus.

3:15 The religious leaders thought they had put an end to Jesus when they crucified him. But their confidence was shaken when Peter told them that Jesus was alive again and that this time they could not harm him. Peter's message emphasized that (1) the people and their religious leaders killed Jesus (3:17), (2) God brought him back to life, and (3) the apostles were witnesses of this fact. After pointing out the sin and injustice of these leaders, Peter showed the significance of the Resurrection, God's triumph and power over death.

3:16 Jesus, not the apostles, received the glory for the healing of the lame man. In those days a man's name represented his character; it stood for his authority and power. By using Jesus' name, Peter showed who gave him the authority and power to heal. The apostles did not emphasize what *they* could do but what God could do through them. Jesus' name is not to be used as magic—it must be used in faith. When we pray in Jesus' name, we must remember that it is Christ himself, not merely the sound of his name, who gives our prayers their power.

3:18 These prophecies are found in Psalm 22 and Isaiah 50:6 and Isaiah 53. Peter was explaining the kind of Messiah God had sent to earth. The Jews expected a great ruler, not a suffering servant.

3:19 John the Baptist prepared the way for Jesus by preaching that people should turn from their sins. The apostles' message of salvation also included the call to turn from sin—acknowledging personal sin and repenting of it. Many people want the benefits of being identified with Christ without admitting their own disobedience and turning from sin. The key to forgiveness is confessing your sin and turning from it (see 2:38).

3:19, 20 When we turn from sin, God promises not only to cleanse us of our sins but to bring spiritual refreshment. Turning away from sin may at first seem painful because it is hard to break old habits and give up certain sins. But God will give you a

your sins and turn to God, so you can be cleansed of your sins. 20 Then wonderful times
of refreshment will come from the presence of the Lord, and he will send Jesus your
Messiah to you again. 21 For he must remain in heaven until the time for the final
restoration of all things, as God promised long ago through his prophets. 22 Moses said,
'The Lord your God will raise up a Prophet like me from among your own people. Listen
carefully to everything he tells you.'* 23 Then Moses said, 'Anyone who will not listen
to that Prophet will be cut off from God's people and utterly destroyed.'*
24 "Starting with Samuel, every prophet spoke about what is happening today. 25 You
are the children of those prophets, and you are included in the covenant God promised
to your ancestors. For God said to Abraham, 'Through your descendants all the families
on earth will be blessed.'* 26 When God raised up his servant, he sent him first to you
people of Israel, to bless you by turning each of you back from your sinful ways."

Peter and John before the Council

4 While Peter and John were speaking to the people, the leading priests, the captain
of the Temple guard, and some of the Sadducees came over to them. 2 They were
very disturbed that Peter and John were claiming, on the authority of Jesus, that there is
a resurrection of the dead. 3 They arrested them and, since it was already evening, jailed
them until morning. 4 But many of the people who heard their message believed it, so
that the number of believers totaled about five thousand men, not counting women and
children.*
5 The next day the council of all the rulers and elders and teachers of religious law met
in Jerusalem. 6 Annas the high priest was there, along with Caiaphas, John, Alexander,

3:21 Luke 1:70
3:22 †Deut 18:15, 18; John 1:20-21; 7:40-41, 52
3:23 †Lev 23:29; †Deut 18:19
3:25 †Gen 22:18; 26:4; Rom 9:4-8
3:26 Acts 13:46; Rom 1:16
4:1 Luke 22:4
4:3 Acts 5:18
4:4 Acts 4:21
4:6 Matt 26:3; Luke 3:2

3:22 Deut 18:15. **3:23** Deut 18:19; Lev 23:29. **3:25** Gen 22:18. **4:4** Greek *5,000 adult males.*

better way. As Hosea promised, "Oh, that we might know the LORD! Let us press on to know him! Then he will respond to us as surely as the arrival of dawn or the coming of rains in early spring" (Hosea 6:3). Do you feel a need to be refreshed?

3:21 The time when God will bring the "final restoration of all things" refers to the Second Coming, the Last Judgment, and the removal of sin from the world.

3:21, 22 Most Jews thought that Joshua was this prophet predicted by Moses (Deuteronomy 18:15). Peter was saying that the prophet was Jesus Christ. Peter wanted to show them that their long-awaited Messiah had come! He and all the apostles were calling the Jewish nation to realize what they had done to their Messiah, to repent, and to believe. From this point on in Acts, we see many Jews rejecting the Good News. So the message went also to the Gentiles, many of whom were open to receive Jesus.

3:24 The prophet Samuel lived during the transition between the judges and the kings of Israel, and he was seen as the first in a succession of prophets. He anointed David king, founding David's royal line, from which the Messiah eventually came. All the prophets pointed to a future Messiah. For more on Samuel, see his Profile in 1 Samuel 8.

3:25 God promised Abraham that he would bless the world through Abraham's descendants, the Jewish race (Genesis 12:3), from which the Messiah would come. God intended the Jewish nation to be a separate and holy nation that would teach the world about God, introduce the Messiah, and then carry on his work in the world. After the days of Solomon, the nation gave up its mission to tell the world about God. Here, too, in apostolic times as well as in the time Jesus spent on earth, Israel rejected its Messiah.

4:1 These leading priests had special influence and were often close relatives of the high priest. The captain of the Temple guard was the leader of the guards who were stationed around the Temple to ensure order. The Sadducees were members of a small but powerful Jewish religious sect that did not believe in the resurrection of the dead. They were the religious leaders who stood to gain financially by cooperating with the Romans. Most of those who engineered and carried out Jesus' arrest and crucifixion were from these three groups.

4:2, 3 Peter and John spoke to the people during the afternoon prayer time. The Sadducees moved in quickly to investigate. Because they did not believe in the resurrection, they were understandably disturbed with what the apostles were saying. Peter and John were refuting one of their fundamental beliefs and thus threatening their authority as religious teachers. Even though the nation was under Roman rule, the Sadducees had almost unlimited power over the Temple grounds. Thus, they were able to arrest Peter and John for no other reason than teaching something that contradicted their beliefs.

4:3 Not often will sharing the Good News send us to jail as it did Peter and John. Still, we run risks in trying to win others to Christ. We might be willing to face a night in jail if it would bring 5,000 people to Christ, but shouldn't we also be willing to suffer for the sake of even one? What do you risk in witnessing—rejection, persecution? Whatever the risks, realize that nothing done for God is ever wasted.

4:5, 6 The rulers, elders, and teachers of religious law made up the Jewish high council—the same council that had condemned Jesus to death (Luke 22:66). It had 70 members plus the current high priest, who presided over the group. The Sadducees held a majority in this ruling group. These were the wealthy, intellectual, and powerful men of Jerusalem. Jesus' followers stood before this high council just as he had.

4:6 Annas had been deposed as high priest by the Romans, who then appointed Caiaphas, Annas's son-in-law, in his place. But because the Jews considered the office of high priest a lifetime position, they still called Annas by that title and gave him respect and authority within the high council. Annas and Caiaphas had played significant roles in Jesus' trial (John 18:24, 28). It did not please them that the man they thought they had sacrificed for the good of the nation (John 11:49-51) had followers who were just as persistent and promised to be just as troublesome as he was.

4:7 Matt 21:23
and other relatives of the high priest. [7]They brought in the two disciples and demanded,
"By what power, or in whose name, have you done this?"
[8]Then Peter, filled with the Holy Spirit, said to them, "Leaders and elders of our
nation, [9]are we being questioned because we've done a good deed for a crippled man?
4:10 Acts 2:24; 3:6
Do you want to know how he was healed? [10]Let me clearly state to you and to all the
4:11 Ps 118:22 Isa 28:16 Matt 21:42 1 Pet 2:4, 7
people of Israel that he was healed in the name and power of Jesus Christ from Nazareth,
the man you crucified, but whom God raised from the dead. [11]For Jesus is the one
referred to in the Scriptures, where it says,

'The stone that you builders rejected
has now become the cornerstone.'*

4:12 Matt 1:21 Acts 10:43 1 Tim 2:5
[12]There is salvation in no one else! There is no other name in all of heaven for people
to call on to save them."
[13]The members of the council were amazed when they saw the boldness of Peter and
4:13 Matt 11:25
John, for they could see that they were ordinary men who had had no special training. They
also recognized them as men who had been with Jesus. [14]But since the man who had been
4:15 Acts 5:34-35
healed was standing right there among them, the council had nothing to say. [15]So they sent
Peter and John out of the council chamber* and conferred among themselves.
4:16 John 11:47 Acts 3:6-10
[16]"What should we do with these men?" they asked each other. "We can't deny they
have done a miraculous sign, and everybody in Jerusalem knows about it. [17]But perhaps
4:17-19 Acts 5:28-29
we can stop them from spreading their propaganda. We'll warn them not to speak to
anyone in Jesus' name again." [18]So they called the apostles back in and told them never
again to speak or teach about Jesus.
[19]But Peter and John replied, "Do you think God wants us to obey you rather than
4:20 1 Jn 1:1, 3
him? [20]We cannot stop telling about the wonderful things we have seen and heard."
[21]The council then threatened them further, but they finally let them go because they
didn't know how to punish them without starting a riot. For everyone was praising God
[22]for this miraculous sign—the healing of a man who had been lame for more than forty
years.

The Believers Pray for Courage

[23]As soon as they were freed, Peter and John found the other believers and told them
4:24 †Exod 20:11 †Ps 146:6
what the leading priests and elders had said. [24]Then all the believers were united as they

4:11 Ps 118:22. **4:15** Greek *the Sanhedrin.*

4:7 The high council asked Peter and John by what power they had healed the man (3:6, 7) and by what authority they preached (3:12-26). The actions and words of Peter and John threatened these religious leaders, who, for the most part, were more interested in their reputations and positions than in God. Through the help of the Holy Spirit (Mark 13:11), Peter spoke boldly before the council, actually putting the council on trial by showing them that the one they had crucified had risen again. Instead of being defensive, the apostles went on the offensive, boldly speaking out for God and presenting the Good News to these leaders.

4:11 The cornerstone unites two walls at the corner of a building and holds the building together. Peter said that the Jews rejected Jesus, but now Christ had become the cornerstone of the church (Psalm 118:22; Mark 12:10; 1 Peter 2:7). Without him there would be no church because it wouldn't be able to stand.

4:12 Many people react negatively to the fact that there is no other name than that of Jesus to call on for salvation. Yet this is not something the church decided; it is the specific teaching of Jesus himself (John 14:6). If God designated Jesus to be the Savior of the world, no one else can be his equal. Christians are to be open-minded on many issues but not on how we are saved from sin. No other religious teacher could die for our sins; no other religious teacher came to earth as God's only Son; no other religious teacher rose from the dead. Our focus should be on Jesus, whom God provided as the way to have an eternal relationship with himself. There is no other name or way!

4:13 Knowing that Peter and John were unschooled, the council was amazed at what being with Jesus had done for them. A changed life convinces people of Christ's power. One of your greatest testimonies is the difference others see in your life and attitudes since you have believed in Christ.

4:13-18 Although the evidence was overwhelming and irrefutable (changed lives and a healed man), the religious leaders refused to believe in Christ and continued to try to suppress the truth. Don't be surprised if some people reject you and your positive witness for Christ. When minds are closed, even the clearest presentation of the facts can't open them. But don't give up either. Pray for those people and continue to spread the Good News.

4:20 We may sometimes be afraid to share our faith in Christ because people may feel uncomfortable or reject us. But Peter and John's zeal for the Lord was so strong that they could not keep quiet, even when threatened. If your courage to witness for God has weakened, pray that your boldness may increase. Remember Jesus' promise, "If anyone acknowledges me publicly here on earth, I will openly acknowledge that person before my Father in heaven" (Matthew 10:32).

4:24-30 Notice how the believers prayed. First, they praised God; then they told God their specific problem and asked for his help. They did not ask God to remove the problem but to help them deal with it. This is a model for us to follow when we pray. We may ask God to remove our problems, and he may choose to do so. But we must recognize that often he will leave a problem but give us the strength and courage to deal with it.

lifted their voices in prayer: "O Sovereign Lord, Creator of heaven and earth, the sea,
and everything in them—25 you spoke long ago by the Holy Spirit through our ancestor
King David, your servant, saying,

'Why did the nations rage?
Why did the people waste their time with futile plans?
26 The kings of the earth prepared for battle;
the rulers gathered together
against the Lord
and against his Messiah.'*

27 "That is what has happened here in this city! For Herod Antipas, Pontius Pilate the
governor, the Gentiles, and the people of Israel were all united against Jesus, your holy
servant, whom you anointed. 28 In fact, everything they did occurred according to your
eternal will and plan. 29 And now, O Lord, hear their threats, and give your servants great
boldness in their preaching. 30 Send your healing power; may miraculous signs and
wonders be done through the name of your holy servant Jesus."
31 After this prayer, the building where they were meeting shook, and they were all
filled with the Holy Spirit. And they preached God's message with boldness.

The Believers Share Their Possessions

32 All the believers were of one heart and mind, and they felt that what they owned was
not their own; they shared everything they had. 33 And the apostles gave powerful
witness to the resurrection of the Lord Jesus, and God's great favor was upon them all.
34 There was no poverty among them, because people who owned land or houses sold
them 35 and brought the money to the apostles to give to others in need.
36 For instance, there was Joseph, the one the apostles nicknamed Barnabas (which means
"Son of Encouragement"). He was from the tribe of Levi and came from the island of
Cyprus. 37 He sold a field he owned and brought the money to the apostles for those in need.

Ananias and Sapphira

5 There was also a man named Ananias who, with his wife, Sapphira, sold some
property. 2 He brought part of the money to the apostles, but he claimed it was the
full amount. His wife had agreed to this deception.

4:25-26 Ps 2:1-2.

4:25-26 †Ps 2:1-2
4:27 Isa 61:1; Acts 3:13
4:28 Acts 2:23
4:29 Eph 6:19
4:30 Acts 5:12
4:31 Acts 2:4; 16:26
4:32 Acts 2:44
4:33-35 Acts 2:45-47
4:36 Acts 9:27; 11:19-30; 12:25; 13:2
5:2 Acts 4:34-35, 37

4:27 Herod Antipas had been appointed by the Romans to rule over the territory of Galilee. For more information on Herod, see his Profile in Mark 6. Pontius Pilate was the Roman governor over Judea. He bowed to pressure from the crowd and sentenced Jesus to death. For more information on Pilate, see his Profile in Mark 15.

4:28 God is the sovereign Lord of all events, who rules history to fulfill his purpose. What his will determines, his power carries out. No army, government, or council can stand in God's way.

4:29-31 Boldness is not reckless impulsiveness. Boldness requires courage to press on through our fears and do what we know is right. How can we be more bold? Like the disciples, we need to pray with others for that courage. To gain boldness, you can (1) pray for the power of the Holy Spirit to give you courage, (2) look for opportunities in your family and neighborhood to talk about Christ, (3) realize that rejection, social discomfort, and embarrassment are not necessarily persecution, and (4) start where you are by being bolder in small ways.

4:32 Differences of opinion are inevitable among human personalities and can actually be helpful if handled well. But spiritual unity is essential—loyalty, commitment, and love for God and his Word. Without spiritual unity, the church could not survive. Paul wrote the letter of 1 Corinthians to urge the church in Corinth toward greater unity.

4:32 None of these Christians felt that what they had was their own, and so they were able to give and share, eliminating poverty among them. They would not let a brother or sister suffer when others had plenty. How do you feel about your possessions? We should adopt the attitude that everything we have comes from God, and we are only sharing what is already his.

4:32-35 The early church was able to share possessions and property as a result of the unity brought by the Holy Spirit working in and through the believers' lives. This way of living is different from communism because (1) the sharing was voluntary; (2) it didn't involve *all* private property but only as much as was needed; (3) it was not a membership requirement in order to be a part of the church. The spiritual unity and generosity of these early believers attracted others to them. This organizational structure is not a biblical command, but it offers vital principles for us to follow.

4:36 Barnabas (Joseph) was a respected leader of the church. He was a Levite by birth, a member of the Jewish tribe that carried out Temple duties. But his family had moved to Cyprus, so Barnabas didn't serve in the Temple. He traveled with Paul on Paul's first missionary journey (13:1ff). For more information on Barnabas, see his Profile in chapter 13.

5:1ff In Acts 5:1–8:3 we see both internal and external problems facing the early church. Inside, there were dishonesty (5:1-11), greed (5:3), and administrative headaches (6:1-7). Outside, the church was being pressured by persecution. While church leaders were careful and sensitive in dealing with the internal problems, there was not much they could do to prevent the external pressures. Through it all, the leaders kept their focus on what was most important—spreading the Good News of Jesus Christ.

5:3 Deut 23:21 John 13:2 [3]Then Peter said, "Ananias, why has Satan filled your heart? You lied to the Holy
Spirit, and you kept some of the money for yourself. [4]The property was yours to sell or
not sell, as you wished. And after selling it, the money was yours to give away. How
could you do a thing like this? You weren't lying to us but to God."

5:5 Acts 2:43 [5]As soon as Ananias heard these words, he fell to the floor and died. Everyone who
heard about it was terrified. [6]Then some young men wrapped him in a sheet and took
him out and buried him.

[7]About three hours later his wife came in, not knowing what had happened. [8]Peter
asked her, "Was this the price you and your husband received for your land?"

"Yes," she replied, "that was the price."

5:9 1 Cor 10:9 [9]And Peter said, "How could the two of you even think of doing a thing like
this—conspiring together to test the Spirit of the Lord? Just outside that door are the
young men who buried your husband, and they will carry you out, too."

[10]Instantly, she fell to the floor and died. When the young men came in and saw that
she was dead, they carried her out and buried her beside her husband. [11]Great fear
gripped the entire church and all others who heard what had happened.

The Apostles Heal Many

5:12 Mark 16:15-20 John 10:23 Acts 3:10 Heb 2:4 [12]Meanwhile, the apostles were performing many miraculous signs and wonders among the
people. And the believers were meeting regularly at the Temple in the area known as
Solomon's Colonnade. [13]No one else dared to join them, though everyone had high regard
5:13 Acts 2:47 for them. [14]And more and more people believed and were brought to the Lord—crowds of
both men and women. [15]As a result of the apostles' work, sick people were brought out into
the streets on beds and mats so that Peter's shadow might fall across some of them as he
went by. [16]Crowds came in from the villages around Jerusalem, bringing their sick and
those possessed by evil spirits, and they were all healed.

The Apostles Meet Opposition

5:17 Acts 4:1, 2 [17]The high priest and his friends, who were Sadducees, reacted with violent jealousy.
[18]They arrested the apostles and put them in the jail. [19]But an angel of the Lord came at

---

5:3 Even after the Holy Spirit had come, the believers were not immune to Satan's temptations. Although Satan was defeated by Christ at the cross, he was still actively trying to make the believers stumble—as he does today (Ephesians 6:12; 1 Peter 5:8). Satan's overthrow is inevitable, but it will not occur until the last days, when Christ returns to judge the world (Revelation 20:10).

5:3ff The sin Ananias and Sapphira committed was not stinginess or holding back part of the money—it was their choice whether or not to sell the land and how much to give. Their sin was lying to God and God's people, saying they gave the whole amount but holding back some for themselves and trying to make themselves appear more generous than they really were. This act was judged harshly because dishonesty, greed, and covetousness are destructive in a church, preventing the Holy Spirit from working effectively. All lying is bad, but when we lie to try to deceive God and his people about our relationship with him, we destroy our testimony for Christ.

5:11 God's judgment of Ananias and Sapphira produced shock and fear among the believers, making them realize how seriously God regards sin in the church.

5:12 Solomon's Colonnade was part of the Temple complex built by King Herod the Great in an attempt to strengthen his relationship with the Jews. A colonnade is an entrance or porch supported by columns. Jesus taught and performed miracles in the Temple many times. When the apostles went to the Temple, they were undoubtedly in close proximity to the same religious leaders who had conspired to put Jesus to death.

5:13 Although many people greatly respected the apostles, they did not dare join them in the Temple or work beside them. Some may have been afraid to face the same kind of persecution the apostles had just faced (4:17), while others may have feared a similar fate as the one that fell on Ananias and Sapphira.

5:14 What makes Christianity attractive? It is easy to be drawn to churches because of programs, good speakers, size, beautiful facilities, or fellowship. People were attracted to the early church by expressions of God's power at work; the generosity, sincerity, honesty, and unity of the members; and the character of the leaders. Have our standards slipped? God wants to add believers to his *church*, not just newer and better programs or larger and fancier facilities.

5:15 People who passed within Peter's shadow were healed, not by Peter's shadow, but by God's power working through Peter.

5:16 What did these miraculous healings do for the early church? (1) They attracted new believers; (2) they confirmed the truth of the apostles' teaching; and (3) they demonstrated that the power of the Messiah, who had been crucified and risen, was now with his followers.

5:17 The religious leaders were jealous; Peter and the apostles were already commanding more respect than they had ever received. The difference, however, was that the religious leaders demanded respect and reverence for themselves; the apostles' goal was to bring respect and reverence for God. The apostles were respected, not because they demanded it, but because they deserved it.

5:17, 18 The apostles experienced power to do miracles, great boldness in preaching, and God's presence in their lives; yet they were not free from hatred and persecution. They were arrested, put in jail, beaten, and slandered by community leaders. Faith in God does not make troubles disappear; it makes troubles appear less frightening because it puts them in the right perspective. Don't expect everyone to react favorably when you share something as dynamic as your faith in Christ. Some will be jealous, afraid, or threatened. Expect some negative reactions, and remember that you must be more concerned about serving God than about the reactions of people (see 5:29).

night, opened the gates of the jail, and brought them out. Then he told them, 20“Go to
the Temple and give the people this message of life!” 21So the apostles entered the
Temple about daybreak and immediately began teaching.
When the high priest and his officials arrived, they convened the high council,* along
with all the elders of Israel. Then they sent for the apostles to be brought for trial. 22But
when the Temple guards went to the jail, the men were gone. So they returned to the
council and reported, 23“The jail was locked, with the guards standing outside, but when
we opened the gates, no one was there!”
24When the captain of the Temple guard and the leading priests heard this, they were
perplexed, wondering where it would all end. 25Then someone arrived with the news
that the men they had jailed were out in the Temple, teaching the people.
26The captain went with his Temple guards and arrested them, but without violence,
for they were afraid the people would kill them if they treated the apostles roughly.
27Then they brought the apostles in before the council. 28“Didn’t we tell you never
again to teach in this man’s name?” the high priest demanded. “Instead, you have
filled all Jerusalem with your teaching about Jesus, and you intend to blame us for his
death!”
29But Peter and the apostles replied, “We must obey God rather than human authority.
30The God of our ancestors raised Jesus from the dead after you killed him by crucifying
him. 31Then God put him in the place of honor at his right hand as Prince and Savior. He
did this to give the people of Israel an opportunity to turn from their sins and turn to God
so their sins would be forgiven. 32We are witnesses of these things and so is the Holy
Spirit, who is given by God to those who obey him.”
33At this, the high council was furious and decided to kill them. 34But one member
had a different perspective. He was a Pharisee named Gamaliel, who was an expert on
religious law and was very popular with the people. He stood up and ordered that the
apostles be sent outside the council chamber for a while. 35Then he addressed his
colleagues as follows: “Men of Israel, take care what you are planning to do to these
men! 36Some time ago there was that fellow Theudas, who pretended to be someone
great. About four hundred others joined him, but he was killed, and his followers went
their various ways. The whole movement came to nothing. 37After him, at the time of the
census, there was Judas of Galilee. He got some people to follow him, but he was killed,
too, and all his followers were scattered.

5:19 Acts 12:7-10
5:20 John 6:63, 68
5:21 Acts 4:5-6
5:24 Acts 4:1
5:26 Matt 14:5; 21:26
5:28 Matt 23:35; 27:25 Acts 2:23; 4:18; 7:52
5:29 Acts 4:19
5:30 Acts 10:39
5:31 Acts 2:33 Heb 2:10
5:32 Luke 24:28 John 15:26-27
5:33 Acts 2:37; 7:54
5:34 Acts 22:3
5:36 Acts 21:38
5:37 Luke 2:1-2; 13:1-2

5:21 Greek *Sanhedrin;* also in 5:27, 41.

5:21 The 70 men of the high council (also called the Sanhedrin) met to question the apostles. This was going to be no small trial. The religious leaders would do anything to stop these apostles from challenging their authority, threatening their secure position, and exposing their hypocritical motives to the people.

5:21 The Temple at daybreak was a busy place. Many people stopped at the Temple to pray and worship at sunrise. The apostles were already there, ready to tell them the Good News of new life in Jesus Christ.

5:21 Suppose someone threatened to kill you if you didn’t stop talking about God. You might be tempted to keep quiet. But after being threatened by powerful leaders, arrested, jailed, and miraculously released, the apostles went back to preaching. This was nothing less than God’s power working through them (4:13)! When we are convinced of the truth of Christ’s resurrection and have experienced the presence and power of his Holy Spirit, we will also have the confidence to speak out for Christ.

5:29 The apostles knew their priorities. While we should try to live at peace with everyone (Romans 12:18), conflict with the world and its authorities is sometimes inevitable for a Christian (John 15:18). There will be situations where you cannot obey both God and people. Then you must obey God and trust his Word. Let Jesus’ words in Luke 6:22 encourage you: “God blesses you who are hated and excluded and mocked and cursed because you are identified with me, the Son of Man.”

5:34 The Pharisees were the other major party in the Jewish high council with the Sadducees (5:17). The Pharisees were the strict keepers of the law—not only God’s law but hundreds of other rules they had added to God’s law. They were careful about outward purity, but many had hearts full of impure motives. Jesus confronted the Pharisees often during his ministry on earth.

5:34 Gamaliel was an unexpected ally for the apostles, although he probably did not support their teachings. He was a distinguished member of the high council and a teacher. While Gamaliel may have saved the apostles’ lives, his real intentions probably were to prevent a division in the council and to avoid arousing the Romans. The apostles were popular among the people, and killing them might start a riot. Gamaliel’s advice to the council gave the apostles some breathing room to continue their work. The council decided to wait, hoping that this would all fade away harmlessly. They couldn’t have been more wrong. Ironically, Paul, later one of the greatest apostles, had been one of Gamaliel’s students (22:3).

5:39 Prov 21:30 Isa 46:10
5:40 Matt 10:17 Mark 13:9
5:41 Matt 5:10-12 John 15:21 1 Pet 4:13
5:42 Acts 2:46

38“So my advice is, leave these men alone. If they are teaching and doing these things
merely on their own, it will soon be overthrown. 39But if it is of God, you will not be
able to stop them. You may even find yourselves fighting against God.”
40The council accepted his advice. They called in the apostles and had them flogged.
Then they ordered them never again to speak in the name of Jesus, and they let them go.
41The apostles left the high council rejoicing that God had counted them worthy to suffer
dishonor for the name of Jesus. 42And every day, in the Temple and in their homes,* they
continued to teach and preach this message: “The Messiah you are looking for is Jesus.”

Seven Men Chosen to Serve

6:1 Acts 2:45; 4:35 1 Tim 5:3
6:3 Acts 1:16 1 Tim 3:7-8
6:4 Acts 1:14
6:5 Acts 21:8

6 But as the believers* rapidly multiplied, there were rumblings of discontent. Those
who spoke Greek complained against those who spoke Hebrew, saying that their
widows were being discriminated against in the daily distribution of food. 2So the
Twelve called a meeting of all the believers.
“We apostles should spend our time preaching and teaching the word of God, not
administering a food program,” they said. 3“Now look around among yourselves,
friends,* and select seven men who are well respected and are full of the Holy Spirit and
wisdom. We will put them in charge of this business. 4Then we can spend our time in
prayer and preaching and teaching the word.”
5This idea pleased the whole group, and they chose the following: Stephen (a man
full of faith and the Holy Spirit), Philip, Procorus, Nicanor, Timon, Parmenas, and

5:42 Greek *from house to house.* **6:1** Greek *disciples;* also in 6:2, 7. **6:3** Greek *brothers.*

5:39 Gamaliel presented some sound advice about reacting to religious movements. Unless adherents in these groups endorse obviously dangerous doctrines or practices, it is often wiser to be tolerant rather than repressive. Sometimes only time will tell if they are merely the work of humans or if God is trying to say something through them. The next time a group promotes differing religious ideas, consider Gamaliel's advice, just in case you “find yourselves fighting against God.”

5:40-42 Peter and John were warned repeatedly not to preach, but they continued in spite of the threats. We, too, should live as Christ has asked us to, sharing our faith no matter what the cost. We may not be beaten or thrown in jail, but we may be ridiculed, ostracized, or slandered. To what extent are you willing to suffer for the sake of sharing the Good News with others?

5:41 Have you ever thought of persecution as a blessing, as something worth rejoicing about? This beating suffered by Peter and John was the first time any of the apostles had been physically abused for their faith. These men knew how Jesus had suffered, and they praised God that he had allowed them to be persecuted like their Lord. If you are mocked or persecuted for your faith, it isn't because you're doing something wrong but because God has counted you “worthy to suffer dishonor for the name of Jesus.”

5:42 Home Bible studies are not new. As the believers needed to grow in their new faith, home Bible studies met their needs, as well as serving as a means to introduce new people to the Christian faith. During later times of persecution, meeting in homes became the primary method of passing on Bible knowledge. Christians throughout the world still use this approach when under persecution and as a way to build up believers.

6:1 When we read the descriptions of the early church—the miracles, the sharing and generosity, the fellowship—we may wish we could have been a part of this “perfect” church. In reality, the early church had problems just as we do today. No church has ever been or will ever be perfect until Christ and his followers are united at his second coming. All churches have problems. If your church's shortcomings distress you, ask yourself: Would a perfect church allow me to be a member? Then do what you can to make your church better. A church does not have to be perfect to advance the cause of Christ.

6:1ff Another internal problem developed in the early church. The Hebraic Jews, native Jewish Christians, spoke Hebrew. The Grecian Jews, Greek-speaking Christians, were probably Jews from other lands who were converted at Pentecost. The Greek-speaking Christians complained that their widows were being unfairly treated. This favoritism was probably not intentional but was more likely caused by the language barrier. To correct the situation, the apostles put seven respected Greek-speaking men in charge of the food distribution program. This solved the problem and allowed the apostles to keep their focus on teaching and preaching the Good News about Jesus.

6:2 “The Twelve” are the 11 original disciples and Matthias, who was chosen to replace Judas Iscariot (1:26).

6:2-4 As the early church increased in size, so did its needs. One great need was to organize the distribution of food to the poor. The apostles needed to focus on preaching, so they chose others to administer the food program. Each person has a vital part to play in the life of the church (see 1 Corinthians 12). If you are in a position of leadership and find yourself overwhelmed by responsibilities, determine *your* God-given abilities and priorities and then find others to help. If you are not in leadership, you have gifts that can be used by God in various areas of the church's ministry. Offer these gifts in service to him.

6:3 This administrative task was not taken lightly. Notice the requirements for the men who were to handle the food program: They were to be well respected and full of the Holy Spirit and wisdom. People who carry heavy responsibilities and work closely with others should have these qualities. We must look for spiritually mature and wise men and women to lead our churches.

6:4 The apostles' priorities were correct. The ministry of the Word should never be neglected because of administrative burdens. Pastors should not try, or be expected to try, to do everything. Instead, the work of the church should be spread out among its members.

Nicolas of Antioch (a Gentile convert to the Jewish faith, who had now become a
Christian). 6 These seven were presented to the apostles, who prayed for them as they
laid their hands on them.
7 God's message was preached in ever-widening circles. The number of believers
greatly increased in Jerusalem, and many of the Jewish priests were converted, too.

Stephen Is Arrested

8 Stephen, a man full of God's grace and power, performed amazing miracles and signs
among the people. 9 But one day some men from the Synagogue of Freed Slaves, as it
was called, started to debate with him. They were Jews from Cyrene, Alexandria, Cilicia,
and the province of Asia. 10 None of them was able to stand against the wisdom and Spirit
by which Stephen spoke.
11 So they persuaded some men to lie about Stephen, saying, "We heard him blaspheme Moses, and even God." 12 Naturally, this roused the crowds, the elders, and the
teachers of religious law. So they arrested Stephen and brought him before the high
council.* 13 The lying witnesses said, "This man is always speaking against the Temple
and against the law of Moses. 14 We have heard him say that this Jesus of Nazareth will
destroy the Temple and change the customs Moses handed down to us." 15 At this point
everyone in the council stared at Stephen because his face became as bright as an angel's.

Stephen Addresses the Council

7 Then the high priest asked Stephen, "Are these accusations true?"
2 This was Stephen's reply: "Brothers and honorable fathers, listen to me. Our
glorious God appeared to our ancestor Abraham in Mesopotamia before he moved to
Haran.* 3 God told him, 'Leave your native land and your relatives, and come to the land
that I will show you.'* 4 So Abraham left the land of the Chaldeans and lived in Haran
until his father died. Then God brought him here to the land where you now live. 5 But
God gave him no inheritance here, not even one square foot of land. God did promise,
however, that eventually the whole country would belong to Abraham and his descendants—though he had no children yet. 6 But God also told him that his descendants would
live in a foreign country where they would be mistreated as slaves for four hundred years.

6:6 Num 8:10; Acts 1:24; 13:3; 1 Tim 4:14
6:7 Acts 12:24; 19:20; 21:20
6:9 Matt 27:32
6:10 Luke 21:15
6:11 Matt 26:59-61
6:13 Acts 7:48; 21:28
6:14 John 2:19-21; Acts 21:21
7:2 Gen 11:31–12:1; 15:7; Acts 22:1
7:3 †Gen 12:1
7:4 Gen 12:5; Heb 11:8
7:5 †Gen 12:7; 13:15; 15:2, 18; 17:8; 24:7
7:6 †Gen 15:13-14

6:12 Greek *Sanhedrin;* also in 6:15. **7:2** *Mesopotamia* was the region now called Iraq. *Haran* was a city in what is now called Syria. **7:3** Gen 12:1.

6:6 Spiritual leadership is serious business and must not be taken lightly by the church or its leaders. In the early church, the chosen men were commissioned (set apart by prayer and laying on of hands) by the apostles. Laying hands on someone, an ancient Jewish practice, was a way to set a person apart for special service (see Numbers 27:23; Deuteronomy 34:9).

6:7 Jesus had told the apostles that they were to witness first in Jerusalem (1:8). In a short time, their message had infiltrated the entire city and all levels of society. Even some priests were being converted, an obvious violation of the wishes of the high council that would endanger their position.

6:7 The word of God spread like ripples on a pond where, from a single center, each wave touches the next, spreading wider and farther. The Good News still spreads this way today. You don't have to change the world single-handedly; it is enough just to be part of the wave, touching those around you, who in turn will touch others until all have felt the movement. Don't ever feel that your part is insignificant or unimportant.

6:8-10 The most important prerequisite for any kind of Christian service is to be filled with faith and the power of the Holy Spirit. By the Spirit's power, Stephen was a wise servant (6:3), miracle worker (6:8), and evangelist (6:10). By the Spirit's power, you can exercise the gifts God has given you.

6:9 This was a group of Jewish slaves who had been freed by Rome and had formed their own synagogue in Jerusalem.

6:11 These men lied about Stephen, causing him to be arrested and brought before the Jewish high council. The Sadducees, the dominant party in the council, accepted and studied only the writings of Moses (Genesis—Deuteronomy). In their view, to speak blasphemy against Moses was a crime. But from Stephen's speech (chapter 7), we learn that this accusation was false. Stephen based his review of Israel's history on Moses' writings.

6:14 When Stephen was brought before the council of religious leaders, the accusation against him was the same that the religious leaders had used against Jesus (Matthew 26:59-61). The group falsely accused Stephen of wanting to change Moses' customs, because they knew that the Sadducees, who controlled the council, believed *only* in Moses' laws.

7:1 This high priest was probably Caiaphas, the same man who had earlier questioned and condemned Jesus (John 18:24).

7:2ff Stephen launched into a long speech about Israel's relationship with God. From Old Testament history he showed that the Jews had constantly rejected God's message and his prophets and that this council had rejected the Messiah, God's Son. He made three main points: (1) Israel's history is the history of God's acts in the world; (2) people worshiped God long before there was a Temple, because God does not live in a Temple; and (3) Jesus' death was just one more example of Israel's rebellion against and rejection of God.

7:2ff Stephen didn't really defend himself. Instead, he took the offensive, seizing the opportunity to summarize his teaching about Jesus. Stephen was accusing these religious leaders of failing to obey God's laws—the laws they prided themselves in following so meticulously. This was the same accusation that Jesus had leveled against them. When we witness for Christ, we don't need to be on the defensive. Instead, we can simply share our faith.

7:7
†Exod 3:12
7:8
Gen 17:10-14; 21:2-4; 25:26; 35:23-26
7:9
Gen 37:28; 39:2
Ps 105:17
7:10
Gen 41:37-43
Ps 105:21
7:11
Gen 41:54

7 'But I will punish the nation that enslaves them,' God told him, 'and in the end they will
come out and worship me in this place.'* 8 God also gave Abraham the covenant of
circumcision at that time. And so Isaac, Abraham's son, was circumcised when he was
eight days old. Isaac became the father of Jacob, and Jacob was the father of the twelve
patriarchs of the Jewish nation.
9 "These sons of Jacob were very jealous of their brother Joseph, and they sold him to
be a slave in Egypt. But God was with him 10 and delivered him from his anguish. And
God gave him favor before Pharaoh, king of Egypt. God also gave Joseph unusual
wisdom, so that Pharaoh appointed him governor over all of Egypt and put him in charge
of all the affairs of the palace.
11 "But a famine came upon Egypt and Canaan. There was great misery for our

7:5-7 Gen 12:7; 15:13-14; Exod 3:12.

STEPHEN

Around the world, the gospel has most often taken root in places prepared by the blood of martyrs. Before people can *give* their lives for the gospel, however, they must first *live* their lives for the gospel. One way God trains his servants is to place them in insignificant positions. Their desire to serve Christ is translated into the reality of serving others. Stephen was an effective administrator and messenger before becoming a martyr.

Stephen was named one of the managers of food distribution in the early church. Long before violent persecution broke out against Christians, there was already social ostracism. Jews who accepted Jesus as Messiah were usually cut off from their families. As a result, the believers depended on each other for support. The sharing of homes, food, and resources was both a practical and necessary mark of the early church. Eventually, the number of believers made it necessary to organize the sharing. People were being overlooked. There were complaints. Those chosen to help manage were chosen for their integrity, wisdom, and sensitivity to God.

Stephen, besides being a good administrator, was also a powerful speaker. When confronted in the Temple by various antagonistic groups, Stephen's logic in responding was convincing. This is clear from the defense he made before the high council. He presented a summary of the Jews' own history and made powerful applications that stung his listeners. During his defense Stephen must have known he was speaking his own death sentence. Members of the council could not stand to have their evil motives exposed. They stoned him to death while he prayed for their forgiveness. His final words show how much like Jesus he had become in a short time. His death had a lasting impact on young Saul (Paul) of Tarsus, who would move from being a violent persecutor of Christians to being one of the greatest champions of the gospel the church has known.

Stephen's life is a continual challenge to all Christians. Because he was the first to die for the faith, his sacrifice raises questions: How many risks do we take in being Jesus' followers? Would we be willing to die for him? Are we really willing to live for him?

Strengths and accomplishments
- One of seven leaders chosen to supervise food distribution to the needy in the early church
- Known for his spiritual qualities of faith, wisdom, grace, and power, and for the Spirit's presence in his life
- Outstanding leader, teacher, and debater
- First to give his life for the gospel

Lessons from his life
- Striving for excellence in small assignments prepares one for greater responsibilities
- Real understanding of God always leads to practical and compassionate actions toward people

Vital statistics
- Church responsibilities: Deacon—distributing food to the needy
- Contemporaries: Paul, Caiaphas, Gamaliel, the apostles

Key verses
"And as they stoned him, Stephen prayed, 'Lord Jesus, receive my spirit.' And he fell to his knees, shouting, 'Lord, don't charge them with this sin!' And with that, he died" (Acts 7:59, 60).

Stephen's story is told in Acts 6:3—8:2. He is also mentioned in Acts 11:19; 22:20.

7:8 Circumcision was a sign of the promise or covenant God made with Abraham and the entire nation of Israel (Genesis 17:9-13). Because Stephen summarized Israel's history, he told how this covenant fared during that time. Stephen pointed out that God always had kept his side of the promise, but Israel had failed again and again to uphold its end. Although the Jews in Stephen's day still circumcised their baby boys, they failed to obey God. The people's hearts were far from God. Their lack of faith and lack of obedience showed that they had failed to keep their part of the covenant.

ancestors, as they ran out of food. 12Jacob heard that there was still grain in Egypt, so he
sent his sons* to buy some. 13The second time they went, Joseph revealed his identity
to his brothers, and they were introduced to Pharaoh. 14Then Joseph sent for his father,
Jacob, and all his relatives to come to Egypt, seventy-five persons in all. 15So Jacob went
to Egypt. He died there, as did all his sons. 16All of them were taken to Shechem and
buried in the tomb Abraham had bought from the sons of Hamor in Shechem.
17"As the time drew near when God would fulfill his promise to Abraham, the number
of our people in Egypt greatly increased. 18But then a new king came to the throne of
Egypt who knew nothing about Joseph. 19This king plotted against our people and forced
parents to abandon their newborn babies so they would die.
20"At that time Moses was born—a beautiful child in God's eyes. His parents cared
for him at home for three months. 21When at last they had to abandon him, Pharaoh's
daughter found him and raised him as her own son. 22Moses was taught all the wisdom
of the Egyptians, and he became mighty in both speech and action.
23"One day when he was forty years old, he decided to visit his relatives, the people
of Israel. 24During this visit, he saw an Egyptian mistreating a man of Israel. So Moses
came to his defense and avenged him, killing the Egyptian. 25Moses assumed his
brothers would realize that God had sent him to rescue them, but they didn't.
26"The next day he visited them again and saw two men of Israel fighting. He tried to
be a peacemaker. 'Men,' he said, 'you are brothers. Why are you hurting each other?'
27"But the man in the wrong pushed Moses aside and told him to mind his own
business. 'Who made you a ruler and judge over us?' he asked. 28'Are you going to kill
me as you killed that Egyptian yesterday?' 29When Moses heard that, he fled the country
and lived as a foreigner in the land of Midian, where his two sons were born.
30"Forty years later, in the desert near Mount Sinai, an angel appeared to Moses in the
flame of a burning bush. 31Moses saw it and wondered what it was. As he went to see,
the voice of the Lord called out to him, 32'I am the God of your ancestors—the God of
Abraham, Isaac, and Jacob.' Moses shook with terror and dared not look.
33"And the Lord said to him, 'Take off your sandals, for you are standing on holy
ground. 34You can be sure that I have seen the misery of my people in Egypt. I have
heard their cries. So I have come to rescue them. Now go, for I will send you to Egypt.'*
35And so God sent back the same man his people had previously rejected by demanding,
'Who made you a ruler and judge over us?' Through the angel who appeared to him in
the burning bush, Moses was sent to be their ruler and savior. 36And by means of many
miraculous signs and wonders, he led them out of Egypt, through the Red Sea, and back
and forth through the wilderness for forty years.
37"Moses himself told the people of Israel, 'God will raise up a Prophet like me from
among your own people.'* 38Moses was with the assembly of God's people in the
wilderness. He was the mediator between the people of Israel and the angel who gave
him life-giving words on Mount Sinai to pass on to us.
39"But our ancestors rejected Moses and wanted to return to Egypt. 40They told Aaron,
'Make us some gods who can lead us, for we don't know what has become of this Moses,
who brought us out of Egypt.' 41So they made an idol shaped like a calf, and they

7:12 Gen 42:1-2
7:13 Gen 45:1-4
7:14 Gen 45:9-10; 46:26-27; Deut 10:22
7:15 Gen 46:5-7; 49:33; Exod 1:6
7:16 Gen 23:16-20
7:17-18 †Exod 1:7-8; Ps 105:24
7:19 Exod 1:10-11, 22
7:20 Exod 2:2; Heb 11:23
7:21 Exod 2:3-10
7:22 1 Kgs 4:30; Isa 19:11
7:23-24 Exod 2:11-12
7:26-28 †Exod 2:13-14
7:29 Exod 2:15
7:30-31 †Exod 3:1-4
7:32-34 †Exod 3:4-10
7:35 †Exod 2:14
7:36 Exod 7:3; 12:41
7:37 †Deut 18:15; Acts 3:22
7:38 Exod 19:1-6; Deut 32:45-47
7:39 Num 14:3
7:40 †Exod 32:1, 23

7:12 Greek *our fathers;* also in 7:15. **7:31-34** Exod 3:5-10. **7:37** Deut 18:15.

7:17 Stephen's review of Jewish history gives a clear testimony of God's faithfulness and sovereignty. Despite the continued failures of his chosen people and the swirling world events, God was working out his plan. When faced by a confusing array of circumstances, remember that (1) God is in control—nothing surprises him; (2) this world is not all there is—it will pass away, but God is eternal; (3) God is just, and he will make things right—punishing the wicked and rewarding the faithful; (4) God wants to use you (like Joseph, Moses, and Stephen) to make a difference in the world.

7:37 The Jews originally thought this "Prophet" was Joshua. But Moses was prophesying about the coming Messiah (Deuteronomy 18:15). Peter also quoted this verse in referring to the Messiah (3:22).

7:38 Stephen used the word *ekklesia* (translated "assembly") to describe the congregation or people of God in the wilderness. This word means "called-out ones" and was used by the first-century Christians to describe their own community or "assembly." Stephen's point was that the giving of the law through Moses to the Jews was the sign of the covenant. By *obedience,* then, they would continue to be God's covenant people. But because they disobeyed (7:39), they broke the covenant and forfeited their right to be the chosen people.

7:38 From Galatians 3:19 and Hebrews 2:2, it appears that God had given the law to Moses through angels. Exodus 31:18 says God wrote the Ten Commandments himself ("written by the finger of God"). Apparently God used angelic messengers as mediators to deliver his law to Moses.

7:42-43 Amos 5:25-27
sacrificed to it and rejoiced in this thing they had made. 42 Then God turned away from
them and gave them up to serve the sun, moon, and stars as their gods! In the book of the
prophets it is written,

'Was it to me you were bringing sacrifices
during those forty years in the wilderness, Israel?
43 No, your real interest was in your pagan gods—
the shrine of Molech,
the star god Rephan,
and the images you made to worship them.
So I will send you into captivity
far away in Babylon.'*

7:44 Exod 25:9, 40; Heb 8:5
44 "Our ancestors carried the Tabernacle* with them through the wilderness. It was
constructed in exact accordance with the plan shown to Moses by God. 45 Years later,
7:45 Josh 3:14-17; 18:1; 23:9; 2 Sam 7:2, 6
when Joshua led the battles against the Gentile nations that God drove out of this land,
the Tabernacle was taken with them into their new territory. And it was used there until
the time of King David.
7:46 2 Sam 7:2-16; 1 Kgs 8:17; Ps 132:1-5
46 "David found favor with God and asked for the privilege of building a permanent
Temple for the God of Jacob.* 47 But it was Solomon who actually built it. 48 However,
the Most High doesn't live in temples made by human hands. As the prophet says,

7:47 1 Kgs 6:1-38
49 'Heaven is my throne,
7:48 2 Chr 2:6; Isa 57:15; Eph 2:22; 1 Pet 2:5
and the earth is my footstool.
Could you ever build me a temple as good as that?'
asks the Lord.
7:49-50 †Isa 66:1-2
'Could you build a dwelling place for me?
50 Didn't I make everything in heaven and earth?'*

51 "You stubborn people! You are heathen at heart and deaf to the truth. Must you forever
7:51 Exod 32:9; 33:3, 5
resist the Holy Spirit? But your ancestors did, and so do you! 52 Name one prophet your
7:52 Matt 23:30-34
ancestors didn't persecute! They even killed the ones who predicted the coming of the
Righteous One—the Messiah whom you betrayed and murdered. 53 You deliberately
7:53 Gal 3:19
disobeyed God's law, though you received it from the hands of angels.*"

54 The Jewish leaders were infuriated by Stephen's accusation, and they shook their
7:55 Heb 1:3, 13
fists in rage.* 55 But Stephen, full of the Holy Spirit, gazed steadily upward into heaven
and saw the glory of God, and he saw Jesus standing in the place of honor at God's right
7:56 Matt 3:16
hand. 56 And he told them, "Look, I see the heavens opened and the Son of Man standing
in the place of honor at God's right hand!"

7:42-43 Amos 5:25-27. **7:44** Greek *the tent of witness.* **7:46** Some manuscripts read *the house of Jacob.* **7:49-50** Isa 66:1-2. **7:53** Greek *received the Law as it was ordained by angels.* **7:54** Greek *they were grinding their teeth against him.*

THE EFFECTS OF STEPHEN'S DEATH

Stephen's death was not in vain. Below are some of the events that were by-products (either directly or indirectly) of the persecution that began with Stephen's martyrdom.

1. Philip's evangelistic tour (Acts 8:4–40)
2. Paul's (Saul's) conversion (Acts 9:1–30)
3. Peter's missionary tour (Acts 9:32—11:18)
4. The church in Antioch in Syria founded (Acts 11:19ff)

7:43 Here Stephen gave more details of the idolatry referred to in 7:40. These were idols worshiped by Israel during their wilderness wanderings (Exodus 32:4). Molech was the god associated with child sacrifice, and Rephan was an Egyptian god. Amos also names Assyrian deities worshiped by Israel (Amos 5:25-27).

7:44-50 Stephen had been accused of speaking against the Temple (6:13). Although he recognized the importance of the Temple, he knew that it was not more important than God. God is not limited; he lives not only in a house of worship but also in hearts of faith that are open to receive him (Isaiah 66:1, 2). Solomon knew this when he prayed at the dedication of the Temple (2 Chronicles 6:18). God wants to live in us. Is he living in you?

7:52 Indeed, many prophets were persecuted and killed: Uriah (Jeremiah 26:20-23); Jeremiah (Jeremiah 38:1-6); Isaiah (tradition says he was killed by King Manasseh; see 2 Kings 21:16); Amos (Amos 7:10-13); Zechariah (not the author of the Bible book but the son of Jehoiada the priest; see 2 Chronicles 24:20-22); Elijah (1 Kings 19:1, 2). Jesus also told a parable about how the Jews had constantly rejected God's messages and persecuted his messengers (Luke 20:9-19).

7:55-58 Stephen saw the glory of God and Jesus, the Messiah, standing at God's right hand. Stephen's words are similar to Jesus' words spoken before the high council (Matthew 26:64; Mark 14:62; Luke 22:69). Stephen's vision supported Jesus' claim and angered

57 Then they put their hands over their ears, and drowning out his voice with their shouts,
they rushed at him. 58 They dragged him out of the city and began to stone him. The official
witnesses took off their coats and laid them at the feet of a young man named Saul.*
59 And as they stoned him, Stephen prayed, "Lord Jesus, receive my spirit." 60 And he
fell to his knees, shouting, "Lord, don't charge them with this sin!" And with that, he died.

7:58 Lev 24:14-16 Deut 17:7
7:59 Ps 31:5 Luke 23:46
7:60 Luke 23:34

8 Saul was one of the official witnesses at the killing of Stephen.

8:1 Acts 7:58

2. Expansion of the church

Persecution Scatters the Believers

A great wave of persecution began that day, sweeping over the church in Jerusalem, and
all the believers except the apostles fled into Judea and Samaria. 2 (Some godly people
came and buried Stephen with loud weeping.) 3 Saul was going everywhere to devastate
the church. He went from house to house, dragging out both men and women to throw
them into jail.

8:3 Acts 9:1; 22:4; 26:9-11 1 Cor 15:9 Gal 1:13

Philip Preaches in Samaria

4 But the believers who had fled Jerusalem went everywhere preaching the Good News
about Jesus. 5 Philip, for example, went to the city of Samaria and told the people there about

8:4 Acts 8:1; 11:19
8:5 Acts 6:5; 21:8

7:58 *Saul* is later called Paul; see 13:9.

PHILIP'S MINISTRY
To escape persecution in Jerusalem, Philip fled to Samaria, where he continued preaching the gospel. While he was there, an angel commanded him to meet an Ethiopian official on the road between Jerusalem and Gaza. The man became a believer before continuing on to Ethiopia. Philip then went from Azotus to Caesarea.

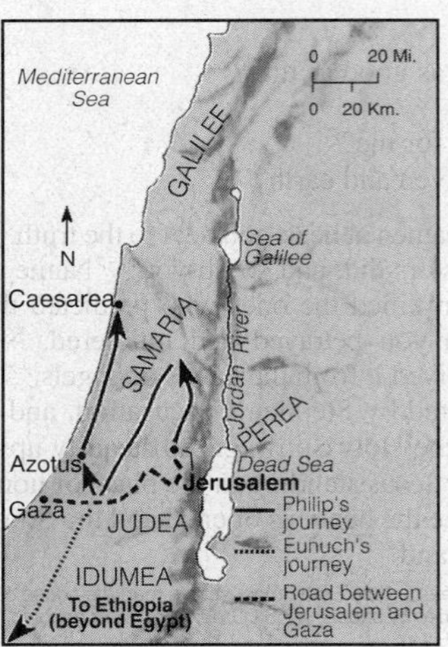

the Jewish leaders who had condemned Jesus to death for blasphemy. They would not tolerate Stephen's words, so they dragged him out and killed him. People may not kill us for witnessing about Christ, but they may let us know they don't want to hear the truth and try to silence us. Keep honoring God in your conduct and words; though many may turn against you and your message, some will follow Christ. Remember, Stephen's death had a profound impact on Paul, who later became the world's greatest missionary. Even those who oppose you now may later turn to Christ.

7:58 Saul is also called Paul (see 13:9), the great missionary who wrote many of the letters in the New Testament. Saul was his Hebrew name; Paul, his Greek name, was used as he began his ministry to the Gentiles. When Luke introduces him, Paul was going everywhere persecuting Jesus' followers. This is in great contrast to the Paul about whom Luke wrote for most of the book of Acts, describing him as a devoted follower of Christ and a gifted preacher. Paul was uniquely qualified to talk to the Jews about Jesus because he had once persecuted those who believed in him and understood how the opposition felt. Paul is a powerful example of a person who was thought impossible for God to reach and change.

7:59 The penalty for blasphemy, speaking irreverently about God, was death by stoning (Leviticus 24:14). The religious leaders, who were furious, had Stephen stoned without a trial. They did not understand that Stephen's words were true because they were not seeking the truth. They only wanted support for their own views.

7:60 As Stephen died, he spoke words very similar to Jesus' words on the cross (Luke 23:34). The early believers were glad to suffer as Jesus had suffered because that meant they were counted worthy (5:41). Stephen was ready to suffer like Jesus, even to the point of asking forgiveness for his murderers. Such a forgiving response comes only from the Holy Spirit. The Spirit can also help us respond as Stephen did with love for our enemies (Luke 6:27). How would you react if someone hurt you because of what you believed?

8:1-4 Persecution forced the Christians out of Jerusalem and into Judea and Samaria, thus fulfilling the second part of Jesus' command (see 1:8). The persecution helped spread the Good News. God would bring great results from the believers' suffering.

8:4 Persecution forced the believers out of their homes in Jerusalem, and along with them went the Good News. Sometimes we have to become uncomfortable before we'll move. We may not want to experience it, but discomfort may be the best thing for us because God may be working through our hurts. When you are tempted to complain about uncomfortable or painful circumstances, stop and ask if God might be preparing you for a special task.

8:5 This is not the apostle Philip (see John 1:43, 44) but a Greek-speaking Jew, "full of the Holy Spirit and wisdom" (6:3), who was one of the seven men chosen to help with the food distribution program in the church (6:5).

8:5 Israel had been divided into three main regions: Galilee in the north, Samaria in the middle, and Judea in the south. The city of Samaria (in the region of Samaria) had been the capital of the northern kingdom of Israel in the days of the divided kingdom before it was conquered by Assyria in 722 B.C. During that war, the Assyrian king took many captives, leaving only the poorest people in the land and resettling it with foreigners. These foreigners intermarried with the Jews who were left, and the mixed race became known as Samaritans. The Samaritans were considered half-breeds by the "pure" Jews in the southern kingdom of Judah, and there was intense hatred between the two groups. But Jesus himself went into Samaria (John 4), and he commanded his followers to spread the Good News there (1:8).

8:7 Matt 10:1; Mark 6:7; 16:17
8:9 Acts 5:36; 13:6
8:12 Acts 2:38
8:13 Acts 19:11
8:14 Acts 8:1
8:15 Acts 2:38; 19:2
8:16 Acts 10:44

the Messiah. 6 Crowds listened intently to what he had to say because of the miracles he did.
7 Many evil spirits were cast out, screaming as they left their victims. And many who had
been paralyzed or lame were healed. 8 So there was great joy in that city.
9 A man named Simon had been a sorcerer there for many years, claiming to be
someone great. 10 The Samaritan people, from the least to the greatest, often spoke of
him as "the Great One—the Power of God." 11 He was very influential because of the
magic he performed. 12 But now the people believed Philip's message of Good News
concerning the Kingdom of God and the name of Jesus Christ. As a result, many men
and women were baptized. 13 Then Simon himself believed and was baptized. He began
following Philip wherever he went, and he was amazed by the great miracles and signs
Philip performed.
14 When the apostles back in Jerusalem heard that the people of Samaria had accepted
God's message, they sent Peter and John there. 15 As soon as they arrived, they prayed
for these new Christians to receive the Holy Spirit. 16 The Holy Spirit had not yet come

MISSIONARIES OF THE NEW TESTAMENT AND THEIR JOURNEYS

Name	*Journey's Purpose*	*Scripture Reference in Acts*
Philip	One of the first to preach the gospel outside Jerusalem	8:4–40
Peter and John	Visited new Samaritan believers to encourage them	8:14–25
Paul (journey to Damascus)	Set out to capture Christians but was captured by Christ	9:1–25
Peter	Led by God to one of the first Gentile families to become Christians—Cornelius's family	9:32—10:48
Barnabas	Went to Antioch as an encourager; traveled on to Tarsus to bring Paul back to Jerusalem from Antioch	11:25–30
Barnabas, Paul, John Mark	Left Antioch for Cyprus, Pamphylia, and Galatia on the first missionary journey	13:1—14:28
Barnabas and John Mark	Left Antioch for Cyprus after a break with Paul	15:36–41
Paul, Silas, Timothy, Luke	Left Antioch to revisit churches in Galatia; then traveled on to Asia, Macedonia, and Achaia on the second missionary journey	15:36—18:22
Apollos	Left Alexandria for Ephesus; learned the complete gospel story from Priscilla and Aquila; preached in Athens and Corinth	18:24–28
Paul, Timothy, Erastus	Revisited churches in Galatia, Asia, Macedonia, and Achaia on the third major missionary journey	18:23; 19:1—21:14

8:7 Jesus encountered and drove out many evil spirits during his ministry on earth. Evil spirits, or demons, are ruled by Satan. Most scholars believe that they are fallen angels who joined Satan in his rebellion against God. They can cause a person to be mute, deaf, blind, or insane and also tempt people to sin. Although they can be powerful, they are not able to read our mind and cannot be everywhere at once. Demons are real and active, but Jesus has given authority over them to his followers. Although Satan is allowed to work in our world, God is in complete control. He can drive demons out and end their destructive work in people's lives. Eventually Satan and his demons will be thrown into the lake of fire, forever ending their evil work in the world (Revelation 20:10).

8:9-11 In the days of the early church, sorcerers and magicians were numerous and influential. They worked wonders, performed healings and exorcisms, and practiced astrology. Their wonders may simply have been magic tricks, or the sorcerers may have been empowered by Satan (Matthew 24:24; 2 Thessalonians 2:9). Simon had done so many wonders that some even thought that he was the Messiah; but his powers did not come from God (see 8:18-24).

8:14 Peter and John were sent to Samaria to find out whether or not the Samaritans were truly becoming believers. The Jewish Christians, even the apostles, were still unsure whether Gentiles (non-Jews) and half-Jews could receive the Holy Spirit. It wasn't until Peter's experience with Cornelius (chapter 10) that the apostles became fully convinced that the Holy Spirit was for all people. It was John who had asked Jesus if they should call fire down from heaven to burn up a Samaritan village that refused to welcome them (Luke 9:51-55). Here he and Peter went to the Samaritans to pray with them.

8:15-17 This was a crucial moment for the spread of the Good News and for the growth of the church. Peter and John had to go to Samaria to help keep this new group of believers from becoming separated from other believers. When Peter and John saw the Lord working in these people, they were assured that the Holy Spirit worked through *all* believers—Gentiles and mixed races as well as "pure" Jews.

upon any of them, for they had only been baptized in the name of the Lord Jesus. 17 Then
Peter and John laid their hands upon these believers, and they received the Holy Spirit.
18 When Simon saw that the Holy Spirit was given when the apostles placed their hands
upon people's heads, he offered money to buy this power. 19 "Let me have this power, too,"
he exclaimed, "so that when I lay my hands on people, they will receive the Holy Spirit!"
20 But Peter replied, "May your money perish with you for thinking God's gift can be
bought! 21 You can have no part in this, for your heart is not right before God. 22 Turn
from your wickedness and pray to the Lord. Perhaps he will forgive your evil thoughts,
23 for I can see that you are full of bitterness and held captive by sin."
24 "Pray to the Lord for me," Simon exclaimed, "that these terrible things won't
happen to me!"
25 After testifying and preaching the word of the Lord in Samaria, Peter and John
returned to Jerusalem. And they stopped in many Samaritan villages along the way to
preach the Good News to them, too.

Philip and the Ethiopian Eunuch

26 As for Philip, an angel of the Lord said to him, "Go south* down the desert road that
runs from Jerusalem to Gaza." 27 So he did, and he met the treasurer of Ethiopia, a eunuch
of great authority under the queen of Ethiopia.* The eunuch had gone to Jerusalem to
worship, 28 and he was now returning. Seated in his carriage, he was reading aloud from
the book of the prophet Isaiah.
29 The Holy Spirit said to Philip, "Go over and walk along beside the carriage."
30 Philip ran over and heard the man reading from the prophet Isaiah; so he asked, "Do
you understand what you are reading?"
31 The man replied, "How can I, when there is no one to instruct me?" And he begged
Philip to come up into the carriage and sit with him. 32 The passage of Scripture he had
been reading was this:

"He was led as a sheep to the slaughter.
And as a lamb is silent before the shearers,
he did not open his mouth.
33 He was humiliated and received no justice.
Who can speak of his descendants?
For his life was taken from the earth."*

8:17 Acts 6:6; 19:6
8:20 Matt 10:8; Acts 2:38
8:21 Ps 78:37
8:22 Acts 2:38
8:23 Deut 29:17-18; Isa 58:6
8:24 Exod 8:8; Num 21:7
8:26 Acts 5:19; 6:5
8:27 1 Kgs 8:41-43; Ps 68:31; Isa 56:3-5; Zeph 3:10
8:32-33 †Isa 53:7-8

8:26 Or *Go at noon.* **8:27** Greek *under the Candace, the queen of Ethiopia.* **8:32-33** Isa 53:7-8.

8:15-17 Many scholars believe that God chose to have a dramatic filling of his Spirit as a sign at this special moment in history—the spread of the Good News into Samaria through the powerful, effective preaching of believers. Normally, the Holy Spirit enters a person's life at conversion. This was a special event. The pouring out of the Spirit would happen again with Cornelius and his family (10:44-47), a sign that the uncircumcised Gentiles could receive the Good News.

8:18-23 "Everything has a price" seems to be true in our world of bribes, wealth, and materialism. Simon thought he could buy the Holy Spirit's power, but Peter harshly rebuked him. The only way to receive God's power is to do what Peter told Simon to do—turn from sin, ask God for forgiveness, and be filled with his Spirit. No amount of money can buy salvation, forgiveness of sin, or God's power. These are only gained by repentance and belief in Christ as Savior.

8:24 The last time a parent or friend rebuked you, were you hurt, angry, or defensive? Learn a lesson from Simon and his reaction to what Peter told him. He exclaimed, "Pray to the Lord for me." If you are rebuked for a serious mistake, it is for your good. Admit your error, repent quickly, and ask for prayer.

8:26 Philip was having a successful preaching ministry to great crowds in Samaria (8:5-8), but he obediently left that ministry to travel on a desert road. Because Philip went where God sent him, Ethiopia was opened up to the Good News. Follow God's leading, even if it seems like a demotion. At first you may not understand his plans, but the results will prove that God's way is right.

8:27 Ethiopia is located in Africa south of Egypt. The eunuch was obviously very dedicated to God because he had traveled such a long distance to worship in Jerusalem. The Jews had contact with Ethiopia in ancient days (Psalm 68:31; Jeremiah 38:7), so this man may have been a Gentile convert to Judaism. Because he was in charge of the treasury of Ethiopia, this man's conversion brought Christianity into the power structures of another government. This is the beginning of the witness "to the ends of the earth" (1:8). See the prophecy in Isaiah 56:3-8 for words about foreigners and eunuchs.

8:29-35 Philip found the Ethiopian man reading Scripture. Taking advantage of this opportunity to explain the Good News, Philip asked the man if he understood what he was reading. Philip (1) followed the Spirit's leading, (2) began the discussion from where the man was (immersed in the prophecies of Isaiah), and (3) explained how Jesus Christ fulfilled Isaiah's prophecies. When we share the Good News, we should start where the other person's concerns are focused. Then we can bring the Good News to bear on those concerns.

8:30, 31 The eunuch asked Philip to explain a passage of Scripture that he did not understand. When we have trouble understanding the Bible, we should ask others to help us. We must never let our insecurity or pride get in the way of understanding God's Word.

8:35 Luke 24:27 Acts 18:28

[34]The eunuch asked Philip, "Was Isaiah talking about himself or someone else?" [35]So
Philip began with this same Scripture and then used many others to tell him the Good
News about Jesus.

8:36 Acts 10:47

[36]As they rode along, they came to some water, and the eunuch said, "Look! There's
some water! Why can't I be baptized?"* [38]He ordered the carriage to stop, and they went
down into the water, and Philip baptized him.

8:39 1 Kgs 18:12 2 Kgs 2:16 Ezek 3:12

[39]When they came up out of the water, the Spirit of the Lord caught Philip away. The
eunuch never saw him again but went on his way rejoicing. [40]Meanwhile, Philip found
himself farther north at the city of Azotus! He preached the Good News there and in
every city along the way until he came to Caesarea.

8:36 Some manuscripts add verse 37, *"You can," Philip answered, "if you believe with all your heart." And the eunuch replied, "I believe that Jesus Christ is the Son of God."*

PHILIP

Jesus' last words to his followers were a command to take the gospel everywhere, but they seemed reluctant to leave Jerusalem. It took intense persecution to scatter the believers from Jerusalem and into Judea and Samaria, where Jesus had instructed them to go. Philip, one of the deacons in charge of food distribution, left Jerusalem and, like most Jewish Christians, spread the gospel wherever he went; but unlike most of them, he did not limit his audience to other Jews. He went directly to Samaria, the last place many Jews would go, due to age-old prejudice.

The Samaritans responded in large numbers. When word got back to Jerusalem, Peter and John were sent to evaluate Philip's ministry. They quickly became involved themselves, seeing firsthand God's acceptance of those who previously were considered unacceptable.

In the middle of all this success and excitement, God directed Philip out to the desert for an appointment with an Ethiopian eunuch, another foreigner, who had been in Jerusalem. Philip went immediately. His effectiveness in sharing the gospel with this man placed a Christian in a significant position in a distant country and may well have had an effect on an entire nation.

Philip ended up in Caesarea, where events allowed him to be Paul's host many years later. Paul, who as the leading persecutor of the Christians had been instrumental in pushing Philip and others out of Jerusalem, had himself become an effective believer. The conversion of the Gentiles begun by Philip was continued across the entire Roman Empire by Paul.

Whether or not you are a follower of Christ, Philip's life presents a challenge. To those still outside the gospel, he is a reminder that the gospel is for you also. To those who have accepted Christ, he is a reminder that we are not free to disqualify anyone from hearing about Jesus. How much like Philip would your neighbors say you are?

Strengths and accomplishments
- One of the seven organizers of food distribution in the early church
- Became an evangelist, one of the first traveling missionaries
- One of the first to obey Jesus' command to take the gospel to all people
- A careful student of the Bible who could explain its meaning clearly

Lessons from his life
- God finds great and various uses for those willing to obey wholeheartedly
- The gospel is universal Good News
- The whole Bible, not just the New Testament, helps us understand more about Jesus
- Both mass response (the Samaritans) and individual response (the man from Ethiopia) to the gospel are valuable

Vital statistics
- Occupations: Deacon, evangelist
- Relatives: Four daughters
- Contemporaries: Paul, Stephen, the apostles

Key verse
"So Philip began with this same Scripture and then used many others to tell him the Good News about Jesus" (Acts 8:35).

Philip's story is told in Acts 6:1–7; 8:5–40; 21:8–10.

8:35 Some think that the Old Testament is not relevant today, but Philip led this man to faith in Jesus Christ by using the Old Testament. Jesus Christ is found in the pages of both the Old and New Testaments. God's entire Word is applicable to all people in all ages. Don't avoid or neglect to use the Old Testament. It, too, is God's Word.

8:38 Baptism was a sign of identification with Christ and with the Christian community. Although there were no witnesses besides Philip, it was still important for the eunuch to take this step.

8:39, 40 Why was Philip suddenly transported to a different city? This miraculous sign showed the urgency of bringing the Gentiles to belief in Christ. Azotus is Ashdod, one of the ancient Philistine capitals. Philip probably lived in Caesarea for the next 20 years (21:8).

Saul's Conversion

9 Meanwhile, Saul was uttering threats with every breath. He was eager to destroy the
Lord's followers,* so he went to the high priest. 2He requested letters addressed to
the synagogues in Damascus, asking their cooperation in the arrest of any followers of
the Way he found there. He wanted to bring them—both men and women—back to
Jerusalem in chains.
3As he was nearing Damascus on this mission, a brilliant light from heaven suddenly
beamed down upon him! 4He fell to the ground and heard a voice saying to him, "Saul!
Saul! Why are you persecuting me?"
5"Who are you, sir?" Saul asked.
And the voice replied, "I am Jesus, the one you are persecuting! 6Now get up and go
into the city, and you will be told what you are to do."
7The men with Saul stood speechless with surprise, for they heard the sound of
someone's voice, but they saw no one! 8As Saul picked himself up off the ground, he
found that he was blind. 9So his companions led him by the hand to Damascus. He
remained there blind for three days. And all that time he went without food and water.
10Now there was a believer* in Damascus named Ananias. The Lord spoke to him in
a vision, calling, "Ananias!"
"Yes, Lord!" he replied.
11The Lord said, "Go over to Straight Street, to the house of Judas. When you arrive,
ask for Saul of Tarsus. He is praying to me right now. 12I have shown him a vision of a
man named Ananias coming in and laying his hands on him so that he can see again."
13"But Lord," exclaimed Ananias, "I've heard about the terrible things this man has
done to the believers in Jerusalem! 14And we hear that he is authorized by the leading
priests to arrest every believer in Damascus."
15But the Lord said, "Go and do what I say. For Saul is my chosen instrument to take

9:1-29 //Acts 22:3-21; 26:9-18
9:1 Acts 8:3
9:2 Acts 9:14; 22:4
9:3 Acts 22:6-7; 26:12-13; 1 Cor 15:8
9:5 Acts 5:39
9:7 Dan 10:7; Acts 22:9; 26:14
9:10 Acts 10:3; 11:5; 12:9; 22:12
9:11 Acts 21:39
9:13 Acts 26:10
9:14 1 Cor 1:2
9:15 Acts 13:2; Rom 1:1; Gal 1:15-16; 1 Tim 1:12

9:1 Greek *disciples.* **9:10** Greek *disciple;* also in 9:36.

9:2 Saul (later called Paul) was so zealous for his Jewish beliefs that he began a persecution campaign against anyone who believed in Christ ("followers of the Way"). Why would the Jews in Jerusalem want to persecute Christians as far away as Damascus? There are several possibilities: (1) to seize the Christians who had fled, (2) to prevent the spread of Christianity to other major cities, (3) to keep the Christians from causing any trouble with Rome, (4) to advance Saul's career and build his reputation as a true Pharisee, zealous for the law, (5) to unify the factions of Judaism by giving them a common enemy.

9:2-5 As Saul traveled to Damascus, pursuing Christians, he was confronted by the risen Christ and brought face to face with the truth of the Good News. Sometimes God breaks into a life in a spectacular manner, and sometimes conversion is a quiet experience. Beware of people who insist that you must have a particular type of conversion experience. The right way to come to faith in Jesus is whatever way God brings *you.*

9:3 Damascus, a key commercial city, was located about 150 miles northeast of Jerusalem in the Roman province of Syria. Several trade routes linked Damascus to other cities throughout the Roman world. Saul may have thought that by stamping out Christianity in Damascus, he could prevent its spread to other areas.

9:3-5 Paul refers to this experience as the start of his new life in Christ (1 Corinthians 9:1; 15:8; Galatians 1:15, 16). At the center of this wonderful experience was Jesus Christ. Paul did not see a vision; he saw the risen Christ himself (9:17). Paul acknowledged Jesus as Lord, confessed his own sin, surrendered his life to Christ, and resolved to obey him. True conversion comes from a personal encounter with Jesus Christ and leads to a new life in relationship with him.

9:5 Saul thought he was pursuing heretics, but he was persecuting Jesus himself. Anyone who persecutes believers today is also guilty of persecuting Jesus (see Matthew 25:40, 45), because believers are the body of Christ on earth.

9:13, 14 "Not him, Lord; that's impossible. He could never become a Christian!" In essence, that's what Ananias said when God told him of Saul's conversion. After all, Saul had pursued believers to their death. Despite these understandable feelings, Ananias obeyed God and ministered to Saul. We must not limit God—he can do anything. We must obey and follow God's leading, even when he leads us to difficult people and places.

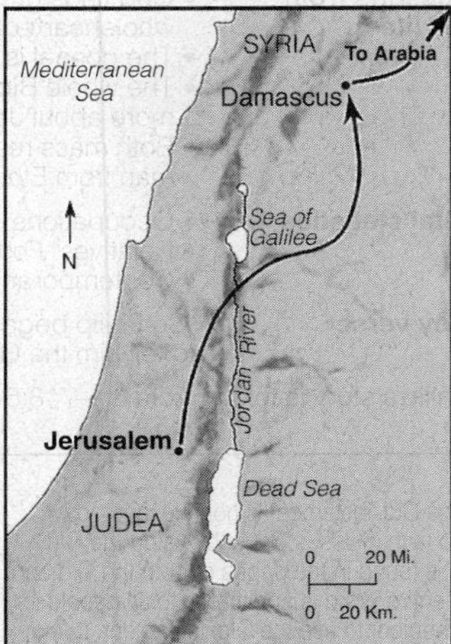

SAUL TRAVELS TO DAMASCUS
Many Christians fled Jerusalem when persecution began after Stephen's death, seeking refuge in other cities and countries. Saul tracked them down, even traveling 150 miles to Damascus in Syria to bring Christians back in chains to Jerusalem. But as he neared the ancient city, he discovered that God had other plans for him (9:15).

9:15, 16 Faith in Christ brings great blessings but often great suffering, too. Paul would suffer for his faith (see 2 Corinthians

9:16 Acts 20:23; 21:11; 2 Cor 11:23-27 — my message to the Gentiles and to kings, as well as to the people of Israel. 16 And I will
show him how much he must suffer for me."
9:17 Acts 13:52; 22:12-13; 1 Cor 9:1; 15:8 — 17 So Ananias went and found Saul. He laid his hands on him and said, "Brother Saul,
the Lord Jesus, who appeared to you on the road, has sent me so that you may get your
sight back and be filled with the Holy Spirit." 18 Instantly something like scales fell from

PAUL

No person, apart from Jesus himself, shaped the history of Christianity like the apostle Paul. Even before he was a believer, his actions were significant. His frenzied persecution of Christians following Stephen's death got the church started in obeying Christ's final command to take the gospel worldwide. Paul's personal encounter with Jesus changed his life. He never lost his fierce intensity, but from then on it was channeled for the gospel.

Paul was very religious. His training under Gamaliel was the finest available. His intentions and efforts were sincere. He was a good Pharisee who knew the Bible and sincerely believed that this Christian movement was dangerous to Judaism. Thus, Paul hated the Christian faith and persecuted Christians without mercy.

Paul got permission to travel to Damascus to capture Christians and bring them back to Jerusalem. But God stopped him in his hurried tracks on the Damascus road. Paul personally met Jesus Christ, and his life was never again the same.

Until Paul's conversion, little had been done about carrying the gospel to non-Jews. Philip had preached in Samaria and to an Ethiopian man; Cornelius, a Gentile, was converted under Peter; and in Antioch in Syria, some Greeks had joined the believers. When Barnabas was sent from Jerusalem to check on this situation, he went to Tarsus to find Paul and bring him to Antioch, and together they worked among the believers there. They were then sent on a missionary journey, the first of three Paul would take that would carry the gospel across the Roman Empire.

The thorny issue of whether Gentile believers had to obey Jewish laws before they could become Christians caused many problems in the early church. Paul worked hard to convince the Jews that Gentiles were acceptable to God, but he spent even more time convincing the Gentiles that they were acceptable to God. The lives Paul touched were changed and challenged by meeting Christ through him.

God did not waste any part of Paul—his background, his training, his citizenship, his mind, or even his weaknesses. Are you willing to let God do the same for you? You will never know all he can do with you until you allow him to have all that you are!

Strengths and accomplishments
- Transformed by God from a persecutor of Christians to a preacher for Christ
- Preached for Christ throughout the Roman Empire on three missionary journeys
- Wrote letters to various churches, which became part of the New Testament
- Was never afraid to face an issue head-on and deal with it
- Was sensitive to God's leading and, despite his strong personality, always did as God directed
- Is often called the apostle to the Gentiles

Weaknesses and mistakes
- Witnessed and approved of Stephen's stoning
- Set out to destroy Christianity by persecuting Christians

Lessons from his life
- The Good News is that forgiveness and eternal life are available to all people and are gifts of God's grace through faith in Christ
- Obedience results from a relationship with God, but obedience will never create or earn that relationship
- Real freedom doesn't come until we no longer have to prove our freedom
- God does not waste our time; he will use our past and present so we may serve him with our future

Vital statistics
- Where: Born in Tarsus but became a world traveler for Christ
- Occupations: Trained as a Pharisee, learned the tentmaking trade, served as a missionary
- Contemporaries: Gamaliel, Stephen, the apostles, Luke, Barnabas, Timothy

Key verses
"For to me, living is for Christ, and dying is even better. Yet if I live, that means fruitful service for Christ. I really don't know which is better. I'm torn between two desires: Sometimes I want to live, and sometimes I long to go and be with Christ. That would be far better for me, but it is better for you that I live" (Philippians 1:21–24).

Paul's story is told in Acts 7:58—28:31 and throughout his New Testament letters.

Saul's eyes, and he regained his sight. Then he got up and was baptized. 19Afterward he 9:19
ate some food and was strengthened. Acts 26:20

Saul in Damascus and Jerusalem

Saul stayed with the believers* in Damascus for a few days. 20And immediately he began
preaching about Jesus in the synagogues, saying, "He is indeed the Son of God!"
21All who heard him were amazed. "Isn't this the same man who persecuted Jesus' 9:21
followers with such devastation in Jerusalem?" they asked. "And we understand that he Acts 8:3
came here to arrest them and take them in chains to the leading priests."
22Saul's preaching became more and more powerful, and the Jews in Damascus 9:22
couldn't refute his proofs that Jesus was indeed the Messiah. 23After a while the Jewish Acts 18:28
leaders decided to kill him. 24But Saul was told about their plot, and that they were 9:23 Acts 23:12
watching for him day and night at the city gate so they could murder him. 25So during 9:24
the night, some of the other believers* let him down in a large basket through an opening Acts 20:3; 23:16, 20
in the city wall. 2 Cor 11:32
26When Saul arrived in Jerusalem, he tried to meet with the believers, but they were 9:25
all afraid of him. They thought he was only pretending to be a believer! 27Then 1 Sam 19:12 2 Cor 11:33
Barnabas brought him to the apostles and told them how Saul had seen the Lord on 9:26
the way to Damascus. Barnabas also told them what the Lord had said to Saul and Acts 22:17 Gal 1:17-18
how he boldly preached in the name of Jesus in Damascus. 28Then the apostles 9:27
accepted Saul, and after that he was constantly with them in Jerusalem, preaching Acts 4:36

9:19 Greek *disciples;* also in 9:26. **9:25** Greek *his disciples.*

11:23-27). God calls us to commitment, not to comfort. He promises to be with us *through* suffering and hardship, not to spare us from them.

9:17 Ananias found Saul, as he had been instructed, and greeted him as "Brother Saul." Ananias feared this meeting because Saul had come to Damascus to capture the believers and take them as prisoners to Jerusalem (9:2). But in obedience to the Holy Spirit, Ananias greeted Saul lovingly. It is not always easy to show love to others, especially when we are afraid of them or doubt their motives. Nevertheless we must follow Jesus' command (John 13:34) and Ananias's example, showing loving acceptance to other believers.

9:17, 18 Although there is no mention of a special filling of the Holy Spirit for Saul, his changed life and subsequent accomplishments bear strong witness to the Holy Spirit's presence and power in his life. Evidently, the Holy Spirit filled Saul when he received his sight and was baptized. See the second note on 8:15-17 for more on the filling of the Holy Spirit.

9:20 Immediately after receiving his sight and spending some time with the believers in Damascus, Saul went to the synagogue to tell the Jews about Jesus Christ. Some Christians counsel new believers to wait until they are thoroughly grounded in their faith before attempting to share the Good News. Saul spent time with other believers to learn about Jesus before beginning his worldwide ministry, but he did not wait to witness. Although we should not rush into a ministry unprepared, we do not need to wait before telling others what has happened to us.

9:21, 22 Saul's arguments were powerful because he was a brilliant scholar. But what was more convincing was his changed life. People knew that what he taught was real because they could see the evidence in the way he lived. It is important to know what the Bible teaches and how to defend the faith, but your words should be backed up with a changed life.

9:23 According to Galatians 1:17, 18, Paul left Damascus and traveled to Arabia, the desert region just southeast of Damascus, where he lived for three years. It is unclear whether his three-year stay occurred between verses 22 and 23 or between verses 25 and 26. Some commentators say that "after a while" could mean a long period of time. They suggest that when Paul re-[turn]ed to Damascus, the governor under Aretas ordered his arrest (2 Corinthians 11:32) in an effort to keep peace with influential Jews.

The other possibility is that Paul's night escape occurred during his first stay in Damascus, just after his conversion, when the Pharisees were especially upset over his defection from their ranks. He would have fled to Arabia to spend time alone with God and to let the Jewish religious leaders cool down. Regardless of which theory is correct, there was a period of at least three years between Paul's conversion (9:3-6) and his trip to Jerusalem (9:26).

9:26, 27 It is difficult to change your reputation, and Saul had a terrible reputation with the Christians. But Barnabas, a Jewish convert (mentioned in 4:36), became the bridge between Saul and the apostles. New Christians (especially those with tarnished reputations) need sponsors, people who will come alongside, encourage, teach, and introduce them to other believers. Find ways that you can become a Barnabas to new believers.

9:27 Galatians 1:18, 19 explains that Paul was in Jerusalem only 15 days and that he met only with Peter and James.

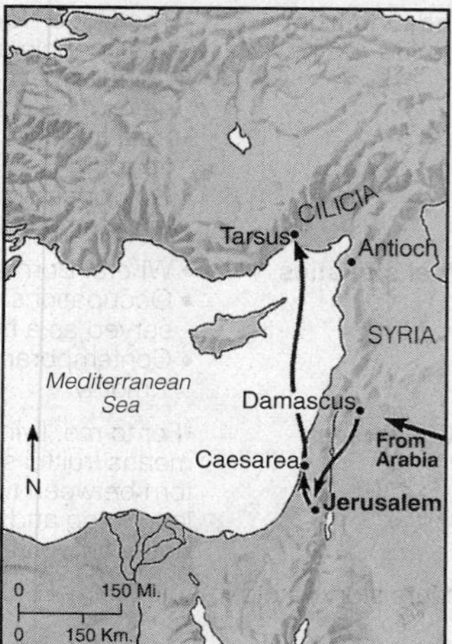

SAUL'S RETURN TO TARSUS
At least three years elapsed between Acts 9:22 and 9:26. After time alone in Arabia (see Galatians 1:16–18), Saul (Paul) returned to Damascus and then to Jerusalem. The apostles were reluctant to believe that this former persecutor could have become one of them. He escaped to Caesarea, where he caught a ship and returned to Tarsus.

boldly in the name of the Lord. [29] He debated with some Greek-speaking Jews, but
they plotted to murder him. [30] When the believers* heard about it, however, they took
him to Caesarea and sent him on to his hometown of Tarsus.
9:31 Acts 8:1 [31] The church then had peace throughout Judea, Galilee, and Samaria, and it grew in
strength and numbers. The believers were walking in the fear of the Lord and in the
comfort of the Holy Spirit.

9:30 Greek *brothers.*

GREAT ESCAPES IN THE BIBLE

Who escaped	*Reference*	*What happened*	*What the escape accomplished*	*Application*
Jacob	Genesis 31:1–55	Fled from his father-in-law, Laban, after almost 20 years of service	Allowed Jacob to return home for Isaac's death and for reconcilation with Esau, his brother	A time away from home often puts the really important things into perspective
Moses	Exodus 2:11–15	Fled Egypt after killing an Egyptian in defense of a fellow Israelite	Saved his own life and began another part of God's training	God fits even our mistakes into his plan
Israelites	Exodus 12:28–42	Escaped Egypt after 430 years, most of that time in slavery	God confirmed his choice of Abraham's descendants	God will not forget his promises
Spies	Joshua 2:1–24	Escaped searchers in Jericho by hiding in Rahab's house	Prepared the destruction of Jericho and preserved Rahab, who would become one of David's ancestors—as well as an ancestor of Jesus	God's plan weaves lives together in a pattern beyond our understanding
Ehud	Judges 3:15–30	Escaped undetected after assassinating the Moabite king Eglon	Broke the control of Moab over Israel and began 80 years of peace	Punishments by God are often swift and deadly
Samson	Judges 16:1–3	Escaped a locked city by ripping the gates from their hinges	Merely postponed Samson's self-destruction because of his lack of self-control	Without dependence on God and his guidance, even great ability is wasted
Elijah	1 Kings 19:1–18	Fled into the wilderness out of fear of Queen Jezebel	Preserved Elijah's life but also displayed his human weakness	Even at moments of real success, our personal weaknesses are our greatest challenges
Saul (Paul)	Acts 9:23–25	Lowered over the wall in a basket to get out of Damascus	Saved this new Christian for great service to God	God has a purpose for every life, which leads to a real adventure for those willing to cooperate
Peter	Acts 12:1–11	Freed from prison by an angel	Saved Peter for God's further plans for his life	God can use extraordinary means to carry out his plan—often when we least expect it
Paul and Silas	Acts 16:22–40	Chains loosened and doors opened by an earthquake, but they chose not to leave the prison	Pointed out the powerlessness of humans before God	When our dependence and attention are focused on God rather than our problems, he is able to offer help in unexpected ways

9:29, 30 In these short sentences we can see two characteristics of Paul, even as a new believer in Christ: He was bold, and he stirred up controversy. These would characterize Paul's ministry the rest of his life.

9:30 Saul's visit to Tarsus helped quiet conflicts with the Jews and allowed him time to prove his commitment. After Saul, the most zealous persecutor, was converted, the church enjoyed a brief time of peace.

Peter Heals Aeneas and Raises Dorcas

32 Peter traveled from place to place to visit the believers, and in his travels he came to the **9:32** Acts 8:14
Lord's people in the town of Lydda. 33 There he met a man named Aeneas, who had been
paralyzed and bedridden for eight years. 34 Peter said to him, "Aeneas, Jesus Christ heals **9:34** Acts 3:6; 4:10
you! Get up and make your bed!" And he was healed instantly. 35 Then the whole population **9:35**
of Lydda and Sharon turned to the Lord when they saw Aeneas walking around. Acts 2:41
36 There was a believer in Joppa named Tabitha (which in Greek is Dorcas*). She was **9:36** 1 Tim 2:10
always doing kind things for others and helping the poor. 37 About this time she became Titus 3:8
ill and died. Her friends prepared her for burial and laid her in an upstairs room. 38 But
they had heard that Peter was nearby at Lydda, so they sent two men to beg him, "Please
come as soon as possible!"
39 So Peter returned with them; and as soon as he arrived, they took him to the upstairs
room. The room was filled with widows who were weeping and showing him the coats and
other garments Dorcas had made for them. 40 But Peter asked them all to leave the room; **9:40** 1 Kgs 17:19-23
then he knelt and prayed. Turning to the body he said, "Get up, Tabitha." And she opened 2 Kgs 4:32-36 Matt 9:25
her eyes! When she saw Peter, she sat up! 41 He gave her his hand and helped her up. Then John 11:43
he called in the widows and all the believers, and he showed them that she was alive. **9:42** Acts 2:41
42 The news raced through the whole town, and many believed in the Lord. 43 And **9:43**
Peter stayed a long time in Joppa, living with Simon, a leatherworker. Acts 10:6

Cornelius Calls for Peter

10 In Caesarea there lived a Roman army officer named Cornelius, who was a captain **10:1-2** Acts 8:40; 27:1, 3
of the Italian Regiment. 2 He was a devout man who feared the God of Israel, as
did his entire household. He gave generously to charity and was a man who regularly
prayed to God. 3 One afternoon about three o'clock, he had a vision in which he saw an **10:3**
angel of God coming toward him. "Cornelius!" the angel said. Acts 3:1
4 Cornelius stared at him in terror. "What is it, sir?" he asked the angel. **10:4** 2 Chr 7:15 Rev 8:4

9:36 The names *Tabitha* in Aramaic and *Dorcas* in Greek both mean "gazelle."

PETER'S MINISTRY
Peter traveled to the ancient crossroads town of Lydda, where he healed crippled Aeneas. The believers in Joppa, an old port city, sent for him after a wonderful woman died. Peter went and brought her back to life. While in Joppa, Peter had a vision that led him to take the gospel to Cornelius, a Gentile, in Caesarea.

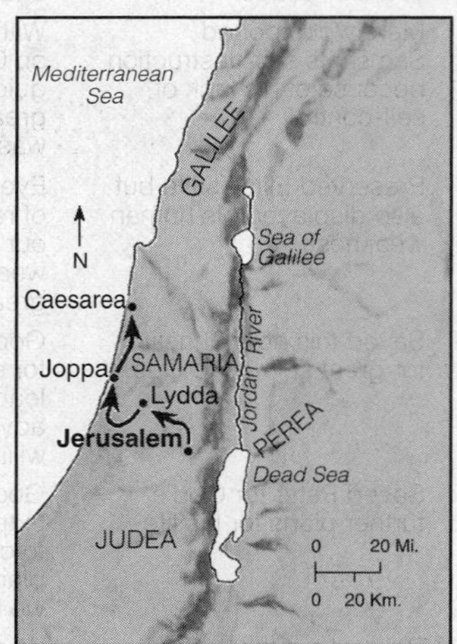

9:36 The important harbor city of Joppa sits 125 feet above sea level overlooking the Mediterranean Sea. Joppa was the town into which the cedars of Lebanon had been floated to be shipped to Jerusalem for use in the Temple construction (2 Chronicles 2:16; Ezra 3:7). The prophet Jonah left the port of Joppa on his ill-fated trip (Jonah 1:3).

9:36-42 Tabitha made an enormous impact on her community by "always doing kind things for others and helping the poor," by making coats and other garments (9:39). When she died, the room was filled with mourners, very likely many of the people she had helped. And when she was brought back to life, the news raced through the town. God uses great preachers like Peter and Paul, but he also uses those who have gifts of kindness like Tabitha. Rather than wishing you had other gifts, make good use of the gifts God has given you.

9:43 In Joppa, Peter stayed at the home of Simon, a leatherworker. Leatherworkers made animal hides into leather. It is significant that Peter was at Simon's house, because leatherworking involved contact with dead animals, and Jewish law considered it an "unclean" job. Peter was already beginning to break down his prejudice against people who were not of his kind and who had customs that did not adhere to Jewish religious traditions.

10:1 This Caesarea, sometimes called Palestinian Caesarea, was located on the coast of the Mediterranean Sea, 32 miles north of Joppa. The largest and most important port city on the Mediterranean in Palestine, it served as the capital of the Roman province of Judea. This was the first city to have Gentile Christians and a non-Jewish church.

10:1 This Roman officer was a commander of 100 soldiers. Although stationed in Caesarea, Cornelius would probably return soon to Rome. Thus, his conversion was a major stepping-stone for spreading the Good News to the empire's capital city.

10:2 What will happen to the heathen who have never heard about Christ? This question is often asked about God's justice. Cornelius wasn't a believer in Christ, but he was seeking God and was reverent and generous. Therefore, God sent Peter to tell Cornelius about Christ. This shows that God "rewards those who sincerely seek him" (Hebrews 11:6). Those who sincerely seek God will find him! God made Cornelius's knowledge complete.

10:4 God saw Cornelius's sincere faith. His prayers and generous giving had not gone unnoticed by God. God answers the sincere prayers of those who seek him by sending the right person or the right information at the right time.

And the angel replied, "Your prayers and gifts to the poor have not gone unnoticed by
10:6 Acts 9:43 God! [5]Now send some men down to Joppa to find a man named Simon Peter. [6]He is staying
with Simon, a leatherworker who lives near the shore. Ask him to come and visit you."
[7]As soon as the angel was gone, Cornelius called two of his household servants and a
devout soldier, one of his personal attendants. [8]He told them what had happened and sent
them off to Joppa.

Peter Visits Cornelius

10:9-32 //Acts 11:5-14 [9]The next day as Cornelius's messengers were nearing the city, Peter went up to the flat roof
10:11 Ezek 1:1-3 Matt 3:16 Acts 7:56 to pray. It was about noon, [10]and he was hungry. But while lunch was being prepared, he
fell into a trance. [11]He saw the sky open, and something like a large sheet was let down by
its four corners. [12]In the sheet were all sorts of animals, reptiles, and birds. [13]Then a voice
said to him, "Get up, Peter; kill and eat them."

CORNELIUS

The early days of Christianity were exciting as God's Spirit moved and people's lives were changed. Converts were pouring in from surprising backgrounds. Even the dreaded Saul (Paul) became a Christian, and non-Jews were responding to the Good News about Jesus. Among the first of these was the Roman captain Cornelius.

Because of frequent outbreaks of violence, Roman soldiers had to be stationed throughout Israel to keep the peace. But most Romans, hated as conquerors, did not get along well in the nation. As an army officer, Cornelius was in a difficult position. He represented Rome, but his home was in Caesarea. During his years in Israel, he had himself been conquered by the God of Israel. He had a reputation as a godly man who put his faith into action, and he was respected by the Jews.

Four significant aspects of Cornelius's character are noted in Acts: (1) He actively sought God, (2) he revered God, (3) he was generous in meeting other people's needs, and (4) he prayed. God told him to send for Peter, because Peter would give him more knowledge about the God he was already seeking to please.

When Peter entered Cornelius's home, Peter broke a whole list of Jewish rules. Peter confessed he wasn't comfortable, but here was an eager audience, and he couldn't hold back his message. He had no sooner started sharing the gospel when God gave overwhelming approval by filling that Roman family with his Holy Spirit. Peter saw he had no choice but to baptize them and welcome them as equals in the growing Christian church. Another step had been taken in carrying the gospel to the whole world.

Cornelius is a welcome example of God's willingness to use extraordinary means to reach those who desire to know him. He does not play favorites, and he does not hide from those who want to find him. God sent his Son because he loves the whole world—and that includes Peter, Cornelius, and you.

Strengths and accomplishments
- A godly and generous Roman
- Although an officer in the occupying army, he seems to have been well-respected by the Jews
- He responded to God and encouraged his family to do the same
- His conversion helped the young church realize that the Good News was for all people, both Jews and Gentiles

Lessons from his life
- God reaches those who want to know him
- The gospel is for all people
- There are people everywhere eager to believe
- When we are willing to seek the truth and be obedient to the light God gives us, God will reward us richly

Vital statistics
- Where: Caesarea
- Occupation: Roman officer
- Contemporaries: Peter, Philip, the apostles

Key verse
"He was a devout man who feared the God of Israel, as did his entire household. He gave generously to charity and was a man who regularly prayed to God" (Acts 10:2).

Cornelius's story is told in Acts 10:1—11:18.

10:12 According to Jewish law, certain foods were forbidden to be eaten (see Leviticus 11). The food laws made it difficult for Jews to eat with Gentiles without risking defilement. In fact, the Gentiles themselves were often seen as "unclean." Peter's vision meant that he should not look upon the Gentiles as inferior people whom God would not redeem. Before having the vision, Peter would have thought that a Gentile Roman officer could not accept Christ. Afterward he understood that it was his responsibility to go with the messengers into a Gentile home and tell Cornelius the Good News of salvation in Jesus Christ.

[14]"Never, Lord," Peter declared. "I have never in all my life eaten anything forbidden by our Jewish laws.*"

[15]The voice spoke again, "If God says something is acceptable, don't say it isn't."* [16]The same vision was repeated three times. Then the sheet was pulled up again to heaven.

[17]Peter was very perplexed. What could the vision mean? Just then the men sent by Cornelius found the house and stood outside at the gate. [18]They asked if this was the place where Simon Peter was staying. [19]Meanwhile, as Peter was puzzling over the vision, the Holy Spirit said to him, "Three men have come looking for you. [20]Go down and go with them without hesitation. All is well, for I have sent them."

[21]So Peter went down and said, "I'm the man you are looking for. Why have you come?"

[22]They said, "We were sent by Cornelius, a Roman officer. He is a devout man who fears the God of Israel and is well respected by all the Jews. A holy angel instructed him to send for you so you can go to his house and give him a message." [23]So Peter invited the men to be his guests for the night. The next day he went with them, accompanied by some other believers* from Joppa.

[24]They arrived in Caesarea the following day. Cornelius was waiting for him and had called together his relatives and close friends to meet Peter. [25]As Peter entered his home, Cornelius fell to the floor before him in worship. [26]But Peter pulled him up and said, "Stand up! I'm a human being like you!" [27]So Cornelius got up, and they talked together and went inside where the others were assembled.

[28]Peter told them, "You know it is against the Jewish laws for me to come into a Gentile home like this. But God has shown me that I should never think of anyone as impure. [29]So I came as soon as I was sent for. Now tell me why you sent for me."

[30]Cornelius replied, "Four days ago I was praying in my house at three o'clock in the afternoon. Suddenly, a man in dazzling clothes was standing in front of me. [31]He told me, 'Cornelius, your prayers have been heard, and your gifts to the poor have been noticed by God! [32]Now send some men to Joppa and summon Simon Peter. He is staying in the home of Simon, a leatherworker who lives near the shore.' [33]So I sent for you at once, and it was good of you to come. Now here we are, waiting before God to hear the message the Lord has given you."

The Gentiles Hear the Good News

[34]Then Peter replied, "I see very clearly that God doesn't show partiality. [35]In every nation he accepts those who fear him and do what is right. [36]I'm sure you have heard about the Good News for the people of Israel—that there is peace with God through Jesus Christ, who is Lord of all. [37]You know what happened all through Judea, beginning in Galilee after John the Baptist began preaching. [38]And no doubt you know that God anointed Jesus of Nazareth with the Holy Spirit and with power. Then Jesus went around doing good and healing all who were oppressed by the Devil, for God was with him.

[39]"And we apostles are witnesses of all he did throughout Israel and in Jerusalem.

10:14 Greek *anything common and unclean.* **10:15** Greek *"What God calls clean you must not call unclean."*
10:23 Greek *brothers.*

10:14 Lev 11:1-47; Ezek 4:14
10:15 Matt 15:11; Rom 14:14, 17, 20; 1 Cor 10:25; 1 Tim 4:3-4; Titus 1:15
10:19 Acts 11:12; 13:2
10:20 Acts 15:7-9
10:22 Acts 10:2
10:23 Acts 10:45; 11:12
10:24 Acts 8:40
10:25-26 Acts 14:13-15; Rev 19:10; 22:9
10:28 John 4:9; Acts 11:3; 15:9
10:30-33 Acts 10:1-8
10:34 Deut 10:17; Rom 2:11; Col 3:25
10:35 Acts 15:9
10:36 Rom 5:1; Eph 2:17
10:38 Luke 4:18-19
10:39 Luke 24:48

10:25, 26 This act of worship could have caused Peter to become arrogant. After all, a Roman officer was bowing before him. Instead, Peter pointed Cornelius to Christ. We, too, should remember our mortality whenever we are flattered or honored, and use the opportunity to give glory to God.

10:34, 35 Perhaps the greatest barrier to the spread of the Good News in the first century was the Jewish-Gentile conflict. Most of the early believers were Jewish, and to them it was scandalous even to think of associating with Gentiles. But God told Peter to take the Good News to a Roman, and Peter obeyed despite his background and personal feelings. (Later Peter struggled with this again—see Galatians 2:11-14.) God was making it clear that the Good News of Christ is for everyone! We should not allow any barrier—language, culture, prejudice, geography, economic level, or educational level—to keep us from telling others about Christ.

10:35 In every nation there are hearts restless for God, ready to receive the Good News—but someone must take it to them. Seeking God is not enough—people must find him. How then shall seekers find God without someone to point the way? Is God asking you to show someone the way to him? (See Romans 10:14, 15.)

10:37-43 Peter's brief and powerful sermon contains a concise statement of the Good News: Jesus' perfect life of servanthood; his death on the cross; his resurrection, personally witnessed and experienced by Peter; Jesus' fulfillment of the Scriptures; and the necessity of personal faith in him. A sermon or witness for Christ does not need to be long to be effective. It should be Spirit led and should center on Christ, the way and the truth and the life.

10:40-41 John 21:12-13 They put him to death by crucifying him, 40but God raised him to life three days later.
Then God allowed him to appear, 41not to the general public,* but to us whom God had
chosen beforehand to be his witnesses. We were those who ate and drank with him after
10:42 Matt 28:19 2 Cor 5:10 he rose from the dead. 42And he ordered us to preach everywhere and to testify that Jesus
is ordained of God to be the judge of all—the living and the dead. 43He is the one all the
10:43 Isa 53:11 Jer 31:34 prophets testified about, saying that everyone who believes in him will have their sins
forgiven through his name."

The Gentiles Receive the Holy Spirit

10:44 Acts 11:15; 15:8 44Even as Peter was saying these things, the Holy Spirit fell upon all who had heard the
message. 45The Jewish believers who came with Peter were amazed that the gift of the
10:46 Mark 16:17 Acts 2:4; 19:6 Holy Spirit had been poured out upon the Gentiles, too. 46And there could be no doubt
about it, for they heard them speaking in tongues and praising God.
10:47 Acts 8:36; 11:17 Then Peter asked, 47"Can anyone object to their being baptized, now that they have
received the Holy Spirit just as we did?" 48So he gave orders for them to be baptized in
10:48 Acts 2:38; 19:5 the name of Jesus Christ. Afterward Cornelius asked him to stay with them for several
days.

Peter Explains His Actions

11 Soon the news reached the apostles and other believers* in Judea that the Gentiles
had received the word of God. 2But when Peter arrived back in Jerusalem, some
11:3 Acts 10:28 Gal 2:12 of the Jewish believers* criticized him. 3"You entered the home of Gentiles* and even
ate with them!" they said.
11:5-14 //Acts 10:9-32 4Then Peter told them exactly what had happened. 5"One day in Joppa," he said,
"while I was praying, I went into a trance and saw a vision. Something like a large sheet
was let down by its four corners from the sky. And it came right down to me. 6When I
looked inside the sheet, I saw all sorts of small animals, wild animals, reptiles, and birds
that we are not allowed to eat. 7And I heard a voice say, 'Get up, Peter; kill and eat them.'
8"'Never, Lord,' I replied. 'I have never eaten anything forbidden by our Jewish
laws.*'
9"But the voice from heaven came again, 'If God says something is acceptable, don't
say it isn't.'*

10:41 Greek *the people.* **11:1** Greek *brothers;* also in 11:29b. **11:2** Greek *those of the circumcision.* **11:3** Greek *of uncircumcised men.* **11:8** Greek *anything common or unclean.* **11:9** Greek *'What God calls clean you must not call unclean.'*

10:43 Two examples of prophets testifying about Jesus and his forgiveness of sins are Isaiah 52:13–53:12 and Ezekiel 36:25, 26.

10:45 Cornelius and Peter were very different people. Cornelius was wealthy, a Gentile, and a military man. Peter was a Jewish fisherman turned preacher. But God's plan included both of them. In Cornelius's house that day, a new chapter in Christian history was written as a Jewish Christian leader and a Gentile Christian convert each discovered something significant about the other. Cornelius needed Peter in order to hear the Good News and know the way of salvation. Peter needed Cornelius in order to know that Gentiles were included in God's plan. You and another believer may also need each other to understand how God works!

10:47, 48 In this case, the people were baptized *after* they received the Holy Spirit, publicly declaring their allegiance to Christ and identification with the Christian community.

10:48 Cornelius wanted Peter to stay with him for several days. He was a new believer and realized his need for teaching and fellowship. Are you as eager to learn more about Christ? Recognize your need to be with mature Christians, and strive to learn from them.

11:1 A Gentile was anyone who was not a Jew. Most Jewish believers thought that God offered salvation only to the Jews because God had given his law to them (Exodus 19–20). A group in Jerusalem believed that Gentiles could be saved, but only if they followed all the Jewish laws and traditions—in essence, if they became Jews. Both were mistaken. God chose the Jews and taught them his laws so they could bring the message of salvation to *all* people (see Genesis 12:3; Psalm 22:27; Isaiah 42:4; 49:6; 56:3-7; 60:1-3; Jeremiah 16:19-21; Zechariah 2:11; Malachi 1:11; Romans 15:9-12).

11:2-18 When Peter brought the news of Cornelius's conversion back to Jerusalem, the believers were shocked that Peter had eaten with Gentiles. After they heard the whole story, however, they praised God (11:18). Their reactions teach us how to handle disagreements with other Christians. Before judging the behavior of fellow believers, it is important to hear them out. The Holy Spirit may have something important to teach us through them.

11:8 God had promised throughout Scripture that he would reach the nations. This began with his general promise to Abraham (Genesis 12:3; 18:18) and became very specific in Malachi's statement: "But my name is honored by people of other nations from morning till night" (Malachi 1:11). But this was an extremely difficult truth for Jews, even Jewish believers, to accept. The Jewish believers understood how certain prophecies were fulfilled in Christ, but they overlooked other Old Testament teachings. Too often we are inclined to accept only the parts of God's Word that appeal to us and support our own agendas, ignoring the teachings we don't like. We must accept all of God's Word as absolute truth.

10 “This happened three times before the sheet and all it contained was pulled back up
to heaven. 11 Just then three men who had been sent from Caesarea arrived at the house
where I was staying. 12 The Holy Spirit told me to go with them and not to worry about
their being Gentiles. These six brothers here accompanied me, and we soon arrived at
the home of the man who had sent for us. 13 He told us how an angel had appeared to him
in his home and had told him, ‘Send messengers to Joppa to find Simon Peter. 14 He will
tell you how you and all your household will be saved!’

15 “Well, I began telling them the Good News, but just as I was getting started, the
Holy Spirit fell on them, just as he fell on us at the beginning. 16 Then I thought of the
Lord’s words when he said, ‘John baptized with* water, but you will be baptized with
the Holy Spirit.’ 17 And since God gave these Gentiles the same gift he gave us when we
believed in the Lord Jesus Christ, who was I to argue?”

18 When the others heard this, all their objections were answered and they began
praising God. They said, “God has also given the Gentiles the privilege of turning from
sin and receiving eternal life.”

The Church in Antioch of Syria

19 Meanwhile, the believers who had fled from Jerusalem during the persecution after
Stephen’s death traveled as far as Phoenicia, Cyprus, and Antioch of Syria. They
preached the Good News, but only to Jews. 20 However, some of the believers who went
to Antioch from Cyprus and Cyrene began preaching to Gentiles* about the Lord Jesus.
21 The power of the Lord was upon them, and large numbers of these Gentiles believed
and turned to the Lord.

22 When the church at Jerusalem heard what had happened, they sent Barnabas to

11:12 Acts 10:23, 45
11:13 Acts 10:30-32
11:14 Acts 10:22, 44; 16:31
11:15 Acts 2:4
11:16 Acts 1:5
11:17 Acts 10:47
11:18 Acts 13:48
11:19 Acts 8:1-4; 13:1; 14:25-27; 15:3
11:21 Luke 1:66 Acts 2:41
11:22 Acts 4:36

11:16 Or *in;* also in 11:16b. **11:20** Greek *the Greeks;* other manuscripts read *the Hellenists.*

BARNABAS AND SAUL IN ANTIOCH

Persecution scattered the believers into Phoenicia, Cyprus, and Antioch, and the gospel went with them. Most spoke only to Jews, but in Antioch, some Gentiles were converted. The church sent Barnabas to investigate, and he was pleased with what he found. Barnabas went to Tarsus to bring Saul (Paul) back to Antioch.

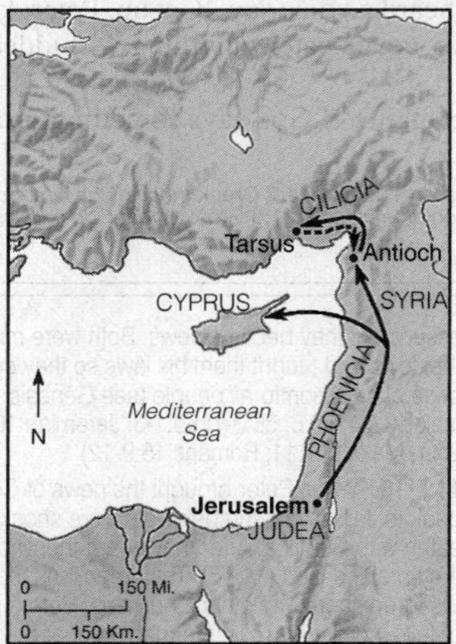

11:12ff Peter’s defense for eating with Gentiles was a simple restatement of what happened. He brought six witnesses with him to back him up, and then he quoted Jesus’ promise about the coming of the Holy Spirit (11:16). These Gentiles’ lives had been changed, and that was all the evidence Peter and the other believers needed. Changed lives are an equally powerful evidence today.

11:16 Jesus had also demonstrated clearly that he and his message were for all people. He preached in Samaria (John 4:1-42); in the region of the Gerasenes, populated by Greeks (Mark 5:1-20); and he even reached out to Romans (Luke 7:1-10). The apostles shouldn’t have been surprised that they were called to do the same.

11:18 The intellectual questions ended, and the theological discussion stopped with the report that God had given the Holy Spirit to the Gentiles. This was a turning point for the early church. They had to accept those whom God had chosen, even if they were Gentiles. But joy over the conversion of Gentiles was not unanimous. This continued to be a struggle for some Jewish Christians throughout the first century.

11:19-21 When the church accepted Peter’s testimony that the Good News was also for Gentiles, Christianity exploded into Gentile areas, and large numbers became believers. The seeds of this missionary work had been sown after Stephen’s death when many believing Jews were persecuted and scattered, settling in faraway cities and spreading the Good News.

11:20, 21 It was in Antioch that Christianity was launched on its worldwide mission and where the believers aggressively preached to the Gentiles (non-Jews who did not worship God). Philip had preached in Samaria, but the Samaritans were part Jewish (8:5); Peter preached to Cornelius, but he already worshiped God (10:2). Believers who were scattered after the outbreak of persecution in Jerusalem spread the Good News to other Jews in the lands they fled to (11:19). At this time, the believers began actively sharing the Good News with Gentiles.

11:22 With the exception of Jerusalem, Antioch of Syria played a more important role in the early church than any other city. After Rome and Alexandria, Antioch was the largest city in the Roman world. In Antioch the first Gentile church was founded, and there the believers were first called Christians (11:26). Paul used the city as his home base during his missionary journeys. Antioch was the center of worship for several pagan cults that promoted sexual immorality and other forms of evil common to pagan religions. It was also a vital commercial center—the gateway to the eastern world. Antioch was a key city both to Rome and to the early church.

11:22-26 Barnabas gives us a wonderful example of how to help new Christians. He demonstrated strong faith; he ministered joyfully with kindness and encouragement; he taught new believers further lessons about God (see 9:26-30). Remember Barnabas when you see new believers, and think of ways to help them grow in their faith.

11:23 Acts 13:43; 14:26; 15:40; 20:24
11:24 Acts 2:41
11:25 Acts 9:30

Antioch. 23 When he arrived and saw this proof of God's favor, he was filled with joy, and
he encouraged the believers to stay true to the Lord. 24 Barnabas was a good man, full of
the Holy Spirit and strong in faith. And large numbers of people were brought to the Lord.
25 Then Barnabas went on to Tarsus to find Saul. 26 When he found him, he brought
him back to Antioch. Both of them stayed there with the church for a full year, teaching
great numbers of people. (It was there at Antioch that the believers* were first called
Christians.)

11:26 Greek *disciples;* also in 11:29a.

HEROD AGRIPPA I

For good or evil, families have lasting and powerful influence on their children. Traits and qualities are passed on to the next generation, and often the mistakes and sins of the parents are repeated by the children. Four generations of the Herod family are mentioned in the Bible. Each leader left his evil mark: Herod the Great murdered Bethlehem's children; Herod Antipas was involved in Jesus' trial and John the Baptist's execution; Herod Agrippa I murdered the apostle James; and Herod Agrippa II was one of Paul's judges.

Herod Agrippa I related fairly well to his Jewish subjects. Because he had a Jewish grandmother of royal blood (Mariamne), he was grudgingly accepted by the people. Although as a youth he had been temporarily imprisoned by the emperor Tiberias, he was now trusted by Rome and got along well with the emperors Caligula and Claudius.

An unexpected opportunity for Herod to gain new favor with the Jews was created by the Christian movement. Gentiles began to be accepted into the church in large numbers. Many Jews had been tolerating this new movement as a sect within Judaism, but its rapid growth alarmed them. Persecution of Christians was revived, and even the apostles were not spared. James was killed, and Peter was thrown into prison.

But soon Herod made a fatal error. During a visit to Caesarea, the people called him a god, and he accepted their praise. Herod was immediately struck with a painful disease, and he died within a week.

Like his grandfather, uncle, and son after him, Herod Agrippa I came close to the truth but missed it. Because religion was important only as an aspect of politics, he had no reverence and no qualms about taking praise that only God should receive. His mistake is a common one. Whenever we become proud of our own abilities and accomplishments, not recognizing them as gifts from God, we repeat Herod's sin.

Strengths and accomplishments
- Capable administrator and negotiator
- Managed to maintain good relations with the Jews in his region and with Rome

Weaknesses and mistakes
- Arranged the murder of the apostle James
- Imprisoned Peter with plans to execute him
- Allowed the people to praise him as a god

Lessons from his life
- Those who set themselves against God are doomed to ultimate failure
- There is great danger in accepting praise that only God deserves
- Family traits can influence children toward great good or great evil

Vital statistics
- Where: Jerusalem
- Occupation: Roman-appointed king of the Jews
- Relatives: Grandfather: Herod the Great. Father: Aristobulus. Uncle: Herod Antipas. Sister: Herodias. Wife: Cypros. Son: Herod Agrippa II. Daughters: Bernice, Mariamne, Drusilla
- Contemporaries: Emperors Tiberias, Caligula, and Claudius. James, Peter, the apostles.

Key verse
"Instantly, an angel of the Lord struck Herod with a sickness, because he accepted the people's worship instead of giving the glory to God. So he was consumed with worms and died" (Acts 12:23).

Herod Agrippa I's story is told in Acts 12:1–23.

11:25 Saul had been sent to his home in Tarsus for protection after his conversion caused an uproar among the Jewish leaders in Jerusalem (9:26-30). He stayed there for several years before Barnabas brought him to help the church at Antioch.

11:26 The young church at Antioch was a curious mixture of Jews (who spoke Greek or Aramaic) and Gentiles. It is significant that this is the first place where the believers were called Christians (or "Christ-ones"), because all they had in common was Christ—not race, culture, or even language. Christ's love crosses all boundaries and unites all people.

11:26 Barnabas and Saul stayed at Antioch for a full year, teaching the new believers. They could have left for other cities, but they saw the importance of follow-up and training. Have you helped someone believe in God? Spend time teaching and encouraging that person. Are you a new believer? Remember, you are just beginning your Christian life. Your faith needs to grow and mature through consistent Bible study and teaching.

27 During this time, some prophets traveled from Jerusalem to Antioch. 28 One of them 11:27
named Agabus stood up in one of the meetings to predict by the Spirit that a great famine Acts 13:1; 15:32
was coming upon the entire Roman world. (This was fulfilled during the reign of 11:29 Rom 15:26
Claudius.) 29 So the believers in Antioch decided to send relief to the believers in Judea,
everyone giving as much as they could. 30 This they did, entrusting their gifts to Barnabas 11:30 Acts 12:25 1 Pet 5:1
and Saul to take to the elders of the church in Jerusalem.

James Is Killed and Peter Is Imprisoned

12 About that time King Herod Agrippa* began to persecute some believers in the 12:2 Matt 4:21; 20:23
church. 2 He had the apostle James (John's brother) killed with a sword. 3 When
Herod saw how much this pleased the Jewish leaders, he arrested Peter during the 12:4-10 Acts 5:18-25
Passover celebration* 4 and imprisoned him, placing him under the guard of four squads 12:5 Eph 6:18
of four soldiers each. Herod's intention was to bring Peter out for public trial after the
Passover. 5 But while Peter was in prison, the church prayed very earnestly for him. 12:7 Acts 5:19

Peter's Miraculous Escape from Prison

6 The night before Peter was to be placed on trial, he was asleep, chained between two
soldiers, with others standing guard at the prison gate. 7 Suddenly, there was a bright light
in the cell, and an angel of the Lord stood before Peter. The angel tapped him on the side
to awaken him and said, "Quick! Get up!" And the chains fell off his wrists. 8 Then the
angel told him, "Get dressed and put on your sandals." And he did. "Now put on your
coat and follow me," the angel ordered.

9 So Peter left the cell, following the angel. But all the time he thought it was a vision. 12:9 Acts 9:10
He didn't realize it was really happening. 10 They passed the first and second guard posts
and came to the iron gate to the street, and this opened to them all by itself. So they passed 12:10 Acts 5:19; 16:26
through and started walking down the street, and then the angel suddenly left him.

11 Peter finally realized what had happened. "It's really true!" he said to himself. "The 12:11 Ps 34:7
Lord has sent his angel and saved me from Herod and from what the Jews were hoping Dan 3:28; 6:22
to do to me!" 2 Pet 2:9

12:1 Greek *Herod the king.* He was the nephew of Herod Antipas and a grandson of Herod the Great. **12:3** Greek *the days of unleavened bread.*

11:27, 28 Prophets were found not only in the Old Testament but also in the early church. Their role was to present God's will to the people and to instruct them in God's word. Sometimes, like Agabus, they also had the gift of predicting the future.

11:28, 29 There were serious food shortages during the reign of the Roman emperor Claudius (A.D. 41–54) because of a drought that had extended across much of the Roman Empire for many years. It is significant that the church in Antioch assisted the church in Jerusalem. The daughter church had grown enough to be able to help the established church.

11:29 The people of Antioch were motivated to give generously because they cared about the needs of others. This is the "cheerful" giving that the Bible commends (2 Corinthians 9:7). Reluctant giving reflects a lack of concern for people. Focus your concern on the needy, and you will be motivated to give.

11:30 Elders were appointed to manage the affairs of the congregation. At this point, not much is known about their responsibilities, but it appears that their main role was to respond to the believers' needs.

12:1 King Herod Agrippa I was the son of Aristobulus and grandson of Herod the Great. His sister was Herodias, who was responsible for the death of John the Baptist (see Mark 6:17-28). Herod Agrippa I was part Jewish. The Romans had appointed him to rule over most of Palestine, including the territories of Galilee, Perea, Judea, and Samaria. He persecuted the Christians in order to please the Jewish leaders who opposed them, hoping that would solidify his position. Agrippa I died suddenly in A.D. 44 (see 12:20-23). His death was also recorded by the historian Josephus.

12:2 James and John were two of the original 12 disciples who followed Jesus. They had asked Jesus for special recognition in his Kingdom (Mark 10:35-40). Jesus said that to be a part of his Kingdom would mean suffering with Jesus (drink from the same cup—Mark 10:38, 39). James and John did indeed suffer—Herod executed James, and later John was exiled (see Revelation 1:9).

12:2-11 Why did God allow James to die and yet miraculously save Peter? Life is full of difficult questions like this. Why is one child physically disabled and another child athletically gifted? Why do people die before realizing their potential? These are questions we cannot possibly answer in this life because we do not see all that God sees. He has chosen to allow evil in this world for a time. But we can trust God's leading because he has promised to destroy all evil eventually. In the meantime, we know that God will help us use our suffering to strengthen us and glorify him. For more on this question, see the notes on Job 1:1ff; 2:10; 3:23-26.

12:3 Peter was arrested during the Festival of Unleavened Bread, the week-long festival directly following Passover. This was a strategic move, since more Jews were in the city than usual, and Herod could impress the most people.

12:5 Herod's plan undoubtedly was to execute Peter, but the believers were praying for Peter's safety. The earnest prayer of the church significantly affected the outcome of these events. Prayer changes things, so pray often and with confidence.

12:7 God sent an angel to rescue Peter. Angels are God's messengers. They are divinely created beings with supernatural power, and they sometimes take on human appearance in order to talk to people. Angels should not be worshiped because they are not divine. They are God's servants, just as we are.

12:12 Acts 12:25; 15:37 Col 4:10 1 Pet 5:13

12 After a little thought, he went to the home of Mary, the mother of John Mark, where
many were gathered for prayer. 13 He knocked at the door in the gate, and a servant girl
named Rhoda came to open it. 14 When she recognized Peter's voice, she was so
overjoyed that, instead of opening the door, she ran back inside and told everyone, "Peter
is standing at the door!"

12:15 Matt 18:10

15 "You're out of your mind," they said. When she insisted, they decided, "It must be
his angel."
16 Meanwhile, Peter continued knocking. When they finally went out and opened the

---

JOHN MARK

Mistakes are effective teachers. Their consequences have a way of making lessons painfully clear. But those who learn from their mistakes are wise. John Mark was a good learner who just needed some time and encouragement.

Mark was eager to do the right thing, but he had trouble staying with a task. In his Gospel, Mark mentions a young man (probably referring to himself) who fled in such fear during Jesus' arrest that he left his clothes behind. This tendency to run showed up later when Paul and Barnabas took him as their assistant on their first missionary journey. At their second stop, Mark left them and returned to Jerusalem. It was a decision Paul did not easily accept. In preparing for their second journey two years later, Barnabas again suggested Mark as a traveling companion, but Paul flatly refused. As a result, the team was divided. Barnabas took Mark with him, and Paul chose Silas. Barnabas was patient with Mark, and the young man repaid his investment. Paul and Mark were later reunited, and the older apostle became a close friend of the young disciple.

Mark was a valuable companion to three early Christian leaders: Barnabas, Paul, and Peter. The material in Mark's Gospel seems to have come mostly from Peter. Mark's role as an assistant allowed him to be an observer. He heard Peter's accounts of the years with Jesus over and over, and he was one of the first to put Jesus' life in writing.

Barnabas played a key role in Mark's life. He stood beside the young man despite his failure, giving him patient encouragement. Mark challenges us to learn from our mistakes and appreciate the patience of others. Is there a "Barnabas" in your life you need to thank for his or her encouragement to you?

Strengths and accomplishments
- Wrote the Gospel of Mark
- Provided the family home as one of the main meeting places for the Christians in Jerusalem
- Persisted beyond his youthful mistakes
- Was an assistant and traveling companion to three of the greatest early missionaries

Weaknesses and mistakes
- Probably the nameless young man described in the Gospel of Mark who fled in panic when Jesus was arrested
- Left Paul and Barnabas for unknown reasons during the first missionary journey

Lessons from his life
- Personal maturity usually comes from a combination of time and mistakes
- Mistakes are not usually as important as what can be learned from them
- Effective living is not measured as much by what we accomplish as by what we overcome in order to accomplish it
- Encouragement can change a person's life

Vital statistics
- Where: Jerusalem
- Occupations: Missionary-in-training, Gospel writer, traveling companion
- Relatives: Mother: Mary. Cousin: Barnabas
- Contemporaries: Paul, Peter, Timothy, Luke, Silas

Key verse
"Only Luke is with me. Bring Mark with you when you come, for he will be helpful to me" (Paul writing in 2 Timothy 4:11).

John Mark's story is told in Acts 12:25—13:13 and 15:36–39. He is also mentioned in Colossians 4:10; 2 Timothy 4:11; Philemon 1:24; 1 Peter 5:13.

12:12 John Mark wrote the Gospel of Mark. His mother's house was large enough to accommodate a meeting of many believers. An upstairs room in this house may have been the location of Jesus' Last Supper with his disciples (Luke 22:8ff).

12:13-15 The prayers of the group of believers were answered, even as they prayed. But when the answer arrived at the door, they didn't believe it. We should be people of faith who believe that God answers the prayers of those who seek his will. When you pray, believe you'll get an answer. And when the answer comes, don't be surprised; be thankful!

door, they were amazed. [17]He motioned for them to quiet down and told them what had 12:17 Acts 15:13; 21:18
happened and how the Lord had led him out of jail. "Tell James and the other brothers
what happened," he said. And then he went to another place.
[18]At dawn, there was a great commotion among the soldiers about what had happened 12:19
to Peter. [19]Herod Agrippa ordered a thorough search for him. When he couldn't be found, Acts 8:40; 16:27
Herod interrogated the guards and sentenced them to death. Afterward Herod left Judea
to stay in Caesarea for a while.

The Death of Herod Agrippa

[20]Now Herod was very angry with the people of Tyre and Sidon. So they sent a
delegation to make peace with him because their cities were dependent upon Herod's
country for their food. They made friends with Blastus, Herod's personal assistant, [21]and
an appointment with Herod was granted. When the day arrived, Herod put on his royal
robes, sat on his throne, and made a speech to them. [22]The people gave him a great 12:22 Ezek 28:2
ovation, shouting, "It is the voice of a god, not of a man!" 12:23
[23]Instantly, an angel of the Lord struck Herod with a sickness, because he accepted 1 Sam 25:38
the people's worship instead of giving the glory to God. So he was consumed with worms 2 Sam 24:16-17 2 Kgs 19:35
and died. Dan 5:20
[24]But God's Good News was spreading rapidly, and there were many new believers. 12:24 Acts 6:7; 19:20
[25]When Barnabas and Saul had finished their mission in Jerusalem, they returned to 12:25
Antioch, taking John Mark with them. Acts 11:29-30

B. PAUL'S MINISTRY (13:1—28:31)

The book focuses now on the ministry to the Gentiles and the spread of the church around the world, and Paul replaces Peter as the central figure in the book. Paul completes three missionary journeys and ends up being imprisoned in Jerusalem and transported to Rome. The book of Acts ends abruptly, showing that the history of the church is not yet complete. We are to be a part of the sequel.

1. First missionary journey

Barnabas and Saul Are Sent Out

13 Among the prophets and teachers of the church at Antioch of Syria were Barnabas, 13:1
Simeon (called "the black man"*), Lucius (from Cyrene), Manaen (the childhood Acts 11:27 Rom 16:21
companion of King Herod Antipas*), and Saul. [2]One day as these men were worshiping 13:2 Gal 1:15-16

13:1a Greek *who was called Niger.* **13:1b** Greek *Herod the tetrarch.*

12:17 This James was Jesus' brother, who became a leader in the Jerusalem church (15:13; Galatians 1:19). The James who was killed (12:2) was John's brother and one of the original 12 disciples.

12:19 Under Roman law, guards who allowed a prisoner to escape were subject to the same punishment the prisoner was to receive. Thus, these 16 guards were sentenced to death.

12:19 The Jews considered Jerusalem their capital, but the Romans made Caesarea their headquarters in Palestine. That is where Herod Agrippa I lived.

12:20 These coastal cities, Tyre and Sidon, were free and self-governing but economically dependent on Judea (see the map in the introduction to Acts for their location). We don't know why Herod had quarreled with them, but now representatives from those cities were trying to appease him through his personal assistant.

12:23 Herod died a horrible death accompanied by intense pain; he was literally eaten alive, from the inside out, by worms. To be eaten by worms was considered to be one of the most disgraceful ways to die. Pride is a serious sin, and in this case, God chose to punish it immediately. God does not immediately punish all sin, but he *will* bring all to judgment (Hebrews 9:27). Accept Christ's offer of forgiveness today. No one can afford to wait.

12:25 John Mark was Barnabas's cousin (Colossians 4:10). His mother, Mary, often opened her home to the apostles (12:12), so John Mark would have been exposed to most of the great men and teachings of the early church. Later, John Mark joined Paul and Barnabas on their first missionary journey, but for unknown reasons, he left them in the middle of the trip. John Mark was criticized by Paul for abandoning the mission (15:37-39), but he wrote the Gospel of Mark and was later acclaimed by Paul as a vital help in the growth of the early church (2 Timothy 4:11).

13:1 What variety there is in the church! The common thread among these five men was their deep faith in Christ. We must never exclude anyone whom Christ has called to follow him.

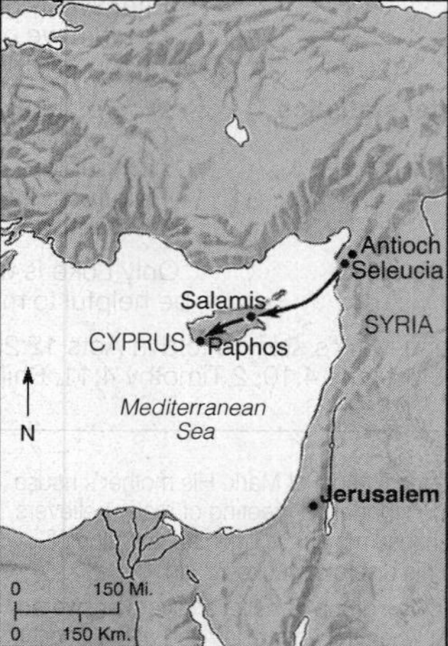

MINISTRY IN CYPRUS
The leaders of the church in Antioch chose Paul and Barnabas to take the gospel westward. Along with John Mark, they boarded ship at Seleucia and set out across the Mediterranean for Cyprus. They preached in Salamis, the largest city, and went across the island to Paphos.

13:3 Acts 6:6 the Lord and fasting, the Holy Spirit said, "Dedicate Barnabas and Saul for the special
work I have for them." 3So after more fasting and prayer, the men laid their hands on
them and sent them on their way.

Paul's First Missionary Journey

13:5 Acts 9:20; 12:12 4Sent out by the Holy Spirit, Saul and Barnabas went down to the seaport of Seleucia
and then sailed for the island of Cyprus. 5There, in the town of Salamis, they went to the

---

BARNABAS

Every group needs an "encourager," because everyone needs encouragement at one time or another. However, the value of encouragement is often missed because it tends to be private rather than public. In fact, people most need encouragement when they feel most alone. A man named Joseph was such an encourager that he earned the nickname "Son of Encouragement," or Barnabas, from the Jerusalem Christians.

Barnabas was drawn to people he could encourage, and he was a great help to those around him. It is delightful that wherever Barnabas encouraged Christians, non-Christians flocked to become believers!

Barnabas's actions were crucial to the early church. In a way, we can thank him for most of the New Testament. God used his relationship with Paul at one point and with Mark at another to keep these two men going when either might have failed. Barnabas did wonders with encouragement!

When Paul arrived in Jerusalem for the first time following his conversion, the local Christians were understandably reluctant to welcome him. They thought his story was a trick to capture more Christians. Only Barnabas proved willing to risk his life to meet with Paul and then convince the others that their former enemy was now a vibrant believer in Jesus. We can only wonder what might have happened to Paul without Barnabas.

It was Barnabas who encouraged Mark to go with him and Paul to Antioch. Mark joined them on their first missionary journey but decided during the trip to return home. Later, Barnabas wanted to invite Mark to join them for another journey, but Paul would not agree. As a result, the partners went separate ways, Barnabas with Mark and Paul with Silas. This actually doubled the missionary effort. Barnabas's patient encouragement was confirmed by Mark's eventual effective ministry. Paul and Mark were later reunited in missionary efforts.

As Barnabas's life shows, we are often presented with situations where there is someone who needs encouragement. Our tendency, however, is to criticize instead. It may be important at times to point out someone's shortcomings, but before we have the right to do this, we must build that person's trust through encouragement. Will you take the opportunity to encourage those with whom you come in contact today?

Strengths and accomplishments
- One of the first to sell possessions to help the Christians in Jerusalem
- First to travel with Paul as a missionary team
- Was an encourager, as his nickname shows, and thus one of the most quietly influential people in the early days of Christianity
- Called an apostle, although not one of the original 12

Weakness and mistake
- With Peter, temporarily stayed aloof from Gentile believers until Paul corrected him

Lessons from his life
- Encouragement is one of the most effective ways to help
- Sooner or later, true obedience to God will involve risk
- There is always someone who needs encouragement

Vital statistics
- Where: Cyprus, Jerusalem, Antioch
- Occupations: Missionary, teacher
- Relatives: Aunt: Mary. Cousin: John Mark
- Contemporaries: Peter, Silas, Paul, Herod Agrippa I

Key verses
"When he arrived and saw this proof of God's favor, he was filled with joy, and he encouraged the believers to stay true to the Lord. Barnabas was a good man, full of the Holy Spirit and strong in faith. And large numbers of people were brought to the Lord" (Acts 11:23, 24).

Barnabas's story is told in Acts 4:36, 37; 9:27—15:39. He is also mentioned in 1 Corinthians 9:6; Galatians 2:1, 9, 13; Colossians 4:10.

13:2, 3 The church dedicated Barnabas and Saul to the work God had for them. To *dedicate* means "to set apart" for a special purpose. We, too, should dedicate our pastors, missionaries, and Christian workers for their tasks. We can also dedicate ourselves to use our time, money, and talents for God's work. Ask God what he wants you to set apart for him.

13:2, 3 This was the beginning of Saul's (Paul, see 13:9) first missionary journey. The church was involved in sending Paul and Barnabas, but it was God's plan. Why did Paul and Barnabas go where they did? (1) The Holy Spirit led them. (2) They followed the communication routes of the Roman Empire, making travel easier. (3) They visited key population and cultural centers to reach as many people as possible. (4) They went to cities with synagogues, speaking first to the Jews in hopes that they would see Jesus as the Messiah and help spread the Good News to everyone.

13:4 Located in the Mediterranean Sea, the island of Cyprus, with a large Jewish population, was Barnabas's home. Their first stop was in familiar territory.

Jewish synagogues and preached the word of God. (John Mark went with them as their
assistant.)
6 Afterward they preached from town to town across the entire island until finally they **13:6**
reached Paphos, where they met a Jewish sorcerer, a false prophet named Bar-Jesus. 7 He Matt 7:15
had attached himself to the governor, Sergius Paulus, a man of considerable insight and Acts 8:9
understanding. The governor invited Barnabas and Saul to visit him, for he wanted to
hear the word of God. 8 But Elymas, the sorcerer (as his name means in Greek), interfered **13:8**
and urged the governor to pay no attention to what Saul and Barnabas said. He was trying 2 Tim 3:8
to turn the governor away from the Christian faith.
9 Then Saul, also known as Paul, filled with the Holy Spirit, looked the sorcerer in the **13:9**
eye and said, 10 "You son of the Devil, full of every sort of trickery and villainy, enemy Acts 2:4
of all that is good, will you never stop perverting the true ways of the Lord? 11 And now **13:10**
the Lord has laid his hand of punishment upon you, and you will be stricken awhile with Hos 14:9 Matt 13:38 John 8:44
blindness." Instantly mist and darkness fell upon him, and he began wandering around **13:11**
begging for someone to take his hand and lead him. 12 When the governor saw what had 2 Kgs 6:18
happened, he believed and was astonished at what he learned about the Lord. Acts 9:8

Paul Preaches in Antioch of Pisidia

13 Now Paul and those with him left Paphos by ship for Pamphylia,* landing at the port **13:13**
town of Perga. There John Mark left them and returned to Jerusalem. 14 But Barnabas Acts 12:12; 15:38
and Paul traveled inland to Antioch of Pisidia.* **13:14** Acts 14:19, 21
On the Sabbath they went to the synagogue for the services. 15 After the usual **13:15** Acts 15:21

13:13-14 *Pamphylia* and *Pisidia* were districts in the land now called Turkey.

13:6, 7 Sergius Paulus functioned as the governor of the island. Such leaders often kept private sorcerers. Bar-Jesus realized that if Sergius Paulus believed in Jesus, he would soon be out of a job.

13:9, 10 Here is where Saul is first called Paul.

13:10 The Holy Spirit led Paul to confront Bar-Jesus with his sin. There is a time to be nice and a time to confront. Ask God to show you the difference and to give you the courage to do what is right.

13:13 No reason is given why John Mark left Paul and Barnabas. Some suggestions are: (1) He was homesick; (2) he resented the change in leadership from Barnabas (his cousin) to Paul; (3) he became ill (an illness that may have affected all of them—see Galatians 4:13); (4) he was unable to withstand the rigors and dangers of the missionary journey; (5) he may have planned to go only that far but had not communicated this to Paul and Barnabas. Paul implicitly accused John Mark of lacking courage and commitment, refusing to take him along on another journey (see 15:37, 38). It is clear from Paul's later letters, however, that he grew to respect Mark (Colossians 4:10) and that he needed Mark in his work (2 Timothy 4:11).

13:14 This is Antioch of Pisidia, not the Antioch of Syria, where there was already a flourishing church (11:26). This Antioch, in the region of Pisidia, was a hub of good roads and trade, with a large Jewish population.

13:14 When they went to a new city to witness for Christ, Paul and Barnabas went first to the synagogue. The Jews who were there believed in God and diligently studied the Scriptures. Tragically, however, many could not accept Jesus as the promised Messiah because they had the wrong idea of what kind of Messiah he would be. He was not, as they desired, a military king who would overthrow Rome's control but a servant-king who would defeat sin in people's hearts. (Only later, when Christ returns, will he judge the nations of the world.) Paul and Barnabas did not separate themselves from the synagogues but tried to show clearly that the very Scriptures the Jews studied pointed to Jesus.

13:14, 15 What happened in a synagogue service? First, the *Shema* was recited (this is Deuteronomy 6:4, which Jews repeated several times daily). Certain prayers were spoken; then there was a reading from the law (the books of Genesis through Deuteronomy), a reading from the Prophets intending to illustrate the law, and a sermon. Those in charge of the service decided who was to lead the service and give the sermon. A different person was chosen to lead each week. Since it was customary for the synagogue leader to invite visiting rabbis to speak, Paul and Barnabas usually had an open door when they first went to a synagogue. But as soon as they spoke about Jesus as Messiah, the door would slam shut. They were usually not invited back by the religious leaders, and sometimes they were thrown out of town!

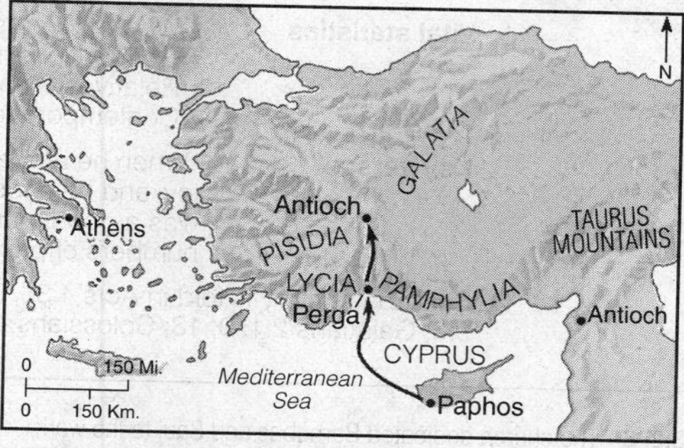

MINISTRY IN PAMPHYLIA AND GALATIA Paul, Barnabas, and John Mark left Paphos and landed at Perga in the humid region of Pamphylia, a narrow strip of land between the sea and the Taurus Mountains. John Mark left them in Perga, but Paul and Barnabas traveled up the steep road into the higher elevation of Pisidia in Galatia. When the Jews rejected his message, Paul preached to Gentiles, and the Jews drove Paul and Barnabas out of the Pisidian city of Antioch.

readings from the books of Moses and from the Prophets, those in charge of the service
sent them this message: "Brothers, if you have any word of encouragement for us, come
and give it!"
16 So Paul stood, lifted his hand to quiet them, and started speaking. "People of Israel,"
he said, "and you devout Gentiles who fear the God of Israel, listen to me.
17 "The God of this nation of Israel chose our ancestors and made them prosper in
Egypt. Then he powerfully led them out of their slavery. 18 He put up with them* through
forty years of wandering around in the wilderness. 19 Then he destroyed seven nations in
Canaan and gave their land to Israel as an inheritance. 20 All this took about 450 years.
After that, judges ruled until the time of Samuel the prophet. 21 Then the people begged
for a king, and God gave them Saul son of Kish, a man of the tribe of Benjamin, who
reigned for forty years. 22 But God removed him from the kingship and replaced him with
David, a man about whom God said, 'David son of Jesse is a man after my own heart,
for he will do everything I want him to.'*
23 "And it is one of King David's descendants, Jesus, who is God's promised Savior
of Israel! 24 But before he came, John the Baptist preached the need for everyone in Israel
to turn from sin and turn to God and be baptized. 25 As John was finishing his ministry
he asked, 'Do you think I am the Messiah? No! But he is coming soon—and I am not
even worthy to be his slave.'*
26 "Brothers—you sons of Abraham, and also all of you devout Gentiles who fear the
God of Israel—this salvation is for us! 27 The people in Jerusalem and their leaders
fulfilled prophecy by condemning Jesus to death. They didn't recognize him or realize
that he is the one the prophets had written about, though they hear the prophets' words
read every Sabbath. 28 They found no just cause to execute him, but they asked Pilate to
have him killed anyway.
29 "When they had fulfilled all the prophecies concerning his death, they took him
down from the cross and placed him in a tomb. 30 But God raised him from the dead!
31 And he appeared over a period of many days to those who had gone with him from
Galilee to Jerusalem—these are his witnesses to the people of Israel.
32 "And now Barnabas and I are here to bring you this Good News. God's promise to
our ancestors has come true in our own time, 33 in that God raised Jesus. This is what the
second psalm is talking about when it says concerning Jesus,

'You are my Son.
Today I have become your Father.*'

34 For God had promised to raise him from the dead, never again to die. This is stated
in the Scripture that says, 'I will give you the sacred blessings I promised to David.'*
35 Another psalm explains more fully, saying, 'You will not allow your Holy One to rot
in the grave.'* 36 Now this is not a reference to David, for after David had served his
generation according to the will of God, he died and was buried, and his body decayed.
37 No, it was a reference to someone else—someone whom God raised and whose body
did not decay.
38 "Brothers, listen! In this man Jesus there is forgiveness for your sins. 39 Everyone
who believes in him is freed from all guilt and declared right with God—something the

13:16 Acts 12:17; 13:26
13:17 Exod 6:6-7; Deut 7:6-8
13:18 Exod 16:35; Num 14:34
13:19 Deut 7:1
13:20 Judg 2:16; 1 Sam 3:20
13:21 1 Sam 8:5; 9:1-2; 10:21-24
13:22 †1 Sam 13:14; 1 Sam 16:1, 13; †Ps 89:21
13:23 2 Sam 7:12; Isa 11:1; Luke 2:11
13:24 Mark 1:4-5
13:25 Mark 1:7; John 1:20
13:27 Acts 3:17
13:28 Matt 27:22-23; Acts 3:14
13:29 Matt 27:59-60; Luke 23:52-53
13:30 Matt 28:6; Acts 2:24
13:31 Luke 24:48; Acts 1:11; 1 Cor 15:5
13:32 Rom 1:2-4
13:33 †Ps 2:7; Heb 1:5; 5:5
13:34 †Isa 55:3
13:35 †Ps 16:10
13:36 1 Kgs 2:10
13:37 Acts 2:24
13:38 Luke 24:27
13:39 Rom 3:28; 10:4

13:18 Other manuscripts read *He cared for them;* compare Deut 1:31. **13:22** 1 Sam 13:14. **13:25** Greek *to untie his sandals.* **13:33** Or *Today I reveal you as my Son.* Ps 2:7. **13:34** Isa 55:3. **13:35** Ps 16:10.

13:16ff Paul's message to the Jews in the synagogue in Antioch began with an emphasis on God's covenant with Israel. This was a point of agreement, because all Jews were proud to be God's chosen people. Then Paul went on to explain how the Good News fulfilled the covenant. Some Jews found this message hard to swallow.

13:23-31 Because Paul was speaking to devout Jews, he began by reminding them about the covenant, Abraham, David, and other familiar themes. Later, when speaking to the Greek philosophers in Athens (17:22-32), he would begin by talking about what he had observed in their city. In both cases, however, he centered the sermon around Christ and emphasized the Resurrection. When you share the Good News, begin where your audience is—then tell them about Christ.

13:38, 39 This is the focus of the Good News: Forgiveness of sins and freedom from guilt are available through faith in Christ to all people—including *you.* Have you received this forgiveness? Are you refreshed each day by the thought that you are right with God?

Jewish law could never do. 40Be careful! Don't let the prophets' words apply to you. For
they said,

41 'Look you mockers,
be amazed and die!
For I am doing something in your own day,
something you wouldn't believe
even if someone told you about it.'*"

13:41 †Hab 1:5

42As Paul and Barnabas left the synagogue that day, the people asked them to return
again and speak about these things the next week. 43Many Jews and godly converts to
Judaism who worshiped at the synagogue followed Paul and Barnabas, and the two men
urged them, "By God's grace, remain faithful."

Paul Turns to the Gentiles

44The following week almost the entire city turned out to hear them preach the word of
the Lord. 45But when the Jewish leaders saw the crowds, they were jealous; so they
slandered Paul and argued against whatever he said.

13:45 Acts 8:6 1 Pet 4:4 Jude 1:10

46Then Paul and Barnabas spoke out boldly and declared, "It was necessary that this
Good News from God be given first to you Jews. But since you have rejected it and
judged yourselves unworthy of eternal life—well, we will offer it to Gentiles. 47For this
is as the Lord commanded us when he said,

13:46 Acts 18:6

13:47 †Isa 49:6 Luke 2:32

'I have made you a light to the Gentiles,
to bring salvation to the farthest corners of the earth.'*"

48When the Gentiles heard this, they were very glad and thanked the Lord for his
message; and all who were appointed to eternal life became believers. 49So the Lord's
message spread throughout that region.

13:48 Rom 8:29-30 Eph 1:4-5, 11 1 Pet 1:2

50Then the Jewish leaders stirred up both the influential religious women and the
leaders of the city, and they incited a mob against Paul and Barnabas and ran them out
of town. 51But they shook off the dust of their feet against them and went to the city of
Iconium. 52And the believers* were filled with joy and with the Holy Spirit.

13:51 Matt 10:14 Mark 6:11 Luke 9:5; 10:11 Acts 18:6

13:52 1 Pet 1:8

13:41 Hab 1:5. **13:47** Isa 49:6. **13:52** Greek *the disciples.*

13:42-45 The Jewish leaders undoubtedly brought theological arguments against Paul and Barnabas, but Luke tells us that the real reason for their hostility was that "they were jealous." When we see others succeeding where we haven't or receiving the affirmation we crave, it is hard to rejoice with them. Jealousy is our natural reaction. But how tragic it is when our own jealous feelings make us try to stop God's work. If a work is God's work, rejoice in it—no matter who is doing it.

13:46 Why was it necessary for the Good News to go first to the Jews? God planned that through the Jewish nation *all* the world would come to know God (Genesis 12:3). Paul, a Jew himself, loved his people (Romans 9:1-5) and wanted to give them every opportunity to join him in proclaiming God's salvation. Unfortunately, many Jews did not recognize Jesus as Messiah, and they did not understand that God was offering salvation to anyone, Jew or Gentile, who comes to him through faith in Christ.

13:47 God had planned for Israel to be this light (Isaiah 49:6). Through Israel came Jesus, the light of the nations (Luke 2:32). This light would spread out and enlighten the Gentiles.

13:50 Instead of accepting the truth, the Jewish leaders stirred up opposition and ran Paul and Barnabas out of town. When confronted by a disturbing truth, people often turn away and refuse to listen. When God's Spirit points out needed changes in our life, we must listen to him. Otherwise we may be pushing the truth so far away that it no longer affects us.

13:51 Often Jews would shake the dust off their feet when leaving a Gentile town on the way back to their own land. This symbolized cleansing themselves from the contamination of those who did not worship God. For Paul and Barnabas to do this to Jews demonstrated that Jews who rejected the Good News were not truly part of Israel and were no better than pagans. Jesus had told his disciples to shake from their feet the dust of any town that would not accept or listen to them (Mark 6:11). The disciples were not to blame if the message was rejected, as long as they had faithfully presented it. When we share Christ carefully and sensitively, God does not hold us responsible for the other person's decision.

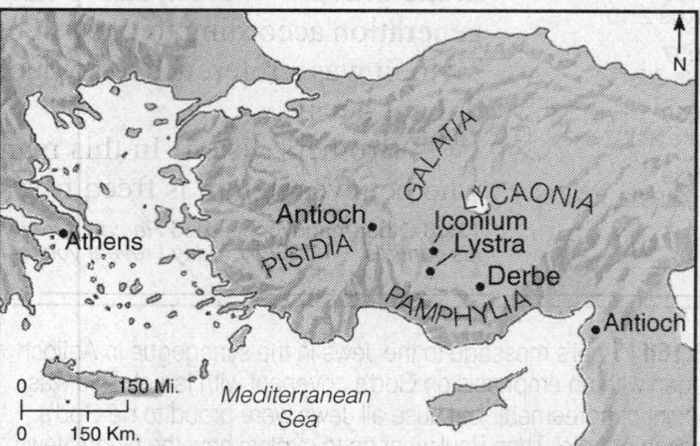

CONTINUED MINISTRY IN GALATIA Paul and Barnabas, thrown out of Antioch in Pisidia, descended the mountains, going east into Lycaonia. They went first to Iconium, a commercial center on the road between Asia and Syria. After preaching there, they had to flee to Lystra, 25 miles south. Paul was stoned in Lystra, but he and Barnabas traveled the 50 miles to Derbe, a border town. The pair then boldly retraced their steps.

Paul and Barnabas in Iconium

14:1 Acts 13:45
14:2 2 Tim 3:11
14:3 Heb 2:4
14:4 Acts 28:24
14:5 Acts 14:19; 20:3; 2 Tim 3:11
14:6 Matt 10:23

14 In Iconium,* Paul and Barnabas went together to the synagogue and preached with
such power that a great number of both Jews and Gentiles believed. 2But the Jews
who spurned God's message stirred up distrust among the Gentiles against Paul and
Barnabas, saying all sorts of evil things about them. 3The apostles stayed there a long time,
preaching boldly about the grace of the Lord. The Lord proved their message was true by
giving them power to do miraculous signs and wonders. 4But the people of the city were
divided in their opinion about them. Some sided with the Jews, and some with the apostles.
5A mob of Gentiles and Jews, along with their leaders, decided to attack and stone
them. 6When the apostles learned of it, they fled for their lives. They went to the region
of Lycaonia, to the cities of Lystra and Derbe and the surrounding area, 7and they
preached the Good News there.

Paul and Barnabas in Lystra and Derbe

14:8 Acts 3:2
14:10 Acts 3:8
14:11 Acts 28:6

8While they were at Lystra, Paul and Barnabas came upon a man with crippled feet. He
had been that way from birth, so he had never walked. 9He was listening as Paul
preached, and Paul noticed him and realized he had faith to be healed. 10So Paul called
to him in a loud voice, "Stand up!" And the man jumped to his feet and started walking.
11When the listening crowd saw what Paul had done, they shouted in their local
dialect, "These men are gods in human bodies!" 12They decided that Barnabas was the
Greek god Zeus and that Paul, because he was the chief speaker, was Hermes. 13The
temple of Zeus was located on the outskirts of the city. The priest of the temple and the
crowd brought oxen and wreaths of flowers, and they prepared to sacrifice to the apostles
at the city gates.
14But when Barnabas and Paul heard what was happening, they tore their clothing in
dismay and ran out among the people, shouting, 15"Friends,* why are you doing this? We
are merely human beings like yourselves! We have come to bring you the Good News that
you should turn from these worthless things to the living God, who made heaven and earth,
the sea, and everything in them. 16In earlier days he permitted all the nations to go their
own ways, 17but he never left himself without a witness. There were always his reminders,
such as sending you rain and good crops and giving you food and joyful hearts." 18But
even so, Paul and Barnabas could scarcely restrain the people from sacrificing to them.

14:15 Exod 20:11; Ps 146:6; Matt 16:16; Acts 10:26; 1 Thes 1:9; Rev 14:7
14:16 Ps 81:12
14:17 Ps 147:8; Rom 1:20

14:1 *Iconium,* as well as *Lystra* and *Derbe* (14:6), were cities in the land now called Turkey. 14:15 Greek *Men.*

14:3, 4 We may wish we could perform a miraculous act that would convince everyone once and for all that Jesus is the Lord. But we see here that even if we could perform a miracle, it wouldn't convince everyone. God gave these men power to do great wonders as confirmation of the message of grace, but people were still divided. Don't spend your time and energy wishing for miracles. Sow your seeds of the Good News on the best ground you can find in the best way you can, and leave the convincing to the Holy Spirit.

14:6 Iconium (14:1), Lystra, and Derbe were three cities Paul visited in the southern part of the region of Galatia. Paul probably wrote a letter to these churches—the letter to the Galatians—because many Jewish Christians were claiming that non-Jewish Christians couldn't be saved unless they followed Jewish laws and customs. Paul's letter refuted this and brought the believers back to a right understanding of faith in Jesus (see Galatians 3:3, 5). Paul may have written his letter soon after leaving the region (see the note on 14:28).

14:11, 12 Zeus and Hermes (also known as Jupiter and Mercury) were two popular gods in the Roman world. People from Lystra claimed that these gods had once visited their city. According to legend, no one offered them hospitality except an old couple, so Zeus and Hermes killed the rest of the people and rewarded the old couple. When the citizens of Lystra saw the miracles of Paul and Barnabas, they assumed that the gods were revisiting them. Remembering the story of what had happened to the previous citizens, they immediately honored Paul and Barnabas and showered them with gifts.

14:15-18 Responding to the people of Lystra, Paul and Barnabas reminded them that God never leaves himself "without a witness." Rain and good crops, for example, are evidence of his goodness. Later Paul wrote that this evidence in nature leaves people without an excuse for unbelief (Romans 1:20). When in doubt about God, look around and you will see abundant evidence that he is at work in our world.

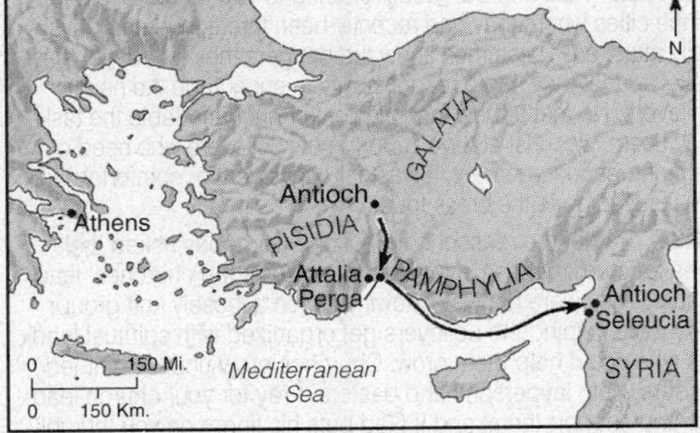

THE END OF THE FIRST JOURNEY From Antioch in Pisidia, Paul and Barnabas went down the mountains back to Pamphylia on the coast. Stopping first in Perga, where they had landed, they went west to Attalia, the main port that sent goods from Asia to Syria and Egypt. There they found a ship bound for Seleucia, the port of Antioch in Syria. This ended their first missionary journey.

19 Now some Jews arrived from Antioch and Iconium and turned the crowds into a
murderous mob. They stoned Paul and dragged him out of the city, apparently dead.
20 But as the believers* stood around him, he got up and went back into the city. The next
day he left with Barnabas for Derbe.

Paul and Barnabas Return to Antioch of Syria

21 After preaching the Good News in Derbe and making many disciples, Paul and
Barnabas returned again to Lystra, Iconium, and Antioch of Pisidia, 22 where they
strengthened the believers. They encouraged them to continue in the faith, reminding
them that they must enter into the Kingdom of God through many tribulations. 23 Paul
and Barnabas also appointed elders in every church and prayed for them with fasting,
turning them over to the care of the Lord, in whom they had come to trust. 24 Then they
traveled back through Pisidia to Pamphylia. 25 They preached again in Perga, then went
on to Attalia.

26 Finally, they returned by ship to Antioch of Syria, where their journey had begun
and where they had been committed to the grace of God for the work they had now
completed. 27 Upon arriving in Antioch, they called the church together and reported
about their trip, telling all that God had done and how he had opened the door of faith to
the Gentiles, too. 28 And they stayed there with the believers in Antioch for a long time.

2. The council at Jerusalem

15 While Paul and Barnabas were at Antioch of Syria, some men from Judea arrived
and began to teach the Christians*: "Unless you keep the ancient Jewish custom
of circumcision taught by Moses, you cannot be saved." 2 Paul and Barnabas, disagreeing

14:19 Acts 13:45; 2 Cor 11:25; 2 Tim 3:11
14:20 Acts 11:26
14:22 1 Tim 3:3; 2 Tim 3:12
14:23 Acts 13:13
14:26 Acts 13:1-3
14:27 1 Cor 16:9; Col 4:3; Rev 3:8
15:1 Lev 12:3; Gal 5:2
15:2 Acts 11:30; Gal 2:1-10

14:20 Greek *disciples;* also in 14:22, 28. 15:1 Greek *brothers;* also in 15:32, 33.

14:18, 19 Only days after the people in Lystra had thought that Paul and Barnabas were gods and wanted to offer sacrifices to them, they stoned Paul and left him for dead. That's human nature. Jesus understood how fickle crowds can be (John 2:24, 25). When many people approve of us, we feel good, but that should never cloud our thinking or affect our decisions. We should not live to please the crowd—especially in our spiritual life. Be like Jesus. Know the nature of the crowd and don't put your trust in it. Put your trust in God alone.

14:18-20 Paul and Barnabas were persistent in their preaching of the Good News, considering the cost to themselves to be nothing in comparison with obedience to Christ. They had just narrowly escaped being stoned in Iconium (14:1-7), but Jews from Antioch and Iconium tracked Paul down, stoned him, and left him for dead. But Paul got up and went back into the city to preach the Good News. That's true commitment! Being a disciple of Christ calls for total commitment. As Christians, we no longer belong to ourselves but to our Lord, for whom we are called to suffer.

14:21, 22 Paul and Barnabas returned to visit the believers in all the cities where they had recently been threatened and physically attacked. These men knew the dangers they faced, yet they believed that they had a responsibility to encourage the new believers. No matter how inconvenient or uncomfortable the task may seem, we must always support new believers who need our help and encouragement. It was not convenient or comfortable for Jesus to go to the cross for us!

14:23 Part of the reason that Paul and Barnabas risked their lives to return to these cities was to organize the churches' leadership. They were not just following up on a loosely knit group; they were helping the believers get organized with spiritual leaders who could help them grow. Churches grow under Spirit-led leaders, both laypersons and pastors. Pray for your church leaders and support them; and if God puts his finger on you, humbly accept the responsibility of a leadership role in your church.

14:28 Paul probably wrote his letter to the Galatians while he was staying in Antioch (A.D. 48 or 49) after completing his first missionary journey. There are several theories as to what part of Galatia Paul was addressing, but most agree that Iconium, Lystra, and Derbe were part of that region for which the letter was intended. Galatians was probably written before the Jerusalem council (Acts 15), because in the letter the question of whether Gentile believers should be required to follow Jewish law was not yet resolved. The council met to solve that problem.

15:1 The real problem for the Jewish Christians was not whether Gentiles could be saved but whether Gentiles had to adhere to the laws of Moses. The test of following these laws was circumcision. The Jewish Christians were worried because soon there would be more Gentile than Jewish Christians. And they were afraid of weakening moral standards among believers if they did not follow Jewish laws. Paul, Barnabas, and the other church leaders believed that the Old Testament law was very important, but it was not a prerequisite to salvation. The law cannot save; only by grace through faith in Jesus Christ can a person be saved.

15:1ff The delegates to the council at Jerusalem came from the churches in Jerusalem and Antioch. The conversion of Gentiles was raising an urgent question for the early church: Do the Gentiles have to adhere to the laws of Moses and other Jewish traditions to be saved? One group of Jewish Christians insisted that following the law, including submitting to the rite of circumcision, was necessary for salvation. The Gentiles, however, did not think they needed to become Jewish first in order to become Christians. So Paul and Barnabas discussed this problem with the leaders of the church. The council upheld the conviction expressed by Paul and Barnabas that following the Jewish laws, including being circumcised, was not essential for salvation.

15:2 The question of whether the Gentile believers should obey the law of Moses to be saved was an important one. The controversy intensified largely due to the success of the new Gentile churches. The conservatives in the Jerusalem church were led by converted Pharisees (15:5), who preferred a legalistic religion to one based on faith alone. If the conservatives had won, the Gentiles would have been required to convert to Judaism and be circumcised. This would have seriously confined Christianity to simply being another sect within Judaism. There is something of a "Pharisee" in each one of us. We may unwittingly mistake upholding tradition, structure, and legal requirements for obeying God. Make sure the Good News brings freedom and life to those you are trying to reach.

with them, argued forcefully and at length. Finally, Paul and Barnabas were sent to
Jerusalem, accompanied by some local believers, to talk to the apostles and elders about
this question. 3The church sent the delegates to Jerusalem, and they stopped along the
way in Phoenicia and Samaria to visit the believers.* They told them—much to everyone's joy—that the Gentiles, too, were being converted.
4When they arrived in Jerusalem, Paul and Barnabas were welcomed by the whole
church, including the apostles and elders. They reported on what God had been doing
through their ministry. 5But then some of the men who had been Pharisees before their
conversion stood up and declared that all Gentile converts must be circumcised and be
required to follow the law of Moses.
6So the apostles and church elders got together to decide this question. 7At the
meeting, after a long discussion, Peter stood and addressed them as follows: "Brothers,

15:3 Acts 11:19; 14:27
15:5 Acts 15:11
15:7-8 Acts 2:4; 10:44; 11:15

15:3 Greek *brothers;* also in 15:23, 36, 40.

THE FIRST CHURCH CONFERENCE

Group	*Position*	*Reasons*
Judaizers (some Jewish Christians)	Gentiles must become Jewish first to be eligible for salvation	1. They were devout, practicing Jews who found it difficult to set aside a tradition of gaining merit with God by keeping the law. 2. They thought grace was too easy for the Gentiles. 3. They were afraid of seeming too non-Jewish in the practice of their new faith—which could lead to death. 4. The demands on the Gentiles were a way of maintaining control and authority in the movement.
Gentile Christians	Faith in Christ as Savior is the only requirement for salvation	1. To submit to Jewish demands would be to doubt what God had already done for them by grace alone. 2. They resisted exchanging their pagan rituals for a system of Jewish rituals—neither of which had power to save. 3. They sought to obey Christ by baptism (rather than by circumcision) as a sign of their new faith.
Peter and James	Faith is the only requirement, but there must be evidence of change by rejecting the old life-style	1. They tried to distinguish between what was true from God's Word and what was just human tradition. 2. They had Christ's command to preach to all the world. 3. They wanted to preserve unity. 4. They saw that Christianity could never survive as just a sect within Judaism.

As long as most of the first Christians were Jewish, there was little difficulty in welcoming new believers; however, Gentiles (non-Jews) began to accept Jesus' offer of salvation. The evidence in their lives and the presence of God's Spirit in them showed that God was accepting them. Some of the early Christians believed that non-Jewish Christians needed to meet certain conditions before they could be worthy to accept Christ. The issue could have destroyed the church, so a conference was called in Jerusalem, and the issue was formally settled there, although it continued to be a problem for many years following. Above is an outline of the three points of view at the conference.

15:2ff It is helpful to see how the churches in Antioch and Jerusalem resolved their conflict: (1) The church in Antioch sent a delegation to help seek a solution; (2) the delegates met with the church leaders to give their reports and set another date to continue the discussion; (3) Paul and Barnabas gave their report; (4) James summarized the reports and drew up the decision; (5) everyone agreed to abide by the decision; (6) the council sent a letter with delegates back to Antioch to report the decision.

This is a wise way to handle conflicts within the church. Problems must be confronted, and all sides of the argument must be given a fair hearing. The discussion should be held in the presence of leaders who are spiritually mature and trustworthy to make wise decisions. Everyone should then abide by the decisions.

you all know that God chose me from among you some time ago to preach to the Gentiles
so that they could hear the Good News and believe. [8]God, who knows people's hearts,
confirmed that he accepts Gentiles by giving them the Holy Spirit, just as he gave him
to us. [9]He made no distinction between us and them, for he also cleansed their hearts
through faith. [10]Why are you now questioning God's way by burdening the Gentile
believers* with a yoke that neither we nor our ancestors were able to bear? [11]We believe
that we are all saved the same way, by the special favor of the Lord Jesus."
[12]There was no further discussion, and everyone listened as Barnabas and Paul told
about the miraculous signs and wonders God had done through them among the Gentiles.
[13]When they had finished, James stood and said, "Brothers, listen to me. [14]Peter* has
told you about the time God first visited the Gentiles to take from them a people for
himself. [15]And this conversion of Gentiles agrees with what the prophets predicted. For
instance, it is written:

16 'Afterward I will return,
and I will restore the fallen kingdom of David.
From the ruins I will rebuild it,
and I will restore it,
17 so that the rest of humanity might find the Lord,
including the Gentiles—
all those I have called to be mine.
This is what the Lord says,
18 he who made these things known long ago.'*

[19]And so my judgment is that we should stop troubling the Gentiles who turn to God,
[20]except that we should write to them and tell them to abstain from eating meat
sacrificed to idols, from sexual immorality, and from consuming blood or eating the
meat of strangled animals. [21]For these laws of Moses have been preached in Jewish
synagogues in every city on every Sabbath for many generations."

The Letter for Gentile Believers

[22]Then the apostles and elders and the whole church in Jerusalem chose delegates, and
they sent them to Antioch of Syria with Paul and Barnabas to report on this decision. The

15:9 Acts 10:43; Rom 10:12
15:10 Matt 23:4; Gal 5:1
15:11 Rom 3:24; Eph 2:5-8
15:12 Acts 14:27; 15:4
15:13 Acts 12:17
15:14 Acts 15:7-9
15:16-17 †Amos 9:11-12
15:18 †Isa 45:21
15:20 Gen 9:4; Exod 20:3-4; Lev 3:17; Deut 12:16; 1 Cor 8:7; 10:7
15:21 Acts 13:15
15:22 Acts 15:27; 16:19; 1 Pet 5:12

15:10 Greek *disciples.* **15:14** Greek *Simon.* **15:16-18** Amos 9:11-12; Isa 45:21.

THE JERUSALEM COUNCIL
A dispute arose when some Judeans taught that Gentile believers had to be circumcised to be saved. Paul and Barnabas went to Jerusalem to discuss this situation with the leaders there. After the Jerusalem council made its decision, Paul and Barnabas returned to Antioch with the news.

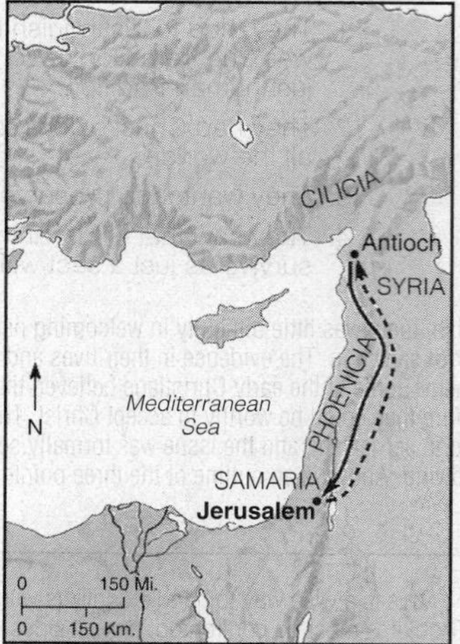

15:10 If the law was a yoke that the Jews could not bear, how did having the law help them throughout their history? Paul wrote that the law was a guide that pointed out their sins so they could repent and return to God and right living (see Galatians 3:24, 25). It was, and still is, impossible to obey the law completely.

15:13 This James is Jesus' brother. He became the leader of the church in Jerusalem and wrote the book of James.

15:20, 21 James's judgment was that Gentile believers did not have to be circumcised, but they should stay away from food sacrificed to idols, from sexual immorality (a common part of idol worship), and from consuming blood (reflecting the biblical teaching that the life is in the blood—Leviticus 17:14) or eating meat of strangled animals. If Gentile Christians would abstain from these practices, they would please God and get along better with their Jewish brothers and sisters in Christ. Of course, there were other actions inappropriate for believers, but the Jews were especially concerned about these four. This compromise helped the church grow unhindered by the cultural differences of Jews and Gentiles. When we share our message across cultural and economic boundaries, we must be sure that the requirements for faith we set up are God's, not people's.

15:22 Apostleship was not a church office but a position and function based on specific gifts. Elders were appointed to lead and manage the church. In this meeting, apostles submitted to the judgment of an elder—James, Jesus' brother.

15:22 Later, Silas accompanied Paul on Paul's second missionary journey in place of Barnabas, who visited different cities with John Mark.

men chosen were two of the church leaders—Judas (also called Barsabbas) and Silas.
23 This is the letter they took along with them:

> "This letter is from the apostles and elders, your brothers in Jerusalem. It is written
> to the Gentile believers in Antioch, Syria, and Cilicia. Greetings!
> **15:24** Gal 1:7; 5:10 24 "We understand that some men from here have troubled you and upset you
> with their teaching, but they had no such instructions from us. 25 So it seemed good
> to us, having unanimously agreed on our decision, to send you these official
> **15:26** Acts 14:19; 1 Cor 15:30 representatives, along with our beloved Barnabas and Paul, 26 who have risked their
> lives for the sake of our Lord Jesus Christ. 27 So we are sending Judas and Silas to
> tell you what we have decided concerning your question.
> 28 "For it seemed good to the Holy Spirit and to us to lay no greater burden on
> **15:29** Gen 9:4; Lev 17:10-14 you than these requirements: 29 You must abstain from eating food offered to idols,
> from consuming blood or eating the meat of strangled animals, and from sexual
> immorality. If you do this, you will do well. Farewell."

30 The four messengers went at once to Antioch, where they called a general meeting
of the Christians and delivered the letter. 31 And there was great joy throughout the church
that day as they read this encouraging message.
15:32 Acts 11:27; 13:1 32 Then Judas and Silas, both being prophets, spoke extensively to the Christians,
encouraging and strengthening their faith. 33 They stayed for a while, and then Judas
and Silas were sent back to Jerusalem, with the blessings of the Christians, to those who
had sent them.* 35 Paul and Barnabas stayed in Antioch to assist many others who were
teaching and preaching the word of the Lord there.

3. Second missionary journey

Paul and Barnabas Separate

15:36 Acts 13:4, 13-14, 51; 14:1, 6, 24-25 36 After some time Paul said to Barnabas, "Let's return to each city where we
previously preached the word of the Lord, to see how the new believers are getting
15:37 Acts 12:12, 25 along." 37 Barnabas agreed and wanted to take along John Mark. 38 But Paul disagreed
strongly, since John Mark had deserted them in Pamphylia and had not shared in their
15:38 Acts 13:13 work. 39 Their disagreement over this was so sharp that they separated. Barnabas took
John Mark with him and sailed for Cyprus. 40 Paul chose Silas, and the believers sent
them off, entrusting them to the Lord's grace. 41 So they traveled throughout Syria and
Cilicia to strengthen the churches there.

15:33 Some manuscripts add verse 34, *But Silas decided to stay there.*

15:23-29 This letter answered their questions and brought great joy to the Gentile Christians in Antioch (15:31). Beautifully written, it appeals to the Holy Spirit's guidance and explains what is to be done as though the readers already knew it. It is helpful when believers learn to be careful not only in what they say but also in how they say it. We may be correct in our content, but we can lose our audience by our tone of voice or by our attitude.

15:31 The debate over circumcision could have split the church, but Paul, Barnabas, and the Jews in Antioch made the right decision—they sought counsel from the church leaders and from God's Word. Our differences should be settled the same way—by seeking wise counsel and abiding by the decisions. Don't let disagreements divide you from other believers.

15:36-39 Paul and Barnabas disagreed sharply over Mark. Paul didn't want to take him along because he had left them earlier (13:13). This disagreement caused the two great preachers to form two teams, opening up two missionary endeavors instead of one. God works even through conflict and disagreements. Later, Mark became vital to Paul's ministry (Colossians 4:10). Christians do not always agree, but problems can be solved by agreeing to disagree and letting God work his will.

15:40 Paul's second missionary journey, this time with Silas as his partner, began approximately three years after his first one ended. The two visited many of the cities covered on Paul's first journey, plus others. This journey laid the groundwork for the church in Greece.

15:40 Silas had been involved in the Jerusalem council and was one of the two men chosen to represent the Jerusalem church by taking the letter and decision back to Antioch (15:22). Paul, from the Antioch church, chose Silas, from the Jerusalem church, and they traveled together to many cities to spread the Good News. This teamwork demonstrated the church's unity after the decision at the Jerusalem council.

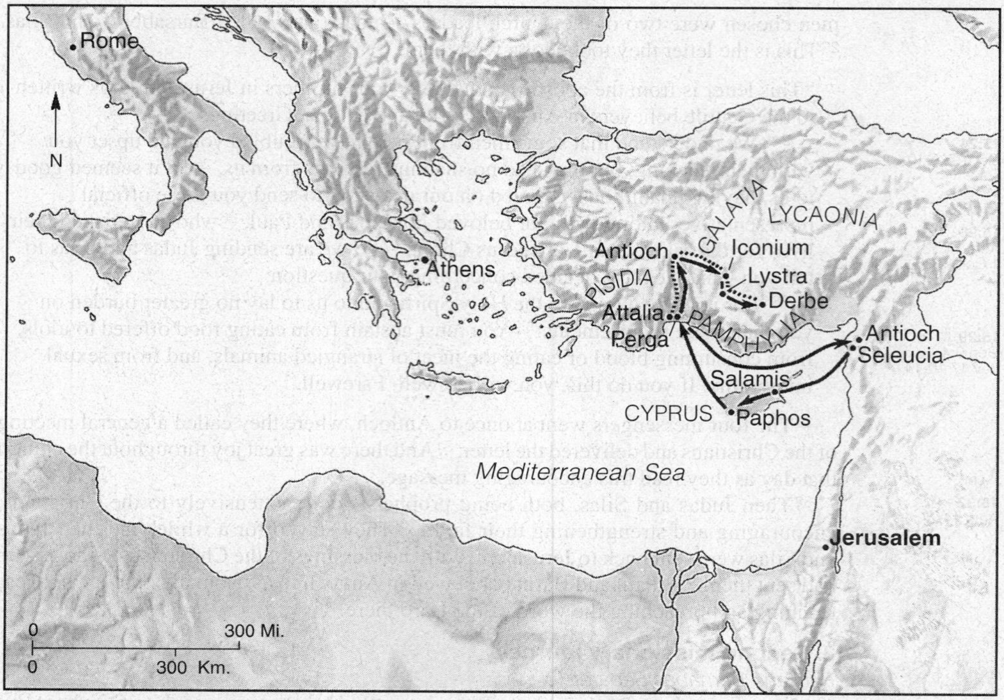

Rome
N
Athens
GALATIA
LYCAONIA
Antioch
Iconium
Lystra
Derbe
PISIDIA
Attalia
Perga
PAMPHYLIA
Antioch
Seleucia
Salamis
CYPRUS
Paphos
Mediterranean Sea
Jerusalem
0 300 Mi.
0 300 Km.

PAUL'S FIRST MISSIONARY JOURNEY (ACTS 13:1—14:28)

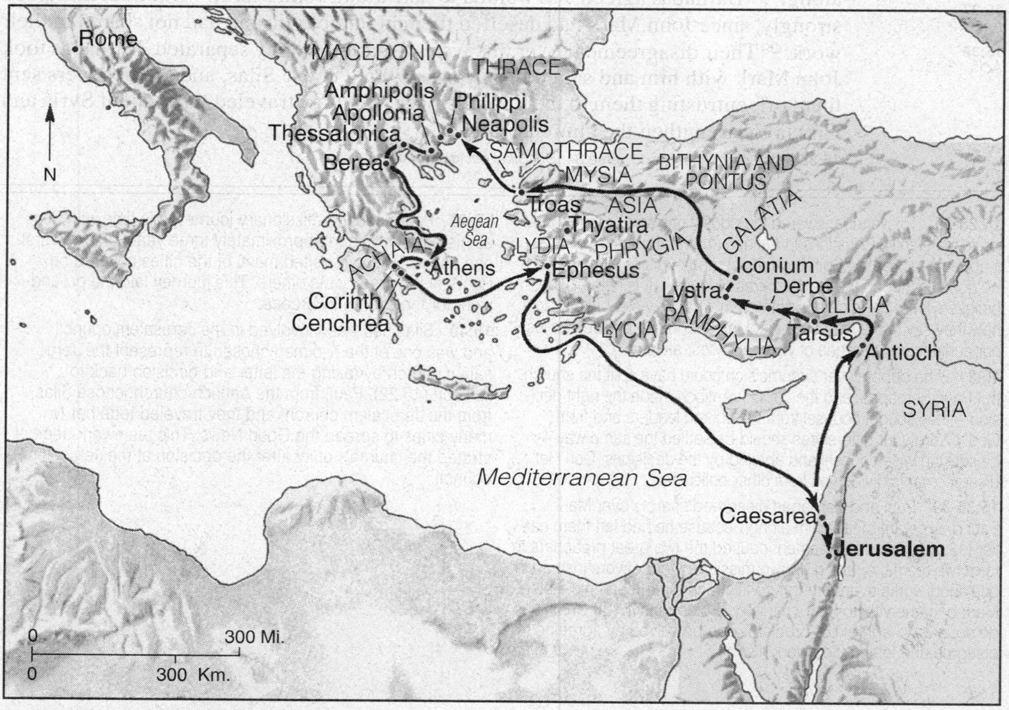

Rome
MACEDONIA
THRACE
Amphipolis
Philippi
Apollonia
Neapolis
Thessalonica
SAMOTHRACE
Berea
N
MYSIA
BITHYNIA AND PONTUS
Troas
ASIA
Aegean Sea
Thyatira
GALATIA
LYDIA
PHRYGIA
ACHAIA
Athens
Ephesus
Iconium
Derbe
Lystra
CILICIA
Corinth
Cenchrea
LYCIA
PAMPHYLIA
Tarsus
Antioch
SYRIA
Mediterranean Sea
Caesarea
Jerusalem
0 300 Mi.
0 300 Km.

PAUL'S SECOND MISSIONARY JOURNEY (ACTS 15:36—18:22)

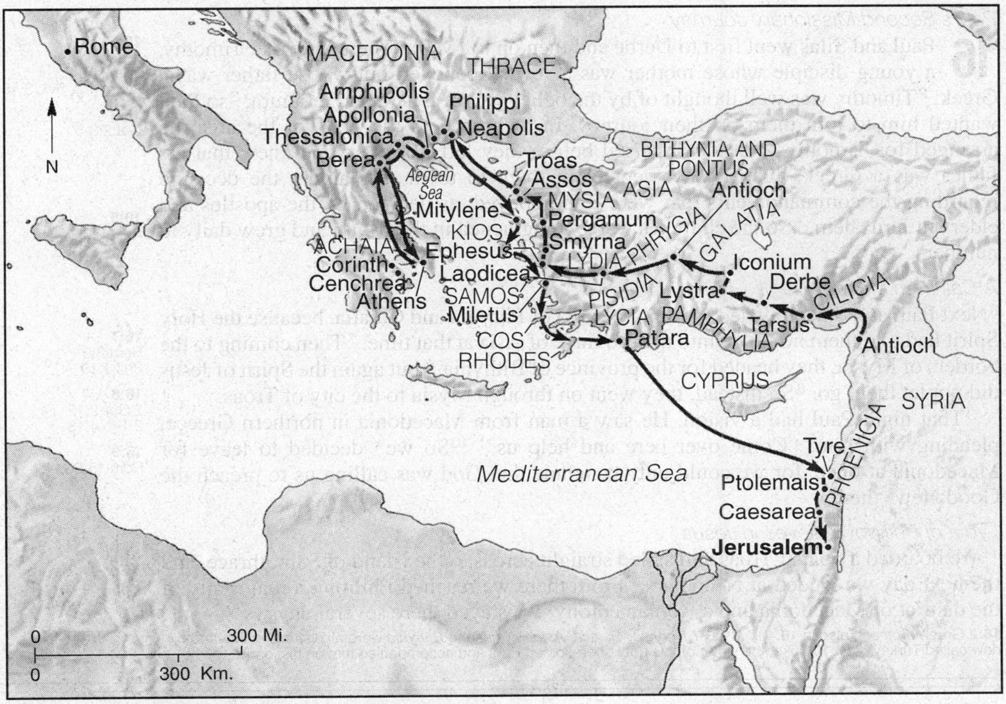

PAUL'S THIRD MISSIONARY JOURNEY (ACTS 18:23—21:16)

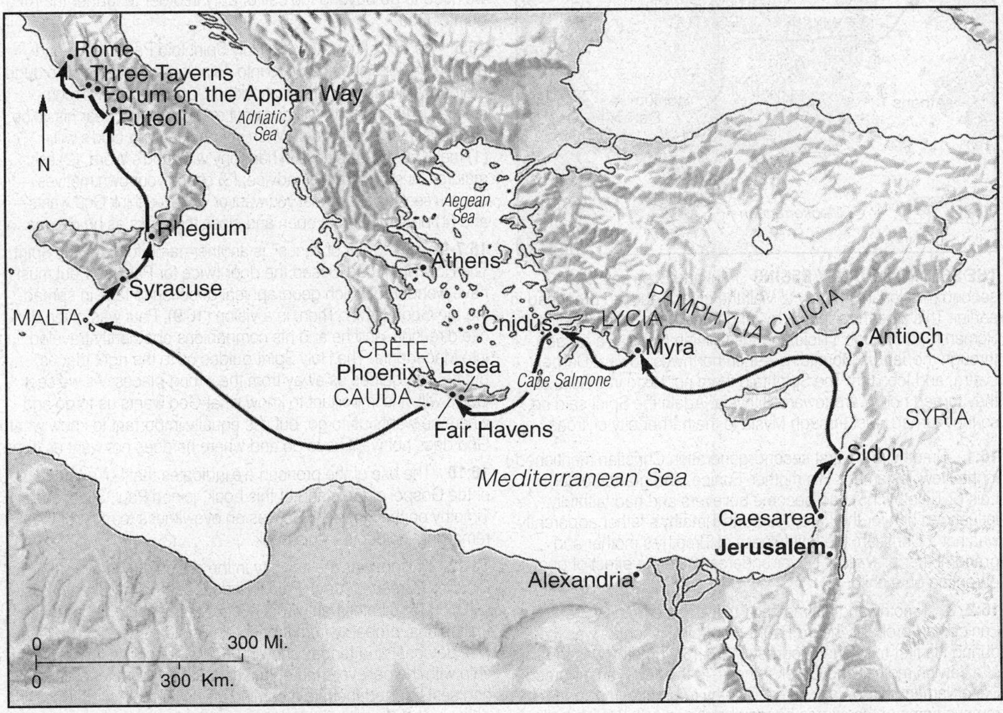

PAUL'S JOURNEY TO ROME (ACTS 21:17—28:31)

Paul's Second Missionary Journey

16 Paul and Silas went first to Derbe and then on to Lystra. There they met Timothy,
a young disciple whose mother was a Jewish believer, but whose father was a
Greek. [2]Timothy was well thought of by the believers* in Lystra and Iconium, [3]so Paul
wanted him to join them on their journey. In deference to the Jews of the area, he
arranged for Timothy to be circumcised before they left, for everyone knew that his
father was a Greek. [4]Then they went from town to town, explaining the decision
regarding the commandments that were to be obeyed, as decided by the apostles and
elders in Jerusalem. [5]So the churches were strengthened in their faith and grew daily in
numbers.

A Call from Macedonia

[6]Next Paul and Silas traveled through the area of Phrygia and Galatia, because the Holy
Spirit had told them not to go into the province of Asia at that time. [7]Then coming to the
borders of Mysia, they headed for the province of Bithynia,* but again the Spirit of Jesus
did not let them go. [8]So instead, they went on through Mysia to the city of Troas.
[9]That night Paul had a vision. He saw a man from Macedonia in northern Greece,
pleading with him, "Come over here and help us." [10]So we* decided to leave for
Macedonia at once, for we could only conclude that God was calling us to preach the
Good News there.

Lydia of Philippi Believes in Jesus

[11]We boarded a boat at Troas and sailed straight across to the island of Samothrace, and
the next day we landed at Neapolis. [12]From there we reached Philippi, a major city of
the district of Macedonia and a Roman colony; we stayed there several days.

16:2 Greek *brothers;* also in 16:40. **16:6-7** *Phrygia, Galatia, Asia, Mysia,* and *Bithynia* were all districts in the land now called Turkey. **16:10** Luke, the writer of this book, here joined Paul and accompanied him on his journey.

16:1 Acts 14:6; Phil 2:19-22; 2 Tim 1:2, 5-6; 3:15
16:3 Gal 2:3-5
16:5 Acts 9:31
16:7 Rom 8:9; Phil 1:19
16:8 2 Cor 2:12; 2 Tim 4:13
16:9 Rom 15:26
16:11 2 Cor 2:12
16:12 Phil 1:1; 1 Thes 2:2

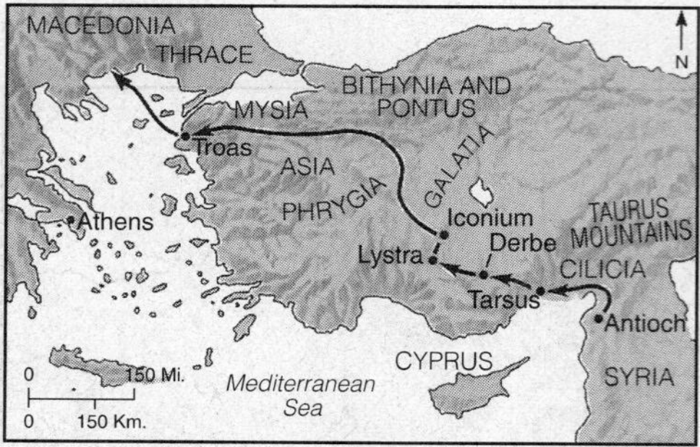

THE SECOND JOURNEY BEGINS Paul and Silas set out on a second missionary journey to visit the cities Paul had preached in earlier. This time they set out by land rather than sea, traveling the Roman road through Cilicia and the Cilician Gates—a gorge through the Taurus Mountains—then northwest toward Derbe, Lystra, and Iconium. The Spirit told them not to go into Asia, so they turned northward toward Bithynia. Again the Spirit said no, so they turned west through Mysia to the harbor city of Troas.

16:1 Timothy is the first second-generation Christian mentioned in the New Testament. His mother, Eunice, and grandmother Lois (2 Timothy 1:5) had become believers and had faithfully influenced him for the Lord. Although Timothy's father apparently was not a Christian, the faithfulness of Timothy's mother and grandmother prevailed. Never underestimate the effect of godly parenting on a child.

16:2, 3 Timothy and his mother, Eunice, were from Lystra. Eunice had probably heard Paul's preaching when he was there during his first missionary journey (14:6-18). Timothy was the son of a Jewish mother and Greek father—to the Jews, a half-breed like a Samaritan. So Paul asked Timothy to be circumcised to remove some of the stigma he may have had with Jewish believers. Timothy was not required to be circumcised (the Jerusalem council had decided that—chapter 15), but he voluntarily did this to overcome any barriers to his witness for Christ. Sometimes we need to go beyond the call of duty in order to further the Kingdom of God.

16:6 We don't know how the Holy Spirit told Paul that he and his companions should not go into Asia. It may have been through a prophet, a vision, an inner conviction, or some other circumstance. To know God's will does not mean we must hear his voice. He leads in different ways. When you are seeking God's will, (1) make sure your plan is in harmony with God's Word; (2) ask mature Christians for their advice; (3) check your own motives—are you seeking to do what you want or what you think God wants?—and (4) pray for God to open and close the doors as he desires.

16:7-9 The "Spirit of Jesus" is another name for the Holy Spirit. The Holy Spirit had closed the door twice for Paul, so Paul must have wondered which geographical direction to take in spreading the Good News. Then, in a vision (16:9), Paul was given definite direction, and he and his companions obediently traveled into Macedonia. The Holy Spirit guides us to the right places, but he also guides us away from the wrong places. As we seek God's will, it is important to know what God wants us to do and where he wants us to go, but it is equally important to know what God does not want us to do and where he does not want us to go.

16:10 The use of the pronoun *we* indicates that Luke, the author of the Gospel of Luke and of this book, joined Paul, Silas, and Timothy on their journey. He was an eyewitness to most of the remaining incidents in this book.

16:12 Philippi was the key city in the region of Macedonia (northern Greece today). Paul founded a church during this visit (A.D. 50–51). Later, Paul wrote a letter to the church, the book of Philippians, probably from a prison in Rome (A.D. 61). The letter was personal and tender, showing Paul's deep love for and friendship with the believers there. In it he thanked them for a gift they had sent, alerted them to a coming visit by Timothy and Epaphroditus, urged the church to clear up any disunity, and encouraged the believers not to give in to persecution.

[13]On the Sabbath we went a little way outside the city to a riverbank, where we
supposed that some people met for prayer, and we sat down to speak with some women
who had come together. [14]One of them was Lydia from Thyatira, a merchant of expensive
purple cloth. She was a worshiper of God. As she listened to us, the Lord opened her heart,
and she accepted what Paul was saying. [15]She was baptized along with other members of

16:14
Rev 1:11; 2:18, 24

SILAS

The lives of the first Christian missionaries can be described with many words, but *boring* is not one of them. There were days of great excitement as men and women who had never heard of Jesus responded to the gospel. There were dangerous journeys over land and sea. Health risks and hunger were part of the daily routine. And there was open and hostile resistance to Christianity in many cities. Silas was one of the first missionaries, and he found out that serving Jesus Christ was certainly not boring!

Silas's name appears in Acts at the end of the first church council on the Jewish/Gentile problem. The majority of early Christians were Jews who realized that Jesus was the fulfillment of God's Old Testament promises to his people; however, the universal application of those promises had been overlooked. Thus, many felt that becoming Jewish was a prerequisite to becoming a Christian. The idea that God could accept a Gentile pagan was too incredible. But Gentiles began to accept Christ as Savior, and the transformation of their lives and the presence of God's Spirit confirmed their conversions. Some Jews were still reluctant, though, and insisted these new Christians take on various Jewish customs. The issue came to a boiling point at the Jerusalem council but was peacefully resolved. Silas was one of the representatives from Jerusalem sent with Paul and Barnabas back to Antioch with an official letter of welcome and acceptance to the Gentile Christians. Having fulfilled this mission, Silas returned to Jerusalem. Within a short time, however, he was back in Antioch at Paul's request to join him on his second missionary journey.

Paul, Silas, and Timothy began a far-ranging ministry that included some exciting adventures. Paul and Silas spent a night singing in a Philippian jail after being severely beaten. An earthquake, the loosing of their chains, and the resulting panic led to the conversion of their jailer. Later, they narrowly missed another beating in Thessalonica, prevented by an evening escape. In Berea there was more trouble, but Silas and Timothy stayed to teach the young believers, while Paul traveled on to Athens. The team was finally reunited in Corinth. In each place they visited, they left behind a small group of Christians.

Silas leaves the story as suddenly as he entered it. Peter mentions him as the co-author of 1 Peter, but we do not know when he joined Peter. He was an effective believer before leaving Jerusalem, and he doubtless continued to minister after his work with Paul was completed. He took advantage of opportunities to serve God and was not discouraged by the setbacks and opposition he met along the way. Silas, though not the most famous of the early missionaries, was certainly a hero worth imitating.

Strengths and accomplishments
- A leader in the Jerusalem church
- Represented the church in carrying the "acceptance letter" prepared by the Jerusalem council to the Gentile believers in Antioch
- Was closely associated with Paul from the second missionary journey on
- Sang songs of praise to God while in jail with Paul in Philippi,
- Worked as a writing secretary for both Paul and Peter

Lessons from his life
- Partnership is a significant part of effective ministry
- God never guarantees that his servants will not suffer
- Obedience to God will often mean giving up what makes us feel secure

Vital statistics
- Where: Roman citizen living in Jerusalem
- Occupation: One of the first career missionaries
- Contemporaries: Paul, Timothy, Peter, Mark, Barnabas

Key verses
"So it seemed good to us, having unanimously agreed on our decision, to send you these official representatives, along with our beloved Barnabas and Paul, who have risked their lives for the sake of our Lord Jesus Christ. So we are sending Judas and Silas to tell you what we have decided concerning your question" (Acts 15:25–27).

Silas's story is told in Acts 15:22—19:10. He is also mentioned in 2 Corinthians 1:19; 1 Thessalonians 1:1; 2 Thessalonians 1:1; 1 Peter 5:12.

16:13 Inscribed on the arches outside the city of Philippi was a prohibition against bringing an unrecognized religion into the city; therefore, this prayer meeting was held outside the city, beside the river.

16:13, 14 After following the Holy Spirit's leading into Macedonia, Paul made his first evangelistic contact with a small group of women. Paul never allowed gender or cultural boundaries to keep him from preaching the Good News. He preached to these women, and Lydia, an influential merchant, believed. This opened the way for ministry in that region. God often worked in and through women in the early church.

16:14 Lydia was a merchant of purple cloth, so she was probably wealthy. Purple cloth was valuable and expensive. It was often worn as a sign of nobility or royalty.

16:14ff Luke highlights the stories of three individuals who became believers through Paul's ministry in Philippi: Lydia, the

her household, and she asked us to be her guests. "If you agree that I am faithful to the
Lord," she said, "come and stay at my home." And she urged us until we did.

Paul and Silas in Prison

[16]One day as we were going down to the place of prayer, we met a demon-possessed **16:16** Deut 18:10-11
slave girl. She was a fortune-teller who earned a lot of money for her masters. [17]She 1 Sam 28:3, 7
followed along behind us shouting, "These men are servants of the Most High God, and
they have come to tell you how to be saved."

[18]This went on day after day until Paul got so exasperated that he turned and spoke to **16:18**
the demon within her. "I command you in the name of Jesus Christ to come out of her," Mark 16:17 Acts 19:13
he said. And instantly it left her.

[19]Her masters' hopes of wealth were now shattered, so they grabbed Paul and Silas
and dragged them before the authorities at the marketplace. [20]"The whole city is in an **16:20**
uproar because of these Jews!" they shouted. [21]"They are teaching the people to do Acts 17:6 **16:21**
things that are against Roman customs." Esth 3:8

[22]A mob quickly formed against Paul and Silas, and the city officials ordered them **16:22**
stripped and beaten with wooden rods. [23]They were severely beaten, and then they were 2 Cor 11:25 1 Thes 2:2
thrown into prison. The jailer was ordered to make sure they didn't escape. [24]So he took
no chances but put them into the inner dungeon and clamped their feet in the stocks.

[25]Around midnight, Paul and Silas were praying and singing hymns to God, and the **16:25**
other prisoners were listening. [26]Suddenly, there was a great earthquake, and the prison Eph 5:19 **16:26**
was shaken to its foundations. All the doors flew open, and the chains of every prisoner Acts 5:19; 12:10
fell off! [27]The jailer woke up to see the prison doors wide open. He assumed the **16:27**
prisoners had escaped, so he drew his sword to kill himself. [28]But Paul shouted to him, Acts 12:18-19
"Don't do it! We are all here!"

[29]Trembling with fear, the jailer called for lights and ran to the dungeon and fell down **16:30**
before Paul and Silas. [30]He brought them out and asked, "Sirs, what must I do to be saved?" Acts 2:37

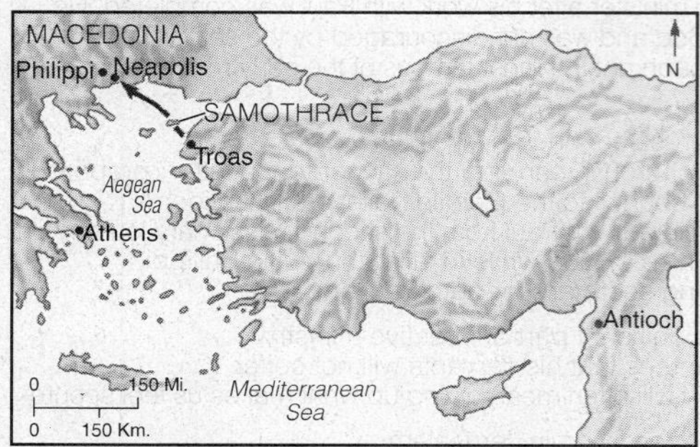

PAUL TRAVELS TO MACEDONIA At Troas, Paul received the Macedonian call (16:9), and he, Silas, Timothy, and Luke boarded a ship. They sailed to the island of Samothrace, then on to Neapolis, the port for the city of Philippi. Philippi sat on the Egnatian Way, a main transportation artery connecting the eastern provinces with Italy.

influential businesswoman (16:14), the demon-possessed slave girl (16:16-18), and the jailer (16:27-30). The Good News was affecting all strata of society, just as it does today.

16:15 Why was Lydia's household baptized after Lydia responded in faith to the Good News? Baptism was a public sign of identification with Christ and the Christian community. Although all members of her household may not have chosen to follow Christ (we don't know), it was now a Christian home.

16:16 This girl's fortune-telling ability came from evil spirits. Fortune-telling was a common practice in Greek and Roman culture. There were many superstitious methods by which people thought they could foretell future events, from interpreting omens in nature to communicating with the spirits of the dead. This young slave girl had an evil spirit, and she made her master rich by interpreting signs and telling people their fortunes. The master was exploiting her unfortunate condition for personal gain.

16:17, 18 What the slave girl said was true, although the source of her knowledge was a demon. Why did a demon announce the truth about Paul, and why did this annoy Paul? If Paul accepted the demon's words, he would appear to be linking the Good News with demon-related activities. This would damage his message about Christ. Truth and evil do not mix.

16:22-25 Paul and Silas were stripped, beaten, and placed in stocks in the inner cell. Despite this dismal situation, they praised God, praying and singing as the other prisoners listened. No matter what our circumstances, we should praise God. Others may come to Christ because of our example.

16:24 Stocks were made of two boards joined with iron clamps, leaving holes just big enough for the ankles. The prisoner's legs were placed across the lower board, and then the upper board was closed over them. Sometimes both wrists and ankles were placed in stocks. Paul and Silas, who had committed no crime and who were peaceful men, were put in stocks designed for holding the most dangerous prisoners in absolute security.

16:27 The jailer drew his sword to kill himself because jailers were responsible for their prisoners and would be held accountable for their escape.

16:30, 31 Paul and Silas's reputation in Philippi was well known. When the jailer realized his own true condition and need, he risked everything to find the answer. The Good News of salvation is simply expressed: Believe in the Lord Jesus, and you will be saved (see Romans 10:9; 1 Corinthians 12:3; Ephesians 2:8, 9; Philippians 2:11). When we recognize Jesus as Lord and trust in him with our entire life, salvation is assured to us. If you have never trusted in Jesus to save you, do so quickly. Your life can be filled with joy, just as the jailer's was (16:34).

16:31 John 3:15; Acts 11:14

31 They replied, "Believe on the Lord Jesus and you will be saved, along with your
entire household." 32 Then they shared the word of the Lord with him and all who lived
in his household. 33 That same hour the jailer washed their wounds, and he and
everyone in his household were immediately baptized. 34 Then he brought them into his
house and set a meal before them. He and his entire household rejoiced because they
all believed in God.
35 The next morning the city officials sent the police to tell the jailer, "Let those men
go!" 36 So the jailer told Paul, "You and Silas are free to leave. Go in peace."

16:37 Acts 22:25

37 But Paul replied, "They have publicly beaten us without trial and jailed us—and we
are Roman citizens. So now they want us to leave secretly? Certainly not! Let them come
themselves to release us!"

16:38 Acts 22:29
16:39 Matt 8:34
16:40 Acts 16:14

38 When the police made their report, the city officials were alarmed to learn that Paul
and Silas were Roman citizens. 39 They came to the jail and apologized to them. Then
they brought them out and begged them to leave the city. 40 Paul and Silas then returned
to the home of Lydia, where they met with the believers and encouraged them once more
before leaving town.

Paul Preaches in Thessalonica

17:2 Acts 9:20; 13:14; 17:10, 17
17:3 Luke 24:26; Acts 3:18; 9:22; 18:5

17 Now Paul and Silas traveled through the towns of Amphipolis and Apollonia
and came to Thessalonica, where there was a Jewish synagogue. 2 As was Paul's
custom, he went to the synagogue service, and for three Sabbaths in a row he
interpreted the Scriptures to the people. 3 He was explaining and proving the prophecies about the sufferings of the Messiah and his rising from the dead. He said, "This

THE BOOKS OF THE NEW TESTAMENT: WHEN WERE THEY WRITTEN? Dates are approximate.

Book	Date	Book	Date	Book	Date
Galatians	49 A.D.	Philemon	60	Acts	66/68
James	49	Philippians	61	2 Peter	66/68
1, 2 Thessalonians	51/52	Matthew	61/64	2 Timothy	66/67
1, 2 Corinthians	55	Luke	61/64	Hebrews	68/70
Romans	57	1 Timothy	64	John	85
Mark	58/60	Titus	64	1, 2, 3 John	85/90
Ephesians	60	1 Peter	64/65	Revelation	95
Colossians	60	Jude	65		

16:31-34 Paul and Silas took the family unit seriously. So the offer of salvation was made to the jailer's entire household—family and servants. Yet it was not the jailer's faith that saved them; they all needed to come to Jesus in faith and believe in him in the same way the jailer had. His entire family did believe and all were saved. Pray that God will use you to introduce Jesus to your family and that they will come to believe in him.

16:37 Paul refused to take his freedom and run. He wanted to teach the city officials in Philippi a lesson and to protect the other believers from the treatment he and Silas had received. The word would spread that Paul and Silas had been found innocent and freed by the leaders, expressing the truth that believers should not be persecuted—especially if they were Roman citizens.

16:38 Roman citizenship carried with it certain privileges. These Philippian authorities were alarmed because it was illegal to whip a Roman citizen. In addition, every citizen had the right to a fair trial, which Paul and Silas had not been given.

17:1 Thessalonica was one of the wealthiest and most influential cities in Macedonia. This is the first city Paul visited where his teachings attracted a large group of socially prominent citizens. The church he planted grew quickly, but from A.D. 50 to 51, Paul was forced out of the city by a mob (17:5, 6, 10). Paul later sent Timothy back to Thessalonica to see how the Christians were doing. Soon afterward, Paul wrote two letters to the Thessalonian believers (1 and 2 Thessalonians), encouraging them to remain faithful and to refuse to listen to false teachers who tried to refute their beliefs.

17:1, 2 A synagogue, a group of Jews who gathered for teaching and prayer, could be established wherever there were 10 Jewish males. Paul's regular practice was to preach in synagogues as long as the Jews allowed it. Often those who weren't Jews would come to these services and hear Paul's preaching. For a description of a synagogue service, see the note on 13:14, 15.

17:2, 3 When Paul spoke in the synagogues, he wisely began by talking about Old Testament writings and explaining how the Messiah fulfilled them, moving from the known to the unknown. This is a good strategy for us. When we witness for Christ, we should begin where people are, affirming the truth they do know, and then we can present Christ, the one who is truth.

MINISTRY IN MACEDONIA
Luke stayed in Philippi while Paul, Silas, and Timothy continued on the Egnatian Way to Amphipolis, Apollonia, and Thessalonica. But trouble arose in Thessalonica, and they fled to Berea. When their enemies from Thessalonica pursued them, Paul set out by sea to Athens, leaving Silas and Timothy to encourage the believers.

Jesus I'm telling you about is the Messiah." 4 Some who listened were persuaded and
became converts, including a large number of godly Greek men and also many
important women of the city.*
5 But the Jewish leaders were jealous, so they gathered some worthless fellows from the 17:5 Rom 16:21
streets to form a mob and start a riot. They attacked the home of Jason, searching for Paul 1 Thes 2:14
and Silas so they could drag them out to the crowd.* 6 Not finding them there, they dragged 17:6
out Jason and some of the other believers* instead and took them before the city council. Acts 16:20, 21
"Paul and Silas have turned the rest of the world upside down, and now they are here
disturbing our city," they shouted. 7 "And Jason has let them into his home. They are all 17:7 Luke 23:2
guilty of treason against Caesar, for they profess allegiance to another king, Jesus." John 19:12
8 The people of the city, as well as the city officials, were thrown into turmoil by these
reports. 9 But the officials released Jason and the other believers after they had posted bail.

Paul and Silas in Berea

10 That very night the believers sent Paul and Silas to Berea. When they arrived there,
they went to the synagogue. 11 And the people of Berea were more open-minded than 17:11
those in Thessalonica, and they listened eagerly to Paul's message. They searched the John 5:39
Scriptures day after day to check up on Paul and Silas, to see if they were really teaching
the truth. 12 As a result, many Jews believed, as did some of the prominent Greek women
and many men.
13 But when some Jews in Thessalonica learned that Paul was preaching the word of 17:13 Acts 14:19
God in Berea, they went there and stirred up trouble. 14 The believers acted at once, 17:14
sending Paul on to the coast, while Silas and Timothy remained behind. 15 Those Matt 10:23
escorting Paul went with him to Athens; then they returned to Berea with a message for 17:15 Acts 18:5
Silas and Timothy to hurry and join him. 1 Thes 3:1

Paul Preaches in Athens

16 While Paul was waiting for them in Athens, he was deeply troubled by all the idols
he saw everywhere in the city. 17 He went to the synagogue to debate with the Jews 17:17
and the God-fearing Gentiles, and he spoke daily in the public square to all who Acts 18:19
happened to be there.
18 He also had a debate with some of the Epicurean and Stoic philosophers. When he 17:18 1 Cor 1:22

17:4 Some manuscripts read *many of the wives of the leading men.* **17:5** Or *the city council.* **17:6** Greek *brothers;* also in 17:10, 14.

17:5 The Jewish leaders didn't refute the theology of Paul and Silas, but they were jealous of the popularity of these itinerant preachers. Their motives for causing the riot were rooted in personal jealousy, not doctrinal purity.

17:6 We don't know much about Jason except that he evidently was the local host and sponsor of Paul and Silas; thus, he took the heat for all the problems. Jason is just one of many "unsung heroes" who faithfully played their part to help spread the Good News. Because of Jason's courage, Paul and Silas were able to minister more effectively. You may not receive much attention (in fact, you may receive only grief) for your service for Christ. But God wants to use you. Lives will be changed because of your courage and faithfulness.

17:6 What a reputation these early Christians had! The power of the Good News revolutionized lives, broke down all social barriers, threw open prison doors, caused people to care deeply for one another, and stirred them to worship God. Our world needs to be turned upside down, to be transformed. The Good News is not in the business of merely improving programs and encouraging good conduct but of dynamically transforming lives. Take courage and ask God how you can help spread his Good News all over *your* world.

17:7 The Jewish leaders had to concoct charges against Paul and Silas that would be heard by the city government. The Romans did not care about theological disagreements between the Jews and these preachers. Treason, however, was a serious offense in the Roman Empire. Although Paul and Silas were not advocating rebellion against Roman law, their loyalty to another king sounded suspicious.

17:8, 9 Jason posted bail—putting up cash for freedom. By doing so, he promised that the trouble would cease or his own property and possibly his own life would be taken.

17:11 How do you evaluate sermons and teachings? The people in Berea searched the Scriptures for themselves to verify the message they heard. Always compare what you hear with what the Bible says. A preacher or teacher who gives God's true message will never contradict or explain away anything that is found in God's Word.

17:15 Athens, with its magnificent buildings and many gods, was a center for Greek culture, philosophy, and education. Philosophers and educated men were always ready to hear something new, so they invited Paul to speak to them at the meeting of the Council of Philosophers (17:18, 19).

17:18 The Epicureans and Stoics were the dominant philosophers in Greek culture. The Epicureans believed that seeking happiness or pleasure was the primary goal of life. By contrast, the Stoics placed thinking above feeling and tried to live in harmony with nature and reason, suppressing their desire for pleasure. Thus, they were very disciplined.

told them about Jesus and his resurrection, they said, "This babbler has picked up some
strange ideas." Others said, "He's pushing some foreign religion."
19 Then they took him to the Council of Philosophers.* "Come and tell us more about
this new religion," they said. 20 "You are saying some rather startling things, and we want
to know what it's all about." 21 (It should be explained that all the Athenians as well as
the foreigners in Athens seemed to spend all their time discussing the latest ideas.)
22 So Paul, standing before the Council,* addressed them as follows: "Men of Athens,

17:19 Greek *the Areopagus.* **17:22** Or *in the middle of Mars Hill;* Greek reads *in the middle of the Areopagus.*

LUKE

One of the essential qualities of a good doctor is compassion. People need to know that their doctor cares. Even if he or she doesn't know what is wrong or isn't sure what to do, real concern is always a doctor's good medicine. Doctor Luke was a person of compassion.

Although we know few facts of his life, Luke has left us a strong impression of himself by what he wrote. In his Gospel, he emphasizes Jesus Christ's compassion. He vividly recorded both the power demonstrated by Christ's life and the care with which Christ treated people. Luke highlighted the relationships Jesus had with women. His writing in Acts is full of sharp verbal pictures of real people caught up in the greatest events of history.

Luke was also a doctor. He had a traveling medical practice as Paul's companion. Since the gospel was often welcomed with whips and stones, the doctor was undoubtedly seldom without patients. It is even possible that Paul's "thorn in the flesh" was some kind of physical ailment that needed Luke's regular attention. Paul deeply appreciated Luke's skills and faithfulness.

God also made special use of Luke as the historian of the early church. Repeatedly, the details of Luke's descriptions have been proven accurate. The first words in his Gospel indicate his interest in the truth.

Luke's compassion reflected his Lord's. Luke's skill as a doctor helped Paul. His passion for the facts as he recorded the life of Christ, the spread of the early church, and the lives of Christianity's missionaries gives us dependable sources for the basis of our faith. He accomplished all this while staying out of the spotlight. Perhaps his greatest example is the challenge to greatness even when we are not the center of attention.

Strengths and accomplishments
- A humble, faithful, and useful companion of Paul
- A well-educated and trained physician
- A careful and exact historian
- Writer of both the Gospel of Luke and the book of Acts

Lessons from his life
- The words we leave behind will be a lasting picture of who we are
- Even the most successful person needs the personal care of others
- Excellence is shown by how we work when no one is noticing

Vital statistics
- Where: Probably met Paul in Troas
- Occupations: Doctor, historian, traveling companion
- Contemporaries: Paul, Timothy, Silas, Peter

Key verses
"Many people have written accounts about the events that took place among us. They used as their source material the reports circulating among us from the early disciples and other eyewitnesses of what God has done in fulfillment of his promises. Having carefully investigated all these accounts from the beginning, I have decided to write a careful summary for you, to reassure you of the truth of all you were taught" (Luke 1:1–4).

Luke includes himself in the *we* sections of Acts 16—28. He is also mentioned in Luke 1:3; Acts 1:1; Colossians 4:14; 2 Timothy 4:11; Philemon 1:24.

17:19 For a time the Council met on a low hill in Athens near the Acropolis. As Paul stood there and spoke about the one true God, his audience could look down on the city and see the many idols representing gods that Paul knew were worthless.

17:22 Paul was well prepared to speak to this group. He came from Tarsus, an educational center, and had the training and knowledge to present his beliefs clearly and persuasively. Paul was a rabbi, taught by the finest scholar of his day, Gamaliel, and he had spent much of his life thinking and reasoning through the Scriptures.

It is not enough to teach or preach with conviction. Like Paul, we must be prepared. The more we know about the Bible, what it means, and how to apply it to our life, the more convincing our words will be. This does not mean that we should avoid presenting the Good News until we feel adequately prepared. We should use what we have learned but always seek to know more in order to be an effective witness and be able to respond to people's questions and arguments.

17:22ff Paul's address is a good example of how to communicate the Good News. Paul did not begin by reciting Jewish history, as he usually did, for this would have been meaningless to his Greek audience. He began by building a case for the one true God, using examples they understood (17:22, 23). Then he established common ground by emphasizing what they agreed on about God (17:24-29). Finally, he moved his message to the person of Christ, centering on the Resurrection (17:30, 31). When you witness to others, you can use Paul's approach: Use examples, establish common ground, and then move people toward a decision about Jesus Christ.

I notice that you are very religious, 23 for as I was walking along I saw your many altars.
And one of them had this inscription on it—'To an Unknown God.' You have been
worshiping him without knowing who he is, and now I wish to tell you about him.
24 "He is the God who made the world and everything in it. Since he is Lord of heaven
and earth, he doesn't live in man-made temples, 25 and human hands can't serve his
needs—for he has no needs. He himself gives life and breath to everything, and he satisfies
every need there is. 26 From one man he created all the nations throughout the whole earth.
He decided beforehand which should rise and fall, and he determined their boundaries.
27 "His purpose in all of this was that the nations should seek after God and perhaps
feel their way toward him and find him—though he is not far from any one of us. 28 For
in him we live and move and exist. As one of your own poets says, 'We are his offspring.'
29 And since this is true, we shouldn't think of God as an idol designed by craftsmen from
gold or silver or stone. 30 God overlooked people's former ignorance about these things,
but now he commands everyone everywhere to turn away from idols and turn to him.*
31 For he has set a day for judging the world with justice by the man he has appointed,
and he proved to everyone who this is by raising him from the dead."
32 When they heard Paul speak of the resurrection of a person who had been dead,

17:23 John 4:22
17:24 1 Kgs 8:27; Isa 42:5; Acts 7:48
17:25 Ps 50:12; Isa 42:5
17:26 Deut 32:8
17:27 Isa 55:6; Jer 23:23-24
17:29 Isa 40:18-25; Rom 1:23
17:30 Acts 14:16
17:31 Pss 9:9; 96:13; Acts 10:42

17:30 Greek *everywhere to repent.*

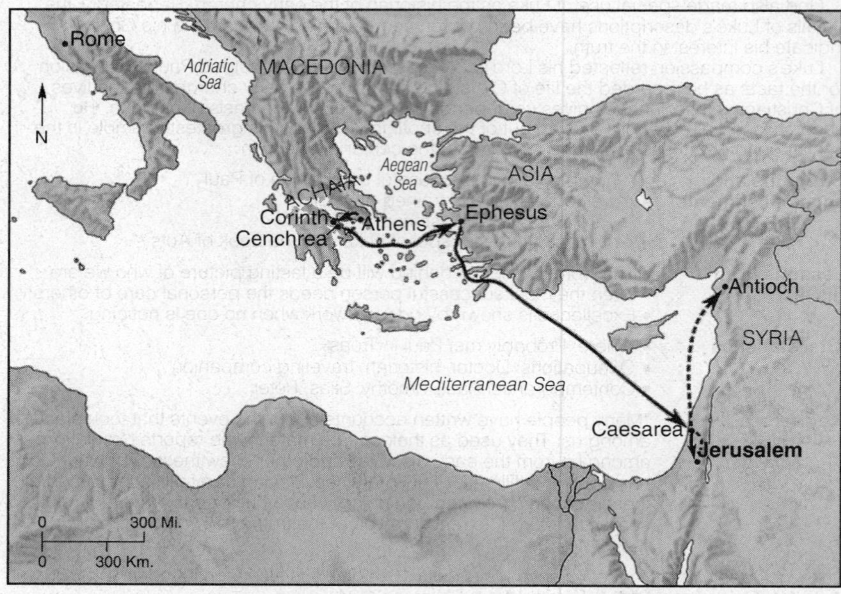

MINISTRY IN CORINTH AND EPHESUS
Paul left Athens and traveled on to Corinth, one of the greatest commercial centers of the empire, located on a narrow neck of land offering direct passage between the Aegean and Adriatic seas. When Paul left from the port of Corinth at Cenchrea, he visited Ephesus. He then traveled to Caesarea, from where he went on to Jerusalem to report on his trip before returning to Antioch.

17:23 The Athenians had built an idol to the unknown god for fear of missing blessings or receiving punishment. Paul's opening statement to the men of Athens was about their unknown god. Paul was not endorsing this god but using the inscription as a point of entry for his witness to the one true God.

17:23 Paul explained the one true God to these educated men of Athens; although these men were, in general, very religious, they did not know God. Today we have a "Christian" society, but to most people, God is still unknown. We need to proclaim who he is and make clear what he did for everyone through his Son, Jesus Christ. We cannot assume that even religious people around us truly know Jesus or understand the importance of faith in him.

17:27, 28 God is known in his creation, and he is close to every one of us. But he is not trapped in his creation—he is transcendent. God is the Creator, not the creation. This means that God is sovereign and in control, while at the same time he is close and personal. Let the Creator of the universe rule your life.

17:30, 31 Paul did not leave his message unfinished. He confronted his listeners with Jesus' resurrection and its meaning to all people—either blessing or punishment. The Greeks had no concept of judgment. Most of them preferred worshiping many gods instead of just one, and the concept of resurrection was unbelievable and offensive to them. Paul did not hold back the truth, however, no matter what they might think of it. Paul often changed his approach to fit his audience, but he never changed his basic message.

17:32-34 Paul's speech received a mixed reaction: Some laughed, some wanted more information, and a few believed. Don't hesitate to tell others about Christ because you fear that some will not believe you. Don't expect a unanimously positive response to your witnessing. Even if only a few believe, it's worth the effort.

some laughed, but others said, "We want to hear more about this later." 33 That ended
Paul's discussion with them, 34 but some joined him and became believers. Among
them were Dionysius, a member of the Council,* a woman named Damaris, and
others.

Paul Meets Priscilla and Aquila in Corinth

18:2 Rom 16:3; 1 Cor 16:19
18:3 Acts 20:34; 1 Cor 4:12; 9:15

18 Then Paul left Athens and went to Corinth.* 2 There he became acquainted with
a Jew named Aquila, born in Pontus, who had recently arrived from Italy with
his wife, Priscilla. They had been expelled from Italy as a result of Claudius Caesar's
order to deport all Jews from Rome. 3 Paul lived and worked with them, for they were
tentmakers* just as he was.

17:34 Greek *an Areopagite.* **18:1** *Athens* and *Corinth* were major cities in Achaia, the region on the southern end of the Greek peninsula. **18:3** Or *leatherworkers.*

AQUILA, PRISCILLA

Some married couples know how to make the most of life. They complement each other, capitalize on each other's strengths, and form an effective team. Their united efforts affect those around them. Aquila and Priscilla were such a couple. They are never mentioned separately in the Bible. In marriage and ministry, they operated as one.

Priscilla and Aquila met Paul in Corinth during his second missionary journey. They had just been expelled from Rome by Emperor Claudius's decree against Jews. Their home was as movable as the tents they made to support themselves. They opened their home to Paul, and he joined them in tentmaking. He shared with them his wealth of spiritual wisdom.

Priscilla and Aquila made the most of their spiritual education. They listened carefully to sermons and evaluated what they heard. When they heard Apollos speak, they were impressed by his ability but realized that his information was not complete. Instead of open confrontation, the couple quietly took Apollos home and shared with him what he needed to know. Until then, Apollos had only been aware of John the Baptist's message about Christ. Priscilla and Aquila told him about Jesus' life, death, and resurrection, and the reality of God's indwelling Spirit. He continued to preach powerfully—but now with the full story.

As for Priscilla and Aquila, they went on using their home as a warm place for training and worship. Back in Rome years later, they hosted one of the house churches that developed.

In an age when the focus is mostly on what happens *between* husband and wife, Aquila and Priscilla are an example of what can happen *through* a husband and wife. Their effectiveness together is the result of their good relationship with each other. Their hospitality opened the doorway of salvation to many. The Christian home is still one of the best tools for spreading the gospel. Do guests find Christ in your home?

Strengths and accomplishments
- Outstanding husband/wife team who ministered in the early church
- Supported themselves by tentmaking while serving Christ
- Close friends of Paul
- Explained to Apollos the full message of Christ

Lessons from their lives
- Couples can have an effective ministry together
- The home is a valuable tool for evangelism
- Every believer needs to be well educated in the faith, whatever his or her role in the church

Vital statistics
- Where: Originally from Rome, moved to Corinth, then Ephesus
- Occupation: Tentmakers
- Contemporaries: Emperor Claudius, Paul, Timothy, Apollos

Key verses
"Greet Priscilla and Aquila. They have been co-workers in my ministry for Christ Jesus. In fact, they risked their lives for me. I am not the only one who is thankful to them; so are all the Gentile churches" (Romans 16:3, 4).

Their story is told in Acts 18. They are also mentioned in Romans 16:3–5; 1 Corinthians 16:19; 2 Timothy 4:19.

18:1 Corinth was the political and commercial center of Greece, surpassing Athens in importance. It had a reputation for great wickedness and immorality. A temple to Aphrodite, goddess of love and war, had been built on the large hill behind the city. In this popular religion, people worshiped the goddess by giving money to the temple and taking part in sexual acts with male and female temple prostitutes. Paul found Corinth a challenge and a great ministry opportunity. Later, he would write a series of letters to the Corinthians dealing in part with the problems of immorality. Two of these letters are 1 and 2 Corinthians.

18:2, 3 Each Jewish boy learned a trade and tried to earn his living with it. Paul and Aquila had been trained in tentmaking, cutting and sewing the woven cloth of goats' hair into tents. Tents were used to house soldiers, and so these tents may have been sold to the Roman army. As a tentmaker, Paul was able to go wherever God led him, carrying his livelihood with him. The word *tentmaker* in Greek was also used to describe a leatherworker.

[4]Each Sabbath found Paul at the synagogue, trying to convince the Jews and Greeks
alike. [5]And after Silas and Timothy came down from Macedonia, Paul spent his full time **18:5** Acts 17:3; 18:28
preaching and testifying to the Jews, telling them, "The Messiah you are looking for is
Jesus." [6]But when the Jews opposed him and insulted him, Paul shook the dust from his **18:6** Matt 10:14
robe and said, "Your blood be upon your own heads—I am innocent. From now on I will Acts 13:45-46;
go to the Gentiles." 20:26
[7]After that he stayed with Titius Justus, a Gentile who worshiped God and lived next
door to the synagogue. [8]Crispus, the leader of the synagogue, and all his household **18:8**
believed in the Lord. Many others in Corinth also became believers and were baptized. 1 Cor 1:14
[9]One night the Lord spoke to Paul in a vision and told him, "Don't be afraid! Speak **18:9-10** Isa 41:10
out! Don't be silent! [10]For I am with you, and no one will harm you because many people Jer 1:18
here in this city belong to me." [11]So Paul stayed there for the next year and a half,
teaching the word of God.
[12]But when Gallio became governor of Achaia, some Jews rose in concerted action **18:12**
against Paul and brought him before the governor for judgment. [13]They accused Paul of Rom 15:26 1 Thes 1:7-8
"persuading people to worship God in ways that are contrary to the law." [14]But just as
Paul started to make his defense, Gallio turned to Paul's accusers and said, "Listen, you
Jews, if this were a case involving some wrongdoing or a serious crime, I would be
obliged to listen to you. [15]But since it is merely a question of words and names and your **18:15**
Jewish laws, you take care of it. I refuse to judge such matters." [16]And he drove them John 18:31
out of the courtroom. [17]The mob had grabbed Sosthenes, the leader of the synagogue, **18:17** Acts 18:8
and had beaten him right there in the courtroom. But Gallio paid no attention. 1 Cor 1:1

Paul Returns to Antioch of Syria

[18]Paul stayed in Corinth for some time after that and then said good-bye to the Christians* **18:18** Num 6:18
and sailed for the coast of Syria, taking Priscilla and Aquila with him. (Earlier, at Cenchrea, Acts 21:24
Paul had shaved his head according to Jewish custom, for he had taken a vow.) [19]When they Rom 16:1
arrived at the port of Ephesus, Paul left the others behind. But while he was there, he went **18:19** Eph 1:1
to the synagogue to debate with the Jews. [20]They asked him to stay longer, but he declined. Rev 1:11; 2:1
[21]So he left, saying, "I will come back later,* God willing." Then he set sail from Ephesus. **18:21** Jas 4:15

18:18 Greek *brothers;* also in 18:27. **18:21** Some manuscripts read *"I must by all means be at Jerusalem for the upcoming festival, but I will come back later."*

18:6 Paul told the Jews he had done all he could for them. Because they rejected Jesus as their Messiah, he would go to the Gentiles, who would be more receptive.

18:10 In a vision, Christ told Paul that he had many people in Corinth. Sometimes we can feel alone or isolated, especially when we see wickedness all around us or are persecuted for our faith. Usually, however, there are others in the neighborhood or community who also follow Christ. Ask God to lead you to them.

18:10, 11 Others who became Christians in Corinth were Phoebe (Romans 16:1—Cenchrea was the port city of Corinth), Tertius (Romans 16:22), Erastus (Romans 16:23), Quartus (Romans 16:23), Chloe (1 Corinthians 1:11), Gaius (1 Corinthians 1:14), Stephanas and his household (1 Corinthians 16:15), Fortunatus (1 Corinthians 16:17), and Achaicus (1 Corinthians 16:17).

18:11 During the year and a half that Paul stayed in wicked Corinth, he established a church and wrote two letters to the believers in Thessalonica (the books of 1 and 2 Thessalonians). Although Paul had been in Thessalonica for only a short time (17:1-15), he commended the believers there for their loving deeds, strong faith, and endurance inspired by hope. While encouraging them to stay away from immorality, he dealt with the themes of salvation, suffering, and the second coming of Jesus Christ. Paul told them to continue to work hard while they awaited Christ's return.

18:12 Gallio served as proconsul of Achaia (modern Greece) in A.D. 51 and was the brother of Seneca the philosopher. He became consul in A.D. 55.

18:13 Paul was charged with promoting a religion not approved by Roman law. This charge amounted to treason. Paul was not encouraging obedience to a human king other than Caesar (see 17:7), nor was he speaking against the Roman Empire. Instead, he was speaking about Christ's eternal Kingdom.

18:14-16 This was an important judicial decision for the spread of the Good News in the Roman Empire. Judaism was a recognized religion under Roman law. As long as Christians were seen as part of Judaism, the court refused to hear cases brought against them. If they had claimed to be a new religion, they could easily have been outlawed by the government. In effect, Gallio was saying, "I don't understand all your terminology and finer points of theology. Handle the matter yourself and don't bother me."

18:17 Crispus had been the leader of the synagogue, but he and his family were converted and joined the Christians (18:8). Sosthenes was chosen to take his place. The mob could have been Greeks venting their feelings against the Jews for causing turmoil, or the crowd may have included some Jews. In any case, they beat Sosthenes for losing the case and leaving the synagogue worse off than before. A person named Sosthenes is mentioned in 1 Corinthians 1:1, and many believe this was the same man who, in time, became a convert and a companion of Paul.

18:18 This vow Paul took was probably a temporary Nazirite vow that ended with shaving of the head and offering the hair as a sacrifice (Numbers 6:18).

18:22 Acts 8:40; 11:19
18:23 Acts 16:6
18:24 Acts 19:1; 1 Cor 1:12; 4:6; 16:12; Titus 3:13
18:25 Acts 19:3

22 The next stop was at the port of Caesarea. From there he went up and visited the church
at Jerusalem* and then went back to Antioch.
23 After spending some time in Antioch, Paul went back to Galatia and Phrygia,
visiting all the believers,* encouraging them and helping them to grow in the Lord.

Apollos Instructed at Ephesus

24 Meanwhile, a Jew named Apollos, an eloquent speaker who knew the Scriptures well, had
just arrived in Ephesus from Alexandria in Egypt. 25 He had been taught the way of the Lord
and talked to others with great enthusiasm and accuracy about Jesus. However, he knew
only about John's baptism. 26 When Priscilla and Aquila heard him preaching boldly in the
synagogue, they took him aside and explained the way of God more accurately.

18:22 Greek *the church.* **18:23** Greek *disciples;* also in 18:27.

APOLLOS

Some people have an amazing natural talent for public speaking. Some even have a great message to go along with it. When Apollos arrived in Ephesus shortly after Paul's departure, he made an immediate impact. He spoke boldly in public, interpreting and applying the Old Testament Scriptures effectively. He debated opponents of Christianity forcefully and effectively. It didn't take long for him to be noticed by Priscilla and Aquila.

The couple quickly realized that Apollos did not have the whole story. His preaching was based on the Old Testament and John the Baptist's message. He was probably urging people to repent and prepare for the coming Messiah. Priscilla and Aquila took him home with them and brought him up to date on all that had happened. As they told him of the life of Jesus, his death and resurrection, and the coming of the Holy Spirit, Apollos must have seen Scripture after Scripture become clear. He was filled with new energy and boldness now that he knew the complete gospel.

Apollos next decided to travel to Achaia. His friends in Ephesus were able to send along a glowing letter of introduction. He quickly became the verbal champion of the Christians in Corinth, debating the opponents of the gospel in public. As often happens, Apollos's abilities eventually created a problem. Some of the Corinthians began to follow Apollos rather than his message. Paul had to confront the Corinthians about their divisiveness. They had been forming little groups named after their favorite preacher. Apollos left Corinth and hesitated to return. Paul wrote warmly of Apollos as a fellow minister who had "watered" the seeds of the gospel that Paul had planted in Corinth. Paul last mentions Apollos briefly to Titus. Apollos was still a traveling representative of the gospel who deserved Titus's help.

Although his natural abilities could have made him proud, Apollos proved himself willing to learn. God used Priscilla and Aquila, fresh from months of learning from Paul, to give Apollos the complete gospel. Because Apollos did not hesitate to be a student, he became an even better teacher. How much does your willingness to learn affect God's efforts to help you become all he wants you to be?

Strengths and accomplishments
- A gifted and persuasive preacher and apologist in the early church
- Willing to be taught
- One of the possible candidates for the unknown author of Hebrews

Lessons from his life
- Effective communication of the gospel includes an accurate message delivered with God's power
- A clear verbal defense of the gospel can be a real encouragement to believers, while convincing unbelievers of its truth

Vital statistics
- Where: From Alexandria in Egypt
- Occupations: Traveling preacher, apologist
- Contemporaries: Priscilla, Aquila, Paul

Key verses
"He had been taught the way of the Lord and talked to others with great enthusiasm and accuracy about Jesus. However, he knew only about John's baptism. When Priscilla and Aquila heard him preaching boldly in the synagogue, they took him aside and explained the way of God more accurately" (Acts 18:25, 26).

Apollos's story is told in Acts 18:24—19:1. He is also mentioned in 1 Corinthians 1:12; 3:4–6, 22; 4:1, 6; 16:12; Titus 3:13.

18:22 This verse marks the end of Paul's second missionary journey and the beginning of the third, which lasted from A.D. 53 to 57. Leaving the church at Antioch (his home base), Paul headed toward Ephesus, but along the way he revisited the churches in Galatia and Phrygia (18:23). The heart of this trip was a lengthy stay (two to three years) in Ephesus. Before returning to Jerusalem, he also visited believers in Macedonia and Greece.

18:24-26 Apollos had heard only what John the Baptist had said about Jesus (see Luke 3:1-18), so his message was not the complete story. John focused on repentance from sin, the first step. But the whole message is to repent from sin and then believe in Christ. Apollos did not know about Jesus' life, crucifixion, and resurrection. Nor did he know about the coming of the Holy Spirit. Priscilla and Aquila explained the way of salvation to him.

[27]Apollos had been thinking about going to Achaia, and the Christians in Ephesus 18:27
encouraged him in this. They wrote to the believers in Achaia, asking them to welcome 2 Cor 3:1
him. When he arrived there, he proved to be of great benefit to those who, by God's
grace, had believed. [28]He refuted all the Jews with powerful arguments in public debate.
Using the Scriptures, he explained to them, "The Messiah you are looking for is Jesus." 18:28 Acts 9:22

4. Third missionary journey

19 While Apollos was in Corinth, Paul traveled through the interior provinces. 19:1
Finally, he came to Ephesus, where he found several believers.* [2]"Did you receive Acts 18:24
the Holy Spirit when you believed?" he asked them. 19:2 John 7:39; 20:22
"No," they replied, "we don't know what you mean. We haven't even heard that there Acts 8:16
is a Holy Spirit."
[3]"Then what baptism did you experience?" he asked. 19:3
And they replied, "The baptism of John." Acts 18:25
[4]Paul said, "John's baptism was to demonstrate a desire to turn from sin and turn to 19:4 Mark 1:4
God. John himself told the people to believe in Jesus, the one John said would come later." 19:5
[5]As soon as they heard this, they were baptized in the name of the Lord Jesus. [6]Then Acts 8:12, 16; 10:48
when Paul laid his hands on them, the Holy Spirit came on them, and they spoke in other Gal 3:27
tongues and prophesied. [7]There were about twelve men in all. 19:6 Acts 2:4; 10:44, 46

Paul Ministers in Ephesus

[8]Then Paul went to the synagogue and preached boldly for the next three months, 19:8
arguing persuasively about the Kingdom of God. [9]But some rejected his message and Acts 28:23

19:1 Greek *disciples;* also in 19:9, 30.

18:27, 28 Apollos was from Alexandria in Egypt, the second most important city in the Roman Empire, and the home of a great university. There was a thriving Jewish population in Alexandria. Apollos was a scholar, orator, and debater; and after his knowledge about Christ was made more complete, God greatly used these gifts to strengthen and encourage the church. Reason is a powerful tool in the right hands and in the right situation. Apollos used the gift of reason to convince many in Greece of the truth of the Good News. You don't have to turn off your mind when you turn to Christ. If you have an ability in logic or debate, use it to bring others to God.

18:27, 28 Not all the work of a minister or missionary is drudgery, setback, or suffering. Chapter 18 is triumphant, showing victories in key cities and the addition of exciting new leaders such as Priscilla, Aquila, and Apollos to the church. Rejoice in the victories Christ brings, and don't let the hazards create a negative mind-set.

19:1 Ephesus was the capital and leading business center of the Roman province of Asia (part of present-day Turkey). A hub of sea and land transportation, it ranked with Antioch in Syria and Alexandria in Egypt as one of the great cities on the Mediterranean Sea. Paul stayed in Ephesus for a little over two years. There he wrote his first letter to the Corinthians to counter several problems the church in Corinth was facing. Later, while imprisoned in Rome, Paul wrote a letter to the Ephesian church (the book of Ephesians).

19:2-4 John's baptism was a sign of repentance from sin only, not a sign of new life in Christ. Like Apollos (18:24-26), these Ephesian believers needed further instruction about the message and ministry of Jesus Christ. They believed in Jesus as the Messiah, but they did not understand the significance of the work of the Holy Spirit. Becoming a Christian involves turning from sin (repentance) and turning to Christ (faith). These "believers" were incomplete.

In the book of Acts, believers received the Holy Spirit in a variety of ways. Usually the Holy Spirit would fill a person as soon as he or she professed faith in Christ. Here that filling happened later because these disciples' knowledge was incomplete. God was confirming to these believers, who did not initially know about the Holy Spirit, that they were a part of the church. The Holy Spirit's filling endorsed them as believers.

Pentecost was the formal outpouring of the Holy Spirit on the church. The other outpourings in the book of Acts were God's way of uniting new believers to the church. The mark of the true church is not merely right doctrine but right actions, the true evidence of the Holy Spirit's work.

19:6 When Paul laid his hands on these disciples, they received the Holy Spirit, just as the disciples did at Pentecost, and there were outward, visible signs of the Holy Spirit's presence. This also happened when the Holy Spirit came on the Gentiles (non-Jews, see 10:45-47).

19:9 Paul spoke in a lecture hall at this school. Such halls were used in the morning for teaching philosophy, but they were empty during the hot part of the day (about 11 A.M. to 4 P.M.). Because many people did not work during those hours, they would come to hear Paul's preaching.

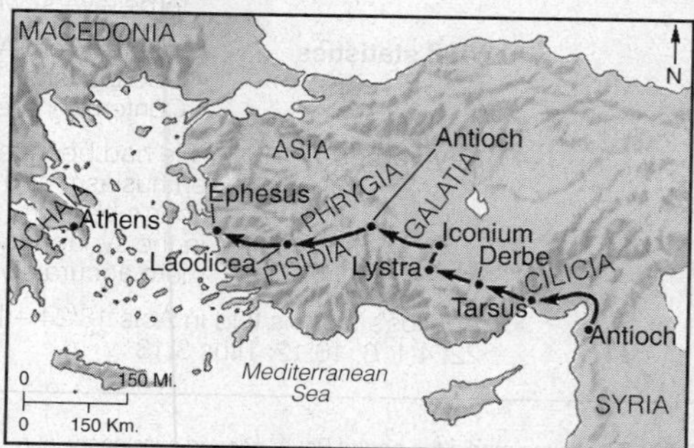

PAUL TAKES A THIRD JOURNEY What prompted Paul's third journey may have been the need to correct any misunderstandings in the churches Paul had planted. So he hurried north, then west, returning to many of the cities he had previously visited. This time, however, he stayed on a more direct westward route toward Ephesus.

19:10 Acts 20:31
19:11 Mark 16:20; Acts 18:3
19:12 Acts 5:15-16
19:13 Matt 12:27; Mark 9:38; Luke 9:49
19:15 Mark 1:24, 34; Luke 4:34, 41
19:17 Acts 5:5, 11
19:19 Deut 18:10-14
19:20 Acts 6:7; 12:24
19:21 Acts 23:11; Rom 15:25; 1 Cor 16:5
19:22 Rom 16:23; 2 Tim 4:20
19:23 2 Cor 1:8
19:24 Acts 16:16
19:26 Ps 115:4; Isa 44:10-20; Jer 10:3-5; Acts 17:29; 1 Cor 8:4

publicly spoke against the Way, so Paul left the synagogue and took the believers with
him. Then he began preaching daily at the lecture hall of Tyrannus. 10 This went on for
the next two years, so that people throughout the province of Asia—both Jews and
Greeks—heard the Lord's message.
11 God gave Paul the power to do unusual miracles, 12 so that even when handkerchiefs
or cloths that had touched his skin were placed on sick people, they were healed of their
diseases, and any evil spirits within them came out.
13 A team of Jews who were traveling from town to town casting out evil spirits tried
to use the name of the Lord Jesus. The incantation they used was this: "I command you
by Jesus, whom Paul preaches, to come out!" 14 Seven sons of Sceva, a leading priest,
were doing this. 15 But when they tried it on a man possessed by an evil spirit, the spirit
replied, "I know Jesus, and I know Paul. But who are you?" 16 And he leaped on them
and attacked them with such violence that they fled from the house, naked and badly
injured.
17 The story of what happened spread quickly all through Ephesus, to Jews and Greeks
alike. A solemn fear descended on the city, and the name of the Lord Jesus was greatly
honored. 18 Many who became believers confessed their sinful practices. 19 A number of
them who had been practicing magic brought their incantation books and burned them
at a public bonfire. The value of the books was several million dollars.* 20 So the message
about the Lord spread widely and had a powerful effect.

The Riot in Ephesus

21 Afterward Paul felt impelled by the Holy Spirit* to go over to Macedonia and Achaia
before returning to Jerusalem. "And after that," he said, "I must go on to Rome!" 22 He
sent his two assistants, Timothy and Erastus, on ahead to Macedonia while he stayed
awhile longer in the province of Asia.
23 But about that time, serious trouble developed in Ephesus concerning the Way. 24 It
began with Demetrius, a silversmith who had a large business manufacturing silver
shrines of the Greek goddess Artemis.* He kept many craftsmen busy. 25 He called the
craftsmen together, along with others employed in related trades, and addressed them as
follows:
"Gentlemen, you know that our wealth comes from this business. 26 As you have seen
and heard, this man Paul has persuaded many people that handmade gods aren't gods at

19:19 Greek *50,000 pieces of silver,* each of which was the equivalent of a day's wage. **19:21** Or *purposed in his spirit.* **19:24** *Artemis* is otherwise known as Diana.

19:10 "The province of Asia" refers to Asia Minor or modern-day Turkey. During this time, Paul and his co-workers spread the Good News throughout the land.

19:13 These Jews traveled from town to town making a living by claiming to heal people and drive out demons. Often they would recite a whole list of names in their incantation to be sure of including the right deity. Here they were trying to use Jesus' name in an effort to match Paul's power.

19:13-16 Many Ephesians engaged in exorcism and occult practices for profit (see 19:18, 19). The sons of Sceva were impressed by Paul, whose power to drive out demons came from God's Holy Spirit, not from witchcraft, and was obviously more powerful than theirs. They discovered, however, that no one can control or duplicate God's power. These men were calling on the name of Jesus without knowing him personally. The power to change people comes from Christ. It cannot be tapped by reciting his name like a magic charm. God works his power only through those he chooses.

19:18, 19 Ephesus was a center for black magic and other occult practices. The people cooked up magical formulas to give them wealth, happiness, and success in marriage. Superstition and sorcery were commonplace. God clearly forbids such practices (Deuteronomy 18:9-13). You cannot be a believer and hold on to the occult, black magic, or sorcery. Once you begin to dabble in these areas, it is extremely easy to become obsessed by them because Satan is very powerful. But God's power is even greater (1 John 4:4; Revelation 20:10). If you are mixed up in the occult, learn a lesson from the Ephesians and get rid of anything that could keep you trapped in such practices.

19:21 Why did Paul say he had to go to Rome? Wherever he went, he could see Rome's influence. Paul wanted to take the message of Christ to the world's center of influence and power.

19:22 Paul later wrote letters to Timothy: the books of 1 and 2 Timothy. Erastus was a committed follower of Christ who was not only Paul's helpful assistant but also Corinth's city treasurer (see Romans 16:23).

19:23 "The Way" refers to those who followed the way of Christ—the Christians.

19:24 Artemis was a goddess of fertility. She was represented by a carved female figure with many breasts. A large statue of her (which was said to have come from heaven, 19:35) was in the great temple at Ephesus. That temple was one of the wonders of the ancient world. The festival of Artemis involved wild orgies and carousing. Obviously the religious and commercial life of Ephesus reflected the city's worship of this pagan deity.

19:25-27 When Paul preached in Ephesus, Demetrius and his fellow craftsmen did not quarrel with his doctrine. Their anger boiled because his preaching threatened their profits. They made silver shrines of the Ephesian goddess Artemis. The craftsmen knew that if people started believing in God and discarding the idols, their livelihood would suffer.

all. And this is happening not only here in Ephesus but throughout the entire province!
[27]Of course, I'm not just talking about the loss of public respect for our business. I'm
also concerned that the temple of the great goddess Artemis will lose its influence and
that Artemis—this magnificent goddess worshiped throughout the province of Asia and
all around the world—will be robbed of her prestige!"
[28]At this their anger boiled, and they began shouting, "Great is Artemis of the **19:28** Acts 18:19
Ephesians!" [29]A crowd began to gather, and soon the city was filled with confusion. **19:29** Acts 20:4; Rom 16:23; 1 Cor 1:14; Col 4:10; Phlm 1:24
Everyone rushed to the amphitheater, dragging along Gaius and Aristarchus, who were
Paul's traveling companions from Macedonia. [30]Paul wanted to go in, but the believers
wouldn't let him. [31]Some of the officials of the province, friends of Paul, also sent a
message to him, begging him not to risk his life by entering the amphitheater.
[32]Inside, the people were all shouting, some one thing and some another. Everything **19:32** Acts 21:34
was in confusion. In fact, most of them didn't even know why they were there.
[33]Alexander was thrust forward by some of the Jews, who encouraged him to explain **19:33** 1 Tim 1:20
the situation. He motioned for silence and tried to speak in defense. [34]But when the
crowd realized he was a Jew, they started shouting again and kept it up for two hours:
"Great is Artemis of the Ephesians! Great is Artemis of the Ephesians!"
[35]At last the mayor was able to quiet them down enough to speak. "Citizens of
Ephesus," he said. "Everyone knows that Ephesus is the official guardian of the temple of
the great Artemis, whose image fell down to us from heaven. [36]Since this is an indisput-
able fact, you shouldn't be disturbed, no matter what is said. Don't do anything rash. [37]You
have brought these men here, but they have stolen nothing from the temple and have not **19:37** Rom 2:22
spoken against our goddess. [38]If Demetrius and the craftsmen have a case against them, **19:38** Acts 13:7
the courts are in session and the judges can take the case at once. Let them go through legal
channels. [39]And if there are complaints about other matters, they can be settled in a legal
assembly. [40]I am afraid we are in danger of being charged with rioting by the Roman
government, since there is no cause for all this commotion. And if Rome demands an
explanation, we won't know what to say." [41]Then he dismissed them, and they dispersed.

Paul Goes to Macedonia and Greece

20 When it was all over, Paul sent for the believers* and encouraged them. Then he **20:1** Acts 16:9-10
said good-bye and left for Macedonia. [2]Along the way, he encouraged the
believers in all the towns he passed through. Then he traveled down to Greece, [3]where **20:3** Acts 9:23-24; 23:12; 2 Cor 11:26
he stayed for three months. He was preparing to sail back to Syria when he discovered
a plot by some Jews against his life, so he decided to return through Macedonia.

20:1 Greek *disciples.*

19:27 Demetrius's strategy for stirring up a riot was to appeal to his fellow workmen's love of money and then to encourage them to hide their greed behind the mask of patriotism and religious loyalty. The rioters couldn't see the selfish motives for their rioting; instead, they saw themselves as heroes for the sake of their land and beliefs.

19:29 Paul often sought others to help him in his work. On this occasion, his traveling companions were Aristarchus (who would accompany him on other journeys; see 20:3, 4 and 27:1, 2), and Gaius (probably not the same Gaius mentioned in Romans 16:23 and 1 Corinthians 1:14).

19:30 Paul wanted to go to the amphitheater to defend his companions, but the other believers wouldn't let him go, fearing for his safety.

19:31 These officials of the province were government officials, responsible for the religious and political order of the region. Paul's message had reached all levels of society, crossing all social barriers and giving Paul friends in high places.

19:33, 34 The mob had become anti-Jewish as well as anti-Christian. This Alexander may have been pushed forward by the Jews as a spokesman to explain that the Jews had no part in the Christian community and thus were not involved in the economic problem of the silversmiths.

19:40 The city of Ephesus was under the domination of the Roman Empire. The main responsibility of the local city leaders was simply to maintain peace and order. If they failed to control the people, Rome would remove the appointed officials from office. The entire town could also be put under martial law, taking away many civic freedoms.

19:41 The riot in Ephesus convinced Paul that it was time to move on. But it also showed that the law still provided some protection for Christians as they challenged the worship of the goddess Artemis and the most idolatrous religion in Asia.

20:1-3 While in Greece, Paul spent much of his time in Corinth. From there he wrote the letter to the Romans. Although Paul had not yet been to Rome, believers had already started a church there (2:10; 18:2). Paul wrote to tell the church that he planned to visit the Roman believers. The letter to the Romans is a theological essay on the meaning of faith and salvation, an explanation of the relation between Jews and Gentiles in Christ, and a list of practical guidelines for the church.

20:4 Acts 16:1; 19:29; 21:29 Eph 6:21 2 Tim 4:20 Titus 3:12
20:6 Acts 16:8, 10

4Several men were traveling with him. They were Sopater of Berea, the son of
Pyrrhus; Aristarchus and Secundus, from Thessalonica; Gaius, from Derbe; Timothy;
and Tychicus and Trophimus, who were from the province of Asia. 5They went ahead
and waited for us at Troas. 6As soon as the Passover season* ended, we boarded a ship
at Philippi in Macedonia and five days later arrived in Troas, where we stayed a week.

Paul's Final Visit to Troas

20:7 Acts 2:42, 46 1 Cor 16:2 Rev 1:10
20:10 1 Kgs 17:21 2 Kgs 4:34 Matt 9:23-24

7On the first day of the week, we gathered to observe the Lord's Supper.* Paul was
preaching; and since he was leaving the next day, he talked until midnight. 8The upstairs
room where we met was lighted with many flickering lamps. 9As Paul spoke on and on,
a young man named Eutychus, sitting on the windowsill, became very drowsy. Finally,
he sank into a deep sleep and fell three stories to his death below. 10Paul went down, bent
over him, and took him into his arms. "Don't worry," he said, "he's alive!" 11Then they
all went back upstairs and ate the Lord's Supper together.* And Paul continued talking
to them until dawn; then he left. 12Meanwhile, the young man was taken home unhurt,
and everyone was greatly relieved.

Paul Meets the Ephesian Elders

20:15 2 Tim 4:20
20:18 Acts 18:19-21; 19:1-41

13Paul went by land to Assos, where he had arranged for us to join him, and we went on
ahead by ship. 14He joined us there and we sailed together to Mitylene. 15The next day
we passed the island of Kios. The following day, we crossed to the island of Samos. And
a day later we arrived at Miletus.
16Paul had decided against stopping at Ephesus this time because he didn't want to
spend further time in the province of Asia. He was hurrying to get to Jerusalem, if
possible, for the Festival of Pentecost. 17But when we landed at Miletus, he sent a
message to the elders of the church at Ephesus, asking them to come down to meet him.
18When they arrived he declared, "You know that from the day I set foot in the

20:6 Greek *the days of unleavened bread.* **20:7** Greek *to break bread.* **20:11** Greek *broke the bread.*

20:4 These men who were traveling with Paul represented churches that Paul had started in Asia. Each man was carrying an offering from his home church to be given to the believers in Jerusalem. By having each man deliver the gift, the gifts had a personal touch, and the unity of the believers was strengthened. This was also an effective way to teach the church about giving, because the men were able to report back to their churches the way God was working through their giving. Paul discussed this gift in one of his letters to the Corinthian church (see 2 Corinthians 8:1-21).

20:5, 6 The use of *us* and *we* shows that this is where Luke again joins the group. The last *we* was in chapter 16.

20:6 Jewish believers celebrated the Passover (which was immediately followed by the Festival of Unleavened Bread) according to Moses' instructions (see Exodus 12:43-51) even if they couldn't be at Jerusalem for the occasion.

20:8, 9 The "flickering lamps" were candles in lanterns. The combination of the heat from the candles and the number of people gathered in the upstairs room probably made the room very warm. This no doubt helped Eutychus fall asleep, as well as the fact that Paul spoke for a long time. Eutychus was probably between the ages of 8 to14 years old (the age of a "young man").

20:16 Paul had missed attending the Passover in Jerusalem, so he was especially interested in arriving on time for Pentecost, which was 50 days after Passover. He was carrying with him gifts for the Jerusalem believers from churches in Asia and Greece (see Romans 15:25, 26; 1 Corinthians 16:1ff; 2 Corinthians 8–9). The Jerusalem church was experiencing difficult times. Paul may have been anxious to deliver this gift to the believers at Pentecost because it was a day of celebration and thanksgiving to God for his provision.

20:18-21 The way of the believer is not an easy road; being a Christian does not solve or remove all problems. Paul served humbly and "with tears," but he never quit, never gave up. The message of salvation was so important that he never missed an opportunity to share it. And although he preached his message in different ways to fit different audiences, the message remained the same: Turn away from sin and turn to Christ by faith. The Christian life will have its rough times, its tears, and its sorrows, as well as its joys, but we should always be ready to tell others what good things God has done for us. His blessings far outweigh life's difficulties.

THROUGH MACEDONIA AND ACHAIA
A riot in Ephesus sent Paul to Troas, then through Macedonia to the region of Achaia. In Achaia he went to Corinth to deal with problems there. Paul had planned to sail from Corinth straight to Antioch in Syria, but a plot against his life was discovered. So he retraced his steps through Macedonia.

province of Asia until now 19I have done the Lord's work humbly—yes, and with tears.
I have endured the trials that came to me from the plots of the Jews. 20Yet I never shrank
from telling you the truth, either publicly or in your homes. 21I have had one message
for Jews and Gentiles alike—the necessity of turning from sin and turning to God, and
of faith in our Lord Jesus.
22"And now I am going to Jerusalem, drawn there irresistibly by the Holy Spirit,* not
knowing what awaits me, 23except that the Holy Spirit has told me in city after city that
jail and suffering lie ahead. 24But my life is worth nothing unless I use it for doing the
work assigned me by the Lord Jesus—the work of telling others the Good News about
God's wonderful kindness and love.
25"And now I know that none of you to whom I have preached the Kingdom will ever
see me again. 26Let me say plainly that I have been faithful. No one's damnation can be
blamed on me,* 27for I didn't shrink from declaring all that God wants for you.
28"And now beware! Be sure that you feed and shepherd God's flock—his church,
purchased with his blood—over whom the Holy Spirit has appointed you as elders.*
29I know full well that false teachers, like vicious wolves, will come in among you after
I leave, not sparing the flock. 30Even some of you will distort the truth in order to draw
a following. 31Watch out! Remember the three years I was with you—my constant watch
and care over you night and day, and my many tears for you.
32"And now I entrust you to God and the word of his grace—his message that is able
to build you up and give you an inheritance with all those he has set apart for himself.
33"I have never coveted anyone's money or fine clothing. 34You know that these
hands of mine have worked to pay my own way, and I have even supplied the needs of
those who were with me. 35And I have been a constant example of how you can help the
poor by working hard. You should remember the words of the Lord Jesus: 'It is more
blessed to give than to receive.'"
36When he had finished speaking, he knelt and prayed with them. 37They wept aloud
as they embraced him in farewell, 38sad most of all because he had said that they would
never see him again. Then they accompanied him down to the ship.

20:22 Or *by my spirit,* or *by an inner compulsion;* Greek reads *by the spirit.* **20:26** Greek *I am innocent of the blood of all.* **20:28** Greek *overseers.*

20:21 Acts 2:38; 26:18
20:22 Acts 19:21
20:23 Acts 9:16; 21:4, 11
20:24 Acts 21:13; 2 Tim 4:7
20:26 Acts 18:6
20:28 Ps 74:2; John 21:15-17; 1 Pet 5:2
20:29 Matt 7:15; John 10:12
20:30 1 Jn 2:19
20:31 Acts 19:10
20:32 Deut 33:3-4; Acts 26:18; Eph 1:18; Col 1:12; 3:24; 1 Pet 1:4
20:33 1 Sam 12:3; 1 Cor 9:11; 2 Cor 7:2; 11:9; 12:14-17
20:34 Acts 18:3; 1 Cor 4:12; 1 Thes 2:9
20:35 1 Thes 4:11
20:36 Acts 21:5

PAUL TRAVELS FROM TROAS TO MILETUS
From Troas, Paul traveled overland to Assos, then boarded a ship to Mitylene and Samos on its way to Miletus. He summoned the elders of the Ephesian church to say farewell to them, because he knew he would probably not see them again.

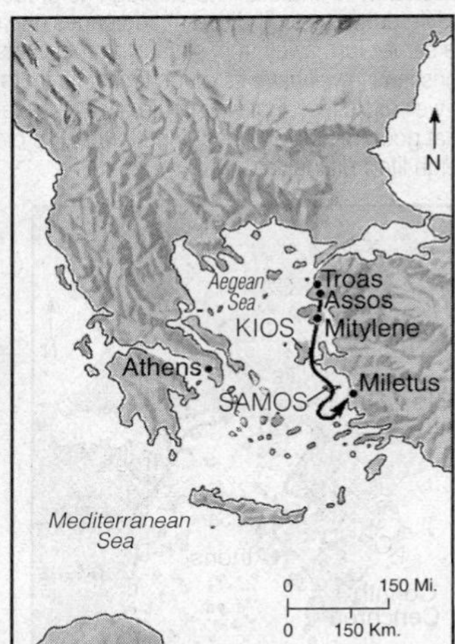

20:23 The Holy Spirit showed Paul that he would be imprisoned and experience suffering. Even knowing this, Paul did not shrink from fulfilling his mission. His strong character was a good example to the Ephesian elders, some of whom would also suffer for Christ.

20:24 We often feel that life is a failure unless we're getting a lot out of it: recognition, fun, money, success. But Paul considered life worth *nothing* unless he used it for God's work. What he put *into* life was far more important than what he got out. Which is more important to you—what you get out of life, or what you put into it?

20:24 Single-mindedness is a quality needed by anyone who wishes to do God's work. Paul was a single-minded person, and the most important goal of his life was to tell others about Christ (Philippians 3:7-13). It is no wonder that Paul was the greatest missionary who ever lived. God is looking for more men and women who will focus on that one great task God has given them to do.

20:31, 36-38 Paul's relationship with these believers is a beautiful example of Christian fellowship. He had cared for them and loved them, even cried over their needs. They responded with love and care for him and sorrow over his leaving. They had prayed together and comforted one another. Like Paul, you can build strong relationships with other Christians by sharing, caring, sorrowing, rejoicing, and praying with them. You will gather others around you only by giving yourself away to them.

20:33 Paul was satisfied with whatever he had, wherever he was, as long as he could do God's work. Examine your attitudes toward wealth and comfort. If you focus more on what you don't have than on what you do have, it's time to reexamine your priorities and put God's work back in first place.

20:34 Paul was a tentmaker, and he supported himself with this trade. Paul did not work to become rich but to be free from being dependent on anyone. He supported himself as well as others who traveled with him (he mentions this in some of his letters; see Philippians 4:11-13; 1 Thessalonians 2:9).

20:35 These words of Jesus are not recorded in the Gospels. Obviously, not all of Jesus' words were written down (John 21:25); this saying may have been passed on orally through the apostles.

Paul's Journey to Jerusalem

21 After saying farewell to the Ephesian elders, we sailed straight to the island of
Cos. The next day we reached Rhodes and then went to Patara. 2There we
boarded a ship sailing for the Syrian province of Phoenicia. 3We sighted the island of
Cyprus, passed it on our left, and landed at the harbor of Tyre, in Syria, where the ship
was to unload. 4We went ashore, found the local believers,* and stayed with them a
week. These disciples prophesied through the Holy Spirit that Paul should not go on
to Jerusalem. 5When we returned to the ship at the end of the week, the entire
congregation, including wives and children, came down to the shore with us. There
we knelt, prayed, 6and said our farewells. Then we went aboard, and they returned
home.

7The next stop after leaving Tyre was Ptolemais, where we greeted the believers* but
stayed only one day. 8Then we went on to Caesarea and stayed at the home of Philip the
Evangelist, one of the seven men who had been chosen to distribute food. 9He had four
unmarried daughters who had the gift of prophecy.

10During our stay of several days, a man named Agabus, who also had the gift of
prophecy, arrived from Judea. 11When he visited us, he took Paul's belt and bound his
own feet and hands with it. Then he said, "The Holy Spirit declares, 'So shall the owner
of this belt be bound by the Jewish leaders in Jerusalem and turned over to the Romans.'"
12When we heard this, we who were traveling with him, as well as the local believers,
begged Paul not to go on to Jerusalem.

21:1 Acts 16:10
21:4 Acts 20:23; 21:11
21:5 Acts 20:36
21:8 Acts 6:5; 8:26, 40; Eph 4:11; 2 Tim 4:5
21:9 Joel 2:28; Acts 2:17
21:10 Acts 11:28
21:11 Acts 20:23; 21:33

21:4 Greek *disciples;* also in 21:16. **21:7** Greek *brothers;* also in 21:17.

PAUL RETURNS TO JERUSALEM
The ship sailed from Miletus to Cos, Rhodes, and Patara. Paul and his companions then boarded a cargo ship bound for Phoenicia. They passed Cyprus and landed at Tyre, then Ptolemais, and finally Caesarea, where Paul disembarked and returned by land to Jerusalem.

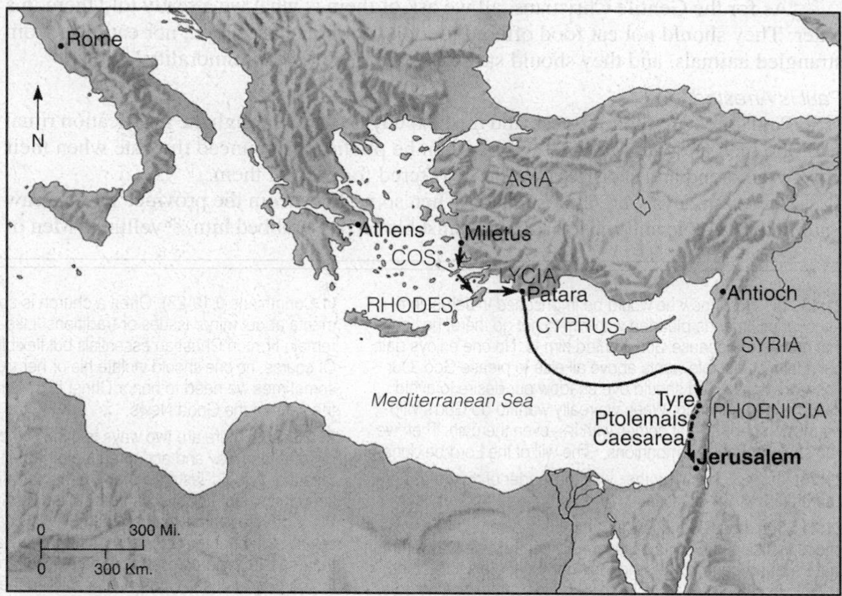

21:4 Did Paul disobey the Holy Spirit by going to Jerusalem? No. More likely, the Holy Spirit warned these believers about the suffering that Paul would face in Jerusalem. They drew the conclusion that he should not go there because of that danger. This is supported by 21:10-12, where the local believers, after hearing that Paul would be turned over to the Romans, begged him to turn back.

21:8 This is the Philip mentioned in 6:5 and 8:26-40.

21:9 Obviously the gift of prophecy was given to both men and women. Women actively participated in God's work (2:17; Philippians 4:3). Other women who prophesied include Miriam (Exodus 15:20), Deborah (Judges 4:4), Huldah (2 Kings 22:14), Isaiah's wife (Isaiah 8:3), and Anna (Luke 2:36-38).

21:10 Fifteen years earlier, Agabus had predicted the famine in Jerusalem (11:27-29).

13 But he said, "Why all this weeping? You are breaking my heart! For I am ready not only to be jailed at Jerusalem but also to die for the sake of the Lord Jesus." 14 When it was clear that we couldn't persuade him, we gave up and said, "The will of the Lord be done."

5. Paul on trial

Paul Arrives at Jerusalem

15 Shortly afterward we packed our things and left for Jerusalem. 16 Some believers from Caesarea accompanied us, and they took us to the home of Mnason, a man originally from Cyprus and one of the early disciples. 17 All the believers in Jerusalem welcomed us cordially.

18 The next day Paul went in with us to meet with James, and all the elders of the Jerusalem church were present. 19 After greetings were exchanged, Paul gave a detailed account of the things God had accomplished among the Gentiles through his ministry.

20 After hearing this, they praised God. But then they said, "You know, dear brother, how many thousands of Jews have also believed, and they all take the law of Moses very seriously. 21 Our Jewish Christians here at Jerusalem have been told that you are teaching all the Jews living in the Gentile world to turn their backs on the laws of Moses. They say that you teach people not to circumcise their children or follow other Jewish customs. 22 Now what can be done? For they will certainly hear that you have come.

23 "Here's our suggestion. We have four men here who have taken a vow and are preparing to shave their heads. 24 Go with them to the Temple and join them in the purification ceremony, and pay for them to have their heads shaved. Then everyone will know that the rumors are all false and that you yourself observe the Jewish laws.

25 "As for the Gentile Christians, all we ask of them is what we already told them in a letter: They should not eat food offered to idols, nor consume blood, nor eat meat from strangled animals, and they should stay away from all sexual immorality."

Paul Is Arrested

26 So Paul agreed to their request, and the next day he went through the purification ritual with the men and went to the Temple. Then he publicly announced the date when their vows would end and sacrifices would be offered for each of them.

27 The seven days were almost ended when some Jews from the province of Asia saw Paul in the Temple and roused a mob against him. They grabbed him, 28 yelling, "Men of

21:13 Acts 20:24
21:14 Matt 26:39
21:19 Acts 15:12
21:20 Acts 15:1, 5; Gal 3:10-11
21:21 Acts 16:3; Gal 2:3
21:23 Acts 18:18
21:24 Num 6:5, 13-20
21:25 Acts 15:19-29
21:26 Num 6:1-21; 1 Cor 9:20
21:27 Acts 24:18; 26:21
21:28 Matt 24:15; Acts 6:13; 24:5-6

21:13, 14 Paul knew he would be imprisoned in Jerusalem. Although his friends pleaded with him to not go there, he knew that he had to because God wanted him to. No one enjoys pain, but a faithful disciple wants above all else to please God. Our desire to please God should overshadow our desire to avoid hardship and suffering. When we really want to do God's will, we must accept all that comes with it—even the pain. Then we can say with Paul's companions, "The will of the Lord be done."

21:18 James, Jesus' brother, was the leader of the Jerusalem church (15:13-21; Galatians 1:19; 2:9).

21:21 The Jerusalem council (Acts 15) had settled the issue of circumcision of Gentile believers. Evidently there was a rumor that Paul had gone far beyond their decision, even forbidding Jews to circumcise their children. This, of course, was not true, and so Paul willingly submitted to Jewish custom to show that he was not working against the council's decision and that he was still Jewish in his life-style. Sometimes we must go the second mile to avoid offending others, especially when doing so would hinder God's work.

21:23, 24 Because Paul was going to participate with the four men in the vow (apparently he was asked to pay for some of the required expenses), he would need to take part in the purification ceremony for entering the Temple (Numbers 6:9-20). Paul submitted himself to this Jewish custom to keep peace in the Jerusalem church. Although Paul was a man of strong convictions, he was willing to compromise on nonessential points, becoming all things to all people so that he might save some (1 Corinthians 9:19-23). Often a church is split over disagreements about minor issues or traditions. Like Paul, we should remain firm on Christian essentials but flexible on nonessentials. Of course, no one should violate his or her true convictions, but sometimes we need to honor Christ by mutual submission for the sake of the Good News.

21:23, 24 There are two ways to think of the Jewish laws. Paul rejected one way and accepted the other. (1) Paul rejected the idea that the Old Testament laws bring salvation to those who keep them. Our salvation is freely given by God's gracious act. We receive salvation through faith. The laws are of no value for salvation except to show us our sin. (2) Paul accepted the view that the Old Testament laws prepare us for and teach us about the coming of Jesus Christ. Christ fulfilled the law and released us from its burden of guilt. But the law still teaches us many valuable principles and gives us guidelines for grateful living. Paul was not observing the laws in order to be saved. He was simply keeping the laws as custom to avoid offending those he wished to reach with the Good News (see Romans 3:21-31; 7:4-6; 13:9, 10). For more on the law, see Galatians 3:23-29; 4:21-31, and the chart in Galatians 4.

21:28, 29 These Jews knew how effective Paul's work had been in Asia. Their strategy was to discredit Paul so that his work would be weakened. Be alert when you hear accusations against God's workers. Someone may be trying to discredit them or to hinder their work. Keep an open mind and pray for the workers. They will be strengthened by your support.

Israel! Help! This is the man who teaches against our people and tells everybody to
disobey the Jewish laws. He speaks against the Temple—and he even defiles it by bringing
21:29 Acts 20:4 Gentiles in!" 29(For earlier that day they had seen him in the city with Trophimus, a Gentile
2 Tim 4:20 from Ephesus,* and they assumed Paul had taken him into the Temple.)
30The whole population of the city was rocked by these accusations, and a great riot
followed. Paul was dragged out of the Temple, and immediately the gates were closed
behind him. 31As they were trying to kill him, word reached the commander of the
21:32 Acts 23:27 Roman regiment that all Jerusalem was in an uproar. 32He immediately called out his
soldiers and officers and ran down among the crowd. When the mob saw the commander
21:33 Acts 20:23 and the troops coming, they stopped beating Paul. 33The commander arrested him and
Eph 6:20 ordered him bound with two chains. Then he asked the crowd who he was and what he
had done. 34Some shouted one thing and some another. He couldn't find out the truth in
21:36 Luke 23:18 all the uproar and confusion, so he ordered Paul to be taken to the fortress. 35As they
John 19:15 Acts 22:22 reached the stairs, the mob grew so violent the soldiers had to lift Paul to their shoulders
to protect him. 36And the crowd followed behind shouting, "Kill him, kill him!"

Paul Speaks to the Crowd

37As Paul was about to be taken inside, he said to the commander, "May I have a word
with you?"
"Do you know Greek?" the commander asked, surprised. 38"Aren't you the Egyptian
who led a rebellion some time ago and took four thousand members of the Assassins out
into the desert?"
21:39 Acts 9:11; 22:3 39"No," Paul replied, "I am a Jew from Tarsus in Cilicia, which is an important city.
21:40 Acts 26:14 Please, let me talk to these people." 40The commander agreed, so Paul stood on the stairs
and motioned to the people to be quiet. Soon a deep silence enveloped the crowd, and
he addressed them in their own language, Aramaic.*

22:1 Acts 7:2 **22** "Brothers and esteemed fathers," Paul said, "listen to me as I offer my defense."
2When they heard him speaking in their own language,* the silence was even
22:3-21 //Acts 9:1-29; 26:9-18 greater. 3"I am a Jew, born in Tarsus, a city in Cilicia, and I was brought up and educated
here in Jerusalem under Gamaliel. At his feet I learned to follow our Jewish laws and
22:3 Acts 5:34-40 Rom 10:2 customs very carefully. I became very zealous to honor God in everything I did, just as
all of you are today. 4And I persecuted the followers of the Way, hounding some to death,
22:4 Acts 8:3; 9:2 binding and delivering both men and women to prison. 5The high priest and the whole
council of leaders can testify that this is so. For I received letters from them to our Jewish
brothers in Damascus, authorizing me to bring the Christians from there to Jerusalem, in
chains, to be punished.
22:6 Acts 9:2-8; 26:12-13 6"As I was on the road, nearing Damascus, about noon a very bright light from heaven

21:29 Greek *Trophimus, the Ephesian.* **21:40** Or *Hebrew.* **22:2** Greek *in Aramaic.*

21:31 Because Jerusalem was under Roman control, an uproar in the city would be investigated by Roman authorities. The commander of the troops at this time was Claudius Lysias (23:26). He was head of a regiment (a special group, part of a legion) of Roman soldiers and was the senior Roman official in Jerusalem.

21:37, 38 By speaking in Greek, Paul showed that he was a cultured, educated man and not just a common rebel starting riots in the streets. The language grabbed the commander's attention and gave Paul protection and the opportunity to give his defense.

21:37, 38 The historian Josephus wrote of an Egyptian who led a revolt of 4,000 people in Jerusalem in A.D. 54 and then disappeared. The commander assumed that Paul was this rebel.

21:40–22:2 Paul was probably speaking in Aramaic, the common language among Palestinian Jews. He used Aramaic not only to communicate in the language of his listeners but also to show that he was a devout Jew and had respect for the Jewish laws and customs. Paul spoke Greek to the Roman officials and Aramaic to the Jews. To minister to people most effectively, use their language.

22:3 Gamaliel was the most honored rabbi of the first century. He was well known and respected as an expert on religious law and as a voice for moderation (5:34). Paul was showing his credentials as a well-educated man trained under the most respected Jewish rabbi.

22:3, 4 By saying that at one time he was as zealous for God as any of his listeners, Paul was acknowledging their sincere motives behind their desire to kill him, pointing out that he had done the same to Christian leaders a few years earlier. Paul always tried to establish common ground with his audience before launching into a full-scale defense of Christianity. When you witness for Christ, first identify yourself with your audience. They are much more likely to listen if they feel a common bond with you.

22:6ff After gaining a hearing and establishing common ground with his audience, Paul gave his testimony. He shared how he had come to faith in Christ. Sound reasoning is good, but it is also important to simply share what Christ has done in our life. But no matter how we present the message, not everyone will accept it, as Paul knew. We must faithfully and responsibly present the Good News and leave the results to God.

suddenly shone around me. 7I fell to the ground and heard a voice saying to me, 'Saul, Saul, why are you persecuting me?'

8"'Who are you, sir?' I asked. And he replied, 'I am Jesus of Nazareth, the one you are persecuting.' 9The people with me saw the light but didn't hear the voice.

10"I said, 'What shall I do, Lord?' And the Lord told me, 'Get up and go into Damascus, and there you will be told all that you are to do.'

11"I was blinded by the intense light and had to be led into Damascus by my companions. 12A man named Ananias lived there. He was a godly man in his devotion to the law, and he was well thought of by all the Jews of Damascus. 13He came to me and stood beside me and said, 'Brother Saul, receive your sight.' And that very hour I could see him!

14"Then he told me, 'The God of our ancestors has chosen you to know his will and to see the Righteous One and hear him speak. 15You are to take his message everywhere, telling the whole world what you have seen and heard. 16And now, why delay? Get up and be baptized, and have your sins washed away, calling on the name of the Lord.'

17"One day after I returned to Jerusalem, I was praying in the Temple, and I fell into a trance. 18I saw a vision of Jesus saying to me, 'Hurry! Leave Jerusalem, for the people here won't believe you when you give them your testimony about me.'

19"'But Lord,' I argued, 'they certainly know that I imprisoned and beat those in every synagogue who believed on you. 20And when your witness Stephen was killed, I was standing there agreeing. I kept the coats they laid aside as they stoned him.'

21"But the Lord said to me, 'Leave Jerusalem, for I will send you far away to the Gentiles!'"

22The crowd listened until Paul came to that word; then with one voice they shouted, "Away with such a fellow! Kill him! He isn't fit to live!" 23They yelled, threw off their coats, and tossed handfuls of dust into the air.

Paul Reveals His Roman Citizenship

24The commander brought Paul inside and ordered him lashed with whips to make him confess his crime. He wanted to find out why the crowd had become so furious. 25As they tied Paul down to lash him, Paul said to the officer standing there, "Is it legal for you to whip a Roman citizen who hasn't even been tried?"

26The officer went to the commander and asked, "What are you doing? This man is a Roman citizen!"

27So the commander went over and asked Paul, "Tell me, are you a Roman citizen?"

"Yes, I certainly am," Paul replied.

28"I am, too," the commander muttered, "and it cost me plenty!"

"But I am a citizen by birth!"

29The soldiers who were about to interrogate Paul quickly withdrew when they heard he was a Roman citizen, and the commander was frightened because he had ordered him bound and whipped.

Paul before the High Council

30The next day the commander freed Paul from his chains and ordered the leading priests into session with the Jewish high council.* He had Paul brought in before them to try to find out what the trouble was all about.

22:9 Acts 9:7; 26:13
22:11 Acts 9:8
22:12 Acts 9:17
22:14 Acts 3:13; 1 Cor 15:8
22:15 Acts 26:16
22:16 Acts 2:38; Rom 10:13; 1 Cor 6:11; Heb 10:22
22:19 Acts 8:3; 22:4-5; 26:9-11
22:20 Acts 7:57–8:1
22:21 Acts 9:15; 13:2; Rom 15:15-16
22:22 Acts 21:36; 25:24
22:25 Acts 16:37
22:29 Acts 16:38

22:30 Greek *Sanhedrin.*

22:21, 22 These people listened intently to Paul, but the word *Gentiles* brought out all their anger and exposed their pride. They were supposed to be a light to the Gentiles, telling them about the one true God. But they had renounced that mission by becoming separatist and exclusive. God's plan, however, would not be thwarted; the Gentiles were hearing the Good News through Jewish Christians, such as Paul and Peter.

22:25-28 Paul's question stopped the officer because by law a Roman citizen could not be punished until he had been proven guilty of a crime. Paul was born a Roman citizen, whereas the commander had purchased his citizenship. Buying citizenship was a common practice and a good source of income for the Roman government. Bought citizenship was considered inferior to citizenship by birth.

22:30 Paul used his times of persecution as an opportunity to witness. Even his enemies were creating a platform for him to address the entire Jewish high council. If we are sensitive to the Holy Spirit's leading, we will see increased opportunities to share our faith, even in the face of opposition.

23:1
Acts 24:16
1 Cor 4:4
2 Cor 1:12
1 Tim 3:9
Heb 13:18
1 Pet 3:16, 21

23:2
John 18:22
Acts 24:1

23:3
Lev 19:15
Ezek 13:10-15
John 7:51

23:5
†Exod 22:28

23:6
Acts 26:5
Phil 3:5

23:8
Matt 22:23
Mark 12:18
Luke 20:27

23:9
Acts 22:7; 25:25

23 Gazing intently at the high council,* Paul began: "Brothers, I have always lived
before God in all good conscience!"
2 Instantly Ananias the high priest commanded those close to Paul to slap him on the
mouth. 3 But Paul said to him, "God will slap you, you whitewashed wall! What kind of
judge are you to break the law yourself by ordering me struck like that?"
4 Those standing near Paul said to him, "Is that the way to talk to God's high priest?"
5 "I'm sorry, brothers. I didn't realize he was the high priest," Paul replied, "for the
Scriptures say, 'Do not speak evil of anyone who rules over you.'*"
6 Paul realized that some members of the high council were Sadducees and some were
Pharisees, so he shouted, "Brothers, I am a Pharisee, as were all my ancestors! And I am
on trial because my hope is in the resurrection of the dead!"
7 This divided the council—the Pharisees against the Sadducees—8 for the Sadducees
say there is no resurrection or angels or spirits, but the Pharisees believe in all of these.
9 So a great clamor arose. Some of the teachers of religious law who were Pharisees
jumped up to argue that Paul was all right. "We see nothing wrong with him," they
shouted. "Perhaps a spirit or an angel spoke to him." 10 The shouting grew louder and
louder, and the men were tugging at Paul from both sides, pulling him this way and that.

23:1 Greek *Sanhedrin;* also in 23:6, 15, 20, 28. **23:5** Exod 22:28.

UNSUNG HEROES IN ACTS

When we think of the success of the early church, we often think of the work of the apostles. But the church could have died if it hadn't been for the unsung heroes, the men and women who through some small but committed act moved the church forward.

Hero	*Reference*	*Heroic Action*
Crippled man	3:9–12	After his healing, he praised God. As the crowds gathered to see what happened, Peter used the opportunity to tell many about Jesus.
Five deacons	6:2–5	Everyone has heard of Stephen, and many know of Philip, but there were five other men chosen to be deacons. They not only laid the foundation for service in the church, but their hard work also gave the apostles the time they needed to preach the gospel.
Ananias	9:10–19	He had the responsibility of being the first to demonstrate Christ's love to Saul (Paul) after his conversion.
Cornelius	10:30–35	His example showed Peter that the gospel was for *all* people, Jews and Gentiles.
Rhoda	12:13–15	Her persistence brought Peter inside Mary's home, where he would be safe.
James	15:13–21	He took command of the Jerusalem council and had the courage and discernment to help form a decision that would affect literally millions of Christians over many generations.
Lydia	16:13–15	She opened her home to Paul, from which he led many to Christ and founded a church in Philippi.
Jason	17:5–9	He risked his life for the gospel by allowing Paul to stay in his home. He stood up for what was true and right, even though he faced persecution for it.
Paul's nephew	23:16–24	He saved Paul's life by telling officials of a murder plot.
Julius	27:1, 43	He spared Paul when the other soldiers wanted to kill him.

23:2-5 Josephus, a respected first-century historian, described Ananias as profane, greedy, and hot-tempered. Paul's outburst came as a result of the illegal command that Ananias had given. Ananias had violated Jewish law by assuming that Paul was guilty without a trial and ordering his punishment (see Deuteronomy 19:15). Paul didn't recognize Ananias as the high priest, probably because Ananias's command broke the law he was pledged to represent. As Christians, we are to represent Christ. If someone around us says, "I didn't know you were a Christian," we have failed to represent him as we should. We are not merely Christ's followers; we are his representative to others.

23:6-8 The Sadducees and Pharisees were two groups of religious leaders but with strikingly different beliefs. The Pharisees believed in a bodily resurrection, but the Sadducees did not. The Sadducees adhered only to Genesis through Deuteronomy, which contain no explicit teaching on resurrection. Paul's words moved the debate away from himself and toward their festering controversy about the resurrection. The Jewish council was split.

23:6-8 Paul's sudden insight that the council was a mixture of Sadducees and Pharisees is an example of the insight that Jesus promises to believers (Mark 13:9-11). God will help us when we are under fire for our faith. Like Paul, we should always be ready to present our testimony. The Holy Spirit will give us the courage to speak boldly.

Finally, the commander, fearing they would tear him apart, ordered his soldiers to take
him away from them and bring him back to the fortress.
11 That night the Lord appeared to Paul and said, "Be encouraged, Paul. Just as you
have told the people about me here in Jerusalem, you must preach the Good News in
Rome."

23:11 Acts 18:9; 27:24; 28:23

The Plan to Kill Paul

12 The next morning a group of Jews got together and bound themselves with an oath to
neither eat nor drink until they had killed Paul. 13 There were more than forty of them.
14 They went to the leading priests and other leaders and told them what they had done.
"We have bound ourselves under oath to neither eat nor drink until we have killed Paul.
15 You and the high council should tell the commander to bring Paul back to the council
again," they requested. "Pretend you want to examine his case more fully. We will kill
him on the way."

23:12 Acts 9:23

23:14-15 Acts 25:3

16 But Paul's nephew heard of their plan and went to the fortress and told Paul. 17 Paul
called one of the officers and said, "Take this young man to the commander. He has
something important to tell him."
18 So the officer did, explaining, "Paul, the prisoner, called me over and asked me to
bring this young man to you because he has something to tell you."
19 The commander took him by the arm, led him aside, and asked, "What is it you want
to tell me?"
20 Paul's nephew told him, "Some Jews are going to ask you to bring Paul before the
Jewish high council tomorrow, pretending they want to get some more information.
21 But don't do it! There are more than forty men hiding along the way ready to jump him
and kill him. They have vowed not to eat or drink until they kill him. They are ready,
expecting you to agree to their request."
22 "Don't let a soul know you told me this," the commander warned the young man as
he sent him away.

23:16 Acts 21:34

Paul Is Sent to Caesarea

23 Then the commander called two of his officers and ordered, "Get two hundred soldiers
ready to leave for Caesarea at nine o'clock tonight. Also take two hundred spearmen and
seventy horsemen. 24 Provide horses for Paul to ride, and get him safely to Governor
Felix." 25 Then he wrote this letter to the governor:

23:23 Acts 8:40

IMPRISONMENT IN CAESAREA
Paul brought news of his third journey to the elders of the Jerusalem church, who rejoiced at his ministry. But Paul's presence soon stirred up the Jews, who persuaded the Romans to arrest him. A plot to kill Paul was uncovered, so Paul was taken by night to Antipatris and then transferred to the provincial prison in Caesarea.

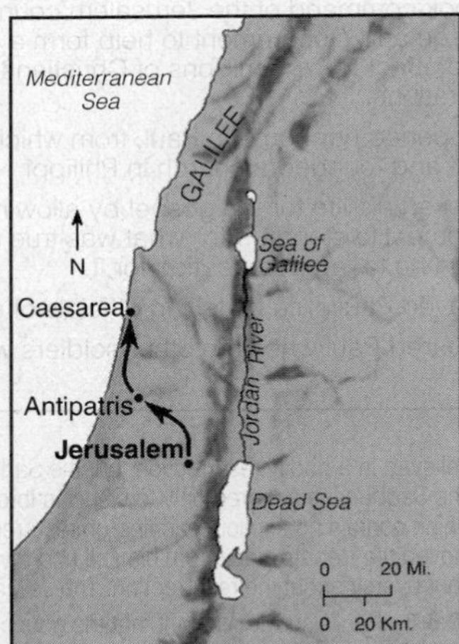

23:14, 15 When the Pharisee/Sadducee controversy died down, the religious leaders refocused their attention on Paul. To these leaders, politics and position had become more important than God. They were ready to plan another murder, just as they had done with Jesus. But as always, God was in control.

23:16 This is the only biblical reference to a member of Paul's family. Some scholars believe that Paul's family had disowned him when he became a Christian. Paul wrote of having suffered the loss of everything for Christ (Philippians 3:8). His nephew was able to see him, even though Paul was in protective custody, because Roman prisoners were accessible to their relatives and friends, who could bring them food and other amenities.

23:16-22 It is easy to overlook children, assuming that they aren't old enough to do much for the Lord. But this young boy played an important part in protecting Paul's life. God can use anyone, of any age, who is willing to yield to him. Jesus made it clear that children are important (Matthew 18:2-6). Give children the importance God gives them.

23:23, 24 The Roman commander ordered Paul sent to Caesarea. Jerusalem was the seat of Jewish government, but Caesarea was the Roman headquarters for the area. God works in amazing and amusing ways. There were infinite possibilities of ways God could use to get Paul to Caesarea, but he chose to use the Roman army to deliver Paul from his enemies. God's ways are not our ways. Ours are limited; his are not. Don't limit God by asking him to respond your way. When God intervenes, things will work out much better than you could ever anticipate.

26 “From Claudius Lysias, to his Excellency, Governor Felix. Greetings! 27 This man was seized by some Jews, and they were about to kill him when I arrived with the troops. When I learned that he was a Roman citizen, I removed him to safety. 28 Then I took him to their high council to try to find out what he had done. 29 I soon discovered it was something regarding their religious law—certainly nothing worthy of imprisonment or death. 30 But when I was informed of a plot to kill him, I immediately sent him on to you. I have told his accusers to bring their charges before you.”

31 So that night, as ordered, the soldiers took Paul as far as Antipatris. 32 They returned to the fortress the next morning, while the horsemen took him on to Caesarea. 33 When they arrived in Caesarea, they presented Paul and the letter to Governor Felix. 34 He read it and then asked Paul what province he was from. “Cilicia,” Paul answered.

35 “I will hear your case myself when your accusers arrive,” the governor told him. Then the governor ordered him kept in the prison at Herod’s headquarters.

Paul Appears before Felix

24 Five days later Ananias, the high priest, arrived with some of the Jewish leaders and the lawyer* Tertullus, to press charges against Paul. 2 When Paul was called in, Tertullus laid charges against Paul in the following address to the governor:

“Your Excellency, you have given peace to us Jews and have enacted reforms for us. 3 And for all of this we are very grateful to you. 4 But lest I bore you, kindly give me your attention for only a moment as I briefly outline our case against this man. 5 For we have found him to be a troublemaker, a man who is constantly inciting the Jews throughout the world to riots and rebellions against the Roman government. He is a ringleader of the sect known as the Nazarenes. 6 Moreover he was trying to defile the Temple when we arrested him.* 8 You can find out the truth of our accusations by examining him yourself.” 9 Then the other Jews chimed in, declaring that everything Tertullus said was true.

10 Now it was Paul’s turn. The governor motioned for him to rise and speak. Paul said, “I know, sir, that you have been a judge of Jewish affairs for many years, and this gives me confidence as I make my defense. 11 You can quickly discover that it was no more than twelve days ago that I arrived in Jerusalem to worship at the Temple. 12 I didn’t argue with anyone in the Temple, nor did I incite a riot in any synagogue or on the streets of the city. 13 These men certainly cannot prove the things they accuse me of doing.

14 “But I admit that I follow the Way, which they call a sect. I worship the God of our ancestors, and I firmly believe the Jewish law and everything written in the books of prophecy. 15 I have hope in God, just as these men do, that he will raise both the righteous

23:27 Acts 21:30-33; 22:25-29
23:28 Acts 22:30
23:29 Acts 18:14-15; 25:18-19; 26:31; 28:18
23:30 Acts 24:19; 25:16
23:33 Acts 8:40
23:34 Acts 6:9; 21:39; 22:3
23:35 Acts 25:16
24:1 Acts 23:2, 24-30, 35
24:3 Acts 23:26; 26:25
24:5 Mark 1:24; Acts 16:20; 17:6; 24:14
24:6 Acts 21:28, 30
24:9 1 Thes 2:16
24:11 Acts 21:27
24:13 Acts 25:7
24:14 Acts 9:2; 26:22
24:15 Dan 12:2; Matt 22:31-32; John 5:28-29; Acts 23:6; 28:20

24:1 Greek *some elders and an orator.* **24:6** Some manuscripts add *We would have judged him by our law, 7 but Lysias, the commander of the garrison, came and took him violently away from us, 8 commanding his accusers to come before you.*

23:26 Felix was the Roman governor of Judea from A.D. 52 to 59. This was the same position Pontius Pilate had held. While the Jews were given much freedom to govern themselves, the governor ran the army, kept the peace, and gathered the taxes.

23:26 How did Luke know what was written in the letter from Claudius Lysias? In his concern for historical accuracy, Luke used many sources to make sure that his writings were correct (see Luke 1:1-4). This letter was probably read aloud in court when Paul came before Felix to answer the Jews' accusations. Also, because Paul was a Roman citizen, a copy may have been given to him as a courtesy.

24:1 The accusers arrived: Ananias, the high priest; Tertullus, the lawyer; and several Jewish leaders. They traveled 60 miles to Caesarea, the Roman center of government, to bring their false accusations against Paul. Their murder plot had failed (23:12-15), but they persisted in trying to kill him. This attempt at murder was both premeditated and persistent.

24:2ff Tertullus was a special orator called to present the religious leaders' case before the Roman governor. He made three accusations against Paul: (1) He was a troublemaker, stirring up riots among the Jews around the world; (2) he was the ringleader of an unrecognized religious sect, which was against Roman law; and (3) he had tried to desecrate the Temple. The religious leaders hoped that these accusations would persuade Felix to execute Paul in order to keep the peace in Palestine.

24:5 While the charge that Paul was a troublemaker was insulting to Paul, it was too vague to be a substantive legal charge. "The Nazarenes" referred to the Christians—named here after Jesus' hometown of Nazareth.

24:10ff Tertullus and the religious leaders seemed to have a strong argument against Paul, but Paul refuted their accusations point by point. Paul was also able to present the Good News through his defense. Paul's accusers were unable to present specific evidence to support their general accusations. For example, Paul was accused of starting trouble among the Jews in the province of Asia (24:18, 19), but the Jews in the province of Asia (western Turkey) were not present to confirm this. This is another example of Paul using every opportunity to witness for Christ (see 24:14, 24).

and the ungodly. 16 Because of this, I always try to maintain a clear conscience before God and everyone else.

17 "After several years away, I returned to Jerusalem with money to aid my people and to offer sacrifices to God. 18 My accusers saw me in the Temple as I was completing a purification ritual. There was no crowd around me and no rioting. 19 But some Jews from the province of Asia were there—and they ought to be here to bring charges if they have anything against me! 20 Ask these men here what wrongdoing the Jewish high council* found in me, 21 except for one thing I said when I shouted out, 'I am on trial before you today because I believe in the resurrection of the dead!'"

22 Felix, who was quite familiar with the Way, adjourned the hearing and said, "Wait until Lysias, the garrison commander, arrives. Then I will decide the case." 23 He ordered an officer to keep Paul in custody but to give him some freedom and allow his friends to visit him and take care of his needs.

24 A few days later Felix came with his wife, Drusilla, who was Jewish. Sending for Paul, they listened as he told them about faith in Christ Jesus. 25 As he reasoned with them about righteousness and self-control and the judgment to come, Felix was terrified. "Go away for now," he replied. "When it is more convenient, I'll call for you again." 26 He also hoped that Paul would bribe him, so he sent for him quite often and talked with him.

27 Two years went by in this way; then Felix was succeeded by Porcius Festus. And because Felix wanted to gain favor with the Jewish leaders, he left Paul in prison.

Paul Appears before Festus

25 Three days after Festus arrived in Caesarea to take over his new responsibilities, he left for Jerusalem, 2 where the leading priests and other Jewish leaders met with him and made their accusations against Paul. 3 They asked Festus as a favor to transfer Paul to Jerusalem. (Their plan was to waylay and kill him.) 4 But Festus replied that Paul was at Caesarea and he himself would be returning there soon. 5 So he said, "Those of you in authority can return with me. If Paul has done anything wrong, you can make your accusations."

6 Eight or ten days later he returned to Caesarea, and on the following day Paul's trial began. 7 On Paul's arrival in court, the Jewish leaders from Jerusalem gathered around and made many serious accusations they couldn't prove. 8 Paul denied the charges. "I am not guilty," he said. "I have committed no crime against the Jewish laws or the Temple or the Roman government."

9 Then Festus, wanting to please the Jews, asked him, "Are you willing to go to Jerusalem and stand trial before me there?"

10 But Paul replied, "No! This is the official Roman court, so I ought to be tried right

24:16 Acts 23:1
24:17 Acts 11:29-30; Rom 15:25-28; 1 Cor 16:1-4; 2 Cor 8:1-4; Gal 2:10
24:18 Acts 21:26-27
24:21 Acts 23:6
24:23 Acts 27:3; 28:16, 30
24:25 Acts 10:42; Gal 5:23; 2 Pet 1:6
24:27 Acts 25:9, 14
25:1 Acts 24:27
25:2 Acts 24:1; 25:15
25:3 Acts 23:15
25:5 Acts 23:30
25:6 Acts 25:17
25:7 Acts 24:5-6, 13
25:8 Acts 6:13; 24:12; 28:17
25:9 Acts 24:27
25:10 Acts 25:21

24:20 Greek *Sanhedrin.*

24:22 Felix had been governor for six years and would have known about the Christians ("the Way"), a topic of conversation among the Romans leaders. The Christians' peaceful life-styles had already proven to the Romans that Christians didn't go around starting riots.

24:25 Paul's talk with Felix became so personal that Felix grew fearful. Felix, like Herod Antipas (Mark 6:17, 18), had taken another man's wife. Paul's words were interesting until they focused on "righteousness and self-control and the judgment to come." Many people will be glad to discuss the Good News with you as long as it doesn't touch their lives too personally. When it does, some will resist or run. But this is what the Good News is all about—God's power to change lives. The Good News is not effective until it moves from principles and doctrine into a life-changing dynamic. When someone resists or runs from your witness, you have undoubtedly succeeded in making the Good News personal.

24:27 Felix lost his job as governor and was called back to Rome. Porcius Festus took over as governor in late 59 or early 60. He was more just than Felix, who had kept Paul in prison for two years, in hopes that perhaps Paul would bribe him and that, by detaining Paul, the Jews would be kept happy. When Festus came into office, he immediately ordered Paul's trial to resume.

24:27 The Jews were in the majority, and the Roman political leaders wanted to defer to them to help keep the peace. Paul seemed to incite problems among the Jews everywhere he went. By keeping him in prison, Felix left office on good terms with the Jews.

25:1-9 Although two years had passed, the Jewish leaders still were looking for a way to kill Paul. They told Festus about Paul and tried to convince him to hold the trial in Jerusalem (so they could prepare an ambush). But God and Paul thwarted their schemes again.

25:10, 11 Every Roman citizen had the right to appeal to Caesar. This didn't mean that Caesar himself would hear the case but that the citizen's case would be tried by the highest courts in the empire. Festus saw Paul's appeal as a way to send him out of the country and thus pacify the Jews. Paul wanted to go to Rome to preach the Good News (Romans 1:10), and he knew that his appeal would give him the opportunity. To go to Rome as a prisoner was better than not to go there at all.

25:11 Acts 26:32; 28:19 here. You know very well I am not guilty. [11]If I have done something worthy of death, I
don't refuse to die. But if I am innocent, neither you nor anyone else has a right to turn
me over to these men to kill me. I appeal to Caesar!"
[12]Festus conferred with his advisers and then replied, "Very well! You have appealed
to Caesar, and to Caesar you shall go!"
[13]A few days later King Agrippa arrived with his sister, Bernice,* to pay their respects
25:14 Acts 24:27 to Festus. [14]During their stay of several days, Festus discussed Paul's case with the king.
25:15 Acts 25:1-2 "There is a prisoner here," he told him, "whose case was left for me by Felix. [15]When I
was in Jerusalem, the leading priests and other Jewish leaders pressed charges against
25:16 Acts 23:30 him and asked me to sentence him. [16]Of course, I quickly pointed out to them that Roman
law does not convict people without a trial. They are given an opportunity to defend
themselves face to face with their accusers.
[17]"When they came here for the trial, I called the case the very next day and ordered

25:13 Greek *Agrippa the king and Bernice arrived.*

HEROD AGRIPPA II

Like great-grandfather, like grandfather; like father, like son—this tells the story of Herod Agrippa II. He inherited the character flaws of generations of powerful men. Each son followed his father in weaknesses, mistakes, and missed opportunities to know God. Each generation had a confrontation with God but failed to realize the importance of the moment. Herod Agrippa's great-uncle, Herod Antipas, actually met Jesus during his trial but failed to see Jesus for who he was. Agrippa II heard the gospel from Paul but considered the message mild entertainment. He found it humorous that Paul actually tried to convince him to become a Christian.

Like so many before and after, Agrippa II stopped within hearing distance of the Kingdom of God. He left himself without excuse. He heard the gospel but decided it wasn't worth responding to personally. Unfortunately, his mistake isn't uncommon. Many who read his story also will not believe. Their problem, like his, is not really that the gospel isn't convincing or that they don't need to know God personally; it is that they choose not to respond.

What has been your response to the gospel? Has it turned your life around and given you the hope of eternal life, or has it been a message to resist or reject? Perhaps it has just been entertainment. It may seem like too great a price to give God control of your life, but the price is minimal compared to living apart from him for eternity because you have chosen not to be his child.

Strengths and accomplishments
- Last of the Herod dynasty that ruled parts of Palestine from 40 B.C. to A.D. 100
- Continued his father's success in mediating between Rome and Palestine
- Continued the family tradition of building and improving cities

Weaknesses and mistakes
- Was not convinced by the gospel and consciously rejected it
- Carried on an incestuous relationship with his sister Bernice

Lessons from his life
- Families pass on both positive and negative influences to children
- There are no guarantees of multiple opportunities to respond to God

Vital statistics
- Occupation: Ruler of northern and eastern Palestine
- Relatives: Great-grandfather: Herod the Great. Father: Herod Agrippa I. Great-uncle: Herod Antipas. Sisters: Bernice, Drusilla
- Contemporaries: Paul, Felix, Festus, Peter, Luke

Key verse "Agrippa interrupted him. 'Do you think you can make me a Christian so quickly?' " (Acts 26:28).

Herod Agrippa II's story is told in Acts 25:13—26:32.

25:11 Paul knew that he was innocent of the charges against him and could appeal to Caesar's judgment. He knew his rights as a Roman citizen and as an innocent person. Paul had met his responsibilities as a Roman, and so he had the opportunity to claim Rome's protection. The good reputation and clear conscience that result from our walk with God can help us remain guiltless before God and blameless before the world.

25:13 This was Herod Agrippa II, son of Herod Agrippa I and a descendant of Herod the Great. He had power over the Temple, controlled the Temple treasury, and could appoint and remove the high priest. Bernice was the sister of Herod Agrippa II. She married her uncle, Herod Chalcis, became a mistress to her brother Agrippa II, and then became mistress to the emperor Vespasian's son, Titus. Here Agrippa and Bernice were making an official visit to Festus. Agrippa, of Jewish descent, could help clarify Paul's case for the Roman governor. Agrippa and Festus were anxious to cooperate in governing their neighboring territories.

Paul brought in. [18]But the accusations made against him weren't at all what I expected.
[19]It was something about their religion and about someone called Jesus who died, but
whom Paul insists is alive. [20]I was perplexed as to how to conduct an investigation of
this kind, and I asked him whether he would be willing to stand trial on these charges in
Jerusalem. [21]But Paul appealed to the emperor. So I ordered him back to jail until I could
arrange to send him to Caesar."

[22]"I'd like to hear the man myself," Agrippa said.

And Festus replied, "You shall—tomorrow!"

Paul Speaks to Agrippa

[23]So the next day Agrippa and Bernice arrived at the auditorium with great pomp,
accompanied by military officers and prominent men of the city. Festus ordered that Paul
be brought in. [24]Then Festus said, "King Agrippa and all present, this is the man whose
death is demanded both by the local Jews and by those in Jerusalem. [25]But in my opinion
he has done nothing worthy of death. However, he appealed his case to the emperor, and
I decided to send him. [26]But what shall I write the emperor? For there is no real charge
against him. So I have brought him before all of you, and especially you, King Agrippa,
so that after we examine him, I might have something to write. [27]For it doesn't seem
reasonable to send a prisoner to the emperor without specifying the charges against
him!"

26 Then Agrippa said to Paul, "You may speak in your defense."

So Paul, with a gesture of his hand, started his defense: [2]"I am fortunate, King
Agrippa, that you are the one hearing my defense against all these accusations made by
the Jewish leaders, [3]for I know you are an expert on Jewish customs and controversies.
Now please listen to me patiently!

[4]"As the Jewish leaders are well aware, I was given a thorough Jewish training from
my earliest childhood among my own people and in Jerusalem. [5]If they would admit
it, they know that I have been a member of the Pharisees, the strictest sect of our
religion. [6]Now I am on trial because I am looking forward to the fulfillment of God's
promise made to our ancestors. [7]In fact, that is why the twelve tribes of Israel worship
God night and day, and they share the same hope I have. Yet, O king, they say it is
wrong for me to have this hope! [8]Why does it seem incredible to any of you that God
can raise the dead?

[9]"I used to believe that I ought to do everything I could to oppose the followers of
Jesus of Nazareth.* [10]Authorized by the leading priests, I caused many of the believers
in Jerusalem to be sent to prison. And I cast my vote against them when they were
condemned to death. [11]Many times I had them whipped in the synagogues to try to get
them to curse Christ. I was so violently opposed to them that I even hounded them in
distant cities of foreign lands.

[12]"One day I was on such a mission to Damascus, armed with the authority and
commission of the leading priests. [13]About noon, Your Majesty, a light from heaven
brighter than the sun shone down on me and my companions. [14]We all fell down, and I
heard a voice saying to me in Aramaic,* 'Saul, Saul, why are you persecuting me? It is
hard for you to fight against my will.*'

[15]"'Who are you, sir?' I asked.

"And the Lord replied, 'I am Jesus, the one you are persecuting. [16]Now stand up! For
I have appeared to you to appoint you as my servant and my witness. You are to tell the

26:9 Greek *oppose the name of Jesus the Nazarene.* **26:14a** Or *Hebrew.* **26:14b** Greek *It is hard for you to kick against the oxgoads.*

25:18-19 Acts 18:14-15; 23:29
25:21 Acts 25:11-12
25:22 Acts 9:15
25:24 Acts 22:22
25:25 Acts 23:9
26:4 Gal 1:13; Phil 3:5-6
26:6 Gen 3:15; 22:18; 26:4; Deut 18:15; Isa 7:14; 9:6-7; Jer 23:5-6; 33:14; Ezek 34:23; 37:24; Dan 9:24; Mal 3:1; 4:2; Acts 13:32; 23:6
26:7 Phil 3:11; 1 Thes 3:10
26:8 Dan 12:2; Acts 23:6
26:9 John 15:21; 16:2; 1 Tim 1:13
26:10 Acts 8:3; 22:4-5
26:12-18 //Acts 9:1-19; 22:6-16
26:14 Acts 9:7
26:16 Acts 22:14-15; Gal 1:12; Col 1:25; 1 Tim 1:12

25:19 Even though Festus knew little about Christianity, he somehow sensed that the Resurrection was central to Christian belief.

25:23ff Paul was in prison, but that didn't stop him from making the most of his situation. Military officers and prominent city leaders met in the auditorium with Agrippa to hear this case. Paul saw this new audience as yet another opportunity to present the Good News. Rather than complain about your present situation, look for ways to use every opportunity to serve God and share him with others. Your problems may be opportunities in disguise.

26:3ff This speech is a good example of Paul's powerful oratory. Beginning with a compliment to Agrippa, he told his story, including the resurrection of Christ, and the royal audience was spellbound.

26:17 Acts 13:46-48; 22:21 Rom 11:13; 15:16 Gal 1:15-16; 2:7-9 1 Tim 2:7 2 Tim 1:11
26:18 Isa 35:5; 42:7, 16; 61:1 Luke 1:77, 79 Eph 1:11; 5:8 Col 1:13 1 Pet 2:9
26:20 Matt 3:8 Acts 9:19-29
26:21 Acts 21:30-31
26:22 Luke 24:27, 44
26:23 Isa 42:6; 49:6 Luke 24:46-47 Rom 1:3-4 1 Cor 15:20 Col 1:18 Rev 1:5
26:24 1 Cor 4:10
26:26 John 18:20 Acts 26:3
26:31 Acts 23:9, 29
26:32 Acts 25:11

world about this experience and about other times I will appear to you. 17 And I will
protect you from both your own people and the Gentiles. Yes, I am going to send you to
the Gentiles, 18 to open their eyes so they may turn from darkness to light, and from the
power of Satan to God. Then they will receive forgiveness for their sins and be given a
place among God's people, who are set apart by faith in me.'

19 "And so, O King Agrippa, I was not disobedient to that vision from heaven. 20 I
preached first to those in Damascus, then in Jerusalem and throughout all Judea, and also
to the Gentiles, that all must turn from their sins and turn to God—and prove they have
changed by the good things they do. 21 Some Jews arrested me in the Temple for
preaching this, and they tried to kill me. 22 But God protected me so that I am still alive
today to tell these facts to everyone, from the least to the greatest. I teach nothing except
what the prophets and Moses said would happen—23 that the Messiah would suffer and
be the first to rise from the dead as a light to Jews and Gentiles alike."

24 Suddenly, Festus shouted, "Paul, you are insane. Too much study has made you
crazy!"

25 But Paul replied, "I am not insane, Most Excellent Festus. I am speaking the sober
truth. 26 And King Agrippa knows about these things. I speak frankly, for I am sure these
events are all familiar to him, for they were not done in a corner! 27 King Agrippa, do you
believe the prophets? I know you do—"

28 Agrippa interrupted him. "Do you think you can make me a Christian so quickly?"*

29 Paul replied, "Whether quickly or not, I pray to God that both you and everyone
here in this audience might become the same as I am, except for these chains."

30 Then the king, the governor, Bernice, and all the others stood and left. 31 As they talked
it over they agreed, "This man hasn't done anything worthy of death or imprisonment."
32 And Agrippa said to Festus, "He could be set free if he hadn't appealed to Caesar!"

Paul Sails for Rome

27:1 Acts 25:12
27:2 Acts 19:29; 20:4
27:3 Matt 11:21 Acts 24:23; 27:43; 28:2, 16

27 When the time came, we set sail for Italy. Paul and several other prisoners were
placed in the custody of an army officer named Julius, a captain of the Imperial
Regiment. 2 And Aristarchus, a Macedonian from Thessalonica, was also with us. We left
on a boat whose home port was Adramyttium; it was scheduled to make several stops at
ports along the coast of the province of Asia.

3 The next day when we docked at Sidon, Julius was very kind to Paul and let him go
ashore to visit with friends so they could provide for his needs. 4 Putting out to sea from
there, we encountered headwinds that made it difficult to keep the ship on course, so we
sailed north of Cyprus between the island and the mainland. 5 We passed along the coast

26:28 Or *"A little more, and your arguments would make me a Christian."*

26:17, 18 Paul took every opportunity to remind his audience that the Gentiles had an equal share in God's inheritance. This inheritance is the promise and blessing of the covenant that God made with Abraham (see Ephesians 2:19; 1 Peter 1:3, 4). Paul's mission was to preach the Good News to the Gentiles.

26:24 Paul was risking his life for a message that was offensive to the Jews and unbelievable to the Gentiles. Jesus received the same response to his message (Mark 3:21; John 10:20). To a worldly, materialistic mind, it seems insane to risk so much to gain what seems to be so little. But as you follow Christ, you soon discover that one's most prized possessions cannot compare to even the smallest eternal reward.

26:26 Paul was appealing to the *facts:* People were still alive who had heard Jesus and seen his miracles; the empty tomb could still be seen; and the Christian message was turning the world upside down (17:6). The history of Jesus' life and the early church are facts that still confront us today. We still have eyewitness accounts of Jesus' life recorded in the Bible as well as historical and archaeological records of the early church to study. Examine the events and facts as verified by many witnesses. Strengthen your faith with the truth of these accounts.

26:28, 29 Agrippa responded to Paul's presentation with a sarcastic remark. Paul didn't react to the brush-off but made a personal appeal to which he hoped all his listeners would respond. Paul's response is a good example for us as we tell others about God's plan of salvation. A sincere personal appeal or personal testimony can show the depth of our concern and break through hardened hearts.

26:28, 29 Paul's heart is revealed here in his words: He was more concerned for the salvation of these strangers than for the removal of his own chains. Ask God to give you a burning desire to see others come to Christ—a desire so strong that it overshadows your problems.

27:1, 2 Use of the pronoun *we* indicates that Luke accompanied Paul on this journey. Aristarchus is the man who was dragged into the theater at the beginning of the riot in Ephesus (19:29; 20:4; Philemon 1:24).

27:1-3 Julius, a hardened Roman army officer, was assigned to guard Paul. Obviously he had to remain close to Paul at all times. Through this contact, Julius developed a respect for Paul. He gave Paul a certain amount of freedom (27:3) and later spared his life (27:43). How would your character look, up close and personal?

of the provinces of Cilicia and Pamphylia, landing at Myra, in the province of Lycia.
[6]There the officer found an Egyptian ship from Alexandria that was bound for Italy, and 27:6
he put us on board. Acts 28:11
[7]We had several days of rough sailing, and after great difficulty we finally neared
Cnidus. But the wind was against us, so we sailed down to the leeward side of Crete, past
the cape of Salmone. [8]We struggled along the coast with great difficulty and finally
arrived at Fair Havens, near the city of Lasea. [9]We had lost a lot of time. The weather 27:9
was becoming dangerous for long voyages by then because it was so late in the fall,* and Lev 16:29-31
Paul spoke to the ship's officers about it.

[10]"Sirs," he said, "I believe there is trouble ahead if we go on—shipwreck, loss of
cargo, injuries, and danger to our lives." [11]But the officer in charge of the prisoners
listened more to the ship's captain and the owner than to Paul. [12]And since Fair Havens
was an exposed harbor—a poor place to spend the winter—most of the crew wanted to
go to Phoenix, farther up the coast of Crete, and spend the winter there. Phoenix was a
good harbor with only a southwest and northwest exposure.

The Storm at Sea

[13]When a light wind began blowing from the south, the sailors thought they could make
it. So they pulled up anchor and sailed along close to shore. [14]But the weather changed 27:14
abruptly, and a wind of typhoon strength (a "northeaster," they called it) caught the ship Mark 4:37
and blew it out to sea. [15]They couldn't turn the ship into the wind, so they gave up and
let it run before the gale.

[16]We sailed behind a small island named Cauda,* where with great difficulty we
hoisted aboard the lifeboat that was being towed behind us. [17]Then we banded the ship

27:9 Greek *because the fast was now already gone by.* This fast happened on the Day of Atonement (*Yom Kippur*), which occurred in late September or early October. **27:16** Some manuscripts read *Clauda.*

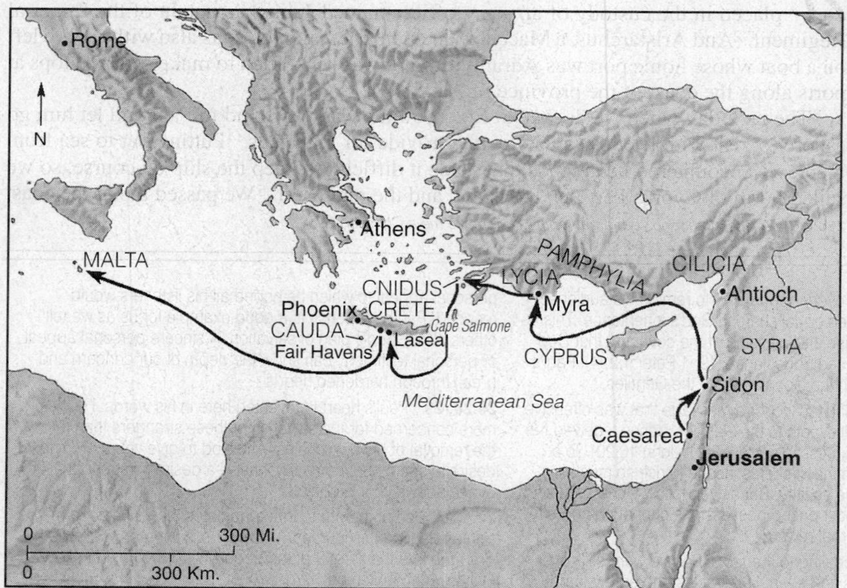

THE TRIP TOWARD ROME Paul began his 2,000-mile trip to Rome at Caesarea. To avoid the open seas, the ship followed the coastline. At Myra, Paul was put on a vessel bound for Italy. It arrived with difficulty at Cnidus, then went to Crete, landing at the port of Fair Havens. The next stop was Phoenix, but the ship was blown south around the island of Cauda, then drifted for two weeks until it was shipwrecked on the island of Malta.

27:9 Ships in ancient times had no compasses and navigated by the stars. Overcast weather made sailing almost impossible and very dangerous. Sailing was doubtful in September and impossible by November. This event occurred in October (A.D. 59).

27:12 Although this was not the best time to sail, the ship's captain and the owner of the ship didn't want to spend the winter in Lasea, or Fair Havens, and so the pilot took a chance. At first the winds and weather were favorable, but then the deadly storm arose.

27:17 Banding the ship with ropes meant passing ropes under the ship to hold it together. Syrtis was on the northern coast of Africa.

with ropes to strengthen the hull. The sailors were afraid of being driven across to the
sandbars of Syrtis off the African coast, so they lowered the sea anchor and were thus
driven before the wind.
[18]The next day, as gale-force winds continued to batter the ship, the crew began
throwing the cargo overboard. [19]The following day they even threw out the ship's
equipment and anything else they could lay their hands on. [20]The terrible storm raged
unabated for many days, blotting out the sun and the stars, until at last all hope was gone.
[21]No one had eaten for a long time. Finally, Paul called the crew together and said,
"Men, you should have listened to me in the first place and not left Fair Havens. You
would have avoided all this injury and loss. [22]But take courage! None of you will lose
your lives, even though the ship will go down. [23]For last night an angel of the God to
whom I belong and whom I serve stood beside me, [24]and he said, 'Don't be afraid, Paul,
for you will surely stand trial before Caesar! What's more, God in his goodness has
granted safety to everyone sailing with you.' [25]So take courage! For I believe God. It
will be just as he said. [26]But we will be shipwrecked on an island."

27:18 Jon 1:5
27:21 Acts 27:10
27:23 Acts 18:9; 23:11; 2 Tim 4:17
27:24 Acts 23:11
27:25 Rom 4:20-21
27:26 Acts 28:1

The Shipwreck

[27]About midnight on the fourteenth night of the storm, as we were being driven across
the Sea of Adria,* the sailors sensed land was near. [28]They took soundings and found
the water was only 120 feet deep. A little later they sounded again and found only
90 feet.* [29]At this rate they were afraid we would soon be driven against the rocks along

27:27 The *Sea of Adria* is in the central Mediterranean; it is not to be confused with the Adriatic Sea. **27:28** Greek *20 fathoms . . . 15 fathoms* [37 meters . . . 27 meters].

PAUL'S JOURNEY TO ROME

One of Paul's most important journeys was to Rome, but he didn't get there the way he expected. It turned out to be more of a legal journey than a missionary journey. Through a series of legal trials and transactions, Paul was delivered to Rome, where his presentation of the gospel would even penetrate the walls of the emperor's palace. Sometimes when our plans don't work out as we want them to, they work out even better than we expected.

Reference	*What Happened*
21:30–34	When Paul arrived in Jerusalem, a riot broke out. Seeing the riot, Roman soldiers put Paul into protective custody. Paul asked for a chance to defend himself to the people. His speech was interrupted by the crowd when he told about what God was doing in the lives of Gentiles.
22:24, 25	A Roman commander ordered a beating to get a confession from Paul. Paul claimed Roman citizenship and escaped the whip.
22:30	Paul was brought before the Jewish high council. Because of his Roman citizenship, he was rescued from the religious leaders who wanted to kill him.
23:10	The Roman commander put Paul back under protective custody.
23:21–24	Due to a plot to kill Paul, the commander transferred him to Caesarea, which was under Governor Felix's control.
23:35	Paul was in prison until the Jews arrived to accuse him. Paul defended himself before Felix.
24:25, 26	Paul was in prison for two years, speaking occasionally to Felix and Drusilla.
24:27	Felix was replaced by Festus.
25:1, 10	New accusations were brought against Paul—Jews wanted him back in Jerusalem for a trial. Paul claimed his right to a hearing before Caesar.
25:12	Festus promised to send him to Rome.
25:13, 14	Festus discussed Paul's case with Herod Agrippa II.
26:1	Agrippa and Festus heard Paul speak. Paul again told his story.
26:24–28	Agrippa interrupted with a sarcastic rejection of the gospel.
26:30–32	Group consensus was that Paul was guilty of nothing and could have been released if he had not appealed to Rome.
27:1, 2	Paul left for Rome, courtesy of the Roman Empire.

27:21 Why would Paul talk to the crew this way? Paul was not taunting them with an "I told you so" but was reminding them that, with God's guidance, he had predicted this very problem (27:10). In the future, they listened to him (27:30-32), and their lives were spared because of it.

27:27 The Sea of Adria referred to the central part of the Mediterranean Sea between Italy, Crete, and the northern coast of Africa.

27:28 Soundings were made by throwing a weighted, marked line into the water. When the lead hit the bottom, sailors could tell the depth of the water from the marks on the rope.

the shore, so they threw out four anchors from the stern and prayed for daylight. 30Then
the sailors tried to abandon the ship; they lowered the lifeboat as though they were going
to put out anchors from the prow. 31But Paul said to the commanding officer and the
soldiers, "You will all die unless the sailors stay aboard." 32So the soldiers cut the ropes
and let the boat fall off.
33As the darkness gave way to the early morning light, Paul begged everyone to eat.
"You haven't touched food for two weeks," he said. 34"Please eat something now for
your own good. For not a hair of your heads will perish." 35Then he took some bread,
gave thanks to God before them all, and broke off a piece and ate it. 36Then everyone
was encouraged, 37and all 276 of us began eating—for that is the number we had aboard.
38After eating, the crew lightened the ship further by throwing the cargo of wheat
overboard.
39When morning dawned, they didn't recognize the coastline, but they saw a bay with
a beach and wondered if they could get between the rocks and get the ship safely to shore.
40So they cut off the anchors and left them in the sea. Then they lowered the rudders,
raised the foresail, and headed toward shore. 41But the ship hit a shoal and ran aground.
The bow of the ship stuck fast, while the stern was repeatedly smashed by the force of
the waves and began to break apart.
42The soldiers wanted to kill the prisoners to make sure they didn't swim ashore and
escape. 43But the commanding officer wanted to spare Paul, so he didn't let them carry
out their plan. Then he ordered all who could swim to jump overboard first and make for
land, 44and he told the others to try for it on planks and debris from the broken ship. So
everyone escaped safely ashore!

27:34 Matt 10:30 Luke 12:7
27:35 Matt 14:19
27:38 Jon 1:5 Acts 27:18
27:41 2 Cor 11:25
27:43-44 Acts 27:22, 24

Paul on the Island of Malta

28 Once we were safe on shore, we learned that we were on the island of Malta. 2The
people of the island were very kind to us. It was cold and rainy, so they built a fire
on the shore to welcome us and warm us.
3As Paul gathered an armful of sticks and was laying them on the fire, a poisonous
snake, driven out by the heat, fastened itself onto his hand. 4The people of the island saw
it hanging there and said to each other, "A murderer, no doubt! Though he escaped the
sea, justice will not permit him to live." 5But Paul shook off the snake into the fire and
was unharmed. 6The people waited for him to swell up or suddenly drop dead. But when
they had waited a long time and saw no harm come to him, they changed their minds and
decided he was a god.
7Near the shore where we landed was an estate belonging to Publius, the chief official

28:1 Acts 27:26, 39
28:4 Luke 13:2, 4
28:5 Mark 16:18 Luke 10:19
28:6 Acts 14:11

PAUL ARRIVES IN ROME
The shipwreck occurred on Malta, where the ship's company spent three months. Finally, another ship gave them passage for the 100 miles to Syracuse, capital of Sicily, then sailed on to Rhegium, finally dropping anchor at Puteoli. Paul was taken to the Forum on the Appian Way and to The Three Taverns before arriving in Rome.

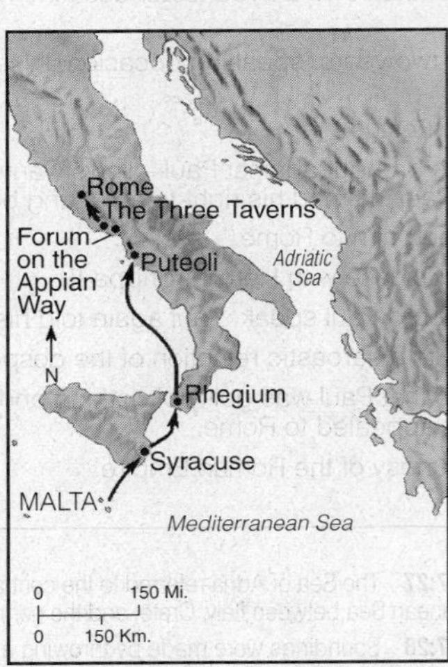

27:42, 43 The soldiers would pay with their own lives if any of their prisoners escaped. Their instinctive reaction was to kill the prisoners so they wouldn't get away. Julius, the officer, was impressed with Paul and wanted to save his life. Julius was the highest ranking official, and therefore he could make this decision. This act preserved Paul for his later ministry in Rome and fulfilled Paul's prediction that all the people on the ship would be saved (27:22).

28:1 The island of Malta is 60 miles south of Sicily. It had excellent harbors and was ideally located for trade.

28:2 The islanders on Malta were of Phoenician ancestry.

28:3 God had promised safe passage to Paul (27:23-25), and he would let nothing stop his servant. The poisonous snake that bit Paul was unable to harm him. Our life is in God's hands, to continue on or to come to an end in his good timing. God still had work for Paul to do.

28:6 These people were very superstitious and believed in many gods. When they saw that Paul was unhurt by the poisonous snake, they thought he was a god. A similar assessment is reported in 14:11-18.

28:7, 8 Paul continued to minister to others, even as a shipwrecked prisoner. On this trip alone, the Roman army officer, the chief official of Malta, and many others were affected. It is no wonder that the Good News spread like wildfire.

28:8 Jas 5:14-15 of the island. He welcomed us courteously and fed us for three days. 8As it happened,
Publius's father was ill with fever and dysentery. Paul went in and prayed for him, and
laying his hands on him, he healed him. 9Then all the other sick people on the island
came and were cured. 10As a result we were showered with honors, and when the time
came to sail, people put on board all sorts of things we would need for the trip.

Paul Arrives at Rome

28:11 Acts 27:6 11It was three months after the shipwreck that we set sail on another ship that had
wintered at the island—an Alexandrian ship with the twin gods* as its figurehead. 12Our
first stop was Syracuse,* where we stayed three days. 13From there we sailed across to
Rhegium.* A day later a south wind began blowing, so the following day we sailed up
the coast to Puteoli. 14There we found some believers,* who invited us to stay with them
seven days. And so we came to Rome.
15The believers in Rome had heard we were coming, and they came to meet us at the
Forum* on the Appian Way. Others joined us at The Three Taverns.* When Paul saw
them, he thanked God and took courage.
28:16 Acts 24:33; 27:3 16When we arrived in Rome, Paul was permitted to have his own private lodging,
though he was guarded by a soldier.

Paul Preaches at Rome under Guard

28:17 Acts 24:12-13; 25:8 17Three days after Paul's arrival, he called together the local Jewish leaders. He said to
them, "Brothers, I was arrested in Jerusalem and handed over to the Roman government,
28:18 Acts 23:29 even though I had done nothing against our people or the customs of our ancestors. 18The
Romans tried me and wanted to release me, for they found no cause for the death
28:19 Acts 25:11 sentence. 19But when the Jewish leaders protested the decision, I felt it necessary to
28:20 Acts 26:6 appeal to Caesar, even though I had no desire to press charges against my own people.
20I asked you to come here today so we could get acquainted and so I could tell you that
I am bound with this chain because I believe that the hope of Israel—the Messiah—has
already come."
21They replied, "We have heard nothing against you. We have had no letters from
28:22 Acts 24:14 Judea or reports from anyone who has arrived here. 22But we want to hear what you
believe, for the only thing we know about these Christians* is that they are denounced
everywhere."
23So a time was set, and on that day a large number of people came to Paul's house.
He told them about the Kingdom of God and taught them about Jesus from the
Scriptures—from the five books of Moses and the books of the prophets. He began
28:24 Acts 14:4 lecturing in the morning and went on into the evening. 24Some believed and some didn't.
25But after they had argued back and forth among themselves, they left with this final
word from Paul: "The Holy Spirit was right when he said to our ancestors through Isaiah
the prophet,

28:11 The *twin gods* were the Roman gods Castor and Pollux. **28:12** *Syracuse* was on the island of Sicily. **28:13** *Rhegium* was on the southern tip of Italy. **28:14** Greek *brothers;* also in 28:15. **28:15a** *The Forum* was about 43 miles (70 kilometers) from Rome. **28:15b** *The Three Taverns* was about 35 miles (57 kilometers) from Rome. **28:22** Greek *this sect.*

28:15 Where did the Roman believers come from? The Good News message had spread to Rome by various methods. Many Jews who lived in Rome visited Jerusalem for religious festivals. Some were present at Pentecost (2:10), believed in Jesus, and brought the message back to Rome. Also, Paul had written his letter to the Romans before he visited there.

28:15 The Forum on the Appian Way was a town about 43 miles south of Rome; The Three Taverns was located about 35 miles south of Rome. A *tavern* was a shop or a place that provided food and lodging for travelers. The Christians openly went to meet Paul and encourage him.

28:17 The decree of Claudius expelling Jews from Rome (18:2) must have been temporary because Jewish leaders were back in Rome.

28:17-20 Paul wanted to preach the Good News in Rome, and he eventually got there—in chains, through shipwreck, and after many trials. Although he may have wished for an easier passage, he knew that God had blessed him greatly in allowing him to meet the believers in Rome and preach the message to both Jews and Gentiles in that great city. In all things, God worked for Paul's good (Romans 8:28). You can trust him to do the same for you. God may not make you comfortable or secure, but he will provide the opportunity to do his work.

28:22 Christians were denounced everywhere by the Romans because they were seen as a threat to the Roman establishment. They believed in one God, whereas the Romans had many gods, including Caesar. The Christians were committed to an authority higher than Caesar.

28:23 Paul used the Old Testament to teach the Jews that Jesus was the Messiah, the fulfillment of God's promises. The book of Romans, written 10 years earlier, reveals the ongoing dialogue that Paul had with the Jews in Rome.

26 'Go and say to my people,
You will hear my words,
but you will not understand;
you will see what I do,
but you will not perceive its meaning.
27 For the hearts of these people are hardened,
and their ears cannot hear,
and they have closed their eyes—
so their eyes cannot see,
and their ears cannot hear,
and their hearts cannot understand,
and they cannot turn to me
and let me heal them.'*

28 So I want you to realize that this salvation from God is also available to the Gentiles,
and they will accept it."*
30 For the next two years, Paul lived in his own rented house.* He welcomed all who
visited him, 31 proclaiming the Kingdom of God with all boldness and teaching about the
Lord Jesus Christ. And no one tried to stop him.

28:26-27 †Isa 6:9-10 John 12:39-40

28:28 Pss 67:2; 98:3 Luke 3:6 Acts 13:46

28:30 Acts 28:16

28:26-27 Isa 6:9-10. **28:28** Some manuscripts add verse 29, *And when he had said these words, the Jews departed, greatly disagreeing with each other.* **28:30** Or *at his own expense.*

28:30 While Paul was under house arrest, he did more than speak to the Jews. He wrote letters, commonly called his Prison Letters, to the Ephesians, Colossians, and Philippians. He also wrote personal letters, such as the one to Philemon. Luke was with Paul in Rome (2 Timothy 4:11). Timothy often visited him (Philippians 1:1; Colossians 1:1; Philemon 1:1), as did Tychicus (Ephesians 6:21), Epaphroditus (Philippians 4:18), and Mark (Colossians 4:10). Paul witnessed to the whole Roman guard (Philippians 1:13) and was involved with the Roman believers.

28:30 Tradition says that Paul was released after two years of house arrest in Rome and then set off on a fourth missionary journey. Some reasons for this tradition are as follows: (1) Luke does not give us an account of his trial before Caesar, and Luke was a detailed chronicler; (2) the prosecution had two years to bring the case to trial, and time may have run out; (3) in his letter to the Philippians, written during his imprisonment in Rome, Paul implied that he would soon be released and would do further traveling; (4) Paul mentions several places where he intended to take the Good News, but he never visited those places in his first three journeys; and (5) early Christian literature talks plainly about other travels by Paul.

It may be that during Paul's time of freedom, he continued to travel extensively, even going to Spain (see Romans 15:24, 28) and back to the churches in Greece. The books of 1 Timothy and Titus were written during this time. Later, Paul was imprisoned again, probably in Rome, where he wrote his last letter (2 Timothy).

28:31 Why does the book of Acts end here and so abruptly? The book is not about the life of Paul but about the spread of the Good News, and that had been clearly presented. God apparently thought it was not necessary for someone to write an additional book describing the continuing history of the early church. Now that the Good News had been preached and established at the center of trade and government, it would spread across the world.

28:31 The book of Acts deals with the history of the Christian church and its expansion in ever-widening circles touching Jerusalem, Antioch, Ephesus, and Rome—the most influential cities in the Western world. Acts also shows the mighty miracles and testimonies of the heroes and martyrs of the early church—Peter, Stephen, James, Paul. All the ministry was prompted and held together by the Holy Spirit working in the lives of ordinary people—merchants, travelers, slaves, jailers, church leaders, males, females, Gentiles, Jews, rich, poor. Many unsung heroes of the faith continued the work, through the Holy Spirit, in succeeding generations, changing the world with a changeless message: Jesus Christ is Savior and Lord of all who call on him. Today we can be the unsung heroes in the continuing story of the spread of the Good News. It is that same message that we Christians are to take to our world so that many more may hear and believe.

ROMANS

KNOWLEDGEABLE and experienced, the district attorney makes his case. Calling key witnesses to the stand, he presents the evidence. After discrediting the testimonies of witnesses for the defense by skillfully cross-examining them, he concludes with an airtight summary and stirring challenge for the jury. The announced verdict is no surprise. "Guilty" states the foreman, and justice is served.

The apostle Paul was intelligent, articulate, and committed to his calling. Like a skilled lawyer, he presented the case for the gospel clearly and forthrightly in his letter to the believers in Rome.

Paul had heard of the church at Rome, but he had never been there, nor had any of the other apostles. Evidently the church had been started by Jews who had come to faith during Pentecost (Acts 2). They spread the gospel on their return to Rome, and the church grew.

Although many barriers separated them, Paul felt a bond with these believers in Rome. They were his brothers and sisters in Christ, and he longed to see them face to face. He had never met most of the believers there, yet he loved them. He sent this letter to introduce himself and to make a clear declaration of the faith.

After a brief introduction, Paul presents the facts of the gospel (1:3) and declares his allegiance to it (1:16, 17). He continues by building an airtight case for the lostness of humanity and the necessity for God's intervention (1:18—3:20).

Then Paul presents the Good News: Salvation is available to all, regardless of a person's identity, sin, or heritage. We are saved by *grace* (unearned, undeserved favor from God) through *faith* (complete trust) in Christ and his finished work. Through him we can stand before God justified, "not guilty" (3:21—5:21). With this foundation Paul moves directly into a discussion of the freedom that comes from being saved—freedom from the power of sin (6:1–23), freedom from the domination of the law (7:1–25), freedom to become like Christ and discover God's limitless love (8:1–39).

Speaking directly to his Jewish brothers and sisters, Paul shares his concern for them and explains how they fit into God's plan (9:1—11:12). God has made the way for Jews and Gentiles to be united in the body of Christ; both groups can praise God for his wisdom and love (11:13–36).

Paul explains what it means to live in complete submission to Christ: Use spiritual gifts to serve others (12:3–8), genuinely love others (12:9–21), and be good citizens (13:1–14). Freedom must be guided by love as we build each other up in the faith, being sensitive and helpful to those who are weak (14:1—15:4). Paul stresses unity, especially between Gentiles and Jews (15:5–13). He concludes by reviewing his reasons for writing, outlining his personal plans (15:22–33), greeting his friends, and giving a few final thoughts and greetings from his traveling companions (16:1–27).

As you read Romans, reexamine your commitment to Christ, and reconfirm your relationships with other believers in Christ's body.

VITAL STATISTICS

PURPOSE:
To introduce Paul to the Romans and to give a sample of his message before he arrives in Rome

AUTHOR:
Paul

TO WHOM WRITTEN:
The Christians in Rome and believers everywhere

DATE WRITTEN:
About A.D. 57, from Corinth, as Paul was preparing for his visit to Jerusalem.

SETTING:
Apparently Paul had finished his work in the east, and he planned to visit Rome on his way to Spain after first bringing a collection to Jerusalem for the poor Christians there (15:23–28). The Roman church was mostly Jewish but also contained a great number of Gentiles.

KEY VERSE:
"Therefore, since we have been made right in God's sight by faith, we have peace with God because of what Jesus Christ our Lord has done for us" (5:1).

KEY PEOPLE:
Paul, Phoebe

KEY PLACE:
Rome

SPECIAL FEATURES:
Paul wrote Romans as an organized and carefully presented statement of his faith—it does not have the form of a typical letter. He does, however, spend considerable time greeting people in Rome at the end of the letter.

THE BLUEPRINT

A. WHAT TO BELIEVE (1:1—11:36)
1. Sinfulness of humankind
2. Forgiveness of sin through Christ
3. Freedom from sin's grasp
4. Israel's past, present, and future

Paul clearly sets forth the foundations of the Christian faith. All people are sinful; Christ died to forgive sin; we are made right with God through faith; this begins a new life with a new relationship with God. Like a sports team that constantly reviews the basics, we will be greatly helped in our faith by keeping close to these foundations. If we study Romans carefully, we will never be at a loss to know what to believe.

B. HOW TO BEHAVE (12:1—16:27)
1. Personal responsibility
2. Personal notes

Paul gives clear, practical guidelines for the believers in Rome. The Christian life is not abstract theology unconnected with life, but it has practical implications that will affect how we choose to behave each day. It is not enough merely to know the gospel; we must let it transform our life and let God impact every aspect of our lives.

MEGATHEMES

THEME	EXPLANATION	IMPORTANCE
Sin	Sin means refusing to do God's will and failing to do all that God wants. Since Adam's rebellion against God, our nature is to disobey him. Our sin cuts us off from God. Sin causes us to want to live our own way rather than God's way. Because God is morally perfect, just, and fair, he is right to condemn sin.	Each person has sinned, either by rebelling against God or by ignoring his will. No matter what our background or how hard we try to live good and moral lives, we cannot earn salvation or remove our sin. Only Christ can save us.
Salvation	Our sin points out our need to be forgiven and cleansed. Although we don't deserve it, God, in his kindness, reached out to love and forgive us. He provides the way for us to be saved. Christ's death paid the penalty for our sin.	It is good news that God saves us from our sin. But in order to enter into a wonderful new relationship with God, we must believe that Jesus died for us and that he forgives all our sin.
Growth	By God's power, believers are sanctified—made holy. This means we are set apart from sin, enabled to obey and to become more like Christ. When we are growing in our relationship with Christ, the Holy Spirit frees us from the demands of the law and from fear of judgment.	Because we are free from sin's control, the law's demands, and fear of God's punishment, we can grow in our relationship with Christ. By trusting in the Holy Spirit and allowing him to help us, we can overcome sin and temptation.
Sovereignty	God oversees and cares about his people—past, present, and future. God's ways of dealing with people are always fair. Because God is in charge of all creation, he can save whomever he wills.	Because of God's mercy, both Jews and Gentiles can be saved. We all must respond to his mercy and accept his gracious offer of forgiveness. Because he is sovereign, let him reign in your heart.
Service	When our purpose is to give credit to God for his love, power, and perfection in all we do, we can serve him properly. Serving him unifies all believers and enables them to show love and sensitivity to others.	None of us can be fully Christlike by ourselves—it takes the entire body of Christ to fully express Christ. By actively and vigorously building up other believers, Christians can be a symphony of service to God.

A. WHAT TO BELIEVE (1:1—11:36)

Paul begins his message to the Romans by vividly portraying the sinfulness of all people, explaining how forgiveness is available through faith in Christ, and showing what believers experience in life through their new faith. In this section, we learn of the centrality of faith to becoming a Christian and to living the Christian life. Apart from faith, we have no hope in life.

1. Sinfulness of humankind

Greetings from Paul

1 This letter is from Paul, Jesus Christ's slave, chosen by God to be an apostle and sent
out to preach his Good News. [2]This Good News was promised long ago by God
through his prophets in the holy Scriptures. [3]It is the Good News about his Son, Jesus,

1:3 Matt 1:1; 22:42 Rom 9:5 2 Tim 2:8

1:1 Paul wrote this letter to the church in Rome. Neither he nor the other church leaders, James and Peter, had yet been to Rome. Most likely, the Roman church had been established by believers who had been at Jerusalem for Pentecost (Acts 2:10) and by travelers who had heard the Good News in other places and had brought it back to Rome (for example, Priscilla and Aquila, Acts 18:2; Romans 16:3-5). Paul wrote the letter to the Romans during his ministry in Corinth (at the end of his

1:4 Acts 13:33 Rom 8:11
1:5 Acts 9:15 Rom 16:26 Gal 1:16 Eph 3:8-9

who came as a man, born into King David's royal family line. [4]And Jesus Christ our Lord
was shown to be the Son of God when God powerfully raised him from the dead by
means of the Holy Spirit.* [5]Through Christ, God has given us the privilege and authority
to tell Gentiles everywhere what God has done for them, so that they will believe and
obey him, bringing glory to his name.

1:4 Or *the Spirit of holiness.*

THE GOSPEL GOES TO ROME
When Paul wrote his letter to the church in Rome, he had not yet been there, but he had taken the gospel "from Jerusalem clear over into Illyricum" (15:19). He planned to visit and preach in Rome one day and hoped to continue to take the gospel farther west—even to Spain.

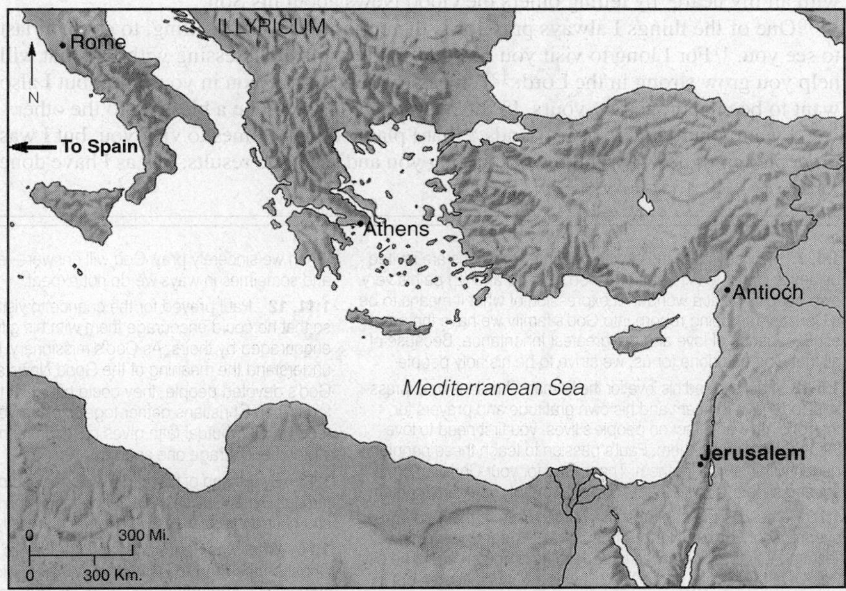

third missionary journey just before returning to Jerusalem; Acts 20:3; Romans 15:25) to encourage the believers and to express his desire to visit them someday (within three years he would). The Roman church had no New Testament because the Gospels were not yet being circulated in their final written form. Thus, this letter may well have been the first piece of Christian literature the Roman believers had seen. Written to both Jewish and Gentile Christians, the letter to the Romans is a systematic presentation of the Christian faith.

1:1 When Paul, a devout Jew who had at first persecuted the Christians, became a believer, God used him to spread the Good News throughout the world. Although he was a prisoner, Paul did eventually preach in Rome (Acts 28), perhaps even to Caesar himself. Paul's Profile is found in Acts 9.

1:1 Paul humbly calls himself Jesus Christ's slave and an apostle ("one who is sent"). For a Roman citizen—which Paul was—to choose to be a slave was unthinkable. But Paul chose to be completely dependent on and obedient to his beloved Master. What is your attitude toward Christ, your Master? Our willingness to serve and obey Jesus Christ enables us to be useful and usable servants to do work for him—work that really matters.

1:2 Some of the prophecies predicting the Good News regarding Jesus Christ are found in Genesis 12:3; Psalms 16:10; 40:6-10; 118:22; Isaiah 11:1ff; Zechariah 9:9-11; 12:10; Malachi 4:1-6.

1:3, 4 Paul states that Jesus is the Son of God, the promised Messiah, and the resurrected Lord. Paul calls Jesus a descendant of King David to emphasize that Jesus truly had fulfilled the Old Testament Scriptures predicting that the Messiah would come from David's line. With this statement of faith, Paul declares his agreement with the teaching of all Scripture and of the apostles.

1:3-5 Here Paul summarizes the Good News about Jesus Christ, who (1) came as a human by natural descent, (2) was part of the Jewish royal line through David, (3) died and was raised from the dead, and (4) opened the door for God's grace and kindness to be poured out on us. The book of Romans is an expansion of these themes.

1:5, 6 Christians have both a privilege and a great responsibility. Paul and the apostles received the privilege of being called, but they also received the authority and the responsibility to share with others what God has done. God also graciously forgives our sins when we believe in him as Lord. In doing this, we are committing ourselves to begin a new life. Paul's new life also involved a God-given responsibility: to witness about God's Good News to the world as a missionary. God may or may not call you to be a foreign missionary, but he does call you (and all believers) to be Christ's ambassador and to witness to the changed life that Jesus Christ has begun in you.

[6]You are among those who have been called to belong to Jesus Christ, [7]dear friends
in Rome. God loves you dearly, and he has called you to be his very own people.
May grace and peace be yours from God our Father and the Lord Jesus Christ.

God's Good News

[8]Let me say first of all that your faith in God is becoming known throughout the world.
How I thank God through Jesus Christ for each one of you. [9]God knows how often I
pray for you. Day and night I bring you and your needs in prayer to God, whom I serve
with all my heart* by telling others the Good News about his Son.
[10]One of the things I always pray for is the opportunity, God willing, to come at last
to see you. [11]For I long to visit you so I can share a spiritual blessing with you that will
help you grow strong in the Lord. [12]I'm eager to encourage you in your faith, but I also
want to be encouraged by yours. In this way, each of us will be a blessing to the other.
[13]I want you to know, dear friends,* that I planned many times to visit you, but I was
prevented until now. I want to work among you and see good results, just as I have done

1:7 1 Cor 1:2; 2 Cor 1:1; Gal 1:3; Eph 1:1
1:8 Rom 16:19; 1 Thes 1:8
1:9 Eph 1:16; Phil 1:8; 1 Thes 2:5; 2 Tim 1:3
1:10 Rom 15:23, 32
1:11 Rom 15:23
1:13 John 15:16; Rom 15:22

1:9 Or *in my spirit.* **1:13** Greek *brothers.*

1:6, 7 Paul says that those who become Christians are invited by Jesus Christ to (1) belong to God's family, and (2) be his very own people. What a wonderful expression of what it means to be a Christian! In being reborn into God's family we have the greatest experience of love and the greatest inheritance. Because of all that God has done for us, we strive to be his holy people.

1:6-12 Paul showed his love for the Roman Christians by expressing God's love for them and his own gratitude and prayers for them. To have an effect on people's lives, you first need to love them and believe in them. Paul's passion to teach these people began with his love for them. Thank God for your Christian brothers and sisters, and let them know how deeply you care for them.

1:7 Rome was the capital of the Roman Empire that had spread over most of Europe, North Africa, and the Near East. In New Testament times, Rome was experiencing a golden age. The city was wealthy, literary, and artistic. It was a cultural center, but it was also morally decadent. The Romans worshiped many pagan gods, and even some of the emperors were worshiped. In stark contrast to the Romans, the followers of Christ believed in only one God and lived by his high moral standards.

1:7 Christianity was at odds with the Romans' dependence on military strength. Many Romans were naively pragmatic, believing that any means to accomplish the intended task was good. And for them, nothing worked better than physical might. The Romans trusted in their strong military power to protect them against all enemies. Christians in every age need to be reminded that God is the only permanent source of our security and salvation, and at the same time he is "our Father"!

1:8 Paul uses the phrase "I thank God through Jesus Christ" to emphasize the point that Christ is the one and only mediator between us and God. Through Christ, God sends his love and forgiveness to us; through Christ, we send our thanks to God (see 1 Timothy 2:5).

1:8 The Roman Christians, at the Western world's political power center, were highly visible. Fortunately, their reputation was excellent; their strong faith was making itself known around the world. When people talk about your congregation or your denomination, what do they say? Are their comments accurate? Would you rather they noticed other features? What is the best way to get the public to recognize your faith?

1:9, 10 When you pray continually about a concern, don't be surprised at how God answers. Paul prayed to visit Rome so he could teach the Christians there. When he finally arrived in Rome, it was as a prisoner (see Acts 28:16). Paul prayed for a safe trip, and he did arrive safely—after getting arrested, slapped in the face, shipwrecked, and bitten by a poisonous snake. God's ways of answering our prayers are often far from what we expect. When we sincerely pray, God will answer—although in his timing and someimes in ways we do not expect.

1:11, 12 Paul prayed for the chance to visit these Christians so that he could encourage them with his gift of faith and be encouraged by theirs. As God's missionary, he could help them understand the meaning of the Good News about Jesus. As God's devoted people, they could offer him fellowship and comfort. When Christians gather together, everyone should give *and* receive. Our mutual faith gives us a common bond to be a blessing and encourage one another.

1:13 By the end of his third missionary journey, Paul had traveled through Syria, Galatia, Asia, Macedonia, and Achaia. The churches in these areas were made up mostly of Gentile believers.

1:14 What was Paul's obligation? After his experience with Christ on the road to Damascus (Acts 9), his whole life was consumed with spreading the Good News of salvation. His obligation was to people of the entire world. He met his obligation by proclaiming Christ's salvation to people—across all cultural, social, racial, and economic lines, both Jews and Gentiles,. We also are obligated to Christ because he took the punishment we deserve for our sins. Although we cannot repay Christ for all he has done, we can demonstrate our gratitude by showing his love to others.

1:16 Paul was not ashamed because his message was the Good News about Christ. It was a message of salvation, it had life-changing power, and it was for everyone. When you are tempted to be ashamed, remember what the Good News is all about. If you focus on God and on what God is doing in the world rather than on your own inadequacy, you won't be ashamed or embarrassed.

1:16 Why did the message go to the Jews first? They had been God's special people for more than 2,000 years, ever since God chose Abraham and promised great blessings to his descendants (Genesis 12:1-3). God did not choose the Jews because they deserved to be chosen (Deuteronomy 7:7, 8; 9:4-6) but because he wanted to show his love and mercy to them, for it would be through them that his Messiah would come into the world. God chose them, not to play favorites, but so that they would tell the world about his plan of salvation.

For centuries the Jews had been learning about God by obeying his laws, keeping his festivals, and living according to his moral principles. Often they would forget God's promises and laws; often they would have to be disciplined; but still they had a precious heritage of belief in the one true God. Of all the people on earth, the Jews should have been the most ready to welcome the Messiah and to understand his mission and message—and some of them did (see Luke 2:25, 36-38). Of course, the disciples and the great apostle Paul were faithful Jews who recognized in Jesus God's most precious gift to the human race.

1:14 1 Cor 9:16
1:16 Acts 3:26; 1 Cor 1:18, 24
1:17 †Hab 2:4; Rom 3:21-22; Gal 3:11; Heb 10:38
1:18 Eph 5:6; Col 3:6

among other Gentiles. [14]For I have a great sense of obligation to people in our culture
and to people in other cultures,* to the educated and uneducated alike. [15]So I am eager
to come to you in Rome, too, to preach God's Good News.
[16]For I am not ashamed of this Good News about Christ. It is the power of God at
work, saving everyone who believes—Jews first and also Gentiles. [17]This Good News
tells us how God makes us right in his sight. This is accomplished from start to finish by
faith. As the Scriptures say, "It is through faith that a righteous person has life."*

God's Anger at Sin

[18]But God shows his anger from heaven against all sinful, wicked people who push the
truth away from themselves.* [19]For the truth about God is known to them instinctively.*

1:14 Greek *to Greeks and to barbarians.* **1:17** Hab 2:4. **1:18** Or *who prevent the truth from being known.* **1:19** Greek *is manifest in them.*

FAITH

Faith is a word with many meanings. It can mean faithfulness (Matthew 24:45). It can mean absolute trust, as shown by some of the people who came to Jesus for healing (Luke 7:2–10). It can mean confident hope (Hebrews 11:1). Or, as James points out, it can even mean a barren belief that does not result in good deeds (James 2:14–26). What does Paul mean when, in Romans, he speaks of "saving faith"?

We must be very careful to understand faith as Paul uses the word because he ties faith so closely to salvation. It is *not* something we must do in order to earn salvation—if that were true, then faith would be just one more deed, and Paul clearly states that human deeds can never save us (Galatians 2:16). Instead, faith is a gift God gives us *because* he is saving us (Ephesians 2:8). It is God's grace, not our faith, that saves us. In his mercy, however, when he saves us, he gives us faith—a relationship with his Son that helps us become like him. Through the faith he gives us, he carries us from death into life (John 5:24).

Even in Old Testament times, grace, not deeds, was the basis of salvation. As Hebrews points out, "it is not possible for the blood of bulls and goats to take away sins" (10:4). God intended for his people to look beyond the animal sacrifices to him, but all too often they instead put their confidence in fulfilling the requirements of the law—that is, performing the required sacrifices. When Jesus triumphed over death, he cancelled the charges against us and opened the way to the Father (Colossians 2:12–15). Because he is merciful, he offers us faith. How tragic if we turn faith into a deed and try to develop it on our own! We can never come to God through our own faith any more than his Old Testament people could come through their own sacrifices. Instead, we must accept his gracious offer with thanksgiving and allow him to plant the seed of faith within us.

1:16 Jews and Christians alike stood against the idolatrous Roman religions, and Roman officials often confused the two groups. This was especially easy to do since the Christian church in Rome could have been originally composed of Jewish converts who had attended Pentecost in Jerusalem (see Acts 2:1ff). By the time Paul wrote this letter to the Romans, however, many Gentiles had joined the church. The Jews and the Gentiles needed to know the relationship between Judaism and Christianity.

1:17 The Good News shows us both how righteous God is in his plan for us to be saved and also how we may be made fit for eternal life. By trusting Christ, our relationship with God is made right. "From start to finish," God declares us to be right with him because of faith and faith alone.

1:17 Paul is quoting Habakkuk 2:4. Habakkuk may have understood "has life" to mean this present life only. But Paul extends this statement to include eternal life. As we trust God, we are saved; we find life both now and forever.

1:18 Why is God angry at sinful people? Because they have substituted the truth about him with a fantasy of their own imagination (1:25). They have stifled the truth God naturally reveals to all people in order to believe anything that supports their own self-centered life-styles. God cannot tolerate sin because his nature is morally perfect. He cannot ignore or condone willful rebellion. God wants to remove the sin and restore the sinner—and he is able to, as long as the sinner does not stubbornly distort or reject the truth. But God shows his anger against those who persist in sinning. Make sure you are not pursuing a fantasy rather than the true God. Don't suppress the truth about him merely to protect your own life-style.

1:18ff Romans 1:18–3:20 develops Paul's argument that no one can claim by their own efforts or merit to be good in God's sight—not the masses, not the Romans, not even the Jews. All people everywhere deserve God's condemnation for their sin.

1:18-20 Does anyone have an excuse for not believing in God? The Bible answers an emphatic *no.* God has revealed what he is like in and through his creation. Every person, therefore, either accepts or rejects God. Don't be fooled. When the day comes for God to judge your response to him, no excuses will be accepted. Begin today to give your devotion and worship to him.

1:18-20 In these verses, Paul answers a common objection: How could a loving God send anyone to hell, especially someone who has never heard about Christ? In fact, says Paul, God has revealed himself plainly in the creation to *all* people. And yet people reject even this basic knowledge of God. Also, all people have an inner sense of what God requires, but they choose not to live up to it. Put another way, people's moral standards are always better than their behavior. If people suppress God's truth in order to live their own way, they have no excuse. They know the truth, and they will have to endure the consequences of ignoring it.

1:18-20 Some people wonder why we need missionaries if people can know about God through nature (the creation). The answer: (1) Although people know that God exists, their wickedness blinds them to the truth. Missionaries sensitively expose their sin and point them to Christ. (2) Although people may believe there is a God, they refuse to commit themselves to him. Missionaries help

God has put this knowledge in their hearts. 20 From the time the world was created, 1:20
people have seen the earth and sky and all that God made. They can clearly see his Job 12:7-9 Ps 19:1
invisible qualities—his eternal power and divine nature. So they have no excuse whatsoever for not knowing God.
21 Yes, they knew God, but they wouldn't worship him as God or even give him thanks. 1:21
And they began to think up foolish ideas of what God was like. The result was that their 2 Kgs 17:15 Eph 4:17-18
minds became dark and confused. 22 Claiming to be wise, they became utter fools 1:22
instead. 23 And instead of worshiping the glorious, ever-living God, they worshiped idols Jer 10:14
made to look like mere people, or birds and animals and snakes. 1 Cor 1:20 1:23
24 So God let them go ahead and do whatever shameful things their hearts desired. As Deut 4:15-19
a result, they did vile and degrading things with each other's bodies. 25 Instead of Ps 106:20
believing what they knew was the truth about God, they deliberately chose to believe 1:24 Acts 14:16
lies. So they worshiped the things God made but not the Creator himself, who is to be
praised forever. Amen.
26 That is why God abandoned them to their shameful desires. Even the women turned 1:26 1 Thes 4:5

---

persuade them by sharing God's Word and by pointing out the dangerous consequences of their actions. (3) Missionaries help the church obey the great commission of our Lord (Matthew 28:19, 20). (4) Most important, although nature reveals God, people need to be told about Jesus and how, through him, they can have a personal relationship with God.

Knowing that God exists is not enough. People must learn that God is loving and that he sent his Son to demonstrate his love for us (5:8). They must be shown how to accept God's forgiveness of their sins. (See also 10:14, 15.)

1:20 What kind of God does nature reveal? Nature shows us a God of might, intelligence, and intricate detail; a God of order and beauty; a God who controls powerful forces. That is *general* revelation. Through *special* revelation (the Bible and the coming of Jesus), we learn about God's love and forgiveness and the promise of eternal life. God has graciously given us many sources that we might come to believe in him.

1:20 God reveals his divine nature and personal qualities through creation, even though creation's testimony has been distorted by the Fall. Adam's sin resulted in a divine curse upon the whole natural order (Genesis 3:17-19); thorns and thistles were an immediate result, and natural disasters have been common from Adam's day to ours. In Romans 8:19-21, Paul says that nature itself is eagerly awaiting its own redemption from the effects of sin (see Revelation 22:3).

1:21-23 How could intelligent people turn to idolatry? Idolatry begins when people reject what they know about God. Instead of looking to him as the creator and sustainer of life, they see themselves as the center of the universe. They soon invent "gods" that are convenient projections of their own selfish ideas. These gods may be wooden figures, or they may also be goals or things we pursue, such as money, power, or possessions. They may even be misrepresentations of God himself—making God in our image, instead of the reverse. The common denominator is this: Idolaters worship the things God made rather than God himself. Is there anything you feel you can't live without? Is there any priority greater than God? Do you have a dream you would sacrifice everything to realize? Does God take first place in your life? Do you worship God or idols of your own making?

1:21-32 Paul clearly portrays the inevitable downward spiral into sin. First, people reject God; next, they make up their own ideas of what a god should be and do; then they fall into every kind of wickedness: greed, hate, envy, murder, fighting, deception, malicious behavior, and gossip. Finally, they grow to hate God and encourage others to do so. God does not cause this steady progression toward evil. Rather, when people reject him, he allows them to live as they choose. God gives them over to or permits them to experience the natural consequences of their sin. Once caught in the downward spiral, no one can pull himself or herself out. Sinners must trust Christ alone to deliver them from destruction.

1:23 When Paul says that people worshiped idols made to look like people or animals instead of worshiping God, he seems to deliberately state people's wickedness in the terms used in the Genesis narrative of Adam's fall (see Genesis 3:1-24). When people worship the creature instead of the Creator, they lose sight of their own identity as those who are higher than the animals—made in the image of God.

1:24-32 These people chose to reject God, and God allowed them to do it. God does not usually stop us from making wrong choices. He lets us choose independence from him, even though he knows that in time we will become slaves to our own rebellious life-style and lose our freedom not to sin. Does life without God look like freedom to you? Look more closely. There is no worse slavery than slavery to sin.

1:25 People tend to believe lies that reinforce their own selfish, personal beliefs. Today, more than ever, we need to know what the basis is for our beliefs. With TV, music, movies, and the rest of the media often presenting sinful life-styles and unwholesome values, we find ourselves constantly bombarded by attitudes and beliefs that are totally opposed to the Bible. Be careful about what influences you to form your opinions. The Bible is the only standard of truth. Evaluate all other opinions in light of its teachings.

1:26, 27 God's plan for sexual relationships is his ideal for his creation. Unfortunately, sin distorts the natural use of God's gifts. Sin often means not only denying God but also denying the way we are made. When people say that any sex act is acceptable as long as nobody gets hurt, they are fooling themselves. In the long run (and often in the short run), sin hurts people—individuals, families, whole societies. How sad it is that people who worship the things God made instead of the Creator so often distort and destroy the very things they claim to value!

1:26, 27 Homosexuality (to turn against or abandon natural relations of sex) was as widespread in Paul's day as it is in ours. Many pagan practices encouraged it. God is willing to receive anyone who comes to him in faith, and Christians should love and accept others no matter what their background. Yet, homosexuality is strictly forbidden in Scripture (Leviticus 18:22). Homosexuality is considered an acceptable practice by many in our world today—even by some churches. But society does not set the standard for God's law. Homosexuals believe that their desires are normal and that they have a right to express them. But God does not encourage us to fulfill all our desires (even normal ones). Those desires that violate his laws must be controlled.

If you have these desires, you can and must resist acting

1:27 Lev 18:22; 20:13; 1 Cor 6:9
against the natural way to have sex and instead indulged in sex with each other. 27 And
the men, instead of having normal sexual relationships with women, burned with lust for
each other. Men did shameful things with other men and, as a result, suffered within
themselves the penalty they so richly deserved.
28 When they refused to acknowledge God, he abandoned them to their evil minds and
let them do things that should never be done. 29 Their lives became full of every kind of
wickedness, sin, greed, hate, envy, murder, fighting, deception, malicious behavior, and
1:30 2 Tim 3:2
gossip. 30 They are backstabbers, haters of God, insolent, proud, and boastful. They are
forever inventing new ways of sinning and are disobedient to their parents. 31 They refuse
1:31 2 Tim 3:3
to understand, break their promises, and are heartless and unforgiving. 32 They are fully
1:32 Rom 6:23
aware of God's death penalty for those who do these things, yet they go right ahead and
do them anyway. And, worse yet, they encourage others to do them, too.

God's Judgment of Sin

2:1 Matt 7:1
2 You may be saying, "What terrible people you have been talking about!" But you
are just as bad, and you have no excuse! When you say they are wicked and
should be punished, you are condemning yourself, for you do these very same things.
2 And we know that God, in his justice, will punish anyone who does such things. 3 Do
you think that God will judge and condemn others for doing them and not judge you
2:4 Rom 9:22; 2 Pet 3:9, 15
when you do them, too? 4 Don't you realize how kind, tolerant, and patient God is with
you? Or don't you care? Can't you see how kind he has been in giving you time to
turn from your sin?
2:5 Ps 110:5
5 But no, you won't listen. So you are storing up terrible punishment for yourself
because of your stubbornness in refusing to turn from your sin. For there is going to come

---

SALVATION'S FREEWAY

Romans 3:23	Everyone has sinned.
Romans 6:23	The penalty for our sin is death.
Romans 5:8	Jesus Christ died for sin.
Romans 10:8–10	To be forgiven for our sin, we must believe and confess that Jesus is Lord. Salvation comes through Jesus Christ.

---

upon them. Consciously avoid places or activities you know will kindle temptations. Don't underestimate the power of Satan to tempt you, or the potential for serious harm if you continue to yield to these temptations. Remember, God can and will forgive sexual sins just as he forgives other sins. Surrender yourself to God, asking him to show you the way out of sin and into the light of his freedom and his love. Prayer, Bible study, and loving support of Christians in a Bible-believing church can help you to gain strength to resist these powerful temptations. If you are already deeply involved in homosexual behavior, seek help from a trustworthy, professional, Christian counselor.

1:32 How were these people aware of God's death penalty? All human beings, who are created in God's image, have a basic moral nature and a conscience. This truth is understood beyond religious circles. Psychologists, for example, say that the rare person who has no conscience has a serious personality disorder that is extremely difficult to treat. Most people instinctively know when they do wrong—but they may not care. Some people will even risk an early death for the freedom to indulge their desires now. "I know it's wrong, but I really want it," they say; or "I know it's dangerous, but it's worth the risk." For such people, part of the "fun" is going against God's law, the community's moral standards, common sense, or their own sense of right and wrong. But deep down inside they know that sin deserves the punishment of death (6:23).

2:1 Whenever we find ourselves feeling justifiably angry about someone's sin, we should be careful. We need to speak out against sin, but we must do so in a spirit of humility. Often the sins we notice most clearly in others are the ones that have taken root in us. If we look closely at ourselves, we may find that we are committing the same sins in more socially acceptable forms. For example, a person who gossips may be very critical of others who gossip about him or her.

2:1ff When Paul's letter was read in the Roman church, no doubt many heads nodded as he condemned idol worshipers, homosexual practices, and violent people. But what surprise his listeners must have felt when he turned on them and said in effect, "You are just as bad, and you have no excuse!" Paul was emphatically stressing that we have all sinned repeatedly, and there is no way apart from Christ to be saved from sin's consequences.

2:4 In his kindness, God holds back his judgment, giving people time to turn from their sin. It is easy to mistake God's patience for approval of the wrong way we are living. Self-evaluation is difficult, and it is even more difficult to bring ourselves to God and let him tell us where we need to change. But as Christians we must ask God to point out our sins, so that he can heal them. Unfortunately, we are more likely to be amazed at God's patience with others than humbled at his patience with us.

2:5-11 Although God does not usually punish us immediately for sin, his eventual judgment is certain. We don't know exactly when it will happen, but we know that no one will escape that final encounter with the Creator. For more on judgment, see John 12:48 and Revelation 20:11-15.

a day of judgment when God, the just judge of all the world, 6will judge all people
according to what they have done. 7He will give eternal life to those who persist in doing
what is good, seeking after the glory and honor and immortality that God offers. 8But he
will pour out his anger and wrath on those who live for themselves, who refuse to obey
the truth and practice evil deeds. 9There will be trouble and calamity for everyone who
keeps on sinning—for the Jew first and also for the Gentile. 10But there will be glory
and honor and peace from God for all who do good—for the Jew first and also for the
Gentile. 11For God does not show favoritism.

12God will punish the Gentiles when they sin, even though they never had God's
written law. And he will punish the Jews when they sin, for they do have the law. 13For
it is not merely knowing the law that brings God's approval. Those who obey the law
will be declared right in God's sight. 14Even when Gentiles, who do not have God's
written law, instinctively follow what the law says, they show that in their hearts they
know right from wrong. 15They demonstrate that God's law is written within them, for
their own consciences either accuse them or tell them they are doing what is right. 16The
day will surely come when God, by Jesus Christ, will judge everyone's secret life. This
is my message.

The Jews and the Law

17If you are a Jew, you are relying on God's law for your special relationship with
him. You boast that all is well between yourself and God. 18Yes, you know what he
wants; you know right from wrong because you have been taught his law. 19You are
convinced that you are a guide for the blind and a beacon light for people who are lost
in darkness without God. 20You think you can instruct the ignorant and teach children
the ways of God. For you are certain that in God's law you have complete knowledge
and truth.

21Well then, if you teach others, why don't you teach yourself? You tell others not to
steal, but do you steal? 22You say it is wrong to commit adultery, but do you do it? You
condemn idolatry, but do you steal from pagan temples? 23You are so proud of knowing
the law, but you dishonor God by breaking it. 24No wonder the Scriptures say, "The
world blasphemes the name of God because of you."*

2:6 †Ps 62:12; Matt 16:27
2:7 Matt 25:46; 2 Tim 4:14
2:8 2 Thes 2:12
2:11 Gal 2:6; Eph 6:9; Col 3:25
2:13 Matt 7:21; John 13:17; Jas 1:22-25
2:14 Acts 10:35
2:16 Acts 10:42; Rom 16:25; 2 Tim 2:8
2:17 Mic 3:11
2:20 2 Tim 3:5
2:21 Matt 23:3-4
2:24 †Isa 52:5; Ezek 36:20

2:24 Isa 52:5.

2:7 Paul says that those who patiently and persistently *do* God's will find eternal life. He is not contradicting his previous statement that salvation comes by faith alone (1:16, 17). We are not saved by good deeds, but when we commit our life fully to God, we want to please him and do his will. As such, our good deeds are a grateful *response* to what God has done, not a prerequisite to earning his favor.

2:12-15 People are condemned not for what they don't know but for what they do with what they know. Those who know God's written Word and his law will be judged by them. Those who have never seen a Bible still know right from wrong, and they will be judged because they violated those standards that their own consciences dictated. God's law is written within them.

2:12-15 If you traveled around the world, you would find evidence in every society and culture of God's moral law. For example, all cultures prohibit murder, and yet in all societies that law has been broken. We belong to a stubborn, sinful race. We know what is right, but we insist on doing what is wrong. It is not enough to know what is right; we must also do it. Admit to yourself and to God that you frequently fail to live up to your own standards (much less to God's standards). That's the first step to forgiveness and healing.

2:17ff Paul continues to argue that all stand guilty before God. After describing the fate of the unbelieving, pagan Gentiles, he moves to admonish God's people. Despite their knowledge of God's will, they were guilty because they, too, refuse to live by it. Those of us who have grown up in Christian families may know what God's Word says. But Paul says that if we do not live up to what we know, we are no better off than the heathen.

2:21, 22 Paul explained to the Jews that they needed to teach *themselves,* not others, by their law. They knew the law so well that they had learned how to excuse their own actions while criticizing others. But the law is more than a set of rules—it is a guideline for living according to God's will. It is also a reminder that we cannot please God without a proper relationship to him. As Jesus pointed out, withholding what rightfully belongs to someone else is stealing (Mark 7:9-13), and anyone who even looks at a woman with lust in his eye has committed adultery with her in his heart (Matthew 5:27, 28). Before we accuse others, we must look at ourselves and see if sin, in any form, exists within us.

2:21-27 These verses are a scathing criticism of hypocrisy. It is much easier to tell others how to behave than to behave properly ourselves. It is easier to say the right words than to allow them to take root in our own life. Do you ever advise others to do something you are unwilling to do yourself? Make sure that your actions match your words.

2:24 If you claim to be one of God's people, your life should reflect what God is like. When you disobey God, you dishonor his name. People may even blaspheme or profane God's name because of you. What do people think about God as they watch your life?

2:25 Gal 5:3 — 25 The Jewish ceremony of circumcision is worth something only if you obey God's
law. But if you don't obey God's law, you are no better off than an uncircumcised
Gentile. 26 And if the Gentiles obey God's law, won't God give them all the rights and
2:28 Matt 3:9; John 8:39; Gal 6:15 — honors of being his own people? 27 In fact, uncircumcised Gentiles who keep God's law
will be much better off than you Jews who are circumcised and know so much about
God's law but don't obey it.
2:29 Deut 30:6; John 5:44; Rom 7:6; 2 Cor 3:6; 10:18; Phil 3:3; Col 2:11; 1 Pet 3:4 — 28 For you are not a true Jew just because you were born of Jewish parents or because
you have gone through the Jewish ceremony of circumcision. 29 No, a true Jew is one
whose heart is right with God. And true circumcision is not a cutting of the body but a
change of heart produced by God's Spirit. Whoever has that kind of change seeks praise
from God, not from people.

God Remains Faithful

3 Then what's the advantage of being a Jew? Is there any value in the Jewish ceremony
3:2 Deut 4:7-8; Ps 147:19-20; Acts 7:38 — of circumcision? 2 Yes, being a Jew has many advantages. First of all, the Jews were
entrusted with the whole revelation of God.*
3 True, some of them were unfaithful; but just because they broke their promises, does
3:4 †Ps 51:4 — that mean God will break his promises? 4 Of course not! Though everyone else in the
world is a liar, God is true. As the Scriptures say, "He will be proved right in what he
says, and he will win his case in court."*

3:2 Greek *the oracles of God.* **3:4** Ps 51:4.

CRUCIAL CONCEPTS IN ROMANS

ELECTION Romans 9:10–13	God's choice of an individual or group for a specific purpose or destiny.
JUSTIFICATION Romans 4:25; 5:18	God's act of declaring us "not guilty" for our sins, making us "right" with him.
PROPITIATION Romans 3:25	The removal of God's punishment for sin through the perfect sacrifice of Jesus Christ.
REDEMPTION Romans 3:24; 8:23	Jesus Christ has paid the price so we can go free. The price of sin is death; Jesus paid the price.
SANCTIFICATION Romans 5:2; 15:16	Becoming more and more like Jesus Christ through the work of the Holy Spirit.
GLORIFICATION Romans 8:18, 19, 30	The ultimate state of the believer after death when he or she becomes like Christ (1 John 3:2).

2:25-29 *Circumcision* refers to the sign of God's special covenant with his people. Submitting to this rite was required for all Jewish males (Genesis 17:9-14). According to Paul, being a circumcised Jew meant nothing if the person didn't obey God's laws. On the other hand, the uncircumcised Gentiles would receive God's love and approval if they kept God's law. Paul goes on to explain that a true Jew (one who pleases God) is not someone who has been circumcised but someone whose heart is right with God and obeys him.

2:28, 29 To be a Jew meant you were in God's family, an heir to all his promises. Yet Paul made it clear that membership in God's family is based on internal, not external, qualities. All whose hearts are right with God are real Jews—that is, part of God's family (see also Galatians 3:7). Attending church or being baptized, confirmed, or accepted for membership is not enough, just as submitting to circumcision was not enough for the Jews. God desires our heartfelt devotion and obedience (see also Deuteronomy 10:16; Jeremiah 4:4).

3:1ff In this chapter Paul contends that everyone stands guilty before God. Paul has dismantled the common excuses of people who refuse to admit they are sinners: (1) "There is no God" or "I follow my conscience" (1:18-32); (2) "I'm not as bad as other people" (2:1-16); (3) "I'm a church member" or "I'm a religious person" (2:17-29). No one will be exempt from God's judgment of sin. Every person must accept the fact that he or she is sinful and condemned before God and receive God's wonderful gift of salvation.

3:1ff What a depressing picture Paul is painting! All of us—pagan Gentiles, humanitarians, and religious people—are condemned by our own actions. The law, which God gave to show the way to live, holds up our evil deeds to public view. Is there any hope for us? Yes, says Paul. The law condemns us, it is true, but the law is not the basis of our hope. God himself is. He, in his righteousness and wonderful love, offers us eternal life. We receive our salvation not through law but through faith in Jesus Christ. We do not—cannot—earn it; we accept it as a gift from our loving heavenly Father.

3:2 The Jewish nation had many advantages. (1) They were entrusted with God's laws ("the whole revelation of God," Exodus 19–20; Deuteronomy 4:8). (2) They were the race through whom the Messiah came to earth (Isaiah 11:1-10; Matthew 1:1-17). (3) They were the beneficiaries of covenants with God himself (Genesis 17:1-16; Exodus 19:3-6). But these privileges did not make them better than anyone else (see 3:9). In fact, because of them the Jews were even more responsible to live up to God's requirements.

5“But,” some say, “our sins serve a good purpose, for people will see God’s goodness
when he declares us sinners to be innocent. Isn’t it unfair, then, for God to punish us?”
(That is actually the way some people talk.) 6Of course not! If God is not just, how is he
qualified to judge the world? 7“But,” some might still argue, “how can God judge and
condemn me as a sinner if my dishonesty highlights his truthfulness and brings him more
glory?” 8If you follow that kind of thinking, however, you might as well say that the
more we sin the better it is! Those who say such things deserve to be condemned, yet
some slander me by saying this is what I preach!

3:5 Rom 5:8; Gal 3:15
3:7 Rom 9:19
3:8 Rom 6:1

All People Are Sinners

9Well then, are we Jews better than others?* No, not at all, for we have already shown
that all people, whether Jews or Gentiles, are under the power of sin. 10As the
Scriptures say,

“No one is good—
  not even one.
11 No one has real understanding;
  no one is seeking God.
12 All have turned away from God;
  all have gone wrong.
No one does good,
  not even one.”*
13 “Their talk is foul, like the stench from an open grave.
  Their speech is filled with lies.”
“The poison of a deadly snake drips from their lips.”*
14 “Their mouths are full of cursing and bitterness.”*
15 “They are quick to commit murder.
16 Wherever they go, destruction and misery follow them.
17 They do not know what true peace is.”*
18 “They have no fear of God to restrain them.”*

19Obviously, the law applies to those to whom it was given, for its purpose is to
keep people from having excuses and to bring the entire world into judgment before
God. 20For no one can ever be made right in God’s sight by doing what his law
commands. For the more we know God’s law, the clearer it becomes that we aren’t
obeying it.

3:9 Rom 1:18–2:24
3:10-12 †Pss 14:1-3; 53:1-3
3:13 †Pss 5:9; 140:3
3:14 †Ps 10:7
3:15-17 †Isa 59:7-8
3:18 †Ps 36:1
3:19 Rom 2:12
3:20 Ps 143:2; Rom 4:15; 7:7; Gal 2:16; 3:11

3:9 Greek *Are we better?* **3:10-12** Pss 14:1-3; 53:1-3. **3:13** Pss 5:9; 140:3. **3:14** Ps 10:7. **3:15-17** Isa 59:7-8. **3:18** Ps 36:1.

3:5-8 Some may think they don’t have to worry about sin because (1) it’s God’s job to forgive; (2) God is so loving that he won’t judge us; (3) sin isn’t so bad—it teaches us valuable lessons; or (4) we need to stay in touch with the culture around us. It is far too easy to take God’s grace for granted. But God cannot overlook sin. No matter how many excuses they make, sinners will have to answer to God for their sin.

3:10-12 Paul is referring to Psalm 14:1-3. “No one is good” means “no one is innocent.” Every person is valuable in God’s eyes because God created us in his image, and he loves us. But no one is good enough (that is, no one can earn right standing with God). Though valuable, we have fallen into sin. But God, through Jesus his Son, has redeemed us and offers to forgive us if we turn to him in faith.

3:10-18 Paul uses these Old Testament references to show that humanity in general, in its present sinful condition, is unacceptable before God. Have you ever thought to yourself, “Well, I’m not too bad. I’m a pretty good person”? Look at these verses and see if any of them apply to you. Have you ever lied? Have you ever hurt someone’s feelings by your words or tone of voice? Are you bitter toward anyone? Do you become angry with those who strongly disagree with you? In thought, word, and deed, you, like everyone else in the world, stand guilty before God. We must remember who we are in his sight—alienated sinners. Don’t deny that you are a sinner. Instead, allow your desperate need to point you toward Christ.

3:19 The last time someone accused you of wrongdoing, what was your reaction? Denial, argument, and defensiveness? The entire world will be silent before almighty God. No excuses or arguments will remain. Have you reached the point with God where you are ready to hang up your defenses and await his decision? If you haven’t, stop now and admit your sin to him. If you have, the following verses are truly good news for you!

3:20, 31 In these verses we see two functions of God’s law. First, it shows us where we go wrong. Because of the law, we know that we are helpless sinners and that we must come to Jesus Christ for mercy. Second, the moral code revealed in the law can serve to guide our actions by holding up God’s moral standards. We do not earn salvation by keeping the law (no one except Christ ever kept or could keep God’s law perfectly), but we do please God when our life conforms to his revealed will for us.

2. Forgiveness of sin through Christ

Christ Took Our Punishment

21 But now God has shown us a different way of being right in his sight—not by obeying
the law but by the way promised in the Scriptures long ago. 22 We are made right in God's
sight when we trust in Jesus Christ to take away our sins. And we all can be saved in this
same way, no matter who we are or what we have done.
23 For all have sinned; all fall short of God's glorious standard. 24 Yet now God in his
gracious kindness declares us not guilty. He has done this through Christ Jesus, who has
freed us by taking away our sins. 25 For God sent Jesus to take the punishment for our
sins and to satisfy God's anger against us. We are made right with God when we believe
that Jesus shed his blood, sacrificing his life for us. God was being entirely fair and just
when he did not punish those who sinned in former times. 26 And he is entirely fair and
just in this present time when he declares sinners to be right in his sight because they
believe in Jesus.
27 Can we boast, then, that we have done anything to be accepted by God? No, because
our acquittal is not based on our good deeds. It is based on our faith. 28 So we are made
right with God through faith and not by obeying the law.
29 After all, God is not the God of the Jews only, is he? Isn't he also the God of the
Gentiles? Of course he is. 30 There is only one God, and there is only one way of being
accepted by him. He makes people right with himself only by faith, whether they are
Jews or Gentiles. 31 Well then, if we emphasize faith, does this mean that we can forget
about the law? Of course not! In fact, only when we have faith do we truly fulfill the
law.

3:21 Rom 1:2, 17; 9:30
3:22 Rom 4:11; 10:4, 12; Gal 2:16; Col 3:11
3:24 Eph 2:8; Heb 9:12
3:25 Lev 16:10; Heb 9:12-14; 1 Pet 1:19; 1 Jn 4:10
3:27 Rom 2:17; 4:2; 1 Cor 1:29-31
3:28 Acts 13:39
3:29 Rom 10:12; Gal 3:28
3:31 Matt 5:17

3:21-29 After all this bad news about our sinfulness and God's condemnation, Paul gives the wonderful news. There is a way to be declared not guilty—by trusting Jesus Christ to take away our sins. Trusting means putting our confidence in Christ to forgive our sins, to make us right with God, and to empower us to live the way he taught us. God's solution is available to all of us regardless of our background or past behavior.

3:23 Some sins seem bigger than others because their obvious consequences are much more serious. Murder, for example, seems to us to be worse than hatred, and adultery seems worse than pride. But this does not mean that because we only commit "little" sins we deserve eternal life. All sins make us sinners, and all sins cut us off from our holy God. All sins, therefore, lead to death (because they disqualify us from living with God), regardless of how great or small they seem. Don't minimize "little" sins or overrate "big" sins. They all separate us from God, but they all can be forgiven.

3:24 Paul explains that God declares us not guilty. When a judge in a court of law declares the defendant not guilty, all the charges are removed from his record. Legally, it is as if the person had never been accused. When God forgives our sins, our record is wiped clean. From his perspective, it is as though we had never sinned.

3:24 Christ set sinners free from slavery to sin. In Old Testament times, a person's debts could result in his being sold as a slave. The next of kin could redeem him—buy his freedom. Christ purchased our freedom and the price was his life.

3:25 Christ died in our place, for our sins. God is justifiably angry at sinners. They have rebelled against him and cut themselves off from his life-giving power. But God declares Christ's death to be the appropriate, designated sacrifice for our sin. Christ then stands in our place, having paid the penalty of death for our sin, and he completely satisfies God's demands. His sacrifice brings pardon, deliverance, and freedom.

3:25, 26 What happened to people who lived before Christ came and died for sin? If God condemned sinners, was he being unfair? If he saved the righteous, was Christ's sacrifice unnecessary? Paul shows that God forgave all human sin at the cross of Jesus. Old Testament believers looked forward in faith to Christ's coming and were saved, even though they did not know Jesus' name or the details of his earthly life. Unlike the Old Testament believers, you know about the God who loved the world so much that he gave his own Son (John 3:16). Have you put your trust in him?

3:27, 28 Most religions require specific duties that must be performed to make a person acceptable to a god. Christianity is unique in that no good deed that we do will make us right with God. No amount of human achievement or personal goodness will close the gap between God's moral perfection and our imperfect daily performance. Good deeds are important, but they will not earn us eternal life. We are saved only by trusting in what God has done for us (see Ephesians 2:8-10).

3:28 Why does God save us by faith alone? (1) Faith eliminates the pride of human effort, because faith is not a deed that we do. (2) Faith exalts what God has done, not what we do. (3) Faith admits that we can't keep the law or measure up to God's standards—we need help. (4) Faith is based on our relationship with God, not our performance for God.

3:31 There were some misunderstandings between the Jewish and Gentile Christians in Rome. Worried Jewish Christians were asking Paul, "Does faith wipe out everything Judaism stands for? Does it cancel our Scriptures, put an end to our customs, declare that God is no longer working through us?" (This is essentially the question used to open chapter 3.) "Absolutely not!" says Paul. When we understand the way of salvation through faith, we understand the Jewish religion better. We know why Abraham was chosen, why the law was given, and why God worked patiently with Israel for centuries. Faith does not wipe out the Old Testament. Rather, it makes God's dealings with the Jewish people understandable. In chapter 4, Paul will expand on this theme (see also 5:20, 21; 8:3, 4; 13:9, 10; Galatians 3:24-29; and 1 Timothy 1:8 for more on this concept).

The Faith of Abraham

4 Abraham was, humanly speaking, the founder of our Jewish nation. What were his
experiences concerning this question of being saved by faith? 2 Was it because of his
good deeds that God accepted him? If so, he would have had something to boast about.
But from God's point of view Abraham had no basis at all for pride. 3 For the Scriptures
tell us, "Abraham believed God, so God declared him to be righteous."*
4 When people work, their wages are not a gift. Workers earn what they receive. 5 But
people are declared righteous because of their faith, not because of their work.
6 King David spoke of this, describing the happiness of an undeserving sinner who is
declared to be righteous:

7 "Oh, what joy for those whose disobedience is forgiven,
  whose sins are put out of sight.
8 Yes, what joy for those
  whose sin is no longer counted against them by the Lord."*

9 Now then, is this blessing only for the Jews, or is it for Gentiles, too? Well, what
about Abraham? We have been saying he was declared righteous by God because of his
faith. 10 But how did his faith help him? Was he declared righteous only after he had been
circumcised, or was it before he was circumcised? The answer is that God accepted him
first, and then he was circumcised later!
11 The circumcision ceremony was a sign that Abraham already had faith and that God
had already accepted him and declared him to be righteous—even before he was
circumcised. So Abraham is the spiritual father of those who have faith but have not been
circumcised. They are made right with God by faith. 12 And Abraham is also the spiritual
father of those who have been circumcised, but only if they have the same kind of faith
Abraham had before he was circumcised.
13 It is clear, then, that God's promise to give the whole earth to Abraham and his
descendants was not based on obedience to God's law, but on the new relationship with
God that comes by faith. 14 So if you claim that God's promise is for those who obey
God's law and think they are "good enough" in God's sight, then you are saying that faith
is useless. And in that case, the promise is also meaningless. 15 But the law brings
punishment on those who try to obey it. (The only way to avoid breaking the law is to
have no law to break!)

4:2 1 Cor 1:31
4:3 †Gen 15:6 Gal 3:6 Jas 2:23
4:4 Rom 11:6 Gal 2:16
4:7-8 †Ps 32:1-2 2 Cor 5:19
4:9 †Gen 15:6 Rom 3:30
4:11 Gen 17:10-11
4:13 Gen 18:18; 22:17-18 Gal 3:29
4:14 Gal 3:18
4:15 Rom 3:20; 7:12 1 Cor 15:55-56 Gal 3:10

4:3 Gen 15:6. **4:7-8** Ps 32:1-2.

4:1-3 The Jews were proud to be called children of Abraham. Paul uses Abraham as a good example of someone who was saved by faith. By emphasizing faith, Paul is not saying that God's law is unimportant (4:13) but that it is impossible to be saved simply by obeying it. For more about Abraham, see his Profile in Genesis 18.

4:4 This verse means that if a person could earn right standing with God by being good, the granting of that gift wouldn't be a free act; it would be an obligation. Our self-reliance is futile; all we can do is cast ourselves on God's mercy and grace.

4:5 When some people learn that they are saved by God through faith, they start to worry. "Do I have enough faith?" they wonder. "Is my faith strong enough to save me?" These people miss the point. It is Jesus Christ who saves us, not *our* feelings or actions, and he is strong enough to save us no matter how weak our faith is. Jesus offers us salvation as a gift because he loves us, not because we have earned it through our powerful faith. What, then, is the role of faith? Faith is believing and trusting in Jesus Christ and reaching out to accept his wonderful gift of salvation.

4:6-8 What can we do to get rid of guilt? King David was guilty of terrible sins—adultery, murder, lying—and yet he experienced the joy of forgiveness. We, too, can have this joy when we (1) quit denying our guilt and recognize that we have sinned, (2) admit our guilt to God and ask for his forgiveness, and (3) let go of our guilt and believe that God has forgiven us. This can be difficult when a sin has taken root in our life over many years, when it is very serious, or when it involves others. We must remember that Jesus is willing and able to forgive every sin. In view of the tremendous price he paid on the cross, it is arrogant to think that there is any sin too great for him to forgive. Even though our faith is weak, our conscience is sensitive, and our memory haunts us, God's Word declares that sins confessed are sins forgiven (1 John 1:9).

4:10 Circumcision was a sign to others and a personal seal or certification for the Jews that they were God's special people. Circumcision of all Jewish boys set apart the Jewish people from the nations that worshiped other gods; thus, it was a very important ceremony. God gave the blessing and the command for this ceremony to Abraham (Genesis 17:9-14).

4:10-12 Rituals did not earn any reward for Abraham; he had been blessed long before the circumcision ceremony was introduced. Abraham found favor with God by faith alone, before he was circumcised. Genesis 12:1-3 tells of God's call to Abraham when he was 75 years old; the circumcision ceremony was introduced when he was 99 (Genesis 17:1-14). Ceremonies and rituals serve as reminders of our faith as well as instruct new or young believers. But we should not think that they give us any special merit before God. They are outward signs and seals that demonstrate inner belief and trust. The focus of our faith should be on Christ and his saving work, not on our own actions.

4:16 Gal 3:7 — 16 So that's why faith is the key! God's promise is given to us as a free gift. And we
are certain to receive it, whether or not we follow Jewish customs, if we have faith like
4:17 †Gen 17:5 — Abraham's. For Abraham is the father of all who believe. 17 That is what the Scriptures
Isa 48:13 — mean when God told him, "I have made you the father of many nations."* This happened
John 5:21 — because Abraham believed in the God who brings the dead back to life and who brings
1 Cor 1:28 — into existence what didn't exist before.
4:18 †Gen 15:5 — 18 When God promised Abraham that he would become the father of many nations,
Abraham believed him. God had also said, "Your descendants will be as numerous as
4:19 †Gen 17:17; 18:11 — the stars,"* even though such a promise seemed utterly impossible! 19 And Abraham's
Heb 11:11 — faith did not weaken, even though he knew that he was too old to be a father at the age
of one hundred and that Sarah, his wife, had never been able to have children.
20 Abraham never wavered in believing God's promise. In fact, his faith grew stronger,
4:22 †Gen 15:6 — and in this he brought glory to God. 21 He was absolutely convinced that God was able
Rom 4:3 — to do anything he promised. 22 And because of Abraham's faith, God declared him to be
4:24 1 Pet 1:21 — righteous.
23 Now this wonderful truth—that God declared him to be righteous—wasn't just for
4:25 Isa 53:4-5 — Abraham's benefit. 24 It was for us, too, assuring us that God will also declare us to be
Rom 8:30 — righteous if we believe in God, who brought Jesus our Lord back from the dead. 25 He
1 Cor 15:17 — was handed over to die because of our sins, and he was raised from the dead to make us
2 Cor 5:15 — right with God.
1 Pet 1:21

Faith Brings Joy

5:1 Rom 3:28 — **5** Therefore, since we have been made right in God's sight by faith, we have peace
with God because of what Jesus Christ our Lord has done for us. 2 Because of our
5:2 Eph 2:18; 3:12 — faith, Christ has brought us into this place of highest privilege where we now stand, and
we confidently and joyfully look forward to sharing God's glory.

4:17 Gen 17:5. **4:18** Gen 15:5.

WHAT WE HAVE AS CHILDREN

What we have as Adam's children	*What we have as God's children*
Ruin 5:9	Rescue 5:8
Sin 5:12, 15, 21	Righteousness 5:18
Death 5:12, 16, 21	Eternal life 5:17, 21
Separation from God 5:18	Relationship with God 5:11, 19
Disobedience 5:12, 19	Obedience 5:19
Judgment 5:18	Deliverance 5:10, 11
Law 5:20	Grace 5:20

4:16 Paul explains that Abraham had pleased God through Abraham's faith alone before he had ever heard about the rituals that would become so important to the Jewish people. We, too, are saved by faith plus nothing. It is not by loving God and doing good that we are saved; neither is it by faith plus love or by faith plus good deeds. We are saved only through faith in Christ, trusting him to forgive all our sins. For more on Abraham, see his Profile in Genesis 18.

4:17 The promise (or covenant) God gave Abraham stated that Abraham would be the father of many nations (Genesis 17:2-4) and that the entire world would be blessed through him (Genesis 12:3). This promise was fulfilled in Jesus Christ. Jesus was from Abraham's line, and truly the whole world was blessed through him.

4:21 Abraham never doubted that God would fulfill his promise. Abraham's life was marked by mistakes, sins, and failures as well as by wisdom and goodness, but he consistently trusted God. His faith was strengthened by the obstacles he faced, and his life was an example of faith in action. If he had looked only at his own resources for subduing Canaan and founding a nation, he would have given up in despair. But Abraham looked to God, obeyed him, and waited for God to fulfill his word.

4:25 When we accept Jesus Christ as our Savior, an exchange takes place. We give him our sins, and he forgives us and makes us right with God (see 2 Corinthians 5:21). There is nothing we can do to earn this. Only through Christ can we be made right in God's eyes. What an incredible bargain this is for us! But sadly, many still choose to pass up this gift to continue "enjoying" their sin.

5:1 We now have peace *with God,* which may differ from peaceful feelings such as calmness and tranquility. Peace with God means that we have been reconciled with him. There is no more hostility between us, no sin blocking our relationship with him. Peace with God is possible only because Jesus paid the price for our sins through his death on the cross.

5:1-5 These verses introduce a section that contains some difficult concepts. To understand the next four chapters, it helps to keep in mind the two-sided reality of the Christian life. On the one hand, we are complete in Christ (our acceptance with him is secure). On the other hand, we are growing in Christ (we are becoming more and more like him). At one and the same time we have the status of kings and the duties of slaves. We feel both the presence of Christ and the pressure of sin. We enjoy the peace that comes from being made right with God, but we still face daily problems that often help us grow. If we remember these two sides of the Christian life, we will not grow discouraged

[3]We can rejoice, too, when we run into problems and trials, for we know that they are
good for us—they help us learn to endure. [4]And endurance develops strength of
character in us, and character strengthens our confident expectation of salvation. [5]And
this expectation will not disappoint us. For we know how dearly God loves us, because
he has given us the Holy Spirit to fill our hearts with his love.
[6]When we were utterly helpless, Christ came at just the right time and died for us
sinners. [7]Now, no one is likely to die for a good person, though someone might be willing
to die for a person who is especially good. [8]But God showed his great love for us by
sending Christ to die for us while we were still sinners. [9]And since we have been made
right in God's sight by the blood of Christ, he will certainly save us from God's judgment.
[10]For since we were restored to friendship with God by the death of his Son while we were
still his enemies, we will certainly be delivered from eternal punishment by his life. [11]So
now we can rejoice in our wonderful new relationship with God—all because of what our
Lord Jesus Christ has done for us in making us friends of God.

5:3 Matt 5:12
5:5 2 Cor 1:22; Gal 4:6; Eph 1:13; Phil 1:20
5:6 Gal 4:4; Eph 5:2
5:8 John 3:16; 1 Jn 4:10
5:9 Rom 1:18; 2:5, 8
5:10 Rom 8:34; 2 Cor 5:18-19; Eph 2:3

Adam and Christ Contrasted

[12]When Adam sinned, sin entered the entire human race. Adam's sin brought death, so
death spread to everyone, for everyone sinned. [13]Yes, people sinned even before the law
was given. And though there was no law to break, since it had not yet been given, [14]they
all died anyway—even though they did not disobey an explicit commandment of God,
as Adam did. What a contrast between Adam and Christ, who was yet to come! [15]And

5:12 Gen 2:17; 3:19; 1 Cor 15:21-22
5:13 Rom 4:15
5:14 1 Cor 15:22, 45

as we face temptations and problems. Instead, we will learn to depend on the power available to us from Christ, who lives in us by the Holy Spirit.

5:2 Paul states that, as believers, we now stand in a place of highest privilege. Not only has God declared us not guilty; he has drawn us close to himself. Instead of being enemies, we have become his friends—in fact, his own children (John 15:15; Galatians 4:5).

5:3, 4 For first-century Christians, suffering was the rule rather than the exception. Paul tells us that in the future we will *become*, but until then we must *overcome*. This means we will experience difficulties that help us grow. We rejoice in suffering, not because we like pain or deny its tragedy, but because we know God is using life's difficulties and Satan's attacks to build our character. The problems that we run into will develop our perseverance—which in turn will strengthen our character, deepen our trust in God, and give us greater confidence about the future. You probably find your patience tested in some way every day. Thank God for those opportunities to grow, and deal with them in his strength (see also James 1:2-4; 1 Peter 1:6, 7).

5:5, 6 All three members of the Trinity are involved in salvation. The Father loved us so much that he sent his Son to bridge the gap between us (John 3:16). The Father and the Son send the Holy Spirit to fill our life with love and to enable us to live by his power (Acts 1:8). With all this loving care, how can we do less than serve him completely!

5:6 We were weak and helpless because we could do nothing on our own to save ourselves. Someone had to come and rescue us. Christ came at exactly the right time in history—according to God's own schedule. God controls all history, and he controlled the timing, method, and events surrounding Jesus' death.

5:8 *While we were still sinners*—these are amazing words. God sent Jesus Christ to die for us, not because we were good enough, but just because he loved us. Whenever you feel uncertain about God's love for you, remember that he loved you even before you turned to him.

5:9, 10 The love that caused Christ to die is the same love that sends the Holy Spirit to live in us and guide us every day. The power that raised Christ from the dead is the same power that saved you and is available to you in your daily life. Be assured that, having begun a life with Christ, you have a reserve of power and love to call on each day for help to meet every challenge or trial. You can pray for God's power and love as you need it.

5:11 God is holy, and he will not be associated with sin. All people are sinful and so they are separated from God. In addition, all sin deserves punishment. Instead of punishing us with the death we deserve, however, Christ took our sins upon himself and took our punishment by dying on the cross. Now we can rejoice in God. Through faith in *Christ's* work, we become close to God (friends) rather than being enemies and outcasts.

5:12 How can we be declared guilty for something Adam did thousands of years ago? Many feel it isn't fair for God to judge us because of Adam's sin. Yet each of us confirms our heritage with Adam by our own sins every day. We have the same sinful nature and are prone to rebel against God, and we are judged for the sins *we* commit. Because we are sinners, it isn't fairness we need—it is mercy.

5:13, 14 Paul has shown that keeping the law does not bring salvation. Here he adds that breaking the law is not what brings death. Death is the result of Adam's sin and of the sins we all commit, even if they don't resemble Adam's. Paul reminds his readers that for thousands of years the law had not yet been explicitly given, and yet people died. The law was added, he explains in 5:20, to help people see their sinfulness, to show them the seriousness of their offenses, and to drive them to God for mercy and pardon. This was true in Moses' day, and it is still true today. Sin is a deep discrepancy between who we are and who we were created to be. The law points out our sin and places the responsibility for it squarely on our shoulders. But the law offers no remedy. When we are convicted of sin, we must turn to Jesus Christ for healing.

5:14 Adam was the counterpart of Christ. Just as Adam was a representative of created humanity, so is Christ the representative of a new spiritual humanity.

5:15-19 We were all born into Adam's physical family—the family line that leads to certain death. All of us have reaped the results of Adam's sin. We have inherited his guilt, a sinful nature (the tendency to sin), and God's punishment. Because of Jesus, however, we can trade judgment for forgiveness. Christ offers us the opportunity to be born into his spiritual family—the family line that begins with forgiveness and leads to eternal life. If we do nothing, we receive death through Adam; but if we come to God by faith, we receive life through Christ. To which family line do you now belong?

what a difference between our sin and God's generous gift of forgiveness. For this one
man, Adam, brought death to many through his sin. But this other man, Jesus Christ,
brought forgiveness to many through God's bountiful gift. [16]And the result of God's
gracious gift is very different from the result of that one man's sin. For Adam's sin led
to condemnation, but we have the free gift of being accepted by God, even though we
5:17 are guilty of many sins. [17]The sin of this one man, Adam, caused death to rule over us,
1 Cor 15:21 but all who receive God's wonderful, gracious gift of righteousness will live in triumph
over sin and death through this one man, Jesus Christ.
5:18 [18]Yes, Adam's one sin brought condemnation upon everyone, but Christ's one act of
Isa 53:11; 1 Cor 15:22 righteousness makes all people right in God's sight and gives them life. [19]Because one
5:19 person disobeyed God, many people became sinners. But because one other person
Phil 2:8 obeyed God, many people will be made right in God's sight.
5:20 [20]God's law was given so that all people could see how sinful they were. But as people
Rom 4:15; 7:8; Gal 3:19 sinned more and more, God's wonderful kindness became more abundant. [21]So just as
5:21 sin ruled over all people and brought them to death, now God's wonderful kindness rules
Rom 6:23 instead, giving us right standing with God and resulting in eternal life through Jesus
Christ our Lord.

3. Freedom from sin's grasp

Sin's Power Is Broken

6:1 **6** Well then, should we keep on sinning so that God can show us more and more
Rom 3:5-8 kindness and forgiveness? [2]Of course not! Since we have died to sin, how can we
6:2 Rom 8:13 continue to live in it? [3]Or have you forgotten that when we became Christians and were
Col 2:20; 3:3 baptized to become one with Christ Jesus, we died with him? [4]For we died and were
6:4 Eph 4:22-24 buried with Christ by baptism. And just as Christ was raised from the dead by the
Col 2:12; 3:10 glorious power of the Father, now we also may live new lives.

WHAT HAS GOD DONE ABOUT SIN?	He has given us . . .		Principle	Importance
	New life	6:2, 3	Sin's power is broken.	We can be certain that sin's power is broken.
		6:4	Sin-loving nature is buried.	
		6:6	You are no longer under sin's control.	
	New nature	6:5	Now you share his new life.	We can see ourselves as unresponsive to the old power and alive to the new.
		6:11	Look upon your old self as dead; instead, be alive to God.	
	New freedom	6:12	Do not let sin control you.	We can commit ourselves to obey Christ in perfect freedom.
		6:13	Give yourselves completely to God.	
		6:14	You are free.	
		6:16	You can choose your own master.	

5:17 What a promise this is to those who love Christ! We can triumph over sin's power and death's threats through the power of Jesus Christ. See 8:17 for more on our privileged position in Christ.

5:20 As a sinner, separated from God, you see his law from below, as a ladder to be climbed to get to God. Perhaps you have repeatedly tried to climb it, only to fall to the ground every time you have advanced one or two rungs. Or perhaps the sheer height of the ladder seems so overwhelming that you have never even started up. In either case, what relief you should feel to see Jesus offering with open arms to lift you above the ladder of the law, to take you directly to God! Once Jesus lifts you into God's presence, you are free to obey—out of love, not necessity, and through God's power, not your own. You know that if you stumble, you will not fall back to the ground. Instead, you will be caught and held in Christ's loving arms.

6:1–8:39 This section deals with *sanctification*—the change God makes in our life as we grow in the faith. Chapter 6 explains that believers are free from sin's control. Chapter 7 discusses the continuing struggle believers have with sin. Chapter 8 describes how we can have victory over sin.

6:1, 2 If God loves to forgive, why not give him more to forgive? If forgiveness is guaranteed, do we have the freedom to sin as much as we want to? Paul's forceful answer is *Of course not!* Such an attitude—deciding ahead of time to take advantage of God—shows that a person does not understand the seriousness of sin. God's forgiveness does not make sin less serious; his Son's death for sin shows us the dreadful seriousness of sin. Jesus paid with his life so we could be forgiven. The availability of God's mercy must not become an excuse for careless living and moral laxness.

6:1-4 In the church of Paul's day, immersion was the usual form of baptism; that is, new Christians were completely "buried" in water. They understood baptism to symbolize the death and burial of the old way of life. Coming up out of the water symbolized resurrection to new life with Christ. If we think of our old, sinful life as dead and buried, we have a powerful motive to resist sin. We can consciously choose to treat the desires and temptations of the old nature as if they were dead. Then we can continue to enjoy our wonderful new life with Jesus (see Galatians 3:27 and Colossians 2:12 and 3:1-4 for more on this concept).

5 Since we have been united with him in his death, we will also be raised as he was.
6 Our old sinful selves were crucified with Christ so that sin might lose its power in our
lives. We are no longer slaves to sin. 7 For when we died with Christ we were set free
from the power of sin. 8 And since we died with Christ, we know we will also share his
new life. 9 We are sure of this because Christ rose from the dead, and he will never die
again. Death no longer has any power over him. 10 He died once to defeat sin, and now
he lives for the glory of God. 11 So you should consider yourselves dead to sin and able
to live for the glory of God through Christ Jesus.
12 Do not let sin control the way you live;* do not give in to its lustful desires. 13 Do
not let any part of your body become a tool of wickedness, to be used for sinning. Instead,
give yourselves completely to God since you have been given new life. And use your
whole body as a tool to do what is right for the glory of God. 14 Sin is no longer your
master, for you are no longer subject to the law, which enslaves you to sin. Instead, you
are free by God's grace.

Freedom to Obey God

15 So since God's grace has set us free from the law, does this mean we can go on sinning?
Of course not! 16 Don't you realize that whatever you choose to obey becomes your
master? You can choose sin, which leads to death, or you can choose to obey God and
receive his approval. 17 Thank God! Once you were slaves of sin, but now you have
obeyed with all your heart the new teaching God has given you. 18 Now you are free from
sin, your old master, and you have become slaves to your new master, righteousness.
19 I speak this way, using the illustration of slaves and masters, because it is easy to
understand. Before, you let yourselves be slaves of impurity and lawlessness. Now you
must choose to be slaves of righteousness so that you will become holy.
20 In those days, when you were slaves of sin, you weren't concerned with doing what
was right. 21 And what was the result? It was not good, since now you are ashamed of the
things you used to do, things that end in eternal doom. 22 But now you are free from the

6:5 Phil 3:10-11; Col 2:12; 3:1
6:6 Gal 2:20; 5:24; Col 2:12
6:7 1 Pet 4:1
6:11 Rom 7:4; Col 2:20; 3:3
6:13 Rom 12:1; 2 Cor 5:14
6:14 Rom 7:4, 6; 8:2, 12; Gal 5:18; 1 Jn 3:16
6:16 John 8:34; 2 Pet 2:19
6:17 2 Tim 1:13
6:18 John 8:32
6:21 Rom 7:5; 8:6, 13
6:22 John 8:32; Rom 8:2; 1 Cor 7:22; 1 Pet 1:9; 2:16

6:12 Or *Do not let sin reign in your body, which is subject to death.*

6:5ff Because we are united with Christ in his death, our evil desires and bondage to sin died with him. Now, united by faith with him in his resurrection life, we have unbroken fellowship with God and freedom from sin's hold on us. For more on the difference between our new life in Christ and our old sinful nature, read Ephesians 4:21-24 and Colossians 3:3-15.

6:6, 7 The power of sin over us died with Christ on the cross. Our "old sinful selves," our sinful nature, died once and for all, so we are freed from its power. The "power of sin" refers to our rebellious sin-loving nature inherited from Adam. Though we often willingly cooperate with our sinful nature, it is not us but the sin in us that is evil. And it is this power of sin at work in our life that is defeated. Paul has already stated that through faith in Christ we stand acquitted, "not guilty" before God. Here Paul emphasizes that we need no longer live under sin's power. God does not take us out of the world or make us robots—we will still feel like sinning, and sometimes we will sin. The difference is that before we were saved we were slaves to our sinful nature, but now we can choose to live for Christ (see Galatians 2:20).

6:8, 9 Because of Christ's death and resurrection, his followers need never fear death. That assurance frees us to enjoy fellowship with him and to do his will. This will affect all our activities—work and worship, play, Bible study, quiet times, and times of caring for others. When you know that you don't have to fear death, you will experience a new vigor in life.

6:11 "Consider yourselves dead to sin" means that we should regard our old sinful nature as dead and unresponsive to sin. Because of our union and identification with Christ, we no longer want to pursue our old plans, desires, and goals. Now we want to live for the glory of God. As we start this new life, the Holy Spirit will help us become all that Christ wants us to be.

6:14, 15 If we're no longer under the law but under grace, are we now free to sin and disregard the Ten Commandments? Paul says, "Of course not!" When we were under the law, sin was our master—the law does not justify us or help us overcome sin. But now that we are bound to Christ, he is our Master, and he gives us power to do good rather than evil.

6:16-18 All people have a master and pattern themselves after him. Without Jesus, we would have no choice; we would be enslaved to sin, and the results would be guilt, suffering, and separation from God. Thanks to Jesus, however, we can now choose God as our Master. Following him, we can enjoy new life and learn how to work for him. Are you still serving your first master, sin? Or have you chosen God?

6:17 To "obey with all your heart" means to give yourself fully to God, to love him "with all your heart, all your soul, and all your mind" (Matthew 22:37). And yet so often our efforts to know and obey God's commands can best be described as "halfhearted." How do you rate your heart's obedience? God wants to give you the power to obey him with all your heart.

6:17 The "new teaching" given to them is the Good News that Jesus died for their sins and was raised to give them new life. Many believe that this refers to the early church's statement of faith found in 1 Corinthians 15:1-11.

6:19-22 It is impossible to be neutral. Every person has a master—either God or sin. A Christian is not someone who cannot sin but someone who is no longer a slave to sin. He or she belongs to God.

6:23 Matt 25:46 John 3:16; 17:2 Rom 5:21 Gal 6:8

power of sin and have become slaves of God. Now you do those things that lead to
holiness and result in eternal life. 23 For the wages of sin is death, but the free gift of God
is eternal life through Christ Jesus our Lord.

No Longer Bound to the Law

7:2 1 Cor 7:39

7 Now, dear friends*—you who are familiar with the law—don't you know that the
law applies only to a person who is still living? 2 Let me illustrate. When a woman
marries, the law binds her to her husband as long as he is alive. But if he dies, the laws

7:3 Luke 16:18

of marriage no longer apply to her. 3 So while her husband is alive, she would be
committing adultery if she married another man. But if her husband dies, she is free from
that law and does not commit adultery when she remarries.

7:4 Rom 6:6; 8:2 Gal 5:18 Col 2:14 1 Pet 2:24

4 So then, dear friends, the point is this: The law no longer holds you in its power,
because you died to its power when you died with Christ on the cross. And now you are
united with the one who was raised from the dead. As a result, you can produce good

7:5 Rom 6:21; 8:8 Gal 5:19-21

fruit, that is, good deeds for God. 5 When we were controlled by our old nature, sinful
desires were at work within us, and the law aroused these evil desires that produced
sinful deeds, resulting in death. 6 But now we have been released from the law, for we

7:6 2 Cor 3:6 Gal 5:22 Phil 3:3

died with Christ, and we are no longer captive to its power. Now we can really serve God,
not in the old way by obeying the letter of the law, but in the new way, by the Spirit.

God's Law Reveals Our Sin

7:7 †Exod 20:17 †Deut 5:21 Rom 4:15

7 Well then, am I suggesting that the law of God is evil? Of course not! The law is not
sinful, but it was the law that showed me my sin. I would never have known that coveting
is wrong if the law had not said, "Do not covet."* 8 But sin took advantage of this law

7:8 Rom 4:15

and aroused all kinds of forbidden desires within me! If there were no law, sin would not
have that power.

7:1 Greek *brothers;* also in 7:4. **7:7** Exod 20:17; Deut 5:21.

6:23 You are free to choose between two masters: sin or Christ Jesus. The wages of sin is eternal death. That is all you can expect or hope for in life without God. By choosing Christ as your master, you receive his gift of eternal life—new life with God that begins on earth and continues forever with God. What choice have you made?

6:23 Eternal life is a gift from God. If it is a gift, then it is not something that we earn, nor something that must be paid back. Consider the foolishness of someone who receives a gift given out of love and then offers to pay for it. A gift cannot be purchased by the recipient. A more appropriate response to a loved one who offers a gift is graceful acceptance with gratitude. Our salvation is a gift of God, not something of our own doing (Ephesians 2:8, 9). He saved us because of his mercy, not because of any good things that we have done (Titus 3:5). How much more we should accept with thanksgiving the gift that God has freely given to us.

7:1ff Paul shows that the law is powerless to save the sinner (7:7-14), the lawkeeper (7:15-22), and even the person with a new nature (7:23-25). The sinner is condemned by the law; the lawkeeper can't live up to it; and the person with the new nature finds his or her obedience to the law sabotaged by the effects of the old nature. Once again Paul declares that salvation cannot be found by obeying the law. No matter who we are, only Jesus Christ can set us free.

7:2-6 Paul uses marriage to illustrate our relationship to the law. When a spouse dies, the law of marriage no longer applies. Because we have died with Christ, the law can no longer condemn us. Since we are united with Christ, his Spirit enables us to produce good deeds for God. We now serve God, not by obeying a set of rules, but out of renewed hearts and minds that overflow with love for him.

7:4 When a person dies to the old life and accepts Christ as Savior, a new life begins. An unbeliever's life is centered on his or her own personal gratification. Those who don't follow Christ have only their own self-determination as their source of power. By contrast, God is at the center of a Christian's life. God supplies the power for a Christian's daily living. Believers find that their whole way of looking at the world changes when they come to Christ.

7:6 Some people try to earn their way to God by keeping a set of rules (obeying the Ten Commandments, attending church faithfully, or doing good deeds), but all they earn for their efforts is frustration and discouragement. However, because of Christ's sacrifice, the way to God is already open, and we can become his children simply by putting our faith in him. No longer trying to reach God by keeping rules, we can become more and more like Jesus as we live for him day by day. Let the Holy Spirit turn your eyes away from your own performance and toward Jesus. He will free you to serve him out of love and gratitude. This is living "in the new way, by the Spirit."

7:6 Keeping the rules, laws, and customs of Christianity doesn't save us. Even if we could keep our actions pure, we would still be doomed because our heart and mind are perverse and rebellious. Like Paul, we can find no relief in the synagogue or church until we look to Jesus Christ himself for our salvation—which he gives us freely. When we do come to Jesus, we are flooded with relief and gratitude. Will we keep the rules any better? Most likely, but we will be motivated by love and gratitude, not by the desire to get God's approval. We will not be merely submitting to an external code but willingly and lovingly be seeking to do God's will.

9 I felt fine when I did not understand what the law demanded. But when I learned the
truth, I realized I had broken the law and was a sinner, doomed to die. 10 So the good law,
which was supposed to show me the way of life, instead gave me the death penalty. 11 Sin
took advantage of the law and fooled me; it took the good law and used it to make me
guilty of death. 12 But still, the law itself is holy and right and good.
13 But how can that be? Did the law, which is good, cause my doom? Of course not!
Sin used what was good to bring about my condemnation. So we can see how terrible
sin really is. It uses God's good commandment for its own evil purposes.

Struggling with Sin

14 The law is good, then. The trouble is not with the law but with me, because I am sold
into slavery, with sin as my master. 15 I don't understand myself at all, for I really want
to do what is right, but I don't do it. Instead, I do the very thing I hate. 16 I know perfectly
well that what I am doing is wrong, and my bad conscience shows that I agree that the
law is good. 17 But I can't help myself, because it is sin inside me that makes me do these
evil things.
18 I know I am rotten through and through so far as my old sinful nature is concerned. No
matter which way I turn, I can't make myself do right. I want to, but I can't. 19 When I want
to do good, I don't. And when I try not to do wrong, I do it anyway. 20 But if I am doing
what I don't want to do, I am not really the one doing it; the sin within me is doing it.
21 It seems to be a fact of life that when I want to do what is right, I inevitably do what
is wrong. 22 I love God's law with all my heart. 23 But there is another law at work within
me that is at war with my mind. This law wins the fight and makes me a slave to the sin
that is still within me. 24 Oh, what a miserable person I am! Who will free me from this
life that is dominated by sin?* 25 Thank God! The answer is in Jesus Christ our Lord. So

7:10 Lev 18:5; Rom 10:5; 2 Cor 3:7; Gal 3:12
7:11 Gen 3:13; Heb 3:13
7:12 1 Tim 1:8
7:14 1 Kgs 21:20-25; Rom 3:9; 6:6
7:15 Gal 5:17
7:18 Gen 6:5; 8:21; John 3:6; Rom 8:3
7:22 Pss 1:2; 40:8; Eph 3:16
7:23 Gal 5:17; Jas 4:1; 1 Pet 2:11
7:24 Rom 6:6; 8:2
7:25 Rom 6:16, 22; 1 Cor 15:57; 2 Cor 2:14

7:24 Greek *from this body of death?*

7:9-11 Where there is no law, there is no sin, because people cannot know that their actions are sinful unless a law forbids those actions. God's law makes people realize that they are sinners doomed to die, yet it offers no help. Sin is real, and it is dangerous. Imagine a sunny day at the beach. You plunge into the surf; then you notice a sign on the pier: "No swimming. Sharks." Your day is ruined. Is it the sign's fault? Are you angry with the people who put it up? The law is like the sign. It is essential, and we are grateful for it—but it doesn't get rid of the sharks.

7:11, 12 Sin deceives people by misusing the law. The law was holy, expressing God's nature and will for people. In the Garden of Eden (Genesis 3), the serpent deceived Eve, changing her focus from the freedom she had to the one restriction God had made. Ever since then, we have all been rebels. Sin looks good to us precisely because God has said it is wrong. Instead of paying attention to his warnings, we use them as a "to do" list. When we are tempted to rebel, we need to look at the law from a wider perspective—in the light of God's grace and mercy. If we focus on his great love for us, we will understand that he only restricts us from actions and attitudes that ultimately will harm us.

7:14 "I am sold into slavery, with sin as my master" may be a reference to the old nature that seeks to rebel and be independent of God. If I, being a Christian, try to struggle with sin in my own strength, I will slip into the grasp of sin's power.

7:15 Paul shares three lessons that he learned in trying to deal with his old sinful desires: (1) Knowledge is not the answer (7:9). Paul felt fine as long as he did not understand what the law demanded. When he learned the truth, he knew he was doomed. (2) Self-determination (struggling in one's own strength) doesn't succeed (7:15). Paul found himself sinning in ways that weren't even attractive to him. (3) Becoming a Christian does not stamp out all sin and temptation from a person's life (7:22-25).

Being born again takes a moment of faith, but becoming like Christ is a lifelong process. Paul compares Christian growth to a strenuous race or fight (1 Corinthians 9:24-27; 2 Timothy 4:7). Thus, as Paul has been emphasizing since the beginning of this letter, *no one* in the world is innocent; no one deserves to be saved—not the pagan who doesn't know God's laws, not the Christian or Jew who knows them and tries to keep them. All of us must depend totally on the work of Christ for our salvation. We cannot earn it by our good behavior.

7:15 This is more than the cry of one desperate man; it describes the experience of all Christians struggling against sin or trying to please God by keeping rules and laws without the Spirit's help. We must never underestimate the power of sin and attempt to fight it in our own strength. Satan is a crafty tempter, and we have an amazing ability to make excuses. Instead of trying to overcome sin with our own human willpower, we must take hold of God's provision for victory over sin: the Holy Spirit, who lives within us and gives us power. And when we fall, he lovingly reaches out to help us up.

7:17-20 "The devil made me do it." "I didn't do it; the sin within me did it." These sound like good excuses for sin, but we are responsible for our actions. We must never use the power of sin or Satan as an excuse, because they are defeated enemies. Without Christ's help, sin is stronger than we are, and sometimes we are unable to defend ourselves against its attacks. That is why we should never stand up to sin all alone. Jesus Christ, who has conquered sin once and for all, promises to fight by our side. If we look to him for help, we will not have to give in to sin.

7:23-25 The "law at work within" is the sin nature deep within us. This is our vulnerability to sin; it refers to everything within us that is more loyal to our old way of selfish living than to God.

7:23-25 This inward struggle with sin was as real for Paul as it is for us. From Paul we learn what to do about it. Whenever Paul felt lost, he would return to the beginning of his spiritual life, remembering that he had already been freed by Jesus Christ. When you feel confused and overwhelmed by sin's appeal, follow Paul's example: Thank God that he has given you freedom through Jesus Christ. Let the reality of Christ's power lift you up to real victory over sin.

you see how it is: In my mind I really want to obey God's law, but because of my sinful
nature I am a slave to sin.

Life in the Spirit

8 So now there is no condemnation for those who belong to Christ Jesus. 2For the
power* of the life-giving Spirit has freed you* through Christ Jesus from the power
of sin that leads to death. 3The law of Moses could not save us, because of our sinful
nature. But God put into effect a different plan to save us. He sent his own Son in a human
body like ours, except that ours are sinful. God destroyed sin's control over us by giving
his Son as a sacrifice for our sins. 4He did this so that the requirement of the law would
be fully accomplished for us* who no longer follow our sinful nature but instead follow
the Spirit.

5Those who are dominated by the sinful nature think about sinful things, but those
who are controlled by the Holy Spirit think about things that please the Spirit. 6If your
sinful nature controls your mind, there is death. But if the Holy Spirit controls your mind,
there is life and peace. 7For the sinful nature is always hostile to God. It never did obey
God's laws, and it never will. 8That's why those who are still under the control of their
sinful nature can never please God.

9But you are not controlled by your sinful nature. You are controlled by the Spirit if
you have the Spirit of God living in you. (And remember that those who do not have the
Spirit of Christ living in them are not Christians at all.) 10Since Christ lives within you,
even though your body will die because of sin, your spirit is alive* because you have
been made right with God. 11The Spirit of God, who raised Jesus from the dead, lives in
you. And just as he raised Christ from the dead, he will give life to your mortal body by
this same Spirit living within you.

12So, dear Christian friends,* you have no obligation whatsoever to do what your
sinful nature urges you to do. 13For if you keep on following it, you will perish. But if
through the power of the Holy Spirit you turn from it* and its evil deeds, you will live.
14For all who are led by the Spirit of God are children of God.

8:1 Rom 8:34
8:2 Rom 8:11; 2 Cor 3:6; Gal 2:19; 5:1
8:3 Acts 13:38; 2 Cor 5:21; Phil 2:7; Heb 2:14; 4:15
8:4 Gal 5:16, 25
8:5 Gal 5:19-22
8:6 Rom 6:23; Gal 6:8
8:9 John 14:17-18, 23; Gal 4:6; Phil 1:19; 1 Pet 1:11
8:10 John 14:20; 15:5; 17:23, 26; 2 Cor 13:5; Col 1:26-27
8:11 Rom 6:5; 1 Cor 6:14; 15:45
8:13 Gal 6:8; Col 3:5
8:14 John 1:12; Gal 3:26; Rev 21:7

8:2a Greek *the law;* also in 8:2b. **8:2b** Some manuscripts read *me.* **8:4** Or *accomplished by us.* **8:10** Or *the Spirit will bring you eternal life.* **8:12** Greek *brothers.* **8:13** Greek *put it to death.*

8:1 "Not guilty; let him go free." What would those words mean to you if you were on death row? The fact is that the whole human race *is* on death row, justly condemned for repeatedly breaking God's holy law. Without Jesus we would have no hope at all. But thank God! He has declared us not guilty and has offered us freedom from sin and power to do his will.

8:2 This life-giving Spirit is the Holy Spirit. He was present at the creation of the world (Genesis 1:2), and he is the power behind the rebirth of every Christian. He gives us the power we need to live the Christian life. For more about the Holy Spirit, read the notes on John 3:6; Acts 1:3; 1:4, 5; 1:5.

8:3 Jesus gave himself as a sacrifice for our sins. In Old Testament times, animal sacrifices were continually offered at the Temple. The sacrifices showed the Israelites the seriousness of sin: Blood had to be shed before sins could be pardoned (see Leviticus 17:11). But the blood of animals could not really remove sins (Hebrews 10:4). The sacrifices could only point to Jesus' sacrifice, which paid the penalty for all sins.

8:5, 6 Paul divides people into two categories: those who let themselves be controlled by their sinful nature and those who follow after the Holy Spirit. All of us would be in the first category if Jesus hadn't offered us a way out. Once we have said yes to Jesus, we will want to continue following him, because his way brings life and peace. Daily we must consciously choose to center our life on God. Use the Bible to discover God's guidelines, and then follow them. In every perplexing situation, ask yourself, What would Jesus want me to do? When the Holy Spirit points out what is right, do it eagerly. For more on our sinful natures versus our new life in Christ, see 6:6-8; Ephesians 4:22-24; Colossians 3:3-15.

8:9 Have you ever worried about whether or not you really are a Christian? A Christian is anyone who has the Spirit of God living in him or her. If you have sincerely trusted Christ for your salvation and acknowledged him as Lord, then the Holy Spirit lives within you and you are a Christian. You can be assured that you have the Holy Spirit because Jesus promised that he would send him. Since you now believe that Jesus Christ is God's Son and that eternal life comes through him (1 John 5:5), you will begin to act as Christ directs (Romans 8:5; Galatians 5:22, 23); you will find help in your daily problems and in your praying (Romans 8:26, 27); you will be empowered to serve God and do his will (Acts 1:8; Romans 12:6ff); and you will become part of God's plan to build up his church (Ephesians 4:12, 13).

8:11 The Holy Spirit is God's promise or guarantee of eternal life for those who believe in him. The Spirit is within us now by faith, and by faith we are certain to live with Christ forever. See Romans 8:23; 1 Corinthians 6:14; 2 Corinthians 4:14; 1 Thessalonians 4:14.

8:13 When we turn away from sin's appeal in the Holy Spirit's power, regarding sin as dead, we can ignore temptation when it comes (see 6:11; Galatians 5:24).

8:14-17 Paul uses adoption to illustrate the believer's new relationship with God. In Roman culture, the adopted person lost all rights in his old family and gained all the rights of a legitimate child in his new family. He became a full heir to his new father's estate. Likewise, when a person becomes a Christian, he or she gains all the privileges and responsibilities of a child in God's family. One of these outstanding privileges is being led by the Spirit (see Galatians 4:5, 6). We may not always feel as though we belong to God, but the Holy Spirit is our witness. His inward presence reminds us of who we are and encourages us with God's love (5:5).

8:14-17 We are no longer like "cowering and fearful slaves"; instead, we are the Master's children. What a privilege! Because we are God's children, we share in great treasures as co-heirs.

15 So you should not be like cowering, fearful slaves. You should behave instead like
God's very own children, adopted into his family—calling him "Father, dear Father."*
16 For his Holy Spirit speaks to us deep in our hearts and tells us that we are God's
children. 17 And since we are his children, we will share his treasures—for everything
God gives to his Son, Christ, is ours, too. But if we are to share his glory, we must also
share his suffering.

The Future Glory

18 Yet what we suffer now is nothing compared to the glory he will give us later. 19 For
all creation is waiting eagerly for that future day when God will reveal who his children
really are. 20 Against its will, everything on earth was subjected to God's curse. 21 All
creation anticipates the day when it will join God's children in glorious freedom from
death and decay. 22 For we know that all creation has been groaning as in the pains of
childbirth right up to the present time. 23 And even we Christians, although we have the
Holy Spirit within us as a foretaste of future glory, also groan to be released from pain
and suffering. We, too, wait anxiously for that day when God will give us our full rights
as his children, including the new bodies he has promised us. 24 Now that we are saved,
we eagerly look forward to this freedom. For if you already have something, you don't
need to hope for it. 25 But if we look forward to something we don't have yet, we must
wait patiently and confidently.
26 And the Holy Spirit helps us in our distress. For we don't even know what we should
pray for, nor how we should pray. But the Holy Spirit prays for us with groanings that cannot
be expressed in words. 27 And the Father who knows all hearts knows what the Spirit is
saying, for the Spirit pleads for us believers in harmony with God's own will. 28 And we
know that God causes everything to work together* for the good of those who love God

8:15 Gal 4:5-6
8:16 2 Cor 1:22; Eph 1:13
8:17 Gal 3:29; 4:7
8:18 2 Cor 4:17; Col 3:4; 1 Pet 1:6-7
8:19 2 Pet 3:13; 1 Jn 3:2
8:20 Gen 3:17-19
8:21 Acts 3:21; 2 Pet 3:13; Rev 21:1
8:22 Jer 12:4
8:23 2 Cor 1:22; 5:5; Phil 3:21
8:26 John 14:16
8:27 1 Cor 4:5
8:28 Eph 1:11; 3:11; 2 Tim 1:9

8:15 Greek *"Abba, Father." Abba* is an Aramaic term for "father." **8:28** Some manuscripts read *And we know that everything works together.*

God has already given us his best gifts: his Son, forgiveness, and eternal life; and he encourages us to ask him for whatever we need.

8:17 There is a price for being identified with Jesus. Along with the great treasures, Paul mentions the suffering that Christians must face. What kinds of suffering are we to endure? For first-century believers, there was economic and social persecution, and some even faced death. We, too, must pay a price for following Jesus. In many parts of today's world, Christians face pressures just as severe as those faced by Christ's first followers. Even in countries where Christianity is tolerated or encouraged, Christians must not become complacent. To live as Jesus did—serving others, giving up one's rights, resisting pressures to conform to the world—always exacts a price. Nothing we suffer, however, can compare to the great price that Jesus paid to save us.

8:19-22 Sin has caused all creation to fall from the perfect state in which God created it. The world is in bondage to death and decay so that it cannot fulfill its intended purpose. One day all creation will be liberated and transformed. Until that time it waits in eager expectation for the resurrection of God's children.

8:19-22 Christians see the world as it is—physically decaying and spiritually infected with sin. But Christians do not need to be pessimistic, because they have hope for future glory. They look forward to the new heaven and new earth that God has promised, and they wait for God's new order that will free the world of sin, sickness, and evil. In the meantime, Christians go with Christ into the world where they heal people's bodies and souls and fight the evil effects of sin in the world.

8:23 We will be resurrected with bodies, glorified bodies like the body Christ now has in heaven (see 1 Corinthians 15:25-58). We have the "foretaste," the first installment or down payment of future glory—the Holy Spirit—as a guarantee of our resurrection life (see 2 Corinthians 1:22; 5:5; Ephesians 1:14).

8:24, 25 It is natural for children to trust their parents, even though parents sometimes fail to keep their promises. Our heavenly Father, however, never makes promises he won't keep. Nevertheless his plan may take more time than we expect. Rather than acting like impatient children as we wait for God's will to unfold, we need to have confidence in God's perfect timing and wisdom.

8:24, 25 In Romans, Paul presents the idea that salvation is past, present, and future. It is past because we *were* saved the moment we believed in Jesus Christ as Savior (3:21-26; 5:1-11; 6:1-11, 22, 23); our new life (eternal life) begins at that moment. And it is present because we *are being* saved; this is the process of sanctification (see the note on 6:1–8:39). But at the same time, we have not fully received all the benefits and blessings of salvation that will be ours when Christ's new Kingdom is completely established. That's our future salvation. While we can be confident of our salvation, we still look ahead with hope and trust toward that complete change of body and personality that lies beyond this life, when we will be like Christ (1 John 3:2).

8:26, 27 As a believer, you are not left to your own resources to cope with problems. Even when you don't know the right words to pray, the Holy Spirit prays with and for you, and God answers. With God helping you pray, you don't need to be afraid to come before him. Ask the Holy Spirit to intercede for you "in harmony with God's own will." Then, when you bring your requests to God, trust that he will always do what is best.

8:28 God works in "everything"—not just isolated incidents—for our good. This does not mean that all that happens to us is good. Evil is prevalent in our fallen world, but God is able to turn every circumstance around for our long-range good. Note that God is not working to make us happy but to fulfill his purpose. Note also that this promise is not for everybody. It can be claimed only by those who love God and are called by him, that is, those whom the Holy Spirit convinces to receive Christ. Such people have a new perspective, a new mind-set. They trust in God, not in worldly treasures; their security is in heaven, not on earth. Their faith in God does not waver in pain and persecution because they know God is with them.

8:29 Eph 1:5; Col 1:18; 2 Tim 2:19; Heb 1:6; 1 Pet 1:2

and are called according to his purpose for them. 29 For God knew his people in advance,
and he chose them to become like his Son, so that his Son would be the firstborn, with many
brothers and sisters. 30 And having chosen them, he called them to come to him. And he gave
them right standing with himself, and he promised them his glory.

Nothing Can Separate Us from God's Love

8:31 Ps 118:6
8:32 John 3:16; Rom 4:25; 5:8
8:33 Isa 50:8
8:34 Ps 110:1; 1 Jn 2:1
8:35 1 Cor 4:11; 2 Cor 11:26-27
8:36 †Ps 44:22
8:37 John 16:33; 1 Cor 15:57; 1 Jn 5:4
8:38 John 10:28; Col 3:3
8:39 Rom 5:3-8

31 What can we say about such wonderful things as these? If God is for us, who can ever
be against us? 32 Since God did not spare even his own Son but gave him up for us all,
won't God, who gave us Christ, also give us everything else?

33 Who dares accuse us whom God has chosen for his own? Will God? No! He is the
one who has given us right standing with himself. 34 Who then will condemn us? Will
Christ Jesus? No, for he is the one who died for us and was raised to life for us and is
sitting at the place of highest honor next to God, pleading for us.

35 Can anything ever separate us from Christ's love? Does it mean he no longer loves
us if we have trouble or calamity, or are persecuted, or are hungry or cold or in danger
or threatened with death? 36 (Even the Scriptures say, "For your sake we are killed every
day; we are being slaughtered like sheep."*) 37 No, despite all these things, overwhelming victory is ours through Christ, who loved us.

38 And I am convinced that nothing can ever separate us from his love. Death can't,
and life can't. The angels can't, and the demons can't. Our fears for today, our worries
about tomorrow, and even the powers of hell can't keep God's love away. 39 Whether we
are high above the sky or in the deepest ocean, nothing in all creation will ever be able
to separate us from the love of God that is revealed in Christ Jesus our Lord.

4. Israel's past, present, and future

God's Selection of Israel

9:1 1 Tim 2:7
9:3 Exod 32:32

9 In the presence of Christ, I speak with utter truthfulness—I do not lie—and my
conscience and the Holy Spirit confirm that what I am saying is true. 2 My heart is
filled with bitter sorrow and unending grief 3 for my people, my Jewish brothers and

8:36 Ps 44:22.

8:29 God's ultimate goal for us is to make us like Christ (1 John 3:2). As we become more and more like him, we discover our true selves, the persons we were created to be. How can we become like Christ? By reading and heeding the Word, by studying his life on earth through the Gospels, by spending time in prayer, by being filled with his Spirit, and by doing his work in the world.

8:29, 30 Some believe these verses mean that before the beginning of the world, God chose certain people to receive his gift of salvation. They point to verses such as Ephesians 1:11, which says that God "chose us from the beginning, and all things happen just as he decided long ago." Others believe that God *knew in advance* who would respond to him, and upon those he set his mark (he chose them). What is clear is that God's *purpose* for people was not an afterthought; it was settled before the foundation of the world. People are to serve and honor God. If you have believed in Christ, you can rejoice in the fact that God has always known you. God's love is eternal. His wisdom and power are supreme. He will guide and protect you until you one day stand in his presence.

8:30 *Called* means "summoned or invited." For more on "right standing" (also called justification) and receiving his glory, see the chart in chapter 3.

8:31-34 Do you ever think that because you aren't good enough for God, he will not save you? Do you ever feel as if salvation is for everyone else but you? Then these verses are especially for you. If God gave his Son for you, he isn't going to hold back the gift of salvation! If Christ gave his life for you, he isn't going to turn around and condemn you! He will not withhold anything you need to live for him. The book of Romans is more than a theological explanation of God's redeeming grace—it is a letter of comfort and confidence addressed to you.

8:34 Paul says that Jesus is pleading for us in heaven. God has acquitted us and has removed our sin and guilt, so it is Satan, not God, who accuses us. When he does, Jesus, our advocate, sits at God's right hand to present our case. For more on the concept of Christ as our advocate, see the notes on Hebrews 4:14; 4:15.

8:35, 36 These words were written to a church that would soon undergo terrible persecution. In just a few years, Paul's hypothetical situations would turn into painful realities. This passage reaffirms God's profound love for his people. No matter what happens to us, no matter where we are, we can never be separated from his love. Suffering should not drive us away from God but help us to identify with him and allow his love to heal us.

8:35-39 These verses contain one of the most comforting promises in all Scripture. Believers have always had to face hardships in many forms: persecution, illness, imprisonment, and even death. These sometimes cause them to fear that they have been abandoned by Christ. But Paul exclaims that it is *impossible* to be separated from Christ. His death for us is proof of his unconquerable love. Nothing can separate us from Christ's presence . God tells us how great his love is so that we will feel totally secure in him. If we believe these overwhelming assurances, we will not be afraid.

8:38 *Powers* are unseen forces of evil in the universe, forces like Satan and his fallen angels (see Ephesians 6:12). In Christ we are super-conquerors, and his love will protect us from any such forces.

9:1-3 Paul expressed concern for his Jewish "brothers and sisters" by saying that he would willingly take their punishment if that would save them. While the only one who can save us is Christ, Paul showed a rare depth of love. Like Jesus, he was willing to sacrifice so others would be saved. How concerned are you for those who don't know Christ? Are you willing to sacrifice your time, money, energy, comfort, and safety to see them come to faith in Jesus?

sisters. I would be willing to be forever cursed—cut off from Christ!—if that would save
them. [4]They are the people of Israel, chosen to be God's special children. God revealed
his glory to them. He made covenants with them and gave his law to them. They have
the privilege of worshiping him and receiving his wonderful promises. [5]Their ancestors
were great people of God, and Christ himself was a Jew as far as his human nature is
concerned. And he is God, who rules over everything and is worthy of eternal praise!
Amen.*

[6]Well then, has God failed to fulfill his promise to the Jews? No, for not everyone born
into a Jewish family is truly a Jew! [7]Just the fact that they are descendants of Abraham
doesn't make them truly Abraham's children. For the Scriptures say, "Isaac is the son
through whom your descendants will be counted,"* though Abraham had other children,
too. [8]This means that Abraham's physical descendants are not necessarily children of
God. It is the children of the promise who are considered to be Abraham's children. [9]For
God had promised, "Next year I will return, and Sarah will have a son."*

[10]This son was our ancestor Isaac. When he grew up, he married Rebekah, who gave
birth to twins. [11]But before they were born, before they had done anything good or bad,
she received a message from God. (This message proves that God chooses according to
his own plan, [12]not according to our good or bad works.) She was told, "The descendants
of your older son will serve the descendants of your younger son."* [13]In the words of
the Scriptures, "I loved Jacob, but I rejected Esau."*

[14]What can we say? Was God being unfair? Of course not! [15]For God said to Moses,

"I will show mercy to anyone I choose,
and I will show compassion to anyone I choose."*

[16]So receiving God's promise is not up to us. We can't get it by choosing it or working
hard for it. God will show mercy to anyone he chooses.

[17]For the Scriptures say that God told Pharaoh, "I have appointed you for the very
purpose of displaying my power in you, and so that my fame might spread throughout
the earth."* [18]So you see, God shows mercy to some just because he wants to, and he
chooses to make some people refuse to listen.

[19]Well then, you might say, "Why does God blame people for not listening? Haven't
they simply done what he made them do?"

[20]No, don't say that. Who are you, a mere human being, to criticize God? Should the
thing that was created say to the one who made it, "Why have you made me like this?"
[21]When a potter makes jars out of clay, doesn't he have a right to use the same lump of
clay to make one jar for decoration and another to throw garbage into? [22]God has every

9:4 Exod 4:22; Deut 4:13; 7:6; Eph 2:12
9:5 John 1:1, 18; Rom 1:3; Titus 2:13; 2 Pet 1:1; 1 Jn 5:20
9:6 Num 23:19; Rom 2:28; Gal 6:16
9:7 †Gen 21:12; Heb 11:18
9:8 Rom 8:14; Gal 3:16; 4:23
9:9 †Gen 18:10, 14
9:10 Gen 25:21
9:12 †Gen 25:23
9:13 †Mal 1:2-3
9:14 Deut 32:4
9:15 †Exod 33:19
9:16 Eph 2:8
9:17 †Exod 9:16
9:18 Exod 4:21; 14:4; Josh 11:20; Rom 11:25
9:20 Isa 29:16; 45:9
9:21 Jer 18:6; 2 Tim 2:20
9:22 Jer 50:25

9:5 Or *May God, who rules over everything, be praised forever. Amen.* **9:7** Gen 21:12. **9:9** Gen 18:10, 14. **9:12** Gen 25:23. **9:13** Mal 1:2-3. **9:15** Exod 33:19. **9:17** Exod 9:16.

9:4 The Jews viewed God's choosing of Israel in the Old Testament as being like adoption. They were undeserving and without rights as natural children. Yet God adopted them and granted them the status of his sons and daughters.

9:6 God's word in the form of beautiful covenant promises came to Abraham. Covenant people, the true children of Abraham, are not just his biological descendants. They are all those who trust in God and in what Jesus Christ has done for them (see also 2:29; Galatians 3:7).

9:11 The Jews were proud of the fact that their lineage came from Isaac, whose mother was Sarah (Abraham's legitimate wife), rather than Ishmael, whose mother was Hagar (Sarah's servant). Paul asserts that no one can claim to be chosen by God because of his or her heritage or good deeds. God freely chooses to save whomever he wills. The doctrine of election teaches that it is God's sovereign choice to save us by his goodness and mercy, not by our own merit.

9:12-14 Was it right for God to choose Jacob, the younger, to be over Esau? In Malachi 1:2, 3, the statement "I showed my love for you by loving your ancestor Jacob. Yet Esau was Jacob's brother, and I rejected Esau" refers to the nations of Israel and Edom rather than to the individual brothers. God chose Jacob to continue the family line of the faithful because he knew his heart was for God. But he did not exclude Esau from knowing and loving him. Keep in mind the kind of God we worship: He is sovereign; he is not arbitrary; in all things he works for our good; he is trustworthy; he will save all who believe in him. When we understand these qualities of God, we know that his choices are good even if we don't understand all his reasons.

9:17, 18 Paul quotes from Exodus 9:16, where God foretold how Pharaoh would be used to declare God's power. Paul uses this argument to show that salvation was God's work, not people's. God's judgment on Pharaoh's sin was to harden his heart, to confirm his disobedience, so that the consequences of his rebellion would be his own punishment.

9:21 With this illustration, Paul is not saying that some of us are worth more than others but that the Creator has control over the created object. The created object, therefore, has no right to demand anything from its Creator—its very existence depends on him. Keeping this perspective removes any temptation to have pride in personal achievement.

right to exercise his judgment and his power, but he also has the right to be very patient
9:23 Rom 8:30 with those who are the objects of his judgment and are fit only for destruction. 23 He also
has the right to pour out the riches of his glory upon those he prepared to be the objects
9:24 Rom 3:29 of his mercy—24 even upon us, whom he selected, both from the Jews and from the
Gentiles.

9:25 †Hos 2:23 25 Concerning the Gentiles, God says in the prophecy of Hosea,

"Those who were not my people,
I will now call my people.
And I will love those
whom I did not love before."*

9:26 †Hos 1:10 26 And,

"Once they were told,
'You are not my people.'
But now he will say,
'You are children of the living God.'"*

9:27 †Isa 10:22 †Hos 2:1 27 Concerning Israel, Isaiah the prophet cried out,

"Though the people of Israel are as numerous as the sand on the seashore,
only a small number will be saved.
9:28 †Isa 10:22-23; 28:22 28 For the Lord will carry out his sentence upon the earth
quickly and with finality."*

9:29 †Isa 1:9 29 And Isaiah said in another place,

"If the Lord Almighty
had not spared a few of us,
we would have been wiped out
as completely as Sodom and Gomorrah."*

Israel's Unbelief

9:30 Gal 2:16 Heb 11:7 30 Well then, what shall we say about these things? Just this: The Gentiles have been made
right with God by faith, even though they were not seeking him. 31 But the Jews, who
9:31 Isa 51:1 Rom 10:2-3 Gal 5:4 tried so hard to get right with God by keeping the law, never succeeded. 32 Why not?
Because they were trying to get right with God by keeping the law and being good
instead of by depending on faith. They stumbled over the great rock in their path. 33 God
9:33 Rom 10:11 1 Pet 2:6, 8 warned them of this in the Scriptures when he said,

9:25 Hos 2:23. **9:26** Hos 1:10. **9:27-28** Isa 10:22-23. **9:29** Isa 1:9.

9:25, 26 About seven hundred years before Jesus' birth, Hosea told of God's intention to restore his people. Paul applies Hosea's message to God's intention to bring Gentiles into his family after the Jews rejected his plan. Verse 25 is a quotation from Hosea 2:23 and verse 26 is from Hosea 1:10.

9:27-29 Isaiah prophesied that only a small number of God's original people, the Jews, would be saved. Paul saw this happening in every city where he preached. Even though he went to the Jews first, relatively few ever accepted the message. Verses 27 and 28 are based on Isaiah 10:22, 23; and 9:29 is from Isaiah 1:9.

9:31-33 Sometimes we are like these people, trying to get right with God by keeping his laws. We may think that attending church, doing church work, giving offerings, and being nice will be enough. After all, we've played by the rules, haven't we? But Paul's words sting—this approach never succeeds. Paul explains that God's plan is not for those who try to earn his favor by being good; it is for those who realize that they can never be good enough and so must depend on Christ. We can be saved only by putting our faith in what Jesus Christ has done. If we do that, we will never be disappointed.

9:32 The Jews had a worthy goal—to honor God. But they tried to achieve it the wrong way—by rigid and painstaking obedience to the law. Thus, some of them became more dedicated to the law than to God. They thought that if they kept the law, God would have to accept them as his people. But God cannot be controlled. The Jews did not see that their Scriptures, the Old Testament, taught that salvation depended on faith, not on human effort (see Genesis 15:6).

9:32 The "rock" they stumbled over was Jesus. The Jews did not believe in him, because he didn't meet their expectations for the Messiah. Some people still stumble over Christ because salvation by faith doesn't make sense to them. They think they must earn their way to God, or perhaps God will simply overlook their sins. Others stumble over Christ because his values are the opposite of the world's. He asks for humility, and many are unwilling to humble themselves before him. He requires obedience, and many refuse to put their wills at his disposal.

"I am placing a stone in Jerusalem* that causes people to stumble,
 and a rock that makes them fall.*
But anyone who believes in him
 will not be disappointed.*"

10 Dear friends,* the longing of my heart and my prayer to God is that the Jewish
people might be saved. [2]I know what enthusiasm they have for God, but it is 10:2 Acts 22:3
misdirected zeal. [3]For they don't understand God's way of making people right with
himself. Instead, they are clinging to their own way of getting right with God by trying 10:3 Rom 9:31-32
to keep the law. They won't go along with God's way. [4]For Christ has accomplished the 10:4 Gal 3:24
whole purpose* of the law. All who believe in him are made right with God.

Salvation Is for Everyone

[5]For Moses wrote that the law's way of making a person right with God requires 10:5 †Lev 18:5
obedience to all of its commands.* [6]But the way of getting right with God through faith Ezek 20:11, 13, 21 Rom 7:10
says, "You don't need to go to heaven" (to find Christ and bring him down to help you).
[7]And it says, "You don't need to go to the place of the dead" (to bring Christ back to life 10:6-8 †Deut 30:12-14
again). [8]Salvation that comes from trusting Christ—which is the message we preach—is
already within easy reach. In fact, the Scriptures say, "The message is close at hand; it
is on your lips and in your heart."*

[9]For if you confess with your mouth that Jesus is Lord and believe in your heart that 10:9 Matt 10:32
God raised him from the dead, you will be saved. [10]For it is by believing in your heart
that you are made right with God, and it is by confessing with your mouth that you are
saved. [11]As the Scriptures tell us, "Anyone who believes in him will not be disap- 10:11 †Isa 28:16
pointed.*" [12]Jew and Gentile are the same in this respect. They all have the same Lord, Rom 9:33
who generously gives his riches to all who ask for them. [13]For "Anyone who calls on 10:12 Acts 15:9
the name of the Lord will be saved."* Eph 2:4-7

[14]But how can they call on him to save them unless they believe in him? And how can 10:13 †Joel 2:32
they believe in him if they have never heard about him? And how can they hear about Acts 2:21
him unless someone tells them? [15]And how will anyone go and tell them without being 10:15 †Isa 52:7 †Nah 1:15

9:33a Greek *in Zion.* **9:33b** Isa 8:14. **9:33c** Or *will not be put to shame.* Isa 28:16. **10:1** Greek *Brothers.* **10:4** Or *the end.* **10:5** Lev 18:5. **10:6-8** Deut 30:12-14. **10:11** Or *will not be put to shame.* Isa 28:16. **10:13** Joel 2:32.

10:1 What will happen to the Jewish people who believe in God but not in Christ? Since they believe in the same God, won't they be saved? If that were true, Paul would not have worked so hard and sacrificed so much to teach them about Christ. Because Jesus is the most complete revelation of God, we cannot fully know God apart from Christ; and because God appointed Jesus to bring God and people together, we cannot come to God by another way. The Jews, like everyone else, must find salvation through Jesus Christ (John 14:6; Acts 4:12). Like Paul, we should pray that all Jews might be saved and lovingly share the Good News with them.

10:3-5 Rather than living by faith in God, the Jews established customs and traditions (in addition to God's law) to try to make themselves acceptable in God's sight. But human effort, no matter how sincere, can never substitute for the righteousness God offers us by faith. The only way to *earn* salvation is to be perfect—and that is impossible. We can only hold out our empty hands and receive salvation as a gift.

10:4 Christ accomplished the whole purpose of the law in two ways: He fulfills the purpose and goal of the law (Matthew 5:17) in that he perfectly exemplified God's desires on earth. But he is also the termination of the law because in comparison to Christ, the law is powerless to save.

10:5 In order to be saved by the law, a person would have to live a perfect life, not sinning once. Why did God give the law when he knew people couldn't keep it? According to Paul, one reason the law was given was to show people how guilty they are (Galatians 3:19). The law was a shadow of Christ—that is, the sacrificial system educated the people so that when the true sacrifice came, they would be able to understand his work (Hebrews 10:1-4). The system of ceremonial laws was to last until the coming of Christ. The law points to Christ, the reason for all those animal sacrifices.

10:6-8 Paul adapts Moses' farewell challenge from Deuteronomy 30:11-14 to apply to Christ. Christ has provided our salvation through his incarnation (God in human form) and resurrection. God's salvation is right in front of us. He will come to us wherever we are. All we need to do is to respond and accept his gift of salvation.

10:8-12 Have you ever been asked, "How do I become a Christian?" These verses give you the beautiful answer: Salvation is as close as your own lips and heart. People think it must be a complicated process, but it is not. If we believe in our heart and say with our mouth that Christ is the risen Lord, we will be saved.

10:11 This verse must be read in context. Paul is not saying Christians will never be disappointed. There will be times when people will let us down or circumstances take a turn for the worse. Paul is saying that God will keep his side of the bargain: Those who call on him will be saved. God will never fail to provide for those who believe.

10:14, 15 We must take God's great message of salvation to others so that they can respond to the Good News. How will your loved ones and neighbors hear it unless someone tells them? Is God calling you to take a part in making his message known in your community? Think of one person who needs to hear the Good News, and think of something you can do to help him or her hear it. Then take that step as soon as possible.

sent? That is what the Scriptures mean when they say, "How beautiful are the feet of
those who bring good news!"*

10:16 †Isa 53:1 John 12:38 Heb 4:2

16 But not everyone welcomes the Good News, for Isaiah the prophet said, "Lord, who
has believed our message?"* 17 Yet faith comes from listening to this message of good
news—the Good News about Christ.

10:17 Gal 3:2, 5 Col 3:16

18 But what about the Jews? Have they actually heard the message? Yes, they have:

10:18 †Ps 19:4

"The message of God's creation has gone out to everyone,
and its words to all the world."*

10:19 †Deut 32:21

19 But did the people of Israel really understand? Yes, they did, for even in the time of
Moses, God had said,

"I will rouse your jealousy by blessing other nations.
I will make you angry by blessing the foolish Gentiles."*

10:20 †Isa 65:1 Rom 9:30

20 And later Isaiah spoke boldly for God:

"I was found by people
who were not looking for me.
I showed myself to those
who were not asking for me."*

10:21 †Isa 65:2

21 But regarding Israel, God said,
"All day long I opened my arms to them,
but they kept disobeying me and arguing with me."*

God's Mercy on Israel

11:1 Phil 3:5

11 I ask, then, has God rejected his people, the Jews? Of course not! Remember that
I myself am a Jew, a descendant of Abraham and a member of the tribe of
Benjamin.

11:2 1 Sam 12:22

2 No, God has not rejected his own people, whom he chose from the very beginning.
Do you remember what the Scriptures say about this? Elijah the prophet complained to

11:3 †1 Kgs 19:10, 14

God about the people of Israel and said, 3 "Lord, they have killed your prophets and torn
down your altars. I alone am left, and now they are trying to kill me, too."*

11:4 †1 Kgs 19:18

4 And do you remember God's reply? He said, "You are not the only one left. I have
seven thousand others who have never bowed down to Baal!"*

11:5 Rom 9:27

5 It is the same today, for not all the Jews have turned away from God. A few* are being
saved as a result of God's kindness in choosing them. 6 And if they are saved by God's

11:6 Rom 4:4

kindness, then it is not by their good works. For in that case, God's wonderful kindness
would not be what it really is—free and undeserved.

11:7 Rom 9:31

7 So this is the situation: Most of the Jews have not found the favor of God they are

10:15 Isa 52:7. **10:16** Isa 53:1. **10:18** Ps 19:4. **10:19** Deut 32:21. **10:20** Isa 65:1. **10:21** Isa 65:2. **11:3** 1 Kgs 19:10, 14. **11:4** 1 Kgs 19:18. **11:5** Greek *A remnant.*

10:18-20 Many Jews who looked for the Messiah refused to believe in him when he came. God offered his salvation to the Gentiles ("other nations" and "people who were not looking for me"); thus, many Gentiles who didn't even know about a Messiah found and believed in him. Some religious people are spiritually blind, while those who have never been in a church are sometimes the most responsive to God's message. Because appearances are deceiving, and we can't see into people's hearts, beware of judging beforehand who will respond to the Good News and who will not.

11:1ff In this chapter Paul points out that not *all* Jews have rejected God's message of salvation. There are still a faithful few (11:5). Paul himself, after all, was a Jew, and so were Jesus' disciples and nearly all of the early Christian missionaries.

11:2 Elijah was a great reforming prophet who challenged the northern kingdom of Israel to repent. See his Profile in 1 Kings 18 for more information.

11:2 God chose the Jews ("his own people") to be the people through whom the rest of the world could find salvation. But this did not mean the entire Jewish nation would be saved; only those who were faithful to God were considered true Jews (11:5). We are saved through faith in Christ, not because we are part of a nation, religion, or family. On whom or on what are you depending for salvation?

11:6 Do you think it's easier for God to love you when you're good? Do you secretly suspect that God chose you because you deserved it? Do you think some people's behavior is so bad that God couldn't possibly save them? If you ever think this way, you don't entirely understand that salvation is by grace, a free gift. It cannot be earned, in whole or in part; it can only be accepted with thankfulness and praise.

11:7 "The rest were made unresponsive" was God's punishment for their sin. It was a confirmation of their own stubbornness. In judging them, God removed their ability to see and hear and to turn from sin; thus, they would experience the consequences of their rebellion.

looking for so earnestly. A few have—the ones God has chosen—but the rest were made
unresponsive. [8]As the Scriptures say,

"God has put them into a deep sleep.
To this very day he has shut their eyes so they do not see,
and closed their ears so they do not hear."*

[9]David spoke of this same thing when he said,

"Let their bountiful table become a snare,
a trap that makes them think all is well.
Let their blessings cause them to stumble.
10 Let their eyes go blind so they cannot see,
and let their backs grow weaker and weaker."*

[11]Did God's people stumble and fall beyond recovery? Of course not! His purpose
was to make his salvation available to the Gentiles, and then the Jews would be jealous
and want it for themselves. [12]Now if the Gentiles were enriched because the Jews turned
down God's offer of salvation, think how much greater a blessing the world will share
when the Jews finally accept it.

[13]I am saying all of this especially for you Gentiles. God has appointed me as the
apostle to the Gentiles. I lay great stress on this, [14]for I want to find a way to make the
Jews want what you Gentiles have, and in that way I might save some of them. [15]For
since the Jews' rejection meant that God offered salvation to the rest of the world, how
much more wonderful their acceptance will be. It will be life for those who were dead!
[16]And since Abraham and the other patriarchs were holy, their children will also be
holy.* For if the roots of the tree are holy, the branches will be, too.

[17]But some of these branches from Abraham's tree, some of the Jews, have been
broken off. And you Gentiles, who were branches from a wild olive tree, were grafted
in. So now you also receive the blessing God has promised Abraham and his children,
sharing in God's rich nourishment of his special olive tree. [18]But you must be careful
not to brag about being grafted in to replace the branches that were broken off.
Remember, you are just a branch, not the root.

[19]"Well," you may say, "those branches were broken off to make room for me." [20]Yes,
but remember—those branches, the Jews, were broken off because they didn't believe
God, and you are there because you do believe. Don't think highly of yourself, but fear
what could happen. [21]For if God did not spare the branches he put there in the first place,
he won't spare you either.

11:8 †Deut 29:4 †Isa 29:10 Matt 13:14 John 12:40 Acts 28:26-27

11:9-10 †Ps 69:22-23

11:11 Acts 13:46; 18:6

11:14 1 Cor 9:20 2 Tim 1:9

11:15 Luke 15:24, 32 Rom 5:10

11:16 Num 15:18-21

11:17 Jer 11:16 Eph 2:11-16

11:18 John 4:22

11:20 Rom 12:16

11:8 Deut 29:4; Isa 29:10. **11:9-10** Ps 69:22-23. **11:16** Greek *If the dough offered as firstfruits is holy, so is the whole lump.*

11:8-10 These verses describe the punishment for unresponsive hearts predicted by the prophet Isaiah (Isaiah 6:9-13). If people refuse to hear God's Good News, they eventually will be unable to understand it. Paul saw this happening in the Jewish congregations he visited on his missionary journeys. (Verse 8 is based on Deuteronomy 29:4 and Isaiah 29:10. Verses 9 and 10 are from Psalm 69:22, 23.)

11:11ff Paul had a vision of a church where all Jews and Gentiles would be united in their love of God and in obedience to Christ. While respecting God's law, this ideal church would look to Christ alone for salvation. A person's ethnic background and social status would be irrelevant (see Galatians 3:28). What mattered would be his or her faith in Christ.

But Paul's vision has not yet been realized. For the most part, Jewish people have rejected the Good News. They have depended on their heritage for salvation, and they do not have the heart of obedience that was so important to the Old Testament prophets and to Paul. Once Gentiles became dominant in many of the Christian churches, they began rejecting Jews and even persecuting them. Unfortunately, this practice has recurred through the centuries.

True Christians should not persecute others. Both Gentiles and Jews have done so much to damage the cause of Christ, whom they claim to serve, that Paul's vision often seems impossible to fulfill. Yet God chose the Jews, just as he chose the Gentiles, and he is still working to unite Jew and Gentile so they become a holy temple where God lives by his Spirit (see Ephesians 2:11-22).

11:13-15 Paul was appointed as an apostle to the Gentiles. He reminded his Jewish brothers and sisters of this fact, hoping that they, too, would want to be saved. The Jews had been rejected, and, thus, Gentiles were being offered salvation. But when a Jew comes to Christ, there is great rejoicing, as if a dead person had come back to life.

11:16-24 Speaking to Gentile Christians, Paul warns them not to feel superior because God rejected some Jews. Abraham's faith is like the root of a productive tree, and the Jewish people are the tree's natural branches. Because of faithlessness, some of the Jews have been broken off, and Gentile believers, who were branches from a wild olive tree, have been grafted in. Both Jews and Gentiles share the tree's nourishment based on faith in God; neither can rest on heritage or culture for salvation.

11:22 John 15:2, 14; Heb 3:14
11:23 2 Cor 3:14-16

22 Notice how God is both kind and severe. He is severe to those who disobeyed, but
kind to you as you continue to trust in his kindness. But if you stop trusting, you also
will be cut off. 23 And if the Jews turn from their unbelief, God will graft them back into
the tree again. He has the power to do it.
24 For if God was willing to take you who were, by nature, branches from a wild olive
tree and graft you into his own good tree—a very unusual thing to do—he will be far
more eager to graft the Jews back into the tree where they belong.

God's Mercy Is for Everyone

11:25 Luke 21:24; Rom 12:16
11:26-27 Ps 14:7; †Isa 59:20-21; Jer 31:31-34; Heb 8:8; 10:16

25 I want you to understand this mystery, dear friends,* so that you will not feel proud
and start bragging. Some of the Jews have hard hearts, but this will last only until the
complete number of Gentiles comes to Christ. 26 And so all Israel will be saved. Do you
remember what the prophets said about this?

> "A Deliverer will come from Jerusalem,*
> and he will turn Israel* from all ungodliness.
> 27 And then I will keep my covenant with them
> and take away their sins."*

11:29 Heb 7:21
11:32 Gal 3:22; 1 Tim 2:4
11:33 Isa 45:15; 55:8
11:34 Job 15:8; 36:22; †Isa 40:13-14; Jer 23:18; 1 Cor 2:16
11:35 †Job 41:3
11:36 1 Cor 8:6

28 Many of the Jews are now enemies of the Good News. But this has been to your
benefit, for God has given his gifts to you Gentiles. Yet the Jews are still his chosen
people because of his promises to Abraham, Isaac, and Jacob. 29 For God's gifts and his
call can never be withdrawn. 30 Once, you Gentiles were rebels against God, but when
the Jews refused his mercy, God was merciful to you instead. 31 And now, in the same
way, the Jews are the rebels, and God's mercy has come to you. But someday they,* too,
will share in God's mercy. 32 For God has imprisoned all people in their own disobedience so he could have mercy on everyone.
33 Oh, what a wonderful God we have! How great are his riches and wisdom and
knowledge! How impossible it is for us to understand his decisions and his methods!
34 For who can know what the Lord is thinking? Who knows enough to be his counselor?* 35 And who could ever give him so much that he would have to pay it back? 36 For
everything comes from him; everything exists by his power and is intended for his glory.
To him be glory evermore. Amen.

11:25 Greek *brothers.* **11:26a** Greek *from Zion.* **11:26b** Greek *Jacob.* **11:26-27** Isa 59:20-21. **11:31** Some manuscripts read *But now they;* other manuscripts read *But they.* **11:34** See Isa 40:13.

11:22 "Continue to trust in his kindness" refers to steadfast perseverance in faith. Steadfastness is a proof of the reality of faith and a by-product of salvation, not a means to it.

11:26 Some say the phrase "and so all Israel will be saved" means that the majority of Jews in the final generation before Christ's return will turn to Christ for salvation. Others say that Paul is using the term *Israel* to refer to the "spiritual" nation of Israel, which is comprised of Jews and Gentiles who have received salvation through faith in Christ. Thus, "all Israel" (or all believers) will receive God's promised gift of salvation. Still others say that "all Israel" means Israel as a whole will have a role in Christ's Kingdom. The Jews' identity as a people won't be discarded. God chose the nation of Israel, and he has never rejected it. He also chose the church, through Jesus Christ, and he will never reject it either. This does not mean, of course, that all Jews or all church members will be saved. It is possible to be Jewish or to belong to a church without ever responding in faith. But just because some people have rejected Christ does not mean that God stops working with either Israel or the church. He continues to offer salvation freely to all. Still others say that the phrase "and so" means "in this way" or "this is how," referring to the necessity of faith in Christ.

11:28-32 In this passage Paul shows how the Jews and the Gentiles benefit each other. Whenever God shows mercy to one group, the other shares the blessing. In God's original plan, the Jews would be the source of God's blessing to the Gentiles (see Genesis 12:3). When the Jews neglected this mission, God blessed the Gentiles anyway through the Jewish Messiah. He still maintained his love for the Jews because of his promises to Abraham, Isaac, and Jacob. But someday all faithful Jews will share in God's mercy. God's plans will not be thwarted: He will "have mercy on everyone." For a beautiful picture of Jews and Gentiles experiencing rich blessings, see Isaiah 60.

11:29 The privileges and invitation of God given to Israel can never be withdrawn.

11:33 This doxology is a prayer of praise to God for the wisdom of his plan. Although God's method and means are beyond our comprehension, God himself is not arbitrary. He governs the universe and our life in perfect wisdom, justice, and love.

11:34, 35 The implication of these questions is that no one has fully understood the mind of the Lord. No one has been his counselor. And God owes nothing to any one of us. Isaiah and Jeremiah asked similar questions to show that we are unable to give advice to God or criticize his ways (Isaiah 40:13; Jeremiah 23:18). God alone is the possessor of absolute power and absolute wisdom.

11:36 In the final analysis, all of us are absolutely dependent on God. He is the source of all things, including ourselves. He is the power that sustains and rules the world that we live in. And God works out all things to bring glory to himself. The all-powerful God deserves our praise.

B. HOW TO BEHAVE (12:1—16:27)

Moving from the theological to the practical, Paul gives guidelines for living as a redeemed people in a fallen world. We are to give ourselves to Christ as living sacrifices, obey the government, love our neighbors, and take special care of those who are weak in the faith. He closes with personal remarks. Throughout this section, we learn how to live our faith each day.

1. Personal responsibility

A Living Sacrifice to God

12 And so, dear Christian friends,* I plead with you to give your bodies to God. Let **12:1**
them be a living and holy sacrifice—the kind he will accept. When you think of Rom 6:13
what he has done for you, is this too much to ask? [2]Don't copy the behavior and customs 1 Pet 2:5
of this world, but let God transform you into a new person by changing the way you **12:2** Gal 1:4
think. Then you will know what God wants you to do, and you will know how good and Eph 4:23 Col 3:10
pleasing and perfect his will really is.
[3]As God's messenger, I give each of you this warning: Be honest in your estimate of **12:3** 1 Cor 12:11
yourselves, measuring your value by how much faith God has given you. [4]Just as our Eph 4:7
bodies have many parts and each part has a special function, [5]so it is with Christ's body. **12:4**
We are all parts of his one body, and each of us has different work to do. And since we 1 Cor 12:12
are all one body in Christ, we belong to each other, and each of us needs all the others. **12:5** 1 Cor 12:27 Eph 4:25
[6]God has given each of us the ability to do certain things well. So if God has given **12:6-8**
you the ability to prophesy, speak out when you have faith that God is speaking through 1 Cor 12:4-11
you. [7]If your gift is that of serving others, serve them well. If you are a teacher, do a good 1 Pet 4:10-11
job of teaching. [8]If your gift is to encourage others, do it! If you have money, share it
generously. If God has given you leadership ability, take the responsibility seriously. And
if you have a gift for showing kindness to others, do it gladly.

12:1 Greek *brothers.*

12:1 When sacrificing an animal according to God's law, a priest would kill the animal, cut it in pieces, and place it on the altar. Sacrifice was important, but even in the Old Testament God made it clear that obedience from the heart was much more important (see 1 Samuel 15:22; Psalm 40:6; Amos 5:21-24). God wants us to offer ourselves, not animals, as *living* sacrifices—daily laying aside our own desires to follow him, putting all our energy and resources at his disposal and trusting him to guide us. We do this out of gratitude that our sins have been forgiven.

12:1, 2 God has good, pleasing, and perfect plans for his children. He wants us to be transformed people with renewed minds, living to honor and obey him. Because he wants only what is best for us, and because he gave his Son to make our new life possible, we should joyfully give ourselves as living sacrifices for his service.

12:2 Paul warned Christians: "Don't copy the behavior and customs of this world" that are usually selfish and often corrupting. Wise Christians decide that much worldly behavior is off-limits for them. Our refusal to conform to this world's values, however, must go even deeper than just behavior and customs; it must be firmly planted in our mind: "Let God transform you into a new person by changing the way you think." It is possible to avoid most worldly customs and still be proud, covetous, selfish, stubborn, and arrogant. Only when the Holy Spirit renews, reeducates, and redirects our mind are we truly transformed (see 8:5).

12:3 Healthy self-esteem is important because some of us think too little of ourselves; on the other hand, some of us overestimate ourselves. The key to an honest and accurate self-evaluation is knowing the basis of our self-worth—our identity in Christ. Apart from him, we aren't capable of very much by eternal standards; in him, we are valuable and capable of worthy service. Evaluating yourself by the worldly standards of success and achievement can cause you to think too much about your worth in the eyes of others and thus miss your true value in God's eyes.

12:4, 5 Paul uses the concept of the human body to teach how Christians should live and work together. Just as the parts of the body function under the direction of the brain, so Christians are to work together under the command and authority of Jesus Christ (see 1 Corinthians 12:12-31; Ephesians 4:1-16).

12:4-8 God gives us gifts so we can build up his church. To use them effectively, we must (1) realize that all gifts and abilities come from God; (2) understand that not everyone has the same gifts; (3) know who we are and what we do best; (4) dedicate our gifts to God's service and not to our personal success; (5) be willing to utilize our gifts wholeheartedly, not holding back anything from God's service.

12:6 God's gifts differ in nature, power, and effectiveness according to his wisdom and graciousness, not according to our faith. God will give spiritual power necessary and appropriate to carry out each responsibility. We cannot, by our own effort or willpower, drum up more ability and thus be more effective teachers or servants. These are God's gifts to his church, and he gives faith and power as he wills. Our role is to be faithful and to seek ways to serve others with what Christ has given us.

12:6 "Prophesying" in Scripture is not always predicting the future. Often it means preaching God's messages (1 Corinthians 14:1-3).

12:6-8 Look at this list of gifts and imagine the kinds of people who would have each gift. Prophets are often bold and articulate. Servers (those in ministry) are faithful and loyal. Teachers are clear thinkers. Encouragers know how to motivate others. Givers are generous and trusting. Leaders are good organizers and managers. Those who show kindness are caring people who are happy to give their time to others. It would be difficult for one person to embody all these gifts. An assertive prophet would not usually make a good counselor, and a generous giver might fail as a leader. When you identify your own gifts (and this list is far from complete), ask how you can use them to build up God's family. At the same time, realize that your gifts can't do the work of the church all alone. Be thankful for people whose gifts are completely different from yours. Let your strengths balance their weaknesses, and be grateful that their abilities make up for your deficiencies. Together you can build Christ's church.

12:9 Amos 5:15; 1 Tim 1:5
12:10 John 13:34; Phil 2:3; 1 Thes 4:9; 2 Pet 1:7
12:11 Acts 18:25; 20:19; Rev 3:15
12:12 Rom 5:2; Heb 10:32, 36
12:13 Heb 13:2
12:14 Matt 5:44
12:15 Job 30:25
12:16 Prov 3:7; Isa 5:21
12:17 Prov 3:4; 20:22; 1 Thes 5:15
12:19 †Deut 32:35
12:20 †Prov 25:21-22; Matt 5:44

9 Don't just pretend that you love others. Really love them. Hate what is wrong.
Stand on the side of the good. 10 Love each other with genuine affection, and take
delight in honoring each other. 11 Never be lazy in your work, but serve the Lord
enthusiastically.
12 Be glad for all God is planning for you. Be patient in trouble, and always be
prayerful. 13 When God's children are in need, be the one to help them out. And get
into the habit of inviting guests home for dinner or, if they need lodging, for the
night.
14 If people persecute you because you are a Christian, don't curse them; pray that God
will bless them. 15 When others are happy, be happy with them. If they are sad, share their
sorrow. 16 Live in harmony with each other. Don't try to act important, but enjoy the
company of ordinary people. And don't think you know it all!
17 Never pay back evil for evil to anyone. Do things in such a way that everyone can
see you are honorable. 18 Do your part to live in peace with everyone, as much as
possible.
19 Dear friends, never avenge yourselves. Leave that to God. For it is written,

"I will take vengeance;
I will repay those who deserve it,"*
says the Lord.

20 Instead, do what the Scriptures say:

"If your enemies are hungry, feed them.
If they are thirsty, give them something to drink,
and they will be ashamed of what they have done to you."*

21 Don't let evil get the best of you, but conquer evil by doing good.

12:19 Deut 32:35. **12:20** Greek *and you will heap burning coals on their heads.* Prov 25:21-22.

12:9 Most of us have learned how to be courteous to others—how to speak kindly, avoid hurting their feelings, and appear to take an interest in them. We may even be skilled in pretending to show compassion when we hear of others' needs, or to become indignant when we learn of injustice. But God calls us to real and sincere love that goes far beyond being hypocritical and polite. Sincere love requires concentration and effort. It means helping others become better people. It demands our time, money, and personal involvement. No individual has the capacity to express love to a whole community, but the body of Christ in your town does. Look for people who need your love, and look for ways you and your fellow believers can love your community for Christ.

12:10 We can honor others in one of two ways. One involves ulterior motives. We honor our bosses so they will reward us, our employees so they will work harder, the wealthy so they will contribute to our cause, the powerful so they will use their power for us and not against us. God's way involves love. As Christians, we honor people because they have been created in God's image, because they are our brothers and sisters in Christ, and because they have a unique contribution to make to Christ's church. Does God's way of honoring others sound too difficult for your competitive nature? Why not try to outdo one another in showing honor? Put others first!

12:13 Christian hospitality differs from social entertaining. Entertaining focuses on the host: The home must be spotless; the food must be well prepared and abundant; the host must appear relaxed and good-natured. Hospitality, by contrast, focuses on the guests' needs, such as a place to stay, nourishing food, a listening ear, or just acceptance. Hospitality can happen in a messy home. It can happen around a dinner table where the main dish is canned soup. It can even happen while the host and the guest are doing chores together. Don't hesitate to offer hospitality just because you are too tired, too busy, or not wealthy enough to entertain.

12:17-21 These verses summarize the core of Christian living. If we love someone the way Christ loves us, we will be willing to forgive. If we have experienced God's grace, we will want to pass it on to others. And remember, grace is *undeserved* favor. By giving an enemy a drink, we're not excusing his misdeeds. We're recognizing him, forgiving him, and loving him in spite of his sins—just as Christ did for us.

12:19-21 In this day of lawsuits and incessant demands for legal rights, Paul's command sounds almost impossible. When someone hurts you deeply, instead of giving him what he deserves, Paul says to befriend him. Why does Paul tell us to forgive our enemies? (1) Forgiveness may break a cycle of retaliation and lead to mutual reconciliation. (2) It may make the enemy feel ashamed and change his or her ways. (3) By contrast, repaying evil for evil hurts you just as much as it hurts your enemy. Even if your enemy never repents, forgiving him or her will free you of a heavy load of bitterness.

12:19-21 Forgiveness involves both attitudes and actions. If you find it difficult to *feel* forgiving toward someone who has hurt you, try responding with kind actions. If appropriate, tell this person that you would like to heal your relationship. Lend a helping hand. Send him or her a gift. Smile at him or her. Many times you will discover that right actions lead to right feelings.

Respect for Authority

13 1Obey the government, for God is the one who put it there. All governments have
been placed in power by God. 2So those who refuse to obey the laws of the land
are refusing to obey God, and punishment will follow. 3For the authorities do not frighten
people who are doing right, but they frighten those who do wrong. So do what they say,
and you will get along well. 4The authorities are sent by God to help you. But if you are
doing something wrong, of course you should be afraid, for you will be punished. The
authorities are established by God for that very purpose, to punish those who do wrong.
5So you must obey the government for two reasons: to keep from being punished and to
keep a clear conscience.

6Pay your taxes, too, for these same reasons. For government workers need to be paid so
they can keep on doing the work God intended them to do. 7Give to everyone what you owe
them: Pay your taxes and import duties, and give respect and honor to all to whom it is due.

Love Fulfills God's Requirements

8Pay all your debts, except the debt of love for others. You can never finish paying that!
If you love your neighbor, you will fulfill all the requirements of God's law. 9For the
commandments against adultery and murder and stealing and coveting—and any other
commandment—are all summed up in this one commandment: "Love your neighbor as
yourself."* 10Love does no wrong to anyone, so love satisfies all of God's requirements.

11Another reason for right living is that you know how late it is; time is running out.
Wake up, for the coming of our salvation is nearer now than when we first believed. 12The
night is almost gone; the day of salvation will soon be here. So don't live in darkness. Get
rid of your evil deeds. Shed them like dirty clothes. Clothe yourselves with the armor of
right living, as those who live in the light. 13We should be decent and true in everything

13:1 Dan 2:21; John 19:11; Titus 3:1
13:3 1 Pet 2:13-14
13:5 1 Pet 2:13
13:7 Matt 22:21; Mark 12:17; Luke 20:25
13:8 Matt 5:34; John 13:34
13:9 †Exod 20:13-15, 17; †Lev 19:18; †Deut 5:17-19, 21
13:11 1 Cor 7:29-31; 1 Thes 5:5-6; Jas 5:8; 1 Pet 4:7
13:12 Eph 5:11; 6:13; 1 Thes 5:8

13:9 Lev 19:18.

13:1 Are there times when we should not obey the government? We should never allow government to force us to disobey God. Jesus and his apostles never disobeyed the government for personal reasons; when they disobeyed, it was in order to follow God's moral standards. Their disobedience was not cheap: They were threatened, beaten, thrown into jail, tortured, and executed for their convictions. Like them, if we are compelled to disobey, we must be ready to accept the consequences.

13:1ff Christians understand Romans 13 in different ways. All Christians agree that we are to live at peace with the state as long as the state allows us to live by our religious convictions. For hundreds of years, however, there have been at least three interpretations of how we are to do this:

(1) Some Christians believe that the state is so corrupt that Christians should have as little to do with it as possible. Although they should be good citizens as long as they can do so without compromising their beliefs, they should not work for the government, vote in elections, or serve in the military.

(2) Others believe that God has given the state authority in certain areas and the church authority in others. Christians can be loyal to both and can work for either. They should not, however, confuse the two. In this view, church and state are concerned with two totally different spheres—the spiritual and the physical—and thus complement each other but do not work together.

(3) Still others believe that Christians have a responsibility to make the state better. They can do this politically, by electing Christian or other high-principled leaders. They can also do this morally, by serving as an influence for good in society. In this view, church and state ideally work together for the good of all.

None of these views advocate rebelling against or refusing to obey the government's laws or regulations unless those laws clearly require you to violate the moral standards revealed by God. Wherever we find ourselves, we must be responsible citizens, as well as responsible Christians.

13:3, 4 When authorities are unjust, upright people are afraid. In these verses, Paul is talking about authorities who are doing their duty. When these officials are just, people who are doing right have nothing to fear.

13:8 Why is love for others called a debt? We are permanently in debt to Christ for the lavish love he has poured out on us. The only way we can even begin to repay this debt is by loving others in turn. Because Christ's love will always be infinitely greater than ours, we will always have the obligation to love our neighbors.

13:9 Somehow many of us have gotten the idea that self-love is wrong. But if this were the case, it would be pointless to love our neighbors as ourselves. But Paul explains what he means by self-love. Even if you have low self-esteem, you probably don't willingly let yourself go hungry. You take care of your body and may even exercise. You clothe yourself reasonably well. You make sure there's a roof over your head. You try not to let yourself be cheated or injured. This is the kind of love we need to have for our neighbors. Do we see that others are fed, clothed, and housed as well as they can be? Are we concerned about issues of social justice? Loving others as ourselves means actively working to see that their needs are met. Interestingly, people who focus on others rather than on themselves rarely suffer from low self-esteem.

13:10 Christians must obey the law of love, which supersedes both religious and civil laws. How easy it is to excuse our indifference to others merely because we have no legal obligation to help them and even to justify harming them if our actions are technically legal! But Jesus does not leave loopholes in the law of love. Whenever love demands it, we are to go beyond human legal requirements and imitate the God of love. See James 2:8, 9; 4:11 and 1 Peter 2:16, 17 for more about this law of love.

13:12-14 The "night" refers to the present evil time. The "day" refers to the time of Christ's return. Some people are surprised that Paul lists fighting and jealousy with the gross and obvious sins of drunkenness and immorality. Like Jesus in his Sermon on the Mount (Matthew 5–7), Paul considers attitudes as important as actions. Just as hatred leads to murder, so jealousy leads to strife and lust to adultery. When Christ returns, he wants to find his people clean on the inside as well as on the outside.

13:13
Luke 21:34
Eph 5:18

we do, so that everyone can approve of our behavior. Don't participate in wild parties and
getting drunk, or in adultery and immoral living, or in fighting and jealousy. 14 But let the
Lord Jesus Christ take control of you, and don't think of ways to indulge your evil desires.

The Danger of Criticism

14:1
1 Cor 9:22
14:2
1 Cor 10:25-27
14:3
Col 2:16
14:4
Matt 7:1
14:5
Gal 4:10
14:6
1 Cor 10:30
14:7
2 Cor 5:15
Gal 2:20
14:8
Phil 1:20
1 Thes 5:10
14:9
Rev 1:18
14:10
Matt 25:31-32
Acts 17:31
2 Cor 5:10
14:11
†Isa 45:23; 49:18

14 Accept Christians who are weak in faith, and don't argue with them about what
they think is right or wrong. 2 For instance, one person believes it is all right to eat
anything. But another believer who has a sensitive conscience will eat only vegetables.
3 Those who think it is all right to eat anything must not look down on those who won't.
And those who won't eat certain foods must not condemn those who do, for God has
accepted them. 4 Who are you to condemn God's servants? They are responsible to the
Lord, so let him tell them whether they are right or wrong. The Lord's power will help
them do as they should.
5 In the same way, some think one day is more holy than another day, while others
think every day is alike. Each person should have a personal conviction about this matter.
6 Those who have a special day for worshiping the Lord are trying to honor him. Those
who eat all kinds of food do so to honor the Lord, since they give thanks to God before
eating. And those who won't eat everything also want to please the Lord and give thanks
to God. 7 For we are not our own masters when we live or when we die. 8 While we live,
we live to please the Lord. And when we die, we go to be with the Lord. So in life and
in death, we belong to the Lord. 9 Christ died and rose again for this very purpose, so that
he might be Lord of those who are alive and of those who have died.
10 So why do you condemn another Christian*? Why do you look down on another
Christian? Remember, each of us will stand personally before the judgment seat of God.
11 For the Scriptures say,

14:10 Greek *your brother;* also in 14:10b, 13, 15, 21.

13:14 How do we let the Lord Jesus Christ take control of us? First, we identify with Christ by being baptized (Galatians 3:27). This shows our solidarity with other Christians and with the death, burial, and resurrection of Jesus Christ. Second, we exemplify the qualities Jesus showed while he was here on earth (love, humility, truth, service). In a sense, we role-play what Jesus would do in our situation (see Ephesians 4:24-32; Colossians 3:10-17). We also must avoid those situations that open the door to gratifying sinful desires.

14:1 Who is weak in faith and who is strong? We are all weak in some areas and strong in others. Our faith is strong in an area if we can survive contact with worldly people without falling into their patterns. It is weak in an area if we must avoid certain activities, people, or places in order to protect our spiritual life. It is important to take self-inventory in order to find out our strengths and weaknesses. Whenever in doubt, we should ask, Can I do that without sinning? Can I influence others for good, rather than being influenced by them?

In areas of strength, we should not fear being defiled by the world; rather we should go and serve God. In areas of weakness, we need to be cautious. If we have a strong faith but shelter it, we are not doing Christ's work in the world. If we have a weak faith but expose it, we are being extremely foolish.

14:1 This verse assumes there will be differences of opinion in the church about what is right or wrong. Paul says we are not to quarrel about issues that are matters of opinion. Differences should not be feared or avoided but accepted and handled with love. Don't expect everyone, even in the best possible church, to agree on every subject. Through sharing ideas we can come to a fuller understanding of what the Bible teaches. Accept, listen to, and respect others. Differences of opinion need not cause division. They can be a source of learning and richness in our relationships.

14:1ff What is weak faith? Paul is speaking about immature faith that has not yet developed the muscle it needs to stand against external pressures. For example, if a person who once worshiped idols became a Christian, he might understand perfectly well that Christ saved him through faith and that idols have no real power. Still, because of his past associations, he might be badly shaken if he unknowingly ate meat that had been used in idol worship. If a person who once worshiped God on the required Jewish holy days became a Christian, he might well know that Christ saved him through faith, not through his keeping of the law. Still, when the festival days came, he might feel empty and unfaithful if he didn't dedicate those days to God.

Paul responds to both weak brothers in love. Both are acting according to their consciences, but their honest convictions do not need to be made into rules for the church. Certainly some issues are central to the faith and worth fighting for, but many are based on individual differences and should not be legislated. Our principle should be: In essentials, unity; in nonessentials, liberty; in everything, love.

14:2 Eating "anything" may refer to a strong Christian being free from dietary restrictions, or it may refer to his eating meat offered to idols. The person weaker in the faith, however, may eat only vegetables and refuse to eat meat that has been offered to idols. But how would Christians end up eating meat that had been offered to idols? The ancient system of sacrifice was at the center of the religious, social, and domestic life of the Roman world. After a sacrifice was presented to a god in a pagan temple, only part of it was burned. The remainder was often sent to the market to be sold. Thus, a Christian might easily—even unknowingly—buy such meat in the marketplace or eat it at the home of a friend. Should a Christian question the source of his meat? Some thought there was nothing wrong with eating meat that had been offered to idols because idols were worthless. Others carefully checked the source of their meat or gave up meat altogether, in order to avoid a guilty conscience. The problem was especially acute for Christians who had once been idol worshipers. For them, such a strong reminder of their pagan days might weaken their newfound faith. Paul also deals with this problem in 1 Corinthians 8.

14:10-12 Each person is accountable to Christ, not to others. While the church must be uncompromising in its stand against activities that are expressly forbidden by Scripture (adultery, homosexuality, murder, theft), it should not create additional rules and regulations and give them equal standing with God's law.

"'As surely as I live,' says the Lord,
'every knee will bow to me
and every tongue will confess allegiance to God.'"*

12 Yes, each of us will have to give a personal account to God. 13 So don't condemn each
other anymore. Decide instead to live in such a way that you will not put an obstacle in
another Christian's path.
14 I know and am perfectly sure on the authority of the Lord Jesus that no food, in and
of itself, is wrong to eat. But if someone believes it is wrong, then for that person it is
wrong. 15 And if another Christian is distressed by what you eat, you are not acting in
love if you eat it. Don't let your eating ruin someone for whom Christ died. 16 Then you
will not be condemned for doing something you know is all right.
17 For the Kingdom of God is not a matter of what we eat or drink, but of living a life
of goodness and peace and joy in the Holy Spirit. 18 If you serve Christ with this attitude,
you will please God. And other people will approve of you, too. 19 So then, let us aim for
harmony in the church and try to build each other up.
20 Don't tear apart the work of God over what you eat. Remember, there is nothing
wrong with these things in themselves. But it is wrong to eat anything if it makes another
person stumble. 21 Don't eat meat or drink wine or do anything else if it might cause
another Christian to stumble. 22 You may have the faith to believe that there is nothing
wrong with what you are doing, but keep it between yourself and God. Blessed are those
who do not condemn themselves by doing something they know is all right. 23 But if
people have doubts about whether they should eat something, they shouldn't eat it. They
would be condemned for not acting in faith before God. If you do anything you believe
is not right, you are sinning.

Living to Please Others

15 We may know that these things make no difference, but we cannot just go ahead
and do them to please ourselves. We must be considerate of the doubts and fears
of those who think these things are wrong. 2 We should please others. If we do what helps
them, we will build them up in the Lord. 3 For even Christ didn't please himself. As the
Scriptures say, "Those who insult you are also insulting me."* 4 Such things were written

14:11 Isa 45:23. **15:3** Ps 69:9.

14:12 Gal 6:5
14:13 Matt 7:1; 2 Cor 6:3
14:14 Acts 10:15; 1 Cor 8:7
14:15 1 Cor 8:11-13
14:16 1 Cor 10:30; Titus 2:5
14:17 Rom 15:13; Gal 5:22
14:19 Rom 12:18; 15:2
14:20 Acts 10:15; 1 Cor 8:9-12
14:21 1 Cor 8:13
14:22 1 Jn 3:21
15:2 Rom 14:19; 1 Cor 9:19; 10:24; Gal 6:2
15:3 †Ps 69:9
15:4 Rom 4:23-24; 2 Tim 3:16

Many times Christians base their moral judgments on opinion, personal dislikes, or cultural bias rather than on the Word of God. When they do this, they show that their own faith is weak; they do not think that God is powerful enough to guide his children. When we stand before God and give a personal account of our life, we won't be worried about what our Christian neighbor has done (see 2 Corinthians 5:10).

14:13 Both strong and weak Christians can cause their brothers and sisters to stumble. The strong but insensitive Christian may flaunt his or her freedom and intentionally offend others' consciences. The scrupulous but weak Christian may try to fence others in with petty rules and regulations, thus causing dissension. Paul wants his readers to be both strong in the faith and sensitive to others' needs. Because we are all strong in some areas and weak in others, we need to constantly monitor the effects of our behavior on others.

14:13ff Some Christians use an invisible weaker brother to support their own opinions, prejudices, or standards. "You must live by these standards," they say, "or you will be offending the weaker brother." In truth, the person would often be offending no one but the speaker. While Paul urges us to be sensitive to those whose faith may be harmed by our actions, we should not sacrifice our liberty in Christ just to satisfy the selfish motives of those who are trying to force their opinions on us. Neither fear them nor criticize them, but follow Christ as closely as you can.

14:14 At the Jerusalem council (Acts 15), the Jewish church in Jerusalem asked the Gentile church in Antioch not to eat meat that had been sacrificed to idols. Paul was at the Jerusalem council, and he accepted this request, not because he felt that eating such meat was wrong in itself, but because this practice would deeply offend many Jewish believers. Paul did not think the issue was worth dividing the church over; his desire was to promote unity.

14:20, 21 Sin is not just a private matter. Everything we do affects others, and we have to think of them constantly. God created us to be interdependent, not independent. We who are strong in our faith must, without pride or condescension, treat others with love, patience, and self-restraint.

14:23 We try to steer clear of actions forbidden by Scripture, of course, but sometimes Scripture is silent. Then we should follow our consciences. "If you do anything you believe is not right, you are sinning" means that to go against a conviction will leave a person with a guilty or uneasy conscience. When God shows us that something is wrong for us, we should avoid it. But we should not look down on other Christians who exercise their freedom in those areas.

15:2 If we merely set out to please our neighbors, we will be people pleasers. Paul was opposed to that (see Galatians 1:10). We are to set aside willfulness and self-pleasing actions for the sake of building others up. Our Christian convictions must not be a disguise for coldhearted treatment of our brothers and sisters.

15:4 The knowledge of the Scriptures affects our attitude toward the present and the future. The more we know about what God has done in years past, the greater the confidence we have about what he will do in the days ahead. We need to diligently read our Bibles so we may have confidence that God's will is best for us.

in the Scriptures long ago to teach us. They give us hope and encouragement as we wait
patiently for God's promises.

15:5 1 Cor 1:10 2 Cor 1:3 5May God, who gives this patience and encouragement, help you live in complete
harmony with each other—each with the attitude of Christ Jesus toward the other. 6Then
15:6 Rev 1:6 all of you can join together with one voice, giving praise and glory to God, the Father of
our Lord Jesus Christ.

15:7 Rom 14:1 7So accept each other just as Christ has accepted you; then God will be glorified.
15:8 Matt 15:24 Acts 3:25-26 2 Cor 1:20 8Remember that Christ came as a servant to the Jews to show that God is true to the
promises he made to their ancestors. 9And he came so the Gentiles might also give glory
to God for his mercies to them. That is what the psalmist meant when he wrote:

15:9 †2 Sam 22:50 †Ps 18:49 "I will praise you among the Gentiles;
I will sing praises to your name."*

15:10 †Deut 32:43 10And in another place it is written,

"Rejoice, O you Gentiles,
along with his people, the Jews."*

15:11 †Ps 117:1 11And yet again,

"Praise the Lord, all you Gentiles;
praise him, all you people of the earth."*

15:12 †Isa 11:10 Rev 5:5; 22:16 12And the prophet Isaiah said,

"The heir to David's throne* will come,
and he will rule over the Gentiles.
They will place their hopes on him."*

13So I pray that God, who gives you hope, will keep you happy and full of peace as
you believe in him. May you overflow with hope through the power of the Holy Spirit.

2. Personal notes

Paul's Reason for Writing

15:14 2 Pet 1:12 14I am fully convinced, dear friends,* that you are full of goodness. You know these things
15:15 Rom 1:5; 12:3 so well that you are able to teach others all about them. 15Even so, I have been bold enough
to emphasize some of these points, knowing that all you need is this reminder from me. For
15:16 Phil 2:17 I am, by God's grace, 16a special messenger from Christ Jesus to you Gentiles. I bring you
the Good News and offer you up as a fragrant sacrifice to God so that you might be pure
15:17 Phil 3:3 and pleasing to him by the Holy Spirit. 17So it is right for me to be enthusiastic about all
15:18 Rom 1:5 Christ Jesus has done through me in my service to God. 18I dare not boast of anything else.
I have brought the Gentiles to God by my message and by the way I lived before them. 19I
15:19 Acts 19:11 1 Cor 2:4 1 Thes 1:5 have won them over by the miracles done through me as signs from God—all by the power
of God's Spirit. In this way, I have fully presented the Good News of Christ all the way from
Jerusalem clear over into Illyricum.*
15:20 Rom 1:15 1 Cor 3:10 2 Cor 10:13, 15 20My ambition has always been to preach the Good News where the name of Christ
has never been heard, rather than where a church has already been started by someone
15:21 †Isa 52:15 else. 21I have been following the plan spoken of in the Scriptures, where it says,

15:9 Ps 18:49. **15:10** Deut 32:43. **15:11** Ps 117:1. **15:12a** Greek *The root of Jesse.* **15:12b** Isa 11:10. **15:14** Greek *brothers;* also in 15:30. **15:19** *Illyricum* was a region northeast of Italy.

15:5-7 Just as we take Jesus' view on the authority of Scripture, the nature of heaven, and the resurrection, we are to have his attitude of love toward other Christians as well. As we grow in faith and come to know Jesus better, we will become more capable of maintaining this attitude of loving unity throughout each day. Christ's attitude is explained in more detail in Philippians 2.

15:17 Paul was enthusiastic about what God had done through him. Being proud of God's work is not a sin—it is worship. If you are not sure whether your pride is selfish or not, ask yourself this question: Am I just as proud of what God is doing through other people as of what he is doing through me?

15:19 Illyricum was a Roman territory on the Adriatic Sea between present-day Italy and Greece. It covered much the same territory as present-day Yugoslavia. See the map in chapter 1.

15:20-22 Paul wanted to visit the church at Rome, but he had delayed his visit because he had heard many good reports about the believers there and knew they were doing well on their own. It was more important for him to preach in areas that had not yet heard the Good News.

"Those who have never been told about him will see,
and those who have never heard of him will understand."*

22 In fact, my visit to you has been delayed so long because I have been preaching in these
places.

Paul's Travel Plans

23 But now I have finished my work in these regions, and after all these long years of
waiting, I am eager to visit you. 24 I am planning to go to Spain, and when I do, I will
stop off in Rome. And after I have enjoyed your fellowship for a little while, you can
send me on my way again.
25 But before I come, I must go down to Jerusalem to take a gift to the Christians there.
26 For you see, the believers in Greece* have eagerly taken up an offering for the
Christians in Jerusalem, who are going through such hard times. 27 They were very glad
to do this because they feel they owe a real debt to them. Since the Gentiles received the
wonderful spiritual blessings of the Good News from the Jewish Christians, they feel the
least they can do in return is help them financially. 28 As soon as I have delivered this
money and completed this good deed of theirs, I will come to see you on my way to
Spain. 29 And I am sure that when I come, Christ will give me a great blessing for you.
30 Dear friends, I urge you in the name of our Lord Jesus Christ to join me in my
struggle by praying to God for me. Do this because of your love for me, given to you by
the Holy Spirit. 31 Pray that I will be rescued from those in Judea who refuse to obey God.
Pray also that the Christians there will be willing to accept the donation I am bringing
them. 32 Then, by the will of God, I will be able to come to you with a happy heart, and
we will be an encouragement to each other.
33 And now may God, who gives us his peace, be with you all. Amen.

Paul Greets His Friends

16 Our sister Phoebe, a deacon in the church in Cenchrea, will be coming to see you
soon. 2 Receive her in the Lord, as one who is worthy of high honor. Help her in
every way you can, for she has helped many in their needs, including me.
3 Greet Priscilla and Aquila. They have been co-workers in my ministry for Christ Jesus.
4 In fact, they risked their lives for me. I am not the only one who is thankful to them; so are
all the Gentile churches. 5 Please give my greetings to the church that meets in their home.
Greet my dear friend Epenetus. He was the very first person to become a Christian in
the province of Asia. 6 Give my greetings to Mary, who has worked so hard for your

15:22 Rom 1:10-13; 1 Thes 2:18
15:23 Acts 19:21; Rom 1:10-11
15:24 1 Cor 16:6
15:25 Acts 19:21; 20:22
15:26 1 Cor 16:1; 2 Cor 8:1; 9:2
15:27 1 Cor 9:11
15:29 Rom 1:10-11
15:30 2 Cor 1:11; Col 1:8; 4:12
15:31 2 Thes 3:2
15:32 Phlm 1:7
15:33 Rom 16:20; Heb 13:20
16:1 Acts 18:18
16:2 Phil 2:29
16:5 1 Cor 16:15, 19; Col 4:15; Phlm 1:2

15:21 Isa 52:15. **15:26** Greek *Macedonia and Achaia,* the northern and southern regions of Greece.

15:23, 24 Paul was referring to the completion of his work in Corinth, the city from which he most likely wrote this letter. Most of Paul's three-month stay in Achaia (see Acts 20:3) was probably spent in Corinth. He believed that he had accomplished what God wanted him to do there, and he was looking forward to taking the Good News to new lands west of Rome. When Paul eventually went to Rome, however, it was as a prisoner (see Acts 28). Tradition says that Paul was released for a time and that he used this opportunity to go to Spain to preach the Good News. This journey is not mentioned in the book of Acts.

15:28 Paul's future plan was to go to Spain because Spain was at the very western end of the civilized world. He wanted to bring Christianity there. Also, Spain had many great minds and influential leaders in the Roman world (Lucan, Martial, Hadrian), and perhaps Paul thought Christianity would advance greatly in such an atmosphere.

15:30 Too often we view prayer as a time for comfort, reflection, or making our requests known to God. But here Paul urges believers to join in his struggle by means of prayer. Prayer is also a weapon in all believers' armor as we intercede for others who join in the fight against Satan. Do your prayers reflect that urgency?

15:33 This phrase sounds like it should signal the end of the letter, and it does pronounce the end of Paul's teaching. He concludes his letter, then, with personal greetings and remarks.

16:1, 2 Phoebe was known as a "deacon," or servant and helper. Apparently she was a wealthy person who helped support Paul's ministry. Phoebe was highly regarded in the church, and she may have delivered this letter from Corinth to Rome. This provides evidence that women had important roles in the early church. Cenchrea, the town where Phoebe lived, was the eastern port of Corinth, six miles from the city center.

16:3 Priscilla and Aquila were a married couple who had become Paul's close friends. They, along with all other Jews, had been expelled from Rome by the emperor (Acts 18:2, 3) and had moved to Corinth. There they met Paul and invited him to live with them. They were Christians before they met Paul and probably told him much about the Roman church. Like Paul, Priscilla and Aquila were missionaries. They helped believers in Ephesus (Acts 18:18-28), in Rome when they were allowed to return, and again at Ephesus (2 Timothy 4:19).

16:5ff Paul's personal greetings went to Romans and Greeks, Jews and Gentiles, men and women, prisoners and prominent citizens. The church's base was broad, crossing cultural, social, and economic lines. From this list we learn that the Christian community was mobile. Though Paul had not yet been to Rome, he had met these people in other places on his journeys.

benefit. 7 Then there are Andronicus and Junia,* my relatives,* who were in prison with
me. They are respected among the apostles and became Christians before I did. Please
give them my greetings. 8 Say hello to Ampliatus, whom I love as one of the Lord's own
children, 9 and Urbanus, our co-worker in Christ, and beloved Stachys.
10 Give my greetings to Apelles, a good man whom Christ approves. And give my best
regards to the members of the household of Aristobulus. 11 Greet Herodion, my relative.*
Greet the Christians in the household of Narcissus. 12 Say hello to Tryphena and
Tryphosa, the Lord's workers, and to dear Persis, who has worked so hard for the Lord.
13 Greet Rufus, whom the Lord picked out to be his very own; and also his dear mother,
who has been a mother to me.
14 And please give my greetings to Asyncritus, Phlegon, Hermes, Patrobas, Hermas,
and the other Christians* who are with them. 15 Give my greetings to Philologus, Julia,
Nereus and his sister, and to Olympas and all the other believers who are with them.
16 Greet each other in Christian love.* All the churches of Christ send you their greetings.

Paul's Final Instructions

17 And now I make one more appeal, my dear brothers and sisters. Watch out for people
who cause divisions and upset people's faith by teaching things that are contrary to what
you have been taught. Stay away from them. 18 Such people are not serving Christ our
Lord; they are serving their own personal interests. By smooth talk and glowing words
they deceive innocent people. 19 But everyone knows that you are obedient to the Lord.
This makes me very happy. I want you to see clearly what is right and to stay innocent
of any wrong. 20 The God of peace will soon crush Satan under your feet. May the grace
of our Lord Jesus Christ be with you.
21 Timothy, my fellow worker, and Lucius, Jason, and Sosipater, my relatives, send
you their good wishes.
22 I, Tertius, the one who is writing this letter for Paul, send my greetings, too, as a
Christian brother.
23 Gaius says hello to you. I am his guest, and the church meets here in his home. Erastus,
the city treasurer, sends you his greetings, and so does Quartus, a Christian brother.*
25 God is able to make you strong, just as the Good News says. It is the message about
Jesus Christ and his plan for you Gentiles, a plan kept secret from the beginning of time.
26 But now as the prophets* foretold and as the eternal God has commanded, this
message is made known to all Gentiles everywhere, so that they might believe and obey
Christ. 27 To God, who alone is wise, be the glory forever through Jesus Christ. Amen.

16:7 Rom 16:11, 21; Col 4:10; Phlm 1:23
16:10 Acts 11:14
16:11 Rom 16:7, 21
16:13 Mark 15:21; 2 Jn 1:1
16:16 1 Cor 16:20; 1 Thes 5:26; 1 Pet 5:14
16:17 1 Cor 5:9, 11; 2 Thes 3:6; 2 Tim 3:5; Titus 3:10; 2 Jn 1:10
16:18 Phil 3:19; Col 2:4; 2 Pet 2:3
16:19 Matt 10:16
16:20 Gen 3:15
16:21 Acts 13:1; 16:1; 17:5
16:25 1 Cor 2:1; Eph 1:9; 3:3-5; Col 1:26-27; 2:2; 2 Tim 1:9-10; 1 Pet 1:20
16:26 Rom 1:2, 5
16:27 Rom 11:36

16:7a Or *Junias;* some manuscripts read *Julia.* **16:7b** Or *compatriots;* also in 16:21. **16:11** Or *compatriot.* **16:14** Greek *brothers.* **16:16** Greek *with a sacred kiss.* **16:23** Some manuscripts add verse 24, *May the grace of our Lord Jesus Christ be with you all. Amen.* **16:26** Greek *the prophetic writings.*

16:7 The fact that Andronicus and Junias were "respected among the apostles" could mean they had distinguished themselves as apostles. They may have been a husband and wife team. Paul's reference to them as relatives (see also 16:21) could mean that they were from the same tribe as Paul.

16:17-20 When we read books or listen to sermons, we should check the content of what is written or said so that we won't be fooled by smooth talk and glowing words. Christians who study God's Word, asking him to reveal the truth, will not be fooled, even though superficial Christians may easily be taken in. For an example of believers who carefully checked God's Word, see Acts 17:10-12.

16:21 Timothy was a key person in the growth of the early church, traveling with Paul on his second missionary journey (Acts 16:1-3). Later Paul wrote two letters to him as he worked to strengthen the churches in Ephesus—1 and 2 Timothy. See his Profile in the book of 1 Timothy.

16:25-27 Paul exclaims that it is wonderful to be alive when the plan, God's secret—his way of saving the Gentiles—is becoming known throughout the world! All the Old Testament prophecies were coming true, and God was using Paul as his instrument to tell this Good News.

16:25-27 As Jerusalem was the center of Jewish life, Rome was the world's political, religious, social, and economic center. There the major governmental decisions were made, and from there the Good News spread to the ends of the earth. The church in Rome was a cosmopolitan mixture of Jews, Gentiles, slaves, free people, men, women, Roman citizens, and world travelers; therefore, it had potential for both great influence and great conflict.

Paul had not yet been to Rome to meet all the Christians there, and, of course, he has not yet met us. We, too, live in a cosmopolitan setting with the entire world open to us. We also have the potential for both widespread influence and wrenching conflict. Listen carefully to Paul's teachings about unity, service, and love so you may apply them.

1 CORINTHIANS

VITAL STATISTICS

PURPOSE:
To identify problems in the Corinthian church, to offer solutions, and to teach the believers how to live for Christ in a corrupt society

AUTHOR:
Paul

TO WHOM WRITTEN:
The church in Corinth and Christians everywhere

DATE WRITTEN:
Approximately A.D. 55, near the end of Paul's three-year ministry in Ephesus, during his third missionary journey

SETTING:
Corinth was a major cosmopolitan city, a seaport and major trade center—the most important city in Achaia. It was also filled with idolatry and immorality. The church was largely made up of Gentiles. Paul had established this church on his second missionary journey.

KEY VERSE:
"Now, dear brothers and sisters, I appeal to you by the authority of the Lord Jesus Christ to stop arguing among yourselves. Let there be real harmony so there won't be divisions in the church. I plead with you to be of one mind, united in thought and purpose" (1:10).

KEY PEOPLE:
Paul, Timothy, members of Chloe's household

KEY PLACES:
Worship meetings in Corinth

SPECIAL FEATURES:
This is a strong, straightforward letter.

ON A bed of grass, a chameleon's skin turns green. On the earth, it becomes brown. The animal changes to match the environment. Many creatures blend into nature with God-given camouflage suits to aid their survival. It's natural to fit in and adapt to the environment. But followers of Christ are *new creations,* born from above and changed from within, with values and life-styles that confront the world and clash with accepted morals. True believers don't blend in very well.

The Christians in Corinth were struggling with their environment. Surrounded by corruption and every conceivable sin, they felt the pressure to adapt. They knew they were free in Christ, but what did this freedom mean? How should they view idols or sexuality? What should they do about marriage, women in the church, and the gifts of the Spirit? These were more than theoretical questions—the church was being undermined by immorality and spiritual immaturity. The believers' faith was being tried in the crucible of immoral Corinth, and some of them were failing the test.

Paul heard of their struggles and wrote this letter to address their problems, heal their divisions, and answer their questions. Paul confronted them with their sin and their need for corrective action and clear commitment to Christ.

After a brief introduction (1:1–9), Paul immediately turns to the question of unity (1:10—4:21). He emphasizes the clear and simple gospel message around which all believers should rally; he explains the role of church leaders; and he urges them to grow up in their faith.

Paul then deals with the immorality of certain church members and the issue of lawsuits among Christians (5:1—6:8). He tells them to exercise church discipline and to settle their internal matters themselves. Because so many of the problems in the Corinthian church involved sex, Paul denounces sexual sin in the strongest possible terms (6:9–20).

Next, Paul answers some questions that the Corinthians had. Because prostitution and immorality were pervasive, marriages in Corinth were in shambles, and Christians weren't sure how to react. Paul gives pointed and practical answers (7:1–40). Concerning the question of meat sacrificed to idols, Paul suggests that they show complete commitment to Christ and sensitivity to other believers, especially weaker brothers and sisters (8:1—11:2).

Paul goes on to talk about worship, and he carefully explains the role of women, the Lord's Supper, and spiritual gifts (11:3—14:40). Sandwiched in the middle of this section is his magnificent description of the greatest gift—love (chapter 13). Then Paul concludes with a discussion of the resurrection (15:1–58), some final thoughts, greetings, and a benediction (16:1–24).

In this letter Paul confronted the Corinthians about their sins and shortcomings. And 1 Corinthians calls all Christians to be careful not to blend in with the world and accept its values and life-styles. We must live Christ-centered, blameless, loving lives that make a difference for God. As you read 1 Corinthians, examine your values in light of complete commitment to Christ.

THE BLUEPRINT

A. PAUL ADDRESSES CHURCH PROBLEMS (1:1—6:20) 1. Divisions in the church 2. Disorder in the church	Without Paul's presence, the Corinthian church had fallen into divisiveness and disorder. This resulted in many problems, which Paul addressed squarely. We must be concerned for unity and order in our local churches, but we should not mistake inactivity for order and cordiality for unity. We, too, must squarely address problems in our churches.
B. PAUL ANSWERS CHURCH QUESTIONS (7:1—16:24) 1. Instruction on Christian marriage 2. Instruction on Christian freedom 3. Instruction on public worship 4. Instruction on the resurrection	The Corinthians had sent Paul a list of questions, and he answered them in a way meant to correct abuses in the church and to show how important it is that they live what they believe. Paul gives us a Christian approach to problem solving. He analyzed the problem thoroughly to uncover the underlying issue and then highlighted the biblical values that should guide our actions.

MEGATHEMES

THEME	EXPLANATION	IMPORTANCE
Loyalties	The Corinthians were rallying around various church leaders and teachers—Peter, Paul, and Apollos. These loyalties led to intellectual pride and created a spirit of division in the church.	Our loyalty to human leaders or human wisdom must never divide Christians into camps. We must care for our fellow believers, not fight with them. Your allegiance must be to Christ. Let him lead you.
Immorality	Paul received a report of uncorrected sexual sin in the church at Corinth. The people had grown indifferent to immorality. Others had misconceptions about marriage. We are to live morally, keeping our bodies for God's service at all times.	Christians must never compromise with sinful ideas and practices. We should not blend in with people around us. You must live up to God's standard of morality and not condone immoral behavior, even if society accepts it.
Freedom	Paul taught freedom of choice on practices not expressly forbidden in Scripture. Some believers felt certain actions—like eating the meat of animals used in pagan rituals—were corrupt by association. Others felt free to participate in such actions without feeling that they had sinned.	We are free in Christ, yet we must not abuse our Christian freedom by being inconsiderate and insensitive to others. We must never encourage others to do something they feel is wrong just because we have done it. Let love guide your behavior.
Worship	Paul addressed disorder in worship. People were taking the Lord's Supper without first confessing sin. There was misuse of spiritual gifts and confusion over women's roles in the church.	Worship must be carried out properly and in an orderly manner. Everything we do to worship God should be done in a manner worthy of his high honor. Make sure that worship is harmonious, useful, and edifying to all believers.
Resurrection	Some people denied that Christ rose from the dead. Others felt that people would not physically be resurrected. Christ's resurrection assures us that we will have new, living bodies after we die. The hope of the resurrection forms the secret of Christian confidence.	Since we will be raised again to life after we die, our life is not in vain. We must stay faithful to God in our morality and our service. We are to live today knowing we will spend eternity with Christ.

A. PAUL ADDRESSES CHURCH PROBLEMS (1:1—6:20)

Through various sources, Paul had received reports of problems in the Corinthian church, including jealousy, divisiveness, sexual immorality, and failure to discipline members. Churches today must also address the problems they face. We can learn a great deal by observing how Paul handled these delicate situations.

Greetings from Paul

1 This letter is from Paul, chosen by the will of God to be an apostle of Christ Jesus, and from our brother Sosthenes. **1:1** Acts 18:17 Rom 1:1

2 We are writing to the church of God in Corinth, you who have been called by God
to be his own holy people. He made you holy by means of Christ Jesus, just as he did **1:2** Rom 8:28; 10:12-13 2 Tim 2:22

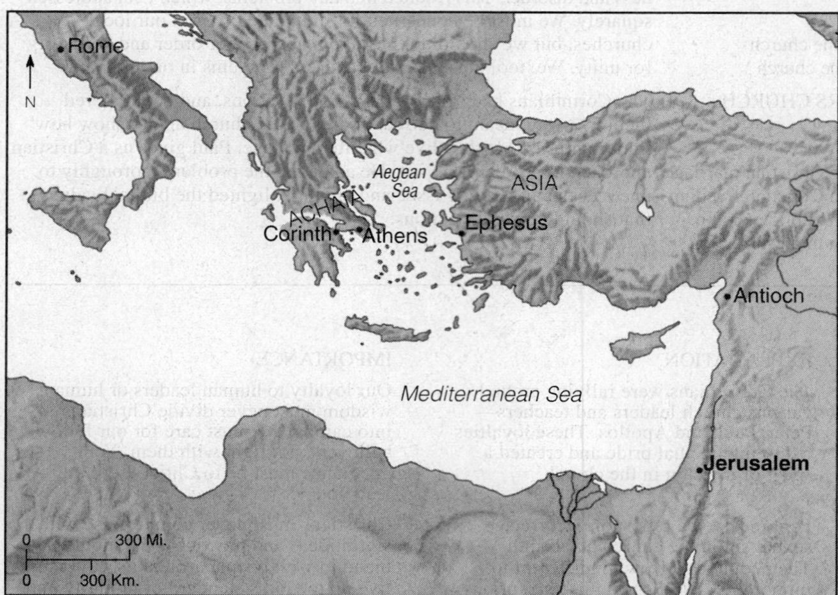

CORINTH AND EPHESUS Paul wrote this letter to Corinth during his three-year visit in Ephesus on his third missionary journey. The two cities sat across from each other on the Aegean Sea—both were busy and important ports. Titus may have carried this letter from Ephesus to Corinth (2 Corinthians 12:18).

1:1 Paul wrote this letter to the church in Corinth while he was visiting Ephesus during his third missionary journey (Acts 19:1–20:1). Corinth and Ephesus faced each other across the Aegean Sea. Paul knew the Corinthian church well because he had spent 18 months in Corinth during his second missionary journey (Acts 18:1-18). While in Ephesus, he had heard about problems in Corinth (1:11). About the same time, a delegation from the Corinthian church had visited Paul to ask his advice about their conflicts (16:17). Paul's purpose for writing was to correct those problems and to answer questions church members had asked in a previous letter (7:1).

1:1 Paul was given a special calling from God to preach about Jesus Christ. Each Christian has a job to do, a role to take, or a contribution to make. One assignment may seem more spectacular than another, but all are necessary to carry out God's greater plans for his church and for his world (12:12-27). Be available to God by placing your gifts at his service. Then as you discover what he calls you to do, be ready to do it.

1:1 Sosthenes may have been Paul's secretary who wrote down this letter as Paul dictated it. He was probably the Jewish synagogue leader in Corinth (Acts 18:17) who had been beaten during an attack on Paul and then later became a believer. Sosthenes was well known to the members of the Corinthian church, and so Paul included his familiar name in the opening of the letter.

1:2 Corinth, a giant cultural melting pot with a great diversity of wealth, religions, and moral standards, had a reputation for being fiercely independent and as decadent as any city in the world. The Romans had destroyed Corinth in 146 B.C. after a rebellion. But in 46 B.C., the Roman emperor Julius Caesar rebuilt it because of its strategic seaport. By Paul's day (A.D. 50), the Romans had made Corinth the capital of Achaia (present-day Greece). It was a large city, offering Rome great profits through trade as well as the military protection of its ports. But the city's prosperity made it ripe for all sorts of corruption. Idolatry flourished, and there were more than a dozen pagan temples employing at least a thousand prostitutes. Corinth's reputation was such that prostitutes in other cities began to be called "Corinthian girls."

1:2 A personal invitation makes a person feel wanted and welcome. We are "called by God to be his own holy people." God personally invites us to be citizens of his eternal Kingdom. Jesus Christ, God's Son, is the only one who can bring us into this glorious Kingdom because he is the only one who removes our sins. "To be made holy" (or sanctified) means that we are chosen or set apart by Christ for his service. We accept God's invitation by accepting his Son, Jesus Christ, and by trusting in the work he did on the cross to forgive our sins.

1:2 This was probably not meant to be a private letter; rather, it may have been circulated to other churches in nearby cities. Although it deals with specific issues facing the church at Corinth, all believers can learn from it. The Corinthian church

all Christians everywhere—whoever calls upon the name of Jesus Christ, our Lord
and theirs.

1:3 Rom 1:7

3May God our Father and the Lord Jesus Christ give you his grace and peace.

Paul Gives Thanks to God

1:5 2 Cor 8:7; 9:11
1:7 Rom 8:19, 23; Phil 3:20; 2 Thes 1:7; Titus 2:13; 2 Pet 3:12
1:8 Phil 1:6; 1 Thes 3:13; 5:23

4I can never stop thanking God for all the generous gifts he has given you, now that you
belong to Christ Jesus. 5He has enriched your church with the gifts of eloquence and
every kind of knowledge. 6This shows that what I told you about Christ is true. 7Now
you have every spiritual gift you need as you eagerly wait for the return of our Lord Jesus
Christ. 8He will keep you strong right up to the end, and he will keep you free from all
blame on the great day when our Lord Jesus Christ returns. 9God will surely do this for
you, for he always does just what he says, and he is the one who invited you into this
wonderful friendship with his Son, Jesus Christ our Lord.

1. Divisions in the church

1:10 Rom 15:5; 1 Cor 11:18

10Now, dear brothers and sisters, I appeal to you by the authority of the Lord Jesus Christ
to stop arguing among yourselves. Let there be real harmony so there won't be divisions
in the church. I plead with you to be of one mind, united in thought and purpose. 11For
some members of Chloe's household have told me about your arguments, dear friends.*

1:11 Greek *my brothers.*

HIGHLIGHTS OF 1 CORINTHIANS		
	The Meaning of the Cross 1:18—2:16	Be considerate of one another because of what Christ has done for us. There is no place for pride or a know-it-all attitude. We are to have the mind of Christ.
	The Story of the Last Supper 11:23–29	The Last Supper is a time of reflection on Christ's final words to his disciples before he died on the cross; we must celebrate this in an orderly and correct manner.
	The Poem of Love 13:1–13	Love is to guide all we do. We have different gifts, abilities, likes, dislikes—but we are called, without exception, to love.
	The Christian's Destiny 15:42–58	We are promised by Christ, who died for us, that as he came back to life after death, so our perishable bodies will be exchanged for heavenly bodies. Then we will live and reign with Christ.

included a great cross section of believers—wealthy merchants, common laborers, former temple prostitutes, and middle-class families. Because of the wide diversity of people and backgrounds, Paul takes great pains to stress the need for both spiritual unity and Christlike character.

1:3 Grace is God's free gift of salvation given to us in Christ. Receiving it brings us peace (see Romans 5:1). In a world of noise, confusion, and relentless pressures, people long for peace. Many give up the search, thinking it impossible to find, but true peace of heart and mind is available to us through faith in Jesus Christ.

1:4-6 In this letter, Paul wrote some strong words to the Corinthians, but he began on a positive note of thanksgiving. He affirmed their privilege of belonging to the Lord and receiving his generous gifts: the power to speak out for him and understand his truth. When we must correct others, it helps to begin by affirming what God has already accomplished in them.

1:7 The Corinthian church members had all the spiritual gifts they needed to live the Christian life, to witness for Christ, and to stand against the paganism and immorality of Corinth. But instead of using what God had given them, they were arguing over which gifts were more important. Paul addresses this issue in depth in chapters 12–14.

1:7-9 Paul guaranteed the Corinthian believers that God would consider them "free from all blame" when Christ returns (see Ephesians 1:7-10). This guarantee was not because of their great gifts or their shining performance, but because of what Jesus Christ accomplished for them through his death and resurrection. *All* who have received the Lord Jesus as their Savior will be considered blameless when he returns (see also 1 Thessalonians 3:13; Hebrews 9:28). If you have faith in Christ, even if it is weak, you *are* and *will be* saved.

1:10 Paul founded the church in Corinth on his second missionary journey. Eighteen months after he left, arguments and divisions arose, and some church members slipped back into an immoral life-style. Paul wrote this letter to address the problems and to clear up confusion about right and wrong so that they would remove the immorality from among them. The Corinthian people had a reputation for jumping from fad to fad; Paul wanted to keep Christianity from degenerating into just another fad.

1:10 By saying "brothers and sisters," Paul is emphasizing that all Christians are part of God's family. Believers share a unity that runs even deeper than that of blood brothers and sisters.

1:10, 11 To "let there be real harmony," allow for no "divisions" and "be of one mind, united in thought and purpose" does not require everyone to believe exactly the same. There is a difference between having opposing viewpoints and being divisive. A group of people will not completely agree on every issue, but they can work together harmoniously if they agree on what truly matters: Jesus Christ is Lord of all. In your church, speak and behave in a way that will reduce arguments and increase harmony. Petty differences should never divide Christians.

12 Some of you are saying, "I am a follower of Paul." Others are saying, "I follow
Apollos," or "I follow Peter,*" or "I follow only Christ." 13 Can Christ be divided into
pieces?
Was I, Paul, crucified for you? Were any of you baptized in the name of Paul? 14 I thank
God that I did not baptize any of you except Crispus and Gaius, 15 for now no one can
say they were baptized in my name. 16 (Oh yes, I also baptized the household of
Stephanas. I don't remember baptizing anyone else.) 17 For Christ didn't send me to
baptize, but to preach the Good News—and not with clever speeches and high-sounding
ideas, for fear that the cross of Christ would lose its power.

The Wisdom of God

18 I know very well how foolish the message of the cross sounds to those who are on the
road to destruction. But we who are being saved recognize this message as the very
power of God. 19 As the Scriptures say,

"I will destroy human wisdom
and discard their most brilliant ideas."*

20 So where does this leave the philosophers, the scholars, and the world's brilliant
debaters? God has made them all look foolish and has shown their wisdom to be useless
nonsense. 21 Since God in his wisdom saw to it that the world would never find him
through human wisdom, he has used our foolish preaching to save all who believe.
22 God's way seems foolish to the Jews because they want a sign from heaven to prove
it is true. And it is foolish to the Greeks because they believe only what agrees with their
own wisdom. 23 So when we preach that Christ was crucified, the Jews are offended, and
the Gentiles say it's all nonsense. 24 But to those called by God to salvation, both Jews
and Gentiles,* Christ is the mighty power of God and the wonderful wisdom of God.

1:12 John 1:42, Acts 18:24, 1 Cor 3:4
1:14 Acts 18:8; 19:29, Rom 16:23
1:17 Matt 28:19, John 4:2, Acts 26:17, 2 Cor 10:10; 11:16
1:18 Rom 1:16, 1 Cor 2:14, 2 Cor 2:15; 4:3
1:19 †Isa 29:14
1:20 Job 12:17, Isa 19:11-12; 33:18; 44:25, 1 Cor 2:6, 8
1:21 Matt 11:25
1:22 Matt 12:38
1:23 1 Cor 2:2
1:24 Col 2:3

1:12 Greek *Cephas.* **1:19** Isa 29:14. **1:24** Greek *Greeks.*

1:12ff In this large and diverse Corinthian church, the believers favored different preachers. Because there was as yet no written New Testament, the believers depended heavily on preaching and teaching for spiritual insight into the meaning of the Old Testament. Some followed Paul, who had founded their church; some who had heard Peter in Jerusalem followed him; others listened only to Apollos, an eloquent and popular preacher who had had a dynamic ministry in Corinth (Acts 18:24; 19:1). Although these three preachers were united in their message, their personalities attracted different people. At this time the church was in danger of dividing. By mentioning Jesus Christ 10 times in the first 10 verses, Paul makes it clear who it is all preachers and teachers should emphasize. God's message is much more important than any human messenger.

1:12, 13 Paul wondered whether the Corinthians' quarrels had "divided" Christ into pieces. This is a graphic picture of what happens when the church (the body of Christ) is divided. With the many churches and styles of worship available today, we could get caught up in the same game of "my preacher is better than yours!" To do so would divide Christ again. But Christ is not divided, and his true followers should not allow anything to divide them. Don't let your appreciation for any teacher, preacher, or author lead you into pride. Our allegiance must be to Christ and to the unity that he desires.

1:17 When Paul said that Christ didn't send him to baptize, he wasn't minimizing the importance of baptism. Baptism was commanded by Jesus himself (Matthew 28:19) and practiced by the early church (Acts 2:41). Paul was emphasizing that no one person should do everything. Paul's gift was preaching, and that's what he did. Christian ministry should be a team effort; no preacher or teacher is a complete link between God and people, and no individual can do all that the apostles did. We must be content to operate within the gifts God has given to us, and carry out his plan wholeheartedly. (For more on different gifts, see chapters 12 and 13.)

1:17 Some speakers use impressive words, but they are weak on content. Paul stressed solid content and practical help for his listeners. He wanted them to be impressed with his *message,* not just his style (see 2:1-5). You don't need to be a great speaker with a large vocabulary to share the Good News effectively. The persuasive power is in the story, not the storyteller. Paul was not against those who carefully prepare what they say (see 2:6) but against those who try to impress others with their knowledge or speaking ability.

1:19 Paul summarizes Isaiah 29:14 to emphasize a point Jesus often made: God's way of thinking is not like the world's way (normal human wisdom). And God offers eternal life, which the world can never give. We can spend a lifetime accumulating wisdom and yet never learn how to have a personal relationship with God. We must come to the crucified and risen Christ to receive eternal life and the joy of a personal relationship with our Savior.

1:22-24 Many Jews considered the Good News of Jesus Christ to be foolish, because they thought the Messiah would be a conquering king accompanied by signs and miracles. Jesus had not restored David's throne as they expected. Besides, he was executed as a criminal, and how could a criminal be a savior? Greeks, too, considered the Good News foolish: They did not believe in a bodily resurrection, they did not see in Jesus the powerful characteristics of their mythological gods, and they thought no reputable person would be crucified. To them, death was defeat, not victory.

The Good News of Jesus Christ still sounds foolish to many. Our society worships power, influence, and wealth. Jesus came as a humble, poor servant, and he offers his Kingdom to those who have faith, not to those who do all kinds of good deeds to try to earn salvation. This looks foolish to the world, but Christ is the mighty power of God, the only way we can be saved. Knowing Christ personally is the greatest wisdom anyone can have.

25 This "foolish" plan of God is far wiser than the wisest of human plans, and God's
weakness is far stronger than the greatest of human strength.
26 Remember, dear brothers and sisters, that few of you were wise in the world's eyes,
or powerful, or wealthy when God called you. 27 Instead, God deliberately chose things
the world considers foolish in order to shame those who think they are wise. And he
chose those who are powerless to shame those who are powerful. 28 God chose things
despised by the world, things counted as nothing at all, and used them to bring to
nothing what the world considers important, 29 so that no one can ever boast in the
presence of God.
30 God alone made it possible for you to be in Christ Jesus. For our benefit God made
Christ to be wisdom itself. He is the one who made us acceptable to God. He made us
pure and holy, and he gave himself to purchase our freedom. 31 As the Scriptures say,

> "The person who wishes to boast
> should boast only of what the Lord has done."*

Paul Preaches Wisdom

2 Dear brothers and sisters, when I first came to you I didn't use lofty words and
brilliant ideas to tell you God's message.* 2 For I decided to concentrate only on
Jesus Christ and his death on the cross. 3 I came to you in weakness—timid and
trembling. 4 And my message and my preaching were very plain. I did not use wise and
persuasive speeches, but the Holy Spirit was powerful among you. 5 I did this so that you
might trust the power of God rather than human wisdom.
6 Yet when I am among mature Christians, I do speak with words of wisdom, but not
the kind of wisdom that belongs to this world, and not the kind that appeals to the rulers
of this world, who are being brought to nothing. 7 No, the wisdom we speak of is the
secret wisdom of God,* which was hidden in former times, though he made it for our
benefit before the world began. 8 But the rulers of this world have not understood it; if

1:25 2 Cor 13:4
1:26 Matt 11:25; John 7:48; Jas 2:1-5
1:27 1 Cor 3:18-19
1:28 Rom 4:17
1:29 Eph 2:9
1:30 Jer 23:5-6; Rom 3:24; 2 Cor 5:21
1:31 †Jer 9:24; 2 Cor 10:17
2:1 1 Cor 1:17
2:3 2 Cor 10:1; Gal 4:13
2:4 1 Cor 4:20
2:5 2 Cor 4:7; 6:7
2:6 Eph 4:13; Phil 3:15; Heb 5:14
2:7 Rom 16:25
2:8 Jas 2:1

1:31 Jer 9:24. **2:1** Greek *mystery;* other manuscripts read *testimony.* **2:7** Greek *we speak God's wisdom in a mystery.*

1:25 The message of Christ's death for sins sounds foolish to those who don't believe. Death seems to be the end of the road, the ultimate weakness. But Jesus did not stay dead. His resurrection demonstrated his power even over death. And he will save us from eternal death and give us everlasting life if we trust him as Savior and Lord. This sounds so simple that many people won't accept it. They try other ways to obtain eternal life (being good, being wise, etc.). But all their attempts are futile. The "foolish" people who simply accept Christ's offer are actually the wisest of all, because they alone will live eternally with God.

1:27 Is Christianity against rational thinking? Christians clearly do believe in using their minds to weigh the evidence and make wise choices. Paul is declaring that no amount of human knowledge can replace or bypass Christ's work on the cross. If it could, Christ would be accessible only to the intellectually gifted and well educated and not to ordinary people or to children.

1:28-31 Paul continues to emphasize that the way to receive salvation is so simple that *any* person who wants to can understand it. Skill and wisdom do not get a person into God's Kingdom—simple faith does. So no one can boast that personal achievements helped him or her secure eternal life. Salvation is totally from God through Jesus' death. There is *nothing* we can do to earn our salvation; we need only to accept what Jesus has already done for us.

1:30 God is our source and the reason for our personal relationship with Christ. Our union and identification with Christ results in our having God's wisdom (Colossians 2:3), being acceptable to God (2 Corinthians 5:21), being pure (1 Thessalonians 4:3-7), and having the penalty for our sins paid by Jesus (Mark 10:45).

2:1 Paul is referring to his first visit to Corinth during his second missionary journey (A.D. 51), when he founded the church (Acts 18:1ff).

2:1-5 A brilliant scholar, Paul could have overwhelmed his listeners with intellectual arguments. Instead, he shared the simple message of Jesus Christ by allowing the Holy Spirit to guide his words. In sharing the Good News with others, we should follow Paul's example and keep our message simple and basic. The Holy Spirit will give power to our words and use them to bring glory to Jesus.

2:4 Paul's confidence was not in his keen intellect or speaking ability but in his knowledge that the Holy Spirit was helping and guiding him. Paul is not denying the importance of study and preparation for preaching; he had a thorough education in the Scriptures. Effective preaching results from studious preparation and reliance on the work of the Holy Spirit. Don't use Paul's statement as an excuse for not studying or preparing.

2:7 God's "secret wisdom . . . which was hidden" was his offer of salvation to all people. Originally unknown to humanity, this plan became crystal clear when Jesus rose from the dead. His resurrection proved that he had power over sin and death and could offer us this power as well (see also 1 Peter 1:10-12 and the first note on Romans 16:25-27). God's plan, however, is still hidden to unbelievers because they either refuse to accept it, choose to ignore it, or simply haven't heard about it.

2:8 Jesus was misunderstood and rejected by those whom the world considered wise and great. He was put to death by the rulers in Palestine—the high priest, King Herod, Pilate, and the Pharisees and Sadducees. Jesus' rejection by these rulers had been predicted in Isaiah 53:3 and Zechariah 12:10, 11.

they had, they would never have crucified our glorious Lord. [9]That is what the Scriptures
mean when they say,

"No eye has seen, no ear has heard,
  and no mind has imagined
what God has prepared
  for those who love him."*

[10]But we know these things because God has revealed them to us by his Spirit, and his
Spirit searches out everything and shows us even God's deep secrets. [11]No one can know
what anyone else is really thinking except that person alone, and no one can know God's
thoughts except God's own Spirit. [12]And God has actually given us his Spirit (not the
world's spirit) so we can know the wonderful things God has freely given us. [13]When
we tell you this, we do not use words of human wisdom. We speak words given to us by
the Spirit, using the Spirit's words to explain spiritual truths.* [14]But people who aren't
Christians can't understand these truths from God's Spirit. It all sounds foolish to them
because only those who have the Spirit can understand what the Spirit means. [15]We who
have the Spirit understand these things, but others can't understand us at all. [16]How
could they? For,

"Who can know what the Lord is thinking?
  Who can give him counsel?"*

But we can understand these things, for we have the mind of Christ.

Paul and Apollos, Servants of Christ

3 Dear brothers and sisters, when I was with you I couldn't talk to you as I would to
mature Christians. I had to talk as though you belonged to this world or as though
you were infants in the Christian life.* [2]I had to feed you with milk and not with solid
food, because you couldn't handle anything stronger. And you still aren't ready, [3]for you
are still controlled by your own sinful desires. You are jealous of one another and quarrel
with each other. Doesn't that prove you are controlled by your own desires? You are
acting like people who don't belong to the Lord. [4]When one of you says, "I am a follower
of Paul," and another says, "I prefer Apollos," aren't you acting like those who are not
Christians?*

2:9 †Isa 64:4; 65:17
2:10 Matt 11:25; 13:11; John 14:26; 15:26; 16:13-15; 1 Jn 2:27
2:11 Prov 20:27; Jer 17:9; Rom 11:33
2:12 John 16:13-15; Rom 8:15; 1 Cor 1:27
2:13 1 Cor 1:17; 2:4; 2 Pet 1:20-21
2:14 John 8:47; 14:17; Jude 1:19
2:15 1 Cor 3:1; Gal 6:1; 1 Jn 2:20
2:16 †Isa 40:13; Rom 11:34
3:1 Gal 6:1; Eph 4:14
3:2 John 16:2; Heb 5:12-13; 1 Pet 2:2
3:3 Rom 13:13; 1 Cor 1:10-11; 11:18
3:4 1 Cor 1:12

2:9 Isa 64:4. **2:13** Or *explaining spiritual truths in spiritual language,* or *explaining spiritual truths to spiritual people.*
2:16 Isa 40:13. **3:1** Greek *in Christ.* **3:4** Greek *aren't you merely human?*

2:9 We cannot imagine all that God has in store for us, both in this life and for eternity. He will create a new heaven and a new earth (Isaiah 65:17; Revelation 21:1), and we will live with him forever. Until then, his Holy Spirit comforts and guides us. Knowing the wonderful and eternal future that awaits us gives us hope and courage to press on in this life, to endure hardship, and to avoid giving in to temptation. This world is not all there is. The best is yet to come.

2:10 "God's deep secrets" refers to God's unfathomable nature and his wonderful plan—Jesus' death and resurrection—and to the promise of salvation, revealed only to those who believe that what God says is true. Those who believe in Christ's death and resurrection and put their faith in him will know all they need to know to be saved. This knowledge, however, can't be grasped by even the wisest people unless they accept God's message. All who reject God's message are foolish, no matter how wise the world thinks they are.

2:13 Paul's words are authoritative because their source was the Holy Spirit. Paul was not merely giving his own personal views or his personal impression of what God had said. Under the inspiration of the Holy Spirit, he wrote the very thoughts and words of God.

2:14, 15 Non-Christians cannot understand spiritual truths, and they cannot grasp the concept that God's Spirit lives in believers. Don't expect most people to approve of or understand your decision to follow Christ. It all seems so silly to them. Just as a tone-deaf person cannot appreciate fine music, the person who rejects Christ cannot understand truths from God's Spirit. With the lines of communication broken, he or she won't be able to hear what God is saying to him or her.

2:15, 16 No one can know what the Lord is thinking (Romans 11:34), but through the guidance of the Holy Spirit, believers have insight into some of God's plans, thoughts, and actions. They, in fact, have "the mind of Christ." Through the Holy Spirit, we can begin to know God's thoughts, talk with him, and expect his answers to our prayers. Are you spending enough time with Christ to have his very mind in you? An intimate relationship with Christ comes only from spending time consistently in his presence and in his Word. Read Philippians 2:5ff for more on the mind of Christ.

3:1-3 Paul called the Corinthians infants in the Christian life because they were not yet spiritually healthy and mature. The proof was that they quarreled like children, allowing divisions to distract them. Immature Christians are "worldly," controlled by their own desires; mature believers are in tune with God's desires. How much influence do your desires have on your life? Your goal should be to let God's desires be yours. Being controlled by your own desires will stunt your growth.

3:5 Acts 18:24; Rom 12:3, 6; 2 Cor 6:4
3:6 Acts 18:4-11
3:8 Pss 18:20; 62:12
3:9 Isa 61:3; Eph 2:20-22; 1 Pet 2:5
3:10 Rom 15:20
3:11 Isa 28:16; Eph 2:20; 1 Pet 2:4-6
3:13 1 Cor 4:5; 2 Tim 1:12, 18; 4:8
3:15 Jude 1:23
3:16 1 Cor 6:19; 2 Cor 6:16
3:17 Eph 2:21-22
3:18 Isa 5:21; 1 Cor 8:2; Gal 6:3
3:19 †Job 5:13; 1 Cor 1:20, 27

[5]Who is Apollos, and who is Paul, that we should be the cause of such quarrels? Why, we're only servants. Through us God caused you to believe. Each of us did the work the Lord gave us. [6]My job was to plant the seed in your hearts, and Apollos watered it, but it was God, not we, who made it grow. [7]The ones who do the planting or watering aren't important, but God is important because he is the one who makes the seed grow. [8]The one who plants and the one who waters work as a team with the same purpose. Yet they will be rewarded individually, according to their own hard work. [9]We work together as partners who belong to God. You are God's field, God's building—not ours.

[10]Because of God's special favor to me, I have laid the foundation like an expert builder. Now others are building on it. But whoever is building on this foundation must be very careful. [11]For no one can lay any other foundation than the one we already have—Jesus Christ. [12]Now anyone who builds on that foundation may use gold, silver, jewels, wood, hay, or straw. [13]But there is going to come a time of testing at the judgment day to see what kind of work each builder has done. Everyone's work will be put through the fire to see whether or not it keeps its value. [14]If the work survives the fire, that builder will receive a reward. [15]But if the work is burned up, the builder will suffer great loss. The builders themselves will be saved, but like someone escaping through a wall of flames.

[16]Don't you realize that all of you together are the temple of God and that the Spirit of God lives in* you? [17]God will bring ruin upon anyone who ruins this temple. For God's temple is holy, and you Christians are that temple.

[18]Stop fooling yourselves. If you think you are wise by this world's standards, you will have to become a fool so you can become wise by God's standards. [19]For the wisdom of this world is foolishness to God. As the Scriptures say,

"God catches those who think they are wise
in their own cleverness."*

3:16 Or *among*. **3:19** Job 5:13.

3:6 Paul planted the seed of the Good News message in people's hearts. He was a missionary pioneer; he brought the message of salvation. Apollos watered the seed. He helped the believers grow stronger in the faith. Paul founded the church in Corinth, and Apollos built on that foundation. Tragically, the believers in Corinth had split into factions, pledging loyalty to different teachers (see 1:11-13). After the preachers' work is completed, God is the one who makes Christians grow. Our leaders should certainly be respected, but we should never place them on pedestals that create barriers between people or set them up as a substitute for Christ.

3:7-9 God's work involves many different individuals with a variety of gifts and abilities. There are no superstars in this task, only team members performing their own special roles. We can become useful members of God's team by setting aside our desires to receive glory for what we do. Don't seek the praise that comes from people—it is comparatively worthless. Instead, seek approval from God.

3:10, 11 The foundation of the church—of all believers—is Jesus Christ. Paul laid this foundation (by preaching Christ) when he began the church at Corinth. Whoever builds the church—officers, teachers, preachers, parents, and others—must build with high-quality materials (right doctrine and right living, 3:12ff) that meet God's standards. Paul is not criticizing Apollos but challenging future church leaders to have sound preaching and teaching.

3:10-17 In the church built on Jesus Christ, each church member should be mature, spiritually sensitive, and doctrinally sound. However, the Corinthian church was filled with those whose work was "wood, hay, and straw," members who were immature, insensitive to one another, and vulnerable to wrong doctrine (3:1-4). No wonder they had so many problems. Local church members should be deeply committed to Christ. Can your Christian character stand the test?

3:11 A building is only as solid as its foundation. The foundation of our life is Jesus Christ; he is our base, our reason for being. Everything we are and do must fit into the pattern provided by him. Are you building your life on the only real and lasting foundation, or are you building on a faulty foundation, such as wealth, security, success, or fame?

3:13-15 Two sure ways to destroy a building are to tamper with the foundation and to build with inferior materials. The church must be built on Christ, not on any other person or principle. Christ will evaluate each minister's contribution to the life of the church, and judgment day will reveal the sincerity of each person's work. God will determine whether or not a person has been faithful to Jesus' instructions. Good work will be rewarded; unfaithful or inferior work will be discounted. "The builders themselves will be saved, but like someone escaping through a wall of flames" means that unfaithful workers will be saved, but only by the skin of their teeth. All their accomplishments will count for nothing.

3:16, 17 Just as our bodies are the "temple of the Holy Spirit" (6:19), the local church or Christian community is God's temple. Just as the Jews' Temple in Jerusalem was not to be destroyed, the church is not to be spoiled and ruined by divisions, controversy, or other sins as members come together to worship God.

3:18-21 Paul was not telling the Corinthian believers to neglect the pursuit of knowledge. He was warning them not to glory in the wisdom of this age. God's way of thinking is far above ours; he knows all the futile thoughts of the "wise." The Corinthians were boasting about the wisdom of their leaders and teachers. Their pride made them value the messenger more than the message. We are not to put our trust in anyone but God.

20 And again,

"The Lord knows the thoughts of the wise,
that they are worthless."*

21 So don't take pride in following a particular leader. Everything belongs to you: 22 Paul
and Apollos and Peter*; the whole world and life and death; the present and the future.
Everything belongs to you, 23 and you belong to Christ, and Christ belongs to God.

Paul and the Corinthians

4 So look at Apollos and me as mere servants of Christ who have been put in charge
of explaining God's secrets. 2 Now, a person who is put in charge as a manager must
be faithful. 3 What about me? Have I been faithful? Well, it matters very little what you
or anyone else thinks. I don't even trust my own judgment on this point. 4 My conscience
is clear, but that isn't what matters. It is the Lord himself who will examine me and
decide.

5 So be careful not to jump to conclusions before the Lord returns as to whether or not
someone is faithful. When the Lord comes, he will bring our deepest secrets to light and
will reveal our private motives. And then God will give to everyone whatever praise is
due.

6 Dear brothers and sisters, I have used Apollos and myself to illustrate what I've been
saying. If you pay attention to the Scriptures,* you won't brag about one of your leaders
at the expense of another. 7 What makes you better than anyone else? What do you have
that God hasn't given you? And if all you have is from God, why boast as though you
have accomplished something on your own?

8 You think you already have everything you need! You are already rich! Without us
you have become kings! I wish you really were on your thrones already, for then we
would be reigning with you! 9 But sometimes I think God has put us apostles on display,
like prisoners of war at the end of a victor's parade, condemned to die. We have become
a spectacle to the entire world—to people and angels alike.

10 Our dedication to Christ makes us look like fools, but you are so wise! We are weak,
but you are so powerful! You are well thought of, but we are laughed at. 11 To this very
hour we go hungry and thirsty, without enough clothes to keep us warm. We have
endured many beatings, and we have no homes of our own. 12 We have worked wearily
with our own hands to earn our living. We bless those who curse us. We are patient with
those who abuse us. 13 We respond gently when evil things are said about us. Yet we are
treated like the world's garbage, like everybody's trash—right up to the present moment.

14 I am not writing these things to shame you, but to warn you as my beloved children.

3:20 Ps 94:11. **3:22** Greek *Cephas.* **4:6** Or *You must learn not to go beyond "what is written," so that.*

3:20 †Ps 94:11
3:21 Rom 8:32
3:22 Rom 8:38
3:23 1 Cor 11:3
4:1 Rom 16:25; Titus 1:7
4:2 Luke 12:42
4:4 Ps 143:2
4:5 Matt 7:1; 1 Cor 3:8; 2 Cor 5:10; Rev 20:12
4:6 1 Cor 1:12, 31
4:7 John 3:27; Rom 12:3, 6
4:8 Rev 3:17, 21
4:9 Rom 8:36; Heb 10:33
4:10 1 Cor 1:18; 3:18; 2 Cor 11:19
4:11 Acts 23:2; Rom 8:35; 2 Cor 11:23-27
4:12 Matt 5:44; Acts 18:3; 1 Pet 3:9
4:13 Lam 3:45
4:14 1 Cor 6:5; 15:34; 2 Cor 6:13

3:22 Paul says that both life and death are ours. While nonbelievers are victims of life, swept along by its current and wondering if there is meaning to it, believers can use life well because they understand its true purpose. Nonbelievers can only fear death. For believers, however, death holds no terrors because Christ has conquered all fears (see 1 John 4:18). Death is only the beginning of eternal life with God.

4:1, 2 Paul urged the Corinthians to think of him, Peter, and Apollos as mere servants of Christ entrusted with the secret things of God (see the note on 2:7). A servant does what his master tells him to do. We must do what God tells us to do in the Bible and through his Holy Spirit. Each day God presents us with needs and opportunities that challenge us to do what we know is right.

4:5 It is tempting to judge fellow Christians, evaluating whether or not they are good followers of Christ. But only God knows a person's heart, and he is the only one with the right to judge. Paul's warning to the Corinthians should also warn us. We are to confront those who are sinning (see 5:12, 13), but we must not judge who is a better servant for Christ. When you judge someone, you invariably consider yourself better—and that is arrogant.

4:6, 7 How easy it is for us to become attached to a spiritual leader. When someone has helped us, it's natural to feel loyalty. But Paul warns against having such pride in our favorite leaders that we cause divisions in the church. Any true spiritual leader is a representative of Christ and has nothing to offer that God hasn't given him or her. Don't let your loyalty cause strife, slander, or broken relationships. Make sure that your deepest loyalties are to Christ and not to his human agents. Those who spend more time in debating church leadership than in declaring Christ's message don't have the mind of Christ.

4:6-13 The Corinthians had split into various cliques, each following its favorite preacher (Paul, Apollos, Peter, etc.). Each clique really believed it was the only one to have the whole truth and thus felt spiritually proud. But Paul told the groups not to boast about being tied to a particular preacher, because each preacher was simply a humble servant who had suffered for the same message of salvation in Jesus Christ. No preacher of God has more status than another.

4:15 Gal 4:19
4:16 1 Cor 11:1; Phil 3:17; 1 Thes 1:6
4:17 Acts 16:1; 19:22; 1 Tim 1:2
4:19 Acts 18:21; 1 Cor 16:5; 2 Cor 1:15-16
4:20 1 Cor 2:4
4:21 2 Cor 1:23; 2:1

15 For even if you had ten thousand others to teach you about Christ, you have only one
spiritual father. For I became your father in Christ Jesus when I preached the Good News
to you. 16 So I ask you to follow my example and do as I do.
17 That is the very reason I am sending Timothy—to help you do this. For he is my
beloved and trustworthy child in the Lord. He will remind you of what I teach about
Christ Jesus in all the churches wherever I go.
18 I know that some of you have become arrogant, thinking I will never visit you again.
19 But I will come—and soon—if the Lord will let me, and then I'll find out whether these
arrogant people are just big talkers or whether they really have God's power. 20 For the
Kingdom of God is not just fancy talk; it is living by God's power. 21 Which do you choose?
Should I come with punishment and scolding, or should I come with quiet love and
gentleness?

2. Disorder in the church

Paul Condemns Spiritual Pride

5:1 Lev 18:7-8; Deut 22:30; 27:20; Eph 5:3
5:3 Col 2:5

5 I can hardly believe the report about the sexual immorality going on among you,
something so evil that even the pagans don't do it. I am told that you have a man in
your church who is living in sin with his father's wife. 2 And you are so proud of
yourselves! Why aren't you mourning in sorrow and shame? And why haven't you
removed this man from your fellowship?
3 Even though I am not there with you in person, I am with you in the Spirit.* Concerning

5:3 Or *in spirit.*

CHURCH DISCIPLINE
The church, at times, must exercise discipline toward members who have sinned. But church discipline must be handled carefully, straightforwardly, and lovingly.

Situations	*Steps* (Matthew 18:15–17)
Unintentional error and/or private sin	1. Go to the brother or sister; show the fault to him or her in private.
Public sin and/or those done flagrantly and arrogantly	2. If he/she does not listen, go with one or two witnesses.
	3. If he/she refuses to listen, take the matter before the church.

After these steps have been carried out, the next steps are

1. Remove the one in error from the fellowship (1 Corinthians 5:2–13).
2. The church gives united disapproval, but forgiveness and comfort are in order if he/she chooses to repent (2 Corinthians 2:5–8).
3. Do not associate with the disobedient person; and if you must, speak to him/her as one who needs a warning (2 Thessalonians 3:14, 15).
4. After two warnings, reject the person from the fellowship (Titus 3:10).

4:15 Paul was calling attention to his special role as the Corinthians' spiritual father. In an attempt to unify the church, Paul appealed to his relationship with them. By *father,* he meant he was the church's founder. Because he started the church, he could be trusted to have its best interests at heart. Paul's tough words were motivated by love—like the love a good father has for his children (see also 1 Thessalonians 2:11).

4:16 Paul told the Corinthians to follow his example. He was able to make this statement because he walked close to God, spent time in God's Word and in prayer, and was aware of God's presence in his life at all times. God was Paul's example; therefore, Paul's life could be an example to other Christians. Paul wasn't expecting others to imitate everything he did, but they should imitate those aspects of his beliefs and conduct that were modeling Christ's way of living.

4:17 Timothy had traveled with Paul on Paul's second missionary journey (see Acts 16:1-3) and was a key person in the growth of the early church. Timothy probably did not deliver this letter to Corinth but more likely arrived there shortly after the letter came (see 16:10). Timothy's role was to see that Paul's advice was read and implemented. Then he was to return to Paul and report on the church's progress.

4:18-20 Some people talk a lot about faith, but that's all it is—talk. They may know all the right words to say, but their lives don't reflect God's power. Paul says that the Kingdom of God is to be *lived,* not just discussed. There is a big difference between knowing the right words and living them out. Don't be content to have the right answers about Christ. Let your life show that God's power is really working in you.

4:19 It is not known whether Paul ever returned to Corinth, but it is likely. In 2 Corinthians 2:1, he writes that he decided not to make "another painful visit," implying that he had had a previous painful confrontation with the Corinthian believers (see 2 Corinthians 12:14; 13:1; and the note on 2 Corinthians 2:1).

5:1ff The church must discipline flagrant sin among its members. Such sins left unchecked can polarize and paralyze a church. The correction, however, should never be vengeful. Instead, it should be given to help bring about a cure. The Corinthian believers had refused to deal with a specific sin in the church: A man was having an affair with his mother (or stepmother). The church was ignoring the situation, and Paul was saying that it had a responsibility to maintain the standards of morality found in God's commandments. God tells us not to judge others. But he also tells us not to tolerate flagrant sin because allowing such sin to go undisciplined will have a dangerous effect on other believers (5:6).

the one who has done this, I have already passed judgment 4in the name of the Lord Jesus.
You are to call a meeting of the church,* and I will be there in spirit, and the power of the
Lord Jesus will be with you as you meet. 5Then you must cast this man out of the church
and into Satan's hands, so that his sinful nature will be destroyed* and he himself* will be
saved when the Lord returns.

6How terrible that you should boast about your spirituality, and yet you let this sort of
thing go on. Don't you realize that if even one person is allowed to go on sinning, soon
all will be affected? 7Remove this wicked person from among you so that you can stay
pure.* Christ, our Passover Lamb, has been sacrificed for us. 8So let us celebrate the
festival, not by eating the old bread* of wickedness and evil, but by eating the new bread*
of purity and truth.

9When I wrote to you before, I told you not to associate with people who indulge in
sexual sin. 10But I wasn't talking about unbelievers who indulge in sexual sin, or who
are greedy or are swindlers or idol worshipers. You would have to leave this world to
avoid people like that. 11What I meant was that you are not to associate with anyone who
claims to be a Christian* yet indulges in sexual sin, or is greedy, or worships idols, or is
abusive, or a drunkard, or a swindler. Don't even eat with such people.

12It isn't my responsibility to judge outsiders, but it certainly is your job to judge those
inside the church who are sinning in these ways. 13God will judge those on the outside;
but as the Scriptures say, "You must remove the evil person from among you."*

Avoiding Lawsuits with Christians

6 When you have something against another Christian, why do you file a lawsuit and ask
a secular court to decide the matter, instead of taking it to other Christians to decide
who is right? 2Don't you know that someday we Christians are going to judge the world?

5:4 2 Thes 3:6
5:5 1 Tim 1:20
5:6 Matt 16:6, 12; Gal 5:9
5:7 Exod 12:3-6, 21; Isa 53:7; 1 Pet 1:19; Rev 5:6
5:8 Exod 12:15-19; Deut 16:3
5:9 2 Cor 6:14
5:10 John 17:15
5:11 Rom 16:17; 2 Thes 3:6; 2 Jn 1:10
5:12 Mark 4:11
5:13 †Deut 17:7; 19:19; 21:21, 24; 24:7
6:1 Matt 18:17
6:2 Dan 7:22; Luke 22:30; Rev 3:21

5:4 Or *In the name of the Lord Jesus, you are to call a meeting of the church.* **5:5a** Or *so that he will die;* Greek reads *for the destruction of the flesh.* **5:5b** Greek *and the spirit.* **5:6-7** Greek *Don't you realize that even a little leaven spreads quickly through the whole batch of dough? 7Purge out the old leaven so that you can be a new batch of dough, just as you are already unleavened.* **5:8a** Greek *not with old leaven.* **5:8b** Greek *but with unleavened [bread].* **5:11** Greek *a brother.* **5:13** Deut 17:7.

5:5 To cast this man "into Satan's hands" means to exclude him from the fellowship of believers. Without the spiritual support of Christians, this man would be left alone with his sin and Satan, and perhaps this would drive him to repentance. "So that his sinful nature will be destroyed" states the hope that the experience would bring him to God to destroy his sinful nature through his turning from sin. *Sinful nature* could mean his body or flesh. This alternative translation would imply that Satan would afflict him physically and thus bring him to God. Putting someone out of the church should be a last resort in disciplinary action. It should not be done out of vengeance but out of love, just as parents punish children to correct and restore them. The church's role should be to help, not hurt, offenders, motivating them to repent of their sins and to return to the fellowship of the church.

5:6 Paul was writing to those who wanted to ignore this church problem. They didn't realize that allowing public sin to exist in the church affects all its members. Paul does not expect anyone to be sinless—all believers struggle with sin daily. Instead, he is speaking against those who deliberately sin, feel no guilt, and refuse to repent. This kind of sin cannot be tolerated in the church because it affects others. We have a responsibility to other believers. Blatant sins, left uncorrected, confuse and divide the congregation. While believers should encourage, pray for, and build up one another, they must also be intolerant of sin that jeopardizes the spiritual health of the church.

5:7, 8 As the Hebrews prepared for their exodus from slavery in Egypt, they were commanded to prepare bread without yeast because they didn't have time to wait for it to rise. And because yeast also was a symbol of sin, they were commanded to sweep all of it out of the house (Exodus 12:15; 13:7). Christ is our Passover lamb, the perfect sacrifice for our sin. Because he has delivered us from the slavery of sin, we should have nothing to do with the sins of the past ("old bread").

5:9 Paul is referring to an earlier letter to the Corinthian church, often called the lost letter because it has not been preserved.

5:10, 11 Paul makes it clear that we should not disassociate ourselves from unbelievers—otherwise we could not carry out Christ's command to tell them about salvation (Matthew 28:18-20). But we are to distance ourselves from the person who claims to be a Christian, yet indulges in sins explicitly forbidden in Scripture by rationalizing his or her actions. By rationalizing sin, a person harms others for whom Christ died and dims the image of God in himself or herself. A church that includes such a person is hardly fit to be the light of the world. To do so would distort the picture of Christ it presents to the world. Church leaders must be ready to correct, in love, for the sake of spiritual unity.

5:12 The Bible consistently tells us not to criticize people by gossiping or making rash judgments. At the same time, however, we are to judge and deal with sin that can hurt others. Paul's instructions should not be used to handle trivial matters or to take revenge; nor should they be applied to individual problems between believers. These verses are instructions for dealing with open sin in the church by a person who claims to be a Christian and yet who sins without remorse. The church is to confront and discipline such a person in love. Also see the notes on 4:5 and 5:1ff.

6:1-6 In chapter 5, Paul explained what to do with open immorality in the congregation. In chapter 6, he teaches how the congregation should handle smaller problems between believers. Society has set up a legal system in which disagreements can be resolved in courts. But Paul declares that Christians should not have to go to a secular court to resolve their differences. As Christians, we have the Holy Spirit and the mind of Christ, so why should we turn to those who lack God's wisdom? Because of all that we have been given as believers, and because of the authority that we will have in the future to judge the world and the angels, we should be

And since you are going to judge the world, can't you decide these little things among
yourselves? 3 Don't you realize that we Christians will judge angels? So you should surely
be able to resolve ordinary disagreements here on earth. 4 If you have legal disputes about
such matters, why do you go to outside judges who are not respected by the church? 5 I am
saying this to shame you. Isn't there anyone in all the church who is wise enough to decide
these arguments? 6 But instead, one Christian* sues another—right in front of unbelievers!
7 To have such lawsuits at all is a real defeat for you. Why not just accept the injustice
and leave it at that? Why not let yourselves be cheated? 8 But instead, you yourselves are
the ones who do wrong and cheat even your own Christian brothers and sisters.

Avoiding Sexual Sin

9 Don't you know that those who do wrong will have no share in the Kingdom of God?
Don't fool yourselves. Those who indulge in sexual sin, who are idol worshipers,
adulterers, male prostitutes, homosexuals, 10 thieves, greedy people, drunkards, abusers,
and swindlers—none of these will have a share in the Kingdom of God. 11 There was a
time when some of you were just like that, but now your sins have been washed away,*
and you have been set apart for God. You have been made right with God because of
what the Lord Jesus Christ and the Spirit of our God have done for you.
12 You may say, "I am allowed to do anything." But I reply, "Not everything is good
for you." And even though "I am allowed to do anything," I must not become a slave to
anything. 13 You say, "Food is for the stomach, and the stomach is for food." This is true,

6:3 2 Pet 2:4; Jude 1:6
6:5 1 Cor 4:14
6:7 Matt 5:39; 1 Thes 5:15; 1 Pet 3:9
6:8 1 Thes 4:6
6:9-10 Gal 5:19-21; Eph 5:5; Rev 22:15
6:11 Acts 22:16; Rom 8:30; 1 Cor 1:2, 30
6:12 1 Cor 10:23
6:13 Col 2:22; 1 Thes 4:3-5

6:6 Greek *one brother.* **6:11** Or *you have been cleansed.*

able to deal with disputes among ourselves. See John 5:22 and Revelation 3:21 for more on judging the world. Judging angels is mentioned in 2 Peter 2:4 and Jude 1:6.

6:6-8 Why did Paul say that Christians should not take their disagreements to unbelivers in secular courts? (1) If the judge and jury are not Christians, they are not likely to be sensitive to Christian values. (2) The basis for going to court is often revenge; this should never be a Christian's motive. (3) Lawsuits harm the cause of Christ and make the church look bad, causing unbelievers to focus on its problems rather than on its purpose.

6:9-11 Paul is describing characteristics of unbelievers. He doesn't mean that all those who have indulged in sexual sin or who have been idol worshipers, adulterers, male prostitutes, homosexuals, thieves, greedy people, drunkards, abusers, and swindlers are automatically and irrevocably excluded from heaven. Christians come out of all kinds of different backgrounds, including these. They may still struggle with evil desires, but they should not continue in these practices. In 6:11, Paul clearly states that even those who sin in these ways can have their lives changed by Christ. However, those who say that they are Christians but persist in these practices with no sign of remorse will not inherit the Kingdom of God. Such people need to reevaluate their lives to see if they truly believe in Christ.

6:9-11 In a permissive society it is easy for Christians to overlook or tolerate some immoral behavior (greed, drunkenness, etc.) while remaining outraged at others (homosexuality, thievery). We must not participate in sin or condone it in any way; we cannot be selective about what we condemn or excuse. Staying away from more "acceptable" forms of sin is difficult, but it is no harder for us than it was for the Corinthians. God expects his followers in any age to have high standards.

6:11 Paul emphasizes God's action in making believers new people. The three aspects of God's work are all part of our salvation: Our sins were washed away, we were set apart for special use (sanctified), and we have been made right with God (justified).

6:12 Apparently the church had been quoting and misapplying the words "I am allowed to do anything." Some Christians in Corinth were excusing their sins by saying that (1) Christ had taken away all sin, and so they had complete freedom to live as they pleased, or (2) what they were doing was not strictly forbidden by Scripture. Paul answered both these excuses: (1) While Christ has taken away our sin, this does not give us freedom to go on doing what we know is wrong. The New Testament specifically forbids many sins (see 6:9, 10) that were originally prohibited in the Old Testament (see Romans 12:9-21; 13:8-10). (2) Some actions are not sinful in themselves, but they are not appropriate because they can control our life and lead us away from God. (3) Some actions may hurt others. Anything we do that hurts rather than helps others is not right.

6:12, 13 Many of the world's religions teach that the soul or spirit is important but the body is not; and Christianity has sometimes been influenced by these ideas. In truth, however, Christianity takes very seriously the realm of the physical. We worship a God who created a physical world and pronounced it good. He promises us a new earth, where real people will have transformed physical lives—not a pink cloud where disembodied souls listen to harp music. At the heart of Christianity is the story of God himself taking on flesh and blood and coming to live with us, offering both physical healing and spiritual restoration.

We humans, like Adam, are a combination of dust and spirit. Just as our spirits affect our bodies, so our physical bodies affect our spirits. We cannot commit sin with our bodies without damaging our souls because our bodies and souls are inseparably joined. In the new earth we will have resurrection bodies that are not corrupted by sin. Then we will enjoy the fullness of our salvation.

6:12, 13 Freedom is a mark of the Christian faith—freedom from sin and guilt, and freedom to use and enjoy anything that comes from God. But Christians should not abuse this freedom and hurt themselves or others. Drinking too much leads to alcoholism; gluttony leads to obesity. Be careful that what God has allowed you to enjoy doesn't grow into a bad habit that controls you. For more about Christian freedom and everyday behavior, read chapter 8.

6:13 Sexual immorality is a temptation that is always before us. In movies and on television, sex outside marriage is treated as a normal, even desirable, part of life, while marriage is often shown as confining and joyless. We can even be looked down on by others if we are suspected of being pure. But God does not forbid sexual sin just to be difficult. He knows its power to destroy us physically and spiritually. No one should underestimate the power of sexual immorality. It has devastated countless lives and destroyed families, churches, communities, and even nations. God wants to protect us from damaging ourselves and others, and so he offers to fill us—our loneliness, our desires—with himself.

though someday God will do away with both of them. But our bodies were not made for
sexual immorality. They were made for the Lord, and the Lord cares about our bodies.
[14]And God will raise our bodies from the dead by his marvelous power, just as he raised
our Lord from the dead. [15]Don't you realize that your bodies are actually parts of Christ?
Should a man take his body, which belongs to Christ, and join it to a prostitute? Never!
[16]And don't you know that if a man joins himself to a prostitute, he becomes one body
with her? For the Scriptures say, "The two are united into one."* [17]But the person who
is joined to the Lord becomes one spirit with him.

[18]Run away from sexual sin! No other sin so clearly affects the body as this one does.
For sexual immorality is a sin against your own body. [19]Or don't you know that your
body is the temple of the Holy Spirit, who lives in you and was given to you by God?
You do not belong to yourself, [20]for God bought you with a high price. So you must
honor God with your body.

6:14 Acts 2:24 Rom 6:5 1 Cor 15:15, 20 Eph 1:19-20
6:17 John 17:21-23 Rom 8:9-11, 16 2 Cor 3:17 Gal 2:20
6:18 1 Thes 4:3-4
6:19 Rom 14:7-8 1 Cor 3:16 2 Cor 6:16
6:20 Phil 1:20 1 Pet 1:18-19

B. PAUL ANSWERS CHURCH QUESTIONS (7:1—16:24)

After discussing disorder in the church, Paul moves to the list of questions that the Corinthians had sent him, including subjects of marriage, singleness, eating meat offered to idols, propriety in worship, orderliness in the Lord's Supper, spiritual gifts, and the resurrection. Questions that plague churches today are remarkably similar to these, so we can receive specific guidance in these areas from this letter.

1. Instruction on Christian marriage

7 Now about the questions you asked in your letter. Yes, it is good to live a celibate
life. [2]But because there is so much sexual immorality, each man should have his own
wife, and each woman should have her own husband.

[3]The husband should not deprive his wife of sexual intimacy, which is her right as a
married woman, nor should the wife deprive her husband. [4]The wife gives authority over

7:1 1 Cor 7:8, 26
7:3 Exod 21:10 1 Pet 3:7

6:16 Gen 2:24.

6:15-17 This teaching about sexual immorality and prostitutes was especially important for the Corinthian church because the temple of the love goddess Aphrodite was in Corinth. This temple employed more than a thousand prostitutes as priestesses, and sex was part of the worship ritual. Paul clearly stated that Christians are to have no part in sexual immorality, even if it is acceptable and popular in our culture.

6:18 Christians are free to be all they can be for God, but they are not free *from* God. God created sex to be a beautiful and essential ingredient of marriage, but sexual sin—sex outside the marriage relationship—*always* hurts someone. It hurts God because it shows that we prefer following our own desires instead of the leading of the Holy Spirit. It hurts others because it violates the commitment so necessary to a relationship. It often brings disease to our bodies. And it deeply affects our personality, which responds in anguish when we harm ourselves physically and spiritually.

6:19, 20 What did Paul mean when he said that our body belongs to God? Many people say they have the right to do whatever they want with their own bodies. Although they think that this is freedom, they are really enslaved to their own desires. When we become Christians, the Holy Spirit comes to live in us. Therefore, we no longer own our bodies. That God bought us "with a high price" refers to slaves purchased at an auction. Christ's death freed us from sin but also obligates us to his service. If you live in a building owned by someone else, you try not to violate the building's rules. Because your body belongs to God, you must not violate his standards for living.

7:1 The Corinthians had written to Paul, asking him several questions relating to the Christian life and problems in the church. The first question was whether it was good to be married. Paul answers this and other questions in the remainder of this letter.

7:1ff Christians in Corinth were surrounded by sexual temptation. The city had a reputation even among pagans for sexual immorality and religious prostitution. It was to this kind of society that Paul delivered these instructions on sex and marriage. The Corinthians needed special, specific instructions because of their culture's immoral standards. For more on Paul's teaching about marriage, see Ephesians 5.

7:3-5 Sexual temptations are difficult to withstand because they appeal to the normal and natural desires that God has given us. Marriage provides God's way to satisfy these natural sexual desires and to strengthen the partners against temptation. Married couples have the responsibility to care for each other; therefore, husbands and wives should not withhold themselves sexually from one another but should fulfill each other's needs and desires. (See also the note on 10:13.)

7:3-11 The Corinthian church was in turmoil because of the immorality of the culture around them. Some Greeks, in rejecting immorality, rejected sex and marriage altogether. The Corinthian Christians wondered if this was what they should do also, so they asked Paul several questions: "Because sex is perverted, shouldn't we also abstain in marriage?" "If my spouse is unsaved, should I seek a divorce?" "Should unmarried people and widows remain unmarried?" Paul answered many of these questions by saying, "For now, stay put. Be content in the situation where God has placed you. If you're married, don't seek to be single. If you're single, don't seek to be married. Live God's way, one day at a time, and he will show you what to do."

7:4 Spiritually, our bodies belong to God when we become Christians because Jesus Christ bought us by paying the price to release us from sin (see 6:19, 20). Physically, our bodies belong to our spouses because God designed marriage so that, through the union of husband and wife, the two become one (Genesis 2:24). Paul stressed complete equality in sexual relationships. Neither male nor female should seek dominance or autonomy.

her body to her husband, and the husband also gives authority over his body to his wife.
7:5 1 Thes 3:5 5So do not deprive each other of sexual relations. The only exception to this rule would
be the agreement of both husband and wife to refrain from sexual intimacy for a limited
time, so they can give themselves more completely to prayer. Afterward they should
come together again so that Satan won't be able to tempt them because of their lack of
7:6 2 Cor 8:8 self-control. 6This is only my suggestion. It's not meant to be an absolute rule. 7I wish
7:7 Matt 19:11-12; 1 Cor 9:5; 12:11 everyone could get along without marrying, just as I do. But we are not all the same. God
gives some the gift of marriage, and to others he gives the gift of singleness.
8Now I say to those who aren't married and to widows—it's better to stay unmarried,
7:9 1 Tim 5:14 just as I am. 9But if they can't control themselves, they should go ahead and marry. It's
better to marry than to burn with lust.
7:10 Mal 2:14-16; Matt 5:32; 19:9; Mark 10:10-12; Luke 16:18 10Now, for those who are married I have a command that comes not from me, but from
the Lord.* A wife must not leave her husband. 11But if she does leave him, let her remain
single or else go back to him. And the husband must not leave his wife.
7:12 2 Cor 11:17 12Now, I will speak to the rest of you, though I do not have a direct command from
the Lord. If a Christian man* has a wife who is an unbeliever and she is willing to
continue living with him, he must not leave her. 13And if a Christian woman has a
husband who is an unbeliever, and he is willing to continue living with her, she must not
7:14 Mal 2:15 leave him. 14For the Christian wife brings holiness to her marriage, and the Christian
husband brings holiness to his marriage. Otherwise, your children would not have a
7:15 Rom 14:19 godly influence, but now they are set apart for him. 15(But if the husband or wife who
isn't a Christian insists on leaving, let them go. In such cases the Christian husband or
7:16 Rom 11:14; 1 Pet 3:1 wife is not required to stay with them, for God wants his children to live in peace.) 16You
wives must remember that your husbands might be converted because of you. And you
husbands must remember that your wives might be converted because of you.
7:17 1 Cor 4:17; 14:33 17You must accept whatever situation the Lord has put you in, and continue on as you

7:10 See Matt 5:32; 19:9; Mark 10:11-12; Luke 16:18. **7:12** Greek *a brother.*

7:7 Both marriage and singleness are gifts from God. One is not morally better than the other, and both are valuable to accomplishing God's purposes. It is important for us, therefore, to accept our present situation. When Paul said he wished that all people were like him (unmarried), he was expressing his desire that more people would devote themselves *completely* to the ministry without the added concerns of a spouse and family, as he had done. He was not criticizing marriage—after all, it is God's created way of providing companionship and populating the earth.

7:9 Sexual pressure is not the best motive for getting married, but it is better to marry the right person than to "burn with lust." Many new believers in Corinth thought that all sex was wrong, and so engaged couples were deciding not to get married. In this passage, Paul was telling couples who wanted to marry that they should not frustrate their normal sexual drives by avoiding marriage. This does not mean, however, that people who have trouble controlling themselves should marry the first person who comes along. It is better to deal with the pressure of desire than to deal with an unhappy marriage.

7:12 Paul's "command" about the permanence of marriage (7:10) comes from the Old Testament (Genesis 2:24) and from Jesus (Mark 10:2-12). His *suggestion* in this verse is based on God's command, and Paul applies it to the situation the Corinthians were facing. Paul ranked the command above the suggestion because one is an eternal principle while the other is a specific application. Nevertheless, for people in similar situations, Paul's suggestion is the best advice they will get. Paul was a man of God, an apostle, and he had the mind of Christ.

7:12-14 Because of their desire to serve Christ, some people in the Corinthian church thought they ought to divorce their pagan spouses and marry Christians. But Paul affirmed the marriage commitment. God's ideal is for husbands and wives to stay together—even when one spouse is not a believer. The Christian spouse should try to win the other to Christ. It would be easy to rationalize leaving; however, Paul makes a strong case for staying with the unbelieving spouse and being a positive influence on the marriage. Paul, like Jesus, believed that marriage is permanent (see Mark 10:1-9).

7:14 The blessings that flow to believers don't stop there but extend to others. God regards the marriage as set apart for his use by the presence of one Christian spouse. The other does not receive salvation automatically but is blessed by this relationship. The children of such a marriage have a godly influence and are set apart (because of God's blessing on the family unit) until they are old enough to make their own decision for Christ.

7:15, 16 This verse is misused by some as a loophole to get out of marriage. But Paul's statements were given to encourage the Christian spouse to try to get along with the unbeliever and make the marriage work. If, however, the unbelieving spouse insists on leaving, Paul said to let him or her go. The only alternative would be for the Christian to deny his or her faith to preserve the marriage, and that would be worse than dissolving the marriage. Paul's chief purpose in writing this was to urge the married couples to seek unity, not separation (see 7:17; 1 Peter 3:1, 2).

7:17 Apparently the Corinthians were ready to make wholesale changes without thinking through the ramifications. Paul was writing to say that people should be Christians where they are. You can do God's work and demonstrate your faith *anywhere.* If you became a Christian after marriage, and your spouse is not a believer, remember that you don't have to be married to a Christian to live for Christ. Don't assume that you are in the wrong place or stuck with the wrong person. You may be just where God wants you (see 7:20).

were when God first called you. This is my rule for all the churches. 18 For instance, a — 7:18 Acts 15:1-19
man who was circumcised before he became a believer should not try to reverse it. And — Gal 5:2
the man who was uncircumcised when he became a believer should not be circumcised
now. 19 For it makes no difference whether or not a man has been circumcised. The — 7:19 Rom 2:25-27
important thing is to keep God's commandments. — Gal 5:6; 6:15
20 You should continue on as you were when God called you. 21 Are you a slave? Don't — Col 3:11
let that worry you—but if you get a chance to be free, take it. 22 And remember, if you — 7:22 John 8:36
were a slave when the Lord called you, the Lord has now set you free from the awful — Eph 6:6; 1 Pet 2:16
power of sin. And if you were free when the Lord called you, you are now a slave of — 7:23
Christ. 23 God purchased you at a high price. Don't be enslaved by the world.* 24 So, dear — 1 Cor 6:20
brothers and sisters, whatever situation you were in when you became a believer, stay — 1 Pet 1:18
there in your new relationship with God.
25 Now, about the young women who are not yet married. I do not have a command — 7:25 2 Cor 4:1
from the Lord for them. But the Lord in his kindness has given me wisdom that can be — 1 Tim 1:12-13
trusted, and I will share it with you. 26 Because of the present crisis,* I think it is best to
remain just as you are. 27 If you have a wife, do not end the marriage. If you do not have
a wife, do not get married. 28 But if you do get married, it is not a sin. And if a young
woman gets married, it is not a sin. However, I am trying to spare you the extra problems
that come with marriage.
29 Now let me say this, dear brothers and sisters: The time that remains is very short, so — 7:29 Rom 13:11
husbands should not let marriage be their major concern. 30 Happiness or sadness or wealth
should not keep anyone from doing God's work. 31 Those in frequent contact with the things — 7:31 1 Jn 2:17
of the world should make good use of them without becoming attached to them, for this
world and all it contains will pass away. 32 In everything you do, I want you to be free from
the concerns of this life. An unmarried man can spend his time doing the Lord's work and
thinking how to please him. 33 But a married man can't do that so well. He has to think about
his earthly responsibilities and how to please his wife. 34 His interests are divided. In the — 7:34 1 Tim 5:5
same way, a woman who is no longer married or has never been married can be more
devoted to the Lord in body and in spirit, while the married woman must be concerned about
her earthly responsibilities and how to please her husband.

7:23 Greek *don't become slaves of people.* **7:26** Or *pressures of life.*

7:18, 19 The ceremony of circumcision was an important part of the Jews' relationship with God. In fact, before Christ came, circumcision was commanded by God for those who claimed to follow him (Genesis 17:9-14). But after Christ's death, circumcision was no longer necessary (Acts 15; Romans 4:9-11; Galatians 5:2-4; Colossians 2:11). Pleasing God and obeying him are more important than observing traditional ceremonies.

7:20 We may become so concerned about what we *could* be doing for God somewhere else that we miss great opportunities right where we are. Paul says that when you become a Christian, you should continue on with the work you have previously been doing—provided it isn't immoral or unethical. Every job can become Christian work when you realize that it can be an opportunity to honor, serve, and speak out for Christ. Because God has placed you where you are, take advantage of every opportunity to serve him there.

7:22 Slavery was common throughout the Roman Empire. Some Christians in the Corinthian church were undoubtedly slaves. Paul said that although they were slaves to other human beings, they were free from the power of sin in their lives. People today are slaves to sin until they commit their lives to Christ, who alone can conquer sin's power. Sin, pride, and fear no longer have any claim over us, just as a slave owner no longer has power over the slaves he has sold. The Bible says we become Christ's slaves when we become Christians (Romans 6:18), but this actually means we gain our freedom, because sin no longer controls us.

7:26 Paul probably foresaw the impending persecution that the Roman government would soon bring upon Christians. He gave this practical advice because being unmarried would mean less suffering and more freedom to throw one's life into the cause of Christ (7:29), even to the point of fearlessly dying for him. Paul's advice reveals his single-minded devotion to spreading the Good News.

7:28 Many people naively think that marriage will solve all their problems. Here are some problems marriage won't solve: (1) loneliness, (2) sexual temptation, (3) one's deepest emotional needs, (4) life's difficulties. Marriage alone does not hold two people together but commitment does—commitment to Christ and to each other despite conflicts and problems. As wonderful as it is, marriage does not automatically solve every problem. Whether married or single, we must be content with our situation and focus on Christ, not on loved ones, to help address our problems.

7:29 Paul urges all believers to make the most of their time before Christ's return. Every person in every generation should have this sense of urgency about telling the Good News to others. Life is short—there's not much time!

7:29-31 Paul urges believers not to regard marriage, home, or financial security as the ultimate goals of life. As much as possible, we should live unhindered by the cares of this world, not getting involved with burdensome mortgages, budgets, investments, or debts that might keep us from doing God's work. A married man or woman, as Paul points out (7:33, 34), must take care of earthly responsibilities but make every effort to keep them modest and manageable.

7:32-34 Some single people feel tremendous pressure to be married. They think their lives can be complete only with a spouse. But Paul underlines one advantage of being single—the potential of a greater focus on Christ and his work. If you are unmarried, use your special opportunity to serve Christ wholeheartedly.

35 I am saying this for your benefit, not to place restrictions on you. I want you to do
whatever will help you serve the Lord best, with as few distractions as possible. 36 But if
a man thinks he ought to marry his fiancée because he has trouble controlling his
passions and time is passing, it is all right; it is not a sin. Let them marry. 37 But if he has
decided firmly not to marry and there is no urgency and he can control his passion, he
does well not to marry. 38 So the person who marries does well, and the person who
doesn't marry does even better.
39 A wife is married to her husband as long as he lives. If her husband dies, she is free
to marry whomever she wishes, but this must be a marriage acceptable to the Lord.*
40 But in my opinion it will be better for her if she doesn't marry again, and I think I am
giving you counsel from God's Spirit when I say this.

7:38 Heb 13:4
7:39 Rom 7:2; 2 Cor 6:14
7:40 1 Cor 7:6, 25

2. Instruction on Christian freedom

Food Sacrificed to Idols

8 Now let's talk about food that has been sacrificed to idols. You think that everyone
should agree with your perfect knowledge. While knowledge may make us feel
important, it is love that really builds up the church. 2 Anyone who claims to know all the
answers doesn't really know very much. 3 But the person who loves God is the one God
knows and cares for.
4 So now, what about it? Should we eat meat that has been sacrificed to idols? Well,
we all know that an idol is not really a god and that there is only one God and no other.
5 According to some people, there are many so-called gods and many lords, both in
heaven and on earth. 6 But we know that there is only one God, the Father, who created

8:1 Acts 15:20, 29
8:2 1 Cor 3:18; 13:8-9; Gal 6:3
8:4 Deut 4:35, 39; 6:4; 1 Cor 10:19
8:6 John 1:3; Acts 17:28; 1 Cor 12:5; Eph 4:5-6; Col 1:16

7:39 Or *but only to a Christian;* Greek reads *but only in the Lord.*

STRONGER, WEAKER BELIEVERS

Advice to	
Stronger believer	Don't be proud of your maturity; don't flaunt your freedom. Act in love so you do not cause a weaker believer to stumble.
Weaker believer	Although you may not feel the same freedom in some areas as in others, take your time, pray to God, but do not force others to adhere to your stipulations. You would hinder other believers by making up rules and standards for how everyone ought to behave. Make sure your convictions are based on God's Word and are not simply an expression of your opinions.
Pastors and leaders	Teach correctly from God's Word, helping Christians to understand what is right and wrong in God's eyes and to see that they can have varied opinions on other issues and still be unified. Don't allow potential problems to get out of hand, causing splits and divisions.

Paul advises those who are more mature in the faith about how they must care about their brothers and sisters in Christ who have more tender consciences; those "weaker" brothers and sisters are advised concerning their growth; and pastors and leaders are instructed on how to deal with the conflicts that easily could arise between these groups.

7:38 When Paul says the unmarried person does even better, he is talking about the potential time available for service to God. The single person does not have the responsibility of caring for a spouse and raising a family. Singleness, however, does not ensure service to God; involvement in service depends on the commitment of the individual.

7:40 Paul's advice comes from the Holy Spirit, who guides and equips both single and married people to fulfill their roles.

8:1 Meat bought in the marketplace was likely to have been offered to an idol in one of the many pagan temples. Animals were brought to a temple, killed before an idol as part of a pagan religious ceremony, and eaten at a feast in the pagan temple or taken to butchers who sold the meat in the marketplace. The believers wondered if, by eating such meat, they were somehow participating in the worship of idols.

8:1-3 Love is more important than knowledge. Knowledge can make us look good and feel important, but we can all too easily develop an arrogant, know-it-all attitude. Many people with strong opinions are unwilling to listen to and learn from God and others. We can obtain God's knowledge only by loving him (see James 3:17, 18). And we can know and be known by God only when we model him by showing love (1 John 4:7, 8).

8:4-9 Paul addressed these words to believers who weren't bothered by eating meat that had been offered to idols. Although idols were phony, and the pagan ritual of sacrificing to them was meaningless, eating such meat offended some Christians with sensitive consciences. Paul said, therefore, that mature believers should avoid eating meat offered to idols if it would violate the conscience of weak Christian.

everything, and we exist for him. And there is only one Lord, Jesus Christ, through whom
God made everything and through whom we have been given life.
7However, not all Christians realize this. Some are accustomed to thinking of idols as
being real, so when they eat food that has been offered to idols, they think of it as the
worship of real gods, and their weak consciences are violated. 8It's true that we can't win
God's approval by what we eat. We don't miss out on anything if we don't eat it, and we
don't gain anything if we do. 9But you must be careful with this freedom of yours. Do
not cause a brother or sister with a weaker conscience to stumble.
10You see, this is what can happen: Weak Christians who think it is wrong to eat this
food will see you eating in the temple of an idol. You know there's nothing wrong with
it, but they will be encouraged to violate their conscience by eating food that has been
dedicated to the idol. 11So because of your superior knowledge, a weak Christian,* for
whom Christ died, will be destroyed. 12And you are sinning against Christ when you sin
against other Christians* by encouraging them to do something they believe is wrong.
13If what I eat is going to make another Christian sin, I will never eat meat again as long
as I live—for I don't want to make another Christian stumble.

Paul Gives Up His Rights

9 Do I not have as much freedom as anyone else?* Am I not an apostle? Haven't I
seen Jesus our Lord with my own eyes? Isn't it because of my hard work that you
are in the Lord? 2Even if others think I am not an apostle, I certainly am to you, for you
are living proof that I am the Lord's apostle.
3This is my answer to those who question my authority as an apostle.* 4Don't we have
the right to live in your homes and share your meals? 5Don't we have the right to bring
a Christian wife* along with us as the other disciples and the Lord's brothers and Peter*
do? 6Or is it only Barnabas and I who have to work to support ourselves? 7What soldier
has to pay his own expenses? And have you ever heard of a farmer who harvests his crop
and doesn't have the right to eat some of it? What shepherd takes care of a flock of sheep
and isn't allowed to drink some of the milk? 8And this isn't merely human opinion.
Doesn't God's law say the same thing? 9For the law of Moses says, "Do not keep an ox
from eating as it treads out the grain."* Do you suppose God was thinking only about
oxen when he said this? 10Wasn't he also speaking to us? Of course he was. Just as farm
workers who plow fields and thresh the grain expect a share of the harvest, Christian
workers should be paid by those they serve.
11We have planted good spiritual seed among you. Is it too much to ask, in return, for
mere food and clothing? 12If you support others who preach to you, shouldn't we have
an even greater right to be supported? Yet we have never used this right. We would rather
put up with anything than put an obstacle in the way of the Good News about Christ.

8:7 Rom 14:14; 1 Cor 10:18
8:8 Rom 14:17
8:9 Rom 14:1, 13, 21; 2 Cor 6:3; Gal 5:13
8:11 Rom 14:15, 20
8:12 Matt 18:6
8:13 Rom 14:21
9:1 Acts 9:3; 18:9; 1 Cor 15:8; 1 Tim 2:7; 2 Tim 1:11
9:2 2 Cor 3:2-3
9:4 Luke 10:8; 1 Cor 9:13-14
9:5 Matt 8:14; 12:46; Mark 6:2-3; Luke 6:15
9:6 2 Thes 3:8-9
9:7 Deut 20:6; Prov 27:18; 1 Cor 3:6, 8; 2 Tim 2:4
9:9 †Deut 25:4; 1 Tim 5:18
9:10 Rom 4:23-24; 2 Tim 2:6
9:11 Rom 15:27
9:12 2 Cor 6:3; 11:7-12

8:11 Greek *brother;* also in 8:13. **8:12** Greek *brothers.* **9:1** Greek *Am I not free?* **9:3** Greek *those who examine me.* **9:5a** Greek *a sister, a wife.* **9:5b** Greek *Cephas.* **9:9** Deut 25:4.

8:10-13 Christian freedom does not mean that anything goes. It means that our salvation is not obtained by good deeds or legalistic rules; it is the free gift of God (Ephesians 2:8, 9). Christian freedom, then, is inseparably tied to Christian responsibility. New believers are often very sensitive to what is right or wrong, what they should or shouldn't do. Some actions may be perfectly all right for us to do but may harm a Christian brother or sister who is still young in the faith and learning what the Christian life is all about. We must be careful not to offend a sensitive or younger Christian or, by our example, cause him or her to sin. When we love others, our freedom should be less important to us than strengthening the faith of a brother or sister in Christ.

9:1 Some Corinthians were questioning Paul's authority and rights as an apostle, so Paul gave his credentials: He actually saw and talked with the resurrected Christ, who called him to be an apostle (see Acts 9:3-18). Such credentials make the advice he gives in this letter more persuasive. In 2 Corinthians 10–13, Paul defends his apostleship in greater detail.

9:1 Changed lives were the evidence that God was using Paul. Does your faith have an impact on others? You can be a life-changer, helping others grow spiritually, if you dedicate yourself to being used by God and letting him make you effective.

9:4ff Paul uses himself as an illustration of giving up personal rights. Paul had the right to hospitality, to be married, and to be paid for his work. But he willingly gave up these rights to win people to Christ. When your focus is on living for Christ, your rights become comparatively unimportant.

9:4-10 Jesus said that workers deserve their wages (Luke 10:7). Paul echoes this thought and urges the church to be sure to pay their Christian workers. We have the responsibility to care for our pastors, teachers, and other spiritual leaders. It is our duty to see that those who serve us in the ministry are fairly and adequately compensated.

9:5 The Lord's brothers attained leadership status in the church at Jerusalem. James (one of Jesus' brothers), for example, led the way to an agreement at the Jerusalem council (Acts 15) and wrote the book of James.

9:13 Lev 6:16, 26; Num 18:8, 31
9:14 Matt 10:10; Luke 10:7; Gal 6:6; 1 Tim 5:18
9:15 Acts 18:3; 2 Cor 11:9-10
9:16 Acts 9:15; Rom 1:14
9:17 Gal 2:7; Eph 3:1-8; Phil 1:16, 17; Col 1:25
9:18 2 Cor 11:7; 12:13
9:19 Gal 5:13
9:20 Acts 16:3; 21:20-26; Rom 11:14
9:21 Rom 2:12, 14; Gal 6:2

13 Don't you know that those who work in the Temple get their meals from the food
brought to the Temple as offerings? And those who serve at the altar get a share of the
sacrificial offerings. 14 In the same way, the Lord gave orders that those who preach the
Good News should be supported by those who benefit from it. 15 Yet I have never used
any of these rights. And I am not writing this to suggest that I would like to start now. In
fact, I would rather die than lose my distinction of preaching without charge. 16 For
preaching the Good News is not something I can boast about. I am compelled by God to
do it. How terrible for me if I didn't do it!

17 If I were doing this of my own free will, then I would deserve payment. But God
has chosen me and given me this sacred trust, and I have no choice. 18 What then is my
pay? It is the satisfaction I get from preaching the Good News without expense to
anyone, never demanding my rights as a preacher.

19 This means I am not bound to obey people just because they pay me, yet I have
become a servant of everyone so that I can bring them to Christ. 20 When I am with the
Jews, I become one of them so that I can bring them to Christ. When I am with those
who follow the Jewish laws, I do the same, even though I am not subject to the law, so
that I can bring them to Christ. 21 When I am with the Gentiles who do not have the
Jewish law,* I fit in with them as much as I can. In this way, I gain their confidence and
bring them to Christ. But I do not discard the law of God; I obey the law of Christ.

22 When I am with those who are oppressed, I share their oppression so that I might bring

9:21 Greek *those without the law.*

WHY WE DON'T GIVE UP

Perseverance, persistence, the prize!! The Christian life was never promised as an easy way to live; instead, Paul constantly reminds us that we must have a purpose and a plan because times will be difficult and Satan will attack. But we never persevere without the promise of a prize—a promise God will keep.

Reference	*The Purpose*	*The Plan*	*The Prize*
1 Corinthians 9:24–27	• Run to get the prize • Run straight to the goal	• Practive strict self-control • Discipline your body, training it	• An eternal prize
Galatians 6:7–10	• Don't get tired of doing good • Don't get discouraged and give up • Do good to everyone	• Live to please the Spirit	• Everlasting life
Ephesians 6:10–20	• Put on all of God's armor • Pray on all occasions	• Use every piece of God's armor to resist the enemy	• Taking our stand against the Devil's strategies
Philippians 3:12–14	• Keep working toward that day when you will be all that Christ Jesus saved me for	• Forget the past; strain to reach the end of the race	• The prize for which God calls us up to heaven
2 Timothy 2:1–13	• Teach these great truths to people who are able to pass them on to others • Be strong in Christ's grace, even when your faith is faltering	• Endure suffering like a soldier, and don't get tied up in worldly affairs • Follow the Lord's rules, as an athlete must do in order to win • Work hard, like a farmer who enjoys the fruit of his labor	• We will live with Christ; we will reign with him • He remains faithful

9:13 As part of their pay, priests in the Temple would receive a portion of the offerings as their food (see Numbers 18:8-24).

9:16 Preaching the Good News was Paul's gift and calling, and he said he couldn't stop preaching even if he wanted to. Paul was driven by the desire to do what God wanted, using his gifts for God's glory. What special gifts has God given you? Are you motivated, like Paul, to honor God with your gifts?

9:19-27 In 9:19-22 Paul asserts that he has freedom to do anything; in 9:24-27 he emphasizes a life of strict discipline. The Christian life involves both freedom and discipline. The goals of Paul's life were to glorify God and bring people to Christ. Thus, he stayed free of any philosophical position or material entanglement that might sidetrack him, while he strictly disciplined himself to carry out his goal. For Paul, both freedom and discipline were important tools to be used in God's service.

9:22, 23 Paul gives several important principles for ministry: (1) Find common ground with those you contact; (2) avoid a know-it-all attitude; (3) make others feel accepted; (4) be sensitive to their needs and concerns; and (5) look for opportunities to tell them about Christ. These principles are just as valid for us as they were for Paul.

them to Christ. Yes, I try to find common ground with everyone so that I might bring them
to Christ. 23I do all this to spread the Good News, and in doing so I enjoy its blessings.
24Remember that in a race everyone runs, but only one person gets the prize. You also
must run in such a way that you will win. 25All athletes practice strict self-control. They
do it to win a prize that will fade away, but we do it for an eternal prize. 26So I run straight
to the goal with purpose in every step. I am not like a boxer who misses his punches.*
27I discipline my body like an athlete, training it to do what it should. Otherwise, I fear
that after preaching to others I myself might be disqualified.

Warnings against Idolatry

10 I don't want you to forget, dear brothers and sisters, what happened to our
ancestors in the wilderness long ago. God guided all of them by sending a cloud
that moved along ahead of them, and he brought them all safely through the waters of
the sea on dry ground. 2As followers of Moses, they were all baptized in the cloud and
the sea. 3And all of them ate the same miraculous* food, 4and all of them drank the same
miraculous water. For they all drank from the miraculous rock that traveled with them,
and that rock was Christ. 5Yet after all this, God was not pleased with most of them, and
he destroyed them in the wilderness.
6These events happened as a warning to us, so that we would not crave evil things as they
did 7or worship idols as some of them did. For the Scriptures say, "The people celebrated
with feasting and drinking, and they indulged themselves in pagan revelry."* 8And we must
not engage in sexual immorality as some of them did, causing 23,000 of them to die in one
day. 9Nor should we put Christ* to the test, as some of them did and then died from
snakebites. 10And don't grumble as some of them did, for that is why God sent his angel of
death to destroy them. 11All these events happened to them as examples for us. They were
written down to warn us, who live at the time when this age is drawing to a close.
12If you think you are standing strong, be careful, for you, too, may fall into the same
sin. 13But remember that the temptations that come into your life are no different from

9:24 Phil 3:14; 2 Tim 4:7
9:25 2 Tim 2:5; 4:8; 1 Pet 5:4
9:26 1 Tim 6:12
9:27 Rom 8:13; 13:14; 2 Cor 13:5
10:1 Exod 13:21-22; 14:15-22
10:3 Exod 16:4, 35; John 6:31-58
10:4 Exod 17:6; Num 20:11; John 6:31-58; 7:37
10:5 Num 14:16, 23
10:6 Num 11:4, 34; Ps 106:14
10:8 †Num 25:1-9
10:9 Exod 17:2; Num 21:5-6
10:10 Num 14:2, 36; 16:41-49
10:13 1 Cor 1:9; 2 Pet 2:9

9:26 Or *I am not just shadowboxing.* **10:3** Greek *spiritual;* also in 10:4. **10:7** Exod 32:6. **10:9** Some manuscripts read *the Lord.*

9:24-27 Winning a race requires purpose and discipline. Paul uses this illustration to explain that the Christian life takes hard work, self-denial, and grueling preparation. As Christians, we are running toward our heavenly reward. The essential disciplines of prayer, Bible study, and worship equip us to run with vigor and stamina. Don't merely observe from the grandstand; don't just turn out to jog a couple of laps each morning. Train diligently—your spiritual progress depends upon it.

9:25 At times we must even give up something good in order to do what God wants. Each person's special duties determine the discipline and denial that he or she must accept. Without a goal, discipline is nothing but self-punishment. With the goal of pleasing God, our denial seems like nothing compared to the eternal, imperishable reward that will be ours.

9:27 When Paul says he might be disqualified, he does not mean that he could lose his salvation but rather that he could lose his privilege of telling others about Christ. It is easy to tell others how to live and then not to take our own advice. We must be careful to practice what we preach.

10:1ff In chapter 9 Paul used himself as an example of a mature Christian who disciplines himself to better serve God. In chapter 10, he uses Israel as an example of spiritual immaturity, shown in their overconfidence and lack of self-discipline.

10:1-5 The cloud and the sea mentioned here refer to Israel's escape from slavery in Egypt when God led them by a cloud and brought them safely through the Red Sea (Exodus 14). The miraculous food and water are the provisions God gave as they traveled through the wilderness (Exodus 15–16).

10:2 "They were all baptized in the cloud and the sea" means that just as we are united in Christ by baptism, so the Israelites were united under Moses' leadership and through the events of the Exodus.

10:7-10 The incident referred to in 10:7 is when the Israelites made a gold calf and worshiped it in the wilderness (Exodus 32). The incident in 10:8 is recorded in Numbers 25:1-9 when the Israelites worshiped Baal of Peor and engaged in sexual immorality with Moabite women. The reference in 10:9 is to the Israelites' complaint about their food (Numbers 21:5, 6). They put the Lord to the test by seeing how far they could go. In 10:10, Paul refers to when the people complained against Moses and Aaron, and the plague that resulted (Numbers 14:2, 36; 16:41-50). The angel of death is also referred to in Exodus 12:23.

10:11 Today's pressures make it easy to ignore or forget the lessons of the past. But Paul cautions us to remember the lessons the Israelites learned about God so we can avoid repeating their errors. The key to remembering is to study the Bible regularly so that these lessons remind us of how God wants us to live. We need not repeat their mistakes!

10:13 In a culture filled with moral depravity and sin-inducing pressures, Paul encouraged the Corinthians about temptation. He said that (1) temptations happen to everyone, so don't feel you've been singled out; (2) others have resisted temptation, and so can you; (3) any temptation can be resisted because God will show you a way out. God will help you in resisting temptation by helping you (1) recognize those people and situations that give you trouble, (2) run from anything you know is wrong, (3) choose to do only what is right, (4) pray for God's help, and (5) seek friends who love God and can offer help when you are tempted. Running from a tempting situation is your first step on the way to victory (see 2 Timothy 2:22).

what others experience. And God is faithful. He will keep the temptation from becoming
so strong that you can't stand up against it. When you are tempted, he will show you a
way out so that you will not give in to it.
14 So, my dear friends, flee from the worship of idols. 15 You are reasonable people.
Decide for yourselves if what I am about to say is true. 16 When we bless the cup at the
Lord's Table, aren't we sharing in the benefits of the blood of Christ? And when we break
the loaf of bread, aren't we sharing in the benefits of the body of Christ? 17 And we all
eat from one loaf, showing that we are one body. 18 And think about the nation of Israel;
all who eat the sacrifices are united by that act.
19 What am I trying to say? Am I saying that the idols to whom the pagans bring
sacrifices are real gods and that these sacrifices are of some value? 20 No, not at all. What
I am saying is that these sacrifices are offered to demons, not to God. And I don't want
any of you to be partners with demons. 21 You cannot drink from the cup of the Lord and
from the cup of demons, too. You cannot eat at the Lord's Table and at the table of
demons, too. 22 What? Do you dare to rouse the Lord's jealousy as Israel did? Do you
think we are stronger than he is?
23 You say, "I am allowed to do anything"—but not everything is helpful. You say, "I
am allowed to do anything"—but not everything is beneficial. 24 Don't think only of your
own good. Think of other Christians and what is best for them.
25 Here's what you should do. You may eat any meat that is sold in the marketplace.

10:14 1 Jn 5:21
10:16 Matt 26:26-28; Acts 2:42; 1 Cor 11:23-26
10:17 Rom 12:5; 1 Cor 12:27; Eph 4:16; Col 3:15
10:18 Lev 7:6, 14-15
10:20 Deut 32:17; Rev 9:20
10:21 2 Cor 6:15-16
10:22 Deut 32:16, 21
10:23 1 Cor 6:12
10:24 Rom 15:1-2
10:25 Acts 10:15; 1 Cor 8:7

MAKING CHOICES ON SENSITIVE ISSUES

If I choose one course of action:

. . . does it help my witness for Christ? (9:19–22)
. . . am I motivated by a desire to help others know Christ? (9:23; 10:33)
. . . does it help me do my best? (9:25)
. . . is it against a specific command in Scripture and would thus cause me to sin? (10:12)
. . . is it the best and most beneficial course of action? (10:23, 33)
. . . am I thinking only of myself, or do I truly care about the other person? (10:24)
. . . am I acting lovingly or selfishly? (10:28–31)
. . . does it glorify God? (10:31)
. . . will it cause someone else to sin? (10:32)

All of us make hundreds of choices every day. Most choices have no right or wrong attached to them—like what you wear or what you eat. But we always face decisions that carry a little more weight. We don't want to do wrong, and we don't want to cause others to do wrong, so how can we make such decisions?

10:14 Idol worship was the major expression of religion in Corinth. There were several pagan temples in the city, and they were very popular. The statues of wood or stone were not evil in themselves, but people gave them credit for what only God could do, such as provide good weather, crops, and children. Idolatry is still a serious problem today, but it takes a different form. We don't put our trust in statues of wood and stone but in paper money and plastic cards. Putting our trust in anything but God is idolatry. Our modern idols are those symbols of power, pleasure, or prestige that we so highly regard. When we understand contemporary parallels to idolatry, Paul's words to "flee from the worship of idols" become much more meaningful.

10:16-21 The idea of unity and fellowship with God through eating a sacrifice was strong in Judaism and Christianity as well as in paganism. In Old Testament days, when a Jew offered a sacrifice, he ate a part of that sacrifice as a way of restoring his unity with God, against whom he had sinned (Deuteronomy 12:17, 18). Similarly, Christians participate in Christ's once-for-all sacrifice at the Lord's Table when they eat the bread and drink from the cup, symbolizing his body and blood. Recent converts from paganism could not help being affected if they knowingly ate with pagans in their feasts the meat offered to idols.

10:21 As followers of Christ we must give him our total allegiance. We cannot, as Paul explains, have a part in "the cup of the Lord and . . . the cup of demons." Eating at the Lord's Table means communing with Christ and identifying with his death. Drinking from the cup of demons means identifying with Satan by worshiping or promoting pagan (or evil) activities. Are you leading two lives, trying to follow both Christ and the crowd? The Bible says that you can't do both at the same time.

10:23, 24 Sometimes it's hard to know when to defer to the weak believer. Paul gives a simple rule of thumb to help in making the decision: We should be sensitive and gracious. While some actions may not be wrong, they may not be in the best interest of others. While we have freedom in Christ, we shouldn't exercise our freedom at the cost of hurting a Christian brother or sister. We are not to consider only ourselves; we must be sensitive to others. For more on the proper attitude toward a weak believer, see the notes on 8:10-13 and Romans 14.

Don't ask whether or not it was offered to idols, and then your conscience won't be
bothered. 26 For "the earth is the Lord's, and everything in it."*
27 If someone who isn't a Christian asks you home for dinner, go ahead; accept the
invitation if you want to. Eat whatever is offered to you and don't ask any questions
about it. Your conscience should not be bothered by this. 28 But suppose someone warns
you that this meat has been offered to an idol. Don't eat it, out of consideration for the
conscience of the one who told you. 29 It might not be a matter of conscience for you, but
it is for the other person.
Now, why should my freedom be limited by what someone else thinks? 30 If I can
thank God for the food and enjoy it, why should I be condemned for eating it?
31 Whatever you eat or drink or whatever you do, you must do all for the glory of God.
32 Don't give offense to Jews or Gentiles or the church of God. 33 That is the plan I follow,
too. I try to please everyone in everything I do. I don't just do what I like or what is best
for me, but what is best for them so they may be saved.

11 And you should follow my example, just as I follow Christ's.

3. Instruction on public worship

Proper Worship

2 I am so glad, dear friends, that you always keep me in your thoughts and you are
following the Christian teaching I passed on to you. 3 But there is one thing I want you
to know: A man is responsible to Christ, a woman is responsible to her husband, and

10:27 Luke 10:8
10:28 Rom 14:16; 1 Cor 8:7, 10-12
10:29 1 Cor 9:1, 19
10:30 1 Tim 4:4
10:31 Col 3:17
10:32 Matt 5:29; Acts 24:16; Rom 14:13; 1 Cor 8:13
10:33 1 Cor 9:20-22
11:1 1 Cor 4:16
11:2 1 Cor 15:2-3; 2 Thes 2:15; 3:6
11:3 Gen 3:16; 1 Cor 3:23; Eph 5:23

10:26 Ps 24:1.

10:25-27 Paul gave one answer to the dilemma: Buy whatever meat is sold at the market without asking whether or not it was offered to idols. It doesn't matter anyway, and no one's conscience would be bothered. When we become too worried about our every action, we become legalistic and cannot enjoy life. Everything belongs to God, and he has given us all things to enjoy. If we know something is a problem, then we can deal with it, but we don't need to go looking for problems.

10:28-33 Why should we be limited by another person's conscience? Simply because we are to do all things for God's glory, even our eating and drinking. Nothing we do should cause another believer to stumble. We do what is best for others, so that they might be saved. On the other hand, Christians should be careful not to have oversensitive consciences. Christian leaders and teachers should teach about the freedom we have in matters not expressly forbidden by Scripture.

10:31 Our actions must be motivated by God's love so that all we do will be for his glory. Keep this as a guiding principle by asking, Is this action glorifying God? or How can I honor God through this action?

10:33 Paul's criterion for all his actions was not what he liked best but what was best for those around him. The opposite approach would be (1) being insensitive and doing what we want, no matter who is hurt by it; (2) being oversensitive and doing nothing, for fear that someone may be displeased; (3) being a "yes person" by going along with everything, trying to gain approval from people rather than from God. In this age of "me first" and "looking out for number one," Paul's startling statement is a good standard. If we make the good of others one of our primary goals, we will develop a serving attitude that pleases God.

11:1 Why did Paul say, "Follow my example"? Paul wasn't being arrogant—he did not think of himself as sinless. At this time, however, the Corinthian believers did not know much about the life and ministry of Christ. Paul could not tell them to imitate Jesus because the Gospels had not yet been written, so they did not know what Jesus was like. The best way to point these new Christians to Christ was to point them to a Christian whom they trusted (see also Galatians 4:12; Philippians 3:17; 1 Thessalonians 1:6; 2:14; 2 Thessalonians 3:7, 9). Paul had been in Corinth almost two years and had built a relationship of trust with many of these new believers.

11:2ff In this section Paul's main concern is irreverence in worship. We need to read it in the context of the situation in Corinth. The matter of wearing hats or head coverings, although seemingly insignificant, had become a big problem because two cultural backgrounds were colliding. Jewish women always covered their heads in worship. For a woman to uncover her head in public was a sign of loose morals. On the other hand, Greek women may have been used to worshiping without head coverings.

In this letter Paul had already spoken about divisions and disorder in the church. Both are involved in this issue. Paul's solution came from his desire for unity among church members and for appropriateness in the worship service. He accepted God's sovereignty in creating the rules for relationships.

11:2-16 This section focuses primarily on proper attitudes and conduct in worship, not on the marriage relationship or on the role of women in the church. While Paul's specific instructions may be cultural (women covering their heads in worship), the principles behind them are timeless: respect for spouse, reverence and appropriateness in worship, and focus of all of life on God. If you are doing something that might easily offend members and divide the church, then change your ways to promote church unity. Paul told the women who were not wearing head coverings to wear them, not because it was a scriptural command, but because it kept the congregation from dividing over a petty issue that served only to take people's minds off Christ.

11:3 The phrase "a woman is responsible to her husband" does not indicate the man's control or supremacy but rather his being her source. Because man was created first, the woman derives her existence from man, as man does from Christ and Christ from God. Evidently Paul was correcting some excesses in worship in which the emancipated Corinthian women were engaging.

11:3 The principle behind Paul's words is *submission,* which is a key element in the smooth functioning of any business, government, or family. God ordained submission in certain relationships to prevent chaos. It is essential to understand that submission is not surrender, withdrawal, or apathy. It does not mean inferiority, because God created all people in his image

Christ is responsible to God. 4 A man dishonors Christ* if he covers his head while
praying or prophesying. 5 But a woman dishonors her husband* if she prays or prophesies without a covering on her head, for this is the same as shaving her head. 6 Yes, if she
refuses to wear a head covering, she should cut off all her hair. And since it is shameful
for a woman to have her hair cut or her head shaved, then she should wear a covering.*
7 A man should not wear anything on his head when worshiping, for man is God's glory,
made in God's own image, but woman is the glory of man. 8 For the first man didn't come
from woman, but the first woman came from man. 9 And man was not made for woman's
benefit, but woman was made for man. 10 So a woman should wear a covering on her
head as a sign of authority because the angels are watching.

11 But in relationships among the Lord's people, women are not independent of men,
and men are not independent of women. 12 For although the first woman came from man,
all men have been born from women ever since, and everything comes from God.

13 What do you think about this? Is it right for a woman to pray to God in public without
covering her head? 14 Isn't it obvious that it's disgraceful for a man to have long hair?
15 And isn't it obvious that long hair is a woman's pride and joy? For it has been given to
her as a covering. 16 But if anyone wants to argue about this, all I can say is that we have
no other custom than this, and all the churches of God feel the same way about it.

Order at the Lord's Supper

17 But now when I mention this next issue, I cannot praise you. For it sounds as if more
harm than good is done when you meet together. 18 First of all, I hear that there are
divisions among you when you meet as a church, and to some extent I believe it. 19 But,
of course, there must be divisions among you so that those of you who are right will be
recognized!

20 It's not the Lord's Supper you are concerned about when you come together. 21 For
I am told that some of you hurry to eat your own meal without sharing with others. As a
result, some go hungry while others get drunk. 22 What? Is this really true? Don't you
have your own homes for eating and drinking? Or do you really want to disgrace the
church of God and shame the poor? What am I supposed to say about these things? Do
you want me to praise you? Well, I certainly do not!

23 For this is what the Lord himself said, and I pass it on to you just as I received it. On

11:5 Acts 21:9
11:7 Gen 1:26; 5:1; 9:6 Jas 3:9
11:8 Gen 2:21-23 1 Tim 2:13
11:9 Gen 2:18
11:12 Rom 11:36
11:16 1 Cor 7:17; 10:32
11:18 1 Cor 1:10-12; 3:3
11:19 1 Jn 2:19
11:21 2 Pet 2:13 Jude 1:12
11:22 1 Cor 10:32 Jas 2:6
11:23-25 †Matt 26:26-28 †Mark 14:22-24 †Luke 22:17-20

11:4 Greek *his head.* **11:5** Greek *her head.* **11:6** Or *then she should have long hair.*

---

and all have equal value. Submission is mutual commitment and cooperation.

Thus, God calls for submission among *equals*. He did not make the man superior; he made a way for a husband and wife to work together. Jesus Christ, although equal with God the Father, submitted to him to carry out the plan for salvation. Likewise, although equal to man under God, the wife should submit to her husband for the sake of their marriage and family. Submission between equals is submission by choice, not by force. We serve God in these relationships by willingly submitting to others in our church, to our spouses, and to our government leaders.

11:9-11 God created lines of authority in order for his created world to function smoothly. Although there must be lines of authority even in marriage, there should *not* be lines of superiority. God created men and women with unique and complementary characteristics. One sex is not better than the other. We must not let the issue of authority and submission become a wedge to destroy oneness in marriage. Instead, we should use our unique gifts to strengthen our marriages and to glorify God.

11:10 This verse may mean that the woman should wear a covering on her head as a sign that she is under the man's authority. This is a fact even the angels understand as they observe Christians in worship. See the note on 11:2ff for an explanation of head coverings.

11:14, 15 In talking about head coverings and length of hair, Paul is saying that believers should look and behave in ways that are honorable in their own culture. In many cultures long hair on men is considered appropriate and masculine. In Corinth, it was thought to be a sign of male prostitution in the pagan temples. And women with short hair were labeled prostitutes. Paul was saying that in the Corinthian culture, Christian women should keep their hair long. If short hair on women was a sign of prostitution, then a Christian woman with short hair would find it difficult to be a believable witness for Jesus Christ. Paul wasn't saying we should adopt all the practices of our culture but that we should avoid appearances and behavior that detract from our ultimate goal of being witnesses for Jesus Christ.

11:17-34 The Lord's Supper (11:20) is a visible representation symbolizing the death of Christ for our sins. It reminds us of Christ's death and the glorious hope of his return. Our participation in it strengthens our faith through fellowship with Christ and with other believers.

11:18, 19 Paul acknowledges that there are differences among church members. When they develop into self-willed divisions, however, they are destructive to the congregation. Those who cause division only serve to highlight those who are genuine believers.

11:21, 22 When the Lord's Supper was celebrated in the early church, it included a feast or fellowship meal followed by the celebration of Communion. In the church in Corinth, the fellowship meal had become a time when some ate and drank excessively while others went hungry. There was little sharing and caring. This certainly did not demonstrate the unity and love that should characterize the church, nor was it a preparation for Communion. Paul condemned these actions and reminded the church of the real purpose of the Lord's Supper.

the night when he was betrayed, the Lord Jesus took a loaf of bread, [24]and when he had
given thanks, he broke it and said, "This is my body, which is given* for you. Do this in
remembrance of me." [25]In the same way, he took the cup of wine after supper, saying, **11:25** Luke 22:20
"This cup is the new covenant between God and you, sealed by the shedding of my blood. 1 Cor 10:16 2 Cor 3:6
Do this in remembrance of me as often as you drink it." [26]For every time you eat this bread **11:26**
and drink this cup, you are announcing the Lord's death until he comes again. Matt 26:69

[27]So if anyone eats this bread or drinks this cup of the Lord unworthily, that person is **11:27**
guilty of sinning against the body and the blood of the Lord. [28]That is why you should Heb 10:29
examine yourself before eating the bread and drinking from the cup. [29]For if you eat the **11:28** Matt 26:22
bread or drink the cup unworthily, not honoring the body of Christ,* you are eating and 2 Cor 13:5
drinking God's judgment upon yourself. [30]That is why many of you are weak and sick
and some have even died.

[31]But if we examine ourselves, we will not be examined by God and judged in this **11:31**
way. [32]But when we are judged and disciplined by the Lord, we will not be condemned 1 Jn 1:9
with the world. [33]So, dear brothers and sisters, when you gather for the Lord's Supper, **11:32** Ps 94:12
wait for each other. [34]If you are really hungry, eat at home so you won't bring judgment Heb 12:5-6
upon yourselves when you meet together. **11:34** 1 Cor 4:19

I'll give you instructions about the other matters after I arrive.

Spiritual Gifts

12 And now, dear brothers and sisters, I will write about the special abilities the Holy **12:1**
Spirit gives to each of us, for I must correct your misunderstandings about them. 1 Cor 14:1
[2]You know that when you were still pagans you were led astray and swept along in **12:2** Hab 2:18-19 1 Thes 1:9

11:24 Some manuscripts read *broken.* **11:29** Greek *the body;* some manuscripts read *the Lord's body.*

11:24, 25 What does the Lord's Supper mean? The early church remembered that Jesus instituted the Lord's Supper on the night of the Passover meal (Luke 22:13-20). Just as Passover celebrated deliverance from slavery in Egypt, so the Lord's Supper celebrates deliverance from sin by Christ's death.

Christians pose several different possibilities for what Christ meant when he said, "This is my body." (1) Some believe that the bread and wine actually become Christ's physical blood and body. (2) Others believe that the bread and wine remain unchanged, but Christ is spiritually present with the bread and wine. (3) Still others believe that the bread and wine symbolize Christ's body and blood. Christians generally agree, however, that participating in the Lord's Supper is an important element in the Christian faith and that Christ's presence, however we understand it, strengthens us spiritually.

11:25 What is this new covenant? In the old covenant, people could approach God only through the priests and the sacrificial system. Jesus' death on the cross ushered in the new covenant or agreement between God and us. Now all people can personally approach God and communicate with him. The people of Israel first entered into this agreement after their exodus from Egypt (Exodus 24), and it was designed to point to the day when Jesus Christ would come. The new covenant completes, rather than replaces, the old covenant, fulfilling everything the old covenant looked forward to (see Jeremiah 31:31-34). Eating the bread and drinking the cup shows that we are remembering Christ's death for us and renewing our commitment to serve him.

11:25 Jesus said, "Do this in remembrance of me as often as you drink it." How do we remember Christ in the Lord's Supper? By thinking about what he did and why he did it. If the Lord's Supper becomes just a ritual or a pious habit, it no longer celebrates Christ's death, and it loses its significance.

11:27ff Paul gives specific instructions on how the Lord's Supper should be observed. (1) We should take the Lord's Supper thoughtfully because we are proclaiming that Christ died for our sins (11:26). (2) We should take it worthily, with due reverence and respect (11:27). (3) We should examine ourselves for any unconfessed sin or resentful attitude and be properly prepared (11:28). (4) We should be considerate of others, waiting until everyone is there and then eating in an orderly and unified manner (11:33).

11:27-34 When Paul said that no one should take the Lord's Supper unworthily, he was speaking to the church members who were participating in it without thinking of its meaning. Those who did so were "guilty of sinning against the body and the blood of the Lord." Instead of honoring his sacrifice, they were sharing in the guilt of those who crucified Christ. In reality, *no one* is worthy to take the Lord's Supper. We are all sinners saved by grace. This is why we should prepare ourselves for Communion through healthy introspection, confession of sin, and resolution of differences with others. These actions remove the barriers that affect our relationship with Christ and with other believers. Awareness of your sin should not keep you away from Communion but drive you to participate in it.

11:29 To not honor the "body of Christ" means not understanding what the Lord's Supper means and not distinguishing it from a normal meal. Those who do so condemn themselves (see 11:27).

11:30 That some of the people had died may have been a special supernatural judgment on the Corinthian church. This type of disciplinary judgment highlights the seriousness of the Communion service. The Lord's Supper is not to be taken lightly; this new covenant cost Jesus his life. It is not a meaningless ritual, but a sacrament given by Christ to help strengthen our faith.

11:34 People should come to this meal desiring to fellowship with other believers and prepare for the Lord's Supper to follow, not to fill up on a big dinner. "If you are really hungry, eat at home" means that they should eat dinner beforehand so as to come to the fellowship meal in the right frame of mind.

12:1ff The spiritual gifts given to each person by the Holy Spirit are special abilities that are to be used to minister to the needs of the body of believers. This chapter is not an exhaustive list of spiritual gifts (see Romans 12; Ephesians 4; 1 Peter 4:10, 11 for more examples). There are many gifts; people have different gifts; some people have more than one gift, and one gift is not superior to another. All spiritual gifts come from the Holy Spirit, and their purpose is to build up Christ's body, the church.

12:1ff Instead of building up and unifying the Corinthian church, the issue of spiritual gifts was splitting it. Spiritual gifts

12:3 John 13:13; 1 Jn 4:2-3
12:4 Rom 12:6; Eph 4:4; Heb 2:4
12:6 Eph 4:6
12:8 1 Cor 2:6
12:9 Matt 17:19-20
12:10 Acts 2:4; Rom 12:6; 1 Cor 14:26-32; Gal 3:5; Eph 4:5; 1 Jn 4:1
12:11 Rom 12:6-8; Eph 4:7
12:12 Rom 12:4-5; 1 Cor 10:17; 12:27
12:13 John 7:37-39; Gal 3:28; Eph 2:18; Col 3:11
12:18 1 Cor 12:28

worshiping speechless idols. 3 So I want you to know how to discern what is truly from
God: No one speaking by the Spirit of God can curse Jesus, and no one is able to say,
"Jesus is Lord," except by the Holy Spirit.
4 Now there are different kinds of spiritual gifts, but it is the same Holy Spirit who is
the source of them all. 5 There are different kinds of service in the church, but it is the
same Lord we are serving. 6 There are different ways God works in our lives, but it is the
same God who does the work through all of us. 7 A spiritual gift is given to each of us as
a means of helping the entire church.
8 To one person the Spirit gives the ability to give wise advice; to another he gives the
gift of special knowledge. 9 The Spirit gives special faith to another, and to someone else
he gives the power to heal the sick. 10 He gives one person the power to perform miracles,
and to another the ability to prophesy. He gives someone else the ability to know whether
it is really the Spirit of God or another spirit that is speaking. Still another person is given
the ability to speak in unknown languages,* and another is given the ability to interpret
what is being said. 11 It is the one and only Holy Spirit who distributes these gifts. He
alone decides which gift each person should have.

One Body with Many Parts

12 The human body has many parts, but the many parts make up only one body. So it is
with the body of Christ. 13 Some of us are Jews, some are Gentiles, some are slaves, and
some are free. But we have all been baptized into Christ's body by one Spirit, and we
have all received the same Spirit.*
14 Yes, the body has many different parts, not just one part. 15 If the foot says, "I am
not a part of the body because I am not a hand," that does not make it any less a part of
the body. 16 And if the ear says, "I am not part of the body because I am only an ear and
not an eye," would that make it any less a part of the body? 17 Suppose the whole body
were an eye—then how would you hear? Or if your whole body were just one big ear,
how could you smell anything?
18 But God made our bodies with many parts, and he has put each part just where he
wants it. 19 What a strange thing a body would be if it had only one part! 20 Yes, there are

12:10 Or *in tongues;* also in 12:28, 30. **12:13** Greek *we were all given one Spirit to drink.*

had become symbols of spiritual power, causing rivalries. Some people thought they were more "spiritual" than others because of their gifts. This was a terrible misuse of spiritual gifts because their purpose is always to help the church function more effectively, not to divide it. We can be divisive if we insist on using our gifts our own way without being sensitive to others. We must never use our gifts as a means of manipulating others or serving our own self-interests.

12:3 Anyone can claim to speak for God, and the world is full of false teachers. Paul gives us a test to help us discern whether or not a messenger is really from God: Does he or she confess Christ as Lord? Don't naively accept the words of all who claim to speak for God; test their credentials by finding out what they teach about Christ.

12:9 All Christians have faith. Some, however, have the spiritual gift of faith, which is an unusual measure of trust in the power of God.

12:10, 11 Prophecy is not just a prediction about the future; it can also mean preaching God's Word with power. Paul discusses speaking in unknown languages and interpreting them in more detail in chapter 14. No matter what gifts a person has, each gift is given by the Holy Spirit. We are responsible to use and sharpen our gifts, but we can take no credit for what God has freely given us.

12:12 Paul compares the body of Christ to a human body. Each part has a specific function that is necessary to the body as a whole. The parts are different for a purpose, and in their differences they must work together. Christians must avoid two common errors: (1) being proud of their abilities, or (2) thinking they have nothing to give to the body of believers. Instead of comparing ourselves to one another, we should use our different gifts, together, to spread the Good News of salvation.

12:13 The church is composed of many types of people from a variety of backgrounds with a multitude of gifts and abilities. It is easy for these differences to divide people, as was the case in Corinth. But despite the differences, all believers have one thing in common—faith in Christ. On this essential truth the church finds unity. All believers are baptized by one Holy Spirit into one body of believers, the church. We don't lose our individual identities, but we have an overriding oneness in Christ. When we become a Christian, the Holy Spirit takes up residence in us, and we are born into God's family. "We have all received the same Spirit" means that each of us has received the same Holy Spirit. As members of God's family, we may have different interests and gifts, but we are united by the Spirit into one spiritual body.

12:14-24 Using the analogy of the body, Paul emphasizes the importance of each church member (see the note on 12:12). If a seemingly insignificant part is taken away, the whole body becomes less effective. Thinking that your gift is more important than someone else's is an expression of spiritual pride. We should not look down on those who seem unimportant, and we should not be jealous of others who have more visible gifts. Instead, we should use the gifts we have been given and encourage others to use theirs. If we don't, the body of believers will be less effective.

many parts, but only one body. 21The eye can never say to the hand, "I don't need you."
The head can't say to the feet, "I don't need you."
22In fact, some of the parts that seem weakest and least important are really the most
necessary. 23And the parts we regard as less honorable are those we clothe with the
greatest care. So we carefully protect from the eyes of others those parts that should not
be seen, 24while other parts do not require this special care. So God has put the body
together in such a way that extra honor and care are given to those parts that have less
dignity. 25This makes for harmony among the members, so that all the members care for
each other equally. 26If one part suffers, all the parts suffer with it, and if one part is
honored, all the parts are glad.
27Now all of you together are Christ's body, and each one of you is a separate and **12:27**
necessary part of it. 28Here is a list of some of the members that God has placed in the Rom 12:5 Eph 1:23; 4:12
body of Christ: Col 1:18, 24

first are apostles, **12:28** Rom 12:6-8
second are prophets, Eph 4:11-12
third are teachers,
then those who do miracles,
those who have the gift of healing,
those who can help others,
those who can get others to work together,
those who speak in unknown languages.

29Is everyone an apostle? Of course not. Is everyone a prophet? No. Are all teachers?
Does everyone have the power to do miracles? 30Does everyone have the gift of healing?
Of course not. Does God give all of us the ability to speak in unknown languages? Can **12:31**
everyone interpret unknown languages? No! 31And in any event, you should desire the 1 Cor 14:1, 39
most helpful gifts.

Love Is the Greatest

First, however, let me tell you about something else that is better than any of them! **13:1** 1 Tim 1:5

13 If I could speak in any language in heaven or on earth* but didn't love others, I would **13:2**
only be making meaningless noise like a loud gong or a clanging cymbal. 2If I had Matt 17:20; 21:21 Mark 11:23
the gift of prophecy, and if I knew all the mysteries of the future and knew everything about 1 Cor 12:9
everything, but didn't love others, what good would I be? And if I had the gift of faith so **13:3**
that I could speak to a mountain and make it move, without love I would be no good to Matt 6:2
anybody. 3If I gave everything I have to the poor and even sacrificed my body, I could boast **13:4** 1 Pet 4:8
about it;* but if I didn't love others, I would be of no value whatsoever. **13:5**
4Love is patient and kind. Love is not jealous or boastful or proud 5or rude. Love 1 Cor 10:24 Phil 2:4
does not demand its own way. Love is not irritable, and it keeps no record of when it **13:6**
has been wronged. 6It is never glad about injustice but rejoices whenever the truth wins 2 Thes 2:12 2 Jn 1:4
3 Jn 1:3-4

13:1 Greek *in tongues of people and angels.* **13:3** Some manuscripts read *and even gave my body to be burned.*

12:25, 26 What is your response when a fellow Christian is honored? How do you respond when someone is suffering? We are to be happy with those who are happy, and if they are sad, share their sorrow (Romans 12:15). Too often, unfortunately, we are jealous of those who rejoice and apathetic toward those who weep. Believers are in the world together—there is no such thing as private or individualistic Christianity. We need to get involved in the lives of others and not just enjoy our own relationship with God.

12:30 Paul discusses the subject of speaking in and interpreting unknown languages in more detail in chapter 14.

12:31 The most helpful gifts are those that are beneficial to the body of Christ. Paul has already made it clear that one gift is not superior to another, but he urges the believers to discover how they can serve Christ's body with the gifts God has given them. Your spiritual gifts are not for your own self-advancement. They were given to you for serving God and enhancing the spiritual growth of the body of believers.

13:1ff In chapter 12 Paul gave evidence of the Corinthians' lack of love in the utilization of spiritual gifts; chapter 13 defines real love; and chapter 14 shows how love works. Love is more important than all the spiritual gifts exercised in the church body. Great faith, acts of dedication or sacrifice, and miracle-working power have little effect without love. Love makes our actions and gifts useful. Although people have different gifts, love is available to everyone.

13:4-7 Our society confuses love and lust. Unlike lust, God's kind of love is directed outward toward others, not inward toward ourselves. It is utterly unselfish. This kind of love goes against our natural inclinations. It is impossible to have this love unless God helps us set aside our own natural desires so that we can love and not expect anything in return. Thus, the more we become like Christ, the more love we will show to others.

13:7 Prov 10:12; Rom 15:1; 1 Pet 4:8
13:10 Phil 3:12
13:11 Ps 131:2
13:12 2 Cor 5:7; 1 Jn 3:2
13:13 Matt 22:37-40; Gal 5:5-6; 1 Thes 1:3; 1 Jn 4:16

out. 7Love never gives up, never loses faith, is always hopeful, and endures through
every circumstance.
8Love will last forever, but prophecy and speaking in unknown languages* and
special knowledge will all disappear. 9Now we know only a little, and even the gift of
prophecy reveals little! 10But when the end comes, these special gifts will all disappear.
11It's like this: When I was a child, I spoke and thought and reasoned as a child does.
But when I grew up, I put away childish things. 12Now we see things imperfectly as in
a poor mirror, but then we will see everything with perfect clarity.* All that I know now
is partial and incomplete, but then I will know everything completely, just as God knows
me now.
13There are three things that will endure—faith, hope, and love—and the greatest of
these is love.

The Gifts of Tongues and Prophecy

14:1 Matt 22:37-40; Rom 12:6; 1 Cor 12:1, 31; 14:39; 16:14; Eph 5:2; Col 3:14; 1 Tim 1:5; Jas 2:8
14:2 Mark 16:17; Acts 2:4; 10:46-47; 19:6
14:3 Rom 14:19
14:4 1 Cor 14:18-19, 26-28
14:5 Num 11:29
14:6 Rom 6:17; Eph 1:17
14:8 Num 10:9; Jer 4:19

14 Let love be your highest goal, but also desire the special abilities the Spirit gives,
especially the gift of prophecy. 2For if your gift is the ability to speak in tongues,*
you will be talking to God but not to people, since they won't be able to understand you.
You will be speaking by the power of the Spirit, but it will all be mysterious. 3But one
who prophesies is helping others grow in the Lord, encouraging and comforting them.
4A person who speaks in tongues is strengthened personally in the Lord, but one who
speaks a word of prophecy strengthens the entire church.
5I wish you all had the gift of speaking in tongues, but even more I wish you were all
able to prophesy. For prophecy is a greater and more useful gift than speaking in tongues,
unless someone interprets what you are saying so that the whole church can get some
good out of it.
6Dear brothers and sisters, if I should come to you talking in an unknown language,*
how would that help you? But if I bring you some revelation or some special knowledge
or some prophecy or some teaching—that is what will help you. 7Even musical instruments like the flute or the harp, though they are lifeless, are examples of the need for
speaking in plain language. For no one will recognize the melody unless the notes are
played clearly. 8And if the bugler doesn't sound a clear call, how will the soldiers know
they are being called to battle? 9And it's the same for you. If you talk to people in a
language they don't understand, how will they know what you mean? You might as well
be talking to an empty room.
10There are so many different languages in the world, and all are excellent for those

13:8 Or *in tongues.* **13:12** Greek *see face to face.* **14:2** Or *in unknown languages;* also in 14:4, 5, 13, 14, 18, 22, 28, 39. **14:6** Or *in tongues;* also in 14:19, 23, 26, 27.

13:10 God gives us spiritual gifts in order to build up, serve, and strengthen fellow Christians—the church. In eternity, we will be made perfect and complete and will be in the very presence of God. We will no longer need spiritual gifts, so they will come to an end.

13:12 Paul offers a glimpse into the future to give us hope that one day we will be complete when we see God face to face. This truth should strengthen our faith. We don't have all the answers now, but one day we will. Someday we will see Christ in person and be able to see with God's perspective.

13:13 In morally corrupt Corinth, love had become a mixed-up term with little meaning. Today people are still confused about love. Love is the greatest of all human qualities, and it is an attribute of God himself (1 John 4:8). Love involves unselfish service to others; to show it gives evidence that you care. *Faith* is the foundation and content of God's message; *hope* is the attitude and focus; *love* is the action. When faith and hope are in line, you are free to love completely because you understand how God loves.

14:1 Prophecy may involve predicting future events, but its main purpose is to communicate God's message to people, providing insight, warning, correction, and encouragement.

14:2 The gift of speaking in tongues (unknown languages) was a concern of the Corinthian church because the use of the gift had caused disorder in worship. Speaking in tongues is a legitimate gift of the Holy Spirit, but the Corinthian believers were using it as a sign of spiritual superiority rather than as a means to spiritual unity. Spiritual gifts are beneficial only when they are properly used to help everyone in the church. We should not exercise them only to make *ourselves* feel good.

14:2ff Paul makes several points about speaking in tongues: (1) It is a spiritual gift from God (14:2); (2) it is a desirable gift even though it isn't a requirement of faith (12:28-31); (3) it is less important than prophecy and teaching (14:4). Although Paul himself spoke in tongues, he stresses prophecy (preaching) because it benefits the whole church, while speaking in tongues primarily benefits the speaker. Public worship must be understandable and edifying to the whole church.

14:7-12 As musical instruments must clearly play each note in order for the music to be recognized, so Paul says words must be preached in the hearers' language in order to be helpful. Because there are many languages in the world (14:10), people sometimes can't understand each other. It is the same with speaking in tongues. Although this gift is helpful to many people in private worship as well as in public worship (with interpretation), Paul says that he would rather speak 5 words that his hearers can understand than 10,000 that they cannot (14:19).

who understand them, [11]but to me they mean nothing. I will not understand people who
speak those languages, and they will not understand me. [12]Since you are so eager to have
spiritual gifts, ask God for those that will be of real help to the whole church.
[13]So anyone who has the gift of speaking in tongues should pray also for the gift of
interpretation in order to tell people plainly what has been said. [14]For if I pray in tongues,
my spirit is praying, but I don't understand what I am saying.
[15]Well then, what shall I do? I will do both. I will pray in the spirit,* and I will pray
in words I understand. I will sing in the spirit, and I will sing in words I understand. [16]For
if you praise God only in the spirit, how can those who don't understand you praise God
along with you? How can they join you in giving thanks when they don't understand
what you are saying? [17]You will be giving thanks very nicely, no doubt, but it doesn't
help the other people present.
[18]I thank God that I speak in tongues more than all of you. [19]But in a church meeting
I would much rather speak five understandable words that will help others than ten
thousand words in an unknown language.
[20]Dear brothers and sisters, don't be childish in your understanding of these things.
Be innocent as babies when it comes to evil, but be mature and wise in understanding
matters of this kind. [21]It is written in the Scriptures,*

"I will speak to my own people
 through unknown languages
 and through the lips of foreigners.
But even then, they will not listen to me,"*
 says the Lord.

[22]So you see that speaking in tongues is a sign, not for believers, but for unbelievers;
prophecy, however, is for the benefit of believers, not unbelievers. [23]Even so, if
unbelievers or people who don't understand these things come into your meeting and
hear everyone talking in an unknown language, they will think you are crazy. [24]But if
all of you are prophesying, and unbelievers or people who don't understand these things
come into your meeting, they will be convicted of sin, and they will be condemned by
what you say. [25]As they listen, their secret thoughts will be laid bare, and they will fall
down on their knees and worship God, declaring, "God is really here among you."

A Call to Orderly Worship

[26]Well, my brothers and sisters, let's summarize what I am saying. When you meet, one
will sing, another will teach, another will tell some special revelation God has given, one
will speak in an unknown language, while another will interpret what is said. But
everything that is done must be useful to all and build them up in the Lord. [27]No more
than two or three should speak in an unknown language. They must speak one at a time,
and someone must be ready to interpret what they are saying. [28]But if no one is present
who can interpret, they must be silent in your church meeting and speak in tongues to
God privately.
[29]Let two or three prophesy, and let the others evaluate what is said. [30]But if someone
is prophesying and another person receives a revelation from the Lord, the one who is

14:12 Rom 14:19; 1 Cor 12:1
14:13 1 Cor 12:10
14:15 Eph 5:19; Col 3:16
14:16 1 Chr 16:36; Neh 8:6; Ps 106:48; Rev 5:14; 7:12
14:17 Rom 14:19
14:20 Eph 4:14; Heb 5:12
14:21 Deut 28:49; †Isa 28:11-12; John 10:34
14:22 1 Cor 14:1
14:23 Acts 2:13
14:24 John 16:8
14:25 Isa 45:14; Zech 8:23
14:26 Rom 14:19; 1 Cor 12:7-10; Eph 4:12; 5:19
14:27 1 Cor 14:2, 5, 13
14:29 1 Cor 12:10; 1 Thes 5:19-21

14:15 Or *in the Spirit;* also in 14:15b, 16. **14:21a** Greek *in the law.* **14:21b** Isa 28:11-12.

14:13-20 If a person has the gift of speaking in tongues, he should also pray for the gift of knowing what he has said (interpretation) so he can tell people afterward. This way, the entire church will be edified by this gift.

14:15 There is a proper place for the intellect in Christianity. In praying and singing, both the mind and the spirit are to be fully engaged. When we sing, we should also think about the meaning of the words. When we pour out our feelings to God in prayer, we should not turn off our capacity to think. True Christianity is neither barren intellectualism nor thoughtless emotionalism. See also Ephesians 1:17, 18; Philippians 1:9-11; Colossians 1:9.

14:22-25 The way the Corinthians were speaking in tongues was helping no one because believers did not understand what was being said, and unbelievers thought that the people speaking in tongues were crazy. Speaking in tongues was supposed to be a *sign* to unbelievers (as it was in Acts 2). After speaking in tongues, believers were supposed to explain what was said and give the credit to God. The unsaved people would then be convinced of a spiritual reality and motivated to look further into the Christian faith. While this is one way to reach unbelievers, Paul says that clear preaching is usually better (14:5).

14:26ff Everything done in worship services must be beneficial to the worshipers. This principle touches every aspect—singing, preaching, and the exercise of spiritual gifts. Those contributing to the service (singers, speakers, readers) must have love as their chief motivation, speaking useful words or participating in a way that will strengthen the faith of other believers.

speaking must stop. 31 In this way, all who prophesy will have a turn to speak, one after
the other, so that everyone will learn and be encouraged. 32 Remember that people who
prophesy are in control of their spirit and can wait their turn. 33 For God is not a God of
disorder but of peace, as in all the other churches.*
34 Women should be silent during the church meetings. It is not proper for them to speak.
They should be submissive, just as the law says. 35 If they have any questions to ask, let them
ask their husbands at home, for it is improper for women to speak in church meetings.*
36 Do you think that the knowledge of God's word begins and ends with you Corinthians? Well, you are mistaken! 37 If you claim to be a prophet or think you are very spiritual,
you should recognize that what I am saying is a command from the Lord himself. 38 But
if you do not recognize this, you will not be recognized.*
39 So, dear brothers and sisters, be eager to prophesy, and don't forbid speaking in
tongues. 40 But be sure that everything is done properly and in order.

4. Instruction on the resurrection

The Resurrection of Christ

15 Now let me remind you, dear brothers and sisters, of the Good News I preached
to you before. You welcomed it then and still do now, for your faith is built on this
wonderful message. 2 And it is this Good News that saves you if you firmly believe
it—unless, of course, you believed something that was never true in the first place.
3 I passed on to you what was most important and what had also been passed on to
me—that Christ died for our sins, just as the Scriptures said. 4 He was buried, and he was
raised from the dead on the third day, as the Scriptures said. 5 He was seen by Peter* and
then by the twelve apostles. 6 After that, he was seen by more than five hundred of his
followers* at one time, most of whom are still alive, though some have died by now.
7 Then he was seen by James and later by all the apostles. 8 Last of all, I saw him, too,
long after the others, as though I had been born at the wrong time. 9 For I am the least of

14:32 1 Jn 4:1
14:33 1 Cor 7:17
14:34 Gen 3:16; Eph 5:22; Col 3:18; 1 Tim 2:11-12; Titus 2:5
14:37 2 Cor 10:7; 1 Jn 4:6
14:39 1 Cor 12:31; 1 Thes 5:20
14:40 1 Cor 14:33; Col 2:5
15:3 Isa 53:5-9; Luke 24:25-27; 1 Pet 2:24
15:4 Ps 16:10; Hos 6:2; Jon 1:17; Luke 24:25-27; John 2:21-22; Acts 2:24-32
15:5 Matt 28:16-17; Mark 16:14; Luke 24:34, 36-43; John 20:19
15:8 Acts 9:3-6; Gal 1:16

14:33 The phrase *as in all the other churches* could be joined to the beginning of 14:34. **14:35** Some manuscripts place verses 34-35 after 14:40. **14:38** Some manuscripts read *If you are ignorant of this, stay in your ignorance.* **15:5** Greek *Cephas.* **15:6** Greek *the brothers.*

14:33 In worship, everything must be done with propriety and in an orderly fashion, especially when the gifts of the Holy Spirit are being exercised. When there is chaos and disorder in the church, God cannot work, for he is not a God of confusion but of peace.

14:34, 35 Does this mean that women should not speak in church services today? It is clear from 11:5 that women prayed and prophesied in public worship. It is also clear in chapters 12–14 that women are given spiritual gifts and are encouraged to exercise them in the body of Christ. Women have much to contribute and can participate in worship services.

In the Corinthian culture, women were not allowed to confront men in public. Apparently some of the women who had become Christians thought that their Christian freedom gave them the right to question the men in public worship. This was causing division in the church. In addition, women of that day did not receive formal religious education as did the men. Women may have been raising questions in the worship services that could have been answered at home without disrupting the services. Paul was asking the women not to flaunt their Christian freedom during worship. The purpose of Paul's words was to promote unity, not to teach about women's roles in the church.

14:40 Worship is vital to the life of an individual and to the whole church. Our church services should be conducted in an orderly way so that we can worship, be taught, and be prepared to serve God. Those who are responsible for planning worship should make sure it has order and direction rather than chaos and confusion.

15:2 Most churches contain people who do not yet believe. Some are moving in the direction of belief, and others are simply pretending. Imposters, however, are not to be removed (see Matthew 13:28, 29), for that is the Lord's work alone. The Good News about Jesus Christ will save us *if* we firmly believe it and faithfully follow it.

15:5-8 There will always be people who say that Jesus didn't rise from the dead. Paul assures us that many people saw Jesus after his resurrection: Peter; the disciples (the Twelve); more than 500 Christian believers (most of whom were still alive when Paul wrote this, although some had died); James (Jesus' half brother); all the apostles; and finally Paul himself. The Resurrection is a historical fact. Don't be discouraged by doubters who deny the Resurrection. Be filled with hope because of the knowledge that one day you, and they, will see the living proof when Christ returns. (For more evidence on the Resurrection, see the chart in Mark 16.)

15:7 This James is Jesus' half brother, who at first did not believe that Jesus was the Messiah (John 7:5). After seeing the resurrected Christ, he became a believer and ultimately a leader of the church in Jerusalem (Acts 15:13). James wrote the New Testament book of James.

15:8, 9 Paul's most important credential of his apostleship was that he was an eyewitness of the risen Christ (see Acts 9:3-6). The other apostles saw Christ in the flesh. Paul was in the next generation of believers—yet Christ appeared to him.

15:9, 10 As a zealous Pharisee, Paul had been an enemy of the Christian church—even to the point of capturing and persecuting believers (see Acts 9:1-3). Thus, he felt unworthy to be called an apostle of Christ. Though undoubtedly the most influential of the apostles, Paul was deeply humble. He knew that he had worked hard and accomplished much but only because God had poured kindness and grace upon him. True humility is not convincing yourself that you are worthless but recognizing God's work in you. It is having God's perspective on who you are and acknowledging his grace in developing your abilities.

all the apostles, and I am not worthy to be called an apostle after the way I persecuted the church of God.

10 But whatever I am now, it is all because God poured out his special favor on me—and not without results. For I have worked harder than all the other apostles, yet it was not I but God who was working through me by his grace. 11 So it makes no difference whether I preach or they preach. The important thing is that you believed what we preached to you.

The Resurrection of the Dead

12 But tell me this—since we preach that Christ rose from the dead, why are some of you saying there will be no resurrection of the dead? 13 For if there is no resurrection of the dead, then Christ has not been raised either. 14 And if Christ was not raised, then all our preaching is useless, and your trust in God is useless. 15 And we apostles would all be lying about God, for we have said that God raised Christ from the grave, but that can't be true if there is no resurrection of the dead. 16 If there is no resurrection of the dead, then Christ has not been raised. 17 And if Christ has not been raised, then your faith is useless, and you are still under condemnation for your sins. 18 In that case, all who have died believing in Christ have perished! 19 And if we have hope in Christ only for this life, we are the most miserable people in the world.

20 But the fact is that Christ has been raised from the dead. He has become the first of a great harvest of those who will be raised to life again.

21 So you see, just as death came into the world through a man, Adam, now the resurrection from the dead has begun through another man, Christ. 22 Everyone dies because all of us are related to Adam, the first man. But all who are related to Christ, the other man, will be given new life. 23 But there is an order to this resurrection: Christ was raised first; then when Christ comes back, all his people will be raised.

24 After that the end will come, when he will turn the Kingdom over to God the Father, having put down all enemies of every kind.* 25 For Christ must reign until he humbles all his enemies beneath his feet. 26 And the last enemy to be destroyed is death. 27 For the Scriptures say, "God has given him authority over all things."* (Of course, when it says "authority over all things," it does not include God himself, who gave Christ his authority.) 28 Then, when he has conquered all things, the Son will present himself to

15:24 Greek *every ruler and every authority and power.* **15:27** Ps 8:6.

15:9 Acts 8:3; 2 Cor 12:11; Eph 3:8
15:10 2 Cor 6:1; 11:5, 23
15:12 Acts 17:32; 23:8; 2 Tim 2:18
15:17 Rom 4:25
15:20 Col 1:18; 1 Pet 1:3; Rev 1:5
15:21 Rom 5:12, 18
15:22 Rom 5:14-18
15:23 1 Thes 4:16
15:24 Dan 2:44; 7:14
15:25 Ps 110:1; Isa 9:7; Matt 22:44
15:26 2 Tim 1:10; Rev 20:14; 21:4
15:27 †Ps 8:6; Matt 28:18; Eph 1:22; Heb 2:8; 1 Pet 3:22
15:28 1 Cor 3:23; Phil 3:21

15:10 Paul wrote of working harder than the other apostles. This was not an arrogant boast, because he knew that his power came from God and that it really didn't matter who worked hardest. Because of his prominent position as a Pharisee, Paul's conversion made him the object of even greater persecution than the other apostles; thus, he had to work harder to preach the same message.

15:12ff Most Greeks did not believe that people's bodies would be resurrected after death. They saw the afterlife as something that happened only to the soul. According to Greek philosophers, the soul was the real person, imprisoned in a physical body, and at death the soul was released. There was no immortality for the body, but the soul entered an eternal state. Christianity, by contrast, affirms that the body and soul will be united after resurrection. The church at Corinth was in the heart of Greek culture. Thus, many believers had a difficult time believing in a bodily resurrection. Paul wrote this part of his letter to clear up this confusion about the resurrection.

15:13-18 The resurrection of Christ is the center of the gospel message. Because Christ rose from the dead as he promised, we know that what he said is true—he is God. Because he rose, we have certainty that our sins are forgiven. Because he rose, he lives and represents us to God. Because he rose and defeated death, we know we will also be raised.

15:19 Why does Paul say believers would be miserable if there were only earthly value to Christianity? In Paul's day, Christianity often brought a person persecution, ostracism from family, and, in many cases, poverty. There were few tangible benefits from being a Christian in that society. It was certainly not a step up the social or career ladder. More important is the fact that if Christ had not been resurrected from the dead, Christians would not be forgiven of their sins or have any hope of eternal life.

15:20 Just as the first part of the harvest was brought to the Temple as an offering (Leviticus 23:10ff) so Christ was the first to rise from the dead and never die again. He is our forerunner, the guarantee of our eventual resurrection to eternal life.

15:21 Death came into the world as a result of Adam and Eve's sin. In Romans 5:12-21, Paul explained why Adam's sin brought sin to all people, how death and sin spread to all humans because of this first sin, and the parallel between Adam's death and Christ's death.

15:24-28 This is not a chronological sequence of events, and no specific time for these events is given. Paul's point is that the resurrected Christ will conquer all evil, including death. See Revelation 20:14 for words about the final destruction of death.

15:25-28 Although God the Father and God the Son are equal, each has a special work to do and an area of sovereign control (15:28). Christ is not inferior to the Father, but his work is to defeat all evil on earth. First, he defeated sin and death on the cross, and in the end he will defeat Satan and all evil. World events may seem out of control, and justice may seem to have vanished. But God is in control, allowing evil to remain for a time until he sends Jesus to earth again. Then he will present to God a perfect new world.

God, so that God, who gave his Son authority over all things, will be utterly supreme
over everything everywhere.
29 If the dead will not be raised, then what point is there in people being baptized for
those who are dead? Why do it unless the dead will someday rise again?
15:30 Rom 8:36; 2 Cor 11:26 30 And why should we ourselves be continually risking our lives, facing death hour by
hour? 31 For I swear, dear friends,* I face death daily. This is as certain as my pride in
15:31 2 Cor 4:10-11 what the Lord Jesus Christ has done in you. 32 And what value was there in fighting wild
15:32 †Isa 22:13; Luke 12:19-21; 2 Cor 1:8 beasts—those men of Ephesus*—if there will be no resurrection from the dead? If there
is no resurrection,

> "Let's feast and get drunk,
> for tomorrow we die!"*

33 Don't be fooled by those who say such things, for "bad company corrupts good
15:34 1 Cor 6:5; Eph 5:14 character." 34 Come to your senses and stop sinning. For to your shame I say that some
of you don't even know God.

The Resurrection Body

15:35 Ezek 37:3 35 But someone may ask, "How will the dead be raised? What kind of bodies will they
15:36 John 12:24 have?" 36 What a foolish question! When you put a seed into the ground, it doesn't
grow into a plant unless it dies first. 37 And what you put in the ground is not the plant
that will grow, but only a dry little seed of wheat or whatever it is you are planting.
15:38 Gen 1:11 38 Then God gives it a new body—just the kind he wants it to have. A different kind
of plant grows from each kind of seed. 39 And just as there are different kinds of seeds
and plants, so also there are different kinds of flesh—whether of humans, animals,
birds, or fish.
40 There are bodies in the heavens, and there are bodies on earth. The glory of the
heavenly bodies is different from the beauty of the earthly bodies. 41 The sun has one

15:31 Greek *brothers.* **15:32a** Greek *fighting wild beasts in Ephesus.* **15:32b** Isa 22:13.

PHYSICAL AND RESURRECTION BODIES

Physical Bodies	*Resurrection Bodies*
Perishable	Imperishable
Sown in dishonor	Raised in glory
Sown in weakness	Raised in power
Natural	Spiritual
From the dust	From heaven

We all have a body—each looks different; each has different strengths and weaknesses. But as physical, earthly bodies, they are all alike. All believers are promised life after death and a body like Christ's (15:49), a resurrection body.

15:29 Some believers were baptized on behalf of others who had died unbaptized. Nothing more is known about this practice, but it obviously affirms a belief in the resurrection. Paul is not promoting baptism for the dead; he is illustrating his argument that the resurrection is a reality.

15:30-34 If death ended it all, enjoying the moment would be all that mattered. But Christians know that there is life beyond the grave and that our life on earth is only a preparation for our life that will never end. What you do today matters for eternity. In light of eternity, sin is a foolish gamble.

15:31, 32 "I face death daily" refers to the dangers Paul encountered daily. The "wild beasts" in Ephesus referred to the savage opposition he had faced there.

15:33 Keeping company with those who deny the resurrection can corrupt good Christian character. Don't let your relationships with unbelievers lead you away from Christ or cause your faith to waver.

15:35ff Paul launches into a discussion about what our resurrected bodies will be like. If you could select your own body, what kind would you choose—strong, athletic, beautiful? Paul explains that we will be recognizable in our resurrected body, yet it will be better than we can imagine, for it will be made to live forever. We will still have our own personality and individuality, but these will be perfected through Christ's work. The Bible does not reveal everything that our resurrected body will be able to do, but we know it will be perfect, without any infirmities (see Philippians 3:21).

15:35ff Paul compares the resurrection with the growth of a seed in a garden. Seeds placed in the ground don't grow unless they "die" first. The plant that grows looks very different from the seed because God gives it a new "body." There are different kinds of bodies—people, animals, fish, birds. Even the angels in heaven have bodies that are different in beauty and glory. Our resurrected body will be very different from our earthly body. It will be a spiritual body full of glory.

kind of glory, while the moon and stars each have another kind. And even the stars differ
from each other in their beauty and brightness.
42 It is the same way for the resurrection of the dead. Our earthly bodies, which die and
decay, will be different when they are resurrected, for they will never die. 43 Our bodies
now disappoint us, but when they are raised, they will be full of glory. They are weak
now, but when they are raised, they will be full of power. 44 They are natural human
bodies now, but when they are raised, they will be spiritual bodies. For just as there are
natural bodies, so also there are spiritual bodies.
45 The Scriptures tell us, "The first man, Adam, became a living person."* But the last
Adam—that is, Christ—is a life-giving Spirit. 46 What came first was the natural body,
then the spiritual body comes later. 47 Adam, the first man, was made from the dust of the
earth, while Christ, the second man, came from heaven. 48 Every human being has an
earthly body just like Adam's, but our heavenly bodies will be just like Christ's. 49 Just
as we are now like Adam, the man of the earth, so we will someday be like Christ, the
man from heaven.
50 What I am saying, dear brothers and sisters, is that flesh and blood cannot inherit
the Kingdom of God. These perishable bodies of ours are not able to live forever.
51 But let me tell you a wonderful secret God has revealed to us. Not all of us will die,
but we will all be transformed. 52 It will happen in a moment, in the blinking of an eye,
when the last trumpet is blown. For when the trumpet sounds, the Christians who have
died* will be raised with transformed bodies. And then we who are living will be
transformed so that we will never die. 53 For our perishable earthly bodies must be
transformed into heavenly bodies that will never die.
54 When this happens—when our perishable earthly bodies have been transformed
into heavenly bodies that will never die—then at last the Scriptures will come true:

"Death is swallowed up in victory.*
55 O death, where is your victory?
O death, where is your sting?"*

56 For sin is the sting that results in death, and the law gives sin its power. 57 How we
thank God, who gives us victory over sin and death through Jesus Christ our Lord!
58 So, my dear brothers and sisters, be strong and steady, always enthusiastic about the
Lord's work, for you know that nothing you do for the Lord is ever useless.

15:42 Dan 12:3; Matt 13:43; 1 Cor 15:50
15:43 Phil 3:20-21; Col 3:4
15:45 †Gen 2:7; John 5:21; 6:63; Rom 8:2; 2 Cor 3:17
15:47 Gen 2:7; 3:19; John 3:13, 31
15:48 Phil 3:20-21
15:49 Gen 5:3; Rom 8:29
15:50 John 3:3, 5
15:51 2 Cor 5:2-4; Phil 3:21; 1 Thes 4:15-17
15:52 Matt 24:31
15:53 2 Cor 5:4
15:54 †Isa 25:8
15:55 †Hos 13:14
15:56 Rom 4:15; 5:12
15:57 Rom 8:37; 1 Jn 5:4
15:58 Rev 14:13

15:45 Gen 2:7. **15:52** Greek *the dead.* **15:54** Isa 25:8. **15:55** Hos 13:14.

15:42-44 Our present body is perishable and prone to decay. Our resurrection body will be transformed. These spiritual body will not be limited by the laws of nature. This does not necessarily mean we'll be superpeople, but our body will be different from and more capable than our present earthly body. Our spiritual body will not be weak, will never get sick, and will never die.

15:45 Because Christ rose from the dead, he is a life-giving spirit. This means that he entered into a new form of existence. He is the source of the spiritual life that will result in our resurrection. Christ's new glorified human body now suits his new glorified life—just as Adam's human body was suitable to his natural life. When we are resurrected, God will give us a transformed, eternal body suited to our new eternal life.

15:50-53 We all face limitations. Some may have physical, mental, or emotional disabilities. Some may be blind, but they can see a new way to live. Some may be deaf, but they can hear God's Good News. Some may be lame, but they can walk in God's love. In addition, they have the encouragement that those disabilities are only temporary. Paul tells us that we all will be given new bodies when Christ returns and that these bodies will be without disabilities, never to die or become sick. This can give us hope in our suffering.

15:51, 52 Christians alive at that day will not have to die but will be transformed immediately. A trumpet blast will usher in the new heaven and earth. The Jews would understand the significance of this because trumpets were always blown to signal the start of great festivals and other extraordinary events (Numbers 10:10).

15:54-56 Satan seemed to be victorious in the Garden of Eden (Genesis 3) and at the cross of Jesus. But God turned Satan's apparent victory into defeat when Jesus Christ rose from the dead (Colossians 2:15; Hebrews 2:14, 15). Thus, death is no longer a source of dread or fear. Christ overcame it, and one day we will also. The law will no longer make sinners out of us who cannot keep it. Death has been defeated, and we have hope beyond the grave.

15:58 Paul says that because of the resurrection, nothing we do is useless. Sometimes we become apathetic about serving the Lord because we don't see any results. Knowing that Christ has won the ultimate victory should affect the way we live right now. Don't let discouragement over an apparent lack of results keep you from doing the work of the Lord enthusiastically as you have opportunity.

16:1 Acts 11:29; 24:17 Rom 15:25-26 2 Cor 8:9 Gal 2:10
16:2 Acts 20:7
16:3 2 Cor 3:1; 8:18-19
16:5 Acts 19:21 1 Cor 4:19
16:6 Rom 15:24 Titus 3:13
16:7 Acts 18:21
16:8 Acts 2:1; 18:19
16:9 Acts 14:27; 19:8-10 2 Cor 2:12
16:10 Acts 16:1
16:11 1 Tim 4:12
16:12 Acts 18:24 1 Cor 1:12
16:13 Eph 6:10 Phil 1:27; 4:1 1 Thes 3:8
16:14 1 Cor 14:1
16:15 1 Cor 1:16
16:16 1 Thes 5:12
16:19 Rom 16:5

The Collection for Jerusalem

16 Now about the money being collected for the Christians in Jerusalem: You should follow the same procedures I gave to the churches in Galatia. [2]On every Lord's Day,* each of you should put aside some amount of money in relation to what you have earned and save it for this offering. Don't wait until I get there and then try to collect it all at once. [3]When I come I will write letters of recommendation for the messengers you choose to deliver your gift to Jerusalem. [4]And if it seems appropriate for me also to go along, then we can travel together.

Paul's Final Instructions

[5]I am coming to visit you after I have been to Macedonia, for I am planning to travel through Macedonia. [6]It could be that I will stay awhile with you, perhaps all winter, and then you can send me on my way to the next destination. [7]This time I don't want to make just a short visit and then go right on. I want to come and stay awhile, if the Lord will let me. [8]In the meantime, I will be staying here at Ephesus until the Festival of Pentecost, [9]for there is a wide-open door for a great work here, and many people are responding. But there are many who oppose me.

[10]When Timothy comes, treat him with respect. He is doing the Lord's work, just as I am. [11]Don't let anyone despise him. Send him on his way with your blessings when he returns to me. I am looking forward to seeing him soon, along with the other believers.*

[12]Now about our brother Apollos—I urged him to visit you along with the other believers, but he was not willing to come right now. He will be seeing you later, when the time is right.

[13]Be on guard. Stand true to what you believe. Be courageous. Be strong. [14]And everything you do must be done with love.

[15]You know that Stephanas and his household were the first to become Christians in Greece,* and they are spending their lives in service to other Christians. I urge you, dear brothers and sisters, [16]to respect them fully and others like them who serve with such real devotion. [17]I am so glad that Stephanas, Fortunatus, and Achaicus have come here. They have been making up for the help you weren't here to give me. [18]They have been a wonderful encouragement to me, as they have been to you, too. You must give proper honor to all who serve so well.

Paul's Final Greetings

[19]The churches here in the province of Asia* greet you heartily in the Lord, along with Aquila and Priscilla and all the others who gather in their home for church meetings.

16:2 Greek *every first day of the week.* **16:11** Greek *the brothers;* also in 16:12, 20. **16:15** Greek *were the firstfruits in Achaia,* the southern region of the Greek peninsula. **16:19** *Asia* was a Roman province in what is now western Turkey.

16:1ff Paul had just said that no good deed is ever useless (15:58). In this chapter he mentions some practical deeds that have value for all Christians.

16:1-4 The Christians in Jerusalem were suffering from poverty and famine, so Paul was collecting money for them (Romans 15:25-31; 2 Corinthians 8:4; 9:1ff). He suggested that believers set aside a certain amount each week and give it to the church until he arrived to take it on to Jerusalem. Paul had planned to go straight to Corinth from Ephesus, but he changed his mind (2 Corinthians 1; 2). When he finally arrived, he took the gift and delivered it to the Jerusalem church (Acts 21:18; 24:17).

16:10, 11 Paul was sending Timothy ahead to Corinth. Paul respected Timothy and had worked closely with him (Philippians 2:22; 1 Timothy 1:2). Although Timothy was young, Paul encouraged the Corinthian church to welcome him because he was doing the Lord's work. God's work is not limited by age. Paul wrote two personal letters to Timothy that have been preserved in the Bible (1 and 2 Timothy).

16:12 Apollos, who had preached in Corinth, was doing evangelistic work in Greece (see Acts 18:24-28; 1 Corinthians 3:3ff). Apollos didn't go to Corinth right away, partly because he knew of the factions there and didn't want to cause any more divisions.

16:13, 14 As the Corinthians awaited Paul's next visit, they were directed to (1) be on their guard against spiritual dangers, (2) stand firm in the faith, (3) be courageous, (4) be strong, and (5) do everything with kindness and in love. Today, as we wait for the return of Christ, we should follow the same instructions.

16:19 Aquila and Priscilla were tentmakers (or leatherworkers) whom Paul had met in Corinth (Acts 18:1-3). They followed Paul to Ephesus and lived there with him, helping to teach others about Jesus (Romans 16:3-5). Many in the Corinthian church would have known this Christian couple. They are also mentioned in Acts 18:18, 26; Romans 16:3; and 2 Timothy 4:19.

[20]The other believers here have asked me to greet you for them. Greet each other in
Christian love.*
[21]Here is my greeting, which I write with my own hand—PAUL.
[22]If anyone does not love the Lord, that person is cursed. Our Lord, come!*
[23]May the grace of the Lord Jesus be with you.
[24]My love to all of you in Christ Jesus.*

16:20 Greek *with a sacred kiss.* **16:22** From Aramaic, *Marana tha.* **16:24** Some manuscripts add *Amen.*

16:20 Rom 16:16
16:21 Gal 6:11; Col 4:18; 2 Thes 3:17; Phlm 1:19
16:22 Gal 1:8-9

16:21 Paul had a helper, or secretary, who wrote down this letter while he dictated. Paul wrote the final words, however, in his own handwriting. This is similar to adding a handwritten postscript (P.S.) to a typewritten letter. It also served to verify that this was a genuine letter from the apostle and not a forgery.

16:22 The Lord Jesus Christ is coming back to earth again. To Paul, this was a wonderful hope, the very best he could look forward to. He was not afraid of seeing Christ—he could hardly wait! Do you share Paul's eager anticipation? Those who love Christ are looking forward to that glorious time of his return (Titus 2:13). To those who do not love the Lord, however, Paul says, let them be cursed.

16:24 The church at Corinth was a church in trouble. Paul lovingly and forcefully confronted them and pointed them back to Christ. He dealt with divisions and conflicts, selfishness, inconsiderate use of freedom, disorder in worship, misuse of spiritual gifts, and wrong attitudes about the resurrection.

In every church, there are problems that create tensions and divisions. We should not ignore or gloss over problems in our churches or in our life. Instead, like Paul, we should deal with problems head-on as they arise. The lesson for us in 1 Corinthians is that unity and love in a church are far more important than leaders and labels.

2 CORINTHIANS

SLITHERING through the centuries, the serpent whispers his smooth-tongued promises, beguiling, deceiving, and tempting—urging men and women to reject God and to follow Satan. Satan's emissaries have been many—false prophets contradicting God's ancient spokesmen, "pious" leaders hurling blasphemous accusations, and heretical teachers infiltrating churches. And the deception continues. Our world is filled with cults, "isms," and ideologies, all claiming to provide the way to God.

Paul constantly struggled with those who would mislead God's people, and he poured his life into spreading the Good News to the uttermost parts of the world. During three missionary trips and other travels, he proclaimed Christ, made converts, and established churches. But often young believers were easy prey for false teachers. False teachers were a constant threat to the gospel and the early church. So Paul had to spend much time warning and correcting these new Christians.

The church at Corinth was weak. Surrounded by idolatry and immorality, they struggled with their Christian faith and life-style. Through personal visits and letters, Paul tried to instruct them in the faith, resolve their conflicts, and solve some of their problems. First Corinthians was sent to deal with specific moral issues in the church and to answer questions about sex, marriage, and tender consciences. That letter confronted the issues directly and was well received by most. But there were false teachers who denied Paul's authority and slandered him. Paul then wrote 2 Corinthians to defend his position and to denounce those who were twisting the truth.

Second Corinthians must have been a difficult letter for Paul to write because he had to list his credentials as an apostle. Paul was reluctant to do so as a humble servant of Christ, but he knew it was necessary. Paul also knew that most of the believers in Corinth had taken his previous words to heart and were beginning to mature in their faith. He affirmed their commitment to Christ.

Second Corinthians begins with Paul reminding his readers of (1) his relationship to them—Paul had always been honest and straightforward with them (1:12–14), (2) his itinerary—he was planning to visit them again (1:15—2:3), and (3) his previous letter (2:4–11). Paul then moves directly to the subject of false teachers (2:17), and he reviews his ministry among the Corinthians to demonstrate the validity of his message and to urge them not to turn away from the truth (3:1—7:16).

Paul next turns to the issue of collecting money for the poor Christians in Jerusalem. He tells them how others have given, and he urges them to show their love in a tangible way as well (8:1—9:15). Paul then gives a strong defense of his authority as a genuine apostle while pointing out the deceptive influence of the false apostles (10:1—13:10).

As you read this intensely personal letter, listen to Paul's words of love and exhortation, and be committed to the truth of God's Word and prepared to reject all false teaching.

VITAL STATISTICS

PURPOSE:
To affirm Paul's ministry, defend his authority as an apostle, and refute the false teachers in Corinth

AUTHOR:
Paul

TO WHOM WRITTEN:
The church in Corinth and Christians everywhere

DATE WRITTEN:
Approximately A.D. 55–57, from Macedonia

SETTING:
Paul had already written three letters to the Corinthians (two are now lost). In 1 Corinthians (the second of these letters), he used strong words to correct and teach. Most of the church had responded in the right spirit; there were, however, those who were denying Paul's authority and questioning his motives.

KEY VERSE:
"We are Christ's ambassadors, and God is using us to speak to you. We urge you, as though Christ himself were here pleading with you, 'Be reconciled to God!'" (5:20).

KEY PEOPLE:
Paul, Timothy, Titus, false teachers

KEY PLACES:
Corinth, Jerusalem

SPECIAL FEATURES:
This is an intensely personal and autobiographical letter.

THE BLUEPRINT

1. Paul explains his actions (1:1—2:11) 2. Paul defends his ministry (2:12—7:16) 3. Paul defends the collection (8:1—9:15) 4. Paul defends his authority (10:1—13:14)	In responding to the attacks on his character and authority, Paul explains the nature of Christian ministry and, as an example, openly shares about his ministry. This is an important letter for all who wish to be involved in any kind of Christian ministry, because it has much to teach us about how we should handle our ministries today. Like Paul, those involved in ministry should be blameless, sincere, confident, caring, open, and willing to suffer for the sake of Christ.

MEGATHEMES

THEME	EXPLANATION	IMPORTANCE
Trials	Paul experienced great suffering, persecution, and opposition in his ministry. He even struggled with a personal weakness—a "thorn" in the flesh. Through it all, Paul affirmed God's faithfulness.	God is faithful. His strength is sufficient for any trial. When trials come, they keep us from pride and teach us dependence on God. He comforts us so we can comfort others.
Church Discipline	Paul defends his role in church discipline. Neither immorality nor false teaching could be ignored. The church was to be neither too lax nor too severe in administering discipline. The church was to restore the corrected person when he or she repented.	The goal of all discipline in the church should be correction, not vengeance. For churches to be effective, they must confront and solve problems, not ignore them. In everything, we must act in love.
Hope	To encourage the Corinthians as they faced trials, Paul reminded them that they would receive new bodies in heaven. This would be a great victory in contrast to their present suffering.	To know we will receive new bodies offers us hope. No matter what adversity we face, we can keep going. Our faithful service will result in triumph.
Giving	Paul organized a collection of funds for the poor in the Jerusalem church. Many of the Asian churches gave money. Paul explains and defends his beliefs about giving, and he urges the Corinthians to follow through on their previous commitment.	Like the Corinthians, we should follow through on our financial commitments. Our giving must be generous, sacrificial, well planned, and based on need. Our generosity not only helps those in need but enables them to thank God.
Sound Doctrine	False teachers were challenging Paul's ministry and authority as an apostle. Paul asserts his authority in order to preserve correct Christian doctrine. His sincerity, his love for Christ, and his concern for the people were his defense.	We should share Paul's concern for correct teaching in our churches. But in so doing, we must share his motivation—love for Christ and people—and his sincerity.

1. Paul explains his actions

Greetings from Paul

1 This letter is from Paul, appointed by God to be an apostle of Christ Jesus, and from our dear brother Timothy. 1:1 1 Cor 1:1 2 Cor 1:19 Eph 1:1
We are writing to God's church in Corinth and to all the Christians throughout Greece.*
2 May God our Father and the Lord Jesus Christ give you his grace and peace. 1:2 Rom 1:7

1:1 Greek *Achaia,* the southern region of the Greek peninsula.

1:1 Paul visited Corinth on his second missionary journey and founded a church there (Acts 18:1ff). He later wrote several letters to the believers in Corinth, two of which are included in the Bible. Paul's first letter to the Corinthians is lost (1 Corinthians 5:9-11), his second letter to them is our book of 1 Corinthians, his third letter is lost (2:6-9; 7:12), and his fourth letter is our book of 2 Corinthians. Second Corinthians was written less than a year after 1 Corinthians.

Paul wrote 1 Corinthians to deal with divisions in the church. When his advice was not taken and their problems weren't solved, Paul visited Corinth a second time. That visit was painful both for Paul and for the church (2:1). He then planned a third visit but delayed it and wrote 2 Corinthians instead. After writing 2 Corinthians, Paul visited Corinth once more (Acts 20:2, 3).

1:1 Paul had great respect for Timothy (see also Philippians 2:19, 20; 1 Timothy 1:2), one of his traveling companions (Acts 16:1-3). Timothy had accompanied Paul to Corinth on his second missionary journey, and Paul had recently sent him there to minister (1 Corinthians 4:17; 16:10). Timothy's report to Paul about the crisis in the Corinthian church prompted Paul to make an unplanned visit to the church to deal with the problem in person (see 2:1). For more information on Timothy, see his Profile in 1 Timothy.

1:1 The Romans had made Corinth the capital of Achaia (the southern half of present-day Greece). The city was a flourishing

God Offers Comfort to All

1:3 Eph 1:3; 1 Pet 1:3
1:4 Isa 51:12; 66:13; 2 Cor 7:6
1:5 2 Cor 4:10; Phil 3:10; Col 1:24
1:6 2 Cor 4:15
1:8 1 Cor 15:23
1:9 Jer 17:5, 7
1:10 2 Tim 4:18; 2 Pet 2:9
1:11 Rom 15:30; 2 Cor 4:15; Phil 1:19

3 All praise to the God and Father of our Lord Jesus Christ. He is the source* of every
mercy and the God who comforts us. 4 He comforts us in all our troubles so that we can
comfort others. When others are troubled, we will be able to give them the same comfort
God has given us. 5 You can be sure that the more we suffer for Christ, the more God will
shower us with his comfort through Christ. 6 So when we are weighed down with
troubles, it is for your benefit and salvation! For when God comforts us, it is so that we,
in turn, can be an encouragement to you. Then you can patiently endure the same things
we suffer. 7 We are confident that as you share in suffering, you will also share God's
comfort.

8 I think you ought to know, dear friends,* about the trouble we went through in the
province of Asia. We were crushed and completely overwhelmed, and we thought we
would never live through it. 9 In fact, we expected to die. But as a result, we learned not
to rely on ourselves, but on God who can raise the dead. 10 And he did deliver us from
mortal danger. And we are confident that he will continue to deliver us. 11 He will rescue
us because you are helping by praying for us. As a result, many will give thanks to God
because so many people's prayers for our safety have been answered.

1:3 Greek *the Father.* **1:8** Greek *brothers.*

DIFFERENCES BETWEEN 1 AND 2 CORINTHIANS

The two letters to the Corinthian church that are found in the Bible are very different, with different tones and focuses.

1 Corinthians	*2 Corinthians*
Practical	Personal
Focuses on the character of the Corinthian church	Focuses on Paul as he bares his soul and tells of his love for the Corinthian church
Deals with questions on marriage, freedom, spiritual gifts, and order in the church	Deals with the problem of false teachers, whereby Paul defends his authority and the truth of his message
Paul instructs in matters concerning the church's well-being	Paul gives his testimony because he knows that acceptance of his advice is vital to the church's well-being
Contains advice to help the church combat the pagan influences in the wicked city of Corinth	Contains testimony to help the church combat the havoc caused by false teachers

trade center because of its seaport. With the thousands of merchants and sailors who disembarked there each year, it had developed a reputation as one of the most immoral cities in the ancient world; its many pagan temples encouraged the practice of sexual immorality along with idol worship. In fact, the Greek word "to Corinthianize" came to mean "to practice sexual immorality." A Christian church in the city would face many pressures and conflicts. For more information on Corinth, see the first note on 1 Corinthians 1:2.

1:3-5 Many think that when God comforts us, our troubles should go away. But if that were always so, people would turn to God only out of a desire to be relieved of pain and not out of love for him. We must understand that being "comforted" can also mean receiving strength, encouragement, and hope to deal with our troubles. The more we suffer, the more comfort God gives us. If you are feeling overhelmed, allow God to comfort you. Remember that every trial you endure will help you comfort other people who are suffering similar troubles.

1:5 Suffering for Christ refers to those afflictions we experience as we serve Christ. At the same time, Christ suffers with his people, since they are united with him. In Acts 9:4, 5 Christ asked Paul why he was persecuting him. This implies that Christ suffered with the early Christians when they were persecuted.

1:6, 7 Paul explains that when he and his companions suffered, it resulted in their "benefit and salvation." But just as God comforted Paul, God would also comfort the Corinthian believers when they suffered for their faith. He would give them the strength to endure.

1:8-10 Paul does not give details about their hardships in Asia, although his accounts of all three missionary journeys record many difficult trials he faced (Acts 13:2–14:28; Acts 15:40–21:17). He does write that they felt that they were going to die and realized that they could do nothing to help themselves—they simply had to rely on God.

1:8-10 We often depend on our own skills and abilities when life seems easy and only turn to God when we feel unable to help ourselves. But as we realize our own powerlessness without him and our need for his constant help in our lives, we come to depend on him more and more. God is our source of power, and we receive his help by keeping in touch with him. With this attitude of dependence, problems will drive us to God rather than away from him. Learn how to rely on God daily.

1:11 Paul requested prayer for himself and his companions as they traveled to spread God's message. Pray for pastors, teachers, missionaries, and others who are spreading the Good News. Satan will challenge anyone making a real difference for God.

Paul's Change of Plans

12 We can say with confidence and a clear conscience that we have been honest* and
sincere in all our dealings. We have depended on God's grace, not on our own earthly
wisdom. That is how we have acted toward everyone, and especially toward you. 13 My
letters have been straightforward, and there is nothing written between the lines and
nothing you can't understand. I hope someday you will fully understand us, 14 even if
you don't fully understand us now. Then on the day when our Lord Jesus comes back
again, you will be proud of us in the same way we are proud of you.

15 Since I was so sure of your understanding and trust, I wanted to give you a double
blessing. 16 I wanted to stop and see you on my way to Macedonia and again on my return
trip. Then you could send me on my way to Judea.

17 You may be asking why I changed my plan. Hadn't I made up my mind yet? Or am
I like people of the world who say yes when they really mean no? 18 As surely as God is
true, I am not that sort of person. My yes means yes 19 because Jesus Christ, the Son of
God, never wavers between yes and no. He is the one whom Timothy, Silas,* and I
preached to you, and he is the divine Yes—God's affirmation. 20 For all of God's
promises have been fulfilled in him. That is why we say "Amen" when we give glory to
God through Christ. 21 It is God who gives us, along with you, the ability to stand firm
for Christ.* He has commissioned us, 22 and he has identified us as his own by placing
the Holy Spirit in our hearts as the first installment of everything he will give us.

23 Now I call upon God as my witness that I am telling the truth. The reason I didn't
return to Corinth was to spare you from a severe rebuke. 24 But that does not mean we
want to tell you exactly how to put your faith into practice.* We want to work together
with you so you will be full of joy as you stand firm in your faith.

2 So I said to myself, "No, I won't do it. I won't make them unhappy with another
painful visit." 2 For if I cause you pain and make you sad, who is going to make me
glad? 3 That is why I wrote as I did in my last letter, so that when I do come, I will not

1:12 Acts 23:1; 1 Cor 1:17; 2 Cor 2:17; 4:15
1:14 2 Cor 5:12; Phil 2:16
1:15 Rom 1:11-13; 1 Cor 4:19
1:16 Acts 19:21; 1 Cor 16:5-6
1:17 2 Cor 5:16
1:19 Acts 18:5; Heb 13:8
1:20 Rom 15:8-9; Rev 3:14
1:21 1 Jn 2:20, 27
1:22 2 Cor 5:5; Eph 1:13-14; 4:30
1:23 1 Cor 4:21
1:24 1 Cor 15:1
2:1 1 Cor 4:21; 2 Cor 12:21
2:2 2 Cor 7:8

1:12 Some manuscripts read *holy.* **1:19** Greek *Silvanus.* **1:21** Or *who has identified us and you as genuine Christians.* **1:24** Greek *want to lord it over your faith.*

1:12-14 Paul knew the importance of honesty and sincerity in word and action, especially in a situation as in Corinth, where constructive criticism was necessary. So Paul did not come with impressive human knowledge (earthly wisdom). God wants us to be real and transparent in all our relationships. If we aren't, we may end up lowering ourselves to spreading rumors, gossiping, and second-guessing.

1:15-17 Paul had recently made a brief, unscheduled visit to Corinth that was very painful for him and the church (see 2:1). After that visit, he told the church when he would return. But Paul changed his original travel plans. Instead of sailing from Ephesus to Corinth before going to Macedonia, he traveled from Ephesus directly to Macedonia, where he wrote a letter to the Corinthians that caused him much anguish and them much sorrow (7:8, 9). He had made his original plans, thinking that the church would have solved its problems. When the time came for Paul's scheduled trip to Corinth, however, the crisis had not been fully resolved (although progress was being made in some areas; 7:11-16). So he wrote a letter instead (2:3, 4; 7:8) because another visit might have only made matters worse. Thus, Paul stayed away from Corinth because he was concerned over the church's unity, not because he was fickle.

1:17-20 Paul's change of plans caused some of his accusers to say that he couldn't be trusted, hoping to undermine his authority. Paul said that he was not the type of person to say yes when he meant no. Paul explained that it was not indecision but concern for their feelings that forced him to change his plans. The reason for his trip—to bring joy (1:24)—could not be accomplished with the present crisis. Paul didn't want to visit them only to rebuke them severely (1:23). Just as the Corinthians could trust God to keep his promises, they could trust Paul as God's representative to keep his. He would still visit them, but at a better time.

1:19, 20 All of God's promises of what the Messiah would be like are fulfilled in Christ ("he is the divine Yes"). Jesus was completely faithful in his ministry; he never sinned (1 Peter 3:18); he faithfully died for us (Hebrews 2:9); and now he faithfully intercedes for us (Romans 8:34; Hebrews 4:14, 15). Because Jesus Christ is faithful, Paul wanted to be faithful in his ministry.

1:21, 22 The Holy Spirit guarantees that we belong to God and will receive all his benefits (Ephesians 1:13, 14). The Holy Spirit guarantees that salvation is ours now, and that we will receive so much more when Christ returns. The great comfort and power the Holy Spirit gives in this life is a foretaste or down payment ("first installment") of the benefits of our eternal life in God's presence. With the privilege of belonging to God comes the responsibility of identifying ourselves as his faithful servants. Don't be ashamed to let others know that you are his.

1:23 The Corinthian church had written to Paul with questions about their faith (see 1 Corinthians 7:1). In response, Paul had written 1 Corinthians. But the church did not follow his instructions.

Paul had planned to visit them again, but instead, he wrote a letter that caused sorrow (7:8, 9) but caused them to change their ways. He didn't want to visit and repeat the same advice for the same problems. He wrote the emotional letter to encourage them to follow the advice that he had already given in previous letters and visits.

2:1 Paul's phrase "another painful visit" indicates that he had already made one difficult trip to Corinth (see the notes on 1:1; 1:15-17) since founding the church. Paul had gone there to deal with those in the church who had been attacking and undermining his authority as an apostle of Jesus Christ, thus confusing other believers.

2:3 Paul's last letter, referred to here, was not the book of 1 Corinthians, but a letter written between 1 and 2 Corinthians,

2:4 2 Cor 2:9; 7:8, 12

be made sad by the very ones who ought to give me the greatest joy. Surely you know
that my happiness depends on your happiness. [4]How painful it was to write that letter!
Heartbroken, I cried over it. I didn't want to hurt you, but I wanted you to know how
very much I love you.

Forgiveness for the Sinner

2:5 1 Cor 5:1-2; 2 Cor 7:11
2:7 Gal 6:1; Eph 4:32
2:9 2 Cor 7:15; 10:6
2:11 2 Cor 4:4; 1 Pet 5:8

[5]I am not overstating it when I say that the man who caused all the trouble hurt your
entire church more than he hurt me. [6]He was punished enough when most of you were
united in your judgment against him. [7]Now it is time to forgive him and comfort him.
Otherwise he may become so discouraged that he won't be able to recover. [8]Now show
him that you still love him.
[9]I wrote to you as I did to find out how far you would go in obeying me. [10]When you
forgive this man, I forgive him, too. And when I forgive him (for whatever is to be
forgiven), I do so with Christ's authority for your benefit, [11]so that Satan will not
outsmart us. For we are very familiar with his evil schemes.

PAUL SEARCHES FOR TITUS
Paul had searched for Titus, hoping to meet him in Troas and receive news about the Corinthian church. When he did not find Titus in Troas, he went on to Macedonia (2:13), most likely to Philippi, where he found Titus.

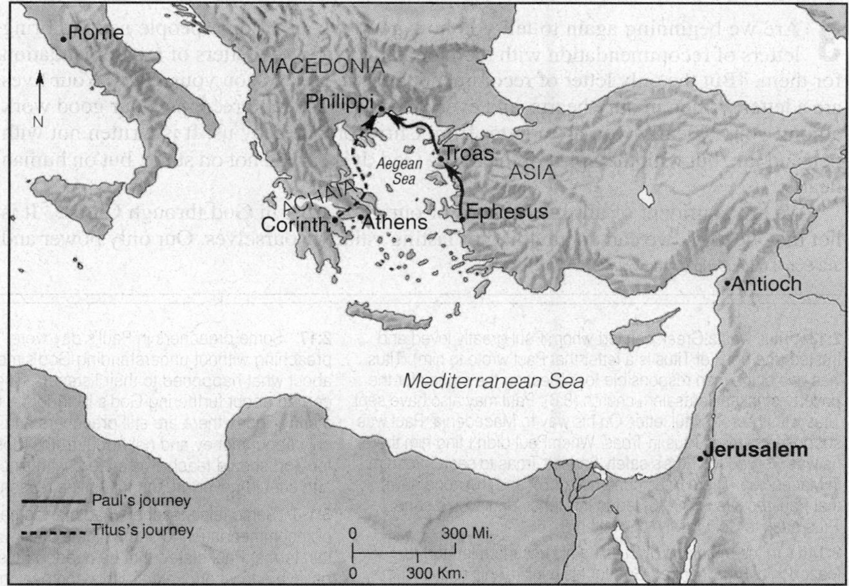

just after his unplanned, painful visit (2:1). Paul refers to this letter again in 7:8.

2:4 Paul did not enjoy reprimanding his friends and fellow believers, but he cared enough about the Corinthians to confront them with their wrongdoing. Proverbs 27:6 says: "Wounds from a friend are better than many kisses from an enemy." Sometimes our friends make choices that we know are wrong. If we ignore their behavior and let them continue in it, we won't be showing love to them. We show love by honestly sharing our concerns in order to help these friends be their very best for God. When we don't make any move to help, we show that we are more concerned about being well liked than about what will happen to them.

2:5-11 Paul explained that it was time to forgive the man who had been punished by the church and had subsequently repented. He needed forgiveness, acceptance, and comfort. Satan would gain an advantage if they permanently separated this man from the congregation rather than forgiving and restoring him. This may have been the man who had required the disciplinary action described in 1 Corinthians 5, or he may have been the chief opponent of Paul who had caused him anguish (2:1-11). The sorrowful letter had finally brought about the repentance of the Corinthians (7:8-14), and their discipline of the man had led to his repentance. Church discipline should seek restoration. Two mistakes in church discipline should be avoided: being too lenient and not correcting mistakes, or being too harsh and not forgiving the sinner. There is a time to confront and a time to comfort.

2:11 We use church discipline to help keep the church pure and to help wayward people repent. But Satan tries to harm the church by tempting it to use discipline in an unforgiving way. This causes those exercising discipline to become proud of their purity, and it causes the person who is being disciplined to become bitter and perhaps leave the church. We must remember that our purpose in discipline is to *restore* a person to the fellowship, not to destroy him or her. We must be cautious that personal anger is not vented under the guise of church discipline.

2. Paul defends his ministry

Ministers of the New Covenant

[12]Well, when I came to the city of Troas to preach the Good News of Christ, the Lord
gave me tremendous opportunities. [13]But I couldn't rest because my dear brother Titus
hadn't yet arrived with a report from you. So I said good-bye and went on to Macedonia
to find him.

[14]But thanks be to God, who made us his captives and leads us along in Christ's
triumphal procession. Now wherever we go he uses us to tell others about the Lord
and to spread the Good News like a sweet perfume. [15]Our lives are a fragrance
presented by Christ to God. But this fragrance is perceived differently by those being
saved and by those perishing. [16]To those who are perishing we are a fearful smell of
death and doom. But to those who are being saved we are a life-giving perfume. And
who is adequate for such a task as this? [17]You see, we are not like those hucksters—
and there are many of them—who preach just to make money. We preach God's
message with sincerity and with Christ's authority. And we know that the God who
sent us is watching us.

2:12 Acts 14:27; 2 Cor 4:3
2:13 2 Cor 7:5-6
2:15 1 Cor 1:18
2:16 Luke 2:34; 2 Cor 3:5-6
2:17 2 Cor 1:12; 12:19

3 Are we beginning again to tell you how good we are? Some people need to bring
letters of recommendation with them or ask you to write letters of recommendation
for them. [2]But the only letter of recommendation we need is you yourselves! Your lives
are a letter written in our* hearts, and everyone can read it and recognize our good work
among you. [3]Clearly, you are a letter from Christ prepared by us. It is written not with
pen and ink, but with the Spirit of the living God. It is carved not on stone, but on human
hearts.

[4]We are confident of all this because of our great trust in God through Christ. [5]It is
not that we think we can do anything of lasting value by ourselves. Our only power and

3:2 Some manuscripts read *your.*

3:1 Acts 18:27; 2 Cor 5:12; 10:12
3:2 1 Cor 9:2
3:3 Exod 24:12; 31:18; 32:15-16; Prov 3:3; Jer 31:33; Ezek 36:26
3:5 1 Cor 15:10; 2 Cor 2:16

2:13 Titus was a Greek convert whom Paul greatly loved and trusted (the book of Titus is a letter that Paul wrote to him). Titus was one of the men responsible for collecting the money for the poverty-stricken Jerusalem church (8:6). Paul may also have sent Titus with the sorrowful letter. On his way to Macedonia, Paul was supposed to meet Titus in Troas. When Paul didn't find him there, he was worried for Titus's safety and left Troas to search for him in Macedonia. There Paul found him (7:6), and the good news that Paul received (7:8-16) led to this letter. Paul would send Titus back to Corinth with this letter (8:16, 17).

2:14ff In the middle of discussing his unscheduled trip to Macedonia, Paul thanked God for his ministry, his relationship with the Corinthian believers, and the way God had used him to help others wherever he went, despite difficulties (2:14–7:4). In 7:5, Paul resumed his story of his trip to Macedonia.

2:14-16 In a Roman triumphal procession, the Roman general would display his treasures and captives amidst a cloud of incense burned for the gods. To the victors, the aroma was sweet; to the captives in the parade, it was the smell of slavery and death. When Christians preach the Good News, it is good news to some and repulsive news to others. Believers recognize the life-giving fragrance of the message. To nonbelievers, however, it smells foul, like death—their own.

2:16, 17 Paul asks "who is adequate" for the task of representing Christ? Our adequacy is always from God (1 Corinthians 15:10; 2 Corinthians 3:5). He has already commissioned and sent us (see Matthew 28:18-20). He has given us the Holy Spirit to enable us to speak with Christ's power. He keeps his eye on us, protecting us as we work for him. As we realize that God has equipped us, we can overcome our feelings of inadequacy. Serving Christ, therefore, requires that we focus on what he can do through us, not on what we can't do by ourselves.

2:17 Some preachers in Paul's day were "hucksters," preaching without understanding God's message or caring about what happened to their listeners. They weren't concerned about furthering God's Kingdom—they just wanted money. Today there are still preachers and teachers who care only about money and not about truth. Those who truly speak for God should teach God's Word with sincerity and integrity and should never preach for selfish reasons (1 Timothy 6:5-10).

3:1-3 Some false teachers had started carrying forged letters of recommendation to authenticate their authority. In no uncertain terms, Paul stated that he needed no such letters. The believers to whom Paul and his companions had preached were enough of a recommendation. Paul did use letters of introduction, however, many times. He wrote them on behalf of Phoebe (Romans 16:1, 2) and Timothy (1 Corinthians 16:10, 11). These letters helped Paul's trusted companions and friends find a welcome in various churches.

3:3 Paul uses powerful imagery from famous Old Testament passages predicting the promised day of new hearts and new beginnings for God's people (see Jeremiah 31:33; Ezekiel 11:19; 36:26). No human being can take credit for this process of conversion. It is the work of God's Spirit. We do not become believers by following some manual or using some technique. Our conversion is a result of God's implanting his Spirit in our heart, giving us new power to live for him.

3:4, 5 Paul was not boasting; he gave God the credit for all his accomplishments. While the false teachers boasted of their own power and success, Paul expressed his humility before God. No one can claim to be adequate without God's help. No one is competent to carry out the responsibilities of God's calling in his or her own strength. Without the Holy Spirit's enabling, our natural talent can carry us only so far. As Christ's witnesses, we need the character and special strength that only God gives.

success come from God. 6 He is the one who has enabled us to represent his new
covenant. This is a covenant, not of written laws, but of the Spirit. The old way ends in
death; in the new way, the Holy Spirit gives life.

The Glory of the New Covenant

7 That old system of law etched in stone led to death, yet it began with such glory that
the people of Israel could not bear to look at Moses' face. For his face shone with the
glory of God, even though the brightness was already fading away. 8 Shouldn't we
expect far greater glory when the Holy Spirit is giving life? 9 If the old covenant,
which brings condemnation, was glorious, how much more glorious is the new
covenant, which makes us right with God! 10 In fact, that first glory was not glorious
at all compared with the overwhelming glory of the new covenant. 11 So if the old
covenant, which has been set aside, was full of glory, then the new covenant, which
remains forever, has far greater glory.

12 Since this new covenant gives us such confidence, we can be very bold. 13 We are
not like Moses, who put a veil over his face so the people of Israel would not see the
glory fading away. 14 But the people's minds were hardened, and even to this day
whenever the old covenant is being read, a veil covers their minds so they cannot
understand the truth. And this veil can be removed only by believing in Christ. 15 Yes,
even today when they read Moses' writings, their hearts are covered with that veil, and
they do not understand.

16 But whenever anyone turns to the Lord, then the veil is taken away. 17 Now, the Lord
is the Spirit, and wherever the Spirit of the Lord is, he gives freedom. 18 And all of us
have had that veil removed so that we can be mirrors that brightly reflect* the glory of
the Lord. And as the Spirit of the Lord works within us, we become more and more like
him and reflect his glory even more.

3:6 Jer 31:31; Luke 22:20; Rom 2:27; 7:6; 8:2; Heb 8:8-13
3:7 Exod 34:29-35
3:9 Deut 27:26; Rom 1:17; 3:21
3:10-11 Exod 34:29-30; John 17:10, 22
3:13 Exod 34:33-35; Rom 11:25
3:14 Acts 13:15; Rom 11:7-8; 2 Cor 4:4
3:16 Isa 25:7; Rom 11:23
3:17 Gal 4:6-7
3:18 Rom 8:29; 2 Cor 4:4, 6

3:18 Or *so that we can see in a mirror.*

3:6 "The old way ends in death; in the new way, the Holy Spirit gives life" means that trying to be saved by keeping the Old Testament laws will end in death. Only by believing in the Lord Jesus Christ can a person receive eternal life through the Holy Spirit. No one but Jesus has ever fulfilled the law perfectly; thus, the whole world is condemned to death. The law makes people realize their sin, but it cannot give life. Under the new covenant, which means promise or agreement, eternal life comes from the Holy Spirit. The Spirit gives new life to all who believe in Christ. The moral law (Ten Commandments) still points out sin and shows us how to obey God, but forgiveness comes only through the grace and mercy of Christ (see Romans 7:10–8:2).

3:7-11 Paul contrasts the glory of the Ten Commandments with the glory of the new covenant. If the law that leads to death was glorious, how much more glorious is God's plan, which gives us life through his Spirit! The sacrifice of Jesus Christ is far superior to the Old Testament system of sacrifice (see Hebrews 8; 10 for a more complete discussion). Christianity is superior to the Judaism of the Old Testament and to any other religion on earth. Because God's plan is far superior by comparison to any other, we dare not reject it or treat it casually.

3:9 Paul is saying that if the old covenant had its glory (and certainly it did), just imagine how glorious the new covenant is. The law was wonderful because, although it condemned us, it pointed us to Christ. But in the new covenant, the law and the promise are fulfilled. Christ has come; by faith we can be made right with God!

3:13-18 When Moses came down Mount Sinai with the Ten Commandments, his face glowed from being in God's presence (Exodus 34:29-35). Moses had to put on a veil to keep the people from being terrified by the brightness of his face and from seeing the radiance fade away. This veil illustrates the fading of the old system and the veiling of the people's minds because of their pride, hardness of heart, and refusal to repent. The veil kept them from understanding references to Christ in the Scriptures. When anyone becomes a Christian, the veil is stripped off (3:16), giving eternal life and freedom from bondage. That person can then be like a mirror reflecting God's glory.

3:17 Those who were trying to be saved by keeping the Old Testament law were soon tied up in rules and ceremonies. But now, through the Holy Spirit, God provides freedom from sin and condemnation (Romans 8:1). When we trust Christ to save us, he removes our heavy burden of trying to please him and our guilt for failing to do so. By trusting Christ we are loved, accepted, forgiven, and freed to live for him. "Wherever the Spirit of the Lord is, he gives freedom."

3:18 The glory that the Spirit imparts to the believer is more excellent and lasts longer than the glory that Moses experienced. By gazing at the nature of God with unveiled minds, we can be more like him. In the Good News, we see the truth about Christ, and it transforms us morally as we understand and apply it. Through learning about Christ's life, we can understand how wonderful God is and what he is really like. As our knowledge deepens, the Holy Spirit helps us to change. Becoming Christlike is a progressive experience (see Romans 8:29; Galatians 4:19; Philippians 3:21; 1 John 3:2). The more closely we follow Christ, the more we will be like him.

Treasure in Perishable Containers

4 And so, since God in his mercy has given us this wonderful ministry, we never give
up. 2 We reject all shameful and underhanded methods. We do not try to trick anyone,
and we do not distort the word of God. We tell the truth before God, and all who are
honest know that.
3 If the Good News we preach is veiled from anyone, it is a sign that they are perishing.
4 Satan, the god of this evil world, has blinded the minds of those who don't believe, so
they are unable to see the glorious light of the Good News that is shining upon them.
They don't understand the message we preach about the glory of Christ, who is the exact
likeness of God.
5 We don't go around preaching about ourselves; we preach Christ Jesus, the Lord. All
we say about ourselves is that we are your servants because of what Jesus has done for
us. 6 For God, who said, "Let there be light in the darkness," has made us understand that
this light is the brightness of the glory of God that is seen in the face of Jesus Christ.
7 But this precious treasure—this light and power that now shine within us—is held in
perishable containers, that is, in our weak bodies.* So everyone can see that our glorious
power is from God and is not our own.
8 We are pressed on every side by troubles, but we are not crushed and broken. We are
perplexed, but we don't give up and quit. 9 We are hunted down, but God never abandons
us. We get knocked down, but we get up again and keep going. 10 Through suffering,
these bodies of ours constantly share in the death of Jesus so that the life of Jesus may
also be seen in our bodies.
11 Yes, we live under constant danger of death because we serve Jesus, so that the life
of Jesus will be obvious in our dying bodies. 12 So we live in the face of death, but it has
resulted in eternal life for you.
13 But we continue to preach because we have the same kind of faith the psalmist had
when he said, "I believed in God, and so I speak."* 14 We know that the same God who
raised our Lord Jesus will also raise us with Jesus and present us to himself along with you.
15 All of these things are for your benefit. And as God's grace brings more and more people
to Christ, there will be great thanksgiving, and God will receive more and more glory.
16 That is why we never give up. Though our bodies are dying, our spirits are* being

4:7 Greek *But we have this treasure in earthen vessels.* **4:13** Ps 116:10. **4:16** Greek *our inner being is.*

4:2 2 Cor 2:17; 1 Thes 2:5
4:3 1 Cor 1:18; 2 Cor 3:14
4:4 John 12:31; 2 Cor 3:14; Col 1:15; Heb 1:3
4:5 1 Cor 9:19; 2 Cor 1:24
4:6 Gen 1:3; Ps 36:9; John 8:12; 12:46; Eph 5:8, 14; 1 Pet 2:9; 2 Pet 1:19
4:7 2 Cor 5:1; 2 Tim 2:20
4:8 2 Cor 7:5
4:9 Rom 8:35
4:10 Rom 8:17; 1 Cor 15:31; Gal 6:17; Phil 3:10; Col 1:24; 2 Tim 2:11; 1 Pet 4:13
4:14 Acts 2:24; 1 Thes 2:19
4:15 2 Cor 1:3-6
4:16 Eph 3:16; Col 3:10

4:2 Preachers, teachers, and anyone else who talks about Jesus Christ must remember that they stand in God's presence—he hears every word. When you tell people about Christ, be careful not to distort the message to please your audience. Proclaim the truth of God's Word.

4:3, 4 The Good News is revealed to everyone, except to those who refuse to believe. Satan is "the god of this evil world." His work is to deceive, and he has blinded those who don't believe in Christ (see 11:14, 15). The allure of money, power, and pleasure blinds people to the light of Christ's Good News. Those who reject Christ and prefer their own pursuits have unknowingly made Satan their god.

4:5 The focus of Paul's preaching was Christ and not himself. When you witness, tell people about what Christ has done and not about your abilities and accomplishments. People must be introduced to Christ, not to you. And if you hear someone preaching about himself or his own ideas rather than about Christ, beware—he is a false teacher.

4:5 Paul willingly served the Corinthian church even though the people must have deeply disappointed him. Serving people requires a sacrifice of time and personal desires. Being Christ's follower means serving others, even when they do not measure up to our expectations.

4:7 The supremely valuable message of salvation in Jesus Christ has been entrusted by God to frail and fallible human beings. Paul's focus, however, was not on the perishable container but on its priceless contents—God's power dwelling in us. Though we are weak, God uses us to spread his Good News, and he gives us power to do his work. Knowing that the power is his, not ours, should keep us from pride and motivate us to keep daily contact with God, our power source. Our responsibility is to let people see God through us.

4:8-12 Paul reminds us that though we may think we are at the end of the rope, we are never at the end of hope. Our perishable body is subject to sin and suffering, but God never abandons us. Because Christ has won the victory over death, we have eternal life. All our risks, humiliations, and trials are opportunities for Christ to demonstrate his power and presence in and through us.

4:15-18 Paul had faced suffering, trials, and distress as he preached the Good News. But he knew that they would one day be over, and he would obtain God's rest and rewards. As we face great troubles, it's easy to focus on the pain rather than on our ultimate goal. Just as athletes concentrate on the finish line and ignore their discomfort, we, too, must focus on the reward for our faith and the joy that lasts forever. No matter what happens to us in this life, we have the assurance of eternal life, when all suffering will end and all sorrow will flee away (Isaiah 35:10).

4:16 It is easy to lose heart and quit. We all have faced problems in our relationships or in our work that have caused us to think about giving up. Rather than quitting when persecution wore him down, Paul concentrated on the inner strength that came from the Holy Spirit (Ephesians 3:16). Don't let fatigue, pain, or criticism force you off the job. Renew your commitment to serving Christ. Don't forsake your eternal reward because of the intensity of today's pain. Your very weakness allows the resurrection power of Christ to strengthen you moment by moment.

4:17 Rom 8:17-18; 1 Pet 1:6-7
4:18 Rom 8:24; 2 Cor 5:7
5:1 1 Cor 15:47; 2 Cor 4:7; 2 Pet 1:13-14
5:2 Rom 8:23; 1 Cor 15:53-54
5:4 1 Cor 15:53-54
5:5 Rom 8:23; 2 Cor 1:22; Eph 1:13-14
5:7 1 Cor 13:12
5:8 Phil 1:23
5:10 Matt 16:27; Acts 10:42
5:12 2 Cor 1:14; 3:1
5:14 Rom 6:6-7; Gal 2:20; Col 3:3

renewed every day. 17 For our present troubles are quite small and won't last very long.
Yet they produce for us an immeasurably great glory that will last forever! 18 So we don't
look at the troubles we can see right now; rather, we look forward to what we have not
yet seen. For the troubles we see will soon be over, but the joys to come will last forever.

New Bodies

5 For we know that when this earthly tent we live in is taken down—when we die and
leave these bodies—we will have a home in heaven, an eternal body made for us by
God himself and not by human hands. 2 We grow weary in our present bodies, and we
long for the day when we will put on our heavenly bodies like new clothing. 3 For we
will not be spirits without bodies, but we will put on new heavenly bodies. 4 Our dying
bodies make us groan and sigh, but it's not that we want to die and have no bodies at all.
We want to slip into our new bodies so that these dying bodies will be swallowed up by
everlasting life. 5 God himself has prepared us for this, and as a guarantee he has given
us his Holy Spirit.

6 So we are always confident, even though we know that as long as we live in these
bodies we are not at home with the Lord. 7 That is why we live by believing and not by
seeing. 8 Yes, we are fully confident, and we would rather be away from these bodies, for
then we will be at home with the Lord. 9 So our aim is to please him always, whether we
are here in this body or away from this body. 10 For we must all stand before Christ to be
judged. We will each receive whatever we deserve for the good or evil we have done in
our bodies.

We Are God's Ambassadors

11 It is because we know this solemn fear of the Lord that we work so hard to persuade
others. God knows we are sincere, and I hope you know this, too. 12 Are we trying to pat
ourselves on the back again? No, we are giving you a reason to be proud of us, so you
can answer those who brag about having a spectacular ministry rather than having a
sincere heart before God. 13 If it seems that we are crazy, it is to bring glory to God. And
if we are in our right minds, it is for your benefit. 14 Whatever we do, it is because Christ's

---

4:17 Our troubles should not diminish our faith or disillusion us. We should realize that there is a purpose in our suffering. Problems and human limitations have several benefits: (1) They remind us of Christ's suffering for us; (2) they keep us from pride; (3) they cause us to look beyond this brief life; (4) they give us opportunities to prove our faith to others; and (5) they give God the opportunity to demonstrate his power. See your troubles as opportunities!

4:18 Our ultimate hope when we are experiencing terrible illness, persecution, or pain is the realization that this life is not all there is—there is life after death! Knowing that we will live forever with God in a place without sin and suffering can help us live above the pain that we face in this life.

5:1-10 Paul contrasts our earthly body and our future resurrection body. Paul clearly states that our present body makes us groan, but when we die we will not be spirits without bodies. We will have new bodies that will be perfect for our everlasting life.

Paul wrote as he did because the church at Corinth was surrounded by Greek culture, and many believers had difficulty with the concept of bodily resurrection because the Greeks did not believe in it. Most saw the afterlife as something that happened only to the soul, with the real person imprisoned in a physical body. They believed that at death the soul was released; there was no immortality for the body, and the soul enters an eternal state. But the Bible teaches that the body and soul are not permanently separated.

Paul describes our resurrected body in more detail in 1 Corinthians 15:46-58. We will still have personalities and recognizable characteristics in our resurrected body, but through Christ's work, our body will be better than we can imagine. The Bible does not tell us everything about our resurrected body, but we know that it will be perfect, without sickness, disease, or pain (see Philippians 3:21; Revelation 21:4).

5:5 The Holy Spirit within us is our guarantee that God will give us an everlasting body at the resurrection (1:22). We have eternity in us now! This truth should give us great courage and patience to endure anything we might have to experience.

5:6-8 Paul was not afraid to die because he was confident of spending eternity with Christ. Of course, facing the unknown may cause us anxiety, and leaving loved ones hurts deeply, but if we believe in Jesus Christ, we can share Paul's hope and confidence of eternal life with Christ.

5:8 For those who believe in Christ, death is only a prelude to eternal life with God. We will continue to live. Let this hope give you confidence and inspire you to faithful service.

5:9, 10 While eternal life is a free gift given on the basis of God's grace (Ephesians 2:8, 9), each of us will still be judged by Christ. He will reward us for how we have lived. God's gracious gift of salvation does not free us from the requirement of faithful obedience. All Christians must give account on the day of judgment of how they have lived (see Matthew 16:27; Romans 14:10-12; 1 Corinthians 3:10-15).

5:12 Those who "brag about having a spectacular ministry rather than having a sincere heart before God" are the false preachers (see 2:17), who were concerned only about getting ahead in this world. They were preaching the Good News for money and popularity, while Paul and his companions were preaching out of concern for eternity. You can identify false preachers by finding out what really motivates them. If they are more concerned about themselves than about Christ, avoid them and their message.

5:13-15 Everything that Paul and his companions did was to honor God. Christ's love controlled their lives. Because Christ died for us, we also are dead to our old life. Like Paul, we should no longer live to please ourselves; we should spend our life pleasing Christ, who died for us and rose from the grave.

love controls us.* Since we believe that Christ died for everyone, we also believe that
we have all died to the old life we used to live.* [15]He died for everyone so that those
who receive his new life will no longer live to please themselves. Instead, they will live
to please Christ, who died and was raised for them.

[16]So we have stopped evaluating others by what the world thinks about them. Once I
mistakenly thought of Christ that way, as though he were merely a human being. How
differently I think about him now! [17]What this means is that those who become
Christians become new persons. They are not the same anymore, for the old life is gone.
A new life has begun!

[18]All this newness of life is from God, who brought us back to himself through what
Christ did. And God has given us the task of reconciling people to him. [19]For God was
in Christ, reconciling the world to himself, no longer counting people's sins against them.
This is the wonderful message he has given us to tell others. [20]We are Christ's ambassadors, and God is using us to speak to you. We urge you, as though Christ himself were
here pleading with you, "Be reconciled to God!" [21]For God made Christ, who never
sinned, to be the offering for our sin, so that we could be made right with God through
Christ.

6 As God's partners,* we beg you not to reject this marvelous message of God's great
kindness. [2]For God says,

"At just the right time, I heard you.
On the day of salvation, I helped you."*

Indeed, God is ready to help you right now. Today is the day of salvation.

Paul's Hardships

[3]We try to live in such a way that no one will be hindered from finding the Lord by the
way we act, and so no one can find fault with our ministry. [4]In everything we do we try
to show that we are true ministers of God. We patiently endure troubles and hardships
and calamities of every kind. [5]We have been beaten, been put in jail, faced angry mobs,
worked to exhaustion, endured sleepless nights, and gone without food. [6]We have
proved ourselves by our purity, our understanding, our patience, our kindness, our
sincere love, and the power of the Holy Spirit.* [7]We have faithfully preached the truth.
God's power has been working in us. We have righteousness as our weapon, both to

5:15 Rom 14:7-9
5:16 2 Cor 10:4
5:17 Isa 65:17; Gal 6:15; Rev 21:5
5:18 Rom 5:10
5:19 Rom 3:24; 4:28
5:20 Eph 6:20
5:21 Isa 53:6, 9; Jer 23:6; Gal 3:13; Heb 4:15; 7:26; 1 Pet 2:22
6:1 1 Cor 3:9; 2 Cor 5:20
6:2 †Isa 49:8
6:3 1 Cor 8:9; 9:12
6:4 2 Cor 4:2
6:5 2 Cor 11:23-27
6:6 1 Tim 4:12
6:7 1 Cor 2:4; 2 Cor 10:4

5:14a Or *urges us on.* **5:14b** Greek *Since one died on behalf of all, then all died.* **6:1** Or *As we work together.* **6:2** Isa 49:8. **6:6** Or *the holiness of spirit.*

5:17 Christians are brand-new people on the *inside.* The Holy Spirit gives them new life, and they are not the same anymore. We are not reformed, rehabilitated, or reeducated—we are re-created (new creations), living in vital union with Christ (Colossians 2:6, 7). At conversion we do not merely turn over a new leaf; we begin a new life under a new Master.

5:18, 19 God brings us back to himself (reconciles us) by blotting out our sins (see also Ephesians 2:13-18) and making us right with him. When we trust in Christ, we are no longer God's enemies, or strangers or foreigners to him. Because we have been reconciled to God, we have the privilege of encouraging others to do the same, and thus we are those who have "the task of reconciling people to him."

5:20 An ambassador is an official representative of one country to another. As believers, we are Christ's ambassadors, sent with his message of reconciliation to the world. An ambassador of reconciliation has an important responsibility. We dare not take this responsibility lightly. How well are you fulfilling your commission as Christ's ambassador?

5:21 When we trust in Christ, we make an exchange: He takes our sin and makes us right with God. Our sin was laid on Christ at his crucifixion. His righteousness is given to us at our conversion. This is what Christians mean by Christ's atonement for sin. In the world, bartering works only when two people exchange goods of relatively equal value. But God offers to trade his righteousness for our sin—something of immeasurable worth for something completely worthless. How grateful we should be for his kindness to us.

6:1 How could the Corinthian believers reject God's message? Perhaps they were doubting Paul and his words, confused by the false teachers, who taught a different message. The people heard God's message but did not let it affect what they said and did. How often do you reject God's message?

6:2 God offers salvation to all people. Many people put off a decision for Christ, thinking that there will be a better time—but they could easily miss their opportunity altogether. There is no time like the present to receive God's forgiveness. Don't let anything hold you back from coming to Christ.

6:3 In everything he did, Paul always considered what his actions communicated about Jesus Christ. If you are a believer, you are a minister for God. In the course of each day, unbelievers observe you. Don't let your careless or undisciplined actions be some person's excuse for rejecting Christ.

6:8 Matt 27:63; 1 Cor 4:10, 13
6:9 Ps 118:18; 2 Cor 1:8-10; 4:10-11
6:10 Acts 3:6; Rom 8:32; 1 Cor 3:21; 2 Cor 8:9
6:11 2 Cor 7:3

attack and to defend ourselves. [8]We serve God whether people honor us or despise us,
whether they slander us or praise us. We are honest, but they call us impostors. [9]We are
well known, but we are treated as unknown. We live close to death, but here we are, still
alive. We have been beaten within an inch of our lives. [10]Our hearts ache, but we always
have joy. We are poor, but we give spiritual riches to others. We own nothing, and yet
we have everything.
[11]Oh, dear Corinthian friends! We have spoken honestly with you. Our hearts are open
to you. [12]If there is a problem between us, it is not because of a lack of love on our part,
but because you have withheld your love from us. [13]I am talking now as I would to my
own children. Open your hearts to us!

The Temple of the Living God

6:14 Eph 5:7, 11; 1 Jn 1:6
6:16 †Lev 26:12; †Jer 32:38; †Ezek 37:27

[14]Don't team up with those who are unbelievers. How can goodness be a partner with
wickedness? How can light live with darkness? [15]What harmony can there be between
Christ and the Devil*? How can a believer be a partner with an unbeliever? [16]And what
union can there be between God's temple and idols? For we are the temple of the living
God. As God said:

"I will live in them
and walk among them.
I will be their God,
and they will be my people.*

6:17 †Isa 52:11; †Ezek 20:34

[17]Therefore, come out from them
and separate yourselves from them, says the Lord.
Don't touch their filthy things,
and I will welcome you.*

6:18 †2 Sam 7:8, 14; Isa 43:6; Jer 31:9

[18]And I will be your Father,
and you will be my sons and daughters,
says the Lord Almighty.*"

7:1 1 Pet 1:15-16

7 Because we have these promises, dear friends, let us cleanse ourselves from
everything that can defile our body or spirit. And let us work toward complete purity
because we fear God.

Paul's Joy at the Church's Repentance

7:2 2 Cor 6:12-13
7:3 2 Cor 6:11-12; Phil 1:7

[2]Please open your hearts to us. We have not done wrong to anyone. We have not led
anyone astray. We have not taken advantage of anyone. [3]I'm not saying this to condemn
you, for I said before that you are in our hearts forever. We live or die together with you.

6:15 Greek *and Beliar.* **6:16** Lev 26:12; Ezek 37:27. **6:17** Isa 52:11; Ezek 20:34. **6:18** 2 Sam 7:14.

6:8-10 What a difference it makes to know Jesus! He cares for us in spite of what the world thinks. Christians don't have to give in to public opinion and pressure. Paul stood faithful to God whether people praised him or slandered him. He remained joyous and content in the most difficult hardships. Don't let circumstances or people's expectations control you. Be firm as you stand true to God, and refuse to compromise his standards for living.

6:11-13 "Our hearts are open to you" means that Paul had told the Corinthian believers his true feelings for them, clearly revealing how much he loved them. The Corinthians were reacting coldly to Paul's words, but Paul explained that his harsh words came from his love for them. It is easy to react against those whom God has placed over us in leadership, rather than to accept their exhortations as a sign of their love for us. We need an open rather than a closed heart toward God's messengers.

6:14-18 Paul urges believers to not form partnerships with unbelievers because this might weaken their Christian commitment, integrity, or standards. It would be a mismatch. Earlier, Paul had explained that this did not mean isolating oneself from unbelievers (see 1 Corinthians 5:9, 10). Paul even urges Christians to stay with their unbelieving spouses (1 Corinthians 7:12, 13). He wanted believers to be active in their witness for Christ to unbelievers but not lock themselves into personal or business relationships that could cause them to compromise their faith. Believers should do everything in their power to avoid situations that could force them to divide their loyalties.

6:14, 15 For those who have discovered God's light, there can be no fellowship or compromise with darkness (1 Corinthians 10:20, 21).

6:17 Separation from the world involves more than keeping our distance from sinners; it means staying close to God. It involves more than avoiding worldly entertainment; it extends to how we spend our time and money. There is no way to separate ourselves totally from all sinful influences. Nevertheless, we are to resist the sin around us, without either giving up or giving in.

7:1 Cleansing is a twofold action: turning *away* from sin, and turning *toward* God. The Corinthians were to have nothing to do with paganism. They were to make a clean break with their past and give themselves to God alone.

4I have the highest confidence in you, and my pride in you is great. You have greatly **7:4**
encouraged me; you have made me happy despite all our troubles. 2 Cor 8:24
5When we arrived in Macedonia there was no rest for us. Outside there was conflict **7:5**
from every direction, and inside there was fear. 6But God, who encourages those who 2 Cor 2:13; 4:8 **7:6**
are discouraged, encouraged us by the arrival of Titus. 7His presence was a joy, but so Isa 49:13
was the news he brought of the encouragement he received from you. When he told me 2 Cor 1:3-4; 2:13
how much you were looking forward to my visit, and how sorry you were about what
had happened, and how loyal your love is for me, I was filled with joy!
8I am no longer sorry that I sent that letter to you, though I was sorry for a time, for I **7:8**
know that it was painful to you for a little while. 9Now I am glad I sent it, not because it 2 Cor 2:2-4
hurt you, but because the pain caused you to have remorse and change your ways. It was
the kind of sorrow God wants his people to have, so you were not harmed by us in any
way. 10For God can use sorrow in our lives to help us turn away from sin and seek **7:10**
salvation. We will never regret that kind of sorrow. But sorrow without repentance is the Matt 27:3-5
kind that results in death.
11Just see what this godly sorrow produced in you! Such earnestness, such concern to
clear yourselves, such indignation, such alarm, such longing to see me, such zeal, and
such a readiness to punish the wrongdoer. You showed that you have done everything
you could to make things right. 12My purpose was not to write about who did the wrong **7:12**
or who was wronged. I wrote to you so that in the sight of God you could show how 1 Cor 5:1-2; 2 Cor 2:3, 9
much you really do care for us. 13We have been encouraged by this. **7:13**
In addition to our own encouragement, we were especially delighted to see how happy 2 Cor 2:13
Titus was at the way you welcomed him and set his mind at ease. 14I had told him how **7:15**
proud I was of you—and you didn't disappoint me. I have always told you the truth, and 2 Cor 2:9; Phil 2:12
now my boasting to Titus has also proved true! 15Now he cares for you more than ever **7:16**
when he remembers the way you listened to him and welcomed him with such respect 2 Cor 2:3; 2 Thes 3:4
and deep concern. 16I am very happy now because I have complete confidence in you. Phlm 1:21

3. Paul defends the collection

A Call to Generous Giving

8 Now I want to tell you, dear friends,* what God in his kindness has done for the **8:1**
churches in Macedonia. 2Though they have been going through much trouble and Acts 16:9 **8:2**
hard times, their wonderful joy and deep poverty have overflowed in rich generosity. 2 Cor 9:11
3For I can testify that they gave not only what they could afford but far more. And they **8:4**
did it of their own free will. 4They begged us again and again for the gracious privilege Acts 24:17; Rom 15:26; 1 Cor 16:1, 3

8:1 Greek *brothers.*

7:5 Here Paul resumed the story that he left in 2:13, where he said he went to Macedonia to look for Titus. Though Paul still had many problems and hardships to face, he still found comfort and joy in the progress of the ministry.

7:8ff "That letter" refers to the third letter (now lost) that Paul had written to the Corinthians. Apparently it had caused the people to begin to change. For an explanation of the chronology of Paul's letters to Corinth, see the first note on 1:1.

7:10 Sorrow for our sins can result in changed behavior. Many people are sorry only for the effects of their sins or for being caught ("sorrow without repentance"). Compare Peter's remorse and repentance with Judas's bitterness and act of suicide. Both denied Christ. One repented and was restored to faith and service; the other took his own life.

7:11 It is difficult to be confronted with our sin and even more difficult to get rid of sin. Paul praised the Corinthians for clearing up an especially troublesome situation (see the note on 2:5-11). Do you tend to be defensive when confronted? Don't let pride keep you from admitting your sins. Accept correction as a tool for your growth, and do all you can to correct problems that are pointed out to you.

8:1ff Paul, writing from Macedonia, hoped that news of the generosity of these churches would encourage the Corinthian believers and motivate them to solve their problems and unite in fellowship.

8:2-5 During his third missionary journey, Paul had collected money for the impoverished believers in Jerusalem. The churches in Macedonia—Philippi, Thessalonica, and Berea—had given money even though they were poor, and they had sacrificially given more than Paul expected. Although they were poor themselves, they wanted to help. The amount we give is not as important as why and how we give. God does not want us to give grudgingly. Instead, he wants us to give as these churches did—out of dedication to Christ, love for fellow believers, the joy of helping those in need, as well as the fact that it was simply the good and right thing to do. How well does your giving measure up to the standards set by the Macedonian churches?

8:3-6 The Kingdom of God spreads through believers' concern and eagerness to help others. Here we see several churches joining to help others beyond their own circle of friends and their own city. Explore ways that you might link up with a ministry outside your city, either through your church or through a Christian organization. By joining with other believers to do God's work, you increase Christian unity and help the Kingdom grow.

of sharing in the gift for the Christians in Jerusalem. 5 Best of all, they went beyond our
highest hopes, for their first action was to dedicate themselves to the Lord and to us for
whatever directions God might give them.
8:6 2 Cor 12:13, 18 — 6 So we have urged Titus, who encouraged your giving in the first place, to return to
8:7 1 Cor 1:5; 16:1-2; 2 Cor 9:8 — you and encourage you to complete your share in this ministry of giving. 7 Since you
excel in so many ways—you have so much faith, such gifted speakers, such knowledge,
such enthusiasm, and such love for us*—now I want you to excel also in this gracious
ministry of giving. 8 I am not saying you must do it, even though the other churches are
eager to do it. This is one way to prove your love is real.
8:9 Matt 8:20; Phil 2:6-7 — 9 You know how full of love and kindness our Lord Jesus Christ was. Though he was very
rich, yet for your sakes he became poor, so that by his poverty he could make you rich.
8:10 2 Cor 9:2 — 10 I suggest that you finish what you started a year ago, for you were the first to propose
this idea, and you were the first to begin doing something about it. 11 Now you should
carry this project through to completion just as enthusiastically as you began it. Give
8:12 Prov 3:27-28; Mark 12:43-44; 2 Cor 9:7 — whatever you can according to what you have. 12 If you are really eager to give, it isn't
important how much you are able to give. God wants you to give what you have, not

8:7 Some manuscripts read *love from us to you.*

PRINCIPLES OF CONFRONTATION IN 2 CORINTHIANS

Method	*Reference*
Be firm and bold	7:9; 10:2
Affirm all you see that is good	7:4
Be accurate and hones	7:14; 8:21
Know the facts	11:22–27
Follow up after the confrontation	7:13; 12:14
Be gentle after being firm	7:15; 13:11–13
Speak words that reflect Christ's message, not your own ideas	10:3; 10:12, 13; 12:19
Use discipline only when all else fails	13:2

Sometimes rebuke is necessary, but it must be used with caution. The purpose of any rebuke, confrontation, or discipline is to help people, not hurt them.

8:7, 8 The Corinthian believers excelled in everything—they had faith, gifted speakers, knowledge, enthusiasm, and love. Paul wanted them to also be leaders in giving. Giving is a natural response of love. Paul did not order the Corinthians to give, but he encouraged them to prove that their love was real. When you love someone, you want to give that person your time and attention and provide for his or her needs. If you refuse to help, your love is not as genuine as you say.

8:9 There is no evidence that Jesus was any poorer than most first-century Palestinians; rather, Jesus became poor by giving up his rights as God and becoming human. In his incarnation, God voluntarily became man—the person Jesus of Nazareth. As a man, Jesus was subject to place, time, and other human limitations. He did not give up his eternal power when he became human, but he did set aside his glory and his rights (see the note on Philippians 2:5-7). In response to the Father's will, he limited his power and knowledge. Christ became "poor" when he became human because he set aside so much. Yet by doing so, he made us "rich" because we received salvation and eternal life.

What made Jesus' humanity unique was his freedom from sin. In Jesus we can see every attribute of God's character. The Incarnation is explained further in these Bible passages: John 1:1-14; Romans 1:2-5; Philippians 2:6-11; 1 Timothy 3:16; Hebrews 2:14; 1 John 1:1-3.

8:10-15 The Christians in the Corinthian church had money, and apparently they had planned to collect money for the Jerusalem church a year previously (see also 9:2). Paul challenges them to act on their plans. Four principles of giving emerge here: (1) Your willingness to give enthusiastically is more important than the amount you give; (2) you should strive to fulfill your financial commitments; (3) if you give to others in need, they will, in turn, help you when you are in need; (4) you should give as a response to Christ, not for anything you can get out of it. How you give reflects your devotion to Christ.

8:12 How do you decide how much to give? What about differences in the financial resources Christians have? Paul gives the Corinthian church several principles to follow: (1) Each person should follow through on previous promises (8:10, 11; 9:3); (2) each person should give as much as he or she is able (8:12; 9:6); (3) each person must make up his or her own mind how much to give (9:7); and (4) each person should give in proportion to what God has given him or her (9:10). God gives to us so that we can give to others.

8:12 Paul says that we should give of what we have, not what we don't have. Sacrificial giving must be responsible. Paul wants believers to give generously, but not to the extent that those who depend on the givers (their families, for example) must go without having their basic needs met. Give until it hurts, but don't give so that it hurts your family and/or relatives who need your financial support.

what you don't have. 13Of course, I don't mean you should give so much that you suffer
from having too little. I only mean that there should be some equality. 14Right now you
have plenty and can help them. Then at some other time they can share with you when
you need it. In this way, everyone's needs will be met. 15Do you remember what the
Scriptures say about this? "Those who gathered a lot had nothing left over, and those
who gathered only a little had enough."*

Titus and His Companions

16I am thankful to God that he has given Titus the same enthusiasm for you that I have.
17He welcomed our request that he visit you again. In fact, he himself was eager to go
and see you. 18We are also sending another brother with Titus. He is highly praised in
all the churches as a preacher of the Good News. 19He was appointed by the churches to
accompany us as we take the offering to Jerusalem*—a service that glorifies the Lord
and shows our eagerness to help. 20By traveling together we will guard against any
suspicion, for we are anxious that no one should find fault with the way we are handling
this generous gift. 21We are careful to be honorable before the Lord, but we also want
everyone else to know we are honorable.

22And we are also sending with them another brother who has been thoroughly tested
and has shown how earnest he is on many occasions. He is now even more enthusiastic
because of his increased confidence in you. 23If anyone asks about Titus, say that he is
my partner who works with me to help you. And these brothers are representatives* of
the churches. They are splendid examples of those who bring glory to Christ. 24So show
them your love, and prove to all the churches that our boasting about you is justified.

The Collection for Christians in Jerusalem

9 I really don't need to write to you about this gift for the Christians in Jerusalem.*
2For I know how eager you are to help, and I have been boasting to our friends in
Macedonia that you Christians in Greece* were ready to send an offering a year ago. In
fact, it was your enthusiasm that stirred up many of them to begin helping. 3But I am
sending these brothers just to be sure that you really are ready, as I told them you would
be, with your money all collected. I don't want it to turn out that I was wrong in my
boasting about you. 4I would be humiliated—and so would you—if some Macedonian
Christians came with me, only to find that you still weren't ready after all I had told them!
5So I thought I should send these brothers ahead of me to make sure the gift you
promised is ready. But I want it to be a willing gift, not one given under pressure.

6Remember this—a farmer who plants only a few seeds will get a small crop. But the
one who plants generously will get a generous crop. 7You must each make up your own
mind as to how much you should give. Don't give reluctantly or in response to pressure.
For God loves the person who gives cheerfully. 8And God will generously provide all
you need. Then you will always have everything you need and plenty left over to share
with others. 9As the Scriptures say,

8:14 Acts 4:34; 2 Cor 9:12
8:15 †Exod 16:18
8:16 2 Cor 2:14
8:18 2 Cor 12:18
8:19 Acts 14:23; 1 Cor 16:3-4
8:21 Prov 3:4; Rom 12:17
8:23 Phil 2:25
8:24 2 Cor 7:4
9:1 Acts 24:17; 2 Cor 8:4, 20
9:2 2 Cor 8:11-12, 19
9:3 1 Cor 16:2; 2 Cor 8:23
9:5 Phil 4:17
9:6 Prov 11:24-25; 22:9; Gal 6:7, 9
9:7 Exod 25:2; Deut 15:7-10; 2 Cor 8:12
9:8 Phil 4:19
9:9 †Ps 112:9

8:15 Exod 16:18. **8:19** See 1 Cor 16:3-4. **8:23** Greek *apostles*. **9:1** Greek *about the offering for the saints*. **9:2** Greek *Achaia*, the southern region of the Greek peninsula.

8:18-21 "Another brother" was traveling with Paul and Titus, a man who was elected by the churches to also take the large financial gift to Jerusalem. Paul explained that by traveling together there could be no suspicion and people would know that the gift was being handled honestly. The church did not need to worry that the bearers of the collection would misuse the money.

9:3-5 Paul reminded the Corinthians to fulfill the commitment that they had already made (see also 8:10-12). They had said that they would collect a financial gift to send to the church in Jerusalem. Paul was sending a few men ahead of him to make sure their gift was ready, so it would be a real gift and not look like people had to give under pressure at the last minute. He was holding them accountable to keep their promise, so that neither Paul nor the Corinthians would be embarrassed.

9:6-8 People may hesitate to give generously to God because they worry about having enough money left over to meet their own needs. Paul assured the Corinthians that God was able to meet their needs. The person who gives only a little will receive only a little in return. Don't let a lack of faith keep you from giving cheerfully and generously.

9:7 Our attitude is more important than the amount we give. We don't have to be embarrassed if we can give only a small gift. God is concerned about *how* we give from the resources we have (see Mark 12:41-44). According to that standard, the giving of the Macedonian churches would be difficult to match (8:3).

9:10 God gives us resources to use and invest for him. Paul uses the illustration of seed to explain that the resources God gives us are not to be hidden, foolishly devoured, or thrown away. Instead, they should be cultivated in order to produce more crops. When we invest what God has given us in his work, he will provide us with even more to give in his service.

"Godly people give generously to the poor.
Their good deeds will never be forgotten."*

9:10 Isa 55:10 Hos 10:12 — 10 For God is the one who gives seed to the farmer and then bread to eat. In the same way,
he will give you many opportunities to do good, and he will produce a great harvest of
generosity* in you.
11 Yes, you will be enriched so that you can give even more generously. And when we
9:11 2 Cor 1:11; 4:15 — take your gifts to those who need them, they will break out in thanksgiving to God. 12 So
9:12 2 Cor 8:14 — two good things will happen—the needs of the Christians in Jerusalem will be met, and
they will joyfully express their thanksgiving to God. 13 You will be glorifying God
through your generous gifts. For your generosity to them will prove that you are obedient
to the Good News of Christ. 14 And they will pray for you with deep affection because
of the wonderful grace of God shown through you.
15 Thank God for his Son—a gift too wonderful for words!*

4. Paul defends his authority

10:1 1 Cor 2:3 2 Cor 10:10 — **10** Now I, Paul, plead with you. I plead with the gentleness and kindness that Christ
himself would use, even though some of you say I am bold in my letters but timid
10:2 1 Cor 4:21 — in person. 2 I hope it won't be necessary, but when I come I may have to be very bold
with those who think we act from purely human motives. 3 We are human, but we don't
10:4 Jer 1:10 Eph 6:13-17 — wage war with human plans and methods. 4 We use God's mighty weapons, not mere
worldly weapons, to knock down the Devil's strongholds. 5 With these weapons we break
10:5 Isa 2:11-12 1 Cor 1:19 — down every proud argument that keeps people from knowing God. With these weapons
we conquer their rebellious ideas, and we teach them to obey Christ. 6 And we will punish
10:6 2 Cor 2:9; 7:15 — those who remained disobedient after the rest of you became loyal and obedient.
7 The trouble with you is that you make your decisions on the basis of appearance.*
10:7 John 7:24 2 Cor 11:23 — You must recognize that we belong to Christ just as much as those who proudly declare
that they belong to Christ. 8 I may seem to be boasting too much about the authority given
10:8 2 Cor 12:6; 13:10 — to us by the Lord. But this authority is to build you up, not to tear you down. And I will
not be put to shame by having my work among you destroyed.

9:9 Ps 112:9. **9:10** Greek *righteousness.* **9:15** Greek *Thank God for his indescribable gift.* **10:7** Or *Look at the obvious facts.*

NEEDS FOR A FUND-RAISING PROJECT

Information	8:4	Enthusiasm	8:7, 8, 11
Definite purpose	8:4	Persistence	8:2ff
Readiness and willingness	9:7	Honesty and integrity	8:21
Dedication	8:5	Accountability	9:3
Leadership	8:7	Someone to keep it moving	8:18–22

The topic of fund-raising is not one to be avoided or one that should embarrass us, but all fund-raising efforts should be planned and conducted responsibly.

9:12-15 Paul emphasizes the spiritual rewards for those who give generously to God's work. We should not expect to become wealthy through giving. Those who receive your gifts will be helped, will praise God, and will pray for you. As you bless others, you will be blessed.

10:1, 2 Paul's opponents questioned his authority. From 7:8-16 we know that the majority of Corinthian believers sided with Paul. However, a minority continued to slander him, saying that he was bold in his letters but had no authority in person. Chapters 10–13 are Paul's response to this charge.

10:3-6 We, like Paul, are merely weak humans, but we don't need to use human plans and methods to win our battles. God's mighty weapons are available to us as we fight against the Devil's "strongholds." The Christian must choose whose methods to use—God's or the world's. Paul assures us that God's mighty weapons—prayer, faith, hope, love, God's Word, the Holy Spirit—are powerful and effective (see Ephesians 6:13-18)! These weapons can break down the proud human arguments against God and the walls that Satan builds to keep people from finding God. When dealing with people's proud arguments that keep them from a relationship with Christ, we may be tempted to use our own methods. But nothing can break down these barriers like God's weapons.

10:5 Paul uses military terminology to describe this warfare against sin and Satan. God must be the commander in chief—even our thoughts must be submitted to his control as we live for him.

10:7-10 Those who opposed Paul portrayed him as weak and powerless, but Paul reminded the Corinthians that he had been given authority by the Lord. False teachers were encouraging the believers to ignore Paul, but Paul explained that the advice in his letters was to be taken seriously. He had authority because he and his companions were the first to bring the Good News to Corinth (10:14). Everyone knew that because of this service, their faith had been built up.

9Now this is not just an attempt to frighten you by my letters. 10For some say, "Don't
worry about Paul. His letters are demanding and forceful, but in person he is weak, and
his speeches are really bad!" 11The ones who say this must realize that we will be just
as demanding and forceful in person as we are in our letters.
12Oh, don't worry; I wouldn't dare say that I am as wonderful as these other men who
tell you how important they are! But they are only comparing themselves with each
other, and measuring themselves by themselves. What foolishness!
13But we will not boast of authority we do not have. Our goal is to stay within the
boundaries of God's plan for us, and this plan includes our working there with you. 14We
are not going too far when we claim authority over you, for we were the first to travel
all the way to you with the Good News of Christ. 15Nor do we claim credit for the work
someone else has done. Instead, we hope that your faith will grow and that our work
among you will be greatly enlarged. 16Then we will be able to go and preach the Good
News in other places that are far beyond you, where no one else is working. Then there
will be no question about being in someone else's territory. 17As the Scriptures say,

"The person who wishes to boast
should boast only of what the Lord has done."*

18When people boast about themselves, it doesn't count for much. But when the Lord
commends someone, that's different!

Paul and the False Apostles

11 I hope you will be patient with me as I keep on talking like a fool. Please bear with
me. 2I am jealous for you with the jealousy of God himself. For I promised you
as a pure bride* to one husband, Christ. 3But I fear that somehow you will be led away
from your pure and simple devotion to Christ, just as Eve was deceived by the serpent.
4You seem to believe whatever anyone tells you, even if they preach about a different
Jesus than the one we preach, or a different Spirit than the one you received, or a different
kind of gospel than the one you believed. 5But I don't think I am inferior to these "super

10:17 Jer 9:24. **11:2** Greek *a virgin.*

10:10 1 Cor 1:17; 2:3; 2 Cor 11:6; Gal 4:13-14
10:11 2 Cor 13:2, 10
10:12 2 Cor 3:1; 5:12
10:13 Rom 12:3
10:14 1 Cor 9:1
10:15 Rom 15:20; 2 Thes 1:3
10:16 Acts 19:21
10:17 †Jer 9:24; 1 Cor 1:31
10:18 Prov 27:2
11:2 Hos 2:19; Eph 5:26-27
11:3 Gen 3:1-6, 13; John 8:44; 1 Tim 2:14
11:4 Rom 8:15; Gal 1:6-8
11:5 Gal 2:6

10:10 Some said that Paul's speaking amounted to nothing. Greece was known for its eloquent and persuasive orators. Evidently, some were judging Paul by comparing him to other speakers they had heard, and Paul was perhaps not the most powerful preacher (although he was an excellent debater). But Paul responded obediently to God's call and thus introduced Christianity to the Roman Empire. Moses and Jeremiah also had problems with speaking (see Exodus 4:10-12; Jeremiah 1:6). Preaching ability is not the first prerequisite of a great leader!

10:12, 13 Paul criticized the false teachers who were trying to prove their goodness by comparing themselves with others rather than with God's standards. When we compare ourselves with others, we may feel proud because we think we're better. But when we measure ourselves against God's standards, it becomes obvious that we have no basis for pride. Don't worry about other people's accomplishments. Instead, ask yourself: How does my life measure up to what God wants? How does my life compare to that of Jesus Christ?

10:17, 18 When we do something well, we want to tell others and be recognized. But recognition is dangerous—it can lead to inflated pride. How much better it is to seek the praise of God rather than the praise of people. Then, when we receive praise, we will be free to give God the credit. What should you change about the way you live in order to receive God's commendation?

11:1 Paul asked the Corinthian believers to bear with him as he talked "like a fool." In other words, Paul felt foolish rehearsing his credentials as a preacher of the Good News (11:16-21). But he thought that he had to do this in order to silence the false teachers (11:13).

11:2 Paul was anxious that the church's love should be for Christ alone, just as a pure bride saves her love for one man only. By "pure bride" he meant one who was unaffected by false doctrine.

11:3 The Corinthians' pure and simple devotion to Christ was being threatened by false teaching. Paul did not want the believers to lose their single-minded love for Christ. Keeping Christ first in our life can be very difficult when we have so many distractions threatening to sidetrack our faith. Just as Eve lost her focus by listening to the serpent, we, too, can lose our focus by letting our life become overcrowded and confused. Is there anything that weakens your commitment to keep Christ first in your life? How can you minimize the distractions that threaten your devotion to him?

11:3, 4 The Corinthian believers fell for smooth talk and messages that sounded good and seemed to make sense. Today there are many false teachings that seem to make sense. Don't believe someone simply because he or she sounds like an authority or says words you like to hear. Search the Bible and check his or her teachings against God's Word. The Bible should be your authoritative guide. Don't listen to any "authoritative preacher" who contradicts God's Word.

11:4 The false teachers distorted the truth about Jesus and ended up preaching a different Jesus, a different spirit than the Holy Spirit, and a different way of salvation. Those who teach anything different from what God's infallible Word says are both mistaken and misleading.

11:5 Paul was saying that these marvelous teachers ("super-apostles") were no better than he was. They may have been more eloquent speakers, but they spoke lies and were servants of Satan.

11:6 1 Cor 1:17 Eph 3:4
11:7 1 Cor 9:12, 18 2 Cor 12:13

apostles." [6]I may not be a trained speaker, but I know what I am talking about. I think
you realize this by now, for we have proved it again and again.
[7]Did I do wrong when I humbled myself and honored you by preaching God's Good
News to you without expecting anything in return? [8]I "robbed" other churches by
accepting their contributions so I could serve you at no cost. [9]And when I was with you

PAUL'S CREDENTIALS
One of Paul's biggest problems with the church in Corinth was his concern that they viewed him as no more than a blustering preacher; thus, they were not taking seriously his advice in his letters and on his visits. Paul addressed this attitude in the letter of 2 Corinthians, pointing out his credentials as an apostle of Christ and why the Corinthians should take his advice.

Reference	Credential
1:1, 21; 4:1	Commissioned by God
1:18; 4:2	Spoke truthfully
1:12	Acted in holiness, sincerity, and dependence on God alone in his dealings with them
1:13, 14	Was straightforward and sincere in his letters
1:22	Had God's Holy Spirit
2:4; 6:11; 11:11	Loved the Corinthian believers
2:17	Spoke with sincerity and Christ's power
3:2, 3	Worked among them and changed their lives
3:4; 12:6	Lived as an example to the believers
4:1, 16	Did not give up
4:2	Taught the Bible with integrity
4:5	Had Christ as the center of his message
4:8–12; 6:4, 5, 9, 10	Endured persecution as he taught the Good News
5:18–20	Was Christ's ambassador, called to tell the Good News
6:3, 4	Tried to live an exemplary life so others would not be kept from God
6:6	Led a pure life, understood the gospel, and displayed patience with the Corinthians
6:7	Was truthful and filled with God's power
6:8	Stood true to God first and always
7:2; 11:7–9	Never corrupted or exploited anyone
8:20, 21	Handled their offering for the Jerusalem believers in a responsible, blameless manner
10:1–6	Used God's weapons, not his own, for God's work
10:7, 8	Was confident that he belonged to Christ
10:12, 13	Would boast not in himself but in the Lord
10:14, 15	Had authority because he taught them the Good News
11:23–33	Endured pain and danger as he fulfilled his calling
12:2–4	Was blessed with an astounding vision
12:7–10	Was constantly humbled by a "thorn" in the flesh that God refused to take away
12:12	Did miracles among them
12:19	Was always motivated to strengthen others spiritually
13:4	Was filled with God's power
13:5, 6	Passed the test
13:9	Was always concerned that his spiritual children become mature believers

11:6 Paul, a brilliant thinker, was not a trained, eloquent speaker. Although his ministry was effective (see Acts 17), he had not been trained in the Greek schools of oratory and speechmaking, as many of the false teachers probably had been. Paul believed in a simple presentation of the Good News (see 1 Corinthians 1:17), and some people thought this showed simple-mindedness. Thus, Paul's speaking performance was often used against him by false teachers. In all our teaching and preaching, content is far more important than the presentation. A simple, clear presentation that helps listeners understand will be of great value.

11:7 The Corinthians may have thought that preachers could be judged by how much money they demanded. A good speaker would charge a large sum, a fair speaker would be a little cheaper, and a poor speaker would speak for free. The false teachers may have argued that because Paul asked no fee for his preaching, he must have been an amateur, with little authority or competence. Believers today must be careful not to assume that every preacher or evangelist who is well known or who demands a large honorarium is superior at teaching God's Word.

11:7-12 Paul could have asked the Corinthian church for financial support. Jesus himself taught that those who minister for God should be supported by the people to whom they minister

and didn't have enough to live on, I did not ask you to help me. For the brothers who came
from Macedonia brought me another gift. I have never yet asked you for any support, and
I never will. 10As surely as the truth of Christ is in me, I will never stop boasting about
this all over Greece.* 11Why? Because I don't love you? God knows I do.
12But I will continue doing this to cut the ground out from under the feet of those who
boast that their work is just like ours. 13These people are false apostles. They have fooled
you by disguising themselves as apostles of Christ. 14But I am not surprised! Even Satan
can disguise himself as an angel of light. 15So it is no wonder his servants can also do it
by pretending to be godly ministers. In the end they will get every bit of punishment their
wicked deeds deserve.

Paul's Many Trials

16Once again, don't think that I have lost my wits to talk like this. But even if you do,
listen to me, as you would to a foolish person, while I also boast a little. 17Such bragging
is not something the Lord wants, but I am acting like a fool. 18And since others boast
about their human achievements, I will, too. 19After all, you, who think you are so wise,
enjoy listening to fools! 20You put up with it when they make you their slaves, take
everything you have, take advantage of you, put on airs, and slap you in the face. 21I'm
ashamed to say that we were not strong enough to do that!

But whatever they dare to boast about—I'm talking like a fool again—I can boast
about it, too. 22They say they are Hebrews, do they? So am I. And they say they are
Israelites? So am I. And they are descendants of Abraham? So am I. 23They say they
serve Christ? I know I sound like a madman, but I have served him far more! I have
worked harder, been put in jail more often, been whipped times without number, and
faced death again and again. 24Five different times the Jews gave me thirty-nine lashes.
25Three times I was beaten with rods. Once I was stoned. Three times I was shipwrecked.
Once I spent a whole night and a day adrift at sea. 26I have traveled many weary miles.
I have faced danger from flooded rivers and from robbers. I have faced danger from my
own people, the Jews, as well as from the Gentiles. I have faced danger in the cities, in
the deserts, and on the stormy seas. And I have faced danger from men who claim to be
Christians but are not.* 27I have lived with weariness and pain and sleepless nights.
Often I have been hungry and thirsty and have gone without food. Often I have shivered
with cold, without enough clothing to keep me warm.

11:10 Greek *Achaia.* **11:26** Greek *from false brothers.*

11:9 2 Cor 12:13
11:11 2 Cor 7:3; 12:15
11:12 1 Cor 9:12
11:13 Rev 2:2
11:15 Phil 3:19
11:16 2 Cor 12:6
11:17 1 Cor 7:12, 25; 2 Cor 7:4
11:18 Phil 3:3-4
11:20 Gal 2:4; 4:9
11:21 2 Cor 10:10
11:22 Rom 11:1; Phil 3:5
11:23 Rom 8:36; 1 Cor 15:10; 16:23; 2 Cor 6:4-5
11:24 Deut 25:3
11:25 Acts 14:19; 16:22; 27:41
11:26 Acts 9:23; 14:5; 20:3; 21:31; Gal 2:4
11:27 1 Cor 4:11; 2 Cor 6:5

(Matthew 10:10). But Paul thought that asking for support in Corinth might be misunderstood. There were many false teachers who hoped to make a good profit from preaching (2:17), and Paul might look like one of them. Paul separated himself completely from those false teachers in order to silence those who only claimed to do God's work.

11:14, 15 One Jewish writing (the Apocalypse of Moses) says that the story of Eve's temptation includes Satan masquerading as an angel. Paul may have been thinking of this story, or he could have been referring to Satan's typical devices. In either case, nothing could be more deceitful than Satan, the prince of darkness (Ephesians 6:12; Colossians 1:13), disguising himself as an angel of light. In the same way, these false apostles were pretending to be apostles of Christ, while in reality they were agents of Satan.

11:14, 15 Satan and his servants can deceive us by appearing to be attractive, good, and moral. Many unsuspecting people follow smooth-talking, Bible-quoting leaders into cults that alienate them from their families and lead them into the practice of immorality and deceit. Don't be fooled by external appearances. Our impressions alone are not an accurate indicator of who is or isn't a true follower of Christ; so it helps to ask these questions: (1) Do the teachings confirm Scripture (Acts 17:11)? (2) Does the teacher affirm and proclaim that Jesus Christ is God, who came into the world as a man to save people from their sins (1 John 4:1-3)? (3) Is the teacher's life-style consistent with biblical morality (Matthew 12:33-37)?

11:22, 23 Paul presented his credentials to counteract the charges that the false teachers were making against him. He felt foolish boasting like this, but his list of credentials would silence any doubts about his authority. Paul wanted to keep the Corinthians from slipping under the spell of the false teachers and turning away from the Good News. Paul also gave a list of his credentials in his letter to the Philippians (see Philippians 3:4-8).

11:23-29 Paul was angry that the false teachers had impressed and deceived the Corinthians (11:13-15). Therefore, he had reestablished his credibility and authority by listing the trials he had endured in his service for Christ. Some of these trials are recorded in the book of Acts (Acts 14:19; 16:22-24). Because Paul wrote this letter during his third missionary journey (Acts 18:23–21:17), his trials weren't over. He would experience yet further difficulties and humiliations for the cause of Christ (see Acts 21:30-33; 22:24-30). Paul was sacrificing his life for the Good News, something the false teachers would never do. The trials and hurts we experience for Christ's sake build our character, demonstrate our faith, and prepare us for further service to the Lord.

11:25 Sea travel was not as safe as it is today. Paul had been shipwrecked three times, and he would face another accident on his voyage to Rome (see Acts 27). By this time, Paul had probably made at least eight or nine voyages.

[28]Then, besides all this, I have the daily burden of how the churches are getting along.
11:29 1 Cor 9:22 [29]Who is weak without my feeling that weakness? Who is led astray, and I do not burn
with anger?
11:30 2 Cor 12:5 [30]If I must boast, I would rather boast about the things that show how weak I am.
11:31 2 Cor 1:23 [31]God, the Father of our Lord Jesus, who is to be praised forever, knows I tell the truth.
[32]When I was in Damascus, the governor under King Aretas kept guards at the city gates
11:32-33 Acts 9:24-25 to catch me. [33]But I was lowered in a basket through a window in the city wall, and that's
how I got away!

Paul's Vision and His Thorn in the Flesh

12:1 Gal 1:12 **12** This boasting is all so foolish, but let me go on. Let me tell about the visions and
revelations I received from the Lord. [2]I* was caught up into the third heaven
fourteen years ago. [3]Whether my body was there or just my spirit, I don't know; only
12:4 Luke 23:43 Rev 2:7 God knows. [4]But I do know that I* was caught up into paradise and heard things so
astounding that they cannot be told. [5]That experience is something worth boasting about,
12:5 2 Cor 11:30 but I am not going to do it. I am going to boast only about my weaknesses. [6]I have plenty
12:6 2 Cor 10:8 to boast about and would be no fool in doing it, because I would be telling the truth. But
I won't do it. I don't want anyone to think more highly of me than what they can actually
12:7 Job 2:6 see in my life and my message, [7]even though I have received wonderful revelations from
God. But to keep me from getting puffed up, I was given a thorn in my flesh, a messenger
from Satan to torment me and keep me from getting proud.
12:8 Matt 26:39, 44 [8]Three different times I begged the Lord to take it away. [9]Each time he said, "My
gracious favor is all you need. My power works best in your weakness." So now I am
12:9 Phil 4:13 glad to boast about my weaknesses, so that the power of Christ may work through me.
12:10 2 Cor 6:4; 13:4 [10]Since I know it is all for Christ's good, I am quite content with my weaknesses and
with insults, hardships, persecutions, and calamities. For when I am weak, then I am
strong.

Paul's Concern for the Corinthians

12:11 2 Cor 11:1, 5 [11]You have made me act like a fool—boasting like this. You ought to be writing
commendations for me, for I am not at all inferior to these "super apostles," even though

12:2 Greek *I know a man in Christ who.* **12:4** Greek *he.*

11:28, 29 Not only did Paul face beatings and dangers, he also carried the daily concern for the young churches, worrying that they were staying true to the Good News and free from false teachings and inner strife. Paul was concerned for individuals in the churches he served. If God has placed you in a position of leadership and authority, treat people with Paul's kind of empathy and concern.

11:32, 33 King Aretas, king of the Nabateans (Edomites) from 9 B.C. to A.D. 40, had appointed a governor to oversee the Nabatean segment of the population in Damascus. Somehow the Jews in Damascus had been able to enlist this governor to help them try to capture Paul (see Acts 9:22-25). Paul gave a "for instance" here, describing his escape from Damascus in a basket lowered from a window in the city wall. Paul recounted this incident to show what he had endured for Christ. The false teachers couldn't make such claims.

12:2, 3 Paul continued his "boasting" by telling about visions and revelations he had received from the Lord. Paul explained that he didn't know if he was taken up in his body or in his spirit, but he had been in paradise ("the third heaven"). This incident cannot be positively identified with a recorded event in Paul's career, although some think this may have been when he was stoned and left for dead (Acts 14:19, 20). Paul told about this incident to show that he had been uniquely touched by God.

12:7, 8 We don't know what Paul's thorn in the flesh was because he doesn't tell us. Some have suggested that it was malaria, epilepsy, or a disease of the eyes (see Galatians 4:13-15). Whatever the case, it was a chronic and debilitating problem, which at times kept him from working. This thorn was a hindrance to his ministry, and he prayed for its removal; but God refused. Paul was a very self-sufficient person, so this thorn must have been difficult for him. It kept Paul humble, reminded him of his need for constant contact with God, and benefited those around him as they saw God at work in his life.

12:9 Although God did not remove Paul's affliction, he promised to demonstrate his power in Paul. The fact that God's power is displayed in our weaknesses should give us courage and hope. As we recognize our limitations, we will depend more on God for our effectiveness rather than on our own energy, effort, or talent. Our limitations not only help develop Christian character but also deepen our worship, because in admitting them, we affirm God's strength.

12:10 When we are strong in abilities or resources, we are tempted to do God's work on our own, and that can lead to pride. When we are weak, allowing God to fill us with *his* power, then we are stronger than we could ever be on our own. God does not intend for us to be weak, passive, or ineffective—life provides enough hindrances and setbacks without us creating them. When those obstacles come, we must depend on God. Only his power will make us effective for him and will help us do work that has lasting value.

12:11-15 Paul was not merely revealing his feelings; he was defending his authority as an apostle of Jesus Christ. Paul was hurt that the church in Corinth doubted and questioned him, so he defended himself for the cause of the Good News, not to satisfy his ego. When you are "put on trial," do you think only about saving your reputation or are you more concerned about what people will think about Christ?

I am nothing at all. [12]When I was with you, I certainly gave you every proof that I am
truly an apostle, sent to you by God himself. For I patiently did many signs and wonders
and miracles among you. [13]The only thing I didn't do, which I do in the other churches,
was to become a burden to you. Please forgive me for this wrong!
[14]Now I am coming to you for the third time, and I will not be a burden to you. I don't
want what you have; I want you. And anyway, little children don't pay for their parents'
food. It's the other way around; parents supply food for their children. [15]I will gladly
spend myself and all I have for your spiritual good, even though it seems that the more
I love you, the less you love me.
[16]Some of you admit I was not a burden to you. But they still think I was sneaky and
took advantage of you by trickery. [17]But how? Did any of the men I sent to you take
advantage of you? [18]When I urged Titus to visit you and sent our other brother with him,
did Titus take advantage of you? No, of course not! For we both have the same Spirit
and walk in each other's steps, doing things the same way.
[19]Perhaps you think we are saying all this just to defend ourselves. That isn't it at all.
We tell you this as Christ's servants, and we know that God is listening. Everything we
do, dear friends, is for your benefit. [20]For I am afraid that when I come to visit you I
won't like what I find, and then you won't like my response. I am afraid that I will find
quarreling, jealousy, outbursts of anger, selfishness, backstabbing, gossip, conceit, and
disorderly behavior. [21]Yes, I am afraid that when I come, God will humble me again
because of you. And I will have to grieve because many of you who sinned earlier have
not repented of your impurity, sexual immorality, and eagerness for lustful pleasure.

Paul's Final Advice

13 This is the third time I am coming to visit you. As the Scriptures say, "The facts
of every case must be established by the testimony of two or three witnesses."* [2]I
have already warned those who had been sinning when I was there on my second visit.
Now I again warn them and all others, just as I did before, that this next time I will not
spare them.
[3]I will give you all the proof you want that Christ speaks through me. Christ is not
weak in his dealings with you; he is a mighty power among you. [4]Although he died on
the cross in weakness, he now lives by the mighty power of God. We, too, are weak, but
we live in him and have God's power—the power we use in dealing with you.
[5]Examine yourselves to see if your faith is really genuine. Test yourselves. If you
cannot tell that Jesus Christ is among you,* it means you have failed the test. [6]I hope you
recognize that we have passed the test and are approved by God.
[7]We pray to God that you will not do anything wrong. We pray this, not to show that
our ministry to you has been successful, but because we want you to do right even if we
ourselves seem to have failed. [8]Our responsibility is never to oppose the truth, but to

12:12 Rom 15:19
12:13 1 Cor 9:12, 18; 2 Cor 11:7
12:14 1 Cor 4:14-15; 2 Cor 13:1
12:15 2 Cor 11:11; Phil 2:17; 1 Thes 2:8
12:16 2 Cor 11:9
12:18 2 Cor 8:6, 16-18
12:19 Rom 9:1
12:20 1 Cor 4:21; 2 Cor 2:1-4
12:21 2 Cor 13:2
13:1 †Deut 19:15; Matt 18:16; 2 Cor 12:14; 1 Tim 5:19
13:2 2 Cor 1:23; 12:21
13:3 Matt 10:20; 1 Cor 5:4
13:4 Rom 1:4; 6:4; Phil 2:7-8; 1 Pet 3:18
13:5 John 14:20; 17:23, 26; Rom 8:10; 1 Cor 11:28; Gal 4:19; Col 1:27
13:8 1 Cor 13:6

13:1 Deut 19:15. **13:5** Or *in you.*

12:13 Paul explained that the only thing he did in the other churches that he didn't do in Corinth was to become a burden—to ask the believers to feed and house him. When he said, "Forgive me for this wrong," he was clearly being sarcastic. He actually did more for the Corinthians than for any other church, but still they misunderstood him.

12:14 Paul had founded the church in Corinth on his first visit there (Acts 18:1). He subsequently made a second visit (2:1). He was planning what would be his third visit (see also 13:1). Paul explained that, as before, he didn't want to be paid, fed, or housed; he only wanted the believers to be nourished with the spiritual food he would feed them.

12:16-19 Although Paul asked nothing of the Corinthian believers, some doubters were still saying that Paul must have been sneaky and made money from them somehow. But Paul again explained that everything he did for the believers was for their edification, not to enrich himself.

12:20, 21 After reading this catalog of sins, it is hard to believe that these are the people that Paul said possessed great gifts and excelled as leaders (8:7). Paul feared that the practices of wicked Corinth had invaded the congregation. He wrote sternly, hoping that they would straighten out their lives before he arrived. We must live differently from unbelievers, not letting secular society dictate how we are to treat others. Don't let culture influence your behavior.

13:2 When Paul arrived the third time in Corinth, he would not be lenient toward unrepentant sinners. His actions could include (1) confronting and publicly denouncing their behavior, (2) exercising church discipline by calling them before the church leaders, or (3) excommunicating them from the church.

13:5 The Corinthians were called to examine and test themselves to see if they really were Christians. Just as we get physical checkups, Paul urges us to give ourselves spiritual checkups. We should look for a growing awareness of Christ's presence and power in our life. Then will we know if we are true Christians or merely impostors. If we're not actively seeking to grow closer to God, we are drawing farther away from him.

13:9 1 Cor 2:3; 4:10
13:10 2 Cor 10:8, 11

stand for the truth at all times. 9We are glad to be weak, if you are really strong. What
we pray for is your restoration to maturity.
10I am writing this to you before I come, hoping that I won't need to deal harshly with
you when I do come. For I want to use the authority the Lord has given me to build you
up, not to tear you down.

Paul's Final Greetings

13:11 Rom 15:33; Phil 4:4
13:12 Rom 16:16; 1 Cor 16:20; 1 Pet 5:14
13:13 Rom 16:20; Phil 2:1

11Dear friends,* I close my letter with these last words: Rejoice. Change your ways.
Encourage each other. Live in harmony and peace. Then the God of love and peace will
be with you.
12Greet each other in Christian love.* All the Christians here send you their greetings.
13May the grace of our Lord Jesus Christ, the love of God, and the fellowship of the
Holy Spirit be with you all.

13:11 Greek *Brothers.* **13:12** Greek *with a sacred kiss.*

13:8, 9 Just as parents want their children to grow into mature adults, so Paul wanted the Corinthians to grow into mature believers. As we share the Good News, our goal should be not merely to see others profess faith or begin attending church but to see them become mature in their faith. Don't set your sights too low.

13:11 Paul's closing words—what he wanted the Corinthians to remember about the needs facing their church—are still fitting for the church today. When these qualities are not present, there are problems that must be dealt with. These traits do not come to a church by glossing over problems, conflicts, and difficulties. They are not produced by neglect, denial, withdrawal, or bitterness. They are the by-products of the extremely hard work of solving problems. Just as Paul and the Corinthians had to hammer out difficulties to bring peace, so we must *apply* the principles of God's Word and not just hear them.

13:14 Paul's farewell blessing invokes all three members of the Trinity: Father (God), Son (Lord Jesus Christ), and Holy Spirit. Although the term *Trinity* is not explicitly used in Scripture, verses such as this one show that it was believed and experienced through knowing God's grace, love, and fellowship. See Luke 1:35—the angel Gabriel's announcement of Jesus' birth to Mary; Matthew 3:17—the Father's voice was heard at the baptism of Jesus; and Matthew 28:19—Jesus' commission to the disciples.

13:14 Paul was dealing with an ongoing problem in the Corinthian church. He could have refused to communicate until they cleared up their situation, but he loved them and reached out to them again with the love of Christ. Love, however, means that sometimes we must confront those we care about. Both authority and personal concern are needed in dealing with people who are ruining their lives with sin. But there are several wrong approaches in confronting others, and these can further break relationships rather than heal them. We can be legalistic and blast people away with the laws they should be obeying. We can turn away from them because we don't want to face the situation. We can isolate them by gossiping about their problem and turning others against them as well. Or, like Paul, we can seek to build relationships by taking a better approach—sharing, communicating, and caring. This is a difficult approach that can drain us emotionally, but it is the best way for other people, and it is the only Christlike way to deal with others' sin.

GALATIANS

VITAL STATISTICS

PURPOSE:
To refute the Judaizers (who taught that Gentile believers must obey the Jewish law in order to be saved), and to call Christians to faith and freedom in Christ

AUTHOR:
Paul

TO WHOM WRITTEN:
The churches in southern Galatia, founded on Paul's first missionary journey (including Iconium, Lystra, Derbe), and Christians everywhere

DATE WRITTEN:
Approximately A.D. 49, from Antioch, prior to the Jerusalem council (A.D. 50)

SETTING:
The most pressing controversy in the early church was the relationship of new believers, particularly Gentiles, to the Jewish laws. This was especially a problem for the converts and for the young churches that Paul had founded on his first missionary journey. Paul wrote to correct this problem. Later, at the council in Jerusalem, the conflict was officially resolved by the church leaders.

KEY VERSE:
"So Christ has really set us free. Now make sure that you stay free, and don't get tied up again in slavery to the law" (5:1).

KEY PEOPLE:
Paul, Peter, Barnabas, Titus, Abraham, false teachers

KEY PLACES:
Galatia, Jerusalem

SPECIAL FEATURES:
This letter is not addressed to any specific body of believers and was probably circulated to several churches in Galatia.

A FAMILY, executing their carefully planned escape at midnight, dashing for the border . . . a man standing outside prison walls, gulping fresh air, awash in the new sun . . . a young woman with every trace of the ravaging drug gone from her system . . . they are FREE! With fresh anticipation, they can begin life anew.

Whether fleeing oppression, stepping out of prison, or breaking a strangling habit, freedom means life. There is nothing so exhilarating as knowing that the past is forgotten and that new options await. People yearn to be free.

The book of Galatians is the charter of Christian freedom. In this profound letter, Paul proclaims the reality of our liberty in Christ—freedom from the law and the power of sin, and freedom to serve our living Lord.

Most of the first converts and early leaders in the church were Jewish Christians who proclaimed Jesus as their Messiah. As Jewish Christians, they struggled with a dual identity: Their Jewishness constrained them to be strict followers of the law; their newfound faith in Christ invited them to celebrate a holy liberty. They wondered how Gentiles (non-Jews) could be part of the Kingdom of Heaven.

This controversy tore the early church. Judaizers—an extremist Jewish faction within the church—taught that Gentile Christians had to submit to Jewish laws and traditions *in addition to* believing in Christ. As a missionary to the Gentiles, Paul had to confront this issue many times.

Galatians was written, therefore, to refute the Judaizers and to call believers back to the pure gospel. The Good News is for all people—Jews and Gentiles alike. Salvation is by God's grace through faith in Christ Jesus *and nothing else.* Faith in Christ means true freedom.

After a brief introduction (1:1–5), Paul addresses those who were accepting the Judaizers' perverted gospel (1:6–9). He summarizes the controversy, including his personal confrontation with Peter and other church leaders (1:10—2:16). He then demonstrates that salvation is by faith alone by alluding to his conversion (2:17–21), appealing to his readers' own experience of the gospel (3:1–5), and showing how the Old Testament teaches about grace (3:6–20). Next, he explains the purpose of God's laws and the relationship between law, God's promises, and Christ (3:21—4:31).

Having laid the foundation, Paul builds his case for Christian liberty. We are saved by faith, not by keeping the law (5:1–12); our freedom means that we are free to love and serve one another, not to do wrong (5:13–26); and Christians should carry each other's burdens and be kind to each other (6:1–10). In 6:11–18, Paul takes the pen into his own hand and shares his final thoughts.

As you read Galatians, try to understand this first-century conflict between grace and law, or faith and deeds, but also be aware of modern parallels. Like Paul, defend the truth of the gospel and reject all those who would add to or twist this truth. You are *free* in Christ—step into the light and celebrate!

THE BLUEPRINT

1. Authenticity of the gospel (1:1—2:21) 2. Superiority of the gospel (3:1—4:31) 3. Freedom of the gospel (5:1—6:18)	In response to attacks from false teachers, Paul wrote to defend his apostleship and the authority of the gospel. The Galatians were beginning to turn from faith to legalism. The struggle between the gospel and legalism is still a relevant issue. Many today would have us return to trying to earn God's favor through following rituals or obeying a set of rules. As Christians, we are not boxed in but set free. To preserve our freedom, we must stay close to Christ and resist any who promote subtle ways for us to earn our salvation.

MEGATHEMES

THEME	EXPLANATION	IMPORTANCE
Law	A group of Jewish teachers insisted that non-Jewish believers must obey Jewish law and traditional rules. They believed a person was saved by following the law of Moses (with emphasis on circumcision, the sign of the covenant), in addition to faith in Christ. Paul opposed them by showing that the law can't save anyone.	We can't be saved by keeping the Old Testament law, even the Ten Commandments. The law served as a guide to point out our need to be forgiven. Christ fulfilled the obligations of the law for us. We must turn to him to be saved. He alone can make us right with God.
Faith	We are saved from God's judgment and penalty for sin by God's gracious gift to us. We receive salvation by faith—trusting in him—not in anything else. Becoming a Christian is in no way based on our initiative, wise choice, or good character. We can be right with God only by believing in him.	Your acceptance with God comes by believing in Christ alone. You must never add to or twist this truth. We are saved by faith, not by the good that we do. Have you placed your whole trust and confidence in Christ? He alone can forgive you and bring you into a relationship with God.
Freedom	Galatians is our charter of Christian freedom. We are not under the jurisdiction of Jewish laws and traditions nor under the authority of Jerusalem. Faith in Christ brings true freedom from sin and from the futile attempt to be right with God by keeping the law.	We are free in Christ, and yet freedom is a privilege. We are not free to disobey Christ or practice immorality, but we are free to serve the risen Christ. Let us use our freedom to love and to serve, not to do wrong.
Holy Spirit	We become Christians through the work of the Holy Spirit. He brings new life; even our faith to believe is a gift from him. The Holy Spirit instructs, guides, leads, and gives us power. He ends our bondage to evil desires, and he creates in us love, joy, peace, and many other wonderful changes.	When the Holy Spirit leads us, he produces his fruit in us. Just as we are saved by faith, not deeds, we also grow by faith. By believing, we can have the Holy Spirit within us, helping us live for Christ. Obey Christ by following the Holy Spirit's leading.

1. Authenticity of the gospel

Greetings from Paul

1 This letter is from Paul, an apostle. I was not appointed by any group or by human
authority. My call is from Jesus Christ himself and from God the Father, who raised
Jesus from the dead.
2All the Christians* here join me in sending greetings to the churches of Galatia.
3May grace and peace be yours from God our Father and from the Lord Jesus Christ.
4He died for our sins, just as God our Father planned, in order to rescue us from this evil
world in which we live. 5That is why all glory belongs to God through all the ages of
eternity. Amen.

1:2 Greek *brothers.*

1:1 Acts 20:24
1:3 Rom 1:7; Phil 1:2; Phlm 1:3
1:4 Rom 4:25; Gal 2:20; 1 Tim 2:6; Titus 2:14
1:5 Rom 11:36

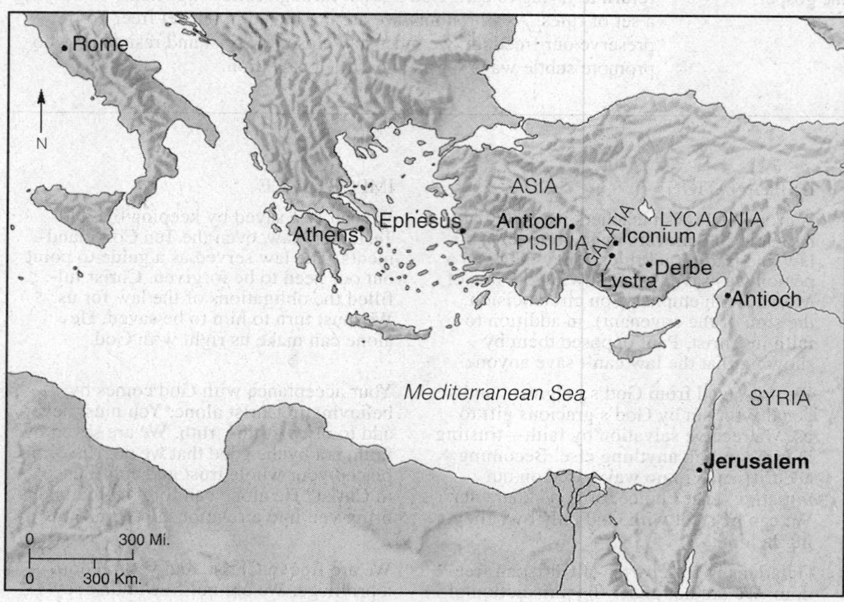

CITIES IN GALATIA
Paul visited several cities in Galatia on each of his three missionary journeys. On his first journey he went through Antioch in Pisidia, Iconium, Lystra, and Derbe, and then retraced his steps; on his second journey he went by land from Antioch of Syria through the four cities in Galatia; on his third journey he also went through those cities on the main route to Ephesus.

1:1 Paul and Barnabas had just completed their first missionary journey (Acts 13:2–14:28). They had visited Iconium, Lystra, and Derbe, cities in the Roman province of Galatia (present-day Turkey). Upon returning to Antioch, Paul was accused by some Jewish Christians of diluting Christianity to make it more appealing to Gentiles. These Jewish Christians disagreed with Paul's statements that Gentiles did not have to follow many of the religious laws that the Jews had obeyed for centuries. Some of Paul's accusers had even followed him to those Galatian cities and had told the Gentile converts they had to be circumcised and follow all the Jewish laws and customs in order to be saved. According to these people, Gentiles had to first become Jews in order to become Christians.

In response to this threat, Paul wrote this letter to the Galatian churches. In it, he explains that following the Old Testament laws, or the Jewish laws, will not bring salvation. A person is saved by grace through faith. Paul wrote this letter about A.D. 49, shortly before the meeting of the Jerusalem council, which settled the law-versus-grace controversy (Acts 15).

1:1 Paul was called to be an apostle by Jesus Christ and God the Father. He presented his credentials at the very outset of this letter because some people in Galatia were questioning his authority.

1:1 For more information about Paul's life, see his Profile in Acts 9. Paul had been a Christian for about 15 years at this time.

1:2 In Paul's time, Galatia was the Roman province located in the center section of present-day Turkey. Much of the region rests on a large and fertile plateau, and large numbers of people had moved to the region because of its favorable agriculture. One of Paul's goals during his missionary journeys was to visit regions with large population centers in order to reach as many people as possible.

1:3-5 God's plan all along was to save us by Jesus' death. We have been rescued from the power of this present evil world—a world ruled by Satan and full of cruelty, tragedy, temptation, and deception. Being rescued from this evil world doesn't mean that we are taken out of it but that we are no longer enslaved to it. You were saved to live for God. Does your life reflect your gratitude for being rescued? Have you transferred your loyalty from this world to Christ?

There Is Only One Good News

1:6 2 Cor 11:4 · **1:7** Acts 15:1, 24; Gal 5:10 · **1:8** 2 Cor 11:14

[6]I am shocked that you are turning away so soon from God, who in his love and mercy
called you to share the eternal life he gives through Christ. You are already following
a different way [7]that pretends to be the Good News but is not the Good News at all.
You are being fooled by those who twist and change the truth concerning Christ.
[8]Let God's curse fall on anyone, including myself, who preaches any other message
than the one we told you about. Even if an angel comes from heaven and preaches any

THE MARKS OF THE TRUE GOSPEL AND OF FALSE GOSPELS

Marks of a false gospel		*Marks of the true gospel*	
2:21	Treats Christ's death as meaningless	1:11, 12	Teaches that the source of the gospel is God
3:12	Says people must obey the law in order to be saved	2:20	Knows that life is obtained through death; we trust in the God who loved us and died for us so that we might die to sin and live for him
4:10	Tries to find favor with God by observing certain rituals	3:14	Explains that all believers have the Holy Spirit through faith
5:4	Counts on keeping laws to erase sin	3:21, 22	Declares that we cannot be saved by keeping laws; the only way of salvation is through faith in Christ, which is available to all
		3:26–28	Says that all believers are one in Christ, so there is no basis for discrimination of any kind
		5:24, 25	Proclaims that we are free from the grip of sin and that the Holy Spirit's power fills and guides us

1:6 Some people were preaching "a different way." They were teaching that to be saved, Gentile believers had to follow Jewish laws and customs, especially the rite of circumcision. Faith in Christ was not enough. This message undermined the truth that salvation is a gift, not a reward for certain deeds. Jesus Christ has made this gift available to all people, not just to Jews. Beware of people who say that we need more than simple faith in Christ to be saved. When people set up additional requirements for salvation, they deny the power of Christ's death on the cross (see 3:1-5).

1:7 The Bible says there is only one way to be forgiven of sin: by believing in Jesus Christ as Savior and Lord. No other person, method, or ritual can give eternal life. Attempting to be open-minded and tolerant, some people assert that all religions are equally valid paths to God. In a free society, people have the right to their religious opinions, but this doesn't guarantee that their ideas are right. God does not accept man-made religion as a substitute for faith in Jesus Christ. He has provided just one way—Jesus Christ (John 14:6).

1:7 Those who had confused the Galatian believers and perverted the Good News were zealous Jewish Christians who believed that the Old Testament practices, such as circumcision and dietary restrictions, were required of all believers. Because these teachers wanted to turn the Gentile Christians into Jews, they were called "Judaizers." Some time after the letter to the Galatians was sent, Paul met with the apostles in Jerusalem to discuss this matter further (see Acts 15).

1:7 Most of the Galatian Christians were Greeks who were unfamiliar with Jewish laws and customs. The Judaizers were an extreme faction of Jewish Christians. Both groups believed in Christ, but their life-styles differed considerably. We do not know why the Judaizers may have traveled no small distance to teach their mistaken notions to the new Gentile converts. They may have been motivated by (1) a sincere wish to integrate Judaism with the new Christian faith, (2) a sincere love for their Jewish heritage, or (3) a jealous desire to destroy Paul's authority. Whether or not these Judaizers were sincere, their teaching threatened these new churches and had to be countered. When Paul said that their teaching twisted and changed the Good News, he was not rejecting everything Jewish. He himself was a Jew who worshiped in the Temple and attended the religious festivals. But he was concerned that *nothing* get in the way of the simple truth of his message—that salvation, for Jews and Gentiles alike, is through faith in Jesus Christ alone.

1:7 A twisting of the truth is more difficult to spot than an outright lie. The Judaizers were twisting the truth about Christ. They claimed to follow him, but they denied that Jesus' work on the cross was sufficient for salvation. There will always be people who twist the Good News. Either they do not understand what the Bible teaches, or they are uncomfortable with the truth as it stands. How can we tell when people are twisting the truth? Before accepting the teachings of any group, find out what the group teaches about Jesus Christ. If their teaching does not match the truth in God's Word, then it is twisted.

1:8, 9 Paul strongly denounced the Judaizers' twisting of the Good News of Christ. He said that even if an angel from heaven came preaching another message, that angel should be "forever cursed." If an angel came preaching another message, he would not be from heaven, no matter how he looked. In 2 Corinthians 11:14, 15, Paul warned that Satan disguises himself as an angel of light. Here he invoked a curse on any angel who spreads a false teaching—a fitting response to an emissary of hell. Paul extended that curse to include himself if he should twist the Good News. His message must never change, for the truth of the Good News never changes. Paul used strong language because he was dealing with a life-and-death issue.

other message, let him be forever cursed. [9]I will say it again: If anyone preaches any
other gospel than the one you welcomed, let God's curse fall upon that person.
[10]Obviously, I'm not trying to be a people pleaser! No, I am trying to please God. If
I were still trying to please people, I would not be Christ's servant.

Paul's Message Comes from Christ

[11]Dear friends,* I solemnly assure you that the Good News of salvation which I preach
is not based on mere human reasoning or logic. [12]For my message came by a direct
revelation from Jesus Christ himself. No one else taught me.

[13]You know what I was like when I followed the Jewish religion—how I violently
persecuted the Christians.* I did my best to get rid of them. [14]I was one of the most
religious Jews of my own age, and I tried as hard as possible to follow all the old
traditions of my religion.

[15]But then something happened! For it pleased God in his kindness to choose me and
call me, even before I was born! What undeserved mercy! [16]Then he revealed his Son
to me* so that I could proclaim the Good News about Jesus to the Gentiles. When all this
happened to me, I did not rush out to consult with anyone else; [17]nor did I go up to
Jerusalem to consult with those who were apostles before I was. No, I went away into
Arabia and later returned to the city of Damascus. [18]It was not until three years later that
I finally went to Jerusalem for a visit with Peter* and stayed there with him for fifteen
days. [19]And the only other apostle I met at that time was James, our Lord's brother. [20]You
must believe what I am saying, for I declare before God that I am not lying. [21]Then after
this visit, I went north into the provinces of Syria and Cilicia. [22]And still the Christians
in the churches in Judea didn't know me personally. [23]All they knew was that people

1:9 Deut 4:2; 12:32; 1 Cor 16:22; Rev 22:18
1:10 1 Thes 2:4
1:12 1 Cor 2:10; Gal 1:1, 15-16; Eph 3:3
1:13 Acts 8:3; 9:21; 22:4-5; 26:4-11
1:14 Acts 22:3
1:15 Acts 9:15
1:16 Rom 1:17; 8:3, 10; Gal 2:9, 20; Col 1:27
1:18 Acts 9:22-23, 26-27
1:19 Matt 13:55; Acts 15:13; Gal 2:9, 12
1:20 Acts 9:30
1:21 Acts 15:2

1:11 Greek *Brothers.* **1:13** Greek *the church of God.* **1:16** Or *in me.* **1:18** Greek *Cephas.*

1:10 Do you spend your life trying to please everybody? Paul had to speak harshly to the Christians in Galatia because they were in serious danger. He did not apologize for his straightforward words, knowing that he could not serve Christ faithfully if he allowed the Galatian Christians to remain on the wrong track. Whose approval are you seeking—others' or God's? Pray for the courage to seek God's approval above anyone else's.

1:11ff Why should the Galatians have listened to Paul instead of the Judaizers? Paul answered this implicit question by furnishing his credentials: His message was received directly from Christ (1:12); he had been an exemplary Jew (1:13, 14); he had had a special conversion experience (1:15, 16; see also Acts 9:1-9); he had been confirmed and accepted in his ministry by the other apostles (1:18, 19; 2:1-9). Paul also presented his credentials to the Corinthian and Philippian churches (2 Corinthians 11–12; Philippians 3:4-9).

1:12 We do not know the details of this revelation. Paul is referring to something other than his experience on the road to Damascus. His point is that his words are more than his own speculations or ideas.

1:13, 14 Paul had been one of the most religious Jews of his day, scrupulously keeping the law and relentlessly persecuting Christians (see Acts 9:1, 2). Before his conversion Paul had been even more zealous for the law than the Judaizers. He had surpassed his contemporaries in religious knowledge and practice. Paul had been sincere in his zeal—but wrong. When he met Jesus Christ, his life changed. He then directed all his energies toward building up the Christian church.

1:14 To be fully Jewish, a person must have descended from Abraham. In addition, a faithful Jew adhered to the Jewish laws and traditions. Gentiles (1:16) are non-Jews, whether in nationality or religion. In Paul's day, Jews thought of all Gentiles as pagans. Jews avoided Gentiles, believing that contact with Gentiles brought spiritual corruption. Although Gentiles could become Jews in religion by undergoing circumcision and by following Jewish laws and customs, they were never fully accepted.

Many Jews had difficulty understanding that God's message is for Jews and Gentiles alike. Some Jews thought that Gentiles had to become Jews before they could become Christians. But God planned to save both Jews and Gentiles. He had revealed this plan through Old Testament prophets (see, for example, Genesis 12:3; Isaiah 42:6; 66:19), and he had fulfilled it through Jesus Christ; he was proclaiming it to the Gentiles through Paul.

1:15, 16 Because God was guiding his ministry, Paul wasn't doing anything that God hadn't already planned and given him power to do. Similarly, God appointed Jeremiah to be his spokesman even before Jeremiah was born (Jeremiah 1:5). God knows you intimately as well, and he chose you to be his even before you were born (see Psalm 139). He wants you to draw close to him and to fulfill the purpose he has for your life.

1:15-24 Paul tells of his conversion to show that his message came directly from God. God commissioned him to preach the Good News to the Gentiles. After his call, Paul did not consult with anyone; instead, he spent three years in Arabia. Then he spoke with Peter and James, but he had no other contact with Jewish Christians for several more years. During those years, Paul preached to the Gentiles the message God had given him. His message did not come from human insight; it came from God.

1:18 This was Paul's first visit to Jerusalem as a Christian, as recorded in Acts 9:26-30.

1:21 Because of opposition in Jerusalem (see Acts 9:29, 30), Paul had gone to Syria and Cilicia. In those remote areas, he had no opportunity to receive instruction from the apostles.

1:23 Acts 9:20 were saying, "The one who used to persecute us now preaches the very faith he tried to
destroy!" 24And they gave glory to God because of me.

The Apostles Accept Paul

2:1 Acts 15:2 **2** Then fourteen years later I went back to Jerusalem again, this time with Barnabas;
and Titus came along, too. 2I went there because God revealed to me that I should
2:2 Gal 1:6 go. While I was there I talked privately with the leaders of the church. I wanted them to
understand what I had been preaching to the Gentiles. I wanted to make sure they did not
2:3 Acts 16:3 disagree, or my ministry would have been useless. 3And they did agree. They did not
even demand that my companion Titus be circumcised, though he was a Gentile.*

2:3 Greek *a Greek.*

JUDAIZERS VERSUS PAUL

What the Judaizers said about Paul	*Paul's defense*
They said he was perverting the truth.	He received his message from Christ himself (1:11, 12).
They said he was a traitor to the Jewish faith.	Paul was one of the most dedicated Jews of his time. Yet, in the midst of one of his most zealous acts, God transformed him through a revelation of the Good News about Jesus (1:13–16; Acts 9:1–30).
They said he compromised and watered down his message for the Gentiles.	The other apostles declared that the message Paul preached was the true gospel (2:1–10).
They said he was disregarding the law of Moses.	Far from degrading the law, Paul puts the law in its proper place. He says it shows people where they have sinned, and it points them to Christ (3:19–29).

As the debate raged between the Gentile Christians and the Judaizers, Paul found it necessary to write to the churches in Galatia. The Judaizers were trying to undermine Paul's authority, and they taught a false gospel. In reply, Paul defended his authority as an apostle and the truth of his message. The debate over Jewish laws and Gentile Christians was officially resolved at the Jerusalem council (Acts 15), yet it continued to be a point of contention after that time.

1:24 Paul's changed life had brought praise from those who saw him or heard about him. His new life had astonished them. They had praised God because only God could have turned this zealous persecutor of Christians into a Christian himself. We may not have had as dramatic a change as Paul, but still our new life should honor God in every way. When people look at you, do they recognize that God has made changes in you? If not, perhaps you are not living as you should.

2:1 Paul was converted around A.D. 35. The 14 years he mentions are probably calculated from the time of his conversion. Therefore, this trip to Jerusalem was not his first. Most likely, he made his first trip to Jerusalem around A.D. 38 (see Acts 9:26-30), and other trips to Jerusalem in approximately A.D. 44 (Acts 11:29, 30; Galatians 2:1-10), A.D. 49/50 (Acts 15), A.D. 52 (Acts 18:22), and A.D. 57 (Acts 21:15ff). Paul probably visited Jerusalem on several other occasions as well.

2:1 Barnabas and Titus were two of Paul's close friends. Barnabas and Paul visited Galatia together on their first missionary journey. Paul wrote a personal letter to Titus, a faithful believer and church leader serving on the island of Crete (see the book of Titus). For more information on Barnabas, see his Profile in Acts 13. For more information on Titus, see the letter Paul wrote to him in the New Testament.

2:1 After his conversion, Paul spent many years preparing for the ministry to which God had called him. This preparation period included time alone with God (1:16, 17), as well as time conferring with other Christians. Often new Christians, in their zeal, want to begin a full-time ministry without investing the necessary time studying the Bible and learning from qualified teachers. We need not wait to share Christ with our friends, but we may need more preparation before embarking on a special ministry, whether volunteer or paid. While we wait for God's timing, we should continue to study, learn, and grow.

2:2 God told Paul, through a revelation, to confer with the church leaders in Jerusalem about the message he was preaching to the Gentiles, so they would understand and approve of what he was doing. The essence of Paul's message to both Jews and Gentiles was that God's salvation is offered to all people regardless of race, sex, nationality, wealth, social standing, educational level, or anything else. Anyone can be forgiven by trusting in Christ (see Romans 10:8-13).

2:2, 3 Even though God had specifically sent him to the Gentiles (Acts 9:15, 16), Paul needed to discuss his message with the leaders of the Jerusalem church (Acts 15). This meeting prevented a major split in the church, and it formally acknowledged the apostles' approval of Paul's preaching. Sometimes we avoid conferring with others because we fear that problems or arguments may develop. Instead, we should openly discuss our plans and actions with friends, counselors, and advisers. Good communication helps everyone understand the situation better, it reduces gossip, and it builds unity in the church.

2:3-5 When Paul took Titus, a Greek Christian, to Jerusalem, the Judaizers ("false" Christians) said that Titus should be circumcised. Paul adamantly refused to give in to their demands. The apostles agreed that circumcision was an unnecessary rite for Gentile converts. Several years later, Paul circumcised Timothy, another Greek Christian (Acts 16:3). Unlike Titus, however, Timothy was half Jewish. Paul did not deny Jews the right to be circumcised; he was simply saying that Gentiles should not be asked to become Jews before becoming Christians.

4 Even that question wouldn't have come up except for some so-called Christians
there—false ones, really*—who came to spy on us and see our freedom in Christ Jesus.
They wanted to force us, like slaves, to follow their Jewish regulations. 5 But we refused
to listen to them for a single moment. We wanted to preserve the truth of the Good News
for you.
6 And the leaders of the church who were there had nothing to add to what I was
preaching. (By the way, their reputation as great leaders made no difference to me, for God
has no favorites.) 7 They saw that God had given me the responsibility of preaching the
Good News to the Gentiles, just as he had given Peter the responsibility of preaching to
the Jews. 8 For the same God who worked through Peter for the benefit of the Jews worked
through me for the benefit of the Gentiles. 9 In fact, James, Peter,* and John, who were
known as pillars of the church, recognized the gift God had given me, and they accepted
Barnabas and me as their co-workers. They encouraged us to keep preaching to the
Gentiles, while they continued their work with the Jews. 10 The only thing they suggested
was that we remember to help the poor, and I have certainly been eager to do that.

Paul Confronts Peter

11 But when Peter came to Antioch, I had to oppose him publicly, speaking strongly
against what he was doing, for it was very wrong. 12 When he first arrived, he ate with
the Gentile Christians, who don't bother with circumcision. But afterward, when some
Jewish friends of James came, Peter wouldn't eat with the Gentiles anymore because he
was afraid of what these legalists would say. 13 Then the other Jewish Christians followed
Peter's hypocrisy, and even Barnabas was influenced to join them in their hypocrisy.

2:4 Gal 1:7; 5:1, 13
2:5 Gal 1:6; 2:14
2:6 Deut 10:17; Acts 10:34; Rom 2:11; 2 Cor 12:11
2:7 Acts 9:15; 22:21; 1 Thes 2:4
2:8 Acts 1:25
2:9 Rom 1:5
2:10 Acts 11:29-30; 24:17
2:12 Acts 11:2-3

2:4 Greek *some false brothers.* **2:9** Greek *Cephas;* also in 2:11, 14.

2:4 These false Christians were most likely from the party of the Pharisees (Acts 15:5). These were the strictest religious leaders of Judaism, some of whom had been converted. We don't know if these were representatives of well-meaning converts or of those trying to pervert Christianity. Most commentators agree that neither Peter nor James had any part in this conspiracy.

2:5 We normally think of taking a stand against those who might lead us into immoral behavior, but Paul had to take a hard line against the most "moral" of people. We must not give in to those who make the keeping of man-made standards a condition for salvation, even when such people are morally upright or in respected positions.

2:6 It's easy to rate people on the basis of their official status and to be intimidated by powerful people. But Paul was not intimidated by these "great leaders" because all believers are equal in Christ. We should show respect for our spiritual leaders, but our ultimate allegiance must be to Christ. We are to serve him with our whole being. God doesn't rate us according to our status; he looks at the attitude of our hearts (1 Samuel 16:7).

2:7-9 The church leaders ("pillars")—James, Peter, and John—realized that God was using Paul to reach the Gentiles, just as Peter was being used so greatly to reach the Jews. After hearing Paul's message, they gave Paul and Barnabas their approval to continue working among the Gentiles.

2:10 The apostles were referring to the poor of Jerusalem. While many Gentile converts were financially comfortable, the Jerusalem church had suffered from the effects of a severe famine in Palestine (see Acts 11:28-30) and was struggling. So on his journeys, Paul had gathered funds for the Jewish Christians (Acts 24:17; Romans 15:25-29; 1 Corinthians 16:1-4; 2 Corinthians 8). The need for believers to care for the poor is a constant theme in Scripture. But often we do nothing, caught up in meeting our own needs and desires. Perhaps we don't see enough poverty to remember the needs of the poor. The world is filled with poor people, here and in other countries. What can you do to help?

2:11 Antioch of Syria (distinguished from Antioch of Pisidia) was a major trade center in the ancient world. Heavily populated by Greeks, it eventually became a strong Christian center. In Antioch the believers were first called Christians (Acts 11:26). Antioch of Syria became the headquarters for the Gentile church and was Paul's base of operations.

2:11ff The Judaizers accused Paul of watering down the Good News to make it easier for Gentiles to accept, while Paul accused the Judaizers of nullifying the truth of the Good News by adding conditions to it. The basis of salvation was the issue: Is salvation through Christ alone, or does it come through Christ *and* adherence to the law? The argument came to a climax when Peter, Paul, the Judaizers, and some Gentile Christians all gathered together in Antioch to share a meal. Peter probably thought that by staying away from the Gentiles, he was promoting harmony—he did not want to offend James and the Jewish Christians. James had a very prominent position and presided over the Jerusalem council (Acts 15). But Paul charged that Peter's action violated the Good News. By joining the Judaizers, Peter implicitly was supporting their claim that Christ was not sufficient for salvation. Compromise is an important element in getting along with others, but we should never compromise the truth of God's Word. If we feel we have to change our Christian beliefs to match those of our companions, we are on dangerous ground.

2:11, 12 Although Peter was a leader of the church, he was acting like a hypocrite. He knew better, yet he was driven by fear of what James and the others would think. Proverbs 29:25 says, "Fearing people is a dangerous trap." Paul knew that he had to confront Peter before his actions damaged the church. So, Paul publicly opposed Peter. Note, however, that Paul did not go to the other leaders, nor did he write letters to the churches telling them not to follow Peter's example. Instead, he opposed Peter face to face. Sometimes sincere Christians, even Christian leaders, make mistakes. And it may take other sincere Christians to get them back on track. If you are convinced that someone is doing harm to himself/herself or the church, try the direct approach. There is no place for backstabbing in the body of Christ.

2:14 Acts 10:28
2:15 Phil 3:4-5
2:16 Acts 15:10-11; Rom 1:17; 3:20, 28; 8:3; Gal 3:11; Eph 2:8
2:19 Rom 6:10-14; 7:4; 2 Cor 5:15
2:20 Rom 6:6; 8:37; Gal 1:4; 1 Tim 2:6; Titus 2:14
2:21 Gal 3:27

14 When I saw that they were not following the truth of the Good News, I said to Peter
in front of all the others, "Since you, a Jew by birth, have discarded the Jewish laws and
are living like a Gentile, why are you trying to make these Gentiles obey the Jewish laws
you abandoned? 15 You and I are Jews by birth, not 'sinners' like the Gentiles. 16 And yet
we Jewish Christians know that we become right with God, not by doing what the law
commands, but by faith in Jesus Christ. So we have believed in Christ Jesus, that we
might be accepted by God because of our faith in Christ—and not because we have
obeyed the law. For no one will ever be saved by obeying the law."*
17 But what if we seek to be made right with God through faith in Christ and then find
out that we are still sinners? Has Christ led us into sin? Of course not! 18 Rather, I make
myself guilty if I rebuild the old system I already tore down. 19 For when I tried to keep
the law, I realized I could never earn God's approval. So I died to the law so that I might
live for God. I have been crucified with Christ. 20 I myself no longer live, but Christ lives
in me. So I live my life in this earthly body by trusting in the Son of God, who loved me
and gave himself for me. 21 I am not one of those who treats the grace of God as
meaningless. For if we could be saved by keeping the law, then there was no need for
Christ to die.

2. Superiority of the gospel

The Law and Faith in Christ

3:1 1 Cor 1:23; Gal 5:7
3:2 Rom 10:17
3:3 Gal 4:9
3:4 2 Jn 1:8

3 Oh, foolish Galatians! What magician has cast an evil spell on you? For you used to
see the meaning of Jesus Christ's death as clearly as though I had shown you a
signboard with a picture of Christ dying on the cross. 2 Let me ask you this one question:
Did you receive the Holy Spirit by keeping the law? Of course not, for the Holy Spirit
came upon you only after you believed the message you heard about Christ. 3 Have you
lost your senses? After starting your Christian lives in the Spirit, why are you now trying
to become perfect by your own human effort? 4 You have suffered so much for the Good
News. Surely it was not in vain, was it? Are you now going to just throw it all away?

2:16 Some translators hold that the quotation extends through verse 14; others through verse 16; and still others through verse 21.

2:15, 16 If observing the Jewish laws cannot justify us, why should we still obey the Ten Commandments and other Old Testament laws? We know that Paul was not saying the law is bad, because in another letter he wrote, "The law itself is holy and right and good" (Romans 7:12). Instead, he is saying that the law can never make us acceptable to God. The law still has an important role to play in the life of a Christian. The law (1) guards us from sin by giving us standards for behavior; (2) convicts us of sin, leaving us the opportunity to ask for God's forgiveness; and (3) drives us to trust in the sufficiency of Christ, because we can never keep the Ten Commandments perfectly. The law cannot possibly save us. But after we become Christians, it can guide us to live as God requires.

2:17-19 Through studying the Old Testament Scriptures, Paul realized that he could not be saved by obeying God's laws. The prophets knew that God's plan of salvation did not rest on keeping the law (see the chart in chapter 4 for references). Because we have all been infected by sin, we cannot keep God's laws perfectly. Fortunately, God has provided a way of salvation that depends on Jesus Christ, not on our own efforts. Even though we know this truth, we must guard against the temptation of using service, good deeds, charitable giving, or any other effort as a substitute for faith.

2:19, 20 How have we been crucified with Christ? *Legally,* God looks at us as if we had died with Christ. Because our sins died with him, we are no longer condemned (Colossians 2:13-15). *Relationally,* we have become one with Christ, and his experiences are ours. Our Christian life began when, in unity with him, we died to our old life (see Romans 6:5-11). *In our daily life,* we must regularly crucify sinful desires that keep us from following Christ. This, too, is a kind of dying with him (Luke 9:23-25).

And yet the focus of Christianity is not dying but living. Because we have been crucified with Christ, we have also been raised with him (Romans 6:5). *Legally,* we have been reconciled with God (2 Corinthians 5:19) and are free to grow into Christ's likeness (Romans 8:29). And *in our daily life,* we have Christ's resurrection power as we continue to fight sin (Ephesians 1:19, 20). We are no longer alone, for Christ lives in us—he is our power for living and our hope for the future (Colossians 1:27).

2:21 Believers today may still be in danger of acting as if Christ died for nothing. How? By replacing Jewish legalism with their own brand of Christian legalism, they are giving people extra laws to obey. By believing they can earn God's favor by what they do, they are not trusting completely in Christ's work on the cross. By struggling to appropriate God's power to change them (sanctification), they are not resting in God's power to save them (justification). If we could be saved by being good, then Christ would not have had to die. But the cross is the only way to salvation.

3:1 The Galatian believers had become fascinated by the false teachers' arguments, almost as though they had been bewitched. Magic was common in Paul's day (Acts 8:9-11; 13:6, 7). Magicians used both optical illusions and Satan's power to perform miracles, and people were drawn into the magicians' mysterious rites without recognizing their dangerous source.

3:2, 3 Some of the believers in Galatia may have been in Jerusalem at Pentecost and received the Holy Spirit there. They knew that they hadn't received God's Spirit by obeying the Jewish laws. Paul stressed that just as they began their Christian lives in the power of the Spirit, so they should grow by the Spirit's power. The Galatians had taken a step backward when they had decided to insist on keeping the Jewish laws. We must realize that we grow spiritually because of God's work in us by his Spirit, not by following special rules.

5 I ask you again, does God give you the Holy Spirit and work miracles among you
because you obey the law of Moses? Of course not! It is because you believe the message
you heard about Christ.
6 In the same way, "Abraham believed God, so God declared him righteous because of
his faith."* 7 The real children of Abraham, then, are all those who put their faith in God.
8 What's more, the Scriptures looked forward to this time when God would accept the
Gentiles, too, on the basis of their faith. God promised this good news to Abraham long
ago when he said, "All nations will be blessed through you."* 9 And so it is: All who put
their faith in Christ share the same blessing Abraham received because of his faith.
10 But those who depend on the law to make them right with God are under his curse,
for the Scriptures say, "Cursed is everyone who does not observe and obey all these
commands that are written in God's Book of the Law."* 11 Consequently, it is clear that no
one can ever be right with God by trying to keep the law. For the Scriptures say, "It is
through faith that a righteous person has life."* 12 How different from this way of faith is
the way of law, which says, "If you wish to find life by obeying the law, you must obey
all of its commands."* 13 But Christ has rescued us from the curse pronounced by the law.
When he was hung on the cross, he took upon himself the curse for our wrongdoing. For
it is written in the Scriptures, "Cursed is everyone who is hung on a tree."* 14 Through the
work of Christ Jesus, God has blessed the Gentiles with the same blessing he promised to
Abraham, and we Christians receive the promised Holy Spirit through faith.

The Law and God's Promises

15 Dear friends,* here's an example from everyday life. Just as no one can set aside or amend
an irrevocable agreement, so it is in this case. 16 God gave the promise to Abraham and his
child.* And notice that it doesn't say the promise was to his children,* as if it meant many
descendants. But the promise was to his child—and that, of course, means Christ. 17 This is
what I am trying to say: The agreement God made with Abraham could not be canceled 430
years later when God gave the law to Moses. God would be breaking his promise. 18 For if

3:5 1 Cor 12:10
3:6 †Gen 15:6; Rom 4:3
3:8 †Gen 12:3; Acts 3:25
3:10 †Deut 27:26; Jer 11:3
3:11 †Hab 2:4; Rom 1:17; Heb 10:38
3:12 †Lev 18:5; Rom 10:5
3:13 †Deut 21:23; Gal 4:5
3:14 Joel 2:28; Acts 2:33
3:15 Heb 9:17
3:16 †Gen 12:7; 13:15; 17:7; 24:7
3:17 Exod 12:40
3:18 Rom 4:14; 11:6

3:6 Gen 15:6. **3:8** Gen 12:3; 18:18; 22:18. **3:10** Deut 27:26. **3:11** Hab 2:4. **3:12** Lev 18:5. **3:13** Deut 21:23. **3:15** Greek *Brothers.* **3:16a** Greek *seed;* also in 3:16c, 19. See Gen 12:7. **3:16b** Greek *seeds.*

3:5 The Galatians knew that they had received the Holy Spirit when they believed, not when they obeyed the law. People still feel insecure in their faith because faith alone seems too easy. People still try to get closer to God by following rules. While certain disciplines (Bible study, prayer) and service may help us grow, they must not take the place of the Holy Spirit in us or become ends in themselves. By asking these questions, Paul hoped to get the Galatians to focus again on Christ as the foundation of their faith.

3:5 The Holy Spirit gives Christians great power to live for God. Some Christians want more than this. They want to live in a state of perpetual excitement. The tedium of everyday living leads them to conclude that something is wrong spiritually. Often the Holy Spirit's greatest work is teaching us to persist, to keep on doing what is right even when it no longer seems interesting or exciting. The Galatians quickly turned from Paul's Good News to the teachings of the newest teachers in town; what they needed was the Holy Spirit's gift of persistence. If the Christian life seems ordinary, you may need the Spirit to stir you up. Every day offers a challenge to live for Christ.

3:6-9 The main argument of the Judaizers was that Gentiles had to become Jews in order to become Christians. Paul exposed the flaw in this argument by showing that real children of Abraham are those who have faith, not those who keep the law. Abraham himself was saved by his faith (Genesis 15:6). All believers in every age and from every nation share Abraham's blessing. This is a comforting promise, a great heritage for us, and a solid foundation for living.

3:10 Paul quoted Deuteronomy 27:26 to prove that, contrary to what the Judaizers claimed, the law cannot justify and save—it can only condemn. Breaking even one commandment brings a person under condemnation. And because everyone has broken the commandments, everyone stands condemned. The law can do nothing to reverse the condemnation (Romans 3:20-24). But Christ took the curse of the law upon himself when he hung on the cross. He did this so we wouldn't have to bear our own punishment. The only condition is that we accept Christ's death on our behalf as the means to be saved (Colossians 1:20-23).

3:11 Trying to be right with God by our own effort doesn't work. Good intentions such as "I'll do better next time" or "I'll never do that again" usually end in failure. Paul points to Habakkuk's declaration (Habakkuk 2:4) that by trusting God—believing in his provision for our sins and living each day in his power—we can break this cycle of failure.

3:17 God kept his promise to Abraham (Genesis 17:7, 8)—he has not revoked it, though thousands of years have passed. He saved Abraham through his faith, and he blessed the world through Abraham by sending the Messiah as one of Abraham's descendants. Circumstances may change, but God remains constant and does not break his promises. He has promised to forgive our sins through Jesus Christ, and we can be sure that he will do so.

3:18, 19 The law has two functions. On the positive side, it reveals the nature and will of God and shows people how to live. On the negative side, it points out people's sins and shows them that it is impossible to please God by trying to obey all his laws completely. God's promise to Abraham dealt with Abraham's faith; the law focuses on actions. The covenant with Abraham shows that faith is the only way to be saved; the law shows how to obey God in grateful response. Faith does not annul the law; but the more we know God, the more we see how sinful we are. Then we are driven to depend on our faith in Christ alone for our salvation.

the inheritance could be received only by keeping the law, then it would not be the result of
accepting God's promise. But God gave it to Abraham as a promise.
19 Well then, why was the law given? It was given to show people how guilty they are.
But this system of law was to last only until the coming of the child to whom God's
promise was made. And there is this further difference. God gave his laws to angels to
give to Moses, who was the mediator between God and the people. 20 Now a mediator is
needed if two people enter into an agreement, but God acted on his own when he made
his promise to Abraham.
21 Well then, is there a conflict between God's law and God's promises? Absolutely
not! If the law could have given us new life, we could have been made right with God
by obeying it. 22 But the Scriptures have declared that we are all prisoners of sin, so the
only way to receive God's promise is to believe in Jesus Christ.
23 Until faith in Christ was shown to us as the way of becoming right with God, we
were guarded by the law. We were kept in protective custody, so to speak, until we could
put our faith in the coming Savior.

God's Children through Faith

24 Let me put it another way. The law was our guardian and teacher to lead us until Christ
came. So now, through faith in Christ, we are made right with God. 25 But now that faith
in Christ has come, we no longer need the law as our guardian. 26 So you are all children
of God through faith in Christ Jesus. 27 And all who have been united with Christ in
baptism have been made like him. 28 There is no longer Jew or Gentile,* slave or free,

3:19 Exod 20:19; Deut 5:5; Acts 7:53; Heb 2:2
3:20 1 Tim 2:5
3:21 Rom 8:2-4
3:22 Rom 3:11-19; 11:32
3:24 Rom 10:4
3:27 Rom 6:3; 13:14
3:28 John 10:16; 17:21; 1 Cor 12:13; Eph 2:14-15; Col 3:11

3:28 Greek *Jew or Greek.*

WHAT IS THE LAW?
Part of the Jewish law included those laws found in the Old Testament. When Paul says that non-Jews (Gentiles) are no longer bound by these laws, he is not saying that the Old Testament laws do not apply to us today. He is saying certain types of laws may not apply to us. In the Old Testament there were three categories of laws:

Ceremonial law	This kind of law relates specifically to Israel's worship (see, for example, Leviticus 1:1–13). Its primary purpose was to point forward to Jesus Christ. Therefore, these laws were no longer necessary after Jesus' death and resurrection. While we are no longer bound by ceremonial laws, the principles behind them—to worship and love a holy God—still apply. The Jewish Christians often accused the Gentile Christians of violating the ceremonial law.
Civil law	This type of law dictated Israel's daily living (see Deuteronomy 24:10, 11, for example). Because modern society and culture are so radically different, some of these guidelines cannot be followed specifically. But the principles behind the commands should guide our conduct. At times, Paul asked Gentile Christians to follow some of these laws, not because they had to, but in order to promote unity.
Moral law	This sort of law is the direct command of God—for example, the Ten Commandments (Exodus 20:1–17). It requires strict obedience. It reveals the nature and will of God, and it still applies to us today. We are to obey this moral law, not to obtain salvation, but to live in ways pleasing to God.

3:19, 20 When God gave his promise to Abraham, he did it by himself alone, without angels or Moses as mediators. Although it is not mentioned in Exodus, Jews believed that the Ten Commandments had been given to Moses by angels (Stephen referred to this in his speech, see Acts 7:38, 53). Paul was showing the superiority of salvation and growth by faith over trying to be saved by keeping the Jewish laws. Christ is the best and only way given by God for us to come to him (1 Timothy 2:5).

3:21, 22 Before faith in Christ delivered us, we were imprisoned by sin, beaten down by past mistakes, and choked by desires that we knew were wrong. God knew we were sin's prisoners, but he provided a way of escape—faith in Jesus Christ. Without Christ, everyone is held in sin's grasp, and only those who place their faith in Christ ever get out of it. Look to Christ—he is reaching out to set you free.

3:24, 25 The picture of the law as a guardian is similar to a tutor giving a young child supervision. We no longer need that kind of supervision. The law teaches us the *need* for salvation; God's grace *gives* us that salvation. The Old Testament still applies today. In it, God reveals his nature, his will for humanity, his moral laws, and his guidelines for living. But we cannot be saved by keeping that law; we must trust in Christ.

3:28 Some Jewish males greeted each new day by praying, "Lord, I thank you that I am not a Gentile, a slave, or a woman." The role of women was enhanced by Christianity. Faith in Christ transcends these differences and makes all believers one in Christ. Make sure you do not impose distinctions that Christ has removed. Because all believers are his heirs, no one is more privileged than or superior to anyone else.

3:28 It's our natural inclination to feel uncomfortable around people who are different from us and to gravitate toward those who are similar to us. But when we allow our differences to separate us from our fellow believers, we are disregarding clear biblical teaching. Make a point to seek out and appreciate people who are not just like you and your friends. You may find that you have a lot in common with them.

male or female. For you are all Christians—you are one in Christ Jesus. [29]And now that
you belong to Christ, you are the true children of Abraham. You are his heirs, and now
all the promises God gave to him belong to you.

4 Think of it this way. If a father dies and leaves great wealth for his young children,
those children are not much better off than slaves until they grow up, even though
they actually own everything their father had. [2]They have to obey their guardians until
they reach whatever age their father set.
[3]And that's the way it was with us before Christ came. We were slaves to the spiritual
powers of this world. [4]But when the right time came, God sent his Son, born of a woman,
subject to the law. [5]God sent him to buy freedom for us who were slaves to the law, so
that he could adopt us as his very own children. [6]And because you Gentiles have become
his children, God has sent the Spirit of his Son into your hearts, and now you can call
God your dear Father.* [7]Now you are no longer a slave but God's own child. And since
you are his child, everything he has belongs to you.

Paul's Concern for the Galatians

[8]Before you Gentiles knew God, you were slaves to so-called gods that do not even exist.
[9]And now that you have found God (or should I say, now that God has found you), why do
you want to go back again and become slaves once more to the weak and useless spiritual
powers of this world? [10]You are trying to find favor with God by what you do or don't do
on certain days or months or seasons or years. [11]I fear for you. I am afraid that all my hard
work for you was worth nothing. [12]Dear friends,* I plead with you to live as I do in freedom
from these things, for I have become like you Gentiles were—free from the law.
You did not mistreat me when I first preached to you. [13]Surely you remember that I
was sick when I first brought you the Good News of Christ. [14]But even though my
sickness was revolting to you, you did not reject me and turn me away. No, you took me
in and cared for me as though I were an angel from God or even Christ Jesus himself.
[15]Where is that joyful spirit we felt together then? In those days, I know you would
gladly have taken out your own eyes and given them to me if it had been possible. [16]Have
I now become your enemy because I am telling you the truth?

3:29 Rom 8:17; Gal 3:16
4:3 Gal 3:23; Col 2:8, 20
4:4 Mark 1:15; John 1:14; Eph 1:10; Heb 2:14
4:5 Rom 8:15; Eph 1:5
4:6 Rom 8:15-16
4:7 Rom 8:17
4:8 2 Chr 13:9; Isa 37:19; Jer 2:11; 1 Cor 8:4-6; 1 Thes 1:9
4:9 Col 2:20
4:10 Rom 14:5; Col 2:16
4:13 1 Cor 2:3
4:14 Matt 10:40
4:16 Amos 5:10

4:6 Greek *into your hearts, crying, "Abba, Father." Abba* is an Aramaic term for "Father." **4:12** Greek *brothers;* also in 4:31.

3:29 The original promise to Abraham was intended for the whole world, not just for Abraham's descendants (see Genesis 12:3). All believers participate in this promise and are blessed as children of Abraham.

4:3-7 Paul uses the illustration of slavery to show that before Christ came and died for sins, people were in bondage to the law. Thinking they could be saved by it, they became enslaved to trying—and failing—to keep it. But we who were once slaves are now God's very own children who have an intimate relationship with him. Because of Christ, there is no reason to be afraid of God. We can come boldly into his presence, knowing that he will welcome us as his family members.

4:4 "When the right time came," God sent Jesus to earth to die for our sins. For centuries the Jews had been wondering when their Messiah would come—but God's timing was perfect. We may sometimes wonder if God will ever respond to our prayers. But we must never doubt him or give up hope. At the right time he will respond. Are you waiting for God's timing? Trust his judgment and trust that he has your best interests in mind.

4:4, 5 Jesus was born of a woman—he was human. He was born as a Jew—he was subject to God's law and fulfilled it perfectly. Thus, Jesus was the perfect sacrifice because, although he was fully human, he never sinned. His death bought freedom for us who were enslaved to sin so that we could be adopted into God's family.

4:5-7 Under Roman law, an adopted child was guaranteed all legal rights to his father's property, even if he was formerly a slave. He was not a second-class son; he was equal to all other sons, biological or adopted, in his father's family. As adopted children of God, we share with Jesus all rights to God's resources. As God's heirs, we can claim what he has provided for us—our full identity as his children (see Romans 8:15-17).

4:13, 14 Paul's illness was a sickness that he was enduring while he visited the Galatian churches. The world is often callous to people's pain and misery. Paul commended the Galatians for not scorning him, even though his condition was a trial to them (he didn't explain what was wrong with him). Such caring was what Jesus meant when he called us to serve the homeless, hungry, sick, and imprisoned as if they were Jesus himself (Matthew 25:34-40). Do you avoid those in pain or those facing difficulty—or are you willing to care for them as if they were Jesus Christ himself?

4:15 Have you lost your joy? Paul sensed that the Galatians had lost the joy of their salvation because of legalism. Legalism can take away joy because (1) it makes people feel guilty rather than loved; (2) it produces self-hatred rather than humility; (3) it stresses performance over relationship; (4) it points out how far short we fall rather than how far we've come because of what Christ did for us. If you feel guilty and inadequate, check your focus. Are you living by faith in Christ or by trying to live up to the demands and expectations of others?

4:16 Paul did not gain great popularity when he rebuked the Galatians for turning away from their first faith in Christ. Human nature hasn't changed much—we still get angry when we're scolded. But don't write off someone who challenges you. There may be truth in what he or she says. Receive his or her words with humility; carefully think them over. If you discover that you need to change an attitude or action, take steps to do it.

4:17 Gal 2:4, 12
4:19 Eph 4:13

[17] Those false teachers who are so anxious to win your favor are not doing it for your
good. They are trying to shut you off from me so that you will pay more attention to
them. [18] Now it's wonderful if you are eager to do good, and especially when I am not
with you. [19] But oh, my dear children! I feel as if I am going through labor pains for you
again, and they will continue until Christ is fully developed in your lives. [20] How I wish

THREE DISTORTIONS OF CHRISTIANITY
Almost from the beginning there were forces at work within Christianity that would have destroyed or sidetracked the movement. Of these, three created many problems then and have continued to reappear in other forms even today. The three aberrations are contrasted to true Christianity.

Group	*Their definition of a Christian*	*Their genuine concern*	*The danger*	*Application question*
Judaized Christianity	Christians are Jews who have recognized Jesus as the promised Savior. Therefore, any Gentile desiring to become a Christian must first become a Jew.	Having a high regard for the Scriptures and God's choice of Jews as his people, they did not want to see God's commands overlooked or broken.	Tends to add human traditions and standards to God's law. Also subtracts from the Scriptures God's clear concern for all nations.	Do you appreciate God's choice of a unique people through whom he offered forgiveness and eternal life to all peoples?
Legalized Christianity	Christians are those who live by a long list of "don'ts." God's favor is earned by good behavior.	Recognized that real change brought about by God should lead to changes in behavior.	Tends to make God's love something to earn rather than to accept freely. Would reduce Christianity to a set of impossible rules and transform the Good News into bad news.	As important as change in action is, can you see that God may be desiring different changes in you than in others?
Lawless Christianity	Christians live above the law. They need no guidelines. God's Word is not as important as our personal sense of God's guidance.	Recognized that forgiveness from God cannot be based on our ability to live up to his perfect standards. It must be received by faith as a gift made possible by Christ's death on the cross.	Forgets that Christians are still human and fail consistently when trying to live only by what they "feel" God wants.	Do you recognize the ongoing need for God's expressed commands as you live out your gratitude for his great salvation?
True Christianity	Christians are those who believe inwardly and outwardly that Jesus' death has allowed God to offer them forgiveness and eternal life as a gift. They have accepted that gift through faith and are seeking to live a life of obedient gratitude for what God has done for them.	Christianity is both private and public, with heart-belief and mouth-confession. Our relationship to God and the power he provides result in obedience. Having received the gift of forgiveness and eternal life, we are now daily challenged to live that life with his help.	Avoids the above dangers.	How would those closest to you describe your Christianity? Do they think you live *so* that God will accept you, or do they know that you live *because* God has accepted you in Christ?

4:17 The false teachers claimed to be religious authorities and experts in Judaism and Christianity. Appealing to the believers' desire to do what was right, they drew quite a following. Paul said, however, that they were wrong and that their motives were selfish. False teachers are often respectable and persuasive. That is why all teachings should be checked against the Bible.

4:19 Paul led many people to Christ and helped them mature spiritually. Perhaps one reason for his success as a spiritual father was the deep concern he felt for his spiritual children; he compared his pain over their faithlessness to the pain of childbirth. We should have the same intense care for those to whom we are spiritual parents. When you lead people to Christ, remember to stand by them to help them grow.

I were there with you right now, so that I could be more gentle with you. But at this
distance I frankly don't know what else to do.

Abraham's Two Children

21 Listen to me, you who want to live under the law. Do you know what the law really
says? 22 The Scriptures say that Abraham had two sons, one from his slave-wife and one **4:22**
from his freeborn wife.* 23 The son of the slave-wife was born in a human attempt to Gen 16:15; 21:2
bring about the fulfillment of God's promise. But the son of the freeborn wife was born **4:23**
as God's own fulfillment of his promise. Rom 9:7-9

24 Now these two women serve as an illustration of God's two covenants. Hagar, the **4:24** Deut 32:2-4
slave-wife, represents Mount Sinai where people first became enslaved to the law. 25 And
now Jerusalem is just like Mount Sinai in Arabia, because she and her children live in **4:26**
slavery. 26 But Sarah, the free woman, represents the heavenly Jerusalem. And she is our Heb 12:22 Rev 3:12; 21:2, 10
mother. 27 That is what Isaiah meant when he prophesied, **4:27** †Isa 54:1

"Rejoice, O childless woman!
Break forth into loud and joyful song,
even though you never gave birth to a child.
For the woman who could bear no children
now has more than all the other women!"*

28 And you, dear brothers and sisters, are children of the promise, just like Isaac. 29 And **4:28** Gal 3:29
we who are born of the Holy Spirit are persecuted by those who want us to keep the law, **4:29**
just as Isaac, the child of promise, was persecuted by Ishmael, the son of the slave-wife. Gen 21:9

30 But what do the Scriptures say about that? "Get rid of the slave and her son, for the **4:30**
son of the slave woman will not share the family inheritance with the free woman's †Gen 21:10
son."* 31 So, dear friends, we are not children of the slave woman, obligated to the law. John 8:35 **4:31**
We are children of the free woman, acceptable to God because of our faith. Gal 3:29

3. Freedom of the gospel

Freedom in Christ

5 So Christ has really set us free. Now make sure that you stay free, and don't get tied **5:1** John 8:32, 36
up again in slavery to the law. Acts 15:10 Gal 2:4

2 Listen! I, Paul, tell you this: If you are counting on circumcision to make you right
with God, then Christ cannot help you. 3 I'll say it again. If you are trying to find favor **5:2** Acts 15:1
with God by being circumcised, you must obey all of the regulations in the whole law of **5:3**
Moses. 4 For if you are trying to make yourselves right with God by keeping the law, you Gal 3:10
have been cut off from Christ! You have fallen away from God's grace.

5 But we who live by the Spirit eagerly wait to receive everything promised to us who **5:5** Rom 8:23-24

4:22 See Gen 16:15; 21:2-3. **4:27** Isa 54:1. **4:30** Gen 21:10.

4:21ff People are saved because of their faith in Christ, not because of what they do. Paul contrasted those who are enslaved to the law (represented by Hagar, the slave-wife) with those who are free from the law (represented by Sarah, the free woman). Hagar's abuse of Sarah (Genesis 16:4) was like the persecution that the Gentile Christians were getting from the Judaizers, who insisted on keeping the law in order to be saved. Eventually Sarah triumphed because God kept his promise to give her a son, just as those who worship Christ in faith will also triumph.

4:24 Paul explained that what happened to Sarah and Hagar is an allegory or picture of the relationship between God and people. Paul was using a type of argument that was common in his day and that was probably being used against him by his opponents.

5:1 Christ died to set us free from sin and from a long list of laws and regulations. Christ came to set us free—not free to do whatever we want because that would lead us back into slavery to our selfish desires. Rather, thanks to Christ, we are now free and able to do what was impossible before—to live unselfishly. Those who appeal to their freedom so that they can have their own way or indulge their own desires are falling back into sin. But it is also wrong to put a burden of lawkeeping on Christians. We must stand against those who would enslave us with rules, methods, or special conditions for being saved or growing in Christ.

5:2-4 Trying to be saved by keeping the law and being saved by grace are two entirely different approaches. "Christ cannot help you" means that Christ's provision for our salvation will not help us if we are trying to save ourselves. Obeying the law does not make it any easier for God to save us. All we can do is accept his gracious gift through faith. Our deeds of service must never be used to try to earn God's love or favor.

5:3, 4 Circumcision was a symbol of having the right background and doing everything required by religion. No amount of work, discipline, or moral behavior can save us. If a person were counting on finding favor with God by being circumcised, he would also have to obey the rest of God's law completely. Trying to save ourselves by keeping all God's laws only separates us from God.

5:6 1 Cor 7:19; 1 Thes 1:3
5:7 1 Cor 9:24
5:8 Rom 8:28
5:9 1 Cor 5:6
5:10 Gal 1:7
5:11 1 Cor 1:23
5:13 1 Pet 2:16
5:14 †Lev 19:18; Rom 13:9

are right with God through faith. 6 For when we place our faith in Christ Jesus, it makes
no difference to God whether we are circumcised or not circumcised. What is important
is faith expressing itself in love.

7 You were getting along so well. Who has interfered with you to hold you back from
following the truth? 8 It certainly isn't God, for he is the one who called you to freedom.
9 But it takes only one wrong person among you to infect all the others—a little yeast
spreads quickly through the whole batch of dough! 10 I am trusting the Lord to bring you
back to believing as I do about these things. God will judge that person, whoever it is,
who has been troubling and confusing you.

11 Dear friends,* if I were still preaching that you must be circumcised—as some say I
do—why would the Jews persecute me? The fact that I am still being persecuted proves that
I am still preaching salvation through the cross of Christ alone. 12 I only wish that those
troublemakers who want to mutilate you by circumcision would mutilate themselves.*

13 For you, dear friends, have been called to live in freedom—not freedom to satisfy
your sinful nature, but freedom to serve one another in love. 14 For the whole law can be
summed up in this one command: "Love your neighbor as yourself."* 15 But if instead
of showing love among yourselves you are always biting and devouring one another,
watch out! Beware of destroying one another.

5:11 Greek *brothers;* also in 5:13. **5:12** Or *castrate themselves;* Greek reads *cut themselves off.* **5:14** Lev 19:18.

VICES AND VIRTUES

The Bible mentions many specific actions and attitudes that are either right or wrong. Look at the list included here. Are there a number of characteristics from the wrong column that are influencing you?

VICES *(Neglecting God and others)*	*VIRTUES* *(The by-products of living for God)*
Sexual immorality *(Galatians 5:19)*	Love *(Galatians 5:22)*
Impure thoughts *(Galatians 5:19)*	Joy *(Galatians 5:22)*
Lust *(Colossians 3:5)*	Peace *(Galatians 5:22)*
Hostility *(Galatians 5:20)*	Patience *(Galatians 5:22)*
Quarreling *(Galatians 5:20)*	Kindness *(Galatians 5:22)*
Jealousy *(Galatians 5:20)*	Goodness *(Galatians 5:22)*
Anger *(Galatians 5:20)*	Faithfulness *(Galatians 5:22)*
Selfish ambition *(Galatians 5:20)*	Gentleness *(Galatians 5:23)*
Divisions *(Galatians 5:20)*	Self-control *(Galatians 5:23)*
Conceit *(2 Corinthians 12:20; Galatians 5:20)*	
Envy *(Galatians 5:21)*	
Murder *(Revelation 22:12–16)*	
Idolatry *(Galatians 5:20; Ephesians 5:5)*	
Demonic activities *(Galatians 5:20)*	
Drunkenness *(Galatians 5:21)*	
Wild living *(Luke 15:13; Galatians 5:21)*	
Cheating *(1 Corinthians 6:8)*	
Adultery *(1 Corinthians 6:9, 10)*	
Homosexuality *(1 Corinthians 6:9, 10)*	
Greed *(1 Corinthians 6:9, 10; Ephesians 5:5)*	
Stealing *(1 Corinthians 6:9, 10)*	
Lying *(Revelation 22:12–16)*	

5:6 We are saved by faith, not by deeds. But love for others and for God is the response of those whom God has forgiven. God's forgiveness is complete, and Jesus said that those who are forgiven much love much (Luke 7:47). Because faith expresses itself through love, you can check your love for others as a way to monitor your faith.

5:9 A little yeast causes a whole lump of dough to rise. It only takes one wrong person to infect all the others.

5:11 Persecution proved that Paul was preaching the true Good News. If he had taught what the false teachers were teaching, no one would be offended. But because he was teaching the truth, he was persecuted by both Jews and Judaizers. Have friends or loved ones rejected you because you have taken a stand for Christ? Jesus said not to be surprised if the world hates you, because it hated him (John 15:18, 19). Just as Paul continued to faithfully proclaim the message about Christ, you should continue doing the ministry God has given you—in spite of the obstacles others may put in your way.

5:13 Paul distinguishes between freedom to sin and freedom to serve. Freedom or license to sin is no freedom at all, because it enslaves you to Satan, others, or your own sinful nature. Christians, by contrast, should not be slaves to sin, because they are free to do right and to glorify God through loving service to others.

5:14, 15 When we are not motivated by love, we become critical of others. We stop looking for good in them and see only their faults. Soon the unity of believers is broken. Have you talked behind someone's back? Have you focused on others' shortcomings instead of their strengths? Remind yourself of Jesus' command to love others as you love yourself (Matthew 22:39). When you begin to feel critical of someone, make a list of that person's positive qualities. If there are problems that need to be addressed, it is better to confront in love than to gossip.

Living by the Spirit's Power

16So I advise you to live according to your new life in the Holy Spirit. Then you won't (5:16 Rom 8:4-6)
be doing what your sinful nature craves. 17The old sinful nature loves to do evil, which
is just opposite from what the Holy Spirit wants. And the Spirit gives us desires that are (5:17 Rom 7:15-23)
opposite from what the sinful nature desires. These two forces are constantly fighting
each other, and your choices are never free from this conflict. 18But when you are (5:18 Rom 6:14; 8:14)
directed by the Holy Spirit, you are no longer subject to the law.
19When you follow the desires of your sinful nature, your lives will produce these evil (5:19-21 Rom 13:12-13; 1 Cor 6:9-10; Eph 5:5; Rev 22:15)
results: sexual immorality, impure thoughts, eagerness for lustful pleasure, 20idolatry,
participation in demonic activities, hostility, quarreling, jealousy, outbursts of anger,
selfish ambition, divisions, the feeling that everyone is wrong except those in your own
little group, 21envy, drunkenness, wild parties, and other kinds of sin. Let me tell you
again, as I have before, that anyone living that sort of life will not inherit the Kingdom
of God.
22But when the Holy Spirit controls our lives, he will produce this kind of fruit in us: (5:22 Eph 5:9)
love, joy, peace, patience, kindness, goodness, faithfulness, 23gentleness, and self-con- (5:24 Rom 6:6; Col 3:5)
trol. Here there is no conflict with the law.
24Those who belong to Christ Jesus have nailed the passions and desires of their sinful
nature to his cross and crucified them there. 25If we are living now by the Holy Spirit, (5:25 Rom 8:4; Gal 5:16)
let us follow the Holy Spirit's leading in every part of our lives. 26Let us not become
conceited, or irritate one another, or be jealous of one another. (5:26 Phil 2:3)

We Reap What We Sow

6 Dear friends, if a Christian* is overcome by some sin, you who are godly should (6:1 1 Cor 2:15; Jas 5:19; 1 Jn 5:16)
gently and humbly help that person back onto the right path. And be careful not to
fall into the same temptation yourself. 2Share each other's troubles and problems, and (6:2 Rom 15:1)

6:1 Greek *Brothers, if a man.*

5:16-18 If your desire is to have the qualities listed in 5:22, 23, then you know that the Holy Spirit is leading you. At the same time, be careful not to confuse your subjective feelings with the Spirit's leading. Being led by the Holy Spirit involves the desire to hear, the readiness to obey God's Word, and the sensitivity to discern between your feelings and his promptings. Live each day controlled and guided by the Holy Spirit. Then the words of Christ will be in your mind, the love of Christ will be behind your actions, and the power of Christ will help you control your selfish desires.

5:17 Paul describes the two forces fighting within us—the Holy Spirit and the sinful nature (our evil desires or inclinations that stem from our body; see also 5:16, 19, 24). Paul is not saying that these forces are equal—the Holy Spirit is infinitely stronger. But if we rely on our own wisdom, we will make wrong choices. If we try to follow the Spirit by our own human effort, we will fail. Our only way to freedom from our evil desires is through the empowering of the Holy Spirit (see Romans 8:9; Ephesians 4:23, 24; Colossians 3:3-8).

5:19-21 We all have evil desires, and we can't ignore them. In order for us to follow the Holy Spirit's guidance, we must deal with them decisively (crucify them—5:24). These desires include obvious sins, such as sexual immorality and demonic activities. They also include less obvious sins, such as hostility, jealousy, and selfish ambition. Those who ignore such sins or refuse to deal with them reveal that they have not received the gift of the Spirit that leads to a transformed life.

5:22, 23 The fruit of the Spirit is the spontaneous work of the Holy Spirit in us. The Spirit produces these character traits that are found in the nature of Christ. They are the by-products of Christ's control—we can't obtain them by *trying* to get them without his help. If we want the fruit of the Spirit to grow in us, we must join our life to his (see John 15:4, 5). We must know him, love him, remember him, and imitate him. As a result, we will fulfill the intended purpose of the law—to love God and our neighbors. Which of these qualities do you want the Spirit to produce in you?

5:23 Because the God who sent the law also sent the Spirit, the by-products of the Spirit-filled life are in perfect harmony with the intent of God's law. A person who exhibits the fruit of the Spirit fulfills the law far better than a person who observes the rituals but has little love in his or her heart.

5:24 In order to accept Christ as Savior, we need to turn from our sins and willingly nail our sinful nature to the cross. This doesn't mean, however, that we will never see traces of its evil desires again. As Christians we still have the capacity to sin, but we have been set free from sin's power over us and no longer have to give in to it. We must daily commit our sinful tendencies to God's control, daily crucify them, and moment by moment draw on the Spirit's power to overcome them (see 2:20; 6:14).

5:25 God is interested in every part of our life, not just the spiritual part. As we live by the Holy Spirit's power, we need to submit every aspect of our life to God: emotional, physical, social, intellectual, vocational. Paul says that because we're saved, we should live like it! The Holy Spirit is the source of your new life, so keep in step with his leading. Don't let anything or anyone else determine your values and standards in any area of your life.

5:26 Everyone needs a certain amount of approval from others. But those who go out of their way to secure honors or to win popularity with a lot of people become conceited and show they are not following the Holy Spirit's leading. Those who look to God for approval won't need to envy others. Because we are God's sons and daughters, we have his Holy Spirit as the loving guarantee of his approval.

6:1-3 No Christian should ever think that he or she is totally independent and doesn't need help from others, and no one should feel excused from the task of helping others. The body of Christ—the church—functions only when the members work together for the common good. Do you know someone who needs help? Is there a Christian brother or sister who needs correction or encouragement? Humbly and gently reach out to that person (John 13:34, 35).

6:3 Rom 12:3; 1 Cor 3:18 · **6:4** 2 Cor 13:5 · **6:6** 1 Cor 9:11, 14 · **6:7** 1 Cor 6:9; 2 Cor 9:6 · **6:8** Job 4:8; Rom 8:13 · **6:9** 2 Thes 3:13 · **6:10** Eph 2:19

in this way obey the law of Christ. [3]If you think you are too important to help someone
in need, you are only fooling yourself. You are really a nobody.
[4]Be sure to do what you should, for then you will enjoy the personal satisfaction of
having done your work well, and you won't need to compare yourself to anyone else.
[5]For we are each responsible for our own conduct.
[6]Those who are taught the word of God should help their teachers by paying them.
[7]Don't be misled. Remember that you can't ignore God and get away with it. You will
always reap what you sow! [8]Those who live only to satisfy their own sinful desires will
harvest the consequences of decay and death. But those who live to please the Spirit
will harvest everlasting life from the Spirit. [9]So don't get tired of doing what is good.
Don't get discouraged and give up, for we will reap a harvest of blessing at the
appropriate time. [10]Whenever we have the opportunity, we should do good to everyone,
especially to our Christian brothers and sisters.

Paul's Final Advice

6:11 1 Cor 16:21 · **6:13** Rom 2:25 · **6:14** Rom 6:2, 6; 1 Cor 2:2; Gal 2:20

[11]Notice what large letters I use as I write these closing words in my own handwriting.
[12]Those who are trying to force you to be circumcised are doing it for just one reason.
They don't want to be persecuted for teaching that the cross of Christ alone can save.
[13]And even those who advocate circumcision don't really keep the whole law. They
only want you to be circumcised so they can brag about it and claim you as their
disciples.
[14]As for me, God forbid that I should boast about anything except the cross of our
Lord Jesus Christ. Because of that cross,* my interest in this world died long ago, and

6:14 Or *Because of him.*

OUR WRONG DESIRES VERSUS THE FRUIT OF THE SPIRIT
The will of the Holy Spirit is in constant opposition to our sinful desires. The two are on opposite sides of the spiritual battle.

Our wrong desires are	*The fruit of the Spirit is*
Evil	Good
Destructive	Productive
Easy to ignite	Difficult to ignite
Difficult to stifle	Easy to stifle
Self-centered	Self-giving
Oppressive and possessive	Liberating and nurturing
Decadent	Uplifting
Sinful	Holy
Deadly	Abundant life

6:4 When you do your very best, you feel good about the results. There is no need to compare yourself with others. People make comparisons for many reasons. Some point out others' flaws in order to feel better about themselves. Others simply want reassurance that they are doing well. When you are tempted to compare, look at Jesus Christ. His example will inspire you to do your very best, and his loving acceptance will comfort you when you fall short of your expectations.

6:6 Paul says that students should take care of the material needs of their teachers (1 Corinthians 9:7-12). It is easy to receive the benefit of good Bible teaching and then to take our spiritual leaders for granted, ignoring their financial and physical needs. We should care for our teachers, not grudgingly or reluctantly, but with a generous spirit, showing honor and appreciation for all they have done (1 Timothy 5:17, 18).

6:7, 8 It would certainly be a surprise if you planted corn and pumpkins came up. It's a natural law to reap what we sow. It's true in other areas, too. If you gossip about your friends, you will lose their friendship. Every action has results. If you plant to please your own desires, you'll reap a crop of sorrow and evil. If you plant to please God, you'll reap joy and everlasting life. What kind of seeds are you sowing?

6:9, 10 It is discouraging to continue to do right and receive no word of thanks or see no tangible results. But Paul challenged the Galatians, and he challenges us to keep on doing good and to trust God for the results. In due time, we will reap a harvest of blessing.

6:11 Up to this point, Paul had probably dictated the letter to a secretary. Here he takes the pen into his own hand to write his final, personal greetings. Paul did this in other letters as well, to add emphasis to his words and to validate that the letter was genuine.

6:13 Some of the Judaizers were emphasizing circumcision as proof of holiness—but ignoring the other Jewish laws. People often choose a certain principle or prohibition and make it the measure of faith. Some may abhor drunkenness but ignore gluttony. Others may despise promiscuity but tolerate prejudice. The Bible in its entirety is our rule of faith and practice. We cannot pick and choose the mandates we will follow.

6:14 The world is full of enticements. Daily we are confronted with subtle cultural pressures and overt propaganda. The only way to escape these destructive influences is to ask God to help crucify our interest in them, just as Paul did. How much do the interests of this world matter to you? (See 2:20 and 5:24 for more on this concept.)

the world's interest in me is also long dead. [15]It doesn't make any difference now
whether we have been circumcised or not. What counts is whether we really have been
changed into new and different people. [16]May God's mercy and peace be upon all those
who live by this principle. They are the new people of God.*
[17]From now on, don't let anyone trouble me with these things. For I bear on my body
the scars that show I belong to Jesus.
[18]My dear Christian friends,* may the grace of our Lord Jesus Christ be with you all.
Amen.

6:15 1 Cor 7:19 2 Cor 5:17 Gal 5:6
6:17 2 Cor 1:5; 4:10
6:18 Rom 16:20 2 Tim 4:22

6:16 Greek *the Israel of God.* **6:18** Greek *Brothers.*

6:15 It is easy to get caught up with the externals. Beware of those who emphasize actions that we should or shouldn't do, with no concern for the inward condition of the heart. Living a good life without an inward change leads to a shallow or empty spiritual walk. What matters to God is that we be completely changed from the inside out (2 Corinthians 5:17).

6:18 Paul's letter to the Galatians boldly declares the freedom of the Christian. Doubtless these early Christians in Galatia wanted to grow in the Christian life, but they were being misled by those who said this could be done only by keeping certain Jewish laws.

How strange it would be for a prisoner who had been set free to walk back into his or her cell and refuse to leave! How strange for an animal, released from a trap, to go back inside it! How sad for a believer to be freed from the bondage of sin, only to return to rigid conformity to a set of rules and regulations!

If you believe in Jesus Christ, you have been set free. Instead of going back into some form of slavery, whether to legalism or to sin, use your freedom to live for Christ and serve him as he desires.

EPHESIANS

OUR churches come in all styles and shapes—secret meetings in homes; wide-open gatherings in amphitheaters; worship services packing thousands into a sanctuary while an overflow crowd watches on closed-circuit television; handfuls who kneel in urban storefronts. Buildings will vary, but the church is not confined to four walls. The church of Jesus Christ is *people,* his people, of every race and nation, who love Christ and are committed to serving him.

The "church age" began at Pentecost (Acts 2). Born in Jerusalem, the church spread rapidly through the ministry of the apostles and the early believers. Fanned by persecution, the gospel flame then spread to other cities and nations. On three courageous journeys, Paul and his associates established local assemblies in scores of Gentile cities.

One of the most prominent of those churches was at Ephesus. It was established in A.D. 53 on Paul's homeward journey to Jerusalem. But Paul returned a year later, on his third missionary trip, and stayed there for three years, preaching and teaching with great effectiveness (Acts 19:1–20). At another time, Paul met with the Ephesian elders, and he sent Timothy to serve as their leader (1 Timothy 1:3). Just a few years later, Paul was sent as a prisoner to Rome. In Rome, he was visited by messengers from various churches, including Tychicus of Ephesus. Paul wrote this letter to the church and sent it with Tychicus. Not written to counteract heresy or to confront any specific problem, Ephesians is a letter of encouragement. In it Paul describes the nature and appearance of the church, and he challenges believers to function as the living body of Christ on earth.

After a warm greeting (1:1, 2), Paul affirms the nature of the church—the glorious fact that believers in Christ have been showered with God's kindness (1:3–8), chosen for greatness (1:9–12), marked with the Holy Spirit (1:13, 14), filled with the Spirit's power (1:15–23), freed from sin's curse and bondage (2:1–10), and brought near to God (2:11–18). As part of God's "household," we stand with the prophets, apostles, Jews, Gentiles, and Christ himself (2:19—3:13). Then, as though overcome with emotion by remembering all that God has done, Paul challenges the Ephesians to live close to Christ, and he breaks into spontaneous praise (3:14–21).

Paul then turns his attention to the implications of being in the body of Christ, the church. Believers should have unity in their commitment to Christ and their use of spiritual gifts (4:1–16). They should have the highest moral standards (4:17—6:9). For the individual, this means rejecting pagan practices (4:17—5:20), and for the family, this means mutual submission and love (5:21—6:9).

Paul then reminds them that the church is in a constant battle with the forces of darkness and that they should use every spiritual weapon at their disposal (6:10–17). He concludes by asking for their prayers, commissioning Tychicus, and giving a benediction (6:18–24).

As you read this masterful description of the church, thank God for the diversity and unity in his family, pray for your brothers and sisters across the world, and draw close to those in your local church.

VITAL STATISTICS

PURPOSE:
To strengthen the believers in Ephesus in their Christian faith by explaining the nature and purpose of the church, the body of Christ

AUTHOR:
Paul

TO WHOM WRITTEN:
The church at Ephesus, and all believers everywhere

DATE WRITTEN:
Approximately A.D. 60, from Rome, during Paul's imprisonment there

SETTING:
The letter was not written to confront any heresy or problem in the churches. It was sent with Tychicus to strengthen and encourage the churches in the area. Paul had spent over three years with the Ephesian church. As a result, he was very close to them. Paul met with the elders of the Ephesian church at Miletus (Acts 20:17–38)—a meeting that was filled with great sadness because he was leaving them for what he thought would be the last time. Because there are no specific references to people or problems in the Ephesian church and because the words "in Ephesus" (1:1) are not present in some early manuscripts, Paul may have intended this to be a circular letter to be read to all the churches in the area.

KEY VERSES:
"We are all one body, we have the same Spirit, and we have all been called to the same glorious future. There is only one Lord, one faith, one baptism, and there is only one God and Father, who is over us all and in us all and living through us all" (4:4–6).

KEY PEOPLE:
Paul, Tychicus

SPECIAL FEATURES:
Several pictures of the church are presented: body, temple, mystery, new man, bride, and soldier. This letter was probably distributed to many of the early churches.

THE BLUEPRINT

1. Unity in Christ (1:1—3:21)
2. Unity in the body of Christ (4:1—6:24)

In this letter, Paul explains the wonderful things that we have received through Christ and refers to the church as a body, a temple, a bride, and a soldier. These all illustrate unity of purpose and show how each individual member is a part that must work together with all the other parts. In our own life, we should work to eradicate all backbiting, gossip, criticism, jealousy, anger, and bitterness, because these are barriers to unity in the church.

MEGATHEMES

THEME	EXPLANATION	IMPORTANCE
God's Purpose	According to God's eternal, loving plan, he directs, carries out, and sustains our salvation.	When we respond to Christ's love by trusting in him, his purpose becomes our mission. Have you committed yourself to fulfilling God's purpose?
Christ the Center	Christ is exalted as the center of the universe and the focus of history. He is the head of the body, the church. He is the Creator and sustainer of all creation.	Because Christ is central to everything, his power must be central in us. Begin by placing all your priorities under his control.
Living Church	Paul describes the nature of the church. The church, under Christ's control, is a living body, a family, a dwelling. God gives believers special abilities by his Holy Spirit to build the church.	We are part of Christ's body, and we must live in vital union with him. Our conduct must be consistent with this living relationship. Use your God-given abilities to equip believers for service. Fulfill your role in the living church.
New Family	Because God through Christ paid our penalty for sin and forgave us, we have been reconciled—brought near to him. We are a new society, a new family. Being united with Christ means we are to treat one another as family members.	We are one family in Christ, so there should be no barriers, no divisions, no basis for discrimination. We all belong to him, so we should live in harmony with one another.
Christian Conduct	Paul encourages all Christians to wise, dynamic Christian living, for with privileges goes family responsibility. As a new community, we are to live by Christ's new standards.	God provides his Holy Spirit to enable us to live his way. To utilize the Spirit's power, we must lay aside our evil desires and draw on the power of his new life. Submit your will to Christ, and seek to love others.

1. Unity in Christ

Greetings from Paul

1 This letter is from Paul, chosen by God to be an apostle of Christ Jesus.
It is written to God's holy people in Ephesus,* who are faithful followers of
Christ Jesus.
2 May grace and peace be yours, sent to you from God our Father and Jesus Christ our
Lord.

1:2 Rom 1:7; Titus 1:4

1:1 Some manuscripts do not include *in Ephesus*.

1:1 Paul wrote this letter to the Ephesian believers and all other believers to give them in-depth teaching about how to nurture and maintain the unity of the church. He wanted to put this important information in written form because he was in prison for preaching the Good News and could not visit the churches himself. The words "in Ephesus" are not present in some early manuscripts. Therefore, this was very likely a circular letter. It was first sent to Ephesus and then circulated to neighboring local churches. Paul mentions no particular problems or local situations, and he offers no personal greetings.

1:1 Paul had been a Christian for nearly 30 years. He had taken three missionary trips and established churches all around the Mediterranean Sea. When he wrote Ephesians, Paul was under house arrest in Rome (see Acts 28:16ff). Though a prisoner, he was free to have visitors and write letters. For more information on Paul, see his Profile in Acts 9.

1:1 Ephesus was one of the five major cities in the Roman Empire, along with Rome, Corinth, Antioch, and Alexandria. Paul first visited Ephesus on his second missionary journey (Acts 18:19-21). During his third missionary journey, he stayed there for almost three years (Acts 19). Paul later met again with the elders of the Ephesian church at Miletus (Acts 20:16-38). Ephesus was a commercial, political, and religious center for all of Asia Minor. The temple to the Greek goddess Artemis (Diana is her Roman equivalent) was located there.

1:1 "Faithful followers of Christ Jesus"—what an excellent reputation! Such a label would be an honor for any believer. What would it take for others to characterize you as a faithful follower of Christ Jesus? Hold fast to your faith, one day at a time; faithfully obey God, even in the details of life. Then, like the Ephesians, you will be known as a person who is faithful to the Lord.

1:4 2 Thes 2:13; 1 Pet 1:2, 20
1:5 Rom 8:15, 29
1:6 Rom 3:24; Col 1:13
1:7 Col 1:14; Heb 9:12

Spiritual Blessings

3 How we praise God, the Father of our Lord Jesus Christ, who has blessed us with
every spiritual blessing in the heavenly realms because we belong to Christ. 4 Long
ago, even before he made the world, God loved us and chose us in Christ to be holy
and without fault in his eyes. 5 His unchanging plan has always been to adopt us into
his own family by bringing us to himself through Jesus Christ. And this gave him great
pleasure.

6 So we praise God for the wonderful kindness he has poured out on us because we
belong to his dearly loved Son. 7 He is so rich in kindness that he purchased our freedom

LOCATION OF EPHESUS
Ephesus was a strategic city, ranking in importance with Alexandria in Egypt and Antioch of Syria as a port. It lay on the most western edge of Asia Minor (modern-day Turkey), the most important port on the Aegean Sea on the main route from Rome to the east.

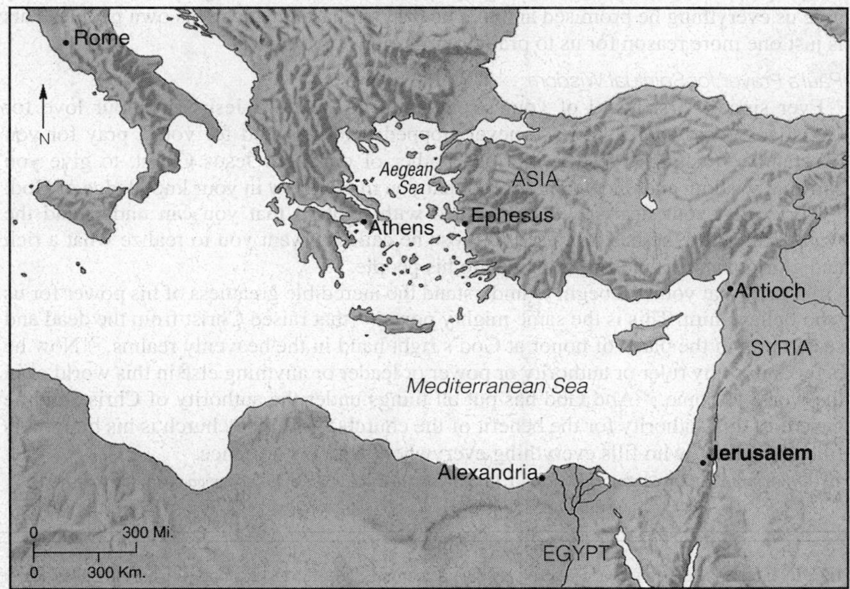

1:3 "Who has blessed us with every spiritual blessing in the heavenly realms" means that in Christ we have all the benefits of knowing God—being chosen for salvation, being adopted as his children, forgiveness, insight, the gifts of the Spirit, power to do God's will, the hope of living forever with Christ. Because we have an intimate relationship with Christ, we can enjoy these blessings now. The "heavenly realms" means that these blessings are eternal, not temporal. The blessings come from Christ's spiritual realm, not the earthly realm of the goddess Artemis. Other references to the heavenly realms in this letter include 1:20; 2:6; 3:10. Such passages reveal Christ in his victorious, exalted role as ruler of all.

1:4 Paul says that God "chose us" to emphasize that salvation depends totally on God. We are not saved because we deserve it but because God is gracious and freely gives salvation. We did not influence God's decision to save us; he saved us according to his plan. Thus, there is no way to take credit for our salvation or to allow room for pride. The mystery of salvation originated in the timeless mind of God long before we existed. It is hard to understand how God could accept us. But because of Christ, we are holy and blameless in his sight. God chose us, and when we belong to him through Jesus Christ, God looks at us as if we had never sinned. All we can do is express our thanks for his wonderful love.

1:5 God's "unchanging plan" is another way of saying that salvation is God's work and not our own doing. In his infinite love, God has adopted us as his own children. Through Jesus' sacrifice, he has brought us into his family and made us heirs along with Jesus (Romans 8:17). In Roman law, adopted children had the same rights and privileges as biological children, even if they had been slaves. Paul uses this term to show how strong our relationship to God is. Have you entered into this loving relationship with God? For more on the meaning of adoption, see Galatians 4:5-7.

1:7 To speak of Jesus' blood was an important first-century way of speaking of Christ's death. His death points to two wonderful truths—redemption and forgiveness. *Redemption* was the price paid to gain freedom for a slave (Leviticus 25:47-54). Through his death, Jesus paid the price to release us from slavery to sin. *Forgiveness* was granted in Old Testament times on the basis of the shedding of animals' blood (Leviticus 17:11). Now we are forgiven on the basis of the shedding of Jesus' blood—he died as the perfect and final sacrifice (see also Romans 5:9; Ephesians 2:13; Colossians 1:20; Hebrews 9:22; 1 Peter 1:19).

1:7, 8 God showered his kindness on us—this is also called God's "grace." This is his voluntary and loving favor given to those he saves. We can't earn salvation, nor do we deserve it. No religious, intellectual, or moral effort can gain it, because it comes only from God's mercy and love. Without God's grace, no person can be saved. To receive it, we must acknowledge that we cannot save ourselves, that only God can save us, and that our only way to receive this loving favor is through faith in Christ.

through the blood of his Son, and our sins are forgiven. 8He has showered his kindness
on us, along with all wisdom and understanding.
9God's secret plan has now been revealed to us; it is a plan centered on Christ,
designed long ago according to his good pleasure. 10And this is his plan: At the right time
he will bring everything together under the authority of Christ—everything in heaven
and on earth. 11Furthermore, because of Christ, we have received an inheritance from
God,* for he chose us from the beginning, and all things happen just as he decided long
ago. 12God's purpose was that we who were the first to trust in Christ should praise our
glorious God. 13And now you also have heard the truth, the Good News that God saves
you. And when you believed in Christ, he identified you as his own by giving you the
Holy Spirit, whom he promised long ago. 14The Spirit is God's guarantee that he will
give us everything he promised and that he has purchased us to be his own people. This
is just one more reason for us to praise our glorious God.

Paul's Prayer for Spiritual Wisdom

15Ever since I first heard of your strong faith in the Lord Jesus and your love for
Christians everywhere, 16I have never stopped thanking God for you. I pray for you
constantly, 17asking God, the glorious Father of our Lord Jesus Christ, to give you
spiritual wisdom and understanding, so that you might grow in your knowledge of God.
18I pray that your hearts will be flooded with light so that you can understand the
wonderful future he has promised to those he called. I want you to realize what a rich
and glorious inheritance he has given to his people.*
19I pray that you will begin to understand the incredible greatness of his power for us
who believe him. This is the same mighty power 20that raised Christ from the dead and
seated him in the place of honor at God's right hand in the heavenly realms. 21Now he
is far above any ruler or authority or power or leader or anything else in this world or in
the world to come. 22And God has put all things under the authority of Christ, and he
gave him this authority for the benefit of the church. 23And the church is his body; it is
filled by Christ, who fills everything everywhere with his presence.

1:11 *Or we have become God's inheritance.* **1:18** *Or realize how much God has been honored by acquiring his people.*

1:9 Rom 16:25; Eph 3:3, 9
1:10 Mark 1:15; Gal 4:4; Col 1:16, 20
1:11 Rom 8:28-29; Eph 3:11
1:12 Eph 1:6, 14
1:13 2 Cor 1:22; Eph 4:30; Col 1:5
1:14 Rom 8:23; 2 Cor 1:22; 5:5
1:16 Col 1:9
1:17 1 Cor 2:9-12
1:18 Acts 26:18; Eph 1:11; 4:4
1:19 Eph 3:7, 16; 6:10; Phil 3:21
1:20 Acts 2:24
1:21 Phil 2:9; Col 1:16; 2:10
1:22 Eph 4:15; Col 1:18; 2:19
1:23 Eph 3:19; 4:10; Col 1:19; 3:11

1:9, 10 God was not intentionally keeping his plan a secret, but his plan for the world could not be fully understood until Christ rose from the dead. His purpose for sending Christ was to unite Jews and Gentiles in one body with Christ as the head. Many people still do not understand God's plan; but at the right time, he will bring us together to be with him forever. Then everyone will understand. On that day, all people will bow to Jesus as Lord, either because they love him or because they fear his power (see Philippians 2:10, 11).

1:11 God's purpose is to offer salvation to the world, just as he planned to do long ago. God is sovereign; he is in charge. When your life seems chaotic, rest in this truth: Jesus is Lord, and God is in control. God's purpose to save you cannot be thwarted, no matter what evil Satan may bring.

1:13, 14 The Holy Spirit is God's guarantee that we belong to him and that he will do what he has promised. The Holy Spirit is like a down payment, a deposit, a validating signature on the contract. The presence of the Holy Spirit in us demonstrates the genuineness of our faith, proves that we are God's children, and secures eternal life for us. His power works in us to transform us now, and what we experience now is a taste of the total change we will experience in eternity.

1:16, 17 Paul prayed that the Ephesians would know Christ better. Christ is our model, and the more we know of him, the more we will be like him. Study Jesus' life in the Gospels to see what he was like on earth nearly 2,000 years ago, and get to know him. Personal knowledge of Christ will change your life.

1:19, 20 The world fears the power of the atom, yet we belong to the God of the universe, who not only created that atomic power but also raised Jesus Christ from the dead. God's incomparably great power is available to help you. There is nothing too difficult for him.

1:20-22 Having been raised from the dead, Christ is now the head of the church, the ultimate authority over the world. Jesus is the Messiah, God's anointed one, the one Israel longed for, the one who would set their broken world right. As Christians we can be confident that God has won the final victory and is in control of everything. We need not fear any dictator or nation or even death or Satan himself. The contract has been signed and sealed; we are waiting just a short while for delivery. Paul says, in Romans 8:37-39, that nothing can separate us from God and his love.

1:22, 23 Christ fills the church with gifts and blessings. The church should be the full expression of Christ, who himself fills everything (see 3:19). When reading Ephesians, it is important to remember that it was written primarily to the entire church, not merely to an individual. Christ is the head, and we are the body of his church (Paul uses this metaphor in Romans 12:4, 5; 1 Corinthians 12:12-27; and Colossians 3:15 as well as throughout the book of Ephesians). The image of the body shows the church's unity. Each member is involved with all the others as they go about doing Christ's work on earth. We should not attempt to work, serve, or worship merely on our own. We need the entire body.

2:1 Eph 2:5 Col 2:13
2:3 Gal 5:24 Col 3:6
2:5 Rom 5:6; 6:4 Eph 2:1 Col 2:13

Made Alive with Christ

2 Once you were dead, doomed forever because of your many sins. 2 You used to live
just like the rest of the world, full of sin, obeying Satan, the mighty prince of the
power of the air. He is the spirit at work in the hearts of those who refuse to obey God.
3 All of us used to live that way, following the passions and desires of our evil nature. We
were born with an evil nature, and we were under God's anger just like everyone else.
4 But God is so rich in mercy, and he loved us so very much, 5 that even while we were
dead because of our sins, he gave us life when he raised Christ from the dead. (It is only
by God's special favor that you have been saved!) 6 For he raised us from the dead along
with Christ, and we are seated with him in the heavenly realms—all because we are one

OUR TRUE IDENTITY IN CHRIST

Romans 3:24	We are justified (declared "not guilty" of sin).
Romans 8:1	No condemnation awaits us.
Romans 8:2	We are set free from the law of sin and death.
1 Corinthians 1:2	We are sanctified (made holy) in Jesus Christ.
1 Corinthians 1:30	We are pure and holy in Christ.
1 Corinthians 15:22	We will be made alive at the resurrection.
2 Corinthians 5:17	We are new persons.
2 Corinthians 5:21	We are made right with God.
Galatians 3:28	We are one in Christ with all other believers.
Ephesians 1:3	We are blessed with every spiritual blessing in Christ.
Ephesians 1:4	We are holy and without fault.
Ephesians 1:5, 6	We are adopted as God's children.
Ephesians 1:7	Our sins are taken away, and we are forgiven.
Ephesians 1:10, 11	We will be brought under Christ's authority.
Ephesians 1:13	We are marked as belonging to God by the Holy Spirit.
Ephesians 2:6	We have been raised up to sit with Christ in the heavenly realms.
Ephesians 2:10	We are God's masterpiece.
Ephesians 2:13	We have been brought near to God.
Ephesians 3:6	We share in the promise in Christ.
Ephesians 3:12	We can come with freedom and confidence into God's presence.
Ephesians 5:29, 30	We are members of Christ's body, the church.
Colossians 2:10	We have been given fullness in Christ.
Colossians 2:11	We are set free from our sinful nature.
2 Timothy 2:10	We will have eternal glory.

2:2 "The mighty prince of the power of the air" is Satan. Paul's readers believed that Satan and the evil spiritual forces inhabited the region between earth and sky. Satan is thus pictured as ruling an evil spiritual kingdom—the demons and those who are against Christ. *Satan* means "the accuser." He is also called the Devil (4:27). In the resurrection, Christ was victorious over Satan and his power. Therefore, Jesus Christ is the permanent ruler of the whole world; Satan is only the temporary ruler of the part of the world that chooses to follow him.

2:3 The fact that all people, without exception, commit sin proves that without Christ we have a sinful nature. We are lost in sin and cannot save ourselves. Does this mean only Christians do good? Of course not—many people do good to others. On a relative scale, many are moral, kind, and law abiding. Comparing these people to criminals, we would say that they are very good indeed. But on God's absolute scale, *no one* is good enough to earn salvation ("dead, doomed forever because of your many sins," 2:1). Only through being united with Christ's perfect life can we become good in God's sight. "Under God's anger" refers to those who are to receive God's wrath because of their rejection of Christ.

2:4, 5 In the previous verses Paul wrote about our old sinful nature (2:1-3). Here Paul emphasizes that we do not need to live any longer under sin's power. The penalty of sin and its power over us were miraculously destroyed by Christ on the cross. Through faith in Christ we stand acquitted, or not guilty, before God (Romans 3:21, 22). God does not take us out of the world or make us robots—we will still feel like sinning, and sometimes we will sin. The difference is that before we became Christians, we were dead in sin and were slaves to our sinful nature. But now we are alive with Christ (see also Galatians 2:20).

2:6 Because of Christ's resurrection, we know that our body will also be raised from the dead (1 Corinthians 15:2-23) and that we have been given the power to live as Christians now (1:19). These ideas are combined in Paul's image of sitting with Christ in "the heavenly realms" (see the note on 1:3). Our eternal life with Christ is certain because we are united in his powerful victory.

with Christ Jesus. [7]And so God can always point to us as examples of the incredible wealth of his favor and kindness toward us, as shown in all he has done for us through Christ Jesus.

[8]God saved you by his special favor when you believed. And you can't take credit for this; it is a gift from God. [9]Salvation is not a reward for the good things we have done, so none of us can boast about it. [10]For we are God's masterpiece. He has created us anew in Christ Jesus, so that we can do the good things he planned for us long ago.

Oneness and Peace in Christ

[11]Don't forget that you Gentiles used to be outsiders by birth. You were called "the uncircumcised ones" by the Jews, who were proud of their circumcision, even though it affected only their bodies and not their hearts. [12]In those days you were living apart from Christ. You were excluded from God's people, Israel, and you did not know the promises God had made to them. You lived in this world without God and without hope. [13]But now you belong to Christ Jesus. Though you once were far away from God, now you have been brought near to him because of the blood of Christ.

[14]For Christ himself has made peace between us Jews and you Gentiles by making us all one people. He has broken down the wall of hostility that used to separate us. [15]By his death he ended the whole system of Jewish law that excluded the Gentiles. His purpose was to make peace between Jews and Gentiles by creating in himself one new person from the two groups. [16]Together as one body, Christ reconciled both groups to God by means of his death, and our hostility toward each other was put to death. [17]He has brought this Good News of peace to you Gentiles who were far away from him, and to us Jews who were near. [18]Now all of us, both Jews and Gentiles, may come to the Father through the same Holy Spirit because of what Christ has done for us.

2:7 Titus 3:4
2:8 John 4:10
2:9 Rom 3:28; 2 Tim 1:9; Titus 3:5
2:11 Col 2:11
2:12 Rom 9:4; 1 Thes 4:13
2:13 Col 1:20
2:14 1 Cor 12:13
2:15 2 Cor 5:17; Gal 3:28; Col 1:21-22; 2:14
2:16 Col 1:20
2:17 Isa 57:19; Zech 9:10
2:18 Eph 3:12; 4:4

2:8, 9 When someone gives you a gift, do you say, "That's very nice—now how much do I owe you?" No, the appropriate response to a gift is "Thank you." Yet how often Christians, even after they have been given the gift of salvation, feel obligated to try to work their way to God. Because our salvation and even our faith are gifts, we should respond with gratitude, praise, and joy.

2:8-10 We become Christians through God's unmerited favor, not as the result of any effort, ability, intelligent choice, or act of service on our part. However, out of gratitude for this free gift, we will seek to help and serve others with kindness, love, and gentleness, and not merely to please ourselves. While no action or work we do can help us obtain salvation, God's intention is that our salvation will result in acts of service. We are not saved merely for our own benefit but to serve Christ and build up the church (4:12).

2:10 We are God's masterpiece (work of art, workmanship). Our salvation is something only God can do. It is his powerful, creative work in us. If God considers us his masterpieces, we dare not treat ourselves or others with disrespect or as inferior work.

2:11-13 Pious Jews considered all non-Jews (Gentiles) ceremonially unclean. They thought of themselves as pure and clean because of their national heritage and religious ceremonies. Paul pointed out that Jews and Gentiles alike were unclean before God and needed to be cleansed by Christ. In order to realize how great a gift salvation is, we need to remember our former natural, unclean condition. Have you ever felt separate, excluded, hopeless? These verses are for you. No one is alienated from Christ's love or from the body of believers.

2:11-13 Jews and Gentiles alike could be guilty of spiritual pride—Jews for thinking their faith and traditions elevated them above everyone else, Gentiles for trusting in their achievements, power, or position. Spiritual pride blinds us to our own faults and magnifies the faults of others. Be careful not to become proud of your salvation. Instead, humbly thank God for what he has done, and encourage others who might be struggling in their faith.

2:11-16 Before Christ's coming, Gentiles and Jews kept apart from one another. Jews considered Gentiles beyond God's saving power and therefore without hope. Gentiles resented Jewish claims. Christ revealed the total sinfulness of both Jews and Gentiles, and then he offered his salvation to both. Only Christ breaks down the walls of prejudice, reconciles all believers to God, and unifies us in one body.

2:14ff Christ has destroyed the barriers people build between themselves. Because these walls have been removed, we can have real unity with people who are not like us. This is true reconciliation. Because of Christ's death, we are all one (2:14); our hostility against each other has been put to death (2:16); we can all have access to the Father by the Holy Spirit (2:18); we are no longer strangers or foreigners to God (2:19); and we are all being built into a holy temple with Christ as our chief cornerstone (2:20, 21).

2:14-22 There are many barriers that can divide us from other Christians: age, appearance, intelligence, political persuasion, economic status, race, theological perspective. One of the best ways to stifle Christ's love is to be friendly with only those people that we like. Fortunately, Christ has knocked down the barriers and has unified all believers in one family. His cross should be the focus of our unity. The Holy Spirit helps us look beyond the barriers to the unity we are called to enjoy.

2:15 By his death, Christ ended the angry resentment between Jews and Gentiles, caused by the Jewish laws that favored the Jews and excluded the Gentiles. Christ died to abolish that whole system of Jewish laws. Then he took the two groups that had been opposed to each other and made them parts of himself. "One new person" means that Christ made a single entity out of the two. Thus, he fused all believers together to become one in himself.

2:17, 18 The Jews were near to God because they already knew of him through the Scriptures and worshiped him in their religious ceremonies. The Gentiles were far away because they knew little or nothing about God. Because neither group could be saved by good deeds, knowledge, or sincerity, both needed to hear about the salvation available through Jesus Christ. Both Jews and Gentiles are now free to come to God through Christ. You have been brought near to him (2:13).

2:20 Isa 28:16 Matt 16:18 Acts 4:11 1 Cor 3:11 1 Pet 2:4-8 Rev 21:14
2:21 1 Cor 3:16 Eph 4:15-16

A Temple for the Lord

19 So now you Gentiles are no longer strangers and foreigners. You are citizens along
with all of God's holy people. You are members of God's family. 20 We are his house,
built on the foundation of the apostles and the prophets. And the cornerstone is Christ
Jesus himself. 21 We who believe are carefully joined together, becoming a holy temple
for the Lord. 22 Through him you Gentiles are also joined together as part of this dwelling
where God lives by his Spirit.

3:1 Eph 4:1 2 Tim 1:8
3:2 Col 1:25
3:3 Eph 1:9-10 Col 1:26
3:5 Eph 1:17
3:6 Eph 2:14-16
3:7 Rom 15:18 Col 1:23, 25
3:8 1 Cor 15:9-10
3:9 Rom 16:25

God's Secret Plan Revealed

3 I, Paul, am a prisoner of Christ Jesus because of my preaching to you Gentiles. 2 As
you already know, God has given me this special ministry of announcing his favor
to you Gentiles. 3 As I briefly mentioned earlier in this letter, God himself revealed his
secret plan to me. 4 As you read what I have written, you will understand what I know
about this plan regarding Christ. 5 God did not reveal it to previous generations, but now
he has revealed it by the Holy Spirit to his holy apostles and prophets.
6 And this is the secret plan: The Gentiles have an equal share with the Jews in all the
riches inherited by God's children. Both groups have believed the Good News, and both
are part of the same body and enjoy together the promise of blessings through Christ
Jesus. 7 By God's special favor and mighty power, I have been given the wonderful
privilege of serving him by spreading this Good News.
8 Just think! Though I did nothing to deserve it, and though I am the least deserving
Christian there is, I was chosen for this special joy of telling the Gentiles about the
endless treasures available to them in Christ. 9 I was chosen to explain to everyone this
plan that God, the Creator of all things, had kept secret from the beginning.

OUR LIVES BEFORE AND AFTER CHRIST

Before	After
Dead because of sin	Made alive with Christ
Under God's anger	Shown God's mercy and given salvation
Followed the ways of the world	Stand for Christ and truth
God's enemies	God's children
Enslaved to Satan	Free in Christ to love, serve, and sit with him
Followed our evil thoughts and desires	Raised up with Christ to glory

2:19-22 A church building is sometimes called God's house. In reality, God's household is not a building but a group of people. He lives in us and shows himself to a watching world through us. People can see that God is love and that Christ is Lord as we live in harmony with each other and in accordance with what God says in his Word. We are citizens of God's Kingdom and members of his household.

2:20 What does it mean to be built on the foundation of the apostles and prophets? It means that the church is not built on modern ideas but rather on the spiritual heritage given to us by the early apostles and prophets of the Christian church.

3:1 Paul was under house arrest in Rome for preaching about Christ. The religious leaders in Jerusalem, who felt threatened by Christ's teachings and didn't believe he was the Messiah, pressured the Romans to arrest Paul and bring him to trial for treason and for causing rebellion among the Jews. Paul had appealed for his case to be heard by the emperor, and he was awaiting trial (see Acts 28:16-31). Even though he was under arrest, Paul maintained his firm belief that God was in control of all that happened to him. Do circumstances make you wonder if God has lost control of this world? Like Paul, remember that no matter what happens, God directs the world's affairs.

3:2, 3 Paul's "special ministry" refers to the special stewardship, trust, or commitment that Paul had been given. He had been assigned the special work of preaching the Good News to the Gentiles, God's great plan shown to Paul in a revelation.

3:5, 6 God's plan was not revealed to previous generations, not because God wanted to keep something from his people, but because he would reveal it to everyone in his perfect timing. God planned to have Jews and Gentiles comprise one body, the church. It was known in the Old Testament that the Gentiles would receive salvation (Isaiah 49:6); but it was never revealed in the Old Testament that all Gentile and Jewish believers would become equal in the body of Christ. Yet this equality was accomplished when Jesus destroyed the "wall of hostility" and created "one new person" (2:14, 15).

3:7 When Paul began spreading the Good News, God gave him the ability to speak effectively. You may not be an apostle or even an evangelist, but God will give you opportunities to tell others about Christ. And with the opportunities he will provide the ability, courage, and power. Whenever an opportunity presents itself, make yourself available to God as his servant. As you focus on the other person and his or her needs, God will communicate your caring attitude. Your words will be natural, loving, and compelling.

3:8 When Paul describes himself as "the least deserving Christian there is," he means that without God's help, he would never be able to do God's work. Yet God chose him to share the Good News with the Gentiles and gave him the power to do it. If we feel that our role is minor, we may be right—except that we have forgotten what a difference God makes. How does God want to use you? Draw on his power, do your part, and faithfully perform the special role God has called you to play in his plan.

10God's purpose was to show his wisdom in all its rich variety to all the rulers and
authorities in the heavenly realms. They will see this when Jews and Gentiles are joined
together in his church. 11This was his plan from all eternity, and it has now been carried
out through Christ Jesus our Lord.
12Because of Christ and our faith in him, we can now come fearlessly into God's
presence, assured of his glad welcome. 13So please don't despair because of what they are
doing to me here. It is for you that I am suffering, so you should feel honored and
encouraged.

Paul's Prayer for Spiritual Empowering

14When I think of the wisdom and scope of God's plan, I fall to my knees and pray to
the Father,* 15the Creator of everything in heaven and on earth. 16I pray that from his
glorious, unlimited resources he will give you mighty inner strength through his Holy
Spirit. 17And I pray that Christ will be more and more at home in your hearts as you trust
in him. May your roots go down deep into the soil of God's marvelous love. 18And may
you have the power to understand, as all God's people should, how wide, how long, how
high, and how deep his love really is. 19May you experience the love of Christ, though
it is so great you will never fully understand it. Then you will be filled with the fullness
of life and power that comes from God.
20Now glory be to God! By his mighty power at work within us, he is able to
accomplish infinitely more than we would ever dare to ask or hope. 21May he be given
glory in the church and in Christ Jesus forever and ever through endless ages. Amen.

2. Unity in the body of Christ

4 Therefore I, a prisoner for serving the Lord, beg you to lead a life worthy of your
calling, for you have been called by God. 2Be humble and gentle. Be patient with
each other, making allowance for each other's faults because of your love. 3Always keep
yourselves united in the Holy Spirit, and bind yourselves together with peace.

3:10 Rom 11:33; 1 Cor 2:7; Eph 1:21; 6:12; 1 Pet 1:12
3:11 Eph 1:11
3:12 Eph 2:18; Heb 4:16
3:14 Phil 2:10
3:16 Phil 4:13, 19; Col 1:11
3:17 John 14:23; Col 2:7
3:18 John 1:16; Col 2:9-10
3:19 Col 2:10
3:20 Eph 1:19-20; Col 1:29
4:1 Eph 3:1; Phil 1:7, 13
4:2 Col 3:12-13
4:3 Col 3:14-15

3:14 Some manuscripts read *the Father of our Lord Jesus Christ.*

3:10 The "rulers and authorities in the heavenly realms" are either angels who are witnesses to these events (see 1 Peter 1:12), or hostile spiritual forces opposed to God (2:2; 6:12).

3:12 It is an awesome privilege to be able to approach God with freedom and confidence. Most of us would be apprehensive in the presence of a powerful ruler. But thanks to Christ, by faith we can enter directly into God's presence through prayer. We know we'll be welcomed with open arms because we are God's children through our union with Christ. Don't be afraid of God. Talk with him about everything. He is waiting to hear from you.

3:13 Why should Paul's suffering make the Ephesians feel honored and encouraged? If Paul had not preached the Good News, he would not be in jail—but then the Ephesians would not have heard the Good News and been converted either. Just as a mother endures the pain of childbirth in order to bring new life into the world, Paul endured the pain of persecution in order to bring new believers to Christ. Obeying Christ is never easy. He calls you to take your cross and follow him (Matthew 16:24)—that is, to be willing to endure pain so that God's message of salvation can reach the entire world. We should feel honored that others have suffered and sacrificed for us so that we might reap the benefit.

3:14, 15 The family of God includes all who have believed in him in the past, all who believe in the present, and all who will believe in the future. We are all a family because we have the same Father. He is the source of all creation, the rightful owner of everything. God promises his love and power to his family, the church (3:16-21). If we want to receive God's blessings, it is important that we stay in contact with other believers in the body of Christ. Those who isolate themselves from God's family and try to go it alone cut themselves off from God's power.

3:17-19 God's love is total, says Paul. It reaches every corner of our experience. It is *wide*—it covers the breadth of our own experience, and it reaches out to the whole world. God's love is *long*—it continues the length of our lives. It is *high*—it rises to the heights of our celebration and elation. His love is *deep*—it reaches to the depths of discouragement, despair, and even death. When you feel shut out or isolated, remember that you can never be lost to God's love. For another prayer about God's immeasurable and inexhaustible love, see Paul's words in Romans 8:38, 39.

3:19 This "fullness" is fully expressed only in Christ (Colossians 2:9, 10). In union with Christ and through his empowering Spirit, we are complete. We have all the fullness of God available to us. But we must appropriate that fullness through faith and through prayer as we daily live for him. Paul's prayer for the Ephesians is also for you. You can ask the Holy Spirit to fill every aspect of your life to the fullest.

3:20, 21 This doxology—prayer of praise to God—ends part 1 of Ephesians. In the first section, Paul described the timeless role of the church. In part 2 (chapters 4–6), he will explain how church members should live in order to bring about the unity God wants. As in most of his books, Paul first lays a doctrinal foundation and then makes practical applications of the truths he has presented.

4:1, 2 God has chosen us to be Christ's representatives on earth. In light of this truth, Paul challenges us to live lives worthy of the calling we have received—the awesome privilege of being called Christ's very own. This includes being humble, gentle, patient, understanding, and peaceful. People are watching your life. Can they see Christ in you? How well are you doing as his representative?

4:1-6 "We are all one body," says Paul. Unity does not just happen; we have to work at it. Often differences among people can lead to division, but this should not be true in the church. Instead of concentrating on what divides us, we should remember what unites us: *one* body, *one* Spirit, *one* future, *one* Lord, *one* faith, *one* baptism, *one* God! Have you learned to appreciate people who are different from you? Can you see how their differing gifts and viewpoints can help the church as it does God's

4:4 Rom 12:5; 1 Cor 12:12-13; Eph 2:16, 18
4:7 Rom 12:3; 1 Cor 12:7
4:9 John 3:13; Acts 2:27; 1 Pet 3:18
4:10 Eph 1:23
4:11 1 Cor 12:28
4:12 1 Cor 12:27
4:13 Eph 1:23; Col 1:28

4 We are all one body, we have the same Spirit, and we have all been called to the same
glorious future. 5 There is only one Lord, one faith, one baptism, 6 and there is only one God
and Father, who is over us all and in us all and living through us all. 7 However, he has given
each one of us a special gift according to the generosity of Christ. 8 That is why the
Scriptures say,

"When he ascended to the heights,
he led a crowd of captives
and gave gifts to his people."*

9 Notice that it says "he ascended." This means that Christ first came down to the lowly
world in which we live.* 10 The same one who came down is the one who ascended
higher than all the heavens, so that his rule might fill the entire universe.
11 He is the one who gave these gifts to the church: the apostles, the prophets, the
evangelists, and the pastors and teachers. 12 Their responsibility is to equip God's people
to do his work and build up the church, the body of Christ, 13 until we come to such unity

4:8 Ps 68:18. **4:9** Or *to the lowest parts of the earth.*

THE ONENESS OF ALL BELIEVERS

Believers are one in	*Our unity is experienced in:*
Body	The fellowship of believers—the church
Spirit	The Holy Spirit, who activates the fellowship
Hope	That glorious future to which we are all called
Lord	Christ, to whom we all belong
Faith	Our singular commitment to Christ
Baptism	Baptism—the sign of entry into the church
God	God, who is our Father who keeps us for eternity

Too often believers are separated because of minor differences in doctrine. But Paul here shows those areas where Christians must agree to attain true unity. When believers have this unity of spirit, petty differences should never be allowed to dissolve that unity.

work? Learn to enjoy the way we members of Christ's body complement one another. (See 1 Corinthians 12:12, 13 for more on this thought.)

4:2 No one is ever going to be perfect here on earth, so we must accept and love other Christians in spite of their faults. When we see faults in fellow believers, we should be patient and gentle. Is there someone whose actions or personality really annoys you? Rather than dwelling on that person's weaknesses or looking for faults, pray for him or her. Then do even more—spend time together and see if you can learn to like him or her.

4:3 To build unity is one of the Holy Spirit's important roles. He leads, but we have to be willing to be led and to do our part to keep the peace. We do that by focusing on God, not on ourselves. For more about who the Holy Spirit is and what he does, see the notes on John 3:6; Acts 1:5; and Ephesians 1:13, 14.

4:4-7 All believers in Christ belong to one body; all are united under one head, Christ himself (see 1 Corinthians 12:12-27). Each believer has God-given abilities that can strengthen the whole body. Your special ability may seem small or large, but it is yours to use in God's service. Ask God to use your unique gifts to contribute to the strength and health of the body of believers.

4:6 God is "over all"—this shows his overruling care (transcendence). He is "in us all" and "living through us all"—this shows his active presence in the world and in the lives of believers (immanence). Any view of God that violates either his transcendence or his immanence does not paint a true picture of God.

4:8 In Psalm 68:18, God is pictured as a conqueror marching to the gates and taking tribute from the fallen city. Paul uses that picture to teach that Christ, in his crucifixion and resurrection, was victorious over Satan. When Christ ascended to heaven, he gave gifts to the church, some of which Paul discusses in 4:11-13.

4:9 The "lowly world" may be (1) the earth itself (lowly by comparison to heaven), (2) the grave, or (3) Hades (many believe Hades is the resting place of souls between death and resurrection). However we understand it, Christ is Lord of the whole universe, past, present, and future. Nothing or no one is hidden from him. The Lord of all came to earth and faced death to rescue all people. No one is beyond his reach.

4:11, 12 Our oneness in Christ does not destroy our individuality. The Holy Spirit has given each Christian special gifts for building up the church. Now that we have these gifts, it is crucial to use them. Are you spiritually mature, exercising the gifts God has given you? If you know what your gifts are, look for opportunities to serve. If you don't know, ask God to show you, perhaps with the help of your minister or Christian friends. Then, as you begin to recognize your special area of service, use your gifts to strengthen and encourage the church.

4:12, 13 God has given his church an enormous responsibility—to make disciples in every nation (Matthew 28:18-20). This involves preaching, teaching, healing, nurturing, giving, administering, building, and many other tasks. If we had to fulfill this command as individuals, we might as well give up without trying— it would be impossible. But God calls us as members of his body. Some of us can do one task; some can do another. Together we can obey God more fully than any of us could alone. It is a human tendency to overestimate what we can do by ourselves and to underestimate what we can do as a group. But as the body of Christ, we can accomplish more together than we would dream possible working by ourselves. Working together, the church can express the fullness of Christ (see the note on 3:19).

in our faith and knowledge of God's Son that we will be mature and full grown in the
Lord, measuring up to the full stature of Christ.
14 Then we will no longer be like children, forever changing our minds about what we
believe because someone has told us something different or because someone has
cleverly lied to us and made the lie sound like the truth. 15 Instead, we will hold to the
truth in love, becoming more and more in every way like Christ, who is the head of his
body, the church. 16 Under his direction, the whole body is fitted together perfectly. As
each part does its own special work, it helps the other parts grow, so that the whole body
is healthy and growing and full of love.

Living as Children of Light

17 With the Lord's authority let me say this: Live no longer as the ungodly* do, for they
are hopelessly confused. 18 Their closed minds are full of darkness; they are far away
from the life of God because they have shut their minds and hardened their hearts against
him. 19 They don't care anymore about right and wrong, and they have given themselves
over to immoral ways. Their lives are filled with all kinds of impurity and greed.
20 But that isn't what you were taught when you learned about Christ. 21 Since you have
heard all about him and have learned the truth that is in Jesus, 22 throw off your old evil
nature and your former way of life, which is rotten through and through, full of lust and
deception. 23 Instead, there must be a spiritual renewal of your thoughts and attitudes.
24 You must display a new nature because you are a new person, created in God's
likeness—righteous, holy, and true.
25 So put away all falsehood and "tell your neighbor the truth"* because we belong to
each other. 26 And "don't sin by letting anger gain control over you."* Don't let the sun
go down while you are still angry, 27 for anger gives a mighty foothold to the Devil.
28 If you are a thief, stop stealing. Begin using your hands for honest work, and then give
generously to others in need. 29 Don't use foul or abusive language. Let everything you say
be good and helpful, so that your words will be an encouragement to those who hear them.

4:17 Greek *Gentiles*. **4:25** Zech 8:16. **4:26** Ps 4:4.

4:14 1 Cor 14:20; Eph 6:11
4:15 Eph 1:22
4:16 Col 2:19
4:17 Rom 1:21; Eph 2:2
4:19 Rom 1:24; Col 3:5
4:22 Rom 6:6; Col 3:5, 8-9; Jas 1:21
4:23 Rom 12:2
4:24 2 Cor 5:17; Col 3:10
4:25 †Zech 8:16; Col 3:8-9
4:28 1 Thes 4:11
4:29 Matt 12:36; Rom 14:19; Col 3:8

4:14-16 Christ is the truth (John 14:6), and the Holy Spirit, who guides the church, is the Spirit of truth (John 16:13). Satan, by contrast, is the father of lies (John 8:44). As followers of Christ, we must be committed to the truth. This means both that our words should be honest and that our actions should reflect Christ's integrity. Holding to the truth in love is not always easy, convenient, or pleasant, but it is necessary if the church is going to do Christ's work in the world.

4:15, 16 Some Christians fear that any mistake will destroy their witness for the Lord. They see their own weaknesses, and they know that many non-Christians seem to have stronger character than they do. How can we grow up into Christ? The answer is that Christ forms us into a body—into a group of individuals who are united in their purpose and in their love for one another and for the Lord. If an individual stumbles, the rest of the group is there to pick that person up and help him or her walk with God again. If a person sins, he or she can find restoration through the church (Galatians 6:1) even as the rest of the body continues to witness to God's truth. As part of Christ's body, do you reflect part of Christ's character and carry out your special role in his work?

4:17 The natural tendency of human beings is to think their way away from God—leaving them "hopelessly confused." Intellectual pride, rationalizations, and excuses all keep people from God. Don't be surprised if people can't grasp the Good News. The Good News will seem foolish to those who forsake faith and rely on their own understanding.

4:17-24 People should be able to see a difference between Christians and non-Christians because of the way Christians live. We are to live full of light (5:8). Paul told the Ephesians to leave behind the old life of sin, since they were followers of Christ. Living the Christian life is a process. Although we have a new nature, we don't automatically think all good thoughts and express all right attitudes when we become new people in Christ. But if we keep listening to God, we will be changing all the time. As you look back over last year, do you see a process of change for the better in your thoughts, attitudes, and actions? Although change may be slow, it comes as you trust God to change you. For more about our new nature as believers, see Romans 6:6; 8:9; Galatians 5:16-26; Colossians 3:3-8.

4:22-24 Our old way of life before we believed in Christ is completely in the past. We should put it behind us like old clothes to be thrown away. When we decide to accept Christ's gift of salvation (2:8-10), it is both a onetime decision, as well as a daily conscious commitment. We are not to be driven by desire and impulse. We must put on the new nature, head in the new direction, and have the new way of thinking that the Holy Spirit gives.

4:25 Lying to each other disrupts unity by creating conflicts and destroying trust. It tears down relationships and leads to open warfare in a church.

4:26, 27 The Bible doesn't tell us that we shouldn't feel angry, but it points out that it is important to handle our anger properly. If vented thoughtlessly, anger can hurt others and destroy relationships. If bottled up inside, it can cause us to become bitter and destroy us from within. Paul tells us to deal with our anger immediately in a way that builds relationships rather than destroys them. If we nurse our anger, we will give Satan an opportunity to divide us. Are you angry with someone right now? What can you do to resolve your differences? Don't let the day end before you begin to work on mending your relationship.

4:28-32 We can bring sorrow to the Holy Spirit by the way we live. Paul warns us against unwholesome language, bitterness, improper use of anger, harsh words, slander, and bad attitudes toward others. Instead of acting that way, we should be forgiving, just as God has forgiven us. Are you bringing sorrow or pleasing

30 And do not bring sorrow to God's Holy Spirit by the way you live. Remember, he
is the one who has identified you as his own, guaranteeing that you will be saved on the
day of redemption.
31 Get rid of all bitterness, rage, anger, harsh words, and slander, as well as all types of
malicious behavior. 32 Instead, be kind to each other, tenderhearted, forgiving one
another, just as God through Christ has forgiven you.

Living in the Light

5 Follow God's example in everything you do, because you are his dear children.
2 Live a life filled with love for others, following the example of Christ, who loved
you and gave himself as a sacrifice to take away your sins. And God was pleased, because
that sacrifice was like sweet perfume to him.
3 Let there be no sexual immorality, impurity, or greed among you. Such sins have no
place among God's people. 4 Obscene stories, foolish talk, and coarse jokes—these are
not for you. Instead, let there be thankfulness to God. 5 You can be sure that no immoral,
impure, or greedy person will inherit the Kingdom of Christ and of God. For a greedy
person is really an idolater who worships the things of this world. 6 Don't be fooled by
those who try to excuse these sins, for the terrible anger of God comes upon all those
who disobey him. 7 Don't participate in the things these people do. 8 For though your
hearts were once full of darkness, now you are full of light from the Lord, and your
behavior should show it! 9 For this light within you produces only what is good and right
and true.
10 Try to find out what is pleasing to the Lord. 11 Take no part in the worthless deeds
of evil and darkness; instead, rebuke and expose them. 12 It is shameful even to talk about
the things that ungodly people do in secret. 13 But when the light shines on them, it
becomes clear how evil these things are. 14 And where your light shines, it will expose
their evil deeds. This is why it is said,

"Awake, O sleeper,
rise up from the dead,
and Christ will give you light."

4:30 Isa 63:10; Eph 1:13-14; 1 Thes 5:19
4:31 Col 3:8; 1 Pet 2:1
4:32 Col 3:12-13
5:1 Matt 5:48
5:2 John 13:34; Gal 1:14; 2:20
5:3 Col 3:5
5:4 Eph 4:29; Col 3:8
5:5 1 Cor 6:9-10; Col 3:5
5:6 Rom 1:18; Col 2:4, 8; 3:6
5:8 John 8:12; Eph 2:2
5:11 Rom 13:12
5:13 John 3:20-21
5:14 Isa 26:19; 51:17; 52:1; 60:1; John 5:25; Rom 13:11

God with your attitudes and actions? Act in love toward your brothers and sisters in Christ, just as God acted in love by sending his Son to die for your sins.

4:30 The Holy Spirit within us is a guarantee that we belong to God. For more on this thought, see the note on 1:13, 14.

4:32 This is Christ's law of forgiveness as taught in the Gospels (Matthew 6:14, 15; 18:35; Mark 11:25). We also see it in the Lord's Prayer—"Forgive us our sins, just as we have forgiven those who have sinned against us." God forgives us, not because we forgive others, but solely because of his great mercy. As we come to understand his mercy, however, we will want to be like him. Having received forgiveness, we will pass it on to others. Those who are unwilling to forgive have not become one with Christ, who was willing to forgive even those who crucified him (Luke 23:34).

5:1, 2 Just as children imitate their parents, we should follow God's example. His great love for us led him to sacrifice himself so that we might live. Our love for others should be of the same kind—a love that goes beyond affection to self-sacrificing service.

5:4 Obscene stories and coarse jokes are so common that we begin to take them for granted. Paul cautions, however, that improper language should have no place in the Christian's conversation because it does not reflect God's gracious presence in us. How can we praise God and remind others of his goodness when we are speaking coarsely?

5:5-7 Paul is not forbidding all contact with unbelievers. Jesus taught his followers to befriend sinners and lead them to him (Luke 5:30-32). Instead, Paul is speaking against condoning the life-style of people who make excuses for bad behavior and recommend its practice to others—whether they are in the church or outside of it. Such people can quickly pollute the church and endanger its unity and purpose. We must befriend unbelievers if we are to lead them to Christ, but we must be wary of those who are viciously evil, immoral, or opposed to all that Christianity stands for. Such people are more likely to influence us for evil than we are likely to influence them for good.

5:8 As people filled with light, our actions should reflect our faith. We should live above reproach morally so that we will reflect God's goodness to others. Jesus stressed this truth in the Sermon on the Mount (Matthew 5:15, 16).

5:10-14 It is important to avoid the "worthless deeds of evil and darkness" (any pleasure or activity that results in sin), but we must go even further. Paul instructs us to expose these deeds, because our silence may be interpreted as approval. God needs people who will take a stand for what is right. Christians must lovingly speak out for what is true and right.

5:14 This is not a direct quote from Scripture but was probably taken from a hymn well known to the Ephesians. The hymn seems to have been based on Isaiah 26:19; 51:17; 52:1; 60:1; and Malachi 4:2. Paul was appealing to the Ephesians to wake up and realize the dangerous condition into which some of them had been slipping.

Living by the Spirit's Power

15So be careful how you live, not as fools but as those who are wise. 16Make the most
of every opportunity for doing good in these evil days. 17Don't act thoughtlessly, but try
to understand what the Lord wants you to do. 18Don't be drunk with wine, because that
will ruin your life. Instead, let the Holy Spirit fill and control you. 19Then you will sing
psalms and hymns and spiritual songs among yourselves, making music to the Lord in
your hearts. 20And you will always give thanks for everything to God the Father in the
name of our Lord Jesus Christ.

Spirit-Guided Relationships: Wives and Husbands

21And further, you will submit to one another out of reverence for Christ. 22You wives
will submit to your husbands as you do to the Lord. 23For a husband is the head of his
wife as Christ is the head of his body, the church; he gave his life to be her Savior. 24As
the church submits to Christ, so you wives must submit to your husbands in everything.
25And you husbands must love your wives with the same love Christ showed the
church. He gave up his life for her 26to make her holy and clean, washed by baptism and
God's word.* 27He did this to present her to himself as a glorious church without a spot
or wrinkle or any other blemish. Instead, she will be holy and without fault. 28In the same

5:16 Col 4:5
5:17 1 Thes 4:3
5:18 Prov 20:1; 23:31
5:19 Col 3:16
5:21 1 Pet 5:5
5:22 Gen 3:16
5:23 1 Cor 11:3
5:26 John 15:3; 17:17 Heb 10:22
5:27 Eph 1:4 Col 1:22

5:26 Greek *having cleansed her by the washing of water with the word.*

5:15, 16 By referring to these days as evil, Paul was communicating his sense of urgency because of evil's pervasiveness. We need the same sense of urgency because our days are also difficult. We must keep our standards high, act wisely, and do good whenever we can.

5:18 Paul contrasts getting drunk with wine, which produces a temporary "high," to being filled with the Spirit, which produces lasting joy. Getting drunk with wine is associated with the old way of life and its selfish desires. In Christ, we have a better joy, higher and longer lasting, to cure our depression, monotony, or tension. We should not be concerned with how much of the Holy Spirit we have but with how much of us the Holy Spirit has. Submit yourself daily to his leading and draw constantly on his power.

5:20 When you feel down, you may find it difficult to give thanks. Take heart—in all things God works for our good if we love him and are called by him (Romans 8:28). Thank God, not for your problems but for the strength he is building in you through the difficult experiences of your life. You can be sure that God's perfect love will see you through.

5:21, 22 Submitting to another person is an often misunderstood concept. It does not mean becoming a doormat. Christ—at whose name "every knee will bow, in heaven and on earth and under the earth" (Philippians 2:10)—submitted his will to the Father, and we honor Christ by following his example. When we submit to God, we become more willing to obey his command to submit to others, that is, to subordinate our rights to theirs. In a marriage relationship, both husband and wife are called to submit. For the wife, this means willingly following her husband's leadership in Christ. For the husband, it means putting aside his own interests in order to care for his wife. Submission is rarely a problem in homes where both partners have a strong relationship with Christ and where each is concerned for the happiness of the other.

5:22-24 In Paul's day, women, children, and slaves were to submit to the head of the family: Slaves would submit until they were freed, male children until they grew up, and women and girls their whole lives. Paul emphasized the equality of all believers in Christ (Galatians 3:28), but he did not suggest overthrowing Roman society to achieve it. Instead, he counseled all believers to submit to one another by choice—wives to husbands and also husbands to wives; slaves to masters and also masters to slaves; children to parents and also parents to children. This kind of mutual submission preserves order and harmony in the family, while it increases love and respect among family members.

5:22-24 Although some people have distorted Paul's teaching on submission by giving unlimited authority to husbands, we cannot get around it: Paul told wives to submit to their husbands. The fact that a teaching is not popular is no reason to discard it. According to the Bible, the man is the spiritual head of the family, and his wife should acknowledge his leadership. But real spiritual leadership involves service. Just as Christ served the disciples, even to the point of washing their feet, so the husband is to serve his wife. A wise and Christ-honoring husband will not take advantage of his leadership role, and a wise and Christ-honoring wife will not try to undermine her husband's leadership. Either approach causes disunity and friction in marriage.

5:22-28 Why did Paul tell wives to submit and husbands to love? Perhaps Christian women, newly freed in Christ, found submission difficult; perhaps Christian men, used to the Roman custom of giving unlimited power to the head of the family, were not used to treating their wives with respect and love. Of course both husbands and wives should submit to each other (5:21), just as both should love each other.

5:25ff Some Christians have thought that Paul was negative about marriage because of the counsel he gave in 1 Corinthians 7:32-38. These verses in Ephesians, however, show a high view of marriage. Here marriage is not a practical necessity or a cure for lust, but a picture of the relationship between Christ and his church! Why the apparent difference? Paul's counsel in 1 Corinthians was designed for a state of emergency during a time of persecution and crisis. Paul's counsel to the Ephesians is more the biblical ideal for marriage. Marriage, for Paul, is a holy union, a living symbol, a precious relationship that needs tender, self-sacrificing care.

5:25-30 Paul devotes twice as many words to telling husbands to love their wives as to telling wives to submit to their husbands. How should a man love his wife? (1) He should be willing to sacrifice everything for her, (2) make her well-being of primary importance, and (3) care for her as he cares for his own body. No wife needs to fear submitting to a man who treats her in this way.

5:26, 27 Christ's death makes the church holy and clean. He cleanses us from the old ways of sin and sets us apart for his special sacred service (Hebrews 10:29; 13:12). Christ cleansed the church by the washing of baptism. Through baptism we are prepared for entrance into the church just as ancient Near Eastern brides were prepared for marriage by a ceremonial bath. It is God's Word that cleanses us (John 17:17; Titus 3:5).

5:29 1 Cor 12:27
5:30 1 Cor 6:15; 12:27
5:31 †Gen 2:24; Matt 19:5
5:33 1 Pet 3:1-2, 5
6:1 Col 3:20
6:2-3 †Exod 20:12; †Deut 5:16; Matt 15:4
6:4 Col 3:21

way, husbands ought to love their wives as they love their own bodies. For a man is
actually loving himself when he loves his wife. 29No one hates his own body but lovingly
cares for it, just as Christ cares for his body, which is the church. 30And we are his body.
31As the Scriptures say, "A man leaves his father and mother and is joined to his wife,
and the two are united into one."* 32This is a great mystery, but it is an illustration of the
way Christ and the church are one. 33So again I say, each man must love his wife as he
loves himself, and the wife must respect her husband.

Children and Parents

6 Children, obey your parents because you belong to the Lord, for this is the right thing
to do. 2"Honor your father and mother." This is the first of the Ten Commandments
that ends with a promise. 3And this is the promise: If you honor your father and mother,
"you will live a long life, full of blessing."*
4And now a word to you fathers. Don't make your children angry by the way you treat
them. Rather, bring them up with the discipline and instruction approved by the Lord.

5:31 Gen 2:24. **6:2-3** Exod 20:12; Deut 5:16.

GOD'S ARMOR FOR US

We are engaged in a spiritual battle—all believers find themselves subject to Satan's attacks because they are no longer on Satan's side. Thus, Paul tells us to use *every piece* of God's armor to resist Satan's attacks and to stand true to God in the midst of those attacks.

Piece of Armor	*Use*	*Application*
Belt	Truth	Satan fights with lies, and sometimes his lies *sound* like truth; but only believers have God's truth, which can defeat Satan's lies.
Body armor	Righteousness	Satan often attacks our heart—the seat of our emotions, self-worth, and trust. God's righteousness is the body armor that protects our heart and ensures his approval. He approves of us because he loves us and sent his Son to die for us.
Shoes	Readiness to spread the Good News	Satan wants us to think that telling others the Good News is a worthless and hopeless task—the size of the task is too big and the negative responses are too much to handle. But the shoes God gives us are the motivation to continue to proclaim the true peace that is available in God—news everyone needs to hear.
Shield	Faith	What *we* see are Satan's attacks in the form of insults, setbacks, and temptations. But the shield of faith protects us from Satan's fiery arrows. With God's perspective, we can see beyond our circumstances and know that ultimate victory is ours.
Helmet	Salvation	Satan wants to make us doubt God, Jesus, and our salvation. The helmet protects our mind from doubting God's saving work for us.
Sword	Word of God	The sword is the only weapon of *offense* in this list of armor. There are times when we need to take the offensive against Satan. When we are tempted, we need to trust in the truth of God's Word.

5:31-33 The union of husband and wife merges two persons in such a way that little can affect one without also affecting the other. Oneness in marriage does not mean losing your personality in the personality of the other. Instead, it means caring for your spouse as you care for yourself, learning to anticipate his or her needs, helping the other person become all he or she can be. The creation story tells of God's plan that husband and wife should be one (Genesis 2:24), and Jesus also referred to this plan (Matthew 19:4-6).

6:1, 2 There is a difference between obeying and honoring. To obey means to do as one is told; to honor means to respect and love. Children are not commanded to disobey God in obeying their parents. Adult children are not asked to be subservient to domineering parents. Children are to obey while under their parents' care, but the responsibility to honor parents is for life.

6:1-4 If our faith in Christ is real, it will usually prove itself at home, in our relationships with those who know us best. Children and parents have a responsibility to each other. Children should honor their parents even if the parents are demanding and unfair. Parents should care gently for their children, even if the children are disobedient and unpleasant. Ideally, of course, Christian parents and Christian children will relate to each other with thoughtfulness and love. This will happen if both parents and children put the others' interests above their own—that is, if they submit to one another.

6:3 Some societies honor their elders. They respect their wisdom, defer to their authority, and pay attention to their comfort and happiness. This is how Christians should act. Where elders are respected, long life is a blessing, not a burden to them.

6:4 The purpose of parental discipline is to help children grow, not to exasperate and provoke them to anger or discouragement (see also Colossians 3:21). Parenting is not easy—it takes lots of patience to raise children in a loving, Christ-honoring manner. But frustration and anger should not be causes for discipline. Instead, parents should act in love, treating their children as Jesus treats the people he loves. This is vital to children's development and to their understanding of what Christ is like.

Slaves and Masters

[5]Slaves, obey your earthly masters with deep respect and fear. Serve them sincerely as
you would serve Christ. [6]Work hard, but not just to please your masters when they are
watching. As slaves of Christ, do the will of God with all your heart. [7]Work with
enthusiasm, as though you were working for the Lord rather than for people. [8]Remember
that the Lord will reward each one of us for the good we do, whether we are slaves or
free.

[9]And in the same way, you masters must treat your slaves right. Don't threaten them;
remember, you both have the same Master in heaven, and he has no favorites.

The Whole Armor of God

[10]A final word: Be strong with the Lord's mighty power. [11]Put on all of God's armor so
that you will be able to stand firm against all strategies and tricks of the Devil. [12]For we
are not fighting against people made of flesh and blood, but against the evil rulers and
authorities of the unseen world, against those mighty powers of darkness who rule this
world, and against wicked spirits in the heavenly realms.

[13]Use every piece of God's armor to resist the enemy in the time of evil, so that after
the battle you will still be standing firm. [14]Stand your ground, putting on the sturdy belt
of truth and the body armor of God's righteousness. [15]For shoes, put on the peace that
comes from the Good News, so that you will be fully prepared.* [16]In every battle you
will need faith as your shield to stop the fiery arrows aimed at you by Satan.* [17]Put on
salvation as your helmet, and take the sword of the Spirit, which is the word of God.
[18]Pray at all times and on every occasion in the power of the Holy Spirit. Stay alert and
be persistent in your prayers for all Christians everywhere.

[19]And pray for me, too. Ask God to give me the right words as I boldly explain God's
secret plan that the Good News is for the Gentiles, too.* [20]I am in chains now for
preaching this message as God's ambassador. But pray that I will keep on speaking
boldly for him, as I should.

6:5-7 //Col 3:22-23 Titus 2:9-10
6:8 Col 3:24-25
6:9 Job 31:13-14 Col 4:1
6:11 Rom 13:12 1 Thes 5:8
6:12 Eph 3:10
6:14 Isa 11:5; 59:17 1 Thes 5:8
6:15 Isa 52:7
6:16 1 Jn 5:4
6:17 Isa 59:17 1 Thes 5:8 Heb 4:12
6:18 Rom 8:26-27 Phil 4:6 Col 4:2-3
6:19 Col 4:3-4

6:15 Or *For shoes, put on the readiness to preach the Good News of peace with God.* **6:16** Greek *by the evil one.* **6:19** Greek *explain the mystery of the gospel.*

6:5 Slaves played a significant part in this society. There were several million of them in the Roman Empire at this time. Because many slaves and owners had become Christians, the early church had to deal straightforwardly with the question of master/slave relations. Paul's statement neither condemns nor condones slavery. Instead, it tells masters and slaves how to live together in Christian households. In Paul's day, women, children, and slaves had few rights. In the church, however, they had freedoms that society denied them. Paul tells husbands, parents, and masters to be caring.

6:6-8 Paul's instructions encourage responsibility and integrity on the job. Christian employees should do their jobs as if Jesus Christ were their supervisor. And Christian employers should treat their employees fairly and with respect. Can you be trusted to do your best, even when the boss is not around? Do you work hard and with enthusiasm? Do you treat your employees as people, not machines? Remember that no matter whom you work for, and no matter who works for you, the one you ultimately should want to please is your Father in heaven.

6:9 Although Christians may be at different levels in earthly society, we are all equal before God. He does not play favorites; no one is more important than anyone else. Paul's letter to Philemon stresses the same point: Philemon, the master, and Onesimus, his slave, were brothers in Christ.

6:10-17 In the Christian life we battle against rulers and authorities (the powerful evil forces of fallen angels headed by Satan, who is a vicious fighter, see 1 Peter 5:8). To withstand their attacks, we must depend on God's strength and use every piece of his armor. Paul is not only giving this counsel to the church, the body of Christ, but to all individuals within the church. The whole body needs to be armed. As you do battle against the "mighty powers of darkness," fight in the strength of the church, whose power comes from the Holy Spirit.

6:12 These who are not "flesh and blood" are demons over whom Satan has control. They are not mere fantasies—they are very real. We face a powerful army whose goal is to defeat Christ's church. When we believe in Christ, these beings become our enemies, and they try every device to turn us away from him and back to sin. Although we are assured of victory, we must engage in the struggle until Christ returns, because Satan is constantly battling against all who are on the Lord's side. We need supernatural power to defeat Satan, and God has provided this by giving us his Holy Spirit within us and his armor surrounding us. If you feel discouraged, remember Jesus' words to Peter: "Upon this rock I will build my church, and all the powers of hell will not conquer it" (Matthew 16:18).

6:18 How can anyone pray at all times? One way is to make quick, brief prayers your habitual response to every situation you meet throughout the day. Another way is to order your life around God's desires and teachings so that your very life becomes a prayer. You don't have to isolate yourself from other people and from daily work in order to pray constantly. You can make prayer your life and your life a prayer while living in a world that needs God's powerful influence. We also should pray for all believers in Christ; so pray for the Christians you know and for the church around the world.

6:19, 20 Undiscouraged and undefeated, Paul wrote powerful letters of encouragement from prison. Paul did not ask the Ephesians to pray that his chains would be removed but that he would continue to speak fearlessly for Christ in spite of them. God can use us in any circumstance to do his will. Even as we pray for a change in our circumstances, we should also pray that God will accomplish his plan through us right where we are. Knowing God's eternal purpose for us will help us through the difficult times.

Final Greetings

6:21
Acts 20:4
2 Tim 4:12
Titus 3:12

6:22
Col 4:7-9

6:23
Gal 6:16
2 Thes 3:16

21 Tychicus, a much loved brother and faithful helper in the Lord's work, will tell you all
about how I am getting along. 22 I am sending him to you for just this purpose. He will
let you know how we are, and he will encourage you.
23 May God give you peace, dear friends,* and love with faith, from God the Father
and the Lord Jesus Christ. 24 May God's grace be upon all who love our Lord Jesus Christ
with an undying love.

6:23 Greek *brothers.*

6:21 Tychicus is also mentioned in Acts 20:4, Colossians 4:7, 2 Timothy 4:12, and Titus 3:12.

6:24 This letter was written to the church at Ephesus, but it was also meant for circulation among other churches. In this letter, Paul highlights the supremacy of Christ, gives information on both the nature of the church and on how church members should live, and stresses the unity of all believers—male, female, parent, child, master, slave—regardless of sex, nationality, or social rank. The home and the church are difficult places to live the Christian life, because our real self comes through to those who know us well. Close relationships between imperfect people can lead to trouble—or to increased faith and deepened dependence on God. We can build unity in our churches through willing submission to Christ's leadership and humble service to one another.

PHILIPPIANS

VITAL STATISTICS

PURPOSE:
To thank the Philippians for the gift they had sent Paul and to strengthen these believers by showing them that true joy comes from Jesus Christ alone

AUTHOR:
Paul

TO WHOM WRITTEN:
All the Christians at Philippi, and all believers everywhere

DATE WRITTEN:
Approximately A.D. 61, from Rome during Paul's imprisonment there

SETTING:
Paul and his companions began the church at Philippi on his second missionary journey (Acts 16:11–40). This was the first church established on the European continent. The Philippian church had sent a gift with Epaphroditus (one of their members) to be delivered to Paul (4:18). Paul was in a Roman prison at the time. He wrote this letter to thank them for their gift and to encourage them in their faith.

KEY VERSE:
"Always be full of joy in the Lord. I say it again—rejoice!" (4:4).

KEY PEOPLE:
Paul, Timothy, Epaphroditus, Euodia, and Syntyche

KEY PLACE:
Philippi

THE WORD *happiness* evokes visions of unwrapping gifts on Christmas morning, strolling hand in hand with the one you love, being surprised on your birthday, responding with unbridled laughter to a comedian, or vacationing in an exotic locale. Everyone wants to be happy; we make chasing this elusive ideal a lifelong pursuit: spending money, collecting things, and searching for new experiences. But if happiness depends on our circumstances, what happens when the toys rust, loved ones die, health deteriorates, money is stolen, and the party's over? Often happiness flees and despair sets in.

In contrast to *happiness* stands *joy.* Running deeper and stronger, joy is the quiet, confident assurance of God's love and work in our life—that he will be there no matter what! Happiness depends on happenings, but joy depends on Christ.

Philippians is Paul's joy letter. The church in that Macedonian city had been a great encouragement to Paul. The Philippian believers had enjoyed a very special relationship with Paul, so he wrote them a personal expression of his love and affection. They had brought him great joy (4:1). Philippians is also a joyful book because it emphasizes the real joy of the Christian life. The concept of *rejoicing* or *joy* appears sixteen times in four chapters, and the pages radiate this positive message, culminating in the exhortation to "always be full of joy in the Lord. I say it again—rejoice!" (4:4).

In a life dedicated to serving Christ, Paul had faced excruciating poverty, abundant wealth, and everything in between. He even wrote this joyful letter from prison. Whatever the circumstances, Paul had learned to be content (4:11, 12), finding real joy as he focused all of his attention and energy on knowing Christ (3:8) and obeying him (3:12, 13).

Paul's desire to know Christ above all else is wonderfully expressed in the following words: "Yes, everything else is worthless when compared with the priceless gain of knowing Christ Jesus my Lord. I have discarded everything else, counting it all as garbage, so that I may have Christ and become one with him. . . . As a result, I can really know Christ and experience the mighty power that raised him from the dead. I can learn what it means to suffer with him, sharing in his death" (3:8–10). May we share Paul's aspiration and seek to know Jesus Christ more and more. Rejoice with Paul in Philippians, and rededicate yourself to finding joy in Christ.

THE BLUEPRINT

1. Joy in suffering (1:1–30)
2. Joy in serving (2:1–30)
3. Joy in believing (3:1—4:1)
4. Joy in giving (4:2–23)

Although Paul was writing from prison, joy is a dominant theme in this letter. The secret of his joy is grounded in his relationship with Christ. People today desperately want to be happy but are tossed and turned by daily successes, failures, and inconveniences. Christians are to be joyful in every circumstance, even when things are going badly, even when we feel like complaining, even when no one else is joyful. Christ still reigns, and we still know him, so we can rejoice at all times.

MEGATHEMES

THEME	EXPLANATION	IMPORTANCE
Humility	Christ showed true humility when he laid aside his rights and privileges as God to become human. He poured out his life to pay the penalty we deserve. Laying aside self-interest is essential to all our relationships.	We are to take Christ's attitude in serving others. We must renounce personal recognition and merit. When we give up our self-interest, we can serve with joy, love, and kindness.
Self-Sacrifice	Christ suffered and died so we might have eternal life. With courage and faithfulness, Paul sacrificed himself for the ministry. He preached the gospel even while he was in prison.	Christ gives us power to lay aside our personal needs and concerns. To utilize his power, we must imitate those leaders who show self-denying concern for others. We dare not be self-centered.
Unity	In every church, in every generation, there are divisive influences (issues, loyalties, and conflicts). In the midst of hardships, it is easy to turn on one another. Paul encouraged the Philippians to agree with one another, stop complaining, and work together.	As believers, we should not contend with one another but unite against a mutual enemy. When we are unified in love, Christ's strength is most abundant. Keep before you the ideals of teamwork, consideration of others, and unselfishness.
Christian Living	Paul shows us how to live successful Christian lives. We can become mature by being so identified with Christ that his attitude of humility and self-sacrifice becomes ours. Christ is both our source of power and our guide.	Developing our character begins with God's work in us. But growth also requires self-discipline, obedience to God's Word, and concentration on our part.
Joy	Believers can have profound contentment, serenity, and peace no matter what happens. This joy comes from knowing Christ personally and from depending on his strength rather than our own.	We can have joy, even in hardship. Joy does not come from outward circumstances but from inward strength. As Christians, we must not rely on what we have or what we experience to give us joy but on Christ within us.

1. Joy in suffering

Greetings from Paul

1 This letter is from Paul and Timothy, slaves of Christ Jesus.
It is written to all of God's people in Philippi, who believe in Christ Jesus, and to
the elders* and deacons.
2 May God our Father and the Lord Jesus Christ give you grace and peace.

1:1 Acts 16:1; 2 Cor 1:1
1:2-3 Rom 1:7-8

Paul's Thanksgiving and Prayer

3 Every time I think of you, I give thanks to my God. 4 I always pray for you, and I make
my requests with a heart full of joy 5 because you have been my partners in spreading the

1:1 Greek *overseers.*

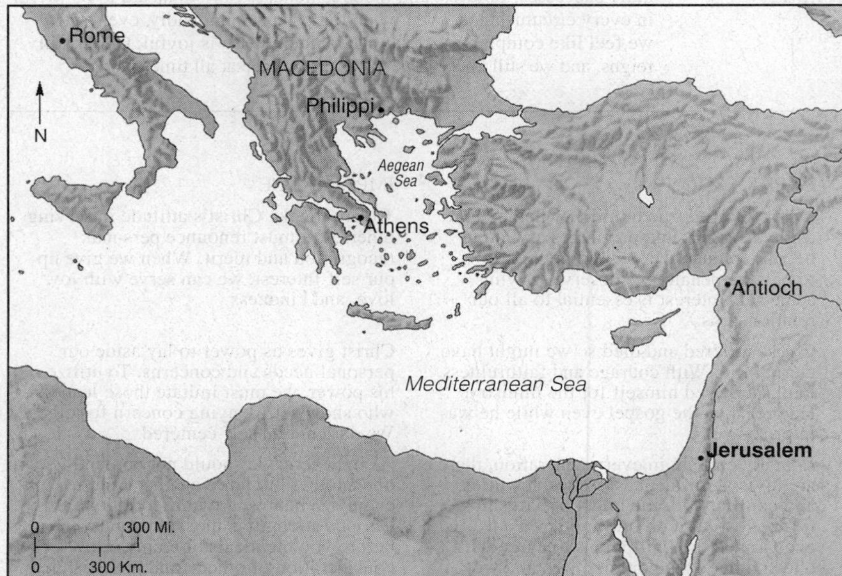

LOCATION OF PHILIPPI
Philippi sat on the Egnatian Way, the main transportation route in Macedonia, an extension of the Appian Way, which joined the eastern empire with Italy.

1:1 This is a personal letter to the Philippians, not intended for general circulation to all the churches, as was the letter to the Ephesians. Paul wanted to thank the believers for helping him when he had a need. He also wanted to tell them why he could be full of joy despite his imprisonment and upcoming trial. In this uplifting letter, Paul counseled the Philippians about humility and unity and warned them about potential problems.

1:1 On Paul's first missionary journey, he visited towns close to his headquarters in Antioch in Syria. On his second and third journeys, he traveled even farther. Because of the great distances between the congregations that Paul had founded, he could no longer personally oversee them all. Thus, he was compelled to write letters to teach and encourage the believers. Fortunately, Paul had a staff of volunteers (including Timothy, Mark, and Epaphras) who personally delivered these letters and often remained with the congregations for a while to teach and encourage them.

1:1 For more information on Paul, see his Profile in Acts 9. Timothy's Profile is found in 1 Timothy 2.

1:1 The Roman colony of Philippi was located in northern Greece (called Macedonia in Paul's day). Philip II of Macedon (the father of Alexander the Great) took the town from ancient Thrace in about 357 B.C., enlarged and strengthened it, and gave it his name. This thriving commercial center sat at the crossroads between Europe and Asia. In about A.D. 50, Paul, Silas, Timothy, and Luke crossed the Aegean Sea from Asia Minor and landed at Philippi (Acts 16:11-40). The church in Philippi consisted mostly of Gentile (non-Jewish) believers. Because they were not familiar with the Old Testament, Paul did not specifically quote any Old Testament passages in this letter.

1:1 Elders (bishops or pastors) and deacons led the early Christian churches. The qualifications and duties of the elders are explained in detail in 1 Timothy 3:1-7 and Titus 1:5-9. The qualifications and duties of deacons are spelled out in 1 Timothy 3:8-13.

1:4 This is the first of many times Paul used the word *joy* in his letter. The Philippians were remembered with joy and thanksgiving whenever Paul prayed. By helping Paul, they were helping Christ's cause. The Philippians were willing to be used by God for whatever he wanted them to do. When others think about you, what comes to their minds? Are you remembered with joy by them? Do your acts of kindness lift up others?

1:4, 5 The Philippians first heard the Good News about 10 years earlier when Paul and his companions visited Philippi (during Paul's second missionary journey) and founded the church there.

1:5 When Paul said that the Philippians were partners in the Good News, he was pointing out their valuable contribution in spreading God's message. They contributed through their

1:6 1 Cor 1:8 Good News about Christ from the time you first heard it until now. 6And I am sure that
God, who began the good work within you, will continue his work until it is finally
finished on that day when Christ Jesus comes back again.
1:7 2 Cor 7:3 7It is right that I should feel as I do about all of you, for you have a very special place
1:8 Rom 1:9 in my heart. We have shared together the blessings of God, both when I was in prison
and when I was out, defending the truth and telling others the Good News. 8God knows
1:9 1 Thes 3:12 how much I love you and long for you with the tender compassion of Christ Jesus. 9I
pray that your love for each other will overflow more and more, and that you will keep
1:10 Rom 12:2; 1 Cor 1:8 on growing in your knowledge and understanding. 10For I want you to understand what
really matters, so that you may live pure and blameless lives until Christ returns. 11May
1:11 John 15:4 you always be filled with the fruit of your salvation*—those good things that are
produced in your life by Jesus Christ—for this will bring much glory and praise to God.

Paul's Joy That Christ Is Preached

1:12 2 Tim 2:9 12And I want you to know, dear friends,* that everything that has happened to me here
1:13 Acts 28:30-31; Eph 3:1; 4:1 has helped to spread the Good News. 13For everyone here, including all the soldiers in
the palace guard, knows that I am in chains because of Christ. 14And because of my
1:14 Phil 1:20 imprisonment, many of the Christians* here have gained confidence and become more
bold in telling others about Christ.

1:11 Greek *the fruit of righteousness.* **1:12** Greek *brothers.* **1:14** Greek *brothers in the Lord.*

---

practical help when Paul was in Philippi and through their financial support when he was in prison. As we help our ministers, missionaries, and evangelists through prayer, hospitality, and financial gifts, we become partners with them.

1:6 The God who began a good work within us continues it throughout our lifetime and will finish it when we meet him face to face. God's work *for* us began when Christ died on the cross in our place. His work *within* us began when we first believed. Now the Holy Spirit lives in us, enabling us to be more like Christ every day. Paul is describing the process of Christian growth and maturity that began when we accepted Jesus and continues until Christ returns.

1:6 Do you sometimes feel as though you aren't making progress in your spiritual life? When God starts a project, he completes it! As with the Philippians, God will help you grow in grace until he has completed his work in your life. When you are discouraged, remember that God won't give up on you. He promises to finish the work he has begun. When you feel incomplete, unfinished, or distressed by your shortcomings, remember God's promise and provision. Don't let your present condition rob you of the joy of knowing Christ or keep you from growing closer to him.

1:7 When he said, "in prison," Paul was probably referring to his imprisonment in Philippi (see Acts 16:22-36). In verses 13 and 14, Paul speaks of his Roman imprisonment. Wherever Paul was, even in prison, he faithfully preached the Good News. Remember Paul's inspiring example when hindrances, small or large, slow down your work for God.

1:7, 8 Have you ever longed to see a friend with whom you share fond memories? Paul had such a longing to see the Christians at Philippi. His love and affection for them was based not merely on past experiences but also on the unity that comes when believers draw upon Christ's love. All Christians are part of God's family and thus share equally in the transforming power of his love. Do you feel a deep love for fellow Christians, friends and strangers alike? Let Christ's love motivate you to love other Christians and to express that love in your actions toward them.

1:9 Often the best way to influence someone is to pray for him or her. Paul's prayer for the Philippians was that they would be unified in love. Their love was to result in greater knowledge of Christ and deeper insight (moral discernment). Their love was not based on feelings but on what Christ had done for them. As you grow in Christ's love, your heart and mind must grow together. Are your love and insight growing?

1:10 Paul prayed that the Philippian believers would have the ability to differentiate between right and wrong, good and bad, vital and trivial. We ought to pray for moral discernment so we can maintain our Christian morals and values. Hebrews 5:14 emphasizes the need for discernment.

1:10 When "Christ returns" refers to the time when God will judge the world through Jesus Christ. We should live each day as though he might return at any moment.

1:11 The "fruit of your salvation" includes all of the character traits flowing from a right relationship with God. There is no other way for us to gain this fruit of righteousness than through Christ. See Galatians 5:22, 23 for the "fruit of the Spirit."

1:12-14 Being imprisoned would cause many people to become bitter or to give up, but Paul saw it as one more opportunity to spread the Good News of Christ. Paul realized that his current circumstances weren't as important as what he did with them. Turning a bad situation into a good one, he reached out to the Roman soldiers who made up the palace guard and encouraged those Christians who were afraid of persecution. We may not be in prison, but we still have plenty of opportunities to be discouraged—times of indecision, financial burdens, family conflict, church conflict, or the loss of our jobs. How we act in such situations will reflect what we believe. Like Paul, look for ways to demonstrate your faith even in bad situations. Whether or not the situation improves, your faith will grow stronger.

1:13 How did Paul end up in chains in a Roman prison? While he was visiting Jerusalem, some Jews had him arrested for preaching the Good News, but he appealed to Caesar to hear his case (Acts 21:15–25:12). He was then escorted by soldiers to Rome, where he was placed under house arrest while awaiting trial—not a trial for breaking civil law, but for proclaiming the Good News of Christ. At that time, the Roman authorities did not consider this to be a serious charge. A few years later, however, Rome would take a different view of Christianity and make every effort to stamp it out of existence. Paul's house arrest allowed him some degree of freedom. He could have visitors, continue to preach, and write letters such as this one. A brief record of Paul's time in Rome is found in Acts 28:11-31. The "palace guard" refers to the elite troops housed in the emperor's palace.

1:14 When we speak fearlessly for Christ or live faithfully for him during difficult situations, we encourage others to do the same. Be an encouragement by the way that you live.

15 Some are preaching out of jealousy and rivalry. But others preach about Christ with 1:15 Phil 2:3
pure motives. 16 They preach because they love me, for they know the Lord brought me
here to defend the Good News. 17 Those others do not have pure motives as they preach 1:17 Acts 21:33
about Christ. They preach with selfish ambition, not sincerely, intending to make my
chains more painful to me. 18 But whether or not their motives are pure, the fact remains
that the message about Christ is being preached, so I rejoice. And I will continue to 1:19
rejoice. 19 For I know that as you pray for me and as the Spirit of Jesus Christ helps me, Job 13:16 2 Cor 1:11
this will all turn out for my deliverance.

Paul's Life for Christ

20 For I live in eager expectation and hope that I will never do anything that causes me 1:20 Rom 5:5; 14:8
shame, but that I will always be bold for Christ, as I have been in the past, and that my 1 Cor 6:20
life will always honor Christ, whether I live or I die. 21 For to me, living is for Christ, and Eph 6:19
dying is even better. 22 Yet if I live, that means fruitful service for Christ. I really don't 1:21 Gal 2:20
know which is better. 23 I'm torn between two desires: Sometimes I want to live, and Col 1:27
sometimes I long to go and be with Christ. That would be far better for me, 24 but it is 1:22 Rom 1:13
better for you that I live.
25 I am convinced of this, so I will continue with you so that you will grow and 1:23 2 Cor 5:8 2 Tim 4:6
experience the joy of your faith. 26 Then when I return to you, you will have even more
reason to boast about what Christ Jesus has done for me. 1:25 Phil 2:24

Live as Citizens of Heaven

27 But whatever happens to me, you must live in a manner worthy of the Good News 1:27 Eph 4:1
about Christ, as citizens of heaven. Then, whether I come and see you again or only hear Phil 4:1-2
about you, I will know that you are standing side by side, fighting together for the Good 1:28 2 Tim 2:11
News. 28 Don't be intimidated by your enemies. This will be a sign to them that they are Heb 13:6
going to be destroyed, but that you are going to be saved, even by God himself. 29 For 1:29 Matt 5:11-12
you have been given not only the privilege of trusting in Christ but also the privilege of
suffering for him. 30 We are in this fight together. You have seen me suffer for him in the 1:30 Acts 16:19-40
past, and you know that I am still in the midst of this great struggle. 1 Thes 2:2

1:15-18 Paul had an amazingly selfless attitude. He knew that some were preaching to build their own reputations, taking advantage of his imprisonment to try to make a name for themselves. Regardless of the motives of these preachers, Paul rejoiced that the Good News was being preached. Some Christians serve for the wrong reasons. Paul wouldn't condone, nor does God excuse, their motives, but we should be glad if God uses their message, regardless of their motives.

1:19-21 This was not Paul's final imprisonment in Rome. But he didn't know that. Awaiting trial, he knew he could either be released or executed. However, he trusted Christ to work it out for his deliverance. Paul's prayer was that when he stood trial, he would speak courageously for Christ and not be timid or ashamed. Whether he lived or died, he wanted to exalt Christ. As it turned out, he was released from this imprisonment but arrested again two or three years later. Only faith in Christ could sustain Paul in such adversity.

1:20, 21 To those who don't believe in God, life on earth is all there is, and so it is natural for them to strive for this world's values: money, popularity, power, pleasure, and prestige. For Paul, however, to live meant to develop eternal values and to tell others about Christ, who alone could help them see life from an eternal perspective. Paul's whole purpose in life was to speak out boldly for Christ and to become more like him. Thus, Paul could confidently say that dying would be even better than living, because in death he would be removed from worldly troubles, and he would see Christ face to face (1 John 3:2, 3). If you're not ready to die, then you're not ready to live. Make certain of your eternal destiny; then you will be free to serve—devoting your life to what really counts, without fear of death.

1:24 Paul had a purpose for living when he served the Philippians and others. We also need a purpose for living that goes beyond providing for our own physical needs. Whom can you serve or help? What is your purpose for living?

1:27 Paul encouraged the believers to be unified, as they stood "side by side, fighting together for the Good News." How sad that much time and effort are lost in some churches by fighting against one another instead of uniting against the real opposition! It takes a courageous church to resist infighting and to maintain the common purpose of serving Christ.

1:29 Paul considered it a privilege to suffer for Christ. We do not by nature consider suffering a privilege. Yet when we suffer, if we faithfully represent Christ, our message and example affect us and others for good (see Acts 5:41). Suffering has these additional benefits: (1) It takes our eyes off of earthly comforts; (2) it weeds out superficial believers; (3) it strengthens the faith of those who endure; (4) it serves as an example to others who may follow us. When we suffer for our faith, it doesn't mean that we have done something wrong. In fact, the opposite is often true—it verifies that we have been faithful. Use suffering to build your character. Don't resent it or let it tear you down.

1:30 Throughout his life Paul suffered for spreading the Good News. Like the Philippians, we are in conflict with anyone who would discredit the saving message of Christ. All true believers are in this fight together, uniting against the same enemy for a common cause.

2:1 2 Cor 13:14; Col 3:12
2:2 1 Pet 3:8
2:3 Rom 12:10; Gal 5:26; 1 Pet 5:5
2:4 1 Cor 10:24
2:6 John 1:1-2; 5:18
2:7 John 1:14; Rom 8:3
2:9 Eph 1:20-21; Heb 1:3-4

2. Joy in serving

Unity through Humility

2 Is there any encouragement from belonging to Christ? Any comfort from his love?
Any fellowship together in the Spirit? Are your hearts tender and sympathetic?
2 Then make me truly happy by agreeing wholeheartedly with each other, loving one
another, and working together with one heart and purpose.
3 Don't be selfish; don't live to make a good impression on others. Be humble, thinking
of others as better than yourself. 4 Don't think only about your own affairs, but be
interested in others, too, and what they are doing.

Christ's Humility and Exaltation

5 Your attitude should be the same that Christ Jesus had. 6 Though he was God, he did not
demand and cling to his rights as God. 7 He made himself nothing;* he took the humble
position of a slave and appeared in human form.* 8 And in human form he obediently
humbled himself even further by dying a criminal's death on a cross. 9 Because of this,

2:7a Or *He laid aside his mighty power and glory.* **2:7b** Greek *and was born in the likeness of men and was found in appearance as a man.*

2:1-5 Many people—even Christians—live only to make a good impression on others or to please themselves. But selfishness brings discord. Paul therefore stressed spiritual unity, asking the Philippians to love one another and to be one in spirit and purpose. When we work together, caring for the problems of others as if they were our problems, we demonstrate Christ's example of putting others first, and we experience unity. Don't be so concerned about making a good impression or meeting your own needs that you strain relationships in God's family.

2:3 Selfishness can ruin a church, but genuine humility can build it. Being humble involves having a true perspective about ourselves (see Romans 12:3). It does not mean that we should put ourselves down. Before God, we are sinners, saved only by God's grace, but we *are* saved and therefore have great worth in God's Kingdom. We are to lay aside selfishness and treat others with respect and common courtesy. Considering others' interests as more important than our own links us with Christ, who was a true example of humility.

2:4 Philippi was a cosmopolitan city. The composition of the church reflected great diversity, with people from a variety of backgrounds and walks of life. Acts 16 gives us some indication of the diverse makeup of this church. The church included Lydia, a Jewish convert from Asia and a wealthy businesswoman (Acts 16:14); the slave girl (Acts 16:16, 17), probably a native Greek; and the jailer serving this colony of the empire, probably a Roman (Acts 16:25-36). With so many different backgrounds among the members, unity must have been difficult to maintain. Although there is no evidence of division in the church, its unity had to be safeguarded (3:2; 4:2). Paul encourages us to guard against any selfishness, prejudice, or jealousy that might lead to dissension. Showing genuine interest in others is a positive step forward in maintaining unity among believers.

2:5 Jesus Christ was humble, willing to give up his rights in order to obey God and serve people. Like Christ, we should have a servant's attitude, serving out of love for God and for others, not out of guilt or fear. Remember, you can choose your attitude. You can approach life expecting to be served, or you can look for opportunities to serve others. See Mark 10:45 for more on Christ's attitude of servanthood.

2:5-7 The Incarnation was the act of the preexistent Son of God voluntarily assuming a human body and human nature. Without ceasing to be God, he became a human being, the man called Jesus. He did not give up his deity to become human, but he set aside the right to his glory and power. In submission to the Father's will, Christ limited his power and knowledge. Jesus of Nazareth was subject to place, time, and many other human limitations. What made his humanity unique was his freedom from sin. In his full humanity, Jesus showed us everything about God's character that can be conveyed in human terms. The Incarnation is explained further in these passages: John 1:1-14; Romans 1:2-5; 2 Corinthians 8:9; 1 Timothy 3:16; Hebrews 2:14; and 1 John 1:1-3.

2:5-11 These verses are probably from a hymn sung by the early Christian church. The passage holds many parallels to the prophecy of the suffering servant in Isaiah 53. As a hymn, it was not meant to be a complete statement about the nature and work of Christ. Several key characteristics of Jesus Christ, however, are praised in this passage: (1) Christ has always existed with God; (2) Christ is equal to God because he *is* God (John 1:1ff; Colossians 1:15-19); (3) though Christ is God, he became a man in order to fulfill God's plan of salvation for all people; (4) Christ did not just have the appearance of being a man—he actually became human to identify with our sins; (5) Christ voluntarily laid aside his divine rights and privileges out of love for his Father; (6) Christ died on the cross for our sins so we wouldn't have to face eternal death; (7) God glorified Christ because of his obedience; (8) God raised Christ to his original position at the Father's right hand, where he will reign forever as our Lord and Judge. How can we do anything less than praise Christ as our Lord and dedicate ourselves to his service!

2:5-11 Often people excuse selfishness, pride, or evil by claiming their rights. They think, "I can cheat on this test; after all, I deserve to pass this class," or "I can spend all this money on myself—I worked hard for it," or "I can get an abortion; I have a right to control my own body." But as believers, we should have a different attitude, one that enables us to lay aside our rights in order to serve others. If we say we follow Christ, we must also say we want to live as he lived. We should develop his attitude of humility as we serve, even when we are not likely to get recognition for our efforts. Are you selfishly clinging to your rights, or are you willing to serve?

2:8 Death on a cross (crucifixion) was the form of capital punishment that Romans used for notorious criminals. It was excruciatingly painful and humiliating. Prisoners were nailed or tied to a cross and left to die. Death might not come for several days, and it usually came by suffocation when the weight of the weakened body made breathing more and more difficult. Jesus died as one who was cursed (Galatians 3:13). How amazing that the perfect man should die this most shameful death so that we would not have to face eternal punishment!

2:9-11 At the Last Judgment, even those who are condemned will recognize Jesus' authority and right to rule. People can choose now to commit their lives to Jesus as Lord or be forced to acknowledge him as Lord when he returns. Christ may return at any moment. Are you prepared to meet him?

God raised him up to the heights of heaven and gave him a name that is above every
other name, [10]so that at the name of Jesus every knee will bow, in heaven and on earth
and under the earth, [11]and every tongue will confess that Jesus Christ is Lord, to the glory
of God the Father.

Shine Brightly for Christ

[12]Dearest friends, you were always so careful to follow my instructions when I was
with you. And now that I am away you must be even more careful to put into action
God's saving work in your lives, obeying God with deep reverence and fear. [13]For
God is working in you, giving you the desire to obey him and the power to do what
pleases him.
[14]In everything you do, stay away from complaining and arguing, [15]so that no one can
speak a word of blame against you. You are to live clean, innocent lives as children of
God in a dark world full of crooked and perverse people. Let your lives shine brightly
before them. [16]Hold tightly to the word of life, so that when Christ returns, I will be
proud that I did not lose the race and that my work was not useless. [17]But even if my life
is to be poured out like a drink offering to complete the sacrifice of your faithful service
(that is, if I am to die for you), I will rejoice, and I want to share my joy with all of you.
[18]And you should be happy about this and rejoice with me.

Paul Commends Timothy

[19]If the Lord Jesus is willing, I hope to send Timothy to you soon. Then when he
comes back, he can cheer me up by telling me how you are getting along. [20]I have no
one else like Timothy, who genuinely cares about your welfare. [21]All the others care
only for themselves and not for what matters to Jesus Christ. [22]But you know how
Timothy has proved himself. Like a son with his father, he has helped me in preaching
the Good News. [23]I hope to send him to you just as soon as I find out what is going
to happen to me here. [24]And I have confidence from the Lord that I myself will come
to see you soon.

2:10 Isa 45:23; Rom 14:11
2:11 John 13:13
2:13 Rom 8:28; 1 Cor 12:6; Heb 13:21
2:14 1 Cor 10:10; 1 Pet 4:9
2:15 Matt 5:45; John 12:36; Eph 5:1
2:16 1 Thes 2:19
2:17 Rom 15:16; 2 Tim 4:6
2:20 1 Cor 16:10
2:21 1 Cor 10:24
2:22 1 Cor 4:17; 1 Tim 1:2
2:24 Phil 1:25

2:12 "Put into action God's saving work in your lives," in light of the preceding exhortation to unity, may mean that the entire church was to work together to rid themselves of divisions and discord. The Philippian Christians needed to be especially careful to obey Christ, now that Paul wasn't there to continually remind them about what was right. We, too, must be careful about what we believe and how we live, especially when we are on our own. In the absence of cherished Christian leaders, we must focus our attention and devotion even more on Christ so that we won't be sidetracked.

2:13 What do we do when we don't feel like obeying? God has not left us alone in our struggles to do his will. He wants to come alongside us and be within us to help. God helps us *desire* to obey him and then gives us the *power* to do what he wants. The secret to a changed life is to submit to God's control and let him work. Next time ask God to help you *desire* to do his will.

2:13 To be like Christ, we must train ourselves to think like Christ. To change our desires to be more like Christ's, we need the power of the indwelling Spirit (1:19), the influence of faithful Christians, obedience to God's Word (not just exposure to it), and sacrificial service. Often it is in *doing* God's will that we gain the *desire* to do it (see 4:8, 9). Do what he wants and trust him to change your desires.

2:14-16 Why are complaining and arguing so harmful? If all that people know about a church is that its members constantly argue, complain, and gossip, they get a false impression of Christ and the Good News. Belief in Christ should unite those who trust him. If your church is always complaining and arguing, it lacks the unifying power of Jesus Christ. Stop arguing with other Christians or complaining about people and conditions within the church and let the world see Christ.

2:14-16 Our life should be characterized by moral purity, patience, and peacefulness, so that we will "shine brightly" in a dark and depraved world. A transformed life is an effective witness to the power of God's Word. Is your life shining brightly, or is it clouded by complaining and arguing? Shine out for God.

2:17 The drink offering was an important part of the sacrificial system of the Jews (for an explanation, see Numbers 28:7). Because this church had little Jewish background, the drink offering may refer to the wine poured out to pagan deities prior to important public events. Paul regarded his life as a sacrifice.

2:17 Even if he had to die, Paul was content, knowing that he had helped the Philippians live for Christ. When you're totally committed to serving Christ, sacrificing to build the faith of others brings a joyous reward.

2:19 Timothy was with Paul in Rome when Paul wrote this letter. He traveled with Paul on his second missionary journey when the church at Philippi was begun. For more information on Timothy, see his Profile in 1 Timothy 2.

2:21 Paul observed that most believers are too preoccupied with their own needs to spend time working for Christ. Don't let your schedule and concerns crowd out your love and Christian service to others.

2:22 Just as a skilled workman trains an apprentice, Paul was preparing Timothy to carry on the ministry in his absence. Whom are you apprenticing for God's work? For more information, see Timothy's Profile in 1 Timothy 2.

2:23 Paul was in prison (either awaiting his trial or its verdict) for preaching about Christ. He was telling the Philippians that when he learned of the court's decision, he would send Timothy to them with the news, and that he would ready to accept whatever came (1:21-26).

Paul Commends Epaphroditus

25 Meanwhile, I thought I should send Epaphroditus back to you. He is a true brother, a
faithful worker, and a courageous soldier. And he was your messenger to help me in my
need. 26 Now I am sending him home again, for he has been longing to see you, and he
was very distressed that you heard he was ill. 27 And he surely was ill; in fact, he almost
died. But God had mercy on him—and also on me, so that I would not have such
unbearable sorrow.

28 So I am all the more anxious to send him back to you, for I know you will be glad
to see him, and that will lighten all my cares. 29 Welcome him with Christian love* and
with great joy, and be sure to honor people like him. 30 For he risked his life for the work
of Christ, and he was at the point of death while trying to do for me the things you
couldn't do because you were far away.

2:25 Phil 4:18
2:26 Phil 1:8
2:29 1 Cor 16:16, 18; 1 Tim 5:17
2:30 1 Cor 16:17

3. Joy in believing

The Priceless Gain of Knowing Christ

3 Whatever happens, dear friends,* may the Lord give you joy. I never get tired of
telling you this. I am doing this for your own good.

2 Watch out for those dogs, those wicked men and their evil deeds, those mutilators
who say you must be circumcised to be saved. 3 For we who worship God in the Spirit*
are the only ones who are truly circumcised. We put no confidence in human effort.
Instead, we boast about what Christ Jesus has done for us.

4 Yet I could have confidence in myself if anyone could. If others have reason for
confidence in their own efforts, I have even more! 5 For I was circumcised when I was
eight days old, having been born into a pure-blooded Jewish family that is a branch of
the tribe of Benjamin. So I am a real Jew if there ever was one! What's more, I was a
member of the Pharisees, who demand the strictest obedience to the Jewish law. 6 And

3:1 Phil 2:18; 4:4
3:2 Ps 22:16, 20; Rev 22:15
3:3 John 4:21-24; Rom 2:29; Gal 6:15; Col 2:11
3:5 Luke 1:59; 2:21; Acts 23:6; Rom 11:1; 2 Cor 11:22
3:6 Acts 8:3; 22:4; 26:9-11; Gal 1:13

2:29 Greek *in the Lord.* **3:1** Greek *brothers;* also in 3:13, 17. **3:3** Or *in spirit;* some manuscripts read *worship by the Spirit of God.*

2:25 Epaphroditus delivered money from the Philippians to Paul; then he returned with this thank-you letter to Philippi. Epaphroditus may have been an elder in Philippi (2:25-30; 4:18) who, while staying with Paul, became ill (2:27, 30). After Epaphroditus recovered, he returned home. He is mentioned only in Philippians.

2:29, 30 The world honors those who are intelligent, beautiful, rich, and powerful. What kind of people should the church honor? Paul indicates that we should honor those who give their lives for the sake of Christ, going where we cannot go ourselves. Our missionaries do that for us today by providing ministry where we are not able to go.

3:1 As a safeguard, Paul reviewed the basics with these believers. The Bible is our safeguard both morally and theologically. When we read it individually and publicly in church, it alerts us to corrections we need to make in our thoughts, attitudes, and actions.

3:2, 3 These "dogs" and "wicked men" were very likely Judaizers—Jewish Christians who wrongly believed that it was essential for Gentiles to follow all the Old Testament Jewish laws, especially submission to the rite of circumcision, in order to receive salvation. Many Judaizers were motivated by spiritual pride. Because they had invested so much time and effort in keeping their laws, they couldn't accept the fact that all their efforts couldn't bring them a step closer to salvation.

Paul criticized the Judaizers because they looked at Christianity backward—thinking that what they *did* (circumcision—cutting or mutilating the flesh) made them believers rather than the free gift of grace given by Christ. What believers do is a *result* of faith, not a *prerequisite* to faith. This had been confirmed by the early church leaders at the Jerusalem council 11 years earlier (Acts 15). Who are the Judaizers of our day? They are those who say that people must add something else to simple faith. No person should add anything to Christ's offer of salvation by grace through faith.

3:2, 3 It is easy to place more emphasis on human effort than on internal faith, but God values the attitude of our heart above all else. Don't judge people's spirituality by their fulfillment of duties or by their level of human activity. And don't think that you will satisfy God by feverishly doing his work. God notices all you do for him and will reward you for it, but only if it comes as a loving response to his free gift of salvation.

3:4-6 At first glance, it looks like Paul is boasting about his achievements. But he is actually doing the opposite, showing that human achievements, no matter how impressive, cannot earn a person salvation and eternal life with God. Paul had impressive credentials: upbringing, nationality, family background, inheritance, orthodoxy, activity, and morality (see 2 Corinthians 11; Galatians 1:13-24, for more of his credentials). However, his conversion to faith in Christ (Acts 9) wasn't based on what he had done but on God's grace. Paul did not depend on his deeds to please God, because even the most impressive credentials fall short of God's holy standards. Are you depending on Christian parents, church affiliation, or just being good to make you right with God? Credentials, accomplishments, or reputation cannot earn salvation. Salvation comes only through faith in Christ.

3:5 Paul belonged to the tribe of Benjamin, a heritage greatly esteemed among the Jews. From this tribe had come Israel's first king, Saul (1 Samuel 10:20-24). The tribes of Benjamin and Judah were the only two tribes to return to Israel after the Exile (Ezra 4:1). Paul was also a Pharisee, a member of a very devout Jewish sect that scrupulously kept its own numerous rules in addition to the laws of Moses. Jewish listeners would have been impressed by both of these credentials.

3:6 Why did Paul, a devout Jewish leader, persecute the church? Agreeing with the leaders of the religious establishment, Paul thought that Christianity was heretical and blasphemous. Because Jesus did not meet his expectations of what the Messiah would be like, Paul assumed that Jesus' claims were false—and therefore wicked. In addition, he saw Christianity as a political menace because it threatened to disrupt the fragile harmony between the Jews and the Roman government.

zealous? Yes, in fact, I harshly persecuted the church. And I obeyed the Jewish law so carefully that I was never accused of any fault.

7I once thought all these things were so very important, but now I consider them worthless because of what Christ has done. 8Yes, everything else is worthless when compared with the priceless gain of knowing Christ Jesus my Lord. I have discarded everything else, counting it all as garbage, so that I may have Christ 9and become one with him. I no longer count on my own goodness or my ability to obey God's law, but I trust Christ to save me. For God's way of making us right with himself depends on faith. 10As a result, I can really know Christ and experience the mighty power that raised him from the dead. I can learn what it means to suffer with him, sharing in his death, 11so that, somehow, I can experience the resurrection from the dead!

Pressing toward the Goal

12I don't mean to say that I have already achieved these things or that I have already reached perfection! But I keep working toward that day when I will finally be all that Christ Jesus saved me for and wants me to be. 13No, dear friends, I am still not all I should be,* but I am focusing all my energies on this one thing: Forgetting the past and looking forward to what lies ahead, 14I strain to reach the end of the race and receive the prize for which God, through Christ Jesus, is calling us up to heaven.*

15I hope all of you who are mature Christians will agree on these things. If you disagree on some point, I believe God will make it plain to you. 16But we must be sure to obey the truth we have learned already.

3:13 Some manuscripts read *I am not all I should be.* **3:14** Or *from heaven.*

3:8
John 17:3
Eph 4:13
2 Pet 3:18

3:9
Rom 1:17; 3:21-22; 9:30; 10:3
Gal 2:16

3:10
Rom 6:3-5; 8:17, 29
Gal 6:17

3:11
Acts 26:8
1 Cor 15:23
Rev 20:5-6

3:12
1 Tim 6:12, 19

3:13
Luke 9:62

3:14
1 Cor 9:24
2 Tim 4:7-8
Heb 12:1

3:15
1 Cor 2:6
Phil 1:9-10

3:16
Gal 6:16

3:7 When Paul spoke of "all these things," he was referring to his credentials, credits, and successes. After showing that he could beat the Judaizers at their own game (being proud of who they were and what they had done), Paul showed that it was the wrong game. Be careful of considering past achievements so important that they get in the way of your relationship with Christ.

3:8 After Paul considered everything he had accomplished in his life, he said that it was all "worthless" when compared with the greatness of knowing Christ. This is a profound statement about values: A person's relationship with Christ is more important than anything else. To know Christ should be our ultimate goal. Consider your values. Do you place anything above your relationship with Christ? If your priorities are wrong, how will you reorder them?

3:9 No amount of law keeping, self-improvement, discipline, or religious effort can make us right with God. Righteousness comes only from God. We are made righteous (receive right standing with him) by trusting in Christ. He exchanges our sin and shortcomings for his complete righteousness. See 2 Corinthians 5:21 for more on Christ's gift of righteousness.

3:9, 10 Paul gave up everything—family, friendship, and freedom—in order to know Christ and his resurrection power. We, too, have access to this knowledge and this power, but we may have to make sacrifices to enjoy it fully. What are you willing to give up in order to know Christ? A crowded schedule in order to set aside a few minutes each day for prayer and Bible study? Your friend's approval? Some of your plans or pleasures? Whatever it is, knowing Christ is more than worth the sacrifice.

3:10 When we become one with Christ by trusting in him, we experience the power that raised him from the dead. That same mighty power will help us live morally renewed and regenerated lives. But before we can walk in newness of life, we must die to sin. Just as the Resurrection gives us Christ's power to live for him, his crucifixion marks the death of our old sinful nature. We can't know the victory of the Resurrection without personally applying the Crucifixion.

3:11 When Paul wrote, "so that, somehow, I can experience the resurrection from the dead," he was not implying uncertainty or doubt. He was unsure of the way that he would meet God, whether by execution or by natural death. He did not doubt that he would be raised, but attainment of it was within God's power and not his own.

3:11 Just as Christ was exalted after his resurrection, so we will one day share Christ's glory (Revelation 22:1-7). Paul knew that he might die soon, but he had faith that he would be raised to life again.

3:12-14 Paul said that his goal was to know Christ, to be like Christ, and to be all Christ had in mind for him. This goal took all of Paul's energies. This is a helpful example for us. We should not let anything take our eyes off our goal—knowing Christ. With the single-mindedness of an athlete in training, we must lay aside everything harmful and forsake anything that may distract us from being effective Christians. What is holding you back?

3:13, 14 Paul had reason to forget the past—he had held the coats of those who stoned Stephen, the first Christian martyr (Acts 7:57, 58, Paul is called Saul here). We have all done things for which we are ashamed, and we live in the tension of what we have been and what we want to be. Because our hope is in Christ, however, we can let go of past guilt and look forward to what God will help us become. Don't dwell on your past. Instead, grow in the knowledge of God by concentrating on your relationship with him *now.* Realize that you are forgiven, and then move on to a life of faith and obedience. Look forward to a fuller and more meaningful life because of your hope in Christ.

3:15, 16 Sometimes trying to live a perfect Christian life can be so difficult that it leaves us drained and discouraged. We may feel so far from perfect that we think we can never please God with our life. Paul used *perfection* (3:12) to mean mature or complete, not flawless in every detail. Those who are mature should press on in the Holy Spirit's power, knowing that Christ will reveal and fill in any discrepancy between what we are and what we should be. Christ's provision is no excuse for lagging devotion, but it provides relief and assurance for those who feel driven.

3:16 Christian maturity involves acting on the guidance that you have already received. We can always make excuses that we still have so much to learn. The instruction for us is to live up to what we already know and live out what we have already learned. We do not have to be sidetracked by an unending search for truth.

3:17 1 Cor 4:16; 1 Pet 5:3
3:18 Gal 6:12
3:20 Eph 2:16, 19; Heb 12:22
3:21 Rom 8:29; 1 Cor 15:28, 43-53

[17]Dear friends, pattern your lives after mine, and learn from those who follow our
example. [18]For I have told you often before, and I say it again with tears in my eyes, that
there are many whose conduct shows they are really enemies of the cross of Christ. [19]Their
future is eternal destruction. Their god is their appetite, they brag about shameful things,
and all they think about is this life here on earth. [20]But we are citizens of heaven, where
the Lord Jesus Christ lives. And we are eagerly waiting for him to return as our Savior.
[21]He will take these weak mortal bodies of ours and change them into glorious bodies like
his own, using the same mighty power that he will use to conquer everything, everywhere.

4:1 Phil 1:8

4 Dear brothers and sisters, I love you and long to see you, for you are my joy and the
reward for my work. So please stay true to the Lord, my dear friends.

4. Joy in giving

Paul's Final Thoughts

4:2 Phil 2:2

[2]And now I want to plead with those two women, Euodia and Syntyche. Please, because
you belong to the Lord, settle your disagreement. [3]And I ask you, my true teammate,*

4:3 Greek *true yokefellow,* or *loyal Syzygus.*

THREE STAGES OF PERFECTION

1. Perfect Relationship	We are perfect because of our eternal union with the infinitely perfect Christ. When we become his children, we are declared "not guilty" and thus righteous because of what Christ, God's beloved Son, has done for us. This perfection is absolute and unchangeable, and it is this perfect relationship that guarantees that we will one day be "completely perfect" (below). See Colossians 2:8–10; Hebrews 10:8–14.
2. Perfect Progress	We can grow and mature spiritually as we continue to trust Christ, learn more about him, draw closer to him, and obey him. Our progress is changeable (in contrast to our relationship, above) because it depends on our daily walk—at times in life we mature more than at other times. But we are growing toward perfection if we "keep working" (Philippians 3:12). These good deeds do not perfect us; rather, as God perfects us, we do good deeds for him. See Philippians 3:1–15.
3. Completely Perfect	When Christ returns to take us into his eternal Kingdom, we will be glorified and made completely perfect. See Philippians 3:20, 21.

All phases of perfection are grounded in faith in Christ and what he has done, not what we can do for him. We cannot perfect ourselves; only God can work in and through us to "continue his work until it is finally finished on that day Christ Jesus comes back again" (1:6).

3:17 Paul challenged the Philippians to pursue Christlikeness by following Paul's own pattern or example. This did not mean, of course, that they should copy everything he did; he had just stated that he was not perfect (3:12). But as he focused his life on being like Christ, so should they. The Gospels may not yet have been in circulation, so Paul could not tell them to read the Bible to see what Christ was like. Therefore, he urged them to imitate him. That Paul could tell people to follow his example is a testimony to his character. Can you do the same? What kind of follower would a new Christian become if he or she imitated you?

3:17-21 Paul criticized not only the Judaizers (see the first note on 3:2, 3) but also self-indulgent Christians, people who claimed to be Christians but didn't live up to Christ's model of servanthood and self-sacrifice. Such people satisfy their own desires before even thinking about the needs of others. Freedom in Christ does not mean freedom to be selfish. It means taking every opportunity to serve and to become the best person you can be.

3:20 Citizens of Philippi had the same rights and privileges as the citizens of Rome because Philippi was a Roman colony. Likewise, we Christians will one day experience all the special privileges of our heavenly citizenship because we belong to Christ. Let us not be so tied to this life that we would be sorry to see Christ return.

3:21 The phrase "weak mortal bodies" does not imply any negative attitude toward the human body. However, the bodies we will receive when we are raised from the dead will be glorious, like Christ's resurrected body. Those who struggle with pain, physical limitations, or disabilities can have wonderful hope in the resurrection. For a more detailed discussion of our new body, see 1 Corinthians 15:35ff and 2 Corinthians 5:1-10.

4:1 How do we "stay true to the Lord"? This refers to what Paul has just taught in 3:20, 21. The way to stay true is to keep our eyes on Christ, to remember that this world is not our home, and to focus on the fact that Christ will bring everything under his control.

4:2, 3 Paul did not warn the Philippian church of doctrinal errors, but he did address some relational problems. These two women had been workers for Christ in the church. Their broken relationship was no small matter, because many had become believers through their efforts. It is possible to believe in Christ, work hard for his Kingdom, and yet have broken relationships with others who are committed to the same cause. But there is no excuse for remaining unreconciled. Do you need to be reconciled to someone today?

to help these women, for they worked hard with me in telling others the Good News.
And they worked with Clement and the rest of my co-workers, whose names are written
in the Book of Life.
4Always be full of joy in the Lord. I say it again—rejoice! 5Let everyone see that you
are considerate in all you do. Remember, the Lord is coming soon.
6Don't worry about anything; instead, pray about everything. Tell God what you need,
and thank him for all he has done. 7If you do this, you will experience God's peace,
which is far more wonderful than the human mind can understand. His peace will guard
your hearts and minds as you live in Christ Jesus.
8And now, dear friends,* let me say one more thing as I close this letter. Fix your
thoughts on what is true and honorable and right. Think about things that are pure and
lovely and admirable. Think about things that are excellent and worthy of praise. 9Keep
putting into practice all you learned from me and heard from me and saw me doing, and
the God of peace will be with you.

Paul's Thanks for Their Gifts

10How grateful I am, and how I praise the Lord that you are concerned about me again.
I know you have always been concerned for me, but for a while you didn't have the
chance to help me. 11Not that I was ever in need, for I have learned how to get along
happily whether I have much or little. 12I know how to live on almost nothing or with

4:4 Phil 3:1
4:5 Heb 10:37; Jas 5:8-9
4:6 Matt 6:25; 1 Pet 5:7
4:7 Isa 26:3; John 14:27
4:9 Rom 15:33; 16:20; 1 Cor 14:33; 1 Thes 5:23
4:11 1 Tim 6:6
4:12 1 Cor 4:11; 2 Cor 11:9

4:8 Greek *brothers.*

4:3 The identity of this "true teammate" remains a mystery. It could be Epaphroditus, the bearer of this letter, or a comrade of Paul in prison. It could also be someone named Syzygus, another way to understand the word for "teammate."

4:3 Those "whose names are written in the Book of Life" are all who are marked for salvation through their faith in Christ (see also Luke 10:17-20; Revelation 20:11-15).

4:4 It seems strange that a man in prison would be telling a church to rejoice. But Paul's attitude teaches us an important lesson: Our inner attitudes do not have to reflect our outward circumstances. Paul was full of joy because he knew that no matter what happened to him, Jesus Christ was with him. Several times in this letter Paul urged the Philippians to be joyful, probably because they needed to hear this. It's easy to get discouraged about unpleasant circumstances or to take unimportant events too seriously. If you haven't been joyful lately, you may not be looking at life from the right perspective.

4:4, 5 Ultimate joy comes from Christ dwelling within us. Christ is near, and at his second coming we will fully realize this ultimate joy. He who lives within us will fulfill his final purposes for us.

4:5 We are to be considerate (reasonable, fair minded, and charitable) to those outside the church, and not just to fellow believers. This means we are not to seek revenge against those who treat us unfairly, nor are we to be overly vocal about our personal rights.

4:6, 7 Imagine never worrying about anything! It seems like an impossibility; we all have worries on the job, in our homes, at school. But Paul's advice is to turn our worries into prayers. Do you want to worry less? Then pray more! Whenever you start to worry, stop and pray.

4:7 God's peace is different from the world's peace (see John 14:27). True peace is not found in positive thinking, in absence of conflict, or in good feelings. It comes from knowing that God is in control. Our citizenship in Christ's Kingdom is sure, our destiny is set, and we can have victory over sin. Let God's peace guard your heart against anxiety.

4:8 What we put into our mind determines what comes out in our words and actions. Paul tells us to program our mind with thoughts that are true, honorable, right, pure, lovely, admirable, excellent, and worthy of praise. Do you have problems with impure thoughts and daydreams? Examine what you are putting into your mind through television, books, conversations, movies, and magazines. Replace harmful input with wholesome material. Above all, read God's Word and pray. Ask God to help you focus your mind on what is good and pure. It takes practice, but it can be done.

4:9 It's not enough to hear or read the Word of God or even to know it well. We must also put it into practice. How easy it is to listen to a sermon and forget what the preacher said. How easy it is to read the Bible and not think about how to live differently. How easy it is to debate what a passage means and not live out that meaning. Exposure to God's Word is not enough. It must lead to obedience.

4:10 In 1 Corinthians 9:11-18, Paul wrote that he didn't accept gifts from the Corinthian church because he didn't want to be accused of preaching only to get money. But Paul maintained that it was a church's responsibility to support God's ministers (1 Corinthians 9:14). He accepted the Philippians' gift because they gave it willingly and because he was in need.

4:10-14 Are you able to get along happily (be content) in any circumstances you face? Paul knew how to be content whether he had plenty or whether he was in need. The secret was drawing on Christ's power for strength. Do you have great needs, or are you discontented because you don't have what you want? Learn to rely on God's promises and Christ's power to help you be content. If you always want more, ask God to remove that desire and teach you contentment in every circumstance. He will supply all your needs, but in a way that he knows is best for you. (See the note on 4:19 for more on God supplying our needs.)

4:12, 13 Paul could get along happily because he could see life from God's point of view. He focused on what he was supposed to *do,* not what he felt he should *have.* Paul had his priorities straight, and he was grateful for everything God had given him. Paul had detached himself from the nonessentials so that he could concentrate on the eternal. Often the desire for more or better possessions is really a longing to fill an empty place in a person's life. To what are you drawn when you feel empty inside? How can you find true contentment? The answer lies in your perspective, your priorities, and your source of power.

4:13 2 Cor 12:9-10 everything. I have learned the secret of living in every situation, whether it is with a full
stomach or empty, with plenty or little. 13 For I can do everything with the help of Christ
4:15 2 Cor 11:8-9 Phil 1:5 who gives me the strength I need. 14 But even so, you have done well to share with me
in my present difficulty.
4:16 Acts 17:1 1 Thes 2:9 15 As you know, you Philippians were the only ones who gave me financial help when
I brought you the Good News and then traveled on from Macedonia. No other church
4:17 1 Cor 9:11 did this. 16 Even when I was in Thessalonica you sent help more than once. 17 I don't say
4:18 2 Cor 9:12 Phil 2:25 this because I want a gift from you. What I want is for you to receive a well-earned
reward because of your kindness.
18 At the moment I have all I need—more than I need! I am generously supplied with
4:19 Ps 23:1 2 Cor 9:8 the gifts you sent me with Epaphroditus. They are a sweet-smelling sacrifice that is
acceptable to God and pleases him. 19 And this same God who takes care of me will
4:20 Rom 11:36 1 Thes 3:13 supply all your needs from his glorious riches, which have been given to us in Christ
Jesus. 20 Now glory be to God our Father forever and ever. Amen.

TRAINING FOR THE CHRISTIAN LIFE

As a great amount of training is needed for athletic activities, so we must train diligently for the Christian life. Such training takes time, dedication, energy, continued practice, and vision. We must all commit ourselves to the Christian life, but we must first know the rules as prescribed in God's Word (2 Timothy 2:5).

Reference	*Metaphors*	*Training*	*Our Goal as Believers*
1 Corinthians 9:24–27	Race	Go into strict training in order to get the prize.	We train ourselves to run the race of life. So we keep our eyes on Christ—the goal—and don't get sidetracked or slowed down. When we do this, we will win a reward in Christ's Kingdom.
Philippians 3:13, 14	Race	Focus all your energies toward winning the race.	Living the Christian life demands all of our energies. We can forget the past and strain to reach the goal because we know Christ promises eternity with him at the race's end.
1 Timothy 4:7–10	Exercise	Spiritual exercise will help you grow in faith and character.	Just as we exercise to keep physically fit, we must also train ourselves to be spiritually fit. As our faith develops, we become better Christians, living in accordance with God's will. Such a life will attract others to Christ and pay dividends in both this life and the next.
2 Timothy 4:7, 8	Fight Race	Fighting the good fight and persevering to the end.	The Christian life is a fight against evil forces from without and temptation from within. If we stay true to God through it all, he promises an end, a rest, and a crown.

4:13 Can we really do everything? The power we receive in union with Christ is sufficient to do his will and to face the challenges that arise from our commitment to doing it. He does not grant us superhuman ability to accomplish anything we can imagine without regard to his interests. As we contend for the faith, we will face troubles, pressures, and trials. As they come, ask Christ to strengthen you.

4:14 The Philippians shared in Paul's financial support while he was in prison.

4:17 When we give to those in need, it not only benefits the receiver but it benefits us as well. It was not the Philippians' gift but their spirit of love and devotion that Paul appreciated most.

4:18 Paul was not referring to a sin offering but to a peace offering, "a sweet-smelling sacrifice that is acceptable to God and pleases him" (Leviticus 7:12-15 contains the instructions for such offerings of thanksgiving). Although the Greek and Roman Christians were not Jews and they had not offered sacrifices according to the Old Testament laws, they were well acquainted with the pagan rituals of offering sacrifices.

4:19 We can trust that God will always meet our needs. Whatever we need on earth he will always supply, even if it is the courage to face death as Paul did. Whatever we need in heaven he will supply. We must remember, however, the difference between our wants and our needs. Most people want to feel good and avoid discomfort or pain. We may not get all that we want. By trusting in Christ, our attitudes and appetites can change from wanting everything to accepting his provision and power to live for him.

Paul's Final Greetings

[21]Give my greetings to all the Christians there. The brothers who are with me here send
you their greetings. [22]And all the other Christians send their greetings, too, especially
those who work in Caesar's palace.
[23]May the grace of the Lord Jesus Christ be with your spirit.

4:22 Phil 1:13
4:23 Rom 16:20; Gal 6:18; 2 Tim 4:22

4:22 There were many Christians in Rome; some were even in Caesar's palace. Perhaps Paul, while awaiting trial, was making converts of the Roman civil service! Paul sent greetings from these Roman Christians to the believers at Philippi. The Good News had spread to all strata of society, linking people who had no other bond but Christ. The Roman Christians and the Philippian Christians were brothers and sisters because of their unity in Christ. Believers today are also linked to others across cultural, economic, and social barriers. Because all believers are brothers and sisters in Christ, let us live like God's true family.

4:23 In many ways the Philippian church was a model congregation. It was made up of many different kinds of people who were learning to work together. But Paul recognized that problems could arise, so in his thank-you letter he prepared the Philippians for difficulties that could crop up within a body of believers. Although a prisoner in Rome, Paul had learned the true secret of joy and peace—imitating Christ and serving others. By focusing our mind on Christ, we will learn unity, humility, joy, and peace. We will also be motivated to live for him. We can live confidently for him because we have "the grace of the Lord Jesus Christ" with us.

COLOSSIANS

REMOVE the head coach, and the team flounders; break the fuel line, and the car won't run; unplug the electrical appliance, and it has no power. Whether for leadership, power, or life, connections are vital!

Colossians is a book of connections. Writing from prison in Rome, Paul combatted false teachings, which had infiltrated the Colossian church. The problem was "syncretism," combining ideas from other philosophies and religions (such as paganism, strains of Judaism, and Greek thought) with Christian truth. The resulting heresy later became known as "Gnosticism," emphasizing special knowledge (*gnosis* in Greek) and denying Christ as God and Savior. To combat this devious error, Paul stressed Christ's deity—his connection with the Father—and his sacrificial death on the cross for sin. Only by being connected with Christ through faith can anyone have eternal life, and only through a continuing connection with him can anyone have power for living. Christ is God incarnate and the *only* way to forgiveness and peace with God the Father. Paul also emphasized believers' connections with each other as Christ's body on earth.

Paul's introduction to the Colossians includes a greeting, a note of thanksgiving, and a prayer for spiritual wisdom and strength for these brothers and sisters in Christ (1:1–12). He then moves into a doctrinal discussion of the person and work of Christ (1:13–23), stating that Christ is "the visual image of the invisible God" (1:15), the Creator (1:16), "the head of the church, which is his body" (1:18), and "the first of all who will rise from the dead" (1:18). His death on the cross makes it possible for us to stand in the presence of God (1:22).

Paul then explains how the world's teachings are totally empty when compared with God's plan, and he challenges the Colossians to reject shallow answers and to live in union with Christ (1:24—2:23).

Against this theological backdrop, Paul turns to practical considerations—what the divinity, death, and resurrection of Jesus should mean to all believers (3:1—4:6). Because our eternal destiny is sure, heaven should fill our thoughts (3:1–4), sexual impurity and other worldly lusts should not be named among us (3:5–8), and truth, love, and peace should mark our life (3:9–15). Our love for Christ should also translate into love for others—friends, fellow believers, spouses, children, parents, slaves, and masters (3:16—4:1). We should constantly communicate with God through prayer (4:2–4), and we should take every opportunity to tell others the Good News (4:5, 6). In Christ we have everything we need for salvation and for living the Christian life.

Paul had probably never visited Colosse, so he concludes this letter with personal comments about their common Christian associations, providing a living lesson of the connectedness of the body of Christ.

Read Colossians as a book for an embattled church in the first century, but read it also for its timeless truths. Gain a fresh appreciation for Christ as the *fullness* of God and the *only* source for living the Christian life. Know that he is your leader, head, and power source, and make sure of your connection to him.

VITAL STATISTICS

PURPOSE:
To combat errors in the church and to show that believers have everything they need in Christ

AUTHOR:
Paul

TO WHOM WRITTEN:
The church at Colosse, a city in Asia Minor, and all believers everywhere

DATE WRITTEN:
Approximately A.D. 60, during Paul's imprisonment in Rome

SETTING:
Paul had never visited Colosse. Evidently the church had been founded by Epaphras and other converts from Paul's missionary travels. The church, however, had been infiltrated by religious relativism, with some believers attempting to combine elements of paganism and secular philosophy with Christian doctrine. Paul confronts these false teachings and affirms the sufficiency of Christ.

KEY VERSES:
"For in Christ the fullness of God lives in a human body, and you are complete through your union with Christ. He is the Lord over every ruler and authority in the universe" (2:9, 10).

KEY PEOPLE:
Paul, Timothy, Tychicus, Onesimus, Aristarchus, Mark, Epaphras

KEY PLACES:
Colosse, Laodicea (4:15, 16)

SPECIAL FEATURES:
Christ is presented as having absolute supremacy and sole sufficiency. Colossians has similarities to Ephesians, probably because it was written at about the same time, but it has a different emphasis.

THE BLUEPRINT

1. What Christ has done (1:1—2:23)
2. What Christians should do (3:1—4:18)

In this letter Paul clearly teaches that Christ has paid for sin, that Christ has reconciled us to God, and that Christ gives us the pattern and the power to grow spiritually. Because Christ is the exact likeness of God, when we learn what he is like, we see what we need to become. Since Christ is Lord over all creation, we should crown him Lord over our life. Since Christ is the head of the body, his church, we should nurture our vital connection to him.

MEGATHEMES

THEME	EXPLANATION	IMPORTANCE
Christ Is God	Jesus Christ is God in the flesh, Lord of all creation, and Lord of the new creation. He is the expressed reflection of the invisible God. He is eternal, preexistent, omnipotent, equal with the Father. He is supreme and complete.	Because Christ is supreme, our life must be Christ-centered. To recognize him as God means to regard our relationship with him as most vital and to make his interests our top priority.
Christ Is Head of the Church	Because Christ is God, he is the head of the church, his true believers. Christ is the founder, the leader, and the highest authority on earth. He requires first place in all our thoughts and activities.	To acknowledge Christ as our head, we must welcome his leadership in all we do or think. No person, group, or church can regard any loyalty as more critical than that of loyalty to Christ.
Union with Christ	Because our sin has been forgiven and we have been reconciled to God, we have a union with Christ that can never be broken. In our faith connection with him, we identify with his death, burial, and resurrection.	We should live in constant contact and communication with God. When we do, we all will be unified with Christ and with one another.
Man-Made Religion	False teachers were promoting a heresy that stressed self-made rules (legalism). They also sought spiritual growth by discipline of the body (asceticism) and visions (mysticism). This search created pride in their self-centered efforts.	We must not cling to our own ideas and try to blend them into Christianity. Nor should we let our hunger for a more fulfilling Christian experience cause us to trust in a teacher, a group, or a system of thought more than in Christ himself. Christ is our hope and our true source of wisdom.

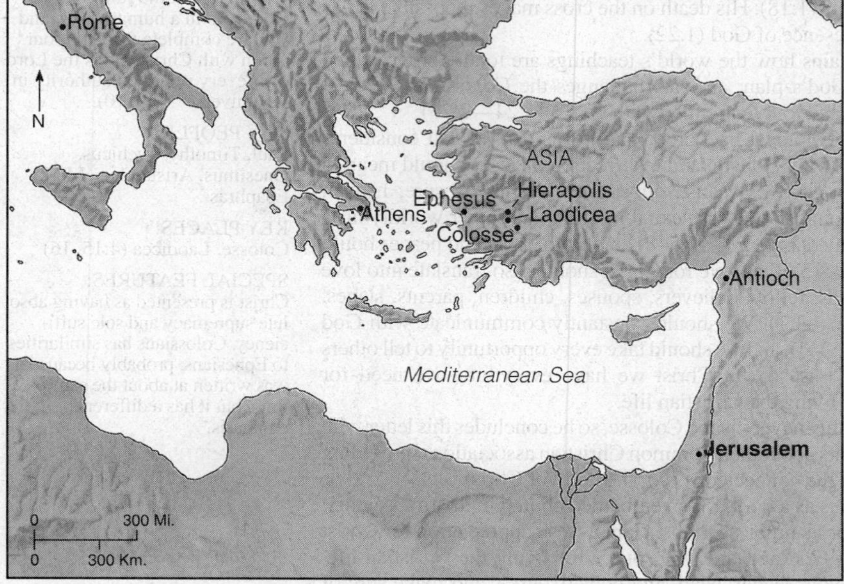

LOCATION OF COLOSSE
Paul had no doubt been through Laodicea on his third missionary journey, as it lay on the main route to Ephesus, but he had never been to Colosse. Though a large city with a significant population, Colosse was smaller and less important than the nearby cities of Laodicea and Hierapolis.

1. What Christ has done

Greetings from Paul

1:1 1 Cor 1:1 Eph 1:1 **1** This letter is from Paul, chosen by God to be an apostle of Christ Jesus, and from
our brother Timothy.
1:2 Rom 1:7 2 It is written to God's holy people in the city of Colosse, who are faithful brothers and
sisters in Christ.
May God our Father give you grace and peace.

Paul's Thanksgiving and Prayer

3 We always pray for you, and we give thanks to God the Father of our Lord Jesus Christ,
1:4 Eph 1:15 4 for we have heard that you trust in Christ Jesus and that you love all of God's people.

THE COLOSSIAN HERESY
Paul answered the various tenets of the Colossian heresy that threatened the church. This heresy was a "mixed bag," containing elements from several different heresies, some of which contradicted each other (as the chart shows).

The Heresy	*Reference*	*Paul's Answer*
Spirit is good; matter is evil.	1:15–20	God created heaven and earth for his glory.
One must follow ceremonies, rituals, and restrictions in order to be saved or perfected.	2:11, 16–23; 3:11	These were only shadows that ended when Christ came. He is all you need to be saved.
One must deny the body and live in strict asceticism.	2:20–23	Asceticism is no help in conquering evil thoughts and desires; instead, it leads to pride.
Angels must be worshiped.	2:18	Angels are not to be worshiped; Christ alone is worthy of worship.
Christ could not be both human and divine.	1:15–20; 2:2, 3	Christ is God in the flesh; he is the eternal one, head of the body, first in everything, supreme.
One must obtain "secret knowledge" in order to be saved or perfected—and this was not available to everyone.	2:2, 18	God's secret is Christ, and he has been revealed to all.
One must adhere to human wisdom, tradition, and philosophies.	2:4, 8–10; 3:15–17	By themselves, these can be misleading and shallow because they have human origin; instead, we should remember what Christ taught and follow his words as our ultimate authority.
It is even better to combine aspects of several religions.	2:10	You have everything when you have Christ; he is all-sufficient.
There is nothing wrong with immorality.	3:1–11	Get rid of sin and evil because you have been chosen by God to live a new life as a representative of the Lord Jesus.

1:1 Colossians, along with Philippians, Ephesians, and Philemon, is called a "Prison Letter" because Paul wrote it from prison in Rome. This prison was actually a house where Paul was kept under close guard at all times (probably chained to a soldier) but given certain freedoms not offered to most prisoners. He was allowed to write letters and to see any visitors he wanted to see.

1:1 Paul was an apostle "chosen by God." Paul often would establish his credentials as chosen and sent by God because he had not been one of the original 12 disciples. *Apostle* means "one sent out by God to preach the gospel." "Chosen by God" means that he was appointed; this was not just a matter of his own personal aspirations.

1:1 Paul mentions Timothy in other New Testament letters as well: 2 Corinthians, Philippians, 1 and 2 Thessalonians, and Philemon. Paul also wrote two letters to Timothy (1 and 2 Timothy). For more information on these men, two of the greatest missionaries of the early church, see Paul's Profile in Acts 9 and Timothy's Profile in 1 Timothy 2.

1:2 The city of Colosse was 100 miles east of Ephesus on the Lycus River. It was not as influential as the nearby city of Laodicea, but as a trading center, it was a crossroads for ideas and religions. Colosse had a large Jewish population—many Jews had fled there when they were forced out of Jerusalem under the persecutions of Antiochus III and IV, almost 200 years before Christ. The church in Colosse had been founded by Epaphras (1:7), one of Paul's converts. Paul had not yet visited this church. His purpose in writing was to refute heretical teachings about Christ that had been causing confusion among the Christians there.

1:2, 3 Letters in Paul's day frequently would begin with identifying the writer and the readers, followed by a greeting of peace. Paul usually would add Christian elements to his greetings, reminding his readers of his call by God to spread the Good News, emphasizing that the authority for his words came from God, and giving thanks for God's blessings.

1:4, 5 Throughout this letter Paul combats a heresy similar to Gnosticism (see the notes on 1:9-14; 1:15-23; 2:4ff). Gnostics believed that it took special knowledge to be accepted by God; for them, even for those who claimed to be Christians, Christ alone was not the way of salvation (1:20). In his introductory comments, therefore, Paul commended the Colossians for their trust (faith), love, and hope as they looked forward to heaven (see 1 Corinthians 13:13). He deliberately omitted the word *knowledge* because of the "special knowledge" aspect of the heresy. It is not *what* we know that brings salvation but *whom* we know. Knowing Christ is knowing God.

5 You do this because you are looking forward to the joys of heaven—as you have been
ever since you first heard the truth of the Good News. 6 This same Good News that came
to you is going out all over the world. It is changing lives everywhere, just as it changed
yours that very first day you heard and understood the truth about God's great kindness
to sinners.
7 Epaphras, our much loved co-worker, was the one who brought you the Good News.
He is Christ's faithful servant, and he is helping us in your place.* 8 He is the one who
told us about the great love for others that the Holy Spirit has given you.
9 So we have continued praying for you ever since we first heard about you. We ask
God to give you a complete understanding of what he wants to do in your lives, and we
ask him to make you wise with spiritual wisdom. 10 Then the way you live will always
honor and please the Lord, and you will continually do good, kind things for others. All
the while, you will learn to know God better and better.
11 We also pray that you will be strengthened with his glorious power so that you
will have all the patience and endurance you need. May you be filled with joy,
12 always thanking the Father, who has enabled you to share the inheritance that
belongs to God's holy people, who live in the light. 13 For he has rescued us from the
one who rules in the kingdom of darkness, and he has brought us into the Kingdom
of his dear Son. 14 God has purchased our freedom with his blood* and has forgiven
all our sins.

1:5 Eph 1:13; 1 Pet 1:4
1:6 Rom 1:13
1:7 Col 4:12; Phlm 1:23
1:9 Eph 1:15-17
1:10 Eph 4:1; Phil 1:27; 1 Thes 2:12
1:11 Eph 3:16
1:12 Acts 26:18; Eph 5:20
1:13 Matt 3:17; Acts 26:18; Eph 1:6; 2:2; 6:12
1:14 Eph 1:7

1:7 Greek *he is ministering on your behalf;* other manuscripts read *he is ministering on our behalf.* **1:14** Some manuscripts do not include *with his blood.*

1:5 When Paul says that we look forward to the joys of heaven, he is emphasizing the security of the believer. Because we know that our future destination and salvation are sure (1 Peter 1:3, 4), we are free to live for Christ and love others. When you find yourself doubting or wavering in your faith or love, remember your destination—heaven.

1:6 Wherever Paul went, he preached the Good News—to Gentile audiences, to hostile Jewish leaders, and even to his Roman guards. Whenever people believed in the message that Paul spoke, they were changed. God's Word is not just for our information, it is for our transformation! Becoming a Christian means beginning a whole new relationship with God, not just turning over a new leaf or determining to do right. New believers have a changed purpose, direction, attitude, and behavior. They are no longer seeking to serve themselves, but they are bearing fruit for God. How is the Good News reaching others through your life?

1:7 Epaphras had founded the church at Colosse while Paul was living in Ephesus (Acts 19:10). Epaphras may have been converted in Ephesus, and then he returned to Colosse, his hometown. For some reason, he visited Rome and, while there, told Paul about the problem of the Colossian heresy. This prompted Paul to write this letter. Epaphras is also mentioned in Philemon 1:23 (the Colossian church met in Philemon's house).

1:8 Because of their love for one another, Christians can have an impact that goes far beyond their neighborhoods and communities. Christian love comes from the Holy Spirit (see Galatians 5:22). The Bible speaks of it as an action and attitude, not just an emotion. Love is a by-product of our new life in Christ (see Romans 5:5; 1 Corinthians 13). Christians have no excuse for not loving, because Christian love is a decision to *act* in the best interests of others.

1:9-14 Paul was exposing a heresy in the Colossian church that was similar to Gnosticism (see the note on 2:4ff for more information). Gnostics valued the accumulation of knowledge, but Paul pointed out that knowledge in itself is empty. To be worth anything, it must lead to a changed life and right living. His prayer for the Colossians has two dimensions: (1) that they might have complete understanding of what God wants to do in their lives, and that they might be wise with spiritual wisdom; (2) that they would continually do good, kind things for others and learn to know God better and better. Knowledge is not merely to be accumulated; it should give us direction for living. Paul wanted the Colossians to be wise, but he also wanted them to *use* their knowledge. Knowledge of God is not a secret that only a few can discover; it is open to everyone. God wants us to learn more about him, and also to put belief into practice by helping others.

1:9-14 Sometimes we wonder how to pray for missionaries and other leaders we have never met. Paul had never met the Colossians, but he faithfully prayed for them. His prayers teach us how to pray for others, whether we know them or not. We can request that they (1) understand what God wants them to do, (2) gain spiritual wisdom, (3) honor and please God, (4) continually do good, kind things for others, (5) learn to know God better and better, (6) be strengthened with God's glorious power, (7) have great patience and endurance, (8) stay full of Christ's joy, and (9) give thanks always. All believers have these same basic needs. When you don't know how to pray for someone, use Paul's prayer pattern for the Colossians.

1:12-14 Paul lists five benefits God gives all believers through Christ: (1) He enabled us to share his inheritance (see also 2 Corinthians 5:21); (2) he rescued us from Satan's kingdom of darkness and made us his children (see also 2:15); (3) he brought us into his eternal Kingdom (see also Ephesians 1:5, 6); (4) he purchased our freedom from sin and judgment with his blood (see also Hebrews 9:12); and (5) he forgave all our sins (see also Ephesians 1:7). Thank God for what you have received in Christ.

1:13 The Colossians feared the unseen forces of darkness, but Paul says that true believers have been transferred from darkness to light, from slavery to freedom, from guilt to forgiveness, and from the power of Satan to the power of God. We have been rescued from a rebel kingdom to serve the rightful King. Our conduct should reflect our new allegiance.

Christ Is Supreme

1:15
John 1:1, 18; 14:9
2 Cor 4:4
Heb 1:3
Rev 3:14

1:16
John 1:3
Heb 1:2

1:18
Acts 4:2; 26:23
Eph 1:22-23
Rev. 1:5

1:21
Rom 5:10
Eph 2:3, 12

15 Christ is the visible image of the invisible God. He existed before God made anything
at all and is supreme over all creation.* 16 Christ is the one through whom God created
everything in heaven and earth. He made the things we can see and the things we can't
see—kings, kingdoms, rulers, and authorities. Everything has been created through him
and for him. 17 He existed before everything else began, and he holds all creation
together.
18 Christ is the head of the church, which is his body. He is the first of all who will rise
from the dead,* so he is first in everything. 19 For God in all his fullness was pleased to
live in Christ, 20 and by him God reconciled everything to himself. He made peace with
everything in heaven and on earth by means of his blood on the cross. 21 This includes

1:15 Greek *He is the firstborn of all creation.* **1:18** Greek *He is the beginning, the firstborn from the dead.*

HOW TO PRAY FOR OTHER CHRISTIANS
How many people in your life could be touched if you prayed in this way?

1. Be thankful for their faith and changed lives (1:3).
2. Ask God to help them know what he wants them to do (1:9).
3. Ask God to give them deep spiritual understanding (1:9).
4. Ask God to help them live for him (1:10).
5. Ask God to give them more knowledge of himself (1:10).
6. Ask God to give them strength for endurance (1:11).
7. Ask God to fill them with joy, strength, and thankfulness (1:11).

1:15, 16 This is one of the strongest statements about the divine nature of Christ found anywhere in the Bible. Jesus is not only equal to God (Philippians 2:6), he *is* God (John 10:30, 38; 12:45; 14:1-11); as the visible image of the invisible God, he is the exact representation of God. He not only reflects God, but he reveals God to us (John 1:18; 14:9); as supreme over all creation, he has all the priority and authority. He came from heaven, not from the dust of the earth (1 Corinthians 15:47), and he is Lord of all (Romans 9:5; 10:11-13; Revelation 1:5; 17:14). He is completely holy (Hebrews 7:26-28; 1 Peter 1:19; 2:22; 1 John 3:5), and he has authority to judge the world (Romans 2:16; 2 Corinthians 5:10; 2 Timothy 4:1). Therefore, Christ is supreme over all creation, including the spirit world. We, like the Colossian believers, must believe in the deity of Jesus Christ (that Jesus is God) or our Christian faith is hollow, misdirected, and meaningless. This is a central truth of Christianity. We must oppose those who say that Jesus was merely a prophet or a good teacher.

1:15-23 In the Colossian church there were several misconceptions about Christ that Paul directly refuted: (1) Believing that matter is evil, false teachers argued that God would not have come to earth as a true human being in bodily form. Paul stated that Christ is the image—the exact likeness—of God and is himself God, and yet he died on the cross as a human being. (2) They believed that God did not create the world because he would not have created evil. Paul proclaimed that Jesus Christ, who was also God in the flesh, is the Creator of both heaven and earth. (3) They said that Christ was not the unique Son of God but rather one of many intermediaries between God and people. Paul explained that Christ existed before anything else and is the firstborn of those resurrected. (4) They refused to see Christ as the source of salvation, insisting that people could find God only through special and secret knowledge. In contrast, Paul openly proclaimed the way of salvation to be through Christ alone. Paul continued to bring the argument back to Christ. When we share the Good News, we, too, must keep the focus on Christ.

1:16 Because the false teachers believed that the physical world was evil, they thought that God himself could not have created it. If Christ were God, they reasoned, he would be in charge only of the spiritual world. But Paul explained that all the kings, kingdoms, rulers, and authorities of both the spiritual and physical worlds were created by and are under the authority of Christ himself. This includes not only the government but also the spiritual world that the heretics were so concerned about. Christ has no equal and no rival. He is the Lord of all.

1:17 God is not only the creator of the world but he is also its sustainer. In him, everything is held together, protected, and prevented from disintegrating into chaos. Because Christ is the sustainer of all life, none of us is independent from him. We are all his servants who must daily trust him to protect us, care for us, and sustain us.

1:18 Christ is the "first of all who will rise from the dead." Jesus was raised from death, and his resurrection proves his lordship over the material world. All who trust in Christ will also defeat death and rise again to live eternally with him (1 Corinthians 15:20; 1 Thessalonians 4:14). Because of Christ's death on the cross, he has been exalted and elevated to the status that was rightfully his (see Philippians 2:5-11). Because Christ is spiritually supreme in the universe, surely we should give him first place in all our thoughts and activities. See the second note on Luke 24:6, 7 for more about the significance of Christ's resurrection.

1:19 By this statement, Paul was refuting the Greek idea that Jesus could not be human and divine at the same time. Christ was fully human; he was also fully divine. Christ has always been God and always will be God. When we have Christ, we have all of God in human form. Don't diminish any aspect of Christ—either his humanity or his divinity.

1:20 Christ's death provided a way for all people to come to God. It cleared away the sin that keeps us from having a right relationship with our creator. This does not mean that everyone has been saved but that the way has been cleared for anyone who will trust Christ to be saved. We can have peace with God and be reconciled to him by accepting Christ, who died in our place. Is there a distance between you and the Creator? Be reconciled to God. Come to him through Christ.

1:21 Because we were alienated from God, we were strangers to his way of thinking and were "enemies." Sin corrupted our way of thinking about God. Wrong thinking leads to sin, which further perverts and destroys our thoughts about him. When we were out of harmony with God, our natural condition was to be totally hostile to his standards. See Romans 1:21-32 for more on the perverted thinking of unbelievers.

1:21, 22 *No one* is good enough to save himself or herself. If we want to live eternally with Christ, we must depend totally on

you who were once so far away from God. You were his enemies, separated from him 1:22
by your evil thoughts and actions, 22 yet now he has brought you back as his friends. He Rom 7:4
has done this through his death on the cross in his own human body. As a result, he has Eph 1:4; 5:27
brought you into the very presence of God, and you are holy and blameless as you stand
before him without a single fault. 23 But you must continue to believe this truth and stand 1:23 Eph 3:17
in it firmly. Don't drift away from the assurance you received when you heard the Good Col 1:5-6
News. The Good News has been preached all over the world, and I, Paul, have been
appointed by God to proclaim it.

Paul's Work for the Church

24 I am glad when I suffer for you in my body, for I am completing what remains of 1:24 Phil 2:17; 3:10
Christ's sufferings for his body, the church. 25 God has given me the responsibility of 2 Tim 1:8
serving his church by proclaiming his message in all its fullness to you Gentiles. 26 This 1:26
message was kept secret for centuries and generations past, but now it has been revealed Rom 16:25-26
to his own holy people. 27 For it has pleased God to tell his people that the riches and Eph 3:3, 5, 9-10
glory of Christ are for you Gentiles, too. For this is the secret: Christ lives in you, and 1:27 Rom 8:10
this is your assurance that you will share in his glory. Eph 3:9
28 So everywhere we go, we tell everyone about Christ. We warn them and teach them 1:28 Eph 4:13
with all the wisdom God has given us, for we want to present them to God, perfect* in 1:29
their relationship to Christ. 29 I work very hard at this, as I depend on Christ's mighty Eph 1:19; 3:7
power that works within me. Phil 4:13

2 I want you to know how much I have agonized for you and for the church at 2:1 Col 4:12-13
Laodicea, and for many other friends who have never known me personally. 2 My 2:2
goal is that they will be encouraged and knit together by strong ties of love. I want them Matt 11:25-27
Eph 1:18-19
Col 2:19

1:28 Or *mature.*

God's grace. This is true whether we have been murderers or honest, hardworking citizens. We have all sinned repeatedly, and *any* sin is enough to cause us to need to come to Jesus Christ for salvation and eternal life. Apart from Christ, there is no way for our sin to be forgiven and removed.

1:22 In order to answer the accusation that Jesus was only a spirit and not a true human being, Paul explained that Jesus' physical body actually died. Jesus suffered death fully as a human so that we could be assured that he died in our place. Jesus faced death as God so we can be assured that his sacrifice was complete and that he truly removed our sin.

1:22, 23 The way to be free from sin is to trust Jesus Christ to take it away. We must stand firmly in the truth of the Good News, putting our confidence in Jesus alone to forgive our sins, to make us right with God, and to empower us to live the way he desires. When a judge in a court of law declares the defendant not guilty, the person is acquitted of all the accusations or charges. Legally, it is as if he or she had never been accused. When God forgives our sins, our record is wiped clean. From his perspective, it is as though we had never sinned. God's solution is available to you. No matter what you have done or what you have been like, God's forgiveness is for you.

1:24 When Paul says, "I am completing what remains of Christ's sufferings," he does not mean that Christ's suffering was inadequate to save him, nor does he mean that there is a predetermined amount of suffering that must be paid by all believers. Paul could be saying that suffering is unavoidable in bringing the Good News of Christ to the world. It is called Christ's suffering because all Christians are related to Christ. When we suffer, Christ feels it with us. But this suffering can be endured joyfully because it changes lives and brings people into God's Kingdom (see 1 Peter 4:1, 2, 12-19). For more about how Paul could rejoice despite his suffering, see the note on Philippians 1:29.

1:26, 27 The false teachers in the Colossian church believed that spiritual perfection was a secret and hidden plan that only a few privileged people could discover. Their secret plan was meant to be exclusive. Paul said that he was proclaiming the word of God in its fullness, not just a part of the plan. He also called God's plan a "message . . . kept secret for centuries and generations past," not in the sense that only a few would understand, but because it was hidden until Christ came. Through Christ it was made open to all. God's secret plan is "Christ lives in you"—God planned to have his Son, Jesus Christ, live in the hearts of all who believe in him—even Gentiles like the Colossians. Do you know Christ? He is not hidden if you will come to him.

1:28, 29 The word *perfect* means "mature or complete," not "flawless." Paul wanted to see each believer mature spiritually. Like Paul, we must work wholeheartedly like an athlete, but we should not strive in our own strength alone. We have the power of God's Spirit working in us. We can learn and grow daily, motivated by love and not by fear or pride, knowing that God gives the energy to become mature.

1:28, 29 Christ's message is for everyone; so everywhere Paul and Timothy went, they brought the Good News to all who would listen. An effective presentation of the Good News includes warning and teaching. The warning is that without Christ, people are doomed to eternal separation from God. The teaching is that salvation is available through faith in Christ. As Christ works in you, tell others about him, warning and teaching them in love. Whom do you know that needs to hear this message?

2:1 Laodicea was located a few miles northwest of Colosse. Like the church at Colosse, the Laodicean church was probably founded by one of Paul's converts while Paul was staying in Ephesus (Acts 19:10). The city was a wealthy center of trade and commerce, but later Christ would criticize the believers at Laodicea for their lukewarm commitment (Revelation 3:14-22). The fact that Paul wanted this letter to be passed on to the Laodicean church (4:16) indicates that false teaching may have spread there as well. Paul was counting on ties of love to bring the churches together to stand against this heresy and to encourage each other to remain true to God's plan of salvation in Christ. Our churches should be encouraging, unified communities, committed to carrying out Christ's work.

2:3 Isa 11:2; Rom 11:33; Eph 3:8, 19
2:5 1 Cor 5:3-4
2:6 Col 1:10
2:7 Eph 2:20; 3:17
2:8 Col 2:4; 1 Tim 6:20
2:9 John 1:14, 16; Col 1:19
2:10 Eph 1:21-22; 3:19

to have full confidence because they have complete understanding of God's secret plan,
which is Christ himself. 3In him lie hidden all the treasures of wisdom and knowledge.
4I am telling you this so that no one will be able to deceive you with persuasive
arguments. 5For though I am far away from you, my heart is with you. And I am very
happy because you are living as you should and because of your strong faith in Christ.

Freedom from Rules and New Life in Christ

6And now, just as you accepted Christ Jesus as your Lord, you must continue to live in
obedience to him. 7Let your roots grow down into him and draw up nourishment from
him, so you will grow in faith, strong and vigorous in the truth you were taught. Let your
lives overflow with thanksgiving for all he has done.
8Don't let anyone lead you astray with empty philosophy and high-sounding nonsense
that come from human thinking and from the evil powers of this world,* and not from
Christ. 9For in Christ the fullness of God lives in a human body,* 10and you are complete
through your union with Christ. He is the Lord over every ruler and authority in the universe.
11When you came to Christ, you were "circumcised," but not by a physical procedure.

2:8 Or *from the basic principles of this world;* also in 2:20. **2:9** Greek *in him dwells all the fullness of the Godhead bodily.*

SALVATION THROUGH FAITH

	Religion by Self-Effort	*Salvation by Faith*
Goal	Please God by our own good deeds	Trust in Christ and then live to please God
Means	Practice, diligent service, discipline, and obedience, in hope of reward	Confess, submit, and commit ourselves to Christ's control
Power	Good, honest effort through self-determination	The Holy Spirit in us helps us do good work for Christ's Kingdom
Control	Self-motivation; self-control	Christ is in us; we are in Christ
Results	Chronic guilt, apathy, depression, failure, constant desire for approval	Joy, thankfulness, love, guidance, service, forgiveness

Salvation by faith in Christ sounds too easy for many people. They would rather think that they have done something to save themselves. Their religion becomes one of self-effort that leads either to disappointment or pride, but finally to eternal death. Christ's simple way is the only way, and it alone leads to eternal life.

2:4ff The problem that Paul was combatting in the Colossian church was similar to Gnosticism (from the Greek word for *knowledge*). This *heresy* (a teaching contrary to biblical doctrine) undermined Christianity in several basic ways: (1) It insisted that important secret knowledge was hidden from most believers; Paul, however, said that Christ provides all the knowledge we need. (2) It taught that the body was evil; Paul countered that God himself lived in a body—that is, he was embodied in Jesus Christ. (3) It contended that Christ only seemed to be human but was not; Paul insisted that Jesus was fully human and fully God.

Gnosticism became fashionable in the second century. Even in Paul's day, these ideas sounded attractive to many, and exposure to such teachings could easily seduce a church that didn't know Christian doctrine well. Similar teachings still pose significant problems for many in the church today. We combat heresy by becoming thoroughly acquainted with God's Word through personal study and sound Bible teaching.

2:6, 7 Receiving Christ as Lord of your life is the beginning of life with Christ. But you must continue to follow his leadership by being rooted, built up, and strengthened in the faith. Christ wants to guide you and help you with your daily problems. You can live for Christ by (1) committing your life and submitting your will to him (Romans 12:1, 2); (2) seeking to learn from him, his life, and his teachings (Colossians 3:16); and (3) recognizing the Holy Spirit's power in you (Acts 1:8; Galatians 5:22).

2:7 Paul uses the illustration of our being rooted in Christ. Just as plants draw nourishment from the soil through their roots, so we draw our life-giving strength from Christ. The more we draw our strength from him, the less we will be fooled by those who falsely claim to have life's answers. If Christ is our strength, we will be free from human regulations.

2:8 Paul writes against any philosophy of life based only on human ideas and experiences. Paul himself was a gifted philosopher, so he is not condemning philosophy. He is condemning teaching that credits humanity, not Christ, with being the answer to life's problems. That approach becomes a false religion. There are many man-made approaches to life's problems that totally disregard God. To resist heresy you must use your mind, keep your eyes on Christ, and study God's Word.

2:9 Again Paul asserts Christ's deity. "In Christ the fullness of God lives in a human body" means that all of God was in Christ's human body. When we have Christ, we have everything we need for salvation and right living. See the note on 1:15, 16 for more on the divine nature of Christ.

2:10 When we know Jesus Christ, we don't need to seek God by means of other religions, cults, or unbiblical philosophies as the Colossians were doing. Christ alone holds the answers to the true meaning of life because he *is* life. Christ is the unique source of knowledge and power for the Christian life. No Christian needs anything in addition to what Christ has provided to be saved. We are complete in him.

2:11 Jewish males were circumcised as a sign of the Jews' covenant with God (Genesis 17:9-14). With the death of Christ, circumcision was no longer necessary. So now our commitment to God is written on our heart, not our body. Christ sets us free from our evil desires by a spiritual operation, not a bodily one. God removes the old nature and gives us a new nature.

It was a spiritual procedure—the cutting away of your sinful nature. 12 For you were
buried with Christ when you were baptized. And with him you were raised to a new life
because you trusted the mighty power of God, who raised Christ from the dead.
13 You were dead because of your sins and because your sinful nature was not yet cut
away. Then God made you alive with Christ. He forgave all our sins. 14 He canceled the
record that contained the charges against us. He took it and destroyed it by nailing it to
Christ's cross. 15 In this way, God disarmed the evil rulers and authorities. He shamed
them publicly by his victory over them on the cross of Christ.
16 So don't let anyone condemn you for what you eat or drink, or for not celebrating
certain holy days or new-moon ceremonies or Sabbaths. 17 For these rules were only
shadows of the real thing, Christ himself. 18 Don't let anyone condemn you by insisting
on self-denial. And don't let anyone say you must worship angels, even though they say
they have had visions about this. These people claim to be so humble, but their sinful
minds have made them proud. 19 But they are not connected to Christ, the head of the
body. For we are joined together in his body by his strong sinews, and we grow only as
we get our nourishment and strength from God.
20 You have died with Christ, and he has set you free from the evil powers of this world.

2:12 Rom 6:5; Eph 1:19-20; 2:6
2:13 Eph 2:1, 5
2:14 Eph 2:15; 1 Pet 2:24
2:15 John 12:31; 2 Cor 2:14; Eph 4:8
2:16 1 Chr 23:31; Rom 14:3, 5
2:17 Heb 8:5; 10:1
2:19 Eph 1:22; 4:15-16
2:20 Rom 6:6; Gal 4:3, 9

2:11, 12 In this passage, circumcision is related to baptism; therefore, some see baptism as the New Testament sign of the covenant, identifying the person with the covenant community. Baptism parallels the death, burial, and resurrection of Christ, and it also portrays the death and burial of our sinful old way of life followed by resurrection to new life in Christ. Remembering that our old sinful life is dead and buried with Christ gives us a powerful motive to resist sin. Not wanting the desires of our past to come back to power again, we can consciously choose to treat our desires as if they were dead. Then we can continue to enjoy our wonderful new life with Christ (see Galatians 3:27 and Colossians 3:1-4).

2:13-15 Before we believed in Christ, our nature was evil. We disobeyed, rebelled, and ignored God (even at our best, we did not love him with all our heart, soul, and mind). The Christian, however, has a new nature. God has crucified the old rebellious nature (Romans 6:6) and replaced it with a new loving nature (Colossians 3:9, 10). The penalty of sin died with Christ on the cross. God has declared us not guilty, and we need no longer live under sin's power. God does not take us out of the world or make us robots—we will still feel like sinning, and sometimes we will sin. The difference is that before we were saved, we were slaves to our sinful nature; but now we are free to live for Christ (see Galatians 2:20).

2:14 The record that was destroyed contained the legal demands of the Old Testament law. The law opposed us by its demands for payment for our sin. Although no one can be saved by merely keeping that record, the moral truths and principles in the Old Testament still teach and guide today.

2:14 We can enjoy our new life in Christ because we have joined him in his death and resurrection. Our evil desires, our bondage to sin, and our love of sin died with him. Now, joining him in his resurrection life, we may have unbroken fellowship with God and freedom from sin. Our debt for sin has been paid in full; our sins are swept away and forgotten by God; and we can be clean and new. For more on the difference between our new life in Christ and our old sinful nature, read Ephesians 4:23, 24 and Colossians 3:3-15.

2:15 Who are these rulers and authorities? Several suggestions have been made, including (1) demonic powers, (2) the gods of the powerful nations, (3) angels (highly regarded by the heretical teachers), or (4) the government of Rome. These rulers and authorities were probably not the demonic forces in 2:10. More likely they are the false teachers who were mediators of the law (Galatians 3:19). The Colossian false teachers were encouraging worship of angels. But at his death, Christ surpassed the position and authority of any angel. So rather than fear angels or worship them, we are to view them as deposed rulers. Paul meant no disrespect toward angels, but he showed that they are not to be compared with Jesus Christ. Some scholars believe these powers are the powers of Rome. By his resurrection, Christ stripped the power away from a world empire that seemed to temporarily defeat him.

2:16 "What you eat or drink" probably refers to the Jewish dietary laws. The festivals mentioned are Jewish holy days celebrated annually, monthly (new moon), and weekly (the Sabbath). These rituals distinguished the Jews from their pagan neighbors. Failure to observe them could be easily noticed by those who were keeping track of what others did. But we should not let ourselves be judged by the opinions of others because Christ has set us free.

2:16, 17 Paul told the Colossian Christians not to let others criticize their diet or their religious ceremonies. Instead of outward observance, believers should focus on faith in Christ alone. Our worship, traditions, and ceremonies can help bring us close to God, but we should never criticize fellow Christians whose traditions and ceremonies differ from ours. More important than how we worship is that we worship Christ. Don't let anyone judge you. You are responsible to Christ.

2:17 Old Testament laws, holidays, and festivals pointed toward Christ. Paul calls them "shadows" of the reality that was to come—Christ himself. When Christ came, he dispelled the shadows. If we have Christ, we have what we need to know and please God.

2:18 The false teachers were proud of their humility! This false humility brought attention and praise to themselves rather than to God. True humility means seeing ourselves as we really are from God's perspective and acting accordingly. People today practice false humility when they talk negatively about themselves so that others will think they are spiritual. False humility is self-centered; true humility is God-centered.

2:18 The false teachers were claiming that God was far away and could be approached only through various levels of angels. They taught that people had to worship angels in order, eventually, to reach God. This is unscriptural; the Bible teaches that angels are God's servants, and it forbids worshiping them (Exodus 20:3, 4; Revelation 22:8, 9). As you grow in your Christian faith, let God's Word be your guide, not the opinions of other people.

2:19 The fundamental problem with the false teachers was that they were not connected to Christ, the head of the body of believers. If they had been joined to him, they could not have taught false doctrine or lived immorally. Anyone who teaches about God without being connected to him by faith should not be trusted.

2:20 The "rules of the world" are the beliefs of pagans. See 2:8 for more on Paul's view of non-Christian philosophy.

So why do you keep on following rules of the world, such as, 21 "Don't handle, don't eat,
2:22 1 Cor 6:13 don't touch." 22 Such rules are mere human teaching about things that are gone as soon
as we use them. 23 These rules may seem wise because they require strong devotion,
2:23 1 Tim 4:3 humility, and severe bodily discipline. But they have no effect when it comes to
conquering a person's evil thoughts and desires.

2. What Christians should do

Living the New Life

3:1 Matt 6:33 Eph 2:6 **3** Since you have been raised to new life with Christ, set your sights on the realities
of heaven, where Christ sits at God's right hand in the place of honor and power.
3:3 Rom 6:2 2 Cor 5:14 2 Let heaven fill your thoughts. Do not think only about things down here on earth.
3 For you died when Christ died, and your real life is hidden with Christ in God. 4 And

---

FROM DEATH TO LIFE

The Bible uses many illustrations to teach what happens when we choose to let Jesus be Lord of our life. Following are some of the most vivid pictures:

1. Because Christ died for us, we have been crucified with him.	Romans 6:2–13; 7:4–6 2 Corinthians 5:14 Galatians 2:20; 5:24; 6:14 Colossians 2:20; 3:3–5 1 Peter 2:24
2. Our old, rebellious nature died with Christ.	Romans 6:6; 7:4–6 Colossians 3:9, 10
3. Christ's resurrection guarantees our new life now and eternal life with him later.	Romans 6:4, 11 Colossians 2:12, 13; 3:1, 3

This process is acted out in baptism (Colossians 2:12), based on our faith in Christ: (1) The old sinful nature dies (crucified). (2) We are ready to receive a new life (buried). (3) Christ gives us new life (resurrected).

2:20; 3:1 How do we die with Christ, and how are we raised with him? When a person becomes a Christian, he or she is given new life through the power of the Holy Spirit. See the notes on 2:11, 12 and 2:13-15 for further information.

2:20-23 People should be able to see a difference between the way Christians and non-Christians live. Still, we should not expect instant maturity in new Christians. Christian growth is a lifelong process. Although we have a new nature, we don't automatically think all good thoughts and have all pure attitudes when we become new people in Christ. But if we keep listening to God, we will be changing all the time. As you look over the last year, what changes for the better have you seen in your thoughts and attitudes? Change may be slow, but your life will change significantly if you trust God to change you.

2:20-23 We cannot reach up to God by following rules of self-denial, by observing rituals, or by practicing religion. Paul isn't saying all rules are bad (see the note on Galatians 2:15, 16). But keeping laws or rules will not earn salvation. The Good News is that God reaches down to human beings, and he asks for our response. Man-made religions focus on human effort; Christianity focuses on Christ's work. Believers must put aside sinful desires, but doing so is the by-product of our new life in Christ, not the reason for our new life. Our salvation does not depend on our own discipline and rule keeping but on the power of Christ's death and resurrection.

2:22, 23 We can guard against man-made religions by asking these questions about any religious group: (1) Does it stress man-made rules and taboos rather than God's grace? (2) Does it foster a critical spirit toward others, or does it exercise discipline discreetly and lovingly? (3) Does it stress formulas, secret knowledge, or special visions more than the Word of God? (4) Does it elevate self-righteousness, honoring those who keep the rules, rather than elevating Christ? (5) Does it neglect Christ's universal church, claiming to be an elite group? (6) Does it teach humiliation of the body as a means to spiritual growth rather than focus on the growth of the whole person? (7) Does it disregard the family rather than hold it in high regard as the Bible does?

2:23 To the Colossians, the discipline demanded by the false teachers seemed good, and legalism still attracts many people today. Following a long list of religious rules requires strong self-discipline and can make a person appear moral, but religious rules cannot change a person's heart. Only the Holy Spirit can do that.

3:1ff In chapter 2, Paul exposed the wrong reasons for self-denial. In chapter 3, he explains true Christian behavior—putting on the new self by accepting Christ and regarding the earthly nature as dead. We change our moral and ethical behavior by letting Christ live within us, so that he can shape us into what we *should* be.

3:1, 2 Setting our sights on heaven means striving to put heaven's priorities into daily practice. Letting heaven fill our thoughts means concentrating on the eternal rather than the temporal. See Philippians 4:7 and Colossians 3:15 for more on Christ's rule in our hearts and minds.

3:2, 3 "For you died" means that we should have as little desire for this world as a dead person would have. The Christian's real home is where Christ life (John 14:2, 3). This truth gives us a different perspective on our life here on earth, looking at life from God's perspective and seeking what he desires. This is the antidote to materialism; we gain the proper perspective on material goods when we take God's view of them. The more we regard the world around us as God does, the more we will live in harmony with him. We must not become too attached to what is only temporary.

3:3 What does it mean that a believer's life is "hidden with Christ"? *Hidden* means "concealed and safe." This is not only a future hope but an accomplished fact right now. Our service and conduct do not earn our salvation, but they are results of our salvation. Take heart that your salvation is sure, and live each day for Christ.

3:4 Christ gives us power to live for him now, and he gives us hope for the future—he will return. In the rest of this chapter Paul explains how Christians should act *now* in order to be prepared for Christ's return.

when Christ, who is your* real life, is revealed to the whole world, you will share in
all his glory.
5 So put to death the sinful, earthly things lurking within you. Have nothing to do with
sexual sin, impurity, lust, and shameful desires. Don't be greedy for the good things of this
life, for that is idolatry. 6 God's terrible anger will come upon those who do such things.
7 You used to do them when your life was still part of this world. 8 But now is the time to
get rid of anger, rage, malicious behavior, slander, and dirty language. 9 Don't lie to each
other, for you have stripped off your old evil nature and all its wicked deeds. 10 In its place
you have clothed yourselves with a brand-new nature that is continually being renewed as
you learn more and more about Christ, who created this new nature within you. 11 In this
new life, it doesn't matter if you are a Jew or a Gentile,* circumcised or uncircumcised,
barbaric, uncivilized,* slave, or free. Christ is all that matters, and he lives in all of us.
12 Since God chose you to be the holy people whom he loves, you must clothe
yourselves with tenderhearted mercy, kindness, humility, gentleness, and patience.
13 You must make allowance for each other's faults and forgive the person who offends
you. Remember, the Lord forgave you, so you must forgive others. 14 And the most
important piece of clothing you must wear is love. Love is what binds us all together in
perfect harmony. 15 And let the peace that comes from Christ rule in your hearts. For as
members of one body you are all called to live in peace. And always be thankful.
16 Let the words of Christ, in all their richness, live in your hearts and make you wise.

3:5 Rom 6:6; 8:13 Gal 5:19-21 Eph 4:19; 5:3, 5
3:7 Eph 2:2
3:8 Eph 4:25-31; 5:4
3:9 Eph 4:25
3:10 Rom 12:2 Eph 2:10; 4:24
3:11 Rom 10:12 1 Cor 12:13 Gal 3:28
3:12 Eph 4:2, 32 1 Pet 1:2
3:13 Eph 4:32; 5:2
3:14 Rom 13:8
3:15 John 14:27 Eph 2:14-16 Phil 4:7

3:4 Some manuscripts read *our.* **3:11a** Greek *Greek.* **3:11b** Greek *Barbarian, Scythian.*

3:5 We should consider ourselves dead and unresponsive to sexual immorality, impurity, lust, shameful desires, and greed. Just like diseased limbs of a tree, these practices must be cut off before they destroy us. We must make a conscious, daily decision to remove anything that supports or feeds these desires and to rely on the Holy Spirit's power.

3:6 "God's terrible anger" refers to God's judgment on these kinds of behavior, culminating with future and final punishment of evil. When tempted to sin, remember that you must one day stand before God.

3:8-10 We must rid ourselves of all evil practices and immorality. Then we can commit ourselves to what Christ teaches. Paul was urging the believers to remain true to their confession of faith. They were to rid themselves of the old life and clothe themselves with the new nature given by Christ. If you have made such a commitment to Christ, are you remaining true to it?

3:9 Lying to one another disrupts unity by destroying trust. It tears down relationships and may lead to serious conflict in a church. So don't exaggerate statistics, pass on rumors or gossip, or say things to build up your own image. Be committed to telling the truth.

3:10 What does it mean to clothe yourself with a brand-new nature? It means that your conduct should match your faith. If you are a Christian, you should act like it. To be a Christian means more than just making good resolutions and having good intentions; it means taking the right actions. This is a straightforward step that is as simple as putting on your clothes.

3:10 Every Christian is in a continuing education program. The more we know of Christ and his work, the more we are being changed to be like him. Because this process is lifelong, we must never stop learning and obeying. There is no justification for drifting along, but there is an incentive to find the rich treasures of growing in him. It takes practice, ongoing review, patience, and concentration to keep in line with his will.

3:11 The Christian church should have no barriers of nationality, race, education level, social standing, wealth, gender, religion, or power. Christ breaks down all barriers and accepts all people who come to him. Nothing should keep us from telling others about Christ or accepting into our fellowship any and all believers (Ephesians 2:14, 15). Christians should be building bridges, not walls.

3:12-17 Paul offers a strategy to help us live for God day by day: (1) Imitate Christ's compassionate, forgiving attitude (3:12, 13); (2) let love guide your life (3:14); (3) let the peace of Christ rule in your heart (3:15); (4) always be thankful (3:15); (5) keep God's Word in you at all times (3:16); (6) live as Jesus Christ's representative (3:17).

3:13 The key to forgiving others is remembering how much God has forgiven you. Is it difficult for you to forgive someone who has wronged you a little when God has forgiven you so much? Realizing God's infinite love and forgiveness can help you love and forgive others.

3:14 All the virtues that Paul encourages us to develop are perfectly bound together by love. As we clothe ourselves with these virtues, the last garment we are to put on is love, which holds all of the others in place. To practice any list of virtues without practicing love will lead to distortion, fragmentation, and stagnation (1 Corinthians 13:3).

3:14, 15 Christians should live in peace. To live in peace does not mean that suddenly all differences of opinion are eliminated, but it does require that loving Christians work together despite their differences. Such love is not a feeling but a decision to meet others' needs (see 1 Corinthians 13). To live in love leads to peace between individuals and among the members of the body of believers. Do problems in your relationships with other Christians cause open conflicts or mutual silence? Consider what you can do to heal those relationships with love.

3:15 The word *rule* comes from the language of athletics: Paul tells us to let Christ's peace be umpire or referee in our heart. Our heart is the center of conflict because there our feelings and desires clash—our fears and hopes, distrust and trust, jealousy and love. How can we deal with these constant conflicts and live as God wants? Paul explains that we must decide between conflicting elements by using the rule of peace. Which choice will promote peace in our souls and in our churches? For more on the peace of Christ, see Philippians 4:7.

3:16 Although the early Christians had access to the Old Testament and freely used it, they did not yet have the New Testament or any other Christian books to study. Their stories and teachings about Christ were memorized and passed on from person to person. Sometimes the teachings were set to music, and so music became an important part of Christian worship and education.

3:17 1 Cor 10:31; Eph 5:20

Use his words to teach and counsel each other. Sing psalms and hymns and spiritual songs
to God with thankful hearts. 17 And whatever you do or say, let it be as a representative of
the Lord Jesus, all the while giving thanks through him to God the Father.

Instructions for Christian Households

3:18 Eph 5:22
3:19 Eph 5:25; 1 Pet 3:7
3:20 Eph 6:1
3:21-25 //Eph 6:4-8
3:25 Acts 10:34

18 You wives must submit to your husbands, as is fitting for those who belong to the Lord.
19 And you husbands must love your wives and never treat them harshly.
20 You children must always obey your parents, for this is what pleases the Lord.
21 Fathers, don't aggravate your children. If you do, they will become discouraged and quit
trying.
22 You slaves must obey your earthly masters in everything you do. Try to please them
all the time, not just when they are watching you. Obey them willingly because of your
reverent fear of the Lord. 23 Work hard and cheerfully at whatever you do, as though you
were working for the Lord rather than for people. 24 Remember that the Lord will give
you an inheritance as your reward, and the Master you are serving is Christ. 25 But if you
do what is wrong, you will be paid back for the wrong you have done. For God has no
favorites who can get away with evil.

4:1 Lev 25:43; Eph 6:9
4:2 Luke 18:1; Eph 6:18; 1 Thes 5:17

4

You slave owners must be just and fair to your slaves. Remember that you also have
a Master—in heaven.

An Encouragement for Prayer

2 Devote yourselves to prayer with an alert mind and a thankful heart. 3 Don't forget to
pray for us, too, that God will give us many opportunities to preach about his secret

SINS VS. SIGNS OF LOVE

Sins of Sexual Attitude and Behavior	*Sins of Speech*	*Signs of Love*
Shameful desires	Anger	Mercy
Sexual sin	Malicious behavior	Kindness
Impurity	Slander	Humility
Lust	Dirty language	Gentleness
Greed	Lying	Patience
		Forgiveness

In Colossians 3:5 Paul tells us to put to death the things found in list 1. In 3:8, 9 he tells us to rid ourselves of the things found in list 2. In 3:12, 13 we're told to practice the things found in list 3. List 1 deals with sins of sexual attitudes and behavior—they are particularly destructive because of what they do to destroy any group or church. List 2 deals with sins of speech—these are the relationship breakers. List 3 contains the relationship builders, which we are to express as members of Christ's body.

3:17 "Whatever you do or say, let it be as a representative of the Lord Jesus" means bringing honor to Christ in every aspect and activity of daily living. As a Christian, you represent Christ at all times—wherever you go and whatever you say. What impression do people have of Christ when they see or talk with you? What changes would you make in your life in order to honor Christ?

3:18–4:1 Paul gives rules for three sets of household relationships: (1) husbands and wives, (2) parents and children, and (3) slave owners and slaves. In each case there is mutual responsibility to submit and love, to obey and encourage, to work hard and be fair. Examine your family and work relationships. Do you relate to others as God intended? See Ephesians 5:21–6:9 for similar instructions.

3:19 Christian marriage involves mutual submission, subordinating our personal desires for the good of the loved one, and submitting ourselves to Christ as Lord. For more on submission, see the notes on Ephesians 5:21-33.

3:20, 21 Children must be handled with care. They need firm discipline administered in love. Don't aggravate them by nagging, deriding, or destroying their self-respect so that they quit trying.

3:22–4:1 Paul does not condemn or condone slavery but explains that Christ transcends all divisions between people. Slaves are told to work hard as though their owner were Christ himself (3:22-25); but owners should be just and fair (4:1). Perhaps Paul was thinking specifically of Onesimus and Philemon—the slave and master whose conflict lay behind the letter to Philemon (see the book of Philemon). Philemon was a slave owner in the Colossian church, and Onesimus had been his slave (4:9).

3:23 Since the Creation, God has given us work to do. If we could regard our work as an act of worship or service to God, such an attitude would take some of the drudgery and boredom out of it. We could work without complaining or resentment if we would treat our job problems as the cost of discipleship.

4:1 Slave owners were to provide what was just and fair. Similarly today, employers should pay fair wages and treat their employees justly. And leaders should take care of their volunteers and not abuse them. If you have responsibility over others, make sure you do what is right and fair. You are accountable to your Master in heaven.

4:2 Have you ever grown tired of praying for something or someone? Paul says we should "devote" ourselves to prayer and be "alert" in prayer. Our persistence is an expression of our faith that God answers our prayers. Faith shouldn't die if the answers come slowly, for the delay may be God's way of working his will in our life. When you feel tired of praying, know that God is present, always listening, always answering—maybe not in ways you had hoped, but in ways that he knows are best.

4:3 The "secret plan" is Christ's Good News of salvation. The

plan—that Christ is also for you Gentiles. That is why I am here in chains. 4 Pray that I
will proclaim this message as clearly as I should.
5 Live wisely among those who are not Christians, and make the most of every
opportunity. 6 Let your conversation be gracious and effective so that you will have the
right answer for everyone.

Paul's Final Instructions and Greetings

7 Tychicus, a much loved brother, will tell you how I am getting along. He is a faithful
helper who serves the Lord with me. 8 I have sent him on this special trip to let you
know how we are doing and to encourage you. 9 I am also sending Onesimus, a faithful
and much loved brother, one of your own people. He and Tychicus will give you all
the latest news.
10 Aristarchus, who is in prison with me, sends you his greetings, and so does Mark,
Barnabas's cousin. And as you were instructed before, make Mark welcome if he comes
your way. 11 Jesus (the one we call Justus) also sends his greetings. These are the only
Jewish Christians among my co-workers; they are working with me here for the
Kingdom of God. And what a comfort they have been!
12 Epaphras, from your city, a servant of Christ Jesus, sends you his greetings. He
always prays earnestly for you, asking God to make you strong and perfect, fully
confident of the whole will of God. 13 I can assure you that he has agonized for you and
also for the Christians in Laodicea and Hierapolis.
14 Dear Doctor Luke sends his greetings, and so does Demas. 15 Please give my greetings

4:4 Eph 6:20
4:5 Eph 5:15-16
4:6 Eph 4:29; 1 Pet 3:15
4:7-8 Acts 20:4; Eph 6:21-22
4:9 Phlm 1:10
4:10 Acts 12:12; 15:37; 19:29; 20:4; 27:2
4:12 Col 1:7; Phlm 1:23
4:13 Col 2:1
4:14 2 Tim 4:10-11; Phlm 1:24
4:15 Rom 16:5

RULES OF SUBMISSION

Wives, submit to your husbands (3:18).	*Husbands,* love your wives and don't be harsh with them (3:19).
Children, obey your parents (3:20).	*Parents,* don't aggravate your children so that they become discouraged (3:21).
Slaves, obey your masters (3:22).	*Masters,* be just and fair to your slaves (4:1).
(*Employees,* work hard for your employers.)	(*Employers,* be just and fair with your employees.)

The New Testament includes many instructions concerning relationships. Most people read these instructions for the other person and ignore the ones that apply to themselves. But you can't control another person's behavior, only your own. Start by following your own instructions and not insisting on the obedience of others first.

whole focus of Paul's life was to tell others about Christ, explaining and preaching this wonderful mystery.

4:4 Paul asked for prayer that he could proclaim the Good News about Christ clearly, and we can request prayer to do the same. No matter what approach to evangelism we use, whether emphasizing life-style and example or whether building relationships, we should never obscure the message of the Good News.

4:5 We should be wise in our contacts with non-Christians, making the most of our opportunities to tell them the Good News of salvation. What opportunities do you have?

4:6 When we tell others about Christ, it is important always to be gracious in what we say. No matter how much sense the message makes, we lose our effectiveness if we are not courteous. Just as we like to be respected, we must respect others if we want them to listen to what we have to say.

4:7 Tychicus was one of Paul's personal representatives and probably the bearer of the letters to the Colossians and Ephesians (see also Ephesians 6:21, 22). He accompanied Paul to Jerusalem with the collection for the church (Acts 20:4).

4:10 Aristarchus was a Thessalonian who accompanied Paul on his third missionary journey. He was with Paul in the riot at Ephesus (Acts 19:29). He and Tychicus were with Paul in Greece (Acts 20:4). Aristarchus went to Rome with Paul (Acts 27:2). Mark started out with Paul and Barnabas on their first missionary journey (Acts 12:25), but he left in the middle of the trip for unknown reasons (Acts 13:13). Barnabas and Mark were relatives, and when Paul refused to take Mark on another journey, Barnabas and Mark journeyed together to preach the Good News (Acts 15:37-41). Mark also worked with Peter (Acts 12:12, 13; 1 Peter 5:13). Later, Mark and Paul were reconciled (Philemon 1:24). Mark wrote the Gospel of Mark. His Profile is in Acts 12.

4:12 Epaphras founded the Colossian church (see the note on 1:7), and his report to Paul in Rome caused Paul to write this letter. Epaphras was a hero of the Colossian church, one of the believers who helped keep the church together despite growing troubles. His earnest prayers for the believers show his deep love and concern for them.

4:13 Laodicea was located a few miles northwest of Colosse; Hierapolis was about five miles north of Laodicea. See the note on 2:1 for more about Laodicea.

4:14 Luke spent much time with Paul, not only accompanying him on most of his third missionary journey but sitting with him in the prison at Rome. Luke wrote the Gospel of Luke and the book of Acts. His Profile is in Acts 16. Demas was faithful for a while, but then he deserted Paul because he "loves the things of this life" (2 Timothy 4:10).

4:15 The early Christians often met in homes. Church buildings were not common until the third century.

to our Christian brothers and sisters at Laodicea, and to Nympha and those who meet in
her house.
16 After you have read this letter, pass it on to the church at Laodicea so they can read
it, too. And you should read the letter I wrote to them. 17 And say to Archippus, "Be sure
to carry out the work the Lord gave you."
18 Here is my greeting in my own handwriting—PAUL.
Remember my chains.
May the grace of God be with you.

4:16 1 Thes 5:27; 2 Thes 3:14
4:17 2 Tim 4:5; Phlm 1:2
4:18 1 Cor 16:21; 2 Thes 3:17

4:16 Some suggest that the letter from Laodicea may be the book of Ephesians, because the letter to the Ephesians was circulated to all the churches in Asia Minor. It is also possible that there was a special letter to the Laodiceans, of which we have no record today. Paul wrote several letters that have been lost (see, for example, 2 Corinthians 2:3 and note).

4:17 Paul's letter to Philemon is also addressed to Archippus (Philemon 1:2). Paul called him a "fellow soldier." He may have been a Roman soldier who had become a member of the Colossian church, or he may have been Philemon's son.

4:17 Paul encouraged Archippus to make sure that he carried out the work he had received in the Lord. There are many ways for us to leave our work unfinished. We can easily get sidetracked morally, we can become exhausted and stop, we can get mad and quit, or we can let it slide and leave it up to others. We should see to it that we finish God's assignments, completing the work we have received.

4:18 Paul usually dictated his letters to a secretary and then often ended with a short note in his own handwriting (see also 1 Corinthians 16:21; Galatians 6:11). This assured the recipients that false teachers were not writing letters in Paul's name. It also gave the letters a personal touch.

4:18 To understand the letter to the Colossians, we need to know that the church was facing pressure from a heresy that promised deeper spiritual life through secret knowledge (an early form of Gnosticism). The false teachers were destroying faith in Christ by undermining Christ's humanity and divinity.

Paul makes it clear in Colossians that Christ alone is the source of our spiritual life, the head of the body of believers. Christ is Lord of both the physical and spiritual worlds. The path to deeper spiritual life is not through religious duties, special knowledge, or secrets; it is only through a clear connection with the Lord Jesus Christ. We must never let anything come between us and our Savior.

1 THESSALONIANS

VITAL STATISTICS

PURPOSE:
To strengthen the Thessalonian Christians in their faith and give them the assurance of Christ's return

AUTHOR:
Paul

TO WHOM WRITTEN:
The church at Thessalonica, and all believers everywhere

DATE WRITTEN:
Approximately A.D. 51 from Corinth; one of Paul's earliest letters

SETTING:
The church at Thessalonica was very young, having been established only two or three years before this letter was written. The Thessalonian Christians needed to mature in their faith. In addition, there was a misunderstanding concerning Christ's second coming—some thought Christ would return immediately, and thus they were confused when their loved ones died because they expected Christ to return beforehand. Also, believers were being persecuted.

KEY VERSE:
"For since we believe that Jesus died and was raised to life again, we also believe that when Jesus comes, God will bring back with Jesus all the Christians who have died" (4:14).

KEY PEOPLE:
Paul, Timothy, Silas

KEY PLACE:
Thessalonica

SPECIAL FEATURES:
Paul received from Timothy a favorable report about the Thessalonians. However, Paul wrote this letter to correct their misconceptions about the resurrection and the second coming of Christ.

SLOWLY they walk, one by one, scattering the leaves and trampling the grass under measured and heavy steps. The minister's words still echoing in their minds, they hear workmen moving toward the terrible place, preparing to cover the casket of their loved one. Death, the enemy, has torn the bonded relationships of family and friends, leaving only memories . . . and tears . . . and loneliness.

But like a golden shaft of sun piercing the winter sky, a singular truth shatters the oppressive gloom: Death is not the end! Christ is the victor over death, and there is hope of the resurrection through him.

As with every member of the human family, first-century Christians came face to face with their mortality. Many of them met early deaths at the hands of those who hated Christ and all allied with him. Whether at the hands of zealous Jews (like Paul before his conversion), angry Greeks, or ruthless Roman authorities, persecution included stonings, beatings, crucifixions, torture, and death. To be a follower of Christ meant to give up everything.

Paul established the church in Thessalonica during his second missionary journey (in about A.D. 51). He wrote this letter a short time later to encourage the young believers there. He wanted to assure them of his love, to praise them for their faithfulness during persecution, and to remind them of their hope—the sure return of their Lord and Savior.

Paul begins this letter with a note of affirmation, thanking God for the strong faith and good reputation of the Thessalonians (1:1–10). Then Paul reviews their relationship—how he and his companions brought the gospel to them (2:1–12), how they accepted the message (2:13–16), and how he longed to be with them again (2:17–20). Because of his concern, Paul sent Timothy to encourage them in their faith (3:1–13).

Paul then presents the core of his message—exhortation and comfort. He challenges them to please God in their daily living by avoiding sexual immorality (4:1–8), loving each other (4:9, 10), and living as good citizens in a sinful world (4:11, 12).

Paul comforts the Thessalonians by reminding them of the hope of the resurrection (4:13–18). Then he warns them to be prepared at all times, for Jesus Christ could return at any moment. When Christ returns, those Christians who are alive and those who have died will be raised to new life (5:1–11).

Paul then gives the Thessalonians a handful of reminders on how to prepare themselves for the Second Coming: Warn the idle (5:14), encourage the timid (5:14), help the weak (5:14), be patient with everyone (5:14), be kind to everyone (5:15), be joyful always (5:16), pray continually (5:17), give thanks (5:18), test everything that is taught (5:20, 21), and avoid evil (5:22). Paul concludes his letter with two benedictions and a request for prayer.

As you read this letter, listen carefully to Paul's practical advice for Christian living. And when burdened by grief and overwhelmed by sorrow, take hope in the reality of Christ's return, the resurrection, and eternal life!

THE BLUEPRINT

1. Faithfulness to the Lord (1:1—3:13) 2. Watchfulness for the Lord (4:1—5:28)	Paul and his companions were faithful to bring the gospel to the Thessalonians in the midst of persecution. The Thessalonians had only recently become Christians, and yet they had remained faithful to the Lord, despite the fact that the apostles were not with them. Others have been faithful in bringing God's Word to us. We must remain faithful and live in the expectation that Christ will return at any time.

MEGATHEMES

THEME	EXPLANATION	IMPORTANCE
Persecution	Paul and the new Christians at Thessalonica experienced persecution because of their faith in Christ. We can expect trials and troubles as well. We need to stand firm in our faith in the midst of trials, being strengthened by the Holy Spirit.	The Holy Spirit helps us to remain strong in faith, able to show genuine love to others and maintain our moral character even when we are being persecuted, slandered, or oppressed.
Paul's Ministry	Paul expressed his concern for this church even while he was being slandered. Paul's commitment to share the gospel in spite of difficult circumstances is a model we should follow.	Paul not only delivered his message, but gave of himself. In our ministries, we must become like Paul—faithful and bold, yet sensitive and self-sacrificing.
Hope	One day all believers, both those who are alive and those who have died, will be united with Christ. To those Christians who die before Christ's return, there is hope—the hope of the resurrection of the body.	If we believe in Christ, we will live with him forever. All those who belong to Jesus Christ—from throughout history—will be present with him at his second coming. We can be confident that we will be with loved ones who have trusted in Christ.
Being Prepared	No one knows the time of Christ's return. We are to live moral and holy lives, ever watchful for his coming. Believers must not neglect daily responsibilities, but always work and live to please the Lord.	The gospel is not only what we believe but also what we must live. The Holy Spirit leads us in faithfulness, so we can avoid lust and fraud. Live as though you expect Christ's return at any time. Don't be caught unprepared.

1. Faithfulness to the Lord

Greetings from Paul

1:1 Acts 17:1; 2 Thes 1:1

1 This letter is from Paul, Silas,* and Timothy.

It is written to the church in Thessalonica, you who belong to God the Father and the Lord Jesus Christ.

May his grace and peace be yours.

1:1 Greek *Silvanus.*

1:1 Paul and his companions probably arrived in Thessalonica in the early summer of A.D. 50. They planted the first Christian church in that city, but had to leave in a hurry because their lives were threatened (Acts 17:1-10). At the first opportunity, probably when he stopped at Corinth, Paul sent Timothy back to Thessalonica to see how the new believers were doing. Timothy returned to Paul with good news: The Christians in Thessalonica were remaining firm in the faith and were unified. But the Thessalonians did have some questions about their new faith. Paul had not had time to answer all their questions during his brief visit, and in the meantime, other questions had arisen. So Paul wrote this letter to answer their questions and to commend them on their faithfulness to Christ.

1:1 For more information on Paul, see his Profile in Acts 9. Timothy's Profile is in 1 Timothy. Silas accompanied Paul on his second missionary journey (Acts 15:36–17:15). He helped Paul

The Faith of the Thessalonian Believers

2We always thank God for all of you and pray for you constantly. 3As we talk to our God
and Father about you, we think of your faithful work, your loving deeds, and your
continual anticipation of the return of our Lord Jesus Christ.
4We know that God loves you, dear brothers and sisters, and that he chose you to be
his own people. 5For when we brought you the Good News, it was not only with words
but also with power, for the Holy Spirit gave you full assurance that what we said was
true. And you know that the way we lived among you was further proof of the truth of
our message. 6So you received the message with joy from the Holy Spirit in spite of the
severe suffering it brought you. In this way, you imitated both us and the Lord. 7As a

1:3 1 Cor 13:13; 2 Thes 1:11
1:4 2 Thes 2:13; 2 Pet 1:10
1:5 1 Cor 2:4-5; 4:20; 2 Thes 3:7
1:6 Acts 17:1-9; 1 Cor 4:16

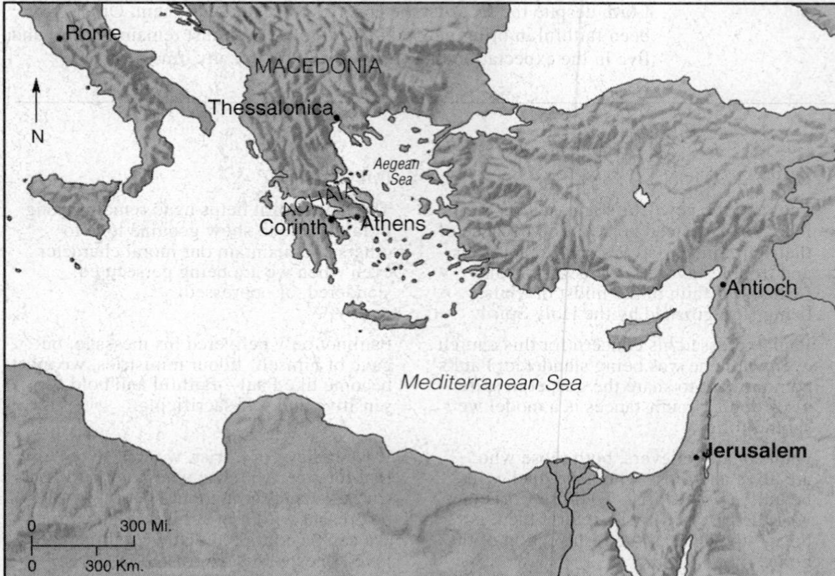

LOCATION OF THESSALONICA
Paul visited Thessalonica on his second and third missionary journeys. It was a seaport and trade center located on the Egnatian Way, a busy international highway. Paul probably wrote his two letters to the Thessalonians from Corinth.

establish the church in Thessalonica (Acts 17:1-9). He is also mentioned in 2 Corinthians 1:19, 2 Thessalonians 1:1, and in 1 Peter 5:12. Silas's Profile is found in Acts 15.

1:1 Thessalonica was the capital and largest city (about 200,000 population) of the Roman province of Macedonia. The most important Roman highway (the Egnatian Way)—extending from Rome all the way to the Orient—went through Thessalonica. This highway, along with the city's thriving seaport, made Thessalonica one of the wealthiest and most flourishing trade centers in the Roman Empire. Recognized as a free city, Thessalonica was allowed self-rule and was exempt from most of the restrictions placed by Rome on other cities in the empire. However, with its international flavor came many pagan religions and cultural influences that challenged the faith of the young Christians there.

1:3 The Thessalonians had stood firm when they were persecuted (1:6; 3:1-4, 7, 8). Paul commended these young Christians for their faithful work, loving deeds, and anticipation of the Lord's return. These characteristics are the marks of effective Christians in any age.

1:5 The Good News came "with power"; it had a powerful effect on the Thessalonians. Whenever the Bible is heard and obeyed, lives are changed! Christianity is more than a collection of interesting facts; it is the power of God to everyone who believes. What has God's power done in your life since you first believed?

1:5 The Holy Spirit changes people when they believe the Good News. When we tell others about Christ, we must depend on the Holy Spirit to open their eyes and convince them that they need salvation. God's power—not our cleverness or persuasion—changes people. Without the work of the Holy Spirit, our words are meaningless. The Holy Spirit not only convicts people of sin but also assures them of the truth of the Good News. (For more information on the Holy Spirit, see John 14:23-26; 15:26, 27; and the notes on John 3:6 and Acts 1:5.)

1:5 Paul wrote, "And you know that the way we lived among you was further proof of the truth of our message." The Thessalonians could see that what Paul, Silas, and Timothy were preaching was true because these men lived it. Does your life confirm or contradict what you say you believe?

1:6 The message of salvation, though welcomed with great joy, brought the Thessalonians severe suffering because it led to persecution from both Jews and Gentiles (3:2-4; Acts 17:5). Having believed the Good News and accepted new life in Christ, apparently many Thessalonians believed that they would be protected from death until Christ returned. Then, when believers began to die under persecution, some Thessalonian Christians started to question their faith. Many of Paul's comments throughout this letter were addressed to these people, as he explained what happens when believers die (see 4:13ff).

1:8 Rom 1:8; 2 Thes 3:1
1:9 Acts 14:15; 1 Cor 12:2
1:10 Phil 3:20; 1 Thes 5:9; Titus 2:13; Heb 9:28; Rev 1:7
2:1 1 Thes 1:5, 9
2:2 Acts 16:22; 17:2; Phil 1:30
2:3 2 Cor 4:2; 2 Pet 1:16
2:4 Gal 1:10; 1 Tim 1:11
2:5 Acts 20:33
2:7 2 Tim 2:24
2:8 2 Cor 12:15
2:9 Acts 18:3; 2 Cor 11:9; 2 Thes 3:8

result, you yourselves became an example to all the Christians in Greece.* 8 And now the
word of the Lord is ringing out from you to people everywhere, even beyond Greece, for
wherever we go we find people telling us about your faith in God. We don't need to tell
them about it, 9 for they themselves keep talking about the wonderful welcome you gave
us and how you turned away from idols to serve the true and living God. 10 And they
speak of how you are looking forward to the coming of God's Son from heaven—Jesus,
whom God raised from the dead. He is the one who has rescued us from the terrors of
the coming judgment.

Paul Remembers His Visit

2 You yourselves know, dear brothers and sisters, that our visit to you was not a failure.
2 You know how badly we had been treated at Philippi just before we came to you
and how much we suffered there. Yet our God gave us the courage to declare his Good
News to you boldly, even though we were surrounded by many who opposed us. 3 So
you can see that we were not preaching with any deceit or impure purposes or trickery.
4 For we speak as messengers who have been approved by God to be entrusted with
the Good News. Our purpose is to please God, not people. He is the one who examines
the motives of our hearts. 5 Never once did we try to win you with flattery, as you very
well know. And God is our witness that we were not just pretending to be your friends
so you would give us money! 6 As for praise, we have never asked for it from you or
anyone else. 7 As apostles of Christ we certainly had a right to make some demands of
you, but we were as gentle among you as a mother* feeding and caring for her own
children. 8 We loved you so much that we gave you not only God's Good News but our
own lives, too.
9 Don't you remember, dear brothers and sisters, how hard we worked among you?
Night and day we toiled to earn a living so that our expenses would not be a burden to

1:7 Greek *Macedonia and Achaia,* the northern and southern regions of Greece; also in 1:8. **2:7** Some manuscripts read *we were as infants among you; we were as a mother.*

1:9, 10 All of us should respond to the Good News as the Thessalonians did: *Turn* to God, *serve* God, and *look forward* to the return of his Son, Christ, from heaven. We should turn from sin to God because Christ is coming to judge the earth. We should be fervent in our service because we have little time before Christ returns. We should be prepared for Christ to return because we don't know when he will come.

1:10 Paul emphasized Christ's second coming throughout this book. Because the Thessalonian church was being persecuted, Paul encouraged them to look forward to the deliverance that Christ would bring. A believer's hope is in the return of Jesus, our great God and Savior (Titus 2:13). Our perspective on life remains incomplete without this hope. Just as surely as Christ was raised from the dead and ascended into heaven, he will return (Acts 1:11).

2:1 "Our visit to you" refers to Paul's first visit to Thessalonica (see Acts 17:1-9).

2:2 The Thessalonians knew that Paul had been imprisoned in Philippi just prior to coming to Thessalonica (see Acts 16:11–17:1). Fear of imprisonment did not keep Paul from preaching the Good News. If God wants us to do something, he will give us the strength and courage to do it despite any obstacles that may come our way.

2:3 This pointed statement may be a response to accusations from the Jewish leaders who had stirred up the crowds (Acts 17:5). Paul did not seek money, fame, or popularity by sharing the Good News. He demonstrated the sincerity of his motives by showing that he and Silas had suffered for sharing the Good News in Philippi. People become involved in ministry for a variety of reasons, not all of them good or pure. When their bad motives are exposed, all of Christ's work suffers. When you get involved in ministry, do so out of love for Christ and others.

2:4-8 In trying to persuade people, we may be tempted to alter our position just enough to make our message more palatable or to use flattery or praise. Paul never changed his *message* to make it more acceptable, but he did tailor his *methods* to each audience. Although our presentation must be altered to be appropriate to the situation, the truth of the Good News must never be compromised.

2:5 It's disgusting to hear a person "butter up" someone. Flattery is phony, and it is a cover-up for a person's real intentions. Christians should not be flatterers. Those who proclaim God's truth have a special responsibility to be honest. Are you honest and straightforward in your words and actions? Or do you tell people what they want to hear in order to get what you want or to get ahead?

2:6-8 When Paul was with the Thessalonians, he didn't flatter them, seek their praise, or become a burden to them. He and Silas completely focused their efforts on presenting God's message of salvation to the Thessalonians. This was important! The Thessalonian believers had their lives changed by God, not Paul; it was Christ's message they believed, not Paul's. When we witness for Christ, our focus should not be on the impression we make. As true ministers of Christ, we should point to him, not to ourselves.

2:7 Gentleness is often overlooked as a personal trait in our society. Power and assertiveness gain more respect, even though no one likes to be bullied. Gentleness is love in action—being considerate, meeting the needs of others, allowing time for the other person to talk, and being willing to learn. It is an essential trait for both men and women. Maintain a gentle attitude in your relationships with others.

2:9 Although Paul had the right to receive financial support from the people he taught, he supported himself as a tentmaker (Acts 18:3) so that he wouldn't be a burden to the new Thessalonian believers.

anyone there as we preached God's Good News among you. 10 You yourselves are our
witnesses—and so is God—that we were pure and honest and faultless toward all of you
believers. 11 And you know that we treated each of you as a father treats his own children.
12 We pleaded with you, encouraged you, and urged you to live your lives in a way that
God would consider worthy. For he called you into his Kingdom to share his glory.

13 And we will never stop thanking God that when we preached his message to you,
you didn't think of the words we spoke as being just our own. You accepted what we said
as the very word of God—which, of course, it was. And this word continues to work in
you who believe.

14 And then, dear brothers and sisters, you suffered persecution from your own
countrymen. In this way, you imitated the believers in God's churches in Judea who,
because of their belief in Christ Jesus, suffered from their own people, the Jews.

15 For some of the Jews had killed their own prophets, and some even killed the Lord
Jesus. Now they have persecuted us and driven us out. They displease God and oppose
everyone 16 by trying to keep us from preaching the Good News to the Gentiles, for fear
some might be saved. By doing this, they continue to pile up their sins. But the anger of
God has caught up with them at last.

Timothy's Good Report about the Church

17 Dear friends,* after we were separated from you for a little while (though our hearts
never left you), we tried very hard to come back because of our intense longing to see
you again. 18 We wanted very much to come, and I, Paul, tried again and again, but Satan
prevented us. 19 After all, what gives us hope and joy, and what is our proud reward and
crown? It is you! Yes, you will bring us much joy as we stand together before our Lord
Jesus when he comes back again. 20 For you are our pride and joy.

3 Finally, when we could stand it no longer, we decided that I should stay alone in
Athens, 2 and we sent Timothy to visit you. He is our co-worker for God and our
brother in proclaiming the Good News of Christ. We sent him to strengthen you, to
encourage you in your faith, 3 and to keep you from becoming disturbed by the troubles

2:10 1 Thes 1:5
2:11 1 Cor 4:14
2:12 Eph 4:1; Col 1:10; 1 Pet 1:15
2:13 1 Thes 1:2; 2 Thes 2:13
2:14 Acts 17:5; 1 Thes 1:6
2:15 Luke 24:20; Acts 2:23; 7:52
2:16 Matt 23:32-33; Acts 13:45, 50; 17:5; 20:3; 21:27; 24:9
2:17 1 Cor 5:3; 1 Thes 3:10
2:18 Rom 1:13; 15:22
2:19 Phil 2:16
2:20 2 Cor 1:14
3:1 Acts 17:15
3:2 Acts 16:1-3
3:3 2 Tim 3:12

2:17 Greek *Brothers.*

2:11 No loving father would neglect the safety of his children, allowing them to walk into circumstances that might be harmful or fatal. In the same way, we must take new believers under our wing until they are mature enough to stand firm in their faith. We must help new Christians become strong enough to influence others for the sake of the Good News.

2:11, 12 By his words and example, Paul encouraged the Thessalonians to live in a way God would consider worthy. Is there anything about your daily life that would embarrass God? What do people think of God from watching you?

2:13 In the New Testament, *the word of God* usually refers to the preaching of the Good News, the Old Testament, or Jesus Christ himself. Today we often apply it only to the Bible. Remember that Jesus Christ himself is the Word (John 1:1).

2:14 Just as the Jewish Christians in Jerusalem were persecuted by other Jews, so the Gentile Christians in Thessalonica were persecuted by their fellow Gentiles. Persecution is discouraging, especially when it comes from your own people. When you take a stand for Christ, you may face opposition, disapproval, and ridicule from your neighbors, friends, and even family members.

2:14 When Paul refers to the Jews, he is talking about certain Jews who opposed his preaching of the Good News. He does not mean all Jews. Many of Paul's converts were Jewish. Paul himself was a Jew (2 Corinthians 11:22).

2:15, 16 Why were so many Jews opposed to Christianity? (1) Although the Jewish religion had been declared legal by the Roman government, it still had a tenuous relationship with the government. At this time, Christianity was viewed as a sect of Judaism. The Jews were afraid that reprisals leveled against the Christians might be expanded to include them. (2) The Jewish leaders thought Jesus was a false prophet, and they didn't want his teachings to spread. (3) They feared that if many Jews were drawn away, their own political position might be weakened. (4) They were proud of their special status as God's chosen people, and they resented the fact that Gentiles could be full members within the Christian church.

2:18 Satan is real. He is called "the god of this evil world" (2 Corinthians 4:4) and "the mighty prince of the power of the air" (Ephesians 2:2). We don't know exactly what hindered Paul from returning to Thessalonica—opposition, illness, travel complications, or a direct attack by Satan—but Satan worked in some way to keep him away. Many of the difficulties that prevent us from accomplishing God's work can be attributed to Satan (see Ephesians 6:12).

2:20 The ultimate reward for Paul's ministry was not money, prestige, or fame, but new believers whose lives had been changed by God through the preaching of the Good News. This was why he longed to see them. No matter what ministry God has given to you, your highest reward and greatest joy should be those who come to believe in Christ and are growing in him.

3:1-3 Some think that troubles are always caused by sin or a lack of faith. Trials may be a part of God's plan for believers. Experiencing problems and persecutions can build character (James 1:2-4), perseverance (Romans 5:3-5), and sensitivity toward others who also face trouble (2 Corinthians 1:3-7). Problems are unavoidable for God's people. Your troubles may be a sign of effective Christian living.

3:1-4 Because Paul could not return to Thessalonica (2:18), he sent Timothy as his representative. According to Acts 17:10, Paul left Thessalonica and went to Berea. When trouble broke out in

3:4 1 Thes 2:14
3:5 Matt 4:3 Phil 2:16
3:6 Acts 18:5
3:7 2 Thes 1:4
3:8 1 Cor 16:13
3:10 1 Thes 2:17 2 Tim 1:3
3:12 Phil 1:9
3:13 Zech 14:5 1 Cor 1:8 1 Thes 1:7, 10; 2:19
4:1 Eph 4:1 2 Thes 3:6
4:2 2 Thes 3:4

you were going through. But, of course, you know that such troubles are going to happen
to us Christians. [4]Even while we were with you, we warned you that troubles would soon
come—and they did, as you well know.
[5]That is why, when I could bear it no longer, I sent Timothy to find out whether your
faith was still strong. I was afraid that the Tempter had gotten the best of you and that all
our work had been useless. [6]Now Timothy has just returned, bringing the good news that
your faith and love are as strong as ever. He reports that you remember our visit with joy
and that you want to see us just as much as we want to see you. [7]So we have been greatly
comforted, dear friends,* in all of our own crushing troubles and suffering, because you
have remained strong in your faith. [8]It gives us new life, knowing you remain strong in
the Lord.
[9]How we thank God for you! Because of you we have great joy in the presence of
God. [10]Night and day we pray earnestly for you, asking God to let us see you again to
fill up anything that may still be missing in your faith.
[11]May God himself, our Father, and our Lord Jesus make it possible for us to come to
you very soon. [12]And may the Lord make your love grow and overflow to each other
and to everyone else, just as our love overflows toward you. [13]As a result, Christ will
make your hearts strong, blameless, and holy when you stand before God our Father on
that day when our Lord Jesus comes with all those who belong to him.

2. Watchfulness for the Lord

Live to Please God

4 Finally, dear brothers and sisters, we urge you in the name of the Lord Jesus to live
in a way that pleases God, as we have taught you. You are doing this already, and
we encourage you to do so more and more. [2]For you remember what we taught you in

3:7 Greek *brothers.*

THE EVENTS OF CHRIST'S RETURN

1. Christ will return visibly, with a commanding shout.
2. There will be an unmistakable call from an angel.
3. There will be a trumpet fanfare such as has never been heard.
4. Believers in Christ who are dead will rise from their graves.
5. Believers who are alive will be caught up in the clouds to meet the Lord.

While Christians have often disagreed about what events will lead up to the return of Christ, there has been less disagreement about what will happen once Christ does return.

Berea, some Christians took Paul to Athens, while Silas and Timothy stayed behind (Acts 17:13-15). Then Paul directed Silas and Timothy to join him in Athens. Later, Paul sent Timothy to encourage the Thessalonian Christians to be strong in their faith in the face of persecution and other troubles.

3:4 Some people turn to God with the hope of escaping suffering on earth. But God doesn't promise that. Instead, he gives us power to grow through our sufferings. The Christian life involves obedience to Christ despite temptations and hardships.

3:5 Satan ("the Tempter") is the most powerful of the evil spirits. His power can affect both the spiritual world (Ephesians 2:1-3; 6:10-12) and the physical world (2 Corinthians 12:7-10). Satan even tempted Jesus (Matthew 4:1-11). But Jesus defeated Satan when he died on the cross for our sins and rose again to bring us new life. At the proper time God will overthrow Satan forever (Revelation 20:7-10).

3:7, 8 During persecution or pressure, believers should encourage one another. Christians who stand firm in the Lord encourage both ministers and teachers (who can see the benefit of their work in those who remain faithful) and also those who are new in their faith (who can learn from the steadfastness of the mature).

3:9, 10 It brings great joy to a Christian to see another person come to faith in Christ and mature in that faith. Paul experienced this joy countless times. He thanked God for those who had come to know Christ and for their strong faith. He also prayed for their continued growth. If there are new Christians who have brought you joy, thank God for them and support them as they continue to grow in the faith.

3:11 Paul wanted to return to Thessalonica. We have no record that he was able to do so; but when he was traveling through Asia on his third journey, he was joined by Aristarchus and Secundus, who were from Thessalonica (Acts 20:4, 5).

3:11-13 "That day when our Lord Jesus comes with all those who belong to him" refers to the second coming of Christ when he will establish his eternal Kingdom. At that time, Christ will gather all believers, those who have died and those who are alive, into one united family under his rule. All believers from all times, including these Thessalonians, will be with Christ in his Kingdom.

3:12 If we are full of God's love, it will overflow to others. It's not enough merely to be courteous to others; we must actively and persistently show love to them. Our love should be growing continually. If your capacity to love has remained unchanged for some time, ask God to fill you again with his never-ending supply. Then look for opportunities to express his love.

4:1-8 Sexual standards were very low in the Roman Empire, and in many societies today, they are not any higher. The temptation to engage in sexual intercourse outside the marriage relationship has always been powerful. Giving in to that temptation can have disastrous results. Sexual sins always hurt someone: individuals, families, businesses, churches. Besides the physical consequences, there are also spiritual consequences. For more on why sexual sin is so harmful, see the note on 1 Corinthians 6:18.

the name of the Lord Jesus. 3 God wants you to be holy, so you should keep clear of all
sexual sin. 4 Then each of you will control your body* and live in holiness and
honor—5 not in lustful passion as the pagans do, in their ignorance of God and his ways.
6 Never cheat another Christian* in this matter by taking his wife, for the Lord avenges
all such sins, as we have solemnly warned you before. 7 God has called us to be holy, not
to live impure lives. 8 Anyone who refuses to live by these rules is not disobeying human
rules but is rejecting God, who gives his Holy Spirit to you.
9 But I don't need to write to you about the Christian love that should be shown among
God's people. For God himself has taught you to love one another. 10 Indeed, your love
is already strong toward all the Christians* in all of Macedonia. Even so, dear friends,*
we beg you to love them more and more. 11 This should be your ambition: to live a quiet
life, minding your own business and working with your hands, just as we commanded
you before. 12 As a result, people who are not Christians will respect the way you live,
and you will not need to depend on others to meet your financial needs.

The Hope of the Resurrection

13 And now, brothers and sisters, I want you to know what will happen to the Christians
who have died so you will not be full of sorrow like people who have no hope. 14 For
since we believe that Jesus died and was raised to life again, we also believe that when
Jesus comes, God will bring back with Jesus all the Christians who have died.
15 I can tell you this directly from the Lord: We who are still living when the Lord
returns will not rise to meet him ahead of those who are in their graves. 16 For the Lord
himself will come down from heaven with a commanding shout, with the call of the
archangel, and with the trumpet call of God. First, all the Christians who have died will
rise from their graves. 17 Then, together with them, we who are still alive and remain on
the earth will be caught up in the clouds to meet the Lord in the air and remain with him
forever. 18 So comfort and encourage each other with these words.

5 I really don't need to write to you about how and when all this will happen, 2 for you
know quite well that the day of the Lord will come unexpectedly, like a thief in the
night. 3 When people are saying, "All is well; everything is peaceful and secure," then

4:3 Heb 10:10; 1 Pet 1:16
4:4 1 Cor 7:2
4:7 Lev 11:44; 2 Thes 2:13-14; 1 Pet 1:15
4:8 Rom 5:5; 1 Jn 3:24
4:9 1 Jn 2:20, 27
4:10 1 Thes 3:12; 2 Thes 3:4
4:11 Eph 4:28; 2 Thes 3:10-12
4:14 Rom 14:9; 1 Cor 15:3-4, 12
4:15 1 Cor 7:10, 25; 15:52
4:16 Matt 24:30; 1 Cor 15:52; 1 Thes 1:10; 2 Thes 1:7
4:17 John 12:26; Acts 1:9; Rev 11:12
5:2 Matt 24:42-44
5:3 Jer 4:10; 6:14; Matt 24:39

4:4 Or *will know how to take a wife for himself;* Greek reads *will know how to possess his own vessel.* **4:6** Greek *a brother.* **4:10a** Greek *the brothers.* **4:10b** Greek *brothers.*

4:1-8 Sexual desires and activities must be placed under Christ's control. God created sex for procreation and pleasure, and as an expression of love between a husband and wife. Sexual experience must be limited to the marriage relationship to avoid hurting ourselves, our relationship to God, and our relationships with others.

4:3 Being made holy is the process of living the Christian life. The Holy Spirit works in us, conforming us to the image of Christ (Romans 8:29).

4:11, 12 There is more to Christian living than simply loving other Christians. We must be responsible in all areas of life. Some of the Thessalonian Christians had adopted a life of idleness, depending on others for handouts. Some Greeks looked down on manual labor. So Paul told the Thessalonians to work hard and live a quiet life. You can't be effective in sharing your faith with others if they don't respect you. Whatever you do, do it faithfully and be a positive force in society.

4:13ff The Thessalonians were wondering why many of their fellow believers had died and what would happen to them when Christ returned. Paul wanted the Thessalonians to understand that death is not the end of the story. When Christ returns, all believers—dead and alive—will be reunited, never to suffer or die again.

4:15 What does Paul mean when he says, "directly from the Lord"? Either this was something that the Lord had revealed directly to Paul, or it was a teaching of Jesus that had been passed along orally by the apostles and other Christians.

4:15-18 Knowing exactly *when* the dead will be raised, in relation to the other events at the Second Coming, is not as important as knowing why Paul wrote these words: to challenge believers to comfort and encourage one another when loved ones die. This passage can be a great comfort when any believer dies. The same love that should unite believers in this life (4:9) will unite believers when Christ returns and reigns for eternity.

4:15-18 Because Jesus Christ came back to life, so will all believers. All Christians, including those living when Christ returns, will live with Christ forever. Therefore, we need not despair when loved ones die or world events take a tragic turn. God will turn our tragedies to triumphs, our poverty to riches, our pain to glory, and our defeat to victory. All believers throughout history will stand reunited in God's very presence, safe and secure. As Paul comforted the Thessalonians with the promise of the resurrection, so we should comfort and reassure each other with this great hope.

4:16 An "archangel" is a high or holy angel appointed to a special task. Michael is the only archangel mentioned in the New Testament (see Jude 1:9).

5:1 "How and when all this will happen" refers to the knowledge of what will happen in the future, specifically at the return of Christ.

5:1-3 Efforts to determine the date of Christ's return are foolish. Don't be misled by anyone who claims to know. We are told here that no one knows and that even believers will be surprised. The Lord will return suddenly and unexpectedly, warns Paul, so be ready! Because no one knows when Jesus will come back to earth, we should be ready at all times. Suppose he were to return today. How would he find you living? Are you ready to meet him? Live each day prepared to welcome Christ.

5:4 1 Jn 2:8
5:5 John 12:36; Eph 5:9
5:7 Acts 2:15
5:8 Isa 59:17; Eph 6:14, 17; 1 Pet 1:13
5:9 1 Thes 1:10; 2 Thes 2:13-14
5:10 Rom 14:8-9

disaster will fall upon them as suddenly as a woman's birth pains begin when her child
is about to be born. And there will be no escape.
4 But you aren't in the dark about these things, dear brothers and sisters, and you won't
be surprised when the day of the Lord comes like a thief. 5 For you are all children of the
light and of the day; we don't belong to darkness and night. 6 So be on your guard, not
asleep like the others. Stay alert and be sober. 7 Night is the time for sleep and the time
when people get drunk. 8 But let us who live in the light think clearly, protected by the
body armor of faith and love, and wearing as our helmet the confidence of our salvation.
9 For God decided to save us through our Lord Jesus Christ, not to pour out his anger on
us. 10 He died for us so that we can live with him forever, whether we are dead or alive
at the time of his return. 11 So encourage each other and build each other up, just as you
are already doing.

CHECKLIST FOR ENCOURAGERS

The command to "encourage" others is found throughout the Bible. In 5:11–23, Paul gives many specific examples of how we can encourage others.

Reference	*Example*	*Suggested Application*
5:11	Build each other up.	Point out to someone a quality you appreciate in him or her.
5:12	Respect leaders.	Look for ways to cooperate.
5:13	Hold leaders in highest regard.	Hold back your next critical comments about those in positions of responsibility. Say "thank you" to your leaders for their efforts.
5:13	Live in peace.	Search for ways to get along with others.
5:14	Warn the lazy.	Challenge someone to join you in a project.
5:14	Encourage the timid.	Encourage those who are timid by reminding them of God's promises.
5:14	Help the weak.	Support those who are weak by loving them and praying for them.
5:14	Be patient.	Think of a situation that tries your patience, and plan ahead of time how you can stay calm.
5:15	Resist revenge.	Instead of planning to get even with those who mistreat you, do good to them.
5:16	Be joyful.	Remember that even in the midst of turmoil, God is in control.
5:17	Pray continually.	God is always with you—talk to him.
5:18	Give thanks.	Make a list of all the gifts God has given you, giving thanks to God for each one.
5:19	Do not stifle the Holy Spirit.	Cooperate with the Spirit the next time he prompts you to participate in a Christian meeting.
5:20	Do not scoff at prophecies.	Receive God's word from those who speak for him.
5:22	Avoid every kind of evil.	Avoid situations where you will be drawn into temptation.
5:23	Count on God's constant help.	Realize that the Christian life is to be lived not in our own strength but through God's power.

5:2 The "day of the Lord" is a future time when God will intervene directly and dramatically in world affairs. Predicted and discussed often in the Old Testament (Isaiah 13:6-12; Joel 2:28-32; Zephaniah 1:14-18), the day of the Lord will include both punishment and blessing. Christ will judge sin and set up his eternal Kingdom.

5:8 For more about the Christian's armor, see Ephesians 6:13-17.

5:9-11 As you near the end of a long race, your legs ache, your throat burns, and your whole body cries out for you to stop. This is when friends and fans are most valuable. Their encouragement helps you push through the pain to the finish line. In the same way, Christians are to encourage one another. A word of encouragement offered at the right moment can be the difference between finishing well and collapsing along the way. Look around you. Be sensitive to others' need for encouragement, and offer supportive words or actions.

Paul's Final Advice

12 Dear brothers and sisters, honor those who are your leaders in the Lord's work. They
work hard among you and warn you against all that is wrong. 13 Think highly of them
and give them your wholehearted love because of their work. And remember to live
peaceably with each other.
14 Brothers and sisters, we urge you to warn those who are lazy. Encourage those who
are timid. Take tender care of those who are weak. Be patient with everyone.
15 See that no one pays back evil for evil, but always try to do good to each other and
to everyone else.
16 Always be joyful. 17 Keep on praying. 18 No matter what happens, always be
thankful, for this is God's will for you who belong to Christ Jesus.
19 Do not stifle the Holy Spirit. 20 Do not scoff at prophecies, 21 but test everything that
is said. Hold on to what is good. 22 Keep away from every kind of evil.

Paul's Final Greetings

23 Now may the God of peace make you holy in every way, and may your whole spirit
and soul and body be kept blameless until that day when our Lord Jesus Christ comes
again. 24 God, who calls you, is faithful; he will do this.
25 Dear brothers and sisters, pray for us.
26 Greet each other in Christian love.*
27 I command you in the name of the Lord to read this letter to all the Christians.*
28 And may the grace of our Lord Jesus Christ be with all of you.

5:26 Greek *Greet all the brothers with a holy kiss.* **5:27** Greek *the brothers.*

5:12 1 Tim 5:17
5:15 Prov 20:22; Rom 12:17; 1 Pet 3:9
5:16 Phil 4:4
5:17 Luke 18:1
5:18 Eph 5:20
5:19 Eph 4:30
5:20 1 Cor 14:1, 39
5:23 Rom 15:33
5:24 1 Cor 1:9
5:27 Col 4:16
5:28 Rom 16:20

5:12 "Those who are your leaders in the Lord's work" probably refers to elders and deacons in the church.

5:12, 13 How can you show respect to your pastor and other church leaders? Express your appreciation, tell them how you have been helped by their leadership and teaching, and thank them for their ministry in your life. If you say nothing, how will they know where you stand? Remember, they need and deserve your support and love.

5:14 Don't loaf around with the lazy; warn them. Don't yell at the timid and weak; encourage and help them. At times it's difficult to distinguish between idleness and timidity. Two people may be doing nothing—one out of laziness and the other out of shyness or fear of doing something wrong. The key to ministry is sensitivity: sensing the condition of each person and offering the appropriate remedy for each situation. You can't effectively help until you know the problem. You can't apply the medicine until you know where the wound is.

5:16-18 Our joy, prayers, and thankfulness should not fluctuate with our circumstances or feelings. Obeying these three commands—be joyful, keep on praying, and be thankful—often goes against our natural inclinations. When we make a conscious decision to do what God says, however, we will begin to see people in a new perspective. When we do God's will, we will find it easier to be joyful and thankful.

5:17 We cannot spend all our time on our knees, but it is possible to have a prayerful attitude at all times. This attitude is built upon acknowledging our dependence on God, realizing his presence within us, and determining to obey him fully. Then we will find it natural to pray frequent, spontaneous, short prayers. A prayerful attitude is not a substitute for regular times of prayer but should be an outgrowth of those times.

5:18 Paul was not teaching that we should thank God *for* everything that happens to us, but *in* everything. Evil does not come from God, so we should not thank him for it. But when evil strikes, we can still be thankful for God's presence and for the good that he will accomplish through the distress.

5:19 By warning us not to "stifle the Holy Spirit," Paul means that we should not ignore or toss aside the gifts the Holy Spirit gives. Here, he mentions prophecy (5:20); in 1 Corinthians 14:39, he mentions speaking in tongues. Sometimes spiritual gifts are controversial, and they may cause division in a church. Rather than trying to solve the problems, some Christians prefer to smother the gifts. This impoverishes the church. We should not stifle the Holy Spirit's work in anyone's life but encourage the full expression of these gifts to benefit the whole body of Christ.

5:20, 21 We shouldn't make fun of those who are called to speak for God ("scoff at prophecies"), but we should always "test everything that is said," checking their words against the Bible. We are on dangerous ground if we scoff at a person who speaks the truth. Instead, we should carefully check out what people say, accepting what is true and rejecting what is false.

5:22-24 As Christians, we cannot avoid every kind of evil because we live in a sinful world. We can, however, make sure that we don't give evil a foothold by avoiding tempting situations and concentrating on obeying God.

5:23 The spirit, soul, and body refer not so much to the distinct parts of a person as to the entire being of a person. This expression is Paul's way of saying that God must be involved in *every* aspect of our life. It is wrong to think that we can separate our spiritual life from everything else, obeying God only in some ethereal sense or living for him only one day each week. Christ must control *all* of us, not just a "religious" part.

5:27 For all the Christians to hear this letter, it had to be read in a public meeting—there were not enough copies to circulate. Paul wanted to make sure that everyone had the opportunity to hear his message because he was answering important questions and offering needed encouragement.

5:28 The Thessalonian church was young, and they needed help and encouragement. Both the persecution they faced and the temptations of their pagan culture were potential problems for these new Christians. Paul wrote, therefore, to strengthen their faith and bolster their resistance to persecution and temptation. We, too, have a responsibility to help new believers—to make sure that they continue in their faith and don't become side-tracked by wrong beliefs or practices. First Thessalonians can better equip us to help our brothers and sisters in Christ.

2 THESSALONIANS

"BUT I thought he said . . . ," "I'm sure he meant . . . ," "It is clear to me that we should . . . ," "I disagree. I think we must . . ."

Effective communication is difficult; often the message sent is *not* the message received in the home, marketplace, neighborhood, or church. Even when clearly stated or written, words can be misinterpreted and misunderstood, especially when filtered through the sieve of prejudices and preconceptions.

Paul faced this problem with the Thessalonians. He had written them earlier to help them grow in the faith, comforting and encouraging them by affirming the reality of Christ's return. Just a few months later, however, word came from Thessalonica that some had misunderstood Paul's teaching about the second coming. His announcement that Christ could come at any moment had caused some to stop working and just wait, rationalizing their idleness by pointing to Paul's teaching. Adding fuel to this fire was the continued persecution of the church. Many felt that indeed this must be the "day of the Lord."

Responding quickly, Paul sent a second letter to this young church. In it he gave further instruction concerning the Second Coming and the day of the Lord (2:1, 2). Second Thessalonians, therefore, continues the subject of 1 Thessalonians and is a call to continued courage and consistent conduct.

The letter begins with Paul's trademark—a personal greeting and a statement of thanksgiving for their faith (1:1–3). He mentions their perseverance in spite of their persecution and trials (1:4) and uses this situation to broach the subject of Christ's return. At that time, Christ will vindicate the righteous who endure and will punish the wicked (1:5–12).

Paul then directly answers the misunderstanding concerning the timing of the events of the end times. He tells them not to listen to rumors and reports that the day of the Lord has already begun (2:1, 2), because a number of events must occur before Christ returns (2:3–12). Meanwhile, they should stand firm for Christ's truth (2:13–15), receive God's encouragement and hope (2:16, 17), pray for strength and for the spread of the Lord's message (3:1–5), and warn those who are idle (3:6–15). Paul ends with personal greetings and a benediction (3:16–18).

Almost 2,000 years later, we stand much closer to the time of Christ's return; but we also would be wrong to see his imminent appearance as an excuse for idle waiting and heavenward gazing. Being prepared for his coming means spreading the gospel, reaching out to those in need, and building the church, his body. As you read 2 Thessalonians, then, see clearly the reality of his return and your responsibility to live for him until that day.

VITAL STATISTICS

PURPOSE:
To clear up the confusion about the second coming of Christ

AUTHOR:
Paul

TO WHOM WRITTEN:
The church at Thessalonica, and all believers everywhere

DATE WRITTEN:
Approximately A.D. 51 or 52, a few months after 1 Thessalonians, from Corinth

SETTING:
Many in the church were confused about the timing of Christ's return. Because of mounting persecution, they thought the day of the Lord must be imminent, and they interpreted Paul's first letter to say that the Second Coming would be at any moment. In light of this misunderstanding, many persisted in being idle and disorderly, with the excuse of waiting for Christ's return.

KEY VERSE:
"May the Lord bring you into an ever deeper understanding of the love of God and the endurance that comes from Christ" (3:5).

KEY PEOPLE:
Paul, Silas, Timothy

KEY PLACE:
Thessalonica

SPECIAL FEATURES:
This is a follow-up letter to 1 Thessalonians. In this letter, Paul indicates various events that must precede the second coming of Christ.

THE BLUEPRINT

1. The bright hope of Christ's return (1:1—2:17)
2. Living in the light of Christ's return (3:1–18)

Paul wrote to encourage those who were facing persecution and to correct a misunderstanding about the timing of Christ's return. The teaching about the Lord's return promoted idleness in this young church. The imminent coming of Christ should never make us idle; we should be even more busy—living purely, using our time well, and working for his Kingdom. We must work not only during easy times when it is convenient but also during difficult times. Christians must patiently watch for Christ's return and work for him while they wait.

MEGATHEMES

THEME	EXPLANATION	IMPORTANCE
Persecution	Paul encouraged the church to persevere in spite of troubles and trials. God will bring victory to his faithful followers and judge those who persecute them.	God promises to reward our faith by giving us his power and helping us bear persecution. Suffering for our faith will strengthen us to serve Christ. We must be faithful to him.
Christ's Return	Since Paul had said that the Lord could come at any moment, some of the Thessalonian believers had stopped working in order to wait for Christ.	Christ will return and bring total victory to all who trust in him. If we are ready, we need not be concerned about *when* he will return. We should stand firm, keep working, and wait for Christ.
Great Rebellion	Before Christ's return, there will be a great rebellion against God led by the man of lawlessness (the Antichrist). God will remove all the restraints on evil before he brings judgment on the rebels. The Antichrist will attempt to deceive many.	We should not be afraid when we see evil increase. God is in control, no matter how evil the world becomes. God guards us during Satan's attacks. We can have victory over evil by remaining faithful to God.
Persistence	Because church members had quit working and become disorderly and disobedient, Paul chastised them for their idleness. He called on them to show courage and true Christian conduct.	We must never get so tired of doing right that we quit. We can be persistent by making the most of our time and talents. Our endurance will be rewarded.

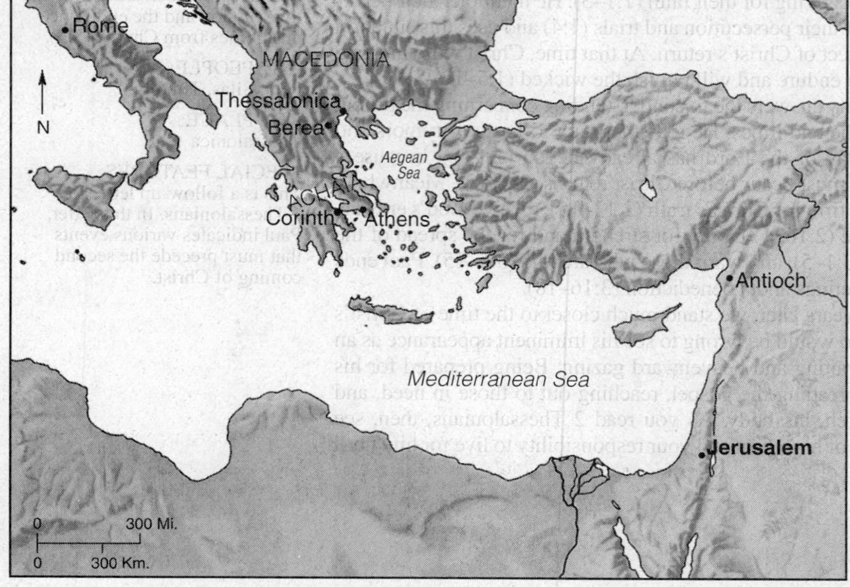

LOCATION OF THESSALONICA
After Paul visited Thessalonica on his second missionary journey, he went on to Berea, Athens, and Corinth (Acts 17—18). From Corinth, Paul wrote his two letters to the Thessalonian church.

1. The bright hope of Christ's return

Greetings from Paul

1 This letter is from Paul, Silas,* and Timothy.
It is written to the church in Thessalonica, you who belong to God our Father and
the Lord Jesus Christ.
2 May God our Father and the Lord Jesus Christ give you grace and peace.

Encouragement during Persecution

3 Dear brothers and sisters, we always thank God for you, as is right, for we are thankful that
your faith is flourishing and you are all growing in love for each other. 4 We proudly tell
God's other churches about your endurance and faithfulness in all the persecutions and
hardships you are suffering. 5 But God will use this persecution to show his justice. For he
will make you worthy of his Kingdom, for which you are suffering, 6 and in his justice he
will punish those who persecute you. 7 And God will provide rest for you who are being
persecuted and also for us when the Lord Jesus appears from heaven. He will come with
his mighty angels, 8 in flaming fire, bringing judgment on those who don't know God and
on those who refuse to obey the Good News of our Lord Jesus. 9 They will be punished with
everlasting destruction, forever separated from the Lord and from his glorious power
10 when he comes to receive glory and praise from his holy people. And you will be among
those praising him on that day, for you believed what we testified about him.
11 And so we keep on praying for you, that our God will make you worthy of the life
to which he called you. And we pray that God, by his power, will fulfill all your good

1:1 Greek *Silvanus.*

1:1 1 Thes 1:1
1:2 Rom 1:7
1:5 Luke 20:35; Phil 1:28; 1 Thes 2:12
1:6 Rom 12:9; Rev 6:10
1:7 Matt 25:31; 1 Thes 4:16
1:8 Ps 79:6; Isa 66:15
1:9 Isa 2:10, 19, 21; 1 Thes 5:3; 2 Thes 2:8
1:10 Ps 88:8; John 17:10; 1 Thes 3:13

1:1 Paul wrote this letter from Corinth less than a year after he wrote 1 Thessalonians. He and his companions, Timothy and Silas, had visited Thessalonica on Paul's second missionary journey (Acts 17:1-10). They established the church there, but Paul had to leave suddenly because of persecution. This prompted him to write his first letter (1 Thessalonians), which contains words of comfort and encouragement. Paul then heard how the Thessalonians had responded to this letter. The good news was that they were continuing to grow in their faith. But the bad news was that false teachings about Christ's return were spreading, leading many to quit their jobs and wait for the end of the world. So Paul wrote to them again. While the purpose of Paul's first letter was to comfort the Thessalonians with the assurance of Christ's second coming, the purpose of his second letter is to correct false teaching about the Second Coming.

1:1 Paul, Silas, and Timothy were together in Corinth (Acts 18:5). Paul wrote this letter on behalf of all three of them. Paul often included Timothy as a co-sender of his letters (see Philippians 1:1; Colossians 1:1; 1 Thessalonians 1:1). For more information about Paul, see his Profile in Acts 9. Timothy's Profile is found in 1 Timothy 2, and Silas's Profile is in Acts 15.

1:1 Thessalonica was the capital and largest city of the Roman province of Macedonia. The most important Roman highway—extending from Rome to the Orient—went through Thessalonica. This highway, along with the city's thriving seaport, made Thessalonica one of the wealthiest and most flourishing trade centers in the Roman Empire. Recognized as a free city, Thessalonica was allowed self-rule and was exempt from most of the restrictions placed by Rome on other cities. Because of this open climate, however, the city had many pagan religions and cultural influences that challenged the Christians' faith.

1:3 Regardless of the contents of Paul's letters, his style was affirming. Paul began most of his letters by stating what he most appreciated about his readers and the joy he felt because of their faith in God. We also should look for ways to encourage and build up other believers.

1:4 The keys to surviving persecution and trials are endurance and faithfulness. When we are faced with crushing troubles, we can have faith that God is using our trials for our good and for his glory. Knowing that God is fair and just will give us patience in our suffering because we know that he has not forgotten us. In God's perfect timing, he will relieve our suffering and punish those who persecute us. Can you trust God's timing?

1:4-6 Paul had been persecuted during his first visit to Thessalonica (Acts 17:5-9). No doubt those who had responded to his message and had become Christians were continuing to be persecuted by both Jews and Gentiles. In Paul's first letter to the Thessalonians, he said that Christ's return would bring deliverance from persecution and judgment on the persecutors. But this caused the people to expect Christ's return right away to rescue and vindicate them. So Paul had to point out that while waiting for God's Kingdom, believers could and should learn perseverance and faith from their suffering.

1:5 As we live for Christ, we will experience troubles because we are trying to be God's people in a perverse world. Some people say that troubles are the result of sin or lack of faith, but Paul teaches that they may be a part of God's plan for believers. Our problems can help us look upward and forward, instead of inward (Mark 13:35, 36; Philippians 3:13, 14); they can build strong character (Romans 5:3, 4); and they can provide us with opportunities to comfort others who also are struggling (2 Corinthians 1:3-5). Your troubles may be an indication that you are taking a stand for Christ.

1:5-7 There are two dimensions of the relief mentioned by Paul. We can gain relief in knowing that our sufferings are strengthening us, making us ready for Christ's Kingdom. We can also gain relief in the fact that one day everyone will stand before God; at that time, wrongs will be righted, judgment will be pronounced, and evil will be terminated.

1:7-9 The "everlasting destruction" that Paul describes is the lake of fire (see Revelation 20:14)—the place of eternal separation from God. Those people who are separated from God in eternity no longer have any hope for salvation.

1:11, 12 As Christians, our calling from God is to become like Christ (Romans 8:29). This is a gradual, lifelong process that will be completed when we see Christ face to face (1 John 3:2). To be "worthy" of this calling means to *want* to do what is right and good (as Christ would). We aren't perfect yet, but we're moving in that direction as God works in us.

intentions and faithful deeds. 12Then everyone will give honor to the name of our Lord **1:12** Isa 66:5
Jesus because of you, and you will be honored along with him. This is all made possible Mal 1:11
because of the undeserved favor of our God and Lord, Jesus Christ.*

Events prior to the Lord's Second Coming

2 And now, brothers and sisters, let us tell you about the coming again of our Lord **2:1**
Jesus Christ and how we will be gathered together to meet him. 2Please don't be so 1 Thes 4:13-17
easily shaken and troubled by those who say that the day of the Lord has already begun. **2:2** 2 Thes 2:15; 3:17
Even if they claim to have had a vision, a revelation, or a letter supposedly from us, don't
believe them. 3Don't be fooled by what they say. **2:3**
For that day will not come until there is a great rebellion against God and the man of 1 Tim 4:1
lawlessness is revealed—the one who brings destruction.* 4He will exalt himself and **2:4**
defy every god there is and tear down every object of adoration and worship. He will Isa 14:13-14 1 Cor 8:5
position himself in the temple of God, claiming that he himself is God. 5Don't you **2:7**
remember that I told you this when I was with you? 6And you know what is holding him Gen 6:3 1 Jn 4:3
back, for he can be revealed only when his time comes. **2:8**
7For this lawlessness is already at work secretly, and it will remain secret until the one Job 4:9
who is holding it back steps out of the way. 8Then the man of lawlessness will be Isa 11:4 Rev 19:15
revealed, whom the Lord Jesus will consume with the breath of his mouth and destroy **2:9**
by the splendor of his coming. 9This evil man will come to do the work of Satan with Matt 24:24 Rev 13:13
counterfeit power and signs and miracles. 10He will use every kind of wicked deception **2:10**

1:12 Or *of our God and the Lord Jesus Christ.* **2:3** Greek *the son of destruction.* 1 Cor 1:18

2:1ff Paul describes the end of the world and Christ's second coming. He says that great suffering and trouble lie ahead, but evil will not prevail, because Christ will return to judge all people. Although Paul presents a few signs of the end times, his emphasis, like Jesus' (Mark 13), is the need for each person to prepare for Christ's return by living rightly day by day. If we are ready, we won't have to be concerned about the preceding events or the timing of Christ's return. God controls all events. (See 1 Thessalonians 4 and 5 for Paul's earlier teaching on this subject.)

2:1, 2 In the Bible, "the day of the Lord" is used in two ways: It can mean the end times (beginning with Christ's birth and continuing until today), and it can mean the final judgment day (in the future). Because some false teachers were saying that judgment day had come, many believers were waiting expectantly for their vindication and for relief from suffering. But judgment day had not yet come; other events would have to happen first.

2:2 "A vision, a revelation, or a letter" could refer to the fact that false teaching had come from (1) someone claiming to have had a divine revelation, (2) someone passing on a teaching as though it were from Paul, or (3) someone distributing a letter supposedly written by Paul.

2:3 Throughout history there have been individuals who epitomized evil and who were hostile to everything Christ stands for (see 1 John 2:18; 4:3; 2 John 1:7). These antichrists have lived in every generation and will continue to work their evil. Then just before Christ's second coming, "the man of lawlessness . . . the one who brings destruction," a completely evil man, will arise. He will be Satan's tool, equipped with Satan's power (2:9). This lawless man will be *the* Antichrist.

It is dangerous, however, to label any person as the Antichrist and to try to predict Christ's coming based on that assumption. Paul mentions the Antichrist, not so we might identify him specifically, but so we might be ready for anything that threatens our faith. If our faith is strong, we don't need to be afraid of what lies ahead, because we know that this lawless man has already been defeated by God, no matter how powerful he becomes or how terrible our situation seems. God is in control, and he will be victorious over the Antichrist. Our task is to be prepared for Christ's return and to spread the Good News so that even more people will also be prepared.

2:3ff When Paul first wrote to the Thessalonians, they were in danger of losing hope in the Second Coming. Then they shifted to the opposite extreme—some of them thought that Jesus would be coming at any minute. Paul tried to restore the balance by describing certain events that would happen before Christ's return.

2:6, 7 What holds back the lawless one? We do not know for certain. Three possibilities have been suggested: (1) government and law, which help to curb evil; (2) the ministry and activity of the church and the effects of the Good News; or (3) the Holy Spirit. The Bible is not clear on who this restrainer is, only that he will not restrain forever. But we should not fear this time when the restraint is removed—God is far stronger than the man of lawlessness, and God will save his people.

2:7 "This lawlessness is already at work secretly" means that the work that this Antichrist will do is already going on. *Secretly* means something no one can discover but something God will reveal. *Lawlessness* is the hidden, subtle, underlying force from which all sin springs. Civilization still has a veneer of decency through law enforcement, education, science, and reason. Although we are horrified by criminal acts, we have yet to see the real horror of complete lawlessness. This will happen when "the one who is holding it back [possibly the Holy Spirit] steps out of the way." Why will God allow this to happen? To show people and nations their own sinfulness, and to show them by bitter experience the true alternative to the lordship of Christ. People totally without God can act no better than vicious animals. Lawlessness, to a certain extent, is already going on, but the man of lawlessness has not yet been revealed.

2:9 This evil man will use "counterfeit power and signs and miracles" to deceive and draw a following. Miracles from God can help strengthen our faith and lead people to Christ, but all miracles are not necessarily from God. Christ's miracles were significant, not just because of their power, but because of their purpose—to help, to heal, and to point us to God. The man of lawlessness will have power to do amazing things, but his power will be from Satan. He will use this power to destroy and to lead people away from God and toward himself. If any so-called religious personality draws attention only to himself or herself, his or her work is not from God.

2:10-12 This man of lawlessness with his power and miracles will deceive those who have refused to believe God's truth. God gives people freedom to turn their backs on him and believe Satan's lies. If they say no to the truth, they will experience the consequences of their sin.

2:11 Rom 1:24, 28 to fool those who are on their way to destruction because they refuse to believe the truth
2 Tim 4:4 that would save them. 11 So God will send great deception upon them, and they will
2:12 Rom 1:18, 32; 2:8 believe all these lies. 12 Then they will be condemned for not believing the truth and for
enjoying the evil they do.

Believers Should Stand Firm

2:13 Deut 33:12 13 As for us, we always thank God for you, dear brothers and sisters loved by the Lord.
Eph 1:4 We are thankful that God chose you to be among the first* to experience salvation, a
salvation that came through the Spirit who makes you holy and by your belief in the truth.
2:14 1 Thes 4:7; 5:9 14 He called you to salvation when we told you the Good News; now you can share in
the glory of our Lord Jesus Christ.
2:15 1 Cor 11:2; 16:13 15 With all these things in mind, dear brothers and sisters, stand firm and keep a strong
2:16 John 3:16 grip on everything we taught you both in person and by letter.
16 May our Lord Jesus Christ and God our Father, who loved us and in his special favor
2:17 1 Thes 3:2; 5:11 gave us everlasting comfort and good hope, 17 comfort your hearts and give you strength
in every good thing you do and say.

2. Living in the light of Christ's return

3:1 1 Thes 1:8; 5:25 *Paul's Request for Prayer*

3 Finally, dear brothers and sisters, I ask you to pray for us. Pray first that the Lord's
3:2 Rom 15:31 message will spread rapidly and be honored wherever it goes, just as when it came
to you. 2 Pray, too, that we will be saved from wicked and evil people, for not everyone
3:3 1 Cor 1:9 believes in the Lord. 3 But the Lord is faithful; he will make you strong and guard you
3:4 1 Thes 4:10 from the evil one.* 4 And we are confident in the Lord that you are practicing the things
we commanded you, and that you always will. 5 May the Lord bring you into an ever
3:5 1 Chr 29:18 deeper understanding of the love of God and the endurance that comes from Christ.

An Exhortation to Proper Living

3:6 Rom 16:17 6 And now, dear brothers and sisters, we give you this command with the authority of our
1 Cor 11:2 Lord Jesus Christ: Stay away from any Christian* who lives in idleness and doesn't
follow the tradition of hard work we gave you. 7 For you know that you ought to follow

2:13 Some manuscripts read *God chose you from the very beginning.* **3:3** Or *from evil.* **3:6** Greek *brother;* also in 3:15.

2:13 Paul consistently taught that salvation begins and ends with God. We can do nothing to be saved on our own merit—we must accept God's gift of salvation (see the note on Ephesians 1:4). There is no other way to receive forgiveness from sin. Paul is encouraging the Thessalonian believers by reminding them that they were chosen by God from the beginning. Being made holy is the process of Christian growth through which the Holy Spirit makes us like Christ (Romans 8:29). See the note on 1:11, 12.

2:14 God worked through Paul and his companions to tell the Good News so that people could share in Christ's glory. It may seem strange that God works through us—fallible, unfaithful, untrustworthy human creatures. But he has given us the fantastic privilege of accomplishing his great mission—telling the world how to find salvation.

2:15 Paul knew that the Thessalonians would face pressure from persecutions, false teachers, worldliness, and apathy to waver from the truth and to leave the faith. So he urged them to "stand firm" and hold on to the truth they had been taught both through his letters and in person. We also may face persecution, false teachings, worldliness, and apathy. We should hold on to the truth of Christ's teachings because our life depends on it. Never forget the reality of Christ's life and love!

3:1-3 Beneath the surface of the routine of daily life, a fierce struggle among invisible spiritual powers is being waged. Our main defense is prayer that God will protect us from the evil one and that he will strengthen us. (See also comments on Ephesians 6:10-19 concerning our armor for spiritual warfare.) The following guidelines can help you prepare for and survive satanic attacks: (1) Take the threat of spiritual attack seriously; (2) pray for strength and help from God; (3) study the Bible to recognize Satan's style and tactics; (4) memorize Scripture so it will be a source of help no matter where you are; (5) associate with those who speak the truth; and (6) practice what you are taught by spiritual leaders.

3:6-10 Paul was writing here about the person who is lazy. Paul explained that when he and his companions were in Thessalonica, they worked hard, buying what they needed rather than becoming a burden to any of the believers. The rule they followed was, "Whoever does not work should not eat." There's a difference between leisure and laziness. Relaxation and recreation provide a necessary and much needed balance to our life; but when it is time to work, Christians should jump right in. We should make the most of our talent and time, doing all we can to provide for ourselves and our dependents. Rest when you should be resting, and work when you should be working.

3:6-15 Some people in the Thessalonian church were falsely teaching that because Christ would return any day, people should set aside their responsibilities, quit work, do no future planning, and just wait for the Lord. But their lack of activity only led them into sin. They became a burden to the church, which was supporting them; they wasted time that could have been used for helping others; and they became meddlers (3:11). These church members may have thought that they were being more spiritual by not working, but Paul tells them to be responsible and get back to work. Being ready for Christ means obeying him in every area of life. Because we know that Christ is coming, we must live in such a way that our faith and our daily practice will please him when he arrives.

our example. We were never lazy when we were with you. 8 We never accepted food from 3:8 Acts 18:3
anyone without paying for it. We worked hard day and night so that we would not be a 1 Thes 2:9
burden to any of you. 9 It wasn't that we didn't have the right to ask you to feed us, but 3:9
we wanted to give you an example to follow. 10 Even while we were with you, we gave Matt 10:10 1 Cor 9:4, 6
you this rule: "Whoever does not work should not eat." 3:10
11 Yet we hear that some of you are living idle lives, refusing to work and wasting time 1 Thes 4:11
meddling in other people's business. 12 In the name of the Lord Jesus Christ, we appeal 3:11 1 Tim 5:13
to such people—no, we command them: Settle down and get to work. Earn your own 3:12
living. 13 And I say to the rest of you, dear brothers and sisters, never get tired of doing 1 Thes 4:11
good.
14 Take note of those who refuse to obey what we say in this letter. Stay away from
them so they will be ashamed. 15 Don't think of them as enemies, but speak to them as 3:15 Gal 6:1
you would to a Christian who needs to be warned. 1 Thes 5:14

Paul's Final Greetings

16 May the Lord of peace himself always give you his peace no matter what happens. The 3:16 Rom 15:33
Lord be with you all.
17 Now here is my greeting, which I write with my own hand—PAUL. I do this at the 3:17 1 Cor 16:21
end of all my letters to prove that they really are from me. Gal 6:11 Col 4:18
18 May the grace of our Lord Jesus Christ be with you all. Phlm 1:19

3:11, 12 An idle person who doesn't work ends up filling his or her time with less than helpful activities, like gossip. Rumors and hearsay are tantalizing, exciting to hear, and make us feel like insiders. But they tear people down. If you often find your nose in other people's business, you may be underemployed. Look for a task to do for Christ or for your family, and get to work.

3:14, 15 Paul counseled the church to stop supporting financially and associating with those who persisted in their idleness. Hunger and loneliness can be very effective ways to make the idle person become productive. Paul was not advising coldness or cruelty, but the kind of tough love that a person would show a brother or sister.

3:18 The book of 2 Thessalonians is especially meaningful for those who are being persecuted or are under pressure because of their faith. In chapter 1 we are told what suffering can do for us. In chapter 2 we are assured of final victory. In chapter 3 we are encouraged to continue living responsibly in spite of difficult circumstances. Christ's return is more than a doctrine; it is a promise. It is not just for the future; it has a vital impact on how we live now.

1 TIMOTHY

WITHOUT trying, we model our values. Parents in particular demonstrate to their children what they consider important and valuable. "Like father, like son" is not just a well-worn cliché; it is a truth repeated in our homes. And experience proves that children often follow the life-styles of their parents, repeating their successes and mistakes.

Timothy is a prime example of one who was influenced by godly relatives. His mother, Eunice, and grandmother Lois were Jewish believers who helped shape his life and promote his spiritual growth (2 Timothy 1:5; 3:15). The first "second generation" Christian mentioned in the New Testament, Timothy became Paul's protégé and pastor of the church at Ephesus. As a young minister, Timothy faced all sorts of pressures, conflicts, and challenges from the church and his surrounding culture. To counsel and encourage Timothy, Paul sent this very personal letter.

Paul wrote 1 Timothy in about A.D. 64, probably just prior to his final Roman imprisonment. Because he had appealed to Caesar, Paul was sent as a prisoner to Rome (see Acts 25—28). Most scholars believe that Paul was released in about A.D. 62 (possibly because the "statute of limitations" had expired), and that during the next few years he was able to travel. During this time, he wrote 1 Timothy and Titus. Soon, however, Emperor Nero began his campaign to eliminate Christianity. It is believed that during this time Paul was imprisoned again and eventually executed. During this second Roman imprisonment, Paul wrote 2 Timothy. Titus and the two letters to Timothy comprise what are called the "Pastoral Letters."

Paul's first letter to Timothy affirms their relationship (1:2). Paul begins his fatherly advice, warning Timothy about false teachers (1:3–11) and urging him to hold on to his faith in Christ (1:12–20). Next, Paul considers public worship, emphasizing the importance of prayer (2:1–7) and order in church meetings (2:8–15). This leads to a discussion of the qualifications of church leaders—elders and deacons. Here Paul lists specific criteria for each office (3:1–16).

Paul speaks again about false teachers, telling Timothy how to recognize them and respond to them (4:1–16). Next, he gives practical advice on pastoral care to the young and old (5:1, 2), widows (5:3–16), elders (5:17–25), and slaves (6:1, 2). Paul concludes by exhorting Timothy to guard his motives (6:3–10), to stand firm in his faith (6:11, 12), to live above reproach (6:13–16), and to minister faithfully (6:17–21).

First Timothy holds many lessons. If you are a church leader, take note of Paul's relationship with this young disciple—his careful counsel and guidance. Measure yourself against the qualifications that Paul gives for overseers and deacons. If you are young in the faith, follow the example of godly Christian leaders like Timothy, who imitated Paul's life. If you are a parent, remind yourself of the profound effect a Christian home can have on family members. A faithful mother and grandmother led Timothy to Christ, and Timothy's ministry helped change the world.

VITAL STATISTICS

PURPOSE:
To give encouragement and instruction to Timothy, a young leader

AUTHOR:
Paul

TO WHOM WRITTEN:
Timothy, young church leaders, and all believers everywhere

DATE WRITTEN:
Approximately A.D. 64, from Rome or Macedonia (possibly Philippi), probably just prior to Paul's final imprisonment in Rome

SETTING:
Timothy was one of Paul's closest companions. Paul had sent Timothy to the church at Ephesus to counter the false teaching that had arisen there (1:3, 4). Timothy probably served for a time as a leader in the church at Ephesus. Paul hoped to visit Timothy (3:14, 15; 4:13), but in the meantime, he wrote this letter to give Timothy practical advice about the ministry.

KEY VERSE:
"Don't let anyone think less of you because you are young. Be an example to all believers in what you teach, in the way you live, in your love, your faith, and your purity" (4:12).

KEY PEOPLE:
Paul, Timothy

KEY PLACE:
Ephesus

SPECIAL FEATURES:
First Timothy is a personal letter and a handbook of church administration and discipline.

THE BLUEPRINT

1. Instructions on right belief (1:1–20)
2. Instructions for the church (2:1—3:16)
3. Instructions for elders (4:1—6:21)

Paul advised Timothy on such practical topics as qualifications for church leaders, public worship, confronting false teaching, and how to treat various groups of people within the church. Right belief and right behavior are critical for anyone who desires to lead or serve effectively in the church. We should all believe rightly, participate in church actively, and minister to one another lovingly.

MEGATHEMES

THEME	EXPLANATION	IMPORTANCE
Sound Doctrine	Paul instructed Timothy to preserve the Christian faith by teaching sound doctrine and modeling right living. Timothy had to oppose false teachers, who were leading church members away from belief in salvation by faith in Jesus Christ alone.	We must know the truth in order to defend it. We must cling to the belief that Christ came to save us. We should stay away from those who twist the words of the Bible for their own purposes.
Public Worship	Prayer in public worship must be done with a proper attitude toward God and fellow believers.	Christian character must be evident in every aspect of worship. We must rid ourselves of any anger, resentment, or offensive behavior that might disrupt worship or damage church unity.
Church Leadership	Paul gives specific instructions concerning the qualifications for church leaders so that the church might honor God and operate smoothly.	Church leaders must be wholly committed to Christ. If you are a new or young Christian, don't be anxious to become a leader in the church. Seek to develop your Christian character first. Be sure to seek God, not your own ambition.
Personal Discipline	It takes discipline to be a leader in the church. Timothy, like all pastors, had to guard his motives, minister faithfully, and live above reproach. Any pastor must keep morally and spiritually fit.	To stay in good spiritual shape, you must discipline yourself to study God's Word and to obey it. Put your spiritual abilities to work!
Caring Church	The church has a responsibility to care for the needs of all its members, especially the sick, the poor, and the widowed. Caring must go beyond good intentions.	Caring for the family of believers demonstrates our Christlike attitude and exhibits genuine love to nonbelievers.

1. Instructions on right belief

Greetings from Paul

1 This letter is from Paul, an apostle of Christ Jesus, appointed by the command of God our Savior and by Christ Jesus our hope.
2 It is written to Timothy, my true child in the faith.
May God our Father and Christ Jesus our Lord give you grace, mercy, and peace.

1:1 Col 1:27; Titus 1:3; 3:4
1:2 Acts 16:1; 2 Tim 1:2; Titus 1:4

1:1 This letter was written to Timothy in A.D. 64 or 65, after Paul's first imprisonment in Rome (Acts 28:16-31). Apparently Paul had been out of prison for several years, and during that time he had revisited many churches in Asia and Macedonia. When he and Timothy returned to Ephesus, they found widespread false teaching in the church. Paul had warned the Ephesian elders to be on guard against the false teachers who inevitably would come after he had left (Acts 20:17-31). Paul sent Timothy to lead the Ephesian church while he moved on to Macedonia. From there Paul wrote this letter of encouragement and instruction to help Timothy deal with the difficult situation in the Ephesian church. Later, Paul was arrested again and brought back to a Roman prison.

1:1 Paul calls himself an *apostle,* meaning "one who is sent." Paul was sent by Jesus Christ to bring the message of salvation to the Gentiles (Acts 9:1-20). For more information on Paul, see his Profile in Acts 9.

1:1 How was Paul an apostle "by the command of God"? In Acts 13:2, the Holy Spirit, through the prophets, said, "Dedicate Barnabas and Saul [Paul] for the special work I have for them." From Romans 16:25, 26 and Titus 1:3, it is obvious that Paul regarded his commission as direct from God.

1:3, 4 Paul first visited Ephesus on his second missionary journey (Acts 18:19-21). Later, on his third missionary journey, he stayed there for almost three years (Acts 19–20). Ephesus, along with Rome, Corinth, Antioch, and Alexandria, was one of the major cities in the Roman Empire. It was a center for the commerce, politics, and religions of Asia Minor, and the location of the temple dedicated to the goddess Artemis (Diana).

1:3 Acts 20:1; Gal 1:6-7; 1 Tim 6:3
1:4 1 Tim 4:7; Titus 3:9
1:5 Rom 13:10; Gal 5:14; 2 Tim 1:5; 2:23
1:6 Titus 1:10
1:9 Gal 3:19; 5:23
1:10 1 Tim 6:3; 2 Tim 4:3; Titus 1:9; 2:1
1:11 Gal 2:7
1:12 Acts 9:15; Gal 1:15-16; Phil 4:13

Warnings against False Teachings

[3]When I left for Macedonia, I urged you to stay there in Ephesus and stop those who are
teaching wrong doctrine. [4]Don't let people waste time in endless speculation over myths
and spiritual pedigrees.* For these things only cause arguments; they don't help people live
a life of faith in God.* [5]The purpose of my instruction is that all the Christians there would
be filled with love that comes from a pure heart, a clear conscience, and sincere faith.
[6]But some teachers have missed this whole point. They have turned away from these
things and spend their time arguing and talking foolishness. [7]They want to be known as
teachers of the law of Moses, but they don't know what they are talking about, even
though they seem so confident. [8]We know these laws are good when they are used as
God intended. [9]But they were not made for people who do what is right. They are for
people who are disobedient and rebellious, who are ungodly and sinful, who consider
nothing sacred and defile what is holy, who murder their father or mother or other people.
[10]These laws are for people who are sexually immoral, for homosexuals and slave
traders, for liars and oath breakers, and for those who do anything else that contradicts
the right teaching [11]that comes from the glorious Good News entrusted to me by our
blessed God.

Paul's Gratitude for God's Mercy

[12]How thankful I am to Christ Jesus our Lord for considering me trustworthy and
appointing me to serve him, [13]even though I used to scoff at the name of Christ. I hunted

1:4a Greek *in myths and endless genealogies, which cause speculation.* **1:4b** Greek *a stewardship of God in faith.*

1:3, 4 The church at Ephesus may have been plagued by the same heresy that was threatening the church at Colosse—the teaching that to be acceptable to God, a person had to discover certain hidden knowledge and had to worship angels (Colossians 2:8, 18). Thinking that it would aid in their salvation, some Ephesians constructed mythical stories based on Old Testament history or genealogies. The false teachers were motivated by their own interests rather than Christ's. They embroiled the church in endless and irrelevant questions and controversies, taking precious time away from the study of the truth. Today we could also enter into worthless and irrelevant discussions, but such disputes quickly crowd out the life-changing message of Christ. Stay away from religious speculation and pointless theological arguments. Such exercises may seem harmless at first, but they have a way of sidetracking us from the central message of the Good News—the person and work of Jesus Christ. And they expend time we should use to share the Good News with others. You should avoid anything that keeps you from doing God's work.

1:3-11 There are many leaders and authorities today who demand allegiance, some of whom would even have us turn from Christ to follow them. When they seem to know the Bible, their influence can be dangerously subtle. How can you recognize false teaching? (1) It promotes controversies instead of helping people come to Jesus (1:4). (2) It is often initiated by those whose motivation is to make a name for themselves (1:7). (3) It will be contrary to the true teaching of the Scriptures (1:6, 7; 4:1-3). To protect yourself from the deception of false teachers, you should learn what the Bible teaches and remain steadfast in your faith in Christ alone.

1:5 The false teachers were motivated by a spirit of curiosity and a desire to gain power and prestige. By contrast, genuine Christian teachers are motivated by sincere faith and a desire to do what is right. It may be exciting to impress people with our great knowledge, but high status based on falsehood is ultimately empty.

1:6 Arguing about details of the Bible can send us off on interesting but irrelevant tangents and cause us to miss the intent of God's message. The false teachers at Ephesus constructed vast speculative systems and then argued about the minor details of their wholly imaginary ideas. We should allow nothing to distract us from the Good News of salvation in Jesus Christ, the main point of Scripture. We should know what the Bible says, apply it to our life daily, and teach it to others. When we do this, we will be able to evaluate all teachings in light of the central truth about Jesus. Don't focus on the minute details of the Bible to the exclusion of the main point God is teaching you.

1:7 Paul was writing against those who were engaging in philosophical speculation based on the Pentateuch (the first five books of the Old Testament, written by Moses).

1:7-11 The false teachers wanted to become famous as teachers of God's law, but they didn't even understand the law's purpose. The law was not meant to give believers a list of commands for every occasion but to show unbelievers their sin and bring them to God. For more of what Paul taught about our relationship to law, see Romans 5:20, 21; 13:9, 10; Galatians 3:24-29.

1:10 There are those who attempt to legitimize homosexuality as an acceptable alternative life-style. Even some Christians say people have a right to choose their sexual preference. But the Bible specifically calls homosexual behavior sin (see Leviticus 18:22; Romans 1:18-32; 1 Corinthians 6:9-11). We must be careful, however, to condemn only the practice and not the people. Those who commit homosexual acts are not to be feared, ridiculed, or hated. They can be forgiven, and their lives can be transformed. The church should be a haven of forgiveness and healing for repentant homosexuals without compromising its stance against homosexual behavior. For more on this subject see the notes on Romans 1:26, 27.

1:12-17 People can feel so guilt-ridden by their past that they think God could never forgive and accept them. But consider Paul's past. He had scoffed at the teachings of Jesus and hunted down and murdered God's people before coming to faith in Christ (Acts 9:1-9). God forgave Paul and used him mightily for his Kingdom. No matter how shameful your past, God also can forgive and use you.

down his people, harming them in every way I could. But God had mercy on me because
I did it in ignorance and unbelief. [14]Oh, how kind and gracious the Lord was! He filled
me completely with faith and the love of Christ Jesus.
[15]This is a true saying, and everyone should believe it: Christ Jesus came into the
world to save sinners—and I was the worst of them all. [16]But that is why God had mercy
on me, so that Christ Jesus could use me as a prime example of his great patience with
even the worst sinners. Then others will realize that they, too, can believe in him and
receive eternal life. [17]Glory and honor to God forever and ever. He is the eternal King,
the unseen one who never dies; he alone is God. Amen.

Timothy's Responsibility

[18]Timothy, my son, here are my instructions for you, based on the prophetic words
spoken about you earlier. May they give you the confidence to fight well in the Lord's
battles. [19]Cling tightly to your faith in Christ, and always keep your conscience clear.
For some people have deliberately violated their consciences; as a result, their faith has
been shipwrecked. [20]Hymenaeus and Alexander are two examples of this. I turned them
over to Satan so they would learn not to blaspheme God.

1:13 Acts 8:3; 26:9; 1 Cor 15:9
1:14 Rom 5:20; 2 Tim 1:13
1:15 Luke 15:2; 19:10; Rom 5:8
1:17 Rom 16:27; 1 Tim 6:15
1:18 1 Tim 6:12
1:19 2 Tim 4:7
1:20 1 Cor 5:5; 2 Tim 2:17; 4:14

2. Instructions for the church

Instructions about Worship

2 I urge you, first of all, to pray for all people. As you make your requests, plead
for God's mercy upon them, and give thanks. [2]Pray this way for kings and all
others who are in authority, so that we can live in peace and quietness, in godliness
and dignity. [3]This is good and pleases God our Savior, [4]for he wants everyone to be

2:2 Rom 13:1
2:4 1 Tim 4:10; 2 Tim 2:25

1:14 We may feel that our faith in God and our love for Christ and for others is inadequate. But we can be confident that Christ will help our faith and love grow as our relationship with him deepens.

1:15 Here Paul summarizes the Good News: Jesus came into the world to save sinners, and no sinner is beyond his saving power. (See Luke 5:32 for Jesus' purpose for being on earth.) Jesus didn't come merely to show us how to live a better life or to challenge us to be better people. He came to offer us salvation that leads to eternal life. Have you accepted his offer?

1:15 Paul calls himself "the worst" of sinners. We think of Paul as a great hero of the faith, but Paul never saw himself that way because he remembered his life before he met Christ. The more Paul understood God's grace, the more he was aware of his own sinfulness. Humility and gratitude should mark the life of every Christian. Never forget that you, too, are a sinner saved by grace.

1:17 This verse is a typical doxology given by Paul as a natural, emotional response to these reflections about the mercy of God. Paul was so moved by God's love that he was able to praise God spontaneously.

1:18 Paul highly valued the gift of prophecy (1 Corinthians 14:1). Through prophecy important messages of warning and encouragement came to the church. Just as pastors are ordained and set apart for ministry in church today, Timothy had been set apart for ministry when elders laid their hands on him (see 4:14). Apparently at this ceremony, several believers had prophesied about Timothy's gifts and strengths. These words from the Lord must have encouraged Timothy throughout his ministry.

1:19 How can you keep your conscience clear? Treasure your faith in Christ more than anything else and do what you know is right. Each time you deliberately ignore your conscience, you are hardening your heart. Over a period of time your capacity to tell right from wrong will diminish. As you walk with God, he will speak to you through your conscience, letting you know the difference between right and wrong. Be sure to act on those inner tugs so that you do what is right—then your conscience will remain clear.

1:20 We don't know who Alexander was—he may have been an associate of Hymenaeus. Hymenaeus's error is explained in 2 Timothy 2:17, 18. He weakened people's faith by teaching that the resurrection had already occurred. Paul says that he turned Hymenaeus over to Satan, meaning that Paul had removed him from the fellowship of the church. Paul did this so that Hymenaeus would see his error and repent. The ultimate purpose of this punishment was correction. The church today is too often lax in disciplining Christians who deliberately sin. Deliberate disobedience should be responded to quickly and sternly to prevent the entire congregation from being affected. But discipline must be done in a way that tries to bring the offender back to Christ and into the loving embrace of the church. The definition of discipline includes these words: strengthening, purifying, training, correcting, perfecting. Condemnation, suspicion, withholding of forgiveness, or permanent exile should not be a part of church discipline.

2:1-4 Although God is all-powerful and all-knowing, he has chosen to let us help him change the world through our prayers. How this works is a mystery to us because of our limited understanding, but it is a reality. Paul urges us to pray for each other and for our leaders in government. Our earnest prayers will have powerful results (James 5:16).

2:2 Paul's command to pray for kings was remarkable considering that Nero, a notoriously cruel ruler, was emperor at this time (A.D. 54–68). When Paul wrote this letter, persecution was a growing threat to believers. Later, when Nero needed a scapegoat for the great fire that destroyed much of Rome in A.D. 64, he blamed the Roman Christians so as to take the focus off himself. Then persecution erupted throughout the Roman Empire. Not only were Christians denied certain privileges in society, some were even publicly butchered, burned, or fed to animals.

2:2 When our life is going along peacefully and quietly, it is difficult to remember to pray for those in authority, because we often take good government for granted. It's easier to remember to pray when we experience problems. But we should pray for those in authority around the world so that their societies will be conducive to the spread of the Good News.

2:4 Both Peter and Paul said that God wants everyone to be saved (see 2 Peter 3:9). This does not mean that all *will* be saved, because the Bible makes it clear that many reject Christ (Matthew 25:31-46; John 12:44-50; Hebrews 10:26-29). The Good News has a universal scope; it is not directed only to people of one race, one sex, or one national background. God

2:5 Rom 3:29-30 saved and to understand the truth. 5For there is only one God and one Mediator who
2:6 Gal 1:4; 2:20 can reconcile God and people. He is the man Christ Jesus. 6He gave his life to
purchase freedom for everyone. This is the message that God gave to the world at the

TIMOTHY

Painful lessons are usually doorways to new opportunities. Even the apostle Paul had much to learn. Shortly after his disappointing experience with John Mark, Paul recruited another eager young man, Timothy, to be his assistant. Paul's intense personality may have been too much for John Mark to handle. It could easily have created the same problem for Timothy. But Paul seems to have learned a lesson in patience from his old friend Barnabas. As a result, Timothy became a "son" to Paul.

Timothy probably became a Christian after Paul's first missionary visit to Lystra (Acts 16:1–5). Timothy already had solid Jewish training in the Scriptures from his mother and grandmother. By Paul's second visit, Timothy had grown into a respected disciple of Jesus. He did not hesitate to join Paul and Silas on their journey. His willingness to be circumcised as an adult is clearly a mark of his commitment. (Timothy's mixed Greek/Jewish background could have created problems on their missionary journeys, because many of their audiences would be made up of Jews who were concerned about the strict keeping of this tradition. Timothy's submission to the rite of circumcision helped to avoid that potential problem.)

Beyond the tensions created by his mixed racial background, Timothy seemed to struggle with a naturally timid character and a sensitivity to his youthfulness. Unfortunately, many who share Timothy's character traits are quickly written off as too great a risk to deserve much responsibility. By God's grace, Paul saw great potential in Timothy. Paul demonstrated his confidence in Timothy by entrusting him with important responsibilities. Paul sent Timothy as his personal representative to Corinth during a particularly tense time (1 Corinthians 4:14–17). Although Timothy was apparently ineffective in that difficult mission, Paul did not give up on him. Timothy continued to travel with Paul.

Our last pictures of Timothy come from the most personal letters in the New Testament: 1 and 2 Timothy. The aging apostle Paul was near the end of his life, but his burning desire to continue his mission had not dimmed. Paul was writing to one of his closest friends—they had traveled, suffered, cried, and laughed together. They shared the intense joy of seeing people respond to the Good News and the agonies of seeing the gospel rejected and distorted. Paul left Timothy in Ephesus to oversee the young church there (1 Timothy 1:3, 4). He wrote to encourage Timothy and give him needed direction. These letters have provided comfort and help to countless other "Timothys" through the years. When you face a challenge that seems beyond your abilities, read 1 and 2 Timothy, and remember that others have shared your experience.

Strengths and accomplishments
- Became a believer during Paul's first missionary journey and joined him for his other two journeys
- Was a respected Christian in his hometown
- Was Paul's special representative on several occasions
- Received two personal letters from Paul
- Probably knew Paul better than any other person, becoming like a son to Paul

Weaknesses and mistakes
- Struggled with a timid and reserved nature
- Allowed others to look down on his youthfulness
- Was apparently unable to correct some of the problems in the church at Corinth when Paul sent him there

Lessons from his life
- Youthfulness should not be an excuse for ineffectiveness
- Our inadequacies and inabilities should not keep us from being available to God

Vital statistics
- Where: Lystra
- Occupations: Missionary, pastor
- Relatives: Mother: Eunice. Grandmother: Lois. Greek father
- Contemporaries: Paul, Silas, Luke, Mark, Peter, Barnabas

Key verses
"I have no one else like Timothy, who genuinely cares about your welfare. All the others care only for themselves and not for what matters to Jesus Christ. But you know how Timothy has proved himself. Like a son with his father, he has helped me in preaching the Good News" (Philippians 2:20–22).

Timothy's story is told in Acts, starting in chapter 16. He is also mentioned in Romans 16:21; 1 Corinthians 4:17; 16:10, 11; 2 Corinthians 1:1, 19; Philippians 1:1; 2:19–23; Colossians 1:1; 1 Thessalonians 1:1–10; 2:3, 4; 3:2–6; 1 and 2 Timothy; Philemon 1; Hebrews 13:23.

loves the whole world and sent his Son to save sinners. Never assume that anyone is outside God's mercy or beyond the reach of his offer of salvation.

2:5, 6 We human beings are separated from God by sin, and only one person in the universe is our mediator and can stand between us and God and bring us together again—Jesus, who is both God and man. Jesus' sacrifice brought new life to all people. Have you let him bring you to the Father?

proper time. 7And I have been chosen—this is the absolute truth—as a preacher and
apostle to teach the Gentiles about faith and truth.
8So wherever you assemble, I want men to pray with holy hands lifted up to God, free
from anger and controversy. 9And I want women to be modest in their appearance. They
should wear decent and appropriate clothing and not draw attention to themselves by the
way they fix their hair or by wearing gold or pearls or expensive clothes. 10For women
who claim to be devoted to God should make themselves attractive by the good things
they do.
11Women should listen and learn quietly and submissively. 12I do not let women teach
men or have authority over them. Let them listen quietly. 13For God made Adam first,
and afterward he made Eve. 14And it was the woman, not Adam, who was deceived by
Satan, and sin was the result. 15But women will be saved through childbearing* and by
continuing to live in faith, love, holiness, and modesty.

2:7 Acts 9:15; 2 Tim 1:1
2:8 Pss 24:4; 63:4
2:9 1 Pet 3:3-5
2:11 1 Cor 14:34
2:12 Eph 5:22
2:13 Gen 1:27; 2:7, 22
2:14 Gen 3:1-6, 13

2:15 Or *will be saved by accepting their role as mothers,* or *will be saved by the birth of the Child.*

2:6 Jesus gave his life as a ransom for our sin (Mark 10:45). A ransom was the price paid to purchase freedom for a slave. Jesus, our mediator, gave his life in exchange for ours. By his death, he paid our penalty for sin and purchased our freedom.

2:7 Paul describes himself as a herald or preacher. He was given the special privilege of announcing the Good News to the Gentiles. He gives his credentials as an apostle in 1 Corinthians 15:7-11.

2:8 Besides displeasing God, anger and controversy make prayer difficult. That is why Jesus said that we should interrupt our prayers, if necessary, to make peace with others (Matthew 5:23, 24). God wants us to obey him immediately and thoroughly. Our goal should be to have a right relationship with God and also with others.

2:9, 10 Apparently some Christian women were trying to gain respect by looking beautiful rather than by becoming Christlike in character. Some may have thought that they could win unbelieving husbands to Christ through their appearance (see Peter's counsel to such women in 1 Peter 3:1-6). It is not unscriptural for a woman to want to be attractive. Beauty, however, begins inside a person. A gentle, modest, loving character gives a light to the face that cannot be duplicated by the best cosmetics and jewelry in the world. A carefully groomed and well-decorated exterior is artificial and cold unless inner beauty is present.

2:9-15 To understand these verses, we must understand the situation in which Paul and Timothy worked. In first-century Jewish culture, women were not allowed to study. When Paul said that women should "learn quietly and submissively," he was offering them an amazing new opportunity. Paul did not want the Ephesian women to teach because they didn't yet have enough knowledge or experience. The Ephesian church had a particular problem with false teachers. Evidently the women were especially susceptible to the false teachings (2 Timothy 3:1-9) because they did not yet have enough biblical knowledge to discern the truth. In addition, some of the women were apparently flaunting their newfound Christian freedom by wearing inappropriate clothing (2:9). Paul was telling Timothy not to put anyone (in this case, women) into a position of leadership who was not yet mature in the faith (see 5:22). The same principle applies to churches today (see the note on 3:6).

2:12 Some interpret this passage to mean that women should never teach in the assembled church; however, commentators point out that Paul did not forbid women from ever teaching. Paul's commended co-worker, Priscilla, taught Apollos, the great preacher (Acts 18:24-26). In addition, Paul frequently mentioned other women who held positions of responsibility in the church. Phoebe worked in the church (Romans 16:1). Mary, Tryphena, Tryphosa and Persis were the Lord's workers (Romans 16:6, 12), as were Euodia and Syntyche (Philippians 4:2). Paul was very likely prohibiting the Ephesian women, not all women, from teaching (see the note on 2:9-15).

2:12 In Paul's reference to women listening and learning quietly and submissively, he is speaking about an attitude of quietness and composure (not total silence). In addition, Paul himself acknowledges that women publicly prayed and prophesied (1 Corinthians 11:5). Apparently, however, the women in the Ephesian church were abusing their newly acquired Christian freedom. Because these women were new converts, they did not yet have the necessary experience, knowledge, or Christian maturity to teach those who already had extensive scriptural education.

2:13, 14 In previous letters Paul had discussed male/female roles in marriage (Ephesians 5:21-33; Colossians 3:18, 19). Here he talks about male/female roles within the church. Some scholars see these verses about Adam and Eve as an illustration of what was happening in the Ephesian church. Just as Eve had been deceived in the Garden of Eden, so the women in the church were being deceived by false teachers. And just as Adam was the first human created by God, so the men in the church in Ephesus should be the first to speak and teach, because they had more training. This view, then, stresses that Paul's teaching here is not universal but applies to churches with similar problems. Other scholars, however, contend that the roles Paul points out are God's design for his created order—God established these roles to maintain harmony in both the family and the church.

2:14 Paul is not excusing Adam for his part in the Fall (Genesis 3:6, 7, 17-19). On the contrary, in his letter to the Romans Paul places the primary blame for humanity's sinful nature on Adam (Romans 5:12-21).

2:15 There are several ways to understand the phrase, being "saved through childbearing": (1) Man sinned and so men were condemned to painful labor. Woman sinned and so women were condemned to pain in childbearing. Both men and women, however, can be saved through trusting Christ and obeying him. (2) Women who fulfill their God-given roles are demonstrating true commitment and obedience to Christ. One of the most important roles for a wife and mother is to care for her family. (3) The childbearing mentioned here refers to the birth of Jesus Christ. Women (and men) are saved spiritually because of the most important birth, that of Christ himself. (4) From the lessons learned through the trials of childbearing, women can develop qualities that teach them about love, trust, submission, and service.

Leaders in the Church

3:1 Acts 20:28
3:2-7 //Titus 1:6-9

3 It is a true saying that if someone wants to be an elder,* he desires an honorable
responsibility. 2For an elder must be a man whose life cannot be spoken against. He
must be faithful to his wife.* He must exhibit self-control, live wisely, and have a good
reputation. He must enjoy having guests in his home and must be able to teach. 3He must
not be a heavy drinker or be violent. He must be gentle, peace loving, and not one who
loves money. 4He must manage his own family well, with children who respect and obey
him. 5For if a man cannot manage his own household, how can he take care of God's
church?

3:7 Mark 4:11; 2 Cor 8:21; 2 Tim 2:26
3:8 Phil 1:1
3:9 1 Tim 1:19

6An elder must not be a new Christian, because he might be proud of being chosen so
soon, and the Devil will use that pride to make him fall.* 7Also, people outside the church
must speak well of him so that he will not fall into the Devil's trap and be disgraced.

8In the same way, deacons must be people who are respected and have integrity. They
must not be heavy drinkers and must not be greedy for money. 9They must be committed
to the revealed truths of the Christian faith and must live with a clear conscience.
10Before they are appointed as deacons, they should be given other responsibilities in
the church as a test of their character and ability. If they do well, then they may serve as
deacons.

11In the same way, their wives* must be respected and must not speak evil of others.
They must exercise self-control and be faithful in everything they do.

12A deacon must be faithful to his wife, and he must manage his children and
household well. 13Those who do well as deacons will be rewarded with respect from
others and will have increased confidence in their faith in Christ Jesus.

The Truths of Our Faith

3:15 Matt 16:16-18; Eph 2:19-21

14I am writing these things to you now, even though I hope to be with you soon, 15so
that if I can't come for a while, you will know how people must conduct themselves in
the household of God. This is the church of the living God, which is the pillar and support
of the truth.

3:1 Greek *overseer;* also in 3:2. **3:2** Greek *be the husband of one wife;* also in 3:12. **3:6** Or *he might fall into the same judgment as the Devil.* **3:11** Or *the women deacons.* The Greek word can be translated *women* or *wives.*

3:1 To be a church leader ("elder") is a heavy responsibility because the church belongs to the living God. Church leaders should not be elected because they are popular, nor should they be allowed to push their way to the top. Instead, they should be chosen by the church because of their respect for the truth, both in what they believe and in how they live.

3:1-13 The word *elder* can refer to a pastor, church leader, or presiding overseer. It is good to want to be a spiritual leader, but the standards are high. Paul enumerates some of the qualifications here. Do you hold a position of spiritual leadership, or would you like to be a leader some day? Check yourself against Paul's standard of excellence. Those with great responsibility must meet high expectations.

3:1-13 The lists of qualifications for church office show that living a blameless and pure life requires effort and self-discipline. All believers, even if they never plan to be church leaders, should strive to follow these guidelines because they are consistent with what God says is true and right. The strength to live according to God's will comes from Christ.

3:2 When Paul says that each elder should be faithful to his wife, he is prohibiting both polygamy and promiscuity. This does not prohibit an unmarried person from becoming an elder or a widowed elder from remarrying.

3:4, 5 Christian workers and volunteers sometimes make the mistake of thinking their work is so important that they are justified in ignoring their families. Spiritual leadership, however, must begin at home. If a man is not willing to care for, discipline, and teach his children, he is not qualified to lead the church. Don't allow your volunteer activities to detract from your family responsibilities.

3:6 New believers should become secure and strong in the faith before taking leadership roles in the church. Too often, when the church is desperate for workers, new believers are placed in positions of responsibility prematurely. New faith needs time to mature. New believers should have a place of service, but they should not be put into leadership positions until they are firmly grounded in their faith, with a solid Christian life-style and a knowledge of the Word of God.

3:6, 7 Younger believers who are selected for office need to beware of the damaging effects of pride. Pride can seduce our emotions and cloud our reason. It can make those who are immature susceptible to the influence of unscrupulous people. Pride and conceit were the Devil's downfall, and he uses pride to trap others.

3:8-13 *Deacon* means "one who serves." This position was possibly begun by the apostles in the Jerusalem church (Acts 6:1-6) to care for the physical needs of the congregation, especially the needs of the Greek-speaking widows. Deacons were leaders in the church, and their qualifications resemble those of the elders. In some churches today, the office of deacon has lost its importance. New Christians are often asked to serve in this position, but that is not the New Testament pattern. Paul says that potential deacons should first be tested before they are asked to serve.

3:11 "Wives" can refer to women helpers or deaconesses. It could also mean wives of deacons or female leaders of the church (such as Phoebe, the deaconess mentioned in Romans 16:1). In either case, Paul expected the behavior of prominent women in the church to be just as responsible and blameless as that of prominent men.

16 Without question, this is the great mystery of our faith:
Christ* appeared in the flesh
and was shown to be righteous by the Spirit.*
He was seen by angels
and was announced to the nations.
He was believed on in the world
and was taken up into heaven.*

3. Instructions for elders

Warnings against False Teachers

4 Now the Holy Spirit tells us clearly that in the last times some will turn away from
what we believe; they will follow lying spirits and teachings that come from demons.
2 These teachers are hypocrites and liars. They pretend to be religious, but their consciences are dead.*
3 They will say it is wrong to be married and wrong to eat certain foods. But God
created those foods to be eaten with thanksgiving by people who know and believe the
truth. 4 Since everything God created is good, we should not reject any of it. We may
receive it gladly, with thankful hearts. 5 For we know it is made holy by the word of God
and prayer.

A Good Servant of Christ Jesus

6 If you explain this to the others, you will be doing your duty as a worthy servant of
Christ Jesus, one who is fed by the message of faith and the true teaching you have
followed. 7 Do not waste time arguing over godless ideas and old wives' tales. Spend
your time and energy in training yourself for spiritual fitness. 8 Physical exercise has
some value, but spiritual exercise is much more important, for it promises a reward in
both this life and the next. 9 This is true, and everyone should accept it. 10 We work hard
and suffer much* in order that people will believe the truth, for our hope is in the living
God, who is the Savior of all people, and particularly of those who believe.

3:16 Isa 7:14; Matt 4:11; John 1:14; Rom 1:3-4; Acts 1:9; 1 Jn 4:2-3; 5:6
4:1 John 16:13; 2 Tim 3:1; 2 Pet 3:3
4:2 Eph 4:19
4:3 Gen 9:3; Rom 14:6; 1 Cor 10:30-31
4:4 Gen 1:31; Acts 10:15
4:6 2 Tim 3:15
4:7 1 Tim 1:4; 2 Tim 2:16; Titus 1:14
4:8 1 Tim 6:6
4:9 1 Tim 1:15
4:10 1 Tim 2:3-4

3:16a Greek *Who;* some manuscripts read *God.* **3:16b** Or *in his spirit.* **3:16c** Greek *in glory.* **4:2** Greek *are seared.* **4:10** Some manuscripts read *and strive.*

3:16 In this short hymn, Paul affirms the humanity and divinity of Christ. By so doing he reveals the heart of the Good News, "the great mystery of our faith" (the secret of how we become godly). "Appeared in the flesh"—Jesus was a man; Jesus' incarnation is the basis of our being right with God. "Was shown to be righteous by the Spirit"—Jesus' resurrection showed that the Holy Spirit's power was in him (Romans 8:11). "Was seen by angels" and "was taken up into heaven"—Jesus is divine. We can't please God on our own; we must depend on Christ. As a man, Jesus lived a perfect life, and so he is a perfect example of how to live. As God, Jesus gives us the power to do what is right. It is possible to live a godly life—through following Christ.

4:1 The "last times" began with Christ's resurrection and will continue until his return when he will set up his Kingdom and judge all humanity.

4:1, 2 False teachers were and still are a threat to the church. Jesus and the apostles repeatedly warned against them (see, for example, Mark 13:21-23; Acts 20:28-31; 2 Thessalonians 2:1-12; 2 Peter 3:3-7). The danger that Timothy faced in Ephesus seems to have come from certain people in the church who were following some Greek philosophers who taught that the body was evil and that only the soul mattered. The false teachers refused to believe that the God of creation was good, because his very contact with the physical world would have soiled him. Though these Greek-influenced church members honored Jesus, they could not believe he was truly human. Paul knew that their teachings, if left unchecked, would greatly distort Christian truth.

It is not enough that a teacher appears to know what he is talking about, is disciplined and moral, or says that he is speaking for God. If his words contradict the Bible, his teaching is false. Like Timothy, we must guard against any teaching that causes believers to dilute or reject any aspect of their faith. Such false teaching can be very direct or extremely subtle.

4:1-5 Paul said the false teachers were hypocritical liars who encouraged people to follow "lying spirits and teachings that come from demons." Satan deceives people by offering a clever imitation of the real thing. The false teachers gave stringent rules (such as forbidding people to marry or to eat certain foods). This made them appear self-disciplined and righteous. Their strict disciplines for the body, however, could not remove sin (see Colossians 2:20-23). We must not be unduly impressed by a teacher's style or credentials; we must look to his teaching about Jesus Christ. His conclusions about Christ show the source of his message.

4:4, 5 In opposition to the false teachers, Paul affirmed that everything God created is good (see Genesis 1). We should ask for God's blessing on his created gifts that give us pleasure and thank him for them. This doesn't mean that we should abuse what God has made (for example, gluttony abuses God's gift of good food, lust abuses God's gift of love, and murder abuses God's gift of life). Instead of abusing, we should enjoy these gifts by using them to serve and honor God. Have you thanked God for the good gifts he has given? Are you using the gifts in ways pleasing to you *and* to God?

4:7-10 Are you in shape both physically and spiritually? In our society, much emphasis is placed on physical fitness, but spiritual health is even more important. Our physical health is susceptible to disease and injury, but faith can sustain us through these tragedies. To train ourselves to be godly, we must develop our faith by using our God-given abilities in the service of the church (see 4:14-16). Are you developing your spiritual muscles?

4:10 Christ is the Savior for all, but his salvation becomes effective only for those who trust him.

4:11 1 Tim 5:7; 6:2
4:12 Titus 2:15
4:13 1 Tim 3:14
4:14 Acts 6:6; 8:17 2 Tim 1:6

11 Teach these things and insist that everyone learn them. 12 Don't let anyone think less
of you because you are young. Be an example to all believers in what you teach, in the
way you live, in your love, your faith, and your purity. 13 Until I get there, focus on
reading the Scriptures to the church, encouraging the believers, and teaching them.
14 Do not neglect the spiritual gift you received through the prophecies spoken to you
when the elders of the church laid their hands on you. 15 Give your complete attention to
these matters. Throw yourself into your tasks so that everyone will see your progress.
16 Keep a close watch on yourself and on your teaching. Stay true to what is right, and
God will save you and those who hear you.

5:1 Lev 19:32 Titus 2:2, 6

5 Never speak harshly to an older man,* but appeal to him respectfully as though he
were your own father. Talk to the younger men as you would to your own brothers.
2 Treat the older women as you would your mother, and treat the younger women with
all purity as your own sisters.

Advice about Widows, Elders, and Slaves

5:4 Eph 6:2 1 Tim 2:3
5:5 Luke 2:37 1 Pet 3:5
5:6 Luke 15:24 Jas 5:5

3 The church should care for any widow who has no one else to care for her. 4 But if she
has children or grandchildren, their first responsibility is to show godliness at home and
repay their parents by taking care of them. This is something that pleases God very much.
5 But a woman who is a true widow, one who is truly alone in this world, has placed
her hope in God. Night and day she asks God for help and spends much time in prayer.
6 But the widow who lives only for pleasure is spiritually dead. 7 Give these instructions
to the church so that the widows you support* will not be criticized.

5:1 Or *an elder.* **5:7** Or *so the church;* Greek reads *so they.*

4:12 Timothy was a young pastor. It would have been easy for older Christians to look down on him because of his youth. He had to earn the respect of his elders by setting an example in his speech, life, love, faith, and purity. Regardless of your age, God can use you. Whether you are young or old, don't think of your age as a handicap. Live so others can see Christ in you.

4:13 The Scriptures that Paul mentions are, in fact, the Old Testament. We must make sure to emphasize the entire Bible, both the Old and the New Testaments. There are rich rewards in studying the people, events, prophecies, and principles of the Old Testament.

4:14 Timothy's commission as a church leader was confirmed by prophecy (see also 1:18) and by the laying on of hands by the elders of the church. He was not a self-appointed leader. If you aspire to church leadership, seek the counsel of mature Christians who know you well and who will hold you accountable.

4:14, 15 As a young leader in a church that had a lot of problems, Timothy may have felt intimidated. But the elders and prophets encouraged him and charged him to use his spiritual gift responsibly. Highly skilled and talented athletes lose their abilities if their muscles aren't toned by constant use, and we will lose our spiritual gifts if we don't put them to work. Our talents are improved by exercise, but failing to use them causes them to waste away from lack of practice and nourishment. What gifts and abilities has God given you? Use them regularly in serving God and others. (See Romans 12:1-8; 2 Timothy 1:6-8 for more on using well the abilities God has given us.)

4:16 We know the importance of watching our life closely. We must be on constant guard against falling into sin that can so easily destroy us. Yet we must watch what we believe ("teaching") just as closely. Wrong beliefs can quickly lead us into sin and heresy. We should be on guard against those who would persuade us that how we live is more important than what we believe. We should persevere in both.

5:2 Men in the ministry can avoid improper attitudes toward women by treating them as family members. If men see women as fellow members in God's family, they will protect them and help them grow spiritually.

5:3ff Paul wanted Christian families to be as self-supporting as possible. He insisted that children and grandchildren take care of the widows in their families (5:4); he suggested that younger widows remarry and start new families (5:14); and he ordered the church not to support lazy members who refused to work (2 Thessalonians 3:10). Nevertheless, when necessary, the believers pooled their resources (Acts 2:44-47); they gave generously to help disaster-ridden churches (1 Corinthians 16:1-4); and they took care of a large number of widows (Acts 6:1-6). The church has always had limited resources, and it has always had to balance financial responsibility with generosity. It only makes sense for members to work as hard as they can and to be as independent as possible, so they can adequately care for themselves and for less fortunate members. When church members are both responsible and generous, everyone's needs will be met.

5:3-5 Because there were no pensions, no social security, no life insurance, and few honorable jobs for women, widows were usually unable to support themselves. The responsibility for caring for the helpless naturally falls first on their families, the people whose lives are most closely linked with theirs. Paul stresses the importance of each family caring for the needs of its widows and not leaving it for the church. The church can then care for those widows who have no families. A widow who had no children or other family members to support her was doomed to poverty. From the beginning, the church took care of its widows, who in turn gave valuable service to the church.

The church should support those who have no families and should also help the elderly, young, disabled, ill, or poverty-stricken with their emotional and spiritual needs. Often families who are caring for their own helpless members have heavy burdens. They may need extra money, a listening ear, a helping hand, or a word of encouragement. Interestingly, those who are helped often turn around and help others, turning the church into more of a caring community. Don't wait for people to ask. Take the initiative and look for ways to serve them.

8 But those who won't care for their own relatives, especially those living in the same
household, have denied what we believe. Such people are worse than unbelievers.
9 A widow who is put on the list for support must be a woman who is at least sixty
years old and was faithful to her husband.* 10 She must be well respected by everyone
because of the good she has done. Has she brought up her children well? Has she been
kind to strangers? Has she served other Christians humbly?* Has she helped those who
are in trouble? Has she always been ready to do good?
11 The younger widows should not be on the list, because their physical desires will
overpower their devotion to Christ and they will want to remarry. 12 Then they would be
guilty of breaking their previous pledge. 13 Besides, they are likely to become lazy and spend
their time gossiping from house to house, getting into other people's business and saying
things they shouldn't. 14 So I advise these younger widows to marry again, have children,
and take care of their own homes. Then the enemy will not be able to say anything against
them. 15 For I am afraid that some of them have already gone astray and now follow Satan.
16 If a Christian woman has relatives who are widows, she must take care of them and
not put the responsibility on the church. Then the church can care for widows who are
truly alone.
17 Elders who do their work well should be paid well,* especially those who work hard
at both preaching and teaching. 18 For the Scripture says, "Do not keep an ox from eating
as it treads out the grain." And in another place, "Those who work deserve their pay!"*
19 Do not listen to complaints against an elder unless there are two or three witnesses
to accuse him. 20 Anyone who sins should be rebuked in front of the whole church so that
others will have a proper fear of God.
21 I solemnly command you in the presence of God and Christ Jesus and the holy
angels to obey these instructions without taking sides or showing special favor to
anyone. 22 Never be in a hurry about appointing an elder. Do not participate in the sins
of others. Keep yourself pure.

5:10 Gen 18:3-4; Acts 9:36
5:13 2 Thes 3:11
5:14 1 Cor 7:9; 1 Tim 6:1
5:15 1 Tim 1:19-20
5:17 Phil 2:29; 1 Thes 5:12
5:18 †Deut 25:4; Matt 10:10; †Luke 10:7; 1 Cor 9:9
5:19 Matt 18:16
5:20 Deut 13:11; Eph 5:11
5:21 1 Tim 6:13
5:22 1 Tim 4:14

5:9 Greek *was the wife of one man.* **5:10** Greek *Has she washed the feet of saints?* **5:17** Greek *should be worthy of double honor.* **5:18** Deut 25:4; Luke 10:7.

5:8 Almost everyone has relatives, family of some kind. Family relationships are so important in God's eyes, Paul says, that a person who neglects his or her family responsibilities has denied the faith. Are you doing your part to meet the needs of those included in your family circle?

5:9-16 Apparently some older widows had been "put on the list for support," meaning that they had taken a vow committing themselves to work for the church in exchange for financial support. Paul lists a few qualifications for these church workers: These widows should be at least 60 years old, should have been faithful to their husbands, and should be well known for their kind deeds. Younger widows should not be included in this group because they might desire to marry again and thus have to break their pledge (5:11, 12).

Three out of four wives today eventually are widowed, so many of the older women in our churches have lost their husbands. Does your church provide an avenue of service for these women? Could you help match their gifts and abilities with your church's needs? Often their maturity and wisdom can be of great service in the church.

5:15 "Gone astray and now follow Satan" refers to the immoral conduct that identified these women with their pagan neighbors.

5:17, 18 Faithful church leaders should be supported and appreciated. Too often they are targets for criticism because the congregation has unrealistic expectations. How do you treat your church leaders? Do you enjoy finding fault, or do you show your appreciation? Do they receive enough financial support to allow them to live without worry and to provide for the needs of their families? Jesus and Paul emphasized the importance of supporting those who lead and teach us (see Galatians 6:6 and the notes on Luke 10:7 and 1 Corinthians 9:4-10).

5:17, 18 Preaching and teaching are closely related. Preaching is proclaiming the Word of God and confronting listeners with the truth of Scripture. Teaching is explaining the truth in Scripture, helping learners understand difficult passages, and helping them apply God's Word to daily life. Paul says that these elders are worthy of double honor. Unfortunately, however, we often take them for granted by not providing adequately for their needs or by subjecting them to heavy criticism. Think of how you can honor your preachers and teachers.

5:19-21 Church leaders are not exempt from sin, faults, and mistakes. But they are often criticized for the wrong reasons—minor imperfections, failure to meet someone's expectations, personality clashes. Thus, Paul said that accusations should not even be heard unless two or three witnesses confirm them. Sometimes church leaders should be confronted about their behavior, and sometimes they should be rebuked. But all rebuking must be done fairly and lovingly and for the purpose of restoration.

5:21 "Holy angels" are all those angels who did not rebel against God like Satan did.

5:21 We must be constantly on guard against favoritism, against giving preferential treatment to some and ignoring others. We live in a society that plays favorites. It's easy to give special treatment to those who are gifted, intelligent, rich, or beautiful without realizing what we are doing. Make sure you honor people for who they are in Christ, not for who they are in the world.

5:22 Paul says that a church should never be hasty about choosing its leaders, especially the pastor, because we may overlook major problems or sins. It is a serious responsibility to choose church leaders. They must have strong faith and be morally upright, having the qualities described in 3:1-13 and Titus 1:5-9. Not everyone who wants to be a church leader is eligible. Be certain of an applicant's qualifications before asking him or her to take a leadership position.

5:23 1 Tim 3:8 23 Don't drink only water. You ought to drink a little wine for the sake of your stomach
5:24-25 because you are sick so often.
Rev 14:13 24 Remember that some people lead sinful lives, and everyone knows they will be
judged. But there are others whose sin will not be revealed until later. 25 In the same way,
everyone knows how much good some people do, but there are others whose good deeds
won't be known until later.

6:1 Eph 6:5 **6** Christians who are slaves should give their masters full respect so that the name of
Titus 2:9-10 God and his teaching will not be shamed. 2 If your master is a Christian, that is no
6:2 1 Tim 4:11 excuse for being disrespectful. You should work all the harder because you are helping
Phlm 1:16 another believer* by your efforts.

False Teaching and True Riches

6:3 1 Tim 1:3, 10 Teach these truths, Timothy, and encourage everyone to obey them. 3 Some false teachers
6:4 may deny these things, but these are the sound, wholesome teachings of the Lord Jesus
2 Tim 2:14 Christ, and they are the foundation for a godly life. 4 Anyone who teaches anything
6:5 2 Tim 3:8; 4:4 different is both conceited and ignorant. Such a person has an unhealthy desire to quibble
Titus 1:14 over the meaning of words. This stirs up arguments ending in jealousy, fighting, slander,
6:6 and evil suspicions. 5 These people always cause trouble. Their minds are corrupt, and
Phil 4:11-12 Heb 13:5 they don't tell the truth. To them religion is just a way to get rich.
6:7 6 Yet true religion with contentment is great wealth. 7 After all, we didn't bring anything
Eccl 5:15 Job 1:21 with us when we came into the world, and we certainly cannot carry anything with us
6:8 when we die. 8 So if we have enough food and clothing, let us be content. 9 But people
Prov 30:8 Heb 13:5 who long to be rich fall into temptation and are trapped by many foolish and harmful
desires that plunge them into ruin and destruction. 10 For the love of money is at the root
6:9 Prov 23:4; 28:22 of all kinds of evil. And some people, craving money, have wandered from the faith and
pierced themselves with many sorrows.

Paul's Final Instructions

6:11 11 But you, Timothy, belong to God; so run from all these evil things, and follow what is
2 Tim 2:22 right and good. Pursue a godly life, along with faith, love, perseverance, and gentleness.
6:12 1 Cor 9:25-26 12 Fight the good fight for what we believe. Hold tightly to the eternal life that God has
2 Tim 4:7

6:2 Greek *a brother.*

5:23 It is unclear why Paul gave this advice to Timothy. Perhaps contaminated water had led to Timothy's indigestion, and so he should stop drinking only water. Whatever the reason, this statement is not an invitation to overindulgence or alcoholism.

5:24, 25 Paul instructs Timothy to choose church leaders carefully because sometimes their sins are not obvious and it takes time for them to be revealed. Church leaders should live lives that are above reproach.

6:1, 2 In Paul's culture there was a great social and legal gulf separating masters and slaves. But as Christians, masters and slaves became spiritual equals, brothers and sisters in Christ Jesus (Galatians 3:28). Paul did not speak against the institution of slavery, but he gave guidelines for Christian slaves and Christian masters. His counsel for the master/slave relationship can be applied to the employer/employee relationship today. Employees should work hard, showing respect for their employers. In turn, employers should be fair (Ephesians 6:5-9; Colossians 3:22–4:15). Our work should reflect our faithfulness to and love for Christ.

6:3-5 Paul told Timothy to stay away from those who just wanted to make money from preaching and from those who strayed from the sound teachings of the Good News into quarrels that caused strife in the church. A person's understanding of the finer points of theology should not become the basis for lording it over others or for making money. Stay away from people who just want to argue.

6:6 This statement is the key to spiritual growth and personal fulfillment. We should honor God and center our desires on him ("true religion," see Matthew 6:33), and we should be content with what God is doing in our life (see Philippians 4:11-13).

6:6-10 Despite overwhelming evidence to the contrary, most people still believe that money brings happiness. Rich people craving greater riches can be caught in an endless cycle that only ends in ruin and destruction. How can you keep away from the love of money? Paul gives us some guidelines: (1) Realize that one day riches will all be gone (6:7, 17); (2) be content with what you have (6:8); (3) monitor what you are willing to do to get more money (6:9, 10); (4) love people more than money (6:11); (5) love God's work more than money (6:11); (6) freely share what you have with others (6:18). (See Proverbs 30:7-9 for more on avoiding the love of money.)

6:8 It is often helpful to distinguish between *needs* and *wants.* We may have all we need to live but let ourselves become anxious and discontent over what we merely want. Like Paul, we can choose to be content without having all that we want. The only alternative is to be a slave to our desires.

6:10 Greed leads to all kinds of evil: marriage problems, robbery, blowups in partnerships. To master greed, you must control it at its root. Get rid of the desire to be rich.

6:11, 12 Paul uses active and forceful verbs to describe the Christian life: run, pursue, fight, hold tightly. Some think Christianity is a passive religion that advocates waiting for God to act. On the contrary, we must have an *active* faith, obeying God with courage and doing what we know is right. Is it time for action on your part? Don't wait—get going!

given you, which you have confessed so well before many witnesses. 13And I command
you before God, who gives life to all, and before Christ Jesus, who gave a good testimony
before Pontius Pilate, 14that you obey his commands with all purity. Then no one can
find fault with you from now until our Lord Jesus Christ returns. 15For at the right time
Christ will be revealed from heaven by the blessed and only almighty God, the King of
kings and Lord of lords. 16He alone can never die, and he lives in light so brilliant that
no human can approach him. No one has ever seen him, nor ever will. To him be honor
and power forever. Amen.
17Tell those who are rich in this world not to be proud and not to trust in their money,
which will soon be gone. But their trust should be in the living God, who richly gives us
all we need for our enjoyment. 18Tell them to use their money to do good. They should
be rich in good works and should give generously to those in need, always being ready
to share with others whatever God has given them. 19By doing this they will be storing
up their treasure as a good foundation for the future so that they may take hold of real
life.
20Timothy, guard what God has entrusted to you. Avoid godless, foolish discussions
with those who oppose you with their so-called knowledge. 21Some people have
wandered from the faith by following such foolishness.

May God's grace be with you all.

6:13 John 18:33-37
6:14 1 Thes 3:13
6:15 Deut 10:17; 1 Tim 1:17; Rev 17:14
6:16 Exod 33:20; Ps 104:2; John 1:18; 5:26; 1 Tim 1:17
6:17 Luke 12:20
6:19 Matt 6:20; 1 Tim 6:12
6:20 2 Tim 1:14; 2:16
6:21 2 Tim 2:18

6:13 Jesus' trial before Pilate is recorded in the Gospels: Matthew 27:11-26; Mark 15:1-15; Luke 23:1-25; John 18:28–19:16.

6:13-16 Paul concludes with a charge to Timothy to obey "his commands," referring to the commands Christ has given to his church or perhaps to Timothy's promise to serve Christ. Timothy's own confession of faith is compared with Christ's before Pilate.

6:17-19 Ephesus was a wealthy city, and the Ephesian church probably had many wealthy members. Paul advised Timothy to deal with any potential problems by teaching that having riches carries great responsibility. Those who have money must be generous, but they must not be arrogant just because they have a lot to give. They must be careful not to put their hope in money instead of in the living God for their security. Even if we don't have material wealth, we can be rich in good deeds. No matter how poor we are, we have something to share with someone.

6:21 The book of 1 Timothy provides guiding principles for local churches, including rules for public worship and qualifications for elders (overseers, pastors), deacons, and special church workers (widows). Paul tells the church leaders to correct incorrect doctrine and to deal lovingly and fairly with all people in the church. The church is not organized simply for the sake of organization but so that Christ can be honored and glorified. While studying these guidelines, don't lose sight of what is most important in the life of the church—knowing God, working together in loving harmony, and taking God's Good News to the world.

2 TIMOTHY

"FAMOUS last words" is more than a cliché. When notable men and women of influence are about to die, the world waits to hear their final words of insight and wisdom. Then those quotes are repeated worldwide. This is also true with a dying loved one. Gathered at his or her side, the family strains to hear every whispered syllable of blessing, encouragement, and advice, knowing that this will be the final message.

One of the most knowledgeable, influential, and beloved men of history is the apostle Paul. And we have his famous last words.

Paul was facing death. He was not dying of a disease in a sterile hospital with loved ones gathered nearby. He was very much alive, but his condition was terminal. Convicted as a follower of Jesus of Nazareth, Paul sat in a cold Roman prison, cut off from the world, with just a visitor or two and his writing materials. Paul knew that soon he would be executed (4:6), and so he wrote his final thoughts to his "son" Timothy, passing to him the torch of leadership, reminding him of what was truly important, and encouraging him in the faith. Imagine how Timothy must have read and reread every word; this was the last message from his beloved mentor, Paul. Because of the situation and the recipient, this is the most intimate and moving of all Paul's letters and his last.

Paul's introduction is tender, and every phrase exudes the love he has for Timothy (1:1–5). He then reminds Timothy of the qualities necessary for a faithful minister of Jesus Christ (1:6—2:13). Timothy should remember his call and use his gifts with boldness (1:6–12), keep to the truth (1:13–18), prepare others to follow him in the ministry (2:1, 2), be disciplined and ready to endure suffering (2:3–7), and keep his eyes and mind focused on Christ (2:8–13). Paul challenges Timothy to hold to sound doctrine, reject error and avoid godless chatter, correctly handle the word of truth (2:14–19), and keep his life pure (2:20–26).

Next, Paul warns Timothy of the opposition that he and other believers would face in the last days from self-centered people who use the church for their own gain and teach false doctrines (3:1–9). Paul tells Timothy to be prepared for these unfaithful people by remembering his example (3:10, 11), understanding the real source of the opposition (3:12, 13), and finding strength and power in the Word of God (3:14–17). Then Paul gives Timothy a stirring charge: to preach the Word (4:1–4) and to fulfill his ministry until the end (4:5–8).

Paul concludes with personal requests and items of information. In these final words, he reveals his loneliness and his strong love for his brothers and sisters in Christ (4:9–22).

There has never been another person like Paul, the missionary apostle. He was a man of deep faith, undying love, constant hope, tenacious conviction, and profound insight. And he was inspired by the Holy Spirit to give us God's message. As you read 2 Timothy, know that you are reading the last words of this great man of God—his last words to Timothy and to all who would claim to follow Christ. Recommit yourself to stand courageously for the truth, knowing the Word and being empowered by the Holy Spirit.

VITAL STATISTICS

PURPOSE:
To give final instructions and encouragement to Timothy, pastor of the church at Ephesus

AUTHOR:
Paul

TO WHOM WRITTEN:
Timothy and all Christians everywhere

DATE WRITTEN:
Approximately A.D. 66 or 67, from prison in Rome. After a year or two of freedom, Paul was arrested again and executed under Emperor Nero.

SETTING:
Paul was virtually alone in prison; only Luke was with him. Paul wrote this letter to pass the torch to the new generation of church leaders. He also asked for visits from his friends and for his scrolls, especially the parchments—possibly parts of the Old Testament, the Gospels, and other biblical manuscripts.

KEY VERSE:
"Work hard so God can approve you. Be a good worker, one who does not need to be ashamed and who correctly explains the word of truth" (2:15).

KEY PEOPLE:
Paul, Timothy, Luke, Mark, and others

KEY PLACES:
Rome, Ephesus

SPECIAL FEATURES:
Because this is Paul's last letter, it reveals his heart and his priorities—sound doctrine, steadfast faith, confident endurance, and lasting love.

THE BLUEPRINT

1. Foundations of Christian service (1:1—2:26)
2. Difficult times for Christian service (3:1—4:22)

Paul gives helpful advice to Timothy to remain solidly grounded in Christian service and to endure suffering during the difficult days to come. It is easy for us to serve Christ for the wrong reasons: because it is exciting, rewarding, or personally enriching. Without a proper foundation, however, we will find it easy to quit during difficult times. All believers need a strong foundation for their service, because Christian service does not get easier as we grow older, and it will become no easier as the time of Christ's return grows closer.

MEGATHEMES

THEME	EXPLANATION	IMPORTANCE
Boldness	In the face of opposition and persecution, Timothy was to carry out his ministry without fear or shame. Paul urged him to utilize boldly the gifts of preaching and teaching that the Holy Spirit had given him.	The Holy Spirit helps us to be wise and strong. God honors our confident testimony even when we suffer. To get over our fear of what people might say or do, we must take our eyes off of people and look only to God.
Faithfulness	Christ was faithful to all of us in dying for our sin. Paul was a faithful minister even when he was in prison. Paul urged Timothy to maintain not only sound doctrine but also loyalty, diligence, and endurance.	We can count on opposition, suffering, and hardship as we serve Christ. But this shows that our faithfulness is having an effect on others. As we trust Christ, he counts us worthy to suffer, and he will give us the strength we need to be steadfast.
Preaching and Teaching	Paul and Timothy were active in preaching and teaching the Good News about Jesus Christ. Paul encouraged Timothy not only to carry the torch of truth but also to train others, passing on to them sound doctrine and enthusiasm for Christ's mission.	We must prepare people to transmit God's Word to others so that they in turn might pass it on. Does your church carefully train others to teach?
Error	In the final days before Christ returns, there will be false teachers, spiritual dropouts, and heretics. The remedy for error is to have a solid program for teaching Christians.	Because of deception and false teaching, we must be disciplined and ready to reject error. Know the Word of God as your sure defense against error and confusion.

1. Foundations of Christian service

Greetings from Paul

1 This letter is from Paul, an apostle of Christ Jesus by God's will, sent out to tell 1:1 John 5:24 Titus 1:1 1 Jn 5:10-11, 20
others about the life he has promised through faith in Christ Jesus.
2 It is written to Timothy, my dear son.
May God our Father and Christ Jesus our Lord give you grace, mercy, and peace. 1:2 1 Tim 1:2

Encouragement to Be Faithful

3 Timothy, I thank God for you. He is the God I serve with a clear conscience, just as my 1:4 Acts 20:37 2 Tim 4:9
ancestors did. Night and day I constantly remember you in my prayers. 4 I long to see

1:1 This letter has a somber tone. Paul was imprisoned for the last time, and he knew he would soon die. Unlike Paul's first imprisonment in Rome, when he was in a house (Acts 28:16, 23, 30) where he continued to teach, this time he was probably confined to a cold dungeon, awaiting his death (4:6-8). Emperor Nero had begun a major persecution in A.D. 64 as part of his plan to pass the blame for the great fire of Rome from himself to the Christians. This persecution spread across the empire and included social ostracism, public torture, and murder. As Paul was waiting to die, he wrote a letter to his dear friend Timothy, a younger man who was like a son to him (1:2). Written in approximately A.D. 66/67, these are the last words we have from Paul.

1:2 Paul's second letter to Timothy was written about two to four years after his first letter. Timothy had been Paul's traveling companion on the second and third missionary journeys, and Paul had left him in Ephesus to help the church there (1 Timothy 1:3, 4). For more information on Timothy, see his Profile in 1 Timothy 2. For more information on the great missionary Paul, see his Profile in Acts 9.

1:3 Paul constantly prayed for Timothy, his friend, his fellow traveler, his son in the faith, and a strong leader in the Christian church. Although the two men were separated from each other, their prayers provided a source of mutual encouragement. We, too, should pray consistently for others, especially for those who do God's work.

1:4 We don't know when Paul and Timothy last parted, but it was probably when Paul was arrested and taken to Rome for his second imprisonment. The tears they shed at parting revealed the depth of their relationship.

you again, for I remember your tears as we parted. And I will be filled with joy when we
are together again.
5 I know that you sincerely trust the Lord, for you have the faith of your mother,
Eunice, and your grandmother, Lois. 6 This is why I remind you to fan into flames the
spiritual gift God gave you when I laid my hands on you. 7 For God has not given us a
spirit of fear and timidity, but of power, love, and self-discipline. 8 So you must never be
ashamed to tell others about our Lord. And don't be ashamed of me, either, even though
I'm in prison for Christ. With the strength God gives you, be ready to suffer with me for
the proclamation of the Good News.
9 It is God who saved us and chose us to live a holy life. He did this not because we
deserved it, but because that was his plan long before the world began—to show his love
and kindness to us through Christ Jesus. 10 And now he has made all of this plain to us
by the coming of Christ Jesus, our Savior, who broke the power of death and showed us
the way to everlasting life through the Good News. 11 And God chose me to be a preacher,
an apostle, and a teacher of this Good News.
12 And that is why I am suffering here in prison. But I am not ashamed of it, for I know
the one in whom I trust, and I am sure that he is able to guard what I have entrusted to
him* until the day of his return.
13 Hold on to the pattern of right teaching you learned from me. And remember to live

1:5 Acts 16:1
1:6 1 Tim 4:14
1:7 Rom 8:15
1:8 Rom 1:16; Eph 3:1; 2 Tim 2:3
1:9 Rom 8:28; 11:14; Eph 2:8-9; Titus 3:5
1:10 1 Cor 15:54
1:11 1 Tim 2:7
1:12 1 Tim 6:20
1:13 Rom 6:17; 1 Tim 1:14

1:12 Or *what has been entrusted to me.*

1:5 Timothy's mother and grandmother, Eunice and Lois, were early Christian converts, possibly through Paul's ministry in their home city, Lystra (Acts 16:1). They had communicated their strong Christian faith to Timothy, even though his father was probably not a believer. Don't hide your light at home; our families are fertile fields for planting seeds of the Good News. Let your parents, children, spouse, brothers, and sisters know of your faith in Jesus, and be sure they see Christ's love, helpfulness, and joy in you.

1:6 At the time of his ordination, Timothy had received special gifts of the Spirit to enable him to serve the church (see 1 Timothy 4:14). In telling Timothy to "fan into flames the spiritual gift God gave you," Paul was encouraging him to persevere. Timothy did not need new revelations or new gifts; he needed the courage and self-discipline to hang on to the truth and to use the gifts he had already received (see 1:13, 14). If Timothy would step out boldly in faith and proclaim the Good News once again, the Holy Spirit would go with him and give him power. When you use the gifts God has given you, you will find that God will give you the power you need.

1:6 Clearly Timothy's spiritual gift had been given to him when Paul and the elders had laid their hands on him and set him apart for ministry (see 1 Timothy 4:14). God gives all Christians gifts to use to build up the body of Christ (see 1 Corinthians 12:4-31), and he gives special gifts to some through church leaders, who serve as God's instruments.

1:6, 7 Timothy was experiencing great opposition to his message and to himself as a leader. His youth, his association with Paul, and his leadership had come under fire from believers and nonbelievers alike. Paul urged him to be bold. When we allow people to intimidate us, we neutralize our effectiveness for God. The power of the Holy Spirit can help us overcome our fear of what some might say or do to us, so that we can continue to do God's work.

1:7 Paul mentions three characteristics of the effective Christian leader: power, love, and self-discipline. These are available to us because the Holy Spirit lives in us. Follow his leading each day so that your life will more fully exhibit these characteristics. See Galatians 5:22, 23 for a list of the by-products of the Holy Spirit's living in us.

1:8 In this time of mounting persecution, Timothy may have been afraid to continue preaching the Good News. His fears were based on fact, because believers were being arrested and executed. Paul told Timothy to expect suffering—Timothy, like Paul, would be jailed for preaching the Good News (Hebrews 13:23). But Paul promised Timothy that God would give him strength and that he would be ready when it was his turn to suffer. Even when there is no persecution, it can be difficult to share our faith in Christ. Fortunately we, like Paul and Timothy, can call on the Holy Spirit to give us courage. Don't be ashamed to testify.

1:9, 10 In these verses Paul gives a brief summary of the Good News. God loves us, chose us, and sent Christ to die for us. We can have eternal life through faith in him, because he broke the power of death with his resurrection. We do not deserve to be saved, but God offers us salvation anyway. What we must do is believe in him and accept his offer.

1:12 Paul was in prison, but that did not stop his ministry. He carried it on through others like Timothy. Paul had lost all his material possessions, but he would never lose his faith. He trusted God to use him regardless of his circumstances. If your situation looks bleak, give your concerns to Christ. He will guard your faith and safely guard all you have entrusted to him until the day of his return. For more on our security in Christ, see Romans 8:38, 39.

1:12 The phrase "guard what I have entrusted to him" could mean: (1) Paul knew that God would guard the souls of those converted through his preaching; (2) Paul trusted God to guard his own soul until Christ's second coming; or (3) Paul was confident that, though he was in prison and facing death, God would carry out the Good News ministry through others such as Timothy. Paul may have expressed his confidence to encourage Timothy, who was undoubtedly discouraged by the problems in Ephesus and fearful of persecution. Even in prison, Paul knew that God was still in control. No matter what setbacks or problems we face, we can trust fully in God.

1:13, 14 Timothy was in a time of transition. He had been Paul's bright young helper; soon he would be on his own as leader of a church in a difficult environment. Although his responsibilities were changing, Timothy was not without help. He had everything he needed to face the future if he would hold on tightly to the Lord's resources. When you are facing difficult transitions, it is good to follow Paul's advice to Timothy and look back at your experience. Who is the foundation of your faith? How can you build on that foundation? What gifts has the Holy Spirit given you? Use the gifts you have already been given.

in the faith and love that you have in Christ Jesus. 14 With the help of the Holy Spirit who **1:14**
lives within us, carefully guard what has been entrusted to you. Rom 8:9, 11, 16 Gal 4:6
15 As you know, all the Christians who came here from the province of Asia have **1:15**
deserted me; even Phygelus and Hermogenes are gone. 16 May the Lord show special 2 Tim 4:10, 16
kindness to Onesiphorus and all his family because he often visited and encouraged **1:16**
me. He was never ashamed of me because I was in prison. 17 When he came to Rome, 2 Tim 4:19
he searched everywhere until he found me. 18 May the Lord show him special **1:18** Heb 6:10
kindness on the day of Christ's return. And you know how much he helped me at
Ephesus.

A Good Soldier of Christ Jesus

2 Timothy, my dear son, be strong with the special favor God gives you in Christ **2:1** Eph 6:10
Jesus. 2 You have heard me teach many things that have been confirmed by many **2:2**
reliable witnesses. Teach these great truths to trustworthy people who are able to pass 2 Tim 1:13
them on to others. **2:3**
3 Endure suffering along with me, as a good soldier of Christ Jesus. 4 And as Christ's 2 Tim 1:8; 4:5
soldier, do not let yourself become tied up in the affairs of this life, for then you cannot **2:5** 1 Cor 9:25
satisfy the one who has enlisted you in his army. 5 Follow the Lord's rules for doing **2:6**
his work, just as an athlete either follows the rules or is disqualified and wins no prize. 1 Cor 9:7, 10
6 Hardworking farmers are the first to enjoy the fruit of their labor. 7 Think about what **2:8**
I am saying. The Lord will give you understanding in all these things. Acts 2:24 Rom 1:3
8 Never forget that Jesus Christ was a man born into King David's family and that **2:9** Eph 3:1
he was raised from the dead. This is the Good News I preach. 9 And because I preach Phil 1:12-14
this Good News, I am suffering and have been chained like a criminal. But the word **2:10**
of God cannot be chained. 10 I am willing to endure anything if it will bring salvation Col 1:24
and eternal glory in Christ Jesus to those God has chosen. **2:11** Rom 6:2-11
11 This is a true saying: 1 Thes 5:10

1:15, 16 Nothing more is known about Phygelus and Hermogenes, who evidently opposed Paul's ministry. These men serve as a warning that even leaders can fall. Onesiphorus was mentioned as a positive example in contrast to these men.

2:1 How can someone be strong with special favor? That "special favor" refers to grace, God's undeserved favor on our behalf. Just as we are saved by God's special favor (Ephesians 2:8, 9), we should live by it (Colossians 2:6). This means trusting completely in Christ and *his* power, and not trying to live for Christ in our strength alone. Receive and utilize Christ's power. He will give you the strength to do his work.

2:2 If the church were to consistently follow this advice, it would expand geometrically as well-taught believers would teach others and commission them, in turn, to teach still others. Disciples need to be equipped to pass on their faith; our work is not done until new believers are able to make disciples of others (see Ephesians 4:12, 13).

2:3-7 As Timothy preached and taught, he would face suffering, but he should be able to endure. Paul used a comparison with soldiers, athletes, and farmers who must discipline themselves and be willing to sacrifice to achieve the results they want. Like soldiers, we have to give up worldly security and endure rigorous discipline. Like athletes, we must train hard and follow the rules. Like farmers, we must work extremely hard and be patient. But we keep going despite suffering because of the thought of victory, the vision of winning, and the hope of harvest. We will see that our suffering is worthwhile when we achieve our goal of glorifying God, winning people to Christ, and one day living eternally with him.

2:7 Paul told Timothy to think about his words, and God would give him understanding. God speaks through the Bible, his Word, but we need to be open and receptive to him. As you read the Bible, ask God to show you his timeless truths and the application to your life. Then consider what you have read by thinking it through and meditating on it. God will give you understanding.

2:8 False teachers were a problem in Ephesus (see Acts 20:29, 30; 1 Timothy 1:3-11). At the heart of false teaching is an incorrect view of Christ. In Timothy's day many asserted that Christ was divine but not human—God but not man. These days we often hear that Jesus was human but not divine—man but not God. Either view destroys the good news that Jesus Christ has taken our sins on himself and has reconciled us to God. In this verse, Paul firmly states that Jesus is fully man ("born into King David's family") and fully God ("raised from the dead"). This is an important doctrine for all Christians. For more on this key concept, see the note on Philippians 2:5-7.

2:9 Paul was in chains in prison because of the Good News he preached. The truth about Jesus is no more popular in our day than in Paul's, but it still reaches receptive hearts. When Paul said that Jesus was God, he angered the Jews who had condemned Jesus for blasphemy; but many Jews became followers of Christ (1 Corinthians 1:24). He angered the Romans who worshiped the emperor as god; but even some in Caesar's household turned to Jesus (Philippians 4:22). When Paul said Jesus was human, he angered the Greeks, who thought divinity was soiled if it had any contact with humanity; still many Greeks accepted the faith (Acts 11:20, 21). The truth that Jesus is one person with two united natures has never been easy to understand, but it is being believed by people every day. Despite the opposition, continue to proclaim Christ. Some will listen and believe.

2:11-13 This is probably an early Christian hymn. God is faithful to his children, and although we may suffer great hardships here, God promises that someday we will live eternally with him. What will this involve? It means believers will live in Christ's Kingdom, and that we will share in the administration of that Kingdom. This truth comforted Paul as he went through suffering and death. Are you facing hardships? Don't turn away from God—he promises you a wonderful future with him. For more information about living eternally with God, see Matthew 16:24-27; 19:28-30; Luke 22:28-30; Romans 5:17; 6:8; 8:10, 11, 17; 1 Corinthians 15:42-58; Colossians 3:3, 4; 1 Thessalonians 4:13-18; Revelation 3:21; 21:1–22:21.

If we die with him,
we will also live with him.
12 If we endure hardship,

2:12
Matt 10:33
Rom 8:17
1 Pet 4:13

we will reign with him.
If we deny him,
he will deny us.
13 If we are unfaithful,

2:13
Num 23:19
Rom 3:3
1 Cor 1:9

he remains faithful,
for he cannot deny himself.

An Approved Worker

14 Remind everyone of these things, and command them in God's name to stop fighting

2:14
1 Tim 1:4; 6:4
Titus 3:9

over words. Such arguments are useless, and they can ruin those who hear them. 15 Work
hard so God can approve you. Be a good worker, one who does not need to be ashamed
and who correctly explains the word of truth. 16 Avoid godless, foolish discussions that

2:17
1 Tim 1:20

lead to more and more ungodliness. 17 This kind of talk spreads like cancer. Hymenaeus
and Philetus are examples of this. 18 They have left the path of truth, preaching the lie

2:18
1 Tim 1:19; 6:21

that the resurrection of the dead has already occurred; and they have undermined the faith
of some.

19 But God's truth stands firm like a foundation stone with this inscription: "The Lord

2:19
†Num 16:5
Isa 52:11
John 10:14

knows those who are his,"* and "Those who claim they belong to the Lord must turn
away from all wickedness."*

20 In a wealthy home some utensils are made of gold and silver, and some are made of

2:20
Rom 9:21

wood and clay. The expensive utensils are used for special occasions, and the cheap ones
are for everyday use. 21 If you keep yourself pure, you will be a utensil God can use for

2:21
2 Tim 3:17

his purpose. Your life will be clean, and you will be ready for the Master to use you for
every good work.

22 Run from anything that stimulates youthful lust. Follow anything that makes you

2:22
1 Tim 6:11

2:19a Num 16:5. **2:19b** See Isa 52:11.

2:13 Jesus is faithful. He will stay by our side even when we have endured so much that we seem to have no faith left. We may be faithless at times, but Jesus is faithful to his promise to be with us "to the end of the age" (Matthew 28:20). Refusing Christ's help will break our communication with God, but he will never turn his back on us even though we may turn our back on him.

2:14-16 Paul urged Timothy to remind the believers not to argue over unimportant details ("fighting over words") or have foolish discussions because such arguments are confusing, useless, and even harmful. False teachers loved to cause strife and divisions by their meaningless quibbling over unimportant details (see 1 Timothy 6:3-5). To explain the word of truth correctly, we must study what the Word of God says so we can understand what it means.

2:15 Because God will examine what kind of workers we have been for him, we should build our life on his Word and build his Word into our life. It alone tells us how to live for him and serve him. Believers who ignore the Bible will certainly be ashamed at the judgment. Consistent and diligent study of God's Word is vital; otherwise we will be lulled into neglecting God and our true purpose for living.

2:16 In important areas of Christian teaching, we must carefully work through our disagreements. But when we bicker long hours over words and theories that are not central to the Christian faith and life, we only provoke anger and hurt feelings. Even if "foolish discussions" reach a resolution, they gain little ground for the Kingdom. Learning and discussing are not bad unless they keep believers constantly focusing on false doctrine or unhelpful trivialities. Don't let anything keep you from your work for and service to God.

2:17, 18 Hymenaeus was also mentioned in 1 Timothy 1:20. Paul had turned Hymenaeus over to Satan because his false teaching concerning the resurrection was destroying some people's faith.

2:18 The false teachers were denying the resurrection of the body. They believed that when a person became a Christian, he or she was spiritually reborn, and that was the only resurrection there would ever be. To them, resurrection was symbolic and spiritual, not physical. Paul clearly taught, however, that believers will be resurrected after they die, and that their bodies as well as their souls will live eternally with Christ (1 Corinthians 15:35ff; 2 Corinthians 5:1-10; 1 Thessalonians 4:15-18). We cannot shape the doctrines of Scripture to match our opinions. If we do, we are putting ourselves above God. Instead, our beliefs should be consistent with God's Word.

2:19 False teachers still spout lies. Some distort the truth, some dilute it, and some simply delete it by saying that God's truth no longer applies. But no matter how many people follow the liars, the solid foundation of God's truth never changes, is never shaken, and will never fade. When we follow God's truth, he will never forsake us.

2:20, 21 Here Paul urged Timothy to be the kind of person Christ could use for his noblest purposes. Don't settle for less than God's highest and best. Allow God to use you as an instrument of his will.

2:22 Running away is sometimes considered cowardly. But wise people realize that removing themselves physically from temptation often can be the most courageous action to take. Timothy, a young man, was warned to run from anything that produced evil thoughts. Do you have a recurring temptation that is difficult to resist? Remove yourself physically from any situation that stimulates your desire to sin. Knowing when to run is as important in spiritual battle as knowing when and how to fight. (See also 1 Timothy 6:11.)

want to do right. Pursue faith and love and peace, and enjoy the companionship of those
who call on the Lord with pure hearts.
23Again I say, don't get involved in foolish, ignorant arguments that only start fights. **2:23** 1 Tim 4:7
24The Lord's servants must not quarrel but must be kind to everyone. They must be able **2:24**
to teach effectively and be patient with difficult people. 25They should gently teach those 1 Tim 3:3; Titus 1:7
who oppose the truth. Perhaps God will change those people's hearts, and they will **2:25**
believe the truth. 26Then they will come to their senses and escape from the Devil's trap. 1 Tim 2:4
For they have been held captive by him to do whatever he wants. **2:26** 1 Tim 3:7

2. Difficult times for Christian service

The Dangers of the Last Days

3 You should also know this, Timothy, that in the last days there will be very difficult **3:1**
times. 2For people will love only themselves and their money. They will be boastful 1 Tim 4:1; Jude 1:18
and proud, scoffing at God, disobedient to their parents, and ungrateful. They will **3:2-3**
consider nothing sacred. 3They will be unloving and unforgiving; they will slander Rom 1:29-31
others and have no self-control; they will be cruel and have no interest in what is good.
4They will betray their friends, be reckless, be puffed up with pride, and love pleasure
rather than God. 5They will act as if they are religious, but they will reject the power that **3:5**
could make them godly. You must stay away from people like that. 1 Tim 2:2
6They are the kind who work their way into people's homes and win the confidence **3:6**
of* vulnerable women who are burdened with the guilt of sin and controlled by many Jude 1:4
desires. 7Such women are forever following new teachings, but they never understand
the truth. 8And these teachers fight the truth just as Jannes and Jambres fought against **3:8** Exod 7:11
Moses. Their minds are depraved, and their faith is counterfeit. 9But they won't get away 1 Tim 6:5
with this for long. Someday everyone will recognize what fools they are, just as **3:9** Exod 8:18; 9:11
happened with Jannes and Jambres.

Paul's Charge to Timothy

10But you know what I teach, Timothy, and how I live, and what my purpose in life is. **3:10** 1 Tim 4:6
You know my faith and how long I have suffered. You know my love and my patient **3:11**
endurance. 11You know how much persecution and suffering I have endured. You know Ps 34:19; Acts 13:14, 50-51; 14:5, 19

3:6 Greek *and take captive.*

2:23-26 As a teacher, Timothy helped those who were confused about the truth. Paul's advice to Timothy, and to all who teach God's truth, is to be kind and gentle, patiently and courteously explaining the truth. Good teaching never promotes quarrels or foolish arguments. Whether you are teaching church school, leading a Bible study, or preaching in church, remember to listen to people's questions and treat them respectfully, while avoiding foolish debates. If you do this, those who oppose you will be more willing to hear what you have to say and perhaps turn from their error.

3:1 Paul's reference to the "last days" reveals his sense of urgency. The last days began after Jesus' resurrection when the Holy Spirit came upon the believers at Pentecost. The "last days" will continue until Christ's second coming. This means that *we* are living in the last days. So we should make the most of the time that God has given us (Ephesians 5:16; Colossians 4:5).

3:1ff In many parts of the world today it is not especially difficult to be a Christian—people aren't jailed for reading the Bible or executed for preaching Christ. But Paul's descriptive list of behavior in the last days describes our society—even, unfortunately, the behavior of many Christians. Check your life against Paul's list. Don't give in to society's pressures. Don't settle for comfort without commitment. Stand up against evil by living as God would have his people live.

3:5 The "act" or appearance of being religious includes going to church, knowing Christian doctrine, using Christian clichés, and following a community's Christian traditions. Such practices can make a person look good, but if the inner attitudes of belief, love, and worship are lacking, the outer appearance is meaningless. Paul warns us not to be deceived by people who only appear to be Christians. It may be difficult to distinguish them from true Christians at first, but their daily behavior will give them away. The characteristics described in 3:2-4 are unmistakable.

3:6, 7 Because of their cultural background, women in the Ephesian church had had no formal religious training. They enjoyed their new freedom to study Christian truths, but their eagerness to learn made them a target for false teachers. Paul warned Timothy to watch out for men who would take advantage of these women. New believers need to grow in their knowledge of the Word, because ignorance can make them vulnerable to deception.

3:7 This verse is not opposing study and learning; it is warning about ineffective learning. It is possible to be a perpetual student and never graduate to putting theory into practice. But honest seekers and true students look for answers. Remember this as you study God's Word. Seek to find God's truth and will for your life.

3:8, 9 According to tradition, Jannes and Jambres were two of the magicians who counterfeited Moses' miracles before Pharaoh (Exodus 7:11, 12). Paul explained that just as Moses exposed and defeated them (Exodus 8:18, 19), God would overthrow the false teachers who were plaguing the Ephesian church.

3:9 Sin has consequences, and no one will get away with it forever. Live each day as if your actions will one day be known to everyone. Now is the time to change anything you wouldn't want revealed later.

3:11 In Lystra, Timothy's hometown, Paul had been stoned and left for dead (Acts 14:19); and this was only one incident among many. In 2 Corinthians 11:23-33 Paul summarized his lifetime of suffering for the sake of the Good News. Paul mentioned his suffering here to contrast his experience with that of the pleasure-seeking false teachers.

all about how I was persecuted in Antioch, Iconium, and Lystra—but the Lord delivered
3:12 John 15:20 Acts 14:22 me from all of it. 12 Yes, and everyone who wants to live a godly life in Christ Jesus will
suffer persecution. 13 But evil people and impostors will flourish. They will go on
deceiving others, and they themselves will be deceived.
3:14 2 Tim 1:13; 2:2 14 But you must remain faithful to the things you have been taught. You know they are
3:15 John 5:39 true, for you know you can trust those who taught you. 15 You have been taught the holy
Scriptures from childhood, and they have given you the wisdom to receive the salvation
3:16 Rom 15:4 2 Pet 1:20-21 that comes by trusting in Christ Jesus. 16 All Scripture is inspired by God and is useful to
teach us what is true and to make us realize what is wrong in our lives. It straightens us
3:17 1 Tim 6:11 2 Tim 2:21 out and teaches us to do what is right. 17 It is God's way of preparing us in every way,
fully equipped for every good thing God wants us to do.

4:1 Acts 10:42 **4** And so I solemnly urge you before God and before Christ Jesus—who will someday
4:2 1 Tim 5:20 Titus 1:13 judge the living and the dead when he appears to set up his Kingdom: 2 Preach the
word of God. Be persistent, whether the time is favorable or not. Patiently correct,
rebuke, and encourage your people with good teaching.
4:3 2 Tim 3:1 3 For a time is coming when people will no longer listen to right teaching. They will
4:4 1 Tim 1:4 follow their own desires and will look for teachers who will tell them whatever they want
to hear. 4 They will reject the truth and follow strange myths.
4:5 2 Tim 1:8 5 But you should keep a clear mind in every situation. Don't be afraid of suffering

---

3:12 In this charge, Paul told Timothy that people who obey God and live for Christ will be persecuted. Don't be surprised when people misunderstand, criticize, and even try to hurt you because of what you believe and how you live. Don't give up. Continue to live as you know you should. God is the only one you need to please.

3:13 Don't expect false teachers and evil people to reform and change on their own. Left alone, they will go from bad to worse. If you have the opportunity, correct them so as to bring them back to faith in Christ. Fight for the truth, especially to protect younger Christians.

3:14 Besieged by false teachers and the inevitable pressures of a growing ministry, Timothy could easily have abandoned his faith or modified his doctrine. Once again Paul counseled Timothy to look to his past and to hold to the basic teachings about Jesus that are eternally true. Like Timothy, we are surrounded by false teachings. But we must not allow our society to distort or crowd out God's eternal truth. Spend time every day reflecting on the foundation of your Christian faith found in God's Word, the great truths that build up your life.

3:15 Timothy was one of the first second-generation Christians: He became a Christian, not because an evangelist preached a powerful sermon, but because his mother and grandmother taught him the holy Scriptures when he was a small child (1:5). A parent's work is vitally important. At home and in church, we should realize that teaching small children is both an opportunity and a responsibility. Jesus wanted little children to come to him (Matthew 19:13-15). Like Timothy's mother and grandmother, Eunice and Lois, do your part in leading children to Christ.

3:15 For Timothy, the "holy Scriptures" were the books of the Old Testament—Genesis to Malachi. The Old Testament is important because it points to Jesus Christ. At the same time, faith in Christ makes the whole Bible intelligible.

3:16 The Bible is not a collection of stories, fables, myths, or merely human ideas about God. It is not a human book. Through the Holy Spirit, God revealed his person and plan to certain believers, who wrote down his message for his people (2 Peter 1:20, 21). This process is known as *inspiration.* The writers wrote from their own personal, historical, and cultural contexts. Although they used their own minds, talents, language, and style, they wrote what God wanted them to write. Scripture is completely trustworthy because God was in control of its writing. Its words are entirely authoritative for our faith and life. The Bible is "God-breathed." Read it, and use its teachings to guide your conduct.

3:16, 17 The whole Bible is God's inspired Word. Because it is inspired and trustworthy, we should *read* it and *apply* it to our life. The Bible is our standard for testing everything else that claims to be true. It is our safeguard against false teaching and our source of guidance for how we should live. It is our only source of knowledge about how we can be saved. God wants to show you what is true and equip you to live for him. How much time do you spend in God's Word? Read it regularly to discover God's truth and to become confident in your life and faith. Develop a plan for reading the whole Bible, not just the familiar passages.

3:17 In our zeal for the *truth* of Scripture, we must never forget its *purpose*—to equip us to do good. We should not study God's Word simply to increase our knowledge or to prepare us to win arguments. We should study the Bible so that we will know how to do Christ's work in the world. Our knowledge of God's Word is not useful unless it strengthens our faith and leads us to do good.

4:1, 2 It was important for Timothy to preach the Good News so that the Christian faith could spread throughout the world. We believe in Christ today because people like Timothy were faithful to their mission. It is still vitally important for believers to spread the Good News. Half the people who have ever lived are alive today, and most of them do not know Christ. He is coming soon, and he wants to find his faithful believers ready for him. It may be inconvenient to take a stand for Christ or to tell others about his love, but preaching the Word of God is the most important responsibility the church and its members have been given. Be prepared for, courageous in, and sensitive to God-given opportunities to tell the Good News.

4:2 We should always be ready to serve God in any situation, whether or not it is convenient. Be sensitive to the opportunities God gives you.

4:2 Paul told Timothy to "correct, rebuke and encourage." It is difficult to accept correction, to be told we have to change. But no matter how much the truth hurts, we must be willing to listen to it so we can more fully obey God.

4:5 To keep cool when you are jarred and jolted by people or circumstances, don't react quickly. In any work of ministry that you undertake, keeping your head makes you morally alert to temptation, resistant to pressure, and vigilant when facing heavy responsibility.

for the Lord. Work at bringing others to Christ. Complete the ministry God has given
you.

Paul's Final Words

6 As for me, my life has already been poured out as an offering to God. The time of my
death is near. 7 I have fought a good fight, I have finished the race, and I have remained
faithful. 8 And now the prize awaits me—the crown of righteousness that the Lord, the
righteous Judge, will give me on that great day of his return. And the prize is not just for
me but for all who eagerly look forward to his glorious return.
9 Please come as soon as you can. 10 Demas has deserted me because he loves the things
of this life and has gone to Thessalonica. Crescens has gone to Galatia, and Titus has
gone to Dalmatia. 11 Only Luke is with me. Bring Mark with you when you come, for he
will be helpful to me. 12 I sent Tychicus to Ephesus. 13 When you come, be sure to bring
the coat I left with Carpus at Troas. Also bring my books, and especially my papers.*
14 Alexander the coppersmith has done me much harm, but the Lord will judge him for
what he has done. 15 Be careful of him, for he fought against everything we said.
16 The first time I was brought before the judge, no one was with me. Everyone had
abandoned me. I hope it will not be counted against them. 17 But the Lord stood with me
and gave me strength, that I might preach the Good News in all its fullness for all the
Gentiles to hear. And he saved me from certain death.* 18 Yes, and the Lord will deliver
me from every evil attack and will bring me safely to his heavenly Kingdom. To God be
the glory forever and ever. Amen.

4:7 1 Cor 9:24-27 Phil 3:12-14 1 Tim 6:12
4:8 1 Cor 9:25 Phil 3:14 Col 1:5 Rev 2:10
4:11 Col 4:10, 14 Phlm 1:24
4:12 Acts 20:4 Eph 6:21-22 Col 4:7-8
4:14 1 Tim 1:20
4:17 Ps 22:21 Dan 6:22 Acts 9:15
4:18 Ps 121:7 Rom 11:36

4:13 Greek *especially the parchments.* **4:17** Greek *from the mouth of a lion.*

4:5-8 As he neared the end of his life, Paul could confidently say he had been faithful to his call. Thus, he faced death calmly, knowing that he would be rewarded by Christ. Is your life preparing you for death? Do you share Paul's confident expectation of meeting Christ? The good news is that the heavenly reward is not just for giants of the faith, like Paul, but for all who are eagerly looking forward to Christ's second coming. Paul gave these words to encourage Timothy and us, so that no matter how difficult the fight seems, we can keep fighting. When we are with Jesus Christ, we will discover that it was all worth it.

4:6 A drink offering consisted of wine poured out on an altar as a sacrifice to God (see Genesis 35:14; Exodus 29:41). Its fragrance was considered pleasing to God. Paul viewed his life as an offering to God.

4:8 In Roman athletic games, a laurel wreath was given to the winners. A symbol of triumph and honor, it was the most coveted prize in ancient Rome. This is probably what Paul was referring to when he spoke of a "crown." But his would be a crown of righteousness. See 2 Corinthians 5:10 and the note on Matthew 19:27 for more on the rewards awaiting us for our faith and deeds. Although Paul would not receive an earthly reward, he would be rewarded in heaven. Whatever we may face—discouragement, persecution, or death—we know our reward is with Christ in heaven.

4:9, 10 Paul was virtually alone and probably lonely. No one had been there at his trial to speak in his defense (4:16), and Demas had left the faith (4:10). Only Luke had returned (4:11).

4:10 Demas had been one of Paul's co-workers (Colossians 4:14; Philemon 1:24), but he had deserted Paul because he loved "the things of this life." In other words, Demas loved worldly values and worldly pleasures. There are two ways to love the world. God loves the world as he created it and as it could be if it were rescued from evil. Others, like Demas, love the world as it is, sin and all. Do you love the world as it could be if justice were done, the hungry were fed, and people loved one another? Or do you love what the world has to offer—wealth, power, pleasure—even if gaining it means hurting people and neglecting the work God has given you to do?

4:11 Crescens and Titus had left, but not for the same reasons as Demas. Paul did not criticize or condemn them.

4:11, 12 Mentioning Demas reminded Paul of more faithful co-workers. Only Luke was with Paul, and Paul was feeling lonely. Tychicus, one of his most trusted companions (Acts 20:4; Ephesians 6:21; Colossians 4:7; Titus 3:12), had already left for Ephesus. Paul missed his young helpers Timothy and Mark. Mark had left Paul and Barnabas on the first missionary journey, and this had greatly upset Paul (Acts 13:13; 15:36-41). But later Mark proved to be a worthy helper, and Paul recognized him as a good friend and trusted Christian leader (Colossians 4:10; Philemon 1:24). Mark wrote the Gospel of Mark.

4:13 Paul's arrest probably occurred so suddenly that he was not allowed to return home to gather his personal belongings. Because he was a prisoner in a damp and chilly dungeon, Paul asked Timothy to bring him his coat. Even more than the coat, Paul wanted his papers (or parchments). These may have included parts of the Old Testament, the Gospels, copies of his own letters, or other important documents.

4:14, 15 Alexander may have been a witness against Paul at his trial. He may have been the Alexander mentioned in 1 Timothy 1:20.

4:17 With his mentor in prison and his church in turmoil, Timothy was probably not feeling very brave. Paul may have been subtly telling Timothy that the Lord had called Timothy to preach and would give him the courage to continue to do so. God always gives us the strength to do what he has commanded. This strength may not be evident, however, until we step out in faith and actually begin doing the task.

4:17 Some have seen this as a reference to Nero throwing Christians to the lions in the Coliseum. More likely, it is Paul's way of describing his deliverance at his first defense (see, for example, Psalm 22:21.

4:18 Here Paul was affirming his belief in eternal life after death. Paul knew the end was near, and he was ready for it. Paul was confident in God's power even as he faced death. Anyone facing a life-and-death struggle can be comforted knowing that God will bring each believer safely through death to his heavenly Kingdom.

Paul's Final Greetings

4:19 Acts 18:2 2 Tim 1:16

4:20 Acts 19:22; 20:4 Rom 16:23

19 Give my greetings to Priscilla and Aquila and those living at the household of
Onesiphorus. 20 Erastus stayed at Corinth, and I left Trophimus sick at Miletus.
21 Hurry so you can get here before winter. Eubulus sends you greetings, and so do
Pudens, Linus, Claudia, and all the brothers and sisters.
22 May the Lord be with your spirit. Grace be with you all.

4:19, 20 Priscilla and Aquila were fellow Christian leaders with whom Paul had lived and worked (Acts 18:2, 3). Onesiphorus visited and encouraged Paul in jail. Erastus was one of Paul's trusted companions (Acts 19:22), as was Trophimus (Acts 20:4; 21:29).

4:19-22 Paul ended the final chapter in his book and in his life by greeting those who were closest to him. Although Paul had spent most of his life traveling, he had developed close and lasting friendships. Too often we rush through our days, barely touching anyone's life. Like Paul, we should take time to weave our life into others' through close personal relationships.

4:22 As Paul reached the end of his life, he could look back and know he had been faithful to God's call. Now it was time to pass the torch to the next generation, preparing leaders to take his place so that the world would continue to hear the life-changing message of Jesus Christ. Timothy was Paul's living legacy, a product of Paul's faithful teaching, discipleship, and example. Because of Paul's work with many believers, including Timothy, the world is full of believers today who are also carrying on the work. What legacy will you leave behind? Whom are you training to carry on your work? It is our responsibility to do all we can to keep the Good News message alive for the next generation.

TITUS

VITAL STATISTICS

PURPOSE:
To advise Titus in his responsibility of supervising the churches on the island of Crete

AUTHOR:
Paul

TO WHOM WRITTEN:
Titus, a Greek, probably converted to Christ through Paul's ministry (he had become Paul's special representative to the island of Crete), and all believers everywhere

DATE WRITTEN:
Approximately A.D. 64, around the same time 1 Timothy was written; probably from Macedonia when Paul traveled between his Roman imprisonments

SETTING:
Paul sent Titus to organize and oversee the churches on Crete. This letter tells Titus how to do this job.

KEY VERSE:
"I left you on the island of Crete so you could complete our work there and appoint elders in each town as I instructed you" (1:5).

KEY PEOPLE:
Paul, Titus

KEY PLACES:
Crete, Nicopolis

SPECIAL FEATURES:
Titus is very similar to 1 Timothy with its instructions to church leaders.

THE VACUUM produced when a strong leader departs can devastate a movement, organization, or institution. Having been dependent on his or her skill, style, and personality, associates and subordinates flounder or vie for control. Soon efficiency and vitality are lost, and decline and demise follow. Often this pattern is repeated in churches. Great speakers and teachers gather a following, and soon a church is flourishing. It is alive, vital, and effective. Lives are being changed and people led into the Kingdom. But when this person leaves or dies, with him or her goes the drive and the heart of the organization.

People flocked to hear Paul's teaching. Educated, articulate, motivated, and filled with the Holy Spirit, this man of God faithfully proclaimed the Good News throughout the Roman Empire; lives were changed and churches begun. But Paul knew that the church must be built on Christ, not on a person. And he knew that eventually he would not be there to build, encourage, discipline, and teach. So he trained young pastors to assume leadership in the churches after he was gone. Paul urged them to center their lives and preaching on the Word of God (2 Timothy 3:16, 17) and to train others to carry on the ministry (2 Timothy 2:2).

Titus was a Greek believer. Taught and nurtured by Paul, he stood before the leaders of the church in Jerusalem as a living example of what Christ was doing among the Gentiles (Galatians 2:1–3). Like Timothy, he was one of Paul's trusted traveling companions and closest friends. Later he became Paul's special ambassador (2 Corinthians 7:5–16) and eventually the overseer of the churches on Crete (Titus 1:5). Slowly and carefully, Paul developed Titus into a mature Christian and a responsible leader. The letter to Titus was a step in this discipleship process. As with Timothy, Paul told Titus how to organize and lead the churches.

Paul begins with a longer than usual greeting and introduction, outlining the leadership progression: Paul's ministry (1:1–3), Titus's responsibilities (1:4, 5), and those leaders whom Titus would appoint and train (1:5). Paul then lists pastoral qualifications (1:6–9) and contrasts faithful elders with the false leaders and teachers (1:10–16).

Next, Paul emphasizes the importance of good deeds in the life of the Christian, telling Titus how to relate to the various age groups in the church (2:2–6). He urges Titus to be a good example of a mature believer (2:7, 8) and to teach with courage and conviction (2:9–15). He then discusses the general responsibilities of Christians in society: Titus should remind the people of these (3:1–8), and he should avoid divisive arguments (3:9–11). Paul concludes with a few matters of itinerary and personal greetings (3:12–15).

Paul's letter to Titus is brief, but it is an important link in the discipleship process, helping a young man grow into leadership in the church. As you read this pastoral letter, you will gain insight into the organization and life of the early church, and you will find principles for structuring contemporary churches. But you should also see how to be a responsible Christian leader. Read the letter to Titus and determine, like Paul, to train men and women to lead and teach others.

THE BLUEPRINT

1. Leadership in the church (1:1–16)
2. Right living in the church (2:1–15)
3. Right living in society (3:1–15)

Paul calls for church order and right living on an island known for laziness, gluttony, lying, and evil. The Christians are to be self-disciplined as individuals, and they must be orderly as people who form one body, the church. We need to obey this message in our day when discipline is not respected or rewarded by our society. Although others may not appreciate our efforts, we must live upright lives, obey the government, and control our speech. We should live together peacefully in the church and be living examples of our faith to contemporary society.

MEGATHEMES

THEME	EXPLANATION	IMPORTANCE
A Good Life	The Good News of salvation is that we can't be saved by living a good life; we are saved only by faith in Jesus Christ. But the gospel transforms people's lives, so that they eventually perform good deeds. Our service won't save us, but we are saved to serve.	A good life is a witness to the gospel's power. As Christians, we must have commitment and discipline to serve. Are you putting your faith into action by serving others?
Character	Titus's responsibility in Crete was to appoint elders to maintain proper organization and discipline, so Paul listed the qualities needed for the eldership. Their conduct in their homes revealed their fitness for service in the church.	It's not enough to be educated or to have a loyal following to be Christ's kind of leader. You must have self-control, spiritual and moral fitness, and Christian character. Who you are is just as important as what you can do.
Church Relationships	Church teaching must relate to various groups. Older Christians were to teach and to be examples to younger men and women. People of every age and group have a lesson to learn and a role to play.	Right living and right relationships go along with right doctrine. Treat relationships with other believers as an outgrowth of your faith.
Citizenship	Christians must be good citizens in society, not just in church. Believers must obey the government and work honestly.	How you fulfill your civic duties is a witness to the watching world. Your community life should reflect Christ's love as much as your church life does.

1. Leadership in the church

Greetings from Paul

1 This letter is from Paul, a slave of God and an apostle of Jesus Christ. I have been
sent to bring faith to those God has chosen and to teach them to know the truth
that shows them how to live godly lives. 2This truth gives them the confidence of
eternal life, which God promised them before the world began—and he cannot lie.
3And now at the right time he has revealed this Good News, and we announce it to
everyone. It is by the command of God our Savior that I have been trusted to do this
work for him.
4This letter is written to Titus, my true child in the faith that we share.
May God the Father and Christ Jesus our Savior give you grace and peace.

1:1 1 Tim 2:4
1:2 2 Tim 1:1, 9; Titus 3:7
1:3 1 Tim 1:1, 11; Titus 2:10
1:4 2 Cor 2:13; 2 Tim 4:10

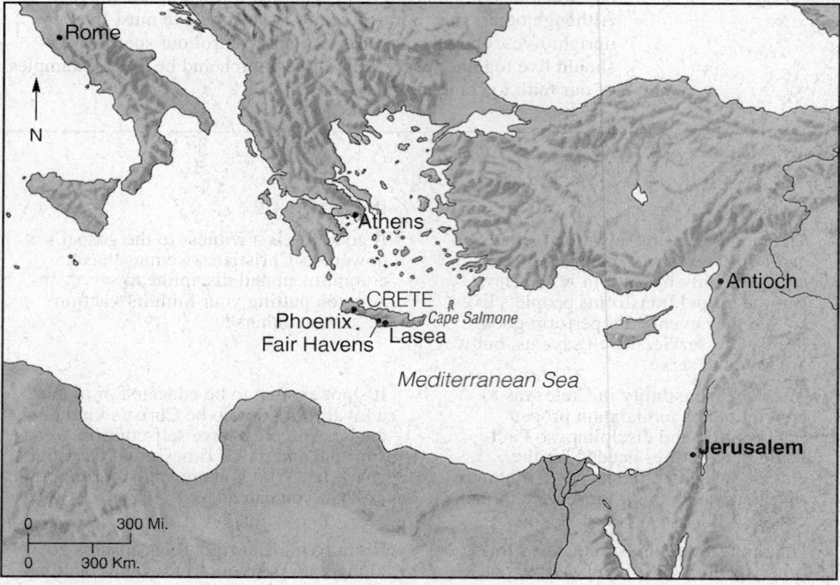

TITUS GOES TO CRETE
Tradition says that after Paul was released from prison in Rome (before his second and final Roman imprisonment), he and Titus traveled together for a while. They stopped in Crete, and when it was time for Paul to go, he left Titus behind to help the churches there.

1:1 Paul wrote this letter between his first and second imprisonments in Rome (before he wrote 2 Timothy) to guide Titus in working with the churches on the island of Crete. Paul had visited Crete with Titus and had left him there to minister (1:5). There was a strong pagan influence on this small island because Crete may have been a training center for Roman soldiers. Therefore, the church in Crete needed strong Christian leadership.

1:1 In one short phrase, Paul gives us insight into his reason for living. He calls himself "a slave of God"—that is, one who was committed to obeying God. This obedience led him to spend his life telling others about Christ. How would you describe your purpose in life? To what are you devoted? For more information on Paul, see his Profile in Acts 9.

1:1 Paul called himself "an apostle." Even though Paul was not one of the original 12, he was specially called by God to bring the Good News to the Gentiles (see Acts 9:1-16 for an account of his call). The word *apostle* means "messenger or missionary." "Those God has chosen" refers to God's choice of his people, the church.

1:2 Apparently lying was commonplace in Crete (1:12). Paul made it clear at the start that God does not lie. The foundation of our faith is trust in God's character. Because God *is* truth, he is the *source* of all truth, and he cannot lie. Believing in him leads to living a God-honoring life-style (1:1). The eternal life that God has promised will be ours because he keeps his promises. Build your faith on the foundation of a trustworthy God who never lies.

1:3 God is called "our Savior," as is Christ Jesus (1:4). "God" here refers to the Father. Jesus did the work of salvation by dying for our sins, and, therefore, he is our Savior. God planned the work of salvation, and he forgives our sins. Both the Father and the Son acted to save us from our sins.

1:4 Titus, a Greek, was one of Paul's most trusted and dependable co-workers. Paul sent Titus to Corinth on several special missions to help the church in its troubles (2 Corinthians 7–8). Paul and Titus also traveled together to Jerusalem (Galatians 2:3) and Crete (1:5). Paul left Titus in Crete to lead the new churches springing up on the island. Titus is last mentioned by Paul in 2 Timothy 4:10, Paul's last recorded letter. Titus had leadership ability, so Paul gave him leadership responsibility, urging him to use his abilities well.

Titus's Work in Crete

1:5 Acts 14:23
1:6-9 //1 Tim 3:2-7; 2 Tim 2:24-26
1:7 1 Cor 4:1
1:9 1 Tim 1:10; 2 Tim 4:3; Titus 2:1
1:10 1 Tim 1:6
1:11 1 Tim 5:13
1:13 1 Tim 5:20
1:14 Col 2:22; 1 Tim 1:4; 4:7; 2 Tim 4:4
1:15 Matt 15:10-11; Rom 14:14-20
1:16 1 Jn 1:6; 2:4

5 I left you on the island of Crete so you could complete our work there and appoint elders
in each town as I instructed you. 6 An elder must be well thought of for his good life. He
must be faithful to his wife,* and his children must be believers who are not wild or
rebellious. 7 An elder* must live a blameless life because he is God's minister. He must
not be arrogant or quick-tempered; he must not be a heavy drinker, violent, or greedy for
money. 8 He must enjoy having guests in his home and must love all that is good. He must
live wisely and be fair. He must live a devout and disciplined life. 9 He must have a strong
and steadfast belief in the trustworthy message he was taught; then he will be able to
encourage others with right teaching and show those who oppose it where they are
wrong.

10 For there are many who rebel against right teaching; they engage in useless talk and
deceive people. This is especially true of those who insist on circumcision for salvation.
11 They must be silenced. By their wrong teaching, they have already turned whole
families away from the truth. Such teachers only want your money. 12 One of their own
men, a prophet from Crete, has said about them, "The people of Crete are all liars; they
are cruel animals and lazy gluttons." 13 This is true. So rebuke them as sternly as
necessary to make them strong in the faith. 14 They must stop listening to Jewish myths
and the commands of people who have turned their backs on the truth.

15 Everything is pure to those whose hearts are pure. But nothing is pure to those who
are corrupt and unbelieving, because their minds and consciences are defiled. 16 Such
people claim they know God, but they deny him by the way they live. They are
despicable and disobedient, worthless for doing anything good.

1:6 Or *have only one wife,* or *be married only once;* Greek reads *be the husband of one wife.* **1:7** Greek *overseer.*

1:5 Crete, a small island in the Mediterranean Sea, had a large population of Jews. The churches there were probably founded by Cretan Jews who had been in Jerusalem at Pentecost (Acts 2:11) more than 30 years before Paul wrote this letter.

1:5 The work that needed completion refers to establishing correct teaching and appointing elders in every town.

1:5 Paul had appointed elders in various churches during his journeys (Acts 14:23). He could not stay in each church, but he knew that these new churches needed strong spiritual leadership. The men chosen were to lead the churches by teaching sound doctrine, helping believers mature spiritually, and equipping them to live for Jesus Christ despite opposition.

1:5-9 Paul briefly described some qualifications that the elders or overseers should have. Paul had given Timothy a similar set of instructions for the church in Ephesus (see 1 Timothy 3:1-7; 5:22). Notice that most of the qualifications involve character, not knowledge or skill. A person's life-style and relationships provide a window into his or her character. Consider these qualifications as you evaluate a person for a position of leadership in your church. It is important to have leaders who can effectively preach God's Word, but it is even more important to have those who can live out God's Word and be examples for others to follow.

1:10 "Those who insist on circumcision for salvation" were the Judaizers, Jews who taught that the Gentiles had to obey all the Jewish laws before they could become Christians. This regulation confused new Christians and caused problems in many churches where Paul had preached the Good News. Paul wrote letters to several churches to help them understand that Gentile believers did not have to become Jews first in order to be Christians; God accepts anyone who comes to him in faith (see Romans 1:17; Galatians 3:2-7). Although the Jerusalem council had dealt with this issue (see Acts 15), devout Jews who refused to believe in Jesus still tried to cause problems in the Christian churches. Church leaders must be alert and take action on anything that divides Christians.

1:10-14 Paul warned Titus to be on the lookout for people who teach wrong doctrines and lead others into error. Some false teachers are simply confused: They speak their misguided opinions without checking them against the Bible. Others have evil motives: They pretend to be Christians only because they can get more money, additional business, or a feeling of power from being a leader in the church. Jesus and the apostles repeatedly warned against false teachers (see Mark 13:22; Acts 20:29; 2 Thessalonians 2:3-12; 2 Peter 3:3-7) because their teachings attack the foundations of truth and integrity upon which the Christian faith is built. You can recognize false teachers because they will (1) focus more attention on themselves than on Christ; (2) ask you to do something that will compromise or dilute your faith; (3) de-emphasize the divine nature of Christ or the inspiration of the Bible; or (4) urge believers to make decisions based more on human judgment than on prayer and biblical guidelines.

1:12 Paul was quoting a line from a poem by Epimenides, a poet and philosopher who had lived in Crete 600 years earlier. Some Cretans had a bad reputation and were known for lying. Paul used this familiar phrase to make the point that Titus's ministry and leadership were very much needed.

1:15 Some people see good all around them, while others see nothing but evil. What is the difference? Our souls become filters through which we perceive goodness or evil. The pure (those who have Christ in control of their lives) learn to see goodness and purity even in this evil world. But corrupt and unbelieving people find evil in everything because their evil minds and hearts color even the good they see and hear. Whatever you choose to fill your mind with will affect the way you think and act. Turn your thoughts to God and his Word, and you will discover more and more goodness, even in this evil world. A mind filled with good has little room for what is evil (see Philippians 4:8).

1:16 Many people claim to know God. How can we know if they really do? We will not know for certain in this life, but a glance at their life-styles will quickly tell us what they value and whether they have ordered their lives around Kingdom priorities. Our conduct speaks volumes about what we believe (see 1 John 2:4-6). What do people know about God and about your faith by watching your life?

2. Right living in the church

Promote Right Teaching

2 But as for you, promote the kind of living that reflects right teaching. [2]Teach the
older men to exercise self-control, to be worthy of respect, and to live wisely. They
must have strong faith and be filled with love and patience.
[3]Similarly, teach the older women to live in a way that is appropriate for someone
serving the Lord. They must not go around speaking evil of others and must not be heavy
drinkers. Instead, they should teach others what is good. [4]These older women must train
the younger women to love their husbands and their children, [5]to live wisely and be pure,
to take care of their homes, to do good, and to be submissive to their husbands. Then
they will not bring shame on the word of God.
[6]In the same way, encourage the young men to live wisely in all they do. [7]And you
yourself must be an example to them by doing good deeds of every kind. Let everything
you do reflect the integrity and seriousness of your teaching. [8]Let your teaching be so
correct that it can't be criticized. Then those who want to argue will be ashamed because
they won't have anything bad to say about us.
[9]Slaves must obey their masters and do their best to please them. They must not talk
back [10]or steal, but they must show themselves to be entirely trustworthy and good. Then
they will make the teaching about God our Savior attractive in every way.
[11]For the grace of God has been revealed, bringing salvation to all people. [12]And we
are instructed to turn from godless living and sinful pleasures. We should live in this evil
world with self-control, right conduct, and devotion to God, [13]while we look forward to
that wonderful event when the glory of our great God and Savior, Jesus Christ, will be
revealed. [14]He gave his life to free us from every kind of sin, to cleanse us, and to make

2:1 1 Tim 1:10; Titus 1:9
2:3 1 Tim 3:8, 11
2:5 Eph 5:22; 1 Tim 5:14
2:7 1 Tim 4:12; 1 Pet 5:3
2:8 1 Pet 2:12
2:9 Eph 6:5
2:11 1 Tim 2:4; 2 Tim 1:10
2:13 John 1:1; 20:28; Rom 9:5; 1 Cor 1:7; Phil 3:20; 2 Pet 1:1; 1 Jn 5:20
2:14 Eph 2:10; 1 Pet 2:9; 1 Jn 1:7

2:1 Notice the emphasis on "right teaching" in Paul's instructions to Titus. This is the *content* of our faith. Believers must be grounded in the truths of the Bible so they won't be swayed by the powerful oratory of false teachers, the possible devastation of tragic circumstances, or the pull of emotions. Learn the Bible, study theology, apply biblical principles, and *do* what you learn.

2:1-8 Having people of all ages in the church makes it strong, but it also brings potential for problems. Paul gave Titus counsel on how to help various groups of people. The older people should teach the younger by words *and* by example. This is how values are passed on from generation to generation. Does your church carry out this basic function?

2:2, 5 Self-control was an important aspect in early Christianity. The Christian community was made up of people from differing backgrounds and viewpoints, making conflict inevitable. Christians existed in a pagan and often hostile world. To stay above reproach, men and women need wisdom and discernment to be discreet and to master their wills, tongues, and passions so that Christ is not dishonored. How is your self-control?

2:3-5 Women who were new Christians were to learn how to have harmony in the home by watching older women who had been Christians for some time. We have the same need today. Young wives and mothers should learn to live in a Christian manner—loving their husbands and caring for their children—through observing exemplary women of God. If you are of an age or in a position where people look up to you, make sure that your example is motivating younger believers to live in a way that honors God.

2:6 This advice given to young men was very important. In ancient Greek society, the role of the husband/father was not viewed as a nurturing role but merely as a functional one. Many young men today have been raised in families where fathers have neglected their responsibilities to their wives and children. Husbands and fathers who are good examples of Christian living are important role models for young men who need to *see* how it is done.

2:7 When Paul encouraged Titus, and through Titus other young men, to be serious, he wanted them to be reverent and purposeful. Christianity should never be intentionally boring or gloomy. Don't let the seriousness of the Good News cause you to repel others by your grim disposition.

2:7, 8 Paul urged Titus to be a good example to those around him so that others might see Titus's good deeds and imitate him. Paul's life would give his words greater impact. If you want someone to act a certain way, be sure that you live that way yourself. Then you will earn the right to be heard, and your life will reinforce what you teach.

2:8 Paul counseled Titus to be above criticism in how he taught. This quality of integrity comes from careful Bible study and listening before speaking. This is especially important when teaching or confronting others about spiritual or moral issues. If we are impulsive, unreasonable, and confusing, we are likely to start arguments rather than to convince people of the truth.

2:9, 10 Slavery was common in Paul's day. Paul did not condemn slavery in any of his letters, but he advised slaves and masters to be loving and responsible in their conduct (see also Ephesians 6:5-9). The standards set by Paul can help any employee/employer relationship. Employees should always do their best work and be trustworthy, not just when the employer is watching. Businesses lose millions of dollars a year to employee theft and time-wasting. If all Christian employees would follow Paul's advice at work, what a transformation it would make!

2:11-14 The power to live as a Christian comes from the Holy Spirit. Because Christ died and rescued us from sin, we are free from sin's control. God gives us the power and understanding to live according to his will and to do good. Then we will look forward to Christ's wonderful return with eager expectation and hope.

2:12 It is not enough to renounce sin and evil desires; we must also live actively for God. To fight against lust, we must say no to temptation, but we must also say yes to active service for Christ.

2:14 Christ's freeing us from sin opens the way for him to purify us. He freed us from sin (redeemed us) by purchasing our release from the captivity of sin with a ransom (see Mark 10:45 for more on Christ as our ransom). We are not only free from the sentence of death for our sin, but we are also purified from sin's influence as we grow in Christ.

2:15 1 Tim 4:12 us his very own people, totally committed to doing what is right. [15]You must teach these
things and encourage your people to do them, correcting them when necessary. You have
the authority to do this, so don't let anyone ignore you or disregard what you say.

3. Right living in society

Do What Is Good

3:1 Rom 13:1 1 Pet 2:13 **3** Remind your people to submit to the government and its officers. They should be
obedient, always ready to do what is good. [2]They must not speak evil of anyone,
3:2 Eph 4:31 and they must avoid quarreling. Instead, they should be gentle and show true humility
to everyone.

3:3 1 Cor 6:11 Eph 5:8 [3]Once we, too, were foolish and disobedient. We were misled by others and became
slaves to many wicked desires and evil pleasures. Our lives were full of evil and envy.
3:5 John 3:5 Eph 2:4, 8 1 Pet 1:3 We hated others, and they hated us.

[4]But then God our Savior showed us his kindness and love. [5]He saved us, not because
of the good things we did, but because of his mercy. He washed away our sins and gave
3:6 Joel 2:28 Rom 5:5 us a new life through the Holy Spirit.* [6]He generously poured out the Spirit upon us
because of what Jesus Christ our Savior did. [7]He declared us not guilty because of his
3:7 Rom 3:24 great kindness. And now we know that we will inherit eternal life. [8]These things I have
3:8 Titus 2:14; 3:14 told you are all true. I want you to insist on them so that everyone who trusts in God will
be careful to do good deeds all the time. These things are good and beneficial for
everyone.

Paul's Final Remarks and Greetings

3:9 2 Tim 2:14, 16, 23 [9]Do not get involved in foolish discussions about spiritual pedigrees* or in quarrels and
3:10 Matt 18:15-17 Rom 16:17 fights about obedience to Jewish laws. These kinds of things are useless and a waste of
time. [10]If anyone is causing divisions among you, give a first and second warning. After
that, have nothing more to do with that person. [11]For people like that have turned away
3:12 Acts 20:4 Eph 6:21-22 2 Tim 4:9, 21 from the truth. They are sinning, and they condemn themselves.
[12]I am planning to send either Artemas or Tychicus to you. As soon as one of them

3:5 Greek *He saved us through the washing of regeneration and renewing of the Holy Spirit.* **3:9** Greek *discussions and genealogies.*

2:15 Paul told Titus to teach the Scriptures as well as to live them. We must also teach, encourage, and correct others when necessary. It is easy to feel afraid when others are older, more influential in the community, or wealthier. Like Titus, we should not let ourselves be threatened when we are trying to minister to others or provide leadership in the church.

3:1, 2 As Christians, our first allegiance is to Jesus as Lord, but we must obey our government and its leaders as well. Christians are not above the law. Obeying the civil law is only the beginning of our Christian responsibility; we must do what we can to be good citizens. In a democracy, this means participation and willingness to serve. (See Acts 5:29 and Romans 13:1ff for more on the Christian's attitude toward government.)

3:3 Following a life of pleasure and giving in to every sensual desire leads to slavery. Many think freedom consists in doing anything they want. But this path leads to a slavish addiction to sensual gratification. A person is no longer free but is a slave to what his or her body dictates (2 Peter 2:19). Christ frees us from the desires and control of sin. Have you been released?

3:3-8 Paul summarized what Christ does for us when he saves us. We move from a life full of sin to one where we are led by God's Holy Spirit. *All* our sins, not merely some, are washed away. Washing refers to the water of baptism, which is a sign of salvation. In becoming a Christian, the believer acknowledges Christ as Lord and recognizes Christ's saving work. We gain eternal life with *all* its treasures. We have a new life through the Holy Spirit, and he continually renews our hearts. None of this occurs because we earned or deserved it; it is all God's gift.

3:4-6 All three persons of the Trinity are mentioned in these verses because all three participate in the work of salvation. Based upon the redemptive work of his Son, the Father forgives us and sends the Holy Spirit to wash away our sins and continually renew us.

3:9 Paul warned Titus, as he warned Timothy, not to get involved in foolish and unprofitable arguments (2 Timothy 2:14). This does not mean we should refuse to study, discuss, and examine different interpretations of difficult Bible passages. Paul is warning against petty quarrels, not honest discussion that leads to wisdom. As foolish arguments develop, it is best to turn the discussion back to a helpful direction or politely excuse yourself.

3:9 The false teachers were basing their heresies on genealogies and speculations about the law (see 1 Timothy 1:3, 4). Similar to the methods used by false teachers in Ephesus and Colosse, they were building their case on genealogies of angels. We should avoid false teachers, not even bothering to get involved in their foolish discussions. Our overreaction can sometimes give more attention to their points of view.

3:9-11 A person must be warned when he or she is causing division that threatens the unity of the church. This should not be a heavy-handed action, but a warning to correct the individual's divisive nature and restore him or her to fellowship. A person who refuses to be corrected should be put outside the fellowship. As Paul said, that person is self-condemned—he or she is sinning and knows it. (See also Matthew 18:15-18 and 2 Thessalonians 3:14, 15 for help in handling such problems in the church.)

3:12 The city of Nicopolis was on the western coast of Greece. Artemas or Tychicus would take over Titus's work on the island of Crete so Titus could meet Paul in Nicopolis. Tychicus was one of Paul's trusted companions (Acts 20:4; Ephesians 6:21; Colossians 4:7). Titus would have to leave soon because sea travel was dangerous in the winter months.

arrives, do your best to meet me at Nicopolis as quickly as you can, for I have decided
to stay there for the winter. 13Do everything you can to help Zenas the lawyer and
Apollos with their trip. See that they are given everything they need. 14For our people
should not have unproductive lives. They must learn to do good by helping others who
have urgent needs.

15Everybody here sends greetings. Please give my greetings to all of the believers who
love us.

May God's grace be with you all.

3:13 Acts 18:24
3:14 Eph 4:28; Titus 2:14; 3:8
3:15 Col 4:18

3:13 Apollos was a famous Christian preacher. A native of Alexandria in North Africa, he became a Christian in Ephesus and was trained by Aquila and Priscilla (Acts 18:24-28; 1 Corinthians 1:12).

3:15 The letters of Paul to Titus and Timothy are his last writings and mark the end of his life and ministry. These letters are rich treasures for us today because they give vital information for church leadership. They provide a strong model for elders, pastors, and other Christian leaders as they develop younger leaders to carry on the work, following Paul's example of preparing Timothy and Titus to carry on his ministry. For practical guidelines on church leadership and problem solving, carefully study the principles found in these letters.

PHILEMON

AT THE foreman's signal, the giant ball is released, and with dynamite force and a reverberating crash, it meets the wall, snapping bricks like twigs and scattering pieces of mortar. Repeatedly, the powerful pendulum works, and soon the barrier has been reduced to rubble. Then it is carted away so that construction can begin.

Life has many walls and fences that divide, separate, and compartmentalize. Not made of wood or stone, they are personal obstructions, blocking people from each other and from God. But Christ came as the great wall remover, tearing down the sin partition that separates us from God and blasting the barriers that keep us from each other. His death and resurrection opened the way to eternal life to bring all who believe into the family of God (see Ephesians 2:14–18).

Roman, Greek, and Jewish cultures were littered with barriers, as society assigned people to classes and expected them to stay in their place—men and women, slave and free, rich and poor, Jews and Gentiles, Greeks and barbarians, pious and pagan. But with the message of Christ, the walls came down, and Paul could declare, "In this new life, it doesn't matter if you are a Jew or a Gentile, circumcised or uncircumcised, barbaric, uncivilized, slave, or free. Christ is all that matters, and he lives in all of us" (Colossians 3:11).

This life-changing truth forms the backdrop for the letter to Philemon. One of three personal letters in the Bible, the letter to Philemon is Paul's personal plea for a slave. Onesimus "belonged" to Philemon, a member of the Colossian church and Paul's friend. But Onesimus, the slave, had stolen from his master and run away. He ran to Rome, where he met Paul, and there he responded to the Good News and came to faith in Christ (1:10). So Paul writes to Philemon and reintroduces Onesimus to him, explaining that he is sending him back, not just as a slave but as a brother (1:11, 12, 16). Tactfully he asks Philemon to accept and forgive his brother (1:10, 14, 15, 20). The barriers of the past and the new ones erected by Onesimus's desertion and theft should divide them no longer—they are one in Christ.

This small book is a masterpiece of grace and tact and a profound demonstration of the power of Christ and of true Christian fellowship in action. What barriers are in your home, neighborhood, and church? What separates you from fellow believers? Is it race? status? wealth? education? personality? As with Philemon, God calls you to seek unity, breaking down those walls and embracing your brothers and sisters in Christ.

VITAL STATISTICS

PURPOSE:
To convince Philemon to forgive his runaway slave, Onesimus, and to accept him as a brother in the faith

AUTHOR:
Paul

TO WHOM WRITTEN:
Philemon, who was probably a wealthy member of the Colossian church, and all believers

DATE WRITTEN:
Approximately A.D. 60, during Paul's first imprisonment in Rome, at about the same time Ephesians and Colossians were written

SETTING:
Slavery was very common in the Roman Empire, and evidently some Christians had slaves. Paul does not condemn the institution of slavery in his writings, but he makes a radical statement by calling this slave Philemon's brother in Christ.

KEY VERSES:
"Perhaps you could think of it this way: Onesimus ran away for a little while so you could have him back forever. He is no longer just a slave; he is a beloved brother, especially to me. Now he will mean much more to you, both as a slave and as a brother in the Lord" (1:15, 16).

KEY PEOPLE: Paul, Philemon, Onesimus

KEY PLACES:
Colosse, Rome

SPECIAL FEATURES:
This is a private, personal letter to a friend.

THE BLUEPRINT

1. Paul's appreciation of Philemon (1:1–7)
2. Paul's appeal for Onesimus (1:8–25)

Paul pleads on behalf of Onesimus, a runaway slave. Paul's intercession for him illustrates what Christ has done for us. As Paul interceded for a slave, so Christ intercedes for us, slaves to sin. As Onesimus was reconciled to Philemon, so we are reconciled to God through Christ. As Paul offered to pay the debts of a slave, so Christ paid our debt of sin. Like Onesimus, we must return to God our Master and serve him.

MEGATHEMES

THEME	EXPLANATION	IMPORTANCE
Forgiveness	Philemon was Paul's friend and the legal owner of the slave Onesimus. Paul asked him not to punish Onesimus but to forgive and restore him as a new Christian brother.	Christian relationships must be full of forgiveness and acceptance. Can you forgive those who have wronged you?
Barriers	Slavery was widespread in the Roman Empire, but no one is lost to God or beyond his love. Slavery was a barrier between people, but Christian love and fellowship are to overcome such barriers.	In Christ we are one family. No walls of racial, economic or political differences should separate us. Let Christ work through you to remove barriers between Christian brothers and sisters.
Respect	Paul was a friend of both Philemon and Onesimus. He had the authority as an apostle to tell Philemon what to do. Yet Paul chose to appeal to his friend in Christian love rather than to order him what to do.	Tactful persuasion accomplishes a great deal more than commands when dealing with people. Remember to exhibit courtesy and respect in your relationships.

1. Paul's appreciation of Philemon

Greetings from Paul

This letter is from Paul, in prison for preaching the Good News about Christ Jesus, and **1:1**
from our brother Timothy. Eph 4:1 Phil 1:7
It is written to Philemon, our much loved co-worker, 2 and to our sister Apphia and to Phlm 1:9, 23
Archippus, a fellow soldier of the cross. I am also writing to the church that meets in **1:2**
your house. Rom 16:5 Phil 2:25
3 May God our Father and the Lord Jesus Christ give you grace and peace. Col 4:17

Paul's Thanksgiving and Prayer

4 I always thank God when I pray for you, Philemon, 5 because I keep hearing of your **1:4**
trust in the Lord Jesus and your love for all of God's people. 6 You are generous because Rom 1:8-9
of your faith. And I am praying that you will really put your generosity to work, for in **1:6** Phil 1:9
so doing you will come to an understanding of all the good things we can do for Christ. **1:7**
7 I myself have gained much joy and comfort from your love, my brother, because your 2 Cor 7:4, 13
kindness has so often refreshed the hearts of God's people.

1:1 Paul wrote this letter from Rome in about A.D. 60, when he was under house arrest (see Acts 28:30, 31). Onesimus was a domestic slave who belonged to Philemon, a wealthy man and a member of the church in Colosse. Onesimus had run away from Philemon and had made his way to Rome, where he met Paul, who apparently led him to Christ (1:10). Paul convinced Onesimus that running from his problems wouldn't solve them, and he persuaded Onesimus to return to his master. Paul wrote this letter to Philemon to ask him to be reconciled to his runaway slave.

1:1 For more information on Paul's life, see his Profile in Acts 9. Timothy's name is included with Paul's in 2 Corinthians, 1 Thessalonians, 2 Thessalonians, Philippians, Colossians, and Philemon—the last three of these letters are from a group known as the "Prison Letters." Timothy was one of Paul's trusted companions; Paul wrote two letters to him—1 and 2 Timothy.

1:1 Philemon was a Greek landowner living in Colosse. He had been converted under Paul's ministry, and the Colossian church met in his home. Onesimus was one of Philemon's slaves.

1:2 Apphia may have been Philemon's wife. Archippus may have been Philemon's son or perhaps an elder in the Colossian church. In either case, Paul included him as a recipient of the letter, possibly so Archippus could read the letter with Philemon and encourage him to take Paul's advice.

1:2 The early churches often would meet in people's homes. Because of sporadic persecutions and the great expense involved, church buildings were typically not constructed at this time.

1:4-7 Paul reflected on Philemon's faith and love. Philemon had opened his heart and his home to the church. We should do likewise, opening ourselves and our homes to others, offering Christian fellowship to refresh people's hearts.

2. Paul's appeal for Onesimus

8 That is why I am boldly asking a favor of you. I could demand it in the name of Christ
1:9 Eph 3:1; 4:1 Phil 1:7 because it is the right thing for you to do, 9 but because of our love, I prefer just to ask
you. So take this as a request from your friend Paul, an old man, now in prison for the
sake of Christ Jesus.
1:10 1 Cor 4:14 Col 4:9 10 My plea is that you show kindness to Onesimus. I think of him as my own son
because he became a believer as a result of my ministry here in prison. 11 Onesimus*
hasn't been of much use to you in the past, but now he is very useful to both of us.
12 I am sending him back to you, and with him comes my own heart.
1:13 Phil 2:30 13 I really wanted to keep him here with me while I am in these chains for preaching
the Good News, and he would have helped me on your behalf. 14 But I didn't want to do
1:14 2 Cor 9:7 1 Pet 5:2 anything without your consent. And I didn't want you to help because you were forced
to do it but because you wanted to. 15 Perhaps you could think of it this way: Onesimus
1:15 Gen 45:5, 8 ran away for a little while so you could have him back forever. 16 He is no longer just a
1:16 Matt 23:8 1 Cor 7:22 1 Tim 6:2 slave; he is a beloved brother, especially to me. Now he will mean much more to you,
both as a slave and as a brother in the Lord.
17 So if you consider me your partner, give him the same welcome you would give me
1:17 2 Cor 8:23 if I were coming. 18 If he has harmed you in any way or stolen anything from you, charge
me for it. 19 I, Paul, write this in my own handwriting: "I will repay it." And I won't
1:19 1 Cor 16:21 mention that you owe me your very soul!
20 Yes, dear brother, please do me this favor for the Lord's sake. Give me this
encouragement in Christ. 21 I am confident as I write this letter that you will do what I
ask and even more!
1:22 Phil 1:25; 2:24 22 Please keep a guest room ready for me, for I am hoping that God will answer your
prayers and let me return to you soon.

11 *Onesimus* means "useful."

1:8, 9 Because Paul was an elder and an apostle, he could have used his authority with Philemon, commanding him to deal kindly with his runaway slave. But Paul based his request not on his own authority but on Philemon's Christian commitment. Paul wanted Philemon's heartfelt, not grudging, obedience. When you know something is right and you have the power to demand it, do you appeal to your authority or to the other person's commitment? Here Paul provides a good example of how to deal with a possible conflict between Christian friends.

1:10 A master had the legal right to kill a runaway slave, so Onesimus feared for his life. Paul wrote this letter to Philemon to help him understand his new relationship with Onesimus. Onesimus was now a Christian brother, not a mere possession.

1:10ff From his prison cell, Paul had led Onesimus to the Lord. Paul asked Philemon to forgive his runaway slave who had become a Christian and, even going beyond forgiveness, to accept Onesimus as a brother. As Christians, we should forgive as we have been forgiven (Matthew 6:12; Ephesians 4:31, 32). True forgiveness means that we treat the one we've forgiven as we would want to be treated. Is there someone you say you have forgiven but who still needs your kindness?

1:11-15 *Onesimus* means "useful." Paul used a play on words, saying that Onesimus had not been much use to Philemon in the past but now had become very useful to both Philemon and Paul. Although Paul wanted to keep Onesimus with him, he was sending Onesimus back, requesting that Philemon accept him not only as a forgiven runaway servant but also as a brother in Christ.

1:15, 16 Slavery was widespread throughout the Roman Empire. In these early days, Christians did not have the political power to change the slavery system. Paul didn't condemn or condone slavery, but he worked to transform relationships. The Good News begins to change social structures by changing the *people* within those structures. (See also 1 Corinthians 7:20-24; Ephesians 6:5-9; Colossians 3:22–4:1 for more on master/slave relationships.)

1:16 What a difference Onesimus's status as a Christian made in his relationship to Philemon. He was no longer merely a slave, but he was also a brother. That meant that both Onesimus and Philemon were members of God's family—equals in Christ. A Christian's status as a member of God's family transcends all other distinctions among believers. Do you look down on any fellow Christians? Remember, they are your equals before Christ (Galatians 3:28). How you treat your brothers and sisters in Christ's family reflects your true Christian commitment.

1:17-19 Paul genuinely loved Onesimus. Paul showed his love by personally guaranteeing payment for any stolen goods or wrongs for which Onesimus might be responsible. Paul's investment in the life of this new believer certainly encouraged and strengthened Onesimus's faith. Are there young believers who need you to demonstrate such self-sacrifice toward them? Be grateful when you can invest in the lives of others, helping them with Bible study, prayer, encouragement, support, and friendship.

1:19 Philemon owed his soul to Paul, meaning that Paul had led Philemon to Christ. Because Paul was Philemon's spiritual father, he was hoping that Philemon would feel a debt of gratitude that he would repay by accepting Onesimus with a spirit of forgiveness.

1:22 Paul was released from prison soon after writing this letter, but the Bible doesn't say whether or not he returned to Colosse.

Paul's Final Greetings

[23]Epaphras, my fellow prisoner in Christ Jesus, sends you his greetings. [24]So do Mark, Aristarchus, Demas, and Luke, my co-workers.

[25]The grace of the Lord Jesus Christ be with your spirit.

1:23 Col 1:7; 4:10

1:25 Gal 6:18

1:23 Epaphras was well known to the Colossians because he had founded the church there (Colossians 1:7). He was a hero to this church, helping to hold it together in spite of growing persecution and struggles with false doctrine. His report to Paul about the problems in Colosse had prompted Paul to write his letter to the Colossians. Epaphras's greetings to the Colossian Christians reveal his deep love for them (Colossians 4:12, 13). He may have been in prison with Paul for preaching the Good News.

1:24 Mark, Aristarchus, Demas, and Luke are also mentioned in Colossians 4:10, 14. Mark had accompanied Paul and Barnabas on their first missionary journey (Acts 12:25ff). Mark also wrote the Gospel of Mark. Luke had accompanied Paul on his third missionary journey and was the writer of the Gospel of Luke and the book of Acts. Demas had been faithful to Paul for a while but then deserted him (see 2 Timothy 4:10).

1:25 Paul urged Philemon to be reconciled to his slave, receiving him as a brother and fellow member of God's family. *Reconciliation* means reestablishing relationship. Christ has reconciled us to God and to others. Many barriers come between people—race, social status, sex, personality differences—but Christ can break down these barriers. Jesus Christ changed Onesimus's relationship to Philemon from slave to brother. Christ can transform our most hopeless relationships into deep and loving friendships.

HEBREWS

CONSCIENTIOUS consumers shop for value, the best products for the money. Wise parents desire only the best for their children, nourishing their growing bodies, minds, and spirits. Individuals with integrity seek the best investment of time, talents, and treasures. In every area, to settle for less would be wasteful, foolish, and irresponsible. Yet it is a natural pull to move toward what is convenient and comfortable.

Judaism was not second-rate or easy. Divinely designed, it was the best religion, expressing true worship and devotion to God. The commandments, the rituals, and the prophets described God's promises and revealed the way to forgiveness and salvation. But Christ came, fulfilling the Law and the Prophets, conquering sin, shattering all barriers to God, freely providing eternal life.

This message was difficult for Jews to accept. Although they had sought the Messiah for centuries, they were entrenched in thinking and worshiping in traditional forms. Following Jesus seemed to repudiate their marvelous heritage and Scriptures. With caution and questions they listened to the gospel, but many rejected it and sought to eliminate this "heresy." Those who did accept Jesus as the Messiah often found themselves slipping back into familiar routines, trying to live a hybrid faith.

Hebrews is a masterful document written to Jews who were evaluating Jesus or struggling with this new faith. The message of Hebrews is that Jesus is better, Christianity is superior, Christ is supreme and completely sufficient for salvation.

Hebrews begins by emphasizing that the old (Judaism) and the new (Christianity) are both religions revealed by God (1:1–3). In the doctrinal section that follows (1:4—10:18), the writer shows how Jesus is superior to angels (1:4—2:18), superior to their leaders (3:1—4:13), and superior to their priests (4:14—7:28). Christianity surpasses Judaism because it has a better covenant (8:1–13), a better sanctuary (9:1–10), and a more sufficient sacrifice for sins (9:11—10:18).

Having established the superiority of Christianity, the writer moves on to the practical implications of following Christ. The readers are exhorted to hold on to their new faith, encourage each other, and look forward to Christ's return (10:19–25). They are warned about the consequences of rejecting Christ's sacrifice (10:26–31) and reminded of the rewards for faithfulness (10:32–39). Then the author explains how to live by faith, giving illustrations of the faithful men and women in Israel's history (11:1–40) and giving encouragement and exhortation for daily living (12:1–17). This section ends by comparing the old covenant with the new (12:18–29). The writer concludes with moral exhortations (13:1–17), a request for prayer (13:18, 19), and a benediction and greetings (13:20–25).

Whatever you are considering as the focus of life, Christ is better. He is the perfect revelation of God, the final and complete sacrifice for sin, the compassionate and understanding mediator, and the *only* way to eternal life. Read Hebrews and begin to see history and life from God's perspective. Then give yourself unreservedly and completely to Christ.

VITAL STATISTICS

PURPOSE:
To present the sufficiency and superiority of Christ

AUTHOR:
Paul, Luke, Barnabas, Apollos, Silas, Philip, Priscilla, and others have been suggested because the name of the author is not given in the biblical text itself. Whoever it was speaks of Timothy as "brother" (13:23).

TO WHOM WRITTEN:
Hebrew Christians (perhaps second-generation Christians, see 2:3) who may have been considering a return to Judaism, perhaps because of immaturity, stemming from a lack of understanding of biblical truths; and all believers in Christ.

DATE WRITTEN:
Probably before the destruction of the Temple in Jerusalem in A.D. 70, because the religious sacrifices and ceremonies are referred to in the book, but no mention is made of the Temple's destruction

SETTING:
These Jewish Christians were probably undergoing fierce persecution, socially and physically, both from Jews and from Romans. Christ had not returned to establish his Kingdom, and the people needed to be reassured that Christianity was true and that Jesus was indeed the Messiah.

KEY VERSE:
"The Son reflects God's own glory, and everything about him represents God exactly. He sustains the universe by the mighty power of his command. After he died to cleanse us from the stain of sin, he sat down in the place of honor at the right hand of the majestic God of heaven" (1:3).

KEY PEOPLE:
Old Testament men and women of faith (chapter 11)

SPECIAL FEATURES:
Although Hebrews is called a "letter" (13:22), it has the form and the content of a sermon.

THE BLUEPRINT

A. THE SUPERIORITY OF CHRIST (1:1—10:18) 1. Christ is greater than the angels 2. Christ is greater than Moses 3. Christ is greater than the Old Testament priesthood 4. The new covenant is greater than the old	The superiority of Christ over everyone and everything is clearly demonstrated by the author. Christianity supersedes all other religions and can never be surpassed. Where can one find anything better than Christ? Living in Christ is having the best there is in life. All competing religions are deceptions or cheap imitations.
B. THE SUPERIORITY OF FAITH (10:19—13:25)	Jews who had become Christians in the first century were tempted to fall back into Judaism because of uncertainty, the security of custom, and persecution. Today believers are also tempted to fall back into legalism, fulfilling minimum religious requirements rather than pressing on in genuine faith. We must strive to live by faith each day.

MEGATHEMES

THEME	EXPLANATION	IMPORTANCE
Christ Is Superior	Hebrews reveals Jesus' true identity as God. Jesus is the ultimate authority. He is greater than any religion or any angel. He is superior to any Jewish leader (such as Abraham, Moses, or Joshua) and superior to any priest. He is the complete revelation of God.	Jesus alone can forgive our sin. He has secured our forgiveness and salvation by his death on the cross. We can find peace with God and real meaning for life by believing in Christ. We should not accept any alternative to or substitute for him.
High Priest	In the Old Testament, the high priest represented the Jews before God. Jesus Christ links us with God. There is no other way to reach God. Because Jesus Christ lived a sinless life, he is the perfect substitute to die for our sin. He is our perfect representative with God.	Jesus guarantees our access to God the Father. He intercedes for us so we can boldly come to the Father with our needs. When we are weak, we can come confidently to God for forgiveness and ask for his help.
Sacrifice	Christ's sacrifice was the ultimate fulfillment of all that the Old Testament sacrifices represented—God's forgiveness for sin. Because Christ is the perfect sacrifice for our sin, our sins are completely forgiven—past, present, and future.	Christ removed sin, which barred us from God's presence and fellowship. But we must accept his sacrifice for us. By believing in him, we are no longer guilty but cleansed and made whole. His sacrifice clears the way for us to have eternal life.
Maturity	Though we are saved from sin when we believe in Christ, we are given the task of going on and growing in our faith. Through our relationship with Christ, we can live blameless lives, be set aside for his special use, and develop maturity.	The process of maturing in our faith takes time. Daily commitment and service produce maturity. When we are mature in our faith, we are not easily swayed or shaken by temptations or worldly concerns.
Faith	Faith is confident trust in God's promises. God's greatest promise is that we can be saved through Jesus.	If we trust in Jesus Christ for our complete salvation, he will transform us completely. A life of obedience and complete trust is pleasing to God.
Endurance	Faith enables Christians to face trials. Genuine faith includes the commitment to stay true to God when we are under fire. Endurance builds character and leads to victory.	We can have victory in our trials if we don't give up or turn our back on Christ. Stay true to Christ and pray for endurance.

A. THE SUPERIORITY OF CHRIST (1:1—10:18)

The relationship of Christianity to Judaism was a critical issue in the early church. The author clears up confusion by carefully explaining how Christ is superior to angels, Moses, and high priests. The new covenant is shown to be far superior to the old. This can be of great encouragement to us and help us avoid drifting away from our faith in Christ.

1. Christ is greater than the angels

Jesus Christ Is God's Son

1:1 Num 12:6-8
1:2 Matt 21:38; John 1:3; 1 Pet 1:20
1:3 Ps 110:1; John 14:9; 2 Cor 4:4; Col 1:15

1 Long ago God spoke many times and in many ways to our ancestors through the
prophets. [2]But now in these final days, he has spoken to us through his Son. God
promised everything to the Son as an inheritance, and through the Son he made the
universe and everything in it. [3]The Son reflects God's own glory, and everything about
him represents God exactly. He sustains the universe by the mighty power of his
command. After he died to cleanse us from the stain of sin, he sat down in the place of
honor at the right hand of the majestic God of heaven.

Christ Is Greater than the Angels

1:5 †Ps 2:7; †2 Sam 7:14

[4]This shows that God's Son is far greater than the angels, just as the name God gave him is
far greater than their names. [5]For God never said to any angel what he said to Jesus:

CHRIST AND THE ANGELS

Hebrews passage	Old Testament passage	How Christ is superior to angels
1: 5, 6	Psalm 2:7	Christ is called "Son" of God, a title never given to an angel.
1:7, 14	Psalm 104:4	Angels are important but are still only servants under God.
1:8, 9	Psalm 45:6	Christ's Kingdom is forever.
1:10	Psalm 102:25	Christ is the Creator of the world.
1:13	Psalm 110:1	Christ is given unique honor by God.

The writer of Hebrews quotes from the Old Testament repeatedly in demonstrating Christ's greatness in comparison to the angels. This audience of first-century Jewish Christians had developed an imbalanced belief in angels and their role. Christ's lordship is affirmed without disrespect to God's valued angelic messengers.

1:1 The book of Hebrews describes in detail how Jesus Christ not only fulfills the promises and prophecies of the Old Testament but is better than everything in the Jewish system of thought. The Jews accepted the Old Testament, but most of them rejected Jesus as the long-awaited Messiah. The recipients of this letter seem to have been Jewish Christians. They were well-versed in Scripture, and they had professed faith in Christ. Whether through doubt, persecution, or false teaching, however, they may have been in danger of giving up their Christian faith and returning to Judaism.

The authorship of this book is uncertain. Several names have been suggested, including Luke, Barnabas, Apollos, Priscilla, and Paul. Most scholars do not believe that Paul was the author, because the writing style of Hebrews is quite different from that of his letters. In addition, Paul identified himself in his other letters and appealed to his authority as an apostle, whereas this writer of Hebrews, who never gives his or her name, appeals to eyewitnesses of Jesus' ministry for authority. Nevertheless, the author of Hebrews evidently knew Paul well. Hebrews was probably written by one of Paul's close associates who often heard him preach.

1:1, 2 God used many approaches to send his messages to people in Old Testament times. He spoke to Isaiah in visions (Isaiah 6), to Jacob in a dream (Genesis 28:10-22), and to Abraham and Moses personally (Genesis 18; Exodus 31:18). Jewish people familiar with these stories would not have found it hard to believe that God was still revealing his will, but it was astonishing for them to think that God had revealed *himself* by speaking through his Son, Jesus Christ. Jesus is the fulfillment and culmination of God's revelation through the centuries. When we know him, we have all we need to be saved from our sin and to have a perfect relationship with God.

1:2, 3 Not only is Jesus the exact representation of God, but he is God himself—the very God who spoke in Old Testament times. He is eternal; he worked with the Father in creating the world (John 1:3; Colossians 1:16). He is the full revelation of God. You can have no clearer view of God than by looking at Christ. Jesus Christ is the complete expression of God in a human body.

1:3 The book of Hebrews links God's saving power with his creative power. In other words, the power that brought the universe into being and that keeps it operating is the very power that cleanses our sins. How mistaken we would be to ever think that God couldn't forgive us. No sin is too big for the Ruler of the universe to handle. He can and will forgive us when we come to him through his Son. That Jesus *sat down* means that the work was complete. Christ's sacrifice was final.

1:4 The superior name that was given to Jesus is "Son of God." This name given to him by his Father is greater than the names and titles of the angels.

1:4ff False teachers in many of the early churches taught that God could be approached only through angels. Instead of worshiping God directly, followers of these heretics revered angels. Hebrews clearly denounces such teaching as false. Some thought of Jesus as the highest angel of God. But Jesus is not a superior angel, and in any case, angels are not to be worshiped (see Colossians 2:18; Revelation 19:1-10). We should not regard any intermediaries or authorities as greater than Christ. Jesus is God. He alone deserves our worship.

1:5, 6 Jesus is God's honored, firstborn Son. In Jewish families the firstborn son held the place of highest privilege and responsibility. The Jewish Christians reading this message would understand that as God's firstborn, Jesus was superior to any created being.

"You are my Son.
Today I have become your Father.*"

And again God said,

"I will be his Father,
and he will be my Son."*

6And then, when he presented his honored* Son to the world, God said, "Let all the
angels of God worship him."* 7God calls his angels

"messengers swift as the wind,
and servants made of flaming fire."*

8But to his Son he says,

"Your throne, O God, endures forever and ever.
Your royal power is expressed in righteousness.
9 You love what is right and hate what is wrong.
Therefore God, your God, has anointed you,
pouring out the oil of joy on you more than on anyone else."*

10And,

"Lord, in the beginning you laid the foundation of the earth,
and the heavens are the work of your hands.
11 Even they will perish, but you remain forever.
They will wear out like old clothing.
12 You will roll them up like an old coat.
They will fade away like old clothing.
But you are always the same;
you will never grow old."*

13And God never said to an angel, as he did to his Son,

"Sit in honor at my right hand
until I humble your enemies,
making them a footstool under your feet."*

14But angels are only servants. They are spirits sent from God to care for those who will
receive salvation.

A Warning against Drifting Away

2 So we must listen very carefully to the truth we have heard, or we may drift away
from it. 2The message God delivered through angels has always proved true, and
the people were punished for every violation of the law and every act of disobedience.

1:6 †Deut 32:43 †Ps 97:7
1:7 †Ps 104:4
1:8-9 †Ps 45:6-7
1:10-12 †Ps 102:25-27
1:13 Ps 110:1 Matt 22:44
1:14 Pss 34:7; 91:11
2:2 Deut 33:2 Acts 7:38, 53 Gal 3:19

1:5a Or *Today I reveal you as my Son.* Ps 2:7. **1:5b** 2 Sam 7:14. **1:6a** Greek *firstborn.* **1:6b** Deut 32:43. **1:7** Ps 104:4. **1:8-9** Ps 45:6-7. **1:10-12** Ps 102:25-27. **1:13** Ps 110:1.

1:10-12 The author of Hebrews quotes Psalm 102:25-27. In the quotation, he regards God as the speaker and applies the words to the Son, Jesus. The earth and the heavens rolled up like a coat reveals that the earth is not permanent or indestructible (a position held by many Greek and Roman philosophies). Jesus' authority is established over all of creation, so we dare not treat any created object or earthly resource as more important than he is.

1:11, 12 Because the readers of Hebrews had experienced the rejection of their fellow Jews, they often felt isolated. Many were tempted to exchange the changeless Christ for their familiar old faith. The writer of Hebrews warned them not to do this: Christ is our *only* security in a changing world. Whatever may happen in this world, Christ remains forever changeless. If we trust him, we are absolutely secure, because we stand on the firmest foundation in the universe—Jesus Christ. A famous hymn captures this truth: "On Christ the solid rock I stand, all other ground is sinking sand."

1:12 What does it mean that Christ is changeless ("you are always the same")? It means that Christ's character will never change. He persistently shows his love to us. He is always fair, just, and merciful to us who are so undeserving. Be thankful that Christ is changeless; he will always help you when you need it and offer forgiveness when you fall.

1:14 Angels are God's messengers, spiritual beings created by God and under his authority (Colossians 1:16). They have several functions: serving believers (1:14), protecting the helpless (Matthew 18:10), proclaiming God's messages (Revelation 14:6-12), and executing God's judgment (Acts 12:1-23; Revelation 20:1-3).

2:1-3 The author called his readers to pay attention to the truth they had heard so that they wouldn't drift away into false teachings. Paying careful attention is hard work. It involves focusing our mind, body, and senses. Listening to Christ means not merely hearing but also obeying (see James 1:22-25). We must listen carefully and be ready to carry out his instructions.

2:3 Heb 1:2; 10:29
3 What makes us think that we can escape if we are indifferent to this great salvation
that was announced by the Lord Jesus himself? It was passed on* to us by those who
2:4 Mark 16:20
heard him speak, 4 and God verified the message by signs and wonders and various
miracles and by giving gifts of the Holy Spirit whenever he chose to do so.

Jesus, the Man

2:5 Heb 6:5
5 And furthermore, the future world we are talking about will not be controlled by angels.
6 For somewhere in the Scriptures it says,

2:6-8 Ps 8:4-6

"What is man that you should think of him,
and the son of man* that you should care for him?
7 For a little while you made him lower than the angels,
and you crowned him with glory and honor.*

2:8 1 Cor 15:27
8 You gave him authority over all things."*

Now when it says "all things," it means nothing is left out. But we have not yet seen all
2:9 Phil 2:6-9
of this happen. 9 What we do see is Jesus, who "for a little while was made lower than
the angels" and now is "crowned with glory and honor" because he suffered death for
2:10 Luke 13:32; 24:46 Acts 3:15 Rom 11:36 Heb 5:9
us. Yes, by God's grace, Jesus tasted death for everyone in all the world. 10 And it was
only right that God—who made everything and for whom everything was made—should
bring his many children into glory. Through the suffering of Jesus, God made him a
perfect leader, one fit to bring them into their salvation.

2:3 Or *and confirmed.* **2:6** Or *Son of Man.* **2:7** Some manuscripts add *You put him in charge of everything you made.* **2:6-8** Ps 8:4-6.

LESSONS FROM CHRIST'S HUMANITY

Christ is the perfect human	
leader	and he wants to lead you
model	and he is worth imitating
sacrifice	and he died for you
conqueror	and he conquered death to give you eternal life
High Priest	and he is merciful, loving, and understanding

God, in Christ, became a living, breathing human being. Hebrews points out many reasons why this is so important.

2:2, 3 "The message God delivered through angels" refers to the teaching that angels, as messengers for God, had brought the law to Moses (see Galatians 3:19). A central theme of Hebrews is that Christ is infinitely greater than all other proposed ways to God. The author was saying that the faith of his Jewish readers was good, but faith must point to Christ. Just as Christ is greater than angels, so Christ's message is more important than theirs. No one will escape God's punishment if he or she is indifferent to the salvation offered by Christ.

2:3 Eyewitnesses to Jesus' ministry had handed down his teachings to the readers of this book. These readers were second-generation believers who had not seen Christ in the flesh. They are like us; we have not seen Jesus personally. We base our belief in Jesus on the eyewitness accounts recorded in the Bible. See John 20:29 for Jesus' encouragement to those who believe without ever having seen him.

2:4 "God verified the message" continues the thought from 2:3. Those who had heard Jesus speak and then had passed on his words also had the truth of their words confirmed by "signs and wonders and various miracles and by giving gifts of the Holy Spirit." In the book of Acts, miracles and gifts of the Spirit authenticated the Good News wherever it was preached (see Acts 9:31-42; 14:1-20). Paul, who discussed spiritual gifts in Romans 12, 1 Corinthians 12–14, and Ephesians 4, taught that their purpose is to build up the church, making it strong and mature. When we see the gifts of the Spirit in an individual or congregation, we know that God is truly present. As we receive God's gifts, we should thank him for them and put them to use in the church.

2:8, 9 God put Jesus in charge of everything, and Jesus revealed himself to us. We do not yet see Jesus reigning on earth, but we can picture him in his heavenly glory. When you are confused by present events and anxious about the future, remember Jesus' true position and authority. He is Lord of all, and one day he will rule on earth as he does now in heaven. This truth can give stability to your decisions day by day.

2:9, 10 God's grace to us led Christ to his death. Jesus did not come into the world to gain status or political power, but to suffer and die so that we could have eternal life ("bring his many children into glory"). If it is difficult for us to identify with Christ's servant attitude, perhaps we need to evaluate our own motives. Are we more interested in power or participation, domination or service, getting or giving?

2:10 How was Jesus made perfect through suffering? Jesus' suffering made him a perfect leader, or pioneer, of our salvation (see the notes on 5:8 and 5:9). Jesus did not need to suffer for his own salvation, because he was God in human form. His perfect obedience (which led him down the road of suffering) demonstrates that he was the complete sacrifice for us. Through suffering, Jesus completed the work necessary for our own salvation. Our suffering can make us more sensitive servants of God. People who have known pain are able to reach out with compassion to others who hurt. If you have suffered, ask God how your experience can be used to help others.

[11]So now Jesus and the ones he makes holy have the same Father. That is why Jesus
is not ashamed to call them his brothers and sisters.* [12]For he said to God,

"I will declare the wonder of your name to my brothers and sisters.*
I will praise you among all your people."

[13]He also said, "I will put my trust in him." And in the same context he said, "Here I
am—together with the children God has given me."*

[14]Because God's children are human beings—made of flesh and blood—Jesus also
became flesh and blood by being born in human form. For only as a human being could
he die, and only by dying could he break the power of the Devil, who had the power of
death. [15]Only in this way could he deliver those who have lived all their lives as slaves
to the fear of dying.

[16]We all know that Jesus came to help the descendants of Abraham, not to help the
angels. [17]Therefore, it was necessary for Jesus to be in every respect like us, his brothers
and sisters, so that he could be our merciful and faithful High Priest before God. He then
could offer a sacrifice that would take away the sins of the people. [18]Since he himself
has gone through suffering and temptation, he is able to help us when we are being
tempted.

2. Christ is greater than Moses

3 And so, dear friends who belong to God* and are bound for heaven, think about this
Jesus whom we declare to be God's Messenger and High Priest. [2]For he was faithful
to God, who appointed him, just as Moses served faithfully and was entrusted with God's
entire house. [3]But Jesus deserves far more glory than Moses, just as a person who builds
a fine house deserves more praise than the house itself. [4]For every house has a builder,
but God is the one who made everything.

2:11 Matt 28:10; John 20:17; Rom 8:29; Heb 10:10; 13:12
2:12 †Ps 22:22
2:13 †Isa 8:17; John 17:11-12
2:14 John 1:14; Rom 8:3; 1 Cor 15:54-57; 2 Tim 1:10; 1 Jn 3:8
2:17 Phil 2:7; Heb 3:1; 4:15; 5:1; 1 Jn 2:2; 4:10
2:18 Heb 4:15; 5:2
3:1 Heb 2:17; 4:14
3:2 Num 12:7-8
3:3 2 Cor 3:7-11

2:11 Greek *his brothers;* also in 2:17. **2:12** Greek *my brothers.* Ps 22:22. **2:13** Isa 8:17-18. **3:1** Greek *holy brothers.*

2:11-13 We who have been set apart for God's service, cleansed, and made holy (sanctified) by Jesus now have the same Father he has, so he has made us his brothers and sisters. Various psalms look forward to Christ and his work in the world. Here the writer quotes a portion of Psalm 22, a messianic psalm. Because God has adopted all believers as his children, Jesus calls them his brothers and sisters.

2:14, 15 Jesus had to become human so that he could die and rise again, in order to destroy the Devil's power over death (Romans 6:5-11). Only then could Christ deliver those who had lived in constant fear of death and free them to live for him. When we belong to God, we need not fear death, because we know that death is only the doorway into eternal life (1 Corinthians 15).

2:14, 15 Christ's death and resurrection set us free from the fear of death because death has been defeated. Every person must die, but death is not the end; instead, it is the doorway to a new life. All who dread death should have the opportunity to know the hope that Christ's victory brings. How can you share this truth with those close to you?

2:16, 17 In the Old Testament, the high priest was the mediator between God and his people. His job was to regularly offer animal sacrifices according to the law and to intercede with God for forgiveness for the people's sins. Jesus Christ is now our High Priest. He came to earth as a human being; therefore, he understands our weaknesses and shows mercy to us. He has *once and for all* paid the penalty for our sins by his own sacrificial death (atonement), and he can be depended on to restore our broken relationship with God. We are released from sin's domination over us when we commit ourselves fully to Christ, trusting completely in what he has done for us (see the note on 4:14 for more about Jesus as the great High Priest).

2:18 Knowing that Christ suffered pain and faced temptation helps us face our trials. Jesus understands our struggles because he faced them as a human being. We can trust Christ to help us survive suffering and overcome temptation. When you face trials, go to Jesus for strength and patience. He understands your needs and is able to help (see 4:14-16).

3:1 This verse would have been especially meaningful to Jewish Christians. For Jews, the highest human authority was the high priest. For Christians, the highest human authorities were God's messengers, the apostles. Jesus, God's Messenger and High Priest, is the ultimate authority in the church.

3:1-6 The author uses different pictures to explain Jesus' relationship to believers: He is (1) the Messenger of God, to whom we should listen; (2) our High Priest, through whom we come to God the Father; and (3) the ruler of God's house ("in charge of the entire household"), whom we should obey. The Bible is filled with different names for and pictures of Jesus Christ, and each one reveals something more about his nature and ministry. What do these images teach you about your relationship with Christ?

3:2, 3 To the Jewish people, Moses was a great hero; he had led their ancestors, the Israelites, from Egyptian bondage to the border of the Promised Land. He also had written the first five books of the Old Testament, and he was the prophet through whom God had given the law; therefore, Moses was the greatest prophet in the Scriptures. But Jesus is worthy of greater honor as the central figure of faith than Moses, who was merely a human servant. Jesus is more than human; he is God himself (1:3). As Moses led the people of Israel out of Egyptian bondage, so Christ leads us out of sin's slavery. Why settle for Moses, the author of Hebrews asks, when you can have Jesus Christ, who appointed Moses?

3:5 Exod 14:31 Num 12:7
3:6 Eph 2:19-22 1 Tim 3:15 1 Pet 2:5
3:7-11 †Ps 95:7-11
3:8 Exod 17:7

5 Moses was certainly faithful in God's house, but only as a servant. His work was an illustration of the truths God would reveal later. 6 But Christ, the faithful Son, was in charge of the entire household. And we are God's household, if we keep up our courage and remain confident in our hope in Christ. 7 That is why the Holy Spirit says,

"Today you must listen to his voice.
8 Don't harden your hearts against him
as Israel did when they rebelled,
when they tested God's patience in the wilderness.
9 There your ancestors tried my patience,
even though they saw my miracles for forty years.
10 So I was angry with them, and I said,
'Their hearts always turn away from me.
They refuse to do what I tell them.'
11 So in my anger I made a vow:
'They will never enter my place of rest.'"*

3:11 Num 14:21-23
3:13 Eph 4:22
3:14 Heb 3:6
3:15 †Ps 95:7-8

12 Be careful then, dear friends.* Make sure that your own hearts are not evil and unbelieving, turning you away from the living God. 13 You must warn each other every day, as long as it is called "today," so that none of you will be deceived by sin and hardened against God. 14 For if we are faithful to the end, trusting God just as firmly as when we first believed, we will share in all that belongs to Christ. 15 But never forget the warning:

"Today you must listen to his voice.
Don't harden your hearts against him
as Israel did when they rebelled."*

3:16-18 Num 14:1-35
3:17 Num 14:29 1 Cor 10:5
3:18 Num 14:22-23

16 And who were those people who rebelled against God, even though they heard his voice? Weren't they the ones Moses led out of Egypt? 17 And who made God angry for forty years? Wasn't it the people who sinned, whose bodies fell in the wilderness? 18 And to whom was God speaking when he vowed that they would never enter his place of rest? He was speaking to those who disobeyed him. 19 So we see that they were not allowed to enter his rest because of their unbelief.

3:7-11 Ps 95:7-11. **3:12** Greek *brothers.* **3:15** Ps 95:7-8.

3:5 Moses was faithful to God's calling not only to deliver Israel but also to prepare the way for the Messiah ("his work was an illustration of the truths God would reveal later"). All the Old Testament believers also served to prepare the way. Thus, knowing the Old Testament is the best foundation for understanding the New Testament. In reading the Old Testament, we see (1) how God used people to accomplish his purposes, (2) how God used events and personalities to illustrate important truths, (3) how, through prophets, God announced the Messiah, and (4) how, through the system of sacrifices, God prepared people to understand the Messiah's work. If you include the Old Testament in your regular Bible reading, the New Testament will grow clearer and more meaningful to you.

3:6 Because Christ lives in us as believers, we can remain courageous and hopeful to the end. We are not saved by being steadfast and firm in our faith, but our courage and hope do reveal that our faith is real. Without this enduring faithfulness, we could easily be blown away by the winds of temptation, false teaching, or persecution (see also 3:14).

3:7-15 In many places, the Bible warns us not to "harden" our hearts. This means stubbornly setting ourselves against God so that we are no longer able to turn to him for forgiveness. The Israelites became hard-hearted when they disobeyed God's command to conquer the Promised Land (see Numbers 13; 14; 20; and Psalm 95). Be careful to obey God's Word, and do not allow your heart to become hardened.

3:11 God's *rest* has several meanings in Scripture: (1) the seventh day of creation and the weekly Sabbath commemorating it (Genesis 2:2; Hebrews 4:4-9); (2) the Promised Land of Canaan (Deuteronomy 12:8-12; Psalm 95); (3) peace with God now because of our relationship with Christ through faith (Matthew 11:28; Hebrews 4:1, 3, 8-11); and (4) our future eternal life with Christ (Hebrews 4:8-11). All of these meanings were probably familiar to the Jewish Christian readers of Hebrews.

3:12-14 Our hearts turn away from the living God when we stubbornly refuse to believe him. If we persist in our unbelief, God will eventually leave us alone in our sin. But God can give us new hearts, new desires, and new spirits (Ezekiel 36:22-27). To prevent having an unbelieving heart, stay in fellowship with other believers, talk daily about your mutual faith, be aware of the deceitfulness of sin (it attracts but also destroys), and encourage each other with love and concern.

3:15-19 The Israelites failed to enter the Promised Land because they did not believe in God's protection, and they did not believe that God would help them conquer the giants in the land (see Numbers 14–5). So God sent them into the wilderness to wander for 40 years. This was an unhappy alternative to the wonderful gift he had planned for them. Lack of trust in God always prevents us from receiving his best.

Promised Rest for God's People

4 God's promise of entering his place of rest still stands, so we ought to tremble with
fear that some of you might fail to get there. [2]For this Good News—that God has 4:2 1 Thes 2:13
prepared a place of rest—has been announced to us just as it was to them. But it did them
no good because they didn't believe what God told them.* [3]For only we who believe can 4:3 †Ps 95:11
enter his place of rest. As for those who didn't believe, God said,

"In my anger I made a vow:
'They will never enter my place of rest,'"*

even though his place of rest has been ready since he made the world. [4]We know it is 4:4 †Gen 2:2
ready because the Scriptures mention the seventh day, saying, "On the seventh day God
rested from all his work."* [5]But in the other passage God said, "They will never enter 4:5 †Ps 95:11
my place of rest."* [6]So God's rest is there for people to enter. But those who formerly 4:6 Heb 3:18
heard the Good News failed to enter because they disobeyed God. [7]So God set another
time for entering his place of rest, and that time is today. God announced this through 4:7 †Ps 95:7-8
David a long time later in the words already quoted:

"Today you must listen to his voice.
Don't harden your hearts against him."*

[8]This new place of rest was not the land of Canaan, where Joshua led them. If it had 4:8 Josh 22:4
been, God would not have spoken later about another day of rest. [9]So there is a special
rest* still waiting for the people of God. [10]For all who enter into God's rest will find 4:10 Gen 2:2 Rev 14:13
rest from their labors, just as God rested after creating the world. [11]Let us do our best to
enter that place of rest. For anyone who disobeys God, as the people of Israel did, will
fall.

[12]For the word of God is full of living power. It is sharper than the sharpest knife, 4:12 Isa 49:2 Jer 23:29 1 Cor 14:24-25 Eph 6:17 1 Pet 1:23
cutting deep into our innermost thoughts and desires. It exposes us for what we really
are. [13]Nothing in all creation can hide from him. Everything is naked and exposed before
his eyes. This is the God to whom we must explain all that we have done. 4:13 2 Chr 16:9 Ps 33:13-15

4:2 Some manuscripts read *they didn't share the faith of those who listened [to God]*. **4:3** Ps 95:11. **4:4** Gen 2:2. **4:5** Ps 95:11. **4:7** Ps 95:7-8. **4:9** Or *Sabbath rest.*

4:1-3 Some of the Jewish Christians who received this letter may have been on the verge of turning back from their promised rest in Christ, just as the people in Moses' day had turned back from the Promised Land. In both cases, the difficulties of the present moment overshadowed the reality of God's promise, and the people doubted that God would fulfill his promises. When we trust our own efforts instead of Christ's power, we, too, are in danger of turning back. Our own efforts are never adequate; only Christ can see us through.

4:2 The Israelites of Moses' day illustrate a problem facing many who fill our churches today. They know a great deal about Christ, but they do not know him personally—they don't combine their knowledge with faith. Let the Good News about Christ benefit your life. Believe in him and then act on what you know. Trust in Christ and do what he says.

4:4 God rested on the seventh day, not because he was tired, but to indicate the completion of creation. The world was perfect, and God was well satisfied with it. This rest is a foretaste of our eternal joy when creation will be renewed and restored, every mark of sin will be removed, and the world will be made perfect again. Our Sabbath-rest in Christ begins when we trust him to complete his good and perfect work in us (see the note on 3:11).

4:6, 7 God had given the Israelites the opportunity to enter Canaan, but they disobeyed and failed to enter (Numbers 13–14). Now God offers us the opportunity to enter his ultimate place of rest—he invites us to come to Christ. To enter his rest, you must believe that God has this relationship in mind for you; you must stop trying to create it; you must trust in Christ for it; and you must determine to obey him. *Today* is the best time to find peace with God. Tomorrow may be too late.

4:8-11 God wants us to enter his rest. For the Israelites of Moses' time, this rest was the earthly rest to be found in the Promised Land. For Christians, it is peace with God now and eternal life on a new earth later. We do not need to wait for the next life to enjoy God's rest and peace; we may have it daily now! Our daily rest in the Lord will not end with death but will become an eternal rest in the place that Christ is preparing for us (John 14:1-4).

4:11 If Jesus has provided for our rest through faith, why must we "do our best to enter that place of rest"? This is not the struggle of doing good in order to obtain salvation, nor is it a mystical struggle to overcome selfishness. It refers to making every effort to appreciate and benefit from what God has already provided. Salvation is not to be taken for granted; to appropriate the gift God offers requires decision and commitment.

4:12 The Word of God is not simply a collection of words from God, a vehicle for communicating ideas; it is living, life-changing, and dynamic as it works in us. With the incisiveness of a surgeon's knife, God's Word reveals who we are and what we are not. It penetrates the core of our moral and spiritual life. It discerns what is within us, both good and evil. The demands of God's Word require decisions. We must not only listen to the Word; we must also let it shape our life.

4:13 Nothing can be hidden from God. He knows about everyone everywhere, and everything about us is wide open to his all-seeing eyes. God sees all we do and knows all we think. Even when we are unaware of his presence, he is there. When we try to hide from him, he sees us. We can have no secrets from God. It is comforting to realize that although God knows us intimately, he still loves us.

3. Christ is greater than the Old Testament priesthood

Christ Is Our High Priest

4:14 Heb 2:17; 3:1
4:15 2 Cor 5:21; Heb 2:17-18
4:16 Heb 7:19

14 That is why we have a great High Priest who has gone to heaven, Jesus the Son of God.
Let us cling to him and never stop trusting him. 15 This High Priest of ours understands
our weaknesses, for he faced all of the same temptations we do, yet he did not sin. 16 So
let us come boldly to the throne of our gracious God. There we will receive his mercy,
and we will find grace to help us when we need it.

5:1 Heb 2:17; 7:27; 8:3
5:2 Heb 2:17; 4:15
5:3 Lev 9:7; 16:6; Heb 7:27; 9:7
5:4 Exod 28:1; Num 14:40
5:5 †Ps 2:7; Acts 13:33; Heb 1:5
5:6 †Ps 110:4

5 Now a high priest is a man chosen to represent other human beings in their dealings
with God. He presents their gifts to God and offers their sacrifices for sins. 2 And
because he is human, he is able to deal gently with the people, though they are ignorant
and wayward. For he is subject to the same weaknesses they have. 3 That is why he has
to offer sacrifices, both for their sins and for his own sins. 4 And no one can become a
high priest simply because he wants such an honor. He has to be called by God for this
work, just as Aaron was.

5 That is why Christ did not exalt himself to become High Priest. No, he was chosen
by God, who said to him,

"You are my Son.
Today I have become your Father.*"

6 And in another passage God said to him,

"You are a priest forever
in the line of Melchizedek."*

5:5 Or *Today I reveal you as my Son.* Ps 2:7. **5:6** Ps 110:4.

THE CHOICES OF MATURITY
One way to evaluate spiritual maturity is by looking at the choices we make. The writer of Hebrews notes many of the ways those choices change with personal growth.

Mature Choices	*Versus*	*Immature Choices*
Teaching others	rather than	just being taught
Developing depth of understanding	rather than	struggling with the basics
Self-evaluation	rather than	self-criticism
Seeking unity	rather than	promoting disunity
Desiring spiritual challenges	rather than	desiring entertainment
Careful study and observation	rather than	opinions and halfhearted efforts
Active faith	rather than	cautious apathy and doubt
Confidence	rather than	fear
Feelings and experiences evaluated in the light of God's Word	rather than	experiences evaluated according to feelings

4:14 Christ is superior to the priests, and his priesthood is superior to their priesthood. To the Jews, the high priest was the highest religious authority in the land. He alone entered the Holy of Holies in the Temple once a year to make atonement for the sins of the whole nation (Leviticus 16). Like the high priest, Jesus mediates between God and us. As humanity's representative, he intercedes for us before God. As God's representative, he assures us of God's forgiveness. Jesus has more authority than the Jewish high priests because he is truly God and truly man. Unlike the high priest, who could go before God only once a year, Christ is always at God's right hand, interceding for us. He is always available to hear us when we pray.

4:15 Jesus is like us because he experienced a full range of temptations throughout his life as a human being. We can be comforted knowing that Jesus faced temptation—he can sympathize with us. We can be encouraged knowing that Jesus faced temptation without giving in to sin. He shows us that we do not have to sin when facing the seductive lure of temptation. Jesus is the only perfect human being who has ever lived.

4:16 Prayer is our approach to God, and we are to come "boldly." Some Christians approach God meekly with heads hung low, afraid to ask him to meet their needs. Others pray flippantly, giving little thought to what they say. Come with reverence because he is your King. But also come with bold assurance because he is your Friend and Counselor.

5:4-6 This chapter stresses both Christ's divine appointment and his humanity. The writer uses two Old Testament verses to show Christ's divine appointment: Psalms 2:7 and 110:4. At the time this book was written, the Romans selected the high priest in Jerusalem. In the Old Testament, however, God chose Aaron, and only Aaron's descendants could be high priests. Christ, like Aaron, was chosen and called by God.

5:6 Melchizedek was a priest of Salem (now called Jerusalem). His Profile is found in Genesis 16. Melchizedek's position is explained in Hebrews 7.

7 While Jesus was here on earth, he offered prayers and pleadings, with a loud cry and
tears, to the one who could deliver him out of death. And God heard his prayers because
of his reverence for God. 8 So even though Jesus was God's Son, he learned obedience
from the things he suffered. 9 In this way, God qualified him as a perfect High Priest, and
he became the source of eternal salvation for all those who obey him. 10 And God
designated him to be a High Priest in the line of Melchizedek.

A Call to Spiritual Growth

11 There is so much more we would like to say about this. But you don't seem to listen,
so it's hard to make you understand. 12 You have been Christians a long time now, and
you ought to be teaching others. Instead, you need someone to teach you again the basic
things a beginner must learn about the Scriptures.* You are like babies who drink only
milk and cannot eat solid food. 13 And a person who is living on milk isn't very far along
in the Christian life and doesn't know much about doing what is right. 14 Solid food is
for those who are mature, who have trained themselves to recognize the difference
between right and wrong and then do what is right.

6 So let us stop going over the basics of Christianity* again and again. Let us go on
instead and become mature in our understanding. Surely we don't need to start all
over again with the importance of turning away from evil deeds and placing our faith in
God. 2 You don't need further instruction about baptisms, the laying on of hands, the
resurrection of the dead, and eternal judgment. 3 And so, God willing, we will move
forward to further understanding.
4 For it is impossible to restore to repentance those who were once enlightened—
those who have experienced the good things of heaven and shared in the Holy Spirit,
5 who have tasted the goodness of the word of God and the power of the age to

5:7 Matt 26:38-46; Mark 14:32-42; Luke 22:39-46
5:8 Phil 2:8; Heb 1:2
5:10 Ps 110:4
5:12 1 Cor 3:2; 1 Pet 2:12
5:13 1 Cor 14:20; Eph 4:14
5:14 Rom 16:19; 1 Cor 2:6
6:1 Phil 3:12-14; Heb 5:12; 9:14
6:2 Acts 2:4; 6:6; 17:18, 32
6:4 John 4:10; Eph 2:8; Heb 10:32
6:5 Ps 34:8; 1 Pet 2:3

5:12 Or *about the oracles of God.* **6:1** Or *the basics about Christ.*

5:7 Jesus was in great agony as he prepared to face death (Luke 22:41-44). Although Jesus cried out to God, asking to be delivered, he was prepared to suffer humiliation, separation from his Father, and death in order to do God's will. At times we will undergo trials, not because we want to suffer, but because we want to obey God. Let Jesus' obedience sustain and encourage you in times of trial. You will be able to face anything if you know that Jesus Christ is with you.

5:7 Have you ever felt that God didn't hear your prayers? Be sure you are praying with reverent submission, willing to do what God wants. God responds to his obedient children.

5:8 Jesus' human life was not a script that he passively followed. It was a life that he chose freely (John 10:17, 18). It was a continuous process of making the will of God the Father his own. Jesus chose to obey, even though obedience led to suffering and death. Because Jesus obeyed perfectly, even under great trial, he can help us obey, no matter how difficult obedience seems to be.

5:9 Christ was always morally perfect. By obeying, he demonstrated his perfection to us, not to God or to himself. In the Bible, *perfect* usually means completeness or maturity. By sharing our experience of suffering, Christ shared our human experience completely. He is now able to offer eternal salvation to those who obey him. See Philippians 2:5-11 for Christ's attitude as he took on human form.

5:12, 13 These Jewish Christians were immature. Some of them should have been teaching others, but they had not even applied the basics to their own lives. They were reluctant to move beyond age-old traditions, established doctrines, and discussion of the basics. They wouldn't be able to understand the high-priestly role of Christ unless they moved out of their comfortable position, cut some of their Jewish ties, and stopped trying to blend in with their culture. Commitment to Christ moves people out of their comfort zones.

5:12-14 In order to grow from infant Christians to mature Christians, we must learn discernment. We must train our conscience, our senses, our mind, and our body to distinguish good from evil. Can you recognize temptation before it traps you? Can you tell the difference between a correct use of Scripture and a mistaken one?

5:14 Our capacity to feast on deeper knowledge of God ("solid food") is determined by our spiritual growth. Too often we want God's banquet before we are spiritually capable of digesting it. As you grow in the Lord and put into practice what you have learned, your capacity to understand will also grow.

6:1, 2 Certain elementary teachings are essential for all believers to understand. Those basics include the importance of faith, the foolishness of trying to be saved by good deeds, the meaning of baptism and spiritual gifts, and the facts of resurrection and eternal life. To go on to maturity in our understanding, we need to move beyond (but not away from) the elementary teachings to a more complete understanding of the faith. And this is what the author intends for them to do (6:3). Mature Christians should be teaching new Christians the basics. Then, acting on what they know, the mature will learn even more from God's Word.

6:3 These Christians needed to move beyond the basics of their faith to an understanding of Christ as the perfect High Priest and the fulfillment of all the Old Testament prophecies. Rather than arguing about the respective merits of Judaism and Christianity, they needed to depend on Christ and live effectively for him.

6:4-6 In the first century, a pagan who investigated Christianity and then went back to paganism made a clean break with the church. But for Jewish Christians who decided to return to Judaism, the break was less obvious. Their life-style remained relatively unchanged. But by deliberately turning away from Christ, they were cutting themselves off from God's forgiveness. Those who persevere in believing are true saints; those who continue to reject Christ are unbelievers, no matter how well they behave.

6:6 Heb 10:26, 29; 2 Pet 2:21; 1 Jn 5:16

come—6 and who then turn away from God. It is impossible to bring such people to
repentance again because they are nailing the Son of God to the cross again by
rejecting him, holding him up to public shame.
7 When the ground soaks up the rain that falls on it and bears a good crop for the

ABRAHAM IN THE NEW TESTAMENT

Abraham was an ancestor of Jesus Christ.	Matthew 1:1, 2, 17; Luke 3:23, 34	Jesus Christ was human; he was born into the line of Abraham, whom God had chosen to be the father of a great nation through which the whole world would be blessed. We are blessed because of what Jesus Christ, Abraham's descendant, did for us.
Abraham was the father of the Jewish nation.	Matthew 3:9; Luke 3:8; Acts 13:26; Romans 4:1; 11:1; 2 Corinthians 11:22; Hebrews 6:13, 14	God wanted to set apart a nation for himself, a nation that would tell the world about him. He began with a man of faith who, though old and childless, believed God's promise of innumerable descendants. We can trust God to do the impossible when we have faith.
Abraham, because of his faith, now sits in the Kingdom with Christ.	Matthew 8:11; Luke 13:28; 16:23–31	Abraham followed God, and now he is enjoying his reward—eternity with God. We will one day meet Abraham because we have been promised eternity as well.
God *is* Abraham's God; thus, Abraham is alive with God.	Matthew 22:32; Mark 12:26; Luke 20:37; Acts 7:32	As Abraham lives forever, we will live forever, because we, like Abraham, have chosen the life of faith.
Abraham received great promises from God.	Luke 1:55, 72, 73; Acts 3:25; 7:17, 18; Galatians 3:6, 14–16; Hebrews 6:13–15	Many of the promises God made to Abraham seemed impossible to be realized, but Abraham trusted God. The promises to believers in God's Word also seem too incredible to believe, but we can trust God to keep all his promises.
Abraham followed God.	Acts 7:2–8; Hebrews 11:8, 17–19	Abraham followed God's leading from his homeland to an unknown territory, which became the Jews' Promised Land. When we follow God, even before he makes all his plans clear to us, we will never be disappointed.
God blessed Abraham because of his faith.	Romans 4; Galatians 3:6–9, 14–29; Hebrews 11:8, 17–19; James 2:21–24	Abraham showed faith in times of disappointment, trial, and testing. Because of Abraham's faith, God counted him righteous and called him his "friend." God accepts us because of our faith.
Abraham is the father of all those who come to God by faith.	Romans 9:6–8; Galatians 3:6–9, 14–29	The Jews are Abraham's children, and Christ was his descendant. We are Christ's brothers and sisters; thus, all believers are Abraham's children and God's children. Abraham was righteous because of his faith; we are made righteous through faith in Christ. The promises made to Abraham apply to us because of Christ.

6:6 This verse points to the danger of the Hebrew Christians' returning to Judaism and thus committing apostasy. Some apply this verse today to superficial believers who renounce their Christianity or to unbelievers who come close to salvation and then turn away. Either way, those who reject Christ will not be saved. Christ died once for all. He will not be crucified again. Apart from his cross, there is no other possible way of salvation. However, the author does not indicate that his readers were in danger of renouncing Christ (see 6:9). He is warning against hardness of heart that would make repentance inconceivable for the sinner.

6:7, 8 Land that produces a good crop receives loving care, but land that produces thistles and thorns has to be burned so

farmer, it has the blessing of God. 8 But if a field bears thistles and thorns, it is useless.
The farmer will condemn that field and burn it.
9 Dear friends, even though we are talking like this, we really don't believe that it
applies to you. We are confident that you are meant for better things, things that come
with salvation. 10 For God is not unfair. He will not forget how hard you have worked for
him and how you have shown your love to him by caring for other Christians, as you
still do. 11 Our great desire is that you will keep right on loving others as long as life lasts,
in order to make certain that what you hope for will come true. 12 Then you will not
become spiritually dull and indifferent. Instead, you will follow the example of those
who are going to inherit God's promises because of their faith and patience.

God's Promises Bring Hope

13 For example, there was God's promise to Abraham. Since there was no one greater to
swear by, God took an oath in his own name, saying:

14 "I will certainly bless you richly,
and I will multiply your descendants into countless millions."*

15 Then Abraham waited patiently, and he received what God had promised.
16 When people take an oath, they call on someone greater than themselves to hold them
to it. And without any question that oath is binding. 17 God also bound himself with an
oath, so that those who received the promise could be perfectly sure that he would never
change his mind. 18 So God has given us both his promise and his oath. These two things
are unchangeable because it is impossible for God to lie. Therefore, we who have fled to
him for refuge can take new courage, for we can hold on to his promise with confidence.
19 This confidence is like a strong and trustworthy anchor for our souls. It leads us
through the curtain of heaven into God's inner sanctuary. 20 Jesus has already gone in
there for us. He has become our eternal High Priest in the line of Melchizedek.

Melchizedek Is Compared to Abraham

7 This Melchizedek was king of the city of Salem and also a priest of God Most High.
When Abraham was returning home after winning a great battle against many kings,
Melchizedek met him and blessed him. 2 Then Abraham took a tenth of all he had won
in the battle and gave it to Melchizedek. His name means "king of justice." He is also
"king of peace" because *Salem* means "peace." 3 There is no record of his father or

6:8 Gen 3:17-18
6:10 Matt 10:40, 42; 1 Thes 1:3
6:11 Heb 3:6; 10:22
6:12 Heb 10:36; 13:7
6:13 †Gen 22:16
6:14 †Gen 22:17
6:15 Gen 21:5
6:17 Ps 110:4; Heb 11:9
6:18 Num 23:19; 1 Sam 15:29; Titus 1:2; Heb 3:6
6:19 Lev 16:2-3, 12, 15; Heb 9:2-3, 7
6:20 Ps 110:4; Heb 4:14; 5:6
7:1-2 †Gen 14:17-20
7:3 Ps 110:4

6:14 Gen 22:17.

the farmer can start over. An unproductive Christian life falls under God's condemnation. We are not saved by deeds or conduct, but what we do is the *evidence* of our faith.

6:10 It's easy to get discouraged, thinking that God has forgotten us. But God is never unjust. He never forgets or overlooks our hard work for him. Presently you may not be receiving rewards and acclaim, but God knows your efforts of love and ministry. Let God's love for you and his intimate knowledge of your service for him bolster you as you face disappointment and rejection here on earth.

6:11, 12 Hope keeps the Christian from becoming lazy or feeling bored. Like an athlete, train hard and run well, remembering the reward that lies ahead (Philippians 3:14).

6:15 Abraham waited patiently; it was 25 years from the time God had promised him a son (Genesis 12:7; 13:14-16; 15:4, 5; 17:16) to Isaac's birth (Genesis 21:1-3). Because our trials and temptations are often so intense, they seem to last for an eternity. Both the Bible and the testimony of mature Christians encourage us to wait for God to act in his timing, even when our needs seem too great to wait any longer.

6:17 God's promises are unchanging and trustworthy because God is unchanging and trustworthy. When promising Abraham a son, God took an oath in his own name. The oath was as good as God's name, and God's name was as good as his divine nature.

6:18, 19 These two unchangeable things are God's promise and his oath. God embodies all truth; therefore, he cannot lie. Because God is truth, you can be secure in his promises; you don't need to wonder if he will change his plans. Our hope is secure and immovable, anchored in God, just as a ship's anchor holds firmly to the seabed. To the true seeker who comes to God in belief, God gives an unconditional promise of acceptance. When you ask God with openness, honesty, and sincerity to save you from your sins, *he will do it.* This truth should give you encouragement, assurance, and confidence.

6:19, 20 A curtain hung across the entrance from the Holy Place to the Most Holy Place, the two innermost rooms of the Temple. This curtain prevented anyone from entering, gazing into, or even getting a fleeting glimpse of the interior of the Most Holy Place (see also 9:1-8). The high priest could enter there only once a year to stand in God's presence and atone for the sins of the entire nation. But Christ is in God's presence at all times, not just once a year, as the High Priest who can continually intercede for us.

7:2ff The writer of Hebrews uses this story from Genesis 14:18-20 to show that Christ is even greater than Abraham, father of the Jewish nation, and Levi (Abraham's descendant). Therefore, the Jewish priesthood (made up of Levi's descendants) was inferior to Melchizedek's priesthood (a type of Christ's priesthood).

7:3-10 Melchizedek was a priest of God Most High (see the note on Genesis 14:18 and his Profile in Genesis 16). He is said to remain a priest forever (see also Psalm 110:4), because his priesthood has no record of beginning or ending. He was a priest of God in Salem (Jerusalem) long before the nation of Israel and the regular priesthood began.

mother or any of his ancestors—no beginning or end to his life. He remains a priest
forever, resembling the Son of God.
7:4 Gen 14:20 — 4 Consider then how great this Melchizedek was. Even Abraham, the great patriarch
of Israel, recognized how great Melchizedek was by giving him a tenth of what he had
7:5 Num 18:21, 26 — taken in battle. 5 Now the priests, who are descendants of Levi, are commanded in the
law of Moses to collect a tithe from all the people, even though they are their own
7:6 Rom 4:13 — relatives.* 6 But Melchizedek, who was not even related to Levi, collected a tenth from
7:7 Gen 14:19 — Abraham. And Melchizedek placed a blessing upon Abraham, the one who had already
received the promises of God. 7 And without question, the person who has the power to
bless is always greater than the person who is blessed.
7:8 Heb 5:6; 6:20 — 8 In the case of Jewish priests, tithes are paid to men who will die. But Melchizedek is
greater than they are, because we are told that he lives on. 9 In addition, we might even
say that Levi's descendants, the ones who collect the tithe, paid a tithe to Melchizedek
through their ancestor Abraham. 10 For although Levi wasn't born yet, the seed from
which he came was in Abraham's loins when Melchizedek collected the tithe from him.
7:11 Ps 110:4; Heb 5:6; 7:17 — 11 And finally, if the priesthood of Levi could have achieved God's purposes—and it
was that priesthood on which the law was based—why did God need to send a different
7:14 Gen 49:10; Isa 11:1; Matt 1:3; 2:6; Luke 3:33; Rom 1:3; Rev 5:5 — priest from the line of Melchizedek, instead of from the line of Levi and Aaron?*
12 And when the priesthood is changed, the law must also be changed to permit it. 13 For
the one we are talking about belongs to a different tribe, whose members do not serve at
the altar. 14 What I mean is, our Lord came from the tribe of Judah, and Moses never
mentioned Judah in connection with the priesthood.

Christ Is like Melchizedek

15 The change in God's law is even more evident from the fact that a different priest, who
is like Melchizedek, has now come. 16 He became a priest, not by meeting the old
requirement of belonging to the tribe of Levi, but by the power of a life that cannot be
7:17 †Ps 110:4; Heb 5:6; 6:20 — destroyed. 17 And the psalmist pointed this out when he said of Christ,

> "You are a priest forever
> in the line of Melchizedek."*

7:18 Rom 8:3 — 18 Yes, the old requirement about the priesthood was set aside because it was weak and
7:19 Rom 3:20; Heb 9:9; 10:19-22 — useless. 19 For the law made nothing perfect, and now a better hope has taken its place.
And that is how we draw near to God.
20 God took an oath that Christ would always be a priest, but he never did this for any
7:21 †Ps 110:4; Heb 5:6; 6:20; 7:17 — other priest. 21 Only to Jesus did he say,

> "The Lord has taken an oath
> and will not break his vow:
> 'You are a priest forever.'"*

7:22 Heb 8:6; 12:24 — 22 Because of God's oath, it is Jesus who guarantees the effectiveness of this better
covenant.

7:5 Greek *their brothers, who are descendants of Abraham.* **7:11** Greek *according to the order of Aaron.* **7:17** Ps 110:4. **7:21** Ps 110:4.

7:11-17 Jesus' high-priestly role was superior to that of any priest of Levi, because the Messiah was a priest of a higher order (Psalm 110:4). If the Jewish priests and their laws had been able to save people, why would God need to send Christ as a priest, who came not from the tribe of Levi (the priestly tribe) but from the tribe of Judah? The animal sacrifices had to be repeated, and they offered only temporary forgiveness; but Christ's sacrifice was offered once, and it offers total and permanent forgiveness. Under the new covenant, the Levitical priesthood was canceled in favor of Christ's role as High Priest. Because Christ is our High Priest, we need to pay attention to him. No minister, leader, or Christian friend can substitute for Christ's work and for his role in our salvation.

7:18, 19 The law was not intended to save people but to point out sin (see Romans 3:20; 5:20) and to point toward Christ (see Galatians 3:24, 25). Salvation comes through Christ, whose sacrifice brings forgiveness for our sins. Being ethical, working diligently to help others, and giving to charitable causes are all commendable, but all of our good deeds cannot save us or make us right with God. There is a "better hope."

7:22-24 This "better covenant" is also called the new covenant or testament. It is new and better because it allows us to go directly to God through Christ. We no longer need to rely on sacrificed animals and mediating priests to obtain God's forgiveness. This new covenant is better because, while all human priests die, Christ lives forever. Priests and sacrifices could not save people, but Christ truly saves. You have access to Christ. He is available to you, but do you go to him with your needs?

23Another difference is that there were many priests under the old system. When
one priest died, another had to take his place. 24But Jesus remains a priest forever;
his priesthood will never end. 25Therefore he is able, once and forever, to save*
everyone who comes to God through him. He lives forever to plead with God on
their behalf.
26He is the kind of high priest we need because he is holy and blameless, unstained
by sin. He has now been set apart from sinners, and he has been given the highest
place of honor in heaven. 27He does not need to offer sacrifices every day like the
other high priests. They did this for their own sins first and then for the sins of the
people. But Jesus did this once for all when he sacrificed himself on the cross.
28Those who were high priests under the law of Moses were limited by human
weakness. But after the law was given, God appointed his Son with an oath, and his
Son has been made perfect forever.

7:24 Isa 9:6-7; Rev 1:18
7:25 Rom 8:34; 1 Jn 2:1
7:26 2 Cor 5:21; Heb 4:14
7:27 Lev 9:7; 16:6, 11, 15; Eph 5:2; Heb 9:12
7:28 Heb 2:10; 5:1-2

4. The new covenant is greater than the old

Christ Is Our High Priest

8 Here is the main point: Our High Priest sat down in the place of highest honor in
heaven, at God's right hand. 2There he ministers in the sacred tent, the true place of
worship that was built by the Lord and not by human hands.
3And since every high priest is required to offer gifts and sacrifices, our High Priest
must make an offering, too. 4If he were here on earth, he would not even be a priest,
since there already are priests who offer the gifts required by the law of Moses. 5They
serve in a place of worship that is only a copy, a shadow of the real one in heaven. For
when Moses was getting ready to build the Tabernacle, God gave him this warning:
"Be sure that you make everything according to the design I have shown you here on
the mountain."* 6But our High Priest has been given a ministry that is far superior to
the ministry of those who serve under the old laws, for he is the one who guarantees
for us a better covenant with God, based on better promises.

8:1 Heb 1:3; 2:17; 4:14; 6:20; 7:26; 9:11
8:2 Num 24:6; Heb 9:11
8:3 Heb 5:1
8:5 †Exod 25:40; 26:30; Col 2:17; Heb 9:23
8:6 Heb 7:22; 9:15; 12:24

7:25 Or *able to save completely.* **8:5** Exod 25:40; 26:30.

7:25 No one can add to what Jesus did to save us; our past, present, and future sins are all forgiven, and Jesus is with the Father as a sign that our sins are forgiven. If you are a Christian, remember that Christ has paid the price for your sins once and for all (see also 9:24-28).

7:25 As our High Priest, Christ is our Advocate, the mediator between us and God. He looks after our interests and intercedes for us with God. The Old Testament high priest went before God once a year to plead for the forgiveness of the nation's sins; Christ makes perpetual intercession before God for us. Christ's continuous presence in heaven with the Father assures us that our sins have been paid for and forgiven (see Romans 8:33, 34; Hebrews 2:17, 18; 4:15, 16; 9:24). This wonderful assurance frees us from guilt and from fear of failure.

7:27 In Old Testament times when animals were sacrificed, they were cut into pieces, the parts were washed, the fat was burned, the blood was sprinkled, and the meat was boiled. Blood was demanded as atonement for sin, and God accepted animal blood to cover the people's sin (Leviticus 17:11). Because of the sacrificial system, the Israelites were generally aware that sin costs someone something and that they themselves were sinful. Many people take Christ's work on the cross for granted. They don't realize how costly it was for Jesus to secure our forgiveness—it cost him his life and painful, temporary separation from his Father (Matthew 27:46; 1 Peter 1:18, 19).

7:27 Because Jesus died *once for all,* he brought the sacrificial system to an end. He forgave sins—past, present, and future. The Jews did not need to go back to the old system because Christ, the perfect sacrifice, completed the work of redemption. You don't have to look for another way to have your sins forgiven—Christ was the final sacrifice for you.

7:28 As we better understand the Jewish sacrificial system, we see that Jesus' death served as the perfect atonement for our sins. His death brings us eternal life. How callous, how cold, how stubborn it would be to refuse God's greatest gift.

8:4 Under the old Jewish system, priests were chosen only from the tribe of Levi, and sacrifices were offered daily on the altar for forgiveness of sins (see 7:12-14). This system would not have allowed Jesus to be a priest, because he was from the tribe of Judah. But his perfect sacrifice ended all need for further priests and sacrifices.

The use of the present tense, "there already are priests who offer the gifts," indicates that this book was written before A.D. 70 when the Temple in Jerusalem was destroyed, ending the sacrifices.

8:5 The pattern for the Tabernacle built by Moses was given by God. It was a pattern of the spiritual reality of Christ's sacrifice, and thus it looked forward to the future reality. There is no Tabernacle in heaven of which the earthly one is a copy, but rather the earthly Tabernacle was an expression of eternal, theological principles. Because the Temple at Jerusalem had not yet been destroyed, using the worship system there as an example would have had a great impact on this original audience.

8:7 Heb 7:11
7 If the first covenant had been faultless, there would have been no need for a second
8:8-12 †Jer 31:31-34
covenant to replace it. 8 But God himself found fault with the old one when he said:

"The day will come, says the Lord,
when I will make a new covenant
with the people of Israel and Judah.
9 This covenant will not be like the one
I made with their ancestors
when I took them by the hand
and led them out of the land of Egypt.
They did not remain faithful to my covenant,
so I turned my back on them, says the Lord.
8:10 Heb 10:16
10 But this is the new covenant I will make
with the people of Israel on that day, says the Lord:
I will put my laws in their minds
so they will understand them,
and I will write them on their hearts
so they will obey them.
I will be their God,
and they will be my people.
8:11 John 6:45
11 And they will not need to teach their neighbors,
nor will they need to teach their family,
saying, 'You should know the Lord.'
For everyone, from the least to the greatest,
will already know me.
8:12 Heb 10:17
12 And I will forgive their wrongdoings,
and I will never again remember their sins."*

8:13 Heb 12:24
13 When God speaks of a new covenant, it means he has made the first one obsolete. It is
now out of date and ready to be put aside.

Old Rules about Worship

9:2 Exod 25:23-40; 26:1-30 Lev 24:5
9 Now in that first covenant between God and Israel, there were regulations for
worship and a sacred tent here on earth. 2 There were two rooms in this tent. In the
first room were a lampstand, a table, and loaves of holy bread on the table. This was
9:3 Exod 26:31-33
called the Holy Place. 3 Then there was a curtain, and behind the curtain was the second
room called the Most Holy Place. 4 In that room were a gold incense altar and a wooden
9:4 Exod 16:33; 25:10-16; 30:1-6 Num 17:8-10 Deut 10:3-5
chest called the Ark of the Covenant, which was covered with gold on all sides. Inside
the Ark were a gold jar containing some manna, Aaron's staff that sprouted leaves, and
the stone tablets of the covenant with the Ten Commandments written on them. 5 The
9:5 Exod 25:17-22
glorious cherubim were above the Ark. Their wings were stretched out over the Ark's
9:6 Num 18:2-6
cover, the place of atonement. But we cannot explain all of these things now.
6 When these things were all in place, the priests went in and out of the first room*
9:7 Exod 30:10 Lev 16:2, 14-15 Heb 5:2-3
regularly as they performed their religious duties. 7 But only the high priest goes into the
Most Holy Place, and only once a year, and always with blood, which he offers to God

8:8-12 Jer 31:31-34. **9:6** Greek *first tent;* also in 9:8.

8:8-12 This passage is a quotation of Jeremiah 31:31-34, which compares the new covenant with the old. The old covenant was the covenant of law between God and Israel. The new and better way is the covenant of grace—Christ's offer to forgive our sins and bring us to God through his sacrificial death. This covenant is new in extent—it goes beyond Israel and Judah to include all the Gentile nations. It is new in application because it is written on our heart and in our mind. It offers a new way to forgiveness, not through animal sacrifice but through faith. Have you entered into this new covenant and begun walking in the better way?

8:10 If our heart is not changed, following God's rules will be unpleasant and difficult. We will rebel against being told how to live. The Holy Spirit, however, gives us new desires, helping us *want* to obey God (see Philippians 2:12, 13). With a new heart, we find that serving God is our greatest joy.

8:10, 11 Under God's new covenant, God's law is inside us. It is no longer an external set of rules and principles. The Holy Spirit reminds us of Christ's words, activates our conscience, influences our motives and desires, and makes us want to obey. Now doing God's will is something we desire with all our heart and mind.

9:5 "Cherubim" are mighty angels.

9:6-8 The high priest could enter the Most Holy Place (9:3), the innermost room of the Tabernacle, one day each year to atone for the nation's sins. The Most Holy Place was a small room that

to cover his own sins and the sins the people have committed in ignorance. [8]By these
regulations the Holy Spirit revealed that the Most Holy Place was not open to the people
as long as the first room and the entire system it represents were still in use.
[9]This is an illustration pointing to the present time. For the gifts and sacrifices that the
priests offer are not able to cleanse the consciences of the people who bring them. [10]For
that old system deals only with food and drink and ritual washing—external regulations
that are in effect only until their limitations can be corrected.

Christ Is the Perfect Sacrifice

[11]So Christ has now become the High Priest over all the good things that have come. He
has entered that great, perfect sanctuary in heaven, not made by human hands and not
part of this created world. [12]Once for all time he took blood into that Most Holy Place,
but not the blood of goats and calves. He took his own blood, and with it he secured our
salvation forever.
[13]Under the old system, the blood of goats and bulls and the ashes of a young cow
could cleanse people's bodies from ritual defilement. [14]Just think how much more the
blood of Christ will purify our hearts from deeds that lead to death so that we can worship
the living God. For by the power of the eternal Spirit, Christ offered himself to God as
a perfect sacrifice for our sins. [15]That is why he is the one who mediates the new
covenant between God and people, so that all who are invited can receive the eternal
inheritance God has promised them. For Christ died to set them free from the penalty of
the sins they had committed under that first covenant.
[16]Now when someone dies and leaves a will, no one gets anything until it is proved
that the person who wrote the will* is dead.* [17]The will goes into effect only after the
death of the person who wrote it. While the person is still alive, no one can use the will
to get any of the things promised to them.
[18]That is why blood was required under the first covenant as a proof of death. [19]For
after Moses had given the people all of God's laws, he took the blood of calves and goats,
along with water, and sprinkled both the book of God's laws and all the people, using
branches of hyssop bushes and scarlet wool. [20]Then he said, "This blood confirms the
covenant God has made with you."* [21]And in the same way, he sprinkled blood on the
sacred tent and on everything used for worship. [22]In fact, we can say that according to
the law of Moses, nearly everything was purified by sprinkling with blood. Without the
shedding of blood, there is no forgiveness of sins.

9:8 John 14:6; Heb 10:19-20
9:9 Heb 5:1; 10:1-2
9:10 Lev 11:2, 25; 15:8; Num 6:3; 19:13
9:11 Heb 8:2; 10:1
9:12 Heb 7:27
9:13 Lev 16:3, 14-15; Num 19:9, 17
9:14 Heb 6:1; 1 Pet 3:18; 1 Jn 1:7
9:15 1 Tim 2:5; Heb 7:22
9:18-19 Exod 24:6-8; Lev 14:4; Num 19:6
9:20 †Exod 24:8; Matt 26:28
9:21 Lev 8:15, 19
9:22 Lev 17:11

9:16a Or *covenant.* **9:16b** Or *Now when someone makes a covenant, it is necessary to ratify it with the death of a sacrifice.* **9:20** Exod 24:8.

---

contained the Ark of the Covenant (a gold-covered chest containing the original stone tablets on which the Ten Commandments were written, a jar of manna, and Aaron's staff). The top of the chest served as the "atonement cover" (the altar) on which the blood would be sprinkled by the high priest on the Day of Atonement. The Most Holy Place was the most sacred spot on earth for the Jews and only the high priest could enter it. The other priests and the common people were forbidden to come into the room. Their only access to God was through the high priest, who would offer a sacrifice and use the animal's blood to atone first for his own sins and then for the people's sins (see also 10:19).

9:10 The people had to keep the Old Testament dietary laws and ceremonial cleansing laws until Christ came with God's new and better way.

9:12 This imagery comes from the Day of Atonement rituals described in Leviticus 16. Through his own death, Christ freed us from the slavery of sin forever.

9:12-14 Though you know Christ, you may believe that you have to work hard to make yourself good enough for God. But rules and rituals have never cleansed people's hearts. By Jesus' blood alone (1) we have our conscience cleansed, (2) we are freed from death's sting and can live to serve God, and (3) we are freed from sin's power. If you are carrying a load of guilt because you are finding that you can't be good enough for God, take another look at Jesus' death and what it means for you. Christ can heal your conscience and deliver you from the frustration of trying to earn God's favor.

9:13, 14 When the people sacrificed animals, God considered the people's faith and obedience, cleansed them from sin, and made them *ceremonially* acceptable according to Old Testament law. But Christ's sacrifice transforms our life and heart and makes us clean on the inside. His sacrifice is infinitely more effective than animal sacrifices. No barrier of sin or weakness on our part can stifle his forgiveness.

9:15 People in Old Testament times were saved through Christ's sacrifice, although that sacrifice had not yet happened. In offering unblemished animal sacrifices, they were anticipating Christ's coming and his death for sin. There was no point in returning to the sacrificial system now that Christ had come and had become the final, perfect sacrifice.

9:22 Why does forgiveness require the shedding of blood? This is no arbitrary decree on the part of a bloodthirsty God, as some have suggested. There is no greater symbol of life than blood; blood keeps us alive. Jesus shed his blood—gave his life—for our sins so that we wouldn't have to experience spiritual death, eternal separation from God. Jesus is the source of life, not death. He gave his own life to pay our penalty for us so that we might live. After shedding his blood for us, Christ rose from the grave and proclaimed victory over sin and death.

9:23 Heb 8:5
9:24 Rom 8:34; Heb 8:2; 9:12; 1 Jn 2:1
9:25 Heb 9:7; 10:19
9:26 1 Cor 10:11; Heb 7:27; 1 Pet 3:18
9:27 Gen 3:19
9:28 Isa 53:12; Phil 3:20; Heb 7:27; 1 Pet 2:24

23 That is why the earthly tent and everything in it—which were copies of things in
heaven—had to be purified by the blood of animals. But the real things in heaven had to
be purified with far better sacrifices than the blood of animals.
24 For Christ has entered into heaven itself to appear now before God as our Advocate.* He did not go into the earthly place of worship, for that was merely a copy of the
real Temple in heaven. 25 Nor did he enter heaven to offer himself again and again, like
the earthly high priest who enters the Most Holy Place year after year to offer the blood
of an animal. 26 If that had been necessary, he would have had to die again and again,
ever since the world began. But no! He came once for all time, at the end of the age, to
remove the power of sin forever by his sacrificial death for us.
27 And just as it is destined that each person dies only once and after that comes
judgment, 28 so also Christ died only once as a sacrifice to take away the sins of many
people. He will come again but not to deal with our sins again. This time he will bring
salvation to all those who are eagerly waiting for him.

Christ's Sacrifice Once for All

10:1 Col 2:17; Heb 7:19; 8:5; 9:11
10:3 Lev 16:34; Heb 9:7
10:4 Lev 16:15, 21; Heb 9:13
10:5-7 †Ps 40:6-8

10 The old system in the law of Moses was only a shadow of the things to come, not
the reality of the good things Christ has done for us. The sacrifices under the old
system were repeated again and again, year after year, but they were never able to
provide perfect cleansing for those who came to worship. 2 If they could have provided
perfect cleansing, the sacrifices would have stopped, for the worshipers would have been
purified once for all time, and their feelings of guilt would have disappeared.
3 But just the opposite happened. Those yearly sacrifices reminded them of their sins
year after year. 4 For it is not possible for the blood of bulls and goats to take away sins.
5 That is why Christ, when he came into the world, said,

"You did not want animal sacrifices and grain offerings.
  But you have given me a body so that I may obey you.
6 No, you were not pleased with animals burned on the altar
  or with other offerings for sin.
7 Then I said, 'Look, I have come to do your will, O God—
  just as it is written about me in the Scriptures.'"*

9:24 Greek *on our behalf.* **10:5-7** Ps 40:6-8.

9:23 In a way that we don't fully understand, the earthly Tabernacle was a copy and symbol of heavenly realities. This purification of the heavenly things can best be understood as referring to Christ's spiritual work for us in heaven (see the note on 8:5).

9:24 Among references to priests, Tabernacles, sacrifices, and other ideas unfamiliar to us, we come to this description of Christ as our Advocate, appearing in God's presence on our behalf. We can relate to this role and be encouraged by it. Christ is on our side at God's side. He is our Lord and Savior. He is not there to convince or remind God that our sins are forgiven but to present both our needs and our service for him as an offering (see 7:25).

9:24-28 All people die physically, but Christ died so that we would not have to die spiritually. We can have wonderful confidence in his saving work for us, doing away with sin—past, present, and future. He has forgiven our past sin—when he died on the cross, he sacrificed himself once for all (9:26); he has given us the Holy Spirit to help us deal with present sin; he appears for us now in heaven as our Advocate (9:24); and he promises to return (9:28) and raise us to eternal life in a world where sin will be banished.

9:26 The "end of the age" refers to the time of Christ's coming to earth in fulfillment of the Old Testament prophecies. Christ ushered in the new era of grace and forgiveness. We are still living in the "end of the age." The day of the Lord has begun and will be completed at Christ's return.

10:3 When people gathered for the offering of sacrifices on the Day of Atonement, they were reminded of their sins, and they undoubtedly felt guilty all over again. What they needed most was forgiveness—the permanent, powerful, sin-destroying forgiveness we have from Christ. When we confess a sin to him, we need never think of it again. Christ has forgiven us, and the sin no longer exists. See 1 John 1:9.

10:4 Animal sacrifices could not take away sins; they provided only a temporary way to deal with sin until Jesus came to deal with sin permanently. How, then, were people forgiven in Old Testament times? Because Old Testament believers were following God's command to offer sacrifices, he graciously forgave them when, by faith, they made their sacrifices. But that practice looked forward to Christ's perfect sacrifice. Christ's way was superior to the Old Testament way because the old way only pointed to what Christ would do to take away sins.

10:5-10 This quotation is not cited in any other New Testament book. However, it is a central teaching of the Old Testament that God desires obedience and a right heart, not empty compliance to the sacrifice system (see the chart in Hosea 7). The writer of Hebrews applies to Christ the words of the psalmist in Psalm 40:6-8. Christ came to offer his body on the cross for us as a sacrifice that is completely acceptable to God. God's new and living way for us to please him is not by keeping laws or even by abstaining from sin. It is by coming to him in faith to be forgiven, and then following him in loving obedience.

10:5-10 The costly sacrifice of an animal's life impressed upon the sinner the seriousness of his or her own sin before God. Because Jesus shed his own blood for us, his sacrifice is infinitely greater than any Old Testament offering. Considering the immeasurable gift he gave us, we should respond by giving him our devotion and service.

8 Christ said, "You did not want animal sacrifices or grain offerings or animals burned
on the altar or other offerings for sin, nor were you pleased with them" (though they are
required by the law of Moses). 9 Then he added, "Look, I have come to do your will."
He cancels the first covenant in order to establish the second. 10 And what God wants is
for us to be made holy by the sacrifice of the body of Jesus Christ once for all time.
11 Under the old covenant, the priest stands before the altar day after day, offering
sacrifices that can never take away sins. 12 But our High Priest offered himself to God as
one sacrifice for sins, good for all time. Then he sat down at the place of highest honor at
God's right hand. 13 There he waits until his enemies are humbled as a footstool under his
feet. 14 For by that one offering he perfected forever all those whom he is making holy.
15 And the Holy Spirit also testifies that this is so. First he says,

16 "This is the new covenant I will make
with my people on that day, says the Lord:
I will put my laws in their hearts
so they will understand them,
and I will write them on their minds
so they will obey them."

17 Then he adds,

"I will never again remember
their sins and lawless deeds."*

18 Now when sins have been forgiven, there is no need to offer any more sacrifices.

10:8 †Ps 40:6
10:10 Eph 5:2; Heb 7:27; 9:12, 28; 1 Pet 2:24
10:11 Heb 5:1
10:12 Ps 110:1; Matt 22:44; Col 3:1; Heb 1:3
10:13 Ps 110:1
10:15 Heb 3:7
10:16-17 †Jer 31:33-34

B. THE SUPERIORITY OF FAITH (10:19—13:25)

Moving from argument to instruction, the author cites many examples of those who have demonstrated faith throughout history. Living by faith is far better than merely fulfilling rituals and rules. This can challenge us to grow in faith and to live in obedience to God each day.

A Call to Persevere

19 And so, dear friends,* we can boldly enter heaven's Most Holy Place because of the
blood of Jesus. 20 This is the new, life-giving way that Christ has opened up for us
through the sacred curtain, by means of his death for us.*

10:19 Eph 3:12
10:20 John 4:6; Heb 6:19; 9:8

10:16-17 Jer 31:33-34. **10:19** Greek *brothers.* **10:20** Greek *his flesh.*

10:9 Cancelling the first covenant in order to establish a far better one meant doing away with the system of sacrifices contained in the ceremonial law. It didn't mean eliminating God's *moral* law (the Ten Commandments). The ceremonial law prepared people for Christ's coming. With Christ's death and resurrection, that system was no longer needed. And through Christ we can fulfill the moral law as we let him live in us.

10:11, 12 Christ's work is contrasted with the work of the Jewish priests. The priests' work was never finished, so they had to stand day after day and offer sacrifices; Christ's sacrifice (dying in our place) is finished, so he is seated. The priests repeated the sacrifices often; Christ sacrificed once for all. The sacrifice system couldn't completely remove sin; Christ's sacrifice effectively cleansed us.

10:12 If the Jewish readers of this book were to return to the old Jewish system, they would be implying that Christ's sacrifice wasn't enough to forgive their sins. Adding anything to his sacrifice or taking anything from it denies its validity. Any system to gain salvation through good deeds is essentially rejecting the significance of Christ's death and spurning the Holy Spirit's work. Beware of anyone who tells you that Christ's sacrifice still leaves you incomplete or that something else is needed to make you acceptable to God. When we believe in Christ, he makes us completely right with God. Our loving relationship leads us to follow him in willing obedience and service. He is pleased with our service, but we cannot be saved by our good deeds.

10:14 We have been made perfect, yet we are being made holy. Through his death and resurrection, Christ, once for all, made his believers perfect in God's sight. At the same time, he is making them holy (progressively cleansed and set apart for his special use) in their daily pilgrimage here. We should not be surprised, ashamed, or shocked that we still need to grow. God is not finished with us. We can encourage this growth process by deliberately applying Scripture to all areas of our life, by accepting the discipline and guidance Christ provides, and by giving him control of our desires and goals.

10:17 The writer concludes his argument with this powerful statement that God will remember our sins no more. Christ forgives completely, so there is no need to confess our past sins repeatedly. As believers, we can be confident that the sins we confess and renounce are forgiven and forgotten.

10:19 The Most Holy Place in the Temple was sealed from view by a curtain (10:20). Only the high priest could enter this holy room, and he did so only once a year on the Day of Atonement when he offered the sacrifice for the nation's sins. But Jesus' death removed the curtain, and all believers may walk into God's presence at any time (see also 6:19, 20).

10:21 Heb 2:17; 3:6
21 And since we have a great High Priest who rules over God's people, 22 let us go right
10:22 Ezek 36:25; Eph 5:26
into the presence of God, with true hearts fully trusting him. For our evil consciences
have been sprinkled with Christ's blood to make us clean, and our bodies have been
washed with pure water.
10:23 1 Cor 1:9; 10:13; Heb 3:6
23 Without wavering, let us hold tightly to the hope we say we have, for God can be
trusted to keep his promise. 24 Think of ways to encourage one another to outbursts of
10:25 Acts 2:42; Heb 3:13
love and good deeds. 25 And let us not neglect our meeting together, as some people do,
but encourage and warn each other, especially now that the day of his coming back again
is drawing near.
10:26 1 Tim 2:4; Heb 6:4-8; 2 Pet 2:20
26 Dear friends, if we deliberately continue sinning after we have received a full
knowledge of the truth, there is no other sacrifice that will cover these sins. 27 There will
10:27 Isa 26:11
be nothing to look forward to but the terrible expectation of God's judgment and the raging
fire that will consume his enemies. 28 Anyone who refused to obey the law of Moses was
10:28 Deut 17:6; 19:5
put to death without mercy on the testimony of two or three witnesses. 29 Think how much
more terrible the punishment will be for those who have trampled on the Son of God and
10:29 Exod 24:8
have treated the blood of the covenant as if it were common and unholy. Such people have
insulted and enraged the Holy Spirit who brings God's mercy to his people.
10:30 †Deut 32:35-36; Ps 135:14
30 For we know the one who said,

> "I will take vengeance.
> I will repay those who deserve it."

He also said,

> "The Lord will judge his own people."*

10:31 2 Cor 5:11
31 It is a terrible thing to fall into the hands of the living God.
32 Don't ever forget those early days when you first learned about Christ. Remember
10:33 1 Cor 4:9; 1 Thes 2:14
how you remained faithful even though it meant terrible suffering. 33 Sometimes you
were exposed to public ridicule and were beaten, and sometimes you helped others who
10:34 Heb 13:3
were suffering the same things. 34 You suffered along with those who were thrown into
jail. When all you owned was taken from you, you accepted it with joy. You knew you
had better things waiting for you in eternity.
35 Do not throw away this confident trust in the Lord, no matter what happens.
10:36 Heb 9:15
Remember the great reward it brings you! 36 Patient endurance is what you need now, so
you will continue to do God's will. Then you will receive all that he has promised.

10:30 Deut 32:35-36.

10:22-25 We have significant privileges associated with our new life in Christ: (1) We have personal access to God through Christ and can draw near to him without an elaborate system (10:22); (2) we may grow in faith, overcome doubts and questions, and deepen our relationship with God (10:23); (3) we may enjoy encouragement from one another (10:24); (4) we may worship together (10:25).

10:25 To neglect Christian meetings is to give up the encouragement and help of other Christians. We gather together to share our faith and to strengthen one another in the Lord. As we get closer to the day when Christ will return, we will face many spiritual struggles, and even times of persecution. Anti-Christian forces will grow in strength. Difficulties should never be excuses for missing church services. Rather, as difficulties arise, we should make an even greater effort to be faithful in attendance.

10:26 When people deliberately reject Christ's offer of salvation, they reject God's most precious gift. They ignore the leading of the Holy Spirit, the one who communicates to us God's saving love. This warning was given to Jewish Christians who were tempted to reject Christ for Judaism, but it applies to anyone who rejects Christ for another religion or, having understood Christ's atoning work, deliberately turns away from it (see also Numbers 15:30, 31 and Mark 3:28-30). The point is that there is no other acceptable sacrifice for sin than the death of Christ on the cross. If someone deliberately rejects the sacrifice of Christ after clearly understanding the Good News teaching about it, then there is no way for that person to be saved, because God has not provided any other name in all of heaven for people to call on to save them (see Acts 4:12).

10:31 This judgment is for those who have rejected God's mercy. For those who accept Christ's love and his salvation, the coming judgment is no cause for worry. Being saved through his grace, they have nothing to fear (see 1 John 4:18).

10:32-36 Hebrews encourages believers to persevere in their Christian faith and conduct when facing persecution and pressure. We don't usually think of suffering as good for us, but it can build our character and our patience. During times of great stress, we may feel God's presence more clearly and find help from Christians we never thought would care. Knowing that Jesus is with us in our suffering and that he will return one day to put an end to all pain helps us grow in our faith and our relationship with him (see Romans 5:3-5).

10:35-38 The writer encourages his readers not to abandon their faith in times of persecution but to show by their endurance that their faith is real. Faith means resting in what Christ has done for us in the past, but it also means trusting him for what he will do for us in the present and in the future (see Romans 8:12-25; Galatians 3:10-13).

37 "For in just a little while,
the Coming One will come and not delay.
38 And a righteous person will live by faith.
But I will have no pleasure in anyone who turns away."*

39 But we are not like those who turn their backs on God and seal their fate. We have faith that assures our salvation.

Great Examples of Faith

11 What is faith? It is the confident assurance that what we hope for is going to
happen. It is the evidence of things we cannot yet see. 2 God gave his approval to
people in days of old because of their faith.
3 By faith we understand that the entire universe was formed at God's command, that
what we now see did not come from anything that can be seen.
4 It was by faith that Abel brought a more acceptable offering to God than Cain did.
God accepted Abel's offering to show that he was a righteous man. And although Abel
is long dead, he still speaks to us because of his faith.
5 It was by faith that Enoch was taken up to heaven without dying—"suddenly he
disappeared because God took him."* But before he was taken up, he was approved as
pleasing to God. 6 So, you see, it is impossible to please God without faith. Anyone who
wants to come to him must believe that there is a God and that he rewards those who
sincerely seek him.
7 It was by faith that Noah built an ark to save his family from the flood. He obeyed
God, who warned him about something that had never happened before. By his faith he
condemned the rest of the world and was made right in God's sight.
8 It was by faith that Abraham obeyed when God called him to leave home and go to
another land that God would give him as his inheritance. He went without knowing
where he was going. 9 And even when he reached the land God promised him, he lived
there by faith—for he was like a foreigner, living in a tent. And so did Isaac and Jacob,
to whom God gave the same promise. 10 Abraham did this because he was confidently
looking forward to a city with eternal foundations, a city designed and built by God.

10:37-38 †Hab 2:3-4; Rom 1:17; Gal 3:11
11:1 Rom 8:24; Heb 3:6, 14
11:3 Gen 1:1-31; Ps 33:6, 9; John 1:3; Rom 1:19-20; Heb 1:2
11:4 Gen 4:3-10
11:5 Gen 5:22-24
11:6 Heb 7:19
11:7 Gen 6:13-22; Rom 3:22; 1 Pet 3:20
11:8 Gen 12:1-5; Acts 7:2-4
11:9 Gen 12:8
11:10 Heb 12:22; Rev 21:2

10:37-38 Hab 2:3-4. **11:5** Gen 5:24.

11:1 Do you remember how you felt when you were very young and your birthday approached? You were excited and anxious. You knew you would certainly receive gifts and other special treats. But some things would be a surprise. Birthdays combine assurance and anticipation, and so does faith! Faith is the conviction based on past experience that God's new and fresh surprises will surely be ours.

11:1 The beginning point of faith is believing in God's character: He *is* who he says. The end point is believing in God's promises: He will *do* what he says. When we believe that God will fulfill his promises even though we don't see those promises materializing yet, we demonstrate true faith (see John 20:24-31).

11:3 God called the universe into existence out of nothing; he declared that it was to be, and it was. Our faith is in the God who created the entire universe by his word. God's word has awesome power. When he speaks, do you listen and respond? How can you better prepare yourself to respond to God's word?

11:4 Cain and Abel were Adam and Eve's first two sons. Abel offered a sacrifice that pleased God, while Cain's sacrifice was unacceptable. Abel's Profile is found in Genesis 5. Cain's Profile is in Genesis 7. Abel's sacrifice (an animal substitute) was more acceptable to God, both because it was a blood sacrifice and, most important, because of Abel's attitude when he offered it.

11:6 Believing that God exists is only the beginning; even the demons believe that much (James 2:19, 20). God will not settle for mere acknowledgment of his existence. He wants a personal, dynamic relationship with you that will transform your life. Those who seek God will find that they are rewarded with his intimate presence.

11:6 Sometimes we wonder about the fate of those who haven't heard of Christ and have not even had a Bible to read. God assures us that all who honestly seek him—who act in faith on the knowledge of God that they possess—will be rewarded. When you tell others the Good News, encourage them to be honest and diligent in their search for truth. Those who hear the Good News are responsible for what they have heard (see 2 Corinthians 6:1, 2).

11:7 Noah experienced rejection because he was different from his neighbors. God commanded him to build a huge boat in the middle of dry land, and although God's command seemed foolish, Noah obeyed. Noah's obedience made him appear strange to his neighbors, just as the new beliefs of Jewish Christians undoubtedly made them stand out. As you obey God, don't be surprised if others regard you as "different." Your obedience makes their disobedience stand out. Remember, if God asks you to do something, he will give you the necessary strength to carry out that task. For more information on Noah, see his Profile in Genesis 8.

11:8-10 Abraham's life was filled with faith. At God's command, he left home and went to another land—obeying without question (Genesis 12:1ff). He believed the covenant that God made with him (Genesis 12:2, 3; 13:14-16; 15:1-6). In obedience to God, Abraham was even willing to sacrifice his son Isaac (Genesis 22:1-19). Do not be surprised if God asks you to give up secure, familiar surroundings in order to carry out his will. For further information on Abraham, see his Profile in Genesis 18.

11:11 Gen 17:19; 21:1-3
11:12 Gen 15:5-6; 22:17; Rom 4:19
11:13 Gen 23:4; Matt 13:17; Heb 11:39
11:14 Heb 13:14
11:15 Gen 24:6-8
11:16 Gen 26:24; Exod 3:6, 15
11:17 Gen 22:1-10; Jas 2:21
11:18 †Gen 21:12
11:19 Rom 4:21
11:20 Gen 27:27-29
11:21 †Gen 47:31; 48:15-16
11:22 Gen 50:24-25; Exod 13:19

11 It was by faith that Sarah together with Abraham was able to have a child, even
though they were too old and Sarah was barren. Abraham believed that God would keep
his promise.* 12 And so a whole nation came from this one man, Abraham, who was too
old to have any children—a nation with so many people that, like the stars of the sky and
the sand on the seashore, there is no way to count them.
13 All these faithful ones died without receiving what God had promised them, but they
saw it all from a distance and welcomed the promises of God. They agreed that they were
no more than foreigners and nomads here on earth. 14 And obviously people who talk like
that are looking forward to a country they can call their own. 15 If they had meant the
country they came from, they would have found a way to go back. 16 But they were
looking for a better place, a heavenly homeland. That is why God is not ashamed to be
called their God, for he has prepared a heavenly city for them.
17 It was by faith that Abraham offered Isaac as a sacrifice when God was testing him.
Abraham, who had received God's promises, was ready to sacrifice his only son, Isaac,
18 though God had promised him, "Isaac is the son through whom your descendants will
be counted."* 19 Abraham assumed that if Isaac died, God was able to bring him back to
life again. And in a sense, Abraham did receive his son back from the dead.
20 It was by faith that Isaac blessed his two sons, Jacob and Esau. He had confidence
in what God was going to do in the future.
21 It was by faith that Jacob, when he was old and dying, blessed each of Joseph's sons
and bowed in worship as he leaned on his staff.
22 And it was by faith that Joseph, when he was about to die, confidently spoke of
God's bringing the people of Israel out of Egypt. He was so sure of it that he commanded
them to carry his bones with them when they left!

11:11 Some manuscripts read *It was by faith that Sarah was able to have a child, even though she was too old and barren. Sarah believed that God would keep his promise.* **11:18** Gen 21:12.

11:11, 12 Sarah was Abraham's wife. They were unable to have children through many years of their marriage. God promised Abraham a son, but Sarah doubted that she could become pregnant in her old age. At first she laughed, but afterward, she believed (Genesis 18). For more information on Sarah, see her Profile in Genesis 19.

11:13 That we are "foreigners and nomads" may be an awareness forced on us by circumstances. It may come late in life or as the result of difficult times. But this world is not our home. We cannot live here forever (see also 1 Peter 1:1). It is best for us not to be so attached to this world's desires and possessions that we can't move out at God's command.

11:13-16 These people of faith died without receiving all that God had promised, but they never lost their vision of heaven ("a better place, a heavenly homeland"). Many Christians become frustrated and defeated because their needs, wants, expectations, and demands are not immediately met when they accept Christ as Savior. They become impatient and want to quit. Are you discouraged because the achievement of your goal seems far away? Take courage from these heroes of faith, who lived and died without seeing the fruit of their faith on earth and yet continued to believe (see 11:36-39).

11:17-19 Abraham was willing to give up his son when God commanded him to do so (Genesis 22:1-19). God did not let Abraham take Isaac's life, because God had given the command in order to test Abraham's faith. Instead of taking Abraham's son, God gave Abraham a whole nation of descendants through Isaac. If you are afraid to trust God with the possession, dream, or person you treasure most, pay attention to Abraham's example. Because Abraham was willing to give up everything for God, he received back more than he could have imagined. What we receive, however, is not always immediate or in the form of material possessions. Material things should be among the least satisfying of rewards. Our best and greatest rewards await us in eternity.

11:20 Isaac was the son who had been promised to Abraham and Sarah in their old age. It was through Isaac that God fulfilled his promise to eventually give Abraham countless descendants. Isaac had twin sons, Jacob and Esau. God chose the younger son, Jacob, through whom to continue the fulfillment of his promise to Abraham. For more information on Isaac, see his Profile in Genesis 19.

11:21 Jacob was Isaac's son and Abraham's grandson. Jacob's sons became the fathers of Israel's 12 tribes. Even when Jacob (also called "Israel") was dying in a strange land, he believed the promise that Abraham's descendants would be like the sand on the seashore and that Israel would become a great nation (Genesis 48:1-22). True faith helps us see beyond the grave. For more information on Jacob and Esau, see their Profiles in Genesis 26 and 25.

11:22 Joseph, one of Jacob's sons, was sold into slavery by his jealous brothers (Genesis 37). Eventually, Joseph was sold again, this time to an official of the Pharaoh of Egypt. Because of Joseph's faithfulness to God, however, he was given a top-ranking position in Egypt. Although Joseph could have used that position to build a personal empire, he remembered God's promise to Abraham. After he had been reconciled to his brothers, Joseph brought his family to be near him and requested that his bones be taken to the Promised Land when the Jews eventually left Egypt (Genesis 50:24, 25). Faith means trusting in God and doing what he wants, regardless of the circumstances or consequences. For more information on Joseph, see his Profile in Genesis 36.

23 It was by faith that Moses' parents hid him for three months. They saw that God had
given them an unusual child, and they were not afraid of what the king might do.
24 It was by faith that Moses, when he grew up, refused to be treated as the son of
Pharaoh's daughter. 25 He chose to share the oppression of God's people instead of
enjoying the fleeting pleasures of sin. 26 He thought it was better to suffer for the sake
of the Messiah than to own the treasures of Egypt, for he was looking ahead to the great
reward that God would give him. 27 It was by faith that Moses left the land of Egypt.
He was not afraid of the king. Moses kept right on going because he kept his eyes on
the one who is invisible. 28 It was by faith that Moses commanded the people of Israel
to keep the Passover and to sprinkle blood on the doorposts so that the angel of death
would not kill their firstborn sons.
29 It was by faith that the people of Israel went right through the Red Sea as though
they were on dry ground. But when the Egyptians followed, they were all drowned.
30 It was by faith that the people of Israel marched around Jericho seven days, and the
walls came crashing down.
31 It was by faith that Rahab the prostitute did not die with all the others in her city who
refused to obey God. For she had given a friendly welcome to the spies.
32 Well, how much more do I need to say? It would take too long to recount the stories
of the faith of Gideon, Barak, Samson, Jephthah, David, Samuel, and all the prophets.
33 By faith these people overthrew kingdoms, ruled with justice, and received what God
had promised them. They shut the mouths of lions, 34 quenched the flames of fire, and
escaped death by the edge of the sword. Their weakness was turned to strength. They
became strong in battle and put whole armies to flight. 35 Women received their loved
ones back again from death.
But others trusted God and were tortured, preferring to die rather than turn from God
and be free. They placed their hope in the resurrection to a better life. 36 Some were

11:23 Exod 1:16, 22; 2:2
11:24 Exod 2:10-12
11:26 Heb 13:13
11:27 Exod 12:50-51
11:28 Exod 12:21-30
11:29 Exod 14:21-31
11:30 Josh 6:12-21
11:31 Josh 2:11-12; 6:21-25 Jas 2:25
11:32 Judg 4–13 1 Sam 1:20; 16:1, 13
11:33 1 Sam 17:34-36 Dan 6:1-27
11:34 2 Kgs 20:7 Dan 3:19-27
11:35 1 Kgs 17:17-24 2 Kgs 4:25-37
11:36 Gen 39:20 Jer 20:2; 37:15

11:23 Moses' parents trusted God to protect their son's life. They were not merely proud parents; they were believers who had faith that God would care for him. As a parent, have you trusted God enough to take care of your children? God has a plan for every person, and your important task is to pray for your children and prepare them to do the work God has planned for them to do. Faith allows us to entrust even our children to God.

11:24-28 Moses became one of Israel's greatest leaders, a prophet and a lawgiver. But when he was born, his people were slaves in Egypt, and the Egyptian officials had ordered that all Hebrew baby boys were to be killed. Moses was spared, however, and Pharaoh's daughter raised Moses in Pharaoh's own household (Exodus 1–2)! It took faith for Moses to give up his place in the palace, but he could do it because he saw the fleeting nature of great wealth and prestige. It is easy to be deceived by the temporary benefits of wealth, popularity, status, and achievement, and to be blind to the long-range benefits of God's Kingdom. Faith helps us look beyond the world's value system to see the eternal values of God's Kingdom. For more information on Moses, see his Profile in Exodus 14.

11:31 When Joshua planned the conquest of Jericho, he sent spies to investigate the fortifications of the city. The spies met Rahab, who had two strikes against her—she was a Gentile and a prostitute. But she showed that she had faith in God by welcoming the spies and by trusting God to spare her and her family when the city was destroyed. Faith helps us turn around and do what is right regardless of our past or the disapproval of others. For more information on Rahab, see her Profile in Joshua 2.

11:32-35 The Old Testament records the lives of the various people who experienced these great victories. Joshua and Deborah overthrew kingdoms (the book of Joshua; Judges 4–5). Nehemiah ruled with justice (the book of Nehemiah). Daniel was saved from the mouths of lions (Daniel 6). Shadrach, Meshach, and Abednego were kept from harm in the flames of a blazing furnace (Daniel 3). Elijah escaped the edge of the swords of evil Queen Jezebel's henchmen (1 Kings 19:2ff). Hezekiah regained strength after sickness (2 Kings 20). Gideon was strong in battle (Judges 7). A widow's son was brought back to life by the prophet Elisha (2 Kings 4:8-37).

We, too, can experience victory through faith in Christ. Our victories over oppressors may be like those of the Old Testament saints, but more likely, our victories will be directly related to the role God wants us to play. Even though our body deteriorates and dies, we will live forever because of Christ. In the promised resurrection, even death will be defeated, and Christ's victory will be made complete.

11:32-40 These verses summarize the lives of other great men and women of faith. Some experienced outstanding victories, even over the threat of death. But others were severely mistreated, tortured, and even killed. Having a steadfast faith in God does not guarantee a happy, carefree life. On the contrary, our faith almost guarantees us some form of abuse from the world. While we are on earth, we may never see the purpose of our suffering. But we know that God will keep his promises to us. Do you believe that God will keep his promises to you?

11:35-39 Many think that pain is the exception in the Christian life. When suffering occurs, they say, "Why me?" They feel as though God deserted them, or perhaps they accuse him of not being as dependable as they thought. In reality, however, we live in an evil world filled with suffering, even for believers. But God is still in control. He allows some Christians to become martyrs for the faith, and he allows others to survive persecution. Rather than asking, "Why me?" it is much more helpful to ask, "Why not me?" Our faith and the values of this world are on a collision course. If we expect pain and suffering to come, we will not be shocked when they hit. But we can also take comfort in knowing that Jesus also suffered. He understands our fears, our weaknesses, and our disappointments (see 2:16-18; 4:14-16). He promised never to leave us (Matthew 28:18-20), and he intercedes on our behalf (7:24, 25). In times of pain, persecution, or suffering, we should trust confidently in Christ.

11:37 1 Kgs 19:10; 2 Chr 24:20-22
11:38 1 Kgs 18:4; 19:9
11:40 Rom 11:26; Rev 6:11

mocked, and their backs were cut open with whips. Others were chained in dungeons.
37 Some died by stoning, and some were sawed in half; others were killed with the sword.
Some went about in skins of sheep and goats, hungry and oppressed and mistreated.
38 They were too good for this world. They wandered over deserts and mountains, hiding
in caves and holes in the ground.
39 All of these people we have mentioned received God's approval because of their
faith, yet none of them received all that God had promised. 40 For God had far better
things in mind for us that would also benefit them, for they can't receive the prize at the
end of the race until we finish the race.*

God's Discipline Proves His Love

12:1 1 Cor 9:24; Phil 3:12-14
12:2 Ps 110:1; Phil 2:8-9; Heb 2:9-10; 1 Pet 1:11
12:4 Heb 10:32-34
12:5-6 †Prov 3:11-12

12 Therefore, since we are surrounded by such a huge crowd of witnesses to the life
of faith, let us strip off every weight that slows us down, especially the sin that so
easily hinders our progress. And let us run with endurance the race that God has set
before us. 2 We do this by keeping our eyes on Jesus, on whom our faith depends from
start to finish.* He was willing to die a shameful death on the cross because of the joy
he knew would be his afterward. Now he is seated in the place of highest honor beside
God's throne in heaven. 3 Think about all he endured when sinful people did such terrible
things to him, so that you don't become weary and give up. 4 After all, you have not yet
given your lives in your struggle against sin.
5 And have you entirely forgotten the encouraging words God spoke to you, his
children? He said,

"My child, don't ignore it when the Lord disciplines you,
and don't be discouraged when he corrects you.
6 For the Lord disciplines those he loves,
and he punishes those he accepts as his children."*

12:6 Rev 3:19
12:7 Deut 8:5; 2 Sam 7:14
12:8 1 Pet 5:9
12:9 Num 16:22; 27:16; Isa 38:16
12:10 2 Pet 1:4

7 As you endure this divine discipline, remember that God is treating you as his own
children. Whoever heard of a child who was never disciplined? 8 If God doesn't discipline you as he does all of his children, it means that you are illegitimate and are not
really his children after all. 9 Since we respect our earthly fathers who disciplined us,
should we not all the more cheerfully submit to the discipline of our heavenly Father and
live forever*?
10 For our earthly fathers disciplined us for a few years, doing the best they knew how.
But God's discipline is always right and good for us because it means we will share in his

11:40 Greek *for us, for they apart from us can't finish.* **12:2** Or *Jesus, the Originator and Perfecter of our faith.* **12:5-6** Prov 3:11-12. **12:9** Or *really live.*

11:39, 40 Hebrews 11 has been called faith's hall of fame. No doubt the author surprised his readers by this conclusion: These mighty Jewish heroes did not receive God's total reward, because they died before Christ came. In God's plan, they and the Christian believers (who were also enduring much testing) would be rewarded together. Once again Hebrews shows that Christianity offers a better way than Judaism.

11:40 There is a solidarity among believers (see 12:23). Old and New Testament believers will be glorified together. Not only are we one in the body of Christ with all those alive, but we are also one with all those who ever lived. It takes all of us to be perfect in him.

12:1 This "huge crowd of witnesses" is composed of the people described in chapter 11. Their faithfulness is a constant encouragement to us. We do not struggle alone, and we are not the first to struggle with the problems we face. Others have run the race and won, and their witness stirs us to run and win also. What an inspiring heritage we have!

12:1-4 The Christian life involves hard work. It requires us to give up whatever endangers our relationship with God, to run patiently, and to struggle against sin with the power of the Holy Spirit. To live effectively, we must keep our eyes on Jesus. We will stumble if we look away from him to stare at ourselves or at the circumstances surrounding us. We should be running for Christ, not ourselves, and we must always keep him in sight.

12:3 When we face hardship and discouragement, it is easy to lose sight of the big picture. But we're not alone; there is help. Many have already made it through life, enduring far more difficult circumstances than we have experienced. Suffering is the training ground for Christian maturity. It develops our patience and makes our final victory sweet.

12:4 These readers were facing difficult times of persecution, but none of them had yet died for their faith. Because they were still alive, the writer urged them to continue to run their race. Just as Christ did not give up, neither should they.

12:5-11 Who loves his child more—the father who allows the child to do what will harm him, or the one who corrects, trains, and even punishes the child to help him learn what is right? It's never pleasant to be corrected and disciplined by God, but his discipline is a sign of his deep love for us. When God corrects you, see it as proof of his love, and ask him what he is trying to teach you.

holiness. 11 No discipline is enjoyable while it is happening—it is painful! But afterward
there will be a quiet harvest of right living for those who are trained in this way.
12 So take a new grip with your tired hands and stand firm on your shaky legs. 13 Mark
out a straight path for your feet. Then those who follow you, though they are weak and
lame, will not stumble and fall but will become strong.

A Call to Listen to God

14 Try to live in peace with everyone, and seek to live a clean and holy life, for those who
are not holy will not see the Lord. 15 Look after each other so that none of you will miss
out on the special favor of God. Watch out that no bitter root of unbelief rises up among
you, for whenever it springs up, many are corrupted by its poison. 16 Make sure that no
one is immoral or godless like Esau. He traded his birthright as the oldest son for a single
meal. 17 And afterward, when he wanted his father's blessing, he was rejected. It was too
late for repentance, even though he wept bitter tears.
18 You have not come to a physical mountain, to a place of flaming fire, darkness, gloom,
and whirlwind, as the Israelites did at Mount Sinai when God gave them his laws. 19 For
they heard an awesome trumpet blast and a voice with a message so terrible that they
begged God to stop speaking. 20 They staggered back under God's command: "If even an
animal touches the mountain, it must be stoned to death."* 21 Moses himself was so
frightened at the sight that he said, "I am terrified and trembling."*
22 No, you have come to Mount Zion, to the city of the living God, the heavenly
Jerusalem, and to thousands of angels in joyful assembly. 23 You have come to the
assembly of God's firstborn children, whose names are written in heaven. You have come
to God himself, who is the judge of all people. And you have come to the spirits of the
redeemed in heaven who have now been made perfect. 24 You have come to Jesus, the one
who mediates the new covenant between God and people, and to the sprinkled blood,
which graciously forgives instead of crying out for vengeance as the blood of Abel did.
25 See to it that you obey God, the one who is speaking to you. For if the people of
Israel did not escape when they refused to listen to Moses, the earthly messenger, how
terrible our danger if we reject the One who speaks to us from heaven! 26 When God
spoke from Mount Sinai his voice shook the earth, but now he makes another promise:

12:11 Jas 3:17-18
12:12 Isa 35:3
12:13 Prov 4:26
12:14 Rom 14:19
12:15 Deut 29:17-18; Heb 4:1
12:16 Gen 25:29-34
12:17 Gen 27:30-40
12:18-19 Exod 19:16-22; 20:18-21; Deut 4:11-12; 5:22-27
12:20 †Exod 19:12-13
12:21 †Deut 9:19
12:22 Gal 4:26; Rev 5:11; 21:2
12:23 Gen 18:25; Phil 3:12
12:24 Gen 4:10; Heb 9:19; 10:22
12:25 Heb 2:1-3; 10:28-29
12:26 Exod 19:18; †Hag 2:6

12:20 Exod 19:13. **12:21** Deut 9:19.

12:11 We may respond to discipline in several ways: (1) We can accept it with resignation; (2) we can accept it with self-pity, thinking we really don't deserve it; (3) we can be angry and resentful toward God; or (4) we can accept it gratefully, as the appropriate response we owe a loving Father.

12:12, 13 God is not only a disciplining parent but also a demanding coach who pushes us to our limits and requires our lives to be disciplined. Although we may not feel strong enough to push on to victory, we will be able to accomplish it as we follow Christ and draw on his strength. Then we can use our growing strength to help those around us who are weak and struggling.

12:12, 13 We must not live with only our own survival in mind. Others will follow our example, and we have a responsibility to them if we are living for Christ, as we claim to be. Does your example make it easier for others to believe in and follow Christ, and to mature in him? Or would those who follow you end up confused and misled?

12:14 The readers were familiar with the ceremonial cleansing ritual that prepared them for worship, and they knew that they had to be holy or clean in order to enter the Temple. Sin always blocks our vision of God; so if we want to see God, we must renounce sin and obey him (see Psalm 24:3, 4). Holiness is coupled with living in peace. A right relationship with God leads to right relationships with fellow believers. Although we will not always feel loving toward all other believers, we must pursue peace as we become more Christlike.

12:15 Like a small root that grows into a great tree, bitterness springs up in our hearts and overshadows even our deepest Christian relationships. A "bitter root" comes when we allow disappointment to grow into resentment, or when we nurse grudges over past hurts. Bitterness brings with it jealousy, dissension, and immorality. When the Holy Spirit fills us, however, he can heal the hurt that causes bitterness.

12:16, 17 Esau's story shows us that mistakes and sins sometimes have lasting consequences (Genesis 25:29-34; 27:36). Even repentance and forgiveness do not always eliminate sin's consequences. How often do you make decisions based on what you want now, rather than on what you need in the long run? Evaluate the long-range effects of your decisions and actions.

12:18-24 What a contrast between the people's terrified approach to God at Mount Sinai and their joyful approach at Mount Zion! What a difference Jesus has made! Before Jesus came, God seemed distant and threatening. After Jesus came, God welcomes us through Christ into his presence. Accept God's invitation!

12:22 As Christians, we are citizens of the heavenly Jerusalem right now; because Christ rules our lives, the Holy Spirit is always with us, and we experience close fellowship with other believers. The full and ultimate rewards and reality of the heavenly Jerusalem are depicted in Revelation 21.

12:27 2 Pet 3:10 "Once again I will shake not only the earth but the heavens also."* 27This means that the
12:28 Dan 2:44 things on earth will be shaken, so that only eternal things will be left.
28Since we are receiving a kingdom that cannot be destroyed, let us be thankful and
please God by worshiping him with holy fear and awe. 29For our God is a consuming fire.

Concluding Words

13:1 Rom 12:10 **13** Continue to love each other with true Christian love.* 2Don't forget to show
hospitality to strangers, for some who have done this have entertained angels
13:2 Gen 18:1-8; 19:1-3 without realizing it! 3Don't forget about those in prison. Suffer with them as though you
13:3 Matt 25:36; Col 4:18; Heb 10:34 were there yourself. Share the sorrow of those being mistreated, as though you feel their
pain in your own bodies.
4Give honor to marriage, and remain faithful to one another in marriage. God will
13:4 1 Cor 7:38 surely judge people who are immoral and those who commit adultery.
13:5 Gen 28:15; †Deut 31:5; Josh 1:5 5Stay away from the love of money; be satisfied with what you have. For God has said,

"I will never fail you.
I will never forsake you."*

13:6 †Ps 118:6 6That is why we can say with confidence,

"The Lord is my helper,
so I will not be afraid.
What can mere mortals do to me?"*

13:7 Heb 6:12 7Remember your leaders who first taught you the word of God. Think of all the good
13:8 Heb 1:12 that has come from their lives, and trust the Lord as they do.
13:9 Eph 4:14; Col 2:7, 16 8Jesus Christ is the same yesterday, today, and forever. 9So do not be attracted by

12:26 Hag 2:6. **13:1** Greek *with brotherly love.* **13:5** Deut 31:6, 8. **13:6** Ps 118:6.

12:27-29 Eventually the world will crumble, and only God's Kingdom will last. Those who follow Christ are part of this unshakable Kingdom, and they will withstand the shaking, sifting, and burning. When we feel unsure about the future, we can take confidence from these verses. No matter what happens here, our future is built on a solid foundation that cannot be destroyed. Don't put your confidence in what will be destroyed; instead, build your life on Christ and his unshakable Kingdom. (See Matthew 7:24-27 for the importance of building on a solid foundation.)

12:29 There is a big difference between the flame of a candle and the roaring blast of a forest fire. We cannot even stand near a raging fire. Even with sophisticated firefighting equipment, a consuming fire is often beyond human control. God is not within our control either. We cannot force him to do anything for us through our prayers. He cannot be contained. Yet, he is a God of compassion. He has saved us from sin, and he will save us from death. But everything that is worthless and sinful will be consumed by the fire of his wrath. Only what is good, dedicated to God, and righteous will remain.

13:1-5 Real love for others produces tangible actions: (1) hospitality to strangers (13:2); (2) empathy for those who are in prison and those who have been mistreated (13:3); (3) respect for your marriage vows (13:4); and (4) contentment with what you have (13:5). Make sure that your love runs deep enough to affect your hospitality, empathy, fidelity, and contentment.

13:2 Three Old Testament people "entertained angels without realizing it": (1) Abraham (Genesis 18:1ff), (2) Gideon (Judges 6:11ff), and (3) Manoah (Judges 13:2ff). Some people say they cannot be hospitable because their homes are not large enough or nice enough. But even if you have no more than a table and two chairs in a rented room, there are people who would be grateful to spend time in your home. Are there visitors to your church with whom you could share a meal? Do you know single people who would enjoy an evening of conversation? Is there any way your home could meet the needs of traveling missionaries? Hospitality simply means making other people feel comfortable and at home.

13:3 We are to have empathy for those in prison, especially for (but not limited to) Christians imprisoned for their faith. Jesus said that his true followers would represent him as they visit those in prison (Matthew 25:36).

13:5 How can we learn to be satisfied with what we have? Strive to live with less rather than desiring more; give away out of your abundance rather than accumulating more; relish what you have rather than resent what you're missing. See God's love expressed in what he has provided, and remember that money and possessions will all pass away. (See Philippians 4:11 for more on contentment, and 1 John 2:17 for the futility of earthly desires.)

13:5, 6 We become content when we realize God's sufficiency for our needs. Christians who become materialistic are saying by their actions that God can't take care of them—or at least that he won't take care of them the way they want. Insecurity can lead to the love of money, whether we are rich or poor. The only antidote is to trust God to meet all our needs.

13:7 If you are a Christian, you owe much to others who have taught you and modeled for you what you needed to know about the Good News and Christian living. Continue following the good examples of those who have invested themselves in you by investing in your life through evangelism, service, and Christian education.

13:8 Though human leaders have much to offer, we must keep our eyes on Christ, our ultimate leader. Unlike any human leaders, he will never change. Christ has been and will be the same forever. In a changing world we can trust our unchanging Lord.

13:9 Apparently some were teaching that keeping the Old Testament ceremonial laws and rituals (such as not eating certain foods) was important for salvation. But these laws were useless for conquering a person's evil thoughts and desires (Colossians 2:23). The laws could influence conduct, but they could not change the heart. Lasting changes in conduct begin when the Holy Spirit lives in each person.

strange, new ideas. Your spiritual strength comes from God's special favor, not from
ceremonial rules about food, which don't help those who follow them.
10 We have an altar from which the priests in the Temple on earth have no right to eat.
11 Under the system of Jewish laws, the high priest brought the blood of animals into the
Holy Place as a sacrifice for sin, but the bodies of the animals were burned outside the
camp. 12 So also Jesus suffered and died outside the city gates in order to make his people
holy by shedding his own blood. 13 So let us go out to him outside the camp and bear the
disgrace he bore. 14 For this world is not our home; we are looking forward to our city in
heaven, which is yet to come.
15 With Jesus' help, let us continually offer our sacrifice of praise to God by proclaiming the glory of his name. 16 Don't forget to do good and to share what you have with
those in need, for such sacrifices are very pleasing to God.
17 Obey your spiritual leaders and do what they say. Their work is to watch over your
souls, and they know they are accountable to God. Give them reason to do this joyfully
and not with sorrow. That would certainly not be for your benefit.
18 Pray for us, for our conscience is clear and we want to live honorably in everything
we do. 19 I especially need your prayers right now so that I can come back to you soon.
20-21 And now, may the God of peace, who brought again from the dead our Lord Jesus,
equip you with all you need for doing his will. May he produce in you, through the power
of Jesus Christ, all that is pleasing to him. Jesus is the great Shepherd of the sheep by an
everlasting covenant, signed with his blood. To him be glory forever and ever. Amen.
22 I urge you, dear friends,* please listen carefully to what I have said in this brief letter.
23 I want you to know that our brother Timothy is now out of jail. If he comes here
soon, I will bring him with me to see you.
24 Give my greetings to all your leaders and to the other believers there. The Christians
from Italy send you their greetings.
25 May God's grace be with you all.

13:10 1 Cor 10:18
13:11 Lev 4:12, 21; 16:27
13:12 John 19:17; Heb 9:12
13:13 Heb 11:26
13:14 Heb 11:10; 12:22
13:15 Ps 50:14; Hos 14:2; 1 Pet 2:5
13:16 Phil 4:18
13:17 Isa 62:6; Ezek 3:17; Acts 20:28
13:19 Phlm 1:22
13:20 Isa 55:3; Jer 32:40; 50:5; Ezek 37:26; Zech 9:11; John 10:11
13:21 Rom 11:36; Phil 2:13
13:22 1 Pet 5:12
13:23 Acts 16:1

13:22 Greek *brothers.*

13:13 The Jewish Christians were being ridiculed and persecuted by Jews who didn't believe in Jesus the Messiah. Most of the book of Hebrews tells them how Christ is greater than the sacrificial system. Here the writer drives home the point of his lengthy argument: It may be necessary to leave the "camp" and suffer with Christ. To be outside the camp meant to be unclean—in the days of the Exodus, those who were ceremonially unclean had to stay outside the camp. But Jesus suffered humiliation and uncleanness outside the Jerusalem gates on their behalf. The time had come for Jewish Christians to declare their loyalty to Christ above any other loyalty, to choose to follow the Messiah whatever suffering that might entail. They needed to move outside the safe confinement of their past, their traditions, and their ceremonies to live for Christ. What holds you back from complete loyalty to Jesus Christ?

13:14 We should not be attached to this world, because all that we are and have here is temporary. Only our relationship with God and our service to him will last. Don't store up your treasures here; store them in heaven (Matthew 6:19-21).

13:15, 16 Since these Jewish Christians, because of their witness to the Messiah, no longer worshiped with other Jews, they should consider praise and acts of service their sacrifices—ones they could offer anywhere, anytime. This must have reminded them of the prophet Hosea's words, "Forgive all our sins and graciously receive us, so that we may offer you the sacrifice of praise" (Hosea 14:2). A "sacrifice of praise" today would include thanking Christ for his sacrifice on the cross and telling others about it. Acts of kindness and sharing are particularly pleasing to God, even when they go unnoticed by others.

13:17 The task of church leaders is to help people mature in Christ. Cooperative followers greatly ease the burden of leadership. Does your conduct give your leaders reason to report joyfully about you?

13:18, 19 The writer recognizes the need for prayer. Christian leaders are especially vulnerable to criticism from others, pride (if they succeed), depression (if they fail), and Satan's constant efforts to destroy their work for God. They desperately need our prayers! For whom should you regularly pray?

13:20, 21 These verses include two significant results of Christ's death and resurrection. God works in us to make us the kind of people that would please him, and he equips us to do the kind of *work* that would please him. Let God change you from within and then use you to help others.

13:23 We have no record of Timothy's imprisonment, but we know that he had been in prison because it states here that he had been released. For more about Timothy, see his Profile in 1 Timothy 2.

13:24, 25 Hebrews is a call to Christian maturity. It was addressed to first-century Jewish Christians, but it applies to Christians of any age or background. Christian maturity means making Christ the beginning and end of our faith. To grow in maturity, we must center our life on him, not depending on religious ritual, not falling back into sin, not trusting in ourselves, and not letting anything come between us and Christ. Christ is sufficient and superior.

JAMES

"MIRACULOUS!" . . . "Revolutionary!" . . . "Greatest ever!" We are inundated by a flood of extravagant claims as we channel surf the television or flip magazine pages. The messages leap out at us. The products assure that they are new, improved, fantastic, and capable of changing our life. For only a few dollars, we can have "cleaner clothes," "whiter teeth," "glamorous hair," and "tastier food." Automobiles, perfume, diet drinks, and mouthwash are guaranteed to bring happiness, friends, and the good life. And just before an election, no one can match the politicians' promises. But talk is cheap, and too often we soon realize that the boasts were hollow, quite far from the truth.

"Jesus is the answer!" . . . "Believe in God!" . . . "Follow me to church!" Christians also make great claims but are often guilty of belying them with their actions. Professing to trust God and to be his people, they cling tightly to the world and its values. Possessing all the right answers, they contradict the gospel with their lives.

With energetic style and crisp, well-chosen words, James confronts this conflict head-on. It is not enough to talk the Christian faith, he says; we must live it. "Dear brothers and sisters, what's the use of saying you have faith if you don't prove it by your actions? That kind of faith can't save anyone" (2:14). The proof of the reality of our faith is a changed life.

Genuine faith will inevitably produce good deeds. This is the central theme of James's letter, around which he supplies practical advice on living the Christian life.

James begins his letter by outlining some general characteristics of the Christian life (1:1–27). Next, he exhorts Christians to act justly in society (2:1–13). He follows this practical advice with a theological discourse on the relationship between faith and action (2:14–26). Then James shows the importance of controlling one's speech (3:1–12). In 3:13–18, James distinguishes two kinds of wisdom—earthly and heavenly. Then he encourages his readers to turn from evil desires and obey God (4:1–12). James reproves those who trust in their own plans and possessions (4:13—5:6). Finally, he exhorts his readers to be patient with each other (5:7–11), to be straightforward in their promises (5:12), to pray for each other (5:13–18), and to help each other remain faithful to God (5:19, 20).

This letter could be considered a how-to book on Christian living. Confrontation, challenges, and a call to commitment await you in its pages. Read James and become a *doer* of the Word (1:22–25).

VITAL STATISTICS

PURPOSE:
To expose hypocritical practices and to teach right Christian behavior

AUTHOR:
James, Jesus' brother, a leader in the Jerusalem church

TO WHOM WRITTEN:
First-century Jewish Christians residing in Gentile communities outside Palestine, and all Christians everywhere

DATE WRITTEN:
Probably A.D. 49, prior to the Jerusalem council held in A.D. 50

SETTING:
This letter expresses James's concern for persecuted Christians who were once part of the Jerusalem church

KEY VERSE:
"Now someone may argue, 'Some people have faith; others have good deeds.' I say, 'I can't see your faith if you don't have good deeds, but I will show you my faith through my good deeds'" (2:18).

THE BLUEPRINT

1. Genuine religion (1:1–27)
2. Genuine faith (2:1—3:12)
3. Genuine wisdom (3:13—5:20)

James wrote to Jewish Christians who had been scattered throughout the Mediterranean world because of persecution. In their hostile surroundings they were tempted to let intellectual agreement pass for true faith. This letter can have rich meaning for us as we are reminded that genuine faith transforms lives. We are encouraged to put our faith into action. It is easy to say we have faith, but true faith will produce loving actions toward others.

MEGATHEMES

THEME	EXPLANATION	IMPORTANCE
Living Faith	James wants believers not only to hear the truth but also to put it into action. He contrasts empty faith (claims without conduct) with faith that works. Commitment to love and to serve others is evidence of true faith.	Living faith makes a difference. Make sure your faith is more than just a statement; it should also result in action. Seek ways of putting your faith to work.
Trials	In the Christian life there are trials and temptations. Successfully overcoming these adversities produces maturity and strong character.	Don't resent troubles when they come. Pray for wisdom; God will supply all you need to face persecution or adversity. He will give you patience and keep you strong in times of trial.
Law of Love	We are saved by God's gracious mercy, not by keeping the law. But Christ gave us a special command: "Love your neighbor as yourself" (Matthew 19:19). We are to love and serve those around us.	Keeping the law of love shows that our faith is vital and real. When we show love to others, we are overcoming our own selfishness.
Wise Speech	Wisdom shows itself in wise speech. God holds us responsible for the results of our destructive words. The wisdom of God that helps control the tongue can help control all our actions.	Accepting God's wisdom will affect your speech. Your words will convey true humility and lead to peace. Think before you speak and allow God to give you self-control.
Wealth	James taught Christians not to compromise with worldly attitudes about wealth. Because the glory of wealth fades, Christians should store up God's treasures through sincere service. Christians must not show partiality to the wealthy or be prejudiced against the poor.	All of us are accountable for how we use what we have. We should not hoard wealth but be generous toward others. In addition, we should not be impressed by the wealthy nor look down on those who are poor.

1. Genuine religion

Greetings from James

1 This letter is from James, a slave of God and of the Lord Jesus Christ. 1:1 Acts 15:23 1 Pet 1:1
It is written to Jewish Christians scattered among the nations.*
Greetings!

Faith and Endurance

2 Dear brothers and sisters, whenever trouble comes your way, let it be an opportunity 1:2 1 Pet 1:6
for joy. 3 For when your faith is tested, your endurance has a chance to grow. 4 So let it 1:3 1 Pet 1:7

1:1 Greek *To the twelve tribes in the dispersion.*

1:1 The writer of this letter, a leader of the church in Jerusalem (see Acts 12:17; 15:13), was James, Jesus' half brother, not James the apostle. The book of James was one of the earliest letters, probably written before A.D. 50. After Stephen was martyred (Acts 7:55–8:3), persecution increased, and Christians in Jerusalem were scattered throughout the Roman world. There were thriving Jewish-Christian communities in Rome, Alexandria, Cyprus, and cities in Greece and Asia Minor. Because these early believers did not have the support of established Christian churches, James wrote to them as a concerned leader, to encourage them in their faith during those difficult times.

1:2, 3 James doesn't say *if* trouble comes your way but *whenever* it does. He assumes that we will have troubles and that it is possible to profit from them. The point is not to pretend to be happy when we face pain but to have a positive outlook ("let it be an opportunity for joy") because of what troubles can produce in our life. James tells us to turn our hardships into times of learning. Tough times can teach us perseverance. For other passages dealing with perseverance (also called patience and steadfastness), see Romans 2:7; 5:3-5; 8:24, 25; 2 Corinthians 6:3-7; 2 Peter 1:2-9.

1:2-4 We can't really know the depth of our character until we see how we react under pressure. It is easy to be kind to others when everything is going well, but can we still be kind when others are treating us unfairly? God wants to make us mature and complete, not to keep us from all pain. Instead of complain-

grow, for when your endurance is fully developed, you will be strong in character and ready for anything.

1:5 Prov 2:3-6 Matt 7:7

5 If you need wisdom—if you want to know what God wants you to do—ask him, and he will gladly tell you. He will not resent your asking. 6 But when you ask him, be sure that you really expect him to answer, for a doubtful mind is as unsettled as a wave of the sea that is driven and tossed by the wind. 7 People like that should not expect to receive anything from the Lord. 8 They can't make up their minds. They waver back and forth in everything they do.

1:6 Matt 21:22 Mark 11:24

1:10-11 Ps 102:4, 11 Isa 40:6-7 1 Pet 1:24

9 Christians who are* poor should be glad, for God has honored them. 10 And those who are rich should be glad, for God has humbled them. They will fade away like a flower in the field. 11 The hot sun rises and dries up the grass; the flower withers, and its beauty fades away. So also, wealthy people will fade away with all of their achievements.

1:12 1 Cor 9:25 2 Tim 4:8 Jas 5:11 Rev 2:10; 3:11

12 God blesses the people who patiently endure testing. Afterward they will receive the crown of life that God has promised to those who love him. 13 And remember, no one who wants to do wrong should ever say, "God is tempting me." God is never tempted to do wrong, and he never tempts anyone else either. 14 Temptation comes from the lure of

1:14 Prov 19:3

1:9 Greek *The brother who is.*

CHAPTER SUMMARY

Chapter 1	Confident Stand	What a Christian has
Chapter 2	Compassionate Service	What a Christian does
Chapter 3	Careful Speech	What a Christian says
Chapter 4	Contrite Submission	What a Christian feels
Chapter 5	Concerned Sharing	What a Christian gives

ing about our struggles, we should see them as opportunities for growth. Thank God for promising to be with you in rough times. Ask him to help you solve your problems or to give you the strength to endure them. Then be patient. God will not leave you alone with your problems; he will stay close and help you grow.

1:5 By "wisdom," James is talking not only about knowledge but about the ability to make wise decisions in difficult circumstances. Whenever we need wisdom, we can pray to God, and he will generously supply what we need. Christians don't have to grope around in the dark, hoping to stumble upon answers. We can ask for God's wisdom to guide our choices.

1:5 *Wisdom* means "practical discernment." It begins with respect for God, leads to right living, and results in increased ability to tell right from wrong. God is willing to give us this wisdom, but we will be unable to receive it if our goals are self-centered instead of God-centered. To learn God's will, we need to read his Word and ask him to show us how to obey it. Then we must do what he tells us.

1:6 We must believe not only in the existence of God but also in his loving care. This includes relying on God and expecting that he will hear and answer when we pray. We must put away our critical attitude when we come to him. God does not grant every thoughtless or selfish request. We must have confidence that God will align our desires with his purposes. For more on this concept, read the note on Matthew 21:22.

1:6 A doubtful mind is not completely convinced that God's way is best. It treats God's Word like any human advice and retains the option to disobey. It vacillates between allegiance to subjective feelings, the world's ideas, and God's commands. If your faith is new, weak, or struggling, remember that you can trust God. Then be loyal to him. To stabilize your wavering or doubtful mind, commit yourself wholeheartedly to God.

1:6-8 If you have ever seen the constant rolling of huge waves at sea, you know how restless they are—subject to the forces of wind, gravity, and tide. Doubt leaves a person as unsettled as the restless waves. If you want to stop being tossed about, rely on God to show you what is best for you. Ask him for wisdom, and trust that he will give it to you. Then your decisions will be sure and solid.

1:9 Christians who aren't in high positions in this world should be glad, because they are great in the Lord's eyes. Such people are often overlooked, even in our churches today, but they are not overlooked by God.

1:9-11 The poor should be glad that riches mean nothing to God; otherwise these people would be considered unworthy. The rich should be glad that money means nothing to God because money is easily lost. We find true wealth by developing our spiritual life, not by developing our financial assets. God is interested in what is lasting (our souls), not in what is temporary (our money and possessions). See Mark 4:18, 19 for Jesus' words on this subject. Strive to treat each person as Christ would treat him or her.

1:10, 11 If wealth, power, and status mean nothing to God, why do we attribute so much importance to them and so much honor to those who possess them? Do your material possessions give you goals and your only reason for living? If they were gone, what would be left? What you have in your heart, not your bank account, matters to God and endures for eternity.

1:12 The crown of life is like the victory wreath given to winning athletes (see 1 Corinthians 9:25). God's crown of life is not glory and honor here on earth but the reward of eternal life—living with God forever. The way to be in God's winners' circle is by loving him and staying faithful even under pressure.

1:12-15 Temptation comes from evil desires inside us, not from God. It begins with an evil thought and becomes sin when we dwell on the thought and allow it to become an action. Like a snowball rolling downhill, sin grows more destructive the more we let it have its way. The best time to stop a temptation is before it is too strong or moving too fast to control. See Matthew 4:1-11; 1 Corinthians 10:13; and 2 Timothy 2:22 for more about escaping temptation.

1:13, 14 People who live for God often wonder why they still have temptations. Does God tempt them? God *tests* people, but he does not *tempt* them by trying to seduce them to sin. God allows Satan to tempt people, however, in order to refine their faith and to help them grow in their dependence on Christ. We can resist the temptation to sin by turning to God for strength and choosing to obey his Word.

our own evil desires. [15]These evil desires lead to evil actions, and evil actions lead to
death. [16]So don't be misled, my dear brothers and sisters.
[17]Whatever is good and perfect comes to us from God above, who created all heaven's
lights.* Unlike them, he never changes or casts shifting shadows. [18]In his goodness he
chose to make us his own children by giving us his true word. And we, out of all creation,
became his choice possession.

Listening and Doing

[19]Dear friends,* be quick to listen, slow to speak, and slow to get angry. [20]Your anger
can never make things right in God's sight.
[21]So get rid of all the filth and evil in your lives, and humbly accept the message God
has planted in your hearts, for it is strong enough to save your souls.
[22]And remember, it is a message to obey, not just to listen to. If you don't obey, you
are only fooling yourself. [23]For if you just listen and don't obey, it is like looking at your
face in a mirror but doing nothing to improve your appearance. [24]You see yourself, walk
away, and forget what you look like. [25]But if you keep looking steadily into God's
perfect law—the law that sets you free—and if you do what it says and don't forget what
you heard, then God will bless you for doing it.
[26]If you claim to be religious but don't control your tongue, you are just fooling
yourself, and your religion is worthless. [27]Pure and lasting religion in the sight of God
our Father means that we must care for orphans and widows in their troubles, and refuse
to let the world corrupt us.

1:16 1 Cor 6:9
1:17 Gen 1:16; Ps 136:7; Matt 7:11
1:18 John 1:13; 1 Pet 1:23
1:19 Prov 10:19; 15:1; Eccl 7:9
1:21 Eph 1:13; 4:22; 1 Pet 2:1
1:22 Matt 7:21, 26; Rom 2:13
1:25 John 13:17; Rom 8:2; Gal 6:2; Jas 2:12; 1 Pet 2:16
1:26 Ps 34:13
1:27 Deut 14:29; 1 Jn 2:15-17

2. Genuine faith

A Warning against Prejudice

2 My dear brothers and sisters, how can you claim that you have faith in our glorious
Lord Jesus Christ if you favor some people more than others?
[2]For instance, suppose someone comes into your meeting* dressed in fancy clothes

2:1 Prov 24:23; Acts 10:34; 1 Cor 2:8

1:17 Greek *from above, from the Father of lights.* **1:19** Greek *Know this, my beloved brothers.* **2:2** Greek *synagogue.*

1:13-15 It is easy to blame others and make excuses for evil thoughts and wrong actions. We use excuses such as: (1) It's the other person's fault; (2) I couldn't help it; (3) everybody's doing it; (4) it was just a mistake; (5) nobody's perfect; (6) the Devil made me do it; (7) I was pressured into it; (8) I didn't know it was wrong; or (9) God is tempting me. A person who makes excuses is trying to shift the blame from himself or herself to something or someone else. A Christian, on the other hand, accepts responsibility for his or her wrongs, confesses them, and asks God for forgiveness.

1:17 The Bible often compares goodness with light and evil with darkness. For other passages where God is pictured as light, see Psalm 27:1, Isaiah 60:19-22, and John 1:1-14.

1:19 When we talk too much and listen too little, we communicate to others that we think our ideas are much more important than theirs. James wisely advises us to reverse this process. Put a mental stopwatch on your conversations, and keep track of how much you talk and how much you listen. When people talk with you, do they feel that their viewpoints and ideas have value?

1:19, 20 These verses speak of anger that erupts when our ego is bruised: *"I am hurt;" "My* opinions are not being heard." When injustice and sin occur, we *should* become angry because others are being hurt. But we should not become angry when we fail to win an argument or when we feel offended or neglected. Selfish anger never helps anybody.

1:21 James advises us to get rid of all that is wrong in our life and "humbly accept" the salvation message we have received, because it alone can save us.

1:22-25 It is important to listen to what God's Word says, but it is much more important to obey it and to *do* what it says. We can measure the effectiveness of our Bible study time by the effect it has on our behavior and attitudes. Do you put into action what you have studied?

1:25 It seems paradoxical that a law could give us freedom, but God's law points out sin in us and gives us the opportunity to ask for God's forgiveness (see Romans 7:7, 8). As Christians, we are saved by God's grace, and salvation frees us from sin's control. As believers, we are free to live as God created us to live. Of course, this does not mean that we are free to do as we please (see 1 Peter 2:16). We are now free to obey God.

1:26 See the notes in chapter 3 for more on taming the tongue. No matter how spiritual we may think we are, we all could control our speech more effectively.

1:27 In the first century, orphans and widows had very little means of economic support. Unless a family member was willing to care for them, they were reduced to begging, selling themselves as slaves, or starving. By caring for these people, the church put God's Word into practice. When we give with no thought of receiving, we show what it means to truly serve others.

1:27 To keep ourselves from letting the world corrupt us, we need to commit ourselves to Christ's ethical and moral system, not the world's. We are not to adapt to the world's value system, which is based on money, power, and pleasure. True faith means nothing if we are contaminated with such values.

2:1ff In this chapter James argues against favoritism and for the necessity of good deeds. He presents three principles of faith: (1) Commitment is an essential part of faith. You cannot be a Christian simply by affirming the right doctrines or agreeing with biblical facts (2:19). You must commit your mind and heart to Christ. (2) Right actions are the natural by-products of true faith. A genuine Christian will have a changed life (2:18). (3) Faith without good deeds doesn't do anybody any good—it is useless (2:14-17). James's teachings are consistent with Paul's teaching that we receive salvation by faith alone. Paul emphasizes the purpose of faith: to bring salvation. James emphasizes the results of faith: a changed life.

2:4 John 7:24
2:5 Luke 6:20; 1 Cor 1:26-28
2:7 Acts 11:26; 1 Pet 4:16
2:8 †Lev 19:18; Matt 7:12; Rom 13:8
2:10 Matt 5:19; Gal 5:3
2:11 †Exod 20:13-14; †Deut 5:17-18; Matt 19:18
2:12 Jas 1:25

and expensive jewelry, and another comes in who is poor and dressed in shabby clothes.
3If you give special attention and a good seat to the rich person, but you say to the poor
one, "You can stand over there, or else sit on the floor"—well, 4doesn't this discrimination show that you are guided by wrong motives?
5Listen to me, dear brothers and sisters. Hasn't God chosen the poor in this world to be
rich in faith? Aren't they the ones who will inherit the kingdom God promised to those who
love him? 6And yet, you insult the poor man! Isn't it the rich who oppress you and drag you
into court? 7Aren't they the ones who slander Jesus Christ, whose noble name you bear?
8Yes indeed, it is good when you truly obey our Lord's royal command found in the
Scriptures: "Love your neighbor as yourself."* 9But if you pay special attention to the
rich, you are committing a sin, for you are guilty of breaking that law.
10And the person who keeps all of the laws except one is as guilty as the person who
has broken all of God's laws. 11For the same God who said, "Do not commit adultery,"
also said, "Do not murder."* So if you murder someone, you have broken the entire law,
even if you do not commit adultery.
12So whenever you speak, or whatever you do, remember that you will be judged by

2:8 Lev 19:18. **2:11** Exod 20:13-14; Deut 5:17-18.

SHOWING FAVORITISM
Why it is wrong to show favoritism to the wealthy:

1. It is inconsistent with Christ's teachings.
2. It results from evil thoughts.
3. It insults people made in God's image.
4. It is a by-product of selfish motives.
5. It goes against the biblical definition of love.
6. It shows a lack of mercy to those less fortunate.
7. It is hypocritical.
8. It is sin.

2:1-7 James condemns acts of favoritism. Often we treat a well-dressed, impressive-looking person better than someone who looks shabby. We do this because we would rather identify with successful people than with apparent failures. The irony, as James reminds us, is that the supposed winners may have gained their impressive life-style at our expense. In addition, the rich find it difficult to identify with the Lord Jesus, who came as a humble servant. Are you easily impressed by status, wealth, or fame? Are you partial to the "haves" while ignoring the "have nots"? This attitude is sinful. God views all people as equals, and if he favors anyone, it is the poor and the powerless. We should follow his example.

2:2-4 Why is it wrong to judge a person by his or her economic status? Wealth may indicate intelligence, wise decisions, and hard work. On the other hand, it may only mean that a person had the good fortune of being born into a wealthy family. Or it may be the sign of greed, dishonesty, or selfishness. By honoring someone just because he or she dresses well, we are making appearance more important than character. Sometimes we do this because (1) poverty makes us uncomfortable; we don't want to face our responsibilities to those who have less than we do; (2) we want to be wealthy, too, and hope to use the rich person as a means to that end; (3) we want the rich person to join our church and help support it financially. All these motives are selfish, stemming from the view that we are superior to the poor person. If we say that Christ is our Lord, then we must live as he requires, showing no favoritism and loving all people regardless of whether they are rich or poor.

2:2-4 We are often partial to the rich because we mistakenly assume that riches are a sign of God's blessing and approval. But God does not promise us earthly rewards or riches; in fact, Christ calls us to be ready to suffer for him and give up everything in order to hold on to eternal life (Matthew 6:19-21; 19:28-30; Luke 12:14-34; Romans 8:15-21; 1 Timothy 6:17-19). We will have untold riches in eternity if we are faithful in our present life (Luke 6:35; John 12:23-25; Galatians 6:7-10; Titus 3:4-8).

2:5 When James speaks about the poor, he is talking about those who have no money and also about those whose simple values are despised by much of our affluent society. Perhaps the "poor" people prefer serving to managing, human relationships to financial security, peace to power. This does not mean that the poor will automatically go to heaven and the rich to hell. Poor people, however, are usually more aware of their powerlessness. Thus, it is often easier for them to acknowledge their need for salvation. One of the greatest barriers to salvation for the rich is pride. For the poor, bitterness can often bar the way to acceptance of salvation.

2:8 The "royal command" is the law of our great King Jesus Christ, who said, "Love each other in the same way that I love you" (John 15:12). This law, originally summarized in Leviticus 19:18, is the basis for all the laws of how people should relate to one another. Christ reinforced this truth in Matthew 22:37-40, and Paul taught it in Romans 13:8 and Galatians 5:14.

2:8, 9 We must treat all people as we would want to be treated. We should not ignore the rich, because then we would be withholding our love. But we must not favor them for what they can do for us, while ignoring the poor who can offer us seemingly so little in return.

2:10 Christians must not use this verse to justify sinning. We dare not say, "Because I can't keep every demand of God, why even try?" James reminds us that if we've broken just one law, we are sinners. We can't decide to keep part of God's law and ignore the rest. You can't break the law a little bit; if you have broken it at all, you need Christ to pay for your sin. Measure yourself, not someone else, against God's standards. Ask for forgiveness where you need it, and then renew your effort to put your faith into practice.

2:12 As Christians, we are saved by God's free gift (grace) through faith, not by keeping the law. But as Christians, we are also required to obey Christ. The apostle Paul taught that "we must all stand before Christ to be judged" (2 Corinthians 5:10) for our conduct. God's grace does not cancel our duty to obey him; it gives our obedience a new basis. The law is no longer an external set of rules, but it is a "law that sets you free"—one we joyfully and willingly carry out, because we love God and have the power of his Holy Spirit (see 1:25).

the law of love, the law that set you free. 13 For there will be no mercy for you if you have
not been merciful to others. But if you have been merciful, then God's mercy toward you
will win out over his judgment against you.

Faith without Good Deeds Is Dead

14 Dear brothers and sisters, what's the use of saying you have faith if you don't prove it
by your actions? That kind of faith can't save anyone. 15 Suppose you see a brother or
sister who needs food or clothing, 16 and you say, "Well, good-bye and God bless you;
stay warm and eat well"—but then you don't give that person any food or clothing. What
good does that do?

17 So you see, it isn't enough just to have faith. Faith that doesn't show itself by good
deeds is no faith at all—it is dead and useless.

18 Now someone may argue, "Some people have faith; others have good deeds." I say,
"I can't see your faith if you don't have good deeds, but I will show you my faith through
my good deeds."

19 Do you still think it's enough just to believe that there is one God? Well, even the
demons believe this, and they tremble in terror! 20 Fool! When will you ever learn that
faith that does not result in good deeds is useless?

21 Don't you remember that our ancestor Abraham was declared right with God
because of what he did when he offered his son Isaac on the altar? 22 You see, he was
trusting God so much that he was willing to do whatever God told him to do. His faith
was made complete by what he did—by his actions. 23 And so it happened just as the
Scriptures say: "Abraham believed God, so God declared him to be righteous."* He was
even called "the friend of God."* 24 So you see, we are made right with God by what we
do, not by faith alone.

25 Rahab the prostitute is another example of this. She was made right with God by her
actions—when she hid those messengers and sent them safely away by a different road.
26 Just as the body is dead without a spirit, so also faith is dead without good deeds.

Controlling the Tongue

3 Dear brothers and sisters, not many of you should become teachers in the church,
for we who teach will be judged by God with greater strictness.

2 We all make many mistakes, but those who control their tongues can also control
themselves in every other way. 3 We can make a large horse turn around and go wherever

2:13 Matt 18:32-35
2:15 Matt 25:35-36
2:16 1 Jn 3:17-18
2:17 Gal 5:6; Jas 2:20, 26
2:18 Matt 7:16-17; Rom 3:28
2:19 Deut 6:4; Matt 8:29
2:20 Gal 5:6; Jas 2:14, 17, 26
2:21 Gen 22:9, 12
2:22 Heb 11:17
2:23 †Gen 15:6; Isa 41:8; Rom 4:3-5
2:25 Josh 2:4, 6, 15; Heb 11:31
2:26 Gal 5:6; Jas 2:14, 17, 20
3:1 Rom 2:21
3:2 Jas 1:4, 26
3:3 Ps 32:9

2:23a Gen 15:6. **2:23b** See Isa 41:8.

2:13 Only God in his mercy can forgive our sins. We can't earn forgiveness by forgiving others. But when we withhold forgiveness from others after having received it ourselves, we show that we don't understand or appreciate God's mercy toward us (see Matthew 6:14, 15; 18:21ff; Ephesians 4:31, 32).

2:14 When someone claims to have faith, what he or she may have is intellectual assent—agreement with a set of Christian teachings—and as such it would be incomplete faith. True faith transforms our conduct as well as our thoughts. If our life remains unchanged, we don't truly believe the truths we claim to believe.

2:17 We cannot earn our salvation by serving and obeying God. But such actions show that our commitment to God is real. Deeds of loving service are not a substitute for, but rather a verification of, our faith in Christ.

2:18 At first glance, this verse seems to contradict Romans 3:28, "We are made right with God through faith and not by obeying the law." Deeper investigation, however, shows that the teachings of James and Paul are not at odds. While it is true that our good deeds can never earn salvation, true faith always results in a changed life and good deeds. Paul speaks against those who try to be saved by deeds instead of true faith; James speaks against those who confuse mere intellectual assent with true faith. After all, even demons know who Jesus is, but they don't obey him (2:19). True faith involves a commitment of your whole self to God.

2:21-24 James says that Abraham was "declared right with God" for what he *did* because he *believed* God (Romans 4:1-5). James and Paul are not contradicting but complementing each other. Let's not conclude that the truth is a blending of these two statements. We are not justified by what we do in any way. True faith always results in good deeds, but the deeds do not justify us. Faith brings us salvation; active obedience demonstrates that our faith is genuine.

2:25 Rahab lived in Jericho, a city the Israelites conquered as they entered the Promised Land (Joshua 2). When Israel's spies came to the city, she hid them and helped them escape. In this way she demonstrated faith in God's purpose for Israel. As a result, she and her family were saved when the city was destroyed. Hebrews 11:31 lists Rahab among the heroes of faith.

3:1 Teaching was a highly valued and respected profession in Jewish culture, and many Jews who embraced Christianity wanted to become teachers. James warned that although it is good to aspire to teach, teachers' responsibility is great because their words and example affect others' spiritual lives. If you are in a teaching or leadership role, how are you affecting those you lead?

3:2, 3 What you say and what you *don't* say are both important. To use proper speech you must not only say the right words at the right time but also not say what you shouldn't. Examples of an untamed tongue include gossiping, putting others down, bragging, manipulating, false teaching, exaggerating, complaining, flattering, and lying. Before you speak, ask, Is what I want to say true? Is it necessary? Is it kind?

3:5 Prov 26:20 — we want by means of a small bit in its mouth. 4And a tiny rudder makes a huge ship turn
wherever the pilot wants it to go, even though the winds are strong. 5So also, the tongue
3:6 Prov 16:27; Matt 12:36-37; 15:11, 18-19 — is a small thing, but what enormous damage it can do. A tiny spark can set a great forest
on fire. 6And the tongue is a flame of fire. It is full of wickedness that can ruin your whole
life. It can turn the entire course of your life into a blazing flame of destruction, for it is
set on fire by hell itself.
3:8 Ps 140:3; Rom 3:13 — 7People can tame all kinds of animals and birds and reptiles and fish, 8but no one can
tame the tongue. It is an uncontrollable evil, full of deadly poison. 9Sometimes it praises
3:9 Gen 1:26-27; 5:1; 1 Cor 11:7 — our Lord and Father, and sometimes it breaks out into curses against those who have been
made in the image of God. 10And so blessing and cursing come pouring out of the same
mouth. Surely, my brothers and sisters, this is not right! 11Does a spring of water bubble
3:12 Matt 7:16 — out with both fresh water and bitter water? 12Can you pick olives from a fig tree or figs
from a grapevine? No, and you can't draw fresh water from a salty pool.

3. Genuine wisdom

True Wisdom Comes from God

3:13 Jas 2:18 — 13If you are wise and understand God's ways, live a life of steady goodness so that only
3:14 2 Cor 12:20 — good deeds will pour forth. And if you don't brag about the good you do, then you will
be truly wise! 14But if you are bitterly jealous and there is selfish ambition in your hearts,
3:15 Jas 1:5, 17 — don't brag about being wise. That is the worst kind of lie. 15For jealousy and selfishness
3:16 1 Cor 3:3; Gal 5:20-21 — are not God's kind of wisdom. Such things are earthly, unspiritual, and motivated by the
Devil. 16For wherever there is jealousy and selfish ambition, there you will find disorder
and every kind of evil.

SPEECH	*When our speech is motivated by*	*It is full of*
	Satan	Bitter jealousy Selfish ambition Earthly concerns and desires Unspiritual thoughts and ideas Disorder Evil
	God and his wisdom	Purity Peace Consideration for others Submission Mercy Sincerity, impartiality Goodness

3:6 James compares the damage the tongue can do to a raging fire—the tongue's wickedness has its source in hell itself. The uncontrolled tongue can do terrible damage. Satan uses the tongue to divide people and pit them against one another. Idle and hateful words are damaging because they spread destruction quickly, and no one can stop the results once they are spoken. We dare not be careless with what we say, thinking we can apologize later, because even if we do, the scars remain. A few words spoken in anger can destroy a relationship that took years to build. Before you speak, remember that words are like fire—you can neither control nor reverse the damage they can do.

3:8 If no human being can control the tongue, why bother trying? Even though we may not achieve perfect control of our tongues, the Holy Spirit will help us learn self-control. Remember that we are not fighting the tongue's fire in our own strength. The Holy Spirit will give us increasing power to monitor and control what we say, so that when we are offended, the Spirit will remind us of God's love, and we won't react in a hateful manner. When we are criticized, the Spirit will heal the hurt and help us to not lash out.

3:9-12 Our contradictory speech often puzzles us. At times our words are right and pleasing to God, but at other times they are violent and destructive. Which of these speech patterns reflects our true identity? We were made in God's image, but the tongue gives us a picture of our basic sinful nature. God works to change us from the inside out. When the Holy Spirit purifies a heart, he gives self-control so that the person will speak words that please God.

3:13-18 Have you ever known anyone who claimed to be wise but who acted foolishly? True wisdom can be measured by a person's character. Just as you can identify a tree by the type of fruit it produces, you can evaluate your wisdom by the way you act. Foolishness leads to disorder, but wisdom leads to peace and goodness. Are you tempted to escalate the conflict, pass on the gossip, or fan the fire of discord? Careful, winsome speech and wise, loving words are the seeds of peace. God loves peacemakers (Matthew 5:9).

3:14, 15 Bitter jealousy and selfish ambition are inspired by the Devil. It is easy for us to be drawn into wrong desires by the pressures of society and sometimes even by well-meaning Christians. By listening to the advice: "Assert yourself," "Go for it," "Set high goals," we can be drawn into greed and destructive competitiveness. Seeking God's wisdom delivers us from the need to compare ourselves to others and to want what they have.

17But the wisdom that comes from heaven is first of all pure. It is also peace loving,
gentle at all times, and willing to yield to others. It is full of mercy and good deeds. It
shows no partiality and is always sincere. 18And those who are peacemakers will plant
seeds of peace and reap a harvest of goodness.

Drawing Close to God

4 What is causing the quarrels and fights among you? Isn't it the whole army of evil
desires at war within you? 2You want what you don't have, so you scheme and kill
to get it. You are jealous for what others have, and you can't possess it, so you fight and
quarrel to take it away from them. And yet the reason you don't have what you want is
that you don't ask God for it. 3And even when you do ask, you don't get it because your
whole motive is wrong—you want only what will give you pleasure.

4You adulterers! Don't you realize that friendship with this world makes you an
enemy of God? I say it again, that if your aim is to enjoy this world, you can't be a friend
of God. 5What do you think the Scriptures mean when they say that the Holy Spirit,
whom God has placed within us, jealously longs for us to be faithful*? 6He gives us more
and more strength to stand against such evil desires. As the Scriptures say,

"God sets himself against the proud,
but he shows favor to the humble."*

7So humble yourselves before God. Resist the Devil, and he will flee from you. 8Draw
close to God, and God will draw close to you. Wash your hands, you sinners; purify your
hearts, you hypocrites. 9Let there be tears for the wrong things you have done. Let there
be sorrow and deep grief. Let there be sadness instead of laughter, and gloom instead of
joy. 10When you bow down before the Lord and admit your dependence on him, he will
lift you up and give you honor.

3:17 Rom 12:9 Heb 12:11
3:18 Matt 5:9 Phil 1:11
4:2 1 Jn 3:15
4:3 1 Jn 3:22; 5:14
4:4 John 15:19 1 Jn 2:15
4:5 1 Cor 6:19 2 Cor 6:16
4:6 †Prov 3:34 Matt 23:12 1 Pet 5:5
4:7 Eph 6:12 1 Pet 5:6-9
4:8 Ps 73:28 Isa 1:16 Zech 1:3 Mal 3:7
4:9 Luke 6:25
4:10 Job 5:11 1 Pet 5:6

4:5 Or *the spirit that God placed within us tends to envy,* or *the Holy Spirit, whom God has placed within us, opposes our envy.* **4:6** Prov 3:34.

4:1-3 Conflicts and disputes among believers are always harmful. James explains that these quarrels result from evil desires battling within us: We want more possessions, more money, higher status, more recognition. When we don't get what we want, we fight in order to have it. Instead of aggressively grabbing what we want, we should submit ourselves to God, ask God to help us get rid of our selfish desires, and trust him to give us what we really need.

4:2, 3 James mentions the most common problems in prayer: not asking, asking for the wrong things, or asking for the wrong reasons. Do you talk to God at all? When you do, what do you talk about? Do you ask only to satisfy your desires? Do you seek God's approval for what you already plan to do? Your prayers will become powerful when you allow God to change your desires so that they perfectly correspond to his will for you (1 John 3:21, 22).

4:3, 4 There is nothing wrong with wanting a pleasurable life. God gives us good gifts that he wants us to enjoy (1:17; Ephesians 4:7; 1 Timothy 4:4, 5). But having friendship with the world involves seeking pleasure at others' expense or at the expense of obeying God. Pleasure that keeps us from pleasing God is sinful; pleasure from God's rich bounty is good.

4:4-6 The cure for evil desires is humility (see Proverbs 16:18, 19; 1 Peter 5:5, 6). Pride makes us self-centered and leads us to conclude that we deserve all we can see, touch, or imagine. It creates greedy appetites for far more than we need. We can be released from our self-centered desires by humbling ourselves before God, realizing that all we really need is his approval. When the Holy Spirit fills us, we see that this world's seductive attractions are only cheap substitutes for what God has to offer.

4:5 This verse may mean that because of our fallen nature, we have a tendency toward envy. James is not quoting a specific verse or passage—he is summing up a teaching of Scripture. See Romans 6:6-8 and Galatians 5:17-21 for more on the human tendency toward envy and discontent.

4:7 Although God and the Devil are at war, we don't have to wait until the end to see who will win. God has *already* defeated Satan (Revelation 12:10-12), and when Christ returns, the Devil and all he stands for will be eliminated forever (Revelation 20:10-15). Satan is here now, however, and he is trying to win us over to his evil cause. With the Holy Spirit's power, we can resist the Devil, and he will flee from us.

4:7-10 How can you draw near to God? James gives five ways: (1) *Humble yourselves before God* (4:7). Yield to his authority and will, commit your life to him and his control, and be willing to follow him. (2) *Resist the Devil* (4:7). Don't allow Satan to entice and tempt you. (3) *Wash your hands* . . . and *purify your hearts* (that is, lead a pure life) (4:8). Be cleansed from sin, replacing your desire to sin with your desire to experience God's purity. (4) *Let there be sorrow and deep grief* for your sins (4:9). Don't be afraid to express deep heartfelt sorrow for what you have done. (5) *Bow down before the Lord,* and he will lift you up (4:10; 1 Peter 5:6).

4:10 Bowing before the Lord means recognizing that our worth comes from God alone. To be humble involves leaning on his power and his guidance, and not going our own independent way. Although we do not deserve God's favor, he wants to lift us up and give us worth and dignity, despite our human shortcomings.

Warning against Judging Others

4:11 Matt 7:1; 2 Cor 12:20; 1 Pet 2:1
4:12 Matt 10:28; Rom 2:1; 14:4; Jas 5:9

11 Don't speak evil against each other, my dear brothers and sisters. If you criticize each
other and condemn each other, then you are criticizing and condemning God's law. But
you are not a judge who can decide whether the law is right or wrong. Your job is to obey
it. 12 God alone, who made the law, can rightly judge among us. He alone has the power
to save or to destroy. So what right do you have to condemn your neighbor?

Warning about Self-Confidence

4:13-14 Prov 27:1; Luke 12:18-20
4:15 Acts 18:21
4:16 1 Cor 5:6
4:17 Luke 12:47

13 Look here, you people who say, "Today or tomorrow we are going to a certain town
and will stay there a year. We will do business there and make a profit." 14 How do you
know what will happen tomorrow? For your life is like the morning fog—it's here a little
while, then it's gone. 15 What you ought to say is, "If the Lord wants us to, we will live
and do this or that." 16 Otherwise you will be boasting about your own plans, and all such
boasting is evil.
17 Remember, it is sin to know what you ought to do and then not do it.

FAITH THAT WORKS
James offers a larger number of similarities to the Sermon on the Mount than any other book in the New Testament. James relied heavily on Jesus' teachings.

Lesson	*Reference*
Whenever trouble comes your way, be joyful.	James 1:2 Matthew 5:10–12
When your endurance is fully developed, you will be strong in character and ready for anything.	James 1:4 Matthew 5:48
Ask God, and he will answer.	James 1:5; 5:15 Matthew 7:7–12
Those who are poor (who don't amount to much by the world's standards) should be glad, for God has honored them.	James 1:9 Matthew 5:3
Watch out for your anger. . . . It can be dangerous.	James 1:20 Matthew 5:22
Be merciful to others, as God is merciful to you.	James 2:13 Matthew 5:7; 6:14
Your faith must express itself in your actions.	James 2:14–16 Matthew 7:21–23
Blessed are the peacemakers; they plant in peace and reap a harvest of goodness.	James 3:17, 18 Matthew 5:9
Friendship with the world makes you an enemy of God.	James 4:4 Matthew 6:24
When you humble yourself and realize your dependence on God, he will lift you up.	James 4:10 Matthew 5:3, 4
Don't speak evil against each other. If you do, you are criticizing God's law.	James 4:11 Matthew 7:1, 2
Treasures on earth will only rot away and be eaten by moths. Store up eternal treasures in heaven.	James 5:2, 3 Matthew 6:19
Be patient in suffering, as God's prophets were patient.	James 5:10 Matthew 5:12
Be honest in your speech; just say a simple yes or no so that you will not sin.	James 5:12 Matthew 5:33–37

4:11, 12 Jesus summarized the law as love for God and neighbor (Matthew 22:37-40), and Paul said that love demonstrated toward a neighbor would fully satisfy the law (Romans 13:6-10). When we fail to love, we are actually breaking God's law. Examine your attitude and actions toward others. Do you build people up or tear them down? When you're ready to criticize someone, remember God's law of love and say something good instead. Saying something beneficial to others will cure you of finding fault and increase your ability to obey God's law of love.

4:13-16 It is good to make plans, but they will disappoint us if we leave God out of them. There is no point in making plans as though God does not exist, because the future is in his hands. What would you like to be doing 10 years from now? one year from now? tomorrow? How will you react if God steps in and rearranges your plans? Plan ahead, but ask for God's guidance. Seek God's will in your planning; he will never disappoint you.

4:14 Life is short no matter how many years we live. Don't be deceived into thinking that you have lots of remaining time to live for Christ, to enjoy your loved ones, or to do what you know you should. Live for God today! Then, no matter when your life ends, you will have fulfilled God's plan for you.

4:17 We tend to think that *doing* wrong is sin. But James tells us that sin is also *not* doing right. (These two kinds of sin are sometimes called sins of commission and sins of omission.) It is a sin to lie; it can also be a sin to know the truth and not tell it. It is a sin to speak evil of someone; it is also a sin to avoid that person when you know he or she needs your friendship. You should

Warning to the Rich

5 Look here, you rich people, weep and groan with anguish because of all the terrible
troubles ahead of you. [2]Your wealth is rotting away, and your fine clothes are
moth-eaten rags. [3]Your gold and silver have become worthless. The very wealth you
were counting on will eat away your flesh in hell.* This treasure you have accumulated
will stand as evidence against you on the day of judgment. [4]For listen! Hear the cries of
the field workers whom you have cheated of their pay. The wages you held back cry out
against you. The cries of the reapers have reached the ears of the Lord Almighty.
[5]You have spent your years on earth in luxury, satisfying your every whim. Now your
hearts are nice and fat, ready for the slaughter. [6]You have condemned and killed good
people who had no power to defend themselves against you.

Patience in Suffering

[7]Dear brothers and sisters, you must be patient as you wait for the Lord's return.
Consider the farmers who eagerly look for the rains in the fall and in the spring. They
patiently wait for the precious harvest to ripen. [8]You, too, must be patient. And take
courage, for the coming of the Lord is near.
[9]Don't grumble about each other, my brothers and sisters, or God will judge you. For
look! The great Judge is coming. He is standing at the door!
[10]For examples of patience in suffering, look at the prophets who spoke in the name
of the Lord. [11]We give great honor to those who endure under suffering. Job is an
example of a man who endured patiently. From his experience we see how the Lord's
plan finally ended in good, for he is full of tenderness and mercy.
[12]But most of all, dear brothers and sisters, never take an oath, by heaven or earth or
anything else. Just say a simple yes or no, so that you will not sin and be condemned for it.

The Power of Prayer

[13]Are any among you suffering? They should keep on praying about it. And those who
have reason to be thankful should continually sing praises to the Lord.
[14]Are any among you sick? They should call for the elders of the church and have

5:1 Prov 11:4, 28; Isa 13:6
5:2 Matt 6:19
5:4 Lev 19:13; Deut 24:14-15; Ps 18:6; Isa 5:9
5:5 Jer 12:3; 25:34; Luke 16:19
5:7 Deut 11:14; Jer 5:24; Joel 2:23
5:8 Rom 13:11-12; Heb 10:37
5:9 Matt 24:33; 1 Cor 4:5; Jas 4:12
5:11 Job 1:20-22; 2:7-10; 42:10-17; Ps 103:8
5:12 Matt 5:34-37
5:13 Col 3:16
5:14 Mark 6:13; Luke 10:34

5:3 Or *will eat your flesh like fire.*

---

be willing to help as the Holy Spirit guides you. If God has directed you to do a kind act, to render a service, or to restore a relationship, do it. You will experience a renewed and refreshed vitality to your Christian faith.

5:1-6 James proclaims the worthlessness of riches, not the worthlessness of the rich. Today's money will be worthless when Christ returns, so we should spend our time accumulating the kind of treasures that will be worthwhile in God's eternal Kingdom. Money is not the problem; Christian leaders need money to live and to support their families; missionaries need money to help them spread the Good News; churches need money to do their work effectively. It is the *love* of money that leads to evil (1 Timothy 6:10) and causes some people to oppress others in order to get more. This is a warning to all Christians who are tempted to adopt worldly standards rather than God's standards (Romans 12:1, 2) as well as an encouragement to all those who are oppressed by the rich. Also read Matthew 6:19-21 to see what Jesus says about riches.

5:6 "Good people" refers to defenseless persons, probably poor laborers. Poor people who could not pay their debts were thrown in prison or forced to sell all their possessions. At times, they were even forced to sell their family members into slavery. With no opportunity to work off their debts, poor people often died of starvation. God called this murder. Hoarding money, exploiting employees, and living self-indulgently will not escape God's notice.

5:7, 8 The farmer must wait patiently for his crops to grow; he cannot hurry the process. But he does not take the summer off and hope that all goes well in the fields. There is much work to do to ensure a good harvest. In the same way, we must wait patiently for Christ's return. We cannot make him come back any sooner. But while we wait, there is much work that we can do to advance God's Kingdom. Both the farmer and the Christian must live by faith, looking toward the future reward for their labors. Don't live as if Christ will never come. Work faithfully to build his Kingdom. The King *will* come when the time is right.

5:9 When things go wrong, we tend to grumble against and blame others for our miseries (see the second note on Genesis 3:11-13). Blaming others is easier than owning our share of the responsibility, but it can be both destructive and sinful. Before you judge others for their shortcomings, remember that Christ the Judge will come to evaluate each of us (Matthew 7:1-5; 25:31-46). He will not let us get away with shifting the blame to others.

5:10, 11 Many prophets suffered and were persecuted, such as Moses, Elijah, and Jeremiah. For a complete list of those persecuted, see the chart in 2 Chronicles 18. For more on the topic of suffering, see the notes on Job 1:1ff; 2:10; 3:23-26; 4:7, 8; 42:17; and Job's Profile in Job 2.

5:12 A person with a reputation for exaggeration or lying often can't get anyone to believe him on his word alone. Christians should never become like that. Always be honest so that others will believe your simple yes or no. By avoiding lies, half-truths, and omissions of the truth, you will become known as a trustworthy person.

5:14, 15 James is referring to someone who is physically ill. In Scripture, oil was both a medicine (see the parable of the Good Samaritan in Luke 10:30-37) and a symbol of the Spirit of God (as used in anointing kings, see 1 Samuel 16:1-13). Thus, oil can represent both the medical and the spiritual spheres of life. Christians should not separate the physical and the spiritual. Jesus Christ is Lord over both the body and the spirit.

5:15 Mark 16:18; Jas 1:6
5:16 Matt 18:15-18; 1 Jn 1:9
5:17 1 Kgs 17:1-7; Luke 4:25
5:18 1 Kgs 18:42-45
5:19 Matt 18:15
5:20 Prov 10:12; 1 Pet 4:8

them pray over them, anointing them with oil in the name of the Lord. 15 And their prayer
offered in faith will heal the sick, and the Lord will make them well. And anyone who
has committed sins will be forgiven.
16 Confess your sins to each other and pray for each other so that you may be healed.
The earnest prayer of a righteous person has great power and wonderful results. 17 Elijah
was as human as we are, and yet when he prayed earnestly that no rain would fall, none
fell for the next three and a half years! 18 Then he prayed for rain, and down it poured.
The grass turned green, and the crops began to grow again.

Restore Wandering Believers

19 My dear brothers and sisters, if anyone among you wanders away from the truth and
is brought back again, 20 you can be sure that the one who brings that person back will
save that sinner from death and bring about the forgiveness of many sins.

5:14, 15 People in the church are not alone. Members of Christ's body should be able to count on others for support and prayer, especially when they are sick or suffering. The elders should be on call to respond to the illness of any member, and the church should be sensitive to the needs of all its members.

5:15 The "prayer offered in faith" does not refer to the faith of the sick person but to the faith of the people praying. God heals, faith doesn't, and all prayers are subject to God's will. But prayer is part of God's healing process.

5:16 Christ has made it possible for us to go directly to God for forgiveness. But confessing our sins to each other still has an important place in the life of the church. (1) If we have sinned against an individual, we must ask him or her to forgive us. (2) If our sin has affected the church, we must confess it publicly. (3) If we need loving support as we struggle with a sin, we should confess that sin to those who are able to provide that support. (4) If we doubt God's forgiveness, after confessing a sin to him, we may wish to confess that sin to a fellow believer for assurance of God's pardon. In Christ's Kingdom, every believer is a priest to other believers (1 Peter 2:9).

5:16-18 The Christian's most powerful resource is communion with God through prayer. The results are often greater than we thought were possible. Some people see prayer as a last resort to be tried when all else fails. This approach is backward. Prayer should come first. Because God's power is infinitely greater than ours, it only makes sense to rely on it—especially because God encourages us to do so.

5:17 For more about the great prophet Elijah, read his Profile in 1 Kings 18.

5:19, 20 Clearly this person who has wandered from the truth is a believer who has fallen into sin—one who is no longer living a life consistent with his or her beliefs. Christians disagree over whether or not it is possible for people to lose their salvation, but all agree that those who fall away from their faith are in serious trouble and need to repent. James urges Christians to help backsliders return to God. By taking the initiative, praying for the person, and acting in love, we can meet the person where he or she is and bring him or her back to God and his forgiveness.

5:20 The book of James emphasizes faith in action. Right living is the evidence and result of faith. The church must serve with compassion, speak lovingly and truthfully, live in obedience to God's commands, and love one another. The body of believers ought to be an example of heaven on earth, drawing people to Christ through love for God and each other. If we truly believe God's Word, we will *live* it day by day. God's Word is not merely something we read or think about, but something we do. Belief, faith, and trust must have hands and feet—ours!

1 PETER

VITAL STATISTICS

PURPOSE:
To offer encouragement to suffering Christians

AUTHOR:
Peter

TO WHOM WRITTEN:
Jewish Christians driven out of Jerusalem and scattered throughout Asia Minor, and all believers everywhere

DATE WRITTEN:
Approximately A.D. 62–64, possibly from Rome

SETTING:
Peter was probably in Rome when the great persecution under Emperor Nero began. (Eventually Peter was executed during this persecution.) Throughout the Roman Empire, Christians were being tortured and killed for their faith, and the church in Jerusalem was being scattered.

KEY VERSE:
"These trials are only to test your faith. . . . So if your faith remains strong after being tried by fiery trials, it will bring you much praise and glory and honor on the day when Jesus Christ is revealed to the whole world" (1:7).

KEY PEOPLE:
Peter, Silas, Mark

KEY PLACES:
Jerusalem, Rome, and the regions of Pontus, Galatia, Cappadocia, Asia Minor, and Bithynia

SPECIAL FEATURES:
Peter used several images that were very special to him because Jesus had used them when he revealed certain truths to Peter. Peter's name (which means "rock") had been given to him by Jesus. Peter's conception of the church—a spiritual house composed of living stones built upon Christ as the foundation—came from Christ. Jesus encouraged Peter to care for the church as a shepherd tending the flock. Thus, it is not surprising to see Peter using living stones (2:5–9) and shepherds and sheep (2:25; 5:2, 4) to describe the church.

CRUSHED, overwhelmed, devastated, torn—these waves of feelings wash over those who suffer, obliterating hope and threatening to destroy them. Suffering has many forms—physical abuse, debilitating disease, social ostracism, persecution. The pain and anguish tempt a person to turn back, to surrender, to give in.

Many first-century followers of Christ were suffering and being abused and persecuted for believing in and obeying Jesus. Beginning in Jerusalem at the hands of their Jewish brothers, the persecution spread to the rest of the world—wherever Christians gathered. It climaxed when Rome determined to rid the empire of the "Christ-ones"—those who would not bow to Caesar.

Peter knew persecution firsthand. Beaten and jailed, Peter had been threatened often. He had seen fellow Christians die and the church scattered. But he knew Christ, and nothing could shake his confidence in his risen Lord. So Peter wrote to the church scattered and suffering for the faith, giving comfort and hope, and urging continued loyalty to Christ.

Peter begins by thanking God for salvation (1:2–6). He explains to his readers that trials will refine their faith (1:7–9). They should believe in spite of their circumstances; for many in past ages believed in God's plan of salvation, even the prophets of old who wrote about it but didn't understand it. But now salvation has been revealed in Christ (1:10–13).

In response to such a great salvation, Peter commands them to live holy lives (1:14–16), to reverently fear and trust God (1:17–21), to be honest and loving (2:1–3), and to become like Christ (2:1–3).

Jesus Christ, as "the living cornerstone" upon whom the church is to be built (2:4, 6), is also the stone that was rejected, causing those who are disobedient to stumble and fall (2:7, 8). But the church, built upon this stone, is to be God's holy priesthood (2:9, 10).

Next, Peter explains how believers should live during difficult times (2:11—4:11). Christians should be above reproach (2:12–17), imitating Christ in all their social roles—masters and servants, husbands and wives, church members and neighbors (2:18—3:17). Christ should be our model for obedience to God in the midst of great suffering (3:18—4:11).

Peter then outlines the right attitude to have about persecution: Expect it (4:12), be thankful for the privilege of suffering for Christ (4:13–18), and trust God for deliverance (4:19).

Next, Peter gives some special instructions: Elders should care for God's flock (5:1–4), younger men should be submissive to those who are older (5:5, 6), and everyone should trust God and resist Satan (5:7–11).

Peter concludes by introducing Silas and by sending personal greetings, possibly from the church in Rome, and from Mark (5:12–14).

When you suffer for doing what is right, remember that following Christ is a costly commitment. When persecuted for your faith, rejoice that you have been counted worthy to suffer for Christ. He suffered for us; as his followers, we should expect nothing less. As you read 1 Peter, remember that trials will come to refine your faith. When they come, remain faithful to God.

THE BLUEPRINT

1. God's great blessings to his people (1:1—2:10) 2. The conduct of God's people in the midst of suffering (2:11—4:19) 3. The shepherding of God's people in the midst of suffering (5:1–14)	Peter wrote to Jewish Christians who were experiencing persecution for their faith. He wrote to comfort them with the hope of eternal life and to challenge them to continue living holy lives. Those who suffer for being Christians become partners with Christ in his suffering. As we suffer, we must remember that Christ is both our hope in the midst of suffering and our example of how to endure suffering faithfully.

MEGATHEMES

THEME	EXPLANATION	IMPORTANCE
Salvation	Our salvation is a gracious gift from God. God chose us out of his love for us, Jesus died to pay the penalty for our sin, and the Holy Spirit cleansed us from sin when we believed. Eternal life is a wonderful gift for those who trust in Christ.	Our safety and security are in God. If we experience joy in relationship with Christ now, how much greater will our joy be when he returns and we see him face to face. Such a hope should motivate us to serve Christ with greater commitment.
Persecution	Peter offers faithful believers comfort and hope. We should expect ridicule, rejection, and suffering because we are Christians. Persecution makes us stronger because it refines our faith. We can face persecution victoriously, as Christ did, if we rely on him.	Christians still suffer for what they believe. We should expect persecution, but we don't have to be terrified by it. The fact that we will live eternally with Christ should give us the confidence, patience, and hope to stand firm even when we are persecuted.
God's Family	We are privileged to belong to God's family, a community with Christ as the founder and foundation. Everyone in this community is related—we are all brothers and sisters, loved equally by God.	Because Christ is the foundation of our family, we must be devoted, loyal, and faithful to him. By obeying him, we show that we are his children. We must accept the challenge to live differently from the society around us.
Family Life	Peter encouraged the wives of unbelievers to submit to their husbands' authority as a means of winning them to Christ. He urged all family members to treat others with sympathy, love, compassion, and humility.	We must treat our families lovingly. Though it's never easy, willing service is the best way to influence loved ones. To gain the strength we need for self-discipline and submission, we need to pray for God's help.
Judgment	God will judge everyone with perfect justice. We all will face God. He will punish evildoers and those who persecute God's people. Those who love him will be rewarded with life forever in his presence.	Because all are accountable to God, we can leave judgment of others to him. We must not hate or resent those who persecute us. We should realize that we will be held responsible for how we live each day.

1. God's great blessings to his people

Greetings from Peter

1 This letter is from Peter, an apostle of Jesus Christ.
I am writing to God's chosen people who are living as foreigners in the lands of 1:2
Pontus, Galatia, Cappadocia, the province of Asia, and Bithynia. 2God the Father chose Rom 8:29 2 Thes 2:13
you long ago, and the Spirit has made you holy. As a result, you have obeyed Jesus Christ Heb 12:24
and are cleansed by his blood.

May you have more and more of God's special favor and wonderful peace.

The Hope of Eternal Life

3All honor to the God and Father of our Lord Jesus Christ, for it is by his boundless 1:4
mercy that God has given us the privilege of being born again. Now we live with a Acts 20:32 Col 1:5, 12
wonderful expectation because Jesus Christ rose again from the dead. 4For God has 2 Tim 4:8
reserved a priceless inheritance for his children. It is kept in heaven for you, pure and 1:5 John 10:28
undefiled, beyond the reach of change and decay. 5And God, in his mighty power, will Phil 4:7

1:1 The apostle Peter wrote this letter to encourage believers who would likely face trials and persecution under Emperor Nero. During most of the first century, Christians were not hunted down and killed throughout the Roman Empire. They could, however, expect social and economic persecution from three main sources: the Romans, the Jews, and their own families. All would very likely be misunderstood; some would be harassed; a few would be tortured and even put to death.

The legal status of Christians in the Roman Empire was unclear. Many Romans still thought of Christians as members of a Jewish sect, and because the Jewish religion was legal, they considered Christianity legal also—as long as Christians complied with the empire's laws. However, if Christians refused to worship the emperor or join the army, or if they were involved in civil disturbances (such as the one in Ephesus recorded in Acts 19:23ff), they might be punished by the civil authorities.

Many Jews did not appreciate being legally associated with Christians. As the book of Acts frequently records, Jews occasionally harmed Christians physically, drove them out of town, or attempted to turn Roman officials against them. Saul, later the great apostle Paul, was an early Jewish persecutor of Christians.

Another source of persecution was the Christian's own family. Under Roman law, the head of the household had absolute authority over all its members. Unless the ruling male became a Christian, the wife, children, and servants who were believers might well face extreme hardship. If they were sent away, they would have no place to turn but the church; if they were beaten, no court of law would uphold their interests.

Peter may have been writing especially for new Christians and those planning to be baptized. Peter wanted to warn them about what lay ahead, and they needed his encouraging words to help them face opposition. This letter is still helpful for any Christians facing trials. Many Christians around the world are living under governments more repressive than the Roman Empire of the first century. Christians everywhere are subject to misunderstanding, ridicule, and even harassment by unbelieving friends, employers, and family members. None of us is exempt from catastrophe, pain, illness, and death—trials that, like persecution, make us lean heavily on God's grace. For today's readers, as well as for Peter's original audience, the theme of this letter is *hope.*

1:1 Peter (also called Simon and Cephas) was one of the 12 disciples chosen by Jesus (Mark 1:16-18; John 1:42) and, with James and John, was part of the inner group that Jesus singled out for special training and fellowship. Peter was one of the first to recognize Jesus as the Messiah, God's Son, and Jesus gave him a special leadership role in the church (Matthew 16:16-19; Luke 22:31, 32; John 21:15-19). Although during Jesus' trial Peter denied knowing Jesus, Peter repented and became a great apostle. For more information on Peter, see his Profile in Matthew 27.

1:1 This letter is addressed to "God's chosen people who are living as foreigners" in various parts of the world—the Jewish Christians scattered throughout the world as a result of persecution against believers in and around Jerusalem. The first believers and leaders of the early church were Jews. When they became Christians, they didn't give up their Jewish heritage, just as you didn't give up your nationality when you became a follower of Christ. Because of persecution, these believers had been scattered throughout the Roman world (this scattering is described in Acts 8:1-4). Persecution didn't stop the spread of the Good News; instead, persecution served as a way to introduce the Good News to the whole empire. Thus, the churches to whom Peter wrote also included Gentile Christians.

1:2 Peter encouraged his readers by this strong declaration that they were *chosen* by God the Father. At one time, only the nation of Israel could claim to be God's chosen people; but through Christ, all believers—Jews and Gentiles—belong to God. Our salvation and security rest in the free and merciful choice of almighty God; no trials or persecutions can take away the eternal life he gives to those who believe in him.

1:2 This verse mentions all three members of the Trinity: God the Father, God the Son (Jesus Christ), and God the Holy Spirit. All members of the Trinity work to bring about our salvation. The Father chose us before we chose him (Ephesians 1:4). Jesus Christ, the Son, died for us while we were still sinners (Romans 5:6-10). The Holy Spirit brings us the benefits of salvation and sets us apart (makes us holy, sanctifies us) for God's service (2 Thessalonians 2:13).

1:3 The term *born again* refers to spiritual birth (regeneration)—the Holy Spirit's act of bringing believers into God's family. Jesus used this concept of new birth when he explained salvation to Nicodemus (see John 3).

1:3-6 Do you need encouragement? Peter's words offer joy and hope in times of trouble, and he bases his confidence on what God has done for us in Christ Jesus. We live with the wonderful expectation of eternal life (1:3). Our hope is not only for the future; eternal life begins when we trust Christ and join God's family. No matter what pain or trial we face in this life, we know that it is not our final experience. Eventually we will live with Christ forever.

1:4 The Jews had looked forward to an inheritance in the Promised Land of Canaan (Numbers 32:19; Deuteronomy 2:12; 19:8). Christians now look forward to a family inheritance in the eternal city of God. God has reserved the inheritance; it will never fade or decay; it will be unstained by sin. The best part is that *you* have an inheritance if you have trusted Christ as your Savior.

1:5 God will help us remain true to our faith through whatever difficult times we must face. The "last day" is the judgment day of Christ described in Romans 14:10 and Revelation 20:11-15. We may have to endure trials, persecution, or violent death, but our souls cannot be harmed if we have accepted Christ's gift of salvation. We know we will receive the promised rewards.

1:6
Rom 5:2
Jas 1:2
1 Pet 4:12

1:7
Job 23:10
Prov 17:3
Isa 48:10
Jas 1:3

1:8
John 20:29
2 Cor 5:7

1:9
Rom 6:22

1:10
Matt 13:17; 26:24

1:11
Isa 53
Luke 24:26
Acts 16:7
2 Pet 1:21

protect you until you receive this salvation, because you are trusting him. It will be
revealed on the last day for all to see. 6 So be truly glad!* There is wonderful joy ahead,
even though it is necessary for you to endure many trials for a while.
7 These trials are only to test your faith, to show that it is strong and pure. It is being
tested as fire tests and purifies gold—and your faith is far more precious to God than
mere gold. So if your faith remains strong after being tried by fiery trials, it will bring
you much praise and glory and honor on the day when Jesus Christ is revealed to the
whole world.
8 You love him even though you have never seen him. Though you do not see him, you
trust him; and even now you are happy with a glorious, inexpressible joy. 9 Your reward
for trusting him will be the salvation of your souls.
10 This salvation was something the prophets wanted to know more about. They
prophesied about this gracious salvation prepared for you, even though they had many
questions as to what it all could mean. 11 They wondered what the Spirit of Christ within

1:6 Or *So you are truly glad.*

THE CHURCHES OF PETER'S LETTER
Peter addressed his letter to the churches located throughout Bithynia, Pontus, Asia, Galatia, and Cappadocia. Paul had evangelized many of these areas; other areas had churches that were begun by the Jews who were in Jerusalem on the day of Pentecost and heard Peter's powerful sermon (see Acts 2:9-11).

1:6 Why were Christians the target of persecution? (1) They refused to worship the emperor as a god and thus were viewed as atheists and traitors. (2) They refused to worship at pagan temples, so business for these moneymaking enterprises dropped wherever Christianity took hold. (3) They didn't support the Roman ideals of self, power, and conquest; and the Romans scorned the Christian ideal of self-sacrificing service. (4) They exposed and rejected the horrible immorality of pagan culture.

1:6, 7 Peter mentions suffering several times in this letter: 1:6, 7; 3:13-17; 4:12-19; 5:9. When he speaks of trials, he is not talking about natural disasters or the experience of God's punishments, but the response of an unbelieving world to people of faith. All believers face such trials when they let their light shine into the darkness. We must accept trials as part of the refining process that burns away impurities and prepares us to meet Christ. Trials teach us patience (Romans 5:3, 4; James 1:2, 3) and help us grow to be the kind of people God wants.

1:7 As gold is heated, impurities float to the top and can be skimmed off. Steel is tempered or strengthened by heating it in fire. Likewise, our trials, struggles, and persecutions refine and strengthen our faith, making us useful to God.

1:10-12 Although the plan of salvation was a mystery to the Old Testament prophets, they still suffered persecution, and some even died for God. In contrast, some Jewish Christians who read Peter's letter had seen Jesus for themselves and knew why he came. They based their assurance on Jesus' death and resurrection. With their firsthand knowledge and personal experience of Jesus, their faith could be even stronger than that of the Old Testament prophets.

1:11 The Spirit of Christ is another name for the Holy Spirit. Before Jesus left his ministry on earth to return to heaven, he promised to send the Holy Spirit, the Counselor, to teach, help, and guide his followers (John 14:15-17, 26; 16:7). The Holy Spirit would tell them all about Jesus and would reveal his glory (John 15:26; 16:14). The Old Testament prophets, writing under the Holy Spirit's inspiration (2 Peter 1:20, 21), described the coming of the Messiah. The New Testament apostles, through the inspiration of the same Spirit, preached the crucified and risen Lord.

them was talking about when he told them in advance about Christ's suffering and his
great glory afterward. They wondered when and to whom all this would happen.
12 They were told that these things would not happen during their lifetime, but many
years later, during yours. And now this Good News has been announced by those who
preached to you in the power of the Holy Spirit sent from heaven. It is all so wonderful
that even the angels are eagerly watching these things happen.

A Call to Holy Living

13 So think clearly and exercise self-control. Look forward to the special blessings that
will come to you at the return of Jesus Christ. 14 Obey God because you are his children.
Don't slip back into your old ways of doing evil; you didn't know any better then. 15 But
now you must be holy in everything you do, just as God—who chose you to be his
children—is holy. 16 For he himself has said, "You must be holy because I am holy."*
17 And remember that the heavenly Father to whom you pray has no favorites when he
judges. He will judge or reward you according to what you do. So you must live in
reverent fear of him during your time as foreigners here on earth. 18 For you know that
God paid a ransom to save you from the empty life you inherited from your ancestors.
And the ransom he paid was not mere gold or silver. 19 He paid for you with the precious
lifeblood of Christ, the sinless, spotless Lamb of God. 20 God chose him for this purpose
long before the world began, but now in these final days, he was sent to the earth for all
to see. And he did this for you.
21 Through Christ you have come to trust in God. And because God raised Christ from
the dead and gave him great glory, your faith and hope can be placed confidently in God.
22 Now you can have sincere love for each other as brothers and sisters because you were
cleansed from your sins when you accepted the truth of the Good News. So see to it that
you really do love each other intensely with all your hearts.*
23 For you have been born again. Your new life did not come from your earthly parents
because the life they gave you will end in death. But this new life will last forever
because it comes from the eternal, living word of God. 24 As the prophet says,

1:16 Lev 11:44-45; 19:2; 20:7. **1:22** Some manuscripts read *with a pure heart.*

1:12 Acts 2:2-4; Eph 3:10
1:14 Rom 12:2; Eph 2:3; 4:17-18; 1 Pet 1:2; 4:2
1:15 2 Cor 7:1; 1 Thes 4:7; 1 Jn 3:3
1:16 †Lev 11:44-45; 19:2; 20:7
1:17 Ps 89:26; Jer 3:19
1:19 Exod 12:5; John 1:29; Heb 9:14
1:20 Acts 2:23; Eph 1:4
1:21 John 14:6; Rom 4:24
1:22 John 13:34; Rom 12:10
1:23 John 1:13; 3:3; Heb 4:12

1:13 The imminent return of Christ should motivate us to live for him. This means being mentally alert ("think clearly"), disciplined ("exercise self-control"), and focused ("look forward"). Are you ready to meet Christ?

1:14-16 The God of Israel and of the Christian church is holy—he sets the standard for morality. Unlike the Roman gods, he is not warlike, adulterous, or spiteful. Unlike the gods of the pagan cults popular in the first century, he is not bloodthirsty or promiscuous. He is a God of mercy and justice who cares personally for each of his followers. Our holy God expects us to imitate him by following his high moral standards and by being both merciful and just.

1:14-16 After people commit their lives to Christ, they sometimes still feel a pull back to their old ways. Peter tells us to be like our heavenly Father—holy in everything we do. Holiness means being totally devoted or dedicated to God, set aside for his special use and set apart from sin and its influence. We're to be set apart and different, not blending in with the crowd, yet not being different just for the sake of being different. God's qualities in our life make us different. Our focus and priorities must be his. All this is in direct contrast to our old ways (1:14). We cannot become holy on our own, but God gives us his Holy Spirit to help us obey and to give us power to overcome sin. Don't use the excuse that you can't help slipping into sin. Rely on God's power to free you from sin's grip.

1:17 "Reverent fear" is not the fear of a slave for a ruthless master but the healthy respect of a believer for the all-powerful God. Because God is the Judge of all the earth, we dare not ignore him or treat him casually. We should not assume that our privileged status as God's children gives us freedom to do whatever we want. We should not be spoiled children but grateful children who love to show respect for our heavenly Father.

1:18, 19 A slave was "ransomed" when someone paid money to buy his or her freedom. God ransomed us from the tyranny of sin, not with money, but with the precious blood of his own Son (Romans 6:6, 7; 1 Corinthians 6:20; Colossians 2:13, 14; Hebrews 9:12). We cannot escape from sin on our own; only the life of God's Son can free us.

1:20 Christ's sacrifice for our sins was not an afterthought, not something God decided to do when the world spun out of control. This plan was set in motion by the all-knowing, eternal God long before the world was created. What a comfort it must have been to Jewish believers to know that Christ's coming and his work of salvation were planned by God long before the world began. This assured them that the law was not being scrapped because it didn't work but that both the law *and* the coming of Christ were part of God's eternal plan.

1:22 "Sincere love" involves selfless giving; a self-centered person can't truly love. God's love and forgiveness free you to take your eyes off yourselves and to meet others' needs. By sacrificing his life, Christ showed that he truly loves you. Now you can love others by following his example and giving of yourself sacrificially.

1:24, 25 Quoting Isaiah 40:6-8, Peter reminds believers that everything in this life—possessions, accomplishments, people—will eventually fade away and disappear. Only God's will, word, and work are permanent. We must stop grasping the temporary and begin focusing our time, money, and energy on the permanent: the Word of God and our eternal life in Christ.

"People are like grass that dies away;
their beauty fades as quickly as the beauty of wildflowers.
The grass withers,
and the flowers fall away.
25 But the word of the Lord will last forever."*

And that word is the Good News that was preached to you.

2:1 Eph 4:22, 31
2:2 1 Cor 3:2; Heb 5:12-13
2:3 †Ps 34:8

2 So get rid of all malicious behavior and deceit. Don't just pretend to be good! Be
done with hypocrisy and jealousy and backstabbing. 2You must crave pure spiritual
milk so that you can grow into the fullness of your salvation. Cry out for this nourishment
as a baby cries for milk, 3now that you have had a taste of the Lord's kindness.

Living Stones for God's House

2:4 Ps 118:22; Isa 28:16; 1 Pet 2:7
2:5 Exod 19:6; Isa 61:6; Eph 2:21-22; 1 Tim 3:15; Heb 13:15; Rev 1:6

4Come to Christ, who is the living cornerstone of God's temple. He was rejected by the
people, but he is precious to God who chose him.
5And now God is building you, as living stones, into his spiritual temple. What's more,
you are God's holy priests, who offer the spiritual sacrifices that please him because of
Jesus Christ. 6As the Scriptures express it,

2:6 †Isa 28:16; Rom 9:32-33; Eph 2:20

"I am placing a stone in Jerusalem,*
a chosen cornerstone,
and anyone who believes in him
will never be disappointed.*"

7Yes, he is very precious to you who believe. But for those who reject him,

2:7 †Ps 118:22; Matt 21:42; Acts 4:11

"The stone that was rejected by the builders
has now become the cornerstone."*

8And the Scriptures also say,

2:8 †Isa 8:14; Luke 2:34; Rom 9:22

"He is the stone that makes people stumble,
the rock that will make them fall."*

1:24-25 Isa 40:6-8. **2:6a** Greek *in Zion.* **2:6b** Or *will never be put to shame.* Isa 28:16. **2:7** Ps 118:22. **2:8** Isa 8:14.

2:2, 3 One characteristic all children share is that they want to grow up—to be like big brother or sister or like their parents. When we are born again, we become spiritual newborn babies. If we are healthy, we will yearn to grow. How sad it is that some people never grow up. The need for milk is a natural instinct for a baby, and it signals the desire for nourishment that will lead to growth. Once we see our need for God's Word and begin to find nourishment in Christ, our spiritual appetite will increase, and we will start to mature. How strong is your desire for God's Word?

2:4-8 In describing the church as God's spiritual temple, Peter drew on several Old Testament texts familiar to his Jewish Christian readers: Psalm 118:22; Isaiah 8:14; 28:16. Peter's readers would have understood the living stones to be Israel; then Peter applied the image of "cornerstone" to Christ. Once again Peter showed that the church does not cancel the Jewish heritage but fulfills it.

2:4-8 Peter portrays the church as a living, spiritual temple, with Christ as the foundation and cornerstone and each believer as a stone. Paul portrays the church as a body, with Christ as the head and each believer as a member (see, for example, Ephesians 4:15, 16). Both pictures emphasize *community.* One stone is not a temple or even a wall; one body part is useless without the others. In our individualistic society, it is easy to forget our interdependence with other Christians. When God calls you to a task, remember that he is also calling others to work with you. Together your individual efforts will be multiplied. Look for those people and join with them to build a beautiful house for God.

2:6 Christians will sometimes be put to shame or face disappointment in this life, but their trust in God is never misplaced. God will not let them down. We can safely put our confidence in him because the eternal life he promises is certain.

2:6-8 No doubt Peter often thought of Jesus' words to him right after he confessed that Jesus was "the Messiah, the Son of the living God": "You are Peter, and upon this rock I will build my church, and all the powers of hell will not conquer it" (Matthew 16:16-18). What is the stone that really counts in the building of the church? Peter answers: Christ himself. What are the characteristics of Christ, the cornerstone? (1) He is completely trustworthy; (2) he is precious to believers; (3) and, though rejected by some, he is the most important part of the church.

2:8 Jesus Christ is called "the stone that makes people stumble, the rock that will make them fall." Some will stumble over Christ because they reject him or refuse to believe that he is who he says he is. But Psalm 118:22 says that "the stone rejected by the builders has now become the cornerstone," the most important part of God's building, the church. In the same way today, people who refuse to believe in Christ have made the greatest mistake of their lives. They have stumbled over the one person who could save them and give meaning to their lives, and they have fallen into God's hands for judgment.

They stumble because they do not listen to God's word or obey it, and so they meet the
fate that has been planned for them.
9 But you are not like that, for you are a chosen people. You are a kingdom of priests,
God's holy nation, his very own possession. This is so you can show others the goodness
of God, for he called you out of the darkness into his wonderful light.

10 "Once you were not a people;
now you are the people of God.
Once you received none of God's mercy;
now you have received his mercy."*

2. The conduct of God's people in the midst of suffering

11 Dear brothers and sisters, you are foreigners and aliens here. So I warn you to keep
away from evil desires because they fight against your very souls. 12 Be careful how you
live among your unbelieving neighbors. Even if they accuse you of doing wrong, they
will see your honorable behavior, and they will believe and give honor to God when he
comes to judge the world.*

Respecting People in Authority

13 For the Lord's sake, accept all authority—the king as head of state, 14 and the officials
he has appointed. For the king has sent them to punish all who do wrong and to honor
those who do right.
15 It is God's will that your good lives should silence those who make foolish
accusations against you. 16 You are not slaves; you are free. But your freedom is not an
excuse to do evil. You are free to live as God's slaves. 17 Show respect for everyone. Love
your Christian brothers and sisters. Fear God. Show respect for the king.

2:9 †Exod 19:5-6; Deut 7:6; 10:15; †Isa 43:20-21; Acts 26:18; 1 Pet 2:5; Rev 1:6
2:10 †Hos 1:6, 9; 2:23; Rom 9:25; 10:19
2:11 Rom 13:14; Gal 5:16; Jas 4:1
2:12 Phil 2:15; Titus 2:14
2:13-14 Rom 13:1-7; Titus 3:1
2:15 1 Pet 2:12; 3:17
2:16 Gal 5:13
2:17 Prov 24:21; Rom 12:10; 13:7

2:10 Hos 1:6, 9; 2:23. **2:12** Or *on the day of visitation.*

2:9 Christians sometimes speak of "the priesthood of all believers." In Old Testament times, people did not approach God directly. A priest acted as intermediary between God and sinful human beings. With Christ's victory on the cross, that pattern changed. Now we can come directly into God's presence without fear (Hebrews 4:16), and we are given the responsibility of bringing others to him also (2 Corinthians 5:18-21). When we are united with Christ as members of his body, we join in his priestly work of reconciling God and people.

2:9, 10 People often base their self-concept on their accomplishments. But our relationship with Christ is far more important than our jobs, successes, wealth, or knowledge. We have been chosen by God as his very own, and we have been called to represent him to others. Remember that your value comes from being one of God's children, not from what you can achieve. You have worth because of what *God does,* not because of what you do.

2:11 As believers, we are "foreigners and aliens" in this world because our real home is with God. Heaven is not the pink-cloud-and-harp existence popular in cartoons. Heaven is where God lives. Life in heaven operates according to God's principles and values, and it is eternal and unshakable. The Kingdom of Heaven came to earth in the symbolism of the Jewish sanctuary (the Tabernacle and Temple), where God's presence dwelt. It came in a fuller way in the person of Jesus Christ: "God with us." It spread through the entire world as the Holy Spirit came to live in every believer.

Someday, after God judges and destroys all sin, the Kingdom of Heaven will rule every corner of this earth. John saw this day in a vision, and he cried out, "Look, the home of God is now among his people! He will live with them, and they will be his people. God himself will be with them" (Revelation 21:3). Our true loyalty should be to our citizenship in heaven, not to our citizenship here, because the earth will be destroyed. Our loyalty should be to God's truth, his way of life, and his dedicated people. Because we are loyal to God, we often will feel like strangers in a world that would prefer to ignore God.

2:12 Peter's advice sounds like Jesus' in Matthew 5:16: If your actions are above reproach, even hostile people will end up praising God. Peter's readers were scattered among unbelieving Gentiles, who were inclined to believe and spread vicious lies about Christians. Gracious, godly, and winsome behavior on the part of Christians could show these rumors to be false and might even win some of the unsaved critics to the Lord. Don't write off people because they misunderstand Christianity; instead, show them Christ by your life. The day may come when those who criticize you will praise God with you.

2:13-17 When Peter told his readers to submit to the civil authorities, he was speaking of the Roman Empire under Nero, a notoriously cruel tyrant. Obviously he was not telling believers to compromise their consciences; as Peter had told the high priest years before, "We must obey God rather than human authority" (Acts 5:29). But in most aspects of daily life, it was possible and desirable for Christians to live according to the law of their land. Today, some Christians live in freedom while others live under repressive governments. All are commanded to cooperate with the rulers as far as conscience will allow. We are to do this "for the Lord's sake"—so that his Good News and his people will be respected. If we are to be persecuted, it should be for obeying God, not for breaking moral or civil laws. For more about the Christian's relationship to government, see the note on Romans 13:1ff.

2:16 We are free from keeping the law as a way to earn salvation. However, we are still to obey, out of gratitude for our free salvation, the teachings of the Ten Commandments, for they are an expression of God's will for us.

Slaves

18 You who are slaves must accept the authority of your masters. Do whatever they tell
you—not only if they are kind and reasonable, but even if they are harsh. 19 For God is
pleased with you when, for the sake of your conscience, you patiently endure unfair
treatment. 20 Of course, you get no credit for being patient if you are beaten for doing
wrong. But if you suffer for doing right and are patient beneath the blows, God is pleased
with you.
21 This suffering is all part of what God has called you to. Christ, who suffered for you,
is your example. Follow in his steps. 22 He never sinned, and he never deceived anyone.
23 He did not retaliate when he was insulted. When he suffered, he did not threaten to get
even. He left his case in the hands of God, who always judges fairly. 24 He personally
carried away our sins in his own body on the cross so we can be dead to sin and live for
what is right. You have been healed by his wounds! 25 Once you were wandering like lost
sheep. But now you have turned to your Shepherd, the Guardian of your souls.

Wives

3 In the same way, you wives must accept the authority of your husbands, even those
who refuse to accept the Good News. Your godly lives will speak to them better than
any words. They will be won over 2 by watching your pure, godly behavior.
3 Don't be concerned about the outward beauty that depends on fancy hairstyles,
expensive jewelry, or beautiful clothes. 4 You should be known for the beauty that comes
from within, the unfading beauty of a gentle and quiet spirit, which is so precious to God.

2:18 Eph 6:5; Jas 3:17
2:20 1 Pet 3:14, 17
2:21 Acts 14:22; 1 Pet 3:9, 18
2:23 Isa 53:7; 1 Pet 3:9
2:24 †Isa 53:4, 12
2:25 †Isa 53:6; Heb 13:20; 1 Pet 5:4
3:1 1 Cor 7:16; 9:19; 1 Pet 2:18
3:3 Isa 3:18-23; 1 Tim 2:9
3:4 Rom 2:29; 7:22

SUBMISSION
Submission is

Functional .....a distinguishing of our roles and the work we are called to do
Relational ......a loving acknowledgment of another's value as a person
Reciprocal .....a mutual, humble cooperation with one another
Universal ......an acknowledgment by the church of the all-encompassing lordship of Jesus Christ

Submission is voluntarily cooperating with someone, first out of love and respect for God and then out of love and respect for that person. Submitting to nonbelievers is difficult, but it is a vital part of leading them to Jesus Christ. We are not called to submit to nonbelievers to the point that we compromise our relationship with God, but we must look for every opportunity to humbly serve in the power of God's Spirit.

2:18-21 Many Christians were household slaves. It would be easy for them to submit to masters who were gentle and kind. But Peter encouraged loyalty and perseverance even in the face of unjust treatment. In the same way, we should submit to our employers, whether they are considerate or harsh. By so doing, we may win them to Christ by our good example. Paul gave similar advice in his letters (see Ephesians 6:5-9; Colossians 3:22–4:15), as did Jesus (Matthew 5:46; Luke 6:32-36).

2:21, 22 We may suffer for many reasons. Some suffering is the direct result of our own sin; some happens because of our foolishness; and some is the result of living in a fallen world. Peter is writing about suffering that comes as a result of doing good. Christ never sinned, and yet he suffered so that we could be set free. When we follow Christ's example and live for others, we, too, may suffer. Our goal should be to face suffering as he did—with patience, calmness, and confidence that God is in control of the future.

2:21-25 Peter had learned about suffering from Jesus. He knew that Jesus' suffering was part of God's plan (Matthew 16:21-23; Luke 24:25-27, 44-47) and was intended to save us (Matthew 20:28; 26:28). He also knew that all who follow Jesus must be prepared to suffer (Mark 8:34, 35). Peter learned these truths from Jesus and passed them on to us.

2:24 Christ died for *our* sins, in *our* place, so we would not have to suffer the punishment we deserve. This is called "substitutionary atonement."

3:1ff When a man became a Christian, he usually would bring his whole family into the church with him (see, for example, the story of the conversion of the Philippian jailer in Acts 16:29-34). By contrast, a woman who became a Christian usually came into the church alone. Under Roman law, the husband and father had absolute authority over all members of his household, including his wife. Demanding her rights as a free woman in Christ could endanger her marriage if her husband disapproved. Peter reassured Christian women who were married to unbelievers that they did not need to preach to their husbands. Under the circumstances, their best approach would be one of godly behavior: They should show their husbands the kind of self-giving love that Christ showed the church. By being exemplary wives, they would please their husbands. At the very least, the men might then allow them to continue practicing their "strange" religion. At best, their husbands would join them and become Christians, too.

3:1-7 A changed life speaks loudly and clearly, and it is often the most effective way to influence a family member. Peter instructs Christian wives to develop inner beauty rather than being overly concerned about their outward appearance. Their husbands will be won over by their love rather than by their looks. Live your Christian faith quietly and consistently in your home, so that your family will see Christ in you.

3:3 We should not be obsessed by fashion, but neither should we be so unconcerned that we do not bother to care for ourselves. Hygiene, neatness, and grooming are important, but even more important are a person's attitude and inner spirit. True beauty begins inside.

5 That is the way the holy women of old made themselves beautiful. They trusted God
and accepted the authority of their husbands. 6 For instance, Sarah obeyed her husband,
Abraham, when she called him her master. You are her daughters when you do what is
right without fear of what your husbands might do.

Husbands

7 In the same way, you husbands must give honor to your wives. Treat her with understanding as you live together. She may be weaker than you are, but she is your equal
partner in God's gift of new life. If you don't treat her as you should, your prayers will
not be heard.

All Christians

8 Finally, all of you should be of one mind, full of sympathy toward each other, loving
one another with tender hearts and humble minds. 9 Don't repay evil for evil. Don't
retaliate when people say unkind things about you. Instead, pay them back with a
blessing. That is what God wants you to do, and he will bless you for it. 10 For the
Scriptures say,

"If you want a happy life and good days,
keep your tongue from speaking evil,
and keep your lips from telling lies.
11 Turn away from evil and do good.
Work hard at living in peace with others.
12 The eyes of the Lord watch over those who do right,
and his ears are open to their prayers.
But the Lord turns his face
against those who do evil."*

3:10-12 Ps 34:12-16.

3:5 1 Tim 5:5
3:6 Gen 18:12
3:7 Eph 5:25; Col 3:19
3:8 Rom 15:5; Eph 4:2, 32
3:9 Matt 5:44; Luke 6:48; Rom 12:17; 1 Thes 5:15; Heb 6:14
3:10-12 †Ps 34:12-16

3:5 To be submissive to another's authority means to cooperate voluntarily out of love and respect for God and for that person. Ideally, submission is mutual ("Submit to one another out of reverence for Christ"—Ephesians 5:21). Even when it is one-sided, however, the expression of submission can be an effective Christian strategy. Jesus Christ submitted to death so that we could be saved; we may sometimes have to submit to unpleasant circumstances so that others will see Christ in us. (Christian submission never requires us to disobey God or to participate in what our conscience forbids.) One-sided submission requires tremendous strength. We could not do it without the power of the Holy Spirit working in us.

3:7 When Peter calls women the "weaker" partners, he does not imply moral or intellectual inferiority but is recognizing women's physical limitations. Women in his day, if unprotected by men, were vulnerable to attack, abuse, and financial disaster. Women's lives may be easier today, but women are still vulnerable to criminal attack and family abuse. And in spite of increased opportunities in the workplace, many women still earn less than men, and the vast majority of the nations' poor are single mothers and their children. A man who honors his wife as a member of the weaker sex will protect, respect, help, and stay with her. He will not expect her to work full-time outside the home and full-time at home; he will lighten her load wherever he can. He will be sensitive to her needs, and he will relate to her with courtesy, consideration, insight, and tact.

3:7 If a man is not considerate and respectful of his wife, his prayers will not be heard, because a living relationship with God depends on right relationships with others. Jesus said that if you have a problem with a fellow believer, you must make it right with that person before coming to worship (Matthew 5:23, 24). This principle carries over into family relationships. If men use their position to mistreat their wives, their prayers will not be heard.

3:8 Peter lists five key elements that should characterize any group of believers: (1) one mind—pursuing the same goals; (2) sympathy—being responsive to others' needs; (3) love—seeing and treating each other as brothers and sisters; (4) tenderness—being affectionately sensitive and caring; and (5) humility—being willing to encourage one another and rejoice in each other's successes. These five qualities go a long way toward helping believers serve God effectively.

3:8, 9 Peter developed the qualities of tenderness and humility the hard way. In his early days with Christ, these attitudes did not come naturally to his impulsive, strong-willed personality (see Mark 8:31-33; John 13:6-9 for examples of Peter's blustering). But the Holy Spirit changed Peter, molding his strong personality to God's use and teaching him tenderness and humility.

3:9 In our fallen world, it is often deemed acceptable by some to tear people down verbally or to get back at them if we feel hurt. Peter, remembering Jesus' teaching to turn the other cheek (Matthew 5:39), encourages his readers to pay back wrongs with a blessing, such as praying for the offenders. In God's Kingdom, revenge is unacceptable behavior, as is insulting a person, no matter how indirectly it is done. Rise above getting back at those who hurt you. Instead of reacting angrily to these people, pray for them.

3:10 For more about controlling your tongue, see the notes in James 3:2-18.

3:11 Too often we see peace as merely the absence of conflict, and we think of peacemaking as a passive role. But an effective peacemaker actively pursues peace by building good relationships, knowing that peace is a by-product of commitment. The peacemaker anticipates problems and deals with them before they occur. When conflicts arise, they are brought into the open and dealt with before they grow unmanageable. Making peace can be harder work than waging war, but it results in life and happiness.

3:13 Titus 2:14
3:14-15 †Isa 8:12-13
3:15 Col 4:6
3:16 1 Pet 2:12
3:17 1 Pet 2:20; 4:15-16
3:18 Eph 2:18; Heb 9:26, 28
3:19 1 Pet 4:6
3:20 Gen 6:1–7:24
3:21 Heb 9:13; 10:22
3:22 Matt 28:18; Mark 16:19; Rom 8:38; Heb 1:4, 6; 4:14

Suffering for Doing Good

13 Now, who will want to harm you if you are eager to do good? 14 But even if you suffer for doing what is right, God will reward you for it. So don't be afraid and don't worry. 15 Instead, you must worship Christ as Lord of your life. And if you are asked about your Christian hope, always be ready to explain it. 16 But you must do this in a gentle and respectful way. Keep your conscience clear. Then if people speak evil against you, they will be ashamed when they see what a good life you live because you belong to Christ. 17 Remember, it is better to suffer for doing good, if that is what God wants, than to suffer for doing wrong!

18 Christ also suffered when he died for our sins once for all time. He never sinned, but he died for sinners that he might bring us safely home to God. He suffered physical death, but he was raised to life in the Spirit.*

19 So he went and preached to the spirits in prison—20 those who disobeyed God long ago when God waited patiently while Noah was building his boat. Only eight people were saved from drowning in that terrible flood.* 21 And this is a picture of baptism, which now saves you by the power of Jesus Christ's resurrection. Baptism is not a removal of dirt from your body; it is an appeal to God from* a clean conscience.

22 Now Christ has gone to heaven. He is seated in the place of honor next to God, and all the angels and authorities and powers are bowing before him.

4:1 Rom 6:7; Gal 2:20; Col 3:5; 1 Pet 2:21
4:2 Rom 6:2; 1 Pet 1:14
4:3 Rom 13:13; Eph 2:2

Living for God

4 So then, since Christ suffered physical pain, you must arm yourselves with the same attitude he had, and be ready to suffer, too. For if you are willing to suffer for Christ, you have decided to stop sinning. 2 And you won't spend the rest of your life chasing after evil desires, but you will be anxious to do the will of God. 3 You have had enough in the past of the evil things that godless people enjoy—their immorality and lust, their feasting and drunkenness and wild parties, and their terrible worship of idols.

4 Of course, your former friends are very surprised when you no longer join them in

3:18 Or *spirit.* **3:20** Greek *saved through water.* **3:21** Or *for.*

3:14, 15 Rather than fear our enemies, we are to quietly trust in God as the Lord of all. We must believe that Christ is truly in control of all events. When he rules our thoughts and emotions, we cannot be shaken by anything our enemies may do.

3:15 Some Christians believe that faith is a personal matter that should be kept to oneself. It is true that we shouldn't be boisterous or obnoxious in sharing our faith, but we should always be ready to give an answer, gently and respectfully, when asked about our faith, our life-style, or our Christian perspective. Can others see your hope in Christ? Are you prepared to tell them what Christ has done in your life?

3:16 You may not be able to keep people from speaking evil against you, but you can at least stop supplying them with ammunition. As long as you do what is right, their accusations will be empty and only embarrass them. Keep your conduct above criticism!

3:18-20 The meaning of preaching "to the spirits in prison" is not completely clear, and commentators have explained it in different ways. The traditional interpretation is that Christ, between his death and resurrection, announced salvation to God's faithful followers who had been waiting for their salvation during the whole Old Testament era. Matthew records that when Jesus died, "tombs opened. Many bodies of godly men and women who had died were raised from the dead after Jesus' resurrection. They left the cemetery, went into the holy city of Jerusalem, and appeared to many people" (Matthew 27:52, 53). A few commentators think that this passage says that Christ's Spirit was in Noah as Noah preached to those imprisoned by sin (but now in hell). Still others hold that Christ went to Hades to proclaim his victory and final condemnation to the fallen angels imprisoned there since Noah's day (see 2 Peter 2:4).

In any case, the passage shows that Christ's Good News of salvation and victory is not limited. It has been preached in the past as well as in the present; it has gone to the dead as well as to the living. God has given everyone the opportunity to come to him, but this does not imply a second chance for those who reject Christ in this life.

3:21 Peter says that Noah's salvation from the Flood symbolized baptism, a ceremony involving water. In baptism we identify with Jesus Christ, who separates us from the lost and gives us new life. It is not the ceremony that saves us but faith in Christ's death and resurrection. Baptism is a symbol of the transformation that happens in the hearts of those who believe (Romans 6:3-5; Galatians 3:27; Colossians 2:12). By identifying themselves with Christ through baptism, Peter's readers could resist turning back, even under the pressure of persecution. Public baptism would keep them from the temptation to renounce their faith.

4:1, 2 Some people will do anything to avoid pain. As followers of Christ, however, we should be willing and prepared to do God's will and to suffer for it if necessary. Sin loses its power to defeat us in our suffering if we focus on Christ and what he wants us to do. When we are in pain or our life is in jeopardy, our real values clearly show up, and sinful pleasures seem less important. If anyone is willing to suffer for Christ by doing the will of God, that person has made a clean break with sin.

4:3, 4 A person whose life changes radically at conversion may experience contempt from old friends. He may be scorned not only because he refuses to participate in certain activities but also because his priorities have changed and he is now heading in the opposite direction. His very life incriminates their sinful activities. Mature Christians should help new believers resist such pressures of opposition by encouraging them to be faithful to Christ.

the wicked things they do, and they say evil things about you. [5]But just remember that
they will have to face God, who will judge everyone, both the living and the dead. [6]That
is why the Good News was preached even to those who have died—so that although their
bodies were punished with death, they could still live in the spirit as God does.
[7]The end of the world is coming soon. Therefore, be earnest and disciplined in your
prayers. [8]Most important of all, continue to show deep love for each other, for love
covers a multitude of sins. [9]Cheerfully share your home with those who need a meal or
a place to stay.
[10]God has given gifts to each of you from his great variety of spiritual gifts. Manage
them well so that God's generosity can flow through you. [11]Are you called to be a
speaker? Then speak as though God himself were speaking through you. Are you called
to help others? Do it with all the strength and energy that God supplies. Then God will
be given glory in everything through Jesus Christ. All glory and power belong to him
forever and ever. Amen.

Suffering for Being a Christian

[12]Dear friends, don't be surprised at the fiery trials you are going through, as if
something strange were happening to you. [13]Instead, be very glad—because these trials
will make you partners with Christ in his suffering, and afterward you will have the
wonderful joy of sharing his glory when it is displayed to all the world.
[14]Be happy if you are insulted for being a Christian, for then the glorious Spirit of God
will come upon you. [15]If you suffer, however, it must not be for murder, stealing, making
trouble, or prying into other people's affairs. [16]But it is no shame to suffer for being a
Christian. Praise God for the privilege of being called by his wonderful name! [17]For the
time has come for judgment, and it must begin first among God's own children. And if
even we Christians must be judged, what terrible fate awaits those who have never
believed God's Good News? [18]And

4:5 Acts 10:42
4:6 1 Pet 3:19
4:7 Rom 13:11-12
4:8 Prov 10:12; Jas 5:20; 1 Pet 1:22
4:10 Rom 12:6-8
4:11 1 Cor 10:31
4:12 1 Pet 1:6-7
4:13 Rom 8:17; 2 Cor 1:5
4:14 Matt 5:11; John 15:21
4:15 1 Thes 4:11; 2 Thes 3:11; 1 Tim 5:13
4:17 Ezek 9:6; 2 Thes 1:8

4:5 The basis of salvation is our belief in Jesus (Acts 16:31), but the basis for judgment is how we have lived. Those who inflict persecution are marked for punishment when they stand before God. Believers have nothing to fear, however, because Jesus will be the final Judge over all (John 5:22; 2 Timothy 4:1).

4:5, 6 Many people in the early church had concerns about life after death. In Thessalonica, Christians worried that loved ones who died before Christ's return might never see Christ (1 Thessalonians 4:13-18). Peter's readers needed to be reminded that the dead (both the faithful and their oppressors) would be judged. The judgment will be perfectly fair, he pointed out, because even the dead have heard the Good News (see also 3:18, 19). The Good News was first announced when Jesus Christ preached on the earth, but it has been operating since before the creation of the world (Ephesians 1:4), and it affects all people, the dead as well as the living.

4:7-9 We should live expectantly because Christ is coming soon. Getting ready to meet Christ involves continually growing in love for God and for others (see Jesus' summary of the law in Matthew 22:37-40). It is important to pray regularly and to reach out to needy people. Your possessions, status, and power will mean nothing in God's Kingdom, but you will spend eternity with other people. Invest your time and talents where they will make an eternal difference.

4:9 For more about hospitality, see the note on Romans 12:13.

4:10, 11 Some people, well aware of their abilities, believe that they have the right to use their abilities as they please. Others feel that they have no special talents at all. Peter addresses both groups in these verses. Everyone has some gifts; find yours and use them. All our abilities should be used in serving others; none are for our own exclusive enjoyment. Peter mentions speaking and serving. Paul lists these and other abilities in Romans 12:6-8, 1 Corinthians 12:8-11, and Ephesians 4:11.

4:11 How is God glorified when we use our abilities? When we use them as he directs, to help others, they will see Jesus in us and glorify him for the help they have received. Peter may have been thinking of Jesus' words, "Let your good deeds shine out for all to see, so that everyone will praise your heavenly Father" (Matthew 5:16).

4:14-16 Again Peter brings to mind Jesus' words: "God blesses you when you are mocked and persecuted and lied about because you are my followers"(Matthew 5:11). Christ will send his Spirit to strengthen those who are persecuted for their faith. This does not mean that all suffering is the result of good Christian conduct. Sometimes a person will grumble, "He's just picking on me because I'm a Christian," when it is obvious to everyone else that the person's own unpleasant behavior is the cause of his or her problems. It may take careful thought or wise counsel to determine the real cause of our suffering. We can be assured, however, that whenever we suffer because of our loyalty to Christ, he will be with us all the way.

4:16 It is not shameful to suffer for being a Christian. When Peter and John were persecuted for preaching the Good News, they rejoiced because such persecution was a mark of God's approval of their work (Acts 5:41). Don't seek out suffering, and don't try to avoid it. Instead, keep on doing what is right whether or not it brings suffering.

4:17, 18 This refers not to final judgment but to God's refining discipline (Hebrews 12:7). God often allows believers to sin and then experience the consequences. He does this for several reasons: (1) to show us our potential for sinning, (2) to encourage us to turn from sin and more constantly depend on him, (3) to prepare us to face other, even stronger temptations in the future, and (4) to help us stay faithful and keep on trusting him. If believers need earthly discipline (judgment) from God, how much more will unbelievers receive it? If the righteous are barely saved (only because of God's mercy), what chance do those have who reject Christ?

4:18 †Prov 11:31 Luke 23:31
4:19 Ps 31:5 1 Pet 2:20

> "If the righteous are barely saved,
> what chance will the godless and sinners have?"*

19 So if you are suffering according to God's will, keep on doing what is right, and trust
yourself to the God who made you, for he will never fail you.

3. The shepherding of God's people in the midst of suffering

Advice for Elders and Young Men

5:1 Luke 24:48 Rev 1:9
5:2 John 21:16 Acts 20:28
5:3 2 Cor 1:24 Phil 3:17 Titus 2:7
5:4 1 Cor 9:25 Heb 13:20
5:5 †Prov 3:34 Jas 4:6
5:6 Jas 4:10
5:7 Ps 55:22 Matt 6:25 Heb 13:5
5:8 Job 1:7 Jas 4:7
5:9 Eph 6:11-13 Jas 4:7

5 And now, a word to you who are elders in the churches. I, too, am an elder and a
witness to the sufferings of Christ. And I, too, will share his glory and his honor
when he returns. As a fellow elder, this is my appeal to you: 2 Care for the flock of God
entrusted to you. Watch over it willingly, not grudgingly—not for what you will get out
of it, but because you are eager to serve God. 3 Don't lord it over the people assigned to
your care, but lead them by your good example. 4 And when the head Shepherd comes,
your reward will be a never-ending share in his glory and honor.
5 You younger men, accept the authority of the elders. And all of you, serve each other
in humility, for

> "God sets himself against the proud,
> but he shows favor to the humble."*

6 So humble yourselves under the mighty power of God, and in his good time he will
honor you. 7 Give all your worries and cares to God, for he cares about what happens to
you.
8 Be careful! Watch out for attacks from the Devil, your great enemy. He prowls around
like a roaring lion, looking for some victim to devour. 9 Take a firm stand against him,
and be strong in your faith. Remember that Christians* all over the world are going
through the same kind of suffering you are.

4:18 Prov 11:31. **5:5** Prov 3:34. **5:9** Greek *your brothers.*

4:19 God created the world, and he has faithfully ordered it and kept it since the Creation. Because we know that God is faithful, we can count on him to fulfill his promises to us. If God can oversee the forces of nature, surely he can see us through the trials we face.

5:1 Elders were church officers providing supervision, protection, discipline, instruction, and direction for the other believers. *Elder* simply means "older." Both Greeks and Jews gave positions of great honor to wise older men, and the Christian church continued this pattern of leadership. Elders carried great responsibility, and they were expected to be good examples.

5:1, 2 Peter, one of Jesus' 12 disciples, was one of the three who saw Christ's glory at the Transfiguration (Mark 9:1-13; 2 Peter 1:16-18). Often the spokesman for the apostles, Peter witnessed Jesus' death and resurrection, preached at Pentecost, and became a pillar of the Jerusalem church. But writing to the elders, he identified himself as a fellow elder, not a superior. He asked them to "care for the flock of God," exactly what Jesus had told him to do (John 21:15-17). Peter was taking his own advice as he worked along with the other elders in caring for God's faithful people. His identification with the elders is a good example of Christian leadership, showing that authority is based on service, not power (Mark 10:42-45).

5:2-5 Peter describes several characteristics of good leaders in the church: (1) They realize they are caring for God's flock, not their own; (2) they lead out of eagerness to serve, not out of obligation; (3) they are concerned for what they can give, not for what they can get; (4) they lead by example, not force. All of us lead others in some way. Whatever our role, our leadership should be in line with these characteristics.

5:4 The head Shepherd is Jesus Christ. This refers to his second coming, when he will judge all people.

5:5 Both young and old can benefit from Peter's instructions. Pride often keeps older people from trying to understand young people and keeps young people from listening to those who are older. Peter told both young and old to be humble and to serve each other. Young men should follow the leadership of older men, who should lead by example. Respect those who are older than you, listen to those younger than you, and be humble enough to admit that you can learn from others.

5:6 We often worry about our position and status, hoping to get proper recognition for what we do. But Peter advises us to remember that God's recognition counts more than human praise. God is able and willing to bless us according to his timing. Humbly obey God regardless of present circumstances, and in his good time—either in this life or in the next—he will honor you.

5:7 Carrying your worries, stresses, and daily struggles by yourself shows that you have not trusted God fully with your life. It takes humility, however, to recognize that God cares, to admit your need, and to let others in God's family help you. Sometimes we think that struggles caused by our own sin and foolishness are not God's concern. But when we turn to God in repentance, he will bear the weight even of those struggles. Letting God have your anxieties calls for action, not passivity. Don't submit to circumstances but to the Lord, who controls circumstances.

5:8, 9 Lions attack sick, young, or straggling animals; they choose victims who are alone or not alert. Peter warns us to watch out for Satan when we are suffering or being persecuted. Feeling alone, weak, helpless, and cut off from other believers, so focused on our troubles that we forget to watch for danger, we are especially vulnerable to Satan's attacks. During times of suffering, seek other Christians for support. Keep your eyes on Christ, and resist the Devil. Then, says James, "he will flee from you" (James 4:7).

10In his kindness God called you to his eternal glory by means of Jesus Christ. After
you have suffered a little while, he will restore, support, and strengthen you, and he will
place you on a firm foundation. 11All power is his forever and ever. Amen.

5:10 1 Thes 2:12, 17; 2 Tim 2:10; 1 Pet 1:6

Peter's Final Greetings

12I have written this short letter to you with the help of Silas,* whom I consider a faithful
brother. My purpose in writing is to encourage you and assure you that the grace of God
is with you no matter what happens.
13Your sister church here in Rome* sends you greetings, and so does my son Mark.
14Greet each other in Christian love.*
Peace be to all of you who are in Christ.

5:12 Acts 15:22; Heb 13:22
5:13 Acts 12:12
5:14 Rom 16:16; Eph 6:23

5:12 Greek *Silvanus.* **5:13** Greek *The elect one in Babylon.* Babylon was probably a code name for Rome.
5:14 Greek *with a kiss of love.*

5:10 When we are suffering, we often feel as though our pain will never end. Peter gave these faithful Christians a broader perspective. In comparison with eternity, their suffering would last only "a little while." Some of Peter's readers would be strengthened and delivered in their own lifetimes. Others would be released from their suffering through death. All of God's faithful followers are assured of an eternal life with Christ, where there will be no suffering (Revelation 21:4).

5:12 Silas was one of the men chosen to deliver the letter from the Jerusalem council to the church in Antioch (Acts 15:22). He accompanied Paul on his second missionary journey (Acts 15:40–18:11), is mentioned by Paul in the salutation of Paul's letters to the Thessalonians (1 Thessalonians 1:1; 2 Thessalonians 1:1), and ministered with Timothy in Corinth (2 Corinthians 1:19).

5:13 Mark, also called John Mark, was known to many of this letter's readers because he had traveled widely (Acts 12:25–13:13; 15:36-41) and was recognized as a leader in the church (Colossians 4:10; Philemon 1:24). Mark was probably with the disciples at the time of Jesus' arrest (Mark 14:51, 52). Tradition holds that Peter was Mark's main source of information when Mark wrote his Gospel.

5:14 Peter wrote this letter just before the cruel emperor Nero began persecuting Christians in Rome and throughout the empire. Afraid for his life, Peter had three times denied even knowing Jesus (John 18:15-27). But here, having learned how to stand firm in an evil world, he encouraged other Christians who were facing persecution for their faith. Peter was martyred for his faith because he lived by the words he wrote. Those who stand for Christ will be persecuted because the world is ruled by Christ's greatest enemy. But just as the small group of early believers stood against persecution, so we must be willing to stand for our faith with the patience, endurance, and courage that Peter exhibited.

2 PETER

WARNINGS have many forms: lights, signs, sights, sounds, smells, feelings, and written words. With varied focus, their purpose is the same—to advise alertness and give notice of imminent danger. Responses to these warnings will also vary—from disregard and neglect to evasive or corrective action. How a person reacts to a warning is usually determined by the situation and the source. One reacts differently to an impending storm than to an onrushing automobile, and the counsel of a trusted friend is heeded more than advice from a stranger or the fearful imaginings of a child.

Second Peter is a letter of warning—from an authority none other than the courageous, experienced, and faithful apostle. And it is the last communication from this great warrior of Christ. Soon thereafter he would die, martyred for his faith.

Previously Peter had written to comfort and encourage believers in the midst of suffering and persecution—an external onslaught. But three years later, in this letter containing his last words, he wrote to warn them of an internal attack—complacency and heresy. He spoke of holding fast to the nonnegotiable facts of the faith, of growing and maturing in the faith, and of rejecting all who would distort the truth. To follow this advice would ensure Christ-honoring individuals and Christ-centered churches.

After a brief greeting (1:1), Peter gives the antidote for stagnancy and shortsightedness in the Christian life (1:2–11). Then he explains that his days are numbered (1:12–15) and that the believers should listen to his messages and the words of Scripture (1:16–21).

Next, Peter gives a blunt warning about false teachers (2:1–22). They will become prevalent in the last days (2:1, 2), they will do or say anything for money (2:3), they will spurn the things of God (2:2, 10, 11), they will do whatever they feel like doing (2:12–17), they will be proud and boastful (2:18, 19), and they will be judged and punished by God (2:3–10, 20–22).

Peter concludes his brief letter by explaining why he has written it (3:1–18): to remind them of the words of the prophets and apostles that predicted the coming of false teachers, to give the reasons for the delay in Christ's return (3:1–13), and to encourage them to beware of heresies and to grow in their faith (3:14–18).

Addressed to those who "share the same precious faith," 2 Peter could have been written to us. Our world is filled with false prophets and teachers, who claim to have the truth and who clamor for attention and allegiance. Listen carefully to Peter's message and heed his warning. Determine to grow in your knowledge of Christ and to reject all those who preach anything inconsistent with God's Word.

VITAL STATISTICS

PURPOSE:
To warn Christians about false teachers and to exhort them to grow in their faith in and knowledge of Christ

AUTHOR:
Peter

TO WHOM WRITTEN:
The church at large and all believers everywhere

DATE WRITTEN:
Approximately A.D. 67, three years after 1 Peter was written, possibly from Rome

SETTING:
Peter knew that his time on earth was limited (1:13, 14), so he wrote about what was on his heart, warning believers of what would happen when he was gone—especially about the presence of false teachers. He reminded his readers of the unchanging truth of the gospel.

KEY VERSE:
"As we know Jesus better, his divine power gives us everything we need for living a godly life. He has called us to receive his own glory and goodness!" (1:3).

KEY PEOPLE:
Peter, Paul

SPECIAL FEATURES:
The date and destination are uncertain, and the authorship has been disputed. Because of this, 2 Peter was the last book admitted to the canon of the New Testament Scripture. Also, there are similarities between 2 Peter and Jude.

THE BLUEPRINT

1. Guidance for growing Christians (1:1–21)
2. Danger to growing Christians (2:1–22)
3. Hope for growing Christians (3:1–18)

While Peter wrote his first letter to teach about handling persecution (trials from without), he wrote this letter to teach about handling heresy (trials from within). False teachers are often subtly deceitful. Believers today must still be vigilant against falling into false doctrine, heresy, and cult activity. This letter gives us clues to help detect false teaching.

MEGATHEMES

THEME	EXPLANATION	IMPORTANCE
Diligence	If our faith is real, it will be evident in our godly behavior. If people are diligent in Christian growth, they won't backslide or be deceived by false teachers.	Growth is essential. It begins with faith and culminates in love for others. To keep growing we need to know God, keep on following him, and remember what he taught us. We must remain diligent in faithful obedience and Christian growth.
False Teachers	Peter warns the church to beware of false teachers. These teachers were proud of their position, promoted sexual sin, and advised against keeping the Ten Commandments. Peter countered them by pointing to the Spirit-inspired Scriptures as our authority.	Christians need discernment to be able to resist false teachers. God can rescue us from their lies if we stay true to his Word, the Bible, and reject those who distort the truth.
Christ's Return	One day Christ will create a new heaven and earth, where we will live forever. As Christians, our hope is in this promise. But with Christ's return comes his judgment on all who refuse to believe.	The cure for complacency, lawlessness, and heresy is found in the confident assurance that Christ will return. God is still giving unbelievers time to repent. To be ready, Christians must keep on trusting and resist the pressure to give up waiting for Christ's return.

1. Guidance for growing Christians

Greetings from Peter

1 This letter is from Simon* Peter, a slave and apostle of Jesus Christist. 1:1
I am writing to all of you who share the same precious faith we have, faith given Rom 1:1, 12 Titus 2:13
to us by Jesus Christ, our God and Savior, who makes us right with God. 1 Pet 1:1
[2]May God bless you with his special favor and wonderful peace as you come to know 1:2 2 Pet 2:20; 3:18
Jesus, our God and Lord,* better and better. Jude 1:2

Growing in the Knowledge of God

[3]As we know Jesus better, his divine power gives us everything we need for living a 1:3 1 Pet 2:9
godly life. He has called us to receive his own glory and goodness! [4]And by that same 1:4
mighty power, he has given us all of his rich and wonderful promises. He has promised 2 Cor 7:1
that you will escape the decadence all around you caused by evil desires and that you Jas 1:27
will share in his divine nature.
[5]So make every effort to apply the benefits of these promises to your life. Then your 1:5
faith will produce a life of moral excellence. A life of moral excellence leads to knowing Col 2:3

1:1 Greek *Simeon.* **1:2** Or *come to know God and Jesus our Lord.*

1:1 First Peter was written just before the time that the Roman emperor Nero began his persecution of Christians. Second Peter was written two or three years later (between A.D. 66 and 68), after persecution had intensified. First Peter was a letter of encouragement to the Christians who suffered, but 2 Peter focuses on the church's internal problems, especially on the false teachers who were causing people to doubt their faith and turn away from Christianity. Second Peter combats their heresies by denouncing the evil motives of the false teachers and reaffirming Christianity's truths—the authority of Scripture, the primacy of faith, and the certainty of Christ's return.

1:2 Many believers want an abundance of God's special favor and peace, but they are unwilling to put forth the effort to get to know him better through Bible study and prayer. To enjoy the privileges God offers us freely, we must "come to know Jesus, our God and Lord, better and better."

1:3, 4 The power to lead a godly life comes from God. Because we don't have the resources to be truly godly, God allows us to "share in his divine nature" in order to keep us from sin and help us live for him. When we are born again, God by his Spirit empowers us with his own goodness. See John 3:6; 14:17-23; 2 Corinthians 5:21; and 1 Peter 1:22, 23.

1:5-9 Faith must be more than belief in certain facts; it must result in action, growth in Christian character, and the practice of moral discipline, or it will die away (James 2:14-17). A life of faith

God better. 6 Knowing God leads to self-control. Self-control leads to patient endurance,
and patient endurance leads to godliness. 7 Godliness leads to love for other Christians,
and finally you will grow to have genuine love for everyone. 8 The more you grow like
this, the more you will become productive and useful in your knowledge of our Lord
Jesus Christ. 9 But those who fail to develop these virtues are blind or, at least, very
shortsighted. They have already forgotten that God has cleansed them from their old life
of sin.

10 So, dear friends,* work hard to prove that you really are among those God has called
and chosen. Doing this, you will never stumble or fall away. 11 And God will open wide
the gates of heaven for you to enter into the eternal Kingdom of our Lord and Savior
Jesus Christ.

Paying Attention to Scripture

12 I plan to keep on reminding you of these things—even though you already know them
and are standing firm in the truth. 13 Yes, I believe I should keep on reminding you of
these things as long as I live. 14 But the Lord Jesus Christ has shown me that my days
here on earth are numbered and I am soon to die.* 15 So I will work hard to make these
things clear to you. I want you to remember them long after I am gone.

16 For we were not making up clever stories when we told you about the power of our
Lord Jesus Christ and his coming again. We have seen his majestic splendor with our
own eyes. 17 And he received honor and glory from God the Father when God's glorious,
majestic voice called down from heaven, "This is my beloved Son; I am fully pleased
with him." 18 We ourselves heard the voice when we were there with him on the holy
mountain.

19 Because of that, we have even greater confidence in the message proclaimed by the
prophets. Pay close attention to what they wrote, for their words are like a light shining
in a dark place—until the day Christ appears and his brilliant light shines in your hearts.*

1:6 Acts 24:25; 1 Cor 9:25; Gal 5:22
1:7 John 13:34-35; Rom 12:10; 1 Pet 1:22
1:8 John 15:2; Col 1:10; 2 Pet 1:2-3
1:10 Rom 8:28; Jude 1:24
1:13-14 John 13:36; 21:18-19; 2 Cor 5:1, 4; 2 Pet 3:1
1:15 Luke 9:31
1:16-18 Matt 17:1-6; Mark 13:26; Luke 9:28-32
1:19 Ps 119:105; Luke 1:78; 2 Cor 4:6; 1 Pet 1:10-12; Rev 22:16

1:10 Greek *brothers.* **1:14** Greek *I must soon put off this earthly tent.* **1:19** Or *until the day dawns and the morning star rises in your hearts.*

---

leads to learning to know God better, self-control, patient endurance, godliness, and loving others. These actions do not come automatically; they require hard work. They are not optional; all of them must be a continual part of the Christian life. We don't finish one and start on the next, but we work on them all together. God empowers and enables us, but he also gives us the responsibility to learn and to grow. We should not be surprised at or resentful of the process.

1:6 False teachers were saying that self-control was not needed because deeds do not help the believer anyway (2:19). It is true that deeds cannot save us, but it is absolutely false to think they are unimportant. We are saved so that we can grow to resemble Christ and serve others. God wants to produce his character in us. But to do this, he demands our discipline and effort. As we obey Christ, who guides us by his Spirit, we will develop self-control not only with respect to food and drink but also with respect to our emotions.

1:9 Our faith must go beyond what we believe; it must become a dynamic part of all we do, resulting in good fruit and spiritual maturity. Salvation does not depend on good deeds, but it results in good deeds. A person who claims to be saved while remaining unchanged does not understand faith or what God has done for him or her.

1:10 Peter wanted to rouse the complacent believers who had listened to the false teachers and believed that because salvation is not based on good deeds they could live any way they wanted. If you truly belong to the Lord, Peter wrote, your hard work will prove it. If you're not working to develop the qualities listed in 1:5-7, maybe you don't belong to him. If you are the Lord's—and your hard work backs up your claim to be chosen by God—you will never be led astray by false teaching or glamorous sin.

1:12-15 Just as coaches constantly review the basics with their teams and good athletes execute the fundamentals, we must not neglect the basics of our faith. An athlete needs constant practice, and we need constant reminders of the fundamentals of our faith and of how we came to believe. Don't allow yourself to be bored or impatient with messages on the basics of the Christian life. Instead, take the attitude of an athlete who continues to practice and refine the basics while learning more advanced skills.

1:13, 14 Peter knew that he would die soon. Many years before, Christ had prepared Peter for the kind of death he would face (see John 21:18, 19). At this time, Peter knew that his death was at hand. Peter was martyred for the faith about A.D. 68. According to one tradition, he was crucified upside down, at his own request, because he did not feel worthy to die in the same manner as his Master.

1:16-18 Peter is referring to the Transfiguration where Jesus' divine identity was revealed to him and two other disciples, James and John (see Matthew 17:1-8; Mark 9:2-8; Luke 9:28-36).

1:16-21 This section is a strong statement on the inspiration of Scripture. Peter affirms that the Old Testament prophets wrote God's messages. He puts himself and the other apostles in the same category because they also proclaim God's truth. The Bible is not a collection of fables or human ideas about God. It is God's very words given *through* people *to* people. Peter emphasized his authority as an eyewitness as well as the God-inspired authority of Scripture to prepare the way for his harsh words against the false teachers. If these wicked men were contradicting the apostles and the Bible, their message could not be from God.

1:19 Christ is a "brilliant light," and when he returns, he will shine in his full glory. Until that day we have Scripture and the Holy Spirit to illuminate it for us and guide us as we seek the truth (see also Luke 1:78; Ephesians 5:14; Revelation 2:28; 22:16).

20 Above all, you must understand that no prophecy in Scripture ever came from the 1:21
prophets themselves* 21 or because they wanted to prophesy. It was the Holy Spirit who 1 Cor 2:13 2 Tim 3:16
moved the prophets to speak from God.

2. Danger to growing Christians

False Teachers

2 But there were also false prophets in Israel, just as there will be false teachers among 2:1
you. They will cleverly teach their destructive heresies about God and even turn Deut 13:1-3
against their Master who bought them. Theirs will be a swift and terrible end. 2 Many will Matt 7:15 1 Tim 4:1
follow their evil teaching and shameful immorality. And because of them, Christ and his Jude 1:4
true way will be slandered. 3 In their greed they will make up clever lies to get hold of 2:3 Rom 16:18
your money. But God condemned them long ago, and their destruction is on the way. 1 Thes 2:5
4 For God did not spare even the angels when they sinned; he threw them into hell,* in 2:4
gloomy caves* and darkness until the judgment day. 5 And God did not spare the ancient Gen 6:1-4 //Jude 1:6
world—except for Noah and his family of seven. Noah warned the world of God's Rev 20:1-2
righteous judgment. Then God destroyed the whole world of ungodly people with a vast 2:5
flood. 6 Later, he turned the cities of Sodom and Gomorrah into heaps of ashes and swept Gen 6:5–8:18 1 Pet 3:20
them off the face of the earth. He made them an example of what will happen to ungodly 2 Pet 3:6
people. 7 But at the same time, God rescued Lot out of Sodom because he was a good man 2:6
who was sick of all the immorality and wickedness around him. 8 Yes, he was a righteous Gen 19:24 Matt 10:15
man who was distressed by the wickedness he saw and heard day after day. Rom 9:29 //Jude 1:7
9 So you see, the Lord knows how to rescue godly people from their trials, even while 2:7
punishing the wicked right up until the day of judgment. 10 He is especially hard on those Gen 19:1-16 2 Pet 3:17
who follow their own evil, lustful desires and who despise authority. These people are 2:9
proud and arrogant, daring even to scoff at the glorious ones* without so much as //Jude 1:6
trembling. 11 But the angels, even though they are far greater in power and strength than 2:10 2 Pet 3:3
these false teachers, never speak out disrespectfully against* the glorious ones. //Jude 1:7-8, 16, 18
12 These false teachers are like unthinking animals, creatures of instinct, who are born 2:11 //Jude 1:9
to be caught and killed. They laugh at the terrifying powers they know so little about, 2:12 //Jude 1:10

1:20 Or *is a matter of one's own interpretation.* **2:4a** Greek *Tartaros.* **2:4b** Some manuscripts read *chains of gloom.* **2:10** *The glorious ones* are probably evil angels; also in 2:11. **2:11** Greek *never bring blasphemous judgment from the Lord against.*

1:20, 21 "It was the Holy Spirit who moved the prophets to speak from God" means that Scripture did not come from the creative work of the prophets' own invention or interpretation. God inspired the writers, so their message is authentic and reliable. God used the talents, education, and cultural background of each writer (they were not mindless robots); and God cooperated with the writers in such a way to ensure that the message he intended was faithfully communicated in the very words they wrote.

2:1 Jesus had told the disciples that false teachers would come (Matthew 24:11; Mark 13:22, 23). Peter had heard these words, and at this time he was seeing them come true. Just as false prophets had contradicted the true prophets in Old Testament times (see, for example, Jeremiah 23:16-40; 28:1-17), telling people only what they wanted to hear, so false teachers were twisting Christ's teachings and the words of his apostles. These teachers were belittling the significance of Jesus' life, death, and resurrection. Some claimed that Jesus couldn't be God; others claimed that he couldn't have been a real man. These teachers allowed and even encouraged all kinds of immorality, especially sexual sin. We must be careful to avoid false teachers today. Any book, tape series, or TV message must be evaluated in the light of God's Word. Beware of special meanings or interpretations that belittle Christ or his work.

2:3 Teachers should be paid by the people they teach, but these false teachers were attempting to make more money by distorting the truth and saying what people wanted to hear. They were more interested in making money than in teaching truth. Peter and Paul both condemned greedy, lying teachers (see 1 Timothy 6:5). Before you send money to any cause, evaluate it carefully. Is the teacher or preacher clearly serving God or promoting his/her own interests? Will the money be used to promote valid ministry, or will it merely finance further promotions?

2:4-6 If God did not spare angels or people who lived before the Flood or the citizens of Sodom and Gomorrah, he would not spare these false teachers. Some people would have us believe that God will save all people because he is so loving. But it is foolish to think that he will cancel the Last Judgment. These three examples should warn us clearly that God judges sin and that unrepentant sinners cannot escape.

2:7-9 Just as God rescued Lot from Sodom, so he is able to rescue us from the temptations and trials we face in a wicked world. Lot was not sinless, but he put his trust in God and was spared when Sodom was destroyed. For more information on Lot, see his Profile in Genesis 14. God also will judge those who cause the temptations and trials, so we need never worry about justice being done.

2:10-12 The "glorious ones" may be angels, all the glories of the unseen world, or more probably, fallen angels. A similar passage is found in Jude 1:8-10. Whoever they are, the false teachers slandered the spiritual realities they did not understand, taking Satan's power lightly and claiming to have the ability to judge evil. Many in our world today mock the supernatural. They deny the reality of the spiritual world and claim that only what can be seen and felt is real. Like the false teachers of Peter's day, they are fools who will be proven wrong in the end. Don't take Satan and his supernatural powers of evil lightly, and don't become arrogant about how defeated he will be. Although Satan will be destroyed completely, he is at work now trying to render Christians complacent and ineffective.

2:13 Rom 13:13; 1 Cor 11:20-21; //Jude 1:12
2:14 Eph 2:3; 2 Pet 2:18; 3:16
2:15 Num 22:5-7, 17; Deut 23:5; //Jude 1:11; Rev 2:14
2:16 Num 22:21-28
2:17 //Jude 1:12-13
2:18 2 Pet 1:4; //Jude 1:16
2:20 Matt 12:45; 2 Pet 1:2, 11; 3:18
2:21 Ezek 18:24; Heb 6:4; 10:26

and they will be destroyed along with them. 13 Their destruction is their reward for the harm they have done. They love to indulge in evil pleasures in broad daylight. They are a disgrace and a stain among you. They revel in deceitfulness while they feast with you. 14 They commit adultery with their eyes, and their lust is never satisfied. They make a game of luring unstable people into sin. They train themselves to be greedy; they are doomed and cursed. 15 They have wandered off the right road and followed the way of Balaam son of Beor,* who loved to earn money by doing wrong. 16 But Balaam was stopped from his mad course when his donkey rebuked him with a human voice.

17 These people are as useless as dried-up springs of water or as clouds blown away by the wind—promising much and delivering nothing. They are doomed to blackest darkness. 18 They brag about themselves with empty, foolish boasting. With lustful desire as their bait, they lure back into sin those who have just escaped from such wicked living. 19 They promise freedom, but they themselves are slaves to sin and corruption. For you are a slave to whatever controls you. 20 And when people escape from the wicked ways of the world by learning about our Lord and Savior Jesus Christ and then get tangled up with sin and become its slave again, they are worse off than before. 21 It would be better if they had never known the right way to live than to know it and then reject the holy commandments that were given to them. 22 They make these proverbs come true: "A dog returns to its vomit,"* and "A washed pig returns to the mud."

3. Hope for growing Christians

The Day of the Lord Is Coming

3:2 //Jude 1:17
3:3 1 Tim 4:1; 2 Pet 2:10; //Jude 1:18
3:4 Isa 5:19; Jer 17:15
3:5 Gen 1:6-9; Heb 11:3
3:6 Gen 7:11-21
3:7 Matt 10:15; 2 Thes 1:7

3 This is my second letter to you, dear friends, and in both of them I have tried to stimulate your wholesome thinking and refresh your memory. 2 I want you to remember and understand what the holy prophets said long ago and what our Lord and Savior commanded through your apostles.

3 First, I want to remind you that in the last days there will be scoffers who will laugh at the truth and do every evil thing they desire. 4 This will be their argument: "Jesus promised to come back, did he? Then where is he? Why, as far back as anyone can remember, everything has remained exactly the same since the world was first created."

5 They deliberately forget that God made the heavens by the word of his command, and he brought the earth up from the water and surrounded it with water. 6 Then he used the water to destroy the world with a mighty flood. 7 And God has also commanded that the heavens and the earth will be consumed by fire on the day of judgment, when ungodly people will perish.

2:15 Other manuscripts read *Bosor.* **2:22** Prov 26:11.

2:13, 14 The feast may have been part of the celebration of the Lord's Supper. The feast was a full meal that ended with Communion. The false teachers, although they were sinning openly, took part in these meals with everyone else in the church. In one of the greatest of hypocritical acts, they attended a sacred feast designed to promote love and unity among believers, while at the same time they gossiped and slandered those who disagreed with their opinions. Paul told the Corinthians, "So if anyone eats this bread or drinks this cup of the Lord unworthily, that person is guilty of sinning against the body and the blood of the Lord" (1 Corinthians 11:27). These men were guilty of more than false teaching and promoting evil pleasures; they were guilty of leading others away from God's Son, Jesus.

2:15 Balaam was hired by a pagan king to curse Israel. He did what God told him to do for a time (Numbers 22–24), but eventually his evil motives and desire for money won out (Numbers 25:1-3; 31:16). Like the false teachers of Peter's day, Balaam used religion for personal advancement, a sin that God does not take lightly.

2:19 A person is a slave to whatever controls him or her. Many believe that freedom means doing anything we want. But no one is ever completely free in that sense. If we refuse to follow God, we will follow our own sinful desires and become enslaved to what our body wants. If we submit our life to Christ, he will free us from slavery to sin. Christ frees us to serve him, a freedom that results in our ultimate good.

2:20-22 Peter is speaking of people who have learned about Christ and how to be saved but then reject the truth and return to their sin. These people are worse off than before because they have rejected the only way out of sin, the only way of salvation. Like someone sinking in quicksand who refuses to grab the rope thrown to him or her, the person who turns away from Christ rejects the only means of escape (see the note on Luke 11:24-26).

3:3, 4 "In the last days" scoffers will say that Jesus is never coming back, but Peter refutes their argument by explaining God's mastery over time. The "last days" is the time between Christ's first and second comings; thus, we, like Peter, live in the last days. We must do the work to which God has called us and believe that he will return as he promised.

3:7 In Noah's day the earth was judged by water; at the Second Coming it will be judged by fire. This fire is described in Revelation 19:20; 20:10-15.

8 But you must not forget, dear friends, that a day is like a thousand years to the Lord,
and a thousand years is like a day. 9 The Lord isn't really being slow about his promise
to return, as some people think. No, he is being patient for your sake. He does not want
anyone to perish, so he is giving more time for everyone to repent. 10 But the day of the
Lord will come as unexpectedly as a thief. Then the heavens will pass away with a
terrible noise, and everything in them will disappear in fire, and the earth and everything
on it will be exposed to judgment.*

11 Since everything around us is going to melt away, what holy, godly lives you should
be living! 12 You should look forward to that day and hurry it along—the day when God
will set the heavens on fire and the elements will melt away in the flames. 13 But we are
looking forward to the new heavens and new earth he has promised, a world where
everyone is right with God.

14 And so, dear friends, while you are waiting for these things to happen, make every
effort to live a pure and blameless life. And be at peace with God.

15 And remember, the Lord is waiting so that people have time to be saved. This is just
as our beloved brother Paul wrote to you with the wisdom God gave him—16 speaking
of these things in all of his letters. Some of his comments are hard to understand, and
those who are ignorant and unstable have twisted his letters around to mean something
quite different from what he meant, just as they do the other parts of Scripture—and the
result is disaster for them.

Peter's Final Words

17 I am warning you ahead of time, dear friends, so that you can watch out and not be
carried away by the errors of these wicked people. I don't want you to lose your own
secure footing. 18 But grow in the special favor and knowledge of our Lord and Savior
Jesus Christ.

To him be all glory and honor, both now and forevermore. Amen.

3:8 Ps 90:4
3:9 Hab 2:3; Rom 2:4; 1 Tim 2:4; Rev 2:21
3:10 Matt 24:43-44; 1 Thes 5:2; Rev 3:3; 16:5
3:12 Ps 50:3; 1 Cor 1:7
3:13 Isa 60:21; 65:17; 66:22; Rev 21:1, 27; 22:15
3:14 1 Thes 3:13; 1 Pet 1:7
3:15 Rom 2:4; Eph 3:3; Col 1:25-27
3:16 2 Pet 2:14
3:17 1 Cor 10:12; 2 Pet 2:18; Rev 2:5
3:18 Rom 11:36; 2 Tim 4:18; 2 Pet 1:2, 11; 2:20

3:10 Some manuscripts read *will be burned up.*

3:8, 9 God may have seemed slow to these believers as they faced persecution every day and longed to be delivered. But God is not slow; he just is not on *our* timetable (Psalm 90:4). Jesus is waiting so that more sinners will repent and turn to him. We must not sit and wait for Christ to return, but we should realize that time is short and we have important work to do. Be ready to meet Christ any time, even today; yet plan your course of service as though he may not return for many years.

3:10, 11 The day of the Lord is the day of God's judgment on the earth. Here it is used in reference to Christ's return. Christ's second coming will be sudden and terrible for those who do not believe in him. But if we are morally clean and spiritually alert, it won't come as a surprise. For other prophetic pictures of the day of the Lord, see Isaiah 34:4; Joel 3:15, 16; Matthew 24; Mark 13; Luke 21; Revelation 6:12-17. Realizing that the earth is going to be burned up, we should put our confidence in what is lasting and eternal and not be bound to earth and its treasures or pursuits. Do you spend more of your time piling up possessions or striving to develop Christlike character?

3:13 God's purpose for people is not destruction but re-creation (see Isaiah 66:22; Revelation 21–22). God will purify the heavens and earth with fire; then he will create them anew. We can joyously look forward to the restoration of God's good world.

3:14 We should not become lazy and complacent because Christ has not yet returned. Instead, we should live in eager expectation of his coming. What would you like to be doing when Christ returns? That is how you should be living each day.

3:15, 16 By the time of Peter's writing, Paul's letters already had a widespread reputation. Notice that Peter spoke of Paul's letters as if they were on a level with "the other parts of Scripture." Already the early church was thinking of Paul's letters as inspired by God.

3:15-18 Peter and Paul had very different backgrounds and personalities, and they preached from different viewpoints. Paul emphasized salvation by grace, not law, while Peter preferred to talk about Christian life and service. The two men did not contradict each other, however, and they always held each other in high esteem. The false teachers intentionally misused Paul's writings by distorting them to condone lawlessness. No doubt this made the teachers popular, because people always like to have their favorite sins justified, but the net effect was to totally destroy Paul's message. Paul may have been thinking of teachers like these when he wrote in Romans 6:15: "So since God's grace has set us free from the law, does this mean we can go on sinning? Of course not!" Peter warned his readers to avoid the mistakes of those wicked teachers by growing in the special favor and knowledge of Jesus. The better we know Jesus, the less attractive false teaching will be.

3:18 Peter concludes this brief letter as he began, urging his readers to grow in the special favor and knowledge of the Lord and Savior Jesus Christ; that is, they were to get to know him better and better. This is the best way to discern false teaching. No matter where we are in our spiritual journey, no matter how mature we are in our faith, the sinful world will always challenge our faith. We still have much room for growth. Every day we need to draw closer to Christ so that we will be prepared to stand for truth in any and all circumstances.

1 JOHN

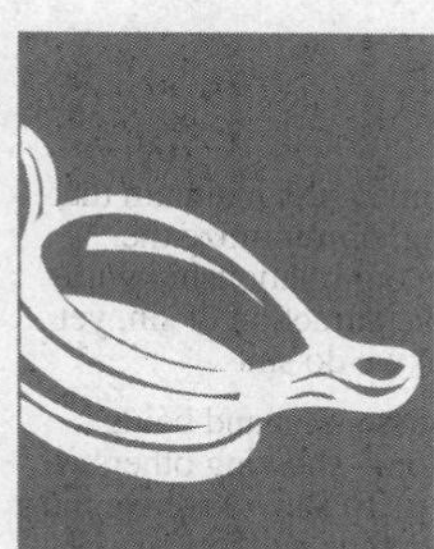

"A GOOD man . . . yes . . . perhaps one of the best who ever lived . . . but just a man," say many. Others disagree, claiming that he suffered from delusions of grandeur—a "messiah complex." And the argument rages over the true identity of this man called Jesus. Suggestions have ranged from "simple teacher" to "egomaniac" and "misguided fool." Whoever he was, all would agree that Jesus left his mark on history.

Hearing these discussions, even Christians can begin to wonder and doubt. Is Jesus really God? Did he come to save sinners like us? Does God care about me?

First John was written to dispel doubts and to build assurance by presenting a clear picture of Christ. Entering history, Jesus was and is God in the flesh and God in focus—seen, heard, and touched by the author of this letter, John the apostle. John walked and talked with Jesus, saw him heal, heard him teach, watched him die, met him arisen, and saw him ascend. John knew God—he had lived with him and had seen him work. And John enjoyed fellowship with the Father and the Son all the days of his life.

The elder statesman in the church, John wrote this letter to his "dear children." In it he presented God as light, as love, and as life. He explained in simple and practical terms what it means to have fellowship with God.

At the same time, false teachers had entered the church, denying the incarnation of Christ. John wrote to correct their serious errors. So John's letter is a model for us to follow as we combat modern heresies.

John opens this letter by giving his credentials as an eyewitness of the Incarnation and by stating his reason for writing (1:1–4). He then presents God as "light," symbolizing absolute purity and holiness (1:5–7), and he explains how believers can walk in the light and have fellowship with God (1:8–10). If they do sin, Christ is their defender (2:1, 2). John urges them to obey Christ fully and to love all the members of God's family (2:3–17). He warns his readers of "antichrists" and the Antichrist who will try to lead them away from the truth (2:18–29).

In the next section, John presents God as "love"—giving, dying, forgiving, and blessing (3:1—4:21). God *is* love, and because God loves us, he calls us his children and makes us like Christ (3:1, 2). This truth should motivate us to live close to him (3:3–6). We can be sure of our family relationship with God when our life is filled with good deeds and love for others (3:7–24). Again, John warns of false teachers who twist the truth. We should reject these false teachers (4:1–6) as we continue to live in God's love (4:7–21).

In the last section, John presents God as "life" (5:1–21). God's life is in his Son. To have his Son is to have eternal life.

Do you know God? Do you know Christ? Do you know that you have eternal life? First John was written to help you know the reality of God in your life through faith in Christ, to assure you that you have eternal life, and to encourage you to remain in fellowship with the God who is light and love. Read this letter written by one overwhelmed by God's love, and with renewed confidence, pass on his love to others.

VITAL STATISTICS

PURPOSE:
To reassure Christians in their faith and to counter false teachings

AUTHOR:
The apostle John

TO WHOM WRITTEN:
The letter is untitled and was written to no particular church. It was sent as a pastoral letter to several Gentile congregations. It was also written to all believers everywhere.

DATE WRITTEN:
Probably between A.D. 85 and 90 from Ephesus

SETTING:
John was an older man and perhaps the only surviving apostle at this time. He had not yet been banished to the island of Patmos, where he would live in exile. As an eyewitness of Christ, he wrote authoritatively to give this new generation of believers assurance and confidence in God and in their faith.

KEY VERSE:
"I write this to you who believe in the Son of God, so that you may know you have eternal life" (5:13).

KEY PEOPLE:
John, Jesus

SPECIAL FEATURES:
John is the apostle of love, and love is mentioned throughout this letter. There are a number of similarities between this letter and John's Gospel—in vocabulary, style, and main ideas. John uses brief statements and simple words, and he features sharp contrasts—light and darkness, truth and error, God and Satan, life and death, love and hate.

THE BLUEPRINT

1. God is light (1:1—2:29)
2. God is love (3:1—4:21)
3. God is life (5:1–21)

John wrote about the most vital aspects of faith so that his readers would know Christian truth from error. He emphasizes the basics of faith so that we can be confident in our faith. In our dark world, God is light. In our cold world, God brings the warmth of love. In our dying world, God brings life. When we lack confidence, these truths bring us certainty.

MEGATHEMES

THEME	EXPLANATION	IMPORTANCE
Sin	Even Christians sin. Sin requires God's forgiveness, and Christ's death provides it for us. Determining to live according to God's standards in the Bible shows that our life is being transformed.	We cannot deny our sin nature, maintain that we are "above" sinning, or minimize the consequences of sin in our relationship with God. We must resist the attraction of sin, yet we must confess when we do sin.
Love	Christ commands us to love others as he loved us. This love is evidence that we are truly saved. God is the Creator of love; he cares that his children love each other.	Love means putting others first and being unselfish. Love is action—showing others we care—not just saying it. To show love we must give sacrificially of our time and money to meet the needs of others.
Family of God	We become God's children by believing in Christ. God's life in us enables us to love our fellow family members.	How we treat others shows who our Father is. Live as a faithful, loving family member.
Truth and Error	Teaching that the physical body does not matter, false teachers encouraged believers to throw off moral restraints. They also taught that Christ wasn't really a man and that we must be saved by having some special mystical knowledge. The result was that people became indifferent to sin.	God is truth and light, so the more we get to know him, the better we can keep focused on the truth. Don't be led astray by any teaching that denies Christ's deity or humanity. Check the message; test the claims.
Assurance	God is in control of heaven and earth. Because his word is true, we can have assurance of eternal life and victory over sin. By faith we can be certain of our eternal destiny with him.	Assurance of our relationship with God is a promise, but it is also a way of life. We build our confidence by trusting in God's Word and in Christ's provision for our sin.

1. God is light

Introduction

1 The one who existed from the beginning* is the one we have heard and seen. We
saw him with our own eyes and touched him with our own hands. He is Jesus Christ,
the Word of life. 2 This one who is life from God was shown to us, and we have seen him.
And now we testify and announce to you that he is the one who is eternal life. He was
with the Father, and then he was shown to us. 3 We are telling you about what we

1:1 John 1:1, 4, 14; 1 Jn 4:14
1:2 John 1:1-4; 19:35; 20:30-31; 1 Jn 5:11, 13, 20

1:1 Greek *What was from the beginning.*

1:1 First John was written by John, one of Jesus' original 12 disciples. He was probably "the disciple Jesus loved" (John 21:20), and along with Peter and James, he had a special relationship with Jesus. This letter was written between A.D. 85 and 90 from Ephesus, before John's exile to the island of Patmos (see Revelation 1:9). Jerusalem had been destroyed in A.D. 70, and Christians were scattered throughout the empire. By the time John wrote this letter, Christianity had been around for more than a generation. It had faced and survived severe persecution. The main problem confronting the church at this time was declining commitment: Many believers were conforming to the world's standards, failing to stand up for Christ and compromising their faith. False teachers were plentiful, and they were accelerating the church's downward slide away from the Christian faith.

John wrote this letter to put believers back on track, to show the difference between light and darkness (truth and error), and to encourage the church to grow in genuine love for God and for one another. He also wrote to assure true believers that they possessed eternal life and to help them know that their faith was genuine—so they could enjoy all the benefits of being God's children. For more about John, see his Profile in John 13.

1:1-5 John opens his first letter to the churches similarly to the way he began his Gospel, emphasizing that Christ ("the Word of life") is eternal, that God came into the world as a human, that he, John, was an eyewitness to Jesus' life, and that Jesus brings light and life.

1:3 As an eyewitness to Jesus' ministry, John was qualified to teach the truth about him. The readers of this letter had not seen and heard Jesus themselves, but they could trust that what John wrote was accurate. We are like those second- and third-generation Christians. Though we have not personally seen, heard, or touched Jesus, we have the New Testament record of his eyewitnesses, and we can trust that they spoke the truth about him. See John 20:29.

1:3, 4 John writes about having fellowship with other believers. There are three principles behind true Christian fellowship:

1:4 John 15:11; 16:24
1:5 John 1:9; 8:12; 1 Tim 6:16
1:6 John 3:19-21; 2 Cor 6:14
1:7 Heb 9:14
1:9 Heb 9:14

ourselves have actually seen and heard, so that you may have fellowship with us. And
our fellowship is with the Father and with his Son, Jesus Christ.
[4]We are writing these things so that our* joy will be complete.

Living in the Light

[5]This is the message he has given us to announce to you: God is light and there is no
darkness in him at all. [6]So we are lying if we say we have fellowship with God but go
on living in spiritual darkness. We are not living in the truth. [7]But if we are living in the
light of God's presence, just as Christ is, then we have fellowship with each other, and
the blood of Jesus, his Son, cleanses us from every sin.
[8]If we say we have no sin, we are only fooling ourselves and refusing to accept the
truth. [9]But if we confess our sins to him, he is faithful and just to forgive us and to cleanse

1:4 Some manuscripts read *your.*

JOHN COUNTERS FALSE TEACHINGS

John counters two major threads in the false teachings of the heretics in this letter:

1:6, 8, 10	They denied the reality of sin. John says that if we continue in sin, we can't claim to belong to God. If we say we have no sin, we are only fooling ourselves and refusing to accept the truth.
2:22; 4:1–3 . . .	They denied that Jesus was the Messiah—God in the flesh. John said that if we believe that Jesus was God incarnate and trust him for our salvation, we are children of God.

First, our fellowship is grounded in the testimony of God's Word. Without this underlying strength, togetherness is impossible. Second, it is mutual, depending on the unity of believers. Third, it is renewed daily through the Holy Spirit. True fellowship combines social and spiritual interaction, and it is made possible only through a living relationship with Christ.

1:5, 6 Light represents what is good, pure, true, holy, and reliable. Darkness represents what is sinful and evil. The statement "God is light" means that God is perfectly holy and true and that he alone can guide us out of the darkness of sin. Light is also related to truth in that light exposes whatever exists, whether it is good or bad. In the dark, good and evil look alike; in the light, they can be clearly distinguished. Just as darkness cannot exist in the presence of light, sin cannot exist in the presence of a holy God. If we want to have a relationship with God, we must put aside our sinful ways of living. To claim that we belong to him but then to go out and live for ourselves is hypocrisy. Christ will expose and judge such deceit.

1:6 Here John was confronting the first of three claims of the false teachers: that we can have fellowship with God and still walk in darkness. False teachers who thought that the physical body was evil or worthless taught one of two approaches to behavior: They insisted on denying bodily desires through rigid discipline, or they approved of gratifying every physical lust because the body was going to be destroyed anyway. Obviously the second approach was more popular! Here John is saying that no one can claim to be a Christian and still live in evil and immorality. We can't love God and court sin at the same time.

1:7 How does Jesus' blood cleanse us from every sin? In Old Testament times, believers symbolically transferred their sins to an animal, which they then sacrificed (see a description of this ceremony in Leviticus 4). The animal died in their place to pay for their sin and to allow them to continue living in God's favor. God graciously forgave them because of their faith in him and because they obeyed his commandments concerning the sacrifice. Those sacrifices anticipated the day when Christ would completely remove sin. Real cleansing from sin came with Jesus, the "Lamb of God who takes away the sin of the world" (John 1:29). Sin, by its very nature, brings death—that is a fact as certain as the law of gravity. Jesus did not die for his own sins; he had none. Instead, by a transaction that we may never fully understand, he died for the sins of the world. When we commit our life to Christ and thus identify ourselves with him, his death becomes ours. He has paid the penalty for our sins, and his blood has purified us. Just as Christ rose from the grave, we rise to a new life of fellowship with him (Romans 6:4).

1:8 Here John was attacking the second claim of the false teachers: that people had no natural tendency toward sin, that they had "no sin," and that they were then incapable of sinning. This idea is at best self-deception and at worst a bald-faced lie. The false teachers refused to take sin seriously. They wanted to be considered Christians, but they saw no need to confess and repent. The death of Christ did not mean much to them because they didn't think they needed it. Instead of repenting and being purified by Christ's blood, they were encouraging sin among believers. In this life we are always capable of sinning, so we should never let down our guard.

1:8-10 The false teachers not only denied that sin breaks our fellowship with God (1:6) and that they had a sinful nature (1:8), but they also denied that their conduct involved any sin at all (1:10). That was a lie that ignored one basic truth: All people are sinners by nature and by practice. At conversion all our sins are forgiven—past, present, and future. Yet even after we become Christians, we still sin and still need to confess. This kind of confession is not offered to gain God's acceptance but to remove the barrier to fellowship that our sin has put between us and him. It is difficult, however, for many people to admit their faults and shortcomings, even to God. It takes humility and honesty to recognize our weaknesses, and most of us would rather pretend that we are strong. But we need not fear revealing our sins to God—he knows them already. He will not push us away, no matter what we've done. Instead, he will draw us to himself.

1:9 Confession is supposed to free us to enjoy fellowship with Christ. It should ease our consciences and lighten our cares. But some Christians do not understand how it works. They feel so guilty that they confess the same sins over and over; then they wonder if they might have forgotten something. Other Christians believe that God forgives them when they confess, but if they died with unconfessed sins, they would be forever lost. These Christians do not understand that God *wants* to forgive us. He allowed his beloved Son to die just so he could offer us pardon. When we come to Christ, he forgives all the sins we have committed or will ever commit. We don't need to confess the sins of the past all over again, and we don't need to fear that God will reject

us from every wrong. [10]If we claim we have not sinned, we are calling God a liar and
showing that his word has no place in our hearts.

2 My dear children, I am writing this to you so that you will not sin. But if you do sin,
there is someone to plead for you before the Father. He is Jesus Christ, the one who
pleases God completely.* [2]He is the sacrifice for our sins. He takes away not only our
sins but the sins of all the world.
[3]And how can we be sure that we belong to him? By obeying his commandments. [4]If
someone says, "I belong to God," but doesn't obey God's commandments, that person
is a liar and does not live in the truth. [5]But those who obey God's word really do love
him. That is the way to know whether or not we live in him. [6]Those who say they live
in God should live their lives as Christ did.

A New Commandment

[7]Dear friends, I am not writing a new commandment, for it is an old one you have always
had, right from the beginning. This commandment—to love one another—is the same
message you heard before. [8]Yet it is also new. This commandment is true in Christ and
is true among you, because the darkness is disappearing and the true light is already
shining.
[9]Anyone who says, "I am in the light" but rejects another Christian* is still in
darkness. [10]But anyone who loves other Christians is walking in the light and does not

1:10 1 Jn 5:10
2:1 1 Tim 2:5; Heb 7:25; 9:24
2:2 John 1:29; Rom 3:25; Heb 2:17; 1 Jn 4:10
2:5 John 14:21, 23
2:6 Matt 11:29; John 13:15; 1 Pet 2:21
2:7 John 13:34; 2 Jn 1:5-6
2:8 John 1:9; 13:34; Rom 13:12; Eph 5:8; 1 Thes 5:5
2:10 Rom 14:13

2:1 Greek *Jesus Christ, the righteous.* **2:9** Greek *hates his brother;* also in 2:11.

us if we don't keep our slate perfectly clean. Of course we should continue to confess our sins, but not because failure to do so will make us lose our salvation. Our relationship with Christ is secure. Instead, we should confess so that we can enjoy maximum fellowship and joy with him.

True confession also involves a commitment not to continue in sin. We wouldn't be genuinely confessing our sins to God if we planned to commit them again and just wanted temporary forgiveness. We should also pray for strength to defeat temptation the next time we face it.

1:9 If God has forgiven us for our sins because of Christ's death, why must we confess our sins? In admitting our sins and receiving Christ's cleansing, we are (1) agreeing with God that our sin truly is sin and that we are willing to turn from it, (2) ensuring that we don't conceal our sins from him and consequently from ourselves, and (3) recognizing our tendency to sin and relying on his power to overcome it.

2:1 John uses "dear children" in a warm, fatherly way. He is not talking down to his readers but is showing affection for them. At this writing, John was a very old man. He had spent almost all his life in ministry, and many of his readers were indeed his spiritual children.

2:1, 2 To people who are feeling guilty and condemned, John offers reassurance. They know they have sinned, and Satan (called "the Accuser" in Revelation 12:10) is demanding the death penalty. When you feel this way, don't give up hope—the best defense attorney in the universe is pleading your case. Jesus Christ, your advocate, your defender, is the Judge's Son. He has already suffered your penalty in your place. You can't be tried for a case that is no longer on the docket. United with Christ, you are as safe as he is. Don't be afraid to ask Christ to plead your case—he has already won it (see Romans 8:33, 34; Hebrews 7:24, 25).

2:2 Jesus Christ is the atoning sacrifice for our sins (see also 4:10). He can stand before God as our mediator because his death satisfied the wrath of God against sin and paid the death penalty for our sin. Thus, Christ both satisfies God's requirement and removes our sin. In him we are forgiven and purified.

2:2 Sometimes it is difficult to forgive those who wrong us. Imagine how hard it would be to forgive everyone, no matter what they had done! This is what God has done in Jesus. No one, no matter what he or she has done, is beyond forgiveness. All a person has to do is turn from all known sin, receive Christ's forgiveness, and commit his or her life to him.

2:3-6 How can you be sure that you belong to Christ? This passage gives two ways to know: if you do what Christ says and live as Christ wants. What does Christ tell us to do? John answers in 3:23: "Believe in the name of his Son, Jesus Christ, and love one another." True Christian faith results in loving behavior; that is why John says that the way we act can give us assurance that we belong to Christ.

2:6 To live as Jesus lived doesn't mean choosing 12 disciples, performing great miracles, and being crucified. We cannot merely copy Christ's life; much of what Jesus did had to do with his identity as God's Son, the fulfillment of his special role in dying for sin, and the cultural context of the first-century Roman world. To walk today as Christ did, we must obey his teachings and follow his example of complete obedience to God and loving service to people.

2:7, 8 The commandment to love others is both old and new. It is old because it comes from the Old Testament (Leviticus 19:18). It is new because Jesus interpreted it in a radically new way (John 13:34, 35). In the Christian church, love is not only expressed by showing respect; it is also expressed through self-sacrifice and servanthood (John 15:13). In fact, it can be defined as "selfless giving," reaching beyond friends to enemies and persecutors (Matthew 5:43-48). Love should be the unifying force and the identifying mark of the Christian community. Love is the key to walking in the light, because we cannot grow spiritually while we hate others. Our growing relationship with God will result in growing relationships with others.

2:9-11 Does this mean that if you dislike someone you aren't a Christian? These verses are not talking about disliking a disagreeable Christian brother or sister. There will always be people we will not like as well as others. John's words focus on the attitude that causes us to ignore or despise others, to treat them as irritants, competitors, or enemies. Christian love is not a feeling but a choice. We can choose to be concerned with people's well-being and treat them with respect, whether or not we feel affection toward them. If we choose to love others, God will help us express our love.

2:11 John 12:35; 2 Cor 4:4; 2 Pet 1:9; 1 Jn 2:9; 3:15

cause anyone to stumble. 11 Those who reject other Christians are wandering in spiritual
darkness and don't know where they are going, for the darkness has made them blind.

2:12 1 Cor 6:11

12 I am writing to you, my dear children, because your sins have been forgiven because of Jesus.

2:13 John 1:1; 16:33; 1 Jn 1:1; 4:4; 5:18

13 I am writing to you who are mature because you know Christ, the one who is from the beginning.

I am writing to you who are young because you have won your battle with Satan.

2:14 John 1:1-2; Eph 6:10; 1 Jn 1:1; 1:10

14 I have written to you, children, because you have known the Father.

I have written to you who are mature because you know Christ, the one who is from the beginning.

I have written to you who are young because you are strong with God's word living in your hearts, and you have won your battle with Satan.

2:15 Rom 12:2; Jas 4:4

2:16 Rom 13:14; Eph 2:3

2:17 Matt 7:21; 1 Cor 7:31

15 Stop loving this evil world and all that it offers you, for when you love the world,
you show that you do not have the love of the Father in you. 16 For the world offers
only the lust for physical pleasure, the lust for everything we see, and pride in our
possessions. These are not from the Father. They are from this evil world. 17 And this
world is fading away, along with everything it craves. But if you do the will of God,
you will live forever.

A BOOK OF CONTRASTS
One of the distinct features of John's writing style was his habit of noting both sides of a conflict. He wrote to show the difference between real Christianity and anything else. Here are some of his favorite contrasts.

Contrast between	*Passage*
Light and darkness	1:5
The new commandment and the old commandment	2:7, 8
Loving the Father and loving the world	2:15, 16
Christ and Antichrist	2:18
Truth and lies	2:20, 21
Children of God and children of the Devil	3:1–10
Eternal life and eternal death	3:14
Love and hatred	3:15, 16
True prophecy and false prophecy	4:1–3
Love and fear	4:18, 19
Having life and not having life	5:11, 12

2:12-14 John was writing to believers of all ages, his "dear children" who had experienced forgiveness through Jesus. Those who were mature in the faith had a long-standing relationship with Christ. The "young" had struggled with Satan's temptations and had won. The children had learned about Christ and were just beginning their spiritual journey. Each stage of life in the Christian pilgrimage builds upon the other. As children learn about Christ, they grow in their ability to win battles with temptation. As young adults move from victory to victory, they grow in their relationship with Christ. Older adults, having known Christ for years, have developed the wisdom needed to teach young people and start the cycle all over again. Has your Christian growth reached the maturity level appropriate for your stage in life?

2:15, 16 Some people think that worldliness is limited to external behavior—the people we associate with, the places we go, the activities we enjoy. Worldliness is also internal because it begins in the heart and is characterized by three attitudes: (1) *the lust for physical pleasure*—preoccupation with gratifying physical desires; (2) *the lust for everything we see*—craving and accumulating things, bowing to the god of materialism; and (3) *pride in our possessions*—obsession with one's status or importance. When the serpent tempted Eve (Genesis 3:6), he tempted her in these areas. Also, when the Devil tempted Jesus in the wilderness, these were his three areas of attack (see Matthew 4:1-11).

By contrast, God values self-control, a spirit of generosity, and a commitment to humble service. It is possible to give the impression of avoiding worldly pleasures while still harboring worldly attitudes in one's heart. It is also possible, like Jesus, to love sinners and spend time with them while maintaining a commitment to the values of God's Kingdom. What values are most important to you? Do your actions reflect the world's values or God's values?

2:17 When our attachment to possessions is strong, it's hard to believe that what we want will one day pass away. It may be even harder to believe that the person who does the will of God will live forever. But this was John's conviction based on the facts of Jesus' life, death, resurrection, and promises. Knowing that this evil world and our desires for its pleasures will end can give us courage to control our greedy, self-indulgent behavior and to continue doing God's will.

18 Dear children, the last hour is here. You have heard that the Antichrist is coming,
and already many such antichrists have appeared. From this we know that the end of the
world has come. 19 These people left our churches because they never really belonged
with us; otherwise they would have stayed with us. When they left us, it proved that they
do not belong with us. 20 But you are not like that, for the Holy Spirit has come upon
you,* and all of you know the truth. 21 So I am writing to you not because you don't know
the truth but because you know the difference between truth and falsehood. 22 And who
is the great liar? The one who says that Jesus is not the Christ. Such people are antichrists,
for they have denied the Father and the Son. 23 Anyone who denies the Son doesn't have
the Father either. But anyone who confesses the Son has the Father also.

24 So you must remain faithful to what you have been taught from the beginning. If
you do, you will continue to live in fellowship with the Son and with the Father. 25 And
in this fellowship we enjoy the eternal life he promised us.

26 I have written these things to you because you need to be aware of those who want
to lead you astray. 27 But you have received the Holy Spirit,* and he lives within you, so
you don't need anyone to teach you what is true. For the Spirit teaches you all things,
and what he teaches is true—it is not a lie. So continue in what he has taught you, and
continue to live in Christ.

28 And now, dear children, continue to live in fellowship with Christ so that when he
returns, you will be full of courage and not shrink back from him in shame. 29 Since we
know that God is always right, we also know that all who do what is right are his children.

2:18 Matt 24:24
2:19 Acts 20:30; 1 Cor 11:19
2:22 1 Jn 4:3
2:23 John 8:19; 17:3; 1 Jn 4:15; 5:1
2:24 1 Jn 4:15; 5:1; 2 Jn 1:9
2:25 John 3:15; 6:40; 17:3
2:26 1 Jn 3:7
2:27 John 14:16, 26; 16:13; 1 Cor 2:10-12; 1 Jn 2:20
2:28 Col 3:4; 1 Thes 2:19; 1 Jn 3:2, 21
2:29 1 Jn 3:7, 10; 4:7

2:20 Greek *But you have an anointing from the Holy One.* **2:27** Greek *the anointing.*

2:18-23 John is talking about the last days, the time between Christ's first and second comings. The first-century readers of 1 John lived in the last days, and so do we. During this time, antichrists (false teachers who pretend to be Christians and who lure weak members away from Christ) will appear. Finally, just before the world ends, one great Antichrist will arise (Revelation 13; 19:20; 20:10). We do not need to fear these evil people, however. The Holy Spirit shows us their errors, so we will not be deceived. However, we must teach God's Word clearly and carefully to the peripheral, weak members among us so that they won't fall prey to these teachers who "come disguised as harmless sheep, but are really wolves that will tear you apart" (Matthew 7:15).

2:19 The antichrists were not total strangers to the church; they once had been in the church, but they did not really belong to it. John does not say why they left; it is clear that their reasons for joining in the first place were wrong. Some people may call themselves Christians for less than the best reasons. Perhaps going to church is a family tradition. Maybe they like the social and business contacts they make there. Or possibly going to church is a long-standing habit, and they have never stopped to ask themselves why they do it. What is your main reason for being a Christian? Unless it is a Christ-centered reason, you may not really belong. You don't have to settle for less than the best. You can become personally acquainted with Jesus Christ and become a loyal, trustworthy follower.

2:20 When a person becomes a Christian, he or she receives the Holy Spirit. One way the Holy Spirit helps the believer and the church is by communicating truth. Jesus is the truth (John 14:6), and the Holy Spirit guides believers to him (John 16:13). People who are opposed to Christ are also opposed to his truth, and the Holy Spirit is not working in their lives. When we are led by the Spirit, we can stand against false teachers and the Antichrist. Ask the Spirit to guide you each day (see 2:27).

2:22, 23 Apparently the antichrists in John's day were claiming faith in God while denying and opposing Christ. To do so, John firmly states, is impossible. Because Jesus is God's Son and the Messiah, to deny Christ is to reject God's way of revealing himself to the world. A person who accepts Christ as God's Son, however, accepts God the Father at the same time. The two are one and cannot be separated. Many cultists today call themselves Christians, but they deny that Jesus is divine. We must expose these heresies and oppose such teachings so that the weak believers among us do not succumb to their teachings.

2:24 These Christians had heard the Good News, very likely from John himself. They knew that Christ was God's Son, that he died for their sins and was raised to give them new life, and that he would return and establish his Kingdom in its fullness. But their fellowship was being infiltrated by teachers who denied these basic doctrines of the Christian faith, and some of the believers were in danger of succumbing to false arguments. John encouraged them to hold on to the Christian truth they heard at the beginning of their walk with Christ. It is important to grow in our knowledge of the Lord, to deepen our understanding through careful study, and to teach these truths to others. But no matter how much we learn, we must never abandon the basic truths about Christ. Jesus will always be God's Son, and his sacrifice for our sins is permanent. No truth will ever contradict these teachings in the Bible.

2:26, 27 Christ had promised to send the Holy Spirit to teach his followers and to remind them of all that Christ had taught (John 14:26). As a result, Christians have the Holy Spirit within them to keep them from going astray. In addition, they have the God-inspired Scriptures, against which they can test questionable teachings. To stay true to Christ, we must follow his Word and his Spirit. Let the Holy Spirit help you discern truth from error. For more about who the Holy Spirit is and what he does, see the notes on John 3:6, Acts 1:5, and Ephesians 1:13, 14.

2:27 Christ lives in us through the Holy Spirit, and we also live in Christ. This means that we place our total trust in him, rely on him for guidance and strength, and live as he wants us to live. It implies a personal, life-giving relationship. John uses the same idea in John 15:5, where he speaks of Christ as the vine and his followers as the branches (see also 3:24; 4:15).

2:28, 29 The visible proof of being a Christian is right behavior. Many people do good deeds but don't have faith in Jesus Christ. Others claim to have faith but rarely produce good deeds. A deficit in either faith or right behavior will be a cause for shame when Christ returns. Because true faith always results in good deeds, those who claim to have faith *and* who consistently do what is right are true believers. Good deeds cannot produce salvation (see Ephesians 2:8, 9), but they are necessary proof that true faith is actually present (James 2:14-17).

2. God is love

Living as Children of God

3 See how very much our heavenly Father loves us, for he allows us to be called his
children, and we really are! But the people who belong to this world don't know
God, so they don't understand that we are his children. 2 Yes, dear friends, we are already
God's children, and we can't even imagine what we will be like when Christ returns. But
we do know that when he comes we will be like him, for we will see him as he really is.
3 And all who believe this will keep themselves pure, just as Christ is pure.
4 Those who sin are opposed to the law of God, for all sin opposes the law of God.
5 And you know that Jesus came to take away our sins, for there is no sin in him. 6 So if
we continue to live in him, we won't sin either. But those who keep on sinning have never
known him or understood who he is.
7 Dear children, don't let anyone deceive you about this: When people do what is right,
it is because they are righteous, even as Christ is righteous. 8 But when people keep on
sinning, it shows they belong to the Devil, who has been sinning since the beginning.
But the Son of God came to destroy these works of the Devil. 9 Those who have been
born into God's family do not sin, because God's life is in them. So they can't keep on
sinning, because they have been born of God. 10 So now we can tell who are children of
God and who are children of the Devil. Anyone who does not obey God's commands
and does not love other Christians* does not belong to God.

Love One Another

11 This is the message we have heard from the beginning: We should love one another. 12 We
must not be like Cain, who belonged to the evil one and killed his brother. And why did he
kill him? Because Cain had been doing what was evil, and his brother had been doing what
was right. 13 So don't be surprised, dear brothers and sisters, if the world hates you.

3:10 Greek *his brother;* also in 3:15.

3:1 John 1:12-13; 16:3; 17:26; Rom 8:16; Eph 1:4-5
3:2 John 17:24; Rom 8:19, 29; 2 Cor 3:18; Phil 3:21
3:4 Matt 7:23
3:5 Isa 53:1-12; John 1:29; 2 Cor 5:21
3:6 Rom 6:14; 1 Jn 3:9
3:8 John 8:44
3:9 Jas 1:18; 1 Pet 1:3
3:10 John 1:12-13
3:11 John 13:34; 15:12; 2 Jn 1:5
3:12 Gen 4:3-8
3:13 John 15:18

3:1 As believers, our self-worth is based on the fact that God loves us and calls us his children. We are his children *now,* not just sometime in the distant future. Knowing that we are his children should encourage us to live as Jesus did. For other references about being part of God's family, see Romans 8:14-17; Galatians 3:26, 27; 4:6, 7.

3:1ff Verse 1 tells us who we are—members of God's family, his children. Verse 2 tells us who we are becoming—reflections of God. The rest of the chapter tells us what we have as we grow to resemble God: (1) victory over sin (3:4-9); (2) love for others (3:10-18); and (3) confidence before God (3:19-24).

3:2, 3 The Christian life is a process of becoming more and more like Christ (see Romans 8:29). This process will not be complete until we see Christ face to face (1 Corinthians 13:12; Philippians 3:21), but knowing that it is our ultimate destiny should motivate us to purify ourselves. To keep pure means to keep morally straight, free from the corruption of sin. God also purifies us, but there is action we must take to remain morally fit (see 1 Timothy 5:22; James 4:8; 1 Peter 1:22).

3:4ff There is a difference between committing a sin and continuing to sin. Even the most faithful believers sometimes commit sins, but they do not cherish a particular sin and choose to commit it. A believer who commits a sin repents, confesses, and finds forgiveness. A person who continues to sin, by contrast, is not sorry for what he or she is doing. Thus, this person never confesses and never receives forgiveness. Such a person is in opposition to God, no matter what religious claims he or she makes.

3:5 Under the Old Testament sacrifice system, a lamb without blemish was offered as a sacrifice for sin. Jesus is "the Lamb of God who takes away the sin of the world" (John 1:29). Because Jesus lived a perfect life and sacrificed himself for our sins, we can be completely forgiven (2:2). We can look back to his death for us and know that we need never suffer eternal death (1 Peter 1:18-20).

3:8, 9 We all have areas where temptation is strong and habits are hard to conquer. These weaknesses give the Devil a foothold, so we must deal with our areas of vulnerability. If we are struggling with a particular sin, however, these verses are not directed at us, even if for the time we seem to keep on sinning. John is not talking about people whose victories are still incomplete; he is talking about people who make a practice of sinning and look for ways to justify it.

Three steps are necessary to find victory over prevailing sin: (1) Seek the power of the Holy Spirit and God's Word; (2) stay away from tempting situations; and (3) seek the help of the body of Christ—be open to their willingness to hold you accountable and to pray for you.

3:9 "They can't keep on sinning" means that true believers do not make a practice of sinning, nor do they become indifferent to God's moral law. All believers still sin, but they are working to gain victory over sin.

3:9 We are "born of God" when the Holy Spirit lives in us and gives us Jesus' new life. Being born again is more than a fresh start; it is a rebirth, receiving a new family name based on Christ's death for us. When this happens, God forgives us and totally accepts us; the Holy Spirit gives us a new mind and heart, lives in us, and begins helping us to become like Christ. Our perspective changes, too, because we have a mind that is renewed day by day by the Holy Spirit (see Romans 12:2; Ephesians 4:22-24). So we must begin to think and act differently. See John 3:1-21 for more on being born again.

3:12, 13 Cain killed his brother, Abel, when God accepted Abel's offering and not his (Genesis 4:1-16). Abel's offering showed that Cain was not giving his best to God, and Cain's jealous anger drove him to murder. People who are morally upright expose and shame those who aren't. If we live for God, the world will often hate us, because we make them painfully aware of their immoral way of living.

14 If we love other Christians,* it proves that we have passed from death to eternal life.
But a person who doesn't love them is still dead. 15 Anyone who hates another Christian
is really a murderer at heart. And you know that murderers don't have eternal life within
them. 16 We know what real love is because Christ gave up his life for us. And so we also
ought to give up our lives for our Christian friends.* 17 But if one of you has enough
money to live well, and sees a brother or sister in need and refuses to help—how can
God's love be in that person?

18 Dear children, let us stop just saying we love each other; let us really show it by our
actions. 19 It is by our actions that we know we are living in the truth, so we will be
confident when we stand before the Lord, 20 even if our hearts condemn us. For God is
greater than our hearts, and he knows everything.

21 Dear friends, if our conscience is clear, we can come to God with bold confidence.
22 And we will receive whatever we request because we obey him and do the things that
please him. 23 And this is his commandment: We must believe in the name of his Son,
Jesus Christ, and love one another, just as he commanded us. 24 Those who obey God's
commandments live in fellowship with him, and he with them. And we know he lives in
us because the Holy Spirit lives in us.

Discerning False Prophets

4 Dear friends, do not believe everyone who claims to speak by the Spirit. You must
test them to see if the spirit they have comes from God. For there are many false
prophets in the world. 2 This is the way to find out if they have the Spirit of God: If a
prophet acknowledges that Jesus Christ became a human being, that person has the Spirit
of God. 3 If a prophet does not acknowledge Jesus, that person is not from God. Such a

3:14 Greek *the brothers.* **3:16** Greek *the brothers.*

3:15 Matt 5:21-22; John 8:44
3:16 John 13:1; 15:13; Phil 2:17
3:17 Deut 15:7-8; Jas 2:15
3:18 Rom 12:9; Jas 1:22
3:19 John 18:37
3:21 Rom 5:1
3:22 Matt 7:7; John 8:29; 14:13
3:23 John 6:29; 13:34
3:24 Rom 8:9
4:1 1 Thes 5:21; 1 Jn 2:18
4:2 John 1:14; 1 Cor 12:3
4:3 2 Jn 1:7

3:15 John echoes Jesus' teaching that whoever hates another person is a murderer at heart (Matthew 5:21, 22). Christianity is a religion of the heart; outward compliance alone is not enough. Bitterness against someone who has wronged you is an evil cancer within you and will eventually destroy you. Don't let a "bitter root" (Hebrews 12:15) grow in you or your church.

3:16 Real love is an action, not a feeling. It produces selfless, sacrificial giving. The greatest act of love is giving oneself for others. How can we "give up our life"? By serving others with no thought of receiving anything in return. Sometimes it is easier to say we'll die for others than to truly live for them—this involves putting others' desires first. Jesus taught this same principle of love in John 15:13.

3:17, 18 These verses give an example of how to give up our life for others—to help those in need. This is strikingly similar to James' teaching (James 2:14-17). How clearly do your actions say you really love others? Are you as generous as you should be with your money, possessions, and time?

3:19, 20 Many are afraid that they don't love others as they should. They feel guilty because they think they are not doing enough to show proper love to Christ. Their consciences bother them. John has these people in mind in this letter. How do we escape the gnawing accusations of our consciences? Not by ignoring them or rationalizing our behavior but by setting our heart on God's love. When we feel guilty, we should remind ourselves that God knows our motives as well as our actions. His voice of assurance is stronger than the accusing voice of our conscience. If we are in Christ, he will not condemn us (Romans 8:1; Hebrews 9:14, 15). So if you are living for the Lord but feeling that you are not good enough, remind yourself that God is greater than your conscience.

3:21, 22 If your conscience is clear, you can come to God without fear, confident that your requests will be heard. John reaffirms Jesus' promise that whatever we ask for will be given to us (Matthew 7:7; see also Matthew 21:22; John 9:31; 15:7). You will receive if you obey and do what pleases him because you will then be asking in line with God's will. Of course this does not mean that you can have anything you want, like instant riches. If you are truly seeking God's will, there are some requests you will not make.

3:23 In the Bible, a person's name stands for his or her character. It represents who he or she really is. We are to believe not only in Jesus' words, but also in his very person as the Son of God. Moreover, to believe "in the name" means to pattern your life after Christ's, to become more like him by uniting yourself with him. And if we are living like Christ, we will "love one another."

3:24 The mutual relationship, living in Christ as he lives in us, shows itself in Christians who keep these three essential commands: (1) Believe in Christ, (2) love the brothers and sisters, and (3) live a morally upright life. The Spirit's presence is not only spiritual and mystical, but it is also practical. Our conduct verifies his presence.

4:1, 2 "Do not believe everyone who claims to speak by the Spirit. You must test them to see if the spirit they have comes from God" means that we shouldn't believe everything we hear just because someone says it is a message from God. There are many ways to test teachers to see if their message is truly from the Lord. One is to check to see if their words match what God says in the Bible. Other tests include their commitment to the body of believers (2:19), their life-style (3:23, 24), and the fruit of their ministry (4:6). But the most important test of all, says John, is what they believe about Christ. Do they teach that Jesus is fully God and fully man? Our world is filled with voices claiming to speak for God. Give them these tests to see if they are indeed speaking God's truth.

4:1-3 Some people believe everything they read or hear. Unfortunately, many ideas printed and taught are not true. Christians should have faith, but they should not be gullible. Verify every message you hear, even if the person who brings it says it's from God. If the message is truly from God, it will be consistent with Christ's teachings.

4:3 The Antichrist will be a person who epitomizes all that is evil, and he will be readily received by an evil world. He is more fully described in 2 Thessalonians 2:3-12 and Revelation 13. The "spirit of the Antichrist" is already here (see the note on 2:18-23).

4:4 John 12:31; Rom 8:31; 1 Jn 2:1
4:5 John 15:19; 17:14, 16
4:6 John 8:47; 14:17; 1 Cor 14:37; 1 Tim 4:1
4:7 1 Jn 2:29; 3:11
4:9 John 3:16
4:10 Rom 5:8, 10; 1 Jn 2:2

person has the spirit of the Antichrist. You have heard that he is going to come into the
world, and he is already here.
4 But you belong to God, my dear children. You have already won your fight with these
false prophets, because the Spirit who lives in you is greater than the spirit who lives in
the world. 5 These people belong to this world, so they speak from the world's viewpoint,
and the world listens to them. 6 But we belong to God; that is why those who know God
listen to us. If they do not belong to God, they do not listen to us. That is how we know
if someone has the Spirit of truth or the spirit of deception.

Loving One Another

7 Dear friends, let us continue to love one another, for love comes from God. Anyone
who loves is born of God and knows God. 8 But anyone who does not love does not know
God—for God is love.
9 God showed how much he loved us by sending his only Son into the world so that
we might have eternal life through him. 10 This is real love. It is not that we loved God,
but that he loved us and sent his Son as a sacrifice to take away our sins.

HERESIES

Most of the eyewitnesses to Jesus' ministry had died by the time John composed this letter. Some of the second- or third-generation Christians began to have doubts about what they had been taught about Jesus. Some Christians with a Greek background had a hard time believing that Jesus was human as well as divine, because in Platonic thought the spirit was all-important. The body was only a prison from which one desired to escape. Heresies developed from a uniting of this kind of Platonic thought and Christianity.

A particularly widespread false teaching, later called *Docetism* (from a Greek word meaning "to seem"), held that Jesus was actually a spirit who only appeared to have a body. In reality he cast no shadow and left no footprints; he was God but not man. Another heretical teaching, related to *Gnosticism* (from a Greek word meaning "knowledge"), held that all physical matter was evil, the spirit was good, and only the intellectually enlightened could enjoy the benefits of religion. Both groups found it hard to believe in a Savior who was fully human.

John answers these false teachers as an eyewitness to Jesus' life on earth. He saw Jesus, talked with him, touched him—he knew that Jesus was more than a mere spirit. In the very first sentence of his letter, John establishes that Jesus had been alive before the world began and also that he lived as a man among men and women. In other words, he was both divine and human.

Through the centuries, many heretics have denied that Jesus was both God and man. In John's day people had trouble believing he was human; today more people have problems seeing him as God. But Jesus' divine-human nature is the pivotal issue of Christianity. Before you accept what religious teachers say about any topic, listen carefully to what they believe about Jesus. To deny either his divinity or his humanity is to consider him less than Christ, the Savior.

4:4 It is easy to be frightened by the wickedness we see all around us and to be overwhelmed by the problems we face. Evil is obviously much stronger than we are. John assures us, however, that God is even stronger. He will conquer all evil—and his Spirit and his Word live in our heart!

4:6 False teachers are popular with the world because, like the false prophets of the Old Testament, they tell people what they want to hear. John warns that Christians who faithfully teach God's Word will not win any popularity contests in the world. People don't want to hear their sins denounced; they don't want to listen to demands that they change their behavior. A false teacher will be well received by non-Christians.

4:7ff Everyone believes that love is important, but love is usually thought of as a feeling. In reality, love is a choice and an action, as 1 Corinthians 13:4-7 shows. God is the source of our love: He loved us enough to sacrifice his Son for us. Jesus is our example of what it means to love; everything he did in life and death was supremely loving. The Holy Spirit gives us the power to love; He lives in our heart and makes us more and more like Christ. God's love always involves a choice and an action, and our love should be like his. How well do you display your love for God in the choices you make and the actions you take?

4:8 John says, "God is love," not "Love is God." Our world, with its shallow and selfish view of love, has turned these words around and contaminated our understanding of love. The world thinks that love is what makes a person feel good and that it is all right to sacrifice moral principles and others' rights in order to obtain such "love." But that isn't real love; it is the exact opposite—selfishness. And God is not that kind of "love." Real love is like God, who is holy, just, and perfect. If we truly know God, we will love as he does.

4:9 Jesus is God's *only* Son. While all believers are sons and daughters of God, only Jesus lives in this special unique relationship (see John 1:18; 3:16).

4:9, 10 Love explains (1) why God creates—because he loves, he creates people to love; (2) why God cares—because he loves them, he cares for sinful people; (3) why we are free to choose—God wants a loving response from us; (4) why Christ died—his love for us caused him to offer a solution to the problem of sin; and (5) why we receive eternal life—God's love expresses itself to us forever.

4:10 Nothing sinful or evil can exist in God's presence. He is absolute goodness. He cannot overlook, condone, or excuse sin as though it never happened. He loves us, but his love does not

[11]Dear friends, since God loved us that much, we surely ought to love each other. [12]No
one has ever seen God. But if we love each other, God lives in us, and his love has been
brought to full expression through us.
[13]And God has given us his Spirit as proof that we live in him and he in us.
[14]Furthermore, we have seen with our own eyes and now testify that the Father sent his
Son to be the Savior of the world. [15]All who proclaim that Jesus is the Son of God have
God living in them, and they live in God. [16]We know how much God loves us, and we
have put our trust in him.
God is love, and all who live in love live in God, and God lives in them. [17]And as we
live in God, our love grows more perfect. So we will not be afraid on the day of judgment,
but we can face him with confidence because we are like Christ here in this world.
[18]Such love has no fear because perfect love expels all fear. If we are afraid, it is for
fear of judgment, and this shows that his love has not been perfected in us. [19]We love
each other* as a result of his loving us first.
[20]If someone says, "I love God," but hates another Christian,* that person is a liar; for
if we don't love people we can see, how can we love God, whom we have not seen?
[21]And God himself has commanded that we must love not only him but our Christian
brothers and sisters, too.

4:11 Matt 18:33
4:12 John 1:18; 14:23; 1 Tim 6:16
4:13 Rom 8:9; 1 Jn 3:24
4:14 John 1:14; 3:17; 4:42; 1 Jn 2:2
4:15 John 6:69; 1 Jn 5:5
4:17 1 Jn 2:5; 3:21
4:18 Rom 8:15
4:20 1 Jn 2:4; 3:17
4:21 Matt 5:43; 22:37-39

3. God is life

Faith in the Son of God

5 Everyone who believes that Jesus is the Christ is a child of God. And everyone who
loves the Father loves his children, too. [2]We know we love God's children if we love
God and obey his commandments. [3]Loving God means keeping his commandments, and
really, that isn't difficult. [4]For every child of God defeats this evil world by trusting
Christ to give the victory. [5]And the ones who win this battle against the world are the
ones who believe that Jesus is the Son of God.
[6]And Jesus Christ was revealed as God's Son by his baptism in water and by shedding

5:1 John 1:13; 3:3; 8:42
5:3 Matt 11:30; John 14:15
5:5 Rom 8:37
5:6 John 1:31-34; 14:7; 19:34-35

4:19 Or *We love him;* Greek reads *We love.* **4:20** Greek *brother.*

make him morally lax. If we trust in Christ, however, we will not have to bear the penalty for our sins (1 Peter 2:24). We will be acquitted (Romans 5:18) by his atoning sacrifice.

4:12 If no one has ever seen God, how can we ever know him? John in his Gospel said, "His only Son, who is himself God, is near to the Father's heart; he has told us about him" (John 1:18). Jesus is the complete expression of God in human form, and he has revealed God to us. When we love one another, the invisible God reveals himself to others through us, and his love is made complete.

4:12 Some people enjoy being with others. They make friends with strangers easily and always are surrounded by many friends. Other people are shy or reserved. They have a few friends, but they are uncomfortable talking with people they don't know or mingling in crowds. Shy people don't need to become extroverts in order to love others. John isn't telling us *how many* people to love, but *how much* to love the people we already know. Our job is to love faithfully the people God has given us to love, whether there are two or two hundred of them. If God sees that we are ready to love others, he will bring them to us. No matter how shy we are, we don't need to be afraid of the love commandment. God provides us the strength to do what he asks.

4:13 When we become Christians, we receive the Holy Spirit. God's presence in our life is proof that we really belong to him. He also gives us the power to love (Romans 5:5; 8:9; 2 Corinthians 1:22). Rely on that power as you reach out to others. As you do so, you will gain confidence. See also Romans 8:16.

4:17 The day of judgment is that time when all people will appear before Christ and be held accountable for their actions. With God living in us through Christ, we have no reason to fear this day because we have been saved from punishment. Instead, we can look forward to the day of judgment because it will mean the end of sin and the beginning of a face-to-face relationship with Jesus Christ.

4:18 If we ever are afraid of the future, eternity, or God's judgment, we can remind ourselves of God's love. We know that he loves us perfectly (Romans 8:38, 39). We can resolve our fears first by focusing on his immeasurable love for us, and then by allowing him to love others through us. His love will quiet your fears and give you confidence.

4:19 God's love is the source of all human love, and it spreads like fire. In loving his children, God kindles a flame in their hearts. In turn, they love others, who are warmed by God's love through them.

4:20, 21 It is easy to say we love God when that love doesn't cost us anything more than weekly attendance at religious services. But the real test of our love for God is how we treat the people right in front of us—our family members and fellow believers. We cannot truly love God while neglecting to love those who are created in his image.

5:1, 2 When we become Christians, we become part of God's family, with fellow believers as our brothers and sisters. It is God who determines who the other family members are, not us. We are simply called to accept and love them. How well do you treat your fellow family members?

5:3, 4 Jesus never promised that obeying him would be easy. But the hard work and self-discipline of serving Christ is no burden to those who love him. And if our load starts to feel heavy, we can always trust Christ to help us bear it (see Matthew 11:28-30).

5:6-8 At this time, there was a false teaching in circulation that said Jesus was "the Christ" only between his baptism and his death—that is, he was merely human until he was baptized, at which time "the Christ" then descended upon him but then later left him before his death on the cross. But if Jesus died only as a

his blood on the cross*—not by water only, but by water and blood. And the Spirit also
gives us the testimony that this is true. 7 So we have these three witnesses*—8 the Spirit, the
water, and the blood—and all three agree. 9 Since we believe human testimony, surely we
can believe the testimony that comes from God. And God has testified about his Son. 10 All
who believe in the Son of God know that this is true. Those who don't believe this are
actually calling God a liar because they don't believe what God has testified about his Son.
11 And this is what God has testified: He has given us eternal life, and this life is in his
Son. 12 So whoever has God's Son has life; whoever does not have his Son does not have life.

Conclusion

13 I write this to you who believe in the Son of God, so that you may know you have
eternal life. 14 And we can be confident that he will listen to us whenever we ask him for
anything in line with his will. 15 And if we know he is listening when we make our
requests, we can be sure that he will give us what we ask for.
16 If you see any Christian* sinning in a way that does not lead to death, you should
pray, and God will give that person life. But there is a sin that leads to death, and I am
not saying you should pray for those who commit it. 17 Every wrong is sin, but not all sin
leads to death.
18 We know that those who have become part of God's family do not make a practice
of sinning, for God's Son holds them securely, and the evil one cannot get his hands on
them. 19 We know that we are children of God and that the world around us is under the
power and control of the evil one. 20 And we know that the Son of God has come, and he
has given us understanding so that we can know the true God. And now we are in God
because we are in his Son, Jesus Christ. He is the only true God, and he is eternal life.
21 Dear children, keep away from anything that might take God's place in your hearts.*

5:9 Matt 3:16-17; John 5:32-37; 8:17-18
5:10 John 3:33; Rom 8:16; Gal 4:6
5:12 John 3:15-16, 36; 5:24; 14:6; 17:2-3; 2 Jn 1:9
5:13 John 20:31
5:14 Matt 7:7; John 14:13; 15:7
5:16 Exod 23:21; Jer 7:16; 14:11; Matt 12:31; Heb 6:4-6; 10:26; Jas 5:15
5:18 John 10:28-29; 1 Jn 2:13; 3:9
5:20 Luke 24:45; John 1:1, 4; 17:3; Rom 9:5; Rev 3:7
5:21 1 Cor 10:14; 1 Thes 1:9

5:6 Greek *This is he who came by water and blood.* **5:7** Some very late manuscripts add *in heaven—the Father, the Word, and the Holy Spirit, and these three are one. And we have three witnesses on earth.* **5:16** Greek *your brother.* **5:21** Greek *keep yourselves from idols.*

---

man, he could not have taken upon himself the sins of the world, and Christianity would be an empty religion. Only an act of God could take away the punishment that we deserve for our sin.

5:7-9 The Gospels twice record God's clear declaration that Jesus was his Son—at Jesus' baptism (Matthew 3:16, 17) and at his transfiguration (Matthew 17:5).

5:12 Whoever believes in God's Son has eternal life. He is all you need. You don't need to *wait* for eternal life because it begins the moment you believe. You don't need to *work* for it because it is already yours. You don't need to *worry* about it because you have been given eternal life by God himself—and it is guaranteed.

5:13 Some people *hope* that they will receive eternal life. John says we can *know* we have it. Our certainty is based on God's promise that he has given us eternal life through his Son. This is true whether you feel close to God or far away from him. Eternal life is not based on feelings but on facts. You can know that you have eternal life if you believe God's truth. If you aren't sure that you are a Christian, ask yourself: Have I honestly committed my life to him as my Savior and Lord? If so, you know by faith that you are indeed a child of God.

5:14, 15 The emphasis here is on God's will, not our will. When we communicate with God, we don't demand what we want; rather we discuss with him what *he* wants for us. If we align our prayers to his will, he will listen; and we can be certain that if he listens, he will give us a definite answer. Start praying with confidence!

5:16, 17 Commentators differ widely in their thoughts about what this sin that leads to death is and whether the death it causes is physical or spiritual. Paul wrote that some Christians had died because they took Communion in an unworthy manner (1 Corinthians 11:27-30), and Ananias and Sapphira were struck dead when they lied to God (Acts 5:1-11). Blasphemy against the Holy Spirit results in spiritual death (Mark 3:29), and the book of Hebrews describes the spiritual death of the person who turns against Christ (Hebrews 6:4-6). John was probably referring to the people who had left the Christian fellowship and joined the antichrists. By rejecting the only way of salvation, these people were putting themselves out of reach of prayer. In most cases, however, even if we knew what the terrible sin is, we would have no sure way of knowing whether a certain person had committed it. Therefore, we should continue praying for our loved ones and for our Christian brothers and sisters, leaving the judgment up to God. Note that John says, "I am not saying you should pray for those who commit it," rather than, "You cannot pray for them." He recognized the lack of certainty.

5:18, 19 Christians commit sins, of course, but they ask God to forgive them, and then they continue serving him. God has freed believers from their slavery to Satan, and he keeps them safe from Satan's continued attacks. The rest of the world does not have the Christian's freedom to obey God. Unless they come to Christ in faith, they have no choice but to obey Satan. There is no middle ground; people either belong to God and obey him, or they live under Satan's control.

5:21 Many things can take God's place in our life. This includes anything that substitutes for the true faith, anything that robs Christ of his full deity and humanity, any human idea that claims to be more authoritative than the Bible, any loyalty that replaces God at the center of our life.

5:21 John presents a clear picture of Christ. What we think about Jesus Christ is central to our teaching, preaching, and living. Jesus is the God-man, fully God and fully human at the same time. He came to earth to die in our place for our sins. Through faith in him, we are given eternal life and the power to do his will. What is your answer to the most important question you could ever ask: Who is Jesus Christ?

2 JOHN

VITAL STATISTICS

PURPOSE:
To emphasize the basics of following Christ—truth and love—and to warn against false teachers

AUTHOR:
The apostle John

TO WHOM WRITTEN:
To "the chosen lady" and her children—or possibly to a local church and all believers everywhere

DATE WRITTEN:
About the same time as 1 John, approximately A.D. 90 from Ephesus

SETTING:
Evidently this woman and her family were involved in one of the churches that John was overseeing—they had developed a strong friendship with John. John was warning her of the false teachers who were becoming prevalent in some of the churches.

KEY VERSE:
"Love means doing what God has commanded us, and he has commanded us to love one another, just as you heard from the beginning" (1:6).

KEY PEOPLE:
John, the chosen lady, and her children

TRUTH and love are frequently discussed in our world but seldom practiced.

From politicians to salesmen, people conveniently ignore or conceal facts and use words to enhance positions or sell products. Perjury is common, and integrity and credibility are endangered species. Words, twisted in meaning and torn from context, have become mere tools for ego building. It is not surprising that we have to "swear" to tell the truth.

And what about love? Our world is filled with its words: Popular songs, greeting cards, media counselors, and romantic novels shower us with notions and dreams of ethereal, idyllic relationships and feelings. Real love, however, is scarce—selfless giving, caring, sharing, and even dying. We yearn to love and be loved but see few living examples of real love. Plentiful are those who grasp, hoard, and watch out for "number one."

Christ is the antithesis of society's prevailing values, that is, falsehood and self-centeredness—for *he is truth and love* in person. Therefore, all who claim loyalty to him must be committed to these ideals—following the truth and living the truth, reflecting love and acting with love toward one another.

The apostle John had seen Truth and Love firsthand—he had been with Jesus. So affected was this disciple that all of his writings, from the Gospel to the book of Revelation, are filled with this theme: Truth and love are vital to the Christian and are inseparable in the Christian life. Second John, his brief letter to a dear friend, is no different. John says to live in the truth and obey God (1:4), watch out for deceivers (1:7), and love God and each other (1:6).

Second John will take just a few minutes to read, but its message should last a lifetime. As you reflect on these few paragraphs penned by the wise and aged follower of Christ, recommit yourself to being a person of truth, of love, and of obedience.

THE BLUEPRINT

1. Watch out for false teachers (1:1–11) 2. John's final words (1:12, 13)	False teachers were a dangerous problem for the church to which John was writing. His warning against showing hospitality to false teachers may sound harsh and unloving to many today. Yet these men were teaching heresy that could seriously harm many believers—for eternity.

MEGATHEMES

THEME	EXPLANATION	IMPORTANCE
Truth	Following God's Word, the Bible, is essential to Christian living because God is truth. Christ's true followers consistently obey his truth.	To be loyal to Christ's teaching, we must seek to know the Bible, but we may never twist its message to our own needs or purposes or encourage others who misuse it.
Love	Christ's command is for Christians to love one another. This is the basic ingredient of true Christianity.	To obey Christ fully, we must believe his command to love others. Helping, giving, and meeting needs put love into practice.
False Leaders	We must be wary of religious leaders who are not true to Christ's teaching. We should not give them a platform to spread false teaching.	Don't encourage those who are opposed to Christ. Politely remove yourself from association with false leaders. Be aware of what is being taught in your church.

1. Watch out for false teachers

Greetings

1:1 (1 Pet 5:13; 1 Jn 3:18; 3 Jn 1:1) This letter is from John the Elder.*
It is written to the chosen lady and to her children,* whom I love in the truth, as does
everyone else who knows God's truth—2 the truth that lives in us and will be in our hearts
forever.
3 May grace, mercy, and peace, which come from God our Father and from Jesus
Christ his Son, be with us who live in truth and love.

1:2 (John 8:32; 14:17; 1 Jn 1:8; 3:18)
1:3 (1 Tim 1:2)

Live in the Truth

4 How happy I was to meet some of your children and find them living in the truth, just
as we have been commanded by the Father.
5 And now I want to urge you, dear lady, that we should love one another. This is not
a new commandment, but one we had from the beginning. 6 Love means doing what God
has commanded us, and he has commanded us to love one another, just as you heard
from the beginning.

1:4 (3 Jn 1:3-4)
1:5 (John 13:34; 15:12; 1 Jn 2:7)
1:6 (John 14:15, 23-24; 1 Jn 2:5, 7; 4:7-12; 5:3)

1a Greek *From the elder.* **1b** Or *the church God has chosen and her members,* or *the chosen Kyria and her children.*

1:1 The "Elder" is John, one of Jesus' 12 disciples and the writer of the Gospel of John, three letters, and the book of Revelation. For more information about John, see his Profile in John 13. This letter was written shortly after 1 John to warn about false teachers. The salutation "to the chosen lady and to her children" could refer to a specific woman or to a church whose identity is no longer known. John may have written this from Ephesus.

1:1-4 The "truth" is the truth about Jesus Christ, as opposed to the lies of the false teachers (see 1 John 2:21-23).

1:5, 6 The statement that Christians should love one another is a recurrent New Testament theme. Yet love for one's neighbor is an old command, first appearing in the third book of Moses (Leviticus 19:18). We can show love in many ways: by avoiding prejudice and discrimination, by accepting people, by listening, helping, giving, serving, and refusing to judge. Knowing God's command is not enough. We must put it into practice, "doing what God has commanded us" (see also Matthew 22:37-39 and 1 John 2:7, 8).

[7]Many deceivers have gone out into the world. They do not believe that Jesus Christ
came to earth in a real body. Such a person is a deceiver and an antichrist. [8]Watch out, so
that you do not lose the prize for which we* have been working so hard. Be diligent so
that you will receive your full reward. [9]For if you wander beyond the teaching of Christ,
you will not have fellowship with God. But if you continue in the teaching of Christ, you
will have fellowship with both the Father and the Son.
[10]If someone comes to your meeting and does not teach the truth about Christ, don't
invite him into your house or encourage him in any way. [11]Anyone who encourages him
becomes a partner in his evil work.

1:7 1 Tim 4:1-5; 2 Pet 2:1-3; 1 Jn 2:18, 26; 4:1-3
1:8 1 Cor 3:8-9
1:9 John 8:31; 1 Jn 2:23
1:10 Rom 16:17; Eph 5:11

2. John's final words

[12]Well, I have much more to say to you, but I don't want to say it in a letter. For I hope
to visit you soon and to talk with you face to face. Then our joy will be complete.
[13]Greetings from the children of your sister,* chosen by God.

1:12 Num 12:8; 1 Jn 1:4; 3 Jn 1:13-14

8 Some manuscripts read *you.* **13** Or *from the members of your sister church.*

1:7 In John's day, many false teachers taught that spirit was good and matter was evil; therefore, they reasoned that Jesus could not have been both God and man. In strong terms, John warns against this kind of teaching. There are still many false teachers who promote an understanding of Jesus that is not biblical. These teachers are dangerous because they distort the truth and undermine the foundations of Christian faith. They may use the right words but change the meanings. The way your teachers live shows a lot about what they believe about Christ. For more on testing teachers, see 1 John 4:1.

1:8 To "receive your full reward" refers not to salvation but to the rewards of loyal service. All who value the truth and persistently hold to it will win their full reward. Those who live for themselves and justify their self-centeredness by teaching false doctrines will lose that reward (see Matthew 7:21-23).

1:10 John instructed the believers not to show hospitality to false teachers. They were to do nothing that would encourage the heretics in their propagation of falsehoods. In addition, if believers were to invite them in, such action would show that they were approving of what the false teachers said and did. It may seem rude to turn people away, even if they are teaching heresy, but how much better it is to be faithful to God than merely courteous to people! John is condemning the support of those who are dedicated to opposing the true teachings of God, not condemning hospitality to unbelievers. John adds that a person who supports a false teacher in any way shares in the teacher's wicked work.

1:10 False teaching is serious business, and we dare not overlook it. It is so serious that John wrote this letter to warn against it. There are so many false teachings in our world that we might be tempted to take many of them lightly. Instead, we should realize the dangers they pose and actively refuse to give heresies any foothold.

3 JOHN

BY special invitation or with a surprise knock, company arrives and with them comes the promise of soiled floors, extra laundry, dirty dishes, altered schedules, personal expense, and inconvenience. From sharing a meal to providing a bed, *hospitality* costs . . . in time, energy, and money. But how we treat others reflects our true values—what is really important to us. Do we see people as objects or inconveniences, or as unique creations of a loving God? And which is more important to God, a person or a carpet? Perhaps the most effective way to demonstrate God's values and Christ's love to others is to invite and welcome guests into our home.

For Gaius, hospitality was a habit, and his reputation for friendship and generosity, especially to traveling teachers and missionaries (1:5), had spread. To affirm and thank Gaius for his Christian lifestyle, and to encourage him in his faith, John wrote this personal note.

John's format for this letter centers around three men: Gaius, the example of one who follows Christ and loves others (1:1–8); Diotrephes, the self-proclaimed church leader who does not reflect God's values (1:9–11); and Demetrius, who also follows the truth (1:12). John encourages Gaius to practice hospitality, continue to walk in the truth, and do what is right.

Although this is a personal letter, we can "look over the shoulder" of Gaius and apply its lessons to our life. As you read 3 John, with which man do you identify? Are you a Gaius, generously giving to others? a Demetrius, loving the truth? or a Diotrephes, looking out for yourself and your "things"? Determine to reflect Christ's values in your relationships, opening your home and touching others with his love.

VITAL STATISTICS

PURPOSE:
To commend Gaius for his hospitality and to encourage him in his Christian life

AUTHOR:
The apostle John

TO WHOM WRITTEN:
Gaius, a prominent Christian in one of the churches known to John, and to all Christians

DATE WRITTEN:
Approximately A.D. 90 from Ephesus

SETTING:
Church leaders traveled from town to town helping to establish new congregations. They depended on the hospitality of fellow believers. Gaius was one who welcomed these leaders into his home.

KEY VERSE:
"Dear friend, you are doing a good work for God when you take care of the traveling teachers who are passing through, even though they are strangers to you" (1:5).

KEY PEOPLE:
John, Gaius, Diotrephes, Demetrius

THE BLUEPRINT

1. God's children live by the standards of the gospel (1:1–12)
2. John's final words (1:13–15)

John wrote to commend Gaius, who was taking care of traveling teachers and missionaries, and to warn against people like Diotrephes, who was proud and refused to listen to spiritual leaders in authority. If we are to live in the truth of the gospel, we must look for ways to support pastors, Christian workers, and missionaries today. All Christians should work together to support God's work both at home and around the world.

MEGATHEMES

THEME	EXPLANATION	IMPORTANCE
Hospitality	John wrote to encourage those who were kind to others. Genuine hospitality for traveling Christian workers was needed then and is still important today.	Faithful Christian teachers and missionaries need our support. Whenever you can extend hospitality to others, it will make you a partner in their ministry.
Pride	Diotrephes not only refused to offer hospitality but also set himself up as a church boss. Pride disqualified him from being a real leader.	Christian leaders must shun pride and its effects on them. Be careful not to misuse your position of leadership.
Faithfulness	Gaius and Demetrius were commended for their faithful work in the church. They were held up as examples of faithful, selfless servants.	Don't take for granted Christian workers who serve faithfully. Be sure to encourage them so they won't grow weary of serving.

1. God's children live by the standards of the gospel

Greetings

This letter is from John the Elder.* 1:1
It is written to Gaius, my dear friend, whom I love in the truth. 2 Jn 1:1
2 Dear friend, I am praying that all is well with you and that your body is as healthy as 1:3 2 Jn 1:4
I know your soul is. 3 Some of the brothers recently returned and made me very happy 1:4
by telling me about your faithfulness and that you are living in the truth. 4 I could have 1 Cor 4:15 Gal 4:19
no greater joy than to hear that my children live in the truth. 1 Jn 2:1

Caring for the Lord's Workers

5 Dear friend, you are doing a good work for God when you take care of the traveling 1:5 Rom 12:13
teachers who are passing through, even though they are strangers to you. 6 They have Heb 13:2
told the church here of your friendship and your loving deeds. You do well to send them 1 Pet 4:10
on their way in a manner that pleases God. 7 For they are traveling for the Lord* and 1:6 Col 1:10
accept nothing from those who are not Christians.* 8 So we ourselves should support Titus 3:13
them so that we may become partners with them for the truth. 1:7 Matt 10:9-14
9 I sent a brief letter to the church about this, but Diotrephes, who loves to be the leader, Mark 6:8-13
does not acknowledge our authority. 10 When I come, I will report some of the things he Luke 9:3-5; 10:4-11 Acts 20:33, 35

1 Greek *From the elder.* **7a** Greek *the Name.* **7b** Greek *from Gentiles.*

1:1 This letter gives us an important glimpse into the life of the early church. Third John, addressed to Gaius, is about the need for showing hospitality to traveling preachers and other believers. It also warns against a would-be church dictator.

1:1 The "Elder," John, was one of Jesus' 12 disciples and the writer of the Gospel of John, three letters, and the book of Revelation. For more information about John, see his Profile in John 13. We have no further information about Gaius, but he is someone whom John loved dearly. Perhaps Gaius had shared his home and hospitality with John at some time during John's travels. If so, John would have appreciated his actions, because traveling preachers depended on expressions of hospitality to survive (see Matthew 10:11-16).

1:2 John was concerned for Gaius's physical *and* spiritual well-being. This was the opposite of the popular heresy that taught the separation of spirit and matter and despised the physical side of life. Today, many people still fall into this way of thinking. This non-Christian attitude logically leads to one of two responses: neglect of the body and physical health, or indulgence of the body's sinful desires. God is concerned for both your body and your soul. As a responsible Christian, you should neither neglect nor indulge yourself but care for your physical needs and discipline your body so that you are at your best for God's service.

1:4 John wrote about "my children" because, as a result of his preaching, he was the spiritual father of many, including Gaius.

1:5 In the church's early days, traveling prophets, evangelists, and teachers were helped on their way by people like Gaius, who housed and fed them. Hospitality is a lost art in many churches today. We would do well to invite more people for meals—fellow church members, young people, traveling missionaries, those in need, visitors. This is an active and much-appreciated way to show your love. In fact, it is probably more important today. Because of our individualistic, self-centered society, there are many lonely people who wonder if anyone cares whether they live or die. If you find such a lonely person, show him or her that *you* care!

1:7 The traveling missionaries neither asked for nor accepted anything from nonbelievers because they didn't want anyone questioning their motives for preaching. God's true preachers do not preach to make money but to express their love for God. It is the church's responsibility to care for Christian workers; this should never be left to nonbelievers.

1:7, 8 When you help someone who is spreading the Good News, you are in a very real way a partner in the ministry. This is the other side of the principle in 2 John 1:10 (see the note there). Not everyone should go to the mission field; those who work for Christ at home are vital to the ministry of those who go and who need support. We can support missionaries by praying for them and by giving them our money, hospitality, and time.

1:9 This letter to which John refers was neither 1 nor 2 John but another letter that no longer exists.

1:10 John 9:22, 34; 2 Jn 1:12; 3 Jn 1:5
1:11 Ps 34:14; 1 Jn 2:29; 3:6, 9-10
1:12 John 19:35; 21:24

is doing and the wicked things he is saying about us. He not only refuses to welcome the
traveling teachers, he also tells others not to help them. And when they do help, he puts
them out of the church.
11 Dear friend, don't let this bad example influence you. Follow only what is good.
Remember that those who do good prove that they are God's children, and those who do
evil prove that they do not know God. 12 But everyone speaks highly of Demetrius, even
truth itself. We ourselves can say the same for him, and you know we speak the truth.

2. John's final words

1:13 Num 12:8; 2 Jn 1:12
1:14 2 Jn 1:12

13 I have much to tell you, but I don't want to do it in a letter. 14 For I hope to see you
soon, and then we will talk face to face.
15 May God's peace be with you.
Your friends here send you their greetings. Please give my personal greetings to each
of our friends there.

1:9, 10 All we know about Diotrephes is that he wanted to control the church. John denounced (1) his refusal to have anything to do with other spiritual leaders, (2) his slander of the leaders, (3) his bad example in refusing to welcome any teachers, and (4) his attempt to excommunicate those who opposed his leadership. Sins such as pride, jealousy, and slander are still present in the church, and when a leader makes a habit of encouraging sin and discouraging right actions, he must be stopped. If no one speaks up, great harm can come to the church. We must confront sin in the church; if we try to avoid it, it will continue to grow. A true Christian leader is a servant, not an autocrat!

1:12 We know nothing about Demetrius except that he may have carried this letter from John to Gaius. The book of Acts mentions an Ephesian silversmith named Demetrius, who opposed Paul (Acts 19:24ff), but this is probably another man. In contrast to the corrupt Diotrephes, Demetrius had a high regard for truth. John personified truth as a witness to Demetrius's character and teaching. In other words, if truth could speak, it would speak on Demetrius's behalf. When Demetrius arrived, Gaius certainly opened his home to him.

1:14 Whereas 2 John emphasizes the need to refuse hospitality to false teachers, 3 John urges continued hospitality to those who teach the truth. Hospitality is a strong sign of support for people and their work. It means giving of your resources to them so their stay will be comfortable and their work and travel easier. Actively look for creative ways to show hospitality to God's workers. It may be in the form of a letter of encouragement, a gift, financial support, an open home, or prayer.

JUDE

VITAL STATISTICS

PURPOSE:
To remind the church of the need for constant vigilance—to keep strong in the faith and to oppose heresy

AUTHOR:
Jude, brother of Jesus and James

TO WHOM WRITTEN:
Jewish Christians and all believers everywhere

DATE WRITTEN:
Approximately A.D. 65

SETTING:
From the first century on, the church has been threatened by heresy and false teaching; we must always be on our guard.

KEY VERSE:
"Dearly loved friends, I had been eagerly planning to write to you about the salvation we all share. But now I find that I must write about something else, urging you to defend the truth of the Good News. God gave this unchanging truth once for all time to his holy people" (1:3).

KEY PEOPLE:
Jude, James, Jesus

TO PROTECT from harm, to guard from attack, to repulse enemies—for centuries rugged defenders have built walls, launched missiles, and waged wars, expending material and human resources in the battle to save nations and cities. And with total commitment and courageous abandon, individuals have fought for their families. It is a rule of life that we fight for survival, defending with all our strength what is most precious to us, from every real or imagined attack.

God's Word and the gift of eternal life have infinite value and have been entrusted to Christ's faithful followers. There are many people who live in opposition to God and his followers. They twist God's truth, seeking to deceive and destroy the unwary. But God's truth must go forth, carried and defended by those who have committed their lives to God's Son. It is an important task, an awesome responsibility, and a profound privilege to have this commission.

This was Jude's message to Christians everywhere. Opposition would come and godless teachers would arise, but Christians should "defend the truth of the Good News" (1:3) by rejecting all falsehood and immorality (1:4–19), remembering God's mighty acts of rescue and punishment (1:5–11, 14–16) and the warnings of the apostles (1:17–19). His readers are to build up their own faith through prayer (1:20), keeping close to Christ (1:21), helping others (1:22, 23), and hating sin (1:23). Then Jude concludes with a glorious benediction of praise to God (1:24, 25).

How much do you value God's Word, the fellowship of the church, and obedience to Jesus Christ? There are many false teachers waiting to destroy your Christ-centered life, the credibility of God's Word, and the unity of the body of Christ. Read Jude and determine to stand firm in your faith and defend God's truth at all costs. *Nothing* is more valuable.

THE BLUEPRINT

1. The danger of false teachers (1:1–16)
2. The duty to fight for God's truth (1:17–25)

Jude wrote to motivate Christians everywhere to action. He wanted them to recognize the dangers of false teaching, to protect themselves and other believers, and to win back those who had already been deceived. Jude was writing against godless teachers who were saying that Christians could do as they pleased without fear of God's punishment. While few teach this heresy openly in the church today, many in the church act as though this were true. This letter contains a warning against living a nominal Christian life.

MEGATHEMES

THEME	EXPLANATION	IMPORTANCE
False Teachers	Jude warns against false teachers and leaders who reject the lordship of Christ, undermine the faith of others, and lead them astray. These leaders and any who follow them will be punished.	We must staunchly defend Christian truth. Make sure that you avoid leaders and teachers who distort the Bible to suit their own purposes. Genuine servants of God will faithfully portray Christ in their words and conduct.
Apostasy	Jude also warns against apostasy—turning away from Christ. We are to remember that God punishes rebellion against him. We must be careful not to drift away from a faithful commitment to Christ.	Those who do not seek to know the truth in God's Word are susceptible to apostasy. Christians must guard against any false teachings that would distract them from the truth preached by the apostles and written in God's Word.

1. The danger of false teachers

Greetings from Jude

1:1 Matt 13:55; Rom 1:1, 6-7; Jas 1:1

1:2 2 Pet 1:2

This letter is from Jude, a slave of Jesus Christ and a brother of James.
I am writing to all who are called to live in the love of God the Father and the care of
Jesus Christ.
2 May you receive more and more of God's mercy, peace, and love.

The Danger of False Teachers

1:3 1 Tim 6:12; Titus 1:4; 2 Pet 3:1-2

1:4 Gal 2:4; 2 Pet 2:1-2; 1 Jn 2:21

3 Dearly loved friends, I had been eagerly planning to write to you about the salvation we
all share. But now I find that I must write about something else, urging you to defend the
truth of the Good News.* God gave this unchanging truth once for all time to his holy
people. 4 I say this because some godless people have wormed their way in among you,

3 Greek *to contend for the faith.*

1:1 Jude's letter focuses on *apostasy*—when people turn away from God's truth and embrace false teachings. Jude reminded his readers of God's judgment on those who had left the faith in the past. This letter is a warning against false teachers—in this case, probably Gnostic teachers (see the note on Colossians 2:4ff for a description of the Gnostic heresy). Gnostics opposed two of the basic tenets of Christianity—the incarnation of Christ and the call to Christian ethics. Jude wrote to combat these false teachings and to encourage true doctrine and right conduct.

1:1 Jude was a brother of James, who was one of the leaders in the early church. Both of these men were Jesus' half brothers. Mary was their mother, and Joseph was their father. Although Mary was Jesus' true mother, God was Jesus' true Father.

1:3 Jude emphasizes the important relationship between correct doctrine and true faith. The truth of the Bible must not be compromised because it gives us the real facts about Jesus and salvation. The Bible is inspired by God and should never be twisted or manipulated; when it is, we can become confused over right and wrong and lose sight of the only path that leads to eternal life. Before writing about salvation, then, Jude felt he had to set his readers back on the right track, calling them back to the basics of their faith. Then the way to salvation would be clearer. "Holy people" refers to all believers.

1:4 Even some of our churches today have false ("godless") teachers who "have wormed their way in" and are twisting the Bible's teachings to justify their own opinions, life-style, or wrong behavior. In doing this, they may gain temporary freedom to do as they wish, but they will discover that in distorting Scripture they are playing with fire. God will judge them for excusing, tolerating, and promoting sin.

1:4 Some people avoid studying the Bible because they think theology is dry and boring. Those who refuse to learn correct doctrine, however, are susceptible to false teaching because they are not fully grounded in God's truth. We must understand the basic doctrines of our faith so that we can recognize false doctrines and prevent wrong teaching from undermining our faith and hurting others.

1:4 Many first-century false teachers were teaching that Christians could do whatever they liked without fear of God's punishment. They had a light view of God's holiness and his justice. Paul refuted this same kind of false teaching in Romans 6:1-23. Even today, some Christians minimize the sinfulness of sin, believing that how they live has little to do with their faith. But what a person truly believes will show up in how he or she acts. Those who truly have faith will show it by their deep respect for God and their sincere desire to live according to the principles in his Word.

saying that God's forgiveness allows us to live immoral lives. The fate of such people was
determined long ago, for they have turned against our only Master and Lord, Jesus Christ.
5 I must remind you—and you know it well—that even though the Lord* rescued the
whole nation of Israel from Egypt, he later destroyed every one of those who did not
remain faithful. 6 And I remind you of the angels who did not stay within the limits of
authority God gave them but left the place where they belonged. God has kept them
chained in prisons of darkness, waiting for the day of judgment. 7 And don't forget the
cities of Sodom and Gomorrah and their neighboring towns, which were filled with
sexual immorality and every kind of sexual perversion. Those cities were destroyed by
fire and are a warning of the eternal fire that will punish all who are evil.
8 Yet these false teachers, who claim authority from their dreams, live immoral lives,
defy authority, and scoff at the power of the glorious ones.* 9 But even Michael, one of
the mightiest of the angels, did not dare accuse Satan of blasphemy, but simply said,
"The Lord rebuke you." (This took place when Michael was arguing with Satan about
Moses' body.) 10 But these people mock and curse the things they do not understand. Like
animals, they do whatever their instincts tell them, and they bring about their own
destruction. 11 How terrible it will be for them! For they follow the evil example of Cain,
who killed his brother. Like Balaam, they will do anything for money. And like Korah,
they will perish because of their rebellion.
12 When these people join you in fellowship meals celebrating the love of the Lord,
they are like dangerous reefs that can shipwreck you.* They are shameless in the way
they care only about themselves. They are like clouds blowing over dry land without
giving rain, promising much but producing nothing. They are like trees without fruit at
harvesttime. They are not only dead but doubly dead, for they have been pulled out by
the roots. 13 They are like wild waves of the sea, churning up the dirty foam of their
shameful deeds. They are wandering stars, heading for everlasting gloom and darkness.
14 Now Enoch, who lived seven generations after Adam, prophesied about these
people. He said,

1:5 Exod 14:21-31 Num 14:29-37 Deut 2:15 1 Cor 10:5-10
1:6 //2 Pet 2:4, 9
1:7 Gen 19:4-25 Matt 10:15 //2 Pet 2:6, 10
1:8 //2 Pet 2:10
1:9 Dan 10:13, 21; 12:1 Zech 3:2 //2 Pet 2:11 Rev 12:7
1:10 //2 Pet 2:12
1:11 Gen 4:3-8 Num 16:1-35; 22:7; 31:16 //2 Pet 2:15-16 1 Jn 3:12 Rev 2:14
1:12 Ezek 34:8 Matt 15:13 1 Cor 11:20-22 //2 Pet 2:13
1:13 Isa 57:20 Phil 3:19 //2 Pet 2:17
1:14 Gen 5:18-24 Deut 33:2 1 Chr 1:1-3 Zech 14:5 Matt 25:31

5 Some manuscripts read *Jesus.* 8 *The glorious ones* are probably evil angels. 12 Or *they are contaminants among you,* or *they are stains.*

1:5-7 Jude gave three examples of rebellion: (1) the nation of Israel—who, although they were delivered from Egypt, refused to trust God and enter the Promised Land (Numbers 14:26-39); (2) the angels—although they were once pure, holy, and living in God's presence, some gave in to pride and joined Satan to rebel against God (2 Peter 2:4); and (3) the cities of Sodom and Gomorrah—the inhabitants were so full of sin that God wiped them off the face of the earth (Genesis 19:1-29). If the chosen people, angels, and sinful cities were punished, how much more would these false teachers be severely judged?

1:7 Many people don't want to believe that God sentences people to "eternal fire" for rejecting him. But this is clearly taught in Scripture. Sinners who don't seek forgiveness from God will face eternal separation from him. Jude gives this warning to all who rebel against, ignore, or reject God.

1:8 The "glorious ones" here are probably angels. Just as the men of Sodom insulted angels (Genesis 19), these false teachers scoffed at any authority. For information on the danger of insulting even the fallen angels, see the note on 2 Peter 2:10-12.

1:9 This incident is not recorded in any other place in Scripture. Moses' death is recorded in Deuteronomy 34. Here Jude may have been making use of an ancient book called *The Assumption of Moses.*

1:10 False teachers claimed that they possessed secret knowledge that gave them authority. Their "knowledge" of God was esoteric—mystical and beyond human understanding. The nature of God *is* beyond our understanding, but God, in his grace, has chosen to reveal himself to us—in his Word, and supremely in Jesus Christ. Therefore, we must seek to know all we can about what he has revealed, even though we cannot fully comprehend God with our finite human mind. Beware of those who claim to have all the answers and who belittle what they do not understand.

1:11 Jude gives three examples of men who did whatever they wanted (1:10): Cain, who murdered his brother out of vengeful jealousy (Genesis 4:1-16); Balaam, who prophesied out of greed, not out of obedience to God's command (Numbers 22–24); and Korah, who rebelled against God's divinely appointed leaders, wanting the power for himself (Numbers 16:1-35). These stories illustrate attitudes that are typical of false teachers—pride, selfishness, jealousy, greed, lust for power, and disregard of God's will.

1:12 When the Lord's Supper was celebrated in the early church, believers ate a full meal before taking part in Communion with the sharing of the bread and wine. The meal was called a "fellowship meal," and it was designed to be a sacred time of fellowship to prepare one's heart for Communion. However, the false teachers were joining these meals, becoming dangers in what should have been a time of rejoicing in the Lord. In several of the churches, however, this meal had turned into a time of gluttony and drunken revelry. In Corinth, for example, some people hastily gobbled food while others went hungry (1 Corinthians 11:20-22). No church function should be an occasion for selfishness, gluttony, greed, disorder, or other sins that destroy unity or take one's mind away from the real purpose for gathering together.

1:12 The false teachers were "doubly dead." They were useless "trees" because they weren't producing fruit; because they weren't even believers, they would be rooted up and burned.

1:14 Enoch is mentioned briefly in Genesis 5:21-24. This quotation is from an apocryphal book called the book of Enoch.

1:14 Other places where Jesus is mentioned as coming with angels ("holy ones") are Matthew 16:27 and 24:31. Daniel 7:10 speaks of God judging humanity in the presence of ten thousand times ten thousand angels.

"Look, the Lord is coming
with thousands of his holy ones.
1:15 2 Pet 2:6-9 — 15 He will bring the people of the world
to judgment.
He will convict the ungodly of all the evil things
they have done in rebellion
and of all the insults that godless sinners
have spoken against him."*

1:16 //2 Pet 2:10, 18 — 16 These people are grumblers and complainers, doing whatever evil they feel like. They
Jude 1:18 — are loudmouthed braggarts, and they flatter others to get favors in return.

2. The duty to fight for God's truth

A Call to Remain Faithful

1:17 Heb 2:3 — 17 But you, my dear friends, must remember what the apostles of our Lord Jesus Christ
2 Pet 3:2 — told you, 18 that in the last times there would be scoffers whose purpose in life is to enjoy
1:18 //2 Pet 3:3 — themselves in every evil way imaginable. 19 Now they are here, and they are the ones
Jude 1:16 — who are creating divisions among you. They live by natural instinct because they do not
1:20 Eph 6:18 — have God's Spirit living in them.
Col 2:7 — 20 But you, dear friends, must continue to build your lives on the foundation of your
1 Thes 5:11 — holy faith. And continue to pray as you are directed by the Holy Spirit.* 21 Live in such
1:21 2 Tim 1:18 — a way that God's love can bless you as you wait for the eternal life that our Lord Jesus
Christ in his mercy is going to give you. 22 Show mercy to those whose faith is
1:23 Amos 4:11 — wavering. 23 Rescue others by snatching them from the flames of judgment. There are
Zech 3:2-5 — still others to whom you need to show mercy, but be careful that you aren't contami-
Rev 3:4 — nated by their sins.*

A Prayer of Praise

1:24 Rom 16:25 — 24 And now, all glory to God, who is able to keep you from stumbling, and who will bring
2 Cor 4:14 — you into his glorious presence innocent of sin and with great joy. 25 All glory to him, who
Phil 1:10; 1 Thes 5:23 — alone is God our Savior, through Jesus Christ our Lord. Yes, glory, majesty, power, and
1:25 Rom 16:27; 2 Pet 3:18 — authority belong to him, in the beginning, now, and forevermore. Amen.

14-15 The quotation comes from the Apocrypha: Enoch 1:9. **20** Greek *Pray in the Holy Spirit.* **23** Greek *mercy, hating even the clothing stained by the flesh.*

1:17 Other apostles also warned about false teachers. See Acts 20:29; 1 Timothy 4:1, 2; 2 Timothy 3:1-5; 2 Peter 2:1-3; 2 John 7.

1:18 The "last times" is a common phrase referring to the time between Jesus' first and second comings. We live in the last times.

1:20 To pray as we are "directed by the Holy Spirit" means to pray in the power and strength of the Holy Spirit. He prays for us (Romans 8:26, 27), opens our mind to Jesus (John 14:26), and teaches us about him (John 15:26).

1:21 John warns his readers to live close to God and his people, not listening to false teachers who would try to pull you away from him (John 15:9, 10).

1:22, 23 Effective witnessing saves people from God's judgment. We witness to some through our compassion and kindness; to others we witness as if we were snatching them from the eternal fire. We are to hate the sin, but we must witness to and love the sinner. Unbelievers, no matter how successful they seem by worldly standards, are lost and in need of salvation. We should not take witnessing lightly—it is a matter of life and death.

1:23 In trying to find common ground with those to whom we witness, we must be careful not to fall into the quicksand of compromise. When reaching out to others, we must be sure that our own footing is safe and secure. Be careful not to become so much like non-Christians that no one can tell who you are or what you believe. Influence them for Christ—don't allow them to influence you to sin!

1:24 As the letter begins, so it ends—with assurance. God keeps believers from falling prey to false teachers. Although false teachers are widespread and dangerous, we don't have to be afraid if we trust God and are rooted and grounded in him.

1:24 To be sinless and perfect ("innocent of sin") will be the ultimate condition of the believer when he or she finally sees Christ face to face. When Christ appears and we are given our new body, we will be like Christ (1 John 3:2). Coming into Christ's presence will be more wonderful than we could ever imagine!

1:25 The audience to whom Jude wrote was vulnerable to heresies and to temptations toward immoral living. Jude encouraged the believers to remain firm in their faith and trust in God's promises for their future. This was all the more important because they were living in a time of increased apostasy. We, too, are living in the last days, much closer to the end than were the original readers of this letter. We, too, are vulnerable to doctrinal error. We, too, are tempted to give in to sin. Although there is much false teaching around us, we need not be afraid or give up in despair—God can keep us from falling, and he guarantees that if we remain faithful, he will bring us into his presence and give us everlasting joy.

REVELATION

VITAL STATISTICS

PURPOSE:
To reveal the full identity of Christ and to give warning and hope to believers

AUTHOR:
The apostle John

TO WHOM WRITTEN:
The seven churches in Asia and all believers everywhere

DATE WRITTEN:
Approximately A.D. 95 from Patmos

SETTING:
Most scholars believe that the seven churches of Asia to whom John writes were experiencing the persecution that took place under Emperor Domitian (A.D. 90–95). It seems that the Roman authorities had exiled John to the island of Patmos (off the coast of Asia). John, who had been an eyewitness of the incarnate Christ, had a vision of the glorified Christ. God also revealed to him what would take place in the future—judgment and the ultimate triumph of God over evil.

KEY VERSE:
"God blesses the one who reads this prophecy to the church, and he blesses all who listen to it and obey what it says. For the time is near when these things will happen" (1:3).

KEY PEOPLE:
John, Jesus

KEY PLACES:
Patmos, the seven churches, the new Jerusalem

SPECIAL FEATURES:
Revelation is written in "apocalyptic" form—a type of Jewish literature that uses symbolic imagery to communicate hope (in the ultimate triumph of God) to those in the midst of persecution. The events are ordered according to literary, rather than strictly chronological, patterns.

WITH tiny wrinkles and cries, he entered the world and, wrapped in strips of cloth, took his first nap on a bed of straw. Subject to time and to parents, he grew to manhood in Roman-occupied Palestine, his gentle hands becoming strong and calloused in Joseph's woodworking shop. As a man, he walked through the countryside and city, touching individuals, preaching to crowds, and training 12 men to carry on his work. At every step he was hounded by those seeking to rid the world of his influence. Finally, falsely accused and tried, he was condemned to a disgraceful execution by foreign hands. And he died—spat upon, cursed, pierced by nails, and hung heavenward for all to deride. Jesus, the God-man, gave his life completely so that all might live.

At God's appointed time, the risen and ascended Lord Jesus will burst onto the world scene. Then everyone will know that Jesus is Lord of the universe! Those who love him will rejoice, greeting their Savior with hearts overflowing into songs of praise. But his enemies will be filled with fear. Allied with Satan, the enemies of Christ will marshal their legions against Christ and his armies. But who can withstand God's wrath? Christ will win the battle and reign victorious forever! Jesus, the humble suffering servant, is also the powerful, conquering King and Judge.

Revelation is a book of hope. John, the beloved apostle and eyewitness of Jesus, proclaimed that the victorious Lord would surely return to vindicate the righteous and judge the wicked. But Revelation is also a book of warning. Things were not as they should have been in the churches, so Christ called the members to commit themselves to live in righteousness.

Although Jesus gave this revelation of himself to John nearly 2,000 years ago, it still stands as a comfort and challenge to God's people today. We can take heart as we understand John's vision of hope: Christ will return to rescue his people and settle accounts with all who defy him.

John begins this book by explaining how he received this revelation from God (1:1–20). He then records specific messages from Jesus to the seven churches in Asia (2:1—3:22). Suddenly, the scene shifts as a mosaic of dramatic and majestic images bursts into view before John's eyes. This series of visions portrays the future rise of evil, culminating in the Antichrist (4:1—18:24). Then follows John's recounting of the triumph of the King of kings, the wedding of the Lamb, the final judgment, and the coming of the new Jerusalem (19:1—22:5). Revelation concludes with the promise of Christ's soon return (22:6–21), and John breathes a prayer that has been echoed by Christians through the centuries: "Amen! Come, Lord Jesus!" (22:20).

As you read the book of Revelation, marvel with John at the wondrous panorama of God's revealed plan. Listen as Christ warns the churches, and root out any sin that blocks your relationship with him. Be full of hope, knowing that God is in control, Christ's victory is assured, and all who trust him will be saved.

THE BLUEPRINT

A. LETTERS TO THE CHURCHES (1:1—3:22)	The vision John received opens with instructions for him to write to seven churches. He both commends them for their strengths and warns them about their flaws. Each letter was directed to a church then in existence but also speaks to conditions in the church throughout history. Both in the church and in our individual lives, we must constantly fight against the temptation to become loveless, immoral, lenient, compromising, lifeless, or casual about our faith. The letters make it clear how our Lord feels about these qualities.
B. MESSAGE FOR THE CHURCH (4:1—22:21) 1. Worshiping God in heaven 2. Opening the seven seals 3. Sounding the seven trumpets 4. Observing the great conflict 5. Pouring out the seven plagues 6. Seizing the final victory 7. Making all things new	This revelation is both a warning to Christians who have grown apathetic and an encouragement to those who are faithfully enduring the struggles in this world. It reassures us that good will triumph over evil, gives us hope as we face difficult times, and gives guidance when we are wavering in our faith. Christ's message to the church is a message of hope for all believers in every generation.

MEGATHEMES

THEME	EXPLANATION	IMPORTANCE
God's Sovereignty	God is sovereign. He is greater than any power in the universe. God is not to be compared with any leader, government, or religion. He controls history for the purpose of uniting true believers in loving fellowship with him.	Though Satan's power may temporarily increase, we are not to be led astray. God is all-powerful. He is in control. He will bring his true family safely into eternal life. Because he cares for us, we can trust him with our very life.
Christ's Return	Christ came to earth as a "Lamb," the symbol of his perfect sacrifice for our sin. He will return as the triumphant "Lion," the rightful ruler and conqueror. He will defeat Satan, settle accounts with all those who reject him, and bring his faithful people into eternity.	Assurance of Christ's return gives suffering Christians the strength to endure. We can look forward to his return as king and judge. Since no one knows the time when he will appear, we must be ready at all times by keeping our faith strong.
God's Faithful People	John wrote to encourage the church to resist the demands to worship the Roman emperor. He warns all God's faithful people to be devoted only to Christ. Revelation identifies who the faithful people are and what they should be doing until Christ returns.	You can take your place in the ranks of God's faithful people by believing in Christ. Victory is sure for those who resist temptation and make loyalty to Christ their top priority.
Judgment	One day God's anger toward sin will be fully and completely unleashed. Satan will be defeated with all of his agents. False religion will be destroyed. God will reward the faithful with eternal life, but all who refuse to believe in him will face eternal punishment.	Evil and injustice will not prevail forever. God's final judgment will put an end to these. We need to be certain of our commitment to Jesus if we want to escape this great final judgment. No one who rejects Christ will escape God's punishment.
Hope	One day God will create a new heaven and a new earth. All believers will live with him forever in perfect peace and security. Those who have already died will be raised to life. These promises for the future bring us hope.	Our great hope is that what Christ promises will come true. When we have confidence in our final destination, we can follow Christ with unwavering dedication no matter what we must face. We can be encouraged by hoping in Christ's return.

A. LETTERS TO THE CHURCHES (1:1—3:22)

Near the end of his life, John received a vision from Christ, which he recorded for the benefit of the seven churches in Asia and for Christians throughout history. This is the only book in the Bible that promises a blessing to those who listen to its words and do what it says.

Prologue

1 This is a revelation from* Jesus Christ, which God gave him concerning the events
that will happen soon. An angel was sent to God's servant John so that John could
share the revelation with God's other servants. 2 John faithfully reported the word of God
and the testimony of Jesus Christ—everything he saw.

1:1 Or *of.*

1:1 Dan 2:28-29, 45; John 12:49; 17:8; Rev 1:19; 5:7; 17:1; 22:6, 8, 16

1:2 Rev 1:9; 6:9

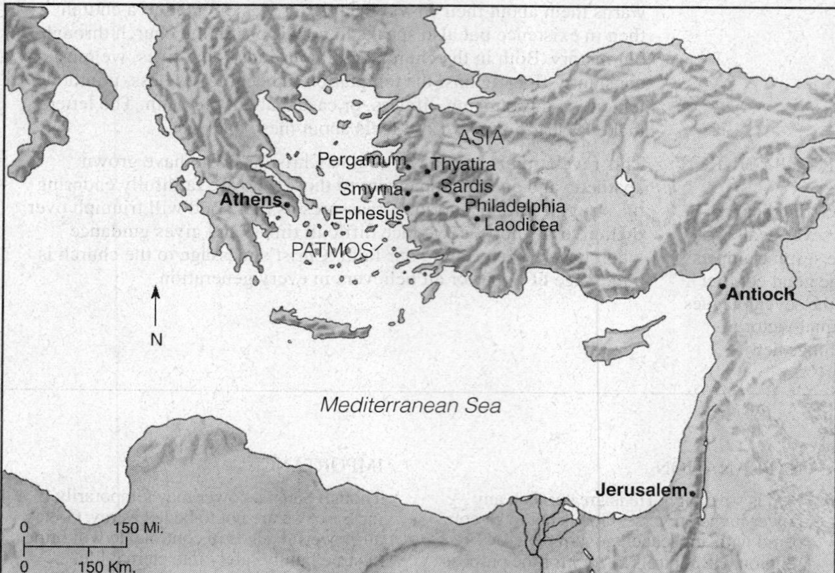

THE SEVEN CHURCHES The seven churches were located on a major Roman road. A letter carrier would leave the island of Patmos (where John was exiled), arriving first at Ephesus. He would travel north to Smyrna and Pergamum, turn southeast to Thyatira, and continue on to Sardis, Philadelphia, and Laodicea—in the exact order in which the letters were dictated.

1:1 Revelation is a book about the future *and* about the present. It offers future hope to all believers, especially those who have suffered for their faith, by proclaiming Christ's final victory over evil and the reality of eternal life with him. It also gives present guidance as it teaches us about Jesus Christ and how we should live for him now. Through graphic pictures we learn that (1) Jesus Christ is coming again, (2) evil will be judged, and (3) the dead will be raised to judgment, resulting in eternal life or eternal destruction.

1:1 According to tradition, John, the author, was the only one of Jesus' original 12 disciples who was not killed for the faith. He also wrote the Gospel of John and the letters of 1, 2, and 3 John. When he wrote Revelation, John was in exile on the island of Patmos in the Aegean Sea, sent there by the Romans for his witness about Jesus Christ. For more information on John, see his Profile in John 13.

1:1 This book is the revelation *from, concerning,* and *of* Jesus Christ. God gave the revelation of his plan to Jesus Christ, who, in turn, revealed it to John. The book of Revelation unveils Christ's full identity and God's plan for the end of the world, and it focuses on Jesus Christ, his second coming, his victory over evil, and the establishment of his Kingdom. As you read and study Revelation, don't focus so much on the timetable of the events or the details of John's imagery that you miss the main message—the infinite love, power, and justice of the Lord Jesus Christ.

1:1 The book of Revelation is *apocalyptic* (meaning uncovered, unveiled, or revealed) in style. This style of ancient literature usually featured spectacular and mysterious imagery, and such literature was written under the name of an ancient hero. John was acquainted with Jewish apocalyptic works, but his book is different in several ways: (1) He uses his own name rather than the name of an ancient hero; (2) he denounces evil and exhorts people to high Christian standards; (3) he offers hope rather than gloom. John was not a psychic attempting to predict the future; he was a prophet of God describing what God had shown him.

1:1 For more about angels, see the note on 5:11.

1:1 Jesus gave his message to John in a revelation (or vision), allowing John to see and record certain future events so they could be an encouragement to all believers. The vision includes many signs and symbols that convey the essence of what is to happen. What John saw, in most cases, was indescribable, so he used illustrations to show what it was *like.* When reading this symbolic language, we don't have to understand every detail—John himself didn't. Instead, realize that John's imagery shows us that Christ is indeed the glorious and victorious Lord of all.

1:3
Rev 22:7, 10

3 God blesses the one who reads this prophecy to the church, and he blesses all who
listen to it and obey what it says. For the time is near when these things will happen.

1:4
Exod 3:14
Rev 1:8; 3:1; 4:5, 8; 5:6; 11:17; 16:5

1:5
Ps 89:27
Isa 40:2
Col 1:18
Rev 3:14; 19:11, 16

John's Greeting to the Seven Churches

4 This letter is from John to the seven churches in the province of Asia. Grace and peace
from the one who is, who always was, and who is still to come; from the sevenfold
Spirit* before his throne; 5 and from Jesus Christ, who is the faithful witness to these
things, the first to rise from the dead, and the commander of all the rulers of the world.
All praise to him who loves us and has freed us from our sins by shedding his blood

1:4 Greek *the seven spirits.*

INTERPRETING THE BOOK OF REVELATION
Over the centuries, four main approaches to interpreting the book of Revelation have developed. Each approach has had capable supporters, but none has proved itself the only way to read this book. However, the most basic application question for each approach can be summarized by asking yourself, Will this help me become a better follower of Jesus Christ today?

Approach	*Description*	*Challenge*	*Caution*
PRETERIST VIEW	John is writing to encourage Christians in his own day who are experiencing persecution from the Roman Empire.	To gain the same kind of encouragement John's first readers gained from the vivid images of God's sovereignty	Do not forget that most biblical prophecy has both an immediate and a future application.
FUTURIST VIEW	Except for the first three chapters, John is describing events that will occur at the end of history.	To see in contemporary events many of the characteristics John describes and realize that the end could come at any time	Do not assume that we have "figured out" the future, since Jesus said that no one will know the day of his return before it happens.
HISTORICIST VIEW	The book of Revelation is a presentation of history from John's day until the second coming of Christ and beyond.	To note the consistency of human evil throughout history and recognize that names may change but the rebellion against God has not	Be careful before identifying current events or leaders as fulfilling aspects of the book of Revelation.
IDEALIST VIEW	The book of Revelation is a symbolic representation of the continual struggle of good and evil. It does not refer to any particular historical events. It is applicable at any point in history.	To gain insight into the past, to prepare for the future, and to live obediently and confidently in the present	Do not avoid the book because it is difficult. Try to understand Revelation within its broader literary context.

1:1-3 The book of Revelation reveals future events, but there is not the gloomy pessimism we might expect. The drama of these unfolding events is spectacular, but there is nothing to fear if you are on the winning side. When you think about the future, walk with confidence because Christ, the victor, walks with you.

1:3 Revelation is a book of prophecy that is both *prediction* (foretelling future events) and *proclamation* (preaching about who God is and what he will do). Prophecy is more than telling the future. Behind the predictions are important principles about God's character and promises. As we read, we will get to know God better so that we can trust him completely.

1:3 The typical news reports—filled with violence, scandal, and political haggling—are depressing, and we may wonder where the world is heading. God's plan for the future, however, provides inspiration and encouragement because we know he will intervene in history to conquer evil. John encourages churches to read this book aloud so everyone can hear it, apply it ("obey" it), and be assured of the fact that God will triumph.

1:3 When John says that "the time is near," he is urging his readers to be ready at all times for the last judgment and the establishment of God's Kingdom. We do not know when these events will occur, but we must always be prepared. They will happen quickly, and there will be no second chance to change sides.

1:4 Jesus told John to write to seven churches that knew and trusted him and had read his earlier letters (see 1:11). The letters were addressed so that they could be read and passed on in a systematic fashion, following the main Roman road clockwise around the province of Asia (now called Turkey).

1:4 The "sevenfold Spirit" is another name for the Holy Spirit. The number seven is used throughout Revelation to symbolize completeness and perfection. For more about the Holy Spirit, see the notes on John 3:6 and Acts 1:5.

1:4-6 The Trinity—the Father ("the one who is, who always was, and who is still to come"), the Holy Spirit ("the sevenfold Spirit"), and the Son (Jesus Christ)—is the source of all truth (John 14:6, 17; 1 John 2:27; Revelation 19:11). Thus, we can be assured that John's message is reliable and is God's word to us.

1:5 Others had risen from the dead—people whom the prophets, Jesus, and the apostles had brought back to life during their ministries—but later those people died again. Jesus was the first who rose from the dead in an imperishable body (1 Corinthians 15:20), never to die again. He is the first to rise from the dead.

1:5, 6 Many hesitate to witness about their faith in Christ because they don't feel the change in their lives has been spectacular enough. But you qualify as a witness for Jesus because of what he has done for you, not because of what you have done for him. Christ demonstrated his great love by setting us free from our sins through his death on the cross ("freed us from our sins by shedding his blood for us"), guaranteeing us a place in his Kingdom, and making us priests to administer God's love to others. The fact that the all-powerful God has offered eternal life to you is nothing short of spectacular.

for us. 6 He has made us his kingdom and his priests who serve before God his Father.
Give to him everlasting glory! He rules forever and ever! Amen!
7 Look! He comes with the clouds of heaven. And everyone will see him—even those
who pierced him. And all the nations of the earth will weep because of him. Yes! Amen!
8 "I am the Alpha and the Omega—the beginning and the end," says the Lord God. "I
am the one who is, who always was, and who is still to come, the Almighty One."

Vision of the Son of Man

9 I am John, your brother. In Jesus we are partners in suffering and in the Kingdom and
in patient endurance. I was exiled to the island of Patmos for preaching the word of God
and speaking about Jesus. 10 It was the Lord's Day, and I was worshiping in the Spirit.*
Suddenly, I heard a loud voice behind me, a voice that sounded like a trumpet blast. 11 It
said, "Write down what you see, and send it to the seven churches: Ephesus, Smyrna,
Pergamum, Thyatira, Sardis, Philadelphia, and Laodicea."
12 When I turned to see who was speaking to me, I saw seven gold lampstands. 13 And
standing in the middle of the lampstands was the Son of Man.* He was wearing a long
robe with a gold sash across his chest. 14 His head and his hair were white like wool, as
white as snow. And his eyes were bright like flames of fire. 15 His feet were as bright as
bronze refined in a furnace, and his voice thundered like mighty ocean waves. 16 He held
seven stars in his right hand, and a sharp two-edged sword came from his mouth. And
his face was as bright as the sun in all its brilliance.
17 When I saw him, I fell at his feet as dead. But he laid his right hand on me and said,
"Don't be afraid! I am the First and the Last. 18 I am the living one who died. Look, I am

1:6 Isa 61:6; 1 Pet 2:5, 9
1:7 Dan 7:13; Zech 12:10; Matt 24:30
1:8 Amos 3:13; 4:13
1:9 Phil 4:14; 2 Tim 2:12
1:11 Rev 1:2, 19; 2:1, 18, 24; 3:1, 4, 7, 14
1:12 Zech 4:2
1:13 Ezek 9:2, 11; Dan 7:13; 10:5
1:14 Dan 7:9; 10:6
1:15 Ezek 1:24; 43:2
1:16 Isa 49:2
1:17 Isa 44:6; 48:12; Dan 8:18

1:10 Or *in spirit.* **1:13** Or *one who looked like a man;* Greek reads *one like a son of man.*

1:5-7 Jesus is portrayed as the all-powerful King, victorious in battle, glorious in peace. He is not just a humble earthly teacher, he is the glorious God. When you read John's description of the vision, keep in mind that his words are not just good advice; they are truth from the King of kings. Don't just read his words for their interesting and amazing portrayal of the future. Let the truth about Christ penetrate your life, deepen your faith in him, and strengthen your commitment to follow him no matter what the cost.

1:7 John is announcing the return of Jesus to earth (see also Matthew 24; Mark 13; 1 Thessalonians 4:15-18). Jesus' second coming will be visible and victorious. All people will see him arrive (Mark 13:26), and they will *know* it is Jesus. When he comes, he will conquer evil and judge all people according to their deeds (20:11-15).

1:7 "Those who pierced him" could refer to the Roman soldiers who pierced Jesus' side as he hung on the cross or to the Jews who were responsible for his death. John saw Jesus' death with his own eyes, and he never forgot the horror of it (see John 19:34, 35; see also Zechariah 12:10).

1:8 Alpha and omega are the first and last letters of the Greek alphabet. The Lord God is the beginning and the end. God the Father is the eternal Lord and Ruler of the past, present, and future (see also 4:8; Isaiah 44:6; 48:12-15). Without him you have nothing that is eternal, nothing that can change your life, nothing that can save you from sin. Is the Lord your reason for living, "the Alpha and the Omega" of your life? Honor the one who is the beginning and the end of all existence, wisdom, and power.

1:9 Patmos was a small rocky island in the Aegean Sea, about 50 miles offshore from the city of Ephesus on the Asia Minor seacoast (see map).

1:9 The Christian church was facing severe persecution. Almost all believers were socially, politically, or economically suffering because of this empire-wide persecution, and some were even being killed for their faith. John was exiled to Patmos because he refused to stop preaching the Good News. We may not face persecution for our faith as the early Christians did, but even with our freedom few of us have the courage to share God's Word with others. If we hesitate to share our faith during easy times, how will we do during times of persecution?

1:12, 13 The seven gold lampstands are the seven churches in Asia (1:11, 20), and Jesus stands among them. No matter what the churches face, Jesus protects them with his all-encompassing love and reassuring power. Through his Spirit, Jesus Christ is still among the churches today. When a church faces persecution, it should remember Christ's deep love and compassion. When a church is troubled by internal strife and conflict, it should remember Christ's concern for purity and his intolerance of sin.

1:13, 14 This "Son of Man" is Jesus himself. The title *Son of Man* occurs many times in the New Testament in reference to Jesus as the Messiah. John recognized Jesus because he lived with him for three years and had seen him both as the Galilean preacher and as the glorified Son of God at the Transfiguration (Matthew 17:1-8). Here Jesus appears as the mighty Son of Man. His white hair indicates his wisdom and divine nature (see also Daniel 7:9); his bright eyes symbolize judgment of all evil; the gold sash across his chest reveals him as the High Priest, who goes into God's presence to obtain forgiveness of sin for those who have believed in him.

1:16 The sword in Jesus' mouth symbolizes the power and force of his message. His words of judgment are as sharp as swords (Isaiah 49:2; Hebrews 4:12).

1:17, 18 As the Roman government stepped up its persecution of Christians, John must have wondered if the church could survive and stand against the opposition. But Jesus appeared in glory and splendor, reassuring John that he and his fellow believers had access to God's strength to face these trials. If you are facing difficult problems, remember that the power available to John and the early church is also available to you (see 1 John 4:4).

1:17, 18 Our sins have convicted and sentenced us, but Jesus holds the keys of death and the grave. He alone can free us from eternal bondage to Satan. He alone has the power and authority to set us free from sin's control. Believers don't have to fear death or the grave because Christ holds the keys to both. All we must do is turn from sin and turn to him in faith. When we attempt to control our life and disregard God, we set a course that leads directly to hell. But when we place our life in Christ's hands, he restores us now and resurrects us later to an eternal, peaceful relationship with him.

1:19 Isa 48:6; Rev 1:1
1:20 Rev 1:4, 12, 16; 2:1; 3:1

alive forever and ever! And I hold the keys of death and the grave.* 19 Write down what
you have seen—both the things that are now happening and the things that will happen
later. 20 This is the meaning of the seven stars you saw in my right hand and the seven
gold lampstands: The seven stars are the angels of* the seven churches, and the seven
lampstands are the seven churches.

The Message to the Church in Ephesus

2:1 Rev 1:12-16, 20; 3:1

2 "Write this letter to the angel of* the church in Ephesus. This is the message from
the one who holds the seven stars in his right hand, the one who walks among the
seven gold lampstands:

1:18 Greek *and Hades.* **1:20** Or *the messengers for.* **2:1** Or *the messenger for;* also in 2:8, 12, 18.

A JOURNEY THROUGH THE BOOK OF REVELATION
Revelation is a complex book, and it has baffled interpreters for centuries. We can avoid a great deal of confusion by understanding the literary structure of this book. This approach will allow us to understand the individual scenes within the overall structure of Revelation and keep us from getting unnecessarily bogged down in the details of each vision. John gives hints throughout the book to indicate a change of scene, a change of subject, or a flashback to an earlier scene.

In chapter 1, John relates the circumstances that led to the writing of this book (1:1–20). In chapters 2 and 3, Jesus gives special messages to the seven churches of Asia Minor (2:1—3:22).

Suddenly, John is caught up into heaven, where he sees a vision of God Almighty on his throne. All of Christ's followers and the heavenly angels are worshiping God (4:1–11). John watches as God gives a scroll with seven seals to the worthy Lamb, Jesus Christ (5:1–14). The Lamb begins to open the seals one by one. As each seal is opened, a new vision appears.

As the first four seals are opened, riders appear on horses of different colors: war, famine, disease, and death are in their path (6:1–8). As the fifth seal is opened, John sees those in heaven who have been martyred for their faith in Christ (6:9–11).

A set of contrasting images appears at the opening of the sixth seal. On one side, there is a great earthquake, stars fall from the sky, and the sky rolls up like a scroll (6:12–17). On the other side, multitudes are before the throne, worshiping and praising God and the Lamb (7:1–17).

Finally, the seventh seal is opened (8:1–5), unveiling a series of God's judgments announced by seven angels with seven trumpets. The first four angels bring hail, fire, a mountain of fire, and a falling star—the sun and moon are darkened (8:6–13). The fifth trumpet announces the coming of locusts with the power to sting (9:1–12). The sixth trumpet heralds the coming of an army of warriors on horses (9:13–21). In 10:1–11, John is given a small scroll to eat. Following this, John is commanded to measure the Temple of God (11:1, 2). He sees two witnesses, who proclaim God's judgment on the earth for three and a half years (11:3–14).

Finally, the seventh trumpet sounds, calling the rival forces of good and evil to the final battle. On one side is Satan and his forces; on the other side stands Jesus Christ with his forces (11:15—13:18). In the midst of this call to battle, John sees three angels announcing the final judgment (14:6–13). Two angels begin to reap this harvest of judgment on the earth (14:14–20). Following on the heels of these two angels are seven more angels, who pour out God's judgment on the earth from seven bowls (15:1—16:21). One of these angels from the group of seven reveals to John a vision of a "great prostitute" called Babylon (symbolizing the Roman Empire), riding a scarlet beast (17:1–18). After the defeat of Babylon (18:1–24), a great multitude in heaven shouts praise to God for his mighty victory (19:1–10).

The final three chapters of the book of Revelation catalog the events that finalize Christ's victory over the enemy: Satan's 1,000-year imprisonment (20:1–10), the final judgment (20:11–15), and the creation of a new earth and a new Jerusalem (21:1—22:6). An angel then gives John final instructions concerning the visions John has seen and what to do once he has written them all down (22:7–11).

Revelation concludes with the promise of Christ's soon return, an offer to drink of the water of life that flows through the great street of the new Jerusalem, and a warning to those who read the book (22:12–21). May we pray with John, "Amen! Come, Lord Jesus!" (22:20).

The Bible ends with a message of warning and hope for men and women of every generation. Christ is victorious, and all evil has been done away with. As you read the book of Revelation, marvel at God's grace in the salvation of the saints and his power over the evil forces of Satan, and remember the hope of this victory to come.

1:20 Who are the "angels of the seven churches"? Some say that they are angels designated to guard the churches; others say that they are elders or pastors of the local churches. Because the seven letters in chapters 2 and 3 contain reprimands, it is doubtful that these angels are heavenly messengers. If these are earthly leaders or messengers, they are accountable to God for the churches they represent.

2:1 Ephesus was the capital of Asia Minor, a center of land and sea trade, and, along with Alexandria and Antioch in Syria, one of the three most influential cities in the eastern part of the Roman Empire. The temple to Artemis, one of the ancient wonders of the world, was located in this city, and a major industry was the manufacture of images of this goddess (see Acts 19:21-41). Paul ministered in Ephesus for three years and warned the Ephesians that false teachers would come and try to draw people away from the faith (see Acts 20:29-31). False teachers did indeed cause problems in the Ephesian church, but the church resisted them, as we can see from Paul's letter

2“I know all the things you do. I have seen your hard work and your patient
endurance. I know you don’t tolerate evil people. You have examined the claims
of those who say they are apostles but are not. You have discovered they are
liars. 3You have patiently suffered for me without quitting. 4But I have this complaint against you. You don’t love me or each other as you did at first! 5Look
how far you have fallen from your first love! Turn back to me again and work as
you did at first. If you don’t, I will come and remove your lampstand from its
place among the churches. 6But there is this about you that is good: You hate the
deeds of the immoral Nicolaitans, just as I do.
7“Anyone who is willing to hear should listen to the Spirit and understand what
the Spirit is saying to the churches. Everyone who is victorious will eat from the
tree of life in the paradise of God.

2:2 2 Cor 11:13; 1 Jn 4:1; Rev 2:19
2:3 John 15:21
2:4 Jer 2:2; Matt 24:12
2:5 Rev 2:16, 22; 3:3, 19
2:6 Ps 139:21
2:7 Gen 2:8-9; 3:22-24; Ezek 31:8-9

to the Ephesians. John spent much of his ministry in this city and knew that they had resisted false teaching (2:2).

2:1 The one who “walks among the seven gold lampstands” (the seven churches) is Jesus (1:11-13). He holds the “seven stars in his right hand” (messengers of the churches), indicating his power and authority over the churches and their leaders. Ephesus had become a large, proud church, and Jesus’ message would remind them that he alone is the head of the body of believers.

2:1ff Does God care about your church? If you are tempted to doubt it, look more closely at these seven letters. The Lord of the universe knew each of these churches and its precise situation. In each letter, Jesus told John to write about specific people, places, and events. He praised believers for their successes and told them how to correct their failures. Just as Jesus cared for each of these churches, he cares for yours. He wants it to reach its greatest potential. The group of believers with whom you worship and serve is God’s vehicle for changing the world. Take it seriously—God does.

2:2 Over a long period of time, the church in Ephesus had steadfastly refused to tolerate sin among its members. This was not easy in a city noted for immoral sexual practices associated with the worship of the goddess Artemis. We also are living in times of widespread sin and sexual immorality. It is popular to be open-minded toward many types of sin, calling them personal choices or alternative life-styles. But when the body of believers begins to tolerate sin in the church, it is lowering the standards and compromising the church’s witness. Remember that God’s approval is infinitely more important than the world’s.

2:2, 3 Christ commended the church at Ephesus for (1) working hard, (2) patiently enduring, (3) not tolerating evil people, (4) critically examining the claims of false apostles, and (5) suffering without quitting. Every church should have these characteristics. But these good efforts should spring from our love for Jesus Christ. Both Jesus and John stressed love for one another as an authentic proof of the Good News (John 13:34; 1 John 3:18, 19). In the battle to maintain sound teaching and moral and doctrinal purity, it is possible to lose a charitable spirit. Prolonged conflict can weaken or destroy our patience and affection. In defending the faith, guard against any structure or rigidity that weakens love.

2:4 Paul had once commended the church at Ephesus for its love for God and others (Ephesians 1:15), but many of the church founders had died, and many of the second-generation believers had lost their zeal for God. They were a busy church—the members did much to benefit themselves and the community—but they were acting out of the wrong motives. Work for God must be motivated by love for God, or it will not last.

2:4, 5 Just as when a man and woman fall in love, so also new believers rejoice at their newfound forgiveness. But when we lose sight of the seriousness of sin, we begin to lose the thrill of our forgiveness (see 2 Peter 1:9). In the first steps of your Christian life, you may have had enthusiasm without knowledge. Do you now have knowledge without enthusiasm? Both are necessary if we are to keep love for God intense and untarnished (see Hebrews 10:32, 35). Do you love God with the same fervor as when you were a new Christian?

2:5 For Jesus to “remove your lampstand from its place” would mean the church would cease to be an effective church. Just as the seven-branched candlestick in the Temple gave light for the priests to see, the churches were to give light to their surrounding communities. But Jesus warned them that their lights could go out. In fact, Jesus himself would extinguish any light that did not fulfill its purpose. The church needed to repent of its sins.

2:6 The Nicolaitans were believers who compromised their faith in order to enjoy some of the sinful practices of Ephesian society. The name *Nicolaitans* is held by some to be roughly the Greek equivalent of the Hebrew word for “Balaamites.” Balaam was a prophet who induced the Israelites to carry out their lustful desires (see 2:14 and Numbers 31:16). When we want to take part in an activity that we know is wrong, we may make excuses to justify our behavior, saying that it isn’t as bad as it seems or that it won’t hurt our faith. Christ has strong words for those who look for excuses to sin.

2:6 Through John, Jesus commended the church at Ephesus for hating the wicked practices of the Nicolaitans. Note that they didn’t hate the people, just their sinful actions. We should accept and love all people and refuse to tolerate any evil. God cannot tolerate sin, and he expects us to stand against it. The world needs Christians who will stand for God’s truth and point people toward right living.

2:7 We are victorious by believing in Christ, persevering, remaining faithful, and living as one who follows Christ. Such a life brings great rewards (21:7).

2:7 Two trees were in the Garden of Eden—the tree of life and the tree of the knowledge of good and evil (see Genesis 2:9). Eating from the tree of life brought eternal life with God; eating from the tree of knowledge brought realization of good and evil. When Adam and Eve ate from the tree of knowledge, they disobeyed God’s command. So they were excluded from Eden and barred from eating from the tree of life. Eventually, evil will be destroyed and believers will be brought into a restored paradise. In the new earth, everyone will eat from the tree of life and live forever.

The Message to the Church in Smyrna

2:8
Rev 1:11, 17-18

8"Write this letter to the angel of the church in Smyrna. This is the message from the one
who is the First and the Last, who died and is alive:

2:9
2 Cor 6:10; 11:14-15
Rev 3:9

2:10
Dan 1:12, 14
Jas 1:12
Rev 3:9; 17:14

2:11
Rev 2:7; 20:6, 14

9"I know about your suffering and your poverty—but you are rich! I know the
slander of those opposing you. They say they are Jews, but they really aren't
because theirs is a synagogue of Satan.
10Don't be afraid of what you are about to
suffer. The Devil will throw some of you into prison and put you to the test. You
will be persecuted for 'ten days.' Remain faithful even when facing death, and I
will give you the crown of life.

11"Anyone who is willing to hear should listen to the Spirit and understand what
the Spirit is saying to the churches. Whoever is victorious will not be hurt by the
second death.

The Message to the Church in Pergamum

2:12
Rev 1:16; 2:16

12"Write this letter to the angel of the church in Pergamum. This is the message from the
one who has a sharp two-edged sword:

THE NAMES OF JESUS

Reference	*Jesus' Name*	*Reference*	*Jesus' Name*
1:13	The Son of Man	7:17	Shepherd
1:17	The First and the Last	12:10	Christ
1:18	The living one who died	19:11	Faithful and True
2:18	The Son of God	19:13	The Word of God
3:14	The faithful and true witness	19:16	King of kings
4:11	Creator	19:16	Lord of lords
5:5	The Lion of the tribe of Judah	22:13	The Alpha and the Omega
5:5	The root of David	22:13	The Beginning and the End
5:6	Lamb	22:16	The bright morning star

Scattered among the vivid images of the book of Revelation is a large collection of names for Jesus. Each one tells something of his character and highlights a particular aspect of his role within God's plan of redemption.

2:8 The city of Smyrna was about 25 miles north of Ephesus. It was nicknamed "Port of Asia" because it had an excellent harbor on the Aegean Sea. The church in this city struggled against two hostile forces: a Jewish population strongly opposed to Christianity, and a non-Jewish population that was loyal to Rome and supported emperor worship. Persecution and suffering were inevitable in an environment like this.

2:9, 10 Persecution comes from Satan, not from God. Satan, the Devil, will cause believers to be thrown into prison and even killed. But believers need not fear death, because it will only result in their receiving the crown of life. Satan may harm their earthly bodies, but he can do them no spiritual harm. The "synagogue of Satan" means that these Jews were serving Satan's purposes, not God's, when they gathered to worship. "Ten days" means that although persecution would be intense, it would be relatively short. It would have a definite beginning and end, and God would remain in complete control.

2:9-11 Pain is part of life, but it is never easy to suffer, no matter what the cause. Jesus commended the church at Smyrna for its faith in suffering. He then encouraged the believers that they need not fear the future if they remained faithful. If you are experiencing difficult times, don't let them turn you away from God. Instead, let them draw you toward greater faithfulness. Trust God and remember your heavenly reward (see also 22:12-14).

2:10 Smyrna was famous for its athletic games. A crown was the victory wreath, the trophy for the champion at the games. If we have been faithful, we will receive the prize of victory—eternal life (James 1:12). The message to the Smyrna church was to remain faithful during suffering because God is in control and his promises are reliable. Jesus never says that by being faithful to him we will avoid troubles, suffering, and persecution. Rather, we must be faithful to him *in* our sufferings. Only then will our faith prove to be genuine. We remain faithful by keeping our eyes on Christ and on what he promises us now and in the future (see Philippians 3:13, 14; 2 Timothy 4:8).

2:11 Believers and unbelievers alike experience physical death. All people will be resurrected, but believers will be resurrected to eternal life with God while unbelievers will be resurrected to be punished with a second death, eternal separation from God (see also 20:14; 21:8, 27; 22:15).

2:12 The city of Pergamum was built on a hill 1,000 feet above the surrounding countryside, creating a natural fortress. It was a sophisticated city, a center of Greek culture and education, with a 200,000-volume library. But it was also the center of four cults, and it rivaled Ephesus in its worship of idols. The city's chief god was Asclepius, whose symbol was a serpent and who was considered the god of healing. People came to Pergamum from all over the world to seek healing from this god.

2:12 Just as the Romans used their swords for authority and judgment, Jesus' sharp two-edged sword represents God's ultimate authority and judgment. It may also represent God's future separation of believers from unbelievers. Unbelievers cannot experience the eternal rewards of living in God's Kingdom.

13 “I know that you live in the city where that great throne of Satan is located,
and yet you have remained loyal to me. And you refused to deny me even when
Antipas, my faithful witness, was martyred among you by Satan’s followers.
14 And yet I have a few complaints against you. You tolerate some among you
who are like Balaam, who showed Balak how to trip up the people of Israel. He
taught them to worship idols by eating food offered to idols and by committing
sexual sin. 15 In the same way, you have some Nicolaitans among you—people
who follow the same teaching and commit the same sins. 16 Repent, or I will
come to you suddenly and fight against them with the sword of my mouth.
17 “Anyone who is willing to hear should listen to the Spirit and understand what the
Spirit is saying to the churches. Everyone who is victorious will eat of the manna that
has been hidden away in heaven. And I will give to each one a white stone, and on the
stone will be engraved a new name that no one knows except the one who receives it.

2:13 Rev 14:12
2:14 Num 31:16; 1 Cor 6:13; 2 Pet 2:15; Jude 1:11
2:15 Rev 2:6
2:16 2 Thes 2:8; Rev 1:16; 2:5; 22:7, 12, 20
2:17 Ps 78:24; Isa 62:2; 65:15; John 6:49-58; Rev 3:12; 19:12

The Message to the Church in Thyatira

18 “Write this letter to the angel of the church in Thyatira. This is the message from the Son
of God, whose eyes are bright like flames of fire, whose feet are like polished bronze:

19 “I know all the things you do—your love, your faith, your service, and your patient
endurance. And I can see your constant improvement in all these things. 20 But I have
this complaint against you. You are permitting that woman—that Jezebel who calls
herself a prophet—to lead my servants astray. She is encouraging them to worship

2:18 Dan 10:6; Rev 1:14-15
2:19 Rev 2:2
2:20 1 Kgs 16:31; 2 Kgs 9:7, 22

2:13 As the center for four idolatrous cults (Zeus, Dionysius, Asclepius, and Athene), Pergamum was called the city “where that great throne of Satan is located.” Surrounded by worship of Satan and the Roman emperor as god, the church at Pergamum refused to renounce its faith, even when Satan’s worshipers martyred one of its members. Standing firm against the strong pressures and temptations of society is never easy, but the alternative is deadly (2:11).

2:13-15 It was not easy to be a Christian in Pergamum. Believers experienced great pressure to compromise or leave the faith. (For information on the Nicolaitans, see the first note on 2:6.) Nothing is known about Antipas except that he did *not* compromise. He was faithful, and he died for his faith. Apparently, however, some in the church were tolerating those who taught or practiced what Christ opposed. Compromise can be defined as a blending of the qualities of two different things or a concession of principles. Cooperate with people as much as you can, but avoid any alliance, partnership, or participation that could lead to immoral practices.

2:14 There is room for differences of opinion among Christians in some areas, but there is no room for heresy and moral impurity. Your town might not participate in idol feasts, but it probably has pornography, sexual sin, cheating, gossiping, and lying. Don’t tolerate sin by bowing to the pressure to be open-minded.

2:14-16 Balak was a king who feared the large number of Israelites traveling through his country, so he hired Balaam to pronounce a curse on them. Balaam refused at first, but an offer of money changed his mind (Numbers 22–24). Later Balaam influenced the Israelites to turn to idol worship (Numbers 31:16; also see 2 Peter 2:15; Jude 1:11). Here Christ rebuked the church for tolerating those who, like Balaam, lead people away from God.

2:16 This sword is God’s judgment against rebellious nations (19:15, 21) and all forms of sin. See also the note on 1:16 and the second note on 2:12.

2:17 This “manna that has been hidden away in heaven” suggests the spiritual nourishment that the faithful believers will receive. As the Israelites traveled toward the Promised Land, God provided manna from heaven for their physical nourishment (Exodus 16:13-18). Jesus, as the bread of life (John 6:51), provides spiritual nourishment that satisfies our deepest hunger.

2:17 It is unclear what the white stones are or exactly what the name on each will be. Because they relate to the hidden manna, they may be symbols of the believer’s eternal nourishment or eternal life. The stones are significant because each will bear the new name of every person who truly believes in Christ. They are the evidence that a person has been accepted by God and declared worthy to receive eternal life. A person’s name represented his or her character. God will give us a new name and a new heart.

2:18 Thyatira was a working person’s town, with many trade guilds for cloth making, dyeing, and pottery. Lydia, Paul’s first convert in Philippi, was a merchant from Thyatira (Acts 16:14). The city was basically secular, with no focus on any particular religion.

2:19 The believers in Thyatira were commended for growing in good deeds. We should not only take comfort in gathering for worship or rejoice when people give their lives to Christ in our church. We should also seek to grow in love, faith, and acts of service. Because the times are critical, we must spend our days wisely and faithfully.

2:20 A woman in the church in Thyatira was teaching that immorality was not a serious matter for believers. Her name may have been Jezebel, or John may have used the name Jezebel to symbolize the kind of evil she was promoting. Jezebel, a pagan queen of Israel, was considered the most evil woman who ever lived (see 1 Kings 19:1, 2; 21:1-15; 2 Kings 9:7-10, 30-37; and her Profile in 1 Kings 21).

2:20 Why is sexual immorality serious? Sex outside marriage always hurts someone. It hurts God because it shows that we prefer to satisfy our desires our own way instead of according to God’s Word or to satisfy them immediately instead of waiting for his timing. It hurts others because it violates the commitment so necessary to a relationship. It hurts us because it often brings disease to our bodies and adversely affects our personalities. Sexual immorality has tremendous power to destroy families, churches, and communities because it destroys the integrity on which these relationships are built. God wants to protect us from hurting ourselves and others; thus, we are to have no part in sexual immorality, even if our culture accepts it.

2:20 In pagan temples, meat was often offered to idols. Then the meat that wasn’t burned was sold to shoppers in the temple marketplace. Eating meat offered to idols wasn’t wrong in itself, but it could violate the conscience of weaker Christian brothers and sisters who would be bothered by it (see 1 Corinthians 8 and the note on Romans 14:2). Jezebel was obviously more concerned about her own selfish pleasure and freedom than about the needs and concerns of fellow believers.

2:21 Rev 9:20
2:22 Rev 17:2; 22:9
2:23 Prov 24:12; Jer 17:10; Matt 16:27; Luke 16:15; Rom 8:27
2:25 Rev 3:11
2:26-27 Ps 2:8-9; Matt 10:22; Rev 12:5
2:28 Rev 22:16
2:29 Rev 2:7
3:1 Rev 1:4, 11, 16; 3:8, 15
3:3 Matt 24:42-44; Luke 22:32; 1 Thes 5:2-6; 2 Pet 3:10; Rev 2:5; 16:15

idols, eat food offered to idols, and commit sexual sin. 21 I gave her time to repent,
but she would not turn away from her immorality. 22 Therefore, I will throw her upon
a sickbed, and she will suffer greatly with all who commit adultery with her, unless
they turn away from all their evil deeds. 23 I will strike her children dead. And all the
churches will know that I am the one who searches out the thoughts and intentions of
every person. And I will give to each of you whatever you deserve. 24 But I also have
a message for the rest of you in Thyatira who have not followed this false teaching
('deeper truths,' as they call them—depths of Satan, really). I will ask nothing more
of you 25 except that you hold tightly to what you have until I come.
26 "To all who are victorious, who obey me to the very end, I will give authority
over all the nations. 27 They will rule the nations with an iron rod and smash them
like clay pots. 28 They will have the same authority I received from my Father, and
I will also give them the morning star! 29 Anyone who is willing to hear should
listen to the Spirit and understand what the Spirit is saying to the churches.

The Message to the Church in Sardis

3 "Write this letter to the angel of* the church in Sardis. This is the message from the
one who has the sevenfold Spirit* of God and the seven stars:

"I know all the things you do, and that you have a reputation for being alive—but
you are dead. 2 Now wake up! Strengthen what little remains, for even what is left
is at the point of death. Your deeds are far from right in the sight of God. 3 Go back

3:1a Or *the messenger for;* also in 3:7, 14. **3:1b** Greek *the seven spirits.*

THE LETTERS TO THE SEVEN CHURCHES

Church	*Reference*	*Commendation*	*Rebuke*	*Action*
Ephesus	2:1–7	Hard work, perseverance	Forsaken first love	Remember and repent
Smyrna	2:8–11	Suffered persecution, poverty	None	Don't fear; be faithful
Pergamum	2:12–17	True to faith	Compromise	Repent
Thyatira	2:18–29	Love, faith, service	Immorality	Repent
Sardis	3:1–6	Effective	Superficial	Wake up; repent
Philadelphia	3:7–13	Faithful	None	Hold on
Laodicea	3:14–22	None	Lukewarm	Be earnest and repent

This summary of the letters to the seven churches shows us the qualities our churches should seek and those we should avoid.

2:21 Jezebel was unwilling to repent. *Repent* means "to change one's mind and to turn from sin" and its disastrous consequences to God and eternal life. In his mercy, God has given us time to decide to follow him. Only our stubborn willfulness stands in the way.

2:23 We cannot hide from Christ; he knows what is in our heart and mind, and still he loves us. The sins we try to hide from God need to be confessed to him.

2:24, 25 The "deeper truths" of Satan were either false teaching advocated by heretics, or secret insights by so-called believers "guaranteed" to promote deeper spiritual life. We should hold tightly to the basics of our Christian faith and view with caution and counsel any new teaching that turns us away from the Bible, the fellowship of our church, or our basic confession of faith.

2:26, 27 Christ says that those who overcome (those who remain faithful until the end and continue to please God) will rule over Christ's enemies and reign with him as he judges evil (see also Psalm 2:8, 9; Isaiah 30:14; Jeremiah 19:11; 1 Corinthians 6:2, 3; Revelation 12:5; 19:15; 20:3, 4 for more about God's judgment).

2:28 Christ is also called the morning star in 22:16. A morning star appears just before dawn, when the night is coldest and darkest. When the world is at its bleakest point, Christ will burst onto the scene, exposing evil with his light of truth and bringing his promised reward.

3:1 The wealthy city of Sardis was actually in two locations. The older section of the city was on a mountain, and when its population outgrew the spot, a newer section was built in the valley below.

3:1 The "sevenfold Spirit" is another name for the Holy Spirit. The seven stars are the messengers, or leaders, of the churches (see the note on 2:1).

3:1 The problem in the Sardis church was not heresy but spiritual death. In spite of its reputation for being active, Sardis was infested with sin. Its deeds were evil, and its clothes soiled. The Spirit has no words of commendation for this church that looked so good on the outside but was so corrupt on the inside.

3:3 The church at Sardis was urged to obey the Christian truth they had heard when they first believed in Christ, to get back to the basics of the faith. It is important to grow in our knowledge of the Lord, to deepen our understanding through careful study. But no matter how much we learn, we must never abandon the basic truths about Jesus. Jesus will always be God's Son, and his sacrifice for our sins is permanent. No new truth from God will ever contradict these fundamental biblical teachings.

to what you heard and believed at first; hold to it firmly and turn to me again. Unless you do, I will come upon you suddenly, as unexpected as a thief.
4“Yet even in Sardis there are some who have not soiled their garments with evil
deeds. They will walk with me in white, for they are worthy. 5All who are victorious will be clothed in white. I will never erase their names from the Book of Life,
but I will announce before my Father and his angels that they are mine. 6Anyone
who is willing to hear should listen to the Spirit and understand what the Spirit is
saying to the churches.

The Message to the Church in Philadelphia

7“Write this letter to the angel of the church in Philadelphia. This is the message from
the one who is holy and true. He is the one who has the key of David. He opens doors,
and no one can shut them; he shuts doors, and no one can open them.

8“I know all the things you do, and I have opened a door for you that no one can
shut. You have little strength, yet you obeyed my word and did not deny me.
9Look! I will force those who belong to Satan—those liars who say they are Jews
but are not—to come and bow down at your feet. They will acknowledge that you
are the ones I love.
10“Because you have obeyed my command to persevere, I will protect you from
the great time of testing that will come upon the whole world to test those who belong to this world. 11Look, I am coming quickly. Hold on to what you have, so that
no one will take away your crown. 12All who are victorious will become pillars in
the Temple of my God, and they will never have to leave it. And I will write my
God’s name on them, and they will be citizens in the city of my God—the new Jerusalem that comes down from heaven from my God. And they will have my new
name inscribed upon them. 13Anyone who is willing to hear should listen to the
Spirit and understand what the Spirit is saying to the churches.

The Message to the Church in Laodicea

14“Write this letter to the angel of the church in Laodicea. This is the message from the
one who is the Amen—the faithful and true witness, the ruler* of God’s creation:

15“I know all the things you do, that you are neither hot nor cold. I wish you were one
or the other! 16But since you are like lukewarm water, I will spit you out of my mouth!

3:4 Jude 1:23
3:5 Exod 32:32-33; Ps 69:28; Matt 10:32; Luke 12:8; Rev 13:8; 17:8; 20:12
3:6 Rev 2:7
3:7 Job 12:14; Isa 22:22; Matt 16:19
3:8 Acts 14:27; Rev 2:13
3:9 Isa 43:4; 49:23; 2 Cor 11:14-15; Rev 2:9
3:10 2 Pet 2:9; Rev 2:10
3:11 Rev 2:25; 22:7, 12, 20
3:12 Ezek 48:35; Gal 4:26; Rev 21:2, 10
3:13 Rev 2:7
3:14 John 1:3; 2 Cor 1:20; Col 1:15-18; Rev 1:5
3:15 Rom 12:11

3:14 Or *the source.*

3:5 To be “clothed in white” means to be set apart for God and made pure. Christ promises future honor and eternal life to those who stand firm in their faith. The names of all believers are registered in the Book of Life. This book symbolizes God’s knowledge of who belongs to him. All such people are guaranteed a listing in the Book of Life and are introduced to the hosts of heaven as belonging to Christ (see Luke 12:8, 9).

3:7 Philadelphia was founded by the citizens of Pergamum. The community was built in a frontier area as a gateway to the central plateau of Asia Minor. Philadelphia’s residents kept barbarians out of the region and brought in Greek culture and language. The city was destroyed by an earthquake in A.D. 17, and aftershocks kept the people so worried that most of them lived outside the city limits.

3:7 The “key of David” represents Christ’s authority to open the door into his future Kingdom. After the door is opened, no one can close it—salvation is assured. Once it is closed, no one can open it—judgment is certain.

3:10 Some believe that “I will protect you from the great time of testing” means there will be a future time of great tribulation from which true believers will be spared. Others interpret this to mean that the church will go through the time of tribulation and that God will keep them strong in the midst of it. Still others believe this refers to times of great distress in general, the church’s suffering through the ages. Whatever the case, our emphasis should be on patiently obeying God no matter what we may face.

3:11 Christians have differing gifts, abilities, experience, and maturity. God doesn’t expect us all to be and act the same, but he does expect us to “hold on” to what we have, to persevere in using our resources for him. The Philadelphians are commended for their effort to obey (3:8) and encouraged to hold tightly to whatever strength they have. You may be a new believer and feel that your faith and spiritual strength are little. Use what you have to live for Christ, and God will commend you.

3:12 The new Jerusalem is the future dwelling of the people of God (21:2). We will have a new citizenship in God’s future Kingdom. Everything will be new, pure, and secure.

3:14 Laodicea was the wealthiest of the seven cities, known for its banking industry, manufacture of wool, and a medical school that produced eye ointment. But the city had always had a problem with its water supply. At one time an aqueduct was built to bring water to the city from hot springs. But by the time the water reached the city, it was neither hot nor refreshingly cool—only lukewarm. The church had become as bland as the tepid water that came into the city.

3:15, 16 Lukewarm water makes a disgusting drink. The church in Laodicea had become lukewarm and thus distasteful and repugnant. The believers didn’t take a stand for anything; indifference had led to idleness. By neglecting to do anything for Christ, the church had become hardened and self-satisfied, and it was destroying itself. There is nothing more disgusting than a half-hearted, nominal Christian who is self-sufficient. Don’t settle for following God halfway. Let Christ fire up your faith and get you into the action.

3:17 Hos 12:8; Zech 11:5; 1 Cor 4:8
3:19 Prov 3:12; 1 Cor 11:32; Heb 12:6; Rev 2:5
3:20 John 14:23
3:21 Matt 19:28; Rev 5:5
3:22 Rev 2:7

17 You say, 'I am rich. I have everything I want. I don't need a thing!' And you don't
realize that you are wretched and miserable and poor and blind and naked. 18 I advise
you to buy gold from me—gold that has been purified by fire. Then you will be rich.
And also buy white garments so you will not be shamed by your nakedness. And buy
ointment for your eyes so you will be able to see. 19 I am the one who corrects and disciplines everyone I love. Be diligent and turn from your indifference.
20 "Look! Here I stand at the door and knock. If you hear me calling and open the
door, I will come in, and we will share a meal as friends. 21 I will invite everyone
who is victorious to sit with me on my throne, just as I was victorious and sat with
my Father on his throne. 22 Anyone who is willing to hear should listen to the Spirit
and understand what the Spirit is saying to the churches."

B. MESSAGE FOR THE CHURCH (4:1—22:21)

Moving from the conditions within the churches in Asia to the future of the universal church, John sees the course of coming events in a way similar to Daniel and Ezekiel. Many of these passages contain clear spiritual teachings, but others seem beyond our ability to understand. The clear teaching of this book is that God will defeat all evil in the end. We must live in obedience to Jesus Christ, the coming Conqueror and Judge.

4:1 Exod 19:20, 24; Ezek 1:1; Dan 2:28-29, 45
4:2 Isa 6:1; Ezek 1:26-27
4:3 Ezek 1:26-28

1. Worshiping God in heaven

4 Then as I looked, I saw a door standing open in heaven, and the same voice I had
heard before spoke to me with the sound of a mighty trumpet blast. The voice
said, "Come up here, and I will show you what must happen after these things." 2 And
instantly I was in the Spirit,* and I saw a throne in heaven and someone sitting on it!
3 The one sitting on the throne was as brilliant as gemstones—jasper and carnelian.

4:2 Or *in spirit.*

3:17 Some believers assume that numerous material possessions are a sign of God's spiritual blessing. Laodicea was a wealthy city, and the church was also wealthy. But what the Laodiceans could see and buy had become more valuable to them than what is unseen and eternal. Wealth, luxury, and ease can make people feel confident, satisfied, and complacent. But no matter how much you possess or how much money you make, you have nothing if you don't have a vital relationship with Christ. How does your current level of wealth affect your spiritual desire? Instead of centering your life primarily on comfort and luxury, find your true riches in Christ.

3:18 Laodicea was known for its great wealth; Christ told the Laodiceans to buy their gold from him (real spiritual treasures). The city was proud of its cloth and dyeing industries; Christ told them to purchase white garments from him (his righteousness). Laodicea prided itself on its precious eye ointment that healed many eye problems; Christ told them to get medicine from him to heal their eyes so they could see the truth (John 9:39). Christ was showing the Laodiceans that true value was not in material possessions but in a right relationship with God. Their possessions and achievements were valueless compared with the everlasting future of Christ's Kingdom.

3:19 God would discipline this lukewarm church unless it turned from its indifference toward him. God's purpose in discipline is not to punish but to bring people back to him. Are you lukewarm in your devotion to God? God may discipline you to help you out of your uncaring attitude, but he uses only loving discipline. You can avoid God's discipline by drawing near to him again through confession, service, worship, and studying his Word. Just as the spark of love can be rekindled in marriage, so the Holy Spirit can reignite our zeal for God when we allow him to work in our heart.

3:20 The Laodicean church was complacent and rich. They felt self-satisfied, but they didn't have Christ's presence among them. Christ knocked at the door of their hearts, but they were so busy enjoying worldly pleasures that they didn't notice that he was trying to enter. The pleasures of this world—money, security, material possessions—can be dangerous, because their temporary satisfaction makes us indifferent to God's offer of lasting satisfaction. If you find yourself feeling indifferent to church, to God, or to the Bible, you have begun to shut God out of your life. Leave the door of your heart constantly open to God, and you won't need to worry about hearing his knock. Letting him in is your only hope for lasting fulfillment.

3:20 Jesus knocks at the door of our heart because he wants to save us and have fellowship with us. He is patient and persistent in trying to get through to us—not breaking and entering, but knocking. He allows us to decide whether or not to open our life to him. Do you intentionally keep his life-changing presence and power on the other side of the door?

3:22 At the end of each letter to these churches, the believers were urged to listen and understand what was written to them. Although a different message was addressed to each church, all the messages contain warnings and principles for everyone. Which letter speaks most directly to your church? Which has the greatest bearing on your own spiritual condition at this time? How will you respond?

4:1 Chapters 4 and 5 record glimpses into Christ's glory. Here we see into the throne room of heaven. God is on the throne and orchestrating all the events that John will record. The world is not spinning out of control; the God of creation will carry out his plans as Christ initiates the final battle with the forces of evil. John shows us heaven before showing us earth so that we will not be frightened by future events.

4:1 The voice John had first heard that sounded like a trumpet blast was the voice of Christ (see 1:10, 11).

4:2 Four times in the book of Revelation John says he was "in the Spirit" (1:10; 4:2; 17:3; 21:10). This expression means that the Holy Spirit was giving him a vision—showing him situations and events he could not have seen with mere human eyesight. All true prophecy comes from God through the Holy Spirit (2 Peter 1:20, 21).

And the glow of an emerald circled his throne like a rainbow. 4 Twenty-four thrones
surrounded him, and twenty-four elders sat on them. They were all clothed in white
and had gold crowns on their heads. 5 And from the throne came flashes of lightning
and the rumble of thunder. And in front of the throne were seven lampstands with
burning flames. They are the seven spirits* of God. 6 In front of the throne was a shiny
sea of glass, sparkling like crystal.
In the center and around the throne were four living beings, each covered with eyes,
front and back. 7 The first of these living beings had the form of a lion; the second
looked like an ox; the third had a human face; and the fourth had the form of an eagle
with wings spread out as though in flight. 8 Each of these living beings had six wings,
and their wings were covered with eyes, inside and out. Day after day and night after
night they keep on saying,

"Holy, holy, holy is the Lord God Almighty—
the one who always was, who is, and who is still to come."

9 Whenever the living beings give glory and honor and thanks to the one sitting on the
throne, the one who lives forever and ever, 10 the twenty-four elders fall down and
worship the one who lives forever and ever. And they lay their crowns before the throne
and say,

11 "You are worthy, O Lord our God,
to receive glory and honor and power.
For you created everything,
and it is for your pleasure that they exist and were created."

The Lamb Opens the Scroll

5 And I saw a scroll in the right hand of the one who was sitting on the throne. There
was writing on the inside and the outside of the scroll, and it was sealed with seven
seals. 2 And I saw a strong angel, who shouted with a loud voice: "Who is worthy to break
the seals on this scroll and unroll it?" 3 But no one in heaven or on earth or under the earth
was able to open the scroll and read it.
4 Then I wept because no one could be found who was worthy to open the scroll and
read it. 5 But one of the twenty-four elders said to me, "Stop weeping! Look, the Lion of

4:4 Isa 24:23; Rev 11:16; 19:4
4:5 Exod 19:16; Ezek 1:13; Zech 4:2; Rev 1:4; 5:6
4:6-7 Ezek 1:5-22; 10:12, 14; Rev 15:7; 19:4
4:8 Isa 6:2; Ezek 1:18; 10:12; Amos 3:13
4:9 Dan 4:34; Rev 4:2; 5:1
4:10 Rev 4:4; 5:8, 14
4:11 Rev 10:6
5:1 Isa 29:11; Ezek 2:9-10; Dan 12:4
5:3 Phil 2:10
5:5 Gen 49:9; Isa 11:1, 10; Heb 7:14

4:5 See 1:4 and 3:1, where the same expression is translated *the sevenfold Spirit.*

4:4 Who are these 24 elders? Because there were 12 tribes of Israel in the Old Testament and 12 apostles in the New Testament, the 24 elders in this vision probably represent all the redeemed of God for all time (both before and after Christ's death and resurrection). They symbolize all those—both Jews and Gentiles—who are now part of God's family. The 24 elders show us that *all* the redeemed of the Lord are worshiping him.

4:5 In Revelation, lightning and thunder are connected with significant events in heaven. They remind us of the lightning and thunder at Mount Sinai when God gave the people his laws (Exodus 19:16). The Old Testament often uses such imagery to reflect God's power and majesty (Psalm 77:18).

4:5 The "seven spirits" is another name for the Holy Spirit. See also Zechariah 4:2-6, where the seven lamps are equated with the one Spirit.

4:6 Glass was very rare in New Testament times, and crystal-clear glass was virtually impossible to find (see 1 Corinthians 13:12). The "sea of glass" highlights both the magnificence and holiness of God.

4:6, 7 Just as the Holy Spirit is seen symbolically in the seven lighted lamps, so the "four living beings" represent the attributes (the qualities and character) of God. These creatures were not real animals. Like the cherubim (the highest order of the angels), they guard God's throne, lead others in worship, and proclaim God's holiness. God's attributes symbolized in the animal-like appearance of these four creatures are majesty and power (the lion), faithfulness (the ox), intelligence (the human), and sovereignty (the eagle). The Old Testament prophet Ezekiel saw four similar creatures in one of his visions (Ezekiel 1:5-10).

4:11 The point of this chapter is summed up in this verse: All creatures in heaven and earth will praise and honor God because he is the creator and sustainer of everything.

5:1 In John's day, books were written on scrolls—pieces of papyrus or vellum up to 30 feet long, rolled up and sealed with clay or wax. The scroll that John sees contains the full account of what God has in store for the world. The seven seals indicate the importance of its contents. The seals are located throughout the scroll so that as each one is broken, more of the scroll can be read to reveal another phase of God's plan for the end of the world. Only Christ is worthy to break the seals and open the scroll (5:3-5).

5:1ff Chapter 5 continues the glimpse into heaven begun in chapter 4.

5:5 The Lion, Jesus, proved himself worthy to break the seals and open the scroll by living a perfect life of obedience to God, dying on the cross for the sins of the world, and rising from the dead to show his power and authority over evil and death. Only Christ conquered sin, death, hell, and Satan himself; so only he can be trusted with the world's future. "Heir to David's throne" refers to Jesus being from David's family line, thus fulfilling the promise of the Messiah in the Old Testament.

5:5, 6 Jesus Christ is pictured as both a Lion (symbolizing his authority and power) and a Lamb (symbolizing his submission to God's will). One of the elders calls John to look at the Lion,

the tribe of Judah, the heir to David's throne,* has conquered. He is worthy to open the
scroll and break its seven seals."
[6]I looked and I saw a Lamb that had been killed but was now standing between the
throne and the four living beings and among the twenty-four elders. He had seven horns
and seven eyes, which are the seven spirits* of God that are sent out into every part of
the earth. [7]He stepped forward and took the scroll from the right hand of the one sitting
on the throne. [8]And as he took the scroll, the four living beings and the twenty-four elders
fell down before the Lamb. Each one had a harp, and they held gold bowls filled with
incense—the prayers of God's people!

5:6 Isa 53:7; Zech 4:10; John 1:29, 36; Rev 1:4; 4:5
5:7 Rev 5:1
5:8 Rev 4:4, 6; 8:3-4; 14:2; 15:2

5:5 Greek *the root of David.* **5:6** See note on 4:5.

EVENTS IN REVELATION DESCRIBED ELSEWHERE IN THE BIBLE

Other Reference	*Revelation Reference*	*Event*
Ezekiel 1:22–28	4:2, 3; 10:1–3	Glowing rainbow around God's throne
Isaiah 53:7	5:6–8	Christ is pictured as a Lamb
Psalm 96	5:9–14	New song
Zechariah 1:7–11; 6:1–8	6:1–8	Horses and riders
Isaiah 2:19–22	6:12; 8:5; 11:13	Earthquake
Joel 2:28–32; Acts 2:14–21	6:12	Moon turns blood red
Mark 13:21–25	6:13	Stars falling from the sky
Isaiah 34:1–4	6:14	Sky rolled up like a scroll
Zephaniah 1:14–18; 1 Thessalonians 5:1–3	6:15–17	God's inescapable wrath
Jeremiah 49:35–39	7:1	Four winds of judgment
Luke 8:26–34	9:1, 2; 17:3–8	Bottomless pit
Joel 1:2—2:11	9:3–11	Plague of locusts
Luke 21:20–24	11:1, 2	Trampling of the holy city of Jerusalem
Zechariah 4	11:3–6	Two olive trees as witnesses
Daniel 7	13:1–10	A beast coming out of the sea
2 Thessalonians 2:7–14	13:11–15	Wondrous signs and miracles done by the evil beast
Jeremiah 25:15–29	14:9–12	Drinking the cup of God's wrath
Isaiah 21:1–10	18:2, 3	"Babylon" falls
Matthew 22:1–14	19:5–8	Wedding feast of the Lamb
Ezekiel 38, 39	20:7–10	Conflict with Gog and Magog
John 5:19–30	20:11–15	Judging of all people
Ezekiel 37:21–28	21:3	God lives among his people
Isaiah 25:1–8	21:4	Our tears will be wiped away forever
Genesis 2:8–14	22:1, 2	Tree of life
1 Corinthians 13:11, 12	22:3–5	We will see God face to face
Daniel 7:18–28	22:5	Believers will reign with God forever

but when John looks he sees a Lamb. Christ the Lamb was the perfect sacrifice for the sins of all; therefore, only he can save us from the terrible events revealed by the scroll. Christ the Lamb won the greatest battle of all. He defeated all the forces of evil by dying on the cross. The role of Christ the Lion will be to lead the battle where Satan is finally defeated (19:19-21). Christ the Lion is victorious because of what Christ the Lamb has already done. We will participate in his victory, not because of our effort or goodness, but because he has promised eternal life to all who believe in him.

5:6 John says the Lamb "had been killed"; the wounds inflicted on Jesus' body during his trial and crucifixion could still be seen (see John 20:24-31). Jesus was called the Lamb of God by John the Baptist (John 1:29). In the Old Testament, lambs were sacrificed to atone for sins; the Lamb of God died as the final sacrifice for all sins (see Isaiah 53:7; Hebrews 10:1-12, 18).

5:6 The horns symbolize strength and power (see 1 Kings 22:11; Zechariah 1:18). Although Christ is a sacrificial lamb, he is in no way weak. He was killed, but now he lives in God's strength and power. In Zechariah 4:2-10, the eyes are equated with the seven lamps and the one Spirit.

[9]And they sang a new song with these words:

"You are worthy to take the scroll
and break its seals and open it.
For you were killed, and your blood has ransomed people for God
from every tribe and language and people and nation.
[10] And you have caused them to become God's kingdom and his priests.
And they will reign* on the earth."

[11]Then I looked again, and I heard the singing of thousands and millions of angels
around the throne and the living beings and the elders. [12]And they sang in a mighty
chorus:

"The Lamb is worthy—the Lamb who was killed.
He is worthy to receive power and riches
and wisdom and strength
and honor and glory and blessing."

[13]And then I heard every creature in heaven and on earth and under the earth and in
the sea. They also sang:

"Blessing and honor and glory and power
belong to the one sitting on the throne
and to the Lamb forever and ever."

[14]And the four living beings said, "Amen!" And the twenty-four elders fell down and
worshiped God and the Lamb.

5:9 Ps 144:9; Rev 14:3
5:10 Exod 19:6; 1 Pet 2:5-9; Rev 1:6; 20:4
5:11 Dan 7:10; Heb 12:22; Rev 4:4, 6
5:12 1 Chr 29:11; Isa 53:7; John 1:29, 36; Rev 4:11
5:13 Phil 2:10; Rev 4:11; 5:7
5:14 Rev 4:6, 9-10

2. Opening the seven seals

The Lamb Breaks the First Six Seals

6 As I watched, the Lamb broke the first of the seven seals on the scroll. Then one of the
four living beings called out with a voice that sounded like thunder, "Come!" [2]I looked
up and saw a white horse. Its rider carried a bow, and a crown was placed on his head. He
rode out to win many battles and gain the victory.

6:1 Rev 5:1, 6
6:2 Zech 1:8; 6:1-3; Rev 14:14; 19:11-12

5:10 Some manuscripts read *they are reigning.*

5:9, 10 People from every nation are praising God before his throne. God's message of salvation and eternal life is not limited to a specific culture, race, or country. Anyone who comes to God in repentance and faith is accepted by him and will be part of his Kingdom. Don't allow prejudice or bias to keep you from sharing Christ with others. Christ welcomes all people into his Kingdom.

5:9, 10 The song of God's people praises Christ's work. He (1) was killed, (2) ransomed them with his blood, (3) gathered them into a Kingdom, (4) made them priests, and (5) appointed them to reign on the earth. Jesus has already died and paid the penalty for sin. He is now gathering us into his Kingdom and making us priests. In the future we will reign with him. Worship God and praise him for what he has done, what he is doing, and what he will do for all who trust in him. When we realize the glorious future that awaits us, we will find the strength to face our present difficulties.

5:10 The believers' song praises Christ for bringing them into the Kingdom and making them kings and priests. While now we are sometimes despised and mocked for our faith (John 15:17-27), in the future we will reign over all the earth (Luke 22:29, 30). Christ's death made all believers priests of God—the channels of blessing between God and people (1 Peter 2:5-9).

5:11 Angels are spiritual beings created by God who help carry out his work on earth. They bring messages (Luke 1:26-28), protect God's people (Daniel 6:22), offer encouragement (Genesis 16:7ff), give guidance (Exodus 14:19), bring punishment (2 Samuel 24:16), patrol the earth (Ezekiel 1:9-14), and fight the forces of evil (2 Kings 6:16-18; Revelation 20:1). There are both good and evil angels (12:7), but because evil angels are allied with Satan, they have considerably less power and authority than good angels. Eventually, the main role of the good angels will be to offer continuous praise to God (see also 19:1-3).

5:14 The scene in chapter 5 shows us that only the Lamb, Jesus Christ, is worthy to open the scroll (the events of history). Jesus, not Satan, holds the future. Jesus Christ is in control, and he alone is worthy to set into motion the events of the last days of history.

6:1ff This is the first of three seven-part judgments. The trumpets (chapters 8–9) and the bowls (chapter 16) are the other two. As each seal is opened, Christ the Lamb sets in motion events that will bring about the end of human history. This scroll is not completely opened until the seventh seal is broken (8:1). The contents of the scroll reveal humankind's depravity and portray God's authority over the events of human history.

6:2ff Four horses appear as the first four seals are opened. The horses represent God's judgment of people's sin and rebellion. God is directing human history—even using his enemies to accomplish his purposes. The four horses are a foretaste of the final judgments yet to come. Some view this chapter as a parallel to the Olivet Discourse (see Matthew 24). The imagery of four horses is also found in Zechariah 6:1-8.

6:2-8 Each of the four horses is a different color. Some assume that the white horse represents victory and that its rider must be Christ (because Christ later rides to victory on a white horse—19:11). But because the other three horses relate to judgment and destruction, this rider on a white horse would most likely not be Christ. The four are part of the unfolding judgment of God, and it would be premature for Christ to ride forth as conqueror. The other horses represent different kinds of judgment: red for warfare and bloodshed; black for famine; pale green for death. The high prices of wheat and barley illustrate famine conditions. But the worst is yet to come.

6:4 Zech 1:8; 6:2; Matt 10:34
6:5 Zech 6:2, 6
6:8 Jer 14:12; 15:2-3; Hos 13:14; Rev 1:18; 20:13
6:9 Exod 29:12; Lev 4:7; Rev 14:18; 20:4
6:10 Ps 79:10; Zech 1:12; Luke 18:7; Rev 3:7, 10; 19:2
6:11 Heb 11:40; Rev 3:4
6:12 Joel 2:10; Matt 24:29; Rev 16:18
6:13 Isa 34:4; Rev 8:10; 9:1
6:14 Ps 46:2; 2 Pet 3:10; Rev 16:20; 20:11; 21:1
6:15 Isa 2:10, 19, 21; Jer 4:29
6:16 Hos 10:8; Luke 23:30
6:17 Joel 2:11; Zeph 1:14-15; Mal 3:2

3 When the Lamb broke the second seal, I heard the second living being say,
"Come!" 4 And another horse appeared, a red one. Its rider was given a mighty sword
and the authority to remove peace from the earth. And there was war and slaughter
everywhere.
5 When the Lamb broke the third seal, I heard the third living being say, "Come!"
And I looked up and saw a black horse, and its rider was holding a pair of scales in his
hand. 6 And a voice from among the four living beings said, "A loaf of wheat bread or
three loaves of barley for a day's pay.* And don't waste* the olive oil and wine."
7 And when the Lamb broke the fourth seal, I heard the fourth living being say,
"Come!" 8 And I looked up and saw a horse whose color was pale green like a corpse.
And Death was the name of its rider, who was followed around by the Grave.* They
were given authority over one-fourth of the earth, to kill with the sword and famine
and disease* and wild animals.
9 And when the Lamb broke the fifth seal, I saw under the altar the souls of all who
had been martyred for the word of God and for being faithful in their witness. 10 They
called loudly to the Lord and said, "O Sovereign Lord, holy and true, how long will
it be before you judge the people who belong to this world for what they have done
to us? When will you avenge our blood against these people?" 11 Then a white robe
was given to each of them. And they were told to rest a little longer until the full
number of the servants of Jesus had been martyred.
12 I watched as the Lamb broke the sixth seal, and there was a great earthquake. The
sun became as dark as black cloth, and the moon became as red as blood. 13 Then the
stars of the sky fell to the earth like green figs falling from trees shaken by mighty winds.
14 And the sky was rolled up like a scroll and taken away. And all of the mountains and
all of the islands disappeared. 15 Then the kings of the earth, the rulers, the generals, the
wealthy people, the people with great power, and every slave and every free person—all
hid themselves in the caves and among the rocks of the mountains. 16 And they cried to
the mountains and the rocks, "Fall on us and hide us from the face of the one who sits
on the throne and from the wrath of the Lamb. 17 For the great day of their wrath has
come, and who will be able to survive?"

6:6a Greek *A choinix of wheat for a denarius, and 3 choinix of barley for a denarius.* **6:6b** Or *hurt* **6:8a** Greek *by Hades.* **6:8b** Greek *death.*

6:8 It is not clear whether "the Grave" was on a separate horse than Death or merely rode along with Death, but the riders described in verses 2-8 are commonly referred to as the four horsemen of the Apocalypse.

6:8 The four riders are given power over one-fourth of the earth, indicating that God is still limiting his judgment—it is not yet complete. With these judgments there is still time for unbelievers to turn to Christ and away from their sin. In this case, the limited punishment not only demonstrates God's wrath on sin but also his merciful love in giving people yet another opportunity to turn to him before he brings final judgment.

6:9 The altar represents the altar of sacrifice in the Temple, where animals were sacrificed to atone for sins. Instead of the animals' blood at the base of the altar, John saw the souls of martyrs who had died for preaching the Good News. These martyrs were told that still more would lose their lives for their belief in Christ (6:11). In the face of warfare, famine, persecution, and death, Christians will be called on to stand firmly for what they believe. Only those who endure to the end will be rewarded by God (Mark 13:13).

6:9-11 The martyrs are eager for God to bring justice to the earth, but they are told to wait. God is not waiting until a certain number is reached, but he is promising that those who suffer and die for their faith will not be forgotten. Rather, they will be singled out by God for special honor. We may wish for justice immediately, as these martyrs did, but we must be patient. God works according to his own timetable, and he promises justice. No suffering for the sake of God's Kingdom, however, is wasted.

6:12 The sixth seal changes the scene back to the physical world. The first five judgments were directed toward specific areas, but this judgment is universal. Everyone will be afraid when the earth itself trembles.

6:15-17 At the sight of God sitting on the throne, all human beings, great and small, will be terrified, calling for the mountains to fall on them so that they will not have to face the judgment of the Lamb. This vivid picture was not intended to frighten believers. For them, the Lamb is a gentle Savior. But those kings, rulers, and generals and other powerful people who previously showed no fear of God and arrogantly flaunted their unbelief will find that they were wrong, and in that day they will have to face God's wrath. No one who has rejected God can survive the day of his wrath, but those who belong to Christ will receive a reward rather than punishment. Do you belong to Christ? If so, you need not fear these final days.

God's People Will Be Preserved

7 Then I saw four angels standing at the four corners of the earth, holding back the
four winds from blowing upon the earth. Not a leaf rustled in the trees, and the sea
became as smooth as glass. 2And I saw another angel coming from the east, carrying the
seal of the living God. And he shouted out to those four angels who had been given power
to injure land and sea, 3"Wait! Don't hurt the land or the sea or the trees until we have
placed the seal of God on the foreheads of his servants."
4And I heard how many were marked with the seal of God. There were 144,000 who
were sealed from all the tribes of Israel:

5 from Judah 12,000
from Reuben 12,000
from Gad 12,000
6 from Asher 12,000
from Naphtali 12,000
from Manasseh 12,000
7 from Simeon 12,000
from Levi 12,000
from Issachar 12,000
8 from Zebulun 12,000
from Joseph 12,000
from Benjamin 12,000

Praise from the Great Multitude

9After this I saw a vast crowd, too great to count, from every nation and tribe and people
and language, standing in front of the throne and before the Lamb. They were clothed in
white and held palm branches in their hands. 10And they were shouting with a mighty
shout, "Salvation comes from our God on the throne and from the Lamb!"
11And all the angels were standing around the throne and around the elders and the four
living beings. And they fell face down before the throne and worshiped God. 12They said,

7:1 Jer 49:36 Ezek 37:9 Dan 7:2 Zech 6:5 Matt 24:31
7:2 Rev 9:4
7:3 Ezek 9:4, 6 Rev 6:6; 9:4; 14:1; 22:4
7:4 Rev 9:16; 14:1, 3
7:9 Rev 3:5; 5:9
7:10 Rev 5:13; 12:10; 19:1; 22:3
7:11 Rev 4:4, 6, 10

7:1ff The sixth seal has been opened, and the people of the earth have tried to hide from God, saying, "Who will be able to survive?" (6:12-17). Just when all hope seems lost, four angels hold back the four winds of judgment until God's people are sealed as his own. Only then will God open the seventh seal (8:1).

7:2 A seal on a scroll or document identified and protected its contents. God places his own seal on his followers, identifying them as his own and guaranteeing his protection over their souls. This shows how valuable we are to him. Our physical bodies may be beaten, maimed, or even destroyed, but *nothing* can harm our souls when we have been sealed by God. See Ephesians 1:13 for the seal of the Holy Spirit.

7:3 God's seal is placed on the foreheads of his servants. This seal is the exact opposite of the mark of the beast explained in 13:16. These two marks place the people in two distinct categories—those owned by God and those owned by Satan.

7:4-8 The number 144,000 is 12 x 12 x 1,000, symbolizing completeness—*all* God's followers will be brought safely to him; not one will be overlooked or forgotten. God seals these believers either by withdrawing them from the earth (this is called the Rapture) or by giving them special strength and courage to make it through this time of great persecution. Even though many believers have to undergo persecution, the seal does not necessarily guarantee protection from physical harm—many will die (see 6:11)—but God will protect them from spiritual harm. No matter what happens, they will be brought to their reward of eternal life. Their destiny is secure. These believers will not fall away from God even though they may undergo intense persecution.

This is not saying that 144,000 individuals must be sealed before the persecution comes, but that when persecution begins, the faithful will have already been sealed (marked by God), and they will remain true to him until the end.

7:4-8 This is a different list from the usual listing of the 12 tribes in the Old Testament, because it is a symbolic list of God's true followers. (1) Judah is mentioned first because Judah is both the tribe of David and of Jesus the Messiah (Genesis 49:8-12; Matthew 1:1). (2) Levi had no tribal allotment because of the Levites' work for God in the Temple (Deuteronomy 18:1), but here the tribe is given a place as a reward for faithfulness. (3) Dan is not mentioned because it was known for rebellion and idolatry, traits unacceptable for God's followers (Genesis 49:17). (4) The two tribes representing Joseph (usually called Ephraim and Manasseh, after Joseph's sons) are here called Joseph and Manasseh because of Ephraim's rebellion. See Genesis 49 for the story of the beginning of these 12 tribes.

7:9 Who is this vast crowd? While some interpreters identify it as the martyrs described in 6:9, it may also be the same group as the 144,000 just mentioned (7:4-8). The 144,000 were sealed by God before the great time of persecution; the vast crowd was brought to eternal life, as God had promised. Before, they were being prepared; now, they are victorious. This crowd in heaven is composed of all those who remained faithful to God throughout the generations. No true believer ever need worry about which group he or she will be in. God includes and protects each of us, and we are guaranteed a place in his presence.

7:10 People try many methods to remove the guilt of sin—good deeds, intellectual pursuits, and even casting blame on others. The crowd in heaven however, praises God, saying that salvation comes from him and from the Lamb. Salvation from sin's penalty can come only through Jesus Christ. Have you had the guilt of sin removed in the only way possible?

7:11 More information about the elders is found in the note on 4:4. The four living beings are explained further in the note on 4:6, 7.

“Amen! Blessing and glory and wisdom
and thanksgiving and honor and power and strength
belong to our God forever and forever. Amen!”

13 Then one of the twenty-four elders asked me, “Who are these who are clothed in
white? Where do they come from?”
14 And I said to him, “Sir, you are the one who knows.”
Then he said to me, “These are the ones coming out of the great tribulation. They
washed their robes in the blood of the Lamb and made them white. 15 That is why they
are standing in front of the throne of God, serving him day and night in his Temple. And
he who sits on the throne will live among them and shelter them. 16 They will never again
be hungry or thirsty, and they will be fully protected from the scorching noontime heat.
17 For the Lamb who stands in front of the throne will be their Shepherd. He will lead
them to the springs of life-giving water. And God will wipe away all their tears.”

The Lamb Breaks the Seventh Seal

8 When the Lamb broke the seventh seal, there was silence throughout heaven for
about half an hour. 2 And I saw the seven angels who stand before God, and they
were given seven trumpets.
3 Then another angel with a gold incense burner came and stood at the altar. And a
great quantity of incense was given to him to mix with the prayers of God’s people, to
be offered on the gold altar before the throne. 4 The smoke of the incense, mixed with
the prayers of the saints, ascended up to God from the altar where the angel had poured
them out. 5 Then the angel filled the incense burner with fire from the altar and threw it
down upon the earth; and thunder crashed, lightning flashed, and there was a terrible
earthquake.

3. Sounding the seven trumpets

The First Four Trumpets

6 Then the seven angels with the seven trumpets prepared to blow their mighty blasts.
7 The first angel blew his trumpet, and hail and fire mixed with blood were thrown
down upon the earth, and one-third of the earth was set on fire. One-third of the trees
were burned, and all the grass was burned.
8 Then the second angel blew his trumpet, and a great mountain of fire was thrown into
the sea. And one-third of the water in the sea became blood. 9 And one-third of all things
living in the sea died. And one-third of all the ships on the sea were destroyed.
10 Then the third angel blew his trumpet, and a great flaming star fell out of the sky,
burning like a torch. It fell upon one-third of the rivers and on the springs of water. 11 The

7:12 Rev 5:12-14
7:13 Rev 6:11; 7:9
7:14 Dan 12:1; Rev 6:11; 22:14
7:15 Rev 4:9; 11:19; 22:3
7:16 Isa 49:10
7:17 Ps 23:1-5; Isa 25:8; 49:10; John 10:11, 14; Rev 21:4, 6; 22:1
8:1 Rev 6:1-17
8:2 Rev 9:1, 13; 1:15
8:3 Exod 30:1-3; Rev 9:13
8:4 Ps 141:2; Rev 5:8; 8:3
8:5 Exod 19:16-19; Lev 16:12; Rev 4:5; 11:19; 16:18
8:7 Ezek 38:22; Joel 3:3; Zech 13:9
8:8 Jer 51:25; Zech 13:9
8:10 Isa 14:12; Rev 6:13; 9:1; 16:4
8:11 Jer 9:15

7:14 “The great tribulation” has been explained in several ways. Some believe it refers to the suffering of believers through the ages; others believe that there is a specific time of intense tribulation yet to come. In either case, these believers come through their times of suffering by remaining loyal to God. Because they remain faithful, God will give them eternal life with him (7:17).

7:14 It is difficult to imagine how blood could make any cloth white, but the blood of Jesus Christ is the world’s greatest purifier because it removes the stain of sin. White symbolizes sinless perfection or holiness, which can be given to people only by the death of the sinless Lamb of God on our behalf. This is a picture of how we are saved through faith (see Isaiah 1:18; Romans 3:21-26).

7:16, 17 God will provide for his children’s needs in their eternal home where there will be no hunger, thirst, or pain, and he will wipe away all tears. When you are suffering or torn apart by sorrow, take comfort in this promise of complete protection and relief.

7:17 In verses 1-8 we see the believers receiving a seal to protect them through a time of great tribulation and suffering; in verses 9-17 we see the believers finally with God in heaven. All who have been faithful through the ages are singing before God’s throne. Their tribulations and sorrows are over: no more tears for sin, for all sins are forgiven; no more tears for suffering, for all suffering is over; no more tears for death, for all believers have been resurrected to die no more.

8:1, 2 When the seventh seal is opened, the seven trumpet judgments are revealed. In the same way, the seventh trumpet will announce the seven bowl judgments in 11:15 and 16:1-21. The trumpet judgments, like the seal judgments, are only partial. God’s final and complete judgment has not yet come.

8:3 An incense burner filled with live coals was used in Temple worship. Incense was poured on the coals, and the sweet-smelling smoke drifted upward, symbolizing believers’ prayers ascending to God (see Exodus 30:7-9).

8:6 The trumpet blasts have three purposes: (1) to warn that judgment is certain, (2) to call the forces of good and evil to battle, and (3) to announce the return of the King, the Messiah. These warnings urge us to make sure our faith is firmly fixed on Christ.

8:7-12 Since only one-third of the earth is destroyed by these trumpet judgments, this is only a partial judgment from God. His full wrath is yet to be unleashed.

name of the star was Bitterness.* It made one-third of the water bitter, and many people
died because the water was so bitter.
12 Then the fourth angel blew his trumpet, and one-third of the sun was struck, and **8:12**
one-third of the moon, and one-third of the stars, and they became dark. And one-third Exod 10:21 Ezek 32:7-8
of the day was dark and one-third of the night also. Rev 6:12-13
13 Then I looked up. And I heard a single eagle crying loudly as it flew through the air, **8:13**
“Terror, terror, terror to all who belong to this world because of what will happen when Rev 3:10; 9:12
the last three angels blow their trumpets.”

The Fifth Trumpet Brings the First Terror

9 Then the fifth angel blew his trumpet, and I saw a star that had fallen to earth from the sky, **9:1** Isa 14:12
and he was given the key to the shaft of the bottomless pit. 2 When he opened it, smoke poured Luke 8:31; 10:18
out as though from a huge furnace, and the sunlight and air were darkened by the smoke. **9:3** Rev 9:5, 10
3 Then locusts came from the smoke and descended on the earth, and they were given
power to sting like scorpions. 4 They were told not to hurt the grass or plants or trees but **9:4**
to attack all the people who did not have the seal of God on their foreheads. 5 They were Ezek 9:4, 6 Rev 7:3
told not to kill them but to torture them for five months with agony like the pain of **9:6**
scorpion stings. 6 In those days people will seek death but will not find it. They will long Job 3:21
to die, but death will flee away! Rev 6:16
7 The locusts looked like horses armed for battle. They had gold crowns on their **9:7** Joel 2:4-5
heads, and they had human faces. 8 Their hair was long like the hair of a woman, and **9:8**
their teeth were like the teeth of a lion. 9 They wore armor made of iron, and their wings Joel 1:6
roared like an army of chariots rushing into battle. 10 They had tails that stung like **9:9** Joel 2:5
scorpions, with power to torture people. This power was given to them for five months. **9:11**
11 Their king is the angel from the bottomless pit; his name in Hebrew is *Abaddon,* and Job 26:6; 28:22
in Greek, *Apollyon*—the Destroyer.
12 The first terror is past, but look, two more terrors are coming!

The Sixth Trumpet Brings the Second Terror

13 Then the sixth angel blew his trumpet, and I heard a voice speaking from the four horns **9:14**
of the gold altar that stands in the presence of God. 14 And the voice spoke to the sixth angel Gen 15:18

8:11 Greek *Wormwood.*

8:13 Habakkuk used the image of an eagle to symbolize swiftness and destruction (see Habakkuk 1:8). The picture here is also of an eagle flying over all the earth, warning of the terrors yet to come. While both believers and unbelievers experience the terrors described in verses 7-12, those “who belong to this world” are the unbelievers who will meet spiritual harm through the next three trumpet judgments. God has guaranteed believers protection from spiritual harm (7:2, 3).

8:13 In 6:10, the martyrs call out to God, “How long will it be before you judge the people who belong to this world for what they have done to us? When will you avenge our blood against these people?” As we see the world’s wickedness, we, too, may cry out to God, “How long?” In the following chapters, the judgment comes at last. We may be distressed and impatient, but God has his plan and his timing, and we must learn to trust him to know what is best. Judgment is coming—be sure of that. Thank God for the time he has given you to turn from sin. Use the available time to work to help others turn to him.

9:1 It is not known whether this “star” that fell from the sky is Satan, a fallen angel, Christ, or a good angel. Most likely it is a good angel, because the key to the shaft of the bottomless pit is normally held by Christ (1:17, 18), and it was temporarily given to this other being from heaven (see also 20:1). This being, whoever he may be, is still under God’s control and authority. The bottomless pit represents the place of the demons and of Satan, the king of demons (9:11). See also Luke 8:31 for another reference to the bottomless pit.

9:3 The prophet Joel described a locust plague as a foreshadowing of the “day of the LORD,” meaning God’s coming judgment (Joel 2:1-10). In the Old Testament, locusts were symbols of destruction because they destroyed vegetation. Here, however, they symbolize an invasion of demons called to torture people who do not believe in God. The limitations placed on the demons (they could only torment people for five months) show that they are under God’s authority.

9:3ff Most likely these locusts are demons—evil spirits ruled by Satan who tempt people to sin. They were not created by Satan, because God is the Creator of all; rather, they are fallen angels who joined Satan in his rebellion. God limits what they can do; they can do nothing without his permission. Their main purpose on earth is to prevent, distort, or destroy people’s relationship with God. Because they are corrupt and degenerate, their appearance reflects the distortion of their spirits. While it is important to recognize their evil activity so we can stay away from them, we must avoid any curiosity about or involvement with demonic forces or with the occult.

9:11 The locust-demons have a leader whose name in Hebrew and in Greek means “Destroyer.” It may be a play on words by John to show that those who worshiped the great god Apollo worshiped only a demon.

9:13 The altar in the Temple had four projections, one at each corner, and these were called the horns of the altar (see Exodus 27:2).

9:14 The word *angels* here means fallen angels or demons. These four unidentified demons will be exceedingly evil and destructive. But note that they do not have the power to release themselves and do their evil work on earth. Instead, they are held back by God and will be released at a specific time, doing only what he allows them to do.

who held the trumpet: "Release the four angels who are bound at the great Euphrates River."
15And the four angels who had been prepared for this hour and day and month and year
were turned loose to kill one-third of all the people on earth. 16They led an army of 200
million mounted troops—I heard an announcement of how many there were.
17And in my vision, I saw the horses and the riders sitting on them. The riders wore
armor that was fiery red and sky blue and yellow. The horses' heads were like the heads
of lions, and fire and smoke and burning sulfur billowed from their mouths. 18One-third
of all the people on earth were killed by these three plagues—by the fire and the smoke
and burning sulfur that came from the mouths of the horses. 19Their power was in their
mouths, but also in their tails. For their tails had heads like snakes, with the power to
injure people.
20But the people who did not die in these plagues still refused to turn from their evil
deeds. They continued to worship demons and idols made of gold, silver, bronze, stone,
and wood—idols that neither see nor hear nor walk! 21And they did not repent of their
murders or their witchcraft or their immorality or their thefts.

The Angel and the Small Scroll

10 Then I saw another mighty angel coming down from heaven, surrounded by a
cloud, with a rainbow over his head. His face shone like the sun, and his feet were
like pillars of fire. 2And in his hand was a small scroll, which he had unrolled. He stood
with his right foot on the sea and his left foot on the land. 3And he gave a great shout,
like the roar of a lion. And when he shouted, the seven thunders answered.
4When the seven thunders spoke, I was about to write. But a voice from heaven called
to me: "Keep secret what the seven thunders said. Do not write it down."
5Then the mighty angel standing on the sea and on the land lifted his right hand to
heaven. 6And he swore an oath in the name of the one who lives forever and ever, who
created heaven and everything in it, the earth and everything in it, and the sea and
everything in it. He said, "God will wait no longer. 7But when the seventh angel blows
his trumpet, God's mysterious plan will be fulfilled. It will happen just as he announced
it to his servants the prophets."
8Then the voice from heaven called to me again: "Go and take the unrolled scroll from
the angel who is standing on the sea and on the land."
9So I approached him and asked him to give me the little scroll. "Yes, take it and eat
it," he said. "At first it will taste like honey, but when you swallow it, it will make your

9:15 Rev 8:7-12; 9:18; 20:7
9:16 Rev 5:11; 7:4
9:17 Job 41:10-12
9:20 Deut 4:28; 32:17; Ps 115:4-7; Dan 5:23; Mic 5:13; Acts 7:41; 1 Cor 10:19-20; Rev 2:21
9:21 Rev 16:9, 11, 21
10:1 Matt 17:2
10:3 Ps 29:3-9
10:4 Dan 8:26; 12:4, 9; Rev 22:10
10:5 Deut 32:40; Dan 12:7
10:6 Gen 14:19, 22; Exod 20:11; Neh 9:6; Ps 146:6
10:7 Dan 9:6, 10; Amos 3:7; Rev 11:15
10:9 Jer 15:16; Ezek 2:8–3:3

9:15 Here one-third of all people are killed. In 6:7, 8, one-fourth of all people were killed. Thus, over one-half of the people in the world will have been killed by God's great judgments. Even more would have been killed if God had not set limits on the destruction.

9:16 In John's day, this number of mounted troops in an army was inconceivable, but today there are countries and alliances that could easily amass this many soldiers. This huge army, led by the four demons, will be sent out to destroy one-third of the earth's population. But the judgment is still not complete.

9:20, 21 These people were so hard-hearted that even plagues did not drive them to God. People don't usually fall into immorality and evil suddenly—they slip into it a little bit at a time until, hardly realizing what has happened, they are irrevocably mired in their wicked ways. Any person who allows sin to take root in his or her life will end up in this predicament. Temptation entertained today becomes sin tomorrow, a habit the next day, then death and separation from God forever (see James 1:15). To think you could never become this evil is the first step toward a hard heart. Acknowledge your need to confess your sin before God.

10:1-6 The purpose of this mighty angel is clear—to announce the final judgments on the earth. His right foot on the sea and left foot on the land (10:2) indicate that his words deal with all creation, not just a limited part as did the seal and trumpet judgments. The seventh trumpet (11:15) will usher in the seven bowl judgments, which will bring an end to the present world. When this universal judgment comes, God's truth will prevail.

10:2 We see two scrolls in Revelation. The first contains a revelation of judgments against evil (5:1ff). The contents of the second small scroll are not indicated, but it also may contain a revelation of judgment.

10:4 Throughout history people have wanted to know what would happen in the future, and God reveals some of it in this book. But John was stopped from revealing certain parts of his vision. An angel also told the prophet Daniel that some visions he saw were not to be revealed yet to everyone (Daniel 12:9), and Jesus told his disciples that the time of the end is known by no one but God (Mark 13:32, 33). God has revealed all we need to know to live for him now. In our desire to be ready for the end, we must not place more emphasis on speculation about the last days than on living for God while we wait.

10:7 When God's plan for human history is completely revealed, all prophecy will be fulfilled. The end of the age will have arrived (see 11:15 and Ephesians 1:9, 10).

10:9, 10 The prophet Ezekiel had a vision in which he was told to eat a scroll filled with judgments against the nation of Israel (Ezekiel 3:1ff). The taste was sweet in his mouth, but the scroll's contents brought destruction—just like the scroll John was told to eat. God's Word is sweet to us as believers because it brings encouragement, but it sours our stomach because of the coming judgment we must pronounce on unbelievers.

stomach sour!" 10So I took the little scroll from the hands of the angel, and I ate it! It was
sweet in my mouth, but it made my stomach sour. 11Then he said to me, "You must
prophesy again about many peoples, nations, languages, and kings."

The Two Witnesses

11 Then I was given a measuring stick, and I was told, "Go and measure the Temple
of God and the altar, and count the number of worshipers. 2But do not measure
the outer courtyard, for it has been turned over to the nations. They will trample the holy
city for 42 months. 3And I will give power to my two witnesses, and they will be clothed
in sackcloth and will prophesy during those 1,260 days."

4These two prophets are the two olive trees and the two lampstands that stand before
the Lord of all the earth. 5If anyone tries to harm them, fire flashes from the mouths of
the prophets and consumes their enemies. This is how anyone who tries to harm them
must die. 6They have power to shut the skies so that no rain will fall for as long as they
prophesy. And they have the power to turn the rivers and oceans into blood, and to send
every kind of plague upon the earth as often as they wish.

7When they complete their testimony, the beast that comes up out of the bottomless
pit will declare war against them. He will conquer them and kill them. 8And their bodies
will lie in the main street of Jerusalem,* the city which is called "Sodom" and "Egypt,"
the city where their Lord was crucified. 9And for three and a half days, all peoples, tribes,
languages, and nations will come to stare at their bodies. No one will be allowed to bury
them. 10All the people who belong to this world will give presents to each other to
celebrate the death of the two prophets who had tormented them.

11But after three and a half days, the spirit of life from God entered them, and they
stood up! And terror struck all who were staring at them. 12Then a loud voice shouted
from heaven, "Come up here!" And they rose to heaven in a cloud as their enemies
watched.

13And in the same hour there was a terrible earthquake that destroyed a tenth of the
city. Seven thousand people died in that earthquake. And everyone who did not die was
terrified and gave glory to the God of heaven.

14The second terror is past, but look, now the third terror is coming quickly.

11:8 Greek *the great city.*

10:11 Jer 1:10; 25:30 Dan 3:4 Rev 5:9
11:1 Ezek 40:3 Rev 21:15
11:2 Ezek 40:17-20 Luke 21:24 Rev 12:6; 13:5
11:3 Rev 2:13
11:4 Zech 4:3, 11, 14
11:5 2 Sam 22:9 2 Kgs 1:10 Jer 5:14
11:6 Exod 7:17-20 1 Kgs 17:1
11:7 Dan 7:21 Rev 13:1, 7
11:8 Isa 1:9-10 Rev 16:19
11:9 Ps 79:2-3
11:10 Neh 8:10, 12
11:11 Ezek 37:5, 10
11:12 2 Kgs 2:11 Acts 1:9 Rev 4:1
11:13 Ezek 38:19-20 Rev 16:9, 11

11:1ff This Temple is most likely a symbol of the church (all true believers), because there will be no Temple in the new Jerusalem (21:22). John measured the Temple to show that God is building walls of protection around his people to spare them from spiritual harm, and that there is a place reserved for all believers who remain faithful to God.

11:2 Those worshiping inside the Temple will be protected spiritually, but those outside will face great suffering. This is a way of saying that true believers will be protected through persecution, but those who refuse to believe will be destroyed.

11:3 These two witnesses bear strong resemblance to Moses and Elijah, two of God's mighty prophets. With God's power, Moses called plagues down upon the nation of Egypt (see Exodus 7–11). Elijah defeated the prophets of Baal (1 Kings 18). Both of these men appeared with Christ at his transfiguration (see Matthew 17:1-7).

11:3 In the book of Revelation, numbers are likely to have symbolic rather than literal meanings. The 42 months or 1,260 days equal 3½ years. As half of the perfect number 7, 3½ can indicate incompletion, imperfection, or even evil. Notice the events predicted for this time period: there is trouble (Daniel 12:7), the holy city is trampled (11:2), the woman takes refuge in the wilderness (12:6), and the Devil-inspired beast exercises his authority (13:5). Some commentators link the 3½ years with the period of famine in the days of Elijah (Luke 4:25; James 5:17). Since Malachi predicted the return of Elijah before the Last Judgment (Malachi 4:5), and since the events in Daniel and Revelation pave the way for the Second Coming, perhaps John was making this connection. It is possible, of course, that the 3½ years are literal. If so, we will clearly recognize when the 3½ years are over! Whether symbolic or literal, however, they indicate that evil's reign will have a definite end.

11:7 This beast could be Satan or an agent of Satan.

11:8, 9 Jerusalem, once the great city and the capital of Israel, is now enemy territory. It is compared with Sodom and with Egypt, both well known for their evil. By the time of John's writing, Jerusalem had been destroyed by the Romans in 70 A.D., nearly a million Jews had been slaughtered, and the Temple treasures had been carried off to Rome.

11:10 The whole world rejoices at the deaths of these two witnesses, who have caused trouble by saying what the people didn't want to hear—words about their sin, their need for repentance, and the coming punishment. Sinful people hate those who call attention to their sin and who urge them to repent. They hated Christ, and they hate his followers (1 John 3:13). When you obey Christ and take a stand against sin, be prepared to experience the world's hatred. But remember that the great reward awaiting you in heaven far outweighs any suffering that you face now.

The Seventh Trumpet Brings the Third Terror

11:15 Ps 10:16; Dan 2:44; 7:14, 27; Rev 10:7; 12:10; 16:17
11:16 Rev 4:4, 10
11:17 Amos 3:13; 4:13; Rev 1:8; 19:6
11:18 Ps 2:1; Rev 10:7; 19:5; 20:12
11:19 2 Chr 5:7; Rev 4:5; 15:5

15 Then the seventh angel blew his trumpet, and there were loud voices shouting in
heaven: "The whole world has now become the kingdom of our Lord and of his Christ,
and he will reign forever and ever."
16 And the twenty-four elders sitting on their thrones before God fell on their faces and
worshiped him. 17 And they said,

"We give thanks to you, Lord God Almighty,
the one who is and who always was,
for now you have assumed your great power
and have begun to reign.
18 The nations were angry with you,
but now the time of your wrath has come.
It is time to judge the dead and reward your servants.
You will reward your prophets and your holy people,
all who fear your name, from the least to the greatest.
And you will destroy all who have caused destruction on the earth."

19 Then, in heaven, the Temple of God was opened and the Ark of his covenant could
be seen inside the Temple. Lightning flashed, thunder crashed and roared; there was a
great hailstorm, and the world was shaken by a mighty earthquake.

4. Observing the great conflict

The Woman and the Dragon

12:2 Isa 26:17; 66:6-9; Mic 4:10
12:3 Dan 7:7, 24; Rev 13:1; 17:3, 7, 12, 16
12:4 Dan 8:10
12:5 Ps 2:9; Rev 2:27; 19:15
12:6 Rev 11:2; 13:5

12 Then I witnessed in heaven an event of great significance. I saw a woman clothed
with the sun, with the moon beneath her feet, and a crown of twelve stars on her head.
2 She was pregnant, and she cried out in the pain of labor as she awaited her delivery.
3 Suddenly, I witnessed in heaven another significant event. I saw a large red dragon
with seven heads and ten horns, with seven crowns on his heads. 4 His tail dragged down
one-third of the stars, which he threw to the earth. He stood before the woman as she was
about to give birth to her child, ready to devour the baby as soon as it was born.
5 She gave birth to a boy who was to rule all nations with an iron rod. And the child was
snatched away from the dragon and was caught up to God and to his throne. 6 And the woman
fled into the wilderness, where God had prepared a place to give her care for 1,260 days.

11:15 The seventh trumpet is sounded, announcing the arrival of the King. There is now no turning back. The coming judgments are no longer partial but complete in their destruction. God is in control, and he unleashes his full wrath on the evil world that refuses to turn to him (9:20, 21). When his wrath begins, there will be no escape.

11:16 For more on the 24 elders, see the note on 4:4.

11:18 In the Bible, God gives rewards to his people according to what they deserve. Throughout the Old Testament, obedience often brought reward in this life (Deuteronomy 28), but obedience and immediate reward are not always linked. If they were, good people would always be rich, and suffering would always be a sign of sin. If we were quickly rewarded for every faithful deed, we would soon think we were pretty good. Before long, we would be doing many good deeds for purely selfish reasons. While it is true that God will reward us for our earthly deeds (see 20:12), our greatest reward will be eternal life in his presence.

11:19 In Old Testament days, the Ark of the Covenant was the most sacred treasure of the Israelite nation. For more information about the Ark, see the note on Exodus 37:1.

12:1–14:20 The seventh trumpet (11:15) ushers in the bowl judgments (15:1–16:21), but in the intervening chapters (12–14), John sees the conflict between God and Satan. He sees the source of all sin, evil, persecution, and suffering on the earth, and he understands why the great battle between the forces of God and Satan must soon take place. In these chapters the nature of evil is exposed, and Satan is seen in all his wickedness.

12:1-6 The woman represents God's faithful people who have been waiting for the Messiah; the crown of 12 stars represents the 12 tribes of Israel. God set apart the Jews for himself (Romans 9:4, 5), and that nation gave birth to the Messiah. The boy (Revelation 12:5) is Jesus, born to a devout Jewish girl named Mary (Luke 1:26-33). Evil King Herod immediately tried to destroy the infant Jesus (Matthew 2:13-20). Herod's desire to kill this newborn king, whom he saw as a threat to his throne, was motivated by Satan (the red dragon), who wanted to kill the world's Savior. The heavenly pageant of Revelation 12 shows that Christ's lowly birth in the town of Bethlehem had cosmic significance.

12:3, 4 The large red dragon, Satan, has seven heads, ten horns, and seven crowns, representing his power and the kingdoms of the world over which he rules. The stars that plunged to earth with him are usually considered to be the angels who fell with Satan and became his demons. According to Hebrew tradition, one-third of all the angels in heaven fell with Satan. For more on demons, see the notes on 9:3ff and Mark 5:1-20.

12:6 The wilderness represents a place of spiritual refuge and protection from Satan. Because God aided the woman's escape into the wilderness, we can be sure that he offers security to all true believers. Satan always attacks God's people, but God keeps them spiritually secure. Some will experience physical harm, but all will be protected from spiritual harm. God will not let Satan take the souls of God's true followers.

12:6 The 1,260 days ($3\frac{1}{2}$ years) is the same length of time that the dragon is allowed to exercise his authority (13:5) and that the holy city is trampled (see the second note on 11:3).

7 Then there was war in heaven. Michael and the angels under his command fought
the dragon and his angels. 8 And the dragon lost the battle and was forced out of heaven.
9 This great dragon—the ancient serpent called the Devil, or Satan, the one deceiving the
whole world—was thrown down to the earth with all his angels.
10 Then I heard a loud voice shouting across the heavens,

> "It has happened at last—the salvation and power and kingdom of our God, and
> the authority of his Christ! For the Accuser has been thrown down to earth—the
> one who accused our brothers and sisters before our God day and night. 11 And they
> have defeated him because of the blood of the Lamb and because of their testimony.
> And they were not afraid to die. 12 Rejoice, O heavens! And you who live in the
> heavens, rejoice! But terror will come on the earth and the sea. For the Devil has
> come down to you in great anger, and he knows that he has little time."

13 And when the dragon realized that he had been thrown down to the earth, he pursued
the woman who had given birth to the child. 14 But she was given two wings like those of a
great eagle. This allowed her to fly to a place prepared for her in the wilderness, where she
would be cared for and protected from the dragon* for a time, times, and half a time.
15 Then the dragon tried to drown the woman with a flood of water that flowed from its
mouth. 16 But the earth helped her by opening its mouth and swallowing the river that
gushed out from the mouth of the dragon. 17 Then the dragon became angry at the woman,
and he declared war against the rest of her children—all who keep God's commandments
and confess that they belong to Jesus.

The Beast out of the Sea

18 Then he stood* waiting on the shore of the sea.

12:7 Dan 10:13; 12:1 Jude 1:9 Rev 12:3

12:9 Gen 3:1 Zech 3:1-2 Matt 4:10 Luke 10:18 Rev 12:3; 20:2-10

12:10 Job 1:9-11 Zech 3:1 Rev 7:10; 11:15

12:11 Rev 2:10; 6:9; 7:14; 15:2

12:12 Rev 8:13; 18:20

12:14 Exod 19:4 Dan 7:25; 12:7 Rev 17:3, 18

12:17 Rev 1:2; 11:7; 13:7

12:14 Greek *the serpent;* also in 12:15. See 12:9. **12:18** Some manuscripts read *Then I stood,* and some translations put this entire sentence into 13:1.

12:7 This event fulfills Daniel 12:1ff. Michael is a high-ranking angel. One of his responsibilities is to guard God's community of believers.

12:7ff Much more happened at Christ's birth, death, and resurrection than most people realize. A war between the forces of good and evil was under way. With Christ's resurrection, Satan's ultimate defeat was assured. Some believe that Satan's fall to earth took place at Jesus' resurrection or ascension and that the 1,260 days (3½ years) is a symbolic way of referring to the time between Christ's first and second comings. Others say that Satan's defeat will occur in the middle of a literal seven-year tribulation period, following the rapture of the church and preceding the second coming of Christ and the beginning of Christ's 1,000-year reign. Whatever the case, we must remember that Christ is victorious—Satan has already been defeated because of Christ's death on the cross (12:10-12).

12:9 The Devil is not a symbol or legend; he is very real. Originally Satan was an angel of God, but through his own pride, he became corrupt. The Devil is God's enemy, and he constantly tries to hinder God's work, but he is limited by God's power and can do only what he is permitted to do (Job 1:6–2:8). The name *Satan* means "Accuser" (12:10). He actively looks for people to attack (1 Peter 5:8, 9). Satan likes to pursue believers who are vulnerable in their faith, who are spiritually weak, or who are isolated from other believers.

Even though God permits the Devil to do his work in this world, God is still in control. And Jesus has complete power over Satan—he defeated Satan when he died and rose again for the sins of everyone. One day Satan will be bound forever, never again to do his evil work (see 20:10).

12:10 Many believe that until this time, Satan still had access to God (see the note on Job 1:7ff). But here his access is forever barred (see also 9:1). He can no longer accuse people before God (see how Satan made accusations about Job before God in Job 1:6ff).

12:11 The critical blow to Satan came when the Lamb, Jesus Christ, shed his blood for our sins. The victory is won by sacrifice—Christ's death in our place to pay the penalty for our sin, and the sacrifices we make because of our faith in him. As we face the battle with Satan, we should not fear it or try to escape from it, but we should loyally serve Christ, who alone brings victory (see Romans 8:34-39).

12:12 The Devil begins to step up his persecution because he knows that "he has little time." We are living in the last days, and Satan's work has become more intense. Even though the Devil is very powerful, as we can see by the condition of our world, he is always under God's control. One of the reasons God allows Satan to work evil and bring temptation is so that those who pretend to be Christ's followers will be weeded out from Christ's true believers. Knowing that the last great confrontation with Jesus is near, Satan is desperately trying to recruit as great an enemy force as possible for this final battle.

12:17 While the woman (12:1) represents faithful Jews and the child (12:5) represents Christ, the rest of her children could be either Jewish believers or, most likely, all believers.

12:17 The apostle Paul tells us that we are in a spiritual battle (Ephesians 6:10-12). John says that the war is still being waged, but the outcome has already been determined. Satan and his followers have been defeated and will be destroyed. Nevertheless Satan is battling daily to bring more into his ranks and to keep his own from defecting to God's side. Those who belong to Christ have gone into battle on God's side, and he has guaranteed them victory. God will not lose the war, but we must make certain not to lose the battle for our own souls. Don't waver in your commitment to Christ. A great spiritual battle is being fought, and there is no time for indecision.

13:1 Dan 7:2-8; Rev 17:12
13:2 Dan 7:4-6; Rev 2:13; 12:3
13:3 2 Thes 2:9-12; Rev 17:8
13:5 Dan 7:8, 11, 20, 25; 11:36; 2 Thes 2:4; Rev 11:2
13:7 Rev 5:9; 11:7
13:8 Dan 12:1
13:10 Jer 15:2; 43:11; Matt 26:52; Heb 6:12

13 And now in my vision I saw a beast rising up out of the sea. It had seven heads
and ten horns, with ten crowns on its horns. And written on each head were names
that blasphemed God. 2 This beast looked like a leopard, but it had bear's feet and a lion's
mouth! And the dragon gave him his own power and throne and great authority.
3 I saw that one of the heads of the beast seemed wounded beyond recovery—but the
fatal wound was healed! All the world marveled at this miracle and followed the beast
in awe. 4 They worshiped the dragon for giving the beast such power, and they worshiped
the beast. "Is there anyone as great as the beast?" they exclaimed. "Who is able to fight
against him?"
5 Then the beast was allowed to speak great blasphemies against God. And he was
given authority to do what he wanted for forty-two months. 6 And he spoke terrible words
of blasphemy against God, slandering his name and all who live in heaven, who are his
temple. 7 And the beast was allowed to wage war against God's holy people and to
overcome them. And he was given authority to rule over every tribe and people and
language and nation. 8 And all the people who belong to this world worshiped the beast.
They are the ones whose names were not written in the Book of Life, which belongs to
the Lamb who was killed before the world was made.
9 Anyone who is willing to hear should listen and understand. 10 The people who are
destined for prison will be arrested and taken away. Those who are destined for death

SATAN'S WORK IN THE WORLD

His hatred for Christ	12:13
His hatred for God's people	12:17
His power and authority	13:2
His popularity among unbelievers	13:4
His blasphemy against God	13:6
His war against believers	13:7
His ability to deceive	13:14

13:1 This beast was initially identified with Rome because the Roman Empire, in its early days, encouraged an evil life-style, persecuted believers, and opposed God and his followers. But the beast also symbolizes the Antichrist—not Satan, but someone under Satan's power and control. This Antichrist looks like a combination of the four beasts that Daniel saw centuries earlier in a vision (Daniel 7). As the dragon (12:17) is in opposition to God, so the beast from the sea is against Christ and may be seen as Satan's false messiah. The early Roman Empire was strong and also anti-Christ (or against Christ's standards); many other individual powers throughout history have been anti-Christ. Many Christians believe that Satan's evil will culminate in a final Antichrist, one who will focus all the powers of evil against Jesus Christ and his followers.

13:1ff Chapter 13 introduces Satan's (the dragon's) two evil accomplices: (1) the beast out of the sea (13:1ff) and (2) the beast out of the earth (13:11ff). Together, the three evil beings form an unholy trinity in direct opposition to the Holy Trinity of God the Father, God the Son, and God the Holy Spirit.

When Satan tempted Jesus in the wilderness, he wanted Jesus to show his power by turning stones into bread, to do miracles by jumping from a high place, and to gain political power by worshiping him (see Matthew 4:1-11). Satan's plan was to rule the world through Jesus, but Jesus refused to do Satan's bidding. Thus, Satan turns to the fearsome beasts described in Revelation. To the beast out of the sea he gives political power. To the beast out of the earth he gives power to do miracles. Both beasts work together to capture the control of the whole world. This unholy trinity—the dragon, the beast out of the sea, and the false prophet (see 16:13)—unite in a desperate attempt to overthrow God, but their efforts are doomed to failure. See what becomes of them in 19:19-21 and 20:10.

13:3ff Because the beast, the Antichrist, is a false messiah, he will be a counterfeit of Christ and will even stage a false resurrection (13:14). People will follow and worship him because they will be awed by his power and miracles (13:3, 4). He will unite the world under his leadership (13:7, 8), and he will control the world economy (13:16, 17). People are impressed by power and will follow those who display it forcefully or offer it to their followers. But those who follow the beast will only be fooling themselves: He will use his power to manipulate others, to point to himself, and to promote evil plans. God, by contrast, uses his infinitely greater power to love and to build up. Don't be misled by claims of great miracles or reports about a resurrection or reincarnation of someone claiming to be Christ. When Jesus returns, he will reveal himself to everyone (Matthew 24:23-28).

13:5 The power given to the beast will be limited by God. He will allow the beast to exercise authority only for a short time. Even while the beast is in power, God will still be in control (11:15; 12:10-12).

13:7 The beast will conquer God's people and rule over them, but he will not be able to harm them spiritually. He will establish worldwide dominance and demand that everyone worship him. And many *will* worship him—everyone except true believers. Refusal to worship the beast will result in temporary suffering for God's people, but they will be rewarded with eternal life in the end.

13:8 See the note on 3:5 for more information on the Book of Life.

13:10 In this time of persecution, being faithful to Christ could bring imprisonment and even execution. Some believers will be hurt or killed. But all that the beast and his followers will be able to do to believers is harm them physically; no spiritual harm will come to those whose faith in God is sincere. All believers will enter God's presence perfected and purified by the blood of the Lamb (7:9-17).

will be killed. But do not be dismayed, for here is your opportunity to have endurance
and faith.

The Beast out of the Earth

11 Then I saw another beast come up out of the earth. He had two horns like those of a **13:11** Rev 13:1, 4
lamb, and he spoke with the voice of a dragon. 12 He exercised all the authority of the **13:12**
first beast. And he required all the earth and those who belong to this world to worship Rev 14:9; 19:20
the first beast, whose death-wound had been healed. 13 He did astounding miracles, such **13:13** 1 Kgs 18:24-39
as making fire flash down to earth from heaven while everyone was watching. 14 And Matt 24:24 2 Thes 2:9
with all the miracles he was allowed to perform on behalf of the first beast, he deceived Rev 19:20
all the people who belong to this world. He ordered the people of the world to make a **13:14** 2 Thes 2:9
great statue of the first beast, who was fatally wounded and then came back to life. 15 He Rev 12:9; 13:3, 12
was permitted to give life to this statue so that it could speak. Then the statue commanded **13:15** Dan 3:3-6
that anyone refusing to worship it must die. Rev 20:4

16 He required everyone—great and small, rich and poor, slave and free—to be **13:16**
given a mark on the right hand or on the forehead. 17 And no one could buy or sell Rev 14:9; 19:18
anything without that mark, which was either the name of the beast or the number **13:17** Rev 14:9, 11; 16:2;
representing his name. 18 Wisdom is needed to understand this. Let the one who has 19:20; 20:4
understanding solve the number of the beast, for it is the number of a man.* His **13:18**
number is 666.* Rev 17:9

The Lamb and the 144,000

14 Then I saw the Lamb standing on Mount Zion, and with him were 144,000 who **14:1** Rev 3:12; 7:4
had his name and his Father's name written on their foreheads. 2 And I heard a **14:2**
sound from heaven like the roaring of a great waterfall or the rolling of mighty thunder. Rev 1:15; 19:6
It was like the sound of many harpists playing together.

3 This great choir sang a wonderful new song in front of the throne of God and before **14:3** Rev 4:4, 6
the four living beings and the twenty-four elders. And no one could learn this song except

13:18a Or *of humanity.* **13:18b** Some manuscripts read *616.*

13:10 The times of great persecution that John saw will provide an opportunity for believers to exercise patient endurance and faithfulness. The tough times we face right now are also opportunities for spiritual growth. Don't fall into Satan's trap and turn away from God when hard times come. Instead, use those tough times as opportunities for growth.

13:11ff The first beast came out of the sea (13:1), but this second beast comes out of the earth. Later identified as the false prophet (16:13; 19:20), he is a counterfeit of the Holy Spirit. He seems to do good, but the purpose of his miracles is to deceive.

13:14 Throughout the Bible we see miracles performed as proofs of God's power, love, and authority. But here we see counterfeit miracles performed to deceive. This is a reminder of Pharaoh's magicians, who duplicated Moses' signs in Egypt. True signs and miracles point us to Jesus Christ, but miracles alone can be deceptive. That is why we must ask with respect to each miracle we see: Is this consistent with what God says in the Bible? The second beast here gains influence through the signs and wonders that he can perform on behalf of the first beast. The second beast orders the people to worship a statue in honor of the first beast—a direct flouting of the second commandment (Exodus 20:4-6). Allowing the Bible to guide our faith and practice will keep us from being deceived by false signs, however convincing they appear to be. Any teaching that contradicts God's Word is false.

13:16, 17 In every generation, Christians need to maintain a healthy skepticism about society's pleasures and rewards. In our educational, economic, and civic structures, there are incentives and rewards. Cooperating Christians must always support what is good and healthy about our society, but we must stand against sin. In some cases, such as Satan's system described here, the system or structure becomes so evil that there is no way to cooperate with it.

13:16-18 This mark of the beast is designed to mock the seal that God places on his followers (7:2, 3). Just as God marks his people to save them, so Satan's beast marks his people to save them from the persecution that Satan will inflict upon God's followers. Identifying this particular mark is not as important as identifying the purpose of the mark. Those who accept it show their allegiance to Satan, their willingness to operate within the economic system he promotes, and their rebellion against God. To refuse the mark means to commit oneself entirely to God, preferring death to compromising one's faith in Christ.

13:18 The meaning of this number has been discussed more than that of any other part of the book of Revelation. The three sixes have been said to represent many things, including the number of a man or the unholy trinity of Satan, the first beast, and the false prophet (16:13). If the number seven is considered to be the perfect number in the Bible, and if three sevens represent complete perfection, then the number 666 falls completely short of perfection. The first readers of this book probably applied the number to the emperor Nero, who symbolized all the evils of the Roman Empire. (The Greek letters of Nero's name represent numbers that total 666.) Whatever specific application the number is given, the number symbolizes the worldwide dominion and complete evil of this unholy trinity designed to undo Christ's work and overthrow him.

14:1ff Chapter 13 described the onslaught of evil that will occur when Satan and his helpers control the world. Chapter 14 gives a glimpse into eternity to show believers what awaits them if they endure. The Lamb is the Messiah. Mount Zion, often another name for Jerusalem, the capital of Israel, is contrasted with the worldly empire. The 144,000 represent believers who have endured persecutions on earth and now are ready to enjoy the eternal benefits and blessings of life with God forever. The three angels contrast the destiny of believers with that of unbelievers.

14:4 2 Cor 11:2
14:5 Isa 53:9; Zeph 3:13; 1 Pet 2:22
14:6 Rev 5:9
14:7 Acts 4:24; Rev 15:4
14:8 Isa 21:9; Jer 51:8; Rev 16:19; 17:5; 18:2, 10
14:9 Rev 13:12-17
14:10 Ps 75:8; Isa 51:17, 22; Jer 25:15; Rev 16:19; 19:20; 20:10; 21:8
14:11 Isa 34:10; Rev 13:12-17
14:12 Rev 2:13; 12:17; 13:10
14:13 Heb 4:10

those 144,000 who had been redeemed from the earth. [4]For they are spiritually undefiled, pure as virgins,* following the Lamb wherever he goes. They have been purchased
from among the people on the earth as a special offering* to God and to the Lamb. [5]No
falsehood can be charged against them; they are blameless.

The Three Angels

[6]And I saw another angel flying through the heavens, carrying the everlasting Good
News to preach to the people who belong to this world—to every nation, tribe, language,
and people. [7]"Fear God," he shouted. "Give glory to him. For the time has come when
he will sit as judge. Worship him who made heaven and earth, the sea, and all the springs
of water."
[8]Then another angel followed him through the skies, shouting, "Babylon is fallen—
that great city is fallen—because she seduced the nations of the world and made them
drink the wine of her passionate immorality."
[9]Then a third angel followed them, shouting, "Anyone who worships the beast and
his statue or who accepts his mark on the forehead or the hand [10]must drink the wine of
God's wrath. It is poured out undiluted into God's cup of wrath. And they will be
tormented with fire and burning sulfur in the presence of the holy angels and the Lamb.
[11]The smoke of their torment rises forever and ever, and they will have no relief day or
night, for they have worshiped the beast and his statue and have accepted the mark of his
name. [12]Let this encourage God's holy people to endure persecution patiently and
remain firm to the end, obeying his commands and trusting in Jesus."
[13]And I heard a voice from heaven saying, "Write this down: Blessed are those who
die in the Lord from now on. Yes, says the Spirit, they are blessed indeed, for they will
rest from all their toils and trials; for their good deeds follow them!"

14:4a Greek *they are virgins who have not defiled themselves with women.* **14:4b** Greek *as firstfruits.*

14:4 These people are true believers whose robes have been washed and made white in Christ's blood (7:14) through his death ("purchased from among the people on the earth"). In the Old Testament, idolatry was often portrayed as spiritual adultery (see the book of Hosea). Their purity is best understood symbolically, meaning that they are free from involvement with the pagan world system. These believers are spiritually pure: They have remained faithful to Christ, they have followed him exclusively, and they have received God's reward for staying committed to him. The "special offering" refers to the act of dedicating the first part (firstfruits) of the harvest as holy to God (Exodus 23:19; see also James 1:18).

14:6, 7 Some believe that this is a final, worldwide appeal to all people to recognize the one true God. No one will have the excuse of never hearing God's truth. Others, however, see this as an announcement of judgment rather than as an appeal. The people of the world have had their chance to proclaim their allegiance to God, and now God's great judgment is about to begin. If you are reading this, you have already heard God's truth. You know that God's final judgment will not be put off forever. Have you joyfully received the everlasting Good News? Have you confessed your sins and trusted in Christ to save you? If so, you have nothing to fear from God's judgment. The Judge of all the earth is your Savior!

14:8 Babylon was the name of both an evil city and an immoral empire, a world center for idol worship. Babylon ransacked Jerusalem and carried the people of Judah into captivity (see 2 Kings 25 and 2 Chronicles 36). Just as Babylon was the Jews' worst enemy, the Roman Empire was the worst enemy of the early Christians. John, who probably did not dare speak against Rome openly, applied the name *Babylon* to this enemy of God's people (Rome)—and, by extension, to all God's enemies of all times.

14:9-11 Those who worship the beast, accept his mark on their foreheads, and operate according to his world economic system will ultimately face God's judgment. Our world values money, power, and pleasure over God's leadership. To get what the world values, many people deny God and violate Christian principles. Thus, they must drink of the wine of God's wrath (see Psalm 75; Isaiah 51:17).

14:11 The ultimate result of sin is unending separation from God. Because human beings are created in God's image with an inborn thirst for fellowship with him, separation from God will be the ultimate torment and misery. Sin always brings misery, but in this life we can choose to repent and restore our relationship with God. In eternity there will no longer be opportunity for repentance. If in this life we choose to be independent of God, in the next life we will be separated from him forever. Nobody is forced to choose eternal separation from God, and nobody suffers this fate by accident. Jesus invites all of us to open the door of our heart to him (3:20). If we do this, we will enjoy everlasting fellowship with him.

14:12 This news about God's ultimate triumph should encourage God's people to remain faithful through every trial and persecution. They can do this, God promises, by trusting in Jesus and obeying the commands found in his Word. The secret to enduring, therefore, is trust and obedience. Trust God to give you patience to endure even the small trials you face daily; obey him even when obedience is unattractive or dangerous.

14:13 While it is true that money, fame, and belongings can't be taken with us from this life, God's people *can* produce fruit that survives even death. God will remember our love, kindness, and faithfulness, and those who accept Christ through our witness will join us in the new earth. Be sure that your values are in line with God's values, and decide today to produce fruit that lasts forever.

The Harvest of the Earth
14 Then I saw the Son of Man* sitting on a white cloud. He had a gold crown on his head
and a sharp sickle in his hand.
15 Then an angel came from the Temple and called out in a loud voice to the one sitting
on the cloud, "Use the sickle, for the time has come for you to harvest; the crop is ripe on
the earth." 16 So the one sitting on the cloud swung his sickle over the earth, and the whole
earth was harvested.
17 After that, another angel came from the Temple in heaven, and he also had a sharp
sickle. 18 Then another angel, who has power to destroy the world with fire, shouted to
the angel with the sickle, "Use your sickle now to gather the clusters of grapes from the
vines of the earth, for they are fully ripe for judgment." 19 So the angel swung his sickle
on the earth and loaded the grapes into the great winepress of God's wrath. 20 And the
grapes were trodden in the winepress outside the city, and blood flowed from the
winepress in a stream about 180 miles* long and as high as a horse's bridle.

14:14 Dan 7:13; Rev 1:13; 6:2
14:15 Joel 3:13; Matt 13:39-40; Mark 4:29
14:18 Joel 3:13; Rev 6:9; 8:3; 14:15
14:19 Isa 63:2-3; Rev 19:15
14:20 Gen 49:11; Isa 63:3; Lam 1:15; Rev 19:15

5. Pouring out the seven plagues

The Song of Moses and of the Lamb

15 Then I saw in heaven another significant event, and it was great and marvelous.
Seven angels were holding the seven last plagues, which would bring God's wrath
to completion. 2 I saw before me what seemed to be a crystal sea mixed with fire. And
on it stood all the people who had been victorious over the beast and his statue and the
number representing his name. They were all holding harps that God had given them.
3 And they were singing the song of Moses, the servant of God, and the song of the Lamb:

"Great and marvelous are your actions,
  Lord God Almighty.
Just and true are your ways,
  O King of the nations.*
4 Who will not fear, O Lord, and glorify your name?
  For you alone are holy.
All nations will come and worship before you,
  for your righteous deeds have been revealed."

15:1 Lev 26:21; Rev 15:6; 16:1; 21:9
15:2 Rev 4:6
15:3 Exod 15:1; Deut 32:4; Ps 145:17; Jer 10:7; Amos 3:13; 4:13; Rev 1:8; 4:8
15:4 Ps 86:9; Jer 10:6-7; Mal 1:11

The Seven Bowls of the Seven Plagues
5 Then I looked and saw that the Temple in heaven, God's Tabernacle, was thrown wide
open! 6 The seven angels who were holding the bowls of the seven plagues came from
the Temple, clothed in spotless white linen* with gold belts across their chests. 7 And one
of the four living beings handed each of the seven angels a gold bowl filled with the
terrible wrath of God, who lives forever and forever. 8 The Temple was filled with smoke

15:5 Exod 38:21; Rev 11:19
15:6 Lev 26:21
15:8 Exod 40:34; 1 Kgs 8:10-11; 2 Chr 5:13-14; Isa 6:4

14:14 Or *one who looked like a man;* Greek reads *one like a son of man.* **14:20** Greek *1,600 stadia* [296 kilometers]. **15:3** Some manuscripts read *King of the ages;* other manuscripts read *King of the saints.* **15:6** Some manuscripts read *in bright and sparkling stone.*

14:14-16 This is an image of judgment: Christ is separating the faithful from the unfaithful like a farmer harvesting his crops. This is a time of joy for the Christians who have been persecuted and martyred—they will receive their long-awaited reward. Christians should not fear the Last Judgment. Jesus said, "I assure you, those who listen to my message and believe in God who sent me have eternal life. They will never be condemned for their sins, but they have already passed from death into life" (John 5:24).

14:19 A winepress was a large vat or trough where grapes were collected and then crushed. The juice flowed out of a duct that led into a large holding vat. The winepress is often used in the Bible as a symbol of God's wrath and judgment against sin (Isaiah 63:3-6; Lamentations 1:15; Joel 3:12, 13).

14:20 The distance of 180 miles is approximately the north-south length of Palestine.

15:1 The seven last plagues are also called the seven bowl judgments. They actually begin in chapter 16. Unlike the previous plagues, these are universal, and they will culminate in the abolition of all evil and the end of the world.

15:2 This is similar to the "sea of glass" described in 4:6, located before the throne of God. Here it is mixed with fire to represent wrath and judgment. Those who stand beside it are victorious over Satan and his evil beast.

15:3, 4 The song of Moses celebrated Israel's deliverance from Egypt (Exodus 15). The song of the Lamb celebrates the ultimate deliverance of God's people from the power of Satan.

15:5-8 This imagery brings us back to the time of the Exodus in the wilderness when the Ark of the Covenant (the symbol of God's presence among his people) resided in the Tabernacle. The angels coming out of the Temple are clothed in spotless white linen with gold belts across their chests. Their garments, reminiscent of the high priest's clothing, show that they are free from corruption, immorality, and injustice. The smoke that fills the Temple is the manifestation of God's glory and power. There is no escape from this judgment.

15:8 Our eternal reign with Christ won't begin until all evil is destroyed by his judgment. The faithful must wait for his timetable to be revealed.

from God's glory and power. No one could enter the Temple until the seven angels had
completed pouring out the seven plagues.

16 Then I heard a mighty voice shouting from the Temple to the seven angels, "Now
go your ways and empty out the seven bowls of God's wrath on the earth."
2 So the first angel left the Temple and poured out his bowl over the earth, and horrible,
malignant sores broke out on everyone who had the mark of the beast and who worshiped
his statue.
3 Then the second angel poured out his bowl on the sea, and it became like the blood
of a corpse. And everything in the sea died.
4 Then the third angel poured out his bowl on the rivers and springs, and they became
blood. 5 And I heard the angel who had authority over all water saying, "You are just in
sending this judgment, O Holy One, who is and who always was. 6 For your holy people
and your prophets have been killed, and their blood was poured out on the earth. So you
have given their murderers blood to drink. It is their just reward." 7 And I heard a voice
from the altar saying, "Yes, Lord God Almighty, your punishments are true and just."
8 Then the fourth angel poured out his bowl on the sun, causing it to scorch everyone
with its fire. 9 Everyone was burned by this blast of heat, and they cursed the name of
God, who sent all of these plagues. They did not repent and give him glory.
10 Then the fifth angel poured out his bowl on the throne of the beast, and his kingdom
was plunged into darkness. And his subjects ground their teeth in anguish, 11 and they
cursed the God of heaven for their pains and sores. But they refused to repent of all their
evil deeds.
12 Then the sixth angel poured out his bowl on the great Euphrates River, and it dried
up so that the kings from the east could march their armies westward without hindrance.
13 And I saw three evil spirits that looked like frogs leap from the mouth of the dragon, the
beast, and the false prophet. 14 These miracle-working demons caused all the rulers of the
world to gather for battle against the Lord on that great judgment day of God Almighty.

15 "Take note: I will come as unexpectedly as a thief! Blessed are all who are watching for me, who keep their robes ready so they will not need to walk naked and
ashamed."

16 And they gathered all the rulers and their armies to a place called *Armageddon* in
Hebrew.

16:1 Isa 66:6; Zeph 3:8
16:2 Exod 9:9-11
16:3 Exod 7:17-21
16:4 Exod 7:17-21; Ps 78:44
16:5 Rev 1:4, 8; 4:8; 11:17
16:6 Ps 79:3; Isa 49:26
16:7 Rev 1:8; 6:9; 14:18; 15:3; 19:2
16:10 Exod 10:21; Isa 8:22; Rev 8:12; 9:2; 13:2
16:11 Rev 9:20-21
16:12 Isa 11:15-16; 44:27; Jer 50:38; 51:36
16:13 Rev 12:3; 13:1, 11-17
16:14 Rev 6:17; 17:14; 19:19
16:15 1 Thes 5:2; Rev 3:3, 18
16:16 Judg 5:19; 2 Kgs 9:27; 23:29; Zech 12:11

16:1ff The bowl judgments are God's final and complete judgments on the earth. The end has come. There are many similarities between the bowl judgments and the trumpet judgments (8:6–11:19), but there are three main differences: (1) These judgments are complete whereas the trumpet judgments are partial; (2) the trumpet judgments still give unbelievers the opportunity to repent, but the bowl judgments do not; and (3) people are indirectly affected by several of the trumpet judgments but directly attacked by all the bowl judgments.

16:7 The significance of the altar itself responding is that *everyone and everything* will be praising God, acknowledging his righteousness and perfect justice.

16:9-21 We know that the people realize that these judgments come from God because they curse him for sending them. But they still refuse to recognize God's authority and repent of their sins. Christians should not be surprised at the hostility and hardness of heart of unbelievers. Even when the power of God is fully and completely revealed, many will still refuse to repent. If you find yourself ignoring God more and more, turn back to him now before your heart becomes too hard to repent (see the note on 9:20, 21 for more on hard hearts).

16:12 The Euphrates River was a natural protective boundary against the empires to the east (Babylon, Assyria, Persia). If it dried up, nothing could hold back invading armies. The armies from the east symbolize unhindered judgment.

16:13, 14 These evil spirits performing miraculous signs, who come out of the mouths of the unholy trinity, unite the rulers of the world for battle against God. The imagery of the demons coming out of the mouths of the three evil rulers signifies the verbal enticements and propaganda that will draw many people to their evil cause. For more about demons, see the note on 9:3ff.

16:15 Christ will return unexpectedly (1 Thessalonians 5:1-6), so we must be ready when he returns. We can prepare ourselves by standing firm in temptation and by being committed to God's moral standards. In what ways does your life show either your readiness or your lack of preparation for Christ's return?

16:16 This battlefield called Armageddon is near the city of Megiddo (southeast of the modern port of Haifa), which guarded a large plain in northern Israel. It is a strategic location near a prominent international highway leading north from Egypt through Israel, along the coast, and on to Babylon. Megiddo overlooked the entire plain southward toward Galilee and westward toward the mountains of Gilboa.

16:16 Sinful people will unite to fight against God in a final display of rebellion. Many are already united against Christ and his people—those who stand for truth, peace, justice, and morality. Your personal battle with evil foreshadows the great battle pictured here, where God will meet evil and destroy it once and for all. Be strong and courageous as you battle against sin and evil: You are fighting on the winning side.

17 Then the seventh angel poured out his bowl into the air. And a mighty shout came
from the throne of the Temple in heaven, saying, "It is finished!" 18 Then the thunder
crashed and rolled, and lightning flashed. And there was an earthquake greater than ever
before in human history. 19 The great city of Babylon split into three pieces, and cities
around the world fell into heaps of rubble. And so God remembered all of Babylon's sins,
and he made her drink the cup that was filled with the wine of his fierce wrath. 20 And
every island disappeared, and all the mountains were leveled. 21 There was a terrible
hailstorm, and hailstones weighing seventy-five pounds* fell from the sky onto the
people below. They cursed God because of the hailstorm, which was a very terrible
plague.

16:17 Isa 66:6; Rev 11:15; 21:6
16:18 Dan 12:1; Matt 24:21; Rev 4:5; 6:12
16:19 Rev 14:8, 10
16:20 Rev 6:14; 20:11
16:21 Exod 9:23-25; Rev 11:19; 16:9, 11

6. Seizing the final victory

The Great Prostitute

17 One of the seven angels who had poured out the seven bowls came over and spoke
to me. "Come with me," he said, "and I will show you the judgment that is going
to come on the great prostitute, who sits on many waters. 2 The rulers of the world have
had immoral relations with her, and the people who belong to this world have been made
drunk by the wine of her immorality."
3 So the angel took me in spirit* into the wilderness. There I saw a woman sitting on
a scarlet beast that had seven heads and ten horns, written all over with blasphemies
against God. 4 The woman wore purple and scarlet clothing and beautiful jewelry made
of gold and precious gems and pearls. She held in her hand a gold goblet full of
obscenities and the impurities of her immorality. 5 A mysterious name was written on her
forehead: "Babylon the Great, Mother of All Prostitutes and Obscenities in the World."
6 I could see that she was drunk—drunk with the blood of God's holy people who were
witnesses for Jesus. I stared at her completely amazed.
7 "Why are you so amazed?" the angel asked. "I will tell you the mystery of this
woman and of the beast with seven heads and ten horns. 8 The beast you saw was alive
but isn't now. And yet he will soon come up out of the bottomless pit and go to eternal
destruction. And the people who belong to this world, whose names were not written in
the Book of Life from before the world began, will be amazed at the reappearance of this
beast who had died.
9 "And now understand this: The seven heads of the beast represent the seven hills of
the city where this woman rules. They also represent seven kings. 10 Five kings have
already fallen, the sixth now reigns, and the seventh is yet to come, but his reign will be
brief. 11 The scarlet beast that was alive and then died is the eighth king. He is like the

17:1 Jer 51:13; Rev 17:15; 19:2
17:2 Jer 51:7; Rev 14:8; 18:3
17:3 Rev 1:10; 12:6; 13:1
17:4 Jer 51:7; Ezek 28:13
17:5 2 Thes 2:7; Rev 17:2, 7
17:6 Rev 16:6; 18:24
17:8 Dan 12:1; Rev 11:7; 13:1, 3
17:9 Rev 13:18

16:21 Greek *1 talent* [34 kilograms]. **17:3** Or *in the Spirit.*

16:17-21 For more information on Babylon and what it represents in Revelation, see the note on 14:8. The city's division into three sections is a symbol of its complete destruction.

17:1ff The destruction of Babylon mentioned in 16:17-21 is now described in greater detail. The "great prostitute," called Babylon, represents the early Roman Empire with its many gods and the blood of Christian martyrs on its hands. The water stands for either sea commerce or a well-watered (well-provisioned) city. The great prostitute represents the seductiveness of the governmental system that uses immoral means to gain its own pleasure, prosperity, and advantage. In contrast to the prostitute, Christ's bride, the church, is pure and obedient (19:6-9). The wicked city of Babylon contrasts with the heavenly city of Jerusalem (21:10–22:5). The original readers probably rather quickly identified Babylon with Rome, but Babylon also symbolizes any system that is hostile to God (see 17:5).

17:3 The scarlet beast is either the dragon of 12:3 or the beast out of the sea described in 13:1.

17:6 Throughout history, people have been killed for their faith. Over the last century, millions have been killed by oppressive governments, and many of those victims were believers. The woman's drunkenness shows her pleasure in her evil accomplishments and her false feeling of triumph over the church. But every martyr who has fallen before her sword has only served to strengthen the faith of the church.

17:8 In chapter 12 we met the dragon (Satan). In chapter 13 we saw the beast from the sea and the power he received from Satan. In chapters 14–16 we see God's great judgments. In this chapter, a scarlet beast similar to the beast and the dragon appears as an ally of the great prostitute. The beast was alive, died, and then came back to life. The beast's resurrection symbolizes the persistence of evil. This resurgence of evil power will convince many to join forces with the beast, but those who choose the side of evil condemn themselves to the Devil's fate—eternal torment.

17:8 For more information on the Book of Life, see the note on 3:5.

17:9-11 Here John is referring to Rome, the city famous for its seven hills. Many say that this city also symbolized all evil in the world—any person, religion, group, government, or structure that opposed Christ. Whatever view is taken of the seven hills and seven kings, this section indicates the climax of Satan's struggle against God. Evil's power is limited, and its destruction is on the horizon.

17:12 Dan 7:20, 24; Rev 18:10, 17, 19
17:14 Matt 22:14; 1 Tim 6:15
17:15 Isa 8:7; Jer 47:2; Rev 13:7; 17:1
17:16 Lev 21:9; Ezek 16:37, 39; Rev 18:8, 19
17:17 Rev 10:7; 17:13
17:18 Rev 16:19

other seven, and he, too, will go to his doom. 12 His ten horns are ten kings who have not
yet risen to power; they will be appointed to their kingdoms for one brief moment to
reign with the beast. 13 They will all agree to give their power and authority to him.
14 Together they will wage war against the Lamb, but the Lamb will defeat them because
he is Lord over all lords and King over all kings, and his people are the called and chosen
and faithful ones."

15 And the angel said to me, "The waters where the prostitute is sitting represent masses
of people of every nation and language. 16 The scarlet beast and his ten horns—which
represent ten kings who will reign with him—all hate the prostitute. They will strip her
naked, eat her flesh, and burn her remains with fire. 17 For God has put a plan into their
minds, a plan that will carry out his purposes. They will mutually agree to give their
authority to the scarlet beast, and so the words of God will be fulfilled. 18 And this woman
you saw in your vision represents the great city that rules over the kings of the earth."

The Fall of Babylon

18:2 Isa 13:19-22; 21:9; Jer 50:39
18:3 Ezek 27:9-25
18:4 Isa 48:20; 52:11; Jer 51:6, 9, 45
18:5 Jer 51:9
18:6 Jer 50:15, 29
18:7 Isa 47:8
18:8 Isa 47:9; Jer 50:31-34

18 After all this I saw another angel come down from heaven with great authority, and
the earth grew bright with his splendor. 2 He gave a mighty shout, "Babylon is
fallen—that great city is fallen! She has become the hideout of demons and evil spirits, a
nest for filthy buzzards, and a den for dreadful beasts. 3 For all the nations have drunk the
wine of her passionate immorality. The rulers of the world have committed adultery with
her, and merchants throughout the world have grown rich as a result of her luxurious living."

4 Then I heard another voice calling from heaven, "Come away from her, my people.
Do not take part in her sins, or you will be punished with her. 5 For her sins are piled as
high as heaven, and God is ready to judge her for her evil deeds. 6 Do to her as she has
done to your people. Give her a double penalty for all her evil deeds. She brewed a cup
of terror for others, so give her twice as much as she gave out. 7 She has lived in luxury
and pleasure, so match it now with torments and sorrows. She boasts, 'I am queen on my
throne. I am no helpless widow. I will not experience sorrow.' 8 Therefore, the sorrows

---

HOW CAN A PERSON KEEP AWAY FROM THE EVIL SYSTEM?
Here are some suggestions:

1. People must always be more important than products.
2. Keep away from pride in your own programs, plans, and successes.
3. Remember that God's will and Word must never be compromised.
4. People must always be considered above the making of money.
5. Do what is right, no matter what the cost.
6. Be involved in businesses that provide worthwhile products or services—not just things that feed the world's desires.

17:12 The 10 horns represent kings of nations yet to arise. Rome will be followed by other powers. Rome is a good example of how the Antichrist's system will work, demanding complete allegiance and ruling by raw power, oppression, and slavery. Whoever the 10 kings are, they will give their power to the Antichrist and make war against the Lamb.

17:16 In a dramatic turn of events, the prostitute's allies turn on her and destroy her. This is how evil operates. Destructive by its very nature, it discards its own adherents when they cease to serve its purposes. An unholy alliance is an uneasy alliance because each partner puts its own interests first.

17:17 No matter what happens, we must trust that God is still in charge, that God overrules all the plans and intrigues of the evil one, and that God's plans will happen just as he says. God even uses people opposed to him as tools to execute his will. Although he allows evil to permeate this present world, the new earth will never know sin.

18:1ff This chapter shows the complete destruction of Babylon, John's metaphorical name for the evil world power and all it represents. Everything that tries to block God's purposes will come to a violent end. For more information on how the book of Revelation uses the name *Babylon,* see the note on 14:8.

18:2, 3 Merchants in the Roman Empire grew rich by exploiting the sinful pleasures of their society. Many businesspeople today do the same thing. Businesses and governments are often based on greed, money, and power. Many bright individuals are tempted to take advantage of an evil system to enrich themselves. Christians are warned to stay free from the lure of money, status, and the good life. We are to live according to the values Christ exemplified: service, giving, self-sacrifice, obedience, and truth.

18:4-8 The people of Babylon had lived in luxury and pleasure. The city boasted, "I am queen on my throne. . . . I will not experience sorrow." The powerful, wealthy people of this world are susceptible to this same attitude. A person who is financially comfortable often feels invulnerable, secure, and in control, feeling no need for God or anyone else. This kind of attitude defies God, and his judgment against it is harsh. We are told to avoid Babylon's sins. If you are financially secure, don't become complacent and deluded by the myth of self-sufficiency. Use your resources to help others and advance God's Kingdom.

of death and mourning and famine will overtake her in a single day. She will be utterly
consumed by fire, for the Lord God who judges her is mighty."
9And the rulers of the world who took part in her immoral acts and enjoyed her great
luxury will mourn for her as they see the smoke rising from her charred remains. 10They
will stand at a distance, terrified by her great torment. They will cry out, "How terrible, how
terrible for Babylon, that great city! In one single moment God's judgment came on her."
11The merchants of the world will weep and mourn for her, for there is no one left to
buy their goods. 12She bought great quantities of gold, silver, jewels, pearls, fine linen,
purple dye, silk, scarlet cloth, every kind of perfumed wood, ivory goods, objects made
of expensive wood, bronze, iron, and marble. 13She also bought cinnamon, spice,
incense, myrrh, frankincense, wine, olive oil, fine flour, wheat, cattle, sheep, horses,
chariots, and slaves—yes, she even traded in human lives.
14"All the fancy things you loved so much are gone," they cry. "The luxuries and
splendor that you prized so much will never be yours again. They are gone forever."
15The merchants who became wealthy by selling her these things will stand at a
distance, terrified by her great torment. They will weep and cry. 16"How terrible, how
terrible for that great city! She was so beautiful—like a woman clothed in finest purple
and scarlet linens, decked out with gold and precious stones and pearls! 17And in one
single moment all the wealth of the city is gone!"
And all the shipowners and captains of the merchant ships and their crews will stand at
a distance. 18They will weep as they watch the smoke ascend, and they will say, "Where in
all the world is there another city like this?" 19And they will throw dust on their heads to
show their great sorrow. And they will say, "How terrible, how terrible for the great city!
She made us all rich from her great wealth. And now in a single hour it is all gone."
20But you, O heaven, rejoice over her fate. And you also rejoice, O holy people of God
and apostles and prophets! For at last God has judged her on your behalf.
21Then a mighty angel picked up a boulder as large as a great millstone. He threw it into
the ocean and shouted, "Babylon, the great city, will be thrown down as violently as I have
thrown away this stone, and she will disappear forever. 22Never again will the sound of
music be heard there—no more harps, songs, flutes, or trumpets. There will be no industry
of any kind, and no more milling of grain. 23Her nights will be dark, without a single lamp.
There will be no happy voices of brides and grooms. This will happen because her
merchants, who were the greatest in the world, deceived the nations with her sorceries. 24In
her streets the blood of the prophets was spilled. She was the one who slaughtered God's
people all over the world."

Songs of Victory in Heaven

19 After this, I heard the sound of a vast crowd in heaven shouting, "Hallelujah!
Salvation is from our God. Glory and power belong to him alone. 2His judgments
are just and true. He has punished the great prostitute who corrupted the earth with her

18:9 Ps 58:10 Ezek 26:16 Rev 17:2
18:10 Ezek 26:17 Rev 14:8
18:11 Ezek 27:27, 36 Rev 18:3
18:12-13 Ezek 27:12-22
18:15 Ezek 27:36
18:16 Rev 17:4
18:17 Ezek 27:27-29 Rev 17:16
18:18 Ezek 27:32 Rev 13:4
18:19 Ezek 27:30-34
18:20 Jer 51:48 Rev 12:12; 19:2
18:21 Jer 51:63
18:22 Ezek 26:13
18:23 Jer 7:34; 16:9; 25:10 Nah 3:4
18:24 Jer 51:49 Matt 23:35-37 Rev 16:6; 17:6
19:1 Rev 4:11; 7:10; 12:10

18:9, 10 Those who are tied to the world's system will lose everything when it collapses. What they have worked for a lifetime to build up will be destroyed in one hour. Those who work only for material rewards will have nothing when they die or when their possessions are destroyed. What can we take with us to the new earth? Our faith, our Christian character, and our relationships with other believers. These are more important than any amount of money, power, or pleasure.

18:9-19 Those who are in control of various parts of the economic system will mourn at Babylon's fall. The political leaders will mourn because they were the overseers of Babylon's wealth and were in a position to enrich themselves greatly. The merchants will mourn because Babylon, the greatest customer for their goods, will be gone. The sea captains will no longer have anywhere to bring their goods because the merchants will have nowhere to sell them. The fall of the evil world system affects all who enjoyed and depended on it. No one will remain unaffected by Babylon's fall.

18:11-13 This list of various merchandise illustrates the extreme materialism of this society. Few of these goods are necessities—most are luxuries. The society had become so self-indulgent that people were willing to use evil means to gratify their desires. Even people had become commodities—people were sold as slaves to Babylon.

18:11-19 God's people should not live for money, because money will be worthless in eternity. And they should keep on guard constantly against greed, a sin that is always ready to take over their lives.

19:1ff Praise is the heartfelt response to God by those who love him. The more you get to know God and realize what he has done, the more you will respond with praise. Praise is at the heart of true worship. Let your praise of God flow out of your realization of who he is and how much he loves you.

19:1, 2 The identity of this great prostitute is explained in the note on 17:1ff.

19:1-8 A vast crowd in heaven initiates the chorus of praise to God for his victory (19:1-3). Then the 24 elders (identified in the note on 4:4) join the chorus (19:4). Finally, the great choir of heaven once again praises God—the wedding of the Lamb

19:3 Isa 34:10; Rev 14:11
19:4 Rev 4:4, 6, 10
19:5 Pss 115:13; 134:1; 135:1; Rev 11:18
19:6 Rev 11:15
19:7 Matt 22:2; 25:10; Eph 5:32; Rev 21:2, 9
19:9 Luke 14:15; Rev 21:5; 22:6
19:10 Acts 10:25-26; Rev 22:8-9
19:11 Isa 11:4; Rev 1:14; 3:14
19:12 Rev 2:17
19:13 Isa 63:1-3; John 1:1, 14; 1 Jn 1:1-2
19:14 Rev 3:4
19:15 Isa 11:4; 63:3; 2 Thes 2:8; Rev 2:27; 14:20
19:16 Rev 17:14
19:17-18 Ezek 39:17-20

immorality, and he has avenged the murder of his servants." 3 Again and again their
voices rang, "Hallelujah! The smoke from that city ascends forever and forever!"
4 Then the twenty-four elders and the four living beings fell down and worshiped God,
who was sitting on the throne. They cried out, "Amen! Hallelujah!"
5 And from the throne came a voice that said, "Praise our God, all his servants, from
the least to the greatest, all who fear him."
6 Then I heard again what sounded like the shout of a huge crowd, or the roar of mighty
ocean waves, or the crash of loud thunder: "Hallelujah! For the Lord our God, the Almighty,
reigns. 7 Let us be glad and rejoice and honor him. For the time has come for the wedding
feast of the Lamb, and his bride has prepared herself. 8 She is permitted to wear the finest
white linen." (Fine linen represents the good deeds done by the people of God.)
9 And the angel said, "Write this: Blessed are those who are invited to the wedding
feast of the Lamb." And he added, "These are true words that come from God."
10 Then I fell down at his feet to worship him, but he said, "No, don't worship me. For
I am a servant of God, just like you and other believers* who testify of their faith in Jesus.
Worship God. For the essence of prophecy is to give a clear witness for Jesus.*"

The Rider on the White Horse

11 Then I saw heaven opened, and a white horse was standing there. And the one sitting
on the horse was named Faithful and True. For he judges fairly and then goes to war.
12 His eyes were bright like flames of fire, and on his head were many crowns. A name
was written on him, and only he knew what it meant. 13 He was clothed with a robe
dipped in blood, and his title was the Word of God. 14 The armies of heaven, dressed in
pure white linen, followed him on white horses. 15 From his mouth came a sharp sword,
and with it he struck down the nations. He ruled them with an iron rod, and he trod the
winepress of the fierce wrath of almighty God. 16 On his robe and thigh was written this
title: King of kings and Lord of lords.
17 Then I saw an angel standing in the sun, shouting to the vultures flying high in the
sky: "Come! Gather together for the great banquet God has prepared. 18 Come and eat
the flesh of kings, captains, and strong warriors; of horses and their riders; and of all
humanity, both free and slave, small and great."
19 Then I saw the beast gathering the kings of the earth and their armies in order to fight

19:10a Greek *brothers.* **19:10b** Or *is the message confirmed by Jesus.*

---

has come (19:6-8). See Matthew 25:1-13 where Christ compares the coming of his Kingdom to a wedding for which we must be prepared.

19:7, 8 This is the culmination of human history—the judgment of the wicked and the wedding of the Lamb and his bride, the church. The church consists of all faithful believers from all time. The bride's clothing stands in sharp contrast to the gaudy clothing of the great prostitute of 17:4 and 18:16. The bride's clothing represents the good deeds of the believers. These good deeds are not done by believers to their merit, but they reflect the work of Christ to save us (7:9, 14).

19:10 The angel did not accept John's homage and worship because only God is worthy of worship. Like John, it would be easy for us to become overwhelmed by this prophetic pageant. But Jesus is the central focus of God's revelation and his redemptive plan (as announced by the prophets). As you read the book of Revelation, don't get bogged down in all the details of the awesome visions; remember that the overarching theme in all the visions is the ultimate victory of Jesus Christ over evil.

19:11 The name "Faithful and True" contrasts with the faithless and deceitful Babylon described in chapter 18.

19:11-21 John's vision shifts again. Heaven opens, and Jesus appears—this time not as a Lamb but as a warrior on a white horse (symbolizing victory). Jesus came first as a Lamb to be a sacrifice for sin, but he will return as a conqueror and king to execute judgment (2 Thessalonians 1:7-10). Jesus' first coming brought forgiveness; his second will bring judgment. The battle lines have been drawn between God and evil, and the world is waiting for the King to ride onto the field.

19:12 Although Jesus is called "Faithful and True" (19:11), "Word of God" (19:13), and "King of kings and Lord of lords" (19:16), this verse implies that no name can do him justice. He is greater than any description or expression the human mind can devise.

19:13 For more about the symbolism of Jesus' clothes being dipped in blood, see the second note on 7:14.

19:16 This title indicates our God's sovereignty. Most of the world is worshiping the beast, the Antichrist, whom they believe has all power and authority. Then suddenly out of heaven ride Christ and his army of angels—the "King of kings and Lord of lords." His entrance signals the end of the false powers.

19:17 This "great banquet" is a grim contrast to the wedding feast of the Lamb (19:9). One is a celebration; the other is devastation.

19:19 The beast is identified in the note on 13:1.

19:19-21 The battle lines have been drawn, and the greatest confrontation in the history of the world is about to begin. The beast (the Antichrist) and the false prophet have gathered the governments and armies of the earth under the Antichrist's rule. The enemy armies believe they have come of their own volition; in reality, God has summoned them to battle in order to defeat them. That they would even presume to fight against God shows how their pride and rebellion have distorted their thinking. There really is no fight, however, because the victory was won when Jesus died on the cross for sin and rose from the dead. Thus, the evil leaders are immediately captured and sent to their punishment, and the forces of evil are annihilated.

against the one sitting on the horse and his army. 20 And the beast was captured, and with
him the false prophet who did mighty miracles on behalf of the beast—miracles that
deceived all who had accepted the mark of the beast and who worshiped his statue. Both
the beast and his false prophet were thrown alive into the lake of fire that burns with sulfur.
21 Their entire army was killed by the sharp sword that came out of the mouth of the one
riding the white horse. And all the vultures of the sky gorged themselves on the dead bodies.

19:20 Isa 30:33; Dan 7:11; Rev 13:12-16; 20:10, 14-15; 21:8

The Thousand Years

20 Then I saw an angel come down from heaven with the key to the bottomless pit
and a heavy chain in his hand. 2 He seized the dragon—that old serpent, the Devil,
Satan—and bound him in chains for a thousand years. 3 The angel threw him into the
bottomless pit, which he then shut and locked so Satan could not deceive the nations
anymore until the thousand years were finished. Afterward he would be released again
for a little while.

4 Then I saw thrones, and the people sitting on them had been given the authority to
judge. And I saw the souls of those who had been beheaded for their testimony about
Jesus, for proclaiming the word of God. And I saw the souls of those who had not
worshiped the beast or his statue, nor accepted his mark on their forehead or their hands.
They came to life again, and they reigned with Christ for a thousand years. 5 This is the
first resurrection. (The rest of the dead did not come back to life until the thousand years
had ended.) 6 Blessed and holy are those who share in the first resurrection. For them the
second death holds no power, but they will be priests of God and of Christ and will reign
with him a thousand years.

20:1 Rev 1:18; 10:1
20:2 Rev 12:9
20:3 2 Pet 2:4; Jude 1:6
20:4 Dan 7:9, 22, 27; Matt 19:28; Rev 13:12-16
20:5 Ezek 37:10; Luke 14:14
20:6 1 Pet 2:5, 9; Rev 1:6; 5:10; 20:14

The Defeat of Satan

7 When the thousand years end, Satan will be let out of his prison. 8 He will go out to
deceive the nations from every corner of the earth, which are called Gog and Magog. He
will gather them together for battle—a mighty host, as numberless as sand along the

20:7 Rev 20:2
20:8 Ezek 7:2; 38:2

19:20 The lake of fire that burns with sulfur is the final destination of the wicked. This lake is different from the bottomless pit referred to in 9:1. The Antichrist and the false prophet are thrown into the lake of fire. Then their leader, Satan himself, will be thrown into that lake (20:10), and finally death and the grave (20:14). Afterward, everyone whose name is not recorded in the Book of Life will be thrown into the lake of fire (20:15).

20:1 The angel and the bottomless pit are explained in the notes on 9:1 and 19:20.

20:2 The dragon, Satan, is discussed in more detail in the notes on 12:3, 4 and 12:9. The dragon is not bound as punishment—that occurs in 20:10—but so that he cannot deceive the nations.

20:2-4 The 1,000 years are often referred to as the *Millennium* (Latin for 1,000). Just how and when this 1,000 years takes place is understood differently among Christian scholars. The three major positions on this issue are called postmillennialism, premillennialism, and amillennialism.

(1) *Postmillennialism* looks for a literal 1,000-year period of peace on earth ushered in by the church. At the end of the 1,000 years, Satan will be unleashed once more, but then Christ will return to defeat him and reign forever. Christ's second coming will not occur until after the 1,000-year period.

(2) *Premillennialism* also views the 1,000 years as a literal time period but holds that Christ's second coming initiates his 1,000-year reign and that this reign occurs before the final removal of Satan.

(3) *Amillennialism* understands the 1,000-year period to be symbolic of the time between Christ's ascension and his return. This Millennium is the reign of Christ in the hearts of believers and in his church; thus, it is another way of referring to the church age. This period will end with the second coming of Christ.

These different views about the Millennium need not cause division and controversy in the church because each view acknowledges what is most crucial to Christianity: Christ will return, defeat Satan, and reign forever! Whatever and whenever the Millennium is, Jesus Christ will unite all believers; therefore, we should not let this issue divide us.

20:3 John doesn't say why God once again sets Satan free, but it is part of God's plan for judging the world. Perhaps it is to expose those who rebel against God in their hearts and confirm those who are truly faithful to God. Whatever the reason, Satan's release results in the final destruction of all evil (20:12-15).

20:4 The beast's mark is explained in the note on 13:16-18.

20:5, 6 Christians hold two basic views concerning this first resurrection: (1) Some believe that the first resurrection is spiritual (in our heart at salvation) and that the Millennium is our spiritual reign with Christ between his first and second comings. During this time, we are priests of God because Christ reigns in our hearts. In this view, the second resurrection is the bodily resurrection of all people for judgment. (2) Others believe that the first resurrection occurs after Satan has been set aside. It is a physical resurrection of believers, who then reign with Christ on the earth for a literal 1,000 years. The second resurrection occurs at the end of this Millennium in order to judge unbelievers who have died.

20:6 The second death is spiritual death—everlasting separation from God (see 21:8).

20:7-9 Gog and Magog symbolize all the forces of evil that band together to battle God. Noah's son Japheth had a son named Magog (Genesis 10:2). Ezekiel presents Gog as a leader of forces against Israel (Ezekiel 38–39).

20:9 Ps 87:2 Ezek 38:22; 39:6
shore. 9 And I saw them as they went up on the broad plain of the earth and surrounded
God's people and the beloved city. But fire from heaven came down on the attacking
armies and consumed them.

20:10 Rev 14:10; 19:20; 20:15
10 Then the Devil, who betrayed them, was thrown into the lake of fire that burns with
sulfur, joining the beast and the false prophet. There they will be tormented day and night
forever and ever.

The Final Judgment

20:11-12 Dan 7:9-10 Matt 25:31-46
11 And I saw a great white throne, and I saw the one who was sitting on it. The earth and sky
fled from his presence, but they found no place to hide. 12 I saw the dead, both great and
20:13 Isa 26:19 Matt 16:27 John 5:28 Rev 1:18
small, standing before God's throne. And the books were opened, including the Book of
Life. And the dead were judged according to the things written in the books, according to
what they had done. 13 The sea gave up the dead in it, and death and the grave* gave up the
20:14 1 Cor 15:26, 55 Rev 19:20
dead in them. They were all judged according to their deeds. 14 And death and the grave were
thrown into the lake of fire. This is the second death—the lake of fire. 15 And anyone whose
name was not found recorded in the Book of Life was thrown into the lake of fire.

7. Making all things new

The New Jerusalem

21:1 Isa 65:17; 66:22
21 Then I saw a new heaven and a new earth, for the old heaven and the old earth had
21:2 Isa 52:1; 61:10
disappeared. And the sea was also gone. 2 And I saw the holy city, the new Jerusalem,
coming down from God out of heaven like a beautiful bride prepared for her husband.

20:13 Greek *and Hades;* also in 20:14.

THE BEGINNING AND THE END

Genesis	*Revelation*
The sun is created.	The sun is not needed.
Satan is victorious.	Satan is defeated.
Sin enters the human race.	Sin is banished.
People run and hide from God.	People are invited to live with God forever.
People are cursed.	The curse is removed.
Tears are shed, with sorrow for sin.	No more sin, no more tears or sorrow.
The garden and earth are cursed.	God's city is glorified; the earth is made new.
Paradise is lost.	Paradise is regained.
People are doomed to death.	Death is defeated; believers live forever with God.

The Bible records for us the beginning of the world and the end of the world. The story of mankind, from beginning to end—from the fall into sin to redemption and God's ultimate victory over evil—is found in the pages of the Bible.

20:9 This is not a typical battle where the outcome is in doubt during the heat of the conflict. Here there is no contest. Two mighty forces of evil—those of the beast (19:19) and of Satan (20:8)—unite to do battle against God. The Bible uses just two verses to describe each battle: The evil beast and his forces are captured and thrown into the lake of fire (19:20, 21), and fire from heaven devours Satan and his attacking armies (20:9, 10). For God, it is as easy as that. There will be no doubt, no worry, no second thoughts for believers about whether they have chosen the right side. If you are with God, you will experience this tremendous victory with Christ.

20:10 Satan's power is not eternal—he will meet his doom. He began his evil work in people at the beginning (Genesis 3:1-6) and continues it today, but he will be destroyed when he is thrown into the lake of fire. The Devil will be released from the bottomless pit ("his prison," 20:7), but he will never be released from the lake of fire. He will never be a threat to anyone again.

20:12-15 At the judgment, the books are opened. They represent God's judgment, and in them are recorded the deeds of everyone, good or evil. We are not saved by deeds, but deeds are seen as clear evidence of a person's actual relationship with God. The Book of Life contains the names of those who have put their trust in Christ to save them.

20:14 Death and the grave are thrown into the lake of fire. God's judgment is finished. The lake of fire is the ultimate destination of everything wicked—Satan, the beast, the false prophet, the demons, death, the grave, and all those whose names are not recorded in the Book of Life because they did not place their faith in Jesus Christ. John's vision does not permit any gray areas in God's judgment. If by faith we have not identified with Christ, confessing him as Lord, there will be no hope, no second chance, no other appeal.

21:1 The earth as we know it will not last forever, but after God's great judgment, he will create a new earth (see Romans 8:18-21; 2 Peter 3:7-13). God had also promised Isaiah that he would create a new and eternal earth (Isaiah 65:17; 66:22). The sea in John's time was viewed as dangerous and changeable. It was also the source of the beast (13:1). We don't know how the new earth will look or where it will be, but God and his followers—those whose names are written in the Book of Life—will be united to live there forever. Will you be there?

21:2, 3 The new Jerusalem is where God lives among his people. Instead of our going up to meet him, he comes down

3 I heard a loud shout from the throne, saying, "Look, the home of God is now among
his people! He will live with them, and they will be his people. God himself will be with
them.* 4 He will remove all of their sorrows, and there will be no more death or sorrow
or crying or pain. For the old world and its evils are gone forever."
5 And the one sitting on the throne said, "Look, I am making all things new!" And then
he said to me, "Write this down, for what I tell you is trustworthy and true." 6 And he
also said, "It is finished! I am the Alpha and the Omega—the Beginning and the End. To
all who are thirsty I will give the springs of the water of life without charge! 7 All who
are victorious will inherit all these blessings, and I will be their God, and they will be my
children. 8 But cowards who turn away from me, and unbelievers, and the corrupt, and
murderers, and the immoral, and those who practice witchcraft, and idol worshipers, and
all liars—their doom is in the lake that burns with fire and sulfur. This is the second
death."
9 Then one of the seven angels who held the seven bowls containing the seven last
plagues came and said to me, "Come with me! I will show you the bride, the wife of the
Lamb."
10 So he took me in spirit* to a great, high mountain, and he showed me the holy city,
Jerusalem, descending out of heaven from God. 11 It was filled with the glory of God and
sparkled like a precious gem, crystal clear like jasper. 12 Its walls were broad and high,
with twelve gates guarded by twelve angels. And the names of the twelve tribes of Israel
were written on the gates. 13 There were three gates on each side—east, north, south, and
west. 14 The wall of the city had twelve foundation stones, and on them were written the
names of the twelve apostles of the Lamb.
15 The angel who talked to me held in his hand a gold measuring stick to measure the
city, its gates, and its wall. 16 When he measured it, he found it was a square, as wide as
it was long. In fact, it was in the form of a cube, for its length and width and height were
each 1,400 miles.* 17 Then he measured the walls and found them to be 216 feet thick*
(the angel used a standard human measure).

21:3 Some manuscripts read *God himself will be with them, their God.* **21:10** Or *in the Spirit.* **21:16** Greek *12,000 stadia* [2,220 kilometers]. **21:17** Greek *144 cubits* [65 meters].

21:3 2 Chr 6:18 Ezek 37:27 Zech 2:10 2 Cor 6:16
21:4 Isa 25:8; 35:10; 43:18; 65:19
21:5 Isa 43:19 2 Cor 5:17
21:6 Rev 1:8; 22:13
21:7 2 Sam 7:14 Rom 8:14 2 Cor 6:16
21:8 Ps 5:6 1 Cor 6:9 Eph 5:5
21:9 Rev 15:1, 7; 19:7
21:10 Ezek 40:1-2 Rev 1:10; 17:3
21:11 Isa 60:1-2, 19 Ezek 43:2 Rev 4:3
21:12 Exod 28:21 Ezek 48:30-34 Rev 22:14
21:14 Eph 2:20 Heb 11:10
21:15 Ezek 40:3, 5
21:16-17 Ezek 48:16-17

to be with us, just as God became man in Jesus Christ and lived among us (John 1:14). Wherever God reigns, there is peace, security, and love.

21:3, 4 Have you ever wondered what eternity will be like? The "holy city, the new Jerusalem" is described as the place where God will "remove all . . . sorrows." Forevermore, there will be no death, sorrow, crying, or pain. What a wonderful truth! No matter what you are going through, it's not the last word—God has written the final chapter, and it is about true fulfillment and eternal joy for those who love him. We do not know as much as we would like, but it is enough to know that eternity with God will be more wonderful than we could ever imagine.

21:5 God is the Creator. The Bible begins with the majestic story of his creation of the universe, and it concludes with his creation of a new heaven and a new earth. This is a tremendous hope and encouragement for the believer. When we are with God, with our sins forgiven and our future secure, we will be like Christ. We will be made perfect like him.

21:6 Just as God finished the work of creation (Genesis 2:1-3) and Jesus finished the work of redemption (John 19:30), so the Trinity will finish the entire plan of salvation by inviting the redeemed into a new creation.

21:6 For more about the water of life, see the note on 22:1.

21:7, 8 The "cowards" are not those who are fainthearted in their faith or who sometimes doubt or question but those who turn back from following God. They are not brave enough to stand up for Christ; they are not humble enough to accept his authority over their lives. They are put in the same list as the unbelieving, the corrupt, the murderers, the immoral, the idolaters, the liars, and those practicing magic arts.

People who are victorious "endure to the end" (Mark 13:13). They will receive the blessings that God promised: (1) eating from the tree of life (Revelation 2:7), (2) escaping from the lake of fire (the "second death," 2:11), (3) receiving a special name (2:17), (4) having authority over the nations (2:26), (5) being included in the Book of Life (3:5), (6) being a pillar in God's spiritual temple (3:12), and (7) sitting with Christ on his throne (3:21). Those who can endure the testing of evil and remain faithful will be rewarded by God.

21:8 The lake is explained in the notes on 19:20 and 20:14. The second death is spiritual death, meaning either eternal torment or destruction. In either case, it is permanent separation from God.

21:10ff The rest of the chapter is a stunning description of the new city of God. The vision is symbolic and shows us that our new home with God will defy description. We will not be disappointed by it in any way.

21:12-14 The new Jerusalem is a picture of God's future home for his people. The 12 tribes of Israel (21:12) probably represent all the faithful in the Old Testament; the 12 apostles (21:14) represent the church. Thus, both believing Gentiles and Jews who have been faithful to God will live together in the new earth.

21:15-17 The city's measurements are symbolic of a place that will hold all God's people. These measurements are all multiples of 12, the number for God's people: There were 12 tribes in Israel, and 12 apostles who started the church. The walls are 144 (12 x 12) cubits (200 feet) thick; There are 12 layers in the walls, and 12 gates in the city; and the height, length, and breadth are all the same, 12,000 stadia (1,400 miles). The new Jerusalem is a perfect cube, the same shape as the Most Holy Place in the Temple (1 Kings 6:20). These measurements illustrate that this new home will be perfect for us.

21:19 Exod 28:17-20; Isa 54:11-12; Ezek 28:13
21:21 Isa 54:12
21:22 John 4:21-24; 17:21-24
21:23 Isa 60:19-20
21:24 Isa 60:3, 5
21:25 Isa 60:11; Zech 14:7
21:27 Isa 52:1

18 The wall was made of jasper, and the city was pure gold, as clear as glass. 19 The
wall of the city was built on foundation stones inlaid with twelve gems: the first was
jasper, the second sapphire, the third agate, the fourth emerald, 20 the fifth onyx, the sixth
carnelian, the seventh chrysolite, the eighth beryl, the ninth topaz, the tenth chrysoprase,
the eleventh jacinth, the twelfth amethyst.
21 The twelve gates were made of pearls—each gate from a single pearl! And the main
street was pure gold, as clear as glass.
22 No temple could be seen in the city, for the Lord God Almighty and the Lamb are its
temple. 23 And the city has no need of sun or moon, for the glory of God illuminates the
city, and the Lamb is its light. 24 The nations of the earth will walk in its light, and the rulers
of the world will come and bring their glory to it. 25 Its gates never close at the end of day
because there is no night. 26 And all the nations will bring their glory and honor into the
city. 27 Nothing evil will be allowed to enter—no one who practices shameful idolatry and
dishonesty—but only those whose names are written in the Lamb's Book of Life.

22:1 Ezek 47:1; Joel 3:18; Zech 14:8; John 7:37-39
22:2 Gen 2:9; Ezek 47:12

22

And the angel showed me a pure river with the water of life, clear as crystal,
flowing from the throne of God and of the Lamb, 2 coursing down the center of
the main street. On each side of the river grew a tree of life, bearing twelve crops of
fruit,* with a fresh crop each month. The leaves were used for medicine to heal the
nations.

22:2 Or *12 kinds of fruit.*

WHAT WE KNOW ABOUT ETERNITY

Description	*Reference*
A place prepared for us	John 14:2, 3
Unlimited by physical properties (1 Corinthians 15:35–49)	John 20:19, 26
Like Jesus	1 John 3:2
New bodies	1 Corinthians 15
A wonderful experience	1 Corinthians 2:9
A new environment	Revelation 21:1
A new experience of God's presence (1 Corinthians 13:12)	Revelation 21:3
New emotions	Revelation 21:4
No more death	Revelation 21:4

The Bible devotes much less space to describing eternity than it does to convincing people that eternal life is available as a free gift from God. Most of the brief descriptions of eternity would be more accurately called hints, since they use terms and ideas from present experience to describe what we cannot fully grasp until we are there ourselves. These references hint at aspects of what our future will be like if we have accepted Christ's gift of eternal life.

21:18-21 The picture of walls made of jewels reveals that the new Jerusalem will be a place of purity and durability—it will last forever.

21:22-24 The Temple, the center of God's presence among his people, was the primary place of worship. No temple is needed in the new city, however, because God's presence will be everywhere. He will be worshiped throughout the city, and nothing will hinder us from being with him.

21:25-27 Not everyone will be allowed into the new Jerusalem, but "only those whose names are written in the Lamb's Book of Life." (The Book of Life is explained in the notes on 3:5 and 20:12-15.) Don't think that you will get in because of your background, personality, or good behavior. Eternal life is available to you only because of what Jesus, the Lamb, has done. Trust him today to secure your citizenship in his new creation.

22:1 The water of life is a symbol of eternal life. Jesus used this same image with the Samaritan woman (John 4:7-14). It pictures the fullness of life with God and the eternal blessings that come when we believe in him and allow him to satisfy our spiritual thirst (see 22:17).

22:2 This tree of life is like the tree of life in the Garden of Eden (Genesis 2:9). After Adam and Eve sinned, they were forbidden to eat from the tree of life because they could not have eternal life as long as they were under sin's control. But because of the forgiveness of sin through the blood of Jesus, there will be no evil or sin in this city. We will be able to eat freely from the tree of life when sin's control over us is destroyed and our eternity with God is secure.

22:2 Why would the nations need to be healed if all evil is gone? John is quoting from Ezekiel 47:12, where water flowing from the Temple produces trees with healing leaves. He is not implying that there will be illness in the new earth; he is emphasizing that the water of life produces health and strength wherever it goes.

3 No longer will anything be cursed. For the throne of God and of the Lamb will be
there, and his servants will worship him. 4 And they will see his face, and his name will
be written on their foreheads. 5 And there will be no night there—no need for lamps or
sun—for the Lord God will shine on them. And they will reign forever and ever.

6 Then the angel said to me, "These words are trustworthy and true: 'The Lord God,
who tells his prophets what the future holds, has sent his angel to tell you what will
happen soon.'"

Jesus Is Coming

7 "Look, I am coming soon! Blessed are those who obey the prophecy written in
this scroll."

8 I, John, am the one who saw and heard all these things. And when I saw and heard
these things, I fell down to worship the angel who showed them to me. 9 But again he
said, "No, don't worship me. I am a servant of God, just like you and your brothers the
prophets, as well as all who obey what is written in this scroll. Worship God!"

10 Then he instructed me, "Do not seal up the prophetic words you have written, for
the time is near. 11 Let the one who is doing wrong continue to do wrong; the one who is
vile, continue to be vile; the one who is good, continue to do good; and the one who is
holy, continue in holiness."

12 "See, I am coming soon, and my reward is with me, to repay all according to
their deeds. 13 I am the Alpha and the Omega, the First and the Last, the Beginning and the End."

14 Blessed are those who wash their robes so they can enter through the gates of the
city and eat the fruit from the tree of life. 15 Outside the city are the dogs—the sorcerers,
the sexually immoral, the murderers, the idol worshipers, and all who love to live a lie.

16 "I, Jesus, have sent my angel to give you this message for the churches. I am both
the source of David and the heir to his throne.* I am the bright morning star."

17 The Spirit and the bride say, "Come." Let each one who hears them say, "Come."

22:3 Zech 14:11
22:4 Pss 17:15; 42:2 Matt 5:8
22:5 Isa 60:19-20 Dan 7:18, 27 Zech 14:7
22:8 1 Jn 1:1-3
22:11 Ezek 3:27 Dan 12:10
22:12 Matt 16:27
22:13 Rev 1:8, 17; 21:6
22:14 Gen 2:9; 3:22 Ezek 47:12 Rev 2:7; 21:12, 27
22:15 1 Cor 6:9-10 Gal 5:19-21 Rev 21:8
22:16 Num 24:17 Isa 11:1, 10 Matt 1:1 Rom 1:3
22:17 Isa 55:1 John 7:37-39

22:16 Greek *I am the root and offspring of David.*

22:3 "No longer will anything be cursed" means that nothing accursed will be in God's presence. This fulfills Zechariah's prophecy (see Zechariah 14:11).

22:8, 9 Hearing or reading an eyewitness account is the next best thing to seeing the event yourself. John witnessed the events reported in Revelation and wrote them down so we could see and believe as he did. If you have read this far, you have seen. Have you also believed?

22:8, 9 The first of the Ten Commandments is "Do not worship any other gods besides me" (Exodus 20:3). Jesus said that the greatest command of Moses' laws was "You must love the Lord your God with all your heart, all your soul, and all your mind" (Matthew 22:37). Here, at the end of the Bible, this truth is reiterated. The angel instructs John to "worship God!" God alone is worthy of our worship and adoration. He is above all creation, even the angels. Are there people, ideas, goals, or possessions that occupy the central place in your life, crowding God out? Worship *only* God by allowing nothing to distract you from your devotion to him.

22:10, 11 The angel tells John what to do after his vision is over. Instead of sealing up what he has written, as Daniel was commanded to do (Daniel 12:4-12), the book is to be left open so that all can read and understand. Daniel's message was sealed because it was not a message for Daniel's time. But the book of Revelation was a message for John's time, and it is relevant today. As Christ's return gets closer, there is a greater polarization between God's followers and Satan's followers. We must read the book of Revelation, hear its message, and be prepared for Christ's imminent return.

22:12-14 Those who wash their robes are those who seek to purify themselves from a sinful way of life. They strive daily to remain faithful and ready for Christ's return. This concept is also explained in the second note on 7:14.

22:14 In Eden, Adam and Eve were barred from any access to the tree of life because of their sin (Genesis 3:22-24). In the new earth, God's people will eat from the tree of life because their sins have been removed by Christ's death and resurrection. Those who eat the fruit of this tree will live forever. If Jesus has forgiven your sins, you will have the right to eat from this tree. For more on this concept, see the first note on 22:2.

22:15 The exact location of these sinners is not known, nor is it relevant. They are outside. They were judged and condemned in 21:8. The emphasis is that nothing evil and no sinner will be in God's presence to corrupt or harm any of the faithful.

22:16 Jesus is both David's "source" and "heir." As the Creator of all, Jesus existed long before David. As a human, however, he was one of David's direct descendants (see Isaiah 11:1-5; Matthew 1:1-17). As the Messiah, he is the "bright morning star," the light of salvation to all.

22:17 Both the Holy Spirit and the bride, the church, extend the invitation to all the world to come to Jesus and experience the joys of salvation in Christ.

22:17 When Jesus met the Samaritan woman at the well, he told her of the living water that he could supply (John 4:10-15). This image is used again as Christ invites anyone to come and drink of the water of life. The Good News is unlimited in scope—all people everywhere may come. Salvation cannot be earned, but God gives it freely. We live in a world desperately thirsty for living water, and many are dying of thirst. But it's still not too late. Let us invite everyone to come and drink.

22:18
Deut 4:2; 12:32
Prov 30:6
Rev 15:6–16:21
22:19
Gen 2:9; 3:22
Ezek 47:12
Rev 2:7; 22:14
22:20
1 Cor 16:22
22:21
Rom 16:20
2 Thes 3:18

Let the thirsty ones come—anyone who wants to. Let them come and drink the water of
life without charge. 18And I solemnly declare to everyone who hears the prophetic words
of this book: If anyone adds anything to what is written here, God will add to that person
the plagues described in this book. 19And if anyone removes any of the words of this
prophetic book, God will remove that person's share in the tree of life and in the holy
city that are described in this book.

20He who is the faithful witness to all these things says, "Yes, I am coming soon!"
Amen! Come, Lord Jesus!

21The grace of the Lord Jesus be with you all.

22:18, 19 This warning is given to those who might purposefully distort the message in this book. Moses gave a similar warning in Deuteronomy 4:1-4. We, too, must handle the Bible with care and great respect so that we do not distort its message, even unintentionally. We should be quick to put its principles into practice in our life. No human explanation or interpretation of God's Word should be elevated to the same authority as the text itself.

22:20 We don't know the day or the hour, but Jesus is coming soon and unexpectedly. This is good news to those who trust him, but a terrible message for those who have rejected him and stand under judgment. *Soon* means "at any moment," and we must be ready for him, always prepared for his return. Would Jesus' sudden appearance catch you off guard?

22:21 Revelation closes human history as Genesis opened it—in paradise. But there is one distinct difference in Revelation—evil is gone forever. Genesis describes Adam and Eve walking and talking with God; Revelation describes people worshiping God face to face. Genesis describes a garden with an evil serpent; Revelation describes a perfect city with no evil. The Garden of Eden was destroyed by sin; but paradise is re-created in the new Jerusalem.

The book of Revelation ends with an urgent plea: "Come, Lord Jesus!" In a world of problems, persecution, evil, and immorality, Christ calls us to endure in our faith. Our efforts to better our world are important, but their results cannot compare with the transformation that Jesus will bring about when he returns. He alone controls human history, forgives sin, and will re-create the earth and bring lasting peace.

Revelation is, above all, a book of hope. It shows that no matter what happens on earth, God is in control. It promises that evil will not last forever. And it depicts the wonderful reward that is waiting for all those who believe in Jesus Christ as Savior and Lord.

TABLE OF WEIGHTS AND MEASURES

WEIGHT	talent	75 pounds	34 kilograms
	mina	1.25 pounds	600 grams
	shekel	0.4 ounces	11.4 grams
	pim	0.25 ounces	8 grams
	beka	0.2 ounces	5.7 grams
	gerah	0.02 ounces	0.6 grams
DISTANCE	long cubit	21 inches	53 centimeters
	cubit	18 inches	45 centimeters
	span	9 inches	23 centimeters
	handbreadth	3 inches	8 centimeters
CAPACITY			
Dry Measure	cor/homer	5 bushels	182 liters
	lethek	2.5 bushels	91 liters
	ephah	0.5 bushels	18 liters
	seah	5 quarts	6 liters
	omer	2 quarts	2 liters
	cab	1 quart	1.3 liters
Liquid Measure	bath	5.5 gallons	21 liters
	hin	1 gallon	3.8 liters
	log	0.3 quarts	0.3 liters

JANUARY 1 . . . Day 1 . . . . . Genesis 1:1–2:3
2 . . . Day 2 . . . . . Genesis 2:15–3:24
3 . . . Day 3 . . . . . Genesis 4:1-16
4 . . . Day 4 . . . . . Genesis 6:9-22
5 . . . Day 5 . . . . . Genesis 7:1-24
6 . . . Day 6 . . . . . Genesis 8:1-22
7 . . . Day 7 . . . . . Genesis 9:1-17
8 . . . Day 8 . . . . . Genesis 11:1-9
9 . . . Day 9 . . . . . Genesis 12:1-9; 17:1-8
10 . . . Day 10 . . . . Genesis 18:1-15
11 . . . Day 11 . . . . Genesis 19:15-29
12 . . . Day 12 . . . . Genesis 21:8-21
13 . . . Day 13 . . . . Genesis 22:1-19
14 . . . Day 14 . . . . Genesis 24:1-27
15 . . . Day 15 . . . . Genesis 24:28-67
16 . . . Day 16 . . . . Genesis 25:19-34
17 . . . Day 17 . . . . Genesis 27:1-40
18 . . . Day 18 . . . . Genesis 28:10-22
19 . . . Day 19 . . . . Genesis 29:14-30
20 . . . Day 20 . . . . Genesis 32:1–33:16
21 . . . Day 21 . . . . Genesis 37:1-36
22 . . . Day 22 . . . . Genesis 39:1-23
23 . . . Day 23 . . . . Genesis 40:1-23
24 . . . Day 24 . . . . Genesis 41:1-36
25 . . . Day 25 . . . . Genesis 41:37-57
26 . . . Day 26 . . . . Genesis 42:1-38
27 . . . Day 27 . . . . Genesis 43:1-34
28 . . . Day 28 . . . . Genesis 44:1-34
29 . . . Day 29 . . . . Genesis 45:1-28
30 . . . Day 30 . . . . Genesis 49:1-33
31 . . . Day 31 . . . . Exodus 1:8–2:10
FEBRUARY 1 . . . Day 32 . . . . Exodus 2:11-25
2 . . . Day 33 . . . . Exodus 3:1-22
3 . . . Day 34 . . . . Exodus 4:1-17
4 . . . Day 35 . . . . Exodus 5:1-23
5 . . . Day 36 . . . . Exodus 6:1-13
6 . . . Day 37 . . . . Exodus 7:1-14
7 . . . Day 38 . . . . Exodus 7:15–9:7
8 . . . Day 39 . . . . Exodus 9:8–10:29
9 . . . Day 40 . . . . Exodus 11:1-10; 12:29-36
10 . . . Day 41 . . . . Exodus 13:17–14:31
11 . . . Day 42 . . . . Exodus 15:22-27; 17:1-7
12 . . . Day 43 . . . . Exodus 16:1-36
13 . . . Day 44 . . . . Exodus 18:1-27
14 . . . Day 45 . . . . Exodus 19:1-25
15 . . . Day 46 . . . . Exodus 20:1-22
16 . . . Day 47 . . . . Exodus 32:1-29
17 . . . Day 48 . . . . Exodus 40:1-38
18 . . . Day 49 . . . . Numbers 12:1-16
19 . . . Day 50 . . . . Numbers 13:1–14:4
20 . . . Day 51 . . . . Numbers 14:5-45
21 . . . Day 52 . . . . Numbers 21:4-9
22 . . . Day 53 . . . . Numbers 22:5-38
23 . . . Day 54 . . . . Deuteronomy 29:1-29
24 . . . Day 55 . . . . Deuteronomy 30:1-20
25 . . . Day 56 . . . . Deuteronomy 31:1-8
26 . . . Day 57 . . . . Deuteronomy 34:1-12
27 . . . Day 58 . . . . Joshua 1:1-18
28 . . . Day 59 . . . . Joshua 2:1-24
MARCH 1 . . . Day 60 . . . . Joshua 3:1-17
2 . . . Day 61 . . . . Joshua 5:13–6:27
3 . . . Day 62 . . . . Joshua 7:1-26
4 . . . Day 63 . . . . Joshua 10:1-15
5 . . . Day 64 . . . . Joshua 23:1-16
6 . . . Day 65 . . . . Joshua 24:1-31
7 . . . Day 66 . . . . Judges 4:4-24
8 . . . Day 67 . . . . Judges 6:1-40
9 . . . Day 68 . . . . Judges 7:1-25
10 . . . Day 69 . . . . Judges 13:1-25
11 . . . Day 70 . . . . Judges 14:1-20
12 . . . Day 71 . . . . Judges 15:1-20
13 . . . Day 72 . . . . Judges 16:1-21
14 . . . Day 73 . . . . Judges 16:22-31
15 . . . Day 74 . . . . Ruth 1:1-22
16 . . . Day 75 . . . . Ruth 2:1-23
17 . . . Day 76 . . . . Ruth 3:1-18
18 . . . Day 77 . . . . Ruth 4:1-22
19 . . . Day 78 . . . . 1 Samuel 1:1-28
20 . . . Day 79 . . . . 1 Samuel 3:1-21
21 . . . Day 80 . . . . 1 Samuel 8:1-5
22 . . . Day 81 . . . . 1 Samuel 8:6-22
23 . . . Day 82 . . . . 1 Samuel 9:1-21
24 . . . Day 83 . . . . 1 Samuel 10:1-27
25 . . . Day 84 . . . . 1 Samuel 14:1-23

26 . . . Day 85 . . . . 1 Samuel 16:1-13
27 . . . Day 86 . . . . 1 Samuel 17:1-31
28 . . . Day 87 . . . . 1 Samuel 17:32-58
29 . . . Day 88 . . . . 1 Samuel 18:1-30
30 . . . Day 89 . . . . 1 Samuel 20:1-42
31 . . . Day 90 . . . . 1 Samuel 24:1-22
APRIL 1 . . . Day 91 . . . . 1 Samuel 25:1-42
2 . . . Day 92 . . . . 1 Samuel 28:1-25
3 . . . Day 93 . . . . 2 Samuel 5:1-12
4 . . . Day 94 . . . . 2 Samuel 9:1-13
5 . . . Day 95 . . . . 2 Samuel 11:1-27
6 . . . Day 96 . . . . 2 Samuel 12:1-25
7 . . . Day 97 . . . . 2 Samuel 13:1-19
8 . . . Day 98 . . . . 2 Samuel 13:20-39
9 . . . Day 99 . . . . 2 Samuel 15:1-37
10 . . . Day 100 . . . 2 Samuel 18:1-18
11 . . . Day 101 . . . 1 Kings 1:5-27
12 . . . Day 102 . . . 1 Kings 1:28-53
13 . . . Day 103 . . . 1 Kings 3:1-15
14 . . . Day 104 . . . 1 Kings 3:16-28
15 . . . Day 105 . . . 1 Kings 6:1-38
16 . . . Day 106 . . . 1 Kings 10:1-13
17 . . . Day 107 . . . 1 Kings 12:1-24
18 . . . Day 108 . . . 1 Kings 17:1-24
19 . . . Day 109 . . . 1 Kings 18:16-46
20 . . . Day 110 . . . 1 Kings 19:1-21
21 . . . Day 111 . . . 1 Kings 21:1-29
22 . . . Day 112 . . . 1 Kings 22:29-40
23 . . . Day 113 . . . 2 Kings 2:1-12
24 . . . Day 114 . . . 2 Kings 2:13-25
25 . . . Day 115 . . . 2 Kings 5:1-27
26 . . . Day 116 . . . 2 Kings 11:1-21
27 . . . Day 117 . . . 2 Kings 22:1–23:3
28 . . . Day 118 . . . Ezra 3:7-13
29 . . . Day 119 . . . Nehemiah 2:1-20
30 . . . Day 120 . . . Nehemiah 5:1-19
MAY 1 . . . Day 121 . . . Nehemiah 8:1-18
2 . . . Day 122 . . . Esther 1:1-22
3 . . . Day 123 . . . Esther 2:1-23
4 . . . Day 124 . . . Esther 3:1-15
5 . . . Day 125 . . . Esther 4:1-17
6 . . . Day 126 . . . Esther 5:1-14
7 . . . Day 127 . . . Esther 6:1–7:10
8 . . . Day 128 . . . Job 1:1-22
9 . . . Day 129 . . . Job 2:1-13
10 . . . Day 130 . . . Job 38:1-41
11 . . . Day 131 . . . Job 42:1-17
12 . . . Day 132 . . . Psalm 1:1-6
13 . . . Day 133 . . . . Psalm 8:1-9
14 . . . Day 134 . . . . Psalm 23:1-6
15 . . . Day 135 . . . . Psalm 51:1-19
16 . . . Day 136 . . . . Psalm 103:1-22
17 . . . Day 137 . . . . Psalm 139:1-24
18 . . . Day 138 . . . . Psalm 145:1-21
19 . . . Day 139 . . . . Proverbs 4:1-27
20 . . . Day 140 . . . . Proverbs 5:1-23
21 . . . Day 141 . . . . Ecclesiastes 12:1-14
22 . . . Day 142 . . . . Isaiah 6:1-13
23 . . . Day 143 . . . . Isaiah 53:1-12
24 . . . Day 144 . . . . Jeremiah 1:1-9
25 . . . Day 145 . . . . Jeremiah 36:1-32
26 . . . Day 146 . . . . Jeremiah 38:1-13
27 . . . Day 147 . . . . Ezekiel 37:1-14
28 . . . Day 148 . . . . Daniel 1:1-21
29 . . . Day 149 . . . . Daniel 2:1-24
30 . . . Day 150 . . . . Daniel 2:25-49
31 . . . Day 151 . . . . Daniel 3:1-30
JUNE 1 . . . Day 152 . . . . Daniel 5:1-30
2 . . . Day 153 . . . . Daniel 6:1-28
3 . . . Day 154 . . . . Jonah 1:1–2:10
4 . . . Day 155 . . . . Jonah 3:1–4:11
5 . . . Day 156 . . . . John 1:1-18
6 . . . Day 157 . . . . Luke 1:5-25
7 . . . Day 158 . . . . Luke 1:26-56
8 . . . Day 159 . . . . Luke 1:57-80
9 . . . Day 160 . . . . Matthew 1:1-25
10 . . . Day 161 . . . . Luke 2:1-20
11 . . . Day 162 . . . . Luke 2:21-39
12 . . . Day 163 . . . . Matthew 2:1-12
13 . . . Day 164 . . . . Matthew 2:13-23
14 . . . Day 165 . . . . Luke 2:41-52
15 . . . Day 166 . . . . Mark 1:1-13
16 . . . Day 167 . . . . John 1:19-34
17 . . . Day 168 . . . . John 1:35-51
18 . . . Day 169 . . . . John 2:1-25
19 . . . Day 170 . . . . John 3:1-21
20 . . . Day 171 . . . . John 3:22-36
21 . . . Day 172 . . . . John 4:1-42
22 . . . Day 173 . . . . John 4:43-54
23 . . . Day 174 . . . . Luke 4:16-30
24 . . . Day 175 . . . . Mark 1:16-39
25 . . . Day 176 . . . . Luke 5:1-39
26 . . . Day 177 . . . . John 5:1-47
27 . . . Day 178 . . . . Mark 2:23–3:19
28 . . . Day 179 . . . . Matthew 5:1-16
29 . . . Day 180 . . . . Matthew 5:17-30

30 . . . Day 181 . . . Matthew 5:31-48
JULY 1 . . . Day 182 . . . Matthew 6:1-18
2 . . . Day 183 . . . Matthew 6:19-34
3 . . . Day 184 . . . Matthew 7:1-12
4 . . . Day 185 . . . Matthew 7:13-29
5 . . . Day 186 . . . Luke 7:1-17
6 . . . Day 187 . . . Matthew 11:1-30
7 . . . Day 188 . . . Luke 7:36–8:3
8 . . . Day 189 . . . Matthew 12:22-50
9 . . . Day 190 . . . Mark 4:1-29
10 . . . Day 191 . . . Matthew 13:24-43
11 . . . Day 192 . . . Matthew 13:44-52
12 . . . Day 193 . . . Luke 8:22-56
13 . . . Day 194 . . . Matthew 9:27-38
14 . . . Day 195 . . . Mark 6:1-13
15 . . . Day 196 . . . Matthew 10:16-42
16 . . . Day 197 . . . Mark 6:14-29
17 . . . Day 198 . . . Matthew 14:13-36
18 . . . Day 199 . . . John 6:22-40
19 . . . Day 200 . . . John 6:41-71
20 . . . Day 201 . . . Mark 7:1-37
21 . . . Day 202 . . . Matthew 15:32–16:12
22 . . . Day 203 . . . Mark 8:22–9:1
23 . . . Day 204 . . . Luke 9:28-45
24 . . . Day 205 . . . Matthew 17:24–18:6
25 . . . Day 206 . . . Mark 9:38-50
26 . . . Day 207 . . . Matthew 18:10-22
27 . . . Day 208 . . . John 7:1-31
28 . . . Day 209 . . . John 7:32-53
29 . . . Day 210 . . . John 8:1-20
30 . . . Day 211 . . . John 8:21-59
31 . . . Day 212 . . . Luke 10:1-24
AUGUST 1 . . . Day 213 . . . Luke 10:25-42
2 . . . Day 214 . . . Luke 11:1-13
3 . . . Day 215 . . . Luke 11:14-32
4 . . . Day 216 . . . Luke 11:33-54
5 . . . Day 217 . . . Luke 12:1-21
6 . . . Day 218 . . . Luke 12:22-48
7 . . . Day 219 . . . Luke 12:49-59
8 . . . Day 220 . . . Luke 13:1-21
9 . . . Day 221 . . . John 9:1-41
10 . . . Day 222 . . . John 10:1-18
11 . . . Day 223 . . . Luke 13:22-35
12 . . . Day 224 . . . Luke 14:1-14
13 . . . Day 225 . . . Luke 14:15-35
14 . . . Day 226 . . . Luke 15:1-10
15 . . . Day 227 . . . Luke 15:11-32
16 . . . Day 228 . . . Luke 16:1-18
17 . . . Day 229 . . . Luke 16:19-31
18 . . . Day 230 . . . John 11:1-36
19 . . . Day 231 . . . John 11:37-57
20 . . . Day 232 . . . Luke 17:1-19
21 . . . Day 233 . . . Luke 17:20-37
22 . . . Day 234 . . . Luke 18:1-14
23 . . . Day 235 . . . Mark 10:1-16
24 . . . Day 236 . . . Mark 10:17-31
25 . . . Day 237 . . . Matthew 20:1-19
26 . . . Day 238 . . . Mark 10:35-52
27 . . . Day 239 . . . Luke 19:1-27
28 . . . Day 240 . . . John 12:1-11
29 . . . Day 241 . . . Matthew 21:1-17
30 . . . Day 242 . . . John 12:20-36
31 . . . Day 243 . . . John 12:37-50
SEPTEMBER 1 . . . Day 244 . . . Mark 11:20-33
2 . . . Day 245 . . . Matthew 21:28-46
3 . . . Day 246 . . . Matthew 22:1-14
4 . . . Day 247 . . . Luke 20:20-40
5 . . . Day 248 . . . Mark 12:28-37
6 . . . Day 249 . . . Matthew 23:1-39
7 . . . Day 250 . . . Luke 21:1-24
8 . . . Day 251 . . . Luke 21:25-38
9 . . . Day 252 . . . Matthew 25:1-30
10 . . . Day 253 . . . Matthew 25:31-46
11 . . . Day 254 . . . Luke 22:1-13
12 . . . Day 255 . . . John 13:1-20
13 . . . Day 256 . . . John 13:21-38
14 . . . Day 257 . . . John 14:1-14
15 . . . Day 258 . . . John 14:15-31
16 . . . Day 259 . . . John 15:1-16
17 . . . Day 260 . . . John 15:17–16:4
18 . . . Day 261 . . . John 16:5-33
19 . . . Day 262 . . . John 17:1-26
20 . . . Day 263 . . . Mark 14:26-52
21 . . . Day 264 . . . John 18:1-24
22 . . . Day 265 . . . Matthew 26:57-75
23 . . . Day 266 . . . Matthew 27:1-10
24 . . . Day 267 . . . Luke 23:1-12
25 . . . Day 268 . . . Mark 15:6-24
26 . . . Day 269 . . . Luke 23:32-49
27 . . . Day 270 . . . Matthew 27:57-66
28 . . . Day 271 . . . John 20:1-18
29 . . . Day 272 . . . Matthew 28:8-15
30 . . . Day 273 . . . Luke 24:13-43
OCTOBER 1 . . . Day 274 . . . John 20:24–21:14
2 . . . Day 275 . . . John 21:15-25
3 . . . Day 276 . . . Matthew 28:16-20

4 . . . Day 277 . . . Luke 24:44-53
5 . . . Day 278 . . . Acts 1:1-11
6 . . . Day 279 . . . Acts 1:12-26
7 . . . Day 280 . . . Acts 2:1-13
8 . . . Day 281 . . . Acts 2:14-40
9 . . . Day 282 . . . Acts 2:41–3:11
10 . . . Day 283 . . . Acts 3:12–4:4
11 . . . Day 284 . . . Acts 4:5-22
12 . . . Day 285 . . . Acts 4:23-37
13 . . . Day 286 . . . Acts 5:1-16
14 . . . Day 287 . . . Acts 5:17-42
15 . . . Day 288 . . . Acts 6:1-15
16 . . . Day 289 . . . Acts 7:1-29
17 . . . Day 290 . . . Acts 7:30-60
18 . . . Day 291 . . . Acts 8:1-25
19 . . . Day 292 . . . Acts 8:26-40
20 . . . Day 293 . . . Acts 9:1-19
21 . . . Day 294 . . . Acts 9:20-31
22 . . . Day 295 . . . Acts 9:32-42
23 . . . Day 296 . . . Acts 10:1-23
24 . . . Day 297 . . . Acts 10:24-48
25 . . . Day 298 . . . Acts 11:1-18
26 . . . Day 299 . . . Acts 11:19-29
27 . . . Day 300 . . . Acts 12:1-25
28 . . . Day 301 . . . Acts 13:1-12
29 . . . Day 302 . . . Acts 14:1-28
30 . . . Day 303 . . . Acts 15:1-21
31 . . . Day 304 . . . Acts 15:22-41
NOVEMBER 1 . . . Day 305 . . . Acts 16:1-15
2 . . . Day 306 . . . Acts 16:16-40
3 . . . Day 307 . . . Acts 17:1-15
4 . . . Day 308 . . . Acts 17:16-34
5 . . . Day 309 . . . Acts 19:1-20
6 . . . Day 310 . . . Acts 19:21-41
7 . . . Day 311. . . . Acts 20:1-12
8 . . . Day 312 . . . Acts 20:13-38
9 . . . Day 313 . . . Acts 21:1-17
10 . . . Day 314 . . . Acts 21:18-36
11 . . . Day 315 . . . Acts 21:37–22:29
12 . . . Day 316 . . . Acts 22:30–23:22
13 . . . Day 317 . . . Acts 23:23–24:27
14 . . . Day 318 . . . Acts 25:1-27
15 . . . Day 319 . . . Acts 26:1-32
16 . . . Day 320 . . . Acts 27:1-26
17 . . . Day 321 . . . Acts 27:27-44
18 . . . Day 322. . . . Acts 28:1-14
19 . . . Day 323. . . . Acts 28:15-31
20 . . . Day 324. . . . Romans 5:1-11
21 . . . Day 325. . . . Romans 8:1-18
22 . . . Day 326. . . . Romans 8:19-39
23 . . . Day 327. . . . Romans 12:1-21
24 . . . Day 328. . . . 1 Corinthians 13:1-13
25 . . . Day 329. . . . 1 Corinthians 15:1-20
26 . . . Day 330. . . . 1 Corinthians 15:42-58
27 . . . Day 331. . . . 2 Corinthians 4:1-18
28 . . . Day 332. . . . Galatians 5:13-26
29 . . . Day 333. . . . Ephesians 1:3-23
30 . . . Day 334. . . . Ephesians 2:1-22
DECEMBER 1 . . . Day 335. . . . Ephesians 4:1-16
2 . . . Day 336. . . . Ephesians 6:10-20
3 . . . Day 337. . . . Philippians 2:1-18
4 . . . Day 338. . . . Philippians 3:1-21
5 . . . Day 339. . . . Colossians 2:1-15
6 . . . Day 340. . . . Colossians 3:1-17
7 . . . Day 341. . . . 1 Thessalonians 1:1-10
8 . . . Day 342. . . . 1 Thessalonians 4:1-18
9 . . . Day 343. . . . 2 Thessalonians 1:1-12
10 . . . Day 344. . . . 2 Thessalonians 3:1-18
11 . . . Day 345. . . . 1 Timothy 4:1-16
12 . . . Day 346. . . . 1 Timothy 6:3-21
13 . . . Day 347. . . . 2 Timothy 1:1-18
14 . . . Day 348. . . . 2 Timothy 3:1-17
15 . . . Day 349. . . . Titus 3:1-11
16 . . . Day 350. . . . Hebrews 10:19-39
17 . . . Day 351. . . . Hebrews 11:1-40
18 . . . Day 352. . . . Hebrews 12:1-13
19 . . . Day 353. . . . James 1:2-27
20 . . . Day 354. . . . James 2:1-13
21 . . . Day 355. . . . James 3:1-12
22 . . . Day 356. . . . 1 Peter 2:1-25
23 . . . Day 357. . . . 1 Peter 3:1-22
24 . . . Day 358. . . . 2 Peter 1:2-21
25 . . . Day 359. . . . 1 John 1:1-10
26 . . . Day 360. . . . 1 John 3:1-24
27 . . . Day 361. . . . 1 John 5:1-21
28 . . . Day 362. . . . Jude 1:17-25
29 . . . Day 363. . . . Revelation 1:1-20
30 . . . Day 364. . . . Revelation 21:1-27
31 . . . Day 365. . . . Revelation 22:1-21

ABBREVIATIONS IN THE INDEX TO NOTES

Following is a list of abbreviations in the Index to Notes:

BOOKS OF THE BIBLE

Genesis	Gn
Exodus	Ex
Leviticus	Lv
Numbers	Nm
Deuteronomy	Dt
Joshua	Jos
Judges	Jgs
Ruth	Ru
1 Samuel	1 Sm
2 Samuel	2 Sm
1 Kings	1 Kgs
2 Kings	2 Kgs
1 Chronicles	1 Chr
2 Chronicles	2 Chr
Ezra	Ezr
Nehemiah	Neh
Esther	Est
Job	Jb
Psalms	Ps
Proverbs	Prv
Ecclesiastes	Eccl
Song of Songs	Song
Isaiah	Is
Jeremiah	Jer
Lamentations	Lam
Ezekiel	Ez
Daniel	Dn
Hosea	Hos
Joel	Jl
Amos	Am
Obadiah	Ob
Jonah	Jon
Micah	Mi
Nahum	Na
Habakkuk	Hb
Zephaniah	Zep
Haggai	Hg
Zechariah	Zec
Malachi	Mal
Matthew	Mt
Mark	Mk
Luke	Lk
John	Jn
Acts	Acts
Romans	Rom
1 Corinthians	1 Cor
2 Corinthians	2 Cor
Galatians	Gal
Ephesians	Eph
Philippians	Phil
Colossians	Col
1 Thessalonians	1 Thes
2 Thessalonians	2 Thes
1 Timothy	1 Tm
2 Timothy	2 Tm
Titus	Ti
Philemon	Phlm
Hebrews	Heb
James	Jas
1 Peter	1 Pt
2 Peter	2 Pt
1 John	1 Jn
2 John	2 Jn
3 John	3 Jn
Jude	Jude
Revelation	Rv

INDEX TO NOTES

This is an index to the notes, charts, maps, and personality profiles in the *Life Application Bible.* Every entry concerning a note has a Bible reference and a page number; every entry concerning a chart, map, or personality profile has a page number. In some instances, a Bible reference is followed by a number in parentheses to indicate that there is more than one note on that particular Scripture. For example, Rv 1:1(2) means that the reader should look up the second note with the heading of 1:1 in Revelation. In most cases, the entries follow in biblical/canonical order (i.e., from Genesis to Revelation). In some cases, however, the entries follow a chronological order—this is especially true with important people in the Bible. Following the general index are special indexes: Index to Charts, Index to Maps, and Index to Personality Profiles. Because of the emphasis on application in the *Life Application Bible,* these indexes are helpful guides for personal and group Bible study, sermon preparation, or teaching.

GOD, KINGDOM OF

GODLINESS

GODS/GODDESSES

GOD'S LAW

GOD'S WILL

GOD'S WORD

GOG

GOLD

GOLDEN CALF

GOLDEN RULE

GOLGOTHA

GOLIATH

GOMER

GOOD, GOODNESS

LIFE, TREE OF

LIGHT

LIMITATIONS

LINEAGE

INDEX TO CHARTS

INDEX TO MAPS

Note: Maps concerning Jesus' ministry are given in chronological order—see Harmony of the Gospels.

INDEX TO PERSONALITY PROFILES

ABBA *Aramaic for "daddy"; see FATHER*

ABIDE(S)(ING) *to remain, stay, or wait; see OBEY or REMAIN*

ABILITY *talent, aptitude, or skill; quality of being able*
giving him great wisdom, *a* . . . Exod 31:3
Holy Spirit gave them this *a* . . . Acts 2:4
given each of us the *a* . . . Rom 12:6
the Spirit gives the *a* . . . 1 Cor 12:8
a to stand firm for Christ . . . 2 Cor 1:21

ABLE *marked by power, intelligence, competence, skill, giftedness*
a to obtain forgiveness for . . . Exod 32:30
never be *a* to rescue you . . . Isa 36:14
No one is *a* to plan his own . . . Jer 10:23
a to stand and face him . . . Mal 3:2
you are *a* to teach others all . . . Rom 15:14
won't be *a* to understand . . . 1 Cor 14:2
a to accomplish infinitely . . . Eph 3:20

ABOMINATION(S) *anything ritually or ethically abhorrent to God; see PROFANE*

ABOUND(ED)(ING) *to have more than an ample supply; see INCREASE*

ABSTAIN *to refrain, keep away, or do without*
a from having sexual . . . Exod 19:15
a from eating meat . . . Acts 15:20

ABUNDANCE, ABUNDANT *great quantity, affluence; more than ample*
a harvests of grain . . . Ps 4:7
feed them from the *a* . . . Ps 36:8
and bless its *a* crops . . . Ps 65:10
a place of great *a* . . . Ps 66:12
May there be *a* prosperity . . . Ps 72:7
you will have *a* joy . . . John 16:24

ACCEPT(ANCE)(ED)(ING)(S) *to receive or approve with favor; dynamic equivalent of justify*
who have *a* his covenant . . . Isa 56:6
offerings, I will not *a* . . . Jer 14:12
I will not *a* your offerings . . . Mal 1:10
disobedient minds to *a* godly . . . Luke 1:17
I am willing to *a* whatever . . . Luke 1:38
no prophet is *a* in his own . . . Luke 4:24
anything to be *a* by God . . . Rom 3:27
a him and declared him to be . . . Rom 4:11
when the Jews finally *a* it . . . Rom 11:12
more wonderful their *a* will be . . . Rom 11:15
sacrifice—the kind he will *a* . . . Rom 12:1
you *a* it with joy . . . Heb 10:34
he punishes those he *a* . . . Heb 12:6

ACCEPTABLE *well-pleasing, favorable, agreeable, welcome*
no more *a* than a human sacrifice . . . Isa 66:3
Abel brought a more *a* . . . Heb 11:4

ACCOMPLISH(ED) *to complete a work, fulfill a plan, or succeed at something*
a his purposes in Jerusalem . . . Isa 10:12
and now you have *a* . . . Isa 25:1
able to *a* infinitely more . . . Eph 3:20

ACCORD(ANCE)(ING) *to be consistent; in agreement or harmony*
occurred *a* to your eternal will . . . Acts 4:28
in exact *a* with the plan . . . Acts 7:44
shaved his head *a* to Jewish . . . Acts 18:18
Give whatever you can *a* . . . 2 Cor 8:11

ACCOUNT(ED) *to reckon or compute; made right (with God); see RIGHT*

ACCOUNT(ING)(S) *description of facts or events; a report; financial transaction*
the *a* of the creation . . . Gen 2:4
demand an *a* from me . . . Job 14:3
give an *a* on judgment day . . . Matt 12:36
bring his *a* up to date . . . Matt 18:23
give a personal *a* to God . . . Rom 14:12

ACCURSED *consigned to destruction; see CURSE or CONDEMN*

ACCUS(ATIONS)(E)(ED)(ER)(ING) *a charge of wrongdoing, often false; to charge with wrongdoing*
judge between . . . *a* and the *a* . . . 2 Chr 6:23
Satan the *A* came with them . . . Job 2:1
you are *a* yourselves of . . . Matt 23:31
leaders made their *a* against . . . Matt 27:12
Don't extort money, and don't *a* . . . Luke 3:14
way to court and you meet your *a* . . . Luke 12:58
you will be *a* before kings . . . Luke 21:12
a him of leading a revolt . . . Luke 23:14
Moses will *a* you! . . . John 5:45
the city was rocked by these *a* . . . Acts 21:30
their own consciences either *a* . . . Rom 2:15

ACHIEVE(D) *to finish; to accomplish; to reach a goal*
until its purpose is *a* . . . Matt 5:18
priesthood of Levi could have *a* . . . Heb 7:11

ACKNOWLEDGE(S) *to express a gratitude or debt; to recognize as valid; to confess (wrongdoing)*
They refuse to *a* its ways . . . Job 24:13
A that the LORD is God! . . . Ps 100:3
you that are near, *a* my might! . . . Isa 33:13
Only *a* your guilt . . . Jer 3:13
A him before he brings darkness . . . Jer 13:16
If anyone *a* me publicly . . . Matt 10:32
they refused to *a* God . . . Rom 1:28

ACQUAINT(ED) *to make familiar; to know firsthand*
They are not *a* with the light . . . Job 24:16
a man of sorrows, *a* . . . Isa 53:3
today so we could get *a* . . . Acts 28:20

ACQUIT(TAL)(TED) *to free from the penalty of a guilty action; (used theologically) to justify or make right with God*
a the one who is innocent . . . 1 Kgs 8:32
would be *a* by my Judge . . . Job 23:7
despises those who *a* the guilty . . . Prov 17:15
a is not based on our good deeds . . . Rom 3:27

ACT(ED)(S) *good work; wicked deed; to behave; to take action or do something*
I *a* in complete innocence! . . . Gen 20:5
awesome power, and terrifying *a* . . . Deut 4:34
have *a* corruptly toward him . . . Deut 32:5
in *The Book of the A* of Solomon . . . 1 Kgs 11:41
you kings, *a* wisely! . . . Ps 2:10
we celebrate your mighty *a* . . . Ps 21:13
for I have *a* with integrity . . . Ps 26:1
no joy for me until he *a* . . . Ps 77:2
time for you to *a* . . . Ps 119:126
participate in *a* of wickedness . . . Ps 141:4
tell its children of your mighty *a* . . . Ps 145:4
attention to their *a* of charity! . . . Matt 6:2
woman they had caught in the *a* . . . John 8:3

ADMONISH(ED) *to warn or give friendly advice; see ENCOURAGE*

ADMONITION *counsel or warning against oversight; see ENCOURAGEMENT*

ADOPT(ED)(ING) *to take another's child into one's own family*
a as my own sons these two boys . . . Gen 48:5
God's very own children, *a* into . . . Rom 8:15

ADULTERER(S)(OUS) *prone to spiritual adultery or idolatry*
The *a* waits for the twilight . . . Job 24:15
in these *a* and sinful days . . . Mark 8:38
idol worshipers, *a*, male prostitutes . . . 1 Cor 6:9

ADULTERY *unlawful sexual relations between a married and an unmarried person; symbolic of idolatry*
Do not commit *a* . . . Exod 20:14
a with her in his heart . . . Matt 5:28
marries another commits *a* . . . Matt 19:9
marries someone else commits *a* . . . Mark 10:11
caught in the act of *a* . . . John 8:3
adultery if she married another . . . Rom 7:3
those who commit *a* . . . Heb 13:4
all who commit *a* with her . . . Rev 2:22

ADVERSARIES *enemies, opponents*
taunt of the enemy, that their *a* . . . Deut 32:27
I will beat down his *a* before him . . . Ps 89:23

ADVERSITY *misfortune, suffering, calamity*
a for food and affliction for drink . . . Isa 30:20

AFFECTION(S) *feeling, desire, disposition, mental state; conviction*
Test my motives and *a* . . . Ps 26:2
Love each other with genuine *a* . . . Rom 12:10
pray for you with deep *a* . . . 2 Cor 9:14

AFFLICT(ED)(ING) *to oppress, trouble, mistreat; to humble, bring low*
will *a* you with the boils of Egypt . . . Deut 28:27
gives justice to the *a* . . . Job 36:6
Don't forget your *a* people . . . Ps 74:19
a ones, who sit in a drunken . . . Isa 51:21
into captivity, *a* and enslaved . . . Lam 1:3

AFFLICTION(S) *great suffering that produces sorrow*
Days of *a* have come upon me . . . Job 30:27
the tune "The Suffering of *A* . . . Ps 88, title
adversity for food and *a* for drink . . . Isa 30:20
a that come from the rod . . . Lam 3:1

AFRAID *fearful or apprehensive about an unwanted or uncertain situation*
I was *a* because I was naked . . . Gen 3:10
the birds and fish will be *a* of you . . . Gen 9:2
Do not be *a*, Abram, for I will . . . Gen 15:1
Joseph's brothers became *a* . . . Gen 50:15
is for me, so I will not be *a* . . . Ps 118:6
do not be *a* of the Assyrians . . . Isa 10:24
I will trust in him and not be *a* . . . Isa 12:2
Don't be *a*, for I am with you . . . Isa 41:10
the angel said, "Do not be *a* . . . Matt 1:20
Why are you *a* . . . Matt 8:26
Don't be *a* . . . Matt 14:27
a the people would kill them . . . Acts 5:26
be *a*, for you will be punished . . . Rom 13:4

AGE *lifetime; to become old*
You will live to a good old *a* . . . Job 5:26
in my old *a*, don't set me aside . . . Ps 71:9

AGE *long period of time; a generation; a measure of history, geology, or culture*
even to the end of the *a* . . . Matt 28:20
this *a* is drawing to a close . . . 1 Cor 10:11
the power of the *a* to come . . . Heb 6:5

ALIEN(S) *foreign or pagan; strangers, sojourners, foreigners; see FOREIGN*

ALIENATE(D) *to make enemies of; to cause a rift; estranged; see SEPARATED*

ALIVE *animate, having life; active; aware*
who were faithful . . . are still *a* . . . Deut 4:4
with all of us who are *a* today . . . Deut 5:3
They are all *a* to him . . . Luke 20:38
who told them Jesus is *a* . . . Luke 24:23
he was actually *a* . . . Acts 1:3
showed them that she was *a* . . . Acts 9:41
whom Paul insists is *a* . . . Acts 25:19
binds her . . . as long as he is *a* . . . Rom 7:2
because of sin, your spirit is *a* . . . Rom 8:10
Lord of those who are *a* . . . Rom 14:9
most of whom are still *a* . . . 1 Cor 15:6
a reputation for being *a* . . . Rev 3:1
The beast you saw was *a* . . . Rev 17:8
thrown *a* into the lake of fire . . . Rev 19:20

ALONE *isolated or solitary; solely or exclusively; without aid or support*
not good for the man to be *a* . . . Gen 2:18
but leave these men *a* . . . Gen 19:8
left Jacob all *a* in the camp . . . Gen 32:24
Joseph is dead, and he *a* is left . . . Gen 42:38
leave us *a* while . . . in Egypt . . . Exod 14:12
trying to do all this *a* . . . Exod 18:14
You *a*, Moses, are allowed . . . Exod 24:2
is our God, the LORD *a* . . . Deut 6:4
I *a* am left, and now . . . 1 Kgs 19:10, 14
You *a* are the LORD . . . Neh 9:6
leave me *a* for these few . . . Job 7:16
go away and leave them *a* . . . Matt 8:34
to a remote area to be *a* . . . Matt 14:13
Jesus was *a* with the twelve . . . Mark 4:10
it will be *a*—a single seed . . . John 12:24
leaving me *a*. Yet I am not *a* . . . John 16:32
leave these men *a* . . . Acts 5:38
he *a* is God . . . 1 Tim 1:17

ALPHA *first letter of Greek alphabet; figurative of beginning or first one*
I am the *A* and the Omega . . . Rev 1:8
I am the *A* and the Omega . . . Rev 21:6
I am the *A* and the Omega, the First . . . Rev 22:13

ALTAR(S) *high place of worship on which sacrifices are offered or incense is burned*
Noah built an *a* . . . Gen 8:20
Abram built an *a* there . . . Gen 12:7
There he built an *a* . . . Gen 13:18
and laid him on the *a* . . . Gen 22:9
Isaac built an *a* there . . . Gen 26:25
built an *a* and called it . . . Gen 33:20
Build *a* in the places . . . Exod 20:24
he built an *a* at the foot . . . Exod 24:4
build the *a*, not for burnt . . . Josh 22:26
David built an *a* there . . . 2 Sam 24:25
the seraphim flew over to the *a* . . . Isa 6:6
the gift on the *a* . . . Matt 23:19
When you swear 'by the *a*,' . . . Matt 23:20
under the *a* the souls of all . . . Rev 6:9

AMBITION *aspiration to achieve a particular goal, good or bad*
a has always been to preach . . . Rom 15:20
anger, selfish *a*, divisions . . . Gal 5:20
with selfish *a*, not sincerely . . . Phil 1:17
your *a*: to live a quiet life . . . 1 Thes 4:11
selfish *a* in your hearts . . . Jas 3:14
jealousy and selfish *a* . . . Jas 3:16

ANGEL(IC)(S) *human or superhuman agent or messenger of God*
I am sending my *a* before . . . Exod 23:20
Manoah asked the *a* . . . Judg 13:17
a came again to present . . . Job 2:1
the *a* of death wait for them . . . Job 33:22
a band of destroying *a* . . . Ps 78:49
highest *a* powers stand in awe . . . Ps 89:7
orders his *a* to protect you . . . Ps 91:11
armies of *a* who serve him . . . Ps 103:21
will punish the fallen *a* . . . Isa 24:21
a of the Lord appeared to him . . . Matt 1:20
the harvesters are the *a* . . . Matt 13:39
with his *a* and will judge . . . Matt 16:27
They will be like the *a* . . . Matt 22:30
thousands of *a* to protect us . . . Matt 26:53
the *a* spoke to the women . . . Matt 28:5
a said, "Don't be afraid . . . Luke 1:13
a who told them Jesus is alive . . . Luke 24:23
She saw two white-robed *a* . . . John 20:12
a of the Lord came at night . . . Acts 5:19
disguise himself as an *a* . . . 2 Cor 11:14
Even if an *a* comes . . . Gal 1:8
must worship *a* . . . Col 2:18
is far greater than the *a* . . . Heb 1:4
entertained *a* without realizing . . . Heb 13:2
spare even the *a* when they sinned . . . 2 Pet 2:4
a who did not stay within the limits . . . Jude 1:6
four *a* standing at the four corners . . . Rev 7:1
seven *a* with the seven trumpets . . . Rev 8:6
fought the dragon and his *a* . . . Rev 12:7
the *a* with the sickle . . . Rev 14:18
a mighty *a* picked up a boulder . . . Rev 18:21
a threw him into the bottomless pit . . . Rev 20:3
twelve gates guarded by twelve *a* . . . Rev 21:12
I fell down to worship the *a* . . . Rev 22:8

ANGER, ANGRY *a strong feeling of displeasure; see FURY and WRATH*
made Cain very *a* and dejected . . . Gen 4:5
don't be *a*, my Lord . . . Gen 18:30
Cursed be their *a*, for it is fierce . . . Gen 49:7
His *a* lasts for a moment . . . Ps 30:5
They made God *a* by building . . . Ps 78:58
how long will you be *a* with us . . . Ps 79:5
Put aside your *a* against us . . . Ps 85:4
gracious God, slow to get *a* . . . Ps 86:15
slow to get *a* and full of . . . Ps 103:8
away from *a*, short-tempered . . . Prov 22:24
right for you to be *a* . . . Jon 4:4
if you are *a* with someone . . . Matt 5:22
sun go down while you are still *a* . . . Eph 4:26
slow to speak, and slow to get *a* . . . Jas 1:19

ANGUISH(ED) *great pain or suffering*
How long must I struggle with *a* . . . Ps 13:2
you care about the *a* of my soul . . . Ps 31:7
My groans come from an *a* heart . . . Ps 38:8
My heart is in *a* . . . Ps 55:4
Jesus was in great *a* of spirit . . . John 13:21
When her child is born, her *a* . . . John 16:21
ground their teeth in *a* . . . Rev 16:10

ANOINT(ED)(ING) *pour oil upon; used for healing or consecration to sacred duty; used for grooming or burial; figurative for divine appointment*
the might of his *a* . . . 1 Sam 2:10
A him to be the leader . . . 1 Sam 9:16
which of his sons to *a* . . . 1 Sam 16:3
you killed the LORD's *a* . . . 2 Sam 1:16
a Jehu . . . and *a* Elisha . . . 1 Kgs 19:16
David had been *a* king over . . . 1 Chr 14:8
love to your *a*, to David . . . Ps 18:50
LORD saves his *a* king . . . Ps 20:6
a my head with oil . . . Ps 23:5
healed many sick people, *a* . . . Mark 6:13
a my body for burial . . . Mark 14:8
a my head, but she has *a* my feet . . . Luke 7:46
Jesus . . . whom you *a* . . . Acts 4:27

ANTICHRIST(S) *opponent of Christ; the personification of evil*
the *A* is coming . . . 1 Jn 2:18
are *a*, for they have denied . . . 1 Jn 2:22
is a deceiver and an *a* . . . 2 Jn 1:7

ANXIETY, ANXIOUS(LY) *uneasy, fearful, or worried about some contingency; eager*
In my *a* I cried out to you . . . Ps 116:11
a working for food to eat . . . Ps 127:2
they *a* search for me . . . Prov 1:28
a to eat this Passover meal . . . Luke 22:15
a to send him back to you . . . Phil 2:28
a to do the will of God . . . 1 Pet 4:2

APOSTLE(S), APOSTLESHIP *messengers or "sent ones"; generally but not exclusively applied to the original twelve followers of Christ and to Paul*
names of the twelve *a* . . . Matt 10:2
twelve of them to be *a* . . . Luke 6:13
an *a* to replace Judas . . . Acts 1:25
a gave powerful witness . . . Acts 4:33
chosen by God to be an *a* . . . Rom 1:1
I am the least of all the *a* . . . 1 Cor 15:9
who were *a* before I was . . . Gal 1:17
on the foundation of the *a* . . . Eph 2:20
a, the prophets, the evangelists . . . Eph 4:11

APPEAR(ANCE)(ED)(S) *to come out of hiding and show up in public view; the outward or visible aspect; to make one's presence known*
so dry ground may *a* . . . Gen 1:9
Let bright lights *a* . . . Gen 1:14
mountain peaks began to *a* . . . Gen 8:5
God had *a* to him there at . . . Gen 35:7
LORD continued to *a* . . . 1 Sam 3:21
Don't judge by his *a* or height . . . 1 Sam 16:7
stand and face him when he *a* . . . Mal 3:2
a changed so that his face . . . Matt 17:2
false prophets will *a* . . . Matt 24:11
an angel of the Lord *a* . . . Luke 1:11
a and began talking with Jesus . . . Luke 9:30
a of the earth and the sky . . . Luke 12:56
Jesus had *a* to them as they . . . Luke 24:35
he will simply *a* . . . John 7:27
Jesus *a* again to the disciples . . . John 21:1
decisions on the basis of *a* . . . 2 Cor 10:7
a slave and *a* in human form . . . Phil 2:7
modest in their *a* . . . 1 Tim 2:9
he *a* to set up his Kingdom . . . 2 Tim 4:1
such antichrists have *a* . . . 1 Jn 2:18

APPOINT(ED)(S)(MENT) *to ordain or designate*
you have *a* as Isaac's wife . . . Gen 24:14
Let Pharaoh *a* officials over . . . Gen 41:34
LORD's *a* annual festivals . . . Lev 23:37
a a new leader for the . . . Num 27:16
he will *a* children to rule . . . Isa 3:4
a me to bring good news . . . Isa 61:1
king *a* Daniel to a high . . . Dan 2:48
faithful to God, who *a* him . . . Heb 3:2
God *a* his Son with an oath . . . Heb 7:28

ARK *commonly, a portable wooden chest, box or coffer; specifically, of Noah, a ship the size of a light cruiser; of the Covenant, a sacred housing for the Law of Moses*
A of acacia wood—a sacred chest . . . Exod 25:10
Bezalel made the *A* out of acacia . . . Exod 37:1
tablets in the sacred chest—the *A* . . . Deut 10:2
priests carrying the *A* of the Covenant . . . Josh 3:3
A of the LORD was carried . . . Josh 6:11
sons of Eli, helped carry the *A* of God . . . 1 Sam 4:4
placed the *A* of God on a new cart . . . 2 Sam 6:3
chest called the *A* of the Covenant . . . Heb 9:4
Noah built an *a* to save his family . . . Heb 11:7
Temple of God was opened and the *A* . . . Rev 11:19

ARM(S) *upper limb of the body; extension or projection of; lineage; figurative of power or might*
Call the Israelites to *a* . . . Exod 17:9
Moses' *a* finally became too tired . . . Exod 17:12
able to bear *a* will cross over . . . Num 32:27
like a lion to tear off an *a* . . . Deut 33:20
Saul sounded the call to *a* . . . 1 Sam 13:3

If my *a* has abused an orphan . . . Job 31:21
the *a* that is raised in violence . . . Job 38:15
Break the *a* of these wicked . . . Ps 10:15
your strong right *a* to save us . . . Ps 60:5
strong right *a* of the LORD . . . Ps 118:15
Every *a* is paralyzed with fear . . . Isa 13:7
his mighty *a* on his enemies . . . Isa 30:30
He will carry the lambs in his *a* . . . Isa 40:11
carry your little sons . . . in their *a* . . . Isa 49:22
I opened my *a* to my own . . . Isa 65:2
His mighty *a* does tremendous . . . Luke 1:51
He took the child in his *a* . . . Luke 2:28

ARM(ED)(S) *to put on armor; to equip*
we will *a* ourselves and lead . . . Num 32:17
God *a* me with strength . . . Ps 18:32
Satan, who is completely *a* . . . Luke 11:21
a with swords and clubs . . . Luke 22:52
a with the authority . . . Acts 26:12
a yourselves with the same . . . 1 Pet 4:1

ARMIES, ARMY *large band of men organized and armed for war; any large multitude devoted to a cause*
Pharaoh's *a*—all his horses . . . Exod 14:9
must not be drafted into the *a* . . . Deut 24:5
able to count his heavenly *a* . . . Job 25:3
Praise him, all the *a* of heaven! . . . Ps 148:2
Assyria's vast *a* is like a glorious . . . Isa 10:18
He sent out his *a* to destroy . . . Matt 22:7
a of heaven, dressed in pure white . . . Rev 19:14
fire . . . down on the attacking *a* . . . Rev 20:9

ARMOR(Y) *weapons of war or self-defense; figurative of spiritual resources; a storehouse or cache of weapons*
man who carried his *a* . . . 1 Sam 14:1
penetrate its double layer of *a* . . . Job 41:13
Put on your *a*, and take up . . . Ps 35:2
His faithful promises are your *a* . . . Ps 91:4
run to the *a* for your weapons . . . Isa 22:8
He also took them to see his *a* . . . Isa 39:2
righteousness as his body *a* . . . Isa 59:17
Put on all of God's *a* . . . Eph 6:11
They wore *a* made of iron . . . Rev 9:9

ASCEND(ED)(ING)(S) *to go or move up*
God has *a* with a mighty shout . . . Ps 47:5
When you *a* to the heights . . . Ps 68:18
I will *a* to heaven . . . Isa 14:13
I am *a* to my Father . . . John 20:17
When he *a* to the heights . . . Eph 4:8
smoke from that city *a* . . . Rev 19:3

ASHAMED *feeling of shame, guilt, or disgrace*
Let them be *a* and terrified . . . Ps 83:17
I will never have to be *a* . . . Ps 119:80
Perhaps then they will be *a* . . . Isa 26:11
a of me and my message . . . Mark 8:38
I, the Son of Man, will be *a* . . . Luke 9:26
not *a* of this Good News . . . Rom 1:16
never be *a* to tell others . . . 2 Tim 1:8
who does not need to be *a* . . . 2 Tim 2:15
God is not *a* to be called . . . Heb 11:16

ASHES *burnt residue or remains of the dead, or anything ruined; denotes grief, repentance, or humiliation*
I am but dust and *a* . . . Gen 18:27
put on sackcloth and *a* . . . Esth 4:1
as he sat among the *a* . . . Job 2:8
about as much value as *a* . . . Job 13:12
I have become as dust and *a* . . . Job 30:19
I sit in dust and *a* to show . . . Job 42:6
a on their heads to show . . . Luke 10:13

ASLEEP *state of bodily rest; figurative for being dull to spiritual things; see SLEEP*
Jonah was sound *a* . . . Jon 1:5
he fell *a*, and an angel . . . Matt 1:20
girl isn't dead; she's only *a* . . . Matt 9:24
disciples and found them *a* . . . Matt 26:40
a, chained between two . . . Acts 12:6
be on your guard, not *a* . . . 1 Thes 5:6

ASSURANCE, ASSURE(D)(S) *to make certain or reassure; characterized by full conviction or confidence*
I *a* you, the wicked cities . . . Matt 10:15
I *a* you that some of you . . . Matt 16:28
Don't drift away from the *a* . . . Col 1:23
lives in you, and this is your *a* . . . Col 1:27
Spirit gave you full *a* . . . 1 Thes 1:5
faith that *a* our salvation . . . Heb 10:39
confident *a* that what we hope . . . Heb 11:1

ASTONISHED *amazed; appalled, horrified; perplexed*
All who pass by will be *a* . . . Jer 18:16
many who heard him were *a* . . . Mark 6:2
were *a* at what they saw . . . Mark 6:51
heard the shepherds' story were *a* . . . Luke 2:18
a at what he learned about . . . Acts 13:12

ATONEMENT *reconciliation; reparation for an offense; cleansing*
young bull as an offering for the *a* . . . Exod 29:36
as your substitute, thus making *a* . . . Lev 1:4
In this way, the priest will make *a* . . . Lev 4:20
blood . . . that brings you *a* . . . Lev 17:11
Day of *A*, when *a* will be made . . . Lev 23:28
the Ark's cover, the place of *a* . . . Heb 9:5

AUTHORITIES, AUTHORITY *the right to govern; the freedom or ability to act*
he taught as one who had real *a* . . . Matt 7:29
By whose *a* did you drive out . . . Matt 21:23
I have been given complete *a* . . . Matt 28:18
I will give you . . . *a* over them . . . Luke 4:6
If you have this *a* from God . . . John 2:18
has given him *a* over everything . . . John 3:35
I don't speak on my own *a* . . . John 12:49
given him *a* over everyone . . . John 17:2
a are sent by God to help you . . . Rom 13:4
by the *a* of the Lord Jesus . . . 1 Cor 1:10
a over her body to her husband . . . 1 Cor 7:4
question my *a* as an apostle . . . 1 Cor 9:3
on her head as a sign of *a* . . . 1 Cor 11:10
You gave him *a* over all things . . . Heb 2:8
did not stay within the limits of *a* . . . Jude 1:6
I will give *a* over all the nations . . . Rev 2:26
had been given the *a* to judge . . . Rev 20:4

AVENGE(S) *to take revenge or punish an evildoer; see VENGEANCE*
relatives may seek to *a* the killing . . . Josh 20:3
never *a* yourselves . . . Rom 12:19
the Lord *a* all such sins . . . 1 Thes 4:6
a our blood against these people? . . . Rev 6:10

AWAKE *to arouse from sleep; to make active; to become alert to*
When I *a*, . . . I will see you face . . . Ps 17:15
a at night, hatching sinful plots . . . Ps 36:4
a through the night, thinking . . . Ps 119:148
stay *a* and be prepared, because . . . Matt 25:13
Couldn't you stay *a* and watch . . . Mark 14:37

AWE(SOME) *characterized by reverential fear*
What an *a* place this is! . . . Gen 28:17
a power, and terrifying acts . . . Deut 4:34
be consumed by this *a* fire . . . Deut 5:25
he is a great and *a* God . . . Deut 7:21
they will stand in *a* of you . . . Deut 28:10
with deepest *a* I will worship . . . Ps 5:7
answer our prayers with *a* deeds . . . Ps 65:5
God is *a* in his sanctuary . . . Ps 68:35
angelic powers stand in *a* of God . . . Ps 89:7
stand in *a* of the God of Israel . . . Isa 29:23
with great wonder and *a* . . . Luke 5:26
with holy fear and *a* . . . Heb 12:28

BABBLE(R) *repetitious or meaningless chatter*
When you pray, don't *b* . . . Matt 6:7
b has picked up some strange . . . Acts 17:18

BABIES, BABY *infant child; youngest of a group; figurative of newborn or immature Christians*
takes your *b* and smashes . . . Ps 137:9
mothers nursing their *b* . . . Matt 24:19
But how can I have a *b* . . . Luke 1:34
my *b* jumped for joy . . . Luke 1:44
the *b* was eight days old . . . Luke 1:59
time came for her *b* to be born . . . Luke 2:6
innocent as *b* . . . 1 Cor 14:20
like *b* who drink only milk . . . Heb 5:12
this nourishment as a *b* . . . 1 Pet 2:2

BACKSLIDER(S) *one who turns back to sin*
B get what they deserve . . . Prov 14:14

BACKSLIDING(S) *a moral lapse; see FAITHLESSNESS*

BALM *a medicinal gum used for healing wounds*
spices, *b*, and myrrh from Gilead . . . Gen 37:25
as gifts—*b*, honey, spices . . . Gen 43:11

BAPTISM(S), BAPTIST, BAPTIZE(D), BAPTIZING *a Christian sacrament; a washing with water for cleansing from sin, linked with repentance and admission into the community of faith; figurative of an ordeal or initiation*
I *b* with water . . . Matt 3:11
Jesus went . . . to be *b* by John . . . Matt 3:13
Did John's *b* come from . . . Matt 21:25
b them in the name of . . . Matt 28:19
Anyone who believes and is *b* . . . Mark 16:16
for they had refused John's *b* . . . Luke 7:30
a terrible *b* ahead of me . . . Luke 12:50
John the *B* was *b* at . . . John 3:23
will be *b* with the Holy Spirit . . . Acts 1:5
turn to God, and be *b* . . . Acts 2:38
Why can't I be *b* . . . Acts 8:36
She was *b* along with other . . . Acts 16:15
he knew only about John's *b* . . . Acts 18:25
b to become one with Christ . . . Rom 6:3
I did not *b* any of you except . . . 1 Cor 1:14
all *b* in the cloud and the sea . . . 1 Cor 10:2
b into Christ's body by one Spirit . . . 1 Cor 12:13
b for those who are dead . . . 1 Cor 15:29
one Lord, one faith, one *b* . . . Eph 4:5
buried with Christ when you were *b* . . . Col 2:12
further instruction about *b* . . . Heb 6:2

BARBARIC *known to speak a foreign (non-Greek) language*
uncircumcised, *b*, uncivilized . . . Col 3:11

BARREN *unproductive, unfruitful, especially in childbearing*
few children and *b* fields . . . Deut 28:18
b woman now has seven . . . 1 Sam 2:5
night be *b*. Let it have no joy . . . Job 3:7
away into a distant, *b* land . . . Isa 22:18
Her *b* wilderness will become . . . Isa 51:3
led us through the *b* wilderness . . . Jer 2:6

BEAR(ERS)(ING)(S), BORE *to carry or support; to suffer under the weight of; to give as testimony*
is too great for me to *b* . . . Gen 4:13
b the mark of my everlasting . . . Gen 17:13
then let me *b* the blame forever . . . Gen 43:9
my representative—he *b* my name . . . Exod 23:21
b the guilt connected with any . . . Exod 28:38
Never . . . *b* a grudge . . . Lev 19:18
for he will *b* all their sins . . . Isa 53:11
He *b* the sins of many . . . Isa 53:12
the coffin . . . and the *b* stopped . . . Luke 7:14
but you can't *b* it now . . . John 16:12
when I could *b* it no longer . . . 1 Thes 3:5
and *b* the disgrace he *b* . . . Heb 13:13

BEAR(ING)(S), BORE, BORN, BORNE *to give birth to or produce; to be productive*
b children with intense pain . . . Gen 3:16

b to them after the Flood . . . Gen 10:1
so she could *b* his children . . . Gen 16:2
your wife, will *b* you a son . . . Gen 17:19
had *b* Nahor eight sons . . . Gen 22:20
she *b* him Zimran, Jokshan, . . . Gen 25:2
the first son she *b* to him . . . Deut 25:6
the new baby she has *b* . . . Deut 28:57
People are *b* for trouble . . . Job 5:7
For I was *b* a sinner . . . Ps 51:5
send your Spirit, new life is *b* . . . Ps 104:30
a brother is *b* to help in time . . . Prov 17:17
new Branch *b* fruit from the old . . . Isa 11:1
Who *b* these children? . . . Isa 49:21
woman who could *b* no children . . . Isa 54:1
May you never *b* fruit . . . Matt 21:19
branches that do *b* fruit . . . John 15:2
b a good crop for the farmer . . . Heb 6:7
tree of life, *b* twelve crops of . . . Rev 22:2

BEAST *devilish creature(s) ravishing the earth during the Tribulation*
b that comes up out of the bottomless . . . Rev 11:7
b come up out of the earth . . . Rev 13:11
the mark of the *b* . . . Rev 16:2
woman sitting on a scarlet *b* . . . Rev 17:3

BEAST(S) *animals, as distinguished from plants or humans; a contemptible person*
a strong *b* of burden . . . Gen 49:14
by the fangs of wild *b* . . . Deut 32:24
It is the king of *b* . . . Job 41:34

BEAUTIFUL(LY), BEAUTIFY, BEAUTY *lovely, handsome, or pleasing to the eye; excellence*
her sister is more *b* than she . . . Judg 15:2
Abigail, was a sensible and *b* . . . 1 Sam 25:3
a woman of unusual *b* . . . 2 Sam 11:2
heart overflows with a *b* thought! . . . Ps 45:1
Mount Zion, the perfection of *b* . . . Ps 50:2
pillars, carved to *b* a palace . . . Ps 144:12
Don't lust for her *b* . . . Prov 6:25
is deceptive, and *b* does not last . . . Prov 31:30
God has made everything *b* . . . Eccl 3:11
O my beloved, you are as *b* as . . . Song 6:4
b will be gone. Only shame . . . Isa 3:24
b fades as quickly as the *b* of flowers . . . Isa 40:6
How *b* on the mountains are . . . Isa 52:7
nothing *b* or majestic about his . . . Isa 53:2
was not dressed as *b* . . . Matt 6:29
tombs—*b* on the outside . . . Matt 23:27

BEG(GAR)(GED)(GING) *to ask for charity or mercy; to ask earnestly for*
b for money and food . . . 1 Sam 2:36
Have I *b* you to use any of . . . Job 6:22
two things I *b* of you . . . Job 13:20
so the demons *b* . . . Matt 8:31
bothering us with all her *b* . . . Matt 15:23
b Jesus to lay his hands . . . Mark 7:32
blind *b* named Bartimaeus . . . Mark 10:46
I'm too proud to *b* . . . Luke 16:3
a diseased *b* named Lazarus . . . Luke 16:20
realized he was the lame *b* . . . Acts 3:10

BEHAVE, BEHAVIOR *to meet a proper standard of conduct; the manner of conducting oneself*
fighting, deception, malicious *b* . . . Rom 1:29
b instead like God's very own . . . Rom 8:15
Don't copy the *b* and customs . . . Rom 12:2
gossip, conceit, and disorderly *b* . . . 2 Cor 12:20
all types of malicious *b* . . . Eph 4:31
get rid of anger, rage, malicious *b* . . . Col 3:8
get rid of all malicious *b* . . . 1 Pet 2:1

BELIEVE(D)(R)(RS)(S), BELIEVING *to trust in; to hold a firm conviction about*
Abram *b* the LORD . . . Gen 15:6
they won't *b* me . . . Exod 3:13
Will they never *b* me . . . Num 14:11
they did not *b* God or trust him . . . Ps 78:22
Only simpletons *b* everything . . . Prov 14:15
Whoever *b* need never run away . . . Isa 28:16
know me, *b* in me, and understand . . . Isa 43:10
What you have *b* has happened . . . Matt 8:13
If another *b* sins against you . . . Matt 18:15
I do *b*, but help me . . . Mark 9:24
prevents them from *b* and . . . Luke 8:12
If I tell you, you won't *b* me . . . Luke 22:67
who *b* him and accepted him . . . John 1:12
who *b* in him will not perish . . . John 3:16
we *b* that you came from God . . . John 16:30
I won't *b* it unless I see . . . John 20:25
by *b* in him you will have life . . . John 20:31
among the community of *b* . . . John 21:23
saving everyone who *b*—Jews . . . Rom 1:16
Instead of *b* what they knew . . . Rom 1:25
Abraham *b* God, so God . . . Rom 4:3
it is by *b* in your heart that you . . . Rom 10:10
If you do anything you *b* is not . . . Rom 14:23
must *b* that there is a God . . . Heb 11:6
even the demons *b* this . . . Jas 2:19

BENEFIT(S) *to favor (another) or gain (for oneself); advantages or blessings*
the abundant *b* . . . Deut 28:47
actions be of *b* to God? . . . Job 22:2
you will be the one to *b* . . . Prov 9:12
b are enjoyed by the servants . . . Isa 54:17
how do you *b* if you gain . . . Matt 16:26
he proved to be of great *b* . . . Acts 18:27
For our *b* God made Christ to . . . 1 Cor 1:30
sharing in the *b* of the blood . . . 1 Cor 10:16
for the *b* of the Gentiles . . . Gal 2:8

BESIEGE(D) *to surround with armed forces*
They went to *b* Samaria . . . 1 Kgs 20:1
against Jerusalem and *b* it . . . 2 Kgs 24:10

BESTOWED *to convey as a gift*
honors are constantly *b* on me . . . Job 29:20
the splendor I *b* on you . . . Ezek 16:14

BETRAY(ED)(ER) *turn your back on a friend; deliver to the enemy*
Son of Man is going to be *b* . . . Matt 17:22
many will turn away . . . and *b* . . . Matt 24:10
will you pay me to *b* Jesus . . . Matt 26:15
how terrible it will be for my *b* . . . Luke 22:22
Jesus knew who would *b* him . . . John 13:11

BEWARE *take heed or be careful*
the time to be careful! *B* that . . . Deut 8:11
B of false prophets who . . . Matt 7:15
B of the yeast of the Pharisees . . . Matt 16:6
watch out! *B* of destroying one . . . Gal 5:15

BIND(ING) *fasten together; see BOUND*
permanent and *b* contract . . . Josh 24:25
heals the brokenhearted, *b* up . . . Ps 147:3
God will break the chains that *b* . . . Isa 9:4
b up your injury . . . Jer 30:13
B him hand and foot . . . Matt 22:13

BIRTHRIGHT *right of firstborn, especially to an inheritance*
trade me your *b* for it . . . Gen 25:31
taking my *b* and now . . . Gen 27:36
his *b* as the oldest son . . . Heb 12:16

BITTER(LY)(NESS) *severe pain, grief, or regret; distasteful*
eat roast lamb with *b* herbs . . . Exod 12:8
couldn't drink it because it was *b* . . . Exod 15:23
Israel spoke *b* against Moses . . . Exod 16:2
make the woman drink the *b* . . . Num 5:24
he broke down and wept *b* . . . 2 Kgs 20:3
I realized how *b* I had become . . . Ps 73:21
he went away, crying *b* . . . Matt 26:75
full of *b* and held captive . . . Acts 8:23
b sorrow and unending grief . . . Rom 9:2
Get rid of all *b*, rage . . . Eph 4:31
no *b* root of unbelief . . . Heb 12:15
fresh water and *b* water? . . . Jas 3:11

BLAME(D) *to find fault with or hold responsible; reproach, censure, or guilt*
then let me bear the *b* forever . . . Gen 43:9
I cannot be *b* for everything . . . Judg 15:3
Why does God *b* people for . . . Rom 9:19

BLAMELESS *innocent; without guilt or censure*
the only *b* man living . . . Gen 6:9
b, a man of complete integrity . . . Job 1:1
b lives and do what is right . . . Ps 15:2
you may live pure and *b* . . . Phil 1:10
you are holy and *b* . . . Col 1:22
kept *b* until that day . . . 1 Thes 5:23
holy and *b*, unstained by sin . . . Heb 7:26

BLASPHEME(D)(R)(S) *to dishonor or revile God*
Do not *b* God or curse . . . Exod 22:28
Take the *b* outside the . . . Lev 24:14
to despise and *b* him . . . 2 Sam 12:14
My name is being *b* all day . . . Isa 52:5
We heard him *b* Moses . . . Acts 6:11
were names that *b* God . . . Rev 13:1

BLASPHEMIES, BLASPHEMY *the words or actions that dishonor God*
except *b* against the Holy . . . Matt 12:31
You have all heard his *b* . . . Matt 26:65
Why do you think this is *b* . . . Mark 2:8
This is *b*! Who but God . . . Luke 5:21
allowed to speak great *b* . . . Rev 13:5
written all over with *b* . . . Rev 17:3

BLEMISH *defect or flaw that seriously impairs or mars*
Since he has a *b*, he may . . . Lev 21:21
spot or wrinkle or any other *b* . . . Eph 5:27

BLESS(ES) *to honor in worship; to offer approval or encouragement*
I will *b* those who *b* you . . . Gen 12:3
As for Ishmael, I will *b* him . . . Gen 17:20
eat it and *b* you instead of Esau . . . Gen 27:10
not let you go unless you *b* me . . . Gen 32:26
May the LORD *b* you . . . Num 6:24
he *b* you only because you *b* him . . . Job 2:4
B Israel, your special possession! . . . Ps 28:9
May God be merciful and *b* us . . . Ps 67:1
Her children stand and *b* her . . . Prov 31:28
From this day onward I will *b* you . . . Hag 2:19
God *b* those who mourn . . . Matt 5:4
B the one who comes . . . Matt 21:9
pray that God will *b* them . . . Rom 12:14
We *b* those who curse us . . . 1 Cor 4:12

BLESSED *happy or wonderful; praiseworthy; bringing pleasure or divine favor*
God *b* the seventh day and . . . Gen 2:3
Melchizedek *b* Abram . . . Gen 14:19
b him with an irrevocable blessing . . . Gen 27:33
Jacob *b* the boys that day . . . Gen 48:20
your God has *b* everything you have . . . Deut 2:7
B be the LORD forever! . . . Ps 89:52
It is more *b* to give . . . Acts 20:35

BLESSING(S) *happiness; praise; divine favor or heavenly reward; the antidote to cursings*
I will make you a *b* . . . Gen 12:2
what good are all your *b* . . . Gen 15:2
God poured out rich *b* on Isaac . . . Gen 25:11
choice between a *b* and a curse . . . Deut 11:26
This is the *b* that Moses . . . Deut 33:1
all the *b* and curses Moses . . . Josh 8:34
My cup overflows with *b* . . . Ps 23:5
their children are a *b* . . . Ps 37:26
his *b*, even life forevermore . . . Ps 133:3
showers of *b* . . . Ezek 34:26
a symbol and a source of *b* . . . Zech 8:13
someone's home, give it your *b* . . . Matt 10:12
asked God's *b* on the food . . . Matt 14:19
same *b* he promised to Abraham . . . Gal 3:14
blessed us with every spiritual *b* . . . Eph 1:3
a long life, full of *b* . . . Eph 6:3

BLIND(ED)(LY)(NESS)(S) *to withhold light from, or pull the wool over; to be without*

sight; lacking spiritual discernment; from God, given as a punishment
b the men of Sodom . . . Gen 19:11
Isaac was old and almost *b* . . . Gen 27:1
bribes *b* the eyes of the wise . . . Deut 16:19
please make them *b* . . . 2 Kgs 6:18
God *b* the eyes of the judges . . . Job 9:24
served as eyes for the *b* . . . Job 29:15
opens the eyes of the *b* . . . Ps 146:8
sees, while the fool is *b* . . . Eccl 2:14
b if you must. You are stupid . . . Isa 29:9
how deaf and *b* you are . . . Isa 42:18
are *b* to every danger . . . Isa 56:10
they wandered *b* through . . . Lam 4:14
b guides leading the *b* . . . Matt 15:14
B guides! How terrible . . . Matt 23:16
brought a *b* man to Jesus . . . Mark 8:22
"Why was this man born *b* . . . John 9:2
Are you saying we are *b* . . . John 9:40
Lord has *b* their eyes and . . . John 12:40
b for three days . . . Acts 9:9
stricken awhile with *b* . . . Acts 13:11
god of this evil world, has *b* . . . 2 Cor 4:4
b or, at least, very shortsighted . . . 2 Pet 1:9

BLOOD(IED)(SHED) *fluid in the circulatory system; signifies human life; kinfolk; of animals, used in priestly sacrifices; of Christ, effective for the forgiveness of sins; on hands or head, symbolic of guilt*
your brother's *b* cries out . . . Gen 4:10
Why should we shed his *b* . . . Gen 37:21
it will turn into *b* . . . Exod 4:9
b on the top and sides of the doorframe . . . Exod 12:23
This *b* confirms the covenant . . . Exod 24:8
b of the sin offering . . . Lev 5:9
b, representing life, that brings . . . Lev 17:11
guilt of *b* on your household . . . Deut 22:8
hands are covered with the *b* . . . Isa 1:15
beaten and *b*, so disfigured . . . Isa 52:14
my *b*, which seals the covenant . . . Matt 26:28
I am innocent of the *b* . . . Matt 27:24
eat my flesh and drink my *b* . . . John 6:54
consuming *b* or eating the meat . . . Acts 15:20
Your *b* be upon your own heads . . . Acts 18:6
shed his *b*, sacrificing his life . . . Rom 3:25
right in God's sight by the *b* . . . Rom 5:9
flesh and *b* cannot inherit . . . 1 Cor 15:50
near to him because of the *b* . . . Eph 2:13
people made of flesh and *b* . . . Eph 6:12
Jesus also became flesh and *b* . . . Heb 2:14
Without the shedding of *b* . . . Heb 9:22
b has ransomed people for God . . . Rev 5:9
washed their robes in the *b* . . . Rev 7:14
defeated him because of the *b* . . . Rev 12:11
a robe dipped in *b* . . . Rev 19:13

BLOT(S)(TED)(TING) *to erase or cover up*
b out every trace of Amalek . . . Exod 17:14
b me out of the record . . . Exod 32:32
b out the stain of my sins . . . Ps 51:1
May his family name be *b* out . . . Ps 109:13
the one who *b* out your sins . . . Isa 43:25
b out the sun and the stars . . . Acts 27:20

BOAST(ED)(FUL)(ING) *to brag; a prideful statement; see PRIDE*
b like a warrior who has . . . 1 Kgs 20:11
b to them about his great . . . Esth 5:11
Listen to their *b* . . . Ps 17:10
we *b* in the LORD our God . . . Ps 20:7
People who *b* of their wealth . . . Ps 49:20
insolent, proud, and *b* . . . Rom 1:30
I dare not *b* of anything else . . . Rom 15:18
How terrible that you should *b* . . . 1 Cor 5:6
Love is not jealous or *b* . . . 1 Cor 13:4
If I must *b*, I would rather *b* . . . 2 Cor 11:30
a fool—*b* like this . . . 2 Cor 12:11
so none of us can *b* . . . Eph 2:9

BODIES, BODY *one's physical essence; a corpse; a group of people*
God formed a man's *b* from . . . Gen 2:7
covered their father's naked *b* . . . Gen 9:23
b will thus bear the mark . . . Gen 17:13
about to die; take my *b* . . . Gen 50:5
its *b* was destroyed by fire . . . Dan 7:11
whole *b* to be thrown into hell . . . Matt 5:29
eye is a lamp for your *b* . . . Matt 6:22
they can only kill your *b* . . . Matt 10:28
eat it, for this is my *b* . . . Matt 26:26
b . . . were raised from the dead . . . Matt 27:52
tomb where they placed his *b* . . . Luke 23:55
Jesus meant his *b* . . . John 2:21
give your *b* to God . . . Rom 12:1
We are all parts of his one *b* . . . Rom 12:5
the Lord cares about our *b* . . . 1 Cor 6:13
b is the temple of the Holy Spirit . . . 1 Cor 6:19
I discipline my *b* like an athlete . . . 1 Cor 9:27
the whole *b* were an eye . . . 1 Cor 12:17
Then God gives it a new *b* . . . 1 Cor 15:38
the church is his *b* . . . Eph 1:23
as they love their own *b* . . . Eph 5:28
our sins in his own *b* . . . 1 Pet 2:24

BOLD(LY)(NESS) *fearless before danger; self-assured; prominent(ly)*
a *b* reproof promotes peace . . . Prov 10:10
the godly are as *b* as lions . . . Prov 28:1
b preached in the name . . . Acts 9:27
Kingdom of God with all *b* . . . Acts 28:31
we can be very *b* . . . 2 Cor 3:12
b in my letters but timid in person . . . 2 Cor 10:1
I will always be *b* for Christ . . . Phil 1:20
come *b* to the throne . . . Heb 4:16
b enter heaven's Most Holy . . . Heb 10:19

BOND(S) *an obligation; a binding agreement or force*
b of love between them . . . 1 Sam 18:1
you have freed me from my *b* . . . Ps 116:16
b of unity between Judah and Israel . . . Zech 11:14

BONDAGE *under captivity, servitude, or compulsion*
keep a fellow Judean in *b* . . . Jer 34:9
b in which Satan has held her . . . Luke 13:16

BOOK(S) *literary work; written records, register, or accounting*
recorded each one in your *b* . . . Ps 56:8
names from the *b* of life . . . Ps 69:28
my life was recorded in your *b* . . . Ps 139:16
the ones recorded in this *b* . . . John 20:30
world could not contain the *b* . . . John 21:25
my *b*, and especially my papers . . . 2 Tim 4:13
the *B* of Life . . . Rev 20:12
the prophetic words of this *b* . . . Rev 22:18

BORN AGAIN *regeneration by the Holy Spirit, analogous to birth*
unless you are *b a* . . . John 3:3
must be *b a* . . . John 3:7
privilege of being *b a* . . . 1 Pet 1:3
you have been *b a* . . . 1 Pet 1:23

BOTTOMLESS *unfathomable; unlimited*
angel from the *b* pit . . . Rev 9:11
beast that comes up out of the *b* pit . . . Rev 11:7
come up out of the *b* pit . . . Rev 17:8
key to the *b* pit . . . Rev 20:1

BOUGHT *to purchase; redeem; hire; bribe; see BUY*
He *b* the plot of land . . . Gen 23:17
wife Michal, for I *b* her with . . . 2 Sam 3:14
God *b* you with a high price . . . 1 Cor 6:20
their Master who *b* them . . . 2 Pet 2:1
She *b* great quantities of . . . Rev 18:12

BOUND *held fast; under physical restraint or moral obligation; see BIND*
b up in the boy's life . . . Gen 44:30
b by their Nazirite vow . . . Num 6:4
b me in heavy chains . . . Lam 3:7
b him and took him to Pilate . . . Matt 27:2
b his own feet and hands . . . Acts 21:11
I am not *b* to obey people . . . 1 Cor 9:19
Satan—and *b* him in chains . . . Rev 20:2

BOUND(ARY)(ARIES)(LESS)(S) *border; limit(less); dividing line*
reaching to the utmost *b* . . . Gen 49:26
Set *b* lines . . . Exod 19:12
these will be the *b* . . . Num 34:2
b for day and night . . . Job 26:10
they act with *b* arrogance . . . Prov 21:24
my love will know no *b* . . . Hos 14:4

BOUNDING *move by leaping*
b over the hills . . . Song 2:8

BOUNTIFUL, BOUNTY *freely and abundantly giving; generosity; crop yield*
eat of the land's *b* . . . Lev 25:7
Share with him some of the *b* . . . Deut 15:14
b harvests of grain . . . 2 Kgs 18:32
will yield its *b* crops . . . Ps 85:12
to enjoy its *b* and goodness . . . Jer 2:7
through God's *b* gift . . . Rom 5:15

BRANCH(ES) *limb of a (family) tree; part of a complex body (of knowledge); figurative of offspring and of disciples (of Christ and his disciples)*
Strip the *b* from the vine . . . Jer 5:10
a righteous *B* on King David's . . . Jer 23:5
versed in every *b* of learning . . . Dan 1:4
birds nested in its *b* . . . Dan 4:12
to bring my servant, the *B* . . . Zech 3:8
vine; you are the *b* . . . John 15:5

BREACH(ED) *broken into; a broken place or gap*
no *b* walls, no forced exile . . . Ps 144:14

BREAD *basic staple in diet of ancient Israel; signififes livelihood*
brought him *b* and wine . . . Gen 14:18
your best flour, and bake some *b* . . . Gen 18:6
gave Esau some *b* and lentil stew . . . Gen 25:34
give us *b*. Why should we die? . . . Gen 47:15
special *B* of the Presence . . . Exod 25:30
loaves of *b* belong to Aaron . . . Lev 24:9
more than *b* for their life . . . Deut 8:3
gave them *b* from heaven . . . Ps 78:24
Stolen *b* tastes sweet . . . Prov 20:17
b for the hungry . . . Isa 55:10
groan as they search for *b* . . . Lam 1:11
stones into loaves of *b* . . . Matt 4:3
if your children ask for a loaf of *b* . . . Matt 7:9
eating, Jesus took *b* . . . Matt 26:26
as he was breaking the *b* . . . Luke 24:35
Philip, where can we buy *b* . . . John 6:5
I am the *b* of life! . . . John 6:48
we break the loaf of *b* . . . 1 Cor 10:16

BREAK(ERS)(ING)(S), BROKE(N) *to fracture; to shatter; to violate or transgress; to burst forth; to separate into parts; to force a way through; to disperse; an eruption, rupture, or interruption in something*
b down the door . . . Gen 19:9
b his wage agreement . . . Gen 31:7
if war *b* out . . . Exod 1:10
of Egypt, causing boils to *b* out . . . Exod 9:9
b camp at Rephidim . . . Exod 19:2
b into a house . . . Exod 22:2
b down their shameful idols . . . Exod 23:24
if you *b* my covenant . . . Lev 26:15
must not *b* any of its bones . . . Num 9:12
b through the enemy lines . . . 2 Kgs 3:26
we are again *b* your commands . . . Ezra 9:14
b our resolve and stop the work . . . Neh 6:9
My flesh *b* open, full of pus . . . Job 7:5
living quietly until he *b* me . . . Job 16:12
his presence *b* through . . . Ps 18:12
as if I were a *b* pot . . . Ps 31:12
my health is *b* . . . Ps 38:7
will not *b* his vow . . . Ps 110:4
before a dispute *b* out . . . Prov 17:14
I will *b* down its walls . . . Isa 5:5
God will *b* the chains . . . Isa 9:4

b into joyful song . . . Isa 52:9
my heart is *b* . . . Jer 8:18
b the yoke that the king . . . Jer 28:4
My heart is *b* over . . . Lam 3:51
b off both its horns . . . Dan 8:7
b the engagement quietly . . . Matt 1:19
where thieves *b* in and steal . . . Matt 6:19
B the loaves into pieces . . . Matt 14:19
as he was *b* the bread . . . Luke 24:35
so they didn't *b* his legs . . . John 19:33
b their promises . . . Rom 1:31
we are not crushed and *b* . . . 2 Cor 4:8
liars and oath *b* . . . 1 Tim 1:10

BROTHER(S) *male family members with the same parents; kinsmen in the extended family, church, or nation; co-workers in ministry; fellow believers, followers, or friends in Christ*
Where is your *b*? . . . Gen 4:9
Yes, he is my *b* . . . Gen 20:5
a *b*—your own mother's son . . . Ps 50:20
b live together in harmony! . . . Ps 133:1
who sows discord among *b* . . . Prov 6:19
a *b* is born to help in . . . Prov 17:17
friend sticks closer than a *b* . . . Prov 18:24
two other *b*, James and John . . . Matt 4:21
Who are my *b*? . . . Matt 12:48
his mother, and his *b* . . . Matt 13:55
there were seven *b* . . . Matt 22:25
on the same level as *b* . . . Matt 23:8
the least of these my *b* . . . Matt 25:40
B will betray *b* to death . . . Mark 13:12
the firstborn, with many *b* . . . Rom 8:29
my people, my Jewish *b* . . . Rom 9:3
dear *b* and sisters, . . . 1 Cor 1:10
even your own Christian *b* . . . 1 Cor 6:8
these *b* are representatives . . . 2 Cor 8:23
b and sisters, are children of . . . Gal 4:28
to call them his *b* . . . Heb 2:11
love for each other as *b* . . . 1 Pet 1:22
our beloved *b* Paul wrote . . . 2 Pet 3:15
the one who accused our *b* . . . Rev 12:10
your *b* the prophets . . . Rev 22:9

BRUISE(D)(S) *to crush or wound; injury*
wound for wound, *b* for bruise . . . Exod 21:25
b his feet with fetters . . . Ps 105:18
with *b*, welts, and infected . . . Isa 1:7

BUILD(ER)(ERS)(ING)(S), BUILT *erect or construct; edify or encourage; walled structure built for permanent use; figurative of the good works and the Church*
Noah *b* an altar . . . Gen 8:20
Let's *b* a great city . . . Gen 11:4
Now *b* a new cart . . . 1 Sam 6:7
this Temple you have *b* . . . 1 Kgs 9:3
stone rejected by the *b* . . . Ps 118:22
Unless the LORD *b* a house . . . Ps 127:1
Wisdom has *b* her spacious . . . Prov 9:1
wise woman *b* her house . . . Prov 14:1
A house is *b* by wisdom . . . Prov 24:3
Israel has *b* many altars . . . Hos 8:11
b a house on solid rock . . . Matt 7:24
the various Temple *b* . . . Matt 24:1
b it again in three days . . . Matt 27:40
tear down my barns and *b* . . . Luke 12:18
try to *b* each other up . . . Rom 14:19
You are God's field, God's *b* . . . 1 Cor 3:9
that *b* will receive a reward . . . 1 Cor 3:14
it is love that really *b* up . . . 1 Cor 8:1
b on the foundation of the . . . Eph 2:20

BURDEN(S) *a (usually) heavy load to be borne—physically, emotionally, or spiritually*
Am I a *b* to you? . . . Job 7:20
a *b* too heavy to bear . . . Ps 38:4
Give your *b* to the LORD . . . Ps 55:22
b I give you is light . . . Matt 11:30
to help ease the *b* . . . Matt 23:4
the daily *b* of how the churches . . . 2 Cor 11:28
not be a *b* to anyone . . . 1 Thes 2:9

BURIED, BURY *interred with funeral ceremonies; figurative of self-denial and submission to Christ*
b Sarah there in Canaan . . . Gen 23:19
do not *b* me in Egypt . . . Gen 47:29
let me return home and *b* . . . Matt 8:21
were *b* with Christ by baptism . . . Rom 6:4
b, and he was raised from the . . . 1 Cor 15:4
you were *b* with Christ . . . Col 2:12

BURN(ED)(ER)(ING)(S)(T) *consume(d) by fire; as sacrifices (burnt offerings); with destructiveness; for purification; in hell; as a martyr; with passion*
rained down fire and *b* . . . Gen 19:24
Sacrifice him there as a *b* . . . Gen 22:2
Bring her out and *b* her! . . . Gen 38:24
Why isn't that bush *b* up? . . . Exod 3:3
If I brought you a *b* offering . . . Ps 51:16
his word *b* in my heart . . . Jer 20:9
Who can survive his *b* fury? . . . Nah 1:6
b the chaff with never-ending fire . . . Luke 3:17
if the work is *b* up . . . 1 Cor 3:15
marry than to *b* with lust . . . 1 Cor 7:9
angel with a gold incense *b* . . . Rev 8:3

BUY(ERS) *see BOUGHT*
to Boaz, "You *b* the land." . . . Ruth 4:8
b and sellers, lenders and . . . Isa 24:2
able to *b* your way out . . . Isa 47:11
no reason for *b* to rejoice . . . Ezek 7:12
enough money to *b* the field . . . Matt 13:44
decided to *b* the potter's field . . . Matt 27:7
b gold from me . . . Rev 3:18

CALAMITY *disaster, distress, or misery caused by grave loss or misfortune*
You have seen my *c* . . . Job 6:21
c waits for them to stumble . . . Job 18:12
spared in times of *c* . . . Job 21:30
to hasten my *c* . . . Job 30:13
C will surely overtake the wicked . . . Ps 34:21
c overcomes you like a storm . . . Prov 1:27
poverty of the poor is their *c* . . . Prov 10:15
C will follow *c* . . . Ezek 7:26
they were suffering such *c* . . . Obad 1:13
loves us if we have trouble or *c* . . . Rom 8:35

CALL(ED)(ING)(S) *to make a request or demand; to designate or name; a divine summons; an occupation or vocation*
God *c* the light "day" . . . Gen 1:5
to see what he would *c* them . . . Gen 2:19
She will be *c* 'woman,' . . . Gen 2:23
Answer me when I *c* . . . Ps 4:1
I will *c* on the LORD . . . Ps 18:3
c yourself a hero, do you? . . . Ps 52:1
c him from the sheep pens . . . Ps 78:70
you alone are *c* the LORD . . . Ps 83:18
God *c* each event back in its turn . . . Eccl 3:15
and will *c* him Immanuel . . . Isa 7:14
c on spirits, mediums, and psychics . . . Isa 19:3
c each by its name . . . Isa 40:26
I have *c* you by name . . . Isa 43:1
C on him now while he is near . . . Isa 55:6
Daniel was *c* Belteshazzar . . . Dan 1:7
Jesus, who is *c* the Messiah . . . Matt 1:16
I *c* my Son out of Egypt . . . Matt 2:15
For I have come to *c* sinners . . . Matt 9:13
Jesus *c* to the crowds and said . . . Matt 15:10
you will be *c* Cephas . . . John 1:42
c his own sheep by name . . . John 10:3
those I have *c* to be mine . . . Acts 15:17
who love him and are *c* by him . . . Rom 8:28
I will now *c* my people . . . Rom 9:25
who *c* on the name of the Lord . . . Rom 10:13
God's gifts and his *c* can never . . . Rom 11:29
c by God to salvation . . . 1 Cor 1:24
c a meeting of the church . . . 1 Cor 5:4
as you were when God *c* you . . . 1 Cor 7:20
c you out of the darkness . . . 1 Pet 2:9
Are you *c* to be a speaker? . . . 1 Pet 4:11
those God has *c* and chosen . . . 2 Pet 1:10

CAPTAIN(S) *leaders with military, naval, prison, police, temple, or civil duties*
Potiphar was *c* of the palace . . . Gen 37:36
Joshua told the *c* of his army . . . Josh 10:24
c to lead his troops . . . 2 Sam 18:1
an army *c* with fifty soldiers . . . 2 Kgs 1:9
Nebuzaradan, *c* of the guard . . . 2 Kgs 25:8
generals and *c* and other officers . . . 1 Chr 26:26
priests and *c* of the Temple . . . Luke 22:4
c of the Temple guard . . . Acts 5:24
Cornelius, who was a *c* . . . Acts 10:1
Julius, a *c* of the Imperial . . . Acts 27:1
the ship's *c* and the owner . . . Acts 27:11
c of the merchant ships . . . Rev 18:17

CAPTIVATED *to be dominated by some special charm*
c by her love . . . Prov 5:19

CAPTIVE(S) *prisoner; (people) held against their will*
all the women and other *c* . . . Gen 14:16
your children would be taken *c* . . . Num 14:31
c to a foreign land . . . 1 Kgs 8:46
c from Jerusalem . . . 2 Kgs 24:14
invaded Judah and taken *c* . . . 2 Chr 28:17
you led a crowd of *c* . . . Ps 68:18
held *c* by his own sins . . . Prov 5:22
c from Jerusalem exiled in . . . Obad 1:20
that *c* will be released . . . Luke 4:18
sword or sent away as *c* . . . Luke 21:24
no longer *c* to its power . . . Rom 7:6
God, who made us his *c* . . . 2 Cor 2:14
he led a crowd of *c* . . . Eph 4:8
held *c* by him to do whatever . . . 2 Tim 2:26

CAPTIVITY *imprisonment, exile; subjection or subservience*
taken into *c* by King Tiglath-pileser . . . 1 Chr 5:6
into *c* under Nebuchadnezzar . . . 1 Chr 6:15
returned from their *c* . . . Ezra 2:1
into *c*, afflicted and enslaved . . . Lam 1:3

CARE(D)(S) *showing due concern, positive regard, or thorough oversight; also its opposite—undue anxiety or worry*
God *c* for you again and again . . . Deut 1:31
life was preserved by your *c* . . . Job 10:12
c about the anguish of my soul . . . Ps 31:7
You *c* for people and animals . . . Ps 36:6
They *c* nothing for God . . . Ps 54:3
I created you and have *c* . . . Isa 46:3
angels came and *c* for Jesus . . . Matt 4:11
more surely *c* for you . . . Luke 12:28
Not that he *c* for the poor . . . John 12:6
Lord *c* about our bodies . . . 1 Cor 6:13
will lighten all my *c* . . . Phil 2:28
take *c* of God's church? . . . 1 Tim 3:5
that you should *c* for him? . . . Heb 2:6
c for orphans and widows . . . Jas 1:27
worries and *c* to God, for he *c* . . . 1 Pet 5:7

CAREFUL(LY) *meticulous; scrupulously attentive; wary*
c to obey the commands . . . Josh 22:3
search *c* for the child . . . Matt 2:8
so *c* to clean the outside . . . Luke 11:39
be *c*, for you too may fall . . . 1 Cor 10:12
Be *c* of him . . . 2 Tim 4:15
Be *c* how you live among . . . 1 Pet 2:12

CARELESS *indifferent; negligent*
c ones will suddenly begin to care . . . Isa 32:10
c ease and drunkenness . . . Luke 21:34

CARNAL(LY) *fleshly, temporal, worldly, or overtly sexual; see SINFUL*

CARRIED, CARRY(ING) *to transport or convey; to sustain the weight of; to bring to a successful end*
and not *c* it through? . . . Num 23:19
too great a burden for me to *c* . . . Deut 1:9
the priests *c* the Ark . . . 1 Kgs 8:6
c away into exile . . . Isa 49:21

it was our weaknesses he *c* . . . Isa 53:4
must *c* out the vows . . . Matt 5:33
c a paralyzed man . . . Mark 2:3
c out his plan to betray Jesus . . . John 13:2
cannot *c* anything with us . . . 1 Tim 6:7

CAST(S)(ING) *to throw off (a restraint); to toss (dice); to form or give shape to; to direct (a shadow, a glance)*
C four rings of gold . . . Exod 25:12
c an idol for themselves . . . Deut 9:12
C lots can end arguments . . . Prov 18:18
where death *c* its shadow . . . Isa 9:2
his anger has *c* a dark shadow . . . Lam 2:1
c out demons in your name . . . Matt 7:22
How can Satan *c* out Satan? . . . Mark 3:23
Jesus *c* a demon out . . . Luke 11:14
I *c* my vote against them . . . Acts 26:10
c this man out of the church . . . 1 Cor 5:5
magician has *c* an evil spell . . . Gal 3:1

CATCH(ES), CAUGHT *to get entangled; to seize and hold firmly; to discover unexpectedly*
a ram *c* by its horns . . . Gen 22:13
first fish you *c* . . . Matt 17:27
evil spirits *c* sight of him . . . Mark 3:11
you will *c* many fish . . . Luke 5:4
let that day *c* you unaware . . . Luke 21:34
c in the act of adultery . . . John 8:3
"God *c* those who . . . 1 Cor 3:19
and was *c* up to God . . . Rev 12:5

CHAFF *husk or seed coverings of wheat*
c, scattered by the wind . . . Ps 1:4
will flee like *c* scattered . . . Isa 17:13
crushed as small as *c* . . . Dan 2:35
like *c* blown by the wind . . . Hos 13:3
mix the wheat you sell with *c* . . . Amos 8:6
separate the *c* from the grain . . . Matt 3:12

CHAIN(ED)(S) *to confine or secure; to obstruct; metal links*
back to Jerusalem in *c* . . . Acts 9:2
c between two soldiers . . . Acts 12:6
except for these *c* . . . Acts 26:29
am in *c* now for preaching . . . Eph 6:20
am in *c* because of Christ . . . Phil 1:13
of God cannot be *c* . . . 2 Tim 2:9
in *c* for a thousand years . . . Rev 20:2

CHANGE(D)(ING)(S) *to transform; to shift, exchange, or transfer*
c into a different person . . . 1 Sam 10:6
nor will he *c* his mind . . . 1 Sam 15:29
law so it cannot be *c* . . . Dan 6:8
c of plans upset Jonah . . . Jon 4:1
c of heart produced by . . . Rom 2:29
by *c* the way you think . . . Rom 12:2
have remorse and *c* your ways . . . 2 Cor 7:9
he would never *c* his mind . . . Heb 6:17
when the priesthood is *c* . . . Heb 7:12

CHARITY *benevolence; kindness; good deeds*
attention to their acts of *c* . . . Matt 6:2
He gave generously to *c* . . . Acts 10:2

CHASTE *consecrated, pure, celibate*
If she is *c* . . . Song 8:9

CHASTEN(ED)(ING)(S) *correct by punishment or discipline; see DISCIPLINE*

CHEER(S), CHEERFUL(LY) *to instill with hope, joy, hilarity, or comfort*
end my sadness and be *c* . . . Job 9:27
renewed hope and *c* . . . Ps 94:19
A *c* look brings joy . . . Prov 15:30
"*C* up," they said . . . Mark 10:49
stones . . . burst into *c* . . . Luke 19:40
loves the person who gives *c* . . . 2 Cor 9:7
c me up by telling me . . . Phil 2:19
Work hard and *c* at . . . Col 3:23

CHIEF *clan leader; of the first order or magnitude*
Pharaoh's *c* cup-bearer and *c* baker . . . Gen 40:1
c administrator over all . . . Num 3:32
presided over them as their *c* . . . Job 29:25
The *c* official renamed them . . . Dan 1:7

CHILD(BEARING)(BIRTH) *act of bringing forth a child; see BEAR or CHILD*
Rachel's pains of *c* . . . Gen 35:16
purification from the blood of *c* . . . Lev 12:4
will be saved through *c* . . . 1 Tim 2:15

CHILD(HOOD)(ISH)(LIKE)(REN) *young person between infancy and youth, not yet of age; adult offspring or descendants; seed; product of; level of dependence, also immaturity; term of endearment, also of rebuke*
from *c* I have cared for orphans . . . Job 31:18
taught *c* and nursing infants . . . Ps 8:2
Come, my *c*, and listen . . . Ps 34:11
taught me from my earliest *c* . . . Ps 71:17
even the *c* not yet born . . . Ps 78:6
protects those of *c* faith . . . Ps 116:6
C are a gift . . . Ps 127:3
like a small *c* is my soul . . . Ps 131:2
Listen, my *c* . . . Prov 1:8
Teach your *c* to choose . . . Prov 22:6
For a *c* is born to us . . . Isa 9:6
virgin will conceive a *c* . . . Matt 1:23
Rachel weeps for her *c* . . . Matt 2:18
be called the *c* of God . . . Matt 5:9
if your *c* ask for a loaf . . . Matt 7:9
revealing it to the *c* . . . Matt 11:25
and become as little *c* . . . Matt 18:3
"Let the *c* come to me . . . Matt 19:14
then died without *c* . . . Mark 12:20
fathers will betray their own *c* . . . Mark 13:12
c grew up healthy and strong . . . Luke 2:40
wombs that have not borne a *c* . . . Luke 23:29
right to become *c* of God . . . John 1:12
I put away *c* things . . . 1 Cor 13:11
c in your understanding . . . 1 Cor 14:20
promise to Abraham and his *c* . . . Gal 3:16
no longer a slave but God's own *c* . . . Gal 4:7
like *c*, forever changing our . . . Eph 4:14
treating you as his own *c* . . . Heb 12:7
writing to you, my dear *c* . . . 1 Jn 2:12
c was snatched away from the dragon . . . Rev 12:5

CHOICE(S) *selection or preference; special, top-rate, prime*
Abel brought several *c* lambs . . . Gen 4:4
Take your *c* of any section . . . Gen 13:9
c sample of the first day's harvest . . . Exod 23:19
c between prosperity and disaster . . . Deut 30:15
c meats have been cooked . . . Matt 22:4
your *c* are never free . . . Gal 5:17
became his *c* possession . . . Jas 1:18

CHOOSE, CHOOSING, CHOSE(N) *decide; selected for a sovereign and redemptive purpose*
Adam *c* a name for each . . . Gen 2:19
He *c* capable men from all . . . Exod 18:25
show mercy to anyone I *c* . . . Exod 33:19
c you to be his own special . . . Deut 14:2
that you would *c* life . . . Deut 30:19
For I have *c* you . . . Isa 41:9
places for the ones he has *c* . . . Mark 10:40
c twelve of them to be apostles . . . Luke 6:13
my Son, my *C* One . . . Luke 9:35
You didn't *c* me. I *c* you . . . John 15:16
you can *c* to obey God . . . Rom 6:16
having *c* them, he called them . . . Rom 8:30
We can't get it by *c* it . . . Rom 9:16
Jews are still his *c* people . . . Rom 11:28
he *c* those who are powerless . . . 1 Cor 1:27
he *c* us from the beginning . . . Eph 1:11
might be proud of being *c* . . . 1 Tim 3:6
Hasn't God *c* the poor . . . Jas 2:5
precious to God who *c* him . . . 1 Pet 2:4
the called and *c* and faithful ones . . . Rev 17:14

CHRIST *Son of God, Messiah, Anointed One*
Jesus *C*, the one you sent . . . John 17:3
by sending *C* to die for us . . . Rom 5:8
in *C* Jesus our Lord . . . Rom 8:39
C himself was a Jew . . . Rom 9:5
his Son, Jesus *C* our Lord . . . 1 Cor 1:9
under the authority of *C* . . . Eph 1:22
confess that Jesus *C* is Lord . . . Phil 2:11
in *C* the fullness of God . . . Col 2:9
C, the sinless, spotless Lamb . . . 1 Pet 1:19
worship *C* as Lord . . . 1 Pet 3:15
Jesus *C*, the Word of life . . . 1 Jn 1:1

CHRISTIAN(ITY)(S) *one(s) belonging to Christ; believer(s); of (or in) the faith; saint(ly) or holy (one) or brother(ly)*
believers were first called *C* . . . Acts 11:26
are not *C* at all . . . Rom 8:9
you condemn another *C* . . . Rom 14:10
first person to become a *C* . . . Rom 16:5
you *C* are that temple . . . 1 Cor 3:17
C wife brings holiness . . . 1 Cor 7:14
Greet each other in *C* love . . . 2 Cor 13:12
so-called *C* there—false ones . . . Gal 2:4
C—you are one in Christ . . . Gal 3:28
I am the least deserving *C* . . . Eph 3:8
the basics of *C* . . . Heb 6:1
with true *C* love . . . Heb 13:1
suffer for being a *C* . . . 1 Pet 4:16

CHURCH(ES) *"assembly" or "called out ones"; the body of believers gathered to worship Jesus (not the building in which they meet)*
this rock I will build my *c* . . . Matt 16:18
take your case to the *c* . . . Matt 18:17
baptized and added to the *c* . . . Acts 2:41
c that meets in their home . . . Rom 16:5
the *c* is his body . . . Eph 1:23
the *c*, which is his body . . . Col 1:18
angels of the seven *c* . . . Rev 1:20

CIRCUMCISE(D), CIRCUMCISION *to cut the foreskin of male children; ceremony signifying Israel's covenant with God; act symbolic of cleansing*
Every male child must be *c* . . . Gen 17:12
be *c* like we are . . . Gen 34:15
c in body but not in spirit . . . Jer 9:25
when the baby was *c* . . . Luke 2:21
ancient Jewish custom of *c* . . . Acts 15:1
you teach people not to *c* . . . Acts 21:21
true *c* is not a cutting . . . Rom 2:29
c ceremony was a sign . . . Rom 4:11
c, though he was a Gentile . . . Gal 2:3
If you are counting on *c* . . . Gal 5:2
proud of their *c* . . . Eph 2:11
must be *c* to be saved . . . Phil 3:2
to Christ, you were "*c*," . . . Col 2:11

CITIES, CITY *central fortified town surrounded by a cluster of unwalled villages; of Jerusalem; figurative of God's presence*
a house inside a walled *c* . . . Lev 25:29
c and towns are fortified . . . Num 13:28
I have never chosen a *c* . . . 1 Kgs 8:16
joy to the *c* of our God . . . Ps 46:4
is the *c* of the great King! . . . Ps 48:2
of Justice and the Faithful *C* . . . Isa 1:26
fairest of Israel's *c* lies . . . Lam 2:1
light of the world—like a *c* . . . Matt 5:14
a *c* designed and built by God . . . Heb 11:10
forward to our *c* in heaven . . . Heb 13:14
great *c* of Babylon split . . . Rev 16:19
the holy *c*, the new Jerusalem . . . Rev 21:2

CITIZEN(S) *person owing allegiance to and deriving protection from a sovereign state*
If any of the *c* of Israel . . . Lev 4:27
the ten leading *c* of a town! . . . Eccl 7:19
registered as *c* of heaven . . . Luke 10:20
But I am a *c* by birth . . . Acts 22:28
You are *c* along with . . . Eph 2:19
we are *c* of heaven . . . Phil 3:20
c in the city of my God . . . Rev 3:12

CLEAN *unadulterated, pure; without guilt or moral corruption; without ceremonial defilement; fit for use or human consumption*
place that is ceremonially *c* . . . Lev 6:11
people who are ceremonially *c* . . . Lev 7:19
what is *c* and may be eaten . . . Lev 11:47
Wash me *c* from my guilt . . . Ps 51:2
Wash yourselves and be *c*! . . . Isa 1:16
home empty, swept, and *c* . . . Matt 12:44
c the outside of the cup . . . Luke 11:39
Not all of you are *c* . . . John 13:11
holy and *c*, washed by baptism . . . Eph 5:26

CLEANSE(D)(S) *to make clean, pure, holy*
an offering to *c* the altar . . . Exod 29:36
C me from these hidden faults . . . Ps 19:12
Who can say, "I have *c* . . . Prov 20:9
be *c* of your sins . . . Acts 3:19
c their hearts through faith . . . Acts 15:9
let us *c* ourselves from . . . 2 Cor 7:1
blood of Jesus, his Son, *c* us . . . 1 Jn 1:7

COMFORT(ED)(S) *to strengthen in body and spirit; to console*
Go to him and *c* him . . . Gen 21:18
she was a special *c* to him . . . Gen 24:67
to *c* and console him . . . Job 2:11
and your staff protect and *c* . . . Ps 23:4
your *c* gave me renewed hope . . . Ps 94:19
it *c* me in all my troubles . . . Ps 119:50
C, *c* my people . . . Isa 40:1
The LORD will *c* Israel . . . Isa 51:3
refusing to be *c* . . . Jer 31:15
No one is here to *c* me . . . Lam 1:16
for they will be *c* . . . Matt 5:4
Any *c* from his love? . . . Phil 2:1
we have been greatly *c* . . . 1 Thes 3:7

COMFORTER *see COUNSELOR or HOLY SPIRIT*

COMMAND(ED)(S) *to issue a charge or directive; religious instruction*
my requirements, *c*, regulations . . . Gen 26:5
just as the LORD had *c* . . . Exod 7:6
love me and obey my *c* . . . Exod 20:6
replace God's *c* with their own . . . Matt 15:9
and your *c* will be obeyed . . . Mark 11:23
and flee at his *c* . . . Luke 4:36
summed up in this one *c* . . . Gal 5:14
obey our Lord's royal *c* . . . Jas 2:8

COMMANDMENT(S) *a gracious provision of God's law or covenant, obeyed as an act of love and devotion; see COMMAND*
the covenant—the Ten *C* . . . Exod 34:28
c of the LORD are right . . . Ps 19:8
if you break the smallest *c* . . . Matt 5:19
No other *c* is greater . . . Mark 12:31
a new *c*: Love each . . . John 13:34
first of the Ten *C* that . . . Eph 6:2
I am not writing a new *c* . . . 1 Jn 2:7

COMMEND(ATIONS)(ED)(S) *to entrust for care or preservation; praiseworthy citation*
people *c* everyone who volunteered . . . Neh 11:2
when the Lord *c* someone . . . 2 Cor 10:18
ought to be writing *c* . . . 2 Cor 12:11

COMMIT(MENT)(S)(TED) *to perpetrate; to obligate or pledge oneself*
c any other similar sin . . . Lev 6:3
c to become someone else's wife . . . Lev 19:20
C everything you do to . . . Ps 37:5
his covenant—the *c* he made . . . Ps 105:8
the man who *c* adultery . . . Prov 6:32
What crime has he *c* . . . Luke 23:22
c to the revealed truths . . . 1 Tim 3:9
sins . . . *c* in ignorance . . . Heb 9:7

COMPANION(S)(SHIP) *close friend or fellow participant*
a *c* who will help him . . . Gen 2:18
and a *c* to ostriches . . . Job 30:29
the *c* of evil people . . . Job 34:8
my equal, my *c* and close friend . . . Ps 55:13
my *c* and loved ones . . . Ps 88:18
Violent people deceive their *c* . . . Prov 16:29
who seek out worthless *c* . . . Prov 28:7
my *c* Titus be circumcised . . . Gal 2:3
c of those who call on . . . 2 Tim 2:22

COMPASSION(ATE) *sympathy, usually granted because of unusual or distressing circumstances*
Have *c* on me, LORD . . . Ps 6:2
your unfailing love and *c* . . . Ps 25:6
Because of your great *c* . . . Ps 51:1
c to those who fear him . . . Ps 103:13
show you his love and *c* . . . Isa 30:18
he brings grief, he also shows *c* . . . Lam 3:32
had *c* on them and healed . . . Matt 14:14
c to anyone I choose . . . Rom 9:15
tender *c* of Christ Jesus . . . Phil 1:8

COMPLAIN(ED)(ERS)(ING)(T)(TS) *to express grief over a perceived injustice; the cause or subject of protest; formal allegation against a party*
Don't I have a right to *c* . . . Job 6:5
I must *c* in my bitterness . . . Job 7:11
"My *c* is with God . . . Job 21:4
I pour out my *c* before him . . . Ps 142:2
you priests, my *c* is with you! . . . Hos 4:4
listen to the LORD's *c*! . . . Mic 6:2
They *c* to their friends . . . Matt 11:16
c bitterly to Jesus' disciples . . . Luke 5:30
who spoke Greek *c* against . . . Acts 6:1
c about other matters . . . Acts 19:39
Elijah the prophet *c* to God . . . Rom 11:2
stay away from *c* and arguing . . . Phil 2:14
c against an elder . . . 1 Tim 5:19
grumblers and *c*, doing whatever evil . . . Jude 1:16

CONCEIVE(D) *to become pregnant; to devise or imagine*
cursed be the night when I was *c* . . . Job 3:3
They *c* trouble and evil . . . Job 15:35
c evil; they are pregnant with trouble . . . Ps 7:14
from the moment my mother *c* me . . . Ps 51:5
The virgin will *c* a child! . . . Isa 7:14
plan *c* behind closed doors . . . Isa 8:12

CONDEMN(ATION)(ED)(ING)(S) *to declare guilty; conviction of guilt; censure*
c those who plan wickedness . . . Prov 12:2
c those who aren't guilty . . . Matt 12:7
justified by them or . . . *c* . . . Matt 12:37
Jesus had been *c* to die . . . Matt 27:3
not . . . to *c* it, but to save it . . . John 3:17
never be *c* for their sins . . . John 5:24
you are *c* yourself . . . Rom 2:1
judge and *c* me as a sinner . . . Rom 3:7
For Adam's sin led to *c* . . . Rom 5:16
now there is no *c* . . . Rom 8:1

CONFESS(ED)(ES)(ION) *to admit or acknowledge (sin or faith); creedal statement*
Ezra prayed and made this *c* . . . Ezra 10:1
When I refused to *c* my sin . . . Ps 32:3
not *c* the sin in my heart . . . Ps 66:18
if they *c* and forsake them . . . Prov 28:13
believers *c* their sinful practices . . . Acts 19:18
if you *c* with your mouth . . . Rom 10:9
every tongue will *c* allegiance . . . Rom 14:11
c that Jesus Christ is Lord . . . Phil 2:11
C your sins to each other . . . Jas 5:16
if we *c* our sins to him . . . 1 Jn 1:9
who *c* the Son has the Father . . . 1 Jn 2:23
and *c* that they belong to Jesus . . . Rev 12:17

CONFIRM(ATION)(ED)(ING)(S) *to strengthen; to remove doubt by authoritative statement or action*
c my everlasting covenant . . . Gen 17:19
public *c* that I dug this well . . . Gen 21:30
blood *c* the covenant . . . Exod 24:8
either *c* or nullify any vows . . . Num 30:13
c you today as his people . . . Deut 29:13
personal *c* of my covenant . . . Isa 42:6
c what they said by . . . signs . . . Mark 16:20
conscience and the Holy Spirit *c* . . . Rom 9:1
c by many reliable witnesses . . . 2 Tim 2:2
blood *c* the covenant . . . Heb 9:20

CONFUSE(D) *to bring to ruin; to mix indiscriminately; perplexed; chaotic*
c the people by giving them . . . Gen 11:9
Can we speak when we are *c* . . . Job 37:20
c their speech, for I see violence . . . Ps 55:9
C and disturbed, Mary tried . . . Luke 1:29
their minds became dark and *c* . . . Rom 1:21

CONFUSION *shame, dishonor, or disgrace; tumult, chaos, or perplexity*
he threw them into *c* . . . Exod 14:24
curses, *c*, and disillusionment . . . Deut 28:20
a day of *c* and terror . . . Isa 22:5
infamous city, filled with *c* . . . Ezek 22:5
the city was filled with *c* . . . Acts 19:29

CONGREGATION *an assembly or gathering (not church)*
in front of the entire *c* . . . Ps 35:18
publicly before the *c* . . . Ps 107:32
c . . . came down to the shore . . . Acts 21:5

CONSCIENCE(S) *one's moral sensitivity or scruples*
lived before God in all good *c* . . . Acts 23:1
c either accuse them or . . . Rom 2:15
c and the Holy Spirit confirm . . . Rom 9:1
believer who has a sensitive *c* . . . Rom 14:2
My *c* is clear . . . 1 Cor 4:4
a weaker *c* to stumble . . . 1 Cor 8:9
clear *c*, and sincere faith . . . 1 Tim 1:5

CONSECRATED *devoted to God; see DEVOTED*

CONSENT(ED) *enthusiastically agree or mutually delight in*
Saul finally *c* . . . 1 Sam 17:37
Will the wild ox *c* to being . . . Job 39:9
to do anything without your *c* . . . Phlm 1:14

CONSOLATION(S) *that which alleviates the grief or sense of loss; just reward; see COMFORT or ENCOURAGEMENT*

CONSOLE(D) *to alleviate the grief or sense of loss; to offer just reward*
traveled . . . to comfort and *c* him . . . Job 2:11
they *c* him and comforted him . . . Job 42:11
a cup of wine to *c* them . . . Jer 16:7

CONSUME(D)(S), CONSUMING *to destroy (as by fire); to waste or burn away*
it *c* them as fire burns straw . . . Exod 15:7
c the burnt offering . . . Lev 9:24
I *c* them; I struck them . . . 2 Sam 22:39
c them with your burning anger . . . Ps 69:24
when disease *c* your body . . . Prov 5:11
He *c* the whole land of Israel . . . Lam 2:3
Jesus will *c* with the breath . . . 2 Thes 2:8
For our God is a *c* fire. . . . Heb 12:29

CONTEMPT *arousing disgust, scorn, disdain*
treat her mistress Sarai with *c* . . . Gen 16:4
treating my regulations with *c* . . . Lev 26:15
those who have treated me with *c* . . . Num 14:23
treated . . . offerings with *c* . . . 1 Sam 2:17
be treated with utter *c* . . . Mark 9:12

CONTENT(MENT) *pleased; satisfied; willing*
"I am *c* just to have you back . . . 2 Sam 19:30
quite *c* with my weaknesses . . . 2 Cor 12:10
true religion with *c* is great . . . 1 Tim 6:6

CONTRITE *grieving and penitent for sin*
whose spirits are *c* and humble . . . Isa 57:15
who have humble and *c* hearts . . . Isa 66:2

CONVICT(ION) *to find or prove guilty of an offense; strong persuasion or opinion*
Never *c* anyone of a crime on . . . Deut 19:15
those who *c* the guilty . . . Prov 24:25
Is it legal to *c* a man before . . . John 7:51

a personal *c* about this matter . . . Rom 14:5
c the ungodly of all the evil . . . Jude 1:15

CORRECT(ED)(ION)(LY)(S) *to set right with remedies, revisions, or reforms; right(ly) or accurate(ly)*
if you refuse to respond *c* . . . Gen 4:7
Ephraim cannot pronounce the word *c* . . . Judg 12:6
they have not worshiped him *c* . . . 2 Kgs 17:26
the joy of those *c* by God! . . . Job 5:17
ignored my advice and rejected the *c* . . . Prov 1:25
just as a father *c* a child . . . Prov 3:12
c of discipline is the way to life . . . Prov 6:23
People who accept *c* . . . Prov 10:17
whoever learns from *c* is wise . . . Prov 15:5
Don't fail to *c* your children . . . Prov 23:13
c your misunderstandings about . . . 1 Cor 12:1
who *c* explains the word of truth . . . 2 Tim 2:15
Patiently *c*, rebuke, and encourage . . . 2 Tim 4:2
Let your teaching be so *c* that . . . Titus 2:8
until their limitations can be *c* . . . Heb 9:10
don't be discouraged when he *c* you . . . Heb 12:5
c and disciplines everyone I love . . . Rev 3:19

CORRUPT(ED)(ION)(S) *to go from good to bad, physically or morally*
earth had become *c* in God's sight . . . Gen 6:11
c . . . violence and depravity . . . Gen 6:12
c and sinful person with a thirst for . . . Job 15:16
are *c*, and their actions are evil . . . Ps 14:1
stay far from *c* speech . . . Prov 4:24
even the courts of law are *c*! . . . Eccl 3:16
bad company *c* good character . . . 1 Cor 15:33
Their minds are *c* . . . 1 Tim 6:5
those who are *c* and unbelieving . . . Titus 1:15
many are *c* by its poison . . . Heb 12:15
refuse to let the world *c* us . . . Jas 1:27
are slaves to sin and *c* . . . 2 Pet 2:19
great prostitute who *c* the earth . . . Rev 19:2

COUNSEL(OR) *advice; policy, plan, or action; one giving such wisdom*
Listen to my *c*, and apply it . . . Job 5:27
with God; *c* and understanding are his . . . Job 12:13
The godly offer good *c* . . . Ps 37:30
keep on guiding me with your *c* . . . Ps 73:24
he will give you another *C* . . . John 14:16
Who knows enough to be his *c* . . . Rom 11:34
Who can give him *c* . . . 1 Cor 2:16
giving you *c* from God's Spirit . . . 1 Cor 7:40
Use his words to teach and *c* . . . Col 3:16

COUNTENANCE *personal bearing or composure; facial expression; see FACE*

COURAGE(OUS) *mental or moral strength*
Be strong and *c* . . . Deut 31:6
and *c*! Do not be afraid . . . Josh 1:9
have *c* because you will have hope . . . Job 11:18
They all lose their *c* . . . Ps 18:45
Be brave and *c* . . . Ps 27:14
c of many people will falter . . . Luke 21:26

COVENANT(S) *mutual agreement or contract (between persons, between nations, or between God and humanity) with conditions and consequences spelled out*
I will remember the eternal *c* . . . Gen 9:16
made a *c* with Abram . . . Gen 15:18
This is my *c* with you . . . Gen 17:4
all those who keep his *c* . . . Ps 25:10
We have not violated your *c* . . . Ps 44:17
Remember your *c* promises . . . Ps 74:20
and broken his everlasting *c* . . . Isa 24:5
personal confirmation of my *c* . . . Isa 42:6
Because they violated their *c* . . . Jer 22:9
I will make a new *c* . . . Jer 31:31
people of the holy *c* . . . Dan 11:28
a *c* with all the wild animals . . . Hos 2:18
like Adam, you broke my *c* and rebelled . . . Hos 6:7
c I made with you, sealed . . . Zech 9:11
The messenger of the *c* . . . Mal 3:1
new *c* to save you—an agreement . . . Luke 22:20
He made *c* with them and . . . Rom 9:4
This cup is the new *c* . . . 1 Cor 11:25
a *c*, not of written laws . . . 2 Cor 3:6
an illustration of God's two *c* . . . Gal 4:24
effectiveness of this better *c* . . . Heb 7:22
need for a second *c* to replace it . . . Heb 8:7
mediates the new *c* between God . . . Heb 9:15

COVER(ED)(ING)(S) *to hide from sight or knowledge; to be of sufficient scope so as to include or top something else; lid or top piece*
you have *c* all their sins . . . Ps 85:2
water that *c* even the mountains . . . Ps 104:6
a cloud above them as a *c* . . . Ps 105:39
He *c* the heavens with clouds . . . Ps 147:8
evil people *c* up their harmful . . . Prov 10:6
but love *c* all offenses . . . Prov 10:12
love and faithfulness *c* sin . . . Prov 16:6
without a *c* on her head . . . 1 Cor 11:5
a veil *c* their minds . . . 2 Cor 3:14
the Ark's *c*, the place of atonement . . . Heb 9:5
no other sacrifice that will *c* these sins . . . Heb 10:26
love *c* a multitude of sins . . . 1 Pet 4:8
four living beings, each *c* with eyes . . . Rev 4:6

COVET(ED)(ING) *to inordinately desire unjust gain or another's property*
Do not *c* your neighbor's house . . . Exod 20:17
have never *c* anyone's money . . . Acts 20:33
never have known that *c* is wrong . . . Rom 7:7
murder and stealing and *c* . . . Rom 13:9

CREATE(D)(S), CREATING *bring into being; form, make, produce*
In the beginning God *c* . . . Gen 1:1
God *c* people in his own image . . . Gen 1:27
c purity in one born impure? . . . Job 14:4
God *c* people to be upright . . . Eccl 7:29
c the light and makes the darkness . . . Isa 45:7
I *c* you and have cared for you . . . Isa 46:3
I am *c* new heavens and a new earth . . . Isa 65:17
c the stars, the Pleiades and Orion . . . Amos 5:8
Are we not all *c* by the same God? . . . Mal 2:10
From the time the world was *c* . . . Rom 1:20
Should the thing that was *c* say . . . Rom 9:20
God, the Father, who *c* everything . . . 1 Cor 8:6
He has *c* us anew in Christ Jesus . . . Eph 2:10
c in himself one new person . . . Eph 2:15
a new person, *c* in God's likeness . . . Eph 4:24
Christ is the one through whom God *c* . . . Col 1:16
Christ, who *c* this new nature . . . Col 3:10
everything God *c* is good . . . 1 Tim 4:4
God rested after *c* the world . . . Heb 4:10
same since the world was first *c* . . . 2 Pet 3:4
For you *c* everything . . . Rev 4:11

CREATION *something that is created; the world; the act of bringing the world into existence; see CREATE*
c of the heavens and the earth . . . Gen 2:1
mysteries hidden since the *c* . . . Matt 13:35
from the beginning of *c* . . . Mark 10:6
all *c* is waiting eagerly for . . . Rom 8:19
nothing in all *c* will ever . . . Rom 8:39
supreme over all *c* . . . Col 1:15
we, out of all *c*, became his choice . . . Jas 1:18

CREATOR *maker; see CREATE*
my *C* would soon do away with me . . . Job 32:22
cause you to forget your *C* . . . Eccl 12:1
the everlasting God, the *C* . . . Isa 40:28
forgotten the LORD, your *C* . . . Isa 51:13
your *C* will be your husband . . . Isa 54:5
the *C* himself, who is to be praised . . . Rom 1:25
God, the *C* of all things . . . Eph 3:9

CREATURE(S) *the whole created universe; human beings; anything animate (not limited to living beings)*
great sea *c* and every sort of fish . . . Gen 1:21
snakes, lizards, and hideous *c* . . . Ezek 8:10
I heard every *c* in heaven and . . . Rev 5:13

CRIME(S), CRIMINAL(S) *an offense; one who has broken the law*
not be held guilty for their *c* . . . Lev 19:17
lust is a shameful sin, a *c* . . . Job 31:11
Don't forgive their *c* and . . . sins . . . Jer 18:23
What *c* have I committed? . . . Jer 37:18
Am I some dangerous *c* . . . Matt 26:55
c in prison, . . . Barabbas . . . Matt 27:16
What *c* has he committed? . . . Luke 23:22
Two others, both *c* . . . Luke 23:32
if he weren't a *c*! . . . John 18:30
a *c*'s death on a cross . . . Phil 2:8
been chained like a *c* . . . 2 Tim 2:9

CROOKED *twisted; out of line; unjust; evil*
they say is *c* and deceitful . . . Ps 36:3
all your dealings are *c* . . . Ps 58:2
as useless as a *c* bow . . . Ps 78:57
What they do is *c* . . . Prov 2:15
She staggers down a *c* trail . . . Prov 5:6
nothing *c* or twisted in it . . . Prov 8:8
those who follow *c* paths . . . Prov 10:9
c heart will not prosper . . . Prov 17:20
straighten out what he has made *c* . . . Eccl 7:13
full of *c* and perverse people . . . Phil 2:15

CROSS(ED)(ING) *to traverse or move across; to fold one (arm) over the other; upright post used as an instrument of death in ancient times; the means by which atonement was made between God and humanity*
I will not *c* this line to harm you . . . Gen 31:52
Jacob *c* his arms as he reached out . . . Gen 48:14
shallow *c* places of the Jordan . . . Josh 2:7
Then all the people *c* over . . . Josh 3:16
refuse to take up your *c* . . . Matt 10:38
c to the other side of the lake . . . Matt 14:22
shoulder your *c*, and follow me . . . Matt 16:24
c land and sea to make one convert . . . Matt 23:15
forced him to carry Jesus' *c* . . . Matt 27:32
nailed him to the *c* and murdered . . . Acts 2:23
you died with Christ on the *c* . . . Rom 7:4
the *c* of Christ would lose its . . . 1 Cor 1:17
on the *c*, he took upon himself . . . Gal 3:13
enemies of the *c* of Christ . . . Phil 3:18
by means of his blood on the *c* . . . Col 1:20
a fellow soldier of the *c* . . . Phlm 1:2
to die a shameful death on the *c* . . . Heb 12:2

CROWN(ED)(ING)(S) *top of the head; a cap or headdress worn by victors, priests, or royalty; to place such a prized emblem upon; to bless or adorn*
on Joseph's head, *c* the brow . . . Deut 33:16
and removed the *c* from my head . . . Job 19:9
you *c* us with glory and honor . . . Ps 8:5
c of finest gold on his head . . . Ps 21:3
c the year with a bountiful . . . Ps 65:11
he *c* the humble with salvation . . . Ps 149:4
c you with grace and clothe you with . . . Prov 1:9
present you with a beautiful *c* . . . Prov 4:9
wife is her husband's joy and *c* . . . Prov 12:4
wise person is *c* with knowledge . . . Prov 14:18
Gray hair is a *c* of glory . . . Prov 16:31
a *c* of long, sharp thorns . . . Matt 27:29
is our proud reward and *c* . . . 1 Thes 2:19
the *c* of righteousness . . . 2 Tim 4:8
Jesus, . . . "*c* with glory and honor" . . . Heb 2:9
on his head were many *c* . . . Rev 19:12

CRUCIFIED, CRUCIFIXION, CRUCIFY (ING) *to execute or nail to the cross; to put to death*

they led him away to be *c* . . . Matt 27:31
shouted, "*C* him! *C* him!" . . . Luke 23:21
forty days after his *c* . . . Acts 1:3
this Jesus whom you *c* . . . Acts 2:36
after you killed him by *c* . . . Acts 5:30
sinful selves were *c* with . . . Rom 6:6
we preach that Christ was *c* . . . 1 Cor 1:23
I have been *c* with Christ . . . Gal 2:19

CUNNING *practical knowledge or skill, with bad connotations*
their *c* schemes are thwarted . . . Job 5:13
the human heart and mind are *c* . . . Ps 64:6

CUP(S) *drinking vessel; figurative of human vessel; token of tangible consolation, salvation of Christ, wrath of God, drunkenness, or fate*
my inheritance, my *c* of blessing . . . Ps 16:5
My *c* overflows with blessings . . . Ps 23:5
LORD holds a *c* in his hand . . . Ps 75:8
a *c* symbolizing his salvation . . . Ps 116:13
the *c* of the LORD's fury . . . Isa 51:17
I set *c* and jugs of wine . . . Jer 35:5
a *c* of deep sorrow to drink . . . Lam 3:15
drink from the same *c* of terror . . . Ezek 23:32
give even a *c* of cold water . . . Matt 10:42
c of sorrow I am about to drink? . . . Matt 20:22
First wash the inside of the *c* . . . Matt 23:26
let this *c* of suffering be taken . . . Matt 26:39
washing *c*, pitchers, and kettles . . . Mark 7:4
he took another *c* of wine . . . Luke 22:20
bless the *c* at the Lord's Table . . . 1 Cor 10:16
This *c* is the new covenant . . . 1 Cor 11:25
undiluted into God's *c* of wrath . . . Rev 14:10

CURSE(D)(S), CURSING *to pronounce a sentence; a condemnation or judgment*
singled out . . . to be *c* . . . Gen 3:14
I will never again *c* the earth . . . Gen 8:21
A *c* on the Canaanites! . . . Gen 9:25
and *c* those who *c* you . . . Gen 12:3
Please come and *c* them for me . . . Num 22:6
c is everyone who *c* you . . . Num 24:9
choice between a blessing and a *c*! . . . Deut 11:26
anyone hanging on a tree is *c* . . . Deut 21:23
C is anyone who . . . . . . Deut 27:15-26
All the *c* written in this book . . . Deut 29:20
Joshua invoked this *c* . . . Josh 6:26
May you be *c*! From now on . . . Josh 9:23
c them. It was Shimei . . . 2 Sam 16:5
C God and die . . . Job 2:9
those *c* by him will die . . . Ps 37:22
This scroll contains the *c* . . . Zech 5:3
symbols of what it means to be *c* . . . Zech 8:13
I will *c* even the blessings you . . . Mal 2:2
Away with you, you *c* ones . . . Matt 25:41
let him be forever *c* . . . Gal 1:8
the law . . . are under his *c* . . . Gal 3:10

DARK(NESS) *devoid of light; nightfall; blackened; in spiritual terms, secret, closed, blinded, or evil; place of punishment (hell)*
a formless mass cloaked in *d* . . . Gen 1:2
Let that day be turned to *d* . . . Job 3:4
d as midnight, a land of utter gloom . . . Job 10:22
through the *d* valley of death . . . Ps 23:4
sat in *d* and deepest gloom . . . Ps 107:10
that *d* is light and light is *d* . . . Isa 5:20
who walk in *d* will see a great . . . Isa 9:2
evil eye . . . plunges you into *d* . . . Matt 6:23
will be cast into outer *d* . . . Matt 8:12
What I tell you now in the *d* . . . Matt 10:27
filled with light, with no *d* . . . Luke 11:36
when the power of *d* reigns . . . Luke 22:53
d fell across the whole land . . . Luke 23:44
light shines through the *d* . . . John 1:5
loved the *d* more than the light . . . John 3:19
How can light live with *d* . . . 2 Cor 6:14
closed minds are full of *d* . . . Eph 4:18
called you out of the *d* . . . 1 Pet 2:9

are doomed to blackest *d* . . . 2 Pet 2:17
no *d* in him at all . . . 1 John 1:5

DEACON(S) *servant; officer of the church*
sister Phoebe, a *d* in the church . . . Rom 16:1
to the elders and *d* . . . Phil 1:1
d must be people who are . . . 1 Tim 3:8
d must be faithful to his wife . . . 1 Tim 3:12

DEAD(LY) *without (physical or spiritual) life; fatal; useless; (un)believers who have died (= "the dead")*
go down to the place of the *d* . . . Ps 139:8
the *d* are better off than the living . . . Eccl 4:2
in a dark place, like a person long *d* . . . Lam 3:6
spiritually *d* care for their own *d* . . . Matt 8:22
girl isn't *d*; she's only asleep . . . Matt 9:24
he will be raised from the *d* . . . Matt 17:23
God of the living, not the *d* . . . Matt 22:32
motionless, and he appeared to be *d* . . . Mark 9:26
He has been raised from the *d* . . . Mark 16:6
the *d* will hear my voice . . . John 5:25
The poison of a *d* snake . . . Rom 3:13
who brings the *d* back to life . . . Rom 4:17
consider yourselves *d* to sin . . . Rom 6:11
life for those who were *d* . . . Rom 11:15
resurrection of the *d* . . . 1 Cor 15:13
you were *d*, doomed forever . . . Eph 2:1
their consciences are *d* . . . 1 Tim 4:2
faith is *d* without good deeds . . . Jas 2:26
evil, full of *d* poison . . . Jas 3:8
the *d* were judged according to . . . Rev 20:12

DEAF *(those) without (physical or spiritual) hearing*
In that day *d* people will hear . . . Isa 29:18
and unstop the ears of the *d* . . . Isa 35:5
in silent awe, *d* to everything . . . Mic 7:16
the lepers are cured, the *d* hear . . . Matt 11:5
d man with a speech impediment . . . Mark 7:32
heathen at heart and *d* to the truth . . . Acts 7:51

DEATH(S) *cessation of (physical or spiritual) life; personification and consequence of evil*
joining his ancestors in *d* . . . Gen 25:8
anything but *d* to separate us . . . Ruth 1:17
in *d* the wicked cease from . . . Job 3:17
crushed, and I am near *d* . . . Job 17:1
D consumes sinners . . . Job 24:19
back from the jaws of *d* . . . Ps 9:13
d itself stared me in the face . . . Ps 18:5
Entering her house leads to *d* . . . Prov 2:18
All who hate me love *d* . . . Prov 8:36
He will swallow up *d* forever! . . . Isa 25:8
he is responsible for their *d* . . . Ezek 33:6
grief to the point of *d* . . . Matt 26:38
passed from *d* into life . . . John 5:24
God's *d* penalty for . . . Rom 1:32
sin brought *d*, so *d* spread . . . Rom 5:12
D no longer has any power . . . Rom 6:9
the wages of sin is *d* . . . Rom 6:23
announcing the Lord's *d* . . . 1 Cor 11:26
O *d*, where is your sting? . . . 1 Cor 15:55
a sin that leads to *d* . . . 1 Jn 5:16
I hold the keys of *d* . . . Rev 1:18
faithful even when facing *d* . . . Rev 2:10
no more *d* or sorrow or . . . Rev 21:4
This is the second *d* . . . Rev 21:8

DEBT(ORS)(S) *what is owing; sense of obligation*
sold as a slave to pay the *d* . . . Exod 22:3
seventh year . . . cancel your *d* . . . Deut 15:1
d owed to us by other Jews . . . Neh 10:31
d of someone you hardly know . . . Prov 6:1
responsible for a neighbor's *d* . . . Prov 17:18
your *d* will rise up in anger . . . Hab 2:7
one of his *d* was brought in . . . Matt 18:24
forgave them both, canceling their *d* . . . Luke 7:42
except the *d* of love for others . . . Rom 13:8

DECEIT(FUL)(FULNESS) *fraud; trickery; lying*
with *d* by tricking you into . . . Num 25:18
a *d* and twisted generation . . . Deut 32:5
their hearts give birth only to *d* . . . Job 15:35
they say is crooked and *d* . . . Ps 36:3
The *d* walk a thorny, treacherous . . . Prov 22:5
planning our *d* lies . . . Isa 59:13
human heart is most *d* . . . Jer 17:9
d or impure purposes or trickery . . . 1 Thes 2:3
all malicious behavior and *d* . . . 1 Pet 2:1
They revel in *d* . . . 2 Pet 2:13

DECEIVE(D)(ER)(ERS)(S), DECEIVING *to lead astray*
Swear . . . you won't *d* me . . . Gen 21:23
he has *d* me twice . . . Gen 27:36
Dinah's brothers *d* Shechem . . . Gen 34:13
d me! You are Saul! . . . 1 Sam 28:12
so as to *d*, if possible . . . Matt 24:24
what that *d* once said . . . Matt 27:63
By smooth talk . . . they *d* . . . Rom 16:18
as Eve was *d* by the serpent . . . 2 Cor 11:3
d you with persuasive arguments . . . Col 2:4
who was *d* by Satan . . . 1 Tim 2:14
They will go on *d* others . . . 2 Tim 3:13
engage in useless talk and *d* . . . Titus 1:10
he never *d* anyone . . . 1 Pet 2:22
don't let anyone *d* you . . . 1 Jn 3:7
Many *d* have gone out into . . . 2 Jn 1:7

DEED(S) *feat or exploit*
recite all your wonderful *d* . . . Ps 40:5
her *d* publicly declare her praise . . . Prov 31:31
woman's *d* will be talked about . . . Matt 26:13
to do good *d* on the Sabbath . . . Mark 3:4
good *d* from a good heart . . . Luke 6:45
which one of these good *d* . . . John 10:32
acquittal is not based on our good *d* . . . Rom 3:27
good fruit, that is, good *d* for God . . . Rom 7:4
Get rid of your evil *d* . . . Rom 13:12
and all its wicked *d* . . . Col 3:9
faithful work, your loving *d* . . . 1 Thes 1:3

DEFILE(D)(MENT)(S) *to make unclean—either physically, sexually, ethically, or ceremonially*
his daughter had been *d* . . . Gen 34:5
with any source of human *d* . . . Lev 5:3
d the place that bears your holy . . . Ps 74:7
not *d* by what you eat . . . Matt 15:11
the thought-life that *d* you . . . Mark 7:20
because it would *d* them . . . John 18:28
that can *d* our body or spirit . . . 2 Cor 7:1
minds and consciences are *d* . . . Titus 1:15
cleanse . . . from ritual *d* . . . Heb 9:13

DELIGHT(ED)(FUL)(ING)(S) *source of great pleasure; to enjoy*
because he *d* in me . . . 2 Sam 22:20
But they *d* in doing . . . Ps 1:2
d in the LORD's perfections . . . Ps 27:4
Take *d* in the LORD . . . Ps 37:4
How *d* and how right! . . . Ps 147:1
corrects a child in whom he *d* . . . Prov 3:12
his constant *d*, rejoicing always . . . Prov 8:30
the City of God's *D* . . . Isa 62:4
your land will be such a *d* . . . Mal 3:12
d to see how happy Titus . . . 2 Cor 7:13

DELIVER(ANCE)(ED)(ER)(ING)(Y) *liberate or redeem from; turn over, give up to; give birth to*
After a very hard *d* . . . Gen 35:17
the time of Tamar's *d* . . . Gen 38:27
d me from my powerful enemies . . . Ps 18:17
eyes strain to see your *d* . . . Ps 119:123
my tower of safety, my *d* . . . Ps 144:2
but *d* us from the evil one . . . Matt 6:13
he *d* Jesus over to them . . . Luke 23:25
d from eternal punishment . . . Rom 5:10
to *d* your gift to Jerusalem . . . 1 Cor 16:3
did *d* us from mortal danger . . . 2 Cor 1:10
all turn out for my *d* . . . Phil 1:19

will *d* me from every evil . . . 2 Tim 4:18
who could *d* him out of death . . . Heb 5:7
promising much and *d* nothing . . . 2 Pet 2:17

DEMON(S) *agent of the Devil; an evil spirit*
possessed by *d,* or were epileptics . . . Matt 4:24
cast out *d* in your name . . . Matt 7:22
empowered by the prince of *d* . . . Matt 9:34
Jesus rebuked the *d* . . . Matt 17:18
the Devil and his *d* . . . Matt 25:41
he had cast out seven *d* . . . Mark 16:9
d threw the man to the floor . . . Luke 4:35
The *d* kept begging Jesus not to . . . Luke 8:31
using your name to cast out *d* . . . Luke 9:49
I have no *d* in me . . . John 8:49
sacrifices are offered to *d* . . . 1 Cor 10:20

DENIED, DENIES, DENY *disavow or refuse to accept as true*
if I grow rich, I may *d* you . . . Prov 30:9
if anyone *d* me here . . . Matt 10:33
you will *d* me three times . . . Matt 26:34
Paul *d* the charges . . . Acts 25:8
have *d* what we believe . . . 1 Tim 5:8
If we *d* him, he will *d* us . . . 2 Tim 2:12
d him by the way they live . . . Titus 1:16
d the Father and the Son . . . 1 Jn 2:22

DEPRAVED, DEPRAVITY *moral corruption; evil; perverted*
violence and *d* everywhere . . . Gen 6:12
d as what they did in Gibeah . . . Hos 9:9
Their minds are *d* . . . 2 Tim 3:8

DESCENDANT(S), DESCENDED *those who came or originated from; offspring, children*
covenant with you and your *d* . . . Gen 9:9
your *d* will be strangers . . . Gen 15:13
mercy on the *d* of Jacob . . . Isa 14:1
d from my friend Abraham . . . Isa 41:8
those who *d* there long ago . . . Ezek 26:20
we are *d* of Abraham . . . John 8:33
to Abraham and his *d* . . . Rom 4:13
The *d* of your older son . . . Rom 9:12
a Jew, a *d* of Abraham . . . Rom 11:1
d of Abraham? So am I . . . 2 Cor 11:22

DESECRATE(D), DESECRATION *to profane something holy or treat it with contempt*
permitting the Sabbath to be *d* . . . Neh 13:18
do not *d* the Sabbath day . . . Isa 56:6
sacrilegious object that causes *d* . . . Dan 9:27; 11:31; 12:11
d the tomb of Edom's king . . . Amos 2:1
sacrilegious object that causes *d* . . . Matt 24:15

DESIRABLE, DESIRE(D)(S) *to have a longing for; the object of that longing; to wish or request*
your *d* will be for your husband . . . Gen 3:16
Potiphar's wife began to *d* him . . . Gen 39:7
If . . . they *d* to do so, . . . Exod 35:21
brag about their evil *d* . . . Ps 10:3
are more *d* than gold . . . Ps 19:10
he will give you your heart's *d* . . . Ps 37:4
you *d* honesty from the heart . . . Ps 51:6
shameful things their hearts *d* . . . Rom 1:24
aroused all kinds of forbidden *d* . . . Rom 7:8
ways to indulge your evil *d* . . . Rom 13:14
d the most helpful gifts . . . 1 Cor 12:31
Spirit gives us *d* that are . . . Gal 5:17
I'm torn between two *d* . . . Phil 1:23
evil *d* lead to evil actions . . . Jas 1:15

DESOLATE(D) *deserted; joyless; alone; barren*
would be cursed and become *d* . . . 2 Kgs 22:19
its Sabbath rest, lying *d* for seventy . . . 2 Chr 36:21
the wastelands, *d* and gloomy . . . Job 30:3
May their homes become *d* . . . Ps 69:25
a *d* ruin, an object of horror . . . Jer 25:18
made me *d,* racked with sickness . . . Lam 1:13
Their farms were *d* . . . Ezek 19:7
cities will be empty and *d* for forty . . . Ezek 29:12
Jerusalem must lie *d* for seventy . . . Dan 9:2
This is a *d* place . . . Matt 14:15
house is . . . empty and *d* . . . Matt 23:38

DESOLATION(S) *sadness; devastation or ruin*
their *d* would last forever . . . Ps 81:15
your lot: *d* and destruction . . . Isa 51:19
d and destruction of war will end . . . Isa 60:18
mock and scorn you in your *d* . . . Ezek 23:32

DESPISE(D)(S) *scorn or regard as unworthy, sometimes with malice or outrage*
is pregnant, and she *d* me . . . Gen 16:5
I am insignificant and *d* . . . Ps 119:141
Shouldn't I *d* those who resist . . . Ps 139:21
fools *d* wisdom and discipline . . . Prov 1:7
It is sin to *d* one's neighbors . . . Prov 14:21
D though you are, O Israel . . . Isa 41:14
one who is *d* and rejected by . . . Isa 49:7
He was *d* and rejected . . . Isa 53:3
devoted to one and *d* the other . . . Matt 6:24
God chose things *d* by the . . . 1 Cor 1:28

DESTROY(ED)(ING)(S) *kill; cause devastation or ruin; the complete consecration of things or people to the* LORD, *either by annihilating them or by giving them as an offering*
I have decided to *d* all . . . Gen 6:13
d both innocent and guilty . . . Gen 18:23
whose people you completely *d* . . . Josh 2:10
The city . . . must be completely *d* . . . Josh 6:17
I have *d* all your enemies . . . 1 Chr 17:8
an angel to *d* Jerusalem . . . 1 Chr 21:15
can *d* much that is good . . . Eccl 9:18
Nothing will hurt or *d* in all . . . Isa 11:9
can *d* both soul and body . . . Matt 10:28
entire human race will be *d* . . . Mark 13:20
to save life or to *d* it? . . . Luke 6:9
and no moth can *d* it . . . Luke 12:33
D this temple, and in three . . . John 2:19
his sinful nature will be *d* . . . 1 Cor 5:5
Beware of *d* one another . . . Gal 5:15
the power to save or to *d* . . . Jas 4:12

DESTRUCTION *place of punishment (hell); see DESTROY*
You will laugh at *d* . . . Job 5:22
path of the wicked leads to *d* . . . Ps 1:6
down to the pit of *d* . . . Ps 55:23
only eternal *d* ahead . . . Ps 92:7
depths of Death and *D* . . . Prov 15:11
Pride goes before *d* . . . Prov 16:18
careful plans for their *d* . . . Lam 2:8
kept from complete *d* . . . Lam 3:22
Their future is eternal *d* . . . Phil 3:19
everlasting *d,* forever separated . . . 2 Thes 1:9

DEVIL *Satan; enemy of God and of everything good; destroyer, tempter, adversary*
to be tempted there by the *D* . . . Matt 4:1
eternal fire prepared for the *D* . . . Matt 25:41
twelve of you, but one is a *d* . . . John 6:70
children of your father the *D* . . . John 8:44
between Christ and the *D* . . . 2 Cor 6:15
strategies and tricks of the *D* . . . Eph 6:11
break the power of the *D* . . . Heb 2:14
Resist the *D,* and he will flee . . . Jas 4:7
Watch out for attacks from the *D* . . . 1 Pet 5:8

DEVOTED, DEVOTION *consecrated or dedicated*
crop will be *d* to the LORD . . . Lev 19:24
a *d* follower of the LORD . . . 1 Kgs 18:3
Protect me, for I am *d* to you . . . Ps 86:2
d myself to your commandments . . . Ps 119:45
I *d* myself to . . . understanding . . . Eccl 1:13
d to one and despise the other . . . Matt 6:24
d themselves to the apostles' teaching . . . Acts 2:42
can be more *d* to the Lord . . . 1 Cor 7:34
who serve with such real *d* . . . 1 Cor 16:16
right conduct, and *d* to God . . . Titus 2:12

DEVOUR(ED)(ING)(S) *to consume by eating; to destroy (as if by eating)*
d everything in sight, like an ox *d* . . . Num 22:4
God is a *d* fire, a jealous God . . . Deut 4:24
Disease eats their skin; death *d* . . . Job 18:13
wildfire will *d* his goods, consuming . . . Job 20:26
who greedily *d* human prey . . . Ps 57:4
Get up! *D* many people! . . . Dan 7:5
It *d* and crushed its victims . . . Dan 7:19
their false religion will *d* them . . . Hos 5:7
biting and *d* one another . . . Gal 5:15
looking for some victim to *d* . . . 1 Pet 5:8
ready to *d* the baby as soon as . . . Rev 12:4

DEVOUT *very religious*
a righteous man and very *d* . . . Luke 2:25
a *d* man who feared the God of . . . Acts 10:2
live a *d* and disciplined life . . . Titus 1:8

DISCERN(MENT) *discover; recognize*
get wisdom, discipline, and *d* . . . Prov 23:23
God's ways are as hard to *d* . . . Eccl 11:5
to *d* what is truly from God . . . 1 Cor 12:3

DISCIPLE(S) *student or follower of some doctrine or teacher*
When John's *d* had gone . . . Matt 11:7
their *d,* . . . supporters of Herod . . . Matt 22:16
said to the crowds and to his *d* . . . Matt 23:1
Come, be my *d* . . . Mark 1:17
John's *d* . . . fast, but your *d* . . . Mark 2:18
truly my *d* if you keep obeying . . . John 8:31
his *d,* but we are disciples of Moses . . . John 9:28
the *d* whom Jesus loved . . . John 21:7
Timothy, a young *d* whose . . . Acts 16:1

DISCIPLINE(D)(S) *to punish or correct with love; to exercise self-control*
and he hasn't *d* them . . . 1 Sam 3:13
God *d* . . . with sickness and pain . . . Job 33:19
get wisdom, *d,* and discernment . . . Prov 23:23
the Lord *d* those he loves . . . Heb 12:6

DISCOURAGE(D) *to deter or hinder; to deprive of courage; see COURAGE or ENCOURAGE*
Are you trying to *d* the rest . . . Num 32:7
Don't be afraid! Don't be *d* . . . Deut 1:21
Otherwise he may become so *d* . . . 2 Cor 2:7
who encourages those who are *d* . . . 2 Cor 7:6
Don't get *d* and give up . . . Gal 6:9
become *d* and quit trying . . . Col 3:21
d when he corrects you . . . Heb 12:5

DISCREET, DISCRETION *showing good judgment; prudent or modest in behavior, speech, and dress*
your *d* that people are made great . . . 1 Chr 29:12
be *d* and will store up knowledge . . . Prov 5:2
woman who . . . lacks *d* . . . Prov 11:22
D is a life-giving fountain . . . Prov 16:22
with wisdom and *d* . . . Dan 2:14

DISGUISE(D) *to mask the identity of; to use pretense or deception*
with a veil to *d* herself . . . Gen 38:14
Saul *d* himself by wearing . . . 1 Sam 28:8
d as harmless sheep . . . Matt 7:15
d himself as an angel . . . 2 Cor 11:14

DISHONOR(S) *to degrade or bring shame upon; see HONOR*
that would *d* his great name . . . 1 Sam 12:22
d my name with your actions . . . Mal 1:12
my Father—and you *d* me . . . John 8:49
to suffer *d* for the name of Jesus . . . Acts 5:41
you *d* God by breaking it . . . Rom 2:23
a woman *d* her husband if . . . 1 Cor 11:5

DISTRESS(ED) *to subject one to grief or misery; a troubling or painful situation*
destined by God to live in *d* . . . Job 3:23
They live in *d* and anguish . . . Job 15:24
I am alone and in deep *d* . . . Ps 25:16

I am weary from *d* . . . Ps 57:6
filled with anguish and deep *d* . . . Matt 26:37
Greatly *d*, one by one . . . Mark 14:19
Holy Spirit helps us in our *d* . . . Rom 8:26

DISTRIBUTE(D)(S), DISTRIBUT(ING)-(ION) *deal out or dispense in proportionate amounts*
d the land among the clans . . . Num 33:54
tenth of your harvest and *d* it . . . 1 Sam 8:15
d the freewill offerings of God . . . 2 Chr 31:14
disciples, who *d* the food . . . Matt 15:36
widows . . . in the daily *d* of food . . . Acts 6:1
men . . . chosen to *d* food . . . Acts 21:8
Holy Spirit who *d* these gifts . . . 1 Cor 12:11

DIVIDE(D)(S), DIVIDING *to separate into parts; partition; distribute; to make distinctions*
d into different language groups . . . Gen 10:25
in the evening he *d* the plunder . . . Gen 49:27
d the money between them . . . Exod 21:35
has *d* but unsplit hooves . . . Lev 11:26
the *d* of the land of Canaan . . . Num 34:29
when he *d* up the human race . . . Deut 32:8
he *d* the sea before them . . . Ps 78:13
A *d* home is also doomed . . . Luke 11:17
d our father's estate with me . . . Luke 12:13
d in their opinion about him . . . John 7:43
d in their opinion about them . . . Acts 14:4
Can Christ be *d* into pieces? . . . 1 Cor 1:13

DIVINATION, DIVINER(S) *predicting the future by inspiration or by special means and omens discernible to sorcerers and magicians (= diviners)*
I have learned by *d* that . . . Gen 30:27
so he did not resort to *d* . . . Num 24:1
judges, prophets, *d*, elders . . . Isa 3:2
call his magicians to use *d* . . . Ezek 21:21

DIVINE *holy; eternal*
filled Bezalel with a *d* spirit . . . Exod 35:31
The king speaks with *d* wisdom . . . Prov 16:10
people do not accept *d* guidance . . . Prov 29:18
full of words with no *d* authority . . . Jer 5:13
his eternal power and *d* nature . . . Rom 1:20
the *d* Yes—God's affirmation . . . 2 Cor 1:19
his *d* power gives us everything . . . 2 Pet 1:3

DIVISION(S) *act or process of dividing, separating, distributing; a portion, part, grouping or distinction; a military unit*
Lead . . . *d* by *d* . . . Exod 6:26
commander of the second *d* . . . 1 Chr 27:4
twenty-four thousand . . . in his *d* . . . 1 Chr 27:4
come to bring strife and *d* . . . Luke 12:51
cause *d* and upset people's faith . . . Rom 16:17
anger, selfish ambition, *d* . . . Gal 5:20
causing *d* among you . . . Titus 3:10

DIVORCE(D)(S) *to dissolve a marriage; to end a relationship*
not marry a widow, a *d* woman . . . Lev 21:14
he writes her a letter of *d* . . . Deut 24:1
I had *d* faithless Israel . . . Jer 3:8
For I hate *d* . . . Mal 2:16
anyone who marries a *d* woman . . . Matt 5:32
d his wife and marries another . . . Matt 19:9
letter of *d* and send her away . . . Mark 10:4

DOUBT(FUL)(LESS)(S) *to lack confidence in; matters of uncertainty*
d torn to pieces by some wild . . . Gen 44:28
Your lives will hang in *d* . . . Deut 28:66
Why did you *d* me? . . . Matt 14:31
but some of them still *d* . . . Matt 28:17
and do not *d* in your heart . . . Mark 11:23
you will know it beyond all *d* . . . Luke 17:24
Why do you *d* who I am? . . . Luke 24:38
d about whether they should eat . . . Rom 14:23
a *d* mind is as unsettled as . . . Jas 1:6

DROSS *waste matter (impurities) from refining metal ore*
Remove the *d* from silver . . . Prov 25:4
They are the *d* that is left over . . . Ezek 22:18
as the *d* is burned away . . . Mal 3:3

DRUNK(ARD)(ARDS), DRUNKEN(NESS) *one who drinks or indulges to excess; intoxicated; saturated*
Noah woke up from his *d* stupor . . . Gen 9:24
make my arrows *d* with blood . . . Deut 32:42
make the rulers of the nations *d* . . . Isa 16:8
Egypt to stagger like a sick *d* . . . Isa 19:14
The earth staggers like a *d* . . . Isa 24:20
pride and joy of the *d* of Israel . . . Isa 28:1
so confused that they will seem *d* . . . Jer 13:13
a *d*, like someone overcome by wine . . . Jer 23:9
reel like a *d* beneath the awful . . . Ezek 23:33
They're *d*, that's all! . . . Acts 2:13
in wild parties and getting *d* . . . Rom 13:13
or is abusive, or a *d* . . . 1 Cor 5:11
Let's feast and get *d* . . . 1 Cor 15:32
d, wild parties, and other . . . Gal 5:21
Don't be *d* with wine . . . Eph 5:18
feasting and *d* and wild . . . 1 Pet 4:3
d by the wine of her immorality . . . Rev 17:2

DUST *specks or clumps of earthy matter; ground or earth*
formed a man's body from the *d* . . . Gen 2:7
to the *d* you will return . . . Gen 3:19
like *d*, they cannot be counted! . . . Gen 13:16
Abram fell face down in the *d* . . . Gen 17:3
humanity would turn again to *d* . . . Job 34:15
in *d* and ashes to show my repentance . . . Job 42:6
a drop in the bucket, *d* on the scales . . . Isa 40:15
He has brought to *d* the kingdom . . . Lam 2:2
throw *d* on their heads in sorrow . . . Lam 2:10
shake off the *d* of that place . . . Matt 10:14
was made from the *d* of the earth . . . 1 Cor 15:47

DUTIES, DUTY *moral or legal obligation; assigned service or task*
priests and judges . . . on *d* . . . Deut 19:17
fulfill the *d* of a brother-in-law . . . Deut 25:5
the rights and *d* of a king . . . 1 Sam 10:25
have simply done our *d* . . . Luke 17:10
d as a worthy servant of Christ . . . 1 Tim 4:6

DWELL(ING)(S) *to stay for a time; to live as a resident*
God, whose *d* is holy . . . Ps 68:5
so they may *d* with me in safety . . . Ps 101:6
the ones who will *d* on high . . . Isa 33:16
d where God lives by his Spirit . . . Eph 2:22

EAR(S) *organ of hearing, expressing the entire faculty of understanding*
pierce his *e* with an awl . . . Exod 21:6
the *e* tests the words it hears . . . Job 12:11
Turn your *e* to listen . . . Ps 71:2
Close their *e*, and shut their . . . Isa 6:10
e are closed, and they cannot . . . Jer 6:10
What I whisper in your *e*, shout . . . Matt 10:27
their *e* cannot hear . . . Matt 13:15
slashed off the right *e* . . . John 18:10
closed their *e* so they . . . Rom 11:8
No eye has seen, no *e* has . . . 1 Cor 2:9
only an *e* and not an eye . . . 1 Cor 12:16

EARNEST(LY)(NESS) *ardent or fervent; zeal*
I *e* search for you . . . Ps 63:1
e I seek for God . . . Isa 26:9
my *e* prayer went out to you . . . Jon 2:7
wear sackcloth and pray *e* . . . Jon 3:8
worshiped the LORD in *e* . . . Hag 1:12
So they *e* begged Jesus . . . Luke 7:4
Such *e*, such concern to . . . 2 Cor 7:11
He always prays *e* for you . . . Col 4:12
e prayer of a righteous . . . Jas 5:16

EARTHLY *belonging to the earth; mundane or worldly; temporal or temporary; human*
I am not an *e* king . . . John 18:36
this *e* tent we live in . . . 2 Cor 5:1
I live my life in this *e* body . . . Gal 2:20
Slaves, obey your *e* masters . . . Eph 6:5
sinful, *e* things lurking within . . . Col 3:5
our *e* fathers who disciplined . . . Heb 12:9
Such things are *e*, unspiritual . . . Jas 3:15
not come from your *e* parents . . . 1 Pet 1:23

EASE(D), EASIER, EASY *rest or leisure; (to make) less difficult*
Even prisoners are at *e* in death . . . Job 3:18
their days of *e* are gone . . . Hos 10:11
e some of his discomfort . . . Jon 4:6
many who choose the *e* way . . . Matt 7:13
Is it *e* to say, 'Your sins . . . Matt 9:5
it is *e* for a camel . . . Matt 19:24
take it *e*! Eat, drink, and be merry! . . . Luke 12:19

ELDER(LY)(S) *older, wise man; ruling body of decision makers invested with authority by virtue of their age, character, or experience*
e people and . . . the aged . . . Lev 19:32
Inquire of your *e* . . . Deut 32:7
rulers and *e* and teachers . . . Acts 4:5
if someone wants to be an *e* . . . 1 Tim 3:1
E who do their work well . . . 1 Tim 5:17
appoint *e* in each town . . . Titus 1:5
call for the *e* of the church . . . Jas 5:14
letter is from John, the *E* . . . 2 Jn 1:1
twenty-four *e* sat on . . . Rev 4:4

ELECT(ION) *chosen or selected by God for a redemptive purpose; see CHOICE or CHOOSE*

ENCOURAGE(D)(MENT)(S) *strengthen or stimulate; to instill with courage*
e many a troubled soul . . . Job 4:3
that *e* me to carry on . . . Job 6:11
e each other to do evil . . . Ps 64:5
means "Son of *E*" . . . Acts 4:36
any word of *e* for us . . . Acts 13:15
he *e* the believers . . . Acts 20:2
If your gift is to *e* others . . . Rom 12:8
hope and *e* as we wait . . . Rom 15:4
will learn and be *e* . . . 1 Cor 14:31

END(S) *cessation, dissolution, death, or destruction; goal or result, toward which some action or agent is heading*
tell us when it will *e* . . . Ps 74:9
my covenant . . . will never *e* . . . Ps 89:28
We *e* our lives with a groan . . . Ps 90:9
drunkards . . . at their wits' *e* . . . Ps 107:27
even forever, to the very *e* . . . Ps 119:112
seems right, but it *e* in death . . . Prov 14:12
e up in the company of the dead . . . Prov 21:16
My righteous rule will never *e* . . . Isa 51:6
mourning will come to an *e* . . . Isa 60:20
until the time of the *e* . . . Dan 12:4
How will all this finally *e* . . . Dan 12:8
harvest is the *e* of the world . . . Matt 13:39
even to the *e* of the age . . . Matt 28:20
sickness will not *e* in death . . . John 11:4
do not *e* the marriage . . . 1 Cor 7:27
e of the world is coming soon . . . 1 Pet 4:7
Theirs will be a swift and terrible *e* . . . 2 Pet 2:1
Omega—the beginning and the *e* . . . Rev 1:8

ENDURANCE, ENDURE(D)(S), ENDURING *to withstand, suffer, or persevere*
You know the insults I *e* . . . Ps 69:19
as solid and *e* as the earth . . . Ps 78:69
His faithful love *e* forever . . . Ps 106:1
who *e* to the end will be . . . Matt 10:22
e through every circumstance . . . 1 Cor 13:7
Patient *e* is what you need . . . Heb 10:36
run with *e* the race . . . Heb 12:1
your *e* is fully developed . . . Jas 1:4
Job . . . who *e* patiently . . . Jas 5:11
e many trials for a while . . . 1 Pet 1:6
patiently *e* unfair treatment . . . 1 Pet 2:19

ENEMIES, ENEMY *foe—personal, national, or spiritual*
I have so many *e* . . . Ps 3:1

My *e* surround me like . . . Ps 22:12, 16
in the presence of my *e* . . . Ps 23:5
If your *e* are hungry . . . Prov 25:21
e is laying siege to Jerusalem . . . Mic 5:1
But I say, love your *e*! . . . Matt 5:44
e came and planted weeds . . . Matt 13:25
while we were still his *e* . . . Rom 5:10
e to be destroyed is death . . . 1 Cor 15:26
Have I now become your *e* . . . Gal 4:16
e of the cross of Christ . . . Phil 3:18
his *e*, separated from him . . . Col 1:21
e are humbled as a footstool . . . Heb 10:13
makes you an *e* of God? . . . Jas 4:4

ENJOY(ED)(ING)(MENT) *delight in; participate in*
What good fellowship we *e* . . . Ps 55:14
e food and drink and to find . . . Eccl 2:24
e your work and accept your lot . . . Eccl 5:19
E prosperity while you can . . . Eccl 7:14
e together the promise of blessings . . . Eph 3:6
e the evil they do . . . 2 Thes 2:12
all we need for our *e* . . . 1 Tim 6:17
e the fleeting pleasures of sin . . . Heb 11:25
e the eternal life he promised . . . 1 Jn 2:25

ENLIGHTENED *shed light upon*
you have *e* my stupidity! . . . Job 26:3
those who were once *e* . . . Heb 6:4

ENVIOUS, ENVIED, ENVY *discontent or resentment because of another's success, advantages, or superiority*
Don't *e* those who do wrong . . . Ps 37:1
For I *e* the proud . . . Ps 73:3
jealous of Moses and *e* of Aaron . . . Ps 106:16
Do not *e* violent people . . . Prov 3:31
had arrested Jesus out of *e* . . . Matt 27:18
lustful pleasure, *e*, slander . . . Mark 7:22
sin, greed, hate, *e*, murder . . . Rom 1:29
e, drunkenness, wild parties . . . Gal 5:21
lives were full of evil and *e* . . . Titus 3:3

ESTABLISH(ED)(ES) *to make firm or stable; to prove*
will *e* you as his holy people . . . Deut 28:9
but he *e* and exalts them . . . Job 36:7
authorities are *e* by God . . . Rom 13:4
every case must be *e* . . . 2 Cor 13:1
the first covenant in order to *e* . . . Heb 10:9

ESTEEM(ED) *to value or appreciate*
may he be *e* by his brothers . . . Deut 33:24
earn *e* by overlooking wrongs . . . Prov 19:11
being held in high *e* is better . . . Prov 22:1

ETERNAL *perpetual; true at all times; characterized by abiding fellowship with God*
evidence of my *e* covenant . . . Gen 9:12
the LORD, the *E* God . . . Gen 21:33
The *e* God is your refuge . . . Deut 33:27
endowed him with *e* blessings . . . Ps 21:6
lives forever from *e* ages past . . . Ps 41:13
only *e* destruction ahead . . . Ps 92:7
must I do to have *e* life? . . . Matt 19:16
e fire prepared for the Devil . . . Matt 25:41
salvation that gives *e* life . . . Mark 16:8
believes in me will have *e* life . . . John 3:15
perpetual spring . . . *e* life . . . John 4:14
done good will rise to *e* life . . . John 5:29
e life to everyone who eats it . . . John 6:50
the Spirit who gives *e* life . . . John 6:63
the words that give *e* life . . . John 6:68
to have *e* life—to know you . . . John 17:3
gift of God is *e* life . . . Rom 6:23
Their future is *e* destruction . . . Phil 3:19
e King, . . . who never dies . . . 1 Tim 1:17
he is the one who is *e* life . . . 1 Jn 1:2

EUNUCH(S) *male attendant, often castrated, implying singular devotion to a master*
e who will serve in the palace . . . Isa 39:7
my blessings are also for the *e* . . . Isa 56:3
Some are born as *e* . . . Matt 19:12
treasurer of Ethiopia, a *e* . . . Acts 8:27

EVANGELIST(S) *preacher of the gospel*
home of Philip the *E* . . . Acts 21:8
apostles, the prophets, the *e* . . . Eph 4:11

EVERLASTING *perpetual or enduring through all time; see ETERNAL*
this *e* covenant between us . . . Gen 17:7
Canaan . . . as an *e* possession . . . Gen 48:4
Mighty God, *E* Father . . . Isa 9:6
name I give them is an *e* . . . Isa 56:5
God will be your *e* light . . . Isa 60:19
and make an *e* covenant . . . Isa 61:8
lives forever. His rule is *e* . . . Dan 4:34
bring in *e* righteousness . . . Dan 9:24
punished with *e* destruction . . . 2 Thes 1:9
e comfort and good hope . . . 2 Thes 2:16
e life through the Good News . . . 2 Tim 1:10
e gloom and darkness . . . Jude 1:13
Give to him *e* glory! . . . Rev 1:6

EVIL *bad, sinful, or morally reprehensible; of the Devil; something that brings sorrow, distress, or misfortune*
knowledge of good and *e* . . . Gen 2:9
consistently and totally *e* . . . Gen 6:5
pay us back for all the *e* . . . Gen 50:15
Israelites did what was *e* . . . Judg 2:11
done *e*, and acted wickedly . . . 1 Kgs 8:47
Solomon did what was *e* . . . 1 Kgs 11:6
Turn back from *e* . . . Job 36:21
The wicked conceive *e* . . . Ps 7:14
keeps you from all *e* . . . Ps 121:7
rescue me from *e* people . . . Ps 140:1
will save you from *e* people . . . Prov 2:12
e people cover up their harmful . . . Prov 10:6, 11
my people have done two *e* things: . . . Jer 2:13
keep quiet, for it is an *e* time . . . Amos 5:13
deliver us from the *e* one . . . Matt 6:13
authority to cast out *e* spirits . . . Matt 10:1
Jesus knew their *e* motives . . . Matt 22:18
for their actions were *e* . . . John 3:19
safe from the *e* one . . . John 17:15
abandoned them to their *e* minds . . . Rom 1:28
that the law of God is *e* . . . Rom 7:7
Never pay back *e* for *e* . . . Rom 12:17
deliver me from every *e* attack . . . 2 Tim 4:18
must not speak *e* of anyone . . . Titus 3:2

EXALT(ED)(ING)(S) *to elevate; to glorify; to raise in rank or power*
God, and I will *e* him! . . . Exod 15:2
rock of my salvation, be *e* . . . 2 Sam 22:47
LORD *e* Solomon . . . 1 Chr 29:25
establishes and *e* them with kings . . . Job 36:7
let us *e* his name together . . . Ps 34:3
you are *e* far above all gods . . . Ps 97:9
prize wisdom, she will *e* you . . . Prov 4:8
will rejoice when I am *e* . . . Isa 13:3
he will be highly *e* . . . Isa 52:13
now the lowly are *e* . . . Ezek 21:26
do as he pleases, *e* himself . . . Dan 11:36
will you be *e* to heaven? . . . Matt 11:23
who humble themselves will be *e* . . . Matt 23:12
e himself and defy every god . . . 2 Thes 2:4
why Christ did not *e* himself . . . Heb 5:5

EXAMPLE(S) *object lesson or warning; same sort, copy, or type*
but don't follow their *e* . . . Matt 23:3
only one *e*. There are many . . . Mark 7:13
would follow his good *e* . . . John 8:39
I have given you an *e* . . . John 13:15
happened to them as *e* . . . 1 Cor 10:11
to give you an *e* to follow . . . 2 Thes 3:9
e of patience in suffering . . . Jas 5:10
your *e*. Follow in his steps . . . 1 Pet 2:21
lead them by your good *e* . . . 1 Pet 5:3
the *e* of Cain . . . Jude 1:11

EXCUSE(D)(S) *to overlook, justify, or make an apology for; the apology or justification offered*
they all began making *e* . . . Luke 14:18
so he asked to be *e* . . . Luke 14:18
have no *e* for their sin . . . John 15:22
no *e* whatsoever for not . . . Rom 1:20
who try to *e* these sins . . . Eph 5:6
no *e* for being disrespectful . . . 1 Tim 6:2

EXECUTE(D)(S) *to inflict or complete (usually judgment); to put to death*
the offender must be *e* . . . Exod 21:23
two groups to be *e* for . . . 2 Sam 8:2
e him for murdering . . . 2 Sam 14:7
e vengeance on the nations . . . Ps 149:7
I will *e* terrible vengeance . . . Ezek 25:17
e all the wise men of Babylon . . . Dan 2:12
Romans are permitted to *e* . . . John 18:31

EXHORT(ED)(ING)(S), EXHORTATION(S) *to excite by argument; urge to good deeds; preach(ing); see ENCOURAGE*

EXPECT(ANTLY)(ATION)(ATIONS)(ED) *to consider probable or certain; hope; assurance*
e me to be the next king . . . 1 Kgs 2:15
e us to leave the city . . . 2 Kgs 7:12
my requests to you and wait *e* . . . Ps 5:3
panting *e*, longing for your . . . Ps 119:131
e of the wicked are all in vain . . . Prov 10:28
wild grapes when I *e* sweet . . . Isa 5:4
things beyond our highest *e* . . . Isa 64:3
Do you really *e* him to listen? . . . Mic 3:4
he eagerly *e* the Messiah . . . Luke 2:25
the Messiah we've been *e* . . . Luke 7:19
will come when least *e* . . . Luke 12:40
confident *e* of salvation . . . Rom 5:4
we *e* far greater glory when . . . 2 Cor 3:8
not *e* to receive anything . . . Jas 1:7
we live with a wonderful *e* . . . 1 Pet 1:3

EYE(S) *organ of (physical and spiritual) sight; also expressing a range of emotions from sorrow and gladness to greed, lust, and understanding*
e will be opened when you eat . . . Gen 3:5
If an *e* is injured . . . Exod 21:24
innocent in the *e* of God? . . . Job 9:2
I will see him with my own *e* . . . Job 19:27
I have seen you with my own *e* . . . Job 42:5
Guard me as the apple of your *e* . . . Ps 17:8
e of the LORD watch over . . . Ps 34:15
my *e* to see the wonderful . . . Ps 119:18
my *e* are not haughty . . . Ps 131:1
may be pure in their own *e* . . . Prov 16:2
Ears to hear and *e* to see . . . Prov 20:12
Your *e* are soft like doves . . . Song 1:15
their ears, and shut their *e* . . . Isa 6:10
have *e* but do not see . . . Jer 5:21
they were covered with *e* . . . Ezek 1:18
the *e* of the LORD . . . Zech 4:10
with lust in his *e* . . . Matt 5:28
e is a lamp for your body . . . Matt 6:22
a speck in your friend's *e* . . . Matt 7:3
Then he touched their *e* . . . Matt 9:29
blessed are your *e*, because . . . Matt 13:16
if your *e* causes you to sin . . . Matt 18:9
the *e* of a needle . . . Luke 18:25
mud over the blind man's *e* . . . John 9:6
shut their *e* so they do not see . . . Rom 11:8
No *e* has seen . . . 1 Cor 2:9
the whole body were an *e* . . . 1 Cor 12:17
in the blinking of an *e* . . . 1 Cor 15:52
taken out your own *e* . . . Gal 4:15
saw him with our own *e* . . . 1 Jn 1:1
e are bright like flames . . . Rev 2:18

FACE *surface; countenance; presence; with perfect clarity or harmony (= "face to face"); to confront*
from the *f* of the earth! . . . Gen 6:13
lovely *f* and shapely figure . . . Gen 29:17
meeting him *f* to *f* . . . Gen 32:20
I have seen God *f* to *f* . . . Gen 32:30
In . . . anger I turned my *f* . . . Isa 54:8
his *f* shone like the sun . . . Matt 17:2
spit in Jesus' *f* and hit him . . . Matt 26:67
His *f* shone like lightning . . . Matt 28:3

never . . . seen him *f* to *f* . . . John 5:37
I *f* death daily . . . 1 Cor 15:31
his *f* shone with the glory . . . 2 Cor 3:7
seen in the *f* of Jesus Christ . . . 2 Cor 4:6
the third had a human *f* . . . Rev 4:7
And they will see his *f* . . . Rev 22:4

FAIL(ED)(ING)(S), FAILURE(S) *fall short; fade away; disappear; disappoint; exception*
reminded of my *f* . . . Gen 41:9
There were crop *f* . . . Gen 41:54
his father was *f* rapidly . . . Gen 48:1
not *f* you or abandon you . . . Josh 1:5
Israelites *f* to drive out the . . . Josh 13:13
He will not *f* you or forsake . . . 1 Chr 28:20
God of Hezekiah will also *f* . . . 2 Chr 32:17
without *f*, provide them with . . . Ezra 6:9
"If you *f* to keep your promise . . . Neh 5:13
bearing fruit each season without *f* . . . Ps 1:3
when my strength is *f* . . . Ps 71:9
he ended their lives in *f* . . . Ps 78:33
Jesus' disciples *f* to follow . . . Mark 7:2
that your faith should not *f* . . . Luke 22:32
it means you have *f* the test . . . 2 Cor 13:5
you might *f* to get there . . . Heb 4:1

FAINT(ED) *to become weak in body and spirit; to lose heart, strength, or courage*
I *f* with longing to enter . . . Ps 84:2
I *f* with longing for your . . . Ps 119:81
I grow *f* when I hear what God . . . Isa 21:3
They will walk and not *f* . . . Isa 40:31
I *f* and lay there . . . Dan 8:18; 10:9
men will grow *f* and weary . . . Amos 8:13
he grew *f* and wished to die . . . Jon 4:8

FAITH *reliance, loyalty, or complete trust in God; a system of religious beliefs*
righteous because of his *f* . . . Gen 15:6
tested Abraham's *f* and obedience . . . Gen 22:1
righteous will live by their *f* . . . Hab 2:4
You have so little *f* . . . Matt 6:30
I haven't seen *f* like this . . . Matt 8:10
if you have *f* and don't doubt . . . Matt 21:21
Do you still not have *f* . . . Mark 4:40
Your *f* has saved you . . . Luke 7:50
We need more *f* . . . Luke 17:5
F in Jesus' name has caused . . . Acts 3:16
convert to the Jewish *f* . . . Acts 6:5
to continue in the *f* . . . Acts 14:22
right with God through *f* . . . Rom 3:28
f, not because of their work . . . Rom 4:5
if we have *f* like Abraham's . . . Rom 4:16
f comes from listening . . . Rom 10:17
Christians who are weak in *f* . . . Rom 14:1
Spirit gives special *f* . . . 1 Cor 12:9
if your *f* is really genuine . . . 2 Cor 13:5
now that *f* in Christ has come . . . Gal 3:25
f expressing itself in love . . . Gal 5:6
There is only one Lord, one *f* . . . Eph 4:5
will need *f* as your shield . . . Eph 6:16
your *f* was still strong . . . 1 Thes 3:5
clear conscience, and sincere *f* . . . 1 Tim 1:5
wandered from the *f* . . . 1 Tim 6:10
to please God without *f* . . . Heb 11:6
when your *f* is tested . . . Jas 1:3
I will show you my *f* . . . Jas 2:18
f given to us by Jesus Christ . . . 2 Pet 1:1
those whose *f* is wavering . . . Jude 1:22

FAITHFUL(LY)(NESS) *firm in adherence, utterly loyal; those who practice faith; see FAITH*
serve me *f* and live . . . Gen 17:1
conditions to test their *f* . . . Exod 15:25
obey his commands, be *f* . . . Josh 22:5
f with all their heart . . . 1 Kgs 2:4
he had proved himself *f* . . . Neh 9:8
The *f* have vanished from . . . Ps 12:1
To the *f* you show yourself *f* . . . Ps 18:25
for you are a *f* God . . . Ps 31:5
I have talked about your *f* . . . Ps 40:10
are *f* to your promises . . . Ps 71:22
F is your very character . . . Ps 89:8
find one who is really *f* . . . Prov 20:6
Great is his *f* . . . Lam 3:23
f and honest and always . . . Dan 6:4
I will be *f* to you . . . Hos 2:20
your *f* and unfailing love . . . Mic 7:20
Jerusalem . . . the *F* City . . . Zech 8:3
a *f*, sensible servant . . . Matt 24:45
you are *f* in small matters . . . Luke 16:10
a manager must be *f* . . . 1 Cor 4:2
And God is *f* . . . 1 Cor 10:13
God, who calls you, is *f* . . . 1 Thes 5:24
your endurance and *f* . . . 2 Thes 1:4
He must be *f* to his wife . . . 1 Tim 3:2
are unfaithful, he remains *f* . . . 2 Tim 2:13
and *f* High Priest . . . Heb 2:17
if we are *f* to the end . . . Heb 3:14
f and just to forgive us . . . 1 Jn 1:9
f even when facing death . . . Rev 2:10
was named *F* and True . . . Rev 19:11

FAITHLESS(NESS) *disloyal; those who abandon the faith or violate a covenant; see FAITH*
turned back and were as *f* as . . . Ps 78:57
your idolatry and *f* . . . Hos 14:4
Nineveh, the beautiful and *f* city . . . Nah 3:4
f to each other, violating . . . Mal 2:10
an evil, *f* generation . . . Matt 12:39
You stubborn, *f* people . . . Luke 9:41

FALL(EN)(ING)(S) *drop down (wounded or dead); descend; lower; fade; collapse; occur by happenstance; occur suddenly or passively; stumble or stray (morally); decline from grace (backslide); the act or event of destruction*
Adam to *f* into a deep sleep . . . Gen 2:21
and haughtiness before a *f* . . . Prov 16:18
LORD determines how they *f* . . . Prov 16:33
your enemies *f* into trouble . . . Prov 24:17
If one person *f* . . . Eccl 4:10
clean as freshly *f* snow . . . Isa 1:18
a rock that makes them *f* . . . Isa 8:14
you are *f* from heaven . . . Isa 14:12
Babylon is *f* . . . Isa 21:9
their wall will soon *f* down . . . Ezek 13:11
tremble at the sound of your *f* . . . Ezek 26:15
After that kingdom has *f* . . . Dan 2:39
it will *f* with a mighty crash . . . Matt 7:27
can *f* to the ground without . . . Matt 10:29
they will both *f* into a ditch . . . Matt 15:14
stars will *f* from the sky . . . Matt 24:29
I saw Satan *f* from . . . Luke 10:18
f on the Sabbath . . . John 7:23
so that you won't *f* away . . . John 16:1
which should rise and *f* . . . Acts 17:26
may *f* into the same sin . . . 1 Cor 10:12
f away from God's grace . . . Gal 5:4
I *f* to my knees and pray . . . Eph 3:14
use that pride to make him *f* . . . 1 Tim 3:6
who disobeys God . . . will *f* . . . Heb 4:11
f into the hands of . . . God . . . Heb 10:31
will not stumble and *f* . . . Heb 12:13
Babylon is *f* . . . Rev 14:8

FALSE(HOOD)(LY) *dishonest; intentionally untrue; misleading; unwise; faithless*
Do not testify *f* . . . Exod 20:16
to swear a *f* . . . Lev 19:12
he knows those who are *f* . . . Job 11:11
I hate every *f* way of life . . . Ps 119:104
a *f* witness tells lies . . . Prov 12:17
exposes the *f* prophets as liars . . . Isa 44:25
stop making *f* accusations . . . Isa 58:9
they will not be *f* again . . . Isa 63:8
foolish things, *f* to the core . . . Lam 2:14
f prophets who come disguised . . . Matt 7:15
f messiahs and *f* prophets . . . Matt 24:24
f apostles. They have fooled . . . 2 Cor 11:13
—*f* ones, really . . . Gal 2:4
So put away all *f* . . . Eph 4:25
f teachers among you . . . 2 Pet 2:1
the beast and his false *f* . . . Rev 19:20

FAMILIES, FAMILY *a household unit of related people, as in a clan*
f of Shem, Ham, and . . . Gen 10:1
All the *f* of the earth . . . Gen 12:3
by their clans and *f* . . . Num 1:2
God of all the *f* of Israel . . . Jer 31:1
all you men of the royal *f* . . . Hos 5:1
will mourn, along with the *f* . . . Zech 12:12

FAMINE(S) *extreme scarcity of food*
a severe *f* in the land . . . Gen 12:10
death in time of *f* . . . Job 5:20
only war, *f*, and disease . . . Jer 14:12
who are destined for *f*, to *f* . . . Jer 15:2
not a *f* of bread or water . . . Amos 8:11
will be *f* and earthquakes . . . Matt 24:7
f swept over the land . . . Luke 15:14
sword and *f* and disease . . . Rev 6:8

FAST(ED)(ING)(S) *to abstain from food*
When I weep and *f* before . . . Ps 69:10
the kind of *f* I want . . . Isa 58:6
mourn and *f* each summer . . . Zech 7:3
The traditional *f* and times . . . Zech 8:19
when you *f*, don't . . . Matt 6:16
but your disciples don't *f* . . . Matt 9:14
were feasting instead of *f* . . . Luke 5:33

FAT(TENED)(TENING) *plump or well filled out; prosperous or fertile; animal grease*
seven *f*, healthy-looking cows . . . Gen 41:2
live off the *f* of the land . . . Gen 45:18
take the *f* of the ram . . . Exod 29:22
the *f* belongs to the LORD . . . Lev 3:16
soon became *f* and unruly; . . . Deut 32:15
oxen, *f* calves, and sheep . . . 1 Kgs 1:19
These *f* cats have everything . . . Ps 73:7
mercenaries . . . like *f* calves . . . Jer 46:21
killed the calf we were *f* . . . Luke 15:27
your hearts are nice and *f* . . . Jas 5:5

FATHER(ED)(S) *male parent; ancestor(s); characteristic of a mentor or provider relationship; name and role for God in relation to the children he fosters/adopts; originator or creator*
why a man leaves his *f* . . . Gen 2:24
f of not just one nation . . . Gen 17:4
the Rock who had *f* you . . . Deut 32:18
replacing his *f*, David . . . 1 Kgs 2:12
My *f*! My *f*! . . . 2 Kgs 2:12
When her *f* and mother . . . Esth 2:7
I was a *f* to the poor . . . Job 29:16
Does the rain have a *f* . . . Job 38:28
Today I have become your *F* . . . Ps 2:7
You are my *F*, my God . . . Ps 89:26
like a *f* to his children . . . Ps 103:13
as a *f* corrects a child . . . Prov 3:12
If you curse your *f* . . . Prov 20:20
Mighty God, Everlasting *F* . . . Isa 9:6
a *f* to the people of Jerusalem . . . Isa 22:21
Surely you are still our *F* . . . Isa 63:16
they say, 'You are my *f*' . . . Jer 2:27
F, you have been my guide . . . Jer 3:4
For I am Israel's *f* . . . Jer 31:9
all children of the same *F* . . . Mal 2:10
as true children of your *F* . . . Matt 5:45
Our *F* in heaven . . . Matt 6:9
f will betray their own . . . Matt 10:21
no one really knows the *F* . . . Matt 11:27
God says, 'Honor your *f* . . . Matt 15:4
on earth as '*F*,' for only God . . . Matt 23:9
division between *f* and son . . . Luke 12:53
spoken of God as his *F* . . . John 5:18
We know his *f* and mother . . . John 6:42
Where is your *f* . . . John 8:19
Our *f* is Abraham . . . John 8:39
children of your *f* the Devil . . . John 8:44
The *F* and I are one . . . John 10:30
to the *F* except through me . . . John 14:6
Abraham is the spiritual *f* of . . . Rom 4:11
calling him "*F*, dear *F*" . . . Rom 8:15
only one God and *F* . . . Eph 4:6
Today I have become your *F* . . . Heb 1:5

FATHERLESS *without a father; orphaned*
Father to the *f*, defender . . . Ps 68:5
May his children become *f* . . . Ps 109:9
rob widows and *f* children! . . . Isa 10:2
We are orphaned and *f* . . . Lam 5:3

FAULT(S) *lack or error; moral weakness less serious than a vice*
Abram, "It's all your *f* . . . Gen 16:5
for something that isn't our *f* . . . Exod 5:16
It's his own *f* . . . Job 19:28
me from these hidden *f* . . . Ps 19:12
wearied me with your *f* . . . Isa 43:24
will be holy and without *f* . . . Eph 5:27
was never accused of any *f* . . . Phil 3:6
allowance for each other's *f* . . . Col 3:13
Then no one can find *f* . . . 1 Tim 6:14

FAVOR(ABLY)(ED)(ITES)(S) *kindness; approval; partiality; friendly regard from a superior; to endow with spiritual blessing or special grace*
caused the Egyptians to look *f* . . . Exod 11:3
slant your testimony in *f* . . . Exod 23:3
seek the *f* of the Almighty . . . Job 8:5
I won't play *f* . . . Job 32:21
have judged in my *f* . . . Ps 9:4
his *f* lasts a lifetime! . . . Ps 30:5
f with both God and people . . . Prov 3:4
f refreshes like a gentle rain . . . Prov 16:15
Greetings, *f* woman! . . . Luke 1:28
to all whom God *f* . . . Luke 2:14
placed his special *f* upon him . . . Luke 2:40
time of the Lord's *f* has come . . . Luke 4:19
God's great *f* was upon them . . . Acts 4:33

FEAR(ED)(FUL)(ING)(S) *to have reverential awe of God; to have a tender conscience; dread or alarm in facing danger; timidity*
you truly *f* God . . . Gen 22:12
because the midwives *f* God . . . Exod 1:17
f that the earth would . . . Num 16:34
tremble with dread and *f* . . . Deut 2:25
hearts have melted in *f* . . . Josh 2:11
Israelites were paralyzed with *f* . . . Josh 7:5
f and worship the LORD . . . 1 Sam 12:14
with depression and *f* . . . 1 Sam 16:14
all the nations to *f* David . . . 1 Chr 14:17
a faithful man who *f* God more . . . Neh 7:2
Yes, Job *f* God, but . . . Job 1:9
my heart will know no *f* . . . Ps 27:3
freeing me from all my *f* . . . Ps 34:4
They have no *f* of God . . . Ps 36:1
those who *f* the LORD . . . Ps 112:1
F of the LORD is . . . Prov 1:7
it means to *f* the LORD . . . Prov 2:5
F people is a dangerous trap . . . Prov 29:25
F God and obey his commands . . . Eccl 12:13
Do not *f* anything except . . . Isa 8:13
f of the LORD is the key . . . Isa 33:6
F not, Jacob, my servant . . . Jer 46:28
who *f* him and loved to . . . Mal 3:16
F only God, who can . . . Matt 10:28
Great *f* swept the crowd . . . Luke 7:16
I *f* neither God nor man . . . Luke 18:4
falter because of the *f* fate . . . Luke 21:26
f gripped the entire church . . . Acts 5:11
walking in the *f* of the Lord . . . Acts 9:31
he accepts those who *f* him . . . Acts 10:35
obey . . . with deep respect and *f* . . . Eph 6:5
have a proper *f* of God . . . 1 Tim 5:20
with holy *f* and awe . . . Heb 12:28
live in reverent *f* of him . . . 1 Pet 1:17
perfect love expels all *f* . . . 1 Jn 4:18

FEAST(ED)(ING)(S) *to enjoy a good meal; banquet*
set a great *f* before them . . . Gen 19:3
they have *f* on prey . . . Num 23:24
f in the presence of . . . Deut 12:7
the *f*, when King Xerxes was . . . Esth 1:10
celebrate these days with *f* . . . Esth 9:22
I, the Son of Man, *f* and . . . Luke 7:34
invited to a wedding *f* . . . Luke 14:8
celebrate the Passover *f* . . . John 18:28
the wedding *f* of the Lamb . . . Rev 19:7

FELLOW *man of lower social class; companion or comrade; associate equal in rank or role*
his *f* tax collectors and . . . Matt 9:10
a *f* servant who owed . . . Matt 18:28
f Jews and residents . . . Acts 2:14
worthless *f* from the streets . . . Acts 17:5
such a *f*! Kill him! . . . Acts 22:22
Timothy, my *f* worker . . . Rom 16:21
a *f* soldier of the cross . . . Phlm 1:2
As a *f* elder . . . 1 Pet 5:1

FELLOWSHIP *friendship; association; company; partnership*
What good *f* we enjoyed . . . Ps 55:14
apostles' teaching and *f* . . . Acts 2:42
I have enjoyed your *f* . . . Rom 15:24
f of the Holy Spirit . . . 2 Cor 13:13
f together in the Spirit? . . . Phil 2:1
if we say we have *f* . . . 1 Jn 1:6
f with both the Father . . . 2 Jn 1:9
join you in *f* meals . . . Jude 1:12

FIGHT(ING)(S) *to actively oppose or combat, as with weapons; to gain by struggle; militarily trained or equipped*
there was a *f* over it . . . Gen 26:21
saw two Hebrew men *f* . . . Exod 2:13
LORD himself will *f* . . . Exod 14:14
When you go out to *f* . . . Deut 20:1
If two Israelite men are *f* . . . Deut 25:11
has the courage to *f* . . . Josh 2:11
thirty thousand *f* men . . . Josh 8:3
uniting to *f* against Israel . . . Josh 11:4
your God *f* for you . . . Josh 23:10
f against our relatives from . . . Judg 20:23
f against the LORD . . . 1 Sam 2:10
Choose someone to *f* for you . . . 1 Sam 17:8
The *f* grew very fierce . . . 1 Sam 31:3
our God will *f* for us! . . . Neh 4:20
if Satan is *f* against himself . . . Mark 3:26
find yourselves *f* against God . . . Acts 5:39
hate, envy, murder, *f* . . . Rom 1:29
This law wins the *f* . . . Rom 7:23
in *f* wild beasts . . . 1 Cor 15:32
f well in the Lord's battles . . . 1 Tim 1:18
F the good *f* for . . . 1 Tim 6:12
I have fought a good *f* . . . 2 Tim 4:7
the quarrels and *f* . . . Jas 4:1

FIND(S), FOUND *to attain or reach (a goal or conclusion); to discover by study or experiment; to experience*
Suppose you *f* fifty innocent . . . Gen 18:24
what the land is like and *f* . . . Num 13:18
your sin will *f* you out . . . Num 32:23
If only I knew where to *f* God . . . Job 23:3
know where to *f* wisdom? . . . Job 28:12
I *f* joy in your commands . . . Ps 119:143
they will not *f* me . . . Prov 1:28
whoever *f* me *f* life . . . Prov 8:35
who *f* a wife *f* a treasure . . . Prov 18:22
I couldn't *f* him anywhere . . . Song 5:6
seek the LORD while you can *f* him . . . Isa 55:6
justice is nowhere to be *f* . . . Isa 59:14
when you *f* him, come . . . Matt 2:8
Everyone who seeks, *f* . . . Matt 7:8
only a few ever *f* it . . . Matt 7:14
will *f* a baby lying . . . Luke 2:12
lost, but now he is *f* . . . Luke 15:24
would *f* the way of peace . . . Luke 19:42
I *f* nothing wrong with . . . Luke 23:4
We have *f* the Messiah . . . John 1:41
the world would never *f* him . . . 1 Cor 1:21
Then no one can *f* fault . . . 1 Tim 6:14
we will *f* grace to help us . . . Heb 4:16

FINISH(ED)(ING) *bring to completion; completed or perfected*
F what they started . . . Matt 23:32
out of money before it was *f* . . . Luke 14:30
and from *f* his work . . . John 4:34
It is *f* . . . John 19:30
As John was *f* his ministry . . . Acts 13:25
I have *f* the race . . . 2 Tim 4:7
until we *f* the race . . . Heb 11:40

FIRE(S) *hot flame and burning light; fiery ordeal; enthusiasm; destructive force; symbolic of hell*
rained down *f* and burning . . . Gen 19:24
as a blazing *f* in a bush . . . Exod 3:2
who answers by setting *f* . . . 1 Kgs 18:24
LORD was not in the *f* . . . 1 Kgs 19:12
The *f* of God has fallen . . . Job 1:16
tested me like gold in a *f* . . . Job 23:10
went through *f* and flood . . . Ps 66:12
F goes forth before him . . . Ps 97:3
Love flashes like *f* . . . Song 8:6
Holy One, will be a flaming *f* . . . Isa 10:17
walk through the *f* of oppression . . . Isa 43:2
LORD is coming with *f* . . . Isa 66:15
burn like an unquenchable *f* . . . Jer 4:4
It's like a *f* in my bones! . . . Jer 20:9
He has sent *f* from heaven . . . Lam 1:13
f has consumed the pastures . . . Joel 1:19
I will send down *f* on . . . Amos 1:4ff
a blazing *f* that refines metal . . . Mal 3:2
Holy Spirit and with *f* . . . Matt 3:11
unquenchable *f* of hell . . . Mark 9:43
I have come to bring *f* . . . Luke 12:49
flames or tongues of *f* . . . Acts 2:3
f, bringing judgment on . . . 2 Thes 1:8
God is a consuming *f* . . . Heb 12:29
tongue is a flame of *f* . . . Jas 3:6
warning of the eternal *f* . . . Jude 1:7
alive into the lake of *f* . . . Rev 19:20

FIRST *highest; earliest; most prominent; preference before something else*
people *f* began to worship . . . Gen 4:26
believe the *f* miraculous sign . . . Exod 4:8
I am the *F* and the Last . . . Isa 44:6
Elijah is indeed coming *f* . . . Matt 17:11
many who are *f* now . . . Matt 20:16
f and greatest commandment . . . Matt 22:38
whoever wants to be *f* must . . . Mark 10:44
must *f* be preached to every . . . Mark 13:10
Jews *f* and also Gentiles . . . Rom 1:16
the *f* woman came from man . . . 1 Cor 11:8
The *f* man, Adam . . . 1 Cor 15:45
so he is *f* in everything . . . Col 1:18
a result of his loving us *f* . . . 1 Jn 4:19
I am the *F* and the Last . . . Rev 1:17
is the *f* resurrection . . . Rev 20:5

FIRSTBORN *eldest; the most prominent; the rightful heir*
selling all his rights as the *f* . . . Gen 25:33
Israel is my *f* son . . . Exod 4:22
the *f* sons will die . . . Exod 11:5
Dedicate to me all the *f* . . . Exod 13:1
money for the *f* sons . . . Num 3:49
At the cost of his *f* son . . . Josh 6:26
his Son would be the *f* . . . Rom 8:29

FIRSTFRUITS *first brought forth; special offering; see OFFERING*

FLATTER(ING)(Y) *to praise excessively out of self-interest*
play favorites or try to *f* . . . Job 32:21
Their speech is filled with *f* . . . Ps 5:9
f lips and insincere hearts . . . Ps 12:2
f of the adulterous woman . . . Prov 2:16
and *f* causes ruin . . . Prov 26:28
take over the kingdom by *f* . . . Dan 11:21
to win you with *f* . . . 1 Thes 2:5
f others to get favors . . . Jude 1:16

FLESH *the meaty part of animal and human bodies; the mortal and weaker or carnal aspect of human nature (the "body" as opposed to the spirit or soul)*
part of my own *f* and bone! . . . Gen 2:23
they are only mortal *f* . . . Gen 6:3

the *f* of his foreskin . . . Gen 17:11
My *f* breaks open . . . Job 7:5
The *f* of your godly ones . . . Ps 79:2
puny *f*, not mighty spirits! . . . Isa 31:3
my skin and *f* grow old . . . Lam 3:4
this bread is my *f* . . . John 6:51
different kinds of *f* . . . 1 Cor 15:39
given a thorn in my *f* . . . 2 Cor 12:7
people made of *f* and blood . . . Eph 6:12
appeared in the *f* . . . 1 Tim 3:16
her *f*, and burn her remains . . . Rev 17:16

FLOURISH(ES)(ING) *grow luxuriantly, prosper, thrive*
f where there is no water? . . . Job 8:11
May all the godly *f* . . . Ps 72:7
it blooms and *f* . . . Ps 90:6
the wicked *f* like weeds . . . Ps 92:7
sons *f* in their youth . . . Ps 144:12
godly *f* like leaves in spring . . . Prov 11:28
your faith is *f* . . . 2 Thes 1:3

FOLLOW(ED)(ERS)(ING)(S) *to pursue or run after; to cling or overtake; to imitate; strive for; attend to*
looked back as she was *f* . . . Gen 19:26
I *f* the LORD . . . Josh 14:8
They immediately *f* him . . . Matt 4:22
because you are my *f* . . . Matt 5:11
I will *f* you no matter . . . Matt 8:19
Matthew got up and *f* him . . . Matt 9:9
but don't *f* their example . . . Matt 23:3
f by a huge crowd . . . Mark 3:7
f the usual Jewish ritual . . . Mark 7:2
your cross, and *f* me . . . Mark 8:34
given up everything to *f* . . . Mark 10:28
Peter *f* far behind . . . Mark 14:54
had been *f* of Jesus . . . Mark 15:41
would *f* his good example . . . John 8:39
They won't *f* a stranger . . . John 10:5
my disciples must come and *f* . . . John 12:26
As *f* of Moses . . . 1 Cor 10:2
give you an example to *f* . . . 2 Thes 3:9
your example. *F* in his steps . . . 1 Pet 2:21
f the beast in awe . . . Rev 13:3
f the Lamb wherever . . . Rev 14:4

FOLLY *lack of good sense; foolishness; wicked or lewd behavior, often with tragic consequences*
charged some of them with *f* . . . Job 4:18
lost because of his incredible *f* . . . Prov 5:23
The woman named *F* . . . Prov 9:13
but fools broadcast their *f* . . . Prov 12:23
confront a fool caught in *f* . . . Prov 17:12

FOOD(S) *something that nourishes, sustains, or supplies energy and vitality*
the fruit trees for your *f* . . . Gen 1:29
you will sweat to produce *f* . . . Gen 3:19
I have given them to you for *f* . . . Gen 9:3
f gave him enough strength . . . 1 Kgs 19:8
she invited him to eat some *f* . . . 2 Kgs 4:8
Use this *f* to make bread . . . Ezek 4:9
daily ration of the best *f* . . . Dan 1:5
f to eat, but not enough to fill . . . Hag 1:6
enough *f* in my Temple . . . Mal 3:10
Give us our *f* for today . . . Matt 6:11
f out here in the wilderness . . . Matt 15:33
worried about having no *f*? . . . Matt 16:8
If you have *f*, share it . . . Luke 3:11
the daily distribution of *f* . . . Acts 6:1
eating *f* offered to idols . . . Acts 15:29
who won't eat certain *f* . . . Rom 14:3
milk and not with solid *f* . . . 1 Cor 3:2
F is for the stomach . . . 1 Cor 6:13
their conscience by eating *f* . . . 1 Cor 8:10
ate the same miraculous *f* . . . 1 Cor 10:3
and cannot eat solid *f* . . . Heb 5:12
old system deals only with *f* . . . Heb 9:10
who needs *f* or clothing . . . Jas 2:15

FOOL(ED)(ING)(S) *one deficient in intellectual, practical, or moral sense; to trick or deceive*
He won't be *f* that easily . . . Gen 27:11
resentment destroys the *f* . . . Job 5:2
f him as easily as you *f* people? . . . Job 13:9
f, outcasts of civilization . . . Job 30:8
You have spoken like a *f* . . . Job 35:16
Only *f* say in their hearts . . . Ps 14:1
were *f* in their rebellion . . . Ps 107:17
f despise wisdom and discipline . . . Prov 1:7
f idle away their time . . . Prov 12:11
F make fun of guilt . . . Prov 14:9
f spend whatever they get . . . Prov 21:20
God takes no pleasure in *f* . . . Eccl 5:4
to *f* with your trick questions? . . . Matt 22:18
they became utter *f* instead . . . Rom 1:22
you will have to become a *f* . . . 1 Cor 3:18
I am acting like a *f* . . . 2 Cor 11:17
you are only *f* yourself . . . Gal 6:3
Don't be *f* by what . . . 2 Thes 2:3
no sin, we are only *f* . . . 1 Jn 1:8

FOOLISH(LY)(NESS) *irreverent, aimless behavior befitting a fool; see FOOL*
isn't right to speak so *f* . . . Job 15:3
God, you know how *f* I am . . . Ps 69:5
so *f* and ignorant . . . Ps 73:22
a *f* child brings grief . . . Prov 10:1
fools spout only *f* . . . Prov 15:2
"*f*" plan of God . . . 1 Cor 1:25
Oh, *f* Galatians! . . . Gal 3:1
Avoid godless, *f* discussions . . . 2 Tim 2:16

FOREIGN(ER)(ERS) *nonresident, alien, or sojourner; pagan*
a stranger in a *f* land . . . Gen 23:4
a stranger in a *f* land . . . Exod 2:22
f and citizens alike . . . Josh 8:33
I am only a *f* . . . Ruth 2:10
when *f* hear of you . . . 2 Chr 6:32
also removed the *f* gods . . . 2 Chr 33:15
They tax the *f* . . . Matt 17:26
Does only this *f* return . . . Luke 17:18
He's pushing some *f* religion . . . Acts 17:18
no longer strangers and *f* . . . Eph 2:19

FORGET(S)(TING), FORGETFULNESS, FORGOT(TEN) *to slip from remembrance; to disregard intentionally; to cease from doing*
f all about Joseph . . . Gen 40:23
God has made me *f* . . . Gen 41:51
not to *f* the LORD . . . Deut 6:12
you *f* the God who . . . Deut 32:18
fate of all who *f* God . . . Job 8:13
how long will you *f* me? . . . Ps 13:1
Has God *f* to be kind? . . . Ps 77:9
They *f* about his power . . . Ps 78:42
I am *f*, cut off . . . Ps 88:5
f the good things he does . . . Ps 103:2
f your commandments . . . Ps 119:141
If I *f* you, O Jerusalem . . . Ps 137:5
My child, never *f* . . . Prov 3:1
both will be *f* . . . Eccl 2:16
cause you to *f* your Creator . . . Eccl 12:1
I will not *f* to help you . . . Isa 44:21
the Lord has *f* us . . . Isa 49:14
you have *f* the LORD . . . Isa 51:13
has not *f* his promise . . . Luke 1:54
completely *f* about justice . . . Luke 11:42
God does not *f* a single . . . Luke 12:6
I don't want you to *f* . . . 1 Cor 10:1
F the past and looking . . . Phil 3:13
never *f* the warning: . . . Heb 3:15
f what you look like . . . Jas 1:24

FORGIVE(N)(NESS)(S) *to pardon or acquit of sins; acquittal; new lease on life*
LORD will *f* her . . . Num 30:5, 8, 12
hear from heaven and *f* . . . 2 Chr 6:25, 27
would not *f* my iniquity . . . Job 10:14
F the rebellious sins . . . Ps 25:7
whose rebellion is *f* . . . Ps 32:1
good, so ready to *f* . . . Ps 86:5
But you offer *f* . . . Ps 130:4
you have not *f* us . . . Lam 3:42
as we have *f* those who . . . Matt 6:12
how often should I *f* . . . Matt 18:21
poured out to *f* the sins . . . Matt 26:28
Who but God can *f* sins! . . . Mark 2:7
first *f* anyone you are . . . Mark 11:25
f anyone's sins, they are *f* . . . John 20:23
sins *f* through his name . . . Acts 10:43
they may receive *f* . . . Acts 26:18
God's generous gift of *f* . . . Rom 5:15
you *f* this man, I *f* him . . . 2 Cor 2:10
there is no *f* of sins . . . Heb 9:22
faithful and just to *f* . . . 1 Jn 1:9

FORM(ED)(ING)(S) *to create, fashion, or give shape to something; the structure, shape, pattern, or appearance of something*
God *f* a man's body from . . . Gen 2:7
a *f* before my eyes . . . Job 4:16
You *f* me with your hands . . . Job 10:8
so the fruit cannot *f* . . . Job 15:33
I, too, was *f* from clay . . . Job 33:6
You *f* the mountains by . . . Ps 65:6
being *f* in utter seclusion . . . Ps 139:15
f me from the beginning . . . Prov 8:22
compared to an idol *f* in a mold . . . Isa 40:19
f me in my mother's womb . . . Isa 49:5
We are all *f* by your hand . . . Isa 64:8
f you in your mother's womb . . . Jer 1:5
f alliances with each . . . Dan 2:43
messages . . . in the *f* of visions . . . Mic 1:1
cannot allow sin in any *f* . . . Hab 1:13
Spirit . . . in the *f* of a dove . . . Luke 3:22
and appeared in human *f* . . . Phil 2:7
living beings had the *f* of a lion . . . Rev 4:7

FORNICATION, FORNICATOR(S) *illicit intercourse (outside wedlock); see IMMORAL*

FORSAKE(N), FORSAKING *to quit, abandon, leave behind, cease from*
doing evil and *f* me . . . Deut 28:20
to *f* evil is real understanding . . . Job 28:28
Why have you *f* me? . . . Ps 22:1
never seen the godly *f* . . . Ps 37:25
if his sons *f* my law . . . Ps 89:30
if they confess and *f* . . . Prov 28:13
the City No Longer *F* . . . Isa 62:12
They have *f* me . . . Jer 2:13
they have *f* the LORD . . . Jer 17:13
Why have you *f* us for so . . . Lam 5:20
God, why have you *f* me? . . . Matt 27:46
I will never *f* you . . . Heb 13:5

FORTUNE-TELLER(S) *one who professes to foretell future events*
consult with sorcerers and *f* . . . Deut 18:14
f and used sorcery . . . 2 Kgs 17:17
enchanters, magicians, or *f* . . . Dan 2:27
end to all witchcraft . . . *f* . . . Mic 5:12
f predict only lies . . . Zech 10:2

FOUND *see FIND*

FOUNDATION(S) *the ground; substructure; basis upon which something is built, supported, or added to*
f for his empire . . . Gen 10:10
f of the mountains . . . Deut 32:22
he will lay its *f* . . . Josh 6:26
f of the heavens shook . . . 2 Sam 22:8
laid the *f* of the Temple . . . Ezra 5:16
Their *f* is dust . . . Job 4:19
f of their lives were . . . Job 22:16
f of law and order . . . Ps 11:3
f of his throne . . . Ps 97:2
f of true wisdom . . . Ps 111:10
the *f* of the world . . . Matt 25:34
house without a *f* . . . Luke 6:49
might complete only the *f* . . . Luke 14:29
can lay any other *f* . . . 1 Cor 3:11
the *f* of the apostles . . . Eph 2:20
a city with eternal *f* . . . Heb 11:10
place you on a firm *f* . . . 1 Pet 5:10
f of your holy faith . . . Jude 1:20
city had twelve *f* stones . . . Rev 21:14

FOUNTAIN(S) *source; spring of water*
a fruitful tree beside a *f* . . . Gen 49:22
you are the *f* of life . . . Ps 36:9
deep *f* of the earth . . . Prov 3:20
wife be a *f* of blessing . . . Prov 5:18
Discretion is a life-giving *f* . . . Prov 16:22
polluting a *f* or muddying a spring . . . Prov 25:26
me—the *f* of living water . . . Jer 2:13

FREE(D)(LY), FREEDOM *voluntary or uncoerced; without restraint or inhibition; gratis or without cost; possessing the rights of citizenship*
You may *f* eat any . . . Gen 2:16
won't be *f* again until you . . . Matt 5:26
Give as *f* as you have received! . . . Matt 10:8
will be *f* from their oppressors . . . Luke 4:18
the truth will set you *f* . . . John 8:32
you are *f* by God's grace . . . Rom 6:14
Who will *f* me from this life . . . Rom 7:24
things God has *f* given us . . . 1 Cor 2:12
f from the concerns of this life . . . 1 Cor 7:32
should my *f* be limited . . . 1 Cor 10:29
our *f* in Christ Jesus . . . Gal 2:4
slave or *f*, male or female . . . Gal 3:28
God has purchased our *f* . . . Col 1:14
f from the evil powers . . . Col 2:20
f from the penalty of the sins . . . Heb 9:15

FRIEND(LY)(S)(SHIP) *intimate associate; association of familiarity and companionship*
he will be *f* to us . . . Gen 32:20
as a man speaks to his *f* . . . Exod 33:11
of your *f* Abraham . . . 2 Chr 20:7
as a person mediates between *f* . . . Job 16:21
my *f* have turned against . . . Job 19:13
the *f* of God was felt . . . Job 29:4
F with the LORD . . . Ps 25:14
his *f* to the godly . . . Prov 3:32
separates the best of *f* . . . Prov 16:28
A *f* is always loyal . . . Prov 17:17
a real *f* sticks closer than . . . Prov 18:24
a *f* of the worst sort of sinners! . . . Matt 11:19
My *f*, go ahead and do . . . Matt 26:50
he won't do it as a *f* . . . Luke 11:8
their lives for their *f* . . . John 15:13
called "the *f* of God." . . . Jas 2:23
f with this world . . . Jas 4:4

FRUITFUL(NESS) *bearing fruit (product of a tree or plant); abundant (at producing work or in bearing children)*
God has made me *f* . . . Gen 41:52
Joseph is a *f* tree . . . Gen 49:22
like *f* gardens by the riverside . . . Num 24:6
He turns the *f* land into . . . Ps 107:34
wife will be like a *f* vine . . . Ps 128:3
and tend its *f* vines . . . Isa 27:3
Ephraim was the most *f* . . . Hos 13:15
pruned for greater *f* . . . John 15:3
f service for Christ . . . Phil 1:22

FULFILL(ED)(ING)(MENT) *to complete or perform as promised; to measure up or satisfy*
I have *f* my contract . . . Gen 29:21
let her *f* the vow or pledge . . . Num 30:5
to *f* the covenant he made . . . Deut 8:18
all Samuel's signs were *f* . . . 1 Sam 10:9
f Jeremiah's prophecy by . . . Ezra 1:1
Cyrus to *f* my righteous purpose . . . Isa 45:13
for the *f* of his promises . . . Isa 62:6
I will *f* all my vows . . . Jon 2:9
when the vision will be *f* . . . Hab 2:3
No, I came to *f* them . . . Matt 5:17
in *f* of his promises . . . Luke 1:2
the Scriptures will be *f* . . . Luke 21:22
f in the Kingdom . . . Luke 22:16
f the prophecy that said . . . John 12:14
f all the requirements of . . . Rom 13:8
promises have been *f* in him . . . 2 Cor 1:20
f all your good intentions . . . 2 Thes 1:11
mysterious plan will be *f* . . . Rev 10:7

FULLNESS *containing all that is wanted, needed, or possible*
gifts of the earth and its *f* . . . Deut 33:16
to give life in all its *f* . . . John 10:10
the *f* of life and power . . . Eph 3:19
For God in all his *f* . . . Col 1:19
in Christ the *f* of God lives . . . Col 2:9
the *f* of your salvation . . . 1 Pet 2:2

FURY *wrath; fierceness; rage; see ANGER*
until your brother's *f* is spent . . . Gen 27:44
day of his *f* and fierce anger . . . Isa 13:9
In my *f* I have trampled my foes . . . Isa 63:3
His *f* is poured out like fire . . . Lam 2:4
Soon I will pour out my *f* . . . Ezek 7:8
Who can survive his burning *f* . . . Nah 1:6
trampled the nations in your *f* . . . Hab 3:12
Act now, before the fierce *f* . . . Zeph 2:2

GAIN(ED) *to win; to derive profit or advantage from; winnings or profits*
if you *g* the whole world . . . Matt 16:26
Felix wanted to *g* favor . . . Acts 24:27
the priceless *g* of knowing Christ . . . Phil 3:8
I myself have *g* much joy . . . Phlm 1:7
win many battles and *g* the victory . . . Rev 6:2

GARDEN(ER)(S) *a planted area where fruits, vegetables, and flowers are cultivated*
God planted a *g* in Eden . . . Gen 2:8
I made *g* and parks . . . Eccl 2:5
You are like a private *g* . . . Song 4:12
Eden, the *g* of God . . . Ezek 28:13
my Father is the *g* . . . John 15:1
She thought he was the *g* . . . John 20:15

GATE(S)(WAY) *opening in a (city) wall, consisting of a door, protected by a series of barriers and flanked towers; the place of judicial decisions, town criers, marketplace trade*
house of God—the *g* to heaven! . . . Gen 28:17
fortified cities with . . . barred *g* . . . Deut 3:5
walls and installing barred *g* . . . 2 Chr 8:5
and the *g* have been burned . . . Neh 1:3
dedicated . . . the *g*, and the wall . . . Neh 12:30
He stood outside the *g* . . . Esth 4:2
g of death . . . . *g* of utter gloom? . . . Job 38:17
Open up, ancient *g*! . . . Ps 24:7
Enter his *g* with thanksgiving . . . Ps 100:4
g and walls of shining gems . . . Isa 54:12
The city *g* are silent . . . Lam 1:4
g to life is small . . . Matt 7:14
rather than going through the *g* . . . John 10:1
he was put beside the Temple *g* . . . Acts 3:2
died outside the city *g* . . . Heb 13:12
twelve *g* guarded by twelve angels . . . Rev 21:12

GATHER(ED)(ING)(S) *to bring together; to reap or harvest; to assemble*
waters beneath the sky be *g* . . . Gen 1:9
g you back from all the nations . . . Deut 30:3
A mob *g* against me . . . Job 16:10
a time to *g* stones . . . Eccl 3:5
I will *g* you and your children . . . Isa 43:5
So I will *g* all nations . . . Isa 66:18
as the crowds were *g* . . . Matt 5:1
where two or three *g* together . . . Matt 18:20
g your children together as a hen . . . Matt 23:37
g crops you didn't cultivate . . . Matt 25:24
be *g* together to meet him . . . 2 Thes 2:1

GAVE, GIVE(N)(S), GIVING *to grant, bestow, convey, offer, provide, or designate; to yield or produce; to suffer the loss of life*
g them to you for food . . . Gen 9:3
the Almighty *g* me life . . . Job 33:4
have *g* him his heart's desire . . . Ps 21:2
I might as well *g* up and die . . . Ps 28:1
will *g* you your heart's desires . . . Ps 37:4
I will *g* it all to you . . . Matt 4:9
will be *g* what you ask for . . . Matt 7:7
We've *g* up everything . . . Matt 19:27
g my life as a ransom for many . . . Matt 20:28
who use well what they are *g* . . . Matt 25:29
g your Father great happiness to *g* . . . Luke 12:32
so loved the world that he *g* . . . John 3:16
the Spirit, who would be *g* . . . John 7:39
My purpose is to *g* life . . . John 10:10
I have *g* you an example . . . John 13:15
I *g* myself entirely to you . . . John 17:19
I'll *g* you what I have . . . Acts 3:6
more blessed to *g* than to . . . Acts 20:35
God, who *g* us Christ, also *g* . . . Rom 8:32
have that God hasn't *g* you? . . . 1 Cor 4:7
who loved me and *g* himself . . . Gal 2:20
g us everything he promised . . . Eph 1:14
g generously to others in need . . . Eph 4:28
God, who richly *g* us all we need . . . 1 Tim 6:17
God has *g* gifts to each . . . 1 Pet 4:10

GENERATION(S) *the whole body of individuals born about the same time (= nation or racial group); the period of time during which those individuals lived (also, age or era); offspring*
covenant between us, *g* after *g* . . . Gen 17:7
so the next *g* might know . . . Ps 78:6
G come and go, but . . . Eccl 1:4
forever, from *g* to *g* . . . Isa 34:17
The *g* born in exile . . . Isa 49:20
fourteen *g* from Abraham . . . Matt 1:17
describe this *g*? . . . Matt 11:16
an evil, faithless *g* . . . Matt 12:39
this *g* will not pass . . . Matt 24:34
g after *g* will call me blessed . . . Luke 1:48
g that has gone astray! . . . Acts 2:40
seven *g* after Adam . . . Jude 1:14

GENTILE(S) *non-Jewish nations, often connoting heathens or pagans*
the *G* . . . will be filled with glory . . . Isa 9:1
you a light to the *G* . . . Isa 49:6
my blessings are for *G*, too . . . Isa 56:3
Galilee where so many *G* live . . . Matt 4:15
to the *G* or the Samaritans . . . Matt 10:5
age of the *G* comes to an end . . . Luke 21:24
a *G* convert to the Jewish faith . . . Acts 6:5
G nations that God drove out . . . Acts 7:45
take my message to the *G* . . . Acts 9:15
poured out upon the *G*, too . . . Acts 10:45
devout *G* who fear the God . . . Acts 13:16
Jews first and also *G* . . . Rom 1:16
Before you *G* knew God . . . Gal 4:8
you *G* used to be outsiders by birth . . . Eph 2:11
Jew or a *G*, . . . uncircumcised . . . Col 3:11

GENTLE(NESS) *kind, mild-mannered*
I am humble and *g* . . . Matt 11:29
I come with quiet love and *g*? . . . 1 Cor 4:21
g, and self-control . . . Gal 5:23
Be humble and *g* . . . Eph 4:2
g among you as a mother . . . 1 Thes 2:7
He must be *g*, peace loving . . . 1 Tim 3:3
It is also peace loving, *g* . . . Jas 3:17
beauty of a *g* and quiet spirit . . . 1 Pet 3:4

GIFT(S) *a present from people to people (often a bribe); a sacrifice from people to God; anything given voluntarily or at no cost; that which is given from God, enabling or empowering his people*
You received *g* from the people . . . Ps 68:18
Children are a *g* from the LORD . . . Ps 127:3
Giving a *g* works wonders . . . Prov 18:16
these are *g* from God . . . Eccl 3:13
his good *g* in the last days . . . Hos 3:5
When you give a *g* to someone . . . Matt 6:2
know how to give good *g* . . . Luke 11:13
knew the *g* God has for you . . . John 4:10
everything I have is a *g* . . . John 17:7
free *g* of God is eternal life . . . Rom 6:23
God has given his *g* to you . . . Rom 11:28
God gives some the *g* of marriage . . . 1 Cor 7:7
different kinds of spiritual *g* . . . 1 Cor 12:4

special abilities, . . . the *g* of prophecy . . . 1 Cor 14:1
privilege of sharing in the *g* . . . 2 Cor 8:4
it is a *g* from God . . . Eph 2:8
gave these *g* to the church . . . Eph 4:11
I want a *g* from you . . . Phil 4:17
not neglect the spiritual *g* . . . 1 Tim 4:14
fan into flames the spiritual *g* . . . 2 Tim 1:6
He presents their *g* to God . . . Heb 5:1
great variety of spiritual *g* . . . 1 Pet 4:10

GLAD(LY)(NESS) *joyful or happy, often with shouts*
be filled with joy and *g* . . . Ps 40:16
be *g* in God's presence . . . Ps 68:3
Worship the LORD with *g* . . . Ps 100:2
We will rejoice and be *g* in it . . . Ps 118:24
Joy and *g* will be found . . . Isa 51:3
will have great joy and *g* . . . Luke 1:14
you *g* honor each other . . . John 5:44
listens *g* to the words of God . . . John 8:47
heard this, they were very *g* . . . Acts 13:48
kindness to others, do it *g* . . . Rom 12:8
all the parts are *g* . . . 1 Cor 12:26

GLORIFIED, GLORIFY(ING) *to bestow honor or praise (as in worship); to magnify; see GLORY*
I will be *g* before all . . . Lev 10:3
g his mighty works, singing . . . Job 36:24
g and honor the King . . . Dan 4:37
I have no wish to *g* myself . . . John 8:50
G your Son so he can . . . John 17:1
then God will be *g* . . . Rom 15:7
g God through your generous . . . 2 Cor 9:13
fear, O Lord, and *g* your name? . . . Rev 15:4

GLORIOUS *possessing or deserving special honor; splendid or magnificent; see GLORY*
God's voice is *g* in the thunder . . . Job 37:5
You are so *g*, so majestic! . . . Ps 45:3
You are their *g* strength . . . Ps 89:17
meditate on your majestic, *g* . . . Ps 145:5
have offended his *g* presence . . . Isa 3:8
I . . . have made you *g* . . . Isa 55:5
I will make my Temple *g* . . . Isa 60:7
fall short of God's *g* standard . . . Rom 3:23
more *g* is the new covenant . . . 2 Cor 3:9
our *g* power is from God . . . 2 Cor 4:7
g church without a spot . . . Eph 5:27
change them into *g* bodies . . . Phil 3:21

GLORY *honor bestowed; splendor or magnificence; a distinguishing quality, asset or attribute; eternity; to boast or take credit for*
g at the expense of Pharaoh . . . Exod 14:4
was filled with the awesome *g* . . . Exod 40:35
give *g* . . . by telling the truth . . . Josh 7:19
Israel's *g* is gone . . . 1 Sam 4:21
crowned us with *g* and honor . . . Ps 8:5
heavens tell of the *g* of God . . . Ps 19:1
Who is the King of *g*? . . . Ps 24:8
gazed upon your power and *g* . . . Ps 63:2
Gray hair is a crown of *g* . . . Prov 16:31
earth is filled with his *g*! . . . Isa 6:3
kings . . . lie in stately *g* . . . Isa 14:8
his *g*, the splendor of our God . . . Isa 35:2
You will *g* in the Holy One . . . Isa 41:16
pride and false *g* of Israel . . . Amos 6:8
the nations . . . all their *g* . . . Matt 4:8
Solomon in all his *g* . . . Matt 6:29
will come in the *g* . . . Matt 16:27
G to God in the highest . . . Luke 2:14
seen his *g*, the *g* of the only Son . . . John 1:14
Jesus' first display of his *g* . . . John 2:11
No, it is for the *g* of God . . . John 11:4
so they are my *g*! . . . John 17:10
brought *g* to his servant Jesus . . . Acts 3:13
heaven and saw the *g* of God . . . Acts 7:55
instead of giving the *g* to God . . . Acts 12:23
he lives for the *g* of God . . . Rom 6:10
the *g* he will give us later . . . Rom 8:18
do all for the *g* of God . . . 1 Cor 10:31
you will share in all his *g* . . . Col 3:4
Son reflects God's own *g* . . . Heb 1:3
bring his many children into *g* . . . Heb 2:10
wonderful joy of sharing his *g* . . . 1 Pet 4:13
all *g* to God, who is able . . . Jude 1:24
worthy . . . to receive *g* and honor . . . Rev 4:11

GNASH(ES)(ING) *grinding or shivering of teeth, possibly from utter despair or extreme cold; expression of (God's) anger*
He *g* his teeth at me . . . Job 16:9
weeping and *g* of teeth . . . Matt 8:12
weeping and *g* of teeth . . . Matt 13:42
g of teeth, for you will see . . . Luke 13:28

GOD *eternal, infinite Spirit; Creator, Redeemer, sovereign Lord*
In the beginning *G* created . . . Gen 1:1
a priest of *G* Most High . . . Gen 14:18
And I will be their *G* . . . Gen 17:8
your *G*, am a jealous *G* . . . Exod 20:5
G is a devouring fire . . . Deut 4:24
If the LORD is *G* . . . 1 Kgs 18:21
G is an awesome *G*, greater than . . . 2 Chr 2:5
"*G* is not a mortal like me . . . Job 9:32
My *G*, my *G*! Why have you . . . Ps 22:1
G is our refuge and strength . . . Ps 46:1
Our *G* is a *G* who saves! . . . Ps 68:20
You are the *G* of miracles . . . Ps 77:14
So merciful, this *G* of ours! . . . Ps 116:5
Mighty *G*, Everlasting Father . . . Isa 9:6
Your *G* is coming! . . . Isa 40:9
Holy One of Israel, the *G* of all . . . Isa 54:5
a *G* in heaven who reveals . . . Dan 2:28
(meaning, *G* is with us) . . . Matt 1:23
I rejoice in *G* my Savior! . . . Luke 1:47
was with *G*, and he was *G* . . . John 1:1
For *G* so loved the . . . John 3:16
G is Spirit . . . John 4:24
mere man, have made yourself *G* . . . John 10:33
My Lord and my *G* . . . John 20:28
To an Unknown *G* . . . Acts 17:23
the world is a liar, *G* is true . . . Rom 3:4
If *G* is for us, who can . . . Rom 8:31
But *G* is so rich in mercy . . . Eph 2:4
Though he was *G*, he did not . . . Phil 2:6
know *G*—for *G* is love . . . 1 Jn 4:8
No one has ever seen *G* . . . 1 Jn 4:12
G himself will be with them . . . Rev 21:3

GOD(S) *impotent pagan deity; image of pagan deity (made of wood, metal, or stone)*
Do not worship any other *g* . . . Exod 20:3
make us some *g* who can . . . Exod 32:1
God is the God of *g* and . . . Deut 10:17
If you . . . serve other *g* . . . Josh 24:20
the *g* of Aram, Sidon, Moab . . . Judg 10:6
g of any other nations ever . . . 2 Kgs 18:33
any *g* as mighty as you? . . . Ps 77:13
You are *g* and children . . . Ps 82:6
make his own *g*—an idol . . . Isa 44:10
Do not be afraid of such *g* . . . Jer 10:5
It is the voice of a *g* . . . Acts 12:22
These men are *g* in . . . Acts 14:11
Satan, the *g* of this evil world . . . 2 Cor 4:4
were slaves to so-called *g* . . . Gal 4:8

GODDESS *female version of a pagan deity; see GOD(S)*
Solomon worshiped Ashtoreth, the *g* . . . 1 Kgs 11:5
Ashtoreth, the detestable *g* . . . 2 Kgs 23:13
shrines of the Greek *g* Artemis . . . Acts 19:24

GODLINESS, GODLY *devotion to God; worthy of God; people who are righteous*
have no place among the *g* . . . Ps 1:5
has set apart the *g* for . . . Ps 4:3
the *g* will flourish like . . . Ps 92:12
the *g* . . . who do right . . . Ps 97:11
g people from righteous Abel to . . . Matt 23:35
at the resurrection of the *g* . . . Luke 14:14
live . . . in *g* and dignity . . . 1 Tim 2:2
show *g* at home . . . 1 Tim 5:4
Pursue a *g* life . . . 1 Tim 6:11
power that could make them *g* . . . 2 Tim 3:5
Your *g* lives will speak . . . 1 Pet 3:1
endurance leads to *g* . . . 2 Pet 1:6

GOOD *kind; profitable; excellent; fitting or appropriate; morally right*
God saw that it was *g* . . . Gen 1:10
into *g* what you meant for evil . . . Gen 50:20
g things from the hand of God . . . Job 2:10
he has been so *g* to me . . . Ps 13:6
are evil; no one does *g*! . . . Ps 14:1
Truly God is *g* to Israel . . . Ps 73:1
approves of those who are *g* . . . Prov 12:2
on both the evil and the *g* . . . Prov 15:3
cheerful heart is *g* medicine . . . Prov 17:22
Learn to do *g*. Seek justice . . . Isa 1:17
his *g* gifts in the last days . . . Hos 3:5
does not produce *g* fruit . . . Matt 3:10
what *g* is salt if it . . . Matt 5:13
g person produces *g* words from a *g* . . . Matt 12:35
Only God is *g* . . . Matt 19:17
Jesus went around doing *g* . . . Acts 10:38
for a person who is especially *g* . . . Rom 5:7
When I want to do *g*, I don't . . . Rom 7:19
conquer evil by doing *g* . . . Rom 12:21
so that we can do the *g* things . . . Eph 2:10
greedy for the *g* things . . . Col 3:5
We know these laws are *g* . . . 1 Tim 1:8
Whatever is *g* and perfect . . . Jas 1:17

GOOD NEWS *news that is kind, profitable, excellent, morally right, and praiseworthy; that is, the gospel of Jesus Christ*
the *G N* about the Kingdom . . . Matt 4:23
G N about Jesus the Messiah . . . Mark 1:1
preach *G N* to the poor . . . Luke 4:18
preaching the *G N* about Jesus . . . Acts 8:4
G N for the people of Israel . . . Acts 10:36
This *G N* was promised long ago . . . Rom 1:2
this *G N*—that God has . . . Heb 4:2
why the *G N* was preached . . . 1 Pet 4:6

GOODNESS *the beneficial quality of something; kindness; see GOOD*
all my *g* pass before you . . . Exod 33:19
Surely your *g* and . . . Ps 23:6
I will see the LORD'S *g* . . . Ps 27:13
Your *g* is so great! . . . Ps 31:19
will see God's *g* when . . . Rom 3:5
living a life of *g* . . . Rom 14:17
g . . . with wickedness? . . . 2 Cor 6:14

GRACE *God's free and unmerited favor toward sinful humanity*
He gives us *g* and glory . . . Ps 84:11
will crown you with *g* . . . Prov 1:9
rains . . . an expression of his *g* . . . Joel 2:23
a spirit of *g* and prayer . . . Zech 12:10
Stephen, a man full of God's *g* . . . Acts 6:8
By God's *g*, remain faithful . . . Acts 13:43
May the *g* of our Lord Jesus . . . Rom 16:20
you have fallen away from God's *g* . . . Gal 5:4
we will find *g* to help us . . . Heb 4:16

GRACIOUS(LY) *abounding in grace and kindness; see GRACE*
children God has *g* given . . . Gen 33:5
the merciful and *g* God . . . Exod 34:6
amazed by the *g* words . . . Luke 4:22
one *g* blessing after another . . . John 1:16
God in his *g* kindness . . . Rom 3:24
result of God's *g* gift . . . Rom 5:16
g privilege of sharing . . . 2 Cor 8:4
My *g* favor is all you need . . . 2 Cor 12:9
Let your conversation be *g* . . . Col 4:6
kind and *g* the Lord was! . . . 1 Tim 1:14
blood, which *g* forgives . . . Heb 12:24
prophesied about this *g* salvation . . . 1 Pet 1:10

GRAVE(S) *burial place; final abode of the dead, both good and wicked; euphemism for Hades, hell, or Sheol.*
stone monument over her *g* . . . Gen 35:20

g where the man of God is . . . 1 Kgs 13:31
relief . . . when they find the *g* . . . Job 3:22
The *g* is ready to receive me . . . Job 17:1
God rescued me from the *g* . . . Job 33:28
can praise you from the *g*? . . . Ps 6:5
g wrapped its ropes around me . . . Ps 18:5
brought me up from the *g* . . . Ps 30:3
put in a rich man's *g* . . . Isa 53:9
ransom them from the *g*? . . . Hos 13:14
like hidden *g* in a field . . . Luke 11:44
the dead in their *g* will hear . . . John 5:28
God raised Christ from the *g* . . . 1 Cor 15:15
keys of death and the *g* . . . Rev 1:18

GRIEF, GRIEV(ED)(ING) *any dire hardship; to cause dire hardship—ailment, injury, distress, vexation, sorrow, or regret*
live in sadness and *g* . . . 1 Sam 2:33
king's deep *g* for his son . . . 2 Sam 19:2
acquainted with bitterest *g* . . . Isa 53:3
and *g* his Holy Spirit . . . Isa 63:10
My soul is crushed with *g* . . . Mark 14:34
disciples, who were *g* . . . Mark 16:10
bitter sorrow and unending *g* . . . Rom 9:2
Let there be sorrow and deep *g* . . . Jas 4:9

GROAN(ED)(ING)(INGS) *sigh, creak, or growling noise, made under duress*
g beneath their burden . . . Exod 2:23
weak and miserable, and I *g* . . . Ps 32:3
all creation has been *g* . . . Rom 8:22
Spirit prays for us with *g* . . . Rom 8:26
dying bodies make us *g* and sigh . . . 2 Cor 5:4

GROUND(S) *soil, earth, or territory; fundamental basis*
so dry *g* may appear . . . Gen 1:9
placed a curse on the *g* . . . Gen 3:17
you are standing on holy *g* . . . Exod 3:5
the hard *g* of your hearts! . . . Jer 4:3
leaving the Temple *g* . . . Matt 24:1
parcel of *g* that Jacob gave . . . John 4:5
spit on the *g*, made mud . . . John 9:6
I try to find common *g* . . . 1 Cor 9:22
put a seed into the *g* . . . 1 Cor 15:36
cut the *g* out from under . . . 2 Cor 11:12
Stand your *g*, putting on . . . Eph 6:14

GUARANTEE(D)(ING)(S) *to assure that some agreement or condition will be fulfilled; to give security for*
covenant . . . by which I will *g* . . . Gen 17:2
I have *g* him an abundance . . . Gen 27:37
I personally *g* his safety . . . Gen 43:9
We offer our own lives as a *g* . . . Josh 2:14
He has *g* his covenant . . . Ps 111:9
as a *g* . . . his Holy Spirit . . . 2 Cor 5:5
The Spirit is God's *g* that . . . Eph 1:14
g that you will be saved . . . Eph 4:30
God's oath, it is Jesus who *g* . . . Heb 7:22

GUILT(Y) *justly chargeable with wrongdoing*
destroy both innocent and *g* . . . Gen 18:23
give us a *g* conscience . . . Gen 37:26
person whom God declares *g* . . . Exod 22:9
laid on him the *g* and sins . . . Isa 53:6
become *g* of murdering . . . Matt 23:35
God . . . declares us not *g* . . . Rom 3:24
g of sinning against the body . . . 1 Cor 11:27
g would have disappeared . . . Heb 10:2
as *g* as the person who . . . Jas 2:10

HANG(ED)(S), HANGING(S), HUNG *to suspend; to execute (on a tree or gallows); to incline downward; to depend; that which hinges on something else*
scarlet rope *h* from the window . . . Josh 2:18
affairs in order, and *h* himself . . . 2 Sam 17:23
white and blue linen *h* . . . Esth 1:6
two men were *h* on a gallows . . . Esth 2:23
God . . . *h* the earth on nothing . . . Job 26:7
went out and *h* himself . . . Matt 27:5
kept guard as he *h* there . . . Matt 27:36
Cursed is everyone who is *h* . . . Gal 3:13

HARD, HARDEN(ED)(S) *difficult or tough; cruel or harsh; (to make) permanent or firm*
how *h* you work! . . . Gen 4:12
too *h* for the LORD? . . . Gen 18:14
your cruelty and my *h* work . . . Gen 31:42
remained *h* and stubborn . . . Exod 7:13
Don't *h* your hearts . . . Ps 95:8
the *h* ground of your hearts! . . . Jer 4:3
fell on the *h* path . . . Matt 13:19
h for a rich person to . . . Matt 19:23
I know you are a *h* man . . . Matt 25:24
hearts were *h* . . . not believe . . . Mark 6:52
is very *h* to understand . . . John 6:60
by choosing it or working *h* . . . Rom 9:16
deceived by sin and *h* . . . Heb 3:13
I have seen your *h* work . . . Rev 2:2

HARVEST(ED)(ERS)(ING)(S)(TIME) *time or fruit of reaping or gathering in a crop—physically or spiritually*
At *h* Cain brought . . . Gen 4:3
springtime and *h*, cold and . . . Gen 8:22
offerings presented at *h* . . . Lev 2:12
not pick up what the *h* drop . . . Lev 19:9
grain *h* from the land . . . Josh 5:11
the field they are *h* . . . Ruth 2:9
They will eat your *h* . . . Jer 5:17
The *h* is finished . . . Jer 8:20
plant or *h* or put food in . . . Matt 6:26
The *h* is so great . . . Matt 9:37
good soil . . . a huge *h* . . . Mark 4:20
h grain on the Sabbath . . . Luke 6:2
are ready now for the *h* . . . John 4:35
time has come for you to *h* . . . Rev 14:15

HATE(D)(FUL)(ERS)(S) *dislike or detest, often with enmity or malice; persecute; strong emotional aversion; detestable*
Esau *h* Jacob because . . . Gen 27:41
his brothers *h* Joseph because . . . Gen 37:4
men who fear God and *h* bribes . . . Exod 18:21
I *h* him. He never prophesies . . . 1 Kgs 22:8
those who *h* them . . . Esth 9:5, 16
I *h* my life. . . . Job 7:16
God *h* me . . . Job 16:9
you *h* all who do evil . . . Ps 5:5
He *h* everyone who loves violence . . . Ps 11:5
and *h* what is wrong . . . Ps 45:7
love the LORD, *h* evil! . . . Ps 97:10
I *h* every false way of life. . . . Ps 119:104
How I *h* discipline! . . . Prov 5:12
six things the LORD *h* . . . Prov 6:16
I *h* pride, arrogance . . . Prov 8:13
with *h* in their hearts . . . Prov 26:24
to love and a time to *h* . . . Eccl 3:8
For I *h* divorce! . . . Mal 2:16
h one and love the other . . . Matt 6:24
world can't *h* you, but it does *h* me . . . John 7:7
it *h* me before it *h* you . . . John 15:18
backstabbers, *h* of God . . . Rom 1:30
No one *h* his own body . . . Eph 5:29
We *h* others, and they *h* us . . . Titus 3:3
but *h* another Christian . . . 1 Jn 4:20

HEAD(S) *top part of the body; seat of the intellect; place of honor; the ranking member; source; authority*
He will crush your *h* . . . Gen 3:15
he saw seven *h* of grain . . . Gen 41:5
If my *h* were shaved . . . Judg 16:17
his *h* and hands had broken off . . . 1 Sam 5:4
h of the table, honoring them . . . 1 Sam 9:22
stood *h* and shoulders above . . . 1 Sam 10:23
My *h* hurts! My *h* hurts! . . . 2 Kgs 4:19
anointing my *h* with oil . . . Ps 23:5
I will hold my *h* high . . . Ps 27:6
coals fall down on their *h* . . . Ps 140:10
heap burning coals on their *h* . . . Prov 25:22
You are sick from *h* to foot . . . Isa 1:6
destroy both the *h* and the tail . . . Isa 9:14
helmet of salvation on his *h* . . . Isa 59:17
the very hairs on your *h* . . . Matt 10:30
on her *h* as a sign of authority . . . 1 Cor 11:10
h can't say to the feet . . . 1 Cor 12:21
husband is the *h* of his wife . . . Eph 5:23

HEAL(ED)(S), HEALTH(Y), HEALING(S) *to mend, cure, make whole; return to original state of health*
Abraham prayed . . . *h* . . . Gen 20:17
dew for *h* crops and good . . . Gen 27:28
they produced *h* offspring . . . Gen 31:38
the LORD who *h* you . . . Exod 15:26
I will keep you *h* . . . Exod 23:25
Those who have been *h* must . . . Lev 14:2
the one who wounds and *h* . . . Deut 32:39
their sins and *h* their land . . . 2 Chr 7:14
take away his *h*, and he . . . Job 2:5
H me, LORD, for my body . . . Ps 6:2
h is broken because of my sins . . . Ps 38:3
my sins and *h* all my diseases . . . Ps 103:3
strike Egypt . . . bring *h* . . . Isa 19:22
it leads to life and *h* . . . Isa 38:16
He was whipped, and we were *h*! . . . Isa 53:5
I will *h* your wayward hearts . . . Jer 3:22
torn us in pieces; now he will *h* . . . Hos 6:1
rise with *h* in his wings . . . Mal 4:2
A *h* tree produces good fruit . . . Matt 7:17
I will come and *h* him . . . Matt 8:7
touch his robe, I will be *h* . . . Matt 9:21
cast out evil spirits and to *h* . . . Matt 10:1
Physician, *h* yourself . . . Luke 4:23
touch of his hand *h* every . . . Luke 4:40
required . . . proof of your *h* . . . Luke 5:14
Aeneas, Jesus Christ *h* you! . . . Acts 9:34
gives the power to *h* the sick . . . 1 Cor 12:9
prayer offered in faith will *h* . . . Jas 5:15
h by his wounds! . . . 1 Pet 2:24
the fatal wound was *h*! . . . Rev 13:3
for medicine to *h* the nations . . . Rev 22:2

HEAR(D)(ING)(S), HEARER(S) *to perceive sound; to be informed of; being obedient or paying heed to; take testimony from and make a legal decision*
I *h* you, so I hid . . . Gen 3:10
h about your misery . . . Gen 16:11
h that I was unloved . . . Gen 29:33
he *h* my loud cries, he ran . . . Gen 39:15
I have *h* that you can . . . Gen 41:15
I have *h* their cries for . . . Exod 3:7
who *h* the words of God . . . Num 24:4, 16
on the day he *h* of it . . . Num 30:5ff
You *h* his words but . . . Deut 4:12
H, O Israel! . . . Deut 6:4
judge on duty will *h* the case . . . Deut 17:9
Have mercy on me and *h* . . . Ps 4:1
The LORD *h* his people . . . Ps 34:17
Ah, I *h* him—my lover! . . . Song 2:8
h with their ears, understand . . . Isa 6:10
and their ears cannot *h* . . . Matt 13:15
Anyone who is willing to *h* . . . Mark 4:9
before he is given a *h*? . . . John 7:51
I say only what I have *h* . . . John 8:26
h me and doesn't obey me . . . John 12:47
how can they *h* about him . . . Rom 10:14
eye has seen, no ear has *h* . . . 1 Cor 2:9
You have *h* me teach . . . 2 Tim 2:2
who formerly *h* the Good News . . . Heb 4:6
don't forget what you *h* . . . Jas 1:25
one we have *h* and seen . . . 1 Jn 1:1
Suddenly, I *h* a loud voice . . . Rev 1:10
willing to *h* . . . Rev 2:7ff; 3:6ff
I saw and *h* these things . . . Rev 22:8

HEART(S) *figuratively, the seat of emotions, thoughts, and intentions; sometimes translated "mind" or "soul"; central or most vital part of something*
It broke his *h* . . . Gen 6:6
strike at the *h* of Egypt . . . Exod 3:20
he hardened his *h* . . . Exod 8:15
I was pouring out my *h* . . . 1 Sam 1:15
God changed his *h* . . . 1 Sam 10:9
Absalom stole the *h* of all . . . 2 Sam 15:6
Solomon, for his *h* had turned . . . 1 Kgs 11:9
have cursed God in their *h* . . . Job 1:5

treasured his word in my h . . . Job 23:12
at night my h instructs me . . . Ps 16:7
My h is sick, withered like . . . Ps 102:4
in the h of Jerusalem . . . Ps 116:19
search for him with all their h . . . Ps 119:2
God knows all h . . . Prov 24:12
the h reflects the person . . . Prov 27:19
eternity in the human h . . . Eccl 3:11
You have ravished my h . . . Song 4:9
is injured, and your h is sick . . . Isa 1:5
Harden the h of these people . . . Isa 6:10
The human h is most deceitful . . . Jer 17:9
his arrows deep into my h . . . Lam 3:13
take away their h of stone . . . Ezek 11:19
a new h and a new spirit . . . Ezek 18:31
turn the h of parents to . . . Mal 4:6
those whose h are pure . . . Matt 5:8
your treasure is, there your h . . . Matt 6:21
from the h come evil thoughts . . . Matt 15:19
h determines what you say . . . Luke 6:45
our h feel strangely warm . . . Luke 24:32
is near to the Father's h . . . John 1:18
eyes and hardened their h . . . John 12:40
take h, because I have overcome . . . John 16:33
has Satan filled your h? . . . Acts 5:3
on your lips and in your h . . . Rom 10:8
minds and hardened their h . . . Eph 4:18
with one h and purpose . . . Phil 2:2
Christ rule in your h . . . Col 3:15
Don't harden your h . . . Heb 3:8

HEAVEN(LY)(S) *sky and stars above; abode of eternal bliss; euphemism for God in his majesty and perfection; celestial; of or pertaining to God in the highest*
God created the h and . . . Gen 1:1
Look up into the h . . . Gen 15:5
the gateway to h! . . . Gen 28:17
food from h for you . . . Exod 16:4
highest h cannot contain you . . . 1 Kgs 8:27
The h will reveal his guilt . . . Job 20:27
LORD still rules from h . . . Ps 11:4
h tell of the glory . . . Ps 19:1
h proclaim his justice . . . Ps 50:6
Let the h be glad . . . Ps 96:11
h declare his righteousness . . . Ps 97:6
love is higher than the h . . . Ps 108:4
for every activity under h . . . Eccl 3:1
for he is in h, and you . . . Eccl 5:2
as the h are higher than . . . Isa 55:9
h . . . your holy, glorious home . . . Isa 63:15
creating new h and a new . . . Isa 65:17
the Kingdom of H is near . . . Matt 3:2
Kingdom of H is given to them . . . Matt 5:3
on earth, just as it is in h . . . Matt 6:10
your h Father will forgive . . . Matt 6:14
powers of h will be shaken . . . Matt 24:29
sign from h to prove yourself . . . Mark 8:11
armies of h—praising God . . . Luke 2:13
The door to h is narrow . . . Luke 13:24
sinned against both h and you . . . Luke 15:18
you will all see h open . . . John 1:51
what is going on in h? . . . John 3:12
the true bread from h . . . John 6:32
H is my throne, and the earth . . . Acts 7:49
blessing in the h realms . . . Eph 1:3
forward to the joys of h . . . Col 1:5
have a Master—in h . . . Col 4:1
he has prepared a h city . . . Heb 11:16
the h will pass away . . . 2 Pet 3:10
a door standing open in h . . . Rev 4:1
silence throughout h . . . Rev 8:1
Then there was war in h . . . Rev 12:7
a new h and a new earth . . . Rev 21:1

HEIR(S) *son of an owner of property; one who inherits; see INHERITANCE*
servant will not be your h . . . Gen 15:4
will be your brother's h . . . Gen 38:8
must be h for the survivors . . . Judg 21:17
The h to David's throne . . . Rom 15:12
You are his h . . . Gal 3:29

HELL *abode of the dead; place of punishment; personification of evil; lowest place one can go*
fire that destroys to h . . . Job 31:12
to death; it is the road to h . . . Prov 2:18
in danger of the fires of h . . . Matt 5:22
The highway to h is broad . . . Matt 7:13
both soul and body in h . . . Matt 10:28
all the powers of h . . . Matt 16:18
escape the judgment of h . . . Matt 23:33
h, 'where the worm never dies . . . Mark 9:47-48
then throw them into h . . . Luke 12:5
h can't keep God's love away . . . Rom 8:38
set on fire by h itself . . . Jas 3:6

HELP(ED)(ER)(FUL)(ING)(S) *to come to one's aid; those who give aid (co-workers)*
companion who will h him . . . Gen 2:18
God h you in everything . . . Gen 21:22
h yourself to the water . . . Ruth 2:9
angels, but they give you no h . . . Job 5:1
I cry out for h, but . . . Job 19:7
I h the poor . . . the orphans . . . Job 29:12
You have always been my h . . . Ps 27:9
always ready to h in times of . . . Ps 46:1
LORD, H! . . . Ps 107:6ff
all human h is useless . . . Ps 108:12
He is your h . . . your shield . . . Ps 115:9-11
Our h is from the LORD . . . Ps 124:8
strengthen you. I will h . . . Isa 41:10
an idol that cannot h . . . Isa 44:10
day of salvation, I will h . . . Isa 49:8
who isn't h me opposes me . . . Matt 12:30
but h me not to doubt! . . . Mark 9:24
has h his servant Israel! . . . Luke 1:54
I have no one to h me . . . John 5:7
Spirit h us in our distress . . . Rom 8:26
but not everything is h . . . 1 Cor 10:23
spiritual gift . . . a means of h . . . 1 Cor 12:7
find grace to h us . . . Heb 4:16
The Lord is my h . . . Heb 13:6

HELPLESS *without any aid, comfort, or chance of success*
His h cries touched her . . . Exod 2:6
h, without any chance . . . Job 6:13
searching for some h victim . . . Ps 10:8
The h put their trust in you . . . Ps 10:14

HIGH(ER)(EST)(LY) *tall; elevated (places); lofty or noble; foremost in rank; of greater value than average, usual, or expected (prices)*
the h position I have today . . . Gen 50:20
climbed h up the mountain . . . Exod 24:18
next h priest after Aaron . . . Exod 29:30
free with your heads held h . . . Lev 26:13
walls of their towns rise h . . . Deut 1:28
The complex was three stories h . . . 1 Kgs 6:6
shrines at the pagan h places . . . 1 Kgs 12:31
h than the heavens . . . Job 22:12
They may rise h, but . . . Job 24:22
from the Almighty on h? . . . Job 31:2
unfailing love of the Most H . . . Ps 21:7
above the h heavens . . . Ps 57:5, 11
the Most H, supreme over all . . . Ps 83:18
he will be h exalted . . . Isa 52:13
worship . . . on every h hill . . . Jer 17:2
the Most H rules over the . . . Dan 4:17
Don't think h of yourself . . . Rom 11:20
God bought you with a h price . . . 1 Cor 6:20
beyond our h hopes . . . 2 Cor 8:5
think more h of me than . . . 2 Cor 12:6
faithful H Priest before God . . . Heb 2:17

HOLIER, HOLY *consecrated or set aside for sacred use (as opposed to pagan or common use); standing apart from sin and evil; characteristic of God, especially the third person of the Trinity; see SPIRIT*
seventh day and declared it h . . . Gen 2:3
you are standing on h ground . . . Exod 3:5
day of rest, a h Sabbath . . . Exod 16:23
of priests, my h nation . . . Exod 19:6
separate the H Place from . . . Exod 26:33
Set them apart as h . . . Exod 28:41
be h because I . . . am h . . . Lev 19:2
a h man of God . . . 2 Kgs 4:9
the H One of Israel! . . . 2 Kgs 19:22
the h vessels of God . . . 1 Chr 22:19
h race has become polluted . . . Ezra 9:2
in Jerusalem, my h city . . . Ps 2:6
is in his h Temple . . . Ps 11:4
from his h heaven . . . Ps 20:6
may stand in his h place? . . . Ps 24:3
they sang, "H, h, h . . . Isa 6:3
baptize you with the H Spirit . . . Matt 3:11
what is h to unholy people . . . Matt 7:6
blasphemy against the H Spirit . . . Matt 12:31
baby born to you will be h . . . Luke 1:35
the H One sent from God . . . Luke 4:34
Father give the H Spirit . . . Luke 11:13
H Spirit has come . . . Acts 1:8
rejected this h, righteous one . . . Acts 3:14
promised . . . in the h Scriptures . . . Rom 1:2
so that you will become h . . . Rom 6:19
their children will also be h . . . Rom 11:16
h and without fault in his eyes . . . Eph 1:4
hearts strong, blameless, and h . . . 1 Thes 3:13
and shared in the H Spirit . . . Heb 6:4
made h by the sacrifice . . . Heb 10:10
be h because I am h . . . 1 Pet 1:16
one who is h and true . . . Rev 3:7
presence of the h angels . . . Rev 14:10
For you alone are h . . . Rev 15:4

HOLINESS *sanctity or purity; see HOLY*
glorious in h like you . . . Exod 15:11
promised this by his h . . . Ps 60:6
in my h I cannot lie . . . Ps 89:35
the h of the Holy One . . . Isa 29:23
named the Highway of H . . . Isa 35:8
in h and righteousness forever . . . Luke 1:75
things that lead to h . . . Rom 6:22
we will share in his h . . . Heb 12:10
who is holy, continue in h . . . Rev 22:11

HOME(S) *living quarters; family-style social unit; place of origin, destiny, or comfort; see HOUSE*
began their long journey h . . . Gen 14:11
for your childhood h . . . Gen 31:30
Come h with me . . . Prov 9:4, 16
be at h among the wise . . . Prov 15:31
A person who strays from h . . . Prov 27:8
A city or h divided against itself . . . Matt 12:25
Nazareth, his boyhood h . . . Luke 4:16
many rooms in my Father's h . . . John 14:2
either publicly or in your h . . . Acts 20:20
to take care of their h . . . Titus 2:5
this world is not our h . . . Heb 13:14

HONOR(ABLE)(ED)(ING)(S) *of God, to reverence his majesty or splendor; of man, to respect or esteem; having a renowned reputation or social standing; from God, to receive physical or spiritual blessing*
an h prince among us . . . Gen 23:6
Now he will h me . . . Gen 30:20
how h you really are . . . Gen 42:19
h this, my last request: . . . Gen 47:29
H your father and mother . . . Exod 20:12
So h the LORD . . . Josh 24:14
stripped me of my h . . . Job 19:9
New h . . . bestowed on me . . . Job 29:20
Give h to the LORD . . . Ps 29:1, 2
I will be h by every . . . Ps 46:10
rescue them and h them . . . Ps 91:15
Sit in h at my right . . . Ps 110:1
h his godly ones . . . Ps 148:14
H . . . with your wealth . . . Prov 3:9
humility precedes h . . . Prov 15:33
God gives great wealth and h . . . Eccl 6:2
You are h, and I love you . . . Isa 43:4
not h me with sacrifices . . . Isa 43:23
days of glory, pomp, and h . . . Isa 47:1
I will give him the h . . . Isa 53:12
the h and respect I deserve? . . . Mal 1:6
may your name be h . . . Matt 6:9

A prophet is *h* . . . Matt 13:57
h me with their words, but . . . Matt 15:8
What an *h* this is . . . Luke 1:43
Jesus as the guest of *h* . . . Luke 5:29
h the Son, just as they *h* . . . John 5:23
give respect and *h* to . . . Rom 13:7
not *h* the body of Christ . . . 1 Cor 11:29
parts we regard as less *h* . . . 1 Cor 12:23
live in holiness and *h* . . . 1 Thes 4:4
an *h* responsibility . . . 1 Tim 3:1
place of *h* in heaven . . . Heb 7:26
Give *h* to marriage . . . Heb 13:4
give glory and *h* and thanks . . . Rev 4:9

HOPE(D)(FUL)(S) *confident trust with the expectation of fulfillment*
the focus of all Israel's *h* . . . 1 Sam 9:20
But the wicked will lose *h* . . . Job 11:20
so you destroy people's *h* . . . Job 14:19
my *h* will go down with me . . . Job 17:16
what *h* do the godless have . . . Job 27:8
the *h* of the poor will not . . . Ps 9:18
for I put my *h* in you . . . Ps 25:21
where do I put my *h*? . . . Ps 39:7
O Lord, you alone are my *h* . . . Ps 71:5
put my *h* in your word . . . Ps 119:74, 81
for they have no *h* . . . Eccl 9:3
all who *h* for deliverance . . . Isa 51:1
O LORD, the *h* of Israel . . . Jer 17:13
to give you a future and a *h* . . . Jer 29:11
dare to *h* when I remember this . . . Lam 3:21
you don't need to *h* for it . . . Rom 8:24
May you overflow with *h* . . . Rom 15:13
never loses faith, is always *h* . . . 1 Cor 13:7
h in Christ only for this life . . . 1 Cor 15:19
without God and without *h* . . . Eph 2:12
I live in eager expectation and *h* . . . Phil 1:20
like people who have no *h* . . . 1 Thes 4:13
I *h* to be with you soon . . . 1 Tim 3:14
what you *h* for will come true . . . Heb 6:11
assurance that what we *h* for . . . Heb 11:1
asked about your Christian *h* . . . 1 Pet 3:15

HORROR(S) *"woe" or ruinous trouble; feelings of intense fear, dread, or aversion*
object of *h* and disgust to . . . Deut 18:12
view them with utter *h* . . . Isa 66:24
What *h* await you, Korazin . . . Matt 11:21
beginning of the *h* to come . . . Matt 24:8
days of greater *h* than . . . Mark 13:19
you may escape these *h* . . . Luke 21:36
God released him from the *h* of death . . . Acts 2:24

HOSTILE, HOSTILITY *unfriendly, even antagonistic; overt acts of killing or enmity*
h toward me and refuse to . . . Lev 26:21
full expression to my *h* . . . Lev 26:41
premeditated *h* . . . is murder . . . Num 35:20
you show yourself *h* . . . 2 Sam 22:27
rise up to punish *h* nations . . . Ps 59:5
all his fury, rage, and *h* . . . Ps 78:49
sinful nature is always *h* to God . . . Rom 8:7
demonic activities, *h*, quarreling . . . Gal 5:20
broken down the wall of *h* . . . Eph 2:14

HOUR(S) *time of day; a (short) unit or passage of time; indefinite time, even the end times*
worked only one *h*, and yet . . . Matt 20:12
no one knows the day or the *h* . . . Matt 24:36
day or *h* of my return . . . Matt 25:13
watch with me even one *h*? . . . Matt 26:40
twelve *h* of daylight every day . . . John 11:9
Jesus knew that his *h* had come . . . John 13:1
facing death *h* by *h* . . . 1 Cor 15:30
the last *h* is here . . . 1 Jn 2:18
silence . . . for about half an *h* . . . Rev 8:1

HOUSE(HOLD)(S) *living quarters; extended family unit, including ancestors and descendants; place of worship; see HOME*
Leave . . . your father's *h* . . . Gen 12:1
h, 318 of them in all . . . Gen 14:14
h of God—the gateway . . . Gen 28:17
Go to the prostitute's *h* . . . Josh 6:22
first thing coming out of my *h* . . . Judg 11:31
wind . . . hit the *h* on all sides . . . Job 1:19
live in the *h* of the LORD . . . Ps 23:6
live in the *h* of the LORD . . . Ps 27:4
Passion for your *h* . . . Ps 69:9
gatekeeper in the *h* of my God . . . Ps 84:10
Entering her *h* leads to death . . . Prov 2:18
A *h* is built by wisdom . . . Prov 24:3
before building your *h* . . . Prov 24:27
As you enter the *h* of God . . . Eccl 5:1
Enlarge your *h*; build an addition . . . Isa 54:2
rebuild . . . your *h* from precious . . . Isa 54:11
who builds a *h* on solid rock . . . Matt 7:24
enemies . . . in your own *h*! . . . Matt 10:36
enter a strong man's *h* and . . . Matt 12:29
Father's *h* into a marketplace . . . John 2:16
saved, . . . your entire *h* . . . Acts 16:31
cannot manage his own *h* . . . 1 Tim 3:5
gossiping from *h* to *h* . . . 1 Tim 5:13
church that meets in your *h* . . . Phlm 1:2
entrusted with God's entire *h* . . . Heb 3:2

HUMAN(ITY)(LY)(S) *mortal; men and women collectively; finite*
the struggle of all *h*? . . . Job 7:1
How frail is *h* . . . Job 14:1
mere *h* that you should care . . . Ps 8:4
an animal instead of a *h* . . . Dan 4:16
was, *h* speaking, the founder . . . Rom 4:1
I will destroy *h* wisdom . . . 1 Cor 1:19
as though he were merely a *h* . . . 2 Cor 5:16

HUMBLE(D)(S) *to not think too highly of oneself; to bring low or prostrate; can imply lower social or economic status; meek or gentle; see HUMILITY*
On that day you must *h* . . . Lev 23:27, 32
Moses was more *h* than any . . . Num 12:3
He has *h* me . . . Job 30:11
leads the *h* in what is right . . . Ps 25:9
h those who hate us . . . Ps 44:7
spirits are contrite and *h* . . . Isa 57:15
until he *h* all his enemies . . . 1 Cor 15:25
h, thinking of others as better . . . Phil 2:3
he shows favor to the *h* . . . Jas 4:6
So *h* yourselves under . . . God . . . 1 Pet 5:6

HUMILIATE(D), HUMILIATION *to shame; disgrace or dishonor*
h as evidence of my sin . . . Job 19:5
but you *h* the proud . . . Ps 18:27
made you despised and *h* . . . Mal 2:9
h and received no justice . . . Acts 8:33

HUMILITY *show of submission or meekness; see HUMBLE*
require strong devotion, *h* . . . Col 2:23
clothe yourselves with . . . *h* . . . Col 3:12
show true *h* to everyone . . . Titus 3:2

HUNGER, HUNGRY *to crave food; any craving or strong desire*
food for the *h* . . . Job 22:7
fills the *h* with good things . . . Ps 107:9
you satisfy the *h* and thirst . . . Ps 145:16
They will neither *h* nor thirst . . . Isa 49:10
I was *h*, and you fed me . . . Matt 25:35
blesses you who are *h* now . . . Luke 6:21
will ever be *h* again . . . John 6:35
If your enemies are *h* . . . Rom 12:20
some go *h* while others . . . 1 Cor 11:21
They will never again be *h* . . . Rev 7:16

HUSBAND(S) *head of family; protector and provider; figurative of Christ*
desire will be for your *h* . . . Gen 3:16
Her *h* can trust her . . . Prov 31:11
your Creator will be your *h* . . . Isa 54:5
you have had five *h* . . . John 4:18
law binds her to her *h* . . . Rom 7:2
h should not deprive . . . 1 Cor 7:3
h must love your wives . . . Eph 5:25
be submissive to their *h* . . . Titus 2:5
you *h* must give honor to . . . 1 Pet 3:7
bride prepared for her *h* . . . Rev 21:2

HYPOCRISY, HYPOCRITE(S) *acting a part in a play; pretense of piety; pretender; false or godless; feigning to be what one is not*
time with liars . . . *h* . . . Ps 26:4
h, speaking wickedness with lies . . . Isa 9:17
h who love to pray publicly . . . Matt 6:5
H! First get rid of the log . . . Matt 7:5
H! . . . careful to tithe . . . Matt 23:23
Pharisees—beware of their *h* . . . Luke 12:1
followed Peter's *h* . . . Gal 2:13
purify your hearts, you *h* . . . Jas 4:8
Be done with *h* and jealousy . . . 1 Pet 2:1

I AM *personal name of God; title or saying by which Jesus identified himself*
God replied, "*I A* THE ONE WHO ALWAYS IS. . . . Exod 3:14
Jesus told her, "*I a* the Messiah!" . . . John 4:26
I a the bread of life . . . John 6:35
I a the light of the world . . . John 8:12
I a the gate for the sheep . . . John 10:7
I a the good shepherd . . . John 10:11
I a the resurrection . . . John 11:25
I a the way, the truth, and . . . John 14:6
I a the true vine . . . John 15:1

IDLE(NESS) *not employed or useful for work; inactivity; uselessness; laziness*
only fools *i* away their time . . . Prov 12:11
You sing *i* songs . . . Amos 6:5
account . . . of every *i* word . . . Matt 12:36
in *i* and doesn't . . . work . . . 2 Thes 3:6

IDOL(S) *image(s) of a false god; see GOD(S)*
Do not make *i* of any kind . . . Exod 20:4
The land is filled with *i* . . . Isa 2:8
set up *i* in their hearts . . . Ezek 14:3
i made of gold, silver, bronze . . . Dan 5:4
destroy all your *i* and sacred . . . Mic 5:13
Can an *i* speak for God? . . . Hab 2:19
they worshiped *i* made . . . Rom 1:23
an *i* is not really a god . . . 1 Cor 8:4
godless people enjoy . . . *i* . . . 1 Pet 4:3
i that neither see nor hear nor walk! . . . Rev 9:20

IDOLATER(S), IDOLATRY *worshipers of idols; blind worship of an undeserving object*
sins of *i* that Jeroboam . . . 1 Kgs 15:26, 34
an end to lewdness and *i* . . . Ezek 23:48
she is married to *i* . . . Hos 4:17
heal . . . your *i* and faithlessness . . . Hos 14:4
a greedy person is really an *i* . . . Eph 5:5
one who practices shameful *i* . . . Rev 21:27

IGNORANCE, IGNORANT, IGNORE *without knowledge or comprehension; stupidity; unaware; inattention (accidental)*
was done in *i* . . . Acts 3:17
overlooked people's former *i* . . . Acts 17:30
i God and get away with it . . . Gal 6:7
i of God and his ways . . . 1 Thes 4:5
both conceited and *i* . . . 1 Tim 6:4
they are *i* and wayward . . . Heb 5:2
sins . . . committed in *i* . . . Heb 9:7
are *i* and unstable . . . 2 Pet 3:16

IMAGE(S) *man-made figure; God-given likeness or reflection*
in our *i*, to be like ourselves . . . Gen 1:26
Seth was the very *i* of his father . . . Gen 5:3
kill a person . . . made in God's *i* . . . Gen 9:6
cut down their carved *i* . . . Exod 34:13
the *i* King Nebuchadnezzar had . . . Dan 3:3
ask speechless stone *i* to . . . Hab 2:19
visible *i* of the invisible God . . . Col 1:15

IMMORAL(ITY) *behavior conflicting with traditional (biblical) moral values*
adultery, all other sexual *i* . . . Matt 15:19
in adultery and *i* living . . . Rom 13:13
laws are for . . . sexually *i* . . . 1 Tim 1:10

godless people enjoy . . . *i* . . . 1 Pet 4:3
Gomorrah . . . filled with sexual *i* . . . Jude 1:7

IMMORTALITY *imperishable; exempt from death*
honor and *i* that God offers . . . Rom 2:7

INCREASE(D)(S), INCREASING *to multiply, augment, enrich; profit or harvest yield; that which is over and above in number, amount, or intensity*
birds *i* and fill the earth . . . Gen 1:22
Jacob's flocks *i* rapidly . . . Gen 30:43
the *i* burden of their slavery . . . Exod 6:9
its yield will be *i* . . . Lev 19:25
And if your wealth *i* . . . Ps 62:10
will he *i* your punishment? . . . Ps 120:3
wicked are in authority, sin *i* . . . Prov 29:16
number of believers greatly *i* . . . Acts 6:7
i confidence in their faith . . . 1 Tim 3:13

INHERIT(ANCE)(ED) *to receive as a legacy or promise; to take possession as a rightful heir; a possession or estate; see HEIR*
Eliezer . . . will *i* all my wealth . . . Gen 15:2
share the family *i* with . . . Gen 21:10
Ephraim and Manasseh . . . will *i* . . . Gen 48:5
priests will receive no *i* . . . Num 18:20
give his *i* to his daughters . . . Num 27:8
i from the Almighty . . . Job 27:13
the nations as your *i* . . . Ps 2:8
you alone are my *i* . . . Ps 16:5
Promised Land as our *i* . . . Ps 47:4
The wise *i* honor . . . Prov 3:35
Those who love me *i* wealth . . . Prov 8:21
rise again to receive the *i* . . . Dan 12:13
i the Kingdom prepared for . . . Matt 25:34
God gave him no *i* . . . Acts 7:5
and give you an *i* . . . Acts 20:32
flesh and blood cannot *i* . . . 1 Cor 15:50
will not *i* the Kingdom . . . Gal 5:21
riches *i* by God's children . . . Eph 3:6
we will *i* eternal life . . . Titus 3:7
to the Son as an *i* . . . Heb 1:2
i God's promises because . . . Heb 6:12
i for his children . . . 1 Pet 1:4
who are victorious will *i* . . . Rev 21:7

INIQUITY *sin, implying perversion of heart and wickedness of purpose*
pardon our *i* and our sins . . . Exod 34:9
you would not forgive my *i* . . . Job 10:14
would cover over my *i* . . . Job 14:17

INNOCENCE, INNOCENT *regarded as righteous, having a clean record and no reason for punishment; of "blood," refers to a guiltless person or a child*
destroy both *i* and guilty . . . Gen 18:23
How can we prove our *i*? . . . Gen 44:16
land to your *i* children . . . Deut 1:39
guilt of murdering an *i* . . . Deut 21:8
guilty and who is *i* . . . 1 Sam 14:41
my *i* in his sight . . . 2 Sam 22:25
Yet I am *i* . . . Job 16:17
I will defend my *i* . . . Job 27:5
I am pure; I am *i* . . . Job 33:9
i, . . . those who do right . . . Ps 17:2
free of guilt and *i* of . . . Ps 19:13
the blood of *i* children . . . Jer 19:4
found *i* in his sight . . . Dan 6:22
betrayed an *i* man . . . Matt 27:4
But if I am *i* . . . Acts 25:11

INTEGRITY *honesty; without compromise or corruption*
twisted . . . without *i* . . . Deut 32:20
man of complete *i* . . . Job 1:1, 8; 2:3
pure and live with complete *i* . . . Job 8:6
to those with *i* you show *i* . . . Ps 18:25
i and honesty protect me . . . Ps 25:21
life of *i* in my own home . . . Ps 101:2
Happy are people of *i* . . . Ps 119:1
The godly walk with *i* . . . Prov 20:7
deacons must . . . have *i* . . . 1 Tim 3:8

INTERCEDE(D) *to mediate or plead another's case for justice or mercy*
if someone sins . . . who can *i*? . . . 1 Sam 2:25
for Joab to ask him to *i* . . . 2 Sam 14:29
messenger . . . to *i* for a person . . . Job 33:23
and *i* for sinners . . . Isa 53:12

INTERPRET(ED)(ERS)(ING)(S), INTERPRETATION(S) *explain; translate*
i dreams is God's business . . . Gen 40:8
speaking to them through an *i* . . . Gen 42:23
i the law and reached a verdict . . . Deut 17:11
i omens, or engage in witchcraft . . . Deut 18:10
i dreams, explain riddles . . . Dan 5:12
give *i* and solve . . . Dan 5:16
fortune-tellers . . . *i* of dreams . . . Zech 10:2
given the ability to *i* . . . 1 Cor 12:10
i what you are saying . . . 1 Cor 14:5
for the gift of *i* . . . 1 Cor 14:13

INVISIBLE *hidden; imperceptible*
clearly see his *i* qualities . . . Rom 1:20
visible image of the *i* God . . . Col 1:15
eyes on the one who is *i* . . . Heb 11:27

IRON *metal used in instruments of war, farming, and building; symbolic of strength for both security and destruction*
hammer, ax, or any other *i* . . . 1 Kgs 6:7
so much *i* and bronze that . . . 1 Chr 22:14
how to dig *i* from the earth . . . Job 28:2
break them with an *i* rod . . . Ps 2:9
As *i* sharpens *i*, a friend . . . Prov 27:17
its legs were of *i* . . . Dan 2:33
rule the nations with an *i* rod . . . Rev 2:27
They wore armor made of *i* . . . Rev 9:9

ISRAEL(ITES) *name given to Isaac's son Jacob, and to his descendants*
Your name . . . is now *I* . . . Gen 32:28
Hear, O *I*! . . . Deut 6:4
I my servant, Jacob my chosen . . . Isa 41:8
he will persuade many *I* . . . Luke 1:16
judging the twelve tribes of *I* . . . Luke 22:30
I, chosen to be God's special . . . Rom 9:4
so all *I* will be saved . . . Rom 11:26

JEALOUS(Y) *attitude of God and man, positive and negative, implying vigilance and zeal for or envy of*
brothers were *j* of Joseph . . . Gen 37:11
a *j* God who will not share . . . Exod 20:5
a devouring fire, a *j* God . . . Deut 4:24
His anger and *j* will . . . Deut 29:20
They stirred up his *j* . . . Deut 32:16
its *j* is as enduring as . . . Song 8:6
the Jews would be *j* . . . Rom 11:11
You are *j* of one another . . . 1 Cor 3:3
to rouse the Lord's *j* . . . 1 Cor 10:22
I am *j* for you with the *j* of God . . . 2 Cor 11:2

JESUS *name given to the Messiah or Savior, meaning "Yahweh Saves"*
J, for he will save his people . . . Matt 1:21
J, the King of the Jews . . . Matt 27:37
Good News about *J* the Messiah . . . Mark 1:1
J, Son of David, have mercy . . . Mark 10:47
When *J* was twelve years old . . . Luke 2:42
J, the son of Joseph from . . . John 1:45
J told her, "I am the Messiah!" . . . John 4:26
J is the Messiah, the Son . . . John 20:31
made this *J* . . . Lord and . . . Acts 2:36
believed in the Lord *J* Christ . . . Acts 11:17
confess . . . that *J* is Lord . . . Rom 10:9
concentrate only on *J* Christ . . . 1 Cor 2:2
cornerstone is Christ *J* . . . Eph 2:20
What we do see is *J* . . . Heb 2:9
keeping our eyes on *J* . . . Heb 12:2
I, *J*, have sent my angel . . . Rev 22:16

JOY(OUS)(S), JOYFUL(LY) *emotion evoked by well-being, success, or good fortune; characterized by gladness or delight*
celebrated *j* for another week . . . 2 Chr 30:23
j shouting and weeping . . . Ezra 3:13
was then dedicated with great *j* . . . Ezra 6:16
the *j* of those corrected by God! . . . Job 5:17
God will receive him with *j* . . . Job 33:26
j comes with the morning . . . Ps 30:5
Let us give a *j* shout . . . Ps 95:1
wise child brings *j* to a father . . . Prov 10:1
given them reasons for *j* . . . Eccl 5:20
All the *j* of life will be gone . . . Isa 24:7
You will live in *j* and peace . . . Isa 55:12
famous city, a city of *j* . . . Jer 49:25
J of All the Earth . . . Lam 2:15
they were filled with *j*! . . . Matt 2:10
hear . . . and receive it with *j* . . . Matt 13:20
but also filled with great *j* . . . Matt 28:8
my baby jumped for *j* . . . Luke 1:44
j . . . when even one sinner . . . Luke 15:10
Yes, your *j* will overflow! . . . John 15:11
j when they saw their Lord! . . . John 20:20
Where is that *j* spirit . . . Gal 4:15
fruit in us: love, *j*, peace . . . Gal 5:22
you are our pride and *j* . . . 1 Thes 2:20
the *j* he knew would be his . . . Heb 12:2
let it be an opportunity for *j* . . . Jas 1:2

JUDGE(D)(S), JUDGING *(those who) pass sentence, punish or condemn; one in a cycle of charismatic deliverers of ancient Israel; see JUDGMENT*
the *J* of all the earth . . . Gen 18:25
LORD raised up *j* . . . Judg 2:16
a prophet who had become a *j* . . . Judg 4:4
coming to *j* the earth . . . 1 Chr 16:33
Do you *j* the people fairly? . . . Ps 58:1
our *j*, our lawgiver, and our king . . . Isa 33:22
j the great people of the world . . . Isa 40:23
He will *j* all the people . . . Jer 25:31
the Ancient One sat down to *j* . . . Dan 7:9
Stop *j* others, and you . . . Matt 7:1
who made me a *j* over you . . . Luke 12:14
a lesson from this evil *j* . . . Luke 18:6
but I am not *j* anyone . . . John 8:15
to save . . . not to *j* . . . John 12:47
the just *j* of all the world . . . Rom 2:5
your job to *j* those inside . . . 1 Cor 5:12
stand before Christ to be *j* . . . 2 Cor 5:10
j the living and the dead . . . 2 Tim 4:1
The great *J* is coming . . . Jas 5:9
no favorites when he *j* . . . 1 Pet 1:17
j the dead and reward your . . . Rev 11:18

JUDGMENT(S) *a ruling or moral decision by a ruler (often God), a judge, or an individual; see JUDGE*
redeem you with . . . acts of *j* . . . Exod 6:6
to flee God's coming *j* . . . Luke 3:7
leaves all *j* to his Son . . . John 5:22
time of *j* . . . has come . . . John 12:31
the *j* seat of God . . . Rom 14:10
I have already passed *j* . . . 1 Cor 5:3
after that comes *j* . . . Heb 9:27
time has come for *j* . . . 1 Pet 4:17
His *j* are just and true . . . Rev 19:2

JUST(LY) *honest; conforming to a standard of correctness; faithful to the original design*
do what is right and *j* . . . Gen 18:19
Can a mortal be *j* and upright . . . Job 4:17
a *j* and blameless man . . . Job 12:4
a God who judges *j* . . . Ps 58:11
Be *j* and fair to all . . . Isa 56:1
You are perfectly *j* in this . . . Hab 1:13
verdicts . . . that are *j* . . . Zech 8:16
her fiancé, being a *j* man . . . Matt 1:19
If God is not *j*, how . . . Rom 3:6
J and true are your ways . . . Rev 15:3

JUSTICE *the administration of law that determines what is right, based on principles of equity and correctness, and rewards accordingly*
not tolerate perverted *j* . . . 2 Chr 19:7
Almighty cannot twist *j* . . . Job 34:12
will judge the world with *j* . . . Ps 9:8
the *j* of your cause . . . Ps 37:6

j being miscarried . . . Eccl 5:8
the measuring line of *j* . . . Isa 28:17
reveal *j* to the nations . . . Isa 42:1
my *j* will become a light . . . Isa 51:4
j is nowhere to be found . . . Isa 59:14
a mighty flood of *j* . . . Amos 5:24
Where is the God of *j* . . . Mal 2:17
proclaim *j* to the nations . . . Matt 12:18
widow . . . appealing for *j* . . . Luke 18:3
humiliated and received no *j* . . . Acts 8:33
God, in his *j*, will punish . . . Rom 2:2
king of *j* . . . Heb 7:2

JUSTIFIED, JUSTIFY *defend; acquit; see MADE RIGHT (with God)*
anxious to see you *j* . . . Job 33:32
j by them or . . . condemned . . . Matt 12:37
man wanted to *j* his actions . . . Luke 10:29
returned home *j* before God . . . Luke 18:14
boasting about you is *j* . . . 2 Cor 8:24

KEY(S) *instrument that opens (or locks) doors or gates; symbolic of authority, power, and control*
the *k* of the Kingdom . . . Matt 16:19
you hide the *k* to knowledge . . . Luke 11:52
k of death and the grave . . . Rev 1:18
has the *k* of David . . . Rev 3:7

KILL(ED)(ING)(S) *to take or deprive of life; if by accident, this is manslaughter; if deliberately, this is murder*
Cain attacked and *k* his brother . . . Gen 4:8
who murders must be *k* . . . Gen 9:5
gain by *k* our brother? . . . Gen 37:26
Moses *k* the Egyptian . . . Exod 2:12
k all the firstborn sons . . . Exod 12:12
deliberately attacks and *k* . . . Exod 21:14
k even your brothers, friends . . . Exod 32:27
k us here in this wilderness . . . Num 16:13
who accidentally *k* someone . . . Num 35:15
the one who *k* and gives life . . . Deut 32:39
Uriah the Hittite was *k*, too . . . 2 Sam 11:21
Am I God, that I can *k* . . . 2 Kgs 5:7
jealousy *k* the simple . . . Job 5:2
God might *k* me . . . Job 13:15
For your sake we are *k* . . . Ps 44:22
the tongue can *k* or nourish . . . Prov 18:21
A time to *k* . . . Eccl 3:3
They can only *k* your body . . . Matt 10:28
He will be *k*, but three days . . . Matt 17:23
will *k* some by crucifixion . . . Matt 23:34
k him and get the estate . . . Luke 20:14
you are trying to *k* me . . . John 7:19
You *k* the author of life . . . Acts 3:15
Get up, Peter; *k* and eat . . . Acts 10:13
For your sake we are *k* . . . Rom 8:36
Jews . . . *k* the Lord Jesus . . . 1 Thes 2:15
army was *k* by the sharp sword . . . Rev 19:21

KIND(LY)(NESS) *benevolent; favorably disposed; gentle; forbearing*
k to me and saved my life . . . Gen 19:19
shown *k* to my master . . . Gen 24:14
but I will remember your *k* . . . Ps 42:6
Has God forgotten to be *k*? . . . Ps 77:9
loving and *k* to thousands . . . Jer 32:18
no *k*, no knowledge of God . . . Hos 4:1
k only to your friends . . . Matt 5:47
How *k* the Lord is! . . . Luke 1:25
he is *k* to the unthankful . . . Luke 6:35
She was always doing *k* . . . Acts 9:36
k give me your attention . . . Acts 24:4
k, tolerant, and patient God . . . Rom 2:4
God is both *k* and severe . . . Rom 11:22
Love is patient and *k* . . . 1 Cor 13:4
reject . . . God's great *k* . . . 2 Cor 6:1
patience, *k*, goodness . . . Gal 5:22
k to each other, tenderhearted . . . Eph 4:32
God's great *k* to sinners . . . Col 1:6
clothe yourselves with . . . *k* . . . Col 3:12
Has she been *k* to strangers? . . . 1 Tim 5:10
k to us through Christ . . . 2 Tim 1:19

KING(S) *sovereign ruler (often God); chief among competitors; see KINGDOM*
to their *k*, the pharaoh . . . Gen 12:15
The *k* of Sodom, Gomorrah . . . Gen 14:3
K will be among them! . . . Gen 17:6
In those days Israel had no *k* . . . Judg 17:6
We want a *k* instead! . . . 1 Sam 10:19
Long live *K* Adonijah! . . . 1 Kgs 1:25
It is the *k* of beasts . . . Job 41:34
my chosen *k* on the throne . . . Ps 2:6
let the *K* of glory enter . . . Ps 24:7, 9
You, O God, are my *k* . . . Ps 74:12
God is *K* in every generation! . . . Ps 146:10
Because of me, *k* reign . . . Prov 8:15
Never make light of the *k* . . . Eccl 10:20
a righteous *k* is coming! . . . Isa 32:1
judge, our lawgiver, and our *k* . . . Isa 33:22
He is the everlasting *K*! . . . Jer 10:10
Israel will be . . . without a *k* . . . Hos 3:4
We have no *k* because . . . Hos 10:3
the LORD will be *k* . . . Zech 14:9
Hail! *K* of the Jews! . . . Matt 27:29
the promised *K* to come . . . Luke 2:38
k have longed to see . . . Luke 10:24
I am not an earthly *k* . . . John 18:36
Without us . . . become *k*! . . . 1 Cor 4:8
almighty God, the *K* of kings . . . 1 Tim 6:15
His ten horns are ten *k* . . . Rev 17:12
K of *k* and Lord of lords . . . Rev 19:16

KINGDOM(S) *rule or realm; dominion of a king*
God of all the *k* . . . 2 Kgs 19:15
is your *k*. We adore you . . . 1 Chr 29:11
Israel became his *k* . . . Ps 114:2
your *k* is an everlasting *k* . . . Ps 145:13
this *k* will be divided . . . Dan 2:41
the Most High rules . . . *k* . . . Dan 4:17
K of Heaven is near . . . Matt 3:2
live for . . . the *K* of God . . . Matt 6:33
the secrets of the *K* . . . Matt 13:11
not fit for the *K* of God . . . Luke 9:62
the *K* of God is near! . . . Luke 10:11
K of God is among you . . . Luke 17:21
can never see the *K* . . . John 3:3
my *K* is not of this world . . . John 18:36
the *K* of God is not . . . Rom 14:17
will not inherit the *K* . . . Gal 5:21
no immoral . . . inherit the *K* . . . Eph 5:5
these people overthrew *k* . . . Heb 11:33
He has made us his *k* . . . Rev 1:6

KISS(ED)(ES)(ING) *salute (or caress) with the lips; to embrace; expression of Christian love (= "sacred kiss")*
k me, my son . . . Gen 27:26
Then Jacob *k* Rachel . . . Gen 29:11
Joseph *k* each of his brothers . . . Gen 45:15
Righteousness and peace have *k*! . . . Ps 85:10
Wounds . . . better than many *k* . . . Prov 27:6
May your *k* be as exciting as . . . Song 7:9
and *k* the calf-idols!" . . . Hos 13:2
give him the *k* of greeting . . . Matt 26:48
she kept *k* his feet . . . Luke 7:38
embraced him, and *k* him . . . Luke 15:20

KNEW, KNOW(ING)(N)(S) *to be intimately familiar with; to discern, recognize, regard, acknowledge, pay heed to, approve, learn*
like God, *k* everything . . . Gen 3:5
now you will be *k* as Abraham . . . Gen 17:5
I *k* what the dream means . . . Gen 40:12
I don't *k* the LORD . . . Exod 5:2
k that I am the LORD . . . Exod 8:22
God who *k* your deeds . . . 1 Sam 2:3
I *k* that my Redeemer lives . . . Job 19:25
k what is right from wrong . . . Ps 37:30
You *k* my every thought . . . Ps 139:2
nor do I *k* the Holy One . . . Prov 30:3
I *k* you before I formed you . . . Jer 1:5
that they truly *k* me . . . Jer 9:24
what it means to *k* me? . . . Jer 22:16
I *k* the plans I have for you . . . Jer 29:11
k exactly what you need . . . Matt 6:8
I never *k* you. Go away . . . Matt 7:23
no one *k* the day or . . . Matt 24:36
I don't even *k* the man . . . Matt 26:72
I am telling you what we *k* . . . John 3:11
How does he *k* so much . . . John 7:15
If you *k* me, then you . . . John 8:19
k my own sheep, and they *k* me . . . John 10:14
eternal life—to *k* you . . . John 17:3
you *k* I love you . . . John 21:15-17
they are not for you to *k* . . . Acts 1:7
I *k* Jesus, and I know Paul . . . Acts 19:15
merely *k* the law . . . Rom 2:13
God *k* his people in advance . . . Rom 8:29
Now we *k* only a little . . . 1 Cor 13:9
Before you Gentiles *k* God . . . Gal 4:8
priceless gain of *k* Christ . . . Phil 3:8
Lord *k* those who are his . . . 2 Tim 2:19
you *k* what I teach, Timothy . . . 2 Tim 3:10
leads to *k* God better . . . 2 Pet 1:5
we *k* he lives in us . . . 1 Jn 3:24

KNOWLEDGE(ABLE) *learning; awareness; sum of what is known; see KNOW*
the *k* of good and evil . . . Gen 2:9
Such *k* is higher than . . . Job 11:8
good judgment and *k* . . . Ps 119:66
Such *k* is too wonderful . . . Ps 139:6
people treasure *k* . . . Prov 10:14
wise and *k* leaders . . . Prov 28:2
k only increases sorrow . . . Eccl 1:18
God gives wisdom, *k* . . . Eccl 2:26
k to the scholars . . . Dan 2:21
k will increase . . . Dan 12:4
complete *k* and truth . . . Rom 2:20
every kind of *k* . . . 1 Cor 1:5
special *k* will all disappear . . . 1 Cor 13:8
faith and *k* of God's Son . . . Eph 4:13
with their so-called *k* . . . 1 Tim 6:20
full *k* of the truth . . . Heb 10:26
special favor and *k* . . . 2 Pet 3:18

LABOR(ERS)(S) *work that produces goods and services; the product of that work; strenuous effort*
painful *l* of farming this . . . Gen 5:29
take advantage of poor *l* . . . Deut 24:14
the forced *l* that Solomon . . . 1 Kgs 9:15
His *l* will not be rewarded . . . Job 20:18
with the fruit of your *l* . . . Ps 104:13
they *l* hard all summer . . . Prov 6:8
reward for all my *l* . . . Eccl 2:10
experiencing the pains of *l* . . . John 16:21
going through *l* pains for you . . . Gal 4:19
enjoy the fruit of their *l* . . . 2 Tim 2:6
find rest from their *l* . . . Heb 4:10
cried out in the pain of *l* . . . Rev 12:2

LAMENT(S) *to regret strongly; a loud mourning or wailing*
l the fate of Jephthah's daughter . . . Judg 11:40
songs of sorrow . . . *Book of L* . . . 2 Chr 35:25
I wail and *l* for Jazer . . . Isa 16:9
teach one another how to *l* . . . Jer 9:20
will you *l* and mourn? . . . Jer 47:5

LANGUAGE(S) *audible, meaningful sound; dialect or manner of speech peculiar to a certain people; a special language gift given by the Holy Spirit*
each tribe with its own *l* . . . Gen 10:5
divided into different *l* groups . . . Gen 10:25
by giving them many *l* . . . Gen 11:9
all races and nations and *l* . . . Dan 3:4; 5:19
speak in unknown *l* . . . 1 Cor 12:10, 28, 30
If I could speak in any *l* . . . 1 Cor 13:1
talking in an unknown *l* . . . 1 Cor 14:6
speaking in plain *l* . . . 1 Cor 14:7
Don't use foul or abusive *l* . . . Eph 4:29
slander, and dirty *l* . . . Col 3:8
from every tribe and *l* . . . Rev 5:9
from every . . . people and *l* . . . Rev 7:9

LAUGH(ED)(ING)(S)(TER) *to show mirth or joy; to despise or mock something*

/to himself in disbelief . . . Gen 17:17
Why did Sarah / . . . Gen 18:13
despises you and / at you . . . 2 Kgs 19:21
You will / at destruction . . . Job 5:22
fill your mouth with / . . . Job 8:21
People jeer and / at me . . . Job 16:10
heaven /. The Lord scoffs at . . . Ps 2:4
But the Lord just / . . . Ps 37:13
/ ends, the grief remains . . . Prov 14:13
to cry and a time to / . . . Eccl 3:4
Sorrow is better than / . . . Eccl 7:3
A party gives / . . . Eccl 10:19
you will / with joy . . . Luke 6:21
/ will turn to mourning . . . Luke 6:25
the leaders / and scoffed . . . Luke 23:35
sadness instead of / . . . Jas 4:9

LAW(S) *words of Moses; a binding decree; a universal principle; governing authority*
commands, regulations, and / . . . Gen 26:5
marry Tamar, as our / requires . . . Gen 38:8
Joseph then made it a / . . . Gen 47:26
This / applies to everyone . . . Exod 12:49
written in the Book of the *L* . . . Josh 8:31
/ . . . contained in the whole / . . . 2 Kgs 17:13
his covenant—all the / . . . 2 Kgs 18:12
found the Book of the *L* . . . 2 Kgs 22:8
a scribe, well-versed in the / . . . Ezra 7:6
/ of the Persians and Medes . . . Esth 1:19
He made the / of the rain . . . Job 28:26
the / of the universe . . . Job 38:33
they think about his / . . . Ps 1:2
foundations of / and order . . . Ps 11:3
/ of the LORD is perfect . . . Ps 19:7
Oh, how I love your /! . . . Ps 119:97
LORD has magnified his / . . . Isa 42:21
cherish my / in your hearts . . . Isa 51:7
the / is no more . . . Lam 2:9
The / has become paralyzed . . . Hab 1:4
to abolish the / of Moses . . . Matt 5:17
/ of Moses says . . . Matt 5:21ff
the / has lost its force . . . Luke 16:17
they never had God's written / . . . Rom 2:12
the more we know God's / . . . Rom 3:20
to avoid breaking the / . . . Rom 4:15
no longer subject to the / . . . Rom 6:14
I died to the / so that . . . Gal 2:19
we were guarded by the / . . . Gal 3:23
his Son . . . subject to the / . . . Gal 4:4
Under the system of Jewish / . . . Heb 13:11
perfect / . . . sets you free . . . Jas 1:25

LEAD(ING)(S), LEADER(S)(SHIP) *to guide by direction or example; to go through; to go first; to result in; chief among others*
the / of different clans . . . Gen 36:15
The / of the Philistines . . . Judg 16:5
path of the wicked / to . . . Ps 1:6
L me in the right path . . . Ps 5:8
Those who / blameless lives . . . Ps 15:2
surefooted as a deer, / me . . . Ps 18:33
/ me beside peaceful streams . . . Ps 23:2
/ me to a glorious destiny . . . Ps 73:24
/ Israel like a flock . . . Ps 80:1
Pride / to disgrace . . . Prov 11:2
/ them beside cool waters . . . Isa 49:10
a / among the nations . . . Isa 55:4
blind guides / the blind . . . Matt 15:14
Whoever wants to be a / . . . Mark 10:43
The / priests and . . . Luke 22:2
by name and / them out . . . John 10:3
If God has given you / . . . Rom 12:8
to / us until Christ came . . . Gal 3:24
follow the Holy Spirit's / . . . Gal 5:25
/ a life worthy of your calling . . . Eph 4:1
/ them by your good example . . . 1 Pet 5:3

LEARN(ED)(ING) *to discover or come to know; to develop the habit of; instruction or education*
/ together what is good . . . Job 34:4
who do evil never /? . . . Ps 14:4; 54:4
I want you to / this lesson . . . Prov 6:9
wise person makes / a joy . . . Prov 15:2
L to do good . . . Isa 1:17
not / this from any human . . . Matt 16:17
/ a lesson from the fig tree . . . Matt 24:32
Gamaliel. At his feet I / . . . Acts 22:3
I / that he was a Roman . . . Acts 23:27
prophesy . . . that everyone will / . . . 1 Cor 14:31
when you / about Christ . . . Eph 4:20
obey the truth we have / . . . Phil 3:16
teaching you / from me . . . 2 Tim 1:13

LEPERS, LEPROSY, LEPROUS *sufferer from a severe contagious skin disease; of houses and clothing, an infectious mildew; figurative of a morally or spiritually plague-like influence*
white as snow with / . . . Exod 4:6
white as snow with / . . . Num 12:10
Naaman . . . suffered from / . . . 2 Kgs 5:1
Gehazi . . . was / . . . 2 Kgs 5:27
King Uzziah had / . . . 2 Chr 26:21
have been healed of / . . . Matt 8:4
the many / in Israel . . . Luke 4:27
an advanced case of / . . . Luke 5:12
the / are cured . . . Luke 7:22

LETTER(S) *written communication; unit of the alphabet*
he writes her a / of divorce . . . Deut 24:1
/, telling King Artaxerxes . . . Ezra 4:8
Your Majesty, give me / . . . Neh 2:7
sent many threatening / . . . Neh 6:19
The / decreed that all Jews . . . Esth 3:13
because of Mordecai's / . . . Esth 9:26
you asked in your / . . . 1 Cor 7:1
you are a / from Christ . . . 2 Cor 3:3
His / are demanding . . . 2 Cor 10:10
what large / I use . . . Gal 6:11
vision, a revelation, or a / . . . 2 Thes 2:2

LIFE *living beings; the animation, sustenance or vitality of something; a manner of living; period from birth to death; spiritual existence transcending death; salvation; see LIVE, LIVING*
will be masters over all / . . . Gen 1:26
into it the breath of / . . . Gen 2:7
the tree of / . . . Gen 2:9; 3:22, 24
All your / you will struggle . . . Gen 3:17
/ of any creature is in its blood . . . Lev 17:11
bread for their /; real / comes . . . Deut 8:3
Your rule should be / for / . . . Deut 19:21
choice . . . between / and death . . . Deut 30:15
But spare his / . . . Job 2:6
/ is long and hard . . . Job 7:1
my / is but a breath . . . Job 7:7
and clean up your / . . . Job 22:23
getting into a / of evil . . . Job 36:21
You will show me the way of / . . . Ps 16:11
Wisdom is a tree of / . . . Prov 3:18
whoever finds me finds / . . . Prov 8:35
Real / is not measured by . . . Luke 12:15
L itself was in him . . . John 1:4
Spirit who gives eternal / . . . John 6:63
I lay down my / for . . . John 10:15
the resurrection and the / . . . John 11:25
eternal / through Christ . . . Rom 6:23
fullness of / . . . from God . . . Eph 3:19
/ is like the morning fog . . . Jas 4:14
the one who is eternal / . . . 1 Jn 1:2
the Lamb's Book of *L* . . . Rev 21:27
fruit from the tree of / . . . Rev 22:14

LIGHT *daytime; brightness; illumination; spiritual enlightenment; exposure to the truth and justice*
Let there be / . . . Gen 1:3
rebel against the / . . . Job 24:13
waited for the /, but darkness . . . Job 30:26
God, you / up my darkness . . . Ps 18:28
The LORD is my / . . . Ps 27:1
Your word . . . a / for my path . . . Ps 119:105
the sinner's / is snuffed . . . Prov 13:9
walk in the / of the LORD! . . . Isa 2:5
will see a great / . . . Isa 9:2
my justice will become a / . . . Isa 51:4
nations will come to your / . . . Isa 60:3
the / of the world . . . Matt 5:14
He is a / to reveal God . . . Luke 2:32
John himself was not the / . . . John 1:8
They hate the / because . . . John 3:20
I am the / of the . . . John 8:12
this / is . . . the glory of God . . . 2 Cor 4:6
full of / from the Lord . . . Eph 5:8
children of the / and . . . 1 Thes 5:5
called . . . into his wonderful / . . . 1 Pet 2:9
God is / . . . no darkness in him . . . 1 Jn 1:5
and the Lamb is its / . . . Rev 21:23

LION(ESS)(S) *a wild beast with a threatening roar; symbolic of a strong and fierce enemy*
Judah is a young /, . . . a / . . . Gen 49:9
a / . . . , drinking the blood . . . Num 23:24
What is stronger than a /? . . . Judg 14:18
they have the heart of a / . . . 2 Sam 17:10
Benaiah . . . chased a / . . . 2 Sam 23:20
made twelve other / figures . . . 1 Kgs 10:20
/ came out and killed him . . . 1 Kgs 13:24
LORD sent / among . . . 2 Kgs 17:25
safe among /, and a little child . . . Isa 11:6
the face of a / . . . Ezek 1:10; 10:14
your mother? A / among /! . . . Ezek 19:2
thrown to the / . . . Dan 6:7, 12
first beast was like a / . . . Dan 7:4
shut the mouths of / . . . Heb 11:33
the Devil . . . like a roaring / . . . 1 Pet 5:8
first . . . had the form of a / . . . Rev 4:7

LIVE(D)(S), LIVING *to be alive or come to life; to endure a period of time (a life span); to attain eternal life; animate life; see LIFE*
man became a / person . . . Gen 2:7
Then they will / forever! . . . Gen 3:22
herdsmen who / in tents . . . Gen 4:20
Adam / another 800 years . . . Gen 5:4
how to conduct their / . . . Exod 18:20
will live long and prosperous / . . . Deut 5:33
Why did my mother let me /? . . . Job 3:12
I do not want to go on / . . . Job 7:16
decided the length of our / . . . Job 14:5
If mortals die, can they / . . . Job 14:14
I know that my Redeemer / . . . Job 19:25
not found among the / . . . Job 28:13
Come back to me and /! . . . Amos 5:4
righteous will / by their faith . . . Hab 2:4
God of the /, not the dead . . . Matt 22:32
in him we / and move and . . . Acts 17:28
those who / for themselves . . . Rom 2:8
can we continue to / in it? . . . Rom 6:2
a / and holy sacrifice . . . Rom 12:1
but Christ / in me . . . Gal 2:20
/ now by the Holy Spirit . . . Gal 5:25
to me, / is for Christ . . . Phil 1:21
word of God is full of / power . . . Heb 4:12
should / their / as Christ did . . . 1 Jn 2:6

LOINS *literally, lower part of the back between ribs and hip area; symbolic of readiness, strength, or reproductivity*
two kidneys . . . near the / . . . Lev 3:4, 15; 4:9; 7:4
Crush the / of their enemies . . . Deut 33:11
the seed . . . in Abraham's / . . . Heb 7:10

LORD *traditionally rendered, Jehovah (Hebrew = Yahweh); the sovereign God Almighty*
The *L* . . . has sent me . . . Exod 3:15
I am the *L* . . . Lev 19:12ff
The *L* is our God, the *L* alone . . . Deut 6:4
You alone are the *L* . . . Neh 9:6
L Almighty—he is the King . . . Ps 24:10
How kind the *L* is! . . . Ps 116:5
the *L* is a faithful God . . . Isa 30:18
The *L* Is Our Righteousness . . . Jer 23:6
provoked the *L*, so their Lord . . . Hos 12:14

LORD(ING)(S) *honored one or a superior; master (to a slave); king or ruler; to exercise authority; see MASTER*
speak further to my *L* . . . Gen 18:27
My *l*, . . . be my guests . . . Gen 19:2
L, will you kill an innocent . . . Gen 20:4
They are gifts, my *l* . . . Gen 33:8
O *L*, I'm just not . . . Exod 4:10
still *l* it over my people . . . Exod 9:17
to Moses, "Oh, my *l*! Please . . . Num 12:11
Give thanks to the *L* of *l* . . . Ps 136:3
my *l* the king, I beg you . . . Jer 37:20
The *L*, the LORD Almighty . . . Jer 46:10
My *l* the king has ordered . . . Dan 1:10
God of gods, the *L* over kings . . . Dan 2:47
L our God is merciful and . . . Dan 9:9
Do not test the *L* your God . . . Matt 4:7
tyrants, and officials *l* it over . . . Matt 20:25
just say, 'The *L* needs it . . . Mark 11:3
The *L* our God is the one . . . Mark 12:29
Praise the *L*, the God of . . . Luke 1:68
yes, the Messiah, the *L* . . . Luke 2:11
The *L* has really risen! . . . Luke 24:34
call me 'Teacher' and '*L*,' . . . John 13:13
Jesus Christ, who is *L* of all . . . Acts 10:36
if you confess . . . Jesus is *L* . . . Rom 10:9
so-called gods and many *l* . . . 1 Cor 8:5
say, "Jesus is *L*," . . . 1 Cor 12:3
the *L* is the Spirit . . . 2 Cor 3:17
that Jesus Christ is *L* . . . Phil 2:11
Don't *l* it over the people . . . 1 Pet 5:3
our only Master and *L*, Jesus . . . Jude 1:4
he is *L* over all *l* . . . Rev 17:14
L our God, the Almighty, reigns . . . Rev 19:6

LOST *no longer possessed or known; beyond reach; ruined emotionally, physically, or morally; lacking assurance of eternal salvation*
time *l* because of the injury . . . Exod 21:19
l heart and were paralyzed . . . Josh 5:1
l even to God on high . . . Job 3:4
those who had *l* hope . . . Job 29:13
wandered in the desert, *l* . . . Ps 107:4
wandered away like a *l* sheep . . . Ps 119:176
l sheep . . . have *l* their way . . . Jer 50:6
your memory *l* to history . . . Ezek 21:32
I will search for my *l* ones . . . Ezek 34:16
Israel—God's *l* sheep . . . Matt 10:6
hundred sheep, and one . . . is *l* . . . Matt 18:12
l sinner who returns to God . . . Luke 15:7
was *l*, but now he is found . . . Luke 15:24
not one was *l*, except . . . John 17:12
l in darkness without God . . . Rom 2:19

LOTS *small stones or other devices used for making choices, much like throwing dice or drawing straws*
sacred *l* to determine which goat . . . Lev 16:8
the LORD's will by . . . *l* . . . Num 27:21
inheritance by means of sacred *l* . . . Josh 14:2
cast sacred *l* . . . to decide . . . Josh 18:6
cast sacred *l* to determine when . . . Neh 10:34
they cast *l*, and . . . Matthias . . . Acts 1:26

LOVE(D)(RS)(S) *the ultimate expression of God's loyalty, purity, and mercy extended toward his people—to be reflected in human relationships of brotherly concern, marital fidelity, and adoration of God*
l your neighbor as yourself . . . Lev 19:18
your magnificent, unfailing *l* . . . Num 14:19
Because he *l* your ancestors . . . Deut 4:37
l the LORD your God . . . Deut 6:5
a sign of his unfailing *l* . . . Job 37:13
LORD corrects those he *l* . . . Prov 3:12
always be captivated by her *l* . . . Prov 5:19
I *l* all who *l* me . . . Prov 8:17
but *l* covers all offenses . . . Prov 10:12
A time to *l* . . . Eccl 3:8
your *l* is sweeter than wine . . . Song 1:2
not to awaken *l* until . . . Song 2:7; 3:5; 8:4
prostituted yourself with many *l* . . . Jer 3:2
I have taken away my unfailing *l* . . . Jer 16:5
"Name your daughter . . . 'Not *l* . . . Hos 1:6
I'll run after other *l* . . . Hos 2:5
I have *l* you deeply . . . Mal 1:2
I say, *l* your enemies! . . . Matt 5:44
If you *l* your father or . . . Matt 10:37
Who . . . *l* him more . . . Luke 7:42
God so *l* the world . . . John 3:16
have God's *l* within you . . . John 5:42
Those who *l* their life . . . John 12:25
L each other. Just as I have *l* . . . John 13:34
as the Father has *l* me . . . John 15:9
how dearly God *l* us . . . Rom 5:5
except the debt of *l* . . . Rom 13:8
but didn't *l* others . . . 1 Cor 13:1, 2
greatest of these is *l* . . . 1 Cor 13:13
Christ's *l* controls us . . . 2 Cor 5:14
Son of God, who *l* me . . . Gal 2:20
husbands must *l* your wives . . . Eph 5:25
l . . . from a pure heart . . . 1 Tim 1:5
l of money is at the root . . . 1 Tim 6:10
l . . . with true Christian love . . . Heb 13:1
l covers a multitude of sins . . . 1 Pet 4:8
when you *l* the world . . . 1 Jn 2:15
know God— for God is *l* . . . 1 Jn 4:8
perfect *l* expels all fear . . . 1 Jn 4:18
fallen from your first *l*! . . . Rev 2:4

LUST(FUL)(S) *inordinate desire or craving*
if your eye . . . causes you to *l* . . . Matt 5:29
burned with *l* for each other . . . Rom 1:27
give in to its *l* desires . . . Rom 6:12
better to marry than . . . *l* . . . 1 Cor 7:9
eagerness for *l* pleasure . . . Gal 5:19
l passion as the pagans . . . 1 Thes 4:5
Run from . . . youthful *l* . . . 2 Tim 2:22
l, their feasting and drunkenness . . . 1 Pet 4:3
l for everything we see . . . 1 Jn 2:16

MADE, MAKE(R), MAKING *to create, prepare, or fashion; to force; to bring about; to render*
God said, "Let us *m* people . . . Gen 1:26
m you a blessing to others . . . Gen 12:2
Do not *m* idols . . . Exod 20:4
m me willing to obey you . . . Ps 51:12
clay pot ever argue with its *m* . . . Isa 45:9
Can people *m* their own god? . . . Jer 16:20
They are *m* up everything . . . Jer 23:16
M of the heavens and earth . . . Jer 33:2
have both forgotten their *M* . . . Hos 8:14
Nothing exists that he didn't *m* . . . John 1:3
m holy by the word of God . . . 1 Tim 4:5
Jesus and the ones he *m* holy . . . Heb 2:11
m everything according to . . . Heb 8:5
those whom he is *m* holy . . . Heb 10:14

MADE RIGHT *to justify, to inherit righteousness, or to be put in a right relationship with God*
ever be *m r* in God's sight . . . Rom 3:20
are *m r* in God's sight . . . Rom 3:22
have been *m r* in God's sight . . . Rom 5:1, 9
will be *m r* in God's sight . . . Rom 5:19
was *m r* in God's sight . . . Heb 11:7

MAGNIFICENCE, MAGNIFICENT *great splendor; grand or lavish*
m . . . with milk and honey . . . Num 13:27
your *m*, unfailing love . . . Num 14:19
It is *m* in elevation . . . Ps 48:2
I will build a *m* palace . . . Jer 22:14
the *m* I gave this tree . . . Ezek 31:9
Artemis—this *m* goddess . . . Acts 19:27

MANAGE(R), MANAGING *to steward the resources of another; a person put in charge*
m my household and organize . . . Gen 41:40
Chuza, Herod's business *m* . . . Luke 8:3
the responsibility of *m* . . . Luke 12:42
hired a *m* to handle his . . . Luke 16:1
a *m* must be faithful . . . 1 Cor 4:2
must *m* his own family well . . . 1 Tim 3:4

MANNA *in Hebrew, the word means "What is it?"; miraculous supply of food given to Israel in the wilderness; symbolic of spiritual nourishment*
m . . . was white like coriander seed . . . Exod 16:31
Israel ate *m* for forty years . . . Exod 16:35
nothing to eat but this *m*! . . . Num 11:6
our ancestors ate *m* . . . bread . . . John 6:31

MARRI(AGE)(ED)(ES), MARRY(ING) *unite(d) in wedlock; figurative of any close union (often with God)*
Abram *m* Sarai, . . . Nahor *m* Milcah . . . Gen 11:29
isn't a man . . . for us to *m* . . . Gen 19:31
that woman you took is *m* . . . Gen 20:3
his mother arranged a *m* . . . Gen 21:21
I'd rather die than see Jacob *m* . . . Gen 27:46
must *m* within their tribe . . . Num 36:8
m her and . . . do not like her . . . Deut 21:14
must *m* . . . because he violated her . . . Deut 22:29
polluted by these mixed *m* . . . Ezra 9:2
men who had *m* pagan wives . . . Ezra 10:17
sinful deed . . . *m* foreign women? . . . Neh 13:27
Let us all *m* you! . . . Isa 4:1
and she *m* someone else . . . Jer 3:1
Do not *m* . . . in this place . . . Jer 16:2
M, and have children. . . . Multiply! . . . Jer 29:6
m vows. I made a covenant . . . Ezek 16:8
Mary, was engaged to be *m* . . . Matt 1:18
anyone who *m* a divorced . . . Matt 5:32
m another commits adultery . . . Matt 19:9
brother should *m* the widow . . . Matt 22:24
get along without *m* . . . 1 Cor 7:7
a *m* acceptable to the Lord . . . 1 Cor 7:39
it is wrong to be *m* . . . 1 Tim 4:3
Give honor to *m* . . . Heb 13:4

MASTER(S) *one in authority or leadership; employer; teacher; lord or Lord; to exercise authority or expertise*
They will be *m* over all life . . . Gen 1:26
husband, he will be your *m* . . . Gen 3:16
when my *m*—my husband . . . Gen 18:12
Joseph says: God has made me *m* . . . Gen 45:9
slave will belong to his *m* . . . Exod 21:6
he is a *m* at every craft! . . . Exod 31:5
not greater than the *m* . . . Matt 10:24
am *m* even of the Sabbath . . . Matt 12:8
M, M, we're going to drown! . . . Luke 8:24
can serve two *m* . . . Luke 16:13
Jesus, *M*, have mercy . . . Luke 17:13
the *m* . . . is served by his . . . Luke 22:27
not greater than the *m* . . . John 13:16
If your *m* is a Christian . . . 1 Tim 6:2
ready for the *M* to use you . . . 2 Tim 2:21

MEASURE(D)(S), MEASURING *an adequate or due portion; a basis or standard for comparison; to gauge or regulate the specific dimensions of*
container used to *m* . . . Exod 16:36
value in silver as *m* by . . . Lev 5:15
m length, weight, or volume . . . Lev 19:35
use honest weights and *m* . . . Deut 25:15
he saw wisdom and *m* it . . . Job 28:27
I will *m* out the valley . . . Ps 60:6
Ten *m* . . . yield only one *m* . . . Isa 5:10
the *m* line of justice . . . Isa 28:17
m off the heavens . . . Isa 40:12
m out your grain in false measures . . . Amos 8:5
gained by dishonestly *m* . . . Mic 6:10
m you use in judging others . . . Matt 7:2
m by how much we own . . . Luke 12:15
Spirit is upon him without *m* . . . John 3:34
m your value by . . . Rom 12:3
comparing . . . *m* themselves . . . 2 Cor 10:12

MEDITATE(S), MEDITAT(ING)(ION) *to contemplate*
curses . . . *m* on them as you . . . Deut 30:1
M on it day and night . . . Josh 1:8

and *m* in his Temple . . . Ps 27:4
we *m* on your unfailing love . . . Ps 48:9
I lie awake thinking of you, *m* . . . Ps 63:6
I will *m* on your principles . . . Ps 119:23

MEDIUM(S) *a psychic; one through whom it is thought the dead communicate with the living*
Do not rely on *m* . . . Lev 19:31
following *m* or psychics . . . Lev 20:6
act as *m* . . . a capital offense . . . Lev 20:27
m . . . call forth the spirits . . . Deut 18:11
There is a *m* at Endor . . . 1 Sam 28:7
Manasseh . . . consulted with *m* . . . 2 Kgs 21:6
the future by consulting *m* . . . Isa 8:19
call on spirits, *m*, and psychics . . . Isa 19:3

MEMBER(S) *part of a larger whole*
seventy *m* of Jacob's family . . . Gen 46:27
m of Chloe's household . . . 1 Cor 1:11
harmony among the *m* . . . 1 Cor 12:25
are *m* of God's family . . . Eph 2:19
a *m* of the Pharisees . . . Phil 3:5
m of one body . . . in peace . . . Col 3:15

MEMORIAL *remembrance; reputation; testimonial*
pillow . . . as a *m* pillar . . . Gen 28:18
manna . . . as a treasured *m* . . . Exod 16:32
the ephod as *m* stones . . . Exod 28:12
stones to build a *m* . . . Josh 4:6
m and a name far greater . . . Isa 56:5
crown will be a *m* in the . . . Zech 6:14
m decorations on the walls . . . Luke 21:5

MERCIES, MERCIFUL, MERCY *forgiving; compassionate; withholding of the punishment or judgment our sins deserve*
for the LORD was *m* . . . Gen 19:16
I will hear, for I am very *m* . . . Exod 22:27
the *m* and gracious God . . . Exod 34:6
m—he will not abandon . . . Deut 4:31
at your *m*—do whatever . . . Josh 9:25
in *m* and have heard their cry . . . 1 Sam 9:16
for his *m* is very great . . . 1 Chr 21:13
he is so just and *m* . . . Job 37:23
So in your *m*, save me . . . Ps 26:11
LORD, have *m* on me . . . Ps 41:10
I will wait for your *m* . . . Ps 52:9
he was *m* and forgave . . . Ps 78:38
m and . . . slow to get angry . . . Ps 103:8
I want you to be *m* . . . Hos 6:6
Maybe he will have *m* . . . Jon 1:6
to love *m*, and to walk . . . Mic 6:8
who are *m* . . . will be shown *m* . . . Matt 5:7
His *m* . . . to all who fear him . . . Luke 1:50
The one who showed him *m* . . . Luke 10:37
Master, have *m* on us! . . . Luke 17:13
m to me . . . a sinner . . . Luke 18:13
I will show *m* to anyone . . . Rom 9:15
the Jews refused his *m* . . . Rom 11:30
He is the source of every *m* . . . 2 Cor 1:3
What undeserved *m*! . . . Gal 1:15
God is so rich in *m* . . . Eph 2:4
why God had *m* on me . . . 1 Tim 1:16
if you have not been *m* . . . Jas 2:13

MESSIAH *see CHRIST*
Are you really the *M* . . . Matt 11:3
You are the *M* . . . Matt 16:16
claiming to be the *M* . . . Luke 21:8
he is the *M*, a king . . . Luke 23:2
We have found the *M* . . . John 1:41
the *M* . . . called Christ . . . John 4:25

MIGHT(IER)(ILY)(Y) *strength; power; authority; very great; extraordinary*
God stationed *m* angelic . . . Gen 3:24
rain fell in *m* torrents . . . Gen 7:11
"like Nimrod, a *m* hunter . . . Gen 10:9
make you into a *m* nation . . . Gen 17:2
strengthened by the *M* One . . . Gen 49:24
redeem you with *m* power . . . Exod 6:6
a *m* shout. Then the walls . . . Josh 6:5
the *m* of the LORD . . . Josh 9:9
He performed *m* miracles . . . Josh 24:17
Samson . . . with all his *m* . . . Judg 16:29
God came *m* upon Saul . . . 1 Sam 11:6
LORD came *m* upon . . . 1 Sam 16:13
the *m* heroes have fallen! . . . 2 Sam 1:19
God is so wise and so *m* . . . Job 9:4
The LORD, strong and *m* . . . Ps 24:8
wise man is *m* than a strong . . . Prov 24:5
He is a *m* savior . . . Zeph 3:17
weakest . . . as *m* as King David! . . . Zech 12:8
fall with a *m* crash . . . Matt 7:27
For he, the *M* One, is holy . . . Luke 1:49
He was a *m* teacher . . . Luke 24:19
Christ is the *m* power of God . . . 1 Cor 1:24
We use God's *m* weapons . . . 2 Cor 10:4
This is the same *m* power . . . Eph 1:19
m powers of darkness . . . Eph 6:12

MILK *from goats, used for food and drink; figurative of abundant produce, prosperity, spiritual food, or salvation*
flowing with *m* and honey . . . Exod 3:8, 17
a young goat in its mother's *m* . . . Exod 23:19
flowing with *m* and honey . . . Num 13:27
wine or *m*—it's all free! . . . Isa 55:1
the hills will flow with *m* . . . Joel 3:18
with *m* and not with solid . . . 1 Cor 3:2
to drink some of the *m*? . . . 1 Cor 9:7
like babies who drink only *m* . . . Heb 5:12
must crave pure spiritual *m* . . . 1 Pet 2:2

MIND(S) *the part of humans that engages in conscious thinking, feeling, and decision making; in the Bible, mind is akin to the heart, not the brain*
closed their *m* to understanding . . . Job 17:4
his *m* concerning me . . . Job 23:13
I will speak my *m* . . . Job 32:17
you look deep within the *m* . . . Ps 7:9
human heart and *m* are cunning . . . Ps 64:6
set their *m* on a pilgrimage . . . Ps 84:5
My *m* reels; my heart races . . . Isa 21:4
put my laws in their *m* . . . Jer 31:33
He's out of his *m* . . . Mark 3:21
flashed through Peter's *m* . . . Mark 14:72
love the Lord . . . all your *m* . . . Luke 10:27
opened their *m* to understand . . . Luke 24:45
m became dark and confused . . . Rom 1:21
at war with my *m* . . . Rom 7:23
Spirit controls your *m* . . . Rom 8:6
one *m*, united in thought and . . . 1 Cor 1:10
for we have the *m* of Christ . . . 1 Cor 2:16
peace will guard your . . . *m* . . . Phil 4:7
m and consciences are defiled . . . Titus 1:15
of one *m*, full of sympathy . . . 1 Pet 3:8

MINISTER(ED)(ING)(S), MINISTRIES, MINISTRY *one who serves or assists another of higher rank; exercise of one's gifts and resources*
my priests and will *m* to me . . . Exod 28:1
stand in his presence, to *m* . . . 2 Chr 29:11
Levitical priests who *m* . . . Jer 33:21, 22
clothes they wore while *m* . . . Ezek 42:14
Millions of angels *m* to him . . . Dan 7:10
Judas the traitor in this *m* . . . Acts 1:25
co-workers in my *m* . . . Rom 16:3
we are true *m* of God . . . 2 Cor 6:4
pretending to be godly *m* . . . 2 Cor 11:15
Complete the *m* God has given . . . 2 Tim 4:5
a believer as a result of my *m* . . . Phlm 1:10
a *m* that is far superior to the *m* . . . Heb 8:6

MISERABLE, MISERY *wretched; object of pity; suffering or distress—physical, emotional, and spiritual*
has heard about your *m* . . . Gen 16:11
Esau's wives made life *m* . . . Gen 26:35
the *m* of my people in Egypt . . . Exod 3:7
put me out of my *m* . . . 2 Sam 1:9
I am filled with shame and *m* . . . Job 10:15
spared this *m* existence . . . Job 10:19
What *m* comforters you are! . . . Job 16:2
M has drained my strength . . . Ps 31:10
I was weak and *m* . . . Ps 32:3
gladness in proportion to . . . *m*! . . . Ps 90:15
destruction and *m* follow them . . . Rom 3:16
what a *m* person I am! . . . Rom 7:24
we are the most *m* . . . 1 Cor 15:19

MORTAL(S) *(merely) human; subject to death*
m flesh . . . live no more than . . . Gen 6:3
Can a *m* be just and upright . . . Job 4:17
What are mere *m* . . . Job 7:17
give life to your *m* body . . . Rom 8:11
deliver us from *m* danger . . . 2 Cor 1:10
take these weak *m* bodies . . . Phil 3:21

MOURN(ED)(ER)(ERS)(ING)(S) *to grieve; sorrow*
people *m* greatly because . . . 1 Sam 6:19
m long enough for Saul . . . 1 Sam 16:1
m and wept and fasted . . . 2 Sam 1:12
in *m*; wear *m* clothes . . . 2 Sam 14:2
with no one to *m* them . . . Job 27:15
who comforts those who *m* . . . Job 29:25
turned my *m* into joyful . . . Ps 30:11
at death's door . . . the *m* . . . Eccl 12:5
Jerusalem will weep and *m* . . . Isa 3:26
called you to weep and *m* . . . Isa 22:12
merrymakers will sigh and *m* . . . Isa 24:7
I, Daniel, had been in *m* . . . Dan 10:2
m unrestrained. Rachel weeps . . . Matt 2:18
God blesses those who *m* . . . Matt 5:4
m in sorrow and shame? . . . 1 Cor 5:2
the sorrows of death and *m* . . . Rev 18:8

MULTIPLY, MULTIPLI(ED)(ES) *increase greatly in extent or number*
m and fill the earth . . . Gen 1:28
m my wounds without cause . . . Job 9:17
you will flourish and *m* . . . Isa 37:31
smallest family will *m* into . . . Isa 60:22
Marry, and have children. . . . *m*! . . . Jer 29:6
as the believers rapidly *m* . . . Acts 6:1

MURDER(ED)(ER)(S) *the personal, intentional killing of another person*
person who *m* must be killed . . . Gen 9:5
die because we *m* him . . . Gen 42:22
Do not *m* . . . Exod 20:13
will repay him for the *m* . . . 1 Kgs 2:32
m he committed at Jezreel . . . Hos 1:4
'Do not *m*. If you commit *m* . . . Matt 5:21
evil thoughts, *m*, adultery . . . Matt 15:19
a *m* from the beginning . . . John 8:44
Messiah whom you . . . *m* . . . Acts 7:52
quick to commit *m* . . . Rom 3:15
he has avenged the *m* . . . Rev 19:2

MYSTERI(ES)(IOUS), MYSTERY *secret; riddle; miracle*
solve the *m* of God? . . . Job 11:7
in strange and *m* ways . . . Isa 45:15
He reveals deep and *m* . . . Dan 2:22
m hidden since the creation . . . Matt 13:35
to understand this *m* . . . Rom 11:25
if I knew all the *m* . . . 1 Cor 13:2
This is a great *m* . . . Eph 5:32
great *m* of our faith . . . 1 Tim 3:16
God's *m* plan will . . . Rev 10:7
A *m* name . . . "Babylon . . . Rev 17:5

NAKED(NESS) *nude, without clothes; exposed; exposure*
and his wife were both *n* . . . Gen 2:25
felt shame at their *n* . . . Gen 3:7
covered their father's *n* . . . Gen 9:23
n from my mother's womb . . . Job 1:21
I was *n*, and you . . . Matt 25:36
n and exposed before his eyes . . . Heb 4:13
shamed by your *n* . . . Rev 3:18
strip her *n*, eat her flesh . . . Rev 17:16

NAME(D)(S) *to call by surname or designation; to appoint; authority; one's identity or reputation*
n the dry ground "land" . . . Gen 1:10

gave *n* to all the livestock . . . Gen 2:20
She *n* him Seth . . . Gen 4:25
His *n* became proverbial . . . Gen 10:9
I am changing your *n* . . . Gen 17:5
No wonder his *n* is Jacob . . . Gen 27:36
n will no longer be Jacob . . . Gen 32:28
This will be my *n* forever . . . Exod 3:15
Do not misuse the *n* . . . Exod 20:7
preserve his brother's *n* in Israel . . . Deut 25:7
all who love your *n* may . . . Ps 5:11
For the honor of your *n* . . . Ps 31:3
Erase their *n* from . . . Ps 69:28
that bears your holy *n* . . . Ps 74:7
I called you by *n* . . . Isa 45:4
I have sworn by my own *n* . . . Isa 45:23
My *n* is being blasphemed . . . Isa 52:5
calls on the *n* of the LORD . . . Joel 2:32
They will call on my *n* . . . Zech 13:9
may your *n* be honored . . . Matt 6:9
in your *n*, . . . in your *n*, . . . in your *n* . . . Matt 7:22
his *n* will be the hope . . . Matt 12:21
many will come in my *n* . . . Matt 24:5
calls his own sheep by *n* . . . John 10:3
The *n* of Jesus has healed . . . Acts 3:16
no other *n* in all of heaven . . . Acts 4:12
a *n* that is above every other *n* . . . Phil 2:9
n God gave him is far greater . . . Heb 1:4
write my God's *n* on them . . . Rev 3:12
144,000 who had his *n* . . . Rev 14:1
A *n* was written on him . . . Rev 19:12

NATION(S) *group of people defined by geography or ethnicity*
languages, territories, and *n* . . . Gen 10:20, 31
the father of a great *n* . . . Gen 12:2
that all the *n* of the earth . . . Josh 4:24
Why do the *n* rage? . . . Ps 2:1
He rules all the *n* . . . Ps 22:28
drove out the pagan *n* . . . Ps 44:2
Godliness exalts a *n* . . . Prov 14:34
house of prayer for all *n* . . . Isa 56:7
will become a mighty *n* . . . Isa 60:22
a *n*, . . . a country ever come . . . Isa 66:8
unify them into one *n* . . . Ezek 37:22
stands guard over your *n* . . . Dan 12:1
n and kingdoms . . . war . . . Matt 24:7
disciples of all the *n* . . . Matt 28:19
to reveal God to the *n* . . . Luke 2:32
by blessing other *n* . . . Rom 10:19
They will rule the *n* . . . Rev 2:27
language and people and *n* . . . Rev 5:9
from every *n* and tribe . . . Rev 7:9
many peoples, *n*, languages . . . Rev 10:11
to rule over every . . . *n* . . . Rev 13:7
medicine to heal the *n* . . . Rev 22:2

NATURAL(LY) *in conformity to laws of nature, or operating only in the physical realm (as opposed to spiritual principles or the supernatural realm); as expected (in accord with the usual course of things)*
Joseph *n* . . . a favorite . . . Gen 39:4
the *n* talented craftsmen . . . Exod 31:6
that dies a *n* death . . . Ezek 44:31
the *n* way to have sex . . . Rom 1:26
n bodies, so also . . . spiritual . . . 1 Cor 15:44
They live by *n* instinct . . . Jude 1:19

NATURE *inherent character or essence; given by God at birth*
acted contrary to *n* . . . Lev 20:12
reject . . . the laws of *n*! . . . Jer 31:36
eternal power and divine *n* . . . Rom 1:20
controlled by our old *n*, sinful . . . Rom 7:5
sinful *n* is always hostile to God . . . Rom 8:7
a Jew as far as his human *n* . . . Rom 9:5
sinful *n* loves to do evil . . . Gal 5:17
born with an evil *n* . . . Eph 2:3
will share in his divine *n* . . . 2 Pet 1:4

NEGLECT(ED) *disregard; overlook; ignore*
You *n* the Rock who . . . Deut 32:18
Don't *n* your mother's teaching . . . Prov 1:8
don't *n* your mother's teaching . . . Prov 6:20
not *n* the spiritual gift . . . 1 Tim 4:14
not *n* our meeting together . . . Heb 10:25

NEIGHBOR(HOOD)(S) *close friend; (adjacent) member of the community*
hitting your *n* like that? . . . Exod 2:13
ask their Egyptian *n* . . . Exod 11:2
another family in the *n* . . . Exod 12:4
testify falsely against your *n* . . . Exod 20:16
love your *n* as yourself . . . Lev 19:18
from your friends and *n* . . . 2 Kgs 4:3
If you can help your *n* . . . Prov 3:28
your *n* into your home . . . Zech 3:10
Moses says, 'Love your *n*' . . . Matt 5:43
And who is my *n* . . . Luke 10:29
Love your *n* as yourself . . . Rom 13:9
tell your *n* the truth . . . Eph 4:25

NEW(NESS) *fresh; original; different than before; successor; unfamiliar*
explore the *n* possessions . . . Gen 13:17
remind each *n* generation of . . . Lev 23:43
if the original owner . . . *n* owner . . . Lev 25:28
always open to *n* ideas . . . Prov 18:15
Nothing under the sun is truly *n* . . . Eccl 1:9
will find *n* strength . . . Isa 40:31
I am creating *n* heavens and a *n* . . . Isa 65:17
put a *n* spirit within them . . . Ezek 11:19
N wine must be stored in *n* wineskins . . . Matt 9:17
the day I drink it *n* with you . . . Matt 26:29
a *n* commandment: Love . . . John 13:34
you have been given *n* life . . . Rom 6:13
Christians become *n* persons . . . 2 Cor 5:17
I will make a *n* covenant . . . Heb 8:8
the *n* heavens and *n* earth . . . 2 Pet 3:13
a *n* name that no one knows . . . Rev 2:17
I saw a *n* heaven and a *n* earth . . . Rev 21:1
I am making all things *n*! . . . Rev 21:5

NEWS *fresh, original, or unfamiliar story of note; see GOOD NEWS*
'Saul is dead,' . . . good *n* . . . 2 Sam 4:10
good man . . . with good *n* . . . 2 Sam 18:27
You must have good *n* . . . 1 Kgs 1:42
the good *n* that he saves . . . 1 Chr 16:23
good *n* hidden in my heart . . . Ps 40:10
the good *n* that he saves . . . Ps 96:2
good *n* makes for good health . . . Prov 15:30
Good *n* from far away . . . Prov 25:25
good *n* . . . from the mountaintops! . . . Isa 40:9
bring good *n* to the poor . . . Isa 61:1
good *n* . . . a message of peace . . . Nah 1:15
the *n* that Jesus was . . . John 12:12

NIGHT *period of darkness between sunrise and sunset; figurative of suffering and sorrow, or the reign of sin and immorality*
God called . . . the darkness "*n*." . . . Gen 1:5
This *n* had been reserved . . . Exod 12:42
a pillar of fire at *n* . . . Exod 13:21
gives songs in the *n*? . . . Job 35:10
Weeping may go on all *n* . . . Ps 30:5
Darkness as black as *n* . . . Isa 60:2
he prayed to God all *n* . . . Luke 6:12
quickly . . . before the *n* falls . . . John 9:4
Nicodemus . . . to Jesus at *n* . . . John 19:39
The *n* is almost gone . . . Rom 13:12
like a thief in the *n* . . . 1 Thes 5:2
because there is no *n* . . . Rev 21:25

OATH(S) *an appeal to God to witness the truth of some statement*
Beersheba—"well of the *o*" . . . Gen 21:31
a vow . . . a pledge under *o* . . . Num 30:2
a peace treaty . . . with a binding *o* . . . Josh 9:15
o David and Jonathan had sworn . . . 2 Sam 21:7
I have sworn this *o* to him . . . Ps 89:3
promised with an *o* to give her . . . Matt 14:7
Peter denied . . . with an *o* . . . Matt 26:72

OBEDIENCE, OBEDIENT(LY), OBEY(ED)-(ING) *submissive to authority; comply with orders; fulfill one's responsibility*
o the terms of the covenant . . . Gen 17:9
who love me and *o* my commands . . . Deut 5:10
We will *o* him alone . . . Josh 24:24
O is far better than sacrifice . . . 1 Sam 15:22
stay pure? By *o* your word . . . Ps 119:9
wind and weather that *o* him . . . Ps 148:8
o your father's commands . . . Prov 6:20
If you will only *o* me . . . Isa 1:19
unless you *o* God better than . . . Matt 5:20
decisive issue is whether they *o* . . . Matt 7:21
Teach these new disciples to *o* . . . Matt 28:20
and was *o* to them . . . Luke 2:51
even the winds and waves *o* . . . Luke 8:25
We must *o* God rather than . . . Acts 5:29
who refuse to *o* the truth . . . Rom 2:8
because one other person *o* . . . Rom 5:19
have *o* with all your heart . . . Rom 6:17
It never did *o* God's laws . . . Rom 8:7
O the government, for God . . . Rom 13:1
you are *o* to the Lord . . . Rom 16:19
I *o* the law of Christ . . . 1 Cor 9:21
Children, *o* your parents . . . Eph 6:1
he *o* humbled himself . . . Phil 2:8
I *o* the Jewish law . . . Phil 3:6
Slaves must *o* their masters . . . Titus 2:9
Jesus . . . learned *o* from . . . Heb 5:8
See to it that you *o* God . . . Heb 12:25
Sarah *o* her husband . . . 1 Pet 3:6

OBSERVANCE, OBSERVE(D)(S) *to notice or consider; to keep or comply with; to watch over or protect*
God *o* all this corruption . . . Gen 6:12
must be *o* for seven days . . . Deut 16:13
another *o* . . . they fasted . . . Neh 9:1
From his throne he *o* all . . . Ps 33:14
for wisdom, I tried to *o* . . . Eccl 8:16
to *o* the Lord's Supper . . . Acts 20:7
who does not *o* and obey all . . . Gal 3:10

OFFEND(ED)(ER)(S) *sin against; to cause a scandal; to stumble or be a stumbling block*
the *o* must be punished . . . Exod 21:23
have I *o* your father . . . 1 Sam 20:1
anything in me that *o* you . . . Ps 139:24
o his glorious presence . . . Isa 3:8
those who are not *o* by me . . . Matt 11:6
you *o* the Pharisees by . . . Matt 15:12
we don't want to *o* them . . . Matt 17:27
Does this *o* you? . . . John 6:61
the Jews are *o* . . . 1 Cor 1:23
forgive the person who *o* . . . Col 3:13

OFFENSE(S) *displeasure; an occasion for stumbling or being a stumbling block because of sin*
an *o* against the LORD . . . Lev 5:19
guilty of a capital *o* . . . Lev 20:9ff
love covers all *o* . . . Prov 10:12
I have scattered your *o* like . . . Isa 44:22
Don't give *o* to Jews or . . . 1 Cor 10:32

OFFER(ED)(S), OFFERING(S) *present for acceptance; gift or sacrifice of various kinds*
LORD accepted Abel's *o* . . . Gen 4:4
burnt *o* on Isaac's shoulders . . . Gen 22:6
so we can *o* sacrifices . . . Exod 5:3, 17
o a burnt *o* for each . . . Job 1:5
o a burnt *o* for yourselves . . . Job 42:8
no delight in sacrifices or *o* . . . Ps 40:6
mindless *o* to God are evil . . . Eccl 5:1
his life is made an *o* for sin . . . Isa 53:10
o your sacrifices to the idols . . . Amos 4:4
Then come and *o* your sacrifice . . . Matt 5:24
immortality that God *o* . . . Rom 2:7
God's *o* of salvation . . . Rom 11:12
an *o* for the Christians . . . Rom 15:26
Eat whatever is *o* . . . 1 Cor 10:27
my life . . . an *o* to God . . . 2 Tim 4:6
required to *o* gifts and sacrifices . . . Heb 8:3

Christ *o* himself to God . . . Heb 9:14
o our sacrifice of praise . . . Heb 13:15

OFFSPRING *children or descendants*
your *o* and her *o* will be enemies . . . Gen 3:15
a mother animal and her *o* . . . Lev 22:28
o of adulterers and prostitutes! . . . Isa 57:3
We are his *o* . . . Acts 17:28

OLD(ER)(EST) *aged; former (associated with the past); worn out; obsolete (invalid)*
in legends of *o* . . . Gen 6:4
he died at a ripe *o* age . . . Gen 25:8
o son will serve the . . . younger . . . Gen 25:23
Rebekah's *o* nurse, Deborah . . . Gen 35:8
from the *o* son of Pharaoh . . . Exod 11:5
I think of the good *o* days . . . Ps 77:5
made him *o* before his time . . . Ps 89:45
gray hair . . . splendor of the *o* . . . Prov 20:29
when they are *o*, they will . . . Prov 22:6
new wine into *o* wineskins . . . Matt 9:17
o than the law of Moses . . . John 7:22
o enough to speak for himself . . . John 9:21, 23
your *o* men will dream dreams . . . Acts 2:17
Our *o* sinful selves were crucified . . . Rom 6:6
the *o* life is gone. A new life . . . 2 Cor 5:17
stripped off your *o* evil nature . . . Col 3:9
Never speak harshly to an *o* . . . 1 Tim 5:1
found fault with the *o* one . . . Heb 8:8

ONE *of the same (stuff); singular; first (in a series); unique*
the two are united into *o* . . . Gen 2:24
not a single *o* survived . . . Exod 14:28
the testimony of only *o* witness . . . Deut 17:6
three shrines—*o* for you, *o* for . . . Mark 9:5
the two are united into *o* . . . Mark 10:8
You lack only *o* thing . . . Mark 10:21
my Son, my Chosen *O* . . . Luke 9:35
be *o* flock with *o* shepherd . . . John 10:16
The Father and I are *o* . . . John 10:30
be *o*, just as you and I are *o* . . . John 17:21
you are *o* in Christ Jesus . . . Gal 3:28
o new person from the two . . . Eph 2:15
o Lord, *o* faith, *o* baptism . . . Eph 4:5
only *o* God and *o* Mediator . . . 1 Tim 2:5

OPEN(ED)(ING)(LY)(S) *set free; make accessible; in plain view; to move (as a door); to expound or explain*
eyes will be *o* when you eat . . . Gen 3:5
o in the sight of all Israel . . . 2 Sam 12:12
like *o* a floodgate . . . Prov 17:14
always *o* to new ideas . . . Prov 18:15
An *o* rebuke is better . . . Prov 27:5
o the eyes of the blind . . . Isa 42:7
he did not *o* his mouth . . . Isa 53:7
I *o* my arms to my own . . . Isa 65:2
and the door will be *o* . . . Matt 7:7
he *o* their minds to . . . Luke 24:45
you will all see heaven *o* . . . John 1:51
his ears are *o* to their prayers . . . 1 Pet 3:12
He *o* doors, . . . he shuts doors . . . Rev 3:7
Then I saw heaven *o* . . . Rev 19:11

OPPORTUNIT(Y)(IES) *favorable circumstance or advantage*
o to do even more mighty . . . Exod 11:9
many *o* to do good . . . 2 Cor 9:10
Whenever we have the *o* . . . Gal 6:10
the most of every *o* . . . Eph 5:16
let it be an *o* for joy . . . Jas 1:2

OPPRESS(ED)(ES)(ING)(ORS) *to treat cruelly or unjustly*
they will be *o* as slaves . . . Gen 15:13
o them with heavy tasks . . . Exod 3:9
Aram was *o* Israel . . . 2 Kgs 13:4
do you gain by *o* me? . . . Job 10:3
so just . . . he does not *o* . . . Job 37:23
and to crush their *o* . . . Ps 72:4
the rights of the *o* . . . Ps 82:3
the tears of the *o* . . . Eccl 4:1
was *o* and treated harshly . . . Isa 53:7
o widows, orphans, foreigners . . . Zech 7:10

were *o* by the Devil . . . Acts 10:38
the rich who *o* you . . . Jas 2:6

OPPRESSION *unjust or abusive exercise of authority or power*
rescue you from the *o* . . . Exod 3:17
burdened by *o* and suffering . . . Judg 2:18
He will save them from *o* . . . Ps 72:14
Rescue me from the *o* . . . Ps 119:134
I observed all the *o* . . . Eccl 4:1
instead he heard cries of *o* . . . Isa 5:7
I share their *o* so that . . . 1 Cor 9:22
He chose to share the *o* . . . Heb 11:25

ORDAIN(ED) *to arrange; prepare; establish something; appoint someone to a specific duty or office; to set apart (certain days or feasts) for religious observance; of God, to make an authoritative decree*
then anoint and *o* them . . . Exod 28:41
offering *o* at Mount Sinai . . . Num 28:6
o priests from the rank and . . . 1 Kgs 12:31
o . . . angelic guardian . . . Ezek 28:14
o of God to be the judge . . . Acts 10:42

OUTWARD(LY) *of or pertaining to the body and its physical features (as opposed to inner character); external*
People judge by *o* appearance . . . 1 Sam 16:7
look like upright people *o* . . . Matt 23:28
o beauty . . . fancy hairstyles . . . 1 Pet 3:3

OVERCOME *to gain the better of or superior position over; conquer*
your descendants *o* . . . Gen 24:60
o with emotion . . . Gen 43:30
o with emotion . . . 2 Sam 18:33
I have *o* the world . . . John 16:33
is *o* by some sin . . . Gal 6:1
beast was allowed . . . to *o* . . . Rev 13:7

OVERTHREW, OVERTHROW(N)(S) *conquer; upset*
o those who rose against . . . Exod 15:7
he *o* the mighty . . . Job 12:19
to destroy and *o* them . . . Jer 1:10
LORD *o* without mercy . . . Jer 20:16
I *o* it, destroyed it . . . Jer 31:28
and truth was *o* . . . Dan 8:12
I will *o* royal thrones . . . Hag 2:22
By faith these people *o* . . . Heb 11:33

PACIFI(ED)(ES) *to reduce anger or make peace with*
the king's anger was *p* . . . Esth 7:10
a secret bribe *p* fury . . . Prov 21:14

PAIN(ED)(FUL)(S) *physical, mental, or emotional suffering*
bear children with intense *p* . . . Gen 3:16
Honest words are *p* . . . Job 6:25
with sickness and *p* . . . Job 33:19
Feel my *p* and see my . . . Ps 25:18
eases their *p* and discomfort . . . Ps 41:3
I am suffering and in *p* . . . Ps 69:29
how bitter . . . , how *p* . . . Ps 73:21
filled with *p* and grief . . . Eccl 2:23
banish grief and *p*, but . . . Eccl 11:10
harvest will be . . . incurable *p* . . . Isa 17:11
had enough *p* already? . . . Jer 45:3
mortally wounded, groaning in *p* . . . Ezek 30:24
creation . . . in the *p* of childbirth . . . Rom 8:22
make my chains more *p* . . . Phil 1:17
as a woman's birth *p* . . . 1 Thes 5:3
discipline . . . is *p*! . . . Heb 12:11
Christ suffered physical *p* . . . 1 Pet 4:1
like the *p* of scorpion stings . . . Rev 9:5
no more death or . . . *p* . . . Rev 21:4

PARABLE(S) *brief narrative story told with earthly analogies to illustrate a spiritual truth*
speak to you in a *p* . . . Ps 78:2
p, wise sayings, and riddles . . . Prov 1:6
in *p* . . . mysteries hidden . . . Matt 13:35
he taught only with *p* . . . Mark 4:34

PARDON(ED)(S) *a judicial act by an appropriate authority (God) to relieve a guilty party of punishment*
Why not just *p* my sin . . . Job 7:21
in him will be freely *p* . . . Ps 34:22
Jerusalem. . . . her sins are *p* . . . Isa 40:2
for he will abundantly *p* . . . Isa 55:7
crimes . . . not yet *p* . . . Joel 3:21
another God like you, who *p* . . . Mic 7:18

PARTIAL(ITY) *incomplete; inclined to favor*
because of their father's *p* . . . Gen 37:4
no *p* and takes no bribes . . . Deut 10:17
God doesn't show *p* . . . Acts 10:34
All that I know now is *p* . . . 1 Cor 13:12
wisdom . . . shows no *p* . . . Jas 3:17

PASSOVER *the historic event (when God's judgment passed over the Hebrews); a commemorative meal and public festival observed by Jews; the prototype OT sacrifice for which Christ is the NT fulfillment*
this is the LORD's *P* . . . Exod 12:11
always celebrate the *P* at . . . Deut 16:1
P . . . marked their exodus . . . Josh 5:10
But not during the *P* . . . Matt 26:5
Unleavened Bread . . . the *P* . . . Luke 22:1
Christ, our *P* Lamb . . . 1 Cor 5:7
Israel to keep the *P* . . . Heb 11:28

PATIENCE, PATIENT(LY) *longsuffering; endurance; forbearance; characterized by this divine virtue or spiritual fruit*
My lord, . . . Be *p* . . . Gen 44:18
be *p* and let me say a word? . . . Job 4:2
Wait *p* for the LORD . . . Ps 27:14
wait *p* for him to act . . . Ps 37:7
they tested God's *p* . . . Ps 78:41
your ancestors tried my *p* . . . Ps 95:9
better to be *p* than powerful . . . Prov 16:32
Be *p* and I will pay it . . . Matt 18:29
kind, tolerant, and *p* God is . . . Rom 2:4
p with . . . his judgment . . . Rom 9:22
Be *p* in trouble . . . Rom 12:12
all the *p* and endurance . . . Col 1:11
Be *p* with everyone . . . 1 Thes 5:14
who *p* endure testing . . . Jas 1:12
partners . . . in *p* endurance . . . Rev 1:9

PEACE(FUL) *calm repose; eternal rest (after death); free of strife or discord; harmony in personal relationship, especially with God*
present a *p* offering . . . Lev 3:1, 6
his favor and give you his *p* . . . Num 6:26
make a *p* treaty with us . . . Josh 9:6
p in the land for forty . . . Judg 3:11; 5:31
at *p* now, asleep and at rest . . . Job 3:13
you will have *p* at last . . . Job 22:21
leads me beside *p* streams . . . Ps 23:2
Work hard at living in *p* . . . Ps 34:14
he speaks *p* to his people . . . Ps 85:8
Pray for the *p* of Jerusalem . . . Ps 122:6
happiness and *p* of mind . . . Prov 29:17
war and a time for *p* . . . Eccl 3:8
Father, Prince of *P* . . . Isa 9:6
p government will never end . . . Isa 9:7
You will keep in perfect *p* . . . Isa 26:3
beaten that we might have *p* . . . Isa 53:5
assurances of *p* . . . Jer 6:14; 8:11
p and prosperity of Babylon . . . Jer 29:7
bringing a message of *p* . . . Nah 1:15
and *p* on earth to all . . . Luke 2:14
come to bring *p* to the earth? . . . Luke 12:51
p is hidden from you . . . Luke 19:42
P be with you . . . Luke 24:36
the *p* I give isn't like . . . John 14:27
you may have *p* in me . . . John 16:33
May grace and *p* be yours . . . Rom 1:7
we have *p* with God . . . Rom 5:1
live in *p* with everyone . . . Rom 12:18
his children to live in *p* . . . 1 Cor 7:15
fruit in us: love, joy, *p* . . . Gal 5:22
Christ himself has made *p* . . . Eph 2:14
His *p* will guard your hearts . . . Phil 4:7

p that comes from Christ . . . Col 3:15
Pursue faith and love and *p* . . . 2 Tim 2:22
wisdom . . . is also *p* loving . . . Jas 3:17

PEOPLE *humanity; clan or kinfolk; nation; body of persons united by common roots or culture*
God said, "Let us make *p* . . . Gen 1:26
make you my own special *p* . . . Exod 6:7
the *p* of Shechem . . . Judg 9:2ff
Your *p* will be my *p* . . . Ruth 1:16
We are his *p*, the sheep . . . Ps 100:3
God's purpose . . . *p* should fear him . . . Eccl 3:14
Blessed be Egypt, my *p* . . . Isa 19:25
and they will be my *p* . . . Jer 31:1, 33
and they will be my *p* . . . Ezek 37:27
preparing the *p* for his arrival . . . Luke 1:17
the Gentiles . . . a *p* for himself . . . Acts 15:14
not my *p*, I will now call my people . . . Rom 9:25
and they will be my *p* . . . 2 Cor 6:16
will judge his own *p* . . . Heb 10:30
P are like grass . . . 1 Pet 1:24
now you are the *p* of God . . . 1 Pet 2:10
from every . . . *p* and nation . . . Rev 5:9
God is now among his *p*! . . . Rev 21:3

PERFECT(ED)(ION) *(brought to) wholeness and completeness; describes whatever level of maturity or morality can be expected given human nature*
you're as *p* as an angel . . . 1 Sam 29:9
Absalom . . . the *p* specimen . . . 2 Sam 14:25
Mount Zion, the *p* of beauty . . . Ps 50:2
devised the *p* plan! . . . Ps 64:6
Even *p* has its limits . . . Ps 119:96
Your decrees are *p* . . . Ps 119:138
Compared to you, no one is *p* . . . Ps 143:2
be *p*, even as your Father . . . is *p* . . . Matt 5:48
all being *p* into one . . . John 17:23
know how . . . *p* his will . . . Rom 12:2
become *p* by your own . . . Gal 3:3
already reached *p*! . . . Phil 3:12
present them to God, *p* . . . Col 1:28
the law made nothing *p* . . . Heb 7:19
the redeemed . . . made *p* . . . Heb 12:23
Whatever is good and *p* . . . Jas 1:17
p love expels all fear . . . 1 Jn 4:18
his love . . . *p* in us . . . 1 Jn 4:18

PERISH(ABLE)(ING) *to be lost or destroyed in either the physical or spiritual sense; pass away*
Does the innocent person *p*? . . . Job 4:7
But the wicked will *p* . . . Ps 37:20
their hopes all *p* . . . Prov 11:7
house of the wicked will *p* . . . Prov 14:11
justice for those who are *p* . . . Prov 31:8
die at birth or *p* in the womb . . . Hos 9:11
that even one . . . should *p* . . . Matt 18:14
not *p* but have eternal life . . . John 3:16
p things like food . . . John 6:27
following it, you will *p* . . . Rom 8:13
our *p* earthly bodies . . . 1 Cor 15:53
being saved and by those *p* . . . 2 Cor 2:15
He does not want anyone to *p* . . . 2 Pet 3:9

PERSECUTE(D)(S), PERSECUTION(S), PERSECUTORS *to pursue (the wicked); to afflict or mock (the righteous)*
your enemies and *p* . . . Deut 30:7
you *p* me as God does? . . . Job 19:22
cruel toward me. You *p* me . . . Job 30:21
he *p* the poor and needy . . . Ps 109:16
Many *p* and trouble me . . . Ps 119:157
blesses those who are *p* . . . Matt 5:10
p in one town, flee . . . Matt 10:23
arrested, *p*, and killed . . . Matt 24:9
Since they *p* me . . . John 15:20
great wave of *p* . . . Acts 8:1
insults, hardships, *p* . . . 2 Cor 12:10
I violently *p* the Christians . . . Gal 1:13
Isaac . . . was *p* by Ishmael . . . Gal 4:29
endure *p* patiently . . . Rev 14:12

PERSEVERANCE, PERSEVERE *enduring hardships with patience*
with faith, love, *p*, and . . . 1 Tim 6:11
my command to *p* . . . Rev 3:10

PERSIST(ED)(ENT) *to continue in the face of obstacles*
But Aaron and Moses *p* . . . Exod 5:3
because of her *p* nagging . . . Judg 14:17
p in all the evil ways . . . 2 Kgs 17:22
who despise *p* sinners . . . Ps 15:4
p in doing what is good . . . Rom 2:7
p in your prayers . . . Eph 6:18

PERVERSE, PERVERSION, PERVERT(ED)(ING) *to corrupt or misuse; cause to turn aside from what is correct, reasonable, or morally right*
this is a terrible *p* . . . Lev 18:23
bribes and *p* justice . . . 1 Sam 8:3
not tolerate *p* justice . . . 2 Chr 19:7
how they *p* the truth! . . . Job 17:12
I will reject *p* ideas . . . Ps 101:4
p talk . . . corrupt speech . . . Prov 4:24
p hearts plot evil . . . Prov 6:14
trickery to *p* justice . . . Isa 29:21
p justice in the courts . . . Lam 3:36
p the true ways of . . . Acts 13:10
crooked and *p* people . . . Phil 2:15

PIECE(S) *parcel or part; standardized unit; portion or morsel; broken bit or fragment; a coin (Greek = denarii; Hebrew = shekel, or some fraction thereof)*
thousand *p* of silver . . . Gen 20:16
p of land for a burial plot . . . Gen 23:4
I have one small silver *p* . . . 1 Sam 9:8
Samuel cut Agag to *p* . . . 1 Sam 15:33
a single *p* of bread . . . 1 Kgs 17:12
two bulls . . . cut it into *p* . . . 1 Kgs 18:23
smashed the idols to *p* . . . 2 Kgs 11:18
a *p* of broken pottery . . . Job 2:8
No, I will say my *p* . . . Job 32:17
for my wages thirty *p* . . . Zech 11:12
Breaking the loaves into *p* . . . Matt 14:19
gave him thirty *p* of silver . . . Matt 26:15
two *p* of silver . . . Luke 10:35
gave him a *p* of broiled fish . . . Luke 24:42
Can Christ be divided into *p*? . . . 1 Cor 1:13

PILGRIM(AGE)(S) *journey with a religious purpose; figurative for the human life span*
a *p* to Jerusalem . . . Ps 84:5
the years of my *p* . . . Ps 119:54
group of *p* to Jerusalem . . . Isa 30:29

PILLAR(S) *architectural support; sacred stone slabs (built to pagan deities); memorial pile of stones; miraculous cloud by day and fire by night; figurative of church leaders*
she became a *p* of salt . . . Gen 19:26
pillow . . . as a memorial *p* . . . Gen 28:18
p to mark the place . . . Gen 35:14
a *p* of cloud . . . a *p* of fire . . . Exod 13:21
the sacred *p* they worship . . . Exod 34:13
shatter their sacred *p* . . . Deut 7:5
Samson . . . between the two *p* . . . Judg 16:25
down the sacred *p* of Baal . . . 2 Kgs 3:2
p—righteousness and justice . . . Ps 89:14
as *p* of the church . . . Gal 2:9
p and support of the truth . . . 1 Tim 3:15
victorious will become *p* . . . Rev 3:12

PIT(S) *natural or dug-out cavity in the earth; burial grave; figurative of danger (especially sexual sin)*
valley was filled with tar *p* . . . Gen 14:10
throw him into a deep *p* . . . Gen 37:20
They dig a *p* to trap others . . . Ps 7:15
nations have fallen into the *p* . . . Ps 9:15
into the *p* of death . . . Ps 30:3
the *p* they dug for me . . . Ps 35:8
out of the *p* of despair . . . Ps 40:2
down into the *p* of death . . . Prov 1:12
A prostitute is a deep *p* . . . Prov 23:27
a land of deserts and *p* . . . Jer 2:6
angel from the bottomless *p* . . . Rev 9:11
beast . . . of the bottomless *p* . . . Rev 11:7
key to the bottomless *p* . . . Rev 20:1

PITIED, PITY *to sympathize; full of compassion*
have no *p*. Do not spare . . . Deut 13:8
You must never show *p* . . . Deut 19:21
he *p* them in their distress . . . Ps 106:44
even yet God will have *p* . . . Jon 3:9
I will no longer have *p* . . . Zech 11:6
great *p* for the crowds . . . Matt 9:36
filled with *p* . . . and forgave . . . Matt 18:27

PLAGUE(D)(S) *calamity or epidemic of infectious disease, issued by God in judgment*
LORD will send a deadly *p* . . . Exod 9:3
LORD sent a great *p* upon . . . Exod 32:35
destroy them with a *p* . . . Num 14:12
These *p* will be intense . . . Deut 28:59
p with problems like everyone . . . Ps 73:5
protect you from the fatal *p* . . . Ps 91:3
Phinehas . . . the *p* was stopped . . . Ps 106:30
killed by these three *p* . . . Rev 9:18
p . . . bring God's wrath . . . Rev 15:1
God, who sent all of these *p* . . . Rev 16:9
the *p* described in this book . . . Rev 22:18

PLANT(ED)(S) *a young tree or herb; to sow with seeds; to establish*
grass and seed-bearing *p* . . . Gen 1:11
God *p* a garden in Eden . . . Gen 2:8
After the Flood, Noah . . . *p* . . . Gen 9:20
They are like trees *p* . . . Ps 1:3
to *p* and a time to harvest . . . Eccl 3:2
I will *p* them there . . . Isa 60:21
has *p* them like . . . oaks . . . Isa 61:3
When I *p* you, I chose . . . Jer 2:21
A farmer went out to *p* . . . Matt 13:3
Every *p* not *p* by my heavenly . . . Matt 15:13
harvesting crops you didn't *p* . . . Luke 19:21
to *p* the seed in your hearts . . . 1 Cor 3:6

PLEASE(D)(S), PLEASING *make glad; satisfy*
was *p* with the sacrifice . . . Gen 8:21
if it *p* you . . . Gen 18:3
you are *p* with me . . . Ps 41:11
p with worthy sacrifices . . . Ps 51:19
I am fully *p* with him . . . Matt 3:17
things that *p* the Spirit . . . Rom 8:5
p and perfect his will . . . Rom 12:2
we live to *p* the Lord . . . Rom 14:8
We should *p* others . . . Rom 15:2
thinking how to *p* him . . . 1 Cor 7:32
God was not *p* with . . . 1 Cor 10:5
acceptable to God and *p* him . . . Phil 4:18
impossible to *p* God without . . . Heb 11:6

PLEASURE(S) *desire or inclination; that which pleases or delights*
no *p* in your offerings . . . Lev 26:31
take no *p* in wickedness . . . Ps 5:4
godly people . . . I take *p* in . . . Ps 16:3
love *p* become poor . . . Prov 21:17
cares and riches and *p* of . . . Luke 8:14
no *p* in anyone who turns . . . Heb 10:38
the fleeting *p* of sin . . . Heb 11:25
only what will give you *p* . . . Jas 4:3

PLUNDER(ED)(ER)(ERS)(ING)(S) *to pillage or ransack; the loot, spoils, or booty from pillaging; to take advantage of*
Gad will be *p* by . . . Gen 49:19
you will *p* the Egyptians! . . . Exod 3:22
all their wealth as *p* . . . Num 31:9
Why did you rush for the *p* . . . 1 Sam 15:19
they can't have any of the *p* . . . 1 Sam 30:22
people who are left . . . as *p* . . . 2 Kgs 21:14
they did not take any *p* . . . Esth 9:10, 16
our enemies have been *p* . . . Ps 76:5
Why has Israel become . . . *p* . . . Jer 2:14
Those who *p* you will be *p* . . . Jer 30:16

POOR(EST) *characterized by poverty or insufficient resources; humble; those deserving of pity or mercy; see POVERTY*
should be no *p* among you . . . Deut 15:4
makes one *p* and another rich . . . 1 Sam 2:7
only the *p* people were left . . . 2 Kgs 24:14
at last the *p* have hope . . . Job 5:16
I helped the *p* . . . Job 29:12
I am *p* and needy . . . Ps 40:17
Help him to defend the *p* . . . Ps 72:4
Rescue the *p* and helpless . . . Ps 82:4
Lazy people are soon *p* . . . Prov 10:4
those who oppress the *p* . . . Prov 14:31
better to be *p* and honest . . . Prov 19:1; 28:6
The wise are often *p* . . . Eccl 9:11
by being merciful to the *p* . . . Dan 4:27
give the money to the *p* . . . Matt 19:21
You will always have the *p* . . . Matt 26:11
preach Good News to the *p* . . . Luke 4:18
a *p* widow came by . . . Luke 21:2
p, but we give spiritual riches . . . 2 Cor 6:10
for your sakes he became *p* . . . 2 Cor 8:9
remember to help the *p* . . . Gal 2:10
Hasn't God chosen the *p* . . . Jas 2:5
wretched and miserable and *p* . . . Rev 3:17

PORTION(ED) *share; one's lot, destiny, or rightful heritage*
I give you an extra *p* . . . Gen 48:22
the customary double *p* . . . Deut 21:17
only one *p* of land . . . Josh 17:14
inherit a double *p* of . . . joy . . . Isa 61:7
p out drop by drop . . . Ezek 4:16

POSSESS(ED) *to seize, gain, or take (control of); to own; see POSSESSION*
to *p* all the land I swore . . . Josh 1:6
those who trust . . . will *p* . . . Ps 37:9
will *p* the land and inherit . . . Isa 57:13
a man *p* by a demon . . . Luke 4:33
give . . . what you greedily *p* . . . Luke 11:41

POSSESSION(S) *property owned; an entitlement; see POSSESS*
land . . . as a permanent *p* . . . Gen 13:15
Jacob took all his *p* with . . . Gen 31:21
Canaan as your special *p* . . . 1 Chr 16:18
Israel, your special *p*! . . . Ps 28:9
my teachings as . . . precious *p* . . . Prov 7:2
Abraham . . . gained *p* of . . . Ezek 33:24
sold their *p* and shared . . . Acts 2:45
became his choice *p* . . . Jas 1:18
pride in our *p* . . . 1 Jn 2:16

POUND(ING)(S) *unit of weights and measures; to beat something repeatedly*
seventy-five *p* of pure gold . . . Exod 25:39
oceans roar as they *p* the shore . . . Ps 93:3
oppresses . . . like a *p* rain . . . Prov 28:3
outweigh a *p* of wisdom . . . Eccl 10:1
them ten *p* of silver . . . Luke 19:13
p of embalming ointment . . . John 19:39

POVERTY *having few or insufficient resources; indigence*
will come to utter *p* . . . Gen 45:11
If any . . . fall into *p* . . . Lev 25:35
sleep, you will end in *p* . . . Prov 20:13
shortcuts lead to *p* . . . Prov 21:5
p will stalk the land . . . Isa 17:4
no *p* among them . . . Acts 4:34
deep *p* . . . rich generosity . . . 2 Cor 8:2
so that by his *p* he could . . . 2 Cor 8:9
your *p*—but you are rich! . . . Rev 2:9

POWER(S)(FUL) *the ability (the right, the strength, or the authority) to do, act, or accomplish something*
growing more and more *p* . . . Exod 1:20
mighty *p* and great acts of . . . Exod 6:6
that you might see my *p* . . . Exod 9:16
so that all . . . know the *p* of . . . Josh 4:24
rescue me from your *p* . . . Job 10:7
God has them in his *p* . . . Job 12:6
the *p* . . . who are privileged . . . Job 22:8
God is *p* and dreadful . . . Job 25:2
of the LORD is *p* . . . Ps 29:4
your faithfulness and saving *p* . . . Ps 40:10
royal *p* is expressed in justice . . . Ps 45:6
His *p* is absolute! . . . Ps 147:5
better to be patient than *p* . . . Prov 16:32
in my *p*, . . . by my authority . . . Zech 10:12
He gets his *p* from Satan . . . Matt 12:24
don't know the *p* of God . . . Matt 22:29
filled with the Holy Spirit's *p* . . . Luke 4:14
healing *p* went out from him . . . Luke 6:19
He has no *p* over me . . . John 14:30
the *p* to release you or to . . . John 19:10
you will receive *p* . . . Acts 1:8
Let me have this *p*, too . . . Acts 8:19
It is the *p* of God at work . . . Rom 1:16
as the very *p* of God . . . 1 Cor 1:18
my weaknesses, so that the *p* . . . 2 Cor 12:9
This is the same mighty *p* . . . Eph 1:19
in the *p* of the Holy Spirit . . . Eph 6:18
the evil *p* of this world . . . Col 2:20
a spirit of . . . of *p*, love . . . 2 Tim 1:7
break the *p* of the Devil . . . Heb 2:14
the *p* of the age to come . . . Heb 6:5
honor and glory and *p* . . . Rev 5:13

PRAISE(D)(S), PRAISING *to worship, commend, or give honor to; an expression of the same*
sang her *p* to their king . . . Gen 12:15
Now I will *p* the LORD . . . Gen 29:35
did they not *p* me for . . . Job 31:20
they *p* the greedy and curse . . . Ps 10:3
P . . . Honor . . . Show him reverence . . . Ps 22:23
how I *p* you! . . . Ps 63:3
sing your *p* . . . in glorious songs . . . Ps 66:4
He is most worthy of *p*! . . . Ps 145:3
everything that lives sing *p* . . . Ps 150:6
Don't *p* yourself; let others . . . Prov 27:2
Her husband *p* her: . . . Prov 31:28
We *p* his love even more . . . Song 1:4
p instead of despair . . . Isa 61:3
Jerusalem the object of *p* . . . Isa 62:7
My *p* are for you alone! . . . Jer 17:14
I *p* and worshiped the Most . . . Dan 4:34
The master was full of *p* . . . Matt 25:21
Oh, how I *p* the Lord . . . Luke 1:46
in the Temple, *p* God . . . Luke 24:53
P God! . . . Hail to the King . . . John 12:13
loved human *p* more than . . . John 12:43
seeks *p* from God . . . Rom 2:29
whatever *p* is due . . . 1 Cor 4:5
So we *p* God for . . . Eph 1:6
offer our sacrifice of *p* . . . Heb 13:15
P our God, all his . . . Rev 19:5

PRAY(ED)(ING)(S) *to intercede with or make petition to God*
Abraham *p* . . . God healed . . . Gen 20:17
never *p* to or swear by . . . Exod 23:13
P that the LORD will . . . Num 21:7
But if you *p* to God . . . Job 8:5
they wouldn't think of *p* . . . Ps 14:4
I sing his songs, *p* to God . . . Ps 42:8
anyone who *p* to anyone . . . Dan 6:7
and *p* to your god! . . . Jon 1:6
When you *p*, don't . . . Matt 6:5, 7
Keep alert and *p* . . . Matt 26:41
he *p* to God all night . . . Luke 6:12
Lord, teach us to *p* . . . Luke 11:1
He *p* more fervently . . . Luke 22:44
Holy Spirit *p* for us . . . Rom 8:26
I *p* for you constantly . . . Eph 1:16
instead, *p* about everything . . . Phil 4:6
p earnestly for you . . . Col 4:12
Keep on *p* . . . 1 Thes 5:17
Then he *p* for rain . . . Jas 5:18

PRAYER(FUL)(S) *conversation with God—in praise, thanksgiving, or intercession; see PRAY*
God answered his *p* . . . Judg 13:9
p made in this place . . . 2 Chr 7:15
and my *p* is pure . . . Job 16:17
Pay attention to my *p* . . . Ps 17:1
in *p* to foreign gods . . . Ps 44:20
my cry! Hear my *p*! . . . Ps 61:1
for you answer our *p* . . . Ps 65:2
my *p* as incense offered . . . Ps 141:2
but he hears the *p* . . . Prov 15:29
though you offer many *p* . . . Isa 1:15
called a place of *p* . . . Matt 21:13
p boxes with Scripture . . . Matt 23:5
pleaded in *p* for you . . . Luke 22:32
My *p* is not for . . . John 17:9
spend our time in *p* . . . Acts 6:4
after more fasting and *p* . . . Acts 13:3
and always be *p* . . . Rom 12:12
p offered in faith . . . Jas 5:15
p will not be heard . . . 1 Pet 3:7
incense—the *p* of . . . Rev 5:8

PREACH(ED)(ER)(ES)(ING) *to proclaim news or deliver a sermon*
Stop *p* against my . . . Amos 7:16
I'll *p* to you . . . Mic 2:11
His *p* will turn . . . Mal 4:6
p . . . Good News . . . Matt 4:23
teaching and *p* in towns . . . Matt 11:1
first be *p* to every nation . . . Mark 13:10
he has appointed me to *p* . . . Luke 4:18
Your duty is to go and *p* . . . Luke 9:60
he *p* the truth . . . John 5:33
boldness in their *p* . . . Acts 4:29
p the word of the Lord . . . Acts 8:25
he began *p* daily . . . Acts 19:9
Paul, . . . sent out to *p* . . . Rom 1:1
to baptize, but to *p* . . . 1 Cor 1:17
support others who *p* . . . 1 Cor 9:12
whether I *p* or they *p* . . . 1 Cor 15:11
p about a different Jesus . . . 2 Cor 11:4
p any other gospel . . . Gal 1:9
a *p* and apostle to teach . . . 1 Tim 2:7
P the word of God . . . 2 Tim 4:2

PREMEDITATED *to think about one's actions beforehand*
p hostility . . . is murder . . . Num 35:20
without *p* hostility . . . Num 35:22

PRESENCE *company; nearness; (symbolic of) God-with-us*
banished . . . from your *p* . . . Gen 4:14
stood in Pharaoh's *p* . . . Gen 41:14
see your glorious *p* . . . Exod 33:18
glorious *p* . . . appeared . . . Num 16:19, 42
an oath in the *p* of the . . . Josh 9:19
the Bread of the *P* . . . 2 Chr 29:18
Satan left the LORD's *p* . . . Job 1:12
so terrified in his *p* . . . Job 23:15
is naked in God's *p* . . . Job 26:6
Who may enter your *p* . . . Ps 15:1
the joy of your *p* . . . Ps 16:11
get away from your *p*! . . . Ps 139:7
will live in your *p* . . . Ps 140:13
in terror at my *p* . . . Ezek 38:20
joy in the *p* of God's . . . Luke 15:10
joy in your *p* . . . Acts 2:28
fills . . . with his *p* . . . Eph 1:23
into the very *p* of God . . . Col 1:22

PRESENT(ED)(S) *to introduce, often for commissioning; to offer or make a gift of; near at hand; here and now*
gave valuable *p* to her . . . Gen 24:53
p themselves at the . . . Deut 31:14
They will *p* incense . . . Deut 33:10
angels came to *p* themselves . . . Job 1:6
p your case to him . . . Job 5:8
p to the apostles . . . Acts 6:6
the elders . . . were *p* . . . Acts 21:18
just in this *p* time . . . Rom 3:26
fully *p* the Good News . . . Rom 15:19
life and death; the *p* and . . . 1 Cor 3:22
Because of the *p* crisis . . . 1 Cor 7:26
to *p* her to himself as . . . Eph 5:27
give *p* . . . to celebrate . . . Rev 11:10

PRESERVE(D)(S) *to protect; to maintain*
to *p* your lives . . . Gen 45:5
May they *p* my name . . . Gen 48:16
p for his descendants . . . Exod 29:29
You have *p* my life . . . Ps 41:12
I will *p* an heir for him . . . Ps 89:29
P me from . . . violent . . . Ps 140:1, 4
Disregarding . . . faults *p* love . . . Prov 17:9
and the wineskins are *p* . . . Matt 9:17
to *p* the truth . . . Gal 2:5

PRIDE *inordinate self-esteem or conceit; disdainful treatment of others; object of boasting; see PROUD or BOAST*
your *p* and dishonesty . . . 1 Sam 17:29
p and joy, O Israel . . . 2 Sam 1:19
p like a jeweled necklace . . . Ps 73:6
not endure conceit and *p* . . . Ps 101:5
oldest child . . . the *p* and joy . . . Ps 105:36
Now swallow your *p* . . . Prov 6:3
That is why I hate *p* . . . Prov 8:13
P goes before destruction . . . Prov 16:18
Sodom's sins were *p* . . . Ezek 16:49
hardened with *p* . . . Dan 5:20
destroy the *p* of the Philistines . . . Zech 9:6
you are our *p* and joy . . . 1 Thes 2:20
the Devil will use that *p* . . . 1 Tim 3:6
p in our possessions . . . 1 Jn 2:16

PRIEST(HOOD)(S) *a descendant of Aaron through Levi in charge of Israel's sacrificial system of worship; the privilege of intercession, granted to all believers under Christ, the great High Priest*
Melchizedek, . . . a *p* of God . . . Gen 14:18
Jethro, the *p* of Midian . . . Exod 18:1
kingdom of *p*, my holy . . . Exod 19:6
set Aaron apart . . . as a *p* . . . Exod 28:3
Levitical *p* carrying the Ark . . . Josh 3:3
Samuel . . . assisted Eli the *p* . . . 1 Sam 2:11
a *p* forever in the line of . . . Ps 110:4
Jeshua the high *p* . . . you other *p* . . . Zech 3:8
rule as king . . . also serve as *p* . . . Zech 6:13
p are the messengers of . . . Mic 2:7
p on duty in the Temple . . . Matt 12:5
betrayed to the leading *p* . . . Matt 20:18
Caiaphas, who was high *p* . . . John 11:49
p forever in the line of . . . Heb 5:6; 7:17
his *p* will never end . . . Heb 7:24
High *P* . . . at God's right . . . Heb 8:1
High *P* over all the good . . . Heb 9:11
you are God's holy *p* . . . 1 Pet 2:5
his kingdom and his *p* . . . Rev 1:6

PRISON(ER)(ERS) *state or place of confinement; (those in) captivity*
Are my daughters *p* . . . Gen 31:26
the *p* where the king's *p* . . . Gen 39:20
the *p* disappeared! . . . 1 Kgs 20:40
he sets the *p* free . . . Ps 68:6
p . . . condemned to die . . . Ps 102:20
free the captives from *p* . . . Isa 42:7
p and trial . . . to his death . . . Isa 53:8
free your *p* from death . . . Zech 9:11
I was in *p* and you . . . Matt 25:36
to release one *p* . . . Mark 15:6
Herod put John in *p* . . . Luke 3:20

PROCLAIM(ED)(ING) *announce; see also PREACH*
p the news of Saul's . . . 1 Sam 31:9
he *p* Ishbosheth king . . . 2 Sam 2:9
the heavens *p* his justice . . . Ps 50:6
I publicly *p* bold promises . . . Isa 45:19
my law will be *p* . . . Isa 51:4
p my every word . . . Jer 23:28
kingdoms will *p* war . . . Mark 13:8
to *p* that captives will . . . Luke 4:18
p the Kingdom of God . . . Acts 28:31
p the Good News . . . Gal 1:16

PROFANE(D), PROFAN(ING)(ITY) *secular or common; unholy or ceremonially unclean; to defile, blaspheme, or do something totally irreverent*
p the name of your God . . . Lev 18:21
sin of *p* what is holy . . . Lev 19:8
defiled my sanctuary and *p* . . . Lev 20:3
mock me with . . . *p* . . . Ps 35:16
you *p* my Temple . . . Ezek 44:7

PROFIT(S) *gain, benefit, or usefulness*
p of wisdom is better than . . . Prov 3:14
Work brings *p*, but . . . Prov 14:23
to find out . . . their *p* . . . Luke 19:15
and make a *p* . . . Jas 4:13

PROMISE(D)(S) *to covenant, pledge, or give assurance*
I solemnly *p* never to . . . Gen 9:11
all that I have *p* . . . Gen 18:19
p to give this land . . . Gen 24:7
wonderful *p* to Israel! . . . Num 10:29
never enter the *P* Land! . . . Deut 1:37
you *p* me that my son . . . 1 Kgs 1:13
fulfill through you the *p* . . . 1 Kgs 6:12
You keep your *p* . . . 1 Kgs 8:23
dangerous to make a rash *p* . . . Prov 20:25
don't make rash *p* to God . . . Eccl 5:2
I publicly proclaim bold *p* . . . Isa 45:19
p with an oath . . . Acts 2:30
This *p* is to you . . . Acts 2:39
fulfillment of God's *p* . . . Acts 26:6
God's *p* to give the whole . . . Rom 4:13
p have been fulfilled . . . 2 Cor 1:20
the *p* was to . . . Christ . . . Gal 3:16
to inherit God's *p* . . . Heb 6:12
God would keep his *p* . . . Heb 11:11
all that God had *p* . . . Heb 11:39
the benefits of these *p* . . . 2 Pet 1:5

PROPHECY, PROPHECIES *the spoken or written word from God; to forthtell (consoling or corrective material) and foretell (predictive material); see PROPHET*
the prophets give false *p* . . . Jer 5:31
If I had the gift of *p* . . . 1 Cor 13:2
a word of *p* strengthens . . . 1 Cor 14:4
Do not scoff at *p* . . . 1 Thes 5:20
no *p* in Scripture ever . . . 2 Pet 1:20
the essence of *p* is . . . Rev 19:10

PROPHESIED, PROPHESIES, PROPHESY *to issue a prophecy; see PROPHECY*
sons and daughters will *p* . . . Joel 2:28
Lord, we *p* in your name . . . Matt 7:22
P to us, you Messiah! . . . Matt 26:68
sons and daughters will *p* . . . Acts 2:17
if she prays or *p* . . . 1 Cor 11:5

PROPHET(S) *an interpreter of the times and of people's hearts; one who issues an oracle or "the word of the Lord"; see PROPHESY*
false *p* or dreamers . . . Deut 13:5
raise . . . a *p* like me . . . Deut 18:15
but Baal has 450 *p* . . . 1 Kgs 18:22
anoint Elisha . . . my *p* . . . 1 Kgs 19:16
tell the *p*, "Shut up! . . . Isa 30:10
The *p* are crazy! . . . Hos 9:7
I sent my *p* to warn you . . . Hos 12:10
a *p* full of lies . . . Mic 2:11
sending you the *p* Elijah . . . Mal 4:5
the law and the *p* . . . Matt 7:12
If you welcome a *p* . . . Matt 10:41
A *p* is honored . . . Matt 13:57
Jesus, the *p* from Nazareth . . . Matt 21:11
who murdered the *p* . . . Matt 23:31
many false *p* will appear . . . Matt 24:11
A mighty *p* has risen . . . Luke 7:16
a *p* of God to be killed . . . Luke 13:33
Are you the *P* . . . John 1:21
Surely, he is the *P* . . . John 6:14
predicted . . . by the *p* Joel . . . Acts 2:16
raise up a *P* like me . . . Acts 3:22; 7:37
one all the *p* testified . . . Acts 10:43
do you believe the *p*? . . . Acts 26:27
Is everyone a *p*? . . . 1 Cor 12:29
the apostles, the *p* . . . Eph 4:11
proclaimed by the *p* . . . 2 Pet 1:19
many false *p* in the world . . . 1 Jn 4:1
the blood of the *p* . . . Rev 18:24
with him the false *p* . . . Rev 19:20

PROPITIATION *sacrifice of Christ, which appeases or turns aside divine wrath; see SACRIFICE*

PROSPER(ED)(ING)(ITY)(OUS)(S) *to succeed or thrive; to become strong and flourish; to cause others to succeed; (economic) well-being; see PEACE*
He's well and *p* . . . Gen 29:6
seven years of *p* . . . Gen 41:26
they began to *p* there . . . Gen 47:27
descendants would *p* forever . . . Deut 5:29
filled with large, *p* cities . . . Deut 6:10
obey . . . so that you will *p* . . . Deut 29:9
envy as I pour out *p* . . . 1 Sam 2:32
You have made him *p* . . . Job 1:10
his *p* will not endure . . . Job 20:21
with success and *p* . . . Ps 21:3
When I was *p* I said . . . Ps 30:6
evil people who *p* . . . Ps 37:7
p despite their wickedness . . . Ps 73:3
May all who love this city *p* . . . Ps 122:6
Upright citizens . . . make it *p* . . . Prov 11:11
Hard work means *p* . . . Prov 12:11
See, my servant will *p* . . . Isa 52:13
LORD's plan will *p* . . . Isa 53:10
peace and *p* of Babylon . . . Jer 29:7
who are satisfied and *p* now . . . Luke 6:25
made them *p* in Egypt . . . Acts 13:17

PROUD *presumptuous, arrogant, haughty; see PRIDE*
silence their *p* tongues . . . Ps 12:3
no confidence in the *p* . . . Ps 40:4
not endure conceit and *p* . . . Ps 101:5
distance from the *p* . . . Ps 138:6
p will be punished . . . Prov 16:5
scatters the *p* . . . Luke 1:51
p of being chosen so soon . . . 1 Tim 3:6
God . . . against the *p* . . . 1 Pet 5:5

PROVERB(S) *wise sayings, usually short and pithy, that have become old adages or famous bywords*
three thousand *p* . . . 1 Kgs 4:32
p in a fool's mouth . . . Prov 26:9
Teacher collected . . . *p* . . . Eccl 12:9
make these *p* come true . . . 2 Pet 2:22

PROVIDE, PROVISION(S) *to furnish or supply, implying foresight in making provision for the future*
God will *p* a lamb . . . Gen 22:8
The LORD Will *P* . . . Gen 22:14
p for their journey . . . Gen 42:25
God will generously *p* . . . 2 Cor 9:8
God will *p* rest . . . 2 Thes 1:7
sacrifices . . . never able to *p* . . . Heb 10:1

PROVOKE(D) *incite to anger, often implying blasphemy or rebellion*
O God . . . *p* you to anger . . . Neh 4:5
has *p* his fury . . . Jer 7:29

PRUDENT *discretion; discreet*
p person foresees the danger . . . Prov 22:3

PSYCHIC(S) *a medium; fortune-teller; one through whom it is thought the dead communicate with the living; see MEDIUM*
Do not rely on mediums or *p* . . . Lev 19:31
p must be put to death . . . Lev 20:27
Manasseh . . . mediums and *p* . . . 2 Kgs 21:6
find out the future . . . *p* . . . Isa 8:19
call on spirits, mediums, and *p* . . . Isa 19:3

PUNISH(ED)(ES)(ING)(MENT) *to impose a penalty to fit the crime: from corrective measures (fines or scolding) and corporal punishment (spanking or whipping) to capital punishment and eternal damnation*

serpent . . . you will be *p* . . . Gen 3:14
Cain . . . *p* is too great . . . Gen 4:13
he does not hesitate to *p* . . . Deut 7:10
wrong to . . . *p* nobles for . . . Prov 17:26
Should I not *p* them . . . Jer 5:9
into eternal *p* . . . Matt 25:46
he was *p* enough . . . 2 Cor 2:6
p with everlasting destruction . . . 2 Thes 1:9
more terrible the *p* . . . Heb 10:29
p all who do wrong . . . 1 Pet 2:14
while *p* the wicked . . . 2 Pet 2:9

PURE *free of contamination or impurities; ritually clean; guileless; faultless; guiltless; chaste; see CLEAN*
Ark's cover . . . of *p* gold . . . Exod 25:17
My teaching is *p* . . . Job 11:4
Can a mortal be *p* . . . Job 15:14
LORD's promises are *p* . . . Ps 12:6
p in their own eyes . . . Prov 16:2
feel *p* but they are filthy . . . Prov 30:12
things that are *p* . . . Phil 4:8
Keep yourself *p* . . . 1 Tim 5:22
p . . . hearts are *p* . . . Titus 1:15
first of all *p* . . . Jas 3:17
p spiritual milk . . . 1 Pet 2:2
just as Christ is *p* . . . 1 Jn 3:3

PURGE *to clear of something unwanted; cleanse or purify; see REFINE*
p away Israel's sin . . . Isa 27:9
p you of your wickedness . . . Ezek 22:15
P out the old leaven . . . 1 Cor 5:7

PURIFIED, PURIFY, PURIFICATION *to make pure or remove (physical or moral) blemishes; make ritually clean; see REFINE*
p the altar . . . Exod 30:10
water of *p* . . . Num 19:12
p by the water . . . Num 31:23
P me from my sins . . . Ps 51:7
p by sprinkling with blood . . . Heb 9:22
p your hearts . . . Jas 4:8

PURSUE(D) *to follow in order to seize, overtake, or kill; to seek*
P a godly life . . . 1 Tim 6:11
P faith and love and peace . . . 2 Tim 2:22
dragon . . . *p* the woman . . . Rev 12:13

QUARREL(S)(ING) *angry contention; complaint; grudge*
jealous of one another and *q* . . . 1 Cor 3:3
afraid that I will find *q* . . . 2 Cor 12:20
Lord's servants must not *q* . . . 2 Tim 2:24
q . . . about . . . Jewish laws . . . Titus 3:9

QUENCH(ED) *to put out or extinguish (as with a damper such as water)*
Many waters cannot *q* love . . . Song 8:7
q the smallest hope . . . Matt 12:20
q the flames of fire . . . Heb 11:33

QUIET(NESS) *peaceful; calm or still*
In *q* and confidence . . . Isa 30:15
Q and confidence . . . Isa 32:17
live a *q* life . . . 1 Thes 4:11
a gentle and *q* spirit . . . 1 Pet 3:4

RACE *an athletic contest; an ethnic classification*
women of the human *r* . . . Gen 6:2
on the entire human *r* . . . Ps 14:2
athlete eager to run the *r* . . . Ps 19:5
doesn't always win the *r* . . . Eccl 9:11
sin entered the entire human *r* . . . Rom 5:12
in a *r* everyone runs . . . 1 Cor 9:24
I have finished the *r* . . . 2 Tim 4:7
run with endurance the *r* . . . Heb 12:1

RAIN(ED)(S) *precipitation; to pour upon*
God had not sent any *r* . . . Gen 2:5
forty days and forty nights of *r* . . . Gen 7:4
r . . . are an expression of his grace . . . Joel 2:23
sends *r* on the just and the unjust . . . Matt 5:45
r comes . . . house, it won't collapse . . . Matt 7:25
fire and burning sulfur *r* down . . . Luke 17:29
ground soaks up the *r* . . . Heb 6:7
prayed . . . no *r* would fall . . . Jas 5:17

RAISE(D)(S) *to recall from death, to rear, lift up*
r them for myself . . . Hos 2:23
R the battle cry . . . Hos 5:8
r a thriving crop of sins . . . Hos10:13
r the dead . . . Matt 10:8
be killed . . . be *r* . . . Matt 16:21
in three days I will *r* . . . John 2:19
God . . . *r* him from the dead . . . Rom 1:4
r . . . to make us right with God . . . Rom 4:25
just as Christ was *r* . . . Rom 6:4
Spirit of God who *r* . . . Rom 8:11
if Christ was not *r* . . . 1 Cor 15:14
How will the dead be *r*? . . . 1 Cor 15:35
Christians . . . will be *r* . . . 1 Cor 15:52
but on God who can *r* . . . 2 Cor 1:9
r us from the dead . . . Eph 2:6

RANSOM(ED) *price paid to obtain release from a binding obligation*
each man . . . must pay a *r* . . . Exod 30:12
r payment for . . . murderers . . . Num 35:31
the rich can pay a *r* . . . Prov 13:8
r . . . return to Jerusalem . . . Isa 35:10
to give my life as a *r* . . . Mark 10:45
God paid a *r* to save you . . . 1 Pet 1:18
blood has *r* people for God . . . Rev 5:9

READ(ER)(ING)(S) *learning from what's written; reciting*
r their future in the stars . . . Jer 10:2
r the messages from the Lord . . . Jer 36:6
r, pay attention . . . Mark 13:14
stood up to *r* the Scriptures . . . Luke 4:16
r from the prophet Isaiah . . . Acts 8:30
Your lives are a letter . . . *r* . . . 2 Cor 3:2
God blesses the one who *r* . . . Rev 1:3

REAP(ED)(ERS)(ING)(S) *to harvest (crops, sin, souls); to receive fruit of one's labor*
r what you sow . . . Gal 6:7

REASON(ED) *to discuss or dispute; to argue rationally; justification*
Job fears God, but not without good *r* . . . Job 1:9
answer God . . . *r* with him . . . Job 9:14

REBEL(LED)(LING)(LION)(LIOUS) *to take up arms against; to oppose, disobey, renounce*
in the thirteenth year they *r* . . . Gen 14:4
Do not *r* against the Lord . . . Num 14:9
r against the Most High . . . Ps 78:17
they have *r* . . . Isa 65:2
Israel . . . *r* . . . wilderness . . . Heb 3:8

REBUKE(D)(S) *to reprove or reprimand; to turn back or keep down*
wise, when *r* . . . Prov 9:8
open *r* . . . hidden love . . . Prov 27:5
r the winds and the . . . Matt 8:26
he *r* them for their unbelief . . . Mark 16:14
believer sins, *r* him . . . Luke 17:3
sins should be *r* . . . 1 Tim 5:20
Balaam . . . donkey *r* him . . . 2 Pet 2:16
The Lord *r* you . . . Jude 1:9

RECEIVE(D)(S) *to acquire or take possession of; to believe or accept as true; welcome*
r the same reward . . . Matt 10:41
believe, you will *r* . . . Matt 21:22
the world . . . cannot *r* . . . John 14:17
Ask . . . and you will *r* . . . John 16:24
R the Holy Spirit . . . John 20:22
Lord Jesus, *r* . . . Acts 7:59
R the Holy Spirit . . . Acts 19:2
just as I *r* it . . . 1 Cor 11:23
r the Spirit . . . Gal 3:2
should not expect to *r* . . . Jas 1:7

RECONCILE(D), RECONCILIATION, RECONCILING *to restore harmony between persons, especially between God and human beings*
be *r* to that person . . . Matt 5:24
God was in Christ *r* . . . 2 Cor 5:19
Be *r* to God! . . . 2 Cor 5:20
Christ *r* . . . to God . . . Eph 2:16

REDEEM(ED)(ER)(ING), REDEMPTION *to buy back, repurchase; to save by payment of a ransom; to rescue from trouble or sin*
I know that my *R* lives . . . Job 19:25
But . . . God will *r* my life . . . Ps 49:15
Lord *r* you . . . Ps 107:2
r will follow it . . . Isa 35:9
I can *r* you . . . Isa 52:3
our *R* from ages past . . . Isa 63:16
and *r* them . . . Luke 1:68
on the day of *r* . . . Eph 4:30

REFINE(D)(S) *to remove impurities from metal; figurative of purifying God's people of sin*
just as gold and silver are *r* . . . Zech 13:9
blazing fire that *r* . . . Mal 3:2

REFRESH(ED)(ES)(ING) *to restore, revive, renew, encourage*
messengers are as *r* . . . Prov 25:13
times of *r* will come . . . Acts 3:20

REFUGE *sanctuary, shelter, or safety*
designate cities of *r* . . . Num 35:11
eternal God is your *r* . . . Deut 33:27
God is our *r* and . . . Ps 46:1
fled to him for *r* . . . Heb 6:18

REIGN(ED)(S) *to rule supreme*
God of Israel *r* . . . Isa 52:7
And He will *r* . . . Luke 1:33
r with you . . . 1 Cor 4:8
For Christ must *r* until he . . . 1 Cor 15:25
Lord our God . . . *r* . . . Rev 19:6
r with Christ . . . Rev 20:4

REJOICE(D)(S), REJOICING *to take joy in or give joy to; to take possession of*
Let the godly *r* . . . Ps 68:3
and the earth *r* . . . Ps 96:11
Let the earth *r*! . . . Ps 97:1
We will *r* and be glad . . . Ps 118:24
your heart will *r* . . . Isa 66:14
I *r* in God my Savior . . . Luke 1:47
Abraham *r* . . . John 8:56
but the world will *r* . . . John 16:20
r . . . worthy to suffer . . . Acts 5:41
went on his way *r* . . . Acts 8:39
r . . . problems and trials . . . Rom 5:3
r whenever the truth wins . . . 1 Cor 13:6
preached, so I *r* . . . Phil 1:18
so I will *r* . . . Phil 2:17
I say it again—*r*! . . . Phil 4:4

RELY, RELIABLE *trust, trustworthy*
Do not *r* on mediums . . . Lev 19:31
r on his unfailing love . . . Ps 33:18
a *r* messenger brings healing . . . Prov 13:17
r on your God . . . Isa 50:10
learned not to *r* on ourselves . . . 2 Cor 1:9
confirmed by many *r* witnesses . . . 2 Tim 2:2

REMAIN(S) *to survive (as) the undestroyed part; to abide or continue unchanged*
the earth *r* . . . Gen 8:22
r guilty because you . . . see . . . John 9:41
If I want him to *r* . . . John 21:22
strengthen what . . . *r* . . . Rev 3:2

REMEMBER(ED), REMEMBRANCE *to bring to mind; to be guided by or act in accord with*
God *r* Noah . . . Gen 8:1
r his covenant promise . . . Exod 2:24
R to observe the Sabbath . . . Exod 20:8
never again *r* their sins . . . Jer 31:34
r your mercy . . . Hab 3:2

r his sacred covenant . . . Luke 1:72
R . . . Lot's wife . . . Luke 17:32
do this in *r* of me . . . Luke 22:19
r the words of the . . . Acts 20:35
Do this in *r* of me . . . 1 Cor 11:24
never again *r* their sins . . . Heb 8:12
R your leaders . . . Heb 13:7

REMNANT *something left over; few people left who gathered together after God scattered them into exile*
a *r* of my people . . . 2 Kgs 19:31
A *r* . . . will return . . . Isa 10:21

RENEW(ED)(ING) *regenerate or restore; make new spiritually*
R a right spirit . . . Ps 51:10
my youth is *r* . . . Ps 103:5
our spirits are being *r* . . . 2 Cor 4:16
r . . . thoughts and attitudes . . . Eph 4:23

REPENT(ANCE)(ED)(S) *to be sorry; change heart and behavior; a moral U-turn from sin to God*
ashes to show my *r* . . . Job 42:6
because they *r* . . . Matt 12:41
impossible . . . to *r* again . . . Heb 6:6
too late for *r* . . . Heb 12:17
time for everyone to *r* . . . 2 Pet 3:9

REQUIRE(D)(S), REQUIREMENT(S) *ask; demand; necessary condition*
don't *r* burnt offerings . . . Ps 40:6
what he *r* . . . Mic 6:8
Much is *r* from those . . . Luke 12:48

RESPECT(ED) *to give particular attention or esteem*
r our earthly fathers . . . Heb 12:9

REST(ED)(S) *peace of mind or spirit; to repose; to take relief or respite; remainder; freedom from activity or labor; see REMAIN or SABBATH*
seventh day . . . God *r* . . . Gen 2:2
seventh day . . . of total *r* . . . Exod 31:15
Ark . . . could *r* . . . 1 Chr 28:2
fly away and *r* . . . Ps 55:6
r in their own land . . . Isa 28:12
and I will give you *r* . . . Matt 11:28
never enter my . . . *r* . . . Heb 3:11
his place of *r* . . . Heb 4:3
a special *r* still waiting . . . Heb 4:9
told to *r* . . . Rev 6:11
r from all their toils . . . Rev 14:13
The *r* of the dead . . . Rev 20:5

RESTORATION, RESTORE(D)(R)(S) *replace; renew; revive; return*
r your youth . . . Ruth 4:15
towns . . . were *r* to Israel . . . 1 Sam 7:14
God to *r* my hand . . . 1 Kgs 13:6
God will . . . *r* him . . . Job 33:26
R to me again the joy . . . Ps 51:12
free Israel now and *r* . . . Acts 1:6
time for the final *r* . . . Acts 3:21

RESURRECTION *rising from the dead with new life*
to her, "I am the *r* . . . John 11:25
Jesus and his *r* . . . Acts 17:18
saying there will be no *r* . . . 1 Cor 15:12
hope in the *r* . . . Heb 11:35
This is the first *r* . . . Rev 20:5

RETURN(ED)(ING)(S) *to go back in thought or practice; to repent; to reciprocate*
As a dog *r* to its . . . Prov 26:11
R to me . . . Zech 1:3
it says, 'I will *r* . . . Matt 12:44
A dog *r* to its . . . 2 Pet 2:22

REVEAL(ED)(S), REVELATION *disclose; the making known of divine truth— in nature, through Christ, through Scripture, and by God's Spirit of truth*
r things belong to us . . . Deut 29:29
the Son chooses to *r* him . . . Matt 11:27
r from Jesus Christ . . . Gal 1:12
r his Son to me . . . Gal 1:16
God himself *r* . . . Eph 3:3
man of lawlessness will be *r* . . . 2 Thes 2:8
will be *r* on the . . . 1 Pet 1:5

REWARD(ED)(S) *recompense; positive consequence*
your *r* will be great . . . Gen 15:1
brings his *r* with him . . . Isa 40:10
great *r* awaits you . . . Matt 5:12
received all the *r* . . . Matt 6:2
will surely be *r* . . . Matt 10:42
r individually, according to their . . . 1 Cor 3:8
looking forward to the great *r* . . . Heb 11:26
my *r* is with me . . . Rev 22:12

RICH(LY) *to be well endowed; wealthy; see WEALTH*
Abram was very *r* . . . Gen 13:2
r rule the poor . . . Prov 22:7
r . . . picture themselves as wise . . . Prov 28:11
make fun of a *r* man . . . Eccl 10:20
it is hard for a *r* . . . Matt 19:23
you who are *r* . . . Luke 6:24
the *r* man's table . . . Luke 16:21
because he was very *r* . . . Luke 18:23
You are already *r*! . . . 1 Cor 4:8
Though he was very *r* . . . 2 Cor 8:9
words of Christ . . . their *r* . . . Col 3:16
those who are *r* . . . 1 Tim 6:17
poor . . . to be *r* . . . Jas 2:5
You say, 'I am *r* . . . Rev 3:17

RICHES *wealth; abundant resources; see WEALTH*
r and honor . . . are mine . . . Prov 8:18
R won't help . . . Prov 11:4
Lord lead to *r* . . . Prov 22:4
r don't last forever . . . Prov 27:24
pour out the *r* of his glory . . . Rom 9:23
r and glorious inheritance . . . Eph 1:18
r and wisdom and strength . . . Rev 5:12

RIGHT(LY)(S) *correct or moral behavior; righteous; located opposite of left; legal claim; to become justified in a genuine and intimate relationship with God; see MADE RIGHT*
the *r* of the firstborn . . . Deut 21:17
Lord, "Sit in honor at my *r* . . . Ps 110:1
path . . . that seems *r* . . . Prov 14:12
the *r* of the poor . . . Jer 5:28
what your *r* hand is doing . . . Matt 6:3
he gave the *r* to become . . . John 1:12
your heart is not *r* . . . Acts 8:21
r hand of the majestic God . . . Heb 1:3

RIGHTEOUS(LY) *of God, an absolute quality of moral standards; of man, a limited or relative quality, corresponding to a standard of rightness or obligations to God and other persons; see RIGHT, RIGHTEOUSNESS*
declared him *r* . . . Gen 15:6
the *r* will be happy . . . Job 22:19
The Lord loves the *r* . . . Ps 146:8
r are rewarded . . . Prov 11:31
the prayers of the *r* . . . Prov 15:29
r person will live by faith . . . Heb 10:38
God declared him to be *r* . . . Jas 2:23
prayer of a *r* person . . . Jas 5:16
the *r* are barely saved . . . 1 Pet 4:18
God's *r* judgment . . . 2 Pet 2:5
even as Christ is *r* . . . 1 Jn 3:7

RIGHTEOUSNESS *living by a divine or moral law; free from guilt or sin; see RIGHT, RIGHTEOUS*
R covered me like a robe . . . Job 29:14
R goes . . . before him . . . Ps 85:13
r never fails . . . Ps 111:3
Lord is the source of . . . *r* . . . Isa 45:24
r will last forever . . . Isa 51:8
you consider so *r* . . . Isa 57:12
r shines like the dawn . . . Isa 62:1
The Lord is Our *R* . . . Jer 23:6
who turn many to *r* . . . Dan 12:3
r . . . triumph over sin . . . Rom 5:17
armor of God's *r* . . . Eph 6:14

RISE(N), ROSE *to take up arms (uprising); to ascend or extend above other objects; to return from the dead; to assume an upright position; to get up from bed*
pleas . . . *r* up to God . . . Exod 2:23
Esther . . . *r* and stood before him . . . Esth 8:4
anger *r* up against them . . . Jer 44:3
third day he will *r* . . . Luke 18:33
The Lord has really *r* . . . Luke 24:34
be the first to *r* . . . Acts 26:23
Christ died and *r* . . . Rom 14:9
because Jesus Christ *r* again . . . 1 Pet 1:3
r to heaven in a cloud . . . Rev 11:12

ROCK *stone; cliff; figurative of shelter, safety, or sustenance*
Strike the *r* . . . Exod 17:6
and struck the *r* . . . Num 20:11
r of our enemies . . . Deut 32:31
The Lord is my *r* . . . 2 Sam 22:2
You are my *r* . . . Ps 31:3
r of safety . . . Ps 61:2
the *R* who can hide you . . . Isa 17:10
shadow of a large *r* . . . Isa 32:2
house on solid *r* . . . Matt 7:24
Peter, and upon this *r* . . . Matt 16:18
r that makes them fall . . . Rom 9:33
drank from . . . *r* . . . 1 Cor 10:4

ROD *used as a walking stick, a club or weapon, a shepherd's crook, a paddling device, a royal scepter, a measuring stick, figurative of divine authority; often translated "staff"; see STAFF*
Your *r* and your staff . . . Ps 23:4
tape and a measuring *r* . . . Ezek 40:3
rule . . . with an iron *r* . . . Rev 2:27

ROOT(ED)(S) *the source of life; to pull up and destroy; to be firmly established*
their *r* will rot . . . Isa 5:24
r had no nourishment . . . Matt 13:6
r go down deep . . . Eph 3:17
r grow down into him . . . Col 2:7
of money is at the *r* . . . 1 Tim 6:10
Watch out that no bitter *r* . . . Heb 12:15

RULE(S), RULING *to exercise leadership over; see REIGN*
that the Most High *r* . . . Dan 4:17
Christ *r* in your hearts . . . Col 3:15

RULER(S) *person with authority; tribal chief; prince or king; city magistrate; powerful spiritual beings; God himself*
the *r* plot together . . . Ps 2:2
Bethlehem . . . *r* of Israel will come . . . Mic 5:2
council of all the *r*, . . . Acts 4:5
Who made you a *r* . . . Acts 7:27
the *r* of this world . . . 1 Cor 2:8
against the evil *r* . . . Eph 6:12

SABBATH(S) *cessation of activity; a holy day set aside to honor God*
a day of rest, a holy *S* . . . Exod 16:23
Remember to observe the *S* . . . Exod 20:8
am master even of the *S* . . . Matt 12:8
S was made to benefit people . . . Mark 2:27

SACRIFICE(D)(S) *worship offering; devotion to God; a submitting or putting to death*
s you want is a broken spirit . . . Ps 51:17
s their sons and their daughters . . . Ps 106:37
when we give him *s* . . . Prov 21:3
I am sick of your *s* . . . Isa 1:11
goats and rams for a *s* . . . Isa 34:6
their *s* are all meaningless . . . Hos 8:13
leave your *s* there beside . . . Matt 5:24
I don't want your *s* . . . Matt 9:13

gave himself as a *s* . . . Eph 5:2
does not need to offer *s* . . . Heb 7:27
remove . . . sin forever by his *s* . . . Heb 9:26
no other *s* that will cover . . . Heb 10:26
continually offer our *s* of praise . . . Heb 13:15
spiritual *s* that please him . . . 1 Pet 2:5

SAINTS *"holy ones" who consecrate themselves for God's service; Christians—all those "in Christ"; angels or martyrs; see SANCTIFY*
may your *s* rejoice in your goodness . . . 2 Chr 6:41

SALVATION *deliverance from slavery (to Egyptians, to sin) or from some great distress by the intervention of God*
my light and my *s* . . . Ps 27:1
joyful in the God of my *s* . . . Hab 3:18
s in no one else . . . Acts 4:12
Today is the day of *s*. . . . 2 Cor 6:2
the first to experience *s* . . . 2 Thes 2:13
indifferent to this great *s* . . . Heb 2:3

SANCTIFICATION, SANCTIFIED, SANCTIFIES, SANCTIFY *to cleanse or set apart for sacred use; to declare or make holy; see SET APART*
the Tabernacle will be *s* . . . Exod 29:43
S them to make them entirely holy. . . . Exod 30:29

SANCTUARY *tabernacle; refuge; enclosed area; place of sanctity and beauty*
they must not approach the *s* . . . Num 4:20
for they have defiled the *s* . . . Num 19:20
are in his *s* . . . Ps 96:6
I will be a *s* to you . . . Ezek 11:16
smile again on your desolate *s* . . . Dan 9:17
into God's inner *s* . . . Heb 6:19

SATAN *"adversary" of God; personification of evil; see DEVIL*
S the Accuser came with them. . . . Job 1:6
Get out of here, *S* . . . Matt 4:10
Get away from me, *S*! . . . Matt 16:23
How can *S* cast out . . . Mark 3:23
S has asked to have all . . . Luke 22:31
the work of *S* . . . 2 Thes 2:9
depths of *S* . . . Rev 2:24
S will be let out . . . Rev 20:7

SATISFIED, SATISFIES, SATISFY *to please or appease; to fulfill an obligation*
I will be fully *s* . . . Ps 17:15
S us in the morning . . . Ps 90:14
s them with a long life . . . Ps 91:16
he *s* the thirsty . . . Ps 107:9
that are never *s* . . . Prov 30:15
he will be *s* . . . Isa 53:11

SAVE(D)(S) *rescue or preserve from danger; deliver from sin*
S me because of your . . . love . . . Ps 6:4
not too weak to *s* you . . . Isa 59:1
now let them *s* you . . . Hos 13:10
s his people from their sins . . . Matt 1:21
have come to *s* the lost . . . Matt 18:11
He *s* others . . . Matt 27:42
will be *s* from our enemies . . . Luke 1:71
Your faith has *s* you . . . Luke 7:50
let him *s* himself if . . . Luke 23:35
but to *s* it . . . John 3:17
I have come to *s* the world . . . John 12:47
S yourselves from this generation . . . Acts 2:40
what must I do to be *s* . . . Acts 16:30
this Good News that *s* you . . . 1 Cor 15:2
God *s* you by his special favor . . . Eph 2:8
the world to *s* sinners . . . 1 Tim 1:15
He *s* us . . . his mercy . . . Titus 3:5
baptism, which now *s* you . . . 1 Pet 3:21

SAVIOR *one who delivers (from trouble, sin, or judgment)*
I, the Lord, am your *S* . . . Isa 60:16
our *S* in times of trouble . . . Jer 14:8
I rejoice in God my *S* . . . Luke 1:47
The *S* . . . has been born tonight . . . Luke 2:11
God's promised *S* of Israel . . . Acts 13:23
God, who is the *S* . . . 1 Tim 4:10
our great God and *S* . . . Titus 2:13

SCATTER(ED)(S) *to disperse or distribute irregularly*
I will *s* you among the . . . Lev 26:33
Israelites . . . have been *s* . . . Jer 50:17
the sheep will be *s* . . . Mark 14:27

SCHEME(D)(R)(S) *to make plans, always with a negative connotation*
is simply a human *s* . . . 1 Sam 26:19
their evil *s* will never succeed . . . Ps 21:11
fret about their wicked *s* . . . Ps 37:7
you will devise a wicked *s* . . . Ezek 38:10

SCOFF(ER)(ERS) *to mock or deride*
join in with *s* . . . Ps 1:1
the *s* of the proud . . . Ps 123:4
They *s* at kings . . . Hab 1:10
s who will laugh at the truth . . . 2 Pet 3:3

SCORN *to ridicule, laugh at, or make light of*
My friends *s* me . . . Job 16:20
an object of *s* and derision . . . Ps 44:13
the *s* of foreign nations . . . Ezek 34:29

SCRIPTURE(S) *the Law; the writings of Moses; the entire collection of sacred books*
to fulfill what the *S* say . . . Mark 14:49
You search the *S* . . . John 5:39
the *S* cannot be altered . . . John 10:35
They searched the *S* . . . Acts 17:11
the *S* tell us, Abraham believed . . . Rom 4:3
All *S* is inspired by God . . . 2 Tim 3:16
the other parts of *S* . . . 2 Pet 3:16

SEAL(ED)(S) *to confirm, certify, or make secure; a closure device that prevents entry; symbol or mark of office*
s them with his *s* . . . 1 Kgs 21:8
it was *s* with seven *S* . . . Rev 5:1

SEARCH(ED)(ES)(ING), SEARCHLIGHT *to investigate or examine thoroughly in an effort to find or verify something*
to *s* for food . . . Job 24:5
The Lord's *s* penetrates . . . Prov 20:27
s the Scriptures . . . John 5:39
s the Scriptures day after day . . . Acts 17:11
his Spirit *s* out everything . . . 1 Cor 2:10

SECRET(LY)(S) *hidden or unexplained; private; covertly; something kept from the knowledge of others*
s things that belong . . . Deut 29:29
he knows the *s* . . . Ps 44:21
your Father, who knows all *s* . . . Matt 6:6
will judge everyone's *s* life . . . Rom 2:16

SEED(S) *grain; descendants; symbolic of a small beginning with big promise*
white like coriander *s* . . . Exod 16:31
a holy *s* that will grow . . . Isa 6:13
producing *s* for the farmer . . . Isa 55:10
planting *s* of peace . . . Zech 8:12
good *s* represents the people . . . Matt 13:38
some *s* fell on a footpath . . . Mark 4:4

SEEK(ING)(S) *search for; request; aim or try*
s my face and turn . . . 2 Chr 7:14
S the Lord while you . . . Isa 55:6
have come to *s* and save . . . Luke 19:10
no one is *s* God . . . Rom 3:11

SEND(ING)(S), SENT *dispatch a messenger; cause (him) to go; to pour out*
and *s* her away . . . Deut 24:1
when the Lord *s* rain . . . 1 Kgs 17:14
continued to *s* my prophets . . . Jer 7:25
s rain on the just and . . . Matt 5:45
s you out as sheep . . . Matt 10:16
As the Father has *s* me . . . John 20:21
He *s* his own Son . . . Rom 8:3
without being *s* . . . Rom 10:15

SEPARATE(D)(S), SEPARATION *set apart or dedicate for a special purpose; to block off; to sever an association; to go in different directions*
and we will *s* . . . Gen 13:9
s themselves from all foreigners . . . Neh 9:2
s close friends . . . Prov 17:9
s the wicked people from the godly . . . Matt 13:49
let no one *s* them . . . Matt 19:6
s us from Christ's love . . . Rom 8:35
hostility that used to *s* us . . . Eph 2:14

SERVANT(S) *one who performs tasks under the direction of another*
A *s* who is pampered . . . Prov 29:21
a *s* respects his master . . . Mal 1:6
good and faithful *s* . . . Matt 25:21
s who have . . . done our duty . . . Luke 17:10

SERVE(D)(S), SERVICE, SERVING *to meet the needs of and subject one's will to that of another*
s Baal and worshiped him . . . 1 Kgs 22:53
not to be *s*, but to *s* . . . Matt 20:28
s the Lord enthusiastically . . . Rom 12:11
s one another in love . . . Gal 5:13

SET APART *to sanctify; to declare or make holy*
s a from the common people . . . Exod 28:1
s a as holy to the LORD . . . Exod 29:21
those he has *s a* . . . Acts 20:32
you have been *s a* . . . 1 Cor 6:11
they are *s a* for him . . . 1 Cor 7:14
s a from sinners . . . Heb 7:26

SHAME(FUL) *objective situation and subjective emotion of public disgrace and humiliation, often suffered at the hands of an enemy; see ASHAMED*
will not be put to *s* . . . Rom 9:33
in order to *s* those . . . 1 Cor 1:27
It is *s* even to talk . . . Eph 5:12
they brag about *s* things . . . Phil 3:19

SHARE(D)(S), SHARING *portion or allotment (of an inheritance); to participate in or give to*
We *s* and *s* alike . . . 1 Sam 30:24
fully *s* its joy . . . Prov 14:10
s . . . in my present difficulty . . . Phil 4:14
s what you have . . . Heb 13:16

SHEEP *small domesticated animal, representing wealth and livelihood to many Israelites; figurative of God's people*
strayed away like *s* . . . Isa 53:6
the *s* will be scattered . . . Zech 13:7
like *s* without a shepherd . . . Matt 9:36
If you had one hundred *s* . . . Luke 15:4
I know my own *s* . . . John 10:14
a *s* to the slaughter . . . Acts 8:32

SHELTER(S) *something that protects; a position of protection; to place under protection*
a *s* for the oppressed . . . Ps 9:9
the *s* of your presence . . . Ps 31:20
humanity finds *s* in the shadow . . . Ps 36:7
time for the Festival of *S* . . . John 7:2
live among them and *s* them . . . Rev 7:15

SHEPHERD(S) *caretaker of sheep; figurative of political and religious leaders, especially those who care for God's people*
The Lord is my *s* . . . Ps 23:1
feed his flock like a *s* . . . Isa 40:11
Their *s* have led them astray . . . Jer 50:6
Shouldn't *s* feed their sheep? . . . Ezek 34:2
God will strike the *S* . . . Matt 26:31
I am the good *s* . . . John 10:11
Jesus is the great *S* . . . Heb 13:20

SHIELD(S) *defensive armor; figurative of one's security in the Lord*
s and . . . my salvation . . . 2 Sam 22:3

Uzziah provided . . . *s*, spears, helmets, . . . 2 Chr 26:14
my strength, my *s* . . . Ps 28:7
He will *s* you . . . Ps 91:4
faith as your *s* . . . Eph 6:16

SHRINE(S) *a place where sacred objects are placed and/or a place set aside for worship*
I will destroy your pagan *s* . . . Lev 26:30
Micah set up a *s* . . . Judg 17:5
Solomon built such *s* . . . 1 Kgs 11:8
Hezekiah tear down his *s* . . . Isa 36:7
whores and *s* prostitutes . . . Hos 4:14
I'll make three *s* . . . Matt 17:4
s of the Greek goddess Artemis . . . Acts 19:24

SICK(NESS)(NESSES) *illness; bad health*
can endure a *s* body . . . Prov 18:14
He took our *s* . . . Matt 8:17
I was *s*, and you cared . . . Matt 25:36
Lazarus's *s* will not . . . John 11:4
their prayer . . . will heal the *s* . . . Jas 5:15

SIGN(S) *pointing to or indicative of something larger or more important; linked with "wonders" and "miracles"*
s to mark off the seasons . . . Gen 1:14
Lord himself will choose the *s* . . . Isa 7:14
the only *s* I will give . . . Matt 12:39
obvious *s* of the times . . . Matt 16:3
many other miraculous *s* . . . John 20:30
s through him . . . Acts 2:22
they want a *s* from heaven . . . 1 Cor 1:22
I patiently did many *s* . . . 2 Cor 12:12

SIMPLE(TONS) *foolishness or lack of good sense; absense of pretense or hypocrisy; one who is simple*
making wise the *s* . . . Ps 19:7
You *s* . . . Prov 1:22
pure and *s* devotion to Christ . . . 2 Cor 11:3

SIN(S)(NED)(NING)(FUL) *moral evil; transgression of or rebellion against God's laws; perversion of the heart; missing the mark; see SINNER*
you will have *s* . . . Num 32:23
Don't *s* by letting anger . . . Ps 4:4
Keep me from deliberate *s* . . . Ps 19:13
Against you . . . have I *s* . . . Ps 51:4
our secret *s* . . . you see them . . . Ps 90:8
He bore the *s* of many . . . Isa 53:12
The person who *s* . . . Ezek 18:4
If another believer *s* against you . . . Matt 18:15
Father, I have *s* . . . Luke 15:18
who takes away the *s* . . . John 1:29
those who have never *s* . . . John 8:7
convince the world of its *s* . . . John 16:8
For all have *s* . . . Rom 3:23
Adam's *s* brought death . . . Rom 5:12
go on *s* . . . Rom 6:15
how terrible *s* really is . . . Rom 7:13
Christ died for our *s* . . . 1 Cor 15:3
the offering for our *s* . . . 2 Cor 5:21
our *s* are forgiven . . . Eph 1:7
yet he did not *s* . . . Heb 4:15
it is *s* to know . . . Jas 4:17
if we confess our *s* . . . 1 Jn 1:9
the *s* of all the world . . . 1 Jn 2:2
they can't keep on *s* . . . 1 Jn 3:9

SINNER(S) *those guilty of sin; see SIN*
or stand around with *s* . . . Ps 1:1
I have come to call *s* . . . Matt 9:13
I'm too much of a *s* . . . Luke 5:8
one lost *s* who returns to God . . . Luke 15:7
while we were still *s* . . . Rom 5:8
many people became *s* . . . Rom 5:19
save *s* . . . I was the worst . . . 1 Tim 1:15
set apart from *s* . . . Heb 7:26
the godless and *s* . . . 1 Pet 4:18

SLANDER(ED)(ERS)(EROUSLY)(S) *to speak critically of another person with the intent to hurt or defame*
Ziba has *s* me . . . 2 Sam 19:27
people who *s* their neighbors . . . Ps 101:5
to *s* is to be a fool . . . Prov 10:18
yet some *s* me . . . Rom 3:8
they will *s* others . . . 2 Tim 3:3

SLEEP(ING), SLEPT *natural or induced state of rest; mental dullness or laziness; euphemism for death; see ASLEEP*
God caused . . . a deep *s* . . . Gen 2:21
I lay down and *s* . . . Ps 3:5
never tires and never *s* . . . Ps 121:4
found them *s* . . . Matt 26:44

SLOW *not hasty; gentle*
s to become angry . . . Neh 9:17
he is *s* to get angry . . . Ps 103:8
s to speak, and *s* to get angry . . . Jas 1:19

SOBER *abstaining from alcohol; under self-control; of sound moral quality*
Stay alert and be *s* . . . 1 Thes 5:6

SOLDIER(S) *person on active military duty*
I have authority over my *s* . . . Matt 8:9
asked some *s* . . . Luke 3:14
The *s* mocked him . . . Luke 23:36
The *s* made a crown . . . John 19:2
When the *s* had crucified . . . John 19:23
Endure suffering . . . as a good *s* . . . 2 Tim 2:3

SON(S) *a parent's male child or descendant further removed; spiritual heir (of Christ); relationship of Jesus to the heavenly Father*
You are my *s* . . . Ps 2:7
a *s* is given to us . . . Isa 9:6
Your *s* are coming . . . Isa 60:4
like a *s* of the gods . . . Dan 3:25
And she will have a *s* . . . Matt 1:21
This is my beloved *S* . . . Matt 3:17
Why . . . bothering us, *S* of God? . . . Matt 8:29
You are the Messiah, the *S* . . . Matt 16:16
Whose *s* is he? . . . Matt 22:42
When the *S* of Man returns . . . Matt 24:37
I am the *S* of God. . . . Matt 27:43
Jesus the Messiah, the *S* of God. . . . Mark 1:1
the only *s* of a widow . . . Luke 7:12
his only *S*, who is himself . . . John 1:18
S can do nothing by himself . . . John 5:19
Woman, he is your *s* . . . John 19:26
Jesus Christ is the *S* of God . . . Acts 8:37
giving his *S* as a sacrifice . . . Rom 8:3
God did not spare . . . his own *S* . . . Rom 8:32
trusting in the *S* of God . . . Gal 2:20
his *S*, born of a woman . . . Gal 4:4
knowledge of God's *S* . . . Eph 4:13
You are my *S* . . . Heb 1:5
even though Jesus was God's *S* . . . Heb 5:8
resembling the *S* of God . . . Heb 7:3
This is my beloved *S* . . . 2 Pet 1:17
Anyone who denies the *S* . . . 1 Jn 2:23
was the *S* of Man . . . Rev 1:13

SORROW(FUL)(S) *mental, physical, or emotional anguish*
will be filled with *s* . . . Ps 16:4
he adds no *s* with it . . . Prov 10:22
despised and rejected, a man of *s* . . . Isa 53:3
God can use *s* . . . 2 Cor 7:10
not be full of *s* . . . 1 Thes 4:13
no more death or *s* . . . Rev 21:4

SORRY *full of regret, sometimes shame*
the Lord was *s* he had . . . Gen 6:6
the king was very *s* . . . Mark 6:26

SOUL(S) *the individual's essential self, life, or being*
with . . . all your *s* . . . Deut 6:5
in the bitterness of my *s* . . . Job 10:1
you will not leave my *s* . . . Ps 16:10
reviving the *s* . . . Ps 19:7
food . . . good for the *s* . . . Isa 55:2
they cannot touch your *s* . . . Matt 10:28
worth more than your *s* . . . Matt 16:26
all your *s* . . . Matt 22:37
s and body be kept blameless . . . 1 Thes 5:23
strong enough to save your *s* . . . Jas 1:21
body is as healthy as . . . *s* . . . 3 Jn 1:2

SOW(ER)(N)(S) *to scatter grain seeds in planting a crop, illustrating the principle of cause and effect*
They *s* their fields . . . Ps 107:37
a person who *s* discord . . . Prov 6:19
always plow and never *s* . . . Isa 28:24
the farmer *s* grain . . . Matt 13:18
reap what you *s* . . . Gal 6:7

SPARE(S) *to refrain from attacking, destroying, or penalizing; over and above what is needed*
s it for their sakes . . . Gen 18:24
have food enough to *s* . . . Luke 15:17
Since God did not *s* . . . Rom 8:32
I will not *s* them. . . . 2 Cor 13:2
God did not *s* . . . the angels . . . 2 Pet 2:4

SPEND, SPENT *to use up or pay out; to exhaust or consume*
They *s* their days in prosperity . . . Job 21:13
Why *s* your money on food . . . Isa 55:2
and had *s* everything she had . . . Mark 5:26

SPIRIT *"wind" or "breath"; a supernatural being; the third member of the Trinity, with God the Father and Jesus the Son*
And the *S* of God was . . . Gen 1:2
My *S* will not put up . . . Gen 6:3
I will put the *S* upon . . . Num 11:17
His *S* will make it . . . true . . . Isa 34:16
I have put my *S* . . . Isa 42:1
The *S* of the Sovereign Lord . . . Isa 61:1
The *S* came into me . . . Ezek 2:2
I will put my *S* in you . . . Ezek 36:27
the *S* of God descending . . . Matt 3:16
I will put my *S* . . . Matt 12:18
Holy *S* descending like a dove . . . Mark 1:10
For God is *S* . . . John 4:24
He is the Holy *S* . . . John 14:17
S of God living in you . . . Rom 8:9
the *S* pleads for us . . . Rom 8:27
it is the same Holy *S* . . . 1 Cor 12:4
the Holy *S* gives life . . . 2 Cor 3:6
your Christian lives in the *S* . . . Gal 3:3
by giving you the Holy *S* . . . Eph 1:13
the Holy *S* tells us clearly . . . 1 Tim 4:1
the Holy *S* . . . jealously longs . . . Jas 4:5
raised to life in the *S* . . . 1 Pet 3:18
S also gives us the testimony . . . 1 Jn 5:6
I was worshiping in the *S* . . . Rev 1:10
The *S* and the bride say . . . Rev 22:17

SPIRIT(S) *"wind" or "breath"; invisible, nonmaterial part of man (as opposed to body or flesh); an evil presence that can possess or influence a person; an attitude, mood, or disposition*
a double share of your *s* . . . 2 Kgs 2:9
Boaz . . . was in good *s* . . . Ruth 3:7
A *s* swept past my face. . . . Job 4:15
I entrust my *s* into your hand . . . Ps 31:5
penetrates the human *s* . . . Prov 20:27
the *s* will return to God . . . Eccl 12:7
a new heart and a new *s* . . . Ezek 18:31
All the *s* fled when . . . Matt 8:16
S of deafness and muteness . . . Mark 9:25
though the *s* is willing . . . Mark 14:38
the *s* and power of Elijah . . . Luke 1:17
entrust my *s* into your hands . . . Luke 23:46
Perhaps a *s* . . . spoke to him. . . . Acts 23:9
if the *s* they have . . . 1 Jn 4:1

SPIRITUAL(LY) *having to do with the spirit, usually God's Spirit; see SPIRIT*
They are *s* prostitutes . . . Exod 34:15
people living in *s* darkness . . . Jon 4:11
the *s* body comes later . . . 1 Cor 15:46
and *s* songs . . . Eph 5:19
lives only for pleasure is *s* dead . . . 1 Tim 5:6
into his *s* temple . . . 1 Pet 2:5

SPOT(S) *blemish*
cut the *s* from the clothing . . . Lev 13:56
Can a leopard take away its *s*? . . . Jer 13:23
without a *s* or wrinkle . . . Eph 5:27

STAFF *see ROD*
Your rod and your *s* . . . Ps 23:4
Jacob . . . leaned on his *s* . . . Heb 11:21

STAND(ING)(S) *remain erect; maintain one's position; endure*
No one will . . . *s* against you . . . Deut 7:24
he will *s* upon the earth . . . Job 19:25
Who will be able to *s* . . . Mal 3:2
the Son of Man *s* . . . Acts 7:56
If you think you are *s* strong . . . 1 Cor 10:12
s true to what you believe . . . 1 Cor 16:13
s firm in your faith . . . 2 Cor 1:24
you will still be *s* firm . . . Eph 6:13
I *s* at the door and knock . . . Rev 3:20

STATUTES *laws or decrees*
I turned to follow your *s* . . . Ps 119:59

STEADFAST *loyal; stable in faith and practice; see UNFAILING*
a strong and *s* belief . . . Titus 1:9

STONE(D)(S), STONING, STONY *hardened mineral or rock; figurative of Christ, of hardened hearts; method of execution*
Jacob set up a *s* pillar . . . Gen 35:14
This *s* has heard everything . . . Josh 24:27
The *s* rejected by the builders . . . Ps 118:22
a foundation *s* in Jerusalem . . . Isa 28:16
your *s* hearts of sin . . . Ezek 36:26
change these *s* here into children . . . Matt 3:9
change these *s* into loaves . . . Matt 4:3
do you give them a *s* . . . Matt 7:9
Anyone who stumbles over that *s* . . . Matt 21:44
The *s* rejected by the builders . . . Luke 20:17
And as they *s* him . . . Acts 7:59
Some died by *s* . . . Heb 11:37
building you, as living *s* . . . 1 Pet 2:5

STRAIGHT *free of curves, dips, or obstacles*
Make a *s*, smooth road . . . Isa 40:3
Mark out a *s* path . . . Heb 12:13

STRANGE(R)(RS) *foreigner or outsider, as opposed to the native; see FOREIGN*
I have been a *s* . . . Exod 2:22
I was a *s* . . . Matt 25:35
They won't follow a *s* . . . John 10:5
no longer *s* and foreigners . . . Eph 2:19
as if something *s* were happening . . . 1 Pet 4:12

STRENGTH(EN)(ENED)(ENING)(ENS) *capacity for endurance or exertion; the power of a person or of God, measured variously in terms of wealth, wisdom, military might, or physical prowess*
No one will succeed by *s* . . . 1 Sam 2:9
God is our refuge and *s* . . . Ps 46:1
clothed with *s* and dignity . . . Prov 31:25
s those who have tired hands . . . Isa 35:3
he offers *s* to the weak . . . Isa 40:29
you are my *s* and fortress . . . Jer 16:19
s and build up your brothers . . . Luke 22:32
where they *s* the believers . . . Acts 14:22
Christ who gives me the *s* . . . Phil 4:13
and gave me *s* . . . 2 Tim 4:17
S what little remains . . . Rev 3:2

STRONG(HOLD) *place or means of protection, safety, or refuge; see STRENGTH*
my God is my . . . *s* . . . Ps 18:2
The Lord *s* and mighty . . . Ps 24:8
s is your hand! . . . Ps 89:13
Satan . . . the *s* one . . . Luke 11:21
I am weak, then I am *s* . . . 2 Cor 12:10
Be *s* with the Lord's . . . Eph 6:10
They became *s* in battle . . . Heb 11:34

STUMBLE(D)(S), STUMBLING *to contend; in opposition against*
stone that causes people to *s* . . . Isa 8:14
caused many to *s* into sin . . . Mal 2:8
that causes people to *s* . . . Rom 9:33
Did God's people *s* . . . Rom 11:11
brother or sister . . . to *s* . . . 1 Cor 8:9
stone that makes people *s* . . . 1 Pet 2:8
able to keep you from *s* . . . Jude 1:24

SUBJECT(ED) *to bring under control or dominion of another*
are *s* to the same laws . . . Num 15:15
everything . . . *s* to God's curse . . . Rom 8:20
Son . . . *s* to the law . . . Gal 4:4

SUBMISSION, SUBMISSIVE, SUBMIT-(TING) *to be subject to or accountable to another—God, society, or fellow believers*
Return to your mistress and *s* . . . Gen 16:9
s yourselves to the Lord . . . 2 Chr 30:8
good for the young to *s* . . . Lam 3:27
s to one another . . . Eph 5:21
s to your husbands . . . Eph 5:22

SUCCEED(ING), SUCCESS(FUL) *to inherit or follow after, as the one next in line; attaining a favorable outcome— victory, wealth, preeminence*
Give me *s* and show kindness . . . Gen 24:12
wisdom; it helps you *s* . . . Eccl 10:10
against the Babylonians . . . never *s* . . . Jer 32:5

SUFFER(ED)(ING)(INGS)(S) *to endure hardship or experience loss*
the Messiah would have to *s* . . . Luke 24:26
what we *s* now is nothing . . . Rom 8:18
the privilege of *s* . . . Phil 1:29
Through the *s* of Jesus . . . Heb 2:10
Are any among you *s*? . . . Jas 5:13
After you have *s* . . . 1 Pet 5:10

SURE(LY) *inevitable; with certainty*
may be *s* that your sin . . . Num 32:23
S your goodness and unfailing love . . . Ps 23:6

SWEAR(ING)(S), SWORE, SWORN *affirm by a solemn oath or binding commitment*
Because you have obeyed . . . I *s* . . . Gen 22:16
I have *s* . . . Every knee . . . Isa 45:23
but to *s* . . . is binding . . . Matt 23:18
I *s* by God, I don't know . . . Matt 26:74
no one greater to *s* by . . . Heb 6:13

SWELL(ING) *to become puffed up or overgrown (in size, volume, pride)*
their feet did not *s* . . . Neh 9:21
the *s* Jordan rushes down . . . Job 40:23
people waited for him to *s* . . . Acts 28:6

SWORD(S) *handheld weapon with a long blade; figurative for war or persecution by government, also of God's word in spiritual warfare*
a flaming *s* . . . guarding the way . . . Gen 3:24
beat their *s* into plowshares . . . Isa 2:4
The *s* of the Lord . . . Isa 34:6
A *s* is being sharpened . . . Ezek 21:9
I will remove . . . *s* and bows . . . Hos 2:18
I came to bring a *s* . . . Matt 10:34
Those who use the *s* . . . Matt 26:52
the *s* of the Spirit . . . Eph 6:17
From his mouth came a sharp *s* . . . Rev 19:15

TABERNACLE *"tent of witness"; portable shrine or tent designated for the worship of God; metaphor for God dwelling among his people*
this *T* and its furnishings . . . Exod 25:9
T filled with . . . glory of the LORD . . . Exod 40:35
maintained the LORD's *T* . . . Num 31:47
presented themselves at the *T* . . . Deut 31:14
LORD lives among us in his *T* . . . Josh 22:19
ancestors carried the *T* . . . Acts 7:44
Temple in heaven, God's *T* . . . Rev 15:5

TABLE(S) *furniture item used for eating, moneychangers, and ritual vessels*
placed the *t* in the Tabernacle . . . Exod 40:22
Feast at my banquet *t* . . . Ezek 39:20
knocked over the *t* . . . Matt 21:12
dogs under the *t* . . . Mark 7:28
bountiful *t* become a snare . . . Rom 11:9
at the Lord's *T* . . . 1 Cor 10:16

TABLET(S) *surface for writing*
t of stone . . . inscribed with . . . Exod 24:12
large, clear letters on a *t* . . . Hab 2:2
motioned for a writing *t* . . . Luke 1:63
stone *t* of the covenant . . . Heb 9:4

TALENT(ED) *a natural ability*
naturally *t* craftsmen . . . Exod 31:6
a *t* harp player . . . 1 Sam 16:18
no *t* at all for doing right! . . . Jer 4:22

TAUGHT, TEACH(ER)(ERS)(ES)(ING) *impart knowledge by precept, example, or experience*
t my laws to their children . . . Deut 4:10
t you what is good and right . . . 1 Sam 12:23
T them to do what is right . . . 1 Kgs 8:36
Who is a *t* like him? . . . Job 36:22
T me how to live . . . Ps 27:11
t you to fear the LORD . . . Ps 34:11
t me to be wise in my inmost being . . . Ps 51:6
t your ways to sinners . . . Ps 51:13
T me your ways, O LORD . . . Ps 86:11
T me to do your will . . . Ps 143:10
T your children . . . Prov 22:6
LORD Almighty is a wonderful *t* . . . Isa 28:29
Anyone who listens to my *t* . . . Matt 7:24
not greater than the *t* . . . Matt 10:24
Let me *t* you . . . Matt 11:29
t them about the Kingdom . . . Luke 9:11
T, what must I do . . . Luke 10:25
Lord, *t* us to pray . . . Luke 11:1
the Holy Spirit will *t* you . . . Luke 12:12
false *t* . . . will come in among you . . . Acts 20:29
third are *t* . . . 1 Cor 12:28
another will *t* . . . 1 Cor 14:26
we *t* them to obey Christ . . . 2 Cor 10:5
law was our guardian and *t* . . . Gal 3:24
and the pastors and *t* . . . Eph 4:11
warn them and *t* them . . . Col 1:28
t and counsel each other . . . Col 3:16
and must be able to *t* . . . 1 Tim 3:2
encouraging . . . and *t* them . . . 1 Tim 4:13
T the older men . . . Titus 2:2
Let your *t* be so correct . . . Titus 2:8
there will be false *t* . . . 2 Pet 2:1
the Spirit *t* you all things . . . 1 Jn 2:27

TEMPLE(S) *first built in Solomon's reign as a permanent worship center, which was destroyed, then rebuilt under Herod's reign; figurative of the human body and of Christ*
finished building the *T* . . . 1 Kgs 6:14
beautify the *T* of the . . . Ezra 7:27
I will worship at your *T* . . . Ps 5:7
LORD is in his holy *T* . . . Ps 11:4
In the last days, the *T* . . . Isa 2:2
the *T* be restored . . . Isa 44:28
one . . . greater than the *T*! . . . Matt 12:6
T will be a place of prayer . . . Luke 19:45
Destroy this *t* . . . John 2:19
t made by human hands . . . Acts 7:48
Christians are that *t* . . . 1 Cor 3:17
your body is the *t* . . . 1 Cor 6:19
becoming a holy *t* . . . Eph 2:21
position himself in the *t* . . . 2 Thes 2:4
living cornerstone of God's *t* . . . 1 Pet 2:4
into his spiritual *t* . . . 1 Pet 2:5
pillars in the *T* of my God . . . Rev 3:12
the Lamb are its *t* . . . Rev 21:22

TEMPT(ATION)(ED)(ER)(S) *entice to sin; put to the test, make a trial of*
I would be *t* to destroy you . . . Exod 33:3
don't let us yield to *t* . . . Matt 6:13
forty days, being *t* by Satan . . . Mark 1:13

don't let us yield to *t* . . . Luke 11:4
will always be *t* to sin . . . Luke 17:1
t from becoming so strong . . . 1 Cor 10:13
not to fall into the same *t* . . . Gal 6:1
faced all of the same *t* . . . Heb 4:15
T comes from the lure . . . Jas 1:14

TENT(S) *portable housing made of cloth or skins; figurative of the mortal body; see TABERNACLE*
Lot moved his *t* . . . Gen 13:12
went into Rachel's *t* . . . Gen 31:33
t of the Tabernacle . . . Num 3:25
How beautiful are your *t* . . . Num 24:5
Sisera ran to the *t* of Jael . . . Judg 4:17
t of the godly will flourish . . . Prov 14:11
like a shepherd's *t* in a storm . . . Isa 38:12
earthly *t* we live in . . . 2 Cor 5:1
ministers in the sacred *t* . . . Heb 8:2

TENTH *one-tenth of any property or produce; see TITHE*
gave Melchizedek a *t* . . . Gen 14:20
to the Levites a *t* of everything . . . Neh 10:37
A *t* of the people . . . live there . . . Neh 11:1
I give you a *t* of my income . . . Luke 18:12

TERRIBLE *dreadful; awesome*
sent a *t* plague . . . Gen 12:17
t swarms of flies . . . Exod 8:24
t sin against the LORD . . . Deut 9:16
t day of his fury . . . Isa 13:9
die from *t* diseases . . . Jer 16:4
t day of the LORD . . . Joel 2:31
how *t* sin really is . . . Rom 7:13
a swift and *t* end . . . 2 Pet 2:1
there was a *t* earthquake . . . Rev 11:13
t wrath of God . . . Rev 15:7
how *t* for Babylon . . . Rev 18:10

TERRIFIED, TERRIFYING *filled with fear or dread*
a *t* vision of darkness . . . Gen 15:12
Moses was *t* . . . Exod 4:3
end this *t* thunder and hail . . . Exod 9:28
great and *t* wilderness . . . Deut 1:19
t them with his fierce fury . . . Ps 2:5
t news I have heard . . . Ezek 21:7
fourth beast, *t*, dreadful . . . Dan 7:7
t and began to sink . . . Matt 14:30
Everyone . . . was *t* . . . Acts 5:5
t by her great torment . . . Rev 18:10

TERROR(S) *fear or dread*
t and dread will overcome them . . . Exod 15:16
trembled and shook with *t* . . . Job 4:14
I am surrounded by *t* . . . Ps 31:13
t of death overpowers me . . . Ps 55:4
Do not be afraid of the *t* . . . Ps 91:5
rescued us from the *t* . . . 1 Thes 1:10
demons . . . tremble in *t*! . . . Jas 2:19
The first *t* is past . . . Rev 9:12
t will come on the earth . . . Rev 12:12

TEST(ED)(ING)(S) *a trial intended to ascertain quality, value, or character; to examine*
God *t* Abraham's faith . . . Gen 22:1
why are you *t* the LORD? . . . Exod 17:2
t me like gold in a fire . . . Job 23:10
You have *t* my thoughts . . . Ps 17:3
T my motives . . . Ps 26:2
t me and know my thoughts . . . Ps 139:23
Do not *t* the Lord . . . Matt 4:7
the hot winds of *t* . . . Luke 8:13
stood up to *t* Jesus . . . Luke 10:25
to *t* the Spirit of the Lord? . . . Acts 5:9
t at the judgment day . . . 1 Cor 3:13
T yourselves . . . 2 Cor 13:5
t everything that is said . . . 1 Thes 5:21
a *t* of their character . . . 1 Tim 3:10
when God was *t* him . . . Heb 11:17
when your faith is *t* . . . Jas 1:3
patiently endure *t* . . . Jas 1:12
trials are only to *t* your faith . . . 1 Pet 1:7

You must *t* them . . . 1 Jn 4:1
the great time of *t* . . . Rev 3:10

TESTIFIED, TESTIFIES, TESTIFY(ING) *to bear witness or give evidence*
Do not *t* falsely . . . Exod 20:16
t that he is the Son of God. . . . John 1:33
t that the Father has sent me. . . . John 5:36
t and preaching the word . . . Acts 8:25
one all the prophets *t* about . . . Acts 10:43
Holy Spirit also *t* . . . Heb 10:15
t that the Father sent his . . . 1 Jn 4:14
who *t* of their faith in Jesus . . . Rev 19:10

TESTIMONY *the evidence given by a witness; the tablets upon which the Ten Commandments ("Ark of the Testimony") were written; see TESTIFY*
do not be swayed in your *t* . . . Exod 23:2
witnesses . . . slant your *t* . . . Job 13:8
earth will give *t* against him . . . Job 20:27
believe because of his *t* . . . John 1:6
the *t* of John . . . John 1:19
my *t* would not be valid . . . John 5:31
because of their *t* . . . John 17:20
Spirit also gives us the *t* . . . 1 Jn 5:6
the *t* of Jesus Christ . . . Rev 1:2
beheaded for their *t* . . . Rev 20:4

THANK(ED)(ING), THANKS(GIVING) *to acknowledge God's goodness*
t offerings to the LORD . . . Exod 29:28
I will *t* the LORD . . . Ps 7:17
singing a song of *t* . . . Ps 26:7
I will give you *t* forever! . . . Ps 30:12
giving *t* is a sacrifice . . . Ps 50:23
come before him with *t* . . . Ps 95:2
Enter his gates with *t* . . . Ps 100:4
t the Lord for his message . . . Acts 13:48
I *t* God . . . for each one of you . . . Rom 1:8
T God for his Son . . . 2 Cor 9:15
give *t* for everything . . . Eph 5:20
t him for all he has done . . . Phil 4:6
always *t* the Father . . . Col 1:12
lives overflow with *t* . . . Col 2:7

THINK(ING)(S) *to reflect or meditate; to conceive or imagine; to suspect; to have an opinion*
they *t* about his law . . . Ps 1:2
mortals that you should *t* of us . . . Ps 8:4
always *t* of your decrees . . . Ps 119:99
godly *t* before speaking . . . Prov 15:28
t he must be a prophet . . . John 9:17
Don't *t* highly of yourself . . . Rom 11:20
changing the way you *t* . . . Rom 12:2
If you *t* you are wise . . . 1 Cor 3:18
t you are standing strong . . . 1 Cor 10:12
T about things that are pure . . . Phil 4:8
So *t* clearly . . . 1 Pet 1:13

THIRST(S)(Y) *desire or need to drink; any ardent desire or craving*
I *t* for God . . . Ps 42:2
My soul *t* for you . . . Ps 63:1
hungry and *t* for justice . . . Matt 5:6
never be *t* again . . . John 4:15
If you are *t*, . . . John 7:37
never again be hungry or *t* . . . Rev 7:16
Let the *t* ones come . . . Rev 22:17

THORN(S)(Y) *spiny plants; extreme difficulty*
It will grow *t* and thistles . . . Gen 3:18
t, treacherous road . . . Prov 22:5
threats are sharp as *t* . . . Ezek 2:6
Other seeds fell among *t* . . . Matt 13:7
crown of *t* . . . John 19:5
a *t* in my flesh, . . . 2 Cor 12:7

THOUGHT(S) *plan; product of thinking; see THINK*
all their *t* were . . . evil . . . Gen 6:5
tested my *t* . . . Ps 17:3
the *t* of my heart . . . Ps 19:14
You know my every *t* . . . Ps 139:2

t are completely different . . . Isa 55:8
the heart come evil *t* . . . Matt 15:19
Jesus . . . answered his *t* . . . Luke 7:40
Jesus knew their *t* . . . Luke 9:47
your heart and *t* will also . . . Luke 12:34
t he was the Messiah . . . Luke 24:21
knows the *t* of the wise . . . 1 Cor 3:20
t . . . as a child . . . 1 Cor 13:11

THRESH(ING) *to separate the grain from the husks; to strike repeatedly*
t season will extend . . . Lev 26:5
t all his crops . . . Isa 28:27
You will be a new *t* instrument . . . Isa 41:15
wheat on a *t* floor . . . Jer 51:33
as farm workers . . . *t* the grain . . . 1 Cor 9:10

THRONE(S) *seat of power for king or deity*
Saul . . . on Israel's *t* . . . 1 Sam 14:47
Your *t*, O God, endures . . . Ps 45:6
sitting on a lofty *t* . . . Isa 6:1
Heaven is my *t* . . . Isa 66:1
heaven is God's *t* . . . Matt 5:34
t of his ancestor David . . . Luke 1:32
Your *t*, O God, endures . . . Heb 1:8
come boldly to the *t* . . . Heb 4:16
sit with me on my *t* . . . Rev 3:21
I saw a great white *t* . . . Rev 20:11

TIME(S) *the occasion or duration of an event; the duration between redemptive events*
t came, she gave birth . . . Gen 4:1
while there is *t* . . . Ps 32:6
obvious signs of the *t*! . . . Matt 16:3
Christ came . . . right *t* . . . Rom 5:6
right *t*, I heard you . . . 2 Cor 6:2
right *t* he will bring . . . Eph 1:10
last days . . . very difficult *t* . . . 2 Tim 3:1
for the *t* is near . . . Rev 1:3
gave her *t* to repent . . . Rev 2:21

TITHE(S) *(to offer) one-tenth of any property or produce; see TENTH*
offer a special *t* . . . Deut 26:12
Bring all the *t* . . . Mal 3:10
For you are careful to *t* . . . Matt 23:23
paid a *t* to Melchizedek . . . Heb 7:9

TONGUE(S) *part of the mouth that enables speech; dialect or language of a people; a special gift of speech given by the Holy Spirit*
far from accusing *t* . . . Ps 31:20
May my *t* stick . . . Ps 137:6
t of fire appeared . . . Acts 2:3
the gift of speaking in *t* . . . 1 Cor 14:5, 13
every *t* will confess . . . Phil 2:11
control your *t* . . . Jas 1:26
no one can tame the *t* . . . Jas 3:8

TORMENT(ED)(ORS) *acute suffering or pain, often linked to divine judgment*
our captors . . . *t* requested . . . Ps 137:3
A murderer's *t* conscience . . . Prov 28:17
smoke of their *t* . . . Rev 14:11
t day and night forever . . . Rev 20:10

TOUCH(ED)(ES) *perceive by feeling; lay hands upon; reach out or come in contact with; have an influence upon*
t it, or we will die . . . Gen 3:3
no evil can *t* you . . . Job 5:19
man's . . . head *t* the clouds . . . Job 20:6
burst into flame at his *t* . . . Ps 104:32
He *t* my lips with it . . . Isa 6:7
LORD *t* my mouth . . . Jer 1:9
If I could just *t* his robe . . . Matt 9:21
Jesus *t* him . . . Mark 1:41
"Who *t* me?" . . . Luke 8:45
don't eat, don't *t* . . . Col 2:21
t him with our own hands . . . 1 Jn 1:1

TRADITION(S) *handing down of stories and customs by oral means or by example, usually without written records*
disobey our age-old *t*? . . . Matt 15:2

old *t* of my religion . . . Gal 1:14
t of hard work . . . 2 Thes 3:6

TRAIN(ED)(ING)(S) *to instruct as a disciple or apprentice; see TEACH*
my body like an athlete, *t* . . . 1 Cor 9:27
may not be a *t* speaker . . . 2 Cor 11:6
t yourself for spiritual fitness . . . 1 Tim 4:7
older women must *t* . . . Titus 2:4
t in this way . . . Heb 12:11

TRANSFORM(ED)(ING)(S) *changed (outward appearance or inner character); see CHANGE*
let God *t* you . . . Rom 12:2

TREASURE(D)(R)(S) *any collection of valuable objects; see WEALTH*
than for hidden *t* . . . Job 3:21
t this word in my heart . . . Job 23:12
I will give you *t* . . . Isa 45:3
Don't store up *t* . . . Matt 6:19
have *t* in heaven . . . Matt 19:21
Erastus, the city *t* . . . Rom 16:23
But this precious *t* . . . 2 Cor 4:7
lie hidden all the *t* . . . Col 2:3
than to own the *t* . . . Heb 11:26

TREE(S) *woody perennial plants, many of which produce crops; highly treasured natural resource; often linked with worship of pagan gods; symbolic of a growing believer*
fruit *t* for your food . . . Gen 1:29
all the *t* in the fields . . . Exod 10:5
do not destroy the *t* . . . Deut 20:19
Asherah poles . . . under every green *t* . . . 1 Kgs 14:23
sacrifices . . . under every green *t* . . . 2 Kgs 16:4
t planted along the riverbank . . . Ps 1:3
thriving like mighty *t* . . . Ps 37:35
live as long as *t* . . . Isa 65:22
healthy *t* produces good fruit . . . Matt 7:17
A *t* is identified . . . Luke 6:44
like *t* without fruit . . . Jude 1:12
t until we have placed the seal . . . Rev 7:3
the river grew a *t* of life . . . Rev 22:2

TRIAL(S) *legal proceeding based in court; trouble of a general sort, often a punishment or testing from God*
I cannot . . . take him to *t* . . . Job 9:32
even strangers received a fair *t* . . . Job 29:16
the *t* the LORD had . . . Job 42:11
prison and *t* . . . to his death . . . Isa 53:8
earth you will have many *t* . . . John 16:33
we run into problems and *t* . . . Rom 5:3

TRIBE(S) *family divisions, usually within Israel, but also of other ethnic peoples*
t with its own language . . . Gen 10:5
founders of twelve *t* . . . Gen 25:16
of the *t* of Judah . . . Exod 31:2
a Jew . . . of the *t* of Benjamin . . . Rom 11:1
born into . . . the *t* of Benjamin . . . Phil 3:5
belongs to a different *t* . . . Heb 7:13
Lion of the *t* of Judah . . . Rev 5:5
ransomed people . . . from every *t* . . . Rev 5:9
from every nation and *t* . . . Rev 7:9
authority to rule over every *t* . . . Rev 13:7

TRIBULATION(S) *trouble of a general sort, often a punishment or testing from God; a period of unparalleled ("great") suffering in the last days*
enter . . . through many *t* . . . Acts 14:22
coming out of the great *t* . . . Rev 7:14

TROUBLE(D)(S) *to disturb mentally or physically; affliction; see TRIAL*
how full of *t*! . . . Job 14:1
from all its *t* . . . Ps 25:22
conceal me there when *t* . . . Ps 27:5
aren't *t* like other people . . . Ps 73:5
will be with them in *t* . . . Ps 91:15
Savior in times of *t*! . . . Jer 14:8
so easily shaken and *t* . . . 2 Thes 2:2

whenever *t* comes your way . . . Jas 1:2
widows in their *t* . . . Jas 1:27
must not be for . . . making *t* . . . 1 Pet 4:15

TRUE, TRUTH *in accord with the reality (natural and special) revealed by God; accurate and trustworthy for all people, time, situations*
these reports are *t* . . . Gen 18:21
your law is perfectly *t* . . . Ps 119:142
T falls dead in the streets . . . Isa 59:14
by the God of *t* . . . Isa 65:16
his acts are just and *t* . . . Dan 4:37
and he is *t* . . . John 7:28
the *t* will set you free . . . John 8:32
I am the way, the *t* . . . John 14:6
guide you into all *t* . . . John 16:13
"What is *t*?" Pilate asked . . . John 18:38
who push the *t* away . . . Rom 1:18
God is *t* . . . Rom 3:4
hold to the *t* in love . . . Eph 4:15
sturdy belt of *t* . . . Eph 6:14
thoughts on what is *t* . . . Phil 4:8
is the absolute *t* . . . 1 Tim 2:7
those who oppose the *t* . . . 2 Tim 2:25
never understand the *t* . . . 2 Tim 3:7
know we are living in the *t* . . . 1 Jn 3:19
know the *t* God . . . 1 Jn 5:20
the *t* that lives in us . . . 2 Jn 1:2
living in the *t* . . . 2 Jn 1:4
God gave this unchanging *t* . . . Jude 1:3
one who is holy and *t* . . . Rev 3:7
t are your ways . . . Rev 15:3
what I tell you is . . . *t* . . . Rev 21:5

TRUST(ED)(ING)(S) *to hope; to place one's confidence in*
those who *t* the LORD . . . Ps 32:10
T in the LORD . . . Ps 37:3
T in the LORD with all . . . Prov 3:5
He *t* God . . . Matt 27:43
those who *t* him . . . John 3:18
If you *t* me . . . John 12:44
when we *t* in Jesus . . . Rom 3:22
I will put my *t* in him . . . Heb 2:13
never stop *t* him . . . Heb 4:14
God can be *t* . . . Heb 10:23
t Christ to give the victory . . . 1 Jn 5:4

TURN(ED)(ING)(S) *to convert or change allegiance; to return or change direction; to face away; to divert one's attention from; to become or transform; to bend or shape*
we *t* around and set out . . . Deut 2:1
A gentle answer *t* away . . . Prov 15:1
t away from the LORD . . . Isa 1:4
t away from your idols . . . Ezek 14:6
right cheek, *t* the other . . . Matt 5:39
t from darkness to . . . Acts 26:18
shocked that you are *t* . . . Gal 1:6
t away from idols . . . 1 Thes 1:9
t to your Shepherd . . . 1 Pet 2:25
T away from evil . . . 1 Pet 3:11
T back to me again . . . Rev 2:5

UNBELIEF, UNBELIEVERS, UNBELIEVNG *skeptical about matters of religious truth*
because of their *u* . . . Matt 13:58
those who are *u* . . . 2 Cor 6:14
in ignorance and *u* . . . 1 Tim 1:13
those who are . . . *u* . . . Titus 1:15
because of their *u* . . . Heb 3:19
But cowards . . . and *u* . . . Rev 21:8

UNDERSTAND(ING) *to comprehend, realize, or be familiar with*
one with real *u* . . . Ps 14:2
His *u* is beyond . . . Ps 147:5
not depend on your own *u* . . . Prov 3:5
people who cherish *u* . . . Prov 19:8
you will not *u* . . . Isa 6:9
depths of his *u* . . . Isa 40:28
Don't you *u*? . . . Matt 15:16
Why can't you *u* . . . John 8:43
hearts cannot *u* . . . Acts 28:27

No one has real *u* . . . Rom 3:11
pray in words I *u* . . . 1 Cor 14:15
Lord will give you *u* . . . 2 Tim 2:7
wise and *u* God's ways . . . Jas 3:13
comments are hard to *u* . . . 2 Pet 3:16

UNDERWORLD *place of destruction (Hebrew = "Sheol"); see HELL*
It is deeper than the *u* . . . Job 11:8
The *u* is naked in God's presence . . . Job 26:6

UNFAILING *certain; reliable; steadfast*
not worthy of . . . *u* love . . . Gen 32:10
rich in *u* love, forgiving . . . Num 14:18
showed me your *u* love . . . Job 10:12
we meditate on your *u* love . . . Ps 48:9
because of your *u* love . . . Ps 51:1
With *u* love I have drawn . . . Jer 31:3
u love and faithfulness . . . John 1:14

UNFAIR(LY) *without equal justice*
If I have been *u* to . . . Job 31:13
justice to all who are treated *u* . . . Ps 103:6
he must never judge *u* . . . Prov 16:10
Friend, I haven't been *u*! . . . Matt 20:13
Lord, doesn't it seem *u* . . . Luke 10:40
Isn't it *u*, then, for God . . . Rom 3:5
Was God being *u*? . . . Rom 9:14
For God is not *u* . . . Heb 6:10
endure *u* treatment . . . 1 Pet 2:19

UNFAITHFUL *stubborn disbelief and disloyalty; adulterous; see UNBELIEF*
Saul died because he was *u* . . . 1 Chr 10:13
u to your God . . . Hos 9:1
some of them were *u* . . . Rom 3:3
If we are *u* . . . 2 Tim 2:13

UNGODLINESS, UNGODLY *wicked behavior; godless; all nonbelievers as a class; see WICKED*
the wickedness of the *u* . . . Ps 7:9
Defend me . . . *u* people . . . Ps 43:1
turn Israel from all *u* . . . Rom 11:26
Live no longer as the *u* . . . Eph 4:17
things that *u* people . . . Eph 5:12
are *u* and sinful . . . 1 Tim 1:9
more and more *u* . . . 2 Tim 2:16
world of *u* people . . . 2 Pet 2:5
when *u* people will perish . . . 2 Pet 3:7
will convict the *u* . . . Jude 1:15

UNITE(D), UNITY *to cause something to adhere to another; in one accord or one spirit*
the two are *u* into one . . . Gen 2:24
intermarry . . . and *u* with you . . . Gen 34:16
Judah and Israel will *u* . . . Hos 1:11
u with him in his death . . . Rom 6:5
one mind, *u* in thought . . . 1 Cor 1:10
two are *u* into one . . . 1 Cor 6:16
u with Christ in baptism . . . Gal 3:27
u in the Holy Spirit . . . Eph 4:3
such *u* in our faith . . . Eph 4:13

UNIVERSE *cosmos; the whole body of things created; population*
know the laws of the *u* . . . Job 38:33
rule might fill the entire *u* . . . Eph 4:10
ruler and authority in the *u* . . . Col 2:10
u was formed at God's command . . . Heb 11:3

UNQUENCHABLE *that which cannot be put out or extinguished; see QUENCH*
thrown into the *u* fire . . . Matt 18:8
the *u* fires of hell . . . Mark 9:43

UNWORTH(ILY)(Y) *without merit, undeserving*
u of eternal life . . . Acts 13:46
cup of the Lord *u* . . . 1 Cor 11:27

UPHOLD *to sustain or support; to defend*
u the rights of the oppressed . . . Ps 82:3
I will *u* you with my victorious . . . Isa 41:10
honest lives and *u* justice . . . Jer 4:2

UPRIGHT *those who do right—as citizens, and in relation to God*
to declare that he is *u* . . . Job 33:23
righteous, and those who are *u* . . . Ps 94:15
the *u* will live in the land . . . Prov 2:21
protects the *u* but destroys . . . Prov 10:29
u citizens bless a city . . . Prov 11:11

UPSET *to disturb the well-being or harmony*
This *u* Abraham very much . . . Gen 21:11
Joseph was *u* when he . . . Gen 48:17
"Don't get *u*, sir," Aaron replied . . . Exod 32:22
Martha, you are so *u* over . . . Luke 10:41
cause divisions and *u* people's faith . . . Rom 16:17

USEFUL *capable; powerful*
is a greater and more *u* gift . . . 1 Cor 14:5
be *u* to all and build them up . . . 1 Cor 14:26
Scripture is inspired by God and is *u* . . . 2 Tim 3:16
productive and *u* in your . . . 2 Pet 1:8

USELESS *in vain or futile; inept or powerless*
their wisdom to be *u* nonsense . . . 1 Cor 1:20
then all our preaching is *u* . . . 1 Cor 15:14
do for the Lord is ever *u* . . . 1 Cor 15:58
my ministry would have been *u* . . . Gal 2:2
weak and *u* spiritual powers . . . Gal 4:9
my work was not *u* . . . Phil 2:16
Such arguments are *u* . . . 2 Tim 2:14
no faith at all—it is dead and *u* . . . Jas 2:17

VEIL(ED)(S) *multicolored curtain dividing the Holy of Holies from the people; a facial covering for modesty, used by Middle Eastern women*
covered herself with a *v* . . . Gen 38:14
Moses . . . put a *v* over his face . . . Exod 34:33
furnish them with magic *v* . . . Ezek 13:18
hearts are covered with that *v* . . . 2 Cor 3:15
If the Good News we preach is *v* . . . 2 Cor 4:3

VENGEANCE *punishment in relation to or consequence for wrongdoing*
I will take *v* . . . Deut 32:35
execute *v* on the nations . . . Ps 149:7
I will take *v* . . . Heb 10:30
instead of crying out for *v* . . . Heb 12:24

VIRTUOUS *moral worth or excellence*
find *v* and capable wife? . . . Prov 31:10
many *v* and capable women . . . Prov 31:29

VISION(S) *a visual form of divine revelation, including dreams, that consists of symbolic images, often accompanied by their interpretation*
spoke to Abram in a *v* . . . Gen 15:1
a terrifying *v* of darkness . . . Gen 15:12
v concerning Judah . . . Isa 1:1
vanish like a *v* in the night . . . Isa 29:7
Daniel . . . of *v* and dreams . . . Dan 1:17
young men will see *v* . . . Joel 2:28
into a trance and saw a *v* . . . Acts 11:5
to that *v* from heaven . . . Acts 26:19
in my *v*, I saw the horses . . . Rev 9:17
woman you saw in your *v* . . . Rev 17:18

VOICE(S) *verbal communication by human and divine means*
listen to his *v* today! . . . Ps 95:7
a *v* shouting in the wilderness . . . Matt 3:3
a *v* from heaven said . . . Matt 3:17
they recognize his *v* . . . John 10:4
join together with one *v* . . . Rom 15:6
listen to his *v* . . . Heb 3:15
there were loud *v* . . . Rev 11:15

VOW(ED)(S) *(to offer a) binding promise or pledge*
Jacob made this *v* . . . Gen 28:20
special *v* to dedicate someone . . . Lev 27:2
present in connection with *v* . . . Num 29:39
When you make a *v* to the . . . Deut 23:21
Jephthah made a *v* . . . Judg 11:30
And she made this *v* . . . 1 Sam 1:11
because you have *v* before God . . . Eccl 8:2
for he had taken a *v* . . . Acts 18:18

WAGE(S) *reward or payment for one's work*
For the *w* of sin is . . . Rom 6:23
the *w* you held back . . . Jas 5:4

WAIL(ING) *a loud plaintive cry of mourning in response to death or destruction*
completely destroyed . . . So I *w* . . . Isa 16:9
Jesus saw . . . the weeping and *w* . . . Mark 5:38
Jesus saw . . . the other people *w* . . . John 11:33

WAIT(ED)(ING)(S) *to stay, serve, or attend to; attitude of watchfulness*
why should I *w* . . . Lord . . . 2 Kgs 6:33
w patiently for him . . . Ps 37:7
w . . . for the Lord . . . Ps 40:1
those who *w* on the . . . Isa 40:31
all creation is *w* . . . Rom 8:19
We too, *w* anxiously . . . Rom 8:23
salvation to all . . . *w* . . . Heb 9:28
he *w* until his enemies . . . Heb 10:13
God *w* . . . while Noah . . . 1 Pet 3:20

WALK(ED)(ING) *traverse or advance by steps; conduct, lifestyle, or way of life; accompany on foot*
w through the dark valley . . . Ps 23:4
The people who *w* . . . Isa 9:2
This is the way . . . *w* here . . . Isa 30:21
be weary. They will *w* . . . Isa 40:31
w humbly with your God . . . Mic 6:8
w to the village of Emmaus . . . Luke 24:13
sleeping mat, and *w* . . . John 5:8
light will shine. *W* in it . . . John 12:35
will *w* with me in white . . . Rev 3:4

WANDER(ED)(ERS)(ING)(S) *stray; meander; slow and aimless movement; flitting from place to place*
w in the wilderness . . . Num 14:33
love to *w* far from me . . . Jer 14:10
Israel . . . will be *w* . . . Hos 9:17
w over deserts and . . . Heb 11:38
anyone . . . *w* away from the truth . . . Jas 5:19
w stars, heading for . . . darkness . . . Jude 1:13

WANT *to desire or wish; to lack or do without*
doesn't *w* to marry her . . . Deut 25:8
I *w* you to be free . . . 1 Cor 7:32

WARN(ED)(ING) *to advise beforehand, usually with alarm*
Time and again I *w* you . . . Isa 48:3
blows the alarm to *w* . . . Ezek 33:3
w them in a dream . . . Matt 2:12
Who *w* you to flee . . . Matt 3:7
w them and teach them . . . Col 1:28
w of the eternal fire . . . Jude 1:7

WASH(ED)(ING)(INGS) *to cleanse—of physical, ceremonial, or spiritual significance; see BAPTIZE*
w myself with soap and water . . . Job 9:30
W me clean . . . Ps 51:2
Pilate . . . *w* his hands . . . Matt 27:24
w in the pool of Siloam . . . John 9:7
w the disciples' feet . . . John 13:5
your sins *w* away . . . Acts 22:16
sins have been *w* away . . . 1 Cor 6:11
w away our sins . . . Titus 3:5
ritual *w*— external regulations . . . Heb 9:10

WATCH(ED)(FUL)(ING) *to diligently wait or keep guard; to observe; surveillance or the act of keeping awake and diligent*
I continued to *w* . . . Dan 7:11
Pharisees *w* . . . Jesus . . . Luke 6:7
all who are *w* . . . Rev 16:15

WATCHMAN, WATCHMEN *person or group posted to be on the lookout for enemies*
abandoned like a *w*'s shelter . . . Isa 1:8
Jerusalem, I have posted *w* on your . . . Isa 62:6
appointed you as a *w* . . . Ezek 3:17

WATER(ED)(ING)(S) *precious resource for drink and irrigation, usually associated with blessing*
Eden, *w* the garden . . . Gen 2:10
drew me out of deep *w* . . . Ps 18:16
life is poured out like *w* . . . Ps 22:14
mountains tremble as the *w* surge . . . Ps 46:3
give you abundant *w* . . . Isa 44:3
fountain of living *w* . . . Jer 2:13
I baptize with *w* . . . John 1:26
give you living *w* . . . John 4:10
rivers of living *w* . . . John 7:38
plant . . . Apollos *w* . . . 1 Cor 3:6
fresh *w* from a salty pool . . . Jas 3:12
witnesses . . . the Spirit, the *w* . . . 1 Jn 5:8
springs of live-giving *w* . . . Rev 7:17
drink the *w* of life . . . Rev 22:17

WEAK(ER)(NESS) *feeble; frail; not (as) able to withstand persuasion or temptation*
strength to the *w* . . . Isa 40:29
knees will be as *w* . . . Ezek 7:17
the body is *w* . . . Matt 26:41
Accept Christians who are *w* . . . Rom 14:1
We are *w* . . . 1 Cor 4:10
For when I am *w* . . . 2 Cor 12:10
w was turned to strength . . . Heb 11:34
society considers her the *w* . . . 1 Pet 3:7

WEALTH(Y) *riches; financial or spiritual affluence; valuables*
will inherit all my *w* . . . Gen 15:2
w and influential man . . . Boaz . . . Ruth 2:1
trusted in your *w* . . . Jer 48:7
the lure of *w* . . . Matt 13:25
few of you were *w* . . . 1 Cor 1:26
w of his favor and kindness . . . Eph 2:7
Your *w* is rotting away . . . Jas 5:2

WEARY *exhausted of strength, endurance, vigor, vision*
run and not grow *w* . . . Isa 40:31
w me with your faults . . . Isa 43:24
Jesus . . . sat *w* beside the well . . . John 4:6

WEEDS *undesirable growth surrounding a plant; something harmful or obnoxious*
perverted justice . . . like poisonous *w* . . . Hos 10:4
planted *w* among the wheat . . . Matt 13:25
w are the people who . . . Matt 13:38

WEEP(ING) *to cry aloud, often linked with prayer and repentance; see WAIL*
in mourning . . . begin to *w* . . . Gen 37:35
place where he could *w* . . . Gen 42:24
w, "O my son Absalom . . . 2 Sam 19:4
joyful shouting and *w* . . . Ezra 3:13
w may go on all night . . . Ps 30:5
you will *w* no more . . . Isa 30:19
w and gnashing of teeth . . . Matt 8:12
God blesses you who *w* . . . Luke 6:21
Daughters of Jerusalem, don't *w* . . . Luke 23:28

WEIGH(ED)(S) *to estimate, evaluate, or consider; to balance opposing factors; determine weight*
you have been *w* . . . Dan 5:27
w down with troubles . . . 2 Cor 1:6

WEIGHT *heaviness; hindrance*
strip off every *w* . . . Heb 12:1

WHIRLWIND *any violent, damage-producing storm; figurative of an invading army; see WIND*
Job from the *w* . . . Job 38:1
harvest the *w* . . . Hos 8:7
his power in the *w* . . . Nah 1:3
scattered them as with a *w* . . . Zech 7:14
flaming fire . . . and *w* . . . Heb 12:18

WHISPER(ED)(ING)(S) *evil speech linked with backbiting, gossip, and the rumor mill; a minor or softer reflection of the original noise*
after the fire . . . a gentle *w* . . . 1 Kgs 19:12
w in my ear . . . Job 4:12
merely a *w* of his power . . . Job 26:14

He *w* in their ear and terrifies . . . Job 33:16
Sin *w* to the wicked . . . Ps 36:1
All who hate me *w* about me . . . Ps 41:7
enemies are *w* against me . . . Ps 71:10
calmed the storm to a *w* . . . Ps 107:29
my enemies *w* and mutter . . . Lam 3:62

WHOLE *sound or unimpaired; complete, entire, or undivided*
w world spoke a single language . . . Gen 11:1
the *w* revelation of God . . . Rom 3:2
leaven . . . *w* batch of dough . . . 1 Cor 5:7
w body were an eye . . . 1 Cor 12:17
obey . . . *w* law of Moses . . . Gal 5:3

WICKED(NESS) *a principle of evil or power of evildoers; working contrary to law and wreaking havoc in the world*
observed the extent . . . *w* . . . Gen 6:5
w will perish . . . 1 Sam 2:9
w will disappear . . . Ps 37:10
in the homes of *w* . . . Ps 84:10
turn from their *w* deeds . . . Isa 55:7
and desperately *w* . . . Jer 17:9
full of greed and *w* . . . Luke 11:39
every kind of *w* . . . Rom 1:29

WIDOW(S) *a woman whose husband has died*
the orphans and *w* . . . Ps 146:9
Jerusalem . . . like a *w* . . . Lam 1:1
poor *w* . . . two pennies . . . Mark 12:42
Greek complained . . . *w* . . . Acts 6:1
church should care for . . . *w* . . . 1 Tim 5:3
care for orphans and *w* . . . Jas 1:27

WIFE, WIVES *a married woman*
joined to his *w* . . . Gen 2:24
listened to your *w* . . . Gen 3:17
Sarah, your *w* . . . Gen 17:19
w . . . for my son Isaac . . . Gen 24:4
w finds a treasure . . . Prov 18:22
an understanding *w* . . . Prov 19:14
divorces his *w* . . . Mark 10:11
Remember . . . Lot's *w* . . . Luke 17:32
husbands, love your *w* . . . Eph 5:25
w must be respected . . . 1 Tim 3:11
faithful to his *w* . . . Titus 1:6
w of the Lamb . . . Rev 21:9

WILDERNESS *any desolate, barren, or unpopulated area, usually linked with danger*
three-day journey into the *w* . . . Exod 3:18
died . . . in the *w* . . . Num 14:2
great and terrifying *w* . . . Deut 1:19
voice shouting in the *w* . . . Matt 3:3
w to hear him preach . . . Matt 3:5
Jesus was led . . . *w* . . . Matt 4:1
pole in the *w* . . . John 3:14

WILL(ING)(INGLY) *decision-making capacity, indicating a power of choice*
your *w* be done . . . Matt 6:10
spirit is *w* . . . Matt 26:41
your *w* not mine . . . Luke 22:42
do the *w* of God . . . John 6:38
know . . . his *w* . . . Rom 12:2
doing his *w* . . . Heb 13:21
Watch over it *w* . . . 1 Pet 5:2

WIND(S)(STORM) *stirring of the air by nature, seasonal or stormy; see WHIRLWIND*
chaff scattered by the *w* . . . Ps 1:4
w and waves obey . . . Matt 8:27
reed, moved by . . . *w* . . . Matt 11:7
hear the *w* but . . . John 3:8
roaring of a mighty *w* . . . Acts 2:2

WINE *fermented grape juice, linked positively with blessings and negatively with strong drink*
W produces mockers . . . Prov 20:1
love is sweeter than *w* . . . Song 1:2
w or milk . . . free . . . Isa 55:1
new *w* into old wineskins . . . Matt 9:17
soldiers gave him *w* . . . Matt 27:34
He must never touch *w* . . . Luke 1:15
he took a cup of *w* . . . Luke 22:17
w supply ran out . . . John 2:3
Don't be drunk with *w* . . . Eph 5:18

WING(S) *feathered appendage of a bird, figurative of freedom and strength from God*
under whose *w* you have . . . Ruth 2:12
cherubim . . . each *w* . . . 1 Kgs 6:24
the shadow of your *w* . . . Ps 17:8; 36:7
w like a dove . . . Ps 55:6
on *w* like eagles . . . Isa 40:31
rise with healing in his *w* . . . Mal 4:2
hen . . . beneath her *w* . . . Matt 23:37
eagle with *w* spread . . . Rev 4:7

WISDOM *ability to discern right from wrong; see WISE*
display your *w* . . . Deut 4:6
only fools despise *w* . . . Prov 1:7
impressed with your own *w* . . . Prov 3:7
person who finds *w* . . . Prov 3:13
is the beginning of *w* . . . Prov 9:10
w is shown . . . Matt 11:19
Jesus grew in . . . *w* . . . Luke 2:52
riches and *w* and knowledge . . . Rom 11:33
w of this world . . . 1 Cor 3:19
our own earthly *w* . . . 2 Cor 1:12
all the treasures of *w* . . . Col 2:3
If you need *w* . . . Jas 1:5
power and riches and *w* . . . Rev 5:12

WISE(LY)(R) *marked by sound judgment, moral sense, prudence; see WISDOM*
He was *w* than anyone else . . . 1 Kgs 4:31
Learn to be *w* . . . Prov 4:5
who save lives are *w* . . . Prov 11:30
foolish, and five were *w* . . . Matt 25:2
God, who alone is *w* . . . Rom 16:27
plan of God . . . *w* . . . 1 Cor 1:25
those who are *w* . . . Eph 5:15
w to receive the salvation . . . 2 Tim 3:15

WITNESS(ES) *person who gives testimony; something of memorial significance*
as a *w* of our vows . . . Gen 31:52
But you are my *w* . . . Isa 43:10
What need . . . for other *w* . . . Luke 22:71
only a *w* to the light . . . John 1:8
confessed . . . before many *w* . . . 1 Tim 6:12
huge crowd of *w* . . . Heb 12:1
Christ, . . . the faithful *w* . . . Rev 1:5

WONDER(S) *mighty works, akin to miracles*
trials, miraculous signs, *w* . . . Deut 4:34
I will do *w* . . . Isa 29:14
cause *w* in the heavens . . . Joel 2:30
w God had done through them . . . Acts 15:12
signs and *w* and miracles . . . 2 Cor 12:12

WONDERFUL(LY) *marked by a marvelous, amazing, or extraordinary quality*
too *w* for me . . . Job 42:3
making me so *w* complex . . . Ps 139:14
royal titles: *W* Counselor . . . Isa 9:6
Peter . . . "Lord, this is *w* . . . Matt 17:4

WORD *special revelation from God*
hidden your *w* in my heart . . . Ps 119:11
w is a lamp for my feet . . . Ps 119:105
w of God proves true . . . Prov 30:5
w of our God stands . . . Isa 40:8
every idle *w* . . . Matt 12:36
beginning the *W* already existed . . . John 1:1
W became human . . . John 1:14
your *w* of truth . . . John 17:17
Let the *w* of Christ . . . Col 3:16
not only with *w* . . . power . . . 1 Thes 1:5
For the *w* of God is . . . Heb 4:12
eternal, living *w* of God . . . 1 Pet 1:23
title was the *W* of God . . . Rev 19:13

WORDS *ordinary speech; special revelation*
May the *w* of my mouth . . . Ps 19:14
wise teacher's *w* . . . Eccl 12:11
my *w* will remain forever . . . Matt 24:35
You alone have the *w* . . . John 6:68

WORK *one's occupation; physical or creative effort*
God rested from all his *w* . . . Gen 2:2
people had *w* . . . Neh 4:6
the *w* of your fingers . . . Ps 8:3
people go off to their *w* . . . Ps 104:23
all *w* comes to an end . . . John 9:4
everything to *w* together . . . Rom 8:28
not by their good *w* . . . Rom 11:6
tear apart the *w* . . . Rom 14:20
w together as partners . . . 1 Cor 3:9
enthusiastic about the Lord's *w* . . . 1 Cor 15:58
Whoever does not *w* . . . 2 Thes 3:10

WORKER(S) *laborers*
the *w* are so few . . . Matt 9:37
w for his vineyard. . . . Matt 20:1
w . . . not . . . ashamed . . . 2 Tim 2:15

WORKS *of God, acts or deeds performed, with redemptive significance; of humankind, efforts to do good and please God, but which do not earn salvation*
same *w* . . . and even greater . . . John 14:12
not according to our . . . *w* . . . Rom 9:12
different ways God *w* . . . 1 Cor 12:6

WORLD *the earth and its inhabitants; this current age and its value system*
The field is the *w* . . . Matt 13:38
w didn't recognize him . . . John 1:10
God so loved the *w* . . . John 3:16
w can't hate you . . . John 7:7
You are of this *w* . . . John 8:23
I have overcome the *w* . . . John 16:33
entire *w* into judgment . . . Rom 3:19
Don't copy . . . this *w* . . . Rom 12:2
things the *w* considers foolish . . . 1 Cor 1:27
death came into the *w* . . . 1 Cor 15:21
Christ, reconciling the *w* to himself . . . 2 Cor 5:19
live in this evil *w* . . . Titus 2:12
Stop loving this evil *w* . . . 1 Jn 2:15
w is fading away . . . 1 Jn 2:17

WORSHIP(ED) *the appropriate response to God's self-revelation*
bowed their heads and *w* . . . Exod 4:31
Do not *w* any other gods . . . Exod 20:3
return to Jerusalem to *w* . . . Isa 27:13
come to *w* him . . . Matt 2:2
Samaritans . . . *w* . . . John 4:22
hear those who *w* him . . . John 9:31
the angels of God *w* him . . . Heb 1:6
on their faces and *w* . . . Rev 11:16

WORTHY *deserving—usually of praise, sometimes of punishment; see UNWORTHY*
a life *w* of your calling . . . Eph 4:1
w . . . to receive glory . . . Rev 4:11
The Lamb is *w* . . . Rev 5:12

WOUND(ED)(S) *physical, mental, or emotional hurt*
W from a friend . . . Prov 27:6
w and crushed for our sins . . . Isa 53:5
w so incurable . . . Jer 15:18
w beyond recovery . . . Rev 13:3

WRATH *extreme displeasure, anger, hostility; God's response to sin; see ANGER*
w is like a flood . . . Prov 27:4
bring God's *w* to completion . . . Rev 15:1
wine of his fierce *w* . . . Rev 16:19

WRETCHED *a most pitiable state of affairs*
realize that you are *w* . . . Rev 3:17

WRITE, WRITING(S), WRITTEN, WROTE *to inscribe or engrave; to record; inscription*
w by the finger of God . . . Exod 31:18
w by God himself *w* . . . Exod 32:16
as Jeremiah dictated, Baruch *w* . . . Jer 36:4
don't believe what he *w* . . . John 5:47

Jesus stooped down and *w* . . . John 8:6
What I have *w* . . . John 19:22
I *w* . . . in my own handwriting . . . Gal 6:11
w them on their hearts . . . Heb 8:10
the angel said, "*W* this . . . Rev 19:9

WRONG(DOING)(ED)(S) *injurious or unjust action; willful violation of rights*
seen the *w* done . . . Lam 3:59
hasn't done anything *w* . . . Luke 23:41
the man in the *w* . . . Acts 7:27
case involving some *w* . . . Acts 18:14
I try not to do *w* . . . Rom 7:19
We have not done *w* . . . 2 Cor 7:2
paid back for the *w* . . . Col 3:25

YES *used as a function word to indicate agreement or emphasis; affirmative*
Y, I know you are innocent . . . Gen 20:6
Just say a simple, '*Y*' . . . or 'No' . . . Matt 5:37

YOKE(D) *wooden crossbar linking two load-pulling animals together; figurative of linkages between people*
never been *y* to a plow . . . Num 19:2
Take my *y* upon you . . . Matt 11:29

YOUTH(FUL)(S) *young person between the age of infancy and marriage*
rebellious sins of my *y* . . . Ps 25:7
y . . . threat of meaninglessness . . . Eccl 11:10
even *y* will become exhausted . . . Isa 40:30
Run from . . . *y* lust . . . 2 Tim 2:22

ZEAL(OUS) *devoted; filled with earnestness, enthusiasm or passion*
it is a misdirected *z* . . . Rom 10:2
such *z*, and such a readiness . . . 2 Cor 7:11
And *z*? Yes, in fact . . . Phil 3:6

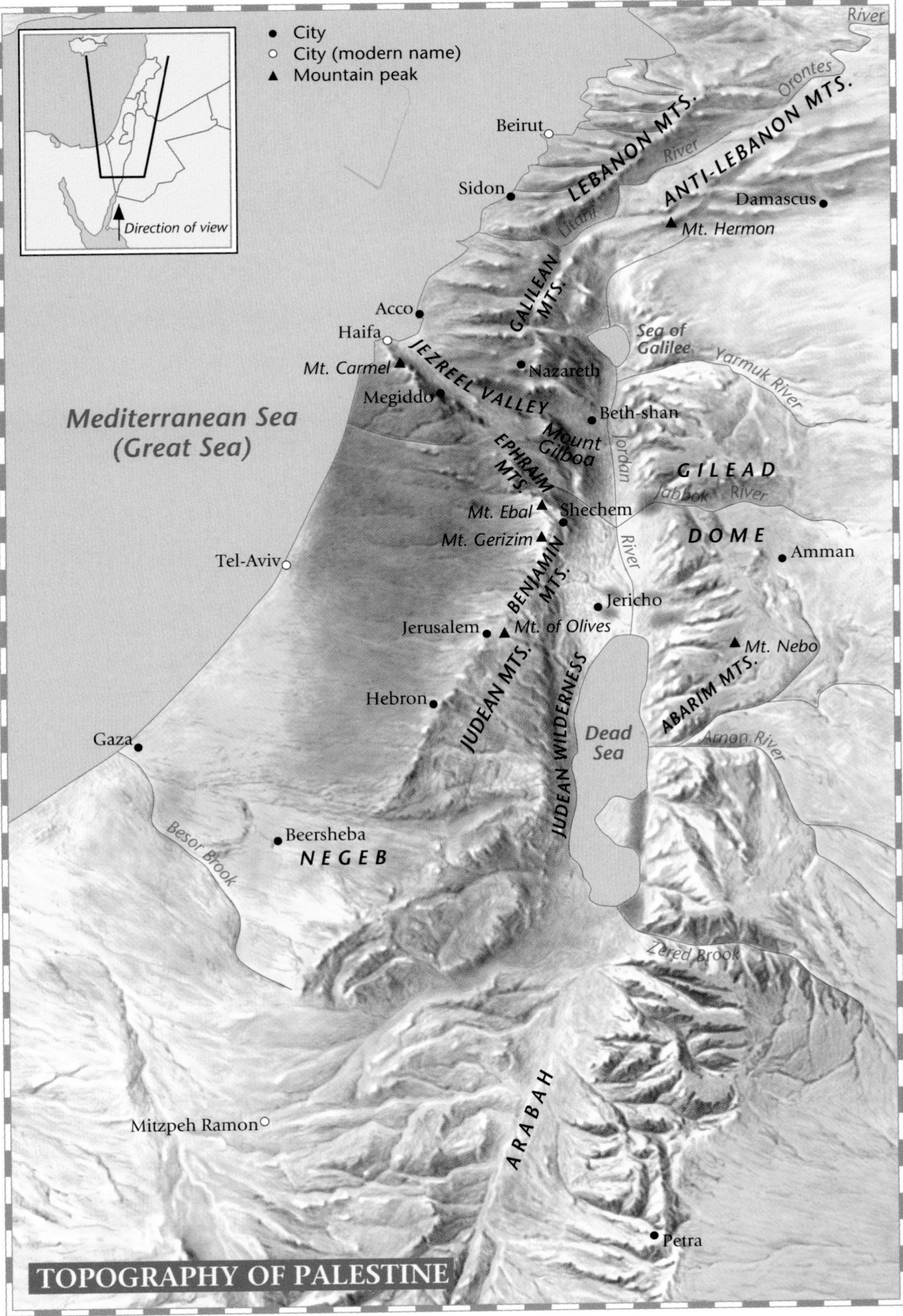

TOPOGRAPHY OF PALESTINE
Direction of view
City
City (modern name)
Mountain peak
River
Orontes
Beirut
LEBANON MTS.
ANTI-LEBANON MTS.
River
Sidon
Damascus
Litani
Mt. Hermon
GALILEAN MTS.
Acco
Haifa
Sea of Galilee
Yarmuk River
JEZREEL VALLEY
Mt. Carmel
Nazareth
Megiddo
Beth-shan
Mediterranean Sea (Great Sea)
Mount Gilboa
EPHRAIM MTS.
Jordan
GILEAD
Jabbok River
Mt. Ebal
Shechem
Mt. Gerizim
DOME
River
Amman
Tel-Aviv
BENJAMIN MTS.
Jericho
Jerusalem
Mt. of Olives
Mt. Nebo
JUDEAN MTS.
JUDEAN WILDERNESS
ABARIM MTS.
Hebron
Dead Sea
Gaza
Arnon River
Besor Brook
Beersheba
NEGEB
Zered Brook
ARABAH
Mitzpeh Ramon
Petra

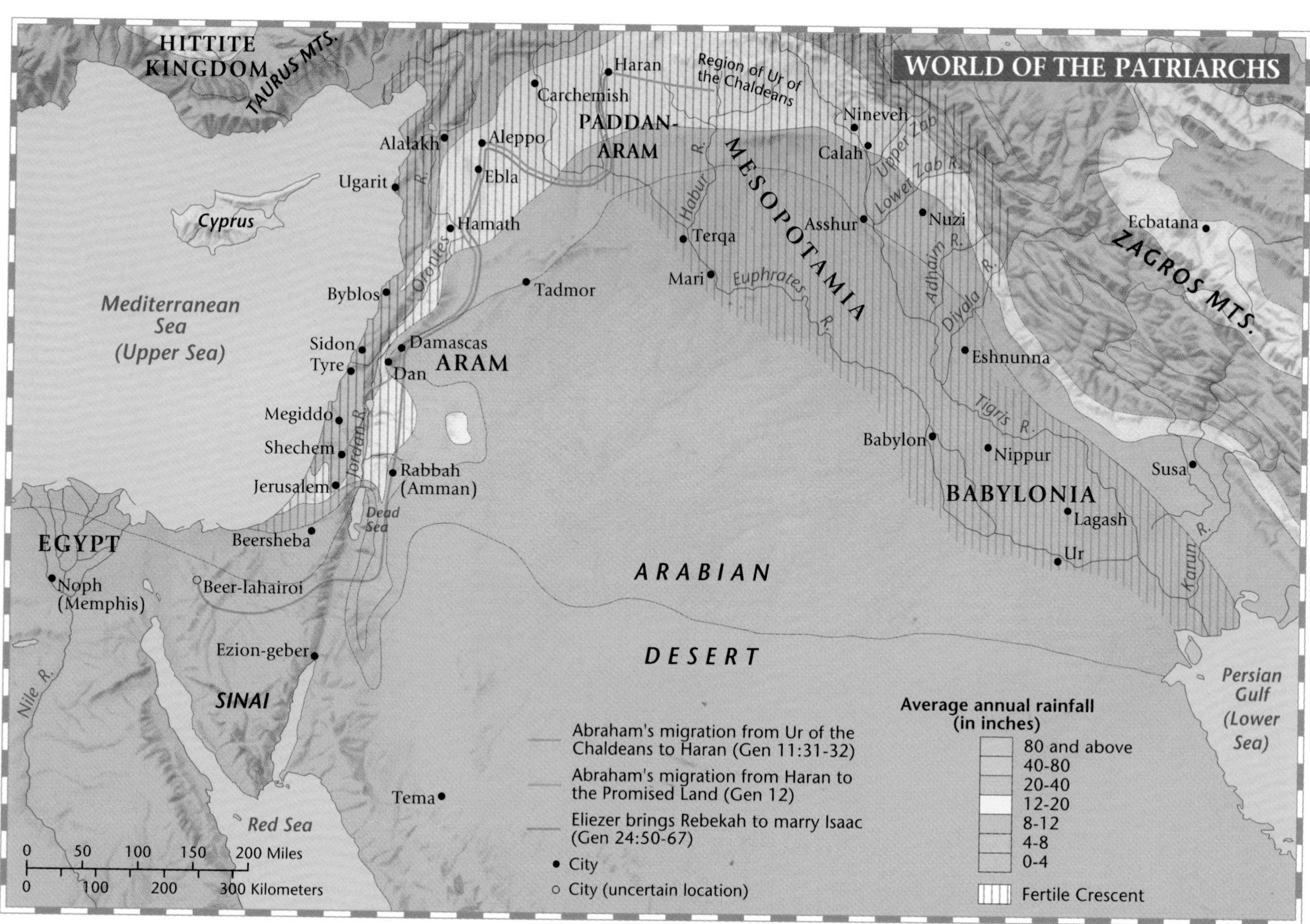

WORLD OF THE PATRIARCHS
HITTITE KINGDOM
TAURUS MTS.
Haran
Region of Ur of the Chaldeans
Carchemish
PADDAN-ARAM
Nineveh
Calah
Upper Zab
Lower Zab R.
Alalakh
Aleppo
Ebla
Ugarit
R.
MESOPOTAMIA
Habur
R.
Cyprus
Hamath
Asshur
Nuzi
Adhaim R.
R.
Terqa
Ecbatana
ZAGROS MTS.
Orontes
Byblos
Tadmor
Mari
Euphrates
R.
Diyala
Mediterranean Sea (Upper Sea)
Sidon
Tyre
Damascas
Dan
ARAM
Eshnunna
Tigris R.
Megiddo
Shechem
Jordan R.
Babylon
Nippur
Jerusalem
Rabbah (Amman)
Susa
BABYLONIA
Dead Sea
Lagash
EGYPT
Beersheba
Ur
Karun
R.
ARABIAN
Noph (Memphis)
Beer-lahairoi
Ezion-geber
DESERT
Nile R.
SINAI
Persian Gulf (Lower Sea)
Tema
Red Sea
Abraham's migration from Ur of the Chaldeans to Haran (Gen 11:31-32)
Abraham's migration from Haran to the Promised Land (Gen 12)
Eliezer brings Rebekah to marry Isaac (Gen 24:50-67)
City
City (uncertain location)
Average annual rainfall (in inches)
80 and above
40-80
20-40
12-20
8-12
4-8
0-4
Fertile Crescent
0 50 100 150 200 Miles
0 100 200 300 Kilometers

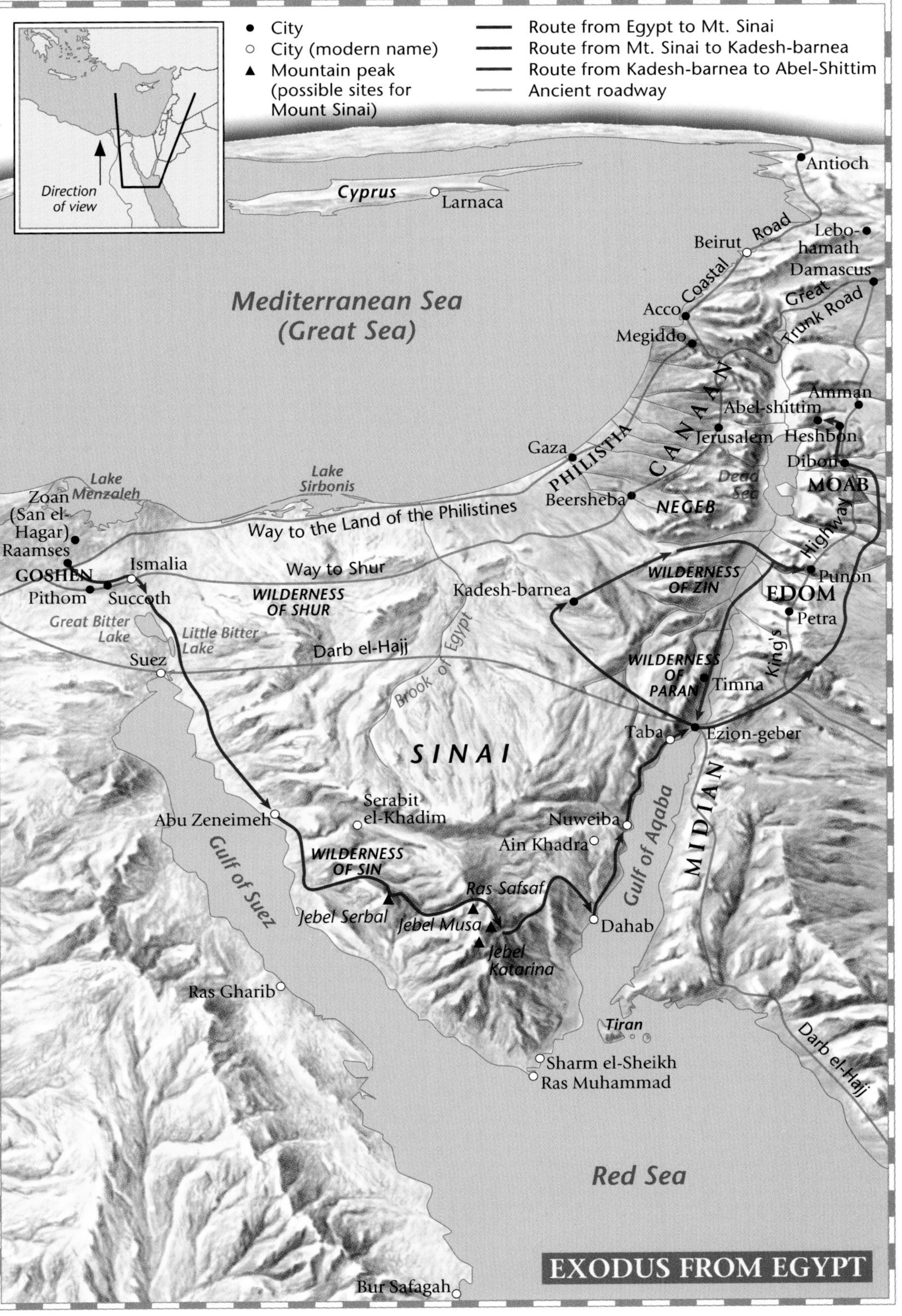

City
City (modern name)
Mountain peak (possible sites for Mount Sinai)
Route from Egypt to Mt. Sinai
Route from Mt. Sinai to Kadesh-barnea
Route from Kadesh-barnea to Abel-Shittim
Ancient roadway
Direction of view
Mediterranean Sea (Great Sea)
Cyprus
Larnaca
Antioch
Beirut
Coastal Road
Lebo-hamath
Damascus
Great Trunk Road
Acco
Megiddo
CANAAN
Amman
Abel-shittim
Jerusalem
Heshbon
Gaza
PHILISTIA
Dibon
Dead Sea
MOAB
Beersheba
NEGEB
Lake Menzaleh
Lake Sirbonis
Zoan (San el-Hagar)
Way to the Land of the Philistines
Raamses
Ismalia
GOSHEN
Way to Shur
WILDERNESS OF ZIN
Punon
Kadesh-barnea
EDOM
Pithom
Succoth
WILDERNESS OF SHUR
Highway
Petra
Great Bitter Lake
Little Bitter Lake
King's
Darb el-Hajj
Brook of Egypt
WILDERNESS OF PARAN
Timna
Suez
Taba
Ezion-geber
SINAI
MIDIAN
Serabit el-Khadim
Abu Zeneimeh
Nuweiba
Ain Khadra
Gulf of Aqaba
Gulf of Suez
WILDERNESS OF SIN
Ras Safsaf
Jebel Serbal
Jebel Musa
Dahab
Jebel Katarina
Ras Gharib
Tiran
Sharm el-Sheikh
Ras Muhammad
Darb el-Hajj
Red Sea
Bur Safagah

EXODUS FROM EGYPT

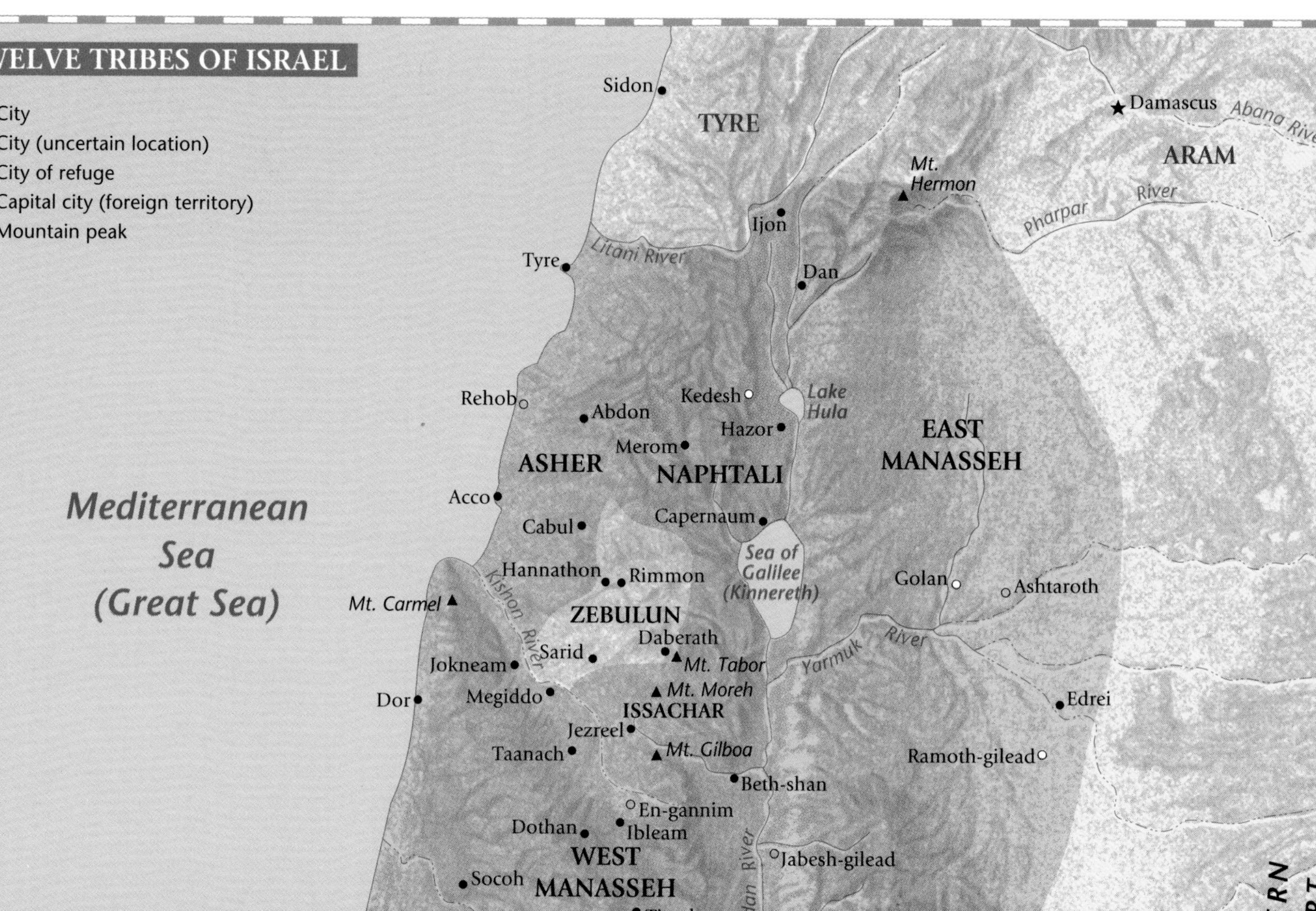

TWELVE TRIBES OF ISRAEL
City
City (uncertain location)
City of refuge
Capital city (foreign territory)
Mountain peak
Mediterranean Sea (Great Sea)
Sidon
TYRE
Tyre
Litani River
Ijon
Dan
Mt. Hermon
Damascus
Abana River
ARAM
Pharpar River
Rehob
Abdon
Kedesh
Lake Hula
Hazor
Merom
ASHER
NAPHTALI
EAST MANASSEH
Acco
Cabul
Capernaum
Sea of Galilee (Kinnereth)
Hannathon
Rimmon
Golan
Ashtaroth
Mt. Carmel
Kishon River
ZEBULUN
Daberath
Sarid
Mt. Tabor
Yarmuk River
Jokneam
Mt. Moreh
Dor
Megiddo
ISSACHAR
Edrei
Jezreel
Taanach
Mt. Gilboa
Ramoth-gilead
Beth-shan
En-gannim
Dothan
Ibleam
WEST MANASSEH
Jordan River
Jabesh-gilead
Socoh
Samaria
Tirzah
Mt. Ebal
Mahanaim

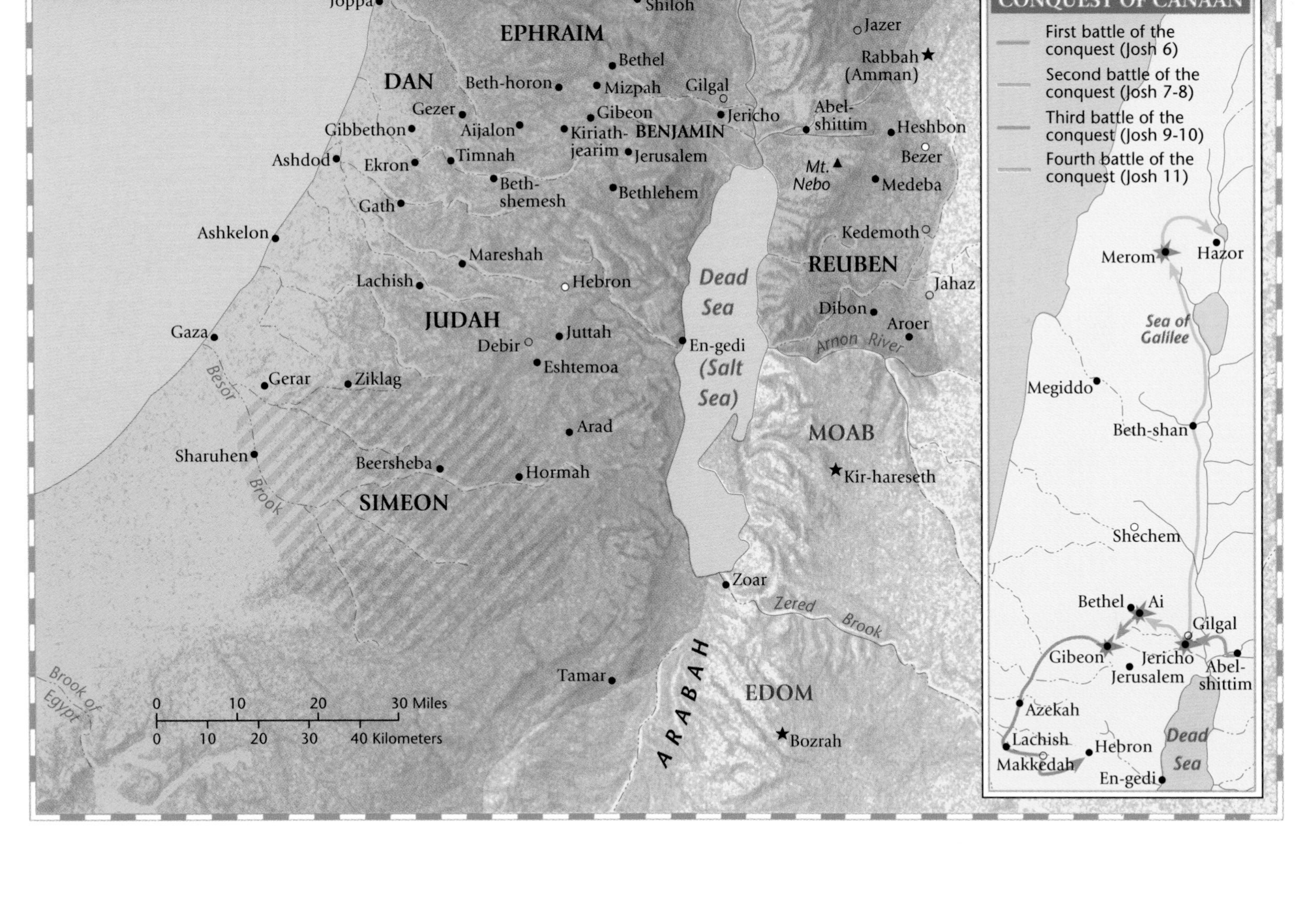

CONQUEST OF CANAAN
First battle of the conquest (Josh 6)
Second battle of the conquest (Josh 7-8)
Third battle of the conquest (Josh 9-10)
Fourth battle of the conquest (Josh 11)
Merom
Hazor
Sea of Galilee
Megiddo
Beth-shan
Shechem
Bethel
Ai
Gilgal
Gibeon
Jericho
Abel-shittim
Jerusalem
Azekah
Lachish
Makkedah
Hebron
Dead Sea
En-gedi
Joppa
Shiloh
EPHRAIM
Jazer
Rabbah (Amman)
Bethel
DAN
Beth-horon
Mizpah
Gilgal
Gezer
Gibeon
Jericho
Abel-shittim
Heshbon
Gibbethon
Aijalon
Kiriath-jearim
BENJAMIN
Jerusalem
Bezer
Ashdod
Ekron
Timnah
Mt. Nebo
Medeba
Beth-shemesh
Bethlehem
Gath
Ashkelon
Kedemoth
Mareshah
REUBEN
Lachish
Hebron
Dead Sea
Jahaz
JUDAH
Dibon
Gaza
Debir
Juttah
En-gedi
Aroer
(Salt Sea)
Arnon River
Eshtemoa
Besor
Gerar
Ziklag
Arad
MOAB
Sharuhen
Beersheba
Hormah
Kir-hareseth
Brook
SIMEON
Zoar
Zered
Brook
Tamar
ARABAH
EDOM
Brook of Egypt
0 10 20 30 Miles
0 10 20 30 40 Kilometers
Bozrah

UNITED KINGDOM
0 40 Miles
0 40 Kilometers
Aleppo
YAMHAD
Euphrates R.
Tiphsah
Cyprus
Hamath
HAMATH
Arvad
Tadmor
Byblos
Lebo-hamath
PHOENICIA
Mediterranean Sea (Great Sea)
Damascus
ARAM
Tyre
Dan
Hazor
Sea of Galilee (Kinnereth)
Dor
Megiddo
Jordan R.
Shechem
AMMON
Joppa
Gezer
Rabbah (Amman)
PHILISTIA
Gaza
Jerusalem
Dead Sea (Salt Sea)
Raphia
MOAB
Beersheba
AMALEK
Petra
EDOM
Kadesh-barnea
Ezion-geber
Gulf of Aqaba
SINAI
EASTERN DESERT
Kingdom of Saul
Kingdom of David
Kingdom of Solomon
DIVIDED KINGDOM
0 25 50 Miles
0 25 50 Kilometers
AMURRU
Great Trunk Road
Hamath
HAMATH
Qatna
Mediterranean Sea (Great Sea)
Arvad
Kadesh
Orontes R.
Coastal Road
PHOENICIA
Sadad
Byblos
Lebo-hamath
Berothai
Sidon
Damascus
Litani R.
Tyre
Dan
Kedesh
ARAM
Hazor
Sea of Galilee (Kinnereth)
Acco
Dor
Ashtaroth
Megiddo
Ramoth-gilead
Salecah
Beth-shan
Jordan R.
Road
Jabbok R.
Shechem
Joppa
ISRAEL
Rabbah (Amman)
Gezer
Gibeah
AMMON
Ashdod
Jerusalem
Medeba
Gath
Highway
Lachish
Dead Sea (Salt Sea)
Gaza
Hebron
Aroer
Trunk
Raphia
JUDAH
MOAB
Beersheba
Kir-hareseth (Kir-moab)
Great
PHILISTIA
NEGEV
Brook of Egypt
King's
Bozrah
Kadesh-barnea
Petra
EDOM
Territory periodically contested by Edom and Judah
WILDERNESS OF ZIN
EASTERN DESERT
Ezion-geber
Gulf of Aqaba
SINAI

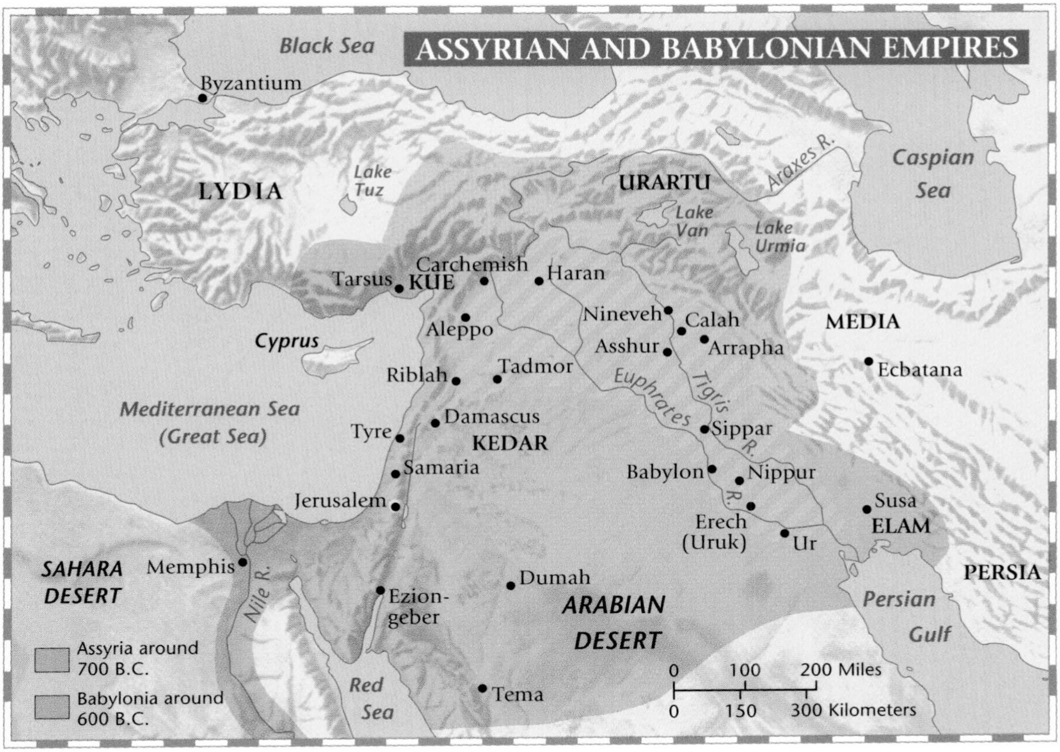

ASSYRIAN AND BABYLONIAN EMPIRES

Black Sea
Byzantium
Caspian Sea
Araxes R.
LYDIA
Lake Tuz
URARTU
Lake Van
Lake Urmia
Carchemish
Tarsus
KUE
Haran
Nineveh
Calah
Aleppo
MEDIA
Cyprus
Asshur
Arrapha
Ecbatana
Riblah
Tadmor
Euphrates
Tigris R.
Mediterranean Sea
(Great Sea)
Damascus
Tyre
KEDAR
Sippar
Samaria
Babylon
Nippur
Jerusalem
R.
Susa
Erech
(Uruk)
ELAM
Ur
SAHARA DESERT
Memphis
Nile R.
PERSIA
Dumah
Ezion-geber
ARABIAN DESERT
Persian Gulf
Assyria around 700 B.C.
Babylonia around 600 B.C.
Red Sea
Tema
0 100 200 Miles
0 150 300 Kilometers

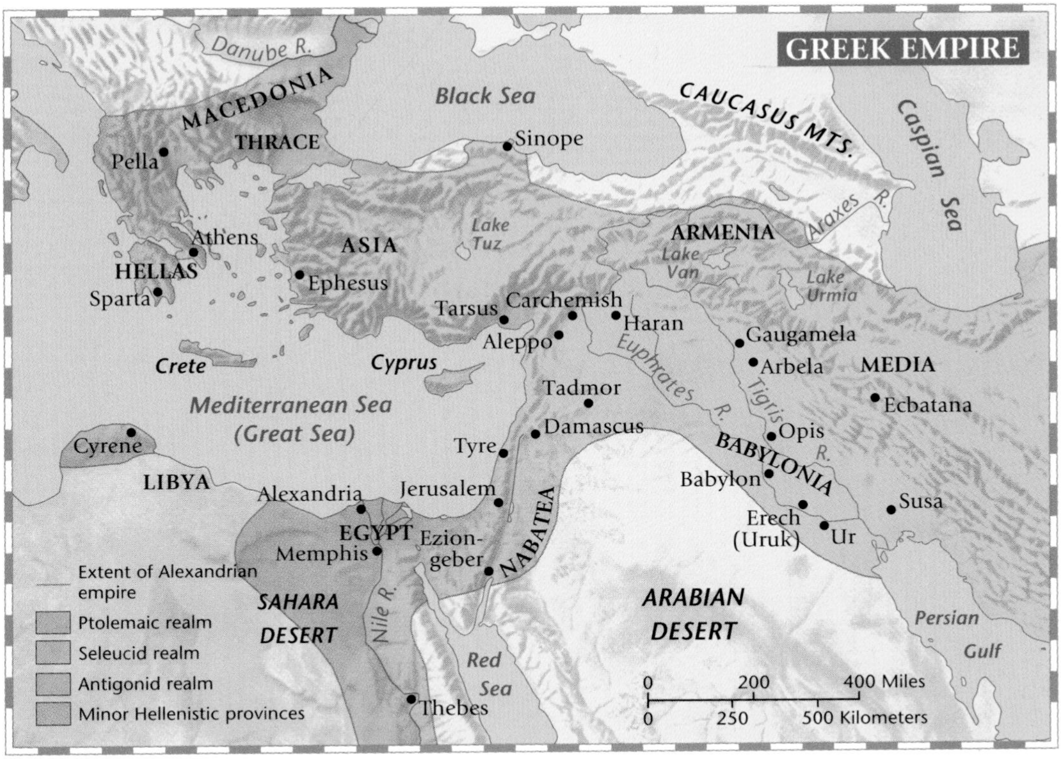

GREEK EMPIRE

Danube R.
MACEDONIA
Black Sea
CAUCASUS MTS.
Caspian Sea
THRACE
Sinope
Pella
Araxes R.
Lake Tuz
ARMENIA
Athens
ASIA
Lake Van
HELLAS
Lake Urmia
Ephesus
Sparta
Tarsus
Carchemish
Haran
Aleppo
Gaugamela
Crete
Cyprus
Arbela
MEDIA
Euphrates R.
Tigris R.
Tadmor
Ecbatana
Mediterranean Sea
(Great Sea)
Damascus
Opis
Cyrene
Tyre
BABYLONIA
LIBYA
Babylon
Alexandria
Jerusalem
Susa
EGYPT
Erech
(Uruk)
Ur
Memphis
Ezion-geber
NABATEA
Extent of Alexandrian empire
SAHARA DESERT
ARABIAN DESERT
Ptolemaic realm
Nile R.
Persian Gulf
Seleucid realm
Red Sea
Antigonid realm
0 200 400 Miles
Minor Hellenistic provinces
Thebes
0 250 500 Kilometers

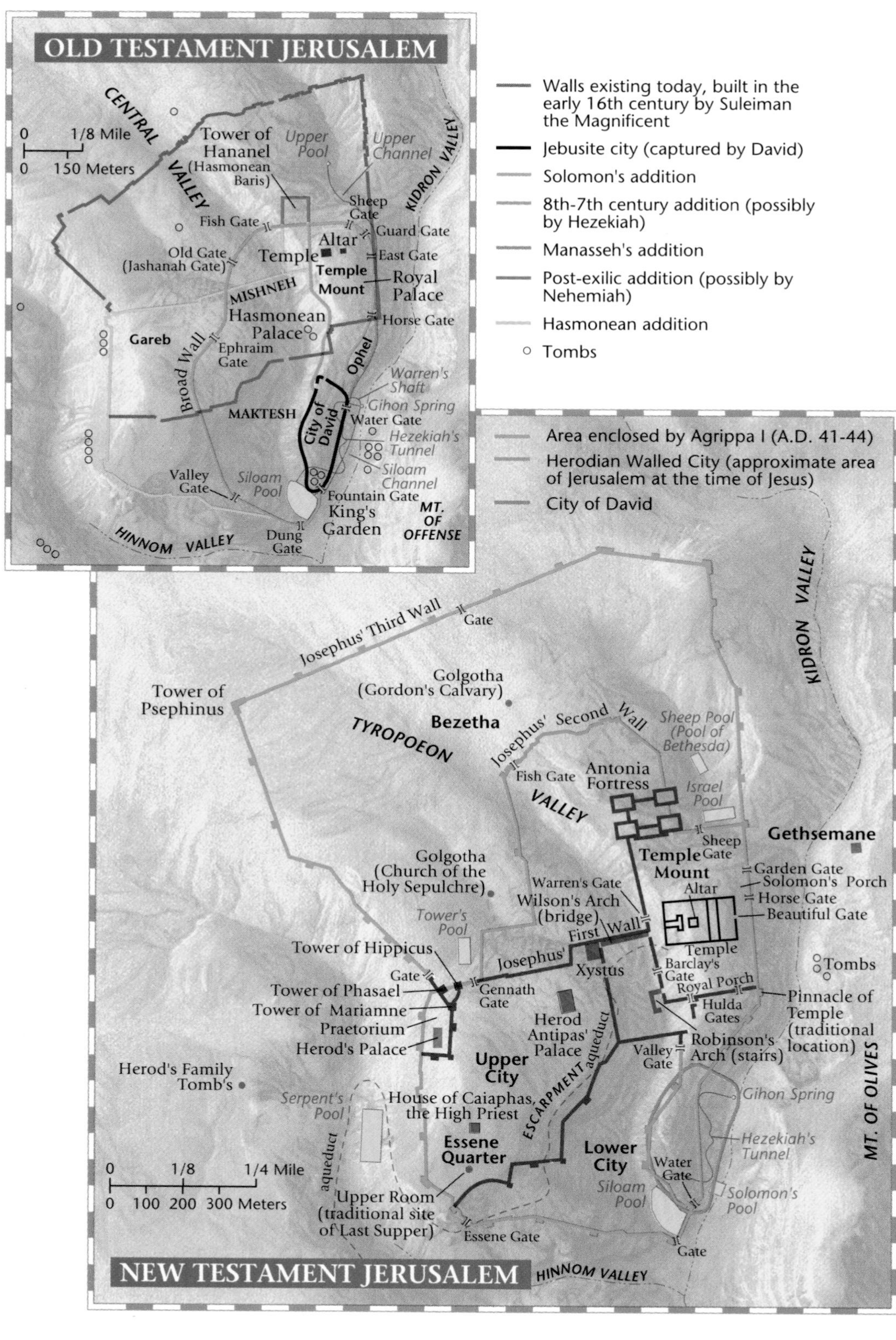
OLD TESTAMENT JERUSALEM
Walls existing today, built in the early 16th century by Suleiman the Magnificent
Jebusite city (captured by David)
Solomon's addition
8th-7th century addition (possibly by Hezekiah)
Manasseh's addition
Post-exilic addition (possibly by Nehemiah)
Hasmonean addition
Tombs
0 1/8 Mile
0 150 Meters
CENTRAL VALLEY
Tower of Hananel (Hasmonean Baris)
Upper Pool
Upper Channel
KIDRON VALLEY
Sheep Gate
Fish Gate
Guard Gate
Altar
Temple
East Gate
Old Gate (Jashanah Gate)
Temple Mount
Royal Palace
MISHNEH
Hasmonean Palace
Horse Gate
Gareb
Broad Wall
Ephraim Gate
Ophel
Warren's Shaft
Gihon Spring
MAKTESH
City of David
Water Gate
Hezekiah's Tunnel
Siloam Channel
Valley Gate
Siloam Pool
Fountain Gate
King's Garden
MT. OF OFFENSE
HINNOM VALLEY
Dung Gate
Area enclosed by Agrippa I (A.D. 41-44)
Herodian Walled City (approximate area of Jerusalem at the time of Jesus)
City of David
KIDRON VALLEY
Josephus' Third Wall
Gate
Golgotha (Gordon's Calvary)
Tower of Psephinus
Bezetha
TYROPOEON VALLEY
Josephus' Second Wall
Sheep Pool (Pool of Bethesda)
Fish Gate
Antonia Fortress
Israel Pool
Gethsemane
Sheep Gate
Temple Mount
Golgotha (Church of the Holy Sepulchre)
Warren's Gate
Wilson's Arch (bridge)
Garden Gate
Solomon's Porch
Altar
Horse Gate
Beautiful Gate
Tower's Pool
Josephus' First Wall
Temple
Tower of Hippicus
Xystus
Barclay's Gate
Tombs
Gate
Tower of Phasael
Gennath Gate
Royal Porch
Pinnacle of Temple (traditional location)
Tower of Mariamne
Praetorium
Herod Antipas' Palace
Hulda Gates
Herod's Palace
Robinson's Arch (stairs)
Valley Gate
Upper City
Herod's Family Tomb's
ESCARPMENT aqueduct
Serpent's Pool
House of Caiaphas, the High Priest
Gihon Spring
MT. OF OLIVES
Hezekiah's Tunnel
Essene Quarter
Lower City
0 1/8 1/4 Mile
0 100 200 300 Meters
aqueduct
Water Gate
Siloam Pool
Solomon's Pool
Upper Room (traditional site of Last Supper)
Essene Gate
Gate
NEW TESTAMENT JERUSALEM
HINNOM VALLEY

ROMAN DIVISION OF PALESTINE
0 10 20 30 Miles
0 10 20 30 40 Kilometers
Mediterranean Sea (Great Sea)
PHOENICIA
ABILENE
Abila
Abana
ITUREA
Mt. Hermon
Damascus
SYRIA
Pharpar R.
Sidon
Litani R.
Coastal Road
Tyre
Caesarea Philippi
GAULANITIS
Cadasa (Kedesh)
Lake Hula
Mt. Meron
Thella
TRACHONITIS
Raphana
GALILEE
Korazin
Capernaum
Bethsaida
Gennesaret
Gergesa
Magdala
Sea of Galilee (Kinnereth)
Tiberias
Hippus
Ptolemais (Acco)
Mt. Carmel
BATANEA
Gebae
Mt. Tabor
Yarmuk R.
Kishon R.
Dora
Nain
Gadara
Abila
Edrei
AURANITIS
DECAPOLIS
Caesarea
Great Trunk Road
Dothan
Scythopolis (Beth-shan)
Pella
Dion
SAMARIA
Gerasa
Sebaste (Samaria)
Mt. Ebal
Sychar
Amathus
Jabbok R.
Yarkon R.
Mt. Gerizim
Antipatris (Aphek)
Alexandrium
Joppa
Jordan R.
PEREA
Lydda (Lod)
Ephraim
Philadelphia (Amman)
Bethel
Tyrus
Jericho
Abila
Azotus (Ashdod)
Jamnia
Jerusalem
Cyprus
Esbus (Heshbon)
Mt. of Olives
Bethany
Medeba
Hyrcania
Bethlehem
Herodium
Ascalon
JUDEA
Marisa
Machaerus
Adora
Hebron
Dead Sea (Salt Sea)
Gaza
En-gedi
Arnon R.
King's Highway
NABATEA
Raphia
Arad
Masada
Besor Brook
Beersheba
IDUMEA
Malatha
Division of Herod's Kingdom to his three sons
Territory of Archelaus
Territory of Herod Antipas
Territory of Philip
Territory of the Proconsul of Syria
City
Decapolis city
Herodian fortress
Decapolis city (uncertain location)
Mountain peak
Extent of Herod the Great's kingdom

MINISTRY OF JESUS

Chronologically speaking, it is not possible to sequentially arrange the events in the life of Christ in any definitive way; none of the New Testament gospels follows an overtly chronological pattern. Accordingly, the arrangement here follows a geographic order, basically proceeding from north to south on the map. Because the gospel of Matthew most frequently contains information cited here, and because it is the most geographically particularistic gospel, synoptic passages are keyed to the book of Matthew, except where they are unattested there or where more pertinent information about the event cited is available in another gospel.

A. *Region of Tyre:* Gentile woman's daughter healed (Mt 15:21-28)

B. *Caesarea Philippi:* Peter's great declaration (Mt 16:13-20)

C. *Mt. Meron/Mt. Tabor/Mt. Hermon:* (1) possible location of Transfiguration (Mt 17:1-13); (2) demon-possessed boy healed nearby (Mt 17:14-21)

D. *Cana of Galilee:* (1) water changed to wine (Jn 2:1-11); (2) Capernaum official's son healed (Jn 4:46-54)

E. *Gennesaret:* (1) possible location of feeding of multitudes (Mt 14:13-21; 15:32-39); (2) many healings (Mk 6:53-56)

F. *Area of Korazin:* (1) judgment pronounced on the cities of Korazin, Bethsaida, and Capernaum (Mt 11:20-24); (2) possible area of Sermon on the Mount (Mt 5-7)

G. *Capernaum:* (1) catch of fish (Lk 5:1-11); (2) evil spirit cast out (Mk 1:21-28); (3) Sermon on the Mount (Mt 5-7); (4) Peter's mother-in-law healed (Mt 8:5-13); (5) Roman officer's servant healed (Mt 8:5-13); (6) paralyzed man healed (Mk 2:1-12); (7) woman with a hemorrhage healed (Mk 5:25-34); (8) Jairus's daughter raised (Lk 8:40-56); (9) two blind men healed (Mt 9:27-31); (10) a mute, demon-possessed man healed (Mt 9:32-34); (11) the twelve apostles sentout (Mt 10:1-15); (12) man with deformed hand healed (Mt 12:9-13); (13) another demon-possessed man healed (Mt 12:22-37); (14) Temple tax provided (Mt 17:24-27); (15) Bread of Life discourse (Jn 6:22-59)

H. *Bethsaida:* (1) possible location of feeding of multitudes (Mt 14:13-21; 15:32-39); (2) blind man healed (Mk 8:22-26)

I. *Sea of Galilee near Bethsaida:* walking on water (Mt 14:22-33)

J. *Sea of Galilee:* storm quieted (Mt 8:23-27)

K. *Gergesa/Gadara:* possible location of casting out demons, which enter pigs; the pigs then rush down a steep bank and drown (Lk 8:26-39)

L. *Nazareth:* (1) childhood home (Mt 2:19-23); (2) rejected by townspeople (Lk 4:16-30)

M. *Nain:* widow's son raised (Lk 7:11-17)

N. *Region of Galilee:* (1) leper cleansed (Mk 1:40-45); (2) post-resurrection appearances to the disciples (Mt 28:16-20)

O. *Region of Ten Towns:* many healings (Mt 15:29-31; Mk 7:31-37)

P. *Region between Galilee and Samaria:* (1) refused entry into village (Lk 9:51-56); (2) ten lepers healed (Lk 17:11-19)

Q. *Sychar:* woman at the well of Samaria (Jn 4:1-42)

R. *Ephraim:* enters into seclusion with the disciples (Jn 11:54)

S. *Region of Perea:* (1) teaching on marriage (Mt 19:1-12); (2) possible location of healing of woman with infirmity (Lk 13:10-13); (3) possible location of healing of man with swollen limbs (Lk 14:1-6); (4) possible location ofthe rich young ruler (Lk 18:18-30)

T. *Jericho:* (1) Bartimaeus healed (Mk 10:46-52); (2) Zacchaeus converted (Lk 19:1-10)

U. *Bethany:* (1) Lazarus raised (Jn 11:1-44); (2) anointing of Mary (Jn 12:1-11)

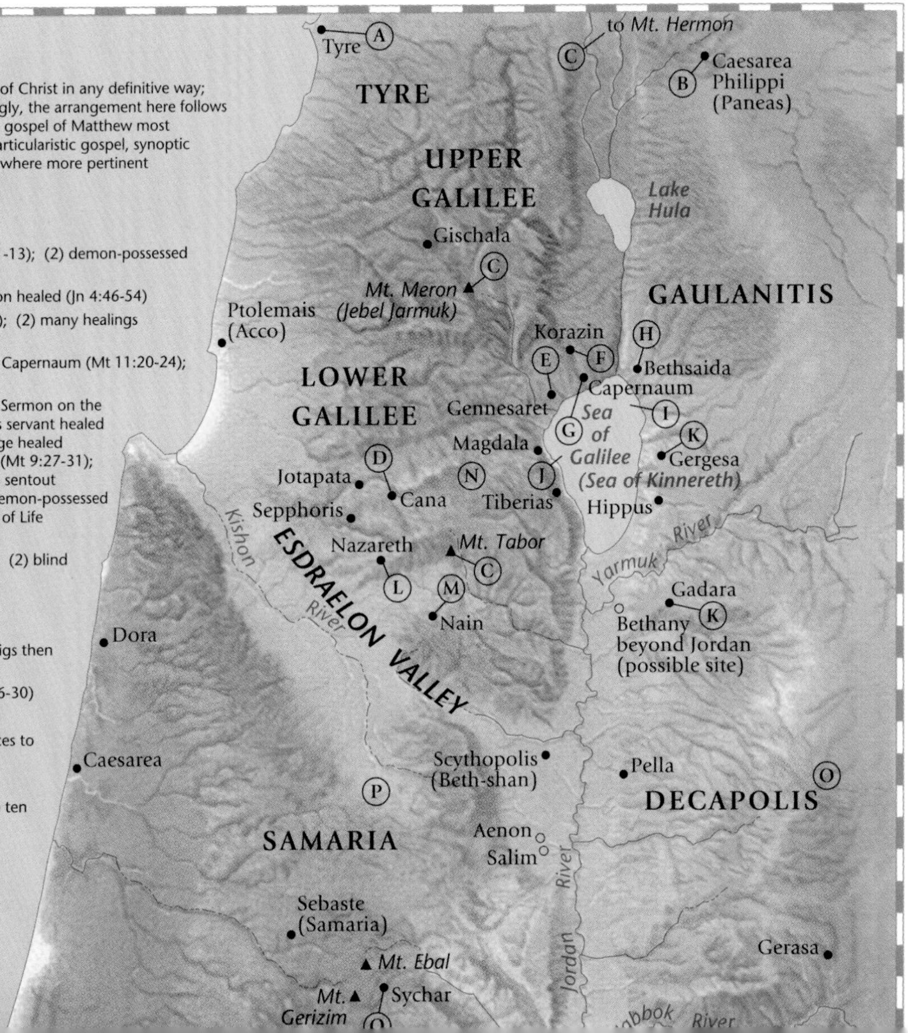

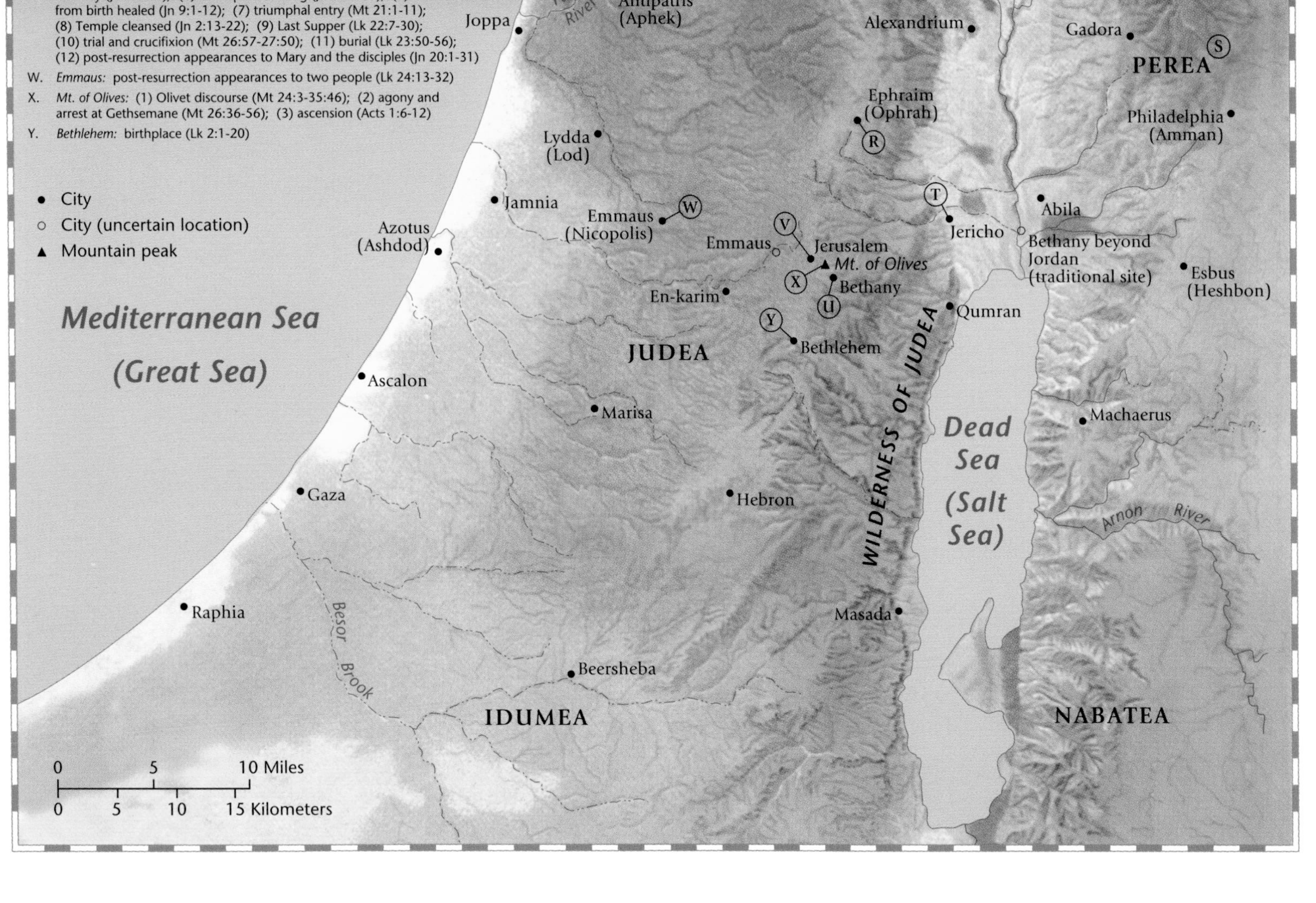
adultery (Jn 8:2-11); (5) attempted stoning (Jn 8:12-59); (6) man blind
from birth healed (Jn 9:1-12); (7) triumphal entry (Mt 21:1-11);
(8) Temple cleansed (Jn 2:13-22); (9) Last Supper (Lk 22:7-30);
(10) trial and crucifixion (Mt 26:57-27:50); (11) burial (Lk 23:50-56);
(12) post-resurrection appearances to Mary and the disciples (Jn 20:1-31)
W. *Emmaus:* post-resurrection appearances to two people (Lk 24:13-32)
X. *Mt. of Olives:* (1) Olivet discourse (Mt 24:3-35:46); (2) agony and arrest at Gethsemane (Mt 26:36-56); (3) ascension (Acts 1:6-12)
Y. *Bethlehem:* birthplace (Lk 2:1-20)
● City
○ City (uncertain location)
▲ Mountain peak
Mediterranean Sea
(Great Sea)
Joppa
River
Antipatris
(Aphek)
Alexandrium
Gadora
S
PEREA
Ephraim
(Ophrah)
R
Philadelphia
(Amman)
Lydda
(Lod)
Jamnia
Emmaus
(Nicopolis)
W
T
Abila
Azotus
(Ashdod)
V
Jericho
Emmaus
Jerusalem
Mt. of Olives
Bethany beyond
Jordan
(traditional site)
X
Bethany
Esbus
(Heshbon)
En-karim
U
Qumran
Y
Bethlehem
JUDEA
WILDERNESS OF JUDEA
Ascalon
Marisa
Machaerus
Dead
Sea
(Salt
Sea)
Gaza
Hebron
Arnon River
Raphia
Masada
Besor Brook
Beersheba
IDUMEA
NABATEA
0 5 10 Miles
0 5 10 15 Kilometers

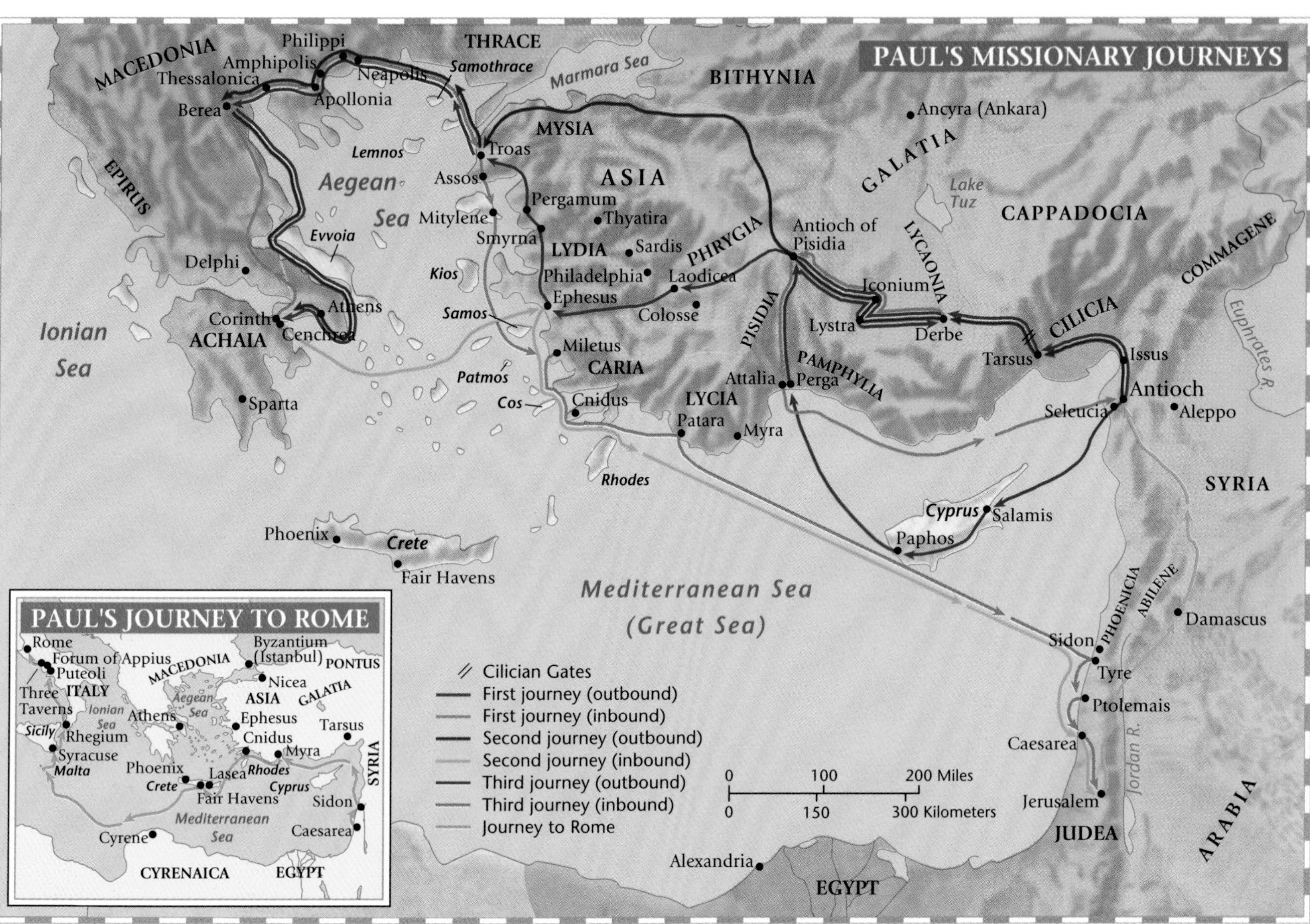
PAUL'S MISSIONARY JOURNEYS
MACEDONIA
THRACE
Philippi
Amphipolis
Thessalonica
Neapolis
Apollonia
Berea
Samothrace
Marmara Sea
BITHYNIA
Ancyra (Ankara)
MYSIA
Troas
Lemnos
EPIRUS
Aegean
Sea
Assos
ASIA
GALATIA
Lake
Tuz
CAPPADOCIA
Pergamum
Mitylene
Thyatira
Smyrna
LYDIA
Sardis
PHRYGIA
Antioch of
Pisidia
LYCAONIA
COMMAGENE
Evvoia
Delphi
Kios
Philadelphia
Laodicea
Ephesus
Iconium
Colosse
Athens
Corinth
Cenchrea
Samos
Ionian
Sea
ACHAIA
Lystra
Derbe
CILICIA
PISIDIA
Euphrates R.
Miletus
Tarsus
Issus
CARIA
PAMPHYLIA
Attalia
Perga
Patmos
Antioch
Sparta
Cos
Cnidus
LYCIA
Seleucia
Aleppo
Patara
Myra
Rhodes
SYRIA
Cyprus
Salamis
Phoenix
Crete
Paphos
Fair Havens
Mediterranean Sea
(Great Sea)
PHOENICIA
ABILENE
Damascus
Sidon
Tyre
Ptolemais
Caesarea
Jordan R.
Jerusalem
JUDEA
ARABIA
Alexandria
EGYPT
Cilician Gates
First journey (outbound)
First journey (inbound)
Second journey (outbound)
Second journey (inbound)
Third journey (outbound)
Third journey (inbound)
Journey to Rome
0
100
200 Miles
0
150
300 Kilometers
PAUL'S JOURNEY TO ROME
Rome
Forum of Appius
Puteoli
Three Taverns
ITALY
MACEDONIA
Byzantium
(Istanbul)
PONTUS
Nicea
ASIA
GALATIA
Aegean
Sea
Ionian
Sea
Athens
Ephesus
Tarsus
Sicily
Rhegium
Cnidus
Syracuse
Myra
Malta
Phoenix
Lasea
Rhodes
SYRIA
Crete
Cyprus
Fair Havens
Sidon
Mediterranean
Sea
Cyrene
Caesarea
CYRENAICA
EGYPT

ROMAN EMPIRE AND SPREAD OF CHRISTIANITY

- ● Christian community established during the first century
- ○ Christian community established during the second century
- The Roman Empire
- Provincial boundary

0 250 500 Miles
0 250 500 Kilometers

German Sea
Atlantic Ocean
BRITANNIA
London
GERMANIA
Cologne
Mainz
Trier
BELGICA
Rhine R.
Loire R.
GALLIA
Lyons
Vienne
Rhone
RAETIA
NORICUM
PANNONIA
DACIA
Danube R.
HISPANIA
Leon
Astorga
Saragossa
Merida
Corduba
Hispalis
GIBRALTAR
Balearic Is.
Corsica
Sardinia
ITALIA
Rome
Ostia
Antium
Puteoli
Pompeii
Adriatic Sea
Tyrrhenian Sea
Sicily
Syracuse
Malta
Solona
DALMATIA
MOESIA
THRACE
MACEDONIA
EPIRUS
ACHAIA
Black Sea
PONTUS
BITHYNIA
GALATIA
CAPPADOCIA
COMMAGENE
CILICIA
PAMPHYLIA
LYCIA
ASIA
Cyprus
Crete
Mediterranean Sea
(Great Sea)
Carthage
Uthina
Hadrumetum
Cirta
Lambesis
Madaurus
NUMIDIA
AFRICA
TRIPOLITANIA
SAHARA DESERT
Cyrene
CYRENAICA
Alexandria
Naucratis
Memphis
Babylon
EGYPT
Nile R.
Red Sea
ARMENIA
Caspian Sea
Malatya
Beit Zabde
Samsat
Edessa
Nisibis
PARTHIA
MESOPOTAMIA
Euphrates R.
Tigris R.
Dura-Europos
SYRIA
Beirut
Sidon
Tyre
Damascus
Bethsaida
Ptolemais
Capernaum
Caesarea
Joppa
Bostra
Pella
Jerusalem
Gaza
Philadelphia
Neapolis
JUDEA
NABATEA (ARABIA)
Jamnia
Persian Gulf
ARABIAN DESERT

Debeltum
THRACE
Byzantium
Black Sea
Ionopolis
Sinope
Amastris
Amisus
Nicomedia
Ancyra
Caesarea Mazaca
Thessalonica
Philippi
Edessa
Berea
Apollonia
MACEDONIA
Aegean Sea
Larissa
Troas
Thyatira
Pergamum
ASIA
Sardis
Antioch in Pisidia
Philadelphia
Tralles
Magnesia
Ephesus
Miletus
Laodicea
Colosse
Lystra
Iconium
Derbe
Tarsus
Antioch
Apamea
Laodicea
Perga
Corinth
Athens
Same
ACHAIA
Cenchrea
Sparta
Rhodes
Myra
Salamis
Crete
Cnossus
Gortyna
Mediterranean Sea (Great Sea)
Paphos
Cyprus
Tripolis

TIMELINE OF BIBLICAL EVENTS

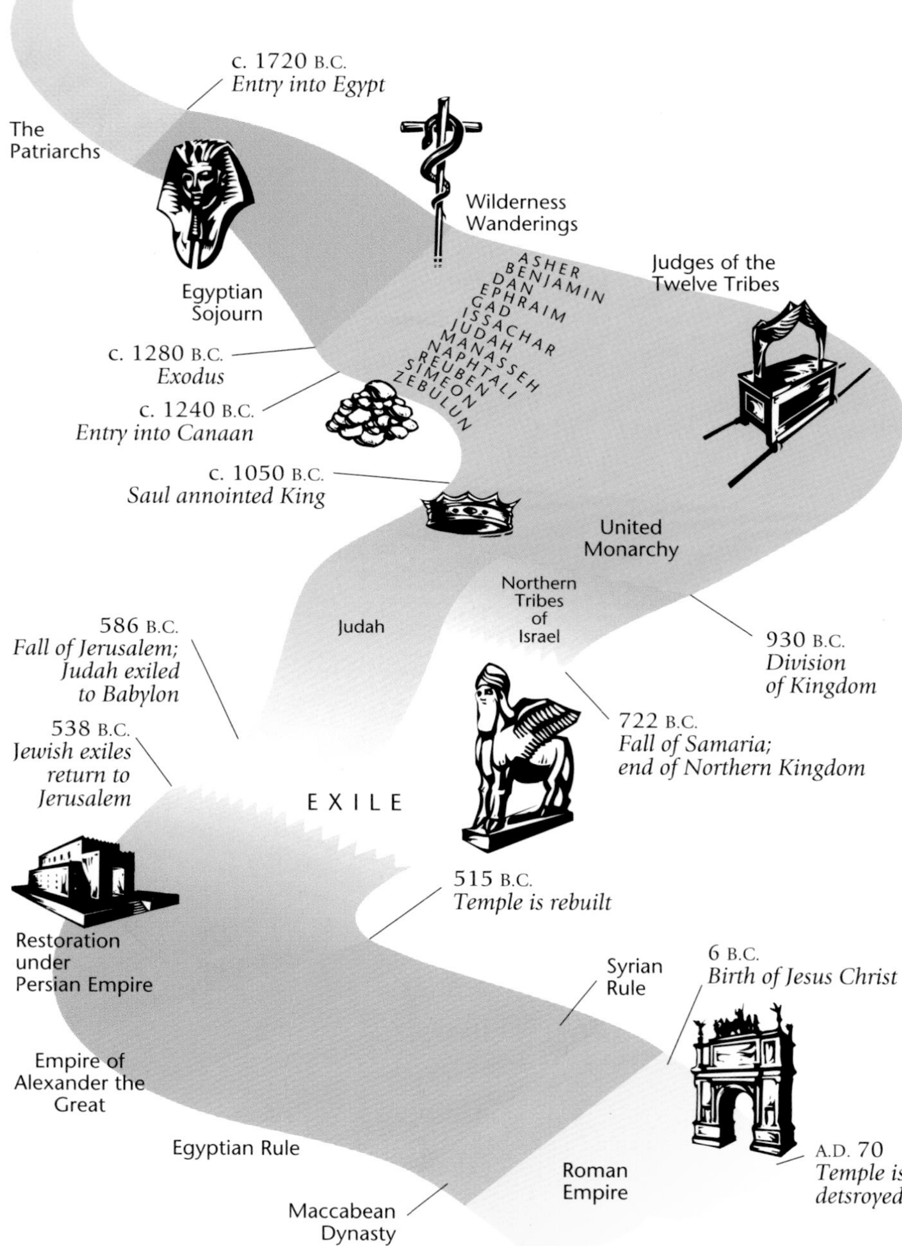

c. 2000 B.C.
Abraham leaves Ur
c. 1720 B.C.
Entry into Egypt
The Patriarchs
Wilderness Wanderings
Egyptian Sojourn
ASHER
BENJAMIN
DAN
EPHRAIM
GAD
ISSACHAR
JUDAH
MANASSEH
NAPHTALI
REUBEN
SIMEON
ZEBULUN
Judges of the Twelve Tribes
c. 1280 B.C.
Exodus
c. 1240 B.C.
Entry into Canaan
c. 1050 B.C.
Saul annointed King
United Monarchy
Northern Tribes of Israel
Judah
586 B.C.
Fall of Jerusalem; Judah exiled to Babylon
930 B.C.
Division of Kingdom
538 B.C.
Jewish exiles return to Jerusalem
722 B.C.
Fall of Samaria; end of Northern Kingdom
EXILE
515 B.C.
Temple is rebuilt
Restoration under Persian Empire
Syrian Rule
6 B.C.
Birth of Jesus Christ
Empire of Alexander the Great
Egyptian Rule
A.D. 70
Temple is detsroyed
Roman Empire
Maccabean Dynasty

THE TEMPLE IN NEW TESTAMENT TIMES

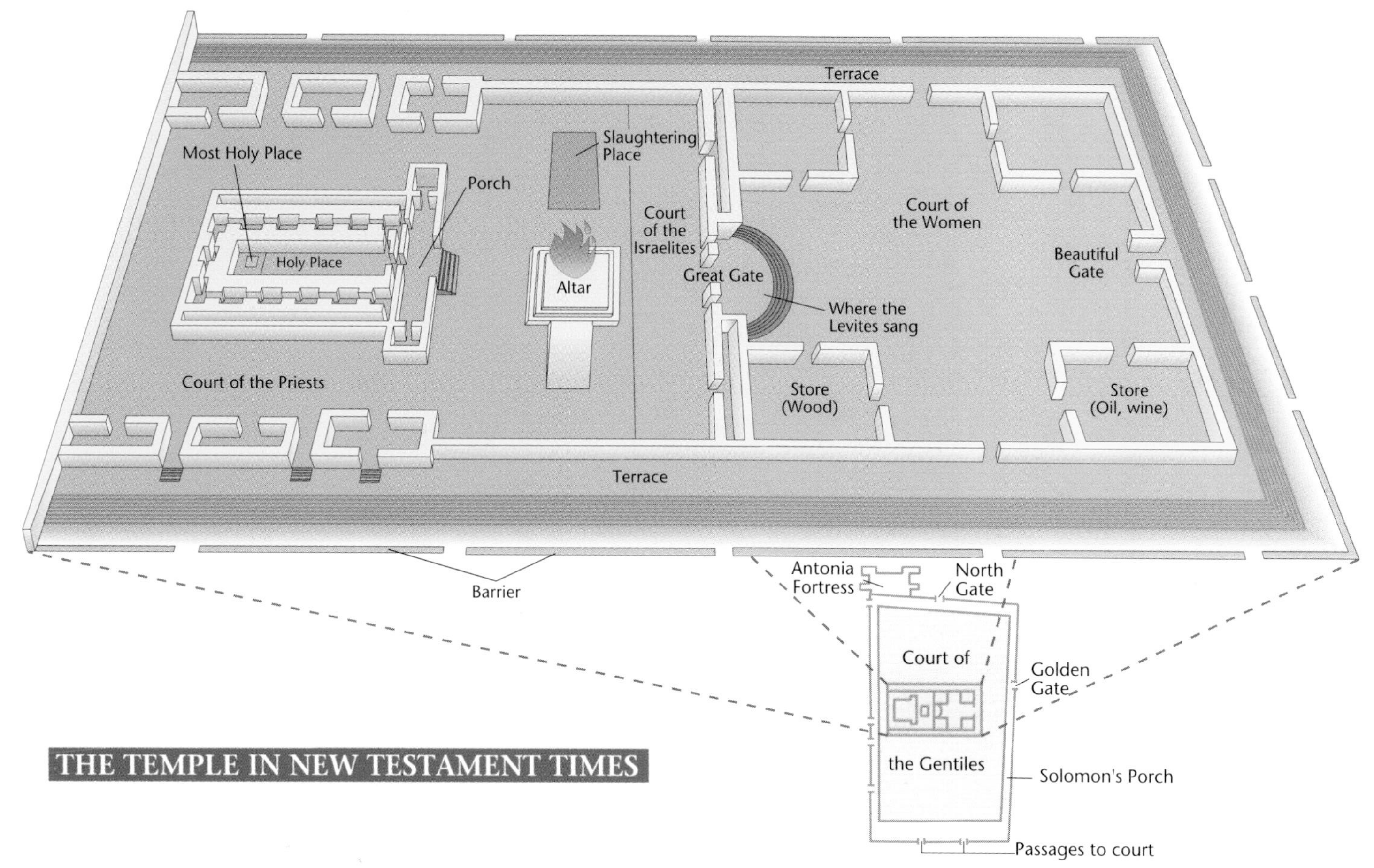

Terrace
Most Holy Place
Slaughtering Place
Porch
Court of the Israelites
Court of the Women
Holy Place
Altar
Great Gate
Beautiful Gate
Where the Levites sang
Court of the Priests
Store (Wood)
Store (Oil, wine)
Terrace
Barrier
Antonia Fortress
North Gate
Court of
Golden Gate
the Gentiles
Solomon's Porch
Passages to court

Note the comparative size of Israel to the state of Florida